WEBSTER'S NEW WORLD™

Concise Spanish Dictionary

Second Edition

WILEY

Wiley Publishing, Inc.

For general information on our other products and services or to obtain technical support, please contact our Customer Care Department within the U.S. at 800-762-2974, outside the U.S. at 317-572-3993, or fax 317-572-4002.

Wiley also publishes its books in a variety of electronic formats. Some content that appears in print may not be available in electronic books. For more information about Wiley products, please visit our web site at www.wiley.com.

Library of Congress Control Number: 2005938171

ISBN-13 978-0-471-74836-6
ISBN-10 0-471-74836-6

Designed and typeset by Chambers Harrap Publishers Ltd., Edinburgh.

Manufactured in the United States of America

10 9 8 7 6 5 4 3 2

Contents
Índice

Preface   iv
Prefacio   v

Structure of Entries   vi-vii
Estructura de las entradas

Spanish Pronunciation Guide   viii-ix
Pronunciación del inglés   x-xi

Abbreviations and symbols   xii-xiv
Abreviaturas y símbolos

SPANISH-ENGLISH DICTIONARY   1-522
DICCIONARIO ESPAÑOL-INGLÉS

Supplement
Suplemento

     Spanish Verbs   (3)-(18)
     Verbos irregulares ingleses   (19)-(21)
     Communication Guide   (23)-(72)
     Guía de comunicación

ENGLISH-SPANISH DICTIONARY   1-528
DICCIONARIO INGLÉS-ESPAÑOL

Preface

The Webster's New World Concise Spanish Dictionary has been expanded and thoroughly revised and updated for this new edition. American English is used on both sides of the dictionary.

The vocabulary is up-to-date, including current computing, Internet and cell phone vocabulary, as well as specialist vocabulary from a wide range of fields including law, medicine, finance and business, education and the media. New terms include: **blogger, phishing, ringtone** and **netiqueta, tarjeta SIM, armas de destrucción masiva.**

Colloquial and slang language is well represented in both Spanish and English. Such items are clearly labeled and appropriately translated to guide the user.

The coverage of Latin American Spanish has been greatly improved with the help of specialist consultants. Detailed labeling shows in which country or region a given word, sense or expression is used. Expressions restricted only or mainly to Spain are also clearly marked.

The layout is clear and easy to use, and a supplement includes tables of Spanish irregular verbs, and a guide to communication in Spanish.

Prefacio

Les presentamos una nueva edición del diccionario Webster's New World Concise de español-inglés, inglés-español aumentada, revisada y actualizada.

En ella se recoge el vocabulario más actual, incluyendo terminología de computación, Internet y telefonía celular, además de términos especializados de un amplio abanico de campos como derecho, medicina, negocios y finanzas, educación y medios de comunicación. Se incluyen neologismos como: **blogger, phishing, ringtone** y **netiqueta, tarjeta SIM, armas de destrucción masiva**.

También se halla bien representado el lenguaje coloquial y el argot tanto español como inglés: los términos que corresponden a dichos registros se han marcado claramente y llevan la traducción apropiada para guiar al usuario.

El español de América se recoge ampliamente en esta edición y las marcas de región utilizadas indican específicamente en qué país de América se usa una determinada palabra, acepción o expresión. Por otra parte, las palabras y expresiones que se usan exclusivamente en España también aparecen marcadas como tales.

Esta es una obra fácil de usar por su clara presentación. Incluye además un suplemento con las conjugaciones de los verbos irregulares españoles e ingleses y una guía de comunicación en inglés.

Structure of Entries
Estructura de las entradas

major ['meɪdʒə(r)] **1** *n* (**a**) *Mil* comandante *mf*; **m. general** general *mf* de división (**b**) *Univ (subject)* especialidad *f* **2** *adj* (**a**) *(important)* importante, de primer orden; **of m. importance** de enorme importancia; **m. league** *(in baseball)* = liga profesional de béisbol estadounidense; *Fig* **a m. league company** una de las grandes empresas del sector (**b**) *Mus* mayor **3** *vi Univ* **to m. in** *(subject)* especializarse en

Field labels indicate senses belonging to a particular subject area
Indicadores de campo semántico para los términos especializados

Headword abbreviated to first letter in examples
En los ejemplos sólo aparece la inicial de la palabra de la entrada

management ['mænɪdʒmənt] *n* (**a**) *(activity) (of company, project)* dirección *f*, gestión *f*; *(of economy, resources)* gestión *f*, administración *f*; **m. consultant** consultor(ora) *m,f* en administración de empresas; **m. studies** estudios *mpl* de gestión empresarial *or* administración de empresas; **m. style** estilo *m* de dirección (**b**) *(managers, employers)* **the m.** la dirección; **under new m.** *(sign)* nuevos propietarios; **m. and unions** la patronal y los sindicatos; **m. buyout** = adquisición de una empresa por sus directivos; **m. team** equipo *m* de dirección

Compounds placed under first element and listed in alphabetical order
Las unidades formadas por más de una palabra aparecen en la entrada correspondiente al primer elemento y ordenadas alfabéticamente

Phonetics shown in full for all headwords
Todas las entradas llevan la transcripción fonética completa

melt [melt] **1** *vt* derretir, fundir; *Fig (sb's resistance)* vencer **2** *vi* derretirse, fundirse; **it melts in the mouth** se funde en la boca; **to m. into thin air** esfumarse
►**melt away** *vi (snow)* derretirse; *(crowd)* dispersarse, disgregarse; *(objections, opposition)* disiparse, desvanecerse
►**melt down** *vt sep (metal)* fundir

New grammatical category introduced by bold numeral, placed on new line
Cada categoría gramatical aparece precedida por un número en negrita en un nuevo párrafo

Gender of noun translations shown in italic
El género de las traducciones se indica en letra cursiva

minute¹ ['mɪnɪt] **1** *n* (**a**) *(of time)* minuto *m*; **it's ten minutes to three** son las tres menos diez; **it's ten minutes past three** son las tres y diez; **wait a m.!** espera un momento!; **just a m.** un momento; **go downstairs this m.!** baja ahora mismo!; **the m. my back was turned she...** en cuanto me di la vuelta, ella... **he'll be here any m.** llegará en cualquier momento; **it'll be ready in a m.** estará listo en un minuto *or* momento; **I've just popped in for a m.** sólo me quedaré un momento; **until/at the last m.** hasta/en el último momento; **m. hand** *(of watch)* minutero *m*; **m. steak** filete *m* muy fino (**b**) *(note)* nota *f*; **minutes** *(of meeting)* acta *f*, actas *fpl* **2** *vt (make note of)* hacer constar en acta; **the meeting will be minuted** se levantará acta de la reunión
minute² [maɪ'njuːt] *adj* (**a**) *(small)* diminuto(a), minúsculo(a); *(increase, improvement)* mínimo(a) (**b**) *(detailed) (examination)* minucioso(a)

Phrasal verbs introduced by ►
Los verbos con partícula vienen precedidos por el símbolo ►

Superscript number marks homographs
Las formas homógrafas aparecen numeradas

Feminine inflections shown consistently
Se muestran todas las terminaciones femeninas

Sense indicators shown in italic in brackets
Los indicadores semánticos van entre paréntesis y en cursiva

Full form of all abbreviations given, with translation
En las abreviaturas siempre se da la forma completa, así como una traducción

MIPS *Comptr (abbr* **million instructions per second***)* millón *m* de instrucciones por segundo

This label means that the translation also works in a figurative sense
La traducción funciona también en sentido figurado

mirage ['mɪrɑːʒ] *n also Fig* espejismo *m*

vi

AA. EE. (*abrev de* **Asuntos Exteriores**) Ministerio de AA. EE. Ministry of Foreign Affairs, ≃ State Department

abatible *adj* **mesa a.** foldaway table; **asientos abatibles** *(en coche)* = seats that tip forward or fold flat

abarcar [59] *vt* (**a**) *(incluir)* to embrace, to cover; *Prov* **quien mucho abarca poco aprieta** don't bite off more than you can chew (**b**) *(ver)* to be able to see, to have a view of; **desde la torre se abarca todo el valle** you can see the whole valley from the tower

abril *nm* April; **tiene catorce abriles** he is fourteen (years of age); *Prov* **en a., aguas mil** March winds, April showers; *ver también* **septiembre**

abstenerse [65] *vpr* (**a**) *(guardarse)* to abstain (**de** from); **se abstuvo de mencionar su embarazo** she refrained from mentioning her pregnancy (**b**) *(en votación)* to abstain; **me abstuve en las últimas elecciones** I didn't vote in the last election

abuso *nm* (**a**) *(uso excesivo)* abuse (**de** of); **a. de confianza** breach of confidence; *Der* **abusos deshonestos** indecent assault; **a. de poder** abuse of power; **abusos sexuales** sexual abuse (**b**) *(escándalo)* scandal, sin

aciago, -a *adj Formal* black, fateful; **un día a.** a fateful day

acojonante *adj Esp muy Fam* (**a**) *(impresionante)* damn fine (**b**) *(que da miedo)* damn scary

actualidad *nf* (**a**) *(momento presente)* current situation; **la a. política** the current political situation; **cuentan en la a. con un millón de socios** they currently have a million members; **estas piezas en la a. se fabrican en serie** these parts are mass-produced nowadays (**b**) *(de asunto, noticia)* topicality; **estar de a.** to be topical; **una noticia de rabiosa a.** an extremely topical news item; **temas de a.** current affairs (**c**) *(noticia)* news *(singular)*; **la a. informativa** the news; **la a. deportiva** the sports news; **ser a.** to be making the news (**d**) *(vigencia)* relevance to modern society; **sus libros siguen teniendo gran a.** her books are still very relevant today

afiche *nm Am* poster

ají (*pl* **ajís 0 ajíes**) *nm Andes, RP* *(pimiento)* chilli (pepper); *(salsa)* = sauce made from oil, vinegar, garlic and chilli

alberca *nf* (**a**) *(depósito)* water tank (**b**) *Col, Méx* *(piscina)* swimming pool

albergar [40] **1** *vt* (**a**) *(personas)* to accommodate, to put up (**b**) *(odio)* to harbor; *(esperanzas)* to cherish
2 albergarse *vpr* to stay; **en qué hotel se albergan** what hotel are they staying in

albor *nm* (**a**) *Literario (blancura)* whiteness (**b**) *Formal (luz del alba)* first light of day (**c**) **albores** *(principio)* dawn, earliest days; **los albores de la civilización** the dawn of civilization

antigualla *nf Pey (cosa)* museum piece; *(persona)* old fogy, old fossil

Spanish Pronunciation Guide

The following table is based on IPA (the International Phonetic Alphabet) with certain modifications and attempts to give an approximate idea of the Spanish sound system as compared with that of English.

Letter	Phonetic symbol	Examples
Vowels:		
a	[a]	gato, amar, mesa
e	[e]	estrella, vez, firme
i	[i]	inicuo, iris
o	[o]	bolo, cómodo, oso
u	[u]	turuta, puro, tribu
y	[i]	y
Diphthongs:		
ai, ay	[ai]	baile, hay
au	[au]	fauna
ei, ey	[ei]	peine, ley
eu	[eu]	feudo
oi, oy	[oi]	boina, hoy
Semi-consonants:		
u	[w]	buey, cuando, fuiste
i	[j]	viernes, vicio, ciudad
y	[j]	yermo, ayer, rey
Consonants:		
b	[b]	boda, burro, ambos
	[β]	haba, traba
c	[k]	cabeza, cuco, acoso, frac
	[θ]	cecina, cielo
ch	[tʃ]	chepa, ocho
d	[d]	dedo, andar
	[ð]	dedo, abad
f	[f]	fiesta, afición
g	[g]	gas, rango, gula
	[ɣ]	agua, agosto, lagar
	[χ]	genio, legión
h	-	hambre, ahíto
j	[χ]	jabón, ajo, carcajada
k	[k]	kilo, kimono
l	[l]	labio, hábil, elegante
l	[j]	lluvia, calle
m	[m]	mano, amigo, hambre
n	[n]	nata, ratón, antes, enemigo

Letter	Phonetic symbol	Examples
ñ	[ɲ]	año
p	[p]	pipa, pelo
q	[k]	quiosco, querer, alambique
r(r)	[r]	pero, correr, padre
	[rr]	roer, honrado, perro
s	[s]	sauna, asado, cortés
t	[t]	teja, están, atraco
v	[b]	verbena, vena
	[β]	ave, vivo
w	[b]	wagón, waterpolo
x	[ks]	éxito, examen
z	[I]	zorro, azul, caza, soez

Stress rules:	Examples:
• If a word ends in a vowel, **-n** or **-s**, the stress should fall on the second last syllable	mano, examen, bocadillos
• If a word has any other ending, the stress falls on the last syllable	hablar, Madrid, ayer
• Exceptions to these rules carry a written accent on the stressed syllable	cómodo, legión, hábil

Pronunciación del inglés

Para ilustrar la pronunciación inglesa, en este diccionario utilizamos los símbolos del AFI (Alfabeto Fonético Internacional). En el siguiente cuadro, para cada sonido del inglés hay ejemplos de palabras en inglés y palabras en español donde aparece un sonido similar. En los casos en los que no hay sonido similar en español, ofrecemos una explicación de cómo se pronuncian.

Carácter AFI	Ejemplo en inglés	Ejemplo en español
Consonantes		
[b]	babble	bebé
[d]	dig	dedo
[dʒ]	giant, jig	se pronuncia como "gi" en italiano - Giovanna
[f]	fit, physics	faro
[g]	grey, big	gris
[h]	happy	"h" aspirada
[j]	yellow	se pronuncia como "y" o "ll" en España - yo, lluvia
[k]	clay, kick	clic
[l]	lip	labio
	pill	papel
[m]	mummy	mamá
[n]	nip, pin	nada
[ŋ]	sing	se pronuncia como "n" antes de "c" - banco
[p]	pip	papá
[r]	rig, write	sonido entre "r" y "rr"
[s]	sick, science	sapo
[ʃ]	ship, nation	show
[t]	tip, butt	tela
[tʃ]	chip, batch	chaucha
[θ]	thick	zapato (como se pronuncia en España)
[ð]	this	hada
[v]	vague, give	vida
[w]	wit, why	whisky
[z]	zip, physics	"s" con sonido zumbante
[ʒ]	pleasure	se pronuncia como "y" o "ll" en el Río de la Plata - yo, lluvia
[χ]	loch	jota
Vocales		
[æ]	rag	se pronuncia "a" con posición bucal para "e"
[ɑː]	large, half	"a" alargada
[ʌ]	cup	"a" breve y cerrada
[e]	set	elefante
[ɜː]	curtain, were	se pronuncia "e" con posición bucal entre "o" y "e"

Carácter AFI	Ejemplo en inglés	Ejemplo en español
[ə]	utter	se pronuncia "e" con posición bucal para "o"
[ɪ]	big, women	"i" breve, a medio camino entre "e" e "i"
[iː]	leak, wee	"i" muy alargada
[ɒ]	lock	"o" abierta
[ɔː]	wall, cork	"o" cerrada y alargada
[ʊ]	put, look	"u" breve
[uː]	moon	"u" muy alargada
Diptongos		
[aɪ]	why, high, lie	aire
[aʊ]	how	aura
[eə]	bear	"ea" pronunciado muy brevemente y con sonido de "e" más marcado que el de "a"
[eɪ]	day, make, main	reina
[əʊ]	show, go	"ou" como en COU
[ɪə]	here, gear	"hielo" pronunciado con el sonido de "i" más marcado y alargado que el de "e"
[ɔɪ]	boy, soil	voy
[ʊə]	poor	"cuerno" pronunciado con el sonido de "u" más marcado y alargado que el de "e"

Abbreviations and Symbols
Abreviaturas y símbolos

English	Abbrev	Spanish
cultural equivalent [introduces a translation which has a roughly equivalent status in the target language]	≃	equivalente cultural [precede a una traducción con connotaciones equivalentes en la lengua de destino]
gloss [introduces an explanation]	=	glosa [precede a una explicación]
abbreviation	*abbr/abrev*	abreviatura
adjective	*adj*	adjetivo
adverb	*adv*	adverbio
agriculture	*Agr*	agricultura
Latin American Spanish	*Am*	español de América
anatomy	*Anat*	anatomía
Andean Spanish (Bolivia, Chile, Colombia, Ecuador, Peru)	*Andes*	español andino (Bolivia, Chile, Colombia, Ecuador, Perú)
architecture	*Archit*	arquitectura
Argentinian Spanish	*Arg*	español de Argentina
architecture	*Arquit*	arquitectura
article	*art*	artículo
astronomy	*Astron*	astronomía
automobiles	*Aut*	automóbiles
auxiliary	*aux*	auxiliar
aviation	*Av*	aviación
biochemistry	*Biochem*	bioquímica
biology	*Biol*	biología
biochemistry	*Bioquím*	bioquímica
Bolivian Spanish	*Bol*	español de Bolivia
stock exchange	*Bolsa*	bolsa
botany	*Bot*	botánica
Central American Spanish	*CAm*	español centroamericano
Caribbean Spanish (Cuba, Puerto Rico, Dominican Republic, Venezuela)	*Carib*	español caribeño (Cuba, Puerto Rico, República Dominicana, Venezuela)
chemistry	*Chem*	química
Chilean Spanish	*Chile*	español de Chile
cinema	*Cin*	cine
Colombian Spanish	*Col*	español de Colombia
commerce	*Com*	comercio
computing	*Comptr*	informática
conjunction	*conj*	conjunción
construction	*Constr*	construcción
Costa Rican Spanish	*CRica*	español de Costa Rica
Cono Sur Spanish	*CSur*	español del Cono Sur
Cuban Spanish	*Cuba*	español de Cuba
cooking	*Culin*	cocina
sport	*Dep*	deporte
law	*Der*	derecho
economics	*Econ*	economía
Ecuadoran Spanish	*Ecuad*	español de Ecuador
education	*Educ*	educación
electricity & electronics	*Elec*	electricidad y electrónica
Peninsular Spanish	*Esp*	español de España
especially	*esp*	especialmente
specialist term	*Espec*	término especializado

euphemism	*Euph/Euf*	eufemismo
exclamation	*exclam*	interjección
feminine	*f*	femenino
informal	*Fam*	familiar
pharmacy	*Farm*	farmacia
rail	*Ferroc*	ferrocarril
figurative	*Fig*	sentido figurado
finance	*Fin*	finanzas
physics	*Fís*	física
physiology	*Fisiol*	fisiología
photography	*Fot*	fotografía
geography	*Geog*	geografía
geology	*Geol*	geología
geometry	*Geom*	geometría
grammar	*Gram*	gramática
Guatemalan Spanish	*Guat*	español de Guatemala
history	*Hist*	historia
humorous	*Hum*	humorístico
industry	*Ind*	industria
computing	*Inform*	informática
interjection	*interj*	interjección
invariable	*inv*	invariable
journalism	*Journ*	periodismo
linguistics	*Ling*	lingüística
literature	*Lit*	literatura
adjectival phrase	*loc adj*	locución adjetiva
adverbial phrase	*loc adv*	ocución adverbial
conjunctive phrase	*loc conj*	locución conjuntiva
prepositional phrase	*loc prep*	locución prepositiva
masculine	*m*	masculino
mathematics	*Math, Mat*	matemáticas
mechanics	*Mec*	mecánica
medicine	*Med*	medicina
weather	*Met, Meteo*	meteorología
Mexican Spanish	*Méx*	español de México
masculine or feminine noun [different form in the feminine]	*m,f*	nombre masculino o femenino [forma femenina diferente]
masculine or feminine noun [same form for both genders]	*mf*	nombre masculino o femenino [formas idénticas]
military	*Mil*	militar
mining	*Min*	minería
mythology	*Mitol*	mitología
marketing	*Mktg*	marketing
music	*Mus, Mús*	música
noun	*n*	nombre
shipping	*Naut, Náut*	náutica
feminine noun	*nf*	nombre femenino
plural feminine noun	*nfpl*	nombre femenino plural
Nicaraguan Spanish	*Nic*	español de Nicaragua
masculine noun	*nm*	nombre masculino
masculine or feminine noun [different form in the feminine]	*nm,f*	nombre masculino o femenino [forma femenina diferente]
masculine or feminine noun [same form for both genders]	*nmf*	nombre masculino o femenino [formas idénticas]
plural masculine noun	*nmpl*	nombre masculino plural
plural noun	*npl*	nombre plural
proper noun	*n pr*	nombre propio
numeral	*núm*	número
Panamanian Spanish	*Pan*	español de Panamá
Paraguayan Spanish	*Par*	español de Paraguay
parliament	*Parl*	parlamento
pejorative	*Pej/Pey*	peyorativo
Peruvian Spanish	*Perú*	español de Perú

philosophy	*Phil*	filosofía
photography	*Phot*	fotografía
physics	*Phys*	física
physiology	*Physiol*	fisiología
plural	*pl*	plural
politics	*Pol*	política
past participle	*pp*	participio pasado
preposition	*prep*	preposición
Puerto Rican Spanish	*PRico*	español de Puerto Rico
proper noun	*pr n*	nombre propio
pronoun	*pron*	pronombre
proverb	*Prov*	proverbio
psychology	*Psy, Psi*	psicología
past tense	*pt*	pretérito
chemistry	*Quím*	química
radio	*Rad*	radio
rail	*Rail*	ferrocarril
Dominican Spanish	*RDom*	español de la República Dominicana
religion	*Rel*	religión
River Plate Spanish (Argentina, Uruguay, Paraguay)	*RP*	español de los países ribereños del Río de la Plata (Argentina, Uruguay y Paraguay)
Salvadoran Spanish	*Salv*	español de El Salvador
school	*Sch*	escuela
Scottish English	*Scot*	inglés de Escocia
specialist term	*Spec*	término especializado
stock exchange	*St Exch*	bolsa
bullfighting	*Taurom*	tauromaquia
technology	*Tech, Tec*	tecnología
telecommunications	*Tel*	telecomunicaciones
textiles	*Tex*	textiles
television	*TV*	televisión
printing	*Typ*	imprenta
university	*Univ*	universidad
Uruguayan Spanish	*Urug*	español de Uruguay
verb	*v*	verbo
Venezuelan Spanish	*Ven*	español de Venezuela
intransitive verb	*vi*	verbo intransitivo
pronominal verb	*vpr*	verbo pronominal
transitive verb	*vt*	verbo transitivo
inseparable phrasal verb [phrasal verb where the verb and the adverb or preposition cannot be separated, eg **go into**: he **went into** the store]	*vt insep*	verbo transitivo con partícula inseparable [por ejemplo, **go into** (entrar en): he **went into** the store (entró en la tienda)]
separable phrasal verb [phrasal verb where the verb and the adverb or preposition can be separated, eg **bring out**: they **brought** a new model **out** or they **brought out** a new model]	*vt sep*	verbo transitivo con partícula separable [por ejemplo, **bring out** (sacar): they **brought** a new model **out** or they **brought** out a new model (sacaron un modelo nuevo)]
vulgar	*Vulg*	vulgar
zoology	*Zool*	zoología

A

A, **a** [a] *nf (letra)* A, a

a *prep*

> **a** combines with the article **el** to form the contraction **al** (e.g. **al centro** to the center).

(**a**) *(dirección)* to; **voy a Tijuana** I'm going to Tijuana; **me voy al extranjero** I'm going abroad; **llegó a Puebla/a la fiesta** he arrived in Puebla/at the party

(**b**) *(posición)* **está a la derecha/izquierda** it's on the right/left; **a orillas del mar** by the sea

(**c**) *(distancia)* **está a más de 100 kilómetros** it's more than 100 kilometers away; **de Monterrey a Durango** from Monterrey to Durango

(**d**) *(periodo de tiempo)* **a las pocas semanas** a few weeks later; **al mes de casados** a month after they were married; **al día siguiente** the following day

(**e**) *(momento preciso)* at; **a las siete** at seven o'clock; **a los once años** at the age of eleven; **al caer la noche** at nightfall; **al oír la noticia se desmayó** on hearing the news, she fainted

(**f**) *(frecuencia)* per, every; **40 horas a la semana** 40 hours per *o* a week; **tres veces al día** three times a day

(**g**) *(con complemento indirecto)* to; **dáselo a Juan** give it to Juan; **dile a Juan que venga** tell Juan to come

(**h**) *(con complemento directo)* **quiere a sus hijos/su gato** she loves her children/her cat; **me cuidan como a un enfermo** they look after me as if I was an invalid

(**i**) *(cantidad, medida, precio)* **a cientos/miles/docenas** by the hundred/thousand/dozen; **la leche se vende a litros** milk is sold by the liter; **a.... kilómetros por hora** at... kilometers per *o* an hour; **¿a cuánto están las peras?** how much are the pears?; **tiene las peras a 2 euros** she's selling pears for *o* at 2 euros; **ganaron tres a cero** they won three to nothing

(**j**) *(modo)* **lo hace a la antigua** he does it the old way; **a lo bestia** rudely; **a lo grande** in style; **a lo Mozart** after Mozart; **a escondidas** secretly; *Culin* **merluza a la vasca/gallega** Basque-style/Galician-style hake

(**k**) *(instrumento)* **escribir a máquina** to type; **a lápiz** in pencil; **a mano** by hand; **olla a presión** pressure cooker

(**l**) *(finalidad)* to; **entró a pagar** he came in to pay; **aprender a nadar** to learn to swim

(**m**) *(complemento de nombre)* **sueldo a convenir** salary to be agreed; **temas a tratar** matters to be discussed

(**n**) *(condición)* **a no ser por mí, hubieses fracasado** if it hadn't been *o* had it not been for me, you would have failed

(**o**) *(en oraciones imperativas)* **¡a la cama!** go to bed!; **¡a callar todo el mundo!** quiet, everyone!; **¡a bailar!** let's dance!; **¡a trabajar!** let's get to work!

(**p**) *(en busca de)* **ir a por pan** to go for bread

(**q**) *(indica desafío)* **¿a que no lo haces?** I bet you won't do it!

AA 1 *nmpl (abrev de* **Alcohólicos Anónimos**) AA

2 *nfpl (abrev de* **Aerolíneas Argentinas**) = Argentinian state airline

AA. EE. *(abrev de* **Asuntos Exteriores**) **Ministerio de AA. EE.** Ministry of Foreign Affairs, ≃ State Department

ababol *nm* poppy

ábaco *nm* abacus

abad *nm* abbot

abadejo *nm* cod

abadesa *nf* abbess

abadía *nf* abbey

abajeño, -a, abajero, -a *Am* **1** *adj* lowland

2 *nm,f* lowlander

abajo 1 *adv* (**a**) *(posición)* *(en general)* below; *(en edificio)* downstairs; **de a.** bottom; **el estante de a.** the bottom shelf; **vive (en el piso de) a.** she lives downstairs; **está aquí/allí a.** it's down here/there; **si no quieres subir hasta la cumbre, espérame a.** if you don't want to climb to the top, wait for me at the bottom; **a. del todo** right at the bottom; **más a.** further down; **la parte de a.** the bottom

(**b**) *(dirección)* down; **ve a.** *(en edificio)* go downstairs; **hacia** *o* **para a.** down, downward; **calle/escaleras a.** down the street/the stairs; **tres portales más a.** three doors further along

(**c**) *(en una escala)* **niños de diez años para a.** children aged ten or under; **de tenientes para a.** everyone of the rank of lieutenant and below; **a. de** less than

(**d**) *(en un texto)* below; **el a. citado** the undermentioned; **el a. firmante** the undersigned

(**e**) *Am* **a. de** below, under

2 *interj* **¡a....!** down with...!; **¡a. la dictadura!** down with the dictatorship!

abalanzarse [14] *vpr* **a. hacia** to rush toward; **a. sobre** to pounce on

abalear *vt Andes, CAm, Ven* to shoot at

abalorio *nm* (**a**) *(cuenta)* glass bead (**b**) *(bisutería)* trinket

abanderado *nm también Fig* standard-bearer

abandonado, -a *adj* (**a**) *(desierto)* deserted (**b**) *(desamparado)* abandoned (**c**) *(descuidado)* *(persona)* unkempt; *(jardín, casa)* neglected

abandonar 1 *vt* (**a**) *(lugar)* to leave; *(barco, vehículo)* to abandon (**b**) *(persona)* to leave; *(hijo, animal)* to abandon (**c**) *(estudios)* to give up; *(proyecto)* to abandon; **abandonó la carrera en el tercer año** she dropped out of college in her third year, she gave up her studies in her third year

2 abandonarse *vpr (de aspecto)* to neglect oneself, to let oneself go; **abandonarse a** *(desesperación, dolor)* to succumb to; *(placer, sentidos)* to abandon oneself to; *(vicio)* to give oneself over to

abandono *nm* (**a**) *(de lugar, profesión, cónyuge)* leaving; *(de hijo, proyecto)* abandonment; *Dep* **ganar por a.** to win by default; *Der* **a. de hogar** desertion *(of family, spouse)* (**b**) *(descuido)* *(de aspecto, jardín)* state of abandon; *(de obligaciones)* neglect

abanicar [59] **1** *vt* to fan

2 abanicarse *vpr* to fan oneself; **se abanicó la cara** she fanned her face

abanico nm (**a**) (para abanicarse) fan; **hizo un a. con los naipes** he fanned out the cards (**b**) (gama) range

abaratar 1 vt (precio, coste) to bring down, to reduce; (artículo) to reduce the price of

2 abaratarse vpr to go down in price, to become cheaper

abarca nf = type of sandal worn by country people

abarcar [59] vt (**a**) (incluir) to embrace, to cover; Prov **quien mucho abarca poco aprieta** don't bite off more than you can chew (**b**) (ver) to be able to see, to have a view of; **desde la torre se abarca todo el valle** you can see the whole valley from the tower

abaritonado, -a adj Mús baritone

abarque etc ver **abarcar**

abarquillar 1 vt (madera) to warp

2 abarquillarse vpr (madera) to warp

abarrotado, -a adj (teatro, autobús) packed (**de** with); (desván, baúl) crammed (**de** with)

abarrotar vt (teatro, autobús) to pack (**de** o **con** with); (desván, baúl) to cram full (**de** o **con** of)

abarrotería nf CAm, Méx grocery store

abarrotero, -a nm,f CAm, Méx grocer

abarrotes nmpl CAm, Méx groceries; **tienda de a.** grocery store

abastecedor, -ora nm,f supplier

abastecer [46] **1** vt to supply (**de** with); **a. de agua a la ciudad** to supply the city with water; **esa región nos abastece de materias primas** that region supplies o provides us with raw materials

2 abastecerse vpr to stock up (**de** on)

abastecimiento nm supplying; **se ha interrumpido el a.** they've cut off the supply; **a. de aguas** water supply

abasto nm **no dar a.** to be unable to cope; **no da a. con tanto trabajo** she can't cope with so much work

abate nm abbé (title given to French or Italian priest)

abatible adj **mesa a.** foldaway table; **asientos abatibles** (en coche) = seats that tip forward or fold flat

abatido, -a adj dejected, downhearted

abatimiento nm (desánimo) low spirits, dejection

abatir 1 vt (**a**) (derribar) (muro) to knock down; (avión) to shoot down (**b**) (desanimar) to depress, to dishearten; **no te dejes a. por tan poca cosa** don't let something so trivial get you down

2 abatirse vpr (**a**) (caer) **abatirse sobre algo/alguien** to pounce on sth/sb (**b**) (desanimarse) to become dejected o disheartened

abdicación nf (de monarca) abdication

abdicar [59] **1** vt **a. el trono (en alguien)** to abdicate the throne (in favor of sb)

2 vi to abdicate; Fig **a. de** (principios, ideales) to renounce

abdomen nm (de persona, insecto) abdomen

abdominal 1 adj abdominal; **dolores abdominales** abdominal pains

2 abdominales nmpl sit-ups

abductor nm Anat abductor

abecé nm también Fig ABC

abecedario nm (**a**) (alfabeto) alphabet (**b**) (libro) spelling book

abedul nm birch (tree)

abeja nf bee; **a. obrera** worker bee; **a. reina** queen bee

abejaruco nm bee-eater

abejorro nm bumblebee

Abel n pr Abel

aberración nf (**a**) (desviación de la norma) **me parece una a.** I find it ridiculous; **echó gaseosa al champán, ¡qué a.!** he put lemonade in the champagne? that's sacrilege!; **a. sexual** sexual perversion (**b**) Fot aberration

aberrante adj (**a**) (absurdo) ridiculous, idiotic (**b**) (perverso) perverse

abertura nf (**a**) (agujero) opening; (ranura) crack (**b**) Fot aperture; **a. del diafragma** aperture

abertzale [aβerˈtʃale] adj & nmf Esp Pol (radical) Basque nationalist

abeto nm fir

abiertamente adv (claramente) openly

abierto, -a 1 participio ver **abrir**

2 adj (**a**) (puerta, boca, tienda) open; **dejar el grifo a.** to leave the faucet on o running; **bien** o **muy a.** wide open; **a. al público** open to the public; **a. al tráfico** open to traffic; **a. de nueve a cinco** open from nine to five; **a. hasta tarde** open late; **a. toda la noche** o **las 24 horas** open all night (**b**) (liberal) open-minded; **estar a. a cualquier sugerencia** to be open to suggestions

abigarrado, -a adj (**a**) (mezclado) **la habitación está a.** the room is a real jumble of different things (**b**) (multicolor) multicolored

abisal adj **fosa a.** ocean trough; **pez a.** abyssal fish

abismal adj (diferencia, distancia) vast, colossal

abismar 1 vt Formal **a. a alguien en la desesperación** to plunge sb into despair

2 abismarse vpr **abismarse en** (lectura) to become engrossed in

abismo nm (**a**) (profundidad) abyss; Fig **estar al borde del a.** to be on the brink of ruin o disaster (**b**) (diferencia) gulf; **entre su sueldo y el mío hay un a.** there's a huge difference between our salaries

Abiyán n Abidjan

abjurar Formal **1** vt (fe, creencias) to abjure, to renounce

2 vi **a. de** (fe, creencias) to abjure, to renounce

ablación nf Med (de tejido, órgano) excision, surgical removal; **a. del clítoris** female circumcision

ablandamiento nm también Fig softening

ablandar 1 vt también Fig to soften

2 ablandarse vpr (material) to soften, to become softer; Fig (actitud, rigor) to soften; **su padre se ablandó cuando la vio llorar** her father relented when he saw her cry

ablativo nm Gram ablative; **a. absoluto** ablative absolute

abluciones nfpl ablutions

ablusado, -a adj (vestido, camisa) loose, baggy

abnegación nf abnegation, self-denial

abnegado, -a adj selfless, unselfish

abobado, -a adj Fam (**a**) (estupefacto) blank, uncomprehending (**b**) (estúpido) stupid

abocado, -a adj destined (**a** to)

abocar [59] vi **a. en un fracaso** to end in failure

abochornado, -a adj embarrassed

abochornar 1 vt to embarrass

2 abochornarse vpr to get embarrassed

abofetear vt to slap (on the face)

abogacía nf legal profession

abogado, -a nm,f (**a**) Der attorney, lawyer; **a. criminalista** criminal lawyer; **a. defensor** counsel for the defense; **a. del estado** public prosecutor; **a. laboralista** labor lawyer; **a. de oficio** legal aid lawyer; **a. en prácticas** articled clerk (**b**) (intercesor) intermediary; (defensor) advocate; **a. del diablo** devil's advocate

abogar [40] vi (**a**) Der **a. por alguien** to represent sb (**b**) (defender) **a. por algo** to advocate sth; **a. por alguien** to stand up for sb, to defend sb

abolengo nm lineage; **de (rancio) a.** of noble lineage

abolición nf abolition

abolicionismo nm Hist abolitionism (opposition to slavery)

abolicionista adj & nmf Hist abolitionist

abolir vt to abolish

abolladura nf dent

abollar 1 vt to dent

2 abollarse vpr to get dented

abombado, -a adj (hacia fuera) buckled; **la lata está un poco abombada** the can has buckled slightly outward

abombar 1 vt to buckle (outward)

2 abombarse vpr to buckle (outward)

abominable adj abominable; **el a. hombre de las nieves** the abominable snowman

abominación nf abomination

abominar 1 vt (detestar) to abhor, to abominate

2 vi **a. de** (condenar) to condemn, to criticize

abonable adj Fin (pagadero) payable

abonado, -a nm,f (a telefónica, revista) subscriber; (al fútbol, teatro) season-ticket holder

abonar 1 vt (a) (pagar) (factura, cuenta) to pay; **a. algo en la cuenta de alguien** to credit sb's account with sth (b) (tierra) to fertilize

2 abonarse vpr (a revista) to subscribe (a to); (al fútbol, teatro) to buy a season ticket (a for)

abonero, -a nm,f Méx hawker, street trader

abono nm (a) (pase) season ticket; **un a. de diez viajes** a ten-journey ticket; **a. transporte** travel pass (for bus, train and subway) (b) (fertilizante) fertilizer (c) (pago) payment (d) Com credit entry (e) Méx (plazo) installment; **pagar en abonos** to pay by installments

abordable adj (persona) approachable; (tema) that can be tackled; (tarea) manageable

abordaje nm Náut boarding

abordar vt (a) (barco) to board (in attack) (b) (persona) to approach (c) (tema, tarea) to tackle (d) Méx, Ven (avión, barco) to board; (tren, autobús) to get on; (automóvil) to get into

aborigen adj (indígena) indigenous; (de Australia) Aboriginal; **aborígenes** (población indígena) indigenous population; (de Australia) Aborigenes

aborrecer [46] vt to abhor, to loathe

aborrecible adj abhorrent, loathsome

aborrecimiento nm loathing, hatred

aborregado, -a adj (a) Fam (adocenado) **estar a.** to be like a sheep (b) **cielo a.** mackerel sky

abortar 1 vt (feto) to abort; Fig (hacer fracasar) to foil

2 vi Med (espontáneamente) to have a miscarriage, to miscarry; (intencionadamente) to have an abortion

abortista adj & nmf abortionist

abortivo nm abortifacient

aborto nm (a) (espontáneo) miscarriage; (intencionado) abortion; **a. clandestino** backstreet abortion (b) muy Fam (persona fea) freak; (idiota) moron

abotargado, -a adj (a) (hinchado) swollen; (cara) puffy (b) (atontado) **tengo la mente abotargada** my mind has gone fuzzy

abotargarse [40] vpr to swell (up)

abotonar 1 vt to button up

2 abotonarse vpr to do one's buttons up; **abotonarse la camisa** to button one's shirt up

abovedado, -a adj Arquit vaulted

abracadabra nm abracadabra

abrace etc ver **abrazar**

abrasador, -ora adj burning

abrasar 1 vt (quemar) (casa, bosque) to burn down; (persona, mano, garganta) to burn; (desecar) to scorch; **el sol abrasó los campos** the sun parched the fields

2 vi (café, sopa) to be boiling hot; **este sol abrasa** the sun is really hot today

3 abrasarse vpr (casa, bosque) to burn down; (persona) to burn oneself; **me abrasé los brazos** I burned my arms; **los**

campos se abrasaron con el calor the heat parched the fields

abrasión nf (a) (fricción) abrasion (b) Med (por fricción) abrasion; (por agente corrosivo) burn

abrasivo, -a 1 adj abrasive

2 nm abrasive

abrazadera nf Tec brace, bracket; (en carpintería) clamp

abrazar [14] **1** vt (rodear con los brazos) to hug, to embrace; Fig (doctrina) to embrace; Fig (profesión) to go into

2 abrazarse vpr to hug, to embrace; **abrazarse a alguien** to hug sb, to cling to sb; **se abrazaron con pasión** they embraced passionately

abrazo nm embrace, hug; **un (fuerte) a.** (en cartas) Yours, Best wishes

abrebotellas nm inv bottle opener

abrecartas nm inv paper knife, letter opener

abrelatas nm inv can opener

abrevadero nm (construido) drinking trough; (natural) watering place

abrevar vt to water, to give water to

abreviación nf (de texto) abridgment

abreviado, -a adj (texto) abridged

abreviar 1 vt (proceso, explicación) to shorten; (texto) to abridge; (palabra) to abbreviate; (viaje, estancia) to cut short

2 vi (darse prisa) to hurry up; **para a.** (al hacer algo) to keep it quick; (al narrar algo) to cut a long story short

abreviatura nf abbreviation

abridor nm (a) (abrebotellas) (bottle) opener (b) (abrelatas) (can) opener

abrigado, -a adj (persona) well wrapped-up; (prenda) warm

abrigador, -ora nm,f Méx Der accessory (after the fact)

abrigar [40] **1** vt (a) (persona) (arropar) to wrap up; (calentar) to keep warm (b) (tener) (esperanza) to cherish; (sospechas, malas intenciones) to harbor

2 vi (ropa, manta) to be warm; **esta chaqueta no abriga nada** this jacket is useless at keeping you warm

3 abrigarse vpr (a) (arroparse) to wrap up (b) (resguardarse) to shelter (de from)

abrigo nm (a) (prenda) coat, overcoat; **a. de piel** fur coat (b) (refugio) shelter; **al a. de** (peligro, ataque) safe from; (lluvia, viento) sheltered from; (ley) under the protection of

abrigue etc ver **abrigar**

abril nm April; **tiene catorce abriles** he is fourteen (years of age); Prov **en a., aguas mil** March winds, April showers; ver también **septiembre**

abrillantador nm polish; **a. de metales** metal polish; **a. de muebles** furniture polish

abrillantar vt to polish

abrir 1 vt (a) (en general) to open; (alas) to spread; (melón) to cut open; (agua, gas) to turn on; (cerradura) to unlock, to open; (cremallera) to undo (b) (túnel) to dig; (canal, camino) to build; (agujero, surco) to make; **le abrieron la cabeza de un botellazo** they smashed his head open with a bottle; también Fig **a. paso** o **camino** to clear the way (c) (negocio, colegio, mercado) to open (d) (apetito) to whet; **la natación abre el apetito** swimming makes you hungry (e) (encabezar) (lista) to head; (manifestación) to lead (f) **a. fuego** (sobre o contra) to open fire (on)

2 vi (a) (en general) to open; **la tienda abre a las cinco** the store opens at five (o'clock) (b) (abrir la puerta) to open the door; **¡abra, policía!** open up, it's the police!

3 abrirse vpr (a) (puerta, caja) to open; **este bote no se abre** this jar won't open; **se te ha abierto la camisa** your shirt has come undone (b) (empezar) (película, función) to open, to begin (c) (sincerarse) to open up; **abrirse a alguien** to open up to sb, to confide in sb; **abrirse más a la gente** to be more open with people (d) (posibilidades) to open up (e) *(cielo)* to clear (**f**) *(rajarse)* to split open; **se cayó del caballo y se abrió la cabeza** she fell off her horse and split her head open (**g**) *también Fig* **abrirse paso** *o* **camino** to make one's way (**h**) *Fam (irse)* to clear off

abrochadora *nf RP (para papeles)* stapler

abrochar 1 *vt* (**a**) *(botones, camisa)* to do up; *(cinturón)* to fasten (**b**) *RP (papeles)* to staple

2 abrocharse *vpr (botones, camisa)* to do up; *(cinturón)* to fasten; **abrocharse la camisa** to do up one's shirt; **¡abróchate!** *(el abrigo)* do your coat up!; **abróchense los cinturones de seguridad** fasten your seatbelts

abrogar [40] *vt Der* to abrogate, to repeal

abroncar [59] *vt* (**a**) *(reprender)* to tell off (**b**) *(abuchear)* to boo

abrótano *nm* southernwood

abrumador, -ora *adj* overwhelming

abrumar *vt (agobiar)* to overwhelm

abrupto, -a *adj (escarpado)* sheer; *(accidentado)* rugged

ABS *nm (abrev de* **antilock braking system)** ABS; **frenos A.** antilock brakes

absceso *nm Med* abscess

abscisa *nf Mat* x-axis

absenta *nf (bebida)* absinthe

absentismo *nm Esp* (**a**) *(de terrateniente)* absentee landownership (**b**) *(de trabajador)* **a. laboral** *(justificado)* absence from work; *(injustificado)* absenteeism

ábside *nm Arquit* apse

absolución *nf* (**a**) *Der* acquittal (**b**) *Rel* absolution

absolutismo *nm* absolutism

absolutista *adj & nmf* absolutist

absoluto, -a 1 *adj (no relativo)* absolute; *(completo)* total, absolute

2 en absoluto *loc adv* **nada en a.** nothing at all; **no me gustó en a.** I didn't like it at all; **¿te gusta?/¿te importa? — en a.** do you like it?/do you mind? — not at all

absolver [41] *vt* (**a**) *Der* to acquit (**b**) *Rel* to absolve

absorbente *adj (esponja, material)* absorbent; *(persona, carácter)* demanding; *(actividad)* absorbing

absorber *vt* (**a**) *(líquido, gas)* to absorb; **esta aspiradora no absorbe el polvo muy bien** this vacuum doesn't pick up dust very well; **esta crema se absorbe muy bien** this cream works into the skin very well (**b**) *(consumir)* to take up, to soak up; **esta tarea absorbe mucho tiempo** this task takes up a lot of time (**c**) *(atraer, dominar)* **este trabajo me absorbe mucho** this job takes up a lot of my time; **su mujer le absorbe mucho** his wife is very demanding; **la televisión los absorbe** television dominates their lives (**d**) *(empresa)* to absorb by merger

absorción *nf* (**a**) *(de líquido, gas)* absorption (**b**) *(de empresa)* absorption (by merger)

absorto, -a *adj* absorbed (**en** in)

abstemio, -a 1 *adj* teetotal

2 *nm,f* teetotaler

abstención *nf* abstention; **hubo mucha a.** *(en elecciones)* there was a low turnout

abstencionismo *nm Pol* abstentionism

abstenerse [65] *vpr* (**a**) *(guardarse)* to abstain (**de** from); **se abstuvo de mencionar su embarazo** she refrained from mentioning her pregnancy (**b**) *(en votación)* to abstain; **me abstuve en las últimas elecciones** I didn't vote in the last election

abstinencia *nf* abstinence

abstracción *nf* abstraction

abstracto, -a 1 *adj* abstract

2 *nm* **en a.** in the abstract

abstraer [66] **1** *vt* to consider separately, to detach

2 abstraerse *vpr* to detach oneself (**de** from)

abstraído, -a *adj* lost in thought

abstruso, -a *adj* abstruse

abstuviera *etc ver* **abstenerse**

absuelto, -a *participio ver* **absolver**

absuelvo *etc ver* **absolver**

absurdo, -a 1 *adj* absurd; **lo a. sería que no lo hicieras** it would be absurd for you not to do it

2 *nm* **decir/hacer un a.** to say/do something ridiculous *o* idiotic; **reducción al a.** reductio ad absurdum

abubilla *nf* hoopoe

abuchear *vt* to boo

abucheo *nm* booing

Abu Dabi *n* Abu Dhabi

abuelo, -a *nm,f* (**a**) *(familiar)* grandfather, *f* grandmother; **abuelos** grandparents; *Fam* **¡cuéntaselo a tu abuela!** you're pulling my leg!; *Fam* **éramos pocos y parió la abuela** that was all we needed; *Fam* **no necesitar abuela** to be full of oneself (**b**) *(anciano) (hombre)* old man, old person; *(mujer)* old woman, old person

abuhardillado, -a *adj* **habitación abuhardillada** attic room

abulense 1 *adj* of/from Avila

2 *nmf* person from Avila

abulia *nf* apathy, lethargy

abúlico, -a 1 *adj* apathetic, lethargic

2 *nm,f* apathetic *o* lethargic person

abultado, -a *adj (paquete)* bulky; *(labios)* thick; *(frente)* prominent; **estómago a.** potbelly; **ganaron por una abultada mayoría** they won by a large majority

abultamiento *nm (bulto)* bulkiness

abultar 1 *vt (hinchar) (mejillas)* to puff out; *(cifras, consecuencias)* to exaggerate

2 *vi (ocupar mucho espacio)* to be bulky; *(formar un bulto)* to bulge; **el equipaje abulta mucho** the luggage takes up a lot of room

abundamiento *nm Formal* **a mayor a., presenté las cifras** I provided the figures for further clarification

abundancia *nf* (**a**) *(gran cantidad)* abundance; **en a.** in abundance (**b**) *(riqueza)* plenty, prosperity; **nadar** *o* **vivir en la a.** to be filthy rich

abundante *adj* abundant

abundar *vi* (**a**) *(ser abundante)* to abound; **aquí abundan los camaleones** there are lots of chameleons here (**b**) **a. en** *(tener)* to be rich in; **la región abunda en recursos naturales** the region is rich in natural resources (**c**) **a. en** *(insistir)* to insist on; **en su discurso abundó en la necesidad de recortar gastos** in her speech she insisted on the need to cut costs (**d**) **a. en** *(estar de acuerdo)* to agree completely with

aburguesado, -a *adj* bourgeois

aburguesamiento *nm* bourgeoisification

aburguesarse *vpr* to adopt middle-class ways; **se han aburguesado mucho desde que se casaron** they've become very bourgeois *o* middle-class since they married

aburrido, -a 1 *adj* (**a**) *(harto, fastidiado)* bored; **estar a. de hacer algo** to be fed up with doing sth; *Fam* **estar a. como un hongo** to be bored stiff (**b**) *(que aburre)* boring

2 *nm,f* bore; **¡eres un a.!** you're so boring!

aburrimiento *nm* boredom

aburrir 1 *vt* to bore; **este trabajo me aburre** this job is boring; **aburre a todo el mundo con sus batallitas** he bores everyone with his old stories

2 aburrirse *vpr* to get bored; *(estar aburrido)* to be bored; *(hartarse)* to be bored sick (**de** of); *Fam* **aburrirse como una ostra** to be bored stiff

abusado, -a *Méx Fam* **1** *adj* smart, sharp

2 *interj* **¡a.!** look out!

abusar *vi (excederse)* to go too far; **a. de algo** to abuse sth; **a. del alcohol** to drink to excess; **puedes comer dulces, pero**

sin a. you can eat sweets, but don't overdo it; **a. de alguien** *(aprovecharse)* to take advantage of sb; *(sexualmente)* to sexually abuse sb

abusivo, -a *adj (trato)* very bad, appalling; *(precio)* extortionate

abuso *nm* (a) *(uso excesivo)* abuse (**de** of); **a. de confianza** breach of confidence; *Der* **abusos deshonestos** indecent assault; **a. de poder** abuse of power; **abusos sexuales** sexual abuse (b) *(escándalo)* scandal, sin

abusón, -ona *Esp Fam* **1** *adj (caradura)* selfish; *(matón)* bullying

2 *nm,f (caradura)* selfish person; *(matón)* bully

abyección *nf Formal (bajeza)* vileness; *(pobreza)* wretchedness

abyecto, -a *adj Formal (malo)* vile; *(pobre)* wretched

a. C. *(abrev de* **antes de Cristo**) BC

ACA ['aka] *nm (abrev de* **Automóvil Club Argentino**) = Argentinian automobile association, ≃ AAA

acá *adv* (a) *(lugar)* here; **de a. para allá** back and forth; **más a.** closer; **¡ven a.!** come (over) here! (b) *(tiempo)* **de una semana a.** during the last week; **de un tiempo a.** recently

acabado, -a **1** *adj* (a) *(terminado)* finished (b) *(completo)* perfect, consummate (c) *(fracasado)* finished, ruined

2 *nm (de producto)* finish; *(de piso)* décor; **a. mate/satinado** matt/satin finish

acabar **1** *vt (terminar)* to finish; *(consumir) (provisiones, dinero)* to use up; **hemos acabado el trabajo** we've finished the work; **acabó sus días en el exilio** he ended his days in exile

2 *vi* (a) *(terminar)* to finish, to end; **el asunto acabó mal** the affair finished *o* ended badly; **a. bien** *(película)* to have a happy ending; **cuando acabes, avísame** tell me when you've finished; **a. de trabajar/comer** to finish working/eating; **el cuchillo acaba en punta** the knife ends in a point; *Fam* **¡acabáramos!** at last!, about time!

(b) **a. de hacer algo** *(haber hecho recientemente)* to have just done sth; **acabo de llegar** I've just arrived

(c) **a. con** *(poner fin a)* to put an end to; *(enemigo)* to destroy; *(salud)* to ruin; **acabaron con todas las provisiones** they used up all the provisions; **a. con la paciencia de alguien** to exhaust sb's patience; **a. con alguien** *(matar)* to kill sb; **ese niño va a a. conmigo** that boy will be the death of me!

(d) **a. por hacer algo** to end up doing sth; **acabarán por llamar** *o* **llamando** they'll call eventually *o* sooner or later

(e) *(tener un fin determinado)* to end up; **a. loco** to end up (going) mad; **ese acabará en la cárcel** he'll end up in jail

(f) **no acabo de entenderlo** I can't quite understand it; **no acaba de gustarme del todo** I just don't really like it

(g) **de nunca a.** never-ending; **este proyecto es el cuento de nunca a.** this project just seems to go on and on

3 acabarse *vpr* (a) *(agotarse)* to be used up, to be gone; **se ha acabado la comida** there's no more food left; **se (nos) ha acabado la leche** the milk has run out, we've run out of milk (b) *(terminar) (guerra, película)* to finish, to be over (c) *(consumir) (comida)* to eat up; **¡acábatelo todo y no dejes ni una miga!** make sure you eat it all up! (d) **¡se acabó!** *(¡basta ya!)* that's enough!; **¡cómprate uno nuevo y se acabó!** buy a new one and have done with it

acabóse *nm* **¡es el a.!** it really is the limit!

acacia *nf* acacia

academia *nf* (a) *(colegio)* school, academy; **a. de idiomas** language school; **a. militar** military academy (b) *(sociedad)* academy

academicismo *nm* academicism

académico, -a 1 *adj* academic

2 *nm,f* academician

acaecer [46] *vi Formal* to take place, to occur

acallar *vt* to silence

acalorado, -a *adj* (a) *(por calor)* hot (b) *(por esfuerzo)* flushed (with effort) (c) *(apasionado) (debate)* heated; *(persona)* hot under the collar; *(defensor)* fervent

acalorar 1 *vt* (a) *(dar calor)* to (make) warm (b) *(excitar)* **a. a alguien** to make sb hot under the collar

2 acalorarse *vpr* (a) *(sentir más calor)* to get hot (b) *(excitarse)* to get hot under the collar

acampada *nf (acción)* camping; **ir/estar de a.** to go/be camping; **zona de a. libre** *(en letrero)* free campsite

acampanado, -a *adj (pantalones)* flared

acampar *vi* to camp

acanalado, -a *adj (columna)* fluted; *(tejido)* ribbed; *(hierro)* corrugated

acanalar *vt* (a) *(terreno)* to dig channels in (b) *(plancha)* to corrugate

acantilado *nm* cliff

acanto *nm* acanthus

acantonamiento *nm Mil (acción)* billeting; *(lugar)* billet

acantonar *Mil* *vt* to billet

2 acantonarse *vpr* to be billeted

acaparador, -ora 1 *adj* greedy

2 *nm,f* hoarder

acaparamiento *nm (monopolio)* monopolization; *(en tiempo de escasez)* hoarding

acaparar *vt* (a) *(monopolizar)* to monopolize; *(mercado)* to corner; **acaparaba las miradas de todos** all eyes were upon her; **los atletas alemanes acapararon las medallas** the German athletes swept the board (b) *(aprovisionarse de)* to hoard

acápite *nm Am* paragraph

acaramelado, -a *adj* (a) *Fam (pareja)* lovey-dovey (b) *Fam (afectado)* sugary (sweet) (c) *(con caramelo)* covered in caramel

acariciar 1 *vt* (a) *(persona)* to caress; *(animal, pelo, piel)* to stroke; **la brisa acariciaba su piel** the breeze caressed her skin (b) *(idea, proyecto)* to cherish

2 acariciarse *vpr (mutuamente)* to caress (each other); **se acarició el pelo** she stroked her hair

ácaro *nm* mite

acarrear *vt* (a) *(transportar)* to carry; *(carbón)* to haul (b) *(ocasionar)* to give rise to

acartonado, -a *adj (persona, piel)* wizened

acartonarse *vpr* to become wizened

acaso 1 *adv* perhaps; **¿a. no lo sabías?** are you trying to tell me you didn't know?

2 si acaso *loc adv* **si a. lo vieras...** if you should see him...; **¿te traigo algo? — si a., una botella de vino** can I get you anything? — you could get me a bottle of wine, if you like

3 por si acaso *loc adv* (just) in case

acatamiento *nm* compliance (**de** with)

acatar *vt (normas)* to respect, to comply with; *(órdenes)* to obey

acatarrado, -a *adj* **estar a.** to have a cold

acatarrarse *vpr* to catch a cold

acaudalado, -a *adj* well-to-do, wealthy

acaudillar *vt también Fig* to lead

acceder *vi* (a) *(consentir)* to agree (**a algo/a hacer algo** to sth/to do sth); **a. a una petición** to grant a request (b) *(tener acceso)* **a. a algo** to enter sth, to gain entry to sth (c) *(alcanzar)* **a. al trono** to accede to the throne; **a. al poder** to come to power; **accedió al cargo de presidente** he became president

accesible *adj* (a) *(lugar)* accessible (b) *(persona)* approachable

accésit *nm inv* runner-up prize

acceso *nm* (a) *(entrada)* entrance (**a** to) (b) *(paso)* access (**a** to) (c) *(carretera)* approach road (d) *(ataque)* fit; *(de fiebre, gripe)* bout; **un a. de tos** a fit of coughing

accesorio, -a 1 *adj* incidental, of secondary importance
2 *nm (utensilio)* accessory; **accesorios** *(de moda, automóvil)* accessories; **accesorios opcionales** optional extras

accidentado, -a 1 *adj* **(a)** *(vida)* turbulent; *(viaje)* eventful **(b)** *(terreno, camino)* rough, rugged
2 *nm,f* injured person, victim

accidental *adj* **(a)** *(no esencial)* incidental, of secondary importance **(b)** *(imprevisto)* chance, unforeseen

accidentarse *vpr* to be involved in *o* have an accident

accidente *nm* **(a)** *(suceso)* accident; **tener** *o* **sufrir un a.** to have an accident; **por a.** by accident, accidentally; **a. aéreo** plane crash; **a. de carretera** road *o* traffic accident; **a. de circulación** road *o* traffic accident; **a. de coche** car crash; **a. ferroviario** railroad accident, train crash; **a. laboral** industrial accident; **a. mortal** fatal accident; **a. de trabajo** industrial accident; **a. de tráfico** road *o* traffic accident **(b)** *(irregularidad)* **los accidentes del terreno** the unevenness of the terrain; **a. geográfico** geographical feature

acción *nf* **(a)** *(efecto de hacer)* action; **rocas erosionadas por la a. del viento** rocks eroded by the wind; **en a.** in action, in operation; **entrar** *o* **ponerse en a.** *(persona)* to go into action; **pasar a la a.** to take action **(b)** *(hecho)* deed, act; **una buena a.** a good deed; *Rel* **a. de gracias** thanksgiving; **a. de guerra** act of war **(c)** *Fin* share; **acciones en cartera** stock in portfolio; **acciones ordinariarias** common stocks; **a. de oro** golden share; **acciones preferentes** preferred stock **(d)** *(de relato, película)* action; **la a. tiene lugar en Venezuela** the action takes place in Venezuela; **película de a.** action movie **(e)** *Der* **iniciar acciones legales contra alguien** to take legal action against sb; **a. popular** action brought by the people

accionamiento *nm* activation

accionar 1 *vt* **(a)** *(mecanismo, palanca)* to activate **(b)** *Am Der* to bring a suit against
2 *vi (gesticular)* to gesture, to gesticulate

accionariado *nm Fin* stockholders

accionista *nmf Fin* stockholder

Accra *n* Accra

acebo *nm (hojas)* holly; *(árbol)* holly bush *o* tree

acebuche *nm* wild olive tree

acechanza *nf* observation, surveillance

acechar *vt* to watch, to spy on; **el cazador acechaba a su presa** the hunter was stalking his prey

acecho *nm* observation, surveillance; **estar al a. de** to lie in wait for; *Fig* to be on the lookout for

acedera *nf* sorrel

acéfalo, -a *adj (estado, organización)* leaderless

aceitar *vt (motor)* to lubricate; *(comida)* to pour oil onto

aceite *nm* oil; **a. de cacahuete/colza** peanut/rapeseed oil; **a. esencial** essential oil; **a. de girasol** sunflower oil; **a. de hígado de bacalao** cod-liver oil; **a. de linaza/maíz/oliva/sésamo** linseed/corn/olive/sesame oil; **a. vegetal** vegetable oil

aceitera *nf* oilcan; **aceiteras** cruet set *(for oil and vinegar)*

aceitoso, -a *adj* oily

aceituna *nf* olive; **a. rellena** stuffed olive

aceitunado, -a *adj* olive; **piel aceitunada** olive skin

aceitunero, -a *nm,f* **(a)** *(recogedor)* olive picker **(b)** *(vendedor)* olive merchant

aceituno *nm* olive tree

aceleración *nf* acceleration

acelerada *nf Am* acceleration, burst of speed

acelerado, -a *adj* rapid, quick; *Fís* accelerated; *Fam Fig* **estar a.** to be hyper

acelerador, -ora 1 *adj* accelerating
2 *nm (de coche)* accelerator; **pisar el a.** to step on the accelerator; *Fig* to step on it; *Fís* **a. de partículas** particle accelerator

acelerar 1 *vt (proceso)* to speed up; *(vehículo)* to accelerate; *(motor)* to gun
2 *vi (conductor)* to accelerate
3 acelerarse *vpr (proceso)* to speed up; *(motor)* to accelerate; *Fam Fig (persona)* to get hyper

acelerón *nm (de corredor, coche)* burst of speed; **dar un a.** *(conductor, coche)* to speed up; *Fig* to get a move on

acelga *nf* chard

acendrado, -a *adj Formal* untarnished, pure

acendrar *vt Formal (cualidad, sentimiento)* to refine

acento *nm* **(a)** *(entonación)* accent; **tener a. cubano** to have a Cuban accent **(b)** *(ortográfico)* accent **(c)** **poner el a. en algo** *(enfatizar)* to emphasize sth

acentuación *nf* **(a)** *(de palabra, sílaba)* accentuation **(b)** *(intensificación)* intensification; *(de problema)* worsening; **una a. de las actitudes racistas** a rise in racist attitudes

acentuado, -a *adj* **(a)** *(sílaba)* stressed; *(vocal) (con tilde)* accented **(b)** *(marcado)* marked, distinct

acentuar [4] **1** *vt* **(a)** *(palabra, letra) (al escribir)* to accent, to put an accent on; *(al hablar)* to stress **(b)** *(intensificar)* to accentuate; **la inflación acentuó la crisis** inflation made the recession even worse **(c)** *(recalcar)* to stress, to emphasize; **a. la necesidad de hacer algo** to emphasize the need to do sth
2 acentuarse *vpr* **(a)** *(intensificarse)* to deepen, to increase **(b)** *(llevar acento)* **las consonantes nunca se acentúan** consonants never have an accent

acepción *nf (de palabra, frase)* meaning, sense

aceptable *adj* acceptable

aceptación *nf* **(a)** *(aprobación)* acceptance **(b)** *(éxito)* success, popularity; **tener gran a.** to be very popular

aceptar *vt* to accept; **no aceptaron sus condiciones** they didn't accept his conditions; **no se aceptan cheques** *(en letrero)* we do not take checks; **se aceptan donativos** *(en letrero)* donations welcome

acequia *nf* irrigation channel *o* ditch

acera *nf* **(a)** *(para peatones)* sidewalk **(b)** *(lado de la calle)* side of the street; *Fam* **ser de la otra a.** *(ser homosexual)* to be one of them

acerado, -a *adj* **(a)** *(con acero)* containing steel **(b)** *(fuerte, resistente)* steely, tough **(c)** *(mordaz)* cutting, biting

acerar *vt* **(a)** *(poner aceras)* to pave **(b)** *(convertir en acero)* to turn into steel

acerbo, -a *adj Formal* **(a)** *(áspero)* bitter **(b)** *(mordaz)* caustic, cutting

acerca: acerca de *loc prep* about

acercamiento *nm (de personas, estados)* rapprochement; *(de suceso, fecha)* approach

acercar [59] **1** *vt* **(a)** *(aproximar)* to bring nearer; **acerca la mesa a la pared** *(sin tocar la pared)* move the table closer to the wall; *(tocando la pared)* push *o* move the table up against the wall; **acércame el pan** could you pass me the bread? **(b)** *(llevar)* **la acercó a la estación en moto** he gave her a ride *o* lift to the station on his bike **(c)** *(personas, posturas)* **la desgracia común los acercó** shared misfortune brought them together; **han acercado posturas tras dos semanas de negociaciones** after two weeks of negotiations the two sides are now closer to each other
2 acercarse *vpr* **(a)** *(aproximarse)* to come closer, to approach; **acércate a ver esto** come and have a look at this; **no te acerques al precipicio** don't go near the edge; *Fig* **se acercó a él en busca de protección** she turned to him for protection
(b) *(ir)* to go; *(venir)* to come; **se acercó a la tienda a por pan** she popped out to the stores for some bread; **acércate por aquí un día de estos** come over and see us some time
(c) *(tiempo)* to draw nearer, to approach; **se acerca la**

Navidad Christmas is coming; **nos acercamos al verano** it will soon be summer

(d) *(parecerse)* **acercarse a** to resemble; **su estilo se acerca más a la poesía que a la prosa** his style is closer to poetry than to prose

(e) *(en negociaciones) (países, bandos)* to come closer; **sus posturas se han acercado mucho en las últimas semanas** the differences between them have narrowed considerably over recent weeks

acería *nf* steelworks *(singular)*

acerico *nm* pincushion

acero *nm* steel; **a. galvanizado** galvanized steel; **a. inoxidable** stainless steel; **a. de tungsteno** tungsten steel

acerque *etc ver* **acercar**

acérrimo, -a *adj (defensor)* die-hard, fervent; *(enemigo)* bitter

acertado, -a *adj* **(a)** *(certero) (respuesta)* correct; *(disparo)* on target; *(comentario)* appropriate **(b)** *(oportuno)* good, clever

acertante 1 *adj* winning

2 *nmf* winner; **los máximos acertantes** *(de quiniela, lotería)* the jackpot winners

acertar [3] **1** *vt* **(a)** *(adivinar)* to guess (correctly); **acerté dos respuestas** I got two answers right **(b)** *(blanco)* to hit

2 *vi* **(a)** *(al contestar, adivinar)* to be right; *(al escoger, decidir)* to make a good choice; **acerté a la primera** I got it right first time; **acertó al elegir esa profesión** she made the right decision when she chose that career; **acertaste con su regalo** you chose her present well, you chose just the right present for her **(b)** *(conseguir)* **a. a hacer algo** to manage to do sth; **no acierto a entenderlo** I can't understand it at all; **acertaba a pasar por allí** she happened to pass that way **(c)** *(hallar)* **a. con** to find

acertijo *nm* riddle

acervo *nm* **a. cultural** *(de una nación, región)* cultural heritage; *Pol* **a. comunitario** acquis communautaire; **a. popular** popular culture

acetato *nm Quím* acetate

acético, -a *adj Quím* acetic

acetileno *nm Quím* acetylene

acetona *nf Quím* acetone; *(quitaesmaltes)* nail-polish remover

achacable *adj* attributable **(a** to)

achacar [59] *vt* to attribute **(a** to)

achacoso, -a *adj* **(a)** *(persona)* frail **(b)** *(cosa)* faulty, defective

achampañado, -a *adj* sparkling

achantar *Fam* **1** *vt* to scare

2 *achantarse* *vpr* to be scared

achaparrado, -a *adj* squat

achaque 1 *ver* **achacar**

2 *nm* ailment, complaint

achatado, -a *adj* flattened; **la Tierra está achatada por los polos** the Earth is flattened at the poles

achatar 1 *vt* to flatten

2 *achatarse* *vpr* to level out

achicar [59] **1** *vt* **(a)** *(empequeñecer)* to make smaller; *Fig (acobardar)* to intimidate **(b)** *(agua) (de barco)* to bale out; *(de mina)* to pump out

2 *achicarse* *vpr (acobardarse)* to be intimidated

achicharrado, -a *adj (quemado)* burned to a crisp; *(acalorado)* boiling (hot)

achicharrante *adj (calor, sol)* boiling

achicharrar 1 *vt* **(a)** *(quemar)* to burn **(b)** *(a preguntas)* to plague, to overwhelm **(a** with)

2 *vi (sol, calor)* to be boiling

3 *achicharrarse* *vpr Fam (quemarse)* to fry, to get burned; *(de calor)* to be boiling (hot)

achicoria *nf* chicory

achinado, -a *adj* **(a)** *(ojos)* slanting **(b)** *(persona)* Chinese-looking **(c)** *RP (aindiado)* Indian-looking

achique 1 *ver* **achicar**

2 *nm Náut* baling out

achispado, -a *adj Fam* tipsy

achispar 1 *vt* to make tipsy

2 *achisparse* *vpr* to get tipsy

acholado, -a *adj Bol, Chile, Perú Pey (físicamente)* Indian-looking, mestizo; *(culturalmente)* = who has adopted Indian ways

achuchado, -a *adj Esp Fam* hard, tough; **la vida está muy achuchada** life is very hard, money is tight

achuchar *vt Fam* **(a)** *(abrazar)* to hug **(b)** *(presionar)* to be on at, to badger

achuchón *nm Fam* **(a)** *(abrazo)* big hug **(b)** *(indisposición)* mild illness; **le dio un a.** he got sick

achulado, -a *adj Esp* cocky

achunchar *Andes Fam* **1** *vt (avergonzar)* to shame

2 *achuncharse* *vpr (avergonzarse)* to be ashamed

achurar *vt RP Fam* **(a)** *(acuchillar)* to stab to death **(b)** *(animal)* to disembowel

achuras *nfpl Perú, RP* (dish of) offal

aciago, -a *adj Formal* black, fateful; **un día a.** a fateful day

acicalado, -a *adj* dapper

acicalar 1 *vt* to do up

2 *acicalarse* *vpr* to do oneself up

acicate *nm* **(a)** *(espuela)* spur **(b)** *(estímulo)* incentive

acidez *nf* acidity; **a. (de estómago)** heartburn

acid house *nm* acid house

ácido, -a 1 *adj (bebida, sabor, carácter)* acid, sour; *Quím* acidic

2 *nm* **(a)** *Quím* acid; **á. desoxirribonucleico** deoxyribonucleic acid; **á. graso** fatty acid; **á. sulfúrico** sulfuric acid **(b)** *Fam (droga)* acid

acierto 1 *ver* **acertar**

2 *nm* **(a)** *(a pregunta)* correct answer **(b)** *(en quinielas)* = correct prediction of results in soccer pools entry **(c)** *(habilidad, tino)* good *o* sound judgment; **fue un a. vender las acciones** it was a good *o* smart idea to sell the stocks

ácimo *adj (pan)* unleavened

acimut *nm Astron* azimuth

aclamación *nf* acclamation, acclaim; **por a.** unanimously

aclamar *vt* to acclaim; **fue aclamado emperador** he was acclaimed emperor

aclaración *nf* explanation, clarification

aclarado *nm Esp* rinsing; **dar un a. a algo** to rinse sth, to give sth a rinse

aclarar 1 *vt* **(a)** *Esp (enjuagar)* to rinse **(b)** *(explicar)* to clarify, to explain; **aclaremos una cosa** let's get one thing clear **(c)** *(color)* to make lighter; **el sol aclara el pelo** the sun makes one's hair lighter **(d)** *(lo espeso) (chocolate, sopa)* to thin (down); *(bosque)* to thin out

2 *v impersonal* **ya aclaraba** *(amanecía)* it was getting light; *(se despejaba)* the sky was clearing

3 *aclararse* *vpr* **(a)** *(entender)* to understand; **no me aclaro con este programa** I can't get the hang of this program; **a ver si nos aclaramos** let's see if we can get this straight; **con tres monedas diferentes no hay quién se aclare** with three different currencies nobody knows where they are **(b)** *(explicarse)* **se aclaró la situación** the situation became clear **(c)** *(tener las cosas claras)* **mi jefe no se aclara** my boss doesn't know what he wants **(d)** **aclararse la garganta** to clear one's throat **(e)** **aclararse el pelo** *(de color)* to dye one's hair a lighter color

aclaratorio, -a *adj* explanatory

aclimatación *nf* acclimatization

aclimatar 1 *vt (planta, animal)* to acclimatize **(a** to)

2 *aclimatarse* *vpr* **(a)** *(planta, animal)* to acclimatize **(a** to) **(b)** *(acostumbrarse)* to settle in; **aclimatarse a algo** to get used to sth

acné *nm Med* **a. (juvenil)** acne

ACNUR [ak'nur] *nf (abrev de* **Alto Comisionado de las Naciones Unidas para los Refugiados***)* UNHCR

acobardar 1 *vt* to frighten, to scare
    2 acobardarse *vpr* to get frightened *o* scared; **acobardarse ante algo** to shrink back from sth

acodado, -a *adj* **(a)** *(persona)* leaning (on his/her elbows) **(b)** *(cañería)* elbowed

acodarse *vpr* to lean (**en** on)

acogedor, -ora *adj (país, persona)* friendly, welcoming; *(casa, ambiente)* cozy

acoger [52] **1** *vt* **(a)** *(recibir) (persona)* to welcome; *(idea, noticia)* to receive **(b)** *(dar refugio a)* to take in; **Suecia acogió a los refugiados políticos** Sweden took in the political refugees; **que Dios lo/la acoja en su seno** God rest his/her soul
    2 acogerse *vpr* **acogerse a** *(ley, derecho)* to take refuge in, to have recourse to; **acogerse a un plan de pensiones** to sign up for a pension scheme

acogida *nf* **(a)** *(de persona)* welcome, reception; *(de idea, película)* reception; **tener buena/mala a.** to be well/badly received, to go down well/badly **(b) a. (familiar)** fostering; **familia/hogar de a.** foster parents/home

acojo *ver* **acoger**

acojonado, -a *adj Esp muy Fam* **está acojonada ante la entrevista del martes** she's crapping herself about her interview on Tuesday

acojonante *adj Esp muy Fam* **(a)** *(impresionante)* damn fine **(b)** *(que da miedo)* damn scary

acojonar *Esp muy Fam* **1** *vt* **(a)** *(asustar)* **a. a alguien** to scare the crap out of sb **(b)** *(impresionar)* **nos acojonó con su última película** we were damn impressed by his last movie
    2 *vi (asustar)* to be damn scary
    3 acojonarse *vpr* **me acojoné y no se lo dije** I crapped out of telling her

acojono *nm Esp muy Fam* **me entró un a. terrible** I started crapping myself

acolchado, -a *adj* padded

acolchar *vt* to pad

acólito *nm* **(a)** *(seguidor)* acolyte **(b)** *(monaguillo)* altar boy

acollarar *vt CSur (unir)* to tie together

acomedido, -a *adj Andes, CAm, Méx* accommodating, obliging

acometer 1 *vt* **(a)** *(atacar)* to attack; **le acometió el sueño** he was overcome by tiredness **(b)** *(emprender)* to undertake
    2 *vi (embestir)* **a. contra** to hurtle into

acometida *nf* **(a)** *(ataque)* attack, charge **(b)** *(de luz, gas)* (utilities) connection

acomodadizo, -a *adj* accommodating, easygoing

acomodado, -a *adj* **(a)** *(rico)* well-off, well-to-do **(b)** *(instalado)* ensconced

acomodador, -ora *nm,f Cine & Teatro* usher, *f* usherette

acomodar 1 *vt* **(a)** *(instalar) (persona)* to seat, to install; *(cosa)* to place **(b)** *(adaptar)* to fit
    2 acomodarse *vpr* **(a)** *(instalarse)* to make oneself comfortable; **se acomodó en el sillón** he settled down in the armchair **(b)** *(adaptarse)* to adapt **(a** to); **el presupuesto deberá acomodarse a nuestras necesidades** our budget should meet our needs

acomodaticio, -a *adj (complaciente)* accommodating, easygoing

acomodo *nm* **(a)** *(alojamiento)* accommodations; *Fig* **dar a. a algo** to allow for sth, to take sth into account **(b)** *CSur, Méx (influencia)* wire-pulling, influence; *Méx (empleo temporal)* seasonal job

acompañado, -a *adj* accompanied (**de** by)

acompañamiento *nm* **(a)** *(comitiva) (en entierro)* cortege; *(de rey)* retinue **(b)** *Culin & Mús* accompaniment

acompañante *nmf* companion

acompañar 1 *vt* **(a)** *(ir con)* to go with, to accompany; **su esposa lo acompaña en todos sus viajes** his wife goes with him on all his trips; **a. a alguien a la puerta** to show sb out; **a. a alguien a casa** to walk sb home **(b)** *(hacer compañía)* **a. a alguien** to keep sb company; **la radio me acompaña mucho** I listen to the radio for company **(c)** *(compartir emociones con)* **a. en algo a alguien** to be with sb in sth; **le acompaño en el sentimiento** (you have) my condolences **(d)** *(adjuntar)* to enclose; **acompañó la solicitud de** *o* **con su curriculum vitae** he sent his résumé along with the application **(e)** *(con música)* to accompany **(f)** *(añadir)* **a. la carne con verduras** to serve the meat with vegetables
    2 *vi (hacer compañía)* to provide company
    3 acompañarse *vpr Mús* **canta y se acompaña con el piano** she sings and accompanies herself on the piano

acompasado, -a *adj (crecimiento, desarrollo)* steady; *(pasos)* measured

acompasar *vt* **a. algo** to synchronize sth (**a** with)

acomplejado, -a 1 *adj* **está a. por su calvicie** he has a complex about his bald patch
    2 *nm,f* **es un a.** he has got a complex

acomplejar 1 *vt* to give a complex
    2 acomplejarse *vpr* to develop a complex

Aconcagua *nm* **el A.** Aconcagua

acondicionado, -a *adj* **(a)** *(equipado)* equipped; **estar bien/mal a.** to be in a fit/no fit state **(b) aire a.** air-conditioning

acondicionador *nm (de aire)* air-conditioner

acondicionamiento *nm (reforma)* conversion, upgrading

acondicionar *vt* **(a)** *(reformar)* to convert, to upgrade **(b)** *(preparar)* to prepare, to get ready

aconfesional *adj* secular

acongojado, -a *adj (apenado)* distressed, anguished

acongojar 1 *vt* to distress, to cause anguish to
    2 acongojarse *vpr* to be distressed

aconsejable *adj* advisable

aconsejar *vt* **(a)** *(dar consejos)* **a. a alguien (que haga algo)** to advise sb (to do sth); **le pedí que me aconsejara (acerca de)** I asked him for advice (about); **¿y tú qué me aconsejas que haga?** and what do you think I should do?, and what would your advice be?; **los expertos aconsejan beber dos litros de agua al día** experts recommend that you drink two liters of water a day **(b)** *(hacer aconsejable)* to make advisable; **la delicadeza de la situación aconseja actuar con prudencia** the delicacy of the situation makes caution advisable

acontecer [46] *vi* to take place, to happen

acontecimiento *nm* event; **esto es todo un a.** this is quite an event *o* occasion!; **adelantarse a los acontecimientos** *(precipitarse)* to jump the gun; *(prevenir)* to take preemptive measures

acopiar *vt* to gather

acopio *nm* stock, store; **hacer a. de** *(existencias, comestibles)* to stock up on; *(valor, paciencia)* to summon up

acoplable *adj* attachable (**a** to)

acoplamiento *nm (de piezas)* attachment, connection; *(de módulo espacial)* docking

acoplar 1 *vt* **(a)** *(encajar)* to attach, to fit together **(b)** *(adaptar)* to adapt, to fit
    2 acoplarse *vpr* **(a)** *(adaptarse)* to adjust (**a** to); *(mutuamente)* to adjust to each other **(b)** *(encajar)* to fit together; **acoplarse a algo** to fit sth **(c)** *(micrófono)* to give feedback

acoquinado, -a *adj Fam* timid, nervous

acoquinar *Fam* **1** *vt* to scare
    2 acoquinarse *vpr* to be scared

acorazado, -a 1 *adj* armor-plated
2 *nm (buque de guerra)* battleship

acorazar [14] *vt* to armor-plate, to armor

acordar [63] **1** *vt* **(a)** *(ponerse de acuerdo en)* to agree (on); **a. hacer algo** to agree to do sth; **acordaron que lo harían** they agreed to do it **(b)** *Am (conceder)* to award **(c)** *Am (recordar)* to remind; **acuérdame de llamar** remind me to call
2 acordarse *vpr* **acordarse (de algo/de hacer algo)** to remember (sth/to do sth); **si mal no me acuerdo** if I remember correctly, if my memory serves me right; *Fam* **¡te vas a a.!** *(como amenaza)* you're in for it!, you'll catch it!

acorde 1 *adj (conforme)* in agreement; **estar a. con** to be in keeping with
2 *nm Mús* chord

acordeón *nm* **(a)** *(instrumento)* accordion **(b)** *Col, Méx Fam (en examen)* crib

acordeonista *nmf* accordionist

acordonado, -a *adj* cordoned off

acordonar *vt* **(a)** *(cercar)* to cordon off **(b)** *(atar)* to do o lace up

acornear *vt* to gore

acorralamiento *nm (de malhechor, animal de caza)* cornering

acorralar *vt también Fig* to corner

acortar 1 *vt (longitud, cuerda)* to shorten; *(falda, pantalón)* to take up; *(reunión, viaje)* to cut short
2 *vi* **por este camino acortaremos** we'll get there quicker this way
3 acortarse *vpr (días)* to get shorter

acosado, -a *adj* hounded, pursued

acosador, -ora *adj* relentless, persistent

acosamiento *nm* harassment

acosar *vt* **(a)** *(perseguir)* to pursue relentlessly **(b)** *(hostigar)* to harass

acoso *nm* **(a)** *(persecución)* relentless pursuit **(b)** *(hostigamiento)* harassment; **a. y derribo** constant harrying; **a. sexual** sexual harassment

acostado, -a *adj (en la cama)* in bed; *(tumbado)* lying down

acostar [63] **1** *vt* **(a)** *(en la cama)* to put to bed **(b)** *Náut* to bring alongside
2 acostarse *vpr (irse a la cama)* to go to bed; *(tumbarse)* to lie down; **suele acostarse tarde** he usually goes to bed late; *Fam* **acostarse con alguien** *(tener relaciones sexuales)* to sleep with sb

acostumbrado, -a *adj* **(a)** *(habitual)* usual **(b)** *(habituado)* **estamos acostumbrados** we're used to it; **estar a. a algo/ a hacer algo** to be used to sth/to doing sth

acostumbrar 1 *vt (habituar)* **a. a alguien a algo/a hacer algo** to get sb used to sth/to doing sth
2 *vi (soler)* **a. a hacer algo** to be in the habit of doing sth; **acostumbra a trabajar los sábados** he usually works on Saturdays
3 acostumbrarse *vpr (habituarse)* **te acostumbrarás pronto** you'll soon get used to it; **acostumbrarse a algo/a hacer algo** to get used to sth/to doing sth

acotación *nf (nota)* note in the margin; *Teatro* stage direction

acotado, -a *adj* enclosed

acotamiento *nm* **(a)** *(de terreno, campo)* enclosing, demarcation **(b)** *Méx (arcén)* shoulder

acotar *vt* **(a)** *(terreno, campo)* to enclose, to demarcate; *(tema, competencias)* to delimit **(b)** *(texto)* to write notes in the margin of

acotejar *vt Andes, Carib* to arrange

ACP *(abrev de* **África, el Caribe y el Pacífico)** ACP; **países A.** ACP countries

ácrata *adj & nmf Pol* anarchist

acre 1 *adj* **(a)** *(olor)* acrid, pungent; *(sabor)* bitter **(b)** *(brusco, desagradable)* caustic
2 *nm* acre

acrecentar [3] **1** *vt* to increase
2 acrecentarse *vpr* to increase

acreditación *nf (de periodista)* press card; *(de diplomático)* credentials

acreditado, -a *adj* **(a)** *(médico, abogado)* distinguished; *(marca)* reputable **(b)** *(embajador, representante)* accredited

acreditar *vt* **(a)** *(certificar)* to certify; *(autorizar)* to authorize, to entitle **(b)** *(demostrar)* to prove, to confirm **(c)** *(dar fama a)* to do credit to **(d)** *(embajador)* to accredit **(e)** *Fin* to credit

acreedor, -ora 1 *adj* **hacerse a. de algo** to earn sth
2 *nm,f Fin* creditor

acribillado, -a *adj* **a. a balazos** riddled with bullets

acribillar *vt* to perforate, to pepper with holes; **a. a alguien a balazos** to riddle sb with bullets; **me han acribillado los mosquitos** the mosquitoes have bitten me all over; *Fig* **a. a alguien a preguntas** to fire questions at sb

acrílico, -a 1 *adj* acrylic
2 *nm Arte* painting done in acrylics

acrimonia *nf (aspereza)* acrimony

acriollarse *vpr Am* to adopt local ways

acrisolado, -a *adj* proven, tried and tested

acristalado, -a *adj (terraza, galería)* glazed

acristalar *vt* to glaze

acrítico, -a *adj* uncritical

acritud *nf (aspereza)* acrimony

acrobacia *nf* **(a)** *(en circo)* acrobatics **(b)** *(de avión)* aerobatic maneuver; *Fig* **hacer acrobacias con las cifras** to massage the figures

acróbata *nmf* acrobat

acrobático, -a *adj (ejercicios, espectáculo)* acrobatic

acrónimo *nm* acronym

acrópolis *nf inv* acropolis

acróstico *nm* acrostic

acta *nf* **(a)** **a.(s)** *(de junta, reunión)* minutes; *(de congreso)* proceedings; **constar en a.** to be recorded in the minutes; **levantar a.** to take the minutes **(b)** *(certificado)* certificate; **a. de defunción** death certificate; **a. notarial** affidavit; **a. (de nombramiento)** certificate of appointment

actinia *nf* sea anemone

actitud *nf* **(a)** *(disposición de ánimo)* attitude; **con esa a. no vamos a ninguna parte** we won't get anywhere with that attitude **(b)** *(postura)* posture, position; **el león estaba en a. vigilante** the lion had adopted an alert pose

activación *nf* stimulation

activar *vt (alarma, mecanismo)* to activate; *(explosivo)* to detonate; *(economía)* to stimulate

actividad *nf* activity; **desplegar una gran a.** to be in a flurry of activity; **en a.** active; *Educ* **actividades extra-escolares** extracurricular activities; **actividades para el tiempo libre** leisure activities

activismo *nm Pol* activism

activista *nmf Pol* activist

activo, -a 1 *adj* **(a)** *(dinámico)* active **(b)** *(que trabaja)* working; **en a.** *(en funciones)* on active service; **todavía está en a.** he's still working **(c)** *Gram* active **(d)** *(volcán)* active
2 *nm Fin* assets; **a. circulante** current assets; **a. disponible** liquid assets; **a. fijo** fixed assets; **a. financiero** financial assets; **a. inmovilizado** fixed assets, tangible assets; **activos intangibles** invisible assets; **a. líquido** liquid assets

acto *nm* **(a)** *(acción)* act; **no es responsable de sus actos** he's not responsible for his actions; **hacer a. de presencia** to show one's face; **a. de fe** act of faith; **a. reflejo** reflex action; **a. sexual** sexual act **(b)** *(ceremonia)* ceremony; **actos culturales** cultural events; **a. electoral** election rally **(c)** *Teatro* act **(d)** *(expresiones)* **a. seguido** immediately after; **en el a.** on the spot, there and then; **reparaciones en el a.** repairs done while you wait

actor *nm* actor; **a. de cine** movie actor; **a. de reparto** *o* **secundario** supporting actor

actriz *nf* actress; **a. de cine** movie actress

actuación *nf* (**a**) *(conducta, proceder)* conduct, behavior (**b**) *(interpretación)* performance; **a. estelar** star turn; **a. de gala** gala performance; **a. en vivo** live performance (**c**) *Der* **actuaciones** proceedings

actual *adj* (**a**) *(del momento presente)* present, current; **el a. alcalde** the present *o* current mayor; **las tendencias actuales de la moda** current fashion trends; **el a. campeón del mundo** the current *o* reigning world champion (**b**) *(de moda)* modern, present-day; **tiene un diseño muy a.** it has a very modern *o* up-to-date design (**c**) *(de interés)* topical; **un tema muy a.** a very topical issue

actualidad *nf* (**a**) *(momento presente)* current situation; **la a. política** the current political situation; **cuentan en la a. con un millón de socios** they currently have a million members; **estas piezas en la a. se fabrican en serie** these parts are mass-produced nowadays (**b**) *(de asunto, noticia)* topicality; **estar de a.** to be topical; **una noticia de rabiosa a.** an extremely topical news item; **temas de a.** current affairs (**c**) *(noticia)* news *(singular)*; **la a. informativa** the news; **la a. deportiva** the sports news; **ser a.** to be making the news (**d**) *(vigencia)* relevance to modern society; **sus libros siguen teniendo gran a.** her books are still very relevant today

actualización *nf* *(de información, datos)* updating; *(de tecnología, industria)* modernization; *Inform (de software, hardware)* upgrade

actualizar [14] *vt (información, datos)* to update; *(tecnología, industria)* to modernize; *Inform (nueva versión)* to upgrade

actualmente *adv* (**a**) *(en estos tiempos)* these days, nowadays; **a. casi nadie viaja en burro** hardly anyone travels by donkey nowadays (**b**) *(en este momento)* at the (present) moment; **su padre está a. en paradero desconocido** his father's present whereabouts are unknown

actuar [4] *vi* (**a**) *(obrar, producir efecto)* to act; **actúa de** *o* **como escudo** it acts *o* serves as a shield; **este tranquilizante actúa directamente sobre los centros nerviosos** this tranquilizer acts directly on the nerve centers (**b**) *Der* to undertake proceedings (**c**) *(en película, teatro)* to perform, to act; **en esta película actúa Victoria Abril** Victoria Abril appears in this movie

actuario, -a *nm,f* (**a**) *Der* clerk of the court (**b**) *Fin* **a. de seguros** actuary

acuarela *nf (técnica, pintura)* watercolor

acuarelista *nmf (pintor)* watercolorist

acuario 1 *nm* (**a**) *(edificio, pecera grande)* aquarium; *(pecera)* fish tank (**b**) *(zodiaco)* Aquarius; *Esp* **ser a.** to be (an) Aquarius
 2 *nmf Esp (persona)* Aquarius

acuartelamiento *nm Mil* (**a**) *(acción)* confinement to barracks (**b**) *(lugar)* barracks

acuartelar *vt Mil* (**a**) *(alojar)* to quarter (**b**) *(retener)* to confine to barracks

acuático, -a *adj* aquatic

acuchillador *nm (de suelos)* floor sander

acuchillar *vt* (**a**) *(apuñalar)* to stab (**b**) *(suelo de madera)* to sand

acuciante *adj* urgent, pressing

acuciar *vt* (**a**) *(instar)* to goad; **el deseo me acuciaba** I was driven by desire (**b**) *(ser urgente)* **le acucia encontrar un nuevo trabajo** he urgently needs to find a new job

acuclillarse *vpr (agacharse)* to squat (down)

acudir *vi* (**a**) *(ir)* to go; *(venir)* to come; **a. a una cita/un mitin** to turn up for an appointment/at a rally; **nadie acudió a mi llamada de auxilio** no one answered my cry for help; *Fig* **a. a la mente** to come to mind (**b**) *(recurrir)* **a. a**

alguien to turn to sb; **si necesitas ayuda, puedes a. a mí** if you need help you can come to *o* ask me

acueducto *nm* aqueduct

acuerdo 1 *ver* **acordar**
 2 *nm* (**a**) *(pacto)* agreement; **llegar a un a.** to reach (an) agreement; **A. General sobre Aranceles y Comercio** General Agreement on Tariffs and Trade; *Ind* **a. marco** framework agreement; *Ind* **a. sobre productividad** productivity agreement; **a. tácito** tacit agreement (**b**) *Am (recuerdo)* **hazme a. de comprar pan** remind me to buy some bread
 3 de acuerdo *loc adv* (**a**) *(bien)* all right (**b**) **de a. con** *(conforme a)* in accordance with; **estar de a. (con alguien/en hacer algo)** to agree (with sb/to do sth); **ponerse de a. (con alguien)** to agree (with sb), to come to an agreement (with sb); **de común a.** by common consent

acuesto *etc ver* **acostar**

acuicultivo *nm* hydroponics *(singular)*

acuicultura *nf (explotación de recursos)* aquiculture, aquaculture; *(de peces)* fish farming

acuífero *nm Geol* aquifer

acumulación *nf* accumulation

acumulador *nm Elec* accumulator, storage battery; **a. de calor** (electric thermal) storage heater

acumular 1 *vt* to accumulate; **le gusta a. recuerdos de sus viajes** she likes collecting souvenirs of her trips
 2 acumularse *vpr* to accumulate, to build up; **se me acumula el trabajo** work is piling up on me

acumulativo, -a *adj* cumulative

acunar *vt (en cuna)* to rock; *(en brazos)* to cradle

acuñar *vt (moneda)* to mint; *(palabra)* to coin

acuoso, -a *adj* (**a**) *(que contiene agua)* watery (**b**) *(jugoso)* juicy

acupuntor, -ora *nm,f* acupuncturist

acupuntura *nf* acupuncture

acurrucarse [59] *vpr* to crouch down; *(por frío)* to huddle up; *(por miedo)* to cower; **se acurrucó en un sillón** he curled up in an armchair

acusación *nf* (**a**) *(inculpación)* charge (**b**) *Der* **la a.** the prosecution; **a. particular** private action

acusado, -a 1 *adj (marcado)* marked, distinct
 2 *nm,f (procesado)* accused, defendant

acusador, -ora *adj* accusing

acusar 1 *vt* (**a**) *(culpar)* to accuse; *Der* to charge; **lo acusaron de asesinato** he was accused of *o* charged with murder (**b**) *(mostrar)* to show; **su rostro acusaba el paso del tiempo** his face showed the passage of time; **a. el golpe** to show the effects; **su espalda acusó el esfuerzo** the effort had taken its toll on his back (**c**) *(recibo)* to acknowledge; **acusamos la recepción del paquete** we acknowledge receipt of your package
 2 acusarse *vpr* (**a**) *(mutuamente)* to blame one another (**de** for) (**b**) *(uno mismo)* **acusarse de haber hecho algo** to confess to having done sth

acusativo *nm Gram* accusative

acusatorio, -a *adj Der* accusatory

acuse *nm* **a. de recibo** acknowledgment of receipt

acusica *nmf Fam* telltale

acústica *nf* (**a**) *(ciencia)* acoustics *(singular)* (**b**) *(de local)* acoustics

acústico, -a *adj* acoustic

ADA ['aða] *nf (abrev de* **Ayuda del Automovilista***)* = Spanish motoring association, ≃ AAA

adagio *nm* (**a**) *(sentencia breve)* adage (**b**) *Mús* adagio

adalid *nm* champion

Adán *n pr* Adam

adán *nm Fam* ragamuffin, scruffy man; *Fam* **ir hecho un a.** to be scruffily dressed, to go about in rags

adaptable *adj* adaptable

adaptación *nf* (**a**) *(acomodación)* adaptation (**a** to); **a. al medio** adaptation to the environment (**b**) *(de libro, obra de teatro)* adaptation; **la película es una buena a. del libro** the movie is a good adaptation of the book

adaptado, -a *adj* suited (**a** to)

adaptador *nm Elec* adapter

adaptar 1 *vt* (**a**) *(modificar)* to adapt (**a** to); **un modelo adaptado a condiciones desérticas** a model adapted to suit desert conditions (**b**) *(libro, obra de teatro)* to adapt (**a** for)

2 adaptarse *vpr* to adjust (**a** to); **no se ha adaptado al clima local** he hasn't adjusted *o* got used to the local climate; **el nuevo local se adapta a las necesidades de la tienda** the new premises meet *o* are well suited to the store's requirements

Addis Abeba *n* Addis Ababa

adecentar 1 *vt* to tidy up

2 adecentarse *vpr* to smarten oneself up

adecuación *nf Formal (idoneidad, conveniencia)* suitability

adecuado, -a *adj* appropriate, suitable

adecuar 1 *vt* to adapt

2 adecuarse *vpr (ser apropiado)* to be appropriate (**a** for); **el programa puede adecuarse a las necesidades del cliente** the program can be adapted to the customer's needs; **este apartamento se adecua a nuestras necesidades** this apartment is well suited to *o* meets our needs

adefesio *nm Fam* (**a**) *(persona)* fright, sight (**b**) *(cosa)* eyesore, monstrosity

a. de JC. *(abrev de* **antes de Jesucristo**) BC

adelantado, -a 1 *adj* advanced; **Galileo fue un hombre a. a su tiempo** Galileo was a man ahead of his time; **llevo el reloj a.** my watch is fast

2 por adelantado *loc adv* in advance

adelantamiento *nm (en carretera)* overtaking

adelantar 1 *vt* (**a**) *(vehículo, competidor)* to overtake
(**b**) *(mover hacia adelante)* to move forward; *(pie, reloj)* to put forward; **adelantó su coche para que yo pudiera aparcar** she moved her car forward so I could park
(**c**) *(en el tiempo) (reunión, viaje)* to bring forward; **me quedaré en la oficina para a. el trabajo** I'm going to stay on late at the office to get ahead with my work
(**d**) *(dinero)* to pay in advance; **pedí que me adelantaran la mitad del sueldo de julio** I asked for an advance of half of my wages for July
(**e**) *(información)* to release; **el gobierno adelantará los primeros resultados a las ocho** the government will announce the first results at eight o'clock; **no podemos a. nada más por el momento** we can't tell you *o* say any more for the time being
(**f**) *(mejorar)* to promote, to advance; **¿qué adelantas con eso?** what do you hope to gain *o* achieve by that?

2 *vi* (**a**) *(progresar)* to make progress; **la informática ha adelantado mucho en la última década** there has been a lot of progress in information technology over the past decade
(**b**) *(reloj)* to be fast (**c**) *(en carretera)* to overtake; **prohibido a.** *(en señal)* no overtaking

3 adelantarse *vpr* (**a**) *(en el tiempo)* to be early; *(frío, verano)* to arrive early; **este año se ha adelantado la primavera** spring has come early this year (**b**) *(en el espacio)* to go on ahead; **me adelanto para comprar el pan** I'll go on ahead and buy the bread (**c**) *(reloj)* to gain; **mi reloj se adelanta cinco minutos al día** my watch is gaining five minutes a day (**d**) *(anticiparse)* **adelantarse a alguien** to beat sb to it; **se adelantó a mis deseos** she anticipated my wishes; **se adelantaron a la competencia** they stole a march on their rivals

adelante 1 *adv* forward, ahead; **(de ahora) en a.** from now on; **más a.** *(en el tiempo)* later (on); *(en el espacio)* further on;

sacar a. *(proyecto, empresa)* to rescue; **salimos a.** we put our problems behind us; *Am* **a. de** in front of

2 *interj* **¡a.!** *(¡siga!)* go ahead!; *(¡pase!)* come in!

adelanto *nm (técnico, de dinero)* advance

adelfa *nf* oleander

adelgazamiento *nm* slimming

adelgazante *adj* slimming

adelgazar [14] **1** *vt (kilos)* to lose

2 *vi* to lose weight, to slim

ademán *nm (gesto) (con las manos)* gesture; *(con la cara)* face, expression; **hizo a. de decir algo/huir** he made as if to say sth/run away

además *adv* moreover, besides; *(también)* also; **a. hay que tener en cuenta que...** it should, moreover, be remembered that...; **es guapa y a. inteligente** she's beautiful, and clever too; **no sólo es demasiado grande, sino que a. te queda mal** it's not just that it's too big, it doesn't suit you either; **a. de** as well as; **a. de simpático es inteligente** as well as being nice, he's intelligent

ADENA [a'ðena] *nf (abrev de* **Asociación para la Defensa de la Naturaleza**) = Spanish nature conservancy organization

adentrarse *vpr* **a. en** *(jungla, barrio)* to go deep into; *(asunto)* to study in depth

adentro 1 *adv* inside; **quédate a. y no salgas** stay inside *o* indoors and don't go out; **le clavó el cuchillo muy a.** he plunged the knife deep into her; **tierra a.** inland; **mar a.** out to sea; *Am* **a. de** inside

2 adentros *nmpl* **para mis/tus/etc adentros** *(pensar, decir)* to myself/yourself/etc; **sonrió para sus adentros** he smiled to himself

adepto, -a 1 *adj (partidario)* supporting; **ser a. a** to be a follower of

2 *nm,f* follower (**a** *o* **de** of)

aderezar [14] *vt* (**a**) *(sazonar) (ensalada)* to dress; *(comida)* to season (**b**) *(conversación)* to liven up, to spice up

aderezo *nm* (**a**) *(aliño) (de ensalada)* dressing; *(de comida)* seasoning (**b**) *(adorno)* adornment

adeudar *vt* (**a**) *(deber)* to owe (**b**) *Fin* to debit; **a. 500 euros a una cuenta** to debit 500 euros to an account

2 adeudarse *vpr* to get into debt

adeudo *nm* (**a**) *Fin* debit (**b**) *Méx (deuda)* debt

adherencia *nf* (**a**) *(de sustancia, superficie)* stickiness, adhesion; *Aut (de ruedas)* road-hugging (**b**) *(parte añadida)* appendage

adherente *adj* adhesive, sticky

adherir [62] **1** *vt* to stick

2 adherirse *vpr* (**a**) *(pegarse)* to stick (**b**) **adherirse a** *(opinión, idea)* to adhere to; *(partido, asociación)* to join

adhesión *nf* (**a**) *(a opinión, idea)* support (**a** of) (**b**) *(a una organización)* entry (**a** into)

adhesivo, -a 1 *adj* adhesive

2 *nm* (**a**) *(pegatina)* sticker (**b**) *(sustancia)* adhesive

adhiero *etc ver* **adherir**

adhiriera *etc ver* **adherir**

ad hoc *adj* ad hoc; **una medida a.** an ad hoc measure

adicción *nf* addiction (**a** to)

adición *nf* addition

adicional *adj* additional

adictivo, -a *adj* addictive

adicto, -a 1 *adj* addicted (**a** to)

2 *nm,f* addict; **un a. a la heroína/al tabaco** a heroin/nicotine addict

adiestrador, -ora *nm,f (de animales)* trainer; **a. de perros** dog handler

adiestramiento *nm* training

adiestrar *vt* to train; **a. a alguien en algo/para hacer algo** to train sb in sth/to do sth

adinerado, -a *adj* wealthy

adiós (*pl* **adioses**) **1** *nm* goodbye; *Fig* **decirle a. a algo** to wave o kiss sth goodbye; **a. a mi esperado fin de semana tranquilo** there go my hopes of a quiet weekend
  2 *interj* **¡a.!** goodbye!; *(al cruzarse con alguien)* hello!

adiposidad *nf Med* fattiness

adiposo, -a *adj Med* fatty

aditamento *nm (complemento)* accessory; *(cosa añadida)* addition

aditivo *nm* additive

adivinador, -ora *nm,f* fortune-teller

adivinanza *nf* riddle

adivinar 1 *vt* **(a)** *(acertar)* to guess; **¡adivina en qué mano está la moneda!** guess which hand the coin is in!; **adivinó el acertijo** he worked out the riddle **(b)** *(predecir)* to foretell; *(el futuro)* to tell **(c)** *(entrever)* **la propuesta deja a. las verdaderas intenciones de los generales** this proposal reveals the generals' true intentions
  2 adivinarse *vpr (vislumbrarse)* to be visible; **el castillo apenas se adivinaba en la lejanía** the castle could just be made out in the distance

adivino, -a *nm,f* fortune-teller; **no soy a.** I'm not psychic

adjetivar *vt Gram* to use adjectivally

adjetivo, -a 1 *adj* adjectival
  2 *nm Gram* adjective; **a. calificativo** qualifying adjective; **a. demostrativo** demonstrative adjective; **a. numeral** quantitative adjective

adjudicación *nf* awarding; *Com* **a. por concurso público** competitive tendering

adjudicar [59] **1** *vt (asignar)* to award
  2 adjudicarse *vpr (apropiarse)* to take for oneself

adjudicatario, -a *nm,f* awardee

adjuntar *vt* to enclose *(in letter)*

adjunto, -a 1 *adj* **(a)** *(incluido)* enclosed; **a. le remito…** please find enclosed… **(b)** *(auxiliar)* assistant; **profesor a.** assistant professor
  2 *nm,f (auxiliar)* assistant

adlátere *nmf Formal* cohort, acolyte

adminículo *nm* gadget

administración *nf* **(a)** *(de empresa)* administration, management; **a. de recursos** resource management **(b)** *(oficina)* manager's office; **la A.** *(Gobierno)* the Administration; **a. de justicia** legal system; **a. local** local government; **a. pública** civil service **(c)** *(de medicamentos)* administering

administrador, -ora 1 *nm,f (de empresa)* manager; *(de bienes ajenos)* administrator
  2 *nm Inform* **a. de archivos** file manager

administrar 1 *vt* **(a)** *(empresa, finca)* to manage, to run; *(casa)* to run; *(país)* to govern, to run; *(recursos)* to manage; **a. justicia** to administer justice **(b)** *(medicamento, sacramentos)* to administer
  2 administrarse *vpr (organizar dinero)* to manage one's finances

administrativo, -a 1 *adj* administrative
  2 *nm,f* white-collar worker

admirable *adj* admirable

admiración *nf* **(a)** *(sentimiento)* admiration **(b)** *(signo ortográfico)* exclamation point

admirador, -ora *nm,f* admirer

admirar 1 *vt* **(a)** *(personaje, obra de arte)* to admire; **lo admiro por su honradez** I admire his honesty; **ser de a.** to be admirable **(b)** *(sorprender)* to amaze; **me admira su descaro** I can't believe his cheek
  2 admirarse *vpr* to be amazed; **admirarse de algo** to be amazed at sth

admisibilidad *nf* acceptability

admisible *adj* acceptable

admisión *nf (de persona)* admission; *(de solicitudes)* acceptance; **reservado el derecho de a.** *(en letrero)* the management reserves the right to refuse admission

admitir *vt* **(a)** *(dejar entrar)* to admit, to allow in; **a. a alguien en** to admit sb to; **no se admiten perros** *(en letrero)* no dogs; **no se admite la entrada a menores de dieciocho años** *(en letrero)* no admittance for under-eighteens
  (b) *(reconocer)* to admit; **admito que estaba equivocado** I admit I was wrong
  (c) *(aceptar)* to accept; **admitimos todas las tarjetas de crédito** we accept all credit cards
  (d) *(permitir, tolerar)* to allow, to permit; **no admite ni un error** he won't stand for a single mistake
  (e) *(tener capacidad para)* to hold; **la sala admite doscientas personas** the room holds o has room for two hundred people

admón. *(abrev de* **administración**) admin.

admonición *nf Formal* warning

admonitorio, -a *adj Formal* warning; **voz admonitoria** voice with a note of warning

ADN *nm (abrev de* **ácido desoxirribonucleico**) DNA

ad nauseam *adv* ad nauseam

adobado, -a *adj* marinated

adobar *vt* to marinate

adobe *nm* adobe

adobo *nm (acción)* marinating; *(salsa)* marinade; **en a.** marinated

adocenado, -a *adj* mediocre, run-of-the-mill

adocenarse *vpr* to lapse into mediocrity

adoctrinamiento *nm (de ideas)* indoctrination; *(enseñanza)* instruction

adoctrinar *vt (inculcar ideas)* to indoctrinate; *(enseñar)* to instruct

adolecer [46] *vi* **a. de** *(enfermedad)* to suffer from; *(defecto)* to be guilty of

adolescencia *nf* adolescence

adolescente *adj & nmf* adolescent

adonde 1 *adv* where; **la ciudad a. vamos** the city we are going to
  2 *prep Fam (a casa de)* **vamos a. la abuela** we're going to granny's

adónde *ver* **dónde**

adondequiera *adv* wherever

adonis *nm inv* Adonis, handsome young man

adopción *nf (de hijo, moda, decisión)* adoption; **Uruguay es mi país de a.** Uruguay is my adopted country

adoptar *vt* **(a)** *(hijo, nacionalidad)* to adopt **(b)** *(medida, decisión)* to take; **a. medidas para luchar contra el desempleo** to take measures to combat unemployment **(c)** *(forma)* **el insecto adopta la forma de una bola para protegerse** the insect curls itself into a ball in order to protect itself; **su timidez adopta la forma de agresividad** his shyness manifests itself as aggressiveness

adoptivo, -a *adj (hijo, país)* adopted; *(padre)* adoptive

adoquín *nm* **(a)** *(piedra)* cobblestone **(b)** *Fam (persona)* blockhead

adoquinado, -a 1 *adj* cobbled
  2 *nm* **(a)** *(suelo)* cobbles **(b)** *(acción)* cobbling

adoquinar *vt* to cobble

adorable *adj (persona)* adorable; *(lugar, película)* wonderful

adoración *nf (de dios, ídolo)* adoration, worship; *(de persona, comida)* adoration; **sentir a. por alguien** to worship sb; *Rel* **la A. de los Reyes Magos** the Adoration of the Magi

adormecer [46] **1** *vt* **(a)** *(producir sueño)* to lull to sleep **(b)** *(aplacar) (miedo, ira)* to calm; *(pena, dolor)* to alleviate, to lessen
  2 adormecerse *vpr* to nod off, to drop off

adormidera *nf* poppy

adormilado, -a *adj (dormido)* dozing; *(con sueño)* sleepy

adormilarse *vpr* to doze

adornado, -a *adj* decorated

adornar 1 *vt* (**a**) *(decorar)* to decorate (**b**) *(aderezar)* to adorn (**con** with)

    2 *vi* to be decorative; **hace falta algo que adorne** we need to add some sort of decorative touch

adorno *nm* decoration; **de a.** *(árbol, figura)* decorative; *Fam Fig* **estar de a.** *(persona)* to be a waste of space

adosado, -a *adj (casa)* semidetached

adosar *vt* **a. algo a algo** to push sth up against sth

adquirir [5] *vt* (**a**) *(comprar)* to acquire, to purchase (**b**) *(conseguir) (conocimientos, hábito, cultura)* to acquire; *(éxito, popularidad)* to achieve

adquisición *nf* (**a**) *(compra, cosa comprada)* purchase; **ser una buena/mala a.** to be a good/bad buy (**b**) *(de conocimiento, hábito)* acquisition

adquisitivo, -a *adj* **poder a.** purchasing power

adrede *adv* on purpose, deliberately

adrenalina *nf Med* adrenalin

Adriático *nm* **el (mar) A.** the Adriatic (Sea)

adscribir 1 *vt* (**a**) *(asignar)* to assign (**b**) *(destinar)* to appoint

    2 adscribirse *vpr* **adscribirse a** *(grupo, partido)* to become a member of; *(ideología)* to subscribe to

adscrito, -a 1 *participio ver* **adscribir**

    2 *adj* assigned

ADSL *nm (abrev de* **asymmetric digital subscriber line**) ADSL

aduana *nf* customs; **derechos de a.** customs duty; **pasar por la a.** to go through customs

aduanero, -a 1 *adj* customs; **controles aduaneros** customs controls

    2 *nm,f* customs officer

aducir [18] *vt (motivo, pretexto)* to give, to furnish; **"estaba muy cansado", adujo** "I was very tired," he explained

adueñarse *vpr* **a. de** *(apoderarse de)* to take over, to take control of; *Fig (dominar)* to take hold of; **el pánico se adueñó de ellos** panic took hold of them

adujera *etc ver* **aducir**

adulación *nf* flattery

adulador, -ora 1 *adj* flattering

    2 *nm,f* flatterer

adular *vt* to flatter

adulón, -ona *nm,f* toady

adulteración *nf* adulteration

adulterar *vt* (**a**) *(alimento)* to adulterate (**b**) *(falsear)* to doctor, to distort

adulterio *nm* adultery

adúltero, -a 1 *adj* adulterous

    2 *nm,f* adulterer, *f* adulteress

adulto, -a 1 *adj* adult; **la edad adulta** adult age, adulthood

    2 *nm,f* adult; **película para adultos** adult movie

adusto, -a *adj* dour

aduzco *ver* **aducir**

advenedizo, -a *adj & nm,f* upstart

advenimiento *nm (llegada)* advent; *(ascenso al trono)* accession

adventismo *nm* (Seventh-Day) Adventism

adventista *adj & nmf* (Seventh-Day) Adventist

adverbial *adj Gram* adverbial

adverbio *nm Gram* adverb; **a. de cantidad/lugar/modo/ tiempo** adverb of degree/place/manner/time

adversario, -a *nm,f* adversary

adversativo, -a *adj Gram* adversative

adversidad *nf* adversity

adverso, -a *adj (condiciones)* adverse; *(destino)* unkind; *(suerte)* bad; *(viento)* unfavorable

advertencia *nf* warning; **una a.** a word of warning; **servir de a.** to serve as a warning; **a. previa** advance warning

advertir [62] *vt* (**a**) *(notar)* to notice (**b**) *(prevenir, avisar)* to warn; **me advirtió del peligro** he warned me of the danger; **te advierto que no me sorprende** mind you, it doesn't surprise me

adviento *nm Rel* Advent

advierto *etc ver* **advertir**

advirtiera *etc ver* **advertir**

adyacente *adj* adjacent

AEE *nf (abrev de* **Agencia Espacial Europea**) ESA

Aenor *nf (abrev de* **Asociación Española para la Normalización y Certificación**) = Spanish body which certifies quality and safety standards for manufactured goods, ≃ ANSI

aeración *nf* aeration

aéreo, -a *adj (del aire)* aerial; *(de la aviación)* air; **base aérea** airbase; **controlador a.** air traffic controller

aerobic, aeróbic *nm* aerobics *(singular)*

aeróbico, -a *adj* aerobic

aerobio, -a *adj Biol* aerobic

aeroclub (*pl* **aeroclubes** *o* **aeroclubs**) *nm* flying club

aerodeslizador *nm* hovercraft

aerodinámica *nf* aerodynamics *(singular)*

aerodinámico, -a *adj* (**a**) *Fís* aerodynamic (**b**) *(forma, línea)* streamlined

aeródromo *nm* airfield

aeroembolismo *nm Med* decompression sickness

aeroespacial *adj* aerospace

aerofaro *nm Av* beacon

aerógrafo *nm Arte* airbrush

aerolínea *nf* airline

aerolito *nm* aerolite

aeromodelismo *nm* airplane modeling

aeromozo, -a *nm,f Am* (air) steward, *f* (air) stewardess *or* hostess

aeronauta *nmf* aeronaut

aeronáutica *nf* aeronautics *(singular)*

aeronáutico, -a *adj* aeronautic

aeronaval *adj* **fuerzas aeronavales** air and sea forces

aeronave *nf (avión, helicóptero)* aircraft; *(dirigible)* airship

aeroplano *nm* airplane

aeropuerto *nm* airport

aerosol *nm* aerosol (spray)

aerospacial *adj* aerospace

aerostático, -a *adj* **globo a.** hot-air balloon

aerostato, aeróstato *nm* hot-air balloon

aerotaxi *nm* light aircraft *(for hire)*

aerotransportado, -a *adj (tropas, polen)* airborne

aerotransportar *vt* to airlift

afabilidad *nf* affability

afable *adj* affable

afamado, -a *adj* famous

afán *nm* (**a**) *(esfuerzo)* hard work; **con a.** energetically, enthusiastically (**b**) *(anhelo)* urge (**c**) **lo único que le mueve es el a. de lucro** he's only interested in money

afanador, -ora *nm,f Méx* cleaner

afanar 1 *vt Fam (robar)* to pinch, to swipe

    2 afanarse *vpr (esforzarse)* to do everything one can

afanoso, -a *adj (trabajador, diligente)* keen, eager

afasia *nf Psi* aphasia

afear *vt* to make ugly, to scar; **a. a alguien su conducta** *(criticar)* to condemn sb's behavior

afección *nf* complaint, disease; **a. cutánea/intestinal/del riñón** skin/bowel/kidney complaint

afectación *nf* affectation

afectado, -a 1 *adj* (**a**) *(amanerado)* affected (**b**) *(afligido)* upset, badly affected

  2 *nm,f* victim; **los afectados por las inundaciones serán indemnizados** the people affected by the floods will receive compensation

afectar *vt* (**a**) *(influir)* to affect; **las medidas afectan a los pensionistas** the measures affect pensioners (**b**) *(afligir)* to upset, to affect badly; **le afectó mucho la muerte de su hermano** his brother's death hit him hard (**c**) *(alterar)* to damage; **a esta madera le afecta mucho la humedad** this wood is easily damaged by damp (**d**) *(simular)* to affect, to feign; **afectó enfado** he feigned *o* affected anger

afectísimo, -a *adj (en carta)* **suyo a.** Best wishes

afectividad *nf* emotions; **la a. en el niño** the emotional world of the child

afectivo, -a *adj (emocional)* emotional; **tener problemas afectivos** to have emotional problems

afecto *nm* affection, fondness; **sentir a. por alguien** to be fond of sb

afectuosamente *adv (en carta)* (yours) affectionately

afectuoso, -a *adj* affectionate, loving

afeitada *nf Am (del pelo, barba)* shave

afeitado *nm* (**a**) *(del pelo)* shave; **un a. suave** a smooth shave (**b**) *Taurom* = blunting of the bull's horns for safety reasons

afeitar 1 *vt* (**a**) *(barba, pelo, persona)* to shave (**b**) *Taurom* = to blunt the bull's horns for safety reasons

  2 afeitarse *vpr (uno mismo)* to shave; **se afeitó la barba** he shaved his beard off; **se afeitó las piernas** she shaved her legs

afeite *nm Anticuado (cosmético)* makeup; **no usa afeites** she doesn't use any makeup

afelpado, -a *adj* plush

afeminado, -a 1 *adj* effeminate

  2 *nm* effeminate man

afeminarse *vpr* to become effeminate

aferrar 1 *vt* to grab (hold of)

  2 aferrarse *vpr también Fig* **aferrarse a algo** to cling to sth

affaire [a'fer] *nm* affair

affmo., -a., afmo., -a. *(abrev de* **afectísimo, -a)** *(en carta)* **suyo a.** *(si se desconoce el nombre del destinatario)* yours faithfully; *(si se conoce el nombre del destinatario)* yours sincerely

Afganistán *n* Afghanistan

afgano, -a *adj & nm,f* Afghan

afianzamiento *nm* (**a**) *(de construcción)* reinforcement (**b**) *(de situación, relación)* consolidation

afianzar [14] **1** *vt* (**a**) *(construcción)* to reinforce (**b**) *(situación, relación)* to consolidate

  2 afianzarse *vpr* to steady oneself; **se afianzó en su opinión** he became more convinced of his opinion; **afianzarse en una posición** to establish oneself in a position

afiche *nm Am* poster

afición *nf* (**a**) *(inclinación)* fondness, liking; **por a.** as a hobby; **tener a. a algo** to be keen on sth (**b**) *(aficionados)* fans; **la a. futbolística** soccer fans; **la a. taurina** followers of bullfighting

aficionado, -a 1 *adj* (**a**) *(interesado)* keen; **ser a. a algo** to be keen on sth; **el público a. al cine** the moviegoing public (**b**) *(no profesional)* amateur

  2 *nm,f* (**a**) *(interesado)* fan; **los aficionados a los toros** followers of bullfighting, bullfighting fans; **un a. al cine** a keen moviegoer; **un gran a. a la música clásica** a great lover of classical music (**b**) *(no profesional)* amateur; **un trabajo de aficionados** an amateurish piece of work

aficionar 1 *vt* **a. a alguien a algo** to make sb keen on sth

  2 aficionarse *vpr* to become keen (**a** on)

afijo, -a *Gram* **1** *adj* affixed

  2 *nm* affix

afilado, -a 1 *adj* (**a**) *(cuchillo, punta)* sharp (**b**) *(dedos, rasgos)* pointed (**c**) *(comentario, crítica)* cutting

  2 *nm* sharpening

afilador, -ora 1 *adj* sharpening

  2 *nm,f (persona)* knife grinder

  3 *nm (objeto)* sharpener; **a. de cuchillos** knife sharpener

afilalápices *nm inv* pencil sharpener

afilar 1 *vt (cuchillo, lápiz)* to sharpen; **piedra de a.** whetstone, grindstone

  2 afilarse *vpr (nariz, dedos)* to taper

afiliación *nf* (**a**) *(acción)* joining (**b**) *(efecto)* membership

afiliado, -a *nm,f* member (**a** of)

afiliarse *vpr* **a. a un partido** to join a party

afín *adj* similar; **su postura es a. a la nuestra** his opinion is close to ours

afinador, -ora *nm,f (de instrumentos)* tuner; **a. de pianos** piano tuner

afinar 1 *vt* (**a**) *Mús (instrumento)* to tune; **a. la voz** to sing in tune (**b**) *(perfeccionar, mejorar)* to fine-tune; **a. la puntería** to improve one's aim (**c**) *(pulir)* to refine

  2 *vi (cantar)* to sing in tune

afincarse [59] *vpr* to settle (**en** in)

afinidad *nf* (**a**) *(gen) & Quím* affinity (**b**) *(parentesco)* **por a.** by marriage

afinque *etc ver* **afincarse**

afirmación *nf* statement, assertion

afirmar 1 *vt* (**a**) *(decir)* to say, to declare; **afirmó que...** he stated that...; **afirmó haber hablado con ella** he said *o* stated that he had talked to her (**b**) *(reforzar)* to reinforce

  2 *vi (asentir)* to agree, to consent; **a. con la cabeza** to nod (in agreement)

  3 afirmarse *vpr* (**a**) *(asegurarse)* **afirmarse en los estribos** to steady oneself in the stirrups (**b**) *(ratificarse)* **afirmarse en algo** to reaffirm sth

afirmativa *nf* affirmative

afirmativo, -a *adj* affirmative; **una respuesta afirmativa** an affirmative answer

aflautado, -a *adj* high-pitched

aflicción *nf* suffering, sorrow

afligir [24] **1** *vt (causar daño)* to afflict; *(causar pena)* to distress

  2 afligirse *vpr* to be distressed (**por** by)

aflojar 1 *vt* (**a**) *(presión, tensión)* to reduce; *(cinturón, corbata)* to loosen; *(cuerda)* to slacken (**b**) *Fam (dinero)* to fork out

  2 *vi* (**a**) *(disminuir)* to abate, to die down (**b**) *(ceder)* to ease off

  3 aflojarse *vpr (presión, cinturón)* to come loose; *(cuerda)* to slacken

afloramiento *nm (de mineral)* outcrop

aflorar *vi* (**a**) *(surgir)* to (come to the) surface, to show; **a. a la superficie** to come to the surface (**b**) *(mineral)* to outcrop

afluencia *nf* (**a**) *(concurrencia)* influx; **hubo una gran a. de público** the attendance was high (**b**) *(abundancia)* abundance

afluente *nm* tributary

afluir [36] *vi (gente)* to flock (**a** to); *(río)* to flow (**a** into); *(sangre, fluido)* to flow (**a** to)

afluyo *etc ver* **afluir**

afmo., -a. = affmo.

afonía *nf* **tener a.** to have lost one's voice

afónico, -a *adj* **quedarse a.** to lose one's voice

aforado, -a *nm,f Der (parlamentario)* = person enjoying parliamentary immunity

aforar *vt Tec* to gauge

aforismo *nm* aphorism

aforo *nm (de teatro, plaza de toros)* seating capacity

afortunadamente *adv* fortunately, luckily

afortunado, -a 1 *adj* (**a**) *(persona)* lucky, fortunate (**b**) *(coincidencia, frase)* happy, felicitous
2 *nm,f (persona)* lucky person; *(en lotería)* lucky winner
afrancesado, -a 1 *adj* Frenchified
2 *nm,f Hist* = supporter of the French during the Peninsular War
afrenta *nf (ofensa, agravio)* affront
afrentar *vt (ofender)* to affront
África *n* Africa; **Á. del Norte** North Africa; **Á. Occidental** West Africa; **Á. Oriental** East Africa; **el Á. subsahariana** sub-Saharan Africa
africada *nf Ling* affricate
africado, -a *adj Ling* affricative
africanismo *nm* Africanism
africano, -a *adj & nm,f* African; **a. occidental** West African
afrikaans *nm (idioma)* Afrikaans
afrikáner *adj & nmf* Afrikaner
afro *adj inv* afro; **un peinado a.** an afro (hairstyle)
afroamericano, -a *adj & nm,f* Afro-American, African-American
afrodisíaco, -a, afrodisiaco, -a *adj & nm* aphrodisiac
afrontar *vt (hacer frente a)* to face; **a. las consecuencias** to face (up to) the consequences; **afrontó la situación con entereza** she faced up squarely to the situation
afrutado, -a *adj* fruity
afta *nf Med* mouth ulcer
after, after hour(s) ['after 'awars] *nm inv Fam* = club which opens well after midnight and stays open into the following morning
after shave ['after seif] *nm* aftershave
afuera 1 *adv* outside; **hace frío a.** it's cold outside; **vamos a. a pasear** let's go out for a walk; **por (la parte de) a.** on the outside; *Am* **a. de** outside
2 *nfpl* **las afueras** the outskirts; **en las afueras** on the outskirts
agachadiza *nf* snipe
agachar 1 *vt* to lower; **a. la cabeza** *(por vergüenza, deferencia)* to bow one's head; *(para evitar un puñetazo, pelota, bala)* to duck (one's head); **agacha la cabeza, que no me dejas ver** move your head down a bit, I can't see
2 agacharse *vpr (en cuclillas)* to crouch down; *(inclinarse)* to bend down; **nos agachamos al empezar el tiroteo** we ducked down when the shooting began
agalla 1 *nf* (**a**) *(de pez)* gill (**b**) *(de árbol)* gall
2 agallas *nfpl (valor)* guts, pluck; **tener agallas para hacer algo** to have the guts to do sth
ágape *nm* banquet, feast
agarrada *nf Fam* row, bust-up
agarradera *nf Am* handle
agarradero *nm* (**a**) *(asa)* hold (**b**) *Fam (pretexto)* pretext, excuse
agarrado, -a 1 *adj* (**a**) *(asido)* **me tenía a. de un brazo/del cuello** he had me by the arm/the throat; **agarrados del brazo** arm in arm; **agarrados de la mano** hand in hand (**b**) *Fam (tacaño)* tight, stingy
2 *nm Fam (baile)* slow dance
agarrar 1 *vt* (**a**) *(asir)* to grab; **me agarró de la cintura** he grabbed me by the waist (**b**) *(atrapar) (ladrón)* to catch; **¡si la agarro, la mato!** if I catch her I'll kill her!; **me agarró desprevenido** he caught me off guard (**c**) *Esp Fam (enfermedad)* to catch (**d**) *Am (tren, avión, autobús)* to get, to take (**e**) *(expresiones) Fam* **agarrarla, a. una buena** to get sloshed; **esto no hay por dónde agarrarlo** this is a mess!
2 *vi* (**a**) *(tinte)* to take; *(planta)* to take root (**b**) *Am (encaminarse)* **a. para** to head for; **agarró para la izquierda** he took a left
3 agarrarse *vpr* (**a**) *(sujetarse)* to hold on; **agarrarse de** to

hold on to; *Fam Fig* **¡agárrate!** guess what! (**b**) *(pegarse)* to stick; **el arroz se ha agarrado a la cazuela** the rice has stuck to the pot (**c**) *Fam (pelearse)* to scrap, to have a fight; *Am* **agarrarse a golpes** to get into a fistfight (**d**) *(pretextar)* **agarrarse a algo** to use sth as an excuse
agarrón *nm* (**a**) *(tirón)* pull, tug (**b**) *Am Fam (altercado)* scrap, fight
agarrotamiento *nm* stiffness, tenseness
agarrotar 1 *vt* (**a**) *(parte del cuerpo)* to cut off the circulation in (**b**) *(ejecutar con garrote)* to garotte
2 agarrotarse *vpr (parte del cuerpo)* to go stiff; *(mecanismo)* to seize up
agasajar *vt* to lavish attention on, to treat like a king; **a. a alguien con algo** to lavish sth upon sb
agasajo *nm* lavish attention
ágata *nf* agate
agave *nm* agave
agazapado, -a *adj* crouching
agazaparse *vpr (ocultarse)* to crouch (down)
agencia *nf* (**a**) *(empresa)* agency; **a. de aduanas** customs agency; **a. de colocación** employment agency *o* bureau; **a. de contactos** escort agency; **a. inmobiliaria** real estate office; **a. matrimonial** marriage bureau; **a. de noticias** news agency; **a. de prensa** press agency; **a. de publicidad** advertising agency; **a. de seguros** insurance company; **a. de viajes** travel agency (**b**) *(organismo)* agency; *Esp* **la A. Tributaria** ≃ the IRS (**c**) *(sucursal)* branch
agenciar 1 *vt* **a. algo a alguien** to fix sb up with sth
2 agenciarse *vpr* to get hold of, to fix oneself up with
agenda *nf* (**a**) *(de notas, fechas)* diary; *(de anillas)* Filofax®; **a. (de direcciones)** address book; **a. electrónica** electronic personal organizer (**b**) *(de trabajo, reunión)* agenda
agente 1 *nmf* (**a**) *(representante)* agent; **a. de cambio (y bolsa)** stockbroker; **a. comercial** broker; **a. en exclusiva** sole agent; **a. inmobiliario(a)** real estate agent; **a. libre de seguros** insurance broker; **a. marítimo(a)** shipping agent (**b**) *(funcionario)* officer; **a. de aduanas** customs officer; **a. doble** double agent; **a. especial** special agent; **a. de inmigración** immigration officer; **a. de policía** police officer, policeman, *f* policewoman; **a. secreto** secret agent; **a. de seguridad** security officer
2 *nm* (**a**) *(causa activa)* agent (**b**) *Econ* **agentes económicos** social partners
agigantar *vt* to blow up, to magnify
ágil *adj (movimiento, persona)* agile; *(estilo, lenguaje)* fluent; *(respuesta, mente)* nimble, sharp
agilidad *nf* agility; **a. mental** mental agility
agilipollado, -a *adj Esp muy Fam* **estar a.** *(estúpido)* to be dumb *o* daft; *(atontado)* to be out of it
agilizar [14] *vt* to speed up
agio *nm Econ* agio
agiotaje *nm Econ* agiotage, speculation
agitación *nf* (**a**) *(de las aguas)* choppiness (**b**) *(intranquilidad)* restlessness, agitation (**c**) *(jaleo)* racket, commotion (**d**) *(conflicto)* unrest
agitado, -a *adj (persona)* upset, agitated; *(mar)* rough, choppy
agitador, -ora *nm,f* agitator; **a. (de masas)** rabble rouser
agitanado, -a *adj* gypsy-like
agitar 1 *vt* (**a**) *(sacudir)* to shake; *(remover)* to stir; **a. los brazos/un pañuelo** to wave one's arms/a handkerchief; **agítese antes de usar** shake before use (**b**) *(poner nervioso a)* to get worked up; *(inquietar)* to worry, to upset (**c**) *(masas, pueblo)* to stir up
2 agitarse *vpr* (**a**) *(moverse)* to move, shake (**b**) *(ponerse nervioso)* to get worked up; *(inquietarse)* to become agitated
aglomeración *nf (de objetos, sustancia)* buildup; *(de gente)* crowd; **a. urbana** urban sprawl

aglomerado *nm (de madera)* chipboard

aglomerar 1 *vt* to bring together

2 aglomerarse *vpr* to amass

aglutinante 1 *adj* (**a**) *(sustancia)* binding (**b**) *Ling* agglutinative

2 *nm* binding agent

aglutinar 1 *vt (aunar, reunir) (personas)* to unite, to bring together; *(ideas, esfuerzos)* to pool

2 aglutinarse *vpr (pegarse)* to bind (together); *(agruparse)* to gather, to come together

agnosticismo *nm* agnosticism

agnóstico, -a *adj & nm,f* agnostic

agobiado, -a *adj (trabajo)* snowed under (**de** with); *(problemas)* weighed down (**de** with)

agobiante *adj (presión, trabajo, persona)* overwhelming; *(calor)* oppressive

agobiar 1 *vt* to overwhelm

2 agobiarse *vpr* to feel overwhelmed; **¡no te agobies!** don't worry!

agobio *nm* (**a**) *(físico)* choking, suffocation; **¡qué a.!** it's stifling! (**b**) *(psíquico)* pressure; **¡qué a.!** this is murder *o* a nightmare!

agolparse *vpr (gente)* to crowd around; *(sangre)* to rush; *(problemas)* to come to a head

agonía *nf* (**a**) *(del moribundo)* death throes (**b**) *(decadencia)* decline, dying days (**c**) *(pena)* agony

agónico, -a *adj también Fig* dying

agonizante *adj también Fig* dying

agonizar [14] *vi* (**a**) *(expirar)* to be dying (**b**) *(extinguirse)* to fizzle out (**c**) *(sufrir)* to be in agony

ágora *nf Hist* agora

agorafobia *nf* agoraphobia

agorar [6] *vt* to predict

agorero, -a *nm,f* prophet of doom

agostado, -a *adj* parched

agosto *nm (mes)* August; *Fig* **hacer el a.** to line one's pockets; *ver también* **septiembre**

agotado, -a *adj* (**a**) *(persona, animal)* exhausted; **estar a. de hacer algo** to be tired out from doing sth (**b**) *(producto)* out of stock, sold out (**c**) *(pila, batería)* flat

agotador, -ora *adj* exhausting

agotamiento *nm* (**a**) *(cansancio)* exhaustion; **a. nervioso** nervous exhaustion (**b**) *(de producto)* sellout; *(de reservas)* exhaustion

agotar 1 *vt* (**a**) *(cansar)* to exhaust (**b**) *(producto)* to sell out of; *(agua)* to use up, to run out of; *(recursos)* to exhaust, to use up; **este niño me agota** this child tires me out

2 agotarse *vpr* (**a**) *(cansarse)* to tire oneself out (**b**) *(acabarse)* to run out; *(libro, disco, entradas)* to sell out; *(pila, batería)* to go flat; **las entradas se agotaron en seguida** the tickets sold out almost immediately

agraciado, -a 1 *adj* (**a**) *(atractivo)* attractive, fetching (**b**) *(afortunado)* **a. con algo** lucky enough to win sth

2 *nm,f (afortunado)* lucky winner

agraciar *vt* (**a**) *(embellecer)* to make more attractive (**b**) *(conceder una gracia)* to pardon (**c**) *Formal (premiar)* to reward

agradable *adj* (**a**) *(persona)* pleasant; **son muy agradables** they're very pleasant (**b**) *(clima, temperatura)* pleasant; *(olor, sabor, película, ciudad)* nice, pleasant; **es muy a. al tacto** it feels very nice; **¡qué sorpresa tan a.!** what a nice *o* pleasant surprise!

agradar 1 *vi* to be pleasant; **siempre trata de a.** she always tries to please

2 *vt* to please; **me agradó recibir tu carta** I was pleased to receive your card

agradecer [46] *vt* (**a**) *(sujeto persona)* **a. algo a alguien** *(dar las gracias)* to thank sb for sth; *(estar agradecido)* to be grateful to

sb for sth; **quisiera agradecerles su presencia aquí** I would like to thank you for coming *o* being here; **te lo agradezco mucho** I'm very grateful to you; **le agradezco su interés** thank you for your interest (**b**) *(sujeto: cosa)* **esa pared agradecería una mano de pintura** that wall could do with a lick of paint

agradecido, -a *adj* grateful; **estar muy a. (por algo)** to be very grateful (for sth); **ser muy a.** *(cosa)* to be very pleasing

agradecimiento *nm* gratitude

agrado *nm (gusto)* pleasure; **esto no es de mi a.** this is not to my liking

agrandar 1 *vt (en general)* to make bigger; *(imagen)* to magnify

2 agrandarse *vpr* to get bigger

agrario, -a *adj (reforma)* agrarian; *(producto, política)* agricultural

agravación *nf*, **agravamiento** *nm* worsening, exacerbation

agravante 1 *adj* aggravating

2 *nm o nf (problema)* additional problem; *Der* aggravating circumstance

agravar 1 *vt (situación, enfermedad)* to aggravate

2 agravarse *vpr* to get worse, to worsen

agraviado, -a *adj* offended; **sentirse a. (por algo)** to feel offended (by sth)

agraviar *vt* to offend

agravio *nm* (**a**) *(ofensa)* offense, insult (**b**) *(perjuicio)* wrong; **a. comparativo** unequal treatment

agredido, -a *nm,f* victim

agredir *vt* to attack

agregación *nf* addition

agregado, -a 1 *adj (añadido)* added on

2 *nm,f* (**a**) *Educ* assistant teacher (**b**) *(de embajada)* attaché; **a. cultural** cultural attaché

3 *nm* (**a**) *(conjunto)* aggregate; *(añadido)* addition (**b**) *Econ* aggregate

agregar [40] *vt* to add (**a** to)

agresión *nf (ataque)* act of aggression, attack; **sufrir una a.** to be the victim of an attack

agresividad *nf* aggression

agresivo, -a *adj también Fig* aggressive

agresor, -ora *nm,f* attacker, assailant

agreste *adj (abrupto, rocoso)* rough, rugged; *(basto, rudo)* coarse, uncouth

agriar [32] **1** *vt (vino, leche)* to (turn) sour; *(carácter)* to sour, to embitter

2 agriarse *vpr (vino, leche)* to turn sour; *(carácter)* to become embittered

agrícola *adj (sector, política)* agricultural; **región a.** farming region

agricultor, -ora *nm,f* farmer

agricultura *nf* agriculture; **a. extensiva/intensiva** extensive/intensive farming

agridulce *adj* bittersweet; *Culin* sweet-and-sour

agrietado, -a *adj (muro, tierra, plato)* cracked, covered with cracks; *(labios, piel)* chapped

agrietar 1 *vt (muro, tierra, plato)* to crack; *(labios, piel)* to chap

2 agrietarse *vpr (muro, tierra, plato)* to crack; *(labios, piel)* to chap

agrimensor, -ora *nm,f* surveyor

agrio, -a 1 *adj* (**a**) *(ácido)* sour (**b**) *(discusión)* bitter

2 agrios *nmpl* citrus fruits

agriparse *vpr Andes, Méx* to catch the flu

agro *nm* agricultural sector; **el a. español** Spanish agriculture

agroalimentario, -a *adj* **sector a.** food-processing industry

agroindustria *nf* agribusiness

agronomía *nf* agronomy

agrónomo, -a *nm,f* agronomist

agropecuario, -a *adj* **sector a.** farming and livestock sector

agroturismo *nm* rural tourism

agrupación *nf* (a) *(asociación)* group, association (b) *(agrupamiento)* grouping

agrupamiento *nm (concentración)* grouping

agrupar 1 *vt* to group (together)

2 agruparse *vpr (congregarse)* to gather (**en torno a** round); *(unirse)* to form a group

agua *nf* (a) *(líquido)* water; **a. de colonia** eau de cologne; **a. corriente** running water; **a. destilada** distilled water; **a. dulce** fresh water; **a. embotellada** bottled water; **a. del grifo** tap water; **a. con hielo** iced water; **a. de lavanda** lavender water; **aguas menores** urine; **a. mineral (sin gas/con gas)** (still/sparkling) mineral water; **a. oxigenada** hydrogen peroxide; **a. potable** drinking water; **aguas residuales** sewage; **a. salada** saltwater; **aguas termales** thermal spring waters; **aguas territoriales** territorial waters

(b) *(de tejado)* slope; **un tejado de dos aguas** a ridged roof

(c) **aguas** *(en diamante, tela)* water

(d) *(expresiones)* **claro como el a.** as clear as day; *Méx Fam* **como a. para chocolate** hopping mad, fizzing; *Fig* **estar con el a. al cuello** to be up to one's neck (in it); *Náut* **hacer a.** to leak; *Fig* to go under; **la empresa está haciendo a.** the company is going under; *Fig* **nadar entre dos aguas** to sit on the fence; **quedar en a. de borrajas** to come to nothing; **ha roto aguas** her waters have broken; *Fig* **eso es a. pasada** that's water over the dam; **venir como a. de mayo** to be a godsend

aguacate *nm (fruto)* avocado (pear); *(árbol)* avocado (tree)

aguacero *nm* shower

aguachento, -a, *adj Am* watery

aguachirle *nf Esp Fam* **este café es un a.** this coffee tastes like dishwater

aguacil *nm RP* dragonfly

aguada *nf Arte* gouache

aguadilla *nf Esp Fam* ducking

aguado, -a *adj (con demasiada agua)* watery; *(diluido a propósito)* watered-down

aguafiestas *nmf inv* spoilsport

aguafuerte *nm Arte* etching

aguamanil *nm* ewer and basin

aguamarina *nf* aquamarine

aguamiel *nm* (a) *Am (bebida)* = water mixed with honey or, in Mexico, cane syrup (b) *Carib, Méx (jugo)* = sap of the agave cactus used to make alcoholic drinks

aguanieve *nf* sleet; **está cayendo a.** it's sleeting

aguantar 1 *vt* (a) *(peso, presión)* to bear; **está aguantando bien las presiones** she's holding *o* bearing up well under the pressure; **esa estantería no va a a. el peso de los libros** that shelf won't take the weight of the books

(b) *(tolerar, soportar)* to bear, to stand; **no lo aguanto** I can't bear him; **no sé cómo la aguantas** I don't know how you put up with her; **no sabe a. una broma** he doesn't know how to take a joke

(c) *(sostener)* to hold; **aguanta los libros mientras limpio la estantería** hold the books while I dust the shelf

(d) *(contener) (respiración, mirada)* to hold; **apenas pude a. la risa** it was all I could do not to laugh

(e) *(durar)* **no creo que aguante mucho tiempo** I don't think he'll be able to last long

(f) *Méx, RP (esperar)* to wait for

2 *vi* (a) *(tiempo)* to hold on; **aguanta un poco más** hold on a bit longer; **no aguanto más** I can't take any more (b) *(resistir)* to last; **estas botas aguantarán hasta el año que viene**

these boots should last me till next year; **a. hasta el final** to stay the course *o* the distance

3 aguantarse *vpr* (a) *(contenerse)* to restrain oneself, to hold oneself back (b) *(resignarse)* **tendrán que aguantarse** they'll just have to put up with it, too bad

aguante *nm* (a) *(paciencia)* self-restraint, tolerance (b) *(resistencia)* strength; *(de persona)* stamina

aguar [11] **1** *vt* (a) *(mezclar con agua)* to water down; **a. el vino** to water the wine (b) *(estropear)* to spoil, to ruin; **la noticia nos aguó la fiesta** the news spoiled our enjoyment

2 aguarse *vpr* to be spoiled

aguardar *vt* to wait for, to await

aguardentoso, -a *adj* (a) *(voz)* hoarse, gravelly (b) *Ecuad (ebrio)* drunk

aguardiente *nm* spirit, liquor

aguarrás *nm* turpentine

aguaturma *nf* Jerusalem artichoke

aguce *etc ver* **aguzar**

aguda *nf* word stressed on the last syllable

agudeza *nf* (a) *(de vista, olfato)* keenness (b) *(mental)* sharpness, shrewdness (c) *(de filo, punta)* sharpness (d) *(dicho ingenioso)* witticism

agudizar [14] **1** *vt* (a) *(sentido)* to make keener; *(mente)* to sharpen; **a. el ingenio** to sharpen one's wits (b) *(problema, crisis)* to exacerbate, to make worse; **el frío agudizó el dolor** the cold made the pain worse

2 agudizarse *vpr* (a) *(problema, crisis)* to get worse (b) *(ingenio)* to get sharper

agudo, -a *adj* (a) *(vista, olfato)* keen (b) *(crisis, problema, enfermedad)* serious, acute (c) *(dolor)* sharp (d) *(sonido)* high, high-pitched (e) *(perspicaz)* keen, sharp; *(ingenioso)* witty (f) *Gram (palabra)* stressed on the last syllable (g) *(filo, punta)* sharp

agüe *etc ver* **aguar**

agüero *nm* **de buen/mal a.** that bodes well/ill

aguerrido, -a *adj (valiente)* battle-hardened; *(experimentado)* veteran

aguijar *vt (caballo)* to spur; *(buey)* to goad

aguijón *nm* (a) *(de insecto, escorpión)* sting (b) *(vara afilada)* goad (c) *(estímulo)* spur, stimulus

aguijonear *vt* (a) *(animal)* to goad on (b) *(estimular)* to drive on; **a. a alguien para que haga algo** to spur sb on to do sth

águila *nf (ave)* eagle; *Fig* **ser un á.** *(ser vivo, listo)* to be sharp *o* perceptive; *Méx* **¿á. o sol?** heads or tails?; **á. imperial** Spanish imperial eagle; **á. real** golden eagle

aguileño, -a *adj* aquiline

aguilucho *nm* (a) *(polluelo de águila)* eaglet (b) *(ave rapaz)* harrier

aguinaldo *nm* (a) *(propina)* = tip given at Christmas (b) *Am (paga extra)* = extra month's pay at Christmas

aguja *nf* (a) *(de coser, jeringuilla)* needle; *(de hacer punto)* knitting needle; *(de tocadiscos)* stylus, needle; **es como buscar una a. en un pajar** it's like looking for a needle in a haystack; **a. de ganchillo** crochet hook; **a. hipodérmica** hypodermic needle; **a. de punto** knitting needle (b) *(de reloj)* hand; *(de brújula)* pointer; *(de iglesia)* spire (c) *(de conífera)* needle; **a. de pino** pine needle (d) *Ferroc* point (e) **agujas** *(de res)* ribs

agujerear 1 *vt* to make a hole/holes in

2 agujerearse *vpr* **se me han agujereado los pantalones** I've got a hole in my pants

agujero *nm* (a) *(hueco, abertura)* hole; **a. de bala** bullet hole; *Astron* **a. negro** black hole (b) *(deuda)* deficit; **hay un a. de cien millones** a hundred million are unaccounted for

agujetas *nfpl* (a) *(en los músculos)* **tener a.** to feel stiff (b) *Méx* shoelaces

agustino, -a *adj & nm,f Rel* Augustinian

aguzar [14] *vt* (**a**) *(apetito)* to whet; *(ingenio, oído)* to sharpen (**b**) *(afilar)* to sharpen

ah *interj (admiración)* ooh!; *(sorpresa)* oh!; *(pena)* ah!; *(al caer en la cuenta de algo)* ah, I see!

ahí *adv* (**a**) *(lugar determinado)* there; **a. arriba/abajo** up/down there; **ponlo a.** put it over there; **vino por a.** he came that way; **¡a. tienes!** here *o* there you are!; **a. vienen los niños** here *o* there come the children; **a. mismo** right there (**b**) *(lugar indeterminado)* **a. es donde te equivocas** that's where you are mistaken; **la solución está a.** that's where the solution lies; **andan por a. diciendo tonterías** they're going around talking nonsense; **está por a.** *(en lugar indeterminado)* she's around (somewhere); *(en la calle)* she's out; **por a.** *(aproximadamente eso)* something like that (**c**) **a. que…** *(por eso)* that's why…; **es un mandón, de a. que no lo aguante nadie** he's very bossy, that's why nobody likes him; **de a. su enfado** that's why she was so angry (**d**) *(momento)* then; **de a. en adelante** from then on

ahijado, -a *nm,f (de padrinos)* godson, *f* goddaughter; *Fig (protegido)* protégé, *f* protégée

ahijar *vt* to adopt

ahínco *nm* enthusiasm, devotion; **con a.** *(estudiar, trabajar)* hard, enthusiastically; *(solicitar)* insistently

ahíto, -a *adj* **estar a. de algo** *(saciado)* to be full of sth; *(harto)* to have had enough of sth

ahogadilla *nf* ducking

ahogado, -a 1 *adj* (**a**) *(en el agua)* drowned (**b**) *(falto de aliento)* *(respiración)* labored; *(grito)* muffled; *(persona)* out of breath
   2 *nm,f* drowned person
   3 *nm Andes, Méx (guiso)* stew; *(sofrito)* = mixture of onion, garlic, peppers, etc, fried together as base for stews

ahogar [40] **1** *vt* (**a**) *(asfixiar) (en el agua)* to drown; *(cubriendo la boca y nariz)* to smother, to suffocate (**b**) *(estrangular)* to strangle (**c**) *(extinguir)* to extinguish, to put out (**d**) *(dominar) (levantamiento)* to put down, to quell; *(pena)* to hold back, to contain; **ahogó sus penas** *(con la bebida)* he drowned his sorrows (**e**) *Aut (vehículo)* to flood
   2 ahogarse *vpr* (**a**) *(en el agua)* to drown; *(asfixiarse)* to suffocate; *Fig* **ahogarse en un vaso de agua** to make a simple task difficult (**b**) *(de calor)* to be stifled (**c**) *Aut (motor)* to flood

ahogo *nm* (**a**) *(asfixia)* breathlessness, difficulty in breathing (**b**) *(angustia)* anguish, distress (**c**) *(económico)* financial difficulty

ahogue *etc ver* **ahogar**

ahondar 1 *vt (hoyo, túnel)* to deepen
   2 *vi* **a. en** *(penetrar)* to penetrate deep into; *(profundizar)* to study in depth

ahora 1 *adv* (**a**) *(en el presente)* now; **a. mismo** right now; **a. es el momento de…** now is the time to…; **a. o nunca** it's now or never; **a partir de a., de a. en adelante** from now on; **a. que lo dices,…** now (that) you mention it,…; **a. que soy más viejo, ya no pienso igual** now (that) I'm older I think differently; **hasta a. sólo se han presentado dos voluntarios** so far only two people have volunteered; **por a.** for the time being
   (**b**) *(pronto)* **a. cuando venga descubriremos la verdad** we'll find out the truth in a moment, when she gets here; **a. voy, déjame terminar** let me finish, I'm coming in a minute; **justo a. iba a llamarte** I was just about to phone you this minute
   (**c**) *(hace poco)* just now, a few minutes ago; **he leído tu mensaje a.** I've just read your message; **se acaban de marchar a. mismo** they just left a few moments ago, they've just left
   2 *conj* (**a**) *(ya… ya)* **a. habla, a. canta** one minute she's talking, the next she's singing (**b**) *(pero)* but, however; **a. bien** but

ahorcado, -a *nm,f* hanged man, *f* hanged woman

ahorcamiento *nm* hanging

ahorcar [59] **1** *vt* to hang; **a. los hábitos** to give up the cloth, to leave the clergy
   2 ahorcarse *vpr* to hang oneself

ahorita, ahoritita *adv Am salvo RP Fam* (right) now

ahorque *etc ver* **ahorcar**

ahorrador, -ora 1 *adj* thrifty, careful with money
   2 *nm,f* thrifty person

ahorrar 1 *vt* (**a**) *(guardar)* to save (**b**) *(evitar)* **ahórrame los detalles** spare me the details
   2 ahorrarse *vpr* **ahorrarse la molestia (de hacer algo)** to save oneself the trouble (of doing sth); **me ahorré un viaje** I saved myself a journey

ahorrativo, -a *adj (persona)* thrifty; *(medida)* money-saving

ahorrista *nmf RP* saver

ahorro *nm* saving; **ahorros** savings

ahuecar [59] **1** *vt* (**a**) *(poner hueco) (manos)* to cup; *(tronco)* to hollow out (**b**) *(mullir) (colchón)* to plump up; *(tierra)* to hoe; *Fam* **a. el ala** to clear off
   2 *vi Fam (irse)* to clear off
   3 ahuecarse *vpr (persona)* to puff up *(with pride)*

ahuevar *vt* **1** *CAm, Ecuad, Perú Fam* **a. a alguien** *(volver tonto)* to leave sb lost for words; *(acobardar)* to scare sb
   2 ahuevarse *vpr (atontarse)* to be lost for words

ahumado, -a 1 *adj (alimento, cristal)* smoked
   2 *nm* smoking

ahumar 1 *vt* (**a**) *(jamón, pescado)* to smoke (**b**) *(lugar)* to fill with smoke
   2 ahumarse *vpr (ennegrecerse de humo)* to become blackened with smoke

ahuyama = **auyama**

ahuyentar *vt (espantar, asustar)* to scare away; *Fig (apartar)* to drive away; **el elevado precio ahuyentó a los compradores** the high price put buyers off

AI *nf (abrev de* **Amnistía Internacional***)* AI

AID *nf (abrev de* **Asociación Internacional de Desarrollo***)* IDA

AIEA *nf (abrev de* **Agencia Internacional de Energía Atómica***)* IAEA

aikido *nm* aikido

aimara *adj & nmf* Aymara

aindiado, -a *adj* Indian *(used of American Indians)*

airado, -a *adj* angry

airar 1 *vt* to anger, to make angry
   2 airarse *vpr* to get angry

airbag ['erβaɣ, air'βaɣ] *(pl* **airbags***) nm (en vehículo)* air bag

aire *nm* (**a**) *(fluido)* air; **al a. libre** in the open air; **con el pecho al a.** bare-chested; **cambiar de aires** to have a change of scene; **dejar algo en el a.** to leave sth up in the air; **estar en el a.** to be in the air; **saltar** *o* **volar por los aires** to be blown sky high; **tomar el a.** to go for a breath of fresh air; **a mi a.** in my own way; **a. acondicionado** air-conditioning; **a. comprimido** compressed air; **a. puro** fresh air; **a. viciado** foul air
   (**b**) *(viento)* wind; *(corriente)* draft; **hoy hace mucho a.** it's very windy today
   (**c**) *(aspecto)* air, appearance; *(parecido)* **tiene un a. a su madre** she has something of her mother; **aires** *(vanidad)* airs; **darse aires (de algo)** to put on airs (about sth)

aireación *nf* ventilation

aireado, -a *adj* airy

airear 1 *vt (ventilar)* to air; *(contar)* to air (publicly)
   2 airearse *vpr* to get a breath of fresh air

airoso, -a *adj* (**a**) *(garboso)* graceful, elegant (**b**) *(triunfante)* **salir a. de algo** to come out of sth with flying colors

aislacionismo *nm Pol* isolationism

aislado, -a *adj* (**a**) *(lugar, suceso)* isolated (**b**) *(cable, pared)* insulated

aislamiento *nm* (**a**) *(de lugar, persona)* isolation (**b**) *(de cable, vivienda)* insulation; **a. de doble pared** cavity wall insulation

aislante 1 *adj* insulating
2 *nm* insulating material

aislar 1 *vt* (**a**) *(persona)* to isolate (**b**) *(del frío, de la electricidad)* to insulate; *(del ruido)* to soundproof (**c**) *(lugar)* to cut off; **la nevada aisló la comarca del resto del país** the snow cut the area off from the rest of the country (**d**) *(virus)* to isolate
2 *vi* **estas ventanas aíslan muy bien del frío/ruido** these windows are very good at keeping the cold/noise out
3 aislarse *vpr* to isolate oneself, to cut oneself off (**de** from)

aizkolari *nm* = competitor in the rural Basque sport of chopping felled tree trunks

ajá *interj* **¡a.!** *(sorpresa)* aha!

ajado, -a *adj (flor)* withered; *(persona)* wizened

ajar 1 *vt (flores)* to wither, to cause to fade; *(piel)* to wrinkle; *(colores)* to cause to fade; *(ropa)* to wear out
2 ajarse *vpr (flores)* to fade, to wither; *(piel)* to wrinkle, to become wrinkled; *(belleza, juventud)* to fade

ajardinado, -a *adj* landscaped

a. JC. *(abrev de **antes de Jesucristo**)* BC

ajedrea *nf* savory *(plant)*

ajedrecista *nmf* chess player

ajedrez *nm inv* chess

ajenjo *nm* (**a**) *(planta)* wormwood, absinthe (**b**) *(licor)* absinthe

ajeno, -a *adj* (**a**) *(de otro)* of others; **jugar en campo a.** to play away from home (**b**) *(no relacionado)* **es un problema a. a la sociedad de hoy** it's a problem that no longer exists in today's society; **esto es a. a nuestro departamento** our department doesn't deal with that; **por causas ajenas a nuestra voluntad** for reasons beyond our control (**c**) *(no enterado, indiferente)* **era ajena a lo que estaba ocurriendo** she had no knowledge of what was happening

ajete *nm* = green stalk of young garlic plant; **revuelto de ajetes** = dish of scrambled egg with garlic stalks

ajetreado, -a *adj* busy; **he tenido un día muy a.** I've had a very busy day

ajetreo *nm (gestiones, molestias)* running around, hard work; *(actividad)* (hustle and) bustle

ají *(pl **ajís** o **ajíes**)* *nm Andes, RP (pimiento)* chilli (pepper); *(salsa)* = sauce made from oil, vinegar, garlic and chilli

ajiaceite *nm* = sauce made from garlic and olive oil

ajiaco *nm Andes, Carib (estofado)* = chilli-based stew

ajillo *nm* **al a.** = in a sauce made with oil, garlic and sometimes chilli

ajo *nm* garlic; *Culin* **a. blanco** cold garlic soup; **a. tierno** = green stalk of young garlic plant; *Fam* **¡a. y agua!** too bad!, tough!; *Fig* **andar** o **estar en el a.** to be in on it

ajuar *nm* (**a**) *(de casa)* furnishings (**b**) *(de novia)* trousseau

ajuntar *Fam* **1** *vt (lenguaje infantil)* **¿me ajuntas?** will you be my friend again?
2 ajuntarse *vpr (irse a vivir juntos)* to move in together

ajustable *adj* adjustable; **sábana a.** fitted sheet

ajustado, -a 1 *adj* (**a**) *(ceñido) (ropa)* tight-fitting; *(tuerca, pieza)* tight; *(resultado, final)* close (**b**) *(justo)* correct, right; *(precio)* reasonable
2 *nm* fitting

ajustador, -ora 1 *adj* adjusting
2 *nm,f Imprenta* typesetter

ajustar 1 *vt* (**a**) *(encajar) (piezas de motor)* to fit; *(puerta, ventana)* to push to (**b**) *(arreglar)* to adjust (**c**) *(apretar)* to tighten; **ajusta bien la tapa** screw the lid on tight (**d**) *(pactar) (matrimonio)* to arrange; *(pleito)* to settle; *(paz)* to negotiate; *(precio)* to fix, to agree
2 *vi (venir justo)* to fit properly, to be a good fit; **la ventana no**

ajusta bien the window won't close properly
3 ajustarse *vpr* (**a**) *(encajarse)* to fit; *Fig* **tu relato no se ajusta a la verdad** your account is at variance with the truth, your account doesn't match the facts (**b**) *(adaptarse)* to fit in (**a** with); **tu plan no se ajusta a nuestras necesidades** your plan doesn't meet our needs; **tenemos que ajustarnos al presupuesto del que disponemos** we have to keep within the limits of our budget

ajuste *nm (de pieza)* fitting; *(de mecanismo)* adjustment; *(de salario)* agreement; **a. de cuentas** settling of scores

ajusticiar *vt* to execute

al *ver* **a, el**

Alá *nm* Allah

ala 1 *nf* (**a**) *(de ave, avión)* wing; **cortar las alas a alguien** to clip sb's wings; *Dep* **a. delta** *(aparato)* hang glider (**b**) *(parte lateral) (de tejado)* eaves; *(de sombrero)* brim; *(de nariz)* side; *(de mesa)* leaf (**c**) *(de edificio, partido)* wing
2 *nmf Dep* winger, wing

alabanza *nf* praise

alabar 1 *vt* to praise; *Fam* **¡alabado sea (el Señor)!** thank heavens!
2 alabarse *vpr* to boast; **se alaba de valiente** he is always boasting about how brave he is

alabarda *nf* halberd

alabardero *nm* halberdier

alabastro *nm* alabaster

alabear 1 *vt* to warp
2 alabearse *vpr* to warp

alacena *nf* (**a**) *(mueble)* kitchen cupboard (**b**) *(en la pared)* wall cupboard

alacrán *nm* scorpion

alado, -a *adj (con alas)* winged; *(ligero)* swift, fleet

ALALC *nf Antes (abrev de **Asociación Latinoamericana de Libre Comercio**)* LAFTA

alambicado, -a *adj* elaborate, involved

alambicar [59] *vt (destilar)* to distill; *(complicar)* to overcomplicate

alambique *nm* still

alambrada *nf* wire fence

alambrar *vt* to fence with wire

alambre *nm* wire; **a. de espino** o **de púas** barbed wire

alameda *nf* (**a**) *(sitio con álamos)* poplar grove (**b**) *(paseo)* tree-lined avenue

álamo *nm* poplar

alano *nm (perro)* mastiff

alante *Fam* = **adelante**

alarde *nm* show o display (**de** of); **hacer a. de algo** to show sth off, to flaunt sth

alardear *vi* **a. de** to show off about

alargadera *nf* extension lead o cable

alargado, -a *adj* long

alargador *nm* extension lead o cable

alargamiento *nm* extension, lengthening

alargar [40] **1** *vt* (**a**) *(ropa)* to lengthen (**b**) *(viaje, visita, plazo)* to extend; **el árbitro alargó el primer tiempo cinco minutos** *(soccer)* the referee added five minutes' stoppage time to the end of the first half (**c**) *(brazo, mano)* to stretch out; **a. el brazo** to stretch out one's arm (**d**) *(pasar)* **a. algo a alguien** to pass sth (over) to sb
2 alargarse *vpr (hacerse más largo)* to get longer; *(hacerse muy largo)* to go on for ages; **la reunión se alargó hasta el alba** the meeting went on o stretched on until dawn

alarido *nm* shriek, howl

alarma *nf* alarm; *Mil* call to arms; **dar la a.** to raise the alarm; **cundió la a.** panic spread; **a. antirrobo** burglar alarm; **a. contra incendios** fire alarm

alarmante *adj* alarming

alarmar 1 *vt (avisar)* to alert; *(asustar)* to alarm
  2 alarmarse *vpr (inquietarse)* to be alarmed

alarmismo *nm* alarmism

alarmista *nmf* alarmist

Alaska *n* Alaska

alavés, -esa 1 *adj* of/from Alava
  2 *nm,f* person from Alava

alazán, -ana 1 *adj* chestnut
  2 *nm,f* chestnut (horse)

alba *nf* (a) *(amanecer)* dawn, daybreak; **al a.** at dawn (b) *(vestidura)* alb

albacea *nmf Der* executor, *f* executrix

albaceteño, -a 1 *adj* of/from Albacete
  2 *nm,f* person from Albacete

albahaca *nf* basil

albanés, -esa 1 *adj & nm,f* Albanian
  2 *nm (lengua)* Albanian

Albania *n* Albania

albañil *nm* bricklayer

albañilería *nf* (a) *(oficio)* bricklaying (b) *(obra)* brickwork

albarán *nm Esp Com* delivery receipt

albaricoque *nm Esp* apricot

albaricoquero *nm Esp* apricot tree

albatros *nm inv* albatross

albedrío *nm (antojo, elección)* fancy, whim; **a su a.** as takes his/her fancy; *Filosofía* **libre a.** free will; **a su libre a.** of his/her own free will

alberca *nf* (a) *(depósito)* water tank (b) *Col, Méx (piscina)* swimming pool

albérchigo *nm* peach tree

albergar [40] **1** *vt* (a) *(personas)* to accommodate, to put up (b) *(odio)* to harbor; *(esperanzas)* to cherish
  2 albergarse *vpr* to stay; **¿en qué hotel se albergan?** what hotel are they staying in?

albergue *nm (alojamiento)* accommodations, lodgings; *(de montaña)* shelter, refuge; **a. de juventud** *o* **juvenil** youth hostel; *RP* **a. transitorio** hourly hotel

alberguista *nmf* youth hosteler

albino, -a *adj & nm,f* albino

albo, -a *adj Literario* white

albóndiga *nf* meatball

albor *nm* (a) *Literario (blancura)* whiteness (b) *Formal (luz del alba)* first light of day (c) **albores** *(principio)* dawn, earliest days; **los albores de la civilización** the dawn of civilization

alborada *nf* (a) *(amanecer)* dawn, daybreak (b) *Mús* = popular song sung at dawn (c) *Mil* reveille

alborear *v impersonal* **empezaba a a.** dawn was breaking

albornoz *nm* bathrobe

alborotado, -a *adj (agitado)* rowdy; *(pelo)* messed up, tousled; **los niños están alborotados con la excursión** the children are all excited about the trip; **los ánimos están alborotados** feelings are running high

alborotador, -ora 1 *adj* rowdy
  2 *nm,f* troublemaker

alborotar 1 *vt (perturbar)* to disturb, to unsettle; *(amotinar)* to stir up, to rouse; *(desordenar)* to mess up; **el viento le alborotó el pelo** the wind messed up her hair
  2 *vi* to be rowdy; **¡niños, no alborotéis!** calm down, children!
  3 alborotarse *vpr (perturbarse)* to get worked up

alboroto *nm* (a) *(ruido)* din (b) *(jaleo)* fuss, to-do

alborozado, -a *adj* overjoyed, delighted

alborozar [14] *vt* to delight

alborozo *nm* delight, joy

albricias *interj* **¡a.!** great!, fantastic!

albufera *nf* lagoon

álbum *nm* album; **á. de autógrafos** autograph album; **á. de fotos/sellos** photo/stamp album

albúmina *nf Quím* albumin

albuminoide *adj Quím* albuminoid

albur *nm* (a) *(pez)* bleak (b) *(azar)* chance (c) *Méx, RDom (juego de palabras)* pun; *(doble sentido)* double meaning

alburear *vi Méx Fam* to pun, to make a pun

ALCA ['alka] *nf (abrev de* **Área de Libre Comercio de las Américas***)* FTAA

alcachofa *nf* (a) *(planta)* artichoke (b) *Esp (pieza) (de regadera)* rose, sprinkler; *(de ducha)* shower head

alcahuete, -a *nm,f* (a) *(mediador)* lover's go-between (b) *(chismoso)* gossipmonger

alcaide *nm* prison governor

alcalde, -esa *nm,f* mayor, *f* mayoress

alcaldía *nf* (a) *(cargo)* mayoralty (b) *(sede)* mayor's office (c) *(término municipal)* municipality

álcali *nm Quím* alkali

alcalino, -a *adj Quím* alkaline

alcaloide *nm Quím* alkaloid

alcance *nm* (a) *(de arma, misil, emisora)* range; **de corto/largo a.** short-/long-range (b) *(de persona)* **a mi a.** within my reach; **al a. de la mano** within arm's reach; **al a. de la vista** within sight; **dar a. a alguien** to catch up with sb; **fuera del a. de** beyond the reach of (c) *(de reformas, medidas)* scope, extent; **de a.** important (d) *(inteligencia)* **de pocos alcances** slow, dim-witted

alcancía *nf esp Am* money box

alcanfor *nm* camphor

alcantarilla *nf (conducto)* sewer; *(boca)* drain

alcantarillado *nm* sewers, sewage system

alcanzar [14] **1** *vt* (a) *(igualarse con)* to catch up with; **¿a que no me alcanzas?** bet you can't catch me!
  (b) *(llegar a)* to reach; **a. la meta** to reach the finishing line; **lo alcancé con una escalera** I used a ladder to reach it; **alcanzó la costa a nado** he swam to the coast; **este coche alcanza los 200 km/h** this car can do up to *o* reach 200 km/h; **el desempleo ha alcanzado un máximo histórico** unemployment is at *o* has reached an all-time high
  (c) *(lograr) (objetivo)* to achieve; **a. la fama/el éxito** to achieve fame/success
  (d) *(entregar)* **alcánzame ese jarrón, que no llego hasta el estante** could you get that vase down for me, I can't reach the shelf
  (e) *(golpear, dar)* to hit; **le alcanzaron dos disparos** he was hit by two shots
  2 *vi* (a) *(ser suficiente)* **a. para algo/alguien** to be enough for sth/sb; **a. para hacer algo** to be enough to do sth; **no sé si alcanzará para todos** I don't know if there'll be enough for everyone (b) *(poder)* **a. a hacer algo** to be able to do sth; **alcancé a verlo unos segundos** I managed to see him for a few seconds; **no alcanzo a comprender por qué** I can't begin to understand why (c) *(llegar)* **no alcanzo** I can't reach it; **hasta donde alcanza la vista** as far as the eye can see

alcaparra *nf* caper

alcatraz *nm* gannet

alcaucil *nm RP (alcachofa)* artichoke

alcayata *nf* hook

alcazaba *nf* citadel

alcázar *nm* fortress

alce 1 *ver* **alzar**
  2 *nm* elk, moose

alcista *adj Fin* **mercado a.** bull market

alcoba *nf* bedroom

alcohol *nm* alcohol; **a. desinfectante** surgical alcohol; *Quím* **a. etílico** ethyl alcohol; **a. de quemar** methylated spirits

alcoholemia *nf* blood alcohol level; **test de a.** Breathalyzer® test

alcohólico, -a *adj & nm,f* alcoholic

alcoholímetro *nm* (**a**) *(para bebida)* alcoholometer (**b**) *(para la sangre)* drunkometer

alcoholismo *nm* alcoholism

alcoholizado, -a *adj* **estar a.** to be an alcoholic

alcoholizar [14] **1** *vt* to turn into an alcoholic
 2 alcoholizarse *vpr* to become an alcoholic

alcornoque *nm* (**a**) *(árbol)* cork oak; *(madera)* cork, corkwood (**b**) *(persona)* idiot, fool

alcotán *nm* hobby *(bird)*

alcurnia *nf* lineage, descent

aldaba *nf* (**a**) *(llamador)* door knocker (**b**) *(pestillo)* latch

aldabonazo *nm* loud knock *(with door knocker)*; *Fig* **ser un a.** to be a bombshell

aldea *nf* small village; **la a. global** the global village

aldeano, -a 1 *adj (pueblerino, rústico)* rustic
 2 *nm,f* villager

aldehído *nm Quím* aldehyde

ale *interj* ¡a.! come on!

aleación *nf* (**a**) *(acción)* alloying (**b**) *(producto)* alloy

alear *vt* to alloy

aleatorio, -a *adj* random

alebrestarse *vpr Col* (**a**) *(rebelarse)* to rebel (**b**) *(ponerse nervioso)* to get worked up

aleccionador, -ora *adj* (**a**) *(instructivo)* instructive (**b**) *(ejemplar)* exemplary

aleccionar *vt* to instruct, to teach

aledaño, -a 1 *adj* adjacent
 2 aledaños *nmpl* surrounding area; **en los aledaños del estadio** in the vicinity of the stadium

alegación *nf* allegation

alegar [40] **1** *vt (motivos, pruebas)* to put forward; **a. que** to claim (that)
 2 *vi Am (quejarse)* to complain

alegato *nm Der* plea; *Fig* **hacer un a. a favor de/en contra de** to make a case for/against

alegoría *nf* allegory

alegórico, -a *adj* allegorical

alegrar 1 *vt* (**a**) *(persona)* to cheer up, to make happy; *(fiesta)* to liven up; **le alegró mucho su visita** his visit really cheered her up; **me alegró el día** it made my day (**b**) *(habitación, decoración)* to brighten up (**c**) *(emborrachar)* to make tipsy
 2 alegrarse *vpr* (**a**) *(sentir alegría)* to be pleased (**de algo/por alguien** about sth/for sb); **me alegro de que me hagas esa pregunta** I'm glad you asked me that; **me alegro!** good! (**b**) *(emborracharse)* to get tipsy

alegre *adj* (**a**) *(contento)* happy; *(irreflexivo)* happy-go-lucky; **una mujer de vida a.** a loose woman (**b**) *(que da alegría)* cheerful, bright (**c**) *(borracho)* tipsy

alegremente *adv (con alegría)* happily, joyfully; *(irreflexivamente)* blithely

alegría *nf* (**a**) *(gozo)* happiness, joy; *(motivo de gozo)* joy; **con a.** happily, joyfully (**b**) *(irresponsabilidad)* rashness, recklessness; **gastaron el dinero con demasiada a.** they spent the money too freely

alegro *adv & nm Mús* allegro

alegrón *nm* pleasant surprise

alegue *etc ver* **alegar**

alejado, -a *adj* distant (**de** from)

alejamiento *nm* (**a**) *(lejanía)* remoteness (**b**) *(distancia)* distance (**c**) *(separación) (de objetos)* separation; *(entre personas)* estrangement

Alejandría *n* Alexandria

alejar 1 *vt (poner más lejos)* to move away; *(ahuyentar) (sospechas, temores)* to allay
 2 alejarse *vpr* (**a**) *(ponerse más lejos)* to go away (**de** from); *(retirarse)* to leave; **se alejaron demasiado del refugio** they strayed too far from the shelter; **¡aléjate de mí!** go away! (**b**) *(distanciarse)* to grow apart; **se fue alejando de sus amigos** he grew apart from his friends

alelado, -a *adj* stupid

alelar *vt* to daze, to stupefy

aleluya 1 *nm o nf* hallelujah
 2 *interj* ¡a.! hallelujah!

alemán, -ana 1 *adj & nm,f* German
 2 *nm (lengua)* German

Alemania *n* Germany; *Antes* **A. Occidental/Oriental** West/East Germany

alentador, -ora *adj* encouraging

alentar [3] **1** *vt (animar)* to encourage
 2 alentarse *vpr Andes, Méx, Ven (recuperarse)* to recover, to get better

alerce *nm* larch

alergeno, alérgeno *nm Med* allergen

alergia *nf también Fig* allergy; **tener a. a algo** to be allergic to sth; **a. a la primavera** *o* **al polen** hay fever

alérgico, -a *adj también Fig* allergic (**a** to)

alero *nm* (**a**) *(del tejado)* eaves (**b**) *Dep* winger, wing (**c**) *Aut* wing

alerón *nm* (**a**) *Av* aileron (**b**) *Esp Fam (axila)* armpit

alerta 1 *adj inv & adv* alert
 2 *nf* alert; **a. roja** red alert
 3 *interj* ¡a.! watch *o* look out!

alertar *vt* to alert (**de** about, to)

aleta *nf* (**a**) *(de pez)* fin (**b**) *(de buzo, foca)* flipper (**c**) *(de coche)* wing (**d**) *(de nariz)* flared part

aletargado, -a *adj* drowsy, lethargic

aletargar [40] **1** *vt* to make drowsy, to send to sleep
 2 aletargarse *vpr (adormecerse)* to become drowsy; *(hibernar)* to hibernate

aletear *vi (ave)* to flap its wings

aleteo *nm* flapping *(of wings)*

Aleutianas *nfpl* **las (Islas) A.** the Aleutian Islands, the Aleutians

alevín *nm* (**a**) *(cría de pez)* fry, young fish (**b**) *(persona)* novice, beginner (**c**) *Dep* **alevines** juniors *(youngest category of players)*

alevosía *nf* (**a**) *(premeditación)* premeditation; **con premeditación y a.** with malice aforethought (**b**) *(traición)* treachery

alevoso, -a *adj* (**a**) *(premeditado)* premeditated (**b**) *(traidor)* treacherous

alfa *nf Fís & Mat* alpha; **a. y omega** beginning and end

alfabético, -a *adj* alphabetical

alfabetización *nf* (**a**) *(de personas) (acción)* teaching to read and write; *(estado)* literacy (**b**) *(de palabras, letras)* alphabetization

alfabetizar [14] *vt* (**a**) *(personas)* to teach to read and write (**b**) *(palabras, letras)* to put into alphabetical order

alfabeto *nm* alphabet; **a. Morse** Morse code

alfajor *nm* (**a**) *(de ajonjolí)* = crumbly shortbread, flavored with sesame seeds (**b**) *(en Argentina)* = small sponge cake filled with creamy toffee

alfalfa *nf* alfalfa

alfanje *nm* scimitar

alfanumérico, -a *adj Inform* alphanumeric

alfaque *nm* sandbank, bar

alfarería *nf* (**a**) *(técnica)* pottery (**b**) *(lugar)* potter's, pottery shop

alfarero, -a *nm,f* potter

alféizar *nm* windowsill

alfeñique *nm (persona)* weakling

alférez *nm Mil* second lieutenant

alfil *nm (pieza de ajedrez)* bishop

alfiler *nm* (a) *(para coser)* pin; *Andes, CSur, Ven* **a. de gancho** safety pin; **no cabe ni un a.** it's jam-packed; *Fig* **prendido con alfileres** sketchy (b) *(joya)* brooch, pin; **a. de corbata** tiepin

alfiletero *nm* pin box

alfombra *nf (grande)* carpet; *(pequeña)* rug; *Am salvo RP* wall-to-wall carpet; **una a. de flores** a carpet of flowers; **a. voladora** magic carpet

alfombrar *vt* to carpet

alfombrilla *nf (alfombra pequeña)* rug; *(felpudo)* doormat; *Inform (para ratón)* mouse mat; **a. (de baño)** bath mat

alforja *nf* (a) *(de persona)* knapsack (b) *(de caballo)* saddlebag

alga *nf* algas *(plantas de mar)* seaweed; *Biol (microscópicas)* algae; **un a.** a piece of seaweed

algarabía *nf* (a) *(habla confusa)* gibberish (b) *(alboroto)* racket

algarada *nf* racket, din

algarroba *nf* (a) *(planta)* vetch (b) *(fruto)* carob *o* locust bean

algarrobo *nm* carob tree

algazara *nf* racket, uproar

álgebra *nf* algebra; **á. elemental** elementary algebra

algebraico, -a *adj* algebraic

álgido, -a *adj (culminante)* critical; **en el punto á. del conflicto** at the height of the conflict

algo 1 *pron* (a) *(alguna cosa)* something; *(en interrogativas)* anything; **¿te pasa a.?** is anything the matter?; **a. es a.** something is better than nothing; **a. así, a. por el estilo** something like that; **a. así como…** something like…; **por a. lo habrá dicho** he must have said it for a reason (b) *(cantidad pequeña)* a bit, a little; **a. de** some (c) *Fam (ataque)* **te va a dar a. como sigas trabajando así** you'll make yourself ill if you go on working like that; **¡a mí me va a dar a.!** *(de risa)* I'm going to injure myself (laughing)!; *(de enfado)* this is going to drive me mad! (d) *(cosa importante)* something; **se cree que es a.** he thinks he's something (special)

2 *adv (un poco)* a bit; **es a. más grande** it's a bit bigger

algodón *nm* cotton; **a. (hidrófilo)** absorbent cotton; **una camisa de a.** a cotton shirt; *Fig* **criado entre algodones** pampered; **a. dulce** cotton candy

algodonero, -a *adj* cotton; **la industria algodonera** the cotton industry

algodonoso, -a *adj* fluffy; **nubes algodonosas** cotton clouds

algoritmo *nm Mat* algorithm

alguacil *nm* (a) *(del ayuntamiento)* mayor's assistant (b) *(del juzgado)* bailiff

alguacilillo *nm Taurom* = mounted official at bullfight

alguien *pron* (a) *(alguna persona)* someone, somebody; *(en interrogativas)* anyone, anybody; **¿hay a. ahí?** is anyone there? (b) *(persona de importancia)* somebody; **se cree a.** she thinks she's somebody (special)

alguno, -a

---

algún is used instead of **alguno** before masculine singular nouns (e.g. **algún día** some day).

---

1 *adj* (a) *(indeterminado)* some; *(en interrogativas)* any; **¿tienes algún libro?** do you have any books?; **algún día** some *o* one day; **compró algunas cosas** he bought some things; **algunas mañanas no me apetece levantarme** some mornings I don't feel like getting up; **algunos amigos míos** some of my friends; **ha surgido algún (que otro) problema** the odd problem has come up; **algún idiota dejó la puerta abierta** some fool left the door open (b) *(ninguno)* any; **no tengo interés a. (en hacerlo)** I'm not in the least (bit) interested (in doing it)

2 *pron* (a) *(persona)* someone, somebody; *(plural)* some people; *(en interrogativas)* anyone, anybody; **¿conociste a algunos?** did you get to know any?; **algunos de** some *o* a few of; **algunos de nosotros** a few of us (b) *(cosa)* the odd one; *(plural)* some, a few; *(en interrogativas)* any; **me salió mal a.** I got the odd one wrong; **algunos de** some *o* a few of

alhaja *nf (joya)* jewel; *(objeto de valor)* treasure; *(persona)* gem; *Irónico* **¡menuda a.!** he's a right one!

alharaca *nf* fuss; **hacer alharacas** to kick up a fuss

alhelí *(pl alhelíes)* *nm* wallflower

alheña *nf* privet

aliado, -a 1 *adj* allied

2 *nm,f* ally; *Hist* **los Aliados** the Allies

alianza *nf* (a) *(pacto, parentesco)* alliance (b) *(anillo)* wedding ring

aliar [32] **1** *vt (naciones)* to ally (**con** with); *(cualidades)* to combine

2 aliarse *vpr* to form an alliance (**con** with)

alias *adv & nm inv (gen) & Inform* alias

alicaído, -a *adj* (a) *(triste)* depressed (b) *(débil)* weak

alicantino, -a 1 *adj* of/from Alicante

2 *nm,f* person from Alicante

alicatado *nm Esp* tiling

alicatar *vt Esp* to tile

alicate *nm* (a) **alicates** *(herramienta)* pliers (b) *Am (para uñas)* nail clippers

aliciente *nm* (a) *(incentivo)* incentive (b) *(atractivo)* attraction

alícuota *adj Mat* aliquot

alienación *nf* (a) *(sentimiento)* alienation (b) *(trastorno psíquico)* derangement, madness

alienado, -a 1 *adj* insane

2 *nm,f* insane person, lunatic

alienante *adj* alienating

alienar *vt* (a) *(enajenar)* to derange, to drive mad (b) *Filosofía* to alienate

alienígena *nmf* alien

aliento 1 *ver* alentar

2 *nm* (a) *(respiración)* breath; **cobrar a.** to catch one's breath; **sin a.** breathless; **a. fétido** foul breath (b) *(ánimo)* strength

aligerar 1 *vt* (a) *(peso)* to lighten; *Fig (pena)* to relieve, to ease (b) *(ritmo)* to speed up; **a. el paso** to quicken one's pace

2 *vi (darse prisa)* to hurry up; **aligera, que llegamos tarde** hurry up, or we'll be late

alijo *nm* contraband; **a. de drogas** consignment of drugs

alimaña *nf* pest *(animal)*

alimentación *nf* (a) *(acción)* feeding (b) *(comida)* food; **el sector de la a.** the food industry; **tienda de a.** grocery store (c) *(régimen alimenticio)* diet; **una a. equilibrada** a balanced diet (d) *Tec* feed, input; *Inform* **a. de papel** paper feed

alimentador, -ora 1 *adj Tec* feeding

2 *nm Tec* feed, feeder; **a. de corriente** power supply unit; *Inform* **a. de papel** paper feed

alimentar 1 *vt* (a) *(dar comida)* to feed; **tengo cinco hijos que a.** I've got five kids to feed (b) *(dar energía, material)* to feed; **la lectura alimenta el espíritu** reading improves your mind (c) *(motor, vehículo)* to fuel

2 *vi* to be nourishing; **los garbanzos alimentan mucho** chickpeas are very nutritious

3 alimentarse *vpr* **alimentarse de** to live on

alimentario, -a *adj* food; **la industria alimentaria** the food industry

alimenticio, -a *adj* nourishing; **productos alimenticios** foodstuffs

alimento *nm* food; **la lectura es un a. para el espíritu** reading improves your mind; **alimentos grasos** fatty foods

alimoche *nm* Egyptian vulture

alimón: al alimón *loc adv Esp* jointly, together

alineación nf (**a**) (colocación en línea) alignment (**b**) Dep (composición de equipo) lineup

alineado, -a adj (**a**) (en línea recta) lined up (**b**) Dep (en equipo) selected (**c**) Pol **países no alineados** nonaligned countries

alineamiento nm alignment; Pol **no a.** nonalignment

alinear 1 vt (**a**) (colocar en línea) to line up (**b**) Dep (seleccionar) to include in the starting lineup

2 alinearse vpr Pol to align

aliñar vt (ensalada) to dress; (carne) to season

aliño nm (para ensalada) dressing; (para carne) seasoning

alioli nm garlic mayonnaise

alirón nm interj ¡a.! hooray!

alisar vt to smooth (down)

alisio Meteo **1** adj **vientos alisios** trade winds

2 nm trade wind

aliso nm alder

alistamiento nm Mil enlistment

alistarse vpr (**a**) Mil to enlist (**b**) Am (prepararse) to get ready

aliteración nf alliteration

alivianarse vpr (**a**) Am (tranquilizarse) to take it easy (**b**) Méx (ser comprensivo) **ya se alivianó y sí va a participar** he's come around and he WILL be taking part

aliviar vt (**a**) (atenuar) to soothe (**b**) (aligerar) (persona) to relieve; (carga) to lighten

alivio nm relief; **de a.** (terrible) dreadful

aljibe nm (**a**) (de agua) cistern (**b**) Náut tanker

allá adv (**a**) (indica espacio) over there; **no te pongas tan a., que no te oigo** don't stand so far away, I can't hear you; **a. donde sea posible** wherever possible; **a. abajo/arriba** down/up there; **a. lejos** right back there; **hacia a.** that way, in that direction; **más a.** further on; **más a. de** beyond; **échate para a.** move over

(**b**) (tiempo) **a. por los años cincuenta** back in the 50s; **a. para el mes de agosto** around August some time

(**c**) (en frases) **a. él/ella** that's his/her problem; **a. cada cual** each person will have to decide for themselves; **el más a.** the great beyond; **no ser muy a.** to be nothing special; **no encontrarse** o **sentirse muy a.** to feel a bit funny

allanamiento nm Esp (sin autorización) forceful entry; Am (con autorización) raid; Der **a. de morada** breaking and entering

allanar vt (**a**) (terreno) to flatten, to level; Fig (dificultad) to overcome; **allanarle el camino a alguien** to smooth the way for sb (**b**) (irrumpir en) to break into; Am (hacer una redada en) to raid; **las tropas allanaron las viviendas de los campesinos** the troops sacked the peasants' houses

allegado, -a 1 adj close

2 nm,f (**a**) (familiar) relative (**b**) (amigo) close friend

allende prep Literario beyond; **a. los mares** across the seas

allí adv there; **a. abajo/arriba** down/up there; **a. mismo** right there; **está por a.** it's around there somewhere

alma nf (**a**) (espíritu) soul; **sentir algo en el a.** to be truly sorry about sth; **agradecer algo en el a.** to be deeply grateful for sth; **lo que dijo me llegó al a.** her words really struck home; **se le cayó el a. a los pies** his heart sank; **como a. en pena** like a lost soul; **como a. que lleva el diablo** like a bat out of hell; Fig **el a. de la fiesta** the life and soul of the party; Fig **el a. del proyecto** the driving force behind the project

(**b**) (persona) soul; **un pueblo de doce mil almas** a town of twelve thousand people; **no se ve un a.** there isn't a soul to be seen; **almas gemelas** kindred spirits (**c**) (de cañón) bore

almacén nm (**a**) (depósito) warehouse; **a. de mercancías** freight depot (**b**) (grandes) almacenes department store (**c**) Andes, RP (de alimentos) grocery store

almacenaje nm storage

almacenamiento nm (gen) & Inform storage

almacenar vt (**a**) (guardar) (gen) & Inform to store (**b**) (reunir) to collect

almanaque nm (**a**) (calendario) calendar (**b**) (publicación anual) almanac

almeja nf clam

almena nf almenas battlements

almendra nf almond

almendrado, -a 1 adj almond-shaped; **ojos almendrados** almond eyes

2 nm Culin almond paste

almendro nm almond (tree)

almendruco nm green almond

almeriense 1 adj of/from Almería

2 nm,f person from Almería

almíbar nm syrup

almibarado, -a adj (**a**) (con almíbar) covered in syrup (**b**) (afectado) syrupy, sugary

almibarar vt to cover in syrup

almidón nm starch

almidonado, -a 1 adj starched

2 nm starching

almidonar vt to starch

alminar nm minaret

almirantazgo nm (**a**) (dignidad) rank of admiral (**b**) (de la Armada) Admiralty

almirante nm admiral

almirez nm mortar

almizcle nm musk

almizclero nm musk deer

almohada nf pillow; Fig **consultarlo con la a.** to sleep on it

almohadilla nf (**a**) (cojín) small cushion (**b**) (de animal) pad

almohadillado, -a adj padded

almohadón nm cushion

almoneda nf (**a**) (subasta) auction (**b**) (local) discount store

almorávide adj & nmf Almoravid

almorranas nfpl piles

almorzar [31] **1** vt (a mediodía) to have for lunch; (a media mañana) to have as a mid-morning snack; **los viernes almuerzan pescado** on Fridays they have fish for lunch

2 vi (a mediodía) to have lunch; (a media mañana) to have a mid-morning snack

almuerzo nm (a mediodía) lunch; (a media mañana) mid-morning snack; **a. tipo bufé** buffet lunch; **a. de trabajo** working lunch

aló interj Andes, Carib (al teléfono) hello

alocado, -a 1 adj crazy

2 nm,f **es un a.** he's crazy

alocución nf address, speech

aloe, áloe nm common aloe

alojamiento nm accommodations; **dar a. a** to put up; **a. y comida** board and lodging

alojar 1 vt to put up

2 alojarse vpr (**a**) (hospedarse) to stay (**b**) (introducirse) to lodge; **la bala se alojó en el pulmón derecho** the bullet lodged in her right lung

alondra nf lark

alopatía nf allopathy

alopecia nf hair loss, Espec alopecia

alpaca nf alpaca

alpargata nf espadrille

Alpes nmpl **los A.** the Alps

alpinismo nm mountaineering, mountain climbing

alpinista nmf mountaineer

alpino, -a adj Alpine

alpiste nm (**a**) (planta) canary grass (**b**) (semilla) birdseed

alquería nf Esp farmstead

alquilado, -a *adj (vehículo, casa, aparato)* rented; *(vehículo con chófer, traje)* hired

alquilar *vt* (**a**) *(dejar en alquiler) (vivienda, oficina, aparato)* to rent (out); *(vehículo, traje)* to hire out; **le alquilamos nuestra casa** we rented our house (out) to him; **se alquila** *(en letrero)* for rent (**b**) *(tomar en alquiler) (vehículo, vivienda, aparato)* to rent; *(vehículo con chófer, traje)* to hire

alquiler *nm* (**a**) *(acción) (de vehículo, vivienda, aparato)* renting; *(vehículo con chófer)*hiring; **¿está en venta o en a.?** is it for sale or to rent?; **coche de a.** rental car; **tenemos viviendas de a.** we have homes to rent; **a. de coches** car rental; *Ind* **a. de equipo** plant leasing (**b**) *(precio) (de vivienda, oficina)* rent; *(de aparato)* rental; *(de vehículo)* rental charge

alquimia *nf* alchemy

alquimista *nmf* alchemist

alquitrán *nm* tar; **a. mineral** coal tar

alquitranar *vt* to tar

alrededor 1 *adv* (**a**) *(en torno)* around; **a. de** around; **de a.** surrounding (**b**) *(aproximadamente)* **a. de** around

2 *nm* **miré a mi a.** I looked around (me); **alrededores** surrounding area

Alsacia *nf* Alsace

alsaciano, -a *adj & nm,f* Alsatian

alta *nf* (**a**) *(del hospital)* **a. (médica)** discharge; **dar de a. a alguien, dar el a. a alguien** to discharge sb (from hospital) (**b**) *(en una asociación)* membership; **darse de a. (en)** to become a member (of); **dar de a. a alguien** to enroll sb; *(en teléfono, Internet)* to connect sb

altanería *nf* haughtiness

altanero, -a *adj* haughty

altar *nm* altar; *Fig* **conducir** *o* **llevar a alguien al a.** to lead sb down the aisle; **a. mayor** high altar

altavoz *nm (para anuncios)* loudspeaker; *(de tocadiscos)* speaker

alteración *nf* (**a**) *(cambio)* alteration (**b**) *(excitación)* agitation (**c**) *(alboroto)* disturbance; **a. del orden público** breach of the peace

alterado, -a *adj* (**a**) *(cambiado)* altered, changed (**b**) *(perturbado)* disturbed, upset; *(enfadado)* angry, annoyed; **los niños están muy alterados con la llegada de las vacaciones** the children are rather overexcited with the holidays coming up

alterar 1 *vt* (**a**) *(cambiar)* to alter; **a. el orden de las palabras** to change the order of the words; **esto altera nuestros planes** that changes our plans (**b**) *(perturbar) (persona)* to agitate, to fluster; **le alteran mucho los cambios** change upsets him a lot (**c**) *(orden público)* to disrupt; **fue detenido por a. el orden público** he was arrested for causing a breach of the peace (**d**) *(estropear)* **el calor alteró los alimentos** the heat made the food spoil

2 alterarse *vpr* (**a**) *(perturbarse)* to get agitated *o* flustered (**b**) *(estropearse)* to spoil

altercado *nm* argument, row

álter ego *nm* alter ego

alternador *nm Elec* alternator

alternancia *nf* alternation

alternar 1 *vt* to alternate; **alterna el estudio con la diversión** she alternates studying with having fun

2 *vi* (**a**) *(relacionarse)* to socialize (**con** with); **no suelen a. mucho** they don't usually socialize much (**b**) *(sucederse)* **a. con** to alternate with

3 alternarse *vpr* (**a**) *(en el tiempo)* to take turns; **los dos partidos se alternan en el poder** the two parties take turns in office (**b**) *(en el espacio)* to alternate

alternativa *nf* (**a**) *(opción)* alternative; **a. de poder** alternative party of government (**b**) *Taurom* = ceremony in which bullfighter shares the kill with his novice, accepting

him as a professional; **tomar la a.** to become a professional bullfighter

alternativamente *adv* alternately

alternativo, -a *adj* (**a**) *(movimiento)* alternating (**b**) *(posibilidad)* alternative (**c**) *(cine, teatro)* alternative

alterne *nm* **bar de a.** = bar where women encourage people to drink in return for a commission

alterno, -a *adj* alternate; *Elec* alternating

alteza *nf (de sentimientos)* loftiness; **A.** *(tratamiento)* Highness; **Su A. Real** His/Her Royal Highness

altibajos *nmpl (del terreno)* unevenness; *(de la vida)* ups and downs

altillo *nm* (**a**) *(desván)* attic, loft (**b**) *Esp (armario)* = small storage cupboard above head height, usually above another cupboard (**c**) *(cerro)* hillock

altímetro *nm* altimeter

altiplanicie *nf*, **altiplano** *nm* high plateau

altísimo, -a 1 *adj (precios, costes)* sky high

2 el A. *Rel* the Most High

altisonante *adj* high-sounding

altitud *nf* altitude; **a. por encima del nivel del mar** altitude above sea level

altivez *nf* haughtiness

altivo, -a *adj* haughty

alto, -a 1 *adj* (**a**) *(persona, árbol, edificio)* tall; *(montaña)* high (**b**) *(indica posición elevada)* high; *(piso)* top, upper; **en lo a. de** at the top of

(**c**) *(cantidad, intensidad)* high; **tiene la fiebre alta** her temperature is high, she has a high temperature; **pasar algo por a.** to pass over sth; **hacer algo por todo lo a.** to do sth in (great) style; **a. horno** blast furnace; *Inform* **alta resolución** high resolution; **alta traición** high treason; **a. voltaje** high voltage

(**d**) *(en una escala)* high; **de a. nivel** *(delegación)* high-level; **un a. dirigente** a high-ranking leader; **alta cocina** haute cuisine; *Mil* **a. mando** *(jefatura)* high command; *(persona)* high-ranking officer; **alta sociedad** high society

(**e**) *(sonido, voz)* loud; **en voz alta** in a loud voice

(**f**) *Geog* upper; **el A. Egipto** Upper Egypt

(**g**) *(hora)* late; **a altas horas de la noche** late at night

2 *nm* (**a**) *(altura)* height; **mide 2 metros de a.** *(cosa)* it's 2 meters high; *(persona)* he's 2 meters tall (**b**) *(lugar elevado)* height; **en lo a. de** at the top of; **los Altos del Golán** the Golan Heights (**c**) *(detención)* stop; **hacer un a.** to make a stop; **dar el a. a alguien** to challenge sb; **a. el fuego** *(cese de hostilidades)* ceasefire

3 *adv* (**a**) *(arriba)* high (up) (**b**) *(hablar)* loud

4 *interj* **¡a.!** halt!, stop!; **¡a.! ¿quién va?** halt! who goes there?; **¡a. ahí!** *(a un fugitivo)* stop!

altoparlante *nm Am* loudspeaker

altozano *nm* hillock

altramuz *nm* lupin

altruismo *nm* altruism

altruista 1 *adj* altruistic

2 *nmf* altruist

altura *nf* (**a**) *(de persona, cosa)* height; **tiene 2 metros de a.** *(persona)* he's 2 meters tall; *(cosa)* it's 2 meters high

(**b**) *(posición)* height; **a la a. de los ojos** at eye level; **pon los dos altavoces a la misma a.** put both speakers level with each other; **el tráfico está congestionado a la a. del ayuntamiento** there's a traffic jam in the area of the town hall

(**c**) *(altitud)* height; **Tegucigalpa está a 1.000 m de a.** Tegucigalpa is 1,000 m above sea level; **ganar** *o* **tomar a.** *(avión)* to climb; **perder a.** *(avión)* to lose height; **se esperan nevadas en alturas superiores a los 800 metros** snow is forecast on high ground above 800 meters; *Fig* **las alturas** *(el cielo)* Heaven (**d**) *(nivel)* **a la a. de** on a par with; **estar a la a. de las circunstancias** to be worthy of the occasion, to be equal to the challenge

(**e**) *(tiempo)* **a estas alturas** by now; **si a estas alturas no te has decidido…** if you haven't decided by now…; **a estas alturas del año ya es muy tarde para ponerse a estudiar** it's a bit late in the year to start studying

alubia *nf* bean; **a. blanca** cannellini bean; **a. roja** kidney bean

alucinación *nf* hallucination

alucinado, -a *adj* (**a**) *Med* hallucinating (**b**) *Fam (sorprendido)* staggered

alucinante *adj* (**a**) *Med* hallucinatory (**b**) *Fam (extraordinario)* amazing, awesome

alucinar 1 *vi* (**a**) *Med* to hallucinate (**b**) *Fam* **¡tú alucinas!** you must be dreaming!; **¡yo alucino!** I can't believe it!

2 *vt Fam* (**a**) *(seducir)* to hypnotize, to captivate (**b**) *(gustar)* **le alucinan las motos** he's crazy about motorbikes

alucine *nm Fam* **¡qué a.!** that's amazing!; **un a. de moto** a humdinger of a bike

alucinógeno, -a 1 *adj* hallucinogenic

2 *nm* hallucinogen

alud *nm también Fig* avalanche

aludido, -a *nm,f* **el a.** the aforesaid; **darse por a.** *(ofenderse)* to take it personally; *(reaccionar)* to take the hint

aludir *vi* **a. a algo** *(sin mencionar)* to allude to sth; *(mencionando)* to refer to sth

alumbrado *nm* lighting; **a. público** streetlighting

alumbramiento *nm* (**a**) *(con luz)* lighting (**b**) *(parto)* delivery

alumbrar 1 *vt* (**a**) *(iluminar)* to light up (**b**) *(dar a luz)* to give birth to

2 *vi (iluminar)* to give light

aluminio *nm* aluminum

aluminosis *nf inv Constr* = structural weakness of buildings as a result of inadequate building materials containing aluminium

alumnado *nm (de escuela)* pupils; *(de universidad)* students

alumno, -a *nm,f (de escuela, profesor particular)* pupil; *(de universidad)* student; **a. externo** day pupil

alunado, -a *adj RP* annoyed, in a bad mood

alunizaje *nm* landing on the moon, lunar landing

alunizar [14] *vi* to land on the moon

alusión *nf (sin mencionar)* allusion; *(mencionando)* reference; **hacer a. a** *(sin mencionar)* to allude to; *(mencionando)* to refer to

alusivo, -a *adj* allusive

aluvión *nm* (**a**) *(de agua)* flood; **un a. de críticas** a battery of criticism; **un a. de insultos** a torrent of abuse (**b**) *Geol (sedimento)* alluvium; **tierras de a.** alluvial deposits

alveolar *adj Anat & Ling* alveolar

alveolo, alvéolo *nm* (**a**) *(de panal)* cell (**b**) *Anat* alveolus

alza *nf* (**a**) *(subida)* rise; **en a.** *Fin* rising; *Fig* gaining in popularity; **jugar al a.** *Fin* to bull the market (**b**) *(de zapato)* raised insole

alzacuello *nm (en traje eclesiástico)* dog collar

alzada *nf* (**a**) *(de caballo)* height (**b**) *Der* appeal

alzado, -a 1 *adj* (**a**) *(militar)* rebel (**b**) *(precio)* fixed; **a tanto a.** *(modo de pago)* in a single payment

2 *nm (proyección vertical)* elevation

alzamiento *nm* uprising, revolt; *Hist* **el A. Nacional** = Francoist term for the 1936 rebellion against the Spanish Republican Government

alzar [14] **1** *vt* (**a**) *(levantar)* to lift, to raise; *(voz)* to raise; *(cuello de abrigo)* to turn up (**b**) *(aumentar)* to raise (**c**) *(construir)* to erect (**d**) *(sublevar)* to stir up, to raise

2 alzarse *vpr* (**a**) *(levantarse)* to rise (**b**) *(sublevarse)* to rise up, to revolt; **alzarse en armas** to take up arms (**c**) *(conseguir)* **alzarse con la victoria** to win, to be victorious; **los**

ladrones se alzaron con un cuantioso botín the thieves made off with a large sum

Alzheimer *nm* (**mal** *o* **enfermedad de**) **A.** Alzheimer's (disease)

AM *(abrev de amplitude modulation)* AM

a.m. *(abrev de ante meridiem)* am

ama *nf* (**a**) *(dueña)* owner (**b**) *(de criado)* mistress; **a. de casa** housewife; **a. de cría** wet nurse; **a. de llaves** housekeeper

amabilidad *nf* kindness; **¿tendría la a. de…?** would you be so kind as to…?

amabilísimo, -a *superlativo ver* **amable**

amable *adj* kind; **¿sería tan a. de…?** would you be so kind as to…?

amado, -a 1 *adj* **mis seres amados** my loved ones

2 *nm,f* loved one

amaestrado, -a *adj (animal)* trained; *(en circo)* performing

amaestrar *vt* to train

amagar [40] **1** *vt* (**a**) **le amagó un golpe** he made as if to hit him; **amagó una sonrisa** she gave a hint of a smile (**b**) *(dar indicios de)* to show signs of

2 *vi (tormenta)* to be imminent, to threaten

amago *nm* (**a**) *(en boxeo)* feint; **hizo a. de darle un puñetazo** she made as if to punch him; **hizo a. de salir corriendo** he made as if to run off (**b**) *(indicio)* sign, hint; **tuve un a. de gripe** I felt like I had a bout of flu coming on

amague *etc ver* **amagar**

amainar 1 *vt Náut* to take in

2 *vi también Fig* to abate, to die down

amalgama *nf también Fig* amalgam

amalgamar *vt también Fig* to amalgamate

amamantar *vt (animal)* to suckle; *(bebé)* to breast-feed

amancebamiento *nm* living together, cohabitation

amancebarse *vpr* to live together, to cohabit

amanecer [46] **1** *nm* dawn; **al a.** at dawn

2 *v impersonal* **amaneció a las siete** dawn broke at seven

3 *vi (en un lugar)* to see in the dawn; **amanecimos en Estambul** we arrived in Istanbul at dawn; *Am* **¿cómo amaneciste?** how did you sleep?

amanerado, -a *adj* (**a**) *(afeminado)* effeminate (**b**) *(afectado)* mannered, affected

amaneramiento *nm* (**a**) *(afeminamiento)* effeminacy (**b**) *(afectación)* affectation

amanerarse *vpr* (**a**) *(afeminarse)* to become effeminate (**b**) *(volverse afectado)* to become affected

amanita *nf* amanita

amansadora *nf RP Fam* tedious wait

amansar 1 *vt (animal)* to tame; *(persona)* to calm down; *(pasiones)* to calm; **la música amansa a las fieras** music hath charms to soothe the savage beast

2 amansarse *vpr* to calm down

amante *nmf* (**a**) *(querido)* lover (**b**) *(aficionado)* **ser a. de algo/de hacer algo** to be keen on sth/doing sth; **los amantes del arte** art lovers; **los amantes del bricolage** do-it-yourself enthusiasts; **un a. de la naturaleza** a nature lover

amanuense *nmf* scribe

amañado, -a *adj (elecciones, resultado)* rigged

amañar 1 *vt (elecciones, resultado)* to rig; *(documento)* to doctor

2 amañarse *vpr* to manage

amaño *nm (treta)* ruse, trick

amapola *nf* poppy

amar 1 *vt* to love; **ama a tu prójimo como a ti mismo** love thy neighbor as thyself

2 amarse *vpr* **se aman** they love each other

amaraje *nm (de hidroavión)* landing at sea; *(de vehículo espacial)* splashdown

amaranto *nm* amaranth

amarar *vi (hidroavión)* to land at sea; *(vehículo espacial)* to splash down

amargado, -a 1 *adj (resentido)* bitter; **estar a. de la vida** to be bitter and twisted
2 *nm,f* bitter person

amargar [40] **1** *vt (día, vacaciones)* to spoil, to ruin; **a. la vida a alguien** to make sb's life hell
2 amargarse *vpr (alimento, persona)* to become bitter; **no te amargues por eso** don't let it bother you

amargo, -a *adj (sabor, recuerdo, persona)* bitter

amargor *nm (sabor)* bitterness

amargue *etc ver* **amargar**

amargura *nf (disgusto)* sorrow

amariconado, -a *Fam Pey* **1** *adj (afeminado)* limp-wristed, faggy
2 *nm (delicado)* wimp

amarillear 1 *vt* to turn yellow
2 *vi* to (turn) yellow

amarillento, -a *adj* yellowish

amarillismo *nm Prensa* sensationalism

amarillo, -a 1 *adj* (**a**) *(color)* yellow; **a. canario** canary yellow; **a. limón** lemon (colored) (**b**) *Prensa* sensationalist (**c**) *Ind* **sindicato a.** = union controlled by the employers
2 *nm (color)* yellow

amariposado, -a *adj Fam (afeminado)* effeminate

amarra *nf Náut* mooring rope; **largar** *o* **soltar amarras** to cast off; *Fig* **tener amarras** *(contactos)* to have connections, to have friends in high places

amarradero *nm Náut (poste)* bollard; *(argolla)* mooring ring

amarrar 1 *vt* (**a**) *Náut* to moor (**b**) *(atar)* to tie (up); **a. algo/a alguien a algo** to tie sth/sb to sth
2 amarrarse *vpr Am salvo RP (pelo)* to tie up; *(cordones)* to tie

amarre *nm Náut* mooring

amarrete *Andes, RP Fam* **1** *adj* stingy, tight
2 *nmf* stingy person, miser

amartelado, -a *adj (ojos, mirada)* adoring; **están amartelados** they are very much in love

amartillar *vt (arma)* to cock

amasar *vt* (**a**) *(masa)* to knead; *(yeso)* to mix (**b**) *(riquezas)* to amass

amasiato *nm CAm, Chile, Méx* **vivir en a.** to live together

amasijo *nm (mezcla)* hodgepodge

amasio, -a *nm,f CAm, Méx* common-law husband, *f* common-law wife

amateur [ama'ter] *(pl* **amateurs***) adj & nmf* amateur

amatista *nf* amethyst

amazacotado, -a *adj (comida)* stodgy

amazona *nf* (**a**) *(jinete)* horsewoman (**b**) *Mitol* Amazon

Amazonas *nm* **el A.** the Amazon

Amazonia *nf* **la A.** the Amazon

amazónico, -a *adj (selva, región)* Amazon; *(tribu, cultura)* Amazonian

ambages *nmpl* **sin a.** without beating about the bush

ámbar *nm* amber

ambarino, -a *adj* amber

Amberes *n* Antwerp

ambición *nf* ambition

ambicionar *vt* to have as one's ambition; **ambiciona el puesto de presidente** it is his ambition to become president

ambicioso, -a 1 *adj* ambitious
2 *nm,f* ambitious person

ambidextro, -a, ambidiestro, -a 1 *adj* ambidextrous
2 *nm,f* ambidextrous person

ambientación *nf* (**a**) *Cine, Lit & Teatro* setting (**b**) *Rad* sound effects

ambientador *nm (de aire)* air freshener

ambiental *adj* (**a**) *(físico, atmosférico)* ambient (**b**) *(del medio ambiente)* environmental

ambientar 1 *vt* (**a**) **la película/historia está ambientada en...** the movie/story is set in... (**b**) *(iluminar)* to light; *(decorar)* to decorate
2 ambientarse *vpr (acostumbrarse)* to settle down *(in new place, job)*

ambiente 1 *adj* ambient
2 *nm* (**a**) *(entorno)* atmosphere; **se respira una enorme tensión en el a.** the tension (in the atmosphere) is palpable; **abre la ventana, el a. está muy cargado** open the window, it's very stuffy in here (**b**) *(animación)* life, atmosphere; **en esta discoteca no hay a.** there's no atmosphere in this disco (**c**) *Esp Fam* **el a.** *(homosexual)* the gay scene (**d**) *Andes, RP (habitación)* room

ambigú *(pl* **ambigús** *o* **ambigúes***) nm* buffet

ambigüedad *nf* ambiguity

ambiguo, -a *adj* (**a**) ambiguous (**b**) *Gram* **sustantivo a.** noun that may be either masculine or feminine

ámbito *nm* (**a**) *(espacio, límites)* confines, scope; **una ley de á. provincial** a law which is applicable at provincial level; **dentro del á. de** within the scope of; **fuera del á. de** outside the realm of; **á. de influencia** sphere of influence (**b**) *(ambiente)* world, circles

ambivalencia *nf* ambivalence

ambivalente *adj* ambivalent

ambos, -as 1 *adj pl* both; **a. actores resultaron premiados** both actors received an award, the two actors both received an award
2 *pron pl* both (of them); **me gustan a.** I like both of them, I like them both

ambrosía *nf Mitol* ambrosia

ambulancia *nf* ambulance

ambulante *adj* traveling; **vendedor a.** peddler, hawker; **prohibida la venta a.** *(en letrero)* no soliciting

ambulatorio, -a 1 *adj* **tratamiento a.** outpatient treatment
2 *nm* clinic, health center

ameba *nf* amoeba

amedrentar 1 *vt* to scare, to frighten
2 amedrentarse *vpr* to get scared *o* frightened

amén 1 *interj* amen; *Fig* **decir a. a** to accept unquestioningly; *Fig* **en un decir a.** in the twinkling of an eye
2 amén de *loc adv (además de)* in addition to

amenaza *nf* threat; **a. de bomba** bomb scare; **a. de muerte** death threat

amenazador, -ora *adj* threatening, menacing

amenazante *adj* threatening, menacing

amenazar [14] **1** *vt* (**a**) *(persona)* to threaten; **a. a alguien con hacer algo** to threaten sb with doing sth; **a. a alguien con el despido/de muerte** to threaten to fire/kill sb (**b**) *(dar señales de)* **esos nubarrones amenazan lluvia** those dark clouds are threatening rain; **esa casa amenaza ruina** that house is in danger of collapsing
2 *v impersonal* **amenaza lluvia/tormenta** it looks like it's going to rain/there's going to be a storm

amenidad *nf* (**a**) *(entretenimiento)* entertaining qualities (**b**) *(agrado)* pleasantness

amenizar [14] *vt* to liven up

ameno, -a *adj* (**a**) *(entretenido)* entertaining (**b**) *(placentero)* pleasant

amenorrea *nf Med* amenorrhea

América *n (continente)* the Americas, America; *Am (Latinoamérica)* Latin America; **A. Central** Central America; **A. del Sur/Norte** South/North America

americana *nf (chaqueta)* jacket

americanada *nf Fam Pey (película)* typical Hollywood movie

americanismo *nm* (**a**) *(carácter)* American character (**b**) *Ling* Americanism

americanizar [14] **1** *vt* to Americanize
  2 americanizarse *vpr* to become Americanized

americano, -a *adj & nm,f* American

amerindio, -a *adj & nm,f* American Indian, Amerindian

ameritar *vt Am* to deserve

amerizaje *nm (de hidroavión)* landing at sea; *(de vehículo espacial)* splashdown

amerizar [14] *vi (hidroavión)* to land at sea; *(vehículo espacial)* to splash down

ametralladora *nf* machine gun

ametrallar *vt* (**a**) *(con ametralladora)* to machine-gun (**b**) *(con metralla)* to shower with shrapnel

amianto *nm* asbestos

amigable *adj* amicable

amígdala *nf* tonsil

amigdalitis *nf inv Med* tonsillitis

amigo, -a 1 *adj* (**a**) *(no enemigo)* friendly; **México y otros países amigos** Mexico and other friendly nations; **un pintor a. me lo regaló** a painter friend of mine gave it to me (**b**) *(aficionado)* **ser a. de algo/hacer algo** to be keen on sth/doing sth; **a. de la buena mesa** partial to good food
  2 *nm,f* (**a**) *(persona)* friend; **hacerse a. de** to make friends with; **hacerse amigos** to become friends; *Fam* **los amigos de lo ajeno** the light-fingered; **un a. del colegio** a school friend; **un a. íntimo** a close friend (**b**) *Fam (compañero, novio)* partner (**c**) *(tratamiento)* (my) friend; **¡a., eso es otra cuestión!** that's another matter, my friend!

amigote, amiguete *nm Fam* pal, buddy

amiguismo *nm* **hay mucho a.** there are always jobs for the boys

amilanamiento *nm* **su a. le impedía hablar** he was so intimidated he couldn't speak

amilanar 1 *vt* (**a**) *(intimidar)* to intimidate (**b**) *(desanimar)* to discourage
  2 amilanarse *vpr (acobardarse)* to be discouraged, to lose heart

aminoácido *nm Biol* amino acid

aminorar 1 *vt* to reduce
  2 *vi* to decrease, to diminish

amistad *nf* friendship; **hacer** *o* **trabar a. (con)** to make friends (with); **amistades** friends

amistoso, -a 1 *adj* friendly; *Dep* **un partido a.** a friendly
  2 *nm Dep* friendly

amnesia *nf Psi* amnesia

amnésico, -a *Psi* **1** *adj* amnesic, amnesiac
  2 *nm,f* amnesiac

amniocentesis *nf inv Med* amniocentesis

amniótico, -a *adj Med* amniotic; **líquido a.** amniotic fluid

amnistía *nf* amnesty; **a. fiscal** = amnesty during which people guilty of tax evasion may pay what they owe without being prosecuted; **A. Internacional** Amnesty International

amnistiar [32] *vt* to grant amnesty to

amo *nm* (**a**) *(dueño)* owner (**b**) *(de criado)* master; *Fam* **ser el a. del cotarro** to rule the roost

amodorrado, -a *adj* drowsy

amodorrarse *vpr* to get drowsy

amolar [63] *Fam* **1** *vt* to irritate, to annoy
  2 amolarse *vpr Am* to become irritated *o* annoyed

amoldable *adj* adaptable; **ser a. a** to be able to adapt to

amoldar 1 *vt (adaptar)* to adapt (**a** to)
  2 amoldarse *vpr (adaptarse)* to adapt (**a** to)

amonal *nm* ammonal

amonestación *nf* (**a**) *(reprimenda)* reprimand (**b**) *Dep* warning (**c**) **amonestaciones** *(para matrimonio)* banns

amonestar *vt* (**a**) *(reprender)* to reprimand (**b**) *Dep* to caution (**c**) *(para matrimonio)* to publish the banns of

amoniacal *adj* with ammonia

amoníaco, amoniaco *nm (gas)* ammonia; *(líquido)* liquid ammonia

amontillado 1 *adj* **vino a.** amontillado, = medium-dry sherry
  2 *nm* amontillado, = medium-dry sherry

amontonar 1 *vt (apilar)* to pile up; *(reunir)* to accumulate
  2 amontonarse *vpr (personas)* to form a crowd; *(problemas, trabajo)* to pile up; *(ideas, solicitudes)* to come thick and fast

amor *nm* (**a**) *(sentimiento)* love; **hacer el a.** to make love; **de mil amores** with pleasure; **por a. al arte** for the love of it; **¡por a. de Dios!** for God's sake!; **al a. de la lumbre** *o* **del fuego** by the fireside; **a. libre** free love; **a. platónico** platonic love; **a. propio** pride (**b**) *(persona amada)* love; **su primer a.** his first love; **el a. de mi vida** the love of my life; **un antiguo a.** an old flame (**c**) *(esmero)* devotion; **escribe con a. su última novela** she's lovingly crafting her latest novel

amoral *adj* amoral

amoralidad *nf* amorality

amoratado, -a *adj (de frío)* blue; *(por golpes)* black and blue

amoratarse *vpr (por el frío)* to turn blue; *(por golpes)* to turn black and blue

amordazar [14] *vt (persona)* to gag; *(perro)* to muzzle; **a. a la prensa** to gag the press

amorfo, -a *adj* (**a**) *(sin forma)* amorphous (**b**) *(persona)* lacking in character

amorío *nm* fling

amoroso, -a *adj (trato, sentimiento)* loving; **carta/relación amorosa** love letter/affair

amortajar *vt (difunto)* to shroud

amortiguación *nf* (**a**) *(de ruido)* muffling; *(de golpe)* softening, cushioning (**b**) *Aut* shock absorbers

amortiguador, -ora 1 *adj (de ruido)* muffling; *(de golpe)* softening, cushioning
  2 *nm Aut* shock absorber

amortiguar [11] **1** *vt (ruido)* to muffle; *(golpe)* to soften, to cushion
  2 amortiguarse *vpr (ruido)* to die away; *(golpe)* to be cushioned

amortizable *adj Fin (bonos, acciones)* redeemable

amortización *nf Fin (de deuda, préstamo)* repayment, paying-off; *(de inversión, capital)* recouping; *(de bonos, acciones)* redemption; *(de bienes de equipo)* depreciation

amortizar [14] *vt* (**a**) *(sacar provecho)* to get one's money's worth out of (**b**) *Fin (deuda, préstamo)* to repay, to pay off; *(inversión, capital)* to recoup; *(bonos, acciones)* to redeem; *(bienes de equipo)* to depreciate (**c**) *(puesto de trabajo)* to abolish, to do away with

amoscarse [59] *vpr Fam* to get in a huff

amotinado, -a *adj & nm,f* rebel, insurgent

amotinamiento *nm (de subordinados)* rebellion, uprising; *(de marineros)* mutiny

amotinar 1 *vt (a subordinados)* to incite to riot; *(a marineros)* to incite to mutiny
  2 amotinarse *vpr (subordinados)* to riot; *(marineros)* to mutiny

amovible *adj (cargo)* revocable

amparar 1 *vt (proteger)* to protect; *(dar cobijo a)* to give shelter to, to take in; **ese derecho lo ampara la Constitución** that right is enshrined in the Constitution
  2 ampararse *vpr (cobijarse)* **ampararse de** to (take) shelter from; **ampararse en una ley** to have recourse to a

law; **se ampara en la excusa de que no sabía nada** she uses her ignorance as an excuse

amparo *nm* protection; **al a. de** *(persona, caridad)* with the help of; *(ley)* under the protection of

amperaje *nm Elec* amperage

amperímetro *nm Elec* ammeter

amperio *nm Elec* amp, ampere

ampliable *adj (plazo)* extendible; *Inform* expandable

ampliación *nf* (a) *(aumento)* expansion; *(de edificio, plazo)* extension; *Fin* **a. de capital** stock issue (b) *Fot* enlargement

ampliadora *nf Fot* enlarger

ampliamente *adv* (a) *(con espacio)* easily; **aquí cabe todo a.** there's more than enough room for everything here (b) *(extensamente) (aceptado, admitido)* widely

ampliar [32] *vt* (a) *(agrandar)* to expand; *(local, vivienda, plazo)* to extend (b) *Fot* to enlarge, to blow up (c) *(estudios)* to further, to continue

amplificación *nf* amplification

amplificador *nm Elec* amplifier

amplificar [59] *vt* to amplify

amplio, -a *adj* (a) *(sala, maletero)* roomy, spacious; *(avenida, gama)* wide (b) *(ropa)* loose (c) *(explicación, cobertura)* comprehensive; **en el sentido más a. de la palabra** in the broadest sense of the word (d) **de amplias miras** broad-minded

amplitud *nf* (a) *(espaciosidad)* roominess, spaciousness; *(de avenida)* wideness (b) *(de ropa)* looseness (c) *(extensión)* extent, comprehensiveness; **a. de miras** broad-mindedness (d) *Fís* **a. de onda** amplitude

ampolla *nf* (a) *(en piel)* blister; *Fig* **levantar ampollas** to create bad feeling (b) *(para inyecciones)* ampoule; *(frasco)* vial

ampollarse *vpr* to blister; **se me han ampollado los pies** I've got blisters on my feet

ampulosidad *nf* pomposity

ampuloso, -a *adj* pompous

amputación *nf* amputation

amputar *vt* to amputate

Amsterdam *n* Amsterdam

amueblado, -a 1 *adj (piso)* furnished

   2 *nm RP* room hired for sex

amueblar *vt* to furnish

amuermar *Esp Fam* **1** *vt (aburrir)* to bore senseless

   2 amuermarse *vpr (aburrirse)* to get bored senseless; *(adormilarse)* to get sleepy

amuleto *nm (antiguo)* amulet; *(de la suerte)* lucky charm

amurallado, -a *adj* walled

amurallar *vt* to build a wall around

anabaptista *adj & nmf* Anabaptist

anabolismo *nm Biol* anabolism

anabolizante 1 *adj* anabolic

   2 *nm* anabolic steroid

anacarado, -a *adj* pearly

anacardo *nm* cashew (nut)

anaconda *nf* anaconda

anacoreta *nmf* anchorite, hermit

anacrónico, -a *adj* anachronistic

anacronismo *nm* anachronism

ánade *nm* duck

anaerobio, -a *adj Biol* anaerobic

anáfora *nf Gram* anaphora

anagrama *nm* anagram

anal *adj Anat* anal

anales *nmpl también Fig* annals

analfabetismo *nm* illiteracy

analfabeto, -a *adj & nm,f* illiterate

analgesia *nf* analgesia

analgésico, -a *adj & nm* analgesic

análisis *nm inv* (a) *(estudio)* analysis; *Fin* **a. coste-beneficio** cost-benefit analysis; **a. gramatical** sentence analysis; **a. de mercado** market analysis; **a. sintáctico** syntactic analysis (b) *(prueba médica)* test; **a. clínico** (clinical) test; **a. de orina** urine analysis; **a. de sangre** blood test

analista *nmf* analyst; *Inform* (computer) analyst; **a. financiero** *o* **de inversiones** investment analyst; **a. de mercados** market analyst; **a. de sistemas** systems analyst

analítica *nf Med* clinical testing

analítico, -a *adj* analytical

analizar [14] *vt* to analyze; **a. sintácticamente la siguiente oración** parse the following sentence

analogía *nf* similarity; **por a.** by analogy

analógico, -a *adj* (a) *(análogo)* analogous, similar (b) *Inform & Tec* analog

análogo, -a *adj* analogous *o* similar (**a** to)

ananá, ananás *nm RP* pineapple

anaquel *nm* shelf

anaranjado, -a *adj* orange

anarco *Fam* **1** *adj* anarchistic

   2 *nmf* anarchist

anarcosindicalismo *nm Pol* anarcho-syndicalism

anarcosindicalista *adj & nmf Pol* anarcho-syndicalist

anarquía *nf* (a) *(falta de gobierno)* anarchy (b) *(doctrina política)* anarchism (c) *(desorden)* chaos, anarchy

anárquico, -a *adj* anarchic

anarquismo *nm Pol* anarchism

anarquista *adj & nmf* anarchist

anatema *nm Rel* curse, anathema; *Fig* curse

anatematizar *vt* to condemn

anatomía *nf* anatomy

anatómico, -a *adj* (a) *Anat* anatomical (b) *(asiento, diseño, calzado)* orthopedic

anca *nf* haunch; **ancas de rana** frogs' legs

ancestral *adj (costumbre)* age-old

ancestro *nm* ancestor

ancho, -a 1 *adj* (a) *(abertura, carretera, río)* wide; *(ropa)* loose-fitting; **te está a.** it's too big for you; **había rocas a lo a. de la carretera** there were rocks across the middle of the road (b) *Esp (persona) (satisfecha, orgullosa)* smug, self-satisfied; **lo dijo delante de todos y se quedó tan a.** he said it in front of everyone, just like that; *Irónico* **¡se habrá quedado a. con la tontería que ha dicho!** he must be delighted with himself for making that stupid remark; **a mis/tus anchas** at ease

   2 *nm* width; **¿cuánto mide** *o* **tiene de a.?** how wide is it?; **tener 5 metros de a.** to be 5 meters wide; *Inform* **a. de banda** bandwidth; *Ferroc* **a. de vía** gauge

anchoa *nf* anchovy

anchura *nf* width

anciano, -a 1 *adj* old

   2 *nm,f (hombre)* old man, old person; *(mujer)* old woman, old person; **los ancianos** the elderly, old people

   3 *nm (de tribu)* elder

ancla *nf* anchor; **echar/levar anclas** to drop/weigh anchor

anclado, -a *adj* **una aldea anclada en el pasado** a village stuck in the past

anclaje *nm Náut* anchoring; *Tec* **los anclajes de una grúa** the moorings of a crane

anclar *vi* to (drop) anchor

áncora *nf* anchor

anda *interj* (a) *(indica sorpresa)* **¡a.!** gosh!; **¡a. la osa!** good grief! (b) *(por favor)* go on! (c) *(venga)* come on! (d) **¡a. ya!** *(negativa despectiva)* get away!, come off it!

andadas *nfpl Fam* **volver a las a.** to return to one's bad old ways

andaderas *nfpl* baby walker

andador, -ora 1 *adj* fond of walking

2 *nm (tacataca)* baby walker; *(para adultos)* (adult) walker

andadura *nf* **la a. de un país** the evolution of a country; **su a. por Europa** his travels through Europe

ándale *interj CAm, Méx Fam* **¡á.!** come on!

Andalucía *n* Andalusia

andalucismo *nm* **(a)** *Pol (doctrina)* = doctrine favoring Andalusian autonomy **(b)** *(palabra)* = Andalusian word or expression

andalusí *Hist* **1** *adj* Moorish

2 *nmf* Moor, = of or related to the Arab empire of Al-Andalus in southern Spain (711–1492)

andaluz, -uza *adj & nm,f* Andalusian

andamiaje *nm* scaffolding; *Fig* structure, framework

andamio *nm* scaffold

andanada *nf* **(a)** *(gen) & Mil* broadside **(b)** *Taurom* = covered stand in a bullring

andando *interj* **¡a.!** come on!, let's get a move on!

andante *adv* **(a)** *(que anda)* walking **(b)** *Mús* andante

andanzas *nfpl* adventures

andar [7] **1** *vi* **(a)** *esp Esp (caminar)* to walk; **¿fuiste en autobús o andando?** did you go by bus or on foot?, did you go by bus or did you walk?; **a. por la calle** to walk in the street

(b) *(funcionar)* to work, to go; **el reloj no anda** the clock has stopped; **las cosas andan mal** things are going badly; **los negocios andan muy bien** business is going very well

(c) *(estar)* to be; **¿qué tal andas?** how are you (doing)?; **a. preocupado** to be worried; **creo que anda por el almacén** I think he is somewhere in the warehouse; **a. haciendo algo** to be doing sth; **anda explicando sus aventuras** he's talking about his adventures; **a. tras algo/alguien** to be after sth/sb; **de a. por casa** *(explicación, método)* basic, rough and ready; **mi ropa de a. por casa** my clothes for wearing around the house

(d) *(ocuparse)* **a. en** *(asuntos, líos)* to be involved in; *(papeleos, negocios)* to be busy with

(e) *(hurgar)* **a. en** to rummage around in; **¿quién ha andado en mis papeles?** who has been messing around with my papers?

(f) *(indica acción)* **en ese país andan a tiros** in that country they go around shooting one another; **andan a voces todo el día** they spend the whole day shouting at each other

(g) *(alcanzar, rondar)* **a. por** to be about; **anda por los sesenta** he's about sixty; **debe de a. por el medio millón** it must be *o* cost about half a million

(h) *Fam (enredar)* **a. con algo** to play with sth

2 *vt* **(a)** *(recorrer)* to go, to travel; **anduvimos 15 kilómetros** we walked (for) 15 kilometers **(b)** *CAm (llevar puesto)* to wear **(c)** *CAm (llevar)* to carry

3 andarse *vpr* **(a)** *(obrar)* **andarse con cuidado/misterios** to be careful/secretive; **andarse con rodeos, andarse por las ramas** to beat around the bush **(b) todo se andará** all in good time **(c)** *Am (marcharse)* to go, to leave; **¡ándate de una vez!** go away!

4 *nm* gait, walk; **andares** *(de persona)* gait; **tener andares de** to walk like

andarín, -ina *adj* **ser muy a.** to be a very keen walker

andas *nfpl* **llevar a alguien en a.** to give sb a fireman's seat carry

ándele *interj CAm, Méx Fam* **¡á.!** come on!

andén *nm* **(a)** *Ferroc* platform **(b)** *Andes, CAm (acera)* sidewalk

Andes *nmpl* **los A.** the Andes

andinismo *nm Am* mountaineering

andinista *nmf Am* mountaineer

andino, -a *adj & nm,f* Andean

Andorra *n* Andorra

andorrano, -a *adj & nm,f* Andorran

andrajo *nm (harapo)* rag

andrajoso, -a 1 *adj* ragged

2 *nm,f* person dressed in rags

andrógeno *nm* androgen

andrógino, -a 1 *adj* androgynous

2 *nm* hermaphrodite

androide *nm (autómata)* android

andurriales *nmpl* remote place; **¿qué haces por estos a.?** what are you doing as far off the beaten track as this?

anduviera *etc ver* **andar**

anea *nf* cattail; **silla de a.** chair with a wickerwork seat

anécdota *nf* anecdote

anecdotario *nm* collection of anecdotes

anecdótico, -a *adj* **(a)** *(con historietas)* anecdotal **(b)** *(no esencial)* incidental

anegar [40] **1** *vt* **(a)** *(inundar)* to flood **(b)** *(ahogar) (planta)* to drown

2 anegarse *vpr* **(a)** *(inundarse)* to flood; **sus ojos se anegaron de lágrimas** tears welled up in his eyes **(b)** *(ahogarse)* to drown

anejo, -a 1 *adj (edificio)* connected (**a** to); *(documento)* attached (**a** to)

2 *nm* annex

anemia *nf Med* anemia

anémico, -a *Med* **1** *adj* anemic

2 *nm,f* anemia sufferer

anemómetro *nm* wind gauge, *Espec* anemometer

anémona *nf (planta)* anemone; **a. de mar** sea anemone

anestesia *nf Med (técnica)* anesthesia; *(sustancia)* anesthetic; **a. general** general anesthesia/anesthetic; **a. local** local anesthesia/anesthetic

anestesiar *vt Med* to anesthetize, to place under anesthetic

anestésico, -a *adj & nm Med* anesthetic

anestesista *nmf* anesthetist

Aneto *nm* **el A.** Aneto

aneurisma *nm Med* aneurysm

anexar *vt (documento)* to attach

anexión *nf* annexation

anexionar *vt* to annex

anexionista *nmf Pol* annexationist

anexo, -a 1 *adj (edificio)* connected; *(documento)* attached

2 *nm* annex

anfeta *nf Fam* tab of speed

anfetamina *nf* amphetamine

anfibio, -a 1 *adj también Fig* amphibious

2 *nm* amphibian

anfiteatro *nm* **(a)** *(en teatro)* circle; *(en cine)* balcony **(b)** *(romano)* amphitheater

anfitrión, -ona 1 *adj* host; **país a.** host country

2 *nm,f* host, *f* hostess

ánfora *nf* **(a)** *(cántaro)* amphora **(b)** *Méx, Perú (electoral)* ballot box

ángel *nm* angel; **á. custodio** *o* **de la guarda** guardian angel; **tener á.** to have something special; **¡eres un á.!** you're an angel!

angélica *nf* angelica

angelical *adj* angelic

angelote *nm* **(a)** *(estatua)* large figure of an angel **(b)** *(niño)* chubby child

ángelus *nm inv Rel* Angelus

angina *nf* **(a) anginas** *(amigdalitis)* sore throat; **tener anginas** to have a sore throat **(b) a. de pecho** angina (pectoris)

anglicanismo *nm Rel* Anglicanism

anglicano, -a *adj & nm,f Rel* Anglican

anglicismo *nm* anglicism

angloamericano, -a *adj & nm,f* Anglo-American

anglófilo, -a *adj & nm,f* anglophile

anglofobia *nf* anglophobia

anglófobo, -a *adj & nm,f* anglophobe

anglófono, -a, angloparlante 1 *adj* English-speaking, anglophone

2 *nm,f* English speaker, anglophone

anglosajón, -ona *adj & nm,f* Anglo-Saxon

Angola *n* Angola

angoleño, -a, angolano, -a *adj & nm,f* Angolan

angora *nf (de conejo)* angora; *(de cabra)* mohair

angosto, -a *adj* narrow

angostura *nf* **(a)** *(estrechez)* narrowness **(b)** *(extracto)* angostura

ángstrom *(pl ángstroms) nm Fís* angstrom

anguila *nf* eel; **a. de mar** conger eel

angula *nf* elver

angular 1 *adj* angular

2 *nm Fot* **gran a.** wide-angle lens

ángulo *nm* **(a)** *(figura geométrica)* angle; **á. agudo/obtuso/ recto** acute/obtuse/right angle; *Mil* **á. de mira** line of sight; *Aut* **á. muerto** blind spot; *Mil* **á. de tiro** elevation **(b)** *(rincón)* corner

anguloso, -a *adj* angular

angurria *nf Am* **(a)** *(hambre)* hunger **(b)** *(codicia, avidez)* greed

angustia *nf* **(a)** *(aflicción)* anxiety **(b)** *Psi* distress

angustiado, -a *adj* anguished, distressed

angustiar 1 *vt* to distress

2 angustiarse *vpr (agobiarse)* to get worried (**por** about)

angustioso, -a *adj (espera, momentos)* anxious; *(situación, noticia)* distressing

anhelante *adj* longing (**por algo/por hacer algo** for sth/to do sth)

anhelar *vt* to long *o* wish for; **a. hacer algo** to long to do sth

anhelo *nm* longing

anhídrido *nm Quím* anhydride; **a. carbónico** carbon dioxide

anidar *vi* **(a)** *(pájaro)* to nest **(b)** *(sentimiento)* **a. en** to find a place in

anilina *nf Quím* aniline

anilla *nf* ring; **anillas** *Dep* rings

anillar *vt* **(a)** *(sujetar)* to fasten with rings **(b)** *(aves)* to ring

anillo *nm* **(a)** *(de dedo, cortina)* ring; **a. de boda** wedding ring; *Fam Fig* **me viene como a. al dedo** *(cosa)* it's just what I needed; **me vienes como a. al dedo, necesitaba un fontanero** how lucky that you should have come, I was looking for a plumber!; *Fam Fig* **no se me van a caer los anillos** it won't hurt me (to do it); **a. de compromiso** *o* **de pedida** engagement ring **(b)** *Zool* annulus **(c)** *(de planeta)* ring

ánima *nf* soul; **á. bendita** soul in purgatory

animación *nf* **(a)** *(alegría)* liveliness **(b)** *(bullicio)* hustle and bustle, activity **(c)** *Cine* animation

animado, -a *adj* **(a)** *(con buen ánimo)* cheerful **(b)** *(divertido)* lively **(c)** *Cine* animated

animador, -ora *nm,f* **(a)** *(en espectáculo)* master of ceremonies **(b)** *(en fiesta de niños)* children's entertainer **(c)** *(en deporte)* cheerleader

animadversión *nf* animosity

animal 1 *adj* **(a)** *(instintos, funciones)* animal; **el reino a.** the animal kingdom **(b)** *(persona) (basto)* rough; *(ignorante)* ignorant

2 *nm* animal; **a. de carga** beast of burden; **a. de compañía** pet; **a. doméstico** *(de granja)* farm animal; *(de compañía)* pet; **a. protegido** protected species

3 *nmf (persona)* animal, brute

animalada *nf* **decir/hacer una a.** to say/do something outrageous

animar 1 *vt* **(a)** *(alegrar) (persona)* to cheer up; *(fuego, diálogo, fiesta)* to liven up; **tu regalo le animó mucho** your present really cheered her up; **los fans animaban a su equipo** the fans were cheering their team on **(b)** *(estimular)* to encourage; **a. a alguien a hacer algo** to encourage sb to do sth **(c)** *(impulsar)* to motivate, to drive; **no le anima ningún afán de riqueza** she's not driven by any desire to be rich

2 animarse *vpr* **(a)** *(persona)* to cheer up; *(fiesta, ambiente)* to liven up; **¡anímate!** cheer up! **(b)** *(decidir)* **¿quién se anima a subir hasta la cumbre?** who's up for climbing right to the top?; **no me animo a decírselo** I can't bring myself to tell her

anímico, -a *adj* **estado a.** state of mind

animismo *nm* animism

ánimo 1 *nm* **(a)** *(aliento)* encouragement; **dar ánimos a alguien** to encourage sb **(b)** *(energía)* energy, vitality; *(humor)* disposition; **¡levanta ese á.!** cheer up!; **no tiene ánimos para nada** she doesn't feel like doing anything; **los ánimos estaban revueltos** feelings were running high **(c)** *(intención)* **con/sin á. de** with/without the intention of; **lo hice sin á. de ofenderte** I didn't mean to offend you; **sin á. de lucro** *(organización)* not-for-profit **(d)** *(valor)* courage **(e)** *(alma)* mind

2 *interj* **¡á.!** *(¡anímate!)* cheer up!; *(¡adelante!)* come on!

animosidad *nf* animosity

animoso, -a *adj (valiente)* courageous; *(decidido)* undaunted

aniñado, -a *adj (comportamiento)* childish; *(voz, rostro)* childlike

aniquilación *nf* annihilation

aniquilar *vt* to annihilate, to wipe out

anís *(pl anises) nm* **(a)** *(planta)* anise **(b)** *(grano)* aniseed **(c)** *(licor)* anisette

anisete *nm* anisette

aniversario *nm (de muerte, fundación, suceso)* anniversary; *(cumpleaños)* birthday; **a. de boda** wedding anniversary

Ankara *n* Ankara

ano *nm* anus

anoche *adv* last night; **antes de a.** the night before last

anochecer [46] **1** *nm* dusk, nightfall; **al a.** at dusk

2 *v impersonal* to get dark; **anochecía** it was getting dark

3 *vi* **a. en algún sitio** to be somewhere at nightfall

anodino, -a *adj* unremarkable

ánodo *nm Elec* anode

anomalía *nf* anomaly

anómalo, -a *adj* anomalous

anonadado, -a *adj* **(a)** *(sorprendido)* astonished, bewildered **(b)** *(abatido)* stunned

anonadamiento *nm* astonishment, bewilderment

anonadar 1 *vt* **(a)** *(sorprender)* to astonish, to bewilder **(b)** *(abatir)* to stun

2 anonadarse *vpr* **(a)** *(sorprenderse)* to be astonished, to be bewildered **(b)** *(abatirse)* to be stunned

anonimato *nm* anonymity; **permanecer en el a.** to remain nameless; **vivir en el a.** to live out of the public eye; **salir del a.** to reveal one's identity

anónimo, -a 1 *adj* anonymous

2 *nm* anonymous letter

anorak *(pl anoraks) nm* anorak

anorexia *nf Med* anorexia; **a. nerviosa** anorexia nervosa

anoréxico, -a *adj & nm,f* anorexic

anormal 1 *adj* **(a)** *(anómalo)* abnormal **(b)** *(subnormal)* subnormal; *(como insulto)* moronic

2 *nmf (persona)* subnormal person; *(como insulto)* moron

anormalidad *nf* **(a)** *(anomalía)* abnormality **(b)** *(defecto físico o psíquico)* handicap, disability

anotación *nf (nota escrita)* note; *(en registro)* entry; *Com* **a. contable** book entry

anotar *vt* (**a**) *(escribir)* to note down, to make a note of (**b**) *(tantos)* to score

anovulatorio, -a 1 *adj (anticonceptivo)* anovulatory

2 *nm (anticonceptivo)* anovulant

anquilosamiento *nm* (**a**) *(de articulación)* paralysis (**b**) *(de economía, ciencia)* stagnation

anquilosar 1 *vt* (**a**) *(articulación)* to paralyze (**b**) *(economía, ciencia)* to cause to stagnate

2 anquilosarse *vpr* (**a**) *(articulación)* to become paralyzed (**b**) *(economía, ciencia)* to stagnate

ánsar *nm* goose

ansarón *nm* gosling

ansia *nf* (**a**) *(afán)* longing, yearning (**de** for) (**b**) *(ansiedad)* anxiousness; *(angustia)* anguish; **ansias** *(náuseas)* sickness, nausea

ansiar [32] *vt* **a. algo** to long for sth; **a. hacer algo** to long to do sth

ansiedad *nf* (**a**) *(inquietud)* anxiety; **con a.** anxiously (**b**) *Psi* nervous tension

ansiolítico, -a *adj & nm Med* sedative, *Espec* anxiolytic

ansioso, -a *adj* (**a**) *(impaciente)* impatient; **estar a. por** *o* **de hacer algo** to be impatient to do sth (**b**) *(angustiado)* in anguish

antagónico, -a *adj* antagonistic

antagonismo *nm* antagonism

antagonista *nmf* opponent

antaño *adv* in days gone by

antártico, -a 1 *adj* Antarctic

2 *nm* **el A.** the Antarctic; **el océano Glacial A.** the Antarctic Ocean

Antártida *nf* **la A.** the Antarctic

ante¹ *nm* (**a**) *(piel)* suede (**b**) *(animal)* elk, moose

ante² *prep* (**a**) *(delante de, en presencia de)* before; **a. mis propios ojos** before my very eyes (**b**) *(frente a) (hecho, circunstancia)* in the face of (**c**) *(respecto de)* compared to; **su opinión prevaleció a. la mía** his opinion prevailed over mine; **a. todo** *(sobre todo)* above all; *(en primer lugar)* first of all

anteanoche *adv* the night before last

anteayer *adv* the day before yesterday

antebrazo *nm* forearm

antecámara *nf* antechamber

antecedente 1 *adj* preceding, previous

2 *nm* (**a**) *(precedente)* precedent (**b**) *Gram & Mat* antecedent

3 antecedentes *nmpl (de asunto)* background; **poner a alguien en antecedentes de** *(informar)* to fill sb in on; **antecedentes penales** *o* **policiales** criminal record

anteceder *vt* to come before, to precede

antecesor, -ora *nm,f (predecesor)* predecessor; **antecesores** *(antepasados)* ancestors

antedicho, -a *adj* aforementioned

antediluviano, -a *adj también Fig* antediluvian

antelación *nf* **con a.** in advance; **con dos horas de a.** two hours in advance

antemano *adv* **de a.** beforehand, in advance

antena *nf* (**a**) *Rad & TV* aerial, antenna; **estar/salir en a.** to be/go on the air; **a. colectiva** = aerial shared by all the inhabitants of a block of flats, CATV; **a. parabólica** satellite dish (**b**) *(de animal)* antenna

anteojeras *nfpl* blinders

anteojos *nmpl* (**a**) *(prismáticos)* binoculars (**b**) *(quevedos)* pince-nez (**c**) *Am (gafas)* spectacles, glasses

antepasado, -a *nm,f* ancestor

antepecho *nm (de puente)* parapet; *(de ventana)* sill

antepenúltimo, -a *adj & nm,f* last but two

anteponer [50] **1** *vt* **a. algo a algo** to put sth before sth

2 anteponerse *vpr* **anteponerse a algo** to come before sth

anteproyecto *nm* draft; *Pol* **a. de ley** draft bill

antepuesto, -a *participio ver* **anteponer**

anterior *adj* (**a**) *(previo)* previous (**a** to); **un modelo muy parecido al a.** a model which is very similar to the previous *o* last one; **el año a.** the year before, the previous year (**b**) *(delantero)* front; **la parte a. de un edificio** the front of a building

anterioridad *nf* **con a.** beforehand; **con a. a** before, prior to

anteriormente *adv* previously

antes 1 *adv* (**a**) *(en el tiempo)* before; *(antaño)* formerly, in the past; **no importa si vienes a.** it doesn't matter if you come earlier; **ya no nado como a.** I can't swim as I used to; **mucho/poco a.** long/shortly before; **lo a. posible** as soon as possible; **a. de Cristo** before Christ, BC; **a. de tiempo** ahead of time; **a. de hacer algo** before doing sth; **a. de que** before; **a. de que llegaras** before you arrived; **de a.** *(antiguo)* old; *(anterior)* previous

(**b**) *(en el espacio)* before; **me bajo dos pisos a.** I get off two floors before (you); **a. de** before

(**c**) *(primero)* first; **esta señora está a.** this lady is first; **entraron a. que yo** they went in in front of me

(**d**) *(expresa preferencia)* **a.... que** rather... than; **prefiero la sierra a. que el mar** I like the mountains better than the sea; **iría a la cárcel a. que mentir** I'd rather go to prison than lie; **a. que nada** *(expresando preferencia)* above all, first and foremost

2 antes bien, antes al contrario *loc adv* on the contrary

antesala *nf* anteroom; *Fig* **estar en la a. de** to be on the verge of; **hacer a.** *(esperar)* to wait

antevíspera *nf* day before yesterday; **la a. de...** two days before...

antiabortista 1 *adj* antiabortion, pro-life

2 *nmf* antiabortion *o* pro-life campaigner

antiácido, -a *adj & nm (medicamento)* antacid

antiadherente *adj* nonstick

antiaéreo, -a *adj* antiaircraft

antiamericano, -a *adj* anti-American

antiarrugas *adj inv* anti-wrinkle

antibalas, antibala *adj inv* bulletproof

antibiótico, -a *adj & nm* antibiotic

antibloqueo 1 *adj inv* **frenos a.** antilock brakes

2 *nm inv* antilock braking system

anticancerígeno *nm* cancer drug

anticarro *adj inv* antitank

anticaspa *adj* antidandruff; **champú a.** (anti)dandruff shampoo

anticatarral 1 *adj* **medicamento a.** cold remedy

2 *nm* cold remedy

anticelulítico, -a *adj* anticellulite

antichoque *adj* shockproof

anticiclón *nm Meteo* anticyclone

anticipación *nf* earliness; **con a.** in advance; **con un mes de a.** a month in advance; **con a. a** prior to

anticipadamente *adv* in advance, beforehand

anticipado, -a *adj (elecciones)* early; *(pago)* advance; **por a.** in advance

anticipar 1 *vt* (**a**) *(prever)* to anticipate (**b**) *(adelantar)* to bring forward (**c**) *(pago)* to pay in advance (**d**) *(información)* **no te puedo a. nada** I can't tell you anything just now

2 anticiparse *vpr* (**a**) *(suceder antes)* to arrive early; **se anticipó a su tiempo** he was ahead of his time (**b**) *(adelantarse)* **anticiparse a alguien** to beat sb to it

anticipo *nm* (**a**) *(de dinero)* advance (**b**) *(presagio)* foretaste

anticlerical *adj* anticlerical

anticlericalismo *nm* anticlericalism

anticlímax *nm inv (en obra, película)* aftermath *(of climax)*

anticoagulante *adj & nm Med* anticoagulant

anticomunismo *nm* anticommunism

anticomunista *adj & nmf* anticommunist

anticoncepción *nf* contraception

anticonceptivo, -a *adj & nm* contraceptive

anticonformismo *nm* nonconformism

anticongelante *adj & nm* antifreeze

anticonstitucional *adj Der* unconstitutional

anticonstitucionalidad *nf Der* unconstitutional nature

anticorrosivo, -a 1 *adj* anticorrosive
   2 *nm* anticorrosive substance

anticorrupción *adj inv* anticorruption

anticristo *nm* Antichrist

anticuado, -a *adj* old-fashioned

anticuario, -a 1 *nm,f (comerciante)* antique dealer; *(experto)* antiquarian
   2 *nm (establecimiento)* antique store

anticuerpo *nm Med* antibody

antidemocrático, -a *adj* undemocratic

antideportivo, -a *adj* unsporting, unsportsmanlike

antidepresivo, -a 1 *adj* antidepressant
   2 *nm* antidepressant (drug)

antideslizante *adj Aut (ruedas)* nonskid

antideslumbrante *adj* antidazzle, antiglare

antidisturbios 1 *adj inv* riot; **material a.** riot gear
   2 *nmpl (policía)* riot police

antidopaje *nm Dep* dope tests

antidoping [anti'ðopin] *adj Dep* doping; **prueba a.** doping test

antídoto *nm* antidote

antidroga *adj* antidrug; **la lucha a.** the fight against drugs

antidumping [anti'ðumpin] *adj Econ (medidas, leyes)* antidumping

antier *adv esp Am Fam* the day before yesterday

antiestético, -a *adj* unsightly

antifascista *adj & nmf* antifascist

antifaz *nm* mask

antigás *adj inv* gas; **careta a.** gas mask

antígeno *nm Med* antigen

antiglobalización *nf* antiglobalization

antigripal 1 *adj* designed to combat flu
   2 *nm* flu remedy

antigualla *nf Pey (cosa)* museum piece; *(persona)* old fogy, old fossil

antiguamente *adv (hace mucho)* long ago; *(previamente)* formerly

Antigua y Barbuda *n* Antigua and Barbuda

antigubernamental *adj* antigovernment

antigüedad *nf* (a) *(edad)* antiquity; *Hist* **la A. (clásica)** (Classical) Antiquity (b) *(veteranía)* seniority; **a. en la empresa** length of service (c) **antigüedades** *(objetos)* antiques

antiguo, -a 1 *adj* (a) *(viejo)* old; *(inmemorial)* ancient; **a. alumno** ex-pupil, former pupil, alumnus; **la antigua Roma** ancient Rome; **el A. Testamento** the Old Testament (b) *(anterior, previo)* former; **el a. régimen** the former regime; *Hist* the ancien régime (c) *(veterano)* senior (d) *(pasado de moda)* old-fashioned; **a la antigua** in an old-fashioned way
   2 *nm,f* (a) *(persona)* old-fashioned person; **su tío es un a.** her uncle is very old-fashioned (b) **los antiguos** *(de la Antigüedad)* the ancients

antihéroe *nm* antihero

antihielo *nm* deicer

antihigiénico, -a *adj* unhygienic

antihistamínico *nm (medicamento)* antihistamine

antiinflacionista *adj Econ* anti-inflationary

antiinflamatorio, -a 1 *adj* anti-inflammatory
   2 *nm* anti-inflammatory drug

antillano, -a 1 *adj* West Indian, of/from the Caribbean
   2 *nm,f* West Indian, person from the Caribbean

Antillas *nfpl* **las A.** the West Indies

antílope *nm* antelope

antimateria *nf Fís* antimatter

antimilitarismo *nm* antimilitarism

antimilitarista *adj & nmf* antimilitarist

antimisil *nm Mil* antimissile

antimonio *nm Quím* antimony

antimonopolio *adj inv Econ* antitrust

antinatural *adj* unnatural

antiniebla *adj inv Aut* **faros a.** fog lights

antioxidante 1 *adj (contra el óxido)* antirust; *(contra la oxidación)* antioxidant
   2 *nm (contra el óxido)* rustproofing agent; *(contra la oxidación)* antioxidant

antipapa *nm* antipope

antiparasitario, -a 1 *adj (para perro, gato)* **collar a.** flea collar; **pastillas antiparasitarias** worming tablets
   2 *nm* (a) *(para perro, gato) (collar)* flea collar; *(pastilla)* (b) *Tel* suppressor

antiparras *nfpl* (a) *CSur (de esquiar, nadar, protectoras)* goggles (b) *Esp Fam* specs

antipatía *nf* dislike; **tener a. a alguien** to dislike sb

antipático, -a 1 *adj* unpleasant
   2 *nm,f* unpleasant person

antipirético, -a *adj & nm (medicamento)* antipyretic

antípodas *nfpl* **las a.** the Antipodes

antiquísimo, -a *superlativo ver* **antiguo**

antirreflectante *adj* nonreflective

antirreglamentario, -a *adj* against the rules; **un procedimiento a.** a procedure which contravenes the rules

antirrobo 1 *adj inv* antitheft; **dispositivo a.** antitheft device
   2 *nm (en coche)* antitheft device; *(en edificio)* burglar alarm

antisemita 1 *adj* anti-Semitic
   2 *nmf* anti-Semite

antisemitismo *nm* anti-Semitism

antiséptico, -a *adj & nm* antiseptic

antisocial *adj* antisocial

antitanque *adj Mil* antitank

antiterrorismo *nm* fight against terrorism

antiterrorista *adj* antiterrorist

antítesis *nf inv* antithesis

antitetánico, -a *adj* antitetanus

antitético, -a *adj Formal* antithetical

antivirus *nm inv Inform* antivirus system

antojadizo, -a *adj* capricious

antojarse *vpr* (a) *(capricho)* **se le antojaron esos zapatos** she fancied those shoes; **se le ha antojado ir al cine** he felt like going to a movie; **cuando se me antoje** when I feel like it (b) *(posibilidad)* **se me antoja que…** I have a feeling that… (c) *Méx (apetecer)* to feel like, to want

antojitos *nmpl Ecuad, Méx* snacks, tapas

antojo *nm* (a) *(capricho)* whim; *(de embarazada)* craving; **a mi/tu a.** my/your (own) way (b) *(lunar)* birthmark

antología *nf* anthology; **de a.** memorable, unforgettable

antológico, -a *adj* (a) *(recopilador)* anthological (b) *(inolvidable)* memorable, unforgettable

antonimia *nf Gram* antonymy

antónimo *nm* antonym

antonomasia *nf* **por a.** par excellence

antorcha *nf* torch; **a. olímpica** Olympic torch

antracita *nf* anthracite

ántrax *nm inv Med (por estafilococo)* carbuncle; *(por bacilo)* anthrax

antro *nm Fam Pey* dive, dump; **un a. de depravación** a den of iniquity

antropocéntrico, -a *adj* anthropocentric

antropocentrismo *nm* anthropocentrism

antropofagia *nf* anthropophagy, cannibalism

antropófago, -a 1 *adj* anthropophagous
2 *nm,f* cannibal

antropología *nf* anthropology

antropológico, -a *adj* anthropological

antropólogo, -a *nm,f* anthropologist

antropomórfico, -a *adj* anthropomorphic

antropomorfo, -a *adj* anthropomorphous

anual *adj* annual

anualidad *nf* annuity, yearly payment

anualmente *adv* annually, yearly

anuario *nm* yearbook

anudar 1 *vt* to knot, to tie in a knot
2 anudarse *vpr (atarse)* to get into a knot; **anudarse los cordones** to tie one's (shoe)laces

anuencia *nf Formal* consent, approval

anulación *nf* (a) *(cancelación)* cancellation; *(de ley)* repeal; *(de matrimonio, contrato)* annulment (b) *Dep (de un partido)* calling-off; *(de un gol)* disallowing; *(de un resultado)* declaration as void

anular¹ 1 *adj (en forma de anillo)* ring-shaped; **dedo a.** ring finger
2 *nm (dedo)* ring finger

anular² *vt* (a) *(cancelar)* to cancel; *(ley)* to repeal; *(matrimonio, contrato)* to annul (b) *Dep (partido)* to call off; *(gol)* to disallow; *(resultado)* to declare void (c) *(reprimir)* to repress

anunciación *nf* announcement; *Rel* **A.** Annunciation

anunciante 1 *adj* advertising
2 *nmf* advertiser

anunciar 1 *vt* (a) *(notificar)* to announce; **hoy anuncian los resultados** the results are announced today (b) *(hacer publicidad de)* to advertise (c) *(presagiar)* to herald; **esas nubes anuncian tormenta** by the look of those clouds, it's going to rain
2 anunciarse *vpr* (a) *(con publicidad)* to advertise (**en** in) (b) *(presentarse)* **las elecciones se anuncian reñidas** the election promises to be a hard-fought one

anuncio *nm* (a) *(notificación)* announcement; *(cartel, aviso)* notice; *(póster)* poster (b) **a. (publicitario)** advertisement, ad; **anuncios por palabras** classified ads (c) *(presagio)* sign, herald

anverso *nm (de moneda)* head, obverse; *(de hoja)* front

anzuelo *nm* (fish) hook; *Fam Fig* bait; **tragarse el a.** to take the bait

añadido, -a 1 *adj* added (**a** to)
2 *nm* addition

añadidura *nf* addition; **por a.** in addition

añadir *vt* to add; **a ese precio hay que a. el impuesto de venta** you have to add sales tax to that price; **"y estará acabado el próximo año", añadió** "and it will be finished next year," she added

añagaza *nf* trick, ruse

añejo, -a *adj* (a) *(vino, licor)* mature (b) *(costumbre)* long-established

añicos *nmpl* **hacer algo a.** to smash sth to pieces, to shatter sth; **hacerse a.** to shatter

añil *adj & nm* indigo

año *nm* (a) *(periodo)* year; **en el a. 1972** in 1972; **los años 30** the thirties; **a. académico** academic year; **a. bisiesto** leap year; *Am* **a. calendario** calendar year; **a. escolar** school year; **a. fiscal** tax year, fiscal *o* financial year; *Astron* **a. luz** light-year; *Fig* **estar a años luz de** to be light-years away from; **a. nuevo** New Year; **¡feliz a. nuevo!** Happy New Year!; *Fam* **el a. de la pera** the year dot; **a. sabático** sabbatical (year); **a. solar** solar year (b) **años** *(edad)* age; **¿cuántos años tienes?** how old are you?; **cumplir años** to have one's birthday; **cumplo años el 25** it's my birthday on the 25th; **estar entrado en años** to be getting on; **te has quitado años de encima** *(rejuvenecer)* you look much younger

añojo *nm (animal)* yearling; *(carne)* veal *(from a yearling calf)*

añoranza *nf (persona, pasado)* nostalgia (**de** for); *(hogar, país)* homesickness (**de** for)

añorar *vt* to miss

aorta *nf Anat* aorta

aovado, -a *adj* egg-shaped

aovar *vi (aves, reptiles)* to lay eggs; *(peces)* to spawn

APA ['apa] *nf (abrev de* **Asociación de Padres de Alumnos**) = Spanish association for parents of schoolchildren, ≃ PTA

apabullante *adj* overwhelming

apabullar 1 *vt* to overwhelm
2 apabullarse *vpr* to be overwhelmed

apacentar [3] *vt* to graze

apachurrar *vt Fam* to squash, to crush

apacible *adj (temperamento, trato)* mild, gentle; *(lugar, ambiente)* pleasant

apaciento *etc ver* **apacentar**

apaciguador, -ora *adj* calming

apaciguamiento *nm* calming; *Pol* appeasement

apaciguar [11] **1** *vt (tranquilizar)* to calm down; *(dolor)* to soothe
2 apaciguarse *vpr (tranquilizarse)* to calm down; *(dolor)* to abate

apadrinar *vt* (a) *(niño)* to act as a godparent to (b) *(artista)* to sponsor

apagado, -a *adj* (a) *(luz, fuego)* out; *(aparato)* off (b) *(color, persona)* subdued (c) *(sonido)* dull, muffled; *(voz)* low, quiet

apagar [40] **1** *vt* (a) *(fuego, incendio)* to put out; *(luz)* to switch off; *(vela)* to extinguish; *(aparato)* to turn *o* switch off; **a. el fuego de la cocina** to turn *o* switch off the stove; **"por favor apaguen sus cigarrillos"** "please extinguish your cigarettes" (b) *(sed)* to quench; *(dolor)* to get rid of; *(color)* to soften; *(sonido)* to muffle
2 apagarse *vpr* (a) *(fuego, vela, luz)* to go out; **tarda un par de minutos en apagarse** *(aparato)* it takes a couple of minutes to switch itself off (b) *(sed)* to be quenched; *(dolor, rencor)* to die down; *(color)* to fade; *(sonido)* to die away; *(brillo)* to become dull; *(ilusión)* to die, to be extinguished

apagón *nm* power cut

apague *etc ver* **apagar**

apaisado, -a *adj Inform* landscape; **un cuadro/espejo a.** a painting/mirror which is wider than it is high

apalabrar *vt (concertar)* to make a verbal agreement regarding; *(contratar)* to engage on the basis of a verbal agreement

Apalaches *nmpl* **los A.** the Appalachians

apalancado, -a *adj Esp Fam* **se pasó la tarde a. delante del televisor** he spent the afternoon lounging in front of the television

apalancamiento *nm* (a) *Econ* leverage (b) *Fam* lounging (about)

apalancar [59] **1** *vt (para abrir)* to lever open; *(para mover)* to lever
2 apalancarse *vpr Esp Fam (apoltronarse)* to install oneself

apalear *vt* to beat up

apantallar *vt Méx* to impress

apañado, -a *adj Fam (hábil, mañoso)* clever, resourceful;

estar a. to have had it; **¡estamos apañados!** we've had it!

apañar *Fam* **1** *vt* (**a**) *(reparar)* to mend (**b**) *(amañar)* to fix, to arrange

2 apañarse *vpr Esp (arreglarse)* to cope, to manage; **se apaña con muy poco dinero** she gets by on very little money; **apañárselas (para hacer algo)** to manage (to do sth)

apaño *nm Fam* (**a**) *(reparación)* patch (**b**) *(chanchullo)* fix, shady deal (**c**) *(acuerdo)* compromise

apapachado, -a *adj Méx Fam* pampered, spoiled

apapachador, -ora *adj Méx Fam* comforting

apapachar *vt Méx Fam (mimar)* to cuddle; *(consentir)* to spoil

apapachos *nmpl Méx Fam* cuddles

aparador *nm* (**a**) *(mueble)* sideboard (**b**) *(escaparate)* store window

aparato *nm* (**a**) *(máquina)* machine; *(electrodoméstico)* appliance; **a. de diálisis** kidney machine; **aparatos gimnásticos** *(en competición, escuela)* apparatus; **a. de radio** radio; **a. de televisión** television set; **a. de vídeo** video *o* videocassette recorder

(**b**) *(teléfono)* **¡al a.!** speaking!

(**c**) *(avión)* plane

(**d**) *Med (prótesis)* aid; *(para dientes)* braces

(**e**) *Anat* system; **a. circulatorio** circulatory system; **a. digestivo** digestive system; **a. reproductor** reproductive system; **a. respiratorio** respiratory system; **a. urinario** urinary tract

(**f**) *Pol* machinery

(**g**) *(ostentación)* pomp, ostentation

(**h**) *Meteo* **a. eléctrico** thunder and lightning

aparatoso, -a *adj* (**a**) *(ostentoso)* ostentatious, showy (**b**) *(espectacular)* spectacular

aparcacoches *nmf inv Esp (en hotel, discoteca)* parking valet

aparcamiento *nm Esp (para muchos vehículos)* parking lot; *(hueco)* parking place; **a. subterráneo** underground parking garage

aparcar [59] **1** *vt Esp (estacionar)* to park; *Fig (posponer)* to shelve

2 *vi* to park

aparcero, -a *nm,f* sharecropper

apareamiento *nm* mating

aparear 1 *vt (animales)* to mate

2 aparearse *vpr (animales)* to mate

aparecer [46] **1** *vi* (**a**) *(ante la vista)* to appear; *(publicación)* to come out; **su número de teléfono no aparece en la guía** her phone number isn't (listed) in the phone book (**b**) *(algo perdido)* to turn up; **¿ya ha aparecido el perro?** has the dog been found yet? (**c**) *(persona)* to appear; *Fam* **a. por** *(lugar)* to turn up at

2 aparecerse *vpr* (**a**) *(santo)* to appear; **se le apareció la Virgen** the Virgin Mary appeared to him; *Fam Fig* he had a real stroke of luck (**b**) *Am Fam (persona)* to turn up; **siempre se aparece sucio** he always turns up dirty

aparecido, -a *nm,f* ghost

aparejado, -a *adj* **llevar** *o* **traer a.** *(conllevar)* to entail

aparejador, -ora *nm,f* general contractor

aparejar *vt* (**a**) *(preparar)* to get ready, to prepare (**b**) *(caballerías)* to harness (**c**) *Náut* to rig (out)

aparejo *nm* (**a**) *(de caballerías)* harness (**b**) *(de pesca)* tackle (**c**) *Tec* block and tackle (**d**) *Náut* rigging; **aparejos** equipment

aparentar 1 *vt* (**a**) *(parecer)* to look, to seem; **no aparenta más de treinta** she doesn't look more than thirty (**b**) *(fingir)* to feign; **aparentó estar enfadado** he pretended to be angry, he feigned anger

2 *vi (presumir)* to show off; **viste así sólo para a.** she just dresses like that to show off

aparente *adj* (**a**) *(falso, supuesto)* apparent (**b**) *(visible)* visible (**c**) *(llamativo)* striking

aparentemente *adv* apparently, seemingly; **a. fácil/inocente** apparently easy/innocent

aparición *nf (de persona, cosa)* appearance; *(de ser sobrenatural)* apparition

apariencia *nf* (**a**) *(aspecto)* appearance; **en a.** apparently; **guardar las apariencias** to keep up appearances; **las apariencias engañan** appearances can be deceptive (**b**) *(falsedad)* illusion

aparque *etc ver* **aparcar**

apartado, -a 1 *adj* (**a**) *(separado)* **a. de** away from (**b**) *(alejado)* remote

2 *nm (párrafo)* paragraph; *(sección)* section; *Col, Ecuad* **a. aéreo** Post Office box, PO Box; **a. de correos** PO Box; **a. de correos número 126** PO Box 126

apartamento *nm esp Am (en edificio)* apartment; *Esp (más pequeño)* apartment

apartar 1 *vt* (**a**) *(alejar)* to move away; *(quitar)* to remove; **el polémico ministro ha sido apartado de su cargo** the controversial minister has been removed from office; **a. la mirada** to look away (**b**) *(separar)* to separate (**c**) *(escoger)* to take, to select; **ya he apartado la ropa para el viaje** I've already put out the clothes for the journey

2 apartarse *vpr* (**a**) *(hacerse a un lado)* to move to one side, to move out of the way; **¡apártense, es una emergencia!** make way, it's an emergency!; **se apartó para dejarme pasar** he stood aside to let me pass (**b**) *(separarse) (dos personas)* to separate, to move away from each other; **apartarse de** *(grupo, lugar)* to move away from; *(tema)* to get away from; *(mundo, sociedad)* to cut oneself off from; **nos apartamos de la carretera** we left the road

aparte 1 *adv* (**a**) *(en otro lugar, a un lado)* aside, to one side; **bromas a.** joking apart (**b**) *(por separado)* separately; **la bufanda envuélvala a., es para regalar** please wrap the scarf up separately, it's a gift (**c**) *(además)* besides; **y a. tiene otro todoterreno** and she has another four-wheel drive besides *o* too; **a. de** *(excepto)* apart from, except from; **a. de feo…** besides being ugly…

2 *adj inv* separate; **lo guardaré en un cajón a.** I'll keep it in a separate drawer; **ser caso** *o* **capítulo a.** to be a different matter

3 *nm* (**a**) *(párrafo)* new paragraph (**b**) *Teatro* aside

apartheid [apar'xeið] *(pl* **apartheids)** *nm Pol* apartheid

aparthotel, apartahotel *nm* = hotel with kitchenette facilities

apasionado, -a 1 *adj* passionate

2 *nm,f* lover, enthusiast

apasionamiento *nm* passion, enthusiasm; **con a.** passionately

apasionante *adj* fascinating

apasionar 1 *vt* to fascinate; **le apasiona la música** he's mad about music

2 apasionarse *vpr* to get excited; **apasionarse por** to be mad about

apatía *nf* apathy

apático, -a 1 *adj* apathetic

2 *nm,f* apathetic person

apátrida 1 *adj* stateless

2 *nmf* stateless person

apdo. *(abrev de* **apartado)** PO Box; **a. de correos 8000** PO Box 8000

apeadero *nm (de tren)* = minor train stop with no permanent buildings

apear 1 *vt* (**a**) *(bajar)* to take down (**b**) *Fam (disuadir)* **a. a alguien de** to talk sb out of; **no pudimos apearle de su idea** we couldn't get him to give up his idea

2 apearse *vpr* (**a**) *(bajarse)* **apearse (de)** *(tren)* to alight (from), to get off; *(coche, autobús)* to get out (of); *(caballo)* to dismount (from) (**b**) *Fam* **apearse de** *(abandonar) (idea)* to give up; *Fam Fig* **apearse del burro** to back down

apechugar [40] *vi Fam* **a. con** to put up with

apedrear *vt (persona)* to stone; *(cosa)* to throw stones at

apegarse [40] *vpr* **a. a** to become fond of

apego *nm* fondness, attachment; **tener/tomar a. a** to be/become fond of

apelación *nf* appeal

apelar *vi* (**a**) *Der* to (lodge an) appeal; **a. ante/contra** to appeal to/against (**b**) *(recurrir)* **a. a** *(persona)* to go to; *(sentido común, bondad)* to appeal to; *(violencia)* to resort to

apelativo *nm* (**a**) *(nombre)* name; **más conocido con el a. de…** better known by the name of…, better known as… (**b**) *Ling* form of address; **un a. cariñoso** an affectionate form of address, a term of endearment

apellidarse *vpr* **se apellida Suárez** his surname is Suárez

apellido *nm* surname, family name; **a. de soltera** maiden name

apelmazado, -a *adj (pelo)* matted; *(arroz, bizcocho)* stodgy; **el jersey está todo a.** the sweater has lost its fluffiness

apelmazar [14] **1** *vt (jersey, pelo)* to matt; *(arroz, bizcocho)* to make stodgy
   2 apelmazarse *vpr (jersey, pelo)* to get matted; *(arroz, bizcocho)* to go stodgy

apelotonar 1 *vt* to bundle up
   2 apelotonarse *vpr (gente)* to crowd together

apenado, -a *adj* (**a**) *(entristecido)* sad (**b**) *Am salvo RP (avergonzado)* ashamed, embarrassed

apenar 1 *vt (entristecer)* to sadden
   2 apenarse *vpr* (**a**) *(entristecerse)* to be saddened (**b**) *Am salvo RP (avergonzarse)* to be ashamed, to be embarrassed

apenas *adv* (**a**) *(casi no)* scarcely, hardly; **a. me puedo mover** I can hardly move (**b**) *(tan sólo)* only; **hace a. dos minutos** only two minutes ago (**c**) *(tan pronto como)* as soon as; **a. llegó, sonó el teléfono** no sooner had he arrived than the phone rang

apencar [59] *vi Fam* **a. con** *(trabajo)* to take on; *(responsabilidad)* to shoulder; *(consecuencias, dificultad)* to live with

apéndice *nm (gen) & Anat* appendix

apendicitis *nf inv Med* appendicitis

Apeninos *nmpl* **los A.** the Appenines

apercibir 1 *vt (reprender, advertir)* to reprimand, to give a warning to; *Der* to issue with a warning
   2 apercibirse *vpr* **apercibirse de algo** to notice sth; **no se apercibió de mi llegada** he didn't notice my arrival

apergaminado, -a *adj (piel, papel)* parchment-like

apergaminarse *vpr (piel)* to become parchment-like

aperitivo *nm (bebida)* aperitif; *(comida)* appetizer; *(pincho con una bebida)* bar snack

aperos *nmpl* (**a**) **a. (de labranza)** farming implements (**b**) *Andes, RP (arneses)* riding gear, trappings

apertura *nf* (**a**) *(acción de abrir)* opening; *(de año académico, temporada)* start (**b**) *Dep (en fútbol americano, rugby)* kickoff; *(en ajedrez)* opening (move) (**c**) *Pol (liberalización)* liberalization

aperturismo *nm Pol* progressive policies

aperturista *adj & nmf Pol* progressive

apesadumbrado, -a *adj (apenado)* grieving, sorrowful

apesadumbrar 1 *vt* to sadden
   2 apesadumbrarse *vpr* to be saddened

apestado, -a *nm,f* plague victim

apestar 1 *vi* to stink (**a** of); **huele que apesta** it stinks to high heaven
   2 *vt* (**a**) *(hacer que huela mal)* to stink up (**b**) *(contagiar la peste)* to infect with the plague

apestoso, -a *adj* foul

apetecer [46] **1** *vi Esp* **¿te apetece un café?** do you want a coffee?; **me apetece salir** I feel like going out

2 *vt* **tenían todo cuanto apetecían** they had everything they wanted

apetecible *adj (comida)* appetizing, tempting; *(vacaciones)* desirable

apetito *nm* appetite; **abrir el a.** to whet one's appetite; **perder el a.** to lose one's appetite; **tener a.** to be hungry; **un a. voraz** a keen appetite

apetitoso, -a *adj* (**a**) *(comida)* appetizing, tempting (**b**) *(oferta, empleo)* tempting

apiadar 1 *vt* to earn the pity of
   2 apiadarse *vpr* to show compassion; **apiadarse de** to take pity on

ápice *nm* (**a**) *(vértice) (de montaña)* peak; *(de hoja, lengua)* tip (**b**) *(punto culminante)* peak, height (**c**) *(pizca)* iota; **ni un á.** not a single bit; **no cedió un á.** he didn't budge an inch

apícola *adj* **la industria a.** the beekeeping industry

apicultor, -ora *nm,f* beekeeper

apicultura *nf* beekeeping

apilar 1 *vt* to pile up
   2 apilarse *vpr* to pile up

apiñado, -a *adj (apretado)* packed, crammed

apiñar 1 *vt* to pack
   2 apiñarse *vpr (agolparse)* to crowd together; *(para protegerse, por miedo)* to huddle together; **apiñarse en torno a algo/alguien** to huddle around sth/sb

apio *nm* celery

apisonadora *nf* steamroller

apisonar *vt (con vehículo apisonadora)* to roll; *(con apisonadora manual)* to tamp down

aplacar [59] **1** *vt (persona, ánimos)* to placate; *(hambre)* to satisfy; *(sed)* to quench; *(dolor)* to ease
   2 aplacarse *vpr (persona, ánimos)* to calm down; *(dolor)* to abate

aplace *etc ver* **aplazar**

aplanadora *nf Am (vehículo)* steamroller

aplanar *vt* to level

aplaque *etc ver* **aplacar**

aplastamiento *nm* squashing, crushing

aplastante *adj (victoria, derrota)* crushing, overwhelming; *(mayoría, superioridad)* overwhelming

aplastar *vt (por el peso)* to squash, to crush; *Fig (derrotar)* to crush

aplatanado, -a *adj Esp, Méx Fam* listless

aplatanar *Esp, Méx Fam* **1** *vt* to make listless; **este calor me aplatana** this heat makes me feel listless
   2 aplatanarse *vpr* to become listless

aplaudir 1 *vt* to applaud; **aplaudo su propuesta** I applaud your proposal
   2 *vi* to applaud, to clap

aplauso *nm (ovación)* round of applause; *Fig (alabanza)* applause; **aplausos** applause

aplazamiento *nm* postponement

aplazar [14] **1** *vt* to postpone
   2 *vi RP (en examen)* to fail

aplicable *adj* applicable (**a** to)

aplicación *nf* (**a**) *(uso, utilidad)* application, use; *Inform* application (**b**) *(al estudio)* application (**c**) *(decoración)* appliqué

aplicado, -a *adj* (**a**) *(estudioso)* diligent (**b**) *(ciencia)* applied

aplicar [59] **1** *vt (técnica, pintura, teoría)* to apply; *(nombre, calificativo)* to give, to apply
   2 aplicarse *vpr* (**a**) *(esmerarse)* to apply oneself (**en algo** to sth); **se aplicó mucho en los estudios** he applied himself very hard to his studies (**b**) *(concernir)* **aplicarse a** to apply to (**c**) *(a uno mismo)* … **¡y aplícate eso a ti también!** …and that goes for you as well!

aplique *nm* wall lamp

aplomo *nm* composure; **perder el a.** to lose one's composure

apnea *nf* (**a**) *Med* apnea; **a. del sueño** sleep apnea (**b**) *Dep* (*buceo*) free diving

apocado, -a *adj* timid

apocalipsis *nm inv* calamity; **A.** Apocalypse

apocalíptico, -a *adj* apocalyptic

apocamiento *nm* timidity

apocarse [59] *vpr* (*intimidarse*) to be frightened; (*humillarse*) to humble oneself

apocopar *vt Gram* to apocopate

apócope *nf Gram* apocope

apócrifo, -a *adj* apocryphal

apodar 1 *vt* to nickname
    2 apodarse *vpr* to be nicknamed

apoderado, -a *nm,f* (**a**) *Der* (official) representative (**b**) *Taurom* agent, manager

apoderarse *vpr* (**a**) **a. de** (*adueñarse de*) to seize; **los sublevados se apoderaron del aeropuerto** the rebels took control of *o* seized the airport (**b**) **a. de** (*dominar*) to take hold of, to grip; **el miedo se apoderó de él** he was overcome with *o* by fear

apodo *nm* nickname

apogeo *nm* height, apogee; **está en (pleno) a.** it is at its height

apolillado, -a *adj también Fig* moth-eaten

apolillar 1 *vt* to eat holes in
    2 apolillarse *vpr* to get moth-eaten

apolíneo, -a *adj* ravishing, stunning; **un joven a.** a young Adonis

apolítico, -a *adj* apolitical

apología *nf* apology, eulogy; *Der* **a. del terrorismo** defense of terrorism

apoltronarse *vpr* (**a**) (*hacerse sedentario*) to become less active; **desde que se casaron se han apoltronado mucho** they've been going out a lot less since they got married (**b**) (*acomodarse*) **a. en** to lounge in

apoplejía *nf Med* apoplexy

apopléjico, -a, apoplético, -a *adj* apoplectic

apoquinar *vt & vi Esp Fam* to fork out

aporrear *vt* (*puerta*) to bang on; **a. el piano** to bang *o* plonk away on the piano

aportación *nf* (**a**) (*suministro*) provision (**b**) (*contribución*) contribution; **hacer una a.** to contribute

aportar *vt* (**a**) (*proporcionar*) to provide (**b**) (*contribuir con*) to contribute

aporte *nm* (**a**) (*aportación*) contribution; **a. vitamínico** vitamin content (**b**) *RP* (*a seguridad social*) social security contribution

aposentar 1 *vt* to put up, to lodge
    2 aposentarse *vpr* to take up lodgings

aposento *nm* (**a**) (*habitación*) room; *Anticuado & Hum* **se retiró a sus aposentos** she withdrew (to her chamber) (**b**) (*alojamiento*) lodgings

aposición *nf Gram* apposition

apósito *nm* dressing

aposta *adv Esp* on purpose, intentionally

apostante *nmf* (*que apuesta*) bettor, better; (*en lotería*) lottery player

apostar [63] **1** *vt* (**a**) (*jugarse*) to bet; **te apuesto una cena a que gana el Madrid** I bet you the price of a dinner that Madrid will win (**b**) (*emplazar*) to post
    2 *vi* to bet (**por** on); **apuesto a que no viene** I bet he doesn't come
    3 apostarse *vpr* (**a**) (*jugarse*) to bet; **apostarse algo con alguien** to bet sb sth (**b**) (*colocarse*) to station oneself

apostasía *nf* apostasy

apóstata *nmf* apostate

apostatar *vi* to apostatize

a posteriori *adv* with hindsight; **habrá que juzgarlo a.** we'll have to judge it after the event

apostilla *nf* (*nota*) note; (*comentario*) comment

apostillar *vt* (*anotar*) to annotate; (*añadir*) to add

apóstol *nm también Fig* apostle

apostolado *nm Rel* (**a**) (*de apóstol*) apostolate (**b**) (*de ideales*) mission

apostólico, -a *adj Rel* apostolic

apóstrofe *nm o nf Lit* apostrophe

apóstrofo *nm Gram* apostrophe

apostura *nf* dashing appearance

apoteósico, -a *adj* tremendous; **un final a.** a grand finale

apoteosis *nf inv* (*final*) grand finale

apoyabrazos *nm inv* armrest

apoyacabezas *nm inv* headrest

apoyamuñecas *nm inv* wrist rest

apoyar 1 *vt* (**a**) (*inclinar*) to lean, to rest; **apoya la cabeza en mi hombro** rest your head on my shoulder; **apoyó la bicicleta contra la pared** she leaned the bicycle against the wall (**b**) (*respaldar*) to support; **lo apoyó mucho durante su depresión** she gave him a lot of support when he was depressed
    2 apoyarse *vpr* (**a**) (*sostenerse*) **apoyarse en** to lean on; **la anciana se apoyaba en un bastón** the old woman was leaning on a walking stick (**b**) (*basarse*) **apoyarse en** (*sujeto: tesis, conclusiones*) to be based on; (*sujeto: persona*) to base one's arguments on (**c**) (*buscar respaldo*) **apoyarse en** to rely on (**d**) (*respaldarse mutuamente*) to support one another

apoyo *nm también Fig* support

APRA ['apra] *nf* (*abrev de* **Alianza Popular Revolucionaria Americana**) = Peruvian political party to the center-right of the political spectrum

apreciable *adj* (**a**) (*perceptible*) appreciable, significant (**b**) (*estimable*) worthy

apreciación *nf* (**a**) (*estimación*) evaluation, assessment (**b**) *Fin* (*de moneda*) appreciation

apreciado, -a *adj* (**a**) (*querido*) esteemed, highly regarded (**b**) (*valorado*) prized (**por** by)

apreciar 1 *vt* (**a**) (*valorar*) to appreciate; **aprecio mucho tu ayuda** I really appreciate your help (**b**) (*sentir afecto por*) to be fond of (**c**) (*percibir*) to detect, to notice; **apreciaron una mejora significativa** they detected *o* noticed a significant improvement; **para a. mejor los detalles** to be able to see the detail better
    2 apreciarse *vpr* (**a**) *Fin* (*moneda*) to appreciate (**b**) (*notarse*) to be noticeable; **no se apreciaba ninguna diferencia entre los dos** there was no noticeable difference between them; **en el gráfico se aprecia un incremento espectacular de los ingresos** in the graph we can see a spectacular growth in income, the graph shows a spectacular growth in income

aprecio *nm* esteem; **sentir a. por alguien** to think highly of sb

aprehender *vt* (**a**) (*atrapar*) (*persona*) to apprehend; (*alijo, mercancía*) to seize (**b**) (*comprender*) to take in

aprehensión *nf* (*de persona*) arrest, capture; (*de alijo, mercancía*) seizure

apremiante *adj* pressing, urgent

apremiar 1 *vt* (**a**) (*meter prisa*) **a. a alguien para que haga algo** to urge sb to do sth (**b**) (*obligar*) **a. a alguien a hacer algo** to compel sb to do sth
    2 *vi* (*ser urgente*) to be pressing; **¡el tiempo apremia!** we're running out of time, time is short

apremio *nm* (**a**) (*urgencia*) urgency (**b**) *Der* writ

aprender 1 *vt* (*adquirir conocimientos de*) to learn; (*memorizar*) to memorize; **a. a hacer algo** to learn to do sth; *Fig* **aprendieron la lección** they learned their lesson

2 *vi* to learn; **¡para que aprendas!** that'll teach you!

3 aprenderse *vpr (memorizar)* to memorize; **aprenderse algo de memoria** to learn sth by heart

aprendiz, -iza *nm,f* **(a)** *(ayudante)* apprentice, trainee **(b)** *(novato)* beginner

aprendizaje *nm* **(a)** *(adquisición de conocimientos)* learning; **el a. de idiomas** language learning **(b)** *(tiempo, situación)* apprenticeship

aprensión *nf (miedo)* apprehension **(por** about); *(escrúpulo)* squeamishness **(por** about)

aprensivo, -a *adj* **(a)** *(miedoso)* apprehensive **(b)** *(escrupuloso)* squeamish **(c)** *(hipocondríaco)* hypochondriac

apresar *vt (presa)* to catch; *(delincuente)* to catch, to capture

apres-ski *adj inv & nm* après-ski

aprestar 1 *vt* **(a)** *(preparar)* to prepare, to get ready **(b)** *(tela)* to size

2 aprestarse *vpr* **aprestarse a hacer algo** to get ready to do sth

apresto *nm (rigidez de la tela)* stiffness; *(sustancia)* size; **el almidón da a. a las telas** starch is used to stiffen cloth

apresurado, -a *adj* hasty, hurried

apresuramiento *nm* haste

apresurar 1 *vt* to hurry along, to speed up; **a. a alguien para que haga algo** to try to make sb do sth more quickly

2 apresurarse *vpr* to hurry; **apresurarse a hacer algo** to rush to do sth; **se apresuró a aclarar que no sabía nada** she was quick to point out that she knew nothing

apretado, -a *adj* **(a)** *(ropa)* tight; *(triunfo)* narrow; *(esprint)* close; *(caligrafía)* cramped **(b)** *(estrujado)* cramped; **íbamos un poco apretados en el coche** it was sort of a squeeze in the car

apretar [3] **1** *vt* **(a)** *(oprimir) (botón, tecla)* to press; *(gatillo)* to pull, to squeeze; *(nudo, tuerca, cinturón)* to tighten; *(acelerador)* to step on; **me aprietan las botas** my boots are too tight **(b)** *(juntar) (dientes)* to grit; *(labios)* to press together; *(puño)* to clench **(c)** *(estrechar)* to squeeze; *(abrazar)* to hug; **a. la mano a alguien** to shake sb's hand **(d)** **a. el paso** to quicken one's pace **(e)** *(presionar)* to press; **lo están apretando para que acepte la oferta** they are pressing him *o* putting pressure on him to accept the offer

2 *vi (calor, lluvia)* to get worse, to intensify

3 apretarse *vpr (agolparse)* to crowd together; *(acercarse)* to squeeze up; *Fig* **apretarse el cinturón** to tighten one's belt

apretón *nm (estrechamiento)* squeeze; **a. de manos** handshake; **apretones** crush; **hubo apretones para entrar** there was a crush to get in

apretujar 1 *vt (aplastar)* to squash; *(hacer una bola con)* to screw up

2 apretujarse *vpr (en banco, autobús)* to squeeze together; *(por frío)* to huddle up

apretujón *nm (abrazo)* bear hug; **hubo apretujones para entrar en el cine** there was a crush to get into the movie theater

apretura *nf (estrechez)* crush; *Fig* **pasar apreturas** to be hard up

aprieta *etc ver* **apretar**

aprieto *nm* fix, difficult situation; **poner en un a. a alguien** to put sb in a difficult position; **estar en un a.** to be in a fix

a priori *adv* in advance, a priori

apriorístico, -a *adj* **hacer juicios apriorísticos** to prejudge things

aprisa *adv* quickly

aprisco *nm* fold, pen

aprisionar *vt* **(a)** *(encarcelar)* to imprison **(b)** *(inmovilizar)* **a. a alguien con cadenas** to put sb in chains; **quedaron aprisionados bajo los escombros** they were trapped under the rubble

aprobación *nf* approval

aprobado, -a 1 *adj (aceptado)* approved

2 *nm Educ* pass; *Fam* **un a. raspado** *o* **por los pelos** a bare pass

aprobar [63] *vt* **(a)** *(proyecto, medida)* to approve; *(ley, moción)* to pass **(b)** *(examen, asignatura)* to pass; **me han aprobado en química** I passed my chemistry exam **(c)** *(comportamiento)* to approve of

aprobatorio, -a *adj (gesto, mirada)* approving

aprontarse *vpr RP* to get ready

apropiación *nf (incautación, ocupación)* appropriation; *(robo)* theft; *Der* **a. indebida** embezzlement

apropiado, -a *adj* suitable, appropriate

apropiar 1 *vt* to adapt **(a** to)

2 apropiarse *vpr* **apropiarse de** *(tomar posesión de)* to appropriate; *(robar)* to steal

aprovechable *adj* usable

aprovechado, -a 1 *adj* **(a)** *(caradura)* **es muy a.** he's a real opportunist, he always has an eye for the main chance **(b)** *(bien empleado) (tiempo)* well-spent; *(espacio)* well-planned **(c)** *(aplicado)* diligent

2 *nm,f (caradura)* sponger

aprovechamiento *nm* **(a)** *(utilización)* use **(b)** *(en el estudio)* progress, improvement

aprovechar 1 *vt* **(a)** *(tiempo, dinero)* to make the most of; *(oferta, ocasión)* to take advantage of; *(conocimientos, experiencia)* to use, to make use of; **me gustaría a. esta oportunidad para...** I'd like to take this opportunity to...; **a. que...** to make the most of the fact that... **(b)** *(lo inservible)* to put to good use; **no tires los restos de la paella, los aprovecharé para hacer sopa** don't throw what's left of the paella away, I'll use it to make a soup

2 *vi* **aprovecha mientras puedas** make the most of it *o* enjoy it while you can; **¡cómo aprovechas para comer chocolate, ahora que no te ve nadie!** you're really making the most of the opportunity to eat chocolate while nobody can see you!; **¡que aproveche!** enjoy your meal!

3 aprovecharse *vpr* **(a)** *(sacar provecho)* to take advantage **(de** of); **se aprovechó de que nadie vigilaba para salir sin pagar** she took advantage of the fact that nobody was watching to leave without paying **(b)** *(abusar de alguien)* to take advantage **(de** of); **fue acusado de aprovecharse de una menor** he was accused of child abuse

aprovisionamiento *nm* supplying

aprovisionar 1 *vt* to supply

2 aprovisionarse *vpr* **aprovisionarse de algo** to stock up on sth

aprox. *(abrev de* **aproximadamente)** approx.

aproximación *nf* **(a)** *(acercamiento)* approach; *(en cálculo)* approximation; *(de países)* rapprochement; *(de puntos de vista)* converging **(b)** *(en lotería)* = consolation prize given to numbers immediately before and after the winning number

aproximadamente *adv* approximately

aproximado, -a *adj* approximate

aproximar 1 *vt* to move closer; **aproxima la mesa a la puerta** move the table closer to *o* over toward the door; **un intento de a. posturas** an attempt at a rapprochement *o* to bring the two sides closer together

2 aproximarse *vpr* **(a)** *(en el espacio)* to approach, to come closer; **el autobús se aproximaba a la parada** the bus was approaching the stop; **el déficit se aproxima a los seis millones** the deficit is close to six million **(b)** *(en el tiempo)* **se aproximan las vacaciones** the vacations are drawing nearer *o* approaching

aproximativo, -a *adj* approximate, rough

apruebo *etc ver* **aprobar**

aptitud *nf* ability, aptitude; **tener a. para algo** to have an aptitude for sth

apto, -a *adj (adecuado, conveniente)* suitable (**para** for); *(capacitado) (intelectualmente)* capable, able; *(físicamente)* fit; *Cine* **a./no a. para menores** suitable/unsuitable for children

apuesta 1 *ver* **apostar**

2 *nf* bet

apuesto, -a *adj* dashing

apunar *Andes* **1** *vt* to cause to have altitude sickness

2 apunarse *vpr* to get altitude sickness

apuntador, -ora *nm,f Teatro* prompter

apuntalamiento *nm también Fig* underpinning

apuntalar *vt también Fig* to underpin

apuntar 1 *vt* **(a)** *(anotar)* to make a note of, to note down; **a. a alguien** *(en lista)* to put sb down (**en** on); *(en curso)* to put sb's name down (**en** *o* **a** for), to sign sb up (**en** *o* **a** for); **he apuntado a mi hijo a clases de natación** I've put my son's name down for swimming lessons, I've signed my son up for swimming lessons; **apúntamelo (en la cuenta)** put it on my account

(b) *(dirigir) (dedo)* to point; *(arma)* to aim; **a. a alguien** *(con el dedo)* to point at sb; *(con un arma)* to aim at sb; **a. una pistola hacia alguien, a. a alguien con una pistola** to aim a gun at sb

(c) *Teatro* to prompt; **fue expulsada de clase por a. las respuestas a un compañero** she was thrown out of the classroom for whispering the answers to a classmate

(d) *(sugerir)* to hint at; *(indicar)* to point out

2 *vi* **(a)** *(vislumbrarse)* to appear; *(día)* to break **(b)** *(indicar)* **a. a** to point to; **todo apunta a que ganará Brasil** everything points to a win for Brazil

3 apuntarse *vpr* **(a)** *(en lista)* to put one's name down; *(en curso)* to enroll; **me he apuntado a** *o* **en un curso de alemán** I've enrolled on a German course **(b)** *(participar)* to join in (**a hacer algo** doing sth); **yo me apunto** I'm in; *Esp Fam* **ese se apunta a un bombardeo** he's game for anything **(c)** *(tantos, éxitos)* to score, to notch up; *Fam* **¡apúntate diez!** *(al acertar)* bingo!

apunte *nm* **(a)** *(nota)* note **(b)** *(boceto)* sketch **(c)** *Com* entry **(d)** *Teatro* prompt; **apuntes** *(en colegio, universidad)* notes; **tomar apuntes** to take notes

apuñalamiento *nm* stabbing

apuñalar *vt* to stab

apurado, -a *adj* **(a)** *(necesitado)* in need; **a. de** short of **(b)** *(avergonzado)* embarrassed **(c)** *(difícil)* awkward, difficult; **una situación apurada** a tricky situation **(d)** *Esp (afeitado)* smooth, close **(e)** *Am (con prisa)* **estar a.** to be in a hurry

apurar 1 *vt* **(a)** *(agotar)* to finish off; *(existencias, la paciencia)* to exhaust **(b)** *(meter prisa)* to hurry **(c)** *(preocupar)* to trouble **(d)** *(avergonzar)* to embarrass

2 apurarse *vpr* **(a)** *Esp, Méx (preocuparse)* to worry (**por** about) **(b)** *(darse prisa)* to hurry

apuro *nm* **(a)** *(dificultad)* fix, difficult situation; **estar en un a.** to be in a tight spot **(b)** *(penuria)* **pasar apuros** to undergo *o* experience hardship **(c)** *(vergüenza)* embarrassment; **me da a. (decírselo)** I'm embarrassed (to tell her) **(d)** *Am (prisa)* **tener a.** to be in a hurry

aquejado, -a *adj* **a. de** suffering from

aquejar *vt* to afflict; **le aquejan varias enfermedades** he suffers from a number of illnesses

aquel, aquella *(pl* **aquellos, -ellas)** *adj demostrativo* that; *(plural)* those

aquél, -élla *(pl* **aquéllos, -éllas)** *pron demostrativo*

Note that **aquél** and its various forms can be written without an accent when there is no risk of confusion with the adjective.

(a) *(ese)* that (one); *(plural)* those (ones); **este cuadro me gusta pero a. del fondo no** I like this picture, but I don't like that one at the back; **a. fue mi último día en Nueva York** that was my last day in New York **(b)** *(nombrado antes)* the former; **teníamos un coche y una moto, ésta estropeada y a. sin gasolina** we had a car and a motorbike, the former was out of gas, the latter had broken down **(c)** *(con oraciones relativas)* whoever, anyone who; **a. que quiera hablar que levante la mano** whoever wishes *o* anyone wishing to speak should raise their hand; **aquéllos que...** those who...

aquelarre *nm* coven

aquella *ver* **aquel**

aquélla *ver* **aquél**

aquello *pron demostrativo* that; **no consiguió saber si a. lo dijo en serio** he never found out whether she meant those words *o* that seriously; **a. de su mujer es una mentira** all that about his wife is a lie

aquellos, -ellas *ver* **aquel**

aquéllos, -éllas *ver* **aquél**

aquí *adv* **(a)** *(indica lugar)* here; **a. abajo/arriba** down/up here; **a. dentro/fuera** in/out here; **a. mismo** right here; **a. y ahora** here and now; **a. y allá** here and there; **a. está** it/he is; **a. tienes** here you are!; **a. viene** here it/he comes; **de a. para allá** *(de un lado a otro)* to and fro; **por a.** over here; **por a. cerca** nearby, not far from here

(b) *(ahora)* now; **de a. a mañana** between now and tomorrow; **de a. a poco** shortly, soon; **de a. a un mes** a month from now, in a month; **de a. en adelante** from now on

(c) *(en tiempo pasado)* **a. empezaron los problemas** that was when the problems started

(d) de a. que *(por eso)* hence, therefore

aquiescencia *nf Formal* approval

aquietar 1 *vt* to calm down

2 aquietarse *vpr* to calm down

aquilatar *vt (metales, joyas)* to assay; *Fig (examinar)* to assess

aquilino, -a *adj (nariz)* aquiline

ara *nf Formal (losa)* altar stone; *(altar)* altar; **en aras de** for the sake of

árabe 1 *adj* Arab, Arabian

2 *nmf (persona)* Arab

3 *nm (lengua)* Arabic

arabesco *nm* arabesque

Arabia Saudí, Arabia Saudita *n* Saudi Arabia

arábigo, -a *adj (de Arabia)* Arab, Arabian; *(numeración)* Arabic

arabista *nmf* Arabist

arácnido *nm* arachnid

arado *nm* plow; *Fam* **es más bruto** *o* **bestia que un a.** he's a complete Neanderthal

Aragón *n* Aragon

aragonés, -esa *adj & nm,f* Aragonese

Aral *nm* **el mar de A.** the Aral Sea

arameo *nm (lengua)* Aramaic

arancel *nm Com* tariff; **a. aduanero** customs duty

arancelario, -a *adj Com* tariff; **barreras (no) arancelarias** (non) tariff barriers

arándano *nm* bilberry, blueberry

arandela *nf (pieza)* washer

araña *nf* **(a)** *(animal)* spider; **a. de mar** spider crab **(b)** *(lámpara)* chandelier

arañar *vt (raspar)* to scratch; *Fig (reunir, conseguir)* to scrape together

arañazo *nm* scratch

arar *vt* to plow

araucano, -a *adj & nm,f* Araucanian

araucaria *nf* monkey puzzle tree

arbitraje nm (**a**) Dep (en fútbol, baloncesto) refereeing; (en tenis, voleibol) umpiring (**b**) Der arbitration

arbitral adj (**a**) Dep **una polémica decisión a.** a controversial decision by the referee (**b**) Der **procedimiento a.** arbitration process

arbitrar 1 vt (**a**) Dep (en fútbol americano, baloncesto) to referee; (en tenis, béisbol, voleibol) to umpire (**b**) (medidas, recursos) to bring together (**c**) Der to arbitrate
  2 vi (**a**) Dep (en fútboll americano, baloncesto) to referee; (en tenis, béisbol, voleibol) to umpire (**b**) Der to arbitrate

arbitrariedad nf (**a**) (cualidad) arbitrariness (**b**) (acción) arbitrary action

arbitrario, -a adj arbitrary

arbitrio nm (decisión) judgment; **dejar algo al a. de alguien** to leave sth to sb's discretion; **arbitrios** (impuestos) taxes

árbitro, -a nm,f (**a**) Dep referee; (en tenis, béisbol, críquet) umpire (**b**) Der arbitrator

árbol nm (**a**) tree; **á. frutal** fruit tree; **á. de Navidad** Christmas tree; **á. genealógico** family tree (**b**) Tec shaft; **á. de levas** camshaft (**c**) Náut mast

arbolado, -a 1 adj (**a**) (terreno) wooded; (calle) tree-lined (**b**) (mar) tempestuous
  2 nm woodland

arboladura nf Náut masts and spars

arboleda nf grove, woods

arbotante nm (**a**) Arquit flying buttress (**b**) Méx (poste) (de luz) lamppost; (de teléfono) telephone pole

arbusto nm bush, shrub

arca nf (**a**) (arcón) chest; Fig **arcas** (fondos) coffers; Fig **las arcas públicas** the Treasury (**b**) (barco) **a. de Noé** Noah's Ark

arcada nf (**a**) (de estómago) **me dieron arcadas** I retched (**b**) Arquit (arcos) arcade; (de puente) arch

arcaico, -a adj archaic

arcaísmo nm archaism

arcaizante adj archaizing

arcángel nm archangel

arcano, -a 1 adj arcane
  2 nm (misterio) mystery

arce nm maple

arcén nm Esp shoulder

archiconocido, -a adj very well-known

archidiócesis nf inv archdiocese

archiduque, -esa nm,f archduke, f archduchess

archimillonario, -a nm,f multimillionaire

archipiélago nm archipelago

archisabido, -a adj very well-known

archivador, -ora 1 nm,f archivist
  2 nm (mueble) filing cabinet

archivar vt (gen) & Inform to file; Fig (olvidar) to push to the back of one's mind

archivo nm (**a**) (lugar) archive; (documentos) archives; TV **imágenes de a.** library pictures (**b**) (informe, ficha) file (**c**) Inform file

arcilla nf clay

arcilloso, -a adj clay-like, clayey; **suelo a.** clayey soil

arcipreste nm archpriest

arco nm (**a**) (gen) & Arquit (forma) arch; **a. apuntado** Gothic arch; **a. de herradura** horseshoe arch; **a. iris** rainbow; **a. de medio punto** semicircular arch; **a. triunfal** triumphal arch (**b**) (para flechas) bow (**c**) Mús (de instrumento) bow (**d**) Geom arc (**e**) esp Am Dep (portería) goal, goal mouth

arcón nm large chest

arder vi (**a**) (quemarse) (bosque, casa) to burn; **la iglesia está ardiendo** the church is burning o on fire; Fam Fig **con eso va que arde** that's more than enough (**b**) (estar caliente) (café, sopa) to be boiling hot; Fig **¡está que arde!** (persona) he's

fuming; (reunión) it's getting pretty heated (**c**) (sentir ardor) **le arde la cara** her face is burning (**d**) (por deseos) **a. de rabia** to burn with rage; **a. en deseos de hacer algo** to be dying to do sth (**e**) (por agitación) **la ciudad ardía en fiestas** the city was one great party

ardid nm ruse, trick

ardiente adj (en llamas) burning; (líquido) scalding; (deseo) burning; (admirador, defensor) ardent

ardientemente adv ardently, fervently

ardilla nf squirrel; **a. gris** gray squirrel

ardite nm **no vale un a.** it isn't worth a plug nickel

ardor nm (calor) heat; (quemazón) burning (sensation); (entusiasmo) fervor; **a. de estómago** heartburn

ardoroso, -a adj ardent, fervent

arduo, -a adj arduous

área nf (**a**) (zona) area; **á. de descanso** (en carretera) rest area; **á. metropolitana** metropolitan area; Econ **á. de libre cambio** free exchange area; **á. de servicio** (en carretera) service area (**b**) (ámbito) area; **la investigación en áreas como la inteligencia artificial** research in areas such as artificial intelligence (**c**) (medida) are, = 100 m^2 (**d**) Geom (superficie) area (**e**) (in soccer) **á. (de penalty** o **castigo)** (penalty) area

areca nf (árbol) areca, betel palm; (fruto) betel nut

arena nf (**a**) (de playa) sand; **arenas movedizas** quicksand (**b**) (escenario de la lucha) arena; **la a. política** the political arena (**c**) Taurom bullring

arenal nm area of sandy ground

arenga nf harangue

arengar [40] vt to harangue

arenilla nf (polvo) dust; **arenillas** (cálculos de la vejiga) bladder stones

arenisca nf sandstone

arenoso, -a adj sandy

arenque nm herring

arepa nf Carib, Col = pancake made of ground cornmeal

arete nm Andes, Méx (pendiente) earring; Esp (en forma de aro) hoop earring

argamasa nf mortar

Argel n Algiers

Argelia n Algeria

argelino, -a adj & nm,f Algerian

argentífero, -a adj silver-bearing

Argentina nf (la) A. Argentina

argentinismo nm = word peculiar to Argentinian Spanish

argentino, -a adj & nm,f Argentinian

argolla nf (**a**) (aro) (large) ring (**b**) Andes, Méx (alianza) wedding ring

argonauta nm Argonaut

argot (pl argots) nm (popular) slang; (técnico) jargon

argucia nf sophism

argüir [8] 1 vt (**a**) Formal (argumentar) to argue (**b**) (demostrar) to prove, to demonstrate (**c**) (deducir) to deduce
  2 vi (argumentar) to argue

argumentación nf line of argument

argumentar 1 vt (alegar) to argue (**que** that); **no argumentó bien su hipótesis** he didn't argue his theory very well
  2 vi (discutir) to argue

argumento nm (**a**) (razonamiento) argument; **un a. a favor de/en contra de hacer algo** an argument for/against doing sth (**b**) (trama) plot

arguya ver argüir

arguyera ver argüir

aria nf (de ópera) aria

aridez nf (de terreno, clima) aridity, dryness

árido, -a 1 *adj (terreno, clima)* arid, dry; *(libro, tema)* dry
  2 áridos *nmpl* dry goods

aries 1 *nm inv* Aries; *Esp* **ser a.** to be (an) Aries
  2 *nmf inv Esp (persona)* Aries

ariete *nm Hist & Mil* battering ram; *(in soccer)* center forward

ario, -a *adj & nm,f* Aryan

arisco, -a *adj* surly

arista *nf* edge

aristocracia *nf* aristocracy

aristócrata *nmf* aristocrat

aristocrático, -a *adj* aristocratic

aristotélico, -a *adj & nm,f Filosofía* Aristotelian

aritmética *nf* arithmetic; **a. parlamentaria** parliamentary arithmetic

aritmético, -a *adj* arithmetic(al)

arlequín *nm* harlequin

arma *nf* (**a**) *(instrumento)* arm, weapon; **alzarse en armas** to rise up in arms; **presentar/rendir armas** to present/ surrender arms; *Fig* **ser de armas tomar** to be someone to be reckoned with; **a. biológica** biological weapon; **a. blanca** blade *(weapon with a sharp blade)*; *Fig* **a. de doble filo** double-edged sword; **a. de fuego** firearm; **a. homicida** murder weapon; **a. nuclear** nuclear weapon; **a. química** chemical weapon; **a. secreta** secret weapon (**b**) *(medio)* weapon; **la vacuna será una poderosa a. contra la malaria** the vaccine will be a powerful weapon against malaria (**c**) **las armas** *(profesión)* the military career, the Army

armada *nf* (marina) navy; *(escuadra)* fleet; **la A.** the Navy; *Hist* **la A. Invencible** the Spanish Armada

armadillo *nm* armadillo

armado, -a *adj* (**a**) *(con armas)* armed (**b**) *(con armazón)* reinforced

armador, -ora *nm,f (dueño)* shipowner; *(constructor)* ship- builder

armadura *nf* (**a**) *(de guerrero)* armor; *(traje completo)* suit of armor (**b**) *(de barco, tejado)* framework

armamentista, armamentístico, -a *adj* arms; **carre- ra a.** arms race

armamento *nm* (**a**) *(armas)* arms (**b**) *(acción)* arming

armar 1 *vt* (**a**) *(montar) (mueble, modelo)* to assemble; *(tienda)* to pitch (**b**) *(ejército, personas)* to arm (**c**) *(fusil, pistola)* to load (**d**) *Fam (lío, escándalo)* to cause; **armarla** to cause trouble; **armó una buena con sus comentarios** she really went and did it with the comments she made
  2 armarse *vpr* (**a**) *(con armas)* to arm oneself; *Fig* **armarse de** *(valor, paciencia)* to summon up (**b**) *Fam (organizarse)* **se armó un gran escándalo** there was a huge fuss; **la que se va a a. cuando se entere tu padre** all hell's going to break loose when your father finds out; **se armó la gorda** *o* **la de Troya** all hell broke loose

armario *nm (para objetos)* cupboard; *(para ropa)* wardrobe; *Fam Fig* **salir del a.** to come out of the closet; **a. empo- trado** built-in cupboard/wardrobe

armatoste *nm (mueble, objeto)* unwieldy object; *(máquina)* contraption

armazón *nm o nf (estructura)* framework, frame; *(de avión, coche)* chassis; *(de edificio)* skeleton

Armenia *n* Armenia

armenio, -a *adj & nm,f* Armenian

armería *nf* (**a**) *(depósito)* armory (**b**) *(tienda)* gunsmith's (store) (**c**) *(arte)* gunsmith's craft

armero *nm (fabricante)* gunsmith; *Mil* armorer

armiño *nm (piel)* ermine; *(animal)* stoat

armisticio *nm* armistice

armonía *nf* harmony

armónica *nf* harmonica, mouth organ

armónico, -a 1 *adj* harmonic
  2 *nm Mús* harmonic

armonio *nm* harmonium

armonioso, -a *adj* harmonious

armonización *nf* harmonization

armonizar [14] **1** *vt* (**a**) *(concordar)* to match; **a. las políticas de los Estados miembros** to harmonize the policies of the member states (**b**) *Mús* to harmonize
  2 *vi (concordar)* **a. con** to match

ARN *nm (abrev de* **ácido ribonucleico**) RNA

arnés *(pl* **arneses**) *nm* armor; **arneses** *(de animales)* trappings, harness

árnica *nf* arnica

aro *nm* (**a**) *(círculo)* hoop; *Tec* ring; **los aros olímpicos** the Olympic rings; *Fig* **pasar por el a.** to knuckle under; **un sostén de aros** an underwired bra (**b**) *Am (pendiente)* earring; *Esp (en forma de aro)* hoop earring

aroma *nm (de café)* aroma; *(de flores)* scent; *(de vino)* bouquet; **a. artificial** artificial flavoring

aromaterapia *nf* aromatherapy

aromático, -a *adj* aromatic

aromatizante *nm* flavoring

aromatizar [14] *vt (con perfume)* to perfume; *(comida)* to flavor

arpa *nf* harp; **a. de boca** Jew's harp

arpegio *nm Mús* arpeggio

arpía *nf Mitol* harpy; *Fig* old hag

arpillera *nf* sacking, burlap

arpón *nm* harpoon

arponear *vt* to harpoon

arquear 1 *vt (madera)* to warp; *(vara, fusta)* to flex; *(cejas, espalda)* to arch; **el gato arqueó el lomo** the cat arched its back
  2 arquearse *vpr* to warp

arqueo *nm* (**a**) *(de cejas, espalda, lomo)* arching (**b**) *Com* tallying up (**c**) *Náut* registered tonnage

arqueología *nf* archaeology

arqueológico, -a *adj* archaeological

arqueólogo, -a *nm,f* archaeologist

arquero, -a *nm,f* (**a**) *Dep & Mil (tirador)* archer (**b**) *(tesorero)* treasurer (**c**) *Am Dep (portero)* goalkeeper

arqueta *nf* casket

arquetípico, -a *adj* archetypal

arquetipo *nm* archetype

arquitecto, -a *nm,f* architect

arquitectónico, -a *adj* architectural

arquitectura *nf (gen) & Inform* architecture

arquitrabe *nm Arquit* architrave

arquivolta *nf Arquit* archivolt

arrabal *nm (barrio pobre)* slum; *(barrio periférico)* outlying district

arrabalero, -a *adj Esp (barriobajero)* rough, coarse

arracimarse *vpr* to cluster together

arraigado, -a *adj (costumbre, idea)* deeply rooted; *(persona)* established

arraigar [40] **1** *vt* to establish
  2 *vi también Fig* to take root
  3 arraigarse *vpr (establecerse)* to settle down

arraigo *nm* roots; **tener mucho a.** to be deeply rooted

arramblar *vi* **a. con** *(destruir)* to sweep away; *Fam (arrebatar)* to make off with

arrancada *nf* sudden start

arrancar [59] **1** *vt* (**a**) *(sacar de su sitio) (árbol)* to uproot; *(malas hierbas, flor)* to pull up; *(cable, página, pelo)* to tear out; *(cartel, cortinas)* to tear down; *(muela)* to pull out, to extract; *(ojos)* to gouge out; *Fig* **a. a alguien de un sitio** to shift sb from somewhere (**b**) *(arrebatar)* **a. algo a alguien** to grab *o* snatch sth from sb; **a. algo de las manos de alguien** to snatch sth out of sb's hands (**c**) *(poner en marcha) (coche, máquina)* to start; *Inform* to start up, to boot (up) (**d**) *(obtener)* **a. algo a alguien** *(confesión, promesa, secreto)* to extract sth from sb; *(sonrisa, dinero, ovación)* to get sth out of sb; *(suspiro, carcajada)* to bring sth from sb

2 *vi* (**a**) *(partir)* to set off (**b**) *(máquina, coche)* to start (**c**) *(provenir)* **a. de** to stem from

3 arrancarse *vpr Chile (salir corriendo)* to rush off

arranque *nm* (**a**) *(comienzo)* start (**b**) *Aut (motor)* starter (motor); **a. eléctrico** electrical starting (**c**) *(arrebato)* fit; **en un a. de ira/generosidad** in a fit of anger/generosity

arras *nfpl* (**a**) *(fianza)* deposit (**b**) *(en boda)* = coins given by the bridegroom to the bride

arrasar 1 *vt* to destroy, to devastate

2 *vi Fam (triunfar)* **el equipo brasileño arrasó en la primera fase** the Brazilian team swept everything before it in the first stage; **esa película arrasó en toda Europa** the movie was a massive success throughout Europe

arrastrado, -a 1 *adj* (**a**) *(vida)* miserable, wretched (**b**) *Méx, RP (servil)* groveler

2 *nm,f Méx, RP (persona servil)* groveler

arrastrar 1 *vt* (**a**) *(objeto, pies) (gen) & Inform* to drag; *(carro, vagón)* to pull; **el viento arrastró las hojas** the wind blew the leaves along; *Inform* **a. y soltar** to drag and drop (**b**) *(convencer)* to win over, to sway; **a. a alguien a algo/a hacer algo** to lead sb into sth/to do sth; **dejarse a. por algo/alguien** to allow oneself to be swayed by sth/sb (**c**) *(soportar)* **arrastra una vida miserable** she leads a miserable life; **arrastra muchas deudas** he has a lot of debts hanging over him (**d**) *(al hablar)* **arrastra las erres** he rolls his r's

2 *vi (rozar el suelo)* to drag along the ground; **te arrastra el vestido** your dress is dragging on the ground

3 arrastrarse *vpr* (**a**) *(por el suelo)* to crawl; **los soldados se arrastraban por el barro** the soldiers crawled through the mud (**b**) *(humillarse)* to grovel; **se arrastró ante ella** he groveled to her

arrastre *nm* (**a**) *(acarreo)* dragging; *Esp Fam Fig* **estar para el a.** to have had it (**b**) *(pesca)* trawling

arrayán *nm* myrtle

arre *interj* **¡a.!** gee up!

arrear *vt* (**a**) *(azuzar)* to gee up (**b**) *(propinar)* to give; **a. una bofetada a alguien** to give sb a thump (**c**) *(poner arreos)* to harness

arrebatado, -a *adj* (**a**) *(impetuoso)* impulsive, impetuous (**b**) *(iracundo)* enraged

arrebatador, -ora *adj* captivating

arrebatar 1 *vt* (**a**) *(quitar)* **a. algo a alguien** to snatch sth from sb (**b**) *(cautivar)* to captivate

2 arrebatarse *vpr (enfurecerse)* to get furious

arrebato *nm* (**a**) *(arranque)* fit, outburst; **un a. de amor** a crush (**b**) *(furia)* rage, fury

arrebol *nm* (**a**) *(de cara)* rosiness, ruddiness (**b**) *(de nubes)* red glow

arrebolado, -a *adj* blushing

arrebujar 1 *vt* (**a**) *(amontonar)* to bundle (up) (**b**) *(arropar)* to wrap up (warmly)

2 arrebujarse *vpr (aroparse)* to wrap oneself up; *(encogerse)* to huddle up

arrechar *CAm, Col, Méx, Ven Vulg* **1** *vt* to make horny, to turn on

2 arrecharse *vpr* to get horny

arrecho, -a *adj* (**a**) *CAm, Col, Méx, Ven Vulg (sexualmente)* horny (**b**) *CAm, Méx, Ven Fam (furioso)* mad, furious

arrechucho *nm Fam* **me dio un a.** I was ill, I wasn't feeling too well

arreciar *vi (temporal, lluvia)* to get worse; *(críticas)* to intensify

arrecife *nm* reef; **a. de coral** coral reef

arredrar 1 *vt* to put off, to frighten off; **no le arredra nada** nothing puts him off

2 arredrarse *vpr* **arredrarse ante** to be put *o* frightened off by

arreglado, -a *adj* (**a**) *(reparado)* fixed, repaired; *(ropa)* mended (**b**) *(ordenado)* tidy (**c**) *(bien vestido)* smart (**d**) *(solucionado)* sorted out; **¡y asunto a.!** that's that!; *Fig* **estamos arreglados** we're really done for (**e**) *(precio)* reasonable

arreglar 1 *vt* (**a**) *(reparar)* to fix, to repair; *(ropa) (estrechar)* to take in; *(agrandar)* to let out (**b**) *(ordenar)* to tidy (up) (**c**) *(solucionar)* to sort out; **todo arreglado, podemos pasar** everything's been sorted out now, we can go in (**d**) *Mús* to arrange (**e**) *(acicalar)* to smarten up; *(cabello)* to do; **arregla a los niños, que vamos a dar un paseo** get the children ready, we're going for a walk (**f**) *Fam (escarmentar)* **¡ya te arreglaré yo!** I'm going to straighten you out!

2 *vi Am (quedar)* **¿cómo vas a ir? — ya arreglé con Carlos** how are you going? — I've already arranged to go with Carlos

3 arreglarse *vpr* (**a**) *(asunto, problema)* to sort itself out; **no llores, todo se arreglará** don't cry, it'll all sort itself out *o* work out in the end (**b**) *(tiempo)* to improve, to get better; **si se arregla el día saldremos de excursión** if the weather improves *o* gets better we can go on a trip somewhere (**c**) *(apañarse)* to make do (**con algo** with sth); **arreglárselas (para hacer algo)** to manage (to do sth); **nos las arreglamos como pudimos** we did the best we could; **¡arréglatelas como puedas!** that's your problem! (**d**) *(acicalarse)* to smarten up

arreglista *nmf Mús (musical)* arranger

arreglo *nm* (**a**) *(reparación)* mending, repair; **hacer un a. a** *(ropa) (estrechar)* to take in; *(agrandar)* to let out (**b**) *(solución)* settlement (**c**) *(acuerdo)* agreement; **llegar a un a.** to reach agreement; **con a. a** in accordance with; **un a. pacífico de las diferencias** an amicable settlement of differences (**d**) *Mús* **arreglos musicales** musical arrangements

arrejuntarse *vpr Fam (pareja)* to shack up together

arrellanarse *vpr* to settle back

arremangado, -a *adj* rolled-up

arremangar [40] *Fam* **1** *vt* to roll up

2 arremangarse *vpr* to roll up one's sleeves

arremeter *vi* **a. contra** to attack

arremetida *nf* attack

arremolinarse *vpr (agua, hojas)* to swirl (about); **a. alrededor de** *o* **en torno a** *(personas)* to mill around, to crowd around

arrendador, -ora *nm,f Der* lessor

arrendamiento *nm Der* (**a**) *(acción)* renting, leasing; **contrato de a.** lease (**b**) *(precio)* rent

arrendar [3] *vt Der* (**a**) *(dar en arriendo)* to let, to lease (**b**) *(tomar en arriendo)* to rent, to lease; *Am* **se arrienda** *(en letrero)* for *o* to rent

arrendatario, -a *Der* **1** *adj* leasing

2 *nm,f* leaseholder, tenant

arreos *nmpl* harness

arrepanchigarse [40] *vpr Fam* to stretch out, to sprawl

arrepentido, -a 1 *adj* repentant

2 *nm,f* (**a**) *Rel* penitent (**b**) *Pol* = person who renounces terrorist activities

arrepentimiento *nm (de pecado, crimen)* repentance

arrepentirse [62] *vpr* (**a**) *(lamentar) (de acción)* to regret it; *(de pecado, crimen)* to repent; **a. de algo/de haber hecho algo** *(acción)* to regret sth/having done sth; *(pecado, crimen)* to repent (of) sth/having done sth; **ven a Florida, no te arrepentirás** come to Florida, you won't regret it; **como no**

me hagas caso, te arrepentirás you'll be sorry if you don't listen to me, if you don't listen to me you'll live to regret it (**b**) *(volverse atrás)* **al final, me arrepentí y no fui** in the end, I decided not to go; **no te arrepientas en el último momento** don't change your mind at the last minute

arrestado, -a 1 *adj* under arrest

2 *nm,f* detainee, person under arrest

arrestar *vt* to arrest

arresto *nm* (**a**) *(detención)* arrest; *Der* **a. domiciliario** house arrest (**b**) **arrestos** courage; **tener arrestos para hacer algo** to have the courage to do sth

arriar [32] *vt* *(velas)* to lower

arriate *nm* (flower) bed

arriba 1 *adv* (**a**) *(posición) (en general)* above; *(en edificio)* upstairs; **te esperaremos a., en la cumbre** we'll wait for you up at the top; **el estante de a.** the top shelf; **el apartamento de a.** *(el siguiente)* the upstairs apartment; *(el último)* the top apartment; **vive a.** she lives upstairs; **está aquí/allí a.** it's up here/there; **a. del todo** right at the top; **más a.** further up; **ponlo un poco más a.** put it a bit higher up

(**b**) *(dirección)* up; **ve a.** *(en edificio)* go upstairs; **hacia** *o* **para a.** up, upward; **calle/escaleras a.** up the street/stairs

(**c**) *(en un texto)* above; **el a. mencionado...** the above-mentioned...

(**d**) *(en una escala)* **personas de metro y medio para a.** people of one and a half meters or over; **a. de** more than

(**e**) *(expresiones)* **de a. abajo** *(cosa)* from top to bottom; *(persona)* from head to toe; **mirar a alguien de a. abajo** *(con desdén)* to look sb up and down

(**f**) *Am* **a. de** *(encima de)* above

2 *interj* **¡a., que se hace tarde!** come on, get up, it's getting late!; **¡a. los mineros!** back the miners!; **¡a. las manos!** hands up!

arribar *vi* **a. a** *(lugar)* to reach; **a. a puerto** to reach port

arribista *nmf* *(profesionalmente)* careerist; *(socialmente)* social climber

arriende *etc ver* **arrendar**

arriendo *nm* *Der* (**a**) *(acción)* leasing (**b**) *(precio)* rent

arriero, -a *nm,f* muleteer

arriesgado, -a *adj* (**a**) *(peligroso)* risky (**b**) *(osado)* daring

arriesgar [40] **1** *vt* *(exponer a peligro)* to risk; *(proponer)* to venture, to suggest

2 arriesgarse *vpr* to take risks/a risk; **no quiero arriesgarme** I don't want to risk it

arrimar 1 *vt* (**a**) *(acercar)* to move *o* bring closer; **a. algo a algo** *(pared, mesa)* to move sth up against sth; *Fam Fig* **a. el hombro** to lend a hand, to pitch in (**b**) *(arrinconar)* to put away

2 arrimarse *vpr* (**a**) *(acercarse)* to come closer; **arrimaos que no cabemos** move up or we won't all fit in; **arrimarse a algo** *(acercándose)* to move closer to sth; *(apoyándose)* to lean on sth (**b**) *(ampararse)* **arrimarse a alguien** to seek sb's protection; *Prov* **quien a buen árbol se arrima (buena sombra le cobija)** it pays to have friends in high places

arrinconado, -a *adj* *(acorralado)* cornered; *(abandonado)* discarded, forgotten

arrinconar *vt* (**a**) *(apartar)* to put in a corner; *(dar de lado)* **a. a alguien** to leave sb out in the cold (**b**) *(abandonar)* to discard (**c**) *(acorralar)* to (back into a) corner

arritmia *nf Med* arrhythmia

arrítmico, -a *adj* arrhythmic

arroba *nf* (**a**) *Inform (en dirección de correo electrónico)* at, @ symbol (**b**) *(peso)* = 11.5 kg; *Fig* **por arrobas** by the sackful

arrobado, -a *adj* enraptured

arrobamiento *nm* rapture

arrobar 1 *vt* to captivate

2 arrobarse *vpr* to go into raptures

arrobo *nm* rapture

arrocero, -a 1 *adj* rice; **una región arrocera** a rice-growing region

2 *nm,f* rice grower

arrodillarse *vpr* to kneel down; *Fig* to go down on one's knees, to grovel

arrogancia *nf* arrogance

arrogante *adj* arrogant

arrogarse [40] *vpr* to assume, to claim for oneself

arrojadizo, -a *adj* **utilizar algo como arma arrojadiza** *(botella, ladrillo)* to use sth as a missile

arrojado, -a *adj* bold, fearless

arrojar 1 *vt* (**a**) *(lanzar)* to throw; *(con violencia)* to hurl, to fling (**b**) *(despedir)* *(humo)* to send out; *(olor)* to give off; *(lava)* to spew out; *Fig* **a. luz sobre algo** to throw light on sth (**c**) *(echar)* **a. a alguien de** to throw sb out of (**d**) *(resultado)* **las cuentas arrojaban un déficit de 5.000 millones** the accounts showed a deficit of five billion; **el resultado arroja dudas sobre la popularidad del gobierno** the result casts doubt on the government's popularity (**e**) *(vomitar)* to throw up

2 arrojarse *vpr* to hurl oneself; **arrojarse en los brazos de alguien** to fling *o* throw oneself at sb; **se arrojaron al río** they threw themselves *o* jumped into the river

arrojo *nm* courage, fearlessness

arrollador, -ora *adj* *(victoria, superioridad)* overwhelming; *(belleza, personalidad)* dazzling

arrollar *vt* (**a**) *(enrollar)* to roll (up) (**b**) *(atropellar)* to knock down, to run over (**c**) *(tirar)* *(sujeto: agua, viento)* to sweep away (**d**) *(vencer)* to crush

arropar 1 *vt* *(con ropa)* to wrap up; *(en cama)* to tuck up; *(proteger)* to protect

2 arroparse *vpr* to wrap oneself up

arrorró *(pl* **arrorroes**) *nm Andes, RP Fam* lullaby

arrostrar *vt* to face up to

arroyo *nm* (**a**) *(riachuelo)* stream (**b**) *(de la calle)* gutter; *Fig* **sacar a alguien del a.** to drag sb out of the gutter

arroz *nm* rice; **a. blanco** boiled rice; **a. integral** brown rice; **a. con leche** rice pudding; *Fig* **¡que si quieres a., Catalina!** for all the good that did!

arrozal *nm* rice field

arruga *nf* *(en ropa, papel)* crease; *(en piel)* wrinkle, line

arrugar [40] **1** *vt* *(ropa, papel)* to crease, to crumple; *(piel)* to wrinkle

2 arrugarse *vpr* (**a**) *(ropa)* to get creased; *(piel)* to get wrinkled (**b**) *Fam (acobardarse)* to be intimidated; **no se arrugaron** they were undaunted

arruinado, -a *adj* ruined

arruinar 1 *vt también Fig* to ruin

2 arruinarse *vpr* to go bankrupt, to be ruined

arrullar 1 *vt* to lull to sleep

2 arrullarse *vpr* *(animales)* to coo; *Fam (personas)* to whisper sweet nothings

arrullo *nm* *(de palomas)* cooing; *(nana)* lullaby; *(de agua, olas)* murmur

arrumaco *nm Fam* **hacerse arrumacos** *(amantes)* to kiss and cuddle; **hacer arrumacos a** *(bebé)* to coo at

arrumbar *vt* to put away

arrume *nm Col,Ven* pile

arsenal *nm* (**a**) *Esp (de barcos)* shipyard (**b**) *(de armas)* arsenal (**c**) *(de cosas, pruebas)* array

arsénico *nm Quím* arsenic

art. *(abrev de* **artículo**) art.

arte *nm o nf* (**a**) *(creación estética)* art; **a. abstracto** abstract art; **a. dramático** drama; **a. figurativo** figurative art; **a. floral** flower arranging; **bellas artes** fine arts; **artes gráficas** graphic arts; **artes interpretativas** performing arts; **artes**

liberales liberal arts; **artes marciales** martial arts; **(escuela de) artes y oficios** technical college; **artes plásticas** visual arts; **a. pop** pop art

(**b**) *(habilidad)* artistry; **el a. de la la conversación** the art of conversation

(**c**) *(astucia)* artfulness, cunning; **malas artes** trickery

(**d**) *(expresiones)* **no tener a. ni parte en** to have nothing whatsoever to do with; **como por a. de birlibirloque** *o* **de magia** as if by magic

artefacto *nm* device; *RP* **a. eléctrico** electrical household appliance; **a. explosivo** explosive device; *RP* **artefactos de iluminación** light fittings and fixtures

artemisa, artemisia *nf (hierba)* mugwort

arteria *nf también Fig* artery

arterial *adj* arterial

arterioesclerosis, arteriosclerosis *nf inv Med* arteriosclerosis

artero, -a *adj* cunning, sly

artesa *nf* trough

artesanado *nm* (**a**) *(artesanos)* craftsmen (**b**) *(arte)* artisanship, artisanry

artesanal *adj (queso, miel)* handmade, produced using traditional methods; *(zapatos)* handcrafted; *(agricultura, método)* traditional

artesanía *nf* (**a**) *(arte)* craftsmanship; **taller de a.** crafts workshop; **objetos de a.** crafts, handicrafts (**b**) *(productos)* crafts, handicrafts; **feria de a.** craft fair

artesano, -a 1 *adj (queso, miel)* handmade, produced using traditional methods; *(zapatos)* handcrafted; *(agricultura, método)* traditional

2 *nm,f* craftsman, *f* craftswoman

artesiano, -a *adj* **pozo a.** artesian well

artesonado *nm Arquit* coffered ceiling

ártico, -a 1 *adj* arctic; **el océano (Glacial) Á.** the Arctic Ocean

2 *nm* **el Á.** the Arctic

articulación *nf* (**a**) *Anat & Tec* joint; **a. de la cadera** hip joint (**b**) *Ling* articulation (**c**) *(estructuración)* coordination

articulado, -a *adj* articulated

articular *vt* (**a**) *(piezas)* to articulate (**b**) *(palabras)* to articulate; **no pude a. palabra** I couldn't utter *o* say a word (**c**) *(plan, política)* to develop, to produce; **esta reforma está articulada en torno a tres principios** this reform is structured around *o* built on three principles (**d**) *(ley, contrato)* to break down into separate articles

articulista *nmf* feature writer

artículo *nm* (**a**) *Gram* article; **a. definido** definite article; **a. determinado** definite article; **a. indefinido** indefinite article; **a. indeterminado** indefinite article (**b**) *(periodístico)* article; *(de diccionario)* entry; **a. de fondo** editorial (**c**) *Com* article, item; **a. básico** basic product; **a. de importación** import; **a. líder** product leader; **a. de primera necesidad** basic commodity; **artículos de regalo** gift items; **artículos de viaje** travel accessories (**d**) *Rel & Fig* **a. de fe** article of faith; **tomar algo como a. de fe** to take sth as gospel

artífice *nmf* architect

artificial *adj* artificial

artificiero *nm (desactivador)* bomb disposal expert

artificio *nm* (**a**) *(aparato)* device (**b**) *(falsedad)* artifice; *(artimaña)* trick; *Fin* **artificios contables** creative accounting

artificioso, -a *adj (engañoso)* deceptive

artillería *nf Mil* artillery; **a. ligera** light artillery

artillero *nm Mil* artilleryman

artilugio *nm* gadget, contrivance

artimaña *nf* trick, ruse

artista *nmf (creador)* artist; *(de espectáculos)* artiste; **es una a. en la cocina** she is a superb cook; **a. gráfico** graphic artist; **a. invitado** guest artist

artístico, -a *adj* artistic

artrítico, -a *adj & nm,f* arthritic

artritis *nf inv Med* arthritis

artrópodo *nm Zool* arthropod

artrosis *nf inv Med* arthrosis

arveja *nf RP* pea

arzobispado *nm* archbishopric

arzobispal *adj* archiepiscopal

arzobispo *nm* archbishop

as *nm* (**a**) *(carta, dado)* ace (**b**) *(campeón)* **un a. del volante** an ace driver; **ser un a.** to be brilliant

asa *nf* handle

asado *nm* (**a**) *(carne)* roast (**b**) *Col, CSur (barbacoa)* barbecue

asador *nm* (**a**) *(aparato)* roaster (**b**) *(varilla)* spit (**c**) *(restaurante)* grill, grillroom

asaduras *nfpl (de cordero, ternera)* offal; *(de pollo, pavo)* giblets

asaetear *vt (disparar)* to shoot arrows at; *(matar)* to kill with arrows

asalariado, -a 1 *adj* salaried

2 *nm,f* salaried employee

asalariar *vt* to take on

asalmonado, -a *adj (trucha, color)* salmon

asaltante *nmf (agresor)* attacker; *(atracador)* robber

asaltar *vt* (**a**) *(atacar)* to attack; *(castillo, ciudad)* to storm (**b**) *(robar)* to rob (**c**) *(sujeto: dudas)* to seize; **iba a ir pero al final le asaltaron las dudas** he was going to go, but he was seized by doubts at the last minute; **le asaltó el pánico** he was overcome by panic (**d**) *(importunar)* **los periodistas asaltaron al actor a preguntas** the journalists bombarded the actor with questions

asalto *nm* (**a**) *(ataque)* attack; *(de castillo, ciudad)* storming; **tomar algo por a.** to storm sth (**b**) *(robo)* robbery (**c**) *Dep (en boxeo)* round

asamblea *nf (reunión)* meeting; *(de trabajadores)* mass meeting; *(cuerpo político)* assembly; **a. general** general meeting; **A. General** *(de la ONU)* General Assembly; **a. general anual** annual general meeting; **a. plenaria** plenary assembly; **a. de trabajadores** works meeting

asambleario, -a *adj* **reunión asamblearia** full meeting; **decisión asamblearia** decision taken by a meeting

asar 1 *vt (alimentos) (al horno)* to roast; *(a la parrilla)* to grill; *Fam (importunar)* **a. a alguien a preguntas** to grill sb with questions

2 asarse *vpr (persona)* to be boiling hot

asaz *adv Anticuado & Hum* very, exceedingly

asbestosis *nf inv Med* asbestosis

ascendencia *nf (linaje)* descent; *(extracción social)* extraction; *(influencia)* ascendancy

ascendente 1 *adj* rising

2 *nm (en astrología)* ascendant

ascender [64] **1** *vi* (**a**) *(subir)* to go up, to climb (**b**) *(aumentar, elevarse)* to rise, to go up (**c**) *(en empleo, deportes)* to be promoted (**a** to) (**d**) *(a totalizar)* to come *o* amount to

2 *vt* **a. a alguien** (**a**) to promote sb (to)

ascendiente 1 *nmf (antepasado)* ancestor

2 *nm (influencia)* influence

ascensión *nf* ascent; *Rel* **A.** Ascension

ascenso *nm* (**a**) *(en empleo, deportes)* promotion (**b**) *(a montaña)* ascent (**c**) *(de precios, temperaturas)* rise

ascensor *nm* elevator

ascensorista *nmf* elevator attendant

asceta *nmf* ascetic

ascético, -a *adj* ascetic

ascetismo *nm* asceticism

ASCII ['asθi] *nm Inform (abrev de* **American Standard Code for Information Interchange**) ASCII

asco *nm* (**a**) *(sensación)* disgust, revulsion; **me da a.** I find it disgusting; **las anguilas me dan a.** I find eels disgusting; **¡me das a.!** you make me sick!; **siento a.** I feel sick; **¡qué a.!** how disgusting!; **tener a. a algo** to find sth disgusting; **hacer ascos a** to turn one's nose up at; **no le hace ascos a nada/nadie** he won't turn down anything/anyone (**b**) *Fam (persona, cosa)* **ser un a.** to be the pits; **es un a. de lugar** it's a hole; **estar hecho un a.** *(cosa)* to be filthy; *(persona)* to be a real sight; **¡qué a. de tiempo!** what foul weather!; **¡qué a. de vida!** what a life!

ascórbico *adj Quím* ascorbic

ascua *nf* ember; **siempre quieren arrimar el a. a su sardina** they always put themselves first; **tener a alguien en ascuas** to keep sb on tenterhooks

aseado, -a *adj (limpio)* clean; *(arreglado)* smart

ASEAN [ase'an] *(abrev de* **Asociación de Naciones del Sudeste Asiático)** ASEAN

asear 1 *vt* to clean

2 asearse *vpr* to get washed and dressed

asechanza *nf* snare

asediar *vt Mil* to lay siege to; *Fig* to pester, to badger

asedio *nm Mil* siege; *Fig* pestering, badgering

asegurado, -a *nm,f* policy holder

asegurador, -ora 1 *adj* insurance; **compañía aseguradora** insurance company

2 *nm,f* insurer

asegurar 1 *vt* (**a**) *(fijar)* to secure (**b**) *(garantizar)* to assure; **te lo aseguro** I assure you; **a. a alguien que…** to assure sb that…; **el gobierno aseguró que no subiría los impuestos** the government promised it would not increase taxes; **¿y quién me asegura que no me está mintiendo?** and what guarantee do I have he isn't lying to me? (**c**) *(contra riesgos)* to insure (**contra** against); **a. algo a todo riesgo** to take out comprehensive insurance on sth; **a. algo en** *(cantidad)* to insure sth for

2 asegurarse *vpr* (**a**) *(cerciorarse)* **asegurarse de que…** to make sure that…; **asegúrate de cerrar la puerta** make sure you close the door (**b**) *Fin* to insure oneself, to take out an insurance policy

asemejar 1 *vi* **a. a** to be similar to, to be like

2 asemejarse *vpr* to be similar; **asemejarse a** to be similar to

asentado, -a *adj (establecido)* settled, established

asentamiento *nm (de población)* settlement

asentar [3] **1** *vt* (**a**) *(instalar) (empresa, campamento)* to set up; *(comunidad, pueblo)* to settle (**b**) *(asegurar) (cimientos)* to lay

2 asentarse *vpr* (**a**) *(instalarse)* to settle down (**b**) *(sedimentarse)* to settle

asentimiento *nm* approval, assent

asentir [62] *vi* (**a**) *(estar conforme)* to agree (**a** to) (**b**) *(afirmar con la cabeza)* to nod

aseo *nm* (**a**) *(limpieza) (acción)* cleaning; *(cualidad)* cleanliness; **a. personal** personal cleanliness *o* hygiene (**b**) *Esp (habitación)* bathroom; **aseos** rest room, toilets; **aseos públicos** public rest rooms

asepsia *nf Med* asepsis; *(indiferencia)* detachment

aséptico, -a *adj Med* aseptic; *(indiferente)* detached

asequible *adj* (**a**) *(accesible, comprensible)* accessible (**b**) *(razonable) (precio, producto)* affordable

aserción *nf* assertion

aserradero *nm* sawmill

aserrar [3] *vt* to saw

aserto *nm* assertion

asesinar *vt (persona)* to murder; *(rey, jefe de Estado)* to assassinate

asesinato *nm (de persona)* murder; *(de rey, jefe de Estado)*

assassination; **un a. a sangre fría** a cold-blooded murder

asesino, -a 1 *adj también Fig* murderous

2 *nm,f (de persona)* murderer, *f* murderess; *(de rey, jefe de Estado)* assassin; **a. profesional** professional killer; **a. en serie** serial killer; **a. a sueldo** contract killer

asesor, -ora *nm,f* adviser; **a. de imagen** image consultant; **a. financiero** financial adviser; **a. fiscal** tax adviser

asesoramiento *nm* advice; *(de empresa)* consultancy

asesorar 1 *vt* to advise; *(empresa)* to provide with consultancy services

2 asesorarse *vpr* to seek advice; **asesorarse de** *o* **con** to consult

asesoría *nf* consultancy; **a. fiscal** tax consultancy; **a. jurídica** *o* **legal** legal advice

asestar *vt (golpe)* to deal; *(tiro)* to fire

aseveración *nf* assertion

aseverar *vt* to assert

asexuado, -a *adj* asexual

asexual *adj* asexual

asfaltado *nm (acción)* asphalting, surfacing; *(asfalto)* asphalt, (road) surface

asfaltadora *nf* (road) surfacer

asfaltar *vt* to asphalt, to surface

asfalto *nm* asphalt

asfixia *nf* asphyxiation, suffocation

asfixiante *adj* asphyxiating; *(calor)* stifling

asfixiar 1 *vt (ahogar)* to asphyxiate, to suffocate; *(agobiar)* to overwhelm

2 asfixiarse *vpr (ahogarse)* to asphyxiate, to suffocate; *(agobiarse)* to be overwhelmed; **¡aquí me asfixio!** *(de calor)* I'm suffocating in here!

así 1 *adv (de este modo)* this way, like this; *(de ese modo)* that way, like that; **ellos lo hicieron a.** they did it this way; **¿a. me agradeces todo lo que he hecho por ti?** is this how you thank me for everything I've done for you?; **a. no vamos a ninguna parte** we're not getting anywhere like this; **era a. de largo** it was this/that long; **es a. de fácil** it's as easy as that; **a. es/era/fue como…** that is/was how…; **a. a.** *(no muy bien)* so-so; **algo a.** *(algo parecido)* something like that; **a. como** *(también)* as well as; *(tal como)* just as; **¡no puedes marcharte a. como a.!** you can't leave just like that!; **algo a. como** *(algo igual a)* something like; **a. es** *(para asentir)* that is correct; **¡a. me gusta!** that's what I like (to see)!; **y a. sucesivamente** and so on, and so forth; **y a. todos los días** and the same thing happens day after day; **a. y todo, aun a.** even so

2 *conj* (**a**) *(aunque)* even if; **a. tenga que…** even if I have to… (**b**) *Am (aun si)* even if; **no nos lo dirá, a. le paguemos** he won't tell us, even if we pay him

3 *adj inv (como éste)* like this; *(como ése)* like that; **no seas a.** don't be like that

4 así que *loc conj (de modo que)* so; *(tan pronto como)* as soon as; **la película empieza dentro de media hora, a. que no te entretengas** the movie starts in half an hour, so don't be long; **a. que tengamos los resultados del análisis, le citaremos para la visita** as soon as we have the results of the test we'll make an appointment for you

5 así pues *loc conj* so, therefore

Asia *n* Asia; **A. Menor** Asia Minor

asiático, -a *adj & nm,f* Asian, Asiatic

asidero *nm (agarradero)* handle; *Fig (apoyo)* support

asiduidad *nf* frequency

asiduo, -a *adj & nm,f* regular

asienta (**a**) *ver* **asentar** (**b**) *ver* **asentir**

asiento *nm* (**a**) *(silla, butaca)* seat; **tomar a.** to sit down; **a. abatible** = seat that tips forward or folds flat; **a. delantero** *(en coche)* front seat; **a. de pasillo** *(en avión)* aisle seat; **a.**

reclinable reclining seat; **a. trasero** back seat; **a. de ventana** *(en avión)* window seat **(b)** *(base)* bottom **(c)** *Com* entry; **a. contable** book entry

asierre *ver* aserrar

asignación *nf* **(a)** *(atribución)* allocation **(b)** *(sueldo)* salary

asignar *vt* **(a)** *(atribuir)* **a. algo a alguien** to assign *o* allocate sth to sb **(b)** *(destinar)* **a. a alguien a** to assign sb to

asignatura *nf Educ* subject; **a. optativa** optional subject; **a. pendiente** subject which a pupil has to retake; *Fig* unresolved matter; **asignaturas troncales** core curriculum

asilado, -a *nm,f* **a. (político)** political refugee

asilar *vt* *(huérfano, anciano)* to put into a home; *(refugiado político)* to grant political asylum to

asilo *nm* **(a)** *(hospicio)* home; **a. de ancianos** nursing home **(b)** *(refugio)* refuge, sanctuary; *Fig (amparo)* asylum; **a. político** political asylum

asilvestrado, -a *adj* feral

asimetría *nf* asymmetry

asimétrico, -a *adj* asymmetric(al)

asimilación *nf* **(a)** *(gen) & Ling* assimilation **(b)** *(comparación)* comparison **(c)** *(equiparación)* granting of equal rights

asimilar 1 *vt* **(a)** *(idea, conocimientos, alimentos)* to assimilate **(b)** *(comparar)* to compare **(c)** *(equiparar)* to grant equal rights to

2 asimilarse *vpr Ling* to become assimilated; **asimilarse a algo** *(parecerse)* to resemble sth

asimismo *adv (también)* also, as well; *(a principio de frase)* likewise

asíncrono, -a *adj Inform* asynchronous

asintiera *ver* asentir

asir [9] **1** *vt* to grasp, to take hold of

2 asirse *vpr también Fig* to cling (**a** to)

asirio, -a *adj & nm,f Hist* Assyrian

asistencia *nf* **(a)** *(ayuda)* assistance; **a. letrada** *o* **jurídica** legal advice; **a. jurídica de oficio** legal aid; **a. médica** medical attention; **a. pública** social security; **a. sanitaria** health care; **a. social** social work; **a. técnica** technical assistance **(b)** *(presencia) (acción)* attendance; *(hecho)* presence **(c)** *(afluencia)* attendance **(d)** *Dep* assist

asistencial *adj Med* health care; **servicios asistenciales** health-care services

asistenta *nf Esp* cleaning lady, cleaning woman

asistente *nmf* **(a)** *(ayudante)* assistant, helper; **a. social** social worker **(b)** *(presente)* person present; **los asistentes** *(el público)* the audience

asistido, -a *adj* **a. por ordenador** computer-assisted; **dirección asistida** power steering

asistir 1 *vt* **(a)** *(ayudar)* to attend to; **le asiste el doctor Jiménez** he is being treated by Dr Jiménez **(b)** *(acompañar)* to accompany

2 *vi* to attend; **a. a un acto** to attend an event

asma *nf Med* asthma

asmático, -a *adj & nm,f* asthmatic

asno *nm* **(a)** *(animal)* ass **(b)** *Fam (necio)* ass

asociación *nf* association; **a. de consumidores** consumer association; **A. Europea de Libre Comercio** European Free Trade Association; **a. de ideas** association of ideas; **a. de vecinos** residents' association

asociacionismo *nm* **una época caracterizada por el a.** a period which saw the formation of many organizations

asociado, -a 1 *adj* **(a)** *(relacionado)* associated **(b)** *(miembro)* associate

2 *nm,f* **(a)** *(miembro)* associate, partner **(b)** *Educ* associate professor

asocial *adj* asocial

asociar 1 *vt* **(a)** *(relacionar)* to associate **(b)** *Com* to take into partnership

2 asociarse *vpr* to form a partnership

asociativo, -a *adj* associative

asolado, -a *adj* devastated

asolar *vt* to devastate

asolearse *vpr Andes, Méx, RP* to bask in the sun

asomar 1 *vt* **a. la cabeza por la ventana** to stick one's head out of the window; **asomaron el bebé al balcón** they took the baby out onto the balcony

2 *vi (sobresalir)* to stick up; **asoma el día** day is breaking

3 asomarse *vpr* **asomarse a la ventana** to stick one's head out of the window; **asomarse al balcón** to go out onto the balcony, to appear on the balcony; **prohibido asomarse por la ventanilla** *(en letrero)* do not lean out of the window

asombrar 1 *vt (causar admiración)* to amaze; *(causar sorpresa)* to surprise

2 asombrarse *vpr (sentir admiración)* to be amazed (**de** at); *(sentir sorpresa)* to be surprised (**de** at)

asombro *nm (admiración)* amazement; *(sorpresa)* surprise

asombroso, -a *adj (sensacional)* amazing; *(sorprendente)* surprising

asomo *nm (indicio)* trace, hint; *(de esperanza)* glimmer; **ni por a.** not under any circumstances

asonancia *nf (en poesía)* assonance

asonante *adj (rima)* assonant

asorochar *Andes* **1** *vt* to cause to have altitude sickness

2 asorocharse *vpr* to get altitude sickness

aspa *nf (figura)* X-shaped cross; *(de molino)* arm

aspaviento *nm* furious gesticulations

aspecto *nm* **(a)** *(apariencia)* appearance; **tener buen a.** *(persona)* to look well; *(comida)* to look nice; **tiene mal a.** *(persona)* he doesn't look well; *(comida)* it doesn't look very nice; **tenía a. de vagabundo** he looked like a tramp **(b)** *(faceta)* aspect; **bajo este a.** from this angle; **en todos los aspectos** in every respect

aspereza *nf* roughness; *Fig* sharpness, sourness; **limar asperezas** to smooth things over

áspero, -a *adj (rugoso)* rough; *(desagradable) (sabor)* sharp, sour; *(persona, carácter)* sour, unpleasant; **una áspera disputa** *(entre grupos)* a bitter dispute

aspersión *nf (de jardín)* sprinkling; *(de cultivos)* spraying; **riego por a.** spraying *(of garden or field with sprinkler)*

aspersor *nm (para jardín)* sprinkler; *(para cultivos)* sprayer

áspid *nm* asp

aspillera *nf (abertura)* loophole, crenel

aspiración *nf* **(a)** *(pretensión)* aspiration **(b)** *(de aire) (por una persona)* breathing in; *(por una máquina)* suction

aspiradora *nf*, **aspirador** *nm* vacuum cleaner; **pasar la a.** to vacuum

aspirante 1 *adj (persona)* aspiring

2 *nmf* candidate (**a** for); *(en deportes, concursos)* contender (**a** for); **un a. a actor/político** a would-be actor/politician

aspirar 1 *vt* **(a)** *(aire) (sujeto: persona)* to breathe in, to inhale; *(sujeto: máquina)* to suck in **(b)** *(limpiar con aspirador)* to vacuum **(c)** *Ling* to aspirate

2 *vi* **a. a algo** *(ansiar)* to aspire to sth; **aspira a (ser) ministro** he aspires to become a minister

aspirina *nf* aspirin

asquear *vt* to disgust, to make sick

asquerosidad *nf* disgusting *o* revolting thing

asqueroso, -a *adj* disgusting, revolting

asta *nf* **(a)** *(de bandera)* flagpole, mast; **a media a.** at half-mast **(b)** *(de lanza)* shaft; *(de brocha)* handle **(c)** *(de toro)* horn

astado *nm Taurom* bull

astenia *nf (debilidad)* fatigue, *Med* asthenia

asténico, -a *adj (débil)* easily fatigued, *Med* asthenic

asterisco *nm* asterisk

asteroide *nm* asteroid

astigmatismo *nm Med* astigmatism

astil *nm (de hacha, pico)* haft; *(de azada)* handle

astilla *nf* splinter; *Fig* **hacer astillas** to smash to smithereens

astillar 1 *vt (mueble)* to splinter; *(tronco)* to chop up
 2 astillarse *vpr* to splinter

astillero *nm* shipyard

astracán *nm* astrakhan

astracanada *nf Fam* farce

astrágalo *nm* (**a**) *Anat* anklebone, *Espec* astragalus (**b**) *Arquit* astragal

astral *adj* astral

astringente *adj* astringent

astro *nm Astron* heavenly body; *Fig* star

astrofísica *nf* astrophysics *(singular)*

astrolabio *nm* astrolabe

astrología *nf* astrology

astrólogo, -a *nm,f* astrologer

astronauta *nmf* astronaut

astronáutica *nf* astronautics *(singular)*

astronave *nf* spacecraft, spaceship

astronomía *nf* astronomy

astronómico, -a *adj también Fig* astronomical

astrónomo, -a *nm,f* astronomer

astroso, -a *adj (andrajoso)* shabby, ragged

astucia *nf (trampas)* cunning; *(sagacidad)* astuteness

asturiano, -a *adj & nm,f* Asturian

Asturias *n* Asturias

astuto, -a *adj (ladino, tramposo)* cunning; *(sagaz, listo)* astute

asuelo *etc ver* **asolar**

asueto *nm* break, rest; **unos días de a.** a few days off

asumir *vt* (**a**) *(adoptar)* to assume; **el descontento asumió caracteres alarmantes** the discontent began to take on alarming proportions (**b**) *(aceptar)* to accept; **a. la responsabilidad de algo** to take on responsibility for sth

asunceño, -a 1 *adj* of/from Asunción
 2 *nm,f* person from Asunción

Asunción *n* Asunción

asunción *nf* assumption; *Rel* **la A.** the Assumption

asunto *nm* (**a**) *(cuestión)* matter; *(problema)* issue; **necesitamos hablar de un a. importante** we need to talk about an important matter; **anda metido en un a. turbio** he's mixed up *o* involved in a questionable affair; **no es a. tuyo** it's none of your business; **el a. es que...** the thing is that...; **¡...y a. concluido!** and that's that!; *Pol* **asuntos exteriores** foreign affairs; **asuntos a tratar** agenda (**b**) *(de obra, libro)* theme (**c**) *(romance)* affair

asustadizo, -a *adj* easily frightened

asustado, -a *adj* frightened, scared

asustar 1 *vt* to frighten, to scare; **¡me has asustado!** you gave me a fright!; **me asusta pensar que pueda tener razón** the scary thing is she may be right
 2 asustarse *vpr* (**a**) *(tener miedo)* to be frightened (**de** of); **me asusté al verlo** I got a shock when I saw him (**b**) *(preocuparse)* to get worried; **no te asustes, seguro que no le ha pasado nada grave** don't get worried, I'm sure nothing bad has happened to him

Atacama *nm* **el (desierto de) A.** the Atacama (Desert)

atacante 1 *adj* attacking
 2 *nmf (agresor)* attacker
 3 *nm (en fútbol)* forward

atacar [59] *vt* (**a**) *(acometer)* to attack; **esta enfermedad ataca el sistema respiratorio** this disease attacks the respiratory system (**b**) *Dep* to attack (**c**) *(criticar)* to attack (**d**) *(afectar)* **le atacó la risa/fiebre** he had a fit of laughter/a bout of fever (**e**) *(poner nervioso)* **ese ruido me ataca (los nervios)** that noise gets on my nerves (**f**) *(corroer)* to corrode

atado *nm* bundle

atadura *nf también Fig* tie

atajar 1 *vi (acortar)* to take a shortcut (**por** through); **si bajas por aquí atajas** it's quicker if you go down this way
 2 *vt* (**a**) *(contener)* to put a stop to; *(hemorragia, inundación)* to stem; **las medidas pretenden a. el problema de la evasión de impuestos** the measures are intended to put a stop to the problem of tax evasion (**b**) *Am (agarrar)* to catch

atajo *nm* (**a**) *(camino corto, medio rápido)* shortcut *o Esp* **coger un a.** to take a shortcut (**b**) *Esp Pey (panda)* bunch

atalaya *nf (torre)* watchtower; *(altura)* vantage point

atañer *vi* (**a**) *(concernir)* **a. a** to concern; **en lo que atañe a este asunto** as far as this subject is concerned (**b**) *(corresponder)* **a. a** to be the responsibility of

ataque 1 *ver* **atacar**
 2 *nm* (**a**) *(acometida)* attack; **¡al a.!** charge!; **a. aéreo** air raid; **a. preventivo** preemptive strike (**b**) *Dep* attack (**c**) *(crítica)* attack; **lanzó duros ataques contra el presidente** she launched several harsh attacks on the president (**d**) *(acceso)* fit; **le dio un a. de risa** he had a fit of the giggles; **a. cardíaco** *o* **al corazón** heart attack; **a. epiléptico** epileptic fit; **a. de nervios** attack of nerves; **a. de pánico** panic attack

atar 1 *vt* (**a**) *(unir) (nudo, cuerda)* to tie; *Fig* **a. cabos** to put two and two together (**b**) *(con cuerdas) (persona caballo, barco)* to tie up; **lo ataron de pies y manos** they tied his hands and feet; **esa cláusula nos ata las manos** our hands are tied by that clause; *Fig* **a. corto a alguien** to keep a tight rein on sb (**c**) *(constreñir)* to tie down; **su trabajo le ata mucho** her work takes up a lot of her time
 2 atarse *vpr* (**a**) *(uno mismo)* to tie oneself down (**b**) **se ató el pelo** she tied her hair up; **atarse los zapatos** to tie one's shoes *o* shoelaces

atarazana *nf* shipyard

atardecer [46] **1** *nm* dusk
 2 *v impersonal* to get dark; **está atardeciendo** it's getting dark

atareado, -a *adj* busy

atascar [59] **1** *vt* to block (up)
 2 atascarse *vpr (obstruirse)* to get blocked up; *Fig (detenerse)* to get stuck; *(al hablar)* to dry up

atasco *nm (obstrucción)* blockage; *(de vehículos)* traffic jam

atasque *etc ver* **atascar**

ataúd *nm* coffin

ataviar [32] **1** *vt* to dress up
 2 ataviarse *vpr* to dress up

atávico, -a *adj* atavistic

atavío *nm* (**a**) *(adorno)* adornment (**b**) *(indumentaria)* attire; **llevaba sus mejores atavíos** she was wearing her finest attire

ate *nm Méx* quince jelly

ateísmo *nm* atheism

atemorizado, -a *adj* frightened

atemorizar [14] **1** *vt* to frighten
 2 atemorizarse *vpr* to get frightened

atemperar *vt (críticas, protestas)* to temper, to tone down; *(ánimos, nervios)* to calm

atemporal *adj* timeless

Atenas *n* Athens

atenazar [14] *vt* (**a**) *(sujetar)* to clench (**b**) *Fig* **el miedo la atenazaba** she was gripped by fear

atención 1 *nf* (**a**) *(interés)* attention; **escucha con a.** listen carefully; **a la a. de** for the attention of; **llamar la a.** *(atraer)* to attract attention; **lo que más me llamó la a. fue...** what struck me most was...; **al principio no me llamó la a.** at first I didn't notice anything unusual; **llamar la a. a**

alguien *(amonestar)* to tell sb off; **poner** *o* **prestar a.** to pay attention

(**b**) *(cortesía)* attentiveness; **en a. a** *(teniendo en cuenta)* out of consideration for; *(en honor a)* in honor of; **atenciones** attentions, attentiveness; **nos colmaron de atenciones** they waited on us hand and foot; **deshacerse en atenciones con** to lavish attention on

(**c**) *(servicio)* **horario de a. al público** opening hours; **a. al cliente** customer service, customer care; **a. hospitalaria** hospital care; **a. sanitaria** health care

2 *interj* **¡a.!** *(en aeropuerto, conferencia)* your attention please!

atender [64] **1** *vt* (**a**) *(satisfacer) (petición, ruego)* to attend to; *(consejo, instrucciones)* to heed; *(propuesta)* to agree to (**b**) *(cuidar de) (necesitados, invitados)* to look after; *(enfermo)* to care for; *(cliente)* to serve; **¿le atienden?** are you being served?

2 *vi* (**a**) *(estar atento)* to pay attention (**a** to) (**b**) *(considerar)* **atendiendo a...** taking into account... (**c**) *(llamarse) (animales)* **a. por** to answer to the name of

ateneo *nm* athenaeum

atenerse [65] *vpr* (**a**) **a. a** *(promesa, orden)* to stick to; *(ley, normas)* to observe, to abide by (**b**) **a. a** *(consecuencias)* to bear in mind

ateniense *adj & nmf* Athenian

atentado *nm* **a. contra alguien** attempt on sb's life; **a. contra algo** crime against sth; **a. (terrorista)** terrorist attack; **sufrir un a. (terrorista)** to be the victim of a terrorist attack

atentamente *adv* (**a**) *(con atención, cortesía)* attentively; **mire a.** watch carefully (**b**) *(en cartas)* Yours (sincerely/faithfully)

atentar *vi* **a. contra (la vida de) alguien** to make an attempt on sb's life; **a. contra algo** *(principio)* to be a crime against sth

atento, -a *adj* (**a**) *(pendiente)* attentive; **estar a. a** *(explicación, programa, lección)* to pay attention to; *(ruido, sonido)* to listen out for; *(acontecimientos, cambios, avances)* to keep up with (**b**) *(cortés)* considerate, thoughtful

atenuación *nf (de dolor)* easing, alleviation; *(de sonido, luz)* attenuation

atenuante *nm Der* extenuating circumstance

atenuar [4] **1** *vt (disminuir, suavizar)* to diminish; *(dolor)* to ease, to alleviate; *(sonido, luz)* to attenuate

2 atenuarse *vpr (disminuir, suavizarse)* to lessen, to diminish

ateo, -a 1 *adj* atheistic

2 *nm,f* atheist

aterciopelado, -a *adj* velvety

aterido, -a *adj* freezing; **a. de frío** shaking *o* shivering with cold

aterirse *vpr* to be freezing

aterrado, -a *adj* terror-stricken

aterrador, -ora *adj* terrifying

aterrar 1 *vt* to terrify

2 aterrarse *vpr* to be terrified

aterrizaje *nm (de avión)* landing; **a. de emergencia** emergency landing; **a. forzoso** forced landing

aterrizar [14] *vi (avión)* to land; *(persona)* to turn up; *Hum (objeto)* to land; **el tapón aterrizó en mi plato** the cork landed on my plate

aterrorizado, -a *adj* terrified, terrorized

aterrorizar [14] **1** *vt* to terrify; **me aterrorizan las arañas** I'm terrified of spiders; **el atracador aterrorizaba a sus víctimas** the robber terrorized his victims

2 aterrorizarse *vpr* to be terrified

atesorar *vt (riquezas)* to amass; *(virtudes)* to be blessed with

atestado *nm* official report

atestar *vt* (**a**) *(llenar)* to pack, to cram (**b**) *Der* to testify to

atestiguar [11] *vt* to testify to

atezado, -a *adj* tanned

atiborrar *Fam* **1** *vt* to stuff full

2 atiborrarse *vpr* to stuff one's face (**de** with)

atice *etc ver* **atizar**

ático *nm (piso)* = attic apartment, usually with a roof terrace; *(desván)* attic

atiendo *etc ver* **atender**

atigrado, -a *adj (gato)* tabby

atildado, -a *adj* smart, spruce

atildar 1 *vt (acicalar)* to smarten up

2 atildarse *vpr* to smarten oneself up

atinado, -a *adj* (**a**) *(respuesta)* correct; *(comentario)* appropriate (**b**) *(oportuno)* good, clever

atinar *vi (adivinar)* to guess correctly; *(dar en el blanco)* to hit the target; **a. a hacer algo** to succeed in doing sth; **a. con** to hit upon

atingencia *nf Arg, CAm, Chile, Méx (relación)* connection

atípico, -a *adj* atypical

atiplado, -a *adj* shrill

atisbar *vt* (**a**) *(divisar, prever)* to make out (**b**) *(acechar)* to observe, to spy on

atisbo *nm (indicio)* trace, hint; *(de esperanza)* glimmer

atizador *nm* poker

atizar [14] **1** *vt* (**a**) *(fuego)* to poke, to stir (**b**) *(sospechas, discordias)* to stir up (**c**) *Esp (persona)* **me atizó bien fuerte** *(un golpe)* he hit me really hard; *(una paliza)* he gave me a good hiding

2 atizarse *vpr Fam (comida, bebida)* to guzzle

atlante *nm Arquit* atlas, telamon

atlántico, -a 1 *adj* Atlantic; **el océano A.** the Atlantic (Ocean)

2 *nm* **el A.** the Atlantic (Ocean)

atlantismo *nm Pol* pro-NATO stance

atlas *nm inv* atlas

atleta *nmf* athlete; **un a. completo** an all-around athlete

atlético, -a *adj* athletic

atletismo *nm* athletics; **a. en pista cubierta** indoor athletics

atmósfera *nf también Fig* atmosphere

atmosférico, -a *adj* atmospheric

atole *nm CAm, Méx* = drink made of cornstarch

atolladero *nm (apuro)* fix, jam; **meter en/sacar de un a. a alguien** to put sb in/get sb out of a tight spot

atolón *nm* atoll

atolondrado, -a 1 *adj* (**a**) *(precipitado)* hasty, disorganized (**b**) *(aturdido)* bewildered

2 *nm,f (precipitado)* hasty *o* disorganized person

atolondramiento *nm* (**a**) *(precipitación)* haste, disorganization (**b**) *(aturdimiento)* bewilderment

atolondrar 1 *vt* to bewilder; **me atolondra tanto griterío** all this shouting is making my head spin

2 atolondrarse *vpr (por golpe)* to be stunned; *(por griterío, confusión)* to be bewildered; **se atolondró con el golpe** she was stunned by the blow

atómico, -a *adj (energía, armas)* atomic, nuclear; *(central)* nuclear; **núcleo a.** (atomic) nucleus

atomización *nf* atomization

atomizador *nm* atomizer, spray

atomizar [14] *vt (líquido)* to atomize

átomo *nm también Fig* atom; **á. gramo** gram-atom

atonal *adj Mús* atonal

atonalidad *nf Mús* atonality

atonía *nf (de mercado, economía)* sluggishness

atónito, -a *adj* astonished, astounded

átono, -a *adj* atonic

atontado, -a 1 *adj* **(a)** *(aturdido)* dazed, stunned **(b)** *(tonto)* stupid

2 *nm,f* idiot, half-wit

atontamiento *nm* **(a)** *(aturdimiento)* confusion, bewilderment **(b)** *(alelamiento)* **¡tengo un a. hoy!** I really can't think straight today!

atontar *vt* **(a)** *(aturdir)* to daze, to stun **(b)** *(volver tonto)* to dull the mind of

atontolinar *Fam vt* to daze, to stun

atorar 1 *vt* to obstruct, to clog

2 atorarse *vpr* **(a)** *(atragantarse)* to choke **(con** on) **(b)** *(cortarse, trabarse)* to get stuck **(c)** *Am (atascarse)* to get blocked, to get clogged up **(d)** *Am (meterse en un lío)* to get into a mess

atormentado, -a *adj* tormented

atormentar *vt* to torture; *Fig* to torment

atornillar *vt* to screw

atorrante *RP* **1** *adj* lazy

2 *nmf* layabout

atosigamiento *nm* urging, pressing

atosigar [40] *vt (con prisas)* to harass; *(con exigencias)* to pester, to badger

atrabiliario, -a *adj* foul-tempered, bilious

atracadero *nm* landing stage

atracador, -ora *nm,f (de banco)* bank robber; *(en la calle)* mugger

atracar [59] **1** *vt (banco)* to rob; *(persona)* to mug

2 *vi Náut* to dock **(en** at)

3 atracarse *vpr* to eat one's fill **(de** of)

atracción *nf* **(a)** *(física, magnética)* attraction; **a. gravitatoria** gravitational pull **(b)** *(atractivo)* attractiveness, charm **(c)** *(espectáculo)* act **(d)** *(centro de atención)* center of attention; **a. turística** tourist attraction **(e)** *(diversión infantil)* fairground attraction

atraco *nm* robbery; **a. a mano armada** armed robbery; **¿1.000 euros por eso? ¡menudo a.!** 1,000 euros for that? that's daylight robbery!

atracón *nm Fam* feast; **darse un a. de algo** *(comida)* to stuff one's face with sth; *(películas, televisión)* to overdose on sth

atractivo, -a 1 *adj* attractive

2 *nm (de persona)* attractiveness, charm; *(de cosa)* attraction; **a. sexual** sex appeal

atraer [66] **1** *vt* **(a)** *(causar acercamiento)* to attract; *(atención)* to attract, to draw; **lo atrajo hacia sí tirándole de la corbata** she pulled him toward her by his tie **(b)** *(gustar)* to attract; **la miel atrae a las moscas** honey attracts flies; **me atrae tu hermana** I'm attracted to your sister, I find your sister attractive; **no me atrae mucho la comida china** I'm not too keen on Chinese food; **no me atrae mucho la idea** the idea doesn't appeal to me much; **la asistencia de personajes famosos atrajo a gran cantidad de público** the presence of the famous drew huge crowds

2 atraerse *vpr (mutuamente)* to attract one another

atragantarse *vpr* to choke **(con** on); *Fig* **se me ha atragantado este libro/tipo** I can't stand that book/guy

atraiga *etc ver* **atraer**

atrajera *etc ver* **atraer**

atrancar [59] **1** *vt* **(a)** *(cerrar)* to bar **(b)** *(obstruir)* to block

2 atrancarse *vpr* **(a)** *(encerrarse)* to lock oneself in **(b)** *(atascarse)* to get blocked **(c)** *(al hablar, escribir)* to dry up

atrapamoscas *nf inv (planta)* Venus flytrap

atrapar *vt (agarrar, alcanzar)* to catch

atraque *ver* **atracar**

atrás 1 *adv* **(a)** *(posición)* behind, at the back; **la falda es más larga por a.** the skirt is longer at the back; **el asiento de a.** the back seat; **dejar a alguien a.** to leave sb behind; **quedarse a.** to fall behind; *Méx Fam Fig* **estar hasta a.**

(borracho) to be plastered **(b)** *(movimiento)* backward; **echarse para a.** to move backward; **dar un paso a.** to take a step backward; **hacia a.** backward **(c)** *(en el tiempo)* earlier; **habían casado tres años a.** they had married three years earlier; **cuarenta años a. pocos tenían televisores** not many people had televisions forty years ago **(d)** *Am* **a. de** behind

2 *interj* **¡a.!** get back!

atrasado, -a *adj* **(a)** *(en el tiempo)* delayed; *(reloj)* slow; *(pago)* overdue, late; **vamos atrasados en este proyecto** we're behind schedule on this project; **número a.** back number; **mi reloj va a.** my watch is slow; *Am* **mi vuelo salió a.** my flight was delayed, my flight departed late **(b)** *(en evolución, capacidad)* backward; **las regiones más atrasadas del país** the most backward regions of the country

atrasar 1 *vt (retrasar) (cita, reloj)* to put back; *(poner más atrás)* to move (further) back

2 *vi (reloj)* to be slow

3 atrasarse *vpr* **(a)** *(en el tiempo)* to be late **(b)** *(quedarse atrás)* to fall behind **(c)** *(reloj)* to lose time; **mi reloj se atrasa 5 minutos al día** my watch loses 5 minutes a day **(d)** *(llegar tarde)* to be delayed; **su vuelo se atrasó** her flight was delayed; **se atrasaron media hora** they were delayed by half an hour; **nos atrasamos hablando con mi tía** we got held up talking to my aunt

atraso *nm* **(a)** *(del reloj)* slowness **(b)** *(de evolución)* backwardness **(c)** *Fin* **atrasos** arrears

atravesado, -a *adj* **hay un árbol a. en la carretera** there's a tree lying across the road; *Fam Fig* **tengo a. a Tomás** I can't stand Tomás

atravesar [3] **1** *vt* **(a)** *(interponer)* to put across **(b)** *(cruzar)* to cross; **atravesó el río a nado** she swam across the river; **atravesó la calle corriendo** he ran across the street **(c)** *(traspasar)* to pass *o* go through; **la bala le atravesó un pulmón** the bullet went through one of his lungs; **el río atraviesa el pueblo** the river goes *o* runs through the village **(d)** *(pasar)* to go through, to experience; **a. una mala racha** to be going through a bad spell; **atraviesan un buen momento** things are going well for them at the moment

2 atravesarse *vpr* **se nos atravesó una moto** a motorbike crossed in front of us; **se le atravesó una espina en la garganta** he got a fish bone caught in his throat; *Fam Fig* **se me ha atravesado la vecina** I can't stand my neighbor

atrayente *adj* attractive

atrechar *vi PRico Fam* to take a shortcut

atreverse *vpr* to dare **(a hacer algo** to do sth); **a. a algo** to be bold enough for sth; **a. con alguien** to take sb on; **¡atrévete y verás!** just you dare and see what happens!

atrevido, -a 1 *adj (osado)* daring; *(caradura)* cheeky

2 *nm,f (osado)* daring person; *(caradura)* cheeky person

atrevimiento *nm* **(a)** *(osadía)* daring **(b)** *(insolencia)* cheek

atrezo *nm Teatro & Cine* props

atribución *nf* **(a)** *(imputación)* attribution **(b)** *(competencia)* responsibility, duty

atribuir [36] **1** *vt* **a. algo a** to attribute sth to; **un cuadro atribuido a Goya** a painting attributed to Goya; **atribuyen la autoría del delito al contable** they think the accountant committed the crime

2 atribuirse *vpr (méritos)* to claim to have; *(poderes)* to assume for oneself; *(culpa)* to take, to accept; **se atribuye el éxito de la película** she is claiming the credit for the movie's success; **se atribuyó la autoría del secuestro** he admitted to having carried out the kidnapping

atribulado, -a *adj* distressed

atribular *Formal* **1** *vt* to distress

2 atribularse *vpr* to be distressed

atributivo, -a *adj Gram* attributive

atributo *nm* attribute

atril *nm (para libros)* lectern; *(para partituras)* music stand

atrincherado, -a *adj* entrenched, dug in; *(en una postura)* entrenched

atrincherarse *vpr* **(a)** *Mil* to entrench oneself, to dig oneself in **(b)** *(en una postura)* **se atrincheró en su oposición a la propuesta** he persisted in his opposition to the proposal; **se atrincheraron en su postura** *(en negociación)* they dug their heels in and refused to give up their position

atrio *nm* **(a)** *(pórtico)* portico **(b)** *(patio interior)* atrium

atrocidad *nf (cualidad)* barbarity; *(acción)* atrocity; **me parece una a. que no tengan calefacción** I think it's terrible *o* awful that they don't have heating

atrofia *nf Med* atrophy; *Fig* deterioration

atrofiado, -a *adj también Fig* atrophied

atrofiar 1 *vt Med* to atrophy; *Fig* to weaken
    2 atrofiarse *vpr Med* to atrophy; *Fig* to deteriorate, to become atrophied

atronador, -ora *adj* deafening

atropellado, -a *adj* hasty

atropellar 1 *vt* **(a)** *(sujeto: vehículo)* to run over; **le atropelló un coche** he was knocked down *o* run over by a car **(b)** *también Fig (sujeto: persona)* to trample on
    2 atropellarse *vpr (al hablar)* to trip over one's words

atropello *nm* **(a)** *(por vehículo)* running over **(b)** *(moral)* abuse **(c)** *(precipitación)* **con a.** hastily

atroz *adj* terrible, awful; **hace un frío a.** it's terribly *o* awfully cold

ATS *nmf Esp (abrev de* **ayudante técnico sanitario)** qualified nurse

attaché [ata'tʃe] *nm* attaché case

atte. *(abrev de* **atentamente)** Yours faithfully/sincerely

atuendo *nm* attire

atufar *Fam* **1** *vi* to stink; **¡huele que atufa!** it really stinks!
    2 *vt (persona)* to overpower

atún *nm* tuna

aturdido, -a *adj* dazed

aturdimiento *nm* **(a)** *(desconcierto)* bewilderment, confusion **(b)** *(torpeza mental)* slowness

aturdir 1 *vt (sujeto: golpe, noticia)* to stun; *(sujeto: alcohol)* to fuddle; *(sujeto: ruido, luz)* to confuse, to bewilder
    2 aturdirse *vpr (por golpe, noticia)* to be stunned; *(por alcohol)* to get fuddled; *(con ruido, luz)* to get confused

aturullar *Fam* **1** *vt* to fluster
    2 aturrullarse *vpr* to get flustered

atusarse *vpr* to preen oneself; **a. el bigote/pelo** to smooth one's mustache/hair

audacia *nf (valentía)* daring, boldness; *(descaro)* gall, cheek

audaz *adj* daring, bold

audible *adj* audible

audición *nf* **(a)** *(acción de oír)* hearing **(b)** *Mús & Teatro* audition

audiencia *nf* **(a)** *(público, recepción)* audience; **dar a.** to grant an audience **(b)** *Der (juicio)* hearing; *(tribunal, edificio)* court; **a. provincial** provincial court; **A. Nacional** = court in Madrid dealing with cases that cannot be dealt with at regional level; **a. pública** public hearing

audífono 1 *nm (para sordos)* hearing aid
    2 audífonos *nmpl Am (para música)* headphones

audímetro *nm TV* audiometer, audience-monitoring device

audiolibro *nm* audiobook, talking book

audiometría *nf* audiometry

audiómetro *nm* audiometer

audiovisual *adj* audiovisual

auditar *vt Fin* to audit

auditivo, -a *adj Anat* **pabellón a.** (outer) ear

auditor, -ora *nm,f Fin* auditor

auditoría *nf Fin* **(a)** *(profesión)* auditing **(b)** *(despacho)* auditor's, auditing company **(c)** *(balance)* audit; **a. externa/interna** external/internal audit

auditorio *nm* **(a)** *(público)* audience **(b)** *(lugar)* auditorium

auge *nm (gen) & Econ* boom; **estar en (pleno) a.** to be booming

augurar *vt (sujeto: persona)* to predict; *(sujeto: suceso)* to augur

augurio *nm* omen, sign

augusto, -a *adj* august

aula *nf (de escuela)* classroom; *(de universidad)* lecture room; **a. magna** great hall

aulaga *nf* gorse

aullar *vi* to howl

aullido *nm* howl

aumentar 1 *vt* to increase; **a. la producción** to increase production; **la lente aumenta la imagen** the lens magnifies the image; **me han aumentado el sueldo** my salary has been raised; **aumentó casi 10 kilos** he put on almost 10 kilos
    2 *vi (temperatura, gastos, sueldo, tensión)* to increase, to rise; *(velocidad)* to increase; **a. de peso/tamaño** to increase in weight/size; **a. de precio** to go up *o* increase in price; **el desempleo aumentó en un 4 por ciento** unemployment rose *o* increased by 4 percent

aumentativo, -a *adj & nm* augmentative

aumento *nm* **(a)** *(de temperatura, gastos, tensión)* increase, rise; *(de velocidad)* increase; **un a. del 10 por ciento** a 10 percent increase; **un a. de los precios** a price rise; **las temperaturas experimentarán un ligero a.** temperatures will rise slightly; **ir en a.** to be on the increase; **a. lineal** *(de sueldo)* across-the-board pay raise; **a. de sueldo** pay raise **(b)** *(en óptica)* **una lente de 20 aumentos** a lens of magnification x 20

aun 1 *conj* even; **a. estando cansado, lo hizo** even though he was tired, he did it; **ni a. puesta de puntillas logra ver** she can't see, even on tiptoe; **a. así** even so; **a. así, deberías decirle algo** even so, you ought to say something to her; **ni a. así lograron la victoria** even then they still didn't manage to win
    2 *adv* even; **a. los más fuertes lloran** even the strongest people cry
    3 aun cuando *loc conj (incluso si)* even if; *(a pesar de que)* even though, although; **no mentiría a. cuando le fuera en ello la vida** she wouldn't lie even if her life depended on it

aún *adv* **(a)** *(con afirmación)* still; *(con negación)* yet, still; **a. respira** he's still breathing; **están a. aquí** they are still here; **a. no** not yet; **a. no lo he recibido** I still haven't got it, I haven't got it yet; **¿a. no has terminado?** haven't you finished yet?; **si nos sobrara el tiempo, a., pero no nos sobra** if we had plenty of time, maybe, but we don't **(b)** *(incluso)* even; **a. más** even more; **si ganamos, lo pasaremos a. mejor que ayer** if we win, we'll have an even better time than yesterday

aunar 1 *vt* to join, to pool; **a. esfuerzos** to join forces
    2 aunarse *vpr (aliarse)* to unite

aunque *conj* **(a)** *(a pesar de que)* even though, although; *(incluso si)* even if; **tendrás que venir a. no quieras** you'll have to come, even if you don't want to; **a. es caro, me lo voy a comprar** although it's expensive I'm going to buy it, I'm going to buy it even though it's expensive **(b)** *(pero)* although; **es lista, a. un poco perezosa** she's clever, although *o* if a little lazy

aúpa *interj Esp* **(a)** **¡a.!** *(¡levántate!)* get up!; *(al coger a un niño en brazos)* upsy-daisy! **(b)** *(¡viva!)* **¡a. (el) Atleti!** back the Athletic! **(c)** *Fam* **una comida de a.** a brilliant meal; *Fam* **un susto de a.** a hell of a fright

au pair [o'per] (*pl* **au pairs**) *nf* au pair

aupar 1 *vt (subir)* to help up; *(coger en brazos)* to lift up in one's arms; *(animar)* to cheer on
  2 auparse *vpr* to climb up

aura *nf* (a) *(halo) (gen) & Med* aura (b) *(viento)* gentle breeze

áureo, -a *adj* golden

aureola *nf Astron & Rel* halo; *(fama)* aura

aurícula *nf Anat (del corazón)* auricle, atrium

auricular 1 *adj* auricular
  2 *nm (de teléfono)* receiver; **auriculares** *(cascos)* headphones

aurífero *adj* gold-bearing

aurora *nf* first light of dawn; **al despuntar** *o* **romper la a.** at dawn; **a. boreal** aurora borealis, northern lights

auscultación *nf Med* auscultation

auscultar *vt Med* **a. a alguien** to listen to sb's chest *(with a stethoscope)*

ausencia *nf* absence; **brillar por su a.** to be conspicuous by one's/its absence; **en a. de** in the absence of; **si llama alguien en mi a., toma el recado** if anyone calls while I'm out, take a message

ausentarse *vpr* to go away

ausente 1 *adj* (a) *(no presente)* absent; **estará a. todo el día** he'll be away all day (b) *(distraído)* absentminded
  2 *nmf* (a) *(no presente)* **hay varios ausentes** there are a number of absentees; **criticó a los ausentes** she criticized the people who weren't there (b) *Der* missing person

auspiciar *vt (apoyar)* to back

auspicio *nm (protección)* protection; **bajo los auspicios de** under the auspices of; **auspicios** *(señales)* omens

austeridad *nf* austerity

austero, -a *adj* austere; **adoptar un presupuesto a.** to limit budgetary expenditure

austral 1 *adj* southern
  2 *nm Antes (moneda)* austral

Australia *n* Australia

australiano, -a *adj & nm,f* Australian

Austria *n* Austria

austriaco, -a *adj & nm,f* Austrian

autarquía *nf* (a) *Econ* autarky, self-sufficiency (b) *Pol* autarchy

autárquico, -a *adj* (a) *Econ* autarkic, self-sufficient (b) *Pol* autarchical

autenticar [59] *vt Der (firma, documento)* to authenticate

autenticidad *nf* authenticity

auténtico, -a *adj* genuine, real; **ser a.** to be genuine; **un a. imbécil** a real idiot

autentificar [59] *vt* to authenticate

autismo *nm Psi* autism

autista *Psi* **1** *adj* autistic
  2 *nmf* autistic person

autito *nm CSur* **autitos chocadores** bumper cars

auto *nm* (a) *(coche)* car; **autos de choque** bumper cars (b) *Der* **a. (judicial)** judicial decree; **a. de procesamiento** indictment; **autos** case documents; **constar en autos** to be recorded in the case documents; **la noche de autos** the night of the crime (c) *Hist* **a. de fe** auto-da-fé *(public punishment of heretics by the Inquisition)* (d) *Lit (mystery)* play; **a. de Navidad** Nativity play

autoabastecerse *vpr (ser autosuficiente)* to be self-sufficient **(de** in)

autoabastecimiento *nm* self-sufficiency

autoadhesivo, -a *adj* self-adhesive

autoafirmación *nf* assertiveness

autoalimentación *nf Inform* automatic paper feed

autoaprendizaje *nm* self-directed learning; **un libro de a.** a teach-yourself book

autoayuda *nf* self-help

autobanco *nm* drive-in bank

autobiografía *nf* autobiography

autobiográfico, -a *adj* autobiographical

autobombo *nm Fam* **darse a.** to blow one's own trumpet

autobronceador *nm* self-tanning cream

autobús (*pl* **autobuses**) *nm* bus

autocar *nm Esp (vehículo)* bus

autocaravana *nf Esp* RV, motor home

autocartera *nf Fin* treasury stock

autocensura *nf* self-censorship

autocine *nm* drive-in (movie)

autoclave *nm Med* autoclave, sterilizing unit

autocomplacencia *nf* self-satisfaction

autocomplaciente *adj* self-satisfied

autocontrol *nm* self-control

autocracia *nf Pol* autocracy

autócrata *nmf Pol* autocrat

autocrático, -a *adj* autocratic

autocrítica *nf* self-criticism

autocrítico, -a *adj* self-critical

autóctono, -a 1 *adj* indigenous, native
  2 *nm,f* native

autodefensa *nf* self-defense

autodefinido *nm* = type of crossword

autodestrucción *nf* self-destruction

autodestruirse *vpr* to self-destruct

autodeterminación *nf Pol* self-determination

autodiagnóstico *nm Inform* self-test

autodidacta 1 *adj* self-taught
  2 *nmf* self-taught person

autodirigido, -a *adj* guided

autodisciplina *nf* self-discipline

autodominio *nm* self-control

autódromo *nm* auto-racing circuit

autoedición *nf Inform* desktop publishing

autoempleo *nm* self-employment

autoencendido *nm Aut* automatic ignition

autoescuela *nf* driving school

autoestima *nf* self-esteem

autoestop *nm* hitchhiking; **hacer a.** to hitchhike

autoestopista *nmf* hitchhiker

autoexec [auto'eksek] *nm Inform* autoexec file

autofinanciación *nf Fin* self-financing

autofocus *nm inv* autofocus

autogestión *nf* self-management

autogestionar 1 *vt* **autogestionan sus fondos** they manage their own finances
  2 autogestionarse *vpr* (a) *(empresa)* to manage itself (b) *(región, país)* to govern itself

autogiro *nm* autogiro

autogobierno *nm Pol* self-government, self-rule

autogol *nm (en fútbol)* own goal

autógrafo *nm* autograph

autoinculparse *vpr* **a. de algo** to incriminate oneself of sth

autoinmune *adj Med* autoimmune

autómata *nm también Fig* automaton, robot

automáticamente *adv* automatically

automático, -a 1 *adj* automatic
  2 *nm (cierre)* snap fastener

automatismo *nm* automatism

automatización *nf* automation

automatizar [14] *vt* to automate

automedicarse [59] *vpr* to self-administer medicine

automoción *nf (sector)* automobile *o* car industry

automotor, -triz *adj* self-propelled

automóvil *nm* automobile, car

automovilismo *nm* motoring; *Dep* auto racing

automovilista *nmf* motorist, driver

automovilístico, -a *adj* motor; *Dep* auto-racing; **industria automovilística** automobile *o* car industry

autonomía *nf* (**a**) *Pol (facultad)* autonomy; *(territorio)* autonomous region; **quieren la a.** they want home rule (**b**) *(de persona)* independence (**c**) *(de vehículo)* range; *(de videocámara)* recording time; *(de computadora portátil, teléfono móvil)* battery life; **a. de vuelo** range

autonómico, -a *adj Pol* autonomous

autonomismo *nm Pol* autonomy movement

autonomista *adj & nmf Pol* autonomist

autónomo, -a 1 *adj* (**a**) *Pol* autonomous (**b**) *(trabajador)* self-employed; *(traductor, periodista)* freelance

   2 *nm,f (trabajador)* self-employed person; *(traductor, periodista)* freelance(r)

autopista *nf* freeway; **a. de peaje,** *Méx* **a. de cuota** turnpike; **a. de información** information superhighway

autoproclamarse *vpr* to proclaim oneself

autopropulsado, -a *adj* self-propelled

autopropulsión *nf* self-propulsion

autopsia *nf Med* autopsy, postmortem

autor, -ora *nm,f (de libro)* author; *(de cuadro)* painter; *(de canción)* writer; *(de sinfonía)* composer; *(de crimen, fechoría)* perpetrator; *(de gol)* scorer; *Der* **a. material del hecho** actual perpetrator of the crime

autoría *nf (de obra)* authorship; *(de crimen)* perpetration

autoridad *nf* (**a**) *(poder)* authority; **impusieron su a.** they imposed their authority; **a. moral** moral authority (**b**) *(persona al mando)* **las autoridades militares/religiosas** the military/religious authorities; **entregarse a las autoridades** *(a la policía)* to give oneself up; **la a.** the authorities (**c**) *(eminencia)* authority; **es una a. en historia** he is an authority on history (**d**) *(control, dominio)* authority; **habla siempre con mucha a.** she always talks with great authority

autoritariamente *adv* in an authoritarian way, dictatorially

autoritario, -a *adj & nm,f* authoritarian

autoritarismo *nm Pol* authoritarianism

autorización *nf* authorization; **dar a. a alguien (para hacer algo)** to authorize sb (to do sth); **pedir a. para hacer algo** to request authorization to do sth; **tenemos a. para usar la sala** we have been authorized *o* we have permission to use the hall; **necesitan la a. de sus padres** they need their parents' consent

autorizado, -a *adj* (**a**) *(permitido a)* authorized (**b**) *(digno de crédito)* authoritative

autorizar [14] *vt* (**a**) *(dar permiso a)* to allow; *(en situaciones oficiales)* to authorize; **a. la publicación de un informe** to authorize the publication of a report; **autoricé a mi hermano para que recogiera el paquete** I authorized my brother to collect the package (**b**) *(capacitar)* **su cargo no lo autoriza para insultarme** his position doesn't give him the right to insult me; **este título nos autoriza para ejercer en la UE** this qualification allows us to practice in the EU

autorradio *nm o nf* car radio

autorregulación *nf* self-regulation

autorretrato *nm* self-portrait

autoservicio *nm* (**a**) *(restaurante)* self-service restaurant (**b**) *(supermercado)* supermarket

autostop *nm* hitchhiking; **hacer a.** to hitchhike

autostopista *nmf* hitchhiker

autosuficiencia *nf* self-sufficiency

autosuficiente *adj* self-sufficient

autosugestión *nf* autosuggestion

autosugestionarse *vpr* to convince oneself (**de** of)

autovacuna *nf Med* autoinoculation

autovía *nf* divided highway

auxiliar 1 *adj (gen) & Gram* auxiliary

   2 *nmf* assistant; **a. administrativo** administrative assistant; **a. de vuelo** flight attendant

   3 *nm Gram* auxiliary

   4 *vt* to assist, to help

auxilio *nm* assistance, help; **una llamada de a.** a call for help; **grité pidiendo a.** I shouted for help; **pedir/prestar a.** to call for/give help; **acudir en a. de alguien** to come to sb's assistance; **primeros auxilios** first aid

auyama, ahuyama *nf Carib, Col* pumpkin

av. *(abrev de* **avenida)** Ave

aval *nm* (**a**) *(documento)* guarantee, reference; **a. bancario** bank guarantee (**b**) *(respaldo)* backing

avalancha *nf también Fig* avalanche

avalar *vt (préstamo, crédito)* to guarantee; **su reputación lo avala** his reputation speaks for itself

avalista *nmf* guarantor

avance 1 *ver* **avanzar**

   2 *nm* (**a**) *(movimiento hacia delante)* advance; **avances científicos** scientific advances (**b**) *Fin (anticipo)* advance payment (**c**) *Rad & TV (de futura programación)* preview; **a. informativo** *(resumen)* news summary; *(por noticia de última hora)* news flash

avanzada 1 *nf Mil* advance patrol

   2 de avanzada *loc adj Am (tecnología)* cutting-edge; *(ideas)* avant-garde

avanzadilla *nf* advance party; *Mil* advance patrol

avanzado, -a 1 *adj (adelantado)* advanced; *(progresista)* progressive

   2 *nm,f* person ahead of his/her time

avanzar [14] **1** *vi* (**a**) *(moverse)* to advance; **las tropas continúan avanzando** the troops are still advancing; **el tráfico no avanzaba** the traffic wasn't moving (**b**) *(progresar)* to make progress; **está avanzando mucho en sus estudios** she's making very good progress with her studies; **esta tecnología avanza a gran velocidad** this technology is developing very quickly (**c**) *(tiempo)* to pass; **el tiempo avanza muy deprisa** time passes quickly; **a medida que avanza el siglo** as the century draws on

   2 *vt* (**a**) *(adelantar)* to move forward (**b**) *(noticias)* **a. algo a alguien** to inform sb of sth in advance

avaricia *nf* greed, avarice; **la a. rompe el saco** greed doesn't pay; *Fam* **ser feo/pesado con a.** to be ugly/boring in the extreme

avaricioso, -a 1 *adj* avaricious, miserly

   2 *nm,f* miser

avariento, -a 1 *adj* avaricious, miserly

   2 *nm,f* miser

avaro, -a 1 *adj* miserly, stingy

   2 *nm,f* miser

avasallador, -ora 1 *adj* overwhelming

   2 *nm,f* slave driver

avasallamiento *nm (de pueblo)* subjugation

avasallar 1 *vt* (**a**) *(dominar)* **dejarse a.** to let oneself be pushed *o* ordered around (**b**) *(rival, oponente)* to overwhelm (**c**) *(pueblo)* to subjugate

   2 *vi* **va por la vida avasallando** he'll trample over people to get what he wants

avatar *nm* vagary, sudden change; **los avatares de la vida** the ups and downs of life

Avda., avda. *(abrev de* **avenida)** Ave

AVE *nm (abrev de* **alta velocidad española)** = Spanish high-speed train

ave 1 *nf (animal)* bird; **el Ave Fénix** the phoenix; **a. del Paraíso** bird of paradise; *Fig* **ser un a. de paso** to be a rolling stone; **a. de presa** bird of prey; *también Fig* **a. rapaz** *o* **de rapiña** bird of prey

2 *interj* **¡Ave María Purísima!** *(indica sorpresa)* saints preserve us!

avecinarse *vpr* to be on the way; **¡la que se nos avecina!** are we in for it!

avefría *nf* lapwing

avejentado, -a *adj (persona, cuero)* aged

avejentar 1 *vt* to age, to put years on

2 avejentarse *vpr* to age

avellana *nf* hazelnut

avellano *nm* hazel (tree)

avemaría *nf (oración)* Hail Mary

avena *nf* **(a)** *(planta)* oat **(b)** *(grano)* oats

avenencia *nf (acuerdo)* compromise

avenida *nf* **(a)** *(calle)* avenue **(b)** *(crecida de río)* flood

avenido, -a *adj* **bien/mal avenidos** on good/bad terms

avenirse [69] *vpr* **(a)** *(llevarse bien)* to get on (well) **(b)** *(ponerse de acuerdo)* to come to an agreement; **a. a algo/a hacer algo** to agree on sth/to do sth

aventajado, -a *adj (adelantado)* outstanding

aventajar *vt (rebasar)* to overtake; *(estar por delante de)* to be ahead of; **a. a alguien en algo** to surpass sb in sth

aventar [3] **1** *vt* **(a)** *(abanicar)* to fan **(b)** *(trigo)* to winnow **(c)** *Andes, CAm, Méx Fam (tirar)* to throw; *(empujar)* to push, to shove

2 aventarse *vpr Méx* **(a)** *(tirarse)* to throw oneself **(b)** *(atreverse)* to dare **(a** to)

aventón *nm CAm, Méx, Perú* **(a)** *(en vehículo)* **pedir/dar a.** to hitch/give a ride *o* lift **(b)** *(empujón)* push, shove

aventura *nf* **(a)** *(suceso, empresa)* adventure; **embarcarse en una a.** to set off on an adventure **(b)** *(relación amorosa)* affair

aventurado, -a *adj* risky

aventurar 1 *vt (opinión)* to venture, to hazard

2 aventurarse *vpr* to take a risk/risks; **aventurarse a hacer algo** to dare to do sth

aventurero, -a 1 *adj* adventurous

2 *nm,f* adventurer, *f* adventuress

avergonzado, -a *adj (humillado, dolido)* ashamed; *(abochornado)* embarrassed

avergonzar [10] **1** *vt (deshonrar, humillar)* to shame; *(abochornar)* to embarrass; **el comportamiento de mi marido me avergüenza** I feel embarrassed by my husband's behavior

2 avergonzarse *vpr (por remordimiento)* to be ashamed **(de** of); *(por timidez)* to be embarrassed **(de** about); **me avergüenzo de haberla insultado** I'm ashamed to have insulted her

avería *nf (de máquina)* fault; *(de coche)* breakdown; **llamar a averías** *(para coche)* to call the garage; *(para aparato)* to call the repair service; *Fam* **hacerse una a.** *(herida)* to hurt oneself

averiado, -a *adj (máquina)* out of order; *(coche)* broken down

averiar [32] **1** *vt* to damage

2 averiarse *vpr (máquina, coche)* to break down

averiguación *nf* investigation; **hacer averiguaciones** to make inquiries

averiguar [11] *vt* to find out

aversión *nf* aversion; **tener a.** to feel aversion toward

avestruz *nm* ostrich; **la política/táctica del a.** burying one's head in the sand

avezado, -a *adj* accustomed **(a** to)

aviación *nf* **(a)** *(navegación)* aviation; **a.** civil aviation **(b)** *(ejército)* air force

aviador, -ora *nm,f* pilot

aviar [32] **1** *vt (comida)* to prepare; *Fam* **estar aviado** to be in a mess

2 aviarse *vpr Fam (manejarse)* to manage; **se las avía muy bien solo** he manages very well on his own

avícola *adj* poultry; **granja a.** poultry farm

avicultor, -ora *nm,f* poultry breeder, poultry farmer

avicultura *nf* poultry farming

ávidamente *adv* avidly, eagerly

avidez *nf* eagerness

ávido, -a *adj* eager **(de** for)

aviento *etc ver* **aventar**

avieso, -a *adj (malo)* evil, twisted

avinagrado, -a *adj también Fig* sour

avinagrar 1 *vt (vino, alimento)* to sour, to make sour

2 avinagrarse *vpr* **(a)** *(vino, alimento)* to go sour **(b)** *(persona, carácter)* to become sour; **se le avinagró el carácter** she became bitter

avío *nm* **(a)** *(preparativo)* preparation **(b)** *(víveres)* provisions; *Fam* **avíos** *(equipo)* things, kit

avión *nm* **(a)** *(aeronave)* plane, airplane; **en a.** by plane; **por a.** *(en un sobre)* airmail; **a. de carga** cargo plane; **a. espía** *o* **de espionaje** spy plane; **a. nodriza** supply plane; **a. a reacción** jet **(b)** *(pájaro)* house martin

avioneta *nf* light aircraft

avisar 1 *vt* **(a)** *(informar)* **a. a alguien de algo** to let sb know sth, to tell sb sth; **llamó para a. que llegaría tarde** she called to say she would be late **(b)** *(advertir)* to warn **(de** of); **yo ya te había avisado** I did warn you; **estás avisado** you've been warned **(c)** *(llamar)* to call, to send for; **hay que a. al electricista** we'll have to call the electrician; **corre, avisa a la policía** go and get the police

2 *vi* **entró sin a.** he came in without knocking; **avisa cuando acabes** let me/us/etc know when you've finished

aviso *nm* **(a)** *(advertencia, amenaza)* warning; **andar sobre a.** to be on the alert; **estar sobre a.** to be forewarned; **poner sobre a. a alguien** to warn sb; **¡que te sirva de a.!** let that be a warning to you!; **a. de bomba** bomb warning

(b) *(notificación)* notice; *(en teatros, aeropuertos)* call; **hasta nuevo a.** until further notice; **llegó sin previo a.** he arrived without warning; **último a. para los pasajeros del vuelo IB 257** last call for passengers of flight IB 257; *Com* **a. de vencimiento** due-date reminder

(c) *Taurom* = warning to matador not to delay the kill any longer

(d) *Am (anuncio)* advertisement, advert

avispa *nf* wasp

avispado, -a *adj Fam* sharp, quick-witted

avispero *nm* **(a)** *(nido)* wasp's nest **(b)** *Fam (lío)* mess; **meterse en un a.** to get into a mess

avistar *vt* to sight, to make out

avitaminosis *nf inv Med* vitamin deficiency

avituallamiento *nm* provisioning

avituallar *vt* to provide with food

avivar 1 *vt (sentimiento)* to rekindle; *(color)* to brighten; *(fuego)* to stoke up

2 avivarse *vpr (sentimiento)* to be rekindled; *(color)* to brighten; *(fuego)* to flare up

avizor *adj* **estar ojo a.** to be on the lookout

avutarda *nf* great bustard

axial *adj* axial

axila *nf* armpit

axioma *nm* axiom

axiomático, -a *adj* axiomatic

ay *(pl* **ayes) 1** *nm* groan

2 *interj* **¡ay!** *(dolor físico)* ouch!; *(sorpresa, pena)* oh!; **¡ay de ti si te cojo!** heaven help you if I catch you!

aya *nf* governess

ayatola, ayatolá *nm* ayatollah

ayer 1 *adv* **(a)** yesterday; **a. por la mañana** yesterday morning; **a. (por la) noche** last night (**b**) *(en el pasado)* in the past

   2 *nm* **el a.** yesteryear

aymara *adj, nm & nmf* Aymara

ayo *nm (tutor)* tutor

ayuda *nf* (**a**) *(asistencia)* help, assistance; **acudir en a. de alguien** to come/go to sb's assistance; **nos fuiste de gran a.** you were a great help to us; **no me sirvió de mucha a.** it wasn't much help to me; **prestar a.** to help, to assist; **a. en carretera** emergency road service (**b**) *(económica, alimenticia)* aid; **a. al desarrollo** development aid; **a. humanitaria** humanitarian aid (**c**) *(limosna)* **una a., por favor** could you spare me some change, please?

ayudante *adj & nmf* assistant; **a. de laboratorio** laboratory assistant

ayudar 1 *vt* to help; **a. a alguien a hacer algo** to help sb (to) do sth; **¿en qué puedo ayudarle?** how can I help you?

   2 *vi* to help; **¿puedo a.?** can I help?

   3 ayudarse *vpr* **ayudarse de** *o* **con** to make use of

ayunar *vi* to fast

ayunas *nfpl* **estar en a.** *(sin comer)* not to have eaten; *Fig (sin enterarse)* to be in the dark

ayuno *nm* fast; **hacer a.** to fast

ayuntamiento *nm* (**a**) *(corporación)* city council (**b**) *(edificio)* city hall

azabache *nm* jet; **negro como el a.** jet-black

azada *nf* hoe

azadón *nm* (large) hoe

azafata *nf* **a. (de vuelo)** air stewardess, air hostess; **a. de exposiciones y congresos** (conference) hostess; **a. de tierra** ground attendant

azafrán *nm (condimento)* saffron

azahar *nm (del naranjo)* orange blossom; *(del limonero)* lemon blossom

azalea *nf* azalea

azar *nm* chance, fate; **al a.** at random; **por (puro) a.** by (pure) chance

azarar 1 *vt (avergonzar)* to embarrass, to fluster; **a. a alguien** *(ruborizar)* to make sb blush

   2 azararse *vpr (avergonzarse)* to be embarrassed, to be flustered; *(ruborizarse)* to blush

azaroso, -a *adj (vida, viaje)* eventful

Azerbaiyán *n* Azerbaijan

azerbaiyano, -a *adj & nm,f* Azerbaijani

azerí *(pl* **azeríes)** *adj & nm* Azeri

ázimo *adj (pan)* unleavened

azimut *(pl* **azimutes)** *nm Astron* azimuth

azogue *nm Anticuado* quicksilver, mercury

azor *nm* goshawk

azorado, -a *adj* embarrassed, flustered

azoramiento *nm* embarrassment

azorar 1 *vt* to embarrass

   2 azorarse *vpr* to be embarrassed

Azores *nfpl* **las A.** the Azores

azotaina *nf Fam* **dar una a. a alguien** to give sb a good smacking

azotar *vt (pegar, golpear)* to beat; *(en el trasero)* to smack, to slap; *(con látigo)* to whip; *Fig* **la epidemia azotó la región** the region was devastated by the epidemic

azote *nm* (**a**) *(utensilio para golpear)* whip, scourge (**b**) *(latigazo)* lash; *(golpe)* blow; *(en el trasero)* smack, slap; *Fig (calamidad)* scourge

azotea *nf (de edificio)* terraced roof; *Fam Fig* **estar mal de la a.** to be funny in the head

azteca 1 *adj* Aztec; *Fam* **el equipo a.** the Mexican team

   2 *nmf* Aztec

   3 *nm (lengua)* Nahuatl, Aztec

azúcar *nm o nf* sugar; **a. blanquilla** granulated sugar; **a. cande** sugar candy, rock candy; **a. de caña** cane sugar; *Chile* **a. flor** confectioner's sugar; *Esp, Méx* **a. glas** confectioner's sugar; *RP* **a. impalpable** confectioner's sugar; *Esp* **a. de lustre** confectioner's sugar; **a. moreno** brown sugar

azucarado, -a *adj* sweet, sugary

azucarar 1 *vt* (**a**) *(endulzar)* to sugarcoat, to sugar (**b**) *Pey (suavizar)* to sweeten

   2 azucararse *vpr Am (cristalizar)* to crystallize

azucarera *nf (fábrica)* sugar refinery; *(recipiente)* sugar bowl

azucarero, -a 1 *adj* sugar; **la industria azucarera** the sugar industry

   2 *nm* sugar bowl

azucarillo *nm* (**a**) *Culin* lemon candy (**b**) *(terrón)* sugar lump

azuce *etc ver* **azuzar**

azucena *nf* white lily

azufre *nm* sulfur

azul *adj & nm* blue; **a. celeste/marino/eléctrico** sky/navy/electric blue; **a. (de) cobalto** cobalt blue; **a. turquesa** turquoise

azulado, -a *adj* bluish

azulejo *nm* (glazed) tile

azulete *nm (para lavar)* blue

azulgrana *adj inv Dep* = relating to Barcelona soccer club

azuzar [14] *vt (animal)* to set on; *(persona)* to egg on

B

B, b [*Esp* be, *Am* be('larva)] *nf (letra)* B, b

baba *nf* (a) *(saliva) (de niño)* dribble; *(de adulto)* spittle, saliva; *(de animal)* slobber (b) *(de caracol)* slime (c) *Fam* **se le cae la b. con su hija** she drools over her daughter; *Fam* **tener mala b.** to be a nasty piece of work

babear *vi* (a) *(niño)* to dribble (b) *(adulto, animal)* to slobber (c) *Fig* to drool

babel *nm o nf Fam* **el debate se convirtió en una b.** the debate degenerated into noisy chaos

babero *nm* bib

babi *nm Esp Fam* = child's overalls

Babia *nf* **estar o quedarse en B.** to have one's head in the clouds

Babilonia *n Hist* Babylon

babilónico, -a *adj* (a) *Hist* Babylonian (b) *(fastuoso)* lavish

bable *nm* = Asturian dialect

babor *nm* port; **a b.** to port

babosa *nf Zool* slug

babosada *nf CAm, Méx Fam (disparate)* daft thing; **no digas babosadas** don't talk bull *o* rubbish!

babosear 1 *vt* to slobber on *o* all over
　　2 *vi CAm, Méx Fam* to talk bull *o* rubbish

baboso, -a 1 *adj* (a) *(niño)* dribbling; *(adulto, animal)* slobbering (b) *Am Fam (tonto)* daft, stupid (c) *Fam (despreciable)* slimy
　　2 *nm,f Fam* (a) *(persona despreciable)* creep (b) *Am (tonto)* twit, idiot

babucha *nf (zapatilla)* slipper; *(árabe)* Moorish slipper

baca *nf* roof rack

bacaladero, -a 1 *adj* cod-fishing; **la flota bacaladera** the cod-fishing fleet
　　2 *nm* cod-fishing boat

bacaladilla *nf* blue whiting

bacalao *nm* cod; *Culin* **b. a la vizcaína** = Basque dish of salt cod cooked in a tomato and red pepper sauce; *Culin* **b. al pil-pil** = Basque dish of salt cod cooked with olive oil and garlic; **b. salado** salt cod; *Esp Fam Fig* **partir** *o* **cortar el b.** to call the shots

bacán *Fam* **1** *adj* (a) *Cuba, Perú (bueno)* cool, wicked (b) *RP (caro)* steep
　　2 *nm RP (rico)* dandy; **como un b.** like a real gentleman

bacanal *nf* orgy

bacarrá, bacará *nm* baccarat

bache *nm* (a) *(en carretera)* pothole (b) *(en un vuelo)* air pocket (c) *(dificultades)* bad time

bachiller *nmf* = person who has passed the "bachillerato"

bachillerato *nm* = Spanish course of secondary studies for academically orientated 16- to 18-year-olds

bacilo *nm* bacillus; **b. de Koch** tubercle bacillus

bacín *nm*, **bacinilla** *nf* chamber pot

backgammon *nm* backgammon

bacon ['beikon] *nm inv Esp (Canadian)* bacon; **b. entreverado** bacon

bacteria *nf* germ; **bacterias** germs, bacteria

bacteriano, -a *adj* bacterial

bactericida 1 *adj* bactericidal
　　2 *nm* bactericide

bacteriología *nf* bacteriology

bacteriológico, -a *adj* **guerra bacteriológica** germ *o* bacteriological warfare

bacteriólogo, -a *nm,f* bacteriologist

báculo *nm* (a) *(de obispo)* crosier (b) *(sostén)* support; **ella será el b. de mi vejez** she'll comfort me in my old age

badajo *nm* clapper *(of bell)*

badajocense 1 *adj* of/from Badajoz
　　2 *nm,f* person from Badajoz

badana *nf (de sombrero)* hatband; *Esp Fam* **zurrarle a alguien la b.** to tan sb's hide

badén *nm* (a) *(de carretera)* ditch (b) *(cauce)* channel

bádminton *nm inv* badminton

bafle *(pl* **bafles)**, **baffle** ['bafle] *(pl* **baffles)** *nm* loudspeaker

bagaje *nm* background; **b. cultural** cultural baggage

bagatela *nf* trifle

Bagdad *n* Baghdad

bagre *nm* (a) *(pez)* catfish (b) *Fam Pey Andes, RP (mujer)* hag, dog; *Andes (hombre)* ugly mug (c) *CRica Pey (prostituta)* prostitute (d) *CAm (persona astuta)* astute person (e) *Andes (persona desagradable)* fool, idiot

Bahamas *nfpl* **las B.** the Bahamas

bahía *nf* bay

Bahráin *n* Bahrain

Baikal *nm* **el (lago) B.** Lake Baikal

bailable *adj* danceable; **música b.** music you can dance to

bailaor, -ora *nm,f* flamenco dancer

bailar 1 *vt* to dance; **b. una rumba** to dance a rumba; **es difícil b. esta música** it's difficult to dance to this music; *Fam Fig* **que me quiten lo bailado** no one can take away the good times
　　2 *vi* (a) *(danzar)* to dance; **¿bailas?** would you like to dance?; **sacar a alguien a b.** to ask sb to dance *o* for a dance; *Fam Fig* **es otro que tal baila** he's just the same, he's no different (b) *(no encajar)* to be loose; **le baila un diente** he has a loose tooth; **los pies me bailan (en los zapatos)** my shoes are too big

bailarín, -ina *nm,f* dancer; *(de ballet)* ballet dancer

baile *nm* (a) *(pieza, arte)* dance; **b. clásico** ballet; **b. regional** regional folk dancing; **b. de salón** ballroom and Latin dance *o* dancing; **¿me concede este b.?** may I have (the pleasure of) this dance? (b) *(fiesta)* ball (c) *(en contabilidad)* **b. de cifras** number transposition (d) *Med* **b. de San Vito** St Vitus' dance

bailongo *nm Fam* bop, boogie

bailotear *vi Fam* to bop, to boogie

bailoteo *nm Fam* bopping

baja *nf* (a) *(descenso)* drop, fall; **redondear el precio a la b.** to round the price down; **el precio del cacao sigue a la b.** the price of cocoa is continuing to fall; **tendencia a la b.** downward trend; *Fin* **jugar a la b.** to bear the market (**b**) *(cese) (forzado)* layoff; **dar de b. a alguien** *(en empresa)* to lay sb off; *(en club, sindicato)* to expel sb; **darse de b. (de)** *(dimitir)* to resign (from); *(salirse)* to drop out (of); *(de subscripción)* to unsubscribe (from) (**c**) *Esp (por enfermedad) (permiso)* sick leave; *(documento)* sick note, doctor's certificate; **estar/darse de b.** to be on/take sick leave; **b. por maternidad** maternity leave (**d**) *Mil* loss, casualty; **bajas civiles** civilian casualties

bajada *nf* (**a**) *(descenso)* descent; **cuando veníamos de b.** on our way (back) down; **b. de bandera** *(de taxi)* minimum fare (**b**) *(pendiente)* (downward) slope (**c**) *(disminución)* decrease, drop; **b. de los precios** *(caída)* drop *o* fall in prices; *(rebaja)* reduction in prices

bajamar *nf* low tide

bajante *nmf (tubería)* drainpipe

bajar 1 *vt* (**a**) *(poner abajo) (libro, cuadro)* to take/bring down; *(telón, ventanilla, mano)* to lower; **ayúdame a b. la caja** *(desde lo alto)* help me get the box down; *(al piso de abajo)* help carry the box downstairs (**b**) *(descender) (montaña, escaleras)* to go/come down; **bajó las escaleras a toda velocidad** she ran down the stairs as fast as she could (**c**) *(precios, inflación, hinchazón)* to reduce; *(música, volumen, radio)* to turn down; *(fiebre)* to bring down; **b. el fuego (de la cocina)** to reduce the heat (**d**) *(ojos, cabeza, voz)* to lower (**e**) *Fam Inform* to download

2 *vi* (**a**) **b. (de)** *(coche)* to get out (of); *(moto, bicicleta, tren, avión)* to get off; *(caballo)* to get off, to dismount; *(árbol, escalera, silla, mesa)* to come/get down (from); **bajo en la próxima parada** I'm getting off at the next stop (**b**) *(descender)* to go/come down; **b. en ascensor** to go/come down in the elevator; **b. por la escalera** to go/come down the stairs; **b. (a) por algo** to go out and get sth; **b. corriendo** to run down (**c**) *(disminuir)* to fall, to drop; *(fiebre, hinchazón)* to go/come down; **bajó la gasolina** the price of gasoline fell; **este modelo ha bajado de precio** this model has gone down in price, the price of this model has gone down; **bajó la Bolsa** stock prices fell; **las acciones de C & C han bajado** C & C stock prices have fallen

3 bajarse *vpr* (**a**) **bajarse (de)** *(coche)* to get out (of); *(moto, bicicleta, tren, avión)* to get off; *(caballo)* to get off, to dismount; *(árbol, escalera, silla)* to come/get down (from); **nos bajamos en la próxima** we get off at the next stop (**b**) *Fam (ir, venir)* to come/go down; **bájate a la playa conmigo** come down to the beach with me (**c**) *Fam Inform* to download; **me he bajado un juego estupendo** I've downloaded an excellent game onto my computer

bajativo *nm Andes, RP (licor)* digestive liqueur; *(tisana)* herbal tea

bajel *nm Literario* vessel, ship

bajero, -a *adj* lower; *(sábana)* bottom

bajeza *nf* (**a**) *(cualidad)* baseness (**b**) *(acción)* vile deed

bajial *nm Méx, Perú* lowland

bajinis *nm Fam* **decir algo por lo b.** to whisper sth, to say sth under one's breath

bajío *nm* sandbank

bajista 1 *adj Fin* bearish; **mercado b.** bear market
2 *nmf Mús* bass player, bassist

bajo, -a 1 *adj* (**a**) *(objeto, cifra)* low; *(persona, estatura)* short; **planta baja** first floor; **me lo dijo por lo b.** he said it to me under his breath; **tirando por lo b.** at least, at the minimum (**b**) *(cabeza)* bowed; *(ojos)* downcast; **paseaba con la cabeza baja** she was walking with her head down (**c**) *(poco audible)* low; *(sonido)* soft, faint; **en voz baja** softly, in a low voice; **pon la música más baja, por favor** turn the music down, please; **por lo b.** *(en voz baja)* in an undertone; *(en secreto)* secretly (**d**) *(territorio, época)* lower; **el b. Amazonas** the

lower Amazon; **la baja Edad Media** the late Middle Ages (**e**) *(pobre)* lower-class (**f**) *(vil)* base

2 *nm* (**a**) *(planta baja) (piso)* first-floor apartment; **los bajos** the first floor (**b**) *Mús (instrumento, cantante)* bass; *(instrumentista)* bassist (**c**) *(de ropa)* hem (**d**) *Aut* **bajos** *(de vehículo)* underside

3 *adv* (**a**) *(hablar)* quietly, softly; **¡habla más b.!** keep your voice down! (**b**) *(caer, volar)* low; *Fig* **¡qué b. has caído!** how low you have sunk!

4 *prep* (**a**) *(debajo de)* under; **b. cero** below zero; *Fig* **b. cuerda** *o* **mano** secretly, in an underhand manner (**b**) *(sometido a)* under; **b. control** under control; **b. el régimen de Franco** under Franco's regime; **prohibido aparcar b. multa de 100 euros** no parking – penalty 100 euros

bajón *nm* slump; **dar un b.** to slump

bajonazo *nm* **dar un b.** *(salud)* to get worse; *(ventas)* to decline

bajorrelieve *nm* bas-relief

bajura *nf* **pesca de b.** coastal fishing

bakalao *Esp Fam* **1** *adj* dance
2 *nm (música)* dance (music)

bala *nf* (**a**) *(proyectil)* bullet; **entró como una b.** she rushed in; **salió como una b.** he shot off; **b. de goma** plastic bullet; *Fam Fig* **b. perdida** good-for-nothing (**b**) *(fardo)* bale

balacear *vt Am (tirotear)* to shoot

balacera *nf Am* shoot-out

balada *nf* ballad

baladí *(pl* **baladíes**) *adj* trivial

baladrón, -ona *nm,f* braggart

baladronada *nf* boast

balalaika, balalaica *nf* balalaika

balance *nm* (**a**) *Fin (documento)* balance sheet; *(operación)* balance; **b. consolidado** consolidated balance sheet; *Am* **b. de pagos** balance of payments (**b**) *(resultado)* outcome; **hacer b. (de)** to take stock (of); **el accidente tuvo un b. de seis heridos** a total of six people were wounded in the accident

balancear 1 *vt (cuna)* to rock; *(columpio)* to swing
2 balancearse *vpr (en columpio, hamaca)* to swing; *(de pie)* to sway; *(en cuna, mecedora)* to rock; *(barco)* to roll

balanceo *nm* (**a**) *(de columpio, hamaca)* swinging; *(de cuna, mecedora)* rocking; *(de barco)* roll (**b**) *Am Aut* wheel balance

balancín *nm* (**a**) *(mecedora)* rocking chair; *(en el jardín)* swing hammock (**b**) *(columpio)* seesaw (**c**) *Aut* rocker arm

balandrista *nmf* yachtsman, *f* yachtswoman

balandro *nm* yacht

balanza *nf* (**a**) *(báscula)* scales; **b. de cocina** kitchen scales; **b. de precisión** precision balance; **la b. se inclinó a nuestro favor** the balance *o* scales tipped in our favor (**b**) *Fin* **b. comercial/de pagos** balance of trade/payments

balar *vi* to bleat

balarrasa *nm Fam* good-for-nothing

balaustrada *nf* balustrade; *(de escalera)* banister

balazo *nm (disparo)* shot; *(herida)* bullet wound

balbucear *vi & vt* to babble

balbuceo *nm* babbling

balbucir *vi & vt* to babble

Balcanes *nmpl* **los B.** the Balkans

balcánico, -a *adj* Balkan

balcanización *nf Pol* balkanization

balcón *nm* (**a**) *(terraza)* balcony (**b**) *(mirador)* vantage point

balconada *nf (balcón corrido)* long balcony *(running across building)*

balda *nf Esp* shelf

baldado, -a *adj* (**a**) *(tullido)* crippled (**b**) *Esp Fam (exhausto)* shattered

baldar 1 *vt* to cripple
2 baldarse *vpr* to injure oneself
balde *nm* pail, bucket; **de b.** free (of charge); **estar de b.** *(estar sin hacer nada)* to be hanging around doing nothing; **en b.** in vain
baldear *vt* to sluice down
baldío, -a 1 *adj* (a) *(sin cultivar)* uncultivated; *(no cultivable)* barren; **un terreno b.** an area of wasteland (b) *(inútil)* fruitless
2 *nm Méx, RP (terreno)* vacant lot
baldón *nm* **ser un b. para** to bring shame upon
baldosa *nf (en casa, edificio)* floor tile; *(en la acera)* paving stone
baldosín *nm* tile
baleado *nm Am* **el saldo fue de tres baleados** three people suffered bullet wounds
balear 1 *vt Am* to shoot
2 *adj* Balearic; **el archipiélago b.** the Balearic Islands
3 *nmf* = person from the Balearic Islands
Baleares *nfpl* **las B.** the Balearic Islands
baleárico, -a *adj* Balearic
balero *nm* (a) *(juguete) Méx, RP* cup and ball (b) *Méx (articulación)* bearing
Bali *n* Bali
balido *nm* bleat, bleating
balín *nm* pellet
balística *nf* ballistics *(singular)*
balístico, -a *adj* ballistic
baliza *nf Náut* marker buoy; *Av* beacon; *Aut* warning light *(for roadworks)*
balizamiento *nm Náut* marker buoys; *Av* beacons; *Aut* warning lights *(for roadworks)*
balizar [14] *vt Náut* to mark out with buoys; *Av* to mark out with beacons; *Aut* to mark out with warning lights
ballena *nf* (a) *(animal)* whale; **b. azul** blue whale (b) *(varilla) (de corsé)* stay
ballenato *nm* whale calf
ballenero, -a 1 *adj* whaling; **barco b.** whaler, whaling ship
2 *nm (barco)* whaler, whaling ship
ballesta *nf* (a) *Hist* crossbow (b) *Aut* (suspension) spring
ballet [ba'le] *(pl* **ballets)** *nm* ballet
balneario *nm* (a) *(de baños medicinales)* spa (b) *Am (centro turístico)* seaside resort
balompié *nm* soccer
balón *nm (pelota)* ball; **echar balones fuera** to evade the issue; **b. de oxígeno** oxygen bag; *Fig* shot in the arm
balonazo *nm* **rompió la ventana de un b.** he smashed the window with the ball; **me dio un b. en la cara** he hit me right in the face with the ball
baloncestista *nmf* basketball player
baloncestístico, -a *adj* basketball
baloncesto *nm* basketball
balonmano *nm* handball
balonvolea *nm* volleyball
balotaje *nm Am* runoff, = second round of voting
balsa *nf* (a) *(embarcación)* raft (b) *(estanque)* pond, pool; *Fig* **ser una b. de aceite** *(mar)* to be as calm as a millpond; *(reunión)* to go smoothly
balsámico, -a *adj* balsamic
bálsamo *nm* (a) *Med* balsam (b) *(alivio)* balm
balsero, -a *nm,f* = refugee fleeing Cuba on a raft
báltico 1 *adj (país, mar)* Baltic
2 *nm* **el B.** the Baltic (Sea)
baluarte *nm* (a) *(fortificación)* bulwark (b) *Fig (bastión)* bastion, stronghold
bamba *nf* (a) *(bollo)* = small cake filled with cream (b) *(composición musical)* bamba (c) *Esp* **bambas** *(zapatillas de deporte)* sneakers

bambalina *nf* backdrop; *Fig* **entre bambalinas** backstage
bambolear 1 *vt* to shake
2 bambolearse *vpr (árbol, persona)* to sway; *(mesa, silla)* to wobble; *(tren, autobús)* to shake and vibrate
bamboleo *nm (de árbol, persona)* swaying; *(de mesa, silla)* wobbling; *(de tren, autobús)* shaking and vibrating
bambú *(pl* **bambúes** *o* **bambús)** *nm* bamboo
banal *adj* banal
banalidad *nf* banality
banalizar [14] *vt* to trivialize
banana *nf* banana; **b. split** banana split
bananero, -a 1 *adj* banana; **república bananera** banana republic
2 *nm (árbol)* banana tree
banano *nm* banana tree
banca *nf* (a) *(actividad)* banking; **b. electrónica** electronic banking; **b. por Internet** Internet banking (b) *(institución)* **la b.** the banks (c) *(en juegos)* bank; **hacer saltar la b.** to break the bank (d) *(asiento)* bench
bancal *nm Agr (terraza)* terrace; *(parcela)* plot
bancario, -a *adj* bank; **crédito b.** bank loan; **sector b.** banking sector
bancarrota *nf* bankruptcy; **estar en b.** to be bankrupt; **ir a la b.** to go bankrupt
banco *nm* (a) *(asiento)* bench; *(de iglesia)* pew; *Pol* **b. azul** = seats in Spanish parliament where government ministers sit; **b. de remo** rowing machine (b) *(institución financiera)* bank; **B. Central Europeo** European Central Bank; **el B. Mundial** the World Bank (c) *(de peces)* shoal (d) *(depósito)* bank; *Inform* **b. de datos** data bank; **b. de sangre** blood bank; **b. de esperma** sperm bank (e) *(de carpintero, artesano)* workbench (f) *Tec* **b. de pruebas** test bench; *Fig* testing ground (g) **b. de arena** sandbank; **b. de hielo** pack ice; **b. de niebla** fog bank
banda *nf* (a) *(de personas) (cuadrilla)* gang; *Mús* band; **b. armada** terrorist organization (b) *(faja)* sash; *(cinta)* ribbon; *(franja)* stripe; **b. magnética** magnetic strip; **b. sonora** *(de película)* sound track; *(en carretera)* rumble strip (c) *Fin (tramo)* band; **b. impositiva** tax bracket; **b. salarial** wage bracket, salary band (d) *Rad* wave band; *Tel* **b. ancha** broadband; **b. de frecuencias** frequency (band) (e) *(en fútbol)* **línea de b.** touchline; **saque de b.** throw-in; **avanzar por la b.** to come/go down the wing (f) *(en billar)* cushion (g) **cerrarse en b.** to dig one's heels in
bandada *nf (de aves)* flock; *(de peces)* shoal
bandazo *nm (del barco)* lurch; **dar bandazos** *(barco, borracho)* to lurch; *(ir sin rumbo)* to chop and change; **dar un b.** *(con el volante)* to swerve violently
bandear 1 *vt* to buffet
2 bandearse *vpr* to look after oneself, to cope
bandeja *nf* tray; *Fig* **servir** *o* **poner algo a alguien en b.** to hand sth to sb on a plate; *Inform* **b. del papel** paper tray
bandera *nf* flag; **jurar b.** to swear allegiance (to the flag); **la b. pirata** the Jolly Roger; **b. blanca** white flag; *Esp Fam* **de b.** *(magnífico)* fantastic, terrific
banderazo *nm Dep* **b. de llegada** waving of flag *(as racing car or bike crosses finishing line)*; **b. de salida** starting signal *(with flag)*
banderilla *nf* (a) *Taurom* banderilla, = barbed dart thrust into bull's back (b) *Esp (aperitivo)* = hors d'oeuvre of pickles and olives on a cocktail stick
banderillear *vi Taurom* to stick "banderillas" in the bull's back
banderillero, -a *nm,f Taurom* banderillero, = bullfighter's assistant who sticks "banderillas" into the bull
banderín *nm* (a) *(bandera)* pennant (b) *Mil* pennant-bearer
banderola *nf* pennant
bandidaje *nm* banditry

bandido, -a *nm,f (delincuente)* bandit; *(granuja)* rascal, scamp; **ese tendero es un b.** that storekeeper is a shark

bando *nm* (a) *(facción)* side; **pasarse al otro b.** to change sides (b) *(edicto) (de alcalde)* edict

bandolera *nf (correa)* bandoleer; **en b.** slung across one's chest

bandolerismo *nm* banditry

bandolero, -a *nm,f* bandit

bandoneón *nm* bandoneon, = musical instrument, similar to accordion, used in tango music

bandurria *nf* = small 12-stringed guitar

Bangkok *n* Bangkok

Bangladesh [bangla'deʃ] *n* Bangladesh

Bangui *n* Bangui

banjo ['banjo] *nm* banjo

Banjul [ban'jul] *n* Banjul

banquero, -a *nm,f* banker

banqueta *nf* (a) *(asiento)* stool (b) *CAm, Méx (acera)* sidewalk

banquete *nm (comida)* banquet; **b. de boda** wedding breakfast; **b. eucarístico** holy communion

banquillo *nm (asiento)* low stool; *Dep* bench; *Der* **b. de los acusados** dock

banquina *nf RP (arcén)* shoulder

banquito *nm RP* stool

bantú *(pl* **bantúes)** *nm (pueblo)* Bantu

bañadera *nf* (a) *Arg (bañera)* bath (b) *RP (vehículo)* = old-fashioned school bus

bañado *nm Bol, RP (terreno)* marshy area

bañado, -a *adj* (a) **b. en oro/plata** gold-/silver-plated (b) **b. en sudor** bathed in sweat

bañador *nm Esp (de mujer)* swimsuit; *(de hombre)* swimming trunks

bañar 1 *vt* (a) *(asear)* to give a bath to; *Med* to bathe (b) *(remojar)* to soak (c) *(revestir)* to coat (d) *(sujeto: río)* to flow through; **el Índico baña las costas del país** the Indian Ocean laps the coast of the country (e) *(sujeto: sol, luz)* to bathe

2 bañarse *vpr* (a) *(en el baño)* to have *o* take a bath (b) *(en playa, piscina)* to go for a swim; **prohibido bañarse** *(en letrero)* no bathing (c) *Am (ducharse)* to have a shower

bañera *nf* bathtub, bath

bañista *nmf* bather

baño *nm* (a) *(acción) (en bañera)* bath; *(en playa, piscina)* swim; **darse un b.** *(en bañera)* to have *o* take a bath; *(en playa, piscina)* to go for a swim; *Esp Fig* **dar un b. a alguien** to take sb to the cleaners; **b. de asiento** hip bath; **b. María** bain Marie; **b. de espuma** bubble bath; **b. turco** Turkish bath; **b. de vapor** steam bath (b) *(bañera)* bathtub, bath (c) *(cuarto de aseo)* bathroom; **una casa con tres baños** a three-bathroom house (d) *(servicios)* bathroom, washroom, toilet; **necesito ir al b.** I need to go to the bathroom *o* toilet (e) **baños** *(balneario)* spa; **baños termales** thermal baths (f) *Am (ducha)* shower; **darse un b.** to have a shower (g) *(vahos)* inhalation (h) *(capa)* coat

baobab *(pl* **baobabs)** *nm* baobab (tree)

baptista *adj & nmf* Baptist

baptisterio *nm* baptistry

baquelita *nf* Bakelite®

baqueta *nf* (a) *(de fusil)* ramrod; *Fig* **tratar** *o* **llevar a la b.** to treat harshly (b) *Mús* drumstick

baquetazo *nm Fam* (a) *(golpe)* thump; **tratar a alguien a baquetazos** to treat sb like dirt (b) *(caída)* fall; **darse** *o* **pegarse un b.** to give oneself a real thump, to have a nasty fall

baqueteado, -a *adj Fam* **estar muy b.** to have been to the school of hard knocks

baquetear *vt Fam (maltratar, molestar)* to push around

bar *nm* bar; **ir de bares** to go out drinking, to go on a barhop

barahúnda *nf* racket, din

baraja *nf* deck *o* pack (of cards); *Fig* **jugar con dos barajas** to play a double game

barajar *vt* (a) *(cartas)* to shuffle (b) *(considerar) (nombres, posibilidades)* to consider; *(datos, cifras)* to mention

baranda, *Esp* **barandilla** *nf* handrail

barata *nf* (a) *Méx (rebaja)* sale (b) *Chile (insecto)* cockroach

baratija *nf* trinket, knickknack

baratillo *nm* (a) *(género)* junk (b) *(tienda)* junk shop; *(mercadillo)* flea market

barato, -a 1 *adj* (a) *(objeto)* cheap; **lo b. sale caro** buying cheap is a false economy (b) *(sentimentalismo)* cheap; *(literatura)* trashy

2 *adv* cheap, cheaply; **me costó b.** it was cheap, I got it cheap; **vender algo b.** to sell sth cheaply; **en este bar se come muy b.** you can eat very cheaply in this bar, the food's very cheap in this bar

barba *nf* beard; **apurarse la b.** to shave close; **dejarse b.** to grow a beard; **barbas** *(de persona)* beard; *(de pez)* barbel; **un hombre con toda la b.** a real man; *Esp* **por b.** *(cada uno)* per head; **lo hizo en sus (propias) barbas** he did it right under her nose; **reírse de alguien en sus propias barbas** to laugh in sb's face; **b. incipiente** stubble

barbacoa *nf* barbecue; **hacer una b.** to have a barbecue

Barbados *n* Barbados

barbaridad *nf* (a) *(cualidad)* cruelty (b) *(disparate)* stupid thing; **¡qué b.!** that's ridiculous! (c) *(montón)* **una b. (de)** tons (of); **se gastó una b.** she spent a fortune

barbarie *nf* (a) *(crueldad) (cualidad)* cruelty, savagery; *(acción)* atrocity (b) *(incultura)* barbarism

barbarismo *nm* (a) *(extranjerismo)* foreign word *(that has not yet been fully accepted as part of the language)* (b) *(incorrección)* substandard usage

bárbaro, -a 1 *adj* (a) *Hist* barbarian (b) *(cruel)* barbaric, cruel (c) *(bruto)* uncouth, coarse (d) *Fam (extraordinario)* brilliant, great

2 *nm,f Hist* barbarian

3 *adv Fam (magníficamente)* **pasarlo b.** to have a wild time

barbear *vt CAm, Méx* to flatter, to butter up

barbechar *vt Agr* (a) *(no cultivar)* to leave fallow (b) *(arar)* to plow for sowing

barbecho *nm (sistema)* land set aside; *(terreno)* fallow field; **tierras en b.** fallow land

barbería *nf* barbershop

barbero *nm* barber

barbilampiño, -a 1 *adj* smooth-faced, beardless

2 *nm* beardless man

barbilla *nf* chin

barbitúrico *nm* barbiturate

barbo *nm* barbel; **b. de mar** red mullet

barboquejo *nm* chinstrap

barbotar *vi & vt* to mutter

barbudo, -a 1 *adj* bearded; **la mujer barbuda** *(en circo)* the bearded woman

2 *nm* man with a beard

barbullar *vi* to jabber

barca *nf* dinghy, small boat; **b. de remos** rowboat

barcarola *nf* barcarole, gondolier's song

barcaza *nf* barge, lighter

Barcelona *n* Barcelona

barcelonés, -esa 1 *adj* of/from Barcelona

2 *nm,f* person from Barcelona

barco *nm (más pequeño)* boat; *(de gran tamaño)* ship; **en b.** by boat; **b. de carga** cargo boat *o* ship; **b. cisterna** tanker; **b. de guerra** warship; **b. mercante** cargo ship; **b. de pesca** *o* **pesquero** fishing boat; **b. de recreo** pleasure boat; **b. torpedero** torpedo boat; **b. de vapor** steamer, steamboat; **b. de vela** sailing ship

bardo *nm* bard

baremo *nm (escala)* scale; *(norma)* yardstick

bareto *nm Esp Fam (bar)* juice joint

bario *nm* barium

barítono *nm* baritone

barlovento *nm* windward (side)

barman *(pl* **barmans)** *nm* bartender

Barna. *abrev de* **Barcelona**

barniz *nm (para madera)* varnish; *(para cerámica)* glaze

barnizado, -a 1 *adj (madera)* varnished; *(cerámica)* glazed
    2 *nm (acción) (de madera)* varnishing; *(de cerámica)* glazing

barnizador, -ora *nm,f* French polisher

barnizar [14] *vt (madera)* to varnish; *(cerámica)* to glaze

barómetro *nm* barometer

barón *nm* baron

baronesa *nf* baroness

barquero, -a *nm,f* boatman, *f* boatwoman

barquilla *nf (de globo)* basket

barquillo *nm (plano)* wafer; *(cono)* cone; *(enrollado)* rolled wafer

barra *nf* **(a)** *(pieza alargada)* bar; *(pieza redonda)* rod; *(de hielo)* block; *(para cortinas)* rod; *(de bicicleta)* crossbar; **b. espaciadora** space bar; **b. de labios** lipstick; **b. (de pan)** baguette, French loaf
    (b) *(de bar, café)* bar *(counter)*; **b. americana** = bar where hostesses chat with clients; **b. libre** = unlimited drink for a fixed price
    (c) *(para bailarines)* bar
    (d) *Dep* **b. fija** horizontal bar; **barras paralelas** parallel bars
    (e) *(signo gráfico)* slash, oblique
    (f) *Inform* **b. de herramientas** tool bar; **b. de menús** menu bar; **b. de tareas** task bar
    (g) no se paró en barras he stopped at nothing to get what he wanted
    (h) *RP Fam (grupo de amigos)* gang; *Andes, RP (público)* crowd, spectators; **b. brava** = group of violent soccer supporters

barrabasada *nf Fam* **hacer barrabasadas** to get up to mischief; **aquello fue una b.** that was a really mischievous thing to do

barraca *nf* **(a)** *(chabola)* shack **(b)** *(caseta de feria)* stall **(c)** *(en Valencia y Murcia)* thatched farmhouse

barracón *nm* large hut

barragana *nf (concubina)* concubine

barranca *nf* **(a)** *(precipicio)* precipice; *(hondonada)* ravine; *(menos profunda)* gully **(b)** *RP (cuesta)* hill; **ir(se) b. abajo** to go downhill

barranco *nm (precipicio)* precipice; *(hondonada)* ravine; *(menos profunda)* gully

barranquismo *nm Dep* canyoning

barraquismo *nm* **erradicar el b.** to deal with the shantytown problem

barreminas *nm inv* minesweeper

barrena *nf* **(a)** *(herramienta)* drill **(b) entrar en b.** *Av* to go into a spin; *(persona, gobierno)* to totter

barrenar *vt* **(a)** *(taladrar)* to drill **(b)** *(frustrar)* to scupper

barrendero, -a *nm,f* street sweeper

barreno *nm* **(a)** *(instrumento)* large drill **(b)** *(agujero) (para explosiones)* blast hole

barreño *nm Esp* dish-washing bowl

barrer 1 *vt* **(a)** *(con escoba)* to sweep **(b)** *(sujeto: viento, olas)* to sweep away; **el huracán barrió todo a su paso** the hurricane destroyed everything in its path **(c)** *Inform & Med (con escáner)* to scan **(d)** *Fam (derrotar)* to thrash, to annihilate
    2 *vi* **b. con** *(llevarse)* to finish off, to make short work of; *Fig* **b. hacia** *o* **para adentro** to look after number one

barrera *nf* **(a)** *(obstáculo)* barrier; *Ferroc* crossing gate; *(de campo, casa)* fence; *Fig* **poner barreras a algo** to erect barriers against sth, to hinder sth; **barreras arancelarias** tariff barriers; **b. del sonido** sound barrier **(b)** *Taurom* = barrier around the edge of a bullring **(c)** *Dep (de jugadores)* wall

barriada *nf (barrio)* neighborhood, area; *Am* shantytown

barrica *nf* keg

barricada *nf* barricade

barrida *nf* **dar una b. a algo** to give sth a sweeping

barrido *nm* **(a)** *(con escoba)* **dar un b. a algo** to give sth a sweeping; *Fig* **servir** *o* **valer tanto para un b. como para un fregado** *(persona)* to be a jack-of-all-trades **(b)** *Inform & Med* scan, scanning **(c)** *Cine* pan, panning

barriga *nf* belly; **echar b.** to get a paunch; *Fig* **rascarse** *o* **tocarse la b.** to twiddle one's thumbs, to laze around

barrigazo *nm Fam* **darse un b.** to fall flat on one's face

barrigón, -ona, barrigudo, -a *Fam* **1** *adj* paunchy
    2 *nm,f (persona)* portly person
    3 *nm (barriga)* big belly

barril *nm* barrel; **de b.** *(bebida)* draft

barrila *nf Fam* **dar la b.** to go on and on

barrilete *nm* **(a)** *(de revólver)* chamber **(b)** *Arg (cometa)* kite

barrillo *nm (granito)* blackhead

barrio *nm* area, district, neighborhood; **los barrios bajos** the rough parts of town; **de b.** *(cine, tienda)* local; *Esp Fam Fig* **mandar a alguien al otro b.** to do sb in, to kill sb; **b. chino** *(de chinos)* Chinatown; *Esp (de prostitución)* red-light district; **b. comercial/periférico** shopping/outlying district; **b. latino** Latin Quarter

barriobajero, -a *Pey* **1** *adj* **un chico b.** a lout; **ese acento es muy b.** that accent is very common *o* vulgar
    2 *nm,f* lout

barrizal *nm* mire

barro *nm* **(a)** *(fango)* mud **(b)** *(arcilla)* clay; **una figurita de b.** a clay figure **(c)** *(grano)* blackhead **(d) arrastrarse por el b.** to abase oneself

barroco, -a 1 *adj* **(a)** *Arte* baroque **(b)** *(recargado)* ornate
    2 *nm Arte* baroque

barroquismo *nm Arte* baroque style

barrote *nm* bar; **estar entre barrotes** *(en prisión)* to be behind bars

barruntar *vt (presentir)* to suspect

barrunto *nm* **(a)** *(presentimiento)* suspicion **(b)** *(indicio)* sign, indication

bartola *nf Fam* **tumbarse a la b.** to lounge around

bártulos *nmpl* things, bits and pieces; *Fam Fig* **liar los b.** to pack one's bags

barullento, -a *adj RP Fam* noisy

barullo *nm Fam* **(a)** *(ruido)* din, racket; **armar b.** to make a racket **(b)** *(desorden)* mess

basa *nf Arquit* base

basalto *nm* basalt

basamento *nm Arquit* base, plinth

basar 1 *vt* **b. algo en** to base sth on
    2 basarse *vpr* **basarse en** *(persona)* to base one's argument on; *(teoría, obra)* to be based on; **¿en qué te basas (para decir eso)?** what basis do you have for saying that?

basca *nf* **(a)** *Esp Fam (de amigos)* crowd **(b) bascas** *(náuseas)* nausea; *(ganas de vomitar)* retching

báscula *nf* scales; **b. de baño/de precisión** bathroom/precision scales

basculador *nm* dump truck

bascular *vi* to tilt

base 1 *nf* **(a)** *(parte inferior) (de edificio)* foundations; **b. de maquillaje** foundation (cream)
    (b) *(fundamento, origen)* basis; **el petróleo es la b. de su economía** their economy is based on oil; **ese argumento**

se cae por su b. that argument is built on sand; **partimos de la b. de que...** we assume that...; **sentar las bases para** to lay the foundations of; *Fin* **b. imponible** taxable income

(**c**) *(de partido, sindicato)* **las bases** the grass roots, the rank and file; **militante/afiliado de b.** grass-roots member

(**d**) *(militar, científica)* base; **b. aérea** air base; **b. espacial** space station; **b. de lanzamiento** launch site; **b. naval** naval base; **b. de operaciones** operational base

(**e**) *Quím* base

(**f**) *Mat & Geom* base

(**g**) *Inform* **b. de datos** database; **b. de datos documental/relacional** documentary/relational database

(**h**) **bases** *(para prueba, concurso)* rules

(**i**) *(en béisbol)* base

2 a base de *loc prep* by (means of); **a b. de no hacer nada** by not doing anything; **me alimento a b. de verduras** I live on vegetables; *Esp Fam* **los niños disfrutaron a b. de bien** the children had a great time

BASIC, basic ['beisik] *nm Inform* BASIC

básico, -a *adj (gen) & Quím* basic; **lo b. de** the basics of

Basilea *n* Basel, Basle

basílica *nf* basilica

basilisco *nm Fam Fig* **ponerse hecho un b.** to go mad, to fly into a rage

basket, *Am* **básquet** *nm* basketball

básquetbol *nm Am* basketball

basquetbolista *nmf Am* basketball player

basset *(pl* **bassets** *o* **basset)** *nm* basset hound

basta *interj* **¡b.!** that's enough!; **¡b. de chistes/tonterías!** that's enough jokes/of this nonsense!

bastante 1 *adj* (**a**) *(suficiente)* enough; **no tengo dinero b.** I haven't got enough money (**b**) *(mucho)* **tengo b. frío** I'm quite *o* pretty cold; **bastantes libros** quite a lot of books, a fair number of books

2 *adv* (**a**) *(suficientemente)* **es lo b. lista para...** she's smart enough to... (**b**) *(considerablemente) (+adjetivo, adverbio)* quite, pretty; *(+verbo)* quite a lot; **es b. fácil** it's pretty *o* quite easy; **b. mejor** quite a lot better; **me gustó b.** I enjoyed it quite a lot

3 *pron* **éramos bastantes** there were quite a few *o* a lot of us

bastar 1 *vi* to be enough; **estos dos me bastan, con estos dos me basta** these two are enough for me, these two will do me; **con ocho basta** eight will be enough; **basta con que se lo digas** it's enough for you to tell her; **un pavo de ese tamaño basta y sobra para seis personas** a turkey that size will be more than enough for six people; **basta que salga a la calle para que se ponga a llover** all I have to do is go out into the street for it to start raining

2 bastarse *vpr* **él solo se basta para terminar el trabajo** he'll be able to finish the work himself; **yo me basto y me sobro para hacer este trabajo** I'm more than capable of doing this job on my own

bastardía *nf* bastardy

bastardilla 1 *adj* **letra b.** italics

2 *nf* italics

bastardo, -a 1 *adj (hijo)* bastard

2 *nm,f* (**a**) *(hijo)* bastard (**b**) *muy Fam (insulto)* bastard, swine

bastedad *nf* coarseness

bastidor *nm* (**a**) *(armazón)* frame; *(para bordar)* embroidery frame (**b**) *Esp Aut* chassis (**c**) *Náut* screw propeller's frame (**d**) *Teatro* **bastidores** wings; *Fig* **entre bastidores** behind the scenes

bastilla *nf (dobladillo)* hem

bastión *nm también Fig* bastion

basto, -a 1 *adj* coarse

2 bastos *nmpl (naipes)* = suit in Spanish deck of cards, with the symbol of a wooden club

bastón *nm* (**a**) *(para andar)* walking stick; **usar b.** to walk

with a stick (**b**) *(de mando)* baton; *Fig* **empuñar el b.** to take the helm (**c**) *(para esquiar)* ski pole

bastonazo *nm* blow (with a stick)

bastoncillo *nm (para los oídos)* cotton swab, Q-tip®

basura *nf* (**a**) *(desechos)* garbage, trash, rubbish; *(en la calle)* litter; **sacar la b.** to take out the garbage *o* trash; **el parque estaba lleno de b.** the park was full of litter; **b. orgánica** organic waste; **b. radiactiva** radioactive waste (**b**) *(recipiente)* garbage *o* trash can; **tirar algo a la b.** to throw sth away (**c**) *(bazofia)* garbage, trash, rubbish; **este artículo es una b.** this article is trash

basurero *nm* (**a**) *(persona)* garbageman, garbage collector (**b**) *(vertedero)* garbage dump

bata *nf* (**a**) *(de casa)* housecoat; *(para baño, al levantarse)* dressing gown (**b**) *(de trabajo)* overalls; *(de médico)* white coat; *(de laboratorio)* lab coat

batacazo *nm* bump, bang

batahola *nf* row, rumpus

batalla *nf* battle; **de b.** *(de uso diario)* everyday; **b. campal** pitched battle; **b. naval** naval *o* sea battle

batallador, -ora *adj* battling; **es muy b.** he's a real fighter

batallar *vi* (**a**) *(con armas)* to fight (**b**) *(con esfuerzo)* to battle

batallita *nf Fam* **contar batallitas** to go on about the old times

batallón *nm* (**a**) *Mil* battalion (**b**) *(grupo numeroso)* crowd

batata *nf Esp, Arg, Col, Ven* sweet potato

bate *nm Dep* bat

bateador, -ora *nm,f (en béisbol)* batter; *(en críquet)* batsman, *f* batswoman

batear *Dep* **1** *vt* to hit

2 *vi* to bat

batel *nm* small boat

batería 1 *nf* (**a**) *Elec & Mil* battery; **b. solar** solar cell (**b**) *Mús* drums (**c**) *Teatro* footlights (**d**) *(conjunto)* set; *(de preguntas)* barrage; **b. de cocina** cookware set; **una b. de pruebas** a battery of tests (**e**) **aparcado en b.** parked at an angle to the sidewalk

2 *nmf* drummer

baterista *nmf Am* drummer

batiborrillo, batiburrillo *nm* jumble

batida *nf* (**a**) *(de caza)* beat (**b**) *(de policía)* combing, search

batido, -a 1 *adj* (**a**) *(nata)* whipped; *(claras)* whisked (**b**) *(senda, camino)* well-trodden

2 *nm* (**a**) *(acción de batir)* beating (**b**) *(bebida)* milk shake

batidor *nm* (**a**) *(aparato manual)* whisk (**b**) *(en caza)* beater (**c**) *Mil* scout

batidora *nf (eléctrica)* mixer

batiente *nm* (**a**) *(de puerta)* jamb; *(de ventana)* frame (**b**) *(costa)* shoreline

batín *nm* dressing gown, robe

batir 1 *vt* (**a**) *(mezclar) (huevos, mezcla líquida)* to beat, to whisk; *(nata)* to whip (**b**) *(golpear)* to beat against; **las olas batían las rocas** the waves beat against the rocks; **el viento batía las ventanas** the windows were banging in the wind (**c**) *(alas)* to flap, to beat (**d**) *(derrotar)* to beat; *(récord)* to break (**e**) *(explorar)* to comb, to search

2 *vi (sol, lluvia)* to beat down

3 batirse *vpr* (**a**) *(luchar)* to fight; **batirse en duelo** to fight a duel (**b**) *(puerta)* to slam shut (**c**) *también Fig* **batirse en retirada** to beat a retreat

batiscafo *nm* bathyscaphe

batista *nf* batiste, cambric

batracio *nm* amphibian

baturro, -a 1 *adj* Aragonese

2 *nm,f* Aragonese peasant

batuta *nf* baton; *Fig* **llevar la b.** to call the tune

baudio *nm Inform* baud

baúl *nm* (**a**) *(cofre)* trunk (**b**) *Arg, Col (maletero)* trunk

bauprés *(pl* **baupreses**) *nm Náut* bowsprit

bautismal *adj* baptismal

bautismo *nm* baptism; **b. de fuego** baptism of fire

Bautista *nm Rel* **el B.** John the Baptist

bautizar [14] *vt* (**a**) *Rel* to baptize, to christen (**b**) *(denominar, poner mote a)* to christen (**c**) *Fam (aguar)* to dilute

bautizo *nm (ceremonia)* baptism, christening; *(fiesta)* christening party

bauxita *nf* bauxite

bávaro, -a *adj & nm,f* Bavarian

Baviera *n* Bavaria

baya *nf* berry

bayeta *nf* (**a**) *(tejido)* flannel (**b**) *(para limpiar)* cloth; **b. de gamuza** chamois

bayonesa *nf (bollo)* = pastry filled with strands of crystallized pumpkin

bayoneta *nf* (**a**) *(arma)* bayonet (**b**) **bombilla de b.** = light bulb locked into socket with two projecting pins

baza *nf* (**a**) *(en naipes)* trick; *Fig* **jugó bien sus bazas** she played her cards right; *Fig* **están jugando su última b.** they're playing their last card; **no pude meter b. (en la conversación)** I couldn't get a word in sideways; **siempre trata de meter b. (en la conversación)** she's always trying to butt in (**b**) *(ventaja)* advantage; **la gran b. del producto es su reducido precio** the product's great advantage is its low price; **el delantero ruso es la gran b. del equipo** the Russian forward is the team's main weapon

bazar *nm* bazaar

bazo *nm* spleen

bazofia *nf* (**a**) *(comida)* pig swill (**b**) *(libro, película)* **ser (una) b.** to be garbage *o* trash

bazuca, bazooka *nm* bazooka

BBS *nf Inform (abrev de* **Bulletin Board Service**) BBS

BCE *nm (abrev de* **Banco Central Europeo**) ECB

bearnesa *nf Culin* **salsa b.** bearnaise sauce

beatería *nf* devoutness

beatificación *nf* beatification

beatificar [59] *vt* to beatify

beatitud *nf* beatitude

beato, -a 1 *adj* (**a**) *(beatificado)* blessed (**b**) *(piadoso)* devout (**c**) *(santurrón)* sanctimonious

2 *nm,f* (**a**) *Rel* beatified person (**b**) *(piadoso)* devout person (**c**) *(santurrón)* sanctimonious person

bebe, -a *nm,f Andes, RP Fam* baby

bebé *nm* baby; **b. probeta** test-tube baby

bebedero *nm* (**a**) *(de jaula)* water dish (**b**) *(abrevadero)* drinking trough (**c**) *Méx, RP (fuente)* drinking fountain

bebedizo *nm* potion; *(de amor)* love potion

bebedor, -ora *nm,f (borrachín)* heavy drinker

beber 1 *vt* (**a**) *(líquido)* to drink (**b**) *(absorber) (palabras, consejos)* to lap up; *(sabiduría, información)* to draw, to acquire

2 *vi* (**a**) *(tomar líquido)* to drink; **b. de una fuente** to drink from a fountain (**b**) *(tomar alcohol)* to drink; **bebí más de la cuenta** I had one too many (**c**) *(brindar)* **b. a la salud de alguien** to drink to sb's health; **b. por algo** to drink to sth

bebida *nf* drink; **darse** *o* **entregarse a la b.** to take to drink *o* the bottle; **el problema de la b.** the problem of alcoholism *o* drinking

bebido, -a *adj* drunk

beca *nf (del gobierno)* grant; *(de organización privada)* scholarship; **b. de investigación** research grant/scholarship

becada *nf* woodcock

becado, -a 1 *adj* **alumno b.** *(por el gobierno)* grant holder; *(por organización privada)* scholarship holder

2 *nm,f esp Am (del gobierno)* grant holder; *(de organización privada)* scholarship holder

becar [59] *vt (sujeto: gobierno)* to award a grant to; *(sujeto: organización privada)* to award a scholarship to

becario, -a *nm,f* (**a**) *(estudiante) (del gobierno)* grant holder; *(de organización privada)* scholarship holder (**b**) *(en prácticas)* person on work experience, intern

becerrada *nf* = bullfight with young bulls

becerro, -a *nm,f* calf

bechamel *nf* béchamel (sauce)

bedel *nm* janitor

beduino, -a *adj & nm,f* Bedouin

befa *nf* jeer; **hacer b. de** to jeer at

begonia *nf* begonia

beicon *nm Esp* bacon

beige [beis] *adj & nm* beige

Beijing [bei'jin] *n* Beijing

Beirut *n* Beirut

beis *adj inv & nm inv Esp* beige

béisbol *nm* baseball

beisbolista 1 *adj* baseball

2 *nmf* baseball player

bel canto *nm inv* bel canto

beldad *nf Formal Hum* fairness, beauty

Belén *n* Bethlehem

belén *nm* (**a**) *(de Navidad)* crib, Nativity scene (**b**) *Fam (desorden)* bedlam (**c**) *(embrollo)* mess; **meterse en belenes** to get mixed up in trouble

belfos *nmpl* horse's lips

belga *adj & nmf* Belgian

Bélgica *n* Belgium

Belgrado *n* Belgrade

Belice *n* Belize

beliceño, -a *adj & nm,f* Belizean

belicismo *nm* warmongering

belicista 1 *adj* belligerent

2 *nmf* warmonger

bélico, -a *adj* **conflicto b.** military conflict; **esfuerzo b.** war effort; **espiral bélica** spiral toward war

belicosidad *nf* bellicosity

belicoso, -a *adj* bellicose; *Fig* aggressive

beligerancia *nf* belligerence

beligerante *adj & nmf* belligerent

bellaco, -a *nm,f* villain, scoundrel

belladona *nf* belladonna, deadly nightshade

bellaquería *nf* wickedness, roguery; **ser una b.** to be a wicked thing to do

belleza *nf* beauty

bello, -a *adj* beautiful; **bellas artes** fine arts; **el b. sexo** the fair sex

bellota *nf* acorn

bemol *Mús* **1** *adj* flat

2 *nm* flat; **doble b.** double flat; *Fig* **tener (muchos) bemoles** *(ser difícil)* to be tricky; *(tener valor)* to have guts; *(ser un abuso)* to go too far

benceno *nm Quím* benzene

bencina *nf* (**a**) *Quím* benzine (**b**) *Chile (gasolina)* gas

bendecir [51] *vt* to bless; **b. la mesa** to say grace

bendición *nf* blessing; **ser una b. de Dios** to be wonderful; *Rel* **bendiciones (nupciales)** *(boda)* wedding

bendigo *ver* bendecir

bendijera *etc ver* bendecir

bendito, -a 1 *adj* (**a**) *(santo)* holy; *(alma)* blessed; *Fam Fig* **¡b. sea Dios!** thank goodness! (**b**) *(dichoso)* lucky (**c**) *(para enfatizar)* blessed; **ya está otra vez con esa bendita historia** there he goes again with the same blessed story!

2 *nm, f* simple soul; **dormir como un b.** to sleep like a baby
benedictino, -a *adj & nm, f Rel* Benedictine
benefactor, -ora 1 *adj* beneficent
  2 *nm, f* benefactor, *f* benefactress
beneficencia *nf* charity
beneficiar 1 *vt* to benefit
  2 beneficiarse *vpr* to benefit; **beneficiarse de algo** to do well out of sth; *Esp Fam* **beneficiarse a alguien** to have sb
beneficiario, -a *nm, f (de seguro)* beneficiary; *(de cheque)* payee
beneficio *nm* **(a)** *(bien)* benefit; **a b. de** *(gala, concierto)* in aid of; **en b. de** for the good of; **en b. de todos** in everyone's interest; **en b. propio** for one's own good **(b)** *(ganancia)* profit; **b. bruto/neto** gross/net profit
beneficioso, -a *adj* beneficial **(para** to)
benéfico, -a *adj* **(a)** *(favorable)* beneficial **(b)** *(de caridad)* charity; **rifa benéfica** charity raffle; **organización benéfica** charity, charitable organization
Benelux *nm (abrev de* **België-Nederland-Luxembourg)** **el B.** Benelux
Benemérita *nf Esp* **la B.** = name given to the "Guardia Civil"
benemérito, -a *adj* worthy
beneplácito *nm* consent
benevolencia *nf* benevolence
benevolente, benévolo, -a *adj* benevolent
bengala *nf* **(a)** *(de señalización)* flare **(b)** *(de fiesta)* sparkler
bengalí *(pl* **bengalíes** *o* **bengalís)** *adj & nmf* Bengali
benignidad *nf* **(a)** *(de persona, carácter, enfermedad)* benign nature **(b)** *(de clima, temperatura)* mildness
benigno, -a *adj* **(a)** *(persona, carácter, enfermedad)* benign **(b)** *(clima, temperatura)* mild
Benín *n* Benin
benjamín, -ina *nm, f* youngest child
benzol *nm Quím* benzol
beodo, -a *adj & nm, f* drunk
beque *etc ver* **becar**
berberecho *nm* cockle
berberisco *adj & nmf* Berber
berbiquí *(pl* **berbiquíes** *o* **berbiquís)** *nm* brace and bit
bereber 1 *adj & nmf* Berber
  2 *nm (lengua)* Berber
berenjena *nf* eggplant
berenjenal *nm Fam (enredo)* mess; **meterse en un b.** to get oneself into a right mess
bergamota *nf* bergamot
bergantín *nm* brigantine
beriberi *nm Med* beriberi
berilio *nm Quím* beryllium
Berlín *n* Berlin
berlina *nf* four-door sedan
berlinés, -esa 1 *adj* of/from Berlin
  2 *nm, f* Berliner
bermejo, -a *adj* reddish
bermellón *adj inv & nm* vermilion
Bermudas *nfpl* **las B.** Bermuda
bermudas *nfpl* Bermuda shorts
Berna *n* Berne
berrear *vi* **(a)** *(animal)* to bellow; *(niño)* to howl **(b)** *Fam (cantar mal)* to screech, to howl
berreta *adj RP Fam* cheapo, crappy
berrido *nm* **(a)** **dar berridos/un b.** *(animal)* to bellow; *(niño)* to howl **(b)** *Fam (cantar mal)* **dar berridos** to screech
berrinche *nm Fam* tantrum; *Esp* **coger** *o Am* **hacer un b.** to throw a tantrum
berro *nm* watercress
berza *nf* cabbage; *Esp Fam* **hoy está con la b.** *(atontado)* he's not with it today

berzas, berzotas *nmf inv Fam* thickhead
besamanos *nm inv* hand-kissing
besamel *nf* béchamel sauce
besar 1 *vt* to kiss
  2 besarse *vpr* to kiss
beso *nm* kiss; **dar un b. a alguien** to give sb a kiss, to kiss sb; **le dio un b. en los labios** he kissed her on the lips; **un b., muchos besos** *(en carta)* love; **Marisa te manda besos** Marisa sends her love; **comerse a besos a alguien** to smother sb with kisses; **b. con lengua** French kiss
bestia 1 *adj* **(a)** *(bruto)* **es tan b. que quería meter el piano por la ventana** he's such an oaf, he wanted to try and get the piano in through the window; **un chiste muy b.** a really gross joke **(b)** *(violento)* **es muy b. con su mujer** he's a real brute to his wife; **¡qué tipo más b.!** what a brute *o* thug! **(c)** *(ignorante)* thick **(d)** *(extraordinario)* amazing; **¡qué b., regateó a seis jugadores él solito!** wow *o* that's amazing, he beat six players all by himself! **(e)** *Fam* **a lo b.: comer a lo b.** to stuff one's face; **cerró la puerta a lo b.** he slammed the door
  2 *nmf* **(a)** *(bruto)* oaf **(b)** *(ignorante)* brute **(c)** *(violento)* brute
  3 *nf (animal)* beast; **b. de carga** beast of burden; **b. negra** bête noire
bestiada *nf Esp Fam* **(a)** *(barbaridad)* **decir/hacer una b.** to say/do something stupid **(b)** **una b. de** *(muchos)* tons *o* stacks of
bestial *adj* **(a)** *(brutal)* animal, brutal; *(apetito)* tremendous **(b)** *Fam (formidable)* terrific
bestialidad *nf* **(a)** *(brutalidad)* brutality **(b)** *Fam (barbaridad)* **decir/hacer una b.** to say/do something stupid **(c)** *Fam (montón)* **una b. de** tons *o* stacks of
bestiario *nm Lit* bestiary
best-seller [bes'seler] *(pl* **best-sellers)** *nm* best seller
besucón, -ona *Fam* **1** *adj* kissy
  2 *nm, f* kissy person
besugo *nm (pescado)* sea bream; *Esp Fam (persona)* idiot
besuquear *Fam* **1** *vt* to smother with kisses
  2 besuquearse *vpr* to smooch
besuqueo *nm Fam* smooching
beta *nf* beta
betabel *nf Méx* beet
betarraga *nf Andes* beet
bético, -a *adj* **(a)** *(andaluz)* Andalusian **(b)** *Dep* = of/relating to Real Betis soccer club
betún *nm* **(a)** *(para calzado)* shoe polish **(b)** *Quím* bitumen; **b. de Judea** asphalt
bi- *prefijo* bi-
bianual *adj* **(a)** *(dos veces al año)* biannual, twice-yearly **(b)** *(cada dos años)* biennial
biberón *nm* (baby's) bottle; **dar el b. a** to bottle-feed
Biblia *nf* Bible; *Fam* **ser la B. en verso** to be endless
bíblico, -a *adj* biblical
bibliobús *(pl* **bibliobuses)** *nm Esp* mobile library
bibliófilo, -a *nm, f (a) (coleccionista)* book collector **(b)** *(lector)* book lover
bibliografía *nf* bibliography
bibliográfico, -a *adj* bibliographic
bibliógrafo, -a *nm, f* bibliographer
bibliorato *nm CSur* file
biblioteca *nf* **(a)** *(lugar, conjunto de libros)* library; **b. ambulante/pública** mobile/public library; **b. de préstamo** lending library **(b)** *(mueble)* bookcase
bibliotecario, -a *nm, f* librarian
biblioteconomía *nf* librarianship, library science
bicameral *adj Pol* bicameral, two-chamber; **sistema b.** two-chamber *o* bicameral system

bicampeón, -ona *nm,f* two-times *o* twice champion

bicarbonato *nm* (**a**) *(medicamento)* **b. (sódico)** bicarbonate of soda (**b**) *Quím* bicarbonate; **b. sódico** *o* **de sodio** sodium bicarbonate

bicéfalo, -a *adj* two-headed, *Espec* bicephalous

bicentenario *nm* bicentenary

bíceps *nm inv* biceps

bicha *nf Fam* snake

bicharraco *nm Fam* (**a**) *(animal)* disgusting creature (**b**) *(persona mala)* unpleasant person

bicho *nm Fam* (**a**) *(animal)* beast, animal; *(insecto)* bug; **¿qué b. le ha picado?** what's eating him? (**b**) *(persona)* **(mal) b.** unpleasant person; **b. raro** weirdo; **siempre está intentando ligar con todo b. viviente** he'll try to make out with anything that moves; **no hay b. viviente que se coma esto** there isn't a creature alive that would eat that (**c**) *(pillo)* little terror

bici *nf Fam* bike

bicicleta *nf* bicycle; **b. de carreras** racing bicycle; **b. estática** exercise bike; **b. de montaña** mountain bike

bicicross *nm* cyclo-cross

bicoca *nf Fam (compra, alquiler)* bargain; *Esp (trabajo)* cushy thing

bidé, bidet *nm* bidet

bidimensional *adj* two-dimensional

bidón *nm (barril)* drum; *(lata)* (jerry) can; *(de plástico)* plastic jerry can, = large water container with handle

biela *nf* connecting rod

Bielorrusia *n* Belarus

bielorruso, -a *adj & nm,f* Belorussian

biempensante, bienpensante 1 *adj* right-thinking; **la sociedad b.** respectable society

2 *nmf* **los biempensantes** right-thinking *o* respectable people

bien 1 *adj inv (respetable)* **una familia b.** a good family; *Pey* **niño b.** rich kid

2 *nm* (**a**) *(concepto abstracto)* good; **el b. y el mal** good and evil; **hacer el b.** to do good (deeds) (**b**) *(provecho)* good; **esto te hará b.** this will do you good; **por el b. de** for the sake of; **lo hice por tu b.** I did it for your own good (**c**) *(nota)* good, = mark between 5.9 and 7 out of 10

3 bienes *nmpl* (**a**) *(patrimonio)* property; **bienes de capital** capital assets; **bienes gananciales** shared possessions; **bienes inmuebles** real estate, real property; **bienes muebles** personal property; **bienes raíces** real estate, real property (**b**) *(productos)* goods; **bienes de consumo** consumer goods; **bienes de equipo** capital goods; **bienes de producción** industrial goods

4 *adv* (**a**) *(debidamente, adecuadamente)* well; **¿cómo estás? — b., gracias** how are you? — fine, thanks; **hacer algo b.** to do sth well; **has hecho b.** you did the right thing; **¡b. hecho!** well done!; **habla inglés b.** she speaks English well; **cierra b. la puerta** shut the door properly; **hiciste b. en decírmelo** you were right to tell me; **¿vamos b. de gasolina?** are we doing all right for gas?, have we got plenty of gas?

(**b**) *(expresa opinión favorable)* **me cayó muy b.** I liked her a lot; **estar b.** *(de aspecto)* to be nice; *(de salud)* to be *o* feel well; *(de calidad)* to be good; *(de comodidad)* to be comfortable; **este traje te está b.** this suit looks good on you; **está b. que te vayas, pero antes despídete** it's all right for you to go, but say goodbye first; **oler/saber b.** to smell/taste nice *o* good; **pasarlo b.** to have a good time; **sentar b. a alguien** *(ropa)* to suit sb; *(comida)* to agree with sb; *(comentario)* to please sb

(**c**) *(muy, bastante)* very; **hoy me he levantado b. temprano** I got up nice and early today; **quiero un vaso de agua b. fría** I'd like a nice cold glass of water

(**d**) *(vale, de acuerdo)* all right, OK; **¿nos vamos? — b.** shall we go? — all right

(**e**) *(de buena gana, fácilmente)* quite happily; **ella b. que lo haría, pero no le dejan** she'd be happy to do it, but they won't let her

(**f**) *(expresiones)* **¡b. por...** three cheers for...; **¡está b.!** *(bueno, vale)* all right then!; *(es suficiente)* that's enough; **¡ya está b.!** that's enough!; **estar a b. con alguien** to be on good terms with sb; **más b.** rather; **no estoy contento, más b. estupefacto** I'm not so much happy as stunned; **¡muy b.!** very good!, excellent!; **¡pues (sí que) estamos b.!** that's all we needed!; **tener a b. hacer algo** to be good enough to do sth

5 *conj* **b.... b.** either... or; **dáselo b. a mi hermano, b. a mi padre** either give it to my brother or my father

6 no bien *loc conj* no sooner, as soon as; **no b. me había marchado cuando empezaron a...** no sooner had I gone than they started...

7 si bien *loc conj* although, even though

8 *interj* (**a**) **¡b.!** *(aprobación)* good!, great!; **hoy saldremos al recreo media hora antes — ¡b.!** break time will be half an hour earlier today — great! (**b**) *(enlazando)* **y b., ¿qué te ha parecido?** well *o* so, what did you think of it?; **y b., ¿a qué estás esperando?** well, what are you waiting for?

bienal 1 *adj* biennial

2 *nf* biennial exhibition

bienaventurado, -a *nm,f Rel* blessed person

bienaventuranza *nf* (**a**) *Rel* divine vision; **bienaventuranzas** Beatitudes (**b**) *(felicidad)* happiness

bienestar *nm* well-being

bienhablado, -a *adj* well-spoken

bienhechor, -ora 1 *adj* beneficial

2 *nm,f* benefactor, *f* benefactress

bienintencionado, -a *adj* well-intentioned

bienio *nm* (**a**) *(periodo)* two years (**b**) *(aumento de sueldo)* two-yearly increment

bienpensante = **biempensante**

bienvenida *nf* welcome; **dar la b. a alguien** to welcome sb

bienvenido, -a *adj* welcome; **¡b.!** welcome!

bies *nm inv* bias binding; **al b.** *(costura)* on the bias

bifásico, -a *adj Elec* two-phase; **sistema b.** AC system

bife *nm Andes, RP* steak

bífido, -a *adj* forked

bífidus *nm inv* bifidus

bifocal 1 *adj* bifocal

2 bifocales *nfpl (gafas)* bifocals

bifurcación *nf* fork; *Tel* bifurcation

bifurcarse [59] *vpr* to fork

bigamia *nf* bigamy

bígamo, -a 1 *adj* bigamous

2 *nm,f* bigamist

bígaro *nm* winkle

bigote *nm* mustache; *Esp Fam* **de bigotes** fantastic

bigotudo, -a *adj* with a big mustache

bigudí *(pl* **bigudís** *o* **bigudíes)** *nm* curler

bikini *nm (bañador)* bikini

bilabial *adj & nf Ling* bilabial

bilateral *adj* bilateral

bilbaíno, -a 1 *adj* of/from Bilbao

2 *nm,f* person from Bilbao

biliar *adj Anat* bile; **conducto b.** bile duct; **vesícula b.** gall bladder

bilingüe *adj* bilingual

bilingüismo *nm* bilingualism

bilioso, -a *adj también Fig* bilious

bilirrubina *nf Bioquím* bilirubin

bilis *nf inv también Fig* bile; *Fig* **tragar b.** to grin and bear it

billar *nm* (**a**) *(juego)* billiards *(singular)*; **b. americano** pool; **b.**

romano bar billiards (**b**) *(mesa)* billiard table (**c**) *(sala)* billiard hall

billete *nm* (**a**) *(de banco)* bill; **b. de banco** banknote (**b**) *Esp (de transporte)* ticket; **b. de avión** plane ticket; **b. abierto** open ticket; **b. de ida** *(en avión)* one-way (ticket); **b. de ida y vuelta** round-trip (ticket); **b. sencillo** one-way (ticket) (**c**) *Esp, Cuba (de cine, teatro)* ticket; **no hay billetes** *(en letrero)* sold out (**d**) *(de rifa)* ticket; **b. de lotería** lottery ticket

billetera *nf,* **billetero** *nm* wallet, billfold

billón *núm* trillion; *ver también* **seis**

bimensual *adj* twice-monthly

bimestral *adj* two-monthly

bimestre *nm* two months

bimotor 1 *adj* twin-engine(d); **avión b.** twin-engine(d) plane
    2 *nm* twin-engine(d) plane

binario, -a *adj (gen) & Inform* binary

bingo *nm* (**a**) *(juego)* bingo (**b**) *(sala)* bingo hall (**c**) *(premio)* full row

binoculares *nmpl (prismáticos)* binoculars; *(de ópera, teatro)* opera glasses

binomio *nm* (**a**) *Mat* binomial (**b**) *(de personas)* pairing

biocombustible *nm* biofuel

biodegradable *adj* biodegradable

biodiversidad *nf* biodiversity

bioética *nf* bioethics *(singular)*

biofísica *nf* biophysics *(singular)*

biofísico, -a *adj* biophysical

biografía *nf* biography

biográfico, -a *adj* biographical

biógrafo, -a *nm,f (persona)* biographer

bioingeniería *nf* bioengineering

biología *nf* biology

biológico, -a *adj* biological

biólogo, -a *nm,f* biologist

biomasa *nf Biol* biomass

biombo *nm* (folding) screen

biopsia *nf* biopsy

bioquímica *nf (ciencia)* biochemistry

bioquímico, -a 1 *adj* biochemical
    2 *nm,f (persona)* biochemist

biorritmo *nm* biorhythm

biosfera *nf* biosphere

biotecnología *nf* biotechnology

bioterrorismo *nm* bioterrorism

bióxido *nm Quím* dioxide; **b. de carbono** carbon dioxide

bipartidismo *nm Pol* two-party system

bipartidista *adj Pol* **sistema b.** two-party system

bipartito, -a *adj* bipartite

bípedo, -a 1 *adj* two-legged
    2 *nm,f* biped

biplano *nm* biplane

biplaza 1 *adj* **vehículo b.** two-seater
    2 *nm* two-seater

bipolar *adj* bipolar

biquini *nm (bañador)* bikini

birlar *vt Fam* to pinch

birlibirloque *nm Esp* **como por arte de b.** as if by magic

Birmania *n Antes* Burma

birmano, -a *Antes* **1** *adj & nm,f* Burmese
    2 *nm (lengua)* Burmese

birome *nm o nf CSur* Biro®

birra *nf Fam* beer, brew

birrete *nm* (**a**) *(de clérigo)* biretta (**b**) *(de catedrático)* mortarboard (**c**) *(de abogados, jueces)* = cap worn by judges and lawyers

birria *nf Fam (persona)* drip; **una b. de jugador** a useless

player; **esta película es una b.** this movie is a load of garbage *o* rubbish

birrioso, -a *adj Fam (malo)* pathetic; *(escaso)* measly

biruji *nm Fam* **¡qué b. hace!** it's freezing cold!

bis 1 *adj inv* **viven en el 150 b.** they live at 150a
    2 *nm* encore
    3 *adv Mús (para repetir)* bis

bisabuelo, -a *nm,f* great-grandfather, *f* great-grandmother; **bisabuelos** great-grandparents

bisagra *nf* hinge

bisbisar, bisbisear *vt* to mutter

bisbiseo *nm* muttering

biscote *nm Esp* piece of Melba toast

bisección *nf Mat* bisection

bisectriz *nf Mat* bisector

bisel *nm* bevel

biselado, -a 1 *adj* beveled
    2 *nm* beveling

biselar *vt* to bevel

bisemanal *adj* twice-weekly

bisexual *adj & nmf* bisexual

bisexualidad *nf* bisexuality

bisiesto *adj* **año b.** leap year

bisílabo, -a *adj* two-syllabled

bismuto *nm Quím* bismuth

bisnieto, -a *nm,f (varón)* great-grandson, great-grandchild; *(hembra)* great-granddaughter, great-grandchild; **bisnietos** great-grandchildren

bisonte *nm* bison

bisoñé *nm* toupee

bisoño, -a *nm,f* novice

Bissau *n* Bissau

bistec *(pl* **bistecs***) nm* steak

bisturí *(pl* **bisturíes***) nm* scalpel

bisutería *nf* imitation jewelry

bit *(pl* **bits***) nm Inform* bit

bitácora *nf* (**a**) *Náut* binnacle (**b**) *Inform* blog

bíter, bitter *nm* bitters *(singular)*

bituminoso, -a *adj* bituminous

bivalente *adj Quím* bivalent

bizantino, -a 1 *adj* (**a**) *Hist* Byzantine (**b**) *(discusión, razonamiento)* hair-splitting
    2 *nm,f* Byzantine

bizarría *nf* (**a**) *(valor)* bravery (**b**) *(generosidad)* generosity

bizarro, -a *adj* (**a**) *(valiente)* brave, valiant (**b**) *(generoso)* generous

bizco, -a 1 *adj* cross-eyed
    2 *nm,f* cross-eyed person

bizcocho *nm (de repostería)* sponge

bizquear *vi* to squint

bizquera *nf* squint

blablablá *nm Fam* blah, blah-blah

blanca *nf Mús* half note; *(en ajedrez, damas)* white (piece); *Esp Fig* **estar** *o* **quedarse sin b.** to be flat broke

Blancanieves *n pr* Snow White

blanco, -a 1 *adj* white; **se quedó b. del susto** *(pálido)* she turned white *o* pale with fear; **página/verso en b.** blank page/verse; **se quedó con la mente en b.** his mind went blank; **una noche en b.** a sleepless night
    2 *nm,f (persona)* white; **los blancos** whites
    3 *nm* (**a**) *(color)* white; **el b. es mi color favorito** white is my favorite color; **b. del ojo** white of the eye (**b**) *(diana)* target; **dar en el b.** to hit the target; *Fig* to hit the nail on the head (**c**) *(objetivo)* target; *(de miradas)* object; **se convirtió en el b. de la crítica** he became the target of criticism (**d**) *(espacio vacío)* blank (space) (**e**) *(vino)* white wine

blancor *nm*, **blancura** *nf* whiteness

blancuzco, -a *adj* off-white

blandengue *adj también Fig* weak

blandir *vt* to brandish

blando, -a *adj* (a) *(suave, mullido)* soft (b) *(persona) (indulgente)* soft, lenient

blandura *nf* (a) *(calidad de suave, mullido)* softness (b) *(debilidad)* weakness; *(indulgencia)* leniency

blanqueador, -ora 1 *adj* **líquido b.** whitener

   2 *nm (líquido)* whitener

blanquear *vt* (a) *(ropa)* to whiten; *(con lejía)* to bleach (b) *(con cal)* to whitewash (c) *(dinero)* to launder

blanquecino, -a *adj* off-white

blanqueo *nm* (a) *(de ropa)* whitening; *(con lejía)* bleaching (b) *(encalado)* whitewashing (c) *(de dinero)* laundering

blanquillo *nm* (a) *CAm, Méx* egg (b) *Andes* white peach

blasfemar *vi* (a) *Rel* to blaspheme (**contra** against) (b) *(maldecir)* to swear, to curse

blasfemia *nf* (a) *Rel* blasphemy (b) *(palabrota)* curse (c) *(injuria)* **es una b. hablar así de...** it's sacrilege to talk like that about...

blasfemo, -a 1 *adj* blasphemous

   2 *nm,f* blasphemer

blasón *nm (escudo)* coat of arms; *Fig (orgullo)* honor, glory

blaugrana *adj inv Dep* = of/relating to Barcelona soccer club

blazer ['bleiser] *(pl* **blazers***) nm* blazer

bledo *nm Fam* **me importa un b.** I don't give a damn

blenorragia *nf Med* blennorrhagia

blenorrea *nf Med* blennorrhea

blindado, -a 1 *adj (puerta)* armor-plated; *Mil* armored; **coche b.** bulletproof car; *Mil* **carro b.** armored vehicle; *Mil* **columna blindada** armored column

   2 *nm Mil (vehículo)* armored vehicle

blindaje *nm (de puerta)* armor-plating; *(de coche)* armor

blindar *vt* to armor-plate

bloc *(pl* **blocs***) nm* pad; **b. de dibujo** sketch pad; **b. de notas** notepad

blocaje *nm (en hockey, fútbol)* bodycheck

blocar [59] *vt Dep* to block; *(en hockey, fútbol)* to bodycheck

blog [bloɣ] *(pl* **blogs***) nm Inform* blog

blonda *nf (encaje)* lace trim

bloque 1 *ver* **blocar**

   2 *nm* (a) *(pieza)* block (b) *(edificio)* block; **un b. de apartamentos** an apartment block; **un b. de oficinas** an office block (c) *Inform* block (d) *Pol* bloc; **en b.** en masse; *Hist* **el b. del Este** the Eastern bloc (e) *Tec* cylinder block

bloquear 1 *vt* (a) *(comunicaciones, carreteras) (por nieve, inundación)* to block; **los manifestantes bloqueaban la salida de la fábrica** the demonstrators were blocking the exit to the factory (b) *(con ejército, barcos)* to blockade (c) *Fin (cuentas)* to freeze (d) *(acuerdo)* to block (e) *(mecanismo)* to jam; **la centralita del ministerio está bloqueada** the ministry's switchboard is jammed (f) *Dep* to block (g) *Inform (archivo)* to lock (h) *Aut* to lock

   2 bloquearse *vpr* (a) *(atascarse)* to be stuck (b) *(persona)* to freeze; **cuando está estresado se bloquea** he just freezes when he's under stress (c) *Aut (dirección)* to lock; *(frenos)* to jam (d) *Inform (pantalla)* to freeze

bloqueo *nm* (a) *(con ejército, barcos)* blockade; **b. naval** naval blockade (b) *Econ* blockade; **b. económico** economic blockade (c) *(de mecanismo)* jamming (d) *Fin (de cuentas)* freeze, freezing (e) *Dep (de jugador)* block (f) **b. mental** mental block (g) *Inform (en archivo)* lock

blues [blus] *nm inv Mús* blues

blúmer *(pl* **blúmers** *o* **blúmeres***) nm CAm, Carib* panties

blusa *nf* blouse

blusón *nm* smock

bluyín *nm*, **bluyines** *nmpl Andes, Ven* jeans

BNG *nm (abrev de* **Bloque Nacionalista Gallego***)* = Galician nationalist party

boa 1 *nf (serpiente)* boa; **b. constrictor** boa constrictor

   2 *nm (prenda)* (feather) boa

boatiné *nm* padded fabric; **una bata de b.** a quilted dressing gown

boato *nm* show, ostentation

bobada, bobería *nf* **decir/hacer una b.** to say/do something stupid; **decir bobadas** to talk nonsense; **hacer bobadas** to mess around

bobalicón, -ona *Fam* **1** *adj* simple

   2 *nm,f* simpleton

bobería = **bobada**

bóbilis *adv Esp Fam* **de b. b.** *(de balde)* for free, for nothing; *(sin esfuerzo)* without trying

bobina *nf* (a) *(de cordel, cable, papel)* reel; *(en máquina de coser)* bobbin (b) *Elec* coil

bobinar *vt* to wind

bobo, -a 1 *adj* (a) *(tonto)* stupid, daft (b) *(ingenuo)* naive, simple

   2 *nm,f* (a) *(tonto)* fool, idiot (b) *(ingenuo)* simpleton

bobsleigh ['boβslei] *(pl* **bobsleighs***) nm* bobsled, bobsleigh

boca *nf* (a) *(de persona, animal)* mouth; **b. arriba/abajo** up/down; **(respiración) b. a b.** mouth-to-mouth resuscitation; **hacer el b. a b. a alguien** to give sb mouth-to-mouth resuscitation, to give sb the kiss of life

   (b) *(entrada) (de botella, túnel)* mouth; *(de buzón)* slot; *(de cañón)* muzzle; *(de escenario)* stage door; *(de puerto)* entrance; *Fam* **a b. de jarro** point-blank; **b. del estómago** pit of the stomach; **b. de incendios** fire hydrant; **b. de metro** subway entrance; **b. de riego** hydrant

   (c) *(persona)* **una b. más para alimentar** one more mouth to feed

   (d) *(expresiones)* **abrir** *o* **hacer b.** to whet one's appetite; **andar** *o* **ir de b. en b.** to be on everyone's lips; *Fam* **cerrar la b. a alguien** to make sb shut up; *Fam* **¡cállate** *o* **cierra la b.!** shut up!; **no decir esta b. es mía** not to open one's mouth; **se me hace la b. agua** it makes my mouth water; **meterse en la b. del lobo** to put one's head into the lion's mouth; **por la b. muere el pez** silence is golden; **a pedir de b.** perfectly; **quedarse con la b. abierta** to be left speechless; **me lo has quitado de la b.** you took the words right out of my mouth; **tapar la b. a alguien** to silence sb

bocacalle *nf (entrada)* entrance *(to a street)*; *(calle)* side street; **gire en la tercera b.** take the third turning

bocadillo *nm* (a) *Esp (comida)* (filled) roll (b) *(en cómic)* speech bubble, balloon

bocado *nm* (a) *(comida)* mouthful; **no probar b.** *(por desgana)* not to touch one's food; **no he probado b. en todo el día** I haven't had a bite to eat all day (b) *(mordisco)* bite (c) **b. de Adán** Adam's apple

bocajarro: a bocajarro *loc adv (disparar)* at point-blank range; **decir algo a b.** to say sth straight out

bocamanga *nf* cuff

bocanada *nf (de líquido)* mouthful; *(de humo)* puff; *(de viento)* gust

boca-oreja *nm* word of mouth

bocata *nm Esp Fam* (filled) roll

bocazas *nmf inv Fam* bigmouth, blabbermouth

boceto *nm* sketch, rough outline

bocha *nf (bolo)* bowl; **bochas** *(juego)* lawn bowling

bochar *vt RP Fam (en examen)* to fail

bochinche *nm Am Fam (ruido)* racket; *(alboroto)* fuss

bochinchero, -a *adj Am Fam* rowdy

bochorno *nm* (a) *(calor)* stifling *o* muggy heat (b) *(vergüenza)* embarrassment

bochornoso, -a *adj* (**a**) *(tiempo)* stifling, muggy (**b**) *(vergonzoso)* embarrassing

bocina *nf* (**a**) *Aut* horn (**b**) *Méx (megáfono)* loudspeaker; *(del teléfono)* mouthpiece

bocinazo *nm Aut* honk

bocio *nm Med* goiter

bock [bok] *(pl* **bocks)** *nm* stein

boda *nf* wedding; **bodas de diamante** *(de matrimonio)* diamond wedding; *(de organización, evento)* diamond jubilee; **bodas de oro** *(de matrimonio)* golden wedding; *(de organización, evento)* golden jubilee; **bodas de plata** *(de matrimonio)* silver wedding; *(de organización, evento)* silver jubilee

bodega *nf* (**a**) *(cava)* wine cellar (**b**) *(tienda)* wine store; *(taberna)* bar *(mainly selling wine)* (**c**) *(en buque, avión)* hold (**d**) *CAm, Carib (colmado)* small grocery store (**e**) *Méx (almacén)* store

bodegón *nm* (**a**) *Arte* still life (**b**) *(taberna)* tavern, inn

bodeguero, -a *nm,f (dueño)* = owner of a wine cellar

bodrio *nm Fam (comida)* slop, pig swill; **ser un b.** *(película, novela, cuadro)* to be trash *o* rubbish; **¡qué b.!** what a load of trash *o* rubbish!

body ['boði] *(pl* **bodies)** *nm* body *(garment)*

BOE ['boe] *nm (abrev de* **Boletín Oficial del Estado)** official Spanish gazette, = daily state publication, giving details of legislation, etc

bóer *nmf* Boer

bofe *nm Fam* **echar el b.** *o* **los bofes** to puff and pant

bofetada *nf* slap (in the face); **dar una b. a alguien** to slap sb (in the face); *Esp Fig* **darse de bofetadas con algo** *(no armonizar)* to clash with sth

bofetón *nm* hard slap (in the face)

bofia *nf Esp Fam* **la b.** the cops

boga *nf* **estar en b.** to be in vogue

bogar [40] *vi* (**a**) *(remar)* to row (**b**) *(navegar)* to sail

bogavante *nm* lobster

Bogotá *n* Bogota

bogotano, -a 1 *adj* of/from Bogotá
2 *nm,f* person from Bogotá

bogue *etc ver* **bogar**

bohemia *nf* bohemian lifestyle

bohemio, -a 1 *adj* (**a**) *(aspecto, vida, barrio)* bohemian (**b**) *(de Bohemia)* Bohemian
2 *nm,f* (**a**) *(artista, vividor)* bohemian (**b**) *(de Bohemia)* Bohemian

bohío *nm Carib* hut

boicot *(pl* **boicots)** *nm* boycott

boicotear *vt* to boycott

boicoteo *nm* boycott

boina *nf* beret

boîte [bwat] *nf* nightclub

boj *nm* (**a**) *(árbol)* box (**b**) *(madera)* boxwood

bol *nm* bowl

bola *nf* (**a**) *(esfera)* ball; *(canica)* marble; *(de helado)* scoop; **b. de alcanfor** mothball; **b. de billar** billiard ball; **b. de cristal** crystal ball; **b. del mundo** globe; **b. de naftalina** mothball; **b. de nieve** snowball; *Fig* **convertirse en una b. de nieve** to snowball; **b. de partido** *(en tenis)* match point (**b**) *Fam (mentira)* fib; **contar bolas** to fib, to tell fibs (**c**) *Fam* rumor; **corre la b. por ahí de que te has echado novio** they say you've got yourself a boyfriend (**d**) *muy Fam* **bolas** *(testículos)* balls; **en bolas** *(desnudo)* stark-naked; *Fig* **no rascar b.** to get everything wrong (**e**) *Am (betún)* shoe polish

bolada *nf CSur Fam* opportunity

bolchevique *adj & nmf* Bolshevik

bolchevismo *nm* Bolshevism

boldo *nm (infusión)* boldo, = type of herbal tea

boleador *nm Am (de zapatos)* shoeshine

boleadoras *nfpl* bolas, = set of three ropes, weighted at the ends, used by Argentinian gauchos for capturing cattle by entangling their legs

bolear *vt Méx* to shine, to polish

bolera *nf* bowling alley

bolero *nm* bolero

boleta *nf* (**a**) *(para entrar)* (admission) ticket (**b**) *Cuba, Méx, RP (para votar)* ballot, voting slip (**c**) *CAm, CSur (multa)* parking ticket (**d**) *Méx (de calificaciones)* report card

boletería *nf Am (de cine, teatro)* box office; *(de estación)* ticket office

boletero, -a *nm,f Am* box office attendant

boletín *nm* journal, periodical; **b. de evaluación** report card; **b. informativo** news bulletin; **b. meteorológico** weather forecast; **b. de noticias** news bulletin; **b. de prensa** press release; **B. Oficial del Estado** official Spanish gazette, = daily state publication, giving details of legislation, etc; **b. de suscripción** subscription form

boleto *nm* (**a**) *(de lotería, rifa)* ticket; *(de quinielas)* coupon; **b. de apuestas** betting slip (**b**) *Am (para transporte)* ticket; **b. de ida y vuelta,** *Méx* **b. redondo** round-trip (ticket) (**c**) *Col, Méx (para espectáculo)* ticket (**d**) *Méx Fam (asunto, problema)* **es mi b.** it's my business

boli *nm Esp Fam* Biro®

boliche *nm* (**a**) *(en petanca)* jack (**b**) *(bolos)* tenpin bowling (**c**) *(bolera)* bowling alley (**d**) *CSur (tienda)* small grocery store

bólido *nm* racing car; *Fig* **ir como un b.** to go at a rate of knots

bolígrafo *nm* ballpoint pen, Biro®

bolillo *nm* (**a**) *(en costura)* bobbin (**b**) *Méx (panecillo)* bread roll

bolinga *Esp Fam* **1** *adj (borracho)* plastered
2 *nm (persona)* boozer
3 *nf* **agarrar una b.** to get plastered

bolitas *nfpl CSur* marbles

bolívar *nm* bolivar

Bolivia *n* Bolivia

boliviano, -a *adj & nm,f* Bolivian

bollera *nf muy Fam* dike

bollería *nf* (**a**) *(tienda)* cake shop (**b**) *(productos)* cakes

bollo *nm* (**a**) *(para comer)* *(de pan)* (bread) roll; *(dulce)* bun (**b**) *(abolladura)* dent; *Esp (abultamiento)* bump (**c**) *Fam (persona atractiva)* dish, gorgeous guy/woman; **ser un b.** to be quite nice

bolo *nm* (**a**) *Dep (pieza)* bowling pin; **(el juego de) los bolos** (tenpin) bowling (**b**) *Esp Fam (actuación)* gig (**c**) *CAm Fam (borracho)* boozer

bolsa *nf* (**a**) *(recipiente)* bag; **b. de agua caliente** hot-water bottle; **b. de aire** air pocket; **b. de aseo** toilet bag; **b. de (la) basura** trash can liner; **b. de la compra** shopping bag; **b. de deportes** sports bag; *Am* **b. de dormir** sleeping bag; **b. de mano** (piece *o* item of) hand luggage; **b. de papel** paper bag; **b. de plástico** *(en tiendas)* shopping *o* plastic bag; *Fig* **b. de pobreza** deprived area; **b. de viaje** travel bag
(**b**) *Fin* **b. (de valores)** stock exchange, stock market; **la B. de Madrid** the Madrid Stock Exchange; **la b. ha subido/bajado** stock prices have gone up/down; **jugar a la b.** to speculate on the stock market
(**c**) *(bolso)* *(de dinero)* purse, pocketbook; **¡la b. o la vida!** your money or your life!
(**d**) **b. de trabajo** *(en universidad, organización)* = list of job openings and searches; *(en periódico)* jobs section
(**e**) *Min (de mineral, aire)* pocket
(**f**) *Anat* sac
(**g**) *Educ (beca)* **b. de estudios** (study) grant
(**h**) *CAm, Méx, Perú (bolsillo)* pocket
(**i**) *Méx (bolso)* purse, handbag

bolsillo *nm* pocket; **calculadora de b.** pocket calculator; **edición de b.** pocket edition; **lo pagué de mi b.** I paid for it out of my own pocket; **meterse** *o* **tener a alguien en el b.** to have sb eating out of one's hand; *Fam* **rascarse el b.** to fork out

bolsista *nmf* (a) *Fin* stockbroker (b) *CAm, Méx (carterista)* pickpocket

bolsístico, -a *adj Fin* stock market; **actividad bolsística** activity on the stock market

bolso *nm* bag; *Esp (de mujer)* purse, handbag; **b. de viaje** overnight bag

boludear *vi RP Fam (hacer tonterías)* to mess around *o* about

boludez *nf RP Fam* (a) *(acto, dicho)* **¡qué b.!** what a damn stupid thing to do/say! (b) *(cosa insignificante)* silly little thing

boludo, -a *RP Fam* **1** *adj* (a) *(estúpido)* damn stupid (b) *(perezoso)* bone lazy
  2 *nm,f* (c) *(estúpido)* jerk (d) *(perezoso)* lazybones

bomba 1 *nf* (a) *(explosivo)* bomb; **poner una b.** to plant a bomb; **b. atómica** atom *o* nuclear bomb; **b. fétida** stink bomb; **b. de hidrógeno** hydrogen bomb; **b. de humo** smoke bomb; **b. incendiaria** gasoline bomb; **b. lacrimógena** tear-gas grenade; **b. de mano** (hand) grenade; **b. de neutrones** neutron bomb; *también Fig* **b. de relojería** time bomb (b) *(de agua, de bicicleta)* pump; *Med* **b. de cobalto** cobalt bomb; **b. hidráulica** hydraulic pump; **b. de pie** foot pump (c) *(acontecimiento)* bombshell; **caer como una b.** to be a bombshell (d) *(en piscina)* **tirarse en b.** to do a bomb (e) *Chile, Ecuad, Ven (gasolinera)* gas station (f) *Fam* **la fiesta de anoche fue la b.** the party last night was something else
  2 *adv Esp Fam* **pasarlo b.** to have a great time

bombacha *nf RP* (a) *(braga)* panties (b) **bombachas** *(pantalones)* = loose pants worn by gauchos

bombachos *nmpl* baggy pants *o* pants

bombardear *vt también Fig* to bombard

bombardeo *nm* bombardment; **b. aéreo** air raid; *Fís* **b. atómico** bombardment in a particle accelerator

bombardero *nm (avión)* bomber

bombazo *nm (explosión)* explosion, blast; *(noticia)* bombshell

bombear *vt (gen) & Dep* to pump

bombeo *nm* (a) *(de líquido)* pumping (b) *(abombamiento)* bulge

bombero, -a *nm,f* (a) *(de incendios)* firefighter, fireman, *f* firewoman; *Esp* **tener ideas de b.** to have crazy ideas (b) *Ven (de gasolinera)* gas-pump attendant

bombilla *nf* (a) *Esp (de lámpara)* light bulb (b) *RP (para mate)* = tube for drinking maté (c) *Méx (cucharón)* ladle

bombillo *nm CAm, Carib, Col, Méx* light bulb

bombín *nm* bowler (hat)

bombita *nf RP* light bulb

bombo *nm* (a) *Mús* bass drum; *Fam* **tengo la cabeza como un b.** my head is throbbing; *Fam* **estar con b.** to be pregnant (b) *Fam (elogio)* hype; **a b. y platillo** with a lot of hype; **le están dando mucho b. a la nueva película** the new movie is getting a lot of hype (c) *Tec* drum

bombón *nm* (a) *(dulce)* chocolate (b) *Fam (mujer)* sweetie, stunner

bombona *nf* cylinder; **b. de butano** (butane) gas cylinder; **b. de gas** gas cylinder; **b. de oxígeno** oxygen bottle *o* cylinder

bombonería *nf* candy store

bonachón, -ona 1 *adj* kindly
  2 *nm,f* kindly person

bonaerense 1 *adj* of/from Buenos Aires
  2 *nmf* person from Buenos Aires

bonancible *adj (tiempo)* fair; *(mar)* calm

bonanza *nf* (a) *(de tiempo)* fair weather; *(de mar)* calm at sea (b) *(prosperidad)* prosperity

bondad *nf (cualidad)* goodness; *(inclinación)* kindness; **tener**
la **b. de hacer algo** to be kind enough to do sth

bondadoso, -a *adj* kind, good-natured

bonete *nm (eclesiástico)* biretta; *(universitario)* mortarboard

bongó *nm* bongo (drum)

boniato *nm Esp, Cuba, Urug* sweet potato

bonificación *nf* (a) *(oferta especial)* bonus; *(descuento)* discount (b) *(mejora)* improvement

bonificar [59] *vt* (a) *(descontar)* to give a discount of (b) *(mejorar)* to improve

bonito, -a 1 *adj* (a) *(lindo)* pretty; *(agradable)* nice; **es la canción más bonita del disco** it's the most beautiful song on the record (b) *(grande)* **recibió una bonita suma** she got a tidy sum of money (c) *Irónico* **¡muy b.!** great!, wonderful!; **¿te parece b. lo que has hecho?** are you proud of what you've done, then?
  2 *adv Am* (a) *(bien)* well (b) *(mucho)* a lot
  3 *nm (pez)* bonito *(type of tuna)*

Bonn *n* Bonn

bono *nm* (a) *(vale)* voucher (b) *Fin* bond; **b. basura/de caja** junk/short-term bond; **b. del Estado/del tesoro** government/treasury bond

bonobús *(pl* bonobuses*)* *nm Esp* = multiple-journey bus ticket

bonoloto *nm* = Spanish state-run lottery

bonotrén *nm Esp* = multiple-journey railroad ticket

bonsái *nm* bonsai

bonzo *nm* (a) *(budista)* Buddhist monk, bonze (b) **quemarse a lo b.** to set oneself alight

boñiga *nf* cowpat

booleano, -a *adj Mat & Inform* Boolean

boom [bum] *(pl* booms*)* *nm* boom

boqueada *nf* **dar las (últimas) boqueadas** to breathe one's last

boquear *vi* to breathe one's last

boquera *nf* = cracked lip in the corner of one's mouth

boquerón *nm* (fresh) anchovy; **boquerones en vinagre** pickled anchovy fillets

boquete *nm* hole

boquiabierto, -a *adj* open-mouthed; *Fig* astounded, speechless

boquilla *nf* (a) *(para fumar)* cigarette holder (b) *(de pipa, instrumento musical)* mouthpiece (c) *(de tubo, aparato)* nozzle (d) *Fam* **es todo de b.** it's all hot air

Borbón *n pr* Bourbon; **los Borbones** the Bourbons

borbónico, -a *adj* Bourbon

borbotear, borbotar *vi* to bubble

borboteo *nm* bubbling

borbotón *nm* **salir a borbotones** to gush out

borda *nf Náut* gunwale; *Fig* **tirar** *o* **echar algo por la b.** to throw sth overboard; **un fuera b.** *(barco)* an outboard motorboat; *(motor)* an outboard motor

bordado, -a 1 *adj* embroidered; *Esp Fig* **el discurso/examen le salió b.** his speech/the exam went like a dream
  2 *nm* embroidery

bordar *vt (coser)* to embroider; *Fig (hacer bien)* to do excellently; **la actriz borda el papel de Cleopatra** the actress is outstanding in the role of Cleopatra

borde 1 *adj Esp Fam (antipático)* **eres muy b.** you're a real SOB; **no te pongas b. que casi no te he tocado** there's no need to get in a huff, I hardly touched you
  2 *nmf Esp Fam (antipático)* SOB
  3 *nm (límite)* edge; *(de carretera)* side; *(de río)* bank; *(de vaso, botella)* rim; **(lleno) hasta el b.** full to the brim; **al b. del mar** by the sea; **estoy al b. de un ataque de nervios** I'm going to go out of my head in a minute; *Fig* **estar al b. del abismo** to be on the brink of ruin *o* disaster; *Méx* **b. (de la banqueta)** curb

bordeado, -a *adj* **b. de** lined with; **un camino b. de árboles** a tree-lined path

bordear *vt* (**a**) *(estar alrededor de)* to border; *(moverse alrededor de)* to skirt (round) (**b**) *(rozar)* to be close to

bordillo *nm* curb

bordo *nm Náut & Av* **a b.** on board; **bienvenidos a b.** welcome aboard

bordó *adj inv & nm RP* burgundy

boreal *adj* northern

borgoña *nm* burgundy

bórico *adj* boric

borla *nf (de flecos)* tassel; *(pompón)* pom-pom

borne *nm Elec* terminal

Borneo *n* Borneo

boro *nm Quím* boron

borra *nf (lana basta)* flock

borrachera *nf* (**a**) *(embriaguez)* drunkenness; **tener/ cogerse una b.** to be/get drunk (**b**) *(emoción)* intoxication

borrachín, -ina *nm,f Fam* boozer

borracho, -a 1 *adj* (**a**) *(ebrio)* drunk (**b**) *(emocionado)* **b. de** drunk *o* intoxicated with
2 *nm,f (persona)* drunk
3 *nm (bizcocho)* ≃ baba (au rhum), = sponge cake soaked in alcohol

borrado *nm Inform* clearing

borrador *nm* (**a**) *(escrito)* rough draft (**b**) *(para pizarra)* blackboard eraser; *(goma de borrar)* eraser

borraja *nf* borage

borrar 1 *vt* (**a**) *(hacer desaparecer) (con goma)* to erase; *(en ordenador)* to delete; *(en casete)* to erase; *Fig* **b. a algo/ alguien del mapa** to wipe sth/sb off the map (**b**) *(tachar)* to cross out; *(de lista)* to take off (**c**) *(pizarra)* to wipe, to dust (**d**) *(olvidar)* to erase; **el tiempo borró el recuerdo de aquel desastre** with time, he was able to erase the disaster from his memory (**e**) *Méx, RP Fam (no hacer caso a)* to ignore
2 borrarse *vpr* (**a**) *(desaparecer)* to disappear; **se bloqueó el ordenador y se borraron algunos documentos** when the computer crashed, certain files were lost; *Fig* **se borró del mapa** he dropped out of sight, he disappeared from circulation (**b**) *(olvidarse)* to be wiped away; **se le borró de la mente** he forgot all about it (**c**) *(de lista)* to take one's name off; **me he borrado de las clases** I've stopped going to those classes

borrasca *nf (tormenta)* thunderstorm; *Meteo (baja presión)* area of low pressure

borrascoso, -a *adj (tiempo)* stormy; *(vida, reunión, relación)* stormy, tempestuous

borrego, -a *nm,f* (**a**) *(animal)* lamb (**b**) *Fam Pey (persona)* **todos le siguen como borregos** they all follow him like sheep

borreguil *adj también Fig* sheep-like

borrico, -a 1 *adj* dim-witted, dim
2 *nm,f* donkey; *Fig* dimwit, dunce

borriquero *adj* **cardo b.** cotton thistle

borriqueta *nf* trestle

borrón *nm (de tinta)* blot; *Fig* blemish; **hacer b. y cuenta nueva** to wipe the slate clean

borronear *vt* (**a**) *(garabatear)* to scribble on (**b**) *(escribir deprisa)* to scribble

borroso, -a *adj (foto, visión)* blurred; *(escritura, texto)* smudgy

boscoso, -a *adj* wooded, woody

Bósforo *nm* **el B.** the Bosphorus

Bosnia *n* Bosnia

Bosnia(-Herzegóvina) *n* Bosnia (and Herzegovina)

bosnio, -a *adj & nm,f* Bosnian

bosque *nm (pequeño)* wood; *(grande)* forest

bosquejar *vt (esbozar)* to sketch (out); *(dar una idea de)* to give a rough outline of

bosquejo *nm (esbozo)* sketch; *(de idea, tema, situación)* rough outline

bosquimano, -a *nm,f* Bushman

bossa nova [bosaˈnoβa] *nf* bossa nova

bosta *nf* cow dung

bostezar [14] *vi* to yawn

bostezo *nm* yawn

bota *nf* (**a**) *(calzado)* boot; *Fig* **morir con las botas puestas** to die with one's boots on; *Fam Fig* **ponerse las botas** *(comiendo)* to stuff one's face; **con este negocio nos vamos a poner las botas** we're going to make a fortune with this business; **botas de agua** gumboots, Wellingtons; **botas camperas** cowboy boots; **botas de esquí** ski boots; **botas de fútbol** soccer shoes; **botas de goma** rubber boots, Wellingtons; **botas de montaña** climbing boots; **botas de montar** riding boots (**b**) *(de vino)* = small leather container in which wine is kept

botadura *nf* launching

botafumeiro *nm* censer

botana *nf Méx* snack, tapa

botánica *nf (ciencia)* botany

botánico, -a 1 *adj* botanical
2 *nm,f (persona)* botanist

botanista *nmf* botanist

botar 1 *vt* (**a**) *(pelota)* to bounce (**b**) *(barco)* to launch (**c**) *Fam (despedir)* to throw *o* kick out (**d**) *Dep (córner)* to take (**e**) *Am salvo RP (tirar)* to throw away; *(volcar, derribar)* to knock over
2 *vi* (**a**) *Esp (saltar)* to jump; *Fam Fig* **está que bota** he is hopping mad (**b**) *(pelota)* to bounce
3 botarse *vpr Am salvo RP (tirarse)* to jump; **botarse al agua** to jump into the water; *(de cabeza)* to dive into the water

botarate *nm Fam* madcap

botavara *nf Náut* boom

bote *nm* (**a**) *(envase) (tarro)* jar; *Esp (lata)* can, tin; *(de champú, pastillas)* bottle; *Am* **b. de la basura** garbage can, trash can; **b. de humo** smoke canister (**b**) *(barca)* boat; **b. de remos** rowboat; **b. salvavidas** lifeboat (**c**) *(salto)* jump; **dar botes** *(saltar)* to jump up and down; *(tren, coche)* to bump up and down; **pegar un b.** *(de susto)* to jump, to give a start (**d**) *(de pelota)* bounce; **dar un b., dar botes** to bounce (**e**) *(propinas)* tips; **el cambio, para el b.** keep the change (**f**) *(en lotería)* rollover jackpot (**g**) *Méx, Ven Fam (cárcel)* joint (**h**) *(expresiones)* **a b. pronto** *(sin pensar)* off the top of one's head; *Esp* **chupar del b.** to feather one's nest; **de b. en b.** chockablock; *Esp* **tener en el b. a alguien** to have sb eating out of one's hand

botella *nf* (**a**) *(recipiente)* bottle; **una b. de champán/leche** *(recipiente)* a champagne/milk bottle; *(contenido)* a bottle of champagne/milk; **en b.** bottled; **darle a la b.** *(beber alcohol)* to be a heavy drinker; **b. de oxígeno** oxygen bottle *o* cylinder (**b**) *Cuba (autostop)* **dar b. a alguien** to give sb a ride; **hacer b.** to hitchhike

botellazo *nm* blow with a bottle

botellero *nm* wine rack

botellín *nm (de cerveza)* small bottle *(0.2 liter)*

botellón *nm Esp Fam* = informal street gathering where young people meet to drink and socialize

botica *nf Anticuado* pharmacy, drugstore

boticario, -a *nm,f Anticuado* pharmacist, druggist

botija *nmf Urug Fam (muchacho)* kid

botijo *nm* = earthenware vessel with a spout used for drinking water

botín *nm* (**a**) *(de guerra, atraco)* plunder, loot; **repartirse el b.** to share out the spoils (**b**) *(calzado)* ankle boot; *Am (de fútbol)* boot

botiquín *nm (caja)* first-aid kit; *(mueble)* first-aid cupboard; *(enfermería)* sick bay

botón 1 *nm* (**a**) *(para abrochar)* button; *Fig* **esto es sólo un b. de muestra** this is just one example; *Fig* **la cena no fue más que un b. de muestra de la cocina local** the meal was no more than a taster *o* sample of the local cuisine (**b**) *(de aparato)* button; *(de timbre)* buzzer; **el b. de pausa/de rebobinado** the pause/rewind button; **darle al b.** to press the button
2 botones *nm inv (de hotel)* bellboy, bellhop

botonadura *nf* buttons

botonear *vi RP Fam* **b. (a alguien)** to squeal (on sb), to snitch (on sb)

Botsuana *n* Botswana

botulismo *nm* botulism

bouquet [bu'ke] *(pl bouquets) nm* bouquet

bourbon ['burβon] *(pl bourbons) nm* bourbon

boutique [bu'tik] *nf* boutique

bóveda *nf Arquit* vault; **b. celeste** firmament; **b. craneal** cranial vault

bovino, -a *adj* bovine; **ganado b.** cattle

box *nm* (**a**) *(de caballo)* stall (**b**) *(de coches)* pit; **entrar en boxes** to make a pit stop (**c**) *Am (boxeo)* boxing

boxeador, -ora *nm,f* boxer

boxear *vi* to box

boxeo *nm* boxing

bóxer *(pl bóxers) nm* (**a**) *(perro)* boxer (**b**) *(calzoncillo)* boxer shorts

boya *nf* (**a**) *(en el mar)* buoy (**b**) *(de una red)* float

boyante *adj* (**a**) *(feliz)* happy (**b**) *(próspero) (empresa, negocio)* prosperous; *(economía, comercio)* buoyant

boy scout [bojes'kaut] *(pl boy scouts) nm* Boy Scout

bozal *nm* (**a**) *(para perro)* muzzle (**b**) *Am (cabestro)* halter

bozo *nm (bigote)* down *(on upper lip)*

bracear *vi* (**a**) *(mover los brazos)* to wave one's arms about (**b**) *(nadar)* to swim

bracero *nm* (**a**) *(jornalero)* day laborer (**b**) *Am (emigrante)* wetback

braga *nf*, **bragas** *nfpl Esp (de mujer)* panties; **unas bragas** a pair of panties; *Fam* **estar hecho una b.** to be whacked; *Fam* **coger** *o* **pillar a alguien en bragas** to catch sb unprepared; **¿la capital de Chad? ¡me pillas en bragas!** the capital of Chad? you've got me there!

bragado, -a *adj (persona)* gutsy

bragazas *nm inv Fam* henpecked man

braguero *nm* truss

bragueta *nf* zipper, flies

braguetazo *nm Esp Fam* marriage for money

brahmán *nm* Brahman

brahmanismo *nm* Brahmanism

braille ['braile] *nm* Braille

brainstorming [brein'stormin] *(pl brainstormings) nm* brainstorming session

bramán *nm* Brahman

bramanismo *nm* Brahmanism

bramante *nm* cord

bramar *vi* (**a**) *(animal)* to bellow (**b**) *(mar)* to roar; *(viento)* to howl (**c**) *(persona) (de dolor)* to groan; *(de ira)* to roar

bramido *nm* (**a**) *(de animal)* bellow (**b**) *(de mar)* roar; *(viento)* howling (**c**) *(de persona) (por dolor)* groan; *(por ira)* roar

brandy *(pl brandies) nm* brandy

branquias *nfpl* gills

brasa *nf* (**a**) *(del fuego)* ember; *Culin* **a la b.** barbecued (**b**) *Esp Fam* **dar la b.** to go on and on (**a/con** at/about)

brasear *vt* to barbecue

brasero *nm* brazier

brasier *nm Carib, Col, Méx* bra

Brasil *nm* (**el**) **B.** Brazil

brasileño, -a *adj & nm,f* Brazilian

brasilero, -a *adj & nm,f RP* Brazilian

Brasilia *n* Brasilia

Bratislava *n* Bratislava

bravatas *nfpl* (**a**) *(amenazas)* threats (**b**) *(fanfarronería)* bravado

braveza *nf (de persona)* bravery; *(del viento, mar)* fierceness, fury

bravío, -a *adj (caballo, toro)* spirited; *(persona)* free-spirited; *(mar)* choppy, rough

bravo, -a 1 *adj* (**a**) *(valiente)* brave (**b**) *(violento)* fierce (**c**) *Am salvo RP (airado)* angry; **ponerse b.** to get angry (**d**) *(animal, planta)* wild (**e**) *(mar)* rough
2 *interj* **¡b.!** bravo!
3 a la brava *loc adv Méx Fam (con descuido)* in a slapdash way

bravucón, -ona 1 *adj* swaggering
2 *nm,f* braggart

bravuconada *nf* show of bravado

bravuconear *vi* to brag

bravuconería *nf* bravado

bravura *nf* (**a**) *(de persona)* bravery (**b**) *(de animal)* ferocity

braza *nf* (**a**) *Esp Dep* breaststroke; **nadar a b.** to do the breaststroke (**b**) *(medida)* fathom

brazada *nf* stroke

brazalete *nm* (**a**) *(en la muñeca)* bracelet (**b**) *(en el brazo, para nadar)* armband

brazo *nm* (**a**) *(de persona, sillón)* arm; *(de animal)* foreleg; **paseaba del b. de su novio** she was walking arm in arm with her boyfriend; **agárrate de mi b.** hold onto my arm; **cogidos del b.** arm in arm; **en brazos** in one's arms; **con los brazos abiertos** with open arms; *Fig* **echarse en brazos de alguien** to throw oneself at sb; **luchar a b. partido** *(con empeño)* to fight tooth and nail; *Fig* **quedarse de brazos cruzados** to sit back and do nothing; **no dio su b. a torcer** he didn't budge an inch, he didn't allow himself to be persuaded; **ser el b. derecho de alguien** to be sb's right-hand man (*f* woman); **b. de gitano** jelly roll
(**b**) *(de árbol, río, candelabro)* branch; *(de grúa)* boom, jib; **el b. político de ETA** the political wing of ETA
(**c**) *(trabajador)* hand
(**d**) *Geog* **b. de mar** arm *(of the sea)*

Brazzaville [bratsa'βil] *n* Brazzaville

brea *nf (sustancia)* tar; *(para barco)* pitch

break [breik] *(pl breaks) nm Dep* **punto de b.** break point

brear *vt Esp Fam (a palos)* to bash in; **b. a preguntas** to bombard with questions

brebaje *nm* concoction, foul drink

brecha *nf* (**a**) *(abertura)* hole, opening; **la b. entre ricos y pobres** the gulf *o* gap between rich and poor (**b**) *(herida)* gash; **hacerse una b. en la cabeza** to cut one's head, to split one's head open (**c**) *Mil* breach (**d**) *(expresiones)* **abrir b. en un mercado** to break into a market; **seguir en la b.** to keep at it

brécol *nm* broccoli

brega *nf (lucha)* struggle, fight

bregar [40] *vi* (**a**) *(luchar)* to struggle, to fight (**b**) *(trabajar)* to work hard (**c**) *(reñir)* to quarrel

breña *nf* scrub

Bretaña *n* Brittany

brete *nm* fix, difficulty; **estar en un b.** to be in a fix; **poner a alguien en un b.** to put sb in a difficult position

bretel *nm CSur* strap; **sin breteles** *(vestido)* strapless

bretón, -ona 1 *adj & nm,f* Breton
2 *nm (lengua)* Breton

breva *nf* (**a**) *(fruta)* early fig (**b**) *(cigarro)* flat cigar (**c**) *Esp Fam*

¡no caerá esa b.! some chance (of that happening)!

breve 1 *adj* (**a**) *(corto)* brief; **seré b.** I shall be brief; **en b.** *(pronto)* shortly; *(en pocas palabras)* in short; **en breves instantes** in a few moments (**b**) *(sílaba, vocal)* short
2 *nf Mús* breve

brevedad *nf* shortness; **a o con la mayor b.** as soon as possible

brevet *nm* (**a**) *Chile (de avión)* pilot's license (**b**) *Bol, Ecuad, Perú (de automóvil)* driver's license (**c**) *RP (de velero)* sailing license

breviario *nm* (**a**) *Rel* breviary (**b**) *(compendio)* compendium

brezal *nm* moorland, moors

brezo *nm* heather

briago, -a *adj Méx Fam* plastered, blitzed

bribón, -ona *nm,f* scoundrel, rogue

bribonada *nf* **ser una b.** to be a roguish thing to do; **bribonadas** roguery

bricolaje *nm* home improvement

brida *nf* (**a**) *(de caballo)* bridle (**b**) *(de tubo)* bracket, collar (**c**) *Med* adhesion

bridge [britʃ] *nm* bridge

brigada 1 *nm Mil* warrant officer
2 *nf* (**a**) *Mil* brigade (**b**) *(equipo)* squad, team; **b. anticorrupción** fraud squad; **b. antidisturbios/antidroga** riot/drug squad; **b. de delitos económicos** fraud squad; **b. de estupefacientes** drug squad

brigadier *nm* brigadier

brigadista *nmf Hist* = member or veteran of the International Brigades during the Spanish Civil War

brillante 1 *adj* (**a**) *(reluciente) (luz, astro)* shining; *(metal, zapatos, pelo)* shiny; *(ojos, sonrisa, diamante)* sparkling (**b**) *(magnífico)* brilliant; **el pianista estuvo b.** the pianist was outstanding
2 *nm* diamond

brillantez *nf (de persona)* brilliance; **hacer algo con b.** to do sth outstandingly

brillantina *nf* hair cream, Brylcreem®

brillar *vi también Fig* to shine; **b. por su ausencia** to be conspicuous by its/one's absence; *Fig* **b. con luz propia** to be outstanding

brillo *nm* (**a**) *(resplandor) (de luz)* brilliance; *(de estrellas)* shining; *(de zapatos)* shine; **sacar b. a** to polish, to shine (**b**) *(lucimiento)* splendor, brilliance

brilloso, -a *adj Am* shining

brincar [59] *vi (saltar)* to skip (about); **b. de alegría** to jump for joy; *Esp Fig* **está que brinca** *(enfadado)* he's hopping mad

brinco *nm* jump; **se levantó del asiento de un b.** she jumped up from her seat; **pegar o dar un b.** to jump, to give a start; **daba brincos de alegría** she was jumping for joy; **el corazón me dio un b. cuando oí su voz** my heart skipped a beat when I heard his voice; *Fig* **en un b.** in a second, quickly

brindar 1 *vi* to drink a toast; **b. por algo/alguien** to drink to sth/sb; **b. a la salud de alguien** to drink to sb's health
2 *vt* to offer; **me brindó su casa** he offered me the use of his house; **el ayuntamiento brindó todos los medios a su disposición** the city council made available all the means at its disposal; **quiero agradecer la confianza que me brindan** I would like to thank you for the confidence you are showing in me; **b. el triunfo a alguien** to dedicate one's victory to sb; **su visita me brindó la ocasión de conocerlo mejor** his visit gave me the opportunity to get to know him better
3 brindarse *vpr* **brindarse a hacer algo** to offer to do sth

brindis *nm inv* toast

brinque *etc ver* **brincar**

brío *nm (energía, decisión)* spirit, verve

brioche *nm* brioche

brioso, -a *adj* spirited, lively

brisa *nf* breeze; **b. marina** sea breeze

brisca *nf* = card game where each player gets three cards and one suit is trumps

británico, -a 1 *adj* British
2 *nm,f* British person, Briton; **los británicos** the British

brizna *nf* (**a**) *(filamento) (de hierba)* blade; *(de tabaco)* strand (**b**) *(un poco)* trace, bit

broca *nf* (drill) bit

brocado *nm* brocade

brocal *nm* curb, parapet

brocha *nf* brush; **b. de afeitar** shaving brush

brochazo *nm* brushstroke

broche *nm* (**a**) *(en collar, pulsera)* clasp, fastener (**b**) *(joya)* brooch; *Fig* **b. de oro** final flourish (**c**) *RP (grapa)* staple (**d**) *Méx, Urug (para el pelo)* barrette (**e**) *Arg (para la ropa)* peg, clothespin

brocheta *nf Culin* shish kebab; *(aguja)* skewer

brócoli *nm* broccoli

bróker *nmf* broker

broma *nf (ocurrencia, chiste)* joke; *(jugarreta)* prank, practical joke; **gastar una b. a alguien** to play a joke/prank on sb; **en o de b.** as a joke; **bromas aparte** joking apart; **entre bromas y veras** half joking; **fuera de b.** joking apart; **no estar para bromas** not to be in the mood for jokes; **tomar algo a b.** not to take sth seriously; **ni en o de b.** no way, not on your life; *Fam Irónico* **me salió la b. por 800 euros** it cost me the tidy sum of 800 euros; **b. de mal gusto** bad joke; **b. pesada** nasty practical joke

bromear *vi* to joke; **con la religión no se bromea** religion isn't something to be taken lightly

bromista 1 *adj* **ser muy b.** to be a real joker
2 *nmf* joker

bromo *nm Quím* bromine

bromuro *nm Quím* bromide

bronca *nf* (**a**) *(jaleo)* row; **armar (una) b.** to kick up a row; **buscar b.** to look for trouble (**b**) *Esp (crítica)* scolding, telling-off; **echar una b. a alguien** to tell sb off (**c**) *RP (rabia)* **me da b.** it makes me mad (**d**) *Méx Fam (dificultad)* snag, problem; **fue una b. poder mudarme** moving was no picnic

bronce *nm* (**a**) *(aleación)* bronze; **Bulgaria se llevó el b.** Bulgaria won (the) bronze (**b**) *(estatua)* bronze (statue)

bronceado, -a 1 *adj* tanned
2 *nm* tan

bronceador, -ora 1 *adj* **crema bronceadora** suntan cream
2 *nm (loción)* suntan lotion; *(crema)* suntan cream

broncear 1 *vt* to tan
2 broncearse *vpr* to get a tan

bronco, -a *adj* (**a**) *(grave) (voz)* harsh; *(tos)* throaty (**b**) *(brusco)* gruff, surly (**c**) *(tosco)* rough; *(paisaje, peñascos)* rugged

bronconeumonía *nf Med* bronchopneumonia

bronquial *adj* bronchial

bronquio *nm* bronchial tube

bronquiolo *nm Anat* bronchiole

bronquitis *nf inv* bronchitis

broquel *nm (escudo)* small shield; *Fig (amparo)* shield

brotar 1 *vi* (**a**) *(planta)* to sprout, to bud; **ya le están brotando las flores al árbol** the tree is already beginning to flower (**b**) *(agua, sangre) (suavemente)* to flow; *(con violencia)* to spout; **la sangre brotaba a borbotones de la herida** blood was gushing from the wound; **b. de** to well up out of; **le brotaron las lágrimas** tears welled up in her eyes (**c**) *(esperanza, sospechas, pasiones)* **entre los dos brotó una profunda amistad** a deep friendship sprang up between them; **brotaron sospechas de que hubiera habido un fraude** suspicions of fraud started to emerge (**d**) *(en la piel)* **le brotó un sarpullido** he broke out in a rash

2 brotarse *vpr Am (salir sarpullidos)* to come out in a rash

brote *nm (de planta)* bud, shoot; *(inicio)* sign, hint; *(de enfermedad)* outbreak; **brotes de soja** bean sprouts

broza *nf* (a) *(maleza)* brush, scrub (b) *(relleno)* waffle

bruces: de bruces *loc adv* face down; **se cayó de b.** he fell headlong, he fell flat on his face; *Fig* **darse de b. con algo/ alguien** to find oneself face-to-face with sth/sb

bruja 1 *nf* (a) *(hechicera)* witch, sorceress (b) *Fam (mujer fea)* hag; *(mujer mala)* (old) witch

2 *adj CAm, Carib, Méx (sin dinero) Fam* **estar b.** to be broke

Brujas *n* Bruges

brujería *nf* witchcraft, sorcery

brujo, -a 1 *adj (hechicero)* enchanting, captivating

2 *nm* wizard, sorcerer

brújula *nf* compass

bruma *nf (niebla)* mist; *(en el mar)* sea mist

brumoso, -a *adj* misty

Brunei *n* Brunei

bruñido *nm* polishing

bruñir *vt* to polish

brusco, -a 1 *adj* (a) *(repentino, imprevisto)* sudden, abrupt (b) *(tosco, grosero)* brusque

2 *nm,f* brusque person

Bruselas *n* Brussels

bruselense 1 *adj* of/from Brussels

2 *nmf* person from Brussels

brusquedad *nf* (a) *(imprevisión)* suddenness, abruptness (b) *(grosería)* brusqueness

brut *nm inv* brut

brutal *adj* (a) *(violento)* brutal (b) *Fam (extraordinario)* wicked, brutal

brutalidad *nf* (a) *(cualidad)* brutality (b) *(acción)* brutal act

bruto, -a 1 *adj* (a) *(violento)* rough; *(torpe)* clumsy; *(ignorante)* thick, stupid; *(maleducado)* rude (b) *(sin tratar)* **en b.** *(diamante)* uncut; *(petróleo)* crude (c) *(sueldo, peso)* gross; **gana 30.000 euros brutos al mes** she earns 30,000 euros a month gross

2 *nm,f* brute

Bs.As. *(abrev de* **Buenos Aires***)* Buenos Aires

bubónico, -a *adj Med (peste)* bubonic

bucal *adj* oral

bucanero *nm* buccaneer

Bucarest *n* Bucharest

buceador, -ora *nm,f* (underwater) diver; **b. de profundidad** deep-sea diver

bucear *vi* (a) *(en agua)* to swim underwater, to dive (b) *(investigar)* **b. en** to delve into

buceo *nm* (underwater) diving

buche *nm* (a) *(de ave)* crop (b) *(de animal)* maw (c) *Fam (de persona)* belly; **llenar el b.** to fill one's belly (d) *(trago)* **tomó un b. de agua** he took *o* drank a mouthful of water

bucle *nm* (a) *(de pelo)* curl, ringlet (b) *Aut & Inform* loop

bucólico, -a *adj* (a) *(campestre)* **un paisaje b.** a charmingly rural landscape (b) *Lit* bucolic

Buda *n pr* Buddha

Budapest *n* Budapest

budín *nm (pastel)* pudding; *Am* **b. de pan** bread pudding

budismo *nm* Buddhism

budista *adj & nmf* Buddhist

buen *ver* bueno

buenamente *adv* **hice lo que b. pude** I did what I could, I did as much as I could

buenaventura *nf*

(a) *(adivinación)* fortune; **leer** *o* **decir la b. a alguien** to tell sb's fortune (b) *(suerte)* good luck

bueno, -a

---

buen is used instead of **bueno** before masculine singular nouns (e.g. **buen hombre** good man). The comparative form of **bueno** is **mejor** (better), and the superlative form is **el mejor** (masculine) or **la mejor** (feminine) (the best).

1 *adj* (a) *(en general)* good; **buenas noticias** good news; **la cena estaba muy buena** the meal was very good; **hacer ejercicio es b. para la salud** exercise is good for your health

(b) *(bondadoso)* kind, good; **ser b. con alguien** to be good to sb; **¡sé b.!** be good!

(c) *(curado, sano)* well, all right; **ya estoy b.** I'm all right now; **todavía no estoy b. del todo** I'm not completely better *o* recovered yet; **ponerse b.** to get well

(d) *(apacible)* nice, fine; **buen tiempo** good *o* fine weather; **hizo buen tiempo** the weather was good

(e) *(uso enfático)* **tiene una buena cantidad de libros** she has a large amount of books, she has several books; **un buen susto** a real fright; **un buen día** one fine day

(f) *Fam (atractivo)* **estar b.** to quite nice, to be tasty; **¡qué b. está tu vecino!** your neighbor's gorgeous *o* a real hunk!

(g) *Irónico (muy malo)* fine; **¡buen amigo te has echado!** some friend he is!; **¡buena la has armado** *o* **hecho!** you've really gone and done it now!; *Irónico* **estaría b.** that would really cap it all; **librarse de una buena** to have a lucky *o* narrow escape; **te has metido en una buena** this is a fine mess you've got *o* gotten yourself into!; *Fig* **poner b. a alguien** to criticize sb harshly

(h) *(en saludos)* **¡buenas!** hello!; **¡buenas!, ¿qué tal?** hi *o* hello, how are you?

(i) *(en frases)* **¡buen provecho!** enjoy your meal!; **¡buen viaje!** have a good trip!; **de buen ver** good-looking, attractive; **de buenas a primeras** *(de repente)* all of a sudden; *(a simple vista)* at first sight, on the face of it; **estar de buenas** to be in a good mood; **lo b. es que...** the best thing about it is that...; **por las buenas** willingly

2 *nm,f Cine* **el b.** the goody; **los buenos siempre ganan** the good guys always win

3 *adv* (a) *(vale, de acuerdo)* all right, OK (b) *(pues)* well (c) *Am (bien)* **¡qué b.!** (that's) great!

4 *interj Col, Méx (al teléfono)* **¡b.!** hello

Buenos Aires *n* Buenos Aires

buey *(pl* bueyes*)* *nm* (a) *(mamífero)* ox (b) *(crustáceo)* edible crab

búfalo *nm* buffalo

bufanda *nf* scarf

bufar *vi (toro, caballo)* to snort; *(gato)* to hiss; *(persona)* **está que bufa** he's furious

bufé *(pl* bufés*)*, **buffet** *(pl* buffets*)* *nm* (a) *(en restaurante)* buffet (b) *(mueble)* sideboard

búfer *(pl* búfers*)* *nm Inform* buffer

bufete *nm* lawyer's practice

buffer ['bafer] *(pl* buffers*)* *nm Inform* buffer

buffet = bufé

bufido *nm* (a) *(de toro, caballo)* snort; *(de gato)* hiss (b) *Fam (de persona)* snarl of anger

bufo, -a *adj (gen) & Mús* comic

bufón *nm* buffoon, jester

bufonada *nf* jape; **bufonadas** buffoonery

bug [bʌɪ] *(pl* bugs*)* *nm Inform* bug

buga *nm Esp Fam (coche)* wheels

buganvilla *nf* bougainvillea

buhardilla *nf* (a) *(habitación)* attic (b) *(ventana)* dormer (window)

búho *nm* owl

buhonero, -a *nm,f* hawker, peddler

buitre 1 *nm* vulture

2 *adj Fam* greedy

bujía *nf Aut* spark plug

bula nf (documento) (papal) bull

bulbo nm Anat & Bot bulb; **b. raquídeo** medulla oblongata, rachidian bulb

buldog (pl **buldogs**) nm bulldog

buldózer (pl **buldozers**) nm bulldozer

bulerías nfpl = popular Andalusian song and dance

bulevar nm boulevard

Bulgaria n Bulgaria

búlgaro, -a 1 adj & nm,f Bulgarian
   2 nm (lengua) Bulgarian

bulimia nf bulimia

bulímico, -a adj bulimic

bulín nm RP Fam bachelor pad

bulla nf Fam (a) (ruido) racket, uproar; **armar b.** to kick up a racket (b) Esp (prisa) **meter b. a alguien** to hurry sb up

bullabesa nf Culin bouillabaisse

bullanga nf merrymaking

bullanguero, -a adj **ser muy b.** to love a good time, to love partying

bulldog [bul'doɣ] (pl **bulldogs**) nm bulldog

bulldozer [bul'doθer] (pl **bulldozers**) nm bulldozer

bullicio nm (de ciudad, mercado) hustle and bustle; (de multitud) hubbub

bullicioso, -a 1 adj (a) (agitado) (reunión, multitud) noisy; (calle, mercado) busy, bustling (b) (inquieto) rowdy, boisterous
   2 nm,f boisterous person

bullir vi (a) (hervir) to boil; (burbujear) to bubble (b) (multitud) to bustle; (ratas, hormigas) to swarm; (mar) to boil; **b. de** to seethe with; **la calle bullía de gente** the street was swarming with people

bulo nm false rumor

bulto 1 nm (a) (volumen) bulk, size; **hacer mucho b.** to take up a lot of space; Fig **hacer b.** to make up the numbers; **un error de b.** a glaring error; Fig **escurrir el b.** (trabajo) to shirk; (cuestión) to evade the issue (b) (abombamiento) (en rodilla, superficie) bump; (en maleta, bolsillo) bulge; **me ha salido un b. en el brazo** I've got a lump on my arm (c) (forma imprecisa) blurred shape (d) (paquete) package; (maleta) item of luggage; (fardo) bundle; **¿dónde puedo dejar mis bultos?** where can I put my luggage o bags?; **b. de mano** piece o item of hand luggage
   2 a bulto loc adv approximately, roughly

bumerán nm boomerang

bungaló (pl **bungalós**), **bungalow** [bunga'lo] (pl **bungalows**) nm bungalow

búnker nm (a) (refugio) bunker (b) Esp Pol reactionary forces

buñuelo nm Culin (dulce) doughnut; (de bacalao) dumpling; **b. de viento** doughnut

BUP [bup] nm Antes (abrev de **Bachillerato Unificado Polivalente**) = academically orientated Spanish secondary school course for pupils aged 14-17

buque nm ship; **b. de carga** cargo ship; **b. de guerra** warship; **b. mercante** merchant ship; **b. nodriza** supply ship; **b. de pasajeros** passenger ship, liner; **b. de salvamento** salvage vessel

buqué nm bouquet

burbuja nf bubble; **hacer burbujas** to bubble; **con burbujas** (bebida) fizzy; **sin burbujas** (bebida) still; **b. inmobiliaria** property bubble

burbujear vi to bubble

burbujeo nm bubbling

burdel nm brothel

Burdeos n Bordeaux

burdeos 1 adj inv maroon
   2 nm inv Bordeaux

burdo, -a adj (lenguaje, modales) crude, coarse; (tela) coarse

burgalés, -esa 1 adj of/from Burgos
   2 nm,f person from Burgos

búrger, burguer ['burɣer] nm Fam burger bar o restaurant

burgués, -esa 1 adj middle-class, bourgeois
   2 nm,f member of the middle class; Hist & Pol member of the bourgeoisie

burguesía nf middle class; Hist & Pol bourgeoisie; **alta b.** upper middle class; Hist & Pol haute bourgeoisie

Burkina Faso n Burkina Faso

burla nf (a) (mofa) taunt; **hacer b. de** to mock (b) (broma) joke (c) (engaño) trick

burladero nm Taurom = wooden board behind which the bullfighter can hide from the bull

burlador nm Casanova, Don Juan

burlar 1 vt (esquivar) to evade; (ley) to flout; **consiguió b. a sus perseguidores** she managed to outwit her pursuers; Fig **burla burlando** without anyone noticing
   2 burlarse vpr to mock; **burlarse de algo/alguien** to mock sth/sb, to make fun of sth/sb; **burlarse de las leyes** to flout the law

burlesco, -a adj (tono) jocular; Lit burlesque

burlete nm weather strip o stripping

burlón, -ona adj (a) (bromista) waggish, fond of telling jokes (b) (sarcástico) mocking

buró nm (a) (escritorio) bureau, writing desk (b) Pol executive committee (c) Méx (mesa de noche) bedside table

burocracia nf bureaucracy; **ya no hay tanta b. para sacarse el pasaporte** there isn't so much red tape involved in getting a passport any more

burócrata nmf bureaucrat

burocrático, -a adj bureaucratic

burocratización nf bureaucratization

burocratizar [14] vt to bureaucratize

burrada nf (a) (tontería) **decir/hacer una b.** to say/do something stupid; **decir burradas** to talk nonsense; **hacer burradas** to act stupidly (b) Esp Fam (cantidad) **una b. (de)** tons (of), masses (of)

burrito nm CAm, Méx burrito

burro, -a 1 adj Fam (necio) stupid, dim (b) (tosco) rough, oafish; **¡qué b. eres!** you're such an oaf! (c) (terco) pigheaded
   2 nm,f (a) (animal) donkey; Fam **no ver tres en un b.** to be as blind as a bat (b) Fam (necio) ass, dimwit (c) Fam (trabajador) **b. (de carga)** workhorse; **trabaja como una burra** she works like a slave
   3 nm (a) Carib, Méx (escalera) stepladder (b) Méx (para planchar) ironing board

bursátil adj **mercado b.** stock market

Burundi n Burundi

bus nm (a) Inform bus (b) Fam (autobús) bus; **en b.** by bus

busca 1 nf search; **(ir) en b. de** (to go) in search of; **orden de b. y captura** arrest warrant; **en b. y captura** on the run (from the police)
   2 nm Esp (buscapersonas) pager

buscador, -ora 1 nm,f (persona) hunter; **b. de oro** gold prospector
   2 nm Inform (en Internet) search engine

buscapersonas nm inv pager

buscapiés nm inv firecracker, jumping jack

buscapleitos nmf inv troubleseeker

buscar [59] **1** vt (a) (para encontrar) to look for; (provecho, beneficio propio) to seek; **busco piso en esta zona** I am looking for an apartment in this area; **estoy buscando trabajo** I'm looking for work; **se fue a b. fortuna a América** he went to seek his fortune in America
   (b) (recoger) to pick up; **voy a b. el periódico** I'm going for the paper o to get the paper; **ir a b. a alguien** to pick sb up; **pasará a buscarnos a las nueve** she'll pick us up at nine

(**c**) *(en diccionario, índice, horario)* to look up

(**d**) *(intentar conseguir)* **siempre busca quedar bien con todos** she always tries to please everybody; **no sé qué está buscando con esa actitud** I don't know what he is hoping to achieve with that attitude; **con estas medidas buscan reducir la inflación** these measures are intended to reduce inflation, with these measures they are seeking to reduce inflation

(**e**) *Inform* to search for

(**f**) *Fam (provocar)* to push, to try the patience of; **b. bronca/ camorra** to look for trouble

2 *vi* to look

3 buscarse *vpr* (**a**) *(castigo, desgracia)* **buscársela** to be asking for it (**b**) *Fam* **se está buscando problemas** she's asking for trouble; **buscarse la vida** *(ganarse el sustento)* to seek one's fortune; *(arreglárselas uno solo)* to look after oneself (**c**) **se busca camarero** *(en letrero)* waiter wanted; **se busca: pastor alemán** lost: German shepherd

buscavidas *nmf inv Fam* (**a**) *(ambicioso)* go-getter (**b**) *(entrometido)* nosy person

buscón, -ona *nm,f (estafador)* swindler

buscona *nf Fam (prostituta)* whore

buseta *nf Col, CRica, Ecuad, Ven* minibus

busque *etc ver* **buscar**

búsqueda *nf* search

busto *nm* (**a**) *(pecho)* chest; *(de mujer)* bust (**b**) *(escultura)* bust

butaca *nf* (**a**) *(mueble)* armchair (**b**) *(localidad)* seat

butacón *nm* large easy chair

Bután *n* Bhutan

butanero, -a *nm,f* = person who delivers gas cylinders

butano *nm* butane (gas)

buten: de buten *loc adv Esp Fam* wicked, terrific

butifarra *nf* = type of Catalan pork sausage

butrón *nm Esp* **método del b.** = method of carrying out a robbery involving gaining access via a hole made in the adjoining building

butronero, -a *nm,f Esp* = robber who breaks in through a hole made from inside an adjoining building

buzo *nm* (**a**) *(persona)* diver (**b**) *Arg (sudadera)* sweatshirt; *(chandal)* tracksuit

buzón *nm* (**a**) mailbox, postbox; **echar algo al b.** to mail sth, to post sth; *RP Fam* **venderle un b. a alguien** to rip sb off (**b**) *Inform (de correo electrónico)* (electronic) mailbox, e-mail address; **b. de entrada** inbox

buzoneo *nm* leafleting

bypass [bai'pas] *nm Med* heart bypass operation

byte [bait] *nm Inform* byte

C

C, c [θe] *nf (letra)* C, c

c., c/ *(abrev de* **calle**) St

c/ *(abrev de* **cuenta**) a/c

cabal 1 *adj* (**a**) *(honrado)* upright, honest (**b**) *(exacto)* exact; *(completo)* complete; **a los nueve meses cabales** at exactly nine months

   2 cabales *nmpl* **no estar en sus cabales** not to be in one's right mind

cábala *nf (doctrina)* kabbalah; *Fig* **hacer cábalas** *(conjeturas)* to speculate, to guess

cabalgadura *nf* mount

cabalgar [40] *vi* to ride

cabalgata *nf Esp* cavalcade, procession; **la c. de los Reyes Magos** = procession to celebrate the journey of the Three Kings, on January 5

cabalista *nmf* kabbalist

cabalístico, -a *adj (de cábala)* kabbalistic; *Fig (oculto)* mysterious

caballa *nf* mackerel

caballar *adj* equine, horse; *Agr* **ganado c.** horses

caballeresco, -a *adj (persona, modales)* chivalrous; *(literatura)* chivalric

caballería *nf* (**a**) *(animal)* mount, horse (**b**) *(cuerpo militar)* cavalry (**c**) **novela de c.** courtly romance

caballeriza *nf* stable

caballerizo *nm* groom, stable boy

caballero 1 *adj (cortés)* gentlemanly

   2 *nm* (**a**) *(señor)* gentleman; *(al dirigir la palabra)* sir; **ser todo un c.** to be a real gentleman; **caballeros** *(en letrero) (en aseos)* gents; *(en grandes almacenes)* menswear (**b**) *(miembro de una orden)* knight; **armar c. a alguien** to knight sb; **c. andante** knight errant (**c**) *(noble)* nobleman

caballerosidad *nf* gentlemanliness

caballeroso, -a *adj* chivalrous, gentlemanly

caballete *nm* (**a**) *(de pintor)* easel (**b**) *(de mesa)* trestle (**c**) *(de nariz)* bridge (**d**) *(de tejado)* ridge

caballito 1 *nm* small horse, pony; **llevar a alguien a c.** to give sb a piggyback ride; **c. del diablo** dragonfly; **c. de mar** sea horse

   2 caballitos *nmpl (de feria)* merry-go-round, carousel

caballo *nm* (**a**) *(animal)* horse; **montar a c.** to ride; **a c.** on horseback; *Fig* **estar a c. entre dos cosas** to be halfway between two things; **vive a c. entre Madrid y Bruselas** she lives part of the time in Madrid and part of the time in Brussels; *Prov* **a c. regalado no le mires el diente** don't look a gift horse in the mouth; **c. de batalla** *(dificultad, escollo)* bone of contention; *(objetivo, obsesión)* hobbyhorse; **c. de carreras** racehorse; **c. de Troya** Trojan Horse (**b**) *(pieza de ajedrez)* knight (**c**) *(naipe)* = card in Spanish deck with a picture of a knight, equivalent to queen in standard deck (**d**) *Tec* **c. (de fuerza** *o* **de vapor)** horsepower (**e**) *Fam (heroína)* smack, horse (**f**) *Dep* **c. con arcos** pommel horse; **c. sin arcos** vaulting horse

cabaña *nf* (**a**) *(choza)* hut, cabin (**b**) *(ganado)* livestock (**c**) *Méx (de fútbol)* goal

cabaré *(pl* **cabarés**), **cabaret** *(pl* **cabarets**) *nm* cabaret

cabaretera *nf* cabaret artist(e)

cabás *(pl* **cabases**) *nm* = plastic/metal case with handle used by schoolgirls for carrying lunch, etc

cabecear *vi* (**a**) *(dormitar)* to nod (off) (**b**) *(persona) (negando)* to shake one's head (**c**) *(caballo)* to toss its head (**d**) *(en fútbol)* to head the ball (**e**) *(balancearse) (barco)* to pitch

cabeceo *nm (con sueño)* nodding; *(de caballo)* tossing

cabecera *nf* (**a**) *(de fila, de mesa)* head; *(de cama)* headboard (**b**) *Esp (de texto)* heading; *(de periódico)* masthead (**c**) *(de río)* headwaters

cabecero *nm (de cama)* headboard

cabecilla *nmf* ringleader

cabellera *nf* head of hair; **cortar la c. a** to scalp

cabello *nm* hair; *Culin* **c. de ángel** = preserve made of strands of pumpkin in syrup

cabelludo, -a *adj* hairy

caber [12] *vi* (**a**) *(entrar, pasar)* to fit (**en** in *o* into); **c. por** to go through; **caben cinco personas** there is room for five people; **no cabía ni un alfiler** the place was packed; **no me cabe en el dedo** it won't fit (on) my finger; **no quiero postre, no me cabe nada más** I don't want a dessert, I couldn't eat another thing, I've no room left for a dessert

   (**b**) *Mat* **nueve entre tres caben a tres** three into nine goes three times; **tres entre cinco no caben** five into three won't go

   (**c**) *(ser posible)* to be possible; **cabe la posibilidad de que no pueda venir** (it is possible that) he might not come; **cabe destacar que…** it's worth pointing out that…; **cabe preguntarse si…** one might ask whether…

   (**d**) *(corresponder)* **c. a alguien** to be sb's duty *o* honor, to fall to sb

   (**e**) *(expresiones)* **dentro de lo que cabe** *(en cierto modo)* up to a point, to some extent; **no c. en sí de alegría** to be beside oneself with joy

cabestrante *nm* capstan

cabestrillo *nm* **en c.** in a sling

cabestro *nm* (**a**) *(cuerda)* halter (**b**) *(animal)* leading ox

cabeza 1 *nf* (**a**) *(de persona, animal, clavo, fémur)* head; **me duele la c.** I've got a headache; **lavarse la c.** to wash one's hair; **por c.** per head; **tirarse de c. (al agua)** to dive (into the water); **c. de ajo** head of garlic; *(gen) & Inform* **c. (lectora)** head; **c. nuclear** nuclear warhead

   (**b**) *(población)* **c. de partido** ≃ county seat

   (**c**) *(expresiones)* **c. abajo** upside down; **c. arriba** the right way up; **a la** *o* **en c.** *(en competición)* in front, in the lead; *(en lista)* at the top *o* head; **alzar** *o* **levantar c.** to get back on one's feet, to recover; **andar** *o* **estar mal de la c.** to be funny in the head; **no me cabe en la c.** I simply can't understand it; *Fam* **calentar la c. a alguien** to drive sb mad; **con la c. (bien) alta** with one's head held high; **de c.** at once, without thinking twice; **ir de c. a** to head straight for; **meterle algo en la c. a alguien** to put sth into sb's head; **se le ha metido en la c. que…** he has got it into his head that…; **obrar con c.** to use one's head; **se me pasó por la c.** it crossed my mind; **perder la c.** to lose one's head; **romperse la c.** to rack *o* cudgel one's brains; **sentar la c.** to settle down; **se le subió a la c.** it went to his head; **tener la c. llena de pájaros** to have one's head in the clouds; **esa chica tiene mucha c.** that girl has got brains; **traer de c. a alguien** to drive sb mad; **venir a la c.** to come to mind

2 *nmf Fam* **c. de chorlito** scatterbrain; *Fam* **es un c. cuadrada** *o* **dura** he's got his ideas and he won't listen to anyone else; **c. de familia** head of the family; *Pol* **c. de lista** = person who heads a party's list of candidates; **c. rapada** skinhead; *Dep* **c. de serie** seed; **c. de turco** scapegoat

cabezada *nf* **(a)** *(de sueño)* **dar cabezadas** to nod off; **echar** *o* **dar una c.** to have a nap **(b)** *(golpe)* headbutt

cabezal *nm* **(a)** *(de aparato)* head **(b)** *(almohada)* bolster

cabezazo *nm (golpe)* (con la cabeza) headbutt; *(en la cabeza)* blow *o* bump on the head; *(en fútbol)* header

cabezón, -ona 1 *adj* **(a)** *(persona)* **ser c.** *(de cabeza grande)* to have a big head; *(terco)* to be pigheaded *o* stubborn **(b)** *Fam (vino)* rough; **este vino es muy c.** this wine will give you a nasty hangover

2 *nm,f (terco)* pigheaded *o* stubborn person

cabezonería *nf Fam* pigheadedness, stubbornness

cabezota *Fam* **1** *adj* pigheaded, stubborn

2 *nmf* pigheaded *o* stubborn person

cabezudo, -a 1 *adj Fam* pigheaded, stubborn

2 *nm,f Fam* pigheaded *o* stubborn person

3 cabezudos *nmpl (en fiesta)* = giant-headed carnival figures

cabida *nf* capacity; **un auditorio con c. para 5.000 espectadores** an auditorium which has room for *o* holds 5,000 people; **dar c. a, tener c. para** to hold, to have room for; **dar c. a** to allow; **tener c. en** to have a place in

cabildo *nm* **(a)** *(municipio)* ≃ city council **(b)** *(de eclesiásticos)* chapter **(c)** *(sala)* chapter house

cabina *nf (cuartito)* booth, cabin; *(de avión) (del piloto)* flight deck, cockpit; *(de los pasajeros)* (passenger) cabin; *(de camión)* cab; **c. de comentaristas** *(en estadio)* commentary booth; **c. electoral** polling *o* voting booth; **c. espacial** space cabin; **c. de proyección** projection booth; **c. telefónica** *(con puerta)* phone booth

cabinero, a *nm,f Col* flight attendant

cabizbajo, -a *adj* crestfallen, downcast

cable *nm* **(a)** *Elec & Inform (para conectar)* cable, lead; *(dentro de aparato)* wire; *Fam Fig* **se le cruzaron los cables** *(se confundió)* he got mixed up; **se le cruzaron los cables y la pegó** in a moment of madness, he hit her; *Fam Fig* **echar un c.** to help out, to lend a hand **(b)** *(de puente)* cable **(c)** *(de fibra óptica)* cable; **televisión por c.** cable television; **c. de fibra óptica** fiber-optic cable

cableado, -a *Inform* **1** *adj* hardwired

2 *nm* hardwiring

cablegrafiar [32] *vt* to cable

cablegrama *nm* cable, telegram

cablevisión *nf* cable television

cabo 1 *nm* **(a)** *(cuerda)* rope **(b)** *Mil* corporal; **c. primero** = military rank between corporal and sergeant **(c)** *Geog* cape; **el C. de Buena Esperanza** the Cape of Good Hope **(d)** *(trozo)* bit, piece; *(trozo final)* stub, stump; *(de cuerda)* end **(e)** *(expresiones)* **al fin y al c.** after all; **atar cabos** to put two and two together; **c. suelto** loose end; **no dejar ningún c. suelto** to tie up all the loose ends; **de c. a rabo** from beginning to end; **estar al c. de la calle** to be well-informed; **llevar algo a c.** to carry sth out

2 al cabo de *loc prep (después de)* after; **al c. de una semana** after a week, a week later

cabotaje *nm* coastal shipping

Cabo Verde *n* Cape Verde

caboverdiano, -a *adj & nm,f* Cape Verdean

cabra *nf* goat; **c. de angora** angora goat; **c. montés** wild goat; **pie** *o* **pata de c.** crowbar, jimmy; *Fam* **estar como una c.** to be out of one's head; *Prov* **la c. siempre tira al monte** you can't make a leopard change his spots

cabrales *nm inv* = Asturian cheese similar to Roquefort

cabré *etc ver* **caber**

cabrear *muy Fam* **1** *vt* **c. a alguien** to piss sb off

2 cabrearse *vpr* to get really pissed (**con** with)

cabreo *nm muy Fam* rage, fit; **agarrar** *o Esp* **coger un c.** to get really pissed off *o* pissed

cabrero, -a *nm,f* goatherd

cabrestante *nm* capstan

cabría *etc ver* **caber**

cabrilla *nf* **(a)** *(pez)* cabrilla **(b)** *(ola)* **cabrillas** white horses, foam-crested waves

cabrío *adj* **macho c.** billy goat

cabriola *nf* prance; **hacer cabriolas** to prance around

cabriolé *nm* **(a)** *(automóvil)* convertible **(b)** *(carruaje)* cabriolet

cabritas *nfpl Chile* popcorn

cabritilla *nf* kid, kidskin

cabrito *nm* **(a)** *(animal)* kid (goat) **(b)** *Fam Euf (insulto)* son of a gun

cabro, -a *nm,f Chile Fam* kid

cabrón, -ona 1 *adj* **(a)** *Vulg* **¡qué c. eres!** you bastard! **(b)** *Méx muy Fam (difícil)* goddamn difficult; **el examen estuvo bien c.** the exam was a bitch

2 *nm,f* **(a)** *Vulg (insulto)* bastard, *f* bitch, asshole **(b)** *Méx Fam (genio)* whiz, ace **(c)** *Méx muy Fam (tío)* guy

3 *nm* **(a)** *Vulg (cornudo)* cuckold **(b)** *(animal)* billy goat

cabronada *nf Vulg* **hacerle una c. a alguien** to be a bastard to sb

cabronazo *nm Vulg* bastard

cabuya *nf CAm, Col,Ven* rope

caca *nf Fam* **(a)** *(excremento)* poop; **hacer c.** to do a poop; *Esp* **una c. de vaca** a cow pie **(b)** *(cosa sucia)* nasty *o* dirty thing **(c)** *(cosa mala)* **este libro es una c.** this book is garbage

cacahuete, *CAm, Méx,* **cacahuate** *nm* **(a)** *(fruto)* peanut **(b)** *(planta)* peanut

cacao *nm* **(a)** *(bebida) (caliente)* cocoa; *(fría)* chocolate milk **(b)** *(semilla)* cocoa (bean) **(c)** *(árbol)* cacao **(d)** *(para labios)* lip salve **(e)** *Fam (confusión)* chaos, mess; *(jaleo)* fuss, rumpus; **c. mental** mental confusion; **tener un c. mental** to be at sixes and sevens

cacarear 1 *vt Fam* **(a)** *(jactarse de)* to boast about **(b)** *(pregonar)* to blab about

2 *vi (gallo)* to cluck, to cackle

cacareo *nm* clucking

cacatúa *nf* **(a)** *(ave)* cockatoo **(b)** *Fam (mujer vieja)* old bat

cace *etc ver* **cazar**

cacereño, -a 1 *adj* of/from Cáceres

2 *nm,f* person from Cáceres

Cáceres *n* Cáceres

cacería *nf (a caballo)* hunt; *(con fusiles)* shoot

cacerola *nf* pot, pan

cacerolear *vi RP* = to protest (against government economic policy) by banging on pots and pans to complain about food shortages

cacha *nf* **(a)** *Fam (muslo)* thigh **(b)** *(mango) (de cuchillo)* handle; *(de pistola)* butt

cachaco, -a 1 *adj* **(a)** *Col (de Bogotá)* of/from Bogotá **(b)** *Andes,Ven* foppish

2 *nm,f Col (de Bogotá)* person from Bogotá

cachalote *nm* sperm whale

cachar *vt* (**a**) *CAm, Ecuad, RP (burlarse de)* to tease (**b**) *Am (cornear)* to gore (**c**) *Nic, RP Fam (agarrar)* to grab (**d**) *Am Fam (sorprender, atrapar)* to catch (**e**) *CSur Fam (entender)* to understand, to get (**f**) *CAm Fam (robar)* to swipe, to pinch

cacharrazo *nm Fam* thump; **pegarse un c.** *(al caer)* to bang oneself; *(en coche)* to have a smash

cacharrería *nf* = store selling terracotta cookware, flowerpots etc

cacharro *nm* (**a**) *(recipiente)* pot; **fregar los cacharros** to do the dishes (**b**) *Fam (trasto)* piece of junk; **tendremos que tirar todos estos cacharros** we'll have to throw all this junk out (**c**) *Fam (máquina)* crock; *(coche)* jalopy

cachas *Esp Fam* **1** *adj inv* **estar c.** to be well-built

2 *nm inv (hombre fuerte)* he-man, strong man

cachaza *nf Fam* **tener c.** to be laid-back

caché *(pl* **cachés**), **cachet** [ka'tʃe] *(pl* **cachets**) *nm* (**a**) *(tarifa de artista)* fee (**b**) *(distinción)* cachet (**c**) *Inform* **(memoria) c.** cache (memory)

cachear *vt* to frisk

cachemir *nm,* **cachemira** *nf* cashmere

Cachemira *n* Kashmir

cacheo *nm* **someter a alguien a un c.** to frisk sb

cachet = **caché**

cachetada *nf Fam* slap

cachete *nm* (**a**) *(moflete)* chubby cheek (**b**) *(bofetada)* slap

cachetear *vt* to slap

cachimba *nf* pipe

cachiporra *nf Fam (garrote)* club, cudgel; *(de policía)* truncheon

cachirulo *nm* (**a**) *(chisme)* thingamajig (**b**) *(pañuelo)* = headscarf worn by men as part of traditional Aragonese costume

cachivache *nm Fam* knickknack

cacho *nm* (**a**) *Fam (pedazo)* piece, bit (**b**) *Andes,Ven (asta)* horn (**c**) *Esp Fam (como intensificador)* **¡c. tonto!** you idiot!

cachondearse *vpr Esp Fam* **c. de alguien** to make a fool out of sb

cachondeo *nm Esp Fam* (**a**) *(diversión)* **ser un c.** to be a laugh; **irse de c.** to go out on the town (**b**) *Pey (cosa poco seria)* joke; **tomarse algo a c.** to treat sth as a joke

cachondo, -a 1 *adj* (**a**) *Esp Fam (divertido)* **ser c.** to be funny (**b**) *Esp, Méx muy Fam (excitado)* **estar c.** to be horny; **poner c.** to turn on; **ponerse c.** to get horny *o* turned on

2 *nm,f Esp Fam* **es un c. (mental)** he's always fooling around

cachorro, -a *nm,f (de perro)* pup, puppy; *(de gato)* kitten; *(de león, lobo, oso)* cub

cacique *nm* (**a**) *(jefe local)* cacique, local political boss; *Fig Pey (déspota)* petty tyrant (**b**) *(jefe indio)* chief, cacique

caciquil *adj Fig Pey* despotic

caciquismo *nm* caciquism

caco *nm Fam* thief

cacofonía *nf* cacophony

cacofónico, -a *adj* cacophonous

cacto *nm,* **cactus** *nm inv* cactus

cacumen *nm Fam (ingenio)* brains, wits

CAD [kað] *nm (abrev de* **computer aided design***)* CAD

cada *adj inv* (**a**) *(en general)* each; *(con números, tiempo)* every; **c. dos meses** every two months; **c. cosa a su tiempo** one thing at a time; **c. cual** each one, everyone; **¿c. cuánto?** how often?; **c. uno de** each of; **c. uno a lo suyo** everyone should get on with their own business; **c. vez** every time, each time (**b**) *(valor progresivo)* **c. vez más** more and more; **c. vez más largo** longer and longer; **c. día más** more and more each

day (**c**) *(valor enfático)* such; **¡se pone c. sombrero!** she wears such hats!; **¡tiene c. cosa!** the things he comes up with!

cadalso *nm* scaffold

cadáver *nm* corpse, (dead) body; **por encima de mi c.** over my dead body

cadavérico, -a *adj* cadaverous; *(pálido)* deathly pale

caddy *(pl* **caddies***) nm* caddy

cadena *nf* (**a**) *(de eslabones)* chain; **reacción en c.** chain reaction; *Aut* **cadenas** (tire) chains; *Fig* **rompió sus cadenas** he broke out of his chains; **tirar de la c.** *(de lavabo)* to flush the toilet, to pull the toilet chain; **c. alimentaria** *o* **alimenticia** food chain; **c. hotelera** hotel chain; **c. montañosa** mountain range; **c. perpetua** life imprisonment; **c. de tiendas** chain of stores (**b**) *TV* channel; *Rad* station; **¿en qué c. dan la película?** what channel is the movie on? (**c**) *(de proceso industrial)* line; **c. de montaje** assembly line; **c. de producción** production line (**d**) *(aparato de música)* **c. (de música** *o* **musical)** sound system

cadencia *nf* rhythm, cadence

cadencioso, -a *adj* rhythmical

cadeneta *nf* chain stitch

cadera *nf* hip

cadete *nm* cadet

cadie *nm* caddy

cadmio *nm Quím* cadmium

caducado, -a *adj (carné, pasaporte)* out-of-date; *(alimento, medicamento)* past its use-by date

caducar [59] *vi (carné, ley, pasaporte)* to expire; *(alimento, medicamento)* to pass its use-by date

caducidad *nf* expiry; **fecha de c.** *(de carné, pasaporte)* expiry date; *(de alimento, medicamento)* use-by date

caducifolio, -a *adj* deciduous

caduco, -a *adj* (**a**) *(persona)* decrepit; *(idea, moda)* outmoded; *(perecedero)* perishable (**b**) *Bot* **de hoja caduca** deciduous

caduque *etc ver* **caducar**

caer [13] **1** *vi* (**a**) *(hacia abajo)* to fall; *(diente, pelo)* to fall out; **tropezó y cayó al suelo** she tripped and fell (over *o* down); **c. de un tejado/árbol** to fall from a roof/tree; **c. rodando por la escalera** to fall down the stairs; **dejar c. algo** *(objeto)* to drop sth

(**b**) *(lluvia, nieve)* to fall; **cayeron cuatro gotas** there were a few spots of rain

(**c**) *(sol)* to go down, to set; **al c. el día** *o* **la tarde** at dusk; **al c. el sol** at sunset

(**d**) *Esp (estar, quedar)* **cae cerca de aquí** it's not far from here; **eso cae fuera de mis competencias** that is *o* falls outside my remit

(**e**) *(darse cuenta)* **c. (en algo)** *(recordar)* to be able to remember (sth); **no dije nada porque no caí** I didn't say anything because it didn't occur to me to do so; **¡ahora caigo!** *(lo entiendo)* I see it now!; *(lo recuerdo)* now I remember!; *Esp* **no caigo** I give up, I don't know; **c. en la cuenta** *(entender)* to realize, to understand

(**f**) *(coincidir) (fecha)* **c.en** to fall on; **cae en domingo** it falls on a Sunday

(**g**) *(picar) (en trampa, broma)* to fall for it

(**h**) *Am (visitar)* to drop in

(**i**) *(expresiones)* **c. (muy) bajo** to sink (very) low; **c. bien/mal** *(comentario, noticia)* to go down well/badly; **me cae bien/mal** *(persona)* I like/don't like him; **c. sobre alguien** *(ladrón)* to pounce *o* fall upon sb; **la desgracia cayó sobre él** he was overtaken by misfortune; **se proseguirá con la investigación caiga quien caiga** the investigation will proceed no matter who might be implicated *o* even if it means that heads will roll; **dejarse c. por casa de alguien** to drop by sb's house; **dejar c. que** *(comentar)* to let drop that; **estar al**

c. *(persona)* to be about to arrive; *(acontecimiento)* to be about to happen

2 caerse *vpr* **(a)** *(persona)* to fall over o down; **caerse de algo** to fall from sth **(b)** *(objeto)* to drop, to fall; *(árbol)* to fall; **se me cayó el libro** I dropped the book **(c)** *(diente, pelo)* to fall out; *(botón)* to fall off; *(cuadro)* to fall down; **se me ha caído un diente** one of my teeth has fallen out **(d)** *(falda, pantalones)* to fall down; **se te caen los pantalones** your pants are falling down **(e)** *Fam Inform (red de ordenadores)* to go down; **la red se ha caído** the network is down

café 1 *nm* **(a)** *(bebida)* coffee; **c. americano** large weak black coffee; **c. cortado** coffee with a dash of milk; **c. expreso** expresso; **c. instantáneo** o **soluble** instant coffee; **c. irlandés** Irish coffee; **c. con leche** coffee with milk; **c. molido** ground coffee; *Am* **c. negro** black coffee; *Andes* **c. perfumado** coffee with alcohol; *Esp* **c. solo**, *Andes, Ven* **c. tinto** black coffee **(b)** *(establecimiento)* café

2 *adj inv (color)* coffee-colored

cafeína *nf* caffeine

cafetal *nm* coffee plantation

cafetera *nf* **(a)** *(italiana)* = screw-together stove-top coffee percolator; *(eléctrica)* (filter) coffee machine; *(en bares)* expresso machine; **c. de émbolo** French press **(b)** *Fam (aparato viejo)* piece of junk

cafetería *nf* cafe

cafetero, -a 1 *adj* **(a)** *(de café)* coffee; *(país)* coffee-producing; **producción cafetera** coffee production **(b)** *(bebedor de café)* fond of coffee

2 *nm,f* *(cultivador)* coffee grower; *(comerciante)* coffee merchant

cafeto *nm* coffee bush

cafiche *nm* *Perú Fam* pimp

caficultor, -ora *nm,f CAm, Col, Méx* coffee grower

cafre 1 *adj* brutish

2 *nmf* brute

cagada *nf* **(a)** *muy Fam (equivocación)* foul-up **(b)** *Fam (excremento)* shit

cagado, -a *nm,f muy Fam (cobarde)* yellow-belly, chicken

cagalera *nf Fam (diarrea)* the runs

cagar [40] **1** *vi Fam (defecar)* to shit, to crap

2 *vt muy Fam* **cagarla** *(estropear)* to ball (it) up; **¡la has cagado!** *(estás en un lío)* you're in deep shit o up shit creek

3 cagarse *vpr Fam* to crap oneself; *Vulg* **¡me cago en la hostia!** fucking hell!; **¡me cago en diez** o **en la mar** o **en la leche!** goddamn it!; *muy Fam* **hace un frío que te cagas** it's goddamn freezing!

cagarruta *nf* dropping

cagón, -ona *adj Fam* **(a)** *(que caga)* shitty **(b)** *(miedica)* chicken, cowardly

cague 1 *ver* **cagar**

2 *nm Fam (miedo)* **¡me entró un c.!** I was scared as hell!

cagueta *Fam* **1** *adj* chicken, cowardly

2 *nmf* chicken, coward

caída *nf* **(a)** *(de hojas, persona, imperio)* fall; *(de diente, pelo)* loss; **a la c. de la tarde** at nightfall; **c. libre** free fall **(b)** *(de paro, precios, terreno)* drop **(de in) (c)** *(de tela, vestido)* drape **(d)** *Fam Inform (de red de ordenadores)* crash

caído, -a 1 *adj* **(a)** *(árbol, hoja)* fallen **(b)** *(decaído)* low

2 *nmpl* **los caídos** the fallen

caigo *ver* **caer**

caimán *nm* alligator, cayman

Caín *n pr* Cain; *Fam Fig* **pasar las de C.** to have a hell of a time

Cairo *nm* **El C.** Cairo

caja *nf* **(a)** *(recipiente)* box; *(para transporte, embalaje)* crate; **una c. de cervezas** a crate of beer; **c. de cambios** gearbox; **c. de cerillas** matchbox, box of matches; *Elec* **c. de herramientas** toolbox; **c. de música** music box; **c. negra** black box, flight

recorder; *Fig* **la c. de Pandora** Pandora's box; *Fam Fig* **la c. tonta** the box, the boob tube; **c. torácica** thorax **(b)** *(para dinero)* cash box; *(en tienda, supermercado)* till; *(en banco)* cashier's desk; *Com* **hacer c.** to count the day's cash; *Esp* **c. de ahorros** savings bank; **c. fuerte** o **de caudales** safe, strongbox; **c. rápida** express checkout; **c. registradora** cash register **(c)** *(ataúd)* coffin **(d)** *(de violín, guitarra)* body

cajero, -a 1 *nm,f (en tienda)* cashier; *(en banco)* teller

2 *nm* **c. (automático)** ATM, automated teller machine, cash dispenser

cajetilla *nf (de cigarrillos)* pack

cajista *nmf Imprenta* typesetter

cajón *nm (de mueble)* drawer; *Fig* **c. de sastre** muddle, jumble; *Fam Fig* **eso es de c.** that goes without saying

cajonera *nf* chest of drawers

cajuela *nf CAm, Méx (maletero)* trunk

cal *nf* **(a)** *(pintura)* whitewash **(b)** *(en polvo)* lime; **el agua tiene mucha c.** the water is very hard; **c. viva** lime; **cerrar a c. y canto** to shut tight o firmly; **con este hombre, es una de c. y otra de arena** you never know with that man, he's nice one minute and horrible the next

cala *nf* **(a)** *(bahía pequeña)* cove **(b)** *(del barco)* hold **(c)** *(de fruta)* sample slice **(d)** *Bot* arum lily **(e)** *Esp Antes Fam (dinero)* peseta

calabacín *nm*, *Méx* **calabacita** *nf* zucchini

calabaza *nf* pumpkin, gourd; *Fam Fig* **dar calabazas a alguien** *(a pretendiente)* to turn sb down; *(en exámenes)* to fail o flunk sb

calabobos *nm inv* drizzle

calabozo *nm* cell

calada *nf* **(a)** *(inmersión)* soaking **(b)** *Esp (de cigarrillo)* drag; **dar una c.** to take a drag

caladero *nm* fishing grounds, fishery

calado, -a 1 *adj* **(a)** *(empapado)* soaked; **c. hasta los huesos** soaked to the skin **(b)** *(en costura)* embroidered *(with openwork)*

2 *nm* **(a)** *Náut* draft **(b)** *(bordado)* openwork

calafatear *vt* to caulk

calamar *nm* squid; **calamares en su tinta** squid cooked in its own ink; **calamares a la romana** squid rings fried in batter

calambre *nm* **(a)** *(descarga eléctrica)* (electric) shock **(b)** *(contracción muscular)* cramp; **me dio un c. en la pierna** I got a cramp in my leg

calamidad *nf* calamity; **pasar calamidades** to suffer great hardship; *Fig* **ser una c.** to be a dead loss

calamitoso, -a *adj* calamitous

cálamo *nm* **(a)** *(planta)* calamus **(b)** *(pluma)* pen

calandria *nf (pájaro)* calandra lark

calaña *nf Pey* **de esa c.** of that ilk

calar 1 *vt* **(a)** *(empapar)* to soak **(b)** *(adivinar) (persona)* to see through **(c)** *(gorro, sombrero)* to jam on **(d)** *(fruta)* to cut a sample of **(e)** *(perforar)* to perforate, to pierce

2 *vi* **(a)** *Náut* to draw **(b)** *(ser permeable)* **estos zapatos calan** these shoes let in water; *Fig* **c. hondo en** *(penetrar)* to have a great impact on

3 calarse *vpr* **(a)** *(empaparse)* to get soaked **(b)** *Esp (motor)* to stall

calato, -a *adj Perú (desnudo)* naked

calavera 1 *nf* **(a)** *(cráneo)* skull **(b)** *Méx Aut* **calaveras** taillights **(c)** *Méx (dulce)* sugar skull

2 *nm (libertino)* rake

calcado, -a *adj* traced; **ser c. a alguien** to be the spitting image of sb

calcamonía *nf Fam* transfer, decal

calcañal, calcañar *nm* heel

calcar [59] *vt* **(a)** *(dibujo)* to trace **(b)** *(imitar)* to copy

calcáreo, -a *adj (terreno)* chalky; **aguas calcáreas** hard water

calce 1 *ver* **calzar**
  2 *nm (cuña)* wedge
calceta *nf* stocking; **hacer c.** to knit
calcetar *vi* to knit
calcetín *nm* sock
calcificación *nf* calcification
calcificarse [59] *vpr* to calcify
calcinación *nf* burning
calcinado, -a *adj* charred, burned
calcinar *vt* to burn, to char
calcio *nm Quím* calcium
calco *nm* (**a**) *(reproducción)* tracing; **papel de c.** carbon paper (**b**) *(imitación)* carbon copy; **es un c. de** it's a carbon copy of (**c**) *Ling* calque, loan translation
calcografía *nf* chalcography
calcomanía *nf* transfer, decal
calculador, -ora *adj también Fig* calculating
calculadora *nf* calculator; **c. de bolsillo** pocket calculator; **c. programable** programmable calculator
calcular *vt* (**a**) *(cantidades)* to calculate; **c. mal** to miscalculate (**b**) *(suponer)* to reckon; **le calculo sesenta años** I reckon he's about sixty (**c**) *(pensar, considerar)* **está todo cuidadosamente calculado** everything has been carefully worked out; **no calculó las consecuencias de sus actos** he didn't foresee the consequences of his actions (**d**) *(imaginar)* to imagine; **calcula la sorpresa que se llevó cuando se lo dijimos** just imagine how surprised he was when we told him
cálculo *nm* (**a**) *(operación)* calculation; **hacer cálculos mentales** to do mental arithmetic; **hacer cálculos** to do some calculations (**b**) *(ciencia)* calculus; **c. diferencial/infinitesimal/integral** differential/infinitesimal/integral calculus (**c**) *(evaluación)* estimate; **c. de probabilidades** probability theory (**d**) *Med* stone, calculus; **c. biliar** gallstone; **c. renal** kidney stone
Calcuta *n* Calcutta
caldas *nfpl* hot springs
caldear *vt* (**a**) *(calentar)* to heat (up) (**b**) *(excitar)* to warm up, to liven up
caldera *nf* boiler; **c. de vapor** steam boiler
caldereta *nf (de pescado)* fish stew; *(de carne)* meat stew
calderilla *nf* small change
caldero *nm* cauldron
calderón *nm Mús* pause
caldo *nm* (**a**) *(para cocinar)* stock; *(sopa)* broth; *Esp Fam Fig* **poner a alguien a c.** *(criticar)* to criticize sb; *(reñir)* to give sb a telling off (**b**) *(vino)* wine (**c**) **c. de cultivo** *Biol* culture medium; *Fig (condición idónea)* breeding ground
caldoso, -a *adj (comida)* with lots of stock; **estar demasiado c.** to be watery
calé *adj & nmf* gypsy
calefacción *nf* heating; **c. central** central heating
calefaccionar *vt CSur* to heat (up), to warm (up)
calefactor *nm* heater
calefón *nm CSur* water heater
caleidoscopio *nm* kaleidoscope
calendario *nm* calendar; **c. escolar/laboral** school/working year
caléndula *nf* calendula, pot marigold
calentador *nm* (**a**) *(aparato)* heater; **c. de agua** water heater (**b**) *(prenda)* **calentadores** leg warmers
calentamiento *nm* (**a**) *(subida de temperatura)* heating; **c. global** global warming (**b**) *(ejercicios)* warm-up
calentar [3] **1** *vt* (**a**) *(subir la temperatura de)* to heat (up), to warm (up); *Fig* **c. motores** to warm up (**b**) *(animar)* to liven up (**c**) *Fam (pegar)* to hit, to strike; **¡te voy a c.!** you'll feel the

back of my hand! (**d**) *Fam (sexualmente)* to turn on (**e**) *Fam (agitar)* to make angry, to annoy; **¡me están calentando con tanta provocación!** all their provocation is getting me worked up!
  2 *vi* (**a**) *(dar calor)* to give off heat (**b**) *(entrenarse)* to warm up
  3 calentarse *vpr* (**a**) *(por calor) (persona)* to warm oneself, to get warm; *(cosa)* to heat up (**b**) *Fam (sexualmente)* to get horny (**c**) *Fam (agitarse)* to get angry *o* annoyed
calentón *nm* **dar un c. al arroz** to heat up the rice
calentura *nf* (**a**) *(fiebre)* fever, temperature (**b**) *(herida)* cold sore
calenturiento, -a *adj* feverish; **tener una imaginación calenturienta** *(incontrolada)* to have a wild imagination; *(sexualmente)* to have a dirty mind
calesa *nf* calash
calesita *nfpl RP* merry-go-round, carousel
calibrado *nm,* **calibración** *nf* (**a**) *(medida)* calibration (**b**) *(de arma)* boring
calibrador *nm* calipers
calibrar *vt* (**a**) *(medir)* to calibrate, to gauge (**b**) *(dar calibre a) (arma)* to bore (**c**) *(juzgar, sopesar)* to gauge
calibre *nm* (**a**) *(diámetro) (de pistola)* caliber; *(de alambre)* gauge; *(de tubo)* bore (**b**) *(instrumento)* gauge (**c**) *(tamaño)* size; *(importancia)* importance, significance
calidad *nf* (**a**) *(de producto, servicio)* quality; **un género de (buena) c.** a quality product; **la relación c.-precio** value (for money); **c. de imagen** image quality; **c. de vida** quality of life (**b**) *(clase)* class (**c**) *(condición)* **en c. de** in one's capacity as
cálido, -a *adj* warm
calidoscopio *nm* kaleidoscope
calientapiernas *nmpl* leg warmers
calientapiés *nm inv* foot warmer
calientaplatos *nm inv* hotplate
calientapollas *nf inv Esp Vulg* prick-teaser
caliente 1 *ver* **calentar**
  2 *adj* (**a**) *(a alta temperatura)* hot; *(templado)* warm; *Fig* **en c.** in the heat of the moment (**b**) *(acalorado)* heated (**c**) *Fam (excitado)* horny
caliento *etc ver* **calentar**
califa *nm* caliph
califato *nm* caliphate
calificación *nf Educ* grade
calificado, -a *adj* (**a**) *(importante)* eminent (**b**) *(apto)* qualified
calificar [59] *vt* (**a**) *(denominar)* **c. a alguien de algo** to call sb sth, to describe sb as sth (**b**) *Educ* to grade; **c. a alguien con un suspenso** to fail sb, to give sb a failing grade (**c**) *Gram* to qualify
calificativo, -a 1 *adj* qualifying
  2 *nm* epithet
caligrafía *nf* (**a**) *(arte)* calligraphy (**b**) *(letra)* handwriting
calígrafo, -a *nm,f* calligrapher
calima, calina *nf* haze, mist
calimocho *nm Esp Fam* = drink comprising red wine and cola
calina = **calima**
calipso *nm* calypso
cáliz *nm* (**a**) *Rel* chalice (**b**) *Bot* calyx
caliza *nf* limestone
calizo, -a *adj* chalky
callado, -a *adj* **estar c.** to be quiet *o* silent; **ser c.** to be quiet *o* reserved
callampa *Chile* **1** *nf (seta)* mushroom
  2 callampas *nfpl* shantytown
callandito *adv Fam* on the quiet

callar 1 *vi* (**a**) *(no hablar)* to keep quiet, to be silent; **quien calla otorga** silence signifies consent (**b**) *(dejar de hablar)* to be quiet, to stop talking; **hacer c. a alguien** to silence sb; **mandar c. a alguien** to tell sb to shut up; **¡calla!** shut up!; **¡calla, si eso me lo dijo a mí también!** guess what, he said that to me, too!

2 *vt* (**a**) *(ocultar)* to keep quiet about (**b**) *(acallar)* to silence

3 callarse *vpr* (**a**) *(no hablar)* to keep quiet, to be silent (**b**) *(dejar de hablar)* to be quiet, to stop talking; **¡cállate!** shut up!; **¿te quieres c.?** would you keep quiet? (**c**) *(ocultar)* to keep quiet about; **esa no se calla nada** she always says what she thinks

calle *nf* (**a**) *(en población)* street, road; **salir a la c.** *(salir de casa)* to go out; **¿qué se opina en la c.?** what does the man in the street think?; **el lenguaje de la c.** everyday language; **c. arriba/abajo** up/down the street; **c. cortada (por obras)** *(en letrero)* road closed (for repairs); **c. de dirección única** one-way street; **c. mayor** main street; **c. peatonal** pedestrian zone; **c. principal** main street

(**b**) *Esp (en atletismo, natación)* lane

(**c**) *(expresiones)* **dejar a alguien en la c.** to put sb out of a job; **echar a alguien a la c.** *(de un trabajo)* to fire sb; *(de un lugar público)* to kick *o* throw sb out; **echarse a la c.** *(manifestarse)* to take to the streets; **hacer la c.** *(prostituta)* to walk the streets; **llevarse a alguien de c.** to win sb over; **traer** *o* **llevar a alguien por la c. de la amargura** to drive sb mad

calleja *nf* side street, alley

callejear *vi* to wander the streets

callejero, -a 1 *adj* **hace mucha vida callejera** he likes going out a lot; **disturbios callejeros** street riot; **perro c.** stray dog

2 *nm Esp (guía)* street map

callejón *nm* alley; **c. sin salida** dead end, blind alley; *Fig* blind alley, impasse

callejuela *nf* backstreet, side street

callista *nmf* chiropodist

callo *nm* (**a**) *(dureza)* callus; *(en el pie)* corn; *Fam Fig* **dar el c.** to slog (**b**) *Fam (persona fea)* sight, fright (**c**) *Esp Culin* **callos** tripe; **callos a la madrileña** = tripe cooked with ham, pork sausage, onion and peppers

callosidad *nf* callus; **callosidades** calluses, hard skin

calloso, -a *adj* calloused

calma *nf* (**a**) *(sin ruido o movimiento)* calm; **en c.** calm; **c. chicha** dead calm (**b**) *(sosiego)* tranquility; **perder la c.** to lose one's composure; **tener c.** *(tener paciencia)* to be patient; **tómatelo con c.** take it easy

calmante 1 *adj* sedative, soothing

2 *nm* sedative, painkiller

calmar 1 *vt* (**a**) *(mitigar)* to relieve (**b**) *(tranquilizar)* to calm, to soothe

2 calmarse *vpr (persona, ánimos)* to calm down; *(dolor, tempestad)* to abate

calmoso, -a *adj* calm

caló *nm Esp* Gypsy dialect

calor *nm* (**a**) *(temperatura alta)* heat; *(tibieza)* warmth; **al c. de la lumbre** by the fireside; **este abrigo da mucho c.** this coat is very warm; **entrar en c.** to get warm; *Fig (público, deportista)* to warm up; **hace c.** it's warm *o* hot; **tener c.** to be warm *o* hot; **c. animal** body heat; *Fís* **c. específico** specific heat (**b**) *(afecto, entusiasmo)* warmth; **el c. del público** the warmth of the audience (**c**) *RP* **calores** *(de la menopausia)* hot flushes

caloría *nf* calorie

calórico, -a *adj* caloric

calorífero, -a *adj (que da calor)* heat-producing

calorífico, -a *adj* calorific

calorro, -a *adj & nm,f Fam* = term used to refer to a Spanish Gypsy, which is usually offensive

calostro *nm* colostrum

calque *etc ver* **calcar**

calumnia *nf (oral)* slander; *(escrita)* libel

calumniar *vt (oralmente)* to slander; *(por escrito)* to libel

calumnioso, -a *adj (de palabra)* slanderous; *(por escrito)* libelous

calurosamente *adv (con afecto)* warmly

caluroso, -a *adj* (**a**) *(excesivamente)* hot; *(agradablemente)* warm (**b**) *(afectuoso)* warm (**c**) *Fam* **es muy c.** he doesn't feel the cold

calva *nf (en la cabeza)* bald patch; *(en tejido, terreno)* bare patch

calvados *nm inv* Calvados

calvario *nm (vía crucis)* Calvary, stations of the Cross; *Fig (sufrimiento)* ordeal

calvicie *nf* baldness

calvinismo *nm* Calvinism

calvinista *adj* Calvinist

calvo, -a 1 *adj* bald; **ni tanto ni tan c.** neither one extreme nor the other

2 *nm,f* bald person

calza *nf* (**a**) *(cuña)* wedge, block (**b**) *Anticuado (media)* stocking (**c**) *Col (en diente)* filling

calzada *nf* road (surface), pavement

calzado, -a 1 *adj (con zapatos)* shod

2 *nm* footwear

calzador *nm* shoehorn

calzar [14] *vt* (**a**) *(calzado)* to wear; **calzaba zapatos de ante** she was wearing suede shoes; **¿qué número calza?** what size (shoe) do you take? (**b**) *(poner cuña a)* to wedge, to block (**c**) *Col (muela)* to fill

2 calzarse *vpr* to put one's shoes on; **se calzó las botas** he put on his boots; **¡cálzate!** put your shoes on!

calzo *nm (cuña)* wedge

calzón *nm* (**a**) *Esp Dep* shorts (**b**) *Andes, Méx, RP (bragas)* panties; **calzones** panties (**c**) *Bol, Méx* **calzones** *(calzoncillos)* shorts

calzonazos *nm inv Fam* henpecked husband

calzoncillo *nm*, **calzoncillos** *nmpl (slip)* shorts; *(bóxer)* boxer shorts; **calzoncillos largos** long johns

CAM [kam] *nm (abrev de* **computer aided manufacturing**) CAM

cama *nf* bed; **estar en** *o* **guardar c.** to be confined to bed; **hacer la c.** to make the bed; *Fig* **hacerle** *o* **ponerle la c. a alguien** to plot against sb; **irse a la c.** to go to bed; **c. de agua** water bed; **c. doble** double bed; **c. de hospital** hospital bed; **c. individual** single bed; **c. de matrimonio** double bed; **c. nido** pull-out bed *(under other bed)*; **c. de rayos UVA** tanning bed; **c. turca** divan

camada *nf* litter

camafeo *nm* cameo

camaleón *nm también Fig* chameleon

camaleónico, -a *adj (persona)* chameleon-like

cámara 1 *nf* (**a**) *(sala)* chamber; **c. acorazada** strong room; **c. frigorífica** cold-storage room; **c. de gas** gas chamber; **c. mortuoria** funeral chamber; **c. de torturas** torture chamber

(**b**) *Pol & Com* chamber; **c. alta/baja** upper/lower house; **C. de Comercio** Chamber of Commerce; **c. de compensación** clearinghouse; **C. de los Comunes** House of Commons; **C. de los Lores** House of Lords; **C. de Representantes** House of Representatives

(**c**) *(de fotos, cine)* camera; *también Fig* **a c. lenta** in slow motion; **c. cinematográfica** *o* **de cine** movie camera; **c. digital** digital camera; **c. fotográfica** camera; **c. oscura** camera obscura; **c. de televisión** television camera; **c. de vídeo** video camera; **c. web** web camera, webcam (**d**) *(receptáculo)* chamber; **c. de aire/gas** air/gas chamber; **c. de combustión** combustion chamber; **c. de descompresión** decompression chamber

(**e**) *(de balón, neumático)* inner tube

2 *nmf (persona)* cameraman, *f* camerawoman

camarada *nmf* (**a**) *Pol* comrade (**b**) *(compañero)* colleague

camaradería *nf* camaraderie

camarera *nf Am (azafata)* air hostess

camarero, -a *nm,f* (**a**) *(de restaurante)* waiter, *f* waitress; *(de hotel)* chamberperson, *f* chambermaid (**b**) *(de rey)* chamberlain, *f* lady-in-waiting

camarilla *nf* clique; *Pol* lobby, pressure group

camarista *nmf* (**a**) *Arg (juez)* appeal court judge (**b**) *Méx (en hotel)* chamberperson, *f* chambermaid

camarón *nm* prawn

camarote *nm* cabin

camastro *nm* ramshackle bed

cambalache *nm Fam* (**a**) *(trueque)* swap (**b**) *RP (tienda)* junk shop (**c**) *RP (gran desorden)* chaos

cambiante *adj* changeable

cambiar 1 *vt* (**a**) *(modificar)* to change (**b**) *(intercambiar)* **c. algo (por algo)** to exchange sth (for sth); **c. libras en dólares** to change pounds into dollars; **c. un artículo defectuoso** to exchange a faulty item; **he cambiado mi turno con un compañero** I swapped shifts with a colleague; **¿te importa si te cambio el sitio?** would you mind swapping *o* changing places with me?

2 *vi* (**a**) *(alterarse)* to change; **c. de** to change; **c. de casa** to move (house); **c. de trabajo** to move *o* change jobs (**b**) *Aut (de marchas)* to change gear

3 cambiarse *vpr* **cambiarse (de ropa)** to change (one's clothes); **cambiarse de casa** to move (house); **no me cambiaría por él** I wouldn't be in his shoes!; **¿te importaría cambiarme el sitio?** would you mind swapping *o* changing places with me?

cambiazo *nm Fam* (**a**) *(cambio grande)* radical change (**b**) *(sustitución)* switch *(in order to steal bag, etc)*; *Fig* **dar el c.** to do a switch

cambio 1 *nm* (**a**) *(modificación)* change; **se ha producido un c. de situación** the situation has changed, there has been a change in the situation; **a las primeras de c.** at the first opportunity; **c. climático** *(calentamiento global)* climate change; **c. de domicilio** change of address; **c. horario** *(bianual)* = putting clocks back or forward one hour; **c. de gobierno** change of government; *Aut* **c. de rasante** brow of a hill; **c. de sentido** U-turn

(**b**) *(intercambio)* exchange; **(oficina de) c.** = business that exchanges currencies; **a c. (de)** in exchange *o* return (for); **no pido nada a c.** I'm not asking for anything back *o* in return

(**c**) *(monedas)* change; **nos hemos quedado sin c.(s)** we're out of change; **¿tiene c. de cinco mil?** have you got change for five thousand?; **quédese con el c.** keep the change

(**d**) *Fin (de acciones)* price; *(de divisas)* exchange rate; **libre c.** *(comercio)* free trade; *(de divisas)* floating exchange rates

(**e**) *Aut* **c. automático** automatic transmission; **c. de marchas** *o* **velocidades** *(acción)* gear change; *(palanca)* gear shift

(**f**) *Dep (sustitución)* substitution, change; **hacer un c.** to make a substitution *o* change

2 *interj Rad* **¡c. (y corto)!** over!; **c. y cierro** over and out!

3 en cambio *loc adv (en su lugar)* instead; *(por otra parte)* on the other hand, however

cambista *nmf* money changer

Camboya *n* Cambodia

camboyano, -a *adj & nm,f* Cambodian

cámbrico, -a *adj & nm Geol* Cambrian

cambur *nm Ven* (**a**) *(empleo)* job (**b**) *(empleado)* clerk (**c**) *(plátano)* banana

camelar *vt Fam* (**a**) *(convencer)* to butter up, to win over (**b**) *(enamorar)* to flirt with

camelia *nf* camellia

camelista *Fam* **1** *adj* wheedling, flattering

2 *nmf* flatterer

camellero, -a *nm,f* camel driver

camello, -a *nm,f* (**a**) *(animal)* camel (**b**) *Fam (traficante)* drug pusher *o* dealer

camellón *nm Col, Méx (en avenida)* median (strip)

camelo *nm Fam* (**a**) *(engaño)* **es puro c.** it's just humbug (**b**) *(noticia falsa)* hoax

camembert ['kamember] *(pl* **camemberts)** *nm* camembert

camerino *nm Teatro* dressing room

Camerún *nm* **(el) C.** Cameroon

camerunés, -esa 1 *adj* Cameroon, of/from Cameroon

2 *nm,f* Cameroonian

camilla 1 *nf* stretcher

2 *adj inv* **mesa c.** = round table with heater underneath

camillero, -a *nm,f* stretcher-bearer

caminante *nmf* walker

caminar 1 *vi* (**a**) *(andar)* to walk; **nosotros iremos caminando** we'll walk, we'll go on foot; *Fig* **c. hacia** to head for; **c. hacia el desastre** to be heading for disaster (**b**) *Am (funcionar)* to work

2 *vt (una distancia)* to travel, to cover

caminata *nf* long walk

camino *nm* (**a**) *(sendero)* path, track; *(carretera)* road; **C. de Santiago** *Astron* Milky Way; *Rel* = pilgrimage route to Santiago de Compostela; **c. trillado** well-trodden path

(**b**) *(ruta, vía)* way; **el c. de la estación** the way to the station; **c. de** on the way to; **está c. de la capital** it's on the way to the capital; **a estas horas ya estarán en c.** they'll be on their way by now; **me pilla de c.** it's on my way; **en el** *o* **de c.** on the way; **por este c.** this way

(**c**) *(viaje)* journey; **nos espera un largo c.** we have a long journey ahead of us; **ponerse en c.** to set off

(**d**) **caminos** *(ingeniería)* civil engineering

(**e**) *(expresiones)* **abrir c. a** to clear the way for; **abrirse c.** to get on *o* ahead; **fueron cada cual por su c.** they went their separate ways; **a medio c.** halfway; **estar a medio c.** to be halfway there; **quedarse a medio c.** to stop halfway through; *Fig* **van c. del desastre/éxito** they're on the road to disaster/success

camión *nm* (**a**) *(de mercancías)* truck; *Fam Fig* **estar como un c.** to be gorgeous; **c. de la basura** garbage truck; **c. cisterna** tanker; **c. de mudanzas** moving van, furniture van (**b**) *CAm, Méx (autobús)* bus

camionero, -a *nm,f* (**a**) *(de camión)* trucker (**b**) *CAm, Méx (de autobús)* bus driver

camioneta *nf* van

camisa *nf* (**a**) *(prenda)* shirt; **c. de fuerza** straitjacket (**b**) *(de serpiente)* slough, skin (**c**) *Tec* lining (**d**) *(expresiones)* **jugarse hasta la c.** to stake everything; **meterse en c. de once varas** to complicate matters unnecessarily; **mudar** *o* **cambiar de c.** to change sides; **no le llega la c. al cuerpo** she's scared stiff

camisería *nf (tienda)* shirt shop, outfitter's

camisero, -a *nm,f* (**a**) *(fabricante)* shirtmaker (**b**) *(vendedor)* outfitter

camiseta *nf* (**a**) *(ropa interior)* undershirt (**b**) *(de manga corta)* T-shirt (**c**) *Dep (de tirantes)* vest; *(con mangas)* shirt

camisola *nf* (**a**) *(prenda interior)* camisole (**b**) *Dep* sports shirt

camisón *nm* (**a**) *(de noche)* nightdress (**b**) *Andes, Carib (de mujer)* chemise

camomila *nf* chamomile

camorra *nf* trouble; **buscar c.** to look for trouble

camorrista 1 *adj* belligerent, quarrelsome
 2 *nmf* troublemaker
camote 1 *nm* (a) *Andes, CAm, Méx* sweet potato (b) *Méx Fam (complicación)* mess; **meterse en un c.** to get into a mess *o* pickle (c) *Perú Fam (novio)* lover, sweetheart
 2 *adj* (a) *Andes Fam (enamorado)* **estar c. por** *o* **de alguien** to be madly in love with sb (b) *Méx Fam* **estar camotes** to be wrecked
camp [kamp] *adj inv (estilo, moda)* retro
campal *adj también Fig* **batalla c.** pitched battle
campamento *nm* camp; **c. base** base camp
campana *nf* bell; *Fig* **echar las campanas al vuelo** to jump for joy; *Fam Fig* **oír campanas y no saber dónde** not to know what one is talking about; **c. de buzo** *o* **de salvamento** diving bell; **c. extractora (de humos)** exhaust hood; **campanas tubulares** tubular bells
campanada *nf* (a) *(de campana)* peal (b) *(de reloj)* stroke (c) *(suceso)* sensation; **dar la c.** to make a big splash, to cause a sensation
campanario *nm* belfry, bell tower
campanero, -a *nm,f* bell ringer
campanilla *nf* (a) *(de la puerta)* (small) bell; *(con mango)* handbell (b) *Anat* uvula (c) *(flor)* campanula, bellflower
campanilleo *nm* tinkle, tinkling sound
campante *adj Fam* **estar** *o* **quedarse tan c.** to be quite unruffled
campaña *nf* (a) *(acción organizada)* campaign; **hacer c. (de/contra)** to campaign (for/against); **c. de desprestigio** character assassination; **c. de difamación** smear campaign; **c. electoral** election campaign; **c. de marketing** marketing campaign; **c. publicitaria** advertising campaign (b) *(periodo de pesca)* fishing season; **la c. del atún** the tuna-fishing season (c) *(campo llano)* open countryside (d) *Mil* **hospital de c.** field hospital; **uniforme de c.** combat uniform
campar *vi* **campa por sus respetos** he follows his own rules, he does things his own way
campechanía *nf* geniality, good-natured character
campechano, -a *adj* genial, good-natured
campeón, -ona *nm,f* champion; **c. de liga** league champions
campeonato *nm* championship; *Fam Fig* **de c.** *(bueno)* terrific, great; *(malo)* terrible
campera *nf* (a) *RP (chaqueta)* short leather jacket (b) *Esp* **camperas** *(botas)* cowboy boots
campero, -a 1 *adj Esp* **botas camperas** cowboy boots
 2 *nm Andes* Jeep®
campesinado *nm* peasants, peasantry
campesino, -a 1 *adj (del campo)* rural, country; *(en el pasado, en países pobres)* peasant; **las labores campesinas** farmwork
 2 *nm,f (persona del campo)* country person; *(en el pasado, en países pobres)* peasant
campestre *adj* country; **comida c.** picnic; **fiesta c.** open-air country festival
cámping ['kampin] *(pl* **cámpings)** *nm* (a) *(actividad)* camping; **ir de c.** to go camping; **c. gas** portable gas stove (b) *(terreno)* campsite, campground
campiña *nf* countryside
campista *nmf* camper
campo *nm* (a) *(campiña)* country, countryside; **en mitad del c.** in the middle of the country *o* countryside; **la emigración del c. a la ciudad** migration from rural areas to cities; **c. abierto** open countryside; **a c. traviesa** cross country
 (b) *(terreno, área)* field; *Fig* **dejar el c. libre a algo/alguien** to leave the field clear for sth/sb; **c. de aviación** airfield; **c. de batalla** battlefield; *Fís* **c. magnético** magnetic field; **c. de pruebas** testing ground; **c. de tiro** firing range; **c. visual** field of vision

 (c) *(campamento)* camp; **c. de concentración** concentration camp; **c. de exterminio** death camp; **c. de refugiados** refugee camp; **c. de trabajo** *(de vacaciones)* work camp; *(para prisioneros)* labor camp
 (d) *Esp Dep (de fútbol)* field; *(de tenis)* court; *(de golf)* course; **jugar en c. propio/contrario** to play at home/away (from home); **c. de deportes** sports facility
 (e) *Inform* field
camposanto *nm* cemetery
campus *nm inv* campus
camuflado, -a *adj Mil* camouflaged; *(oculto)* hidden; **un coche c. de la policía** an unmarked police car
camuflaje *nm* camouflage
camuflar *vt* to camouflage
can *nm* hound, dog
cana *nf* (a) gray hair; *Fam* **echar una c. al aire** to let one's hair down; *Fam* **peinar canas** to be getting on, to be old (b) *Andes, Cuba, RP Fam (cárcel)* joint (c) *RP Fam (policía)* **la c.** the cops
Canadá *nm* **(el) C.** Canada
canadiense *adj & nmf* Canadian
canal 1 *nm* (a) *(cauce artificial)* canal; **c. de riego** irrigation channel (b) *Geog (estrecho)* channel, strait; **el C. de la Mancha** the (English) Channel; **el C. de Panamá** the Panama Canal; **el C. de Suez** the Suez Canal (c) *Rad & TV* channel; **cambiar de c.** to switch channels; **c. de pago** subscription channel (d) *Anat* canal, duct (e) *(medio, vía)* channel; *Com* **c. de comercialización** distribution channel
 2 *nm o nf* (a) *(de un tejado)* (valley) gutter (b) *(res)* carcass; **abrir en c.** to slit open; *Fig* to tear apart
canalé *nm* ribbed knitwear
canaleta *nf Bol, CSur* gutter
canalización *nf* (a) *(de territorio, río)* canalization; *(de agua)* piping; **todavía no tienen c. de agua** they're not yet connected to the water mains (b) *(de recursos, esfuerzos)* channeling
canalizar [14] *vt* (a) *(territorio, río)* to canalize; *(agua)* to channel (b) *(recursos, esfuerzos)* to channel
canalla *nmf* swine, dog
canallada *nf* dirty trick
canallesco, -a *adj (acción, intención)* despicable, vile; *(sonrisa)* wicked, evil
canalón *nm (de tejado)* gutter; *(en la pared)* drainpipe
canana *nf* cartridge belt
canapé *nm* (a) *Culin* canapé (b) *(sofá)* sofa, couch
Canarias *nfpl* **las (islas) C.** the Canary Islands, the Canaries
canario, -a 1 *adj* of/from the Canary Islands, Canary
 2 *nm,f (persona)* Canary Islander
 3 *nm (pájaro)* canary
canasta *nf* (a) *(cesto)* (gen) & *Dep* basket; *RP Econ* **el precio de la c. familiar** the cost of the average week's shopping (b) *(juego de naipes)* canasta (c) *Col, Méx (de automóvil)* roof rack
canastero, -a *nm,f* basket weaver
canastilla *nf* (a) *(cesto pequeño)* basket (b) *(de bebé)* layette
canasto *nm* large basket; *Anticuado o Hum* **¡canastos!** *(expresa enfado)* for Heaven's sake!; *(expresa sorpresa)* good heavens!
Canberra *n* Canberra
cancán 1 *nm (baile)* cancan
 2 cancanes *nmpl o nfpl RP (leotardos)* panty hose *(plural)*
cancela *nf* wrought-iron gate
cancelación *nf* (a) *(anulación)* cancellation (b) *(de deuda)* payment, settlement
cancelar *vt* (a) *(anular)* to cancel (b) *(deuda)* to pay, to settle
cáncer 1 *nm* (a) *Med & Fig* cancer; **c. cervical** cervical cancer; **c. de mama** breast cancer; **c. de pulmón** lung cancer (b) *(zodiaco)* Cancer; *Esp* **ser c.** to be (a) Cancer
 2 *nmf Esp (persona)* Cancer, Cancerian

cancerbero *nm (en fútbol)* goalkeeper

canceriano, -a *Am* **1** *adj (zodiaco)* Cancer; **ser c.** to be (a) Cancer

  2 *nm,f (persona)* Cancer, Cancerian

cancerígeno, -a *adj Med* carcinogenic

cancerología *nf Med* oncology

cancerológico, -a *adj Med* oncological

cancerólogo, -a *nm,f Med* cancer specialist, oncologist

canceroso, -a *Med* **1** *adj (úlcera, tejido)* cancerous; *(enfermo)* suffering from cancer

  2 *nm,f (enfermo)* cancer patient

cancha *nf* (**a**) *(de tenis, baloncesto, squash)* court; *Am (de fútbol)* field; *Am (de golf)* course; *RP* **está en su c.** he's in his element; *Chile* **c. de aterrizaje** runway; *Am* **c. de carreras** racetrack (**b**) *Am (descampado)* open space, open ground; *(corral)* fenced yard (**c**) *Andes, PRico Fam (maíz)* toasted corn (**d**) *(expresiones)* **dar c. a alguien** to give sb a chance; *RP Fam* **¡abran c.!** make way!; *RP* **tener c.** to be streetwise *o* savvy

canchero, -a **1** *adj RP Fam* savvy, streetwise

  2 *nm,f* (**a**) *RP Fam (desenvuelto)* savvy *o* streetwise person (**b**) *Am (cuidador)* groundsman, *f* groundswoman

canciller *nm Pol* (**a**) *(de gobierno, embajada)* chancellor (**b**) *(de asuntos exteriores)* foreign minister

cancillería *nf Pol* (**a**) *(de Gobierno)* chancellorship (**b**) *(de embajada)* chancellery (**c**) *(de Asuntos Exteriores)* foreign ministry

canción *nf* song; **la misma c.** the same old story; **c. de amor** love song; **c. de cuna** lullaby; **c. pop** pop song; **c. protesta** protest song

cancionero *nm* songbook

cancro *nm Med* cancer

candado *nm* padlock

candeal *adj* **pan c.** white bread *(of high quality, made from durum wheat)*

candela *nf* (**a**) *(vela)* candle; *Fam (lumbre)* light (**b**) *(fuego)* fire

candelabro *nm* candelabra

candelero *nm* candlestick; **estar en c.** to be in the limelight

candente *adj* (**a**) *(incandescente)* red-hot (**b**) *(actual)* highly topical; **de c. actualidad** highly topical; **tema c.** burning issue

candidato, -a *nm,f* candidate

candidatura *nf* (**a**) *(para un cargo)* candidacy; **presentar uno su c.** to put oneself forward as a candidate for (**b**) *(lista)* list of candidates

candidez *nf* ingenuousness

cándido, -a *adj* ingenuous, simple

candil *nm (lámpara)* oil lamp

candilejas *nfpl* footlights

candombe, candomblé *nm (danza)* = South American carnival dance of African origin; *(tambor)* = drum used in the "candombe" dance

candor *nm* ingenuousness

candoroso, -a *adj* ingenuous, simple

caneca *nf Col (para basura)* trash can

caneco *nm (petaca)* hip flask

canela *nf* cinnamon; *Fig* **ser c. fina** to be sheer class

canelo, -a **1** *adj (caballo, perro)* golden brown

  2 *nm Fam* **hemos hecho el c.** we've been had!

canelones *nmpl Culin* cannelloni

canesú *nm* (**a**) *(de vestido)* bodice (**b**) *(de blusa)* yoke

cangrejo *nm* crab; **c. de río** crayfish

canguelo *nm Fam* **le entró c.** she got in a funk, she freaked out

canguro **1** *nm (animal)* kangaroo

  2 *nmf Esp Fam (persona)* babysitter; **hacer de c.** to babysit

caníbal **1** *adj* cannibalistic

  2 *nmf* cannibal

canibalismo *nm* cannibalism

canica *nf* marble; **las canicas** *(juego)* marbles; **jugar a las canicas** to play marbles

caniche *nm* poodle

canicie *nf* gray hair

canícula *nf* dog days, high summer

canicular *adj* **calor c.** blistering heat

canijo, -a **1** *adj (pequeño)* tiny; *(enfermizo)* sickly

  2 *nm,f* small, sickly person

canilla *nf* (**a**) *Fam (espinilla)* shinbone; *(pierna)* leg (**b**) *Esp (bobina)* bobbin (**c**) *RP (grifo)* faucet

canillera *nf Am* (**a**) *(protección)* shin pad (**b**) *(temblor)* **tenía c.** his legs were trembling *o* shaking

canillita *nm Am* newspaper vendor

canino, -a **1** *adj* canine

  2 *nm (diente)* canine (tooth)

canje *nm* exchange

canjeable *adj* exchangeable

canjear *vt* to exchange

cannabis *nm inv* cannabis

cano, -a *adj* gray *(hair)*

canoa *nf* canoe

canódromo *nm* greyhound track

canon *nm* (**a**) *(norma)* canon (**b**) *(modelo)* ideal (**c**) *(impuesto)* tax (**d**) *Mús* canon (**e**) *Der* **cánones** canon law

canónico, -a *adj* canonical; *Der* **derecho c.** canon law

canónigo *nm* canon

canonización *nf* canonization

canonizar [14] *vt* to canonize

canoso, -a *adj (persona)* gray-haired

canotier [kano'tje] *(pl* **canotiers**) *nm (sombrero)* straw boater

cansado, -a *adj* (**a**) *(fatigado)* tired; **estar c. de algo/de hacer algo** to be tired of sth/of doing sth (**b**) *(pesado, cargante)* tiring

cansador, -ora *adj Andes, RP* boring

cansancio *nm* (**a**) *(fatiga)* tiredness (**b**) *(hastío)* boredom

cansar **1** *vt* to tire (out); **me cansa mucho leer sin gafas** I get very tired if I read without my glasses

  2 *vi* to be tiring; **esta tarea cansa mucho** it's a very tiring job *o* task

  3 cansarse *vpr también Fig* to get tired (**de** of); **los niños se cansan muy pronto de todo** children get tired of things very quickly; **¡ya me he cansado de repetirlo! ¡cállense ahora mismo!** I'm tired of telling you! be quiet this minute!

cansino, -a *adj* lethargic

Cantabria *n* Cantabria

Cantábrico *nm* **el (mar) C.** the Cantabrian Sea

cantábrico, -a *adj* **la cordillera cantábrica** the Cantabrian Mountains

cántabro, -a *adj & nm,f* Cantabrian

cantada *nf Fam Dep* goalkeeping error

cantado, -a *adj Fam* **el resultado está c.** the result is a foregone conclusion

cantaleta *nf Am* **la misma c.** the same old story

cantamañanas *nmf inv* unreliable person

cantante **1** *adj* singing

  2 *nmf* singer; **c. de rock/ópera** rock/opera singer

cantaor, -ora *nm,f* flamenco singer

cantar **1** *vt* (**a**) *(canción)* to sing (**b**) *(bingo, línea, el gordo)* to call (out)

  2 *vi* (**a**) *(persona, ave)* to sing; *(gallo)* to crow; *(insecto)* to chirp (**b**) *Fam (confesar)* to talk (**c**) *Esp Fam (apestar)* to stink; **le cantan los pies** he has smelly feet (**d**) *Esp Fam (desentonar)* to stick out like a sore thumb (**e**) *(alabar)* **c. a** to sing the praises of

3 *nm Lit* poem; *Fam Fig* **eso es otro c.** that's another story

cantarín, -ina *adj (persona)* fond of singing; *(voz)* singsong

cántaro *nm* large pitcher; **a cántaros** in torrents; **llover a cántaros** to rain cats and dogs

cantata *nf* cantata

cantautor, -ora *nm,f* singer-songwriter

cante *nm* **c. (jondo o hondo)** flamenco singing; *Esp Fam* **dar el c.** to stick out a mile

cantegril *nm Urug* shantytown

cantera *nf (de piedra)* quarry; *(de jóvenes promesas)* young blood; **un jugador de la c.** a home-grown o local player

canterano, -a 1 *adj* home-grown

2 *nm,f* home-grown player

cantero *nm Cuba, RP* flower bed

cántico *nm* canticle

cantidad 1 *nf* **(a)** *(medida)* quantity, amount; **¿qué c. de pasta hará falta?** how much pasta will we need? **(b)** *(abundancia)* abundance, large number; **en c.** in abundance; *Fam* **c. de** lots of **(c)** *(número)* number; **sumar dos cantidades** to add two numbers o figures together **(d)** *(suma de dinero)* sum (of money)

2 *adv Esp Fam* really; **me gusta c.** I really like it a lot; **corrimos c.** we did a lot of running

cantiga, cántiga *nf* ballad

cantilena = cantinela

cantimplora *nf* water bottle

cantina *nf (de soldados)* mess; *(en fábrica)* canteen; *(en estación de tren)* buffet

cantinela, cantilena *nf* **la misma c.** the same old story

cantinero, -a *nm,f* canteen manager, *f* canteen manageress

canto *nm* **(a)** *(acción, arte)* singing; *(canción)* song; *Fig* **c. de(l) cisne** swansong; **c. fúnebre** funeral chant; *Fig* **c. del gallo** daybreak; **c. gregoriano** Gregorian chant; **c. guerrero** war song; *Fig* **c. de sirena** wheedling **(b)** *(lado, borde)* edge; *(de cuchillo)* blunt edge; **de c.** sideways; *Fam Fig* **por el c. de un duro** by a hair's breadth **(c)** *(guijarro)* pebble; *Fig* **darse con un c. en los dientes** to consider oneself lucky; **c. rodado** pebble

cantón *nm (territorio)* canton

cantonal *adj* cantonal

cantonera *nf (de esquina, libro)* corner piece

cantor, -ora 1 *adj* singing; **ave cantora** songbird

2 *nm,f* singer

cantoral *nm* choir book

canturrear *vt & vi Fam* to sing softly

canturreo *nm Fam* humming, quiet singing

cánula *nf Med* cannula

canutas *nfpl Esp Fam* **pasarlas c.** to have a rough time

canuto *nm* **(a)** *(tubo)* tube; *Fam Fig* **no sabe hacer la o con un c.** he is as dumb as a stump **(b)** *Fam (porro)* joint

caña *nf* **(a)** *(planta)* cane; *(de río, de estanque)* reed; **c. de azúcar** sugarcane **(b)** *Esp (de cerveza)* small glass of beer **(c)** **c. (de pescar)** fishing rod **(d)** *(de bota)* leg **(e)** *(tuétano)* bone marrow **(f)** *Andes, Cuba, RP (alcohol)* rum **(g)** *(expresiones) Fam* **darle o meterle c. a algo** to get a move on with sth; **meter c. al coche** to step on it; **darle c. a alguien** *(pegarle)* to give sb a beating

cañabrava *nf Cuba, RP* = reed used for building roofs and walls

cañada *nf (camino para ganado)* cattle track; *Cuba (valle)* valley; *RP (arroyo)* creek, stream

cañadón *nm RP* ravine

cáñamo *nm* hemp

cañamón *nm* hempseed

cañaveral *nm* **(a)** *(de juncos)* reedbed **(b)** *Am (de azúcar)* sugarcane plantation

cañería *nf* pipe

cañero, -a 1 *adj Esp Fam (música)* heavy

2 *nm,f Am (trabajador)* sugar plantation worker; *(propietario)* sugar plantation owner

cañí *adj* **(a)** *Fam (folclórico, popular)* = term used to describe the traditional folklore and values of Spain **(b)** *(gitano)* Gypsy

cañizo *nm* wattle

caño *nm (de fuente)* jet

cañón 1 *nm* **(a)** *(arma)* gun; *Hist* cannon **(b)** *(de fusil, pistola)* barrel; *(de chimenea)* flue; *(de órgano)* pipe **(c)** *Geog* canyon; **el (Gran) C. del Colorado** the Grand Canyon

2 *adj Esp Fam* **estar c.** to be gorgeous

cañonazo *nm* **(a)** *(disparo de cañón)* gunshot **(b)** *Fam (en fútbol)* powerful shot

cañonear *vt* to shell

cañonera *nf* gunboat

caoba *nf* mahogany

caolín *nm* kaolin, china clay

caos *nm inv* chaos; **ser un c.** to be in chaos

caótico, -a *adj* chaotic

CAP [kap] *nm (abrev de* **Certificado de Aptitud Pedagógica***)* = Spanish teaching certificate needed to teach in secondary education

cap. *(abrev de* **capítulo***)* ch

capa *nf* **(a)** *(manto)* cloak, cape; *Fam* **andar de c. caída** *(persona)* to be in a bad way; *(negocio)* to be struggling; **defender algo a c. y espada** to defend sth tooth and nail; **hacer de su c. un sayo** to do as one pleases **(b)** *(baño)* *(de barniz, pintura)* coat; *(de chocolate)* coating **(c)** *(estrato)* layer; *Geol* stratum, layer; **c. atmosférica** atmosphere; **una c. de hielo** a film of ice; **c. de ozono** ozone layer; **c. terrestre** Earth's surface **(d)** *(grupo social)* stratum, class **(e)** *Taurom* cape

capacete *nm Carib, Méx (de automóvil)* hood

capacho *nm* wicker basket

capacidad *nf* **(a)** *(cabida)* capacity; **con c. para quinientas personas** with a capacity of five hundred; **este teatro tiene c. para mil doscientos espectadores** this theater can seat one thousand two hundred people; **c. máxima** *(en ascensor)* maximum load; *Inform* **c. de memoria** memory capacity **(b)** *(aptitud, talento, potencial)* ability; **no tener c. para algo/para hacer algo** to be no good at sth/at doing sth; **c. adquisitiva** purchasing power; **c. de concentración** ability to concentrate; **c. ofensiva** firepower

capacitación *nf* training

capacitador, -ora *Am* **1** *adj* **curso c.** training course

2 *nm,f* trainer

capacitar *vt* **c. a alguien para hacer algo** *(habilitar)* to entitle sb to do sth; *(formar)* to train sb to do sth

capado *adj* castrated, gelded

capar *vt* **(a)** *(animal)* to castrate, to geld **(b)** *Col Fam* **c. clase** *(faltar)* to play hooky

caparazón *nm también Fig* shell

capataz, -aza *nm,f* foreman, *f* forewoman

capaz 1 *adj* **(a)** *(apto)* capable; **es un profesor muy c.** he's a very skilled o gifted teacher; **c. de algo/de hacer algo** capable of sth/of doing sth; **es c. de todo con tal de conseguir lo que quiere** he's capable of anything to get what he wants; **¡no serás c. de dejarme sola!** surely you wouldn't leave me all alone! **(b)** *(espacioso)* **muy/poco c.** with a large/small capacity **(c)** *Der* competent

2 *adv Andes, RP Fam (quizá)* maybe; **c. (que) viene Pedro** Pedro might come

capazo *nm (cesta)* large wicker basket

capcioso, -a *adj* disingenuous; **pregunta capciosa** trick question

capea *nf Taurom* = amateur bullfight with young bulls

capear *vt (eludir)* to get out of; **c. el temporal** to ride out *o* weather the storm

capella: a capella *loc adj & adv Mús* a cappella

capellán *nm* chaplain

capelo *nm* **c. (cardenalicio)** cardinal's hat

Caperucita Roja *nf* Little Red Riding Hood

caperuza *nf* (a) *(gorro)* hood (b) *(capuchón)* top, cap

capicúa 1 *adj inv* reversible

2 *nm inv* reversible number

capilar 1 *adj* (a) *(del cabello)* hair; **loción c.** hair lotion (b) *Anat & Fís* capillary

2 *nm Anat* capillary

capilaridad *nf Fís* capillarity, capillary action

capilla *nf* chapel; *Fig* **estar en c.** *(condenado a muerte)* to be awaiting execution; *Fam (en ascuas)* to be on tenterhooks; **c. ardiente** funeral chapel

capirotada *nf Méx* = bread pudding with nuts and raisins

capirotazo *nm* flick

capirote *nm* (a) *(gorro)* hood (b) *Fam* **ser un tonto de c.** to be a complete idiot

cápita *nf* **per c.** per capita

capital 1 *adj* (a) *(importante)* supreme (b) *(principal)* main (c) *Rel (pecado)* deadly

2 *nm Econ & Fin* capital; **c. circulante/fijo/social** working/fixed/equity capital; **c. escriturado** equity capital, capital stock; **c. líquido** liquid assets; **c. bajo riesgo** sum at risk; **c. de riesgo** venture capital, risk capital; **c. social** equity capital

3 *nf (ciudad)* capital

capitalidad *nf Formal* **ostentar la c. de** to be the capital of

capitalino, -a *adj* of the capital (city), capital; **la vida capitalina** life in the capital (city)

capitalismo *nm* capitalism

capitalista *adj & nmf* capitalist

capitalización *nf* capitalization

capitalizar [14] *vt* (a) *Econ* to capitalize (b) *(sacar provecho de)* to capitalize on

capitán, -ana *nm,f (en ejército de tierra)* captain; *(en aviación)* captain; *(en marina)* lieutenant; *Mil* **c. general** general of the army

capitana *nf Náut* flagship

capitanear *vt* (a) *Dep & Mil* to captain (b) *(dirigir)* to head, to lead

capitanía *nf Mil* (a) *(empleo)* captaincy (b) *(oficina)* military headquarters; **c. general** Captaincy General

capitel *nm Arquit* capital

capitolio *nm* (a) *(edificio)* capitol; **el C.** *(en Estados Unidos)* the Capitol (b) *(acrópolis)* acropolis

capitoste *nmf Fam* big wheel, big boss

capitulación *nf* capitulation, surrender; **capitulaciones matrimoniales** marriage contract

capitular *vi* to capitulate, to surrender

capítulo *nm* (a) *(de libro)* chapter; *(de serie)* episode (b) *(tema, sección)* subject; **ser c. aparte** to be another matter (altogether)

capo *nm (de la mafia)* mafia boss, capo

capó *nm* hood

capón *nm* (a) *(animal)* capon (b) *Fam (golpe)* rap on the head

caporal *nm Mil* corporal

capota *nf (de vehículo)* convertible top

capotazo *nm Taurom* = pass with the cape

capote *nm* (a) *(capa)* cape with sleeves; *(militar)* greatcoat (b) *Taurom* cape (c) *Fig* **echar un c. a alguien** to give sb a (helping) hand

capotear *vt Taurom* to distract with the cape

capricho *nm* whim, caprice; **darse un c.** to treat oneself

caprichoso, -a *adj* capricious

capricorniano, -a *Am* **1** *adj (zodiaco)* Capricorn; **ser c.** to be (a) Capricorn

2 *nm,f (persona)* Capricorn

capricornio 1 *nm (zodiaco)* Capricorn; *Esp* **ser c.** to be (a) Capricorn

2 *nmf Esp (persona)* Capricorn

cápsula *nf* (a) *(gen) & Anat* capsule (b) *(tapón)* cap

captación *nf (de adeptos)* recruitment; **c. de fondos** fund raising

captar 1 *vt* (a) *(atraer) (simpatía)* to win; *(interés)* to gain, to capture (b) *(entender)* to grasp (c) *(sintonizar)* to pick up, to receive

2 captarse *vpr (atraer)* to win, to attract

captor, -ora *nm,f* captor

captura *nf* capture

capturar *vt* to capture

capucha *nf* hood

capuchino, -a 1 *adj* Capuchin

2 *nm* (a) *(fraile)* Capuchin (b) *(café)* cappuccino

capuchón *nm* (a) *(de prenda)* hood (b) *(de bolígrafo, pluma)* top, cap

capullo, -a 1 *adj Esp muy Fam* **ser muy c.** to be a real jerk

2 *nm* (a) *(de flor)* bud (b) *(de gusano)* cocoon (c) *Esp Vulg (glande)* head

3 *nm,f Esp muy Fam (insulto)* jerk

caqui 1 *adj inv (color)* khaki

2 *nm* (a) *(fruto)* kaki (b) *(color)* khaki

cara 1 *nf* (a) *(rostro)* face; **esa c. me suena de algo** I remember that face from somewhere, I've seen that face somewhere before

(b) *(persona)* face; **acudieron muchas caras famosas** a lot of famous faces were there

(c) *(lado)* side; *Geom* face; **c. A** *(de disco)* A side

(d) *(de moneda)* heads; **c. o cruz,** *Andes, Ven* **c. o sello,** *RP* **c. o ceca** heads or tails; **echar algo a c. o cruz** to toss (a coin) for sth, to flip a coin for sth

(e) *(parte frontal)* front

(f) *Fam (desvergüenza)* cheek, nerve; **tener (mucha) c., tener la c. muy dura** to have a lot of cheek *o* nerve; **tener la c. de hacer algo** to have the nerve to do sth

(g) *(facciones, aspecto)* **¡alegra esa c.!** cheer up *o* don't look so miserable!; **poner c. de tonto** to make a stupid face; **tener buena/mala c.** *(persona)* to look well/awful; **tener c. de enfadado** to look angry; **tiene c. de ponerse a llover** it looks as if it's going to rain

(h) *(indicando posición)* **c. a** *(frente a)* facing; **c. a c.** face to face; **de c.** *(sol, viento)* in one's face; **de c. a** with a view to

(i) *(expresiones)* **a c. descubierta** openly; **se le cayó la c. de vergüenza** she blushed with shame; **cruzar la c. a alguien** to slap sb in the face; **dar la c.** *(responsabilizarse)* to face up to the consequences; **dar la c. por alguien** to stick up for sb; **decir algo a alguien en** *o* **a la c.** to say sth to sb's face; **echar en c. algo a alguien** to reproach sb for sth; **hacer c. a algo/alguien** to stand up to sth/sb; **por su linda c., por su c. bonita** because his/her face fits; **romper** *o* **partir la c. a alguien** to smash sb's face in; **verse las caras** *(pelearse)* to have it out; *(enfrentarse)* to fight it out

2 *nmf Fam* **c. (dura)** shameless person; **ser un c.** to be shameless

carabela *nf* caravel

carabina *nf* (a) *(arma)* carbine, rifle (b) *Fam Fig (mujer)* chaperone

carabinero *nm* (a) *(en España)* customs policeman (b) *(en Italia)* carabiniere (c) *Chile (policía)* armed policeman

carabo *nm* tawny owl

Caracas *n* Caracas

caracol 1 nm (**a**) (animal) snail (**b**) (concha) shell (**c**) (del oído) cochlea (**d**) (rizo) curl
  2 interj ¡**caracoles!** good grief!

caracola nf conch

caracolada nf Culin = stew made with snails

caracolear vi (caballo) to prance about

caracolillo nm (**a**) (café) pea-bean coffee (**b**) (en la cara) kiss curl

carácter (pl **caracteres**) nm (**a**) (personalidad, modo de ser, genio) character; **tener buen/mal c.** to be good-natured/bad-tempered; **tener mucho c.** to have a strong personality (**b**) (índole, naturaleza) character; **una reunión de c. privado/oficial** a private/official meeting; **solicitaron ayuda con c. de urgencia** they requested urgent assistance (**c**) (de imprenta) character; **escriba en caracteres de imprenta** (en impreso) please print

característica nf (**a**) (rasgo) characteristic, feature (**b**) Am (de teléfono) area code

característico, -a adj characteristic; **este gesto es c. de ella** this gesture is typical o characteristic of her

caracterización nf (**a**) (de personaje) characterization (**b**) (maquillaje) makeup

caracterizar [14] **1** vt (**a**) (definir) to characterize; **con la amabilidad que la caracteriza** with the kindness so typical of her (**b**) (representar) to portray (**c**) (maquillar) to make up
  2 caracterizarse vpr to be characterized (**por** by); **se caracteriza por su bajo consumo de energía** it is notable for its low energy consumption

cadura Fam **1** adj **ser muy c.** to have a lot of cheek o nerve
  2 nmf **ser un(a) c.** to have a lot of cheek o nerve

carajillo nm = black coffee with a dash of brandy or rum

carajo muy Fam **1** nm **me importa un c.** I couldn't give a shit; **irse al c.** (plan, proyecto) to go down the tubes; ¡**vete al c.!** go to hell!
  2 interj ¡**c.!** damn it!

caramba interj ¡**c.!** (sorpresa) good heavens!, jeez!; (enfado) for heaven's sake!

carámbano nm icicle; Fam Fig **estar hecho un c.** to be frozen stiff

carambola nf cannon (in billiards); Fig **de** o **por c.** by a (lucky) fluke; ¡**carambolas!** good heavens!

caramelizar [14] vt (bañar) to cover with caramel

caramelo nm (**a**) (golosina) candy; **un c. de limón** a lemon drop; **un c. de menta** a mint; **c. para la tos** cough candy (**b**) (azúcar fundido) caramel; **calentarlo a punto de c.** heat it until it is about to caramelize

caramillo nm shepherd's flute

carantoñas nfpl **hacer c. a alguien** to butter sb up

caraota nf Ven bean

caraqueño, -a 1 adj of/from Caracas
  2 nm,f person from Caracas

cárate nm karate

carátula nf (**a**) (de libro) front cover; (de disco) jacket (**b**) (máscara) mask (**c**) Méx (de reloj) dial, face

caravana nf (**a**) (remolque) trailer (**b**) (de camellos) caravan; (de carromatos) wagon train (**c**) (de coches) backup (**d**) CSur **caravanas** (pendientes) earrings

caravaning [kara'βanin] (pl **caravanings**) nm trailering

caray interj ¡**c.!** (sorpresa) good heavens!, jeez!; (enfado) damn it!

carbohidrato nm carbohydrate

carbón nm (**a**) (para quemar) coal; **negro como el c.** black as coal; (por el sol) brown as a berry; **c. de leña** o **vegetal** charcoal; **c. mineral** o **de piedra** coal (**b**) (para dibujar) charcoal

carbonatado, -a adj carbonated

carbonato nm Quím carbonate

carboncillo nm charcoal

carbonera nf coal bunker

carbonero, -a 1 adj coal; **industria carbonera** coal industry
  2 nm,f (persona) coal merchant; **la fe del c.** blind faith

carbónico, -a adj carbonic

carbonífero, -a adj & nm Geol (era) Carboniferous

carbonilla nf (**a**) (ceniza) cinder (**b**) (carbón pequeño) small coal

carbonizado, -a adj charred

carbonizar [14] **1** vt to char, to carbonize; **morir carbonizado** to burn to death
  2 carbonizarse vpr to be charred

carbono nm carbon; **c. 14** carbon 14

carburación nf Aut carburation

carburador nm carburetor

carburante nm fuel

carburar 1 vt to carburate
  2 vi Fam to function

carburo nm carbide

carca Fam Pey **1** adj old-fashioned
  2 nmf old fogy

carcaj nm quiver

carcajada nf guffaw; **reír a carcajadas** to roar with laughter

carcajearse vpr to roar with laughter

carcajeo nm roars of laughter

carcamal, Méx, RP **carcamán** nmf Fam Pey old crock

carcasa nf (de CD, ordenador) case; (de máquina) casing

cárcel nf prison; **meter a alguien en la c.** to put sb in prison; **c. de alta seguridad** maximum security prison o jail; **c. de régimen abierto** open prison

carcelario, -a adj prison; **la vida carcelaria** prison life; **régimen c.** prison conditions

carcelero, -a nm,f jailer

carcinógeno, -a 1 adj carcinogenic
  2 nm carcinogen

carcinoma nm Med carcinoma, cancerous tumor

carcoma nf (**a**) (insecto) woodworm (**b**) (polvo) wood dust

carcomer 1 vt también Fig to eat away at
  2 carcomerse vpr (consumirse) to be eaten up o consumed

carcomido, -a adj (madera) worm-eaten

cardado, -a 1 adj (lana) carded; (pelo) teased
  2 nm (de lana) carding; (del pelo) teasing

cardador, -ora nm,f carder

cardamomo nm cardamom

cardán nm Cardan joint

cardar vt (lana) to card; (pelo) to tease

cardenal nm (**a**) Rel cardinal (**b**) (hematoma) bruise

cardenalicio, -a adj **colegio c.** college of cardinals (group); **manto c.** cardinal's robe

cardenillo nm verdigris

cárdeno, -a adj purple

cardiaco, -a, cardíaco, -a adj cardiac; **paro c.** cardiac arrest; **insuficiencia cardiaca** heart failure

cárdigan nm cardigan

cardinal adj cardinal

cardiografía nf cardiography

cardiograma nm electrocardiogram

cardiología nf cardiology

cardiólogo, -a nm,f cardiologist

cardiopatía nf heart condition

cardiorrespiratorio, -a adj Med cardiopulmonary

cardiovascular adj cardiovascular

cardo nm (**a**) (planta) thistle; **c. borriquero** cotton thistle (**b**)

Esp Fam (persona) (fea) ugly mug; *(arisca)* cranky person

carear *vt (testigos, acusados)* to bring face-to-face

carecer [46] *vi* **c. de algo** to lack sth

carenado *nm (de moto)* fairing

carencia *nf (ausencia)* lack; *(defecto)* deficiency; **sufrir carencias afectivas** to be deprived of love and affection; **sufrir muchas carencias** to suffer great need

carenciado, -a *Am* **1** *adj* deprived

2 *nm,f* deprived person

carente *adj* **c. de** lacking (in)

careo *nm (de testigos, acusados)* confrontation; **someter a un c.** to bring face-to-face

carero, -a *Fam* **1** *adj* pricey

2 *nm,f (tendero)* = storekeeper who charges high prices; **el pescadero es un c.** the fish dealer is a bit pricey

carestía *nf (alto precio)* **la c. de la vida** the high cost of living

careta *nf (máscara)* mask; **c. antigás** gas mask

careto *nm Esp Fam (cara)* mug

carey *nm (material)* tortoiseshell; *(tortuga)* sea turtle

carga *nf* **(a)** *(acción)* loading; **zona de c. y descarga** loading zone

(b) *(cargamento) (de avión, barco)* cargo; *(de tren)* freight

(c) *(peso)* load; *Fig (sufrimiento)* burden; **representa una enorme c. para sus hijos** she is a great burden on her children; **llevar la c. de algo** to be responsible for sth; **c. máxima autorizada** maximum authorized load

(d) *(ataque, explosivo)* charge; **¡a la c.!** charge!; *Fig* **volver a la c.** *(insistir)* to insist; *(atacar de nuevo)* to go back on the offensive; **c. explosiva** explosive charge; **c. de profundidad** depth charge

(e) *(de mechero, bolígrafo)* refill

(f) *(de obra, declaraciones)* **un poema con una fuerte c. erótica** a highly erotic poem; **una estatua con una c. simbólica** a statue that is very symbolic

(g) *(impuesto)* tax; **cargas fiscales** taxes; **c. tributaria** levy

(h) *(eléctrica)* charge

cargado, -a *adj* **(a)** *(lleno)* loaded **(de** with); *(arma)* loaded; *Fig* **estar c. de** to have loads of **(b)** *(bebida)* strong **(c)** *(bochornoso) (habitación)* stuffy; *(tiempo)* sultry, close; *(cielo)* overcast **(d)** *Fís (eléctricamente)* charged

cargador *nm* **(a)** *(de arma)* chamber **(b)** *(persona)* loader; **c. de muelle** longshoreman, stevedore **(c)** *(de baterías)* charger

cargamento *nm* cargo

cargante *adj Fam* annoying

cargar [40] **1** *vt* **(a)** *(llenar) (vehículo, arma, cámara)* to load; *(pluma, mechero)* to refill; **c. algo de** to load sth with; **c. algo en un barco/en un camión** to load sth onto a ship/onto a truck; **c. algo demasiado** to overload sth; *Fig* **c. las tintas** to exaggerate, to lay it on thick **(b)** *(peso encima)* **cargué la caja a hombros** I carried the box on my shoulder **(c)** *(adeudar) (importe, factura, deuda)* to charge **(a** to); **c. algo a alguien en su cuenta** to charge sth to sb's account **(d)** *(responsabilidad, tarea)* to give; **siempre le cargan de trabajo** they always give him far too much work to do **(e)** *Elec* to charge **(f)** *Esp Fam (molestar)* to bug; **me carga su pedantería** his pretentiousness really gets on my nerves

2 *vi* **(a)** **c. con** *(paquete, bulto)* to carry; *(coste, responsabilidad)* to bear; *(consecuencias)* to accept; *(culpa)* to get; **hoy me toca a mí c. con los niños** it's my turn to look after the children today **(b)** *(atacar)* **c. (contra)** to charge

3 **cargarse** *vpr* **(a)** *(batería)* to charge **(b)** *(persona)* **cargarse de deudas** to get up to one's neck in debt; **se cargó de hijos** she had a lot of children **(c)** *(lugar)* to get stuffy **(d)** *(parte del cuerpo)* **se me cargan las piernas** my legs get tired; **se me carga la cabeza con tanto ruido** my head's throbbing from all this noise **(e)** *Fam (acabar con) (objeto)* to break; *(plan, empresa)* to ruin; **se cargó el jarrón** he broke

the vase **(f)** *Fam (matar) (persona)* to bump off; *(animal)* to kill **(g)** *Fam (suspender)* to fail; **el profesor se cargó a la mitad de la clase** the teacher failed half the class **(h)** *Esp Fam* **¡te la vas a c.!** you're in for it!

cargo *nm* **(a)** *(cuidado)* charge; **los niños han quedado a mi c.** the children have been left in my care; **las personas a su c.** *(familiares)* his dependents; *(trabajadores)* the people working under him; **estar a c. de algo, tener algo a su c.** to be in charge of sth; **hacerse c. de** *(asumir el control de)* to take charge of; *(ocuparse de)* to take care of; *(comprender)* to understand; **me hago c. de la difícil situación** I am aware of o I realize the difficulty of the situation; **me da c. de conciencia dejarle pagar** I feel bad about letting him pay

(b) *(empleo)* post, position; **ocupa un c. muy importante** she holds a very important position o post; **alto c.** *(persona) (en empresa)* top manager; *(en la Administración)* high-ranking official; **c. público** public office

(c) *Fin* charge; **con c. a** charged to; **correr a c. de** to be borne by; **hacerse c. de** to pay for

(d) *Der (acusación)* charge; **formular graves cargos contra alguien** to bring serious charges against sb

cargosear *vt CSur* to annoy, to pester

cargoso, -a *adj CSur* annoying

carguero *nm* cargo boat

cariacontecido, -a *adj* crestfallen

cariado, -a *adj* decayed

cariar *vt* **1** to cause decay in; **el azúcar caria las muelas** sugar causes tooth decay

2 cariarse *vpr* to decay

cariátide *nf* caryatid

Caribe 1 *adj* **el mar C.** the Caribbean (Sea)

2 *nm* **el C.** the Caribbean (Sea)

caribeño, -a 1 *adj* Caribbean

2 *nm,f* person from the Caribbean

caribú *(pl* **caribús** *o* **caribúes)** *nm* caribou

caricatura *nf* caricature

caricaturesco, -a *adj* caricature; **un retrato c. de la situación** a caricature of the situation

caricaturista *nmf* caricaturist

caricaturizar [14] *vt* to caricature

caricia *nf (a persona)* caress, stroke; *(a animal)* stroke; **hacer caricias/una c. a alguien** to caress sb

Caricom [kari'kom] *nm o nf (abrev de* **Comunidad (Económica) del Caribe)** Caricom

caridad *nf* charity

caries *nf inv* tooth decay; **tengo tres c.** I have three cavities

carillón *nm* carillon

cariñena *nm* = wine from Cariñena, in the province of Zaragoza

cariño *nm* **(a)** *(afecto)* affection; **tener c. a** to be fond of; **tomar c. a** to grow fond of; **tratar a alguien con c.** to be affectionate to(ward) sb **(b)** *(cuidado)* loving care; **tratar algo con c.** to treat sth with loving care **(c)** *(apelativo)* dear, love, honey

cariñoso, -a *adj* affectionate

carioca 1 *adj* of/from Rio de Janeiro

2 *nmf* person from Rio de Janeiro

carisma *nm* charisma

carismático, -a *adj* charismatic

Cáritas *nf* = charitable organization run by the Catholic Church

caritativo, -a *adj* charitable

cariz *nm* look, appearance; **tomar mal/buen c.** to take a turn for the worse/better

carlinga *nf Av (para piloto)* cockpit; *(para pasajeros)* cabin

carlismo *nm Hist* Carlism

carlista *adj & nmf* Carlist

carmelita *adj & nmf* Carmelite

carmesí *(pl carmesíes) adj & nm* crimson

carmín 1 *adj (color)* carmine

2 *nm* **(a)** *(color)* carmine **(b)** *(lápiz de labios)* lipstick

carnada *nf también Fig* bait

carnal 1 *adj* **(a)** *(de la carne)* carnal **(b)** *(parientes)* **primo c.** first cousin; **tío c.** uncle *(not by marriage)*

2 *nm Méx Fam (amigo)* friend, buddy

carnaval *nm* **(a)** *(fiesta)* carnival **(b)** *Rel* Shrovetide

carnavalada *nf Fam* farce

carnavalesco, -a *adj* carnival; **ambiente c.** carnival atmosphere

carnaza *nf también Fig* bait

carne *nf* **(a)** *(alimento)* meat; **c. blanca** white meat; **c. de cerdo,** *Andes* **c. de chancho** pork; **c. de cordero** lamb; *Esp* **c. de membrillo** quince jelly; *Am* **c. molida,** *Esp, RP* **c. picada** mincemeat; **c. roja** red meat; *Méx* **c. de res** beef; **c. de ternera** veal; **c. de vaca** beef **(b)** *(de persona, fruta)* flesh **(c)** *(sensualidad)* flesh; **los placeres de la c.** the pleasures of the flesh **(d)** *(expresiones)* **c. de cañón** cannon fodder; **entrado en carnes** plump; **c. de gallina** goose bumps; **se me pone la c. de gallina al ver esas imágenes** it sends a shiver down my spine when I see those pictures; **en c. y hueso** in person; **ser de c. y hueso** to be human; **en c. viva** raw; **poner toda la c. en el asador** to go for broke

carné *(pl carnés),* **carnet** *(pl carnets) nm* **(a)** *(documento)* card; **c. de conducir** *o RP* **de conductor** driver's license; **c. de estudiante** student card; **c. de identidad** identity card; **c. de socio** membership card **(b)** *(agenda)* notebook

carnear *vt Andes, RP* to slaughter, to butcher

carnero 1 *nm (animal)* ram; *(carne)* mutton

2 *nm,f RP Fam Pey (esquirol)* scab

carnet = carné

carnicería *nf* **(a)** *(tienda)* butcher's **(b)** *(masacre)* massacre, bloodbath; **fue una c.** it was carnage

carnicero, -a 1 *adj (animal)* carnivorous

2 *nm,f también Fig (persona)* butcher

cárnico, -a *adj* meat; **industrias cárnicas** meat industry; **productos cárnicos** meat products

carnitas *nfpl Méx* = small pieces of braised pork

carnívoro, -a 1 *adj* carnivorous

2 *nm* carnivore

carnosidad *nf* fleshy part

carnoso, -a *adj (persona, rodillas)* fleshy; *(labios)* full

caro, -a 1 *adj* **(a)** *(costoso)* expensive; **la vida está muy cara** everything is so expensive **(b)** *Formal (querido)* cherished

2 *adv* **costar c.** to be expensive; *Fig* **pagar c. algo** to pay dearly for sth; *Fig* **un día te va a salir cara tu conducta** you'll pay dearly for this behavior one day; **vender c. algo** to sell sth at a high price; *Fig* not to give sth up easily; **vendieron cara su derrota** their enemy paid a high price for their victory

Carolina *n* **C. del Norte/Sur** North/South Carolina

carolingio, -a *adj & nm,f* Carolingian

carota *nmf Esp Fam* **ser un(a) c.** to have a lot of cheek *o* nerve

carótida *adj & nf* carotid

carozo *nm RP* stone, pit

carpa *nf* **(a)** *(pez)* carp **(b)** *(de circo)* big top; *(en parque, la calle)* large tent *(for events)* **(c)** *Am (tienda de campaña)* tent

carpanta *nf Esp Fam* ravenous hunger

Cárpatos *nmpl* **los C.** the Carpathians

carpeta *nf* file, folder

carpetazo *nm* **dar c. a algo** to shelve sth

carpetovetónico, -a *adj* deeply Spanish

carpintería *nf* **(a)** *(de muebles y utensilios)* carpentry; *(de puertas y ventanas)* joinery **(b)** *(taller)* carpenter's/joiner's shop

carpintero, -a *nm,f (de muebles y utensilios)* carpenter; *(de puertas y ventanas)* joiner

carraca *nf (instrumento)* rattle; *(cosa vieja)* old crock

carraspear *vi* to clear one's throat

carraspeo *nm* cough, clearing of one's throat

carraspera *nf* **tener c.** to have a frog in one's throat

carrera *nf* **(a)** *(acción de correr)* **a la c.** *(corriendo)* running, at a run; *(rápidamente)* fast, quickly; *(alocadamente)* hastily; **dar(se) una c.** to run; **ir a un sitio de una c.** to run somewhere; **tomar c.** to take a run-up

(b) *(competición)* race; **carreras** races, racing; **¿echamos una c.?** shall we race each other?; **c. armamentística** *o* **de armamentos** arms race; **c. de caballos** horse race; **c. de coches** auto race; **c. contrarreloj** *(en ciclismo)* time trial; **la c. espacial** the space race; **c. de fondo** long-distance race; **c. de obstáculos** steeplechase; **c. de relevos** relay (race)

(c) *(estudios)* college course; **hacer la c. de derecho/físicas** to study law/physics (at college); **cuando acabes la c.** when you finish your studies

(d) *(profesión)* career; **hacer c.** *(triunfar)* to succeed (in life)

(e) *Fam* **hacer la c.** *(prostituirse)* to walk the streets

(f) *(trayecto)* route

(g) *(de taxi)* ride; **¿cuánto es la c. a la estación?** what's the fare to the station?

(h) *(en medias)* run

(i) *(calle)* = name of certain Spanish streets

(j) *Tec (de émbolo)* stroke

(k) *(en béisbol)* run

(l) *Col, Méx, Ven (en el pelo)* parting

carrerilla *nf* **tomar** *o Esp* **coger c.** to take a run-up; **decir algo de c.** to reel sth off

carreta *nf* cart

carrete *nm* **(a)** *(de hilo)* bobbin, reel; *(de alambre)* coil; *(de pesca)* reel **(b)** *Fot* roll (of film) **(c)** **dar c. a alguien** to draw sb out

carretera *nf* road; **c. de circunvalación** beltway; **c. comarcal** minor road; *Méx* **c. de cuota** toll road; **c. nacional** ≃ state highway; **c. de peaje** toll road; **c. secundaria** side road

carretero, -a 1 *adj Am* road; **un accidente c.** a road accident

2 *nm Fig* **fumar como un c.** to smoke like a chimney

carretilla *nf* wheelbarrow

carricoche *nm Anticuado* jalopy

carril *nm* **(a)** *(de carretera)* lane; **c. de aceleración** on-ramp; **c. bici** bikeway; **c. bus** bus lane; **c. lento** slow lane; **c. deceleración** off-ramp; **c. rápido** fast lane; **c. de salida** off-ramp **(b)** *(de vía de tren)* rail **(c)** *(de ruedas)* rut

carrillo *nm* cheek; *Fig* **comer a dos carrillos** to cram one's face with food

carrito *nm* **(a)** *(para equipaje, de supermercado)* cart **(b)** *Méx,Ven* **carritos chocones** bumper cars

carrizal *nm* reedbed

carrizo *nm* reed

carro *nm* **(a)** *(vehículo)* cart; *Fig* **aguantar carros y carretas** to put up with a lot; **¡para el c.!** *(espera)* hang on a minute!; **subirse al c. de la tecnología** to sign up for the new technology; *Mil* **c. de combate** tank **(b)** *(carrito)* cart; *(de bebé)* baby carriage; **c. de la compra** shopping cart **(c)** *(de máquina de escribir)* carriage **(d)** *Am salvo RP (automóvil)* car **(e)** *Méx (de tren)* car; **c. comedor** dining car; **c. dormitorio** sleeper

carrocería *nf* bodywork

carromato *nm* wagon

carroña *nf* carrion

carroñero, -a *adj (animal)* carrion-eating

carroza 1 *nf (coche)* carriage
2 *nmf Fam (viejo)* old fogy

carruaje *nm* carriage

carrusel *nm* **(a)** *(tiovivo)* merry-go-round, carousel **(b)** *(de caballos)* dressage, display of horsemanship

carta *nf* **(a)** *(escrito)* letter; **echar una c.** to mail a letter; **c. abierta** *(en periódico)* open letter; **c. de agradecimiento** letter of thanks, thank-you letter; **c. de amor** love letter; **c. bomba** letter bomb; **c. certificada** certified letter; *Com* **c. de crédito** letter of credit; *Am* **c. postal** postcard; **c. de presentación** *(para un tercero)* letter of introduction; *(con currículum)* cover letter; **c. de recomendación** reference (letter); **c. urgente** express letter
(b) *(naipe)* (playing) card; **jugar a las cartas** to play cards; **echar las cartas a alguien** to tell sb's fortune *(with cards)*
(c) *(menú)* menu; **a la c.** *(menú)* à la carte; *(televisión, programación)* pay-per-view; **comer a la c.** to eat à la carte; **c. de vinos** wine list
(d) *(mapa)* map; *Náut* chart; **c. astral** star chart
(e) *(documento)* charter; **cartas credenciales** letters of credence; **C. Magna** *(constitución)* constitution; **c. de naturaleza** naturalization papers; **c. de trabajo** work permit; **c. verde** green card
(f) *(expresiones)* **a c. cabal** through and through; **dar c. blanca a alguien** to give sb carte blanche *o* a free hand; **enseñar las cartas** to show one's hand; **jugarse la última c.** to play one's last card; **jugarse todo a una c.** to put all one's eggs in one basket; **no saber a qué c. quedarse** to be unsure; **poner las cartas boca arriba** *o* **sobre la mesa** to put one's cards on the table; **tomar cartas en un asunto** to intervene in a matter

cartabón *nm* T square

cartagenero, -a 1 *adj* of/from Cartagena
2 *nm,f* person from Cartagena

cartaginés, -esa *adj & nm,f Hist* Carthaginian

cartapacio *nm* **(a)** *(carpeta)* folder **(b)** *(cuaderno)* notebook

cartearse *vpr* to correspond; **nos seguimos carteando** we still write to each other

cartel *nm* **(a)** *(anuncio)* poster; **prohibido fijar carteles** *(en letrero)* posting of flyers prohibited **(b)** *(fama)* **tener buen/mal c.** to be popular/unpopular

cártel *nm* cartel

cartelera *nf* **(a)** *(tablón)* billboard **(b)** *Prensa* entertainments page; **estar en c.** to be showing; **lleva un año en c.** it has been running for a year

cartelero, -a *adj* popular, big-name

cartelista *nmf* poster artist

carteo *nm* correspondence

cárter *nm Aut* housing

cartera *nf* **(a)** *(para dinero)* wallet, billfold **(b)** *(para documentos)* briefcase; *(sin asa)* portfolio; *(de colegial)* satchel; *Fig* **tener algo en c.** to have sth in the pipeline **(c)** *Com, Fin & Pol* portfolio; **c. de pedidos** *(pedidos pendientes)* orders in hand; *(pedidos atrasados)* backlog; **c. de valores** portfolio **(d)** *Andes, RP (bolso)* purse

carterista *nmf* pickpocket

cartero, -a *nm,f* mailman, *f* mailwoman

cartesiano, -a *adj & nm,f Filosofía* Cartesian

cartilaginoso, -a *adj* cartilaginous

cartílago *nm* cartilage

cartilla *nf* **(a)** *(documento)* book; **c. (de ahorros)** savings book; **c. militar** = booklet to say one has completed one's military service; **c. del paro** = registration card issued to the unemployed; **c. de racionamiento** ration book; **c. de la seguridad social** = social security card **(b)** *(para aprender a leer)* primer; *Fig* **leerle la c. a alguien** to read sb the riot act

cartografía *nf* cartography

cartógrafo, -a *nm,f* cartographer

cartomancia *nf* cartomancy, fortune-telling *(with cards)*

cartón *nm* **(a)** *(material)* cardboard; **c. piedra** papier-mâché **(b)** *(de cigarrillos)* carton **(c)** *(de leche, zumo)* carton **(d)** *Méx (tira cómica)* comic strip

cartoné *nm* **en c.** bound in boards

cartonista *nmf Méx* comic-strip artist

cartuchera *nf* cartridge belt

cartucho *nm* **(a)** *(de arma, tinta)* cartridge; *Fig* **quemar el último c.** to play one's last card **(b)** *(envoltorio) (de monedas)* roll; *(cucurucho)* paper cone

cartuja *nf* charterhouse

cartujo, -a 1 *adj* Carthusian
2 *nm* **(a)** *(religioso)* Carthusian **(b)** *(persona retraída)* hermit

cartulina *nf* card, thin cardboard; **una carpeta de c.** a cardboard folder

casa *nf* **(a)** *(edificio)* house; *(piso)* apartment; *Fam* **una mentira como una c.** a whopping great lie; **ser de andar por c.** *(sencillo)* to be simple *o* basic; *Fig* **echar** *o* **tirar la c. por la ventana** to spare no expense; **empezar la c. por el tejado** to put the cart before the horse; **c. adosada** row house; **C. Blanca** White House; **c. de campo** country house; **c. de de muñecas** dollhouse; **c. particular** private house; **C. Rosada** *(en Argentina)* = Argentinian presidential palace; **c. solariega** ancestral home, family seat; **c. unifamiliar** = house (usually detached) on an estate
(b) *(hogar)* home; **en c.** at home; **¿está tu hermano en c.?** is your brother at home?; **buscar c.** to look for somewhere to live; **cambiarse** *o* **mudarse de c.** to move (house); **ir a c.** to go home; **pásate por mi c.** come around to my place
(c) *(familia)* family; *(linaje)* house; *Hist* **la c. de Austria** the Hapsburgs; *Hist* **la c. de Borbón** the Bourbons; **c. real** royal family
(d) *(establecimiento)* company; **¡invita la c.!** it's on the house!; **especialidad/vino de la c.** house specialty/wine; **c. de apuestas** the bookie's; **c. de citas** brothel; **c. de comidas** = cheap restaurant serving simple meals; **c. discográfica** record company; **c. de empeño** pawnshop; **c. de huéspedes** rooming house; *Fig* **¡esto es una c. de locos!** this place is a madhouse!; *Com* **c. matriz** *(de empresa)* head office; *(de grupo de empresas)* parent company; *Vulg* **c. de putas** whorehouse; **c. de socorro** first-aid station
(e) *Dep* home; **jugar en c.** to play at home; **jugar fuera de c.** to play away (from home); **el equipo de c.** the home team

Casablanca *n* Casablanca

casaca *nf (de chaqué)* frock coat; *(chaquetón)* jacket

casación *nf Der* annulment

casadero, -a *adj* marriageable

casado, -a 1 *adj* married (**con** to)
2 *nm,f* married man, *f* married woman; **los recién casados** the newlyweds

casamentero, -a 1 *adj* matchmaking
2 *nm,f* matchmaker

casamiento *nm* wedding, marriage

casanova *nm* Casanova

casar 1 *vt* **(a)** *(en matrimonio)* to marry **(b)** *(unir)* to fit together
2 *vi* to match
3 casarse *vpr* to get married (**con** to); **casarse por la iglesia** to have a church wedding; **casarse por lo civil** to have a civil wedding; *Fig* **no se casa con nadie** he doesn't take sides

cascabel *nm* (small) bell; *Fig* **poner el c. al gato** to bell the cat, to dare to go ahead

cascabeleo *nm* tinkle, jingle

cascada *nf (de agua)* waterfall; **en c.** one after another

cascado, -a *adj* **(a)** *Esp Fam (estropeado)* bust; *(persona)* worn-out **(b)** *(ronco)* rasping

cascajo *nm* rubble; *Fam Fig* **estar hecho un c.** to be a wreck

cascanueces *nm inv* nutcracker

cascar [59] **1** *vt* (**a**) *(romper)* to crack; **c. un huevo** to crack an egg (**b**) *Esp Fam (dañar)* to damage, to harm; *Fig* **cascarla** to kick the bucket (**c**) *Fam (la voz)* to make croaky (**d**) *Fam (pegar)* to thump
  2 *vi Esp Fam (hablar)* to ramble on
  3 cascarse *vpr* (**a**) *(romperse)* to crack (**b**) *Esp Fam* **se le cascó la voz** his voice went croaky

cáscara *nf (de almendra, huevo)* shell; *(de limón, naranja)* peel

cascarilla *nf* husk

cascarón *nm* eggshell; *Fig* **salir del c.** *(independizarse)* to leave the nest; *(abrirse)* to come out of one's shell

cascarrabias *nmf inv* grouch, sourpuss

casco 1 *nm* (**a**) *(para la cabeza)* helmet; *(de motorista)* crash helmet; **cascos azules** U.N. peacekeeping troops, blue berets (**b**) *(de barco)* hull (**c**) *(de ciudad)* **c. antiguo** old (part of) town; **c. urbano** downtown (**d**) *(de caballo)* hoof (**e**) *Esp, Méx (envase)* empty bottle (**f**) *(pedazo)* fragment, piece; *Andes, Cuba, RP (gajo)* segment
  2 cascos *nmpl* (**a**) *Fam (auriculares)* headphones (**b**) *(expresiones)* **calentarse** *o* **romperse los cascos** to rack *o* cudgel one's brains; **ser alegre** *o* **ligero de cascos** *(irresponsable)* to be irresponsible; *(mujer)* to be flighty

cascote *nm* piece of rubble

caserío *nm* (**a**) *(aldea)* hamlet (**b**) *(casa de campo)* country house

casero, -a 1 *adj* (**a**) *(de casa) (comida)* homemade; *(trabajos)* domestic; *(celebración)* family (**b**) *(hogareño)* home-loving
  2 *nm,f* (**a**) *(propietario)* landlord, *f* landlady (**b**) *(encargado)* house agent

caserón *nm* large, rambling house

caseta *nf* (**a**) *(casa pequeña)* hut (**b**) *(en la playa)* beach hut (**c**) *(de feria)* stall, booth (**d**) *(para perro)* kennel

casete 1 *nf (cinta)* cassette
  2 *nm (magnetófono)* cassette *o* tape recorder

cash-flow *nm* cash flow

casi *adv* almost; **c. me muero** I almost *o* nearly died; **no comió c. nada** she ate almost *o* practically nothing; **c. no dormí** I hardly slept at all; **c., c.** almost, just about; **c. nunca** hardly ever; **¿qué te pasa? — ¡c. nada! que me ha dejado mi mujer** what's up? — my wife only went and left me; **lo venden por tres millones — ¡c. nada!** they're selling it for three million — what a bargain!; **c. siempre** almost *o* nearly always

casilla *nf* (**a**) *(de caja, armario)* compartment; *(para cartas)* pigeonhole; *Andes, RP* **c. de correos,** *CAm, Carib, Méx* **c. postal** PO Box (**b**) *(en un impreso)* box (**c**) *(de tablero de juego)* square (**d**) *Méx (de votación)* voting booth (**e**) *Am Inform* **c. de correo de entrada** inbox (**f**) *(expresiones)* **sacar a alguien de sus casillas** to drive sb mad; **salir** *o* **salirse de sus casillas** to fly off the handle

casillero *nm* (**a**) *(mueble)* set of pigeonholes (**b**) *(casilla)* pigeonhole

casino *nm* (**a**) *(para jugar)* casino (**b**) *(asociación)* (social) club

casís *nm inv* (**a**) *(arbusto)* black currant bush (**b**) *(fruto)* black currant (**c**) *(licor)* cassis

caso *nm* (**a**) *(situación, circunstancias)* case; **el c. es que...** *(el hecho es que)* the thing is (that)...; *(lo importante es que)* what matters is (that)...; **el c. Dreyfus** the Dreyfus affair; **en c. afirmativo/negativo** if so/not; **en c. de** in the event of; **en c. de que** if; **(en)** *c.* **de que venga** should she come; **en cualquier** *o* **todo c.** in any event *o* case; **en el mejor/peor de los casos** at best/worst; **en tal** *o* **ese c.** in that case; **en último c.** as a last resort; **ir al c.** to get to the point; **pongamos por c. que...** let's suppose (that)...; **ser un c.** to be a case, to be a right one; **ser un c. perdido** to be a lost

cause; **no venir al c.** to be irrelevant; **c. de conciencia** matter of conscience; **fue un c. de fuerza mayor** it was due to force of circumstances
  (**b**) *(atención)* **hacer c. a** to pay attention to; **hacer c. omiso de** to ignore; **se lo dije, pero ella, ni c.** I told her but she didn't take any notice; **¡ni c.!, ¡no hagas c.!** don't take any notice!; **no me hace ni c.** she doesn't take a bit of notice of me

casona *nf* large house, mansion

casorio *nm Esp Fam* wedding

caspa *nf* (**a**) *(en el pelo)* dandruff (**b**) *Esp Fam* **la c.** *(famosos)* C-list celebs

Caspio 1 *adj* **el mar C.** the Caspian Sea
  2 *nm* **el C.** the Caspian Sea

cáspita *interj Anticuado o Hum* **¡c.!** *(sorpresa)* my goodness!; *(enfado)* darn it!

casposo, -a *adj* (**a**) *(con caspa)* covered in dandruff (**b**) *Esp (música, película)* cheesy; **los famosos casposos** C-list celebs

casposo, -a *adj* (**a**) *(con caspa)* covered in dandruff (**b**) *Esp Fam (música, película)* cheesy; **los famosos casposos** C-list celebs (**c**) *Esp Fam (asqueroso)* disgusting

casque *etc ver* **cascar**

casquería *nf (tienda)* = store selling offal; *(productos)* offal; *Fam Fig* **en esa película sale demasiada c.** that movie is too gory

casquete *nm* (**a**) *(gorro)* skullcap (**b**) **c. esférico** segment of a sphere; **c. polar** polar icecap (**c**) *muy Fam* **echar un c.** to screw

casquillo *nm* (**a**) *(de bala)* case (**b**) *(de lámpara)* socket, lampholder

casquivano, -a *adj Fam (irresponsable)* irresponsible; *(mujer)* flighty

cassette [ka'sete, ka'set] **1** *nf (cinta)* cassette
  2 *nm (magnetófono)* cassette *o* tape recorder

casta *nf* (**a**) *(linaje)* stock, lineage; **de c. le viene al galgo** it runs in the family (**b**) *(especie, calidad)* breed (**c**) *(en la India)* caste

castaña *nf* (**a**) *(fruto)* chestnut; *Fam* **sacarle a alguien las castañas del fuego** to get sb out of trouble; **c. de agua** water chestnut (**b**) *Esp Fam (golpe)* bash (**c**) *Esp Fam (borrachera)* **agarrarse una c.** to get legless (**d**) *Esp Fam (cosa aburrida)* bore; **este libro es una c.** this book is boring

castañazo *nm Fam* bash; **darse un c.** *(golpe)* to bump oneself; *(con el coche)* to have a crash

castañeta *nf Taurom* = bullfighter's ornamental pigtail

castañetear *vi (dientes)* to chatter; **me castañetean las rodillas** my knees are knocking

castañeteo *nm (de castañuelas)* clacking; *(de dientes)* chattering

castaño, -a 1 *adj (color)* chestnut
  2 *nm* (**a**) *(color)* chestnut; *Fig* **pasar de c. oscuro** to be beyond a joke (**b**) *(árbol)* chestnut (tree); **c. de Indias** horse chestnut (tree) (**c**) *(madera)* chestnut

castañuela *nf* castanet; *Fig* **estar como unas castañuelas** to be over the moon

castellanizar [14] *vt* to hispanicize

castellano, -a 1 *adj & nm,f* Castilian
  2 *nm (lengua)* (Castilian) Spanish

castellanohablante, castellanoparlante 1 *adj* Spanish-speaking
  2 *nmf* Spanish speaker

castellano-leonés, -esa 1 *adj* of/from Castilla y León
  2 *nm,f* person from Castilla y León

castellano-manchego, -a 1 *adj* of/from Castilla-La Mancha
  2 *nm,f* person from Castilla-La Mancha

castellanoparlante = **castellanohablante**

castellonense 1 *adj* of/from Castellón
  2 *nm,f* person from Castellón

casticismo *nm* purism

castidad *nf* chastity

castigador, -ora *Fam* **1** *adj* seductive
  2 *nm,f* lady-killer, *f* man-eater

castigar [40] **1** *vt* (**a**) *(imponer castigo a)* to punish; **castigaron a los niños sin cena** they punished the children by sending them to bed without dinner; **lo castigaron con la pena capital** he was given the death penalty (**b**) *Dep* to penalize (**c**) *(piel, salud)* to damage; *(sujeto: sol, viento, epidemia)* to devastate; **una zona castigada por las inundaciones** a region severely hit by the floods (**d**) *(enamorar)* to seduce
  2 castigarse *vpr* to be hard on oneself

castigo *nm* (**a**) *(sanción)* punishment; **c. corporal** corporal punishment; **c. ejemplar** exemplary punishment (**b**) *(daño)* damage; **infligir un duro c. a** to inflict severe damage on (**c**) *Fam (persona)* **¡qué c. de niño/hombre!** what a pain that child/man is! (**d**) *Dep* **máximo c.** penalty; **el árbitro señaló el máximo c.** the referee pointed to the spot

Castilla *n* Castile; **C. la Nueva/la Vieja** New/Old Castile

Castilla-La Mancha *n* Castile and La Mancha

Castilla y León *n* Castile and León

castillo *nm* (**a**) *(edificio)* castle; **hacer castillos en el aire** to build castles in the air; **c. de arena** sand castle; **c. de fuegos artificiales** firework display (**b**) *Náut* **c. de popa** quarterdeck; **c. de proa** forecastle

casting ['kastin] *(pl* **castings**) *nm Cine & Teatro* audition; **hacer un c.** to hold an audition

castizo, -a *adj (lenguaje, palabra)* = derived from popular usage and considered linguistically pure; *(barrio, taberna)* typical; **un andaluz c.** a typical Andalusian

casto, -a *adj* chaste

castor *nm* beaver

castración *nf* castration

castrador, -ora *adj* **una madre castradora** a strong *o* dominant mother

castrar *vt* (**a**) *(animal, persona)* to castrate; *(gato)* to neuter (**b**) *(debilitar)* to sap, to impair

castrense *adj* military

castrismo *nm* Castroism

castrista *adj & nmf* Castroist

casual *adj* accidental; **un encuentro c.** a chance encounter

casualidad *nf* coincidence; **la c. hizo que nos encontráramos** chance brought us together; **dio la c. de que...** it so happened that...; **no es c. que...** it's no coincidence that...; **de c.** by chance; **¿no llevarás por c. un paraguas?** you wouldn't happen to have an umbrella with you?; **¡qué c.!** what a coincidence!

casualmente *adv* by chance

casucha *nf Pey* hovel, dump

casuística *nf Der* case law

casuístico, -a *adj Formal* casuistic

casulla *nf* chasuble

cata *nf* tasting; **c. de vinos** wine tasting

catabolismo *nm* catabolism

cataclismo *nm* cataclysm

catacumbas *nfpl* catacombs

catador, -ora *nm,f* taster

catadura *nf (aspecto)* look, appearance

catafalco *nm* catafalque

catalán, -ana **1** *adj & nm,f* Catalan, Catalonian
  2 *nm (lengua)* Catalan

catalanismo *nm* (**a**) *(palabra)* Catalanism (**b**) *Pol* Catalan nationalism

catalanista *adj & nmf* Catalan nationalist

catalejo *nm* telescope

catalepsia *nf* catalepsy

cataléptico, -a *adj Med* cataleptic; *Fam Fig* half asleep

catalítico, -a *adj Quím* catalytic

catalizador, -ora **1** *adj* (**a**) *Quím* catalytic (**b**) *(impulsor)* **el principio c. del cambio** the catalyst of change
  2 *nm* (**a**) *Quím & Fig* catalyst (**b**) *Aut* catalytic converter

catalizar [14] *vt Quím* to catalyze; *(impulsar)* to provoke

catalogación *nf* cataloguing; **no admitir c.** *(ser extraordinario)* to be hard to categorize

catalogar [40] *vt* (**a**) *(en catálogo)* to catalog (**b**) *(clasificar)* **c. a alguien (de)** to class sb (as)

catálogo *nm* catalog

Cataluña *n* Catalonia

catamarán *nm* catamaran

cataplasma *nf* (**a**) *Med* poultice (**b**) *Fam (pesado)* bore

cataplines *nmpl Fam (testículos)* nuts

cataplum, cataplún *interj* **¡c.!** crash!, bang!

catapulta *nf* catapult

catapultar *vt* to catapult

catapún *Fam* **1** *interj* **¡c.!** *(en lenguaje infantil)* crash!, bang!
  2 *adj inv* **en el año c.** ages ago; **es del año c.** it's ancient

catar *vt* to taste

catarata *nf* (**a**) *(de agua)* waterfall; **las cataratas del Iguazú** the Iguaçu Falls; **las cataratas del Niágara** Niagara Falls (**b**) *Med* cataract

cátaro, -a *Hist adj & nm,f* Cathar

catarro *nm* cold

catarsis *nf inv (purificación)* catharsis

catártico, -a *adj* cathartic

catastral *adj* **registro c.** land record; **valor c.** = value of a property recorded in the land record, ≃ assessed value

catastro *nm* land records

catástrofe *nf* catastrophe; *(accidente de avión, tren)* disaster; **c. ecológica** environmental disaster; **c. natural** natural disaster

catastrófico, -a *adj* catastrophic

catastrofismo *nm (pesimismo)* scaremongering, alarmism

catastrofista *adj & nmf* alarmist

catatónico, -a *adj* (**a**) *(paciente)* catatonic (**b**) *Fam (alterado)* flabbergasted

catavino *nm* wine-tasting glass

catavinos *nmf inv* wine taster

catchup *(pl* **catchups**) *nm* ketchup, catchup

cate *nm Fam* fail

catear *vt* (**a**) *Esp Fam* to fail, to flunk; **he cateado *o* me han cateado la física** I failed *o* flunked physics (**b**) *Am (casa)* to search

catecismo *nm* catechism

cátedra *nf* (**a**) *(cargo) (en universidad)* chair; *(en instituto)* post of head of department (**b**) *(departamento)* department (**c**) **sentar c.** to lay down the law

catedral *nf* cathedral; **una mentira como una c.** a whopping great lie

catedralicio, -a *adj* cathedral; **ciudad catedralicia** cathedral city

catedrático, -a *nm,f (de universidad)* professor; *(de instituto)* head of department

categoría *nf* (**a**) *(clase)* category; **un hotel de primera c.** a top-class hotel; **c. gramatical** part of speech (**b**) *(posición social)* standing; **de c.** important (**c**) *(calidad)* quality; **de (primera) c.** first-class

categóricamente *adv* categorically

categórico, -a *adj* categorical

catequesis *nf inv* catechesis, ≃ Sunday school

catequizar [14] *vt* (**a**) *(enseñar religión)* to instruct in Christian doctrine (**b**) *(adoctrinar)* to convert

catering ['katerin] (*pl* **catering** *o* **caterings**) *nm* catering

caterva *nf* host, multitude

catéter *nm Med* catheter

cateto, -a 1 *adj Pey* uncultured, uncouth
  2 *nm,f Pey* country bumpkin
  3 *nm Geom* cathetus

catire, -a *adj Carib* blond(e)

catódico, -a *adj* cathodic, cathode

cátodo *nm* cathode

catolicismo *nm* Catholicism

católico, -a 1 *adj* Catholic; *Fam Fig* **no estar muy c.** to be under the weather
  2 *nm,f* Catholic

catorce *núm* fourteen; *ver también* **seis**

catorceavo, -a, catorzavo, -a *núm (fracción)* fourteenth; **la catorceava parte** a fourteenth

catre *nm (cama)* camp bed, cot; *Fam* **irse al c.** to hit the sack, to hit the hay

catsup (*pl* **catsups**) *nm Méx* ketchup, catchup

caucásico, -a *adj & nm,f* Caucasian

Cáucaso *nm* **el C.** the Caucasus

cauce *nm* **(a)** *Agr & Fig* channel **(b)** *(de río)* riverbed; **volver a su c.** to return to normal

caucho *nm* **(a)** *(sustancia)* rubber; **c. vulcanizado** vulcanized rubber **(b)** *(planta)* rubber tree

caudal *nm* **(a)** *(cantidad de agua)* flow, volume **(b)** *(capital, abundancia)* wealth

caudaloso, -a *adj* **(a)** *(río)* with a large flow **(b)** *(persona)* wealthy, rich

caudillaje *nm* leadership

caudillo *nm (en la guerra)* leader, head; *Hist* **el C.** = title used to refer to Franco

causa *nf* **(a)** *(origen)* cause; **la relación c.-efecto** the relationship between cause and effect **(b)** *(razón)* reason; **se desconocen las causas del accidente** it is not known what caused the accident; **a** *o* **por c. de** because of; **por c. mayor** for reasons beyond my/our/*etc* control **(c)** *(ideal)* cause; **dieron su vida por la c.** they gave their lives for the cause; **hacer c. común con alguien** to make common cause with sb; **ser una c. perdida** to be a lost cause **(d)** *Der* case

causal *adj* causal

causalidad *nf* causality

causante 1 *adj* **la razón c.** the cause
  2 *nmf* cause; **el c. del accidente** the person responsible for the accident

causar *vt (originar)* to cause; *(impresión)* to make; *(placer)* to give; **el accidente le causó graves lesiones** he was seriously injured in the accident; **el huracán causó estragos en la costa** the hurricane wreaked havoc on the coast; **el terremotó causó dos mil muertos** two thousand people died in the earthquake, the earthquake killed two thousand people

causticidad *nf también Fig* causticity

cáustico, -a *adj también Fig* caustic

cautela *nf* caution, cautiousness; **con c.** cautiously

cautelar *adj* precautionary, preventive

cauteloso, -a 1 *adj* cautious, careful
  2 *nm,f* cautious person

cauterizar [14] *vt* to cauterize

cautivador, -ora 1 *adj* captivating, enchanting
  2 *nm,f* charmer

cautivar *vt* **(a)** *(apresar)* to capture **(b)** *(seducir)* to captivate, to enchant

cautiverio *nm* captivity

cautividad *nf* captivity; **vivir en c.** to live in captivity

cautivo, -a *adj & nm,f* captive

cauto, -a *adj* cautious, careful

cava 1 *nm (bebida)* cava, = Spanish sparkling wine
  2 *nf (bodega)* wine cellar

cavar 1 *vt (hoyo)* to dig; *(con azada)* to hoe; *Fig* **está cavando su propia tumba** she is digging her own grave
  2 *vi (hacer hoyo)* to dig; *(con azada)* to hoe

caverna *nf (cueva)* cave; *(más grande)* cavern

cavernícola *nmf* caveman, *f* cavewoman

cavernoso, -a *adj (voz, tos)* hollow

caviar *nm* caviar

cavidad *nf* cavity; **la c. bucal** the buccal *o* oral cavity

cavilación *nf* deep thought, pondering

cavilar *vi* to think deeply, to ponder

caviloso, -a *adj* thoughtful, pensive

cayado *nm* **(a)** *(de pastor)* crook **(b)** *(de obispo)* crosier

cayena *nf (especia)* cayenne pepper

cayera *etc ver* **caer**

cayo *nm (isla)* key, islet

caza 1 *nf* **(a)** *(acción de cazar)* hunting; **ir de c.** to go hunting; *Fig* **dar c. a** to hunt down; *Fig* **c. de brujas** witch hunt **(b)** *(animales, carne)* game; **c. mayor** big game; **c. menor** small game
  2 *nm (avión)* fighter (plane)

cazabombardero *nm* fighter-bomber

cazador, -ora 1 *adj* hunting
  2 *nm,f (persona)* hunter; **c. furtivo** poacher

cazadora *nf (prenda)* bomber jacket

cazadotes *nm inv* fortune hunter

cazalla *nf (bebida)* = aniseed-flavored spirit

cazar [14] *vt* **(a)** *(animales)* to hunt **(b)** *Fam (pillar, atrapar)* to catch; *(en matrimonio)* to trap; **me has cazado despistado** you've caught me on the hop; **cuando me hablan rápido en inglés no cazo una** when people speak English quickly to me I can't understand a word; *Fig* **cazarlas al vuelo** to be quick on the uptake

cazarrecompensas *nmf inv* bounty hunter

cazatalentos *nmf inv* **(a)** *(de artistas, deportistas)* talent scout **(b)** *(de ejecutivos)* headhunter

cazo *nm* **(a)** *(cacerola)* saucepan; *(cucharón)* ladle **(b)** *Fam (persona fea)* ugly mug

cazoleta *nf* **(a)** *(recipiente)* pot **(b)** *(de pipa)* bowl

cazuela *nf* **(a)** *(recipiente)* pot, saucepan; *(de barro)* earthenware cooking pot **(b)** *(guiso)* casserole, stew; **a la c.** casseroled

cazurro, -a 1 *adj (bruto)* stupid
  2 *nm,f (bruto)* idiot, fool

CC (a) *(abrev de* **código civil**) civil code **(b)** *(abrev de* **código de circulación**) highway code **(c)** *(abrev de* **cuerpo consular**) consular staff

cc *(abrev de* **centímetros cúbicos**) cc

c/c *(abrev de* **cuenta corriente**) a/c

CC.AA. *(abrev de* **Comunidades Autónomas**) = autonomous regions (of Spain)

CC. OO. *(abrev de* **Comisiones Obreras**) = Spanish left-wing trade union

CD 1 *nm* (*pl* **CDs**) *(abrev de* **compact disc**) CD; **CD interactivo** interactive CD
  2 (a) *(abrev de* **club deportivo**) *(en fútbol)* FC **(b)** *(abrev de* **cuerpo diplomático**) CD

CD-i *nm (abrev de* **compact disc interactivo**) CD-i

CD-R *nm (abrev de* **compact disc recordable**) CD-R

CD-ROM ['θeðe'rrom] (*pl* **CD-ROMs**) *nm* CD-ROM

CD-RW *nm (abrev de* **compact disc rewritable**) CD-RW

CE 1 *nm (abrev de* **Consejo de Europa**) CE
  2 *nf Antes (abrev de* **Comunidad Europea**) EC

ce *nf Fig* **ce por be** in great detail

cebada *nf* barley

cebado, -a *adj (gordo)* huge

cebador *nm* (**a**) *(de fluorescente)* ballast (**b**) *(de pólvora)* primer

cebar 1 *vt* (**a**) *(engordar)* to fatten (up) (**b**) *(fuego, caldera)* to stoke, to fuel; *(máquina, arma)* to prime (**c**) *(anzuelo)* to bait (**d**) *RP (mate)* to prepare, to brew

2 cebarse *vpr* **cebarse en** *(ensañarse)* to be merciless with; **la policía se cebó con los manifestantes** the police dealt with the demonstrators brutally

cebiche = **ceviche**

cebo *nm también Fig* bait

cebolla *nf (planta)* onion; *Fam (cabeza)* nut, head

cebolleta *nf* (**a**) *(planta)* scallion, green onion (**b**) *(en vinagre)* (small) pickled onion

cebollino *nm* (**a**) *(planta)* chive; *(cebolleta)* scallion, green onion (**b**) *Fam (necio)* idiot

cebón, -ona 1 *adj* fattened

2 *nm* pig

cebra *nf* zebra; **paso de c.** pedestrian crosswalk

cebú *(pl* **cebúes***) nm* zebu

ceca *nf* mint; *Fam* **ir de la C. a la Meca** to go here, there and everywhere; *RP* **cara o c.** heads or tails

cecear *vi* to lisp

ceceo *nm* lisp

cecina *nf* dried, salted meat

cedazo *nm* sieve

ceder 1 *vt* (**a**) *(traspasar, transferir)* to hand over (**b**) *(conceder)* to give up

2 *vi* (**a**) *(venirse abajo)* to give way; **la puerta finalmente cedió** the door finally gave way (**b**) *(destensarse)* to give, to become loose; **ha cedido el jersey** the jersey has gone baggy (**c**) *(disminuir)* to abate (**d**) *(rendirse)* to give up; **c. a** to give in to; **c. en** to give up on

cedilla *nf* cedilla

cedro *nm* cedar

cédula *nf* document; **c. de citación** summons *(singular)*; **c. de habitabilidad** = certificate stating that a place is habitable; **c. hipotecaria** mortgage bond; *Am* **c. de identidad** identity card; **c. de vecindad** identity card

CEE *nf Antes (abrev de* **Comunidad Económica Europea***)* EEC

cefalea *nf Med* headache

cefalópodo *nm Zool* cephalopod

céfiro *nm (viento)* zephyr

cegador, -ora *adj* blinding

cegar [43] **1** *vt* (**a**) *también Fig* to blind (**b**) *(tapar) (ventana)* to block off; *(tubo)* to block up

2 *vi* to be blinding

3 cegarse *vpr también Fig* to be blinded

cegato, -a *Fam* **1** *adj* shortsighted

2 *nm,f* shortsighted person

cegesimal *adj* = of or relating to cgs units

cegué *etc ver* **cegar**

ceguera *nf también Fig* blindness

CEI ['θei] *nf (abrev de* **Confederación de Estados Independientes***)* CIS

Ceilán *n Antes* Ceylon

ceja *nf* (**a**) *(en la cara)* eyebrow; *Fam Fig* **quemarse las cejas** to burn the midnight oil; *Fam* **se le metió entre c. y c. que…** he got it into his head that…; *Fam* **tener a alguien entre c. y c.** not to be able to stand the sight of sb (**b**) *(de instrumento de cuerda) (puente)* bridge; *(cejilla)* capo

cejar *vi* **c. en** to give up on; **no cejaremos en nuestro empeño (de…)** we will not flag in our efforts (to…)

cejijunto, -a *adj* (**a**) *(persona)* bushy-eyebrowed (**b**) *(gesto)* frowning

cejilla *nf (de guitarra)* capo

celada *nf* (**a**) *(pieza de armadura)* helmet (**b**) *(emboscada)* ambush; *Fig* trick, trap

celador, -ora *nm,f (de colegio)* janitor; *(de hospital)* orderly; *(de prisión)* guard; *(de museo)* attendant

celda *nf (gen) & Inform* cell; **c. de castigo** solitary confinement cell

celdilla *nf (de panal)* cell

celebérrimo, -a *adj* extremely famous

celebración *nf* (**a**) *(festejo)* celebration (**b**) *(de ceremonia, reunión)* holding

celebrar *vt* (**a**) *(festejar)* to celebrate (**b**) *(llevar a cabo)* to hold; *(oficio religioso, misa)* to celebrate; **celebraremos la reunión esta tarde** we'll hold the meeting this afternoon (**c**) *(alegrarse de)* **celebro tu ascenso** I'm delighted by your promotion; **celebro que hayas podido venir** I'm delighted you were able to come (**d**) *(alabar)* to praise, to applaud

2 celebrarse *vpr* (**a**) *(festejarse)* to be celebrated; **esa fiesta se celebra el 25 de Julio** that holiday falls on July 25 (**b**) *(llevarse a cabo)* to take place, to be held

célebre *adj* famous, celebrated

celebridad *nf* (**a**) *(fama)* fame (**b**) *(persona famosa)* celebrity

celeridad *nf* speed; **con c.** rapidly

celeste 1 *adj (del cielo)* celestial, heavenly; **azul c.** sky blue

2 *nm* sky blue

celestial *adj* celestial, heavenly

celestina *nf* lovers' go-between

celibato *nm* celibacy

célibe *adj & nmf* celibate

celo 1 *nm* (**a**) *(esmero)* zeal, keenness (**b**) *(devoción)* devotion (**c**) *(de hembra)* heat; **en c.** in heat (**d**) *Esp (cinta adhesiva)* Scotch® tape (**e**) jealousy

2 celos *nmpl* jealousy; **dar celos a alguien** to make sb jealous; **tener celos de alguien** to be jealous of sb

celofán *nm* cellophane

celosía *nf* lattice window, jalousie

celoso, -a 1 *adj* (**a**) *(con celos)* jealous (**b**) *(cumplidor)* keen, eager

2 *nm,f (con celos)* jealous person

celta 1 *adj* Celtic

2 *nmf (persona)* Celt

3 *nm (lengua)* Celtic

celtíbero, -a, celtibero, -a *adj & nm,f* Celtiberian

céltico, -a *adj* Celtic

célula *nf* cell; **c. fotoeléctrica** photoelectric cell, electric eye; **c. fotovoltaica** photovoltaic cell; **c. madre** stem cell, mother cell

celular *adj Biol* cellular

celulitis *nf inv* cellulite

celuloide *nm* (**a**) *Quím* celluloid (**b**) *(película)* film

celulosa *nf* cellulose

cementerio *nm (de muertos)* cemetery; **c. de automóviles** *o* **coches** junkyard; **c. nuclear** *o* **radiactivo** nuclear dumping ground

cemento *nm* (**a**) *(material)* cement; *(hormigón)* concrete; **c. armado** reinforced concrete (**b**) *Am (para pegar)* glue

cena *nf* dinner, evening meal; **dar una c.** to give a dinner party; **c. de despedida** farewell dinner; *Rel* **la última c.** the Last Supper

cenáculo *nm Formal (grupo)* circle

cenador *nm* arbor, bower

cenagal *nm* bog, marsh

cenagoso, -a *adj* muddy

cenar 1 *vt* to have for dinner

2 *vi* to have dinner; **c. fuera** to eat out, to go out for dinner

cencerro *nm* cowbell; *Fam* **estar como un c.** to be as mad as a hatter

cenefa *nf (en vestido)* border; *(en pared)* frieze

cenetista 1 *adj* = relating to the CNT

   2 *nmf* member of the CNT

cenicero *nm* ashtray

Cenicienta *nf* (la) C. Cinderella

ceniciento, -a *adj* ashen, ash-gray

cenit *nm también Fig* zenith

cenital *adj* **luz c.** light from above

ceniza *nf* ash; **cenizas** *(de cadáver)* ashes

cenizo, -a 1 *adj* ashen, ash-gray

   2 *nm,f Fam (gafe)* jinxed person; **ser un c.** to be jinxed

censar *vt* to take a census of

censo *nm* **(a)** *(padrón)* census; *Esp* **c. electoral** list of registered voters **(b)** *(tributo)* tax **(c)** *Der* lease

censor, -ora *nm,f* **(a)** *(funcionario)* censor **(b)** *(crítico)* critic **(c)** *Esp* **c. (jurado) de cuentas** certified public accountant

censura *nf* **(a)** *(prohibición)* censorship **(b)** *(organismo)* censors **(c)** *(reprobación)* censure, severe criticism **(d)** *Esp Fin* **c. de cuentas** inspection of accounts, audit

censurable *adj* censurable

censurar *vt* **(a)** *(prohibir)* to censor **(b)** *(reprobar)* to criticize severely, to censure

centauro *nm* centaur

centavo, -a 1 *núm* hundredth; **la centava parte** a hundredth

   2 *nm (moneda) (en países anglosajones)* cent; *(en países latinoamericanos)* centavo; **sin un c.** penniless

centella *nf* **(a)** *(rayo)* flash **(b)** *(chispa)* spark **(c)** *(cosa, persona)* **es una c.** he's like lightning; **rápido como una c.** quick as a flash

centellear *vi (luz)* to sparkle; *(estrella)* to twinkle

centelleo *nm (de joya)* sparkle; **el c. de las estrellas/luces** the twinkle *o* twinkling of the stars/lights

centena *nf* hundred; **una c. de coches** a hundred cars

centenar *nm* hundred; **un c. de** a hundred; **a centenares** by the hundreds

centenario, -a 1 *adj (persona)* in his/her hundreds; *(institución, edificio)* century-old

   2 *nm* centenary; **quinto c.** five-hundredth anniversary

centeno *nm* rye

centesimal *adj* centesimal

centésimo, -a *núm* hundredth

centígrado, -a *adj* centigrade; **veinte grados centígrados** twenty degrees centigrade

centigramo *nm* centigram

centilitro *nm* centiliter

centímetro *nm* **(a)** *(medida)* centimeter **(b)** *(cinta)* measuring tape

céntimo *nm (moneda)* cent; *Fig* **estar sin un c.** to be flat broke

centinela *nm* sentry

centollo *nm* spider crab

centrado, -a *adj* **(a)** *(basado)* **c. en** based on **(b)** *(equilibrado)* stable, steady **(c)** *(rueda, cuadro)* centered

central 1 *adj* central

   2 *nf* **(a)** *(oficina)* headquarters, head office; *(de correos, comunicaciones)* main office; **c. telefónica** telephone exchange **(b)** *(de energía)* power station; **c. eléctrica** power station; **c. eólica** wind farm; **c. hidroeléctrica** *o* **hidráulica** hydroelectric power station; **c. nuclear** nuclear power station; **c. térmica** thermal power station **(c)** *Méx* **c. camionera** bus station

   3 *nm Dep* central defender

centralismo *nm Pol* centralism

centralista *adj & nmf Pol* centralist

centralita *nf* switchboard

centralización *nf* centralization

centralizado, -a *adj* centralized

centralizar [14] *vt* to centralize

centrar 1 *vt* **(a)** *(gen) & Dep* to center **(b)** *(persona)* to steady, to make stable **(c)** *(atraer)* to be the center of; **centraba todas las miradas** all eyes were on her

   2 centrarse *vpr* **(a)** *(concentrarse)* **centrarse en** to concentrate *o* focus on **(b)** *(equilibrarse)* to find one's feet

céntrico, -a *adj* central

centrifugado *nm (de ropa)* spin

centrifugadora *nf* **(a)** *(máquina)* centrifuge **(b)** *(para secar ropa)* spin-dryer

centrifugar [40] *vt* **(a)** *Tec* to centrifuge **(b)** *(ropa)* to spin-dry

centrífugo, -a *adj* centrifugal

centrípeto, -a *adj* centripetal

centrismo *nm Pol* centrism

centrista 1 *adj Pol* center, centrist; **un partido c.** a party of the center

   2 *nmf* centrist; **los centristas propusieron una reforma** the center proposed a reform

centro *nm* **(a)** *(punto, área)* center; **c. de atracción** center of attraction; **c. de gravedad** center of gravity; **c. de interés** center of interest; **c. de mesa** centerpiece; **c. nervioso** nerve center; *también Fig* **c. neurálgico** nerve center; **c. óptico** optic center **(b)** *(establecimiento)* center; **c. de acogida** *(para refugiados)* reception center; *(para mujeres maltratadas)* (women's) refuge; **c. de cálculo** computer center; **c. cívico** community center; **c. comercial** shopping center *o* mall; **c. docente** *o* **de enseñanza** educational institution; **c. recreativo** leisure center; **c. de salud** clinic **(c)** *(de ciudad)* city/town center; **me voy al c.** I'm going to town; **c. ciudad** *o* **urbano** *(en letrero)* city/town center **(d)** *Pol* **ser de c.** to be at the center of the political spectrum

centroafricano, -a *adj & nm,f* Central African

Centroamérica *n* Central America

centroamericano, -a *adj & nm,f* Central American

centrocampista *nmf Dep* midfielder

centroderecha *nm* center-right

centroeuropeo, -a *adj & nm,f* Central European

centroizquierda *nm* center-left

centuplicar [59] *vt* to increase a hundredfold

céntuplo 1 *adj* hundredfold

   2 *nm* hundredfold

centuria *nf (siglo, en el ejército romano)* century

centurión *nm Hist* centurion

cenutrio, -a *nm,f Fam (estúpido)* idiot, fool

ceñido, -a *adj* tight

ceñidor *nm* belt

ceñir [47] **1** *vt* **(a)** *(apretar)* to be tight on **(b)** *(abrazar)* to embrace **(c)** *(amoldar)* **c. a** to keep *o* restrict to

   2 ceñirse *vpr* **(a)** *(apretarse)* to tighten **(b)** *(limitarse)* **ceñirse a** to keep *o* stick to

ceño *nm* frown, scowl; **fruncir el c.** to frown, to knit one's brow

ceñudo, -a *adj* frowning, scowling

CEOE ['θeo'e] *nf (abrev de* **Confederación Española de Organizaciones Empresariales***)* = Spanish employers' organization

cepa *nf* **(a)** *(vid)* vine **(b)** *(de vino)* variety **(c)** *(linaje)* stock; **de pura c.** *(auténtico)* real, genuine; *(de pura sangre)* thoroughbred

CEPAL [θe'pal] *nf (abrev de* **Comisión Económica para América Latina***)* ECL

cepillar 1 *vt* **(a)** *(ropa, pelo)* to brush **(b)** *(madera)* to plane **(c)** *Fam (robar)* to pinch; **c. algo a alguien** to pinch sth off sb **(d)** *Esp, Col Fam (adular)* to butter up, to flatter

   2 cepillarse *vpr* **(a)** *(pelo, ropa)* to brush; **cepillarse el pelo** to brush one's hair **(b)** *Fam (comida, trabajo)* to polish off (**c**) *(suspender)* to fail; **se lo cepillaron** they failed him (**d**) *muy Fam* **cepillarse a alguien** *(copular)* to screw sb; *(matar)* to bump sb off

cepillo *nm* (**a**) *(para limpiar)* brush; **c. de dientes** toothbrush; **c. del pelo** hairbrush; **c. de uñas** nailbrush (**b**) *(de carpintero)* plane (**c**) *(de donativos)* collection box, poor box

cepo *nm* (**a**) *(para cazar)* trap (**b**) *(para vehículos)* Denver boot (**c**) *(para sujetar)* clamp (**d**) *(para presos)* stocks

ceporro *nm Fam* idiot, blockhead

CEPYME [θe'pime] *nf (abrev de* **Confederación Española de la Pequeña y Mediana Empresa**) = Spanish confederation of SME's

cera *nf* (**a**) *(sustancia)* wax; *(del oído)* earwax; **hacerse la c.** *(depilarse)* to wax; **c. de abeja** beeswax; **c. depilatoria** hair-removing wax (**b**) *Andes, Méx (vela)* candle

cerámica *nf* (**a**) *(arte)* ceramics *(singular)*, pottery (**b**) *(objeto)* piece of pottery

ceramista *nmf* potter

cerbatana *nf* blowpipe

cerca 1 *nf (valla)* fence; *(muro)* wall
   2 *adv* near, close; **¿está o queda c.?** is it near o nearby?; **c. de** *(en el espacio)* near, close to; *(aproximadamente)* nearly, about; **de c.** *(examinar, mirar)* closely; *(afectar)* deeply; *(vivir)* first-hand; **ver algo/a alguien de c.** to see sth/sb close up; **por aquí c.** nearby; **si no costó dos millones, andará c.** it can't have cost much less than two million

cercado *nm* (**a**) *(valla)* fence (**b**) *(lugar)* enclosure

cercanía *nf (cualidad)* nearness, closeness; **cercanías** *(lugar)* outskirts, suburbs; **en las cercanías de** on the outskirts of; **tren de cercanías** local train

cercano, -a *adj* (**a**) *(pueblo, lugar)* nearby (**b**) *(tiempo)* near (**c**) *(pariente, fuente de información)* close (**a** to)

cercar [59] *vt* (**a**) *(vallar)* to fence (off) (**b**) *(rodear, acorralar)* to surround

cercenar *vt* (**a**) *(extremidad)* to amputate (**b**) *(restringir)* to cut back, to curtail

cerciorarse *vpr* to make sure (**de** of)

cerco *nm* (**a**) *(marca)* circle, ring; **el vaso ha dejado un c. en la mesa** the glass has left a ring on the table (**b**) *(de astro)* halo (**c**) *(asedio)* siege; **poner c. a** to lay siege to

cerda *nf (pelo) (de cerdo, jabalí)* bristle; *(de caballo)* horsehair

cerdada *nf Fam* dirty trick

Cerdeña *n* Sardinia

cerdo, -a 1 *nm,f* (**a**) *(animal)* pig, *f* sow; *Fam* **come como un c.** *(sin modales)* he eats like a pig; *(mucho)* he pigs out; *Fam* **estar como un c.** to be a fat pig (**b**) *Fam (persona)* pig, swine
   2 *nm (carne)* pork

cereal *nm* cereal; **cereales** (breakfast) cereal

cerealero, -a *Am* **1** *adj (región)* cereal-growing; **producción cerealera** cereal production
   2 *nm,f* cereal grower

cerealista *adj (región)* cereal-growing

cerebelo *nm Anat* cerebellum

cerebral *adj Anat & Fig* cerebral; **lesión c.** cerebral lesion

cerebro *nm* (**a**) *(órgano)* brain; **c. electrónico** electronic brain (**b**) *(cabecilla)* brains *(singular)*; *(inteligencia)* brains

ceremonia *nf* (**a**) *(acto)* ceremony; **c. de apertura** opening ceremony; **c. de clausura** closing ceremony; **c. inaugural** opening ceremony; **c. iniciática** o **de iniciación** initiation ceremony (**b**) *(pompa, boato)* ceremony, pomp; **recibieron a los reyes con gran c.** they welcomed the king and queen with great pomp

ceremonial *adj & nm* ceremonial

ceremonioso, -a *adj* ceremonious

cereza *nf* (**a**) *(fruta)* cherry (**b**) *Am (del café)* coffee bean

cerezal *nm* cherry orchard

cerezo *nm* (**a**) *(árbol)* cherry tree (**b**) *(madera)* cherry (wood)

cerilla *nf Esp* match

cerillo *nm CAm, Ecuad, Méx* match

cerner [66], **cernir** [25] **1** *vt* to sieve, to sift
   2 **cernerse** *vpr (ave, avión)* to hover; *(amenaza, peligro)* to loom

cernícalo *nm* (**a**) *(ave)* kestrel (**b**) *Fam (bruto)* brute

cernir = **cerner**

cero 1 *núm* zero; *ver también* **seis**
   2 *nm* (**a**) *(signo)* naught, zero, oh (**b**) *(cantidad)* nothing; *(en fútbol americano, béisbol, fútbol)* nothing, zero; *(en tenis)* love (**c**) *(temperatura)* zero; **sobre/bajo c.** above/below zero; **c. absoluto** absolute zero (**d**) *(expresiones)* **cortarse el pelo al c.** to shave one's head, to cut all one's hair off; **partir de c.** to start from scratch; *Fig* **ser un c. a la izquierda** *(un inútil)* to be useless; *(un don nadie)* to be a nobody

cerque *etc ver* **cercar**

cerquillo *nm Am* bangs

cerquita *adv* very near

cerrado, -a *adj* (**a**) *(al exterior)* closed, shut; *(con llave, pestillo)* locked (**b**) *(tiempo, cielo)* overcast; *(noche)* dark (**c**) *(mentalidad, sociedad)* closed (**a** to) (**d**) *(rodeado)* surrounded; *(por montañas)* walled in (**e**) *(circuito)* closed (**f**) *(curva)* sharp, tight (**g**) *(vocal)* close (**h**) *(acento)* broad, thick

cerradura *nf* lock

cerrajería *nf* (**a**) *(oficio)* locksmithing, locksmithery (**b**) *(local)* locksmith's (store)

cerrajero, -a *nm,f* locksmith

cerrar 1 *vt* (**a**) *(objeto) (en general)* to close; *(puerta, cajón, boca, tienda)* to shut, to close; *(puños)* to clench; *(con llave)* to lock; *(botella, tarro)* to put the lid o top on (**b**) *(negocio, colegio) (a diario)* to close; *(permanentemente)* to close down; **el gobierno cerrará dos centrales nucleares** the government is to close down two nuclear power stations (**c**) *(grifo, llave de gas)* to turn off (**d**) *(agujero, hueco)* to fill, to block (up) (**e**) *(carretera, calle)* to block; **la policía cerró la calle** the police closed off the street; **c. el paso a alguien** to block sb's way (**f**) *(cercar)* to fence (off), to enclose (**g**) *(cicatrizar)* to heal, to close up (**h**) *(terminar)* to close; **c. la marcha** *(ir en última posición)* to bring up the rear; **la orquesta cerraba el desfile** the orchestra closed the procession
   2 *vi* (**a**) *(en general) (puerta, tienda)* to close, to shut; *(con llave, pestillo)* to lock up (**b**) *(persona)* to close the door; **¡cierra, que entra frío!** close the door, you're letting the cold in! (**c**) *(negocio, colegio) (a diario)* to close; *(definitivamente)* to close down; **¿a qué hora cierra?** what time do you close?
   3 **cerrarse** *vpr* (**a**) *(al exterior)* to close, to shut (**b**) *(incomunicarse)* to clam up; **cerrarse a** to close one's mind to (**c**) *(herida)* to heal, to close up (**d**) *(acto, debate, discusión)* to (come to a) close

cerrazón *nf (obstinación)* stubbornness, obstinacy

cerril *adj* (**a**) *(animal)* wild (**b**) *(obstinado)* stubborn, obstinate; *(tosco, grosero)* coarse

cerro *nm* hill; *Esp Fam Fig* **irse por los cerros de Úbeda** to go off at a tangent, to stray from the point

cerrojazo *nm* **dar c. a** *(puerta)* to bolt shut; *(conversación, reunión)* to bring to a halt

cerrojo *nm* bolt; **echar el c.** to bolt the door

certamen *nm* competition, contest

certero, -a *adj* (**a**) *(tiro)* accurate (**b**) *(opinión, respuesta)* correct

certeza *nf* certainty; **tener la c. de que...** to be certain (that)...

certidumbre *nf* certainty

certificación *nf* (**a**) *(hecho)* certification (**b**) *(documento)* certificate

certificado, -a 1 *adj (documento)* certified; *(carta, paquete)* certified

2 *nm* certificate; **c. de calidad** quality guarantee; **c. de defunción** death certificate; *Fin* **c. de depósito** certificate of deposit; **c. de matrimonio** marriage certificate; **c. médico** medical certificate; *Com* **c. de origen** certificate of origin

certificar [59] *vt* (**a**) *(constatar)* to certify (**b**) *(en correos)* to register (**c**) *(sospechas, inocencia)* to confirm

cerumen *nm* earwax

cerval *adj* **miedo c.** terror

cervantino, -a *adj* Cervantine

cervatillo *nm* (small) fawn

cervato *nm* fawn

cervecera *nf* brewery

cervecería *nf* (**a**) *(fábrica)* brewery (**b**) *(bar)* bar

cervecero, -a 1 *adj* brewing; **fábrica cervecera** brewery; **industria cervecera** brewing industry
  2 *nm,f (que hace cerveza)* brewer

cerveza *nf* beer; **c. de barril** draft beer; **c. negra** stout; **c. sin alcohol** alcohol-free beer, nonalcoholic beer

cervical 1 *adj* (**a**) *(del útero)* cervical (**b**) *(del cuello)* neck; **lesión c.** neck injury; **vértebra c.** cervical vertebra
  2 cervicales *nfpl* neck vertebrae

cerviz *nf Anat* nape, back of the neck; *Fig* **bajar** *o* **doblar la c.** *(humillarse)* to bow down, to submit

cesante 1 *adj* (**a**) *(destituido)* dismissed, fired (**b**) *CSur, Méx (parado)* unemployed
  2 *nmf* dismissed civil servant

cesantear *vt Am* to lay off

cesantía *nf* (**a**) *(destitución)* firing (**b**) *Chile, CSur (desempleo)* unemployment

César *n pr Hist* Caesar; *Fig* **dar (a Dios lo que es de Dios y) al C. lo que es del C.** to render unto Caesar the things which are Caesar's (and to God the things which are God's)

cesar 1 *vt (destituir)* to fire; *(alto cargo)* to remove from office
  2 *vi (parar)* to stop *o* cease (**de hacer algo** doing sth); **sin c.** nonstop, incessantly

cesárea *nf Med* caesarean (section)

cese *nm* (**a**) *(detención, paro)* stopping, ceasing (**b**) *(destitución)* firing; *(de alto cargo)* removal from office

cesio *nm* cesium

cesión *nf* cession, transfer; *Der* **c. de bienes** surrender of property

cesionario, -a *nm,f* transferee, assignee

cesionista *nmf Der* transferor, assignor

césped *nm* (**a**) *(hierba)* lawn, grass; **cortar el c.** to mow the lawn, to cut the grass; **prohibido pisar el c.** *(en letrero)* keep off the grass (**b**) *Dep* field; *Am (en tenis)* grass court

cesta *nf* (**a**) *(canasta)* basket; **(el precio de) la c. de la compra** the cost of the average week's shopping; *Inform* **c. (de la compra o de pedidos)** *(en página web)* shopping basket *o* cart (**b**) *Dep* **c. punta** jai alai, = type of pelota

cestería *nf* (**a**) *(oficio)* basket making (**b**) *(tienda)* basket shop

cestero, -a *nm,f* basket weaver

cesto *nm* (**a**) *(cesta)* (large) basket; **c. de la ropa sucia** laundry basket, linen basket (**b**) *Dep (canasta)* basket

cesura *nf* caesura

cetáceo *nm Zool* cetacean

cetme *nm* = light automatic rifle used by Spanish army

cetrería *nf* falconry

cetrino, -a *adj Formal* sallow

cetro *nm* (**a**) *(vara)* scepter; *(reinado)* reign (**b**) *(superioridad)* **ostentar el c. de** to hold the crown of

Ceuta *n* Ceuta

ceutí (*pl* **ceutíes**) **1** *adj* of/from Ceuta
  2 *nmf* person from Ceuta

ceviche, cebiche *nm Andes, Méx* = raw fish marinated in lemon and garlic

cf., cfr. *(abrev de* **confróntese***)* cf

CFC *nmpl (abrev de* **clorofluorocarbonos***)* CFC

cfr. = cf.

cg *(abrev de* **centigramo***)* cg

CGPJ *nm (abrev de* **Consejo General del Poder Judicial***)* = governing body of the Spanish judiciary, elected by the Spanish parliament

Ch, ch [tʃe] *nf* Ch, ch

ch/ *(abrev de* **cheque***)* check

chabacanada *nf* vulgar thing; **ser una c.** to be vulgar

chabacanería *nf* (**a**) *(acción, comentario)* **lo que hizo/dijo fue una c.** what he did/said was vulgar (**b**) *(cualidad)* vulgarity

chabacano, -a 1 *adj* vulgar
  2 *nm Méx (fruta)* apricot; *(árbol)* apricot tree

chabola *nf Esp* shack; **barrio de chabolas** shantytown

chabolismo *nm Esp* **erradicar el c.** to deal with the shantytown problem; **el crecimiento del c.** the growing number of people living in shantytowns

chabolista *nmf Esp* shantytown dweller

chacal *nm* jackal

chacarero, -a *nm,f Andes, RP* farmer

chacha *nf Fam* maid

chachachá *nm* cha-cha

cháchara *nf Fam* chatter; **estar de c.** to have a chatter

chachi *adj inv Esp Fam* cool, neat

chacho *nm Esp Fam* son

chacina *nf* cured *o* prepared pork

chacinería *nf (tienda)* pork butcher's

chacinero, -a *nm,f* pork butcher

chacolí *nm* = light wine from the Basque Country

chacota *nf* **tomar algo a c.** to take sth as a joke

chacra *nf Andes, RP* farm

Chad *nm* **el C.** Chad

chador *nm* chador

chafar 1 *vt* (**a**) *(aplastar)* to flatten (**b**) *(arrugar)* to crease (**c**) *Fam (estropear)* to spoil, to ruin; **el robo nos chafó las vacaciones** the robbery ruined our vacation
  2 chafarse *vpr Fam (estropearse)* to be ruined

chaflán *nm* (**a**) *(de edificio)* corner (**b**) *Geom* bevel

chal *nm* shawl

chala *nf* (**a**) *Andes, RP (de mazorca)* corn husk (**b**) *Chile (sandalia)* leather sandal

chalado, -a *Fam* **1** *adj* crazy, mad; *Fig* **estar c. por algo/alguien** to be crazy about sth/sb
  2 *nm,f* loony

chaladura *nf Fam* (**a**) *(locura)* craziness, madness (**b**) *(enamoramiento)* crazy infatuation

chalán, -ana *nm,f (comerciante)* horse dealer; *Fig* shark, wheeler-dealer

chalana *nf Náut* barge

chaneo *nm (comercio)* horse-dealing; *Fig* horse-trading

chalar *Fam* **1** *vt* to drive around the bend
  2 chalarse *vpr* **chalarse por** to be crazy about

chalé (*pl* **chalés**), **chalet** (*pl* **chalets**) *nm (casa)* detached house (with garden); *(en el campo)* cottage; *(de alta montaña)* chalet; *Esp* **c. adosado** semidetached house

chaleco *nm* vest; *(de punto)* tank top; **c. antibalas** bulletproof vest; *Am* **c. de fuerza** straitjacket; **c. salvavidas** life jacket

chalet = chalé

chalupa *nf Náut* small boat

chamaco, -a *nm,f Méx Fam* kid

chamán *nm* shaman

chamanismo *nm* shamanism

chamarileo *nm* dealing in secondhand goods

chamarilero, -a *nm,f* secondhand dealer

chamarra *nf* jacket

chamba *nf* (**a**) *CAm, Méx, Perú Fam (trabajo)* job (**b**) *Col,Ven (zanja)* ditch

chambelán *nm* chamberlain

chambergo *nm (chaquetón)* short coat

chamizo *nm (choza)* thatched hut; *Fam Pey (lugar)* hovel, dive

champa *nf CAm* (**a**) *(tienda de campaña)* tent (**b**) *(cobertizo)* shed

champán, champaña *nm* champagne

champiñón *nm* mushroom

champú *(pl* **champús** *o* **champúes**) *nm* shampoo

chamuscado, -a *adj (pelo, plumas)* singed; *(tela, papel)* scorched; *(tostada)* burned

chamuscar [59] **1** *vt (pelo, plumas)* to singe; *(tela, papel)* to scorch; *(tostada)* to burn

    2 chamuscarse *vpr (pelo, plumas)* to get singed; *(tela, papel)* to get scorched; *(tostada)* to burn, to get burned

chamusquina *nf Fam Fig* **me huele a c.** it smells a bit fishy to me, I don't like the look of this

chance *nm o nf Am* opportunity, chance; **tener c. de hacer algo** to have the chance to do sth; **¿me das un c.?** can I have a go?

chanchada *nf Am Fam* (**a**) *(porquería)* disgusting habit; **¡no hagas chanchadas!** stop being so disgusting! (**b**) *(jugarreta)* dirty trick

chancho, -a *Am* **1** *adj Fam (sucio)* filthy

    2 *nm* (**a**) *(animal)* pig, *f* sow (**b**) *Fam (persona sucia)* dirty *o* filthy pig

chanchullero, -a *Fam* **1** *adj* crooked, tricky

    2 *nm,f* trickster, crook

chanchullo *nm Fam* swindle, racket

chancla, chancleta *nf (sandalia)* backless sandal; *(para la playa)* thong

chanclo *nm* (**a**) *(de madera)* clog (**b**) *(de plástico)* galosh

chándal *(pl* **chándals**) *nm Esp* tracksuit

changa *nf* (**a**) *Bol, RP (trabajo temporal)* odd job (**b**) *Andes, Cuba (chiste)* joke

changador *nm RP* porter

changarro *nm Méx (tienda)* small store; *(puesto)* stand

chango, -a **1** *adj* (**a**) *Carib (bromista)* playful, joking (**b**) *Chile (fastidioso)* tedious, annoying (**c**) *Méx, PRico* **estar c.** to be cheap and plentiful

    2 *nm,f* (**a**) *Carib (bromista)* joker, prankster (**b**) *Chile (fastidioso)* tedious person (**c**) *Arg, Bol, Méx (muchacho)* youngster

    3 *nm* (**a**) *Méx (mono)* monkey (**b**) *Ven* **changos** *(harapos)* rags

changurro *nm* = typical Basque dish of dressed crab

chanquete *nm* = small translucent fish eaten whole

chantaje *nm* blackmail; **hacer c. a alguien** to blackmail sb; **c. emocional** emotional blackmail

chantajear *vt* to blackmail

chantajista *nmf* blackmailer

chantillí *nm* whipped cream

chanza *nf* joke

chao *interj Fam* **¡c.!** bye!, see you!

chapa *nf* (**a**) *(lámina) (de metal)* sheet, plate; *(de madera)* board; *Aut* bodywork; **taller de c. y pintura** body shop; **c. ondulada** corrugated iron (**b**) *(de botella)* top, cap; **juego de las chapas** = children's game played with bottle tops (**c**) *(insignia)* badge (**d**) *Col, Cuba, Méx (cerradura)* lock (**e**) *RP (de matrícula)* license plate

chapado, -a *adj* (**a**) *(recubierto) (con metal)* plated; *(con madera)* veneered; **c. en oro** gold-plated; **c. a la antigua** stuck in the past, old-fashioned (**b**) *Esp muy Fam (cerrado)* shut, closed

chapapote *nm* oil sludge

chapar **1** *vt* (**a**) *(recubrir) (con metal)* to plate; *(con madera)* to veneer (**b**) *Esp Fam (cerrar)* to shut, to close

    2 *vi Esp Fam (cerrar)* to shut, to close

chaparro, -a **1** *adj* short and squat

    2 *nm,f (persona)* short, squat person

    3 *nm Bot* dwarf oak

chaparrón *nm* (**a**) *(lluvia)* downpour (**b**) *(gran cantidad)* **un c. de críticas** a barrage of criticism; **un c. de solicitudes** a flood of applications

chapear *vt (con metal)* to plate; *(con madera)* to veneer

chapela *nf* beret

chapero *nm Fam* male prostitute

chapista *nmf Aut* panel beater

chapistería *nf (taller)* body shop

chapó *interj* **¡c.!** *(¡bien hecho!)* well done!, bravo!

chapopote *nm Carib, Méx* bitumen, pitch

chapotear *vi* to splash about

chapoteo *nm* splashing

chapucear *vt* to botch (up)

chapucería *nf (job)*

chapucero, -a **1** *adj (trabajo)* shoddy, sloppy; *(persona)* bungling

    2 *nm,f* bungler

chapulín *nm CAm, Méx* grasshopper

chapurrar, chapurrear *vt* to speak badly

chapurreo *nm* jabbering

chapuza **1** *nf* (**a**) *(trabajo mal hecho)* botch (job) (**b**) *(trabajo ocasional)* odd job

    2 chapuzas *nmf inv Fam (persona)* bungler

chapuzón *nm* dip; **darse un c.** to go for a dip

chaqué *nm* morning coat

chaqueta *nf (de traje)* jacket; *(de punto)* cardigan; *Fig* **cambiar(se) de c.** to change sides; **c. de chándal** tracksuit top

chaqueteo *nm Esp* changing sides

chaquetero, -a *adj & nm,f Esp Fam* turncoat

chaquetilla *nf* short jacket

chaquetón *nm* heavy jacket, short coat

charada *nf* = newspaper puzzle in which a word must be guessed, with its meaning and certain syllables given as clues

charanga *nf* (**a**) *(banda)* brass band (**b**) *Fam (fiesta)* party

charango *nm* = small South American guitar, often made from armadillo shell

charca *nf* pool, pond

charco *nm* puddle; *Fam Fig* **cruzar el c.** to cross the pond *o* Atlantic

charcutería *nf* (**a**) *(tienda)* ≃ delicatessen, = store selling cold meats and cheeses (**b**) *(productos)* cold cuts and cheese

charcutero, -a *nm,f* = seller of "charcutería"

charla *nf* (**a**) *(conversación)* chat (**b**) *(conferencia)* talk

charlar *vi* to chat (**sobre** about); **c. con alguien** to chat with sb, to have a chat with sb

charlatán, -ana **1** *adj* talkative

    2 *nm,f* (**a**) *(hablador)* chatterbox (**b**) *Pey (mentiroso)* trickster, charlatan (**c**) *(vendedor)* traveling salesman, *f* traveling saleswoman

charlatanería *nf* (**a**) *Pey (palabrería)* spiel (**b**) *(locuacidad)* talkativeness

charlestón *nm* Charleston

Charlot *n pr* Charlie Chaplin

charlotada *nf Fam* (**a**) *(payasada)* **charlotadas** clowning around (**b**) *Taurom* slapstick bullfight

charlotear *vi* to chat

charloteo *nm* chatting; **estar de c.** to be chatting *o* having a chat

charnego, -a *nm,f* = pejorative term referring to immigrant to Catalonia from another part of Spain

charol *nm (piel)* patent leather

charola *nf Bol, CAm, Méx* tray

charrería *nf Méx* = horse-riding skills as practiced by "charros"

charretera *nf* epaulet

charro, -a 1 *adj* (a) *Esp (salmantino)* Salamancan (b) *(recargado)* gaudy, showy
   2 *nm,f* (a) *Esp (salmantino)* Salamancan (b) *Méx (con traje típico)* = Mexican cowboy/cowgirl in traditional dress (c) *Méx (jinete)* horseman, *f* horsewoman

charrúa *adj inv & nmf inv CSur* Uruguayan

chárter 1 *adj inv* **vuelo c.** charter flight
   2 *nm (pl* **chárters** *o* **chárteres)** charter flight

chasca *nf* (a) *Fam (hoguera)* camp fire (b) *Andes (greña)* mop of hair

chascar [59] **1** *vt (lengua)* to click; *(dedos)* to snap; *(látigo)* to crack
   2 *vi (lengua)* to click

chascarrillo *nm Fam* funny story

chasco *nm* (a) *(decepción)* disappointment; **llevarse un c.** to be disappointed (b) *(burla)* trick; **dar un c. a alguien** to play a trick on sb

chasis *nm inv* (a) *Aut* chassis (b) *Fot* plate holder (c) *Fam (esqueleto)* body

chasque *etc ver* **chascar**

chasquear 1 *vt* (a) *(látigo)* to crack (b) *(lengua)* to click (c) *(engañar)* to play a trick on
   2 *vi (madera)* to crack

chasquido *nm (de látigo, madera, hueso)* crack; *(de lengua, arma)* click; *(de dedos)* snap

chasquilla *nf Chile (flequillo)* bangs

chat *(pl* **chats)** *nm Inform (charla)* chat; *(sala)* Internet chat room

chata *nf (orinal)* bedpan

chatarra *nf* (a) *(metal)* scrap (metal) (b) *(objetos, piezas)* junk (c) *Fam (joyas)* cheap and crummy jewelry; *(condecoraciones)* brass, medals (d) *Fam (monedas)* small change

chatarrería *nf* scrapyard

chatarrero, -a *nm,f* scrap (metal) dealer

chatear *vi* (a) *Inform* to chat (b) *Esp Fam* to go out drinking, to barhop

chateo *nm Esp Fam* **ir de c.** to go out drinking, to barhop

chato, -a 1 *adj* (a) *(nariz)* snub; *(persona)* snub-nosed; *(superficie, objeto)* flat
   2 *nm,f* (a) *(persona)* snub-nosed person (b) *Fam (apelativo)* love, dear
   3 *nm Esp Fam* = small glass of wine

chau *interj Bol, CSur, Perú Fam* **¡c.!** bye!, see you!

chaucha *nf* (a) *Andes, RP (moneda)* coin of little value (b) *Bol, RP (judía verde)* green bean (c) *Andes (patata)* new potato

chauvinismo [tʃoβiˈnismo] *nm* chauvinism

chauvinista [tʃoβiˈnista] **1** *adj* chauvinistic
   2 *nmf* chauvinist

chaval, -a *nm,f (niño)* kid, lad; *(niña)* kid, girl

chavalería *nf* kids

chaveta *nf* (a) *(clavija)* cotter pin (b) *Fam (cabeza)* nut, head; *Fig* **perder la c.** to go off one's rocker (c) *Andes (navaja)* penknife

chavo, a *Fam* **1** *nm,f Méx (chico)* guy, *f* girl; *(novio)* boyfriend, *f* girlfriend
   2 *nm (dinero)* **no tener un c.** to be penniless

chayote *nm CAm, Méx* chayote

che *interj* **¡c.!** *(¡oye!)* hey! *RP Fam (como muletilla)* **¡pero qué hacés, c.!** what do you think you're doing?

checada *nf Andes, CAm, Méx* checkup

checar [59] *vt Andes, CAm, Méx* to check; **chécalo bien** look at that!, check it out!

chechén, -ena *adj & nm,f* Chechen

Chechenia *n* Chechnya

checheno, -a *adj & nm,f* Chechen

checo, -a 1 *adj & nm,f* Czech
   2 *nm (lengua)* Czech

checoslovaco, -a *adj & nm,f Antes* Czechoslovakian, Czechoslovak

Checoslovaquia *n Antes* Czechoslovakia

chef [tʃef] *(pl* **chefs)** *nm* chef

cheli *nm Fam* = slang typical of Madrid

chelín *nm Antes (en Austria)* schilling; *(en el Reino Unido)* shilling

chelo *nm* cello

chepa *nf Fam* hump

cheposo, -a, chepudo, -a *Fam* **1** *adj* humpbacked
   2 *nm,f* hunchback

cheque *nm* check; **extender un c.** to make out a check; *también Fig* **c. en blanco** blank check; **c. cruzado** *o* **barrado** crossed check; **c. sin fondos** bad check; **c. (de) gasolina** gas voucher; **c. nominativo** = check made payable to a specific person; **c. al portador** check payable to the bearer; **c. de viaje** traveler's check

chequear *vt* (a) *Med* **c. a alguien** to examine sb, to give sb a checkup (b) *(comprobar)* to check

chequeo *nm* (a) *Med* checkup; **hacerse un c.** to have a checkup (b) *(comprobación)* check; **hacer un c. (de algo)** to check (sth)

chequera *nf* checkbook

cheto, -a = **concheto**

chévere *adj Am salvo RP Fam* great, fantastic

cheviot *(pl* **cheviots)** *nm* cheviot

chic *adj inv* chic

chica *nf* (a) *(joven)* girl; **mira, c., haz lo que quieras** look, dear *o* darling, you can do what you want; **c. de alterne** = girl who works in bars on a commission basis, encouraging customers to drink, B-girl (b) *(criada)* maid

chicano, -a 1 *adj & nm,f* Chicano, Mexican-American
   2 *nm (lengua)* Chicano

chicarrón, -ona *nm,f Fam* strapping lad, *f* strapping girl

chicha *nf* (a) *Esp Fam (para comer)* meat; *(de persona)* flesh (b) *(bebida)* = alcoholic drink made from fermented corn; *Fam* **no ser ni c. ni limonada** *o* **limoná** to be neither one thing nor the other, to be neither fish nor fowl

chícharo *nm CAm, Méx* pea

chicharra *nf* (a) *Zool* cicada (b) *Méx (timbre)* electric buzzer

chicharro *nm (pez)* horse mackerel

chicharro *nm Am* pea

chicharrón *nm (frito)* pork crackling; **chicharrones** *(embutido)* = cold processed meat made from pork

chiche *nm* (a) *Andes, RP (adorno)* delicate ornament; *Fam (juguete)* toy (b) *CAm, Méx muy Fam (pecho)* tit

chichi *nm* (a) *muy Fam (vulva)* beaver (b) *Méx muy Fam (pecho)* tit

chichón *nm* bump

chichonera *nf (para ciclistas)* hairnet

chicle *nm* chewing gum

chiclé, chicler *nm Aut* jet

chico, -a 1 *adj (pequeño)* small
   2 *nm* (a) *(joven)* boy (b) *(tratamiento)* sonny (c) **c. (de los recados)** *(en oficina)* office boy; *(en tienda)* errand boy

chifa *nm Andes* Chinese restaurant

chifla *nf Fam* **tomarse algo a c.** to treat sth as a joke; **tomarse las cosas a c.** to treat everything as a joke

chiflado, -a *Fam* **1** *adj* crazy, mad
  2 *nm,f* loony

chifladura *nf (locura)* madness; **su última c. son las motos** his latest craze is for motorbikes

chiflar 1 *vt Fam (encantar)* **me chiflan las patatas fritas** I'm mad about French fries
  2 *vi (silbar)* to whistle

chiflido *nm* whistling

chifonier *nm (mueble)* highboy

chigüín *nm CAm* kid

chihuahua *nm* chihuahua

chií *(pl* **chiíes)**, **chiíta** *adj & nmf* Shiite

chilaba *nf* djellaba

chilango, -a *Méx Fam* **1** *adj* of/from Mexico City
  2 *nm,f* person from Mexico City

Chile *n* Chile

chile *nm CAm, Méx* chilli; **c. poblano** = large fresh chilli, similar to a green pepper

chilena *nf* (overhead) scissors kick

chileno, -a *adj & nm,f* Chilean

chilindrón *nm Culin* = seasoning made of tomatoes and peppers

chillar 1 *vi* **(a)** *(gritar) (persona)* to scream, to yell; *(ave, mono)* to screech; *(cerdo)* to squeal; *(ratón)* to squeak **(b)** *(chirriar)* to screech; *(puerta, madera)* to creak; *(bisagra)* to squeak
  2 *vt Fam (reñir)* to yell at

chillido *nm (de persona)* scream, yell; *(de ave, mono)* screech; *(de cerdo)* squeal; *(de ratón)* squeak

chillón, -ona 1 *adj* **(a)** *(voz)* piercing **(b)** *(persona)* noisy, screeching **(c)** *(color)* loud, gaudy
  2 *nm,f* noisy person

chilpayate, -a *nm,f Méx Fam* kid

chimenea *nf* **(a)** *(hogar)* fireplace **(b)** *(tubo)* chimney

chimpancé *nm* chimpanzee

China *nf* **(la) C.** China

china *nf* **(a)** *(piedra)* small stone, pebble; *Fam* **le tocó la c.** he drew the short straw **(b)** *Fam (droga)* deal *(small amount of hash)* **(c)** *Am (india)* Indian woman **(d)** *Arg, Chile (criada)* maid

chinchar *Fam* **1** *vt* to pester, to bug
  2 chincharse *vpr* to put up with it; **¡tú no tienes, para que te chinches!** I've got one and you haven't, so there!

chinche 1 *adj Fam (molesto)* annoying
  2 *nf* **(a)** *(insecto)* bedbug **(b)** *Am (clavo)* thumbtack
  3 *nmf Fam (persona)* pest, pain

chincheta *nf* thumbtack

chinchilla *nf* chinchilla

chinchín *nm* **(a)** *(ruido)* noise of a brass band **(b)** *(brindis)* toast; **¡c.!** here's to you!

chinchón *nm* **(a)** *(bebida)* = aniseed liquor **(b)** *(juego de cartas)* = card game where players aim to collect two sets of three cards

chinchorro *nm* **(a)** *Méx (red)* net **(b)** *Chile, Ven (hamaca)* hammock

chinchoso, -a 1 *adj Fam* annoying
  2 *nm,f* pest, pain

chinero *nm* china o glass cabinet

chinesco, -a *adj* Chinese

chinga *nf* **(a)** *CAm, Ven (colilla)* cigar end **(b)** *Ven (borrachera)* drunkenness **(c)** *CAm, Ven (en el juego)* = fee paid by gamblers **(d)** *Méx muy Fam (paliza)* **me dieron una c.** they kicked the shit out of me **(e)** *Méx muy Fam (trabajo duro)* **es una c.** it's a bitch of a job **(f)** *Méx muy Fam (fastidio)* pain in the ass

chingada *nf Méx Vulg* **¡vete a la c.!** fuck off!; **de la c.** *(muy difícil)* fucking hard

chingadera *nf Méx Fam (contravención)* **¡deja de hacer chingaderas!** stop messing around!

chingado, -a *adj* **(a)** *Esp, Méx muy Fam (estropeado)* bust **(b)** *Méx Vulg (como intensificador)* fucking

chingar [40] **1** *vt Esp, Méx* **(a)** *muy Fam (estropear)* to bust **(b)** *muy Fam (molestar)* **c. a alguien** to get up sb's nose, to piss sb off **(c)** *Vulg (copular)* to fuck; *Méx* **¡chinga tu madre!** fuck you!
  2 *vi Esp, Méx Vulg (copular)* to screw, to fuck
  3 chingarse *vpr Méx muy Fam (estropearse)* to pack in, to conk out

chingo *nm Méx muy Fam* **un c. de** *(un montón de)* a shitload of

chingón, -ona *adj Méx muy Fam (muy bueno)* fantastic, great, neat

chinita *nf* **(a)** *Am (criada)* maid **(b)** *Chile (animal)* ladybug

chino, -a 1 *adj* **(a)** *(de China)* Chinese **(b)** *Am (mestizo)* of mixed race
  2 *nm,f* **(a)** *(de China)* Chinese (man/woman); *Fig* **trabajar como un c.** to slave away **(b)** *Am (mestizo)* person of mixed race
  3 *nm* **(a)** *(lengua)* Chinese; *Fam* **me suena a c.** *(no lo conozco)* I've never heard of it; *(no lo entiendo)* it's all Greek to me **(b)** **chinos** *(juego)* = game in which each player must guess the number of coins or pebbles in the other's hand **(c)** *(pasapuré)* vegetable mill

chip *(pl* **chips)** *nm Inform* chip; **c. de silicio** silicon chip

chipé, chipén *adj inv Fam* brilliant, terrific; **ser de c.** to be brilliant o terrific

chipirón *nm* baby squid

Chipre *n* Cyprus

chipriota *adj & nmf* Cypriot

chiquero *nm Taurom* bull pen

chiquilicuatro *nm* insignificant person, nobody

chiquilín, -ina *nm,f* small boy, *f* small girl

chiquillada *nf (cosa de niños)* childish thing; *(travesura)* childish prank; **hacer una c. (a alguien)** to play a childish prank (on sb)

chiquillería *nf* kids

chiquillo, -a *nm,f* kid

chiquitín, -ina 1 *adj* tiny
  2 *nm,f* tiny tot

chiquito, -a 1 *adj* tiny
  2 *nm Esp (de vino)* = small glass of wine
  3 *nfpl Fig* **no andarse con chiquitas** not to mess around

chiribita *nf (chispa)* spark; *Fam* **ver chiribitas** to see spots in front of one's eyes; **le hacían chiribitas los ojos al verlo** her eyes lit up when she saw him

chirigota *nf Fam* joke

chirimbolo *nm Fam* thingamajig, whatsit

chirimía *nf Mús* shawm

chirimoya *nf* custard apple

chiringuito *nm* **(a)** *(bar)* refreshment counter **(b)** *Fam (negocio)* **montarse un c.** to set up a little business

chiripa *nf Fam* fluke; **de** o **por c.** by luck

chirivía *nf* parsnip

chirla *nf* small clam

chirona *nf Esp Fam* clink, slammer; **en c.** in the clink

chirriar [32] *vi (sonar)* to screech; *(puerta, madera)* to creak; *(bisagra, muelles)* to squeak

chirrido *nm (ruido)* screech; *(de puerta, madera)* creak; *(de bisagra, muelles)* squeak

chiruca® *nf* = canvas hiking boot

chis *interj* **¡c.!** ssh!

chisme *nm* **(a)** *(cotilleo)* rumor, piece of gossip **(b)** *Fam (cosa)* thingamajig, thingy

chismear *vi Fam* to gossip

chismorrear *vi* to spread rumors, to gossip

chismorreo *nm* gossip

chismoso, -a 1 *adj* gossipy
  2 *nm,f* gossip, scandalmonger

chispa *nf* **(a)** *(de fuego, electricidad)* spark; *Fam Fig* **echar chispas** to be hopping mad **(b)** *(pizca)* bit **(c)** *(agudeza, gracia)* sparkle; **esa novela tiene c.** that novel has really got something

chispazo *nm también Fig* spark

chispeante *adj* **(a)** *(que chispea)* that gives off sparks **(b)** *(conversación, discurso, mirada)* sparkling

chispear 1 *vi* **(a)** *(chisporrotear)* to spark **(b)** *(relucir)* to sparkle
  2 *v impersonal (llover)* to spit (with rain); **empezó a c.** a few spots of rain started to fall

chisporrotear *vi (fuego, leña)* to crackle; *(aceite)* to splutter; *(comida)* to sizzle

chisporroteo *nm (de fuego, leña)* crackling; *(de aceite)* spluttering; *(de comida)* sizzling

chisquero *nm* (cigarette) lighter

chist *interj* ¡c.! ssh!

chistar *vi* **sin c.** without a word (of protest)

chiste *nm* **(a)** *(cuento)* joke; **contar chistes** to tell jokes; *Fig* **no tiene ningún c.** there's nothing special about it; **c. verde**, *Méx* **c. colorado** dirty joke **(b)** *Andes, Méx, RP (broma)* joke, prank; **hacerle un c. a alguien** to play a joke o prank on sb

chistera *nf (sombrero)* top hat

chistorra *nf* = type of cured pork sausage typical of Aragon and Navarre

chistoso, -a 1 *adj* funny
  2 *nm,f* amusing o funny person

chistu *nm* Basque flute

chistulari *nmf* "chistu" player

chita *nf Esp Fam* **a la c. callando** quietly, on the quiet

chitón *interj* ¡c.! quiet!

chivar *Esp Fam* **1** *vt* to whisper, to tell secretly
  2 chivarse *vpr (niños)* to tell **(de** on); *(delincuentes)* to squeal **(de** on)

chivatazo *nm Esp Fam* tip-off; **dar el c.** to squeal

chivato, -a 1 *nm,f Esp Fam (delator)* rat; *(acusica)* telltale
  2 *nm* **(a)** *(luz)* warning light; *(alarma)* alarm bell **(b)** *Ven Fam (pez gordo)* big cheese

chivo, -a *nm,f* kid, young goat; **c. expiatorio** scapegoat

chocante *adj* puzzling

chocar [59] **1** *vi* **(a)** *(colisionar)* to crash (**contra** into), to collide (**contra** with); **chocaron dos autobuses** two buses crashed o collided; **la moto chocó contra un árbol** the motorbike hit a tree; **c. de frente con** to have a head-on collision with **(b)** *(enfrentarse)* to clash; **mis ideas siempre han chocado con las suyas** he and I have always had different ideas about things **(c)** *(extrañar)* to surprise, to puzzle; **me choca que no haya llegado ya** I'm surprised o puzzled that she hasn't arrived yet **(d)** *Col, Méx, Ven Fam (molestar)* to annoy, to bug; **me choca que esté siempre controlándome** it really annoys me how he's always watching me
  2 *vt* **(a)** *(manos)* to shake; *Fam* **¡chócala!, ¡choca esos cinco!** put it there! **(b)** *(copas, vasos)* to clink

chochear *vi* **(a)** *(viejo)* to be senile **(b)** *Fam (de cariño)* **c. por alguien** to dote on sb

chochez *nf* **(a)** *(vejez)* senility **(b)** *(dicho, hecho)* **decir/hacer chocheces** to say/do senile things

chocho, -a 1 *adj* **(a)** *(viejo)* senile **(b)** *Fam (encariñado)* soft, doting
  2 *nm* **(a)** *Esp, Méx Vulg (vulva)* beaver **(b)** *Fam (altramuz)* lupine seed *(for eating)*

choclo *nm Andes, RP (maíz)* corn

choclón *nm Chile Fam* crowd

choco[1] *nm (sepia)* cuttlefish

choco[2]**, -a** *adj CAm, Chile, Méx (cojo)* one-legged; *(manco)* one-armed

chocolatada *nf* = afternoon party where people drink thick drinking chocolate

chocolate *nm* **(a)** *(para comer)* chocolate; *(para beber)* **c. (a la taza)** thick drinking chocolate; **c. blanco** white chocolate; **c. con leche** milk chocolate **(b)** *Esp Fam (hachís)* hash

chocolatería *nf* **(a)** *(fábrica)* chocolate factory **(b)** *(establecimiento)* = café where drinking chocolate is served

chocolatero, -a 1 *adj* **ser muy c.** to love chocolate
  2 *nm,f* **(a)** *(aficionado al chocolate)* chocoholic, person fond of chocolate **(b)** *(oficio)* chocolate maker/seller

chocolatina *nf* chocolate bar

chófer *Esp*, **chofer** *Am nmf* chauffeur

chollo *nm Esp Fam* **(a)** *(producto, compra)* bargain **(b)** *(trabajo, situación)* cushy thing

cholo, -a *Am* **1** *adj (mestizo)* mestizo, half-caste
  2 *nm,f* **(a)** *(mestizo)* mestizo, half-caste **(b)** *(indio)* educated indian

chomba *nf RP* polo shirt

chompa *nf Andes* sweater

chompipe *nm CAm* = species of turkey

chonchón *nm Chile* lamp

chongo *nm Méx* **(a)** *(moño)* bun **(b)** *(dulce)* **chongos zamoranos** = dessert made from milk curds, served in syrup

chop [ʃop] *(pl* **chops)** *nm CSur (jarra)* beer mug; *(cerveza)* (mug of) beer

choped, chopped *nm* = type of luncheon meat

chopera *nf* poplar grove

chopito *nm* baby squid

chopo *nm* poplar

chopped = **choped**

choque 1 *ver* **chocar**
  2 *nm* **(a)** *(impacto)* impact; *(de coche, avión)* crash; **c. frontal** head-on collision **(b)** *(enfrentamiento)* clash **(c)** *(impresión)* shock; **c. cultural** culture shock

chorbo, -a *nm,f Esp Fam (chico)* kid; *(adulto)* guy, *f* woman

chorear *vi Fam Chile, Col, Perú, RP (robar)* to pilfer

choriceo *nm Esp Fam (robo)* robbery; *(timo)* rip-off

chorizar [14] *vt Esp Fam* to swipe, to pinch

chorizo *nm* **(a)** *(embutido)* = cured pork sausage, flavored with paprika **(b)** *Esp Fam (ladrón)* thief

chorlito *nm* **(a)** *Zool* plover **(b)** *Fam* **cabeza de c.** scatterbrain

choro *nm Andes* mussel

chorra *Esp Fam* **1** *nmf (tonto)* jerk; **hacer el c.** to mess around
  2 *nf (suerte)* luck

chorrada *nf Esp Fam* **decir una c.** to say something stupid; **chorradas** garbage; **decir chorradas** to talk bull

chorrear 1 *vi* **(a)** *(gotear) (gota a gota)* to drip; *(en un hilo)* to trickle; **estar chorreando** *(estar empapado)* to be soaking o wringing wet **(b)** *(brotar)* to spurt o gush (out)
  2 *vt (sujeto: prenda)* to drip; *(sujeto: persona)* to drip with

chorreo *nm* **(a)** *(goteo) (gota a gota)* dripping; *(en un hilo)* trickling; **un c. de dinero** a steady drain on funds **(b)** *(brote)* spurting, gushing

chorreras *nfpl* frill

chorretón *nm* **(a)** *(chorro)* spurt; **le caían chorretones de helado por la barbilla** he'd got ice cream all over his chin **(b)** *(mancha)* stain

chorro *nm* **(a)** *(de líquido) (borbotón)* jet, spurt; *(hilo)* trickle; **salir a chorros** to spurt o gush out; *Fam Fig* **como los chorros del oro** as clean as a new pin **(b)** *(de luz, gente, preguntas)* stream **(c)** *Méx Fam* **un c. de** a load of, loads of; **tiene un c. de dinero** she has loads of money

chotearse *vpr Fam* to make fun (**de** of)

choteo *nm Fam* joking, kidding; **estar de c.** to be kidding

chotis *nm inv* = dance typical of Madrid

choto, -a *nm,f* (a) *(cabrito)* kid, young goat; *Fam* **estar como una chota** to be crazy, to be off one's rocker (b) *(ternero)* calf

chovinismo *nm* chauvinism

chovinista 1 *adj* chauvinistic

   2 *nmf* chauvinist

choza *nf* hut; **c. de barro** mud hut

christmas ['krismas] *nm inv* Christmas card

chubasco *nm* *(lluvia)* shower; **chubascos ocasionales** occasional showers

chubasquero *nm* raincoat

chúcaro, -a *adj Andes, CAm, RP Fam* wild

chuchería *nf* (a) *(golosina)* candy (b) *(objeto)* trinket

chucho *nm Fam* (a) *(perro)* mutt, dog (b) *RP (susto)* fright; **un c. de frío** a shiver

chueco, -a *adj Am* twisted

chufa *nf* (a) *(planta)* chufa (b) *(tubérculo)* tiger nut

chufla *nf Fam* joke; **estar de c.** to be kidding; **tomarse las cosas a c.** to treat everything as a joke, not to take things seriously

chulada *nf* (a) *(bravuconada)* piece of bravado; **chuladas** bravado (b) *Fam (cosa bonita)* delight, gorgeous thing

chulapo, -a, chulapón, -ona *nm,f* = lower-class native of 18th- and 19th-century Madrid

chulear *Fam* **1** *vt Esp* **c. a una mujer** to live off a woman

   2 chulearse *vpr (fanfarronear)* to be cocky (**de** about); **se está chuleando de que aprobó el examen** he's showing off about having passed the exam

chulería *nf* (a) *(bravuconería)* cockiness (b) *(salero)* charm, winning ways

chulesco, -a *adj* = relating to lower-class Madrid life of the 18th and 19th centuries

chuleta 1 *nf* (a) *(de carne)* chop; **c. de cerdo/cordero** pork/lamb chop (b) *Esp,Ven Fam (en examen)* crib

   2 *nmf Fam (chulo)* cocky person

   3 *adj Fam (chulo)* cocky

chuletada *nf* barbecue

chulo, -a 1 *adj* (a) *Esp (descarado)* cocky; **ponerse c.** to get cocky (b) *Esp, Méx Fam (bonito)* cool, neat

   2 *nm,f* (a) *Esp (descarado)* cocky person (b) *(madrileño)* = lower-class native of 18th- and 19th-century Madrid

   3 *nm (proxeneta)* pimp

chumba *adj*

chumbera *nf* prickly pear cactus

chumbo, -a *adj* **higo c.** prickly pear; **higuera chumba** prickly pear

chuminada *nf Fam* silly thing, trifle

chumino *nm Esp muy Fam* beaver; *Vulg* **no me sale del c.** I can't be fucking well bothered

chungo, -a *Fam* **1** *adj (persona)* horrible, nasty; *(cosa)* lousy; **la cosa está chunga** it's a real bitch

   2 *nf Esp* **tomarse algo a chunga** to take sth as a joke, not to take sth seriously

chupa *nf Esp Fam* coat

chupachups® *nm inv Esp* lollipop

chupacirios *nmf inv Fam Pey* holy Joe

chupada *nf (de helado) (con la lengua)* lick; *(con los labios)* suck; *(de cigarrillo)* puff, drag

chupado, -a *adj* (a) *(delgado)* skinny (b) *Fam (fácil)* **estar c.** to be dead easy *o* a piece of cake

chupamedias *nmf inv Andes, RP,Ven Fam* toady

chupar 1 *vt* (a) *(succionar)* to suck; *(lamer)* to lick; *(fumar)* to puff at (b) *(absorber)* to soak up (c) *Fam (quitar)* **chuparle algo a alguien** to milk sb for sth; **ese hombre le está chupando la sangre** that man is bleeding her dry (d) *Am Fam (beber)* to booze, to tipple

   2 chuparse *vpr* (a) *(succionar)* to suck; **chuparse el dedo** to suck one's thumb; *Fam* **¿te crees que me chupo el dedo?** do you think I was born yesterday?; *Fig* **estar para chuparse los dedos** to be mouthwatering; *Fam* **¡chúpate esa!** take that! (b) *Esp (adelgazar)* to get thinner (c) *Esp Fam (aguantar)* to put up with

chupatintas *nmf inv Pey* pen pusher

chupe *nm Andes, Arg* stew

chupete *nm* (a) *(para bebé)* pacifier (b) *Col (dulce)* lollipop

chupetear *vt* to suck on, to suck away at

chupetín *nm RP (piruleta)* lollipop

chupetón *nm* (a) *(con la lengua)* lick; *(con los labios)* suck; **dar un c. a algo** to lick sth (b) *Esp Fam (moradura en la piel)* lovebite, hickey

chupi *adj Esp Fam* great

chupinazo *nm* (a) *(cañonazo)* cannon shot (b) *Fam Dep (patada)* hard kick; *(a puerta)* screamer, hard shot

chupito *nm* shot

chupón, -ona 1 *nm,f Fam (gorrón)* sponger, cadger

   2 *nm Méx (chupete)* pacifier

chupóptero, -a *nm,f Fam* parasite

churrasco *nm* barbecued *o* grilled meat

churrasquera *nf RP* grill

churrasquería *nf RP* steak house

churrería *nf* = food store or stall selling "churros"

churrero, -a *nm,f* "churros" seller

churrete *nm (chorro)* spurt; *(mancha)* stain

churrigueresco, -a *adj Arte* churrigueresque

churro *nm* (a) *(para comer)* = dough formed into sticks or rings and fried in oil (b) *Fam (fracaso)* botch; **ese dibujo es un c.** that drawing is awful

churruscado, -a *adj (quemado)* burned; *Fam (crujiente)* crispy

churruscar [59] *vt* to burn

churrusco *nm Fam (pan)* piece of burned toast; **¡esto no es una chuleta, es un c.!** this chop is burned to a cinder!

churumbel *nm Esp Fam* kid

chusco, -a 1 *adj* funny

   2 *nm Fam* crust of stale bread

chusma *nf* rabble, mob

chusmear *vi Am Fam* to gossip

chusmerío *nm RP* piece of gossip

chut *(pl* **chuts)** *nm Dep (patada)* kick; *(a puerta)* shot

chutar 1 *vi* (a) *(lanzar la pelota)* to kick the ball; *(a puerta)* to shoot (b) *Esp Fam (funcionar)* to work; **esto va que chuta** it's going great; **con eso va que chuta** that's plenty *o* more than enough

   2 chutarse *vpr Esp Fam* to shoot up

chute *nm Esp Fam* fix

chuzo *nm Fam* **llover a chuzos, caer chuzos de punta** to pour down

CI *nm (abrev de* **cociente de inteligencia)** IQ

CIA ['θia] *nf (abrev de* **Central Intelligence Agency)** CIA

cía., Cía. *(abrev de* **compañía)** Co

cianuro *nm* cyanide

ciática *nf* sciatica

ciático, -a *adj* sciatic

cibercafé, *Fam* **ciber** *nm* cybercafe

ciberdelito *nm* cybercrime

ciberespacio *nm* cyberspace

cibernauta *nmf* cybernaut, netizen, Net user

cibernética *nf* cybernetics *(singular)*

cibernético, -a *adj* cybernetic

ciberokupa *nmf Inform* cybersquatter

ciberokupación *nm Inform* cybersquatting

cibersexo *nm* cybersex

cicatería *nf* stinginess, miserliness

cicatero, -a 1 *adj* stingy, miserly

2 *nm,f* skinflint, miser

cicatriz *nf también Fig* scar

cicatrización *nf* scarring

cicatrizante 1 *adj* healing

2 *nm* healing substance

cicatrizar [14] **1** *vi* to form a scar, to heal (up)

2 *vt* to heal

cicerón *nm* eloquent speaker, orator

cicerone *nmf* guide

ciclamen *nm* cyclamen

cíclico, -a *adj* cyclical

ciclismo *nm* cycling

ciclista 1 *adj* cycling; **equipo c.** cycling team; **prueba c.** cycle race

2 *nmf* cyclist

ciclo *nm* (a) *(periodo)* *(gen)* & *Econ* cycle; **c. menstrual** menstrual cycle; **c. vital** life cycle (b) *(de conferencias, actos)* series

ciclocross *nm* cyclo-cross

ciclomotor *nm* moped

ciclón *nm* cyclone

cíclope *nm* Cyclops

ciclópeo, -a *adj (enorme)* colossal, massive

ciclostil, ciclostilo *nm* cyclostyle

cicloturismo *nm* bicycle touring

cicloturista *nmf* = person on cycling holiday

ciclovía *nf Am (para bicicletas)* bikeway

CICR *nm (abrev de* **Comité Internacional de la Cruz Roja**) IRCC

cicuta *nf* hemlock

ciego, -a 1 *ver* **cegar**

2 *adj* (a) *(sin vista)* blind; **es c. de nacimiento** he was born blind; **quedarse c.** to go blind (b) *(enloquecido)* blinded (**de** by); **c. de ira** blind with rage (c) *(pozo, tubería)* blocked (up) (d) *(total)* *(fe, confianza)* blind; **tengo una confianza ciega en él** I trust him unconditionally (e) *Esp Fam (borracho)* blind drunk; *(drogado)* stoned; **nos pusimos ciegos de cerveza** we got blind drunk on beer

3 *nm,f (invidente)* blind person; **los ciegos** the blind

4 *nm* (a) *Anat* cecum (b) *Esp Fam (de droga)* trip; **tener/cogerse un c.** *(de alcohol)* to be/get blind drunk (c) **los ciegos** *(sorteo de la ONCE)* = lottery organized by Spanish association for the blind

5 a ciegas *loc adv* blindly

ciegue *etc ver* **cegar**

cielo 1 *nm* (a) *(atmósfera)* sky; **mira hacia el c.** look upward; *Min* **a c. abierto** *(a la intemperie)* in the open; *(mina)* opencut (b) *Rel* heaven (c) *(nombre cariñoso)* my love, my dear (d) *(parte superior)* **c. del paladar** roof of the mouth; **c. raso** ceiling (e) *(expresiones)* **como llovido del c.** *(inesperadamente)* out of the blue; *(oportunamente)* at just the right moment; **estar en el séptimo c.** to be in seventh heaven; **se le juntó el c. con la tierra** he lost his nerve; **mover c. y tierra** to move heaven and earth; **ser un c.** to be an angel; **ver el c. abierto** to see one's way out

2 *interj* **¡c. santo!, ¡cielos!** good heavens!

ciempiés *nm inv* centipede

cien *núm* a *o* one hundred; **c. mil** a *o* one hundred thousand; **por c.** percent; **c. por c.** a hundred percent; *ver también* **seis**

ciénaga *nf* marsh, bog

ciencia *nf* (a) *(método, estudio)* science; **a c. cierta** for certain; **no se conoce a c. cierta el número de víctimas** the number of victims isn't known for certain; **ciencias económicas** economics *(singular)*; **ciencias exactas** mathematics *(singular)*; **c. ficción** science fiction; **ciencias de la información** media studies; **ciencias naturales** natural sciences; **ciencias ocultas** occultism; **ciencias políticas** political science; **ciencias sociales** social sciences (b) *(sabiduría)* learning, knowledge; *Hum* **por c. infusa** through divine inspiration; *Fam* **tener poca c.** to be straightforward (c) *Educ* **ciencias** science; **soy de ciencias** I studied science

cieno *nm* mud, sludge

cientificismo *nm* = overemphasis on scientific ideas

científico, -a 1 *adj* scientific

2 *nm,f* scientist

cientista *nmf CSur* **c. social** sociologist

ciento *núm* a *o* one hundred; **c. cincuenta** a *o* one hundred and fifty; **cientos de** hundreds of; **por c.** percent; *Fam Fig* **darle c. y raya a alguien** to run rings around sb; *Fam Fig* **eran c. y la madre** everybody and his dog was there; *ver también* **seis**

ciernes *nmpl* **estar en c.** to be in its infancy; **una campeona en c.** a budding champion; **tenemos un viaje en c.** we're planning a journey

cierno *etc ver* **cerner**

cierre *nm* (a) *(acción de cerrar)* closing, shutting; *(de fábrica)* shutdown; *Rad* & *TV* sign-off; *Ind* **c. patronal** lockout (b) *(mecanismo)* fastener; *Aut* **c. centralizado** automatic locking; **c. de combinación** combination lock; **c. metálico** *(de tienda)* metal shutter (c) *Andes, Méx, RP (cremallera)* zipper; **c.** *Andes, Méx* **relámpago** *o Chile* **eclair** *o Urug* **metálico** zipper

cierto, -a 1 *adj* (a) *(verdadero)* true; **no es c. (que...)** it is not true (that...); **es el hijo de Javier, ¿no es c.?** he's Javier's son, isn't he?; **si bien es c. que...** while it is true that...; **estar en lo c.** to be right; **lo c. es que...** the fact is that... (b) *(seguro)* certain, definite (c) *(algún)* certain; **c. hombre** a certain man; **c. día...** one day...; **en cierta ocasión** once, on one occasion

2 *adv* right, certainly; **por c.** by the way

ciervo, -a *nm,f* (a) *(macho)* deer, stag; *(hembra)* deer, hind (b) *(insecto)* **c. volante** stag beetle

cierzo *nm* north wind

CIF [θif] *nm Esp (abrev de* **código de identificación fiscal**) = number identifying company for tax purposes

cifra *nf* (a) *(signo)* figure; **un código de cuatro cifras** a four-digit code (b) *(cantidad)* number, total; *(de dinero)* sum; **ingresó la c. de un millón de dólares** he deposited the sum of one million dollars; **c. de ventas** sales figures; **c. de negocios** turnover (c) *(código)* **en c.** in code

cifrado, -a *adj* coded, in code

cifrar 1 *vt* (a) *(codificar)* *(mensaje, texto)* to code (b) *(valorar)* *(pérdidas)* to estimate (c) *(reducir)* *(aspiraciones, esperanzas)* to pin, to place; **cifran todas sus esperanzas en el nuevo jugador** they're pinning all their hopes on the new player

2 cifrarse *vpr* (a) **c. en** *(cantidad)* to come to, to amount to (b) **c. en** *(aspiraciones, esperanzas)* to be pinned on

cigala *nf* langoustine, Dublin Bay prawn

cigarra *nf* cicada

cigarrera *nf (caja)* cigar case

cigarrero, -a *nm,f (persona)* cigar maker

cigarrillo *nm* cigarette; **cigarrillos mentolados** menthol cigarettes

cigarro *nm* (a) *(puro)* cigar (b) *(cigarrillo)* cigarette

cigoto *nm Biol* zygote

cigüeña *nf* stork

cigüeñal *nm* crankshaft

cilantro *nm* coriander, cilantro

cilicio *nm (faja, cordón)* spiked belt *(of penitient)*; *(vestidura)* hair shirt

cilindrada *nf* cylinder capacity

cilíndrico, -a *adj* cylindrical

cilindro *nm* cylinder; *(de imprenta)* roller

cima *nf* (**a**) *(cúspide) (de montaña)* peak, summit; *(de árbol)* top (**b**) *(apogeo)* peak, high point; **dar c. a** *(negociaciones, acuerdo)* to conclude

cimarrón, -ona 1 *adj (animal)* feral
2 *nm,f Am Hist (esclavo)* runaway slave

címbalo *nm* cymbal

cimborrio *nm Arquit* cupola

cimbreante *adj* swaying

cimbrear 1 *vt* (**a**) *(vara)* to wave about (**b**) *(caderas)* to sway
2 **cimbrearse** *vpr* to sway

cimentación *nf* (**a**) *(acción)* laying of the foundations (**b**) *(cimientos)* foundations

cimentar [3] *vt* (**a**) *(edificio)* to lay the foundations of; *(ciudad)* to found, to build (**b**) *(idea, paz, fama)* to cement, to consolidate

cimero, -a *adj (alto)* topmost; *Fig (sobresaliente)* foremost, most outstanding

cimiento *etc ver* **cimentar**

cimientos *nmpl* (**a**) *Constr* foundation; *también Fig* **echar los c.** to lay the foundations (**b**) *(base)* basis *singular*

cimitarra *nf* scimitar

cinabrio *nm* cinnabar

cinc *nm* zinc

cincel *nm* chisel

cincelar *vt* to chisel

cincha *nf* girth

cincho *nm* (**a**) *(cinturón)* belt (**b**) *(aro de hierro)* hoop

cinco *núm* five; *Fam* **¡choca esos c.!** put it there!; **c. puertas** four-door hatchback; *ver también* **seis**

cincuenta *núm* fifty; **los (años) c.** the fifties; *ver también* **seis**

cincuentena *nf* fifty; **andará por la c.** he must be about fifty; **una c. de persones** fifty people

cincuentenario *nm* fiftieth anniversary

cincuentón, -ona *nm,f Fam* person in his/her fifties

cine *nm (arte)* cinema; *(edificio)* movie theater; **hacer c.** to make movies; **c. de estreno** first-run movie theater; **c. de verano** open-air movie theater; **c. fórum** film with discussion group; **c. mudo** silent movies; **c. sonoro** talking pictures, talkies

cineasta *nmf* moviemaker, movie director

cineclub *(pl* **cineclubs** *o* **cineclubes)** *nm* (**a**) *(asociación)* film society (**b**) *(sala)* club cinema

cinéfilo, -a *nm,f (que va al cine)* (keen) moviegoer; *(que entiende de cine)* movie buff

cinegética *nf* hunting

cinegético, -a *adj* hunting; **asociación cinegética** hunting club

cinemascope® *nm* Cinemascope®

cinemateca *nf* film library

cinemática *nf Fís* kinematics *(singular)*

cinematografía *nf* moviemaking

cinematográfico, -a *adj* movie; **guión c.** movie script

cinematógrafo *nm* (**a**) *(aparato)* movie projector (**b**) *(local)* movie theater

cinerama® *nm* Cinerama®

cinética *nf* kinetics *(singular)*

cinético, -a *adj* kinetic

cingalés, -esa *adj & nm,f* Sinhalese

cíngaro, -a *adj & nm,f* Tzigane

cínico, -a 1 *adj (desvergonzado)* shameless
2 *nm,f (desvergonzado)* shameless person

cinismo *nm (desvergüenza)* shamelessness

cinta *nf* (**a**) *(de plástico, papel)* strip, band; *(de tela)* ribbon; **c. adhesiva** *o* **autoadhesiva** adhesive tape, Scotch tape®; **c.**

aislante insulating tape; **c. de impresora** printer ribbon; **c. métrica** tape measure; **c. perforada** punched tape (**b**) *(de imagen, sonido, ordenadores)* tape; **c. de audio** audio cassette; **c. digital/magnética** digital/magnetic tape; **c. magnetofónica** recording tape; **c. de vídeo** *o Am* **video** videotape; **c. virgen** blank tape (**c**) *(mecanismo)* belt; **c. transportadora** conveyor belt (**d**) *(película)* movie

cinto *nm* belt

cintura *nf* waist; *Fam Fig* **meter en c.** to bring under control; **c. de avispa** wasp waist

cinturilla *nf* waistband

cinturón *nm* (**a**) *(cinto)* belt; *Fig* **apretarse el c.** to tighten one's belt; *Dep* **c. negro** black belt (**b**) *(área circundante)* belt; **c. industrial** industrial belt; **c. verde** greenbelt (**c**) *(carretera)* beltway (**d**) *(en coche, avión)* **c. de seguridad** seat *o* safety belt

ciñera *etc ver* **ceñir**

ciño *etc ver* **ceñir**

cipote¹ *nm* (**a**) *Fam (bobo)* dimwit, moron (**b**) *Vulg (pene)* prick, cock

cipote², -a *nm,f CAm* kid

ciprés *(pl* **cipreses)** *nm* cypress

circense *adj* circus; **artista c.** circus performer; **espectáculo c.** circus show

circo *nm* (**a**) *(espectáculo)* circus (**b**) *Geol* **c. (glaciar)** cirque, corrie

circuito *nm* (**a**) *Dep & Elec* circuit; **c. cerrado** closed circuit; **c. impreso/integrado** printed/integrated circuit (**b**) *(contorno)* belt (**c**) *(viaje)* tour

circulación *nf* (**a**) *(movimiento) (gen) & Fin* circulation; **tiene problemas de c.** *(de la sangre)* he has bad circulation; *Fin* **c. fiduciaria** *o* **monetaria** paper currency (**b**) *(tráfico)* traffic

circulante *adj Fin* **capital c.** working capital

circular 1 *adj & nf* circular
2 *vi* (**a**) *(líquido)* to flow *o* circulate (**por** through); *(persona)* to move *o* walk (**por** around); *(vehículos)* to drive (**por** along); **este autobús no circula hoy** this bus doesn't run today (**b**) *(de mano en mano)* to circulate; *(moneda)* to be in circulation (**c**) *(difundirse)* to go around

circulatorio, -a *adj* (**a**) *Anat* circulatory (**b**) *(del tráfico)* traffic; **caos c.** traffic chaos

círculo *nm también Fig* circle; **pusieron las sillas en c.** they put the chairs in a circle; **c. de amistades** circle of friends; *Dep* **c. central** center circle; **círculos económicos** economic circles; **c. de lectores** book club; **el C. Polar Antártico/Ártico** the Antarctic/Artic Circle; **círculos políticos** political circles; **c. vicioso** vicious circle

circuncidar *vt* to circumcise

circuncisión *nf* circumcision

circunciso *adj* circumcised

circundante *adj* surrounding

circundar *vt* to surround

circunferencia *nf* circumference

circunflejo *adj* **acento c.** circumflex

circunlocución *nf,* **circunloquio** *nm* circumlocution

circunnavegar [40] *vt* to circumnavigate, to sail around

circunscribir 1 *vt* (**a**) *(limitar)* to restrict, to confine (**b**) *Geom* to circumscribe
2 **circunscribirse** *vpr* to confine oneself (**a** to)

circunscripción *nf* (**a**) *(limitación)* limitation (**b**) *(distrito)* district; *(militar)* division; **c. (electoral)** electoral district

circunscrito, -a 1 *participio ver* **circunscribir**
2 *adj* restricted, limited

circunspección *nf Formal* (**a**) *(comedimiento)* circumspection (**b**) *(seriedad)* graveness, seriousness

circunspecto, -a *adj Formal* (**a**) *(comedido)* circumspect (**b**) *(serio)* grave, serious

circunstancia *nf* circumstance; **en estas circunstancias** under the circumstances; *Fam* **puso cara de circunstancias** his face took on a serious expression *o* turned serious; *Der* **c. agravante/atenuante/eximente** aggravating/extenuating/exonerating circumstance

circunstancial *adj* (a) *(del momento)* chance; **un hecho c.** a chance occurrence; **una decisión c.** an ad hoc decision (b) *Gram* **complemento c.** adjunct

circunvalación *nf* (a) *(acción)* going around (b) *(carretera)* beltway

circunvalar *vt* to go around

circunvolución *nf* (a) *(vuelta)* circumvolution (b) *Anat (cerebral)* convolution

cirílico, -a *adj* Cyrillic

cirio *nm* (a) *(vela)* (wax) candle; **c. pascual** paschal candle (b) *Fam (alboroto)* row, rumpus; **montar un c.** to kick up a row

cirro *nm* Meteo cirrus

cirrosis *nf inv Med* cirrhosis; **c. hepática** cirrhosis of the liver

cirrótico, -a *adj Med* cirrhotic; *Fam Fig* **estar c.** to be an alcoholic

ciruela *nf* plum; **c. claudia** greengage; **c. pasa** prune

ciruelo *nm* plum tree

cirugía *nf* surgery; **c. cardíaca** heart surgery; **c. endoscópica** keyhole surgery; **c. exploratoria** exploratory surgery; **c. estética** cosmetic surgery; **c. plástica** plastic surgery

cirujano, -a *nm,f* surgeon; **c. plástico** plastic surgeon

cisco *nm* (a) *(carbón)* slack; *Fig* **hecho c.** shattered (b) *Fam (alboroto)* row, rumpus

Cisjordania *nf* the West Bank

cisma *nm Rel* schism; *Fig (escisión)* split

cismático, -a *adj & nm,f* schismatic

cisne *nm* swan

cisterciense *adj & nmf* Cistercian

cisterna *nf* (a) *(de retrete)* cistern (b) *(aljibe, tanque)* tank

cistitis *nf inv Med* cystitis

cita *nf* (a) *(entrevista)* appointment; *(de novios)* date; **darse c.** to meet; **tener una c.** to have an appointment; **c. a ciegas** blind date (b) *(referencia)* quotation

citación *nf Der* summons *(singular)*

citar 1 *vt* (a) *(convocar)* to make an appointment with; **me citó a la salida del cine** he arranged to meet me at the exit of the movie theater (b) *(aludir)* to mention; *(textualmente)* to quote; **citó algunos casos** he cited several cases (c) *Der* to summons; **c. a declarar a los procesados** to summons the defendants to give evidence

  2 citarse *vpr* **citarse (con alguien)** to arrange to meet (sb)

cítara *nf* zither

citología *nf* (a) *Med (análisis ginecológico)* smear test; **hacerse una c.** to have a smear test (b) *Biol* cytology

citoplasma *nm Biol* cytoplasm

cítrico, -a 1 *adj* citric

  2 cítricos *nmpl* citrus fruits

CiU [θiu] *nf (abrev de* **Convergència i Unió***)* = Catalan coalition party to the right of the political spectrum

ciudad *nf* (a) *(localidad)* (grande) city; *(pequeña)* town; **C. del Cabo** Cape Town; **c. catedralicia** cathedral town/city; **c. dormitorio** commuter town; **la C. Eterna** the Eternal City; **c. jardín** garden city; **C. de México** Mexico City; **c. natal** hometown; *Méx* **c. perdida** shantytown; **la C. Santa** the Holy City; **c. satélite** satellite city; **C. del Vaticano** Vatican City (b) *(instalaciones)* complex; **c. sanitaria** hospital complex; **c. universitaria** university campus

ciudadanía *nf* (a) *(nacionalidad)* citizenship (b) *(población)* public, citizens

ciudadano, -a 1 *adj (deberes, conciencia)* civic; *(urbano)* city; **vida c.** city life

  2 *nm,f* citizen; **el c. de a pie** the man in the street; **c. de segunda** second-class citizen

ciudadela *nf* citadel, fortress

ciudadrealeño, -a 1 *adj* of/from Ciudad Real

  2 *nm,f* person from Ciudad Real

ciuredano, -a *nm,f Inform* cybernaut, netizen, Net user

cívico, -a *adj (deberes, conciencia)* civic; *(conducta)* public-spirited

civil 1 *adj* civil; **casarse por lo c.** to get married in a civil ceremony

  2 *nmf* (a) *(no militar)* civilian (b) *Fam (Guardia Civil)* = member of the "Guardia Civil"

civilización *nf* civilization

civilizado, -a *adj* civilized

civilizar [14] **1** *vt* to civilize

  2 civilizarse *vpr* to become civilized

civismo *nm* (a) *(urbanidad)* community spirit (b) *(cortesía)* civility, politeness

cizalla *nf* (a) *(herramienta)* shears, metal cutters; *(guillotina)* guillotine (b) *(recortes)* metal cuttings

cizaña *nf Bot* darnel; *Fig* **meter o sembrar c.** to sow discord; *Fig* **separar la c. del buen grano** to separate the wheat from the chaff

cl *(abrev de* **centilitro***)* cl

clamar 1 *vt (exigir)* to cry out for; **c. justicia** to cry out for justice

  2 *vi* (a) *(implorar)* to appeal (b) *(protestar)* to cry out; *Fig* **es como c. en el desierto** it's like talking to a brick wall

clamor *nm* clamor

clamoroso, -a *adj* (a) *(victoria, éxito)* resounding (b) *(protesta, llanto)* loud, clamorous

clan *nm* (a) *(tribu, familia)* clan (b) *(banda)* faction

clandestinidad *nf* secrecy; **en la c.** underground

clandestino, -a *adj* clandestine; *Pol* underground

claque *nf* claque

claqué *nm* tap dancing

claqueta *nf Cine* clapperboards

clara *nf* (a) *(de huevo)* white (b) *Esp Fam (bebida)* shandy

claraboya *nf* skylight

claramente *adv* clearly

clarear 1 *vt* to light up

  2 *v impersonal* (a) *(amanecer)* **empezaba a c.** dawn was breaking (b) *(despejarse)* to clear up, to brighten up; **saldremos cuando claree** we'll go out when it clears up

  3 clarearse *vpr (transparentarse)* to be see-through

clarete 1 *adj* **vino c.** light red wine

  2 *nm* light red wine

claridad *nf* (a) *(transparencia)* clearness, clarity (b) *(luz)* light (c) *(franqueza)* candidness; **ser de una c. meridiana** to be crystal clear (d) *(lucidez)* clarity

clarificación *nf* clarification

clarificador, -ora *adj* clarifying

clarificar [59] *vt* (a) *(aclarar)* to clarify; *(misterio)* to clear up (b) *(purificar)* to refine

clarín 1 *nm (instrumento)* bugle

  2 *nmf (persona)* bugler

clarinete 1 *nm (instrumento)* clarinet

  2 *nmf (persona)* clarinetist

clarinetista *nmf* clarinetist

clarisa *nf Rel* nun of the order of St Clare

clarividencia *nf* farsightedness, perception

clarividente 1 *adj* farsighted, perceptive

  2 *nmf* perceptive person

claro, -a 1 *adj* (a) *(luminoso)* bright; *(color)* light; *(día)* clear (b) *(sonido)* clear; **hablaba con una voz clara** she spoke in a clear voice (**c**) *(diluido) (té, café)* weak; *(salsa)* thin

(**d**) *(poco tupido)* thin, sparse

(**e**) *(persona, explicación, ideas, libro)* clear

(**f**) *(obvio, evidente)* clear; **está c. que…** of course…; **¿está c.?** is that clear?; **dejar algo c.** to make sth clear; **a las claras** clearly; **está más c. que el agua** it's perfectly o crystal clear; **poner algo en c.** to get sth clear, to clear sth up; **sacar algo en c. (de)** to make sth out (from); **tengo c. que no puedo contar con él** one thing I'm quite sure about is that I can't rely on him

2 *nm* (**a**) *(en bosque)* clearing; *(en multitud)* space, gap; *(en cielo nublado)* break in the clouds; **se esperan nubes y claros** it will be cloudy with some bright spells (**b**) **c. de luna** moonlight

3 *adv* clearly; **hablar c.** to speak clearly; **¡c.!** of course!; **¡c. que me gusta!** of course I like it!; **¡c. que sí!** of course!; **¡c. que no!** of course not!

claroscuro *nm* chiaroscuro

clase *nf* (**a**) *(grupo, categoría)* class; **de primera c.** first-class; **de segunda c.** second-class; **c. alta/media** upper/middle class; **las clases dirigentes** the ruling classes; **c. obrera** working class; **clases pasivas** = pensioners and people on benefit; **c. preferente** business class; **c. social** social class; **c. trabajadora** working class; **c. turista** tourist class

(**b**) *(tipo)* sort, kind; **no me gusta esa c. de bromas** I don't like that kind of joke; **toda c. de** all sorts o kinds of

(**c**) *Educ (asignatura, alumnos)* class; *(aula)* classroom; **dar clases** *(en un colegio)* to teach; *(en una universidad)* to lecture; **hoy tengo c.** *(en el colegio)* I have to go to school today; *(en universidad)* I've got lectures today; *Esp* **clases de conducir** driving lessons; **c. de francés/inglés** French/English class; **c. magistral** master class; *Am* **clases de manejar** driving lessons; **clases particulares** private tuition

(**d**) *(estilo)* **tener c.** to have class

clasicismo *nm* (**a**) *Arte & Lit* classicism (**b**) *(carácter de obra, autor)* classical nature

clásico, -a 1 *adj* (**a**) *(de la Antigüedad)* classical (**b**) *(ejemplar, prototípico)* classic (**c**) *(peinado, estilo, música)* classical (**d**) *(habitual)* customary (**e**) *(peculiar)* **c. de** typical of

2 *nm,f (escritor)* classic

clasificación *nf* classification; *Dep* (league) standings; *Fin* **c. de solvencia** credit rating

clasificado *nm Am* classified ad

clasificador, -ora 1 *adj* classifying

2 *nm (mueble)* filing cabinet

clasificadora *nf (máquina)* sorter

clasificar [59] **1** *vt* to classify; **una película clasificada para mayores de 18 años** a movie with an 18 rating

2 *vi Am Dep* to qualify (**para** for)

3 clasificarse *vpr* (**a**) *Dep (ganar acceso)* to qualify (**para** for); **nos hemos clasificado para los cuartos de final** we've got through to o qualified for the quarterfinals (**b**) *(llegar)* **se clasificó en segundo lugar** she came second

clasismo *nm* class discrimination

clasista 1 *adj* class-conscious; *Pey* snobbish

2 *nmf* class-conscious person; *Pey* snob

claudia *adj* **ciruela c.** greengage

claudicación *nf Formal (cesión, rendición)* capitulation, surrender

claudicar [59] *vi Formal (ceder, rendirse)* to capitulate, to give up

claustro *nm* (**a**) *Arquit* cloister (**b**) *(en universidad)* senate (**c**) *(en instituto, colegio) (profesores)* teaching staff, faculty; *(reunión)* ≃ staff meeting, faculty meeting (**d**) **c. materno** *(matriz)* womb

claustrofobia *nf* claustrophobia

claustrofóbico, -a *adj* claustrophobic

cláusula *nf* (**a**) *(disposición)* clause; *Com* **c. de escape** escape clause, opt-out clause; *Com* **c. de penalización** penalty clause (**b**) *Gram* clause

clausura *nf* (**a**) *(acto solemne)* closing ceremony; **discurso/ceremonia de c.** closing speech/ceremony (**b**) *(cierre)* closing down (**c**) *(aislamiento)* enclosed life, enclosure; *Rel* **convento/monja de c.** convent/nun of an enclosed order

clausurar *vt* (**a**) *(acto)* to close, to conclude (**b**) *(local)* to close down

clavada *nf Esp Fam (precio abusivo)* rip-off

clavadista *nmf CAm, Méx* diver

clavado, -a *adj* (**a**) *(con clavos)* nailed (**b**) *(en punto)* **a las cuatro clavadas** at four o'clock on the dot (**c**) *(a la medida)* just right (**d**) *(parecido)* almost identical; **ser c. a alguien** to be the spitting image of sb (**e**) *(fijo)* fixed

clavar 1 *vt* (**a**) *(clavo, estaca)* to drive; *(cuchillo)* to thrust; *(chincheta, alfiler)* to stick (**b**) *(letrero, placa)* to nail, to fix; **clavó la suela de la bota** he nailed on the sole of the boot (**c**) *(mirada, atención)* to fix, to rivet; **c. los ojos** o **la mirada en algo/alguien en** to stare at sth/sb (**d**) *Fam (cobrar)* **me han clavado cien euros** they stung me for a hundred euros; **en esa tienda te clavan** they charge you an arm and a leg in that store

2 clavarse *vpr (hincarse)* **me clavé una astilla en el pie** I got a splinter in my foot

clave 1 *adj inv (fundamental, esencial)* key; **es una fecha c. para la empresa** it's a crucial date for the company

2 *nm Mús* harpsichord

3 *nf* (**a**) *(código)* code; **en c.** in code; **nos mandaron los mensajes en c.** they sent us the messages in code, they sent us coded messages; **c. de acceso** access code (**b**) *(solución)* key; **la c. de la felicidad/del éxito** the key to happiness/success (**c**) *Mús* clef; **c. de fa** bass clef; **c. de sol** treble clef (**d**) *Inform* password

clavecín *nm* spinet

clavel *nm* carnation

clavellina *nf* small carnation, pink

claveteado *nm* studding

clavetear *vt* (**a**) *(adornar con clavos)* to stud (with nails) (**b**) *(poner clavos)* to nail *(roughly)*

clavicémbalo *nm* harpsichord

clavicordio *nm* clavichord

clavícula *nf* collarbone

clavija *nf* (**a**) *Elec* pin; *(de auriculares, teléfono)* jack (**b**) *Mús* peg (**c**) *Fam Fig* **apretar las clavijas a alguien** to put the screws on sb

clavo *nm* (**a**) *(pieza metálica)* nail; *Fam Fig* **agarrarse a un c. ardiendo** to clutch at straws; **estaré allí como un c.** I'll be there on the dot; *Fam* **dar en el c.** to hit the nail on the head (**b**) *(especia)* clove (**c**) *Fam (precio abusivo)* rip-off (**d**) *Med (para huesos)* pin

claxon *nm* horn; **tocar el c.** to sound the horn

clemencia *nf* mercy, clemency

clemente *adj (persona)* merciful, clement; *(invierno)* mild

clementina *nf* clementine

cleptomanía *nf* kleptomania

cleptómano, -a *nm,f* kleptomaniac

clerecía *nf* (**a**) *(clero)* clergy (**b**) *(oficio)* priesthood

clerical 1 *adj* clerical

2 *nmf* clericalist

clérigo *nm (católico)* priest; *(anglicano)* clergyman

clero *nm* clergy

clic *(pl* **clics**), **click** *(pl* **clicks**) *nm Inform* click; **hacer c.** to click; **hacer doble c.** to double click

clicar [59] *Inform* **1** *vt* to click on

2 *vi* to click

cliché *nm* (**a**) *Fot* negative (**b**) *Imprenta* plate (**c**) *(tópico)* cliché

click = clic

cliente, -a *nm,f (de tienda, garaje, bar)* customer; *(de banco, abogado) (gen)* client; *(de hotel)* guest; **el c. siempre tiene razón** the customer is always right

clientela *nf (de tienda, garaje)* customers; *(de banco, abogado)* clients; *(de hotel)* guests; *(de bar, restaurante)* clientele

clientelismo *nm Pol* = practice of giving preferential treatment to a particular interest group in exchange for its support

clima *nm* **(a)** *(atmosférico)* climate; **c. continental** continental climate; **c. mediterráneo** mediterranean climate; **c. tropical** tropical climate **(b)** *(ambiente)* atmosphere; **las negociaciones se desarrollaron en un c. de distensión** the talks took place in a relaxed atmosphere

climaterio *nm Med* menopause

climático, -a *adj* climatic

climatización *nf* air-conditioning

climatizado, -a *adj* air-conditioned; **piscina climatizada** heated swimming pool

climatizar [14] *vt* to air-condition

climatología *nf* **(a)** *(tiempo)* climate **(b)** *(ciencia)* climatology

climatológico, -a *adj* climatological

clímax *nm inv* climax

clínica *nf* clinic; **c. de adelgazamiento** slimming clinic; **c. veterinaria** veterinary surgery

clínico, -a 1 *adj* clinical
    2 *nm,f* doctor

clip *(pl* **clips)** *nm* **(a)** *(para papel)* paper clip **(b)** *(para el pelo)* hairclip **(c)** *(videoclip)* (pop) video

clíper *nm* clipper

clisé *nm* **(a)** *Fot* negative **(b)** *Imprenta* plate **(c)** *(tópico)* cliché

clítoris *nm inv* clitoris

cloaca *nf* sewer

cloch, cloche *(pl* **cloches)** *nm Méx, Ven* clutch

clon *nm* clone

clonación *nf* cloning

clonar *vt* to clone

clónico, -a 1 *adj* cloned
    2 *nm Inform (ordenador)* clone

cloquear *vi* to cluck

cloración *nf* chlorination

clorar *vt* to chlorinate

clorato *nm Quím* chlorate

clorhídrico *adj Quím* **ácido c.** hydrochloric acid

clórico, -a *adj Quím* chloric

cloro *nm* **(a)** *Quím* chlorine **(b)** *CAm, Chile, Méx, Ven (lejía)* bleach

clorofila *nf Bot* chlorophyll

cloroformo *nm Quím* chloroform

cloruro *nm Quím* chloride; **c. de cal** bleaching powder; **c. de sodio** *o* **sódico** sodium chloride

clóset *(pl* **clósets)** *nm Am* built-in cupboard, closet

clown ['klaun, 'kloun] *(pl* **clowns)** *nm* clown

club *(pl* **clubs** *o* **clubes)** *nm* **(a)** *(sociedad)* club; **c. de fans** fan club; **c. de fútbol** soccer club; **c. náutico** yacht club **(b)** *(local de alterne)* = roadside bar and brothel

clueca *adj* broody

cm *(abrev de* **centímetro)** cm

CNI *nm (abrev de* **Centro Nacional de Inteligencia**) = Spanish national intelligence service

CNMV *Esp Fin (abrev de* **Comisión Nacional del Mercado de Valores)** *nf* ≃ SEC

CNT *nf (abrev de* **Confederación Nacional del Trabajo)** = Spanish anarchist trade union federation created in 1911

CNV *nf Arg Fin (abrev de* **Comisión Nacional de Valores)** ≃ SEC

Co. *(abrev de* **compañía)** Co

coacción *nf* coercion

coaccionar *vt* to coerce

coactivo, -a *adj* coercive

coadyuvante *adj* helping, assisting

coadyuvar *vi Formal* **c. en algo/a hacer algo** to contribute to sth/to doing sth

coagulación *nf Med* clotting, coagulation

coagulante *Med* **1** *adj* clotting
    2 *nm* clotting agent

coagular 1 *vt (sangre)* to clot, to coagulate; *(líquido)* to coagulate
    2 coagularse *vpr (sangre)* to clot; *(líquido)* to coagulate

coágulo *nm Med* clot

coalición *nf* coalition

coaligar [40] **1** *vt* to ally, to unite
    2 coligarse *vpr* to unite, to join together

coartada *nf* alibi

coartar *vt* to limit, to restrict

coaseguro *nm* coinsurance

coautor, -ora *nm,f* coauthor

coaxial *adj* coaxial

coba *nf Esp, Méx Fam (halago)* flattery; **dar c. a alguien** *(adular)* to suck up *o* crawl to sb; *(aplacar)* to soft-soap sb

cobalto *nm* cobalt

cobarde 1 *adj* cowardly
    2 *nmf* coward

cobardía *nf* cowardice

cobardica *Fam Pey* **1** *nmf* scaredy-cat
    2 *adj* **ser c.** to be a scaredy-cat

cobaya *nmf también Fig* guinea pig

cobertizo *nm* **(a)** *(tejado adosado)* lean-to **(b)** *(caseta)* shed

cobertor *nm* bedspread

cobertura *nf* **(a)** *(cubierta)* cover **(b)** *(de un servicio)* coverage; **c. informativa** news *o* media coverage; **c. nacional/regional** national/regional coverage **(c)** *(de un seguro)* cover; **c. sanitaria** health cover

cobija *nf Am* blanket

cobijar 1 *vt* **(a)** *(albergar)* to house **(b)** *(proteger)* to shelter
    2 cobijarse *vpr* to take shelter

cobijo *nm* shelter; **dar c. a alguien** to give shelter to sb, to take sb in

cobista *nmf Fam* creep

Cobol *nm Inform* COBOL

cobra *nf* cobra

cobrador, -ora *nm,f (del autobús)* conductor, *f* conductress; *(de deudas, recibos)* collector

cobrar 1 *vt* **(a)** *Com (dinero)* to charge; *(cheque)* to cash; *(deuda)* to collect; **nos cobra 700 euros de alquiler al mes** she charges us 700 euros rent a month, we pay her 700 euros rent a month; **me cobró de más** he overcharged me; **cantidades por c.** amounts due; **¿me cobra?** *(al pagar)* how much do I owe you? **(b)** *(un sueldo)* to earn, to be paid; **cobra un millón al año** she earns a million a year; **está cobrando el paro** he's receiving unemployment benefit **(c)** *(adquirir)* to take on, to acquire; **c. fama** to become famous **(d)** *(sentir)* **cobrarle afecto** *o* **cariño a alguien** to take a liking to sb
    2 *vi* **(a)** *(en el trabajo)* to get paid **(b)** *Fam (recibir una paliza)* **¡vas a c.!** you'll catch it!; **el niño cobró por portarse mal** the child got a beating for being naughty
    3 cobrarse *vpr* **(a)** *(causar)* **el accidente se cobró ocho vidas** eight people were killed in the crash **(b)** *(al pagar)* **¿se cobra?** how much do I owe you?

cobre *nm* copper; *Am Fam* **no tener un c.** to be flat broke

cobrizo, -a *adj (pelo, piel)* copper

cobro *nm (de talón)* cashing; *(de pago)* collection; **llamar a c. revertido a alguien** to call sb collect

coca *nf* (**a**) *(planta)* coca (**b**) *Fam (cocaína)* coke

Coca-Cola® *nf* Coca-Cola®, Coke®

cocaína *nf* cocaine

cocainómano, -a *nm,f* cocaine addict

cocción *nf* *(de alimentos)* cooking; *(en agua)* boiling; *(en horno)* baking

cóccix *nm inv* coccyx

cocear *vi* to kick

cocer [15] **1** *vt* (**a**) *(alimentos)* to cook; *(hervir)* to boil; *(en horno)* to bake (**b**) *(cerámica, ladrillos)* to fire

2 cocerse *vpr (alimentos)* to cook; *(hervir)* to boil; *(en horno)* to bake; *Prov* **en todas partes cuecen habas** it's the same wherever you go; *Fig* **¿qué se cuece por aquí?** what's cooking?, what's going on here?

cochambre *nf* *Fam (suciedad)* filth; *(basura)* garbage

cochambroso, -a *adj Fam* filthy

cochayuyo *nm Chile, Perú* seaweed

coche *nm* (**a**) *(automóvil)* car, automobile; **ir en c.** *(montado)* to go by car; *(conduciendo)* to drive; **viajar en c.** to travel by car; **c. de alquiler** hire car; **c. antiguo** *(de antes de 1930)* vintage car; *(más moderno)* classic car; **c. automático** automatic; **c. bomba** car bomb; **c. de bomberos** fire engine, fire truck; **c. de carreras** racing car; **c. celular** police van; **coches de choque** bumper cars; **c. deportivo** sports car; **c. de empresa** company car; **c. de época** *(de antes de 1930)* vintage car; *(más moderno)* classic car; **c. familiar** station wagon; **c. fúnebre** hearse; **c. de ocasión** used car; **c. patrulla** patrol car; **c. de policía** police car; **c. usado** *o* **de segunda mano** used car

(**b**) *(de caballos)* carriage

(**c**) *(de niño)* baby carriage

(**d**) *(de tren)* coach, car; **c. cama** sleeping car, sleeper; **c. restaurante** restaurant *o* dining car

cochecito *nm (de niño)* baby carriage

cochera *nf (para coches)* garage; *(de autobuses, tranvías)* depot

cochero *nm* coachman

cochinada *nf* (**a**) *(cosa sucia)* filthy thing; **es una c.** it's filthy; **hacer cochinadas** *(porquerías)* to be disgusting; *(sexuales)* to be naughty (**b**) *(grosería)* obscenity, dirty word (**c**) *(mala jugada)* dirty trick

cochinilla *nf* (**a**) *(crustáceo)* wood louse (**b**) *(insecto)* cochineal

cochinillo *nm* suckling pig

cochino, -a 1 *adj (sucio)* filthy; *Fam (maldito)* damned; **¡está obsesionado con el c. dinero!** with him it's always money, money, money!

2 *nm,f (animal)* pig, *f* sow

cocido, -a 1 *adj* (**a**) *(alimentos)* cooked; *(hervido)* boiled (**b**) *(barro)* fired

2 *nm Culin* stew; **c. madrileño** = chickpea stew, containing meat, sausage and potatoes

cociente *nm* quotient; **c. intelectual** IQ

cocina *nf* (**a**) *(habitación)* kitchen (**b**) *(electrodoméstico)* stove; **c. eléctrica/de gas** electric/gas stove (**c**) *(arte)* cooking; **libro de c.** cookbook; **clase de c.** cooking class; **c. casera** home cooking; **c. española** Spanish cuisine *o* cooking

cocinar 1 *vt* to cook; **¿qué se cocina por aquí?** what's cooking?, what's going on here?

2 *vi* to cook

cocinero, -a *nm,f* cook; *Fig* **ha sido c. antes que fraile** he's got experience on the subject

cocinilla 1 *nf (aparato)* portable *o* camp stove

2 *nm Fam (persona)* **es un c.** he's great in the kitchen

cocker ['koker] *(pl* **cockers**) *nm* cocker spaniel

coco *nm* (**a**) *(fruto)* coconut (**b**) *Fam (cabeza)* nut, head; **está mal del c.** he's soft *o* isn't right in the head; **por más vueltas que le doy al c. no consigo entenderlo** I've racked my brains but I still can't understand it; **comerse el c.**

to worry (one's head); **comerle el c. a alguien** *(convencer)* to brainwash sb (**c**) *Fam (fantasma)* bogeyman; **si no te portas bien vendrá el c.** if you're not good the bogeyman will come and get you (**d**) *Biol (bacteria)* coccus

cococha *nf* barbel

cocodrilo *nm* crocodile

cocotero *nm* coconut palm

cóctel, coctel *nm* (**a**) *(bebida, comida)* cocktail; **c. de gambas** shrimp cocktail (**b**) *(reunión)* cocktail party (**c**) **c. molotov** gasoline bomb, Molotov cocktail

coctelera *nf* cocktail shaker

coctelería *nf* cocktail bar

coda *nf Mús* coda

codazo *nm* *(suave)* nudge; *(fuerte)* jab *(with one's elbow)*; **abrirse paso a codazos** to elbow one's way through; **dar un c. a alguien** to nudge/elbow sb

codearse *vpr* to rub shoulders (**con** with)

codeína *nf* codeine

codera *nf* elbow patch

códice *nm* codex

codicia *nf* (**a**) *(de riqueza)* greed (**b**) *(de aprender, saber)* thirst (**de** for)

codiciar *vt* to covet

codicioso, -a *adj* greedy

codificación *nf* (**a**) *(de norma, ley)* codification (**b**) *(de mensaje en clave)* encoding (**c**) *Inform* coding

codificado, -a *adj (emisión de TV)* scrambled

codificador, -ora 1 *adj* codifying

2 *nm (aparato)* scrambler *(for pay TV)*

codificar [59] *vt* (**a**) *(ley)* to codify (**b**) *(un mensaje)* to encode (**c**) *Inform* to code

código *nm (gen) & Inform* code; **c. de acceso** access code; **c. ASCII** ASCII (code); **c. de barras/de señales** bar/signal code; **c. de circulación** highway rules; **c. civil** civil code; **c. de comercio** commercial law; **c. de conducta** code of conduct; *Inform* **códigos de fusión** merge codes; **c. genético** genetic code; **c. máquina** machine code; **c. mercantil** commercial law; **c. Morse** Morse code; **c. penal** penal code; **c. postal** zip code; **c. territorial** area code

codillo *nm* (**a**) *(en un cuadrúpedo)* upper foreleg; *Culin* knuckle of pork (**b**) *(de jamón)* shoulder (**c**) *(de un tubo)* elbow, bend

codirector, -ora *nm,f* codirector

codo *nm* (**a**) *(en brazo)* elbow; **tenía los codos sobre la mesa** he was leaning (with his elbows) on the table; **c. con c., c. a c.** side by side; *Fam Fig* **empinar el c.** to booze; *Fam Fig* **hablar por los codos** to talk nineteen to the dozen, to be a chatterbox; *Fam* **hincar** *o* **romperse los codos** *(estudiar)* to study hard; **se sacó la carrera a base de codos** she got her degree by sheer hard work; *Med* **c. de tenista** tennis elbow (**b**) *(en tubería)* bend; *(pieza)* elbow joint (**c**) *(medida)* cubit

codorniz *nf* quail

COE ['koe] *nm (abrev de* **Comité Olímpico Español***)* Spanish Olympic Committee

coedición *nf* joint publication

coeditar *vt* to publish jointly

coeficiente *nm (índice)* rate; *Mat & Fís* coefficient; *Fin* **c. de caja** cash ratio; **c. intelectual** *o* **de inteligencia** IQ; *Fin* **c. de liquidez** liquidity ratio

coercer [40] *vt* to restrict, to constrain

coerción *nf* coercion

coercitivo, -a *adj* coercive

coetáneo, -a *adj & nm,f* contemporary

coexistencia *nf* coexistence; **c. pacífica** peaceful coexistence

coexistente *adj* coexisting

coexistir *vi* to coexist

cofia *nf (de enfermera, camarera)* cap; *(de monja)* coif

cofrade *nmf (de cofradía religiosa)* brother, *f* sister; *(de cofradía no religiosa)* member

cofradía *nf (religiosa)* brotherhood, *f* sisterhood; *(profesional)* guild

cofre *nm* (**a**) *(arca)* chest, trunk (**b**) *(para joyas)* jewel box

coger [52] **1** *vt* (**a**) *(tomar, agarrar)* to take; **c. a alguien de la mano** to take sb by the hand; **coge esta bolsa un momento** hold this bag a moment; **¿puedes c. el teléfono, por favor?** could you pick the phone up *o* answer the phone, please?

(**b**) *(atrapar) (ladrón, pez, pájaro)* to catch; **¿a que no me coges?** bet you can't catch me!

(**c**) *(alcanzar) (persona, vehículo)* to catch up with

(**d**) *(recoger) (objeto caído)* to pick up; *(frutos, flores)* to pick; **se me ha caído el bolígrafo, ¿me lo puedes c.?** I've dropped my pen, could you pick it up for me?

(**e**) *(quedarse con) (propina, empleo, piso)* to take; **llegaremos pronto para c. buen sitio** we'll get there early to get a good seat

(**f**) *(contratar) (personal)* to take on

(**g**) *(quitar)* to take (**a alguien** from sb); **¿quién me ha cogido el lápiz?** who's taken my pencil?; **te he cogido la calculadora un momento** I've just borrowed your calculator for a moment

(**h**) *(tren, autobús)* to take, to catch; **no me gusta c. el avión** I don't like flying

(**i**) *(contraer) (gripe, resfriado)* to catch, to get; **c. una borrachera** to get drunk; **c. frío** to get cold

(**j**) *(sentir) (manía, odio, afecto)* to start to feel; **c. cariño/miedo a** to become fond/scared of

(**k**) *(cobrar)* **c. fuerzas** to build up one's strength; **c. velocidad** to gather speed

(**l**) *(sujeto: vehículo)* to knock over, to run over; *(sujeto: toro)* to gore

(**m**) *(oír)* to catch; *(entender)* to get; **no cogió el chiste** he didn't get the joke

(**n**) *(sorprender, encontrar)* **c. a alguien haciendo algo** to catch sb doing sth; **c. a alguien desprevenido** to take sb by surprise

(**o**) *(sintonizar) (canal, emisora)* to get, to receive

(**p**) *(abarcar) (espacio)* to cover, to take up

(**q**) *Am Vulg* to screw, to fuck

2 *vi* (**a**) *(situarse)* to be; **coge muy cerca de aquí** it's not very far from here (**b**) *(dirigirse)* **c. a la derecha/la izquierda** to turn right/left (**c**) *(indicando acción repentina)* **cogió y se fue** he upped and went; **de pronto cogió y me insultó** he turned around and insulted me (**d**) *Am Vulg* **c. con alguien** to screw *o* fuck sb

3 cogerse *vpr* (**a**) *(asirse)* **cogerse de** *o* **a algo** to cling to *o* clutch sth (**b**) *(pillarse)* **cogerse los dedos/la falda con la puerta** to catch one's fingers/skirt in the door; *Fam* **cogerse un cabreo** to throw a fit; **cogerse una gripe** to catch the flu (**c**) *(sintonizarse) (canal, emisora)* to get; **desde mi casa no se coge el Canal 5** you can't get Channel 5 from my house

cogestión *nf* joint management, comanagement

cogida *nf (de torero)* goring

cognac [ko'nak] *(pl* **cognacs***)* *nm* brandy, cognac

cognitivo, -a *adj* cognitive

cogollo *nm* (**a**) *(de lechuga)* heart (**b**) *(brote)* shoot

cogorza *nf Fam* **agarrar una c.** to get smashed, to get blind drunk

cogotazo *nm* rabbit punch

cogote *nm Esp* nape, back of the neck

cogulla *nf Rel* habit

cohabitación *nf* cohabitation

cohabitar *vi* to cohabit, to live together

cohecho *nm* bribery

coheredero, -a *nm,f* coheir, *f* coheiress

coherencia *nf (de conducta, estilo)* consistency; *(de razonamiento)* coherence

coherente *adj (conducta, estilo)* consistent; *(razonamiento)* coherent

cohesión *nf* cohesion; **la c. del partido** party unity

cohesionar 1 *vt* to unite

2 cohesionarse *vpr* to unite

cohesivo, -a *adj* cohesive

cohete *nm* rocket; **cohetes** *(fuegos artificiales)* fireworks; **c. espacial** space rocket; **c. propulsor** booster (rocket)

cohibición *nf* inhibition

cohibido, -a *adj* inhibited

cohibir 1 *vt* to inhibit

2 cohibirse *vpr* to become inhibited

cohorte *nf* cohort

COI ['koi] *nm (abrev de* **Comité Olímpico Internacional***)* IOC

coima *nf Andes, RP Fam* bribe

coimear *vt Andes, RP Fam* to bribe

coincidencia *nf* coincidence

coincidir *vi* (**a**) *(superficies, versiones, gustos)* to coincide; **su versión de los hechos no coincide con la de otros testigos** her version of events doesn't coincide with that of other witnesses (**b**) *(estar de acuerdo)* to agree; **coincido contigo en que...** I agree with you that..., I am in agreement with you that... (**c**) *(en un sitio)* **coincidimos en la fiesta** we were both at the party; **coincidí con ella en un congreso** I met her at a conference (**d**) *(en el tiempo)* to coincide; **mi cumpleaños coincide con el primer día de clase** my birthday falls on the first day of classes

coito *nm (sexual)* intercourse

coitus interruptus *nm inv* coitus interruptus

cojear *vi* (**a**) *(persona)* to limp; *Fam Fig* **ya sé de qué pie cojea María** I know Maria's weak points; *Fam Fig* **los dos cojean del mismo pie** they're two of a kind (**b**) *(mueble)* to wobble (**c**) *(argumento)* to be faulty

cojera *nf (acción)* limp; *(estado)* lameness

cojín *nm* cushion

cojinete *nm (en eje)* bearing; *(en un riel de ferrocarril)* chair

cojo, -a 1 *ver* **coger**

2 *adj* (**a**) *(persona)* lame (**b**) *(mueble)* wobbly (**c**) *(razonamiento, frase)* faulty

3 *nm,f* cripple

cojones *nmpl Esp Vulg* balls; **¡ahora lo vas a hacer por c.!** you goddamn well ARE going to do it!; **es bueno/malo de c.** it's goddamn marvelous/awful; **¡no me sale de los c.!** I can't be goddamn bothered!; **tener c.** to have balls; **¡c.!** *(expresa enfado)* for fuck's sake!

cojonudo, -a *adj Esp muy Fam* goddamn brilliant

cojudear *vt Andes Fam* (**a**) *(hacer tonterías)* to mess around (**b**) *(engañar)* to trick

cojudez *nf Andes muy Fam* **decir cojudeces** to talk a load of goddamn nonsense

cojudo, -a *adj Andes muy Fam* goddamn stupid

col *nf* cabbage; **coles de Bruselas** Brussels sprouts; **c. lombarda** red cabbage

cola *nf* (**a**) *(de animal, avión)* tail

(**b**) *(de vestido de novia)* train

(**c**) *(fila)* line; **hay mucha c.** there's a big *o* long line; **hacer** *o* **guardar c.** to stand in line; **me tuve que poner a la c.** I had to join the end of the line; **¡a la c.!** go to the back of the line!; *Inform* **c. de impresión** printing queue

(**d**) *(de clase, lista)* bottom; *(de desfile)* end; **están a la c. del mundo civilizado en cuanto a inversiones educativas** they have the worst record in the civilized world as regards investment in education; **ir a la c. del pelotón** to be one of the tailenders; *Fam* **tener** *o* **traer c.** to have serious consequences *o* repercussions

(**e**) *(pegamento)* glue; *Fam Fig* **no pegan ni con c.** they don't match at all

(**f**) *(bebida)* cola

(**g**) *(peinado)* **c. (de caballo)** ponytail

(**h**) *Fam (pene)* peter

(**i**) *Am Fam (nalgas)* fanny

(**j**) *Ven (autoestop)* **dar la c. a alguien** to give sb a ride; **pedir c.** to hitchhike

colaboración *nf* (**a**) *(cooperación)* collaboration; **hacer algo en c. con alguien** to do sth in collaboration with sb (**b**) *(de prensa)* contribution, article

colaboracionismo *nm Pol* collaborationism

colaboracionista *Pol* **1** *adj* collaborationist

2 *nmf* collaborator

colaborador, -ora 1 *adj* cooperative

2 *nm,f* *(compañero)* associate, colleague; *(de prensa)* contributor, writer; **c. externo** freelancer

colaborar *vi* (**a**) *(ayudar)* to collaborate (**b**) *(en prensa)* **c. en** *o* **con** to write for, to work for (**c**) *(contribuir)* to contribute

colación *nf* (**a**) *(para comer)* snack (**b**) *Fam* **sacar** *o* **traer algo a c.** *(tema)* to bring sth up

colada *nf Esp (ropa)* washing; **hacer la c.** to do the washing

coladero *nm Fam* easy way through

colado, -a *adj* (**a**) *(líquido)* strained (**b**) *Fam (enamorado)* **estar c. por alguien** to have a crush on sb

colador *nm (para líquidos)* strainer, sieve; *(para verdura)* colander

colage *nm* collage

colágeno *nm* collagen

colapsar 1 *vt* to bring to a halt, to stop; **el tráfico ha colapsado las calles** traffic has blocked the streets

2 colapsarse *vpr (mercado)* to collapse; **se ha colapsado el tráfico** traffic has ground to a halt

colapso *nm* (**a**) *Med* collapse, breakdown (**b**) *(de actividad)* stoppage; *(de tráfico)* traffic jam, holdup

colar [63] **1** *vt* (**a**) *(leche, té)* to strain; *(café)* to filter (**b**) *Fam (dinero falso)* to pass off as genuine; *(mentira)* to slip through (**c**) *(en cola)* **me coló** he let me cut in line (**d**) *(en fiesta)* **nos coló en la fiesta** he got us into the party (**e**) *(introducir)* to slip, to squeeze (**por** through)

2 *vi Fam (pasar por bueno)* **esto no colará** this won't hold water

3 colarse *vpr* (**a**) *(líquido)* **colarse por** to seep through (**b**) *(persona) (en un sitio)* to slip, to sneak; *(en una cola)* to cut in line; **colarse en una fiesta** to gate-crash a party; **¡eh, no te cueles!** hey, don't cut in line! (**c**) *Fam (equivocarse)* to slip up

colateral *adj* on either side

colcha *nf* bedspread

colchón *nm* (**a**) *(de cama)* mattress; **c. inflable** *o* **hinchable** air mattress (**b**) *Inform* buffer

colchonero, -a 1 *nm,f* upholsterer, mattressmaker

2 *adj Dep* = relating to Atlético de Madrid soccer club

colchoneta *nf (de playa)* beach mat; *(en gimnasio)* mat

cole *nm Fam* school

colear *vi* (**a**) *(animal)* to wag its tail (**b**) *(asunto, problema)* to drag on

colección *nf también Fig* collection

coleccionable 1 *adj* collectable

2 *nm* = special supplement in serialized form

coleccionar *vt* to collect

coleccionismo *nm* collecting

coleccionista *nmf* collector; **c. de sellos** stamp collector

colecta *nf* collection; **hacer una c.** to collect money, to organize a collection

colectar *vt* to collect

colectividad *nf* community

colectivismo *nm* collectivism

colectivización *nf* collectivization

colectivizar [14] *vt* to collectivize

colectivo, -a 1 *adj* collective

2 *nm* (**a**) *(grupo)* group (**b**) *Andes (taxi)* collective taxi *(with a fixed rate and that travels a fixed route)*; *Arg, Bol (autobús)* minibus

colector, -ora 1 *adj* collecting

2 *nm,f (persona)* collector

3 *nm* (**a**) *(sumidero)* sewer; **c. de basuras** chute (**b**) *Tec (de motor)* manifold (**c**) *(de transistor)* collector

colega *nmf* (**a**) *(compañero profesional)* colleague, coworker (**b**) *(homólogo)* counterpart, opposite number (**c**) *Esp Fam (amigo)* pal, buddy

colegiado, -a 1 *adj* = who belongs to a professional association

2 *nm,f Dep* referee

colegial, -ala *nm,f* schoolboy, *f* schoolgirl; **cartera/ uniforme de c.** school bag/uniform

colegiarse *vpr* = to join a professional association

colegiata *nf* collegiate church

colegiatura *nf* (**a**) *Andes, CAm, Méx (matrícula)* tuition fees (**b**) *Chile, Col, RP (afiliación)* = membership of a professional association

colegio *nm* (**a**) *(escuela)* school; **c. estatal** public school; **c. de monjas** convent school; **c. mixto** mixed *o* coeducational school; **c. nacional** public elementary school; **c. de pago** private school; **c. privado** private school; **c. público** public school (**b**) *(de profesionales)* **c. (profesional)** professional association (**c**) *Pol* **c. electoral** *(lugar)* polling station; *(votantes)* ward (**d**) *Esp* **c. mayor** dormitory, residence hall

colegir [55] *vi* to infer (**de** from), to gather (**de** from); **de ahí se puede c. que** it can thus be inferred that

colegislador, -ora *adj (asamblea)* joint legislative

coleóptero *nm* beetle

cólera 1 *nm Med* cholera

2 *nf (ira)* anger, rage; **montar en c.** to get angry, to lose one's temper

colérico, -a *adj (furioso)* furious; *(irritable)* bad-tempered; **estar c.** to be furious

colesterol *nm* cholesterol

coleta *nf* pigtail; *Fig* **cortarse la c.** to call it a day, to retire

coletazo *nm* flick *o* swish of the tail; *Fig* **está dando (los últimos) coletazos** it's in its death throes

coletilla *nf (de discurso, escrito)* closing comment

colgado, -a *adj* (**a**) *(cuadro, jamón)* hanging (**de** from) (**b**) *(teléfono)* on the hook (**c**) *Fam (atontado, loco)* crazy, daft (**d**) *Fam (abandonado)* **dejar a alguien c.** to leave sb in the lurch (**e**) *Fam (enganchado)* **quedarse c. (con)** to get hooked (on) (**f**) *Fam* **tengo c. el inglés del curso pasado** I flunked my English exam last year

colgador *nm (percha)* hanger, coat hanger; *(gancho)* hook

colgajo *nm* (**a**) *(tela)* hanging piece of material; *(hilo)* loose thread (**b**) *(de piel)* flap

colgante 1 *adj* hanging

2 *nm* pendant

colgar [16] **1** *vt* (**a**) *(suspender, ahorcar)* to hang (**b**) *(teléfono)* **c. el teléfono** to hang up; **me colgó en mitad de la frase** she hung up on me when I was in midsentence (**c**) *(atribuir)* **le colgaron ese apodo en la escuela** he got that nickname at school (**d**) *(abandonar)* to give up; **c. los estudios** to abandon one's studies; **c. los hábitos** to leave the priesthood, to give up the cloth; *Fig (renunciar)* to give up one's job

2 *vi* (**a**) *(pender)* to hang (**de** from) (**b**) *(hablando por teléfono)* to hang up, to put the phone down; **no cuelgue, por favor** hold the line, please

3 colgarse *vpr* (**a**) *(suspenderse)* to hang (**de** from); *(ahorcarse)* to hang oneself (**b**) *Inform (computadora)* to crash

colibrí *(pl* **colibríes** *o* **colibrís**) *nm* hummingbird

cólico *nm* colic; **c. bilioso** bilious attack; **c. hepático** biliary colic; **c. nefrítico** *o* **renal** renal colic

coliflor *nf* cauliflower

coligar [40] **1** *vt* to ally, to unite

2 coligarse *vpr* to unite, to join together

colijo *ver* **colegir**

colilla *nf (de cigarrillo)* (cigarette) butt *o* stub; *(de puro)* (cigar) butt *o* stub

colimba *nf Arg Fam* military service

colín *nm Esp* breadstick

colina *nf* hill

colindante *adj* neighboring, adjacent

colindar *vi* to be adjacent, to adjoin

colirio *nm* eyewash, eyedrops

coliseo *nm* coliseum

colisión *nf (de vehículos)* collision, crash; *(de ideas, intereses)* clash; **c. múltiple** pileup

colisionar *vi* (**a**) *(coche)* to collide (**contra** with), to crash (**contra** into) (**b**) *(ideas)* to clash

colista *nmf (en liga de fútbol)* bottom team; *(en carreras)* tailender

colistero, -a *nm, f Fam Inform* list member

colitis *nf inv (diarrea)* stomach infection

collado *nm (colina)* hill

collage [ko'laʃ] *nm* collage

collar *nm* (**a**) *(para personas)* necklace; **c. de diamantes** diamond necklace; **c. de perlas** pearl necklace (**b**) *(para animales)* collar (**c**) *(abrazadera)* collar, ring

collarín *nm* medical collar

colleja *nf* **dar una c. a alguien** to slap sb *o* give sb a slap on the back of the neck

collera *nf Andes* cuff link

collie ['koli] *nm* collie

colmado, -a 1 *adj* full to the brim (**de** with); **está c. de problemas** he is loaded down with problems

2 *nm* grocer's, grocery store

colmar *vt (recipiente)* to fill (to the brim); *(aspiración, deseo)* to fulfill; **c. a alguien de regalos/elogios** to shower gifts/praise on sb

colmena *nf* beehive

colmenar *nm* apiary

colmenero, -a *nm,f* beekeeper

colmillo *nm (de persona)* canine, eyetooth; *(de perro)* fang; *(de elefante)* tusk; *Fig* **enseñar los colmillos** to show one's teeth

colmo *nm* height; **el c. de la estupidez** the height of stupidity; **es el c. de la locura** it's sheer madness; **para c. de desgracias** to crown it all; **¡eso es el c.!** that's the last straw!

colocación *nf* (**a**) *(acción)* placing, positioning; *(situación)* place, position (**b**) *(empleo)* position, job

colocado, -a *adj* (**a**) *(en lugar)* placed; *(en empleo)* **estar muy bien c.** to have a very good job (**b**) *Fam (drogado)* high, stoned; *(borracho)* blind drunk, smashed

colocar [59] **1** *vt* (**a**) *(en una posición, un lugar)* to place, to put; *(bomba)* to plant; **hay que c. bien ese cuadro, está torcido** that picture needs to be hung properly, it isn't straight; **vuelve a c. ese libro donde estaba** put that book back where it was (**b**) *(invertir)* to place, to invest (**c**) *(en un empleo)* to find a job for; **colocó a su hijo de abogado en su empresa** he found his son a job as a lawyer in his own firm (**d**) *(casar)* to marry off (**e**) *Fam (endilgar)* to palm off; **le colocaron una moto que no funciona** they palmed a motorbike off on him that doesn't work

2 *vi Fam (droga, alcohol)* **este costo coloca cantidad** this hash gives you a real high; **este ponche coloca mucho** this punch is strong stuff

3 colocarse *vpr* (**a**) *(en una posición, un lugar) (de pie)* to stand; *(sentado)* to sit; **colócate en tu asiento** sit in your seat (**b**) *(en un trabajo)* to get a job; **me he colocado de guardia jurado** I've got a job as a security guard (**c**) *Fam (emborracharse)* to get blind drunk *o* smashed; *(drogarse)* to get high *o* stoned

colocón *nm Fam* **llevar un c.** *(de droga)* to be high; *(de bebida)* to be loaded

colofón *nm* (**a**) *(remate, fin)* climax, culmination (**b**) *(de libro)* colophon

coloide *adj* colloid

Colombia *n* Colombia

colombianismo *nm* Colombian expression

colombiano, -a *adj & nm,f* Colombian

colombina *nf Col (dulce)* lollipop

colombino, -a *adj* = relating to Christopher Columbus

Colombo *n* Colombo

colombofilia *nf* pigeon fancying

Colón *n pr* **(Cristóbal) C.** Christopher Columbus

colon *nm* colon; **c. irritable** irritable bowel syndrome

colón *nm* colon *(unit of currency in Costa Rica and El Salvador)*

Colonia *n* Cologne

colonia *nf* (**a**) *(estado dependiente)* colony (**b**) *(de niños)* **c. (de verano)** (summer) camp; **ir de colonias** to go on a summer camp (**c**) *(perfume)* eau de cologne; **me gusta la c. que usa tu novio** I like your boyfriend's aftershave (**d**) *(barrio)* district; *Méx* **c. proletaria** shantytown, slum area

colonial *adj* colonial

colonialismo *nm* colonialism

colonialista *adj & nmf* colonialist

colonización *nf* colonization

colonizador, -ora 1 *adj* colonizing

2 *nm,f* colonizer, colonist

colonizar [14] *vt* to colonize

colono *nm* settler, colonist

coloque *etc ver* **colocar**

coloquial *adj* colloquial

coloquio *nm* (**a**) *(conversación)* conversation (**b**) *(debate)* discussion, debate

color *nm* (**a**) *(que se ve)* color; **¿de qué c.?** what color?; **es c. azul** it's blue; **a todo c.** in full color; **de colores** colorful; **televisión en c.** color television; **colores complementarios** complementary colors; **c. primario** primary color

(**b**) *(aspecto)* tone; **no tienes muy buen c.** you look a bit off-color

(**c**) *(para pintar)* paint; **colores** *(lápices)* colored pencils

(**d**) *(en los naipes)* suit

(**e**) *(raza)* color; **sin distinción de credo ni c.** regardless of creed or color; **de c.** *(persona)* colored

(**f**) *(bandera, camiseta)* **los colores nacionales** the national colors; **defender los colores del Académico** *(el equipo)* to play for Académico

(**g**) *(expresiones)* **dar c. a algo** to color sth in; *Fig* to brighten *o* liven sth up; *Esp Fam* **no hay c.** it's no contest; **sacarle** *o* **salirle a alguien los colores (a la cara)** to make sb blush; **ver las cosas de c. de rosa** to see things through rose-colored *o* rose-tinted spectacles

coloración *nf* (**a**) *(acción)* coloring (**b**) *(color)* coloration, coloring (**c**) *Biol* markings

colorado, -a 1 *adj (color)* red; **ponerse c.** to blush, to go red

2 *nm (color)* red

colorante *nm* coloring

colorear *vt* to color (in)

colorete *nm (maquillaje)* rouge, blusher; *Andes (de labios)* lipstick; **tener coloretes** to be red in the face

colorido *nm* colorfulness; **una fiesta de gran c.** a very colorful local festival

colorín *nm* bright color; **de colorines** brightly colored; **c. colorado, este cuento se ha acabado** and they all lived happily ever after

colorista *adj* coloristic

colosal *adj* (a) *(estatura, tamaño)* colossal (b) *(extraordinario)* great, enormous

coloso *nm (estatua)* colossus; *Fig (cosa, persona)* giant

colt® [kolt] *(pl* **colts**) *nm* Colt®; **un c. del 45** a Colt .45

columna *nf* (a) *(en edificio)* column (b) *(de soldados)* column; **quinta c.** fifth column (c) *(de texto)* column; **la c. de opinión** the opinion column; **un artículo a cuatro columnas** a four-column article (d) *(apoyo)* pillar; **c. vertebral** spinal column (e) *Aut* **c. de dirección** steering column

columnata *nf* colonnade

columnista *nmf* columnist

columpiar 1 *vt* to swing
2 columpiarse *vpr* to swing

columpio *nm* swing; **los columpios** the children's playground

colza *nf* rape; **aceite de c.** rapeseed oil

coma 1 *nm Med* coma; **en c.** in a coma
2 *nf* (a) *Gram* comma; *Fig* **sin faltar una c.** word for word (b) *Mat* **c. (decimal)** ≃ decimal point

comadre *nf (mujer chismosa)* gossip, gossipmonger; *(vecina)* neighbor

comadrear *vi* to gossip

comadreja *nf* weasel

comadreo *nm* gossip

comadrona *nf* midwife

comanche *adj & nf* Comanche

comandancia *nf* (a) *(rango)* command (b) *(edificio)* command headquarters (c) *Méx (de policía)* police station

comandante *nm Mil (rango)* major; *(de un puesto)* commander, commandant; *(de avión)* captain; **c. en jefe** commander-in-chief

comandar *vt Mil* to command

comando *nm* (a) *Mil* commando; **c. suicida** suicide squad; **c. terrorista** terrorist cell (b) *Inform* command

comarca *nf* area, district; **una c. arrocera** a rice-growing region *o* area

comarcal *adj* local; **un problema de ámbito c.** a local problem

comatoso, -a *adj* comatose

comba *nf Esp* (a) *(juego)* skipping; **jugar a la c.** to jump rope (b) *(cuerda)* jump rope

combado, -a *adj* warped

combadura *nf (de alambre, barra)* bend; *(de pared)* bulge; *(de viga)* sag

combar 1 *vt* to warp
2 combarse *vpr* to warp

combate *nm (lucha)* fight; *(batalla)* battle; *también Fig* **dejar a alguien fuera de c.** to knock sb out; **c. de boxeo** boxing match; **c. cuerpo a cuerpo** hand-to-hand combat; **c. de lucha libre** wrestling match

combatiente *nmf* combatant, fighter

combatir 1 *vt* to combat, to fight; **un producto para c. la caries** a product which fights tooth decay
2 *vi* to fight (**contra** against)

combatividad *nf* fighting spirit

combativo, -a *adj* aggressive, combative

combi *nm* (a) *Esp (frigorífico)* freezer (b) *Am (autobús)* minibus

combinación *nf* (a) *(unión)* combination; **una c. explosiva** an explosive combination (b) *(de bebidas)* cocktail (c) *(de caja fuerte)* combination (d) *Quím* compound (e) *(prenda)* slip (f) *(plan)* scheme (g) *(de medios de transporte)* connections; **no hay buena c. para ir de aquí allí** there's no easy way of getting there from here

combinado, -a 1 *adj (con distintos elementos)* combined
2 *nm* (a) *(bebida)* cocktail (b) *Dep* combined team

combinar 1 *vt* (a) *(mezclar)* to combine; **combina lo práctico con lo barato** it is both practical and cheap (b) *(bebidas)* to mix (c) *(colores)* to match (d) *(planificar)* to arrange, to organize
2 *vi (colores, ropa)* **c. con** to go with; **no tengo nada que combine con estos pantalones** I haven't got anything to go *o* that goes with these pants

combinatoria *nf Mat* combinatorial analysis

combustible 1 *adj* combustible
2 *nm* fuel; **c. fósil** fossil fuel; **c. sólido** = coal, wood or other solid used as fuel

combustión *nf* combustion

comecocos *nm inv* (a) *Fam (para convencer)* **este panfleto es un c.** this pamphlet is designed to brainwash you (b) *Fam (cosa difícil de comprender)* mind-bending problem *o* puzzle (c) *(juego)* Pac-Man®

comedero *nm* trough; **c. de pájaros** bird table

comedia *nf* comedy; *Fig (engaño)* farce; **c. musical** musical (comedy)

comediante, -a *nm,f* actor, *f* actress; *Fig (farsante)* fraud

comedido, -a *adj* (a) *(moderado)* moderate, restrained (b) *Am (servicial)* obliging

comedimiento *nm* moderation, restraint

comediógrafo, -a *nm,f* playwright, dramatist

comedirse [47] *vpr* (a) *(moderarse)* to restrain oneself (b) *Am (ofrecerse)* to volunteer oneself

comedor *nm* (a) *(habitación) (de casa)* dining room; *(de fábrica)* canteen (b) *(muebles)* dining-room suite

comendadora *nf* mother superior

comensal *nmf* fellow diner; **los comensales charlaban animadamente** the diners were having a lively conversation

comentar *vt (opinar sobre)* to comment on; *(hablar de)* to discuss

comentario *nm* (a) *(observación)* comment, remark; **hizo un c. muy acertado** she made a very apt remark; **el presidente no quiso hacer comentarios** the president did not wish to (make any) comment; **sin comentarios** no comment; **sobran comentarios** what can you say? (b) *(crítica)* commentary; **c. de texto** literary commentary, textual analysis (c) **comentarios** *(murmuraciones)* gossip

comentarista *nmf* commentator; **c. deportivo** (sports) commentator

comenzar [17] **1** *vt* to start, to begin; **c. diciendo que…** to start *o* begin by saying that…
2 *vi* to start, to begin; **c. a hacer algo** to start doing *o* to do sth; **c. por hacer algo** to begin by doing sth; **"hiena" comienza por hache** "hyena" starts with an "h"; **el partido comenzó tarde** the game started late

comer 1 *vt* (a) *(alimentos)* to eat; *Esp, Méx (al mediodía)* to have for lunch; *esp Andes (a la noche)* to have for dinner; **no come carne casi nunca** she hardly ever eats meat
(b) *(en los juegos de tablero)* to take, to capture; **me comió un alfil** he took one of my bishops
(c) *(consumir)* to eat up; **les come la envidia** they're eaten up with envy; **eso me come mucho tiempo** that takes up a lot of my time
(d) *(expresiones)* **ni come ni deja c.** he's a dog in the manger; **no tengas miedo, nadie te va a c.** don't be afraid, nobody's going to eat you; **sin comerlo ni beberlo** *(algo bueno)*

through no credit of one's own; *(algo malo)* through no fault of one's own

2 *vi (ingerir alimentos)* to eat; *Esp, Méx (al mediodía)* to have lunch; *esp Andes (a la noche)* to have dinner; **¿qué hay de c.?** *(al mediodía)* what's for lunch?; *(a noche)* what's for dinner?; **c. fuera** *(al mediodía)* to go out for lunch; **¡a c., chicos!** lunch is/dinner's/*etc* ready, children!; **dar de c.** to feed

3 comerse *vpr* **(a)** *(alimentos)* to eat; **en ese restaurante se come muy bien** the food is very good at that restaurant; **se comió los tres platos** he had all three courses; **comerse las uñas** to bite one's nails; *Fig* **comerse a alguien con los ojos** *o* **con la mirada** to be unable to keep one's eyes off sb; *Fig* **¿y eso cómo se come?** and what are we/am I supposed to make of that?; *Fam* **tu amigo está para comérselo** your friend's gorgeous

(b) *(desgastar) (recursos)* to eat up; *(metal)* to corrode; **el sol se comió los colores de la ropa** the sun made the clothes fade

(c) *(en los juegos de tablero)* to take, to capture

(d) *(palabras, texto)* to swallow; **se comió un párrafo** she missed out a paragraph; *Fam* **se va a c. sus palabras** she'll have to eat her words

comercial 1 *adj (de empresas)* commercial; *(internacional)* trade; **relaciones comerciales** trade relations

2 *nmf (vendedor, representante)* sales rep

comercialización *nf* marketing

comercializar [14] *vt* to market

comerciante *nmf* tradesman, *f* tradeswoman; *(tendero)* storekeeper; **pequeños comerciantes** small businessmen

comerciar *vi* to trade, to do business; **c. con armas/pieles** to deal *o* trade in arms/furs

comercio *nm* **(a)** *(de productos)* trade; **libre c.** free trade; *Inform* **c. electrónico** e-commerce; **c. exterior/interior** foreign/domestic trade; **c. justo** fair trade; **c. de pieles** fur trade **(b)** *(tienda)* store, shop **(c)** *(conjunto de tiendas)* stores; **el c. cierra mañana por ser festivo** the stores are closed tomorrow because it's a holiday

comestible 1 *adj* edible, eatable

2 comestibles *nmpl* food; **tienda de comestibles** grocer's, grocery store

cometa 1 *nm Astron* comet

2 *nf* kite

cometer *vt (crimen)* to commit; *(error)* to make

cometido *nm* **(a)** *(objetivo)* mission, task **(b)** *(deber)* duty

comezón *nf* **(a)** *(picor)* **tener c.** to have an itch; **tengo c. en la nariz** I've got an itchy nose **(b)** *(remordimiento)* twinge; *(deseo)* urge, itch

cómic *(pl* **cómics)**, **comic** *(pl* **comics)** *nm* comic book

comicidad *nf* humorousness

comicios *nmpl Pol* elections

cómico, -a 1 *adj* **(a)** *(de la comedia)* comedy, comic; **actor c.** comedy actor **(b)** *(gracioso)* comic, comical

2 *nm,f (actor de teatro)* actor, *f* actress; *(humorista)* comedian, comic, *f* comedienne

comida *nf* **(a)** *(alimento)* food; **c. basura** junk food; **c. casera** home cooking; *Méx* **c. chatarra** junk food; *Méx* **c. corrida** *o* **corriente** set meal; **comidas para empresas** business catering; **c. para perros** dog food; **c. preparada** convenience food; **c. rápida** fast food **(b)** *(almuerzo, cena)* meal; *Esp, Méx (al mediodía)* lunch; **c. de Navidad** Christmas dinner; **c. de trabajo** business lunch

comidilla *nf Fam* **ser/convertirse en la c.** to be/become the talk of the town

comidió *etc ver* **comedirse**

comienzo 1 *ver* **comenzar**

2 *nm* start, beginning; **a comienzos del siglo XX** at the beginning of the twentieth century; **dar c. (a algo)** to start (sth), to begin (sth)

comillas *nfpl* quotation marks; **entre c.** in quotation marks

comilón, -ona *Fam* **1** *adj* greedy

2 *nm,f (persona)* greedy pig, glutton

comilona *nf (festín)* blowout

comino *nm (planta)* cumin, cummin; *Fam Fig* **me importa un c.** I don't give a damn; *Fam Fig* **no vale un c.** it isn't worth a plugged nickel

comisaría *nf* **c. (de policía)** police station, precinct, station house

comisario, -a *nm,f* **(a)** *(de policía)* captain **(b)** *(delegado)* commissioner; **c. europeo** European Commissioner; **c. político** political commissar

comisión *nf* **(a)** *(delegación)* committee, commission; **C. Europea** European Commission; **c. investigadora** *o* **de investigación** committee of inquiry; **Comisiones Obreras** = Spanish left-wing trade union; **c. parlamentaria** parliamentary committee; **c. permanente** standing committee; **c. de servicio** special assignment; **c. de trabajo** temporary committee **(b)** *Com* commission; **(trabajar) a c.** (to work) on a commission basis; **cobro de comisiones** *(delito)* acceptance of bribes; **c. bancaria** bank charges **(c)** *(de un delito)* perpetration

comisionado, -a *nm,f* committee member

comisionar *vt* to commission

comisionista *nmf* commission agent

comisura *nf* corner *(of mouth, eyes)*

comité *nm* committee; **c. ejecutivo** executive committee; *Ind* **c. de empresa** employees' group

comitiva *nf* retinue

como 1 *adv* **(a)** *(comparativo)* **ser c. algo** to be like sth; **vive c. un rey** he lives like a king; **lo que dijo fue c. para ruborizarse** his words were enough to make you blush; **tan… c….** as… as…; **es (tan) negro c. el carbón** it's as black as coal

(b) *(de la manera que)* as; **lo he hecho c. es debido** I did it as *o* the way it should be done; **me encanta c. bailas** I love the way you dance; **lo hagamos c. lo hagamos habrá problemas** whichever way we do it there'll be problems

(c) *(según)* as; **c. te decía ayer…** as I was telling you yesterday…

(d) *(en calidad de)* as; **trabaja c. bombero** he works as a fireman; **dieron el dinero c. anticipo** they gave the money as an advance

(e) *(aproximadamente)* about; **me quedan c. mil pesos** I've got about a thousand pesos left; **estamos c. a mitad de camino** we're about halfway there; **tiene un sabor c. a naranja** it tastes a bit like an orange

2 *conj* **(a)** *(ya que) (+ indicativa)* as, since; **c. no llegabas, nos fuimos** as *o* since you didn't arrive, we left **(b)** *Esp (si) (+ subjuntivo)* if; **c. no me hagas caso, lo pasarás mal** if you don't listen to me, there will be trouble **(c)** *(que)* that; **después de tantas veces c. te lo he explicado** after all the times (that) I've explained it to you

3 como que *loc conj* **(a)** *(que)* **le pareció c. que lloraban** it seemed to him (that) they were crying **(b)** *(expresa causa)* **pareces cansado — c. que he trabajado toda la noche** you seem tired — well, I've been up all night working **(c)** *(irónico)* **¡c. que te voy a creer a ti que eres un mentiroso!** as if I'd believe a liar like you!

4 como quiera que *loc conj* **(a)** *(de cualquier modo que)* whichever way, however; **c. quiera que sea** whatever the case may be **(b)** *(dado que)* since, given that

5 como si *loc conj* as if

cómo 1 *adv* **(a)** *(de qué modo, por qué motivo)* how; **¿c. lo has hecho?** how did you do it?; **¿c. son?** what are they like?; **no sé c. has podido decir eso** I don't know how you could say that; **¿c. que no la has visto nunca?** what do you mean you've never seen her?; *Esp* **¿a c. están los tomates?** how much are the tomatoes?; **¿c.?** *(¿qué dices?)* sorry?, what?; *Fam* **¿c. es eso?** *(¿por qué?)* how come? **(b)** *(exclamativo)* how; **¡c. pasan los años!** how time flies!; **¡c. no!** of course!; **¡c.! ¿no te has enterado?** what! you mean you haven't heard?; **está lloviendo, ¡y c.!** it's raining like crazy

2 *nm* **el c. y el porqué** the whys and wherefores

cómoda *nf* chest of drawers

comodidad *nf (estado, cualidad)* comfort; *(conveniencia)* convenience; **para su c.** for your convenience; **comodidades** comforts; **el equipo ganó con c.** the team won comfortably *o* easily

comodín 1 *adj Am (comodón)* comfort-loving

2 *nm (naipe)* joker; *Inform* wild card

cómodo, -a *adj* **(a)** *(confortable)* comfortable; **estar c.** to feel comfortable; **ponte c.** *(como en casa)* make yourself at home **(b)** *(conveniente)* convenient; **es muy c. que te traigan la compra a casa** it's very convenient *o* handy having the shopping delivered to your home **(c)** *(oportuno, fácil)* easy; **es muy c. dejar que los demás decidan todo por ti** it's very easy to let others make all the decisions for you

comodón, -ona 1 *adj (amante de la comodidad)* comfort-loving; *(vago)* laid-back; **no seas c.** don't be so lazy

2 *nm,f (amante de la comodidad)* comfort-lover; *(vago)* laid-back person

comodoro *nm* commodore

comoquiera: comoquiera que *loc conj (de cualquier manera que)* whichever way, however; *(dado que)* since, given that

Comores *nfpl* **las (Islas) C.** the Comoros (Islands)

compa *nmf Fam* pal, buddy

compact = compacto

compactación *nf Inform* compression; **c. de ficheros** zipping

compactar *vt* to compress

compacto, compact ['kompak] *(pl* **compacts)** *nm* **(a)** *(disco)* compact disc, CD **(b)** *(aparato)* compact disc player

compadecer [46] **1** *vt* to pity, to feel sorry for

2 compadecerse *vpr* **compadecerse de** to pity, to feel sorry for

compadre *nm Fam (amigo)* buddy

compadrear *vi RP* to brag, to boast

compadreo *nm (amistad)* friendship

compaginación *nf* **(a)** *(combinación)* reconciling **(b)** *(en imprenta)* page makeup

compaginar 1 *vt* **(a)** *(combinar)* to reconcile **(b)** *(en imprenta)* to make up

2 compaginarse *vpr* **compaginarse con** to square with, to go together with

compañerismo *nm* comradeship

compañero, -a *nm,f* **(a)** *(pareja, acompañante)* companion **(b)** *(colega)* colleague; **fue c. mío en la universidad** he was at college with me; **c. (de clase)** classmate; *Esp* **c. de piso** roommate; **c. (de trabajo)** colleague, fellow worker; **c. de viaje** traveling companion **(c)** *(par)* **el c. de este guante** the glove that goes with this one **(d)** *(camarada)* comrade; **el c. Rodríguez** comrade Rodríguez

compañía *nf* **(a)** *(cercanía)* company; **en c. de** accompanied by, in the company of; **hacer c. a alguien** to keep sb company **(b)** *(acompañante)* company; **andar en malas compañías** to keep bad company; **¿quiénes han sido? — Fernando y c., como de costumbre** who was it? — Fernando and co, as usual **(c)** *(empresa)* company; **c. aérea** airline; **c. discográfica** record company **(d)** *(de teatro, danza)* company; **c. de teatro** theater company **(e)** *(en ejército)* company

comparación *nf* comparison; **en c. con** in comparison with, compared to; **las c. son odiosas** comparisons are odious

comparado, -a *adj* **c. con** compared to; **gramática comparada** comparative grammar

comparar 1 *vt* to compare; **c. algo/a alguien con algo/alguien** to compare sth/sb with sth/sb; **c. precios** to compare prices, to shop around

2 *vi* to compare, to make a comparison; **¡no compares, ésta es mucho más bonita!** don't compare, this one's much nicer!

comparativo, -a *adj & nm* comparative

comparecencia *nf (ante el juez, la prensa)* appearance

comparecer [46] *vi* to appear

compareciente *Der* **1** *adj* appearing

2 *nmf* person appearing

comparsa 1 *nf* **(a)** *Teatro* extras **(b)** *(en carnaval)* = group of people at carnival in same costume and with masks

2 *nmf* **(a)** *Teatro* extra **(b)** *(en carreras, competiciones)* also-ran; **no es más que un c.** he's just there to make up the numbers

compartido, -a *adj (casa, habitación)* shared

compartimentar *vt* to compartmentalize

compartimento, compartimiento *nm* compartment; **c. estanco** watertight compartment; **c. de fumadores** smoking compartment

compartir *vt* **(a)** *(ganancias, gastos)* to share (out) **(b)** *(casa, vehículo)* to share; **c. algo con alguien** to share sth with sb **(c)** *(ideas, pesimismo)* to share; **no comparto tu opinión** I don't share your opinion

compás *(pl* **compases)** *nm* **(a)** *(instrumento)* pair of compasses **(b)** *Náut (brújula)* compass **(c)** *Mús (periodo)* bar; *(ritmo)* rhythm, beat; **al c. (de la música)** in time (with the music); **llevar el c.** to keep time; **perder el c.** to lose the beat **(d)** *Fig* **c. de espera** pause, interlude; **las negociaciones se hallan en un c. de espera** negotiations have been temporarily suspended

compasión *nf* compassion, pity; **disparó sin c. contra los prisioneros** he shot at the prisoners without pity; **tener c. de** to feel sorry for; **¡por c.!** for pity's sake!

compasivo, -a *adj* compassionate, sympathetic

compatibilidad *nf (gen) & Inform* compatibility

compatibilizar [14] *vt* to make compatible

compatible *adj (gen) & Inform* compatible

compatriota *nmf (hombre)* compatriot, fellow countryman; *(mujer)* compatriot, fellow countrywoman

compay *(pl* **compays)** *nm Cuba Fam* friend, buddy

compeler *vt* to compel, to force

compendiar *vt* **(a)** *(cualidades, características)* to epitomize **(b)** *(libro, historia)* to abridge

compendio *nm* **(a)** *(libro)* compendium **(b)** *(síntesis)* epitome, essence

compenetración *nf* mutual understanding

compenetrado, -a *adj* **están muy compenetrados** they understand each other very well; **es un equipo muy c.** they work very well as a team

compenetrarse *vpr* to understand each other

compensación *nf (gen) & Fin* compensation; **en c. (por)** in return (for); **c. bancaria** bank clearing

compensar 1 *vt* **(a)** *(valer la pena)* to make up for; **no me compensa (perder tanto tiempo)** it's not worth my while (wasting all that time) **(b)** *(indemnizar)* **c. a alguien (de o por)** to compensate sb (for)

2 *vi* **no compensa** it's not worth it

competencia *nf* **(a)** *(entre personas, empresas)* competition; **la c.** the competition; **hacer la c. a alguien** to compete with sb; *Com* **c. desleal** unfair competition **(b)** *(incumbencia)* field, province; **no es de mi c.** it's not my responsibility **(c)** *(atribuciones)* **competencias** powers **(d)** *(aptitud)* competence **(e)** *Am (deportiva)* competition

competente *adj* competent; **c. en materia de** responsible for

competer *vi* **c. a** *(incumbir)* to be up to, to be the responsibility of; *(a una autoridad)* to come under the jurisdiction of

competición *nf* competition

competidor, -ora 1 *adj* rival, competing
   2 *nm,f* competitor

competir [47] *vi* (**a**) *(contender)* to compete (**con/por** with/for); **varios grupos compiten por la obtención del contrato** several groups are competing for the contract; **nos es muy difícil c. con las importaciones chinas** we find it very difficult to compete with Chinese imports (**b**) *(igualar)* **c. (con)** to be on a par (with); **compiten en belleza** they rival each other in beauty

competitividad *nf* competitiveness

competitivo, -a *adj* competitive

compilación *nf* *(acción)* compiling; *(colección)* compilation

compilador, -ora 1 *adj* compiling
   2 *nm,f (persona)* compiler
   3 *nm Inform* compiler

compilar *vt (gen) & Inform* to compile

compincharse *vpr* **c. para hacer algo** to plot to do sth

compinche *nmf* buddy

compitiera *etc ver* **competir**

compito *etc ver* **competir**

complacencia *nf* pleasure, satisfaction

complacer [42] **1** *vt* to please; **me complace anunciar...** I am pleased to announce...
   2 complacerse *vpr* **complacerse en hacer algo** to take pleasure in doing sth

complaciente *adj* (**a**) *(amable)* obliging, helpful (**b**) *(indulgente)* indulgent

complejidad *nf* complexity

complejo, -a 1 *adj* complex
   2 *nm* (**a**) *Psi* complex; **c. de culpabilidad** guilt complex; **c. de Edipo** Oedipus complex; **c. de inferioridad** inferiority complex (**b**) *(zona construida)* complex; **c. deportivo** sports complex; **c. industrial** industrial park; **c. residencial** private housing project

complementar 1 *vt* to complement
   2 complementarse *vpr* to complement each other

complementario, -a 1 *adj* complementary
   2 *nm (en lotería)* = complementary number

complemento *nm* (**a**) *(añadido)* complement; **la fruta es el c. ideal de una dieta equilibrada** fruit is the ideal complement to a balanced diet; **c. salarial** bonus, wage supplement; **c. vitamínico** vitamin supplement (**b**) *Gram* object, complement; **c. agente** agent; **c. circunstancial** adjunct; **c. directo/indirecto** direct/indirect object (**c**) **complementos** *(accesorios)* accessories

completamente *adv* completely, totally

completar 1 *vt* to complete
   2 completarse *vpr* to be completed

completo, -a *adj* (**a**) *(entero, perfecto)* complete; **nombre c.** full name; **por c.** completely; **un atleta muy c.** an all-around athlete (**b**) *(lleno)* full; **todos los hoteles de la ciudad están al c.** all the hotels in town are full; **c.** *(en cartel) (hotel)* no vacancies; *(aparcamiento)* full; *(en taquilla)* sold out

complexión *nf* build

complicación *nf* (**a**) *(dificultad)* complication (**b**) *(complejidad)* complexity

complicado, -a *adj* complicated

complicar [59] **1** *vt (dificultar)* to complicate; **complicarle la vida a alguien** to cause sb a lot of trouble
   2 complicarse *vpr (problema)* to become complicated; *(enfermedad)* to get worse; **se están complicando las cosas** things are getting complicated; **la reunión se complicó y terminamos a las once** complications arose

at the meeting and we finished at eleven; **¡no te compliques la vida!** don't complicate matters (unnecessarily)!

cómplice *nmf* accomplice

complicidad *nf* complicity

complot, compló *nm* plot, conspiracy

componenda *nf* shady deal

componente 1 *adj* component, constituent
   2 *nm (gen) & Elec* component; *(persona)* member
   3 *nf* **viento de c. este** easterly wind

componer [50] **1** *vt* (**a**) *(formar, ser parte de)* to make up (**b**) *(música, versos)* to compose (**c**) *(reparar)* to repair (**d**) *(adornar) (cosa)* to deck out, to adorn; *(persona)* to dress up (**e**) *(en imprenta)* to set, to compose (**f**) *Am (hueso)* to set
   2 componerse *vpr* (**a**) *(estar formado)* **componerse de** to be made up of, to consist of (**b**) *(engalanarse)* to dress up (**c**) *Am (mejorar) (persona)* to get better; *(tiempo)* to clear up, to improve (**d**) *(expresiones)* **componérselas (para hacer algo)** to manage (to do sth); **allá se las compongan** that's their problem

comportamiento *nm* behavior

comportar 1 *vt* to involve, to entail
   2 comportarse *vpr* to behave; **comportarse bien** to behave (oneself); **comportarse mal** to behave badly, to misbehave; **compórtate o tendré que castigarte** behave yourself or I'll have to punish you

composición *nf* composition; **hacerse una c. de lugar** to size up the situation

compositor, -ora *nm,f* composer

compost *nm* compost

compostelano, -a 1 *adj* of/from Santiago de Compostela
   2 *nm,f* person from Santiago de Compostela

compostura *nf* (**a**) *(reparación)* repair (**b**) *(de persona, rostro)* composure (**c**) *(en comportamiento)* restraint; **guardar la c.** to show restraint

compota *nf Culin* compote, stewed fruit

compra *nf* purchase; **por la c. de una enciclopedia te regalan un televisor** if you buy an encyclopedia, they'll give you a television free; **esta impresora fue una excelente c.** this printer was a really good buy; **algunos supermercados te llevan la c. a casa** some supermarkets deliver your shopping to your home; **hacer** *Esp* **la c.** *o Am* **las compras** to do the shopping; **ir de compras** to go shopping; **c. al contado** cash purchase; *Am* **c. en cuotas** installment plan; **c. a plazos** installment plan

comprador, -ora 1 *adj* buying, purchasing
   2 *nm,f (adquiriente)* buyer, purchaser; *(en una tienda)* shopper, customer

comprar *vt* (**a**) *(adquirir)* to buy, to purchase; **se lo compré a un vendedor ambulante** I bought it from a street vendor *o* seller; **se lo compraron a Ignacio como regalo de despedida** they bought it for Ignacio as a leaving present (**b**) *(sobornar)* to buy (off), to bribe; **¡el árbitro está comprado!** they've bribed the referee!

compraventa *nf* trading (**de** in); **c. de armas** arms dealing

comprender 1 *vt* (**a**) *(incluir)* to include, to comprise; **el periodo comprendido entre 1995 y 1999** the period from 1995 to 1999, the period between 1995 and 1999 (**b**) *(entender)* to understand; **te comprendo perfectamente** I quite understand; **comprendo que estés triste** I can understand that you're unhappy; **como comprenderás, me enfadé muchísimo** I don't have to tell you I was absolutely furious
   2 comprenderse *vpr (personas)* to understand each other

comprensible *adj* understandable, comprehensible

comprensión *nf* understanding

comprensivo, -a *adj* understanding

compresa *nf* (**a**) *(femenina)* sanitary napkin (**b**) *(para herida)* compress

compresión *nf* compression

compresor, -ora 1 *adj* compressing
2 *nm* compressor

comprimido, -a 1 *adj* compressed
2 *nm* (**a**) *(pastilla)* pill, tablet (**b**) *Perú (en exámenes)* crib

comprimir *vt (gen) & Inform* to compress; **c. un archivo** to zip a file

comprobación *nf* checking

comprobante *nm (documento)* supporting document, proof; *(recibo)* receipt

comprobar [63] *vt* (**a**) *(revisar, averiguar)* to check; **tengo que c. si lo tengo** I have to check *o* see if I've got it; **¿podrías c. a qué hora sale el tren?** could you check what time the train leaves? (**b**) *(demostrar)* to prove; **se ha comprobado que la vacuna es efectiva** the vaccine has been proved to be effective

comprometedor, -ora *adj* compromising

comprometer 1 *vt* (**a**) *(poner en peligro) (éxito, posibilidades)* to jeopardize; *(persona, inversión)* to compromise (**b**) *(avergonzar)* to embarrass; **publicaron unas fotos que lo comprometen** they published some compromising photos of him (**c**) *(hacer responsable)* **c. a alguien (a hacer algo)** to oblige *o* compel sb (to do sth)
2 comprometerse *vpr* (**a**) *(asumir un compromiso)* to commit oneself; **se han comprometido a cumplir el acuerdo de paz** they have committed themselves to fulfilling the peace agreement; **me comprometí a acabarlo cuanto antes** I promised to finish it as soon as possible (**b**) *(ideológicamente, moralmente)* to become involved (**en** in)

comprometido, -a *adj* (**a**) *(con una idea)* committed (**con** to) (**b**) *(situación)* compromising, awkward

compromisario *nm Pol* delegate, representative *(in an election)*

compromiso *nm* (**a**) *(obligación)* commitment; *(acuerdo)* agreement (**b**) *(cita)* engagement; **c. matrimonial** engagement (**c**) *(dificultad)* compromising *o* difficult situation; **poner a alguien en un c.** to put sb in a difficult *o* awkward position

compuerta *nf* sluice, floodgate

compuesto, -a 1 *participio ver* **componer**
2 *adj* (**a**) *(formado)* **c. de** composed of, made up of (**b**) *(múltiple)* compound; **interés c.** compound interest; **ojo c.** compound eye (**c**) *(acicalado)* dressed up
3 *nm Gram & Quím* compound

compulsar *vt* to check against the original

compulsivo, -a *adj* compulsive, urgent

compungido, -a *adj* contrite, remorseful

compusiera *etc ver* **componer**

computable *adj* **gastos computables a efectos fiscales** expenditure taken into account for tax purposes

computación *nf* (**a**) *(cómputo)* calculation, computation (**b**) *Am (informática)* computing

computacional *adj* computational, computer

computadora *nf, esp Am* **computador** *nm* computer

computar *vt* (**a**) *(calcular)* to compute, to calculate (**b**) *(considerar)* to count, to regard as valid

computarizar, computerizar [14] *vt* to computerize

cómputo *nm (recuento)* calculation; *(de votos)* count

comulgar [40] *vi* (**a**) *Rel* to take Communion (**b**) *(estar de acuerdo)* **c. con algo** to share sth

común *adj* (**a**) *(compartido) (amigo, interés)* mutual; *(bienes, pastos)* communal; **hacer algo en c.** to do sth together; **hacer algo de c. acuerdo** to do sth by mutual consent *o* agreement; **tener algo en c.** to have sth in common; **no tengo nada en c. con ella** I have nothing in common with

her (**b**) *(habitual)* common; **fuera de lo c.** out of the ordinary; **poco c.** unusual; **por lo c.** generally (**c**) *(ordinario, vulgar)* ordinary, average

comuna *nf* commune

comunal *adj* communal

comunicación *nf* (**a**) *(contacto, intercambio de información)* communication; **ponerse en c. con alguien** to get in touch with sb; **medios de c. de masas** mass media; **comunicaciones** communications; **se cortó la c. mientras hablábamos** *(por teléfono)* we were cut off; **c. no verbal** nonverbal communication (**b**) *(escrito oficial)* communiqué

comunicado, -a 1 *adj* **bien c.** *(lugar)* well-served, with good connections
2 *nm* announcement, statement; **c. oficial** official communiqué; **c. de prensa** press release

comunicador, -ora *nm, f* communicator

comunicante 1 *adj* communicating
2 *nmf* informant

comunicar [59] **1** *vt* (**a**) *(transmitir) (sentimientos, ideas)* to convey; *(movimiento, virus)* to transmit (**b**) *(información)* **c. algo a alguien** to inform sb of sth, to tell sb sth; **lamentamos tener que comunicarle que...** we regret to inform you that... (**c**) *(conectar)* to connect; **esta carretera comunica los dos pueblos** this road connects the two towns (**d**) *Am (al teléfono)* to call, to telephone
2 *vi* (**a**) *(estar conectado)* **c. con** to lead to; **nuestras habitaciones comunican** there's a door between our two rooms (**b**) *(telefónicamente) (persona)* to get through; *Esp (teléfono)* to be busy; **no consigo c. con él** I can't get through to him; *Esp* **está comunicando** the line's busy
3 comunicarse *vpr* (**a**) *(hablarse)* to communicate (with each other); **se comunican por correo electrónico** they communicate by e-mail (**b**) *(dos lugares)* to be connected (**c**) *(propagarse)* to spread

comunicativo, -a *adj* communicative, open

comunidad *nf* (**a**) *(grupo)* community; **la c. científica/ internacional** the scientific/international community; **C. Andina** Andean Community; *Pol* **c. autónoma** autonomous region, = largest administrative division in Spain, with its own Parliament and a number of devolved powers; *Antes* **C. Europea** European Community; **c. de propietarios** *o* **de vecinos** residents association (**b**) *(cualidad de común) (de ideas, bienes)* communion; **c. de bienes** co-ownership *(between spouses)*

comunión *nf también Fig* communion; *Rel* **hacer la primera c.** to take one's First Communion

comunismo *nm Pol* communism

comunista *adj & nmf Pol* communist

comunitario, -a *adj* (**a**) *(de la comunidad)* community; **espíritu c.** community spirit (**b**) *(de la UE)* Community, of the European Union; **política comunitaria** EU *o* Community policy

con *prep* (**a**) *(en general)* with; **¿c. quién vas?** who are you going with?; **lo ha conseguido c. su esfuerzo** he has achieved it through his own efforts; **una cartera c. varios documentos** a briefcase containing several documents; **c. el tiempo lo olvidé** in time I forgot it
(**b**) *(a pesar de)* in spite of; **c. todo** despite everything; **c. lo estudioso que es, le suspendieron** for all his hard work, they still failed him
(**c**) *(hacia)* **para c.** toward; **es amable para c. todos** she is friendly toward *o* with everyone
(**d**) *(seguido de infinitivo) (para introducir una condición)* by; **c. hacerlo así** by doing it this way; **c. salir a las diez es suficiente** if we leave at ten, we'll have plenty of time
(**e**) *(a condición de que)* **c. (tal) que** *(seguido de subjuntivo)* as long as; **c. que llegue a tiempo me conformo** I don't mind as long as he arrives on time

(f) *(para expresar queja o decepción)* **mira que perder ¡c. lo bien que jugaste!** it's bad luck you lost, you played really well!

conato *nm* attempt; **c. de robo** attempted robbery; **un c. de incendio** the beginnings of a fire

concatenación *nf* succession

concatenar *vt* to link together

concavidad *nf* **(a)** *(cualidad)* concavity **(b)** *(lugar)* hollow

cóncavo, -a *adj* concave

concebir [47] **1** *vt (plan, hijo)* to conceive; *(imaginar)* to imagine
2 *vi* to conceive

conceder *vt* **(a)** *(dar)* to grant; *(premio)* to award; *(importancia)* to give; **me concedió un deseo** he granted me a wish; **le concedí el beneficio de la duda** I gave him the benefit of the doubt; **no concede entrevistas** she doesn't give interviews; **¿me concede cinco minutos?** could you give o spare me five minutes? **(b)** *(asentir)* to admit, to concede

concejal, -ala *nm,f* (city o town) councilor

concejalía *nf* seat on the city o town council

concejo *nm* **(a)** *(ayuntamiento)* (city o town) council **(b)** *(municipio)* municipality

concelebrar *vt Rel* to concelebrate

concentración *nf* **(a)** *(mental)* concentration **(b)** *(densidad)* *(gen)* & *Quím* concentration; *Econ* **c. parcelaria** land consolidation; **c. urbana** conurbation **(c)** *(reunión)* gathering **(d)** *Dep* training camp

concentrado *nm* concentrate

concentrar 1 *vt* **(a)** *(atención, esfuerzos)* to concentrate **(b)** *(gente)* to bring together; *(tropas)* to assemble; **esta zona concentra el 80 por ciento de los casos** 80 percent of the cases occurred in this region
2 concentrarse *vpr* **(a)** *(mentalmente)* to concentrate **(b)** *(disolución)* to become more concentrated **(c)** *(reunirse)* to gather, to congregate

concéntrico, -a *adj* concentric

concepción *nf* conception

concepto *nm* **(a)** *(idea)* concept **(b)** *(opinión)* opinion; **tener buen c. de alguien** to have a high opinion of sb **(c)** *(motivo)* **bajo ningún c.** under no circumstances **(d)** *(de una cuenta)* heading, item; **pagar algo en c. de adelanto** to pay sth in advance

conceptual *adj* conceptual

conceptualismo *nm* conceptualism

conceptualista 1 *adj* conceptualistic
2 *nmf* conceptualist

concerniente *adj* **c. a** concerning, regarding

concernir [25] *v impersonal* to concern; **en lo que concierne a** as regards; **por lo que a mí concierne** as far as I'm concerned

concertación *nf* settlement; *Ind* **c. social** = process of employer-labor-union negotiations

concertado, -a 1 *adj* **(a)** *(acordado)* arranged **(b)** *Esp (colegio)* government-assisted
2 *nm,f CRica,Ven* servant

concertar [3] **1** *vt (precio)* to agree on; *(cita)* to arrange; *(pacto)* to reach
2 *vi (concordar)* to tally (**con** with), to fit in (**con** with)

concertina *nf* concertina

concertino *nm* first violin

concertista *nmf* soloist; **c. de piano** concert pianist

concesión *nf* **(a)** *(de préstamo, licencia)* granting; *(de premio)* awarding **(b)** *(cesión) (gen)* & *Com* concession; **sin hacer concesiones (a)** without making concessions (to)

concesionario, -a *Com* **1** *adj* concessionary
2 *nm,f (persona con derecho exclusivo de venta)* licensed dealer; *(titular de una concesión)* concessionaire, licensee; **c. de automóviles** car dealer *(of particular make)*

concha 1 *nf* **(a)** *(de molusco)* shell **(b)** *(carey)* tortoiseshell **(c)** *Andes, RP Vulg (vulva)* cunt
2 *nmf Andes, RP Vulg* **c. de su madre** motherfucker

conchabarse *vpr Fam* to gang up (**contra** on)

concheto, -a, cheto, -a *RP Fam* **1** *adj* posh
2 *nm,f* rich kid

conchudo, -a *adj* **(a)** *Andes, Méx, Ven Fam (desfachatado)* shameless; *(cómodo)* lazy **(b)** *Méx, Ven Fam (oportunista)* **es muy c.** he always has an eye for the main chance **(c)** *Perú, RP muy Fam (persona despreciable)* **ser muy c.** to be a real jerk

concibiera *etc ver* **concebir**

concibo *etc ver* **concebir**

conciencia, consciencia *nf* **(a)** *(conocimiento)* consciousness, awareness; **tener/tomar c. de** to be/become aware of **(b)** *(moral, integridad)* conscience; **en c.** in all honesty; **me remuerde la c.** I have a guilty conscience; **hacer algo a c.** *(con esmero)* to do sth conscientiously

concienciar, Am concientizar [14] **1** *vt* **c. a alguien de algo** to make sb aware of sth
2 concienciarse, Am concientizarse *vpr* to become aware (**de** of)

concienzudo, -a *adj* conscientious

concierna *etc ver* **concernir**

concierto 1 *ver* **concertar**
2 *nm* **(a)** *(actuación)* concert **(b)** *(composición)* concerto; **c. para viola/piano** viola/piano concerto **(c)** *(acuerdo)* agreement; *Fin* **c. económico** economic agreement o accord **(d)** *(orden)* order

conciliábulo *nm* secret meeting

conciliación *nf* *(en un litigio)* reconciliation; *(en un conflicto laboral)* conciliation

conciliador, -ora *adj* conciliatory

conciliar 1 *adj* conciliar
2 *vt* to reconcile; **c. el sueño** to get to sleep

conciliatorio, -a *adj* conciliatory

concilio *nm* council; *Rel* **c. ecuménico** ecumenical council; *Rel* **C. Vaticano II** Second Vatican Council

concisión *nf* conciseness

conciso, -a *adj* concise

concitar *vt Formal* to stir up, to arouse

conciudadano, -a *nm,f* fellow citizen

cónclave, conclave *nm Rel* conclave; *Fig (reunión)* meeting

concluir [34] **1** *vt* to conclude; **c. haciendo o por hacer algo** to end up doing sth
2 *vi* to (come to an) end

conclusión *nf* conclusion; **en c.** in conclusion; **llegar a una c.** to come to o reach a conclusion; **sacar conclusiones** to draw conclusions; **yo no te voy a decir nada, saca tus propias conclusiones** I'm not saying anything, you can draw your own conclusions; **lo que saqué en c. es que...** I've come to o reached the conclusion that...

concluyente *adj* conclusive

concomerse *vpr* **c. de** *(envidia)* to be green with; *(arrepentimiento)* to be consumed with; *(impaciencia)* to be itching with

concomitancia *nf* concomitance

concomitante *adj* concomitant

concordancia *nf (gen)* & *Gram* agreement

concordar [63] **1** *vt* to reconcile
2 *vi (estar de acuerdo)* to agree o tally (**con** with); *Gram* to agree (**con** with)

concordato *nm* concordat

concordia *nf* harmony

concreción *nf* **(a)** *(de idea, medida)* specificity **(b)** *(de partículas)* concretion

concretar 1 *vt* **(a)** *(precisar)* to specify, to state exactly **(b)** *(reducir a lo esencial)* to summarize

2 concretarse *vpr* (**a**) *(limitarse)* **concretarse a hacer algo** to confine *o* limit oneself to doing sth (**b**) *(materializarse)* to take shape

concreto, -a 1 *adj* (**a**) *(no abstracto)* concrete (**b**) *(determinado)* specific, particular; **en el caso c. de Nicaragua,...** in the specific case of Nicaragua,...; **aún no tenemos una fecha concreta** we don't have a definite date yet; **en c.** *(específicamente)* specifically; *(en resumen)* in short; **nada en c.** nothing definite; **en ningún sitio en c.** nowhere in particular, not in any one place
2 *nm Am (material)* concrete; **c. armado** reinforced concrete

concubina *nf* concubine

concubinato *nm* concubinage

concuerdo *ver* **concordar**

conculcar [59] *vt Formal* to infringe, to break

concuñado, -a *nm,f (hermano del cuñado)* = brother or sister of one's brother-in-law or sister-in-law; *(cónyuge del cuñado)* = spouse of one's brother-in-law or sister-in-law

concupiscencia *nf* concupiscence, lustfulness

concurrencia *nf* (**a**) *(asistencia)* attendance; *(espectadores)* crowd, audience (**b**) *(de sucesos)* concurrence (**c**) *Com* competition; *Der* **no c.** noncompetition clause

concurrente 1 *adj* concurrent
2 *nmf* person present

concurrido, -a *adj (bar, calle)* crowded, busy; *(espectáculo)* well-attended

concurrir *vi* (**a**) *(reunirse)* **c. a algo** to go to sth, to attend sth (**b**) *(influir)* to contribute (**a** to) (**c**) *(participar)* **c. a** *(concurso)* to take part in, to compete in; *(examen)* to take

concursante *nmf (en concurso)* competitor, contestant; *(en oposiciones)* candidate

concursar *vi (competir)* to compete, to participate; *(en oposiciones)* to be a candidate

concurso *nm* (**a**) *(prueba) (literaria, deportiva)* competition; *(de televisión)* game show; **c. de belleza** beauty contest; **c. televisivo** *o* **de televisión** game show (**b**) *(para una obra)* tender; **salir a c. público** to be put out to tender (**c**) *(ayuda)* cooperation

condado *nm (territorio)* county

condal *adj* **la Ciudad C.** Barcelona

conde, -esa *nm,f* count, *f* countess

condecoración *nf (gen) & Mil* decoration

condecorar *vt* to decorate

condena *nf* (**a**) *(judicial)* sentence; **cumplir c.** to serve a sentence (**b**) *(reprobación)* condemnation (**por** of)

condenable *adj* condemnable

condenado, -a 1 *adj* (**a**) *(a una pena)* sentenced; *(a un sufrimiento)* condemned; *(a un olvido)* **c. al olvido** a book destined to be forgotten (**b**) *Fam (maldito)* damned, wretched
2 *nm,f* (**a**) *(a una pena)* convicted person; *(a muerte)* condemned person; *Fam Fig* **correr como un c.** to run like the blazes; *Fam Fig* **trabajar como un c.** to work like a slave (**b**) **los condenados** *(al infierno)* the damned (**c**) *Fam (maldito)* wretch; **ese c. se niega a pagarme** that wretched man refuses to pay me

condenar 1 *vt* (**a**) *(declarar culpable)* to convict (**b**) *(castigar)* **c. a alguien a algo** to sentence sb to sth; **fue condenado a tres años de prisión** he was sentenced to three years in prison (**c**) *(predestinar)* **estar condenado a** to be doomed to; **esa iniciativa está condenada al fracaso** that initiative is doomed to failure (**d**) *(reprobar)* to condemn
2 condenarse *vpr* to be damned

condensación *nf* condensation

condensado, -a *adj* condensed

condensador, -ora 1 *adj* condensing
2 *nm* condenser

condensar *vt también Fig* to condense

condescendencia *nf (benevolencia)* graciousness, kindness; *(altivez)* condescension

condescender [64] *vi* **c. a** *(con amabilidad)* to consent to, to accede to; *(con desprecio)* to deign to, to condescend to

condescendiente *adj* obliging

condestable *nm Hist* constable

condición *nf* (**a**) *(término, estipulación)* condition; **con la** *o* **a c. de que** on condition that; **con una sola c.** on one condition; **sin condiciones** unconditional; **las condiciones de un contrato** the terms of a contract; **condiciones de pago** terms of payment; **c. sine qua non** prerequisite
(**b**) **condiciones** *(circunstancias)* conditions; **condiciones atmosféricas** weather conditions; **condiciones de trabajo** working conditions; **condiciones de vida** living conditions
(**c**) *(estado)* condition; **en buenas/malas condiciones** in good/bad condition; **estar en condiciones de** *o* **para hacer algo** *(físicamente)* to be in a fit state to do sth; *(por la situación)* to be in a position to do sth; **no estar en condiciones** *(vivienda)* to be unfit for living in; *(instalaciones)* to be unfit for use
(**d**) *(naturaleza)* nature; *(clase social)* social class; **de c. humilde** of humble circumstances; **mi c. de mujer...** the fact that I am a woman...
(**e**) *(aptitud)* **tener condiciones para algo/para hacer algo** to have the ability *o* capacity for sth/to do sth

condicionado, -a *adj* conditioned

condicional *adj & nm* conditional

condicionamiento *nm* conditioning

condicionante *nm* determinant

condicionar *vt* **c. algo a algo** to make sth dependent on sth

condimentación *nf* seasoning

condimentar *vt* to season

condimento *nm* seasoning; **añadir condimentos** to add seasoning

condiscípulo, -a *nm,f* schoolmate

condolencia *nf* condolence; **expresó sus condolencias a la viuda** he offered his condolences to the widow

condolerse [41] *vpr* to feel pity (**de** for)

condominio *nm* (**a**) *Der (de un territorio)* condominium; *(de una cosa)* joint ownership (**b**) *Am (edificio)* condominium

condón *nm* condom

condonación *nf (de deuda)* remittance

condonar *vt* (**a**) *(deuda, pena)* to remit (**b**) *(violencia, terrorismo)* to condone

cóndor *nm* condor

conducción *nf* (**a**) *Esp (de vehículo)* driving (**b**) *(por tubería)* piping; *(por cable)* wiring (**c**) *(conducto) (de agua, gas)* pipe; *(de electricidad)* cable (**d**) *(dirección)* management, running

conducente *adj* conducive, leading (**a** to)

conducir [18] **1** *vt* (**a**) *(vehículo)* to drive (**b**) *(dirigir) (empresa)* to manage, to run; *(ejército)* to lead; *(asunto)* to handle (**c**) *(persona)* to lead (**d**) *(por tubería, cable) (calor)* to conduct; *(líquido)* to convey; *(electricidad)* to carry
2 *vi* (**a**) *(en vehículo)* to drive (**b**) *(a sitio, situación)* **c. a** to lead to
3 conducirse *vpr* to behave

conducta *nf* behavior, conduct

conductismo *nm Psi* behaviorism

conductista *nmf Psi* behaviorist

conductividad *nf Fís* conductivity

conducto *nm* (**a**) *(de fluido)* pipe (**b**) *(vía)* channel; **por c. de** through (**c**) *Anat* duct; **c. lacrimal** tear duct

conductor, -ora 1 *adj Fís* conductive
2 *nm,f (de vehículo)* driver; **c. de autobús** bus driver; **c. en prácticas** student driver
3 *nm Fís* conductor

conectado, -a *adj* (**a**) *Elec* connected (**a** to) (**b**) *Inform* online

conectar 1 *vt* to connect sth (**a** *o* **con** (up) to); **el puente conecta la isla con el continente** the bridge connects *o* links the island to the mainland

2 *vi* (**a**) *Rad & TV* **c. con** to go over to (**b**) *(persona)* **c. con alguien** *(ponerse en contacto)* to get in touch with sb; *(entenderse)* to relate to sb (**c**) *(vuelo)* to connect

3 conectarse *vpr (aparato)* to switch (itself) on; **conectarse a Internet** *(por primera vez)* to get connected to the Internet, to go online; *(regularmente)* to access the Internet

conectividad *nf Inform* number of ports

conector *nm (cable)* cable, lead

conejera *nf (madriguera)* (rabbit) warren; *(conejar)* rabbit hutch

conejillo *nm* **c. de Indias** guinea pig

conejo, -a 1 *nm,f* rabbit, *f* doe; *Culin* **c. de angora** Angora rabbit; **c. a la cazadora** = rabbit cooked in olive oil with chopped onion, garlic and parsley

2 *nm Esp muy Fam (vulva)* pussy, beaver

conexión *nf* (**a**) *(vínculo)* connection (**b**) *Elec & Inform* connection; **c. a Internet** Internet conexion (**c**) *Rad & TV* linkup; **c. vía satélite** satellite link (**d**) **tener conexiones** *(amistades influyentes)* to have connections

conexo, -a *adj* related, connected

confabulación *nf* conspiracy

confabularse *vpr* to plot, to conspire

confección *nf* (**a**) *(de ropa)* tailoring, dressmaking; **un traje de c.** a ready-to-wear *o* a ready-made suit (**b**) *(de comida)* preparation, making; *(de lista)* drawing up

confeccionar *vt* (**a**) *(ropa)* to make (up) (**b**) *(lista)* to draw up; *(plato)* to prepare

confederación *nf* confederation; **la C. Helvética** Switzerland

confederado, -a 1 *adj* confederate

2 *nm Hist* Confederate

confederarse *vpr* to confederate, to form a confederation

conferencia *nf* (**a**) *(charla)* lecture; **dar una c.** to give a talk *o* lecture; **c. de prensa** press conference (**b**) *(reunión)* conference (**c**) *(por teléfono)* (long-distance) call

conferenciante *nmf* speaker

conferenciar *vi* to have a discussion

conferencista *nmf Am* speaker

conferir [62] *vt (cualidad)* to give, to lend; **c. algo a alguien** *(honor, dignidad)* to confer *o* bestow sth upon sb; *(responsabilidades)* to give sth to sb

confesar [3] **1** *vt (gen) & Rel* to confess (to); **le confesó antes de morir** he heard his confession before he died; **confieso que te mentí** I admit I lied to you

2 confesarse *vpr Rel* **confesarse (de algo)** to confess (sth)

confesión *nf* (**a**) *(de pecado, crimen)* confession (**b**) *(credo)* religion, (religious) persuasion

confesional *adj* denominational; **Estado c.** = country with an official state religion

confesionario *nm* confessional

confeso, -a *adj* self-confessed

confesor *nm* confessor

confeti *nm* confetti

confiabilidad *nf Am (fiabilidad)* reliability

confiable *adj Am* reliable

confiado, -a *adj (seguro)* (over) confident; *(crédulo)* trusting

confianza *nf* (**a**) *(seguridad)* confidence (**en** in); **tengo c. en que lo conseguirán** I'm confident they'll achieve it; **c. en sí mismo** self-confidence (**b**) *(fe)* trust; **de c.** *(persona)* trustworthy, reliable; *(producto, servicio)* reliable; **una marca de toda c.** a very reliable brand (**c**) *(familiaridad)* familiarity; **amigo de c.** close *o* intimate friend; **tengo mucha c. con él** I

am very close to him; **en c.** in confidence; **puedes hablar con toda c.** you can talk quite freely; *Fam* **donde hay c. da asco** familiarity breeds contempt; **se toma demasiadas confianzas** she's too familiar, she takes too many liberties

confiar [32] **1** *vi* **c. en** to trust; **c. en la suerte** to trust to luck; **confía demasiado en los demás** he is too trusting of others; **no confío en sus intenciones** I don't believe his intentions are honest; **c. en que** to be confident that; **confío en que Dios nos ayudará** I have faith *o* am confident that God will help us

2 *vt* (**a**) *(secreto)* to confide (**b**) *(responsabilidad, persona, asunto)* **c. algo a alguien** to entrust sth to sb

3 confiarse *vpr* (**a**) *(despreocuparse)* to be too sure (of oneself), to be overconfident (**b**) *(sincerarse)* **confiarse a** to confide in

confidencia *nf* confidence, secret

confidencial *adj* confidential

confidencialidad *nf* confidentiality

confidente *nmf* (**a**) *(amigo)* confidant, *f* confidante (**b**) *(policial)* informer

confiero *etc ver* **conferir**

confieso *etc ver* **confesar**

configuración *nf (disposición) (gen) & Inform* configuration; *(del terreno)* lie; *(de la costa)* outline, shape; *(de ciudad)* layout; **c. por defecto** default settings

configurar *vt* (**a**) *(formar)* to shape, to form (**b**) *Inform* to configure

confín *nm* (**a**) *(límite)* border, boundary (**b**) *(extremo) (del reino, universo)* outer reaches; **en los confines de** on the very edge of

confinamiento *nm* (**a**) *(de un detenido)* confinement (**en** to) (**b**) *(de un desterrado)* banishment (**a** *o* **en** to)

confinar *vt* (**a**) *(detener)* to confine (**en** to) (**b**) *(desterrar)* to banish (**a** *o* **en** to)

confiriera *etc ver* **conferir**

confirmación *nf (gen) & Rel* confirmation

confirmar *vt* to confirm

confiscación *nf* confiscation

confiscar [59] *vt* to confiscate

confitado, -a *adj* candied; **frutas confitadas** crystallized fruit

confitar *vt* to candy

confite *nm* candy

confitería *nf* (**a**) *(tienda)* candy store, confectioner's (**b**) *RP (café)* cafe

confitero, -a *nm,f* confectioner

confitura *nf* preserve, jam

conflagración *nf* conflict, war

conflictividad *nf* conflict; **c. laboral** labor unrest

conflictivo, -a *adj (asunto)* controversial; *(situación)* troubled; *(persona)* difficult

conflicto *nm (desacuerdo, lucha)* conflict; *(de intereses, opiniones)* clash; **conflictos** conflict; **entrar en c. con** to be in conflict with; **c. armado** armed conflict; **c. generacional** generation gap; **c. laboral** labor dispute; **c. de intereses** conflict of interests

confluencia *nf* confluence; **la c. de las dos calles** the place where the two roads meet

confluir [34] *vi* (**a**) *(corriente, cauce)* to converge, to meet (**en** at) (**b**) *(personas)* to come together, to gather (**en** in)

conformar 1 *vt (configurar)* to shape

2 conformarse *vpr* **conformarse con** *(suerte, destino)* to resign oneself to; *(apañárselas con)* to make do with; *(contentarse con)* to settle for; **me conformo con lo que tengo** I'm quite happy with what I've got; **no se conforma con cualquier cosa** he won't settle for just anything

conforme 1 *adj* (**a**) *(acorde)* **c. a** in accordance with; **c. al reglamento** in accordance with the rules (**b**) *(de acuerdo)* in agreement (**con** with); **si no estás c., protesta** if you don't agree, say so (**c**) *(contento)* happy (**con** with)

   2 *adv* (**a**) *(a medida que)* as; **c. envejecía** as he got older (**b**) *(como)* exactly as; **te lo cuento c. lo vi** I'm telling you exactly what I saw (**c**) *(en cuanto)* as soon as; **c. amanezca, me iré** I'll leave as soon as it gets light

conformidad *nf (aprobación)* approval; **dio su c.** she gave her consent; **de c. con** in accordance with

conformismo *nm* conformity

conformista *adj & nmf* conformist

confort *(pl* conforts*) nm* comfort; **todo c.** *(en anuncio)* all modern conveniences

confortable *adj* comfortable

confortar *vt* to console, to comfort

confraternidad *nf* brotherhood

confraternizar [14] *vi* to get along (like brothers)

confrontación *nf* (**a**) *(enfrentamiento)* confrontation (**b**) *(comparación)* comparison

confrontar *vt* (**a**) *(enfrentar)* to confront (**b**) *(comparar)* to compare

confucianismo, confucionismo *nm* Confucianism

Confucio *n pr* Confucius

confucionismo = confucianismo

confundido, -a *adj* (**a**) *(avergonzado)* embarrassed (**b**) *(equivocado)* confused

confundir 1 *vt* (**a**) *(trastocar)* **c. una cosa con otra** to mistake one thing for another; **c. dos cosas** to get two things mixed up; **siempre lo confundo con su hermano gemelo** I always mistake him for his twin brother; **creo que me está confundiendo con otro** I think you're confusing me with someone else (**b**) *(liar)* to confuse; **me confundes con tanta información** you're confusing me with all that information (**c**) *(mezclar)* to mix up (**d**) *(abrumar)* to confound

   2 confundirse *vpr* (**a**) *(equivocarse)* to make a mistake; **confundirse de piso/tren** to get the wrong floor/train; **se ha confundido** *(al teléfono)* (you've got the) wrong number; **no te confundas... yo no soy un mentiroso** don't get the wrong idea... I'm no liar (**b**) *(liarse)* to get confused; **me confundo con tanta información** I get confused by all that information (**c**) *(mezclarse) (colores, siluetas)* to merge (**en** into); **confundirse entre la gente** *(personas)* to lose oneself in the crowd

confusión *nf* (**a**) *(desorden, lío)* confusion; **hubo una gran c.** there was great confusion (**b**) *(error)* mix-up; **ha habido una c.** there has been a bit of a mix-up

confusionismo *nm* confusion

confuso, -a *adj* (**a**) *(explicación)* confused (**b**) *(poco claro) (clamor, griterío)* confused; *(contorno, forma)* blurred (**c**) *(turbado)* confused, bewildered

conga *nf* conga

congelación *nf* (**a**) *(de alimentos)* freezing (**b**) *Econ (de precios, salarios)* freeze; **c. de precios** price freeze; **c. salarial** wage freeze

congelado, -a 1 *adj* (**a**) *(alimento, objeto, persona)* frozen (**b**) *(dedos, miembro)* frostbitten (**c**) *Econ (precios, salarios)* frozen (**d**) *TV Cine* **imagen congelada** freeze-frame

   2 congelados *nmpl* frozen foods

congelador *nm* freezer

congelar 1 *vt* (**a**) *(alimento, objeto, persona)* to freeze (**b**) *(dedos, miembro)* to affect with frostbite (**c**) *Econ (precios, salarios)* to freeze; **c. una cuenta bancaria** to freeze a bank account (**d**) *TV & Cine (imagen)* to freeze

   2 congelarse *vpr* (**a**) *(en general)* to freeze; **¡me congelo de frío!** I'm freezing! (**b**) *(dedos, miembro)* to get frostbitten; **se le congelaron los pies y las manos** she got frostbite in her feet and hands

congénere *nmf* **me avergüenzo de mis congéneres** I am ashamed of my kind

congeniar *vi* to get on (**con** with)

congénito, -a *adj* *(enfermedad)* congenital; *(talento, estupidez)* innate

congestión *nf* congestion; **tengo c. nasal** I've got a blocked nose

congestionado, -a *adj (cara)* flushed; *(calle)* congested; *(nariz)* blocked; **tener la nariz congestionada** to have a blocked nose

congestionar 1 *vt* to block

   2 congestionarse *vpr* (**a**) *(calle)* to become congested (**b**) *(cara)* to flush, to turn purple

conglomerado *nm* *Geol & Tec* conglomerate; *(mezcla)* combination

conglomerar *vt Tec* to conglomerate; *(intereses, tendencias)* to unite

Congo *nm* **el C.** *(río)* the Congo (River); *(país)* (the) Congo

congoja *nf* anguish

congoleño, -a *adj & nm,f* Congolese

congraciarse *vpr* **c. con alguien** to win sb over, to get on sb's good side

congratulación *nf Formal* **congratulaciones** congratulations; **recibió la c. del ministro** he received the minister's congratulations

congratular *Formal* **1** *vt* to congratulate (**por** on)

   2 congratularse *vpr* to be pleased (**por** about)

congregación *nf* congregation

congregar [40] **1** *vt* to assemble, to bring together

   2 congregarse *vpr* to assemble, to gather

congresista *nmf* (**a**) *(en un congreso)* delegate (**b**) *(político)* congressman, *f* congresswoman

congreso *nm* (**a**) *(de una especialidad)* conference, congress (**b**) *(asamblea nacional)* **el C. (de los Diputados)** *(en España)* = lower house of Spanish Parliament, ≃ the House of Representatives; **el C.** *(en Estados Unidos)* Congress

congrio *nm* conger eel

congruencia *nf* consistency

congruente *adj* consistent, coherent

cónico, -a *adj* conical

conífera *nf* conifer

conjetura *nf* conjecture; **hacer conjeturas, hacerse una c.** to conjecture

conjeturar *vt* to conjecture about, to make predictions about

conjugación *nf* (**a**) *Gram* conjugation (**b**) *(combinación)* combination; *(de esfuerzos, ideas)* pooling

conjugar [40] *vt* (**a**) *Gram* to conjugate (**b**) *(combinar)* to combine

conjunción *nf* (**a**) *Astron & Gram* conjunction (**b**) *(de circunstancias, hechos)* combination

conjuntado, -a *adj* coordinated

conjuntar *vt* to coordinate

conjuntiva *nf Anat* conjunctiva

conjuntivitis *nf inv* conjunctivitis

conjuntivo, -a *adj* conjunctive

conjunto, -a 1 *adj (acción, esfuerzo)* joint; **cuenta conjunta** joint account

   2 *nm* (**a**) *(agrupación)* collection, group; **un c. de circunstancias** a number of factors (**b**) *(totalidad)* whole; **en c.** overall, as a whole; **c. histórico-artístico** heritage site (**c**) *(de música)* group, band (**d**) *Mat* set; **c. vacío** empty set (**e**) *(de ropa)* outfit

conjura *nf* conspiracy, plot

conjurado, -a *nm,f* plotter, conspirator

conjurar 1 *vt* (**a**) *(exorcizar)* to exorcize; *Fig* **sus palabras conjuraron mi miedo** his words dispelled my fears (**b**) *(un peligro)* to ward off, to avert

2 *vi (conspirar)* to conspire, to plot

3 conjurarse *vpr (conspirar)* to conspire, to plot

conjuro *nm (encantamiento)* spell, incantation; *(exorcismo)* exorcism

conllevar *vt* **(a)** *(implicar)* to involve, to entail **(b)** *(soportar)* to bear

conmemoración *nf* commemoration; **en c. de** in commemoration of

conmemorar *vt* to commemorate

conmemorativo, -a *adj* commemorative

conmensurable *adj* quantifiable

conmigo *pron personal* with me; **c. mismo/misma** with myself; **llevo siempre el pasaporte c.** I always carry my passport on me; **estaba hablando c. mismo** I was talking to myself

conminación *nf* threat

conminar *vt* **(a)** *(forzar)* **c. a alguien a hacer algo** to instruct *o* order sb to do sth **(b)** *(amenazar)* **c. a alguien (con hacer algo)** to threaten sb (with doing sth)

conmiseración *nf* compassion, pity

conmoción *nf* **(a)** *(física o psíquica)* shock; **c. cerebral** concussion **(b)** *(trastorno, disturbio)* upheaval

conmocionar *vt* **(a)** *(psíquicamente)* to shock, to stun **(b)** *(físicamente)* to concuss

conmovedor, -ora *adj* moving, touching

conmover [41] **1** *vt* **(a)** *(emocionar)* to move, to touch **(b)** *(sacudir)* to shake

2 conmoverse *vpr* **(a)** *(emocionarse)* to be moved, to be touched **(b)** *(sacudirse)* to be shaken

conmutación *nf Der* commutation

conmutador *nm* **(a)** *Elec* switch **(b)** *Am (centralita)* switchboard

conmutar *vt Der* to commute

connatural *adj* innate

connivencia *nf* **en c.** in collusion

connotación *nf* connotation; **una c. irónica** a hint of irony

connotar *vt* to suggest, to have connotations of

cono *nm* cone; **el C. Sur** = Chile, Argentina, Paraguay and Uruguay; **c. de señalización** traffic cone

conocedor, -ora *nm,f* expert; **es un gran c. de los vinos franceses** he is a connoisseur of French wine

conocer [19] **1** *vt* **(a)** *(saber cosas acerca de)* to know; **c. algo a fondo** to know sth well; **c. bien un tema** to know a lot about a subject; **darse a c.** to make oneself known; **dieron a c. la noticia a través de la prensa** they announced the news through the press

(b) *(a una persona) (por primera vez)* to meet; *(desde hace tiempo)* to know; **¿conoces a mi jefe?** do you know *o* have you met my boss?; **c. a alguien de vista** to know sb by sight; **c. a alguien de oídas** to have heard of sb; **¿de qué la conoces?** how do you know her?

(c) *(lugar, país) (descubrir)* to get to know, to visit for the first time; *(desde hace tiempo)* to know; **no conozco Rusia** I've never been to Russia; **me gustaría c. Australia** I'd like to go to *o* visit Australia

(d) *(reconocer)* **c. a alguien (por algo)** to recognize sb (by sth)

2 conocerse *vpr* **(a)** *(uno mismo)* to know oneself **(b)** *(dos o más personas) (por primera vez)* to meet, to get to know each other; *(desde hace tiempo)* to know each other; **se conocen de vista** they know each other by sight

3 *v impersonal (parecer)* **se conoce que…** apparently…

conocido, -a 1 *adj* well-known

2 *nm,f* acquaintance

conocimiento *nm* **(a)** *(saber)* knowledge; **hablar/actuar con c. de causa** to know what one is talking about/doing; **poner algo en c. de alguien** to bring sth to sb's attention,

to inform sb of sth; **tener c. de algo** to be aware of sth; **ha llegado a mi c. que estás insatisfecho** it has come to my attention that you are not happy

(b) conocimientos *(nociones)* knowledge; **tengo algunos conocimientos de informática** I have some knowledge of computers, I know a bit about computers

(c) *(sentido, conciencia)* consciousness; **perder/recobrar el c.** to lose/regain consciousness; **estaba tumbado en el suelo, sin c.** he was lying unconscious on the floor

conozco *ver* **conocer**

conque *conj* so; **¿c. te has cansado?** so you're tired, are you?; **¿c. esas tenemos?** so that's what you're up to?

conquense 1 *adj* of/from Cuenca

2 *nmf* person from Cuenca

conquista *nf (de tierras, persona)* conquest; *(de libertad, derecho)* winning

conquistador, -ora 1 *adj (seductor)* seductive

2 *nm,f* **(a)** *(de tierras)* conqueror **(b)** *Hist* conquistador

3 *nm (seductor)* Casanova, lady-killer

conquistar *vt* **(a)** *(tierras)* to conquer **(b)** *(libertad, derechos, simpatía)* to win **(c)** *(seducir)* to win the heart of

consabido, -a *adj (conocido)* well-known; *(habitual)* usual

consagración *nf* **(a)** *Rel* consecration **(b)** *(dedicación)* dedication **(c)** *(reconocimiento)* recognition; **esta obra supuso la c. del joven escritor** this work gained recognition for the young writer

consagrado, -a *adj* **(a)** *Rel* consecrated **(b)** *(dedicado)* dedicated **(c)** *(reconocido)* recognized, established

consagrar 1 *vt* **(a)** *Rel* to consecrate **(b)** *(dedicar) (tiempo, espacio)* to devote; *(monumento, lápida)* to dedicate; **consagró su vida a la literatura** he devoted *o* dedicated his life to literature **(c)** *(acreditar, confirmar)* to confirm, to establish

2 consagrarse *vpr* **(a)** *(dedicarse)* to devote *o* dedicate oneself **(a** to) **(b)** *(alcanzar reconocimiento)* to establish oneself

consanguíneo, -a *adj* related by blood; **hermano c.** half brother *(of same father)*

consanguinidad *nf* blood relationship

consciencia = **conciencia**

consciente *adj* conscious; **estar c.** *(estar despierto)* to be conscious; **ser c. de** to be aware of

consecución *nf (de un deseo)* realization; *(de un objetivo)* attainment; *(de un premio)* winning

consecuencia *nf* **(a)** *(resultado)* consequence; **a** *o* **como c. de** as a consequence *o* result of; **en c.** consequently; **tener consecuencias** to have consequences **(b)** *(coherencia)* consistency; **actuar en c.** to act accordingly; **cuando supo que estaba embarazada actuó en c.** when he found out that she was pregnant he did the decent thing

consecuente *adj (coherente)* consistent; **una persona c.** a person of principle

consecutivo, -a *adj* consecutive; **tres victorias consecutivas** three consecutive victories, three victories in a row; **siete semanas consecutivas** seven consecutive weeks, seven straight weeks

conseguir [61] *vt (obtener)* to obtain, to get; *(un objetivo)* to achieve; **consiguió todo lo que se propuso** she achieved everything she set out to do; **c. hacer algo** to manage to do sth; **no consiguió que me enfadara** she didn't (manage to) get me annoyed

consejería *nf Esp (de comunidad autónoma)* department

consejero, -a *nm,f* **(a)** *(en asuntos personales)* counselor; *(en asuntos técnicos)* adviser, consultant; **c. matrimonial** marriage guidance counselor **(b)** *(de un consejo de administración)* member; *Pol* councilor; *Com* **c. delegado** chief executive (officer), managing director

consejo *nm* **(a)** *(advertencia)* advice; **dar un c.** to give some advice *o* a piece of advice; **te voy a dar un c.** I've got a piece of advice for you; **dar consejos** to give (some) advice; **pedir c. a alguien** to ask sb for advice, to ask (for) sb's advice; **c. médico** medical advice (**b**) *(organismo)* council; *(reunión)* meeting; **c. de administración** board of directors; *(reunión)* board meeting; **c. escolar** board of governors; **C. de Europa** Council of Europe; **c. de ministros** cabinet; *(reunión)* cabinet meeting; **C. de Seguridad** Security Council (**c**) **c. de guerra** court martial

consenso *nm (acuerdo)* consensus; *(consentimiento)* consent

consensuado, -a *adj* approved by consensus

consensual *adj* consensual

consensuar [4] *vt* to approve by consensus

consentido, -a 1 *adj* spoiled
2 *nm,f* spoiled brat

consentimiento *nm* consent; **c. por escrito** written consent

consentir [62] **1** *vt* (**a**) *(tolerar)* to allow, to permit (**b**) *(mimar)* to spoil; **le consienten demasiado** they let him have his own way too much
2 *vi* **c. en algo/en hacer algo** to agree to sth/to do sth; **consintió en que se quedaran** he agreed to let them stay

conserje *nmf (de colegio, ministerio)* doorman; *(de bloque de viviendas)* superintendent, supervisor

conserjería *nf (en colegio, ministerio)* porter's lodge; *(en bloque de viviendas)* superintendent's *o* supervisor's office

conserva *nf* **conservas** canned food; **en c.** canned; **c. de carne** canned meat

conservación *nf* (**a**) *(de costumbres, patrimonio)* conservation; *(de alimentos)* preservation (**b**) *(mantenimiento)* maintenance; **en buen estado de c.** in good condition

conservador, -ora 1 *adj (tradicionalista)* conservative; *(del partido conservador)* Conservative
2 *nm,f* (**a**) *(tradicionalista)* conservative; *(miembro del partido conservador)* Conservative (**b**) *(de museo)* curator

conservadurismo *nm* conservatism

conservante *nm* preservative

conservar 1 *vt* (**a**) *(mantener) (alimento)* to preserve; *(amistad)* to sustain, to keep up; *(salud)* to look after; *(calor)* to retain (**b**) *(guardar) (libros, cartas, secreto)* to keep; **todavía conserva sus primeras zapatillas de ballet** she still has her first ballet shoes; **consérvese en el frigorífico** *(en etiqueta)* keep refrigerated
2 conservarse *vpr* (**a**) *(alimento)* to keep (**b**) *(persona)* **se conserva bien** he's doing well; **se conserva muy joven** she keeps herself looking very young (**c**) *(subsistir)* to survive; **no se conserva ningún escrito de esa época** there are no surviving documents from that time, no document has survived from that time

conservatorio *nm* conservatory, conservatoire

conservero, -a *adj* canning; **la industria conservera** the canning industry

considerable *adj (grande)* considerable; *(importante, eminente)* notable

consideración *nf* (**a**) *(reflexión)* consideration, factor; **debemos tener en cuenta estas consideraciones** we must take these factors into consideration; **tomar en c.** to take into consideration *o* account (**b**) *(respeto)* respect; **en c. a algo** in recognition of sth; **tratar a alguien con c.** to be nice to sb/s (**c**) *(importancia)* **de c.** serious; **hubo varios heridos de c.** several people were seriously injured

considerado, -a *adj (atento)* considerate, thoughtful; *(respetado)* respected, highly regarded

considerar 1 *vt* (**a**) *(pensar en)* to consider; *(juzgar, estimar)* to think; **bien considerado, creo que tienes razón** on reflection, I think you're right (**b**) *(respetar)* to esteem, to treat with respect
2 considerarse *vpr (uno mismo)* to consider oneself; **me considero feliz** I consider myself happy

consiento *etc ver* **consentir**

consigna *nf* (**a**) *(órdenes)* instructions (**b**) *(para el equipaje)* checkroom

consignar *vt* (**a**) *(poner por escrito)* to record, to write down (**b**) *(asignar)* to allocate (**c**) *(mercancía)* to consign, to dispatch (**d**) *(equipaje)* to deposit in the baggage room

consignatario, -a *nm,f* (**a**) *(de una mercancía)* consignee (**b**) *(representante)* **c. de buques** shipping agent

consigo 1 *ver* **conseguir**
2 *pron personal (singular)* with him/her; *(plural)* with them; *(con usted)* with you; *(con uno mismo)* with oneself; **c. mismo/misma** with himself/herself; **lleva siempre el pasaporte c.** she always carries her passport on her; **hablar c. mismo** to talk to oneself

consiguiente *adj* resulting; **con la c. decepción** with the resulting disappointment; **por c.** consequently, therefore

consiguiera *etc ver* **conseguir**

consintiera *etc ver* **consentir**

consistencia *nf también Fig* consistency

consistente *adj* (**a**) *(sólido) (material)* solid (**b**) *(coherente) (argumento)* sound, convincing (**c**) *(compuesto)* **c. en** consisting of

consistir *vi* (**a**) **c. en** *(ser, componerse de)* to consist of; **la oferta consiste en una impresora y un escáner** the offer consists of a printer and a scanner; **¿en qué consiste su problema?** what exactly is your problem?; **su tarea consiste en atender el teléfono** her job simply involves *o* entails answering the phone (**b**) **c. en** *(basarse en)* to lie in, to be based on

consistorial *adj* of the city *o* town council; **casa c.** city *o* town hall

consistorio *nm* city *o* town council

consola *nf* (**a**) *Inform & Tec* console; **c. de videojuegos** video console (**b**) *(mesa)* console table

consolación *nf* consolation

consolador, -ora *adj* consoling, comforting

consolar [63] **1** *vt* to console; **me consuela pensar que podría haber sido peor** it's some consolation to reflect that it could have been worse
2 consolarse *vpr* to console oneself, to take comfort; **¡consuélate! al menos no has suspendido** look on the bright side! at least you didn't fail

consolidación *nf* consolidation

consolidar *vt* to consolidate

consomé *nm* consommé

consonancia *nf* harmony; **en c. con** in keeping with

consonante *nf* consonant

consonántico, -a *adj* consonant, consonantal

consorcio *nm* consortium; **c. bancario** bankers' consortium

consorte *nmf (cónyuge)* spouse; *(príncipe)* consort

conspicuo, -a *adj (evidente)* conspicuous; *(ilustre)* eminent

conspiración *nf* plot, conspiracy

conspirador, -ora *nm,f* conspirator, plotter

conspirar *vi* to conspire, to plot

constancia *nf* (**a**) *(perseverancia) (en una empresa)* perseverance; *(en las ideas, opiniones)* steadfastness; **hacer algo con c.** to persevere with sth (**b**) *(testimonio)* record; **dejar c. de algo** *(registrar)* to put sth on record; *(probar)* to demonstrate sth

constante 1 *adj* (**a**) *(persona) (en una empresa)* persistent; *(en ideas, opiniones)* steadfast (**b**) *(acción)* constant
2 *nf* constant; *Med* **constantes vitales** vital signs; *Med* **mantener las constantes vitales de alguien** to keep sb alive

constar *vi* (**a**) *(información)* to appear (**en** in), to figure (**en** in); **su nombre no consta en esta lista** his name is not on *o* does not appear on this list; **hacer c. algo** to put sth on record; **me consta que...** I am quite sure that...; **que conste que...** let it be clearly understood that..., let there be no doubt that...; **yo no he sido, que conste** let's get one thing clear, it wasn't me **(b)** *(estar constituido por)* **c. de** to consist of

constatación *nf* confirmation

constatar *vt (observar)* to confirm; *(comprobar)* to check

constelación *nf* constellation

consternación *nf* consternation, dismay

consternado, -a *adj* dismayed, extremely upset

consternar *vt* to dismay, to upset

constipado, -a 1 *adj* **estar c.** to have a cold
  2 *nm* cold

constiparse *vpr* to catch a cold

constitución *nf* **(a)** constitution; **tener una c. fuerte/ débil** to have a strong/weak constitution **(b)** *(de un estado)* constitution **(c)** *(creación)* creation, forming **(d)** *(composición)* composition, makeup

constitucional *adj* constitutional

constitucionalidad *nf* constitutionality

constituir [34] *vt* **(a)** *(componer)* to make up **(b)** *(ser)* to be; **constituye una falta grave** it is *o* constitutes a serious misdemeanor; **no creo que constituya ningún obstáculo** I don't think it constitutes an obstacle, I don't see it as an obstacle **(c)** *(crear)* to set up, to constitute

constitutivo, -a *adj* constituent; **elemento c.** constituent element; **ser c. de algo** to constitute sth

constituyente *adj & nm* constituent

constreñir *vt* **(a)** *(obligar)* **c. a alguien a hacer algo** to compel *o* force sb to do sth **(b)** *(oprimir, limitar)* to restrict

constricción *nf* constriction

construcción *nf* **(a)** *(acción) (gen) & Gram* construction; **en c.** under construction **(b)** *(edificio)* building

constructivo, -a *adj* constructive

constructor, -ora 1 *adj* building, construction; **empresa constructora** construction firm, building company
  2 *nm,f (de edificios)* builder

construir [34] *vt (edificio, barco, muro)* to build; *(aviones, coches)* to manufacture; *(frase, teoría)* to construct

consubstancial *adj* **ser c. a algo** to be an integral part of sth

consuegro, -a *nm,f* = father-in-law/mother-in-law of one's son or daughter

consuelo 1 *ver* **consolar**
  2 *nm* consolation, solace

consuetudinario, -a *adj* customary; **derecho c.** common law

cónsul *nm* consul

consulado *nm (oficina)* consulate; *(cargo)* consulship

consular *adj* consular

consulta *nf* **(a)** *(sobre un problema) (acción)* consultation; *(pregunta)* query, inquiry; **hacer una c. a alguien** to seek sb's advice; **libro/obra de c.** reference book/work **(b)** *(despacho de médico)* office; **horas de c.** (doctor's) office hours; **pasar c.** to hold (doctor's) office hours

consultar 1 *vt (dato, fecha)* to look up; *(libro, persona)* to consult; **me consultó antes de hacerlo** *(me pidió consejo)* he consulted me before doing it; *(me pidió permiso)* he asked me before he did it
  2 *vi* **c. con** to consult, to seek advice from

consulting [kon'sultin] *nm* consultancy (firm)

consultivo, -a *adj* consultative, advisory

consultor, -ora *nm,f* consultant; **c. (en administración) de empresas** management consultant

consultoría, consultora *nf* consultancy firm

consultorio *nm* **(a)** *(de un médico)* office **(b)** *(en periódico)* advice column; *(en radio)* = program answering listeners' questions; **c. sentimental** *(en radio)* = phone-in where people get advice on their personal problems **(c)** *(asesoría)* advice bureau

consumación *nf (de matrimonio, proyecto)* consummation; *(de un crimen)* perpetration

consumado, -a *adj* consummate, perfect; **es un granuja c.** he's a real rascal

consumar *vt (realizar completamente)* to complete; *(un crimen)* to perpetrate; *(el matrimonio)* to consummate

consumibles *nmpl* consumables

consumición *nf* **(a)** *(acción)* consumption **(b)** *(bebida)* drink; *(comida)* food; **son diez euros la entrada con c.** it costs ten euros to get in, including the first drink

consumido, -a *adj (flaco)* emaciated

consumidor, -ora *nm,f (de producto)* consumer; *(en bar, restaurante)* patron

consumir 1 *vt* **(a)** *(producto)* to consume; **en casa consumimos mucho aceite de oliva** we use a lot of olive oil at home; **c. drogas** to take drugs; **c. preferentemente antes de...** best before... **(b)** *(gastar)* to use, to consume; **esta estufa consume mucha electricidad** this heater uses a lot of electricity; **mi coche consume cinco litros a los cien** my car does twenty kilometers to the liter **(c)** *(destruir)* *(sujeto: fuego)* to destroy; *(sujeto: enfermedad)* to eat away at; *Fig* **le consumen los celos** he is eaten up by *o* consumed with jealousy
  2 *vi* to consume
  3 consumirse *vpr* **(a)** *(persona)* to waste away; **se consume de envidia** he is eaten up *o* consumed with envy **(b)** *(fuego)* to burn out

consumismo *nm* consumerism

consumista *adj* consumerist, materialistic

consumo *nm* consumption; **bienes/sociedad de c.** consumer goods/society; **se ha disparado el c. de agua mineral** sales of mineral water have shot up; **c. de combustible** fuel consumption; **c. de drogas** drug-taking

consustancial *adj* **ser c. a algo** to be an integral part of sth

contabilidad *nf* **(a)** *(oficio)* accountancy **(b)** *(de persona, empresa)* bookkeeping, accounting; **llevar la c.** to do the accounts; **doble c.** double-entry bookkeeping; **c. de costes** cost accounting

contabilización *nf Com* entering

contabilizar [14] *vt Com* to enter

contable *nmf Esp* accountant

contactar 1 *vt (comunicarse con)* to contact
  2 *vi* **c. con** to contact

contacto *nm* **(a)** *(entre dos cosas, personas)* contact; **perder el c.** to lose touch; **ponerse en c. con** to get in touch with; **c. visual** eye contact **(b)** *Aut* ignition **(c)** *Elec* **hacer c.** to make contact

contactólogo, -a *nm,f* contact-lens specialist

contado, -a 1 *adj* **(a)** *(raro)* rare, infrequent; **en contadas ocasiones** very rarely, on very few occasions **(b)** **había diez personas mal contadas** there were no more than ten people
  2 al contado *loc adv* (in) cash

contador, -ora 1 *nm,f Am (persona)* accountant
  2 *nm (aparato)* meter; **el c. del agua/del gas/de la luz** water/gas/electricity meter

contaduría *nf (oficina)* accountant's office; *(departamento)* accounts office; *Am* **c. general** audit office

contagiar 1 *vt (persona)* to infect; *(enfermedad)* to transmit; **me has contagiado el resfriado** you've given me your cold; **contagió su entusiasmo a sus compañeros** he passed his enthusiasm on to his companions
  2 contagiarse *vpr (enfermedad, risa)* to be contagious;

(persona) to become infected; **me contagié de mi hermano** I caught it from my brother; **se contagió de su optimismo** he infected her with his optimism

contagio *nm* infection, contagion

contagioso, -a *adj (enfermedad)* contagious, infectious; *(risa)* infectious

container *(pl* containers*) nm (para mercancías)* container

contaminación *nf (acción)* contamination; *(del medio ambiente)* pollution; **c. acústica** noise pollution

contaminado, -a *adj (alimento)* contaminated; *(medio ambiente)* polluted

contaminante 1 *adj* contaminating, polluting

2 contaminantes *nmpl* pollutants

contaminar *vt* (**a**) *(envenenar)* to contaminate; *(el medio ambiente)* to pollute (**b**) *(pervertir)* to corrupt

contante *adj Fam* **con dinero c. y sonante** in hard cash

contar [63] **1** *vt* (**a**) *(enumerar)* to count; **se pueden c. con los dedos de una mano** you can count them on (the fingers of) one hand (**b**) *(incluir)* to count; **cuenta también los gastos de desplazamiento** count *o* include travel costs too; **somos 57 sin c. a los niños** there are 57 of us, not counting the children (**c**) *(narrar)* to tell; **cuéntame, ¿cómo te va la vida?** tell me, how are things?

2 *vi* (**a**) *(hacer cálculos)* to count; **sabe c. hasta diez** she can count to ten (**b**) *(importar)* to count; **aquí no cuento para nada** I count for nothing here; **lo que cuenta es...** what matters is... (**c**) **c. con** *(confiar en)* to count on; *(tener, poseer)* to have; *(tener en cuenta)* to take into account; **con esto no contaba** I hadn't reckoned with that; **cuenta con dos horas para hacerlo** he has two hours to do it

3 contarse *vpr* (**a**) *(incluirse)* **se cuentan entre los favoritos** they are among the favorites (**b**) *Fam (al saludarse)* **¿qué (te) cuentas?** how are you doing?

contemplación *nf* (**a**) *(meditación)* contemplation (**b**) *(consideración)* **contemplaciones** consideration; **tratar a alguien sin contemplaciones** not to take into account sb's feelings; **nos echaron sin contemplaciones** they threw us out unceremoniously

contemplar *vt* (**a**) *(opción, posibilidad)* to contemplate, to consider; **está contemplando presentar la dimisión** she is considering handing in her resignation; **la ley contempla varios supuestos** the law provides for *o* covers various cases; **esta propuesta no contempla los ingresos por publicidad** this proposal doesn't take into account income from advertising (**b**) *(paisaje, monumento)* to look at, to contemplate

contemplativo, -a *adj* contemplative

contemporáneo, -a *adj & nm,f* contemporary

contemporizador, -ora 1 *adj* accommodating

2 *nm,f* **es un c.** he's very accommodating

contemporizar [14] *vi* to be accommodating

contención *nf* (**a**) *Constr* **muro de c.** retaining wall (**b**) *(moderación)* restraint, self-restraint

contencioso, -a 1 *adj* (**a**) *(tema, cuestión)* contentious (**b**) *Der* litigious

2 *nm* dispute, conflict

contender [64] *vi (competir)* to contend; *(pelear)* to fight

contendiente 1 *adj (en una competición)* competing; **las partes contendientes** *(en una guerra)* the warring factions; **los ejércitos contendientes** the opposing armies

2 *nmf (en una competición)* contender; *(en una guerra)* warring faction

contenedor, -ora 1 *adj* containing

2 *nm (recipiente grande)* container; *(para escombros)* Dumpster®; **c. de basura** large wheeled garbage can; **c. de vidrio** bottle recycling center

contener [65] **1** *vt* (**a**) *(encerrar)* to contain; **no contiene**

CFC *(en etiqueta)* does not contain CFCs; **¿qué contiene esa maleta?** what's in this suitcase? (**b**) *(detener, reprimir)* to restrain, to hold back; **tuvieron que contenerlo para que no agrediera al fotógrafo** he had to be restrained from attacking the photographer; **no pudo c. la risa/el llanto** he couldn't help laughing/crying

2 contenerse *vpr* to restrain oneself, to hold oneself back; **conseguí contenerme** I managed to restrain myself

contengo *ver* **contener**

contenido *nm (de recipiente, libro)* contents; *(de discurso, redacción)* content

contentar 1 *vt* to please, to keep happy

2 contentarse *vpr* **contentarse con** to make do with, to be satisfied with

contento, -a 1 *adj* (**a**) *(alegre)* happy; **se puso muy c. al ver a sus nietos** he was very happy to see his grandchildren (**b**) *(satisfecho)* pleased; **no c. con insultarlo, le pegó una bofetada** not content with insulting him, he slapped his face; *Fam* **pagamos cada uno la mitad y todos tan contentos** we paid half each and that was us

2 *nm* happiness, joy; **no caber en sí de c.** to be beside oneself with joy

conteo *nm* counting-up

contertulio, -a *nm,f* companion *(at a social gathering)*

contestación *nf* answer

contestador *nm, CSur* **contestadora** *nf* **c. (automático)** answering machine

contestar 1 *vt (responder)* to answer; **c. a una pregunta** to answer a question; **contestó que sí/que no** he said yes/no

2 *vi* (**a**) *(responder)* to answer; **no contestan** *(al teléfono)* there's no reply *o* answer (**b**) *(con insolencia)* to answer back; **¡no contestes a tu madre!** don't answer back to your mother!

contestatario, -a *adj* antiestablishment

contestón, -ona *adj Fam* cheeky; **es muy c.** he's always answering back

contexto *nm* context

contextual *adj* contextual

contextualizar [14] *vt (problema, situación)* to put into perspective *o* context

contextura *nf (estructura)* structure; *(complexión)* build

contienda 1 *ver* **contender**

2 *nf (competición, combate)* contest; *(guerra)* conflict, war

contiene *ver* **contener**

contigo *pron personal* with you; **c. mismo/misma** with yourself; **¿estás hablando c. mismo?** are you talking to yourself?

contigüidad *nf* adjacency

contiguo, -a *adj* adjacent

continencia *nf* continence, self-restraint

continental *adj* continental

continente *nm* (**a**) *Geog* continent (**b**) *(recipiente)* container

contingencia *nf (eventualidad)* eventuality; *Formal (posibilidad)* possibility

contingente 1 *adj Formal* possible; **es un hecho c.** it's not impossible

2 *nm* (**a**) *(grupo)* contingent (**b**) *Com* quota

continuación 1 *nf (de acción, estado)* continuation; *(de novela, película)* sequel

2 a continuación *loc adv* next; **a c. añada una pizca de sal** next, add a pinch of salt; **saludó al presidente y a c. se fue** she greeted the president and then left; **pasaremos a c. a abordar el problema de...** we shall now pass on to address the problem of...; **a c., para todos ustedes, la gran cantante...** and now, we bring you the great singer...

continuar [4] **1** *vt* to continue, to carry on with; **los peregrinos continuaron su camino** the pilgrims went *o* continued on their way

2 *vi* to continue, to go on; **c. haciendo algo** to continue doing *o* to do sth; **continúa lloviendo** it's still raining; **todavía continúa en la empresa** she's still with *o* working for the company; **continuará** *(historia, programa)* to be continued

continuidad *nf (en una sucesión)* continuity; *(permanencia)* continuation; *Formal* **sin solución de c.** without stopping

continuista *nmf Pol* supporter of the status quo

continuo, -a *adj* (a) *(ininterrumpido)* continuous; **las continuas lluvias obligaron a suspender el partido** the constant *o* continuous rain forced them to call off the game (b) *(perseverante)* continual; **me irritan sus continuas preguntas** her continual questioning irritates me

contonearse *vpr (hombre)* to swagger; *(mujer)* to swing one's hips

contoneo *nm (de hombre)* swagger; *(de mujer)* sway of the hips

contornear *vt (seguir el contorno de)* to go around; *(perfilar)* to outline

contorno *nm* (a) *Mat* contour; *(línea)* outline; **c. de cintura** waist (measurement); **c. de pecho** bust (measurement); **el c. accidentado de la isla** the ragged coastline of the island (b) **contornos** *(vecindad)* neighborhood; *(de una ciudad)* outskirts

contorsión *nf* contortion

contorsionarse *vpr (retorcerse)* to do contortions; *(de dolor)* to writhe

contorsionista *nmf* contortionist

contra 1 *prep* against; **un jarabe c. la tos** a cough syrup; **en c.** against; **estar en c. de algo, estar c. algo** to be opposed to sth; **en c. de** *(a diferencia de)* contrary to; **eso va c. el reglamento** that's against regulations

2 *nm* **los pros y los contras** the pros and cons

contraalmirante *nm* rear admiral

contraatacar [59] *vi* to counterattack

contraataque *nm* counterattack

contrabajo 1 *nm (instrumento)* double bass

2 *nmf (instrumentista)* double-bass player, double-bassist

contrabandista *nmf* smuggler

contrabando *nm (acto)* smuggling; *(mercancías)* contraband; **pasar algo de c.** to smuggle sth in; **c. de armas** gunrunning; **tabaco de c.** contraband cigarettes

contracción *nf (gen) & Ling & Med* contraction

contracepción *nf* contraception

contraceptivo, -a *adj* contraceptive

contrachapado, -a 1 *adj* (made of) plywood

2 *nm* plywood

contracorriente *nf* countercurrent; **ir a c.** to go against the current *o* tide

contráctil *adj* contractile

contractual *adj* contractual

contractura *nf (muscular)* cramp

contracultura *nf* counterculture

contracultural *adj* counterculture; **una corriente c.** a counterculture movement

contradecir [51] **1** *vt* to contradict

2 contradecirse *vpr* to contradict oneself

contradicción *nf* contradiction; **estar en c. con** to be in (direct) contradiction to

contradicho, -a *participio ver* **contradecir**

contradictorio, -a *adj* contradictory

contraer [66] **1** *vt* (a) *(encoger)* to contract (b) *(vicio, costumbre)* to acquire (c) *(enfermedad)* to catch (d) **c. matrimonio (con)** to get married (to)

2 contraerse *vpr* to contract

contraespionaje *nm* counterespionage

contrafuerte *nm* (a) *Arquit* buttress (b) *(del calzado)* heel reinforcement (c) *Geog* foothill

contragolpe *nm* counterattack

contrahecho, -a *adj* deformed

contraindicación *nf (en medicamento)* **contraindicaciones: embarazo, diabetes** not to be taken during pregnancy or by diabetics

contraindicado, -a *adj* **está c. beber alcohol durante el embarazo** alcohol should be avoided during pregnancy

contraindicar [59] *vt (médico)* to advise against

contralmirante *nmf* rear admiral

contralor, -ora *nm,f Am (en institución, empresa)* comptroller

contraloría *nf Am (oficina)* comptroller's office

contralto 1 *nm (voz)* contralto

2 *nmf (cantante)* countertenor, *f* contralto

contraluz *nm* back lighting; **a c.** against the light

contramaestre *nm* (a) *Náut* boatswain; *Mil* warrant officer (b) *(capataz)* foreman

contramano: a contramano *loc adv (en sentido contrario)* the wrong way

contraofensiva *nf* counteroffensive

contraoferta *nf* counteroffer

contraorden *nf* countermand

contrapartida *nf* compensation; **como c.** to make up for it

contrapelo: a contrapelo *loc adv (acariciar)* the wrong way; **su intervención iba a c. del resto** his remarks went against the general opinion; **vivir a c.** to have an unconventional lifestyle

contrapesar *vt (físicamente)* to counterbalance; *(contrarrestar)* to compensate for

contrapeso *nm (en ascensores, poleas)* counterweight; *(fuerza que iguala)* counterbalance

contraponer [50] **1** *vt* (a) *(oponer)* **a su postura intransigente contrapusimos una más flexible** we responded to his intransigence by suggesting greater flexibility (b) *(cotejar)* to compare

2 contraponerse *vpr* to be opposed

contraportada *nf (de periódico, revista)* back page; *(de libro)* back cover; *(de disco)* back

contraposición *nf* (a) *(oposición)* conflict (b) *(comparación)* comparison

contraproducente *adj* counterproductive

contraprogramación *nf* = competitive TV scheduling

contrapuesto, -a 1 *participio ver* **contraponer**

2 *adj* conflicting

contrapunto *nm Mús* counterpoint; *(contraste)* contrast

contraria *nf* **llevar la c.** to be awkward *o* contrary; **¡siempre me está llevando la c.!** *(verbalmente)* he's always contradicting me!; *(con acciones)* he always does the opposite of what I tell him!

contrariado, -a *adj* upset

contrariar [32] *vt* (a) *(contradecir)* to go against (b) *(disgustar)* to upset

contrariedad *nf* (a) *(dificultad)* setback (b) *(disgusto)* annoyance (c) *(oposición)* contrary *o* opposing nature

contrario, -a 1 *adj* (a) *(opuesto) (dirección, sentido, idea)* opposite; *(parte)* opposing; *(equipo)* opposing; **todo lo c.** quite the contrary (b) *(desfavorable)* **es c. a nuestros intereses** it goes against our interests (c) **ser c. a algo** to be opposed to sth

2 *nm,f (rival)* opponent

3 *nm (opuesto)* opposite

4 al contrario *loc adv* on the contrary; **no me disgusta, al c., me encanta** I don't dislike it, quite the contrary in fact, I like it; **al c. de mi casa, la suya tiene calefacción central** unlike my house, hers has central heating

5 de lo contrario *loc adv* otherwise

6 por el contrario *loc adv* on the other hand

contrarreembolso *nm* cash on delivery

Contrarreforma *nf Hist* Counter-Reformation

contrarreloj 1 *adj inv Dep* **etapa c.** time trial; *Fig* **trabajar a c.** to work against the clock
   2 *nf inv Dep* time trial

contrarrembolso *nm* cash on delivery

contrarréplica *nf* reply; **en su c., el ministro dijo que…** the minister countered that…

contrarrestar *vt (neutralizar)* to counteract

contrarrevolución *nf* counterrevolution

contrarrevolucionario, -a *adj & nm,f* counter-revolutionary

contrasentido *nm* **hacer/decir eso es un c.** it doesn't make sense to do/say that

contraseña *nf* password

contrastar 1 *vi* to contrast (**con** with)
   2 *vt (comprobar)* to check, to verify

contraste *nm* contrast; **en c. con** *(a diferencia de)* in contrast with *o* to; *(comparado con)* in comparison with

contrata *nf Der* (fixed-price) contract

contratación *nf (de personal)* hiring

contratante *nmf* contracting party

contratar *vt* (**a**) *(obreros, personal, detective)* to hire; *(deportista)* to sign (**b**) *(servicio, obra, mercancía)* **c. algo a alguien** to contract for sth with sb

contraterrorismo *nm* counterterrorism

contraterrorista *adj* counterterrorist

contratiempo *nm (accidente)* mishap; *(dificultad)* setback

contratista *nmf* contractor; **c. de obras** building contractor

contrato *nm Com* contract; **bajo c.** under contract; **c. administrativo** administrative contract; **c. de alquiler** lease, rental agreement; **c. de arrendamiento** lease; **c. basura** short-term contract *(with poor conditions)*; **c. de compraventa** contract of sale; **c. fijo** *o* **indefinido** permanent contract; **c. laboral** *o* **de trabajo** work contract; **c. mercantil** commercial contract; **c. en prácticas** work-experience contract; **c. temporal** temporary *o* short-term contract; **c. verbal** oral contract

contraveneno *nm* antidote

contravenir [69] *vi* **c. a** to contravene

contraventana *nf* shutter

contrayente *nmf Formal* **los contrayentes** the bride and groom

contribución *nf* (**a**) *(aporte)* contribution (**b**) *(impuesto)* tax; **c. directa/indirecta** direct/indirect tax; **c. urbana** = tax for local services

contribuir [34] *vi* (**a**) *(aportar)* to contribute (**a** to); **c. con algo para** to contribute sth toward; **todos contribuyeron al triunfo** everyone contributed to the victory; **sus declaraciones contribuyeron a enrarecer el ambiente** his words served to make the atmosphere tense (**b**) *(pagar impuestos)* to pay taxes

contribuyente *nmf* taxpayer

contrición *nf* contrition

contrincante *nmf* rival, opponent

contrito, -a *adj* (**a**) *(arrepentido)* contrite (**b**) *(triste, compungido)* downcast

control *nm* (**a**) *(dominio)* control; **bajo c.** under control; **fuera de c.** out of control; **perder el c.** *(perder la calma)* to lose one's temper; *Econ* **c. de cambios** exchange control; **c. de la natalidad** birth control

  (**b**) *(verificación)* examination, inspection; **todos los productos pasan un riguroso c.** all the products are rigorously inspected *o* examined; **(bajo) c. médico** (under) medical supervision; **c. antidoping** dope *o* drugs test; **c. de calidad** quality control; **c. de existencias** stock control; *Av* **c. del tráfico aéreo** air traffic control

  (**c**) *(de policía)* checkpoint; **c. de pasaportes** passport control

  (**d**) *(examen)* test, quiz

  (**e**) *(mando)* control; **el c. del encendido/apagado** the on/off switch; **c. remoto** remote control

controlador, -ora *nm,f* controller; **c. aéreo** air traffic controller

controlar 1 *vt* (**a**) *(dominar)* to control (**b**) *(comprobar)* to check (**c**) *(vigilar)* to watch, to keep an eye on
   2 controlarse *vpr* to control oneself, to restrain oneself

controversia *nf* controversy

controvertido, -a *adj* controversial

contubernio *nm* conspiracy

contumacia *nf* obstinacy, stubbornness

contumaz *adj* stubborn, obstinate

contundencia *nf (de golpes)* force; *(de palabras, argumentos)* forcefulness

contundente *adj (arma, objeto)* blunt; *(golpe)* thudding; *(razonamiento, argumento)* forceful

conturbar *vt Formal* to trouble, to perturb

contusión *nf* bruise

contusionar *vt* to bruise

contuviera *etc ver* **contener**

conurbación *nf* conurbation

conurbano *nm RP* suburbs

convalecencia *nf* convalescence

convalecer [46] *vi* to convalesce (**de** after)

convaleciente *adj* convalescent

convalidación *nf Educ (de estudios)* recognition; *(de asignaturas)* validation

convalidar *vt Educ (estudios)* to recognize; *(asignaturas)* to validate

convección *nf Fís* convection

convector *nm* convector; **c. de aire caliente** convection heater

convencer [40] **1** *vt* (**a**) *(persuadir)* to convince; **c. a alguien de algo** to convince sb of sth; **lo convencí para que me dejara ir a la fiesta** I convinced *o* persuaded him to let me go to the party (**b**) *(satisfacer)* **es barato, pero no me acaba de c.** *o* **no me convence del todo** it's certainly cheap, but I'm not totally sure about it

   2 *vi* **su explicación no convenció** his explanation wasn't convincing; **a pesar de ganar, el equipo no convenció** although they won, the team failed to impress

   3 convencerse *vpr* **convéncete, no conseguirás nada actuando así** believe (you) me, you won't get anywhere behaving like that; **convencerse de** to become convinced of

convencimiento *nm (certeza)* conviction; *(acción)* convincing

convención *nf* convention; **la C. de Ginebra** the Geneva Convention

convencional *adj* conventional

convencionalismo *nm* conventionality

convenido, -a *adj* agreed; **hicieron lo c.** they did what they'd agreed

conveniencia *nf* (**a**) *(utilidad)* usefulness; *(oportunidad)* suitability (**b**) *(interés)* convenience; **sólo mira su c.** he only looks after his own interests

conveniente *adj (útil)* useful; *(oportuno)* suitable, appropriate; *(lugar, hora)* convenient; *(aconsejable)* advisable; **sería c. asistir** it would be a good idea to go

convenio *nm* agreement; *Ind* **c. colectivo** collective agreement; **c. salarial** wage agreement *o* settlement

convenir [69] **1** *vi* (**a**) *(venir bien)* to be suitable; **este horario me conviene** these hours suit me; **te convendría dormir unas horas** you would do well to get a few hours' sleep (**b**) *(ser aconsejable)* **conviene analizar la situación** it would be a good idea to analyze the situation; **no conviene que os vean juntos** it wouldn't be a good idea for them to see you together, it would be better if they didn't see you together; **conviene aclarar que...** it should be made clear that... (**c**) *(acordar)* **c. en** to agree on

  2 *vt* to agree on

convento *nm (de monjas)* convent; *(de monjes)* monastery

conventual *adj* **la vida c.** *(de monjas)* convent life; *(de monjes)* monastic life

convergencia *nf* convergence

convergente *adj* converging, convergent

converger [52] *vi* to converge

conversación *nf* conversation; **dar c. a alguien** to keep sb talking; **conversaciones** *(contactos)* talks; **conversaciones de paz** peace talks

conversada *nf Am Fam* chat

conversador, -ora 1 *adj* talkative

  2 *nm,f* conversationalist

conversar *vi* to talk, to converse; **conversaron de** *o* **sobre política durante dos horas** they talked about *o* discussed politics for two hours

conversión *nf* conversion

converso, -a 1 *adj* converted

  2 *nm,f* convert

convertibilidad *nf Econ* convertibility

convertible *adj* convertible

convertir [25] **1** *vt* (**a**) *Rel* to convert (**b**) *(transformar)* **c. algo/a alguien en** to convert sth/sb into, to turn sth/sb into; **convirtió al príncipe en rana** she turned the prince into a frog (**c**) *(medidas)* **c. millas en kilómetros** to convert miles (in)to kilometers; **c. dólares en pesos** to convert dollars into pesos

  2 convertirse *vpr* (**a**) *Rel* to convert (**a** to) (**b**) *(transformarse)* **convertirse en** to become, to turn into

convexidad *nf* convexity

convexo, -a *adj* convex

convicción *nf* conviction; **tener la c. de que** to be convinced that

convicto, -a *adj* convicted

convidado, -a *nm,f* guest; **estuvo en la cena como el c. de piedra** he sat through the whole meal without saying a word

convidar 1 *vt (invitar)* to invite; **c. a alguien a una copa** to stand *o* buy sb a drink; **me convidaron a comer en su casa** they invited me around for a meal

  2 *vi (mover, incitar)* **el buen tiempo convida a salir** this good weather makes you want to get out

conviene *ver* **convenir**

convierta *etc ver* **convertir**

convincente *adj* convincing

conviniera *etc ver* **convenir**

convite *nm* (**a**) *(invitación)* invitation (**b**) *(fiesta)* banquet

convivencia *nf* living together

convivir *vi* to live together; **c. con** to live with

convocar [59] *vt (reunión)* to convene; *(huelga, elecciones)* to call

convocatoria *nf* (**a**) *(anuncio, escrito)* notice; **c. de huelga** strike (action); **llamar a c.** to summon (**b**) *(de examen)* **tengo el inglés en cuarta c.** this is the fourth time I've had to take this English exam

convoy *(pl* **convoyes**) *nm* (**a**) *(de barcos, camiones)* convoy (**b**) *(tren)* train

convulsión *nf* (**a**) *(de músculos)* convulsion (**b**) *(de tierra)* tremor (**c**) *(política, social)* **un periodo de convulsiones** a period of upheaval

convulsionar *vt* to throw into upheaval

convulsivo, -a *adj* convulsive

convulso, -a *adj* convulsed

conyugal *adj* conjugal; **vida c.** married life

cónyuge *nmf* spouse; **los cónyuges** husband and wife

coña *nf Esp muy Fam* (**a**) *(guasa)* joke; **está de c.** she's just messing around; **¡ni de c.!** no goddamn way! (**b**) *(casualidad)* **acertó de c.** it was a total fluke that he got it right (**c**) *(molestia)* drag, pain; **dar la c.** to be a pain

coñac *(pl* **coñacs**)**, coñá** *(pl* **coñá**) *nm* brandy, cognac

coñazo *nm Esp muy Fam* pain, drag; **dar el c.** to be a pain; **ser un c.** to be goddamn boring

coño *esp Esp Vulg* **1** *nm* (**a**) *(vulva)* cunt, twat; **no me sale del c.** I can't be fucking bothered (**b**) *(para enfatizar)* **¿dónde/qué c....?** where/what the fuck...?; **vive en el quinto c.** she lives fucking miles from anywhere

  2 *interj* (**a**) *(enfado)* **¡c.!** for fuck's sake! (**b**) *(sorpresa)* **¡c.!** fucking hell!

cooperación *nf* cooperation

cooperador, -ora *adj* cooperative

cooperante 1 *adj* cooperating

  2 *nmf* (overseas) volunteer worker

cooperar *vi* to cooperate (**con alguien en algo** with sb in sth)

cooperativa *nf* cooperative; **c. agrícola** farming cooperative; **c. de viviendas** housing cooperative

cooperativismo *nm* cooperative movement

cooperativo, -a *adj* cooperative

coordenadas *nfpl* coordinates; *Mat* **c. cartesianas** Cartesian coordinates

coordinación *nf* coordination

coordinado, -a *adj* coordinated

coordinador, -ora 1 *adj* coordinating

  2 *nm,f* coordinator

coordinadora *nf (organización)* grouping

coordinar *vt* (**a**) *(movimientos, gestos)* to coordinate (**b**) *(esfuerzos, medios)* to combine, to pool

copa *nf* (**a**) *(recipiente)* glass; **una c. de champán** a champagne glass (**b**) *(contenido)* glass; **una c. de vino** a glass of wine; **beber una c. de más** to have a drink too many; **ir de copas** to go out drinking; **¿quieres (tomar) una c.?** would you like (to have) a drink? (**c**) *(trofeo, competición)* cup; **la C. del Mundo** the World Cup (**d**) *(de árbol)* top; *Fig* **una mentira como la c. de un pino** a whopper (of a lie) (**e**) *(de sombrero)* crown (**f**) **copas** *(naipes)* = suit in Spanish deck of cards, with the symbol of a goblet

copar *vt* to monopolize

copartícipe *nmf* *(en empresa)* partner; *(en actividad)* participant

copear *vi Fam* to have a few drinks

Copenhague *n* Copenhagen

copeo *nm Fam* drinking; **ir de c.** to go out drinking

copero, -a *adj Dep* **un equipo c.** a good cup-winning team; **partido c.** = game in a cup competition

copete *nm* (**a**) *(de ave)* crest (**b**) *(de pelo)* tuft (**c**) *Fam* **de alto c.** posh

copetín *nm RP (bebida)* aperitif

copia *nf* (**a**) *(reproducción)* copy; **sacar una c.** to make a copy; *Inform* **c. impresa** hard copy; *Inform* **c. de seguridad** backup; **hacer una c. de seguridad de algo** to make a backup of sth (**b**) *(acción)* copying (**c**) *(persona)* (spitting) image

copiador, -ora *adj* copying

copiadora *nf (máquina)* photocopier

copiar 1 *vt (gen)* & *Inform* to copy; **copió lo que yo iba diciendo** he took down what I was saying

  2 *vi (en examen)* to cheat, to copy

copiloto *nmf* copilot

copión, -ona *nm,f Fam (imitador)* copycat; *(en examen)* cheat

copiosamente *adv (llover)* heavily; **llorar c.** to cry one's eyes out

copioso, -a *adj* abundant

copista *nmf* copyist

copistería *nf (tienda)* copy shop

copla *nf* (a) *(canción)* folk song, popular song; *Fig* **ya está otra vez con la misma c.** he's back on his hobbyhorse (b) *(estrofa)* verse, stanza

copo *nm* (a) *(de nieve, cereales)* flake; **copos de avena** rolled oats (b) *(de algodón)* ball

copón *nm Esp muy Fam* **un lío del c.** a hell of a mess; **nos lo pasamos del c.** we had a hell of a good time

coprocesador *nm Inform* coprocessor; **c. matemático** maths coprocessor

coproducción *nf* coproduction

copropiedad *nf (de empresa)* joint ownership, co-ownership; *(multipropiedad)* timesharing

copropietario, -a *nm,f* co-owner, joint owner

coprotagonista *nmf* costar

coprotagonizar [14] *vt* to costar in

copto, -a 1 *adj* Coptic
  2 *nm (lengua)* Coptic

cópula *nf* (a) *(sexual)* copulation (b) *Gram* copula

copulación *nf (gen)* & *Gram* copulation

copular *vi* to copulate

copulativo, -a *adj Gram* copulative

copyright [kopi'rrait] *nm* copyright

coque *nm* coke

coqueta *nf (tocador)* dressing table

coquetear *vi también Fig* to flirt

coqueteo *nm* flirtation

coquetería *nf* coquetry

coqueto, -a *adj* (a) *(persona) (que flirtea)* flirtatious; *(que se arregla mucho)* concerned with one's appearance (b) *(cosa)* charming, delightful

coraje *nm* (a) *(valor)* courage (b) *(rabia)* anger; **me da mucho c.** it makes me furious

coral 1 *adj* choral
  2 *nm* coral
  3 *nf* (a) *(coro)* choir (b) *(composición)* chorale

coralino, -a *adj* coral

Corán *nm Rel* **el C.** the Koran

coránico, -a *adj Rel* Koranic

coraza *nf* (a) *(de soldado)* cuirass (b) *(de tortuga)* shell (c) *(protección)* shield

corazón *nm* (a) *(de persona, animal, lugar)* heart; **en pleno c. de la ciudad** right in the heart of the city; **a c. abierto** *(operación)* open-heart; **padecer del c.** to have heart trouble; *Fig* **con el c. en la mano** frankly, openly; **de (todo) c.** from the bottom of one's heart, quite sincerely; **se me encoge el c. al ver…** it breaks my heart to see…; **romper** *o* **partir el c. a alguien** to break sb's heart; **no tener c.** to have no heart, to be heartless; **tener un c. de oro** to have a heart of gold (b) *(de frutas)* core (c) *(apelativo)* sweetheart; **¡Ana de mi c.!** Ana, sweetheart! (d) *(dedo)* **c.** middle finger (e) *Rel* **Sagrado C.** Sacred Heart

corazonada *nf* (a) *(presentimiento)* feeling, hunch (b) *(impulso)* sudden impulse

corbata *nf* tie; **c. de** *Chile* **humita** *o Ven* **lacito** *o Méx* **moño** *o Esp* **pajarita** bow tie

corbatín *nm CAm, Carib, Col* bow tie

corbeta *nf Mil* corvette

Córcega *n* Corsica

corcel *nm* steed

corchea *nf Mús* eighth note

corchera *nf (en piscina)* lane marker

corchete *nm* (a) *(broche)* hook and eye (b) *(signo ortográfico)* (square) bracket (c) *Chile (grapa)* staple

corchetear *vt Chile* to staple

corchetera *nf Chile* stapler

corcho *nm* cork

corcholata *nf Méx (metal)* bottle top

córcholis *interj (para expresar sorpresa)* **¡c.!** good heavens!

corcova *nf* hump

corcovado, -a *nm,f* hunchback

cordada *nf* = roped party of mountaineers

cordaje *nm* (a) *(de guitarra, raqueta)* strings (b) *Náut* rigging

cordel *nm* cord; **a c.** in a straight line

cordelería *nf (tienda)* = store selling rope, string, etc

cordero, -a *nm,f también Fig* lamb; **C. de Dios** lamb of God

cordial *adj* cordial

cordialidad *nf* cordiality

cordillera *nf* mountain range; *RP* **la C.** the southern Andes; **la C. Cantábrica** the Cantabrian Mountains

cordobés, -esa 1 *adj* of/from Córdoba
  2 *nm,f* person from Córdoba

cordón *nm* (a) *(cuerda) (gen)* & *Anat* cord; *(de zapato)* lace; **c. umbilical** umbilical cord (b) *(cable eléctrico)* flex (c) *(para protección, vigilancia)* cordon; **c. sanitario** cordon sanitaire (d) *CSur (de la vereda)* curb; **aparcar en c.** to park end-to-end

cordura *nf (juicio)* sanity; *(sensatez)* sense

Corea *n* **C. del Norte/del Sur** North/South Korea

coreana *nf (abrigo)* parka, snorkel jacket

coreano, -a *adj* & *nm,f* Korean

corear *vt (exclamando)* to chorus; *(cantando)* to sing

coreografía *nf* choreography

coreógrafo, -a *nm,f* choreographer

corintio, -a *adj* & *nm,f* Corinthian

corista 1 *nmf (en coro)* chorus singer
  2 *nf (en cabaret)* chorus girl

cormorán *nm* cormorant

cornada *nf Taurom* = wound from bull's horns; **el torero recibió tres cornadas** the bullfighter was gored three times

cornamenta *nf* (a) *(de toro)* horns; *(de ciervo)* antlers (b) *Fam (de marido engañado)* cuckold's horns

cornamusa *nf* (a) *(trompeta)* hunting horn (b) *(gaita)* bagpipes

córnea *nf* cornea

cornear *vt* to gore

corneja *nf* crow

córneo, -a *adj* horny

córner *(pl* **córners)** *nm (en fútbol)* corner (kick)

corneta 1 *nf (instrumento)* bugle
  2 *nmf (persona)* bugler

cornete *nm* (a) *Anat* turbinate bone (b) *(helado)* cornet, cone

cornetín 1 *nm (instrumento)* cornet
  2 *nmf (persona)* cornet player

cornflakes® ['konfleks] *nmpl* Cornflakes®

cornisa *nf* (a) *Arquit* cornice (b) *Geog* **la c. cantábrica** the Cantabrian coast

cornucopia *nf* (a) *(espejo)* = small decorative mirror (b) *(cuerno)* cornucopia, horn of plenty

cornudo, -a 1 *adj* (a) *(animal)* horned (b) *Fam (marido)* cuckolded
  2 *nm Fam* cuckold

coro *nm* (a) *(grupo de voces, parte de iglesia)* choir; **contestar a c.** to answer all at once (b) *(de obra musical)* chorus

corola *nf* corolla

corolario *nm* corollary

corona *nf* (a) *(de monarca)* crown (b) **la c.** *(la monarquía)* the Crown (c) *(de flores)* garland; **c. fúnebre/de laurel** funeral/laurel wreath (d) *(de santos)* halo

coronación *nf* (a) *(de monarca)* coronation (b) *(remate, colmo)* culmination

coronamiento *nm* (**a**) *(remate, fin)* culmination (**b**) *Arquit* crown

coronar *vt* (**a**) *(persona)* to crown (**b**) *(terminar)* to complete; *(culminar)* to crown, to cap (**c**) *(cima)* to reach

coronario, -a *adj Anat* coronary

coronel *nm Mil* colonel

coronilla *nf* crown (of the head); *Fam* **estar hasta la c. (de)** to be sick and tired (of)

corotos *nmpl Carib Fam* things, whatnots

corpachón *nm* big body, big frame

corpiño *nm* (**a**) *(de vestido, top)* bodice (**b**) *Arg (sostén)* bra

corporación *nf* corporation; **corporaciones locales** local authorities

corporal *adj (calor)* body; *(trabajo, daño)* physical; *(castigo)* corporal

corporativismo *nm Pol* = self-interested behavior, especially of professional groups

corporativo, -a *adj* corporate

corpóreo, -a *adj* corporeal

corpulencia *nf* corpulence

corpulento, -a *adj* corpulent

corpus *(pl inv o* **corpora)** *nm* corpus

Corpus Christi ['korpus 'kristi] *nm Rel* Corpus Christi

corpúsculo *nm* corpuscle

corral *nm* (**a**) *(para aves)* run; *(para cerdos, ovejas)* pen (**b**) *Hist (para teatro)* = open-air theater in courtyard

corrala *nf* = building with several floors of small apartments on running balconies round a central courtyard

corralito *nm (para niños)* playpen

correa *nf* (**a**) *(de bolso, reloj)* strap; *(cinturón)* belt; *(de perro)* leash, lead (**b**) *Tec* belt; **c. del ventilador** fan belt

correaje *nm (de caballo)* harness; *(de soldado)* equipment belts

corrección *nf* (**a**) *(de error)* correction; *(de examen)* marking; *(de texto)* revision; **c. de pruebas** proofreading (**b**) *(perfección)* correctness (**c**) *(de comportamiento)* correctness, courtesy; **c. política** political correctness (**d**) *(reprimenda)* reprimand

correccional *nm* reformatory, reform school

correctivo, -a 1 *adj* corrective

   2 *nm* punishment

correcto, -a *adj* (**a**) *(resultado, texto, respuesta)* correct (**b**) *(persona)* polite; *(conducta)* proper

corrector, -ora 1 *adj* corrective

   2 *nm,f* **c. de estilo** copy editor; **c. (de pruebas)** proofreader

   3 *nm Inform* **c. de estilo** style-checker; **c. ortográfico** spell-checker

corredera *nf (ranura)* runner; **puerta de c.** sliding door

corredero, -a *adj* sliding

corredizo, -a *adj* **nudo c.** slipknot

corredor, -ora 1 *adj* running; **ave corredora** large flightless bird

   2 *nm,f* (**a**) *(deportista)* runner; **c. de cross** cross-country runner; **c. de fondo** long-distance runner; *Fig* **ser un c. de fondo** to have staying power (**b**) *Fin & Com (intermediario)* **c. de apuestas** bookmaker; **c. de bolsa** stockbroker; **c. de comercio** registered broker; **c. de fincas** land agent; **c. de seguros** insurance broker

   3 *nm (pasillo)* corridor, passage

correduría *nf Com* **c. de seguros** *(oficina)* insurance broker's

corregidor, -ora *nm,f Hist* = magistrate appointed by the king, especially in former Spanish colonies

corregir [55] **1** *vt* (**a**) *(error)* to correct; *(examen)* to mark; **corrígeme si me equivoco, pero creo que...** correct me if I'm wrong, but I think... (**b**) *(reprender)* to reprimand

   2 corregirse *vpr* to change for the better

correlación *nf* correlation

correlacionar *vt* to correlate

correlativo, -a *adj* correlative

correligionario, -a *nm,f (en política, ideología)* person of the same ideological persuasion; *(en religión)* fellow believer; **Churchill y sus correligionarios** Churchill and his fellow conservatives

correo 1 *adj* **tren c.** mail train

   2 *nm* mail; **a vuelta de c.** by return mail; **echar algo al c.** to mail sth; **mandar algo por c.** to send sth by mail; *Esp* **Correos** *(organismo)* the post office; **c. aéreo** airmail; *Inform* **c. basura** junk mail, spam; **c. caracol** snail mail; **c. certificado** registered mail; **c. comercial** direct mail; **c. electrónico** *(sistema)* e-mail, electronic mail; **enviar un c. (electrónico) a alguien** to e-mail sb, to send sb an e-mail; **c. urgente** ≃ special delivery; **c. de voz** voice mail

correoso, -a *adj (carne)* leathery, tough; *(pan)* chewy

correr1 *vi* (**a**) *(persona, animal)* to run; **me gusta c. todas las mañanas** I like to go for a run every morning; **¡corre a pedir ayuda!** run for help!; **a todo c.** at full speed *o* pelt

   (**b**) *(apresurarse)* **¡corre, que vamos a perder el autobús!** hurry up, we're going to miss the bus!; **no corras, que te vas a equivocar** don't rush yourself, or you'll make a mistake

   (**c**) *(conductor)* to drive fast

   (**d**) *(río)* to flow; *(camino, agua del grifo)* to run

   (**e**) *(el tiempo, las horas)* to pass, to go by; **esta última semana ha pasado corriendo** this last week has flown by

   (**f**) *(noticia)* to spread; **corre el rumor de que...** there's a rumor that...

   (**g**) **c. con los gastos (de algo)** to bear the cost (of sth); **c. a cargo de** to be taken care of by

   2 *vt* (**a**) *(recorrer) (una distancia)* to cover; **corrió los 100 metros** he ran the 100 meters (**b**) *(mover) (mesa, silla)* to move *o* pull up; **corre la cabeza, que no veo** move your head out of the way, I can't see (**c**) *(cerrar)* **c. las cortinas** to draw the curtains; **c. el pestillo** to bolt the door (**d**) *(experimentar)* **c. aventuras** to have adventures; **c. peligro** to be in danger; **c. el riesgo de (hacer) algo** to run the risk of (doing) sth (**e**) *Fam Inform (programa, aplicación)* to run

   3 correrse *vpr* (**a**) *(desplazarse) (persona)* to move over; *(cosa)* to slide (**b**) *(pintura, colores)* to run; **se me ha corrido el rímel** my mascara has run (**c**) *Andes, Esp muy Fam* to come; *Esp Fig* **correrse de gusto (con algo)** *(disfrutar)* to get off (on sth)

correría *nf* foray

correspondencia *nf* (**a**) *(relación)* correspondence (**b**) *(correo)* correspondence; **mantengo c. con ella** she and I write to each other; **¿te importaría recogerme mi c.?** would you mind picking up my mail for me? (**c**) *(de metro, tren)* connection; **próxima estación, Sol, c. con línea tres** next stop Sol, change here for line three

corresponder 1 *vi* (**a**) *(compensar)* **c. (con algo) a alguien/algo** to repay sb/sth (with sth); **ella nunca correspondió a mi amor** she never returned my love, she never felt the same way about me (**b**) *(tocar)* **les corresponde un millón a cada uno** they get *o* they're due one million each (**c**) *(coincidir)* to correspond (**a/con** to/with) (**d**) *(competer)* **corresponderle a alguien hacer algo** to be sb's responsibility to do sth (**e**) *(ser adecuado)* to be right *o* fitting; **voy a darle las gracias como corresponde** I'm going to thank him, as is only right

   2 *vt (sentimiento)* to repay; **ella no le correspondía** she didn't feel the same way about him; **amor no correspondido** unrequited love

   3 corresponderse *vpr* (**a**) *(escribirse)* to correspond (**b**) *(amarse)* to love each other

correspondiente *adj* (**a**) *(perteneciente, relativo)* corresponding (**a** to); **trajo todos los documentos correspondientes al tema** he brought all the documents relevant to the subject; **el presupuesto c. al ejercicio de 2001** the budget for 2001 (**b**) *(respectivo)* respective; **cada uno tomó su parte c.** each person took their own share (**c**) *(lógico)* **llegó tarde, con el c. disgusto de sus padres** he arrived late, to the understandable annoyance of his parents

corresponsal *nmf* (**a**) *Prensa* correspondent (**b**) *Com* agent

corresponsalía *nf* post of correspondent

corretaje *nm Com* brokerage

corretear *vi* (**a**) *(correr)* to run around (**b**) *Fam (vagar)* to hang around (**c**) *Méx (adelantar)* to overtake

correveidile *nmf* gossip

corrida *nf* (**a**) *Taurom* bullfight (**b**) *(acción de correr)* run

corrido, -a 1 *adj* (**a**) *(cortinas)* drawn (**b**) *(avergonzado)* embarrassed (**c**) *(continuo)* continuous; **balcón c.** long balcony *(running across building)*; **banco c.** long bench; *Fig* **de c.** by heart; **recitar algo de c.** to recite sth like a parrot
2 *nm (canción mejicana)* Mexican ballad

corriente 1 *adj* (**a**) *(normal)* ordinary, normal; **un reloj normal y c.** an ordinary watch; *Fam* **c. y moliente** run-of-the-mill (**b**) *(agua)* running (**c**) *(mes, año, cuenta)* current
2 *nf* (**a**) *(de río, electricidad)* current; **le dio la c. al tocar el enchufe** she got an electric shock when she touched the socket; **c. alterna/continua** alternating/direct current; **la c. del Golfo** the Gulf Stream (**b**) *(de aire)* draft (**c**) *(tendencia)* trend, current; *(de opinión)* tide; **c. de pensamiento** school of thought (**d**) *(expresiones)* **dejarse llevar de** o **por la c.** to follow the crowd; **ir contra c.** to go against the tide; *Fam* **llevarle** o **seguirle la c. a alguien** to humor sb
3 al corriente *loc adv* **mantener** o **tener al alguien al c. de algo** to keep sb informed about sth; **ponerse al c.** to bring oneself up to date; **está al c. de la noticia** he has heard the news

corrigió *ver* **corregir**

corrijo *ver* **corregir**

corrillo *nm* knot o small group of people; **formar corrillos** to go into huddles

corrimiento *nm* shift, slipping; **c. de tierras** landslide

corro *nm* (**a**) *(círculo)* circle, ring; **en c.** in a circle; **hacer c.** to form a circle (**b**) *Bolsa* ring, pit

corroboración *nf* corroboration

corroborar *vt* to corroborate

corroer [57] *vt* (**a**) *(desgastar)* to corrode; *Geol* to erode (**b**) *(consumir)* to consume, to eat away at; **le corroe la envidia** he's consumed with envy

corromper 1 *vt* (**a**) *(madera)* to rot; *(alimentos)* to turn bad, to spoil (**b**) *(pervertir)* to corrupt (**c**) *(sobornar)* to bribe
2 corromperse *vpr* (**a**) *(pudrirse)* to rot (**b**) *(pervertirse)* to become corrupted

corrosión *nf (desgaste)* corrosion; *(de un metal)* rust; *Geol* erosion

corrosivo, -a *adj también Fig* corrosive

corrupción *nf* (**a**) *(delito, decadencia)* corruption; *Der* **c. de menores** corruption of minors (**b**) *(soborno)* bribery (**c**) *(de una sustancia)* decay

corruptela *nf* corruption

corrupto, -a *adj* corrupt

corruptor, -ora 1 *adj* corrupting
2 *nm,f* corrupter; *Der* **c. de menores** corrupter of minors

corrusco *nm* hard crust

corsario, -a 1 *adj* pirate; **un buque c.** a pirate ship
2 *nm* corsair, pirate

corsé *nm* corset

corsetería *nf* ladies' lingerie store

corso, -a 1 *adj & nm,f* Corsican
2 *nm (dialecto)* Corsican

cortacésped *nm* lawn mower

cortacircuitos *nm inv* circuit breaker

cortado, -a 1 *adj* (**a**) *(labios, manos)* chapped (**b**) *(leche)* sour, spoiled; *(mayonesa)* spoiled (**c**) *Fam (persona)* **estar c.** to be inhibited; **quedarse c.** to be left speechless; **ser c.** to be shy
2 *nm* (**a**) *(café)* = small coffee with just a little milk (**b**) *Fam (persona)* **ser un c.** to be shy

cortador, -ora 1 *adj* cutting
2 *nm (de césped)* lawn mower

cortadora *nf* cutter; **c. de césped** lawn mower

cortadura *nf* cut

cortafuego *nm* firebreak

cortante *adj* (**a**) *(afilado)* sharp (**b**) *(tajante) (frase, estilo)* cutting; *(viento)* biting; *(frío)* bitter

cortapisa *nf* limitation, restriction

cortaplumas *nm inv* penknife

cortapuros *nm inv* cigar cutter

cortar 1 *vt* (**a**) *(seccionar)* to cut; *(en pedazos)* to cut up; *(escindir) (rama, brazo, cabeza)* to cut off; *(talar)* to cut down; **c. una rebanada de pan** to cut a slice of bread; **corta la tarta en cinco partes** divide the cake in five, cut the cake into five slices; **cortarle el pelo a alguien** to cut sb's hair; *Inform* **c. y pegar** cut and paste
(**b**) *(recortar) (tela, figura de papel)* to cut out; *(gastos)* to cut back
(**c**) *(labios, piel)* to crack, to chap
(**d**) *(hender) (aire, olas)* to slice through
(**e**) *(baraja)* to cut
(**f**) *(leche)* to curdle
(**g**) *(interrumpir) (retirada, luz, teléfono)* to cut off; *(carretera)* to block (off); *(hemorragia)* to stop, to staunch; *(discurso, conversación)* to interrupt; **c. el tráfico** to close the road to traffic
(**h**) *(poner fin a) (beca)* to cut; *(abusos)* to put a stop to; **c. un problema de raíz** *(impedirlo)* to nip a problem in the bud; *(erradicarlo)* to root a problem out
(**i**) *Fam (avergonzar)* **este hombre me corta un poco** I find it hard to be myself when that man's around
2 *vi* (**a**) *(producir un corte)* to cut; **estas tijeras no cortan** these scissors don't cut (properly); *Fig* **c. por lo sano** *(aplicar una solución drástica)* to resort to drastic measures; *(para evitar más pérdidas)* to cut one's losses (**b**) *(atajar)* to take a shortcut (**por** through) (**c**) *(terminar una relación)* to split up (**con** with); **corté con mi novio** I've split up with my boyfriend
3 cortarse *vpr* (**a**) *(herirse)* to cut oneself; **cortarse con un cristal** to cut oneself on a piece of glass; **cortarse (en) la cara** to cut one's face; **cortarse el pelo** to have a haircut, to have one's hair cut
(**b**) *(labios, piel)* to become chapped o cracked
(**c**) *(leche)* to curdle
(**d**) *(interrumpirse)* **se cortó la comunicación** I was/we were *etc* cut off; **se te va a c. la digestión** you'll get stomach cramps
(**e**) *Fam (turbarse)* to become tongue-tied; **no te cortes, sírvete lo que te apetezca** don't be shy o polite, take whatever you want; **no se corta a la hora de criticar** he doesn't mince his words o hold back when he has criticisms to make

cortaúñas *nm inv* nail clippers

cortavientos *nm inv* windbreak

corte 1 *nm* (**a**) *(raja)* cut; **se hizo un c. en la rodilla** he cut his knee; **c. y confección** *(para mujeres)* dressmaking; *(para hombres)* tailoring; **c. de pelo** haircut
(**b**) *(retal de tela)* length
(**c**) *(contorno)* shape
(**d**) *(interrupción)* **c. de luz** power cut; **c. de digestión** stomach cramps
(**e**) *(sección)* section
(**f**) *(concepción, estilo)* style
(**g**) *(pausa)* break; **c. publicitario** commercial break

(**h**) *Esp (filo)* (cutting) edge

(**i**) *Am (reducción) (presupuestario, salarial)* cut, cutback

(**j**) *Fam (vergüenza)* embarrassment; **dar c. a alguien** to embarrass sb; **me da c. decírselo** I feel embarrassed to tell him

(**k**) *Fam (respuesta ingeniosa)* put-down; **dar** *o* **pegar un c. a alguien** to cut sb dead

(**l**) **c. de mangas** = obscene gesture involving raising one arm with a clenched fist and placing one's other hand in the crook of one's elbow; *Fig* **hacer un c. de mangas a alguien** ≃ to give sb the finger

2 *nf* (**a**) *(del rey)* court; *Esp* **las Cortes (Generales)** *(cámara legislativa)* the Spanish parliament (**b**) *(galanteo)* **hacer la c. a alguien** to court sb (**c**) *esp Am (tribunal)* court; **C. Penal Internacional** International Criminal Court

cortedad *nf* (**a**) *(de longitud)* shortness; *(de duración)* shortness, brevity (**b**) *(timidez)* shyness; **c. de miras** shortsightedness

cortejar *vt* to court

cortejo *nm* retinue; **c. fúnebre** funeral cortege *o* procession

cortés *(pl* **corteses)** *adj* polite, courteous

cortesana *nf (prostituta)* courtesan

cortesano, -a 1 *adj (modales)* courtly; **la vida cortesana** life at court

2 *nm,f (personaje de la corte)* courtier

cortesía *nf* courtesy; **las trataron con c.** they were treated courteously *o* politely; **por c. de** courtesy of; **tuvo la c. de llamarme** he was kind enough to phone me; **de c.** courtesy; **una visita de c.** a courtesy call; **le daremos diez minutos de c.** we'll give him ten minutes

córtex *nm inv Anat* cortex

corteza *nf* (**a**) *(del árbol)* bark (**b**) *(de pan)* crust; *(de queso, tocino, limón)* rind; *(de naranja)* peel; **cortezas de cerdo** pork cracklings (**c**) *Geol (terrestre)* crust (**d**) *Anat* cortex

cortical *adj* cortical

corticoide *nm* corticoid

cortijo *nm (finca)* farm *(typical of Andalusia and Extremadura)*; *(casa)* farmhouse

cortina *nf (de tela)* curtain; *Fig* **c. de agua** sheet of water; *Am Hist* **c. de hierro** Iron Curtain; *también Fig* **c. de humo** smoke screen

cortinaje *nm* curtains

cortisona *nf* cortisone

corto, -a 1 *adj* (**a**) *(de poca longitud, duración)* short; **las mangas me están cortas** my sleeves are too short; **el paseo se me ha hecho muy c.** the walk seemed to go very quickly (**b**) *(escaso) (raciones)* small, meager; **c. de** *(dinero)* short of; *Fig* **c. de miras** shortsighted; **c. de vista** shortsighted (**c**) *(tonto)* **c. (de alcances)** dim, simple (**d**) *(expresiones)* **ni c. ni perezoso** just like that; **quedarse c.** *(al calcular)* to underestimate; **nos quedamos cortos al comprar pan** we didn't buy enough bread

2 *nm Cine* short (movie)

cortocircuito *nm* short circuit

cortometraje *nm* short (film)

coruñés, -esa 1 *adj* of/from La Coruña

2 *nm,f* person from La Coruña

corva *nf* back of the knee

corvo, -a *adj (curvado)* curved; *(nariz)* hooked

corzo, -a *nm,f* roebuck, *f* roe deer

cosa *nf* (**a**) *(objeto, idea)* thing; **tengo que decirte una c.** I've got something to tell you; **¿quieres alguna c.?** is there anything you want?; **cualquier c.** anything; **no es gran c.** it's not important, it's no big deal; **poca c.** nothing much

(**b**) *(asunto)* **tengo muchas cosas que hacer** I've got a lot (of things) to do; **eso es c. mía** that's my affair *o* business; **eso es c. fácil** that's easy; **cada c. a su tiempo** one thing at a time

(**c**) *(ocurrencia)* funny remark; **¡qué cosas tienes!** you do say some funny things!; **son cosas de mamá** that's just the way Mom is, that's just one of Mom's little idiosyncrasies

(**d**) *Fam (reparo)* **me da c. decírselo** I'm a bit uneasy about telling him

(**e**) *(expresiones)* **c. de** about; **tardará c. de tres semanas** it'll take about three weeks; **se presentó al examen a c. hecha** he took the exam although he knew he was certain to pass; **hacer algo como quien no quiere la c.** *(disimuladamente)* to do sth innocently; *(sin querer)* to do sth almost without realizing it; **como si tal c.** as if nothing had happened; **entre unas cosas y otras** what with one thing and another; **no era c. de presentarse sin avisar** you couldn't just turn up without warning; **tendrá treinta años o c. así** he must be thirty or thereabouts; **y cosas así** and so on; **¡qué c.!** how strange!; **la c. se pone fea** things are getting ugly, there's trouble brewing; **las cosas como son, nunca vas a aprobar ese examen** let's face it, you're never going to pass that exam

cosaco, -a 1 *adj* Cossack

2 *nm,f* Cossack; **beber como un c.** to drink like a fish

coscorrón *nm* bump on the head; **se dio un c.** he bumped his head

cosecante *nf Mat* cosecant

cosecha *nf* (**a**) *Agr* harvest; *Fam Fig* **ser de la (propia) c. de alguien** to be made up *o* invented by sb (**b**) *(del vino)* vintage

cosechadora *nf* combine (harvester)

cosechar 1 *vt* (**a**) *(cultivar)* to grow (**b**) *(recolectar)* to harvest (**c**) *(obtener)* to win, to reap; **su última novela ha cosechado muchos éxitos** his latest novel has been a great success; **cosechó numerosas críticas por sus declaraciones** he received a lot of criticism for his statement; **el equipo cubano cosechó veinte medallas en los campeonatos** the Cuban team picked up twenty medals at the championships

2 *vi* to (bring in the) harvest

cosechero, -a *nm,f (de cereales)* harvester, reaper; *(de frutos)* picker

coseno *nm Mat* cosine

coser 1 *vt* (**a**) *(con hilo)* to sew; **c. un botón** to sew on a button (**b**) *(con grapas)* to staple (together) (**c**) *(expresiones)* **c. a alguien a balazos** to riddle sb with bullets; **c. a cuchilladas** to stab repeatedly

2 *vi* to sew; *Fam Fig* **ser c. y cantar** to be child's play *o* a piece of cake

cosido *nm* stitching

cosmética *nf* cosmetics

cosmético, -a 1 *adj* cosmetic; **productos cosméticos** cosmetics

2 *nm* cosmetic

cósmico, -a *adj* cosmic

cosmogonía *nf* cosmogony

cosmografía *nf* cosmography

cosmología *nf* cosmology

cosmonauta *nmf* cosmonaut

cosmopolita *adj & nmf* cosmopolitan

cosmos *nm inv* cosmos

cosmovisión *nf* world view

coso *nm* (**a**) *Taurom (plaza)* bullring (**b**) *CSur Fam (objeto)* whatnot, thing

cosquillas *nfpl* **hacer c.** to tickle; **tener c.** to be ticklish; *Fig* **buscarle las c. a alguien** to provoke sb, to irritate sb

cosquilleo *nm* tickling sensation

costa *nf* (**a**) *(litoral)* coast; **pasan las vacaciones en la c.** they spend their vacations on the coast; **la C. Azul** the Côte d'Azur; **la C. Brava** the Costa Brava (**b**) *(coste)* **a c. de** at the expense of; **lo hizo a c. de grandes esfuerzos** he did it by dint of much effort; **aún vive a c. de sus padres** he's still living off his parents; **a toda c.** at all costs; *Der* **costas (judiciales)** *(legal)* costs (**c**) **C. de Marfil** Ivory Coast

costado *nm* side; **de c.** sideways

costal 1 *adj Med* rib, costal; **tiene una fractura c.** he has a fractured rib
  2 *nm* sack

costalada *nf,* **costalazo** *nm* heavy fall *(backward)*; **darse una c.** to fall over backward

costanera *nf CSur* promenade

costar [63] *vi* (**a**) *(dinero)* to cost; **¿cuánto cuesta?** how much is it?; **me costó 3.000 pesos** it cost me 3,000 pesos; **costó muy barato** it was very cheap; *Fig* **c. un ojo de la cara** *o* **un riñón** to cost an arm and a leg
  (**b**) *(tiempo)* to take; **nos costó seis horas llegar** it took us six hours to get there
  (**c**) *(ser difícil, penoso)* **me costó decírselo** I found it difficult to tell him; **a este niño le cuesta dormirse** this child has difficulty getting to sleep; **no le habría costado nada ayudarme** it wouldn't have cost him anything to help me; **c. trabajo** to be difficult, to take a lot of work; **me costó (trabajo) acostumbrarme** it took me a while to get used to it; **cuesta (trabajo) abrir esa puerta** this door is difficult to open
  (**d**) *(expresiones)* **c. caro a alguien** to cost sb dearly; **cueste lo que cueste** whatever the cost; **le costó la vida** it cost him his life

Costa Rica *n* Costa Rica

costarricense, costarriqueño, -a *adj & nm,f* Costa Rican

coste *nm Esp (de producción)* cost; *(de un objeto)* price; **c. de distribución** distribution cost; **costes de explotación** operating costs; **costes fijos** fixed costs; **costes indirectos** indirect costs; **costes de mano de obra** labor costs; **c. de sustitución** replacement cost; **c. de la vida** cost of living; **c. unitario** unit cost; **costes variables** variable costs

costear 1 *vt* (**a**) *(pagar)* to pay for (**b**) *Náut (la costa)* to hug, to keep close to
  2 costearse *vpr* **costearse algo** *(pagarse)* to pay for sth oneself; **trabaja para costearse los estudios** she's working to pay for her studies

costeño, -a, costero, -a 1 *adj* coastal; **un pueblo c.** a seaside town
  2 *nm,f Am* = person from the coast

costera *nf Méx* promenade

costero, -a = **costeño**

costilla *nf* (**a**) *Anat & Náut* rib; *Fam* **costillas** *(espalda)* back (**b**) *Culin* cutlet; **costillas de cerdo** pork chops (**c**) *Fam (cónyuge)* better half

costillar *nm (de persona)* ribs, rib cage; *(de carne)* side

costo *nm* (**a**) *(de producción)* cost; *(de un objeto)* price; **c. de distribución** distribution cost; **costos de explotación** operating costs; **costos fijos** fixed costs; **costos indirectos** indirect costs; **costos de mano de obra** labor costs; **c. de sustitución** replacement cost; **c. de la vida** cost of living; **c. unitario** unit cost; **costos variables** variable costs (**b**) *Esp Fam (hachís)* hash

costoso, -a *adj (operación, maquinaria)* expensive; *(trabajo)* exhausting; *(triunfo)* costly

costra *nf (de suciedad, de tierra)* layer, crust; *(de pan)* crust; *(de herida)* scab

costumbre *nf* habit, custom; **tomar/perder la c. de hacer algo** to get into/out of the habit of doing sth; **como de c.** as usual; **la cantidad de c.** the usual amount; **tener la c. de** *o* **tener por c. hacer algo** to be in the habit of doing sth; **costumbres** *(de país, cultura)* customs; *(de persona)* habits; **no hay que perder las buenas costumbres** we don't want to break with tradition

costumbrismo *nm* = literary style that deals with typical regional or national customs

costumbrista *adj (novela)* = describing the customs of a country or region

costura *nf* (**a**) *(labor)* sewing, needlework (**b**) *(en tela)* seam (**c**) *(oficio)* dressmaking; **alta c.** haute couture (**d**) *(cicatriz)* scar

costurera *nf* dressmaker, seamstress

costurero *nm (caja)* sewing box

cota *nf* (**a**) *(altura)* altitude, height above sea level (**b**) *(armadura)* **c. de malla(s)** coat of mail (**c**) *(nivel)* **alcanzar altas cotas de popularidad** to become very popular

cotangente *nf Mat* cotangent

cotarro *nm Fam* riotous gathering; **dirigir el c.** to rule the roost, to be the boss

cotejar *vt* to compare

cotejo *nm* comparison

cotice *etc ver* **cotizar**

cotidianidad *nf (vida cotidiana)* everyday life; *(frecuencia)* commonness

cotidiano, -a *adj* daily; **el trabajo c.** day-to-day tasks; **ser algo c.** to be an everyday occurrence

cotiledón *nm* cotyledon

cotilla *Esp Fam* **1** *adj* gossipy
  2 *nmf* gossip, busybody

cotillear *vi Esp Fam* to gossip

cotilleo *nm Esp Fam* gossip, tittle-tattle; **tengo que contarte un c.** I've got a bit of gossip to tell you

cotillón *nm* = party on New Year's Eve or January 5

cotizable *adj* quotable

cotización *nf* (**a**) *(valor)* value (**b**) *(en Bolsa)* quotation, price (**c**) *(a la seguridad social)* contribution

cotizado, -a *adj* (**a**) *(en Bolsa)* quoted (**b**) *(persona)* sought-after

cotizar [14] **1** *vt* (**a**) *(valorar)* to quote, to price (**b**) *(pagar)* to pay
  2 *vi Com (pagar)* to contribute; **los trabajadores tienen que c. a la seguridad social** employees have to pay Social Security contributions
  3 cotizarse *vpr* (**a**) *(estimarse)* to be valued *o* prized; **el conocimiento de idiomas se cotiza mucho** a knowledge of foreign languages is considered extremely important (**b**) **cotizarse a** *(producto)* to sell for, to fetch; *(bonos, valores)* to be quoted at

coto *nm* preserve; **c. de caza** game preserve; *Fig* **poner c. a** to put a stop to

cotorra *nf* (**a**) *(ave)* parrot (**b**) *Fam (persona)* chatterbox; **hablar como una c.** to talk nineteen to the dozen

cotorrear *vi Fam* to chatter

cotufa *nf* Jerusalem artichoke

coturno *nm* buskin

COU [kou] *nm Antes (abrev de* **Curso de Orientación Universitaria**) = one-year course which prepared pupils aged 17-18 for Spanish university entrance examinations

couché *adj* **papel c.** glossy paper

country ['kauntri] **1** *adj* **estilo c.** country (and western) style
  2 *nm* country (and western) music

covacha *nf* hovel

coxal *adj* hip; **fractura c.** hip fracture

coxis *nm inv* coccyx

coyote *nm* (**a**) *(coyote)* coyote (**b**) *Méx Fam (intermediario)* fixer, middleman

coyotear *vi Méx Fam* to wheel and deal

coyuntura *nf* (**a**) *(situación)* moment; **la c. económica** the economic situation (**b**) *(articulación)* joint

coyuntural *adj* temporary, provisional

coz *nf* kick; *Fam Fig* **tratar a alguien a coces** to treat sb like dirt

CPI *nf* (*abrev de* **Corte Penal Internacional**) ICC

cps *Inform* (*abrev de* **caracteres por segundo**) cps

CPU *nf Inform* (*abrev de* **Central Processing Unit**) CPU

crac (*pl* **cracs**) *nm Fin* crash

crack [krak] (*pl* **cracks**) *nm* (**a**) (*estrella*) star, superstar (**b**) *Fin* crash (**c**) (*droga*) crack

cracker (*pl* **crackers**) *nmf Fam Inform* cracker

crampón *nm* crampon

craneal *adj* cranial

cráneo *nm* cranium, skull; *Fam* **ir de c.** to be doing badly

crápula *nmf* libertine

craso, -a *adj* (**a**) (*grave*) (*error*) serious; (*ignorancia*) astonishing (**b**) (*grueso*) fat

cráter *nm* crater

crayón *nm Méx, Arg* (*lápiz*) wax crayon

creación *nf* creation; **c. de empleo** job creation

creador, -ora 1 *adj* creative

2 *nm,f* creator; **c. gráfico** creator (*of cartoon etc*); **el C.** the Creator

crear 1 *vt* (**a**) (*hacer, producir, originar*) to create; **me crea muchos problemas** it gives me a lot of trouble, it causes me a lot of problems; **Picasso creó escuela** Picasso's works have had a seminal influence (**b**) (*inventar*) to invent (**c**) (*fundar*) to found

2 crearse *vpr* (*inventarse*) **se ha creado un mundo de fantasía** he lives in his own little world; **se crea problemas él solo** he imagines problems where there aren't any

creatividad *nf* creativity

creativo, -a 1 *adj* creative

2 *nm,f* (*en publicidad*) ideas man, *f* ideas woman

crecepelo *nm* hair tonic *o* restorer

crecer [46] **1** *vi* (**a**) (*persona, planta*) to grow (**b**) (*días, noches*) to grow longer (**c**) (*río, marea*) to rise (**d**) (*aumentar*) (*desempleo, valor*) to rise, to increase; (*valor*) to increase (**e**) (*la luna*) to wax

2 crecerse *vpr* to become more self-confident; **crecerse ante las dificultades** to thrive in the face of adversity

creces *nmpl* **le devolvieron con c. el dinero que les prestó** they paid back the money he lent them with interest; **los italianos nos superan con c.** the Italians are a lot better than us; **es el mejor con c.** he is by far the best; **la oferta supera con c. a la demanda** supply far exceeds demand; **cumplió con c. el trabajo que se le encargó** he more than fulfilled the task he had been given

crecida *nf* spate, flood

crecido, -a *adj* (*cantidad*) large; (*hijo*) grown-up

creciente *adj* (*seguridad, confianza*) growing; (*luna*) crescent, waxing

crecimiento *nm* (*desarrollo*) growth; (*de precios*) rise; **c. económico** economic growth; **c. exponencial** exponential growth; **c. sostenible** sustainable growth

credencial 1 *adj* accrediting

2 *nf* (*de acceso a un lugar*) pass; **credenciales (diplomáticas)** credentials

credibilidad *nf* credibility

crediticio, -a *adj* credit; **entidad crediticia** credit institution, lender

crédito *nm* (**a**) (*préstamo*) loan; (**comprar algo**) **a c.** (to buy sth) on credit; **c. bancario** bank loan; **c. blando** soft loan; **c. al consumo** consumer credit; **c. a la exportación** export credit; **c. hipotecario** mortgage (loan); **c. oficial** official credit; **c. personal** personal loan (**b**) (*plazo de préstamo*) credit (**c**) (*confianza*) trust, belief; **digno de c.** trustworthy; **dar c. a algo** to believe sth; **¡no doy c. a mis oídos!** I can't believe my ears! (**d**) (*fama*) standing, reputation (**e**) (*en universidad*) credit (**f**) *Cine* **títulos de c.** credits

credo *nm* (**a**) (*religioso*) creed (**b**) (*ideológico, político*) credo

credulidad *nf* credulity

crédulo, -a 1 *adj* credulous, gullible

2 *nm,f* credulous *o* gullible person

creencia *nf* belief; **cada cual es libre de tener sus creencias** everyone is entitled to their own opinion; **es una c. popular** it's a commonly held opinion

creer [37] **1** *vt* (**a**) (*estar convencido de*) to believe; **créeme, sólo quería ayudar** believe me *o* honestly, I only wanted to help; **¡ya lo creo!** of course! (**b**) (*suponer, pensar*) to think; **no creo, creo que no** I don't think so; **creo que sí** I think so; **creo que ha sido Sara** I think it was Sara; **¡quién lo hubiera creído!** who would have thought it!; **c. a alguien capaz de hacer algo** to believe sb to be capable of doing sth

2 *vi* to believe (**en** in); **debe de ser bastante interesante — no creas,...** it must be very interesting — far from it *o* don't you believe it,...

3 creerse *vpr* (**a**) (*considerarse*) **se cree Dios** he thinks he's God; **¿pero tú quién te has creído que eres?** just who do you think you are? (**b**) (*dar por cierto*) to believe completely; **no me lo creo** *o* **puedo c.** I can't *o* don't believe it

creíble *adj* credible, believable

creído, -a *adj* (*presumido*) conceited

crema 1 *nf* (**a**) (*para la piel, sopa*) cream; **c. de base** foundation cream; **c. de cacao** cocoa butter; **c. de espárragos** cream of asparagus (soup); **c. facial** face cream; **c. hidratante** moisturizer; **c. de manos** hand cream; **c. de marisco** seafood bisque; **c. pastelera** (confectioner's) custard; **c. para zapatos** shoe polish (**b**) *esp Am* (*de leche*) cream; **c. líquida** cream

2 *adj* cream; **color c.** cream(-colored)

cremación *nf* cremation

cremallera *nf* (**a**) (*para cerrar*) zipper (**b**) *Tec* rack

crematístico, -a *adj* financial

crematorio, -a 1 *adj* **horno c.** cremator

2 *nm* crematorium

cremoso, -a *adj* creamy

crepe *nm, Méx* **crepa** *nf* (*torta*) crêpe

crepé *nm* (*tejido*) crepe

crepitar *vi* to crackle

crepuscular *adj* crepuscular, twilight; **luz c.** twilight

crepúsculo *nm* (*al amanecer*) first light; (*al anochecer*) twilight, dusk; *Fig* **en el c. de su vida** in his twilight years

crescendo [kre'ʃendo] *nm Mús & Fig* crescendo; **in c.** growing

creso, -a *adj Fam* **rico y c.** filthy rich

crespo, -a *adj* tightly curled, frizzy

crespón *nm* crepe

cresta *nf* (**a**) (*de gallo*) comb; (*de punk*) Mohican (**b**) (*de ola, montaña*) crest; **estar en la c. (de la ola)** to be riding high

Creta *n* Crete

creta *nf* chalk

cretense *adj & nmf* Cretan

cretino, -a *nm,f* cretin

cretona *nf* cretonne

creyente 1 *adj* **ser c.** to be a believer

2 *nmf* believer

creyera *etc ver* **creer**

crezca *etc ver* **crecer**

cría *nf* (**a**) (*hijo del animal*) young (**b**) (*crianza*) (*de animales*) breeding; (*de plantas*) growing

criadero *nm* (**a**) (*de animales*) farm (*breeding place*); (*de árboles, plantas*) nursery; **c. de ostras** oyster bed (**b**) (*de mineral*) seam

criadillas *nfpl Culin* testicles

criado, -a 1 *adj* brought up; **niño mal c.** spoiled child

2 *nm,f* servant, *f* maid

criador, -ora 1 *adj* producing

2 *nm,f (de animales)* breeder; *(de vinos)* grower

crianza *nf* (a) *(de bebé)* nursing, breast-feeding (b) *(de animales)* breeding, rearing (c) *(del vino)* vintage; **vino de c.** vintage wine (d) *(educación)* breeding

criar [32] 1 *vt* (a) *(animales)* to breed, to rear; *(flores, árboles)* to grow (b) *(educar)* to bring up; **nos criaron en el respeto a los demás** we were brought up to respect others (c) *(amamantar) (sujeto: mujer)* to breast-feed; *(sujeto: animal)* to suckle (d) *(vino)* to mature
  2 **criarse** *vpr* (a) *(crecer)* to grow up; *(educarse)* to be educated; **el cachorro se crió en cautividad** the cub was reared in captivity (b) *(reproducirse)* to breed

criatura *nf* (a) *(niño)* child; *(bebé)* baby (b) *(ser vivo)* creature

criba *nf* (a) *(tamiz)* sieve (b) *(selección)* screening

cribar *vt* (a) *(con tamiz)* to sieve (b) *(seleccionar)* to screen out, to select

Crimea *n* Crimea

crimen *nm* crime; **cometer un c.** to commit a crime; *Fam* **sería un c. dejar al bebé solo** it would be criminal *o* a crime to leave the baby on its own; *Fam* **¡ese corte de pelo es un c.!** that haircut is awful *o* criminal!; **c. de guerra** war crime; **c. organizado** organized crime; **c. pasional** crime of passion, crime passionnel

criminal *adj & nmf* criminal; **c. de guerra** war criminal

criminalidad *nf* (a) *(cualidad)* criminality (b) **(índice de) c.** crime rate

criminalista 1 *adj* criminal; **abogado c.** criminal lawyer
  2 *nmf* criminal lawyer

criminalizar [14] *vt* to criminalize

criminología *nf* criminology

criminólogo, -a *nm,f* criminologist

crin *nf* mane; **cepillo de c.** horsehair brush

crío, -a *nm,f (niño)* kid; **esperan el c. para diciembre** the baby is due in December; **mi abuelo está hecho un c.** my grandfather doesn't look his age at all; **¡no seas c.!** don't be such a baby!, don't be so childish!

criogenia *nf* cryogenics *(singular)*

criollo, -a 1 *adj* (a) *(persona)* = native to Latin America (b) *(comida, lengua)* creole
  2 *nm,f (persona)* = person (black or white) born in Latin America
  3 *nm (idioma)* creole

crioterapia *nf* cryotherapy

cripta *nf* crypt

críptico, -a *adj* cryptic

criptografía *nf* cryptography

criptograma *nm* cryptogram

criptón *nm Quím* krypton

críquet *nm* cricket

crisálida *nf* chrysalis

crisantemo *nm* chrysanthemum

crisis *nf inv (situación difícil)* crisis; **estar en c.** to be in crisis; **c. económica** recession; **c. energética** energy crisis; **c. de identidad** identity crisis; **c. nerviosa** nervous breakdown

crisma[1] *nf Fam* Nut; **romperle la c. a alguien** to smash sb's face in; **romperse la c.** to bash one's head

crisma[2] *nm*, **crismas** *nm inv Esp* Christmas card

crisol *nm (de metales)* crucible; *(lugar donde se mezclan cosas)* melting pot

crispación *nf (de nervios)* tension; *(de músculos)* tenseness

crispado, -a *adj* tense

crispar 1 *vt (los nervios)* to set on edge; *(los músculos)* to tense; *(las manos)* to clench; **este trabajo me crispa los nervios** this work sets my nerves on edge
  2 **crisparse** *vpr* to become tense

cristal *nm* (a) *(mineral)* crystal; **c. líquido** liquid crystal; **c. de**

roca rock crystal (b) *Esp (material)* glass; **el suelo está lleno de cristales** there's glass all over the floor; **c. ahumado** smoked glass; **c. tallado** cut glass; **c. tintado** tinted glass (c) *Esp (de ventana)* (window) pane; *(de gafas)* lens (d) *Esp (espejo)* mirror; **bajar el c.** *(ventanilla)* to open *o* roll down the window

cristalera *nf (puerta)* French window; *(ventana)* large window

cristalería *nf* (a) *(objetos)* glassware; **les regalamos una c.** we gave them a set of glassware (b) *(tienda)* glazier's (shop); *(fábrica)* glassworks *(singular)*

cristalero, -a *nm,f* glazier

cristalino, -a 1 *adj* crystalline
  2 *nm* crystalline lens

cristalización *nf también Fig* crystallization

cristalizar [14] 1 *vi también Fig* to crystallize
  2 **cristalizarse** *vpr* to crystallize; *Fig* **cristalizarse en** to develop into

cristiandad *nf* Christianity, Christendom

cristianismo *nm* Christianity

cristianización *nf* Christianization, conversion to Christianity

cristianizar [14] *vt* to Christianize, to convert to Christianity

cristiano, -a 1 *adj & nm,f* Christian
  2 *nm Fam Fig* **hablar en c.** *(en castellano)* to speak (proper) Spanish; *(en lenguaje comprensible)* to speak clearly

cristo *nm* crucifix; **C.** Christ; **armar un C.** to kick up a fuss; *Fam Fig* **donde C. dio las tres voces/perdió el gorro** way out in the sticks

criterio *nm* (a) *(norma)* criterion (b) *(juicio)* taste, discernment (c) *(opinión)* opinion

crítica *nf* (a) *(juicio, análisis)* review; **esa novela ha recibido muy buenas críticas** that novel has had very good reviews; **c. literaria** literary criticism (b) *(conjunto de críticos)* **la c.** the critics (c) *(ataque)* criticism; **le han llovido muchas críticas** he has received a barrage of criticism; **lanzó duras críticas contra el proyecto** she severely criticized the project

criticable *adj* censurable, open to criticism

criticar [59] 1 *vt* (a) *(censurar)* to criticize (b) *(enjuiciar)* *(literatura, arte)* to review
  2 *vi* to gossip

crítico, -a 1 *adj* critical
  2 *nm,f (persona)* critic

criticón, -ona 1 *adj* nit-picking, overcritical
  2 *nm,f* nit-picker

Croacia *n* Croatia

croar 1 *vi* to croak
  2 *nm* croaking

croata 1 *adj* Croatian
  2 *nmf* Croat, Croatian

crocante 1 *adj RP* crunchy
  2 *nm* almond brittle

crocanti *nm (helado)* = ice cream covered in chocolate and nuts

croché *(pl crochés)*, **crochet** [kro'tʃe] *(pl crochets)* *nm* (a) *(labor)* crochet; **hacer c.** to crochet; **una colcha de c.** a crocheted bedspread (b) *(en boxeo)* hook

croissant [krwa'san] *(pl croissants)* *nm* croissant

croissantería [krwasante'ria] *nf* = shop selling filled croissants

crol *nm Dep* crawl; **nadar a c.** to do the crawl

cromado *nm* chromium plating

Cromañón *nm* Cro-Magnon

cromar *vt* to chrome, to chromium-plate

cromático, -a *adj* chromatic

cromatismo *nm* coloring

cromo *nm* (a) *(metal)* chrome (b) *Esp (estampa)* picture card; **c. repetido** swap

cromosoma *nm* chromosome

cromosómico, -a *adj* chromosomal

crónica *nf* (**a**) *(de la historia)* chronicle (**b**) *(de un periódico)* column; *(de la televisión)* feature, program; **la c. deportiva** the sports news *o* roundup

crónico, -a *adj* chronic

cronicón *nm* = brief, usually anonymous, chronicle

cronista *nmf (historiador)* chronicler; *(periodista) (en televisión)* reporter; *(en periódico)* writer

crono *nm Esp Dep* time

cronoescalada *nf Dep* time-trial climb

cronología *nf* chronology

cronológico, -a *adj* chronological

cronometrador, -ora *nm,f* timekeeper

cronometraje *nm* timing

cronometrar *vt* to time

cronómetro *nm Dep* stopwatch; *Tec* chronometer

cróquet *nm* croquet

croqueta *nf* croquette

croquis *nm inv* sketch

cross *nm inv Dep (carrera)* cross-country race; *(deporte)* cross-country (running)

crótalo *nm* rattlesnake

croupier [kru'pjer] *nm* croupier

cruasán *nm* croissant

cruce 1 *ver* **cruzar**

2 *nm* (**a**) *(de líneas)* crossing, intersection; *(de carreteras)* crossroads; **gira a la derecha en el próximo c.** turn right at the next junction (**b**) *(paso)* crossing; **un c. fronterizo** a border crossing (**c**) *(de animales)* cross; **un c. de fox-terrier y chihuahua** a cross between a fox terrier and a chihuahua (**d**) *(de teléfono)* crossed line; **hay un c. en la línea** we've got *o* there's a crossed phone line (**e**) *(en competición deportiva)* round *(in knockout competition)*; **les tocó el c. más difícil** they got the toughest draw

crucero *nm* (**a**) *(viaje)* cruise (**b**) *(barco)* cruiser (**c**) *(de iglesias)* transept

cruceta *nf* (**a**) *(de una cruz)* crosspiece (**b**) *(en fútbol)* angle *(of crossbar and goalpost)*

crucial *adj* crucial

crucificar [59] *vt* (**a**) *(en una cruz)* to crucify (**b**) *(atormentar)* to torment

crucifijo *nm* crucifix

crucifixión *nf* crucifixion

crucigrama *nm* crossword (puzzle)

cruda *nf Guat, Méx Fam* hangover

crudeza *nf* (**a**) *(de clima)* harshness (**b**) *(de descripción, imágenes)* brutality, harsh realism

crudo, -a 1 *adj* (**a**) *(natural)* raw; *(petróleo)* crude (**b**) *(sin cocer completamente)* undercooked (**c**) *(realidad, clima, tiempo)* harsh; *(novela)* harshly realistic, hard-hitting (**d**) *(cruel)* cruel (**e**) *(color)* beige

2 *nm* crude (oil)

cruel *adj (persona, acción)* cruel; *(dolor)* excruciating, terrible; *(clima)* harsh

crueldad *nf* (**a**) *(de persona, acción)* cruelty; *(del clima)* harshness (**b**) *(acción cruel)* act of cruelty

cruento, -a *adj* bloody

crujido *nm (de madera)* creaking; *(de hojas secas)* crackling; **un c.** *(de madera)* a creak; *(de hojas secas)* a crackle; **el c. de sus pisadas** the crunch of his footsteps

crujiente *adj (patatas fritas)* crunchy; *(madera)* creaky; *(hojas secas)* rustling; *(pan)* crusty

crujir *vi (patatas fritas, nieve)* to crunch; *(madera)* to creak; *(hojas secas)* to crackle; *(dientes)* to grind

crupier *nm* croupier

crustáceo *nm* crustacean

cruz *nf* (**a**) *(forma)* cross; **con los brazos en c.** with one's arms stretched out to the sides; *Fam* **hacerse cruces** to be baffled *o* astounded; *Fam* **hacer c. y raya** to break off relations; **c. gamada** swastika; **c. de Malta** Maltese cross; **la C. Roja** the Red Cross (**b**) *(de una moneda)* tails *(singular)* (**c**) *(aflicción)* burden, torment; **¡qué c.!** what a life!

cruza *nf Am* cross, crossbreed

cruzada *nf también Fig* crusade

cruzado, -a 1 *adj* (**a**) *(cheque, piernas, brazos)* crossed (**b**) *(atravesado)* **c. en la carretera** blocking the road (**c**) *(animal)* crossbred (**d**) *(abrigo, chaqueta)* double-breasted

2 *nm* crusader

cruzar [14] **1** *vt* (**a**) *(calle, río)* to cross; **cruzó la calle corriendo** he ran across the street; **esta carretera cruza varios pueblos** this road goes through several towns; **un río que c. todo el país** a river that flows the length of the country (**b**) *(piernas, brazos)* to cross (**c**) *(animales)* to cross (**d**) *(unas palabras)* to exchange (**e**) *Fam* **cruzarle la cara a alguien** *(pegarle)* to slap sb across the face

2 cruzarse *vpr* (**a**) *(atravesarse)* to cross; **la N-10 no se cruza con la N-20** the N-10 doesn't meet the N-20 at any point; **cruzarse de brazos** to fold one's arms; *Fig (no hacer nada)* to stand back and do nothing (**b**) *(interponerse)* **se me cruzó un perro** a dog ran out in front of me (**c**) *(personas)* **cruzarse con alguien** to pass sb; **ayer me crucé con tu mujer camino trabajo** I saw *o* met your wife yesterday on the way to work

CSCE *nf Antes (abrev de* **Conferencia de Seguridad y Cooperación Europeas***)* CSCE

CSD *nm (abrev de* **Consejo Superior de Deportes***)* = Spanish national sports council

CSIC [θe'sik] *nm (abrev de* **Consejo Superior de Investigaciones Científicas***)* = Spanish council for scientific research

CSN *nm (abrev de* **Consejo de Seguridad Nuclear***)* = Spanish nuclear safety council

cta. *(abrev de* **cuenta***)* a/c

cte. *(abrev de* **corriente***)* inst

CTI [sete'i] *nm Am (abrev de* **centro de tratamiento intensivo***)* ICU

c/u *(abrev de* **cada uno***)* per item

cuaderna *nf Náut* rib

cuaderno *nm (libreta)* notebook; *(de colegial)* exercise book; **c. de anillas** ring binder; *Náut* **c. de bitácora** logbook

cuadra *nf* (**a**) *(de caballos)* stable; *Fam (lugar sucio)* pigsty (**b**) *Am (de edificios)* block

cuadrado, -a 1 *adj* (**a**) *(figura) (gen)* & *Mat* square (**b**) *(persona)* square-built, stocky

2 *nm (gen)* & *Mat* square

cuadragésimo, -a *núm* fortieth

cuadrangular *adj* quadrangular

cuadrángulo *nm* quadrangle

cuadrante *nm* (**a**) *(de círculo)* quadrant (**b**) *(reloj de sol)* sundial

cuadrar 1 *vi* (**a**) *(información, hechos)* to square, to agree (**con** with); **hay algo en su explicación que no cuadra** there's something about his explanation that doesn't add up (**b**) *(números, cuentas)* to tally, to add up; **tus cálculos no cuadran con los míos** your calculations don't tally with mine

2 *vt (dar forma de cuadrado)* to make square, to square off

3 cuadrarse *vpr Mil* to stand to attention

cuadratura *nf Geom* quadrature; **la c. del círculo** squaring the circle

cuádriceps *nm inv* quadriceps

cuadrícula *nf* grid

cuadriculado, -a *adj* squared; *Fam Fig* **ser muy c.** *(rígido)* to have a very rigid mentality

cuadricular *vt* to divide into squares

cuadriga, cuádriga *nf Hist* four-in-hand

cuadrilátero *nm* (a) *Geom* quadrilateral (b) *Dep* ring

cuadrilla *nf* (a) *(de amigos, trabajadores)* group; *(de maleantes)* gang (b) *(de torero)* team of helpers

cuadro *nm* (a) *(cuadrado)* square; *(de flores)* bed; **una camisa a cuadros** a check shirt; *Inform* **c. de diálogo** dialogue box (b) *(pintura)* painting; **un c. de Miró** a painting by Miró (c) *(escena)* scene, spectacle; **después del terremoto, la ciudad presentaba un c. desolador** after the earthquake, the city was a scene of devastation (d) *(equipo)* team; **el c. directivo de una empresa** the management of a company; **c. flamenco** flamenco group (e) *(gráfico)* chart, diagram; **c. sinóptico** tree diagram (f) *(de bicicleta)* frame (g) *(de aparato)* **c. de distribución** switchboard; **c. de mandos** control panel; **c. de fusibles** fuse box (h) *Teatro* scene (i) *Med* **c. (clínico)** symptoms; **presenta un c. de extrema gravedad** her symptoms are extremely serious

cuadrúpedo, -a 1 *adj* four-legged

    2 *nm* quadruped

cuádruple *nm* quadruple

cuadruplicar [59] *vt* to quadruple

cuádruplo *nm* quadruple

cuajada *nf* curd (cheese)

cuajado, -a *adj* (a) *(leche)* curdled (b) *(lleno)* **c. de** full of

cuajar 1 *vt* (a) *(solidificar) (leche)* to curdle; *(sangre)* to clot, to coagulate (b) **c. de** *(llenar)* to fill with; *(cubrir)* to cover with

    2 *vi* (a) *(lograrse) (acuerdo)* to be settled; *(negocio)* to take off, to get going (b) *(ser aceptado) (persona)* to fit in; *(moda)* to catch on (c) *(nieve)* to settle

    3 cuajarse *vpr* (a) *(leche)* to curdle; *(sangre)* to clot, to coagulate (b) *(llenarse)* **cuajarse de** to fill (up) with

cuajo *nm* (a) *(fermento)* rennet (b) **arrancar de c.** *(árbol)* to uproot; *(brazo, cabeza)* to tear right off

cual *pron relativo* **el/la c.** *(de persona) (sujeto)* who; *(complemento)* whom; *(de cosa)* which; **lo c.** which; **conoció a una española, la c. vivía en Buenos Aires** he met a Spanish girl who lived in Buenos Aires; **está muy enfadada, lo c. es comprensible** she's very angry, which is understandable; **todo lo c.** all of which; **sea c. sea** *o* **fuere su decisión** whatever his decision (may be); **los tres son a c. más inteligente** all three are equally intelligent

cuál *pron* (a) *(interrogativo)* what; *(en concreto, especificando)* which one; **¿c. es tu nombre?** what is your name?; **¿c. es la diferencia?** what's the difference?; **no sé cuáles son mejores** I don't know which are best; **¿c. prefieres?** which one do you prefer? (b) *(en oraciones distributivas)* **todos contribuyeron, c. más, c. menos** everyone contributed, although some more than others

cualesquiera *ver* **cualquiera**

cualidad *nf* quality

cualificación *nf* degree of skill *(of a worker)*; **debemos mejorar la c. de los obreros** we have to get a more highly skilled workforce

cualificado, -a *adj* skilled

cualificar [59] *vt* to qualify

cualitativo, -a *adj* qualitative

cualquier *ver* **cualquiera**

cualquiera *(pl* **cualesquiera)**

> **cualquier** is used before singular nouns (e.g. **cualquier hombre** any man).

1 *adj* any; **a cualquier hora** any time; **en cualquier lugar** anywhere; **de cualquier manera** *o* **modo, no pienso ayudar** I've no intention of helping, anyway *o* in any case;

en cualquier momento at any time; **cualquier día vendré a visitarte** I'll drop by one of these days; **no es un escritor c.** he's no ordinary writer

    2 *pron* anyone; **c. te lo dirá** anyone will tell you; **¡c. lo sabe!** who knows!; **¡c. se lo come!** nobody could eat that!; **c. que** *(persona)* anyone who; *(cosa)* whatever; **c. que te vea se reiría** anyone who saw you would laugh; **c. que sea la razón** whatever the reason (may be); **cualesquiera que sean las razones** whatever the reasons (may be)

    3 *nmf* *(don nadie)* nobody

    4 *nf Fam* *(prostituta)* tart

cuan *adv* *(todo lo que)* **se desplomó c. largo era** he fell flat on the ground

cuán *adv* how

cuando 1 *adv* when; **c. me agacho, me duele la espalda** when *o* whenever I bend down, my back hurts; **c. quieras** whenever you like; **de c. en c., de vez en c.** from time to time, now and again; **c. más** at the most; **c. menos** at least; **c. quiera que** whenever

    2 *conj* (a) *(si)* if; **c. tú lo dices será verdad** it must be true if you say so; **no será tan malo c. ha vendido tantas copias** it can't be that bad if it's sold so many copies (b) *(indica contraste)* even though; **no tiene muchos amigos, c. en realidad es una persona muy agradable** he doesn't have a lot of friends, even though he's actually a very nice person

    3 *prep* **c. la guerra** during the war

    4 aun cuando *loc conj* **no mentiría aun c. le fuera en ello la vida** she wouldn't lie even if her life depended on it

cuándo 1 *adv* when; **¿c. vas a venir?** when are you coming?; **quisiera saber c. sale el tren** I'd like to know when *o* at what time the train leaves

    2 *prep* **quemaron ese colegio c. la guerra** that school was burned down during the war

    3 *nm* **ignorará el cómo y el c. de la operación** he won't know how or when the operation will take place

cuantía *nf* *(suma)* amount, quantity; *(alcance)* extent; **una ayuda de una c. sin precisar** an unspecified amount of aid; **todavía no se conoce la c. de los daños** the final cost of the damage is not yet known

cuántica *nf* quantum mechanics *(singular)*

cuántico, -a *adj* quantum; **mecánica/teoría cuántica** quantum mechanics/theory

cuantificable *adj* quantifiable

cuantificar [59] *vt* to quantify

cuantioso, -a *adj* large, substantial

cuantitativo, -a *adj* quantitative

cuanto, -a 1 *adj* (a) *(todo)* **despilfarra c. dinero gana** he squanders all the money he earns; **soporté todas cuantas críticas me hizo** I put up with every single criticism he made of me (b) *(algunos)* **unos cuantos chicos** some *o* a few boys (c) *(+ adverbio) (compara cantidades)* **cuantas más mentiras digas, menos te creerán** the more you lie, the less people will believe you; **cuantos más amigos traigas, tanto mejor** the more friends you bring, the better

    2 *pron relativo* (a) *(todo lo que)* everything, as much as; **come c. quieras** eat as much as you like; **comprendo c. dice** I understand everything he says; **todo c.** everything (b) *(expresa correlación)* **c. más se tiene, más se quiere** the more you have, the more you want (c) **cuantos** *(todos) (personas)* everyone who; *(cosas)* everything (that); **cuantos fueron alabaron el espectáculo** everyone who went said the show was excellent; **dio las gracias a todos cuantos le ayudaron** he thanked everyone who helped him (d) **unos cuantos** *(algunos)* some, a few; **no tengo todos sus libros, sólo unos cuantos** I don't have all of her books, only some *o* a few of them

    3 *adv* *(compara cantidades)* **c. más come, más gordo está**

the more he eats, the fatter he gets; **c. más lo pienso, menos lo entiendo** the more I think about it, the less I understand it; **c. antes** as soon as possible

4 en cuanto *loc adv (tan pronto como)* as soon as; **en c. acabe** as soon as I've finished

5 en cuanto *loc prep* (**a**) *(en calidad de)* as; **en c. cabeza de familia** as head of the family (**b**) **en c. a** as regards; **en c. a tu petición** as regards your request, as far as your request is concerned

cuánto, -a 1 *adj* (**a**) *(interrogativo) (singular)* how much; *(plural)* how many; **¿cuántas manzanas tienes?** how many apples do you have?; **¿c. pan quieres?** how much bread do you want?; **no sé cuántos hombres había** I don't know how many men were there (**b**) *(exclamativo)* what a lot of; **¡cuánta gente (había)!** what a lot of people (were there)!

2 *pron* (**a**) *(interrogativo) (singular)* how much; *(plural)* how many; **¿c. quieres?** how much do you want?; **¿a c. están los tomates?** how much are the tomatoes?; **me gustaría saber c. te costarán** I'd like to know how much they'll cost you; **¿cuántos han venido?** how many came?; **dime cuántas quieres** tell me how many you want (**b**) *(exclamativo)* **¡c. han cambiado las cosas!** how things have changed!; **¡c. me gusta!** I really like it!; **¡cuántos han venido!** so many people have come!

cuáquero, -a *nm,f Rel* Quaker

cuarcita *nf* quartzite

cuarenta *núm* forty; **los (años) c.** the forties; *Fam Fig* **cantar a alguien las c.** to give sb a piece of one's mind; *ver también* **seis**

cuarentavo, -a *núm* fortieth

cuarentena *nf* (**a**) *(por epidemia)* quarantine; **poner en c.** *(enfermos)* to (put in) quarantine; *(noticia)* to put on hold (**b**) *(cuarenta unidades)* forty; **andará por la c.** he must be about forty; **una c. de…** *(unos cuarenta)* about forty…; *(cuarenta)* forty…

cuarentón, -ona *nm,f Fam* person in his/her forties

cuaresma *nf Rel* Lent

cuarta *nf* (**a**) *(palmo)* span (**b**) *Aut* fourth (gear); **meter (la) c.** to go into fourth (gear)

cuarteamiento *nm (resquebrajamiento)* cracking

cuartear 1 *vt* to cut *o* chop up

2 cuartearse *vpr* to crack

cuartel *nm* (**a**) *Mil* barracks; **c. general** headquarters (**b**) *(buen trato)* **guerra sin c.** all-out war; **lucha sin c.** fight to the death

cuartelada *nf* minor military uprising

cuartelazo *nm* military uprising, revolt

cuartelero, -a *adj* (**a**) *Mil* barracks; **vida cuartelera** life in the barracks (**b**) *(lenguaje)* vulgar, coarse

cuartelillo *nm (de la Guardia Civil)* = post of the Guardia Civil

cuarteto *nm* quartet; **c. de cuerda** string quartet

cuartilla *nf* sheet of quarto

cuarto, -a 1 *núm* fourth; **la cuarta parte** a quarter; **el c. poder** *(la prensa)* the Fourth Estate

2 *nm* (**a**) *(parte)* quarter; **un c. de hora** a quarter of an hour; **son las dos y c.** it's a quarter after two; *Fam* **ser tres cuartos de lo mismo** to be exactly the same *o* no different; **c. creciente/menguante** first/last quarter (**b**) *(habitación)* room; **c. de aseo** washroom, small bathroom; **c. de baño** bathroom; **c. de estar** living room; **c. oscuro** *(para fotografía)* darkroom; *RP (para votación)* voting booth (**c**) *(dinero)* **estar sin un c.** to be skint; *Fam* **cuartos** dough, cash (**d**) *Dep* **cuartos de final** quarter finals

cuarzo *nm* quartz

cuate *nmf CAm, Ecuad, Méx (gemelo)* twin; *Fam (amigo)* pal, buddy

cuaternario, -a *Geol* **1** *adj* Quaternary

2 *nm* **el C.** the Quaternary (era)

cuatrero, -a *nm,f (de caballos)* horse thief; *(de ganado)* cattle rustler

cuatrienio *nm* four-year period

cuatrillizo, -a *nm,f* quadruplet, quad

cuatrimestral *adj* (**a**) *(en frecuencia)* four-monthly (**b**) *(en duración)* four-month, lasting four months; *Educ* **asignatura c.** = four-month course in a given subject

cuatrimestre *nm* (period of) four months

cuatrimotor *nm* four-engined plane

cuatripartito, -a *adj* four-part

cuatro 1 *núm* four; *ver también* **seis**

2 *adj (poco)* a few; **hace c. días** a few days ago; *Fam Fig* **c. gatos** hardly a soul; **éramos c. gatos** there were only a handful of us; *Méx Fam* **c. lámparas** *(persona)* four-eyes; *Fam* **c. ojos** *(persona)* four-eyes

3 *nm Carib* = four-stringed guitar

cuatrocientos, -as *núm* four hundred; *ver también* **seis**

Cuba *n* Cuba

cuba *nf* barrel, cask; *Fam* **estar como una c.** to be legless *o* blind drunk

cubalibre *nm (de ron)* rum and cola; *(de ginebra)* gin and cola

cubano, -a *adj & nm,f* Cuban

cubata *nm Fam (combinado)* tall drink; *(de ron)* rum and cola; *(de ginebra)* gin and cola

cubero *nm* **a ojo de buen c.** roughly

cubertera *nf RP (cajón)* cutlery drawer; *(bandeja)* cutlery tray

cubertería *nf* (set of) cutlery

cubeta *nf (cuba pequeña)* bucket, pail; *(de barómetro)* bulb; *Fot* tray

cubetera *nf CSur, Perú* ice (cube) tray

cubicaje *nm Aut* capacity

cúbico, -a *adj* cubic

cubierta *nf* (**a**) *(de libro, cama)* cover (**b**) *(de neumático)* carcass, body (**c**) *(de barco)* deck; **c. de paseo** promenade deck

cubierto, -a 1 *participio ver* **cubrir**

2 *adj* (**a**) *(tapado, recubierto)* covered (**de** with); **estar a c.** *(protegido)* to be under cover; *(con saldo acreedor)* to be in the black; **ponerse a c.** to take cover (**b**) *(cielo)* overcast (**c**) *(vacante)* filled

3 *nm* (**a**) *(pieza de cubertería)* piece of cutlery (**b**) *(juego de cubertería)* set of cutlery (**c**) *(para cada persona)* place setting (**d**) *(comida)* set menu

cubil *nm (de animales)* den, lair; *(de personas)* poky room

cubilete *nm (en juegos)* cup; *(molde)* mold

cubismo *nm Arte* cubism

cubista *adj & nmf Arte* cubist

cubitera *nf* ice bucket

cubito *nm (de hielo)* ice cube

cúbito *nm Anat* ulna

cubo *nm* (**a**) *(recipiente)* bucket; **c. de la basura** *(en la cocina, la calle)* garbage can (**b**) *Geom & Mat* cube; **elevar al c.** to cube (**c**) *(de rueda)* hub

cubrecama *nm* bedspread

cubrir 1 *vt* (**a**) *(tapar, recubrir, recorrer)* to cover; **c. algo de algo** to cover sth with *o* in sth; **c. a alguien de insultos/alabanzas** to heap insults/praise on sb (**b**) *(proteger) (retirada, asegurado)* to cover (**c**) *(puesto, vacante)* to fill (**d**) *(gastos)* to cover; **el presupuesto no cubre todos los gastos** the budget doesn't cover all the expenses; **c. gastos** *(exactamente)* to break even (**e**) *(noticia)* to cover (**f**) *(el macho a la hembra)* **c. a** to mate with

2 cubrirse *vpr* (**a**) *(taparse)* to become covered (**de** with) (**b**) *(protegerse)* to shelter (**de** from) (**c**) *(con sombrero)* to put one's hat on (**d**) *(con ropa)* to cover oneself (**de** with) (**e**) *(cielo)* to cloud over (**f**) *(llenarse)* **cubrirse de gloria** *(triunfar)* to cover oneself in *o* with glory; *Irónico* to land oneself in it

cuca *nf Esp Antes Fam* peseta

cucaña *nf* greasy pole

cucaracha *nf* cockroach

cuchara *nf* **(a)** *(para comer)* spoon; **c. de palo** wooden spoon; **c. sopera** soup spoon **(b)** *(cucharada)* spoonful

cucharada *nf* spoonful; **una c. rasa** a level spoonful

cucharadita *nf* teaspoon, teaspoonful

cucharilla *nf* teaspoon

cucharón *nm* ladle

cucheta *nf RP Náut* berth

cuchichear *vi* to whisper

cuchicheo *nm* whispering

cuchilla *nf* blade; **c. de afeitar** razor blade

cuchillada *nf* *(golpe)* stab; *(herida)* stab wound

cuchillería *nf* **(a)** *(oficio)* cutlery, knifemaking **(b)** *(taller)* cutler's shop

cuchillo *nm* knife; **pasar a c.** to put to the sword; **c. de cocina** kitchen knife; **c. eléctrico** electric carving knife; **c. de monte** hunting knife

cuchipanda *nf Fam* party

cuchitril *nm* hovel

cuchufleta *nf Fam* joke; **estar de c.** to be joking

cuclillas *nfpl* **en c.** squatting; **ponerse en c.** to squat (down)

cuclillo *nm* cuckoo

cuco, -a 1 *adj Fam* **(a)** *(bonito)* pretty **(b)** *Esp (astuto)* shrewd, canny

　2 *nm* cuckoo

cucú *nm* **(a)** *(canto)* cuckoo **(b)** *(reloj)* cuckoo clock

cucurucho *nm* **(a)** *(de papel)* paper cone **(b)** *(para helado)* cornet, cone **(c)** *(gorro)* pointed hat

cuece *ver* **cocer**

cuelgo *etc ver* **colgar**

cuelgue *nm Fam* **(a)** *(por drogas)* high **(b)** *(enamoramiento)* **tener un c. con** *o* **por alguien** to be crazy about sb, to be hooked on sb

cuello *nm* **(a)** *(de persona, animal, botella)* neck; **al c.** around one's neck; *Fig* **estar hasta el c. de algo** to be up to one's eyes in sth; *Fig* **c. de botella** bottleneck **(b)** *(de prendas)* collar; **c. alto** turtleneck; **c. de pico** V-neck; **c. vuelto,** *Am* **c. tortuga** turtleneck **(c)** *Anat* **c. uterino** *o* **del útero** cervix

cuelo *etc ver* **colar**

cuenca *nf* **(a)** *(de río)* basin **(b)** *(del ojo)* (eye) socket **(c)** *(región minera)* **c. (minera)** mining area *o* region

cuenco *nm* earthenware bowl

cuenta 1 *ver* **contar**

　2 *nf* **(a)** *(acción de contar)* count; **echar cuentas** to reckon up; **llevar/perder la c. de** to keep/lose count of; **c. atrás** countdown

　(b) *(cálculo)* sum; *Fam* **c. de la vieja** counting on one's fingers **(c)** *Fin, Com & Inform* account; **abonar/cargar algo en c. a alguien** to credit/debit sth to sb's account; **abrir una c.** to open an account; **llevar las cuentas** to keep the books; **pagar mil euros a c.** to pay a thousand euros down; *Esp* **c. de ahorros** savings account; *Esp* **c. de ahorro vivienda** home loan; **c. bancaria** bank account; **c. comercial** business account; **c. conjunta** joint account; **c. de correo (electrónico)** e-mail account; **c. corriente** checking account; **c. de crédito** account with an overdraft facility; **c. de depósito** deposit account; **c. deudora** overdrawn account; **c. de explotación** operating statement; **c. de inversión** investment account; **c. de pérdidas y ganancias** profit and loss account; **c. a plazo fijo** deposit account

　(d) *(factura)* bill; *(en restaurante)* check; **domiciliar una c.** to pay an account by recurring payments; **pasar la c.** to send the bill; **c. por cobrar/pagar** account receivable/payable; **c. de gastos** expense account

　(e) *(obligación, cuidado)* responsibility; **déjalo de mi c.** leave it to me; **trabajar por c. propia/ajena** to be self-employed/ an employee

　(f) *(de collar, rosario)* bead

　(g) *(expresiones)* **a fin de cuentas** in the end; **ajustarle a alguien las cuentas** to settle an account *o* a score with sb; **caer en la c. de algo** to realize sth; **dar c. de algo** *(comunicar)* to report sth; *(terminar)* to account for sth, to finish sth off; **darse c. de algo** to realize sth; **en resumidas cuentas** in short; **más de la c.** too much; **pedir cuentas a alguien** to call sb to account; **por mi/tu c.** on my/your own; **salir de cuentas** to be due to give birth; **tener en c. algo** to bear sth in mind

cuentagotas *nm inv* dropper; *Fig* **a** *o* **con c.** in dribs and drabs

cuentakilómetros *nm inv Aut (de distancia recorrida)* ≃ odometer; *(de velocidad)* speedometer

cuentapropista *nmf Am* self-employed person

cuentarrevoluciones *nm inv Aut* tachometer

cuentista *nmf* **(a)** *(escritor)* short-story writer **(b)** *Fam (mentiroso)* fibber, storyteller

cuento *nm* **(a)** *(fábula)* tale; **c. de hadas** fairy tale; *Fam* **el c. de la lechera** wishful thinking; **c. popular** folktale **(b)** *(narración)* short story **(c)** *Fam (mentira, exageración)* story, lie; **c. chino** tall story, whopper **(d)** *(expresiones)* **quitarse** *o* **dejarse de cuentos** to stop beating about the bush; **ser el c. de nunca acabar** to be the same old story; **ese tiene mucho c.** he's always putting it on; **venir a c.** to be relevant; **venir con cuentos** to tell fibs *o* stories; **vivir del c.** to live by one's wits

cuerda *nf* **(a)** *(para atar) (fina)* string; *(más gruesa)* rope; **c. floja** tightrope **(b)** *(de instrumento)* string **(c)** *(de reloj)* spring; **dar c. a** *(reloj)* to wind up **(d)** *Geom* chord **(e)** *Anat* **cuerdas vocales** vocal cords **(f)** *(expresiones)* **bajo c.** secretly, in an underhand manner; **estar en la c. floja** to be hanging by a thread; **este conferenciante todavía tiene c. para rato** this speaker looks like he's going to go on for a while yet; **tirar de la c.** to go too far, to push it

cuerdo, -a 1 *adj* **(a)** *(sano de juicio)* sane **(b)** *(sensato)* sensible

　2 *nm,f* sane person

cueriza *nf Andes Fam* beating

cuerno *nm (de animal)* horn; *(de ciervo)* antler; *(de caracol)* horn, feeler; *Fam* **mandar al c. a alguien** to send sb packing; *Fam* **poner cuernos a alguien** to be unfaithful to sb; *(a un hombre)* to cuckold sb; *Geog* **el C. de África** the Horn of Africa

cuero *nm* **(a)** *(material)* leather; **una chamarra de c.** a leather jacket **(b)** *(piel de animal)* skin; *(piel curtida)* hide; **c. cabelludo** scalp; **en cueros (vivos)** stark naked **(c)** *Am (látigo)* whip **(d)** *Ecuad, Ven Pey (mujer)* broad

cuerpo *nm* **(a)** *(en general)* body; **a c.** without a coat on; **de c. entero** *(retrato, espejo)* full-length; **en c. y alma** body and soul; **luchar c. a c.** to fight hand-to-hand; **de c. presente** (lying) in state; **tomar c.** to take shape; **vivir a c. de rey** to live like a king; **¡c. a tierra!** hit the ground!, get down!; **c. celeste** heavenly body; **c. extraño** foreign body; **el c. humano** the human body

　(b) *(parte principal)* main body

　(c) *(consistencia)* thickness; **mover hasta que la mezcla tome c.** stir until the mixture thickens; **el proyecto de nuevo aeropuerto va tomando c.** the new airport project is taking shape

　(d) *(corporación consular, militar)* corps; **c. de bomberos** fire department; **c. diplomático** diplomatic corps; **c. de policía** police force

　(e) *(parte de armario, edificio)* section

　(f) *Der* **c. del delito** corpus delicti, = evidence of a crime or means of perpetrating it

　(g) *Imprenta (de letra)* point

cuervo *nm* raven

cuesco *nm Fam (pedo)* loud fart

cuesta 1 *ver* **costar**

2 *nf* slope; **c. arriba** uphill; **c. abajo** downhill; *Fam Fig* **trabajar los viernes se me hace muy c. arriba** I find working on Fridays heavy going

3 a cuestas *loc adv* on one's back, over one's shoulders

cuestación *nf* collection (for charity)

cuestión *nf* (a) *(pregunta)* question (b) *(problema)* problem (c) *(asunto)* matter, issue; **en c.** in question; **en c. de** *(en materia de)* as regards; **en c. de una hora** in no more than an hour

cuestionable *adj* questionable, debatable

cuestionar 1 *vt* to question

2 cuestionarse *vpr* to (call into) question

cuestionario *nm* questionnaire

cuesto *etc ver* **costar**

cuete *adj Méx Fam* loaded

cueva *nf* cave

cuezo *ver* **cocer**

cuico *nm Méx Fam* cop

cuidado 1 *nm* (a) care; **el c. de la piel/del cabello** skin/hair care; **estar al c. de** to be in charge of; **tener c. con** to be careful with; **eso me tiene** *o* **trae sin c.** I couldn't care less about that; **c. con el perro** *(en letrero)* beware of the dog; **c. con el escalón** *(en letrero)* watch the step; *Med* **cuidados intensivos** intensive care (b) **de c.** *(peligroso)* dangerous; **fue un accidente/una fiesta de c.** *(tremendo)* it was some accident/party

2 *interj* **¡c.!** careful!, look out!

cuidador, -ora *nm,f Dep* trainer

cuidadoso, -a *adj* careful

cuidar 1 *vt (enfermo, niño, casa)* to look after; *(aspecto, ropa)* to take care about; *(detalles)* to pay attention to

2 *vi* **c. de** to look after; **cuida de que no lo haga** make sure she doesn't do it

3 cuidarse *vpr* (a) *(uno mismo)* to take care of *o* to look after oneself; **¡cuídate!** take care! (b) *(tener cuidado)* **cuidarse de algo** to be careful about sth, to take care about sth; **se cuidó mucho de que no la vieran** she took great care to insure that no one saw her; **cuídate mucho de escuchar sus palabras** don't listen to what he says

cuita *nf* trouble, worry

culata *nf* (a) *(de arma)* butt (b) *(de animal)* hindquarters (c) *(de motor)* cylinder head

culatazo *nm (golpe)* blow with the butt of a rifle; *(retroceso)* recoil, kick

culé *adj Fam Dep* = relating to Barcelona soccer club

culebra *nf* snake; **c. de agua** grass snake

culebrón *nm Esp Fam* soap opera

culinario, -a *adj* culinary

culmen *nm* high point

culminación *nf* culmination

culminante *adj* culminating; **punto c.** high point

culminar 1 *vt* to crown (**con** with)

2 *vi* to finish, to culminate

culo *nm Fam o Am Vulg* (a) *(nalgas)* butt; **me caí de c.** I fell flat on my backside; *muy Fam* **ir de c.** *(negocio, país)* to be going down the tubes; **el equipo va de c. este año** the team's doing shit *o* crap this year; *Fig* **ser un c. inquieto** *o* **de mal asiento** *(enredador)* to be fidgety; *(errante)* to be a restless soul; *muy Fam* **vive en el c. del mundo** he lives fucking miles from anywhere (b) *(ano)* asshole; *Esp Vulg* **¡que te den por c.!**, **¡vete a tomar por c.!** fuck off! (c) *(de vaso, botella)* bottom (d) *(líquido)* **queda un c. de vino** there's a drop (or two) of wine left in the bottom

culpa *nf* (a) *(responsabilidad)* **un sentimiento de c.** a feeling of guilt; **echar la c. a alguien (de)** to blame sb (for); **por c.**

de because of; **tener la c. de algo** to be to blame for sth; **¿qué c. tengo yo de que te hayas caído?** it's hardly my fault you fell over, is it?; *Fam* **yo no tengo la c. de que seas tan distraído** it's not my fault you're so absentminded (b) *Rel* **culpas** sins

culpabilidad *nf* guilt

culpabilizar [14] **1** *vt* to blame

2 culpabilizarse *vpr* to accept the blame (**de** for)

culpable 1 *adj* guilty (**de** of); **declarar c. a alguien** to find sb guilty; **declararse c.** to plead guilty; **es c. de varios robos** he is responsible for *o* has committed several robberies; **me siento c. de lo que pasó** I feel responsible for what has happened

2 *nmf* (a) *Der* guilty party; **la policía busca al c. del robo** the police are loking for the person responsible for the robbery (b) *(responsable)* **tú eres el c.** you're to blame

culpar *vt* **c. a alguien (de)** *(atribuir la culpa)* to blame sb (for); *(acusar)* to accuse sb (of)

culteranismo *nm Lit* Gongorism

culterano, -a *Lit* **1** *adj* Gongoristic

2 *nm,f* Gongorist

cultismo *nm* literary *o* learned word

cultivable *adj* cultivable, arable

cultivado, -a *adj* cultivated

cultivador, -ora *nm,f* grower

cultivar 1 *vt* (a) *(tierra)* to farm, to cultivate; *(plantas)* to grow (b) *(amistad, inteligencia)* to cultivate (c) *(arte)* to practice (d) *(germen)* to culture

2 cultivarse *vpr (persona)* to improve oneself

cultivo *nm* (a) *(de tierra)* farming; *(de plantas)* growing (b) *(plantación)* crop (c) *(de gérmenes)* culture

culto, -a 1 *adj (persona)* cultured, educated; *(estilo)* refined; *(palabra)* literary, learned

2 *nm* (a) *(devoción)* worship; **rendir c. a** *(dios)* to worship; *(persona, valentía)* to pay homage *o* tribute to; **c. a la personalidad** personality cult (b) *(religión)* cult

cultura *nf* (a) *(de sociedad)* culture; **c. empresarial** corporate culture (b) *(sabiduría)* learning, knowledge; **c. general** general knowledge

cultural *adj* cultural

culturismo *nm* bodybuilding

culturista *nmf* bodybuilder

culturizar [14] *vt* to educate

cumbia *nf* cumbia, = type of Colombian dance

cumbre 1 *adj* **el momento c. de su carrera** the peak *o* high point of his career; **su obra c.** her most outstanding work

2 *nf* (a) *(de montaña)* summit (b) *(punto culminante)* peak, pinnacle (c) *Pol* summit (conference)

cumpleaños *nm inv* birthday

cumplido, -a 1 *adj* (a) *(orden)* carried out; *(promesa)* kept; *(deber, profecía)* fulfilled; *(plazo)* expired (b) *(completo, lleno)* full, complete (c) *(cortés)* courteous

2 *nm* compliment

cumplidor, -ora 1 *adj* reliable, dependable

2 *nm,f* reliable *o* dependable person

cumplimentar *vt* (a) *(saludar)* to greet (b) *(felicitar)* to congratulate (c) *(cumplir) (orden)* to carry out; *(contrato)* to fulfill

cumplimiento *nm* (a) *(de un deber)* performance; *(de contrato, obligaciones)* fulfillment; *(de la ley)* observance; *(de órdenes)* carrying out; **murió en el c. de su deber** he died in the course of *o* while carrying out his duty; **en c. del artículo 34** in compliance with article 34 (b) *(de promesa)* fulfillment; *(de amenaza)* carrying out (c) *(de condena)* **comenzará el c. de su condena el próximo lunes** he will begin serving his sentence next Monday; **durante el c. del servicio militar** while he was doing his military service (d) *(de plazo)* expiry (e) *(de objetivo)* achievement, fulfillment

cumplir 1 *vt* (**a**) *(deber)* to do, to carry out, to perform; *(contrato, obligaciones)* to fulfill; *(ley)* to observe; *(orden)* to carry out; **los candidatos deben c. los siguientes requisitos** the candidates shall meet *o* satisfy the following requirements

(**b**) *(promesa)* to keep; *(amenaza)* to carry out; **cumplió su deseo de subir al Aconcagua** she fulfilled her wish of climbing the Aconcagua

(**c**) *(años)* to reach; **mañana cumplo 20 años** I'm 20 *o* it's my 20th birthday tomorrow; **cumple años la próxima semana** it's her birthday next week, she has her birthday next week; **¡que cumplas muchos más!** many happy returns!

(**d**) *(condena)* to serve; *(servicio militar)* to do

2 *vi* (**a**) *(plazo, garantía)* to expire

(**b**) *(realizar el deber)* to do one's duty; **c. con alguien** to do one's duty by sb; **para** *o* **por c.** out of politeness; **c. con el deber** to do one's duty; **c. con la palabra** to keep one's word; **yo me limito a c. con mi trabajo** I'm just doing my job

(**c**) *(con norma, condición)* to comply; **este producto no cumple con la normativa europea** this product doesn't comply with *o* meet European standards

(**d**) *(por cortesía)* **lo dijo por c.** she said it because she felt she had to; **acudió a la boda por c. con su hermano** she went to the wedding out of a sense of duty to her brother

3 cumplirse *vpr* (**a**) *(hacerse realidad)* **finalmente se cumplió su deseo** finally her wish was fulfilled, she finally got her wish; **se cumplieron las amenazas y una bomba estalló en el centro de la ciudad** the threats were carried out when a bomb exploded in the city center (**b**) *(plazo)* **mañana se cumple el plazo de presentación de solicitudes** the deadline for applications expires tomorrow; **el próximo año se cumple el primer centenario de su muerte** next year will be the hundredth anniversary of his death

cúmulo *nm* (**a**) *(de objetos)* pile, heap (**b**) *(nube)* cumulus (**c**) *(de circunstancias, asuntos)* accumulation, series

cuna *nf* (**a**) *(de niño)* cot, cradle (**b**) *(de movimiento, civilización)* cradle; *(de persona)* birthplace

cundir *vi* (**a**) *(propagarse)* to spread (**b**) *Esp (dar de sí) (comida, reservas)* to go a long way; *(trabajo, estudio)* to go well; **me cundió mucho el tiempo** I got a lot done

cuneiforme *adj* cuneiform

cuneta *nf (de una carretera)* ditch; *(de una calle)* gutter

cunnilingus *nm inv* cunnilingus

cuña *nf* (**a**) *(pieza)* wedge (**b**) *(de publicidad)* commercial break (**c**) *(orinal)* bedpan (**d**) *Andes, RP (enchufe)* **tener c.** to have friends in high places

cuñado, -a *nm,f* brother-in-law, *f* sister-in-law

cuño *nm* (**a**) *(troquel)* die (**b**) *(sello, impresión)* stamp (**c**) *Fig* **ser de nuevo c.** to be a new coinage

cuota *nf* (**a**) *(contribución) (a entidad, club)* membership fee, subscription; *(de inscripción, conexión)* fee; *(a Hacienda)* tax (payment); **c. de admisión** admission fee (**b**) *(cupo)* quota; **las cuotas lácteas/pesqueras** *(en UE)* milk/fishing quotas; *Econ* **c. de mercado** market share; **c. de pantalla** audience share (**c**) *Am (plazo de pago)* installment (**d**) *Méx (en autopista)* toll

cupé *nm* coupé

cupido *nm (representación del amor)* cupid

cupiera *etc ver* **caber**

cuplé *nm* popular song

cupletista *nmf* "cuplé" singer

cupo 1 *ver* **caber**

2 *nm* (**a**) *(cantidad máxima)* quota (**b**) *(cantidad proporcional)* share; *(de una cosa racionada)* ration

cupón *nm (vale)* coupon; *(de lotería, rifa)* ticket

cúprico, -a *adj Quím* copper; **óxido/sulfato c.** copper oxide/sulfate

cúpula *nf* (**a**) *(bóveda)* dome, cupola (**b**) *(mandos)* leaders

cura 1 *nm* priest

2 *nf* (**a**) *(curación)* recovery (**b**) *(tratamiento)* treatment, cure; **necesitar una c. de sueño** to need a good sleep (**c**) **no tener c.** *(ser incurable)* to be incurable; *Fam (ser incorregible)* to be incorrigible

curación *nf* (**a**) *(de enfermo) (recuperación)* recovery; *(tratamiento)* treatment; *(de herida)* healing (**b**) *(de alimento)* curing

curado, -a 1 *adj (alimento)* cured; *(pieles)* tanned; *Fam* **estar c. de espanto** to be unshockable

2 *nm (de alimentos)* curing; *(de pieles)* tanning

curandería *nf* (**a**) *(medicina popular)* traditional *o* folk medicine (**b**) *Fam Pey (medicina falsa)* quackery

curandero, -a *nm,f* quack

curanto *nm Chile* = stew of meat and shellfish

curar 1 *vt* (**a**) *(sanar)* to cure (**b**) *(herida)* to dress (**c**) *(alimentos)* to cure (**d**) *(pieles)* to tan

2 *vi (enfermo)* to get well, to recover; *(herida)* to heal up

3 curarse *vpr* (**a**) *(sanar)* to recover *(de* from); **curarse en salud** to play safe (**b**) *(alimento)* to cure

curare *nm* curare

curasao *nm* curaçao

curativo, -a *adj* curative

curazao [kuraˈsao] *nm* curaçao

curcuncho *nm Andes Fam* (**a**) *(joroba)* hump (**b**) *(jorobado)* hunchback

curda *nf Fam Esp, RP* **agarrar** *o Esp* **coger una c.** to get plastered

curdo, -a 1 *adj* Kurdish

2 *nm,f (persona)* Kurd

3 *nm (lengua)* Kurdish

cureña *nf* gun carriage

curia *nf* (**a**) *Hist & Rel* curia (**b**) *Der (abogacía)* legal profession

curiosear 1 *vi (fisgonear)* to nose around; *(en tienda)* to browse around

2 *vt (libros, revistas)* to browse through

curiosidad *nf* (**a**) *(deseo de saber)* curiosity; **sentir** *o* **tener c. por** to be curious about (**b**) *(limpieza)* neatness, tidiness

curioso, -a 1 *adj* (**a**) *(por saber, averiguar)* curious, inquisitive (**b**) *(raro)* odd, strange (**c**) *(limpio)* neat, tidy; *(cuidadoso)* careful

2 *nm,f* onlooker

curita *nf Am* Band-Aid®

currante *Esp Fam* **1** *adj* hardworking

2 *nmf* worker

currar *vi Esp Fam* to work

curre *nm Esp Fam* work

currelar *vi Esp Fam* to work

currelo *nm Esp Fam* work

currículum (vitae) [kuˈrrikulum ('bite)] *(pl* **currícula** *o* **currículums (vitae))**, **currículo** *nm* curriculum vitae, résumé

currito, -a *nm,f Esp Fam* (ordinary) worker

curro *nm Esp Fam* work

currusco *nm Fam* crust (of bread)

curry *nm* curry; **pollo al c.** chicken curry

cursar *vt* (**a**) *(estudiar)* to study; **c. estudios de medicina** to study medicine; **cursaba segundo** she was in her second year (**b**) *(enviar)* to send (**c**) *(ordenar)* to give, to issue (**d**) *(tramitar)* to submit

cursi 1 *adj (vestido, canción)* tacky; *(modales, persona)* affected

2 *nmf* affected person

cursilada *nf* **ser una c.** *(acto, comportamiento)* to be affected;

(comentario) to be stupid; *(decoración, objeto)* to be tacky

cursilería *nf* (**a**) **ser una c.** *(acto, comportamiento)* to be affected; *(comentario)* to be stupid; *(decoración, objeto)* to be tacky (**b**) *(cualidad)* tackiness

cursillo *nm* (**a**) *(curso)* short course (**b**) *(conferencias)* series of lectures

cursiva 1 *adj (letra)* italic
2 *nf* italics

curso *nm* (**a**) *(año académico)* year
(**b**) *(lecciones)* course; **un c. de inglés/informática** an English/computing course; **c. por correspondencia** correspondence course; **c. intensivo** crash course
(**c**) *(texto, manual)* textbook
(**d**) *(dirección) (de río, acontecimientos)* course; *(de la economía)* trend; **dar c. a algo** *(dar rienda suelta)* to give free rein to sth; *(tramitar)* to process *o* deal with sth; **en el c. de una semana ha habido tres accidentes** there have been three accidents in the course of a week; **la situación comenzará a mejorar en el c. de un año** the situation will begin to improve within a year; **en c.** *(mes, año)* current; *(trabajo)* in progress; **seguir su c.** to go on, to continue
(**e**) *(circulación)* **moneda de c. legal** legal tender

cursor *nm Inform* cursor

curtido, -a 1 *adj* (**a**) *(piel, cuero)* tanned (**b**) *(experimentado)* seasoned
2 *nm* tanning

curtiembre *nf Andes, RP* tannery

curtir 1 *vt* (**a**) *(piel)* to tan (**b**) *(persona)* to harden
2 curtirse *vpr* (**a**) *(piel)* to tan (**b**) *(persona)* to become hardened

curva *nf* (**a**) *(gráfico, línea, forma)* curve; **c. de aprendizaje** learning curve; *Fam* **c. de la felicidad** *(barriga)* paunch; **c. de nivel** contour line (**b**) *(de carretera, río)* bend; **una carretera con muchas curvas** a winding road (**c**) **curvas** *(de mujer)* curves

curvado, -a *adj (forma)* curved; *(espalda)* bent

curvar 1 *vt (doblar)* to bend; *(espalda, cejas)* to arch
2 curvarse *vpr* to become bent

curvatura *nf* curvature

curvilíneo, -a *adj (en geometría)* curved; *(silueta del cuerpo)* curvaceous

curvo, -a *adj (forma)* curved; *(doblado)* bent

cuscurro *nm (pan frito)* crouton; *(punta de pan)* end *(of baguette)*

cuscús *nm inv* couscous

cúspide *nf* (**a**) *(de montaña)* summit, top (**b**) *(apogeo)* peak, height (**c**) *Geom* apex

custodia *nf* (**a**) *(de cosas)* safekeeping (**b**) *(de personas)* custody; **estar bajo la c. de** to be in the custody of (**c**) *Rel* monstrance

custodiar *vt* (**a**) *(vigilar)* to guard (**b**) *(proteger)* to look after

custodio *nm* guard

cutáneo, -a *adj* skin; **enfermedad cutánea** skin disease; **erupción cutánea** rash

cúter *nm (cuchilla)* mat knife

cutícula *nf* cuticle

cutis *nm inv* skin, complexion

cutre *adj Esp Fam* (**a**) *(de bajo precio, calidad)* cheap and nasty (**b**) *(sórdido)* shabby, dingy (**c**) *(tacaño)* tight, stingy

cutrería, cutrez *nf Esp Fam* shabbiness, dinginess; **este hotel es una c.** this hotel is a dump; **me regaló una c.** he gave me a cheap and nasty present

cuyo, -a *adj (posesión) (por parte de personas)* whose; *(por parte de cosas)* of which, whose; **ésos son los amigos en cuya casa nos hospedamos** those are the friends in whose house we spent the night; **ese señor, c. hijo conociste ayer** that man, whose son you met yesterday; **un equipo cuya principal estrella...** a team, the star player of which *o* whose star player...; **en c. caso** in which case

CV *nm (abrev de* **currículum vitae**) résumé

D

D, d [de] *nf (letra)* D, d

D. *(abrev de* **don***)* ≃ Mr.; *ver* **don**

Dacca *n* Dacca

dactilar *adj* **huella d.** fingerprint

dactilografía *nf* typing

dadá, dadaísmo *nm Arte* Dada, Dadaism

dadaísta *adj & nmf Arte* Dadaist

dádiva *nf (regalo)* gift; *(donativo)* donation

dadivoso, -a *adj* generous

dado¹ *nm* dice, die

dado², -a 1 *adj* given; **dada la naturaleza del caso** given the nature of the case; **en un momento d.** *(en el tiempo)* at a certain point; **ser d. a** to be inclined *o* given to
    2 dado que *loc conj* since, seeing as; **d. que somos tan pocos, se suspende la reunión** seeing as there are so few of us here, the meeting is adjourned

dador, -ora *nm,f* **(a)** *(de letra de cambio)* drawer **(b)** *(de carta)* bearer

daga *nf* dagger

daguerrotipo *nm* daguerreotype

daiquiri *nm* daiquiri

Dakar *n* Dakar

Dakota *n* D. del Norte/Sur North/South Dakota

dalai-lama *nm* Dalai Lama

dale *interj* ¡d.! ¡otra vez con lo mismo! there you go again!; **te digo que pares y tú ¡d. (que d.)!** I've told you to stop, but you just carry on and on!

dalia *nf* dahlia

dálmata *adj & nmf* **(a)** *(persona)* Dalmatian **(b)** *(perro)* Dalmatian

daltónico, -a 1 *adj* color-blind
    2 *nm,f* person with color blindness

daltonismo *nm* color blindness

dama *nf* **(a)** *(mujer)* lady; **d. de honor** *(de novia)* bridesmaid; *(de reina)* lady-in-waiting; **primera d.** *Teatro* leading lady; *Pol* first lady **(b)** *(en juego de damas)* king; *(en ajedrez, naipes)* queen; **damas** *(juego)* checkers *(singular)*

damajuana *nf* demijohn

Damasco *n* Damascus

damasco *nm* **(a)** *(tela)* damask **(b)** *Andes, RP (albaricoque)* apricot

damasquinado *nm* damascene

damero *nm* checkerboard

damisela *nf Anticuado* damsel

damnificado, -a 1 *adj* affected, damaged
    2 *nm,f* victim

damnificar [59] *vt (cosa)* to damage; *(persona)* to harm, to injure

dance *etc ver* **danzar**

dandi, dandy *nm* dandy

danés, -esa 1 *adj* Danish
    2 *nm,f (persona)* Dane
    3 *nm (lengua)* Danish

dantesco, -a *adj también Fig* Dantesque

Danubio *nm* **el D.** the (River) Danube

danza *nf (actividad)* dancing; *(baile)* dance; *Fig* **estar siempre en d.** to be always on the go *o* doing sth; *Fam Fig* **estar metido en d.** to be up to no good; **d. clásica** classical ballet; **d. española** Spanish dance; **d. del vientre** belly dance

danzar [14] *vi (bailar)* to dance; *Fig (ir de un sitio a otro)* to run about

danzarín, -ina 1 *adj* active, lively
    2 *nm,f* dancer

dañado, -a *adj (objeto, vehículo)* damaged

dañar 1 *vt (pieza, objeto)* to damage; *(vista, cosecha)* to harm, to damage; *(persona)* to hurt; **el tabaco daña la salud** tobacco damages your health
    2 dañarse *vpr (cosa)* to become damaged; *(persona)* to injure, to hurt; **se dañó el codo jugando al squash** he hurt his elbow playing squash

dañino, -a *adj* harmful

daño *nm* **(a)** *(dolor)* pain, hurt; **hacer d. a alguien** to hurt sb; **me hacen d. los zapatos** my shoes are hurting me; **hacerse d.** to hurt oneself; **me hice d. en el tobillo** I hurt my ankle; **¿te has hecho d.?** have you hurt yourself?, are you hurt? **(b)** *(perjuicio) (a algo)* damage; *(a alguien)* harm; **los daños se calculan en un millón de pesos** the damage is estimated to be about a million pesos; **el d. ya está hecho** the damage is done; **daños estructurales** structural damage; **daños medioambientales** environmental damage; **daños y perjuicios** damages

dar [20] **1** *vt* **(a)** *(entregar, otorgar)* to give; *(proporcionar)* to give, to provide with; *(naipes)* to deal; **d. algo a alguien** to give sth to sb, to give sb sth; **se lo di a mi hermano** I gave it to my brother
    (b) *(producir)* to give, to produce; *(frutos, flores)* to bear; *(beneficios, intereses)* to yield; **la salsa le da un sabor muy bueno** the sauce gives it a very pleasant taste, the sauce makes it taste very nice
    (c) *(fiesta, cena)* to have, to hold; **d. una cena en honor de alguien** to hold *o* give a dinner in someone's honor
    (d) *(luz, agua, gas) (encender)* to turn *o* switch on; *(suministrar por primera vez)* to connect; *(suministrar tras un corte)* to turn back on
    (e) *Cine, Teatro & TV* to show; *(concierto, interpretación)* to give; **dan una película del oeste** they're showing a western, there's a western on
    (f) *(mostrar)* to show; **d. muestras de sensatez** to show good sense
    (g) *(untar con, aplicar)* **d. barniz a una silla** to varnish a chair
    (h) *(enseñar)* to teach; **d. inglés/historia** to teach English/history
    (i) *(provocar)* **le dio un infarto** he had a heart attack; **me da vergüenza/pena** it makes me ashamed/sad; **me da risa** it

makes me laugh; **me da miedo** it frightens me; *Fam* **si no se calla me va a d. algo** if he doesn't shut up soon, I'll go mad; *Fam* **si sigues trabajando así te va a d. algo** you can't go on working like that

(**j**) *(expresa acción)* **d. un grito** to give a cry; **d. un vistazo a** to have a look at; **darle un golpe/una puñalada a alguien** to hit/stab sb; **voy a d. un paseo** I'm going (to go) for a walk

(**k**) *(considerar)* **d. algo por** to consider sth as; **eso lo doy por hecho** I take that for granted; **d. a alguien por muerto** to give sb up for dead

(**l**) *(expresiones)* **donde las dan las toman** you get what you deserve; **el reloj dio las doce** the clock struck twelve; *Esp Fam* **d. el día a alguien** to ruin sb's day (for them); **es tan pesado que me dio la tarde** he's so boring that he ruined the afternoon for me; **no d. una** to get everything wrong

2 *vi* (**a**) *(repartir)* *(en naipes)* to deal

(**b**) *(horas)* to strike; **dieron las tres en el reloj** three o'clock struck

(**c**) *(golpear)* **le dieron en la cabeza** they hit him on the head; **la piedra dio contra el cristal** the stone hit the window; **como no te portes bien, te voy a d.** if you don't behave, I'll smack you

(**d**) **d. a** *(accionar)* *(llave de paso)* to turn; *(botón, timbre)* to press

(**e**) **d. a** *(estar orientado)* *(sujeto: ventana, balcón)* to look out onto, to overlook; *(sujeto: pasillo, puerta)* to lead to; *(sujeto: casa, fachada)* to face

(**f**) *(encontrar)* **d. con algo/alguien** to find sth/sb; **he dado con la solución** I've hit upon the solution

(**g**) *(proporcionar)* **d. de beber a alguien** to give sb something to drink; **da de mamar a su hijo** she breastfeeds her son

(**h**) *(ser suficiente)* **d. para** to be enough for

(**i**) *(motivar)* **d. que hablar** to set people talking; **aquello me dio que pensar** that made me think

(**j**) *(expresa repetición)* **le dieron de palos** they beat him repeatedly with a stick

(**k**) *(tomar costumbre)* **darle a uno por hacer algo** to get it into one's head to do sth; **le ha dado por la gimnasia** she's taken it into her head to start gymnastics

(**l**) *(expresiones)* **d. de sí** *(ropa, calzado)* to give, to stretch; **no d. más de sí** *o* **para más** *(persona, animal)* not to be up to much anymore

3 darse *vpr* (**a**) *(suceder)* to occur, to happen; **se da pocas veces** it rarely happens; **se dio la circunstancia de que...** it so happened that...

(**b**) *(entregarse)* **darse a la bebida** to take to drink

(**c**) *(golpearse)* **darse contra** *o* **con** to hit; **se dieron contra una farola** they crashed into *o* hit a lamppost

(**d**) *(tener aptitud)* **se me da bien/mal el latín** I'm good/bad at Latin

(**e**) *(considerarse)* **darse por** to consider oneself (to be); **darse por vencido** to give in

(**f**) *(expresiones)* *Esp Fam* **dársela a alguien** *(engañar)* to take sb in; *Fam* **se las da de intelectual/elegante** he fancies himself as an intellectual/a dandy

dardo *nm* dart

dársena *nf* dock

darvinismo *nm* Darwinism

datación *nf (de restos arqueológicos)* dating

datar 1 *vt* to date

2 *vi* **d. de** to date back to, to date from

dátil *nm* (**a**) *Bot & Culin* date (**b**) *Fam* **dátiles** *(dedos)* fingers (**c**) *(animal)* **d. (de mar)** date mussel

dativo *nm Gram* dative

dato *nm (hecho, cifra)* piece of information, fact; **datos** *(información)* information, data; *Inform* data; **datos (personales)** (personal) details

dcha. *(abrev de* **derecha**) rt

d. de JC., d. JC. *(abrev de* **después de Jesucristo**) AD

de *prep*

> **de** combines with the article **el** to form the contraction **del** (e.g. **del hombre** of the man).

(**a**) *(posesión, pertenencia)* of; **el coche de mi padre/mis padres** my father's/parents' car; **es de ella** it's hers; **la pata de la mesa** the table leg

(**b**) *(procedencia, distancia)* from; **salir de casa** to leave home; **soy de Bilbao** I'm from Bilbao; **de la playa al apartamento hay 100 metros** it's 100 meters from the beach to the apartment

(**c**) *(materia)* (made) of; **un vaso de plástico** a plastic cup; **un reloj de oro** a gold watch

(**d**) *(contenido)* **un vaso de agua** a glass of water

(**e**) *(en descripciones)* **una película de terror** a horror movie; **de fácil manejo** user-friendly; **la señora de verde** the lady in green; **el chico de la coleta** the boy with the ponytail; **he comprado las peras de dos dólares el kilo** I bought the pears that were two dollars a kilo; **un sello de 60 céntimos** a 60-cent stamp

(**f**) *(asunto)* about; **hablábamos de ti** we were talking about you; **libros de historia** history books

(**g**) *(uso)* **una bici de carreras** a racer; **ropa de deporte** sportswear

(**h**) *(en calidad de)* as; **trabaja de bombero** he works as a fireman

(**i**) *(tiempo)* *(desde)* from; *(durante)* in; **trabaja de nueve a cinco** she works from nine to five; **de madrugada** early in the morning; **a las cuatro de la tarde** at four in the afternoon; **trabaja de noche y duerme de día** he works at night and sleeps during the day

(**j**) *(causa, modo)* with; **morirse de hambre** to die of hunger; **llorar de alegría** to cry with joy; **de una patada** with a kick; **de una sola vez** in one go; **de tres en tres** three at a time

(**k**) *(con superlativos)* **el mejor de todos** the best of all; **el más importante del mundo** the most important in the world

(**l**) *(en comparaciones)* **más/menos de...** more/less than...

(**m**) *(adjetivo + de + infinitivo)* **es difícil de creer** it's hard to believe

(**n**) *(+ infinitivo)* *(condición)* if; **de ir a verte, sería este domingo** if I do visit you, it'll be this Sunday; **de no ser por ti, me hubiese hundido** if it hadn't been for you, I wouldn't have made it

(**o**) *(el + adjetivo + de)* *(enfatiza cualidad)* **el idiota de tu hermano** your stupid brother

dé *ver* **dar**

deambular *vi* to wander (around)

deán *nm* dean

debacle *nf* debacle

debajo *adv* underneath; **el de d.** the one underneath; **d. vive un pianista** a pianist lives downstairs; **el vecino/la oficina de d.** the neighbor/office downstairs; **d. de** underneath, under; **d. de la mesa/las escaleras** under the table/the stairs; **¿qué llevas d. del abrigo?** what have you got on under your coat?; **llevo una camiseta por d.** I've got a vest on underneath; **por d. de lo normal** below normal; **pasamos por d. del puente** we went under the bridge

debate *nm* debate

debatir 1 *vt* to debate

2 debatirse *vpr (luchar)* to struggle; **debatirse entre la vida y la muerte** to hover between life and death

debe *nm* debit (side); **d. y haber** debit and credit

deber 1 *nm* (**a**) *(obligación)* duty; **los derechos y los deberes de los ciudadanos** citizens' rights and duties (**b**) **deberes** *(trabajo escolar)* homework; **hacer los deberes** to do one's homework

2 *vt* *(adeudar)* to owe; **d. algo a alguien** to owe sb sth, to owe sth to sb; **¿qué** *o* **cuánto le debo?** how much is it?

3 *vi* **(a)** (+ *infinitivo*) *(expresa obligación)* **debo hacerlo** I have to do it, I must do it; **debes dominar tus impulsos** you must *o* should control your impulses; **deberían abolir esa ley** they ought to *o* should abolish that law; **no deberías fumar tanto** you shouldn't smoke so much **(b)** *(expresa posibilidad)* **deben de ser las diez** it must be ten o'clock; **no debe de ser muy mayor** she can't be very old

4 deberse a *vpr* **(a)** *(ser consecuencia de)* to be due to; **y eso, ¿a qué se debe?** and what's the reason for that? **(b)** *(dedicarse a)* to have a responsibility toward

debidamente *adv* properly

debido, -a 1 *adj* **(a)** *(adeudado)* owing, owed **(b)** *(justo, conveniente)* due, proper; **el tema se abordará en su d. momento** the subject will be dealt with in due course; **con el d. respeto, creo que se equivoca** with all due respect, I think you're mistaken; **creo que he comido más de lo d.** I think I've had a bit too much to eat; **como es d.** properly

2 debido a *loc prep* **d. a su enfermedad** owing to *o* because of his illness; **esto es d. a la falta de previsión** this is due to lack of foresight

débil 1 *adj* **(a)** *(persona)* *(sin fuerzas)* weak; *(condescendiente)* lax, lenient; **de constitución d.** prone to illness, sickly; **d. de carácter** of weak character **(b)** *(voz, sonido)* faint; *(luz)* dim; **una d. mejoría** a slight improvement; **una d. brisa movía la cortinas** a slight breeze moved the curtains

2 *nmf* weak person

debilidad *nf* **(a)** *(flojedad)* weakness; **tener d. por** to have a soft spot for; **el chocolate es su d.** he has a weakness for chocolate **(b)** *(condescendencia)* laxness

debilitación *nf*, **debilitamiento** *nm* weakening

debilitante *adj* debilitating

debilitar 1 *vt* to weaken

2 debilitarse *vpr* to become *o* grow weak

debitar *vt* to debit

débito *nm (debe)* debit; *(deuda)* debt; *Am* **d. bancario** regular bank payments

debut *(pl* debuts*)* *nm (de persona)* debut; *(de obra)* premiere; **su d. en sociedad fue brillante** her entry into society was impressive

debutante *nmf* = person making his/her debut

debutar *vi (actor, cantante)* to make one's debut; **la obra debuta en Madrid el día 4** the play opens in Madrid on the fourth

década *nf* decade

decadencia *nf* decadence; **en d.** *(moda)* on the way out; *(cultura, sociedad)* in decline; **la d. del imperio** the decline of the empire

decadente *adj (ambiente)* decadent; *(economía)* in decline

decaedro *nm* decahedron

decaer [13] *vi (debilitarse)* to decline; *(enfermo)* to get weaker; *(salud)* to fail; *(entusiasmo)* to flag; *(empresa)* to go downhill; **¡que no decaiga!** don't lose heart!; **su belleza no ha decaído con los años** her beauty has not faded with the years

decágono *nm* decagon

decaído, -a *adj (desalentado)* gloomy, downhearted; *(débil)* frail

decaigo *ver* **decaer**

decaimiento *nm (desaliento)* gloominess; *(decadencia)* decline; *(falta de fuerzas)* weakness

decalcificar [59] *Med* **1** *vt* to decalcify

2 decalcificarse *vpr* to decalcify, to lose calcium

decalitro *nm* decaliter

decálogo *nm Rel* Decalogue; *Fig (normas)* ten golden *o* basic rules

decámetro *nm* decameter

decanato *nm* **(a)** *(cargo)* deanship **(b)** *(despacho)* dean's office

decano, -a *nm,f* **(a)** *(de corporación, facultad)* dean **(b)** *(veterano) (hombre)* senior member, doyen; *(mujer)* senior member, doyenne

decantar 1 *vt* to decant

2 decantarse *vpr* **(a)** *(inclinarse)* to lean (toward) **(b)** **decantarse por** *(optar por)* to opt for

decapante 1 *adj* **líquido d.** paint stripper

2 *nm* paint stripper

decapar *vt* to strip the paint from

decapitación *nf* decapitation, beheading

decapitar *vt* to decapitate, to behead

decatleta *nmf* decathlete

decatlón *nm* decathlon

decayera *etc ver* **decaer**

deceleración *nf* deceleration

decelerar *vt & vi* to decelerate, to slow down

decena *nf* ten; **una d. de...** *(unas diez)* about ten...; *(diez)* ten...; **las víctimas se cuentan por decenas** there have been dozens of casualties; **estos tornillos se venden por decenas** these screws are sold in tens

decenal *adj* **un plan d.** a ten-year plan; **un premio d.** a prize awarded every ten years

decencia *nf* **(a)** *(decoro)* decency; *(en el vestir)* modesty **(b)** *(dignidad)* dignity

decenio *nm* decade

decente *adj* **(a)** *(digno)* decent; **un sueldo d.** a decent salary *o* wage **(b)** *(en el comportamiento)* proper; *(en el vestir)* modest; **este es un establecimiento d.** this is a respectable establishment **(c)** *(limpio)* clean

decepción *nf* disappointment; **me llevé una gran d. al oír la noticia** I was really disappointed when I heard the news; **su nueva película ha sido una d.** her new movie is disappointing *o* a disappointment

decepcionante *adj* disappointing

decepcionar *vt* to disappoint

deceso *nm* decease, death

dechado *nm* **ser un d. de virtudes** to be a paragon of virtue

decibelio, *Am* **decibel** *nm* decibel

decididamente *adv* **(a)** *(con decisión)* resolutely, with determination **(b)** *(sin duda)* definitely; **d., es buena idea** it's definitely a good idea

decidido, -a *adj* determined

decidir 1 *vt* **(a)** *(tomar una decisión)* to decide; **el juez decidirá si es inocente o no** the judge will decide *o* determine whether or not he is innocent; **d. hacer algo** to decide to do sth **(b)** *(determinar)* to decide; **el voto de la clase media decidió la elección** the middle-class vote decided *o* swung the election

2 *vi* to decide, to choose; **¿a qué restaurante vamos? — tú decides** which restaurant shall we go to? — you decide; **d. entre dos cosas** to choose between two things

3 decidirse *vpr* to decide, to make up one's mind; **¡decídete de una vez!** make up your mind!; **decidirse a hacer algo** to decide to do sth; **si te decides a venir, llámame** if you decide to come, give me a ring; **decidirse por** to decide on, to choose

decigramo *nm* decigram

decilitro *nm* deciliter

décima *nf (en medidas)* tenth; **tiene unas décimas de fiebre** she has a slight fever; **una d. de segundo** a tenth of a second; **ganó por décimas de segundo** he won by tenths of a second

decimal *adj & nm* decimal

decímetro *nm* decimeter

décimo, -a 1 *núm* tenth; **la décima parte** a tenth

2 *nm* (**a**) *(fracción)* tenth (**b**) *(en lotería)* = ticket giving a tenth share in a number entered in the Spanish "Lotería Nacional"

decimoctavo, -a *núm* eighteenth

decimocuarto, -a *núm* fourteenth

decimonónico, -a *adj* (**a**) *(del siglo XIX)* nineteenth-century (**b**) *(anticuado)* old-fashioned

decimonono, -a *núm Formal* nineteenth

decimonoveno, -a *núm* nineteenth

decimoquinto, -a *núm* fifteenth

decimoséptimo, -a *núm* seventeenth

decimosexto, -a *núm* sixteenth

decimotercero, -a *núm* thirteenth

decir [21] **1** *vt* (**a**) *(en general)* to say; **d. que sí/no** to say yes/no; **dice que no viene** she says (that) she is not coming; **¿cómo se dice "estación" en inglés?** how do you say "estación" in English?; **dicen que va a ser un verano muy seco** they say it's going to be a very dry summer

(**b**) *(contar, ordenar)* to tell; **¿quién te lo ha dicho?** who told you that?; **¿qué quieres que te diga?** what do you want me to say?, what can I say?; **d. a alguien que haga algo** to tell sb to do sth; **d. la verdad** to tell the truth

(**c**) *(recitar)* to recite, to read

(**d**) *(revelar)* to tell, to show; **eso lo dice todo** that says it all; **d. mucho (en favor) de** to say a lot for

(**e**) *(llamar)* to call; **le dicen la carretera de la muerte** they call it the road of death

(**f**) *(expresiones)* **d. para sí** to say to oneself; **decirle a alguien cuatro verdades** to tell sb a few home truths; **preocuparse por el qué dirán** to worry about what people will say; **es d.** that is, that's to say; **ni que d. tiene** needless to say; **¡no me digas!** no!, never!; **¡no me digas que no te gusta!** don't tell me you don't like it!; **no me dice nada el tenis** tennis doesn't do anything for me; **no hay más que d.** that's all there is to it, that's that; (**o**) **mejor dicho** or rather; **por decirlo así, por así decirlo** in other words, so to speak; **no está lloviendo mucho que digamos** it's not exactly raining; **querer d.** to mean; **¿qué quieres d. con eso?** what do you mean by that?; *Esp* **¡y que lo digas!** you can say that again!

2 *vi* **como quien dice, como si dijéramos** so to speak; *Esp* **¿diga?, ¿dígame?** *(al teléfono)* hello?

3 decirse *vpr Fam (reflexionar)* to say to oneself

4 es un d. it's not strictly true

decisión *nf* (**a**) *(dictamen, resolución)* decision; **tomar una d.** to make *o* take a decision; **d. por mayoría** majority decision (**b**) *(empeño, tesón)* determination, resolve; *(seguridad, resolución)* decisiveness; **actuar con d.** to act decisively

decisivo, -a *adj* decisive

decisorio, -a *adj* decision-making

declamación *nf* (**a**) *(arte)* declamation (**b**) *(recitación)* recital, recitation

declamar *vt & vi* to declaim, to recite

declaración *nf* (**a**) *(manifestación)* statement; *(afirmación)* declaration; **no hizo declaraciones a los medios de comunicación** he didn't make any statement to the media; **prestar d.** to give evidence; **tomar d. (a)** to take a statement (from); **d. de amor** declaration of love; **d. de guerra** declaration of war; **d. del impuesto sobre la renta** income tax return (**b**) *(comienzo) (de incendio)* outbreak

declarado, -a *adj (manifiesto)* open, professed; **es un homosexual d.** he is openly gay; **hay un odio d. entre ellos** there is open hostility between them

declarante *nmf* witness

declarar 1 *vt (manifestar)* to declare; *(afirmar)* to state, to say; **d. la verdad** to tell the truth; **d. culpable/inocente a alguien** to find sb guilty/not guilty; **¿algo que d.?** *(en aduana)* anything to declare?

2 *vi Der* to testify, to give evidence; **lo llamaron a d.** he was called to give evidence

3 declararse *vpr* (**a**) *(incendio, epidemia)* to break out (**b**) *(confesar el amor)* to declare one's feelings *o* love; **se le ha declarado Fernando** Fernando has declared his love to her (**c**) *(dar una opinión)* **declararse a favor de algo** to say that one supports sth; **declararse en contra de algo** to say one is opposed to sth; **declararse culpable/inocente** to plead guilty/not guilty

declinación *nf* (**a**) *(caída)* decline (**b**) *Gram* declension

declinar 1 *vt (gen) & Gram* to decline; *(responsabilidad)* to disclaim; **declinó amablemente la invitación** he politely declined the invitation

2 *vi (día, tarde)* to draw to a close; *(fiebre)* to subside, to abate; *(economía)* to decline; **su interés por la caza ha declinado** his interest in hunting has declined

declive *nm* (**a**) *(decadencia)* decline, fall; **en d.** in decline (**b**) *(pendiente)* slope; **un terreno en d.** an area of sloping ground

decolaje *nm Am* takeoff

decolar *vi Am* to take off

decoloración *nf (pérdida de color)* discoloration, fading; *(de pelo)* bleaching

decolorante 1 *adj* bleaching

2 *nm* bleaching agent

decolorar 1 *vt* to bleach

2 decolorarse *vpr* to fade; **decolorarse el pelo** to bleach one's hair

decomisar *vt* to confiscate, to seize

decomiso *nm (acción)* confiscation *(by customs)*; **tienda de decomisos** = store selling goods (such as cameras and radios) confiscated by customs

decoración *nf* (**a**) *(acción)* decoration; *(efecto)* decor (**b**) *(adorno)* decorations

decorado *nm Cine & Teatro* set; **decorados** sets, scenery

decorador, -ora *nm,f* interior designer; *Cine & Teatro* set designer

decorar 1 *vt* to decorate

2 *vi* to be decorative

decorativo, -a *adj* decorative

decoro *nm* (**a**) *(pudor)* decency, decorum (**b**) *(dignidad)* dignity; **vivir con d.** to live decently

decoroso, -a *adj (decente)* decent; *(correcto)* seemly, proper

decrecer [46] *vi (disminuir)* to decrease, to decline; *(caudal del río)* to go down; **el paro decreció en un 2 por ciento** unemployment has fallen by 2 percent; **la luna está decreciendo** the moon is on the wane

decreciente *adj* declining, decreasing

decrépito, -a *adj Pey (anciano)* decrepit; *(civilización, industria)* decadent, declining

decrepitud *nf Pey (de un anciano)* decrepitude; *(de una civilización)* decline

decretar *vt* to decree

decretazo *nm Esp Fam Pey* diktat

decreto *nm* decree; **por real d.** by royal decree; **d. ley** decree

decúbito *nm* horizontal position

dedal *nm* thimble

dédalo *nm* labyrinth, maze

dedicación *nf* dedication; **con d. (en) exclusiva** full-time; **trabaja con d.** he works with real dedication

dedicar [59] **1** *vt* (**a**) *(tiempo, dinero, energía)* to devote (**b**) *(espacio, cuarto, solar)* to use; **este solar se dedicará a viviendas** this land will be used for housing (**c**) *(libro, monumento)* to dedicate; **dedicó al público unas palabras de agradecimiento** he addressed a few words of thanks to the audience

2 dedicarse a *vpr* (**a**) *(a una profesión)* **¿a qué se dedica usted?** what do you do for a living?; **se dedica a la**

enseñanza she works as a teacher (**b**) *(a una actividad, persona)* to spend time on; **dejé la empresa para dedicarme a mi familia** I left the company so that I could spend more time with my family; **los domingos me dedico al estudio** I spend Sundays studying

dedicatoria *nf* dedication

dedillo *nm Fam* **saber algo al d.** to know sth inside out

dedique *etc ver* **dedicar**

dedo *nm* (**a**) *(de la mano)* finger; **meterse el d. en la nariz** to pick one's nose; **¡no señales con el d.!** don't point!; **dos dedos de whisky** two fingers of whiskey; **d. anular** ring finger; **d. corazón** *o* **medio** middle finger; **d. gordo** *o* **pulgar** thumb; **d. índice/meñique** index/little finger
  (**b**) *(del pie)* toe; **d. gordo/pequeño** big/little toe
  (**c**) *(expresiones)* **escaparse de entre los dedos** to slip through one's fingers; *Fam* **hacer d., ir a d.** to hitchhike; *Fig* **chuparse el d.** to be a fool; **no creas que me chupo el d.** I wasn't born yesterday, you know; **estar para chuparse los dedos** to be mouthwatering; *Fam* **nadie movió un d. para ayudarme** nobody lifted a finger to help me; **nombrar a alguien a d.** to handpick sb; **no tener dos dedos de frente** to be as thick as two short planks; *Esp* **pillarse** *o* **cogerse los dedos** to get one's fingers burned; **poner el d. en la llaga** to put one's finger on it

deducción *nf* deduction; *Fin* **d. fiscal** tax-deductible expenditure

deducible *adj* (**a**) *(idea)* deducible (**b**) *(dinero)* deductible

deducir [18] *vt* (**a**) *(inferir)* to guess, to deduce; **por la luz dedujo que debía de ser tarde** he could tell by the light that it must be late; **dedujo quién era el asesino** he worked out who the killer was (**b**) *(descontar)* to deduct; **me deducen del sueldo la seguridad social** national health insurance is deducted from my salary

deductivo, -a *adj* deductive

dedujera *etc ver* **deducir**

deduzco *ver* **deducir**

de facto *adj* de facto

defecación *nf* defecation

defecar [59] *vi* to defecate

defección *nf* defection, desertion

defectivo, -a *adj* defective

defecto *nm* (**a**) *(físico)* defect; *(moral)* fault, shortcoming; **no le veo ningún d. a esta casa** I can't see anything wrong with this house; **d. de fábrica** *o* **fabricación** defect in manufacturing; **d. de forma** administrative error; **d. del habla** *o* **de pronunciación** speech defect *o* impediment (**b**) **por d.** by default (**c**) **en su d.** by default; **acuda a la embajada o, en su d., al consulado más cercano** go to the embassy, or, failing that, to the nearest consulate

defectuoso, -a *adj (mercancía)* defective, faulty; *(trabajo)* inaccurate

defender [64] **1** *vt* (**a**) *(país, reo)* to defend; *(amigo)* to stand up for; **d. los intereses de alguien** to defend sb's interests; **defendió su teoría con sólidos argumentos** he supported his theory with sound arguments (**b**) *(proteger) (del frío, calor)* to protect (**de** against)
  2 defenderse *vpr* (**a**) *(protegerse)* to defend oneself (**de** against); **me defendí como pude de sus ataques** I defended myself from his attacks as best I could (**b**) *(apañarse)* to get by; **se defiende bien en su trabajo** he's getting along okay at work; **se defiende en inglés** he can get by in English; **¿qué tal dibujas? — me defiendo** how are you at drawing? — I'm not too bad; **sé defenderme sola** I can look after myself

defendible *adj* defensible

defendido, -a *nm,f (de abogado)* client *(of defense counsel)*

defenestración *nf* dismissal, unceremonious removal

defenestrar *vt* to oust, to dismiss

defensa 1 *nf* (**a**) *(protección)* defense; **en d. de** in defense of; **la d. del medio ambiente** the protection of the environment; **d. personal** self-defense (**b**) *Der* **la d.** *(parte en un juicio)* the defense; **en d. propia, en legítima d.** *(acción)* in self-defense (**c**) **(el Ministerio de) D.** ≃ the Department of Defense (**d**) **defensas** *(sistema inmunitario)* defenses; **tiene las defensas muy bajas** his body's defenses are very low (**e**) *Dep* defense
  2 *nmf Dep* defender; **d. central** central defender, center back

defensiva *nf* defensive; **ponerse/estar a la d.** to go/be on the defensive

defensivo, -a *adj* defensive; **estrategia defensiva** defensive strategy

defensor, -ora 1 *adj* **abogado d.** counsel for the defense
  2 *nm,f (de ideal, persona)* defender; *(abogado)* counsel for the defense; *(adalid)* champion; **un gran d. de la paz** a great campaigner for peace; *Esp* **d. del pueblo** ombudsman; **d. del soldado** = public body created to defend soldiers' rights, especially young soldiers doing military service; **el d. del título** *(el actual campeón)* the defending champion

defeño, -a *nm,f Méx* person from the "Distrito Federal" *(Mexico City)*

deferencia *nf* deference; **por d. a** in deference to

deferente *adj (cortés)* deferential

deferir [62] **1** *vt Der* to refer
  2 *vi* to defer (**a** to)

deficiencia *nf (defecto)* deficiency, shortcoming; *(insuficiencia)* lack

deficiente 1 *adj* (**a**) *(defectuoso) (producto, cantidad, persona)* deficient; *(audición, vista)* defective (**b**) *(mediocre)* poor, unsatisfactory
  2 *nmf* **d. (mental)** mentally handicapped person
  3 *nm Educ* **muy d.** very poor, D

déficit *(pl* **déficits***) nm* (**a**) *Econ* deficit; **d. de la balanza comercial** trade gap; **d. comercial** trade deficit; **d. presupuestario** budget deficit; **d. público** public deficit (**b**) *(falta)* lack, shortage

deficitario, -a *adj (empresa, operación)* loss-making; *(balance)* negative, showing a deficit

defiendo *etc ver* **defender**

definición *nf* (**a**) *(explicación)* definition; **por d.** by definition (**b**) *(descripción)* description (**c**) *(en televisión)* resolution; **alta d.** high resolution

definido, -a *adj* (**a**) *(límite, idea)* (clearly) defined (**b**) *Gram* **artículo d.** definite article

definir 1 *vt* (**a**) *(explicar, precisar)* to define (**b**) *(describir)* to describe
  2 definirse *vpr* to take a clear stance; **no se definió por ninguno de los dos bandos** he took neither side; **el plan no acababa de definirse** the plan had not yet taken any definite shape

definitivamente *adv* (**a**) *(sin duda)* definitely (**b**) *(para siempre)* for good

definitivo, -a 1 *adj* (**a**) *(concluyente, final)* final; **los resultados definitivos** the final results; **la versión definitiva** *(de un texto)* the definitive version (**b**) *(decisivo)* decisive; **su intervención fue definitiva para resolver el conflicto** his intervention was decisive in resolving the conflict
  2 en definitiva *loc adv* in short; **ésta es, en definitiva, la única alternativa que nos queda** this is, in short, the only alternative we have left

deflación *nf Econ* deflation

deflacionista, deflacionario, -a *adj Econ* deflationary

deflagración *nf Formal* deflagration

deflagrar *vi Formal* to deflagrate

defoliación *nf* defoliation

deforestación *nf* deforestation

deforestar *vt* to deforest

deformación *nf (de huesos, objetos)* deformation; *(de imagen, verdad)* distortion; **d. física** (physical) deformity; **tener d. profesional** to be always acting as if one were still at work

deformado, -a *adj* (a) *(cuerpo)* deformed; *(objeto)* misshapen (b) *(imagen, verdad)* distorted

deformar 1 *vt (huesos, objetos)* to deform; *(imagen, verdad)* to distort

2 deformarse *vpr* to go out of shape; **se me ha deformado el jersey al lavarlo** my sweater lost its shape when I washed it

deforme *adj (cuerpo)* deformed, disfigured; *(imagen)* distorted; *(objeto)* misshapen

deformidad *nf* deformity

defraudación *nf (fraude fiscal)* tax evasion

defraudador, -ora 1 *adj (a hacienda)* tax-evading

2 *nm,f (a hacienda)* tax evader

defraudar 1 *vt* (a) *(decepcionar)* to disappoint; **su última película me defraudó mucho** I was very disappointed by his last movie; **creí que podría contar contigo, pero me has defraudado** I thought I could count on you, but you've let me down (b) *(estafar)* to defraud; **d. a Hacienda** to practice tax evasion

2 *vi (decepcionar)* to be disappointing, to disappoint; **reapareció Carreras y no defraudó** Carreras made a reappearance and did not disappoint

defunción *nf* decease, death; **cerrado por d.** *(en letrero)* closed due to bereavement

degeneración *nf* degeneration

degenerado, -a *adj & nm,f* degenerate

degenerar *vi* to degenerate (**en** into)

degenerativo, -a *adj (proceso, enfermedad)* degenerative

deglución *nf* swallowing

deglutir *vt & vi* to swallow

degolladero *nm* slaughterhouse

degollar [6] *vt (cortar la garganta)* to cut *o* slit the throat of; *(decapitar)* to behead; *Fig* **¡como lo pille, lo degüello!** I'll kill him if I catch him!

degollina *nf Esp Fam* bloodbath

degradable *adj* degradable

degradación *nf* (a) *(de moral, naturaleza)* degradation (b) *(de un cargo)* demotion

degradante *adj* degrading

degradar 1 *vt* (a) *(moralmente)* to degrade, to debase (b) *(de un cargo)* to demote

2 degradarse *vpr* to degrade *o* lower oneself

degüello 1 *ver* **degollar**

2 *nm (decapitación)* beheading; *(degolladura)* slaughter; *Fig* **entrar a d.** to storm in ruthlessly

degustación *nf* tasting *(of wines, food)*

degustar *vt* to taste *(wines, food)*

dehesa *nf* meadow

deidad *nf* deity

deificar [59] *vt* to deify

dejada *nf (en tenis)* drop shot

dejadez *nf (abandono)* neglect; *(en aspecto)* slovenliness; *(pereza)* laziness; **no lo hizo por d.** he didn't do it because he couldn't be bothered

dejado, -a 1 *adj* careless; *(aspecto)* slovenly

2 *nm,f (persona)* slovenly person

dejar 1 *vt* (a) *(poner)* to leave, to put; **dejó los papeles en la mesa** he put *o* left the papers on the table; **deja el abrigo en la percha** put your coat on the hanger; **he dejado la moto muy cerca** I've left *o* parked my motorbike nearby

(b) *(encomendar)* **dejarle algo a alguien** to leave sth with sb; **le dejé los niños a mi madre** I left the children with my mother

(c) *Esp (prestar)* **d. algo a alguien** to lend sb sth, to lend sth to sb; **¿me dejas un paraguas?** could you lend me an umbrella?

(d) *(abandonar) (casa, trabajo, país)* to leave; *(tabaco, estudios)* to give up; *(familia)* to abandon; **d. a alguien en algún sitio** *(con el coche)* to drop sb off somewhere; **d. algo por imposible** to give sth up as a lost cause; **d. a alguien atrás** to leave sb behind; **su marido la ha dejado** her husband has left her; **te dejo, tengo que irme** I have to leave you now, I must go

(e) *(permitir)* **d. a alguien hacer algo** to let sb do sth, to allow sb to do sth; **sus gritos no me dejaron dormir** his cries prevented me from sleeping; **déjame a mí** let me do it, leave it to me; **deja que tu hijo venga con nosotros** let your son come with us; **¿me dejas ir?** will you let me go?, can I go?; *Fig* **d. correr algo** to leave sth be; **déjalo estar** leave it as it is, let it be; **dejó pasar tres semanas** he let three weeks go by

(f) *(reservar)* **deja algo de café para mí** leave some coffee for me

(g) *(omitir)* to leave out; **d. algo por *o* sin hacer** to fail to do sth; **dejó lo más importante por resolver** he left the most important question unresolved

(h) *(imperativo) (olvidar)* to forget (about); *(no molestar)* to leave alone *o* in peace; **déjalo, no importa** forget it, it doesn't matter; **¡déjame, que tengo trabajo!** leave me alone, I'm busy!; **déjame tranquilo *o* en paz** leave me alone *o* in peace

(i) *(indica resultado)* **d. algo hecho** to get sth done; **d. algo como nuevo** to leave something as good as new; **el examen me dejó agotado** I was left exhausted by the exam

(j) *(esperar)* **d. que** to wait until; **dejó que acabara de llover para salir** he waited until it had stopped raining before going out

2 *vi* (a) *(parar)* **d. de hacer algo** to stop doing sth; **ha dejado de fumar/beber** he's stopped smoking/drinking; **poco a poco dejaron de llamarse** they gradually stopped phoning one another; **no deja de venir ni un solo día** he never fails to come (b) *(expresando promesa)* **no d. de** to be sure to; **¡no dejes de escribirme!** be sure to write to me! (c) **d. (mucho *o* bastante) que desear** to leave a lot to be desired

3 dejarse *vpr* (a) *(olvidar)* **dejarse algo en algún sitio** to leave sth somewhere (b) *(permitir)* **dejarse engañar** to allow oneself to be taken in; **le quisimos ayudar, pero no se dejó** we wanted to help him, but he wouldn't let us (c) *(no cortarse)* **dejarse la barba** to grow a beard; **dejarse el pelo largo** to grow one's hair long (d) *(cesar)* **dejarse de hacer algo** to stop doing sth; **¡déjate de tonterías!** don't talk nonsense! (e) *(descuidarse)* to let oneself go (f) **dejarse llevar (por algo)** to get carried away (with sth)

deje *nm (acento)* accent

dejo *nm* (a) *(acento)* accent (b) *(sabor)* aftertaste

del *ver* **de**

delación *nf* denunciation

delantal *nm* apron

delante *adv* (a) *(en primer lugar, en la parte delantera)* in front (**de** of); **ve tú d., yo me sentaré detrás** you go in the front, I'll sit at the back; **el de d.** the one in front; **el asiento de d.** the seat in front; **d. de mí/ti** in front of me/you; **lo tienes d. de las narices** it's in front of your nose (b) *(enfrente)* opposite; **d. hay una fábrica** there's a factory opposite

delantera *nf* (a) *(primer puesto)* lead; **coger *o* tomar la d.** to take the lead; **llevar la d.** to be in the lead; **coger *o* tomar la d. a alguien** to beat sb to it (b) *(ventaja)* **nos llevan tres**

minutos de d. they're three minutes ahead of us; **su hermano le lleva la d. en los estudios** his brother is doing better than him at school (**c**) *Dep* forward, forward line (**d**) *Fam (de una mujer)* bust

delantero, -a 1 *adj* front

  2 *nm,f Dep* forward; **d. centro** center forward

delatar 1 *vt* (**a**) *(denunciar)* to denounce; **lo delaté a la policía** I reported him to the police (**b**) *(sujeto: sonrisa, ojos)* to betray, to give away

  2 delatarse *vpr* to give oneself away

delator, -ora *nm,f* informer

delco *nm Esp Aut* distributor

delectación *nf Formal* delight, great pleasure; **con d.** with delight, delightedly

delegación *nf* (**a**) *(autorización, comisión)* delegation; **d. de poderes** devolution (of power) (**b**) *Esp (sucursal)* local office; **D. del Gobierno** = office representing central government in each province; **d. de Hacienda** = head tax office *(in each province)* (**c**) *Méx* **d. de policía** police station

delegado, -a *nm,f* (**a**) *(representante)* delegate; **d. de curso** class representative (**b**) *Com* representative

delegar [38] *vt* **d. algo en alguien** to delegate sth to sb

deleitar 1 *vt* to delight

  2 deleitarse *vpr* **deleitarse con** *o* **en algo** to take pleasure in sth; **deleitarse haciendo algo** to take pleasure in *o* enjoy doing sth

deleite *nm* delight

deletrear *vt* to spell (out)

deleznable *adj (malo)* (*clima, libro, actuación*) appalling; *(excusa, razón)* contemptible

delfín *nm* (**a**) *(animal)* dolphin (**b**) *Hist* dauphin; *(sucesor)* successor

delgadez *nf (en general)* thinness; *(esbeltez)* slimness

delgado, -a *adj (en general)* thin; *(esbelto)* slim, slender

deliberación *nf* deliberation

deliberado, -a *adj* deliberate

deliberar *vi* to deliberate

delicadeza *nf* (**a**) *(miramiento)* (*con cosas*) care; *(con personas)* kindness, attentiveness; **le dio la noticia con d.** he broke the news to her tactfully (**b**) *(finura)* (*de perfume, rostro*) delicacy; *(de persona)* sensitivity (**c**) *(de un asunto, situación)* delicacy

delicado, -a *adj* (**a**) *(objeto, perfume, gusto)* delicate; **una situación delicada** a delicate *o* tricky situation (**b**) *(persona)* *(sensible)* sensitive; *(muy exigente)* fussy; *(educado)* polite; **su estado (de salud) es d.** his condition is delicate; **estar d. de salud** to be in poor health; **estar d. del corazón** to have a weak heart; **¡no seas d., hay que comérselo todo!** don't be so picky, you've got to eat all of it!

delicia *nf* delight; **hacer las delicias de alguien** to delight sb

delicioso, -a *adj (comida)* delicious; *(persona, lugar, clima)* lovely, delightful

delictivo, -a *adj* criminal

delimitación *nf (de terreno)* fixing of the boundaries; *(de funciones)* delimitation

delimitar *vt (terreno)* to set out the boundaries of; *(funciones)* to define

delincuencia *nf* crime; **está aumentando la d.** crime is on the increase; **d. juvenil** juvenile delinquency

delincuente *nmf* criminal; **d. habitual** habitual offender; **d. juvenil** juvenile delinquent

delineación *nf* (**a**) *(trazado)* delineation, outlining (**b**) *(profesión)* technical drawing *o* drafting

delineador, -ra *adj* delineating, outlining

delineante *nmf* draftsman, *f* draftswoman

delinear *vt* (**a**) *(plano)* to draw (**b**) *(proyecto)* to outline

delinquir [22] *vi* to commit a crime

delirante *adj* (**a**) *(persona)* delirious (**b**) *(idea, fiesta)* wild, crazy

delirar *vi (un enfermo, un borracho)* to be delirious; *Fig (decir disparates)* to talk nonsense

delirio *nm (por fiebre, borrachera)* delirium; *(de un enfermo mental)* ravings; **delirios de grandeza** delusions of grandeur

delírium tremens *nm inv* delirium tremens

delito *nm* crime, offense; **cometer un d.** to commit a crime *o* an offense; **no es ningún d. criticar al profesor** it's no crime to criticize the teacher; **d. ecológico** ecological crime; **d. fiscal** tax offense; **d. informático** computer crime; **d. de sangre** violent crime

delta *nm & nf* delta

deltoides *nm inv Anat* deltoid (muscle)

demacrado, -a *adj* gaunt, haggard

demacrar 1 *vt* to make gaunt *o* haggard

  2 demacrarse *vpr* to become gaunt *o* haggard

demagogia *nf* demagoguery

demagógico, -a *adj* demagogic

demagogo, -a *nm,f* demagogue

demanda *nf* (**a**) *(petición)* request; *(reivindicación)* demand; **d. salarial** wage claim; **en d. de** asking for (**b**) *Econ* demand (**c**) *Der* lawsuit; *(por daños y perjuicios)* claim; **presentar una d. contra** to take legal action against; **d. de divorcio** petition for a divorce

demandado, -a *nm,f* defendant

demandante *nmf* plaintiff

demandar *vt* (**a**) *Der* **d. a alguien (por)** to sue sb (for) (**b**) *(pedir)* to ask for, to seek

demarcación *nf* (**a**) *(señalización)* demarcation (**b**) *(territorio)* area; *(jurisdicción)* district

demarcar [59] *vt* to demarcate, to mark out

demarrar *vi Dep* to put on a burst of speed, to put on a spurt

demás *adj* (**a**) *(resto)* **los d. invitados** the other *o* the remaining guests; **lo d.** the rest; **todo lo d.** everything else; **los/las d.** the others, the rest; **¿dónde vamos los d.?** where do the rest of us go?; **los problemas de los d.** other people's business; **se bebió su cerveza y la de los d.** he drank his beer and everyone else's; **por lo d.** apart from that, otherwise; **la casa tiene lavadora, lavaplatos y todo lo d.** the house has a washing machine, a dishwasher and all the rest of it; **y d.** etc. and so on (**b**) *RP Fam (sensacional)* great, cool

demasía: en demasía *loc adv* in excess, too much

demasiado, -a 1 *adj (singular)* too much; *(plural)* too many; **demasiada comida** too much food; **demasiados niños** too many children; **aquí hay d. niño** there are too many kids in here, this place is too full of kids

  2 *adv* too much; *(+adjetivo o adverbio)* too; **habla d.** she talks too much; **iba d. rápido** he was going too fast; **¡esto es d.!** *(el colmo)* this is too much!

  3 *pron* **éramos demasiados** there were too many of us

demencia *nf* madness, insanity; **d. senil** senile dementia

demencial *adj (disparatado)* crazy, mad

demente 1 *adj* mad

  2 *nmf Med* mental patient; *(loco)* lunatic

demérito *nm Formal (desventaja)* disadvantage; **los méritos y deméritos de algo** the merits and demerits of sth

demiurgo *nm* demiurge

democracia *nf* democracy; *Pol* **d. popular** people's democracy

demócrata 1 *adj* democratic; **el partido d.** the Democratic Party

  2 *nmf* democrat; **los demócratas** the Democrats

democratacristiano, -a *adj & nm,f Pol* Christian Democrat

democrático, -a *adj* democratic

democratización *nf* democratization

democratizador, -ora *adj* democratizing; **proceso d.** process of democratization

democratizar [14] *vt* to democratize

democristiano, -a *adj & nm,f Pol* Christian Democrat

demografía *nf* demography

demográfico, -a *adj (estudio, instituto)* demographic; **crecimiento d.** population increase; **explosión demográfica** population explosion

demoledor, -ora *adj (huracán, críticas)* devastating; *(argumento)* overwhelming, crushing

demoler [41] *vt (edificio)* to demolish, to pull down; *(argumento, teoría)* to demolish; *(sistema, organización)* to destroy

demolición *nf (de edificio, argumento)* demolition; *(de sistema, organización)* destruction

demoniaco, -a, demoníaco, -a *adj* devilish, diabolic

demonio *nm* (a) *(diablo)* devil; *Fam* **saber/oler a demonios** to taste/smell disgusting; **se lo llevaban todos los demonios** *(estaba muy enfadado)* he was hopping mad (b) *(para enfatizar)* **¿qué/dónde demonios…?** what/where the hell…?; **¡demonios!** damn (it)!

demora *nf* delay; **sin d.** without delay, immediately

demorar 1 *vt* to delay

2 *vi Am (tardar)* **¡no demores!** don't be late!; **este quitamanchas demora en actuar** this stain remover takes a while to work

3 demorarse *vpr* (a) *(retrasarse)* to be delayed (b) *(detenerse)* to stop (somewhere) (c) *esp Am (llegar tarde)* to be late

demostración *nf* (a) *(muestra)* demonstration; **una d. de cariño** a demonstration of affection (b) *(del funcionamiento)* demonstration; **hacer una d.** *(de cómo funciona algo)* to demonstrate, to give a demonstration; **me hizo una d. de cómo preparar una paella** he showed me how to make a paella (c) *(exhibición)* display; **la policía hizo una d. de fuerza ante los manifestantes** the police made a show of force in front of the demonstrators (d) *(matemática)* proof

demostrar [63] *vt* (a) *(mostrar, exhibir)* to show, to display; **demuestra tener mucho interés (en)** he shows a lot of interest (in) (b) *(funcionamiento, procedimiento)* to demonstrate, to show (c) *(probar)* to demonstrate, to prove

demostrativo, -a *adj* (a) *(representativo)* representative (b) *Gram* demonstrative

demudado, -a *adj* **tenía el rostro d.** his face was pale; **estaba completamente demudada** *(angustiada)* she looked grief-stricken

demudar 1 *vt* to change, to alter

2 demudarse *vpr (tejido)* to change color; *(persona, rostro)* to change expression

demuelo *etc ver* **demoler**

demuestro *etc ver* **demostrar**

denegación *nf* refusal, rejection

denegar [43] *vt* to turn down, to reject

dengue *nm (enfermedad)* dengue

denigrante *adj (humillante)* degrading; *(insultante)* insulting

denigrar *vt (humillar)* to denigrate, to vilify; *(insultar)* to insult

denodado, -a *adj Formal (decidido)* determined; *(valiente)* brave, intrepid

denominación *nf* naming; **D. de Origen** = guarantee of region of origin of a wine or other product

denominador *nm* denominator; *Mat & Fig* **d. común** common denominator

denominar 1 *vt* to call

2 denominarse *vpr* to be called

denostar [63] *vt Formal* to insult

denotar *vt* to indicate, to show

densidad *nf (gen) & Inform* density; **d. de población** population density; *Inform* **alta/doble d.** high/double density

denso, -a *adj (vegetación, humo)* dense; *(líquido, material)* thick; *(tráfico)* heavy; *(libro, película)* difficult to follow, involved

dentado, -a *adj (rueda)* cogged, toothed; *(filo, cuchillo)* serrated; *(sello)* perforated; *(hojas)* dentate

dentadura *nf* (set of) teeth; **d. postiza** false teeth, dentures

dental *adj* dental; **hilo** *o* **seda d.** dental floss

dentellada *nf (mordisco)* bite; *(herida, marca)* toothmark

dentera *nf* **dar d. a alguien** to set sb's teeth on edge

dentición *nf* (a) *(proceso)* teething (b) *(conjunto)* teeth

dentífrico, -a 1 *adj* **pasta dentífrica** toothpaste

2 *nm* toothpaste

dentista *nmf* dentist

dentistería *nf CAm, Col, Ecuad, Ven (consultorio)* dental surgery; *(estudios)* dentistry

dentística *nf Chile, Ecuad* dentistry

dentro *adv* (a) *(en el espacio)* inside; **espera aquí d.** wait in here; **está ahí d.** it's in there; **d. de** in; **d. del coche** in *o* inside the car; **d. de la legalidad** within the law; **d. de lo posible** as far as possible; **d. de lo razonable** within reason; **d. de lo que cabe, no ha sido un mal resultado** all things considered, it wasn't a bad result; **d. de** inside; **el bolsillo de d.** the inside pocket; **hacia/para d.** inward; **por d.** (on the) inside; *Fig* inside, deep down

(b) *(en el tiempo)* **d. de poco/un año** in a while/a year; **d. de los próximos meses** within the next few months; **d. de dos sábados** the Saturday after next, a week Saturday; **la cena estará lista d. de nada** dinner will be ready in a moment *o* very soon

denuedo *nm (valor)* courage; *(esfuerzo)* resolve

denuncia *nf (acusación)* accusation; *(condena)* denunciation; *(a la policía)* complaint; **presentar una d. contra** to file a complaint against

denunciante *nmf* = person who reports a crime

denunciar *vt* (a) *(delito)* to report (to the police); **denunció a su esposo por malos tratos** she reported her husband to the police for ill-treatment (b) *(acusar, reprobar)* to denounce, to condemn (c) *(delatar, revelar)* to indicate, to reveal

deontología *nf* deontology

deontológico, -a *adj* **código d.** code of ethics

D.E.P. *(abrev de* **descanse en paz***)* RIP

deparar *vt* (a) *(traer)* **¿qué nos deparará el futuro?** what will the future bring?, what does the future have in store for us? (b) *(ofrecer)* **d. la ocasión de hacer algo** to provide the opportunity to do sth

departamental *adj* departmental

departamento *nm* (a) *(en oficina, organización, universidad)* department; *(ministerio)* ministry, department; **d. de atención al cliente** customer services (department); **d. de caballeros** menswear department; **d. de marketing** marketing department; **d. de personal** personnel (department) (b) *(división territorial)* administrative district; *(en Francia)* department (c) *(compartimento)* compartment (d) *Arg (apartamento)* apartment

departir *vi* to chat, to talk

depauperación *nf* (a) *(física)* weakening, enfeeblement (b) *(económica)* impoverishment

depauperado, -a *adj* (a) *(físicamente)* enfeebled, debilitated (b) *(económicamente)* impoverished

depauperar *vt* (a) *(físicamente) (persona)* to debilitate, to weaken; *(salud)* to undermine (b) *(económicamente)* to impoverish

dependencia *nf* (a) *(de una persona)* dependence; *(de drogas)* dependency (b) *(departamento)* section; *(sucursal)* branch; **dependencias** *(instalaciones)* outbuildings; **en dependencias policiales** on police premises

depender *vi* to depend; **d. de algo** to depend on sth; **todo depende de lo que decida el juez** everything depends on what the judge decides; **depende…** it depends…; **d. de**

alguien to be dependent on sb; **depende de ti** it's up to you; **si de mí dependiera, el trabajo sería tuyo** if it were up to me, the job would be yours

dependiente, -a 1 *adj* dependent
  2 *nm,f* salesclerk

depilación *nf* hair removal; **d. eléctrica** electrolysis; **d. a la cera** waxing

depiladora *nf* ladies' shaver, hair remover

depilar 1 *vt (piernas, axilas)* to remove the hair from; *(cejas)* to pluck; *(con cera)* to wax
  2 depilarse *vpr* **depilarse las piernas/axilas** *(con maquinilla)* to shave one's legs/armpits; *(con cera)* to wax one's legs/armpits; **depilarse las cejas** to pluck one's eyebrows

depilatorio, -a 1 *adj* hair-removing
  2 *nm* hair remover

deplorable *adj (suceso, comportamiento)* deplorable; *(aspecto)* sorry, pitiful

deplorar *vt* to regret deeply

deponer [50] *vt* **(a)** *(abandonar) (actitud)* to drop, to set aside; *(armas)* to lay down **(b)** *(destituir) (ministro, secretario)* to remove from office; *(líder, rey)* to depose; **d. a alguien de su cargo** to strip sb of his/her office

deportación *nf* deportation

deportado, -a 1 *adj* deported
  2 *nm,f* deportee

deportar *vt* to deport

deporte *nm* sport; **hacer d.** to do *o* play sports; **practicar un d.** to do *o* play a sport; **hacer algo por d.** to do sth for fun; **deportes de aventura** adventure sports; **el d. blanco** skiing; **deportes de competición** competitive sports; **d. de masas** spectator sport

deportista 1 *adj* sporty, sports-loving
  2 *nmf* sportsman, *f* sportswoman

deportividad *nf* sportsmanship

deportivo, -a 1 *adj (conducta, espíritu)* sportsmanlike; **coche d.** sports car; **instalaciones deportivas** sports complex; **periódico d.** sports paper
  2 *nm* sports car

deposición *nf* **(a)** *(destitución) (de ministro, secretario)* removal from office; *(de líder, rey)* overthrow **(b)** *Med* **deposiciones** *(heces)* stools

depositar 1 *vt* **(a)** *(dejar, colocar)* to place; **depositaron su confianza en ella** they placed their trust in her; **había depositado sus ilusiones en su hijo** he had placed all his hopes on his son **(b)** *(en el banco)* to deposit
  2 depositarse *vpr (asentarse)* to settle

depositario, -a *nm,f* **(a)** *(de dinero)* trustee **(b)** *(de confianza)* repository **(c)** *(de mercancías)* depository

depósito *nm* **(a)** *(almacén) (de mercancías)* store, warehouse; *(de armas)* dump, arsenal; **d. de cadáveres** morgue, mortuary **(b)** *(recipiente)* tank; **d. de combustible** fuel tank; **d. de gasolina** gas tank **(c)** *(de dinero)* deposit **(d)** *(de polvo, sedimento)* deposit; **depósitos minerales** mineral deposits **d. legal** = copy of a publication legally required to be sent to the authorities

depravación *nf* depravity

depravado, -a 1 *adj* depraved
  2 *nm,f* depraved person; **ser un d.** to be depraved *o* degenerate

depravar 1 *vt* to corrupt, to deprave
  2 depravarse *vpr* to become depraved

depre *Fam* **1** *adj* **estar d.** to be feeling down
  2 *nf* **tener la d.** to be feeling down

depreciación *nf* depreciation

depreciar 1 *vt* to (cause to) depreciate
  2 depreciarse *vpr* to depreciate

depredación *nf* **(a)** *(entre animales)* hunting, preying on **(b)** *(daño)* depredation, pillaging

depredador, -ora 1 *adj* predatory
  2 *nm,f* predator

depredar *vt (animal)* to prey on; *(piratas, invasores)* to pillage

depresión *nf* **(a)** *(económica, anímica)* depression; **d. nerviosa** nervous breakdown; **d. puerperal** *o* **posparto** postnatal depression **(b)** *(en superficie, terreno)* hollow, depression

depresivo, -a 1 *adj (propenso a la depresión)* depressive; *(deprimente)* depressing
  2 *nm,f (propenso a la depresión)* depressive

depresor, -ora *adj & nm* depressor

deprimente *adj* depressing

deprimido, -a *adj* depressed

deprimir 1 *vt* to depress
  2 deprimirse *vpr* to get depressed

deprisa *adv* fast, quickly; **¡d.!** quick!

depuesto, -a 1 *participio ver* **deponer**
  2 *adj (destituido) (ministro, secretario)* removed from office; *(líder, rey)* deposed

depuración *nf (de agua, metal, gas)* purification; *(de organismo, sociedad)* purge; **d. de aguas residuales** sewage disposal

depurado, -a *adj (estilo)* refined, polished; *(diseño, líneas)* sleek, elegant

depurador, -ora 1 *adj* purifying
  2 *nm* purifier

depuradora *nf (en río)* treatment plant; *(de piscina)* filter system; **d. de aguas** water purification plant

depurar *vt (agua, metal, gas)* to purify; *(organismo, sociedad)* to purge; *(estilo, gusto)* to refine; *Inform* to debug

depusiera *etc ver* **deponer**

derby *nm (en hípica)* derby; *(en fútbol)* (local) derby

derecha *nf* **(a)** *(contrario de izquierda)* right, right-hand side; **a la d. (de)** to the right (of); **a mi/vuestra d.** on my/your right(-hand side); **girar a la d.** to turn right **(b)** *Pol* right (wing); *Esp* **ser de derechas** to be right-wing **(c)** *Esp* **no hacer nada a derechas** to do nothing right

derechazo *nm (en boxeo)* right

derechista 1 *adj* right-wing
  2 *nmf* right-winger

derecho, -a 1 *adj* **(a)** *(vertical)* upright **(b)** *(recto)* straight **(c)** *(de la derecha)* right; **mano/pierna derecha** right hand/leg
  2 *nm* **(a)** *(leyes, estudio)* law; **d. administrativo** administrative law; **d. canónico** canon law; **d. civil** civil law; **d. internacional** international law; **d. laboral** *o* **del trabajo** labor law; **d. mercantil** commercial law; **d. natural** natural law; **d. penal** criminal law
  (b) *(prerrogativa)* right; **tener d. a algo** to have a right to sth; **tener d. a hacer algo** to have the right to do sth; **el d. al voto** the right to vote; **reservado el d. de admisión** the management reserves the right of admission; **¡no hay d.!** it's not fair!; **me queda el d. al pataleo** all I can do now is complain; **derechos de autor** *(potestad)* copyright; **derechos civiles** civil rights; **derechos humanos** human rights
  (c) *(impuesto, tarifa)* **derechos de aduana** customs duty; **derechos de autor** *(dinero)* royalties; **derechos de exportación** export duty; **derechos de importación** import duty; **derechos de inscripción** membership fee; **d. de paso** *(en propiedades)* right of way; **derechos reales** death duty
  (d) *(contrario de revés)* right side; **del d.** right side out
  3 *adv* **(a)** *(en posición vertical)* upright **(b)** *(directamente)* straight; **ir d. a** to go straight to **(c)** *Am (de frente)* straight on, straight ahead

deriva *nf* drift; **a la d.** adrift; **ir a la d.** to drift; *Geol* **d. continental** continental drift

derivación *nf* (a) *(cable, canal, carretera)* branch (b) *Elec* shunt (c) *Gram* derivation

derivada *nf Mat* derivative

derivado, -a 1 *adj Gram* derived

    2 *nm* (a) *(producto)* by-product (b) *Quím* derivative

derivar 1 *vt* (a) *(desviar)* to divert; **derivó el debate hacia otro tema** he steered the debate onto another topic (b) *Mat* to derive

    2 *vi* (a) *(desviarse)* to change direction, to drift (b) *(proceder)* **d. de** to derive from; *Gram* to be derived from (c) *(acabar)* **d. en** to end in

    3 derivarse de *vpr* to be derived from, to come from; **palabras que se derivan del griego** words which come from Greek

dermatitis *nf inv Med* dermatitis

dermatología *nf Med* dermatology

dermatológico, -a *adj Med* dermatological

dermatólogo, -a *nm,f Med* dermatologist

dérmico, -a *adj* skin; **tejido d.** skin tissue

dermis *nf inv Anat* dermis

dermoprotector, -ora *adj* skin-protecting; **crema dermoprotectora** skin cream

derogación *nf Der* repeal

derogar [38] *vt Der (ley)* to repeal

derramamiento *nm* spilling; **d. de sangre** bloodshed

derramar 1 *vt (por accidente)* to spill; *(verter)* to pour; **d. lágrimas/sangre** to shed tears/blood

    2 derramarse *vpr (por accidente)* to spill

derrame *nm* (a) *Med* discharge; **d. cerebral** stroke; **d. sinovial** water on the knee (b) *(de líquido)* spilling; *(de sangre)* shedding

derrapaje *nm* skid

derrapar *vi* to skid; *Fam* **le derrapan las neuronas** he's gone crazy

derrape *nm* skid

derredor *nm* **al** *o* **en d.** around

derrengado, -a *adj Fam (agotado)* exhausted

derrengar *vt (agotar)* to exhaust, to tire out

derretir [47] **1** *vt (licuar)* to melt; *(nieve)* to thaw

    2 derretirse *vpr* (a) *(metal, mantequilla)* to melt; *(hielo, nieve)* to thaw; **la nieve se derrite con el sol** the snow melts in the sunshine (b) *Fam (enamorarse)* to be madly in love (**por** with); *(emocionarse)* **se derrite cada vez que ella lo mira** his heart misses a beat whenever she looks at him

derribar *vt (construcción)* to knock down, to demolish; *(hacer caer)* *(árbol)* to cut down, to fell; *(avión)* to bring down; *(gobierno, gobernante)* to overthrow

derribo *nm (de edificio)* demolition; *(de árbol)* felling; *(de avión)* bringing down; *(de gobierno, gobernante)* overthrow; **material de d.** rubble

derritiera *etc ver* **derretir**

derrito *etc ver* **derretir**

derrocamiento *nm (de gobierno)* toppling, overthrow; *(de rey)* overthrow

derrocar [59] *vt (gobierno)* to topple, to overthrow; *(rey)* to overthrow

derrochador, -ora 1 *adj* wasteful

    2 *nm,f* spendthrift

derrochar *vt* (a) *(malgastar)* to squander, to waste (b) *(rebosar de)* to ooze, to be full of; **derrochaba simpatía** he was incredibly friendly

derroche *nm* (a) *(despilfarro)* waste, squandering; **¡qué d.!** what an awful waste! (b) *(abundancia)* **el concierto fue un d. de técnica, sensibilidad y talento** the concert was a fine display of technique, sensitivity and talent; **la película es todo un d. de imaginación** the movie is prodigiously imaginative

derrota *nf* (a) *(fracaso)* defeat (b) *Náut (rumbo)* course

derrotado, -a *adj* defeated

derrotar *vt* to defeat

derrotero *nm* (a) *(camino)* direction; **tomar diferentes derroteros** to follow a different course (b) *Náut* course

derrotismo *nm* defeatism

derrotista *adj & nmf* defeatist

derruir [34] *vt* to demolish, to knock down

derrumbamiento *nm (de puente, edificio) (por accidente)* collapse; *(intencionado)* demolition; *(de imperio)* fall; *(de empresa)* collapse; *(de persona)* devastation

derrumbar 1 *vt (puente, edificio)* to demolish; *(moralmente)* to destroy, to devastate

    2 derrumbarse *vpr* (a) *(puente, edificio)* to collapse; *(techo)* to fall in, to cave in; **se derrumbó extenuado sobre la cama** he collapsed on the bed exhausted (b) *(persona)* to be devastated; *(esperanzas)* to be shattered; **en la segunda parte el equipo se derrumbó** the team went to pieces in the second half

derrumbe *nm* collapse

desabastecer [46] *vt* **d. a alguien de** to leave sb short of

desabastecido, -a *adj* without supplies; **d. de** short *o* out of

desaborido, -a *Fam* **1** *adj* boring, dull

    2 *nm,f* bore

desabotonar 1 *vt* to unbutton

    2 desabotonarse *vpr (persona)* to undo one's buttons; *(ropa)* to come undone

desabrido, -a *adj (tiempo)* unpleasant, bad; *Esp (persona)* surly; *Esp (tono)* harsh

desabrigarse *vpr* (a) *(en la calle)* **¡no te desabrigues!** make sure you wrap up warmly! (b) *(en la cama)* to throw off the covers

desabrochar 1 *vt* to undo

    2 desabrocharse *vpr (persona)* to undo one's buttons; *(ropa)* to come undone; **se desabrochó el cuello de la camisa** he unbuttoned his shirt collar; **se te ha desabrochado la bragueta** your fly has come undone

desacatar *vt (ley, regla)* to disobey; *(costumbre, persona)* not to respect

desacato *nm* (a) *(falta de respeto)* lack of respect (**a** for), disrespect (**a** for) (b) *Der (al juez, tribunal)* contempt of court; **d. a la autoridad** = refusal to obey an offical

desaceleración *nf* slowing down

desacertado, -a *adj (inoportuno)* unwise, ill-considered; *(erróneo)* mistaken, wrong

desacierto *nm (error)* error

desaconsejar *vt* **d. algo (a alguien)** to advise (sb) against sth; **d. a alguien que haga algo** to advise sb not to do sth

desacoplar *vt Elec* to disconnect; *Tec* to uncouple

desacorde *adj (opiniones)* differing, conflicting

desacostumbrado, -a *adj* unusual, uncommon

desacreditado, -a *adj* discredited

desacreditar 1 *vt* to discredit

    2 desacreditarse *vpr* to become discredited

desactivado, -a 1 *adj* deactivated

    2 *nm* deactivation

desactivar *vt* to defuse

desacuerdo *nm* disagreement; **estar en d. (con)** to disagree (with)

desafecto, -a *adj* hostile (**a** to), disaffected (**a** with)

desafiante *adj* defiant

desafiar [32] *vt* (a) *(persona)* to challenge; **d. a alguien a algo/a que haga algo** to challenge sb to sth/to do sth (b) *(peligro, ley)* to defy

desafinado, -a *adj (instrumento)* out of tune

desafinar vi (instrumento) to be out of tune; (persona) to sing out of tune

desafío nm challenge

desaforadamente adv (**a**) (excesivamente) wildly, to excess (**b**) (con furia) furiously

desaforado, -a adj (**a**) (excesivo) uncontrolled (**b**) (furioso) furious, wild

desafortunadamente adv unfortunately

desafortunado, -a 1 adj (**a**) (desgraciado) unfortunate (**b**) (sin suerte) unlucky
    2 nm,f unlucky person

desafuero nm outrage, atrocity

desagradable 1 adj unpleasant
    2 nmf **son unos desagradables** they're unpleasant people

desagradar vi to displease; **me desagrada su actitud** I don't like her attitude; **me desagradó tener que levantarme tan pronto** I didn't like having to get up so early; **créame, me desagrada mucho tener que decirle esto** believe me, I really don't like to have to say this to you; **a nadie le desagradan los elogios** nobody minds being praised

desagradecido, -a nm,f ungrateful person

desagrado nm displeasure; **con d.** reluctantly

desagraviar vt **d. a alguien por algo** (por una ofensa) to make amends to sb for sth; (por un perjuicio) to compensate sb for sth

desagravio nm **en señal de d.** (in order) to make amends

desaguadero nm drain

desaguar [11] vi (**a**) (bañera, agua) to drain (**b**) (río) **d. en** to flow into

desagüe nm (de calle) drain; (de lavabo, lavadora) waste outlet

desaguisado nm (destrozo) mess; (desorden) shambles (singular); **hacer un d.** to make a mess; **la inauguración fue un verdadero d.** the opening was a shambles

desahogado, -a adj (de espacio) spacious, roomy; (de dinero) well-off, comfortable

desahogar [38] **1** vt (ira) to vent; (pena) to relieve, to ease
    2 desahogarse vpr (contar penas) **desahogarse con alguien** to pour out one's woes o to tell one's troubles to sb; (desfogarse) to let off steam

desahogo nm (alivio) relief, release; (de espacio) space, room; (económico) ease; **vivir con d.** to be comfortably off

desahuciar vt (**a**) (inquilino) to evict (**b**) (enfermo) **d. a alguien** to give up all hope of saving sb

desahucio nm eviction

desairado, -a adj (**a**) (poco airoso) (actuación) unimpressive, unsuccessful (**b**) (humillado) spurned

desairar vt (persona) to snub, to slight; (cosa) not to think much of, to be unimpressed by

desaire nm snub, slight; **hacer un d. a alguien** to snub sb

desajustar 1 vt (piezas) to disturb, to knock out of place
    2 desajustarse vpr **el mecanismo se ha desajustado** the mechanism isn't working properly

desajuste nm (**a**) (de piezas) misalignment; (de máquina) malfunction, fault (**b**) (de declaraciones, versiones) inconsistency; (económico) imbalance

desalar vt (quitar sal a) to remove salt from; (agua) to desalinate, to desalt

desalentar [3] **1** vt to dishearten, to discourage
    2 desalentarse vpr to be discouraged, to lose heart

desaliento nm dismay, dejection

desalinearse vpr to go out of line

desalinizar [14] vt to desalinate, to desalt

desaliñado, -a adj (persona, aspecto) scruffy

desaliño nm (de persona, aspecto) scruffiness

desalmado, -a 1 adj heartless
    2 nm,f heartless person

desalojar vt (**a**) (por emergencia) (edificio, personas) to evacuate (**b**) (por la fuerza) (ocupantes) to eject, to remove; (inquilinos) to evict (**c**) (por propia voluntad) to abandon, to move out of

desalojo nm (**a**) (por emergencia) (de edificio, personas) evacuation (**b**) (por la fuerza) (de ocupantes) ejection, removal; (de inquilinos) eviction

desamarrar vt to cast off

desamor nm (falta de afecto) indifference, coldness; (odio) dislike

desamortización nf (de propiedades) disentailment, alienation

desamortizar [14] vt (propiedades) to disentail, to alienate

desamparado, -a 1 adj (persona) helpless; (lugar) desolate, forsaken
    2 nm,f helpless person

desamparar vt (persona) to abandon

desamparo nm (abandono) abandonment; (aflicción) helplessness

desandar [7] vt (camino) to go back over; **d. lo andado** to retrace one's steps; Fig to go back to square one

desangelado, -a adj (casa, habitación) drab; (acto, celebración) dull, uninspiring

desangrar 1 vt (animal, persona) to bleed; (económicamente) to bleed dry
    2 desangrarse vpr to lose a lot of blood; **murió desangrado** he bled to death

desanimado, -a adj (**a**) (persona) downhearted (**b**) (fiesta, lugar) quiet, lifeless

desanimar 1 vt to discourage
    2 desanimarse vpr to get downhearted o discouraged

desánimo nm (desaliento) dejection

desanudar vt to untie

desapacible adj unpleasant

desaparecer [46] **1** vi (**a**) (de la vista) to disappear; **me ha desaparecido la pluma** my pen has disappeared; **será mejor que desaparezcas de escena durante una temporada** you'd better make yourself scarce for a while; **d. de la faz de la tierra** to vanish from the face of the earth; **¡desaparece de mi vista ahora mismo!** get out of my sight this minute! (**b**) (en guerra, accidente) to go missing
    2 vt Am (persona) = to detain extrajudicially during political repression and possibly kill

desaparecido, -a 1 adj (**a**) (extraviado) missing (**b**) (ya no existente) **el d. John Lennon** the late John Lennon; **la desaparecida Sociedad de Naciones** the now defunct League of Nations
    2 nm,f missing person; **ha habido veinte muertos y tres desaparecidos** twenty people have been killed and three are missing

desaparición nf disappearance

desapasionado, -a adj dispassionate

desapego nm indifference

desapercibido, -a adj unnoticed; **pasar d.** to go unnoticed

desaprensión nf unscrupulousness

desaprensivo, -a nm,f (gamberro) reckless delinquent

desaprobación nf disapproval

desaprobar [63] vt (mostrar disconformidad) to disapprove of; (propuesta, plan) to reject

desaprovechado, -a adj (tiempo, ocasión, talento) wasted; (espacio, recursos, terreno) not put to the best use

desaprovechamiento nm (de tiempo, ocasión, talento) waste; (de espacio, recursos, terreno) failure to exploit fully

desaprovechar vt (tiempo, ocasión, talento) to waste; (espacio, recursos, terreno) to underuse, to fail to exploit fully

desarmable adj (mueble) that can be dismantled

desarmado, -a adj (**a**) (persona) unarmed (**b**) (desmontado) dismantled

desarmador *nm Méx* screwdriver

desarmar *vt* (**a**) *(quitar las armas)* to disarm (**b**) *(desmontar)* to take apart, to dismantle

desarme *nm Mil & Pol* disarmament; **d. nuclear** nuclear disarmament

desarraigado, -a *adj (persona)* uprooted, rootless

desarraigar [38] *vt (vicio, costumbre)* to root out; *(persona, pueblo)* to banish, to drive (out)

desarraigo *nm (de vicio, costumbre)* rooting out; *(de persona, pueblo)* banishment

desarreglado, -a *adj (cuarto, armario, persona)* untidy; *(vida)* disorganized

desarreglar *vt (armario, pelo)* to mess up; *(planes, horario)* to upset

desarreglo *nm (de cuarto, persona)* untidiness; *(de vida)* disorder; **me siento rara, debo de tener un d. hormonal** I'm feeling a bit funny, it must be my hormones

desarrollado, -a *adj* developed

desarrollador, -ora *nm,f Inform* developer; **d. de software** software developer

desarrollar 1 *vt* (**a**) *(mejorar) (crecimiento, país)* to develop; **desarrolló un sexto sentido para las finanzas** she developed *o* acquired a sixth sense for money (**b**) *(exponer) (teoría, tema, fórmula)* to expound, to explain; **¿podrías d. esa idea un poco más?** could you expand on that idea a little more? (**c**) *(realizar) (actividad, trabajo)* to carry out (**d**) *Mat* to expand

2 desarrollarse *vpr* (**a**) *(crecer, mejorar)* to develop (**b**) *(suceder) (reunión)* to take place; *(película)* to be set; **la manifestación se desarrolló sin incidentes** the demonstration went off without incident; **la acción de la novela se desarrolla en el siglo XIX** the novel is set in the 19th century

desarrollismo *nm* = policy of development at all costs

desarrollo *nm* (**a**) *(mejora)* development; **d. del producto** product development; **d. sostenible** sustainable development (**b**) *(crecimiento)* growth

desarropar 1 *vt* to uncover

2 desarroparse *vpr* **se desarropa durante la noche** he kicks off the bedclothes during the night

desarrugar [38] *vt (alisar)* to smooth out; *(planchar)* to iron out the creases in

desarticulación *nf (de huesos)* dislocation; *(de organización, banda)* breaking up

desarticular *vt (huesos)* to dislocate; *(organización, banda)* to break up; *(plan)* to foil

desaseado, -a *adj (sucio)* dirty; *(desarreglado)* untidy

desasistido, -a *adj* **dejar a alguien d.** to leave sb unattended (to)

desasosegado, -a *adj* uneasy, nervous

desasosegar [43] **1** *vt* to disturb, to make uneasy

2 desasosegarse *vpr* to become uneasy

desasosiego *nm* (**a**) *(inquietud)* unease, anxiety (**b**) *(nerviosismo)* nervousness

desastrado, -a *adj (desaseado)* scruffy; *(sucio)* dirty

desastre *nm* disaster; **su madre es un d.** her mother is hopeless; **¡vaya d.!** what a shambles!

desastroso, -a *adj* disastrous

desatar 1 *vt* (**a**) *(nudo, lazo)* to untie; *(paquete)* to undo; *(animal)* to unleash (**b**) *(tormenta, iras, pasión)* to unleash; *(entusiasmo)* to arouse; *(lengua)* to loosen

2 desatarse *vpr* (**a**) *(nudo, lazo)* to come undone (**b**) *(desencadenarse) (tormenta)* to break; *(ira, cólera)* to erupt

desatascador *nm* (sink) plunger

desatascar [59] *vt* to unblock

desatención *nf (falta de atención)* lack of attention; *(descortesía)* discourtesy, impoliteness

desatender [64] *vt* (**a**) *(obligación, persona)* to neglect (**b**) *(ruegos, consejos)* to ignore

desatendido, -a *adj* (**a**) *(obligación, persona)* neglected (**b**) *(maleta, paquete)* unattended (**c**) *(ruegos, consejo)* ignored

desatento, -a *adj (distraído)* inattentive; *(descortés)* impolite

desatinar *vi (al actuar)* to act foolishly; *(al hablar)* to say stupid things

desatino *nm* (**a**) *(estupidez) (al actuar)* foolish action; *(al hablar)* foolish remark (**b**) *(desacierto)* mistake

desatornillador *nm Andes, CAm* screwdriver

desatornillar *vt* to unscrew

desatrancar [59] *vt (puerta, ventana)* to unbolt; *(tubería)* to unblock

desautorizar [14] *vt* (**a**) *(desmentir) (noticia)* to deny (**b**) *(prohibir) (manifestación, huelga)* to ban (**c**) *(desacreditar)* to discredit

desavenencia *nf (desacuerdo)* friction, tension; *(riña)* quarrel

desavenido, -a *adj* at odds (**con** with); **dos familias desavenidas** two families at odds with each other

desavenirse [69] *vpr* to fall out

desaventajado, -a *adj* disadvantaged

desayunar 1 *vi* to have breakfast

2 *vt* to have for breakfast

3 desayunarse *vpr* **se desayunaron con café y tostadas** they had coffee and toast for breakfast

desayuno *nm* breakfast

desazón *nf (ansiedad)* unease, anxiety; *(molestia)* annoyance

desazonar *vt (causar ansiedad)* to worry, to cause anxiety to; *(causar molestia)* to annoy, to upset

desbancar [59] *vt (ocupar el puesto de)* to oust, to replace

desbandada *nf* breaking up, scattering; **en d.** in great disorder

desbandarse *vpr* to scatter

desbarajuste *nm* disorder, confusion; **¡vaya d.!** what a mess!

desbaratado, -a *adj (roto)* wrecked, broken down

desbaratar *vt* to ruin, to wreck

desbarrar *vi Esp* to talk nonsense

desbloquear *vt (cuenta)* to unfreeze; *(país)* to lift the blockade on; *(negociación)* to end the deadlock in

desbocado, -a *adj (caballo)* runaway

desbocarse [59] *vpr (caballo)* to bolt

desbordamiento *nm (de río)* overflowing; *(de sentimiento)* loss of control

desbordante *adj (sentimiento, entusiasmo)* boundless; *(imaginación)* rich

desbordar 1 *vt* (**a**) *(cauce, ribera)* to overflow, to burst (**b**) *(límites, previsiones, capacidad)* to exceed; *(paciencia)* to push beyond the limit (**c**) *(contrario, defensa)* to get past, to pass

2 *vi* **d. de** to overflow with

3 desbordarse *vpr (río)* to flood, to burst its banks; *(bañera)* to overflow; *(pasión, sentimiento)* to erupt

desbravar *vt (ganado)* to tame, to break in

descabalgar [38] *vi* to dismount

descabellado, -a *adj* crazy

descabellar *vt Taurom* to give the coup de grâce to

descabello *nm Taurom* coup de grâce

descabezar [14] *vt* (**a**) *(quitar la cabeza) (persona)* to behead; *(cosa)* to break the head off (**b**) *(quitar la punta) (planta, árbol)* to top

descacharrado, -a *adj Fam* bust

descacharrante *adj Fam* hilarious

descacharrar *vt Fam* to bust

descafeinado, -a 1 *adj* (**a**) *(sin cafeína)* decaffeinated (**b**) *(sin fuerza)* watered down

2 *nm* decaffeinated coffee

descafeinar vt (**a**) *(quitar cafeína)* to decaffeinate (**b**) *(quitar fuerza a)* to water down

descalabrar 1 vt *(herir)* to wound in the head; *Fam (perjudicar)* to do serious damage to
2 descalabrarse vpr to hurt one's head; *Fam* to brain oneself

descalabro nm major setback, disaster

descalcificación nf *Med* loss of calcium

descalcificar [59] *Med* **1** vt to decalcify
2 descalcificarse vpr to decalcify, to lose calcium

descalificación nf (**a**) *(de competición)* disqualification (**b**) *(ofensa)* dismissive insult; **una guerra de descalificaciones** a back-and-forth exchange of insults

descalificar [59] vt (**a**) *(en una competición)* to disqualify (**b**) *(desprestigiar)* to discredit; **descalificó con saña a su oponente** he viciously attacked his opponent

descalzar [14] **1** vt **d. a alguien** to take sb's shoes off
2 descalzarse vpr to take off one's shoes

descalzo, -a adj barefoot

descamación nf *(de la piel)* flaking

descamarse vpr *(piel)* to flake

descaminado, -a adj *(equivocado)* **andar** o **ir d.** to be on the wrong track; *(caminante, excursionista)* to be heading in the wrong direction

descaminar 1 vt *(sujeto: malas compañías)* to lead astray; *(sujeto: guía)* to take the wrong way
2 descaminarse vpr *(por malas compañías)* to go astray; *(en una excursión)* to go the wrong way

descamisado, -a 1 adj (**a**) *(sin camisa)* barechested (**b**) *(pobre)* wretched
2 nm,f (**a**) *(pobre)* poor wretch (**b**) *Arg Hist* = working-class supporter of General Perón and his wife Evita

descampado nm open country; **juegan al fútbol en un d.** they play soccer on an area of wasteland

descansado, -a adj *(actividad)* restful; **estar d.** to be rested o refreshed

descansar 1 vt (**a**) *(reposar)* to rest, to lie; **descansó la cabeza en mi hombro** he laid o rested his head on my shoulder (**b**) *(relajar)* to rest; **dormir descansa la vista** sleep gives your eyes o eyesight a rest
2 vi (**a**) *(reposar)* to rest; **descansó un rato antes de seguir** he rested for a while before continuing; **después de tanto trabajo necesito d.** I need a rest after all that work; **¿paramos a** o **para d.?** how about stopping for a rest?; **necesitas d. de tantas preocupaciones** you need a break from all these worries; **descansaremos en una hora** we'll take a break in an hour; **llevo cuatro horas trabajando sin d.** I've been working for four hours nonstop o without a break (**b**) *(dormir)* to sleep; **¡que descanses!** sleep well! (**c**) *(estar enterrado)* to lie; **que en paz descanse** may he/she rest in peace (**d**) *(viga, teoría)* **d. en** to rest on (**e**) *Mil* **¡descansen!** at ease!

descansillo nm landing

descanso nm (**a**) *(reposo)* rest; **tomarse un d.** to take a rest; **día de d.** day off (**b**) *(pausa)* break; *(en cine)* intermission; *(en teatro)* intermission; *Dep* halftime (**c**) *(alivio)* relief (**d**) *Mil* **adoptar la posición de d.** to stand at ease

descapitalización nf *Fin* undercapitalization

descapitalizar [14] **1** vt *Fin* to undercapitalize
2 descapitalizarse vpr to be undercapitalized

descapotable adj & nm convertible

descarado, -a 1 adj (**a**) *(desvergonzado)* *(persona)* cheeky, impertinent (**b**) *(flagrante)* barefaced, blatant; **¡es un robo d.!** it's daylight robbery! (**c**) *Esp Fam (por supuesto, seguro)* **¡d.!** you bet!
2 nm,f wise guy, smart aleck

descarga nf (**a**) *(de mercancías)* unloading (**b**) *(de electricidad)* shock; **d. eléctrica** electric shock (**c**) *(disparo)* firing, shots (**d**) *Inform* download

descargador, -ora nm,f *(en mercado)* porter; *(en puerto)* longshoreman

descargar [38] **1** vt (**a**) *(vaciar)* to unload; **descargó su cólera sobre mí** he took his anger out on me; **descargó su conciencia en mí** he unburdened his conscience on me (**b**) *(disparar)* to fire (**sobre** at) (**c**) *(puntapié, puñetazo)* to deal, to land; **descargó un golpe contra la mesa** he thumped his fist on the table (**d**) *Elec (pila, batería)* to run down (**e**) *(exonerar)* **d. a alguien de algo** to free o release sb from sth (**f**) *Der (absolver)* **d. a alguien de algo** to clear sb of sth (**g**) *Inform* to download
2 vi to burst; *(tormenta)* to break
3 descargarse vpr (**a**) *(desahogarse)* **descargarse con** o **en alguien** to take it out on sb (**b**) *Der* to clear oneself (**de** of) (**c**) *Elec (pila, batería)* to go flat (**d**) *Inform* to download

descargo nm (**a**) *(excusa)* **d. a** argument against (**b**) *Der* defense; **en su d.** in his/her defense (**c**) *Com (de deuda)* discharge; *(recibo)* receipt

descarnado, -a adj (**a**) *(descripción)* brutal (**b**) *(persona, animal)* scrawny

descaro nm cheek, impertinence

descarozar [14] vt *Andes, RP* to pit, to stone

descarriado, -a adj *(animal)* stray; **anda d. a causa de las malas compañías** he's gone astray because of the bad company he's been keeping

descarriarse [32] vpr *(ovejas, ganado)* to stray; *(persona)* to lose one's way, to go astray

descarrilamiento nm derailment

descarrilar vi to be derailed

descartable *Am* **1** adj *(pañal, jeringuilla, envase)* disposable
2 nm *(pañal)* disposable
3 nf *(jeringuilla)* disposable

descartar 1 vt *(ayuda)* to refuse, to reject; *(posibilidad)* to rule out
2 descartarse vpr **descartarse (de)** to discard

descarte nm *(de naipes)* discard

descascarillado, -a adj *(desconchado)* chipped

descascarillar 1 vt *(pelar)* to hull
2 descascarillarse vpr *(desconcharse)* to chip; **la pared se está descascarillando** the paint is flaking off the wall

descastado, -a nm,f ungrateful person

descatalogado, -a adj *(disco)* discontinued; **está d.** *(libro)* it's no longer in the catalog

descatalogar vt *(libro, disco)* **lo han descatalogado** they've dropped it from their catalog

descendencia nf (**a**) *(hijos)* offspring; *(hijos, nietos)* descendants; **morir sin d.** to die without issue (**b**) *(linaje)* lineage, descent

descendente adj *(número, temperatura)* falling; *(movimiento, dirección)* downward, descending

descender [64] **1** vi (**a**) *(valor, temperatura, nivel)* to fall, to drop; **ha descendido el interés por la política** there is less interest in politics
(**b**) *(de una altura)* to descend; **la niebla descendió sobre el valle** the mist descended on the valley; **el río desciende por el valle** the river runs down the valley
(**c**) *(de vehículo)* **d. de un avión** to get off a plane; **d. de un coche** to get out of a car
(**d**) *(en competición deportiva)* to be relegated; **d. a segunda** to be relegated to the second division; **d. de categoría** to be relegated
(**e**) *(de antepasado)* **d. de** to be descended from
(**f**) *(en estimación)* to go down
2 vt *(bajar)* **descendieron al paciente de la ambulancia**

they took the patient out of the ambulance; **descendió las escaleras rápidamente** she ran down the stairs

descendiente *nmf* descendant

descenso *nm* (**a**) *(en el espacio)* descent (**b**) *(de valor, temperatura, nivel)* drop; **ir en d.** to be decreasing *o* on the decline (**c**) *(prueba de esquí)* downhill (**d**) *(en fútbol)* relegation

descentrado, -a *adj* (**a**) *(geométricamente)* off-center (**b**) *(mentalmente)* unsettled, disorientated

descentralización *nf* decentralization

descentralizar [14] *vt* to decentralize

descentrar *vt* (**a**) *(geométricamente)* to knock off-center (**b**) *(desconcentrar)* to distract

descerebrado, -a *Esp, Andes, RP Fam* **1** *adj* moronic, brainless
     2 *nm,f* moron, halfwit

descerrajar *vt (disparo)* to fire

desciendo *etc ver* **descender**

descifrable *adj (mensaje, jeroglífico)* decipherable; *(letra)* legible

descifrar *vt* (**a**) *(clave, mensaje)* to decipher; **¿has descifrado las instrucciones?** have you managed to make sense of the instructions? (**b**) *(motivos, intenciones)* to work out; *(misterio)* to solve; *(problemas)* to puzzle out

desclasificar [59] *vt* to declassify

desclavar *vt* to unnail

descocado, -a *adj Fam (persona)* carried away; **anoche estaba completamente d.** he was completely over the top last night; **un vestido d.** a provocative dress

descocarse *vpr Fam* to get carried away

descoco *nm* **¡qué d.!** how shameless!

descodificador *nm* decoder

descodificar [59] *vt* to decode

descojonante *adj muy Fam* **ser d.** to be a scream, to make one wet oneself

descojonarse *vpr muy Fam* to wet oneself laughing (**de** at)

descojono, descojone *nm muy Fam* **ser un d.** to be a scream, to make one wet oneself

descolgar [16] **1** *vt* (**a**) *(una cosa colgada)* to take down; **d. la ropa** to take down the washing (**b**) *(teléfono)* to pick up, to take off the hook
     2 descolgarse *vpr* (**a**) *(bajar)* **descolgarse (por algo)** to let oneself down *o* to slide down (sth) (**b**) *(corredor)* *(quedarse atrás)* to fall back behind; **descolgarse de** to break away from (**c**) *Fam (mencionar)* **descolgarse con que** to come out with the idea that

descollar *vi (sobresalir)* to stand out

descolocado, -a *adj (objeto)* out of place; *Fam (confuso)* disorientated, confused

descolocar [59] *vt (objeto)* to put out of place, to disturb; *Fam (persona)* to confuse; **me descolocó totalmente con esa pregunta** I didn't know what to say in reply to his question

descolonización *nf* decolonization

descolonizar [14] *vt* to decolonize

descolorar *vt* to fade

descolorido, -a *adj* faded

descomedido, -a *adj Esp* excessive, uncontrollable

descompasado, -a *adj* excessive, uncontrollable

descompensación *nf* imbalance

descompensado, -a *adj* unbalanced

descompensar *vt* to unbalance

descomponer [50] **1** *vt* (**a**) *(pudrir)* *(fruta)* to rot; *(cadáver)* to decompose; **la humedad descompone ciertos alimentos** dampness makes some foods rot (**b**) *(dividir)* to break down; **d. algo en** to break sth down into (**c**) *(desordenar)* to mess up (**d**) *(estropear)* to damage, to break; **la cena le descompuso el vientre** the dinner gave him an upset stomach; **creo que**

comí algo que me descompuso (el cuerpo) I think I ate something that didn't agree with me (**e**) *(enojar)* to annoy
     2 descomponerse *vpr* (**a**) *(pudrirse)* *(fruta)* to rot; *(cadáver)* to decompose (**b**) *(turbarse, alterarse)* **se le descompuso el rostro** he looked distraught (**c**) *(irritarse)* to get (visibly) annoyed (**d**) *(averiarse)* to break down (**e**) *(estómago)* **se me descompuso el estómago** I had a stomach upset

descomposición *nf* (**a**) *(de elementos)* decomposition (**b**) *(putrefacción)* *(de fruta)* rotting; *(de cadáver)* decomposition; **en avanzado estado de d.** in an advanced state of decomposition (**c**) *(alteración)* distortion (**d**) *Esp (diarrea)* diarrhea

descompostura *nf* (**a**) *(falta de mesura)* lack of respect, rudeness (**b**) *Am (malestar)* unpleasant *o* nasty turn; *(diarrea)* diarrhea (**c**) *Méx, RP (avería)* breakdown

descompresión *nf* decompression

descomprimir *vt (gen)* & *Inform* to decompress

descompuesto, -a 1 *participio ver* **descomponer**
     2 *adj* (**a**) *(putrefacto)* *(fruta)* rotten; *(cadáver)* decomposed (**b**) *(alterado)* *(rostro)* distorted, twisted (**c**) *(con diarrea)* **estar d.** to have an upset stomach

descomunal *adj* tremendous, enormous

desconcentrar 1 *vt* to distract
     2 desconcentrarse *vpr* to get distracted

desconcertado, -a *adj* disconcerted; **estar d.** to be disconcerted *o* thrown

desconcertante *adj* disconcerting

desconcertar [3] **1** *vt* to disconcert, to throw
     2 desconcertarse *vpr* to be thrown *o* bewildered

desconchado, desconchón *nm* **la pared tenía varios desconchados** the plaster had come off the wall in several places; **el plato tenía un d.** the plate was chipped

desconchar 1 *vt* to chip
     2 desconcharse *vpr (pintura)* to flake off; *(loza)* to chip; **la pared se había desconchado en varios sitios** the plaster had come off the wall in several places

desconchinflar *Méx Fam* **1** *vt* to wreck, to bust
     2 desconchinflarse *vpr* to pack up

desconchón = **desconchado**

desconcierto *nm* *(desorden)* disorder; *(desorientación, confusión)* confusion

desconectado, -a *adj (aparato)* unplugged; *Fig* **está muy d. de su familia** he isn't in touch with his family very often

desconectar 1 *vt (aparato)* to switch off; *(línea)* to disconnect; *(desenchufar)* to unplug
     2 *vi Fam (persona)* to switch off; **d. de la realidad** to cut oneself off from one's surroundings
     3 desconectarse *vpr (aislarse, olvidarse)* to forget about one's worries; **desconectarse de algo** to shut sth out, to forget (about) sth

desconfiado, -a 1 *adj* distrustful
     2 *nm,f* distrustful person

desconfianza *nf* distrust

desconfiar [32] *vi* (**a**) **d. de** *(sospechar de)* to distrust; **desconfío de él** I don't trust him (**b**) **d. de** *(no confiar en)* to have no faith in; **desconfío de que venga** I doubt whether he'll come

descongelar *vt* (**a**) *(producto)* to thaw; *(nevera)* to defrost (**b**) *(precios)* to free; *(créditos, salarios)* to unfreeze

descongestión *nf* (**a**) *(nasal)* clearing, decongestion (**b**) **d. del tráfico** clearing up of traffic congestion

descongestionante *adj* decongestive

descongestionar *vt* (**a**) *Med* to clear (**b**) *(calle, centro de ciudad)* to make less congested; **d. el tráfico** to reduce congestion

desconocedor, -ora *adj* unaware (**de** of)

desconocer [19] *vt (ignorar)* not to know; **desconozco quién es/dónde trabaja** I don't know who he is/where he works; **se desconoce su paradero** her whereabouts are unknown; **por causas que aún se desconocen** for reasons as yet unknown *o* which are still unknown

desconocido, -a 1 *adj* **(a)** *(no conocido)* unknown; **lo d.** the unknown; **nació en 1821, de padre d.** he was born in 1821, and it is not known who his father was; **su nombre no me es del todo d.** I've heard his name **(b)** *(extraño)* **no dé su teléfono o dirección a personas desconocidas** don't give your telephone number or address to strangers **(c)** *(muy cambiado)* **estar d.** to have changed beyond all recognition

2 *nm,f* **(a)** *(extraño)* stranger **(b)** *(persona sin fama)* unknown **(c)** *(persona sin identificar)* unidentified person

desconocimiento *nm* ignorance, lack of knowledge

desconsideración *nf* thoughtlessness; **me parece una d. por su parte** I think it is rather thoughtless of him

desconsiderado, -a 1 *adj* thoughtless, inconsiderate

2 *nm,f* thoughtless *o* inconsiderate person

desconsolado, -a *adj* disconsolate

desconsolar [63] *vt* to distress

desconsuelo *nm* distress, grief

descontado, -a 1 *adj* discounted

2 por descontado *loc adv* obviously, needless to say; **dar algo por d.** to take sth for granted

descontaminación *nf* decontamination

descontaminar *vt* to decontaminate

descontar [63] *vt* **(a)** *(una cantidad)* to deduct; **siete, descontando a los profesores** seven, not counting the teachers **(b)** *Com* to discount

descontentar *vt* to upset, to make unhappy

descontento, -a 1 *adj* unhappy, dissatisfied

2 *nm* dissatisfaction

descontrol *nm* lack of control; *Fam* **la fiesta fue un d.** the party was rather wild; *Fam* **su vida es un d.** he leads a very disorganized life

descontrolado, -a *adj* **estar d.** to be out of control

descontrolar 1 *vt Fam* to confuse; **¡no me descontroles!** stop confusing me!; **el cambio de horario me ha descontrolado** the change in the timetable has got me all mixed up

2 *vi Fam* **ese tío descontrola mucho** that guy is pretty wild

3 descontrolarse *vpr (coche, inflación)* to go out of control; *(persona)* to lose control; *Fam (desmadrarse)* to go wild, to go over the top

desconvocar [59] *vt* to cancel, to call off

descorazonador, -ora *adj* discouraging

descorazonamiento *nm* discouragement

descorazonar 1 *vt* to discourage

2 descorazonarse *vpr* to be discouraged, to lose heart

descorchador *nm Andes, RP* corkscrew

descorchar *vt* to uncork

descorrer *vt* **(a)** *(cortinas)* to draw back, to open **(b)** *(cerrojo, pestillo)* to draw back

descortés *(pl* **descorteses)** *adj* rude, discourteous

descortesía *nf* discourtesy

descortezar [14] *vt (árbol)* to strip the bark from; *(pan)* to take the crust off

descoser 1 *vt* to unstitch

2 descoserse *vpr* to come unstitched

descosido, -a 1 *adj* unstitched

2 *nm (roto)* burst seam; **como un d.** *(hablar)* endlessly, nonstop; *(beber, comer)* to excess; *(gritar)* wildly

descoyuntar 1 *vt* to dislocate; *Fam Fig* **no hagas eso, que te vas a d.** don't do that, you'll injure yourself

2 descoyuntarse *vpr* to dislocate

descrédito *nm* discredit; **ir en d. de algo/alguien** to count against sth/sb; **estar en d.** to be discredited

descreído, -a *nm,f* nonbeliever, disbeliever

descreimiento *nm* unbelief

descremado, -a *adj* skimmed

descremar *vt* to skim

describir *vt* to describe

descripción *nf* description; **una d. de los hechos** an account of what happened

descriptivo, -a *adj* descriptive

descrito, -a *participio ver* **describir**

descuajar *vt* **(a)** *(derretir)* to melt **(b)** *(arrancar)* to uproot

descuajaringado, -a, descuajeringado, -a *adj Fam (coche, aparato)* falling to bits

descuajaringar, descuajeringar [38] *Fam* **1** *vt* to break into pieces

2 descuajaringarse *vpr* **(a)** *(descomponerse)* to fall apart *o* to pieces **(b)** *(troncharse de risa)* to fall about laughing

descuartizamiento *nm (de persona)* dismemberment; *(de res)* carving up, quartering

descuartizar [14] *vt (persona)* to dismember; *(res)* to carve up, to quarter

descubierto, -a 1 *participio ver* **descubrir**

2 *adj* **(a)** *(sin cubrir)* uncovered; *(coche)* open; **decir/hacer algo a cara descubierta** to say/do sth openly **(b)** *(cielo)* clear **(c)** *(sin sombrero)* bareheaded

3 *nm* **(a)** *Fin (de empresa)* deficit; *(de cuenta bancaria)* overdraft; **al** *o* **en d.** overdrawn **(b)** *(expresiones)* **al d.** *(al raso)* in the open; **quedar al d.** to be exposed *o* uncovered; **poner al d.** to reveal

descubridor, -ora *nm,f* discoverer

descubrimiento *nm* **(a)** *(de nuevas tierras, invenciones)* discovery **(b)** *(de placa, busto)* unveiling **(c)** *(de complot)* uncovering; *(de asesinos)* detection

descubrir 1 *vt* **(a)** *(hallar)* to discover; *(petróleo)* to strike **(b)** *(destapar) (estatua, placa)* to unveil; *(complot, parte del cuerpo)* to uncover; **la entrevista nos descubrió otra faceta de su personalidad** the interview revealed another aspect of his character; *Fig* **d. el pastel** to let the cat out of the bag, to give the game away **(c)** *(enterarse de)* to discover, to find out; **descubrió que su mujer lo engañaba** he discovered *o* found out that his wife was cheating on him **(d)** *(delatar)* to give away

2 descubrirse *vpr* **(a)** *(quitarse el sombrero)* to take one's hat off; **ante una hazaña así no puedo sino descubrirme** I can only take my hat off to such a feat **(b)** *(parte del cuerpo)* to uncover; **no se les permite descubrirse el rostro** they aren't allowed to uncover their faces

descuelgo *ver* **descolgar**

descuento 1 *ver* **descontar**

2 *nm* discount; **hacer d.** to give a discount; **con d.** at a discount; **un d. del 10 por ciento** 10 percent off

descuerar *vt Chile Fam* to slam, to criticize

descuidado, -a *adj* **(a)** *(desaseado) (persona, aspecto)* untidy; *(jardín)* neglected **(b)** *(negligente)* careless; **es muy d. con sus cosas** he's very careless with his things **(c)** *(distraído)* **estaba d.** he wasn't paying attention

descuidar 1 *vt (desatender)* to neglect

2 *vi (no preocuparse)* not to worry; **apaga la luz cuando te marches — descuida** turn off the light when you leave — don't worry, I will; **descuida, que yo me encargo** don't worry, I'll take care of it

3 descuidarse *vpr* **(a)** *(abandonarse)* to neglect one's appearance; **descuidarse de algo/de hacer algo** to neglect sth/to do sth **(b)** *(despistarse)* **me descuidé un instante y se me fue la bici a la cuneta** I let my attention wander for an instant and the bicycle went into the ditch; **como te**

descuides, ya no hay entradas if you're not careful there won't be any tickets left; **no te puedes d. ni un momento** you've got to be alert all the time; **en cuanto te descuidas se pone a cantar** he'll break into song at the drop of a hat

descuido *nm* (**a**) *(olvido)* oversight; *(error)* slip; **al menor d.** if you let your attention wander for even a moment; **en un d., borré el fichero** I deleted the file by mistake (**b**) *(falta de aseo)* untidiness, slovenliness

desde 1 *prep* (**a**) *(tiempo)* since; **no lo veo d. el mes pasado/ d. ayer** I haven't seen him since last month/yesterday; **d. ahora** from now on; **d. el principio** from the beginning; **d. hace mucho/un mes** for ages/a month; **d.... hasta...** from... until...; **d. el lunes hasta el viernes** from Monday through Friday; **d. entonces** since then; **d. que** since; **d. que murió mi madre** since my mother died; **d. ya** *(inmediatamente)* right now

(**b**) *(espacio)* from; **d. arriba/fuera** from above/the outside; **d.... hasta...** from... to...; **d. aquí hasta el centro** from here to the center (**c**) *(cantidad)* from; **d. 100.000 pesos** from 100,000 pesos

2 desde luego *loc adv* **¡d. luego (que sí)!** of course!; **¡d. luego...!** *(en tono de reproche)* for goodness' sake!; **¡d. luego, tienes cada idea!** you really come out with some funny ideas!

desdecir [51] **1** *vi* **d. de** *(desmerecer)* to be unworthy of; *(no cuadrar con)* not to go with, to clash with

2 desdecirse *vpr* to go back on one's word; **desdecirse de** to go back on

desdén *nm* disdain, contempt

desdentado, -a *adj* toothless

desdeñable *adj* contemptible; **una cantidad nada d.** a considerable amount

desdeñar *vt* to scorn

desdeñoso, -a *adj* scornful, disdainful

desdibujado, -a *adj* blurred

desdibujarse *vpr* to blur, to become blurred

desdice *ver* **desdecir**

desdicha *nf* *(desgracia)* *(situación)* misery; *(suceso)* misfortune; **por d.** unfortunately

desdichado, -a 1 *adj* *(decisión, situación)* unfortunate; *(persona) (sin suerte)* unlucky; *(sin felicidad)* unhappy

2 *nm,f* poor wretch

desdicho, -a *participio ver* **desdecir**

desdigo *ver* **desdecir**

desdijera *etc ver* **desdecir**

desdoblamiento *nm* (**a**) *(de objeto)* unfolding (**b**) *(de imagen, personalidad)* splitting

desdoblar 1 *vt* (**a**) *(servilleta, papel)* to unfold; *(alambre)* to straighten out (**b**) *(dividir)* to split

2 desdoblarse *vpr* (**a**) *(servilleta, papel)* to unfold (**b**) *Fam (multiplicarse)* to be in two places at once

desdoro *nm Formal* disgrace, cause of shame

desdramatizar [14] *vt* to play down

deseable *adj* desirable

desear *vt* (**a**) *(querer)* to want; *(anhelar)* to wish; **¿qué desea?** *(en tienda)* what can I do for you?; **¿desea algo más?** *(en tienda)* would you like anything else?, is that everything?; **desearía estar allí** I wish I was there; **estoy deseando que llegue** I can't wait for her to arrive; **dejar mucho/no dejar nada que d.** to leave much/nothing to be desired; **es de d. que las negociaciones terminen pronto** a quick end to the negotiations would be desirable

(**b**) *(felicidad)* to wish; **te deseo mucha suerte** I wish you the best of luck; **me deseó lo mejor/un buen viaje** he wished me all the best/a pleasant journey

(**c**) *(sexualmente)* to desire

desecación *nf* *(de alimentos, plantas)* drying, *Espec* desiccation; *(de terreno)* draining

desecar [59] **1** *vt (alimentos, plantas)* to dry; *(terreno)* to drain

2 desecarse *vpr (alimentos, plantas)* to dry; *(terreno)* to dry up

desechable *adj (pañal, jeringuilla)* disposable; *(plan, opción)* provisional

desechar *vt* (**a**) *(tirar)* to throw out, to discard (**b**) *(rechazar) (ayuda, oferta)* to refuse, to turn down; *(idea)* to reject; *(plan, proyecto)* to drop (**c**) *(despreciar)* to ignore, to take no notice of

desecho *nm* (**a**) *(objeto usado)* unwanted object; *(ropa)* cast-off; **material de d.** *(residuos)* waste products; *(metal)* scrap (**b**) *(escoria)* dregs; **desechos** *(basura)* garbage, trash; *(residuos)* waste products

desembalar *vt* to unpack

desembarazar [14] **1** *vt (habitación, camino)* to clear; **d. a alguien de algo** to rid sb of sth

2 desembarazarse *vpr* **desembarazarse de** to get rid of

desembarazo *nm* ease

desembarcadero *nm* pier, landing stage

desembarcar [59] **1** *vt (pasajeros)* to disembark; *(mercancías)* to unload

2 *vi* (**a**) *(de barco, avión)* to disembark (**b**) *Am (de autobús, tren)* **d. (de)** to get off

3 desembarcarse *vpr Am* to disembark (**de** from)

desembarco *nm* (**a**) *(de pasajeros)* disembarkation (**b**) *Mil* landing

desembarque *nm (de mercancías)* unloading

desembarrancar [59] *vt* to refloat

desembocadura *nf (de río)* mouth; *(de calle)* opening

desembocar [59] *vi* **d. en** *(río)* to flow into; *(calle)* to lead onto; *(asunto)* to lead to, to result in

desembolsar *vt* to pay out

desembolso *nm* payment; **d. inicial** down payment; **la operación supuso un d. de 100 millones** the operation cost 100 million

desembozar [14] *vt* (**a**) *(rostro)* to unmask, to uncover (**b**) *(cañería)* to unblock

desembragar [38] *vi Aut* to disengage the clutch, to declutch

desembrollar *vt Fam (lío, malentendido)* to straighten out; *(ovillo)* to disentangle

desembuchar *vi Fam* to spit it out

desempacar [59] *vt* to unpack

desempalmar *vt* to disconnect

desempañar *vt (quitar el vaho a) (con trapo)* to wipe the steam off; *(electrónicamente)* to demist

desempaquetar *vt (paquete)* to unwrap; *(caja)* to unpack

desempatar *vi* **todavía no han desempatado** it's still a tie; **jugar para d.** to have a play-off

desempate *nm* **el d. llegó en el minuto treinta con un gol de River Plate** River Plate took the lead in the thirtieth minute; **partido de d.** decider

desempeñar 1 *vt* (**a**) *(función, misión)* to carry out; *(cargo, puesto)* to hold; **desempeña el cargo de tesorero** he holds the post of treasurer (**b**) *(papel)* to play; **desempeñó en muchas ocasiones el papel de Drácula** he played (the part of) Dracula many times (**c**) *(joyas)* to redeem

2 desempeñarse *vpr* to get oneself out of debt

desempeño *nm* (**a**) *(de función)* carrying out; **en el d. de su cargo** in the carrying out of his duties (**b**) *(de papel)* performance (**c**) *(de objeto)* redemption

desempleado, -a 1 *adj* unemployed

2 *nm,f* unemployed person; **los desempleados de larga duración** the long-term unemployed

desempleo *nm* unemployment; **d. de larga duración** long-term unemployment

desempolvar *vt (mueble, jarrón)* to dust; *(recuerdos)* to revive; *Fig* **un día decidió d. su violín** one day he decided to take up the violin again

desenamorarse *vpr* to fall out of love (**de** with)

desencadenante 1 *adj* **los factores desencadenantes de...** the factors which brought about...

   2 *nm* **el d. de la tragedia/guerra** what brought about the tragedy/war

desencadenar 1 *vt* (**a**) *(preso, perro)* to unchain (**b**) *(suceso, polémica)* to give rise to, to spark off; *(pasión, furia)* to unleash; **la medida desencadenó fuertes protestas** the measure provoked furious protests

   2 desencadenarse *vpr* (**a**) *(pasiones, odios, conflicto)* to erupt; *(guerra)* to break out (**b**) *(viento)* to blow up; *(tormenta)* to burst; *(terremoto)* to strike

desencajado, -a *adj* (**a**) *(mueble)* broken; **la puerta está desencajada** the door won't shut properly (**b**) *(rostro)* contorted

desencajar 1 *vt* (**a**) *(mecanismo, piezas) (sin querer)* to knock out of place; *(intencionadamente)* to take apart (**b**) *(cajón, puerta)* to unjam (**c**) *(rostro)* **el terror le desencajó el rostro** his face was contorted with fear

   2 desencajarse *vpr* (**a**) *(piezas)* to come apart (**b**) *(rostro)* to distort, to become distorted (**c**) *(hueso)* to dislocate; **se le ha desencajado la mandíbula** he's dislocated his jaw

desencajonar *vt* to take out of a box

desencantar 1 *vt* (**a**) *(decepcionar)* to disappoint (**b**) *(romper el hechizo)* to disenchant

   2 desencantarse *vpr* to be disappointed

desencanto *nm* disappointment

desenchufar *vt* *(quitar el enchufe)* to unplug; *(apagar)* to switch off

desencolar *vt* to unstick

desencontrarse *vpr CSur* **casi nos desencontramos** we almost missed each other

desencuentro *nm* *(en una cita)* failure to meet up; *(desacuerdo)* disagreement

desenfadado, -a *adj (persona, conducta)* relaxed, easygoing; *(comedia, programa de TV)* lighthearted; *(estilo)* light; *(en el vestir)* casual

desenfado *nm (desenvoltura)* ease; *(desparpajo)* forwardness, uninhibited nature

desenfocado, -a *adj (imagen)* out of focus; *(visión)* blurred; **ver d.** to have blurred vision

desenfocar [59] *vt (objeto)* to focus incorrectly; *(foto)* to take out of focus

desenfrenado, -a *adj (ritmo, baile)* frantic, frenzied; *(comportamiento)* uncontrolled; *(apetito)* insatiable

desenfrenar 1 *vt (caballo)* to unbridle

   2 desenfrenarse *vpr (persona)* to lose one's self-control

desenfreno *nm* (**a**) *(descontrol)* lack of restraint (**b**) *(vicio)* debauchery

desenfundar *vt (pistola)* to draw; *(mueble)* to uncover; **desenfundó el violín** he took the violin out of its case

desenganchar 1 *vt* (**a**) *(vagón)* to uncouple (**b**) *(caballo)* to unhitch (**c**) *(pelo, jersey)* to free

   2 desengancharse *vpr Fam (de un vicio)* to kick the habit

desengañado, -a 1 *adj* disillusioned (**de** with)

   2 *nm,f* person who has been disillusioned *(with life or love)*

desengañar 1 *vt* (**a**) *(a una persona equivocada)* **d. a alguien** to reveal the truth to sb (**b**) *(a una persona esperanzada)* to disillusion

   2 desengañarse *vpr* to become disillusioned (**de** with); **desengáñate** stop kidding yourself

desengaño *nm* disappointment; **llevarse** *o* **sufrir un d. con alguien** to be disappointed in sb; **d. amoroso** unhappy affair

desengarzar [14] *vt (perlas)* to unstring; *(diamante)* to remove from its setting

desengrasar *vt* to remove the grease from

desenlace *nm* denouement, ending

desenlazar [14] *vt (nudo)* to undo; *(brazos)* to unlink; **desenlazó las manos** he unclasped his hands

desenmarañar *vt* (**a**) *(ovillo, pelo)* to untangle (**b**) *(asunto)* to sort out; *(problema)* to resolve

desenmascarar *vt (descubrir)* to unmask

desenredar 1 *vt* (**a**) *(hilos, pelo)* to untangle (**b**) *(asunto)* to sort out; *(problema)* to resolve

   2 desenredarse *vpr* to extricate oneself (**de algo** from sth); **desenredarse el pelo** to unknot one's hair

desenrollar *vt (hilo, cinta)* to unwind; *(persiana)* to roll down; *(pergamino, papel)* to unroll

desenroscar [59] *vt* to unscrew

desensillar *vt* to unsaddle

desentenderse [64] *vpr* to pretend not to hear/know; **d. de** to refuse to have anything to do with

desentendido, -a *adj* **hacerse el d.** to pretend one hasn't noticed/heard sth

desenterrar [3] *vt* (**a**) *(cadáver)* to disinter; *(tesoro, escultura)* to dig up (**b**) *(recordar)* to recall, to revive (**de** from) (**c**) *(sacar a la luz)* **d. viejos rencores** to rake up old quarrels

desentonar *vi* (**a**) *Mús (cantante)* to sing out of tune; *(instrumento)* to be out of tune (**b**) *(color, cortinas, edificio)* to clash (**con** with) (**c**) *(persona, modales)* to be out of place

desentrañar *vt* to unravel, to figure out

desentrenado, -a *adj (bajo de forma)* out of training; *(falto de práctica)* out of practice

desentrenarse *vpr (bajar de forma)* to get out of training

desentubar *vt Fam* **d. a un enfermo** *(sacar tubos)* to remove a tube/tubes from a patient

desentumecer [46] **1** *vt* to stretch

   2 desentumecerse *vpr* to loosen up

desenvainar *vt (espada)* to draw

desenvoltura *nf (al moverse, comportarse)* ease; *(al hablar)* fluency

desenvolver [41] **1** *vt* to unwrap

   2 desenvolverse *vpr* (**a**) *(asunto, proceso)* to progress; *(trama)* to unfold; *(entrevista)* to pass off (**b**) *(persona)* to cope, to manage; **sabe desenvolverse ella sola** she can cope *o* manage by herself; **se desenvuelve muy bien en su nuevo trabajo** he's getting along fine in his new job; **se sabe d. bastante bien en inglés** he can get along pretty well in English

desenvuelto, -a 1 *participio ver* **desenvolver**

   2 *adj (comportamiento, movimiento)* natural, easy; *(al hablar)* fluent

desenzarzar [14] *vt (prenda)* to untangle

deseo *nm* (**a**) *(pasión)* desire; **arder en deseos de hacer algo** to be burning with desire to do sth (**b**) *(anhelo)* wish; **se cumplió mi d.** my wish came true, I got my wish; **pedir/ conceder un d.** to ask for/grant a wish; **tus deseos son órdenes** your wish is my command; **buenos deseos** good intentions; **con mis/nuestros mejores deseos** *(en carta, obsequio)* (with my/our) best wishes

deseoso, -a *adj* **estar d. de algo/de hacer algo** to long for sth/to do sth

deseque *etc ver* **desecar**

desequilibrado, -a 1 *adj* (**a**) *(persona)* unbalanced (**b**) *(balanza, eje)* off-center

   2 *nm,f* madman, *f* madwoman

desequilibrar *vt* (**a**) *(persona, mente)* to unbalance (**b**) *(objeto)* to knock off balance; *(economía)* to upset

desequilibrio *nm* (**a**) *(mecánico, en la dieta)* lack of balance (**b**) *(mental)* mental instability (**c**) *(en la economía)* imbalance

deserción *nf (de soldado)* desertion; *Am* **d. escolar** dropping out of school

desertar *vi (soldado)* to desert; *Fig* **d. de** to abandon; **desertó**

de sus obligaciones he neglected his duties

desértico, -a *adj* (**a**) *(del desierto)* desert; **clima d.** desert climate (**b**) *(despoblado)* deserted

desertificación *nf* desertification

desertización *nf* *(del terreno)* desertification; *(de la población)* depopulation

desertizar [14] **1** *vt* to turn into a desert
   2 desertizarse *vpr* to turn into a desert

desertor, -ora *nm,f* deserter

desesperación *nf* (**a**) *(falta de esperanza)* despair, desperation; **con d.** in despair; **se suicidó presa de la d.** despair drove him to suicide; **me entra la d. cuando pienso en el poco tiempo que nos queda** I start getting *o* feeling desperate when I think of how little time we have left (**b**) *(enojo)* **¡me entra una d. cuando veo estas injusticias!** it makes me mad when I see injustices like these!; **es una d. lo lento que van los trenes** it's maddening how slowly the trains go

desesperado, -a *adj* desperate; **en un intento d. por huir del incendio** in a desperate attempt to escape from the fire; **lo hice porque estaba d.** I did it out of desperation; **gritaba d. que lo ayudaran** he was screaming frantically for them to help him; **(hacer algo) a la desesperada** (to do sth) in desperation

desesperante *adj* infuriating

desesperanza *nf* lack of hope; **cuando la vio besar a Rodrigo, la d. se apoderó de él** when he saw her kiss Rodrigo he gave up hope

desesperanzar [14] **1** *vt* to cause to lose hope
   2 desesperanzarse *vpr* to lose hope

desesperar 1 *vt* (**a**) *(quitar la esperanza a)* to drive to despair (**b**) *(irritar, enojar)* to exasperate, to drive mad
   2 *vi* **d. de hacer algo** to lose all hope of doing sth
   3 desesperarse *vpr* (**a**) *(perder la esperanza)* to be driven to despair (**b**) *(irritarse, enojarse)* to get mad *o* exasperated

desestabilización *nf* destabilization

desestabilizador, -ora *adj* destabilizing

desestabilizar [14] *vt* to destabilize

desestatizar [14] *vt Am* to privatize, to sell off

desestimar *vt* (**a**) *(rechazar)* to turn down (**b**) *(despreciar)* to turn one's nose up at

desfachatez *nf* cheek

desfalcar [59] *vt* to embezzle

desfalco *nm* embezzlement

desfallecer [46] *vi* (**a**) *(debilitarse)* to be exhausted; **d. de** to feel faint from (**b**) *(desmayarse)* to faint

desfallecimiento *nm* (**a**) *(desmayo)* fainting fit (**b**) *(debilidad)* faintness

desfasado, -a *adj* *(persona)* out of touch; *(libro, moda)* out of date; **estar d.** to be out of touch

desfasar *vt Elec* to phase out

desfase *nm (diferencia)* gap; **llevamos un d. de diez años con respecto a Suecia** we are ten years behind Sweden; **d. horario** jet lag

desfavorable *adj* unfavorable

desfavorecer [46] *vt* (**a**) *(perjudicar)* to go against the interest of (**b**) *(sentar mal)* not to suit

desfavorecido, -a *adj* (**a**) *(desaventajado)* disadvantaged (**b**) *(feo)* **salí muy d. en la foto** I came out very badly in the photo

desfiguración *nf (de rostro, cuerpo)* disfigurement; *(de la verdad)* distortion

desfigurado, -a *adj* disfigured

desfigurar *vt (rostro, cuerpo)* to disfigure; *(la verdad)* to distort

desfiladero *nm* narrow mountain pass

desfilar *vi* (**a**) *(gen) & Mil* to parade (**b**) *(marcharse)* to head off, to leave

desfile *nm* (**a**) *Mil* parade, march past (**b**) *(de carrozas)* procession; **d. de modelos** fashion show

desflorar *vt* to deflower

desfogar [38] **1** *vt* to vent
   2 desfogarse *vpr* to let off steam

desfogue *nm* letting off of steam

desfondar 1 *vt* (**a**) *(caja, bolsa)* to knock the bottom out of; **vas a d. la caja si la llenas más** the bottom will fall out of that box if you put any more in it (**b**) *(agotar)* to wear out
   2 desfondarse *vpr (persona)* to become completely exhausted

desforestación *nf* deforestation

desforestar *vt* to deforest

desgajar 1 *vt (página)* to tear out; *(rama)* to break off; *(libro, periódico)* to rip up; *(naranja)* to split into segments
   2 desgajarse *vpr (rama)* to break off; *(hoja)* to fall

desgana *nf, Am* **desgano** *nm* (**a**) *(falta de apetito)* lack of appetite (**b**) *(falta de ánimo)* lack of enthusiasm; **con d.** unenthusiastically

desganado, -a *adj* (**a**) *(sin apetito)* **estar d.** to have lost one's appetite (**b**) *(sin ganas)* listless, apathetic

desgano = desgana

desgañitarse *vpr* to scream oneself hoarse

desgarbado, -a *adj* clumsy, ungainly

desgarrador, -ora *adj* harrowing

desgarrar 1 *vt* to rip; **d. el corazón** to break one's heart
   2 desgarrarse *vpr* to rip

desgarro *nm* tear

desgarrón *nm* big tear

desgastar 1 *vt* to wear out
   2 desgastarse *vpr* to become worn

desgaste *nm* (**a**) *(de tela, muebles)* wear and tear; *(de roca)* erosion; *(de pilas)* running down; *(de cuerdas)* fraying; **el d. de las ruedas** the wear on the tires (**b**) *(de persona)* wear and tear; *(de dirigentes)* losing of one's touch; **el d. de los años** the wear and tear of the years

desglosar *vt* to break down

desglose *nm* breakdown

desgobernar [3] *vt (país)* to govern badly

desgobierno *nm (de país)* misgovernment, misrule

desgracia *nf* (**a**) *(mala suerte)* misfortune; **ha tenido la d. de sufrir dos accidentes aéreos** she's had the misfortune to be in two air accidents; **bastante d. tengo ya con haber perdido mi trabajo** it's bad enough having lost my job; **por d.** unfortunately (**b**) *(catástrofe)* disaster; **desgracias personales** casualties; **es una d. que...** it's a terrible shame that... (**c**) *(expresiones)* **caer en d.** to fall into disgrace; **es la d. de la familia** he's the shame of the family

desgraciadamente *adv* unfortunately

desgraciado, -a 1 *adj* (**a**) *(afectado)* unfortunate (**b**) *(sin suerte)* unlucky (**c**) *(infeliz)* unhappy
   2 *nm,f* (**a**) *(persona sin suerte)* born loser (**b**) *(pobre infeliz)* miserable wretch (**c**) *(canalla)* **el muy d. me robó el ordenador** the swine stole my computer

desgraciar 1 *vt* (**a**) *(cosa)* to spoil (**b**) *(persona) (deshonrar)* to demean; *(herir)* to injure seriously
   2 desgraciarse *vpr (plan, proyecto)* to be a complete disaster, to fall through

desgranar *vt* (**a**) *(insultos, oraciones)* to spout, to come out with (**b**) *(maíz, trigo)* to thresh

desgravable *adj* tax-deductible

desgravación *nf* deduction; **d. fiscal** tax relief

desgravar 1 *vt* to deduct from one's tax bill
   2 *vi* to be tax-deductible

desgreñado, -a *adj* disheveled

desguace *nm* (**a**) *(acción) (de automóviles)* scrapping; *(de buques)* breaking (**b**) *(depósito)* scrap yard

desguarnecer [46] *vt* (**a**) *(quitar los adornos)* to strip (**b**) *Mil* to leave unprotected *o* without troops

desguazar [14] *vt (automóvil)* to scrap; *(buque)* to break up

deshabillé *nm* negligee

deshabitado, -a *adj (casa)* empty, uninhabited; *(región)* uninhabited

deshabitar *vt* (**a**) *(casa)* to leave (**b**) *(territorio)* to depopulate, to empty of people

deshabituar [4] **1** *vt* **d. a alguien (de)** to get sb out of the habit (of)

2 deshabituarse *vpr* to break the habit (**a** of)

deshacer [33] **1** *vt* (**a**) *(nudo, paquete)* to undo; *(tarta, castillo de arena)* to destroy; **d. las maletas** to unpack one's suitcases *o* bags; **tuvo que d. todo el camino porque se había olvidado las llaves en casa** she had to go all the way back because she had left her keys at home

(**b**) *(disolver) (helado, mantequilla)* to melt; *(pastilla, terrón de azúcar)* to dissolve

(**c**) *(despedazar) (libro)* to tear up; *(res, carne)* to cut up

(**d**) *(poner fin a) (contrato, negocio)* to cancel; *(pacto, tratado)* to break; *(plan, intriga)* to foil; *(organización)* to dissolve; **tenemos que d. este lío** we have to sort this problem out

(**e**) *(destruir) (enemigo)* to rout; *(matrimonio)* to ruin

(**f**) *(afligir)* to devastate

2 deshacerse *vpr* (**a**) *(nudo, trenza)* to come undone

(**b**) *(disolverse) (helado, mantequilla, nieve)* to melt; *(pastilla, terrón de azúcar)* to dissolve

(**c**) *(afligirse)* to go to pieces; **se deshizo en lágrimas al enterarse** he dissolved into tears when he found out

(**d**) *(librarse)* **deshacerse de** to get rid of; **se deshicieron de un sofá viejo** they got rid of an old sofa

(**e**) **deshacerse en elogios (con** *o* **hacia alguien)** to lavish praise (on sb)

(**f**) **deshacerse por alguien** *(desvivirse)* to bend over backward for sb; *(estar enamorado)* to be madly in love with sb

desharrapado, -a 1 *adj* ragged

2 *nm,f* person dressed in rags

deshecho, -a 1 *participio ver* **deshacer**

2 *adj* (**a**) *(nudo, paquete)* undone; *(cama)* unmade; *(maleta)* unpacked (**b**) *(derretido) (pastilla, terrón de azúcar)* dissolved; *(helado, mantequilla)* melted (**c**) *(enemigo)* destroyed; *(matrimonio)* ruined (**d**) *(anulado) (contrato, negocio)* canceled; *(pacto, tratado)* broken; *(plan, intriga)* foiled; *(organización)* dissolved (**e**) *(afligido)* devastated; **d. en lágrimas** in floods of tears; **tiene los nervios deshechos** his nerves are in shreds (**f**) *(cansado)* tired out; **la carrera lo dejó d.** the run left him exhausted; **vengo d.** I'm wrecked *o* exhausted

deshelar [3] **1** *vt (nieve, lago, hielo)* to thaw, to melt; *(parabrisas)* to deice

2 deshelarse *vpr* to thaw, to melt

desheredado, -a 1 *adj (excluido de herencia)* disinherited; *(indigente)* underprivileged

2 *nm,f (indigente)* deprived person; **los desheredados** the underprivileged

desheredar *vt* to disinherit

deshice *etc ver* **deshacer**

deshidratación *nf* dehydration

deshidratado, -a *adj* dehydrated

deshidratar 1 *vt* to dehydrate

2 deshidratarse *vpr* to become dehydrated

deshiela *ver* **deshelar**

deshielo *nm* thaw

deshilachado, -a *adj* frayed

deshilachar 1 *vt* to unravel

2 deshilacharse *vpr* to fray

deshilar *vt* to unravel

deshilvanado, -a *adj* (**a**) *(tela)* untacked (**b**) *(discurso, guión)* disjointed

deshilvanar *vt* to untack

deshinchar 1 *vt* (**a**) *(globo, rueda)* to let down, to deflate (**b**) *(hinchazón)* to reduce the swelling in

2 deshincharse *vpr* (**a**) *(globo, hinchazón)* to go down; *(neumático)* to go flat (**b**) *(desanimarse)* to get off one's high horse

deshizo *ver* **deshacer**

deshojar 1 *vt (árbol)* to strip the leaves off; *(flor)* to pull the petals off; *(libro)* to tear the pages out of; **d. una margarita** = to pull the petals off a daisy saying "he/she loves me, he/she loves me not"

2 deshojarse *vpr (árbol)* to shed its leaves; *(flor)* to drop its petals

deshollinador, -ora *nm,f* chimney sweep

deshollinar *vt* to sweep

deshonestidad *nf* dishonesty

deshonesto, -a *adj (sin honradez)* dishonest; *(sin pudor)* indecent; **proposiciones deshonestas** indecent proposals

deshonor *nm,* **deshonra** *nf* dishonor

deshonrar *vt* to dishonor; **con su conducta deshonra a toda la familia** he is dishonoring the entire family with his conduct

deshonroso, -a *adj* dishonorable, shameful

deshora *nf* **a d., a deshoras** *(en momento inoportuno)* at a bad time; *(en horas poco habituales)* at an unearthly hour

deshuesar *vt (carne)* to bone; *(fruto)* to pit

deshumanizar [14] **1** *vt* to dehumanize

2 deshumanizarse *vpr (relaciones)* to become dehumanized; *(persona)* to lose one's humanity

desiderátum *nm inv* greatest wish

desidia *nf (en el trabajo)* carelessness; *(en el aspecto)* slovenliness

desidioso, -a *adj (en el trabajo)* careless; *(en el aspecto)* slovenly

desierto, -a 1 *adj* (**a**) *(vacío)* deserted, empty; **una isla desierta** a desert island; **la ciudad se queda desierta en agosto** the city is deserted in August (**b**) *(vacante) (concurso)* void; *(premio)* deferred; **la plaza quedó desierta** the post was left unfilled

2 *nm* desert; **el d. de Atacama** the Atacama Desert; **el d. del Sahara** the Sahara Desert

designación *nf* (**a**) *(nombre)* designation (**b**) *(nombramiento)* appointment

designar *vt* (**a**) *(nombrar)* to appoint; **han designado a Gómez para el cargo** Gómez has been appointed to the post (**b**) *(fijar, determinar)* to name, to fix; **d. medidas contra la corrupción** to draw up measures against corruption

designio *nm* intention, plan

desigual *adj* (**a**) *(diferente)* different; *(terreno)* uneven (**b**) *(tiempo, persona, humor)* changeable; *(alumno, actuación)* inconsistent; *(lucha)* unevenly matched, unequal; *(tratamiento)* unfair, unequal

desigualdad *nf (económica, social, racial)* inequality; *(diferencia)* difference; *(del terreno)* roughness; *(de carácter)* changeability; *(de actuación, rendimiento)* inconsistency; **acabar con las desigualdades regionales** to put an end to inequalities between the regions

desilusión *nf (chasco)* disappointment; *(estado de ánimo)* disillusionment; **llevarse** *o* **sufrir una d.** to be disappointed; **caer en la d.** to become disillusioned

desilusionado, -a *adj (decepcionado)* disappointed; *(sin ilusiones)* disillusioned; **está muy d. con la política** he's very disillusioned with politics

desilusionar 1 *vt (decepcionar)* to disappoint; *(dejar sin* *ilusiones)* to disillusion; *(desengañar)* to reveal the truth to

2 desilusionarse *vpr (decepcionarse)* to be disappointed; *(quedarse sin ilusiones)* to be disillusioned; *(desengañarse)* to realize the truth

desincentivar *vt* to discourage

desincrustar *vt (tuberías)* to descale

desinencia *nf Gram* ending

desinfección *nf* disinfection

desinfectante *adj & nm (para objetos)* disinfectant; *(para heridas)* antiseptic

desinfectar *vt* to disinfect

desinflado, -a *adj (neumático)* flat

desinflamar 1 *vt* to reduce the inflammation in

2 desinflamarse *vpr* to become less inflamed

desinflar 1 *vt* (a) *(quitar aire)* to let down, to deflate (b) *Fig (quitar importancia)* to play down (c) *(desanimar)* to depress

2 desinflarse *vpr* (a) *(perder aire) (balón)* to go down; *(neumático)* to go flat (b) *(desanimarse)* to get depressed (c) *(achicarse)* to become discouraged, to lose heart

desinformación *nf* misinformation

desinformar *vt* to misinform

desinhibición *nf* lack of inhibition

desinhibido, -a *adj* uninhibited

desinhibir 1 *vt* to free from inhibitions

2 desinhibirse *vpr* to lose one's inhibitions

desintegración *nf* (a) *(de objetos)* disintegration; *Fís* **d. nuclear** nuclear decay (b) *(de grupos, organizaciones)* breaking up

desintegrar 1 *vt* (a) *(objetos)* to disintegrate; *(átomo)* to split (b) *(grupos, organizaciones)* to break up

2 desintegrarse *vpr* (a) *(objetos)* to disintegrate (b) *(grupos, organizaciones)* to break up

desinterés *(pl* **desintereses)** *nm* (a) *(indiferencia)* disinterest, lack of interest (b) *(generosidad)* unselfishness

desinteresado, -a *adj* (a) *(generoso)* unselfish (b) *(indiferente)* uninterested

desinteresarse *vpr* to lose interest (**de** in)

desintoxicación *nf* detoxification; **clínica de d.** *(para alcohólicos)* drying-out clinic

desintoxicar [59] **1** *vt* to detoxify

2 desintoxicarse *vpr (dejar de beber)* to dry out; **se fue al campo para desintoxicarse de la ciudad** he went to the country to get the city out of his system

desinversión *nf Econ* disinvestment, divestment

desinvertir *vt Econ* to disinvest

desistimiento *nm* giving up; *Der* abandonment

desistir *vi* to give up, to stop (**de hacer algo** doing sth)

deslavazado, -a *adj (discurso)* disconnected, rambling

desleal *adj* disloyal (**a** *o* **con** to); **competencia d.** unfair competition

deslealtad *nf* disloyalty

desleír [56] *vt* to dissolve

deslenguado, -a *adj* foul-mouthed

desliar [32] *vt* to unwrap

desligar [38] **1** *vt* (a) *(desatar)* to untie (b) *(separar, diferenciar)* to separate (**de** from)

2 desligarse *vpr* (a) *(desatarse)* to untie oneself (b) *(separarse)* to become separated (**de** from); *(distanciarse)* to distance oneself (**de** from)

deslindar *vt (limitar)* to mark out (the boundaries of); *(separar)* to define

deslió *ver* **desleír**

deslío *etc ver* **desleír**

desliz *nm* slip, error; **tener** *o* **cometer un d.** *(error)* to slip up; *(infidelidad conyugal)* to be unfaithful

deslizamiento *nm* slide, sliding; **d. de tierra** landslide

deslizante *adj* slippery

deslizar [14] **1** *vt* (a) *(mano, objeto)* **d. algo en** to slip sth into; **d. algo por algo** to slide sth along sth; **deslizó la mano por la barandilla** he ran his hand down the banister (b) *(indirecta, comentario)* to let slip in

2 deslizarse *vpr* (a) *(resbalar)* to slide; **el barco se deslizaba por la superficie** the boat slid along the surface; **los esquiadores se deslizaban por la nieve** the skiers slid across the snow; **el patinador se desliza por el hielo** the skater glides across the ice (b) *(introducirse)* **deslizarse en** *(persona)* to slip into; *(error)* to creep into (c) *(sujeto: tiempo, vida)* to slip away *o* by

deslomar 1 *vt (a golpes)* to thrash

2 deslomarse *vpr Fam* to break one's back, to wear oneself out

deslucido, -a *adj* (a) *(sin brillo)* faded; *(plata)* tarnished (b) *(sin gracia) (acto, ceremonia)* dull; *(actuación)* lackluster, uninspired

deslucir [39] *vt (espectáculo)* to spoil, to ruin

deslumbrante *adj (luz, belleza)* dazzling; **estaba d.** she looked stunning

deslumbrar *vt también Fig* to dazzle

deslustrar *vt también Fig* to take the shine off

desmadejado, -a *adj (débil, flojo)* weak, worn out

desmadejar *vt* to wear *o* tire out

desmadrarse *vpr Esp Fam* to go wild

desmadre *nm Fam* (a) *(caos)* chaos, utter confusion (b) *(desenfreno)* **la fiesta fue un d.** the party was really wild

desmán *nm* (a) *(exceso)* excess; **con sus desmanes ahuyenta a mis amigos** his outrageous behavior scares off my friends (b) *(abuso de poder)* abuse (of power)

desmandado, -a *adj (desobediente)* unruly

desmandarse *vpr* (a) *(desobedecer)* to be disobedient (b) *(insubordinarse)* to get out of hand

desmano *nf* **a d.** *(fuera de alcance)* out of reach; *(fuera del camino seguido)* out of the way

desmantelado, -a *adj* dismantled

desmantelamiento *nm (de casa, fábrica)* stripping; *(de organización)* disbanding; *(de arsenal, andamiaje)* dismantling; *(de barco)* unrigging; **el d. de todas las bases militares** the closing of all military bases

desmantelar *vt (casa, fábrica)* to clear out, to strip; *(organización)* to disband; *(arsenal, andamio)* to dismantle; *(barco)* to unrig

desmañado, -a *adj* clumsy, awkward

desmaquillador *nm* makeup remover

desmaquillar 1 *vt* to remove the makeup from

2 desmaquillarse *vpr* to take one's makeup off

desmarcar [59] **1** *vt Dep* to draw the marker away from

2 desmarcarse *vpr* (a) *Dep* to lose one's marker (b) *(apartarse)* **d. de** to distance oneself from

desmarque *nm* (a) *Dep* **realizó un buen d.** he lost his marker well (b) *(alejamiento)* **su d. de la política del gobierno** his disavowal of government policy

desmayado, -a *adj* (a) *(persona)* unconscious; **caer d.** to faint (b) *(color)* pale; *(voz)* faint, weak

desmayar 1 *vi* to lose heart

2 desmayarse *vpr* to faint

desmayo *nm* (a) *(físico)* fainting fit; **sufrir un d.** to faint (b) *(moral)* loss of heart; **sin d.** unfalteringly; **con d.** feebly

desmedido, -a *adj* excessive, disproportionate

desmedirse [47] *vpr* to go too far, to go over the top

desmejorado, -a *adj* poorly, unwell

desmejorar 1 *vt* to spoil

2 *vi* to go downhill, to deteriorate

3 desmejorarse *vpr* to go downhill, to deteriorate

desmelenado, -a *adj* (a) *(persona)* reckless, wild (b) *(cabello)* tousled, disheveled

desmelenar 1 *vt (cabello)* to dishevel
 2 desmelenarse *vpr* to go wild

desmembración *nf*, **desmembramiento** *nm* (**a**) *(de cuerpo)* dismemberment; *(de miembro, extremidad)* loss (**b**) *(de estados, partidos)* breakup

desmembrar [3] **1** *vt* (**a**) *(trocear) (cuerpo)* to dismember; *(miembro, extremidad)* to cut off (**b**) *(disgregar)* to break up
 2 desmembrarse *vpr* to break up; **el Estado se está desmembrando** the state is breaking up *o* falling apart

desmemoriado, -a 1 *adj* forgetful
 2 *nm,f* forgetful person

desmentido *nm* denial

desmentir [62] *vt* (**a**) *(negar)* to deny; **desmintió la noticia** he denied the report (**b**) *(no corresponder)* to belie

desmenuzar [14] **1** *vt* (**a**) *(trocear) (pan, pastel, roca)* to crumble; *(carne)* to chop up; *(papel)* to tear up into little pieces (**b**) *(examinar, analizar)* to scrutinize
 2 desmenuzarse *vpr (pan, pastel, roca)* to crumble

desmerecer [46] **1** *vt* not to deserve, to be unworthy of
 2 *vi* to lose value; **d. (en algo) de alguien** to be inferior to sb (in sth); **ganó el equipo visitante, pero el Bétis no desmereció** the visiting team won, but Bétis gave a good account of themselves

desmesurado, -a *adj (excesivo)* excessive, disproportionate; *(enorme)* enormous

desmidiera *etc ver* **desmedirse**

desmido *etc ver* **desmedirse**

desmiembro *ver* **desmembrar**

desmiento *ver* **desmentir**

desmigajar 1 *vt* to crumble
 2 desmigajarse *vpr* to crumble

desmilitarización *nf (de país, zona)* demilitarization

desmilitarizar [14] *vt* to demilitarize

desmintiera *etc ver* **desmentir**

desmitificación *nf* **la d. del presidente** the removal of the aura surrounding the president

desmitificador, -ora *adj* **revelaciones desmitificadoras de la figura de Gandhi** revelations which shatter the Gandhi myth

desmitificar [59] *vt* **el escándalo desmitificó al presidente** the scandal showed the president had feet of clay

desmochado, -a *adj (árbol)* polled

desmochar *vt (árbol)* to poll

desmontable *adj* that can be dismantled; **una librería d.** a self-assembly bookcase

desmontar 1 *vt* (**a**) *(desarmar) (máquina)* to take apart *o* to pieces; *(motor)* to strip down; *(piezas)* to dismantle; *(rueda)* to remove, to take off; *(tienda de campaña)* to take down; *(arma)* to uncock (**b**) *(de caballo, moto, bicicleta)* to unseat; **el caballo desmontó al jinete** the horse threw its rider; **desmontó al niño de la bicicleta** he took the boy off the bicycle
 2 *vi* **d. de** *(caballo)* to dismount from; *(moto, bicicleta)* to get off; *(coche)* to get out of
 3 desmontarse *vpr* **desmontarse de** *(caballo)* to dismount from; *(moto, bicicleta)* to get off; *(coche)* to get out of

desmonte *nm* (**a**) *(terreno)* **un d.** an area of leveled ground (**b**) *(allanamiento)* leveling (**c**) *(de bosque)* clearing

desmoralización *nf* demoralization

desmoralizado, -a *adj* demoralized

desmoralizador, -ora, desmoralizante *adj* demoralizing

desmoralizar [14] **1** *vt* to demoralize
 2 desmoralizarse *vpr* to become demoralized

desmoronamiento *nm (de edificio, roca, ideales)* crumbling; *(de imperio)* fall

desmoronar 1 *vt (edificio, roca)* to cause to crumble
 2 desmoronarse *vpr* (**a**) *(edificio, roca, ideales)* to crumble,

to fall to pieces (**b**) *(persona)* to go to pieces; *(imperio)* to fall apart

desmotivar *vt* to demotivate

desmovilizar [14] *vt* to demobilize

desnacionalizar [14] *vt* to denationalize, to privatize

desnatado, -a *adj (leche)* skimmed

desnatar *vt* to skim

desnaturalizado, -a *adj (sustancia)* adulterated; *(alcohol)* denatured

desnaturalizar [14] *vt* (**a**) *(sustancia)* to adulterate (**b**) *(persona)* to deny the natural rights of

desnivel *nm* (**a**) *(cultural, social)* inequality, gap (**b**) *(del terreno)* drop; **había un d. de 500 metros** there was a drop of 500 meters

desnivelado, -a *adj (terreno, piso)* uneven; **la mesa está desnivelada** this table isn't level

desnivelar 1 *vt* to make uneven; *(balanza)* to tip
 2 desnivelarse *vpr* to become uneven

desnucar [59] **1** *vt* to break the neck of
 2 desnucarse *vpr* to break one's neck

desnuclearización *nf (de armas)* nuclear disarmament; *(de centrales nucleares)* = getting rid of nuclear power

desnuclearizar [14] *vt* to make nuclear-free

desnudar 1 *vt* (**a**) *(persona)* to undress (**b**) *(cosa)* to strip (**de** of); **desnudó su discurso de toda floritura** he avoided all ornament in his speech
 2 desnudarse *vpr* to undress, to get undressed; **tuvo que desnudarse de cintura para arriba** he had to strip to the waist

desnudez *nf (de persona)* nakedness, nudity; *(de cosa)* bareness

desnudismo *nm* nudism

desnudo, -a 1 *adj* (**a**) *(persona, cuerpo)* naked (**b**) *(salón, hombro, árbol)* bare; *(verdad)* plain; *(paisaje)* bare, barren
 2 *nm* nude; **pintar un d.** to paint a nude

desnutrición *nf* malnutrition

desnutrido, -a *adj* undernourished

desnutrirse *vpr* to become malnourished

desobedecer [46] *vt* to disobey

desobediencia *nf* disobedience; **d. civil** civil disobedience

desobediente *adj* disobedient

desocupado, -a *adj* (**a**) *(persona) (ocioso)* free, unoccupied; *(sin empleo)* unemployed (**b**) *(asiento, cargo)* vacant, unoccupied (**c**) *(tiempo)* free

desocupar *vt (edificio)* to vacate; *(habitación, mesa)* to leave; **si consigo d. una tarde, te llamo** if I can free up an afternoon, I'll call you; **desocupó su silla para cedérsela a la anciana** he gave (up) his seat to the old lady

desodorante 1 *adj* deodorant, deodorizing
 2 *nm* deodorant; *CSur* **d. ambiental** air freshener; **d. de bola** roll-on (deodorant); **d. de barra/de spray** deodorant stick/spray

desodorizar [14] *vt* to deodorize

desoír *vt* not to listen to, to take no notice of; **d. los consejos de alguien** to ignore sb's advice

desolación *nf (destrucción)* desolation; *(desconsuelo)* distress, grief; **sumir en la d.** to devastate

desolado, -a *adj (paraje)* desolate; *(persona)* devastated

desolador, -ora *adj (imagen, espectáculo)* desolate; *(noticia)* devastating

desolar [63] **1** *vt* (**a**) *(destruir)* to devastate, to lay waste (**b**) *(afligir)* to cause anguish to; **la muerte del padre desoló a la familia** the father's death devastated the family
 2 desolarse *vpr* to be devastated

desollar [63] *vt* to skin; *Fig* **si lo pillo, lo desuello** if I catch him I'll skin him alive

desorbitado, -a adj (**a**) (exagerado) disproportionate; (precio) exorbitant (**b**) **con los ojos desorbitados** pop-eyed

desorbitar 1 vt (exagerar) to exaggerate, to blow out of proportion; **la inflación ha desorbitado los precios** inflation has sent prices sky-high

2 desorbitarse vpr **la inflación se ha desorbitado** inflation has gone out of control o through the roof

desorden nm (**a**) (confusión) disorder, chaos; (falta de orden) mess; **tu dormitorio está en d.** your bedroom is in a mess (**b**) **desórdenes** (disturbios) disturbance; **se han producido desórdenes por toda la ciudad** there have been disturbances throughout the city (**c**) (vida desenfrenada) excess (**d**) (alteración física) disorder; **sufre desórdenes nerviosos/estomacales** he has a nervous/stomach complaint

desordenado, -a 1 adj (**a**) (habitación, persona) untidy, messy; (documentos, fichas) jumbled (up) (**b**) (vida, comportamiento) disorganized, messy

2 nm,f untidy person; **es una desordenada** she's very untidy

desordenar vt (habitación, cajón) to mess up; (documentos, fichas) to jumble up; (pelo) to ruffle

desorganización nf disorganization

desorganizado, -a adj disorganized

desorganizar [14] vt to disrupt, to disorganize

desorientación nf (**a**) (en el espacio) disorientation (**b**) (en la mente) confusion

desorientado, -a adj (en el espacio) lost; (confuso) confused; **tiene 98 años y anda ya algo d.** he's 98 and he's a bit confused

desorientar 1 vt (**a**) (en el espacio) to disorient, to mislead (**b**) (en la mente) to confuse

2 desorientarse vpr to lose one's way o bearings

desosar [23] vt (carne) to bone; (fruta) to pit

desovar vi (peces, anfibios) to spawn; (insectos) to lay eggs

desoxirribonucleico adj Quím **ácido d.** deoxyribonucleic acid

despabilado, -a adj (**a**) (despierto) wide-awake (**b**) (listo) smart, quick

despabilar 1 vt (**a**) (despertar) to wake up (**b**) (hacer más avispado) to make streetwise

2 despabilarse vpr (**a**) (despertarse) to wake up (**b**) (darse prisa) to hurry up

despachar 1 vt (**a**) (mercancía) to dispatch (**b**) (en tienda) (cliente) to serve; (entradas, bebidas) to sell; **¿lo despachan?** are you being served? (**c**) Fam (terminar) (trabajo, discurso) to finish off; (comida) to polish off (**d**) (del trabajo) **d. a alguien (de)** to dismiss o fire sb (from) (**e**) (asunto, negocio) to settle (**f**) Am (facturar) to check in

2 vi (**a**) (sobre un asunto) to do business (**b**) (en una tienda) to serve

3 despacharse vpr (hablar francamente) **despacharse con alguien** to give sb a piece of one's mind

despacho nm (**a**) (oficina) office; (en casa) study (**b**) (muebles) set of office furniture (**c**) (comunicación oficial) dispatch (**d**) (venta) sale; (lugar de venta) **d. de billetes/localidades** ticket/box office

despachurrar vt Fam to squash

despacio 1 adv (**a**) (lentamente) slowly (**b**) esp Am (en voz baja, sin hacer ruido) quietly

2 interj **¡d.!** take it easy!

despampanante adj stunning; **una rubia d.** a stunning blonde

despanzurrar 1 vt Fam to cause to burst open

2 despanzurrarse vpr to burst (open); **se ha despanzurrado el sofá** the stuffing is coming out of the sofa

desparejado, -a adj (calcetín, guante) odd

desparejar vt to mix up

desparpajo nm Fam forwardness, self-assurance; **con d.** with assurance, confidently

desparramar 1 vt (líquido) to spill; (objetos) to spread, to scatter

2 desparramarse vpr (líquido) to spill; (objetos, personas) to scatter, to spread out

despatarrarse vpr Fam to open one's legs wide; **se despatarró en el sofá y se quedó dormido** he sprawled out on the sofa and fell asleep

despavorido, -a adj terrified; **salir d.** to rush out in terror

despecharse vpr to get angry

despecho nm (rencor, venganza) spite; (desengaño) bitterness; **(hacer algo) por d.** (to do sth) out of spite; **a d. de** in spite of, despite

despechugado, -a adj Fam (hombre) showing a lot of chest, with one's shirt open; (mujer) showing a lot of cleavage, with a very low neckline

despechugarse [38] vpr Fam to bare one's breast

despectivo, -a adj (**a**) (despreciativo) scornful, contemptuous; **hablar de algo/alguien en tono d.** to speak scornfully o contemptuously about sth/sb (**b**) Gram pejorative

despedazar [14] vt (**a**) (físicamente) to tear apart (**b**) (moralmente) to shatter

despedida nf (**a**) (adiós) goodbye, farewell; **una fiesta/un regalo de d.** a going-away party/present (**b**) (fiesta) farewell party; **d. de soltera** hen party; **d. de soltero** bachelor party

despedido, -a adj (por cierre, reducción de plantilla) redundant; (por razones disciplinarias) fired

despedir [47] **1** vt (**a**) (decir adiós) to say goodbye to; **nos despidió con la mano** he waved goodbye to us; **fuimos a despedirle a la estación** we went to see him off at the station (**b**) (de un empleo) (por cierre, reducción de plantilla) to make redundant, to lay off; (por razones disciplinarias) to fire, to sack (**c**) (lanzar, arrojar) to fling; **salir despedido de/por/hacia algo** to fly out of/through/toward sth (**d**) (difundir, desprender) to give off; **despide un olor insoportable** it gives off an unbearable smell

2 despedirse vpr (decir adiós) to say goodbye (**de** to); **despidieron con un beso** they kissed each other goodbye; **se despide atentamente** (en carta) yours sincerely/faithfully; **si no apruebas, ya puedes despedirte de la moto** if you don't pass, you can kiss the motorbike goodbye

despegable adj detachable

despegado, -a adj cold, detached

despegar [38] **1** vt to unstick

2 vi (**a**) (avión) to take off (**b**) (empresa, equipo) to take off; **la empresa no acaba de d.** the company hasn't really been able to take off

3 despegarse vpr (**a**) (etiqueta, pegatina, sello) to come unstuck (**b**) (persona) **despegarse de alguien** to break away o withdraw from sb; **no se despegó de su novia ni un minuto** he didn't leave his girlfriend's side for a minute

despego nm detachment, indifference

despegue nm (de avión) takeoff; **d. económico** economic takeoff

despeinado, -a adj (por el viento) windswept; (descuidado) disheveled; **estás d.** your hair needs a comb

despeinar 1 vt (pelo) to ruffle; **d. a alguien** to mess up sb's hair; **el viento la había despeinado** the wind had ruffled her hair

2 despeinarse vpr to get one's hair messed up

despejado, -a adj (**a**) (tiempo, día) clear (**b**) (persona, mente) alert (**c**) (espacio) (ancho) spacious; (sin estorbos) clear, uncluttered

despejar 1 *vt* (**a**) *(habitación, mente)* to clear (**b**) *(misterio, incógnita)* to clear up, to put an end to
  2 *v impersonal* to clear up
  3 despejarse *vpr* (**a**) *(persona)* *(espabilarse)* to clear one's head; *(despertarse)* to wake oneself up (**b**) *(tiempo)* to clear up; *(cielo)* to clear

despeje *nm Dep* clearance

despellejar 1 *vt* (**a**) *(animal)* to skin (**b**) *(criticar)* to pull to pieces
  2 despellejarse *vpr* to peel; **se te está despellejando la nariz** your nose is peeling

despelotarse *vpr Esp Fam* (**a**) *(desnudarse)* to strip off (**b**) **d. (de risa)** to laugh one's head off

despelote *nm Fam* (**a**) *Am (caos)* chaos; **se armó un d.** chaos broke out; **ser un d.** *(proyecto, reunión)* to be chaotic (**b**) *(cachondeo)* **tu primo es un d.** your cousin is good fun; **esa película es un d.** that movie is a great laugh *o* a scream

despeluchar 1 *vt* **d. algo** to wear sth threadbare
  2 despelucharse *vpr* to wear threadbare

despenalización *nf* decriminalization

despenalizar [14] *vt* to decriminalize; **d. las drogas blandas** to decriminalize soft drugs

despendolarse *vpr Esp Fam* to go wild

despendole *nm Esp Fam* loss of control; **la fiesta fue un d.** the party was really wild

despensa *nf* larder, pantry

despeñadero *nm* precipice

despeñar 1 *vt* to throw over a cliff
  2 despeñarse *vpr* to fall over a cliff

desperdiciar *vt* *(tiempo, comida)* to waste; *(dinero)* to squander; *(ocasión)* to throw away

desperdicio *nm* (**a**) *(acción)* waste (**b**) *(residuo)* **desperdicios** scraps (**c**) **no tener d.** to be excellent from start to finish

desperdigar [38] **1** *vt* to scatter, to disperse
  2 desperdigarse *vpr* to scatter

desperezarse [14] *vpr* to stretch

desperfecto *nm* *(deterioro)* damage; *(defecto)* flaw, imperfection; **pagar los desperfectos ocasionados** to pay for the damage caused; **sufrir desperfectos** to get damaged

despersonalizar [14] *vt* to depersonalize

despertador *nm* (**a**) *(aparato)* alarm clock; **d. telefónico** alarm call service (**b**) *Arg (en carretera)* speed bump

despertar [3] **1** *vt* (**a**) *(persona, animal)* to wake (up); **despiértame a la seis, por favor** could you wake me (up) at six, please? (**b**) *(reacción)* to arouse; **d. odio/pasión** to arouse hatred/passion; **el ejercicio me despierta el apetito** exercise gives me an appetite; **d. a alguien las ganas de hacer algo** to make sb want to do sth (**c**) *(recuerdo)* to revive, to awaken; **esta canción despierta en mí buenos recuerdos** this song brings back happy memories
  2 *vi* to wake (up)
  3 *nm* awakening
  4 despertarse *vpr* to wake (up)

despiadado, -a *adj* pitiless, merciless

despidiera *etc ver* **despedir**

despido 1 *ver* **despedir**
  2 *nm (expulsión)* dismissal; *(por cierre, reducción de plantilla)* layoff; **d. forzoso** compulsory layoff; **d. improcedente** *(por incumplimiento de contrato)* wrongful dismissal; *(por ir contra el derecho laboral)* illegal dismissal

despiece *nm* cutting-up

despierto, -a 1 *ver* **despertar**
  2 *adj* (**a**) *(sin dormir)* awake (**b**) *(espabilado, listo)* bright, sharp

despilfarrador, -ora 1 *adj* wasteful, spendthrift
  2 *nm,f* spendthrift, squanderer

despilfarrar *vt (dinero)* to squander; *(energía, agua)* to waste

despilfarro *nm (de dinero)* squandering; *(de energía, agua)* waste; **un d.** *(compra)* a waste of money

despintar *vt* to take the paint off

despiojar *vt* to delouse

despiole *nm RP Fam* rumpus, shindy

despiporre *nm Fam* **fue el d.** it was something else

despistado, -a 1 *adj* absentminded; **en ese momento estaba d. y no la vi** I was distracted at the time and didn't see her
  2 *nm,f* scatterbrain

despistar 1 *vt* (**a**) *(dar esquinazo)* to throw off the scent; **despistaron a sus perseguidores** they shook off their pursuers (**b**) *(confundir)* to mislead; *(distraer)* to distract; **el ruido me despista** the noise is distracting me
  2 despistarse *vpr* (**a**) *(perderse)* to lose one's way, to get lost (**b**) *(distraerse)* to get confused

despiste *nm* (**a**) *(distracción)* absentmindedness; *(error)* mistake, slip (**b**) *(persona)* **Marta es un d.** Marta is very absentminded

desplante *nm* rude remark; **hacer un d. a alguien** *(con acciones)* to do something rude to sb; *(con palabras)* to be rude to sb

desplazado, -a *adj (persona)* out of place

desplazamiento *nm* (**a**) *(viaje)* journey; *(traslado)* move; **un d. hacia la derecha/izquierda** *(en política)* a shift to the right/left (**b**) *Náut* displacement

desplazar [14] **1** *vt* (**a**) *(trasladar)* to move (**a** to); **d. algo/a alguien de** to remove sb/sth from (**b**) *(tomar el lugar de)* to take the place of (**c**) *Náut* to displace
  2 desplazarse *vpr (viajar)* to travel; *(moverse)* to move

desplegar [43] *vt* (**a**) *(tela, periódico, mapa)* to unfold; *(alas)* to spread, to open; *(bandera)* to unfurl (**b**) *(cualidad)* to display (**c**) *Mil* to deploy

despliegue *nm* (**a**) *(de cualidad)* display (**b**) *Mil* deployment; **d. de misiles** missile deployment

desplomarse *vpr (caer)* to collapse; *(techo)* to fall in; **se desplomó agotado en el sillón** he collapsed exhausted into the chair

desplome *nm* collapse

desplumar *vt* (**a**) *(ave)* to pluck (**b**) *Fam (estafar)* to fleece

despoblación *nf* depopulation

despoblado, -a 1 *adj* unpopulated, deserted
  2 *nm* deserted spot

despoblar 1 *vt* to depopulate
  2 despoblarse *vpr* to become depopulated

despojar 1 *vt* **d. a alguien de algo** to strip sb of sth
  2 despojarse *vpr* **despojarse de algo** *(bienes, alimentos)* to give sth up; *(ropa, adornos)* to take sth off

despojo *nm* (**a**) *(acción)* stripping, plundering (**b**) **despojos** *(de animales)* offal (**c**) *(cadáver)* **hallaron los despojos del héroe** they found the hero's mortal remains; *Fig* **es un d. humano** he's a (physical/mental) wreck

despolitizar [14] *vt* to depoliticize

desposado, -a *nm,f (hombre)* groom; *(mujer)* bride; **los desposados** the newlyweds

desposar 1 *vt* to marry
  2 desposarse *vpr* to get married, to marry

desposeer [37] *vt* to dispossess

desposeído, -a 1 *adj* (**a**) *(pobre)* poor, dispossessed (**de** of); **un hombre d. de todos sus bienes** a man deprived of all his possessions (**b**) **d. de** *(carente)* lacking (in)
  2 *nm,f* **los desposeídos** the have-nots, the wretched

desposorios *nmpl Formal* (**a**) *(compromiso)* betrothal (**b**) *(matrimonio)* marriage, wedding

déspota *nmf* despot; **es un d. con sus hijos** he's a tyrant with his children

despótico, -a *adj* despotic

despotismo *nm* despotism; *Hist* **d. ilustrado** enlightened despotism

despotricar [59] *vi* to rant on (**contra** at)

despreciable 1 *adj (indigno)* despicable, contemptible; *(de poca importancia)* negligible

2 *nmf* contemptible person, wretch

despreciar *vt* (**a**) *(desdeñar)* to scorn (**b**) *(rechazar)* to spurn

despreciativo, -a *adj* scornful, contemptuous

desprecio *nm* (**a**) *(desdén)* scorn, contempt; **una mirada/un gesto de d.** a scornful *o* contemptuous look/gesture; **con d.** contemptuously, with contempt (**b**) *(acto despreciativo)* snub; **hacer un d. a alguien** to snub sb (**c**) *(desinterés)* disregard; **muestran un d. olímpico por los derechos humanos** they show complete disregard for human rights

desprender 1 *vt* (**a**) *(lo que estaba fijo)* to remove, to detach (**b**) *(olor, luz, calor)* to give off

2 desprenderse *vpr* (**a**) *(soltarse)* to come *o* fall off; **la etiqueta se desprendió del vestido** the label fell off the dress

(**b**) *(deducirse)* **¿qué conclusiones se desprenden de esta decisión?** what conclusions can be drawn from this decision?; **de sus palabras se desprende que…** from his words it is clear *o* it can be seen that…

(**c**) *(librarse)* **desprenderse de** to get rid of

(**d**) *(renunciar)* **desprenderse de algo** to part with sth, to give sth up

(**e**) *(apartarse)* **jamás se desprende de su amuleto** he is never without his lucky charm; **no se desprendía de su madre** she wouldn't leave her mother's side

desprendido, -a *adj (generoso)* generous

desprendimiento *nm* (**a**) *(separación)* detachment; **d. de tierras** landslide; *Med* **d. de retina** detachment of the retina (**b**) *(generosidad)* generosity

despreocupación *nf* lack of concern *o* worry; **con d.** in a carefree manner

despreocupadamente *adv* in a carefree manner

despreocupado, -a *adj (sin preocupaciones)* carefree; *(negligente)* unconcerned

despreocuparse *vpr* **d. de** *(asunto)* to stop worrying about; *(persona)* not to bother about

desprestigiar *vt* to discredit

desprestigio *nm* discredit

despresurización *nf* depressurization; **en caso de d. de la cabina** *(en avión)* if there is a sudden fall in cabin pressure

desprevenido, -a *adj* unprepared; **pillar d. a alguien** to catch sb unawares, to take sb by surprise

desprolijidad *nf RP* untidiness, sloppiness

desprolijo, -a *adj RP (casa)* messy, untidy; *(cuaderno)* untidy; *(en el aspecto)* unkempt, disheveled; *(al hacer las cosas)* sloppy

desproporción *nf* disproportion

desproporcionado, -a *adj* disproportionate

despropósito *nm* stupid remark; **fue un d.** it was a stupid thing to say; **decir despropósitos** to say stupid things, to talk nonsense

desproteger [52] *vt Inform (programa)* to hack into

desprotegido, -a *adj* unprotected

desprovisto, -a *adj* **d. de** lacking in, devoid of

después *adv* (**a**) *(en el tiempo) (más tarde)* later, afterward; *(entonces)* then; *(justo lo siguiente)* next; **ellos llegaron d.** they arrived later; **años d.** years later; **mucho d.** much later; **poco d.** soon after; **llamé primero y d. entré** I knocked first and then I went in; **yo voy d.** it's my turn next; **d. de hacer algo** after doing sth; **d. de que** after; **d. de que te fueras a la cama** after you went to bed; *Fig* **d. de todo** after all; **llegó d. que yo** she arrived after I did *o* after me

(**b**) *(en el espacio)* next, after; **¿qué viene d.?** what comes

next *o* after?; **hay una farmacia y d. está mi casa** there's a drugstore and then there's my house; **varias manzanas d.** several blocks further on; **está 2 kilómetros d. del pueblo** it's 2 kilometers past the village

(**c**) *(en una lista, jerarquía)* further down; **d. de** after; **d. del vino, la cerveza es la bebida más popular** after wine, beer is the most popular drink; **quedó d. del atleta ruso** he finished behind the Russian athlete; **d. de él, nadie lo ha conseguido** since he did it, no one else has

despuntar 1 *vt (romper la punta)* to break the point off; *(desgastar la punta)* to blunt

2 *vi* (**a**) *(flor, capullo)* to bud; *(planta)* to sprout (**b**) *(persona)* to excel, to stand out (**c**) *(alba)* to break; *(día)* to dawn

desquiciado, -a *adj* deranged, unhinged

desquiciar *vt* (**a**) *(puerta, ventana)* to unhinge (**b**) *(persona) (desequilibrar)* to derange, to disturb mentally; *(poner nervioso)* to drive mad

desquitarse *vpr* to get one's own back (**de algo/alguien** for sth/on sb)

desquite *nm* revenge

desratización *nf* rodent extermination

desratizar [14] *vt* to clear of rodents

desregulación *nf* deregulation

desregular *vt* to deregulate

desriñonarse *vpr Fam (esforzarse)* to break one's back

destacable *adj* notable, worthy of comment; **lo más d. de la película fue…** what was most notable about the movie was…

destacado, -a *adj (persona)* distinguished, prominent; *(acto)* outstanding; **una d. autoridad en la materia** a leading authority in the field

destacamento *nm Mil* detachment

destacar [59] **1** *vt* (**a**) *(poner de relieve)* to emphasize, to highlight; **cabe d. que…** it is important to point out that…; **hay que d. el trabajo de los actores** the acting deserves special mention (**b**) *(tropas)* to station; *(corresponsal)* to assign, to send

2 *vi (sobresalir)* to stand out; **destaca entre sus otras novelas por su humor** it stands out among her other novels for *o* because of its humor

3 destacarse *vpr* to stand out (**de/por** from/because of); **el actor se destacó por sus dotes de cómico** the actor was outstanding in comic roles

destajo *nm* piecework; **trabajar a d.** *(por trabajo hecho)* to do piecework; *(mucho)* to work flat out

destapador *nm Am* bottle opener

destapar 1 *vt* (**a**) *(caja, botella)* to open; *(olla)* to take the lid off (**b**) *(oídos)* to unblock (**c**) *(descubrir)* to uncover

2 destaparse *vpr* (**a**) *(desabrigarse)* to lose the covers; **el bebé se destapa por las noches** the baby kicks the blankets off at night (**b**) *(oídos)* to become unblocked (**c**) *(revelarse)* to open up; **al final se destapó el escándalo** in the end the scandal came to light

destape *nm (en revistas)* nude photos; *(en películas, teatro)* striptease

destartalado, -a *adj (viejo, deteriorado)* dilapidated; *(desordenado)* untidy

destellar *vi (diamante, ojos)* to sparkle; *(estrellas)* to twinkle

destello *nm* (**a**) *(de luz)* sparkle; *(de estrella)* twinkle (**b**) *(manifestación momentánea)* glimmer; **un d. de ironía** a hint of irony

destemplado, -a *adj* (**a**) *(persona)* **me siento un poco d.** I'm feeling a bit cold (**b**) *(instrumento)* out of tune (**c**) *(tiempo, clima)* unpleasant (**d**) *(carácter, actitud)* irritable (**e**) *(voz)* sharp

destemplarse *vpr* (**a**) *(enfriarse)* to catch a chill (**b**) *(irritarse)* to get upset (**c**) *(instrumento musical)* to get out of tune

destensar 1 *vt (músculo)* to relax; *(cuerda, cable)* to slacken

2 destensarse *vpr (cuerda, cable)* to slacken, to sag

desteñido, -a *adj (descolorido)* faded; *(manchado)* discolored

desteñir [47] **1** *vt (decolorar)* to fade, to bleach; *(manchar)* to discolor

2 *vi* to run, not to be colorfast; **estos pantalones destiñen** the color in these pants runs

3 desteñirse *vpr* to fade

desternillante *adj* hysterically funny

desternillarse *vpr* **d. de risa** to split one's sides laughing *o* with laughter

desterrar [3] *vt* (**a**) *(persona)* to banish, to exile (**b**) *(idea)* to dismiss; *(costumbre, hábito)* to do away with

destetar *vt* to wean

destete *nm* weaning

destiempo: a destiempo *loc adv* at the wrong time

destierro 1 *ver* **desterrar**

2 *nm (fuera del país)* exile; *(dentro del país)* internal exile; **en el d.** in exile

destilación *nf* distillation

destilar 1 *vt* (**a**) *(agua, alcohol)* to distill (**b**) *(sangre, pus)* to ooze (**c**) *(cualidad, sentimiento)* to exude, to ooze

2 *vi (gotear)* to trickle, to drip

destilería *nf* distillery

destinar *vt* (**a**) **d. algo a** *o* **para** *(cantidad, edificio)* to set sth aside for; *(empleo, cargo)* to assign sth to; *(carta)* to address sth to; *(medidas, programa, publicación)* to aim sth at; **el dinero recogido se destinará a comprar medicinas** the money collected will go to buy medicine (**b**) **d. a alguien a** *(cargo, empleo)* to appoint sb to; *(plaza, lugar)* to post sb to; **está destinado en Colombia** he's been posted *o* sent to Colombia; **estar destinado al éxito/fracaso** to be destined for success/failure

destinatario, -a *nm,f* addressee

destino *nm* (**a**) *(sino)* destiny, fate; **su d. era convertirse en estrella de cine** she was destined to become a movie star (**b**) *(rumbo)* destination; (**ir**) **con d. a** (to be) bound for *o* going to; **un vuelo con d. a…** a flight to…; **el tren con d. a La Paz** the train for La Paz, the La Paz train; **pasajeros con d. a Chicago, embarquen por puerta 6** passengers flying to Chicago, please board at gate 6 (**c**) *(empleo, plaza)* position, post; **le han dado un d. en las Canarias** he's been posted to the Canaries (**d**) *(finalidad)* use, function

destitución *nf* dismissal

destituir [34] *vt* to dismiss

destornillador *nm* (**a**) *Esp, Carib, RP (herramienta)* screwdriver (**b**) *Fam (bebida)* screwdriver

destornillar *vt* to unscrew

destreza *nf* skill, dexterity

destripar *vt* (**a**) *(sacar las tripas a) (animal, persona)* to disembowel; *(pescado)* to gut (**b**) *(colchón, muñeca)* to rip open

destronar *vt (rey)* to dethrone, to depose; *(rival)* to unseat, to replace at the top

destrozado, -a *adj* (**a**) *(mueble)* broken, ruined (**b**) *(persona) (emocionalmente)* shattered, devastated; *(físicamente)* shattered

destrozar [14] *vt* (**a**) *(físicamente) (romper)* to smash; *(estropear)* to ruin (**b**) *(emocionalmente) (persona)* to shatter, to devastate; *(vida)* to ruin

destrozo *nm* damage; **alguien tendrá que pagar los destrozos** someone will have to pay for the damage

destrozón, -ona *Fam* **1** *adj* **ese niño es muy d.** that child is always breaking things; **d. con la ropa** hard on one's clothes

2 *nm,f* **ese niño es un d.** that child is always breaking things

destrucción *nf* destruction

destructivo, -a *adj* destructive

destructor, -ora 1 *adj* destructive

2 *nm Mil* destroyer

destruido, -a *adj RP Fam (persona) (físicamente)* shattered; *(anímicamente)* shattered, devastated

destruir [34] *vt (deshacer)* to destroy; *(casa, argumento)* to demolish; *(proyecto)* to ruin, to wreck; *(ilusión)* to dash

desubicar [59] *vt Andes, RP* to confuse

desunión *nf* (**a**) *(separación)* separation (**b**) *(división, discordia)* disunity

desunir *vt* (**a**) *(separar)* to separate (**b**) *(enemistar) (grupos)* to divide, to cause a rift between

desusado, -a *adj* (**a**) *(pasado de moda)* old-fashioned, obsolete (**b**) *(desacostumbrado)* unusual

desuso *nm* disuse; **caer en d.** to become obsolete, to fall into disuse

desvaído, -a *adj (color)* pale, washed-out; *(forma, contorno)* blurred; *(mirada)* vague

desvalido, -a 1 *adj* needy, destitute

2 *nm,f* needy *o* destitute person

desvalijador, -ora *nm,f (de casas)* burglar

desvalijamiento *nm (de casa)* burglary; *(de persona)* robbery

desvalijar *vt (casa)* to burglarize; *(persona)* to rob; *Fig* **mis nietos me han desvalijado la nevera** my grandchildren have cleaned out my fridge

desvalimiento *nm Formal* destitution

desvalorizar [14] *vt* to devalue

desván *nm* attic, loft

desvanecer [46] **1** *vt* (**a**) *(humo, nubes)* to dissipate, to disperse (**b**) *(sospechas, temores)* to dispel

2 desvanecerse *vpr* (**a**) *(desmayarse)* to faint (**b**) *(humo, nubes, color)* to clear, to disappear; *(sonido, sospechas, temores)* to fade away

desvanecimiento *nm (desmayo)* fainting fit

desvariar [32] *vi (delirar)* to be delirious; *Fam (decir tonterías)* to talk nonsense, to rave; **¡no desvaríes!** don't talk nonsense *o* rubbish!

desvarío *nm* (**a**) *(dicho)* raving; *(hecho)* act of madness (**b**) *(delirio)* delirium

desvelar 1 *vt* (**a**) *(quitar el sueño)* to keep awake (**b**) *(noticia, secreto)* to reveal, to tell

2 desvelarse *vpr* **desvelarse por hacer algo** to make every effort to do sth

desvelo *nm* (**a**) *(insomnio)* sleeplessness, insomnia (**b**) *(esfuerzo, cuidado)* **a pesar de nuestros desvelos…** despite all our care and effort…

desvencijado, -a *adj (silla, mesa)* rickety; *(camión, coche)* battered

desvencijar *vt (romper)* to break; *(desencajar)* to cause to come apart

desventaja *nf* disadvantage; **estar en d.** to be at a disadvantage

desventajoso, -a *adj* disadvantageous, unfavorable

desventura *nf* misfortune

desventurado, -a 1 *adj* unfortunate

2 *nm,f* poor wretch

desvergonzado, -a 1 *adj* shameless, insolent

2 *nm,f* shameless person; **¡habráse visto el d.!** what a bad-mannered lout!

desvergüenza *nf* (**a**) *(atrevimiento, frescura)* shamelessness (**b**) *(dicho)* shameless remark; *(hecho)* shameless act

desvestir [47] **1** *vt* to undress

2 desvestirse *vpr* to undress (oneself)

desviación *nf* (**a**) *(de dirección, cauce, norma)* deviation; *Med* **d. de columna** curvature of the spine (**b**) *(en la carretera)* detour

desviado, -a *adj* (**a**) *(cambiado de dirección)* diverted (**b**) *(ojo)* squinty

desviar [32] **1** *vt (tráfico, río)* to divert; *(dirección)* to change; *(golpe)* to parry; *(pelota, disparo)* to deflect; *(pregunta)* to evade; *(conversación)* to change the direction of; *(mirada, ojos)* to avert

2 desviarse *vpr* **(a)** *(cambiar de dirección) (conductor)* to take a detour; *(vehículo)* to go off course; **desviarse de** to turn off **(b)** *(cambiar)* **desviarse de** *(tema)* to wander *o* digress from; *(propósito, idea)* to lose sight of

desvincular 1 *vt Der (bienes, propiedades)* to disentail

2 desvincularse *vpr* to disassociate oneself **(de** from)

desvío *nm* **(a)** *(en carretera) (salida)* detour; *(por obras, accidente)* detour; **toma el primer d. a la derecha** take the first turnoff to the right; **al llegar al cruce toma el d. de** *o* **a Guadalajara** when you get to the crossroads take the turning for *o* road to Guadalajara; **d. por obras** *(en letrero)* diversion, men at work **(b)** *Tel* **d. de llamada** call transfer

desvirgar [38] *vt* to deflower

desvirtuar [4] *vt (estropear)* to spoil; *(distorsionar)* to distort; **su victoria quedó totalmente desvirtuada** his victory was rendered meaningless; **esta actuación desvirtúa el espíritu del acuerdo** this action violates the spirit of the agreement

desvistiera *etc ver* **desvestir**

desvisto *etc ver* **desvestir**

desvivirse *vpr (desvelarse)* to do everything one can **(por** for); **d. por hacer algo** to bend over backward to do sth

detalladamente *adv* in (great) detail

detallado, -a *adj* detailed, thorough

detallar *vt (historia, hechos)* to detail, to give a rundown of; *(cuenta, gastos)* to itemize

detalle 1 *nm* **(a)** *(pormenor, rasgo)* detail; **con d.** in detail; **dar detalles** to give details; **entrar en detalles** to go into detail; **para más detalles, llame al teléfono...** for more information, call... **(b)** *(obsequio)* gift; **te he traído un d.** I've brought you a little present *o* a little something **(c)** *(atención)* nice gesture *o* thought; **¡pero qué d. ha tenido!** what a nice gesture!, how thoughtful of him/her!; **tener un d. (con alguien)** to be considerate (to sb); **es todo un d.** how courteous *o* considerate

2 al detalle *loc adj & adv Com* retail; **en este almacén no se vende al d.** we don't sell retail in this warehouse

detallista 1 *adj (meticuloso)* painstaking; *(atento)* thoughtful

2 *nmf Com* retailer

detección *nf* detection

detectar *vt* to detect

detective *nmf* detective; **d. privado** private detective

detectivesco, -a *adj* **labor detectivesca** detective work; **novela detectivesca** detective novel

detector, -ora 1 *adj* **aparato d.** detecting equipment

2 *nm* detector; **d. de humo/incendios/mentiras/ metales/minas** smoke/fire/lie/metal/mine detector

detención *nf* **(a)** *(parada)* stopping, holding-up **(b)** *(arresto)* arrest

detener [65] **1** *vt* **(a)** *(parar)* to stop; **consiguieron d. la hemorragia** they managed to stop the bleeding; **estaba decidido, nada podía detenerlo** he had made up his mind, nothing could stop him **(b)** *(arrestar)* to arrest **(c)** *(entretener)* to keep, to delay

2 detenerse *vpr* **(a)** *(pararse)* to stop; **detenerse a hacer algo** to stop to do sth; **se detuvo a hablar con una amiga y llegó tarde** she stopped to talk to a friend and was late **(b)** *(demorarse)* to hang about, to linger; **no te detengas tanto con la presentación y ve al grano** don't spend so much time on the presentation and get to the point

detenidamente *adv* carefully, thoroughly

detenido, -a 1 *adj* **(a)** *(detallado)* careful, thorough; **un examen d.** a careful, detailed examination **(b)** *(arrestado)* **(estar) d.** (to be) under arrest

2 *nm,f* prisoner, person under arrest

detenimiento *nm* **con d.** carefully, thoroughly

detentar *vt* to hold unlawfully; **los militares que detentan el poder en...** the military in power in...

detergente *nm* detergent; **d. para la ropa** washing powder; *Am* **d. para la vajilla** dish liquid; **d. de** *o* **con acción biológica** biological washing powder; **d. líquido** liquid detergent; **d. en polvo** soap powder

deteriorar 1 *vt* to damage, to spoil

2 deteriorarse *vpr (estropearse)* to deteriorate; *(empeorar)* to deteriorate, to get worse

deterioro *nm (daño)* damage; *(empeoramiento)* deterioration; **el d. de la situación** the worsening of *o* deterioration in the situation

determinación *nf* **(a)** *(de precio, fecha)* settling, fixing **(b)** *(resolución)* determination, resolution **(c)** *(decisión)* **tomar una d.** to take a decision

determinado, -a *adj* **(a)** *(concreto)* specific; *(en particular)* particular **(b)** *(resuelto)* determined **(c)** *Gram* definite

determinante 1 *adj* decisive, determining

2 *nm* **(a)** *Gram* determiner **(b)** *Mat* determinant

determinar 1 *vt* **(a)** *(fijar) (fecha, precio)* to settle, to fix; *(lugar)* to decide **(b)** *(averiguar)* to establish, to determine; **d. las causas de la muerte** to establish *o* determine the cause of death **(c)** *(motivar)* to cause, to bring about; **aquello determinó su dimisión** that caused him to resign **(d)** *(decidir)* to decide; **d. hacer algo** to decide to do sth **(e)** *(distinguir)* to distinguish, to discern; **no pude d. quién era** I couldn't make out who he was

2 determinarse *vpr* **determinarse a hacer algo** to make up one's mind to do sth

determinismo *nm* determinism

detestable *adj* detestable

detestar *vt* to detest

detiene *ver* **detener**

detonación *nf (acción)* detonation; *(sonido)* explosion

detonador *nm* detonator

detonante 1 *adj* explosive

2 *nm (explosivo)* explosive; *Fig (desencadenante)* **ser el d. de algo** to spark sth off

detonar *vi* to detonate, to explode

detractor, -ora 1 *adj* disparaging **(de** about)

2 *nm,f* detractor

detrás *adv* **(a)** *(en el espacio)* behind; **tus amigos vienen d.** your friends are coming on behind; **el interruptor está d.** the switch is at the back; **d. de** behind; **d. de alguien** behind sb's back; **deja un espacio d. de la coma** leave a space after the comma; **por d.** at the back; **hablar de alguien por d.** to talk about sb behind his/her back; **andar** *o* **ir d. de alguien/algo** to be after sb/sth **(b)** *(en el orden)* then, afterward; **Portugal y d. Puerto Rico** Portugal and then Puerto Rico; **fuimos pasando uno d. de otro** we went in one after another

detrimento *nm* damage; **en d. de** to the detriment of

detrito *nm*, **detritus** *nm inv Biol* detritus; **detritos** *(residuos)* waste

detuviera *etc ver* **detener**

deuce [djus] *nm Dep* deuce

deuda *nf* debt; **contraer una d.** to get into debt; *Fig* **estar en d. con alguien** to be indebted to sb; **saldar una d.** to pay off *o* settle a debt; **está lleno de deudas** he's heavily *o* deep in debt; *Econ* **d. exterior** *o* **externa** foreign debt; *Econ* **d. interior** *o* **interna** internal debt; **deudas de juego** gambling debts; **d. pública** *(títulos)* government stock; *Econ (concepto)* public debt

deudo, -a *nm,f* relative, relation

deudor, -ora 1 *adj Fin* **saldo d.** debit balance

2 *nm,f* debtor

devaluación *nf* devaluation

devaluado, -a *adj (moneda)* devalued

devaluar [4] **1** *vt* to devalue

 2 devaluarse *vpr* to go down in value

devanar 1 *vt* to wind

 2 devanarse *vpr Fam* **devanarse los sesos** to rack one's brains

devaneo *nm* (**a**) *(distracción)* idle pursuit (**b**) *(coqueteo)* **tener un d. con alguien** *(amoroso)* to have an affair with sb; **me contó sus devaneos con Juan** she told me about her flirtation with Juan; **en su juventud tuvo sus devaneos con la ultraderecha** he flirted with the far right when he was young

devastado, -a *adj* devastated

devastador, -ora *adj* devastating

devastar *vt* to devastate

develar *vt Am (revelar)* to reveal, to disclose; *(inaugurar)* to unveil

devengar [38] *vt (intereses, dividendos)* to yield; *(sueldo)* to earn

devengo 1 *ver* **devengar, devenir**

 2 *nm (cantidad)* amount due

devenir [69] **1** *nm* transformation; **la vida es un continuo d.** life is a continual process of change

 2 *vi (convertirse)* to become, to turn into

devoción *nf* devotion; **tener d. por alguien** to be devoted to sb; **tener d. por algo** to have a passion for sth

devocionario *nm Rel* prayer book

devolución *nf (de objeto)* return; *(de dinero)* refund; *Fin* **d. fiscal** tax rebate *o* refund

devolver [41] **1** *vt* (**a**) *(retornar) (lo entregado o prestado)* to give back (**a** to); *(lo alquilado)* to take back, to return (**a** to); *(producto defectuoso, carta)* to return (**a** to); *(cambio)* to give; **si no queda satisfecho, le devolvemos el dinero** if you're not satisfied, we'll refund you *o* give you back the money; **si ya lo tiene, ¿lo puedo d.?** *(en tienda)* if he already has it, can I bring it back?

 (**b**) *(restablecer)* **el triunfo devolvió la confianza al equipo** the victory gave the team back its confidence

 (**c**) *(corresponder) (favor, visita)* to return; **nunca me devuelves las llamadas** you never call me back

 (**d**) *(pelota)* to pass back

 (**e**) *(vomitar)* to throw *o* bring up

 2 *vi* to throw up; **tener ganas de d.** to feel like throwing up

 3 devolverse *vpr Am salvo RP* to come back

devorar *vt también Fig* to devour; **lo devoraban los celos** he was consumed by jealousy

devoto, -a 1 *adj* (**a**) *(piadoso)* devout; **ser d. de** to have a devotion for (**b**) *(admirador)* devoted (**de** to) (**c**) *(imagen, templo, lugar)* devotional

 2 *nm,f* (**a**) *(beato)* **los devotos** the faithful (**b**) *(admirador)* devotee

devuelta *nf Carib, Col* change

devuelto, -a 1 *participio ver* **devolver**

 2 *nm Fam (vómito)* sick

devuelvo *etc ver* **devolver**

dextrosa *nf Quím* dextrose

deyección *nf Geol (de una montaña)* debris *(singular)*; *(de un volcán)* ejecta *(plural)*; *Med* **deyecciones** stools, feces

DF *nm (abrev de* **Distrito Federal**) *(en México)* Mexico City; *(en Venezuela)* Caracas

dg *(abrev de* **decigramo**) dg

DGI *nf RP (abrev de* **Dirección General Impositiva**) ≃ IRS

di (**a**) *ver* **dar** (**b**) *ver* **decir**

día *nm* (**a**) *(periodo de tiempo)* day; **el referéndum se celebrará el d. 25 de abril** the referendum will take place on April 25; **me voy el d. ocho** I'm going on the eighth; **¿a qué d. estamos?** what day is it today?; **¿qué tal d. hace?** what's the weather like today?; **todos los días** every day; **al d. siguiente** (on) the following day; **el d. que se entere nos mata** when he finds out, he'll kill us; **de d. en d.** from day to day, day by day; **del d.** fresh; **en su d.** in due course; **hoy (en) d.** nowadays; **todo el (santo) d.** all day long; **el d. de mañana** in the future; **d. de los enamorados** (St) Valentine's Day; **d. del espectador** = day when some movie theaters sell tickets at a discount; **d. festivo** (public) holiday; **d. hábil** workday; **el Día del Juicio Final** Judgment Day; *Fam* **hasta el d. del juicio** until doomsday; **d. laborable** working day; **d. lectivo** school *o* teaching day; **d. libre** day off; **d. de Navidad** Christmas Day; *Am* **d. patrio** national holiday *(commemorating important historical event)*

 (**b**) *(luz diurna)* daytime, day; **es de d.** it's daytime; **hacer algo de d.** to do sth in the daytime *o* during the day; **d. y noche** day and night; **en pleno d., a plena luz del d.** in broad daylight

 (**c**) *(expresiones)* **¡buenos días!**, *Am* **¡buen d.!** good morning!; **mañana será otro d.** tomorrow is another day; **no pasar los días para alguien** not to look one's age; **tener un buen/mal d.** to have a good/bad day; **un d. es un d.** this is a special occasion; **el d. menos pensado…** when you least expect it …; **un d. de estos** sometime soon; **un d. sí y otro no** every other day; *Fam* **un d. sí y otro también** every blessed day; **estar/ponerse al d. (de)** to be/get up-to-date (with); **poner algo/a alguien al d.** to update sth/sb; **vivir al d.** to live from hand to mouth; **terminó sus días en la pobreza** he ended his days in poverty; **en aquellos días** in those days

diabetes *nf inv Med* diabetes *(singular)*

diabético, -a *adj & nm,f Med* diabetic

diablillo *nm Fam Fig* little devil

diablo *nm* devil; **pobre d.** poor devil; **tener el d. en el cuerpo, ser la piel del d.** to be a little devil; **mandar al d. a alguien** to send sb packing; **más sabe el d. por viejo que por d.** experience is what really counts; *Fam* **¿dónde/cómo diablos…?** where/how the hell…?; **¡diablos!** damn it!

diablura *nf* prank

diabólico, -a *adj* (**a**) *(del diablo)* diabolic (**b**) *(muy malo, difícil)* diabolical

diábolo *nm* diabolo

diácono *nm Rel* deacon

diacrítico, -a *adj (signo)* diacritical

diacronía *nf* diachrony

diacrónico, -a *adj* diachronic

diadema *nf (joya)* tiara; *(para el pelo)* hair band

diáfano, -a *adj* (**a**) *(casi transparente) (cristal)* (almost) transparent; *(tela)* diaphanous (**b**) *(claro) (luz, cielo, ojos)* clear; *(agua, explicación)* crystal-clear (**c**) *Esp (oficina)* open-plan

diafragma *nm* diaphragm

diagnosis *nf inv* diagnosis

diagnosticar [59] *vt* to diagnose; **le diagnosticaron cáncer** he was diagnosed as having cancer

diagnóstico *nm* diagnosis

diagonal *adj & nf* diagonal; **en d.** diagonally

diagrama *nm* diagram; **d. de barras** bar chart; **d. de flujo** flow diagram *o* chart

dial *nm* dial

dialectal *adj* **variante/expresión d.** dialect variant/ expression

dialéctica *nf* dialectics *(singular)*

dialéctico, -a *adj* dialectic(al)

dialecto *nm* dialect

dialectología *nf* dialectology

diálisis *nf inv Med* dialysis

dialogante *adj* **ser una persona d.** to be open to dialogue

dialogar [38] *vi (hablar)* to have a conversation (**con** with), to talk (**con** to); *(negociar)* to hold a dialogue *o* talks (**con** with)

diálogo *nm (conversación)* conversation; *Lit & Pol* dialogue; *Fam* **d. de besugos** half-witted conversation; **fue un d. de sordos** nobody listened to anyone else; **los diálogos** *(en película, serie)* the dialogue

diamante *nm (gema)* diamond; **diamantes** *(en naipes)* diamonds; **d. en bruto** uncut diamond; *Fig* **ser un d. en bruto** to have a lot of potential

diametralmente *adv* diametrically; **d. opuesto a** diametrically opposed to

diámetro *nm* diameter

diana *nf* (**a**) *(de dardos)* dartboard; **hacer d.** to hit the bull's-eye; **¡d.!** bullseye! (**b**) *(toque de corneta)* reveille; **tocar d.** to sound the reveille

diantre *interj* **¡d.!** dash it!

diapasón *nm Mús* tuning fork

diapositiva *nf* slide, transparency

diariamente *adv* daily, every day

diariero, -a *nm,f Andes, RP* newspaper seller

diario, -a 1 *adj* daily; **a d.** every day; **ropa de d.** everyday clothes

   2 *nm* (**a**) *(periódico)* daily (paper), newspaper; **d. hablado** radio news (bulletin) (**b**) *(relación día a día)* diary; **d. íntimo** (personal) diary; **d. de navegación** logbook; **d. de sesiones** parliamentary report

diarrea *nf Med* diarrhea; *Fam* **tener una d. mental** not to be thinking straight

diáspora *nf* diaspora

diástole *nf* diastole, dilation of the heart

diatriba *nf* diatribe

dibujante *nmf (artista)* drawer, sketcher; *(de dibujos animados, tebeos)* cartoonist; *(de dibujo técnico)* draftsman, *f* draftswoman

dibujar 1 *vt & vi* to draw, to sketch

   2 dibujarse *vpr* (**a**) *(mostrarse, verse)* to be outlined; **la montaña se dibujaba en el horizonte** the mountain was outlined on the horizon (**b**) *(revelarse)* **Fuster se está dibujando como un futuro campeón** Fuster is beginning to look like a future champion

dibujo *nm* (**a**) *(técnica, obra)* drawing; **d. a lápiz/al carboncillo** pencil/charcoal drawing; **d. anatómico** anatomical drawing; *Educ* **d. lineal** = drawing of geometrical figures; **d. técnico** technical drawing; **dibujos animados** cartoons (**b**) *(en tela, prenda)* pattern

dicción *nf* diction

diccionario *nm* dictionary; **d. de sinónimos** thesaurus

dice *ver* **decir**

dicha *nf (felicidad)* joy

dicharachero, -a *adj Fam* talkative

dicho, -a 1 *participio ver* **decir**

   2 *adj* said, aforementioned; **dichos individuos...** the said *o* aforesaid individuals...; **lo d. no significa que...** having said this, it does not mean (that)...; **¡lo d.!** that's settled then!; **o mejor d.** or rather; **d. y hecho** no sooner said than done

   3 *nm* saying; **del d. al hecho hay un gran** *o* **mucho trecho** it's easier said than done

dichoso, -a *adj* (**a**) *(feliz)* happy (**b**) *Fam (para enfatizar)* blessed, confounded; **¡siempre está con la dichosa tele puesta!** he always has that blasted TV on!; **no vamos a resolver nunca este d. asunto** we'll never get to the bottom of this blessed business

diciembre *nm* December; *ver también* **septiembre**

dicotomía *nf* dichotomy

dictado *nm* dictation; **escribir al d.** to take dictation; **obedecer al d. de** to follow the dictates of; **dictados** *(órdenes)* dictates

dictador, -ora *nm,f* dictator

dictadura *nf Pol* dictatorship; **d. del proletariado** dictatorship of the proletariat

dictáfono *nm* Dictaphone®

dictamen *nm (opinión)* opinion, judgment; *(informe)* report

dictaminar *vt* **los expertos dictaminaron que no había peligro** the experts stated that there was no danger; **todavía no se han dictaminado las causas de la enfermedad** the cause of the illness has still not been found *o* determined

dictar *vt* (**a**) *(texto)* to dictate; *Am (clase)* to teach, to give (**b**) *(emitir) (sentencia, fallo)* to pronounce, to pass; *(ley)* to enact; *(decreto)* to issue

dictatorial *adj* dictatorial

didáctica *nf* didactics *(singular)*

didáctico, -a *adj* didactic

diecinueve *núm* nineteen; *ver también* **seis**

diecinueveavo, -a *núm (fracción)* nineteenth; **la diecinueveava parte** a nineteenth

dieciocho *núm* eighteen; *ver también* **seis**

dieciochoavo, -a *núm (fracción)* eighteenth; **la dieciochoava parte** an eighteenth

dieciséis *núm* sixteen; *ver también* **seis**

dieciseisavo, -a *núm (fracción)* sixteenth; **la dieciseisava parte** a sixteenth

diecisiete *núm* seventeen; *ver también* **seis**

diecisieteavo, -a *núm (fracción)* seventeenth; **la diecisieteava parte** a seventeenth

diente *nm* tooth; **se le ha caído un d.** he has lost a tooth; **le está saliendo un d.** he's got a tooth coming through; **armado hasta los dientes** armed to the teeth; **enseñar los dientes** to bare one's teeth; **hablar entre dientes** to mumble, to mutter; **hincar el d. a algo** to sink one's teeth into sth; *Fig* to get one's teeth into sth; **ponerle a alguien los dientes largos** to turn sb green with envy; **me hace rechinar los dientes** it sets my teeth on edge; **d. de ajo** clove of garlic; **d. canino** canine tooth; **d. incisivo** incisor; **d. de leche** milk tooth; **d. de león** *(planta)* dandelion

diera *ver* **dar**

diéresis *nf inv* diaeresis

dieron *ver* **dar**

diesel, diésel *adj* diesel

diestra *nf* right hand; **a la d.** on the right *o* right-hand side

diestro, -a 1 *adj* (**a**) *(mano derecha)* right; *(persona)* right-handed; *Esp* **a d. y siniestro** left, right and center, all over the place (**b**) *(hábil)* skillful (**en** at)

   2 *nm Taurom* matador

dieta *nf* (**a**) *(régimen, alimentación)* diet; **estar a d.** to be on a diet; **poner alguien a d.** to put sb on a diet; **d. equilibrada** balanced diet; **d. macrobiótica** macrobiotic diet (**b**) *Com* **dietas** *(dinero)* expense *o* subsistence allowance; **d. de kilometraje** ≃ mileage allowance

dietario *nm* housekeeping book

dietética *nf* dietetics *(singular)*

dietético, -a *adj* dietetic, dietary

dietista *nmf Am* dietician

diez 1 *núm* ten; *Fam* **una chica d.** a stunning woman, a ten; **los D. Mandamientos** the Ten Commandments; *ver también* **seis**

   2 *nm (nota)* A, top grade

diezmar *vt* to decimate

diezmo *nm Hist* tithe

difamación *nf (verbal)* slander; *(escrita)* libel

difamador, -ora 1 *adj (de palabra)* defamatory, slanderous; *(por escrito)* libelous

   2 *nm,f (de palabra)* slanderer; *(por escrito)* libeler

difamar *vt (verbalmente)* to slander; *(por escrito)* to libel

difamatorio, -a *adj (declaraciones, críticas)* defamatory; *(texto, carta, escrito)* libelous

diferencia *nf* (a) *(disimilitud)* difference; **el problema de esa pareja es la d. de edad** that couple's problem is the difference in their ages; **a d. de** unlike; **establecer o hacer una d. entre** to make a distinction between; **el mejor/peor con d.** by far the best/worst (b) *(desacuerdo)* difference; **tuvieron sus diferencias** they had their differences; **limar diferencias** to settle one's differences (c) *(en suma, resta)* difference; **tendremos que pagar la d.** we'll have to pay the difference; **d. horaria** time difference; **d. salarial** wage differential

diferencial 1 *adj* distinguishing
2 *nm Tec* differential
3 *nf Mat* differential

diferenciar 1 *vt* to distinguish (**de** from)
2 *vi* to distinguish, to differentiate
3 diferenciarse *vpr* (a) *(diferir)* to differ, to be different (**de/en** from/in) (b) *(descollar)* **diferenciarse de** to stand out from

diferendo *nm Andes, RP* dispute

diferente 1 *adj* different (**de** o **a** from o to); **una casa d. de o a la mía** a house different from mine; **yo soy muy d. de** o **a él** I'm very different from him; **por diferentes razones** for a variety of reasons, for various reasons
2 *adv* differently; **se comportan muy d. el uno del otro** they behave very differently (from one another)

diferido *nm TV* **en d.** recorded

diferir [62] **1** *vt (posponer)* to postpone, to put off
2 *vi (diferenciarse)* to differ, to be different; **d. de alguien en algo** to differ from sb in sth

difícil *adj* (a) *(complicado)* difficult; **va a ser d. encontrar un sitio abierto a estas horas** it's going to be difficult o hard to find anywhere that's open at this time; **d. de hacer** difficult to do; **se me hace d. acostumbrarme a madrugar** I can't get used to getting up early; **no me lo pongas d.** don't make things difficult o hard for me; **tiene muy d. encontrar trabajo** it's very difficult o hard for him to find work (b) *(improbable)* unlikely; **es d. que ganen** they are unlikely to win (c) *(rebelde)* difficult, awkward; **es un niño muy d.** he's a very awkward o difficult child; **tener un carácter d.** to be an awkward person, to be difficult to get on with

dificultad *nf* (a) *(calidad de difícil)* difficulty; **el grado de d. de los exámenes** the degree of difficulty of the exams (b) *(obstáculo)* problem; **la d. está en hacerlo sin mojarse los pies** the difficult thing is to do it without getting your feet wet; **encontrar dificultades** to run into trouble o problems; **pasar por dificultades** to suffer hardship

dificultar *vt (estorbar)* to hinder; *(obstruir)* to obstruct

dificultoso, -a *adj* hard, fraught with difficulties

difiero *etc ver* **diferir**

difiriera *etc ver* **diferir**

difteria *nf Med* diphtheria

difuminado, -a *adj* (a) *Arte* stumped (b) *Fot* soft-focus; **en d.** in soft focus (c) *(poco claro)* blurred

difuminar *vt* to blur

difumino *nm Arte* stump, = roll of paper used for blurring chalk or charcoal drawings

difundir 1 *vt (noticia, doctrina, epidemia)* to spread; *(luz, calor)* to diffuse; *(emisión radiofónica)* to broadcast
2 difundirse *vpr (noticia, doctrina, epidemia)* to spread; *(luz, calor)* to be diffused

difunto, -a 1 *adj* deceased, dead; **el d. Sr. Pérez** the late Mr. Pérez
2 *nm,f* **el d.** the deceased

difusión *nf (de cultura, noticia, doctrina)* dissemination; *(de luz, calor, ondas)* diffusion; *(de programa)* broadcasting

difuso, -a *adj (luz)* diffuse; *(estilo, explicación)* wordy

difusor, -ora 1 *adj (medio, agencia)* broadcasting
2 *nm,f* propagator

diga *ver* **decir**

digerir [62] *vt (comida)* to digest; *(noticia, hechos)* to assimilate, to take in

digestión *nf* digestion

digestivo, -a 1 *adj* digestive
2 *nm* digestive (drink)

digiero *etc ver* **digerir**

digiriera *etc ver* **digerir**

digitador, -ora *nm,f Am* keyboarder

digital 1 *adj* (a) *(del dedo)* **huellas digitales** fingerprints (b) *Inform & Tec* digital
2 *nf (planta)* foxglove

digitalización *nf Inform* digitizing

digitalizador *nm Inform* digitizer

digitalizar [14] *vt Inform* to digitize

digitar *vt Am* to key, to type

dígito *nm Mat* digit

dignamente *adv* with dignity, in a dignified manner

dignarse *vpr* **d. (a)** to deign to; **no se dignó (a) contestarme** he didn't deign to reply

dignatario, -a *nm,f* dignitary

dignidad *nf* (a) *(cualidad)* dignity (b) *(cargo)* office (c) *(personalidad)* dignitary

dignificar [59] *vt* to dignify

digno, -a *adj* (a) *(honroso) (actitud, respuesta)* dignified; *(persona)* honorable, noble
(b) *(decente) (sueldo, actuación)* decent, good
(c) *(merecedor)* **d. de** worthy of; **d. de confianza** trustworthy; **d. de elogio** praiseworthy; **no me siento d. de tantos elogios** I don't feel I deserve so much praise; **no eres d. de ella** you're not good enough for her; **d. de mención/de ver** worth mentioning/seeing
(d) *(adecuado)* worthy; **un d. sucesor del ex campeón** a worthy successor to the former champion; **lo recibieron con honores dignos de un rey** they gave him a welcome fit for a king

digo *ver* **decir**

digresión *nf* digression

dije *adj Chile* nice, pleasant

dijera *etc ver* **decir**

dilación *nf* delay; **sin d.** without delay, at once

dilapidar *vt* to squander, to waste

dilatación *nf (de sólido, gas)* expansion; *(de pupila, cuello del útero)* dilation

dilatado, -a *adj* (a) *(pupila, cuello del útero)* dilated (b) *(experiencia)* extensive; **una dilatada trayectoria radiofónica** many years' experience in radio

dilatar 1 *vt* (a) *(sólido, gas)* to expand; *(pupila, cuello del útero)* to dilate; **el calor dilata los cuerpos** heat causes bodies to expand (b) *(prolongar)* to prolong (c) *(demorar)* to delay
2 dilatarse *vpr* (a) *(extenderse)* to expand; *(pupila, cuello de útero)* to dilate; **los cuerpos se dilatan con el calor** bodies expand when heated (b) *(prolongarse)* to be prolonged, to go on; **la reunión se dilató hasta el amanecer** the meeting went on until dawn (c) *(demorarse)* to be delayed

dilatorio, -a *adj Der* dilatory, delaying

dilema *nm* dilemma

diletante *adj & nmf* dilettante

diligencia *nf* (a) *(prontitud)* speed; **actuar con d.** to act speedily (b) *(trámite, gestión)* **diligencias** formalities, official paperwork (c) *(vehículo)* stagecoach (d) *Der* **diligencias** proceedings; **instruir diligencias** to start proceedings

diligente *adj (persona)* efficient, swift; *(respuesta)* prompt

dilucidar *vt* to elucidate

diluido, -a *adj* diluted

diluir [34] **1** *vt* to dilute

2 diluirse *vpr* to dissolve

diluviar *v impersonal* to pour with rain

diluvio *nm también Fig* flood; **el D. Universal** the Flood

diluyera *etc ver* diluir

diluyo *etc ver* diluir

dimanar *vi* **d. de** *(alegría)* to emanate from; *(medidas, consecuencias)* to arise from

dimensión *nf* (**a**) *(en el espacio)* dimension; **una película en tres dimensiones** a 3-D movie (**b**) *(tamaño)* dimension; **una habitación de grandes dimensiones** a large room; **una caja de pequeñas dimensiones** a small box (**c**) *(magnitud)* scale; **las dimensiones de la tragedia** the extent *o* scale of the tragedy; **la d. del problema es tal que…** the scale of the problem is such that…

diminutivo *nm* diminutive

diminuto, -a *adj* tiny, minute

dimisión *nf* resignation; **presentar la d.** to hand in one's resignation

dimisionario, -a **1** *adj* resigning

2 *nm,f* person resigning

dimitir *vi* to resign (**de** from)

dimos *ver* dar

Dinamarca *n* Denmark

dinámica *nf (gen) & Fís* dynamics *(singular)*; **entramos en una d. de desarrollo económico** we are beginning a process of economic development; **d. de grupo** group dynamics

dinámico, -a *adj* dynamic

dinamismo *nm* dynamism

dinamita *nf* dynamite; *Fig* **ese cóctel/jugador es pura d.** that cocktail/player is dynamite

dinamitar *vt* to dynamite

dinamizar [14] *vt* to speed up

dinamo, dínamo *nf Esp* dynamo

dinar *nm* dinar

dinastía *nf* dynasty

dinástico, -a *adj* dynastic

dineral *nm Fam* fortune

dinero *nm* money; **¿pagará con d. o con tarjeta?** will you be paying in cash or by credit card?; **andar bien/mal de d.** to be well off for/short of money; **una familia de d.** a family of means; *Econ* **d. circulante** money in circulation; **d. contante (y sonante)** hard cash; **d. de curso legal** legal tender; **d. en efectivo** cash; **d. electrónico** e-cash; **d. fácil** easy money; **d. falso** counterfeit money; **d. en metálico** cash; **d. negro** undeclared income/payment; **d. sucio** dirty money; **d. suelto** loose change

dinosaurio *nm* dinosaur

dintel *nm Arquit* lintel

diñar *vt Esp Fam* **diñarla** to snuff it

dio *ver* dar

diocesano, -a *adj* diocesan

diócesis *nf inv* diocese

diodo *nm Elec* diode

dioptría *nf* diopter

dios, -osa **1** *nm,f* god, *f* goddess

2 *nm* (**a**) *(ser sobrenatural)* God; **el D. de los cristianos** the Christian God; **a la buena de D.** any old how; *Fam* **se armó la de D. es Cristo** all hell broke loose; **como D. le da a entender** as best one can; **dejado de la mano de D.** godforsaken; *Fam* **hacer algo como D. manda** to do sth properly; *Fam* **tu vecina está como D.** your neighbor's gorgeous; **necesitar D. y ayuda** to have one's work cut out;

sin encomendarse a D. ni al diablo throwing caution to the winds; *Prov* **D. los cría y ellos se juntan** birds of a feather flock together

(**b**) *(en exclamaciones, invocaciones)* **¡D. mío!** good God!, (oh) my God!; **D. sabe, sabe D.** God (alone) knows; **D. dirá** it's in the lap of the gods; **D. mediante, si D. quiere** God willing; **¡D. lo quiera!** let's hope so; **¡D. Santo, ¡Santo D.!, ¿qué vamos a hacer ahora?** oh my God, what are we going to do now?; **¡D. te oiga!** let's hope so!; **¡gracias a D.!** thank heavens!; **¡por D.!** for God's sake!; **que D. te lo pague** God bless you!; **¡vaya por D.!** for Heaven's sake!, honestly!

dióxido *nm Quím* dioxide; **d. de azufre** sulfur dioxide; **d. de carbono** carbon dioxide

dioxina *nf Quím* dioxin

diplodocus *nm inv,* **diplodoco** *nm* diplodocus

diploma *nm* diploma

diplomacia *nf* (**a**) *(tacto)* diplomacy (**b**) *(carrera)* diplomatic service

diplomado, -a **1** *adj* qualified

2 *nm,f* holder of a diploma

diplomar **1** *vt* to grant a diploma to

2 diplomarse *vpr* to graduate, to receive a diploma; **se diplomó en Enfermería** he received a diploma in nursing, he qualified as a nurse

diplomático, -a **1** *adj también Fig* diplomatic

2 *nm,f* diplomat; **d. de carrera** career diplomat

diplomatura *nf Educ* $\simeq$ diploma, = qualification obtained after three years of university study

dipsomanía *nf* dipsomania

díptico *nm Arte* diptych

diptongo *nm* diphthong

diputación *nf* (**a**) *(comisión)* committee; **d. permanente** standing committee (**b**) *Esp (de comunidad autónoma)* = government and administrative body in certain autonomous regions; **d. provincial** = governing body of each province

diputado, -a *nm,f* $\simeq$ representative; **d. por Quintana Roo** $\simeq$ representative for Quintana Roo

dique *nm* (**a**) *(en río)* dike; **d. de contención** dam (**b**) *(en puerto)* dock; **d. seco** dry dock

dirá *ver* decir

dirección *nf* (**a**) *(sentido, rumbo)* direction; **calle de d. única** one-way street; **en d. a** toward, in the direction of; **los trenes con** *o* **en d. a la frontera** trains to the border; **en d. contraria** in the opposite direction; **se fue en d. sur** he went south; **d. prohibida** *(en letrero)* no entry

(**b**) *(domicilio)* address; *Inform* **d. de correo electrónico** e-mail address; **d. electrónica** *(de correo)* e-mail address; *(de página)* web page address; **d. web** web address

(**c**) *(mando) (de empresa, hospital)* management; *(de partido)* leadership; *(de colegio)* headship; *(de periódico)* editorship; *(de una película)* direction; *(de una obra de teatro)* production; *(de una orquesta)* conducting; **estudia d. de cine** he's studying movie directing

(**d**) *(junta directiva)* management; **d. comercial** commercial department; **d. general** head office; **D. General de Tráfico** = government department in charge of road transportation

(**e**) *(de un vehículo)* steering; *Esp* **d. asistida** power steering

direccional **1** *adj* directional

2 *nm o nf Col, Ecuad, Méx (en vehículo)* turn signal

direccionamiento *nm Inform* addressing

direccionar *vt Inform* to address

directa *nf Aut* high gear; **poner** *o* **meter la d.** to go into high gear; *Fig* to really get a move on

directiva *nf* (**a**) *(junta)* board (of directors) (**b**) *(ley de la UE)* directive

directivo, -a **1** *adj* managerial

2 *nm,f (jefe)* manager

directo, -a 1 *adj* (**a**) *(en línea recta)* direct (**b**) *(sin detención)* direct; **no hay tren d. de Barcelona a Roma** there isn't a direct train from Barcelona to Rome (**c**) *(persona, pregunta)* direct; **su lenguaje era d., sin rodeos** her words were direct, she didn't beat about the bush

2 *nm* **en d.** *(retransmisión, concierto)* live

3 *adv* straight; **d. a** straight to

director, -ora *nm,f* (**a**) *(de empresa)* director; *(de hotel, banco)* manager; *(de periódico)* editor; *(de colegio)* principal; **d. adjunto** associate *o* deputy director; **d. comercial** marketing manager; **d. ejecutivo** executive director; **d. espiritual** father confessor; **d. general** chief executive officer; **d. gerente** chief executive; **d. de marketing** marketing manager; **d. de personal** personnel manager; **d. técnico** *(en fútbol)* director of soccer; **d. de tesis** supervisor (**b**) *(de obra artística)* **d. artístico** artistic director; **d. de cine** movie director; **d. de escena** producer, stage manager; **d. de fotografía** director of photography; **d. de orquesta** conductor

directorio *nm (gen) & Inform* directory; *Inform* **d. raíz** root directory

directriz *nf* (**a**) *Mat* directrix (**b**) **directrices** *(normas)* guidelines

dirham (*pl* **dirhams**) *nm* dirham

diría *ver* **decir**

dirigencia *nf Am* leadership

dirigente 1 *adj (en partido)* leading; *(en empresa)* management; **la clase d.** the ruling class

2 *nmf (de partido político)* leader; *(de empresa)* manager; **el máximo d. del partido** the leader of the party

dirigible *nm* airship

dirigir [24] **1** *vt* (**a**) *(conducir) (coche, barco)* to steer; *(avión)* to pilot

(**b**) *(llevar) (empresa, hotel, hospital)* to manage; *(colegio, periódico)* to run; *(partido, revuelta)* to lead; *(expedición)* to head, to lead; *(tesis)* to supervise; **dirige mi tesis, me dirige la tesis** he's supervising my thesis, he's my PhD advisor

(**c**) *(película, obra de teatro)* to direct; *(orquesta)* to conduct

(**d**) *(apuntar)* **dirigió la mirada hacia la puerta** he looked toward the door; **dirige el telescopio al norte** point the telescope toward the north

(**e**) *(dedicar, encaminar)* **nos dirigían miradas de lástima** they were giving us pitying looks, they were looking at us pityingly; **d. unas palabras a alguien** to speak to sb, to address sb; **dirigió sus pasos hacia la casa** he headed toward the house; **no me dirigen la palabra** they don't speak to me; **un programa dirigido a los amantes de la música clásica** a program (intended) for lovers of classical music; **consejos dirigidos a los jóvenes** advice aimed at the young

(**f**) *(carta, paquete)* to address

(**g**) *(guiar) (persona)* to guide

2 dirigirse *vpr* (**a**) *(encaminarse)* **dirigirse a** *o* **hacia** to head for; **¿hacia dónde te diriges?** where are you heading for? (**b**) *(hablar)* **dirigirse a** to address, to speak to (**c**) *(escribir)* **dirigirse a** to write to; **se dirigió a varias empresas por escrito para pedir ayuda financiera** he wrote to several firms asking for financial assistance; **me dirijo a usted para solicitarle…** I'm writing to you to request…; **diríjase al apartado de correos 42** write to P.O. Box 42

dirigismo *nm* state control

dirijo *ver* **dirigir**

dirimir *vt* (**a**) *(resolver)* to resolve (**b**) *(disolver)* to annul, to dissolve

discapacidad *nf* disability, handicap; **las personas con discapacidades físicas** people with physical disabilities, the physically handicapped

discapacitado, -a 1 *adj* disabled, handicapped

2 *nm,f* disabled person, handicapped person; **d. físico** physically handicapped *o* disabled person

discar [59] *vt Andes, RP* to dial

discernimiento *nm* discernment

discernir [25] *vt* to discern, to distinguish; **d. algo de algo** to distinguish sth from sth

disciplina *nf* discipline; **guardar** *o* **mantener la d.** to maintain discipline; **tiene mucha d.** he's very (self-)disciplined; *Pol* **d. de voto** party discipline *(in voting)*

disciplinado, -a *adj* disciplined

disciplinar *vt* to discipline

disciplinario, -a *adj* disciplinary

discípulo, -a *nm,f* disciple

disc-jockey [dis'jokei] *nmf* disc jockey

disco 1 *nm* (**a**) *Anat, Astron & Geom* disk; **d. solar** the sun (**b**) *(de música)* record; *Fam Fig* **ser como un d. rayado** to go on like a broken record; **d. compacto** compact disc; **d. de éxito** hit (record); **d. de larga duración** LP, long-playing record (**c**) *(semáforo)* (traffic) light (**d**) *Dep* discus (**e**) *Inform* disk; **d. de arranque/del sistema** startup/system disk; **d. duro/flexible** hard/floppy disk; **d. magnético** magnetic disk; **d. óptico** optical disk; **d. removible/rígido** removable/hard disk; **d. virtual** virtual disk (**f**) *(del teléfono)* dial

2 *nf Fam (discoteca)* disco

discóbolo *nm* discus thrower

discografía *nf* records previously released *(by an artist or group)*

discográfica *nf Esp* record company

discográfico, -a *adj* record; **casa discográfica** record company; **la industria discográfica** the recording *o* music industry

díscolo, -a *adj* disobedient, rebellious

disconforme *adj* in disagreement; **estar d. con** to disagree with

disconformidad *nf* disagreement

discontinuidad *nf* lack of continuity; **una d. en el crecimiento** a change in the rate of growth

discontinuo, -a *adj (intermitente)* intermittent; **línea discontinua** dotted line

discordancia *nf (de sonidos)* discord; *(de colores)* clash; *(de opiniones)* clash, conflict; **una d. entre los planes y el resultado final** a discrepancy between the plans and the final result

discordante *adj (sonidos)* discordant; *(colores)* clashing; *(opiniones)* conflicting

discordar [63] *vi* (**a**) *(desentonar) (colores, opiniones)* to clash; *(instrumentos)* to be out of tune (**b**) *(discrepar)* **d. de alguien (en)** to disagree with sb (on *o* about)

discorde *adj (colores, opiniones)* clashing; *Mús* discordant

discordia *nf* discord

discoteca *nf* (**a**) *(local)* disco, discotheque (**b**) *(colección)* record collection

discotequero, -a 1 *adj* disco; **música discotequera** disco music

2 *nm,f* nightclubber

discreción *nf* (**a**) *(reserva)* discretion; **tuvo la d. de no mencionarlo** he had the tact not to mention it (**b**) *(voluntad)* **a d.** as much as one wants, freely; **lo dejo a tu d.** I leave it to your discretion; **fuego a d.** fire at will

discrecional *adj (cantidad)* according to taste; *(poderes)* discretionary; **parada d.** *(en autobús)* flag stop

discrepancia *nf (diferencia)* difference, discrepancy; *(desacuerdo)* disagreement

discrepar *vi (diferenciarse)* to differ (**de** from); *(disentir)* to disagree (**de** with)

discreto, -a *adj* (**a**) *(prudente, reservado)* discreet (**b**) *(cantidad)* moderate, modest (**c**) *(no extravagante)* modest;

ropa discreta inconspicuous clothes (**d**) *(normal) (actuación)* fair, reasonable

discriminación *nf* discrimination; **d. positiva** affirmative action; **d. racial** racial discrimination; **d. sexual** sexual discrimination

discriminador, ora 1 *adj (situación, ley)* discriminatory
  2 *nm Elec* discriminator

discriminar *vt* (**a**) *(distinguir)* **d. algo de** to discriminate o distinguish sth from (**b**) *(marginar)* to discriminate against

discriminatorio, -a *adj* discriminatory

disculpa *nf (pretexto)* excuse; *(excusa, perdón)* apology; **dar disculpas** to make excuses; **pedir disculpas a alguien (por)** to apologize to sb (for)

disculpar 1 *vt* to excuse; **disculpen la tardanza** I'm sorry for being late; **d. a alguien (de** o **por algo)** to forgive sb (for sth); **discúlpame por haber olvidado tu cumpleaños** please forgive me for forgetting your birthday
  2 *vi (perdonar)* **disculpa, no era mi intención ofenderte** I'm sorry, I didn't mean to offend you
  3 **disculparse** *vpr* to apologize (**de** o **por** for); **después de su mala actuación, se disculpó con el público** after his bad performance he apologized to the audience

discurrir 1 *vi* (**a**) *(pasar) (personas)* to wander, to walk; *(tiempo, vida, sesión)* to go by, to pass; *(río, tráfico)* to flow (**b**) *(pensar)* to think, to reflect
  2 *vt* to come up with

discurso *nm* (**a**) *(exposición oral)* speech; **dar** o **pronunciar un d. (sobre)** to give o deliver a speech (on); **d. de agradecimiento** speech of thanks; **d. de clausura** closing speech (**b**) *Pey (sermón)* lecture; **me soltó uno de sus discursos** she gave me one of her lectures (**c**) *(ideario)* discourse, ideology (**d**) *(transcurso)* **el d. del tiempo** the passage of time; **con el d. de los años** with the passing years (**e**) *Ling* discourse

discusión *nf (pelea)* argument; *(conversación)* discussion; **eso no admite d.** there's no denying it

discutible *adj* debatable

discutidor, -a 1 *adj* argumentative
  2 *nm,f* argumentative person

discutir 1 *vi* (**a**) *(pelear)* to argue (**de** o **sobre** about); **ha discutido con su hermano** she's had an argument with her brother; **discuten por cualquier tontería** they argue about the least little thing (**b**) *(hablar)* to discuss; **d. de** o **sobre algo** to discuss sth, to talk about sth
  2 *vt* (**a**) *(contradecir)* to dispute; **no te discuto que tengas razón** I don't dispute that you're right (**b**) *(hablar)* to discuss; **eso es mejor que lo discutas con tu padre** you'd be better discussing that with your father

disecado, -a *adj (animal)* stuffed; *(planta)* dried

disecar [59] *vt* (**a**) *(animal)* to stuff; *(planta)* to dry (**b**) *Med (cadáver)* to dissect

disección *nf Med (de cadáver)* dissection

diseccionar *vt* (**a**) *(cadáver, animal)* to dissect (**b**) *Fig (analizar)* to dissect, to analyze in detail

diseminación *nf (de semillas, ideas, culturas)* spreading, dissemination

diseminar *vt (semillas)* to scatter; *(ideas, culturas)* to spread, to disseminate

disensión *nf* disagreement, dissension

disentería *nf* dysentery

disentir [62] *vi* to disagree (**de/en** with/on)

diseñador, -ora *nm,f* designer; **d. gráfico** graphic designer; **d. industrial** industrial designer; **d. de modas** fashion designer

diseñar *vt* to design

diseño *nm* design; **bar de d.** trendy bar; **ropa de d.** designer clothes; *Inform* **d. asistido por ordenador** computer-aided

design; **d. gráfico** graphic design; **d. industrial** industrial design

diseque *etc ver* **disecar**

disertación *nf (oral)* lecture, discourse; *(escrita)* dissertation

disertar *vi* to speak (**sobre** on), to lecture (**sobre** on)

disfraz *nm (traje)* disguise; *(para baile, fiesta)* fancy dress; **llevar un d.** *(para camuflarse)* to wear a disguise; *(para baile, fiesta)* to wear fancy dress; **un d. de bruja/gorila** a witch/gorilla costume

disfrazar [14] **1** *vt* (**a**) *(con traje)* to disguise; **d. a alguien de** to dress sb up as (**b**) *(disimular) (intenciones, verdad, hechos)* to disguise; *(sentimientos, nervios)* to hide; **disfrazó la voz para que no lo reconociera** he disguised his voice so she wouldn't recognize him
  2 **disfrazarse** *vpr (para baile, fiesta)* to wear fancy dress; *(para engañar)* to disguise oneself; **fueron a la fiesta disfrazados** they went to the party in fancy dress; **¿tú a qué te vas a d.?** what are you going to dress up as?; **disfrazarse de princesa** to dress up as a princess

disfrutar 1 *vi* (**a**) *(sentir placer)* to enjoy oneself; **disfruté mucho con el concierto** I enjoyed the concert a lot; **d. de lo lindo** to enjoy oneself very much, to have a great time; **disfruto escuchándoles reír** I enjoy hearing them laugh; **espero que disfruten del espectáculo** I hope you enjoy the show (**b**) *(disponer de)* **d. de algo** to enjoy sth; **disfruta de muy buena salud** he enjoys excellent health; **allá disfrutan de un clima excelente** they have o enjoy an excellent climate there
  2 *vt* to enjoy; **¡que lo disfrutes con salud!** I hope you enjoy it!

disfrute *nm* (**a**) *(placer)* enjoyment (**b**) *(provecho)* benefit, use

disfunción *nf* malfunction

disgregar [38] **1** *vt* (**a**) *(multitud, manifestación)* to disperse, to break up (**b**) *(roca, imperio, Estado)* to break up; *(átomo)* to split
  2 **disgregarse** *vpr* (**a**) *(multitud, manifestación)* to disperse, to break up (**b**) *(roca, imperio, estado)* to break up

disgustado, -a *adj (enojado)* upset

disgustar 1 *vt* (**a**) *(enojarse)* to upset; **le disgustó que olvidáramos su cumpleaños** he was upset that we forgot his birthday (**b**) *(desagradar)* **ese sombrero no me disgusta** that hat's not bad; **me disgusta tener que decirle esto** I don't like to have to say this to you
  2 **disgustarse** *vpr* (**a**) *(sentir enojo)* to get upset (**b**) *(enemistarse)* to fall out

disgusto 1 *nm* (**a**) *(enojo)* **dar un d. a alguien** to upset sb; **¡este niño no nos da más que disgustos!** that child just gives us one headache after another!; **casi nos da un d.** we almost had a tragedy on our hands; **llevarse un d.** to be upset; **¡qué d. me llevé cuando lo supe!** I was so upset when I found out! (**b**) *(pelea)* **tener un d. con alguien** to have a quarrel with sb
  2 a disgusto *loc adv* **estar a d.** to feel uncomfortable o uneasy; **hacer algo a d.** to do sth unwillingly o reluctantly

disidencia *nf (política, religiosa)* dissidence; *(desacuerdo)* disagreement

disidente 1 *adj (en política)* dissident; *(en religión)* dissenting
  2 *nmf (político)* dissident; *(religioso)* dissenter; **un d. soviético** a Soviet dissident

disiento *etc ver* **disentir**

disimulado, -a *adj* hidden, concealed; **hacerse el d.** to pretend not to notice

disimular 1 *vt* to hide, to conceal; **lo disimulas muy mal** you're not very good at hiding it
  2 *vi* to pretend

disimulo *nm* pretense, concealment; **tiró el papel al suelo con d.** she surreptitiously dropped the piece of paper on the floor; **la miró con d.** he sneaked a look at her; **salió con d.**

por la puerta de atrás she sneaked out by the back door

disimulón, -ona *Fam* **1** *adj* sneaky, shifty
2 *nm,f* sneaky o shifty person

disintiera *etc ver* **disentir**

disipar 1 *vt* (**a**) *(dudas, sospechas)* to dispel; *(ilusiones)* to shatter (**b**) *(fortuna, herencia)* to squander, to throw away (**c**) *(niebla, humo, vapor)* to drive o blow away
2 disiparse *vpr* (**a**) *(dudas, sospechas)* to be dispelled; *(ilusiones)* to be shattered (**b**) *(niebla, humo, vapor)* to vanish

diskette [dis'kete, dis'ket] *nm Inform* diskette, floppy disk

dislate *nm* piece of nonsense o absurdity; **su plan es un d.** her plan is absurd

dislexia *nm* dyslexia

disléxico, -a *adj & nm,f* dyslexic

dislocación *nf* dislocation

dislocado, -a *adj (tobillo)* dislocated

dislocar [59] **1** *vt* to dislocate
2 dislocarse *vpr* (**a**) *(articulación)* **se me ha dislocado un codo** I've dislocated an elbow (**b**) *Esp Fam (persona)* to go wild

disminución *nf* decrease, drop

disminuido, -a 1 *adj* handicapped
2 *nm,f* handicapped person; **un d. físico/psíquico** a physically/mentally handicapped person

disminuir [34] **1** *vt* to reduce, to decrease
2 *vi (decrecer)* to decrease; *(precios, temperatura)* to drop, to fall; *(vista, memoria)* to fail; *(días)* to get shorter; *(beneficios)* to fall off

disnea *nf* dyspnea, difficulty in breathing

disociación *nf* dissociation

disociar *vt* to dissociate (**de** from)

disolución *nf* (**a**) *(acción)* dissolving (**b**) *(de manifestación, familia)* breaking up; *(de empresa, partido)* dissolution, winding up; *(de parlamento, matrimonio)* dissolution (**c**) *(mezcla)* solution

disoluto, -a 1 *adj* dissolute
2 *nm,f* dissolute person

disolvente *adj & nm* solvent

disolver [41] **1** *vt* (**a**) *(en líquido)* to dissolve; **d. en leche agitando constantemente** dissolve it in milk, stirring continuously; **d. un caramelo en la boca** to suck candy (**b**) *(reunión, manifestación, familia)* to break up; *(empresa, partido)* to dissolve, to wind up; *(parlamento, matrimonio)* to dissolve
2 disolverse *vpr* (**a**) *(en líquido)* to dissolve; **dejar que la pastilla se disuelva en la boca** *(en prospecto)* allow the tablet to dissolve in your mouth (**b**) *(reunión, manifestación, familia)* to break up

disonante *adj* dissonant, discordant

dispar *adj* disparate, dissimilar

disparadero *nm* **poner a alguien en el d.** to push sb too far

disparado, -a *adj* **salir/entrar d.** to shoot out/in

disparador *nm* (**a**) *(de armas)* trigger (**b**) *Fot* shutter release

disparar 1 *vt* (arma, flecha, persona) to shoot; *(tiro)* to fire
2 *vi* (**a**) *(con arma)* to shoot, to fire; **d. al aire** to shoot in the air; **d. a matar** to shoot to kill; **d. contra el enemigo** to shoot o fire at the enemy; *Fig* **tengo varias preguntas para ti — ¡dispara!** I have several questions for you — fire away! o shoot! (**b**) *(con cámara)* to shoot, to take a photograph
3 dispararse *vpr* (**a**) *(arma)* to go off; **se le disparó el arma** his gun went off (**b**) *(precipitarse) (persona)* to rush off; *(caballo)* to bolt (**c**) *(precios, inflación)* to shoot up

disparatado, -a *adj* absurd, crazy

disparatar *vi* *(decir tonterías)* to talk nonsense; *(hacer tonterías)* to behave foolishly

disparate *nm* (**a**) *(comentario, acción)* silly thing; *(idea)* crazy idea; **¡no digas disparates!** don't talk nonsense!; **hacer un d.** to do something crazy (**b**) *(precio)* **gastar/costar un d.** to spend/cost a ridiculous amount

disparejo, -a *adj esp Am* uneven, variable

disparidad *nf* difference, disparity

disparo *nm* shot

dispendio *nm* extravagance, spending on luxuries

dispendioso, -a *adj* costly, expensive

dispensa *nf* (*de examen)* exemption; *(para casarse)* dispensation

dispensar *vt* (**a**) *(disculpar)* to excuse, to forgive; **¡dispense!** excuse me!, pardon me!, I beg your pardon! (**b**) *(rendir) (honores)* to confer (**a alguien** upon sb); *(bienvenida, ayuda)* to give sth (to sb) (**c**) *(eximir)* to excuse (**de** from), to exempt (**de** from)

dispensario *nm* dispensary

dispepsia *nf* dyspepsia

dispersar 1 *vt* (**a**) *(esparcir) (objetos)* to scatter (**b**) *(disolver) (gentío)* to disperse; *(manifestación)* to break up; *(esfuerzos)* to dissipate
2 dispersarse *vpr* to scatter; *(distraerse)* to let one's attention wander

dispersión *nf* (*de objetos, gente, luz)* scattering; *(de manifestación)* breaking up

disperso, -a *adj* scattered; **chubascos dispersos** scattered showers

display [dis'plei] *nm Inform* display

displicencia *nf* (**a**) *(desagrado)* contempt (**b**) *(negligencia)* carelessness; *(desgana)* lack of enthusiasm

displicente *adj* (**a**) *(desagradable)* contemptuous (**b**) *(negligente)* careless; *(desganado)* unenthusiastic

disponer [50] **1** *vt* (**a**) *(arreglar)* to arrange; **dispuso todo para el viaje** he got everything ready for the journey (**b**) *(cena, comida)* to lay on (**c**) *(decidir) (sujeto: persona)* to decide; *(sujeto: ley)* to stipulate; **el juez dispuso que se cerrara el local** the judge ordered that the premises be closed; **en su testamento dispuso que...** she stated in her will that...; **según lo dispuesto en el artículo 8,...** according to the provisions of Article 8,...
2 *vi* (**a**) *(poseer)* **d. de** to have; **dispongo de todo el tiempo del mundo** I have all the time in the world (**b**) *(usar)* **d. de** to make use of; **dispón de mi casa siempre que quieras** you're welcome in my house whenever you like
3 disponerse *vpr* **disponerse a hacer algo** to prepare o get ready to do sth

disponibilidad *nf* (**a**) *(de plazas, producto)* availability (**b**) *(a ayudar)* readiness to help (**c**) **disponibilidades** *(medios)* financial resources

disponible *adj* available; **no tengo mucho tiempo d.** I don't have much free time

disposición *nf* (**a**) *(colocación)* arrangement, layout (**b**) *(estado)* **estar** o **hallarse en d. de hacer algo** to be prepared o ready to do sth (**c**) *(orden)* order; *(de ley)* provision (**d**) *(uso)* **a d. de** at the disposal of; **poner algo a la d. de alguien** to put sth at sb's disposal (**e**) *(aptitud)* talent; **tiene buena d. para la pintura** he has a natural gift for painting

dispositivo *nm* device; **d. intrauterino** intrauterine device, IUD

dispuesto, -a 1 *participio ver* **disponer**
2 *adj* (**a**) *(preparado)* ready; **estar d. a hacer algo** to be prepared to do sth; **está d. a todo con tal de conseguir lo que quiere** he's prepared to do anything to get what he wants (**b**) *(capaz)* capable; *(a ayudar)* ready to help

dispusiera *etc ver* **disponer**

disputa *nf* dispute

disputar *vt* (**a**) *(cuestión, tema)* to argue about (**b**) *(trofeo, puesto)* to compete for, to dispute; *(carrera, partido)* to compete in; **mañana se disputará la final** the final will take place tomorrow

disquera *nf Am* record company

disquero, -a *adj Am* record; **la industria disquera** the record *o* music industry

disquete *nm Inform* diskette, floppy disk

disquetera *nf Inform* disk drive

disquisición *nf (exposición)* disquisition; **disquisiciones** *(digresiones)* digressions

distancia *nf* (a) *(espacio)* distance; **estábamos a bastante d. del incendio** we were quite a distance from the fire; **¿a qué d. está el próximo pueblo?** how far is the next town?; **está a varios kilómetros de d.** it is several kilometers away; **a d.** from a distance; **mantener a d.** to keep at a distance; **mantenerse a una d. prudencial de** to keep at a safe distance from; **d. de seguridad** safe distance

(b) *(en el tiempo)* gap, space; **está a dos minutos de d. del ciclista francés** he's two minutes away from the French cyclist

(c) *(diferencia)* difference

(d) *(expresiones)* **acortar las distancias** to come closer (to an agreement); **guardar las distancias** to keep one's distance; **salvando las distancias** only up to a point

distanciamiento *nm (afectivo)* distance, coldness; *(de opiniones, posturas)* distancing

distanciar 1 *vt (alejar)* to drive apart; *(rival)* to forge ahead of; **con el tiempo se fueron distanciando** they grew *o* drifted apart as time went on

2 **distanciarse** *vpr (alejarse) (afectivamente)* to grow apart; *(físicamente)* to distance oneself

distante *adj* (a) *(en el espacio)* far away (**de** from) (b) *(en el trato)* distant; **estaba d., con la mirada perdida** he was distant, staring into space

distar *vi* (a) *(hallarse a)* **ese sitio dista varios kilómetros de aquí** that place is several kilometers away from here (b) *(diferenciarse)* **d. de** to be far from

diste *ver* **dar**

distender [64] *vt (situación, relaciones)* to ease; *(cuerda)* to slacken

distendido, -a *adj (informal)* relaxed, informal

distensión *nf* (a) *(entre países)* détente; *(entre personas)* easing of tension (b) *(de arco, cuerda)* slackening (c) *Med (muscular)* strain

distiendo *etc ver* **distender**

distinción *nf* (a) *(diferencia)* distinction; **una d. sutil** a fine distinction; **a d. de** in contrast to, unlike; **sin d.** alike; **sin d. de sexo, raza o religión** without distinction of sex, race or religion; **hacer distinciones en el trato** not to treat everyone the same (b) *(privilegio)* privilege (c) *(modales, elegancia)* refinement, elegance

distingo *nm* reservation; **no hacer distingos** to make no distinctions

distinguido, -a *adj* (a) *(notable)* distinguished (b) *(elegante)* refined

distinguir [26] 1 *vt* (a) *(diferenciar)* to distinguish; **¿tú distingues estas dos camisas?** can you tell the difference between these two shirts?; **me es imposible distinguirlos** I can't tell them apart; **d. algo de algo** to tell sth from sth

(b) *(caracterizar)* to distinguish, to characterize; **d. algo/a alguien de** to distinguish sth/sb from, to set sth/sb apart from

(c) *(premiar)* to honor; **hoy nos distingue con su presencia Don...** today we are honored to have with us Mr....

(d) *(vislumbrar)* to make out; **¿distingues algo?** *(al mirar)* can you see anything?, can you make anything out?

2 *vi* to differentiate, to know the difference (**entre** between)

3 **distinguirse** *vpr* (a) *(destacarse)* to stand out; **se distingue por su elegancia** she is noted for her elegance (b) *(caracterizarse)* to be characterized (**por** by) (c)

(vislumbrarse) to be visible; **desde tan lejos no se distingue nada** you can't see/hear a thing from so far away

distintivo, -a 1 *adj* distinctive; *(señal)* distinguishing

2 *nm* badge

distinto, -a *adj* (a) *(diferente)* different (**de** *o* **a** from *o* to) (b) *(claro)* clear; **claro y d.** perfectly clear (c) **distintos** *(varios)* various; **hay distintas maneras de preparar este plato** there are various different ways of making this dish

distorsión *nf (de imágenes, sonidos, palabras)* distortion

distorsionado, -a *adj* (a) *(sonido)* distorted (b) *(relato, interpretación)* distorted, twisted

distorsionador, -ora *adj* (a) *(efecto)* distorting (b) *(análisis, enfoque)* misleading

distorsionar *vt* to distort

distracción *nf* (a) *(entretenimiento)* entertainment; *(pasatiempo)* hobby, pastime (b) *(despiste)* slip; *(falta de atención)* absentmindedness

distraer [66] 1 *vt* (a) *(divertir)* to amuse, to entertain (b) *(despistar)* to distract; **¡no me distraigas, que estoy trabajando!** don't distract me, I'm working!

2 *vi (entretener)* to be entertaining; **la lectura distrae mucho** reading is fun

3 **distraerse** *vpr* (a) *(divertirse)* to enjoy oneself; *(pasar el tiempo)* to pass the time; **trata de distraerte** try to take your mind off things (b) *(despistarse)* **no te distraigas y haz los deberes** don't get distracted and do your homework; **en este trabajo no puedes distraerte ni un momento** in this job you can't take your mind off what you're doing for a second

distraído, -a 1 *adj* (a) *(entretenido) (libro)* readable; *(programa de TV, película)* watchable; **una tarde/conversación distraída** quite a nice afternoon/conversation (b) *(despistado)* absentminded

2 *nm,f* daydreamer, absentminded person

distribución *nf* (a) *(reparto, división)* distribution; **d. de premios** awards ceremony; **d. de la riqueza** distribution of wealth; **d. de tareas** assignment of duties (b) *(de mercancías)* delivery; **d. comercial** commercial distribution (c) *(de casa, habitaciones)* layout

distribuidor, -ora 1 *adj (entidad)* wholesale; **una red distribuidora** a distribution network

2 *nm,f (repartidor)* deliveryman, *f* deliverywoman; *(vendedor)* sales representative

3 *nm (máquina de tabaco, bebidas)* vending machine; *(cajero automático)* cash dispenser *o* machine

distribuidora *nf (firma)* wholesaler, supplier; *(de películas)* distributor

distribuir [34] 1 *vt* (a) *(repartir)* to distribute; *(carga, trabajo)* to spread; *(pastel, ganancias)* to divide up; *(correo, propaganda)* to deliver; *Com (mercancías, productos)* to distribute; **distribuyen comida entre los pobres** they give out food to the poor, they distribute food among the poor; **d. las tareas** to divide up *o* share out the tasks (b) *(disponer)* **una casa muy bien distribuida** a house with a very nice layout

2 **distribuirse** *vpr* (a) *(repartirse)* **nos distribuimos las tareas domésticas** we share the household chores (b) *(colocarse)* to spread out; **los alumnos se distribuyeron en pequeños grupos** the pupils got themselves into small groups

distributivo, -a *adj* distributive

distrital *adj Am* district; **las autoridades distritales** the district authorities

distrito *nm* district; **d. electoral** constituency; **d. postal** *(número)* zip code

distrofia *nf Med* dystrophy; **d. muscular** muscular dystrophy

disturbio *nm* disturbance; *(violento)* riot; **disturbios callejeros** street disturbances, rioting

disuadir *vt* to dissuade (**de** from)

disuasión *nf* deterrence

disuasivo, -a, disuasorio, -a *adj* deterrent; **elemento d.** deterring factor

disuelto, -a *participio ver* **disolver**

disuelva *etc ver* **disolver**

disyuntiva *nf* straight choice

disyuntivo, -a *adj Gram* disjunctive

DIU [diu] *nm* (*abrev de* **dispositivo intrauterino**) IUD, coil; **ponerse un D.** to have an IUD inserted

diurético, -a *adj & nm* diuretic

diurno, -a *adj* (*de día*) daytime; (*planta, animal*) diurnal; **horas diurnas** daytime *o* daylight hours

divagación *nf* digression

divagar [38] *vi* to digress

diván *nm* divan; (*de psiquiatra*) couch

divergencia *nf* (*de líneas*) divergence; (*de opiniones*) difference of opinion

divergente *adj* (*líneas, calles*) divergent, diverging; (*opiniones*) different, differing

divergir [24] *vi* (*líneas, calles*) to diverge; (*opiniones*) to differ (**en** on)

diversidad *nf* diversity; **d. de opiniones** variety of opinions

diversificación *nf* diversification

diversificar [59] **1** *vt* to diversify
2 diversificarse *vpr* to become more varied, to diversify

diversión *nf* (**a**) (*hecho de divertirse*) enjoyment; **hacer algo por d.** to do sth for enjoyment *o* fun; **un poco de d. no nos vendría mal** we could do with a bit of fun (**b**) (*pasatiempo*) entertainment, amusement; **mi d. favorita es el cine** my favorite pastime is going to the movies

diverso, -a 1 *adj* (*diferente*) different
2 diversos, -as *adj pl* (*varios*) several, various; **diversos motivos** a variety of reasons

divertido, -a *adj* (**a**) (*entretenido*) (*película, libro*) entertaining; (*fiesta*) enjoyable (**b**) (*que hace reír*) funny

divertimento *nm Mús* divertimento; (*novela, película*) entertainment, divertissement

divertir [62] **1** *vt* to entertain, to amuse
2 divertirse *vpr* to enjoy oneself; **se divirtieron muchísimo en la excursión** they had a great time on the trip, they really enjoyed the trip; **se divierte con cualquier cosa** she's easily amused; **¡que te diviertas/os divirtáis!** have a nice time!, enjoy yourself/yourselves!

dividendo *nm Fin & Mat* dividend; **d. a cuenta** interim dividend

dividir 1 *vt* (**a**) (*separar*) to divide (**en/entre** into/between); **el río divide en dos la ciudad** the river divides *o* splits the city in two (**b**) (*repartir*) to share out; **nos dividimos las tareas domésticas** we shared the household chores between us (**c**) (*desunir*) **el testamento dividió a los hermanos** the will set the brothers against one another (**d**) *Mat* to divide by; **d. 12 entre 3** divide 12 by 3; **15 dividido por 3 igual a 5** 15 divided by 3 is 5
2 *vi Mat* to divide
3 dividirse *vpr* to divide (**en** into); **se dividieron en dos grupos** they split into two groups

divierto *etc ver* **divertir**

divieso *nm Med* boil

divinamente *adv también Fig* divinely

divinidad *nf* (*dios*) divinity, god

divino, -a *adj* (**a**) (*de Dios, de los dioses*) divine (**b**) *Fam* (*estupendo*) divine, heavenly; **una casita divina** a darling little house

divirtiera *etc ver* **divertir**

divisa *nf* (**a**) (*moneda*) foreign currency; **d. convertible** convertible currency; **una d. fuerte** a strong currency (**b**) (*distintivo*) emblem

divisar *vt* to spy, to make out; **divisó un barco en la lejanía** he could make out a ship in the distance

divisible *adj* divisible

división *nf* (*repartición*) division; (*partición*) splitting up; **d. acorazada** armored division; **d. del trabajo** division of labor; *Dep* **primera/segunda d.** first/second division

divismo *nm Fig Pey* **están hartos de su d.** they're sick of the way she acts like a prima donna

divisor *nm Mat* divisor; **máximo común d.** greatest common divisor

divisorio, -a *adj* dividing

divo, -a *nm,f* (**a**) *Mús* (*hombre*) opera singer; (*mujer*) diva, prima donna (**b**) (*celebridad*) star; *Fam* **ir de d.** to give oneself airs

divorciado, -a 1 *adj* divorced
2 *nm,f* divorcé, *f* divorcée

divorciar 1 *vt también Fig* to divorce
2 divorciarse *vpr* to get divorced; **sus padres se han divorciado hace poco** his parents (got) divorced recently

divorcio *nm* (**a**) *Der* divorce (**b**) (*diferencia*) difference, inconsistency

divulgación *nf* (*de noticia, secreto*) revelation; (*de rumor*) spreading; (*de cultura, ciencia, doctrina*) popularization; **una obra de d. científica** a work of popular science

divulgar [38] *vt* (*noticia, secreto*) to reveal; (*rumor*) to spread; (*cultura, ciencia, doctrina*) to popularize

divulgativo, -a *adj* popularizing

dizque *adv Andes, Carib, Méx Fam* apparently

d. JC. = **d. de JC.**

dl (*abrev de* **decilitro**) dl

dm (*abrev de* **decímetro**) dm

DNA *nm* (*abrev de* **ácido desoxirribonucleico**) DNA

DNI *nm* (*abrev de* **documento nacional de identidad**) ID card

Dña. (*abrev de* **doña**) ≃ Mrs.

DO (*abrev de* **Denominación de Origen**) = certification that a product comes from a particular region and conforms to certain quality standards

do *nm Mús* C; (*en solfeo*) do; *Fam Fig* **dar el do de pecho** to give one's all

dóberman *nm* Doberman (pinscher)

dobladillo *nm* (*de traje, vestido*) hem; (*de pantalón*) cuff

doblado, -a *adj* (**a**) (*papel, camisa*) folded (**b**) (*voz, película*) dubbed

doblaje *nm* dubbing; **actor de d.** = actor who dubs voices in a foreign-language movie

doblar 1 *vt* (**a**) (*plegar*) to fold (**b**) (*torcer*) to bend; *Fig* **d. el espinazo** (*someterse*) to bend the knee (**c**) (*esquina*) to turn, to go around; **al d. la esquina** when you turn the corner (**d**) (*duplicar*) to double; **dobló la apuesta** he doubled the bet; **su padre le dobla la edad** his father is twice his age (**e**) (*voz, actor*) to dub; **d. una película al español** to dub a movie into Spanish (**f**) (*corredor*) to lap
2 *vi* (**a**) (*girar*) to turn; **dobla en la primera a la derecha** take the first right (**b**) (*campanas*) to toll
3 doblarse *vpr* (*someterse*) **doblarse a** to give in to

doble 1 *adj* double; **d. falta** (*en tenis*) double fault; **d. fondo** false bottom; **d. moral** double standard; **d. personalidad** split personality; **d. sentido** (*de frase*) double meaning; **una calle de d. sentido** a two-way street; **d. techo** (*de tienda de campaña*) tent cover; **d. ventana** secondary glazing
2 *nmf* (*persona parecida*) double; *Cine* stand-in; **buscan a un d. de Groucho Marx** they're looking for a Groucho Marx look-alike; **esa chica es tu d.** that girl is your double
3 *nm* (**a**) (*duplo*) **el d.** twice as much; **8 es el d. de 4** 8 is twice 4; **es el d. de ancho** it's twice as wide; **es el d. de alto que su hijo** he's twice as tall as his son; **gana el d. que**

yo she earns twice as much as I do, she earns double what I do; **el d. de gente** twice as many people; **tiene el d. de habitantes** it has double *o* twice the number of inhabitants (**b**) **dobles** *(en tenis)* doubles; **dobles mixtos** mixed doubles
  4 *adv* double; **trabajar d.** to work twice as hard

doblegar [38] **1** *vt (someter)* to bend, to cause to give in
  2 doblegarse *vpr* to give in (**ante** to), to yield (**ante** to)

doblete *nm* **hacer d.** to have a second job; **hace d. de panadero por las noches** he has a second job as a baker at night

doblez 1 *nm (pliegue)* fold, crease
  2 *nm o nf (falsedad)* deceit

doblón *nm* doubloon

doc. *(abrev de* **documento***)* doc

doce *núm* twelve; **las d. campanadas** the bells *(at New Year)*; **las d. y media** half past twelve; *ver también* **seis**

doceavo, -a *núm (fracción)* twelfth; **la doceava parte** a twelfth

docena *nf* dozen; **una d. de huevos** a dozen eggs; **media d. de niños** half a dozen children; **a docenas** by the dozen

docencia *nf* teaching

docente 1 *adj* teaching; **personal d.** teaching staff
  2 *nmf* teacher

dócil *adj (niño, animal)* obedient; *(persona)* docile, tractable

docilidad *nf* obedience

docto, -a *adj* learned

doctor, -ora *nm,f* (**a**) *(de universidad)* doctor (**en** of); **d. en derecho/psicología (por la Universidad de...)** doctor of law/psychology (from the University of ...); **d. honoris causa** honorary doctor; **ser d. honoris causa** to have an honorary doctorate (**b**) *(médico)* doctor; **la doctora Piñán le atenderá enseguida** Dr Piñán will see you in a minute

doctorado *nm* doctorate

doctoral *adj* doctoral

doctorar 1 *vt* to confer a doctorate on
  2 doctorarse *vpr* to receive *o* earn one's doctorate (**en** in)

doctrina *nf* doctrine

doctrinal *adj* doctrinal

docudrama *nm* docudrama

documentación *nf* (**a**) *(ciencia, manuales de uso)* documentation (**b**) *(identificación personal)* papers

documentado, -a *adj* (**a**) *(informado) (informe, estudio)* researched; *(persona)* informed (**b**) *(con papeles encima)* having identification

documental *adj & nm* documentary

documentalista *nmf* archivist

documentar 1 *vt* (**a**) *(evidenciar)* to document (**b**) *(informar)* to brief
  2 documentarse *vpr* to do research

documento *nm* (**a**) *(escrito)* document; **d. confidencial** restricted document; **d. nacional de identidad** identity card (**b**) *(testimonio)* record

dodecaedro *nm* dodecahedron

dodotis® *nm inv* disposable diaper

dogma *nm Rel & Fig* dogma; **d. de fe** article of faith

dogmático, -a *adj* dogmatic

dogmatismo *nm* dogmatism

dogmatizar [14] *vi* to express oneself dogmatically, to pontificate

dogo *nmf* bull mastiff

dólar *nm* dollar

dolarización *nf Econ* dollarization

dolarizar [14] *vt Econ* to dollarize

dolby® *nm inv* Dolby®

dolencia *nf* complaint, ailment

doler [41] **1** *vi* to hurt; **¿te duele?** does it hurt?; **me duele la**

pierna my leg hurts; **me duele la garganta** I have a sore throat; **me duele la cabeza** I have a headache; **me duele ver tanta injusticia** it pains me to see so much injustice; **le dolió en el alma** it upset her terribly; *Fam Fig* **¡ahí le duele!** that has really got to him!
  2 dolerse *vpr* **dolerse de** *o* **por algo** *(quejarse)* to complain about sth; *(arrepentirse)* to be sorry about sth

dolido, -a *adj* hurt, upset; **estar/sentirse d.** to be/feel hurt

doliente *adj (enfermo)* ill; *(afligido)* grieving

dolmen *nm* dolmen

dolo *nm Der* **hacer algo con d.** to do sth with premeditation *o* wittingly

dolor *nm* (**a**) *(físico)* pain; **siento un d. en el costado** I have a pain in my side; (**tener**) **d. de cabeza** (to have a) headache; **¡este niño no nos da más que dolores de cabeza!** that child does nothing but make trouble for us!; **d. de espalda** back pain; **d. de estómago** stomachache; **dolores menstruales** period pains; **d. de muelas** toothache; **dolores del parto** labor pains (**b**) *(moral)* grief, sorrow; **su fallecimiento nos llena de d.** his death fills us with sorrow

dolorido, -a *adj* (**a**) *(físicamente)* sore; **tener la pierna/ espalda dolorida** to have a sore leg/back (**b**) *(moralmente)* grieving, sorrowing; **estar d.** to be grieving/sorrowing

doloroso, -a *adj (físicamente)* painful; *(moralmente)* distressing

doma *nf (de animales salvajes)* taming; **d. de caballos** breaking-in of horses

domador, -ora *nm,f (de animales salvajes)* tamer; *(de caballos)* breaker; **d. de leones** lion tamer

domar *vt (animales salvajes)* to tame; *(caballo)* to break in; *(personas, pasiones)* to control

domesticado, -a *adj (animal)* tame

domesticar [59] *vt* (**a**) *(animal)* to tame, to domesticate (**b**) *Hum (persona)* to domesticate, to housebreak

doméstico, -a *adj* domestic

domiciliación *nf Esp* **pagar mediante d. (bancaria)** to pay by regular bank payments

domiciliado, -a *adj Esp* **tener el pago del teléfono d.** to pay the phone bill by regular bank payments

domiciliar 1 *vt Esp (pago)* to pay by regular bank payments
  2 domiciliarse *vpr (persona)* to establish residence

domiciliario, -a *adj Der* **arresto d.** house arrest; **asistente d.** in-home help

domicilio *nm* (**a**) *(vivienda)* residence, home; *Dep* **a d.** *(en campo contrario)* away; **servicio a d.** home delivery; **vender a d.** to sell door-to-door; **d. particular** private residence (**b**) *(dirección)* address; **d. fijo** permanent address; **sin d. fijo** no fixed address; **d. fiscal** registered office; **d. social** head office (**c**) *(localidad)* residence

dominación *nf* rule, dominion

dominador, -ora *adj* dominating

dominante *adj* (**a**) *(nación, religión, tendencia)* dominant; *(vientos)* prevailing (**b**) *(persona)* domineering

dominar 1 *vt* (**a**) *(controlar) (pasión, nervios, caballo)* to control; *(situación)* to be in control of; *(incendio)* to bring under control; *(rebelión)* to put down; *(país, territorio)* to dominate, to rule (over); **era imposible d. el vehículo** it was impossible to maintain control of the vehicle
  (**b**) *(sujeto: emoción)* to overcome; **lo dominaba el deseo irrefrenable de besarla** he was overcome by an irresistible desire to kiss her
  (**c**) *(conocer) (técnica, tema)* to master; **domina varias lenguas** she speaks various languages fluently; **ha conseguido d. el inglés en pocos meses** he managed to acquire a good command of English within a few months
  (**d**) *(divisar)* to overlook; **desde aquí se domina todo Guanajuato** you can see the whole of Guanajuato from here

2 *vi (predominar)* to predominate

3 dominarse *vpr* to control oneself

domingo *nm* Sunday; *Rel* **D. de Pentecostés** Pentecost, Whitsunday; *Rel* **D. de Ramos** Palm Sunday; *Rel* **D. de Pascua** o **de Resurrección** Easter Sunday; *ver también* **sábado**

dominguero, -a *nm,f Fam Pey (conductor)* Sunday driver; *(en campo, playa)* day-tripper

Dominica *n* Dominica

dominical *adj* **excursión/suplemento d.** Sunday outing/supplement

dominicano, -a *adj & nm,f* Dominican

dominico, -a *adj & nm,f Rel* Dominican

dominio *nm* **(a)** *(dominación, posesión)* control **(sobre** over) **(b)** *(autoridad)* authority, power **(c)** *(territorio)* domain; *(ámbito)* realm; **dominios** *(territorio)* dominions **(d)** *(conocimiento) (de arte, técnica)* mastery; *(de idiomas)* command **(e) ser del d. público** to be public knowledge **(f)** *Inform* domain

dominó *nm* **(a)** *(juego)* dominoes *(singular)* **(b)** *(fichas)* set of dominoes

domótica *nf* home automation

don *nm* **(a)** *(tratamiento)* **d. Andrés Iturbe** Mr. Andrés Iturbe; *(en cartas)* Andrés Iturbe Esquire; **d. Andrés** Mr. Iturbe **(b)** *(habilidad)* gift; **d. de mando** leadership qualities; **tener el d. de la palabra** *(cualidad humana)* to have the gift of speech; *(de orador)* to be a gifted speaker; **tener d. de gentes** to have a way with people

donación *nf* donation

donador, -ora *nm,f (de sangre, órgano)* donor

donaire *nm (al expresarse)* wit; *(al andar, moverse)* grace

donante *nmf* donor; **d. de órganos** organ donor; **d. de riñón** kidney donor; **d. de sangre** blood donor; **d. de semen** sperm donor

donar *vt* to donate; **d. sangre** to give blood

donativo *nm* donation

doncel *nm Hist* page

doncella *nf* maid

donde

> **donde** combines with the preposition **a** to form **adonde** when following a noun, pronoun or adverb expressing location (e.g. **el sitio adonde vamos** the place where we're going; **es allí adonde iban** that's where they were going).

1 *adv* where; **el bolso está d. lo dejaste** the bag is where you left it; **puedes ir d. quieras** you can go wherever you want; **hasta d.** as far as, up to where; **llegaré hasta d. pueda** I'll get as far as I can; **d. sea posible** wherever possible; **por d.** wherever; **iré por d. me manden** I'll go wherever they send me

2 *pron* where; **la casa d. nací** the house where I was born; **la ciudad de d. viene** the town (where) she comes from, the town from which she comes; **hacia d.** toward where, toward which; **hasta d.** as far as where, as far as which; **de d.** *(de lo cual)* from which

3 *prep (en casa de)* **fui d. mi madre** I went to my mother's

dónde *adv*

> **dónde** can combine with the preposition **a** to form **adónde** (e.g. **¿adónde vamos?** where are we going?).

where; **¿d. está el niño?** where's the child?; **no sé d. se habrá metido** I don't know where she can be; **dime d. lo has escondido** tell me where you've hidden it; **¿d. me llevas?** where are you taking me (to)?; **¿de d. eres?** where are you from?; **¿hacia d. vas?** where are you heading?; **¿por d.?** whereabouts?; **¿por d. se va al teatro?** how do you get

to the theater from here?; **¿por d. has entrado?** where did you come in?

dondequiera *adv* **d. que** wherever; **d. que vayas/mires** wherever you go/look

donjuán, don Juan *nm Fam* ladykiller, Casanova

donostiarra *Esp* **1** *adj* of/from San Sebastian

2 *nmf* person from San Sebastian

dónut® *(pl* **dónuts)** *nm* doughnut

doña *nf* **d. María Rey** Mrs. María Rey; **d. María** Mrs. Rey

dopado, -a *adj (deportista)* = having taken performance-enhancing drugs

dopaje *nm Dep* drug-taking

dopar 1 *vt* to dope

2 doparse *vpr* to take artificial stimulants

doping ['dopin] *(pl* **dopings)** *nm* doping

doquier *adv* **por d.** everywhere

dorada *nf (pez)* gilthead

dorado, -a 1 *adj (objeto, época)* golden

2 *nm (parte dorada)* gilt; **limpiar los dorados** to clean the brass fittings

dorador, -ora *nm,f* gilder

dorar 1 *vt* **(a)** *(cubrir con oro)* to gild; *Fam Fig* **d. la píldora (a alguien)** to sweeten the pill (for sb) **(b)** *(alimento)* to brown **(c)** *(piel)* to turn golden brown

2 dorarse *vpr* **(a)** *(comida)* to brown **(b)** *(piel)* to tan

dórico, -a *adj* Doric

dormido, -a *adj (persona)* asleep; **quedarse d.** to fall asleep **(b)** *(brazo, pierna)* **tengo el pie d.** my foot has gone to sleep

dormilón, -ona *Fam* **1** *adj* fond of sleeping

2 *nm,f (persona)* sleepyhead

dormir [27] **1** *vt* **(a)** *(niño)* to get off to sleep; **d. la siesta** to have an afternoon nap; *Fam* **dormirla, d. la mona** to sleep it off **(b)** *(anestesiar)* **d. a alguien** to put sb to sleep

2 *vi* **(a)** *(reposar)* to sleep; **¿duermes?** are you asleep?; **¡a d.!, ¡es hora de d.!** off to bed!, it's time for bed! **(b)** *(pernoctar)* to spend the night; **dormimos en el autobús** we spent the night on the bus

3 dormirse *vpr* **(a)** *(persona)* to fall asleep **(b)** *(brazo, mano)* to go to sleep; **se me ha dormido la pierna** my leg has gone to sleep **(c)** *(despistarse)* to be slow to react; **¡no te duermas y haz algo!** don't just stand there, do something!

dormitar *vi* to doze

dormitorio *nm* **(a)** *(de casa)* bedroom; *(de colegio)* dormitory; **d. principal** master bedroom **(b)** *(muebles)* bedroom suite

dorsal 1 *adj* dorsal

2 *nm Dep* number *(on player's back)*

dorso *nm* back; **al d., en el d.** on the back; **véase al d.** see overleaf; **el d. de la mano** the back of the hand

DOS [dos] *nm (abrev de* **disk operating system)** DOS

dos *núm* two; **los dos estamos de acuerdo** both of us agree; **es un regalo para los d.** it's a present for both o the two of you; **de d. en d.** in twos, two by two; **en un d. por tres** in no time at all; **cada d. por tres** every five minutes; **ya somos d.** that makes two of us; **dos puntos** colon; *ver también* **seis**

doscientos, -as *núm* two hundred; *ver también* **seis**

dosel *nm* canopy

dosificación *nf* dosage

dosificador *nm* dispenser

dosificar [59] *vt* **(a)** *Quím* to measure out **(b)** *(fuerzas, alimentos)* to use sparingly

dosis *nf inv* **(a)** *(de medicamento, droga)* dose **(b)** *(de paciencia, cariño)* amount; **me encantan los niños, pero en pequeñas d.** I love children, but in small doses

dossier [do'sjer] *nm inv* dossier, file

dotación *nf* **(a)** *(de dinero, armas, medios)* amount granted **(b)** *(personal)* staff, personnel; *(tripulantes)* crew; *(patrulla)* squad

dotado, -a *adj* gifted; **d. de** *(persona)* blessed with; *(edificio, instalación, aparato)* equipped with

dotar *vt* (**a**) *(proveer)* **d. algo de** to provide sth with (**b**) *(tripular)* **d. algo de** to man sth with (**c**) *(conferir)* **d. a algo/alguien de** to endow sth/sb with; **la naturaleza lo dotó de una gran inteligencia** nature had endowed him with great intelligence (**d**) *(dar una dote)* to give a dowry to

dote *nf* *(en boda)* dowry; **dotes** *(aptitud)* qualities; **tener dotes de algo** to have a talent for sth; **dotes de mando** leadership qualities

doy *ver* **dar**

dpi *(abrev de* **dots per inch***)* dpi

dpto. *(abrev de* **departamento***)* dept; **d. de personal** personnel dept

Dr. *(abrev de* **doctor***)* Dr

Dra. *(abrev de* **doctora***)* Dr

dracma *nf Antes* drachma

draconiano, -a *adj* draconian

DRAE ['drae] *nm* *(abrev de* **Diccionario de la Real Academia Española***)* = dictionary of the Spanish Royal Academy

draga *nf (máquina)* dredge; *(barco)* dredger

dragado *nm* dredging

dragaminas *nm inv* minesweeper

dragar [38] *vt* to dredge

drago *nm* dragon tree

dragón *nm* dragon

drague *etc ver* **dragar**

draipen *(pl* **draipenes***) nm RP* fiber-tip pen

drama *nm* (**a**) *(obra)* play (**b**) *(desgracia)* drama; *Fam* **hacer un d. (de algo)** to make a drama (out of sth)

dramático, -a *adj* dramatic

dramatismo *nm* dramatic nature, drama; **con d.** dramatically

dramatizar [14] *vt* to dramatize; *Fam* **¡no hay que d.!** there's no need for melodrama!, don't exaggerate!

dramaturgo, -a *nm,f* playwright, dramatist

dramón *nm Fam* melodrama

drástico, -a *adj* drastic

drenaje *nm* drainage

drenar *vt* to drain

driblar *vt Dep* to dribble

dribling ['driβlin] *(pl* **driblings***) nm Dep (habilidad)* dribbling; *(regate)* dribble

dril *nm (tejido)* drill

drive [draif] *nm* (**a**) *Inform* drive (**b**) *(en tenis, golf)* forehand

driver ['draiβer] *(pl* **drivers***) nm* (**a**) *Inform* driver (**b**) *(en golf)* driver

droga *nf* drug; **la d.** drugs; **d. blanda/dura** soft/hard drug; **drogas sintéticas** *o* **de diseño** designer drugs

drogadicción *nf* drug addiction

drogadicto, -a 1 *adj* addicted to drugs
2 *nm,f* drug addict

drogado, -a *adj* drugged

drogar [38] **1** *vt* to drug
2 drogarse *vpr* to take drugs

drogata *adj & nmf Fam* junkie

drogodependencia *nf* drug dependence, drug addiction

drogodependiente *nmf* drug addict

drogota *adj & nmf Fam* junkie

drogue *etc ver* **drogar**

droguería *nf Esp* = store selling paint, cleaning materials, etc

droguero, -a *nm,f Esp* = owner of a "droguería"

dromedario *nm* dromedary

drugstore ['druɣstor] *nm* = establishment comprising late-night store and bar

druida *nm,* **druidesa** *nf* druid, *f* druidess

dto. *(abrev de* **descuento***)* discount

dual *adj* dual

dualidad *nf* duality

dualismo *nm* dualism

dubitativo, -a *adj* hesitant

Dublín *n* Dublin

dublinés, -esa 1 *adj* of/from Dublin
2 *nm,f* Dubliner

ducado *nm* (**a**) *(tierras)* duchy (**b**) *(moneda)* ducat

ducal *adj* ducal

ducha *nf* shower; **tomar** *o* **darse una d.** to have *o* take a shower; *Fam Fig* **una d. de agua fría** a bucket of cold water

duchar 1 *vt (dar una ducha)* to shower; *Fam (mojar)* to soak; **¡me has duchado entero con tu gaseosa!** you've soaked me with your lemonade!
2 ducharse *vpr* to have a shower

ducho, -a *adj* **ser d. en** *(entendido)* to know a lot about; *(diestro)* to be skilled at

dúctil *adj* (**a**) *(metal)* ductile (**b**) *(persona)* malleable

ductilidad *nf* (**a**) *(de metal)* ductility (**b**) *(de persona)* malleability

duda *nf* doubt; **poner algo en d.** to call sth into question; **sacar a alguien de la d.** to remove sb's doubts; **salir de dudas** to set one's mind at rest; **sin d.** without (a) doubt; **tengo mis dudas** I have my doubts; **¡la d. ofende!** how could you doubt me!; **no cabe d.** there is no doubt about it; **no te quepa d.** don't doubt it, make no mistake about it

dudar 1 *vi* (**a**) *(desconfiar)* **d. de algo/alguien** to have one's doubts about sth/sb; **¿acaso dudas de mí?** don't you trust me then? (**b**) *(no estar seguro)* **d. sobre algo** to be unsure about sth (**c**) *(vacilar)* to hesitate; **d. entre hacer una cosa u otra** to be unsure whether to do one thing or another; **no dudes en venir a preguntarme** don't hesitate to come and ask me
2 *vt* to doubt; **¿vas a venir? — lo dudo** are you going to come? — I doubt it *o* I don't think so; **lo dudo mucho** I very much doubt it; **yo no lo hice — no lo dudo, pero…** I didn't do it — I'm sure you didn't, but…; **dudo que venga** I doubt (whether) he'll come

dudoso, -a *adj* (**a**) *(improbable)* **ser d. (que)** to be doubtful (whether), to be unlikely (that) (**b**) *(vacilante)* hesitant, indecisive (**c**) *(sospechoso)* dubious, suspect; **una broma de gusto d.** a joke in questionable taste

DUE ['due] *nmf Esp* *(abrev de* **diplomado universitario en enfermería***)* graduated nurse

duela *etc ver* **doler**

duelo *nm* (**a**) *(combate)* duel (**b**) *(sentimiento)* grief, sorrow; **en señal de d.** as a sign of mourning

duende *nm* (**a**) *(personaje)* imp, goblin (**b**) *(encanto)* charm

dueño, -a *nm,f (propietario)* owner; *(de piso alquilado)* landlord, *f* landlady; **cambiar de d.** to change hands; **¿tú eres el d. de esta bici?** are you the owner of this bike?; **hacerse d. de algo** *(dominar)* to take control of sth; **ser d. de sí mismo** to be self-possessed; **ser muy d. de hacer algo** to be free to do sth

duermevela *nm* snooze; **en d.** snoozing

duermo *etc ver* **dormir**

Duero *nm* **el D.** the Douro

dueto *nm* duet

dulce 1 *adj* (**a**) *(sabor)* sweet; **le gusta todo lo d.** she loves anything sweet (**b**) *(agua)* fresh (**c**) *(persona, carácter)* sweet, gentle, mild (**d**) *(mirada, sonrisa)* tender; *(voz, sonido, música)* mellow, sweet; *(recuerdo)* sweet; **sus años dulces** his golden years
2 *nm (caramelo, postre)* sweet; *(pastel)* cake, pastry; **me encanta el d.** *(todo lo dulce)* I love sweet things; *Fig* **a nadie le amarga un d.** anything's better than nothing; **d. de membrillo** quince jelly

dulcificar [59] *vt* (**a**) *(endulzar)* to sweeten (**b**) *(suavizar)* to soften

dulzaina *nf* = musical instrument similar to a clarinet, but smaller and higher-pitched, used in folk music

dulzón, -ona *adj* sickly sweet

dulzor *nm* sweetness

dulzura *nf (suavidad)* sweetness; *Fam* **ven aquí, d.** come here, darling *o* sweetheart

dumping ['dumpin] *nm Econ* dumping

duna *nf* dune

dúo *nm* (**a**) *Mús* duet (**b**) *(pareja)* duo; **a d.** together

duodécimo, -a *núm* twelfth

duodenal *adj Anat* duodenal

duodeno *nm Anat* duodenum

dúplex *nm inv* (**a**) *(piso)* duplex (**b**) *Elec* linkup

duplicado, -a 1 *adj* in duplicate
  2 *nm* duplicate, copy
  3 *adv* **(por) d.** (in) duplicate

duplicar [59] **1** *vt* (**a**) *(cantidad)* to double (**b**) *(documento)* to duplicate
  2 duplicarse *vpr* to double

duplicidad *nf* (**a**) *(repetición)* duplication (**b**) *(falsedad)* duplicity

duplo, -a *adj & nm* double

duque, -esa *nm,f* duke, *f* duchess

duración *nf* length

duradero, -a *adj (que permanece)* lasting; *(ropa, zapatos)* hard-wearing

duralex® *nm* = heat-resistant glass

duraluminio® *nm* ≃ Dural®, Duralumin®

durante *prep (mientras)* during; *(en todo el tiempo de)* for; **por favor, desconecten sus teléfonos móviles d. la proyección** please insure cell phones are switched off during the movie; **d. la guerra** during the war; **estuvo sin beber d.**

un año he went (for) a year without drinking; **d. el verano mejoró su situación económica** his financial situation improved over the summer; **d. una hora** for an hour; **d. toda su vida** throughout her life

durar *vi (continuar siendo)* to last; *(permanecer, subsistir)* to remain, to stay; **la leche fresca sólo dura unos pocos días** fresh milk only lasts *o* keeps a few days; **no durará mucho en ese puesto** he won't stay *o* last long in that job; **aquellas botas me duraron tres años** those boots lasted me three years; **¿cuánto dura la película?** how long is the movie?; **aún dura la fiesta** the party's still going on; **aún le dura el enfado** she's still angry

duraznero *nm Am* peach tree

durazno *nm Am* peach

Durex® *nm Méx* Scotch® tape

dureza *nf* (**a**) *(de objeto, metal)* hardness (**b**) *(de clima, persona)* harshness (**c**) *(callosidad)* callus, patch of hard skin

durmiente *adj* sleeping; **la Bella D.** Sleeping Beauty

durmiera *etc ver* **dormir**

duro, -a 1 *adj* (**a**) *(material, superficie)* hard; *(carne)* tough; *(pan)* stale (**b**) *(resistente)* tough (**c**) *(clima)* harsh (**d**) *(palabras, acciones)* harsh; **estuvo muy d. con él** she was very hard on him (**e**) *(expresiones)* **estar a las duras y a las maduras** *(sin rendirse)* to be there through thick and thin; *(sin quejarse)* to take the rough with the smooth; *Fam* **ser d. de mollera** to be thick; *Fam* **ser d. de oído** to be hard of hearing; **ser d. de pelar** to be a hard nut to crack
  2 *nm* (**a**) *Esp Antes (moneda)* five-peseta coin; **cinco duros** *(moneda)* twenty-five peseta coin; **estar sin un d.** to be flat broke (**b**) *(persona)* tough guy
  3 *adv* hard

duty free ['djuti'fri] *(pl* **duty frees**) *nm* duty-free shop

d/v *(abrev de* **días vista**) **15 d.** within 15 days

DVD *nm (pl* **DVDs**) *(abrev de* **Disco Versátil Digital**) DVD

E

E, e [e] *nf (letra)* E, e

e *conj* and

> **e** is used instead of **y** in front of words beginning with **i** or **hi** (e.g. **apoyo e interés** support and interest; **corazón e hígado** heart and liver).

EAU *nmpl (abrev de* **Emiratos Árabes Unidos**) UAE

ebanista *nmf* cabinetmaker

ebanistería *nf* (**a**) *(oficio)* cabinetmaking (**b**) *(taller)* cabinetmaker's

ébano *nm* ebony

ebonita *nf* ebonite, vulcanite

ebrio, -a *adj* (**a**) *(borracho)* drunk (**b**) *(ofuscado)* **e. de** *(ira)* blind with; *(poder)* drunk *o* intoxicated with; **e. de éxito** drunk with success

Ebro *nm* **el E.** the Ebro

ebullición *nf* **en e.** boiling; *Fig* in turmoil

eccema *nm Med* eczema

ECG *nm (abrev de* **electrocardiograma**) ECG

echar 1 *vt* (**a**) *(tirar)* to throw; *(red)* to cast; **e. algo a la basura** to throw sth in the garbage can

(**b**) *(meter)* to put; **echa esos pantalones a la lavadora** put those pants in the washing machine

(**c**) *(añadir) (vino, agua)* to pour (**a** *o* **en** into); *(sal, azúcar)* to add sth (**a** *o* **en** to); **échame más zumo, por favor** could you pour me some more juice, please?

(**d**) *(decir) (discurso)* to give; *(reprimenda)* to dish out

(**e**) *(carta, postal)* to mail; **e. algo al correo** to mail sth, to put sth in the mail, to mail sth

(**f**) *(humo, vapor, chispas)* to give off, to emit; *Fam Fig* **está que echa humo** she's fuming

(**g**) *(hojas, flores)* to sprout, to shoot

(**h**) *(expulsar)* **e. a alguien (de)** to throw sb out (of); **le han echado del partido** he's been expelled from the party

(**i**) *(despedir)* **e. a alguien (de)** to fire sb (from); **¡que lo echen!** fire him!, kick him out!

(**j**) *(accionar)* **e. la llave/el cerrojo** to lock/bolt the door; **e. el freno** to brake, to put the brakes on

(**k**) *(acostar)* to lie (down)

(**l**) *(calcular)* **¿cuántos años le echas?** how old do you reckon he is?; **siempre me echan años de menos** people always think I'm younger than I really am

(**m**) *Fam Esp* **¿qué echan esta noche en la tele?** what's on TV tonight?

(**n**) *(buenaventura)* to tell; **e. las cartas (a alguien)** to read sb's fortune *(in cards)*

(**o**) *(expresiones)* **e. abajo** *(edificio)* to pull down, to demolish; *(gobierno)* to bring down; *(proyecto)* to ruin; **e. a perder** *(vestido, alimentos, plan)* to ruin; *(ocasión)* to waste; **e. de menos** to miss

2 *vi* (**a**) *(encaminarse)* **e. por la calle arriba** to go *o* head up the street (**b**) *(empezar)* **e. a andar** to set off; **e. a correr** to break into a run; **e. a llorar** to burst into tears; **e. a reír** to burst out laughing

3 echarse *vpr* (**a**) *(lanzarse)* **echarse al suelo** to throw oneself on the floor; **se echó a sus brazos** she threw herself into his arms

(**b**) *(acostarse)* to lie down; **me voy a e. un rato** I'm going to have a nap; **echarse a dormir** *(acostarse)* to go to bed

(**c**) *(empezar)* **echarse a hacer algo** to begin to do sth, to start doing sth; **se echó a cantar/reír** he burst into song/laughter

(**d**) *(apartarse)* **echarse a un lado** to move aside; *Fig* **echarse atrás** to back out

(**e**) *(obtener)* **echarse (un) novio** to get oneself a boyfriend

(**f**) **echarse a perder** *(comida)* to spoil; *(plan)* to fall through

echarpe *nm* shawl

eclecticismo *nm* eclecticism

ecléctico, -a *adj & nm,f* eclectic

eclesiástico, -a 1 *adj* ecclesiastical

2 *nm* clergyman

eclipsar 1 *vt (astro, persona)* to eclipse

2 eclipsarse *vpr (astro)* to go into eclipse; *(persona)* to drop out of the limelight

eclipse *nm* eclipse; **e. luna/solar** lunar/solar eclipse; **e. total** total eclipse

eclosión *nf* emergence

eco 1 *nm* (**a**) *(de sonido)* echo; **en este patio hay e.** there's an echo in this courtyard; **oímos el e. de sus voces** we heard the echo of their voices; **hacerse e. de algo** *(dar noticia)* to report sth; *(repetir)* to echo sth; *Fig* **tener e.** to arouse interest (**b**) *(rumor)* rumor; **el e. lejano de los tambores** the distant sound of the drums; **aún resuenan los ecos del escándalo** the scandal still hasn't quite died down; **ecos de sociedad** society column, gossip column

2 *nf Fam (ecografía)* (ultrasound) scan

Ecofin *nm Pol (abrev de* **Consejo de Ministros de Economía y Finanzas**) Ecofin

ecografía *nf Med (técnica)* ultrasound scanning; *(imagen)* ultrasound scan

ecología *nf* ecology

ecológico, -a *adj (medioambiental)* ecological; *(alimentos)* organic; *(detergente)* environmentally friendly

ecologismo *nm* Green movement

ecologista 1 *adj* environmental, ecological

2 *nmf* environmentalist, ecologist

economato *nm* company cooperative store

econometría *nf Econ* econometrics *(singular)*

economía *nf* (**a**) *(actividad productiva)* economy; **e. dirigida** command economy; **e. doméstica** housekeeping; **e. de libre mercado** free-market economy; **e. de mercado** market economy; **e. mixta** mixed economy; **e. planificada** planned economy; **e. de subsistencia** subsistence economy; **e. sumergida** black *o* hidden economy (**b**) *(estudio)* economics *(singular)*; **e. aplicada** applied economics (**c**) *(ahorro)* saving; **por e. de espacio** to save space; **hacer economías** to save

económico, -a *adj* (**a**) *(de la economía) (asunto, doctrina, política)* economic (**b**) *(del dinero) (problemas, situación)* financial (**c**) *(barato)* cheap, low-cost; **te sale más e.** it works out cheaper (**d**) *(que gasta poco) (motor, aparato)* economical; *(persona)* thrifty

economista *nmf* economist

economizar [14] *vt* to save

ecopunto *nm* recycling center

ecosistema *nm* ecosystem

ecotasa *nf* ecotax

ecoturismo *nm* ecotourism

ectoplasma *nm* ectoplasm

ecu *nm Antes (abrev de* **unidad de cuenta europea**) ecu

ecuación *nf Mat* equation; **e. lineal** linear equation; **e. de segundo grado** quadratic equation

Ecuador *n* Ecuador

ecuador *nm* equator; *Fig* **pasar el e.** to pass the halfway point

ecualizador *nm* equalizer; **e. gráfico** graphic equalizer

ecuánime *adj* (**a**) *(en el ánimo)* level-headed (**b**) *(en el juicio)* impartial, fair

ecuanimidad *nf* (**a**) *(del ánimo)* equanimity, composure (**b**) *(del juicio)* impartiality, fairness

ecuatorial *adj* equatorial

ecuatoriano, -a *adj & nm,f* Ecuadorian, Ecuadoran, Ecuadorean

ecuestre *adj* equestrian

ecuménico, -a *adj* ecumenical

eczema *nm Med* eczema

ed. (**a**) *(abrev de* **editor**) ed (**b**) *(abrev de* **edición**) edit

edad *nf* age; **¿qué e. tienes?** how old are you?; **tiene 25 años de e.** she's 25 years old; **una persona de mediana e.** a middle-aged person; **una persona de e.** an elderly person; **¡son cosas de la e.!** it's (just) his/her/their age!; **la tercera e.** *(ancianos)* senior citizens; **la e. antigua** ancient times; **la E. de Bronce** the Bronze Age; **la e. contemporánea** the modern age *(since the French revolution)*; **e. escolar** school age; **e. del juicio** age of reason; **la E. de Hierro** the Iron Age; **la E. Media** the Middle Ages; *Fig* **e. de oro** golden age; *Fam* **e. del pavo** awkward age; **la E. de Piedra** the Stone Age; **e. de la razón** age of reason

edecán *nmf Méx (en congreso)* conference usher; *(acompañante)* escort

edelweiss ['eðelweis] *nm inv* edelweiss

edema *nm Med* edema

edén *nm Rel* Eden; *Fig* paradise

edición *nf* (**a**) *(acción) Imprenta* publication; *Inform, Rad & TV* editing; **e. de Jorge Urrutia** *(en libro)* edited by Jorge Urrutia; **la segunda e. del telediario** ≃ the evening news (**b**) *(ejemplares)* edition; **e. de bolsillo** pocket edition; **e. crítica** critical edition; **e. extraordinaria** special edition; **e. de lujo** deluxe edition; **e. pirata** pirate edition; **e. príncipe** first edition (**c**) *(celebración periódica)* **la e. de los Oscars/del Mundial de 1998** the 1998 Oscars/World Cup; **la décima e. del festival** the tenth festival

edicto *nm* edict

edificación *nf* building

edificante *adj (conducta)* exemplary; *(libro, discurso)* edifying

edificar [59] *vt* (**a**) *(construir)* to build (**b**) *(aleccionar)* to edify

edificio *nm* building; **e. inteligente** intelligent building

edil *nm (city)* councilor

Edimburgo *n* Edinburgh

Edipo *n pr Mitol* Oedipus

editar *vt* (**a**) *(libro, periódico)* to publish; *(disco)* to release (**b**) *Inform, Rad & TV* to edit

editor, -ora 1 *adj* publishing; **empresa editora** publishing company

2 *nm,f* (**a**) *(de libro, periódico)* publisher (**b**) *Rad & TV* editor

3 *nm Inform* editor; **e. de textos** text editor

editorial 1 *adj* **empresa e.** publishing house *o* company

2 *nm Prensa* editorial

3 *nf* publisher, publishing house

editorialista *nmf Prensa* editorial writer

edredón *nm* eiderdown, quilt; **e. (nórdico)** comforter

educación *nf* (**a**) *(enseñanza)* education; **e. de** *o* **para adultos** adult education; **e. a distancia** distance learning; **e. especial** special education; **e. física** physical education; **e. preescolar** nursery education; **e. primaria** primary education; **e. sexual** sex education; **e. secundaria** secondary education; **e. vial** road safety education (**b**) *(modales)* good manners; **no tienes ninguna e.** you have no manners; **¡qué poca e.!** how rude!; **mala e.** bad manners; **es una falta de e., es de mala e.** it's bad manners

educado, -a *adj* polite, well-mannered; **mal e.** rude, ill-mannered

educador, -ora *nm,f* teacher

educar [59] *vt* (**a**) *(enseñar)* to educate (**b**) *(criar)* to bring up (**c**) *(cuerpo, voz, oído)* to train

educativo, -a *adj* educational; **sistema e.** education system

edulcorante 1 *adj* **sustancia e.** sweetener

2 *nm* sweetener

edulcorar *vt* to sweeten

eduque *etc ver* **educar**

EEE *nm (abrev de* **espacio económico europeo**) EEA

EE. UU. *nmpl (abrev de* **Estados Unidos**) USA

efebo *nm* Adonis

efectista *adj* designed for effect, dramatic

efectivamente *adv (en respuestas)* precisely, exactly

efectividad *nf* effectiveness

efectivo, -a 1 *adj (real)* actual, true; **hacer e.** *(realizar)* to carry out; *(dinero, crédito)* to pay; *(cheque)* to cash; **su nombramiento no será e. hasta mañana** her appointment will not take effect until tomorrow

2 *nm* (**a**) *(dinero)* cash; **en e.** in cash (**b**) **efectivos** *(personal)* forces; **efectivos militares** troops; **varios efectivos policiales** a number of policemen

efecto 1 *nm* (**a**) *(consecuencia, resultado)* effect; **con e. desde** with effect from; **hacer e.** to take effect; **surtir e.** to have an effect; **tener e.** *(vigencia)* to come into *o* take effect; **e. dominó** domino effect; **e. invernadero** greenhouse effect; **e. óptico** optical illusion; **efectos secundarios** side effects

(**b**) *(finalidad)* aim, purpose; **al e., a dicho e., a tal e.** to that end; **a efectos de algo** as far as sth is concerned; **a efectos legales,...** as far as the law is concerned,..., in the eyes of the law,...; **a todos los efectos** for all practical purposes

(**c**) *(impresión)* impression; **producir buen/mal e.** to make a good/bad impression

(**d**) *(de balón, bola)* spin; **dar e. a** to put spin on

(**e**) *Com (documento)* bill; **e. de comercio** commercial paper; **e. de favor** accommodation bill

(**f**) *Cine* **efectos especiales** special effects; **efectos sonoros/visuales** sound/visual effects

(**g**) *(posesiones)* **efectos personales** personal possessions *o* effects

2 en efecto *loc adv* indeed; **y, en e., fuimos a visitar la ciudad** and we did indeed visit the city; **¿lo hiciste tú? — en e.** did you do it? — I did indeed *o* indeed I did

efectuar [4] **1** *vt (realizar)* to carry out; *(compra, pago, viaje)* to make; **el tren efectuará su salida a las ocho** the train will depart at eight; **el Papa efectuará una visita oficial a la zona** the Pope will make an official visit to the area

2 efectuarse *vpr* to take place

efeméride *nf (suceso)* major event; *(conmemoración)* anniversary; *Prensa* **efemérides** = list of the day's anniversaries published in a newspaper

efervescencia *nf* (a) *(de líquido)* effervescence; *(de bebida)* fizziness (b) *(agitación, inquietud)* unrest; **estar en plena e.** to be buzzing *o* humming with activity

efervescente *adj (bebida)* fizzy; **aspirina/comprimido e.** soluble aspirin/tablet

eficacia *nf (de persona)* efficiency; *(de medicamento, medida)* effectiveness

eficaz *adj (persona)* efficient; *(medicamento, medida)* effective

eficiencia *nf* efficiency

eficiente *adj* efficient

efigie *nf (imagen)* effigy; *(en monedas)* image, picture

efímero, -a *adj* ephemeral

efluvio *nm (emanación)* vapor; *(aroma)* scent; *(de alegría, simpatía)* aura; **los efluvios de su perfume** the smell of her perfume

EFTA ['efta] *nf (abrev de* **European Free Trade Association)** EFTA

efusión *nf (cordialidad)* effusiveness, warmth

efusividad *nf* effusiveness

efusivo, -a *adj* effusive

EGB *nf Antes (abrev de* **educación general básica)** = stage of Spanish education system for pupils aged 6-14

Egeo *nm* **el (mar) E.** the Aegean (Sea)

egipcio, -a *adj & nm,f* Egyptian

Egipto *n* Egypt

ego *nm* ego

egocéntrico, -a 1 *adj* egocentric, self-centered
    2 *nm,f* egocentric *o* self-centered person

egocentrismo *nm* egocentricity

egoísmo *nm* selfishness, egoism

egoísta 1 *adj* egoistic, selfish
    2 *nmf* egoist, selfish person

ególatra 1 *adj* egotistical
    2 *nmf* egotist

egolatría *nf* egotism

egregio, -a *adj Formal* illustrious

egresado, -a *nm,f Am* (a) *(de escuela)* (high school) graduate (b) *(de universidad)* (college) graduate

egresar *vi Am* to graduate

egreso *nm Am* graduation

eh *interj* ¡eh! hey!

Eire *n Hist* Eire

ej. *(abrev de* **ejemplo)** example, ex

eje *nm* (a) *(de rueda)* axle; *(de máquina)* shaft; *Am* **e. vial** main road (b) *Geom & Astron* axis; **e. de abscisas** x-axis; **e. de ordenadas** y-axis (c) *(idea central)* central idea, basis; **es el e. de la empresa** she holds the company together; **el e. argumental de la novela** the central strand of the novel's plot (d) *Hist* **el Eje** the Axis

ejecución *nf* (a) *(realización)* carrying out; **tuvimos problemas durante la e. de la tarea** we had problems while carrying out the task; **la e. del tenista fue brillante** the tennis player's performance was outstanding (b) *(de condenado)* execution (c) *(de concierto)* performance, rendition (d) *Inform (de un programa)* execution, running

ejecutable *adj* (a) *(realizable)* feasible, practicable (b) *Inform* executable

ejecutar *vt* (a) *(realizar)* to carry out; **e. las órdenes de alguien** to carry out sb's orders (b) *(condenado)* to execute (c) *(concierto)* to perform (d) *Inform (programa)* to execute, to run

ejecutiva *nf (junta)* executive; **la e. del partido socialista** the executive of the socialist party

ejecutivo, -a 1 *adj* executive
    2 *nm,f (persona)* executive; **e. agresivo** aggressively

ambitious executive; **e. de cuentas** account administrator
    3 *nm Pol* **el E.** the government

ejecutor, -ora *nm,f* (a) *Der* executor (b) *(verdugo)* executioner

ejecutoria *nf* (a) *(título)* letters patent of nobility (b) *(historial)* record of accomplishment (c) *Der (sentencia)* final judgment; *(despacho)* writ of execution

ejecutorio, -a *adj Der* final

ejem *interj* ¡e.! hum!, ahem!

ejemplar 1 *adj* exemplary; **castigo e.** exemplary punishment; **fue un marido e.** he was a model husband
    2 *nm* (a) *(de libro)* copy; *(de revista)* issue; *(de moneda)* example; **ejemplares atrasados del "New Yorker"** back issues of the "New Yorker"; **e. de muestra** specimen copy; **e. de regalo** *(libro)* complimentary copy (b) *(de especie, raza)* specimen; **pescó un e. de 200 libras** he caught one weighing 200 lbs; **quedan pocos ejemplares de panda gigante** there are few giant pandas left

ejemplaridad *nf* exemplary nature

ejemplificar [59] *vt* to exemplify

ejemplo *nm* example; **es el vivo e. del optimismo** he's optimism personified; **dar e.** to set an example; **no des mal e. a los niños** don't set the children a bad example; **por e.** for example; **poner un e.** to give an example; **poner de e.** to give as an example; **predicar con el e.** to practice what one preaches; **servir de e.** to serve as an example

ejercer [40] **1** *vt* (a) *(profesión)* to practice; *(cargo)* to hold; **ejerce la medicina** he's in practice as a doctor (b) *(poder, derecho)* to exercise; *(influencia, dominio)* to exert; **e. presión sobre** to put pressure on; **e. influencia (en)** to have an effect *o* influence (on)
    2 *vi* to practice (one's profession); **estudió enfermería, pero no ejerce** she studied as a nurse, but is not working in the profession; **e. de** to practice *o* work as; **ejerce como abogada** she practices as a lawyer, she's a practicing lawyer; **ejerce mucho de jefe** he acts like he's the boss

ejercicio *nm* (a) *(tarea, deporte)* exercise; *Mil* drill; **hacer e.** to (do) exercise; *Rel* **ejercicios espirituales** retreat; **e. físico** physical exercise (b) *(examen)* quiz, test (c) *(de profesión)* practicing; *(de cargo, funciones)* carrying out; **ya no está en e.** he no longer practices (d) *(de poder, derecho)* exercising (e) *Fin* financial year; **e. económico/fiscal** financial/tax year

ejercitar 1 *vt* (a) *(derecho)* to exercise (b) *(idioma)* to practice
    2 ejercitarse *vpr* to train (**en** in)

ejército *nm Mil & Fig* army; **E. del Aire** Air Force; **e. profesional** professional army; **e. regular** regular army; **el E. de Salvación** the Salvation Army; **E. de Tierra** Army *(as opposed to Navy and Air Force)*

ejerzo *ver* **ejercer**

ejido *nm* (a) *Méx (institución)* = system of cooperative land tenure; *(terreno)* = piece of land farmed by a cooperative; *(sociedad)* = farming cooperative (b) *Hist* common land

ejote *nm CAm, Méx* green bean

el *(f* **la,** *mpl* **los,** *fpl* **las)** *art*

---

el is used instead of **la** before feminine nouns which are stressed on the first syllable and begin with **a** or **ha** (e.g. **el agua**, **el hacha**). Note that **el** combines with the prepositions **a** and **de** to produce the contracted forms **al** and **del**.

(a) *(en general)* the; **el coche** the car; **la casa** the house; **los niños** the children; **el agua/hacha/águila** the water/ax/ eagle; **fui a recoger a los niños** I went to pick up the children (b) *(con sustantivo abstracto o sentido genérico)* **el amor** love; **la vida** life; **el hombre** man, human beings; **los niños imitan a los adultos** children copy adults (c) *(indica posesión, pertenencia)* **se partió la pierna** he broke his leg; **se quitó los zapatos** she took her shoes off; **tiene el**

pelo oscuro he has dark hair; **se dieron la mano** they shook hands

(**d**) *(con días de la semana)* **vuelven el sábado** they're coming back on Saturday

(**e**) *(con nombres propios geográficos)* **el Sena** the (River) Seine; **el Everest** (Mount) Everest; **la España de la postguerra** postwar Spain

(**f**) *Fam (con nombre propio de persona)* **llama a la María** call Maria

(**g**) *(con complemento de nombre, especificativo)* **el de** the one with; **he perdido el tren, cogeré el de las nueve** I've missed the train, I'll get the nine o'clock one; **el de azul** *(cosa)* the blue one; *(persona)* the one in blue; **el de aquí** this one here

(**h**) *(con complemento de nombre, posesivo)* **mi hermano y el de Juan** my brother and Juan's

(**i**) *(antes de frase)* **el que** *(cosa)* the one, whichever; *(persona)* whoever; **coge el que quieras** take whichever you like; **el que más corra** whoever runs fastest

(**j**) *(antes de adjetivo)* **prefiero el rojo al azul** I prefer the red one to the blue one

él, ella *pron personal*

> Usually omitted as a personal pronoun in Spanish except for emphasis or contrast.

(**a**) *(sujeto, predicado) (persona)* he, *f* she; *(animal, cosa)* it; **mi hermana es ella** she's the one who is my sister (**b**) *(después de preposición) (complemento)* him, *f* her; **de él** his; **de ella** hers; **voy a ir de vacaciones con ella** I'm going on vacation with her; **díselo a ella** tell it to her; **este regalo es para él** this present is for him

elaboración *nf (de producto)* manufacture; *(de idea)* working out; *(de plan, informe)* drawing up; **de e. casera** homemade; **proceso de e.** *(industrial)* manufacturing process

elaborar *vt (producto)* to make, to manufacture; *(idea)* to work out; *(plan, informe)* to draw up

elasticidad *nf (de un cuerpo)* elasticity; *(de horario, interpretación)* flexibility

elástico, -a 1 *adj (cuerpo)* elastic; *(horario, interpretación)* flexible

2 *nm (cinta)* elastic; *(goma elástica)* rubber band; *(de pantalón, falda)* elastic waistband

Elba *nm* **el E.** the Elbe

E/LE ['ele] *(abrev de* **Español como Lengua Extranjera***)* Spanish as a foreign language

elección *nf* (**a**) *(nombramiento)* election; **la e. del árbitro no llevó mucho tiempo** it didn't take a long time to choose the referee

(**b**) *(opción)* choice; **no tenemos e.** we have no choice; **el color lo dejo a tu e.** I'll leave the (choice of) color up to you; **un regalo de su e.** a gift of his own choosing

(**c**) *Pol* **elecciones** election; **presentarse a las elecciones** to run in the elections; **elecciones autonómicas** elections to the regional parliament; **elecciones generales** elections to the national parliament; ≃ congressional elections; **elecciones municipales** local elections; **elecciones presidenciales** presidential election

eleccionario, -a *adj Am* electoral

electo, -a *adj* elect; **el presidente e.** the president elect

elector, -ora *nm,f* voter, elector

electorado *nm* electorate

electoral *adj* electoral

electoralismo *nm* electioneering

electoralista *adj* electioneering; **una medida e.** a vote-catching measure

electricidad *nf* electricity; **e. estática** static electricity

electricista 1 *adj* electrical

2 *nmf* electrician

eléctrico, -a *adj* electric

electrificación *nf* electrification

electrificar [59] *vt* to electrify

electrizar [14] *vt (exaltar)* to electrify

electrocardiograma *nm* electrocardiogram, ECG; **el e. mostró que tenía problemas de corazón** the ECG revealed that there were problems with his heart

electrochoque *nm* electric shock therapy

electrocución *nf* electrocution

electrocutar 1 *vt* to electrocute

2 electrocutarse *vpr* to electrocute oneself

electrodiálisis *nf inv* electrodialysis

electrodo *nm* electrode

electrodoméstico *nm* electrical (household) appliance

electroencefalógrafo *nm* electroencephalograph

electroencefalograma *nm* electroencephalogram

electrógeno, -a 1 *adj* **grupo e.** generator

2 *nm* generator

electrólisis *nf inv* electrolysis

electrólito *nm* electrolyte

electromagnético, -a *adj* electromagnetic

electromagnetismo *nm* electromagnetism

electromecánica *nf* electromechanics *(singular)*

electrón *nm* electron

electrónica *nf* electronics *(singular)*

electrónico, -a *adj* electronic; **microscopio e.** electron microscope

electroshock [elektro'ʃok] *(pl* **electroshocks***) nm (terapia)* electric shock therapy

electrostática *nf* electrostatics *(singular)*

electrostático, -a *adj* electrostatic

electroterapia *nf* electrotherapy

elefante, -a 1 *nm,f* elephant

2 *nm* **e. marino** elephant seal

elefantiasis *nf inv* elephantiasis

elegancia *nf* (**a**) *(de persona, ropa)* elegance, smartness (**b**) *(de barrio, hotel, fiesta)* smartness (**c**) *(de movimiento, porte)* gracefulness, elegance (**d**) *(de actitud, comportamiento)* graciousness

elegante *adj* (**a**) *(persona, ropa)* elegant, smart; **estás muy e. con ese vestido** you look really smart in that dress; **ponte e., vamos a una boda** make yourself smart, we're going to a wedding (**b**) *(barrio, hotel, fiesta)* smart, chic (**c**) *(movimiento, porte)* graceful, elegant (**d**) *(actitud, comportamiento)* gracious; **fue un gesto poco e. por su parte** it wasn't a very gracious gesture on his part

elegantoso, -a *adj Am Fam* smart

elegía *nf* elegy

elegiaco, -a, elegíaco, -a *adj* elegiac

elegible *adj* eligible

elegido, -a 1 *adj (escogido)* selected, chosen; *Pol* elected

2 *nm,f* person chosen/elected; *Fig* **los elegidos** the chosen few

elegir [55] **1** *vt* (**a**) *(escoger)* to choose, to select; **tiene dos colores a e.** you can choose from two colors; **rojo o verde, ¿cuál eliges?** red or green, which one do you want? (**b**) *(por votación)* to elect; **fue elegido por unanimidad** he was elected unanimously; **ha sido elegida mejor película del año** it was voted best film of the year

2 *vi (escoger)* to choose; **dar a alguien a e. entre varias cosas** to give sb a choice between several things; **hay mucho donde e.** there's a lot to choose from

elemental *adj* (**a**) *(básico)* basic (**b**) *(obvio)* obvious

elemento 1 *nm* (**a**) *(sustancia)* element; **e. químico** chemical element; **estar (uno) en su e.** to be in one's element (**b**) *(factor)* factor; **el e. sorpresa** the surprise factor (**c**) *(en equipo, colectivo) (persona)* individual; *(objeto, característica)* element (**d**) **elementos** *(fundamentos)* rudiments (**e**) **elementos** *(fuerzas atmosféricas)* elements; *Fig* **luchar contra los elementos** to struggle against the elements; **los cuatro elementos** the four elements

2 *nm,f Esp Fam Pey (persona)* **un e. de cuidado** a bad lot; **menuda elementa está hecha** she's a real tearaway

elenco *nm* (**a**) *(reparto)* cast; *(conjunto)* panoply, array; **un e. de estrellas** a galaxy of stars (**b**) *(catálogo)* list, index

elepé *nm* LP (record)

elevación *nf* (**a**) *(de pesos, objetos)* lifting; *(de nivel, altura, precios)* rise (**b**) *(de terreno)* elevation, rise

elevado, -a *adj* (**a**) *(alto)* high; **era de elevada estatura** he was tall in stature; **un e. número de accidentes** a large *o* high number of accidents (**b**) *(noble) (ideal)* lofty, noble (**c**) *(tono, lenguaje)* elevated, sophisticated

elevador *nm* (**a**) *(montacargas)* hoist (**b**) *Méx (ascensor)* elevator

elevadorista *nmf Am (empleado)* elevator operator

elevalunas *nm inv* window handle; **e. eléctrico** electric window

elevar 1 *vt* (**a**) *(levantar) (peso, objeto)* to lift; *(pared)* to build, to put up (**b**) *(aumentar) (precio, cantidad)* to raise (**c**) *Mat* to raise; **e. x al cuadrado/al cubo** to square/cube x; **diez elevado a quince** ten to the fifteenth (power) (**d**) *(subir)* to elevate (**a** to); **lo elevaron a la categoría de héroe** they made him into a hero (**e**) *(propuesta, quejas)* to present

2 elevarse *vpr* (**a**) *(subir)* to rise; **el globo se elevó por los aires** the balloon rose into the air; **elevarse a** *(altura)* to reach (**b**) *(edificio, montaña)* to rise up (**c**) *(aumentar) (precio, temperatura)* to increase, to go up (**d**) **elevarse a** *(gastos, daños)* to amount *o* come to; **el número de muertos se eleva ya a treinta** the number of dead has now risen to thirty

elidir *vt* to elide

eligió *ver* **elegir**

elijo *ver* **elegir**

eliminación *nf* elimination; **e. de residuos** waste disposal

eliminar *vt* *(en juego, deporte)* to eliminate; *(matar)* to eliminate, to get rid of; *(contaminación, enfermedad)* to get rid of

eliminatoria *nf (partido)* game; *(en atletismo)* heat; **e. de copa** *(en fútbol)* cup game

eliminatorio, -a *adj* qualifying; **prueba eliminatoria** *(examen)* selection test; *(en deporte)* qualifying heat

elipse *nf* ellipse

elipsis *nf inv* ellipsis

elipsoide *nm* ellipsoid

elíptico, -a *adj* elliptical

élite, elite *nf* elite; **deportista de é.** top-class sportsman/sportswoman

elitismo *nm* elitism

elitista *adj & nmf* elitist

elixir *nm (remedio milagroso)* elixir; **el e. de la eterna juventud** the elixir of eternal youth; **e. bucal** mouthwash

ella *ver* **él**

ellas *ver* **ellos**

ello *pron personal (neutro)* it; **no nos llevamos bien, pero e. no nos impide formar un buen equipo** we don't get on very well, but it *o* that doesn't stop us from making a good team; **no quiero hablar de e.** I don't want to talk about it; **por e.** for that reason

ellos, ellas *pron personal*

Usually omitted in Spanish except for emphasis or contrast.

(**a**) *(sujeto, predicado)* they; **los invitados son e.** they are the guests, it is they who are the guests (**b**) *(después de preposición) (complemento)* them; **de e.** theirs; **me voy al bar con ellas** I'm going with them to the bar; **díselo a e.** tell it to them

elocución *nf* elocution

elocuencia *nf* eloquence

elocuente *adj* eloquent; **se hizo un silencio e.** there was an eloquent silence; **una mirada e.** a meaningful look

elogiar *vt* to praise

elogio *nm* praise

elogioso, -a *adj* appreciative, eulogistic

elongación *nf* elongation

elote *nm CAm, Méx (mazorca)* corncob, ear of corn; *(granos)* corn

elucidar *vt* to elucidate, to throw light upon

elucubración *nf (reflexión)* reflection, meditation; **eso no son más que elucubraciones suyas** it's all just a lot of crazy ideas he's dreamed up

elucubrar *vt (reflexionar)* to reflect *o* meditate upon; *(teorías, fantasías)* to dream up

eludir *vt (evitar)* to avoid; *(perseguidores)* to escape; **e. a la prensa** to avoid the press

e-mail ['imeil] *(pl e-mails) nm Inform* e-mail

emanación *nf* emanation, emission

emanar 1 *vt (olor, humo)* to emanate, to give off; *(hostilidad)* to emanate; *(alegría, confianza)* to exude, to radiate; **emanaba tristeza por todos los poros** she exuded sadness from every pore

2 *vi* to emanate (**de** from)

emancipación *nf (de mujer, esclavo)* emancipation; *(de menores de edad)* coming of age; *(de país)* obtaining of independence

emancipado, -a *adj (mujer)* emancipated; *(esclavo)* freed, emancipated; *(país)* independent

emancipar 1 *vt (esclavo, pueblo)* to emancipate, to free; *(país)* to grant independence (to)

2 emanciparse *vpr* to become independent

embadurnado, -a *adj* smeared (**de** with)

embadurnar 1 *vt* to smear (**de** with)

2 embadurnarse *vpr* **embadurnarse de** to smear oneself with

embajada *nf* (**a**) *(edificio)* embassy (**b**) *(cargo)* ambassadorship (**c**) *(empleados)* embassy staff

embajador, -ora *nm,f* ambassador

embalaje *nm* (**a**) *(acción)* packing (**b**) *(material)* packaging

embalar 1 *vt* to wrap up, to pack

2 embalarse *vpr (corredor)* to race away; *(vehículo)* to pick up speed; *(entusiasmarse)* to get carried away; **cuando se embala a hablar no hay quien lo pare** once he gets into his stride you can't shut him up

embaldosar *vt (piso)* to tile

embalsamamiento *nm* embalming

embalsamar *vt* to embalm

embalsar 1 *vt* to dam (up)

2 embalsarse *vpr* to collect, to form puddles

embalse *nm* reservoir

embarazada *nf* pregnant woman

embarazado, -a *adj* pregnant; **dejar embarazada a alguien** to get sb pregnant; **estar embarazada de ocho meses** to be eight months pregnant; **quedarse embarazada** to get pregnant

embarazar [14] *vt* (**a**) *(preñar)* to get pregnant (**b**) *(impedir)* to restrict (**c**) *(avergonzar)* to inhibit

embarazo *nm* (**a**) *(preñez)* pregnancy; **e. no deseado** unplanned pregnancy; **e. psicológico** false pregnancy (**b**) *(timidez)* embarrassment (**c**) *(impedimento)* obstacle

embarazoso, -a *adj* awkward, embarrassing

embarcación *nf* boat, vessel

embarcadero *nm* jetty

embarcar [59] **1** *vt* (**a**) *(personas)* to board; *(mercancías)* to load (**b**) *(involucrar)* **e. a alguien en algo** to involve sb in sth

2 *vi* to board; **por favor embarquen por la puerta C** please board the plane at gate C *o* proceed through gate C

3 embarcarse *vpr* (**a**) *(para viajar)* to board; **se embarcó en un mercante rumbo a Australia** he boarded a merchant ship *o* he embarked on a merchant ship bound for Australia (**b**) *(aventurarse)* **embarcarse en algo** to get oneself involved in sth

embargado, -a *adj* **e. por la pena/la alegría** overcome with grief/joy

embargar [38] *vt* (**a**) *Der* to seize, to distrain; **le han embargado todos sus bienes** his property has been seized (**b**) *(sujeto: emoción)* to overcome

embargo 1 *nm* (**a**) *Der* seizure (**b**) *(económico)* embargo; **el e. a Cuba de Estados Unidos** the United States' embargo against Cuba; **e. comercial** trade embargo

2 sin embargo *loc conj* (**a**) *(no obstante)* however, nevertheless; **es, sin e., uno de los mejores jugadores del equipo** nevertheless, he's one of the best players on the team (**b**) *(por el contrario)* on the other hand; **los ingresos han aumentado y, sin e., los gastos se han mantenido al mismo nivel** income has increased, while on the other hand expenses have remained largely the same

embarque *nm (de personas)* boarding; *(de mercancías)* loading; **el e. se realizará por la puerta G** the flight will board at gate G

embarrado, -a *adj* muddy

embarrancar [59] **1** *vi* to run aground

2 embarrancarse *vpr (barco)* to run aground; *(coche)* to get stuck

embarrar 1 *vt* to cover with mud

2 embarrarse *vpr* to get covered in mud

embarullar *Fam* **1** *vt* to mess up

2 embarullarse *vpr* to get into a muddle

embate *nm (del mar)* pounding; *(del destino)* blow; **el e. de las olas** the pounding of the waves

embaucador, -ora 1 *adj* deceitful

2 *nm,f* swindler, confidence man, con man

embaucar [59] *vt* to deceive, to take in; **no te dejes e.** don't (let yourself) be taken in; **e. a alguien en algo** to talk sb into sth

embeber *vt* **1** to soak up

2 embeberse *vpr (ensimismarse)* to become absorbed (**en** in); **se embebió en sus fantasías** he lost himself in his dream world; **me embebí de la poesía de Lorca** I immersed *o* steeped myself in Lorca's poetry

embelesado, -a *adj* spellbound, entranced

embelesar 1 *vt* to captivate; **su belleza lo embelesó** he was enchanted *o* captivated by her beauty

2 embelesarse *vpr* to be captivated

embeleso *nm* (**a**) *(encanto)* enchantment; **lo miraba con e.** she watched him entranced *o* spellbound (**b**) *Cuba (planta)* leadwort

embellecedor *nm (moldura)* chrome; *(tapacubos)* hubcap

embellecer [46] *vt* to adorn, to embellish

embellecimiento *nm* embellishment

embestida *nf (ataque)* attack; *(de toro)* charge; **derribó la puerta de una e.** he broke down the door with a single charge

embestir [47] **1** *vt (lanzarse contra)* to attack; *(sujeto: toro)* to charge; **el coche embistió al árbol** the car smashed into the tree

2 *vi (lanzarse)* to attack; *(toro)* to charge; **el coche embistió contra el árbol** the car smashed into the tree

emblanquecer [46] *vt* to whiten

emblema *nm* (**a**) *(divisa, distintivo)* emblem, badge (**b**) *(símbolo)* symbol

emblemático, -a *adj* symbolic, emblematic; **una figura**

emblemática del Renacimiento a representative figure of the Renaissance

embobar 1 *vt* to absorb, to fascinate; **esa mujer lo tiene embobado** he's crazy about that woman

2 embobarse *vpr* to be captivated *o* fascinated (**con** by)

embocadura *nf* (**a**) *(de río, puerto)* mouth (**b**) *(de instrumento)* mouthpiece

embocar [59] *vt* to enter *(a narrow space)*, to squeeze into

embolado *nm Esp Fam* (**a**) *(mentira)* fib (**b**) *(follón)* jam, mess

embole *nm RP Fam (aburrimiento)* bore

embolia *nf* clot, embolism

émbolo *nm Aut* piston

embolsarse *vpr (ganar)* to make, to earn

embonar *vt Andes, Cuba, Méx Fam (ajustar)* to suit; *(ensamblar)* to join

emborrachar 1 *vt (sujeto: persona)* to get drunk; *(sujeto: bebida)* to make *o* get drunk; **lo emborracharon con champán** they got him drunk on champagne; **emborrachó el bizcocho en jerez** he soaked the sponge cake in sherry; *Fig* **la alegría lo emborrachaba** he was drunk with joy

2 emborracharse *vpr* to get drunk

emborrascarse [59] *vpr* to cloud over, to turn black

emborronar *vt* (**a**) *(garabatear)* to scribble on; *(manchar)* to smudge (**b**) *(escribir de prisa)* to scribble

emboscada *nf también Fig* ambush; **caer en/tender una e.** to walk into/to lay an ambush

emboscar [59] *vt* to ambush

embotado, -a *adj (sentidos)* dulled; *(cabeza)* muzzy

embotamiento *nm* dullness

embotar *vt (sentidos)* to dull; **tenía la mente embotada de tanto estudiar** his mind had been dulled by so much studying

embotellado, -a 1 *adj* bottled

2 *nm* bottling

embotelladora *nf* bottling machine

embotellamiento *nm* (**a**) *(de tráfico)* traffic jam (**b**) *(de líquidos)* bottling

embotellar *vt* (**a**) *(tráfico)* to block (**b**) *(líquido)* to bottle

embozar [14] **1** *vt (rostro)* to cover (up)

2 embozarse *vpr (persona)* to cover one's face

embozo *nm (de sábana)* turnover

embragar [38] *vi* to engage the clutch

embrague *nm* clutch

embravecer [46] **1** *vt* to enrage

2 embravecerse *vpr* (**a**) *(animal, persona)* to become enraged (**b**) *(mar)* to become rough

embravecido, -a *adj* rough

embriagado, -a *adj* intoxicated

embriagador, -ora *adj* intoxicating, heady

embriagar [38] **1** *vt* (**a**) *(extasiar)* to intoxicate (**b**) *(emborrachar)* to make drunk

2 embriagarse *vpr* (**a**) *(extasiarse)* to become drunk (**de** with) (**b**) *(emborracharse)* to get drunk (**con** on)

embriaguez *nf* (**a**) *(borrachera)* drunkenness (**b**) *(éxtasis)* intoxication

embriología *nf* embryology

embrión *nm* embryo

embrionario, -a *adj también Fig* embryonic

embrollar 1 *vt (asunto)* to confuse, to complicate; *(hilos)* to tangle up

2 embrollarse *vpr* to get muddled up *o* confused

embrollo *nm (de hilos)* tangle; *(lío)* mess; *(mentira)* lie

embromado, -a *adj Andes, Carib, RP Fam* (**a**) *(complicado)* tricky (**b**) *(mal)* in a bad way

embromar *Fam vt* (**a**) *(tomar el pelo a)* to make fun of (**b**) *(fastidiar)* to annoy (**c**) *Andes, Carib, RP (estropear)* to ruin

embrujar *vt también Fig* to bewitch

embrujo *nm (maleficio)* curse, spell; *(de ciudad, ojos)* charm, magic

embrutecer [46] **1** *vt* to stultify, to make dull
 2 embrutecerse *vpr* to become stultified

embrutecimiento *nm (acción)* stultification

embuchado, -a *adj* **carne embuchada** cured cold meat

embuchar *vt* **(a)** *Fam (comer)* to wolf down, to gobble up **(b)** *(embutir)* to process into sausages

embudo *nm* funnel

embuste *nm* lie

embustero, -a 1 *adj* lying
 2 *nm,f* liar

embutido *nm* **(a)** *(comida)* cold cured meat **(b)** *(acción)* sausage-making, stuffing

embutir *vt* to stuff; **se embutió en unos pantalones de cuero** he squeezed himself into a pair of leather pants

eme *nf Fam (mierda)* **¡vete a la e.!** take a hike!

emergencia *nf* **(a)** *(urgencia)* emergency; **en caso de e.** in case of emergency **(b)** *(brote)* emergence

emergente *adj* emerging

emerger [52] *vi (salir del agua)* to emerge; *(aparecer)* to come into view, to appear

emérito, -a *adj* emeritus

emerjo *ver* **emerger**

emético, -a *adj & nm Farm* emetic

emigración *nf* **(a)** *(de personas)* emigration; *(de aves)* migration **(b)** *(grupo de personas)* emigrant community

emigrado, -a *nm,f* emigrant

emigrante *adj & nmf* emigrant

emigrar *vi (persona)* to emigrate; *(ave)* to migrate

emilio *nm Fam Inform* e-mail (message)

eminencia *nf (persona)* eminent figure, leading light; *(excelencia)* excellence; **la e. de su obra** the outstanding nature of his work; **e. gris** éminence grise; **Su E.** His Eminence

eminente *adj* **(a)** *(excelente)* eminent **(b)** *(elevado)* high

emir *nm* emir

emirato *nm* emirate; **Emiratos Árabes Unidos** United Arab Emirates

emisario, -a *nm,f* emissary

emisión *nf* **(a)** *(de energía, rayos)* emission **(b)** *(de bonos, sellos, monedas)* issue; *Fin* **e. de obligaciones** debentures issue **(c)** *Rad & TV (transmisión)* broadcasting; *(programa)* program, broadcast

emisor, -ora 1 *adj* **(a)** *(de radio, TV)* transmitting, broadcasting; **una fuente emisora de calor** a heat source **(b)** *(de dinero, bonos)* issuing
 2 *nm* source; **un e. de ondas de radio** a source of radio waves

emisora *nf (de radio)* radio station

emitir 1 *vt* **(a)** *(rayos, calor, sonidos)* to emit **(b)** *(moneda, sellos, bonos)* to issue **(c)** *(expresar) (juicio, opinión)* to express; *(fallo)* to pronounce **(d)** *Rad & TV* to broadcast
 2 *vi* to broadcast

emoción *nf* **(a)** *(conmoción, sentimiento)* emotion; **la e. le impedía hablar** he was so emotional he could hardly speak; **lloraba de e.** he was moved to tears; **temblaba de e.** he was trembling with emotion **(b)** *(expectación)* excitement; **seguían el partido con e.** they followed the game with excitement; **¡qué e.!** how exciting!

emocionado, -a *adj* moved, excited

emocional *adj* emotional

emocionante *adj* **(a)** *(conmovedor)* moving, touching **(b)** *(apasionante)* exciting, thrilling

emocionar 1 *vt* **(a)** *(conmover)* to move **(b)** *(excitar, apasionar)* to thrill, to excite

2 emocionarse *vpr* **(a)** *(conmoverse)* to be moved **(b)** *(excitarse, apasionarse)* to get excited

emolumento *nm* emolument

emoticón, emoticono *nm Inform* smiley

emotividad *nf* emotional impact, emotiveness

emotivo, -a *adj (persona)* emotional; *(escena, palabras)* moving

empacadora *nf Agr* baler, baling machine

empacar [59] *vt* **(a)** *(empaquetar)* to pack **(b)** *Agr* to bale **(c)** *Méx (envasar) (en tarros)* to bottle; *(en latas)* to can, to tin

empachado, -a *adj* **estar e.** *(de comida)* to have indigestion; *Fam* **estar e. de algo** to be fed up with sth, to be sick and tired of sth

empachar 1 *vt* to give indigestion to
 2 empacharse *vpr (sufrir indigestión)* to get indigestion; *(comer demasiado)* to stuff oneself **(de** with); *Fam Fig (hartarse)* to overdose **(de** on)

empacho *nm* **(a)** *(indigestión)* indigestion; **se agarró un e. de pasteles** she gave herself indigestion eating too many cakes **(b)** *Fam (hartura)* **tener (un) e. de** to have had enough *o* one's fill of; **se dio un e. de televisión** he overdosed on television **(c)** *(vergüenza)* embarrassment; **se dirigió a los asistentes sin ningún e.** he addressed the audience without the least embarrassment

empadronamiento *nm* registration on list of voters

empadronar 1 *vt* to enter on the list of registered voters
 2 empadronarse *vpr* to enter oneself on the list of registered voters; **me he empadronado en Madrid** I've got my name on the list of registered voters in Madrid

empalagar [38] **1** *vt* **los bombones me empalagan** I find chocolates sickly; **me empalaga con tanta cortesía** I find his excessive politeness rather cloying
 2 empalagarse *vpr* **empalagarse de** *o* **con** to get sick of

empalago *nm* cloying taste

empalagoso, -a *adj (pastel)* sickly sweet, cloying; *(persona)* smarmy; *(discurso)* syrupy

empalar 1 *vt* to impale
 2 empalarse *vpr Chile (entumecerse)* to become numb *o* stiff

empalizada *nf (cerca)* fence; *Mil* stockade

empalmar 1 *vt* **(a)** *(tubos, cables)* to connect, to join **(b)** *(planes, ideas)* to link **(c)** *(en fútbol)* to volley
 2 *vi* **(a)** *(autocares, trenes)* to connect **(b)** *(carreteras)* to link *o* join (up) **(c)** *(sucederse)* to follow on **(con** from)
 3 empalmarse *vpr Esp Vulg* to get a hard-on

empalme *nm* **(a)** *(entre cables, tubos)* joint, connection **(b)** *(de líneas férreas, carreteras)* junction

empanada *nf* meat/seafood turnover; **e. gallega** = pie typical of Galicia, filled with seafood or meat; *Fam* **tener una e. mental** to be in a real muddle, not to be able to think straight

empanadilla *nf* small turnover

empanado, -a *adj* breaded, covered in breadcrumbs

empanar, *Méx* **empanizar** *vt Culin* to coat in breadcrumbs

empantanado, -a *adj* **(a)** *(inundado)* flooded **(b)** *(atascado)* bogged down

empantanar 1 *vt* to flood
 2 empantanarse *vpr* **(a)** *(inundarse)* to be flooded *o* waterlogged **(b)** *(atascarse)* to get bogged down

empañado, -a *adj* **(a)** *(cristal)* misted *o* steamed up; *(metal)* tarnished; **tenía los ojos empañados por las lágrimas** his eyes were misted over with tears **(b)** *(reputación)* tarnished

empañar 1 *vt* **(a)** *(cristal)* to mist up, to steam up **(b)** *(reputación)* to tarnish; *(felicidad)* to spoil, to cloud
 2 empañarse *vpr* to mist up, to steam up

empapado, -a *adj* soaked, drenched

empapar 1 *vt* **(a)** *(mojar) (material)* to soak; *(persona)* to soak, to drench **(b)** *(absorber)* to soak up

2 empaparse *vpr* (**a**) *(persona, traje)* to get soaked *o* drenched; **me he empapado los zapatos** I've got my shoes soaked (**b**) *(enterarse bien)* **empaparse de** *o* **en** to become imbued with; **se empapó del tema antes de dar la conferencia** he immersed himself in the subject before giving the talk

empapelado *nm* (**a**) *(acción)* papering (**b**) *(papel)* wallpaper

empapelador, -ora *nm,f* paperhanger

empapelar *vt* (**a**) *(pared)* to paper, to wallpaper (**b**) *Esp Fam (delincuente, infractor)* to bust

empaque 1 *ver* **empacar**

2 *nm* (**a**) *(seriedad, solemnidad) (de ocasión)* solemnity; *(de persona)* presence (**b**) *Méx (envase)* packaging

empaquetar *vt* (**a**) *(envolver)* to pack, to package (**b**) *Fam (endilgar)* **empaquetarle algo a alguien** to lumber *o* land sb with sth; **me empaquetaron el trabajo** I was lumbered *o* landed with the job

emparedado, -a 1 *adj* confined

2 *nm* sandwich

emparedamiento *nm (como castigo)* walling up

emparedar *vt (como castigo)* to wall up

emparejamiento *nm* pairing

emparejar 1 *vt* (**a**) *(juntar en pareja) (personas)* to pair off; *(zapatos, calcetines)* to match (up) (**b**) *(nivelar)* to make level

2 emparejarse *vpr (personas)* to find a partner

emparentado, -a *adj* related; **estar e. con alguien** to be related to sb

emparentar [3] *vi* **e. con** to marry into

emparrado *nm* = vines trained on an overhead frame to provide shade in a garden

emparrar *vt* to train

empastar *vt (diente)* to fill

empaste *nm (de diente)* filling

empatado, -a *adj* (**a**) *(partido)* tied; *(equipos)* level; **los dos equipos van empatados en primer lugar** the two are tying for first place (**b**) *(en elecciones, votación)* equally placed, tied

empatar *vi (en partido, elecciones, competición)* to tie; **e. a cero** to tie nothing to nothing; **e. a dos/tres (goles)** to tie two/ three all

empate *nm (en partido, elecciones, competición)* tie; **un e. a cero/dos** a goalless/two-two tie

empatía *nf* empathy

empecé *ver* **empezar**

empecinado, -a *adj* stubborn

empecinamiento *nm* stubbornness

empecinarse *vpr* to insist (**en hacer algo** on doing sth)

empedernido, -a *adj (bebedor, fumador)* heavy; *(criminal, jugador)* hardened

empedrado *nm* paving

empedrar [3] *vt* to pave

empeine *nm (de pie, zapato)* instep

empellón *nm* shove; **abrirse paso a empellones** to get through by pushing and shoving; **echar a alguien a empellones** to remove sb by force

empeñado, -a *adj* (**a**) *(en préstamo)* in pawn (**b**) *(obstinado)* determined; **estar e. en hacer algo** to be determined to do sth

empeñar 1 *vt* (**a**) *(joyas, bienes)* to pawn (**b**) *(palabra)* to give

2 empeñarse *vpr* (**a**) *(obstinarse)* to insist; **empeñarse en hacer algo** *(persistir)* to insist on doing sth; *(estar decidido a)* to be set on doing sth; **se empeñó en que nos quedáramos** he insisted that we stay; **no sé por qué te empeñas en hablar de ello** I don't know why you insist on talking about it (**b**) *(endeudarse)* to get into debt; **se empeñaron hasta las cejas** they got themselves up to their eyeballs in debt

empeño *nm* (**a**) *(de joyas, bienes)* pawning; **casa de empeños**

pawnshop (**b**) *(obstinación)* determination; **tener e. en hacer algo** to be determined to do sth; **poner e. en hacer algo** to make a great effort to do sth, to take pains to do sth; **morir en el e.** to die in the attempt

empeoramiento *nm* worsening, deterioration

empeorar 1 *vi* to get worse, to deteriorate

2 *vt* to make worse

empequeñecer [46] *vt (quitar importancia)* to diminish; *(en una comparación)* to overshadow, to dwarf

emperador *nm* (**a**) *(título)* emperor (**b**) *(pez)* swordfish

emperatriz *nf* empress

emperifollado, -a *adj Fam* dolled up, done up to the nines

emperifollar *Fam* **1** *vt* to doll up

2 emperifollarse *vpr* to doll oneself up

empero *adv Formal* nevertheless, nonetheless

emperrarse *vpr* to insist (**en hacer algo** on doing sth)

empezar [17] **1** *vt* to begin, to start; **empezó la conferencia dando la bienvenida a los asistentes** she began *o* started her speech by welcoming everyone there; **empezaron otra botella de vino** they started *o* opened another bottle of wine

2 *vi* to begin, to start; **la clase empieza a las diez** the class begins *o* starts at ten o'clock; **¡no empieces!, ¡ya hemos discutido este tema lo suficiente!** don't you start, we've spent long enough on this subject already!; **al e. la reunión** when the meeting started *o* began; **e. a hacer algo** to begin *o* start to do sth; **e. por hacer algo** to begin *o* start by doing sth; **para e.** to begin *o* start with

empiece *nm Fam* beginning, start

empiezo *etc ver* **empezar**

empinado, -a *adj* steep

empinar 1 *vt* (**a**) *(inclinar)* to tip up (**b**) *(levantar)* to raise; *Fam* **e. el codo** to bend the elbow

2 empinarse *vpr* (**a**) *(animal)* to stand up on its hind legs (**b**) *(persona)* to stand on tiptoe

empingorotado, -a *adj* stuck-up, posh

empírico, -a 1 *adj* empirical

2 *nm,f* empiricist

empirismo *nm* empiricism

emplasto *nm* (**a**) *Med* poultice (**b**) *Fam (pegote, masa)* sticky *o* gooey mess

emplazamiento *nm* (**a**) *(ubicación)* location (**b**) *Der* summons

emplazar [14] *vt* (**a**) *(situar)* to locate; *Mil* to position (**b**) *(citar)* to summon; *Der* to summons

empleado, -a *nm,f (asalariado)* employee; *(de banco, oficina)* clerk; **e. de aduanas** customs officer; **e. de banca** bank clerk; **empleada de hogar** maid

empleador, -ora *nm,f* employer

emplear 1 *vt* (**a**) *(usar) (objetos, materiales)* to use; *(tiempo)* to spend; **e. algo en hacer algo** to use sth to do sth; **si lo consigo, daré por bien empleado el tiempo** if I manage to do it, I'll regard it as time well spent; *Esp* **le está bien empleado** he deserves it, it serves him right (**b**) *(contratar)* to employ

2 emplearse *vpr* (**a**) *(en un trabajo)* to find a job; **se empleó de camarero** he found a job as a waiter (**b**) *(usarse)* to be used (**c**) *(esforzarse)* **emplearse a fondo** to do one's utmost

empleo *nm* (**a**) *(uso)* use (**b**) *(trabajo)* employment; *(puesto)* job; **estar sin e.** to be out of work; **oficina de e.** $\simeq$ job center; **pleno e.** full employment; **e. compartido** job sharing; **e. comunitario** community service; **e. juvenil** youth employment

emplomadura *nf RP (diente)* filling

emplomar *vt* (**a**) *(cubrir con plomo)* to lead (**b**) *RP (diente)* to fill

emplumar *vt (como adorno)* to adorn with feathers; *(como castigo)* to tar and feather

empobrecer [46] **1** *vt* to impoverish

2 empobrecerse *vpr* to get poorer

empobrecido, -a *adj* impoverished

empobrecimiento *nm* impoverishment

empollar 1 *vt* (**a**) *(huevo)* to incubate (**b**) *Esp Fam (estudiar)* to bone up on

2 *vi Esp Fam* to hit the books

3 empollarse *vpr Esp Fam* to hit the books (on)

empollón, -ona *Esp Fam* **1** *adj* **ser e.** to be a grind

2 *nm,f* grind

empolvarse *vpr* to powder one's face

emponzoñar *vt también Fig* to poison

emporio *nm* = center of commerce, finance etc

emporrado, -a *adj Esp Fam* stoned *(on cannabis)*

emporrarse *vpr Esp Fam* to get stoned *(on cannabis)*

empotrado, -a *adj* built-in

empotrar *vt* to build in

emprendedor, -ora *adj* enterprising

emprender *vt (trabajo)* to start; *(viaje, marcha)* to set off on; **e. el vuelo** to fly off

empresa *nf* (**a**) *(sociedad)* company; **pequeña y mediana e.** small and medium-sized business; **libre e.** free enterprise; **e. conjunta** joint venture; **e. filial** subsidiary; **e. matriz** parent company; **e. privada** private company; **la e. privada** the private sector; **e. pública** public sector firm; **la e. pública** the public sector; **e. punto com** dot com (company); **e. de trabajo temporal** temp agency; **e. de transportes** trucking firm (**b**) *(acción)* enterprise, undertaking; **se embarcó en una peligrosa e.** he embarked on a risky enterprise *o* undertaking

empresariado *nm* employers

empresarial 1 *adj* **estudios empresariales** management *o* business studies

2 empresariales *nfpl Esp* business studies

empresario, -a *nm,f (patrono)* employer; *(hombre, mujer de negocios)* businessman, *f* businesswoman; *(de teatro)* impresario; **pequeño e.** small businessman

empréstito *nm Fin* debenture loan

empujar 1 *vt* (**a**) *(puerta)* to push (open); *(vehículo)* to push (**b**) *(forzar, presionar)* to press; **e. a alguien a que haga algo** to push sb into doing sth; **verse empujado a hacer algo** to find oneself forced *o* having to do sth

2 *vi* to push; **¡eh, sin e.!** hey, stop pushing!; **e.** *(en letrero)* push; **las nuevas generaciones vienen empujando con fuerza** the new generation is making its presence felt

empuje *nm* (**a**) *(presión)* pressure (**b**) *(energía)* energy, drive

empujón *nm* (**a**) *(empellón)* shove, push; **dar un e. a alguien** to give sb a shove *o* push; **abrirse paso a empujones** to shove *o* push one's way through (**b**) *(impulso)* effort; **dar un último e. a** to make one last effort with

empuñadura *nf (de paraguas, bastón)* handle; *(de espada)* hilt

empuñar *vt* to take hold of, to grasp

emulación *nf (gen) & Inform* emulation

emulador *nm Inform* emulator

emular *vt (gen) & Inform* to emulate

émulo, -a *nm,f Formal* rival

emulsión *nf* emulsion

emulsionar *vt* to emulsify

en *prep* (**a**) *(lugar) (en el interior de)* in; *(sobre la superficie de)* on; *(en un punto concreto de)* at; **viven en la capital** they live in the capital; **tiene el dinero en el banco** he keeps his money in the bank; **en la mesa/el plato** on the table/plate; **en casa/el trabajo** at home/work

(**b**) *(dirección)* into; **el avión cayó en el mar** the plane fell into the sea; **entraron en la habitación** they came/went into the room

(**c**) *(tiempo) (mes, año)* in; *(día)* on; **nació en 1953/marzo** she was born in 1953/March; **en Nochebuena** on Christ-

mas Eve; **en Navidades** at Christmas; **en aquella época** at that time, in those days; **en un par de días** in a couple of days

(**d**) *(medio de transporte)* by; **ir en tren/coche/avión/barco** to go by train/car/plane/boat

(**e**) *(modo)* in; **en voz baja** in a low voice; **lo dijo en inglés** she said it in English; **pagar en dólares** to pay in dollars; **la inflación aumentó en un 10 por ciento** inflation increased by 10 percent; **todo se lo gasta en ropa** he spends everything on clothes

(**f**) *(precio)* in; **las ganancias se calculan en millones** profits are calculated in millions; **te lo dejo en 5.000** I'll let you have it for 5,000

(**g**) *(tema)* **es un experto en la materia** he's an expert on the subject; **es doctor en medicina** he's a doctor of medicine

(**h**) *(causa)* from; **lo detecté en su forma de hablar** I could tell from the way he was speaking

(**i**) *(materia)* in, made of; **en seda** in silk

(**j**) *(cualidad)* in terms of; **lo supera en inteligencia** she is more intelligent than he is

enagua *nf*, **enaguas** *nfpl* petticoat

enajenable *adj* transferable, alienable

enajenación *nf*, **enajenamiento** *nm* (**a**) *(locura)* mental derangement, insanity; *(éxtasis)* rapture (**b**) *Der (de una propiedad)* transfer of ownership, alienation

enajenar *vt* (**a**) *(volver loco)* to drive mad; *(extasiar)* to enrapture (**b**) *Der (propiedad)* to transfer ownership of, to alienate

enaltecer [46] *vt* to praise

enamoradizo, -a 1 *adj* **es muy e.** he falls in love very easily

2 *nm,f* person who falls in love easily

enamorado, -a 1 *adj* in love (**de** with)

2 *nm,f* lover

enamoramiento *nm* falling in love; **un e. pasajero** a brief infatuation

enamorar 1 *vt* to win the heart of; **la enamoró** she fell in love with him

2 enamorarse *vpr* to fall in love (**de** with)

enanismo *nm Med* dwarfism

enano, -a 1 *adj* dwarf

2 *nm,f* dwarf; *Fam (niño)* kid; *Fam* **me lo pasé como un e.** I got a real kick out of it

enarbolar *vt (bandera)* to raise, to hoist; *(pancarta)* to hold up; *(arma)* to brandish

enarcar [59] *vt* to arch

enardecer [46] **1** *vt (excitar)* to inflame; *(multitud)* to whip up, to inflame

2 enardecerse to become inflamed

enarque *etc ver* **enarcar**

encabezado *nm Chile, Méx (en periódico)* headline

encabezamiento *nm (de carta, escrito)* heading; *(en periódico)* headline; *(preámbulo)* foreword

encabezar [14] *vt* (**a**) *(artículo de periódico)* to headline; *(libro)* to write the foreword for (**b**) *(lista, carta)* to head (**c**) *(marcha, expedición)* to lead

encabritarse *vpr* (**a**) *(caballo, moto)* to rear up (**b**) *Fam (persona)* to get grouchy

encabronar *Vulg* **1** *vt Esp* to piss off

2 encabronarse *vpr Esp, Méx* to get pissed off

encadenado *nm* (**a**) *Cine* fade, dissolve (**b**) *Constr* buttress

encadenamiento *nm* linking, stringing together

encadenar *vt* (**a**) *(atar)* to chain (up) (**b**) *(enlazar)* to link (together); *(esclavizar)* to chain

encajar 1 *vt* (**a**) *(meter ajustando)* to fit (**en** into) (**b**) *(meter con fuerza)* to push (**en** into) (**c**) *(hueso dislocado)* to set (**d**) *(golpe, noticia, críticas)* to take (**e**) *(soltar)* **e. algo a alguien** *(discurso)* to force sb to listen to *o* sit through sth; *(insultos)* to hurl sth at

sb; **encajarle un golpe a alguien** to land sb a blow
2 *vi* (**a**) *(piezas, objetos)* to fit (**b**) *(hechos, declaraciones, datos)* to match; **e. con algo** to match sth (**c**) *(ser oportuno, adecuado)* to fit nicely (**con** with)

encaje *nm* (**a**) *(ajuste)* insertion, fitting-in (**b**) *(tejido)* lace; **pañuelo/bragas de e.** lace handkerchief/panties

encajonar *vt* (**a**) *(en cajas, cajones)* to pack, to put in boxes (**b**) *(en sitio estrecho)* **e. algo/a alguien (en)** to squeeze sth/sb (into)

encalado, -a 1 *adj* whitewashed
2 *nm* whitewash

encalar *vt* to whitewash

encallado, -a *adj* stranded

encallar *vi* (**a**) *(barco)* to run aground (**b**) *(proceso, proyecto)* to founder

encallecer [46] **1** *vt* *(manos, piel)* to harden; *(persona)* to harden, to make callous
2 encallecerse *vpr* *(manos, piel)* to become calloused *o* hard; *(persona)* to become callous *o* hard

encamarse *vpr* (**a**) *(enfermo)* to take to one's bed (**b**) *muy Fam* **e. con alguien** *(acostarse)* to sleep with sb

encaminar 1 *vt* *(persona, pasos)* to direct; **estar encaminado a hacer algo** *(medidas, actividades)* to be aimed at doing sth
2 encaminarse *vpr* **encaminarse a/hacia** to set off for/ toward

encamotarse *vpr Andes, CAm Fam* to fall in love

encandilado, -a *adj* dazzled, fascinated

encandilar 1 *vt* to dazzle, to impress greatly
2 encandilarse *vpr* to be dazzled

encanecer [46] **1** *vi* to go gray
2 encanecerse *vpr* to go gray

encantado, -a *adj* (**a**) *(contento)* delighted; **e. (de conocerle)** pleased to meet you (**b**) *(hechizado)* *(casa, lugar)* haunted; *(persona)* bewitched

encantador, -ora 1 *adj* delightful, charming
2 *nm,f* **e. de serpientes** snake charmer

encantamiento *nm* enchantment

encantar *vt* (**a**) *(gustar)* **encantarle a alguien algo/hacer algo** to love sth/doing sth; **¡me encanta!** I love it/him/her! (**b**) *(embrujar)* to bewitch, to cast a spell on

encanto *nm* (**a**) *(atractivo)* charm; **ser un e.** to be a treasure *o* delight (**b**) *(apelativo cariñoso)* darling (**c**) *(hechizo)* spell; **como por e.** as if by magic

encañonar *vt* *(persona)* to point a gun at

encapotado, -a *adj* overcast

encapotarse *vpr* to cloud over

encapricharse *vpr* (**a**) *(obstinarse)* **e. con algo/hacer algo** to set one's mind on sth/doing sth (**b**) *Esp* *(sentirse atraído)* **e. de alguien** to become infatuated with sb; **e. de algo** to take a real liking to sth

encapuchado, -a 1 *adj* hooded
2 *nm,f* hooded person

encapuchar 1 *vt* to put a hood on
2 encapucharse *vpr* to put one's hood on

encaramar 1 *vt* to lift up
2 encaramarse *vpr* to climb up (**a** *o* **en** onto)

encarar 1 *vt* (**a**) *(hacer frente a)* to confront, to face up to (**b**) *(poner frente a frente)* to bring face-to-face
2 encararse *vpr* *(enfrentarse)* **encararse a** *o* **con** to stand up to

encarcelación *nf,* **encarcelamiento** *nm* imprisonment

encarcelar *vt* to imprison

encarecer [46] **1** *vt* (**a**) *(productos, precios)* to make more expensive (**b**) *(alabar)* to praise
2 encarecerse *vpr* to become more expensive

encarecidamente *adv* earnestly

encarecimiento *nm* (**a**) *(de producto, coste)* increase in price (**b**) *(empeño)* **con e.** insistently

encargado, -a 1 *adj* responsible (**de** for), in charge (**de** of)
2 *nm,f* person in charge; *Com* manager, *f* manageress

encargar [38] **1** *vt* (**a**) *(poner al cargo)* **e. a alguien de algo** to put sb in charge of sth; **e. a alguien que haga algo** to tell sb to do sth (**b**) *(pedir)* to order; **si no lo tienen, encárgalo** if they haven't got it, order it; **he dejado encargada la comida para las dos** I've booked lunch for two o'clock
2 encargarse *vpr* **encargarse de** *(ocuparse)* to deal with sth; *(estar a cargo de)* to be in charge of; **se encarga de las facturas** she deals with *o* handles the invoicing; **me encargo de abrir la puerta todas las mañanas** I see to it that the door is opened every morning; **yo me encargaré de eso** I'll take care of *o* see to that; **tú encárgate de los niños** you look after the children; **la lluvia se encargó de arruinar el espectáculo** the rain made sure the show was ruined, the rain ruined the show

encargo *nm* (**a**) *(pedido)* order; **por e.** to order; *Esp* **hecho de e.** tailor-made (**b**) *(recado)* errand (**c**) *(tarea)* task, assignment

encariñarse *vpr* **e. con** to become fond of

encarnación *nf* *(personificación)* *(cosa)* embodiment; *(persona)* personification; *Rel* **E.** Incarnation

encarnado, -a 1 *adj* (**a**) *(personificado)* incarnate (**b**) *(color)* red
2 *nm* red

encarnar 1 *vt* *(ideal, doctrina)* to embody; *(personaje, papel)* to play
2 *vi Rel* to become flesh

encarnizado, -a *adj* bloody, bitter

encarnizarse [14] *vpr* **e. con** *(presa)* to fall upon; *(prisionero, enemigo)* to treat savagely

encarpetar *vt* to file away

encarrilar 1 *vt* (**a**) *(tren)* to put back on the rails (**b**) *(negocio, situación)* to put on the right track, to point in the right direction
2 encarrilarse *vpr* to find out what one wants to do in life

encarte *nm* *(en naipes)* lead

encasillamiento *nm* pigeonholing

encasillar *vt* (**a**) *(clasificar)* to pigeonhole; *Teatro* to typecast (**b**) *(poner en casillas)* to put in a box, to enter into a grid

encasquetar 1 *vt* (**a**) *(gorro)* to pull on (**b**) *Fam* *(inculcar)* **e. algo a alguien** *(idea, teoría)* to drum sth into sb; *(discurso, lección)* to force sb to sit through sth (**c**) *Fam* *(endilgar)* **e. algo a alguien** to lumber sb with sth
2 encasquetarse *vpr* *(sombrero)* to pull on

encasquillar 1 *vt* (**a**) *(atascar)* to jam (**b**) *Am* *(herrar)* to shoe
2 encasquillarse *vpr* (**a**) *(atascarse)* to get jammed (**b**) *Cuba Fam* *(acobardarse)* to get scared

encausar *vt Der* to prosecute

encauzar [14] *vt* *(agua)* to channel; *(orientar)* to direct

encebollado, -a *Culin* **1** *adj* cooked with onions
2 *nm* = stew of fish or meat and onions

encebollar *vt Culin* to add onions to

encefálico, -a *adj Anat* **masa encefálica** brain mass

encefalitis *nf inv Med* encephalitis

encéfalo *nm Anat* brain

encefalograma *nm Med* encephalogram

encefalopatía *nf Med* **e. espongiforme bovina** bovine spongiform encephalopathy

enceguecer [46] *vt Am* to blind

encendedor *nm* (cigarette) lighter

encender [64] **1** *vt* (**a**) *(vela, cigarro, chimenea)* to light; **e. una cerilla** to light *o* strike a match (**b**) *(aparato)* to switch on; **enciende la luz, que no veo** switch the light on, I can't see (**c**) *(entusiasmo, ira)* to arouse; *(pasión, discusión)* to inflame
2 encenderse *vpr* (**a**) *(fuego, gas)* to ignite; *(luz, estufa)* to come on (**b**) *(persona, rostro)* to go red, to blush; *(de ira)* to flare up

encendido, -a 1 *adj* (**a**) *(luz, colilla)* burning; **la luz está encendida** the light is on (**b**) *(deseos, mirada, palabras)* passionate, ardent (**c**) *(mejillas)* red, flushed
    2 *nm Aut* ignition

encerado, -a 1 *adj* waxed, polished
    2 *nm* (**a**) *(acción)* waxing, polishing (**b**) *(pizarra)* chalkboard; **salir al e.** to come/go up to the chalkboard

encerar *vt* to wax, to polish

encerrar [3] **1** *vt* (**a**) *(recluir)* to shut up *o* in; *(con llave)* to lock up *o* in; *(en la cárcel)* to lock away *o* up (**b**) *(contener)* to contain; **sus palabras encerraban una amenaza** there was a threat in his words
    2 encerrarse *vpr (recluirse)* to shut oneself away; *(con llave)* to lock oneself away; **se encerró en su casa para acabar la novela** she shut herself away in her house to finish the novel; **se ha encerrado en sí misma y no quiere hablar con nadie** she's withdrawn into her shell and doesn't want to talk to anyone; **los estudiantes se encerraron en la biblioteca** the students occupied the library

encerrona *nf (trampa)* trap

encestar *vt & vi Dep* to score *(in basketball)*

enceste *nm Dep* basket; **¡e. de Johnson!** Johnson scores!

enchapado *nm* veneer

enchapar *RP vt & vi* to plate

encharcado, -a *adj (calle)* covered in puddles; *(campo de juego)* waterlogged

encharcamiento *nm* flooding, swamping

encharcar [59] **1** *vt* to waterlog
    2 encharcarse *vpr* (**a**) *(terreno)* to become waterlogged (**b**) *(pulmones)* to become flooded

enchastrar *vt RP Fam* (**a**) *(ensuciar)* to make dirty (**b**) *(desprestigiar)* to blacken

enchilada *nf CAm, Méx* enchilada, = filled tortilla baked in chili sauce

enchilarse *vpr Méx Fam* to get angry

enchinar *vt Méx* to curl

enchironar *vt Esp Fam* to put away

enchufado, -a *Fam* **1** *adj* **estar e.** = to have got where one is through connections
    2 *nm,f* = person who has got where they are through connections

enchufar *vt* (**a**) *(aparato)* to plug in (**b**) *Fam (colocar en un trabajo)* to pull strings for

enchufe *nm* (**a**) *Elec (macho)* plug; *(hembra)* socket (**b**) *Fam (recomendación)* connections; **tener e.** to have connections; **obtener algo por e.** to get sth by pulling strings *o* through one's connections

enchufismo *nm Fam* string-pulling

encía *nf* gum

encíclica *nf Rel* encyclical; **e. papal** papal encyclical

enciclopedia *nf* encyclopedia

enciclopédico, -a *adj* encyclopedic

enciendo *etc ver* **encender**

encierro 1 *ver* **encerrar**
    2 *nm* (**a**) *(protesta)* sit-in (**b**) *Taurom* running of the bulls

encima *adv* (**a**) *(arriba)* on top; **pásame el de e.** pass me the top one *o* the one on top; **el vecino de e.** the upstairs neighbor; **e. de** *(en lugar superior que)* above; *(sobre, en)* on (top of); **vivo e. de tu casa** I live upstairs from you; **el pan está e. de la nevera** the bread is on (top of) the fridge; *Fig* **estar e. de alguien** to be on at sb; **por e.** *(superficialmente)* superficially; **por e. de** over; *Fig* more than; **vive por e. de sus posibilidades** he lives beyond his means; **por e. de todo** more than anything else
    (**b**) *(en tiempo)* **las elecciones ya están e.** the elections are already upon us; **se nos echó la noche e.** night fell, night descended upon us

(**c**) *(además)* on top of that; **e. de no hacerlo bien…** on top of not doing it well…; **e. de ser tonto, es feo** on top of being stupid, he's also ugly

(**d**) *(sobre sí)* **lleva un abrigo e.** she has a coat on; **ponte algo e., vas a tener frío** put something on, you'll be cold; **¿llevas dinero e.?** have you got any money on you?

encimera *nf Esp (de cocina)* worktable; *(sábana)* top sheet

encimero, -a *adj* top

encina *nf* holm oak

encinar *nm* oak forest/grove

encinta *adj inv* pregnant

enclaustrado, -a *adj* cloistered

enclaustrar 1 *vt* to shut up in a convent
    2 enclaustrarse *vpr* to shut oneself up in a convent; *Fig (encerrarse)* to lock oneself up in a room

enclavado, -a *adj* set, situated

enclavar *vt (clavar)* to nail

enclave *nm* enclave

enclenque *adj* sickly, frail

encofrador, -ora *nm,f* formsetter

encofrar *vt* (**a**) *(en construcción)* to put up formwork for (**b**) *Min* to timber

encoger [52] **1** *vt* (**a**) *(ropa)* to shrink; *Fig* **e. el ánimo a alguien** to discourage sb (**b**) *(miembro, músculo)* to contract
    2 *vi* to shrink; **el algodón encoge al lavarlo** cotton shrinks when you wash it
    3 encogerse *vpr* (**a**) *(ropa)* to shrink (**b**) *(miembro, músculo)* to contract; **encogerse de hombros** to shrug one's shoulders; **se me encoge el corazón de oírla llorar** it makes my heart bleed to hear her cry (**c**) *(apocarse)* to cringe

encogido, -a *adj (tímido)* shy; *(pusilánime)* fearful, fainthearted

encojo *ver* **encoger**

encolado *nm (de material, objeto)* gluing; *(de papel pintado)* pasting

encolar *vt (material, objeto)* to glue; *(papel pintado)* to paste

encolerizar [14] **1** *vt* to infuriate, to enrage
    2 encolerizarse *vpr* to get angry

encomendar [3] **1** *vt* to entrust
    2 encomendarse *vpr* **encomendarse a** *(persona)* to entrust oneself to; *(Dios, santos)* to put one's trust in; *Fam* **(hacer algo) sin encomendarse a Dios ni al diablo** (to do sth) entirely of one's own accord

encomiable *adj* laudable, praiseworthy

encomiar *vt Formal* to praise, to extol

encomienda *nf* (**a**) *(encargo)* assignment, mission (**b**) *Hist* = area of land and its native inhabitants given to a conquistador

encomio *nm Formal* praise; **digno de e.** praiseworthy

enconado, -a *adj (lucha)* bitter; *(partidario)* passionate, ardent

enconar 1 *vt* to inflame
    2 enconarse *vpr* (**a**) *(persona)* to get angry (**b**) *(herida)* to become inflamed

encono *nm* rancor, animosity

encontradizo, -a *adj* **hacerse el e.** to contrive a meeting

encontrado, -a *adj (intereses, opiniones)* conflicting

encontrar [63] **1** *vt* (**a**) *(hallar)* to find; **lo encontré durmiendo** I found him sleeping (**b**) *(dificultades)* to encounter (**c**) *(juzgar, considerar)* to find; **no lo encuentro tan divertido como dice la gente** I don't find it *o* think it is as funny as people say; **no sé qué le encuentran a ese pintor** I don't know what they see in that painter
    2 encontrarse *vpr* (**a**) *(hallarse)* to be; **se encuentra en París** she's in Paris; **fui a visitarle y me encontré con que ya no vivía allí** I went to visit him only to discover that he no longer lived there (**b**) *(de ánimo, salud)* to feel; **¿qué tal te encuentras?** how are you feeling?; **no se encuentra muy**

bien she isn't very well (**c**) *(coincidir)* **encontrarse (con alguien)** to meet (sb); **me encontré con Juan** I ran into *o* met Juan (**d**) *(reunirse)* to meet; **¿dónde nos encontraremos?** where shall we meet? (**e**) *(chocar)* to collide

encontronazo *nm (golpe)* collision, crash

encoñado, -a *adj Esp Vulg* **estar e. con alguien** to have the hots for sb; **estar e. con algo** to be crazy *o* nuts about sth

encoñarse *vpr Esp Vulg* **e. con alguien** to get the hots for sb; **e. con algo** to go crazy *o* nuts about sth

encopetado, -a *adj* posh, upper-class

encorsetar *vt (con corsé)* to corset; *(poner límites)* to straitjacket

encorvado, -a *adj* hunched; **e. por la edad** stooped *o* bowed with age

encorvar 1 *vt* to bend
   2 encorvarse *vpr* to stoop

encrespar 1 *vt* (**a**) *(pelo)* to curl; *(mar)* to make choppy *o* rough (**b**) *(irritar)* to irritate
   2 encresparse *vpr* (**a**) *(mar)* to get rough (**b**) *(persona)* to get irritated

encriptación *nf Inform* encryption

encriptar *vt Inform* to encrypt

encrucijada *nf* crossroads *(singular)*; *Fig* **en una e.** at a crossroads

encuadernación *nf (técnica)* binding; *(taller)* binder's, bookbinder's; **Encuadernaciones Olarte** *(empresa)* Olarte the Bookbinders

encuadernador, -ora *nm,f* bookbinder

encuadernar *vt* to bind

encuadrar *vt* (**a**) *(enmarcar) (cuadro, tema)* to frame (**b**) *(encerrar)* to contain (**c**) *(encajar)* to fit

encuadre *nm Fot* composition

encubierto, -a 1 *participio ver* **encubrir**
   2 *adj (intento)* covert; *(insulto, significado)* hidden

encubridor, -ora 1 *adj* concealing; **no es más que una maniobra encubridora** it's just an attempt to conceal things
   2 *nm,f (de delito)* accessory (**de** to)

encubrimiento *nm (de delito)* concealment; *(de persona)* harboring

encubrir *vt (delito)* to conceal; *(persona)* to harbor

encuentro 1 *ver* **encontrar**
   2 *nm* (**a**) *(acción)* meeting, encounter; **tuvieron un e. fortuito** they had a chance encounter *o* meeting; **fijemos un lugar** *o* **sitio de e.** let's decide on a place to meet; **salir al e. de alguien** *(para recibir)* to go to meet sb; *(para atacar)* to confront sb (**b**) *Dep* game, match (**c**) *(hallazgo)* find

encuesta *nf* (**a**) *(de opinión)* survey, opinion poll (**b**) *(investigación)* investigation, inquiry

encuestado, -a *nm,f* person polled

encuestador, -ora *nm,f* pollster

encuestar *vt* to poll

encumbrado, -a *adj* exalted, distinguished

encumbramiento *nm (acción)* rise; *(posición)* distinguished *o* exalted position

encumbrar 1 *vt* to elevate *o* raise to a higher position
   2 encumbrarse *vpr* to rise to a higher position

encurtidos *nmpl* pickles

encurtir *vt* to pickle

endeble *adj (persona, argumento)* weak, feeble; *(objeto)* fragile

endecasílabo, -a 1 *adj* hendecasyllabic
   2 *nm* hendecasyllabic verse

endemia *nf Med* endemic disease

endémico, -a *adj Med & Fig* endemic

endemoniado, -a 1 *adj* (**a**) *Fam (molesto) (niño)* wicked; *(trabajo)* very tricky (**b**) *(desagradable)* terrible, foul (**c**) *(poseído)* possessed (by the devil)
   2 *nm,f* person possessed by the devil

endenantes *adv Am Fam* before

enderezamiento *nm (acción de poner derecho)* straightening; *(acción de poner vertical)* putting upright

enderezar [14] **1** *vt* (**a**) *(poner derecho)* to straighten; *(poner vertical)* to put upright (**b**) *(corregir)* to set right, to straighten out
   2 enderezarse *vpr (sentado)* to sit up straight; *(de pie)* to stand up straight

endeudado, -a *adj* indebted, in debt

endeudamiento *nm* debt

endeudarse *vpr* to get into debt

endiablado, -a *adj (persona)* wicked; *(tiempo, genio)* foul; *(problema, crucigrama)* fiendishly difficult

endibia *nf* endive

endilgar [38] *vt Fam* **e. algo a alguien** *(sermón, bronca)* to dish sth out to sb; *(bulto, tarea)* to lumber sb with sth

endiñar *vt Esp Fam* **e. algo a alguien** *(golpe)* to land *o* deal sb sth; *(tarea)* to lumber sb with sth

endiosamiento *nm* self-importance, conceit

endiosarse *vpr* to become conceited

endivia *nf* endive

endocrino, -a *Med* **1** *adj* **glándula endocrina** endocrine gland
   2 *nm,f* endocrinologist

endocrinología *nf Med* endocrinology

endocrinólogo, -a *nm,f Med* endocrinologist

endogamia *nf* endogamy

endógeno, -a *adj* endogenous

endomingado, -a *adj Fam* dressed up, dolled up

endomingar [38] *Fam* **1** *vt* to dress up, to doll up
   2 endomingarse *vpr* to get dressed *o* dolled up in one's best clothes

endorfina *nf* endorphin

endosar *vt* (**a**) *(tarea)* **e. algo a alguien** to lumber sb with sth (**b**) *Com* to endorse

endosatario, -a *nm,f Com* endorsee

endoscopia *nf Med* endoscopy

endoscopio *nm Med* endoscope

endoso *nm Com* endorsement

endrina *nf* sloe

endrino *nm* blackthorn, sloe

endrogado, -a *adj CAm, Méx* **estar e.** to be in debt

endrogarse [38] *vpr Chile, Méx, Perú (con deudas)* to get into debt

endulzante *nm* sweetener

endulzar [14] *vt (con azúcar)* to sweeten; *(con dulzura)* to ease, to make more bearable

endurecer [46] *vt* (**a**) *(hacer más duro)* to harden (**b**) *(fortalecer)* to strengthen

endurecimiento *nm también Fig* hardening

enebro *nm* juniper (tree)

eneldo *nm* dill

enema *nf* enema; **poner un e. a alguien** to give sb an enema

enemigo, -a 1 *adj* enemy; **los ejércitos enemigos** the enemy armies; **ser e. de algo** to hate sth
   2 *nm,f (rival)* enemy; **e. encarnizado** sworn enemy; **e. mortal** mortal enemy; **el e. público número uno** public enemy number one
   3 *nm (ejército rival)* enemy; **pasarse al e.** to go over to the enemy

enemistad *nf* enmity; **su e. duraba ya años** they've been enemies for years; **siento una profunda e. hacia ellos** I feel intense hatred for them

enemistado, -a *adj* **dos países enemistados por...** two countries who are enemies because of...; **está e. con sus vecinos** he has fallen out with his neighbors

enemistar 1 *vt* to make enemies of; **el testamento**

enemistó a los hermanos the will set the brothers against each other

2 enemistarse *vpr* to fall out (**con** with); **si Francia se enemistara con Alemania,...** if France were to fall out with Germany,...

energética *nf* energetics *(singular)*

energético, -a *adj* energy; **las legumbres proporcionan un alto aporte e.** pulses provide lots of energy

energía *nf* (**a**) *(para máquina)* energy; **e. alternativa** alternative energy; **e. atómica** nuclear power; **e. eólica** wind power; **e. hidráulica** water power; **e. hidroeléctrica** hydroelectric power; **e. limpia** clean energy; **e. nuclear** nuclear power; **energías renovables** renewable forms of energy; **e. solar** solar energy *o* power; **e. térmica** thermal energy (**b**) *(de persona, respuesta)* strength; **respondió con e.** he responded energetically; **hay que empujar con e.** you have to push hard

enérgico, -a *adj (energético)* energetic; *(carácter)* forceful; *(gesto, medida)* vigorous; *(decisión, postura)* emphatic

energúmeno, -a *nm,f* lunatic; **se puso hecho un e.** he went berserk *o* crazy

enero *nm* January; *ver también* **septiembre**

enervante *adj (debilitador)* draining; *(exasperante)* exasperating

enervar *vt* (**a**) *(debilitar)* to sap, to weaken (**b**) *(poner nervioso)* to exasperate

enésimo, -a *adj* (**a**) *Mat* nth (**b**) *Fig* umpteenth; **por enésima vez** for the umpteenth time

enfadado, -a *adj esp Esp* (**a**) *(irritado)* angry; *(molesto)* annoyed; **estar e. con alguien** to be angry/annoyed with sb (**b**) *(peleado)* **están enfadados desde hace años** they fell out (with each other) years ago

enfadar *esp Esp* **1** *vt (irritar)* to anger; *(molestar)* to annoy

2 enfadarse *vpr* (**a**) *(irritarse)* to get angry (**con** with); *(molestarse)* to get annoyed (**con** with); **se enfada por nada** he gets angry for no reason; **no te enfades, pero creo que te equivocas** don't get annoyed, but I think you're wrong; **no te enfades con quien no tiene la culpa** don't get angry with people if it isn't their fault (**b**) *(pelearse)* to fall out; **se enfadaron por una bobada** they fell out over a silly little thing

enfado *esp Esp nm* (**a**) *(por irritarse)* anger; *(por molestarse)* annoyance (**b**) *(enemistad)* **su e. dura ya años** *(recíproco)* they fell out years ago

enfangar [38] **1** *vt* to cover in mud

2 enfangarse *vpr* (**a**) *(con fango)* to get covered in mud (**b**) *Fam Fig* **enfangarse en un asunto sucio** to get mixed up in shady business

énfasis *nm inv* emphasis; **poner é. en algo** to emphasize sth

enfático, -a *adj* emphatic

enfatizar [14] *vt* to emphasize, to stress

enfermar 1 *vt* (**a**) *(causar enfermedad a)* to make ill (**b**) *(irritar)* **e. a alguien** to get on sb's nerves

2 *vi* to fall ill

3 enfermarse *vpr* to fall ill

enfermedad *nf* illness; **enfermedades del corazón/de la piel** heart/skin diseases; **e. de Alzheimer** Alzheimer's disease; **e. hereditaria** hereditary disease; **e. infecciosa** infectious disease; **e. laboral** industrial disease; **e. mental** mental illness; **e. profesional** occupational disease; **e. de transmisión sexual** sexually transmitted disease; **la e. de las vacas locas** mad cow disease; **e. venérea** venereal disease

enfermería *nf* sick bay

enfermero, -a *nm,f* nurse

enfermizo, -a *adj también Fig* unhealthy

enfermo, -a 1 *adj* ill, sick; **me pone e. su falta de**

puntualidad his lack of punctuality gets on my nerves

2 *nm,f (en general)* sick person; *(en el hospital)* patient; **e. de sida** AIDS sufferer; **e. terminal** terminally ill patient

enfervorizado, -a *adj* wildly enthusiastic; **la multitud enfervorizada animaba a su equipo** the frenzied crowd cheered on their team

enfervorizar [14] *vt* to inflame, to rouse

enfilado, -a *adj* **tener a alguien e.** to have it in for sb

enfilar 1 *vt* (**a**) *(camino)* to go *o* head straight along (**b**) *(arma)* to aim

2 *vi* **e. hacia** to go *o* head straight toward

enfisema *nm* emphysema

enflaquecer [46] **1** *vt* to make thin

2 *vi* to grow thin, to lose weight

enfocar [59] **1** *vt* (**a**) *(imagen, objetivo)* to focus (**b**) *(sujeto: luz, foco)* to shine on (**c**) *(tema, asunto)* to approach, to look at

2 *vi* **e. hacia alguien/algo** *(cámara)* to focus on sb/sth; *(luz)* to shine on sb/sth

enfoque *nm* (**a**) *(de una imagen)* focus (**b**) *(de un asunto)* approach, angle

enfrascado, -a *adj* **estar e. (en)** to be totally absorbed (in)

enfrascar [59] **1** *vt* to bottle

2 enfrascarse *vpr (riña)* to get embroiled (**en** in); *(lectura, conversación)* to become engrossed (**en** in)

enfrentamiento *nm* confrontation

enfrentar 1 *vt* (**a**) *(poner frente a frente)* to bring face-to-face (**b**) *(hacer frente a)* to confront, to face; **enfrentan el futuro con inquietud** they face the future with unease

2 enfrentarse *vpr* (**a**) **enfrentarse a** *(afrontar)* to confront, to face; *(en lucha, conflicto)* to confront; **se enfrentó a su enfermedad con valor** she faced up to her illness bravely; **nos enfrentamos al enemigo** we confronted the enemy (**b**) *(dos bandos)* to meet, to clash; **los dos equipos se enfrentarán por el campeonato** the two teams will play each other for the championship

enfrente *adv* (**a**) *(al otro lado)* opposite; **vive e.** he lives opposite, he lives across from me; **la tienda de e.** the store across the road; **e. de** opposite, facing (**b**) *(en contra)* **tiene a todos e.** everyone's against him

enfriamiento *nm* (**a**) *(catarro)* cold (**b**) *(acción)* cooling; **el e. de las relaciones entre ambos países** the cooling of relations between both countries

enfriar [32] **1** *vt también Fig* to cool

2 *v impersonal* to get colder

3 enfriarse *vpr* (**a**) *(líquido, pasión, amistad)* to cool down (**b**) *(quedarse demasiado frío)* to go cold; **se te va a e. la sopa** your soup is going to get cold (**c**) *(resfriarse)* to catch a cold

enfundar 1 *vt (espada)* to sheathe; *(pistola)* to put away

2 enfundarse *vpr* **enfundarse algo** to wrap oneself up in sth

enfurecer [46] **1** *vt* to infuriate, to madden

2 enfurecerse *vpr (persona)* to get furious; *(mar)* to become rough

enfurecido, -a *adj* (**a**) *(persona)* enraged (**b**) *(mar)* raging

enfurecimiento *nm* anger, fury

enfurruñado, -a *adj* **estar e.** to be sulking

enfurruñarse *vpr Fam* to sulk

engalanado, -a *adj (persona)* dressed up; *(ciudad, coche)* decked out (**con** with)

engalanar 1 *vt* to decorate

2 engalanarse *vpr (persona)* to dress up; *(ciudad)* to be decked out (**con** with)

enganchado, -a *adj* (**a**) *(prendido)* caught; **la bufanda se me quedó enganchada a la puerta** I caught my scarf on the door (**b**) *Fam (adicto)* hooked (**a** on)

enganchar 1 *vt* (**a**) *(agarrar)* *(vagones)* to couple; *(remolque, caballos)* to hitch up; *(pez)* to hook (**b**) *(colgar)* to hang (up) (**c**)

Fam (atraer) **e. a alguien para que haga algo** to rope sb into doing sth (**d**) *Fam (pillar) (empleo, marido)* to land (oneself) (**e**) *Andes, CAm, Méx (contratar)* to hire, to contract

2 *vi Fam (hacer adicto)* to be addictive; **un videojuego de los que enganchan** an addictive video game

3 engancharse *vpr* (**a**) *(prenderse)* **engancharse algo con** *o* **en** to catch sth on; **se le enganchó la falda en las zarzas** she caught her skirt on the brambles; **te has enganchado las medias** you've caught *o* snagged your tights on something (**b**) *(alistarse)* to enlist, to join up (**c**) *Fam (hacerse adicto)* to get hooked (**a** on) (**d**) *Andes, CAm, Méx (para trabajo)* to sign up

enganche *nm* (**a**) *(de trenes)* coupling (**b**) *(gancho)* hook (**c**) *(reclutamiento)* enlistment (**d**) *Méx (depósito)* deposit

enganchón *nm (de ropa, tela)* snag

engañabobos *nm inv Fam* (**a**) *(cosa)* con (trick) (**b**) *(persona)* con man, con artist

engañar 1 *vt* (**a**) *(mentir)* to deceive; **a mí no me engañas, sé que tienes cincuenta años** you can't fool me, I know you're fifty (**b**) *(ser infiel a)* to deceive, to cheat on; **engaña a su marido** she cheats on her husband (**c**) *(estafar)* to cheat, to swindle; **te engañaron vendiéndote esto tan caro** they cheated you if they sold that to you for such a high price; **e. a alguien como a un chino** to take sb for a ride (**d**) *(hacer más llevadero)* to appease; **e. el hambre** to take the edge off one's hunger

2 *vi* to be deceptive *o* misleading; **las apariencias engañan** appearances can be deceptive

3 engañarse *vpr* (**a**) *(hacerse ilusiones)* to delude oneself; **se engaña si cree que...** he's deluding himself if he thinks that...; **no te engañes, ya no lo volverás a ver** don't kid yourself, you'll never see it again now (**b**) *(equivocarse)* to be wrong

engañifa *nf Fam (mentira, broma)* trick; *(estafa)* swindle

engaño *nm* (**a**) *(mentira, broma)* deceit; *(estafa)* swindle; **ha sido víctima de un e. en la compra del terreno** he was swindled over the sale of the land; **no nos llamemos a e., el programa se puede mejorar y mucho** let's not kid ourselves, the program could be a lot better; **que nadie se llame a e., la economía no va bien** let no one have illusions about it, the economy isn't doing well (**b**) *(ardid)* ploy, trick; **las rebajas son un e. para que la gente compre estupideces** the sales are a swindle intended to try to make people buy junk

engañoso, -a *adj (persona, palabras)* deceitful; *(aspecto, apariencia)* deceptive

engarce *nm* setting

engarzar [14] *vt* (**a**) *(encadenar) (abalorios)* to thread; *(perlas)* to string (**b**) *(diamante)* to set (**c**) *(palabras)* to string together

engastar *vt* to set, to mount

engatusador, -ora *Fam* **1** *adj* coaxing, cajoling

2 *nm,f* coaxer

engatusar *vt Fam* to sweet-talk; **e. a alguien para que haga algo** to sweet-talk sb into doing sth

engendrar *vt* (**a**) *(hijo, idea)* to conceive (**b**) *(originar)* to give rise to; **la falta de cariño engendra inseguridad** lack of affection gives rise to insecurity

engendro *nm* (**a**) *(ser deforme)* freak, deformed creature; *(niño)* malformed child (**b**) *(obra fea o mala)* monstrosity

englobar *vt* to include

engolado, -a *adj (presuntuoso)* presumptuous, arrogant; *(pomposo)* pompous, bombastic

engolosinarse *vpr* **e. con** to develop a taste for

engomar *vt* (**a**) *(dar goma)* to put glue on (**b**) *(dar apresto)* to size

engominado, -a *adj (pelo)* slicked-back

engominar *vt* to put hair cream on

engordar 1 *vt* (**a**) *(animal)* to fatten up (**b**) *(aumentar)* to swell

2 *vi* (**a**) *(persona)* to put on weight; **he engordado seis libras** I've put on six pounds (**b**) *(comida, bebida)* to be fattening

engorde *nm* fattening (up)

engorro *nm* nuisance

engorroso, -a *adj (molesto)* bothersome; *(físicamente)* cumbersome

engrampadora *nf RP* stapler

engrampar *vt RP* to staple

engranaje *nm* (**a**) *(acción)* gearing (**b**) *(mecanismo) (de reloj, piñón)* cogs; *(de vehículo)* gears (**c**) *(enlace) (de ideas)* chain, sequence (**d**) *(aparato) (político, burocrático)* machinery

engranar *vt* (**a**) *(piezas)* to engage (**b**) *(ideas)* to link, to connect

engrandecer [46] *vt* (**a**) *(enaltecer)* to exalt (**b**) *(aumentar)* to increase, to enlarge

engrandecimiento *nm* (**a**) *(ensalzamiento)* enhancement (**b**) *(aumento)* increase

engrapadora *nf Am* stapler

engrapar *vt Am* to staple

engrasar *vt (motor)* to lubricate; *(bisagra, mecanismo)* to oil; *(eje)* to grease; *(molde de horno)* to grease, to oil

engrase *nm (de motor)* lubrication; *(de mecanismo)* oiling

engreído, -a 1 *adj* conceited, full of one's own importance

2 *nm,f* conceited person

engrescar [59] *vt* to egg on, to incite

engripado, -a *adj CSur* **estar e.** to have (the) flu

engriparse *vpr CSur* to come down with (the) flu

engrosar [63] *vt (aumentar)* to swell; **la herencia pasó a e. la fortuna familiar** the inheritance went to swell the family fortune

engrudo *nm* paste

enguantarse *vpr* to put one's gloves on

engullir *vt* to gobble up, to wolf down

enharinar *vt* to flour

enhebrar *vt* (**a**) *(aguja)* to thread; *(perlas)* to string (**b**) *(palabras)* to string together

enhiesto, -a *adj (derecho)* erect, upright; *(bandera)* raised

enhorabuena 1 *nf* congratulations; **dar la e. a alguien por algo** to congratulate sb on sth

2 *interj* **¡e. (por...)!** congratulations (on...)!

enigma *nm* enigma

enigmático, -a *adj* enigmatic

enjabonado, -a 1 *adj* soapy

2 *nm* soaping

enjabonar *vt (con jabón)* to soap; *(dar coba)* to soft-soap

enjaezar [14] *vt* to harness *(with decorative harness)*

enjambre *nm también Fig* swarm

enjaulado, -a *adj* caged; *Fig* **como un perro e.** like a caged animal

enjaular *vt (en jaula)* to cage; *Fam (en prisión)* to jail, to lock up

enjoyar 1 *vt* to adorn with jewels

2 enjoyarse *vpr* to put on (one's) jewels

enjuagar [38] **1** *vt* to rinse

2 enjuagarse *vpr* to rinse oneself/one's mouth/one's hands etc; **enjuagarse el pelo** to rinse one's hair

enjuague *nm* rinse; **e. bucal** *(acción)* rinsing of the mouth; *(líquido)* mouthwash

enjugar [38] *vt* (**a**) *(secar)* to dry, to wipe away; **enjugó sus lágrimas** he dried his tears (**b**) *(pagar) (deuda)* to pay off; *(déficit)* to cancel out

enjuiciable *adj* indictable, liable to prosecution

enjuiciamiento *nm* (**a**) *Der* trial (**b**) *(opinión)* judgment

enjuiciar *vt* (**a**) *Der* to try (**b**) *(opinar)* to judge

enjundia *nf* substance; **su último libro tiene mucha e.** there's a lot in her last book

enjuto, -a *adj (delgado)* lean

enlace 1 *ver* **enlazar**

  2 *nm* (a) *(conexión) (gen)* & *Inform* link (b) *(persona)* go-between; *Esp* **e. sindical** shop steward (c) *Quím* bond (d) *(boda)* **e. (matrimonial)** marriage (e) *(de trenes)* connection; **estación de e.** junction; **vía de e.** crossing, crossover

enladrillado *nm* brick paving

enladrillar *vt* to pave with bricks

enlatado, -a 1 *adj* (a) *(en lata)* canned, tinned (b) *TV (programa, música)* prerecorded; *(risa)* canned

  2 enlatados *nmpl Am (comestibles)* groceries

enlatar *vt* to can, to tin

enlazar [14] **1** *vt* **e. algo a** *(atar)* to tie sth up to; *(trabar, relacionar)* to link *o* connect sth with

  2 *vi (trenes)* to connect (**en** at)

  3 enlazarse *vpr* to become linked

enlistar *vt Méx* to list

enlodar *vt* to cover in mud

enloquecedor, -ora *adj* maddening

enloquecer [46] **1** *vt* (a) *(volver loco)* to drive mad (b) *(gustar mucho)* to drive wild *o* crazy; **le enloquece el esquí** she's mad *o* crazy about skiing

  2 *vi* to go mad

enloquecido, -a *adj* mad, crazed

enloquecimiento *nm* madness

enlosar *vt* to pave

enlucir [39] *vt* (a) *(blanquear)* to whitewash (b) *(enyesar)* to plaster (c) *(metales)* to polish

enlutado, -a *adj* in mourning

enlutar *vt* (a) *(vestir de luto)* to dress in mourning (b) *(entristecer)* to cast a shadow over

enmaderar *vt (pared)* to panel; *(suelo)* to lay the floorboards of

enmadrarse *vpr* to become too tied to one's mother

enmarañado, -a *adj* (a) *(pelo)* matted, tangled; *(cable)* tangled (b) *(asunto)* complicated

enmarañar 1 *vt* (a) *(enredar)* to tangle (up) (b) *(complicar)* to complicate, to confuse

  2 enmarañarse *vpr* (a) *(enredarse)* to become tangled (b) *(complicarse)* to become confused *o* complicated

enmarcar [59] **1** *vt* (a) *(cuadro)* to frame (b) *(dar un contexto)* **enmarcan su política energética dentro del respeto al medio ambiente** their energy policy is placed within a framework of respect for the environment

  2 enmarcarse *vpr* **las medidas se enmarcan dentro de la nueva política conciliadora** the measures form part of the new policy of reconciliation; **esta actuación se enmarca dentro de la convención de Viena** this action falls within the provisions of the Vienna convention

enmascarado, -a 1 *adj* masked

  2 *nm,f* masked man, *f* masked woman

enmascarar *vt (rostro)* to mask; *(encubrir)* to disguise

enmendar [3] **1** *vt (error)* to correct; *(ley, dictamen)* to amend; *(comportamiento)* to mend; *(daño, perjuicio)* to redress; **enmendarle la plana a alguien** *(corregir)* to find fault with what sb has done; *(superar)* to go one better than sb

  2 enmendarse *vpr* to mend one's ways

enmienda *nf* (a) *(acción)* **hacer propósito de e.** to promise to mend one's ways (b) *(en un texto)* correction (c) *(de ley, contrato)* amendment

enmiendo *etc ver* **enmendar**

enmohecer [46] **1** *vt (con moho)* to turn moldy; *(metal)* to rust

  2 enmohecerse *vpr (con moho)* to grow moldy; *(metal, conocimientos)* to go rusty

enmohecido, -a *adj (con moho)* moldy; *(metal, conocimientos)* rusty

enmoquetado, -a *adj Esp, RP* **1** *adj* carpeted

  2 *nm* (wall-to-wall) carpeting

enmoquetar *vt Esp, RP* to carpet

enmudecer [46] **1** *vt* to silence

  2 *vi (callarse)* to fall silent, to go quiet; *(perder el habla)* to be struck dumb

enmudecimiento *nm* silence

ennegrecer [46] **1** *vt (poner negro)* to blacken

  2 *vi* to darken

  3 ennegrecerse *vpr (ponerse negro)* to become blackened; **el cielo se ennegreció de repente** the sky suddenly darkened *o* grew dark

ennoblecer [46] *vt (persona)* to ennoble, to dignify; **esas acciones lo ennoblecen** these actions do him credit

enojadizo, -a *adj esp Am* irritable, touchy

enojado, -a *adj esp Am (irritado)* angry; *(molesto)* annoyed

enojar *esp Am* **1** *vt (irritar)* to anger; *(molestar)* to annoy

  2 enojarse *vpr (irritarse)* to get angry (**con** with); *(molestarse)* to get annoyed (**con** with)

enojo *nm esp Am (irritación)* anger; *(molestia)* annoyance

enojoso, -a *adj esp Am (molesto)* annoying; *(delicado, espinoso)* awkward

enología *nf* enology, study of wine

enólogo, -a *nm,f* enologist, wine expert

enorgullecer [46] **1** *vt* to fill with pride

  2 enorgullecerse *vpr* to be proud (**de** of); **me enorgullezco de pertenecer a esta familia** I am proud to be a member of this family

enorme *adj* enormous, huge

enormidad *nf* (a) *(de tamaño)* enormity, hugeness; **me gustó una e.** I liked it enormously (b) *(despropósito)* crass remark/ mistake/ etc

enquistado, -a *adj (odio, costumbre)* deep-rooted, deeply entrenched

enquistamiento *nm Med* encystment

enquistarse *vpr* (a) *Med* to develop into a cyst (b) *(odio, costumbre)* to take root, to become entrenched; *(proceso)* to become bogged down

enraizar [14] *vi (árbol)* to take root; *(persona)* to put down roots

enramada *nf* (a) *(espesura)* branches, canopy (b) *(cobertizo)* bower

enrarecer [46] **1** *vt (situación, ambiente)* to make strained

  2 enrarecerse *vpr (atmósfera)* to become rarefied; *(situación, ambiente)* to become strained

enrarecido, -a *adj* (a) *(aire)* rarefied (b) *(situación, ambiente)* strained, tense

enredadera *nf* creeper

enredador, -ora 1 *adj (travieso)* naughty, mischievous; *(chismoso)* gossiping

  2 *nm,f (travieso)* mischief-maker; *(chismoso)* gossip

enredar 1 *vt* (a) *(madeja, pelo)* to tangle up; *(situación, asunto)* to complicate, to confuse (b) *(implicar)* **e. a alguien (en)** to embroil sb (in), to involve sb (in) (c) *(entretener)* to bother, to annoy

  2 *vi Fam* to get up to mischief; **e. con algo** to fiddle with *o* mess around with sth

  3 enredarse *vpr* (a) *(plantas)* to climb; *(madeja, pelo)* to get tangled up; *(situación, asunto)* to become confused; **la cola de la cometa se enredó en unas ramas** the tail of the kite got tangled in some branches (b) *(meterse)* **enredarse en un asunto** to get mixed up *o* involved in something; **enredarse a hacer algo** to start doing sth (c) *Fam (sentimentalmente)* **enredarse con** to get involved *o* have an affair with

enredo *nm* (a) *(maraña)* tangle, knot (b) *(lío)* mess, complicated affair; *(asunto ilícito)* shady affair; *Teatro & Cine* **comedia de e.** farce (c) *(amoroso)* (love) affair

enrejado *nm* (a) *(barrotes) (de balcón, verja)* railings; *(de jaula, celda, ventana)* bars (b) *(de cañas)* trellis

enrejar vt (ventanas) to bar

enrevesado, -a adj complex, complicated

enriquecedor, -ora adj enriching

enriquecer [46] **1** vt (**a**) (hacer rico) to bring wealth to, to make rich (**b**) (sustancia) to enrich
2 enriquecerse vpr to get rich

enriquecido, -a adj enriched

enriquecimiento nm enrichment

enristrar vt (**a**) (ajos, cebollas) to string (**b**) (lanza) to couch

enrocar [59] **1** vt & vi (en ajedrez) to castle
2 enrocarse vpr to castle

enrojecer [46] **1** vt to redden, to turn red
2 vi (por calor) to flush; (por turbación) to blush
3 enrojecerse vpr (por calor) to flush; (por turbación) to blush

enrojecimiento nm (**a**) (de la piel) redness, red mark (**b**) (de las mejillas) blushing

enrolar 1 vt to enlist
2 enrolarse vpr (en la marina) to enlist (**en** in); **enrolarse en un barco** to join a ship's crew

enrollado, -a adj (**a**) (en forma de rollo) in a roll, rolled up (**b**) Esp Fam (interesante, animado) fun; **es un tío muy e.** he's a great guy, he's really great (**c**) Fam (dedicado, entregado) **están muy enrollados con el parapente** they're into paragliding in a big way (**d**) Fam (en relaciones amorosas) **está e. con una sueca** he's going out with a Swedish woman; **están enrollados desde hace tres años** they've been an item for the last three years

enrollar 1 vt (**a**) (papel, alfombra) to roll up (**b**) Fam (gustar) **me enrolla mucho** I love it, I think it's great
2 enrollarse vpr (**a**) (en sí mismo) (papel) to roll up; (manguera, cuerda) to coil up (**b**) Fam (hablar) to go on (and on); **no te enrolles y dime qué quieres** just get to the point and tell me what you want; **me enrollé demasiado en la tercera pregunta** I spent too much time on the third question; Esp **se enrolla como una persiana** he could talk his head off (**c**) Fam (sexualmente) (hacer el amor) get it on; (besarse, abrazarse) to neck, to make out (**d**) Esp Fam (en el trato) **se enrolla muy bien con los clientes** he gets on very well with the clients

enroque nm (en ajedrez) castle

enroscar [59] vt (**a**) (tuerca) to screw in; (tapa) to screw on (**b**) (enrollar) to roll up; (cuerpo, cola) to curl up

enrulado, -a adj Chile, RP curly

ensaimada nf = cake made of sweet coiled pastry

ensalada nf (**a**) (plato) salad; **e. mixta** mixed salad (**b**) Fam (lío) mishmash

ensaladera nf salad bowl

ensaladilla nf Esp **e. (rusa)** Russian salad, = salad of boiled, diced potatoes and carrots or peas, in mayonnaise

ensalmo nm incantation, spell; **como por e.** as if by magic

ensalzamiento nm praise

ensalzar [14] vt to praise

ensamblado, -a 1 adj (mueble, piezas) assembled
2 nm assembly

ensamblador, -ora 1 nm,f (persona) joiner
2 nm Inform assembler

ensambladura nf, **ensamblaje** nm (acción) assembly; (unión) joint

ensamblar vt (gen) & Inform to assemble; (madera) to join

ensanchamiento nm (de orificio, calle) widening; (de ropa) letting out

ensanchar 1 vt (orificio, calle) to widen; (ropa) to let out; (ciudad) to expand
2 ensancharse vpr (orificio, calle) to widen, to open out

ensanche nm (**a**) (de calle) widening (**b**) (en la ciudad) new suburb

ensangrentado, -a adj bloodstained, covered in blood

ensangrentar [3] vt to cover with blood

ensañamiento nm viciousness, savagery

ensañarse vpr **e. con** to torment, to treat cruelly

ensartado, -a adj (perlas) strung; **trozos de carne ensartados en un pincho** pieces of meat threaded on a skewer

ensartar vt (**a**) (perlas) to string (**b**) (atravesar) (torero) to gore; (puñal) to plunge, to bury; **ensartó las verduras en pinchos** he threaded the vegetables on skewers

ensayar vt (**a**) (experimentar) to test (**b**) Teatro to rehearse

ensayista nmf essayist

ensayo nm (**a**) Teatro rehearsal; **e. general** dress rehearsal (**b**) (prueba) test; **le salió al primer e.** he got it at the first attempt (**c**) Lit essay (**d**) (en rugby) try

enseguida adv (inmediatamente) immediately, at once; (pronto) very soon; **llegará e.** he'll be here any minute now; **vino a las seis, pero se fue e.** he came at six, but he left soon after

ensenada nf cove, inlet

enseña nf ensign

enseñado, -a adj (**a**) (educado) educated (**b**) (perro) housebroken

enseñante nmf teacher

enseñanza nf (educación) education; (instrucción) teaching; **enseñanzas** (de filósofo, profeta) teachings; **se dedica a la e.** he works as a teacher; **un centro de e.** an educational institution; **de cualquier error puede extraerse una e.** there's a lesson to be learned from every mistake you make; **e. a distancia** distance education; **e. estatal** state education; **e. de idiomas** language teaching; **e. media** secondary education; **e. personalizada** personal o individual tutoring; **e. primaria** primary education; **e. privada** private education; **e. pública** state education; **e. secundaria** secondary education; **e. superior** higher education; **e. universitaria** college o university education

enseñar vt (**a**) (instruir, aleccionar) to teach; **enseña inglés en una academia de idiomas** he teaches English in a language school; **e. a alguien a hacer algo** to teach sb (how) to do sth; **la derrota les enseñó a ser más humildes** the defeat taught them some humility (**b**) (mostrar) to show; **enséñame tu vestido nuevo** show me your new dress; **al estirarse, enseñaba el ombligo** when he stretched you could see his belly button; **va enseñando los hombros provocativamente** her shoulders are provocatively uncovered

enseñorearse vpr to take possession (**de** of)

enseres nmpl (**a**) (efectos personales) belongings (**b**) (muebles, accesorios) furnishings

ensillado, -a adj (caballo) saddled

ensillar vt (caballo) to saddle up

ensimismado, -a adj (enfrascado) absorbed; (pensativo) lost in thought

ensimismamiento nm self-absorption

ensimismarse vpr (enfrascarse) to become absorbed; (abstraerse) to lose oneself in thought

ensoberbecer [46] **1** vt to fill with pride
2 ensoberbecerse vpr to become puffed up with pride

ensombrecer [46] **1** vt también Fig to cast a shadow over
2 ensombrecerse vpr to darken

ensoñación nf daydream; **ni por e.** not even in one's wildest dreams

ensopar vt Andes, RP, Ven to soak

ensordecedor, -ora adj deafening

ensordecer [46] **1** vt (**a**) (causar sordera) to cause to go deaf (**b**) (sujeto: sonido) to deafen
2 vi to go deaf

ensordecimiento *nm* deafness

ensortijar *vt* to curl

ensuciar 1 *vt (manchar)* to (make) dirty; *(desprestigiar)* to sully, to tarnish; **e. el nombre de alguien** to sully sb's name *o* reputation

2 ensuciarse *vpr* to get dirty; **la alfombra se ha ensuciado de pintura** the carpet has got paint on it

ensueño *nm también Fig* dream; **de e.** dream, ideal; **tienen una casa de e.** they have a dream house

entablado *nm (armazón)* wooden platform; *(suelo)* floorboards

entablar *vt* **(a)** *(suelo)* to put down floorboards on **(b)** *(iniciar)* *(conversación, amistad)* to strike up; *(negocio)* to start up **(c)** *(entablillar)* to put in a splint

entablillar *vt* to put in a splint

entallado, -a *adj (vestido, chaqueta)* tailored

entallar *vt (prenda)* to take in at the waist

entarimado *nm (plataforma)* wooden platform; *(suelo)* floorboards

entarimar *vt (suelo)* to put down floorboards on

ente *nm* **(a)** *(ser)* being **(b)** *(corporación)* body, organization; **e. público** *(institución)* = state-owned body *o* institution; **el E. público** *(televisión)* = Spanish state broadcasting company **(c)** *Fam (personaje)* oddball

entelequia *nf (fantasía)* pipe dream

entenado, -a *nm,f Méx* stepson, *f* stepdaughter

entendederas *nfpl Fam* brains; **ser corto de e.** to be a bit dim

entendedor, -ora *nm,f Prov* **al buen e. le sobran las palabras** *o* **pocas palabras bastan** a word to the wise is sufficient

entender [64] **1** *vt* **(a)** *(comprender)* to understand; **ahora entiendo lo que quieres decir** now I understand *o* know what you mean; **no te entiendo, habla más despacio** I don't understand you, could you speak more slowly?; **no entiendo cómo puede gustarte Arturo** I don't know what you see in Arturo; **no entiendo nada, ¿no deberían haber llegado ya?** I just can't understand it, surely they were supposed to have arrived by now; **¡no hay quien te entienda!** you're impossible!; **¿tú qué entiendes por "amistad"?** what do you understand by "friendship"?; **dar a e. que...** to imply (that)...; **hasta que no llegue no podemos empezar, ¿entiendes?** we can't start until she gets here, all right?

(b) *(juzgar, opinar)* to think; **yo no lo entiendo así** I don't see it that way

2 *vi* **(a)** *(saber)* **e. de algo** to know about sth; **e. poco/algo de** to know very little/a little about **(b)** *(ocuparse)* **e. de** *o* **en** *(en general)* to deal with

3 entenderse *vpr* **(a)** *(comprenderse)* *(uno mismo)* to know what one means; *(dos personas)* to understand each other; **yo ya me entiendo** I know what I'm doing; **se entienden en inglés** they communicate with each other in English **(b)** *(llevarse bien)* to get on **(c)** *(ponerse de acuerdo)* to reach an agreement **(d)** *Fam (apañarse)* **allá te las entiendas tú con la lavadora** the washing machine's your problem

4 *nm* **a mi e....** the way I see it...

entendido, -a 1 *adj* **(a)** *(comprendido)* understood; **¿e.?** (is that) understood?; **¡e.!** all right!, okay!; **no darse por e.** to pretend one hasn't heard **(b)** *(versado)* expert

2 *nm,f* expert **(en** on)

entendimiento *nm (comprensión)* understanding; *(juicio)* judgment; *(inteligencia)* mind, intellect

entente *nf Pol* entente cordiale; *Com* agreement

enterado, -a 1 *adj* **(a)** *(informado)* **estar e. de algo** to be aware of sth; **darse por e.** to indicate that one is aware of sth; **no darse por e.** to turn a deaf ear **(b)** *(entendido)* well-informed **(en** about)

2 *nm,f Irónico* know-it-all

enterar 1 *vt* **e. a alguien de algo** to inform sb about sth

2 enterarse *vpr* **(a)** *(descubrir, saber)* to find out **(de** about); **como se entere, me mata** if she finds out, she'll kill me; **¿te has enterado del accidente de Ana?** did you hear about Ana's accident?; **¡entérate de una vez!** ¡**yo no soy tu criado!** get this straight, I'm not your servant!

(b) *Fam (comprender)* to get it, to understand; **no te enteras de nada** you don't understand, do you?

(c) *(darse cuenta)* **enterarse (de algo)** to notice (sth); **no se enteró del golpe** he didn't notice the impact

(d) *(expresiones)* **¡para que te enteres!** I'll have you know!, as a matter of fact!; **¡te vas a e.!** you'll know all about it!, you'll catch it!; **¡se va a e. de quién soy yo!** he's going to find out what sort of stuff I'm made of!

entereza *nf (serenidad)* composure, self-possession; *(honradez)* integrity; *(firmeza)* firmness

enternecedor, -ora *adj* touching, moving

enternecer [46] **1** *vt* to move, to touch

2 enternecerse *vpr* to be moved

enternecimiento *nm* **el desamparo de los refugiados consiguió su e.** he softened when he saw how helpless the refugees were

entero, -a 1 *adj* **(a)** *(completo)* whole; **vi la película entera** I watched the whole movie; **el edificio/país e.** the entire *o* whole building/country; **es de mi entera confianza** she has my complete confidence; **por e.** entirely, completely **(b)** *(sin desperfecto)* in one piece; **este cristal está e.** this pane hasn't been broken **(c)** *(sereno)* composed; **se mostró muy e. en el juicio** he was very composed at the trial **(d)** *(honrado)* upright, honest

2 *nm Bolsa* point

enterrador, -ora *nm,f* gravedigger

enterramiento *nm (acción, ceremonia)* burial; *(lugar)* burial site

enterrar [3] **1** *vt* **(a)** *(cadáver, objeto, tesoro)* to bury **(b)** *(olvidar)* to forget about **(c)** *(clavar)* to sink *o* drive in; **le enterró el puñal en el vientre** he plunged the dagger into his belly **(d)** *(sobrevivir)* **enterró a todos sus hermanos** he survived all his brothers

2 enterrarse *vpr Fig* **enterrarse en vida** to hide oneself away

entibiar 1 *vt (enfriar)* to cool; *(templar)* to warm

2 entibiarse *vpr* to cool; **sus relaciones se entibiaron** *(de pareja)* their relationship lost its passion; *(diplomáticas, amistad)* relations between them became more distant

entidad *nf* **(a)** *(corporación)* body; *(empresa)* firm, company; **e. bancaria** bank; **e. de crédito** lending institution **(b)** *(en filosofía)* entity **(c)** *(importancia)* importance; **de e.** of importance

entiendo *etc ver* **entender**

entierro 1 *ver* **enterrar**

2 *nm (acción)* burial; *(ceremonia)* funeral

entlo. *(abrev de* **entresuelo)** mezzanine

entoldado *nm (toldo)* awning; *(para fiestas, bailes)* large tent

entoldar *vt* to cover with an awning

entomología *nf* entomology

entomólogo, -a *nm,f* entomologist

entonación *nf* intonation

entonar 1 *vt* **(a)** *(cantar)* to sing **(b)** *(tonificar)* to pick up; **esta sopa te entonará** this soup will do you the world of good

2 *vi* **(a)** *(al cantar)* to sing in tune **(b)** *(armonizar)* **e. (con algo)** to match (sth)

3 entonarse *vpr* to become tipsy *o* merry; **se entonó con una copa de oporto** he took a glass of port as a pick-me-up

entonces *adv* then; **si no te gusta, e. no vayas** if you don't like it, then don't go; **si no ha llegado, e. tiene que estar en la oficina** if he hasn't arrived yet, then he must still be at the office; **el e. primer ministro** the then prime minister; **desde e.** since then; **en** o **por aquel e.** at that time; **e., ¿vienes o no?** are you coming or not, then?

entontecer [46] *vt* **e. a alguien** to dull sb's brain

entornado, -a *adj (puerta, ventana)* ajar

entornar *vt* to half-close

entorno *nm* environment, surroundings

entorpecer [46] *vt* (a) *(debilitar) (movimientos)* to hinder; *(miembros)* to numb; *(mente)* to cloud (b) *(dificultar)* to obstruct, to hinder; *(tráfico)* to hold up, to slow down

entorpecimiento *nm* (a) *(debilitamiento) (físico)* numbness; *(mental)* haziness (b) *(dificultad)* hindrance; **el accidente provocó un e. del tráfico** the accident caused a holdup in traffic

entrada *nf* (a) *(acción)* entry; *(llegada)* arrival; **prohibida la e.** *(en letrero)* no entry; **hizo una e. espectacular** she made a spectacular entrance

(b) *(lugar)* entrance; *(recibidor)* entrance hall; **e.** *(en letrero)* entrance, way in; **te espero a la e. del cine** I'll meet you outside the movie theater; **e. de artistas** stage door; **e. principal** main entrance

(c) *Tec* inlet, intake

(d) *(en espectáculos) (billete)* ticket; *(recaudación)* receipts, takings; **e. libre** o **gratuita** admission free; **sacar una e.** to buy a ticket; **no hay entradas** *(en letrero)* sold out

(e) *(público)* audience; *Dep* attendance

(f) *Esp (pago inicial)* down payment

(g) *(en contabilidad)* income

(h) *(plato)* appetizer

(i) *(en la frente)* **tener entradas** to have a receding hairline

(j) *(en un diccionario)* entry

(k) *(principio)* beginning, start; **de e. no me gustó, pero…** at first I didn't like it, but…; **me di cuenta de e. de que algo andaba mal** I realized from the start that something was wrong

(l) *Inform* input

entrado, -a *adj* **e. el otoño** once we're into fall; **entrada la noche** once night has set in; **e. en años** elderly; **e. en carnes** portly, rather large

entramado *nm* framework

entramar *vt* to make the framework of

entrampado, -a *adj Fam (endeudado)* **estar e.** to be up to one's neck in debt

entrante 1 *adj (año, mes)* coming; *(presidente, gobierno)* incoming

2 *nm* (a) *Esp (plato)* appetizer (b) *(hueco)* recess

entraña 1 *nf RP* skirt; **churrasco de e.** grilled skirt steak

2 entrañas *nfpl* (a) *(vísceras)* entrails, insides; *Fig* **arrancarle a alguien las entrañas** to break sb's heart; *Fig* **no tener entrañas** to be heartless (b) *(centro, esencia)* heart; **las entrañas de la Tierra** the bowels of the earth

entrañable *adj (persona)* dear; *(amigo)* very dear; *(recuerdo)* fond; *(cariño, amistad)* warm

entrañar *vt* to involve

entrar 1 *vi* (a) *(introducirse) (viniendo)* to enter, to come in; *(yendo)* to enter, to go in; **déjame e.** let me in; **e. en algo** to enter sth, to come/go into sth; **entré por la ventana** I got in through the window

(b) *(penetrar)* to go in; **e. en algo** to go into sth

(c) *(caber)* to fit (**en** in); **esta llave no entra en la cerradura** this key won't fit in the lock; **este anillo no me entra** I can't get this ring on my finger; **el pie no me entra en el zapato** I can't get this shoe on

(d) *(incorporarse)* **e. (en algo)** *(colegio, empresa)* to start (at sth); *(club, partido político)* to join (sth); **e. de** *(botones, ayudante)* to start off as

(e) *(empezar)* **entramos a las nueve** we start at nine o'clock; **e. a hacer algo** to start doing sth; **entró a trabajar hace un mes** he started work a month ago

(f) *(participar)* to join in; **e. en** *(discusión, polémica)* to join in; *(negocio)* to get in on; **no entremos en cuestiones morales** let's not get involved in moral issues; **yo ahí ni entro ni salgo** it has nothing to do with me

(g) *(estar incluido)* **e. en, e. dentro de** to be included in

(h) *(figurar)* **e. en** to belong to; **entro en el grupo de los disconformes** I number among the dissidents

(i) *(periodo de tiempo)* to start; **el verano entra el 21 de junio** summer starts on June 21; **e. en** *(edad, vejez)* to reach; *(año nuevo)* to start

(j) *(cantidad)* **¿cuántos entran en un kilo?** how many do you get to the kilo?

(k) **entrarle a alguien** *(sujeto: estado físico, de ánimo)* **le entraron ganas de hablar** he suddenly felt like talking; **me está entrando frío** I'm getting cold; **me entró mucha pena** I was filled with pity

(l) *(sujeto: concepto, asignatura)* **no le entra la geometría** he can't get the hang of geometry; **no le entra en la cabeza que eso no se hace** he can't seem to get it into his head that that sort of behavior is out

(m) *Aut* to engage; **no entra la tercera** it won't go into third gear

2 *vt* (a) *(introducir)* to bring in (b) *(prenda de vestir)* to take in (c) *(acometer)* to approach, to deal with; **a ése no hay por donde entrarle** there's no way of getting through to him

entre 1 *prep* (a) *(en medio de dos)* between; **e. las diez y las once** between ten and eleven o'clock; **e. paréntesis** in parentheses; **e. nosotros** *(en confianza)* between you and me, between ourselves; **discutían e. sí** they were arguing with each other; **era un color e. verde y azul** the color was somewhere between green and blue; **dudo e. ir o quedarme** I don't know o can't decide whether to go or to stay

(b) *(en medio de muchos)* among, amongst; **estaba e. los asistentes** she was among those present; **estuvo e. los mejores** he was one of o amongst the best; **e. otras cosas** among other things

(c) *(indica colaboración o adición)* **lo hicieron e. tres amigos** the three friends did it between them; **e. hombres y mujeres somos más de cien** there are over a hundred of us, men and women together; **e. una cosa y otra** what with one thing and another; **e. que se levanta y se arregla, se le va media mañana** it takes her half the morning just to get up and get ready

(d) *(en divisiones)* **divide veinte e. cuatro** divide twenty by four; **ocho e. dos cuatro** eight divided by two is four

2 entre tanto *loc adv (mientras tanto)* meanwhile

entreabierto *participio ver* **entreabrir**

entreabrir *vt* to half-open

entreacto *nm* intermission

entrecasa *nf Am* **estar de e.** to be casually dressed; **los guisos de e.** home cooking

entrecejo *nm* = space between the eyebrows; **fruncir el e.** to frown

entrecerrado, -a *adj (puerta, ventana)* half-shut

entrecerrar [3] *vt* to half-close

entrechocar [59] **1** *vt (espadas)* to clash

2 *vi (dientes)* to chatter

entrecomillado, -a 1 *adj* in quotation marks

2 *nm* text in quotation marks

entrecomillar *vt* to put in quotation marks

entrecortado, -a *adj (voz, habla)* faltering; *(respiración)* labored; *(señal, sonido)* intermittent

entrecot *(pl* **entrecots** o **entrecotes)** *nm* entrecôte

entrecruzado, -a *adj* interwoven

entrecruzar [14] **1** *vt (entrelazar)* to interweave; *(dedos)* to link together

2 entrecruzarse *vpr* to interweave; **sus destinos se**

entrecruzaban their destinies were intertwined

entredicho *nm* estar en e. to be in doubt; **poner en e.** to question, to call into question

entrega *nf* (**a**) *(acto de entregar)* handing over; *(de pedido, paquete)* delivery; *(de premios)* presentation; **el acto de e. de los Premios Nobel** the Nobel Prize award ceremony; **no acudió a la e. de premios** he didn't attend the prizegiving ceremony; **hacer e. de algo a alguien** to present sb with sth; **e. a domicilio** home delivery; **e. contra reembolso** cash on delivery (**b**) *(dedicación)* devotion (**a** to) (**c**) *(fascículo)* **por entregas** in installments

entregar [38] **1** *vt (dar)* to hand over; *(pedido, paquete)* to deliver; *(examen, informe)* to hand in; *(persona)* to turn over; **al final del curso te entregan un diploma** you're given a diploma at the end of the course; **el presidente entregó los premios a los ganadores** the president handed out *o* presented the prizes to the winners; **no entregarán a los rehenes hasta que no reciban el rescate** they won't turn over *o* release the hostages until they receive the ransom

2 entregarse *vpr* (**a**) *(rendirse) (soldado, ejército)* to surrender; *(criminal)* to turn oneself in; **se entregó a la policía** he gave himself up to the police (**b**) **entregarse a** *(persona, trabajo)* to devote oneself to; *(vicio, pasión)* to give oneself over to

entreguerras: de entreguerras *loc adj* **periodo/literatura de e.** time/literature between the wars

entrelazar [14] *vt* to interlace, to interlink

entrelínea *nf* space between two lines

entremedias, entremedio *adv* in between

entremés *(pl* entremeses*) nm* (**a**) *Culin* **entremeses** hors d'œuvres (**b**) *Lit* = short, amusing one-act play

entremeter 1 *vt* to insert, to put in

2 entremeterse *vpr (inmiscuirse)* to meddle (**en** in)

entremetido, -a 1 *adj* meddling

2 *nm,f* meddler

entremezclar 1 *vt* to mix up

2 entremezclarse *vpr* to mix

entrenador, -ora *nm,f* trainer; *(seleccionador)* director of football

entrenamiento *nm* training

entrenar 1 *vt & vi* to train

2 entrenarse *vpr* to train

entreoír [44] *vt* to half-hear

entrepierna *nf* crotch; *muy Fam* **pasarse algo por la e.** to piss on sth

entreplanta *nf* mezzanine

entresacar [59] *vt* to pick out

entresijos *nmpl* ins and outs

entresuelo *nm* mezzanine

entretanto 1 *adv* meanwhile

2 *nm* **en el e.** in the meantime

entretecho *nm Arg, Chile, Col, Méx* attic, loft

entretejer *vt* to interweave

entretela *nf (de ropa)* inner lining; **entretelas** *(de persona)* innermost heart

entretención *nf Chile* entertainment

entretener [65] **1** *vt* (**a**) *(despistar)* to distract (**b**) *(retrasar)* to hold up, to keep (**c**) *(divertir)* to entertain (**d**) *(mantener)* to keep alive, to sustain

2 entretenerse *vpr* (**a**) *(despistarse)* to get distracted (**b**) *(retrasarse)* to be held up (**c**) *(divertirse)* to amuse oneself

entretenido, -a *adj* entertaining, enjoyable

entretenimiento *nm* (**a**) *(acción)* entertainment (**b**) *(pasatiempo)* pastime

entretiempo 1 *nm CSur* halftime

2 de entretiempo *loc adj* **ropa de e.** spring/fall clothes

entrever [70] **1** *vt* (**a**) *(vislumbrar)* to barely make out; *(por un*

instante) to glimpse (**b**) *(adivinar)* to see signs of

2 entreverse *vpr* to be barely visible; **no se entreve una solución** there's no sign of a solution

entreverado 1 *adj* **tocino e.** bacon

2 *nm Ven* = roast lamb with salt and vinegar

entreverar *CSur* **1** *vt* to mix

2 entreverarse *vpr* to get tangled

entrevero *nm CSur* tangle, mess

entrevista *nf* interview; **e. en exclusiva** exclusive interview; **e. de trabajo** job interview

entrevistado, -a *nm,f* interviewee

entrevistador, -ora *nm,f* interviewer

entrevistar 1 *vt* to interview

2 entrevistarse *vpr* to have a meeting (**con** with)

entrevisto *participio ver* **entrever**

entristecer [46] **1** *vt* to make sad

2 entristecerse *vpr* to become sad

entristecimiento *nm* sadness

entrometerse *vpr* to interfere (**en** in)

entrometido, -a 1 *adj* interfering

2 *nm,f* meddler

entrometimiento *nm* meddling

entromparse *vpr Fam* to get legless

entroncamiento *nm (parentesco)* relationship, connection

entroncar [59] *vi* (**a**) *(emparentarse)* to become related (**con** to) (**b**) *(trenes)* to connect (**c**) *(relacionarse)* to be related (**con** to)

entronización *nf* coronation, enthronement; *Fig* **sus películas son la e. del mal gusto** his movies are the height of bad taste

entronizar [14] *vt* to crown, to enthrone; *Fig* to exalt, to praise to the skies

entropía *nf Fís* entropy

entubar *vt* to fit tubes to, to tube; *Med* to put tubes/a tube into

entuerto *nm* wrong, injustice; **deshacer entuertos** to right wrongs

entumecer [46] **1** *vt* to numb

2 entumecerse *vpr* to become numb

entumecido, -a *adj* numb

entumecimiento *nm* numbness

enturbiar *también Fig* **1** *vt* to cloud

2 enturbiarse *vpr* to become cloudy

entusiasmado, -a *adj* excited; **estamos entusiasmados con la nueva casa** we're really excited about the new house

entusiasmar 1 *vt* (**a**) *(animar)* to fill with enthusiasm (**b**) *(gustar)* **le entusiasma la música** he loves music

2 entusiasmarse *vpr* to get excited (**con** about)

entusiasmo *nm* enthusiasm; **despertar e. (en alguien)** to arouse (sb's) enthusiasm; **aplaudieron con e.** they applauded enthusiastically

entusiasta 1 *adj* enthusiastic

2 *nmf* enthusiast

entusiástico, -a *adj* enthusiastic

enumeración *nf* enumeration, listing

enumerar *vt* to enumerate, to list

enunciación *nf,* **enunciado** *nm* formulation, enunciation

enunciar *vt* to formulate, to enunciate

envainar *vt* to sheathe

envalentonamiento *nm* boldness

envalentonar 1 *vt* to urge on, to fill with courage

2 envalentonarse *vpr* to become daring

envanecer [46] **1** *vt* to make vain

2 envanecerse *vpr* to become vain

envanecimiento *nm* vanity

envarado, -a 1 *adj* stiff, formal

2 *nm,f* stiff *o* formal person

envasado *nm (en bolsas, cajas)* packing; *(en latas)* canning; *(en botellas)* bottling; **e. al vacío** vacuum-packed

envasar *vt (en bolsas, cajas)* to package; *(en latas)* to can; *(en botellas)* to bottle

envase *nm* (**a**) *(envasado) (en bolsas, cajas)* packing; *(en latas)* canning; *(en botellas)* bottling (**b**) *(recipiente)* container; *(botella)* bottle; **e. desechable** disposable container; **e. sin retorno** nonreturnable bottle; **e. (retornable)** returnable empty bottle

envejecer [46] **1** *vi (hacerse viejo)* to grow old; *(parecer viejo)* to age
    2 *vt* to age

envejecido, -a *adj (de edad)* old; *(de aspecto)* aged

envejecimiento *nm* aging

envenenamiento *nm* poisoning

envenenar 1 *vt* to poison
    2 envenenarse *vpr (persona)* to poison oneself; *(relación)* to become bitter

envergadura *nf* (**a**) *(importancia)* size, extent; *(complejidad)* complexity; **una reforma de gran e.** a wide-ranging reform (**b**) *(de ave, avión)* wingspan

envés *(pl* enveses*) nm (de hoja)* reverse (side), back; *(de tela)* wrong side

enviado, -a *nm,f* (**a**) *Pol* envoy (**b**) *Prensa* correspondent; **e. especial** special correspondent

enviar [32] *vt* (**a**) *(mandar, remitir)* to send; *(por barco)* to ship; *(por fax)* to fax; **te enviaré la información por correo electrónico** I'll e-mail the information to you, I'll send you the information by e-mail; **envíale mis saludos a tu madre** give my regards to your mother (**b**) *(persona)* to send; **lo enviaron de embajador** they sent him as an ambassador; **lo enviaron (a) por agua** they sent him for water

enviciar 1 *vt* to addict, to get hooked
    2 enviciarse *vpr* to become addicted

envidia *nf* envy; **tener e. de** to envy

envidiable *adj* enviable

envidiar *vt* to envy

envidioso, -a 1 *adj* envious
    2 *nm,f* envious person

envilecer [46] **1** *vt* to debase
    2 envilecerse *vpr* to become debased

envilecimiento *nm* debasement

envío *nm* (**a**) *Com* dispatch; *(de correo)* delivery; *(de víveres, mercancías)* consignment (**b**) *(paquete)* package

envite *nm* (**a**) *(en el juego)* raise (**b**) *(ofrecimiento)* offer

enviudar *vi* to be widowed

envoltorio *nm,* **envoltura** *nf* wrapper, wrapping

envolvente *adj* enveloping

envolver [41] **1** *vt* (**a**) *(embalar)* to wrap (up); **envuélvamelo para regalo, por favor** could you giftwrap it, please? (**b**) *(enrollar)* to wind (**c**) *(implicar)* **e. a alguien en** to involve sb in (**d**) *(cubrir, rodear)* to envelop, to cover; **la niebla envolvía el valle** the valley was deep in mist
    2 envolverse *vpr* (**a**) **envolverse en** *o* **con algo** *(cubrirse)* to wrap oneself in sth (**b**) **envolverse en algo** *(involucrarse)* to get involved with sth; **se ha envuelto en un asunto de drogas** he has got involved in something to do with drugs

envuelto *participio ver* **envolver**

envuelvo *etc ver* **envolver**

enyesar *vt (brazo, pierna)* to put in a plaster cast; *(pared)* to plaster

enyetar *vt RP Fam* to jinx

enzarzar [14] **1** *vt* to entangle, to embroil
    2 enzarzarse *vpr* **enzarzarse en** to get entangled *o* embroiled in

enzima *nm o nf* enzyme

eólico, -a *adj* **energía eólica** wind energy

epatar *vt* to shock

e.p.d. *(abrev de* **en paz descanse***)* RIP

épica *nf* epic

epicentro *nm* epicenter

épico, -a *adj* epic

epicureísmo *nm* Epicureanism

epicúreo, -a *adj & nm,f* Epicurean

epidemia *nf* epidemic

epidémico, -a *adj* epidemic

epidemiología *nf Med* epidemiology

epidérmico, -a *adj Anat* epidermic

epidermis *nf inv Anat* epidermis

epidural *adj & nf Med* epidural

Epifanía *nf Rel* Epiphany

epífisis *nf inv Anat* pineal gland

epiglotis *nf inv Anat* epiglottis

epígrafe *nm* heading

epigrafía *nf* epigraphy

epigrama *nm* epigram

epilepsia *nf* epilepsy

epiléptico, -a *adj & nm,f* epileptic

epílogo *nm* epilogue

episcopado *nm* (**a**) *(dignidad)* episcopate, episcopacy (**b**) *(territorio)* diocese

episcopal *adj* episcopal; **la Iglesia E.** the Episcopal Church

episódico, -a *adj* episodic, episodical

episodio *nm* (**a**) *(de serie, libro)* episode (**b**) *(suceso)* event

epistemología *nf* epistemology

epístola *nf* (**a**) *Formal (carta)* epistle (**b**) *Rel* Epistle

epistolar *adj Formal* epistolary

epistolario *nm* collected letters

epitafio *nm* epitaph

epitelio *nm Anat* epithelium

epíteto *nm* epithet

epítome *nm* summary, synopsis

e.p.m. *(abrev de* **en propia mano***)* by hand

época *nf* (**a**) *(periodo)* period; **esa é. de su vida** that period in his life; **en aquella é.** at that time; **hacer é.** to become a symbol of its time; **coche de é.** vintage car; **vestido de é.** period dress (**b**) *(estación)* season; **é. de apareamiento** mating season

epónimo, -a 1 *adj* eponymous
    2 *nm* eponym

epopeya *nf (poema)* epic; *(hazaña)* feat

épsilon *nf* epsilon

equidad *nf* fairness

equidistante *adj* equidistant

equidistar *vi* to be equidistant (**de** from)

équido, -a 1 *adj* equine
    2 *nm* = member of the horse family

equilátero, -a *adj Geom* equilateral

equilibrado, -a *adj* (**a**) *(igualado)* balanced (**b**) *(sensato)* sensible

equilibrar 1 *vt* to balance
    2 equilibrarse *vpr* to balance

equilibrio *nm* balance; **mantener algo en e.** to balance sth; **mantener/perder el e.** to keep/lose one's balance; *Fig* **hacer equilibrios** to perform a balancing act; **hay un e. de fuerzas** the forces are evenly balanced; **e. ecológico** ecological balance; **e. de poder** balance of power

equilibrismo *nm (en trapecio)* trapeze; *(en cuerda)* tightrope walking

equilibrista *nmf (trapecista)* trapeze artist; *(en cuerda)* tightrope walker

equino, -a *adj* equine

equinoccial *adj* equinoctial

equinoccio *nm* equinox

equipaje *nm* baggage; **hacer el e.** to pack; **e. de mano** hand luggage

equipamiento *nm (acción)* equipping; *(equipo)* equipment

equipar 1 *vt* **e. a alguien (de** *o* **con)** *(de instrumentos, herramientas)* to equip sb (with); *(de ropa)* to fit sb out (with)
2 equiparse *vpr* to equip oneself (**de** *o* **con** with)

equiparable *adj* comparable (**a** to)

equiparar 1 *vt* to compare
2 equipararse *vpr* to be compared

equipo *nm* (**a**) *(personas)* team; **trabajar en e.** to work as a team; **e. de rescate** rescue team; **e. de salvamento** rescue team (**b**) *(jugadores)* team; **un e. de béisbol** a baseball team; **e. local/visitante** local/visiting team (**c**) *(equipamiento)* equipment; **e. de oficina** office equipment (**d**) *(de novia)* trousseau; *(de soldado)* kit; *(de colegial)* uniform (**e**) *(de música)* system; **e. de alta fidelidad** hi-fi system; **e. de sonido** sound system

equis 1 *adj* X; **un número e. de personas** x number of people
2 *nf inv* **la letra e.** the letter "x"

equitación *nf (deporte)* horseback riding; *(como arte)* horsemanship, equestrianism

equitativo, -a *adj* fair, evenhanded

equivalencia *nf* equivalence

equivalente *adj & nm* equivalent

equivaler [69] *vi* (**a**) *(ser igual)* to be equivalent (**a** to); **300 pies equivalen a unos 90 metros** 300 feet are equivalent to 90 meters; **un dólar equivale a 100 centavos** there are 100 cents in a dollar (**b**) *(significar)* to amount, to be equivalent (**a** to); **aquello equivaldría a una rendición incondicional** that would amount to an unconditional surrender

equivocación *nf* mistake; **por e.** by mistake

equivocado, -a *adj* mistaken

equivocar [59] **1** *vt* **e. algo con algo** to mistake sth for sth; **e. el camino** to take the wrong road; **equivoqué la fecha** I got the date wrong
2 equivocarse *vpr (estar en un error)* to be wrong; *(cometer un error)* to make a mistake; **te equivocas con tu profesor, no es tan mala persona** you're wrong about your teacher, he's not such a bad person; **te equivocas si crees que me voy a asustar** you're mistaken if you think you're going to frighten me; **se equivocó de nombre/puerta** he got the wrong name/door; **equivocarse en algo** to make a mistake in sth; **se equivocó en la suma** he got the total wrong

equívoco, -a 1 *adj* (**a**) *(ambiguo)* ambiguous, equivocal (**b**) *(sospechoso)* suspicious
2 *nm* misunderstanding

era 1 *ver* **ser**
2 *nf* (**a**) *(periodo)* era; **e. cristiana/geológica** Christian/geological era; **la e. espacial** the space age (**b**) *(para trillar)* threshing floor

erario *nm* funds; **e. público** exchequer

Erasmo *n pr* Erasmus

Erasmus [e'rasmus] *nm inv (abrev de* **European Action Scheme for the Mobility of University Students***)* Erasmus; **un estudiante/una beca E.** an Erasmus student/scholarship

ERE ['ere] *nm Esp Econ (abrev de* **expediente de regulación de empleo***)* layoff plan, workforce adjustment plan

erección *nf* erection

eréctil *adj* erectile

erecto, -a *adj* erect

eremita *nmf* hermit

eres *ver* **ser**

ergio *nm Fís (unidad)* erg

ergonomía *nf* ergonomics *(singular)*

ergonómico, -a *adj* ergonomic

erguido, -a *adj* upright

erguir [28] **1** *vt* to raise
2 erguirse *vpr* to rise up

erial *nm* uncultivated land

erice *etc ver* **erizar**

erigir [24] **1** *vt* (**a**) *(construir)* to erect, to build (**b**) *(nombrar)* to name
2 erigirse *vpr* **erigirse en** to set oneself up as

eritema *nm Med* skin rash

Eritrea *n* Eritrea

erizado, -a *adj* (**a**) *(pelo)* on end; *(con púas, espinas)* spiky (**b**) *(lleno)* **e. de** plagued with

erizar [14] **1** *vt* to cause to stand on end
2 erizarse *vpr (pelo)* to stand on end; *(persona)* to stiffen

erizo 1 *nm* (**a**) *(mamífero)* hedgehog (**b**) *(pez)* puffer fish; **e. de mar** sea urchin
2 *adj* **pez e.** puffer fish

ermita *nf* hermitage

ermitaño, -a *nm,f* hermit

erogación *nf Chile (donativo)* contribution

erogar [38] *vt* (**a**) *Am Formal (gastar)* to spend (**b**) *Chile (donar)* to contribute

erógeno, -a *adj* erogenous

eros *nm inv* eros

erosión *nf* erosion

erosionar 1 *vt* to erode
2 erosionarse *vpr* to erode

erosivo, -a *adj* erosive

erótica *nf* **la e. del poder** the thrill of power

erótico, -a *adj* erotic

erotismo *nm* eroticism

erotizar [14] *vt* to eroticize

erradicación *nf* eradication

erradicar [59] *vt* to eradicate

errado, -a *adj (tiro)* wide of the mark, missed; *(razonamiento)* mistaken

errante *adj* wandering

errar [29] **1** *vt (vocación, camino)* to choose wrongly; *(tiro, golpe)* to miss
2 *vi* (**a**) *(vagar)* to wander (**b**) *(equivocarse)* to make a mistake (**c**) *(al tirar)* to miss

errata *nf* misprint; **fe de erratas** errata *pl*

errático, -a *adj* wandering

erre *nf* **e. que e.** stubbornly

erróneo, -a *adj* mistaken

error *nm* mistake, error; **cometer un e.** to make a mistake; **estar en un e.** to be mistaken; **por e.** by mistake; **salvo e. u omisión** errors and omissions excepted; **e. de bulto** huge *o* big mistake; **e. de cálculo** miscalculation; **e. humano** human error; **e. de imprenta** misprint; **e. judicial** miscarriage of justice

ertzaina [er'tʃaina] *nmf Esp* = member of Basque regional police force

Ertzaintza [er'tʃaintʃa] *nf Esp* = Basque regional police force

eructar *vi* to belch

eructo *nm* belch

erudición *nf* erudition

erudito, -a 1 *adj* erudite
2 *nm,f* scholar

erupción *nf* (**a**) *Geol* eruption; **en e.** erupting (**b**) *Med* **e. (cutánea)** rash

eruptivo, -a *adj (roca)* volcanic; *(volcán)* active

es *ver* **ser**

esa *ver* **ese**[2]

ésa *ver* **ése**

esbeltez *nf* slenderness, slimness

esbelto, -a *adj* slender, slim

esbirro *nm* henchman

esbozar [14] *vt* to sketch, to outline; **e. una sonrisa** to give a hint of a smile

esbozo *nm* sketch, outline

escabechado, -a *Culin* **1** *adj* marinated
  2 *nm* marinade

escabechar *vt Culin* to marinate

escabeche *nm Culin* marinade; **en e.** marinaded

escabechina *nf Fam* (**a**) *(destrozo)* destruction (**b**) *Esp (en examen)* huge number of failures; **fue una e.** it was a massacre

escabroso, -a *adj* (**a**) *(abrupto)* rough (**b**) *(obsceno)* risqué (**c**) *(espinoso)* awkward, thorny

escabullirse *vpr* (**a**) *(desaparecer)* to slip away (**de** from) (**b**) *(escurrirse)* **se me escabulló** he slipped out of my hands

escacharrado, -a *adj Esp Fam* bust

escacharrar *Esp Fam* **1** *vt* to bust
  2 escacharrarse *vpr* to bust

escafandra *nf* diving suit; **e. espacial** spacesuit

escafandrista *nmf* diver

escala *nf* (**a**) *(para medir)* scale; *(de colores)* range; **e. Celsius** Celsius (temperature) scale; **e. de Richter** Richter scale; **e. salarial** salary scale; **e. de valores** set of values (**b**) *(de dibujo, mapa)* scale; **una reproducción a e.** a scale model; **un dibujo a e. natural** a life-size drawing; **a e. mundial** on a worldwide scale; **a gran e.** on a large scale (**c**) *(en vuelo)* stopover; *(en crucero)* port of call; **hacer e.** to stop over; **sin e.** nonstop; **e. técnica** refueling stop (**d**) *Mús* scale (**e**) *(escalera)* ladder

escalada *nf* (**a**) *(de montaña)* climb; **e. en roca** rock climbing (**b**) *(de violencia, precios)* escalation, rise (**de** in)

escalador, -ora *nm,f (montañero, ciclista)* climber

escalafón *nm* scale, ladder

escalar *vt* to climb

escaldado, -a *adj* (**a**) *Culin* scalded (**b**) *(receloso)* wary

escaldar **1** *vt* to scald
  2 escaldarse *vpr* to get burned

escaleno *adj Geom* scalene

escalera *nf* (**a**) *(en edificio)* stairs, staircase; *(de mano)* ladder; **e. de caracol** spiral staircase; **e. de incendios** fire escape; **e. mecánica** escalator; **e. de servicio** service stairs; **e. de tijera** stepladder (**b**) *(en naipes)* run; **e. de color** straight flush

escalerilla *nf (de avión)* stairs

escalfado, -a *adj (huevo)* poached

escalfar *vt* to poach

escalinata *nf* staircase

escalofriante *adj* spine-chilling

escalofrío *nm* shiver; **tener escalofríos** to be shivering; **un e. de temor** a shiver of fear; *Fig* **dar escalofríos a alguien** to give sb the shivers

escalón *nm (peldaño)* step; *(travesaño)* rung; *(categoría, nivel)* grade

escalonado, -a *adj* (**a**) *(en el tiempo)* spread out (**b**) *(terreno)* terraced

escalonar *vt* (**a**) *(en el tiempo)* to spread out (**b**) *(terreno)* to terrace

escalope *nm* escalope

escalpelo *nm* scalpel

escama *nf* (**a**) *(de peces, reptiles)* scale (**b**) *(de jabón, piel)* flake

escamado, -a *adj Fam* suspicious, wary

escamar **1** *vt* (**a**) *(pescado)* to scale (**b**) *Fam (causar recelo a)* to make suspicious
  2 escamarse *vpr Fam* to smell a rat, to get suspicious

escamotear *vt* **e. algo a alguien** *(estafar)* to do *o* swindle sb out of sth; *(hurtar)* to rob sb of sth

escampar *v impersonal* to clear up, to stop raining

escanciar *vt* to serve, to pour out

escandalizar [14] **1** *vt* to scandalize, to shock
  2 escandalizarse *vpr* to be shocked

escándalo *nm* (**a**) *(inmoralidad)* scandal; *(indignación)* outrage; **los sueldos de los políticos son un e.** *o* **de e.** politicians' salaries are a scandal *o* a disgrace; **¡esto es un e.!, quiero que me devuelvan el dinero** this is outrageous! I want my money back; **e. sexual** sex scandal (**b**) *(alboroto)* uproar, racket; **armar un e.** to kick up a fuss

escandaloso, -a **1** *adj* (**a**) *(inmoral)* outrageous, shocking (**b**) *(ruidoso)* very noisy
  2 *nm,f* very noisy *o* loud person

Escandinavia *n* Scandinavia

escandinavo, -a *adj & nm,f* Scandinavian

escanear *vt Inform & Med* to scan

escáner *nm Inform & Med (aparato)* scanner; *Med* **hacer un e. a alguien** to give sb a scan

escaño *nm (cargo, asiento)* seat *(in parliament)*

escapada *nf* (**a**) *(huida)* escape, flight; *Dep* breakaway (**b**) *(viaje)* quick trip

escapar **1** *vi* (**a**) *(huir)* to get away, to escape (**de** from) (**b**) *(en carrera)* to break away (**c**) **dejar e.** *(carcajada, grito, suspiro)* to let out; **no quiero dejar e. esta oportunidad para agradecer...** I don't want to let this opportunity pass by without thanking... (**d**) *(quedar fuera del alcance)* **e. a alguien** to be beyond sb; **ese asunto escapa a mis competencias** that matter is outside my sphere of responsibility
  2 escaparse *vpr* (**a**) *(huir)* to get away, to escape (**de** from); **escaparse de casa** to run away from home; **no te escapes, que quiero hablar contigo** don't run off, I want to talk to you (**b**) *(en carrera)* to break away (**c**) *(gas, agua)* to leak (**d**) *(soltar, perder)* **se me escapó la risa/una palabrota** I let out a laugh/an expletive; **se me escapó el tren** I missed the train; **se me escapó la ocasión** the opportunity slipped by (**e**) *(pasar inadvertido)* **a tu madre no se le escapa nada** your mother doesn't miss a thing

escaparate *nm* (store) window, display window

escaparatismo *nm* window dressing

escaparatista *nmf* window dresser

escapatoria *nf* (**a**) *(fuga)* escape; **no tener e.** to have no way out (**b**) *Fam (evasiva)* way (of getting) out

escape *nm (de gas)* leak; *(de coche)* exhaust; *Esp Fam Fig* **salir a e.** to leave in a rush, to rush off

escapismo *nm* escapism

escapista *adj* escapist

escapulario *nm Rel* scapular

escaquearse *vpr Esp Fam* to duck out; **e. de (hacer) algo** to worm one's way out of (doing) sth; **¡no te escaquees!** don't duck out!

escarabajo *nm* beetle; **e. pelotero** dung beetle

escaramuza *nf Mil & Fig* skirmish

escarapela *nf* rosette, cockade

escarbadientes *nm inv* toothpick

escarbar *vt* to scratch, to scrape

escarceos *nmpl* forays; **e. amorosos** flirtations

escarcha *nf* frost

escarchado, -a *adj (fruta)* candied

escarchar *v impersonal* to freeze (over)

escardar *vt* to weed

escarlata *adj & nm* scarlet

escarlatina *nf* scarlet fever

escarmentar [3] *vi* to learn (one's lesson)

escarmiento *nm* lesson; **dar un e. a alguien** to teach sb a lesson; **servir de e.** to serve as a lesson

escarnecer [46] *vt* to mock, to ridicule

escarnecimiento *nm* mockery, ridicule

escarnio *nm* mockery, ridicule

escarola *nf* (curly) endive

escarpado, -a *adj* *(inclinado)* steep; *(abrupto)* craggy

escarpia *nf* = L-shaped hook for hanging pictures etc

escarpín *nm* **(a)** *Am (de bebé)* bootee **(b)** *(de neopreno)* shoe

escasear *vi* to be scarce, to be in short supply

escasez *nf (insuficiencia)* shortage; *(pobreza)* poverty; **e. de mano de obra** labor shortage

escaso, -a *adj* **(a)** *(conocimientos, recursos)* limited, scant; *(tiempo)* short; *(cantidad, número)* low; *(víveres, trabajo)* scarce, in short supply; *(visibilidad, luz)* poor; **joyas de e. valor** jewelry of scant *o* little value; **andar e. de** to be short of; **voy e. de dinero** I don't have much money **(b)** *(casi completo)* **un metro e.** barely a meter; **dura dos horas escasas** it lasts barely two hours; **a un mes e. de las elecciones** with barely a month to go to the elections

escatimar *vt (gastos, comida)* to be sparing with, to skimp on; *(esfuerzo, energías)* to use as little as possible; **no e. gastos** to spare no expense

escatología *nf (sobre excrementos)* scatology

escatológico, -a *adj (de excrementos)* scatological

escay *nm* leatherette

escayola *nf Constr* plaster of Paris; *Med* plaster; **una e.** a plaster cast

escayolado, -a *adj (brazo, pierna)* in a plaster cast

escayolar *vt* to put in a plaster cast

escayolista *nmf* decorative plasterer

escena *nf* **(a)** *(escenario)* stage; *también Fig* **desaparecer de e.** to leave the stage; **llevar a la e.** to dramatize; **poner en e.** to stage; **puesta en e.** staging; **salir a e.** to go on stage **(b)** *(suceso, acto)* scene; *Fam* **hacer una e.** to make a scene; **me hizo una e. de celos** she treated me to one of her jealous rages

escenario *nm* **(a)** *(tablas, escena)* stage; *Cine & Teatro (ambientación)* setting **(b)** *(de suceso)* scene; **el e. del crimen/ accidente** the scene of the crime/accident

escénico, -a *adj* scenic

escenificación *nf (de novela)* dramatization; *(de obra de teatro)* staging

escenificar [59] *vt (novela)* to dramatize; *(obra de teatro)* to stage

escenografía *nf* set design

escenógrafo, -a *nm,f* set designer

escepticismo *nm* skepticism

escéptico, -a 1 *adj* **(a)** *(filósofo)* skeptic **(b)** *(incrédulo)* skeptical
2 *nm,f* skeptic

escindido, -a *adj* **un grupo e.** a breakaway group

escindir 1 *vt* to split
2 escindirse *vpr* to split (**en** into)

escisión *nf (del átomo)* splitting; *(de partido político)* split

esclarecedor, -ora *adj* illuminating

esclarecer [46] *vt* to clear up, to shed light on; **e. los hechos** to establish the facts

esclarecimiento *nm* clearing up, elucidation

esclava *nf (pulsera)* = metal identity bracelet

esclavina *nf* short cape

esclavismo *nm* (system of) slavery

esclavista 1 *adj* proslavery
2 *nmf* supporter of slavery

esclavitud *nf también Fig* slavery

esclavizar [14] *vt también Fig* to enslave

esclavo, -a 1 *adj* enslaved
2 *nm,f también Fig* slave; **es un e. del trabajo** he's a slave to his work; **es un e. del tabaco** he's addicted to tobacco

esclerosis *nf inv Med* sclerosis; **e. múltiple** multiple sclerosis

esclerótica *nf* sclera, sclerotic

esclusa *nf (de canal)* lock; *(compuerta)* floodgate

escoba *nf* **(a)** *(para barrer)* broom **(b)** *(juego de cartas)* = type of card game

escobazo *nm* blow with a broom; *Fig* **echar a alguien a escobazos** to kick sb out

escobilla *nf* brush

escobón *nm* broom

escocedura *nf* **(a)** *(herida)* sore **(b)** *(sensación)* smarting, stinging

escocer [15] **1** *vi (herida, piel)* to sting; **me escuecen los ojos** my eyes are stinging *o* smarting
2 escocerse *vpr* **escocerse de algo** to be hurt by sth

escocés, -esa 1 *adj* Scottish; **tela escocesa** tartan; **whisky e.** scotch whiskey
2 *nm,f (persona) (hombre)* Scot, Scotsman; *(mujer)* Scot, Scotswoman
3 *nm (lengua)* (Scottish) Gaelic

Escocia *n* Scotland

escocido, -a *adj* **estar e.** *(bebé)* to have diaper rash

escoger [52] **1** *vt* to choose; **tiene dos sabores a e.** there are two flavors to choose from; **tener mucho donde e.** to have plenty of choice
2 *vi* to choose; **tenemos que e. entre tres candidatos** we have to choose between three candidates

escogido, -a *adj (elegido)* selected, chosen; *(selecto)* choice, select

escojo *ver* **escoger**

escolanía *nf* choirboys

escolapio, -a *nm,f* = member of the religious order of the Escuelas Pías

escolar 1 *adj* **edad e.** school age
2 *nmf (niño)* pupil, schoolboy; *(niña)* pupil, schoolgirl

escolaridad *nf* schooling

escolarización *nf* schooling

escolarizar [14] *vt* to provide with schools

escolástica *nf* scholasticism

escolástico, -a *adj* scholastic

escollera *nf* breakwater

escollo *nm (en el mar)* reef; *(obstáculo)* stumbling block

escolta 1 *nf (acompañamiento)* escort
2 *nmf (para protección) (persona, grupo)* bodyguard

escoltar *vt* to escort

escombrera *nf (vertedero)* tip

escombro *nm*, **escombros** *nmpl* rubble, debris *(singular)*

esconder 1 *vt* to hide, to conceal
2 esconderse *vpr* to hide (**de** from); **¡rápido, escóndete!** quick, hide!; **no te escondas de mí** don't hide from me; **detrás de su seriedad se esconde un gran sentido del humor** his seriousness conceals a lively sense of humor

escondidas 1 *nfpl RP* **las e.** hide-and-seek
2 a escondidas *loc adv* in secret

escondido, -a 1 *adj (lugar)* secluded
2 *nm Ven* **el e.** *(juego)* hide-and-seek

escondite *nm* **(a)** *(lugar)* hiding place **(b)** *(juego)* hide-and-seek

escondrijo *nm* hiding place

escoñar *Esp muy Fam* **1** *vt* to bust
2 escoñarse *vpr* to get bust

escopeta *nf* shotgun; **e. de aire comprimido** air gun; **e. de cañones recortados** sawed-off shotgun

escopetado, -a, escopeteado, -a *adj Esp Fam* **salir e.** to shoot off

escopetazo *nm (disparo)* shotgun blast; *(herida)* shotgun wound

escopeteado, -a = **escopetado**

escoplo *nm* chisel

escorar *vi Náut* to list

escorbuto *nm* scurvy

escoria *nf* dregs, scum; **la e. de la sociedad** the dregs of society

escorpiano, -a *Am* **1** *adj (zodiaco)* Scorpio; **ser e.** to be (a) Scorpio
2 *nm,f (persona)* Scorpio

escorpio 1 *nm (zodiaco)* Scorpio; *Esp* **ser e.** to be (a) Scorpio
2 *nmf Esp (persona)* Scorpio

escorpión *nm* scorpion

escorzo *nm* foreshortening; **en e.** foreshortened

escota *nf Náut* sheet

escotado, -a *adj (vestido)* low-cut, low-necked

escotadura *nf* low neckline

escotar *vt* to lower the neckline of

escote 1 *nm (de prendas)* neckline; *(de persona)* cleavage; **un e. pronunciado** a plunging neckline
2 a escote *loc adv Esp* **pagar a e.** to go Dutch

escotilla *nf* hatch, hatchway

escozor *nm* stinging

escriba *nm* scribe

escribanía *nf (profesión)* clerkship; *(útiles de escribir)* inkstand

escribano, -a 1 *nm* **(a)** *Hist* scrivener **(b)** *(ave)* bunting
2 *nm,f Andes, CRica, RP (notario)* notary (public)

escribiente *nmf* clerk

escribir 1 *vt* to write; **hace mucho que no me escribe** she hasn't written to me for a long time
2 *vi* to write; **todavía no ha aprendido a e.** he still hasn't learned (how) to write; **e. a lápiz** to write in pencil; **e. a mano** to write by hand; **e. a máquina** to type
3 escribirse *vpr* **(a)** *(personas)* to write to one another **(b)** *(palabras)* **se escribe con "h"** it is spelled with an "h"

escrito, -a 1 *participio ver* **escribir**
2 *adj* written; **por e.** in writing; *Fig* **estaba e. que acabaría mal** it was fated o destined to end badly
3 *nm (texto, composición)* text; *(documento)* document; *(obra literaria)* writing, work; **envió un e. de protesta al ayuntamiento** he sent a letter of protest to the council

escritor, -ora *nm,f* writer; **e. de novela negra** crime writer

escritorio *nm (mueble)* desk, bureau

escritura *nf* **(a)** *(técnica)* writing **(b)** *(sistema de signos)* script; **e. hebrea** Hebrew script **(c)** *Der* **escrituras** deeds **(d)** *Rel* **Sagrada E., Sagradas Escrituras** Holy Scripture

escriturar *vt Der* to execute (by deed); **la propiedad está escriturada por 50.000 dólares** the official purchase price for the property was 50,000 dollars

escroto *nm* scrotum

escrúpulo *nm* **(a)** *(duda, recelo)* scruple; **sin escrúpulos** unscrupulous **(b)** *(minuciosidad)* scrupulousness, great care **(c)** *(aprensión)* qualm; **le da e.** he has qualms about it

escrupuloso, -a *adj* **(a)** *(minucioso)* scrupulous **(b)** *(aprensivo)* particular, fussy

escrutar *vt* **(a)** *(con la mirada)* to scrutinize, to examine **(b)** *(votos)* to count

escrutinio *nm* count *(of votes)*

escuadra *nf* **(a)** *(regla, plantilla)* set square **(b)** *(de buques)* squadron **(c)** *(de soldados)* squad

escuadrilla *nf (de buques, aviones)* squadron

escuadrón *nm (de aviones)* squadron; **e. de cazas** fighter squadron; **e. de la muerte** death squad

escuálido, -a *adj* emaciated

escualo *nm (tiburón)* shark

escucha *nf* listening-in, monitoring; **estar** *o* **permanecer a la e.** to listen in; **escuchas telefónicas** telephone tapping

escuchar 1 *vt* **(a)** *(sonido)* to listen to **(b)** *(consejo, aviso)* to listen to, to heed; **nunca escucha mis consejos** he never listens to my advice; **tú nunca me escuchas** you never listen to me; **escúchame, eso que quieres es imposible** listen, what you want is impossible
2 *vi* to listen

escuchimizado, -a *Esp Fam* **1** *adj* skinny, thin as a rake
2 *nm,f* skinny person

escudar 1 *vt* to shield
2 escudarse *vpr* **escudarse en algo** to hide behind sth, to use sth as an excuse

escudería *nf* team *(in auto racing)*

escudero *nm* squire

escudilla *nf* deep bowl

escudo *nm* **(a)** *(arma)* shield **(b)** *Antes (moneda)* escudo **(c)** *(emblema)* **e. (de armas)** coat of arms

escudriñar *vt (examinar)* to scrutinize, to examine; *(otear)* to search

escuece *ver* **escocer**

escuela *nf* school; **hacer e.** to have a following; **ser de la vieja e.** to be of the old school; **e. de arte** school of art, art school; **e. de arte dramático** drama school; **e. de bellas artes** art school; **e. de comercio** business school; **e. de hostelería** catering school; *Am* **e. de manejo** driving school; **E. Oficial de Idiomas** = Spanish State language-teaching institute; **e. primaria** elementary school; **e. privada** private school; **e. pública** public school; **e. secundaria** high school; **e. taurina** bullfighting school; **e. universitaria** = section of a university which awards diplomas in a vocational discipline (e.g. engineering, business) after three years of study; **e. de verano** summer school

escueto, -a *adj (sucinto)* concise; *(sobrio)* plain, unadorned

escueza *etc ver* **escocer**

escuincle, -a *Méx Fam* **1** *adj* young
2 *nm,f* nipper, kid

esculcar [59] *vt Am (registrar)* to search

esculpir *vt* to sculpt, to carve

escultor, -ora *nm,f* sculptor, *f* sculptress

escultórico, -a *adj* sculptural

escultura *nf* sculpture; **una e. en mármol** a marble sculpture; **una e. en madera** *(pequeña)* a wood carving; *(grande)* a wooden sculpture

escultural *adj* **(a)** *(en arte)* sculptural **(b)** *(persona)* statuesque

escupidera *nf* spittoon

escupir 1 *vi* to spit
2 *vt (sujeto: persona, animal)* to spit out; *(sujeto: volcán, chimenea)* to belch out; **e. a alguien** to spit at sb; **le escupió en la cara** she spat in his face; **las ametralladoras escupían fuego** the machine guns were blazing away

escupitajo *nm Fam* gob, spit

escurreplatos *nm inv* dish rack, plate rack

escurridero *nm* drainboard

escurridizo, -a *adj también Fig* slippery

escurridor *nm* colander

escurrir 1 *vt (platos, verdura)* to drain; *(ropa)* to wring out; *Fam Fig* **e. el bulto** *(trabajo)* to get out of it; *(cuestión)* to evade the issue
2 *vi* **(a)** *(gotear)* to drip; **deja los platos a e.** leave the dishes to drain **(b)** *(resbalar)* to slide; **una lágrima escurrió por su mejilla** a tear slid down her cheek
3 escurrirse *vpr* **(a)** *Fam (escabullirse)* to get away, to escape **(b)** *(resbalarse)* **se me escurrió de las manos** it slipped through my fingers

escusado *nm Euf* **el e.** *(retrete)* the bathroom

escúter *nm* (motor) scooter

esdrújula *nf Gram* word stressed on the third-to-last syllable

esdrújulo, -a *adj Gram* stressed on the third-to-last syllable

ese[1] *nf (figura)* zigzag; **hacer eses** *(en carretera)* to zigzag; *(al andar)* to stagger about

ese[2]**, -a** *(pl* **esos, -as)** *adj demostrativo* **(a)** *(en general)* that, *pl* those **(b)** *Fam Pey* **el hombre e. no me inspira confianza** I don't trust that man

ése, -a *(pl* **ésos, -as)** *pron demostrativo*

Note that **ése** and its various forms can be written without an accent when there is no risk of confusion with the adjective.

(a) *(en general) (singular)* that one; *(plural)* those (ones); **ponte otro vestido, é. no te queda bien** put on another dress, that one doesn't suit you; **estos pasteles están muy buenos, pero ésos me gustan más** these cakes are very good but I like those ones better **(b)** *Fam* **é. fue el que me pegó** that's the one who hit me **(c)** *(expresiones)* **¡a é.!** stop that man!; **ni por ésas** not even then; **no me lo vendió ni por ésas** even then he wouldn't sell it to me

esencia *nf* essence; **quinta e.** quintessence

esencial *adj* essential; **su participación fue e. en el proyecto** her participation was essential to the project; **lo e.** the fundamental thing; **en lo e. coincidimos** we agree on the basic points *o* the essentials; **no e.** nonessential, inessential

esfera *nf* **(a)** *(figura)* sphere; **e. celeste** celestial sphere; **e. terrestre** (terrestrial) globe **(b)** *(de reloj)* face **(c)** *(círculo social)* circle; **las altas esferas de la política** high political circles

esférico, -a **1** *adj* spherical

2 *nm Dep* ball

esfero *nm*, **esferográfico** *nm Col, Ecuad* ballpoint pen

esfinge *nf* sphinx

esfínter *nm* sphincter

esforzar [31] **1** *vt (voz, vista)* to strain; **tuve que e. la voz** I had to strain my voice

2 esforzarse *vpr* to make an effort; **tienes que esforzarte más si quieres aprobar** you'll have to make more of an effort if you want to pass; **nos esforzamos, pero fue imposible ganarlos** we tried very hard, but they were impossible to beat; **no te esfuerces, no puede oírte** don't bother (shouting), she can't hear you; **esforzarse en** *o* **por hacer algo** to try very hard to do sth, to do one's best to do sth

esfuerzo *nm* effort; **hacer esfuerzos, hacer un e.** to make an effort, to try hard; **estoy haciendo esfuerzos por no llorar** I'm trying hard not to cry; **haz un último e., ya verás como ahora lo consigues** make one last attempt, you'll do it this time!; **sin e.** effortlessly

esfumarse *vpr* **(a)** *(esperanzas, posibilidades)* to fade away **(b)** *Fam (persona)* to vanish, to disappear; **¡esfúmate!** beat it!, get lost!

esgrima *nf* fencing

esgrimir *vt* **(a)** *(arma)* to brandish, to wield **(b)** *(argumento, datos)* to use, to employ

esguince *nm* sprain; **hacerse un e. en el tobillo** to sprain one's ankle; **e. cervical** whiplash (injury)

eslabón *nm (de cadena)* link; **el e. perdido** the missing link

eslabonar *vt también Fig* to link together

eslalon *(pl* **eslalons)** *nm Dep* slalom; **e. gigante** giant slalom

eslavo, -a **1** *adj* slav, Slavonic

2 *nm,f (persona)* Slav

3 *nm (lengua)* Slavonic

eslip *(pl* **eslips)** *nm* briefs

eslogan *nm* slogan

eslora *nf Náut* length

eslovaco, -a **1** *adj & nm,f* Slovak, Slovakian

2 *nm (lengua)* Slovak

Eslovaquia *n* Slovakia

Eslovenia *n* Slovenia

esloveno, -a **1** *adj & nm,f* Slovene

2 *nm (lengua)* Slovene

esmaltado, -a **1** *adj* enameled

2 *nm* enameling

esmaltar *vt* to enamel

esmalte *nm* **(a)** *(en dentadura, cerámica)* enamel; *(de uñas)* nail varnish *o* polish **(b)** *(objeto, joya)* enamel

esmerado, -a *adj (persona)* painstaking, careful; *(trabajo)* carefully done, polished

esmeralda **1** *nf (piedra preciosa)* emerald

2 *adj & nm inv* emerald

esmerarse *vpr (esforzarse)* to take great pains (**en** over)

esmeril *nm* emery

esmerilado, -a *adj (pulido)* polished with emery; *(translúcido)* ground

esmerilar *vt (pulir)* to polish with emery

esmero *nm* great care

esmirriado, -a *adj Fam* puny, weak

esmoquin *nm* tuxedo

esnifada *nf Fam (de cocaína)* snort; *(de cola)* sniff

esnifar *vt Fam (cocaína)* to snort; *(cola)* to sniff

esnob *(pl* **esnobs)** **1** *adj* **es muy e.** he's always trying to look trendy and sophisticated

2 *nmf* = person who wants to appear trendy and sophisticated

esnobismo *nm* **sólo lo hace por e.** he's just doing that because he thinks it's trendy and sophisticated

ESO ['eso] *nf Esp (abrev de* **Enseñanza Secundaria Obligatoria)** = mainstream secondary education for pupils aged 12-16

eso *pron demostrativo (neutro)* that; **e. es la Torre Eiffel** that's the Eiffel Tower; **e. es lo que yo pienso** that's just what I think; **e. que propones es irrealizable** what you're proposing is impossible; **e. de vivir solo no me gusta** I don't like the idea of living on my own; **¡e., e.!** that's right!, yes!; **¡e. es!** that's it; **¿cómo es e.?, ¿y e.?** *(¿por qué?)* how come?; **para e. es mejor no ir** if that's all it is, you might as well not go; **por e. vine** that's why I came; **a e. de** (at) around *o* about; **a e. del mediodía** around about midday; **en e.** just then, at that very moment; **y e. que** even though

esófago *nm* esophagus

esos, -as *ver* **ese**[2]

ésos, -as *ver* **ése**

esotérico, -a *adj* esoteric

esoterismo *nm* **(a)** *(impenetrabilidad)* esoteric nature **(b)** *(ciencias ocultas)* esotericism

espabilado, -a *adj (avispado)* quick-witted, on the ball

espabilar **1** *vt* **(a)** *(despertar)* to wake up **(b)** *(avispar)* **e. a alguien** to sharpen sb's wits

2 espabilarse *vpr* **(a)** *(despertarse)* to wake up, to brighten up **(b)** *(darse prisa)* to get a move on **(c)** *(avisparse)* to sharpen one's wits

espachurrar *Fam* **1** *vt* to squash

2 espachurrarse *vpr* to get squashed

espaciado, -a *adj* at regular intervals

espaciador *nm* space bar

espacial *adj* **coordenadas espaciales** spatial coordinates; **cohete/lanzadera e.** space rocket/shuttle

espaciar *vt* to space out

espacio *nm* **(a)** *(sitio, capacidad, extensión)* space; **no tengo mucho e.** I don't have much room; **a doble e.** *(en texto)* double-spaced; **por e. de** over a period of; **e. aéreo** air space; **e. en blanco** blank; **e. verde** green area *(in town or city)*; **e. vital** living space; *Inform* **e. Web** Web space **(b)** *Astron* **el e. (exterior)** (outer) space; **la conquista del e. es todavía un sueño** the conquest of (outer) space is still a dream **(c)** *Rad & TV (programa independiente)* program; *(dentro de otro programa)* slot; **e. electoral** political advertisement; **e. publicitario** advertising slot

espacioso, -a *adj* spacious

espada 1 *nf* **(a)** *(arma)* sword; **estar entre la e. y la pared** to be between the devil and the deep blue sea; **ser una e. de dos filos** *o* **de doble filo** to be a double-edged *o* two-edged sword; **la e. de Damocles** the sword of Damocles; **el pago de la hipoteca era una e. de Damocles para la familia** the family always had the mortgage payments hanging over them **(b)** *(naipe)* = any card in the "espadas" suit; **espadas** = suit in Spanish deck of cards, with the symbol of a sword
  2 *nm Taurom* matador
  3 *adj inv* **pez e.** swordfish

espadachín *nm* swordsman

espadaña *nf* **(a)** *(planta)* cattail **(b)** *(campanario)* bell gable

espagueti *nm* piece of spaghetti; **espaguetis** spaghetti *(singular)*; *Fam Fig* **estar como un e.** to be as thin as a rail

espalda *nf* **(a)** *(del cuerpo)* back; **caer de e.** to fall flat on one's back; **cargado de espaldas** round-shouldered; **de espaldas a alguien** with one's back turned on sb; **lo vi de espaldas** I saw him from behind; **tumbarse de espaldas** to lie (flat) on one's back; **por la e.** from behind; *Fig* behind one's back; **dar la e. a alguien** to have one's back to sb
  (b) *(expresiones)* **cubrirse las espaldas** to cover oneself; **echarse algo sobre las espaldas** to take sth on; **hablar de alguien a sus espaldas** to talk about sb behind their back; **hacer algo a espaldas de alguien** to do sth behind sb's back; **tirar** *o* **tumbar de espaldas** to be amazing *o* stunning; **volver la e. a alguien** to turn one's back on sb
  (c) *(en natación)* backstroke; **nadar a e.** to do the backstroke

espaldarazo *nm* blow to the back; **eso le dio el e. (definitivo)** that finally earned her widespread recognition

espalderas *nfpl* stall bars

espaldilla *nf* shoulder *(of lamb etc)*

espantada *nf* **dar** *o* **pegar una e.** *(caballo)* to bolt; *Fam Fig* **dar la e.** to split

espantadizo, -a *adj* nervous, easily frightened

espantajo *nm* **(a)** *(espantapájaros)* scarecrow **(b)** *(persona fea)* fright, sight

espantapájaros *nm inv* scarecrow

espantar 1 *vt* **(a)** *(ahuyentar)* to frighten *o* scare away; **espanta a las moscas con el rabo** it keeps the flies off with its tail **(b)** *(asustar)* to frighten, to scare **(c)** *(pasmar)* to appall, to shock
  2 *vi (asustar)* **esa casa espanta sólo de verla** that house is frightening just to look at
  3 espantarse *vpr* **(a)** *(ser ahuyentado)* to get frightened *o* scared **(b)** *(pasmarse)* to be appalled *o* shocked

espanto *nm* **(a)** *(miedo)* fright; **le tiene e. a las arañas** he's frightened of spiders **(b)** *(pasmo)* **¡qué e.!** how terrible!; *Fam* **¡qué e. de traje!** what an awful *o* a frightful suit!; **hacía un calor de e.** the heat was appalling

espantoso, -a *adj* **(a)** *(terrorífico)* horrific **(b)** *(enorme)* terrible **(c)** *(feísimo)* frightful, horrible

España *n* Spain

español, -ola 1 *adj* Spanish
  2 *nm,f (persona)* Spaniard; **los españoles** the Spanish, Spaniards
  3 *nm (lengua)* Spanish

españolada *nf Pey* = exaggerated portrayal of Spain

españolismo *nm* **(a)** *(apego, afecto)* affinity for things

Spanish **(b)** *(carácter, naturaleza)* Spanishness, Spanish character

españolizar [14] **1** *vt* to make Spanish, to Hispanicize
  2 españolizarse *vpr* to adopt Spanish ways

esparadrapo *nm* Band-Aid®

esparcimiento *nm* **(a)** *(diseminación)* scattering **(b)** *(ocio)* relaxation, time off

esparcir [72] **1** *vt (extender)* to spread; *(diseminar)* to scatter
  2 esparcirse *vpr* to spread (out)

espárrago *nm* stalk of asparagus; **espárragos** asparagus; **espárragos trigueros** wild asparagus; *Fam* **¡vete a freír espárragos!** get lost!

esparraguera *nf* asparagus (plant)

espartano, -a 1 *adj (de Esparta)* Spartan; *(sobrio)* spartan
  2 *nm,f* Spartan

esparto *nm* esparto (grass)

espasmo *nm* spasm

espasmódico, -a *adj* spasmodic

espatarrarse *vpr Fam* to sprawl *(with one's legs wide open)*

espátula *nf* **(a)** *Culin & Med* spatula; *Arte* palette knife; *Constr* bricklayer's trowel; *(de empapelador)* stripping knife **(b)** *(ave)* spoonbill

especia *nf* spice; **un plato con muchas especias** a very spicy dish

especial 1 *adj* **(a)** *(adecuado, excepcional)* special; **hoy es un día e., celebramos nuestro aniversario** today's a special day, we're celebrating our anniversary; **tienen e. interés en conocerte** they're especially interested in meeting you; **e. para** specially for **(b)** *(peculiar)* peculiar, strange
  2 *nm (programa)* special; **un e. informativo** a news special
  3 en especial *loc adv* especially, particularly; **¿alguno en e.?** anyone in particular?

especialidad *nf* **(a)** *(culinaria)* specialty, specialty; **e. de la casa** specialty of the house **(b)** *(en estudios)* major; **estudia la e. de derecho canónico** she's specializing in canon law; **este tema no es de mi e.** this subject doesn't come into my specialist field; **son cinco años de carrera y tres de e.** there are five years of university study and three years of specialization

especialista 1 *adj* specializing **(en** in)
  2 *nmf* **(a)** *(experto)* specialist **(en** in) **(b)** *Cine* stuntman, *f* stuntwoman

especialización *nf* specialization

especializado, -a *adj* specialized **(en** in); *(mano de obra)* skilled; **un abogado e. en casos de divorcio** a lawyer specializing in divorce cases

especializar [14] **1** *vt* to specialize
  2 especializarse *vpr* to specialize **(en** in)

especialmente *adv* especially, specially

especie *nf* **(a)** *(animal)* species *(singular)*; **e. endémica** endemic species; **e. protegida** protected species; **e. en vías de extinción** endangered species **(b)** *(clase)* kind, sort; **pagar en e.** to pay in kind

especiería *nf* spice store

especiero *nm* spice rack

especificación *nf* specification

especificar [59] *vt* to specify

especificidad *nf* specificity

específico, -a 1 *adj* specific
  2 *nmpl Med* patent medicine

espécimen *(pl* **especímenes)** *nm* specimen

espectacular *adj* spectacular

espectacularidad *nf* spectacular nature

espectáculo *nm* **(a)** *(función)* show, performance; **espectáculos** *(sección periodística)* entertainment section; **el mundo del e.** (the world of) show business; **e. de guiñol** puppet show; **e. pirotécnico** firework display; **e. de**

variedades variety show (**b**) *(suceso, escena)* sight; **ver cómo le pegaban fue un penoso e.** seeing them hit him was a terrible sight; *Fam* **dar el e.** to cause a scene

espectador *nmf* (**a**) *(de televisión)* viewer; *(de cine, teatro)* member of the audience; *(de espectáculo deportivo)* spectator; **los espectadores** *(de cine, teatro)* the audience (**b**) *(de suceso, discusión)* onlooker; **yo fui un mero e.** I was just an onlooker

espectral *adj* (**a**) *Fís* spectral (**b**) *Fig* ghostly

espectro *nm* (**a**) *Fís* spectrum (**b**) *(fantasma)* specter, ghost

especulación *nf* speculation

especulador, -ora 1 *adj* speculating
2 *nm,f* speculator

especular *vi* (**a**) *(reflexionar, formular hipótesis)* to speculate (**sobre** about) (**b**) **e. en** *(comerciar, traficar)* to speculate on

especulativo, -a *adj* speculative

espejismo *nm* mirage; *Fig* illusion

espejo *nm* mirror; **mirarse al** *o* **en el e.** to look at oneself in the mirror; **como un e.** *(muy limpio)* spotless; **e. lateral** side mirror; **e. retrovisor** rearview mirror

espeleología *nf* spelunking, caving, *Espec* speleology

espeleólogo, -a *nm,f* spelunker, caver, *Espec* speleologist

espeluznante *adj* hair-raising, lurid

espera *nf* wait; **después de una e. prudencial, partimos sin él** after waiting for a reasonable amount of time, we left without him; **la e. se nos hizo interminable** the waiting seemed endless; **en e. de, a la e. de** waiting for, awaiting; **seguimos a la e. de su respuesta** *(en cartas)* we await your reply; **en e. de lo que decida el jurado** while awaiting the jury's decision

esperanto *nm* Esperanto

esperanza *nf* *(deseo, ganas)* hope; *(confianza, expectativas)* expectation; **dar esperanzas a** to encourage, to give hope to; **mantengo la e. de volver a verla** I still hope to see her again; **perder la e.** to lose hope; **tengo e. de que todo se arregle** I have hopes that everything will be sorted out; **tener e. de hacer algo** to hope to be able to do sth; *Prov* **la e. es lo último que se pierde** where there's life there's hope; **e. de vida** life expectancy

esperanzado, -a *adj* hopeful

esperanzador, -ora *adj* encouraging, hopeful

esperanzar [14] **1** *vt* to give hope to, to encourage
2 esperanzarse *vpr* to be encouraged

esperar 1 *vt* (**a**) *(aguardar)* to wait for; **te esperaremos en el aeropuerto** we'll meet you at the airport, we'll be waiting for you at the airport; **e. a que alguien haga algo** to wait for sb to do sth

(**b**) *(tener esperanza de)* to hope; **espero poder ayudar** I hope I can be of some help; **e. que** to hope that; **espero que sí/no** I hope so/not; **e. hacer algo** to hope to do sth

(**c**) *(tener confianza en)* to expect; **no esperábamos esta reacción** we didn't expect this reaction; **e. algo de alguien** to expect sth from sb, to hope for sth from sb; **como era de e.** as was to be expected

(**d**) *(ser inevitable)* to await, to be in store for; **le esperan dificultades** many difficulties await him; *Fam* **¡me espera una buena en casa!** I'm in for it when I get home!

2 *vi (aguardar)* to wait; **espera, que ya voy** wait a minute, I'm coming; *Prov* **quien espera desespera** a watched pot never boils

3 esperarse *vpr* (**a**) *(imaginarse, figurarse)* to expect; **se esperaban lo peor** they expected *o* feared the worst (**b**) *(aguardar)* to wait; **esperarse a que alguien haga algo** to wait for sb to do sth (**c**) *(uso impersonal)* to be expected; **se esperan lluvias en toda la región** rain is expected *o* there will be rain across the whole region; **se espera que acudan varios miles de personas** several thousand people are expected to attend

esperma *nm o nf (semen)* sperm

espermatozoide, espermatozoo *nm* sperm, spermatozoon

espermicida 1 *adj* spermicidal
2 *nm* spermicide

esperpéntico, -a *adj* grotesque

esperpento *nm (persona)* grotesque sight; *(cosa)* absurdity, piece of nonsense

espesar *vt & vi* to thicken

espeso, -a *adj (crema, pintura, muro)* thick; *(bosque, niebla)* dense; *(nieve)* deep

espesor *nm* (**a**) *(grosor)* thickness; **tiene 2 metros de e.** it's 2 meters thick (**b**) *(densidad) (de niebla, bosque)* density; *(de nieve)* depth

espesura *nf* (**a**) *(vegetación)* thicket (**b**) *(grosor)* thickness; *(densidad)* density

espetar *vt* (**a**) *(palabras)* to blurt out, to tell straight out (**b**) *(carne)* to skewer

espía *nmf* spy; **avión e.** spy plane

espiar [32] *vt* to spy on

espiga *nf* (**a**) *(de cereal)* ear (**b**) *(en telas)* herringbone (**c**) *(pieza) (de madera)* peg; *(de hierro)* pin

espigado, -a *adj* (**a**) *(persona)* tall and slim (**b**) *(cereal)* ripe

espigar [38] **1** *vt (información)* to glean
2 espigarse *vpr* (**a**) *(persona)* to shoot up (**b**) *(planta)* to go to seed

espigón *nm* breakwater

espiguilla *nf* herringbone

espín *nm Fís* spin

espina *nf (de pez)* bone; *(de planta)* thorn; *(astilla)* splinter; *Fam* **me da mala e.** it makes me uneasy, there's something fishy about it; **todavía tengo clavada la e. de no haber ido a la universidad** I still feel bad about not having gone to college; *Fig* **sacarse una e.** *(desquitarse)* to settle an old score; *(desahogarse)* to relieve a long-standing frustration; **e. dorsal** spine; *Fig* backbone

espinaca *nf* **e.(s)** spinach

espinal *adj* spinal

espinazo *nm* spine, backbone; *Fig* **doblar el e.** *(humillarse)* to kow-tow; *(trabajar duro)* to put one's back into it

espinilla *nf* (**a**) *(hueso)* shin, shinbone (**b**) *(grano)* blackhead

espinillera *nf* shin guard *o* pad

espino *nm* (**a**) *(planta)* hawthorn (**b**) *(alambre)* barbed wire

espinoso, -a *adj también Fig* thorny

espionaje *nm* espionage; **e. industrial** industrial espionage

espiración *nf* exhalation, breathing out

espiral *nf también Fig* spiral; **en e.** *(escalera, forma)* spiral; *Econ* **e. inflacionaria,** *Esp* **e. inflacionista** inflationary spiral

espirar *vt & vi* to exhale, to breathe out

espiritismo *nm* spiritualism

espiritista *adj* spiritualist

espíritu *nm* (**a**) *(mente, alma)* spirit; *Rel* soul; **E. Santo** Holy Ghost (**b**) *(fantasma)* ghost (**c**) *(actitud)* spirit; **tener e. de contradicción** to be contrary; **e. deportivo** sporting spirit; **e. de equipo** team spirit; **e. de venganza** desire for vengeance (**d**) *(carácter)* spirit; **el e. de la época** the spirit of the age (**e**) *(ánimo)* **levantar el e. a alguien** to lift *o* raise sb's spirits

espiritual *adj & nm* spiritual

espiritualidad *nf* spirituality

espita *nf* spigot, faucet

esplendidez *nf* (**a**) *(generosidad)* generosity (**b**) *(magnificencia)* splendor

espléndido, -a *adj* (**a**) *(magnífico)* splendid, magnificent (**b**) *(generoso)* generous, lavish

esplendor *nm* (a) *(magnificencia)* splendor (b) *(apogeo)* greatness

esplendoroso, -a *adj* magnificent

espliego *nm* lavender

espolear *vt también Fig* to spur on

espoleta *nf (de proyectil)* fuse

espolón *nm* (a) *(de ave)* spur (b) *Arquit* buttress

espolvorear *vt* to dust, to sprinkle

esponja *nf* sponge; **beber como una e.** to drink like a fish

esponjar *vt* to fluff up

esponjosidad *nf (de toalla)* fluffiness; *(de bizcocho)* sponginess

esponjoso, -a *adj (toalla, jersey)* fluffy; *(bizcocho)* light, fluffy

esponsales *nmpl* betrothal

esponsorizar [14] *vt* to sponsor

espontaneidad *nf* spontaneity

espontáneo, -a 1 *adj* spontaneous
2 *nm,f (en los toros)* = spectator who tries to join in a bullfight

espora *nf* spore

esporádico, -a *adj* sporadic

esport [es'por]: **de esport** *loc adj* **chaqueta de e.** sports jacket; **ropa de e.** casual clothes

esposa 1 *nf Am (anillo)* episcopal ring
2 esposas *nfpl (objeto)* handcuffs; **ponerle las e. a alguien** to handcuff sb

esposado, -a *adj* handcuffed

esposar *vt* to handcuff

esposo, -a *nm,f* husband, *f* wife; **los esposos salieron de la iglesia** the couple *o* the newlyweds left the church

espot [es'pot] *(pl* **espots**) *nm* **e. (publicitario)** (television) commercial *o* ad

espray *nm* spray

esprint *(pl* **esprints**) *nm* sprint

esprintar [esprintar] *vi* to sprint

esprínter *nmf* sprinter

espuela *nf* (a) *(en el talón)* spur (b) *Fam (última copa)* **tomar la e.** to have one for the road

espuerta *nf (recipiente)* basket; **a espuertas** by the sackful *o* bucket

espuma *nf (burbujas)* foam; *(de jabón)* lather; *(de olas)* surf; *(de cerveza)* head; *(de un caldo)* scum; *(para pelo)* (styling) mousse; **crecer como la e.** *(negocio)* to go from strength to strength; *también Fig* **echar e. por la boca** to foam at the mouth; **e. de afeitar** shaving foam; **e. de baño** bubble bath; **e. de poliuretano** polyurethane foam

espumadera *nf* skimmer

espumar *vt (caldo)* to skim

espumarajo *nm* froth, foam; *también Fig* **echar espumarajos (por la boca)** to foam at the mouth; **el mar estaba lleno de espumarajos** there was lots of dirty foam on the sea

espumillón *nm* tinsel

espumoso, -a 1 *adj (baño)* foamy, bubbly; *(cerveza)* frothy, foaming; *(vino)* sparkling; *(jabón)* lathery
2 *nm* sparkling wine

espurio, -a *adj (falso)* spurious, false; *(bastardo)* illegitimate

esputar *vi* to cough up *o* spit phlegm

esputo *nm (flema)* spittle; *Med* sputum

esqueje *nm* cutting *(of plant)*

esquela *nf Esp* funeral notice *(in newspaper)*

esquelético, -a *adj Anat* skeletal; *Fam (muy delgado)* skinny; **estar e.** to be extremely thin

esqueleto *nm* (a) *(de persona)* skeleton; *Fam* **menear** *o* **mover el e.** to boogie (on down); **estar como un e.** to be skin and bone (b) *(armazón)* framework; *(de novela, argumento)* outline

esquema *nm (gráfico)* diagram; *(resumen)* outline

esquemático, -a *adj (dibujo, plano)* schematic; **muy e.** *(explicación, resumen)* simplified

esquematizar [14] *vt* (a) *(en forma de gráfico)* to draw a diagram of (b) *(resumir)* to outline

esquí *(pl* **esquíes** *o* **esquís**) *nm* (a) *(tabla)* ski (b) *(deporte)* skiing; **e. acuático** waterskiing; **e. alpino** downhill skiing; **e. de descenso** downhill skiing; **e. de fondo** cross-country skiing; **e. náutico** waterskiing; **e. nórdico** cross-country skiing

esquiador, -ora *nm,f* skier

esquiar [32] *vi* to ski; **van a e. a los Alpes** they're going skiing in the Alps

esquila *nf* (a) *(cencerro)* cowbell; *(campana pequeña)* small bell (b) *(acción de esquilar)* shearing

esquilador, -ora *nm,f* sheepshearer

esquilar *vt* to shear

esquilmar *vt (recursos)* to overexploit

esquimal 1 *adj & nmf* Eskimo
2 *nm (lengua)* Eskimo

esquina *nf* (a) *(en calle)* corner; *también Fig* **a la vuelta de la e.** just around the corner; **doblar la e.** to turn the corner; **en la e.** on the corner; **hacer e. (con)** to be on the corner (of) (b) *(en fútbol)* corner; **saque de e.** corner (kick)

esquinado, -a *adj* on the corner

esquinazo *nm* corner; *Esp* **dar (el) e. a alguien** to give sb the slip

esquirla *nf (de loza, hueso)* splinter

esquirol *nmf Pey* scab

esquivar *vt (persona, discusión)* to avoid; *(golpe)* to dodge

esquivez *nf* shyness

esquivo, -a *adj* shy

esquizofrenia *nf* schizophrenia

esquizofrénico, -a *adj & nm,f* schizophrenic

esquizoide *adj* schizoid

esta *ver* **este**

ésta *ver* **éste**

estabilidad *nf* stability; **e. de precios** price stability

estabilización *nf* stabilization

estabilizador, -ora 1 *adj* stabilizing
2 *nm (de avión, barco)* stabilizer

estabilizante *nm (aditivo)* stabilizer

estabilizar [14] **1** *vt* to stabilize
2 estabilizarse *vpr* to stabilize, to become stable

estable *adj* (a) *(firme)* stable (b) *(permanente) (huésped)* permanent; *(cliente)* regular

establecer [46] **1** *vt* (a) *(fijar, expresar)* to establish; **no lograba e. contacto con la torre de control** he couldn't make *o* establish contact with the control tower; **la policía no ha podido e. la causa de su muerte** the police have been unable to establish *o* determine the cause of death; **las normas del club establecen que...** the club rules state that... (b) *(instalar) (colonia, poblado)* to establish; *(negocio, campamento)* to set up
2 establecerse *vpr* (a) *(instalarse)* to settle; **se establecieron en Madrid** they settled in Madrid, they set up home in Madrid (b) *(poner un negocio)* to set up a business; **voy a establecerme por mi cuenta** I'm going to set up on my own *o* set up my own business

establecido, -a *adj (convencional)* established

establecimiento *nm* (a) *(tienda, organismo)* establishment; **e. de enseñanza** educational institution (b) *(de normas, hechos)* establishment; *(de récord)* setting (c) *(de negocio, colonia)* setting up (d) *(de emigrantes, colonos)* settlement

establo *nm (para caballos)* stable; *(para vacas)* cowshed

estaca *nf* (a) *(para clavar, delimitar)* stake; *(de tienda de* *campaña)* peg; **le clavó una e. en el corazón** she drove a stake through his heart (**b**) *(garrote)* cudgel

estacada *nf* **dejar a alguien en la e.** to leave sb in the lurch; **quedarse en la e.** to be left in the lurch

estación *nf* (**a**) *(edificio)* station; **iré a esperarte a la e.** I'll meet you at the station; **e. de autobuses** bus station; **e. espacial** space station; **e. de esquí** ski resort; **e. meteorológica** weather station; **e. de metro** subway station; **e. de servicio** service station; *Inform* **e. de trabajo** workstation; **e. de tren** railway station (**b**) *(del año, temporada)* season; **la e. de las lluvias** the rainy season

estacional *adj (del año, de temporada)* seasonal

estacionamiento *nm* (**a**) *(acción)* parking; **e. indebido** illegal parking (**b**) *Am (lugar)* parking lot

estacionar 1 *vt (aparcar)* to park; **prohibido e.** *(en letrero)* no parking
2 estacionarse *vpr Am (aparcar)* to park

estacionario, -a *adj (inmóvil)* stationary; *Econ* stagnant

estadía *nf Am* stay; **planeó una e. de tres días en Lima** he planned a three-day stop in Lima

estadio *nm* (**a**) *Dep* stadium; **e. de fútbol** soccer stadium (**b**) *(fase)* stage

estadista *nmf* statesman, *f* stateswoman

estadística *nf* (**a**) *(ciencia)* statistics *(singular)* (**b**) *(dato)* statistic

estadístico, -a 1 *adj* statistical
2 *nm,f* statistician

estado *nm* (**a**) *(situación, condición)* state; **el e. de las carreteras** road conditions; **su e. es grave** *(enfermo)* his condition is serious; **estar en buen/mal e.** *(vehículo, terreno)* to be in good/bad condition; *(alimento, bebida)* to be fresh/spoiled; **en e. de alerta** on (the) alert; **estar en e. (de esperanza** o **buena esperanza)** to be expecting; **quedarse en e.** to become pregnant; **e. anímico** o **de ánimo** state of mind; **e. de bienestar** welfare state; **e. civil** marital status; **en e. de coma** in a coma; **e. de cuentas** statement of accounts; **e. de excepción** o **emergencia** state of emergency; **e. de salud** (state of) health; **e. de sitio** state of siege
(**b**) *(gobierno)* state; **el E.** the state; *Mil* **E. Mayor** general staff
(**c**) *(país, división territorial)* state; **e. policial** police state; **e. satélite** satellite (state); **Estados Unidos de América** United States of America

estadounidense, *Méx* **estadunidense 1** *adj* American; **la política e.** American o US politics
2 *nmf* American

estafa *nf (timo, robo)* swindle; *(a empresa, organización)* fraud

estafador, -ora *nm,f* swindler

estafar *vt (timar, robar)* to swindle; *Com* to defraud; **estafó cien millones a la empresa** he defrauded the company of a hundred million

estafeta *nf* branch post office

estafilococo *nm* staphylococcus

estalactita *nf* stalactite

estalagmita *nf* stalagmite

estalinismo *nm* Stalinism

estalinista *adj* & *nmf* Stalinist

estallar *vi* (**a**) *(explotar) (bomba)* to explode; *(neumático)* to burst; *(volcán)* to erupt; *(cristal)* to shatter; *(olas)* to break, to crash; **si sigo comiendo voy a e.** if I eat any more I'll burst (**b**) *(sonar) (ovación)* to break out; *(látigo)* to crack (**c**) *(guerra, epidemia)* to break out; *(tormenta)* to break; **ha estallado un nuevo escándalo de corrupción** a new corruption scandal has erupted
(**d**) *(expresarse bruscamente)* to blow up, to blow one's top; **se metieron tanto conmigo que al final estallé** they went on at me so much I eventually blew up o blew my top; **e. en**

sollozos to burst into tears; **e. en una carcajada** to burst out laughing; **¡voy a e. de nervios!** I'm so nervous!

estallido *nm* (**a**) *(explosión) (de bomba)* explosion; *(de trueno)* crash; *(de látigo)* crack; **hubo un e. de aplausos** there was a burst of applause (**b**) *(comienzo) (de guerra)* outbreak; **el e. del escándalo provocó su dimisión** he resigned when the scandal broke

Estambul *n* Istanbul

estamento *nm* stratum, class; **el e. eclesiástico/ intelectual** the clergy/the intelligentsia

estampa *nf* (**a**) *(imagen, tarjeta)* picture (**b**) *(aspecto)* appearance (**c**) *(retrato, ejemplo)* image; *Fig* **es la viva e. de su madre** he's the (spitting) image of his mother!; **¡maldita sea su e.!** damn o curse him!

estampación *nf (en tela, papel)* printing; *(en metal)* stamping

estampado, -a 1 *adj* printed
2 *nm* (**a**) *(acción)* printing (**b**) *(dibujo)* (cotton) print

estampar *vt* **1** (**a**) *(imprimir) (en tela, papel)* to print; *(metal)* to stamp (**b**) *(escribir)* **e. la firma** to sign one's name (**c**) *(arrojar)* **e. algo/a alguien contra** to fling sth/sb against, to hurl sth/sb against (**d**) *(dar) (beso)* to plant; *(bofetada)* to land
2 estamparse *vpr (lanzarse, golpearse)* **se estampó contra el muro** he crashed into the wall

estampida *nf* stampede; **de e.** suddenly, in a rush

estampido *nm* report, bang

estampilla *nf* (**a**) *(para marcar)* rubber stamp (**b**) *Am (de correos)* stamp

estampillar *vt (sellar)* to stamp; *(documentos)* to rubber-stamp

estancado, -a *adj (agua)* stagnant; *(situación, proyecto)* at a standstill

estancamiento *nm* stagnation

estancarse [59] *vpr (situación, proceso)* to come to a standstill

estancia *nf* (**a**) *Esp, Méx (tiempo)* stay (**b**) *(habitación)* room (**c**) *CSur (hacienda)* cattle ranch

estanciero, -a *nm,f CSur* ranch owner, rancher

estanco, -a 1 *adj* watertight; **compartimento e.** watertight compartment
2 *nm Esp* tobacconist's

estándar *adj inv* & *nm* standard

estandarización *nf* standardization

estandarizar [14] *vt* to standardize

estandarte *nm* standard, banner

estanflación *nf Econ* stagflation

estanque *nm* (**a**) *(en parque, jardín)* pond; *(para riego)* reservoir (**b**) *Chile (depósito)* tank *(of gas)*

estanquero, -a *nm,f* tobacconist

estante *nm* shelf

estantería *nf (en general)* shelves, shelving; *(para libros)* bookcase

estañar *vt* to tin-plate

estaño *nm* tin

estar [30] **1** *vi* (**a**) *(hallarse)* to be; **¿dónde está la llave?** where is the key?; **¿está María? — no, no está** is Maria there? — no, she's not here
(**b**) *(con fechas)* **¿a qué estamos hoy?** what's the date today?; **hoy estamos a martes/a 15 de julio** today is Tuesday/July 15; **estábamos en octubre** it was October
(**c**) *(quedarse)* to stay, to be; **estaré un par de horas y me iré** I'll stay a couple of hours and then I'll go
(**d**) *(hallarse listo)* to be ready; **¿aún no está ese trabajo?** is that piece of work still not ready?
(**e**) **e. a** *(expresa valores, grados)* to be; **estamos a veinte grados** it's twenty degrees here; **el dólar está a 10 pesos** the dollar is at 10 pesos; **están a dos dólares el kilo** they're two dollars a kilo
(**f**) **e. en** *(consistir)* to be, to lie in; **el problema está en la fecha** the problem is the date

(g) e. para *(servir)* to be (there) for; *(expresa disposición)* to be in the mood for; **para eso están los amigos** that's what friends are for; **para eso estoy** that's what I'm here for; **no estoy para bromas** I'm not in the mood for jokes

(h) e. por *(+ infinitivo) (faltar)* **eso está aún por escribir** that has yet to be written; **eso está por ver** that remains to be seen

(i) e. por *(+ infinitivo) (a punto de)* **e. por hacer algo** to be on the verge of doing sth; **estuve por pegarle** I was on the verge of hitting him

(j) e. sin *(+ infinitivo) (expresa negación)* **estoy sin dormir desde ayer** I haven't slept since yesterday; **está sin acabar** it's not finished

2 *v copulativo* **(a)** *(+ adjetivo) (expresa cualidad, estado)* to be; **los pasteles están ricos** the cakes are delicious; **esta calle está sucia** this street is dirty

(b) *(+ adverbio)* **¡ya está bien!** that's enough (of that)!; *Esp (ropa)* **este traje te está bien** this suit looks good on you

(c) *(+ preposición) (expresa estado)* to be; **e. de mudanza** to be (in the process of) moving; **estamos de suerte** we're in luck; **e. de vacaciones** to be on vacation; **e. de viaje** to be on a trip; **e. en uso** to be in use; **e. en guardia** to be on guard; **estamos sin agua** we have no water, we're without water

(d) *(+ preposición) (expresa apoyo, predilección)* **estoy contigo** I'm on your side; **e. por** to be in favor of

(e) e. de *(expresa ocupación)* to be; **está de cajera** she's a checkout girl

(f) e. que *(+ verbo) (expresa actitud)* **está que muerde porque ha suspendido** he's furious because he failed

3 *v aux* **(a)** *(+ gerundio) (expresa duración)* to be; **están golpeando la puerta** they're banging on the door **(b)** *(+ participio)* to be; **está terminado** it's finished

4 estarse *vpr (permanecer)* to stay; **te puedes e. con nosotros unos días** you can stay *o* spend a few days with us; **¡estate quieto!** keep still!

estarcir *vt* to stencil

estárter *(pl* **estárters)** *nm Aut* choke

estatal *adj* state; **una empresa e.** a state-owned company; **la política e.** government policy

estatalizar [14] *vt* to nationalize

estático, -a *adj* **(a)** *Fís* static **(b)** *(inmóvil)* stock-still

estatismo *nm* **(a)** *Pol* statism, state interventionism **(b)** *(inmovilidad)* stillness

estatizar [14] *vt Am* to nationalize

estatua *nf* statue

estatuilla *nf* statuette

estatura *nf (altura)* height; *(categoría)* stature

estatus *nm inv* status

estatutario, -a *adj* statutory

estatuto *nm (norma)* statute; *(de empresa)* article (of association); *(de ciudad)* bylaw; **e. de autonomía** = legislation devolving powers to an autonomous Spanish region

este[1] 1 *adj (posición, parte)* east, eastern; *(dirección, viento)* easterly

2 *nm* east; **viento del e.** east wind; **ir hacia el e.** to go east(wards); **está al e. de Caracas** it's (to the) east of Caracas; **los países del E.** the countries of Eastern Europe

este[2], -a *(pl* **estos, -as)** *adj demostrativo* **(a)** *(en general)* this; *(plural)* these; **esta camisa** this shirt; **e. año** this year **(b)** *Fam Pey (singular)* that; *(plural)* those; **no soporto a la niña esta** I can't stand that girl **(c)** *Méx, RP (como muletilla)* er, um

éste, -a *(pl* **éstos, -as)** *pron demostrativo*

Note that **éste** and its various forms can be written without an accent when there is no risk of confusion with the adjective.

(a) *(en general)* this one; *(plural)* these (ones); **dame otro boli,**

é. no funciona give me another pen, this one doesn't work; **aquellos cuadros no están mal, aunque éstos me gustan más** those paintings aren't bad, but I like these (ones) better; **ésta ha sido la semana más feliz de mi vida** this has been the happiest week of my life

(b) *(recién mencionado)* the latter; **entraron Juan y Pedro, é. con un abrigo verde** Juan and Pedro came in, the latter wearing a green coat

(c) *Fam (despectivo)* **é. es el que me pegó** this is the guy *or* the one who hit me; **éstos son los culpables de todo lo ocurrido** it's this bunch who are to blame for everything

(d) *Fam* **en éstas** just then, at that very moment

estela *nf (de barco)* wake; *(de avión)* vapor trail; *(de humo, olor)* trail

estelar *adj* **(a)** *Astron* stellar **(b)** *Cine & Teatro* star; **un reparto e.** a star-studded cast

estenografía *nf* shorthand

estenotipia *nf* **(a)** *(arte)* stenotypy **(b)** *(máquina)* stenotype

estenotipista *nmf* stenotypist

estenotipo *nm* stenotype

estentóreo, -a *adj Formal* stentorian

estepa *nf* steppe

éster *nm* ester

estera *nf (tejido)* matting; *(alfombrilla)* mat

estercolero *nm (para estiércol)* dunghill; *(lugar sucio)* pigsty

estéreo *adj inv & nm* stereo

estereofonía *nf* stereo

estereofónico, -a *adj* stereophonic, stereo; **sonido e.** stereo sound

estereoscopio *nm* stereoscope

estereotipado, -a *adj* stereotyped, stereotypical

estereotipar *vt* to stereotype

estereotipo *nm* stereotype

estéril *adj* **(a)** *(persona)* infertile, sterile; *(terreno)* barren, infertile **(b)** *(gasa)* sterilized **(c)** *(inútil)* futile, fruitless

esterilidad *nf* sterility

esterilización *nf* sterilization

esterilizado, -a *adj* sterilized, sterile

esterilizador, -ora *adj* sterilizing

esterilizar [14] *vt* to sterilize

esterilla *nf* beach mat

estérilmente *adv* sterilely

esterlina *adj* **libra e.** pound sterling

esternón *nm* breastbone, *Espec* sternum

esteroide *nm* steroid

estertor *nm* death rattle

esteta *nmf* aesthete

estética *nf* **(a)** *(en filosofía)* aesthetics *(singular)* **(b)** *(belleza)* beauty *(c)* *(estilo)* style; **la e. de los años setenta** the style of the seventies

estetición *(pl* **esteticiéns)** *nmf* beautician

esteticismo *nm* aestheticism

esteticista *nf* beautician

estético, -a *adj* aesthetic

estetoscopio *nm* stethoscope

esthéticienne [esteti'θjen] *nf* beautician

estiba *nf* stowage

estibador, -ora *nm,f* stevedore

estibar *vt* to stow

estiércol *nm (excrementos)* dung; *(abono)* manure

estigma *nm* **(a)** *(marca)* mark, scar **(b)** *(deshonor)* stigma **(c)** *Rel* **estigmas** stigmata

estigmatización *nf (marca)* branding; *(deshonra)* stigmatization

estigmatizar [14] *vt (marcar)* to scar; *(con hierro candente)* to brand; *(deshonrar)* to stigmatize

estilarse *vpr Fam* to be in (fashion)

estilete *nm (daga)* stiletto

estilismo *nm* styling

estilista *nmf* (**a**) *(escritor)* stylist (**b**) *(de moda, accesorios)* stylist

estilística *nf* stylistics *(singular)*

estilístico, -a *adj* stylistic

estilizado, -a *adj (figura, cuerpo)* slim and elegant

estilizar [14] *vt* to stylize

estilo *nm* (**a**) *(artístico, literario)* style; **esa iglesia es de e. gótico** that church was built in the Gothic style; **al e. de** in the style of (**b**) *(manera, carácter)* style; **esa chica tiene mucho e.** that girl has a lot of style; **cada uno tiene un e. de hacer las cosas** we all have our own way of doing things; **e. de vida** lifestyle (**c**) *(en natación)* stroke; **e. libre** freestyle (**d**) *Gram* **e. directo/indirecto** direct/indirect quote (**e**) **algo por el e.** something of the sort; **ser por el e.** to be similar

estilográfica *nf* fountain pen

estima *nf* esteem, respect; **se ganó la e. del público** he earned the public's respect; **tiene una gran e. por su padre** he has great respect for his father; **no te tienen mucha e. por aquí** people don't have a very high opinion of you around here; **tener a alguien en gran *o* alta e.** to hold sb in high esteem

estimable *adj* (**a**) *(cantidad)* considerable (**b**) *(digno de estimación)* worthy of appreciation

estimación *nf* (**a**) *(aprecio)* esteem, respect (**b**) *(valoración)* valuation; *(cálculo aproximado)* estimate (**c**) *(en impuestos)* assessment

estimado, -a *adj* (**a**) *(querido)* esteemed, respected; **e. Señor** *(en carta)* Dear Sir (**b**) *(aproximado)* estimated

estimar 1 *vt* (**a**) *(apreciar) (persona)* to think highly of, to respect; *(cosa)* to value; **estima mucho a sus amigos** he values his friends highly (**b**) *(evaluar)* to value; **e. el valor de algo** to estimate the value of sth; **han estimado que las pérdidas superan los cien millones** the losses are estimated to be over a hundred million (**c**) *(creer)* to consider, to deem; **no estimó necesario realizar declaraciones** she didn't consider *o* deem it necessary to make any statement

    2 estimarse *vpr (tener dignidad)* to have self-respect

estimativo, -a *adj* approximate, rough; **un juicio e. (sobre *o* de)** an evaluation (of)

estimulación *nf* stimulation

estimulador, -ora *adj* encouraging

estimulante 1 *adj* (**a**) *(que anima)* encouraging (**b**) *(que excita)* stimulating

    2 *nm* stimulant

estimular *vt* (**a**) *(animar)* to encourage (**b**) *(excitar)* to stimulate

estímulo *nm* (**a**) *(aliciente)* incentive; *(ánimo)* encouragement (**b**) *(de un órgano)* stimulus

estío *nm Literario* summer

estipendio *nm* remuneration

estipulación *nf* (**a**) *(acuerdo)* agreement (**b**) *Der* stipulation

estipular *vt* to stipulate

estirado, -a *adj* (**a**) *(persona) (altanero)* haughty; *(adusto)* uptight (**b**) *(brazos, piernas)* outstretched (**c**) *(jersey)* baggy, shapeless

estiramiento *nm* stretching

estirar 1 *vt* (**a**) *(alargar)* to stretch; **e. el cuello** to crane one's neck; *Fig* **e. las piernas** to stretch one's legs (**b**) *(desarrugar)* to straighten (**c**) *(dinero)* to make last; *(discurso, tema)* to spin out; **he de e. el sueldo para llegar a fin de mes** it's an effort to make my salary last till the end of the month

    2 *vi* (**a**) *(tirar)* **e. (de)** to pull (**b**) *(agrandarse)* **el jersey ha estirado al lavarlo** the jersey has gone baggy in the wash (**c**) *(crecer)* to shoot up

    3 estirarse *vpr* (**a**) *(desperezarse)* to stretch (**b**) *(tumbarse)* to stretch out (**c**) *(crecer)* to shoot up (**d**) *(agrandarse)* **el jersey se ha estirado al lavarlo** the jersey has gone baggy in the wash (**e**) *Fam (ser generoso)* to splash out; **se estiró y nos invitó a cenar** he splashed out and treated us to dinner

estirón *nm* (**a**) *(acción)* tug, pull (**b**) *(al crecer)* **dar *o* pegar un e.** to shoot up suddenly

estirpe *nf* stock, lineage

estival *adj* summer; **vacaciones estivales** summer vacation

esto *pron demostrativo* (**a**) *(esta cosa)* this thing; **e. es tu regalo de cumpleaños** this is your birthday present; **e. que acabas de decir no tiene sentido** what you've just said doesn't make sense; **e. de trabajar de noche no me gusta** I don't like this business of working at night; **¿para e. me has hecho venir?** you got me to come here for THIS? (**b**) *(expresiones)* **e. es** that is (to say); **a todo e.** *(por cierto)* by the way; **en e.** just then, at that very moment; **por e.** that's why

estocada *nf (en esgrima)* stab; *Taurom* (sword) thrust

Estocolmo *n* Stockholm

estofa *nf* **de baja e.** *(gente)* low-class; *(cosas)* poor-quality

estofado *nm* stew

estofar *vt* to stew

estoicismo *nm* stoicism

estoico, -a 1 *adj* stoic, stoical

    2 *nm* stoic

estola *nf* stole

estomacal 1 *adj (del estómago)* stomach; *(bebida)* digestive; **afección e.** stomach complaint

    2 *nm (bebida)* digestive

estómago *nm* stomach; **con el e. vacío** on an empty stomach; *Fig* **me revuelve el e. ver imágenes de guerra** it turns my stomach to see pictures of war; *Fig* **tener buen *o* mucho e.** to be tough, to be able to stand a lot

estomatología *nf Med* stomatology

Estonia *n* Estonia

estonio, -a *adj & nm,f* Estonian

estopa *nf (fibra)* tow; *(tela)* burlap

estoque *nm* rapier

estoquear *vt* to stab

estor *nm* (Roman) blind

estorbar 1 *vt (molestar)* to bother; *(obstaculizar)* to hinder; **le estorba el flequillo para jugar al tenis** his bangs bother him when he plays tennis; **el abrigo me estorba con tanto calor** I find wearing my coat uncomfortable in this heat; **esta mesa estorba el paso** this table is in people's way

    2 *vi* (**a**) *(estar en medio)* to be in the way; **no hace más que e.** all he does is get in the way (**b**) *(molestar)* **no quites el aire acondicionado, que no estorba** don't turn the air-conditioning off, it's not bothering me

estorbo *nm (obstáculo)* hindrance; *(molestia)* nuisance

estornino *nm* starling

estornudar *vi* to sneeze

estornudo *nm* sneeze

estos, -as *ver* **este**

éstos, -as *ver* **éste**

estoy *ver* **estar**

estrábico, -a 1 *adj* squint-eyed

    2 *nm,f* person with a squint

estrabismo *nm* squint

estrado *nm* platform; **subir al e.** *(orador)* to go up on to the platform; *(testigo)* to take the stand

estrafalario *adj* outlandish, eccentric

estragón *nm* tarragon

estragos *nmpl* **causar *o* hacer e. en** *(físicos)* to wreak havoc with; *(morales)* to destroy, to ruin

estrambótico, -a *adj* outlandish

estramonio *nm* thorn apple

estrangulador, -ora *nm,f* strangler

estrangulamiento *nm* strangulation

estrangular 1 *vt* (**a**) *(ahogar)* to strangle (**b**) *(tubo, conducto)* to constrict; *Med* to strangulate (**c**) *(proyecto)* to stifle, to nip in the bud

2 estrangularse *vpr* to strangle oneself

estraperlista *nmf* black marketeer

estraperlo *nm* black market; **productos de e.** black-market goods

Estrasburgo *n* Strasbourg

estratagema *nf Mil* stratagem; *(astucia)* artifice, trick

estratega *nmf* strategist; **un e. de salón** an armchair strategist

estrategia *nf* strategy; **e. de marketing** marketing strategy

estratégico, -a *adj* strategic

estratificación *nf* stratification

estratificado, -a *adj* stratified

estratificar [59] **1** *vt* to stratify

2 estratificarse *vpr Geol* to form strata; *(sociedad)* to become stratified

estrato *nm Geol, Meteo & Fig* stratum; **los estratos sociales** the social strata

estratosfera *nf* stratosphere

estratosférico, -a *adj* (**a**) *(de la estratosfera)* stratospheric (**b**) *Fam (precio)* astronomical

estrechamente *adv* (**a**) *(íntimamente)* closely; **e. relacionados** closely related (**b**) *(apretadamente)* tightly

estrechamiento *nm* (**a**) *(de calle, tubo)* narrowing (**b**) *(de relaciones entre países)* rapprochement

estrechar 1 *vt* (**a**) *(hacer estrecho)* to narrow; *(ropa)* to take in (**b**) *(relaciones)* to make closer; **ambos países estrecharon sus vínculos de amistad** the two countries strengthened their ties of friendship (**c**) *(apretar)* to squeeze, to hug; **e. la mano a alguien** to shake sb's hand; **la estrechó entre sus brazos** he hugged *o* embraced her

2 estrecharse *vpr* (**a**) *(hacerse estrecho)* to narrow (**b**) *(abrazarse)* to embrace (**c**) *(apretarse)* to squeeze up; **se estrecharon en un fuerte abrazo** they hugged one another tightly; **se estrecharon la mano** they shook hands

estrechez *nf* (**a**) *(falta de anchura)* narrowness; *(falta de espacio)* lack of space; *(de ropa)* tightness; **e. de miras** narrow-mindedness (**b**) *(falta de dinero)* hardship; **pasar estrecheces** to be hard up (**c**) *(intimidad)* closeness

estrecho, -a 1 *adj* (**a**) *(no ancho)* narrow; *(ropa)* tight; **desde que he engordado toda la ropa me está estrecha** since I put on weight, all my clothes have been too tight for me; **íbamos muy estrechos en el autobús** our bus was packed; **e. de miras** narrow-minded (**b**) *(íntimo)* close; **tengo una estrecha relación con él** I have a close relationship with him (**c**) *(rígido)* strict; **serán sometidos a estrecha vigilancia** they will be kept under close *o* strict surveillance

2 *nm,f Fam (persona)* prude

3 *nm Geog* strait; **el E. de Gibraltar** the Strait(s) of Gibraltar; **el E. de Magallanes** the Strait(s) of Magellan

estregar [43] *vt* to rub

estrella 1 *nf* (**a**) *(astro)* star; *(suerte, destino)* fate; *Fig* **ver las estrellas** to see stars; **tener buena/mala e.** to be lucky/unlucky; **e. fugaz** shooting star; **e. polar** Pole Star (**b**) **e. de mar** starfish (**c**) *(artista, deportista)* star; **es la e. del equipo** he's the star of the team; **e. de cine** movie star; **e. invitada** guest star (**d**) *(símbolo)* star; **un hotel de cuatro estrellas** a four-star hotel

2 *adj inv* star; **producto e.** flagship *o* star product

estrellado, -a *adj* (**a**) *(con estrellas)* starry (**b**) *(por la forma)* star-shaped (**c**) *(que ha chocado)* smashed; *Fig* **ha nacido e.** he was born unlucky

estrellar 1 *vt* *(arrojar)* to smash

2 estrellarse *vpr* (**a**) *(chocar) (persona, objeto)* to smash (**contra** against); *(avión, coche)* to crash (**contra** into) (**b**) *(fracasar)* to come to nothing

estrellato *nm* stardom

estrellón *nm Am (choque)* crash

estremecedor, -ora *adj* (**a**) *(ruido)* startling, shocking (**b**) *(por miedo, horror)* terrifying, frightening

estremecer [46] **1** *vt* to shake

2 estremecerse *vpr (de horror, miedo)* to tremble *o* shudder (**de** with); *(de frío)* to shiver (**de** with); **me estremezco sólo de pensarlo** I get the shivers just thinking about it

estremecimiento *nm (de miedo)* shudder; *(de frío)* shiver

estrenar 1 *vt* (**a**) *(objeto)* to use for the first time; *(ropa)* to wear for the first time; *(piso)* to move into; **¿estrenas zapatos, eh?** new shoes, huh?; **los que hoy han estrenado la nueva línea de metro dicen que...** those who have used the new subway line on its first day say that...; **se vende bicicleta, a e.** *(en anuncio)* bike for sale, brand-new (**b**) *(película)* to release, to show for the first time; *(obra de teatro)* to premiere

2 estrenarse *vpr (persona)* to make one's debut, to start; **se estrenó como jugador de fútbol americano ayer** he made his debut as a football player yesterday

estreno *nm* (**a**) *(de cosa)* first use (**b**) *(de espectáculo)* premiere, first night; *(de actor)* debut; **la noche del e.** the opening night

estreñido, -a *adj* constipated

estreñimiento *nm* constipation

estreñir [47] *vt* to constipate

estrépito *nm (ruido)* racket, din; *(ostentación)* fanfare

estrepitoso, -a *adj* (**a**) *(ruidoso)* noisy; *(aplausos)* deafening (**b**) *(derrota)* resounding; *(fracaso)* spectacular

estreptococo *nm Med* streptococcus

estreptomicina *nf Med* streptomycin

estrés *nm inv* stress

estresado, -a *adj* suffering from stress; **estar e.** to be stressed

estresante *adj* stressful

estresar 1 *vt* to cause stress to; **ese ruido me está estresando** that noise is getting on my nerves

2 estresarse *vpr* to stress

estría *nf (surco)* groove; *(en la piel)* stretch mark

estriado, -a *adj* (**a**) *(piel)* stretch-marked (**b**) *(columna)* fluted

estriar [32] **1** *vt* to groove

2 estriarse *vpr (piel)* to become stretch-marked

estribaciones *nfpl* foothills

estribar *vi* **e. en** to lie in, to consist in

estribillo *nm* (**a**) *Mús* chorus; *Lit* refrain (**b**) *Fam (coletilla)* pet word *o* phrase

estribo *nm* (**a**) *(de montura)* stirrup; **perder los estribos** to fly off the handle (**b**) *(de coche, tren)* step

estribor *nm* starboard; **a e.** (to) starboard

estricnina *nf* strychnine

estrictez *nf Am* strictness

estricto, -a *adj* strict

estridencia *nf (de ruido)* stridency, shrillness; *(de colores, comportamiento)* loudness

estridente *adj (ruido)* strident, shrill; *(color)* garish, loud; *(persona, comportamiento)* loud

estrofa *nf* stanza, verse

estrógeno *nm* estrogen

estroncio *nm* strontium

estropajo *nm* scourer

estropajoso, -a *adj* (**a**) *(pelo)* coarse; *(textura)* fibrous;

(carne) dry and chewy **(b)** *(lengua, boca)* dry and pasty

estropeado, -a (a) *adj (aparato)* broken **(b)** *(envejecido)* aged

estropear 1 *vt* **(a)** *(aparato)* to break **(b)** *(ropa, vista)* to ruin; **el exceso de sol estropea la piel** too much sun is bad for the skin **(c)** *(plan, cosecha)* to ruin, to spoil; **siempre tienes que estropearlo todo** you always have to ruin everything **(d)** *(envejecer)* to age

2 estropearse *vpr* **(a)** *(máquina)* to break down; **se me ha estropeado el despertador** my alarm clock is broken; **se ha estropeado el día** the day has turned out badly **(b)** *(comida)* to spoil **(c)** *(persona)* **se ha estropeado mucho con los años** he hasn't aged well **(d)** *(plan)* to fall through

estropicio *nm* **hacer** *o* **causar un e.** to wreak havoc

estructura *nf* structure; **e. profunda/superficial** deep/ surface structure

estructuración *nf* structuring, organization

estructural *adj* structural

estructuralismo *nm* structuralism

estructuralista *adj & nmf* structuralist

estructurar *vt* to structure, to organize

estruendo *nm* **(a)** *(ruido)* din, roar; *(de trueno)* crash **(b)** *(alboroto)* uproar, tumult

estrujar 1 *vt* **(a)** *(limón)* to squeeze; *(trapo, ropa)* to wring (out); *(papel)* to screw up; *(caja)* to crush **(b)** *(persona, mano)* to squeeze; **me estrujó un pie** he squashed my foot; **¡no me estrujes!** don't squash *o* crush me! **(c)** *(sacar partido)* to bleed dry

2 estrujarse *vpr (apretujarse)* to huddle together

estrujón *nm* **(a)** *(abrazo)* bear hug **(b)** *(apretujón)* **hubo muchos estrujones** there was a lot of pushing and shoving

estuario *nm* estuary

estucado *nm* stucco, stuccowork

estucar [59] *vt* to stucco

estuche *nm (de lápices, gafas, reloj)* case; *(de joyas)* box

estuco *nm* stucco

estudiado, -a *adj* studied

estudiante *nmf (de universidad, secundaria)* student; *(de primaria)* schoolchild, pupil; **e. de enfermería** student nurse; **e. universitario** college student

estudiantil *adj* student; **protestas estudiantiles** student protests

estudiar 1 *vt* **(a)** *(carrera, libro, asunto)* to study; **estudia biológicas** he's studying biology; **después de e. tu propuesta he decidido no aceptarla** after studying your proposal, I've decided not to accept it **(b)** *(observar)* to observe

2 *vi* to study; **estudia todas las tardes** he spends every afternoon studying; **estudió con el Presidente** he went to school/college with the President; **¿estudias o trabajas?** do you work or are you a student?

estudio *nm* **(a)** *(actividad)* study; **ha dedicado muchos años al e. del tema** she has studied the subject for many years; **estar en e.** to be under consideration; **e. de campo** field study; **e. de mercado** *(técnica)* market research; *(investigación)* market survey; **e. de viabilidad** feasibility study

(b) estudios *(educación)* studies; **el niño va muy bien en los estudios** the boy is doing very well at school; **tener estudios** to be well-educated; **no tiene estudios** he hasn't had much education; **estudios de posgrado** postgraduate studies; **estudios primarios/secundarios** primary/ secondary education

(c) *(oficina)* study; *(de fotógrafo, pintor)* studio; *(apartamento)* studio apartment

(d) *Cine, Rad & TV* studio; **los estudios de la Metro** the Metro studios; **e. cinematográfico** movie studio; **e. de grabación** recording studio

estudioso, -a 1 *adj* studious

2 *nm,f (especialista)* specialist, expert; **un e. de la naturaleza humana** a student of human nature

estufa *nf (calefacción)* heater; *Méx (cocina)* stove; **e. de gas** gas fire

estulticia *nf Formal* stupidity, foolishness

estupa *nm muy Fam* drug-squad detective, narc

estupefacción *nf* astonishment

estupefaciente *nm* narcotic, drug; **brigada de estupefacientes** drugs squad

estupefacto, -a *adj* astonished; **quedarse e.** to be speechless *o* flabbergasted

estupendamente *adv* wonderfully; **estoy e.** I feel wonderful

estupendo, -a *adj* wonderful, marvelous; **¡e.!** wonderful!, marvelous!

estupidez *nf* **(a)** *(dicho, hecho)* **decir/hacer una e.** to say/do something stupid; **no dice más que estupideces** all she ever talks is nonsense; **hizo la e. de preguntarle al portero** he made the foolish mistake of asking the caretaker; **sería un e. negarlo** it would be foolish to deny it; **¿y por eso se enfada? ¡pues vaya una e.!** he got annoyed about that? how stupid can you get! **(b)** *(cualidad)* stupidity

estúpido, -a 1 *adj* stupid

2 *nm,f* idiot

estupor *nm* astonishment

estupro *nm Der* rape of a minor

esturión *nm* sturgeon

estuviera *etc ver* **estar**

esvástica *nf* swastika

ETA ['eta] *nf (abrev de* **Euskadi Ta Askatasuna)** ETA, = terrorist Basque separatist organization

etano *nm* ethane

etapa *nf* stage; **las últimas etapas** the final stages; **por etapas** in stages; **quemar etapas** to come on in leaps and bounds, to progress rapidly; **está pasando una mala e.** he's going through a bad time; **e. ciclista** stage *(of cycle race)*

etarra 1 *adj* ETA; **el terrorismo e.** ETA terrorism

2 *nmf* member of ETA

ETB *nf (abrev de* **Euskal Telebista)** = Basque television network

etc. *(abrev de* **etcétera)** etc

etcétera 1 *adv* etcetera

2 *nm* **y un largo e. de…** and a long list of…

éter *nm* **(a)** *(gas)* ether **(b)** *Formal (cielo)* **el é.** the ether, the heavens

etéreo, -a *adj* ethereal

eternidad *nf* eternity; *Fam* **hace una e. que no la veo** it's ages since I last saw her

eternizar [14] **1** *vt* **e. algo** to make sth last forever

2 eternizarse *vpr* **eternizarse (haciendo algo)** to spend absolutely ages (doing sth); **la reunión se eternizó** the meeting went on and on

eterno, -a *adj (perpetuo)* eternal; *Fam (larguísimo)* never-ending, interminable; **la eterna canción** the same old story

ética *nf* **(a)** *(en filosofía)* ethics *(singular)* **(b)** *(moralidad)* ethics; **é. profesional** (professional) ethics

ético, -a *adj* ethical

etileno *nm* ethylene

etílico, -a *adj Quím* ethyl; **alcohol e.** ethyl alcohol; **intoxicación etílica** alcohol poisoning

etilismo *nm* intoxication

etilo *nm* ethyl

etimología *nf* etymology

etimológico, -a *adj* etymological

etiología *nf Med* etiology

etíope *adj & nmf* Ethiopian

Etiopía n Ethiopia

etiqueta nf (**a**) (en producto) (pegada o cosida) label; (colgada o atada) tag, label; **cada sobre lleva una e. con la dirección** each envelope has an address label on it; **ponga una e. con su nombre a la maleta** put a label o tag with your name on it on the suitcase; **la e. del precio** the price tag; Fig **colgarle a alguien la e. de…** to label sb as…; **no me gusta poner etiquetas a la gente** I don't like to label people (**b**) (ceremonial) etiquette; **de e.** formal; **vestirse de e.** to wear formal dress (**c**) Inform tag

etiquetado nm labeling

etiquetadora nf pricing gun

etiquetar vt también Fig to label; **e. a alguien de algo** to label sb sth

etiquetero, -a adj ceremonious, formal

etnia nf ethnic group; **una persona de e. oriental** a person of Asian extraction

étnico, -a adj ethnic

etnocentrismo nm ethnocentrism

etnografía nf ethnography

etnográfico, -a adj ethnographic

etnógrafo, -a nm,f ethnographer

etnología nf ethnology

etnológico, -a adj ethnologic, ethnological

etnólogo, -a nm,f ethnologist

etrusco, -a adj & nm,f Etruscan

ETT (pl **ETTs**) nf (abrev de **Empresa de Trabajo Temporal**) temp agency

EUA nmpl (abrev de **Estados Unidos de América**) USA

eucalipto nm eucalyptus

eucaristía nf **la e.** the Eucharist

eucarístico, -a adj Eucharistic

eufemismo nm euphemism

eufemístico, -a adj euphemistic

eufonía nf euphony

euforia nf euphoria, elation

eufórico, -a adj euphoric, elated

Éufrates nm **el É.** the Euphrates

eugenesia nf eugenics (singular)

eunuco nm eunuch

Eurasia n Eurasia

eurasiático, -a adj Eurasian

EURATOM [eura'tom] nf (abrev de **Comunidad Europea de la Energía Atómica**) EURATOM

eureka interj ¡e.! eureka!

Euribor [euri'βor] nm Fin (abrev de **Euro InterBank Offered Rate**) EURIBOR

euritmia nf Med regular heartbeat

euro nm (moneda) Euro

euroasiático, -a adj & nm,f Eurasian

Eurocámara nf European Parliament

eurocomunismo nm Eurocommunism

eurocomunista adj & nmf Eurocommunist

euroconector nm TV = 21-pin connector for linking audio and video equipment to a television set

eurócrata adj & nmf Eurocrat

eurodiputado, -a nm,f Euro-MP, MEP

eurodólar nm Fin Eurodollar

euroejército nm Euro army

euroescéptico, -a adj & nm,f Euroskeptic

euroliga nf (de fútbol) European super league

Europa n Europe; **E. Central** Central Europe; **E. del Este** Eastern Europe; **E. Occidental** Western Europe

europarlamentario, -a nm,f Euro-MP, MEP

europeidad nf Europeanness

europeísmo nm Europeanism

europeísta adj & nmf pro-European

europeización nf Europeanization

europeizar [14] vt to Europeanize

europeo, -a adj & nm,f European

Eurovisión nf Eurovision

Euskadi n the Basque Country

euskera, euskara nm Basque

eutanasia nf euthanasia

Eva n pr Eve

evacuación nf (de zona, edificio, vientre) evacuation

evacuado, -a 1 adj evacuated
2 nm,f evacuee

evacuar vt (edificio, zona) to evacuate; (vientre) to empty, to void

evadido, -a 1 adj (persona) escaped; (divisas, impuestos) evaded
2 nm,f escapee, fugitive

evadir 1 vt (impuestos) to evade; (respuesta, peligro) to avoid
2 evadirse vpr to escape (**de** from)

evaluable adj calculable

evaluación nf (**a**) (de daños, pérdidas, costo) assessment, evaluation; (de empleados) appraisal; **una primera e. de las estadísticas confirma que…** a first assessment of the statistics confirms that…; **hizo una e. positiva de la situación** he gave a positive assessment of the situation; **e. de impacto ambiental** environmental impact assessment; **e. de riesgos** risk assessment (**b**) Educ (acción) assessment; (examen) exam, test; (periodo) = division of school year, of which there may be three to five in total; **e. continua** continuous assessment

evaluador, -ora adj evaluating, evaluative

evaluar [4] vt (**a**) (daños, pérdidas, costo) to assess, to evaluate (**b**) Educ (alumno) to assess, to test; (examen) to grade

evanescencia nf Formal evanescence

evanescente adj Formal evanescent

evangélico, -a adj & nm,f evangelical

evangelio nm Rel gospel; Fig beliefs

evangelista nm Evangelist

evangelización nf evangelization, evangelizing

evangelizador, -ora 1 adj evangelizing
2 nm,f evangelist

evangelizar [14] vt to evangelize

evaporación nf evaporation

evaporar 1 vt to evaporate
2 evaporarse vpr (**a**) (líquido) to evaporate (**b**) Fam (persona, fondos) to disappear into thin air

evasión nf (**a**) (huida) escape (**b**) (de dinero) **e. de capitales** o **divisas** capital flight; **e. fiscal** tax evasion (**c**) (entretenimiento) amusement, recreation; (escapismo) escapism; **literatura de e.** escapist literature

evasiva nf evasive answer; **responder con evasivas** not to give a straight answer

evasivo, -a adj evasive

evasor, -ora 1 adj guilty of evasion
2 nm,f (de la cárcel) jailbreaker

evento nm event

eventual adj (**a**) (no fijo) (trabajador) temporary, casual; (gastos) incidental (**b**) (posible) possible

eventualidad nf (**a**) (temporalidad) temporariness (**b**) (hecho incierto) eventuality; (posibilidad) possibility; **en la e. de que viniera, lo recibiríamos** in the event of his coming, we would receive him

eventualmente adv (por casualidad) by chance; (posiblemente) possibly; **me quedaré una semana, e. dos** I'll stay for a week, or possibly two

Everest nm **el E.** (Mount) Everest

evidencia *nf* (a) *(prueba)* evidence, proof (b) *(claridad)* obviousness; **poner algo en e.** to demonstrate sth; **poner a alguien en e.** to show sb up

evidenciar 1 *vt* to show, to demonstrate

2 evidenciarse *vpr* to be obvious *o* evident

evidente *adj* evident, obvious

evitar 1 *vt* (a) *(impedir) (desastre, accidente)* to avoid, to prevent; **podría haberse evitado esta catástrofe** this disaster could have been avoided *o* prevented; **e. que alguien haga algo** to stop *o* prevent sb from doing sth (b) *(eludir) (cuestión, persona)* to avoid; **Javier siempre evita encontrarse conmigo** Javier always avoids meeting me; **no puede evitarlo** he can't help it (c) *(ahorrar)* to save; **esto me evita tener que ir** this saves me (from) having to go

2 evitarse *vpr* to save; **te evitarás muchos problemas** you'll save yourself a lot of problems

evocación *nf* recollection, evocation

evocador, -ora *adj* evocative

evocar [59] *vt (recordar)* to evoke

evolución *nf* (a) *(progreso) (de sociedad, situación)* evolution; *(de enfermedad)* development, progress; **me preocupa la e. económica del país** I'm worried about where this country's economy is heading (b) *(de especies)* evolution; **la e. de las especies marinas** the evolution of marine life (c) *(movimiento)* **contemplaban las evoluciones del jugador en la banda** they watched the player warming up on the sidelines; **me gusta ver las evoluciones de los aviones en el aeropuerto** I like watching planes taking off and landing at the airport

evolucionar *vi* (a) *(progresar) (sociedad, situación)* to evolve; *(enfermedad)* to develop, to progress; **el paciente no evoluciona** the patient isn't making any progress (b) *Mil* to carry out maneuvers

evolucionismo *nm* evolutionism

evolucionista *adj & nmf* evolutionist

evolutivo, -a *adj* evolutionary

evoque *etc ver* **evocar**

ex 1 *nmf inv (cónyuge)* ex

2 *prefijo* ex-; **el ex presidente** the ex-president, the former president

exabrupto *nm* sharp word *o* remark

exacción *nf (de impuestos, multas)* exaction, collection

exacerbado, -a *adj* **los ánimos estaban exacerbados** tempers were running high

exacerbar *vt* (a) *(agudizar)* to exacerbate, to aggravate (b) *(irritar)* to irritate, to infuriate

exactamente *adv* exactly, precisely

exactas *nfpl* mathematics *(singular)*

exactitud *nf (precisión)* accuracy, precision; *(puntualidad)* punctuality; **no lo sé con e.** I don't know exactly

exacto, -a 1 *adj* (a) *(justo)* exact; **tres metros exactos** exactly three meters (b) *(preciso)* accurate, precise; **no sé la fecha exacta de la boda** I don't know the exact date of the wedding; **para ser exactos** to be precise (c) *(idéntico)* **una copia exacta del original** an exact copy of the original; **es e. a su padre** he looks just like his father

2 *interj* **¡e.!** exactly!, precisely!

exageración *nf* exaggeration; **este precio es una e.** that's a ridiculous price; **su reacción me pareció una e.** I thought his reaction was a bit over the top

exagerado, -a *adj (cifra, reacción, gesto)* exaggerated; *(precio)* exorbitant; **es muy e.** *(en cantidad, valoración)* he exaggerates a lot; *(en reacción)* he overreacts a lot

exagerar 1 *vt* to exaggerate

2 *vi* to exaggerate; **yo creo que exageras** I think you're exaggerating; **no exageremos, no fue para tanto** let's not exaggerate, it wasn't that bad; **tantas precauciones, ¿no**

estás exagerando un poco? aren't you going a bit too far with *o* overdoing it with all these precautions?

exaltación *nf* (a) *(júbilo)* elation, intense excitement; *(acaloramiento)* overexcitement (b) *(ensalzamiento)* exaltation

exaltado, -a 1 *adj (jubiloso)* elated; *(acalorado) (persona)* worked up; *(discusión)* heated; *(excitable)* hotheaded

2 *nm,f (fanático)* fanatic; *Pol* extremist

exaltar 1 *vt* (a) *(elevar)* to promote, to raise (b) *(glorificar)* to exalt

2 exaltarse *vpr* to get excited *o* worked up (**por** about)

examen *nm* (a) *(ejercicio)* exam, examination; **aprobar un e.** to pass an exam; *Esp* **suspender** *o Am* **reprobar un e.** to fail an exam; **hacer un e.** to do *o* take an exam; **poner un e. a alguien** to set *o* give sb an exam; **presentarse a un e.** to take an exam; *Esp* **e. de conducir** driving test; **e. escrito** written examination; **e. de ingreso** entrance examination; *Am* **e. de manejar** driving test; **e. final** final (exam); **e. oral** oral (exam); **e. parcial** end-of-term exam

(b) *(indagación)* consideration, examination; **someter a e.** to examine; **hacer e. de conciencia** to take a good look at oneself; **libre e.** personal interpretation; **e. médico** medical examination *o* checkup

examinador, -ora *nm,f* examiner

examinando, -a *nm,f* examinee, candidate

examinar 1 *vt* to examine

2 examinarse *vpr Esp* to take an exam; **mañana me examino de matemáticas** I've got my math exam tomorrow

exangüe *adj Formal* exhausted

exánime *adj* (a) *(muerto)* dead (b) *(desmayado)* lifeless; *(agotado)* exhausted, worn-out

exasperación *nf* exasperation

exasperante *adj* exasperating, infuriating

exasperar 1 *vt* to exasperate, to infuriate

2 exasperarse *vpr* to get exasperated

Exc. *(abrev de* **Excelencia***)* Excellency

excarcelación *nf* release (from prison)

excarcelar *vt* to release (from prison)

excavación *nf* (a) *(acción)* excavation (b) *(lugar)* dig, excavation; **e. arqueológica** archaeological dig

excavador, -ora 1 *adj* excavating, digging

2 *nm,f (persona)* excavator, digger

excavadora *nf (máquina)* digger

excavar *vt (cavar)* to dig; *(en arqueología)* to excavate

excedencia *nf Esp (de funcionario, empleado)* leave (of absence); *Educ* sabbatical; **un año de e.** a year's leave of absence; *Educ* a year's sabbatical

excedentario, -a *adj* surplus; **la balanza de pagos ha sido excedentaria** the balance of payments has been in surplus

excedente 1 *adj* (a) *(producción)* surplus (b) *Esp (funcionario, empleado)* on leave; *Educ* on sabbatical

2 *nmf Esp (persona)* person on leave

3 *nm Com* surplus; **excedentes agrícolas** agricultural surpluses

exceder 1 *vt* to exceed, to surpass; **e. el límite de velocidad** to exceed *o* go over the speed limit; **excede en dos kilos el peso permitido** it is two kilos over the weight limit; **esto excede mis atribuciones** that is beyond my authority

2 *vi* to be greater; **e. a** *o* **de** to exceed

3 excederse *vpr* (a) *(propasarse)* to go too far *o* overstep the mark (**en** in) (b) *(rebasar el límite)* **se excede en el peso** it's too heavy

excelencia 1 *nf (cualidad)* excellence; **por e.** par excellence

2 *nmf* **Su E.** His Excellency, *f* Her Excellency

excelente *adj* excellent

excelentísimo, -a *adj* most excellent; **el e. ayuntamiento**

de Málaga Malaga city council; **el e. embajador de…** his excellency the ambassador of…

excelso, -a *adj Formal* sublime, elevated

excentricidad *nf* eccentricity

excéntrico, -a *adj & nm,f* eccentric

excepción *nf* exception; **a** *o* **con e. de** with the exception of, except for; **de e.** exceptional; **e. hecha de Pérez** Pérez excepted; **hacer una e.** to make an exception; *Prov* **la e. confirma la regla** the exception proves the rule

excepcional *adj* exceptional

excepto *adv* except (for)

exceptuar [4] *vt* (*excluir*) to exclude (**de** from); (*eximir*) to exempt (**de** from); **exceptuando a…** excluding…; **se exceptúa a los menores de 16 años** children under the age of 16 are exempt

excesivo, -a *adj* excessive

exceso *nm* (**a**) (*demasía*) excess; **en e.** (*fumar, beber, comer*) excessively, to excess; **trabaja en e.** he works too hard; **e. de confianza** overconfidence; **e. de equipaje** excess baggage; **e. de peso** (*obesidad*) excess weight; **e. de velocidad** speeding (**b**) (*abuso*) excess; **denunciaron los excesos de los invasores** they condemned the invaders' excesses *o* atrocities; **cometer un e.** to go too far; **cometer un e. en la bebida/comida** to drink/eat to excess; **los excesos se pagan** we pay for our overindulgence

excipiente *nm* excipient

excisión *nf Med* excision

excitable *adj* excitable

excitación *nf* (**a**) (*nerviosismo*) agitation; (*por enfado, sexo*) arousal (**b**) *Biol & Elec* excitation

excitado, -a *adj* (**a**) (*nervioso*) agitated; (*por enfado, sexo*) aroused (**b**) *Biol & Elec* excited

excitante 1 *adj* (*emocionante*) exciting; (*sexualmente*) arousing; (*café, tabaco*) stimulating
  2 *nm* stimulant

excitar 1 *vt* (**a**) (*inquietar*) to upset, to agitate (**b**) (*estimular*) (*sentidos*) to stimulate; (*apetito*) to whet; (*curiosidad, interés*) to excite; (*sexualmente*) to arouse
  2 excitarse *vpr* (**a**) (*alterarse*) to get worked up *o* excited (**por** about) (**b**) (*sexualmente*) to become aroused

exclamación *nf* (*interjección*) exclamation; (*grito*) cry

exclamar *vt & vi* to exclaim

exclamativo, -a *adj* exclamatory

excluir [34] *vt* (*dejar fuera*) to exclude (**de** from); (*hipótesis, opción*) to rule out; (*hacer imposible*) to preclude

exclusión *nf* exclusion

exclusiva *nf* (**a**) *Prensa* exclusive (**b**) *Com* exclusive *o* sole right; **tenemos la distribución en España en e.** we are the sole distributor in Spain

exclusividad *nf* (**a**) (*de club, ambiente, producto*) exclusiveness (**b**) *Com* (*privilegio*) exclusive *o* sole right

exclusivo, -a *adj* (*club, ambiente, producto*) exclusive

excluyente *adj* excluding

Excmo., Excma. (*abrev de* **Excelentísimo, Excelentísima**) **el E. Ayto. de Málaga** Malaga City Council

excombatiente *nmf* war veteran

excomulgar [38] *vt* to excommunicate

excomunión *nf* excommunication

excoriar *vt* to chafe

excrecencia *nf* growth

excreción *nf* excretion

excremento *nm* **un e. de perro** a piece of dog poop; **excrementos** (*de ave, conejo, oveja*) droppings; (*de persona*) excrement

excretar 1 *vt* (*soltar*) to secrete
  2 *vi* (*evacuar*) to excrete

excretorio, -a *adj* excretory

exculpación *nf* exoneration; *Der* acquittal

exculpar 1 *vt* to exonerate; *Der* to acquit
  2 exculparse *vpr* to declare oneself innocent (**de** of)

exculpatorio, -a *adj* exonerative

excursión *nf* (*viaje*) excursion, trip; **ir de e.** to go on an outing *o* a trip

excursionismo *nm* (*en el campo*) rambling; (*de montaña*) hiking

excursionista *nmf* (*en el campo*) rambler; (*en la montaña*) hiker

excusa *nf* (**a**) (*pretexto, motivo*) excuse (**b**) (*petición de perdón*) apology; **presentó sus excusas** he apologized

excusable *adj* (**a**) (*perdonable*) excusable (**b**) (*evitable*) avoidable

excusado, -a 1 *adj* (**a**) (*disculpado*) excused (**b**) (*inútil*) unnecessary, superfluous; **e. (es) decir que…** needless to say…
  2 *nm Euf* **el e.** (*retrete*) the bathroom

excusar 1 *vt* (**a**) (*disculpar a*) to excuse; (*disculparse por*) to apologize for (**b**) *Esp* (*evitar*) to avoid; **excuso decir que…** there's no need for me to say that…
  2 excusarse *vpr* to apologize, to excuse oneself

execrable *adj* abominable, execrable

execrar *vt Formal* to abhor

exégesis *nf inv* exegesis, explanation

exención *nf* exemption; *Fin* **e. fiscal** tax exemption

exento, -a *adj* exempt; **e. de** (*sin*) free from, without; (*eximido de*) exempt from

exequias *nfpl* funeral

exfoliación *nf* exfoliation

exfoliante 1 *adj* exfoliating
  2 *nm* exfoliating cream/lotion

exfoliar 1 *vt* to exfoliate
  2 exfoliarse *vpr* to exfoliate

exhalación *nf* (**a**) (*emanación*) exhalation, vapor; (*suspiro*) breath (**b**) *Fam Fig* **como una e.** as quick as a flash

exhalar *vt* (**a**) (*aire*) to exhale, to breathe out; (*suspiros*) to heave; **e. el último suspiro** to breathe one's last (breath) (**b**) (*olor, vapor*) to give off

exhaustivo, -a *adj* exhaustive

exhausto, -a *adj* exhausted

exhibición *nf* (**a**) (*demostración*) show, display (**b**) (*deportiva, artística*) exhibition; **e. aérea** air show (**c**) (*de películas*) showing

exhibicionismo *nm* exhibitionism

exhibicionista *nmf* (*que gusta de llamar la atención*) exhibitionist; (*pervertido sexual*) exhibitionist, flasher

exhibir 1 *vt* (**a**) (*cuadros, fotografías*) to exhibit; (*modelos*) to show; (*productos*) to display (**b**) (*joyas, cualidades*) to show off (**c**) (*película*) to show, to screen
  2 exhibirse *vpr* (*alardear*) to show off

exhortación *nf* exhortation

exhortar *vt* **e. a** to exhort to

exhumación *nf* exhumation, disinterment

exhumar *vt* to exhume, to disinter

exigencia *nf* (**a**) (*requisito*) demand, requirement (**b**) (*petición*) demand; **venirle a alguien con exigencias** to make demands on sb

exigente 1 *adj* demanding
  2 *nmf* demanding person

exigible *adj* payable on demand

exigir [24] **1** *vt* (**a**) (*pedir*) to demand; **exijo saber la respuesta** I demand to know the answer; **e. algo de** *o* **a alguien** to demand sth from sb; **exigen una licenciatura** you need to have a degree (**b**) (*requerir, necesitar*) to call for, to require; **este trabajo exige mucha concentración** this work calls for a lot of concentration

2 *vi* to be demanding

exiguo, -a *adj (escaso)* meager, paltry; *(pequeño)* minute

exijo *ver* **exigir**

exiliado, -a 1 *adj* exiled, in exile

2 *nm,f* exile

exiliar 1 *vt* to exile

2 exiliarse *vpr* to go into exile

exilio *nm* exile; **en el e.** in exile

eximente *Der* **1** *adj* absolutory, absolving

2 *nf* case for acquittal

eximio, -a *adj Formal* eminent, illustrious

eximir *vt* to exempt (**de** from)

existencia *nf* (**a**) *(circunstancia de existir)* existence; **se ha confirmado la e. de varios manuscritos inéditos** it has been confirmed that there are several unpublished manuscripts; **este niño me está amargando la e.** that child is making my life a misery (**b**) *Com* **existencias** stock; **quedan muy pocas existencias en el almacén** there's isn't much stock in the warehouse; **en existencias** in stock; **quedarse sin existencias (de algo)** to run out (of sth); **reponer las existencias** to restock

existencial *adj* existential

existencialismo *nm* existentialism

existencialista *adj & nmf* existentialist

existente *adj* existing, existent

existir *vi* (**a**) *(ser real)* to exist; **los gnomos no existen** gnomes don't exist (**b**) *(haber)* to exist; **existe el riesgo de...** there is the risk that...; **existe mucha pobreza** there is a lot of poverty (**c**) *(vivir)* to exist; **mientras yo exista no tienes que preocuparte** you don't have to worry while I'm still here

éxito *nm* (**a**) *(logro, fama)* success; **la fiesta fue un é.** the party was a success; **con é.** successfully; **tener é.** to be successful (**b**) *(libro)* best seller; *(canción)* hit; **de é.** *(libro)* best-selling; *(canción)* hit; **ser un é. (de ventas)** *(libro)* to be a best seller; *(canción)* to be a hit; **un é. de taquilla** a box-office hit

exitoso, -a *adj* successful

ex libris *nm inv* ex libris

éxodo *nm* exodus

exógeno, -a *adj* exogenous

exoneración *nf* (**a**) *(de culpa, responsabilidad)* exoneration; *(de carga, obligación)* freeing (**b**) *(de empleo, cargo)* dismissal

exonerar *vt* **e. a alguien (de)** *(culpa, responsabilidad)* to exonerate sb (from); *(carga, obligación)* to free sb (from); *(empleo, cargo)* to dismiss o remove sb (from)

exorbitante *adj* exorbitant

exorcismo *nm* exorcism

exorcista *nmf* exorcist

exorcizar [14] *vt* to exorcize

exótico, -a *adj* exotic

exotismo *nm* exoticism

expandible *adj Inform* expandible

expandir *(gen) & Inform* **1** *vt* to expand

2 expandirse *vpr* to expand

expansión *nf* (**a**) *(de gas, empresa)* expansion; **en e.** expanding (**b**) *(relajación)* relaxation; *(diversión)* recreation

expansionarse *vpr* (**a**) *(divertirse)* to relax, to let off steam (**b**) *(desarrollarse)* to expand

expansionismo *nm* expansionism

expansionista *adj* expansionist

expansivo, -a *adj (que se extiende)* expansive; *(persona)* open, frank

expatriación *nf* expatriation; *(exilio)* exile

expatriado, -a 1 *adj* **los españoles expatriados**

(emigrantes) expatriate Spaniards; *(exiliados)* Spanish exiles

2 *nm,f (emigrante)* expatriate; *(exiliado)* exile

expatriar [32] **1** *vt (expulsar)* to exile

2 expatriarse *vpr (emigrar)* to leave one's country, to emigrate; *(exiliarse)* to go into exile

expectación *nf* expectancy, anticipation

expectante *adj* expectant

expectativa *nf (esperanza)* hope; *(perspectiva)* prospect; **contra toda e.** against all expectations; **estar a la e.** to wait and see; **estar a la e. de** *(atento)* to be on the lookout for; *(a la espera)* to be hoping for; **e. de vida** life expectancy

expectoración *nf Med* (**a**) *(acción)* expectoration (**b**) *(esputo)* sputum

expectorante *adj & nm* expectorant

expectorar *vi Med* to expectorate

expedición *nf (viaje, grupo)* expedition

expedicionario, -a *adj* expeditionary

expedidor, -ora *nm,f* sender, dispatcher

expedientar *vt (castigar)* to take disciplinary action against; *(llevar a juicio)* to start proceedings against

expediente *nm* (**a**) *(documentación)* documents; *(ficha)* file; *Esp Econ* **e. de regulación de empleo** layoff plan, workforce adjustment plan (**b**) *(historial)* record; *Fam Fig* **cubrir el e.** to do the bare minimum; **hacer algo por cubrir el e.** to do sth for the sake of appearances; **e. académico** academic record, transcript (**c**) *(investigación)* inquiry; **abrir e. a alguien** *(castigar)* to take disciplinary action against sb; *(llevar a juicio)* to start proceedings against sb

expedir [47] *vt (carta, pedido)* to send, to dispatch; *(pasaporte, decreto)* to issue; *(contrato, documento)* to draw up

expeditivo, -a *adj* expeditious; **utilizar métodos expeditivos** to adopt harsh measures

expedito, -a *adj* clear, free; *también Fig* **tener el paso o camino e.** to have one's way clear

expeler *vt* to emit

expendedor, -ora 1 *adj* **máquina expendedora** vending machine

2 *nm,f (de mercancía)* dealer, retailer; *(de lotería)* seller, vendor

expendeduría *nf (estanco)* cigar store

expender *vt* to sell, to retail

expensas: a expensas de *loc prep* at the expense of; **vive a e. de sus abuelos** his grandparents support him financially

experiencia *nf* (**a**) *(veteranía)* experience; **tiene mucha e. en la reparación de lavadoras** he has a lot of experience at repairing washing machines; **e. laboral** work experience (**b**) *(vivencia)* experience; **sé por (propia) e. que este trabajo implica sacrificio** I know from my own experience that this job involves a lot of sacrifices (**c**) *(experimento)* experiment

experimentación *nf* experimentation

experimentado, -a *adj (persona)* experienced; *(método)* tried and tested

experimentador, -ora 1 *adj* experimenting

2 *nm,f* experimenter

experimental *adj* experimental

experimentar 1 *vt* (**a**) *(sensación, efecto)* to experience; *(derrota, pérdidas)* to suffer; **e. frío/calor** to feel cold/hot; **las temperaturas experimentarán un leve ascenso/descenso** we will see a slight rise/fall in temperatures (**b**) *(probar)* to test; *(hacer experimentos con)* to experiment with o on

2 *vi* **e. con** to experiment with o on

experimento *nm* experiment

experto, -a *adj & nm,f* expert

expiación *nf* atonement, expiation

expiar [32] *vt* to atone for, to expiate

expiatorio, -a *adj* expiatory

expidiera *etc ver* **expedir**

expido *etc ver* **expedir**

expiración *nf* expiry

expirar *vi* to expire

explanación *nf* (a) *(allanamiento)* leveling (b) *Formal (explicación)* explanation, explication

explanada *nf* area of flat o level ground

explanar *vt (terreno)* to level

explayarse *vpr* (a) *(divertirse)* to amuse oneself, to enjoy oneself (b) *(hablar mucho)* to talk at length (c) *(desahogarse)* to pour out one's heart (**con** to)

explicación *nf* explanation; **dar/pedir explicaciones** to give/demand an explanation

explicar [59] 1 *vt* (a) *(exponer, contar)* to explain; *(teoría)* to expound; **¿te importaría explicarme qué pasa?** would you mind telling me o explaining what's going on?; **explícame cómo funciona** tell me how it works (b) *(enseñar)* to teach, to lecture in

 2 **explicarse** *vpr* (a) *(comprender)* to understand; **no me lo explico** I can't understand it (b) *(dar explicaciones)* to explain oneself; **a ver, explícate, ¿qué quieres decir con eso?** come on, explain, what do you mean by that?; **no sé si me explico** do you know what I mean? (c) *(expresarse)* to make oneself understood

explicativo, -a *adj* explanatory

explícito, -a *adj* explicit

exploración *nf* (a) *(de territorio)* exploration (b) *Med (interna)* exploration; *(externa)* examination (c) *Min* prospecting

explorador, -ora *nm,f (viajero)* explorer; *(scout)* Boy Scout, f Girl Guide; *Mil* scout

explorar *vt* (a) *(averiguar, reconocer)* to explore; *Mil* to scout (b) *Med (internamente)* to explore; *(externamente)* to examine (c) *Min* to prospect

exploratorio, -a *adj (instrumento, técnica)* exploratory; *(conversaciones)* preliminary

explosión *nf también Fig* explosion; **hacer e.** to explode; **una e. controlada** a controlled explosion; **una e. de colores** a riot of color; **e. atómica** o **nuclear** atomic explosion; **e. demográfica** population explosion

explosionar *vt & vi* to explode, to blow up

explosivo, -a 1 *adj* (a) *(sustancia, artefacto)* explosive (b) *Gram* plosive

 2 *nm* explosive

explotación *nf* (a) *(acción)* exploitation; *(de fábrica, negocio)* running; *(de yacimiento)* mining; *(agrícola)* farming; *(de petróleo)* drilling (b) *(instalaciones)* **e. agrícola** farm; **e. minera** mine; **e. petrolífera** oil field

explotador, -ora 1 *adj* exploiting

 2 *nm,f* exploiter

explotar 1 *vt (persona)* to exploit; *(fábrica)* to run, to operate; *(terreno)* to farm; *(mina)* to work

 2 *vi* to explode

expo *nf (exposición universal)* expo

expoliación *nf* pillaging, plundering

expoliador, -ora 1 *adj* pillaging, plundering

 2 *nm,f* pillager, plunderer

expoliar *vt* to pillage, to plunder

expolio *nm* pillaging, plundering

exponencial *adj & nf* exponential

exponente *nm Mat & Fig* exponent

exponer [50] 1 *vt* (a) *(teoría)* to expound; *(ideas, propuesta)* to set out, to explain (b) *(cuadro, obra)* to exhibit; *(objetos en vitrinas)* to display (c) *(vida, prestigio)* to risk (d) *(parte del cuerpo)* to expose

 2 **exponerse** *vpr (a riesgo)* to run the risk (a of); *(a ataque, crítica)* to expose oneself (a to); **si salimos ahora nos exponemos a que nos caiga un chaparrón** if we go out now we run the risk of getting caught in a downpour; **no se expongan al sol sin la debida protección** do not expose yourself o go out in the sun without proper protection; **ya sabes a lo que te expones** you know what you're letting yourself in for

exportación *nf* (a) *(acción)* export (b) *(mercancías)* exports; *Com* **exportaciones invisibles** invisible exports

exportador, -ora 1 *adj* **país e.** exporting country, exporter

 2 *nm,f* exporter

exportar *vt Com & Inform* to export

exposición *nf* (a) *(de arte)* exhibition; *(de objetos en vitrina)* display; **e. universal** international exposition o exhibition, world's fair (b) *(al sol, calor, radiaciones) & Fot* exposure (c) *(de teoría)* exposition; *(de ideas, propuesta)* setting out, explanation

exposímetro *nm* exposure meter

expositivo, -a *adj* explanatory

expósito, -a *Anticuado* **1** *adj* **niño e.** foundling

 2 *nm,f* foundling

expositor, -ora 1 *adj* exponent

 2 *nm,f (en feria)* exhibitor; *(de teoría)* exponent

exprés *adj inv* (a) *(carta)* ≃ first-class (b) *(café)* expresso

expresado, -a *adj (mencionado)* above-mentioned

expresamente *adv (a propósito)* expressly; *(explícitamente)* explicitly, specifically

expresar 1 *vt (manifestar)* to express; *(mostrar)* to show; **es una sensación rara, no sé cómo expresarlo** it is an odd feeling, I don't know how to express it; **quisiera expresarles mi más sincero agradecimiento** I would like to thank you most sincerely

 2 **expresarse** *vpr* to express oneself; **creo que me he expresado con suficiente claridad** I think I have made myself clear enough

expresión *nf* (a) *(del rostro)* expression (b) *(de ideas, sentimientos)* expression; **reducir a la mínima e.** to cut down to the bare minimum; **e. corporal** self-expression through movement; *Educ* **e. escrita** writing skills (c) *Ling & Mat* expression

expresionismo *nm* expressionism

expresionista *adj & nmf* expressionist

expresividad *nf* expressiveness

expresivo, -a *adj (vivaz, explícito)* expressive; *(cariñoso)* affectionate

expreso, -a 1 *adj (explícito)* specific; *(deliberado)* express; *(claro)* clear

 2 *nm* (a) *(tren)* = slow overnight train (b) *(café)* expresso

 3 *adv* on purpose, expressly

exprimelimones *nm inv* lemon squeezer

exprimidor *nm* squeezer

exprimir *vt* (a) *(fruta)* to squeeze; *(zumo)* to squeeze out (b) *(persona)* to exploit

ex profeso *adv* intentionally, expressly

expropiación *nf* expropriation; **e. forzosa** expropriation

expropiar *vt* to expropriate

expuesto, -a 1 *participio ver* **exponer**

 2 *adj* (a) *(desprotegido)* exposed (a to); **estar e. a** *(viento, lluvia, crítica)* to be exposed to (b) *(arriesgado)* dangerous, risky (c) *(dicho)* stated, expressed (d) *(exhibido)* on display

expugnar *vt Formal* to (take by) storm

expulsar *vt* (a) *(de local, organización)* to throw out; *(de clase)* to send out, to expel; *(de colegio, organización)* to expel (b) *Dep* to send off (c) *(humo)* to emit, to give off; *(objeto, sustancia)* to expel

expulsión *nf* (a) *(de colegio, organización)* expulsion (b) *Dep* sending-off (c) *(de objeto, sustancia)* expulsion

expulsor *nm (en arma de fuego)* ejector

expurgar [38] *vt (texto)* to expurgate

expusiera *etc ver* **exponer**

exquisitez *nf* (a) *(cualidad)* exquisiteness (b) *(cosa)* exquisite thing; *(comida)* delicacy

exquisito, -a *adj (refinado)* exquisite; *(comida)* delicious, sublime

extasiarse [32] *vpr* to go into ecstasies (**ante** *o* **con** over)

éxtasis *nm inv* ecstasy

extemporáneo, -a *adj* (a) *(clima)* unseasonable (b) *(inoportuno)* inopportune, untimely

extender [64] **1** *vt* (a) *(tela, plano, alas)* to spread (out); *(brazos, piernas)* to stretch out; **me extendió la mano** she held out her hand to me (b) *(mantequilla)* to spread; *(pintura)* to smear; *(objetos)* to spread out (c) *(ampliar)* to extend, to widen; **extendieron el castigo a todos los alumnos** the punishment was extended to include all the pupils (d) *(documento)* to draw up; *(certificado)* to issue; **le extenderé un cheque** I'll write you (out) a check, I'll make out a check to you

2 extenderse *vpr* (a) *(ocupar)* **extenderse por** to stretch *o* extend across (b) *(hablar mucho)* to enlarge, to expand (**en** on) (c) *(durar)* to extend, to last (d) *(difundirse)* to spread (**por** across); **el incendio se extendió por el bosque** the fire spread through the forest (e) *(tenderse)* to stretch out

extendido, -a *adj* (a) *(esparcido)* spread out (b) *(abierto)* outstretched, open (c) *(diseminado)* widespread, prevalent

extensible *adj* extensible, extendible

extensión *nf* (a) *(superficie)* area, expanse; **solares con una e. de 500 metros cuadrados** plots with an area of 500 square meters (b) *(amplitud) (de país)* size; *(de conocimientos)* extent; **la novela tiene una e. de 600 páginas** the novel is 600 pages long (c) *(duración)* duration, length (d) *(sentido)* range of meaning; **en toda la e. de la palabra** in every sense of the word; **por e.** by extension (e) *Inform* extension (f) *Tel* extension

extensivo, -a *adj* extensive; **hacer algo e. a** to extend sth to

extenso, -a *adj (país)* vast; *(libro, película)* long

extensor, -ora 1 *adj (músculo)* extensor

2 *nm (aparato)* chest expander

extenuación *nf* severe exhaustion

extenuado, -a *adj* completely exhausted, drained

extenuante *adj* completely exhausting, draining

extenuar [4] **1** *vt* to exhaust completely, to drain

2 extenuarse *vpr* to exhaust oneself, to tire oneself out

exterior 1 *adj* (a) *(de fuera)* outside; *(capa)* outer, exterior; **la parte e. del vehículo** the outside of the vehicle; **apartamento/habitación e.** apartment/room that looks onto the street (b) *(visible)* outward; **su aspecto e. es de calma** she is outwardly calm (c) *(extranjero) (comercio, asuntos)* foreign

2 *nm* (a) *(superficie)* outside; **en el e.** outside (b) *(extranjero)* **en el e.** abroad; **una apertura al e.** an opening to the outside world (c) *Cine* **exteriores** *(escenas)* outside shots; **rodar en exteriores** to film on location

exterioridad *nf* outward appearance

exteriorización *nf* outward demonstration, manifestation

exteriorizar [14] *vt* to show, to reveal

exterminación *nf* extermination

exterminador, -ora *adj* exterminating

exterminar *vt* (a) *(aniquilar)* to exterminate (b) *(devastar)* to destroy, to devastate

exterminio *nm* extermination

externalización *nf Com* outsourcing

externalizar [14] *vt Com* to outsource

externar *vt Méx (emoción, opinión)* to express

externo, -a *adj (de fuera)* external; *(parte, capa)* outer; *(influencia)* outside; *(signo, aspecto)* outward

extiendo *etc ver* **extender**

extinción *nf* (a) *(aniquilación)* extinction; *(de esperanzas)* loss (b) *(de plazos, obligaciones)* termination, end

extinguidor *nm Am* fire extinguisher

extinguir [26] **1** *vt (incendio)* to put out, to extinguish; *(raza)* to wipe out; *(afecto, entusiasmo)* to put an end to

2 extinguirse *vpr (fuego, luz)* to go out; *(animal, raza)* to become extinct, to die out; *(ruido)* to die out; *(afecto)* to die

extinto, -a *adj (especie, volcán)* extinct; **el e. Pedro Bustamante** the late Pedro Bustamante

extintor *nm Esp* fire extinguisher

extirpación *nf Med* removal; *(erradicación)* eradication, stamping-out

extirpar *vt (tumor)* to remove; *(muela)* to extract; *(erradicar)* to eradicate, to stamp out

extornar *vt Com* to rebate

extorno *nm Com* rebate

extorsión *nf Der* extortion

extorsionar *vt Der* to extort

extorsionista *nmf Der* extortionist

extra 1 *adj* (a) *(adicional)* extra; **horas extras** overtime (b) *(de gran calidad)* top quality, superior

2 *nmf Cine* extra

3 *nm (gasto)* extra

4 *nf (gasolina)* premium gas

extra- *prefijo* extra-

extracción *nf* (a) *(de astilla, bala)* removal, extraction; *(de diente)* extraction; *(de carbón)* mining (b) *(en sorteos)* drawing (c) *(origen)* **e. social** social extraction

extractar *vt* to summarize, to shorten

extracto *nm* (a) *(resumen)* summary, résumé; **e. de cuenta** bank statement (b) *(concentrado)* extract; **e. de carne** meat extract

extractor *nm (de humos)* extractor fan

extracurricular *adj Educ* extracurricular

extradición *nf* extradition

extraditable *adj* extraditable

extraditar *vt* to extradite

extraer [66] *vt (obtener, sacar)* to extract (**de** from); *(sangre)* to draw (**de** from); *(carbón)* to mine (**de** from); *(conclusiones)* to come to *o* draw (**de** from)

extraescolar *adj* extracurricular

extrafino, -a *adj* top quality, deluxe

extrajudicial *adj* extrajudicial

extralegal *adj* extralegal

extralimitación *nf* abuse *(of power, authority)*

extralimitarse *vpr* to go too far

extramatrimonial, extramarital *adj* extramarital

extramuros *adv* outside the city *o* town

extranjería *nf* foreign status; *Der* **ley de e.** immigration law

extranjerismo *nm* foreign word

extranjerizar [14] *vt* to introduce foreign customs to

extranjero, -a 1 *adj* foreign

2 *nm,f (persona)* foreigner

3 *nm (territorio)* **ir al e.** to go abroad; **del e.** from abroad; **en** *o* **por el e.** abroad; **viajar por el e.** to travel abroad

extranjis: de extranjis *loc adv Esp Fam* on the quiet

extrañamiento *nm* banishment

extrañar 1 *vt* (a) *(sorprender)* to surprise; **me extraña (que digas esto)** I'm surprised (that you should say that); **no me extraña nada que no haya venido** I'm not in the least surprised he hasn't come (b) *(echar de menos)* to miss; **extraña mucho a sus amigos** she misses her friends a lot (c) *(encontrar extraño)* to find strange, not to be used to; **he dormido mal porque extraño la cama** I slept badly because I'm not used to the bed (d) *(desterrar)* to banish

2 extrañarse *vpr (sorprenderse de)* to be surprised (**de** at)

extrañeza *nf* (a) *(sorpresa)* surprise (b) *(rareza)* strangeness

extraño, -a 1 *adj* (a) *(raro)* strange; **es e. que no hayan llegado ya** it's strange *o* odd they haven't arrived yet; **me**

resulta e. oírte hablar así I find it strange *o* odd to hear you talk like that (**b**) *(ajeno)* detached, uninvolved (**c**) *Med* foreign
2 *nm,f* stranger
3 *nm (movimiento brusco)* **el vehículo hizo un e.** the vehicle went out of control for a second

extraoficial *adj* unofficial

extraordinario, -a 1 *adj* (**a**) *(insólito)* extraordinary; **lo e. es que...** the extraordinary thing is that... (**b**) *(gastos)* additional; *(edición, suplemento)* special
2 *nm* (**a**) *Prensa* special edition (**b**) *(correo)* special delivery

extraparlamentario, -a *adj* extra-parliamentary

extraplano, -a *adj* super-slim, extra-thin

extrapolación *nf* extrapolation

extrapolar *vt* to extrapolate

extrarradio *nm* outskirts, suburbs

extrasensorial *adj* extrasensory

extraterrestre *adj & nmf* extraterrestrial

extraterritorial *adj* extraterritorial

extraterritorialidad *nf* extraterritorial rights

extravagancia *nf* eccentricity

extravagante *adj* eccentric, outlandish

extravasarse *vpr* to flow out

extraversión *nf* extroversion

extravertido, -a *adj & nm,f* extrovert

extraviado, -a *adj (perdido)* lost; *(animal)* stray

extraviar [32] **1** *vt* (**a**) *(objeto)* to lose, to mislay; *(excursionista)* to mislead, to cause to lose one's way (**b**) *(mirada, vista)* to allow to wander
2 extraviarse *vpr (persona)* to get lost; *(objeto)* to be mislaid, to go missing

extravío *nm* (**a**) *(pérdida)* loss, mislaying (**b**) *(desenfreno)* excess

extremado, -a *adj* extreme

Extremadura *n* Extremadura

extremar 1 *vt (precaución, vigilancia)* to maximize
2 extremarse *vpr* to take great pains *o* care

extremaunción *nf Rel* last rites, *Espec* extreme unction

extremeño, -a 1 *adj* of/from Extremadura
2 *nm,f* person from Extremadura

extremidad *nf (extremo)* end; **extremidades** *(del cuerpo)* extremities

extremismo *nm* extremism

extremista *adj & nmf* extremist

extremo, -a 1 *adj (sumo)* extreme; *(en el espacio)* far, furthest; **la extrema izquierda/derecha** the far left/right
2 *nm* (**a**) *(punta)* end; **al otro e. de la calle** the other end of the street
(**b**) *(límite)* extreme; **ir *o* pasar de un e. al otro** to go from one extreme to the other; **no desearía llegar a ese e.** I wouldn't want to go to those lengths; **llegar a extremos ridículos/peligrosos** to reach ridiculous/dangerous extremes; **en último e.** as a last resort
(**c**) *Dep* **e. derecho/izquierdo** outside right/left
(**d**) *(punto, asunto)* issue, question; **...e. que ha sido rechazado por...** ...a claim which has been denied by...; **este e. está aún por confirmar** that remains to be confirmed

extremosidad *nf (efusividad)* effusiveness

extremoso, -a *adj (efusivo)* effusive, gushing

extrínseco, -a *adj* extrinsic

extroversión *nf* extroversion

extrovertido, -a *adj & nm,f* extrovert

exuberancia *nf* exuberance

exuberante *adj* exuberant

exudación *nf Med* exudation

exudar *vt* to exude, to ooze

exultación *nf* exultation

exultante *adj* exultant

exultar *vi* to exult, to rejoice (**de** with)

exvoto *nm* votive offering, ex voto

eyaculación *nf* ejaculation; **e. precoz** premature ejaculation

eyacular *vi* to ejaculate

eyección *nf* ejection, expulsion

eyectar *vt* to eject, to expel

eyector *nm (de armas)* ejector; *(de aire, gases)* extractor

EZLN *nm Méx (abrev de* **Ejército Zapatista de Liberación Nacional***)* Zapatista Army of National Liberation

F

F, f ['efe] *nf (letra)* F, f

f. (a) *(abrev de* **factura***)* inv (b) *(abrev de* **folio***)* f

fa *nm Mús* F; *(en solfeo)* fa

fabada *nf* = Asturian stew made of beans, pork sausage and bacon

fábrica *nf* (a) factory; **f. de papel** paper mill; **f. siderúrgica** iron and steelworks *(singular)*; **es así de f.** it was like that when I bought it (b) *(construcción)* **un muro de f.** *(de ladrillo)* a brick wall; *(de piedra)* a stone wall

fabricación *nf* manufacture; **de f. casera** homemade; **f. en serie** mass production

fabricante 1 *adj* manufacturing; **la empresa f.** the manufacturer

    2 *nmf* manufacturer

fabricar [59] *vt* (a) *(producir)* to manufacture, to make (b) *(construir)* to build, to construct (c) *(inventar)* to fabricate, to make up

fábula *nf* (a) *(relato)* fable; *(leyenda)* legend, myth; **lo pasamos de f.** we had a fabulous *o* fantastic time (b) *(rumor)* piece of gossip

fabulación *nf* invention, fantasy

fabular *vi* to make things up

fabulista *nmf* author of fables

fabuloso, -a *adj* (a) *(muy bueno)* fabulous, fantastic (b) *(ficticio)* mythical, fantastic

facción *nf* (a) *Pol* faction (b) **facciones** *(rasgos)* features; **facciones demacradas** drawn features

faccioso, -a 1 *adj* factious, rebellious

    2 *nm,f* rebel

faceta *nf* facet

facha *Fam* **1** *nf* (a) *(aspecto)* look; **con esta f. no puedo ir a ninguna parte** I can't go anywhere looking like this (b) *(mamarracho)* mess; **vas hecho una f.** you look a mess

    2 *nmf Esp Pey (fascista)* fascist

fachada *nf* (a) *Arquit* facade; **con f. a** facing (b) *(apariencia)* outward appearance; **es pura f.** it's just a show

facial *adj* facial; **rasgos faciales** (facial) features

fácil *adj* (a) *(sencillo)* easy; **f. de hacer/decir** easy to do/say; **dinero f.** easy money (b) *(tratable)* easygoing (c) *(probable)* probable, likely; **es f. que no venga** it's likely she won't come, she probably won't come

facilidad *nf* (a) *(simplicidad)* ease, easiness (b) *(aptitud)* aptitude; **tener f. para algo** to have a gift for sth; **tiene f. de palabra** he's good at expressing himself; **dar facilidades a alguien para hacer algo** to make it easy for sb to do sth; **facilidades de pago** easy (payment) terms

facilitar *vt* (a) *(simplificar)* to facilitate, to make easy; *(posibilitar)* to make possible; **esta máquina nos facilita mucho la tarea** this machine makes the job a lot easier (for us) (b) *(proporcionar)* to provide; **nos facilitaron toda la información que necesitábamos** they provided us with all the information we needed

fácilmente *adv* easily; **tardará f. tres meses** it'll easily take three months

facilón, -ona *adj Fam (muy fácil)* dead easy; *(demasiado simple)* too simple

facineroso, -a *nm,f* miscreant, criminal

facsímil, facsímile 1 *adj* facsimile; **edición f.** facsimile edition

    2 *nm* (a) *(copia)* facsimile (b) *(fax)* facsimile, fax

factible *adj* feasible

fáctico, -a *adj* **los poderes fácticos** the powers that be, the forces of the establishment

factor *nm* factor; **f. (de protección) 30** *(de crema solar)* factor 30 (protection)

factoría *nf (fábrica)* factory

factótum *(pl* **factótums***) nmf* factotum

factura *nf* (a) *(por mercancías, trabajo realizado)* invoice; *(de compra, luz, teléfono)* bill; *Fig* **pasar f.** *(los excesos, años)* to take their toll; **f. detallada** itemized bill; *Com* **f. pro forma** *o* **proforma** pro forma invoice; **f. del gas/del teléfono** gas/phone bill (b) *(hechura)* **de buena/mala f.** well/badly made (c) *Arg (repostería)* cakes and pastries

facturación *nf* (a) *(de equipaje)* *(en aeropuerto)* checking-in; *(en estación)* registration; **mostrador de f.** check-in desk (b) *(ventas)* net revenue (c) *(cobro)* invoicing

facturar *vt* (a) *(equipaje)* *(en aeropuerto)* to check in; *(en estación)* to register (b) *(vender)* to turn over; **facturaron 4.000 millones en 2003** they had a turnover of 4,000 million in 2003 (c) *(cobrar)* **facturarle a alguien algo** to invoice *o* bill sb for sth

facultad *nf* (a) *(capacidad)* faculty; **facultades (mentales)** (mental) faculties; **está empezando a perder facultades** his mind is beginning to go (b) *(universitaria)* faculty; **F. de Filosofía y Letras** Arts Faculty, Faculty of Arts (c) *(poder)* power, right (d) *(propiedad)* property; **tiene la f. de ablandar la madera** it has the property of softening wood

facultar *vt* to authorize; **este título lo faculta para ejercer en Alemania** this qualification allows him to practice in Germany

facultativo, -a 1 *adj* (a) *(voluntario)* optional (b) *(médico)* medical

    2 *nm,f* doctor

FAD [faŏ] *nmpl (abrev de* **Fondos de Ayuda al Desarrollo***)* = Spanish foreign aid fund

fado *nm* fado, = melancholy Portuguese folk song

faena *nf* (a) *(tarea)* task, work; **faenas agrícolas** *o* **del campo** farm work, agricultural work; **faenas domésticas** housework, household chores (b) *Fam (fastidio)* **hacerle una (mala) f. a alguien** to play a dirty trick on sb; **¡qué f.!** what a pain! (c) *Taurom* bullfighter's performance

faenar 1 *vi (pescar)* to fish

    2 *vt RP (ganado)* to slaughter

fagocitar *vt (engullir)* to engulf, to swallow up

fagocito *nm Biol* phagocyte

fagocitosis *nf inv Biol* phagocytosis

fagot 1 *nm (instrumento)* bassoon
  2 *nmf (músico)* bassoonist

Fahrenheit [faren'χait] *adj inv* Fahrenheit

fair play ['ferplei] *nm* fair play

faisán *nm* pheasant

faja *nf* (**a**) *(prenda de mujer)* girdle; *(terapéutica)* (surgical) corset; *(de esmoquin)* cummerbund; *(de campesino)* sash *(wrapped around waist)* (**b**) *(de terreno) (pequeña)* strip; *(grande)* belt (**c**) *(de libro)* band *(around new book)*

fajar 1 *vt* (**a**) *(periódico)* to put a wrapper on; *(libro)* to put a band on (**b**) *Am Fam (acometer)* to attack, to assault (**c**) *RP Fam (timar)* to rip off
  2 fajarse *vpr Am Fam (pegarse)* **se fajaron** they had a scrap

fajín *nm* sash

fajo *nm (de billetes, papel)* wad; *(de leña, cañas)* bundle

fakir *nm* fakir

falacia *nf (mentira)* lie, untruth; *(concepción errónea)* fallacy; **eso es una f.** that's a lie, that's not true

falange *nf* (**a**) *Anat & Mil* phalanx (**b**) *Pol* **la F. (Española)** the Falange

falangismo *nm* Falangist movement

falangista *adj & nmf* Falangist

falaz *adj* false

falda *nf* (**a**) *(prenda)* skirt; *Fam Fig* **estar pegado a las faldas de su madre** to be tied to his/her mother's apron strings; **f. escocesa** kilt; **f. pantalón** culottes (**b**) *(de montaña)* lower slope (**c**) *(regazo)* lap (**d**) **faldas** *(de mesa camilla)* tablecloth

faldero, -a *adj* (**a**) *(dócil)* **perro f.** lapdog (**b**) *(mujeriego)* keen on women

faldón *nm* (**a**) *(de ropa)* tail; *(de cortina, mesa camilla)* folds (**b**) *(de tejado)* gable

falencia *nf Am Com* bankruptcy

falibilidad *nf* fallibility

falible *adj* fallible

fálico, -a *adj* phallic

falla *nf* (**a**) *(defecto)* fault, defect; *Am (error)* mistake (**b**) *Geol* fault (**c**) **las Fallas** *(fiesta)* = celebrations in Valencia during which giant papier-mâché figures are burned

fallar 1 *vt* (**a**) *(equivocar) (respuesta)* to get wrong; *(tiro)* to miss (**b**) *(sentenciar)* to pass sentence on; *(premio)* to award
  2 *vi* (**a**) *(equivocarse)* to get it wrong; *(no acertar)* to miss (**b**) *(fracasar, flaquear)* to fail; *(no funcionar)* to stop working; *(plan)* to go wrong; **este truco nunca falla** this trick never fails; **me fallaron los frenos** my brakes didn't work (**c**) *(decepcionar)* **fallarle a alguien** to let sb down (**d**) *(quebrarse, ceder)* to give way (**e**) *(sentenciar)* **f. a favor/en contra** to find in favor of/against

fallecer [46] *vi* to pass away, to die

fallecido, -a *adj & nm,f* deceased

fallecimiento *nm* decease, death

fallero, -a *adj* = relating to the celebrations in Valencia during which giant papier-mâché figures are burned

fallido, -a *adj (esfuerzo, intento)* unsuccessful, failed; *(esperanza)* vain; *(disparo)* missed

fallo *nm* (**a**) *Esp (error)* mistake; *Dep* miss; **tener un f.** to make a mistake; **un f. humano** a human error; **un f. técnico** a technical fault (**b**) *Esp (defecto)* fault; **tener muchos fallos** to have lots of faults (**c**) *(veredicto)* verdict; *(en concurso)* decision

fallutería *nf RP Fam* hypocrisy

falluto, -a *adj RP Fam* phony, hypocritical

falo *nm* phallus

falocracia *nf* male chauvinism

falócrata *nm* male chauvinist

falsario, -a 1 *adj (persona)* untruthful
  2 *nm,f* liar

falseamiento *nm* falsifying, falsification

falsear *vt (hechos, historia, datos)* to falsify, to distort; *(moneda, firma)* to forge

falsedad *nf* (**a**) *(falta de verdad, autenticidad)* falseness (**b**) *(mentira)* falsehood, lie

falsete *nm* falsetto; **voz de f.** falsetto voice

falsificación *nf* forgery

falsificador, -ora *nm,f* forger

falsificar [59] *vt* to forge

falsilla *nf* guide sheet *(for writing paper)*

falso, -a *adj* (**a**) *(afirmación, información, rumor)* false, untrue; **dar f. testimonio** to give false evidence; **jurar en f.** to commit perjury; **falsa alarma** false alarm; *Ling* **f. amigo** false friend; **falsa modestia** false modesty; **f. techo** false ceiling (**b**) *(dinero, firma, cuadro)* forged; *(joyas)* fake; **un diamante f.** an imitation diamond (**c**) *(hipócrita)* deceitful

falta *nf* (**a**) *(carencia)* lack; *(escasez)* shortage; **hay f. de trabajo** there's a shortage of work; **a f. de** in the absence of; **por f. de** for want o lack of; **fue absuelto por f. de pruebas** he was acquitted for lack of evidence; **es una f. de educación** it's bad manners; **es una f. de respeto** it shows a lack of respect
  (**b**) *(ausencia)* absence; **nadie notó su f.** nobody noticed his/its absence; **echar en f. algo/a alguien** *(notar la ausencia de)* to notice that sth/sb is missing; *(echar de menos)* to miss sth/sb; **sin f.** without fail; **el lunes sin f.** on Monday without fail
  (**c**) **hacer f.** to be necessary; **me hace f. suerte** I need some luck; **me haces mucha f.** I really need you; **si hiciera f., llámanos** if necessary, call us
  (**d**) **f. (de asistencia)** absence; **me han puesto dos faltas este mes** I was marked absent twice this month
  (**e**) *(imperfección)* fault; *(error)* mistake; **sacarle faltas a alguien/algo** to find fault with sb/sth; **f. de ortografía** spelling mistake
  (**f**) *Dep (infracción)* foul; *(en tenis)* fault; **lanzar** o **sacar una f.** to take a free kick; **f. libre directa** direct free kick offense; **f. personal** personal foul
  (**g**) *Der* offense; **f. grave/leve** serious/minor offense
  (**h**) *(en la menstruación)* missed period

faltante *Am* **1** *adj* missing
  2 *nm Com* **f. de caja** cash shortage

faltar *vi* (**a**) *(no haber)* to be lacking, to be needed; **falta aire** there's not enough air; **falta sal** it needs a bit of salt
  (**b**) *(no tener)* **le faltan las fuerzas** he lacks o doesn't have the strength; **le falta experiencia** she lacks experience; **me faltan palabras para expresar mi agradecimiento** I can't find the words to express my gratitude
  (**c**) *(hacer falta)* to be necessary; **me falta tiempo** I need time; **para que su felicidad fuera completa sólo faltaba que viniera su hijo** all it needed to make her happiness complete was for her son to arrive; **¡lo que me faltaba!** that's all I needed!; **sólo le faltó ponerse a llorar** he did everything but burst into tears
  (**d**) *(quedar)* **falta mucho por hacer** there is still a lot to be done; **sólo te falta firmar** all you have to do is sign; **falta un mes para las vacaciones** there's a month to go till the holidays; **¿cuánto falta para Leeds?** how much further is it to Leeds?; **falta poco para que llegue** it won't be long till he arrives; **faltó poco para que le matase** I very nearly killed him
  (**e**) *(estar ausente)* to be absent o missing; **falta Elena** Elena is missing; **el día que yo falte** when I have passed on
  (**f**) *(no acudir)* **sólo faltaron mis padres** only my parents weren't there o failed to turn up; **f. a una cita** not to turn up at an appointment; **¡no faltes (a la cita)!** don't miss it!, be there!; **ha faltado a clase tres veces** she has been absent o off three days
  (**g**) *(no cumplir)* **faltó a su palabra** she went back on her

word, she broke o didn't keep her word; **faltó a su obligación** he neglected his duty; **faltó a la verdad** she wasn't being truthful, she wasn't telling the truth

(**h**) *(expresiones)* **¡no faltaba** o **faltaría más!** *(asentimiento)* of course!; *(rechazo)* **f. a alguien al respeto** to be disrespectful to sb

falto, -a *adj* **f. de** lacking in, short of; **f. de recursos/escrúpulos** lacking means/scruples; **f. de imaginación** unimaginative

faltón, -ona *adj Fam* rude

faltriquera *nf (bolso)* small purse

fama *nf* (**a**) *(renombre)* fame; **tener f.** to be famous o well-known (**b**) *(reputación)* reputation; **buena/mala f.** good/bad reputation; **tener f. de tacaño/generoso** to have a name for being mean/generous

famélico, -a *adj* starving, famished

familia *nf* family; **de buena f.** from a good family; *Fig* **estábamos en f.** there were only a few of us; *Fig* **no te dé vergüenza, que estamos en f.** don't be shy, you're among friends; **ser como de la f.** to be like one of the family; **venir de f.** to run in the family; **f. de acogida** *(de niño)* foster parents; **f. nuclear** nuclear family; **f. numerosa** large family; **la f. política** the in-laws; **la F. Real** the Royal Family

familiar 1 *adj* (**a**) *(de familia)* family; **reunión f.** family gathering (**b**) *(en el trato) (agradable)* friendly; *(en demasía)* overly familiar (**c**) *(lenguaje, estilo)* informal, colloquial (**d**) *(conocido)* familiar; **su cara me es** o **me resulta f.** her face looks familiar (**e**) *(tamaño)* family-sized; **un envase f.** a family pack

2 *nmf* relative, relation

familiaridad *nf* (**a**) *(en el trato)* familiarity (**b**) *(exceso de confianza)* **tomarse muchas familiaridades** to be overly familiar

familiarizado, -a *adj* familiar, conversant (**con** with); **estar f. con algo** to be familiar o conversant with sth

familiarizar [14] **1** *vt* to familiarize (**con** with)

2 familiarizarse *vpr* **familiarizarse con** *(estudiar)* to familiarize oneself with; *(acostumbrarse a)* to get used to

famoso, -a 1 *adj* famous; **es famosa por su belleza** she is famous for her beauty

2 *nm,f* famous person, celebrity

fan *(pl* **fans)** *nmf* fan

fanático, -a 1 *adj* fanatical

2 *nm,f (exaltado)* fanatic; *Dep* fanatical supporter; **es una fanática del cine** she's mad about the movies

fanatismo *nm* fanaticism; **con f.** fanatically

fanatizar [14] *vt* to arouse fanaticism in

fandango *nm (baile)* fandango

fandanguillo *nm* = type of fandango

fané *adj RP* worn out

fanega *nf* = grain measure which varies from region to region

fanfarria *nf* (**a**) *(música)* fanfare; *(banda)* brass band (**b**) *Fam (ostentación)* show, razzmatazz; *(jactancia)* boasting, bragging

fanfarrón, -ona 1 *adj* boastful

2 *nm,f* braggart, show-off

fanfarronada *nf* brag; **decir fanfarronadas** to boast, to brag

fanfarronear *vi* to boast, to brag (**de** about)

fanfarronería *nf* showing-off, bragging

fango *nm* (**a**) *(barro)* mud (**b**) *(deshonra)* **el escándalo le cubrió de f.** the scandal sullied his reputation

fangoso, -a *adj* muddy

fantasear 1 *vi* to fantasize

2 *vt* to imagine, to fantasize about

fantasía *nf* (**a**) *(imaginación)* imagination; *(cosa imaginada)* fantasy; **vive en un mundo de f.** he lives in a world of her own, he lives in a fantasy world; **bisutería de f.** costume

jewelry; **ropa de f.** fancy clothes (**b**) *Mús* fantasia

fantasioso, -a *adj* imaginative

fantasma 1 *adj* (**a**) **pueblo/barco f.** ghost town/ship; **una empresa f.** a bogus company (**b**) *Esp Fam (persona)* **es muy f.** he's a real show-off

2 *nm (espectro)* ghost, phantom

3 *nmf Esp Fam (fanfarrón)* show-off

fantasmada *nf Esp Fam* brag

fantasmagórico, -a *adj* phantasmagoric

fantasmal *adj* ghostly

fantasmón, -ona *nm,f Esp Fam* show-off

fantástico, -a *adj* fantastic

fantochada *nf* crazy o mad thing

fantoche *nm* (**a**) *(títere)* puppet (**b**) *(mamarracho)* (ridiculous) sight

fanzine *nm* fanzine

FAO [fao] *nf (abrev de* **Food and Agriculture Organization**) FAO

faquir *nm* fakir

faradio *nm Elec* farad

farándula *nf* **la f.** the theater, the stage

faraón *nm* pharaoh

faraónico, -a *adj (del faraón)* pharaonic; *(fastuoso)* lavish, magnificent

FARC [fark] *nfpl (abrev de* **Fuerzas Armadas Revolucionarias de Colombia**) Revolutionary Armed Forces of Colombia, = guerrilla group

fardada *nf Esp Fam* showing-off

fardar *vi Esp Fam* **f. de algo** to show (sth) off

fardo *nm* bundle

fardón, -ona *Esp Fam* **1** *adj* flashy

2 *nm,f* show-off

farero, -a *nm,f* lighthouse keeper

farfullar *vt & vi (deprisa)* to gabble; *(con enfado)* to splutter; *(en voz baja)* to mutter, to mumble

faringe *nf* pharynx

faringitis *nf inv* sore throat

fariña *nf Andes, RP* coarse manioc o cassava flour

fariseísmo *nm* hypocrisy

fariseo, -a *nm,f* (**a**) *Hist* Pharisee (**b**) *(hipócrita)* hypocrite

farmacéutico, -a 1 *adj* pharmaceutical

2 *nm,f* pharmacist, druggist

farmacia *nf* (**a**) *(ciencia)* pharmacy (**b**) *(establecimiento)* pharmacy, drugstore; **f. de guardia** o **de turno** = pharmacy open outside normal shopping hours

fármaco *nm* medicine, drug

farmacología *nf* pharmacology

farmacológico, -a *adj* pharmacological

farmacopea *nf* pharmacopoeia

farmacoterapia *nf* = treatment using course of drugs

faro *nm* (**a**) *(para barcos)* lighthouse (**b**) *(de coche)* headlight, headlamp; **f. antiniebla** fog lamp o light

farol *nm* (**a**) *(farola)* streetlamp, streetlight; *(linterna)* lantern, lamp (**b**) *(en el juego)* bluff; **ir de f.** to be bluffing (**c**) *Fam (exageración)* brag

farola *nf (farol)* streetlamp, streetlight; *(poste)* lamppost

farolear *vi Fam* to fib

farolero, -a 1 *adj Fam* boastful

2 *nm,f* (**a**) *(oficio)* lamplighter (**b**) *Fam (fanfarrón)* show-off

farolillo *nm* (**a**) *(de papel)* paper o Chinese lantern (**b**) *(planta)* Canterbury bell

farra *nf* (**a**) *Fam* binge, spree; **ir de f.** to paint the town red (**b**) *Andes, RP* **tomar a alguien para la f.** to make fun of sb

farragoso, -a *adj* confused, rambling

farruco, -a *adj (valiente)* cocky; **ponerse f.** to get cocky

farsa *nf también Fig* farce

farsante 1 *adj* deceitful
2 *nmf* deceitful person; **es un f.** he's a fraud
FAS *nm inv* (*abrev de* **Fondo de Asistencia Social**) = Spanish social welfare fund
fascículo *nm* (*entrega*) part, installment (*of publication*); **por fascículos (semanales/mensuales)** in (weekly/monthly) installments
fascinación *nf* fascination; **sentir f. por algo** to be fascinated by sth
fascinante *adj* fascinating
fascinar *vt* to fascinate; **me fascinan Klee y Kandinsky** I love *o* adore Klee and Kandinsky
fascismo *nm* fascism
fascista *adj & nmf* fascist
fase *nf* phase; **la f. final del campeonato** the final stage of the championship; **el proyecto está en f. de estudio** the project is still being researched
fastidiado, -a *adj Esp Fam* (**a**) (*de salud*) ill; **ando f. del estómago** I've got an upset stomach; **tengo la espalda fastidiada** I've injured my back (**b**) (*estropeado*) **la máquina de café está fastidiada** (*no funciona*) the coffee machine is busted; (*funciona mal*) the coffee machine isn't working properly
fastidiar 1 *vt* (**a**) *Esp* (*estropear*) (*fiesta, vacaciones*) to spoil, to ruin; (*máquina, objeto*) to break (**b**) (*molestar*) to annoy, to bother
2 *vi Esp* **¡no fastidies!** you're having me on!
3 fastidiarse *vpr Esp* (**a**) (*estropearse*) (*fiesta, vacaciones*) to be ruined; (*máquina*) to break down (**b**) (*aguantarse*) to put up with it
fastidio *nm* (**a**) (*molestia*) nuisance, bother (**b**) (*enfado*) annoyance
fastidioso, -a *adj* annoying; **es un dolor muy f.** it's a very annoying *o* irritating pain
fasto *nm* pomp, extravagance
fastuosidad *nf* lavishness, sumptuousness
fastuoso, -a *adj* lavish, sumptuous
fatal 1 *adj* (**a**) (*mortal*) fatal (**b**) *Esp Fam* (*muy malo*) terrible, awful; **lo que has hecho está f.** what you've done is awful *o* terrible (**c**) (*inevitable*) inevitable (**d**) (*seductor*) **mujer f.** femme fatale
2 *adv Esp Fam* (*muy mal*) **me cae f.** I can't stand him; **pasarlo f.** to have a terrible *o* an awful time; **sentirse f.** to feel terrible
fatalidad *nf* (**a**) (*destino*) fate, destiny (**b**) (*desgracia*) misfortune
fatalismo *nm* fatalism
fatalista 1 *adj* fatalistic
2 *nmf* fatalist
fatídico, -a *adj* fateful, ominous
fatiga *nf* (**a**) (*cansancio*) tiredness, fatigue; **f. crónica** chronic fatigue; **f. nerviosa** strain, stress (**b**) (*ahogo*) shortness of breath, breathlessness (**c**) **fatigas** (*penas*) hardships, troubles
fatigado, -a *adj* tired, weary
fatigante *adj* tiring
fatigar [38] **1** *vt* to tire, to weary; **la televisión me fatiga mucho la vista** my eyes get very tired watching television
2 fatigarse *vpr* (*cansarse*) to get tired; (*ahogarse*) to get breathless *o* out of breath
fatigoso, -a *adj* tiring, fatiguing
fatigue *etc ver* **fatigar**
fatuidad *nf* (**a**) (*necedad*) fatuousness, foolishness (**b**) (*vanidad*) conceit
fatuo, -a *adj* (**a**) (*necio*) fatuous, foolish (**b**) (*engreído*) conceited
fauces *nfpl* jaws
fauna *nf* (**a**) (*animales*) fauna (**b**) *Fam* **en ese bar se reúne**

una f. muy rica you find all sorts of people in that bar
fauno *nm* faun
fausto, -a *adj* happy, fortunate
fauvismo [fo'βismo] *nm* fauvism
favela *nf* = Brazilian shantytown
favor *nm* (**a**) (*servicio*) favor; **hacerle un f. a alguien** to do sb a favor; **hágame el f. de cerrar la puerta** would you mind shutting the door, please?; **pedir un f. a alguien** to ask sb a favor; **por f.** please (**b**) (*apoyo*) **estar a f. de** to be in favor of; **en f. de** to the benefit of; **tener a *o* en su f. a alguien** to enjoy sb's support; **tenía a todo el pueblo a su f.** he had the people on his side (**c**) **favores** (*de una mujer*) favors
favorable *adj* (**a**) (*beneficioso*) favorable (**b**) (*partidario*) **ser f. a algo** to be in favor of sth
favorablemente *adv* **el paciente evoluciona f.** the patient is making good progress
favorecedor, -ora *adj* flattering, becoming
favorecer [46] *vt* (**a**) (*beneficiar*) to favor; (*ayudar*) to help, to assist; **esta política favorece a los más pobres** this policy works in favor of the poorest; **les favoreció la suerte** luck was on their side (**b**) (*sentar bien*) to suit; **ese corte de pelo te favorece** that haircut suits you
favorecido, -a *adj* (**a**) (*en foto*) **salir muy f.** to come out really well (**b**) *Am* (*en sorteo*) **resultar f. con** to win
favoritismo *nm* favoritism
favorito, -a *adj & nm,f* favorite
fax *nm* (**a**) (*aparato*) fax (machine); **mandar algo por f.** to fax sth (**b**) (*documento*) fax
faxear *vt Fam* to fax
fayuquero, -a *nm,f Méx Fam* dealer in contraband
faz *nf* (**a**) *Formal* (*cara*) countenance, face (**b**) (*del mundo, de la tierra*) face; **fueron barridos de la f. de la tierra** they were swept off *o* from the face of the earth
fe *nf* (**a**) (*creencia, confianza*) faith; **la fe católica** the Catholic faith; **hacer algo de buena fe** to do sth in good faith; **tener fe en** to have faith in, to believe in; **la fe mueve montañas** faith can move mountains (**b**) (*documento*) certificate; **fe de bautismo** baptismal certificate; **fe de erratas** errata (**c**) **dar fe de que** to testify that
fealdad *nf* (**a**) (*de rostro, paisaje, edificio*) ugliness (**b**) (*de conducta*) unworthiness
febrero *nm* February; *ver también* **septiembre**
febril *adj* (*con fiebre*) feverish; (*actividad*) hectic
febrilmente *adv* hectically
fecal *adj* fecal; **aguas fecales** sewage
fecha *nf* (*día*) date; (*momento actual*) current date; **una f. señalada** an important date; **en f. próxima** in the next few days; **fijar la f. de algo** to set a date for sth; **hasta la f.** to date, so far; **ocurrió por estas fechas** it happened around this time of year; **f. de caducidad** (*de alimentos*) sell-by date; (*de carné, pasaporte*) expiry date; (*de medicamento*) use before date; **f. de entrega** delivery date; **f. límite** deadline; **f. de nacimiento** date of birth; **f. de vencimiento** due date
fechador *nm* postmark
fechar *vt* to date
fechoría *nf* bad deed, misdemeanor; **cometer una f.** to do sth wicked
fécula *nf* starch (*in food*)
fecundación *nf* fertilization; **f. artificial** *o* **asistida** artificial insemination; **f. in vitro** in vitro fertilization
fecundar *vt* (**a**) (*fertilizar*) to fertilize (**b**) (*hacer productivo*) to make fertile
fecundidad *nf* (**a**) (*fertilidad*) fertility (**b**) (*productividad*) productiveness
fecundo, -a *adj* (*tierra, mujer*) fertile; (*artista*) prolific
FEDER ['feðer] *nm* (*abrev de* **Fondo Europeo de Desarrollo Regional**) ERDF

federación *nf* federation; **f. deportiva** sports federation

federal *adj & nmf* federal

federalismo *nm* federalism

federalista *adj & nmf* federalist

federar 1 *vt* to federate
  2 federarse *vpr* (**a**) *(formar federación)* to become *o* form a federation (**b**) *(ingresar en federación)* to join a federation

federativo, -a 1 *adj* federative
  2 *nm,f* member of a federation

feedback ['fiðβak] (*pl* **feedbacks**) *nm* feedback

fehaciente *adj* irrefutable

felación *nf* fellatio

feldespato *nm* feldspar

felicidad *nf* happiness; **¡felicidades!** *(enhorabuena)* congratulations!; *(en cumpleaños)* happy birthday!

felicitación *nf* (**a**) *(acción)* **felicitaciones** congratulations (**b**) *(tarjeta)* greeting card; **f. de cumpleaños** birthday card; **f. de Navidad** Christmas card

felicitar 1 *vt* to congratulate (**por** on); **¡te felicito!** congratulations!; **felicita a Ana, es su cumpleaños** wish Ana well, it's her birthday
  2 felicitarse *vpr* to be pleased *o* glad (**por** about)

félidos *nmpl* felines, cats

feligrés, -esa *nm,f* parishioner; **cuando los feligreses salen de la iglesia** when the congregation comes out of church

feligresía *nf* (**a**) *(feligreses)* parishioners (**b**) *(parroquia)* parish

felino, -a 1 *adj* feline
  2 *nm* feline, cat

feliz *adj* (**a**) *(dichoso, alegre)* happy; **¡f. Navidad!** Happy Christmas!; **¡f. Año Nuevo!** Happy New Year! (**b**) *(afortunado)* lucky (**c**) *(oportuno)* timely

felonía *nf* *(traición)* treachery, betrayal; *(infamia)* vile deed

felpa *nf* *(de seda)* plush; *(de algodón)* toweling

felpudo *nm* doormat

femenino, -a 1 *adj* (**a**) *(de mujer)* women's; *(sexo, órganos sexuales)* female; **baloncesto f.** women's basketball; **un toque f.** a woman's touch; **un programa dirigido al público f.** a program aimed at women (**b**) *(de la feminidad)* feminine
  2 *nm Gram* feminine

fémina *nf* woman, female

feminidad, femineidad *nf* femininity

feminismo *nm* feminism

feminista *adj & nmf* feminist

feminizar [14] *vt* to make feminine

femoral 1 *adj* femoral
  2 *nf* femoral artery

fémur *nm* femur, thighbone

fenecer [46] *vi Formal* to pass away, to die

fenicio, -a 1 *adj & nm,f* Phoenician
  2 *nm (lengua)* Phoenician

fénix *nm inv (ave)* phoenix; **volvió como el ave f.** he rose like a phoenix from the ashes

fenomenal 1 *adj* (**a**) *(magnífico)* great, fantastic (**b**) *(enorme)* phenomenal
  2 *adv Fam* **pasarlo f.** to have a great *o* fantastic time; **me siento f.** I feel great *o* fantastic
  3 *interj* great!, terrific!

fenómeno 1 *nm* (**a**) *(suceso)* phenomenon; **f. metereológico** meteorological phenomenon (**b**) *(monstruo)* freak; **es un f. jugando al tenis** she's an amazing tennis player
  2 *adv Fam* **pasarlo f.** to have a great *o* fantastic time; **me siento f.** I feel great *o* fantastic
  3 *interj* great!, terrific!

fenomenología *nf* phenomenology

fenotipo *nm* phenotype

feo, -a1 *adj* (**a**) *(persona)* ugly; **más f. que picio** as ugly as sin (**b**) *(aspecto, herida, conducta)* nasty; *(tiempo)* foul, horrible; **está metido en un asunto muy f.** he's mixed up in some really nasty business; **ponerse f.** *(situación, tiempo)* to turn nasty; **está f. escupir** it's rude to spit (**c**) *Am (olor, sabor)* unpleasant
  2 *nm,f (persona)* ugly person
  3 *nm (desaire)* slight, insult; **hacer un f. a alguien** to offend *o* slight sb

feraz *adj Literario* fertile, fecund

féretro *nm* coffin

feria *nf* (**a**) *(mercado, exhibición)* fair; **f. de artesanía** craft fair; **f. de ganado** cattle market; **f. del libro** book fair; **f. de muestras** trade fair (**b**) *(fiesta popular)* festival; *(de atracciones)* amusement park; *Méx Fam* **como en f.: en ese negocio le fue como en f.** that deal turned out really badly for him; **F. de Abril** = annual fair in Seville (**c**) *Méx (monedas)* small change; **¿me cambia diez pesos por f.?** could you give me change of ten pesos, please?

feriado, -a *adj Am* **día f.** (public) holiday

ferial *adj* fair; **recinto f.** fairground(s), exhibition area

feriante *nmf (vendedor)* exhibitor *(at trade fair)*

fermentación *nf* fermentation

fermentar *vt & vi también Fig* to ferment

fermento *nm* ferment

ferocidad *nf* ferocity, fierceness

Feroe *nfpl* **las (Islas) F.** the Faeroes, the Faeroe Islands

feromona *nf* pheromone

feroz *adj* (**a**) *(animal, bestia)* fierce, ferocious (**b**) *(criminal, asesino)* cruel, savage (**c**) *(intenso) (dolor, angustia)* terrible; **tenía un hambre f.** he was ravenous *o* starving; **la competencia es f.** the competition is fierce

férreo, -a *adj también Fig* iron; **la vía férrea** the railroad track; **disciplina férrea** iron discipline

ferretería *nf* hardware store

ferretero, -a *nm,f* hardware dealer

férrico, -a *adj* ferric

ferrocarril *nm (sistema, medio)* railroad, railway; *(tren)* train; **por f.** by train

ferrocarrilero, -a = ferroviario

ferroso, -a *adj* ferrous

ferroviario, -a, *Méx* **ferrocarrilero, -a 1** *adj* **línea ferroviaria** railroad *o* railway line; **red ferroviaria** railroad *o* rail(way) network
  2 *nm,f* railroad *o* railway worker

ferry *nm* ferry

fértil *adj también Fig* fertile

fertilidad *nf también Fig* fertility

fertilización *nf* fertilization; *Med* **f. in vitro** in vitro fertilization

fertilizante 1 *adj* fertilizing
  2 *nm* fertilizer

fertilizar [14] *vt* to fertilize

ferviente *adj* fervent

fervor *nm* fervor; **con f.** fervently

fervoroso, -a *adj* fervent

festejar 1 *vt* (**a**) *(celebrar)* to celebrate (**b**) *(agasajar)* to entertain
  2 festejarse *vpr (celebrarse)* to be celebrated

festejo *nm* (**a**) *(fiesta)* party; **festejos** *(celebraciones)* public festivities; **festejos taurinos** bullfights (**b**) *(agasajo)* entertaining

festín *nm* banquet, feast; **darse un f.** to have a feast

festinar *vt Am (apresurar)* to hasten, to hurry up

festival *nm* festival; **f. de cine** film festival

festividad *nf* festivity

festivo, -a *adj* (a) *(de fiesta)* festive; **día f.** (public) holiday (b) *(alegre)* cheerful, jolly; *(chistoso)* funny, witty

festón *nm (en costura)* scallop

festonear *vt (en costura)* to scallop

fetal *adj* fetal

fetén *adj inv Esp Fam* great

fetiche *nm* fetish

fetichismo *nm* fetishism

fetichista 1 *adj* fetishistic
2 *nmf* fetishist

fétido, -a *adj* fetid, foul-smelling

feto *nm* (a) *(embrión)* fetus (b) *Fam (persona fea)* ugly person, fright

feudal *adj* feudal

feudalismo *nm* feudalism

feudo *nm Hist* fief; *Fig (dominio)* domain, area of influence

fez *nm* fez

FF AA *nfpl (abrev de* **Fuerzas Armadas***)* = Spanish armed forces

fiabilidad *nf* reliability

fiable *adj (máquina)* reliable; *(persona)* trustworthy

fiado *nm* **al f.** on credit; **dar f.** to give credit

fiador, -ora *nm,f* guarantor, surety; **salir f. por** to vouch for

fiambre *nm* (a) *(alimento)* cold cut (b) *Fam (cadáver)* stiff, corpse; **dejar f.** to bump off

fiambrera *nf* lunch *o* sandwich box

fiambrería *nf RP* delicatessen

fianza *nf* (a) *(depósito)* deposit (b) *Der* bail; **bajo f.** on bail (c) *(garantía)* security, bond

fiar [32] **1** *vt Com* to sell on credit
2 *vi* (a) *Com* to sell on credit (b) **ser de f.** to be trustworthy
3 fiarse *vpr* **¡no te fíes!** don't be too sure (about it)!; **fiarse de algo/alguien** to trust sth/sb

fiasco *nm* fiasco

fibra *nf* (a) *(de tela, alimenticia)* fiber; *(de madera)* grain; **alimentos ricos en f.** foods rich in fiber; **f. alimenticia** dietary fiber; **f. óptica** optic fiber; **f. sintética** synthetic fiber; **f. de vidrio** fiberglass (b) *(energía)* character, vigor

fibroma *nm Med* fibroma

fibrosis *nf inv Med* fibrosis

fibroso, -a *adj (carne)* chewy, tough; *(persona)* lean; *Anat (tejido)* fibrous

ficción *nf* (a) *(invención)* fiction (b) *(simulación)* pretense, make-believe (c) *(género literario)* fiction; **literatura de f.** fiction

ficha *nf* (a) *(tarjeta)* (index) card; *(con detalles personales)* file, record card; **f. policial** police record; **f. técnica** (technical) specifications (b) *(de guardarropa, aparcamiento)* ticket (c) *(de teléfono)* token (d) *(de juego)* counter; *(de ajedrez, damas)* piece; *(de ruleta)* chip (e) *Dep (contrato)* contract (f) *Inform* card; **f. perforada** perforated card

fichaje *nm Dep (contratación)* signing (up); *(importe)* transfer fee

fichar 1 *vt* (a) *(archivar)* to note down on an index card, to file (b) *(sujeto: policía)* to put on police files *o* records (c) *Dep* to sign up (d) *Fam (pillar)* to sniff out, to see through
2 *vi* (a) *(en el trabajo) (al entrar)* to punch in, to clock in *o* on; *(al salir)* to punch out, to clock out *o* off (b) *Dep* to sign up (**por** for)

fichero *nm (gen) & Inform* file

ficticio, -a *adj* (a) *(imaginario)* fictitious (b) *(convencional)* imaginary

ficus *nm inv* rubber plant

fidedigno, -a *adj* reliable

fideicomisario, -a *nm,f Der* trustee

fideicomiso *nm Der* trust

fidelidad *nf* (a) *(lealtad)* loyalty; *(de cónyuge, perro)* faithfulness; *Com* **f. a la marca** brand loyalty (b) *(precisión)* accuracy; **alta f.** high fidelity

fidelización *nf Com* building of customer loyalty; **programa de f.** loyalty program

fidelizar [14] *vt Com* **f. a los clientes** to build customer loyalty

fideo *nm* noodle; **estar como un f.** to be as thin as a rake

fiduciario, -a *adj & nm,f Der & Econ* fiduciary

fiebre *nf* fever; **tener f.** to have a temperature; **f. aftosa** foot-and-mouth disease; **f. amarilla** yellow fever; **f. del heno** hay fever; **la f. del oro** the gold rush; **f. tifoidea** typhoid (fever)

fiel 1 *adj* (a) *(leal) (amigo, seguidor)* loyal; *(cónyuge, perro)* faithful; **fue siempre f. a sus ideas** he always remained faithful to his ideas (b) *(preciso)* accurate; **un f. reflejo de la realidad** a very accurate picture of reality
2 *nm* (a) *(de balanza)* needle, pointer (b) *Rel* **los fieles** the faithful

fielmente *adv* faithfully

fieltro *nm* felt

fiera 1 *nf (animal)* wild animal; **estar/ponerse hecho una f.** to be/go wild with anger
2 *nmf Esp (persona) (genial)* demon; **es un f. jugando al tenis** he's a demon tennis player

fiero, -a *adj* savage, ferocious

fierro *nm Am* (a) *(hierro)* iron (b) *Fam (arma)* piece

fiesta *nf* (a) *(de pueblo, barrio)* (local) festivities; **el pueblo está en fiestas** the town is holding its annual fair *o* festival; **aguar la f. a alguien** to spoil sb's fun; **f. mayor** = local celebrations for the festival of a town's patron saint; *Esp* **la f. nacional** *(los toros)* bullfighting; **f.(s) patronal(es)** = celebrations for the feast day of a town's patron saint
(b) *(día)* public holiday; **ser f.** to be a public holiday; **hacer f.** to be on holiday; **fiestas** *(vacaciones)* vacation; *Rel* **f. de guardar** holiday of obligation; *Rel* **f. movible** a movable feast
(c) *(reunión)* party; **dar una f. en honor de alguien** to give a party in sb's honor; **f. de disfraces** fancy dress party

fiestero, -a *nm,f* party animal

FIFA ['fifa] *nf (abrev de* **Federación Internacional de Fútbol Asociación***)* FIFA

figura 1 *nf* (a) *(objeto, de persona)* figure; *(forma)* shape; **una f. en la oscuridad** a shadowy form; **f. geométrica** geometrical figure *o* shape; **f. paterna** father figure; **f. de porcelana** china *o* porcelain figure (b) *(personaje destacado)* (well-known) figure; **figuras del mundo del deporte** well-known figures from the sporting world (c) *(en naipes)* face card (d) *Ling* **f. retórica** figure of speech (e) *Der* **f. jurídica** legal concept
2 *nmf Esp Fam* **es un f.** he's really something

figuraciones *nfpl* imaginings; **son f. tuyas** it's all in your imagination

figurado, -a *adj* figurative

figurante, -a *nm,f* extra

figurar 1 *vi* (a) *(aparecer)* to appear, to figure (**en** in); **figura en los títulos de crédito como productor** he appears *o* is listed in the credits as the producer; **figura entre los artistas más destacados de su época** he was one of the most outstanding artists of his day (b) *Fam (destacar, sobresalir)* **le encanta f.** he likes to seem important
2 *vt* (a) *(representar)* to represent (b) *(simular)* to feign, to simulate
3 figurarse *vpr (imaginarse)* to imagine; **me figuro que vendrá en tren** I imagine she'll come by train; **ya me lo figuraba yo** I thought as much; **¿se rió? — figúrate** did she laugh? — and how!

figurativo, -a *adj Arte* figurative

figurín *nm* fashion sketch; *Fig* **ir** *o* **estar hecho un f.** to be dressed up to the nines

figurón *nm Fam* show-off, poser

fijación *nf* (**a**) *(gen) & Fot* fixing (**b**) *(obsesión)* fixation (**c**) **fijaciones** *(en esquí)* bindings

fijador *nm (líquido)* fixative; **f. de pelo** *(crema)* hair gel; *(espray)* hair spray

fijar 1 *vt* (**a**) *(asegurar)* to fix (**a** *o* **en** onto); *(cartel)* to stick up; *(sello)* to stick on; **prohibido f. carteles** *(en letrero)* post no bills (**b**) *(establecer) (fecha, precio)* to set, to fix; *(significado)* to establish; **f. el domicilio** to take up residence; **f. la mirada/la atención en** to fix one's gaze/attention on

  2 fijarse *vpr* (**a**) *(notar)* to pay attention; **fijarse en algo** *(darse cuenta)* to notice sth; *(prestar atención)* to pay attention to sth; **¿no te has fijado en la expresión de su cara?** didn't you notice the expression on her face?; **¡fíjate!** just imagine! (**b**) **fijarse un objetivo** to set oneself a target

fijeza *nf* firmness; **con f.** *(con seguridad)* definitely, for sure; *(con persistencia)* fixedly

Fiji [fiji] *n* Fiji

fijo, -a 1 *adj* (**a**) *(no variable, inmóvil)* fixed; *(sujeto)* firmly attached; **tenía los ojos fijos en él** she didn't take her eyes off him, she had her eyes fixed on him; **no tienen fecha fija para la boda** they haven't set a date for the wedding (**b**) *(empleado, trabajo)* permanent; **estoy f. en la empresa** I've got a permanent job in the company (**c**) *(cliente)* regular

  2 *adv Fam* definitely; **f. que viene** he's definitely coming

fila 1 *nf (hilera)* line; *(de asientos)* row; **en f., en f. india** in line, in single file; **aparcar en doble f.** to double-park; **ponerse en f.** to line up

  2 filas *nfpl* (**a**) *Mil* ranks; *Fig* **cerrar filas** to close ranks; **en filas** doing military service; **llamar a filas a alguien** to call sb up; **romper filas** to fall out (**b**) *(de partido)* ranks; **militaba en las filas socialistas** she was an active member of the socialist party

filamento *nm* filament

filantropía *nf* philanthropy

filantrópico, -a *adj* philanthropic

filantropismo *nm* philanthropy

filántropo, -a *nm,f* philanthropist

filarmónica *nf* philharmonic (orchestra)

filarmónico, -a *adj* philharmonic

filatelia *nf* philately

filatélico, -a 1 *adj* philatelic

  2 *nm,f* philatelist

filete *nm* (**a**) *(grueso)* (fillet) steak; *(delgado)* fillet; *(solomillo)* sirloin (**b**) *(de tornillo)* thread

filetear *vt* (**a**) *(adornar)* to fillet, to decorate with fillets (**b**) *(hacer filetes)* to fillet

filfa *nf Fam* **¡menuda f.!** *(mentira)* what a whopper!; *(engaño)* what a swindle!

filiación *nf* (**a**) *(ficha militar, policial)* record, file (**b**) *Pol* affiliation (**c**) *(parentesco)* relationship

filial 1 *adj* (**a**) *(de hijo)* filial (**b**) *(de empresa)* subsidiary

  2 *nf* subsidiary

filibustero *nm* pirate

filiforme *adj* thread-like

filigrana *nf* (**a**) *(en orfebrería)* filigree (**b**) *(habilidad)* skillful work (**c**) *(en billetes)* watermark

Filipinas *nfpl* **(las) F.** the Philippines *(singular)*

filipino, -a 1 *adj & nm,f* Filipino

  2 *nm (lengua)* Filipino

filisteo, -a *adj & nm,f* Philistine

film *(pl* **films)** *nm* movie

filmación *nf* filming, shooting

filmadora *nf (cámara)* cine camera

filmar *vt* to film, to shoot

filme *nm* movie

filmografía *nf* filmography

filmoteca *nf (archivo)* film library; *(sala de cine)* film institute; **la F. Nacional** the national film archive

filo *nm (borde)* (cutting) edge; **al f. de** just before; **al f. de la medianoche** at the stroke of midnight; *Fig* **de doble f., de dos filos** double-edged

filología *nf* (**a**) *(ciencia)* philology (**b**) *(carrera)* language and literature

filológico, -a *adj* philological

filólogo, -a *nm,f* philologist

filón *nm* (**a**) *(de carbón, oro)* seam (**b**) *(cosa provechosa)* gold mine; **un f. de información** a mine of information

filoso, -a *adj Am* sharp

filosofar *vi* to philosophize

filosofía *nf* (**a**) *(estudio)* philosophy (**b**) *(resignación)* **tomarse algo con f.** to be philosophical about sth

filosófico, -a *adj* philosophical

filósofo, -a *nm,f* philosopher

filoxera *nf* phylloxera

filtración *nf* (**a**) *(de líquido)* filtration (**b**) *(de información)* leak

filtrante *adj* filtering

filtrar 1 *vt* (**a**) *(líquido)* to filter (**b**) *(información)* to leak

  2 filtrarse *vpr* (**a**) *(líquido)* to filter, to seep (**por** through) (**b**) *(información)* to be leaked

filtro *nm* (**a**) *(de café, cigarrillo, aparato, cámara)* filter; **f. del aire** air filter (**b**) *(pócima)* philter

filudo, -a *adj Andes* sharp

fimosis *nf inv Med* phimosis, = condition in which the foreskin is too tight to be retracted

fin *nm* (**a**) *(final)* end; **dar** *o* **poner f. a algo** to put an end to sth; **tocar a su f.** to come to a close; **a fines de** at the end of; **al** *o* **por f.** at last, finally; **a f. de cuentas** after all; **al f. y al cabo** after all; **al f. del mundo** to the end of the earth (and back); **en f.** anyway; **en f., lo volveremos a intentar** well *o* anyway, we can try again; **sin f.** endless; **f. de año** *(Nochevieja)* New Year's Eve; **f. de curso** *(en colegio)* end of the school year; *(en universidad)* end of the academic year; **f. de fiesta** grand finale; **f. de semana** weekend

  (**b**) *(objetivo)* aim, goal; **un f. en sí mismo** an end in itself; **el f. justifica los medios** the end justifies the means; **con este f.** with this aim, to this end; **a f. de** in order to; **a f. de contener la inflación** (in order) to keep inflation down; **un concierto con fines benéficos** a charity concert

finado, -a *nm,f* **el f.** the deceased

final 1 *adj* final, end; **punto f.** end point

  2 *nm* end; **a finales de** at the end of; **al f.** *(en conclusión)* in the end; **ya verás como al f. acepta** she'll agree in the end, you'll see; **al f. de** at the end of; **al f. del pasillo** at the end of the corridor; **f. feliz** happy ending

  3 *nf* final; *Dep* **f. de la copa** cup final

finalidad *nf* aim, purpose

finalista 1 *adj* among the finalists

  2 *nmf* finalist

finalización *nf (terminación)* end; *(de contrato)* termination

finalizar [14] **1** *vt* to finish, to complete

  2 *vi* to end, to finish (**con** in)

finalmente *adv* finally

financiación *nf, Am* **financiamiento** *nm* financing

financiar *vt* to finance

financiera *nf (empresa)* finance company

financiero, -a 1 *adj* financial

  2 *nm,f (persona)* financier

financista *nmf Am* financier

finanzas *nfpl* finance

finar *vi Formal* to pass away

finca *nf (bien inmueble)* property; *(casa de campo)* country residence; *Der* **f. rústica/urbana** property (in the country/city)

fineza *nf (a) (cualidad)* (fine) quality **(b)** *(cortesía)* courtesy

finger ['finger] *(pl* **fingers)** *nm* aerobridge

fingido, -a *adj* feigned, apparent

fingimiento *nm* pretense

fingir [24] **1** *vt* to feign; **fingió no saber nada** he pretended not to know anything
2 *vi* to pretend
3 fingirse *vpr* **se fingió enfermo/cansado** he pretended to be ill/tired

finiquitar *vt Fin (deuda)* to settle; *(trabajador)* to pay off

finiquito *nm Fin (de deuda)* settlement; *(por despido)* layoff settlement

finito, -a *adj* finite

finjo *ver* **fingir**

finlandés, -esa 1 *adj* Finnish
2 *nm,f (persona)* Finn
3 *nm (lengua)* Finnish

Finlandia *n* Finland

fino, -a 1 *adj* **(a)** *(de calidad) (tela, alimentos)* fine, high-quality **(b)** *(delgado)* thin; *(cintura)* slim **(c)** *(manos)* delicate; *(piel)* smooth; *(pelo)* fine **(d)** *(cortés)* refined **(e)** *(oído, olfato)* sharp, keen **(f)** *(gusto, humor, ironía)* refined
2 *nm* dry sherry

finolis *Fam* **1** *adj inv* affected
2 *nmf inv* affected person

fintar 1 *vt* **f. a alguien** *(en esgrima, boxeo)* to feint at sb; *(en fútbol, baloncesto)* to deceive by a feigned pass
2 *vi (en esgrima, boxeo)* to feint; *(en fútbol, baloncesto)* to deceive by feigning a pass

finura *nf (a) (buena calidad)* fineness **(b)** *(delgadez)* thinness **(c)** *(cortesía)* refinement **(d)** *(de oído, olfato)* sharpness, keenness **(e)** *(de gusto, humor, ironía)* refinement

fiordo *nm Geog* fjord

firma *nf (a) (rúbrica)* signature; *(acción)* signing; **estampar la f.** to sign, to write one's signature **(b)** *(empresa)* firm

firmamento *nm* firmament

firmante 1 *adj* signatory
2 *nmf* signatory; **el abajo f.** the undersigned

firmar *vt* to sign; *Fig* **f. algo en blanco** to rubber-stamp sth

firme 1 *adj* **(a)** *(fuerte, sólido)* firm; *(andamio, construcción)* stable **(b)** *(argumento, base)* solid **(c)** *(carácter, actitud, paso)* resolute; *Mil* **¡firmes!** attention! **(d) de f.: trabaja de f. en el nuevo proyecto** he's working full-time on the new project; **un acuerdo en f.** a firm agreement; **una respuesta en f.** a definite answer
2 *adv* hard; **mantenerse f. en** to hold fast to; **se mantuvo f. en su actitud** he refused to give way, he stood his ground
3 *nm (de carretera)* road surface; **f. en mal estado** *(en letrero)* uneven road surface

firmeza *nf* **(a)** *(fortaleza, solidez)* firmness; *(de construcción)* stability **(b)** *(de argumento)* solidity **(c)** *(de carácter, actitud)* resolution

fiscal 1 *adj* fiscal; **año/asesor/fraude f.** tax year/adviser/fraud
2 *nmf Der* ≃ district attorney; **F. General del Estado** ≃ attorney general

fiscalía *nf Der (cargo)* ≃ post of district attorney; *(oficina)* ≃ district attorney's office

fiscalidad *nf* taxation

fiscalización *nf (de acción, persona)* investigation; *(de empresa)* tax investigation; *(de cuentas)* inspection

fiscalizador, -ora *adj Formal* investigating, auditing; **órgano f.** auditing body; **función fiscalizadora** auditing function

fiscalizar [14] *vt (acción, persona)* to inquire into; *(empresa)* to investigate for tax purposes; *(cuentas)* to inspect for tax purposes

fisco *nm* **el f.** the Treasury

fisgar [38] *vi Fam* to pry

fisgón, -ona *Fam* **1** *adj* nosy, prying
2 *nm,f* busybody, meddler

fisgonear *vi Fam* to pry

fisgoneo *nm Fam* prying

fisgue *etc ver* **fisgar**

física *nf (ciencia)* physics *(singular)*; **f. nuclear** nuclear physics

físico, -a 1 *adj* physical
2 *nm,f (persona)* physicist
3 *nm (complexión) (de hombre, atleta)* physique; *(de mujer)* figure; **una modelo con un f. impresionante** a model with a stunning figure

fisiología *nf* physiology

fisiológico, -a *adj* physiological

fisiólogo, -a *nm,f* physiologist

fisión *nf Fís* fission

fisionomía *nf* features, appearance

fisioterapeuta *nmf Med* physiotherapist

fisioterapia *nf Med* physiotherapy

fisonomía *nf* features, appearance

fisonomista *nmf* **ser un buen/mal f.** to be good/bad at remembering faces

fistol *nm Méx (de corbata)* tie pin

fístula *nf Med* fistula

fisura *nf (grieta)* fissure, crack; *(quiebra, ruptura)* crack

fitología *nf* botany

fitoplancton *nm* phytoplankton

fitosanitario, -a *adj* plant health; **control f.** plant health measure

fitoterapia *nf* herbal medicine

Fiyi *n* Fiji

flacidez, flaccidez *nf* flabbiness

flácido, -a, fláccido, -a *adj* flaccid, flabby

flaco, -a *adj (persona)* thin, skinny; *(punto)* weak; **hacer un f. servicio** *o* **favor a alguien** to do sb no favors, to be unhelpful to sb; *Am Fam (como apelativo)* **¿cómo estás, flaca?** hey, how are you doing?

flagelación *nf* flagellation

flagelar 1 *vt* to flagellate
2 flagelarse *vpr* to flagellate oneself

flagelo *nm* **(a)** *(látigo)* whip **(b)** *Biol* flagellum

flagrante *adj* flagrant; *Der* **en f. delito** in flagrante delicto

flamante *adj (vistoso)* resplendent; *(nuevo)* brand-new

flambear *vt Culin* to flambé

flamear *vi* **(a)** *(fuego)* to blaze, to flare up **(b)** *(bandera, vela)* to flap

flamenco, -a 1 *adj* **(a)** *(música, baile)* flamenco; **cante/espectáculo f.** flamenco singing/show **(b)** *(de Flandes)* Flemish
2 *nm,f (de Flandes)* Fleming
3 *nm* **(a)** *(ave)* flamingo **(b)** *(lengua)* Flemish **(c)** *(música, baile)* flamenco

flamencología *nf* study of flamenco

flamencólogo, -a *nm,f* expert in flamenco

flan *nm* crème caramel; **f. de huevo/vainilla** = crème caramel made with egg/vanilla; *Fam* **estar hecho un f., estar como un f.** to be shaking like a jelly, to be a bundle of nerves

flanco *nm* flank

Flandes *n* Flanders

flanera *nf* crème caramel mold

flanquear *vt* to flank

flaquear *vi (fuerzas)* to weaken; *(entusiasmo, equipo)* to flag

flaqueza *nf* weakness

flash [flaʃ, flas] *(pl* **flashes***) nm* (**a**) *Fot* flash (**b**) *(informativo)* news flash (**c**) *Fam (imagen mental)* flash of inspiration; *Esp* **¡me llevé un f.!** I got a bit of a shock!

flashback ['flasβak] *(pl* **flashbacks***) nm Cine* flashback

flato *nm Esp* **tener f.** to have a stitch

flatulencia *nf* flatulence, wind

flatulento, -a *adj* flatulent

flauta *nf* (**a**) *Mús* flute; **f. (dulce)** recorder; **f. travesera** transverse flute (**b**) *CSur Fig Fam* **de la gran f.** tremendous; **¡(la gran) f.!** good grief!, good heavens!

flautín *nm* piccolo

flautista *nmf* flutist, flautist

flebitis *nf inv Med* phlebitis

flebotomía *nf Med* bloodletting

flecha *nf* arrow; *Fig* **como una f.** like a shot

flechado, -a *adj Fam* **salir f.** to shoot out

flechazo *nm* (**a**) *(con saeta)* arrow shot; *(herida)* arrow wound (**b**) *Fam (amoroso)* **fue un f.** it was love at first sight

fleco *nm* (**a**) *(adorno)* fringe; **con flecos** fringed (**b**) *(de tela gastada)* frayed edge (**c**) *Méx (flequillo)* bangs

flema *nf* phlegm

flemático, -a *adj (tranquilo)* phlegmatic

flemón *nm* gumboil

flequillo *nm* bangs

fletamiento *nm (de buque, avión)* charter, chartering

fletán *nm* halibut

fletar *vt (buque, avión)* to charter

flete *nm* (**a**) *(precio)* freightage (**b**) *(carga)* cargo, freight

fletero, -a *adj Am* for hire

flexibilidad *nf* flexibility

flexibilización *nf (de normas)* relaxation; *(del mercado de trabajo)* liberalization

flexibilizar [14] *vt (normas)* to make more flexible; *(mercado de trabajo)* to liberalize

flexible *adj* flexible

flexión *nf* (**a**) *(de brazo, pierna)* bending; **flexiones de brazo** push-ups; **flexiones abdominales** sit-ups (**b**) *Gram* inflection

flexionar *vt* to bend

flexo *nm Esp* adjustable table lamp *o* light

flexor, -ora 1 *adj* flexional

2 *nm* flexor

flipado, -a *adj Esp Fam (asombrado)* flabbergasted; *(drogado)* stoned, high

flipante *adj Esp Fam* cool, wild

flipar *Esp Fam* **1** *vi* (**a**) *(disfrutar)* to have a wild time (**b**) *(asombrarse)* to be flabbergasted (**c**) *(con una droga)* to be stoned *o* high

2 *vt (gustar a)* **me flipan los videojuegos** I'm crazy about video games

3 fliparse *vpr (disfrutar)* to go wild (**con** about)

flipe *nm Esp Fam* **¡qué f.!** what a gas!

flipper *(pl* **flippers***) nm* pinball machine

flirtear *vi* to flirt

flirteo *nm* flirtation, flirting

flojear *vi* (**a**) *(piernas)* to weaken; *(película, libro)* to flag; *(calor, trabajo)* to ease off; *(ventas)* to fall off; **me flojeaban las fuerzas** I was feeling weak; **le flojea la memoria** his memory is going *o* failing (**b**) *(no ser muy apto)* **f. en algo** to get worse at sth (**c**) *Andes Fam (no hacer nada)* to laze around *o* about

flojedad *nf* weakness

flojera *nf Fam* lethargy, feeling of weakness

flojo, -a 1 *adj* (**a**) *(suelto)* loose; **la falda me queda floja** this skirt is too loose for me (**b**) *(débil) (persona, bebida)* weak; *(sonido)* faint; *(salud)* poor; *(viento)* light; **muy Fam me la trae floja** I couldn't give a rat's ass (**c**) *(sin calidad, aptitudes) (obra, actuación, notas)* poor; **estar f. en algo** to be poor *o* weak at sth (**d**) *(mercado, negocio)* slack

2 *nm,f Andes, Méx Fam* layabout, lazybones

flor 1 *nf* (**a**) *(de planta)* flower; **en f.** in flower; **una camisa de flores** a flowery shirt; **echar flores a alguien** to pay sb compliments; *Esp Fam* **ni flores** no idea; *Fig* **ser f. de un día** to be flash in the pan; **f. de azahar** orange blossom; **f. de lis** fleur-de-lis; **flores cortadas** cut flowers; **flores naturales** real flowers; **f. de Pascua** poinsettia, Christmas flower

(**b**) *(lo mejor)* **la f. y nata** the crème de la crème, the cream; **ser la f. de la canela** to be the crème de la crème *o* the cream; **en la f. de la edad** *o* **de la vida** in the prime of life

(**c**) **a f. de agua/tierra** at water/ground level; **tiene una sensibilidad a f. de piel** she's extremely sensitive; **tengo los nervios a f. de piel** my nerves are really on edge

(**d**) *Chile (en uñas)* white spot

2 *adj inv CSur Fam (muy bueno)* great, fantastic

flora *nf* flora; *Med* **f. intestinal** intestinal flora

floración *nf* flowering, blossoming

floral *adj* floral

floreado, -a *adj* flowery

florear *vi CAm* to flower

florecer [46] *vi (dar flor)* to flower; *(prosperar)* to flourish

floreciente *adj (próspero)* flourishing

florecimiento *nm (de planta)* flowering; *(prosperidad)* flourishing

Florencia *n* Florence

florentino, -a *adj & nm,f* Florentine

florero *nm* vase

florete *nm* fencing foil

floricultor, -ora *nm,f* flower grower

floricultura *nf* flower growing

florido, -a *adj (con flores)* flowery; *(estilo, lenguaje)* florid

florín *nm Antes (moneda)* guilder

florista *nmf* florist

floristería *nf* florist's (store)

floritura *nf* flourish

flota *nf (de barcos, vehículos)* fleet; **f. pesquera** fishing fleet

flotabilidad *nf* (**a**) *(en el agua)* buoyancy (**b**) *Econ* floatability

flotación *nf (gen) & Econ* flotation

flotador *nm* (**a**) *(para nadar)* rubber ring (**b**) *(de caña de pescar)* float (**c**) *(de cisternas)* ball cock

flotante *adj (gen) & Econ* floating

flotar 1 *vt Econ* to float

2 *vi* (**a**) *(en líquido, aire)* to float (**b**) *(desconfianza, tensión)* to hang, to hover (**c**) *Econ* to float; **hacer f. una divisa** to float a currency

flote: a flote *loc adv* afloat; **mantenerse a f.** to stay afloat; *Fig* **sacar algo a f.** to get sth back on its feet; *Fig* **salir a f.** to get back on one's feet

flotilla *nf* flotilla

fluctuación *nf* (**a**) *(variación)* fluctuation (**b**) *(vacilación)* wavering

fluctuante *adj* fluctuating

fluctuar [4] *vi* (**a**) *(variar)* to fluctuate (**b**) *(vacilar)* to waver

fluidez *nf* (**a**) *(de sustancia, líquido)* fluidity; *(del tráfico)* free flow (**b**) *(de relaciones)* smoothness (**c**) *(en el lenguaje)* fluency

fluido, -a 1 *adj* (**a**) *(sustancia)* fluid; *(tráfico)* free-flowing (**b**) *(relaciones)* smooth (**c**) *(lenguaje)* fluent

2 *nm* fluid; **f. eléctrico** electric current *o* power

fluir [34] *vi* to flow

flujo *nm* flow; **f. y reflujo** ebb and flow; *Com* **f. de caja** cash flow; **f. migratorio** flow of immigrants; **f. sanguíneo** bloodstream; **f. vaginal** vaginal discharge

flúor *nm* fluorine

fluorescencia *nf* fluorescence

fluorescente 1 *adj* fluorescent
2 *nm* fluorescent tube

fluoruro *nm Quím* fluoride

fluvial *adj* river; **cuenca f.** river basin

flux *nm inv* **(a)** *(en naipes)* flush **(b)** *Carib, Col, Méx (traje)* suit

fluya *etc ver* **fluir**

fluyera *etc ver* **fluir**

FM *nf* (*abrev de* **frecuencia modulada**) FM

FMI *nm* (*abrev de* **Fondo Monetario Internacional**) IMF

fobia *nf* phobia

foca *nf* seal; *Fam Fig* **está como una f.** *(está gorda)* she's like a whale

focal *adj* focal

focalizar [14] *vt* to focus

foco *nm* **(a)** *(centro)* center, focal point; *(de epidemia)* source, breeding ground; **un f. de infecciones** a source of infection; **un f. de rebelión/intrigas** a hotbed of rebellion/intrigue; **un f. de miseria** a severely deprived area **(b)** *(lámpara) (para un punto)* spotlight; *(para una zona)* floodlight **(c)** *Fís & Geom* focus **(d)** *Andes, Méx (bombilla)* light bulb **(e)** *Am (farola)* streetlight **(f)** *Am Aut (car)* headlight

fofo, -a *adj* flabby

fogaje *nm* **(a)** *Cuba, Méx (erupción)* rash **(b)** *Ecuad (llamarada)* blaze **(c)** *Carib (sofoco)* stifling heat

fogata *nf* bonfire, fire

fogón *nm* **(a)** *(para cocinar)* stove **(b)** *(de máquina de vapor)* firebox

fogonazo *nm* flash

fogonero, -a *nm,f* stoker

fogosidad *nf (de persona)* passion; *(de caballo)* spirit

fogoso, -a *adj (persona)* passionate, intense; *(caballo)* spirited, lively

fogueo *nm* **de f.** blank

foie-gras [fwa'ɤras] *nm inv* (pâté de) foie-gras

fol. (*abrev de* **folio**) f

folclore, folclor *nm* folklore

folclórico, -a 1 *adj* traditional, popular
2 *nm,f Esp* = singer of traditional Spanish songs

folclorismo *nm* folklore

fólder *nm Andes, CAm, Méx (carpeta)* folder

foliación *nf* foliation

folículo *nm* follicle; **f. piloso** hair follicle

folio *nm (hoja)* leaf, sheet *(approximately 8.25 x 11.75 inches)*; **tamaño f.** = 8.25 x 11.75 inches *(approximately)*

folk *nm* folk (music)

folklor *nm* folklore

follado, -a *adj Esp muy Fam (con prisa)* **voy f.** I'm rushed of my goddamn feet

follaje *nm* foliage

follar *vi & vt Esp muy Fam* to screw

folletín *nm (melodrama)* melodrama; **de f.** *(vida, incidente)* melodramatic

folletinesco, -a *adj* melodramatic

folleto *nm (turístico, publicitario)* brochure; *(explicativo, de instrucciones)* leaflet

follón 1 *nm Esp Fam* **(a)** *(discusión)* row; **se armó un f.** there was an almighty row **(b)** *(lío)* mess; **¡vaya f.!** what a mess!; **me hice un f. con las listas** I got into a real muddle o mess with the lists
2 follones *nmpl Ecuad (bragas)* panties

follonero, -a *Esp Fam* **1** *adj* **ser muy f.** to be a real troublemaker
2 *nm,f* troublemaker

fomentar *vt* to encourage, to foster

fomento *nm* encouragement, fostering; **Ministerio de F.** Ministry of Public Works

fonación *nf* phonation

fonador, -ora *adj* speech; **el aparato f.** the speech apparatus

fonazo *nm Méx Fam* phone, call

fonda *nf* boardinghouse; **hacer parada y f.** *(para comer)* to stop for something to eat; *(para dormir)* to make an overnight stop

fondeadero *nm* anchorage

fondear 1 *vi* to anchor
2 *vt (sondear)* to sound; *(registrar) (barco)* to search

fondista *nmf* **(a)** *Dep (corredor)* long-distance runner; *(nadador)* long-distance swimmer; *(esquiador)* cross-country skier **(b)** *(propietario de fonda)* landlord, *f* landlady

fondo *nm* **(a)** *(parte inferior)* bottom; **doble f.** false bottom; **fondos** *(de embarcación)* bottom; *Fig* **bajos fondos** underworld; **sin f.** bottomless; **tocar f.** *(embarcación)* to scrape along the seabed/riverbed; *Fig (crisis)* to bottom out; **su popularidad ha tocado f.** their popularity has reached an all-time low o rock bottom
(b) *(de habitación)* back; **al f. de** *(calle, pasillo)* at the end of; *(sala)* at the back of
(c) *(dimensión)* depth; **tener un metro de f.** to be one meter deep
(d) *(de cuadro, foto, tela)* background; **sobre f. negro** on a black background; **al f.** in the background
(e) *(de asunto, problema)* heart, bottom; **llegar al f. de** to get to the heart o bottom of; **el problema de f.** the underlying problem; **la cuestión de f.** the fundamental issue; **en el f.** *(en lo más íntimo)* deep down; *(en lo esencial)* basically
(f) *Fin (de dinero)* fund; **a f. perdido** nonreturnable; **fondos** *(capital)* funds; **estar mal de fondos** *(persona)* to be badly off; *(empresa)* to be short of funds; **recaudar fondos** to raise funds; **f. de amortización** sinking fund; **f. de comercio** goodwill; **f. común** kitty; **f. de garantía de depósito** deposit guarantee fund; **f. de inversión** investment fund; **f. de inversión mobiliaria** mutual fund; **F. Monetario Internacional** International Monetary Fund; **f. de pensiones** pension fund; **fondos reservados** = contingency funds available to ministries, for which they do not have to account publicly
(g) *(de biblioteca, archivo)* catalog, collection; **f. editorial** backlist
(h) *(fundamento)* reason, basis
(i) *(de obra literaria)* substance
(j) *(de una persona)* **tener buen f.** to have a good heart
(k) *Dep (resistencia)* stamina; *(ejercicio)* push-up; **de f.** long-distance; **de medio f.** middle-distance
(l) *Col, Méx (combinación)* petticoat
(m) *(expresiones)* **hacer algo a f.** to do sth thoroughly; **hacer una limpieza a f.** to have a thorough cleaning; **emplearse a f.** to do one's utmost

fondón, -ona *adj Fam* beefy, chunky

fondue [fon'du] *nf Culin (comida)* fondue; *(utensilios)* fondue set

fonema *nm* phoneme

fonendoscopio *nm* stethoscope

fonética *nf (ciencia)* phonetics *(singular)*

fonético, -a *adj* phonetic

fonetista *nmf* phonetician

fónico, -a *adj* phonic

fono *nm Am Fam* phone

fonoaudiología *nf RP* speech therapy

fonoaudiólogo, -a *nm,f RP* speech therapist

fonógrafo *nm* phonograph, gramophone

fonología *nf* phonology

fonometría *nf* phonometry

fonoteca *nf* record library

fontanería *nf* plumbing

fontanero, -a *nm,f* plumber

footing ['futin] *nm* jogging; **hacer f.** to go jogging

foque *nm Náut* jib

forajido, -a *nm,f* outlaw

foral *adj* = relating to ancient regional laws still existing in some parts of Spain

foráneo, -a *adj* foreign

forastero, -a *nm,f* stranger

forcé *ver* **forzar**

forcejear *vi* to struggle

forcejeo *nm* struggle

forcemos *ver* **forzar**

fórceps *nm inv* forceps

forense 1 *adj* forensic; **médico f.** forensic scientist, pathologist
  2 *nmf* forensic scientist, pathologist

forestal *adj* forest; **incendio f.** forest fire; **repoblación f.** reforestation

forfait [for'fait, for'fe] (*pl* **forfaits**) *nm* **(a)** *(para esquiar)* ski pass **(b)** *Dep* default **(c)** *(precio invariable)* fixed rate; **a f.** fixed price

forja *nf (taller)* forge; *también Fig (acción)* forging

forjado, -a *adj (hierro)* wrought

forjador, -ora *nm,f* (metal) forger

forjar 1 *vt* **(a)** *(metal)* to forge **(b)** *(persona, nación)* to create, to form; **las guerras forjan héroes** wars create heroes **(c)** *(mentira)* to invent; *(plan)* to form
  2 forjarse *vpr* **(a)** *(labrarse)* to carve out for oneself **(b)** *(imaginarse)* **forjarse demasiadas ilusiones** to build up false hopes (for oneself) **(c)** *(crearse, originarse)* to be forged; **la revolución se forjó en las minas de carbón** the revolution was forged in the coal mines

forma1 *nf* **(a)** *(figura)* shape, form; **en f. de** in the shape of; **en f. de L** L-shaped; **tener f. ovalada** *o* **de óvalo** to be oval in shape; **formas** *(silueta)* figure, curves
  (b) *(manera)* way, manner; **se puede hacer de varias formas** it can be done in several different ways; **¡qué f. de llover!** it's absolutely pouring down!; **de cualquier f., de todas formas** anyway, in any case; **de esta f.** in this way; **f. de pago** method of payment; **f. de ser: es su f. de ser** that's just the way he is
  (c) *(condición)* **estar en f.** to be fit; **estar en baja/plena f.** *(física)* to be in poor/top shape; *(psicológica)* to be off form/on top form; **mantenerse en f.** to keep fit; **f. física** fitness
  (d) *(manifestación)* form; **la fotografía es una f. de arte** photography is an art form; **formas de vida** life forms
  (e) *(no fondo)* form; **f. y fondo** form and content
  (f) *Rel* host
  (g) *Méx (formulario)* form
  2 formas *nfpl (modales)* manners, social conventions; **guardar las formas** to keep up appearances
  3 de forma que *loc conj* in such a way that, so that; **dobla la camisa de f. que no se arruguen las mangas** fold the shirt so (that) the sleeves don't get creased; **han organizado las conferencias de f. que haya diez minutos de intervalo entre ellas** they've arranged the speeches in such a way that there's a ten-minute break between each one

formación *nf* **(a)** *(creación)* formation **(b)** *(educación)* training; **f. académica** formal education; **f. en el lugar de trabajo** in-company *o* in-house training; **f. profesional** vocational training **(c)** *(conjunto)* grouping; *Mil* formation; **f. política** political party

formador, -ora *adj* forming, constituting

formal *adj* **(a)** *(de la forma, legal)* formal; **ser novios formales** to be engaged **(b)** *(que se porta bien)* well-behaved, good **(c)** *(responsable, fiable)* reliable **(d)** *(serio)* serious, sober

formalidad *nf* **(a)** *(requisito)* formality; **es una mera f.** it's just a formality **(b)** *(educación)* (good) manners **(c)** *(fiabilidad)* reliability **(d)** *(seriedad)* seriousness

formalismo *nm* formalism

formalista 1 *adj* formal
  2 *nmf* formalist

formalización *nf* formalization

formalizar [14] *vt* to formalize

formar 1 *vt* **(a)** *(hacer)* to form; **f. una bola con algo** to make sth into a ball; **f. un equipo** to make up a team; **f. una asociación cultural** to set up a cultural organization; **f. parte de** to form *o* be part of; **forma parte del equipo** she's a member of the team **(b)** *(educar)* to train, to educate **(c)** *Mil* to form up
  2 *vi Mil* to fall in; **¡a f.!** fall in!
  3 formarse *vpr* **(a)** *(hacerse, crearse)* to form; **se formó espuma en la superficie** froth formed on the surface **(b)** *(educarse)* to be trained *o* educated

formateado, -a *Inform* **1** *adj* formatted
  2 *nm (proceso)* formatting

formatear *vt Inform* to format

formateo *nm Inform* formatting

formativo, -a *adj* formative

formato *nm (gen) & Inform* format; **f. apaisado** landscape (orientation); **f. vertical** *o* **de retrato** portrait (orientation)

formica® *nf* Formica®

formidable *adj (enorme)* tremendous; *(extraordinario)* amazing, fantastic

formol *nm* formalin

fórmula *nf* formula; **f. uno** formula one; **f. de cortesía** polite expression; **f. de tratamiento** form of address

formulación *nf* formulation

formular 1 *vt* to formulate; **f. una pregunta** to ask a question; **formuló cuidadosamente su respuesta** she phrased her reply carefully
  2 *vi* to write formulas

formulario *nm* form; **rellenar un f.** to fill in *o* out a form

formulismo *nm (apego) (a las formas)* formalism; *(a las normas)* sticking to the rules

fornicación *nf Formal* fornication

fornicar [59] *vi Formal* to fornicate

fornido, -a *adj* well-built

foro *nm* **(a)** *(tribunal)* court (of law) **(b)** *Teatro* back of the stage **(c)** *(lugar de discusión)* forum; **f. de debate** forum for debate; *Inform* **f. de discusión** discussion group

forofo, -a *nm,f Esp Fam* fan

forrado, -a *adj (libro)* covered; *(ropa)* lined (**de** with); *(asiento)* upholstered; *Fam Fig* **estar f.** to be rolling in it

forraje *nm* fodder, forage

forrar *vt (libro)* to cover; *(ropa)* to line (**de** with); *(asiento)* to upholster
  2 forrarse *vpr Fam (persona)* to make a bundle

forro *nm (de libro)* cover; *(de ropa)* lining; *(de asiento)* upholstery; *Fam* **¡ni por el f.!** no way!; **tela de f.** lining material; **f. polar** fleece jacket

fortachón, -ona *adj* strapping, well-built

fortalecer [46] *vt* to strengthen

fortalecimiento *nm* strengthening

fortaleza *nf* **(a)** *(fuerza) (física)* strength; *(moral, mental)* strength, fortitude **(b)** *(recinto)* fortress

fortificación *nf* fortification

fortificar [59] *vt* to fortify

fortín *nm* small fort

fortísimo, -a *superlativo ver* **fuerte**

fortuito, -a *adj* chance; **encuentro f.** chance encounter

fortuna *nf* (**a**) *(suerte)* (good) luck; **por f.** fortunately, luckily; **probar f.** to try one's luck; **tuvo la mala f. de caerse** he had the misfortune *o* bad luck to fall (**b**) *(destino)* fortune, fate (**c**) *(riqueza)* fortune; **hacer f.** to make one's fortune

forúnculo *nm* boil

forzado, -a *adj* forced; **trabajos forzados** hard labor; **verse f. a hacer algo** to find oneself forced to do sth

forzar [31] *vt* (**a**) *(obligar, empujar)* to force; **f. a alguien a hacer algo** to force sb to do sth; **f. la vista** to strain one's eyes; **f. una cerradura** to force a lock (**b**) *(violar)* to rape

forzoso, -a *adj* *(obligatorio)* obligatory, compulsory; *(inevitable)* inevitable; *(necesario)* necessary

forzudo, -a 1 *adj* strong

    2 *nm,f* strong man, *f* strong woman

fosa *nf* (**a**) *(sepultura)* grave; **f. común** common grave (**b**) *Anat* cavity; **fosas nasales** nostrils (**c**) *(hoyo)* pit; **f. marina** oceanic trench; **f. séptica** septic tank

fosfatar *vt* *(fertilizar)* to fertilize with phosphates

fosfato *nm* phosphate

fosforescencia *nf* phosphorescence

fosforescente *adj* phosphorescent

fosforito *adj* *Esp Fam (color, rotulador)* fluorescent

fósforo *nm* (**a**) *Quím* phosphorus (**b**) *(cerilla)* match

fósil 1 *adj* fossil; **combustible f.** fossil fuel

    2 *nm* fossil; *Fam (viejo)* old fossil

fosilización *nf* fossilization

fosilizado, -a *adj* fossilized

fosilizarse [14] *vpr* *(animal, hueso)* to fossilize; *(persona)* to turn into an old fossil

foso *nm (hoyo)* ditch; *(de castillo)* moat; *(de garaje)* pit; *Dep & Teatro* pit

foto *nf* photo, picture; **sacar una f. a alguien** to take a photo *o* picture of sb

fotocélula *nf* photocell, photoelectric cell

fotocomponer [50] *vt* *Imprenta* to typeset

fotocomposición *nf* *Imprenta* typesetting

fotocopia *nf* (**a**) *(objeto)* photocopy; **hacer una f.** to make *o* take a photocopy (**b**) *(procedimiento)* photocopying

fotocopiadora *nf* *(máquina)* photocopier; *(tienda)* copy shop

fotocopiar *vt* to photocopy

fotoeléctrico, -a *adj* photoelectric

foto-finish, fotofinis *nf inv Dep* photo finish

fotofobia *nf* photophobia

fotogenia *nf* photogenic qualities

fotogénico, -a *adj* photogenic

fotograbado *nm* photogravure

fotografía *nf* (**a**) *(arte)* photography; **f. aérea** aerial photography (**b**) *(objeto)* photograph; **hacer** *o* **sacar una f. a alguien** to take a picture *o* photograph of sb; **f. de carné** passport-sized photograph; **f. de grupo** group photograph

fotografiar [32] *vt* to photograph, to take a photograph of

fotográfico, -a *adj* photographic

fotógrafo, -a *nm,f* photographer; **f. de prensa** press photographer

fotograma *nm* still

fotolito *nm* photolithograph

fotomatón *nm* passport photo machine

fotometría *nf* photometry

fotómetro *nm* light *o* exposure meter

fotomodelo *nmf* photographic model

fotomontaje *nm* photomontage

fotón *nm* *Fís* photon

fotonovela *nf* photo story

fotosensible *adj* photosensitive

fotosíntesis *nf inv* photosynthesis

foulard [fu'lar] *(pl* **foulards)** *nm* scarf

foxterrier [fokste'rrjer, foks'terrjer] *(pl* **foxterriers)** *nm* fox terrier

foxtrot *nm* foxtrot

FP *nf* *(abrev de* **formación profesional)** = vocationally oriented education in Spain for pupils aged 14 and upward

fra. *(abrev de* **factura)** inv

frac *(pl* **fracs)** *nm* tails, dress coat

fracasado, -a 1 *adj* failed

    2 *nm,f* failure

fracasar *vi (intento, persona)* to fail (**como** as); *(producto)* to be a failure; **el modelo fracasó en Europa** the model was a failure in Europe

fracaso *nm* failure; **un rotundo f.** an outright failure; **todo fue un f.** the whole thing was a disaster; **el f. escolar** educational failure, poor performance at school

fracción *nf* (**a**) *(parte, quebrado)* fraction; **f. decimal** decimal fraction (**b**) *Pol* faction

fraccionadora *nf Méx* real estate agent

fraccionamiento *nm* (**a**) *(división)* division, breaking up (**b**) *Méx (urbanización)* housing project

fraccionar *vt* to divide, to break up; *(pago)* to split up into installments

fraccionario, -a *adj (moneda)* fractional

fractal *nm* fractal

fractura *nf* fracture

fracturar 1 *vt* to fracture

    2 fracturarse *vpr* to fracture; **fracturarse un brazo/una pierna** to fracture one's arm/leg

fragancia *nf* fragrance

fragante *adj* fragrant

fraganti *ver* **in fraganti**

fragata *nf* frigate

frágil *adj (objeto)* fragile; *(persona)* frail

fragilidad *nf (de objeto)* fragility; *(de persona)* frailty

fragmentación *nf (rotura)* fragmentation; *(división)* division

fragmentar *vt (romper)* to fragment; *(dividir)* to divide

fragmentario, -a *adj (incompleto)* fragmentary

fragmento *nm* fragment, piece; *(de obra)* excerpt

fragor *nm (de batalla)* clamor; *(de trueno)* crash

fragua *nf* forge

fraguar [11] **1** *vt* (**a**) *(forjar)* to forge (**b**) *(idear)* to think up

    2 *vi* to set, to harden

    3 fraguarse *vpr (tramarse)* to be in the offing; *(crearse, originarse)* to be hatched

fraile *nm* friar

frailecillo *nm* puffin

frambuesa *nf* raspberry

francachela *nf Fam (fiesta)* party; *(comilona)* spread

francés, -esa 1 *adj* French

    2 *nm,f* Frenchman, *f* Frenchwoman; **los franceses** the French; **marcharse** *o* **despedirse a la francesa** to leave without even saying goodbye

    3 *nm (lengua)* French

francesada *nf Fam Pey (costumbre)* Frenchified habit; **¡es una f.!** *(película, libro)* it's typical French trash!

Fráncfort *n* Frankfurt

franchute, -a *nm,f Fam Pey* Frog, = pejorative term referring to a French person

Francia *n* France

franciscano, -a *adj & nm,f* Franciscan

francmasón *nm* Freemason

francmasonería *nf* Freemasonry

francmasónico, -a *adj* Masonic

franco, -a 1 *adj* (**a**) *(sincero)* frank, open; *(directo)* frank (**b**) *(sin obstáculos, gastos)* free; **f. de porte** free shipping; **puerto f.** free port (**c**) *Hist* Frankish

2 *nm,f Hist* Frank

3 *nm* (**a**) *(moneda)* franc; **f. suizo** Swiss franc (**b**) *(lengua)* Frankish

francófilo, -a *adj & nm,f* francophile

francófono, -a 1 *adj* francophone

2 *nm,f* francophone

francotirador, -ora *nm,f* (**a**) *Mil* sniper (**b**) *(rebelde)* maverick

franela *nf* (**a**) *(tejido)* flannel (**b**) *Bol, Col, Ven (sudadera)* sweatshirt; *(camiseta) (interior)* undershirt; *(exterior)* T-shirt (**c**) *RP (trapo)* dustcloth

franja *nf (banda, tira)* strip; *(en bandera, uniforme)* strip; *TV* **f. (horaria) de máxima audiencia** prime time; **la F. de Gaza** the Gaza Strip

franquear *vt* (**a**) *(paso, camino)* to clear (**b**) *(río, montañas)* to negotiate, to cross; *también Fig* **f. el umbral** to cross the threshold (**c**) *(correo)* to attach postage to

franqueo *nm* postage; **f. pagado** postage-paid, postpaid

franqueza *nf* (**a**) *(sinceridad)* frankness, openness (**b**) *(confianza)* familiarity

franquicia *nf* (**a**) *(tienda)* franchise (**b**) *(exención)* exemption; **f. postal** free postage

franquiciado, -a *nm,f Com* franchisee, franchise holder

franquiciador, -ora *nm,f Com* franchiser

franquismo *nm* **el f.** *(régimen)* the Franco regime; *(doctrina)* Franco's doctrine

franquista 1 *adj* pro-Franco, Francoist; **el régimen f.** the Franco regime

2 *nmf* supporter of Franco

frasco *nm* bottle

frase *nf* (**a**) *(oración)* sentence (**b**) *(locución)* expression; **f. hecha** *(modismo)* set phrase; *(tópico)* cliché

fraseología *nf* (**a**) *(estilo)* phraseology (**b**) *(palabrería)* verbiage

fraternal *adj* brotherly, fraternal

fraternidad *nf* brotherhood, fraternity

fraternizar [14] *vi* to get on like brothers

fraterno, -a *adj* brotherly, fraternal

fratricida 1 *adj* fratricidal

2 *nmf* fratricide

fratricidio *nm* fratricide

fraude *nm* fraud; **f. fiscal** tax evasion

fraudulento, -a *adj* fraudulent

fray *nm Rel* brother

frazada *nf Am* blanket; **f. eléctrica** electric blanket

frecuencia *nf* frequency; **con f.** often; **¿con qué f.?** how often?; **alta/baja f.** high/low frequency; **f. modulada, modulación de f.** frequency modulation

frecuentación *nf* frequenting

frecuentado, -a *adj* **una plaza muy frecuentada** a very busy square; **un lugar muy f. por estudiantes** a place which is very popular with students; **un sitio f. por carteristas** a place frequented by pickpockets

frecuentar *vt (lugar)* to frequent; *(persona)* to see, to visit

frecuente *adj (reiterado)* frequent; *(habitual)* common

freelance, free lance ['frilans] *adj* freelance

free shop ['friʃop] *(pl* **free shops***) nm RP* duty-free shop

Freetown ['fritaun] *n* Freetown

freeware ['friwer] *nm Inform* freeware

freezer ['friser] *(pl* **freezers***) nm Am* freezer

fregadera *nf Am salvo RP Fam* pain, drag

fregadero *nm Esp, Méx* (kitchen) sink

fregado, -a 1 *adj Andes, Méx, Ven Fam* (**a**) *(con ser) (persona)*
annoying; *(situación)* tricky (**b**) *(con estar) (objeto)* bust; **¡estoy f.!** I've had it!

2 *nm* (**a**) *(lavado) (de platos, suelo)* wash; *(frotando)* scrub (**b**) *Fam (lío)* mess (**c**) *Fam (discusión)* row, rumpus

fregar [43] **1** *vt* (**a**) *(limpiar)* to wash; **f. los platos** to wash the dishes; **f. el suelo** to mop the floor (**b**) *(frotar)* to scrub (**c**) *Andes, Méx, Ven Fam (molestar)* to bother, to pester; *(estropear)* to bust

2 *vi* (**a**) *(limpiar)* to clean; *(frotar)* to scrub; *(limpiar los platos)* to wash the dishes (**b**) *Andes, Méx, Ven Fam (molestar)* to be a pain; **¡no friegues!** *(expresando sorpresa)* you're kidding!, you can't be serious!

3 fregarse *vpr Andes, Méx, Ven Fam (estropearse)* **se nos han fregado las vacaciones** that's gone and messed our vacation up

fregona *nf* (**a**) *Esp (utensilio)* mop (**b**) *Fam Pey (criada)* skivvy

fregotear *vt Fam* to give a good washing to; **f. el suelo** to give the floor a good mopping

fregué *ver* **fregar**

freidora *nf* deep-fat fryer

freiduría *nf* = store where fried food, especially fish, is cooked and served

freír [56] **1** *vt* (**a**) *(alimento)* to fry (**b**) *Fam (molestar)* **f. a alguien a preguntas** to pester sb with questions (**c**) *Fam (matar)* **f. a alguien (a tiros)** to gun sb down

2 freírse *vpr* to be frying; *Fam* **me estoy friendo (de calor)** I'm boiling *o* roasting

frenada *nf Am* **dar una f.** to brake hard

frenado *nm* braking

frenar 1 *vt* (**a**) *Aut* to brake (**b**) *(contener)* to check; *(disminuir)* to curb, to slow down; **los altos tipos de interés frenan a los inversores** the high interest rates are holding investors back

2 *vi (en vehículo)* to brake

3 frenarse *vpr (contenerse)* to restrain oneself

frenazo *nm* (**a**) *(en vehículo)* **dar un f.** to brake hard (**b**) *(de actividad)* sudden stop

frenesí *(pl* **frenesíes** *o* **frenesís***) nm* frenzy

frenético, -a *adj* (**a**) *(colérico)* furious, mad (**b**) *(enloquecido)* frenzied, frantic

frenillo *nm* frenum

freno 1 *nm* (**a**) *Aut* brake; *Fam* **¡echa el f.!** *(detente, cállate)* clam up!, that's enough of that!; *(no te pases)* don't get carried away!; **pisar el f.** to step on the brakes; **frenos ABS** ABS brakes; **f. automático** automatic brake; **frenos de disco** disc brakes; **f. de mano** emergency brake (**b**) *(de caballerías)* bit (**c**) *(contención)* check; **poner f. a** to put a stop to

2 frenos *nmpl Méx (en dientes)* braces

frenopatía *nf* psychiatry

frenopático, -a 1 *adj* psychiatric

2 *nm Fam (manicomio)* loony bin

frente 1 *nf* forehead; **f. a f.** face-to-face

2 *nm* (**a**) *(parte delantera)* front; **dar un paso al f.** to step forward; **estar al f. de** *(empresa)* to be in charge of, to head; *(manifestación)* to be at the front of, to lead; **de f.** *(hacia delante)* forward; **chocaron de f.** they collided head on; **me encontré de f. con él** I found myself face-to-face with him; **en f.** opposite; **en f. de mi casa** opposite my house; **hacer f. a algo** to face up to sth (**b**) *Mil (de batalla)* front; **hacer** *o* **formar f. común** to make common cause (**c**) *Meteo* front; **f. cálido/frío** warm/cold front

3 *prep* **f. a** *(enfrente de)* opposite; **estamos f. a una revolución científica** we are facing a scientific revolution; **f. a las duras críticas de la oposición,...** in the face of harsh criticism from the opposition,...

fresa[1] *nf* (**a**) *Esp, CAm, Carib, Méx (fruto)* strawberry; *(planta)* strawberry plant (**b**) *(herramienta) (de dentista)* drill; *(de orfebre)* milling cutter

fresa² *Méx Fam* **1** *adj (esnob)* posh
  2 *nm,f* posh person
fresador, -ora *nm,f (persona)* milling machine operator
fresadora *nf (máquina)* milling machine
fresca *nf* (a) *(insolencia)* **soltarle una f.** *o* **cuatro frescas a alguien** to tell sb a few home truths (b) *Pey (mujer)* loose woman
fresco, -a 1 *adj* (a) *(temperatura, aire)* cool; **un vestido f.** a cool dress; **tómate algo f.** have a cold drink
  (b) *(alimento)* fresh
  (c) *(reciente) (pintura, tinta)* wet; **noticias frescas** fresh news
  (d) *(espontáneo)* fresh; **un estilo f.** a refreshing style
  (e) *(caradura)* fresh, forward, cheeky; *Pey (mujer)* loose; **¡qué f.!** what a nerve!
  (f) **tan f.: ha pasado la noche en vela y está tan f.** he was up all night but he's still fresh as a daisy; **no ha estudiado y sigue tan f.** he hasn't studied but he's not in the least bothered; **dijo una tontería enorme y se quedó tan f.** he made an incredibly stupid remark and just carried on as if nothing was wrong
  2 *nm,f (caradura)* forward *o* cheeky person; **es un f.** he's really forward *o* cheeky
  3 *nm* (a) *(frescor)* coolness; **al f.** in a cool place; **hace f.** it's chilly; **tomar el f.** to get a breath of fresh air; *Fam* **me trae al f. lo que digan los demás** I don't give two hoots what people say (b) *Arte* fresco; **al f.** in fresco (c) *Andes, CAm, Méx (refresco)* soft drink
frescor *nm* coolness, freshness
frescura *nf* (a) *(de fruta, verdura)* freshness (b) *(espontaneidad)* freshness (c) *(descaro)* nerve, cheek; **¡qué f.!** what a nerve!
fresno *nm* ash (tree)
fresón *nm* large strawberry
fresquería *nf Am* refreshment stand
freudiano, -a [froi'ðjano] *adj* Freudian
fría 1 *ver* **freír**
  2 *ver* **frío**
frialdad *nf* (a) *(baja temperatura)* coldness (b) *(indiferencia)* coldness; **me trata con mucha f.** he's very cold toward me, he treats me very coldly (c) *(serenidad)* **examinar las cosas con f.** to look at things calmly *o* coolly
fríamente *adv* (a) *(con indiferencia)* coldly, coolly (b) *(con serenidad)* calmly, coolly
fricandó *nm* fricandeau
fricasé *nm* fricassee
fricativa *nf* fricative
fricativo, -a *adj* fricative
fricción *nf* (a) *(rozamiento)* friction (b) *(tensión)* friction (c) *(friega)* rub, massage
friccionar *vt* to rub, to massage
frie *ver* **freír**
friega 1 *ver* **fregar**
  2 *nf* (a) *(masaje)* massage; **dar friegas de alcohol a alguien** to give sb an alcohol rub (b) *Andes, Méx Fam (molestia)* pain, drag; *(zurra)* thrashing, hiding
friegaplatos *nm inv* dishwasher
friera *etc ver* **freír**
frigidez *nf (sexual)* frigidity
frígido, -a *adj* frigid
frigorífico, -a 1 *adj (que produce frío)* **cámara frigorífica** cold store; **camión f.** refrigerated truck
  2 *nm Esp* icebox, refrigerator
frijol, fríjol *nm Am salvo RP* bean
frió *ver* **freír**
frío, -a 1 *ver* **freír**
  2 *adj* (a) *(a baja temperatura)* cold; **hoy está el día f.** it's cold today; **me he quedado f. esperándote** I've gotten cold waiting for you (b) *(tono, color)* cold; **una habitación fría** a

cold *o* unwelcoming room (c) *(indiferente)* cold; **un recibimiento muy f.** a cold *o* frosty reception; **estuvo muy f. conmigo** he was very cold toward me; **es demasiado fría y calculadora** she's too cold and calculating; **dejar a alguien f.** to leave sb cold (d) *(sereno)* cool, calm; **mantener la cabeza fría** to keep a cool head
  3 *nm* (a) *(temperatura, sensación)* cold; *Esp* **coger** *o* *Am* **tomar f.** to catch a chill; *Fam* **¡hace un f. que pela!** it's freezing cold!; *Fam* **pelarse de f.** to be freezing to death; **tener f.** to be cold; *Fig* **no me da ni f. ni calor** I can take it or leave it (b) **en f.: mañana, en f., lo analizarás mejor** tomorrow, in the cold light of day, you'll look at it more clearly; *Esp* **coger a alguien en f.** to catch sb on the hop
friolento, -a *adj Am* sensitive to the cold
friolera *nf Fam* **costó la f. de 2.000 dólares** it cost a cool 2,000 dollars
friolero, -a *Esp* **1** *adj* sensitive to the cold
  2 *nm,f* **es un f.** he really feels the cold
frisar *vt* to be around, to be getting on for *(a certain age)*
Frisbee® ['frisβi] *nm* frisbee®
friso *nm* (a) *Arquit* frieze (b) *(zócalo)* baseboard
frisón, -ona *adj & nm,f* Frisian
fritada *nf* dish of fried food
fritanga *nf Fam Esp* dish of fried food; **olor a f.** smell of frying
frito, -a 1 *participio ver* **freír**
  2 *adj* (a) *(alimento)* fried (b) *Fam (harto)* fed up (to the back teeth); **me tienen f. con tantas quejas** I'm sick (and tired) of all their complaining (c) *Fam (dormido)* flaked out, asleep
  3 *fritos nmpl* fried food
fritura *nf* dish of fried food
frivolidad *nf* frivolity
frívolo, -a *adj* frivolous
frondosidad *nf* leafiness
frondoso, -a *adj (planta, árbol)* leafy; *(bosque)* dense
frontal *adj (ataque)* frontal; *(colisión)* head-on; **la parte f.** the front, the front part
frontera *nf* (a) *(división)* border (b) *(límite)* bounds; **su ambición no tiene fronteras** his ambition is limitless *o* knows no bounds; **la f. entre amor y odio** the dividing line between love and hate
fronterizo, -a *adj* border; **ciudad fronteriza** border town; **conflicto f.** border dispute
frontis *nm inv* facade
frontispicio *nm* (a) *(de edificio) (fachada)* facade; *(remate)* pediment (b) *(de libro)* frontispiece
frontón *nm* (a) *(deporte)* pelota; *(cancha)* pelota court (b) *Arquit* pediment
frotamiento *nm* rubbing
frotar 1 *vt (rozar, masajear)* to rub; *(al fregar)* to scrub
  2 *vi (rozar, masajear)* to rub; *(al fregar)* to scrub
  3 *frotarse vpr* **frotarse las manos** to rub one's hands
frotis *nm inv* smear; **f. cervical** cervical smear
fructífero, -a *adj* fruitful
fructificar [59] *vi también Fig* to bear fruit
fructosa *nf* fructose
fructuoso, -a *adj* fruitful
frugal *adj* frugal
frugalidad *nf* frugality
fruición *nf* gusto, delight
frunce *nm (en tela)* gathering
fruncido, -a 1 *adj* (a) *(tela)* gathered (b) **con el ceño f.** with a frown, frowning
  2 *nm (en tela)* gathering
fruncir [72] *vt* (a) *(tela)* to gather (b) *(labios)* to purse; **f. el ceño** to frown

fruslería *nf* triviality, trifle

frustración *nf* frustration

frustrado, -a *adj (persona)* frustrated; *(plan)* failed

frustrante *adj* frustrating

frustrar 1 *vt* (a) *(persona)* to frustrate (b) *(posibilidades, ilusiones, robo)* to thwart
2 frustrarse *vpr* (a) *(persona)* to get frustrated (b) *(ilusiones)* to be thwarted; *(proyecto)* to fail

fruta *nf* fruit; **f. escarchada** candied *o* crystallized fruit; **f. de la pasión** passion fruit; **f. del tiempo** seasonal fruit, fruit in season

frutal 1 *adj* fruit; **árbol f.** fruit tree
2 *nm* fruit tree

frutera *nf CSur (recipiente)* fruit bowl

frutería *nf* fruit shop

frutero, -a 1 *nm,f (persona)* fruit seller
2 *nm (recipiente)* fruit bowl

frutícola *adj* **la producción f.** fruit production; **una región f.** a fruit-growing region

fruticultura *nf* fruit farming

frutilla *nf Bol, CSur, Ecuad* strawberry

fruto *nm* (a) *(naranja, plátano)* fruit; *(nuez, avellana)* nut; **f. prohibido** forbidden fruit; **frutos secos** dried fruit and nuts (b) *(resultado)* fruit; **fue f. de su empeño** it was the fruit *o* result of her efforts; **dar f.** to bear fruit; **sacar f. a** *o* **de algo** to profit from sth

fu: ni fu ni fa *loc adv Fam* so-so

fucsia 1 *nf (planta)* fuchsia
2 *adj inv & nm inv (color)* fuchsia

fue *ver* **ir, ser**

fuego *nm* (a) *(llamas, hoguera)* fire; **atizar el f.** to poke the fire; **hacer un f.** to make a fire; **pegar f. a algo** to set sth on fire, to set fire to sth; **echar f. por los ojos** to look daggers; *Fig* **jugar con f.** to play with fire; **fuegos artificiales** fireworks; **f. fatuo** will-o'-the-wisp; **f. de San Telmo** St Elmo's fire
(b) *(de cocina)* ring, burner; **apagar/bajar el f.** to turn off/lower the heat; **poner el agua al f. hasta que empiece a hervir** heat the water until it starts to boil; **a f. lento/vivo** over a low/high heat
(c) *(para fumar)* **pedir/dar f.** to ask for/give a light; **¿tiene f.?** have you got a light?
(d) *(disparos)* fire; **abrir** *o* **hacer f.** to fire, to open fire; *Fig* **estar entre dos fuegos** to be between the devil and the deep blue sea; **f. cruzado** cross fire
(e) *(apasionamiento)* passion, ardor; **la distancia avivó el f. de su pasión** distance rekindled the fires of his passion

fuel *nm* fuel oil

fuelle *nm* (a) *(para soplar)* bellows (b) *(de maleta, bolso)* accordion pleats (c) *(entre vagones)* connecting corridor, concertina vestibule

fuel-oil *nm* fuel oil

fuente *nf* (a) *(de agua) (construcción)* fountain; *(manantial)* spring; **f. de agua potable** drinking fountain (b) *(bandeja)* (serving) dish (c) *(origen)* source; **f. de alimentación** *Elec* feed source; *Inform* power supply; **f. de energía** energy source; **f. de energía renovable** renewable energy source; **f. de ingresos** source of income; **f. de riqueza** source of wealth (d) *(de información)* source; **según fuentes del ministerio de Educación,...** according to Ministry of Education sources,...; **fuentes oficiosas/oficiales** unofficial/official sources (e) *Imprenta* font

fuera 1 *ver* **ir, ser**
2 *adv* (a) *(en el exterior)* outside; **hace frío f.** it's cold outside; **f. de la casa** outside the house; **lo echó f.** she threw him out; **salen mucho a comer f.** they eat out a lot; **hacia f.** outward; **por f.** (on the) outside; **sólo vimos la iglesia por f.** we only saw the church from the outside
(b) *(en otro lugar)* away; *(en el extranjero)* abroad; **Ana está f.** *(de viaje)* Ana is away; **de f.** *(extranjero)* from abroad; **a los de f. les sorprende** people who aren't from around here find it strange
(c) *Dep* **el equipo de f.** the away team; **jugar f.** to play away (from home); **f. de banda** out of play; **f. de combate** knocked out; *Fig* out of action; **f. de juego,** *Am* **f. de lugar** offside
(d) **f. de** *(alcance, peligro)* out of; *(cálculos, competencia)* outside; *(excepto)* except for, apart from; **f. de horas de oficina** outside office hours; **f. de la ley** illegal; **estar f. de lugar** to be out of place; **f. de plazo** after the closing date; **f. de peligro** out of danger; **f. de serie** exceptional, out of the ordinary; **ser un f. de serie** to be one of a kind; **estar f. de sí** to be beside oneself (with rage)
3 *interj* **¡f.!** (get) out!; *(en el teatro)* (get) off!; **¡f. de aquí!** get out of my sight!

fueraborda 1 *adj inv* outboard; **motor f.** outboard motor *o* engine; **lancha f.** outboard, boat with outboard motor
2 *nm inv (motor)* outboard motor *o* engine
3 *nf inv (lancha)* outboard, boat with outboard motor

fuerce *ver* **forzar**

fuero *nm* (a) *(ley local)* = ancient regional law still existing in some parts of Spain (b) *(jurisdicción)* code of laws (c) **en su f. interno** in her heart of hearts, deep down

fuerte 1 *adj* (a) *(persona, viento)* strong; *(frío, dolor, color)* intense; *(lluvia, resfriado)* heavy; *(golpe, pelea)* hard; **un medicamento muy f.** a very powerful medicine
(b) *(comida) (pesado)* heavy; *(picante)* hot
(c) *(alto) (sonido)* loud; **está demasiado f.** it's on too loud
(d) *(nudo)* tight
(e) *(influyente, sólido)* strong; **es una empresa f. en el sector** the company's strong in this sector; **una moneda f.** a strong currency
(f) *(grande) (cantidad)* large, considerable; **una f. presencia de artistas europeos** a large contingent of European artists
(g) *(impactante)* **lenguaje f.** strong language; **algunas de las escenas son muy fuertes** some of the scenes are very shocking; *Fam* **¡qué f.!** *(bueno)* wow!, amazing!; *(malo)* how awful!, oh no!
(h) *(versado)* **estar f. en algo** to be good at sth
2 *adv* (a) *(intensamente)* hard; *(abrazar, agarrar)* tight (b) *(abundantemente) (comer)* a lot (c) *(en voz alta)* loudly
3 *nm* (a) *(fortificación)* fort (b) *(punto fuerte)* strong point, forte; **su f. son las matemáticas** math is his forte

fuerza 1 *ver* **forzar**
2 *nf* (a) *(fortaleza)* strength; *(de sonido)* loudness; *(de dolor)* intensity; **tener mucha f.** to be very strong; **recuperar fuerzas** to recover one's strength, to get one's strength back; **sacar fuerzas de flaqueza** to screw up one's courage; **no me siento con fuerzas** I don't feel strong enough; **tener fuerzas para** to have the strength to; **la f. de la costumbre** force of habit; **la f. del destino** the power of destiny; **f. física** strength; *Der* **f. mayor** force majeure; *(en seguros)* act of God; **no llegué por un caso de f. mayor** I didn't make it due to circumstances beyond my control; **f. de voluntad** willpower
(b) *(violencia)* force; **a la f.** *(contra la voluntad)* by force; *(por necesidad)* of necessity; **tuvo que llevarle al colegio a la f.** she had to drag him to school by force; **recurrir a la f.** to resort to force; **a la f. tenía que saber la noticia** she must have known the news; **por la f.** by force; **f. bruta** brute force
(c) *(grupo) Mil* force; **todas las fuerzas políticas** all the political groups; **f. aérea** air force; **Fuerzas Armadas** armed forces; **f. de intervención** troops, forces; **f. de intervención rápida** rapid reaction force; **fuerzas nacionalistas** *(partidos)* nationalist parties; **fuerzas del**

orden público security forces; **fuerzas de pacificación** peacekeeping forces; **fuerzas de seguridad** security forces

(d) *Fís* force; **f. centrífuga/centrípeta** centrifugal/centripetal force; **f. de la gravedad** force of gravity; **f. motriz** driving force

3 a fuerza de *loc prep* by dint of; **a f. de mucho estudiar** by studying hard

4 por fuerza *loc adv* inevitably; **tenía que ocurrir un desastre por f.** a disaster was inevitable; **tengo que salir por f.** I absolutely have to go out

fuese
(a) *ver* **ir** (b) *ver* **ser**

fuet (*pl* **fuets**) *nm* = type of cured pork sausage typical of Catalonia

fuete *nm Am* whip

fuga *nf* (a) *(huida)* escape; **darse a la f.** to take flight; **f. de cerebros** brain drain (b) *(escape)* leak (c) *Mús* fugue

fugacidad *nf* fleeting nature

fugarse [38] *vpr* to escape; **f. de casa** to run away from home; **f. con alguien** to run off with sb

fugaz *adj* fleeting; **una visita f.** a flying visit

fugitivo, -a 1 *adj* (a) *(en fuga)* fleeing (b) *(fugaz)* fleeting
2 *nm,f* fugitive

fugue *etc ver* **fugarse**

führer ['firer] (*pl* **führers**) *nm* führer

fui (a) *ver* **ir** (b) *ver* **ser**

fulana *nf* *(prostituta)* tart, whore

fulano, -a *nm,f* what's his/her name, so-and-so

fular *nm* scarf

fulero, -a *Fam* **1** *adj* (a) *(chapucero)* shoddy (b) *(tramposo)* dishonest
2 *nm,f* trickster

fulgor *nm* shining; *(de disparo)* flash

fulgurante *adj* *(resplandeciente)* flashing; *(rápido)* rapid; **un ascenso/éxito f.** a lightning rise/success

fulgurar *vi* to gleam; *(intermitentemente)* to flash

full *nm* *(en póquer)* full house

fullero, -a *Fam* **1** *adj* cheating, dishonest
2 *nm,f* cheat

fulminante *adj* (a) *(despido, muerte)* sudden; *(enfermedad)* devastating; *(mirada)* withering (b) *(explosivo)* fulminating

fulminar *vt* *(sujeto: enfermedad)* to strike down; **un rayo la fulminó** she was struck by lightning; **f. a alguien con la mirada** to look daggers at sb

fumadero *nm (de opio)* den

fumador, -ora *nm,f* smoker; **f. pasivo** passive smoker; **no f.** nonsmoker

fumar 1 *vt* to smoke
2 *vi* to smoke; **f. como un carretero** to smoke like a chimney
3 fumarse *vpr* (a) *(cigarillo)* to smoke (b) *Esp Fam (clase)* to skip (c) *Esp Fam (fortuna, ahorros)* to blow (d) *RP Fam (persona, situación)* to put up with

fumeta *nmf Fam* pothead, pot smoker

fumigación *nf* fumigation

fumigador *nm* fumigator

fumigar [38] *vt* to fumigate

funambulista *nmf* tightrope walker

función 1 *nf* (a) *(actividad, objetivo)* function; *(trabajo)* duty; **esta pieza desempeña una f. clave** this part has a crucial function o role; **la f. del coordinador** the coordinator's job o function; **director en funciones** acting director; **entrar en funciones** to take up one's duties; **funciones fisiológicas** bodily functions (b) *Teatro* show; **f. benéfica** charity performance, benefit (c) *Mat* function
2 en función de *loc prep* depending on; **estar** o **ir en f.**

de to depend on, to be dependent on

funcional *adj* functional

funcionalidad *nf* functional qualities

funcionalismo *nm* functionalism

funcionamiento *nm* operation, functioning; **explicó el f. de la empresa** he explained how the company works; **entrar/estar en f.** *(sistema)* to come into/be in operation; *(máquina)* to start/be (working o running); **poner algo en f.** *(sistema)* to put sth into operation; *(máquina)* to start sth (working)

funcionar *vi* *(machine)* to work, to run; *(plan, idea, método)* to work; **funciona a pilas** it works o runs off batteries; **no funciona** *(en letrero)* out of order

funcionariado *nm (de la Administración central)* civil service; *(profesor, bombero, enfermero)* public sector workers

funcionario, -a *nm,f (de la Administración central)* civil servant; *(profesor, bombero, enfermero)* public sector worker; **f. de prisiones** prison officer

funda *nf (de sofá, máquina de escribir, guitarra)* cover; *(de almohada)* pillowcase; *(de disco)* sleeve; *(de gafas)* pouch; *(de diente)* cap

fundación *nf* foundation

fundado, -a *adj* (a) *(argumento, idea)* well-founded (b) *(creado, establecido)* founded

fundador, -ora 1 *adj* founding
2 *nm,f* founder

fundamentación *nf* foundation, basis

fundamental *adj* fundamental

fundamentalismo *nm* fundamentalism

fundamentalista *adj & nmf* fundamentalist

fundamentar 1 *vt* (a) *(basar)* to base (b) *Constr* to lay the foundations of
2 fundamentarse *vpr (basarse)* to be based o founded (**en** on)

fundamento *nm* (a) *(base)* foundation, basis (b) *(razón)* reason, grounds; **sin f.** unfounded, groundless; **fundamentos** *(principios)* basic principles; *(cimientos)* foundations

fundar 1 *vt* (a) *(crear)* to found (b) *(basar)* to base (**en** on)
2 fundarse *vpr (basarse)* to be based (**en** on); **¿en qué te fundas para decir eso?** what grounds do you have for saying that?

fundición *nf* (a) *(taller)* foundry (b) *(fusión)* smelting

fundido *nm Cine (apareciendo)* fade-in; *(desapareciendo)* fade-out; **f. en negro** fade-out (to black)

fundillos *nmpl Chile (calzoncillos)* shorts

fundir 1 *vt* (a) *(derretir) (mantequilla, hielo)* to melt; *(hierro, plomo)* to smelt; *(oro)* to melt down (b) *Elec (fusible, bombilla)* to blow (c) *Com* to merge (d) *Cine* to fade (e) *Esp Fam (gastar)* to blow (f) *Am* **f. el motor** to make the engine seize up (g) *Am (arruinar)* to bankrupt, to ruin
2 fundirse *vpr* (a) *Elec* to blow; **se han fundido los plomos** the fuses have gone; **se ha fundido la bombilla de la cocina** the light in the kitchen has gone (b) *(derretirse) (mantequilla, hielo, plomo, hierro)* to melt; *Fig* **se fundieron en un abrazo** they fell into one another's arms (c) *Com* to merge (d) *Am (motor)* to seize up (e) *Esp Fam (gastar)* to blow; **fundirse el sueldo** to blow one's wages (f) *Am Fam (arruinarse) (persona, negocio)* to go bust

fúnebre *adj (misa)* funeral; *(música)* funereal; *(paisaje, expresión)* gloomy; **coche f.** hearse

funeral *nm (misa)* funeral (service o mass); *(entierro, cremación)* funeral

funerala *nf* **a la f.** *(ojo)* black

funeraria *nf* mortician's, funeral home o parlor, undertaker's

funerario, -a *adj* funeral; **rito f.** funeral o funerary rite

funesto, -a *adj* fateful, disastrous

fungible *adj* disposable

fungicida 1 *adj* fungicidal

  2 *nm* fungicide

fungir [24] *vi Méx, Perú* to act, to serve (**de** *o* **como** as)

funicular 1 *adj* funicular

  2 *nm* (**a**) *(por tierra)* funicular (**b**) *(por aire)* cable car

funky ['funki] **1** *adj* **música f.** funk

  2 *nm* funk

furcia *nf Esp Pey* slag, whore

furgón *nm (furgoneta)* van; *(de tren)* wagon, van; **f. de equipajes** caboose

furgoneta *nf* van; **f. de reparto** delivery van

furia *nf* fury; **ponerse hecho una f.** to fly into a rage

furibundo, -a *adj* furious

furioso, -a *adj* furious

furor *nm* (**a**) *(enfado)* fury, rage (**b**) *(ímpetu)* fever, urge (**c**) **hacer f.** to be all the rage

furtivo, -a 1 *adj (mirada, sonrisa)* furtive; **cazador f.** poacher

  2 *nm,f (cazador)* poacher

furúnculo *nm* boil

fusa *nf Mús* thirty-second note

fuseaux [fu'so] *nm inv* ski pants

fuselaje *nm* fuselage

fusible 1 *adj* fusible

  2 *nm* fuse

fusil *nm* rifle

fusilamiento *nm* (**a**) *(ejecución)* execution by firing squad (**b**) *Fam (plagio)* plagiarism

fusilar *vt* (**a**) *(ejecutar)* to execute by firing squad, to shoot (**b**) *Fam (plagiar)* to plagiarize

fusilero *nm* fusilier, rifleman

fusión *nf* (**a**) *(agrupación)* merging; *(de empresas, bancos)* merger; *Inform* merge (**b**) *(de metal, hielo)* melting; *Fís* fusion; **f. nuclear** nuclear fusion

fusionar 1 *vt (gen) & Econ* to merge

  2 fusionarse *vpr (gen) & Econ* to merge

fusta *nf* riding crop *o* whip

fustán *nm Am* petticoat

fuste *nm* shaft

fustigar [38] *vt* (**a**) *(azotar)* to whip (**b**) *(censurar)* to criticize harshly

futbito *nm Bol, Esp* five-a-side

fútbol, *Méx* **futbol** *nm* soccer; **f. americano** football; *Esp* **f. sala** indoor five-a-side

futbolero, -a *Fam* **1** *adj* **es muy f.** he is soccer crazy

  2 *nm,f* soccer fan

futbolín *nm Esp (juego)* foosball

futbolista *nmf* soccer player

futbolístico, -a *adj* soccer; **campeonato f.** soccer championship

fútil *adj* trivial

futilidad *nf* triviality

futón *nm* futon

futre *Andes* **1** *adj* foppish

  2 *nm* dandy

futurible *adj* potential

futurismo *nm* futurism

futurista *adj (diseño, ropa)* futuristic; *Arte* futurist

futuro, -a 1 *adj* future; **futura madre** expectant mother

  2 *nm* (**a**) *(porvenir)* future; **en el f.,...** in future,...; **sin f.** with no future, without prospects; *Fin* **futuros** futures (**b**) *Gram* future; **f. perfecto** future perfect

futurología *nf* futurology

futurólogo, -a *nm,f* futurologist

G

G, g [χe] *nf (letra)* G, g

g *(abrev de* **gramo***)* g

G7 [χe'siete] *nm (abrev de* **Grupo de los Siete***)* G7

G8 [χe'otʃo] *nm (abrev de* **Grupo de los Ocho***)* G8

gabacho, -a *Esp Fam Pey* **1** *adj* Froggy
    2 *nm,f* Frog

gabán *nm* overcoat

gabardina *nf (a) (prenda)* raincoat **(b)** *(tela)* gabardine

gabinete *nm* **(a)** *(despacho)* office **(b)** *(sala)* study **(c)** *(gobierno)* cabinet; **g. en la sombra** shadow cabinet *(in parliamentary system)*

Gabón *n* Gabon

gacela *nf* gazelle

gaceta *nf* gazette

gacetillero, -a *nm,f Fam Anticuado (periodista)* hack

gachas *nfpl Culin* (corn) porridge

gachí *nf Fam* bird, chick

gacho, -a *adj* **(a)** *(caído)* drooping; **caminaba con la cabeza gacha** he was walking along with his head bowed *o* hanging his head **(b)** *Méx Fam (persona)* nasty, rotten **(c)** *Méx Fam (objeto)* awful, ghastly

gachó *nm Fam* guy

gaditano, -a1 *adj* of/from Cadiz
    2 *nm,f* person from Cadiz

gaélico, -a1 *adj* Gaelic
    2 *nm (lengua)* Gaelic

gafado, -a *adj Esp Fam* **estar g.** to be jinxed

gafar *vt Esp Fam* to jinx, to bring bad luck to

gafas *nfpl* glasses; *(protectoras, para nadar)* goggles; *(para submarinismo)* diving mask; **unas g.** a pair of glasses; **g. bifocales** bifocal glasses, bifocals; **g. de esquí** skiing goggles; **g. graduadas** prescription glasses; **g. para leer** reading glasses; **g. oscuras** sunglasses; **g. de sol** sunglasses

gafe *Esp Fam* **1** *adj* jinxed; **ser g.** to be jinxed
    2 *nmf* jinxed person
    3 *nm* **tener el g.** to be jinxed

gafotas *nmf inv Esp Fam* four-eyes

gag *(pl gags) nm (broma)* gag

gaita *nf (a) (instrumento)* bagpipes **(b)** *Esp Fam (pesadez)* drag, pain

gaitero, -a *nm,f* piper

gaje *nm* **gajes del oficio** occupational hazards

gajo *nm* **(a)** *(de naranja, limón)* segment **(b)** *(racimo)* bunch **(c)** *(rama)* broken-off branch

gala *nf* **(a)** *(fiesta)* gala; **cena de g.** black tie dinner, formal dinner; **traje de g.** formal dress; **uniforme de g.** dress uniform **(b)** *(ropa)* **se puso sus mejores galas** she put on her finery **(c)** *Esp (actuación)* gala show *o* performance **(d)** *(expresiones)* **hacer g. de algo** *(preciarse de)* to be proud of sth; *(exhibir)* to demonstrate sth; **tener a g. algo** to be proud of sth

galáctico, -a *adj (de las galaxias)* galactic; *Fam (moderno, futurista)* space-age

galaico, -a *adj Formal* Galician

galán *nm* **(a)** *(hombre atractivo)* attractive young man **(b)** *Teatro* leading man, lead

galante *adj* gallant

galantear *vt* to court, to woo

galanteo *nm* courting, wooing

galantería *nf* **(a)** *(cualidad)* politeness **(b)** *(acción)* gallantry, compliment

galápago *nm* turtle

Galápagos *nfpl* **las (islas) G.** the Galapagos Islands

galardón *nm* award, prize

galardonado, -a *adj* award-winning, prize-winning

galardonar *vt* to award a prize to

galaxia *nf* galaxy

galbana *nf Fam* laziness, sloth

galena *nf* galena, lead sulfide

galeno *nm Anticuado* doctor

galeón *nm* galleon

galeote *nm* galley slave

galera *nf* galley

galerada *nf* galley proof

galería *nf (a) (pasillo)* gallery; *(corredor descubierto)* verandah **(b)** *(local)* **g. de arte** art gallery; **g. comercial** shopping arcade **(c)** *(vulgo)* masses; **hacer algo para la g.** to play to the gallery

galerista *nmf* gallery owner

galerna *nf* strong northwest wind *(on north coast of Spain)*

Gales *n* **(el país de) G.** Wales

galés, -esa1 *adj* Welsh
    2 *nm,f* Welshman, *f* Welshwoman; **los galeses** the Welsh
    3 *nm (lengua)* Welsh

galgo *nm* greyhound; **carreras de galgos** greyhound races; **g. afgano** Afghan hound

Galicia *n* Galicia

galicismo *nm* gallicism

galimatías *nm inv (lenguaje)* gibberish; *(lío)* jumble

gallardete *nm* pennant

gallardía *nf (a) (valentía)* bravery **(b)** *(apostura)* noble bearing

gallardo, -a *adj (a) (valiente)* brave, dashing **(b)** *(bien parecido)* fine-looking, striking

gallear *vi* to strut about, to show off

gallego, -a1 *adj & nm,f* Galician; *CSur, Cuba Fam* Spanish
    2 *nm (lengua)* Galician

galleguismo *nm (palabra, expresión)* Galician expression

galleta *nf* **(a)** *Culin* cookie; **g. para perros** dog biscuit **(b)** *Esp Fam (cachete)* slap, smack; **dar una g. a alguien** to give sb a slap *o* smack **(c)** *Esp (golpe)* **se dieron una g.** *(en automóvil)* they crashed the car; **me di una g. en la rodilla bajando las escaleras** I banged myself on the knee coming down the stairs

gallina 1 *nf* hen; **cría gallinas** *(gallinas, pollos y gallos)* he keeps chickens; *Fam* **la g. ciega** blind man's buff; *Fam Fig* matar la g. de los huevos de oro to kill the goose that lays the golden eggs

2 *nmf Fam (persona)* chicken, coward

gallináceo, -a *adj* gallinaceous

gallinazo *nm Am* vulture

gallinero *nm* (**a**) *(corral)* henhouse (**b**) *Fam Teatro* gods *(singular)* (**c**) *Fam (alboroto)* madhouse

gallito *Fam* **1** *adj (bravucón)* cocky

2 *nm* **es un g.** he's cocky

gallo *nm* (**a**) *(ave)* rooster, cock, cockerel; *Fam Fig* **en menos que canta un g.** in no time at all; **g. de pelea** fighting cock; *Carib* **g. pinto** rice and beans (**b**) *(al cantar)* false note; *(al hablar)* squeak (**c**) *(pez)* John Dory (**d**) *(en boxeo)* **peso g.** bantamweight

galo, -a **1** *adj Hist* Gallic; *(francés)* French

2 *nm,f (persona)* Gaul

galón *nm* (**a**) *(adorno)* braid; *Mil* stripe (**b**) *(medida)* gallon

galopada *nf* gallop

galopante *adj (inflación)* galloping

galopar *vi* to gallop

galope *nm* gallop; **al g.** at a gallop; *también Fig* **a g. tendido** at full gallop

galpón *nm Andes, Carib, RP* shed

galvanización *nf* galvanization

galvanizar [14] *vt* to galvanize

gama *nf (conjunto)* range; *(de colores, modelos)* range; *Mús* scale

gamba *nf* (**a**) *(animal)* shrimp (**b**) *Fam* **meter la g.** to put one's foot in it

gamberrada *nf Esp (acto violento)* act of hooliganism; *(travesura)* loutish act

gamberrismo *nm Esp* hooliganism

gamberro, -a *Esp* **1** *adj* loutish

2 *nm,f (persona)* hooligan, lout; **hacer el g.** to behave loutishly, to cause trouble

Gambia *n* The Gambia

gambito *nm (en ajedrez)* gambit

gameto *nm* gamete

gamín, -ina *nm,f Col* street urchin

gamma *nf* gamma

gamo *nm* fallow deer

gamonal *nm Andes, CAm, Ven* village chief

gamuza *nf* (**a**) *(tejido)* chamois (leather); *(trapo)* duster (**b**) *(animal)* chamois

gana *nf* (**a**) *(afán)* desire, wish (**de** to); **me dan** *o* **entran ganas de llorar** I feel like crying; **tener ganas de (hacer) algo** to feel like (doing) sth; **¡qué ganas tengo de empezar las vacaciones!** I can't wait for the vacation *o* holidays to start!; **no tengo ganas de que me pongan una multa** I don't relish getting a fine; **quedarse con (las) ganas de hacer algo** not to manage to do sth; **de buena g.** willingly; **de mala g.** unwillingly; *Fam* **no me da la g.** I don't feel like it; *Fam* **porque me da la g.** because I feel like it; **hace/come todo lo que le viene en g.** she does/eats whatever she pleases; **¿por qué habrá dicho eso?** — **son ganas de fastidiar** why would he say a thing like that? — he's just being nasty; **tenerle ganas a alguien** *(odiar)* to have it in for sb

(**b**) *(apetito)* appetite; **comer sin ganas** to eat without appetite, to pick at one's food

ganadería *nf* (**a**) *(actividad)* livestock farming; **g. ovina** sheep farming (**b**) *(ganado)* livestock (**c**) *(lugar)* livestock farm

ganadero, -a **1** *adj* livestock-farming; **región ganadera** livestock-farming region

2 *nm,f* livestock farmer

ganado *nm* livestock, stock; **g. ovino** sheep; **g. porcino** pigs; **g. vacuno** cattle

ganador, -ora **1** *adj* winning

2 *nm,f* winner

ganancia *nf (rendimiento)* profit; *(ingreso)* earnings; **ganancias y pérdidas** profit and loss; **g. líquida** net profit

ganancial *adj* **bienes gananciales** shared possessions

ganapán *nm* odd-job man

ganar **1** *vt* (**a**) *(premio, competición)* to win (**b**) *(sueldo, dinero)* to earn; **¿cuánto ganas?** how much do you earn? (**c**) *(peso, tiempo)* to gain; **g. fama** to achieve fame; **en tren ganas una hora** you save an hour by taking the train (**d**) *(derrotar)* to beat; **te voy a g.** I'm going to beat you (**e**) *(conseguir)* **llorando no ganas nada** it's no use crying, crying won't change anything; **¿qué gano yo con eso?** what's in it for me? (**f**) *(aventajar)* **me gana en velocidad** he's faster than me (**g**) *(llegar a) (lugar)* to reach, to make it to (**h**) *(conquistar)* to take, to capture

2 *vi* (**a**) *(vencer)* to win; **ganaron por tres a uno** they won three to one (**b**) *(lograr dinero)* to earn money; *Fam Fig* **no gano para disgustos** I've more than enough worries *o* troubles (**c**) *(mejorar)* to benefit (**con** from); **gana mucho con la barba** he looks a lot better with a beard; **g. en algo** to gain in sth; **ha ganado en amplitud** *(parece mayor)* it looks bigger

3 **ganarse** *vpr* (**a**) *(conquistar) (simpatía, respeto)* to earn; *(persona)* to win over (**b**) *(obtener)* **se gana la vida de barrendero** he earns his living as a street sweeper (**c**) *(merecer)* to deserve; **nos hemos ganado unas vacaciones** we've earned *o* we deserve a vacation

ganchillo *nm (aguja)* crochet hook; *(labor)* crochet; **hacer g.** to crochet

ganchito *nm* (**a**) *Esp (aperitivo)* = cheese-flavored snack made from corn, $\simeq$ Cheeto® (**b**) *RP (grapa)* staple

gancho *nm* (**a**) *(garfio)* hook; *(de percha)* peg; *Esp Fam* **como le eche el g. al que me ha robado la bici…** just wait till I get my hands on whoever stole my bike… (**b**) *(cómplice) (de timador)* decoy (**c**) *Fam (atractivo)* **esa chica tiene mucho g.** that girl is quite something; **tiene g. como relaciones públicas** she has a real gift for public relations

ganchudo, -a *adj* hooked

gandalla *nmf Méx Fam*

(**a**) *(sinvergüenza)* swine (**b**) *(deshonesto)* crook

gandul, -ula **1** *adj* lazy

2 *nm,f* lazybones, layabout

gandulear *vi* to loaf around *o* about

gandulería *nf* idleness

ganga *nf* bargain

Ganges *nm* **el G.** the Ganges

ganglio *nm Anat* **g. (linfático)** lymph node *o* gland

gangoso, -a **1** *adj (voz)* nasal *(caused by cleft palate)*

2 *nm,f* = person with a nasal voice caused by a cleft palate

gangrena *nf* gangrene

gangrenado, -a *adj* gangrenous

gangrenarse *vpr* to become gangrenous

gangrenoso, -a *adj* gangrenous

gángster ['ganster] *(pl* **gángsters** *o* **gángsteres***)* *nm* gangster

gangsterismo [ganste'rismo] *nm* gangsterism

gansada *nf Fam* silly thing

ganso, -a **1** *nm,f* (**a**) *(ave) (hembra)* goose; *(macho)* gander (**b**) *Fam (tonto)* idiot, fool; **hacer el g.** to clown around

2 *adj Fam (alto)* tall; *(grande)* huge

gánster *(pl* **gánsters** *o* **gánsteres***)* *nm* gangster

gansterismo *nm* gangsterism

ganzúa *nf* picklock

gañán *nm* (**a**) *(hombre rudo)* lout, boor (**b**) *(bracero)* farm laborer

gañido *nm* yelp

garabatear *vi & vt* to scribble

garabato *nm* scribble; **hacer garabatos** to scribble

garaje, *Am* **garage** *nm* garage *(for parking)*

garante *nmf* guarantor; **salir g.** to act as guarantor

garantía *nf* **(a)** *(seguro, promesa)* guarantee; **me ha dado su g. de que lo hará** she guaranteed that she'd do it; **de g.** reliable, dependable; **ser g. de algo** to guarantee sth; *Pol* **garantías constitucionales** constitutional rights **(b)** *(de producto)* guarantee, warranty; **viene con una g. de tres años, tiene tres años de g.** it comes with a three-year guarantee *o* warranty, it has a three-year guarantee *o* warranty; **estar en g.** to be under guarantee **(c)** *(fianza)* security; **dejó su reloj como g.** he left his watch as security

garantizado, -a *adj* guaranteed

garantizar [14] *vt* **(a)** *(asegurar)* to guarantee; **te garantizo que te lo devolveré el viernes** I guarantee *o* I assure you I'll give it back to you on Friday; **la central garantiza el suministro eléctrico a la ciudad** the power station ensures the city's supply of electricity **(b)** *(contra riesgo, deterioro)* to guarantee; **les garantizaron el televisor por un año** they guaranteed the television for a year, they gave them a year's guarantee for the television **(c)** *(avalar)* to vouch for

garbanzo *nm* chickpea; *Fam Fig* **ser el g. negro** to be the black sheep

garbeo *nm* *Esp Fam* stroll; **dar un g.** to go for *o* take a stroll

garbo *nm* *(de persona)* grace; *(de escritura)* stylishness, style

garboso, -a *adj* *(persona)* graceful; *(escritura)* stylish

garceta *nf* little egret

gardenia *nf* gardenia

garduña *nf* marten

garete *nm* *Fam* **ir** *o* **irse al g.** *(fracasar)* to go down the drain, to go to pot

garfio *nm* hook

gargajo *nm* phlegm

garganta *nf* **(a)** *Anat* throat; *Fig* **lo tengo atravesado en la g.** he/it sticks in my gullet **(b)** *(desfiladero)* gorge

gargantilla *nf* choker

gargantúa *nm* big eater, glutton

gárgaras *nfpl* gargling; **hacer g.** to gargle; *Fam* **mandar a alguien a hacer g.** to send sb packing; *Fam* **¡vete a hacer g.!** get lost!

gárgola *nf* gargoyle

garita *nf* *(de centinela)* sentry box; *(de conserje)* porter's lodge

garito *nm* *(casa de juego)* gambling den; *Fam (establecimiento)* dive

garnacha *nf (uva)* = purplish grape

Garona *nm* **el G.** the Garonne

garra *nf* *(de mamífero)* claw; *(de ave)* talon, claw; *Fig (de persona)* paw, hand; **caer en las garras de alguien** to fall into sb's clutches; *Fam* **tener g.** *(persona)* to have charisma; *(novela, canción)* to be gripping

garrafa *nf* carafe; *Fam* **de g.** *(bebida alcohólica)* cheap and nasty

garrafal *adj* monumental, enormous

garrafón *nm* demijohn

garrapata *nf* tick

garrapiñado, -a *adj* caramel-coated

garrapiñar *vt (fruta)* to candy; *(almendras)* to coat with caramelized sugar

garrocha *nf (vara)* pike, lance; *Am (de atletismo)* (vaulting) pole

garronear *vt & vi RP Fam* to scrounge, to sponge

garrotazo *nm* blow with a club *o* stick

garrote *nm* **(a)** *(estaca)* club, stick **(b)** *(instrumento de ejecución)* **g.**
(vil) garotte; **dar g. a alguien** to garotte sb **(c)** *Méx (freno)* brake

garrulo, -a *Fam* **1** *adj* coarse, uncouth
2 *nm,f* country bumpkin, yokel, hick

garúa *nf Andes, RP, Ven* drizzle

garza *nf* heron; **g. real** gray heron

garzón, -ona *nm, f Chile* waiter, *f* waitress

gas *nm* **(a)** *(fluido)* gas; **con g.** *(agua, bebida)* carbonated, sparkling; *Esp Fam* **a todo g.** flat out, at top speed; *Esp Fam* **aun jugando a medio g. ganaron** they won even though they weren't really trying; *Esp Fam Fig* **quedarse sin g.** to run out of steam; **g. butano** butane (gas); *Esp* **g. ciudad** coal gas; **g. hilarante** laughing gas; **g. lacrimógeno** tear gas; **g. mostaza** mustard gas; **g. natural** natural gas; *Quím* **g. noble** noble gas **(b) gases** *(en el estómago)* wind

gasa *nf* gauze

gasear *vt* to gas

gaseoducto *nm* gas pipeline

gaseosa *nf* **(a)** *Esp, Arg (bebida transparente)* pop **(b)** *CAm, RP (refresco con gas)* soda

gaseoso, -a *adj (estado)* gaseous; *(bebida)* fizzy

gásfiter *nmf Chile, Perú* plumber

gasfitería *nf Chile, Perú* plumber's (shop)

gasfitero, -a *nm,f Ecuad* plumber

gasificación *nf* gasification

gasificar [59] *vt (convertir en gas)* to gasify; *(bebida)* to carbonate

gasoducto *nm* gas pipeline

gasóleo, gasoil *nm* diesel oil

gasolina *nf* gas, gasoline; **echar** *o* **poner g.** to put some gas in; **g. con/sin plomo** leaded/unleaded gasoline

gasolinera, *Méx* **gasolinería** *nf* gas station

gastado, -a *adj (objeto)* worn out; *(frase, tema)* hackneyed; *(persona)* broken, burned out

gastar 1 *vt* **(a)** *(consumir)* *(dinero, tiempo)* to spend; *(gasolina, electricidad)* to use (up); *(ropa, zapatos)* to wear out **(b)** *(malgastar)* *(dinero, energía)* to waste **(c)** *Esp (tener, usar)* *(ropa)* to wear; *(número de zapatos)* to take; **g. mal genio** to have a bad temper **(d)** *Esp (hacer)* **g. una broma (a alguien)** to play a joke (on sb) **(e)** *Esp* **gastarlas** to carry on, to behave; **¡no sabes cómo se las gastan allí!** you can't imagine how they carry on there!
2 *vi* to spend (money)
3 gastarse *vpr* **(a)** *(deteriorarse, desgastarse)* to wear out **(b)** *(consumirse)* to run out; **se han gastado las pilas** the batteries have run out *o* gone dead **(c)** *(dinero)* to spend; **nos gastamos veinte pesos en comida** we spent twenty pesos on food

gasto *nm (dinero gastado)* spending; *(costo)* expense; **el g. de energía** energy consumption; **el g. educativo/militar** *(de país)* spending on education/defense; **los gastos de la casa** household expenses; **cubrir gastos** to cover costs, to break even; **no reparar en gastos** to spare no expense; **g. corriente** current expenditure; **g. deducible** tax-deductible expense; **g. de defensa** defense spending; **g. de desplazamiento** relocation expenses, settling-in allowance; **gastos de envío** postage and packing; **gastos fijos** fixed charges *o* costs; **gastos generales** general expenses, overhead costs; **gastos de mantenimiento** maintenance costs; **g. público** public expenditure; **gastos de representación** entertainment allowance; **gastos de viaje** travel expenses

gástrico, -a *adj Anat* gastric

gastritis *nf inv Med* gastritis

gastroenteritis *nf inv Med* gastroenteritis

gastrointestinal *adj Anat* gastrointestinal

gastronomía *nf* gastronomy

gastronómico, -a *adj* gastronomic

gastrónomo, -a *nm,f* gourmet, gastronome

gatas: a gatas *loc adv Fam* (**a**) *(a cuatro patas)* on all fours (**b**) *RP (apenas)* barely

gatear *vi* to crawl

gatera *nf* cat flap *o* door

gatillo *nm* trigger

gato, -a 1 *nm,f* cat; *Fam* **dar g. por liebre a alguien** to swindle *o* cheat sb; *Fam* **buscar tres pies al g.** to overcomplicate matters; *Fam Fig* **aquí hay g. encerrado** there's something fishy going on here; *Fam* **llevarse el g. al agua** to pull it off; *Fam Fig* **sólo había cuatro gatos** there was hardly a soul there; **g. montés** wildcat; **g. siamés** Siamese cat

   2 *nm Aut* jack

GATT [gat] *nm* (*abrev de* **General Agreement on Tariffs and Trade**) GATT

gatuno, -a *adj* catlike, feline

gaucho, -a *adj & nm,f* gaucho

gavilán *nm* sparrow hawk

gavilla *nf* sheaf

gaviota *nf* seagull

gay [gai, gei] *adj inv & nmf* gay

gayumbos *nmpl Esp Fam (calzoncillos)* shorts

gazapo *nm* (**a**) *(animal)* young rabbit (**b**) *(error)* misprint

gazmoñería *nf* sanctimoniousness

gazmoño, -a *adj* sanctimonious

gaznate *nm* gullet

gazpacho *nm* gazpacho, = Andalusian soup made from tomatoes, peppers, cucumbers and bread, served chilled

GB (*abrev de* **Gran Bretaña**) GB

géiser *nm* geyser

geisha ['geisa] *nf inv* geisha

gel *nm* gel; **g. de ducha** shower gel; **g. moldeador** styling gel

gelatina *nf (de carne)* gelatine; *(de fruta)* Jell-O®

gelatinoso, -a *adj* gelatinous

gélido, -a *adj* gelid, icy

gema *nf* gem

gemelo, -a 1 *adj* **hermano g.** twin brother, twin; **ser el alma gemela de alguien** to be sb's soul mate

   2 *nm,f (persona)* twin; **g. idéntico** identical twin; **g. monocigótico** identical twin

   3 *nm (músculo)* calf muscle

   4 gemelos *nmpl* (**a**) *(de camisa)* cuff links (**b**) *(prismáticos)* binoculars; *(para teatro)* opera glasses; **unos gemelos** a pair of binoculars/opera glasses

gemido *nm (de persona)* moan, groan; *(de animal)* whine

geminiano, -a *Am* **1** *adj* Gemini; **ser g.** to be (a) Gemini

   2 *nm,f* Gemini

géminis 1 *nm (zodiaco)* Gemini; *Esp* **ser g.** to be (a) Gemini

   2 *nmf Esp (persona)* Gemini

gemir [47] *vi* (**a**) *(persona)* to moan, to groan; *(animal)* to whine (**b**) *(viento)* to howl

gemología *nf* gemology

gen *nm* gene

gendarme *nmf* gendarme

gendarmería *nf* gendarmerie

genealogía *nf* genealogy

genealógico, -a *adj* genealogical

generación *nf* generation; **g. espontánea** spontaneous generation, autogenesis

generacional *adj* **conflicto g.** conflict between the generations, generation gap

generador, -ora 1 *adj* generating

   2 *nm Elec* generator

general 1 *adj (común)* general; **tener nociones generales de griego** to have a general knowledge of Greek; **esa es la**

opinión g. de los que no leen los periódicos that's what people who don't read the papers usually think; **por lo g., en g.** in general, generally; **por lo g., suelo ir en tren** I generally go by train, in general I go by train

   2 *nm Mil* general; **g. de brigada** brigadier general; **g. de división** major general

generala *nf Mil* call to arms

generalidad *nf* (**a**) *(mayoría)* majority (**b**) *(vaguedad)* generalization; **generalidades** *(principios básicos)* basic principles

generalísimo *nm* supreme commander, generalissimo; *Hist* **el G.** = title given to Franco

generalista *adj (médico)* general

Generalitat [jenerali'tat] *nf* = name of the autonomous government of the regions of Catalonia or Valencia

generalización *nf* (**a**) *(comentario)* generalization (**b**) *(extensión) (de conflicto)* escalation, widening; *(de prácticas, enseñanza)* spread

generalizado, -a *adj* widespread

generalizar [14] **1** *vt* to spread, to make widespread

   2 *vi* to generalize

   3 generalizarse *vpr* to become widespread

generalmente *adv* generally

generar *vt (originar, causar)* to generate; *(engendrar)* to create

generativo, -a *adj* generative

generatriz *nf Geom* generatrix

genérico, -a *adj (común)* generic

género *nm* (**a**) *(clase)* kind, type; **es el mejor de su g.** it's the best of its kind; **sin ningún g. de dudas** absolutely without a doubt; **el g. humano** the human race (**b**) *Gram* gender; **de g. ambiguo** = that may be either masculine or feminine; **g. femenino/masculino** feminine/masculine gender (**c**) *Lit* genre (**d**) *Biol* genus (**e**) *Mús* **g. chico** zarzuela, = Spanish light opera; **g. lírico** opera (**f**) *(productos)* merchandise, goods (**g**) *(tejido)* cloth, material

generosidad *nf* generosity

generoso, -a *adj* (**a**) *(persona)* generous; **fue muy g. con sus hermanos** he was very generous to his brothers and sisters; *Irónico* **¡gracias, g.!** thanks, big spender! (**b**) *(abundante)* generous; **una ración generosa** a generous helping

génesis 1 *nf inv* genesis

   2 *nm inv Rel* **el G.** Genesis

genética *nf* genetics *(singular)*

genético, -a *adj* genetic

genial *adj* (**a**) *(artista, escritor)* of genius (**b**) *(estupendo)* great

genialidad *nf* (**a**) *(capacidad)* genius (**b**) *(acción)* stroke of genius

genio *nm* (**a**) *(talento)* genius; **un g. del arte moderno** one of the geniuses of modern art (**b**) *(ser mitológico)* genie (**c**) *(personalidad fuerte)* temper; **tener mucho g.** to be quick-tempered; **tener mal g.** to be bad-tempered (**d**) *(carácter)* nature, disposition

genioso, -a *adj Méx Fam* bad-tempered, moody

genital 1 *adj* genital

   2 genitales *nmpl* genitals

genitivo *nm Gram* genitive

genocidio *nm* genocide

genoma *nm* genome

genómico, -a *adj* genomic

genotipo *nm* genotype

Génova *n* Genoa

genovés, -esa *adj & nm,f* Genoese

gente 1 *nf* (**a**) *(personas)* people; **toda la g.** everyone, everybody; **son buena g.** they're good people; **g. bien** well-to-do people; **g. de bien** decent folk; **g. de la calle** ordinary people; **la g. corriente** the common people; *Esp* **la g. guapa**

the beautiful people, the smart set; **g. menuda** kids (**b**) *Fam (familia)* folks

2 *adj inv Am (amable)* decent

gentil 1 *adj (amable)* kind, nice

2 *nmf Rel* gentile

gentileza *nf* courtesy, kindness; **¿tendría la g. de decirme…?** would you be so kind as to tell me…?; **por g. de** by courtesy of

gentilhombre *nm Hist* gentleman *(in the royal court)*

gentilicio *nm* = term referring to the natives or inhabitants of a particular place

gentío *nm* crowd

gentuza *nf Pey* riffraff, rabble

genuflexión *nf Rel* genuflection; **hacer una g.** to genuflect

genuino, -a *adj* genuine

GEO [χeo] *nm o nmpl (abrev de* **Grupo Especial de Operaciones**) = specially trained police force, ≃ SWAT

geodesia *nf* geodesy

geodinámica *nf* geodynamics *(singular)*

geofísica *nf (ciencia)* geophysics *(singular)*

geofísico, -a 1 *adj* geophysical

2 *nm,f (persona)* geophysicist

geografía *nf* geography; **por toda la g. española** all over Spain; **g. física** physical geography; **g. humana** human geography

geográfico, -a *adj* geographical

geógrafo, -a *nm,f* geographer

geología *nf* geology

geológico, -a *adj* geological

geólogo, -a *nm,f* geologist

geometría *nf* geometry

geométrico, -a *adj* geometric

geopolítica *nf* geopolitics *(singular)*

geopolítico, -a *adj* geopolitical

Georgia *n* Georgia

georgiano, -a 1 *adj & nm,f* Georgian

2 *nm (lengua)* Georgian

geranio *nm* geranium

gerencia *nf* (**a**) *(dirección)* management (**b**) *(cargo)* post of manager (**c**) *(oficina)* manager's office

gerenciar *vt Am* to manage

gerente *nmf* manager, director

geriatra *nmf Med* geriatrician

geriatría *nf Med* geriatrics *(singular)*

geriátrico, -a 1 *adj* geriatric

2 *nm (hospital)* geriatric hospital; *(residencia)* retirement *o* nursing home

gerifalte *nm* (**a**) *(ave)* gyrfalcon (**b**) *(persona)* bigwig

germanía *nf Hist* thieves' slang

germánico, -a 1 *adj (tribus, carácter)* Germanic, Teutonic

2 *nm (lengua)* Germanic

germanismo *nm* Germanism

germanista *nmf* German scholar

germano, -a 1 *adj (alemán)* German; *(tribus, carácter)* Germanic, Teutonic

2 *nm,f (alemán)* German; *Hist* Teuton

germen *nm también Fig* germ; **g. de trigo** wheat germ

germicida 1 *adj* germicidal

2 *nm* germicide

germinación *nf* germination

germinar *vi también Fig* to germinate

gerontocracia *nf* gerontocracy

gerontología *nf Med* gerontology

gerontólogo, -a *nm,f Med* gerontologist

gerundense 1 *adj* of/from Gerona

2 *nmf* person from Gerona

gerundio *nm* gerund

gesta *nf* exploit, feat

gestación *nf* (**a**) *(embarazo)* pregnancy, *Espec* gestation (**b**) *(de idea, proyecto)* gestation

gestar 1 *vi* to gestate

2 gestarse *vpr* **se estaba gestando una nueva era** the seeds of a new era had been sown

gesticulación *nf (de manos, brazos)* gesticulation; *(de cara)* face-pulling

gesticular *vi (con manos, brazos)* to gesticulate; *(con la cara)* to pull faces

gestión *nf* (**a**) *Com & Fin (administración)* management; **g. de cartera** portfolio management; **g. de crisis** crisis management; **g. de empresas** business management; **g. financiera** financial management; **g. de personal** personnel management; **g. política** *(de gobierno, ministro)* conduct in government; **g. de recursos** resource management; **g. de riesgos** risk management

(**b**) *Inform* **g. de ficheros** file management

(**c**) *(diligencia)* **tengo que hacer unas gestiones** I have a few things to do; **las gestiones del negociador fracasaron** the negotiator's efforts came to nothing

gestionar *vt* (**a**) *(tramitar)* to negotiate (**b**) *(administrar)* to manage

gesto *nm* (**a**) *(mueca)* face, grimace; *(ademán)* gesture; **hacer un g.** *(con las manos)* to gesture, to make a gesture; **hacer un g. de asentimiento** *(con la cabeza)* to nod; **torcer el g.** to pull a face *(expressing displeasure)* (**b**) *(acción)* gesture; **un g. de buena voluntad** a goodwill gesture, a gesture of goodwill; **ha sido un g. muy bonito ir a visitarla** visiting her was a very nice gesture

gestor, -ora 1 *adj* **el equipo g.** the management team

2 *nm,f* = person who carries out dealings with public bodies on behalf of private customers or companies, combining the roles of lawyer and accountant; *Fin* **g. de fondos** fund manager

gestoría *nf* = office of a "gestor"

gestual *adj* using gestures

Ghana *n* Ghana

ghanés, -esa *adj & nm,f* Ghanaian

ghetto ['geto] *nm* ghetto

giba *nf (de camello)* hump; *(de persona)* hunchback, hump

giboso, -a 1 *adj* hunchbacked

2 *nm,f* hunchback

Gibraltar *n* Gibraltar

gibraltareño, -a *adj & nm,f* Gibraltarian

GIF [gif] *nm Inform (abrev de* **graphics interchange format**) GIF

gigabyte [χiɣa'βait] *nm Inform* gigabyte

giganta *nf* giantess

gigante 1 *adj* gigantic

2 *nm* giant

gigantesco, -a *adj* gigantic

gigantismo *nm Med* gigantism

gigoló [ʒiɣo'lo] *nm* gigolo

gil, -ila *nm,f CSur Fam* jerk

gilí *Fam* **1** *adj* stupid

2 *nmf* jerk

gilipollada *nf Esp muy Fam* **hacer/decir una g.** to do/say something goddamn stupid

gilipollas, gilipuertas *Esp muy Fam* **1** *adj inv* **ser g.** to be a dork

2 *nmf inv* dork

gilipollez *nf inv Esp muy Fam* **hacer/decir una g.** to do/say something goddamn stupid

gilipuertas *Esp Fam Euf* **1** *adj inv* dumb

2 *nmf inv* dumbo

gima *etc ver* **gemir**

gimiera *etc ver* **gemir**

gimnasia *nf (deporte, ejercicio)* gymnastics *(singular); (asignatura)* PE; **hacer g.** to do exercises; **confundir la g. con la magnesia** to get the wrong end of the stick; **g. correctiva** physiotherapeutic exercises; **g. deportiva** gymnastics; **g. con pesas** weight training; **g. rítmica** rhythmic gymnastics; **g. sueca** free exercise, callisthenics; **g. terapéutica** physiotherapeutic exercises

gimnasio *nm* gymnasium

gimnasta *nmf* gymnast

gimnástico, -a *adj* gymnastic

gimo *etc ver* **gemir**

gimotear *vi* to whine, to whimper

gimoteo *nm* whining, whimpering

gincana *nf (carrera de obstáculos)* gymkhana; *(de automóviles)* rally

Ginebra *n* Geneva

ginebra *nf* gin

ginecología *nf Med* gynecology

ginecológico, -a *adj Med* gynecological

ginecólogo, -a *nm,f Med* gynecologist

ginger ale [jinje'reil] *nm inv* ginger ale

gingival *adj* gum; **una afección g.** a gum infection

gingivitis *nf inv Med* gingivitis

ginseng [jin'sen] *nm* ginseng

gin-tonic, gintonic [jin'tonik] *(pl* **gin-tonics, gintonics** *)* *nm* gin and tonic

gira *nf* tour; **estar de g.** to be on tour

girar 1 *vi* **(a)** *(dar vueltas)* to turn; *(rápidamente)* to spin **(b)** *(doblar)* to turn; **el camino gira a la derecha** the road turns to the right **(c)** *(tratar)* **g. en torno a** *o* **alrededor de** to be centered around, to center on; **el coloquio giró en torno a la pena de muerte** the discussion dealt with the topic of the death penalty **(d)** *Com* to remit payment

2 *vt* **(a)** *(hacer dar vueltas a)* to turn; *(rápidamente)* to spin; **g. la cabeza** to turn one's head **(b)** *Com* to draw **(c)** *(dinero)* to transfer, to remit

3 girarse *vpr (persona)* to turn around

girasol *nm* sunflower

giratorio, -a *adj (puerta)* revolving; *(silla)* swivel

giro *nm* **(a)** *(cambio de dirección)* turn; *Fig* **un g. de 180 grados** a U-turn **(b)** *(postal, telegráfico)* money order; **g. postal** *(postal)* money order **(c)** *(de letras, órdenes de pago)* draft **(d)** *(expresión)* turn of phrase **(e)** *Am (ramo)* industry

GIS [χis] *nm inv Inform (abrev de* **geographical information system***)* GIS

gis *nm Méx* chalk

gitanería *nf* **(a)** *(engaño)* wiliness, craftiness **(b)** *(gitanos)* Gypsies

gitano, -a 1 *adj* **(a)** *(raza, persona)* Gypsy **(b)** wily, crafty

2 *nm,f* Gypsy

glaciación *nf (periodo)* ice age; *(proceso)* glaciation

glacial *adj (época)* glacial; *(viento, acogida)* icy

glaciar 1 *adj* glacial

2 *nm* glacier

gladiador *nm* gladiator

gladiolo, gladíolo *nm* gladiolus

glamour [gla'mur] *nm* glamor

glande *nm Anat* glans (penis)

glándula *nf Anat* gland; **g. endocrina** endocrine gland; **glándulas mamarias** mammary glands; **g. sudorípara** sweat gland

glasé 1 *adj* glacé

2 *nm* glacé silk

glaseado, -a 1 *adj* glacé

2 *nm* glazing

glasear *vt* to glaze

glaucoma *nm Med* glaucoma

glicerina *nf* glycerine

global *adj* global, overall

globalización *nf (mundialización)* globalization

globalizar [14] *vt* to give an overall view of

globo *nm* **(a)** *(la Tierra)* **el g.** the globe; **g. terráqueo** *o* **terrestre** globe **(b)** *(aeróstato, juguete)* balloon; **g. aerostático** hot-air balloon; **g. sonda** weather balloon; *Fig* **lanzar un g. sonda** to fly a kite **(c)** *(lámpara)* round glass lampshade **(d)** *(esfera)* sphere; *Anat* **g. ocular** eyeball

glóbulo *nm Med* blood cell, corpuscle; **g. blanco/rojo** white/red corpuscle, white/red blood cell

gloria *nf* **(a)** *(en religión)* glory **(b)** *(celebridad)* celebrity, star **(c)** *(placer)* delight; **estar en la g.** to be in seventh heaven; **saber a g.** to taste divine *o* heavenly

glorieta *nf* **(a)** *(de jardín)* arbor **(b)** *(plazoleta)* square; *(plazoleta circular)* circus **(c)** *Esp (rotonda)* traffic circle

glorificación *nf* glorification

glorificar [59] *vt* to glorify

glorioso, -a *adj* glorious

glosa *nf* marginal note

glosador, -ora *nm,f* commentator *(on text)*

glosar *vt* **(a)** *(anotar)* to annotate **(b)** *(comentar)* to comment on

glosario *nm* glossary

glotis *nf inv Anat* glottis

glotón, -ona 1 *adj* gluttonous, greedy

2 *nm,f* glutton

glotonería *nf* gluttony, greed

glucemia *nf Med* glycemia

glúcido *nm* carbohydrate

glucosa *nf* glucose

gluten *nm* gluten

glúteo, -a 1 *adj* gluteal

2 *nm* gluteus

gnomo ['nomo] *nm* gnome

gnóstico, -a ['nostiko] *adj & nm,f* gnostic

gobernabilidad *nf* governability

gobernable *adj* governable

gobernación *nf* **(a)** *(gestión)* governing **(b)** *Col (de provincia)* provincial government **(c)** *Méx* **G.** *(ministerio)* ≃ the Department of the Interior

gobernador, -ora 1 *adj* governing

2 *nm,f* governor; *Esp Antes* **g. civil** = person representing the central government in each province

gobernanta *nf (en hotel)* cleaning and laundry staff manageress

gobernante 1 *adj* ruling; **partido g.** governing party

2 *nmf* ruler, leader

gobernar [3] **1** *vt* **(a)** *(regir, dirigir)* to govern, to rule; *(casa, negocio)* to run, to manage; **se deja g. por su marido** she allows herself to be ruled by her husband; **sus sentimientos gobiernan sus acciones** his feelings govern his actions **(b)** *(barco)* to steer; *(avión)* to fly

2 *vi Náut* to steer

Gobi *nm* **el desierto de G.** the Gobi Desert

gobiernista *Andes, Méx* **1** *adj* progovernment

2 *nmf* government supporter

gobierno *nm* **(a)** *(de país, región)* government; **el g. en pleno asistió al acto** all the members of the government attended; **g. autónomo** autonomous government; **g. central** central government; *Esp Antes* **g. civil** = body representing the central government in each province; **g. de coalición** coalition government; *Esp* **g. militar** = body representing the army in each province; **g. provisional** caretaker government; **g. de transición** caretaker *o* interim government

(**b**) *(edificio)* government buildings

(**c**) *(administración, gestión)* running, management

(**d**) *(control)* control

goce 1 *ver* **gozar**

2 *nm* pleasure

godo, -a 1 *adj* Gothic

2 *nm,f Hist* Goth

gofre *nm Esp* waffle

gogó: a gogó *loc adv Esp* **hubo comida/bebida a g.** there was loads of food/drink

gol *nm* goal; *Fig* **meter un g. a alguien** to put one over on sb, to score an advantage over sb; **g. en propia meta** own goal

golazo *nm Fam* amazing goal

goleada *nf* high score, cricket score; **ganar por g.** to score a heavy victory

goleador, -ora *nm,f* goal scorer

golear *vt* to score a lot of goals against, to thrash

golero, -a *nm,f RP* goalkeeper

goleta *nf* schooner

golf *nm* golf

golfa *nf Esp Fam (mujer promiscua)* tart, slag

golfante *nmf* scoundrel, rascal

golfear *vi Fam (hacer el golfo)* to hang out

golfería *nf* (**a**) *(golfos)* layabouts, good-for-nothings (**b**) *(actitud, comportamiento)* loutish behavior

golfista *nmf* golfer

golfístico, -a *adj* golf, golfing

golfo, -a 1 *adj (gamberro)* loutish; *(pillo)* roguish

2 *nm* (**a**) *(gamberro)* lout; *(pillo)* rogue (**b**) *Geog* gulf, bay; **el G. de Bengala** the Bay of Bengal; **el G. de México** the Gulf of Mexico; **el G. Pérsico** the Persian Gulf; **el G. de Vizcaya** the Bay of Biscay

gollete *nm* neck

golondrina *nf* swallow

golondrino *nm Med* boil in the armpit

golosina *nf (dulce)* candy; *(exquisitez)* tidbit, delicacy

goloso, -a 1 *adj* sweet-toothed

2 *nm,f* sweet-toothed person

golpe *nm* (**a**) *(impacto)* blow; *(en puerta)* knock; *(entre coches)* bump, collision; **me di un g. en la rodilla** I banged my knee; **tengo un g. en el brazo** I've banged my arm; **el coche tiene un g. en la puerta** the car door has a dent in it; **moler a alguien a golpes** to beat sb up; *Dep* **un g. bajo** a blow below the belt; *Fig* a low blow; **g. de castigo** *(en rugby)* penalty (kick); **g. franco** free kick

(**b**) *(disgusto)* blow

(**c**) *(atraco)* raid, job, heist; **dar un g.** to do a job

(**d**) *Pol* **g. (de Estado)** coup (d'état)

(**e**) *(ocurrencia)* witticism

(**f**) *(en tenis, golf)* shot

(**g**) *(expresiones)* **errar** *o* **fallar el g.** to miss the mark; *Fam* **dar el g.** to cause a sensation, to be a hit; **no dar** *o* **pegar g.** not to lift a finger, not to do a stroke of work; **de g.** suddenly; *Fam* **de g. y porrazo** without warning, just like that; **de un g.** at *or* in one fell swoop, all at once; **g. de gracia** coup de grâce; **g. de suerte** stroke of luck; **g. de vista** glance; **al primer g. de vista** at a glance

golpear 1 *vt & vi (pegar, impactar)* to hit; *(puerta)* to bang; *(con puño)* to punch

2 golpearse *vpr* to give oneself a bump *o* bang; **se golpeó en la cabeza** he bumped *o* banged his head

golpeteo *nm (de dedos, lluvia)* drumming; *(de puerta, persiana)* banging

golpismo *nm* tendency to military coups

golpista 1 *adj* involved in a military coup; **una intentona g.** an attempted coup

2 *nmf =* person involved in a military coup

golpiza *nf Am* beating

goma *nf* (**a**) *(sustancia)* gum; **g. arábiga** gum arabic; **g. de mascar** chewing gum (**b**) *(tira elástica)* rubber band; **g. elástica** elastic (**c**) *(caucho)* rubber; **g. espuma** foam rubber; **g. de borrar** eraser (**d**) *Fam (preservativo)* rubber

gomaespuma *nf* foam rubber

gomería *nf CSur* tire center

gomero, -a *Am* **1** *nm,f (persona)* rubber-plantation worker

2 *nm (árbol)* rubber tree

gomina *nf* hair gel

gominola *nf* soft fruit candy

gomoso, -a *adj* gummy

gónada *nf Anat* gonad

góndola *nf* (**a**) *(embarcación)* gondola (**b**) *(autobús) Andes (interurbano)* (long-distance) bus; *Bol (urbano)* city bus (**c**) *(en supermercado)* gondola

gondolero *nm* gondolier

gong (*pl* **gongs**) *nm* gong

gonorrea *nf Med* gonorrhea

gordinflón, -ona *Fam* **1** *adj* chubby, tubby

2 *nm,f* fatty

gordo, -a 1 *adj* (**a**) *(persona)* fat; **está más g. que antes** he's put on weight; *Fam* **me cae g.** I can't stand him (**b**) *(grueso)* thick (**c**) *Fam (problema, asunto)* big, serious; **me pasó algo muy g. con él** something very serious happened to me with him; *Fig* **armar la gorda** to kick up a row *o* stink

2 *nm,f (persona obesa)* fat man, *f* fat woman; **los gordos** fat people

3 *nm (en lotería)* first prize, jackpot; **le tocó el g.** he won first prize, he won the jackpot

gordura *nf* fatness, obesity

gore *nm* slasher movies

gorgojo *nm (insecto)* weevil

gorgonzola *nm* gorgonzola

gorgorito *nm* warble; *Fam* **hacer gorgoritos** *(cantar)* to warble

gorgoteo *nm* gurgle, gurgling

gorila *nm* (**a**) *(animal)* gorilla (**b**) *Fam (guardaespaldas)* bodyguard; *Esp (en discoteca, pub)* bouncer

gorjear *vi* to chirp, to twitter

gorjeo *nm* chirping, twittering

gorra *nf* (peaked) cap; *Esp, Méx* **de g.** for free; *Esp, Méx Fam* **vivir de g.** to scrounge; **g. de plato** peaked cap *(of officer)*; **g. de visera** baseball cap

gorrear *vt & vi Fam* to sponge, to scrounge

gorrinada *nf* (**a**) *(guarrada) (acción)* disgusting behavior; *(lugar)* pigpen (**b**) *(mala pasada)* dirty trick

gorrino, -a *nm,f también Fig* pig

gorrión *nm* sparrow; **g. macho** cock sparrow

gorro *nm* cap; *Fam* **estar hasta el g. (de)** to be fed up (with); **g. de baño** *(para piscina)* swimming cap, bathing cap; *(para ducha)* shower cap

gorrón, -ona *Esp, Méx Fam* **1** *adj* sponging, scrounging

2 *nm,f* sponger, scrounger

gorronear *vt & vi Esp, Méx Fam* to sponge, to scrounge

gorronería *nf Esp Fam* sponging, scrounging

góspel *nm Mús* gospel (music)

gota *nf* (**a**) *(de líquido)* drop; *(de sudor)* bead; **no probé una g. de alcohol** I didn't drink a drop of alcohol; **caer cuatro gotas** to spit (with rain); **ni g. (de)** not a drop (of); **no se veía ni g.** you couldn't see a thing; **no corre ni una g. de brisa** there isn't a breath of wind; **no entiendo ni g. de alemán** I don't understand a word of German; **ni g. de**

sentido común not an ounce of common sense; **fue la g. que colma el vaso, fue la última g.** it was the last straw; **como dos gotas de agua** like two peas in a pod; *Fam* **sudar la g. gorda** to sweat blood, to work very hard; *Med* **g. a g.** intravenous drip

  (**b**) *Meteo* **g. fría** = cold front that remains in one place for some time, causing continuous heavy rain

  (**c**) *(enfermedad)* gout

gotear 1 *vi (líquido, grifo)* to drip; *(techo, depósito)* to leak; *Fig* to trickle through

  2 *v impersonal (chispear)* to spit, to drizzle

gotelé *nm* = decorative technique of applying paint to give a roughly textured surface

goteo *nm (de líquido)* dripping; *(de gente, información)* trickle

gotera *nf* (**a**) *(filtración)* leak (**b**) *(mancha)* stain *(left by leaking water)*

gotero *nm* (**a**) *(gota a gota)* (intravenous) drip (**b**) *Am (cuentagotas)* dropper, eyedropper

gótico, -a 1 *adj* Gothic

  2 *nm (arte)* Gothic

gourmet [gur'met] *(pl* **gourmets**) *nmf* gourmet

goyesco, -a *adj* = relating to or like Goya's paintings

gozada *nf Fam* absolute delight; **¡qué g. de coche/película!** what a wonderful car/movie!

gozar [14] *vi* to enjoy oneself; **g. con** to take delight in; **g. de algo** to enjoy sth; **goza de una buena posición social** he has *o* enjoys good social standing; **g. de buena salud** to be in good health; **goza de la confianza del presidente** he is trusted by the president

gozne *nm* hinge

gozo *nm* joy, pleasure; *Fam* **mi g. en un pozo** that's just my (bad) luck

g/p, g.p. *(abrev de* **giro postal***)* MO

grabación *nf* recording; **g. digital** digital recording

grabado *nm (técnica, lámina)* engraving; **g. al aguafuerte** etching; **g. sobre madera** woodcut

grabador, -ora *nm,f (persona)* engraver

grabadora *nf (magnetófono)* tape recorder; **g. de CD** CD writer

grabar 1 *vt* (**a**) *(en metal)* to engrave; *(en madera)* to carve; **grabó su nombre en un tronco** she carved her name on a tree (**b**) *(sonido, cinta)* to record, to tape; **han grabado un nuevo disco** they've recorded a new album (**c**) *Inform (documento)* to save; *(CD-ROM)* to record, to burn (**d**) *(fijar)* **grabado en su memoria** imprinted *o* engraved on his memory; **¡que te quede bien grabado!** don't you forget it!

  2 **grabarse** *vpr* **grabársele a alguien en la memoria** to become imprinted *o* engraved on sb's mind

gracejo *nm* **tener mucho g.** to be a good talker; **contar una historia con g.** to tell a story in an amusing way

gracia 1 *nf* (**a**) *(humor, comicidad)* humor; **¡qué g.!** how funny!; **su voz me hace mucha g.** *(me divierte)* I think he's got a really funny voice, his voice makes me laugh; **mi sombrero le hizo g. a Ana** *(le gustó)* Ana liked my hat; **no me hizo g.** I didn't find it funny; **tener g.** *(ser divertido, curioso)* to be funny

  (**b**) *(arte, habilidad)* skill, natural ability; *Esp* **todavía no le he pillado** *o* **cogido la g. a esta cámara** I still haven't got the hang of using this camera

  (**c**) *(encanto)* grace, elegance; **no consigo verle la g. a este cuadro** I just don't know what people see in this painting; **la g. del plato está en la salsa** the secret of the dish is (in) the sauce

  (**d**) *(ocurrencia)* **no le rías las gracias al niño** don't laugh when the child does/says something silly

  (**e**) *(incordio)* nuisance; **vaya g. tener que salir a mitad de la noche** it's a real nuisance having to go out in the middle of

the night; *Fam* **¡maldita la g. que me hace tener que volverlo a hacer!** it's a real pain having to do it all over again!

  (**f**) *(favor)* favor; *(indulto)* pardon; **caer en g.** to be liked

  (**g**) *Rel* **la g. de Dios** the grace of God

  2 **gracias** *nfpl* thank you, thanks; **gracias a** thanks to; **dar las gracias a alguien (por)** to thank sb (for); **muchas gracias** thank you very much, thanks very much; **gracias por venir** thank you for coming

grácil *adj (armonioso)* graceful; *(delicado)* delicate

gracioso, -a 1 *adj* (**a**) *(divertido)* funny, amusing; **se cree muy g.** he thinks he's really smart (**b**) *(curioso)* funny; **es g. que…** it's funny how… (**c**) *(bonito, atractivo)* pretty

  2 *nm,f (persona divertida)* funny *o* amusing person; *Pey* smart alec, comedian

  3 *nm Teatro* fool, clown

grada *nf* (**a**) *(peldaño)* step (**b**) *Teatro* row (**c**) **gradas** *(en estadio)* = banked area for spectators with standing room only

gradación *nf* scale

graderío *nm Esp (gradas) Teatro* rows; *Dep* = banked area for spectators with standing room only; *(público)* crowd

grado *nm* (**a**) *(unidad)* degree; **g. centígrado** degree centigrade (**b**) *(índice, nivel)* degree; **quemaduras de primer g.** first-degree burns; **mostró un alto g. de preparación** he was very well prepared; **en menor g.** to a lesser extent *o* degree; **en g. sumo** greatly (**c**) *(rango)* grade; *Mil* rank (**d**) *Educ (año)* grade, year, class (**e**) *(voluntad)* **hacer algo de buen/mal g.** to do sth willingly/unwillingly; **te lo prestaré de buen g.** I'd be happy to lend it to you

graduable *adj* adjustable

graduación *nf* (**a**) *(acción)* grading; *(de la vista)* eye test; *(de gafas)* strength (**b**) *Educ* graduation (**c**) *(de bebidas)* strength, proof; **bebidas de alta g.** spirits (**d**) *Mil* rank

graduado, -a 1 *adj* (**a**) *(termómetro)* graduated; **gafas graduadas** prescription glasses; **recipiente g.** *(jarra)* measuring jug (**b**) *(universitario)* graduate

  2 *nm,f (persona)* graduate

  3 *nm Esp Educ* **g. escolar** *(título)* = basic school certificate

gradual *adj* gradual

graduar [4] 1 *vt* (**a**) *(medir)* to gauge, to measure; *(regular)* to regulate; *(vista)* to test (**b**) *(escalonar)* to stagger (**c**) *Educ* to confer a degree on (**d**) *Mil* to confer a rank on, to commission

  2 **graduarse** *vpr* to graduate (**en** in)

graffiti *nm* piece of graffiti; **la pared estaba llena de graffitis** the wall was covered in graffiti

grafía *nf* written symbol

gráfica *nf* graph, chart

gráfico, -a 1 *adj* graphic

  2 *nm (figura)* graph, chart; *(dibujo)* diagram; **g. de barras** bar chart; **g. de sectores** pie chart

grafismo *nm (diseño)* graphics

grafista *nmf* graphic artist *o* designer

grafito *nm* graphite

grafología *nf* graphology

grafólogo, -a *nm,f* graphologist

gragea *nf* (**a**) *(píldora)* pill, tablet (**b**) *(confite)* sugar-coated candy

grajilla *nf* jackdaw

grajo, -a *nm,f* rook

gral. *(abrev de* **general***)* gen

gramática *nf (disciplina, libro)* grammar; *Fam* **tener g. parda** to be streetwise *o* worldly-wise

gramatical *adj* grammatical

gramático, -a 1 *adj* grammatical

  2 *nm,f (persona)* grammarian

gramínea *Bot* 1 *adj* **una planta g.** a grass, *Espec* a gramineous plant

  2 *nf* grass, *Espec* gramineous plant

gramo *nm* gram; *Fig* **no tiene ni un g. de cordura** he hasn't an ounce of good sense

gramófono *nm* gramophone

gramola *nf* gramophone

grampa *nf Am* staple

gran *ver* **grande**

Granada *n* (a) *(en España)* Granada (b) *(en las Antillas)* Grenada

granada *nf* (a) *(fruta)* pomegranate (b) *(proyectil)* grenade; **g. de mano** hand grenade

granadilla *nf* passion fruit

granadina *nf* (a) *(bebida)* grenadine (b) *(cante)* = type of flamenco from Granada

granadino, -a 1 *adj* (a) *(en España)* of/from Granada (b) *(en las Antillas)* Grenadian **2** *nm,f* person from Granada

granado *nm* pomegranate (tree)

granar *vi* to seed

granate 1 *nm* garnet
  2 *adj inv* garnet-colored

grande

> **gran** is used instead of **grande** before singular nouns (e.g. **gran hombre** great man).

1 *adj* (a) *(de tamaño)* big, large; *(de altura)* tall; *(de intensidad, importancia)* great; **este traje me está** *o* **me queda g.** this suit is too big for me; **un gran artista** a great artist; **el gran favorito** the firm favorite; **una gran figura** a big name; **una gran parte de mi trabajo implica…** a large part of my job involves…; **una gran responsabilidad** a heavy responsibility; **a lo g.** in a big way, in style; **grandes almacenes** department store; *Fot* **gran angular** wide-angle lens; **Gran Bretaña** Great Britain; **el Gran Cañón** the Grand Canyon; **gran danés** Great Dane; **gran éxito** *(disco, libro)* smash (hit); **los Grandes Lagos** the Great Lakes; **la Gran Muralla (china)** the Great Wall (of China); **el gran público** the general public; *Esp Com* **gran superficie** hypermarket
  (b) *Méx, RP (de edad)* old
  (c) *RP Fam (fantástico)* fantastic
  (d) *Fam* **pasarlo en g.** to have a great time
2 *nm* (a) *(noble)* grandee (b) *(persona, entidad importante)* **uno de los grandes del sector** one of the major players in the sector; **uno de los grandes de la literatura mexicana** one of the big names in Mexican literature (c) *Fam* **grandes** *(adultos)* grown-ups

grandeza *nf* (a) *(de tamaño)* (great) size; *(esplendor)* magnificence, grandeur; **en toda su g.** in all its splendor *o* grandeur (b) *(de sentimientos)* generosity, graciousness (c) *Esp (aristocracia)* **la g.** the Spanish grandees

grandilocuencia *nf* grandiloquence

grandilocuente *adj* grandiloquent

grandiosidad *nf* grandeur

grandioso, -a *adj* grand, splendid

grandullón, -ona *Fam* **1** *adj* overgrown
  2 *nm,f* big boy, *f* big girl

granel *nm* **a g.** *(sin envase)* loose; *(en gran cantidad)* in bulk; *(en abundancia)* in abundance; **vender/comprar vino a g.** to sell/buy wine from the barrel

granero *nm* granary

granito *nm* granite

granizada *nf* hailstorm

granizado *nm* = drink of flavored crushed ice; **g. de limón/café** = lemon-/coffee-flavored crushed ice drink

granizar [14] *v impersonal* to hail

granizo *nm* hail

granja *nf* farm; **g. avícola** poultry farm; **g. escuela** = farm which schoolchildren visit or stay at to learn about farming life and animals

granjear 1 *vt* (a) *(conquistar)* to earn (b) *Chile (estafar)* to swindle
  2 granjearse *vpr* to gain, to earn

granjearse *vpr* to gain, to earn

granjero, -a *nm,f* farmer

grano *nm* (a) *(de cereal, arena)* grain; **g. de café** coffee bean; **g. de pimienta** peppercorn (b) *(partícula)* grain (c) *(en la piel)* spot, pimple (d) *(expresiones)* **apartar** *o* **separar el g. de la paja** to separate the wheat from the chaff; **aportar** *o* **poner uno su g. de arena** to do one's bit; **ir al g.** to get to the point

granuja *nmf (pillo)* rogue, scoundrel; *(canalla)* trickster, swindler

granujada *nf* dirty trick

granulado, -a 1 *adj* granulated
  2 *nm* granules

gránulo *nm* granule

granuloso, -a *adj* bumpy

grapa *nf (para papeles)* staple; *(para heridas)* stitch, (wire) suture

grapadora *nf* stapler; **g. industrial** staple gun

grapar *vt* to staple

grasa *nf* (a) *(en comestibles)* fat; *(de cerdo)* lard; **g. vegetal** vegetable fat (b) *(lubricante)* grease, oil (c) *(suciedad)* grease

grasiento, -a *adj* greasy

graso, -a *adj (mantecoso)* greasy; *(con alto contenido en grasas)* fatty

grasoso, -a *adj* greasy

gratén *nm Culin* gratin; **al g.** au gratin

gratificación *nf* (a) *(moral)* reward (b) *(monetaria)* bonus

gratificante *adj* rewarding

gratificar [59] *vt (complacer)* to reward; *(retribuir)* to give a bonus to; *(dar propina a)* to tip

gratinado, -a *adj Culin* au gratin

gratinar *vt Culin* to cook au gratin

gratis *adv* free, for nothing; **ser g.** to be free; **me salió g. el viaje** the journey didn't cost me anything

gratitud *nf* gratitude

grato, -a *adj* pleasant; **nos es g. comunicarle que…** we are pleased to inform you that…

gratuito, -a *adj* (a) *(sin dinero)* free (b) *(arbitrario)* gratuitous; *(infundado)* unfair, uncalled for

grava *nf* gravel

gravamen *nm* (a) *(impuesto)* tax (b) *(obligación moral)* burden

gravar *vt* (a) *(con impuestos)* to tax (b) *(agravar)* to worsen

grave 1 *adj* (a) *(enfermedad, situación, error)* serious; *(estilo)* formal; **estar g.** to be seriously ill; **presenta heridas graves** he is seriously injured; **su semblante g. impone respeto** her serious features inspire respect (b) *(sonido, voz)* low, deep (c) *Gram (palabra)* stressed on the second-to-last syllable; *(tilde)* grave
  2 *nf Gram* word stressed on the second-to-last syllable

gravedad *nf* (a) *(cualidad de grave)* seriousness (b) *Fís* gravity

gravidez *nf Formal* pregnancy

grávido, -a *adj Formal* full

gravilla *nf* gravel

gravitación *nf Fís* gravitation

gravitacional *adj* gravitational

gravitar *vi Fís* to gravitate; *Fig* **g. sobre** *(pender)* to hang *o* loom over; *(recaer)* to rest on

gravitatorio, -a *adj* gravitational

gravoso, -a *adj* burdensome; *(costoso)* expensive, costly

graznar *vi (cuervo)* to caw; *(ganso)* to honk; *(pato)* to quack; *(persona)* to squawk

graznido *nm (de cuervo)* caw, cawing; *(de ganso)* honk, honking; *(de pato)* quack, quacking; *(de persona)* squawk, squawking

greca *nf Arquit* fret
Grecia *n* Greece
grecolatino, -a *adj* Greco-Latin
grecorromano, -a *adj* Greco-Roman
gregario, -a *adj* gregarious; **el instinto g.** the herd instinct
gregoriano, -a *adj* Gregorian
grelo *nm* turnip leaf
gremial *adj* (**a**) *Hist* guild; **ordenanzas gremiales** guild statutes (**b**) *Am (sindical)* labor-union; **organización g.** labor-union organization
gremialismo *nm* (**a**) *Pey (corporativismo)* = self-interested behavior, especially of professional groups (**b**) *Am (sindicalismo)* unionism
gremialista *nmf Am* union member
gremio *nm* (**a**) *Hist* guild (**b**) *(conjunto de profesionales)* profession, trade (**c**) *Fam (grupo)* league, club (**d**) *Am (sindicato)* labor union
greña *nf* (**a**) *(pelo enredado)* tangle of hair; **greñas** *(pelo largo)* long hair (**b**) *Fam* **andar a la g. (con alguien)** to be at loggerheads (with sb)
greñudo, -a *adj* with disheveled *o* unkempt hair
gres *nm* stoneware
gresca *nf* row; **se armó una g.** there was a fuss *o* row
griego, -a 1 *adj & nm,f* Greek
   2 *nm (lengua)* Greek
grieta *nf* crack; *(entre montañas)* crevice; *(que deja pasar luz)* chink
grifa *nf Fam* marijuana
grifería *nf* taps
grifero, -a *nm,f Perú* gas-pump attendant
grifo *nm* (**a**) *Esp (llave)* faucet; **g. monomando** = faucet that combines hot and cold water (**b**) *Perú (gasolinera)* gas station
grill [gril] *(pl grills) nm* grill
grillado, -a *adj Esp Fam* crazy, loopy
grillete *nm* shackle
grillo *nm* (**a**) *(insecto)* cricket (**b**) **grillos** *(grilletes)* shackles
grima *nf* (**a**) *(disgusto)* annoyance; **me da g.** he/she/it gets on my nerves (**b**) *(dentera)* **me da g.** he/she/it sets my teeth on edge
gringo, -a *adj & nm,f* gringo
gringolandia *nf Am Fam Hum* Yankeeland
gripa *nf Col, Méx* flu
gripal *adj* flu-like; **síntomas gripales** flu(-like) symptoms
griparse *vpr* to seize up
gripe *nf* flu
griposo, -a *adj* fluey
gris 1 *adj (color)* gray; *(existencia)* gloomy, miserable; *(discurso, persona)* dull, characterless
   2 *nm* (**a**) gray; **g. marengo/perla** dark/pearl gray (**b**) *Esp Fam Antes* **los grises** *(la policía)* the cops
grisáceo, -a *adj* grayish
grisalla *nf Méx* scrap metal
grisear *vi* to become gray
grisú *(pl grisúes) nm Med* firedamp
gritar 1 *vi (hablar alto)* to shout; *(chillar)* to scream; **no grites tanto, habla más bajo** don't shout so much, lower your voice a bit; **gritó de dolor** he screamed in pain
   2 *vt* (**a**) *(en voz alta)* **g. algo a alguien** to shout sth at sb (**b**) *(reñir)* to shout *o* yell at; **¡no me grites!** don't shout *o* yell at me!
griterío *nm* screaming, shouting
grito *nm (chillido)* shout; *(de dolor, miedo)* cry, scream; *(de sorpresa, de animal)* cry; **se escuchaban los gritos de los manifestantes** you could hear the demonstrators chanting; **dar** *o* **pegar un g.** to shout *o* scream (out); *Fam* **a g. limpio** *o* **pelado** at the top of one's voice; **hablar a gritos** to shout, to

talk at the top of one's voice; *Fig* **pedir algo a gritos** to be crying out for sth; *Fam* **poner el g. en el cielo** to hit the roof; **ser el último g.** to be the latest fashion *o* craze, to be the in thing; **g. de dolor** cry of pain; **g. de guerra** war *o* battle cry
gritón, -ona *adj Fam* loudmouthed
groenlandés, -esa 1 *adj* Greenlandic
   2 *nm,f* Greenlander
Groenlandia *n* Greenland
grog *(pl grogs) nm* grog
grogui *adj también Fig* groggy
grosella *nf* **g. (roja)** red currant; **g. negra** black currant; **g. silvestre** gooseberry
grosellero *nm (silvestre)* gooseberry bush
grosería *nf (cualidad)* rudeness; *(acción)* rude thing; *(palabrota)* swear word
grosero, -a 1 *adj* (**a**) *(maleducado)* rude, crude (**b**) *(tosco)* coarse, rough
   2 *nm,f* rude person
grosor *nm* thickness
grosso modo *adv* roughly, in broad terms
grotesco, -a *adj* grotesque
grúa *nf* (**a**) *(máquina)* crane (**b**) *(vehículo)* tow truck
grueso, -a 1 *adj* (**a**) *(espeso)* thick (**b**) *(corpulento)* thickset; *(obeso)* fat (**c**) *(en grano)* coarse; **sal gruesa** coarse salt (**d**) *Meteo* **mar gruesa** stormy *o* heavy sea
   2 *nm* (**a**) *(grosor)* thickness (**b**) *(parte mayor)* **el g. de** the bulk of; **el g. del público ya se ha marchado** most of the crowd has already left
grulla *nf* crane; *Fam Pey* **una vieja g.** *(mujer)* an old bag
grumete *nm* cabin boy
grumo *nm (de líquido)* lump; *(de sangre)* clot
grumoso, -a *adj* lumpy
grunge [grunt∫] *nm* grunge
gruñido *nm (de perro)* growl; *(de cerdo)* grunt; *(de persona)* grumble
gruñir *vi (perro)* to growl; *(cerdo)* to grunt; *(persona)* to grumble
gruñón, -ona 1 *adj* grumpy
   2 *nm,f* old grump
grupa *nf* hindquarters
grupo *nm (conjunto)* group; *(de árboles)* cluster; *(de músicos)* group, band; *Tec* unit, set; **en g.** in a group; **g. de discusión** *Inform* discussion group; *Mktg* focus group; *Elec* **g. electrógeno** generator; *Com* **g. de empresas** (corporate) group; **g. ecologista** environmental group; **g. de estudio** study group; **g. de música pop** pop group; *Inform* **g. de noticias** newsgroup; *Pol* **g. parlamentario** parliamentary group; *Pol* **g. de presión** pressure group, lobby; **g. de riesgo** group at risk; **g. de rock** rock group; *Med* **g. sanguíneo** blood group
grupúsculo *nm* minor group
gruta *nf* grotto
gruyère [gru'jer] **1** *adj* **queso g.** Gruyère cheese
   2 *nm* Gruyère
gta. *abrev de* **glorieta**
guacal *nm* (**a**) *CAm, Méx (calabaza)* pumpkin (**b**) *Carib, Col, Méx (jaula)* cage
guacamayo, -a *nm,f (ave)* macaw
guacamol, guacamole *nm* guacamole, avocado dip
guachafita *nf Col,Ven Fam* racket, uproar
guachimán *nm Am* night watchman
guachinango *nm Méx (pez)* red snapper
guacho, -a *nm,f Andes, CSur Fam* illegitimate child
guadalajareño, -a 1 *adj* of/from Guadalajara
   2 *nm,f* person from Guadalajara
Guadalquivir *nm* **el G.** the Guadalquivir

guadaña *nf* scythe

Guadiana *nm* **el G.** the Guadiana

guagua *nf* (**a**) *Cuba, PRico, RDom (autobús)* bus (**b**) *Andes (niño)* baby

guajira *nf* = Cuban popular song about country life

guajiro, -a *nm,f Cuba Fam* peasant

guajolote *nm CAm, Méx* turkey

gualdo, -a *adj* yellow

guampa *nf Bol, CSur* horn

guanábana *nf Am* soursop

guanajo *nm Carib* turkey

guanche *adj & nmf* guanche, = original inhabitant of the Canary Islands

guano *nm* (**a**) *(abono)* guano (**b**) *Cuba (palmera)* palm tree

guantazo *nm Fam* slap

guante *nm* glove; **arrojar** *o* **tirar el g.** to throw down the gauntlet; **de g. blanco** gentlemanly; *Fam Fig* **echarle el g. a algo/alguien** to get hold of sth/sb, to get one's hands on sth/sb; **estar más suave que un g.** to be as meek as a lamb; **g. de boxeo** boxing glove; **g. de goma** rubber glove

guantera *nf (en coche)* glove compartment

guaperas *Esp Fam* **1** *adj inv* pretty-pretty

2 *nm inv* (**a**) *(presumido)* pretty boy (**b**) *(artista, cantante)* heartthrob

guapetón, -ona *adj Esp Fam* gorgeous

guapo, -a **1** *adj* (**a**) *esp Esp (atractivo)* good-looking; *(hombre)* handsome; *(mujer)* pretty (**b**) *esp Esp (elegante)* smart; **¡qué g. te has puesto!** you look really nice! (**c**) *Esp Fam (muy bueno)* cool, ace (**d**) *Am (valiente)* gutsy; **ser g.** to have guts

2 *nm,f* (**a**) *(valiente)* **a ver quién es el g. que…** let's see who's brave enough to… (**b**) *Esp Fam (apelativo)* pal

guapura *nf (de hombre)* handsomeness; *(de mujer)* prettiness

guaraches *nmpl Méx* sandals *(with a sole made from a tire)*

guarango, -a *adj CSur* coarse, vulgar

guaraní *(pl* **guaraníes***)* **1** *adj & nmf* Guarani

2 *nm* (**a**) *(lengua)* Guarani (**b**) *(moneda)* guarani

guarda **1** *nmf (vigilante)* guard, keeper; **g. forestal** gamekeeper, forest ranger; **g. jurado** security guard

2 *nf* (**a**) *(tutela)* guardianship (**b**) *(de libros)* flyleaf

guardabarrera *nmf Ferroc* grade-crossing keeper

guardabarros *nm inv Esp, Bol, RP (en automóvil, bicicleta)* fender

guardabosque *nmf* forest ranger

guardacoches *nmf inv* parking attendant

guardacostas *nm inv (barco)* Coast Guard boat

guardador, -ora *nm,f* keeper

guardaespaldas *nmf inv* bodyguard

guardafrenos *nmf inv Ferroc* brakeman, *f* brakewoman

guardagujas *nmf inv Ferroc* switchman, *f* switchwoman

guardameta *nmf* goalkeeper

guardamuebles *nm inv* furniture storage warehouse

guardapolvo *nm* overalls

guardar **1** *vt* (**a**) *(conservar)* to keep; *(poner en su sitio)* to put away; **guarda el vestido en el armario** she keeps the dress in the wardrobe; **¡guarda los juguetes!** put your toys away!; **guardo muy buenos recuerdos de mi infancia** I have very good memories of my childhood

(**b**) *(reservar)* to save (**a** *o* **para alguien** for sb); **guarda un poco de pastel para tu hermano** leave *o* save a bit of cake for your brother

(**c**) *(vigilar)* to keep watch over; *(proteger)* to guard

(**d**) *(observar) (ley, norma, fiesta)* to observe; *(secreto, promesa)* to keep; **g. cama** to stay in bed; **g. silencio** to keep quiet; **g. las apariencias** to keep up appearances

(**e**) *Inform* to save

2 guardarse *vpr* (**a**) *(colocar)* **se guardó la pluma en el**

bolsillo she put the pen in her pocket (**b**) *(quedarse con)* **guárdate tu ironía para otro momento** save *o* keep your irony for another occasion (**c**) **guardarse de hacer algo** *(evitar)* to avoid doing sth; *(abstenerse de)* to be careful not to do sth; **me guardaré de criticarle** I'll be careful not to criticize him (**d**) *Fam* **guardársela a alguien** to have it in for sb

guardarropa *nm* (**a**) *(armario)* wardrobe; *(de cine, discoteca)* cloakroom (**b**) *(ropa)* wardrobe

guardarropía *nf Teatro* wardrobe

guardavallas *nmf inv Am* goalkeeper

guardavida *nmf RP* lifeguard

guardería *nf (establecimiento)* nursery; *(en aeropuerto, supermercado)* crèche

guardia **1** *nf* (**a**) *(conjunto de personas)* guard; **la vieja g.** the old guard; **G. Civil** Civil Guard, = armed Spanish police force who patrol rural areas and highways, guard public buildings in cities and police borders and coasts (**b**) *(vigilancia)* watch, guard; **en g.** on guard; **montar (la) g.** to mount guard; **aflojar** *o* **bajar la g.** to lower *o* drop one's guard (**c**) *(turno)* duty; **estar de g.** to be on duty

2 *nmf (persona)* policeman, *f* policewoman; **g. civil** civil guard; **g. municipal** (local) policeman, *f* (local) policewoman; **g. de seguridad** security guard; **g. de tráfico** traffic policeman, *f* traffic policewoman

3 *nm* **g. marina** = sea cadet in final two years of training

guardián, -ana *nm,f (de persona)* guardian; *(de cosa)* watchman, keeper

guarecer [46] **1** *vt* to protect, to shelter (**de** from)

2 guarecerse *vpr* to shelter (**de** from)

guarida *nf (de animal)* lair; *Fig* hideout

guarismo *nm* figure, number

guarnecer [46] *vt* (**a**) *(adornar)* to decorate; *(ropa)* to trim (**b**) *Culin (acompañar)* to garnish (**c**) *Mil (vigilar)* to be garrisoned in

guarnición *nf* (**a**) *(adorno)* decoration; *(de ropa)* trimming (**b**) *Culin* garnish (**c**) *Mil* garrison

guarrada *nf Esp Fam (cosa asquerosa)* filthy thing; *(mala pasada)* filthy *o* dirty trick

guarrería *nf Esp Fam (suciedad)* filth, muck; *(acción)* filthy thing

guarro, -a *Esp* **1** *adj Fam* filthy

2 *nm,f (animal)* pig, *f* sow; *Esp Fam (persona)* filthy *o* dirty pig

guarura *nm Méx Fam* bodyguard

guasa *nf Fam* (**a**) *(gracia)* humor; *(ironía)* irony; **estar de g.** to be joking (**b**) *(pesadez)* **tener mucha g.** to be a pain in the neck

guasca *nf Andes* whip

guasearse *vpr Fam* to poke fun (**de** at)

guasón, -ona **1** *adj* fond of teasing

2 *nm,f* joker, tease

guata *nf* (**a**) *(de algodón)* cotton padding (**b**) *Chile Fam (barriga)* belly

guateado, -a *adj* padded

Guatemala *n* (**a**) *(país)* Guatemala (**b**) *(ciudad)* Guatemala City

guatemalteco, -a *adj & nm,f* Guatemalan

guateque *nm Esp, Cuba, Méx* party

guatón, -ona *adj Andes Fam* potbellied

guau *interj (ladrido)* woof

guay *adj, adv & interj Esp Fam* cool, neat

guayaba *nf (fruta)* guava

guayabera *nf CAm, Carib, Col* = lightweight man's shirt with pockets and sometimes tucks or embroidery, worn outside pants

guayabo, -a *nm* (**a**) *(árbol)* guava tree (**b**) *Andes Fam (resaca)* hangover

Guayana *nf* la G. Francesa French Guiana

guayanés, -esa *adj & nm,f* Guianan, Guianese

guayín *nm Méx Fam* van

gubernamental *adj* government; **política g.** government policy

gubernativo, -a *adj* government; **orden gubernativa** government decree

guepardo *nm* cheetah

güero, -a *adj Méx Fam* blond, *f* blonde, fair-haired

guerra *nf* (a) *(conflicto)* war; *(referido al tipo de conflicto)* warfare; **declarar la g.** to declare war; *Fig* **le tiene la g. declarada a su hermano** he's at daggers drawn with his brother; **en g.** at war; **g. sin cuartel** all-out war; **g. atómica** nuclear war; **g. bacteriológica** germ warfare; **g. civil** civil war; **g. fría** cold war; **g. de las galaxias** star wars; **g. de guerrillas** guerrilla warfare; **g. mundial** world war; **g. de nervios** war of nerves; **g. nuclear** nuclear war; **g. de precios** price war; **g. psicológica** psychological warfare; **g. química** chemical warfare; **g. santa** holy war; **g. sucia** dirty war
(b) *Fam (problemas)* **dar g.** to be a pain, to be annoying; *(niño)* to act up

guerrear *vi* to wage war (**contra** on *o* against)

guerrera *nf (prenda)* (military) jacket

guerrero, -a 1 *adj (belicoso)* warlike; *(peleón)* argumentative, quarrelsome
2 *nm,f* warrior

guerrilla *nf (grupo)* guerrilla group

guerrillero, -a 1 *adj* guerrilla; **ataque g.** guerrilla attack
2 *nm,f* guerrilla

gueto *nm* ghetto

güevón, -ona = **huevón**

güey 1 *nm Méx muy Fam (tonto)* jerk
2 *interj* **¡ay g.!** *(asombro)* goddamn!

guía 1 *nmf (persona)* guide; **g. espiritual** *(persona, libro)* spiritual guide; **g. turístico** tour guide, tourist guide
2 *nf* (a) *(indicación)* guidance (b) *(libro)* guide (book); **g. de carreteras** road atlas; **g. de conversación** phrase book; **g. de ferrocarriles** train timetable; *Esp, RP* **g. telefónica** *o* **de teléfonos** telephone book *o* directory; **g. turística** tourist guide (c) *(de bicicleta)* handlebars (d) *(para cortinas)* rail

guiar [32] **1** *vt* (a) *(indicar dirección)* to guide, to lead; *(aconsejar)* to guide, to direct (b) *Aut* to drive; *Náut* to steer (c) *(plantas, ramas)* to train
2 guiarse *vpr* **guiarse por algo** to be guided by *o* to follow sth; **se guía por el instinto** he's guided by instinct

guija *nf* pebble

guijarro *nm* pebble

guijarroso, -a *adj* pebbly

guillado, -a *adj Fam* crazy

guilladura *nf Fam* craziness

guillotina *nf* guillotine

guillotinar *vt* to guillotine

guinda *nf* morello (cherry); *Fig* **la g.** the finishing touch, the icing on the cake

guindar *Fam* **1** *vt* (a) *Esp (robar)* to pinch; *Esp* **g. algo a alguien** to pinch sth off sb (b) *CAm, Méx, Ven (colgar)* to hang up
2 guindarse *vpr CAm, Méx, Ven (colgarse)* to hang

guindilla *nf* chilli (pepper)

guindo *nm* morello (cherry) tree

guinea *nf* guinea

Guinea-Bissau *n* Guinea-Bissau

Guinea Ecuatorial *n* Equatorial Guinea

guineano, -a *adj & nm,f* Guinean

guiñador *nm Bol* turn signal

guiñapo *nm* (a) *(andrajo)* rag (b) *(persona)* **estar hecho un g.** to be a wreck

guiñar 1 *vt* to wink; **guiñarle un ojo a alguien** to wink at sb
2 guiñarse *vpr* to wink at each other

guiño *nm* wink

guiñol *nm* puppet theater

guiñolesco, -a *adj* farcical

guión *nm* (a) *(resumen)* framework, outline (b) *Cine & TV* script; *Fig* **eso no estaba en el g.** that's not what was agreed on; **g. de cine** movie script (c) *Gram (signo)* hyphen

guionista *nmf* scriptwriter

guipuzcoano, -a 1 *adj* of/from Guipúzcoa
2 *nm,f* person from Guipúzcoa

guiri *Esp Fam* **1** *adj* foreign
2 *nmf* foreigner

guirigay *nm Esp Fam* (a) *(jaleo)* racket (b) *(lenguaje ininteligible)* gibberish

guirlache *nm* almond brittle

guirnalda *nf* garland

guisa *nf* way, manner; **a g. de** by way of, as; **de esta g.** in this way

guisado *nm* stew

guisante *nm esp Esp* pea

guisar 1 *vt & vi* to cook
2 guisarse *vpr Fam (suceder, planearse)* to be cooking, to be going on

guiso *nm* stew

güisqui *nm* whiskey

guita *nf* (a) *Esp, RP Fam (dinero)* dough (b) *(cuerda)* twine, string

guitarra 1 *nf* guitar; **chafar la g. a alguien** to mess things up for sb; **g. acústica** acoustic guitar; **g. eléctrica** electric guitar
2 *nmf* guitarist

guitarrero, -a *nm,f* guitar maker

guitarrista *nmf* guitarist

gula *nf* gluttony

gulasch [gu'las] *nm inv* goulash

gurí, -isa *nm,f RP Fam* kid, child

guripa *nm Esp Fam* cop

gurú, guru *nm* guru

gusa *nf Esp Fam (hambre)* **tener g.** to be starving

gusanillo *nm Fam* **el g. de la conciencia** conscience; **entrarle a uno el g. del viaje** to be bitten by the travel bug; **matar el g.** *(bebiendo)* to have a drink on an empty stomach; *(comiendo)* to have a snack between meals; **sentir un g. en el estómago** to have butterflies (in one's stomach)

gusano *nm* (a) *(animal)* worm; *(de mosca)* maggot; **g. de luz** glowworm; **g. de (la) seda** silkworm (b) *Fam Pey (persona)* worm (c) *Inform* worm

gusarapo, -a *nm,f* creepy-crawly

gustar 1 *vi* (a) *(agradar)* to be pleasing; **me gusta ir al cine** I like going to the movies; **me gustan las novelas** I like novels; **así me gusta, has hecho un buen trabajo** that's what I like to see, you've done a fine job; **hazlo como más te guste** do it whichever way you see fit, do it however you like (b) *(atraer)* **me gusta Andrés** I fancy Andrés; **me gustas mucho** I like you a lot, I really like you (c) *(en fórmulas de cortesía)* **como/cuando guste** as/whenever you wish; **¿gustas?** *(¿quieres?)* would you like some? (d) *Formal* **g. de hacer algo** to like *o* enjoy doing sth
2 *vt (saborear, probar)* to taste, to try

gustativo, -a *adj* taste; **papila gustativa** taste bud

gustazo *nm Fam* great pleasure; **darse el g. de algo/hacer algo** to allow oneself the pleasure of sth/doing sth

gustillo *nm* (a) *(sabor)* aftertaste (b) *(impresión)* **me dejó un g. amargo** it left a bitter taste in my mouth

gusto *nm* (**a**) *(estilo)* taste; *(sabor)* taste, flavor; **una casa decorada con (buen) g.** a tastefully decorated house; **de buen/mal g.** in good/bad taste; *Prov* **sobre gustos no hay nada escrito** there's no accounting for taste, each to his own; **tener buen/mal g.** to have good/bad taste

(**b**) *(placer)* pleasure; **con mucho g.** gladly, with pleasure; **iría con (mucho) g., pero no puedo** I'd love to go but I can't; **da g. estar aquí** it's a real pleasure to be here; **mucho g. — el g. es mío** pleased to meet you — the pleasure's mine; **hacer algo a g.** *(de buena gana)* to do sth willingly *o* gladly; *(cómodamente)* to do sth comfortably; **mucho** *o* **tanto g.** pleased to meet you; **sentirse** *o* **encontrarse** *o* **estar a g.** to feel comfortable *o* at ease; **tomar g. a algo** to take a liking to sth

gustoso, -a *adj* (**a**) *(con placer)* **hacer algo g.** to do sth gladly *o* willingly; **lo habría hecho g., pero no pude** I'd gladly have done it, but I wasn't able to (**b**) *(sabroso)* tasty

gutural *adj* guttural

Guyana *nf* Guyana

Guyana francesa *nf* **la G.** French Guyana

guyanés, -esa *adj & nm,f* Guyanese

gymkhana [jin'kɑnɑ] *nf (carrera de obstáculos)* gymkhana; *(de automóviles)* rally

H

H, h [ˈatʃe] *nf (letra)* H, h; *Fig* **por h o por b** for one reason or another

H *(abrev de* **Hermano***)* Br

h, h. *(abrev de* **hora***)* hr, h

ha 1 *ver* **haber**

  2 *nf (abrev de* **hectárea***)* ha

haba *nf* broad bean

habanera *nf Mús* habanera

habanero, -a *adj* of/from Havana *nm,f* person from Havana

habano *nm* Havana cigar

habeas corpus *nm inv* habeas corpus

haber [1] **1** *v aux* **(a)** *(en tiempos compuestos)* to have; **lo he/había hecho** I have/had done it; **los niños ya han comido** the children have already eaten

  (b) *(expresa reproche)* **h. venido antes** you could have come a bit earlier; **¡haberlo dicho!** why didn't you say so?; **haberme escuchado** I told you (so), you should have listened to me; **de haberlo sabido...** if only I'd known...

  (c) *(expresa obligación)* **h. de hacer algo** to have to do sth; **has de estudiar más** you have to study more; **siempre has de ser tú el que se queje** you always have to be the one to complain

  2 *v impersonal* **(a)** *(existir, estar)* **hay** there is/are; **hay mucha gente en la calle** there are a lot of people in the street; **había/hubo muchos problemas** there were many problems; **habrá dos mil** *(expresa futuro)* there will be two thousand; *(expresa hipótesis)* there must be two thousand; **es un artista donde los haya** he's as good an artist as you'll find; **hay quien dice...** some people say...

  (b) *(expresa obligación)* **hay que hacer más ejercicio** one *o* you should do more exercise; **habrá que soportar su mal humor** we'll have to put up with his bad mood

  (c) *(expresiones)* **algo habrá** there must be something in it; **¡hay que ver!** well I never!; **lo habido y por h.** everything under the sun; **no hay de qué** don't mention it; *Fam* **¿qué hay?** *(saludo)* how are you doing?

  3 *nm* **(a)** *(bienes)* assets **(b)** *(en cuentas, contabilidad)* credit (side)

habichuela *nf Esp, Carib, Col* bean

habido, -a *adj* occurred; **los accidentes habidos este verano** the number of accidents this summer

hábil *adj* **(a)** *(diestro)* skillful; **es muy h. con las manos** he's very good with his hands **(b)** *(utilizable) (lugar)* suitable, fit; **día h.** workday

habilidad *nf (destreza)* skill; **tener h. para algo** to be good at sth; **salió del compromiso con h.** she cleverly extricated herself from the situation

habilidoso, -a *adj* skillful, clever

habilitación *nf* **(a)** *(acondicionamiento)* fitting out **(b)** *Der (autorización)* authorization, right

habilitado, -a 1 *adj Der* authorized

  2 *nm,f* paymaster

habilitar *vt* **(a)** *(acondicionar)* to furnish, to equip; **habilitó el desván para cuarto de huéspedes** he furnished the attic as a guest bedroom **(b)** *Der (autorizar)* to authorize **(c)** *(financiar)* to finance

hábilmente *adv* skillfully

habiloso, -a *adj Chile* shrewd, astute

habitabilidad *nf* habitability; **estar/no estar en condiciones de h.** to be fit/unfit for human habitation

habitable *adj* habitable, inhabitable

habitación *nf (cuarto)* room; *(dormitorio)* bedroom; **h. doble** *(con cama de matrimonio)* double room; *(con dos camas)* twin room; **h. individual** single room; **h. de invitados** spare room

habitacional *adj CSur, Méx* housing; **un complejo h.** a housing project

habitáculo *nm (casa)* dwelling; *(habitación)* room

habitado, -a *adj (región, casa)* inhabited

habitante *nm (de ciudad, país)* inhabitant; *(de barrio)* resident

habitar 1 *vi* to live; **una región sin h.** an unpopulated area

  2 *vt* to live in, to inhabit; **una especie que habita las zonas montañosas** a species found in mountainous areas

hábitat *(pl* **hábitats***) nm* **(a)** *Biol* habitat; **h. marino/urbano** marine/urban habitat **(b)** *(vivienda)* housing conditions

hábito *nm* **(a)** *(costumbre)* habit; **tener el h. de hacer algo** to be in the habit of doing sth; **crear h.** to be addictive **(b)** *(de monje)* habit; **tomar el h.** *o* **los hábitos** *(monja)* to take the veil; *(sacerdote)* to take holy orders

habituación *nf* **(a)** *(a drogas)* addiction **(b)** *(a situación)* **la h. al nuevo trabajo fue difícil** getting used to the new job was difficult

habitual *adj (costumbre, respuesta)* habitual; *(cliente, lector)* regular; **es h.** it's not uncommon, it's normal; **lo h. es dejar propina** it is usual *o* customary to leave a tip; **lo h. en un caso así es llamar a la policía** in a case like this you would normally call the police

habituar [4] **1** *vt* **h. a alguien a** to accustom sb to

  2 habituarse *vpr* **habituarse a** *(acostumbrarse)* to get used *o* accustomed to; *(drogas)* to become addicted to

habla *nf* **(a)** *(idioma)* language; *(dialecto)* dialect; **de h. española** Spanish-speaking; **los países de h. inglesa** English-speaking countries; **el h. popular** the everyday speech **(b)** *(facultad)* speech; **no saben si recuperará el h.** they don't know if she will ever speak again; **quedarse sin h.** to be left speechless **(c)** *Ling* parole **(d)** *(al teléfono)* **estar al h. con alguien** to be on the line to sb; **¿el Sr. Pastor? — al h.** Mr. Pastor? — speaking!

hablador, -ora 1 *adj* talkative

  2 *nm,f* chatterbox

habladurías *nfpl (rumores)* rumors; *(chismes)* gossip; **no son más que h.** it's all just idle gossip

hablante 1 *adj* speaking

2 *nmf* speaker; **h. nativo** native speaker

hablar 1 *vi* **(a)** *(emitir palabras, expresarse)* to speak; **h. en voz alta/baja** to speak loudly/softly; **h. claro** to speak clearly

(b) *(conversar)* to talk **(con** to), to speak **(con** to); **necesito h. contigo** I need to talk *o* speak to you, we need to talk; **h. con alguien por teléfono** to speak to sb on the phone; **h. de algo** to talk about sth

(c) *(confesar)* to talk; **hacer h. a alguien** *(en interrogatorio)* to get sb to talk

(d) *(expresiones)* **h. por h.** to talk for the sake of talking; **h. bien/mal de** to speak well/badly of; **me han hablado muy bien de este restaurante** I've heard a lot of good things about this restaurant, I've heard people speak very highly of this restaurant; **h. de tú a alguien** to address sb as "tú"; **dar que h.** to make people talk; **¡ni h.!** no way!; **no me habla** he's not speaking to me

2 *vt* **(a)** *(idioma)* to speak **(b)** *(asunto)* to discuss; **es mejor que lo hables con él** it would be better if you talked to him about it

3 hablarse *vpr* **(a)** *(dos personas)* to speak (to each other); **no hablarse** not to be speaking, not to be on speaking terms **(b)** *(reflexivo)* **se habla inglés** *(en letrero)* English spoken

habón *nm* *(roncha)* lump *(on skin)*

habrá *ver* **haber**

hacedor, -ora *nm,f* maker; **el H.** the Maker

hacendado, -a *nm,f* landowner

hacendoso, -a *adj* = proud of one's house and its upkeep

hacer [33] **1** *vt* **(a)** *(realizar) (estudios, experimento, favor)* to do; *(viaje, sacrificio, promesa)* to make; *(comunión)* to take; *(pregunta)* to ask; **¿qué haces?** what are you doing?; **tengo mucho que h.** I have a lot to do; **estoy haciendo segundo** I'm in my second year; **¿qué habré hecho con las llaves?** what have I done with the keys?; **la carretera hace una curva** there's a bend in the road

(b) *(elaborar, crear, cocinar)* to make; **h. un vestido/planes** to make a dress/plans; **h. un poema/una sinfonía** to write a poem/a symphony; **h. una fiesta** to have a party; **para h. la carne...** to cook the meat...

(c) *(obtener) (fotocopia)* to make; *(retrato)* to paint; *(fotografía)* to take

(d) *(arreglar) (casa, colada)* to do; *(cama)* to make

(e) *(construir)* to build; **han hecho un edificio nuevo** they've put up a new building

(f) *(movimientos, sonidos, gestos)* to make; **le hice señas** I signaled to her; **h. ruido** to make a noise; **el gato hace "miau"** cats go "meow"

(g) *(practicar) (en general)* to do; *(tenis, fútbol)* to play; **debes h. deporte** you should start doing some sport

(h) *(causar)* **h. daño a alguien** to hurt sb; **me hizo gracia** I thought it was funny

(i) *(transformar en)* **h. a alguien feliz** to make sb happy; **la guerra no le hizo un hombre** the war didn't make him (into) a man; **hizo pedazos el papel** he tore the paper to pieces; **h. de algo/alguien algo** to make sth/sb into sth; **hizo de ella una buena cantante** he made a good singer of her

(j) *(dar aspecto a)* to cause to look *o* seem; **este espejo te hace gordo** that mirror makes you look *o* seem fat

(k) *(comportarse como)* **h. el tonto** to act the fool; **h. el vándalo** to act like a hooligan

(l) *Cine & Teatro (papel)* to play; **hace el papel de la hija del rey** she plays (the part of) the king's daughter

(m) *(suponer)* to think, to reckon; **a estas horas yo te hacía en París** I thought *o* reckoned you'd be in Paris by now

(n) *(ser causa de)* **h. que alguien haga algo** to make sb do sth; **has hecho que se enfadara** you've made him angry; **me hizo reír** it made me laugh

(o) *(mandar)* **h. que se haga algo** to have sth done; **voy a h. teñir este vestido** I'm going to have this dress dyed

2 *vi* **(a)** *(intervenir)* **déjame h. a mí** let me do it **(b)** *Cine & Teatro* **h. de** *(actuar)* to play; *(trabajar)* to act as **(c)** *(aparentar)* **h. como si** to act as if; **haz como que no te importa** act as if you don't care **(d)** *(procurar, intentar)* **h. por h. algo** to try to do sth; **haré por verle esta noche** I'll try to see him tonight **(e)** *Esp* **¿hace?** all right?

3 *v impersonal* **(a)** *(tiempo meteorológico)* **hace frío/sol/viento** it's cold/sunny/windy; **hace buen/mal tiempo** the weather is good/bad; **hace un día precioso** it's a beautiful day **(b)** *(tiempo transcurrido)* **hace diez años** ten years ago; **hace mucho/poco** a long time/not long ago; **hace dos sábados** the Saturday before last; **hace un mes que llegué** it's a month since I arrived; **no la veo desde hace un año** I haven't seen her for a year

4 hacerse *vpr* **(a)** *(guisarse, cocerse)* to cook

(b) *(fabricarse)* to make oneself; **h. un vestido** *(uno mismo)* to make oneself a dress; *(encargarlo)* to have a dress made

(c) *(causarse)* **hacerse daño** to hurt oneself

(d) *(convertirse en)* to become; **hacerse musulmán** to become a Muslim; **hacerse viejo** to grow old

(e) *(resultar)* **se me ha hecho muy corto** it seemed very short

(f) *(crearse en la mente)* **hacerse ilusiones** to get one's hopes up; **hacerse una idea de algo** to imagine what sth is like

(g) *(mostrarse)* **hacerse el gracioso/el simpático** to try to act the comedian/the nice guy; **hacerse el distraído** to pretend to be miles away

(h) *(acostumbrarse)* **hacerse a algo** to get used to sth

(i) *(conseguir)* **hacerse con algo** to get hold of sth

hacha *nf* ax; *Fig* **desenterrar el h. de guerra** to sharpen one's sword; *Fam* **ser un h.** to be a whiz *o* an ace

hachazo *nm* blow of an ax, hack

hache *nf* = the letter "h"; **llamémosle h., llámale h.** call it what you like

hachemita, hachemí *adj & nmf* Hashemite

hachís [χa'tʃis] *nm* hashish

hacia *prep* **(a)** *(dirección)* toward; **h. aquí/allí** this/that way; **h. abajo** downward; **h. arriba** upward; **h. adelante** forward; **h. atrás** backward; **h. la izquierda/derecha** to the left/right

(b) *(tiempo)* around, about; **h. las diez** around *o* about ten o'clock; **empezó a perder la vista h. los sesenta años** he started to lose his sight at around the age of sixty; **h. finales de año** toward the end of the year

(c) *(sentimiento)* toward; **siente hostilidad h. las reformas** he is hostile toward the reforms

(d) *(tendencia)* toward; **un paso más h. la guerra civil** a further step toward civil war

hacienda *nf* **(a)** *(finca)* country estate *o* property **(b)** *(bienes)* property **(c)** *(del Estado)* **(el Ministerio de) H.** ≃ the Department of the Treasury; **pagar a H.** to pay the IRS

hacinamiento *nm* *(de personas)* overcrowding; *(de objetos)* heaping, piling

hacinar 1 *vt* to pile *o* heap (up)

2 hacinarse *vpr* *(gente)* to be crowded together; *(cosas)* to be piled *o* heaped (up)

hacker ['χaker] *(pl* **hackers)** *nmf* *Fam Inform* hacker

hada *nf* fairy; **h. madrina** fairy godmother

hado *nm* fate, destiny

hagiografía *nf* *Rel & Pey* hagiography

hago *ver* **hacer**

Haití *n* Haiti

haitiano, -a *adj & nm,f* Haitian

hala *interj Esp* **¡h.!** *(para dar ánimo, prisa)* come on!; *(para expresar incredulidad)* no!, you're joking!; *(para expresar admiración, sorpresa)* wow!

halagador, -ora 1 *adj* flattering
2 *nm,f* flatterer

halagar [38] *vt* to flatter

halago *nm* flattery

halague *etc ver* **halagar**

halagüeño, -a *adj* **(a)** *(halagador)* flattering **(b)** *(prometedor)* promising, encouraging

halar = **jalar**

halcón *nm (ave)* falcon, hawk

hale *interj Esp* **¡h.!** come on!

hálito *nm* **(a)** *(aliento)* breath **(b)** *Literario (brisa)* zephyr

halitosis *nf inv* bad breath, *Espec* halitosis

hall [χol] *(pl* **halls**) *nm* entrance hall, foyer

hallar 1 *vt (encontrar)* to find; *(averiguar)* to find out
2 hallarse *vpr* **(a)** *(en un lugar) (persona)* to be, to find oneself; *(cosa, edificio)* to be (situated) **(b)** *(en una situación)* to be; **hallarse enfermo** to be ill

hallazgo *nm* **(a)** *(descubrimiento)* discovery **(b)** *(objeto)* find

halo *nm (de astros, santos)* halo; *(de objetos, personas)* aura

halógeno, -a *adj Quím* halogenous; **faros halógenos** halogen headlights; **lámpara halógena** halogen lamp

halterofilia *nf* weight lifting

hamaca *nf* **(a)** *(para colgar)* hammock **(b)** *Esp (tumbona) (silla)* deck chair; *(canapé)* sunlounger **(c)** *RP (columpio)* swing; *(mecedora)* rocking chair

hamacar [59] *RP* **1** *vt (en columpio)* to swing; *(en cuna)* to rock
2 hamacarse *vpr (en columpio)* to swing; *(en cuna)* to rock

hambre *nf* **(a)** *(apetito)* hunger; *(inanición)* starvation; **tener h.** to be hungry; **matar el h.** to satisfy one's hunger; *Fig* **nos mataban de h.** they had us on a starvation diet; **morir o morirse de h.** *(literalmente)* to be starving, to be dying of hunger; *(tener mucha hambre)* to be starving; **pasar h.** to starve; **h. canina** ravenous hunger
(b) *(epidemia)* famine
(c) *(deseo)* **h. de** hunger o thirst for
(d) *(expresiones)* **se junta el h. con las ganas de comer** it's one thing on top of another; **ser más listo que el h.** to be nobody's fool; *Prov* **a buen h. no hay pan duro** *(de comida)* hunger is the best sauce; *(de placeres)* beggars can't be choosers

hambriento, -a 1 *adj* starving
2 *nm,f* starving person; **los hambrientos** the hungry

hambruna *nf* famine

Hamburgo *n* Hamburg

hamburguesa *nf* hamburger, burger

hamburguesería *nf* hamburger joint

hampa *nf* underworld

hampón *nm* thug

hámster ['χamster] *(pl* **hámsters**) *nm* hamster

hándicap ['χandikap] *(pl* **hándicaps**) *nm* handicap

hangar *nm* hangar

Hanoi *n* Hanoi

haragán, -ana 1 *adj* lazy, idle
2 *nm,f* layabout, idler

haraganear *vi* to laze around o about, to lounge around o about

haraganería *nf* laziness, idleness

harakiri *nm* hara-kiri

harapiento, -a *adj* ragged, tattered

harapo *nm* rag, tatter

haraquiri *nm* hara-kiri

Harare *n* Harare

hardware ['χarwer] *nm Inform* hardware

haré *etc ver* **hacer**

harén *nm* harem

harina *nf* flour; *Fig* **ser h. de otro costal** to be a different kettle of fish; **h. de maíz** cornmeal; **h. integral** wholemeal flour

harinoso, -a *adj (consistencia, textura)* floury; *(manzana)* soft

hartar 1 *vt* **(a)** *(atiborrar)* to stuff (full) **(b)** *(fastidiar, cansar)* **h. a alguien** to annoy sb, to get on sb's nerves; **me estás hartando con tantas exigencias** I'm getting fed up with all your demands
2 hartarse *vpr* **(a)** *(atiborrarse)* to stuff o gorge oneself **(b)** *(cansarse)* to get fed up **(de** with) **(c)** *(no parar)* **hartarse de algo** to do sth nonstop

hartazgo, *Esp* **hartón** *Fam nm* fill; **darse un h. (de)** to have one's fill (of)

harto, -a 1 *adj* **(a)** *(de comida)* full **(b)** *(cansado)* tired **(de** of), fed up **(de** with); **me tiene h. con el piano** I'm fed up with him and his piano; **estoy h. de repetírtelo** I'm sick and tired of telling you **(c)** *Am salvo RP (mucho)* a lot of, lots of; **h. dinero** a lot of o lots of money
2 *adv* **(a)** *Esp Formal (muy)* extremely; **es h. frecuente** it's extremely common **(b)** *Am salvo RP (muy)* very, really; **h. grande** very o really big

hartón = **hartazgo**

hash [χaʃ, χas] *nm inv Fam* hashish

hasta 1 *prep* **(a)** *(en el espacio)* as far as, up to; **voy h. la próxima estación** I'm going as far as the next station; **desde aquí h. allí** from here to there **(b)** *(en el tiempo)* until, till; **h. ahora** (up) until now, so far; **h. el final** right up until the end; **h. luego** o **pronto** o **la vista** see you (later); **h. que** until, till; **h. que vuelvas** until you get back **(c)** *(con cantidades)* up to; **un interés de h. el 7 por ciento** interest rates of up to 7 percent
2 *adv (incluso)* even; **h. en verano hace frío** it's even cold in summer

hastiar [32] **1** *vt (aburrir)* to bore; *(asquear)* to sicken, to disgust
2 hastiarse *vpr* **hastiarse de** to tire of, to get fed up with

hastío *nm (tedio)* boredom; *(repugnancia)* disgust

hatajo *nm Pey* load, bunch; **un h. de** *(gamberros)* a bunch of; *(mentiras)* a pack of

hatillo *nm* bundle of clothes

hato *nm* **(a)** *(de ganado)* herd; *(de ovejas)* flock **(b)** *(de ropa)* bundle

Hawai [χaˈwai] *n* Hawaii

hawaiano, -a [χawaiˈano] *adj & nm,f* Hawaiian

haya 1 *ver* **haber**
2 *nf (árbol)* beech (tree); *(madera)* beech (wood)

hayal *nm* beech grove o wood

haz 1 *ver* **hacer**
2 *nm* **(a)** *(de leña)* bundle; *(de cereales)* sheaf **(b)** *(de luz)* beam

hazaña *nf* feat, exploit

hazmerreír *nm* laughing stock

he *ver* **haber**

heavy ['χeβi] *(pl* **heavies** o **heavys**) **1** *adj* **(a)** *(música)* heavy **(b)** *Fam* **¡qué h.!** *(increíble)* (that's) wicked!; *(terrible)* (what a) bummer!
2 *nmf Fam (persona)* heavy-metal fan
3 *nm Mús* **h. (metal)** heavy metal

hebdomadario, -a *adj* weekly

hebilla *nf* buckle

hebra *nf (de hilo, tabaco)* thread; *(de judías, puerros)* string; *Esp Fig* **pegar la h.** to start chatting

hebraico, -a *adj* Hebraic

hebreo, -a 1 *adj & nm,f* Hebrew

  2 *nm (lengua)* Hebrew

hecatombe *nf (desastre)* disaster; *(partido, examen)* massacre; **la inundación causó una h.** the flood caused great loss of life

hechicería *nf* (a) *(arte)* witchcraft, sorcery (b) *(maleficio)* spell

hechicero, -a 1 *adj* enchanting, bewitching

  2 *nm,f (hombre)* wizard, sorcerer; *(mujer)* witch, sorceress; *(de la tribu)* witch doctor, medicine man

hechizar [14] *vt* (a) *(con maleficio)* to cast a spell on (b) *(con encantos)* to bewitch, to captivate

hechizo, -a 1 *adj* Chile, Méx homemade

  2 *nm* (a) *(maleficio)* spell (b) *(encanto)* magic, charm

hecho, -a 1 *participio ver* **hacer**

  2 *adj* (a) *(llevado a cabo)* **lo h., h. está** what is done is done; **¡(eso está) h.!** it's a deal!, you're on!; **tú lo hiciste, así que a lo h., pecho** you did it, so you'll have to take the consequences (b) *(acabado)* mature; **una mujer hecha y derecha** a fully grown woman; **estás h. un artista** you've become quite an artist (c) *(carne)* done; **muy h.** well done; **poco h.** rare

  3 *nm* (a) *(suceso)* event; **h. consumado** fait accompli; **de h.** in fact, actually (b) *(realidad, dato)* fact; **el h. es que…** the fact is that…

hechura *nf* (a) *(de traje)* cut (b) *(forma)* shape

hectárea *nf* hectare

hectolitro *nm* hectoliter

hectómetro *nm* hectometer

heder [64] *vi* (a) *(apestar)* to stink, to reek (b) *(fastidiar)* to be annoying *o* irritating

hediondez *nf* stench, stink

hediondo, -a *adj (de mal olor)* stinking, foul-smelling; *(insoportable)* unbearable

hedonismo *nm* hedonism

hedonista 1 *adj* hedonistic

  2 *nmf* hedonist

hedor *nm* stink, stench

hegemonía *nf (dominación)* dominance; *Pol* hegemony

hegemónico, -a *adj (dominante)* dominant; *(clase, partido)* ruling

hégira, héjira *nf* hegira

helada *nf* frost; **anoche cayó una h.** there was frost last night

heladera *nf CSur (nevera)* fridge

heladería *nf (tienda)* ice-cream parlor; *(puesto)* ice-cream stall

heladero, -a *nm,f* ice-cream seller

helado, -a 1 *adj* (a) *(hecho hielo) (agua)* frozen; *(lago)* frozen over (b) *(muy frío) (manos, agua)* freezing; *(no caliente) (sopa)* stone-cold (c) *(atónito)* dumbfounded, speechless; **¡me dejas h.!** I don't know what to say!

  2 *nm* ice cream; *CSur* **h. de agua** Popsicle®

helador, -ora *adj* freezing

helar [3] **1** *vt* (a) *(líquido)* to freeze (b) *(dejar atónito)* to dumbfound

  2 *v impersonal* **anoche heló** there was a frost last night

  3 helarse *vpr (líquido, persona)* to freeze; **el lago se ha helado** the lake has frozen over; **se helaron las plantas** the plants were caught by the frost; **me hielo de frío** I'm freezing

helecho *nm* fern, bracken

helénico, -a *adj* Hellenic, Greek

helenismo *nm* Hellenism

helenista *nmf* Hellenist

heleno, -a *adj* Hellenic, Greek

hélice *nf* (a) *Tec* propeller (b) *(espiral)* spiral, helix

helicoidal *adj* helicoid, spiral

helicóptero *nm* helicopter

helio *nm* helium

heliocéntrico, -a *adj* heliocentric

helipuerto *nm* heliport

Helsinki *n* Helsinki

helvético, -a *adj & nm,f* Swiss; **Confederación Helvética** *(Suiza)* Swiss Confederation

hematíe *nm* red blood cell

hematología *nf* hematology

hematológico, -a *adj* hematological

hematólogo, -a *nm,f* hematologist

hematoma *nm* bruise

hembra *nf* (a) *Biol* female; *(mujer)* woman; *(niña)* girl (b) *(del enchufe)* socket

hembrilla *nf (de corchete)* eye

hemeroteca *nf* newspaper library *o* archive

hemiciclo *nm* (a) *(semicírculo)* semicircle (b) *(en el parlamento)* floor

hemiplejía, hemiplejia *nf* hemiplegia

hemipléjico, -a *adj & nm,f* hemiplegic

hemisférico, -a *adj* hemispheric

hemisferio *nm* hemisphere; **h. norte** northern hemisphere; **h. sur** southern hemisphere

hemodiálisis *nf inv* kidney dialysis

hemofilia *nf* hemophilia

hemofílico, -a *adj & nm,f* hemophiliac

hemoglobina *nf* hemoglobin

hemograma *nm* blood-test results

hemopatía *nf* blood disease *o* disorder

hemorragia *nf* hemorrhage; **h. nasal** nosebleed; **se puso un torniquete para detener la h.** he put on a tourniquet to stop the bleeding

hemorrágico, -a *adj* hemorrhagic

hemorroides *nfpl* hemorrhoids, piles

henchido, -a *adj* bloated; *Fig* **h. de orgullo** bursting with pride

henchir [47] **1** *vt* to fill (up)

  2 henchirse *vpr* (a) *(hartarse)* to stuff oneself (b) *Fig (llenarse)* to be full **(de** of)

hender [64], **hendir** [62] *vt (carne, piel)* to carve open, to cleave; *(piedra, madera)* to crack open; *(aire, agua)* to cut *o* slice through

hendido, -a *adj* split (open)

hendidura *nf (en carne, piel)* cut, split; *(en piedra, madera)* crack

hendir = **hender**

henequén *n* sisal, henequen

henna ['χena] *nf* henna

heno *nm* hay

hepático, -a *adj* liver; **afección hepática** liver complaint

hepatitis *nf inv* hepatitis

heptagonal *adj* heptagonal

heptágono *nm* heptagon

heráldica *nf* heraldry

heráldico, -a *adj* heraldic

heraldo *nm* herald

herbáceo, -a *adj* herbaceous

herbario *nm (colección)* herbarium

herbicida *nm* weed killer

herbívoro, -a 1 *adj* herbivorous

  2 *nm,f* herbivore

herbolario, -a 1 *nm,f (persona)* herbalist

  2 *nm (tienda)* herbalist's (store)

herboristería *nf* herbalist's (store)

hercio *nm* hertz

hercúleo, -a *adj* very powerful, incredibly strong; *Fig* **un esfuerzo h.** a Herculean effort

Hércules *n* Hercules; **las Columnas de H.** *(el estrecho de Gibraltar)* the Pillars of Hercules

hércules *nm inv* ox, very strong man

heredad *nf* country estate *o* property

heredar *vt* **(a)** *(recibir)* *(dinero, rasgos)* to inherit (**de** from); **heredó el abrigo de su hermano** she inherited the coat from her brother; **un problema heredado del gobierno anterior** a problem inherited from the previous government; **ha heredado la nariz de su madre** he has his mother's nose **(b)** *Méx (legar)* *(dinero)* to bequeath; **su madre le ha heredado la nariz** he has his mother's nose

heredero, -a *nm,f* heir, *f* heiress; **el príncipe h.** the crown prince; **el h. al trono** the heir to the throne

hereditario, -a *adj* hereditary

hereje *nmf (renegado)* heretic; *Fig (irreverente)* iconoclast

herejía *nf (heterodoxia)* heresy; *Fig (insulto)* insult; *(disparate)* outrage

herencia *nf (de bienes)* inheritance; *(de características)* legacy; *Biol* heredity; **recibir una h.** to receive an inheritance

herético, -a *adj* heretical

herida *nf* **(a)** *(lesión)* injury; *(en lucha, atentado)* wound; **h. de bala** bullet *o* gunshot wound **(b)** *(ofensa)* injury, offense; *(pena)* hurt, pain

herido, -a 1 *adj (dañado)* injured; *(en lucha, atentado)* wounded; *(sentimentalmente)* hurt, wounded; **resultaron heridos once civiles** eleven civilians were wounded; **h. de muerte** mortally wounded; **se sintió h. en su amor propio** his pride was hurt
2 *nm,f (persona)* injured person; *(en lucha, atentado)* wounded person; **no hubo heridos** there were no casualties; **los heridos** the injured/the wounded

herir [62] *vt* **(a)** *(físicamente)* to injure; *(en lucha, atentado)* to wound; **lo hirieron en el hombro** he was wounded in the shoulder, he suffered a shoulder wound; **la hirieron de muerte** she was fatally wounded **(b)** *(vista)* to hurt; *(oído)* to pierce; **el nuevo edificio hiere la vista** the new building is an eyesore **(c)** *(sentimentalmente)* to hurt; **lo que dijiste le hirió profundamente** what you said hurt him deeply

hermafrodita *adj & nmf* hermaphrodite

hermanado, -a *adj (unido, ligado)* united (**con** with), joined (**con** to); *(ciudades)* partnered, affiliated

hermanamiento *nm (unión)* union; *(de ciudades)* partnership, affiliation

hermanar 1 *vt (esfuerzos, personas)* to unite; *(ciudades)* to partner *o* affiliate
2 hermanarse *vpr (ciudades)* to be partnered *o* affiliated

hermanastro, -a *nm,f (medio hermano)* half brother, *f* half sister; *(hijo del padrastro/de la madrastra)* stepbrother, *f* stepsister

hermandad *nf* **(a)** *(asociación)* association; *Rel (de hombres)* brotherhood; *(de mujeres)* sisterhood **(b)** *(amistad)* intimacy, close friendship

hermano, -a 1 *adj* **ciudades hermanas** sister cities; **dos pueblos hermanos como México y España** two countries with close ties, such as Mexico and Spain
2 *nm,f* brother, *f* sister; **todos los hermanos se parecen mucho entre sí** all the brothers and sisters look very much alike; **son medio hermanas** they're half sisters; **hermanos gemelos** twin brothers; **h. mayor** older *o* big brother; **hermanos mellizos** twin brothers; **h. menor** younger *o* little brother; **h. político** brother-in-law; **hermanos siameses** Siamese twins

hermenéutica *nf* hermeneutics *(singular)*

hermenéutico, -a *adj* hermeneutic

herméticamente *adv* hermetically; **h. cerrado** hermetically sealed

hermético, -a *adj* **(a)** *(al aire)* airtight, hermetic; *(al agua)* watertight, hermetic **(b)** *(persona)* inscrutable, uncommunicative

hermetismo *nm* **(a)** *(al aire)* airtightness; *(al agua)* watertightness **(b)** *(de persona)* inscrutability, uncommunicativeness

hermoso, -a *adj* **(a)** *(bello)* *(paisaje, paseo, mujer)* beautiful, lovely; *(hombre)* handsome; **¡qué atardecer más h.!** what a beautiful *o* lovely sunset! **(b)** *(grande)* **la casa tiene un salón muy h.** the house has a nice big living room; **cazaron un h. ejemplar** they caught a really big one **(c)** *Fam (gordo, grande)* plump; **el bebé está muy h.** he's a real bouncing baby

hermosura *nf (belleza)* beauty; *(de hombre)* handsomeness

hernia *nf* hernia, rupture; **h. de hiato** hiatus hernia; **h. inguinal** inguinal hernia

herniado, -a 1 *adj* ruptured
2 *nm,f* person suffering from a hernia

herniarse *vpr* **(a)** *Med* to rupture oneself **(b)** *Fam Irónico* **¡cuidado, no te vayas a herniar!** careful! you don't want to strain yourself!

héroe *nm* hero

heroicidad *nf* **(a)** *(cualidad)* heroism **(b)** *(hecho)* heroic deed

heroico, -a *adj* heroic

heroína *nf* **(a)** *(mujer)* heroine **(b)** *(droga)* heroin

heroinomanía *nf* heroin addiction

heroinómano, -a *nm,f* heroin addict

heroísmo *nm* heroism

herpes *nm inv* herpes

herradura *nf* horseshoe

herraje *nm* iron fittings, ironwork

herramienta *nf* tool

herrería *nf* **(a)** *(taller)* smithy, forge **(b)** *(oficio)* blacksmith's trade

herrerillo *nm (carbonero)* great tit; *(común)* blue tit

herrero *nm* blacksmith, smith

herrumbrarse *vpr* to rust, to go rusty

herrumbre *nf* **(a)** *(óxido)* rust **(b)** *(sabor)* iron taste

herrumbroso, -a *adj* rusty

hertz [χerts] *(pl hertzs) nm* hertz

hervidero *nm* **(a)** *(de gente) (muchedumbre)* swarm, throng; *(sitio)* place throbbing *o* swarming with people; **la sala era un h. de periodistas** the hall was swarming with journalists **(b)** *(de pasiones, intrigas)* hotbed

hervido, -a *adj* boiled

hervidor *nm (para agua)* kettle; *(para leche)* milk pan

hervir [62] **1** *vt* to boil
2 *vi* **(a)** *(líquido)* to boil; **h. a borbotones** to be at a rolling boil; *Fig* **le hervía la sangre** his blood was boiling **(b)** *(estar caliente)* to be boiling (hot); **esa sopa está hirviendo** that soup is boiling (hot) **(c)** *(lugar)* **h. de** to swarm with **(d)** *(persona)* **h. en** to be burning with

hervor *nm* boiling; **dar un h. a algo** to blanch sth; **añadir las hierbas durante el h.** add the herbs while it's boiling

heteróclito, -a *adj* heterogeneous

heterodoxia *nf* heterodoxy, unorthodox nature

heterodoxo, -a 1 *adj* heterodox, unorthodox
2 *nm,f* heterodox *o* unorthodox person

heterogeneidad *nf* heterogeneity

heterogéneo, -a *adj* heterogeneous

heteromorfo, -a *adj* heteromorphous

heterosexual *adj & nmf* heterosexual

heterosexualidad *nf* heterosexuality

hexadecimal *adj Inform* hexadecimal

hexaedro *nm* hexahedron, cube

hexagonal *adj* hexagonal

hexágono *nm* hexagon

hez *nf también Fig* dregs; **heces** *(excrementos)* feces, excrement

hg *(abrev de* **hectogramo***)* hg

hiato *nm Gram* hiatus

hibernación *nf (de animales)* hibernation

hibernar *vi* to hibernate

hibisco *nm* hibiscus

hibridación *nf* hybridization

híbrido, -a 1 *adj también Fig* hybrid
　2 *nm (animal, planta)* hybrid; *Fig (mezcla)* cross

hice *etc ver* **hacer**

hidalgo, -a 1 *adj* **(a)** *(noble)* noble **(b)** *(caballeroso)* courteous, gentlemanly
　2 *nm,f* nobleman, *f* noblewoman

hidalguía *nf* **(a)** *(aristocracia)* nobility **(b)** *(caballerosidad)* courtesy, chivalry

hidra *nf* hydra

hidratación *nf (de la piel)* moisturizing; *(de persona)* rehydration; *(de sustancia)* hydration

hidratado, -a *adj (piel)* moist; *Quím* hydrated

hidratante 1 *adj* moisturizing
　2 *nm (crema, loción)* moisturizer

hidratar *vt (piel)* to moisturize; *Quím* to hydrate

hidrato *nm* hydrate; **h. de carbono** carbohydrate

hidráulica *nf* hydraulics *(singular)*

hidráulico, -a *adj* hydraulic

hídrico, -a *adj* hydric

hidroavión *nm* seaplane, hydroplane

hidrocarburo *nm* hydrocarbon

hidrocefalia *nf Med* water on the brain, *Espec* hydrocephalus

hidrodinámica *nf* hydrodynamics *(singular)*

hidrodinámico, -a *adj* hydrodynamic

hidroelectricidad *nf* hydroelectricity

hidroeléctrico, -a *adj* hydroelectric; **central hidroeléctrica** hydroelectric power station

hidrófilo, -a *adj* absorbent; **algodón h.** cotton

hidrofobia *nf* hydrophobia, rabies

hidrófobo, -a *adj* hydrophobic, rabid

hidrófugo, -a *adj (contra filtraciones)* waterproof; *(contra humedad)* damp-proof

hidrogenar *vt* to hydrogenate

hidrógeno *nm* hydrogen

hidrografía *nf* hydrography

hidrográfico, -a *adj* hydrographic

hidrólisis *nf inv* hydrolysis

hidrolizado, -a *adj* hydrolyzed

hidrología *nf* hydrology

hidrológico, -a *adj* hydrologic, hydrological; **un plan h.** a plan for managing water resources

hidromasaje *nm* whirlpool bath, Jacuzzi®

hidromecánico, -a *adj* hydrodynamic, water-powered

hidrometría *nf* hydrometry

hidroplano *nm* **(a)** *(barco)* hydrofoil **(b)** *(avión)* seaplane

hidrosfera *nf* hydrosphere

hidrosoluble *adj* water-soluble

hidrostática *nf* hydrostatics *(singular)*

hidrostático, -a *adj* hydrostatic

hidroterapia *nf* hydrotherapy

hidrovía *nf Am* waterway

hidróxido *nm* hydroxide

hidruro *nm* hydride

hiedra *nf* ivy

hiel *nf* **(a)** *(bilis)* bile **(b)** *(mala intención)* spleen, bitterness

hiela *ver* **helar**

hielera *nf CSur, Méx* cooler, cool box

hielo *nm* ice; **un whisky con h.** a whiskey on the rocks; *Fig* **quedarse de h.** to be stunned *o* speechless; *Fig* **romper el h.** to break the ice

hiena *nf* hyena

hierático, -a *adj (expresión, actitud)* solemn, impassive

hierba, yerba *nf* **(a)** *(planta)* herb; **mala h.** weed; **hierbas aromáticas** aromatic herbs; **h. mate** maté; **hierbas medicinales** medicinal herbs **(b)** *(césped)* grass **(c)** *Fam (marihuana)* grass **(d)** *(expresiones)* **ser mala h.** to be a nasty piece of work; *Prov* **mala h. nunca muere** ill weeds grow apace; **y otras hierbas** and so on

hierbabuena *nf* mint

hierbaluisa *nf* lemon verbena

hiero *etc ver* **herir**

hierro *nm* **(a)** *(metal)* iron; **un h.** a piece of metal; *Fig* **quitarle h. a algo** to play sth down; *Fig* **tener una salud de h.** to have an iron constitution; **h. forjado/fundido** wrought/cast iron **(b)** *(de puñal)* blade; *(de flecha)* point; *Prov* **quien a h. mata a h. muere** he who lives by the sword dies by the sword

hiervo *etc ver* **hervir**

hi-fi ['ifi] *nf (abrev de* **high fidelity***)* hi-fi

higadillo *nm* **higadillos de pollo** chicken livers

hígado *nm* liver; *Fam* **echar los hígados** to nearly kill oneself (with the effort); *Fam* **tener hígados** to have guts

higiene *nf* hygiene; **h. dental** dental hygiene

higiénico, -a *adj* hygienic

higienista *nmf* hygienist; **h. dental** dental hygienist

higienización *nf* sterilization

higienizar [14] **1** *vt (acondicionar)* to improve hygiene in; *(limpiar)* to sanitize
　2 higienizarse *vpr RP Formal* to wash

higo *nm* fig; *Fam Fig* **de higos a brevas** once in a blue moon; *Fam Fig* **estar hecho un h.** *(persona)* to be wrecked; *(cosa)* to be falling apart; **h. chumbo** prickly pear

higrometría *nf* hygrometry

higrómetro *nm* hygrometer

higuera *nf* fig tree; *Fam Fig* **estar en la h.** to have one's head in the clouds; **h. chumba** prickly pear

hijastro, -a *nm,f* stepson, *f* stepdaughter

hijo, -a 1 *nm,f* **(a)** *(descendiente)* son, *f* daughter; **estar esperando un h.** to be expecting (a baby); *Fam* **cualquier *o* todo h. de vecino tiene derecho a trabajar** everyone, no matter who they are, has a right to work; *Fam* **nos gusta salir por la noche, como a cualquier *o* todo h. de vecino** like most people, we like going out in the evening; **h. adoptivo** adopted son; **hija adoptiva** adopted daughter; *Méx Vulg* **h. de la chingada** fucking bastard; motherfucker; **h. ilegítimo *o* natural** illegitimate son; **hija ilegítima *o* natural** illegitimate daughter; *Fam Pey* **h. de papá** rich kid; **h. político** son-in-law; **hija política** daughter-in-law; **h. pródigo** prodigal son; *Vulg* **h. de puta** fucking bastard, motherfucker; *Vulg* **hija de puta** fucking bitch; **h. único** only son; **hija única** only daughter
　(b) *(natural)* native
　(c) *(como forma de dirigirse a alguien)* **¡h., no te pongas así!** don't be like that!; **¡pues h., podrías haber avisado!** you could at least have told me, couldn't you?; **¡hija mía, qué bruta eres!** God, you're stupid!; **¡h., eres el colmo!** you really are the limit!
　2 *nm (hijo o hija)* child; **hijos** children

híjole, híjoles *interj Méx* wow!

hijoputa *nmf Vulg* fucking bastard, motherfucker

hilacha *nf* loose thread

hilada *nf* row

hiladora *nf* spinning machine

hilandería *nf* (a) *(arte)* spinning (b) *(taller)* (spinning) mill

hilandero, -a *nm,f* spinner

hilar *vt (hilo)* to spin; *(ideas, planes)* to think up; *Fig* **h. delgado** *o* **muy fino** to split hairs

hilarante *adj* mirth-provoking; **gas h.** laughing gas

hilaridad *nf* hilarity

hilatura *nf (actividad)* spinning

hilera *nf* row; **en h.** in a row

hilo *nm* (a) *(fibra, hebra)* thread; *Am* **al h.** *(seguidos)* in a row; **colgar** *o* **pender de un h.** to be hanging by a thread; **mover los hilos** to pull some strings; **h. dental** dental floss
  (b) *(tejido)* linen
  (c) *(de metal, teléfono)* wire; **sin hilos** wireless
  (d) *(de agua, sangre)* trickle; **entraba un h. de luz por la ventana** a thin shaft of light came in through the window; **apenas le salía un h. de voz** he was barely able to speak
  (e) *Mús* **h. musical** piped music
  (f) *(de pensamiento)* train; *(de discurso, conversación)* thread; **perder el h.** to lose the thread; **seguir el h.** to follow (the thread); **tomar** *o* **retomar el h. (de la conversación)** to pick up the thread (of the conversation); **esto viene al h. de lo que dijimos ayer** this relates to what we were saying yesterday; **h. argumental** line of argument

hilván *nm* (a) *(costura)* basting (b) *(hilo)* basting stitch

hilvanado *nm* basting

hilvanar *vt* (a) *(ropa)* to baste (b) *(coordinar) (ideas)* to piece together (c) *(improvisar)* to throw together

Himalaya *nm* **el H.** the Himalayas

himen *nm* hymen

himeneo *nm Literario* wedding

himno *nm* hymn; **h. nacional** national anthem

hincapié *nm* **hacer h. en** *(insistir)* to insist on; *(subrayar)* to emphasize, to stress

hincar [59] **1** *vt* **h. algo en** to stick sth into; *Fig* **hincarle el diente a algo** *(empezar)* to get to grips with sth, to get to work on sth
  2 hincarse *vpr* **hincarse de rodillas** to fall to one's knees

hincha 1 *ver* **henchir**
  2 *nmf* (a) *(seguidor)* fan, supporter (b) *RP Fam (persona molesta)* pain, bore
  3 *nf Esp Fam (rabia)* **tener h. a alguien** to have it in for sb

hinchable *adj* inflatable

hinchada *nf* fans

hinchado, -a *adj* (a) *(rueda, globo)* inflated; *(cara, tobillo)* swollen (b) *(persona)* bigheaded, conceited; *(lenguaje, estilo)* bombastic

hinchar 1 *vt* to blow up, to inflate; *Esp Fam Fig* **ya me está hinchando las narices** he's beginning to get up my nose
  2 hincharse *vpr* (a) *(de aire)* to inflate; **el globo se hinchó en pocas horas** the balloon was inflated in a few hours (b) *(pierna, mano)* to swell (up); **se me ha hinchado el brazo** my arm has swollen (up) (c) *(persona)* to get puffed up (d) *(hartarse)* **se hinchó a comer** she stuffed herself; **nos hinchamos de paella** we stuffed ourselves with paella; **nos hinchamos de reír** we laughed ourselves silly

hinchazón *nf* swelling; **ya está bajando la h.** the swelling is already going down

hinchiera *etc ver* **henchir**

hincho *etc ver* **henchir**

hindi *nm* Hindi

hindú *(pl* **hindúes)** *adj & nmf* (a) *(de la India)* Indian (b) *Rel* Hindu

hinduismo *nm* Hinduism

hinojo *nm* fennel

hinque *etc ver* **hincar**

hip *interj* **¡h.!** *(hipido)* hic!; **¡h.! ¡h.! ¡hurra!** hip, hip, hooray!

hipar *vi* to hiccup, to have hiccups

hiper- *prefijo Fam (muy)* mega-; **me ha salido hipercaro** it was megaexpensive; **¡es hiperguapo!** he's a real dish!

híper *nm inv Fam* hypermarket

hiperactividad *nf* hyperactivity

hiperactivo, -a *adj* hyperactive

hipérbaton *(pl* **hipérbatos** *o* **hiperbatones)** *nm Lit* hyperbaton

hipérbola *nf* hyperbola

hipérbole *nf* hyperbole

hiperbólico, -a *adj Mat & Lit* hyperbolic

hiperenlace *nf Inform* hyperlink

hiperfunción *nf Med* increase in normal rate of functioning

hiperglucemia *nf* hyperglycemia

hiperinflación *nf* hyperinflation

hipermercado *nm* hypermarket

hipermétrope 1 *adj* farsighted
  2 *nmf* farsighted person

hipermetropía *nf* farsightedness, hypertropia, *Espec* hyperopia, hypermetropia

hiperrealismo *nm Arte* hyperrealism

hiperrealista *adj & nmf Arte* hyperrealist

hipersensibilidad *nf* hypersensitivity (**a** to)

hipersensible *adj* hypersensitive

hipersónico, -a *adj* hypersonic

hipertensión *nf* high blood pressure

hipertenso, -a 1 *adj* with high blood pressure
  2 *nm,f* person with high blood pressure

hipertermia *nf* hyperthermia

hipertexto *nm Inform* hypertext

hipertextual *adj Inform* **enlace h.** hypertext link

hipertrofia *nf Med* hypertrophy; *Fig (de organización)* overexpansion

hiperventilación *nf Med* hyperventilation

hip-hop ['χipχop] *nm* hip-hop

hípica *nf (carreras de caballos)* horse racing; *(equitación)* show jumping

hípico, -a *adj* **concurso h.** *(de las carreras)* horse races; *(de la equitación)* show jumping

hipido *nm* hiccup

hipismo *nm* horse racing

hipnosis *nf inv* hypnosis

hipnótico, -a 1 *adj* hypnotic
  2 *nm* hypnotic, narcotic

hipnotismo *nm* hypnotism

hipnotizador, -ora 1 *adj (de la hipnosis)* hypnotic; *(fascinante)* spellbinding, mesmerizing
  2 *nm,f* hypnotist

hipnotizar [14] *vt (con hipnosis)* to hypnotize; *(fascinar)* to mesmerize

hipo *nm* hiccups; **tener h.** to have (the) hiccups; *Fig* **quitar el h. a alguien** to take someone's breath away

hipoalergénico, -a *adj* hypoallergenic

hipocalórico, -a *adj (alimento, dieta)* low-calorie

hipocampo *nm (caballito de mar)* sea horse

hipocentro *nm* hypocenter, focus

hipocondría *nf* hypochondria

hipocondriaco, -a *adj & nm,f* hypochondriac

hipocrático, -a *adj* **juramento h.** Hippocratic oath

hipocresía *nf* hypocrisy

hipócrita 1 *adj* hypocritical
  2 *nmf* hypocrite

hipodérmico, -a *adj* hypodermic

hipódromo *nm* racetrack, racecourse

hipófisis *nf inv* pituitary gland

hipofunción *nf Med* decrease in normal rate of functioning

hipoglucemia *nf* hypoglycemia

hipopótamo *nm* hippopotamus

hipotálamo *nm* hypothalamus

hipoteca *nf* mortgage; **levantar una h.** to pay off a mortgage

hipotecable *adj* mortgageable

hipotecar [59] *vt* (**a**) *(bienes)* to mortgage (**b**) *(poner en peligro) (futuro)* to mortgage; *(salud)* to put at risk

hipotecario, -a *adj* mortgage; **crédito h.** mortgage (loan)

hipotensión *nf* low blood pressure

hipotenso, -a 1 *adj* with low blood pressure
2 *nm,f* person with low blood pressure

hipotensor *nm* hypotensive drug

hipotenusa *nf* hypotenuse

hipotermia *nf* hypothermia

hipótesis *nf inv* hypothesis

hipotético, -a *adj* hypothetic, hypothetical

hippy, hippie ['χipi] (*pl* **hippies**) *adj & nmf* hippy

hiriente *adj (palabras)* hurtful, cutting

hiriera *etc ver* **herir**

hirsuto, -a *adj (cabello)* wiry; *(brazo, pecho)* hairy

hirviera *etc ver* **hervir**

hisopo *nm* (**a**) *Rel* aspergillum, sprinkler (**b**) *Bot* hyssop

hispalense *adj & nmf* Sevillian

hispánico, -a *adj & nm,f (de España)* Hispanic; *(hispano-hablante)* Spanish-speaking; **el mundo h.** the Spanish-speaking world

hispanidad *nf (cultura)* Spanishness; *(pueblos)* Spanish-speaking world

hispanismo *nm* (**a**) *(palabra, expresión)* Hispanicism (**b**) *(afición)* = interest in or love of Spain

hispanista *nmf* Hispanist, student of Hispanic culture

hispanizar [14] **1** *vt* to Hispanicize *o* Hispanize
2 hispanizarse *vpr* to become Hispanicized *o* Hispanized

hispano, -a 1 *adj (español)* Spanish; *(hispanoamericano)* Spanish-American; *(en Estados Unidos)* Hispanic
2 *nm,f (español)* Spaniard; *(estadounidense)* Hispanic

Hispanoamérica *n* Spanish America

hispanoamericano, -a 1 *adj* Spanish-American
2 *nm,f* Spanish American

hispanoárabe 1 *adj* Hispano-Arabic
2 *nmf* Spanish Arab

hispanohablante 1 *adj* Spanish-speaking
2 *nmf* Spanish speaker

hispanojudío, -a 1 *adj* Spanish-Jewish
2 *nm,f* Spanish Jew

histamina *nf* histamine

histerectomía *nf* hysterectomy

histeria *nf Med & Fig* hysteria; **h. colectiva** mass hysteria

histérico, -a *adj* (**a**) *Med* hysterical (**b**) *Fam (nervioso)* **estar h.** to be a bag *o* bundle of nerves; **ponerse h.** to get in a flap; **ese ruido me pone h.** that noise really gets on my nerves
2 *nm,f* (**a**) *Med* hysteric (**b**) *Fam (nervioso)* **es un h.** he's always getting in a flap

histerismo *nm* hysteria

histerotomía *nf* hysterotomy

histograma *nm* histogram

histología *nf* histology

historia *nf* (**a**) *(ciencia)* history; **pasar a la h.** to go down in history; **h. antigua/universal** ancient/world history; **h. del arte** art history; **h. natural** natural history

(**b**) *(narración)* story; **una h. de amor/fantasmas** a love/ghost story; **es siempre la misma h.** it's the same old story

(**c**) *Fam (excusa, enredo)* story; **¡déjate de historias!** that's enough of that!; **no me vengas ahora con historias** don't give me that!, you don't expect me to believe that, do you?

(**d**) *Fam (asunto)* **a mí no me enredes en tus historias** don't drag me into your problems; **está metido en una h. muy turbia** he's involved in a very shady business

historiado, -a *adj* gaudy

historiador, -ora *nm,f* historian

historial *nm (ficha)* record; **h. médico** *o* **clínico** medical *o* case history

historicidad *nf* historicity, historical authenticity

historicismo *nm* historicism

histórico, -a *adj* (**a**) *(de la historia) (novela, legado)* historical; *(centro)* historic (**b**) *(verídico)* factual (**c**) *(importante)* historic; **máximo/mínimo h.** all-time high/low

historieta *nf* (**a**) *(chiste)* funny story, anecdote (**b**) *(tira cómica)* comic strip

historiografía *nf* historiography

historiógrafo, -a *nm,f* historiographer

histrión *nm* (**a**) *(actor)* actor (**b**) *(persona afectada)* play-actor

histriónico, -a *adj* histrionic

histrionismo *nm* histrionics

hit [χit] (*pl* **hits**) *nm* hit

hitita *adj & nmf* Hittite

hitleriano, -a [χitle'rjano] *adj & nm,f* Hitlerite

hito *nm también Fig* milestone; **mirar a alguien de h. en h.** to stare at sb

hizo *ver* **hacer**

hl *(abrev de* **hectolitro***)* hl

hm *(abrev de* **hectómetro***)* hm

hnos. *(abrev de* **hermanos***)* bros

hobby ['χoβi] (*pl* **hobbys**) *nm* hobby

hocico *nm* (**a**) *(de perro, zorro)* muzzle; *(de gato, ratón)* nose; *(de cerdo)* snout (**b**) *Fam (de persona) (boca)* rubber lips; *(cara)* mug; **meter los hocicos en un asunto** to stick one's nose into something

hockey ['χokei] *nm* hockey; *Am* **h. sobre césped** field hockey; **h. sobre hielo** hockey; **h. sobre hierba** field hockey; **h. sobre patines** roller hockey

hogar *nm* (**a**) *(casa)* home; *(unidad familiar)* household; **su marido trabaja fuera y ella se ocupa del h.** her husband goes out to work and she's a housewife; **más de la mitad de los hogares del país** in more than half of the households in the country; **los jóvenes sin h.** young homeless people; **h. dulce h.** home sweet home; **h. de acogida** foster home (**b**) *(de chimenea)* fireplace; *(de horno, cocina)* grate

hogareño, -a *adj (persona)* home-loving, homely; *(tarea, economía)* domestic; *(ambiente)* family; **ambiente h.** family atmosphere; **la paz hogareña** domestic bliss

hogaza *nf* large round loaf

hoguera *nf* bonfire; **morir en la h.** to be burned at the stake

hoja *nf* (**a**) *(de planta)* leaf; *(de hierba)* blade; **h. caduca** deciduous leaf; **h. de laurel** bay leaf; **h. de parra** *(en cuadro)* fig leaf; **h. perenne** perennial leaf (**b**) *(de papel)* sheet (of paper); *(de libro)* page; **h. informativa** newsletter; **h. de pedido** order form; **h. de servicios** record (of service), track record (**c**) *(de cuchillo)* blade; **h. de afeitar** razor blade (**d**) *(de puertas, ventanas)* leaf (**e**) *Inform* **h. de cálculo** spreadsheet

hojalata *nf* tin plate

hojalatería *nf* (**a**) *(para hojalata)* tinsmith's (**b**) *Méx (para automóviles) (lugar)* body shop; *(actividad)* panel beating

hojalatero, -a *nm,f* (a) *(para hojalata)* tinsmith (b) *Méx (para automóviles)* panel beater

hojaldre *nm* puff pastry

hojarasca *nf* (a) *(hojas secas)* (dead) leaves; *(frondosidad)* tangle of leaves (b) *(palabrería)* waffle

hojear *vt* to leaf through

hola *interj* ¡h.! *(saludo)* hello!; *RP (al teléfono)* hello?

holá *interj RP (al teléfono)* hello?

Holanda *n* Holland

holandés, -esa 1 *adj* Dutch
2 *nm,f (persona)* Dutchman, *f* Dutchwoman; **los holandeses** the Dutch
3 *nm (lengua)* Dutch

holandesa *nf (hoja de papel)* = piece of paper measuring 22 x 28cm *(approx 8.6 x 11 in)*

holding ['xoldin] *(pl* **holdings**) *nm Com* holding company

holgado, -a *adj* (a) *(ropa)* baggy, loose-fitting; *(habitación, espacio)* roomy (b) *(victoria, situación económica)* comfortable

holganza *nf* idleness

holgar [16] *vi* (a) *(estar ocioso)* to be idle, to be taking one's ease (b) *(sobrar)* to be unnecessary; **huelgan comentarios** one need say no more; **huelga decir que...** needless to say...

holgazán, -ana 1 *adj* idle, good-for-nothing
2 *nm,f* good-for-nothing

holgazanear *vi* to laze about

holgazanería *nf* idleness

holgura *nf* (a) *(de espacio)* room; *(de ropa)* bagginess, looseness; *(entre piezas)* play, give (b) *(bienestar)* comfort, affluence; **vivir con h.** to be comfortably off

holístico, -a *adj* holistic

hollar [63] *vt* to tread (on)

hollejo *nm* skin *(of grape, olive etc)*

hollín *nm* soot

hollywoodiense [xoliβu'ðjense] *adj* Hollywood; **la vida h.** life in Hollywood, the Hollywood scene

holocausto *nm* holocaust

holografía *nf* holography

hológrafo, -a 1 *adj* holographical
2 *nm* holograph

holograma *nm* hologram

hombre 1 *nm* (a) *(varón adulto)* man; **un pobre h.** a nobody; **¡pobre h.!** poor guy!; **de h. a h.** man-to-man; **ser muy h.** to be a (real) man; **ser todo un h., ser un h. de pelo en pecho** to be a real man, to be every inch a man; **h. de acción** man of action; **el h. de la calle** the man in the street; **h. de las cavernas** caveman; **h. lobo** werewolf; **h. de mundo** man of the world; **h. de negocios** businessman; **h. orquesta** one-man band; **h. de paja** front (man), straw man; **h. de palabra** man of his word; **h. rana** frogman; **el h. de a pie** the man in the street; *Fam* **el h. del saco** the bogeyman; **h. del tiempo** weatherman
(b) **el h.** *(la humanidad)* man, mankind
2 *interj Esp* ¡h.! **¡qué alegría verte!** (hey,) how nice to see you!; **¡sí, h.!** sure!; **¡sí, h., que ya voy!** all right, all right, I'm coming!; **h., ¡qué pena!** oh, what a shame!; **pero h., no te pongas así** oh, don't be like that!

hombrear *vi* to act the man

hombrera *nf (de traje, vestido)* shoulder pad; *(de uniforme)* epaulet

hombría *nf* manliness

hombro *nm* shoulder; **al h.** across one's shoulder; **a hombros** over one's shoulders; **encogerse de hombros** to shrug one's shoulders; **arrimar el h.** to lend a hand; **hacer algo h. con h.** to do sth together; **mirar por encima del h. a alguien** to look down one's nose at sb

hombruno, -a *adj* masculine, mannish

homenaje *nm (en honor de alguien)* tribute; *(al soberano)* homage; **partido (de) h.** game honoring sb; **en h. de** *o* **a** in honor of, as a tribute to; **rendir h. a** to pay tribute to

homenajeado, -a 1 *adj* honored
2 *nm,f* guest of honor

homenajear *vt* to pay tribute to, to honor

homeópata *nmf* homeopath

homeopatía *nf* homeopathy

homeopático, -a *adj* homeopathic

homérico, -a *adj Lit* Homeric

homicida 1 *adj (agresión, mirada, intención)* murderous; **arma h.** murder weapon
2 *nmf* murderer

homicidio *nm* homicide, manslaughter

homilía *nf Rel* homily, sermon

homínido *nm* hominid

homoerótico, -a *adj* homoerotic

homofobia *nf* homophobia

homófono, -a *adj Ling* homophonic

homogeneidad *nf* homogeneity

homogeneización *nf* homogenization

homogeneizador, -ora *adj* homogenizing

homogeneizar [14] *vt* to homogenize

homogéneo, -a *adj* homogenous

homógrafo, -a *Ling* **1** *adj* homographic
2 *nm* homograph

homologable *adj* **h.** (a) comparable (to)

homologación *nf* (a) *(equiparación)* bringing into line (b) *(de un producto)* official authorization; *(de un récord)* official confirmation

homologar [38] *vt* (a) *(equiparar)* to bring into line (**con** with), to make comparable (**con** with) (b) *(producto)* to authorize officially; *(récord)* to confirm officially

homólogo, -a 1 *adj* (a) *(semejante)* equivalent (b) *Quím* homologous
2 *nm,f* counterpart

homonimia *nf* homonymy

homónimo, -a 1 *adj* homonymous
2 *nm,f (tocayo)* namesake
3 *nm Ling* homonym

homosexual *adj & nmf* homosexual

homosexualidad *nf* homosexuality

honda *nf* sling

hondo, -a *adj* (a) *también Fig (profundo)* deep; **lo h.** the depths; **calar h. en** to strike a chord with; **en lo más h. de** in the depths of (b) **cante h.** flamenco singing

hondonada *nf* hollow

hondura *nf* depth

Honduras *n* Honduras

hondureño, -a *adj & nm,f* Honduran

honestamente *adv (con honradez)* honestly; *(con decencia)* modestly, decently; *(con justicia)* fairly

honestidad *nf (honradez)* honesty; *(decencia)* modesty, decency; *(justicia)* fairness

honesto, -a *adj (honrado)* honest; *(decente)* modest, decent; *(justo)* fair

hongo 1 *adj* **sombrero h.** derby
2 *nm* (a) *Biol* fungus (b) *esp Am (comestible)* mushroom; *(no comestible)* toadstool (c) **hongos** *(enfermedad)* fungus, fungal infection (d) *(sombrero)* **(sombrero) h.** derby

Honolulú [xonolu'lu] *n* Honolulu

honor *nm* (a) *(cualidad)* honor; **es un h. para mí presentarles a...** it's an honor for me to present to you...; **nos hizo el h. de invitarnos** he did us the honor of inviting us; **hacer h. a** to live up to; **en h. de** in honor of; **en h. a la verdad** to be (quite) honest (b) **honores** *(ceremonial)* honors;

le recibieron con honores de jefe de Estado he was welcomed with all the ceremony befitting a head of state; **hacer los honores de la casa** to do the honors, to look after the guests

honorabilidad *nf* honor

honorable *adj* honorable

honorar *vt* to honor

honorario, -a 1 *adj* honorary
2 honorarios *nmpl* fees

honorífico, -a *adj* honorific

honoris causa *adj* honoris causa

honra *nf* honor; **ser la h. de** to be the pride of; **es la h. de su país** she's the pride *o* toast of her country; **tener algo a mucha h.** to be honored by sth; **¡y a mucha h.!** and proud of it!; **honras fúnebres** funeral

honradez *nf* honesty

honrado, -a *adj* honest

honrar 1 *vt* to honor; **nos honró con su presencia** she honored us with her presence; **su sinceridad le honra** his sincerity does him credit
2 honrarse *vpr* to be honored (**con algo/de hacer algo** by sth/to do sth); **me honro de ser su amigo** I feel honored to be his friend

honrilla *nf* pride, concern about what people say

honroso, -a *adj* (*acto, gesto*) honorable

hooligan ['χulivan] (*pl* **hooligans**) *nmf* (soccer) hooligan

hora *nf* (a) (*sesenta minutos*) hour; **media h.** half an hour; **una h. y media** an hour and a half; **(pagar) por horas** (to pay) by the hour; **horas extraordinarias** overtime; **horas de luz** daylight hours; **horas de oficina/trabajo** office/work hours; **horas de vuelo** flying time; **horas de visita** visiting times
(b) (*en un reloj*) time; **¿qué h. es?** what time is it?; **¿a qué h. sale?** what time does it leave?; **dar la h.** to strike the hour; **poner el reloj en h.** to set one's watch *o* clock; **h. oficial** official time; **h. de salida** departure time
(c) (*momento determinado*) time; **es h. de irse** it's time to go; **a la h.** on time; **a su h.** when the time comes, at the appropriate time; **llegó su h.** (*muerte*) his time has come; **a primera h.** first thing in the morning; **a última h.** (*al final del día*) at the end of the day; (*en el último momento*) at the last moment; *Prensa* **última h.** stop press; **de última h.** (*noticia*) latest, up-to-the-minute; (*preparativos*) last-minute; **h. de cenar** dinnertime; **h. de cierre** closing time; *Am* **h. pico**, *Esp* **h. punta** rush hour
(d) (*cita*) appointment; **pedir/dar h.** to ask for/give an appointment; **tener h. en/con** to have an appointment at/ with
(e) (*expresiones*) **a altas horas de la noche** in the small hours; *Fam* **¡a buenas horas (mangas verdes)!** that's a lot of good now!; **en mala h.** unluckily; *CAm, Méx* **la h. de la h.**, *Esp, Andes, Carib, RP* **la h. de la verdad** the moment of truth; *CAm, Méx* **a la h. de la h.**, *Esp, Andes, Carib, RP* **a la h. de la verdad** when it comes to the crunch; **tener las horas contadas** to have one's days numbered; **¡ya era h.!** and about time too!

horadar *vt* (*perforar*) to pierce; (*con máquina*) to bore through

horario, -a 1 *adj* **aguja horaria** (*de reloj*) hour hand
2 *nm* schedule; **h. de apertura** opening hours; **h. de atención al público** (*en oficina*) opening *o* office hours; **h. comercial** opening hours; **h. flexible** flexitime; **h. intensivo** = workday without a long break for lunch; **h. laboral** work hours; **h. lectivo** class time; **h. de oficina** office hours; **h. partido** = workday with long (two to three hour) lunch break, ending at 7-8pm; **h. previsto** scheduled time; **h. de trabajo** work hours; **h. de trabajo flexible** flexible work hours; **h. de verano** summer opening hours; **h. de visitas** visiting hours

horca *nf* (a) (*patíbulo*) gallows (b) (*herramienta*) pitchfork

horcajadas: a horcajadas *loc adv* astride

horchata *nf* = cold drink made from ground chufa nuts, water and sugar

horchatería *nf* = milk bar where "horchata" is served

horda *nf* horde; **las hordas mongolas** the Mongol hordes

horizontal *adj* horizontal

horizontalidad *nf* flatness

horizonte *nm* (a) (*línea*) horizon; **h. artificial** artificial horizon (b) (*perspectivas*) **un h. poco prometedor** an unpromising outlook; **este proyecto amplía nuestros horizontes** this project represents a widening of our horizons

horma *nf* (*molde*) mold, pattern; (*de zapatos*) shoe tree; (*de sombrero*) hat block; *Fig* **encontrar la h. de su zapato** to meet one's match

hormiga *nf* ant; *Fig* **ser una h.** to be hardworking and thrifty; **h. obrera/reina** worker/queen ant

hormigón *nm* concrete; **h. armado** reinforced concrete

hormigonar *vt* to construct with concrete

hormigonera *nf* concrete mixer

hormiguear *vi* (a) (*dar sensación de hormigueo*) **me hormiguean las piernas** I've got pins and needles in my legs (b) (*moverse, bullir*) to swarm

hormigueo *nm* (a) (*sensación*) pins and needles (b) (*movimiento*) bustle

hormiguero 1 *adj* **oso h.** anteater
2 *nm* ants' nest, ant hill; **Tokio es un h. humano** Tokyo is swarming with people

hormiguita *nf Fam* **ser una h.** to be hardworking and thrifty

hormona *nf* hormone

hormonal *adj* hormonal

hornacina *nf* (vaulted) niche

hornada *nf* (*de pan, cerámica*) batch; (*de jóvenes*) crop

hornear *vt* to bake

hornillo *nm* (*para cocinar*) camping *o* portable stove; (*de laboratorio*) small furnace

horno *nm* (a) *Culin* oven; (*de cerámica, ladrillos*) kiln; **pescado al h.** baked fish; **esta casa es un h. en verano** this house is an oven in summer; *Fam Fig* **no está el h. para bollos** the time is not right; **alto h.** blast furnace; **h. crematorio** crematory; **h. eléctrico** electric oven; **h. microondas** microwave (oven) (b) *Tec* furnace; **altos hornos** (*factoría*) iron and steelworks

horóscopo *nm* (a) (*signo zodiacal*) star sign (b) (*predicción*) horoscope

horquilla *nf* (a) (*para el pelo*) hairpin (b) (*herramienta*) wooden pitchfork

horrendo, -a *adj* (a) (*terrorífico*) horrifying, terrifying (b) (*muy malo*) terrible, awful (c) (*muy feo*) horrible, hideous

hórreo *nm* = raised granary typical of Asturias and Galicia

horrible *adj* (a) (*terrorífico*) horrifying, terrifying (b) (*muy malo*) terrible, awful (c) (*muy feo*) horrible, hideous

horripilante *adj* (a) (*terrorífico*) horrifying, spine-chilling (b) (*muy feo*) horrible, hideous

horripilar *vt* to terrify, to scare to death

horror 1 *nm* (a) (*miedo*) terror, horror; **me da h. pensarlo** just thinking about it gives me the shivers; **¡qué h.!** how awful!; **¡qué h. de día!** what an awful day! (b) (*atrocidad*) atrocity; **los horrores de la guerra** the horrors of war (c) *Fam* **un h.** (*mucho*) an awful lot; **me gusta un h.** I absolutely love it
2 *adv Fam* **horrores** terribly, an awful lot; **me gusta horrores** I absolutely love it

horrorizado, -a *adj* terrified, horrified

horrorizar [14] **1** *vt* to terrify, to horrify
2 horrorizarse *vpr* to be terrified *o* horrified

horroroso, -a adj (a) (terrorífico) horrifying, terrifying (b) (muy malo) appalling, awful (c) (muy feo) horrible, hideous

hortaliza nf (garden) vegetable

hortelano, -a nm,f truck farmer

hortensia nf hydrangea

hortera Esp Fam **1** adj (decoración, ropa, canción) tacky; **es muy h.** he has really tacky taste
2 nmf **ser un h.** to have tacky taste

horterada nf Esp Fam **esa canción es una h.** that song is really tacky

hortícola adj horticultural

horticultor, -ora nm,f horticulturalist

horticultura nf horticulture

hosco, -a adj (persona) sullen, gruff; (lugar) grim, gloomy

hospedaje nm (a) (alojamiento) accommodation, lodgings, accommodations (b) (dinero) (cost of) board and lodging (c) Inform hosting

hospedar 1 vt (a) (persona) to put up (b) Inform to host
2 hospedarse vpr to stay

hospedería nf (lugar de alojamiento) guesthouse; (de convento) hospice

hospiciano, -a nm,f = resident of an orphanage

hospicio nm (para niños) orphanage, children's home; (para pobres) poorhouse

hospital nm hospital; **h. de campaña** field hospital; **h. de maternidad** maternity hospital; **h. psiquiátrico** psychiatric or mental hospital

hospitalario, -a adj (a) (acogedor) hospitable (b) (de hospital) hospital; **atención hospitalaria** hospital care

hospitalidad nf hospitality

hospitalización nf hospitalization

hospitalizar [14] vt to hospitalize, to take o send to the hospital

hosquedad nf sullenness, gruffness

host [χost] (pl **hosts**) nm Inform host

hostal nm guesthouse

hostelería nf catering

hostelero, -a 1 adj catering; **sector h.** catering trade
2 nm,f landlord, f landlady

hostería nf guesthouse

hostia 1 nf (a) Rel host (b) Esp Vulg (golpe) bash, punch; (accidente) smashup (c) Esp Vulg (expresiones) **¿para qué hostias…?** why the hell…?; **había la h. de gente** the place was heaving; **hace un frío de la h.** it's goddamn freezing out there!; **ser la h.** (de bueno) to be goddamn amazing; (de malo) to be goddamn awful; **a toda h.** at full pelt o flat out; **tener mala h.** to be a mean bastard
2 interj Esp Vulg **¡h.!, ¡hostias!** goddamn it!

hostiar vt Vulg to bash

hostigamiento nm harassment

hostigar [38] vt (a) (acosar) to pester, to bother (b) Mil to harass

hostil adj hostile

hostilidad nf (sentimiento) hostility; Mil **hostilidades** hostilities

hostilizar [14] vt to harass

hotel nm hotel

hotelería nf Andes, RP hotel and catering industry

hotelero, -a 1 adj hotel; **hay escasez de plazas hoteleras** there is a shortage of hotel accommodation
2 nm,f (hombre) hotelier, hotel manager; (mujer) hotelier, hotel manageress

hovercraft (pl **hovercrafts**) nm hovercraft

hoy adv (a) (en este día) today; **h. es martes** today is Tuesday, it's Tuesday today; **¿a qué estamos h.?** what's today's date?; **de h. en adelante** from now on; **de h. no pasa, tengo que ordenar esta mesa** it can't wait any longer, I have to tidy this table today; **de h. para mañana** as soon o quickly as possible; **h. por ti y mañana por mí** you can do the same for me sometime (b) (en la actualidad) nowadays, today; **h. día, h. en día** these days, nowadays; **la mujer de h. en día** women today, modern women; **h. por h.** at the present moment, as things are at the moment

hoyo nm (concavidad) hole, pit; (de golf) hole; Fam (sepultura) grave

hoyuelo nm dimple

hoz nf (a) (herramienta) sickle; **la h. y el martillo** the hammer and sickle (b) (barranco) gorge, canyon

HTML nm Inform (abrev de **hypertext markup language**) HTML

HTTP nm Inform (abrev de **hypertext transfer protocol**) HTTP

huacal nm CAm, Col, Méx (a) (jaula) cage (b) (cajón) drawer

huachafería nf Perú Fam (a) (hecho) tacky thing (b) (dicho) awkward comment

huachafo, -a adj Perú Fam tacky

huaso, -a nm,f Andes Fam peasant

hubiera etc ver **haber**

hucha nf Esp money box

hueco, -a 1 adj (a) (vacío) hollow (b) (sonido) resonant, hollow (c) (sin ideas) empty
2 nm (a) (cavidad) hole; (en pared) recess (b) (rato libre) spare moment; **te puedo hacer un h. esta tarde** I can squeeze you in this afternoon (c) (espacio libre) space, gap; (de escalera) well; (de ascensor) shaft; **no había ni un h. en el teatro** there wasn't an empty seat in the theater; **hazme un h. en el sofá** make a bit of room for me on the sofa; **la marcha de los hijos dejó un h. en sus vidas** the children leaving home left a gap in their lives

huecograbado nm photogravure

huela etc ver **oler**

huelga 1 ver **holgar**
2 nf strike; **estar/declararse en h.** to be/to go on strike; **h. de brazos caídos** sit-down (strike); **h. de celo** job action; **h. general** general strike; **h. de hambre** hunger strike; **h. indefinida** indefinite strike; **h. salvaje** wildcat strike; **h. de solidaridad** sympathy strike

huelguista nmf striker

huelguístico, -a adj strike; **convocatoria huelguística** strike call

huella 1 ver **hollar**
2 nf (a) (de persona) footprint; (de animal, rueda) track; Fig **seguir las huellas de alguien** to follow in sb's footsteps; **h. digital** o **dactilar** fingerprint; **h. genética** genetic fingerprint (b) (vestigio) trace (c) (impresión profunda) mark; **dejar h.** to leave one's mark

huérfano, -a adj & nm,f orphan

huero, -a adj (vacío) hollow; (palabras) empty

huerta nf (a) (huerto) truck farm (b) (tierra de regadío) = irrigated crop-growing region

huertano, -a nm,f Esp (murciano) person from Murcia; (valenciano) Valencian

huertero, -a nm,f truck farmer

huerto nm (de hortalizas) vegetable garden; (de frutales) orchard; Fam Fig **llevarse a alguien al h.** to have (one's will and) one's way with sb

hueso nm (a) (del cuerpo) bone; Fam Fig **acabar** o **dar con sus huesos en** to end up in; Fam Fig **calarse hasta los huesos** to get soaked to the skin; Fam Fig **estar en los huesos** to be all skin and bones; Fam Fig **no poder con sus huesos** to be ready to drop, to be exhausted; Fam Fig **ser un h. duro de roer** to be a hard nut to crack; Culin **h. de santo** = small marzipan roll filled with egg yolk (**b**) *(de fruto)* pit; **aceitunas sin h.** pitted olives

(**c**) *Fam (persona)* very strict person; *(asignatura)* difficult subject

(**d**) *Fam* **la sin h.** the tongue

(**e**) *Méx Fam (enchufe)* contacts, influence; *(trabajo fácil)* cushy job

huésped, -eda *nm,f* guest

hueste *nf (ejército)* army; **huestes** *(seguidores)* followers

huesudo, -a *adj* bony

hueva *nf* roe; **huevas de bacalao** cod roe

huevada *nf Andes, RP muy Fam* crap

huevear *vi Andes Fam* to mess around

huevera *nf* (**a**) *(para servir)* egg cup (**b**) *(para guardar)* egg box

huevero, -a *nm,f* egg seller

huevo *nm* (**a**) *(de animales)* egg; *Andes* **h. a la copa** boiled egg; **h. duro** hard-boiled egg; **h. escalfado/frito** poached/fried egg; **h. pasado por agua** soft-boiled egg; **h. de Pascua** Easter egg; **huevos al plato** = eggs cooked in the oven in an earthenware dish; **huevos revueltos** scrambled eggs; *Méx* **h. tibio** boiled egg (**b**) *muy Fam* **huevos** *(testículos)* balls, nuts; **tener huevos** to have balls; **costar un h.** to cost a hell of a lot; **¡y un h.!** my ass!

huevón, -ona, güevón, -ona *muy Fam* **1** *adj* (**a**) *Cuba, Méx (vago)* lazy; **es muy h.** he's so goddamn lazy (**b**) *Andes, Arg,Ven (tonto, torpe)* **es muy h.** he's a jerk

2 *nm,f* (**a**) *Cuba, Méx (vago)* **es un h.** he's so goddamn lazy (**b**) *Andes, Arg,Ven (tonto, torpe)* jerk

hugonote, -a *adj & nm,f* Huguenot

huida *nf* escape, flight

huidizo, -a *adj (esquivo)* shy, elusive; *(frente, mentón)* receding

huir [34] **1** *vi* (**a**) *(escapar) (de enemigo)* to flee (**de** from); *(de cárcel)* to escape (**de** from); **h. del país** to flee the country (**b**) **h. de algo** *(evitar)* to avoid sth, to keep away from sth

2 *vt* to avoid

huiro *nm Chile, Perú* seaweed

hule *nm* oilskin

hulla *nf* soft coal

hullero, -a *adj* soft coal; **producción hullera** soft-coal production

humanidad *nf* humanity; *Educ* **humanidades** humanities

humanismo *nm* humanism

humanista 1 *adj* humanist, humanistic

2 *nmf* humanist

humanístico, -a *adj* humanistic

humanitario, -a *adj* humanitarian

humanitarismo *nm* humanitarianism

humanización *nf* humanization, making more human

humanizar [14] **1** *vt* to humanize, to make more human

2 **humanizarse** *vpr* to become more human

humano, -a 1 *adj* (**a**) *(del hombre)* human (**b**) *(compasivo)* humane

2 *nm* human being; **los humanos** mankind

humareda *nf* cloud of smoke; **¡qué h.!** what a lot of smoke!, it's so smoky!

humazo *nm* cloud of smoke

humeante *adj (que echa humo)* smoking; *(que echa vapor)* steaming

humear *vi (salir humo)* to (give off) smoke; *(salir vapor)* to steam

humedad *nf* (**a**) *(de suelo, tierra)* dampness; *(de pared, techo)* damp; *(de piel, ojos)* moistness; **hay mucha h. en la casa** the house is very damp (**b**) *(de atmósfera)* humidity

humedal *nm* wetland

humedecer [46] **1** *vt* to moisten

2 **humedecerse** *vpr* to become moist; **humedecerse los labios** to moisten one's lips

humedecimiento *nm* moistening

húmedo, -a *adj* (**a**) *(suelo, tierra, casa)* damp; *(piel, ojos)* moist (**b**) *(aire, clima, atmósfera)* humid

húmero *nm Anat* humerus

humidificador *nm* humidifier

humidificar [59] *vt* to humidify

humildad *nf* humility

humilde *adj* humble

humillación *nf* humiliation

humillado, -a *adj* humiliated

humillante *adj* humiliating

humillar 1 *vt* to humiliate

2 **humillarse** *vpr* to humble oneself; **humillarse a hacer algo** *(rebajarse)* to lower oneself to do sth, to stoop to doing sth

humita *nf Chile (pajarita)* bow tie

humo *nm* (**a**) *(producto de combustión)* smoke; *(vapor)* steam; *(de vehículo)* fumes; *Fam Fig* **echar h.** to be fuming, to have smoke coming out of one's ears; *Fam* **se hizo h.** *(desapareció)* he made himself scarce (**b**) **humos** *Fam (soberbia)* **bajarle a alguien los humos** to take sb down a peg or two; **con esa derrota se les han bajado los humos** that defeat has brought them back down to earth; **darse humos** to give oneself airs

humor *nm* (**a**) *(estado de ánimo)* mood; *(carácter)* temperament; **estar de buen/mal h.** to be in a good/bad mood; **estar de un h. de perros** to be in a filthy mood (**b**) *(gracia)* humor; **un programa de h.** a comedy program; **no tiene sentido del h.** she doesn't have a sense of humor; **en vez de enfadarme, me lo tomé con h.** rather than get upset, I just laughed it off; **h. negro** black humor (**c**) *(ganas)* mood; **no estoy de h.** I'm not in the mood; **no está de h. para ponerse a cocinar** she doesn't feel like cooking (**d**) *Anat* humor

humorismo *nm (carácter burlón)* humor; *(en televisión, teatro)* comedy

humorista *nmf (persona burlona)* humorist; *(en televisión, teatro)* comedian, *f* comedienne

humorístico, -a *adj* humorous

humoso, -a *adj* smoky

humus *nm inv* humus

hundimiento *nm (de barco)* sinking; *(ruina)* collapse

hundir 1 *vt* (**a**) *(sumergir)* to sink; *(esconder, introducir)* to bury; **hundió el cuchillo en su espalda** she buried the knife in his back; **hundió los dedos en su cabello** he ran his fingers through her hair (**b**) *(afligir)* to devastate, to destroy; **el anuncio de su muerte hundió a la familia** his family was devastated by the news of his death (**c**) *(hacer fracasar)* to ruin

2 **hundirse** *vpr* (**a**) *(sumergirse)* to sink; *(intencionadamente)* to dive (**b**) *(derrumbarse)* to collapse; *(techo)* to cave in; *Fig* **el estadio se hundió tras el tercer gol del equipo** the stadium went wild after the team scored its third goal (**c**) *(afligirse)* to be devastated; **se hundió tras conocer su despido** he was devastated when he found out that he was being made redundant (**d**) *(fracasar)* to be ruined

húngaro, -a 1 *adj & nm,f* Hungarian

2 *nm (lengua)* Hungarian

Hungría *n* Hungary

huno, -a 1 *adj* Hunnish

2 *nm,f* Hun

huracán *nm* hurricane

huracanado, -a *adj Meteo (viento)* hurricane-force

huraño, -a *adj* unsociable

hurgar [38] **1** *vi (rebuscar)* to rummage around (**en** in); *(con dedo, palo)* to poke around (**en** in)

2 **hurgarse** *vpr* **hurgarse la nariz** to pick one's nose; **hurgarse los bolsillos** to rummage around in one's pockets

hurgón *nm* poker

hurgonear *vt* to poke

hurgue *etc ver* **hurgar**

Hurón *nm* **lago H.** Lake Huron

hurón *nm* (**a**) *(animal)* ferret (**b**) *(persona huraña)* unsociable person; *(persona fisgona)* busybody

hurra *interj* ¡**h.**! hurray!

hurtadillas: a hurtadillas *loc adv* on the sly, stealthily

hurtar *vt* to steal

hurto *nm* theft

húsar *nm Mil* hussar

husmeador, -ora *adj (perro)* sniffer; *(persona)* nosy, prying

husmear 1 *vt (olfatear)* to sniff out, to scent

2 *vi (curiosear)* to nose around

huso *nm (para hilar)* spindle; *(en máquina)* bobbin; **h. horario** time zone

huy *interj* ¡**h.**! *(dolor)* ouch!; *(sorpresa)* gosh!

huyera *etc ver* **huir**

huyo *etc ver* **huir**

I

I, i [i] *nf (letra)* I, i

IAE *nm (abrev de* **Impuesto sobre Actividades Econó-micas)** = Spanish tax paid by professionals and store owners

ib. *(abrev de* **ibídem**) ibid

iba *etc ver* **ir**

ibérico, -a *adj* Iberian

íbero, -a 1 *adj & nm,f* Iberian

   2 *nm (lengua)* Iberian

Iberoamérica *n* Latin America

iberoamericano, -a *adj & nm,f* Latin American

íbice *nm* ibex

ibicenco, -a 1 *adj* of/from Ibiza

   2 *nm,f* person from Ibiza

ibíd. *(abrev de* **ibídem**) ibid

ibídem, ibidem *adv* ibidem, ibid

ibis *nm inv* ibis

ice *etc ver* **izar**

iceberg [iθe'βer] *(pl* **icebergs)** *nm* iceberg

ICI ['iθi] *nm (abrev de* **Instituto de Cooperación Ibero-americana)** Institute for Latin American Cooperation

icónico, -a *adj* iconic

icono *nm* icon

iconoclasta 1 *adj* iconoclastic

   2 *nmf* iconoclast

iconografía *nf* iconography

iconográfico, -a *adj* iconographical

ictericia *nf* jaundice

ictiología *nf* ichthyology

ictus *nm Med* stroke

I+D ['imas'de] *(abrev de* **investigación y desarrollo)** R&D

id *ver* **ir**

id. *(abrev de* **ídem**) id, idem

ida *nf* (**a**) *(viaje)* outward journey; **el viaje de i. lo haremos de noche** we'll travel out there overnight; **a la i. fuimos en tren** we went by train on the way there; **(billete de) i. y vuelta** round-trip (ticket); *Fig* **idas y venidas** comings and goings (**b**) *Dep* **partido de i.** first leg

idea *nf* (**a**) *(concepto, ocurrencia)* idea; **buena/mala i.** good/bad idea; **hacerse una i. de algo** to get an idea of sth; **hacerse a la i. de que** to get used to the idea that; **no tengo ni i. (de)** I don't have a clue (about); *Esp Fig* **tener ideas de bombero** to have wild *o* crazy ideas; **tener i. de cómo hacer algo** to know how to do sth; **tener una ligera i.** to have a vague idea; **i. brillante** brilliant idea, brainwave; **i. fija** obsession; **ser una persona de ideas fijas** to be a person of fixed ideas

   (**b**) *(propósito)* intention; **con la i. de** with the idea *o* intention of; **tener i. de hacer algo** to intend to do sth; **a mala i.** maliciously

   (**c**) *(opinión)* impression; **cambiar de i.** to change one's mind; **ideas** *(ideología)* ideas

ideal *adj & nm* ideal

idealismo *nm* idealism

idealista 1 *adj* idealistic

   2 *nmf* idealist

idealización *nf* idealization

idealizar [14] *vt* to idealize

idear *vt* (**a**) *(planear)* to think up, to devise (**b**) *(inventar)* to invent

ideario *nm* ideology

ídem *pron* ditto; **i. de í.** *(lo mismo)* exactly the same; *(yo también)* same here

idéntico, -a *adj* identical (**a** to); **es i. a su abuelo** *(físicamente)* he's the image of his grandfather; *(en carácter)* he's exactly the same as his grandfather

identidad *nf* (**a**) *(de persona, pueblo)* identity (**b**) *(igualdad)* identical nature

identificador *nm Inform* indentifier; **i. de llamada** caller ID

identificación *nf* identification

identificar [59] **1** *vt* to identify

   2 identificarse *vpr* **identificarse con** *(persona, ideas)* to identify with; **¡identifíquese!** *(diga quién es)* identify yourself!; *(muestre una identificación)* show me some identification!

ideograma *nm* ideogram, ideograph

ideología *nf* ideology

ideológico, -a *adj* ideological

ideólogo, -a *nm,f* ideologist

idílico, -a *adj* idyllic

idilio *nm* love affair

idioma *nm* language

idiomático, -a *adj* idiomatic

idiosincrasia *nf* individual character

idiosincrático, -a *adj* characteristic

idiota 1 *adj* (**a**) *(tonto)* stupid (**b**) *(enfermo)* mentally deficient

   2 *nmf* idiot

idiotez *nf* (**a**) *(bobada)* stupid thing; *(bobería)* stupidity (**b**) *(enfermedad)* mental deficiency

idiotizar [14] *vt* to turn into an idiot, to zombify

ido, -a *adj* mad, touched

idólatra 1 *adj* idolatrous

   2 *nmf* idolater, *f* idolatress; *Fig* idolizer

idolatrar *vt (dios)* to worship; *Fig* to idolize

idolatría *nf (culto)* idolatry; *(admiración ciega)* worship, idolization

ídolo *nm* idol

idoneidad *nf* suitability

idóneo, -a *adj* suitable (**para** for)

iglesia *nf* church; **ir a la i.** to go to church; **con la i. hemos topado** now we're really up against it; **la i. anglicana** the Anglican Church; **i. parroquial** parish church

iglú *(pl* **iglúes)** *nm* igloo

ígneo, -a *adj* igneous

ignición *nf (de motor)* ignition; **la chispa provocó la i. del combustible** the spark ignited the fuel

ignífugo, -a *adj* fireproof, flameproof

ignominia *nf* ignominy

ignominioso, -a *adj* ignominious

ignorancia *nf* ignorance; **i. supina** blind ignorance

ignorante 1 *adj* ignorant; **i. de lo que ocurría** unaware of what was happening
  2 *nmf* ignoramus

ignorar *vt* (**a**) *(desconocer)* not to know, to be ignorant of (**b**) *(no tener en cuenta)* to ignore

ignoto, -a *adj* unknown, undiscovered

igual 1 *adj* (**a**) *(idéntico)* the same (**que** as); **llevan jerseys iguales** they're wearing the same sweater; **son iguales** they're the same; **tengo uno i. que el tuyo** I've got one just like yours; **es i. de grande que el mío** it's as big as mine, it's the same size as mine
  (**b**) *(parecido)* similar (**que** to); **de carácter son iguales** they have very similar characters
  (**c**) *(tal, semejante)* **nunca había visto cosa i.** I'd never seen the like of it
  (**d**) *(equivalente)* equal (**a** to)
  (**e**) *(liso)* even
  (**f**) *(constante) (velocidad)* constant; *(clima, temperatura)* even
  (**g**) *Mat* **A más B es i. a C** A plus B equals C
  (**h**) *Dep* **van iguales** the scores are tied
  2 *nmf* equal; **de i. a i.** as an equal; **sin i.** without equal, unrivaled
  3 *adv* (**a**) *(de la misma manera)* the same; **yo pienso i.** I think the same, I think so too; **es muy alto, al i. que su padre** he's very tall, just like his father; **baila i. que la Pavlova** she dances just like Pavlova; **por i.** equally (**b**) *Esp (posiblemente)* perhaps; **i. llueve** it could well rain; **con suerte, i. llego mañana** with a bit of luck I may arrive tomorrow (**c**) **dar** *o* **ser i. a alguien** *(no importar)* to be all the same to sb; **es** *o* **da i.** it doesn't matter, it doesn't make any difference; **me da i. lo que piense la gente** I don't care what people think

igualación *nf* (**a**) *(de terreno)* leveling; *(de superficie)* smoothing (**b**) *(de cantidades)* equalizing

igualado, -a *adj (terreno)* leveled, level; **de momento van igualados** they're even at the moment

igualar 1 *vt* (**a**) *(hacer igual)* to make equal, to equalize; *Dep* to equalize; **i. algo a** *o* **con** to equate sth with (**b**) *(persona)* to be equal to; **nadie la iguala en generosidad** nobody is as generous as she is (**c**) *(terreno)* to level; *(superficie)* to smooth
  2 igualarse *vpr (cosas diferentes)* to become equal; **igualarse a** *o* **con** *(otra persona, equipo)* to become equal with, to match

igualdad *nf* (**a**) *(equivalencia)* equality; **en i. de condiciones** on equal terms; **i. de derechos** equal rights; **i. de oportunidades** equal opportunities (**b**) *(identidad)* sameness

igualitario, -a *adj* egalitarian

igualitarismo *nm* egalitarianism

igualmente *adv* (**a**) *(también)* also, likewise (**b**) *(fórmula de cortesía)* the same to you, likewise

iguana *nf* iguana

Iguazú *n* **(las cataratas del) I.** the Iguaçu Falls

ijada *nf*, **ijar** *nm* flank, side

ikastola *nf* = primary school in the Basque country where classes are given entirely in Basque

ikurriña *nf* = Basque national flag

ilación *nf* cohesion

ilegal *adj* illegal

ilegalidad *nf* (**a**) *(acción)* unlawful act (**b**) *(cualidad)* illegality; **estar en la i.** to be illegal *o* outside the law

ilegalizar [14] *vt* to ban, to outlaw

ilegible *adj* illegible

ilegitimar *vt (logro)* to invalidate; **su pasado lo ilegitima para ser alcalde** his past makes him unfit to be mayor; **sus infidelidades ilegitiman sus celos** her infidelities deny her the right to be jealous

ilegitimidad *nf* illegitimacy

ilegítimo, -a *adj* illegitimate; **hijo i.** illegitimate child

ileso, -a *adj* unhurt, unharmed; **salir** *o* **resultar i.** to escape unharmed

iletrado, -a *adj & nm,f* illiterate

ilícito, -a *adj* illicit

ilimitado, -a *adj* unlimited, limitless; **poder i.** absolute power

ilocalizable *adj* **se encuentra i.** he cannot be found

ilógico, -a *adj* illogical

iluminación *nf* (**a**) *(luces) (gen)* & *Cine* & *Teatro* lighting; *(acción)* illumination (**b**) *Rel* enlightenment

iluminado, -a 1 *adj* (**a**) *(con luz)* lit (up) (**b**) *Rel* enlightened
  2 *nm,f Rel* enlightened person

iluminador, -ora 1 *adj* illuminating
  2 *nm,f* lighting technician

iluminar 1 *vt* (**a**) *(dar luz a)* to illuminate, to light up; **los focos que iluminan la iglesia** the floodlights which light up the church (**b**) *(adornar con luces)* to light up; **iluminan el castillo por la noche** the castle is lit up at night (**c**) *Rel* to enlighten
  2 *vi* to give light; **la lámpara ilumina muy poco** the lamp doesn't give much light
  3 iluminarse *vpr* (**a**) *(con luz)* to light up (**b**) *(de alegría)* **se le iluminó el rostro** his face lit up (**c**) *Rel* to become enlightened

ilusión *nf* (**a**) *(esperanza)* hope; **la i. de su vida es ir al espacio** his life's dream is to travel into space; **hacerse** *o* **forjarse ilusiones** to build up one's hopes; **no te hagas demasiadas ilusiones** don't get your hopes up too much; **no me hago muchas ilusiones de que me vayan a dar la beca** I'm not too optimistic about getting the grant
  (**b**) *Esp (emoción)* thrill, excitement; **la novia lleva los preparativos de la boda con i.** the bride is very excited about the preparations for the wedding; **¡qué i.!** how exciting!; **me hace mucha i. que vengas** I'm really delighted *o* thrilled that you're coming
  (**c**) *(infundada)* delusion, illusion; *(espejismo)* illusion; **i. óptica** optical illusion

ilusionar 1 *vt* (**a**) *(esperanzar)* **i. a alguien (con algo)** to build up sb's hopes (about sth) (**b**) *(emocionar)* to excite, to thrill
  2 ilusionarse *vpr* (**a**) *(esperanzarse)* to get one's hopes up (**con** about) (**b**) *(emocionarse)* to get excited (**con** about)

ilusionismo *nm* conjuring, magic

ilusionista *nmf* conjurer, magician

iluso, -a 1 *adj* naive
  2 *nm,f* naive person, dreamer

ilusorio, -a *adj* illusory; *(promesa)* empty

ilustración *nf* (**a**) *(estampa, dibujo)* illustration (**b**) *(cultura)* learning; **no tiene mucha i.** he doesn't have much education (**c**) *Hist* **la I.** the Enlightenment

ilustrado, -a *adj* (**a**) *(publicación)* illustrated (**b**) *(persona)* learned (**c**) *Hist* enlightened; **el despotismo i.** enlightened despotism

ilustrador, -ora 1 *adj* illustrative
  2 *nm,f* illustrator

ilustrar *vt* (**a**) *(explicar)* to illustrate, to explain; **i. algo con un ejemplo** to illustrate sth with an example (**b**) *(publicación)* to illustrate (**c**) *(educar)* to enlighten

ilustrativo, -a *adj* illustrative

ilustre *adj* (**a**) *(distinguido)* illustrious, distinguished (**b**) *(título)* **el i. señor alcalde** his Worship, the mayor

Ilustrísimo, -a 1 *adj* **el I. Ayuntamiento de Madrid** the City Council of Madrid

2 *nf* **Su Ilustrísima** Your/His Grace, Your/His Worship

imagen *nf* (**a**) *(figura)* image; **a i. y semejanza de** identical to, exactly the same as; **ser la viva i. de alguien** to be the spitting image of sb

(**b**) *TV* picture; **imágenes de archivo** archive pictures; **imágenes del partido/de la catástrofe** pictures of the game/of the disaster

(**c**) *(apariencia pública)* image; **los casos de corrupción han deteriorado la i. del gobierno** the corruption scandals have tainted the image of the government; **tener buena/mala i.** to have a good/bad image; **i. corporativa** *o* **de empresa** corporate image; **i. de marca** brand image

(**d**) *(estatua)* statue

(**e**) *Lit* image

imaginable *adj* imaginable, conceivable

imaginación *nf* (**a**) *(facultad)* imagination; **un niño con mucha i.** a child with a very vivid imagination, a very imaginative child; **pasar por la i. de alguien** to occur to sb, to cross sb's mind; **no me pasó por la i.** it never occurred to me; **se deja llevar por la i.** he lets his imagination run away with him (**b**) *(idea falsa)* **imaginaciones** delusions, imaginings; **son imaginaciones tuyas** you're just imagining things, it's all in your mind

imaginar 1 *vt* (**a**) *(suponer, visualizar)* to imagine; **imagino que te has enterado de la noticia** I imagine *o* suppose you've heard the news; **no puedes i. cuánto me enfadé** you can't imagine how angry I was (**b**) *(idear)* to think up, to invent

2 imaginarse *vpr* (**a**) *(suponer)* to imagine; **no te llamé porque me imaginé que estabas muy ocupada** I didn't call you because I thought you'd be very busy; **¡imagínate!** just think *o* imagine!; **me imagino que sí** I suppose so; *Fam* **¿te imaginas que viene?** what if he were to come? (**b**) *(visualizar)* to imagine, to picture; **no me lo imagino vestido de indio** I can't imagine *o* picture him dressed as an Indian

imaginaria *nf* *(guardia)* reserve guard, night guard; **estar de i.** to be on night-guard duty

imaginario, -a *adj* imaginary

imaginativo, -a *adj* imaginative

imaginería *nf* religious image-making

imán *nm* (**a**) *(para atraer)* magnet (**b**) *(entre musulmanes)* imam

imantación, imanación *nf* magnetization

imantar, imanar *vt* to magnetize

imbatible *adj* unbeatable

imbatido, -a *adj* unbeaten

imbebible *adj* undrinkable

imbécil 1 *adj* stupid

2 *nmf* idiot

imbecilidad *nf* stupidity; **decir/hacer una i.** to say/do something stupid

imberbe *adj* beardless

imborrable *adj* *(tinta)* indelible; *(recuerdo)* unforgettable

imbricación *nf* overlap

imbricado, -a *adj* overlapping

imbricar [59] *vt* to make overlap

imbuir [34] *vt* to imbue (**de** with)

imitación *nf* imitation; *(de humorista)* impersonation; **a i. de** in imitation of; **piel de i.** imitation leather

imitador, -ora *nm,f* imitator; *(humorista)* impersonator

imitamonas, imitamonos *nmf inv Fam* copycat

imitar *vt (copiar)* to imitate, to copy; *(a personajes famosos)* to impersonate; *(producto, material)* to simulate

imitativo, -a *adj* imitative

impaciencia *nf* impatience

impacientar 1 *vt* to make impatient, to exasperate

2 impacientarse *vpr* to grow impatient

impaciente *adj* impatient; **i. por hacer algo** impatient *o* anxious to do sth

impactante *adj* hard-hitting

impactar 1 *vt (sujeto: noticia)* to have an impact on

2 *vi (bala)* to hit

impacto *nm* (**a**) *(choque)* impact; *(de bala)* hit (**b**) *(señal)* (impact) mark; **i. de bala** bullet hole; **i. ambiental** environmental impact (**c**) *(impresión)* impact, strong impression; **causar un gran i. en alguien** to make a big impact *o* impression on sb

impagable *adj* invaluable

impagado, -a 1 *adj* unpaid

2 *nm* unpaid bill

impago, -a 1 *adj Am (salario, factura)* unpaid

2 *nm* nonpayment; **el i. de una factura** failure to pay a bill

impala *nm* impala

impalpable *adj* impalpable

impar *adj* (**a**) *(número)* odd (**b**) *(sin igual)* unequaled

imparable *adj* unstoppable

imparcial *adj* impartial

imparcialidad *nf* impartiality

impartir *vt* to give; **i. clases** to teach

impasibilidad *nf* impassivity

impasible *adj* impassive

impasse [im'pas] *nm* impasse

impavidez *nf* *(valor)* fearlessness, courage; *(impasibilidad)* impassivity

impávido, -a *adj* *(valeroso)* fearless, courageous; *(impasible)* impassive

impecable *adj* impeccable

impedancia *nf* impedance

impedido, -a 1 *adj* disabled; **estar i. de un brazo** to have the use of only one arm

2 *nm,f* disabled person

impedimenta *nf* baggage, appurtenances

impedimento *nm (obstáculo)* obstacle; *(para el matrimonio)* impediment; **no hay ningún i. para hacerlo** there's no reason why we shouldn't do it

impedir [47] *vt* (**a**) *(imposibilitar)* to prevent; **i. a alguien hacer algo** to prevent sb from doing sth; **la lesión le impedía correr** the injury stopped *o* prevented him from running; **la nieve impidió la celebración del partido** the snow prevented the game from taking place; **impedirle el paso a alguien** to bar sb's way; **si nada lo impide saldremos por la mañana** all being well we'll leave in the morning (**b**) *(dificultar)* to hinder, to obstruct

impeler *vt* (**a**) *(hacer avanzar)* to propel (**b**) *(incitar)* **i. a alguien a algo/hacer algo** to drive sb to sth/to do sth

impenetrabilidad *nf también Fig* impenetrability

impenetrable *adj también Fig* impenetrable

impenitencia *nf* impenitence

impenitente *adj (pecador)* unrepentant, impenitent; *Fig (incorregible)* inveterate

impensable *adj* unthinkable

impensado, -a *adj* unexpected

impepinable *adj Esp Fam (argumento)* undeniable, unanswerable; **¡eso es i.!** that's for sure!

imperante *adj* prevailing

imperar *vi* to prevail

imperativo, -a 1 *adj* (**a**) *(gen)* & *Gram* imperative (**b**) *(autoritario)* imperious

2 *nm (gen)* & *Gram* imperative

imperceptible *adj* imperceptible

imperdible *nm* safety pin

imperdonable *adj* unforgivable

imperecedero, -a *adj (producto)* nonperishable; *(eterno)* immortal, eternal

imperfección *nf* (**a**) *(cualidad)* imperfection (**b**) *(defecto)* flaw, defect

imperfecto, -a 1 *adj (no perfecto)* imperfect; *(defectuoso)* faulty, defective; *Gram* **pretérito i.** (past) imperfect
  2 *nm Gram* imperfect

imperial *adj* imperial

imperialismo *nm* imperialism

imperialista *adj & nmf* imperialist

impericia *nf (torpeza)* lack of skill; *(inexperiencia)* inexperience

imperio *nm* (**a**) *(territorio)* empire (**b**) *(dominio)* rule; **el i. de la ley** the rule of law; **valer un i.** to be worth a fortune (**c**) *(mandato)* emperorship

imperioso, -a *adj* (**a**) *(autoritario)* imperious (**b**) *(apremiante)* urgent, pressing

impermeabilidad *nf* impermeability

impermeabilización *nf* waterproofing

impermeabilizante *adj* waterproofing

impermeabilizar [14] *vt* to (make) waterproof

impermeable 1 *adj* waterproof
  2 *nm* raincoat

impersonal *adj* impersonal

impertérrito, -a *adj (impávido)* unperturbed, unmoved; *(ante peligros)* fearless

impertinencia *nf* (**a**) *(cualidad)* impertinence (**b**) *(comentario)* impertinent remark

impertinente 1 *adj* impertinent; **ponerse i.** to be impertinent *o* rude
  2 *nmf (persona)* impertinent person
  3 impertinentes *nmpl (anteojos)* lorgnette

imperturbabilidad *nf* imperturbability

imperturbable *adj* imperturbable

ímpetu *nm* (**a**) *(brusquedad)* force (**b**) *(energía)* energy; **perder í.** to lose momentum

impetuosidad *nf (precipitación)* impetuosity

impetuoso, -a 1 *adj* (**a**) *(olas, viento, ataque)* violent (**b**) *(persona)* impulsive, impetuous
  2 *nm,f* impulsive person

impidiera *etc ver* **impedir**

impido *etc ver* **impedir**

impío, -a *adj* godless, impious

implacable *adj* implacable, relentless

implantación *nf* (**a**) *(establecimiento)* introduction (**b**) *Biol* implantation (**c**) *Med* insertion

implantar 1 *vt* (**a**) *(establecer)* to introduce (**b**) *Med* to insert
  2 implantarse *vpr* (**a**) *(establecerse)* to be introduced (**b**) *Biol* to become implanted

implante *nm* implant

implementar *vt* to implement

implemento *nm* implement

implicación *nf* (**a**) *(participación)* involvement (**b**) **implicaciones** *(consecuencias)* implications

implicancia *nf CSur* implication

implicar [59] **1** *vt* (**a**) *(involucrar)* to involve (**en** in); *Der* to implicate (**en** in) (**b**) *(significar, suponer)* to mean, to imply
  2 implicarse *vpr Der* to incriminate oneself; **implicarse en** to become involved in

implícito, -a *adj* implicit

imploración *nf* entreaty, plea

implorar *vt* to implore

impoluto, -a *adj (superficie)* spotless; *(blanco)* pure; *(reputación)* unblemished

imponderabilidad *nf* imponderability

imponderable 1 *adj (incalculable)* invaluable; *(imprevisible)* imponderable
  2 *nm* imponderable

imponente *adj* (**a**) *(impresionante)* imposing, impressive (**b**) *Fam (estupendo)* sensational, terrific; **¡la profesora está i.!** the teacher is a stunner!

imponer [50] **1** *vt* (**a**) **i. algo (a alguien)** *(forzar a aceptar)* to impose sth (on sb); **i. respeto** to command respect; **el profesor impuso silencio en la clase** the teacher silenced the class (**b**) *(moda)* to set; *(costumbre)* to introduce
  2 *vi* to be imposing
  3 imponerse *vpr* (**a**) *(hacerse respetar)* to command respect, to show authority (**b**) *(prevalecer)* to prevail (**c**) *(asumir)* *(obligación, tarea)* to take on (**d**) *(ser necesario)* to be necessary (**e**) *Dep* to win, to prevail

imponible *adj Fin* **base i.** taxable income

impopular *adj* unpopular

impopularidad *nf* unpopularity

importación *nf (acción)* importing; *(artículo)* import; **de i.** imported

importado, -a *adj* imported

importador, -ora 1 *adj* importing; **empresa importadora** importer, importing company
  2 *nm,f* importer

importancia *nf* importance; **dar i. a algo** to attach importance to sth; **darse i.** to give oneself airs; **de i.** important, of importance; **no tiene i.** *(no es importante)* it's not important; *(no pasa nada)* it doesn't matter; **sin i.** unimportant; **quitar i. a algo** to play sth down

importante *adj* (**a**) *(destacado, significativo)* important; *(lesión)* serious (**b**) *(cantidad)* considerable

importar 1 *vt* (**a**) *(productos) & Inform* to import (**b**) *(sujeto: factura, coste)* to amount to, to come to
  2 *vi* (**a**) *(preocupar, tener interés)* to matter; **ya no te importo — al contrario, sí que me importas** you don't care about me anymore — on the contrary, you do matter to me; **no me importa lo que piense la gente** I don't care what people think
  (**b**) *(ser importante)* to matter; **lo que importa es que...** what matters *o* the important thing is that...; **no importa** it doesn't matter; **¡qué importa que llueva!** so what if it's raining?
  (**c**) *(incumbir, afectar)* **¡no te importa!** it's none of your business!; **¿a mí qué me importa?** what's that to me?, what do I care?; **¿y a ti qué te importa?** what's it got to do with you?; *Fam* **me importa un bledo** *o* **comino** *o* **pito** I don't give a damn, I couldn't care less
  (**d**) *(molestar)* to mind; **no me importa que venga tu familia** I don't mind if your family comes; **preferiría no salir, si no te importa** I'd rather not go out, if you don't mind *o* if it's all the same to you; **¿le importa que me siente?** do you mind if I sit down?

importe *nm (precio)* price, cost; *(de factura)* total; **i. total** total cost

importunar 1 *vt* to bother, to pester
  2 *vi* to be tiresome *o* a nuisance

importuno, -a *adj* (**a**) *(en mal momento)* inopportune, untimely (**b**) *(molesto)* inconvenient (**c**) *(inadecuado)* inappropriate

imposibilidad *nf* impossibility; **su i. para contestar la pregunta** his inability to answer the question; **i. física** *o* **material** physical impossibility

imposibilitado, -a *adj* disabled; **estar i. para hacer algo** to be unable to do sth

imposibilitar *vt* **i. a alguien (para) hacer algo** to make it impossible for sb to do sth, to prevent sb from doing sth

imposible 1 *adj* (**a**) *(irrealizable)* impossible; **es i. de**

arreglar it's impossible to fix, it can't be fixed; **es i. que se lo haya dicho** he can't possibly have told her; **nos fue i. ir** we were unable to go; **hacer lo i.** to do everything possible and more (**b**) *Fam (insoportable)* unbearable, impossible; **el tráfico en el centro estaba i.** the traffic in the center was impossible *o* a nightmare

   2 *nm* **pedir imposibles** to ask for the impossible

imposición *nf* (**a**) *(obligación)* imposition (**b**) *(impuesto)* tax; **doble i.** double taxation (**c**) *Fin* deposit; **hacer** *o* **efectuar una i.** to make a deposit (**d**) **i. de manos** laying on of hands

impositivo, -a *adj* tax; **política impositiva** tax *o* taxation policy

impostar *vt (la voz)* to make resonate

impostergable *adj* (extremely) urgent, impossible to postpone

impostor, -ora 1 *adj (suplantador)* fraudulent

   2 *nm,f (suplantador)* impostor

impostura *nf* (**a**) *(suplantación)* fraud (**b**) *(calumnia)* slander

impotencia *nf* impotence

impotente 1 *adj* impotent

   2 *nm* impotent man

impracticable *adj* (**a**) *(irrealizable)* impracticable (**b**) *(intransitable)* impassable

imprecación *nf* imprecation

imprecar [59] *vt* to imprecate

imprecatorio, -a *adj* imprecatory

imprecisión *nf* imprecision, vagueness; **contestó con imprecisiones** he gave vague answers

impreciso, -a *adj* imprecise, vague

impredecible *adj (inesperado)* unforeseeable; *(imprevisible)* unpredictable

impregnar 1 *vt* to impregnate (**de** with)

   2 impregnarse *vpr* to become impregnated (**de** with)

impremeditación *nf* lack of premeditation

impremeditado, -a *adj* unpremeditated

imprenta *nf* (**a**) *(máquina)* (printing) press (**b**) *(establecimiento)* printing house

imprescindible *adj* indispensable, essential

impresentable 1 *adj* unpresentable

   2 *nmf* **es un i.** he's a disgrace

impresión *nf* (**a**) *(efecto)* impression; **causar (una) buena/mala i.** to make a good/bad impression; **dar la i. de** to give the impression of; **me dio la i. de que estaban enfadados** I got the impression they were annoyed; **le dio mucha i. ver el cadáver** seeing the body was a real shock to him (**b**) *(opinión)* **me gustaría conocer tu i. del tema** I'd like to know what your thoughts are on the issue; **cambiar impresiones** to compare notes, to exchange views (**c**) *(huella)* imprint; **i. digital** *o* **dactilar** fingerprint (**d**) *Imprenta (acción)* printing; *(edición)* edition

impresionable *adj* impressionable

impresionante *adj (asombroso, extraordinario)* amazing, astonishing; *(maravilloso)* impressive; *(grande)* enormous

impresionar 1 *vt* (**a**) *(maravillar)* to impress; *(emocionar)* to move; *(conmocionar, horrorizar)* to shock (**b**) *Fot* to expose

   2 *vi (maravillar)* to make an impression; *(emocionar)* to be moving; *(conmocionar, horrorizar)* to be shocking

   3 impresionarse *vpr (maravillarse)* to be impressed; *(emocionarse)* to be moved; *(conmocionarse, horrorizarse)* to be shocked

impresionismo *nm* impressionism

impresionista *adj & nmf* impressionist

impreso, -a 1 *participio ver* **imprimir**

   2 *adj* printed

   3 *nm* (**a**) *(texto)* printed sheet; **impresos** *(en sobre)* printed matter (**b**) *(formulario)* form; **i. de inscripción** entry form; **i. de solicitud** application form

impresor, -ora *nm,f (persona)* printer

impresora *nf Inform* printer; **i. de chorro de tinta** ink-jet printer; **i. láser** laser printer; **i. matricial** *o* **de agujas** dot matrix printer; **i. térmica** thermal printer

imprevisible *adj (inesperado)* unforeseeable; *(impredecible)* unpredictable; **el tiempo aquí es muy i.** the weather here is very unpredictable; **una persona i.** an unpredictable person

imprevisión *nf* lack of foresight

imprevisto, -a 1 *adj* unexpected

   2 *nm (hecho)* unforeseen circumstance; **salvo imprevistos** barring accidents; **imprevistos** *(gastos)* unforeseen expenses

imprimir 1 *vt* (**a**) *(libro, documento)* to print; *(huella, paso)* to leave, to make (**b**) *(dar)* **el atleta mexicano imprimió un ritmo endiablado a la carrera** the Mexican athlete set a fiendish pace in the race; **sus dibujos imprimen carácter al libro** her illustrations lend character to the book; **i. velocidad a algo** to speed sth up

   2 *vi* to print

improbabilidad *nf* improbability, unlikelihood

improbable *adj* improbable, unlikely

ímprobo, -a *adj Formal (trabajo, esfuerzo)* Herculean, strenuous

improcedencia *nf* (**a**) *(desacierto)* inappropriateness (**b**) *Der* inadmissibility

improcedente *adj* (**a**) *(inoportuno)* inappropriate (**b**) *Der* inadmissible

improductivo, -a *adj* unproductive

impromptu *nm Mús* impromptu

impronta *nf* mark, impression; **llevar la i. de** to have the hallmarks of

impronunciable *adj* unpronounceable

improperio *nm* insult; **lanzar improperios** to hurl insults

impropiedad *nf* impropriety

impropio, -a *adj* improper (**de** for), unbecoming (**de** to)

improrrogable *adj (plazo)* unextendable; **durante seis días improrrogables** for six days only; **la fecha es i.** the deadline is final

improvisación *nf* improvisation

improvisado, -a *adj (comida, actuación artística)* improvised; *(discurso)* impromptu; *(comentario)* ad-lib; *(cama, refugio)* makeshift

improvisar 1 *vt (discurso, plan)* to improvise; *(comida)* to rustle up, to improvise; **i. una cama** to make (up) a makeshift bed

   2 *vi (músico, orador)* to improvise; *(actor)* to ad-lib

improviso: de improviso *loc adv* unexpectedly, suddenly; **coger a alguien de i.** to catch sb unawares

imprudencia *nf* (**a**) *(falta de prudencia) (en los actos)* carelessness, recklessness; *(en los comentarios)* indiscretion; *Der* **i. temeraria** criminal negligence (**b**) *(acción)* careless *o* reckless act, indiscretion; *(dicho indiscreto)* tactless remark, indiscretion; *(dicho desacertado)* foolish *o* reckless remark

imprudente 1 *adj (en los actos)* careless, rash; *(en los comentarios)* indiscreet; **es muy i.** *(al conducir)* he's a reckless driver

   2 *nmf (en los actos)* rash *o* reckless person; *(en los comentarios)* indiscreet person

impúber 1 *adj* prepubescent

   2 *nmf* prepubescent child

impudicia *nf* immodesty

impúdico, -a *adj* immodest, indecent

impudor *nm* immodesty

impuesto, -a 1 *participio ver* **imponer**

   2 *nm* tax; **i. sobre el capital** capital tax; **i. de circulación** road tax; **i. al consumo** tax on the consumer; **i. directo** direct tax; **i. ecológico** ecotax; **i. indirecto** indirect tax; **i. de lujo** luxury tax; **i. municipal** local tax; **i. sobre el**

patrimonio property tax; **i. sobre las plusvalías** capital gains tax; **i. sobre la renta** income tax; **i. revolucionario** revolutionary tax, = protection money paid by businessmen to terrorists; **i. de sociedades** corporation tax; **i. sobre sucesiones** inheritance tax; *Am* **i. al valor agregado**, *Esp* **i. sobre el valor añadido** value-added tax, $\simeq$ sales tax

impugnable *adj* contestable

impugnación *nf* contestation, challenge

impugnar *vt* to contest, to challenge

impulsar *vt* (**a**) *(empujar)* to propel, to drive (**b**) *(incitar)* **i. a alguien (a algo/a hacer algo)** to drive sb (to sth/to do sth) (**c**) *(promocionar) (economía)* to stimulate; *(amistad)* to foster; **i. las relaciones Norte-Sur** to promote North-South relations; **las claves que impulsan el sector** the key drivers for the industry

impulsividad *nf* impulsiveness

impulsivo, -a 1 *adj* impulsive

    2 *nm,f* impulsive person, hothead

impulso *nm* (**a**) *Fís* impulse (**b**) *(empuje)* momentum; **tomar i.** to take a run-up (**c**) *(estímulo)* stimulus, boost; **la medida supondrá un i. al consumo** the measure will boost consumption; **dar i. a una iniciativa** to encourage *o* promote an initiative (**d**) *(deseo, motivación)* impulse, urge; **un i. me hizo gritar** a sudden impulse made me shout; **mi primer i. fue marcharme** my first instinct was to leave; **se deja llevar por sus impulsos** he acts on impulse

impulsor, -ora 1 *adj* driving; **fuerza impulsora** driving force

    2 *nm,f* dynamic force; **él fue el i. del proyecto** he was the driving force behind the project

impune *adj* unpunished; **quedar i.** to go unpunished

impunemente *adv* with impunity

impunidad *nf* impunity

impuntual *adj* unpunctual

impuntualidad *nf* unpunctuality

impureza *nf* impurity

impuro, -a *adj también Fig* impure

impusiera *etc ver* **imponer**

imputabilidad *nf* imputability

imputable *adj* attributable (**a** to)

imputación *nf* accusation

imputar *vt* (**a**) *(atribuir)* **i. algo a alguien** *(delito)* to accuse sb of sth; *(fracaso, error)* to attribute sth to sb (**b**) *Com* to allocate, to assign

inabarcable *adj* **un concepto i.** a concept which is difficult to grasp

inabordable *adj* inaccessible

inacabable *adj* interminable, endless

inacabado, -a *adj* unfinished

inaccesible *adj* inaccessible

inacción *nf* inaction, inactivity

inaceptable *adj* unacceptable

inactividad *nf* inactivity

inactivo, -a *adj* inactive

inadaptación *nf* maladjustment

inadaptado, -a 1 *adj* maladjusted

    2 *nm,f* misfit

inadecuado, -a *adj (inapropiado)* unsuitable, inappropriate

inadmisible *adj* inadmissible

inadvertido, -a *adj* unnoticed; **pasar i.** to go unnoticed

inagotable *adj* inexhaustible

inaguantable *adj* unbearable

inalámbrico, -a *adj* cordless; *Inform* wireless

in albis *adv* in the dark; **quedarse i.** to be left none the wiser

inalcanzable *adj* unattainable, beyond reach

inalienable *adj* inalienable

inalterable *adj* (**a**) *(salud)* stable; *(amistad)* undying; *(principios)* unshakable; *(decision)* final; **permanecer i.** to remain unchanged (**b**) *(color)* fast (**c**) *(rostro, carácter)* impassive (**d**) *Dep* **el marcador permanece i.** the score remains unchanged

inalterado, -a *adj* unaltered, unchanged

inamovible *adj* immovable, fixed

inane *adj Formal* inane

inanición *nf* starvation; **morir de i.** to die of starvation, to starve to death

inanimado, -a *adj* inanimate

inánime *adj* lifeless

inapagable *adj* inextinguishable

inapelable *adj* (**a**) *Der* not open to appeal (**b**) *(inevitable)* inevitable

inapetencia *nf* lack of appetite

inapetente *adj* lacking in appetite; **estar i.** to have no appetite

inaplazable *adj (reunión, sesión)* that cannot be postponed; *(necesidad)* urgent, pressing

inaplicable *adj* inapplicable, not applicable

inapreciable *adj* (**a**) *(incalculable)* invaluable, inestimable (**b**) *(insignificante)* imperceptible

inapropiado, -a *adj* inappropriate, unsuitable

inarrugable *adj* crease-resistant

inasequible *adj* (**a**) *(por el precio)* prohibitive (**b**) *(inalcanzable)* *(meta, ambición)* unattainable; *(persona)* unapproachable

inastillable *adj* shatterproof

inatacable *adj (fortaleza, país)* unassailable; *(argumento)* irrefutable

inaudible *adj* inaudible

inaudito, -a *adj* unheard-of

inauguración *nf (de edificio, puente, Juegos Olímpicos)* official opening, opening (ceremony); *(de congreso)* opening session

inaugural *adj* opening, inaugural

inaugurar *vt (edificio, congreso)* to (officially) open; *(año académico, época)* to mark the beginning of, to inaugurate; *(estatua)* to unveil

inca *adj & nmf* Inca

incaico, -a *adj* Inca

incalculable *adj* incalculable; **de i. valor** priceless; *Fig* of inestimable value

incalificable *adj* unspeakable, indescribable

incandescencia *nf* incandescence

incandescente *adj* incandescent

incansable *adj* untiring, tireless

incapacidad *nf* (**a**) *(imposibilidad)* inability (**b**) *(falta de aptitud)* incompetence (**c**) *Der* incapacity; **i. laboral** industrial disability

incapacitado, -a 1 *adj Der (para ejercer cargos, votar)* disqualified (**para** from); *(para testar, testificar)* incapacitated; *(para trabajar)* unfit

    2 *nm,f Der* disqualified person, person declared unfit

incapacitar *vt* (**a**) *(sujeto: circunstancias) (para ejercer cargos, votar)* to disqualify (**para** from); *(para trabajar)* to render unfit (**para** for) (**b**) *(sujeto: juez) (para ejercer cargos, votar)* to disqualify (**para** from), to declare disqualified (**para** from); *(para trabajar)* to declare unfit (**para** for *o* to)

incapaz *adj* (**a**) *(no capaz)* incapable (**de** of); **fuimos incapaces de alcanzar la cumbre** we weren't able to *o* didn't manage to reach the top; **es i. de hacer una suma sin equivocarse** he can't do the simplest sum without making a mistake; **es i. de hacer daño a nadie** he would never harm anyone (**b**) *(sin talento)* **i. para** incompetent at, no good at; **soy i. para las sumas** I'm no good at *o* useless at arithmetic problems (**c**) *Der* **declarar i. a alguien** to declare sb incapable *o* unfit

incautación *nf* seizure, confiscation

incautarse *vpr* (**a**) *Der* **i. de** to seize, to confiscate (**b**) *(apoderarse)* **i. de** to grab

incauto, -a 1 *adj* gullible, naive
  2 *nm,f* gullible *o* naive person

incendiar 1 *vt* to set fire to
  2 incendiarse *vpr* to catch fire; **se ha incendiado el bosque** the forest has caught fire *o* is on fire

incendiario, -a 1 *adj (bomba)* incendiary; *(artículo, libro)* inflammatory
  2 *nm,f* arsonist

incendio *nm* fire; **i. forestal** forest fire; **un i. provocado** a case of arson

incensario *nm* censer

incentivar *vt* to encourage

incentivo *nm* incentive; **i. fiscal** tax incentive

incertidumbre *nf* uncertainty

incesante *adj* incessant, ceaseless

incesto *nm* incest

incestuoso, -a *adj* incestuous

incidencia *nf* (**a**) *(repercusión)* impact, effect (**b**) *(suceso)* event; **el viaje transcurrió sin incidencias** the journey passed without incident

incidental *adj* incidental

incidente 1 *adj (luz, rayo)* incident
  2 *nm* incident; **el viaje transcurrió sin incidentes** the journey passed without incident

incidir *vi* **i. en** *(incurrir en)* to fall into, to lapse into; *(insistir en)* to focus on; *(influir en)* to have an impact on, to affect

incienso *nm* incense; **oro, i. y mirra** gold, frankincense and myrrh

incierto, -a *adj* (**a**) *(dudoso)* uncertain (**b**) *(falso)* untrue

incineración *nf (de cadáver)* cremation; *(de basura)* incineration

incinerador *nm (de basura)* incinerator

incinerar *vt (cadáver)* to cremate; *(basura)* to incinerate

incipiente *adj (inicial)* incipient; **una democracia i.** a fledgling democracy; **una amistad i.** a budding friendship

incisión *nf* incision

incisivo, -a 1 *adj* (**a**) *(instrumento)* sharp, cutting (**b**) *(mordaz)* incisive (**c**) *(diente)* incisive
  2 *nm (diente)* incisor

inciso, -a *nm (corto)* comment, passing remark; *(más largo)* digression

incitación *nf* incitement

incitante *adj (insinuante)* provocative; *(interesante)* enticing

incitar *vt (a la violencia)* to incite; **el hambre le incitó a robar** hunger made him steal; **¿qué le incitó a hacerlo?** what made him do it?

incivil *adj* uncivil

incivilizado, -a *adj* uncivilized

inclasificable *adj* unclassifiable

inclemencia *nf* harshness, inclemency; **las inclemencias del tiempo** the inclemency of the weather

inclemente *adj* harsh, inclement

inclinación *nf* (**a**) *(desviación)* slant, inclination; *(de terreno)* slope (**b**) *(afición)* penchant *o* propensity (**a** *o* **por** for); **tiene una i. natural por la música** she has a natural bent for music (**c**) *(cariño)* **i. hacia alguien** fondness toward sb (**d**) *(saludo)* bow; **nos saludó con una i. de cabeza** he greeted us with a nod

inclinado, -a *adj* (**a**) *(terreno)* sloping (**b**) *(cabeza)* bowed; *(objeto)* sloping, at *o* on a slant

inclinar 1 *vt* (**a**) *(doblar)* to bend; *(cabeza)* to bow; *(ladear)* to

tilt; *Fig* **i. la balanza a favor de** to tip the balance in favor of (**b**) *(influir)* **i. a alguien a hacer algo** to persuade sb to do sth
  2 inclinarse *vpr* (**a**) *(doblarse)* to lean; **la grúa se está inclinando peligrosamente** the crane is leaning *o* tilting dangerously; **inclínate hacia adelante** lean forward; *Fig* **la balanza se inclinó a nuestro favor** the balance tipped in our favor (**b**) *(para saludar)* to bow (**ante** before) (**c**) *(tender)* to be *o* feel inclined (**a** to); **me inclino a pensar que no** I'm rather inclined to think not (**d**) *(preferir)* **inclinarse por** to favor, to lean toward

ínclito, -a *adj Formal* illustrious

incluido, -a *adj (franqueo, servicio)* included; **IVA i.** inclusive of VAT; **hasta el 31 de diciembre i.** up to and including December 31

incluir [34] *vt (comprender)* to include; *(adjuntar)* to enclose; **el precio incluye desayuno y cena en el hotel** the price includes breakfast and evening meals at the hotel; **te he incluido en la lista de participantes** I've included *o* put you on the list of participants; **a mí no me incluyas** count me out

inclusa *nf* foundling hospital

inclusión *nf* inclusion

inclusive *adv* inclusive

incluso 1 *adv* even; **me gustó i. a mí** even I liked it; **la comida de ayer estaba buena, la de hoy, mejor i.** yesterday's meal was good, and today's was even better
  2 *prep* even; **todos, i. tú, debemos ayudar** we must all help, even you

incoar *vt* to commence, to initiate

incobrable *adj* irrecoverable

incógnita *nf* (**a**) *Mat* unknown (quantity) (**b**) *(misterio)* mystery

incógnito, -a *adj* unknown; **viajar/estar de i.** to travel/be incognito

incoherencia *nf* (**a**) *(cualidad)* incoherence (**b**) *(comentario)* nonsensical remark

incoherente *adj* (**a**) *(inconexo)* incoherent (**b**) *(inconsecuente)* inconsistent

incoloro, -a *adj también Fig* colorless

incólume *adj Formal* unscathed

incombustible *adj* fire-resistant

incomestible, incomible *adj* inedible

incomodar 1 *vt* (**a**) *(causar molestia)* to bother, to inconvenience (**b**) *(enfadar)* to annoy
  2 incomodarse *vpr (enfadarse)* to get annoyed (**por** about)

incomodidad *nf* (**a**) *(de silla)* uncomfortableness (**b**) *(de situación, persona)* awkwardness, discomfort

incómodo, -a *adj* (**a**) *(silla, postura)* uncomfortable (**b**) *(situación)* awkward, uncomfortable; **una pregunta incómoda** an awkward question; **me resulta i. hablar con ella de estos temas** I find it embarrassing *o* I feel uncomfortable talking to her about these matters; **sentirse i.** to feel awkward *o* uncomfortable

incomparable *adj* incomparable

incomparecencia *nf* failure to appear (in court)

incompatibilidad *nf* incompatibility; *Der* **i. de caracteres** incompatibility

incompatible *adj* incompatible (**con** with)

incompetencia *nf* incompetence

incompetente *adj* incompetent

incompleto, -a *adj* (**a**) *(falto de una parte)* incomplete (**b**) *(inacabado)* unfinished

incomprendido, -a 1 *adj* misunderstood
  2 *nm,f* misunderstood person; **fue siempre un i.** no one ever understood him

incomprensible *adj* incomprehensible

incomprensión *nf* lack of understanding

incomunicación *nf* (**a**) *(falta de comunicación)* lack of communication (**b**) *(de detenido)* solitary confinement (**c**) *(de una localidad)* isolation

incomunicado, -a *adj* **estar i.** *(sin líneas de comunicación)* to be isolated; *(por la nieve)* to be cut off; *(preso)* to be in solitary confinement; *(detenido)* to be held incommunicado

incomunicar [59] *vt (dejar sin líneas de comunicación)* to keep isolated; *(sujeto: la nieve)* to cut off; *(preso)* to place in solitary confinement; *(detenido)* to hold incommunicado

inconcebible *adj* inconceivable

inconcluso, -a *adj* unfinished

inconcreto, -a *adj* vague, imprecise

incondicional 1 *adj (rendición, perdón)* unconditional; *(ayuda)* wholehearted; *(seguidor)* staunch

    2 *nmf* staunch supporter

inconexo, -a *adj (parte)* unconnected; *(pensamiento, texto)* disjointed

inconfesable *adj* shameful

inconformismo *nm* nonconformism

inconformista *adj & nmf* nonconformist

inconfundible *adj* unmistakable

incongruencia *nf (cualidad)* inconsistency; **hacer/decir una i.** *(algo fuera de lugar)* to do/say sth incongruous; *(algo absurdo)* to do/say sth crazy *o* illogical; **lleno de incongruencias** *(relato, libro)* full of inconsistencies

incongruente *adj (fuera de lugar)* incongruous; *(desarti-culado)* inconsistent; *(absurdo)* crazy, illogical

inconmensurable *adj (enorme)* vast, immense

inconmovible *adj* unshakable, unyielding

inconquistable *adj* unassailable, impregnable

inconsciencia *nf* (**a**) *(aturdimiento, desmayo)* unconscious-ness (**b**) *(falta de juicio)* thoughtlessness

inconsciente 1 *adj* (**a**) *(sin conocimiento)* unconscious; **estar i.** to be unconscious; **un acto i.** an unconscious action (**b**) *(irreflexivo)* thoughtless, reckless

    2 *nmf* thoughtless *o* reckless person

    3 *nm Psi* **el i.** the unconscious

inconscientemente *adv (sin darse cuenta)* unconsciously, unwittingly

inconsecuencia *nf* inconsistency

inconsecuente 1 *adj* inconsistent

    2 *nmf* inconsistent person

inconsistencia *nf* flimsiness

inconsistente *adj* flimsy, insubstantial

inconsolable *adj* inconsolable

inconstancia *nf* (**a**) *(en el trabajo, la conducta)* unreliability (**b**) *(de opinión, ideas)* changeability

inconstante *adj* (**a**) *(en el trabajo)* **es muy i.** he never sticks at anything (**b**) *(de opinión, ideas)* changeable, fickle

inconstitucional *adj* unconstitutional

inconstitucionalidad *nf* unconstitutionality

incontable *adj (innumerable)* countless, innumerable

incontaminado, -a *adj* uncontaminated, unpolluted

incontenible *adj (alegría)* unbounded; *(llanto)* uncontrol-lable

incontestable *adj* indisputable, undeniable

incontinencia *nf* (**a**) *(vicio)* lack of restraint (**b**) *Med* incontinence

incontinente *adj* (**a**) *(insaciable)* lacking all restraint (**b**) *Med* incontinent

incontrolable *adj* uncontrollable

incontrolado, -a *adj (velocidad)* furious; *(situación)* out of hand; *(comando)* maverick, not controlled by the leadership; *(aumento de precios)* spiraling

incontrovertible *adj* incontrovertible, indisputable

inconveniencia *nf* (**a**) *(inoportunidad)* inappropriateness (**b**) *(comentario)* tactless remark; *(acto)* faux pas, mistake

inconveniente 1 *adj* inappropriate

    2 *nm* (**a**) *(dificultad)* obstacle, problem; *(objeción)* objection; **han puesto inconvenientes a su nombramiento** they have raised objections to his appointment; **no tener i. en hacer algo** to have no objection to doing sth; **si no tienes i., me voy a marchar** if you don't mind *o* if it's all right by you, I'll leave (**b**) *(desventaja)* disadvantage, drawback; **tiene el i. de que es muy caro** it suffers from the disadvantage *o* drawback of being very expensive

incordiar *vt Esp Fam* to bother, to pester

incordio *nm Esp Fam* pain, nuisance

incorporación *nf (unión, adición)* incorporation (**a** into); **su i. tendrá lugar el día 31** *(a un puesto)* she starts work on the 31st

incorporado, -a *adj Mec* built-in; **llevar** *o* **tener algo i.** to have sth built in

incorporar 1 *vt* (**a**) *(añadir)* to incorporate (**a** into); *Culin* to mix (**a** into); **incorporaron los territorios al imperio** the territories became part of the empire (**b**) *(levantar)* **i. a alguien** to sit sb up

    2 incorporarse *vpr* (**a**) *(unirse) (a equipo)* to join; *(a trabajo)* to start; **incorporarse a filas** to start one's military service (**b**) *(levantarse)* to sit up

incorpóreo, -a *adj* incorporeal, intangible

incorrección *nf* (**a**) *(falta de corrección)* incorrectness; *(error gramatical)* mistake (**b**) *(descortesía)* lack of courtesy, rudeness

incorrecto, -a *adj* (**a**) *(equivocado)* incorrect, wrong (**b**) *(descortés)* rude, impolite

incorregible *adj* incorrigible

incorruptible *adj (substancia)* imperishable; *(persona)* incorruptible

incorrupto, -a *adj (cadáver)* uncorrupted, not decomposed

incredulidad *nf* incredulity

incrédulo, -a 1 *adj* skeptical, incredulous; *Rel* unbelieving

    2 *nm,f* unbeliever

increíble *adj (inconcebible)* unbelievable; *(extraordinario)* incredible; **es i. que pasen cosas así** it's hard to believe that such things can happen

incrementar 1 *vt* to increase

    2 incrementarse *vpr* to increase

incremento *nm (de precios, actividad)* increase; *(de temperatura)* rise

increpar *vt* (**a**) *(reprender)* to reprimand (**b**) *(insultar)* to abuse, to insult

incriminación *nf* accusation

incriminar *vt* to accuse

incriminatorio, -a *adj* incriminating

incruento, -a *adj* bloodless

incrustación *nf* inlay; **un marco con incrustaciones de oro** a frame with a gold inlay *o* inlaid with gold

incrustado, -a *adj* (**a**) *(encajado)* **i. en** fixed into (**b**) **con rubíes incrustados** inlaid with rubies (**c**) *(periodista)* embedded

incrustar 1 *vt (introducir, empotrar)* **i. nácar en la madera** to inlay the wood with mother-of-pearl; *Fam Fig* **me incrustó un codo en el costado** he jabbed *o* rammed his elbow into my ribs

    2 incrustarse *vpr (introducirse, empotrarse)* **la bala se incrustó en el hueso/muro** the bullet embedded itself in the bone/wall; **el coche se incrustó en el muro** the car plowed into the wall; **la cal se había incrustado en las tuberías** the pipes had become scaled

incubación *nf (de huevos, enfermedad)* incubation; **periodo de i.** *(de enfermedad)* incubation period; **i. artificial** artificial incubation

incubadora *nf* incubator

incubar *vt* (**a**) *(huevo)* to incubate (**b**) *(enfermedad)* to be sickening for

incuestionable *adj* *(teoría, razón)* irrefutable; *(deber)* bounden

inculcar [59] *vt* **i. algo a alguien** to instill sth into sb

inculpación *nf* accusation; *Der* charge

inculpado, -a 1 *adj* accused; *Der* charged
2 *nm,f* accused

inculpar *vt (acusar)* to accuse (**de** of); *Der* to charge (**de** with); **todas las pruebas le inculpan** all the evidence points to his guilt

incultivable *adj* uncultivable, unfit for cultivation

inculto, -a 1 *adj* (**a**) *(persona)* uneducated (**b**) *(tierra)* uncultivated
2 *nm,f* ignoramus

incultura *nf* lack of education

incumbencia *nf* **es/no es de nuestra i.** it is/isn't a matter for us, it falls/doesn't fall within our area of responsibility; **no es asunto de tu i.** it's none of your business

incumbir *vi* **i. a alguien** to be a matter for sb, to be within sb's area of responsibility; **esto no te incumbe** this is none of your business

incumplimiento *nm (de deber, obligación)* failure to fulfill; *(de orden, ley)* noncompliance; *(de promesa)* failure to keep; **i. de contrato** breach of contract

incumplir *vt (deber)* to fail to fulfill, to neglect; *(orden, ley)* to fail to comply with; *(promesa)* to break; *(contrato)* to breach

incunable 1 *adj* incunabular
2 *nm* incunabulum

incurable *adj también Fig* incurable

incurrir *vi* **i. en** *(delito, falta)* to commit; *(error)* to make; *(desprecio, castigo)* to incur

incursión *nf* incursion; *Fig* **hicieron una i. en la cocina** they raided the kitchen

indagación *nf* investigation, inquiry

indagar [38] **1** *vt* to investigate, to inquire into
2 *vi* to investigate, to inquire

indebido, -a *adj* (**a**) *(incorrecto)* improper (**b**) *(ilegal)* unlawful, illegal

indecencia *nf* (**a**) *(cualidad)* indecency (**b**) **¡es una i.!** *(es impúdico)* it's not decent!; *(es indignante)* it's outrageous!

indecente *adj* (**a**) *(impúdico)* indecent (**b**) *(indigno)* miserable, wretched

indecible *adj* indescribable, unspeakable

indecisión *nf* indecisiveness

indeciso, -a *adj* (**a**) *(persona) (inseguro)* indecisive; *(que está dudoso)* undecided, unsure; **estar i. sobre algo** to be undecided about sth (**b**) *(pregunta, respuesta)* hesitant; *(resultado)* undecided

indecoroso, -a *adj* unseemly

indefectible *adj Formal* unfailing

indefendible *adj* *(comportamiento, actitud)* indefensible; *(teoría)* untenable

indefensión *nf* defenselessness

indefenso, -a *adj* defenseless

indefinible *adj* indefinable; **de edad i.** of indeterminate age

indefinido, -a *adj* (**a**) *(ilimitado) (tiempo)* indefinite; *(contrato)* open-ended (**b**) *(impreciso)* vague (**c**) *Gram* indefinite

indeleble *adj* indelible

indemne *adj* unhurt, unharmed; **salir i.** to escape unhurt

indemnización *nf (compensación) (por catástrofe)* compensation; *(por despido)* severance pay, layoff pay; *Der* **i. por daños y perjuicios** damages

indemnizar [14] *vt* **i. a alguien (por)** to compensate sb (for)

indemostrable *adj* unprovable

independencia *nf* independence; **con i. de** irrespective *o* regardless of

independentismo *nm* independence movement

independentista 1 *adj* advocating independence
2 *nmf* supporter of independence

independiente *adj* (**a**) *(país, persona)* independent (**b**) *(aparte)* separate

independizar [14] **1** *vt* to grant independence to
2 independizarse *vpr* to become independent (**de** of)

indescifrable *adj* *(código)* unbreakable; *(letra)* indecipherable; *(misterio)* inexplicable, impenetrable

indescriptible *adj* indescribable

indeseable *adj & nmf* undesirable

indestructible *adj* indestructible

indeterminación *nf (indecisión)* indecisiveness

indeterminado, -a *adj* (**a**) *(sin determinar)* indeterminate; **por tiempo i.** indefinitely (**b**) *(impreciso)* vague (**c**) *Gram* **artículo i.** indefinite article

indexación *nf (gen) & Inform* indexing

indexar *vt (gen) & Inform* to index

India *nf* (**la**) **I.** India

indiano, -a 1 *adj* (Latin American) Indian
2 *nm,f* (**a**) *(indígena)* (Latin American) Indian (**b**) *(emigrante)* = Spanish emigrant to Latin America who returned to Spain having made his fortune

indicación *nf* (**a**) *(señal, gesto)* sign, signal (**b**) *(instrucción)* instruction; **pedir/dar indicaciones** *(para llegar a un sitio)* to ask for/give directions (**c**) *(nota, corrección)* note (**d**) *Med* **indicaciones** *(de medicamento)* uses

indicado, -a *adj* (**a**) *(apropiado)* suitable, appropriate; **no es el juguete más i. para un niño de tres años** it's not the most suitable *o* appropiate toy for a three-year-old child; **este no es el momento i. para discutir ese asunto** this is not the right time to talk about this matter; **un método i. únicamente para casos extremos** a method recommended *o* to be used only in extreme cases (**b**) *(marcado)* specified; **se entregará en la fecha indicada por el cliente** it will be delivered on the date specified by the client

indicador, -ora 1 *adj* indicating; **flecha indicadora** indicating arrow
2 *nm* (**a**) *(signo)* indicator; **i. económico** economic indicator (**b**) *Mec* gauge, meter; **i. del nivel de gasolina** fuel gauge

indicar [59] *vt* (**a**) *(señalar)* to indicate; *(sujeto: aguja, flecha)* to read; **todo parece i. que ganará el equipo visitante** everything seems to indicate that the visiting team will win; **me indicó con un gesto que me sentara** she motioned to me to sit down; **esa flecha indica a la derecha** that arrow points to the right; **esa luz indica que le falta agua al motor** that light shows that the engine is low on water (**b**) *(explicar)* to tell, to explain to; **nos indicó el camino del aeropuerto** she told us the way to the airport (**c**) *(prescribir)* to prescribe

indicativo, -a 1 *adj* indicative
2 *nm Gram* indicative

índice *nm* (**a**) *(indicador)* index; *(proporción)* level, rate; **í. de alfabetización** literacy rate; **í. de audiencia** rating; **í. bursátil** stock-market index; **í. del costo** *o Esp* **coste de la vida** cost-of-living index; **í. de desempleo** unemployment rate; **í. de mortalidad** death rate; **í. de natalidad** birth rate; **í. de popularidad** popularity rating; *Esp* **í. de precios al consumo,** *Am* **í. de precios al consumidor** consumer price index
(**b**) *(señal)* sign, indicator; **í. económico** economic indicator
(**c**) *(lista, catálogo)* catalog; *(en libro)* (table of) contents; **í. alfabético** index
(**d**) *(dedo)* index finger

indicio *nm (señal)* sign; *(pista)* clue; *(cantidad pequeña)* trace; **hay indicios de violencia** there are signs of violence

Índico *nm* **el (océano) Í.** the Indian Ocean

indiferencia *nf* indifference

indiferente *adj* indifferent; **me es i.** *(me da igual)* I don't mind, it's all the same to me; *(no me interesa)* I'm not interested in it

indígena 1 *adj* indigenous, native
  2 *nmf* native

indigencia *nf* destitution, poverty

indigenismo *nm* Indianism

indigenista *adj & nmf* Indianist

indigente 1 *adj* destitute, poor
  2 *nmf* poor person

indigestarse *vpr* to get indigestion; **se me ha indigestado el guiso** the stew gave me indigestion; *Fam Fig* **se me ha indigestado esa chica** I can't stomach that girl

indigestión *nf* indigestion; **tener una i.** to have indigestion

indigesto, -a *adj* hard to digest, indigestible

indignación *nf* indignation

indignado, -a *adj* indignant

indignante *adj* shocking, outrageous

indignar 1 *vt* to anger
  2 indignarse *vpr* to get angry *o* indignant (**por** about)

indigno, -a *adj* **(a)** *(impropio, no merecedor)* unworthy (**de** of), not worthy (**de** of); **soy i. de tal honor** I am not worthy of such an honor **(b)** *(degradante)* shameful, appalling

índigo *nm* indigo

indio, -a 1 *adj* Indian
  2 *nm,f* Indian; *Esp Fam* **hacer el i.** to play the fool; **i. americano** native American

indique *etc ver* **indicar**

indirecta *nf* hint; **lanzar una i. a alguien** to drop a hint to sb

indirecto, -a *adj* indirect

indisciplina *nf* indiscipline

indisciplinado, -a 1 *adj* undisciplined
  2 *nm,f* undisciplined person

indiscreción *nf* **(a)** *(cualidad)* indiscretion **(b)** *(comentario)* indiscreet remark; **si no es i.** if you don't mind my asking

indiscreto, -a 1 *adj* indiscreet
  2 *nm,f* indiscreet person

indiscriminado, -a *adj* indiscriminate

indiscutible *adj* indisputable

indisociable *adj* inseparable (**de** from)

indisolubilidad *nf* indissolubility

indisoluble *adj* **(a)** *(sustancia)* insoluble **(b)** *(unión, ley)* indissoluble

indispensable *adj* indispensable, essential; **lo i.** the bare minimum, the (bare) essentials

indisponer [50] **1** *vt* **(a)** *(enfermar)* to make ill, to upset **(b)** *(enemistar)* to set at odds
  2 indisponerse *vpr* **(a)** *(enfermar)* to fall *o* become ill **(b)** *(enemistarse)* to fall out (**con** with)

indisposición *nf* **(a)** *(malestar)* indisposition **(b)** *(reticencia)* unwillingness

indispuesto, -a 1 *participio ver* **indisponer**
  2 *adj* indisposed, unwell; **estar i.** to be unwell *o* indisposed

indistinguible *adj* indistinguishable

indistintamente *adj* **(a)** *(sin distinción)* equally, alike; **se refería a jóvenes y viejos i.** he was referring to young and old alike **(b)** *(sin claridad)* indistinctly

indistinto, -a *adj* **(a)** *(indiferente)* **es i.** it doesn't matter, it makes no difference **(b)** *(cuenta, cartilla)* joint **(c)** *(perfil, figura)* indistinct, blurred

individual 1 *adj* **(a)** *(de uno solo)* individual; *(habitación, cama)* single; *(despacho)* personal; **los derechos individuales** the rights of the individual **(b)** *(prueba, competición)* singles; **competición i.** singles competition
  2 individuales *nmpl Dep* singles

individualidad *nf* individuality

individualismo *nm* individualism

individualista 1 *adj* individualistic
  2 *nmf* individualist

individualizado, -a *adj* individualized

individualizar [14] *vt* **(a)** *(personalizar)* to individualize **(b)** *(caracterizar)* **su imaginación lo individualiza** his imagination singles him out

individuo, -a *nm,f* **(a)** *(ser individual)* person, individual; **los derechos del i.** the rights of the individual **(b)** *(persona desconocida)* person, individual; **dos individuos atracaron un banco** two people *o* individuals robbed a bank **(c)** *(mala persona)* individual; **no me gusta nada el i. con el que sales** I don't like that individual *o* character you're going out with at all **(d)** *(de especie)* **quedan sólo 200 individuos de esta especie** only 200 individuals remain of this species; **cada i. ocupa un territorio** each animal occupies its own territory

indivisibilidad *nf* indivisibility

indivisible *adj* indivisible

indiviso, -a *adj* undivided

indización *nf* indexation

indizar [14] *vt* to index

Indochina *n Antes* Indochina

indochino, -a *adj & nm,f Antes* Indochinese

indocumentado, -a 1 *adj* **(a)** *(sin documentación)* without identity papers; **estar i.** to have no (means of) identification **(b)** *Esp Fam (ignorante)* ignorant
  2 *nm,f Esp Fam (ignorante)* **es un i.** he doesn't know much

indoeuropeo, -a 1 *adj* Indo-European
  2 *nm (lengua)* Indo-European

índole *nf (naturaleza)* nature; *(tipo)* type, kind; **de toda í.** of every kind

indolencia *nf* indolence, laziness

indolente *adj* indolent, lazy

indoloro, -a *adj* painless

indomable *adj* **(a)** *(animal)* untamable **(b)** *(carácter)* rebellious; *(pueblo)* unruly

indomesticable *adj* untamable

indómito, -a *adj* **(a)** *(animal)* untamable **(b)** *(carácter)* rebellious; *(pueblo)* unruly

Indonesia *n* Indonesia

indonesio, -a 1 *adj & nm,f* Indonesian
  2 *nm (lengua)* Indonesian

inducción *nf* **(a)** *(gen) & Fís* induction **(b)** *Der* incitement **(a** to)

inducir [18] *vt* **(a)** *(incitar)* **i. a alguien a algo/a hacer algo** to lead sb into sth/into doing sth; **ello les indujo a pensar que el asesino era el mayordomo** this led them to think that the butler was the murderer; **esa frase puede i. a error** that sentence could be misleading; **sus instrucciones me indujeron a error** her instructions caused *o* led me to make a mistake **(b)** *(deducir)* to infer **(c)** *Fís* to induce

inductivo, -a *adj* inductive

inductor, -ora 1 *adj* instigating
  2 *nm* inductor

indudable *adj* undoubted; **es i. que...** there is no doubt that...

indujera *etc ver* **inducir**

indulgencia *nf* indulgence; **i. plenaria** plenary indulgence

indulgente *adj* indulgent

indultar *vt* to pardon

indulto *nm Der* pardon; **otorgar** *o* **conceder el i. a alguien** to grant sb a pardon

indumentaria *nf* attire

industria *nf* (**a**) *(sector)* industry; **i. alimentaria** food industry; **i. automovilística** *o* **del automóvil** automobile *o* car industry; **i. cinematográfica** *o* **del cine** movie *o* film industry; **i. del ocio** leisure industry; **i. punta** sunrise industry (**b**) *(fábrica)* factory

industrial 1 *adj* industrial
  2 *nmf* industrialist

industrialismo *nm* industrialism

industrialización *nf* industrialization

industrializado, -a *adj* industrialized; **países industrializados** industrialized countries

industrializar [14] **1** *vt* to industrialize
  2 industrializarse *vpr* to become industrialized

industrioso, -a *adj* industrious

induzca *etc ver* inducir

INE ['ine] *nm* (*abrev de* **Instituto Nacional de Estadística**) = organization that publishes official statistics about Spain

inédito, -a *adj* (**a**) *(no publicado)* unpublished (**b**) *(sorprendente)* unheard-of, unprecedented

inefable *adj* indescribable

ineficacia *nf* (**a**) *(bajo rendimiento)* inefficiency (**b**) *(baja efectividad)* ineffectiveness

ineficaz *adj* (**a**) *(de bajo rendimiento)* inefficient (**b**) *(de baja efectividad)* ineffective

ineficiencia *nf* (**a**) *(bajo rendimiento)* inefficiency (**b**) *(baja efectividad)* ineffectiveness

ineficiente *adj* (**a**) *(de bajo rendimiento)* inefficient (**b**) *(de baja efectividad)* ineffective

ineluctable *adj Formal* inevitable, inescapable

ineludible *adj* unavoidable

INEM [i'nem] *nm* (*abrev de* **Instituto Nacional de Empleo**) = Spanish department of employment

inenarrable *adj* indescribable

ineptitud *nf* ineptitude

inepto, -a 1 *adj* inept
  2 *nm,f* inept person

inequívoco, -a *adj* *(apoyo, resultado)* unequivocal; *(señal, voz)* unmistakable

inercia *nf también Fig* inertia; **hacer algo por i.** to do sth out of inertia

inerme *adj* *(sin armas)* unarmed; *(sin defensa)* defenseless

inerte *adj* (**a**) *(materia)* inert (**b**) *(cuerpo, cadáver)* lifeless

inescrutable *adj* (**a**) *(persona, rostro)* inscrutable (**b**) *(misterio, verdad)* impenetrable

inesperado, -a *adj* unexpected

inestabilidad *nf* instability

inestable *adj* unstable; **tiempo i.** changeable weather

inestimable *adj* inestimable, invaluable

inevitable *adj* inevitable

inexactitud *nf* inaccuracy

inexacto, -a *adj* (**a**) *(impreciso)* inaccurate (**b**) *(erróneo)* incorrect, wrong

inexcusable *adj* (**a**) *(imperdonable)* inexcusable (**b**) *(ineludible)* unavoidable

inexistencia *nf* nonexistence

inexistente *adj* nonexistent

inexorabilidad *nf* inexorability

inexorable *adj* *(avance)* inexorable; *(persona)* pitiless, unforgiving

inexperiencia *nf* inexperience

inexperto, -a 1 *adj* (**a**) *(falto de experiencia)* inexperienced (**b**) *(falto de habilidad)* unskillful, inexpert
  2 *nm,f* person without experience

inexplicable *adj* inexplicable

inexpresivo, -a *adj* *(rostro)* expressionless; *(persona, carácter)* undemonstrative

inexpugnable *adj* unassailable, impregnable

inextinguible *adj* *(fuego)* unquenchable; *(sentimiento)* undying

in extremis *adv* right at the very last moment

inextricable *adj* intricate

infalibilidad *nf* infallibility

infalible *adj* infallible

infamar *vt Formal* to defame

infame *adj* vile, base

infamia *nf* (**a**) *(deshonra)* infamy, disgrace (**b**) *(mala acción)* vile *o* base deed

infancia *nf* (**a**) *(periodo)* childhood; **tuvo una i. muy feliz** she had a very happy childhood; **desde su más tierna i.** from early childhood; **un amigo de la i.** a childhood friend (**b**) *(todos los niños)* children *(plural)*; **la salud de la i.** children's health

infante, -a 1 *nm,f* (**a**) *(niño)* infant (**b**) *(hijo del rey)* *(niño)* infante, prince; *(niña)* infanta, princess
  2 *nm* *(soldado)* infantryman

infantería *nf* infantry; **i. de marina** marines; **i. ligera** light infantry

infanticida 1 *adj* infanticidal
  2 *nmf* infanticide, child-murderer

infanticidio *nm* infanticide

infantil *adj* (**a**) *(para niños)* children's; **psicología i.** child psychology (**b**) *(inmaduro)* infantile, childish

infantilismo *nm* infantilism

infantiloide *adj* childlike

infarto *nm* **i. (de miocardio)** heart attack; **le dio un i.** he had a heart attack; *Fam Fig* **casi le dio un i.** she almost had a heart attack *o* a seizure; **i. cerebral** stroke

infatigable *adj* indefatigable, tireless

infatuación *nf* vanity

infatuar [4] *vt* to make conceited

infausto, -a *adj* ill-starred

infección *nf* infection

infeccioso, -a *adj* infectious

infectado, -a *adj* infected

infectar 1 *vt* to infect
  2 infectarse *vpr* to become infected

infecto, -a *adj* (**a**) *(agua, carroña)* putrid (**b**) *(población, zona)* infected (**c**) *(desagradable)* foul, terrible

infecundidad *nf* infertility

infecundo, -a *adj* infertile

infelicidad *nf* unhappiness

infeliz 1 *adj* *(desgraciado)* unhappy; *(ingenuo)* trusting
  2 *nmf* *(ingenuo)* **es un i.** he's a trusting soul; **un pobre i.** a poor wretch

inferior 1 *adj* (**a**) *(de abajo)* bottom; **la mitad i.** the bottom *o* lower half; **la parte i. (de algo)** the bottom (of sth) (**b**) *(menor)* lower (**a** than); **temperaturas inferiores a diez grados** temperatures lower than *o* below ten degrees; **una cifra i. a cien** a figure under *o* below one hundred (**c**) *(peor)* inferior (**a** to); **es i. a la media** it's below average
  2 *nmf* inferior; **trata con desprecio a sus inferiores** he treats those beneath him with contempt

inferioridad *nf* inferiority; **estar en i. de condiciones** to be at a disadvantage; **acabaron el partido en i. numérica** they ended the game with fewer players on the field than their opponents

inferir [62] *vt* (**a**) *(deducir)* to infer (**de** from), to deduce (**de** from) (**b**) *(ocasionar)* *(herida)* to inflict; *(mal)* to cause

infernal *adj también Fig* infernal

infértil *adj (mujer)* infertile; *(campo)* barren, infertile

infertilidad *nf (mujer)* infertility; *(campo)* barrenness, infertility

infestar *vt* to infest; **durante el verano, los turistas infestan la ciudad** in summer the city is overrun by tourists

infidelidad *nf (conyugal)* infidelity; *(a la patria, un amigo)* unfaithfulness, disloyalty

infiel 1 *adj* (**a**) *(desleal) (cónyuge)* unfaithful; *(amigo)* disloyal (**b**) *(inexacto)* inaccurate, unfaithful
2 *nmf Rel* infidel

infiernillo *nm* portable stove

infierno *nm* hell; **su vida con él era un i.** her life with him was hell; *Fam* **en el quinto i.** in the middle of nowhere; *Fam* **irse al i.** to go down the tubes; *Fam* **mandar a alguien al i.** to tell sb to go to hell; *Fam* **¡vete al i.!** go to hell!

infiero *etc ver* **inferir**

infiltración *nf* (**a**) *(de líquido)* seeping (**b**) *(de persona, ideas)* infiltration

infiltrado, -a 1 *adj* infiltrated
2 *nm,f* infiltrator

infiltrar 1 *vt* (**a**) *(inyectar)* to inject (**b**) *(ideas)* to infiltrate
2 infiltrarse en *vpr* to infiltrate

ínfimo, -a *adj (calidad, categoría)* extremely low; *(precio)* giveaway; *(importancia)* minimal

infinidad *nf* **una i. de** an infinite number of; *(mucho)* masses of; **en i. de ocasiones** on countless occasions

infinitesimal *adj* infinitesimal

infinitivo *nm* infinitive

infinito, -a 1 *adj también Fig* infinite; **infinitas veces** hundreds of times
2 *nm* infinity; **el i.** the infinite
3 *adv (mucho)* extremely, infinitely

infiriera *etc ver* **inferir**

inflable *adj* inflatable

inflación *nf Econ* inflation

inflacionario, -a *adj* inflationary

inflacionismo *nm* inflationism

inflacionista *adj* inflationary

inflamable *adj* flammable, inflammable

inflamación *nf Med* inflammation

inflamar 1 *vt* (**a**) *(hinchar) (sujeto: infección, fiebre)* to inflame (**b**) *(con fuego)* to set alight (**c**) *(con pasiones)* to inflame
2 inflamarse *vpr* (**a**) *(hincharse) (por infección)* to become inflamed; *(por golpe)* to swell up; **se me ha inflamado la rodilla por el golpe** my knee has swollen up as a result of the blow (**b**) *(con fuego)* to catch fire, to burst into flames (**c**) *(con pasiones)* to become inflamed; **se inflamó cuando escuchó las noticias** he became inflamed with anger when he heard the news

inflamatorio, -a *adj* inflammatory

inflar 1 *vt* (**a**) *(soplando)* to blow up, to inflate; *(con bomba)* to pump up (**b**) *(exagerar)* to blow up, to exaggerate (**c**) *RP Fam (molestar)* **no me infles** stop bugging me!
2 *vi RP Fam (molestar)* to be a pain
3 inflarse *vpr (hartarse)* to stuff oneself (**de** with)

inflexibilidad *nf también Fig* inflexibility

inflexible *adj también Fig* inflexible

inflexión *nf* inflection

infligir [24] *vt* to inflict; *(castigo)* to impose

influencia *nf* (**a**) *(poder)* influence; **tuvo gran i. sobre el resultado de las elecciones** it had a considerable influence on the result of the election, it heavily influenced the result of the election; **bajo la i. de la anestesia** under (the influence of) the anesthetic (**b**) **influencias** *(contactos)* contacts, pull; **consiguió ese puesto por influencias** she got that job through knowing the right people

influenciar *vt* to influence, to have an influence on

influenza *nf* influenza

influir [34] **1** *vt* to influence
2 *vi* to have influence; **i. en** to influence, to have an influence on

influjo *nm* influence

influyente *adj* influential

infografía *nf (en periódico, revista)* graphics

infopista *nf Inform* information highway

información *nf* (**a**) *(conocimiento)* information; **para mayor i., visite nuestra página web** for more information visit our web page; **para tu i.** for your information; **i. confidencial** inside information; **i. privilegiada** privileged information
(**b**) *Prensa (noticias)* news *(singular)*; *(noticia)* report, piece of news; **hemos recibido informaciones contradictorias sobre el accidente** we have received conflicting reports about the accident; **i. deportiva** sports news; **i. meteorológica** weather report *o* forecast
(**c**) *(oficina)* information office; *(mostrador)* information desk; **Sr. López, acuda a i.** would Mr. López please come to the information desk
(**d**) *(telefónica)* information; **i. horaria** (telephone) time-of-day service

informado, -a *adj (sobre un tema, noticia)* informed; **muy i. (sobre)** well-informed (about)

informador, -ora 1 *adj* informing, reporting
2 *nm,f* reporter; **i. de la policía** police informer

informal *adj* (**a**) *(desenfadado, no solemne)* informal; **una reunión i.** an informal meeting; **vestido de manera i.** casually dressed (**b**) *(irresponsable)* unreliable

informalidad *nf* (**a**) *(desenfado, falta de formalismo)* informality (**b**) *(irresponsabilidad)* unreliability

informante 1 *adj* informing
2 *nmf* informant, informer

informar 1 *vt* **i. a alguien (de)** to inform *o* tell sb (about); **le han informado mal** he has been misinformed; **se ha de i. a los detenidos de sus derechos** when someone is arrested, you have to read them their rights; **¿me podría i. de los horarios de trenes a Boston?** could you tell me the times of the trains to Boston?
2 *vi* to inform; *(periódico)* to report; **según informa nuestro corresponsal,...** according to our correspondent,...
3 informarse *vpr* to find out (details); **me informaré y luego te llamo** I'll call you once I've found out the details; **informarse de** *o* **sobre** to find out about

informática *nf* (**a**) *(tecnología)* computing, information technology, IT; **el departamento de i. de la empresa** the IT department of the company; **la empresa va a invertir más en i.** the company is going to invest more in computers; **no sé nada de i.** I don't know anything about computers; **se requieren conocimientos de i.** candidates should be computer literate (**b**) *(asignatura)* computer science

informático, -a 1 *adj* computer; **red informática** computer network
2 *nm,f (persona)* computer specialist, IT specialist

informativo, -a 1 *adj* informative; **boletín i.** news bulletin; **folleto i.** information leaflet
2 *nm* news (bulletin)

informatización *nf* computerization

informatizado, -a *adj* computerized

informatizar [14] *vt* to computerize

informe 1 *adj* shapeless
2 *nm* (**a**) *(documento, estudio)* report (**b**) *Der* = oral summary of case given to the judge by counsel for defence or prosecution (**c**) **informes** *(información)* information; *(sobre comportamiento)* report; *(para un empleo)* references

infortunado, -a 1 *adj* unfortunate, unlucky; *(encuentro, conversación)* ill-fated

2 *nm,f* unfortunate *o* unlucky person

infortunio *nm (hecho desgraciado)* calamity, misfortune; *(mala suerte)* misfortune, bad luck

Infovía® *nf Inform* = Spanish computer network providing access to Internet servers

infracción *nf (de reglamento)* infringement; **i. de circulación** *o* **tráfico** driving offense

infraccionar *Am* **1** *vt (multar)* to fine

2 *vi (en deporte)* to commit a foul; *(contra la ley)* to offend, to break the law; *(contra reglamento)* to violate the rules

infractor, -ora 1 *adj* offending

2 *nm,f* offender

infraestructura *nf* **(a)** *(de organización, país)* infrastructure **(b)** *(de construcción)* foundations

in fraganti *loc adv* **atrapar a alguien i.** to catch sb red-handed *o* in the act

infrahumano, -a *adj* subhuman

infranqueable *adj (río, abismo)* impassable; *(problema, dificultad)* insurmountable

infrarrojo, -a *adj* infrared

infrautilización *nf* underuse

infrautilizar [14] *vt* to underuse

infravalorado, -a *adj* underrated

infravalorar 1 *vt* to undervalue, to underestimate

2 infravalorarse *vpr* to undervalue oneself

infravivienda *nf* **el problema de la i.** the problem of housing which is unfit for human habitation

infrecuente *adj* infrequent; **no es i.** it's not uncommon *o* unusual

infringir [24] *vt (quebrantar)* to infringe, to break

infructuoso, -a *adj* fruitless, unsuccessful

ínfulas *nfpl* pretensions, presumption; **darse í.** to give oneself airs

infumable *adj* **(a)** *(cigarrillo)* unsmokable **(b)** *Esp, RP Fam (comportamiento)* unbearable, intolerable; *(libro, película)* awful, terrible

infundado, -a *adj* unfounded

infundio *nm Formal* untruth, lie

infundir *vt* **i. algo a alguien** to fill sb with sth, to inspire sth in sb; **i. miedo** to inspire fear

infusión *nf* herbal tea, infusion; **i. de manzanilla** camomile tea

infuso, -a *adj Hum* **por ciencia infusa** through divine inspiration

ingeniar 1 *vt* to invent, to devise

2 ingeniarse *vpr* **ingeniárselas** to manage, to engineer it; **no sé cómo se las ingenia, pero siempre gana él** I don't know how he does it, but he always wins; **ingeniárselas para hacer algo** to manage *o* contrive to do sth; **se las ingenió para no tener que lavar los platos** she managed to wangle her way out of doing the dishes

ingeniería *nf* engineering; *Fig* **una obra de i.** a major operation; **i. civil** civil engineering; **i. electrónica** electrical engineering; **i. genética** genetic engineering; **i. industrial** mechanical engineering; **i. de sistemas** system(s) engineering

ingeniero, -a 1 *nm,f* engineer; **i. agrónomo** agronomist; *Esp* **i. de caminos, canales y puertos** civil engineer; **i. civil** civil engineer; **i. industrial** industrial engineer; **i. de minas** mining engineer; **i. naval** naval engineer; *Inform* **i. de programas** software engineer; **i. químico** chemical engineer; *Inform* **i. de sistemas** systems engineer; **i. de sonido** sound engineer; **i. de telecomunicaciones** telecommunications engineer

2 *nm Am salvo RP* = title used to address businessmen and professionals (even if they are not actually qualified as an engineer)

ingenio *nm* **(a)** *(inteligencia)* ingenuity; **aguzar el i.** to sharpen one's wits **(b)** *(agudeza)* wit, wittiness **(c)** *(máquina)* device

ingenioso, -a *adj (inteligente)* ingenious, clever; *(agudo)* witty

ingente *adj* enormous, huge

ingenuidad *nf* ingenuousness, naivety

ingenuo, -a 1 *adj* naive, ingenuous; **¡no seas i.!** don't be so naive!

2 *nm,f* ingenuous *o* naive person; **hacerse el i.** to act the innocent

ingerir [62] *vt* to consume, to ingest

ingestión *nf* consumption; **en caso de i. accidental** if accidentally swallowed

ingiero *etc ver* **ingerir**

ingiriera *etc ver* **ingerir**

Inglaterra *n* England

ingle *nf* groin

inglés, -esa 1 *adj* English

2 *nm,f (persona)* Englishman, *f* Englishwoman; **los ingleses** the English

3 *nm (lengua)* English

ingobernable *adj (país)* ungovernable; *(niño)* uncontrollable, unmanageable

ingratitud *nf* ingratitude, ungratefulness

ingrato, -a *adj (persona)* ungrateful; *(trabajo)* thankless

ingravidez *nf* weightlessness; **en estado de i.** in conditions of zero gravity

ingrávido, -a *adj* weightless

ingrediente *nm* ingredient

ingresar 1 *vt Esp (dinero)* to deposit, to pay in

2 *vi* **(a)** **i. en** *(asociación, ejército)* to join; *(hospital)* to be admitted to; *(convento, universidad)* to enter; *Esp* **i. cadáver** to be dead on arrival **(b)** *Am* **i. a** *(lugar)* to get into

ingreso *nm* **(a)** *(entrada)* entry, entrance; *(en asociación, ejército)* joining; *(en hospital, universidad)* admission; **examen de i.** entrance exam **(b)** *Esp (de dinero)* deposit **(c)** *Fin* **ingresos** *(sueldo)* income; *(recaudación)* revenue; **ingresos brutos/ netos** gross/net income

inhábil *adj* **(a)** *(torpe)* clumsy, unskillful **(b)** *(incapacitado) (por defecto físico)* unfit; *(por la edad)* disqualified

inhabilitación *nf (incapacitación)* disqualification; *(minusvalía)* disablement

inhabilitar *vt* to disqualify **(para** from)

inhabitable *adj* uninhabitable

inhabitado, -a *adj* uninhabited

inhalación *nf* inhalation

inhalador *nm* inhaler

inhalar *vt* to inhale

inherente *adj* inherent; **ser i. a** to be inherent in *o* to, to be an inherent part of

inhibición *nf* inhibition

inhibir 1 *vt* to inhibit

2 inhibirse *vpr* **(a)** *(cohibirse)* to become inhibited *o* shy **(b)** **inhibirse de** to abstain from, to hold back from

inhóspito, -a *adj* inhospitable

inhumación *nf* burial

inhumano, -a *adj (despiadado)* inhuman; *(desconsiderado)* inhumane

inhumar *vt* to inter, to bury

iniciación *nf* **(a)** *(ceremonia)* initiation **(b)** *(principio)* start, beginning

iniciado, -a 1 *adj* **(a)** *(empezado)* started **(b)** *(neófito)* initiated

2 *nm,f* initiate

inicial *adj & nf* initial

inicialización *nf Inform* initialization

inicializar [14] *vt Inform* to initialize

iniciar 1 *vt (empezar)* to start, to initiate; *(debate, discusión)* to start off; **i. a alguien en algo** to initiate sb into sth

2 iniciarse *vpr (empezar)* to start, to commence; **iniciarse en el estudio de algo** to begin one's studies in sth; **se inició en el piano a los sesenta años** he took up the piano at sixty

iniciático, -a *adj* initiation; **rito i.** initiation rite

iniciativa *nf (propuesta)* proposal, initiative; *(cualidad, capacidad)* initiative; **tener i.** to have initiative; **tomar la i.** to take the initiative; **i. privada** private enterprise

inicio *nm* start, beginning; **el i. de una enfermedad** the onset of a disease

inicuo, -a *adj* iniquitous

inigualable *adj* unrivaled

inigualado, -a *adj* unequaled

inimaginable *adj* unimaginable

inimitable *adj* inimitable

ininteligible *adj* unintelligible

ininterrumpido, -a *adj* uninterrupted, continuous

iniquidad *nf* iniquity

injerencia *nf* interference, meddling

injerir [62] **1** *vt* to introduce, to insert

2 injerirse *vpr (entrometerse)* to interfere (**en** in), to meddle (**en** in)

injertar *vt* to graft

injerto *nm* graft; **i. de piel** skin graft

injiero *etc ver* **injerir**

injiriera *etc ver* **injerir**

injuria *nf (insulto)* insult; *(agravio)* offense; *Der* slander

injuriar *vt (insultar)* to insult, to abuse; *(agraviar)* to offend; *Der* to slander

injurioso, -a *adj* insulting, abusive; *Der* slanderous

injustamente *adv* unfairly, unjustly

injusticia *nf* injustice; **¡es una i.!** *(quejándose)* it's not fair!; *(con indignación)* it's an outrage!

injustificable *adj* unjustifiable

injustificado, -a *adj* unjustified

injusto, -a *adj* unfair, unjust

Inmaculada *nf* la I. the Virgin Mary; **la I. Concepción** the Immaculate Conception

inmaculado, -a *adj* immaculate, spotless

inmadurez *nf* immaturity

inmaduro, -a *adj* (**a**) *(fruta)* unripe (**b**) *(persona)* immature

inmaterial *adj* immaterial

inmediaciones *nfpl (de localidad)* surrounding area; *(de lugar, casa)* vicinity; **en las i. del accidente** in the immediate vicinity of the accident

inmediatamente *adv* immediately, at once

inmediatez *nf* immediateness, immediacy

inmediato, -a *adj* (**a**) *(instantáneo)* immediate; **de i.** immediately, at once (**b**) *(contiguo)* next, adjoining

inmejorable *adj* unbeatable, that cannot be bettered

inmemorial *adj* immemorial; **desde tiempos inmemoriales** from time immemorial

inmensidad *nf* (**a**) *(grandeza)* immensity (**b**) *(multitud)* huge amount, sea

inmenso, -a *adj* (**a**) *(grande)* immense (**b**) *(profundo)* deep; **sintió una inmensa alegría** she felt deeply *o* tremendously happy (**c**) *Fam (fantástico)* marvelous; **el tenor estuvo i.** the tenor was wonderful

inmerecido, -a *adj* undeserved

inmersión *nf (de objeto)* immersion; *(de submarinista, submarino)* dive

inmerso, -a *adj también Fig* immersed (**en** in)

inmigración *nf (movimiento de personas)* immigration; *(oficina)* Immigration

inmigrante *adj & nmf* immigrant

inmigrar *vi* to immigrate

inminencia *nf* imminence

inminente *adj* imminent, impending

inmiscuirse [34] *vpr* to interfere *o* meddle (**en** in)

inmobiliaria *nf* (**a**) *(agencia)* real estate agency (**b**) *(constructora)* construction company

inmobiliario, -a *adj* property, real estate; **agente i.** realtor; **propiedad inmobiliaria** real estate

inmolación *nf* immolation, sacrifice

inmolar 1 *vt* to sacrifice

2 inmolarse *vpr* to sacrifice oneself

inmoral *adj* immoral

inmoralidad *nf* (**a**) *(cualidad)* immorality (**b**) *(acción)* immoral action; **lo que hizo fue una i.** what he did was immoral

inmortal *adj* immortal

inmortalidad *nf* immortality

inmortalizar [14] *vt* to immortalize

inmóvil *adj (quieto)* motionless, still; *(coche, tren)* stationary

inmovilidad *nf* immobility

inmovilismo *nm* defense of the status quo

inmovilizado, -a 1 *adj* immobilized

2 *nm Fin* fixed assets

inmovilizar [14] *vt* to immobilize

inmueble 1 *adj* **bienes inmuebles** real estate

2 *nm (edificio)* building

inmundicia *nf (suciedad)* filth, filthiness; *(basura)* garbage

inmundo, -a *adj* filthy, dirty

inmune *adj* (**a**) *Med & Fig* immune; **ser i. a algo** to be immune to sth; **i. a la crítica** immune to criticism (**b**) *(exento)* exempt

inmunidad *nf* immunity; **i. diplomática** diplomatic immunity; **i. parlamentaria** parliamentary immunity, ≃ congressional immunity

inmunitario, -a *adj Med* immune

inmunizado, -a *adj Med* immunized, inoculated; *Fig* immunized

inmunizar [14] *vt Med & Fig* to immunize (**contra** against)

inmunodeficiencia *nf Med* immunodeficiency

inmunodeficiente *adj Med* immunodeficient

inmunodepresión *nf Med* immunosuppression

inmunodepresor, -ora *adj Med* immunosuppressant

inmunología *nf Med* immunology

inmunológico, -a *adj Med* immune, immunological

inmunoterapia *nf Med* immunotherapy

inmutabilidad *nf* immutability

inmutable *adj* immutable, unchangeable

inmutar 1 *vt* to upset, to perturb

2 inmutarse *vpr* to get upset, to be perturbed; **ni se inmutó** he didn't bat an eyelid

innato, -a *adj* innate; **es i. en él** it comes naturally to him

innecesario, -a *adj* unnecessary

innegable *adj* undeniable

innegociable *adj* unnegotiable, not negotiable

innoble *adj* ignoble

innombrable *adj* unmentionable

innovación *nf* innovation

innovador, -ora 1 *adj* innovative, innovatory

2 *nm,f* innovator

innovar *vt (método, técnica)* to improve on

innumerable *adj* countless, innumerable

inobservancia *nf* breaking, violation

inocencia *nf* innocence

inocentada nf practical joke, trick; **hacerle una i. a alguien** to play a trick o practical joke on sb

inocente 1 adj (**a**) (no culpable) innocent (**b**) (ingenuo) naive, innocent (**c**) (sin maldad) harmless

2 nmf (**a**) (no culpable) innocent person (**b**) (sin maldad) harmless person (**c**) **Día de los Inocentes** December 28, ≃ April Fools' Day

inocuidad nf innocuousness, harmlessness

inocular vt to inoculate

inocuo, -a adj innocuous, harmless

inodoro, -a1 adj odorless

2 nm toilet (bowl)

inofensivo, -a adj inoffensive, harmless

inolvidable adj unforgettable

inoperable adj inoperable

inoperancia nf ineffectiveness

inoperante adj ineffective

inopia nf **estar en la i.** to be miles away, to be daydreaming

inopinado, -a adj unexpected

inoportuno, -a adj (**a**) (en mal momento) inopportune, untimely (**b**) (molesto) inconvenient (**c**) (inadecuado) inappropriate

inorgánico, -a adj inorganic

inoxidable adj (acero) stainless

input ['imput] (pl **inputs**) nm Inform input

inquebrantable adj (fe, amistad) unshakable; (lealtad) unswerving

inquietante adj worrying

inquietar 1 vt to worry, to trouble

2 inquietarse vpr to worry, to get anxious

inquieto, -a adj (**a**) (preocupado) worried, anxious (**por** about) (**b**) (agitado, emprendedor) restless

inquietud nf (preocupación) worry, anxiety; **tener inquietudes** (afán de saber) to have an inquiring mind

inquilino, -a nm,f tenant

inquina nf antipathy, aversion; **tener i. a** to feel aversion toward

inquirir [5] vt to inquire into, to investigate

inquisición nf (**a**) (indagación) inquiry, investigation (**b**) **la I.** (tribunal) the (Spanish) Inquisition

inquisidor, -ora1 adj inquisitive, inquiring

2 nm inquisitor

inquisitivo, -a adj inquisitive

inquisitorial, inquisitorio, -a adj inquisitorial

inri nm Esp Fam Fig **para más i.** to add insult to injury, to crown it all

insaciable adj (apetito, curiosidad) insatiable; (sed) unquenchable

insalubre adj insalubrious, unhealthy

insalubridad nf insalubrity, unhealthiness

Insalud [in'salud] nm Esp (abrev de **Instituto Nacional de la Salud**) ≃ Medicaid

insalvable adj (obstáculo) insuperable, insurmountable

insano, -a adj (no saludable) unhealthy; (loco) insane

insatisfacción nf (**a**) (disgusto, descontento) dissatisfaction (**b**) (falta, carencia) lack of fulfillment

insatisfecho, -a adj (**a**) (descontento) dissatisfied (**de** o **con** with) (**b**) (no saciado) not full, unsatisfied; **quedarse i.** to be left unsatisfied, to be left (still) wanting more

inscribir 1 vt (**a**) (grabar) to engrave (**en** on), inscribe (**en** on) (**b**) (apuntar) **i. algo/a alguien (en)** to register sth/sb (on)

2 inscribirse vpr **inscribirse en** (curso) to enroll in; (asociación, partido) to join

inscripción nf (**a**) Educ registration, enrollment; (en censo, registro) registration; (en concursos) entry; **desde su i.** (en asociación, partido) since he joined; **está abierto el plazo de i.** now enrolling, registration now open (**b**) (escrito) inscription

inscrito, -a participio ver **inscribir**

insecticida 1 adj insecticidal

2 nm insecticide

insectívoro, -a adj insectivorous

insecto nm insect

inseguridad nf (**a**) (falta de confianza) insecurity (**b**) (duda) uncertainty (**c**) (peligro) lack of safety; **i. ciudadana** lack of law and order

inseguro, -a adj (**a**) (sin confianza) insecure (**b**) (dudoso) uncertain (**de** about), unsure (**de** of o about) (**c**) (peligroso) unsafe

inseminación nf insemination; **i. artificial** artificial insemination

inseminar vt to inseminate

insensatez nf foolishness, senselessness; **hacer/decir una i.** to do/say sth foolish

insensato, -a1 adj foolish, senseless

2 nm,f foolish o senseless person, fool; **¡qué has hecho, i.!** what have you done, you fool o maniac?

insensibilidad nf (emocional) insensitivity; (física) numbness

insensibilizar [14] **1** vt Med to numb

2 insensibilizarse vpr (emocionalmente) to become desensitized (**a** to)

insensible adj (**a**) (indiferente) insensitive (**a** to) (**b**) (entumecido) numb (**c**) (imperceptible) imperceptible

inseparable adj inseparable

insepulto, -a adj Formal unburied

inserción nf insertion

insertar vt (gen) & Inform to insert (**en** into)

inservible adj useless, unserviceable

insidia nf (**a**) (trampa) trap, snare (**b**) (mala acción) malicious act

insidioso, -a adj malicious

insigne adj distinguished, illustrious

insignia nf (**a**) (distintivo) badge; Mil insignia (**b**) (bandera) flag, banner

insignificancia nf (**a**) (cualidad) insignificance (**b**) (cosa, hecho) trifle, insignificant thing

insignificante adj insignificant

insinuación nf hint, insinuation; **insinuaciones** (amorosas) innuendo

insinuante adj (mirada, ropa) suggestive; (comentarios) full of innuendo

insinuar [4] **1** vt to hint at, to insinuate; **¿qué insinúas?** what are you suggesting?

2 insinuarse vpr (**a**) (amorosamente) to make advances (**a** to) (**b**) (notarse) **empiezan a insinuarse problemas** it's beginning to look as if there might be problems

insípido, -a adj también Fig insipid

insistencia nf insistence

insistente adj insistent

insistir vi to insist (**en** on); **no insistas, te he dicho que no** don't keep on about it, I've told you the answer is no; **i. en que** to insist o maintain that; **la dirección insiste en que los empleados deben llevar corbata** the management insists on employees wearing a tie; **no sé por qué insiste en llamarme** I don't know why he keeps on o persists in phoning me; **insistió mucho sobre este punto** he laid great stress on this point

in situ adj & adv on the spot

insobornable adj incorruptible

insociable adj unsociable

insolación nf Med sunstroke

insolencia nf insolence; **hacer/decir una i.** to do/say sth insolent

insolente 1 *adj (descarado)* insolent; *(orgulloso)* haughty
2 *nmf* insolent person
insolidaridad *nf* lack of solidarity
insolidario, -a 1 *adj* lacking in solidarity
2 *nm,f* person lacking in solidarity
insólito, -a *adj* very unusual
insoluble *adj* insoluble
insolvencia *nf* insolvency
insolvente *adj* insolvent
insomne *adj & nmf* insomniac
insomnio *nm* insomnia, sleeplessness
insondable *adj también Fig* unfathomable
insonorización *nf* soundproofing
insonorizado, -a *adj* soundproof
insonorizar [14] *vt* to soundproof
insonoro, -a *adj* soundless
insoportable *adj* unbearable, intolerable
insoslayable *adj* inevitable, unavoidable
insospechable *adj* impossible to tell, unforeseeable
insospechado, -a *adj* unexpected, unforeseen
insostenible *adj* untenable
inspección *nf (examen)* inspection; *(policial)* search; **i. de calidad** quality control inspection; *Esp* **i. técnica de vehículos** = annual technical inspection for motor vehicles of five years or more
inspeccionar *vt* to inspect; **la policía inspeccionó la zona** the police searched the area
inspector, -ora *nm,f* inspector; **i. de aduanas** customs official; **i. de Hacienda** tax inspector; **i. de policía** police inspector
inspiración *nf* (a) *(artística)* inspiration; **una i. súbita** a flash of inspiration (b) *(respiración)* inhalation, breath
inspirado, -a *adj* inspired (**en** by)
inspirar 1 *vt* (a) *(sentimientos, ideas)* to inspire; **no me inspira mucha confianza** he doesn't inspire much confidence in me; **me inspira terror** I find him frightening (b) *(respirar)* to inhale, to breathe in
2 inspirarse *vpr* to be inspired (**en** by); **viajó al Caribe para inspirarse** he went to the Caribbean in search of inspiration
instalación *nf (de aparato)* installation; *(de local, puesto)* setting up; **i. eléctrica** wiring; **i. del gas** gas pipes; **instalaciones** *(deportivas, sanitarias)* facilities
instalador, -ora 1 *adj* installing, fitting
2 *nm,f* fitter
instalar 1 *vt* (a) *(montar) (antena, aparato)* to install, to fit; *(local, puesto)* to set up (b) *(situar) (objeto)* to place; *(gente)* to put up
2 instalarse *vpr (establecerse)* **instalarse en** to settle (down) in; *(nueva casa)* to move into; **a falta de dormitorios, se instalaron en el salón** as there were no bedrooms, they put themselves up in the living room
instancia *nf* (a) *(solicitud)* application (form) (b) *(ruego)* request; **a instancias de** at the request *o* bidding of; **en última i.** as a last resort (c) *Der* **juzgado de primera i.** court of first instance
instantánea *nf* snapshot, snap
instantáneo, -a *adj* (a) *(momentáneo)* momentary (b) *(rápido)* instantaneous; **provoca una reacción instantánea** it gets an immediate reaction (c) *(café)* instant
instante *nm* moment, instant; **a cada i.** all the time, constantly; **al i.** instantly, immediately; **en un i.** in a second
instar *vt* **i. a alguien a que haga algo** to urge *o* press sb to do sth
instauración *nf* establishment
instaurar *vt* to establish, to set up

instigación *nf* **por i. de** at the instigation of; **lo acusan de i. a la violencia** he is accused of inciting violence
instigador, -ora 1 *adj* instigating
2 *nm,f* instigator
instigar [38] *vt* **i. a alguien (a que haga algo)** to instigate sb (to do sth); **i. a algo** to incite to sth
instintivo, -a *adj* instinctive
instinto *nm* instinct; **i. maternal/de supervivencia** maternal/survival instinct; **por i.** instinctively
institución *nf* (a) *(organización, tradición)* institution; **i. benéfica** charitable organization; **i. pública** public institution; *Fig* **ser una i.** to be an institution (b) *(de ley, sistema)* introduction; *(de organismo)* establishment; *(de premio)* foundation
institucional *adj* institutional
institucionalizado, -a *adj* institutionalized
institucionalizar [14] *vt* to institutionalize
instituir [34] *vt* (a) *(fundar) (Gobierno)* to establish; *(premio, sociedad)* to found; *(sistema, reglas)* to introduce (b) *(nombrar)* to appoint, to name
instituto *nm* (a) *(corporación)* institute (b) *(centro) Esp (de enseñanza secundaria)* high school; **i. de belleza** beauty salon; *Esp* **i. de Formación Profesional** technical college
institutriz *nf* governess
instrucción *nf* (a) *(conocimientos)* education; *(docencia)* instruction; **i. militar** military training (b) **instrucciones** *(de uso)* instructions; **instrucciones de montaje** assembly instructions (c) *Der (investigación)* preliminary investigation; *(curso del proceso)* proceedings
instructivo, -a *adj (experiencia, narración)* instructive; *(juguete, película)* educational
instructor, -ora 1 *adj* training, instructing
2 *nm,f* instructor, teacher
instruido, -a *adj* educated; **muy i.** well-educated
instruir [34] *vt* (a) *(enseñar)* to instruct (b) *Der* to prepare
instrumental 1 *adj* instrumental
2 *nm* instruments; **i. médico** surgical instruments
instrumentar *vt* (a) *(composición musical)* to orchestrate, to score (b) **i. medidas para hacer algo** to bring in measures to do sth
instrumentista *nmf* (a) *Mús* instrumentalist (b) *Med* OR nurse
instrumento *nm* (a) *(musical)* instrument; **i. de cuerda** stringed instrument; **i. musical** musical instrument; **i. de percusión** percussion instrument; **i. de viento** wind instrument (b) *(herramienta)* tool, instrument; **i. de precisión** precision tool (c) *(medio)* means, tool; **un i. para estimular la demanda** a means of stimulating demand
insubordinación *nf* insubordination
insubordinado, -a 1 *adj* insubordinate
2 *nm,f* insubordinate (person), rebel
insubordinar 1 *vt* to stir up, to incite to rebellion
2 insubordinarse *vpr* to rebel
insubstancial *adj* insubstantial
insubstituible *adj* irreplaceable
insuceso *nm Col, Ecuad, Méx, RP* unfortunate incident
insuficiencia *nf* (a) *(escasez)* lack, shortage (b) *Med* failure, insufficiency; **i. cardiaca/renal** heart/kidney failure
insuficiente 1 *adj* insufficient
2 *nm (nota)* fail
insuflar *vt* to insufflate
insufrible *adj* intolerable, insufferable
ínsula *nf* island
insular 1 *adj* insular, island; **el clima i.** the island climate
2 *nmf* islander
insulina *nf* insulin

insulinodependiente *adj & nmf Med* insulin-dependent

insulso, -a *adj también Fig* bland, insipid

insultante *adj* insulting, offensive

insultar *vt* to insult

insulto *nm* insult; **insultos** verbal abuse

insumisión *nf* (**a**) *Esp Mil* = refusal to do military service or a civilian equivalent (**b**) *(rebeldía)* rebelliousness

insumiso, -a 1 *adj* rebellious

2 *nm,f* (**a**) *Esp Mil* = person who refuses to do military service or a civilian equivalent (**b**) *(rebelde)* rebel

insumos *nmpl Am (bienes)* raw materials; *(suministros)* supplies

insuperable *adj* (**a**) *(inmejorable)* unsurpassable (**b**) *(sin solución)* insurmountable, insuperable

insurgente *adj* insurgent

insurrección *nf* insurrection, revolt

insurrecto, -a *adj & nm,f* insurgent, rebel

insustancial *adj* insubstantial

insustituible *adj* irreplaceable

intachable *adj* irreproachable

intacto, -a *adj* intact; **el autobús quedó i. después del accidente** the bus survived the accident intact; **el partido conserva i. el apoyo de sus votantes** the support of the party's voters has been unaffected

intangible *adj* intangible

integración *nf (gen) & Mat* integration; **i. racial** racial integration

integrado, -a *adj* integrated

integral 1 *adj* (**a**) *(total)* total, complete (**b**) *(sin refinar) (pan, harina, pasta)* whole wheat; *(arroz)* brown (**c**) *(constituyente)* integral; **ser parte i. de algo** to be an integral part of sth (**d**) *Mat* **cálculo i.** integral calculus

2 *nf Mat* integral

íntegramente *adv* wholly, entirely

integrante 1 *adj* integral, constituent; **Estado i. de la UE** member state of the EU; **ser parte i. de algo** to be an integral part of sth

2 *nmf* member

integrar 1 *vt* (**a**) *(gen) & Mat* to integrate (**b**) *(componer)* to make up

2 integrarse *vpr* to integrate; **integrarse en** to become integrated into

integridad *nf* (**a**) *(moral)* integrity (**b**) *(totalidad)* wholeness

integrismo *nm* (**a**) *Pol* reaction, traditionalism (**b**) *Rel* fundamentalism

integrista *adj & nmf* (**a**) *Pol* reactionary, traditionalist (**b**) *Rel* fundamentalist

íntegro, -a *adj* (**a**) *(completo)* whole, entire; **versión íntegra** *(de libro)* unabridged edition; *(de película)* uncut version (**b**) *(honrado)* upright, honorable

intelecto *nm* intellect

intelectual *adj & nmf* intellectual

intelectualidad *nf* intelligentsia, intellectuals

intelectualizar [14] *vt* to intellectualize

inteligencia *nf* intelligence; *Inform* **i. artificial** artificial intelligence

inteligente *adj (gen) & Inform* intelligent

inteligibilidad *nf* intelligibility

inteligible *adj* intelligible

intelligentsia [inteli'ɣensja] *nf* intelligentsia

intemperancia *nf* intemperance, immoderation

intemperie *nf* **a la i.** in the open air

intempestivo, -a *adj (clima, comentario)* harsh; *(hora)* ungodly, unearthly; *(proposición, visita)* inopportune

intemporal *adj* timeless, independent of time

intención *nf* intention; **su i. es volver a presentarse al**

concurso she intends to enter the competition again; **con i.** *(intencionadamente)* intentionally; **tener la i. de** to intend to; **tener buenas/malas intenciones** to have good/bad intentions; **lo dije sin i. de ofender a nadie** it wasn't my intention to offend anyone, I didn't mean any offense; **lo hizo sin mala i.** he didn't mean it maliciously; **la i. es lo que cuenta** it's the thought that counts; **ya veo cuáles son tus intenciones** I see what you're up to now

intencionado, -a *adj* intentional, deliberate; **bien i.** *(acción)* well-meant; *(persona)* well-meaning; **mal i.** *(acción)* ill-meant, ill-intentioned; *(persona)* malevolent

intencional *adj* intentional, deliberate

intencionalidad *nf* intent

intendencia *nf* (**a**) *(militar)* ≃ Quartermaster Corps (**b**) *RP (corporación municipal)* city council (**c**) *Chile (gobernación)* regional government

intendente, -a *nm,f* (**a**) *(militar)* quartermaster (**b**) *RP (alcalde)* mayor (**c**) *Chile (gobernador)* provincial governor

intensidad *nf (fuerza)* intensity; *(de lluvia)* heaviness; *(de luz, color)* brightness; *(de amor)* passion, strength; **de poca i.** *(luz)* dim, weak; **llovía con poca i.** light rain was falling; **i. de corriente** strength of current

intensificación *nf* intensification

intensificar [59] **1** *vt* to intensify

2 intensificarse *vpr* to intensify

intensivo, -a *adj* intensive; **curso i.** intensive course

intenso, -a *adj (mirada, calor)* intense; *(lluvia)* heavy; *(luz, color)* bright; *(amor)* passionate, strong; **poco i.** *(lluvia)* light; *(luz)* dim, weak

intentar *vt* **i. (hacer algo)** to try (to do sth); **¡inténtalo!** have a try *o* go!; **intenta ser más discreto** try to be more discreet; **¡ni lo intentes!** *(advertencia)* don't even try it!; **la próxima vez, intenta que no se te caiga** try not to drop it next time

intento *nm (tentativa)* attempt; **aprobó el examen en el segundo i.** he passed the exam at the second attempt; **lo conseguiré aunque muera en el i.** I'll do it if it kills me; **i. de golpe de Estado** attempted coup; **i. de robo** attempted robbery; **i. de suicidio** suicide attempt

intentona *nf Pol* **i. (golpista)** attempted coup

interacción *nf* interaction

interaccionar *vi* to interact

interactividad *nf* interactivity

interactivo, -a *adj* interactive

interbancario, -a *adj* interbank

intercalar *vt* to insert, to put in

intercambiable *adj* interchangeable

intercambiador *nm Esp (de transportes)* transportation interchange, = station where passengers can change to various other means of transportation

intercambiar *vt* to exchange; *(lugares, posiciones)* to change, to swap

intercambio *nm* exchange; **i. comercial** trade

interceder *vi* **i. (por alguien)** to intercede (on sb's behalf)

interceptar *vt* (**a**) *(detener)* to intercept (**b**) *(obstruir)* to block

interceptor, -ora 1 *adj* intercepting

2 *nm* interceptor

intercesión *nf* intercession

intercesor, -ora 1 *adj* interceding

2 *nm,f* interceder, intercessor

interconexión *nf* interconnection

intercontinental *adj* intercontinental

intercostal *adj* intercostal, between the ribs

interdicción *nf* interdiction

interdisciplinar, interdisciplinario, -a *adj* interdisciplinary

interés (*pl* **intereses**) *nm* (**a**) *(provecho, curiosidad)* interest; **de i.** interesting; **una construcción de i. histórico** a building of historical interest; **hacer algo por el i. de alguien, hacer algo en i. de alguien** to do sth in sb's interest; **poner i. en algo** to take a real interest in sth; **tener i. en** *o* **por** to be interested in; **tengo i. en que venga pronto** it's in my interest that he should come soon

(**b**) *(egoísmo)* self-interest, selfishness; **por i.** out of selfishness; **intereses creados** vested interests

(**c**) **intereses** *(aficiones)* interests; **entre sus intereses se cuentan el golf y la vela** his interests include golf and sailing

(**d**) *Fin* interest; **un préstamo con un i. del 5 por ciento** a loan at 5 percent interest; **intereses atrasados** back interest; **i. bancario** bank interest

interesado, -a 1 *adj* (**a**) *(preocupado, curioso)* interested (**en** *o* **por** in) (**b**) *(egoísta)* selfish, self-interested (**c**) *(implicado)* **las partes interesadas** the interested parties

2 *nm,f* (**a**) *(deseoso, curioso)* interested person; **los interesados** those interested (**b**) *(involucrado)* person concerned; **los interesados** the parties concerned, those involved (**c**) *(egoísta)* selfish *o* self-interested person

interesante *adj* interesting; **¡eso suena muy i.!** that sounds really exciting!

interesar 1 *vt* (**a**) *(atraer el interés)* to interest; **le interesa el arte** she's interested in art; **por si te interesa** in case you're interested; **este asunto nos interesa a todos** this matter concerns us all; **a quien pueda i.** *(en carta)* to whom it may concern (**b**) *(convenir)* to be to the advantage of; **no les interesa que baje el precio** it wouldn't be to their advantage for the price to come down

2 interesarse *vpr* to take an interest (**en** *o* **por** in), to be interested (**en** *o* **por** in); **se interesó por ti/tu salud** she asked about you/your health

interestatal *adj* interstate

interfaz *nf Inform* interface

interfecto, -a *nm,f* *(víctima)* murder victim; *Esp Hum (de quien se habla)* the body in question

interferencia *nf* interference

interferir [62] **1** *vt* (**a**) *Rad, Tel & TV* to jam (**b**) *(interponerse)* to interfere with

2 *vi* to interfere (**en** in)

interfono *nm* intercom

ínterin *nm inv Formal* interim; **en el í.** in the meantime

interina *nf* *(asistenta)* cleaning lady

interinidad *nf* (**a**) *(cualidad)* temporariness (**b**) *(periodo)* (period of) temporary employment

interino, -a 1 *adj (provisional)* temporary; *(presidente, director)* acting; *(gobierno)* interim

2 *nm,f* *(suplente)* stand-in, deputy; *(médico, juez)* locum tenens; *(profesor)* substitute teacher

interior 1 *adj* (**a**) *(de dentro)* inside, inner; *(patio, jardín)* interior, inside; *(habitación, vida)* inner; **ropa i.** underwear (**b**) *Pol (comercio, política)* domestic (**c**) *Geog* inland

2 *nm* (**a**) *(parte de dentro)* interior; **el i. del edificio** the inside of the building; **en el i. de** inside (**b**) *Geog* interior, inland area (**c**) *(de una persona)* inner self, heart; **en mi i.** deep down (**d**) *Col, Ven (calzoncillos)* underpants

3 *nmf Dep (jugador)* central midfielder; **i. derecho/izquierdo** inside right/left

interioridad *nf* *(carácter)* inner self; **interioridades** *(asuntos)* private affairs

interiorismo *nm* interior design

interiorista *nmf* interior designer

interiorización *nf* *(de sentimientos, ideas)* internalization

interiorizar [14] *vt* (**a**) *(asumir, consolidar)* to internalize (**b**) *(no manifestar)* **interioriza sus emociones** he doesn't show his emotions

interjección *nf* interjection

interlineado *nm* spacing between the lines

interlocutor, -ora *nm,f (en negociación, debate)* participant; **su i.** the person she was speaking to

interludio *nm (gen) & Mús* interlude

intermediación *nf* (**a**) *(en conflicto)* intervention, mediation; **por i. de** through the intervention *o* mediation of (**b**) *Fin* intermediation

intermediar *vi* to mediate

intermediario, -a 1 *adj* intermediary

2 *nm,f* intermediary, go-between; *Com* middleman

intermedio, -a 1 *adj* (**a**) *(etapa)* intermediate, halfway; *(calidad)* average; *(tamaño)* medium (**b**) *(tiempo)* intervening; *(espacio)* in between

2 *nm (gen) & Teatro, Cine* intermission; *TV* (commercial) break

interminable *adj* endless, interminable

intermitencia *nf* intermittence, intermittency

intermitente 1 *adj* intermittent

2 *nm Esp, Col (en vehículo)* turn signal

internación *nf CSur* admission

Internacional *nf Pol* International; **la I.** *(himno)* the Internationale

internacional *adj* international

internacionalidad *nf* internationality

internacionalismo *nm* internationalism

internacionalizar [14] *vt* to internationalize

internada *nf Dep* break, breakaway

internado, -a 1 *nm* (**a**) *(colegio)* boarding school (**b**) *(estancia)* *(en manicomio)* confinement; *(en colegio)* boarding

2 *nm,f RP (en hospital)* patient

internamente *adv* internally

internamiento *nm (en manicomio)* confinement; *(en escuela)* boarding; *Pol* internment

internar 1 *vt (en escuela)* to send to boarding school (**en** at); *(en manicomio)* to commit (**en** to); *(en campo de concentración)* to intern (**en** in); *RP (en hospital)* to admit (**en** to)

2 internarse *vpr (en un lugar)* to go *o* penetrate deep (**en** into); *(en un tema)* to become deeply involved (**en** in)

internauta *nmf* cybernaut, netizen, Net user

Internet *nf* the Internet; **está en I.** it's on the Internet

internista *adj & nmf* internist

interno, -a 1 *adj* (**a**) *(de dentro)* internal; **parte interna del cajón** the inside of the box (**b**) *(medicina, hemorragia)* internal (**c**) *Pol* domestic (**d**) *(alumno)* boarding; **estuvo i. en Suiza** he went to a boarding school in Switzerland

2 *nm,f* (**a**) *(alumno)* boarder (**b**) *(preso)* prisoner, inmate

3 *nm RP (de teléfono)* (telephone) extension

interparlamentario, -a *adj* interparliamentary

interpelación *nf* formal question

interpelar *vt* to question

interpersonal *adj* interpersonal

interplanetario, -a *adj* interplanetary

Interpol [inter'pol] *nf (abrev de **International Criminal Police Organization**)* Interpol

interpolación *nf* insertion, inclusion

interpolar *vt* to interpolate, to put in

interponer [50] **1** *vt* (**a**) *(entre dos cosas)* to put *o* place *(between two things)*, to interpose (**b**) *Der* to lodge, to make

2 interponerse *vpr* **interponerse entre** *(estar)* to be placed *o* situated between; *(ponerse)* to come *o* get between; **se interponía una barrera entre ellos** there was a barrier between them; **interponerse entre dos contendientes** to intervene between two opponents

interposición *nf* (**a**) *(entre dos contendientes)* mediation (**b**) *(entre dos cosas)* **la i. del panel evita que llegue el ruido**

the panel serves as a barrier against noise (**c**) *Der* lodging *(of an appeal)*

interpretación *nf* (**a**) *(de ideas, significado)* interpretation (**b**) *(artística)* performance, interpretation; *(de obra musical)* performance, rendition; **estudia i. teatral** she's studying acting (**c**) *(traducción)* interpreting

interpretar *vt* (**a**) *(entender, explicar, traducir)* to interpret (**b**) *(artísticamente) (obra de teatro, sinfonía)* to perform; *(papel)* to play; *(canción)* to sing

interpretativo, -a *adj* (**a**) *(de la interpretación artística)* **tiene mucha capacidad interpretativa para los papeles cómicos** he's very good in comic roles; **el pianista tiene un gran estilo i.** he's a very stylish pianist (**b**) *(del significado)* interpretative

intérprete *nmf* (**a**) *(traductor) & Inform* interpreter (**b**) *(artista)* performer (**c**) *(comentarista)* commentator

interpuesto, -a *participio ver* **interponer**

interracial *adj* interracial

interregno *nm* interregnum

interrelación *nf* interrelation

interrelacionar 1 *vt* to interrelate
   2 interrelacionarse *vpr* to be interrelated

interrogación *nf* (**a**) *(signo)* question mark (**b**) *(pregunta)* question (**c**) *(interrogatorio)* interrogation

interrogador, -ora 1 *adj* questioning
   2 *nm,f (que interroga)* questioner; *(con amenazas)* interrogator

interrogante *nm o nf* (**a**) *(incógnita)* question (**b**) *(signo de interrogación)* question mark

interrogar [38] *vt (preguntar)* to question; *(con amenazas)* to interrogate

interrogativo, -a *adj* interrogative

interrogatorio *nm (preguntas)* questioning; *(con amenazas)* interrogation

interrumpir 1 *vt* (**a**) *(conversación, frase)* to interrupt; **¿interrumpo algo importante?** am I interrupting anything important? (**b**) *(servicio)* to suspend; **el servicio quedó interrumpido durante dos horas** services were suspended for two hours (**c**) *(viaje, vacaciones)* to cut short; **interrumpió sus vacaciones el día 8** he ended his vacation early on the 8th (**d**) *(circulación)* to block
   2 *vi* to interrupt; **espero no i.** I hope I'm not interrupting
   3 interrumpirse *vpr* to be interrupted; *(tráfico)* to be blocked; **se interrumpió para beber agua** she paused to take a drink of water

interrupción *nf* (**a**) *(corte, parada)* interruption; **i. (voluntaria) del embarazo** termination of pregnancy (**b**) *(de discurso, trabajo)* breaking off; *(de viaje, vacaciones)* cutting short (**c**) *(de circulación)* blocking

interruptor *nm* switch; **i. general** main utility switch *(for gas, water or electricity)*

intersección *nf* intersection

intersticio *nm* crack, gap

interurbano, -a *adj* intercity; *Tel* long-distance

intervalo *nm (gen) & Mús* interval; *(en representación)* intermission; **a intervalos** at intervals; **en el i. de un mes** in the space of a month

intervención *nf* (**a**) *(acción, participación)* intervention (**b**) *(discurso)* speech; *(pregunta, comentario)* contribution (**en** to) (**c**) *Fin (de cuentas)* auditing (**d**) *Med* operation (**e**) *Tel* tapping

intervencionismo *nm* interventionism

intervencionista *adj & nmf* interventionist

intervenir [69] **1** *vt* (**a**) *(operar)* **i. (quirúrgicamente)** to operate on (**b**) *(teléfono, línea)* to tap (**c**) *(incautarse de)* to seize (**d**) *Fin (cuentas)* to audit; *Am (empresa)* to put into administration
   2 *vi* (**a**) *(participar)* to take part (**en** in); *(en discusión, debate)* to make a contribution (**en** to); **intervino en varias películas**

cómicas she appeared in several comedy movies; **en la evolución de la economía intervienen muchos factores** several different factors play a part in the state of the economy; **después del presidente intervino el Sr. Ramírez** Mr. Ramírez spoke after the president (**b**) *(interferir, imponer el orden)* to intervene (**en** in) (**c**) *(operar)* **i. (quirúrgicamente)** to operate

interventor, -ora *nm,f* (**a**) *Fin* auditor (**b**) *(de tren)* ticket collector (**c**) *(en elecciones)* canvasser

interviú *nf* interview

intestado, -a *adj & nm,f* intestate

intestinal *adj* intestinal

intestino, -a 1 *adj* internecine
   2 *nm* intestine; **i. delgado/grueso** small/large intestine

intifada *nf* intifada

íntimamente *adv* (**a**) *(privadamente)* privately (**b**) *(a fondo)* intimately; **dos fenómenos í. relacionados** two phenomena which are intimately *o* closely connected (with each other)

intimar *vi* to be/become close (**con** to)

intimidación *nf* intimidation

intimidad *nf* (**a**) *(vida privada)* private life; **en la i.** in private; **violar la i. de alguien** to invade sb's privacy (**b**) *(amistad)* intimacy (**c**) **intimidades** *(asuntos privados)* personal matters

intimidar *vt* to intimidate

intimidatorio, -a *adj* intimidating, threatening

intimista *adj* **pintor i.** painter of domestic scenes; **novela i.** novel of family life

íntimo, -a 1 *adj* (**a**) *(vida, fiesta)* private; *(ambiente, restaurante)* intimate (**b**) *(relación, amistad)* close (**c**) *(sentimiento)* innermost; **en lo (más) í. de su corazón/alma** deep down in her heart/soul
   2 *nm,f* close friend

intitular *vt* to entitle, to call

intocable 1 *adj (persona, institución)* above criticism
   2 *nm (en la India)* untouchable

intolerable *adj (inaceptable, indignante)* intolerable, unacceptable; *(dolor, ruido)* unbearable

intolerancia *nf* intolerance

intolerante 1 *adj* intolerant
   2 *nmf* intolerant person

intoxicación *nf* poisoning; **una i. alimentaria** a bout of food poisoning

intoxicar [59] **1** *vt* to poison
   2 intoxicarse *vpr* to poison oneself

intraducible *adj* untranslatable

intragable *adj Fam (película, libro)* unbearable, awful

intramuros *adv* within the city walls

intramuscular *adj* intramuscular

intranet *(pl* intranets) *nf Inform* intranet

intranquilidad *nf* unease, anxiety

intranquilizar [14] **1** *vt* to worry, to make uneasy
   2 intranquilizarse *vpr* to get worried

intranquilo, -a *adj (preocupado)* worried, uneasy; *(nervioso)* restless

intranscendencia *nf* insignificance, unimportance

intranscendente *adj* insignificant, unimportant

intransferible *adj* nontransferable, untransferable

intransigencia *nf* intransigence

intransigente *adj* intransigent

intransitable *adj* impassable

intransitivo, -a *adj* intransitive

intrascendencia *nf* insignificance, unimportance

intrascendente *adj* insignificant, unimportant

intratable *adj* unsociable, difficult to get on with

intrauterino, -a *adj* intrauterine

intravenoso, -a *adj* intravenous

intrépido, -a *adj* intrepid

intriga *nf* (**a**) *(suspense)* curiosity; **película/novela de i.** thriller; **¡qué i.! ¿qué habrá pasado?** I'm dying to know what's happened! (**b**) *(maquinación)* intrigue (**c**) *(trama)* plot

intrigado, -a *adj* intrigued

intrigante 1 *adj* intriguing

2 *nmf (maquinador)* schemer; *(chismoso)* stirrer

intrigar [38] *vt & vi* to intrigue

intrincado, -a *adj* (**a**) *(bosque)* thick, dense (**b**) *(problema)* intricate

intrincar [59] *vt* to complicate, to confuse

intríngulis *nm inv Fam (dificultad)* snag, catch; *(quid)* nub, crux

intrínseco, -a *adj* intrinsic

intro *nm Inform* enter (key), return (key); **darle al i.** to press enter *o* return

introducción *nf* introduction (**a** to)

introducir [18] **1** *vt* (**a**) *(meter) (llave, carta)* to put in, to insert; *Inform (datos)* to input, to enter; **introduzca su número secreto** enter your PIN number (**b**) *(mercancías)* to bring in, to introduce; **una banda que introduce droga en el país** a gang smuggling drugs into the country (**c**) *(dar a conocer)* **i. a alguien en** to introduce sb to; **i. algo en** to introduce *o* bring sth to

2 introducirse *vpr* **introducirse en** to get into; **los ladrones se introdujeron en la casa por la ventana** the burglars got into the house through the window

introductor, -ora 1 *adj* introductory; **el país i. de esta moda** the country that brought in this fashion

2 *nm,f* introducer

introductorio, -a *adj* introductory

intromisión *nf* intrusion

introspección *nf* introspection

introspectivo, -a *adj* introspective

introvertido, -a *adj & nm,f* introvert

intrusión *nf* intrusion

intrusismo *nm* = illegal practice of a profession

intruso, -a *nm,f* intruder

intubar *vt* to intubate

intuición *nf* intuition; **tener una i.** to have a (gut) feeling

intuir [34] *vt* to know by intuition, to sense

intuitivo, -a *adj* intuitive

intuyera *etc ver* **intuir**

intuyo *etc ver* **intuir**

inuit *(pl* **inuit** *o* **inuits**) *adj & nmf* Inuit

inundación *nf* flood, flooding

inundar 1 *vt (por las aguas)* to flood; *(por turistas, aficionados)* to swamp; *(con quejas, pedidos)* to inundate, to swamp

2 inundarse *vpr (con agua)* to flood; **inundarse de** *(turistas, quejas)* to be inundated *o* swamped with

inusitado, -a *adj* uncommon, rare

inusual *adj* unusual

inútil 1 *adj* (**a**) *(objeto)* useless; *(intento, esfuerzo)* unsuccessful, vain; **sus intentos resultaron inútiles** his attempts were unsuccessful *o* in vain; **es i., ya es demasiado tarde** there's no point, it's too late; **es i. que lo esperes, se ha ido para siempre** there's no point in waiting for him, he's gone for good (**b**) *(inválido)* disabled (**c**) *(no apto)* unfit

2 *nmf* hopeless case, useless person; **es un i.** he's useless *o* hopeless

inutilidad *nf* (**a**) *(falta de utilidad)* uselessness; *(falta de eficacia)* ineffectiveness; *(falta de sentido)* pointlessness (**b**) *(invalidez)* disablement

inutilizar [14] *vt (máquinas, dispositivos)* to disable, to put out of action; **esas cajas inutilizan la habitación de**

huéspedes those boxes are stopping us from using the guest room

invadir *vt* (**a**) *(sujeto: ejército)* to invade; **los turistas invadieron el museo** the tourists flooded the museum (**b**) *(sujeto: sentimiento)* to overcome, to overwhelm; **lo invadió la tristeza** he was overcome by sadness (**c**) *Aut* **i. el carril contrario** to go onto the wrong side of the road

invalidación *nf* invalidation

invalidar *vt (sujeto: circunstancias)* to invalidate; *(sujeto: árbitro, juez)* to declare invalid

invalidez *nf* (**a**) *Med* disablement, disability; **i. permanente/temporal** permanent/temporary disability (**b**) *Der* invalidity

inválido, -a 1 *adj* (**a**) *Med* disabled (**b**) *Der* invalid

2 *nm,f* invalid, disabled person; **los inválidos** the disabled

invalorable *adj CSur* invaluable

invariable *adj* invariable

invasión *nf* invasion

invasor, -ora 1 *adj* invading

2 *nm,f* invader

invectiva *nf* invective

invencible *adj (ejército, enemigo)* invincible; *(timidez)* insurmountable, insuperable

invención *nf* invention

invendible *adj* unsaleable

inventado, -a *adj* made-up

inventar 1 *vt (máquina, sistema)* to invent; *(narración, falsedades)* to make up

2 inventarse *vpr* to make up

inventariar [32] *vt* to make an inventory of

inventario *nm* inventory; *Com* **hacer el i.** to do the inventory *o* stocktaking

inventiva *nf* inventiveness

invento *nm (invención)* invention; *(mentira)* lie, fib

inventor, -ora *nm,f* inventor

invernadero *nm* greenhouse

invernal *adj (de invierno)* winter; *(tiempo, paisaje)* wintry; **temporada i.** winter season

invernar *vi (pasar el invierno)* to (spend the) winter; *(hibernar)* to hibernate

inverosímil *adj* improbable, implausible

inverosimilitud *nf* improbability, implausibility

inversión *nf* (**a**) *(del orden)* inversion (**b**) *(de dinero, tiempo)* investment; **i. de capital** capital investment; **i. del exterior** incoming foreign investment; **inversiones extranjeras** foreign investments; **i. en paraíso fiscal** offshore investment

inversionista *nmf* investor

inverso, -a *adj* opposite; **a la inversa** the other way around; **en orden i.** in reverse *o* inverse order; **contar/escribir en orden i.** to count/write backward; **traducción inversa** translation into a foreign language

inversor, -ora 1 *adj* investing

2 *nm,f Com & Fin* investor

3 *nm Elec* inverter

invertebrado, -a *adj & nm Zool* invertebrate

invertido, -a 1 *adj* (**a**) *(al revés)* reversed, inverted; *(sentido, dirección)* opposite (**b**) *(dinero)* invested (**c**) *(homosexual)* homosexual

2 *nm,f* homosexual

invertir [62] *vt* (**a**) *(orden)* to reverse; *(poner boca abajo)* to turn upside down, to invert (**b**) *(dinero, tiempo, esfuerzo)* to invest (**c**) *(tardar) (tiempo)* to spend

investidura *nf* investiture

investigación *nf* (**a**) *(estudio)* research; **i. científica** scientific research; **i. y desarrollo** research and development

(b) *(indagación)* investigation, inquiry; **la i. del asesinato** the murder inquiry

investigador, -ora 1 *adj* **(a)** *(que estudia)* research; **capacidad investigadora** research capability **(b)** *(que indaga)* investigating

2 *nm,f* **(a)** *(estudioso)* researcher **(b)** *(detective)* investigator; **i. privado** private investigator *o* detective

investigar [38] **1** *vt* **(a)** *(estudiar)* to research **(b)** *(indagar)* to investigate

2 *vi* **(a)** *(estudiar)* to do research **(b)** *(indagar)* to investigate

investir [47] *vt* **i. a alguien de** *o* **con algo** to invest sb with sth

inveterado, -a *adj* deep-rooted

inviabilidad *nf* impracticability

inviable *adj* impractical, unviable

invicto, -a *adj* unconquered, unbeaten

invidencia *nf* blindness

invidente 1 *adj* blind, sightless

2 *nmf* blind *o* sightless person; **los invidentes** the blind

invierno *nm* **(a)** *(estación)* winter; **en i.** in winter, in wintertime; **i. nuclear** nuclear winter **(b)** *(estación lluviosa)* rainy season

invierta *etc ver* **invertir**

inviolabilidad *nf* inviolability

inviolable *adj* inviolable

invirtiera *etc ver* **invertir**

invisible *adj* invisible

invitación *nf* invitation

invitado, -a *nm,f* guest

invitar 1 *vt* **(a)** *(convidar)* **i. a alguien (a algo/a hacer algo)** to invite sb (to sth/to do sth); **me han invitado a una fiesta** I've been invited to a party; **me invitó a entrar** she asked me in **(b)** *(pagar)* **te invito** it's my treat, this one's on me; **i. a alguien a algo** to buy sb sth *(food, drink)*; **me invitó a una cerveza** he bought me a beer; **te invito a cenar fuera** I'll take you out for dinner

2 *vi* **(a)** *(pagar)* to pay; **invito yo** it's my treat, this one's on me; **invita la casa** it's on the house **(b)** *(incitar)* **i. a algo** to encourage sth; **este sol invita a salir** the sun makes you want to go out

in vitro *loc adj & adv* in vitro; **fecundación i.** in vitro fertilization

invocación *nf* invocation

invocar [59] *vt* to invoke

involución *nf* regression, deterioration

involucionar *vi* to regress, to deteriorate

involucionismo *nm* reactionary nature; **las fuerzas del i.** the forces of reaction

involucionista 1 *adj* regressive, reactionary

2 *nmf* reactionary

involucrado, -a *adj* *(en acciones, proyecto, accidente)* involved; *(en delito, escándalo)* implicated

involucrar 1 *vt* **i. a alguien (en)** to involve sb (in)

2 involucrarse *vpr* to get involved **(en** in)

involuntario, -a *adj* *(espontáneo)* involuntary; *(sin querer)* unintentional

invoque *etc ver* **invocar**

invulnerabilidad *nf* invulnerability

invulnerable *adj* immune **(a** to), invulnerable **(a** to)

inyección *nf* **(a)** *(con jeringa)* injection; **poner una i. a alguien** to give sb an injection; **i. intravenosa** intravenous injection **(b)** *Tec & Aut* injection; **motor de i.** fuel-injected engine; **i. de combustible** fuel injection; **i. de tinta** ink-jet **(c)** *(de dinero, humor, vitalidad)* injection; **sus palabras fueron una i. de moral para las tropas** his words were a morale booster for the troops

inyectable 1 *adj* injectable

2 *nm* injection

inyectar 1 *vt* **(a)** *(con jeringa)* to inject; **le inyectaron insulina** they gave him an insulin injection **(b)** *(dinero, humor, vitalidad)* to inject

2 inyectarse *vpr* **inyectarse algo** to inject oneself with sth; **inyectarse drogas** to take drugs intravenously

iodo *nm* iodine

ion *nm* ion

iónico, -a *adj* ionic

ionización *nf* ionization

ionizador *nm* ionizer

ionizar [14] *vt* to ionize

ionosfera *nf* ionosphere

IPC *nm* *(abrev de Esp* **Índice de Precios al Consumo** *o Am* **Índice de Precios al Consumidor)** CPI

ipso facto *adv* immediately

ir [35] **1** *vi* **(a)** *(en general)* to go; **ir hacia el sur/al cine** to go south/to the movies; **ir en autobús/coche** to go by bus/car; **ir andando** to go on foot, to walk; **¡vamos!** let's go!

(b) *(expresa duración gradual)* **ir haciendo algo** to be (gradually) doing sth; **va anocheciendo** it's getting dark; **voy mejorando mi estilo** I'm working on improving my style

(c) *(expresa intención, opinión)* **ir a hacer algo** to be going to do sth; **voy a decírselo a tu padre** I'm going to tell your father; **te voy a echar de menos** I'm going to miss you

(d) *(cambiar)* **ir a mejor/peor** to get better/worse

(e) *(funcionar)* to work; **la manivela va floja** the crank is loose; **la televisión no va** the television isn't working

(f) *(desenvolverse)* to go; **le va bien en su nuevo trabajo** things are going well for him in his new job; **su negocio va mal** his business is going badly; **¿cómo te va?** how are you doing?

(g) *(corresponder)* to go; **estas tazas van con estos platos** these cups go with these saucers

(h) *(colocarse)* to go, to belong; **esto no va ahí** that doesn't go *o* belong there

(i) *Esp (gustar, convenir)* **no me va el pop** I don't like pop music; **ni me va ni me viene** I don't care one way or the other

(j) *(vestir)* **ir en/con** to wear; **iba en camisa y corbata** he was wearing a shirt and tie; **ir de azul/de uniforme** to be dressed in blue/in uniform; **iba hecho un pordiosero** he looked like a beggar

(k) *(vacaciones, tratamiento)* **irle bien a alguien** to do sb good

(l) *(ropa)* **irle (bien) a alguien** to suit sb; **ir con algo** to go with sth; **esta camisa no va con esos pantalones** this shirt doesn't go with these pants

(m) *(expresa apoyo)* **ir con** to support; **voy con el Real Madrid** I support Real Madrid

(n) *(comentario, indirecta)* **ir por alguien** to be meant for sb, to be aimed at sb

(o) *Esp (película, novela)* **ir de** to be about

(p) *Fam Esp* **ir de,** *RP* **irla de** *(persona)* to think oneself; **va de listo** he thinks he's clever; **¿de qué vas?** just who do you think you are?

(q) *Esp (buscar)* **ir (a) por algo/alguien** to go and get sth/sb, to go and fetch sth/sb

(r) *(alcanzar)* **va por el cuarto vaso de vino** he's already on his fourth glass of wine; **vamos por la mitad de la asignatura** we've covered about half the subject

(s) *(expresiones)* **fue y dijo que...** he went and said that...; **ir a lo suyo** to look out for oneself, to look after number one; **¡qué va!** *(por supuesto que no)* not in the least!, not at all!; *(me temo que no)* I'm afraid not; *(no digas tonterías)* don't be ridiculous; *Esp* **ser el no va más** to be the ultimate

2 irse *vpr* **(a)** *(marcharse)* to go, to leave; **irse a** to go to; **¡vete!** go away! **(b)** *(gastarse, desaparecer)* to go; **se ha ido la**

luz there's been a power cut (**c**) **irse abajo** *(edificio)* to fall down; *(negocio)* to collapse; *(planes)* to fall through

IRA ['ira] *nm (abrev de* **Irish Republican Army**) IRA

ira *nf* anger, rage

iracundo, -a *adj (furioso)* angry, irate; *(irascible)* irascible

Irak *n* Iraq

irakí = **iraquí**

Irán *n* Iran

iraní *(pl* **iraníes**) **1** *adj & nmf* Iranian

  2 *nm (lengua)* Iranian

Iraq *n* Iraq

iraquí *(pl* **iraquíes**), **irakí** *(pl* **irakíes**) *adj & nmf* Iraqi

irascible *adj* irascible

iridiscencia *nf* iridescence

iridiscente *adj* iridescent

iridología *nf* iridology

iridólogo, -a *nm,f Med* iridologist

iris *nm inv* iris

Irlanda *n* Ireland; **I. del Norte** Northern Ireland

irlandés, -esa 1 *adj* Irish

  2 *nm,f (persona)* Irishman, *f* Irishwoman; **los irlandeses** the Irish

  3 *nm (lengua)* Irish

ironía *nf* irony

irónico, -a *adj* ironic, ironical

ironizar [14] **1** *vt* to ridicule

  2 *vi* to be ironical (**sobre** about)

IRPF *nm (abrev de* **Impuesto sobre la Renta de las Personas Físicas**) = Spanish personal income tax

irracional *adj* irrational

irracionalidad *nf* irrationality

irradiación *nf* (**a**) *(de luz, calor)* radiation (**b**) *(de cultura, ideas)* dissemination, spreading (**c**) *(de alimentos)* irradiation

irradiar *vt* (**a**) *(luz, calor)* to radiate (**b**) *(alimentos, enfermo, órgano)* to irradiate (**c**) *(simpatía, felicidad)* to radiate

irrazonable *adj* unreasonable

irreal *adj* unreal

irrealidad *nf* unreality

irrealizable *adj (sueño, objetivo)* unattainable; *(plan)* impractical

irrebatible *adj* irrefutable, indisputable

irreconciliable *adj* irreconcilable

irreconocible *adj* unrecognizable

irrecuperable *adj* irretrievable

irreductible *adj* (**a**) *(fenómeno, fracción)* irreducible (**b**) *(país, pueblo)* unconquerable

irreemplazable *adj* irreplaceable

irreflexión *nf* rashness

irreflexivo, -a *adj* rash

irrefrenable *adj* irrepressible, uncontainable

irrefutable *adj* irrefutable

irregular *adj* (**a**) *(no uniforme) (terreno, superficie)* uneven; *(comportamiento)* erratic; **su rendimiento en los estudios es i.** he's inconsistent in his studies (**b**) *(situación)* irregular; **la financiación i. de los partidos** the irregular funding of the parties (**c**) *Ling (verbo)* irregular

irregularidad *nf* (**a**) *(de terreno, superficie)* unevenness (**b**) *(de situación)* irregularity (**c**) *(delito, falta)* irregularity (**d**) *Ling (de verbo)* irregularity

irrelevancia *nf* unimportance, insignificance

irrelevante *adj* unimportant, insignificant

irremediable *adj* unavoidable

irremediablemente *adv* inevitably

irremisible *adj (imperdonable)* unpardonable; *(irremediable)* irremediable

irremplazable *adj* irreplaceable

irreparable *adj* irreparable

irrepetible *adj* unique, unrepeatable

irreprimible *adj* irrepressible

irreprochable *adj* irreproachable

irresistible *adj* irresistible

irresoluble *adj* unsolvable

irresoluto, -a *adj Formal* irresolute

irrespetuoso, -a *adj* disrespectful

irrespirable *adj (aire)* unbreathable; *Fig (ambiente)* oppressive

irresponsabilidad *nf* irresponsibility

irresponsable 1 *adj* irresponsible

  2 *nmf* irresponsible person

irrestricto, -a *adj Am* unconditional, complete

irreverente *adj* irreverent

irreversible *adj* irreversible

irrevocable *adj* irrevocable

irrigación *nf* irrigation

irrigador *nm Med* irrigator

irrigar [38] *vt* to irrigate

irrisorio, -a *adj (excusa, historia)* laughable, risible; **nos ofrecieron un precio i.** we were offered a derisory sum; **una cantidad irrisoria** a ridiculously *o* ludicrously small amount

irritabilidad *nf* irritability

irritable *adj* irritable

irritación *nf* irritation

irritado, -a *adj* (**a**) *(persona)* irritated, annoyed (**b**) *(piel)* irritated

irritante *adj* irritating

irritar 1 *vt* to irritate

  2 irritarse *vpr* (**a**) *(enfadarse)* to get angry *o* annoyed (**b**) *(sujeto: piel)* to become irritated

irrompible *adj* unbreakable

irrumpir *vi* **i. en** *(lugar, vida)* to burst into; *(escena política, pantalla)* to burst onto

irrupción *nf (en lugar)* irruption (**en** into), bursting in; **su i. en la política** his sudden appearance on the political scene; **su i. en mi vida** his sudden entrance into my life

isabelino, -a *adj (en España)* Isabelline; *(en Inglaterra)* Elizabethan

ISBN *nm (abrev de* **International Standard Book Number**) ISBN

isla *nf* (**a**) *island*; **las Islas Baleares** the Balearic Islands; **las Islas Británicas** the British Isles; **las Islas Canarias** the Canary Islands; **i. desierta** desert island; **las Islas Malvinas** the Falkland Islands, the Falklands; **la I. de Man** the Isle of Man; **la I. de Pascua** Easter Island (**b**) *Méx, RP (de árboles)* grove (**c**) *Ven (mediana)* median (strip)

islam *nm* Islam

Islamabad *n* Islamabad

islámico, -a *adj* Islamic

islamismo *nm* Islam

islamizar [14] **1** *vt* to Islamize, to convert to Islam

  2 islamizarse *vpr* to convert to Islam

islandés, -esa 1 *adj* Icelandic

  2 *nm,f (persona)* Icelander

  3 *nm (lengua)* Icelandic

Islandia *n* Iceland

isleño, -a 1 *adj* island; **las costumbres isleñas** the island customs

  2 *nm,f* islander

isleta *nf (en calle)* traffic island

islote *nm* small island

ISO ['iso] *(abrev de* **International Standards Organization**) ISO

isobara, isóbara *nf* isobar

isomorfo, -a *adj* isomorphic

isósceles *adj inv* isosceles

isoterma *nf Meteo (línea)* isotherm

isotérmico, -a, isotermo, -a *adj* **camión i.** refrigerated truck

isotónico, -a *adj* isotonic

isótopo 1 *adj* isotopic
   2 *nm* isotope

Israel *n* Israel

israelí (*pl* **israelíes**) *adj & nmf* Israeli

israelita *adj & nmf* Israelite

istmo *nm* isthmus

Italia *n* Italy

italianismo *nm* Italianism

italianizar [14] *vt* to Italianize

italiano, -a 1 *adj & nm,f* Italian
   2 *nm (lengua)* Italian

itálico, -a *adj & nm,f Hist* Italic

ítem (*pl* **ítems**) *nm* item

iteración *nf* iteration

itinerante *adj (vida)* itinerant; *(exposición)* traveling; *(embajador)* roving

itinerario *nm* route, itinerary

ITV *nf Esp* (*abrev de* **inspección técnica de vehículos**) = annual technical inspection for motor vehicles with an age of five years or more

IU *nf* (*abrev de* **Izquierda Unida**) = Spanish left-wing coalition party

IVA ['iβa] *nm* (*abrev de Esp* **impuesto sobre el valor añadido,** *Am* **impuesto al valor agregado**) value-added tax, ≃ sales tax

izar [14] *vt* to raise, to hoist

izda (*abrev de* **izquierda**) L, l

izquierda *nf* (**a**) *(lado)* left; **a la i. (de)** on *o* to the left (of); **girar a la i.** to turn left (**b**) *(mano)* left hand (**c**) *Pol* left (wing); *Esp* **de izquierdas,** *Am* **de i.** left-wing; **i. radical** hard left (**d**) *(puerta)* **el segundo i.** the left-hand apartment on the third floor

izquierdismo *nm* left-wing views

izquierdista 1 *adj* left-wing
   2 *nmf* left-winger

izquierdo, -a *adj* left; **mano/pierna izquierda** left hand/ leg; **el margen i.** the left-hand margin; **a mano izquierda** on the left-hand side

izquierdoso, -a *adj Fam* leftish

J

J, j ['χota] *nf (letra)* J, j

ja *interj* **¡ja!** ha!

jabalí (*pl* **jabalíes**) *nm* wild boar

jabalina *nf Dep* javelin

jabato, -a 1 *adj Esp Fam (valiente)* brave
  2 *nm* **(a)** *(animal)* young wild boar **(b)** *Esp Fam (valiente)* daredevil

jabón *nm* soap; *Fam Fig* **dar j. a alguien** to soft-soap sb; **j. de afeitar** shaving soap; **j. líquido** liquid soap; **j. de tocador** toilet soap

jabonar *vt* to soap

jaboncillo *nm* tailor's chalk

jabonera *nf* soap dish

jabonoso, -a *adj* soapy

jabugo *nm* = good quality cured ham from Jabugo, similar to Parma ham

jaca *nf (caballo pequeño)* pony; *(yegua)* mare

jacal *nm Méx* hut

jacinto *nm* hyacinth

jaco *nm* **(a)** *(caballo)* nag **(b)** *Fam (heroína)* junk, smack

jacobeo, -a *adj* of/relating to St James; **la ruta jacobea** = pilgrim's route to Santiago de Compostela

jacobinismo *nm Pol* Jacobinism

jacobino, -a *adj & nm,f Pol* Jacobin

jactancia *nf* boasting

jactancioso, -a *adj* boastful

jactarse *vpr* to boast (**de** about *o* of)

jaculatoria *nf Rel* short prayer

jacuzzi [ja'kusi] *nm* Jacuzzi®

jade *nm* jade

jadeante *adj* panting

jadear *vi* to pant

jadeo *nm* panting

jaguar *nm* jaguar

jaiba *nf Am salvo RP* crayfish

jaima *nf* = Bedouin tent

jalada *nf* **(a)** *Méx (tirón)* pull; *(suave)* tug; **dar una j. a algo** to pull sth; *(suavemente)* to tug sth **(b)** *Méx Fam (reprimenda)* telling off; **dar una j. a alguien** to tell sb off **(c)** *Perú Fam (aventón)* ride; **dar una j. a alguien** to give sb a ride

jalar¹, halar 1 *vt* **(a)** *Am salvo RP (tirar de)* to pull; *(suavemente)* to tug; **lo jaló de la manga** she pulled his sleeve **(b)** *Perú Fam (transportar)* to give a ride
  2 *vi Am salvo RP* **(a)** *(tirar)* to pull; **jale** *(en letrero)* pull **(b)** *(irse)* to go

jalar² *Esp Fam* **1** *vt (comer)* to eat
  2 *vi* to eat
  3 jalarse *vpr (comerse)* to eat

jale *nm Méx Fam* work

jalea *nf* jelly; **j. real** royal jelly

jalear *vt* to cheer on

jaleo *nm Fam* **(a)** *(alboroto)* row, rumpus; **armar j.** to kick up a row *o* fuss **(b)** *(lío)* mess, confusion **(c)** *(aplausos, gritos)* cheering

jalón *nm* **(a)** *(vara)* marker pole; *(hito)* landmark, milestone **(b)** *Am salvo RP (tirón)* pull; *(suave)* tug; *(reprimenda)* to give someone a telling off

jalonar *vt (con varas)* to stake *o* mark out; *(señalar)* to mark

Jamaica *n* Jamaica

jamaicano, -a *adj & nm,f* Jamaican

jamás *adv* never; **no lo he visto j.** I've never seen him; **la mejor novela que j. se haya escrito** the best novel ever written; **j. en la vida había visto algo así** never before had I seen such a thing, I'd never seen such a thing in all my life; **nunca j.** never ever; **por siempre j.** for evermore; *Fam* **¡j. de los jamases!** not in a million years!

jamba *nf* jamb, door post

jamelgo *nm Fam* nag

jamón *nm* ham; *Esp Fam* **¡y un j. (con chorreras)!** you've got to be joking!, not on your life!; **j. (de) York** *o* **dulce** (boiled) ham; **j. serrano** cured ham, Parma ham

jamona *Fam* **1** *adj* well-stacked, buxom
  2 *nf* buxom wench, well-stacked woman

jane® *nf Urug* bleach

Japón *nm* **(el) J.** Japan

japonés, -esa 1 *adj & nm,f* Japanese
  2 *nm (lengua)* Japanese

japuta *nf* Ray's bream, Atlantic pomfret

jaque *nm* **j. (al rey)** check; **j. mate** checkmate; *Fig* **tener en j. a alguien** to keep sb in a state of anxiety

jaqueca *nf* migraine; *Fam* **dar j. (a alguien)** to bother (sb), to pester (sb)

jarabe *nm* syrup; **j. para la tos** cough mixture *o* syrup; *Esp Fam* **¡te voy a dar j. de palo!** I'll give you a clip around the ear!; *Fam* **tener mucho j. de pico** to have the gift of the gab, to be a smooth talker

jarana *nf Fam* **(a)** *(juerga)* **estar/irse de j.** to be/go out on the town **(b)** *(alboroto)* rumpus, shindy

jaranero, -a *Fam* **1** *adj* fond of partying
  2 *nm,f* party animal

jarcia *nf Náut* rigging

jardín *nm* yard; **j. botánico** botanic(al) garden; **j. del Edén** Garden of Eden; **j. de infancia** kindergarten, nursery school; **j. zoológico** zoo

jardinera *nf* planter

jardinería *nf* gardening

jardinero, -a *nm,f* gardener; *Culin* **a la jardinera** garnished with vegetables

jarra *nf (para servir)* jug; *(para beber)* tankard; **con los brazos en jarras** *(postura)* hands on hips, with arms akimbo; **j. de cerveza** beer glass; **j. de leche** milk jug

jarrear *v impersonal Fam* **está jarreando** it's coming down in buckets, it's pouring

jarrete *nm* hock

jarro *nm* jug; *Fig* **fue como un j. de agua fría** it was a bolt from the blue; **llover a jarros** to be bucketing down

jarrón *nm* vase

Jartum *n* Khartoum

jaspe *nm* jasper

jaspeado, -a 1 *adj* mottled, speckled

2 *nm* mottling

jaspear *vt* to mottle, to speckle

jauja *nf Fam* paradise, heaven on earth; **ser j.** to be heaven on earth *o* paradise

jaula *nf* cage; *Fig* **j. de oro** gilded cage

jauría *nf (de perros)* pack

Java 1 *nm Inform* Java

2 *n* Java

javanés, -esa *adj & nm,f* Javanese

jazmín *nm* jasmine

jazz [jas] *nm inv* jazz

jazzístico, -a [ja'sistiko] *adj* jazz

JC *(abrev de* **Jesucristo)** JC

je *interj* ¡je! ha!

jeans [jins] *nmpl* jeans; **unos j.** a pair of jeans

jeep [jip] *(pl* **jeeps)** *nm* jeep

jefatura *nf* (a) *(cargo)* leadership (b) *(organismo)* headquarters, head office

jefazo, -a *nm,f Fam* big boss, head honcho

jefe, -a *nm,f* (a) *(persona al mando)* boss; *(de empresa)* manager; *(líder)* leader; *(de tribu, ejército)* chief; *(de departamento)* head; *Mil* **en j.** in chief; **j. de cocina** head chef; **j. de compras** purchasing manager; **j. de estación** stationmaster; **j. de Estado** head of state; **j. del estado mayor** chief of staff; **j. de estudios** director of studies; **j. de gobierno** head of government; **j. de personal** personnel manager; **j. de prensa** press officer; **j. de producción** production manager; **j. de redacción** editor in chief; **j. de ventas** sales manager

(b) *Fam (camarero, conductor)* **j., pónganos dos cervezas** give us two beers, Mac

Jehová *n* Jehovah

jemer *nm* **jemeres rojos** Khmer Rouge

jengibre *nm* ginger

jeque *nm* sheikh

jerarca *nm* high-ranking person, leader

jerarquía *nf* hierarchy; **las altas jerarquías de la nación** the leaders of the nation

jerárquico, -a *adj* hierarchical

jerarquizar [14] *vt* to structure in a hierarchical manner

jerez *nm* sherry; **j. fino** dry sherry

jerga *nf* jargon

jergón *nm* straw mattress

jerifalte *nm* (a) *(ave)* gyrfalcon (b) *(persona)* bigwig

jerigonza *nf (galimatías)* gibberish; *(jerga)* jargon

jeringa *nf* syringe

jeringar *vt Fam (fastidiar)* to bug

jeringuilla *nf* syringe; **j. hipodérmica** hypodermic syringe

jeroglífico, -a 1 *adj* hieroglyphic

2 *nm* (a) *(inscripción)* hieroglyphic (b) *(pasatiempo)* rebus

jersey *(pl* **jerseys** *o* **jerséis)** *nm Esp (prenda)* sweater; **j. de cuello alto** polo neck (sweater)

Jerusalén *n* Jerusalem

Jesucristo *n* Jesus Christ

jesuita *adj & nm Rel* Jesuit

jesuítico, -a *adj (ambiguo, disimulado)* jesuitical, devious

jesús *interj* ¡j.! *(sorpresa)* gosh!, good heavens!; *Esp (tras estornudo)* bless you!; *Fam* **en un decir j.** in the blink of an eye

jet [jet] *(pl* **jets) 1** *nm* jet

2 *nf Esp* **la j.** the jet set

jeta *Fam* **1** *nf (cara)* mug, face; **romperle la j. a alguien** to smash sb's face in; *Esp* **tener (mucha) j.** to be a wise guy

2 *nmf Esp* **ser un j.** to be a wise guy

jet lag ['jetlag] *nm* jet lag

jet-set ['jetset] *Esp nf, Am nm* jet set

jíbaro, -a 1 *adj* Jivaro; **las tribus jíbaras** the Jivaro tribes

2 *nm,f* Jivaro

jibia *nf* cuttlefish

jiennense 1 *adj* of/from Jaén

2 *nmf* person from Jaén

jijona *nm* = type of nougat made in Jijona

jilguero *nm* goldfinch

jilipollada *nf muy Fam* **hacer/decir una j.** to do/say something goddamn stupid

jilipollas *muy Fam* **1** *adj inv* daft, dumb

2 *nmf inv* jerk

jilipollez *muy Fam nf inv* **hacer/decir una j.** to do/say something goddamn stupid

jineta *nf* civet (cat)

jinete *nmf* horseman, *f* horsewoman; **el caballo derribó al j.** the horse threw its rider

jingoísmo *nm Pol* jingoism

jiote *nm Méx* rash

jipioso, -a *adj Fam (de estilo hippie)* hippie

jirafa *nf* (a) *Zool* giraffe (b) *Cine & TV* boom

jirón *nm* (a) *(andrajo)* shred, rag; **hecho jirones** in tatters (b) *Perú (calle)* street

jitomate *nm Méx* tomato

jiu-jitsu [jiu'jitsu] *nm* jujitsu

JJ. OO. *nmpl (abrev de* **Juegos Olímpicos)** Olympic Games

jo *interj Esp Fam Euf* ¡jo! *(fastidio)* sugar!; *(asombro, admiración)* wow!; **¡jo, mamá, yo quiero ir!** but Mom, I want to go!

jobar *interj Esp Fam Euf* ¡j.! Jeez!

jockey ['jokei] *(pl* **jockeys)** *nm* jockey

jocosidad *nf* jocularity

jocoso, -a *adj* jocular

jocundo, -a *adj Formal* jovial, cheerful

joder *Vulg* **1** *vi* (a) *(fastidiar)* to mess around *o* about; **¡no jodas!** *(incredulidad, sorpresa)* no shit! (b) *Esp (copular)* to fuck

2 *vt* (a) *(molestar)* **j. a alguien** to piss sb off (b) *(estropear)* to screw up (c) *Esp (copular con)* to fuck

3 *interj Esp (expresa dolor, enfado, sorpresa)* ¡j.! Christ!, Jesus!

4 joderse *vpr* (a) *(aguantarse)* to fucking well put up with it; **¡que se joda!** he can fuck off!; **¡hay que joderse!** can you fucking believe it? (b) *(estropearse)* **se ha jodido la tele** the TV's screwed up

jodido, -a *adj Vulg* (a) *(físicamente)* screwed; *(anímicamente)* fucked up (b) *(estropeado)* bust (c) *(difícil)* fucking difficult; **es muy j. levantarse a las seis** getting up at six is a real bastard

jodienda *nf Esp Vulg* pain (in the ass)

jofaina *nf* washbowl

jogging ['joɣin] *nm* (a) *(deporte)* jogging (b) *RP (ropa)* tracksuit

Johannesburgo [joχanes'burgo] *n* Johannesburg

joker ['joker] *(pl* **jokers)** *nm* joker *(in cards)*

jolgorio *nm* merrymaking

jolín, jolines *interj Fam* ¡j.!, *(fastidio)* shucks!, blast!; *(sorpresa)* gosh!, wow!

jondo *adj* **cante j.** = traditional flamenco singing

jónico, -a *adj* Ionic

jonrón *nm Am (en béisbol)* home run

jopé *interj Esp Fam* ¡j.! Jeez!

Jordania *n* Jordan

jordano, -a *adj & nm,f* Jordanian

jornada *nf* (a) *(de trabajo)* workday; **j. electoral** polling day; **j. intensiva** = workday from 8 am to 3 pm with only a short lunch break; **j. laboral** workday; **media j.** half day; **j. partida** = workday with long (2-3 hour) lunch break, ending at 7-8 pm; **j. de puertas abiertas** open day, open house; **j. de reflexión** = day immediately before elections when campaigning is forbidden; **jornadas (sobre)** *(congreso)* conference (on) **(b)** *(de viaje)* day's journey **(c)** *Dep* round of games *o* matches, program

jornal *nm* day's wage

jornalero, -a *nm,f* day laborer

joroba *nf* hump

jorobado, -a 1 *adj* **(a)** *(con joroba)* hunchbacked **(b)** *Fam (estropeado)* bust; **tengo el estómago j.** my stomach's acting up

2 *nm,f (con joroba)* hunchback

jorobar 1 *vt Fam* **(a)** *(molestar)* to bug **(b)** *(estropear) (fiesta, planes)* to mess up; *(máquina, objeto)* to bust

2 jorobarse *vpr Fam* **(a)** *(fastidiarse, aguantarse)* **¡pues te jorobas!** you can like it or lump it! **(b)** *(estropearse)* to bust

jorongo *nm Méx* **(a)** *(manta)* blanket **(b)** *(poncho)* poncho

jota *nf* **(a)** = lively folk song and dance, originally from Aragon **(b)** *Fam* **no entender ni j. (de)** *(no comprender)* not to understand a word (of); **no saber ni j. de algo** not to know the first thing about sth; **no ver ni j.** *(por mala vista)* to be as blind as a bat; *(por oscuridad)* not to be able to see a thing

jotero, -a *nm,f* jota dancer/singer

joto *nm Méx Fam Pey* fag

joven 1 *adj* young; **está muy j. para su edad** he looks very young for his age; **esa ropa te hace más j.** those clothes make you look younger; **de j.** as a young man/woman; **la noche es j.** the night is young; **moda j.** youth fashion

2 *nmf* **(a)** *(persona joven)* young man, *f* young woman; **los jóvenes** young people **(b)** *(como apelativo)* **¡oiga, j.!** excuse me young man!

jovenzuelo, -a *nm,f* youngster

jovial *adj* jovial, cheerful

jovialidad *nf* joviality, cheerfulness

joya *nf* jewel; *Fig* gem; **el nuevo empleado es una j.** the new worker is a real gem; **la j. de mi colección** the pride of my collection; **las joyas de la corona** the crown jewels

joyería *nf* **(a)** *(tienda)* jeweler's (shop) **(b)** *(arte, comercio)* jewelry

joyero, -a 1 *nm,f (persona)* jeweler

2 *nm (caja)* jewelry box

joystick ['joistik] *(pl* joysticks) *nm* joystick

Jr. *(abrev de* **júnior)** Jr.

juanete *nm* bunion

jubilación *nf* **(a)** *(retiro)* retirement; **j. anticipada** early retirement **(b)** *(pensión)* pension

jubilado, -a 1 *adj* retired

2 *nm,f* retiree; **club de jubilados** senior citizens' club

jubilar 1 *vt* **j. a alguien (de)** to pension sb off (from), to retire sb (from)

2 jubilarse *vpr* to retire

jubileo *nm Rel* jubilee

júbilo *nm* jubilation, joy

jubiloso, -a *adj* jubilant, joyous

judaico, -a *adj* Judaic, Jewish

judaísmo *nm* Judaism

judas *nm inv* Judas, traitor

judeocristiano, -a *adj* Judeo-Christian

judeoespañol, -ola 1 *adj* Sephardic

2 *nm,f (persona)* Sephardic Jew

3 *nm (lengua)* Sephardi

judería *nf Hist* Jewish ghetto *o* quarter

judía *nf* bean; **j. blanca** haricot bean; *Esp* **j. verde** green bean

judiada *nf Fam* dirty trick

judicatura *nf* **(a)** *(cargo)* office of judge **(b)** *(institución)* judiciary

judicial *adj* judicial

judío, -a 1 *adj* Jewish

2 *nm,f* **(a)** *(hebreo)* Jew, *f* Jewess **(b)** *Fam Pey (tacaño)* skinflint

judo ['juðo] *nm* judo

judogui [ju'ðovi] *nm Dep* judogi, judo outfit

judoka [ju'ðoka] *nmf* judoist, judoka

juego 1 *ver* **jugar**

2 *nm* **(a)** *(deporte, diversión)* game; **j. de azar** game of chance; *Am* **j. de computadora** computer game; **juegos florales** poetry competition; **juegos malabares** juggling; **j. de manos** conjuring trick; **j. de mesa** board game; **Juegos Olímpicos** Olympic Games; *Esp* **j. de ordenador** computer game; **j. de palabras** play on words, pun; **j. de prendas** game of forfeit

(b) *(acción)* play, playing; **estar/poner en j.** to be/put at stake; *Fig* **descubrirle el j. a alguien** to see through sb; *Dep* **fuera de j.** offside; *Fig* **ser un j. de niños** to be child's play; **j. sucio/limpio** foul/clean play

(c) *(con dinero)* gambling; **¡hagan j.!** place your bets!

(d) *(conjunto de objetos)* set; *Esp* **a j. (ropa)** matching; **hacer j. (con)** to match; *Inform* **j. de caracteres** character set; **j. de herramientas** tool kit; **j. de llaves/sábanas** set of keys/sheets; **j. de té/café** tea/coffee service

(e) *(mano) (de cartas)* hand; **me salió un buen j.** I was dealt a good hand

(f) *Am (en feria)* fairground attraction

juegue *etc ver* **jugar**

juerga *nf Fam* lively party, binge; **irse de j.** to go out on the town; **estar de j.** to be partying; **montar una j.** to party; **tomar algo a j.** to take sth as a joke; **¡qué j. nos pasamos anoche con su primo!** what a laugh we had with her cousin last night!

juerguista 1 *adj* **ser muy j.** to be a party animal

2 *nmf* party animal

jueves *nm inv* Thursday; *Fam* **no ser nada del otro j.** to be nothing out of this world; **J. Santo** Maundy Thursday; *ver también* **sábado**

juez *nmf* **(a)** *Der* judge; **j. de instrucción, j. de primera instancia** examining magistrate; **j. de paz** Justice of the Peace **(b)** *Dep (árbitro)* referee; *(en atletismo)* official; **j. árbitro** referee; **j. de línea** *(fútbol, fútbol americano)* linesman; **j. de salida** starter; **j. de silla** umpire

jugada *nf* **(a)** *Dep & (en ajedrez)* move; *(en billar)* shot; **las mejores jugadas del partido** the highlights of the match **(b)** *(treta)* dirty trick; **hacer una mala j. a alguien** to play a dirty trick on sb

jugador, -ora 1 *adj (en deporte)* playing; *(en casino, timba)* gambling

2 *nm,f (en deporte)* player; *(en casino, timba)* gambler; **j. de ajedrez** chess player

jugar [36] **1** *vi* **(a)** *(practicar un deporte, juego)* to play; **j. al ajedrez/a las cartas** to play chess/cards; **j. en un equipo** to play for a team; **j. a las muñecas** to play with one's dolls; **te toca j.** it's your turn *o* go; **j. limpio/sucio** to play clean/dirty **(b)** *(con dinero)* to gamble **(a** on); **j. a la lotería** to play the lottery; **j. a** *o* **en la Bolsa** to speculate (on the Stock Exchange) **(c)** *Fig (ser desconsiderado)* **j. con alguien** to play with sb; **j. con los sentimientos de alguien** to toy with sb's feelings **(d)** *Fig (influir)* **j. a favor de alguien** to work in sb's favor; **el tiempo juega en su contra** time is against her

2 *vt* **(a)** *(partido, juego)* to play; *(ficha, pieza)* to move **(b)** *(dinero)* to gamble **(a** on)

3 jugarse *vpr* **(a)** *(apostarse)* to bet; **me juego lo que quieras a que no vienen** I bet you anything they won't come **(b)** *(arriesgar)* to risk **(c)** **jugársela a alguien** to play a dirty trick on sb

jugarreta *nf Fam* dirty trick

juglar *nm* minstrel

juglaresco, -a *adj* minstrel; **poesía juglaresca** troubadour poetry

jugo *nm* (a) *(líquido)* juice; *Am (de fruta)* juice; **jugos gástricos** gastric juices (b) *Fam (provecho, interés)* meat, substance; **este libro tiene mucho j.** this is a very meaty book, this book has a lot of substance; **sacar j. a algo/alguien** *(aprovechar)* to get the most out of sth/sb

jugosidad *nf* juiciness

jugoso, -a *adj* (a) *(con jugo)* juicy (b) *(cotilleo)* juicy (c) *(sustancioso)* meaty, substantial

jugué *etc ver* **jugar**

juguera *nf CSur* juicer

juguete *nm* (a) *(para niños)* toy; **una pistola/un coche de j.** a toy gun/car; **juguetes bélicos** war toys; **j. educativo** educational toy (b) *(persona, cosa)* **tratar a alguien como un j.** to treat sb as a plaything; **el presidente es un j. en manos de los militares** the president is a puppet of the military

juguetear *vi* to play (around); **j. con algo** to toy with sth

juguetería *nf* toy store

juguetón, -ona *adj* playful

juicio *nm* (a) *Der* trial; **llevar a alguien a j.** to take sb to court; *Rel* **el J. Final** the Last Judgment (b) *(sensatez)* (sound) judgment; *(cordura)* sanity, reason; **estar/no estar en su (sano) j.** to be/not to be in one's right mind; **perder el j.** to lose one's reason, to go mad (c) *(opinión)* opinion; **a mi j.** in my opinion; **no tengo suficientes elementos de j. como para formarme una opinión** I don't have enough information to base an opinion on; **j. de valor** value judgment

juicioso, -a *adj* sensible, wise

julai *nmf Esp Fam (inocente)* fool, mug

julepe *nm* = type of card game

juliana *nf (sopa)* = soup made with chopped vegetables and herbs; **cortar en j.** to cut into julienne strips

julio *nm* (a) *(mes)* July; *ver también* **septiembre** (b) *Fís* joule

jumbo ['jumbo] *nm* jumbo (jet)

jumento, -a *nm,f* ass, donkey

jumper ['jamper] *(pl* **jumpers***) nm CSur, Méx (prenda)* sweater

juncal *nm* bed of rushes

junco *nm* (a) *(planta)* rush, reed (b) *(embarcación)* junk

jungla *nf* jungle

junio *nm* June; *ver también* **septiembre**

júnior *(pl* **júniors***)* **1** *adj* (a) *Dep* under-21 (b) *(hijo)* junior
     2 *nmf Dep* under-21

junta *nf* (a) *(grupo, comité)* committee; *(de empresa, examinadores)* board; **j. directiva** board of directors; **j. de gobierno** = government and administrative body in certain autonomous regions; **j. militar** military junta (b) *(reunión)* meeting; **j. (general) de accionistas** stockholders' meeting; **j. general extraordinaria** extraordinary general meeting (c) *(juntura)* joint; **j. de culata** gasket

juntamente *adv* **j. con** together with

juntar 1 *vt (unir, reunir)* to put together; *(cromos, sellos, monedas)* to collect; *(fondos)* to raise; *(personas)* to bring together; **poco a poco ha juntado una valiosa colección de cuadros** she has gradually put together a valuable collection of paintings; **juntaron todos los departamentos en un solo edificio** they brought all the departments together in a single building
     2 juntarse *vpr* (a) *(unirse) (personas)* to get together; *(ríos, caminos)* to meet (b) *(arrimarse)* to draw *o* move closer (c) *(tener amistad)* **juntarse con** to mix with (d) *(convivir)* **juntarse con alguien** to move in with sb

junto, -a 1 *adj* (a) *(unido, agrupado)* together; **hacer algo juntos** to do sth together; **¿se lo envuelvo todo j.?** shall I wrap everything up together for you?; **no se han casado pero viven juntos** they're not married, but they live together; **nunca he visto tanto niño j.** I've never seen so many children all in one place (b) *(próximo, cercano)* close together; **las casas están muy juntas** the houses are too close together (c) *(al mismo tiempo)* **no puedo atender a tantos clientes juntos** I can't serve all these customers at the same time
     2 junto a *loc prep* next to
     3 junto con *loc conj* together with

juntura *nf* joint

Júpiter *nm* Jupiter

jura *nf (promesa solemne)* oath; *(de un cargo)* swearing in; *Mil* **j. de bandera** oath of allegiance to the flag

jurado, -a 1 *adj (declaración)* sworn; **enemigo j.** sworn enemy
     2 *nm* (a) *(tribunal) (en juicio)* jury; *(en concurso, competición)* (panel of) judges (b) *(miembro) (en juicio)* member of the jury; *(en concurso, competición)* judge

juramentar *vt* to swear in

juramento *nm* (a) *(promesa solemne)* oath; **bajo j.** on *o* under oath; **prestar j.** to take the oath; **tomar j. a alguien** to swear sb in; *Med* **j. hipocrático** Hippocratic oath (b) *(blasfemia)* oath, curse

jurar 1 *vt (prometer solemnemente)* to swear; *(constitución, bandera)* to pledge *o* swear allegiance to; **j. un cargo** to be sworn in; **j. que** to swear that; **j. por...** to swear by...; **te lo juro** I promise, I swear it; **te juro que no ha sido culpa mía** I swear that it wasn't my fault; **habría jurado que era tu hermana** I could have sworn it was your sister
     2 *vi (blasfemar)* to swear; *Fam Fig* **j. en hebreo** *o* **arameo** to swear like a trooper; *Irónico* **no sé mucho alemán — no hace falta que lo jures** I don't know much German — you don't say! *o* tell me something I don't know!

jurásico, -a *adj & nm* Jurassic

jurel *nm* scad, horse mackerel

jurídico, -a *adj* legal

jurisconsulto, -a *nm,f* legal expert, jurist

jurisdicción *nf* jurisdiction

jurisdiccional *adj* jurisdictional; **aguas jurisdiccionales** territorial waters

jurisprudencia *nf (ciencia)* jurisprudence; *(casos previos)* case law; **sentar j.** to set a legal precedent

jurista *nmf* jurist

justa *nf Hist* joust

justamente *adv* (a) *(con justicia)* justly (b) *(exactamente)* exactly; **j., eso es lo que estaba pensando** exactly, that's just what I was thinking

justicia *nf* (a) *(derecho)* justice; *(equidad)* fairness, justice; **administrar j.** to administer justice; **en j.** in (all) fairness; **se le hizo j. entregándole el premio** she received the recognition she deserved when she was awarded the prize; **esa foto no le hace j.** that photo doesn't do him justice; **ser de j.** to be only fair; **j. social** social justice (b) *(sistema de leyes)* **la j.** the law; **tomarse la j. por su mano** to take the law into one's own hands (c) *(organización)* **la j. española** the Spanish legal system; **la persigue la j. británica** she is being sought by the British courts

justiciero, -a *adj* righteous; **ángel j.** avenging angel

justificable *adj* justifiable

justificación *nf (gen) & Imprenta* justification; *Inform* **j. automática** automatic justification

justificado, -a *adj* justified

justificante *nm* written proof, documentary evidence; **j. médico** doctor's note, sick note

justificar [59] **1** *vt* (**a**) *(gen)* & *Imprenta* to justify (**b**) *(excusar)* **j. a alguien** to make excuses for sb

2 justificarse *vpr* (**a**) *(actitud, decisión)* to be justified (**b**) *(persona)* to justify *o* excuse oneself; **justificarse por algo** to excuse oneself for sth; **justificarse con alguien** to make one's excuses to sb

justificativo, -a *adj* providing evidence, supporting

justiprecio *nm* valuation

justo, -a 1 *adj* (**a**) *(equitativo)* fair (**b**) *(merecido) (recompensa, victoria)* deserved; *(castigo)* just (**c**) *(exacto)* exact (**d**) *(idóneo)* right (**e**) *(apretado, ceñido)* tight; **estar** *o* **venir j.** to be a tight fit; **cabemos cinco, pero un poco justos** there's room for five of us, but it's a bit of a squeeze (**f**) *Rel* righteous

2 *nm Rel* **los justos** the righteous; **pagarán justos por pecadores** the innocent will suffer instead of the guilty

3 *adv* (**a**) *(exactamente)* just; **j. a tiempo** just in time, in the nick of time; **j. antes/después** just before/after; **j. detrás/en medio** right behind/in the middle; **¿al lado del puente? — j. ahí** by the bridge? — exactly (**b**) *(precisamente)* just; **j. ahora iba a llamarte** I was just about to phone you; **j. ahora que llego yo se va todo el mundo** everybody's leaving just as I get here

juvenil 1 *adj* youthful; *Dep* **equipo j.** youth team

2 *nmf Dep* **los juveniles** the youth team

juventud *nf* (**a**) *(edad, época)* youth; **en su j.** when she was young, in her youth (**b**) *(los jóvenes)* young people *(plural)*; **la j. ha perdido el respeto por los ancianos** young people no longer respect the elderly; **las juventudes del partido** the youth wing of the party

juzgado *nm* court; **j. de guardia** = court open during the night or at other times when ordinary courts are shut; *Fam* **ser de j. de guardia** to be criminal *o* a crime; **j. de instrucción** court of first instance, ≃ justice court; **j. de lo penal** criminal court; **j. de primera instancia** court of first instance, ≃ justice court

juzgar [38] *vt* (**a**) *Der* to try (**b**) *(enjuiciar)* to judge; *(estimar, considerar)* to consider, to judge; **no tienes derecho a juzgarme** you have no right to judge me; **enseguida juzga a la gente** he's very quick to judge; **j. mal a alguien** to misjudge sb; **a j. por (cómo)** judging by (how)

K

K, k [ka] *nf (letra)* K, k
Kabul *n* Kabul
kafkiano, -a *adj* Kafkaesque
káiser *(pl* **káisers)** *nm* kaiser
kaki 1 *adj inv (color)* khaki
  2 *nm* **(a)** *(fruto)* kaki, sharon fruit **(b)** *(color)* khaki
Kalahari *nm* **el (desierto del) K.** the Kalahari Desert
kamikaze *adj & nmf Mil & Fig* kamikaze
Kampala *n* Kampala
kantiano, -a *adj & nm,f* Kantian
karaoke *nm* karaoke
kárate *nm* karate
karateka *nmf* karateka, karateist
karma *nm* karma
kart *(pl* **karts)** *nm* go-kart
karting *nm* go-kart racing, karting
katiusca, katiuska *nf Esp (bota)* rubber boot
Katmandú *n* Katmandu
kayac *(pl* **kayacs)**, **kayak** *(pl* **kayaks)** *nm* kayak
Kazajistán *n* Kazakhstan
kebab *(pl* **kebabs)** *nm* kebab
kéfir *nm* kefir
kelvin *(pl* **kelvins)** *nm Fís* kelvin; **grados K.** degrees
  Kelvin
kendo *nm* kendo
Kenia *n* Kenya
keniano, -a, keniata *adj & nmf* Kenyan
kepis *nm inv* kepi
kermés [ker'mes] *(pl* **kermeses)**, **kermesse** [ker'mes] *(pl*
  kermesses) *nf* fair, kermis
keroseno, *Am* **kerosén,** *Am* **kerosene** *nm* kerosene
ketchup ['ketʃup] *(pl* **ketchups)** *nm* ketchup, catchup
keynesianismo *nm Econ* Keynesianism
keynesiano, -a *adj Econ* Keynesian
kg *(abrev de* **kilogramo)** kg
kibbutz [ki'βuts] *nm inv* kibbutz
Kiev *n* Kiev
kif *nm* hashish
kikirikí *nm (canto del gallo)* cock-a-doodle-do
kiko *nm* = toasted, salted corn kernels
kilim *(pl* **kilims)** *nm* kilim
Kilimanjaro *nm* **el K.** (Mount) Kilimanjaro
kilo *nm* **(a)** *(peso)* kilo, kilogram **(b)** *Esp Antes Fam (millón)*
  million (pesetas)
kilobyte [kilo'βait] *nm Inform* kilobyte
kilocaloría *nf* kilocalorie
kilogramo *nm* kilogram
kilohercio *nm* kilohertz
kilojulio *nm* kilojoule
kilolitro *nm* kiloliter

kilometraje *nm (de vehículo)* ≃ mileage; *(de carretera)*
  distance in kilometers
kilometrar *vt (carretera)* to mark out the distance (in
  kilometers)
kilométrico, -a *adj* **(a)** *(distancia)* kilometric **(b)** *Fam (largo)*
  truly long
kilómetro *nm* kilometer; **k. cuadrado** square kilometer
kilopondio *nm Fís (unidad)* kilopond
kilovatio *nm* kilowatt; **k. hora** kilowatt-hour
kilovoltio *nm* kilovolt
kimono *nm* kimono
Kingston *n* Kingston
Kinshasa *n* Kinshasa
kiosco, kiosko *nm (tenderete)* kiosk; *(de periódicos)* newsstand, newspaper stand *o* kiosk; **k. de música** bandstand
kiosquero, -a *nm,f* = person selling newspapers, drinks etc
  from a kiosk
Kioto *n* Kyoto
Kirguizistán *n* Kirg(h)izstan
kirial *nm Rel* plainsong book
Kiribati *n* Kiribati
kirsch [kirʃ] *nm* kirsch
kit *(pl* **kits)** *nm (conjunto)* kit, set; *(para montar)* kit
kitsch [kitʃ] *adj inv* kitsch
kiwi *nm* **(a)** *(fruto)* kiwi (fruit) **(b)** *(ave)* kiwi
KKK *nm (abrev de* **Ku-Klux-Klan)** KKK
Kleenex® ['klines, 'klineks] *nm inv* paper handkerchief,
  (paper) tissue
km *(abrev de* **kilómetro)** km
km/h *(abrev de* **kilómetros por hora)** kmh, kmph
knockout [no'kaut] *(pl* **knockouts)** *nm* knockout
KO ['kao] *nm (abrev de* **knockout)** KO; *también Fig* **ganar por**
  KO to win by a knockout
koala *nm* koala (bear)
kopek *(pl* **kopeks)** *nm* kopeck
kosovar 1 *adj* Kosovan
  2 *nmf* Kosovan, Kosovar
Kosovo *n* Kosovo
Kremlin *nm* **el K.** the Kremlin
kril *nm* krill
kriptón *nm Quím* krypton
Kuala Lumpur *n* Kuala Lumpur
kung-fu *nm* kung fu
Kurdistán *nm* Kurdistan
kurdo, -a 1 *adj* Kurdish
  2 *nm,f* Kurd
Kuwait [ku'βait] *n* Kuwait
kuwaití [kuβai'ti] *(pl* **kuwaitíes)** *adj & nmf* Kuwaiti
kv, kW *nm (abrev de* **kilowatio)** kW
kvh, kWh *nm (abrev de* **kilowatio hora)** kWh

L

L, l ['ele] *nf (letra)* L, l

l *(abrev de* **litro**) l

la¹ *nm Mús* A; *(en solfeo)* la

la² 1 *art ver* **el**

  2 *pron ver* **lo¹**

laberíntico, -a *adj también Fig* labyrinthine

laberinto *nm* (**a**) *(mitológico)* labyrinth; *(en jardín)* maze (**b**) *(cosa complicada)* labyrinth, maze

labia *nf Fam* smooth talk; **tener mucha l.** to have the gift of the gab

labial 1 *adj* (**a**) *(de los labios)* lip; **protector l.** lip salve *o* balm (**b**) *Gram* labial

  2 *nf Gram* labial

lábil *adj (sustancia, estructura)* unstable; *(persona, situación)* volatile

labio *nm* (**a**) *(de boca)* lip; *Fig* **no despegar los labios** not to utter a word; **l. leporino** cleft lip, harelip; **leer los labios** to lip-read; **leer los labios a alguien** to read sb's lips; **morderse los labios** to bite one's tongue; *Fig* **estar pendiente de los labios de alguien** to hang on sb's every word (**b**) *(borde)* edge (**c**) *(de vulva)* labium

labiodental *adj & nf* labiodental

labor *nf* (**a**) *(trabajo)* work; *(tarea)* task; **hizo una buena l. al frente de la empresa** she did a good job at the helm of the company; **profesión: sus labores** occupation: housewife; *Fig* **no estar por la l.** *(ser reacio)* not to be keen on the idea; **labores domésticas** household chores; **l. de equipo** teamwork (**b**) *(de costura)* needlework; **l. de encaje** lacemaking; **l. de punto** knitting (**c**) *Agr* **casa de l.** farmhouse; **tierra de l.** agricultural land, arable land

laborable 1 *adj* **día l.** *(hábil)* workday; *(de semana)* weekday

  2 *nm* **este tren circula sólo los laborables** this train only runs on weekdays

laboral *adj (derecho)* labor; *(semana, condiciones)* working

laboralista 1 *adj* **abogado l.** labor lawyer

  2 *nmf* labor lawyer

laboratorio *nm* laboratory; **l. de idiomas** *o* **lenguas** language laboratory

laboriosidad *nf* (**a**) *(dedicación)* application, diligence (**b**) *(dificultad)* laboriousness

laborioso, -a *adj* (**a**) *(aplicado)* hardworking (**b**) *(difícil)* laborious, arduous

laborismo *nm* **el l.** *(ideología)* Labourism; *(movimiento)* the labor movement

laborista 1 *adj* Labour

  2 *nmf* Labour Party supporter *o* member; **los laboristas** Labour

labrador, -ora *nm,f* (**a**) *(agricultor)* farmer; *(trabajador)* farmworker (**b**) *(perro)* Labrador

labranza *nf Agr* **casa de l.** farmhouse; **tierra de l.** agricultural land, arable land

labrar 1 *vt* (**a**) *(campo) (arar)* to plow; *(cultivar)* to cultivate (**b**) *(piedra, metal)* to work (**c**) *(porvenir, fortuna)* to carve out

  2 **labrarse** *vpr* **labrarse un porvenir** to carve out a future for oneself

labriego, -a *nm,f* farmworker

laburar *vi RP Fam* to work

laburo *nm RP Fam* job

laca *nf* (**a**) *(para muebles)* lacquer (**b**) *(para el pelo)* hair spray (**c**) **l. de uñas** nail varnish

lacado *nm* lacquering

lacar [59] *vt* to lacquer

lacayo *nm (criado)* footman; *Fig Pey* lackey

lacerante *adj (dolor)* excruciating, stabbing; *(palabras)* hurtful, cutting; *(grito)* piercing

lacerar *vt* to lacerate; *Fig* to wound

lacio, -a *adj* (**a**) *(cabello) (liso)* straight; *(sin fuerza)* lank (**b**) *(planta)* wilted (**c**) *(sin fuerza)* limp

lacón *nm* shoulder of pork

lacónico, -a *adj* laconic

laconismo *nm* terseness

lacra *nf* (**a**) *(secuela)* **la enfermedad le dejó como l. una cojera** he was left lame by the illness (**b**) *(defecto)* blight

lacrar *vt* to seal with sealing wax

lacre *nm* sealing wax

lacrimal *adj* lacrimal, tear; **conducto l.** tear duct

lacrimógeno, -a *adj* (**a**) *(novela, película)* weepy, tear-jerking (**b**) **gas l.** tear gas

lacrimoso, -a *adj* (**a**) *(ojos)* tearful (**b**) *(historia)* weepy, tear-jerking

lactancia *nf* lactation; **l. artificial** bottle feeding; **l. materna** breast-feeding

lactante *nmf* baby *(not yet eating solid food)*

lácteo, -a *adj* (**a**) *(industria, productos)* dairy (**b**) *(blanco)* milky; **de aspecto l.** milky

láctico, -a *adj* lactic

lactosa *nf* lactose

lacustre *adj (animal, planta)* lake-dwelling, lacustrine; **hábitat l.** lake habitat

ladeado, -a *adj (torcido)* tilted, at an angle; **mételo l.** put it in sideways

ladear 1 *vt* to tilt

  2 **ladearse** *vpr (cuadro)* to tilt; *(persona)* to turn sideways

ladera *nf* slope, mountainside

ladilla *nf* crab (louse)

ladino, -a 1 *adj* (**a**) *(astuto)* crafty (**b**) *(judeoespañol)* Ladino (**c**) *CAm, Méx, Ven (no blanco)* nonwhite

  2 *nm,f CAm, Méx, Ven (no blanco)* = nonwhite Spanish-speaking person

  3 *nm (lengua)* Ladino

lado *nm* (**a**) *(costado, cara, parte)* side; **el cine está a este l. de la calle** the movie theater is on this side of the street; **al l.** *(cerca)* nearby; **al l. de** *(junto a)* beside; **de al l.** next; **la casa de al l.** the house next door; **al otro l. de la calle/frontera,** across the street/border; **en el l. de arriba/abajo** on the top/

bottom; **a ambos lados** on both sides; **de l.** *(torcido)* tilted, at an angle; **mételo de l.** put it in sideways; **dormir de l.** to sleep on one's side; **viento de l.** crosswind; **atravesar algo de l. a l.** to cross sth from one side to the other; **echarse** *o* **hacerse a un l.** to move aside; **por un l.** on the one hand; **por otro l.** on the other hand

(b) *(lugar)* place; **debe de estar en otro l.** it must be somewhere else; **de un l. para** *o* **a otro** to and fro; **por todos lados** everywhere, all around; **iremos cada uno por nuestro l.** we will go our separate ways

(c) *(bando)* side; **y tú ¿de qué l. estás?** whose side are you on?; **ponerse del l. de alguien** to take sb's side

(d) *(expresiones)* **dar de l. a alguien** to cold-shoulder sb; **dejar algo de l.** *o* **a un l.** *(prescindir)* to leave sth to one side; **mirar de l. a alguien** *(despreciar)* to look askance at sb

ladrador, -ora *adj* barking

ladrar *vi también Fig* to bark; *Fam* **está que ladra** he's hopping mad, he's fit to be tied

ladrido *nm también Fig* bark

ladrillo *nm* (a) *Constr* brick (b) *Fam (pesadez)* drag, bore

ladrón, -ona 1 *adj* thieving

2 *nm,f (persona)* thief; *(de bancos)* robber; *(de casas)* burglar; **l. de guante blanco** gentleman burglar *o* thief

3 *nm (para varios enchufes)* adapter

lagar *nm (de vino)* winepress; *(de aceite)* oil press

lagarta *nf Fam Pey (mujer)* scheming woman

lagartija *nf (small)* lizard

lagarto, -a 1 *nm,f (reptil)* lizard

2 *nm Méx (caimán)* alligator

lago *nm* lake

Lagos *n* Lagos

lágrima *nf* tear; **nos costó muchas lágrimas** it caused us a lot of heartache; **deshacerse en lágrimas** to burst into tears; **enjugarse** *o* **secarse las lágrimas** to wipe away *o* dry one's tears; **llorar a l. viva** to cry buckets; **hacer saltar las lágrimas** to bring tears to the eyes; *Fig* **lágrimas de cocodrilo** crocodile tears

lagrimal 1 *adj* lacrimal, tear; **conducto l.** tear duct

2 *nm* corner of the eye

lagrimear *vi (persona)* to weep; *(ojos)* to water

laguna *nf* (a) *(lago)* lagoon (b) *(en colección, memoria)* gap; *(en leyes, reglamento)* loophole

La Habana *n* Havana

La Haya *n* The Hague

laicismo *nm* laicism

laico, -a 1 *adj* lay, secular

2 *nm,f* layman, *f* laywoman

laísmo *nm* = incorrect use of "la" and "las" instead of "le" and "les" as indirect objects

lama *nm* lama

lambada *nf* lambada

lambiscón, -ona *nm,f Méx Fam* toady, yes-man

lambisconear *vt Méx Fam* to suck up to

lamé *nm* lamé

lameculos *nmf inv muy Fam* brownnose, ass-licker

lamentable *adj* (a) *(triste)* terribly sad (b) *(malo)* lamentable, deplorable

lamentación *nf* moaning

lamentar 1 *vt* to regret, to be sorry about; **lo lamento** I'm very sorry; **lamentamos comunicarle...** we regret to inform you...

2 lamentarse *vpr* to complain (**de** *o* **por** about)

lamento *nm* moan, cry of pain

lamer 1 *vt* to lick; *muy Fam Fig* **lamerle el culo a alguien** to lick sb's ass

2 lamerse *vpr* to lick oneself; *Fig* **lamerse las heridas** to lick one's wounds

lametón, lametazo *nm (big)* lick; **dar un l. a algo** to give sth a big lick

lamida *nf* lick; **dar una l. a algo** to lick sth, to give sth a lick

lamido, -a *adj* skinny

lámina *nf* (a) *(plancha)* sheet; *(placa)* plate (b) *(rodaja)* slice (c) *(grabado)* engraving (d) *(dibujo)* plate

laminado, -a 1 *adj* (a) *(reducido a láminas)* rolled (b) *(cubierto por láminas)* laminated

2 *nm* (a) *(reducir a láminas)* rolling (b) *(cubrir con láminas)* lamination

laminador *nm*, **laminadora** *nf* rolling mill

laminar 1 *adj* laminar

2 *vt* (a) *(hacer láminas)* to roll (b) *(cubrir con láminas)* to laminate

lámpara *nf* (a) *(aparato)* lamp; **l. halógena** halogen lamp; **l. de mesa** table lamp; **l. de pie** floor lamp (b) *(bombilla)* bulb (c) *Mec* valve (d) *Fam (mancha)* stain

lamparilla *nf* small lamp

lamparita *nf RP* light bulb

lamparón *nm Fam* stain

lampiño, -a *adj (sin barba)* beardless, smooth-cheeked; *(sin vello)* hairless

lamprea *nf* lamprey

lana 1 *nf* wool; **de l.** woolen; *Prov* **ir a por l. y volver trasquilado** to be hoist with one's own petard; **l. de vidrio** fiberglass

2 *nm Andes, Méx Fam* loot, dough

lanar *adj* wool-bearing; **ganado l.** sheep

lance 1 *ver* **lanzar**

2 *nm* (a) *(en juegos, deportes)* incident; *(acontecimiento)* event (b) *(riña)* dispute

lancero *nm* lancer

lanceta *nf Andes, Méx* sting

lancha *nf* (a) *(embarcación) (grande)* launch; *(pequeña)* boat; **l. de desembarco** landing craft; **l. motora** motor launch, motorboat; **l. neumática** rubber dinghy; **l. patrullera** patrol boat; **l. salvavidas** lifeboat (b) *(piedra)* slab

lancinante *adj Literario* lancing, stabbing

landa *nf* moor

landó *nm* landau

land rover® [lan'rroβer] *(pl* **land rovers)** *nm* Land Rover®

langosta *nf* (a) *(crustáceo)* rock *o* spiny lobster (b) *(insecto)* locust

langostino *nm* king prawn

languidecer [46] *vi (persona)* to languish; *(conversación, entusiasmo)* to flag

languidez *nf (debilidad)* listlessness; *(falta de ánimo)* disinterest

lánguido, -a *adj (débil)* listless; *(falto de ánimo)* disinterested

lanilla *nf* (a) *(pelillo)* nap (b) *(tejido)* flannel

lanolina *nf* lanolin

lanoso, -a, lanudo, -a *adj* woolly

lanza *nf* (a) *(arma) (arrojadiza)* spear; *(en justas, torneos)* lance (b) *(de carruaje)* shaft

lanzacohetes *nm inv* rocket launcher

lanzadera *nf (de telar)* shuttle; **l. espacial** space shuttle

lanzado, -a *adj* (a) *(atrevido)* forward; *(valeroso)* fearless (b) *(rápido)* **ir l.** to hurtle along

lanzador, -ora *nm,f* thrower

lanzagranadas *nm inv* grenade launcher

lanzallamas *nm inv* flamethrower

lanzamiento *nm* (a) *(de objeto)* throwing; *(de cohete)* launching (b) *Dep (con la mano)* throw; *(con el pie)* kick; *(en béisbol)* pitch; **l. de disco** discus; **l. de jabalina** javelin; **l. de martillo** hammer; **l. de peso** shot put (c) *(de producto, artista)* launch; *(de disco)* release; **precio/oferta de l.** introductory price/offer

lanzamisiles *nm inv* rocket launcher

lanzaplatos *nm inv Dep* (clay pigeon) trap

lanzar [14] **1** *vt* (**a**) *(tirar)* to throw; *(con fuerza)* to hurl, to fling; *(de una patada)* to kick; *(bomba)* to drop; *(flecha, misil)* to fire; *(cohete)* to launch; **l. a alguien al mar/río** to throw sb into the sea/river (**b**) *(grito, gemido, aullido)* to let out; *(acusación, insulto)* to hurl; *(suspiro)* to heave; **l. insultos contra alguien** to insult sb (**c**) *Com (producto, artista, periódico)* to launch; *(disco, película)* to release

2 lanzarse *vpr* (**a**) *(tirarse)* to throw oneself; **lanzarse a la piscina/al agua** to jump into the pool/water (**b**) *(abalanzarse)* **lanzarse sobre** to fall upon; **los atracadores se lanzaron sobre él** the robbers fell upon him (**c**) *(empezar)* **decidió lanzarse a la política** she decided to enter the world of politics; **si se confirma la noticia los inversores se lanzarán a vender** if the news is confirmed, investors will not hesitate to start selling

lanzatorpedos *nm inv* torpedo tube

Laos *n* Laos

laosiano, -a *adj & nm,f* Laotian

lapa *nf* (**a**) *Zool* limpet; *Fig* **pegarse como una l.** to cling like a leech (**b**) *Fam (persona)* hanger-on, pest

La Paz *n* La Paz

lapicera *nf CSur* ballpoint (pen), Biro®

lapicero *nm* (**a**) *Esp (lápiz)* pencil (**b**) *Chile (estilográfica)* fountain pen (**c**) *CAm, Perú (bolígrafo)* ballpoint (pen), Biro®

lápida *nf* memorial stone; **l. mortuoria** tombstone

lapidación *nf* stoning

lapidar *vt* to stone

lapidario, -a *adj (frase)* meaningful, oracular

lapislázuli *nm* lapis lazuli

lápiz *nm* pencil; **l. de labios** lipstick; **l. de ojos** eyeliner; *Inform* **l. óptico** light pen

lapo *nm Esp Fam* spit

lapón, -ona 1 *adj & nm,f* Lapp

2 *nm (lengua)* Lapp

Laponia *n* Lapland

lapso *nm* space, interval; **en el l. de unas semanas** in the space of a few weeks

lapsus *nm inv* lapse, slip; **tener un l.** to make a slip of the tongue

laquear *vt* to lacquer

lar 1 *nm* (**a**) *(lumbre)* hearth (**b**) *Mitol* household god

2 lares *nmpl (hogar)* hearth and home; **¿qué haces tú por estos lares?** what are you doing in these parts?

larga *nf* (**a**) *(luz)* high beam; **dar** *o* **poner las largas** to put one's headlights on high beam (**b**) **a la l.** in the long run (**c**) **dar largas a algo** to put sth off; **siempre me está dando largas** he's always putting me off

largar [38] **1** *vt* (**a**) *Fam (dar, decir)* to give; **le largué una bofetada** I gave him a smack (**b**) *(cuerda)* to pay out

2 *vi Esp Fam (hablar)* to yack (away)

3 largarse *vpr Fam* to clear off, to make oneself scarce; **¡me largo!** I'm off!

largavistas *nm inv Bol, CSur* binoculars

largo, -a 1 *adj* (**a**) *(en espacio, tiempo)* long; **estarle l. a alguien** to be too long for sb; **vivió allí largos años** she lived there for many years; **estuvo enfermo l. tiempo** he was ill for a long time; **la película se me hizo muy larga** the movie seemed to drag on forever (**b**) *Fam (alto)* tall (**c**) *(sobrado)* **media hora larga** a good half hour; **debió de costar un millón l.** it must have cost a million and then some (**d**) *(generoso)* **l. en hacer algo** generous in doing sth

2 *nm* (**a**) *(longitud)* length; **¿cuánto mide** *o* **tiene de l.?, ¿cómo es de l.?** how long is it?; **tiene dos metros de l.** it's two meters long; **pasar de l.** to pass by; **vestirse de l.** to dress up, to dress formally; **a lo l.** lengthwise; **a lo l. de dos**

kilómetros for two km; **a lo l. y (a lo) ancho de** right across, throughout (**b**) *(de piscina)* length; **hacer tres largos** to swim *o* do three lengths (**c**) *(mucho tiempo)* **la cosa va para l.** it's going to take a long time (**d**) *(largometraje)* feature

3 *adv* at length; **l. y tendido** at great length

4 *interj* **¡l. de aquí!** clear off!, get out of here!

largometraje *nm* feature

largue *etc ver* **largar**

larguero *nm* (**a**) *Constr* main beam (**b**) *Dep* crossbar

largueza *nf (generosidad)* generosity

larguirucho, -a *adj Fam* lanky

largura *nf* length

laringe *nf* larynx

laringitis *nf inv* laryngitis

laringología *nf* laryngology

laringólogo, -a *nm,f* laryngologist

La Rioja *n* La Rioja

larva *nf* larva

larvado, -a *adj* latent

las 1 *art ver* **el**

2 *pron ver* **lo¹**

lasaña *nf* lasagna, lasagne

lascivia *nf* lasciviousness, lechery

lascivo, -a 1 *adj* lascivious, lewd

2 *nm,f* lascivious *o* lewd person

láser 1 *adj inv* **rayo l.** laser beam

2 *nm inv* laser

laserterapia *nf* laser therapy

lasitud *nf* lassitude

laso, -a *adj* (**a**) *(cansado)* weary (**b**) *(liso)* straight

Las Palmas (de Gran Canaria) *n* Las Palmas

lástima *nf* (**a**) *(compasión)* pity (**b**) *(pena)* shame, pity; **dar l.** to be a crying shame; **da l. ver gente así** it's sad to see people in that state; **¡qué l.!** what a shame *o* pity!; **quedarse hecho una l.** to be a sorry *o* pitiful sight

lastimadura *nf Am* graze

lastimar 1 *vt* to hurt

2 lastimarse *vpr* to hurt oneself

lastimoso, -a, lastimero, -a *adj* pitiful, woeful

lastrar *vt* to ballast

lastre *nm* (**a**) *(peso)* ballast; **soltar l.** to discharge ballast (**b**) *(estorbo)* burden

lata *nf* (**a**) *(envase)* can, tin; *(de bebidas)* can; **en l.** canned, tinned (**b**) *Esp Fam (fastidio)* pain; **levantarse tan temprano es una l.** getting up so early is a real pain; **¡qué l.!** what a pain!; **una l. de libro** a deadly boring book; **dar la l. a alguien** to pester sb

latencia *nf* latency; **periodo de l.** latent period

latente *adj* latent

lateral 1 *adj* (**a**) *(del lado)* lateral; *(puerta, pared)* side (**b**) *(indirecto)* indirect

2 *nm* (**a**) *(lado)* side (**b**) *Dep* **l. derecho/izquierdo** right/left back

látex *nm inv* latex

latido *nm (del corazón)* beat; *(en dedo, herida)* throb, throbbing

latiente *adj (corazón)* beating

latifundio *nm* large rural estate

latifundismo *nm* = system of land tenure characterized by the "latifundio"

latigazo *nm* (**a**) *(golpe)* lash (**b**) *(chasquido)* crack (of the whip) (**c**) *Esp Fam (trago)* swig (**d**) *(dolor)* shooting pain

látigo *nm* whip

latiguillo *nm (palabra, frase)* verbal tic

latín *nm* Latin; **l. clásico/vulgar** Classical/Vulgar Latin; **l. de cocina** *o* **macarrónico** dog Latin; *Fig* **saber (mucho) l.** to be sharp, to be on the ball

latinajo *nm Fam Pey* = Latin word used in an attempt to sound academic

latinismo *nm* Latinism

latinista *nmf* Latinist

latinizar [14] *vt* to Latinize

latino, -a *adj & nm,f* Latin

Latinoamérica *n* Latin America

latinoamericano, -a *adj & nm,f* Latin American

latir *vi* (a) *(corazón)* to beat; **en sus declaraciones late un cierto nerviosismo** there is a certain amount of nervousness lurking in his statements (b) *Méx, Ven (parecer)* **¿vendrá? — me late que sí** will she come? — I have a feeling she will

latitud *nf* (a) *Geog* latitude (b) **latitudes** *(parajes)* region, area

lato, -a *adj Formal* (a) *(discurso)* extensive, lengthy (b) *(sentido)* broad

latón *nm* brass

latoso, -a *Fam* **1** *adj* tiresome, pesky
2 *nm,f* pain (in the neck)

latrocinio *nm* larceny

laúd *nm* lute

laudable *adj* praiseworthy

láudano *nm* laudanum

laudatorio, -a *adj* laudatory

laudo *nm Der* = binding judgment in arbitration

laureado, -a *adj* prize-winning

laurear *vt* **l. a alguien (con)** to honor sb (with)

laurel *nm Bot* laurel; *Culin* bay leaf; *Fig* **laureles** *(honores)* laurels; *Fig* **dormirse en los laureles** to rest on one's laurels

lava *nf* lava

lavable *adj* washable

lavabo *nm* (a) *(objeto)* washbowl (b) *(habitación)* washroom

lavacoches *nmf inv* car washer

lavadero *nm (en casa)* laundry room; *(público)* washing place

lavado *nm* wash, washing; **l. de cerebro** brainwashing; **l. de estómago** stomach pumping; **l. y engrase** *(en garaje)* car wash and lubrication; **l. en seco** dry cleaning

lavadora *nf* washing machine; **poner la l.** to do some washing (in the machine)

lavafrutas *nm inv* ≃ finger bowl

La Valeta *n* Valetta

lavamanos *nm inv* washbowl

lavanda *nf* lavender

lavandería *nf (en hospital, hotel)* laundry; *(automática)* launderette, Laundromat®

lavandero, -a *nm* laundryman, *f* laundress

lavandina *nf (lejía) Arg* bleach

lavaplatos **1** *nmf inv (persona)* dishwasher
2 *nm inv* (a) *(aparato)* dishwasher (b) *Chile, Col, Méx, Ven (lugar)* (kitchen) sink

lavar **1** *vt* (a) *(limpiar)* to wash; **l. a mano** to hand-wash, to wash by hand; **l. y marcar** shampoo and set; **l. en seco** to dry-clean; *Fig* **lavarle el cerebro a alguien** to brainwash sb (b) *(honor)* to clear; *(ofensa)* to make up for
2 *vi* (a) *(detergente)* to get things clean (b) *(hacer la colada)* to do the washing
3 lavarse *vpr* to wash; **espera un momento, que me estoy lavando** hold on a minute, I'm washing *o* I'm getting washed; **lavarse las manos/la cara** to wash one's hands/face; **lavarse los dientes** to brush *o* clean one's teeth

lavarropas *nm inv RP* washing machine

lavaseco *nm Andes* dry cleaner's

lavativa *nf* enema

lavatorio *nm Andes, RP (lavabo)* washbowl

lavavajillas *nm inv (aparato)* dishwasher; *(líquido)* dish soap

laxante **1** *adj* (a) *(medicamento)* laxative (b) *(relajante)* relaxing
2 *nm Med* laxative

laxar *vt (vientre)* to loosen

laxativo, -a *adj & nm* laxative

laxitud *nf (de músculo, cable)* slackness; *(de moral)* laxity

laxo, -a *adj (músculo, cable)* slack; *(moral)* lax

lazada *nf* bow

lazareto *nm* leper colony

lazarillo *nm (persona)* blind person's guide; **(perro) l.** guide dog, seeing-eye dog

lazo **1** *nm* (a) *(atadura)* bow (b) *(cinta)* ribbon (c) *(trampa)* snare; *(de vaquero)* lasso; *Fig* **echar el l. a alguien** to snare sb
2 lazos *nmpl (vínculos)* ties, bonds

LCD *(abrev de* **liquid crystal display***)* LCD

Lda. *(abrev de* **licenciada***)* graduate *(used as title)*

Ldo. *(abrev de* **licenciado***)* graduate *(used as title)*

le *pron personal*

> **se** is used instead of **le** when it is used as an indirect object pronoun before **lo**, **la**, **los** or **las** (e.g. **se lo dije** I said it to him/her; **dáselos** give them to him/her).

(a) *(complemento indirecto) (hombre)* (to) him; *(mujer)* (to) her; *(cosa)* to it; *(usted)* to you; **le expliqué el motivo** I explained the reason to him/her; **le tengo miedo** I'm afraid of him/her; **ya le dije lo que pasaría** *(a usted)* I told you what would happen (b) *Esp (complemento directo)* him; *(usted)* you

leal **1** *adj* loyal (a to)
2 *nmf* loyal supporter (a of)

lealtad *nf* loyalty (a to)

leasing ['lisin] *(pl* **leasings***) nm Fin* leasing

lebrel *nm* whippet

lección *nf* lesson; **una l. de humildad** a humbling experience; **dar a alguien una l.** *(como castigo, advertencia)* to teach sb a lesson; *(como ejemplo)* to give sb a lesson; **servir de l.** to serve as a lesson; **l. magistral** *Mús* master class; *Educ* = lecture given by eminent academic to mark a special occasion; **lecciones de vuelo** flying lessons

lechal **1** *adj* sucking
2 *nm* sucking lamb

lechazo *nm* young lamb

leche *nf* (a) *(de mujer, hembra)* milk; **l. de coco** coconut milk; **l. condensada** condensed milk; **l. descremada** *o* **desnatada** skimmed milk; **l. entera** whole milk; **l. esterilizada/homogeneizada** sterilized/homogenized milk; **l. merengada** = drink made from milk, egg whites, sugar and cinnamon; **l. pasteurizada** pasteurized milk; **l. en polvo** powdered milk; **l. semidesnatada** two-percent milk; **l. UHT** UHT milk
(b) *(loción)* **l. bronceadora** sun lotion; **l. hidratante** moisturizing lotion; **l. limpiadora** cleansing milk
(c) *Esp muy Fam (golpe)* **dar** *o* **pegar una l. a alguien** to belt *o* clobber sb; **darse una l.** to come a cropper; **se dio una l. con el coche** he had a smashup in his car
(d) *Esp muy Fam (expresiones)* **estar de mala l.** to be in a goddamn awful mood; **tener mala l.** *(mala intención)* to be a mean *o* complete bastard; **¡esto es la l.!** *(el colmo)* this is the absolute goddamn limit!; **correr/trabajar a toda l.** *(muy rápido)* to run/work like hell; **¿cuándo/qué/por qué leches…?** when/what/why the hell…?

lechera *nf (para transportar)* milk churn; *(para servir)* milk jug

lechería *nf* dairy

lechero, -a **1** *adj* milk, dairy; **producción lechera** milk production; **vaca lechera** dairy cow
2 *nm,f (persona)* milkman, *f* milkwoman

lecho *nm* (a) *(cama)* bed; **ser un l. de rosas** to be a bed of roses (b) *(de río)* bed (c) *(de mar)* bed, floor (c) *Geol (capa)* layer

lechón *nm* sucking pig

lechoso, -a *adj* milky

lechuga *nf (planta)* lettuce; *Fam* **fresco como una l.** *(sano, lozano)* as fresh as a daisy; **l. iceberg** *o* **repolluda** iceberg lettuce; **l. romana** romaine (lettuce), cos lettuce

lechuza *nf (barn)* owl

lecitina *nf* lecithin

lectivo, -a *adj* school; **durante el horario l.** during school hours

lector, -ora 1 *nm,f* **(a)** *(de libros)* reader **(b)** *Esp Educ* language assistant
2 *nm (aparato)* reader; *Inform* **l. de CD-ROM** CD-ROM drive; **l. de documentos** document reader; **l. óptico** optical scanner; **l. óptico de caracteres** optical character reader

lectorado *nm Esp Educ* = post of language assistant; **hacer un l.** to work as a language assistant

lectura *nf* **(a)** *(de libros)* reading; **l. ligera** light reading **(b)** *Educ (de tesis)* defense **(c)** *(escrito)* reading (matter) **(d)** *(interpretación)* reading, interpretation **(e)** *Inform (de datos)* scanning; **l. óptica** optical scanning

leer [37] **1** *vt* to read; **leo el francés, pero no lo hablo** I can read French, but I can't speak it; **l. el pensamiento a alguien** to read sb's mind
2 *vi* to read; **l. en alto** to read aloud; *Fig* **l. entre líneas** to read between the lines

legación *nf* legation

legado *nm* **(a)** *(herencia)* legacy **(b)** *(representante) (cargo)* legation; *(persona)* legate

legajo *nm* file

legal *adj* **(a)** *(conforme a ley)* legal; **no cumple los requisitos legales** it doesn't meet the legal requirements **(b)** *(relativo a la ley)* legal; **asesoramiento l.** legal advice **(c)** *(forense)* forensic; **medicina l.** legal medicine **(d)** *Esp Fam (de confianza)* honest, decent; **es un tío muy l.** he's a great guy

legalidad *nf* legality

legalismo *nm* fine legal point, legalism

legalista 1 *adj* legalistic
2 *nmf* legalist

legalización *nf* **(a)** *(concesión de estatus legal)* legalization **(b)** *(certificado)* (certificate of) authentication

legalizar [14] *vt* **(a)** *(conceder estatus legal)* to legalize **(b)** *(certificar)* to authenticate

legañas *nfpl* sleep *(in the eyes)*

legañoso, -a *adj* full of sleep

legar [38] *vt* **(a)** *(dejar en herencia)* to bequeath **(b)** *(delegar)* to delegate

legatario, -a *nm,f Der* legatee

legendario, -a *adj* legendary

legible *adj* legible

legión *nf también Fig* legion; **l. extranjera** foreign legion

legionario, -a 1 *adj* legionary
2 *nm Hist* legionary; *Mil* legionnaire

legionella [leχioˈnela] *nf* **(a)** *(enfermedad)* legionnaire's disease **(b)** *(bacteria)* legionella bacterium

legislación *nf* **(a)** *(leyes)* legislation **(b)** *(ciencia)* law

legislador, -ora 1 *adj* legislative
2 *nm,f* legislator

legislar *vi* to legislate

legislativo, -a *adj* legislative

legislatura *nf (periodo)* term of office

legitimación *nf* **(a)** *(legalización)* legitimation **(b)** *(certificación)* authentication

legitimar *vt* **(a)** *(justificar)* to legitimize **(b)** *(autentificar)* to authenticate

legitimidad *nf* legitimacy

legítimo, -a *adj* **(a)** *(lícito, justificado)* legitimate **(b)** *(auténtico)* real, genuine

lego, -a 1 *adj* **(a)** *(profano, laico)* lay **(b)** *(ignorante)* ignorant; **ser l. en** to know nothing about
2 *nm,f* **(a)** *(profano)* layman, *f* laywoman **(b)** *(ignorante)* ignorant person

legrado *nm Med* scraping, curettage

legua *nf* league; **l. marina** marine league; *Fam Fig* **verse a la l.** to stand out a mile

legue *etc ver* **legar**

leguleyo, -a *nm,f Pey* bad lawyer

legumbre *nf* pulse, pod vegetable; **legumbres secas** dried pulses; **legumbres verdes** green vegetables

leguminosa *nf* pulse, legume

lehendakari [lendaˈkari] *nmf* = president of the autonomous Basque government

leído, -a *adj* **(a)** *(obra)* **muy/poco l.** much/little read **(b)** *(persona)* well-read

leísmo *nm Gram* = incorrect use of "le" as direct object instead of "lo"

leitmotiv [leitmoˈtif] *(pl* **leitmotivs)** *nm* leitmotiv

lejanía *nf* distance

lejano, -a *adj* distant; **el L. Oriente** the Far East

lejía *nf* bleach

lejos *adv* **(a)** *(en el espacio)* far (away); **¿está l.?** is it far?; **eso queda muy l.** that's a long way away; **vivo l. del centro** I live a long way from the city center; **a lo l.** in the distance; **de** *o* **desde l.** from a distance; *Fig* **llegará l.** she'll go far **(b)** *(en el pasado)* long ago; **eso queda ya l.** that happened a long time ago **(c)** *(expresiones)* **l. de** far from; **l. de mejorar…** far from getting better…; *Fam* **no es el mejor ni de l.** he's nowhere near *o* nothing like the best

lelo, -a 1 *adj* stupid, slow
2 *nm,f* idiot

lema *nm* **(a)** *(norma)* motto **(b)** *(eslogan político, publicitario)* slogan

Leman *nm* **el lago L.** Lake Geneva

lempira *nm* lempira

lencería *nf* **(a)** *(ropa interior)* lingerie; **departamento de l.** lingerie department **(b)** *(tienda)* lingerie store **(c)** *(género de lienzo)* linen

lengua *nf* **(a)** *(órgano)* tongue; **las malas lenguas dicen que…** according to the gossip…; *Fam* **irse de la l.** to let the cat out of the bag; *Fam* **ir/llegar con la l. fuera** to go along/ arrive puffing and panting; **morderse la l.** to bite one's tongue; **se le trabó la l.** she stumbled over her words; *Fam* **tener la l. muy larga** to be a gossip; *Fam Fig* **tirar a alguien de la l.** to draw sb out; *Esp* **l. de gato** *(de chocolate)* cat's tongue *(chocolate cookie)*; *Fig* **l. de víbora** *o* **viperina** malicious tongue; **l. de tierra** tongue of land
(b) *(idioma, lenguaje)* language; **l. materna** mother tongue; **l. muerta** dead language

lenguado *nm* sole

lenguaje *nm* language; **l. cifrado** code; **l. coloquial/ comercial** colloquial/business language; **l. corporal** body language; **l. gestual** gestures; *Inform* **l. máquina** machine language; *Inform* **l. de alto nivel/de bajo nivel** high-level/ low-level language; *Inform* **l. de programación** programming language; **l. por señas** sign language

lenguaraz *adj* **(a)** *(malhablado)* foul-mouthed **(b)** *(charlatán)* talkative

lengüeta *nf (de instrumento musical, zapato)* tongue

lengüetazo *nm,* **lengüetada** *nf* lick

lenidad *nf Formal* leniency

Leningrado *n Antes* Leningrad

leninismo *nm Pol* Leninism

leninista *adj & nmf Pol* Leninist

lenitivo, -a 1 *adj* soothing, lenitive
2 *nm* **(a)** *(físico)* lenitive **(b)** *(moral)* balm

lenocinio *nm Formal* procuring, pimping; **casa de l.** brothel

lente 1 *nf* lens; *Esp* **lentes de contacto** contact lenses

   2 *nmpl* **lentes** *(gafas)* glasses

lenteja *nf* lentil

lentejuela *nf* sequin; **un vestido de lentejuelas** a sequined dress

lenticular *adj* lenticular

lentilla *nf Esp* contact lens; **lentillas blandas/duras** soft/hard lenses

lentitud *nf* slowness; **con l.** slowly

lento, -a 1 *adj* slow; *(muerte, agonía)* lingering, long drawn out; **una película lenta** a slow movie; **¡qué lentas pasan las horas!** time is passing so slowly!

   2 *adv* slowly

leña *nf* (a) *(madera)* firewood; *Fig* **echar l. al fuego** to add fuel to the flames *o* fire (b) *Fam (golpes)* beating; **dar l. a alguien** to beat sb up

leñador, -ora *nm,f* woodcutter

leñazo *nm Fam (golpe)* bang, bash; *(con el coche)* smashup, crash

leñe *interj Esp Fam* **¡l.!** for heaven's sake!

leñera *nf* woodshed

leñero,-a *Fam Dep* **1** *adj* dirty

   2 *nm,f* dirty player

leño *nm* (a) *(de madera)* log; *Fam* **dormir como un l.** to sleep like a log (b) *Fam (persona)* blockhead

leñoso, -a *adj* woody

leo 1 *nm (zodiaco)* Leo; *Esp* **ser l.** to be (a) Leo

   2 *nmf Esp (persona)* Leo

león, -ona *nm,f (africano) (macho)* lion; *(hembra)* lioness; *Am (puma)* puma; *Prov* **no es tan fiero el l. como lo pintan** he/it/*etc* is not as bad as he/it/*etc* is made out to be; **l. marino** sea lion

leonera *nf (jaula)* lion's cage; *Esp Fam* **este cuarto es una l.** this room is in a real state

leonés, -esa 1 *adj* of/from León

   2 *nm,f* person from León

leonino, -a *adj* (a) *(rostro, aspecto)* leonine (b) *(contrato, condiciones)* one-sided, unfair

leopardo *nm* leopard

leotardos *nmpl* (a) *Esp (medias)* thick tights (b) *(de gimnasta)* leotard

Lepe *n* **saber más que L.** to be very clever *o* astute

lépero, -a *adj CAm, Méx Fam* coarse, vulgar

leporino *adj* **labio l.** cleft lip, harelip

lepra *nf* leprosy

leprosería *nf* leper colony

leproso, -a 1 *adj* leprous

   2 *nm,f* leper

lerdo, -a *Fam* **1** *adj (idiota)* dim, slow-witted; *(torpe)* useless, hopeless

   2 *nm,f (idiota)* fool, idiot; *(torpe)* useless idiot

leridano, -a 1 *adj* of/from Lérida

   2 *nm,f* person from Lérida

les *pron personal pl*

> **se** is used instead of **les** when it is used as an indirect object pronoun before **lo, la, los, las** (**se lo dije** I said it to them; **dáselo** give it to them).

   (a) *(complemento indirecto) (ellos)* (to) them; *(ustedes)* (to) you; **l. expliqué el motivo** I explained the reason to them; **l. tengo miedo** I'm afraid of them; **ya l. dije lo que pasaría** *(a ustedes)* I told you what would happen (b) *Esp (complemento directo) (ellos)* them; *(ustedes)* you

lesbiana *nf* lesbian

lesbianismo *nm* lesbianism

lesbiano, -a, lésbico, -a *adj* lesbian

leseras *nfpl Chile Fam* nonsense

lesión *nf* (a) *(daño físico)* injury; **l. de columna** spinal injury; *Der* **lesiones graves** serious bodily harm (b) *(perjuicio)* damage, harm

lesionado, -a 1 *adj* injured

   2 *nm,f* injured person

lesionar 1 *vt (físicamente)* to injure; *(perjudicar)* to damage, to harm

   2 lesionarse *vpr* to injure oneself

lesivo, -a *adj Formal* damaging, harmful

leso, -a *adj Formal* **crimen de lesa humanidad** crime against humanity; **crimen de lesa patria** high treason

Lesoto *n* Lesotho

letal *adj* lethal

letanía *nf Rel & Fig* litany

letárgico, -a *adj* (a) *Med & Fig* lethargic (b) *Zool* hibernating

letargo *nm* (a) *Med & Fig* lethargy (b) *Zool* hibernation

letón, -ona 1 *adj & nm,f* Latvian

   2 *nm (lengua)* Latvian

Letonia *n* Latvia

letra *nf* (a) *(signo)* letter

   (b) *(escritura, caligrafía)* handwriting; **no entiendo su l.** I can't read his writing *o* handwriting

   (c) *Imprenta* type, typeface; *Fig* **leer la l. pequeña** to read the small print; *Fig* **mandar cuatro letras a alguien** to drop sb a line; **l. cursiva** italic type, italics; **l. de imprenta** *(impresa)* print; *(en formulario)* block capitals; **escriba en l. de imprenta** please write in block capitals; **l. itálica** italic type, italics; **l. de molde** *(impresa)* print; *(en formulario)* block capitals; **l. negrita** bold (face)

   (d) *(texto de canción)* lyrics

   (e) *Com* **l. (de cambio)** bill of exchange; **girar una l.** to draw a bill of exchange; **protestar una l.** to protest a bill; **l. avalada** guaranteed bill of exchange; **l. de cambio a la vista** demand bill, sight bill

   (f) *(sentido)* literal meaning; **seguir instrucciones al pie de la l.** to follow instructions to the letter

   (g) *Educ* **letras** arts; **una asignatura de letras** an arts subject

letrado, -a 1 *adj* learned

   2 *nm,f* lawyer

letrero *nm* sign

letrina *nf* latrine

letrista *nmf* lyricist

leucemia *nf* leukemia

leucocito *nm* leukocyte

leva *nf* (a) *Mil* levy (b) *Náut* weighing anchor (c) *Mec* cam

levadizo, -a *adj* **puente l.** drawbridge

levadura *nf* yeast, leaven; **l. (en polvo)** baking powder; **l. de cerveza** brewer's yeast

levantador, -ora *nm,f Dep* **l. de pesas** weight lifter

levantamiento *nm* (a) *(sublevación)* uprising (b) *(elevación)* raising; *Dep* **l. de pesas** weight lifting (c) *(supresión)* lifting, removal

levantar 1 *vt* (a) *(alzar, elevar)* to raise; *(objeto pesado, capó, trampilla)* to lift (up); **l. algo del suelo** to pick sth up off the ground; **l. a alguien del suelo** to help sb up off the ground; **l. a alguien de la cama** to get sb out of bed; **l. la vista** *o* **mirada** to look up; *Fig* **no ha conseguido l. cabeza** he's still not back to his old self; **l. el ánimo** to cheer up

   (b) *(quitar) (pintura, venda, tapa)* to remove

   (c) *(construir) (edificio, muro)* to build, to raise

   (d) *(retirar) (campamento)* to strike; *(tienda de campaña, tenderete)* to take down

   (e) *(provocar) (protestas, polémica)* to stir up; **l. a alguien contra** to stir sb up against

   (f) *(suprimir) (embargo, prohibición)* to lift; **l. el castigo a alguien** to let sb off

(g) *(sesión) (terminar)* to bring to an end; *(aplazar)* to adjourn; **si no hay más preguntas, se levanta la sesión** *(en reunión)* if there are no more questions, that ends the meeting
(**h**) *(redactar) (acta, atestado)* to draw up
(**i**) *Fam (robar)* to pinch, to swipe
2 levantarse *vpr* (**a**) *(ponerse de pie)* to stand up; *(de la cama)* to get up (**b**) *(elevarse) (sol)* to climb in the sky; *(niebla)* to lift (**c**) *(sublevarse)* to rise up (**d**) *(viento, oleaje)* to get up, to rise

levante *nm* (**a**) *(este)* east; *(región)* east coast; *Geog* **L.** = the coastal provinces of Spain between Catalonia and Andalusia: Castellón, Valencia, Alicante and Murcia (**b**) *(viento)* east wind

levantino, -a 1 *adj* of/from the Levante region of Spain
2 *nm,f* person from the Levante region of Spain

levantisco, -a *adj* restless, turbulent

levar *vt Náut* **l. anclas** to weigh anchor

leve *adj* (**a**) *(suave, sutil)* light; *(olor, sabor, temblor)* slight, faint (**b**) *(pecado, falta, herida)* minor; *(enfermedad)* mild, slight

levedad *nf* (**a**) *(suavidad, sutileza)* lightness (**b**) *(de pecado, falta, herida)* minor nature; *(de enfermedad)* mildness

levita *nf* frock coat
levitación *nf* levitation
levitar *vi* to levitate
lexema *nm Ling* lexeme
lexicalizar [14] *Ling* **1** *vt* to lexicalize
2 lexicalizarse *vpr* to become lexicalized
léxico, -a 1 *adj* lexical
2 *nm (vocabulario)* vocabulary
lexicografía *nf* lexicography
lexicográfico, -a *adj* lexicographical
lexicógrafo, -a *nm,f* lexicographer
lexicología *nf* lexicology
lexicólogo, -a *nm,f* lexicologist
lexicón *nm* lexicon

ley *nf* (**a**) *(norma, precepto)* law; *(parlamentaria)* act; **leyes** *(derecho)* law; *Fam* **ganaron con todas las de la l.** they won fair and square; **de buena l.** reliable, sterling; *Fam* **l. del embudo** one law for oneself and another for everyone else; **l. marcial** martial law; **l. de la oferta y la demanda** law of supply and demand; *Hist* **l. sálica** Salic law; *Hist* **la Ley Seca** Prohibition; **la l. de la selva** the law of the jungle; *Dep* **l. de la ventaja** advantage (law) (**b**) *(de metal precioso)* **de l.** *(oro)* = containing the legal amount of gold; *(plata)* sterling

leyenda *nf* (**a**) *(narración)* legend (**b**) *(inscripción)* inscription, legend

leyera *etc ver* **leer**

liado, -a *adj* (**a**) *(confundido)* befuddled (**b**) *(ocupado)* tied up (**c**) *(involucrado)* involved (**d**) *(complicado)* mixed-up

liana *nf* liana

liante *nmf Esp Fam (persuasivo)* smooth talker; *(enredador)* troublemaker; **claro que me convenció, es un l.** of course he persuaded me, he could talk you into anything!

liar [32] **1** *vt* (**a**) *(atar)* to tie up (**b**) *(cigarrillo)* to roll (**c**) *(envolver)* **l. algo en** *(papel)* to wrap sth up in (**d**) *(involucrar)* **l. a alguien (en)** to get sb mixed up (in) (**e**) *(complicar)* to confuse; **¡ya me has liado!** now you've really got me confused!; **su declaración no hizo más que l. el tema** his statement only complicated *o* confused matters (**f**) *Esp Fam* **liarla** *(meter la pata)* to mess things up; **¡ya la hemos liado!, ¿por qué la invitaste?** you've really gone and done it now, why did you invite her?
2 liarse *vpr* (**a**) *(enredarse)* to get muddled up; **me lié y tardé tres horas en terminar** I got muddled *o* confused and took three hours to finish (**b**) *Esp (empezar)* to begin, to start; **liarse a hacer algo** to start *o* begin doing sth; **se liaron a puñetazos** they set about one another (**c**) *Esp Fam (sentimentalmente)* to get involved (**con** with), to have an affair (**con** with)

libación *nf Literario* libation
libanés, -esa *adj & nm,f* Lebanese
Líbano *nm* **el L.** the Lebanon
libar *vt* to sip, to suck
libelo *nm* lampoon
libélula *nf* dragonfly
liberación *nf* (**a**) *(de ciudad, país)* liberation; *(de rehén, prisionero)* freeing; **l. de la mujer** women's liberation; **l. sexual** sexual liberation (**b**) *(de hipoteca)* redemption
liberado, -a *adj (ciudad, país)* liberated; *(rehén, prisionero)* freed
liberal *adj & nmf* liberal
liberalidad *nf* liberality
liberalismo *nm Pol* liberalism
liberalización *nf* liberalization; *Econ* deregulation
liberalizar [14] *vt* to liberalize; *Econ* to deregulate
liberar 1 *vt (ciudad, país)* to liberate; *(rehén, prisionero)* to free; **l. a alguien de algo** to free sb from sth
2 liberarse *vpr* to liberate oneself; **liberarse de algo** to free *o* liberate oneself from sth
Liberia *n* Liberia
liberiano, -a *adj & nm,f* Liberian
libertad *nf* freedom, liberty; **puede entrar en mi casa con toda l.** she is entirely free to come into my house when she pleases; **dejar** *o* **poner a alguien en l.** to set sb free, to release sb; **estar en l.** to be free; **tener l. para hacer algo** to be free to do sth; **tomarse la l. de hacer algo** to take the liberty of doing sth; **tomarse libertades (con)** to take liberties (with); **l. de cátedra** academic freedom; *Econ* **l. de circulación de capitales/trabajadores** free movement of capital/workers; **l. condicional** parole; **l. de culto** freedom of worship; **l. de expresión** freedom of speech; **l. de imprenta** freedom of the press; **l. de movimientos** freedom of movement; **l. de prensa** freedom of the press; **l. provisional** bail
libertador, -ora 1 *adj* liberating
2 *nm,f* liberator
libertar *vt también Fig* to liberate
libertario, -a *adj & nm,f Pol* libertarian
libertinaje *nm* licentiousness
libertino, -a 1 *adj* licentious
2 *nm,f* libertine
liberto, -a *nm,f Hist* freedman, *f* freedwoman
Libia *n* Libya
libidinoso, -a *adj* libidinous, lewd
libido *nf* libido
libio, -a *adj & nm,f* Libyan
libra *nf* (**a**) *(zodiaco)* Libra; *Esp* **ser l.** to be (a) Libra
2 *nmf Esp (persona)* Libran
3 *nf (unidad de peso, moneda)* pound; **l. esterlina** pound sterling
librado, -a 1 *nm,f Com* drawee
2 *adj* **salir bien l.** to get off lightly; **salir mal l.** to come off badly
librador, -ora *nm,f Com* drawer
libramiento *nm*, **libranza** *nf Com* order of payment
librano, -a *Am* **1** *adj* Libra; **ser l.** to be (a) Libra
2 *nm,f* Libran
librar 1 *vt* (**a**) **l. a alguien (de algo/de hacer algo)** *(eximir)* to free sb (from sth/from doing sth); *(de pagos, impuestos)* to exempt sb (from sth/from doing sth); **¡líbreme Dios!** God *o* Heaven forbid! (**b**) *(entablar) (pelea, lucha)* to engage in; *(batalla, combate)* to join, to wage (**c**) *Com* to draw
2 *vi Esp (no trabajar)* to be off work
3 librarse *vpr* (**a**) *(salvarse)* **librarse (de hacer algo)** to escape (from doing sth); **se libró del servicio militar** he got off having to do military service; **de buena te libraste**

you had a lucky escape (**b**) *(deshacerse)* **librarse de algo/ alguien** to get rid of sth/sb

libre *adj* (**a**) *(no sujeto)* free; *(rato, tiempo)* spare; *(camino, vía)* clear; *(espacio, piso, retrete)* empty, vacant; **un taxi l.** a free *o* empty taxi; **el puesto de tesorero ha quedado l.** the post of treasurer is now vacant; *Dep* **200 metros libres** 200 meters freestyle; **ser l. de** *o* **para hacer algo** to be free to do sth; *Esp* **ir por l.** to go it alone; **l. de** *(sin)* free from; *(exento)* exempt from; *Econ* **l. cambio** free trade; **l. de franqueo** postage-free; **l. de impuestos** tax-free; *Econ* **l. mercado** free market (**b**) *(alumno)* external; **estudiar por l.** to be an external student

librea *nf* livery

librecambio *nm* free trade

librecambismo *nm* free trade

librepensador, -ora 1 *adj* freethinking
    2 *nm,f* freethinker

librepensamiento *nm* freethinking

librería *nf* (**a**) *(tienda)* bookstore, bookshop (**b**) *Esp (mueble)* bookcase (**c**) *Inform* library

librero, -a 1 *nm,f (persona)* bookseller
    2 *nm CAm, Col, Méx (mueble)* bookshelf

libreta *nf* (**a**) *(para escribir)* notebook (**b**) *(de banco)* **l. (de ahorros)** savings book (**c**) *Urug* **l. de manejar** driver's license

libreto *nm* (**a**) *Mús* libretto (**b**) *Am Cine* script

libro *nm* (**a**) *(para leer)* book; *Fam* **ser (como) un l. abierto** to be an open book; *Pol* **l. blanco** (government) white paper; **l. de bolsillo** (pocket-sized) paperback; **l. de cabecera** bedside book; **l. de cocina** cookbook; **l. de consulta** reference book; **l. de cuentos** storybook; **l. de ejercicios** exercise book; **l. electrónico** electronic book; *Educ* **l. de escolaridad** school report; **l. de familia** = document containing personal details of the members of a family; **l. de reclamaciones** complaints book; **l. de registro (de entradas)** register; *Rel* **l. sagrado** Book *(in Bible)*; **l. de texto** textbook; **l. verde** = preliminary government report
    (**b**) *Com* **llevar los libros** to keep the books; **l. de caja** cashbook; **l. de contabilidad** account book

Lic. *(abrev de* **licenciado***)* graduate *(used as title)*

licantropía *nf* lycanthropy

licántropo *nm* werewolf

licencia *nf* (**a**) *(documento)* license, permit; *(autorización)* permission; **l. de armas/caza** gun/hunting license; *Carib, Chile, Ecuad* **l. de conducir**, *Méx* **l. para conducir** driver's license; **l. de exportación/importación** export/import license; **l. fiscal** = official authorization to practice a profession; *Méx* **l. de manejar** *o* **manejo** driver's license; **l. de obras** planning permission; **l. poética** poetic license (**b**) *Mil* leave; **l. absoluta** discharge (**c**) *Am (en el trabajo)* leave (**d**) *(confianza)* liberty; **tomarse licencias con alguien** to take liberties with sb

licenciado, -a 1 *adj Mil* discharged
    2 *nm,f* (**a**) *Educ* graduate; **l. en económicas/derecho** economics/law graduate (**b**) *Mil* discharged soldier (**c**) *Am salvo RP (forma de tratamiento)* = form of address used to indicate respect; **el l. Pérez** Mr. Pérez; **¡por supuesto, l.!** of course, Mr. Pérez, Sir!

licenciamiento *nm Mil* discharge

licenciar 1 *vt* (**a**) *Mil* to discharge (**b**) *Am (en universidad)* to confer a degree on
    2 licenciarse *vpr* (**a**) *(en universidad)* to graduate (**en** in) (**b**) *Mil* to be discharged

licenciatura *nf* degree (**en** *o* **de** in)

licencioso, -a *adj* licentious

liceo *nm* (**a**) *Educ* lycée (**b**) *(de recreo)* social club

licitación *nf* bid, bidding

licitador, -ora *nmf* bidder

licitar *vt* to bid for

lícito, -a *adj* (**a**) *(legal)* lawful (**b**) *(correcto)* right (**c**) *(justo)* fair

licor *nm* spirits, liquor

licorera *nf* (**a**) *(botella)* decanter (**b**) *(mueble)* cocktail cabinet

licorería *nf* (**a**) *(fábrica)* distillery (**b**) *(tienda)* liquor store

licuado *nm Am* milk shake

licuadora *nf Esp (para extraer zumo)* juice extractor, juicer; *Am (para batir)* blender

licuar [4] *vt Culin* to liquidize

licuefacción *nf* liquefaction

lid *nf Anticuado* fight; *Fig* **en buena l.** in a fair contest; **un experto en estas lides** an old hand in these matters

líder 1 *adj* leading
    2 *nmf* leader; *Com* **l. del mercado** market leader

liderar *vt* to lead

liderazgo, liderato *nm* (**a**) *(primer puesto)* lead; *(en liga)* first place (**b**) *(dirección)* leadership

lidia *nf* (**a**) *(arte)* bullfighting (**b**) *(corrida)* bullfight

lidiador, -ora *nm,f Taurom* bullfighter

lidiar 1 *vi (luchar)* to struggle (**con** with)
    2 *vt Taurom* to fight

liebre *nf* hare; *Fig* **correr como una l.** to run like a hare; *Fig* **levantar la l.** to let the cat out of the bag

Liechtenstein ['litχenstein] *n* Liechtenstein

liendre *nf* nit

lienzo *nm* (**a**) *(tela)* (coarse) cloth; *(paño)* piece of cloth (**b**) *(para pintar)* canvas (**c**) *(cuadro)* painting

lifting ['liftin] *(pl* **liftings***) nm* face-lift

liga *nf* (**a**) *(confederación, agrupación) & Dep* league (**b**) *(para medias) (elástico)* garter; *(colgante)* garter

ligadura *nf* (**a**) *Med & Mús* ligature; *Med* **l. de trompas** tubal ligation (**b**) *(atadura)* bond, tie

ligamento *nm Anat* ligament; **rotura de ligamentos** torn ligaments

ligar [38] **1** *vt* (**a**) *(unir, aglutinar)* to bind; *(atar)* to tie (up); *(salsa)* to thicken; *Med* to put a ligature on (**b**) *Mús* to slur
    2 *vi Fam (encontrar pareja)* to score; **l. con alguien** *(entablar relaciones)* to make out with sb
    3 ligarse *vpr Esp Fam* **ligarse a alguien** to make out with sb

ligazón *nf* link, connection

ligereza *nf* (**a**) *(levedad)* lightness; *(de dolor)* slightness (**b**) *(agilidad)* agility (**c**) *(rapidez)* speed (**d**) *(irreflexión)* rashness; **fue una l. decir eso** it was rash *o* reckless to say that

ligero, -a 1 *adj* (**a**) *(leve)* light; *(dolor, rumor, descenso)* slight; *(traje, tela)* thin; **ir** *o* **viajar l. de equipaje** to travel light; **un l. gusto a ajo** a hint of garlic; **una ligera gripe** a touch of flu; **l. de ropa** scantily dressed *o* clad (**b**) *(ágil)* agile, nimble (**c**) *(rápido)* quick, swift; **caminar a paso l.** to walk at a brisk pace
    2 a la ligera *loc adv* **hacer algo a la ligera** to do sth without much thought; **juzgar a la ligera** to be superficial in one's judgments; **tomarse algo a la ligera** not to take sth seriously

light [lait] *adj inv (comida)* low-calorie; *(refresco)* diet; *(cigarrillos)* light

ligón, -ona *Esp Fam* **1** *adj* **es muy l.** he's always getting off with somebody or other
    2 *nm,f* goer, raver

ligoteo *nm Esp Fam* **salir de l.** to go out to score

ligue 1 *ver* **ligar**
    2 *nm Esp Fam* (**a**) *(acción)* **salir de l.** to go out to score (**b**) *(novio)* squeeze

liguero, -a 1 *adj Dep* league; **partido l.** league game
    2 *nm* garter belt

liguilla *nf Dep* mini-league, round-robin tournament

lija *nf* (a) *(papel)* sandpaper (b) *(pez)* dogfish
lijadora *nf* sander
lijar *vt* to sand down
lila 1 *nf (flor)* lilac
　2 *adj inv & nm (color)* lilac
liliputiense 1 *adj* dwarfish
　2 *nmf* midget
Lima *n* Lima
lima *nf* (a) *(herramienta)* file; **l. de uñas** nail file; *Fam* **comer como una l.** to eat like a horse (b) *(fruto)* lime
limaco *nm* slug
limadora *nf* polisher
limadura *nf* filing
limar *vt (pulir)* to file down; *Fig (perfeccionar)* to polish, to add the finishing touches to
limbo *nm* (a) *Rel* limbo; *Fam* **estar en el l.** to be miles away (b) *Astron & Bot* limb
limeño, -a 1 *adj* of/from Lima
　2 *nm,f* person from Lima
limitación *nf* (a) *(restricción)* limitation, limit; **l. de velocidad** speed limit (b) *(de distrito)* boundaries
limitado, -a *adj* (a) *(restringido) (espacio, acceso)* limited; **disponemos de un espacio muy l.** we have very limited space; **tienen un acceso l. a los servicios sanitarios** they have limited access to health-care services; **el problema no está l. a un solo país** the problem is not limited *o* restricted to just one country (b) *(poco dotado) (alumno, artista)* of limited ability; **como cantante es muy l.** he has limited ability as a singer
limitar 1 *vt* (a) *(restringir)* to limit, to restrict; **han limitado la velocidad máxima a cuarenta por hora** they've restricted the speed limit to forty kilometres an hour; **este sueldo tan bajo me limita mucho** I can't do very much on such a low salary (b) *(terreno)* to mark out (c) *(atribuciones, derechos)* to set out, to define
　2 *vi* to border (**con** on)
　3 limitarse *vpr* **limitarse a** to limit oneself to; **me limitaré a enumerar los puntos principales** I will restrict myself to a description of the main points; **se limitó a recordarnos nuestros derechos** he merely *o* just reminded us of our rights; **limítate a ayudar** just concentrate on helping
límite 1 *adj inv* (a) *(precio, velocidad, edad)* maximum (b) *(situación)* extreme; *(caso)* borderline
　2 *nm* (a) *(tope)* limit; **al l.** at the limit; **dentro de un l.** within limits; **su pasión no tiene l.** her passion knows no bounds; **estoy al l. de mis fuerzas** I've reached the limit of my strength; **me dejan estar conectado a Internet sin l. de tiempo** I have unlimited access to the Internet; *Fin* **l. de crédito** credit limit; **l. de edad** age limit; **l. de velocidad** speed limit (b) *(confín)* boundary
limítrofe *adj (país, territorio)* bordering; *(terreno, finca)* neighboring
limo *nm* mud *(from bed of river, lake)*
limón *nm* lemon
limonada *nf (natural)* lemonade; *(refresco)* lemon soda
limonar *nm* lemon grove
limonero *nm* lemon tree
limosna *nf* (a) *Rel* alms (b) *(a un mendigo)* **dar l.** to give money; **pedir l.** to beg; *Fig* to ask for charity
limosnear *vi* to beg
limpia *nmf Fam (limpiabotas)* shoeshine
limpiabotas *nmf inv* shoeshine
limpiacristales *nm inv* window-cleaning fluid
limpiador, -ora 1 *adj* cleaning
　2 *nm,f* cleaner
limpiamente *adv* (a) *(con destreza)* cleanly (b) *(honradamente)* honestly

limpiametales *nm inv* metal polish
limpiaparabrisas *nm inv* windshield wiper
limpiar 1 *vt* (a) *(quitar la suciedad)* to clean; *(con trapo)* to wipe; *(mancha)* to wipe away; *(zapatos)* to polish; **limpia la mesa de migas** clean *o* wipe the crumbs off the table (b) *(desembarazar)* **l. algo de algo** to clear sth of sth (c) *Fam (en el juego)* to clean out (d) *Fam (robar)* to swipe, to pinch
　2 *vi* to clean
　3 limpiarse *vpr* to clean *o* wipe oneself; **límpiate esa mancha** wipe that stain off yourself; **se limpió con una servilleta** she wiped herself with a napkin; **límpiate la nariz** wipe your nose
limpiavidrios *nm inv Am* window-cleaning fluid
límpido, -a *adj Formal* limpid
limpieza *nf* (a) *(cualidad)* cleanliness; *Hist* **l. de sangre** racial purity (b) *(acción)* cleaning; **hacer la l.** to do the cleaning; **l. en seco** dry cleaning; **l. étnica** ethnic cleansing (c) *(destreza)* skill, cleanness
limpio, -a 1 *adj* (a) *(sin suciedad)* clean; *(cielo, imagen)* clear (b) *(neto) (sueldo)* net (c) *(honrado)* honest; *(intenciones)* honorable; *(juego)* clean (d) *(sin culpa)* **estar l.** to be in the clear; **l. de culpa/sospecha** free of blame/suspicion (e) *Fam (sin dinero)* broke (f) *(expresiones)* **a puñetazo l.** with bare fists; **abrió la puerta a patada limpia** he kicked down the door
　2 *adv* cleanly, fair; **pasar** *Esp* **a** *o Am* **en l.**, **poner en l.** to make a fair copy of, to write out neatly; **sacar algo en l. de** to make sth out from
limpión *nm Carib, Col (paño)* cleaning rag
limusina *nf* limousine
linaje *nm* lineage
linaza *nf* linseed
lince *nm* lynx; **ser un l. (para algo)** to be very sharp (at sth)
linchamiento *nm* lynching
linchar *vt* to lynch; **l. a alguien** to lynch sb
lindante *adj* **l. (con)** *(terreno)* bordering; *(conceptos, ideas)* bordering (on)
lindar *vi* **l. con** *(terreno)* to adjoin, to be next to; *(conceptos, ideas)* to border on
linde *nm o nf* boundary
lindero *nm* boundary
lindeza *nf* (a) *(belleza)* prettiness (b) *Irónico* **lindezas** *(insultos)* insults
lindo, -a 1 *adj esp Am* pretty, lovely; *Fam* **de lo l.** a great deal
　2 *adv Am* very well, beautifully
línea *nf* (a) *(raya, trazo, límite)* line; *Aut* **l. continua** solid white line; *Fin* **l. de crédito** credit line, line of credit; **l. divisoria** dividing line; **l. de flotación** waterline; **l. de mira** line of fire; **l. de puntos** dotted line; **líneas paralelas** parallel lines; **l. recta** straight line; **l. de tiro** line of fire
　(b) *(de telecomunicaciones)* line; **no hay l.** the line's dead
　(c) *(en deportes)* line; **l. de banda** sideline, touchline; **l. de meta** *(en fútbol, fútbol americano)* goal line; *(en carrera)* finishing line; **l. de salida** starting line; **l. de saque** *o* **servicio** baseline, service line
　(d) *(en comercio)* line; **l. de productos** line of products
　(e) *(silueta)* figure; **guardar la l.** to watch one's figure; **un coche de l. aerodinámica** a streamlined car
　(f) *(estilo)* style; **de l. clásica** classical; **eso está muy en su l.** that's just his style; **l. de conducta** course of action
　(g) *(ruta)* **una nueva l. de autobús** a new bus route; **l. aérea** airline
　(h) *Inform* **en l.** online; **fuera de l.** off-line
　(i) *(expresiones)* **en líneas generales** in broad terms; **de primera l.** first-rate; **en toda la l.** *(completamente)* all along the line; **leer entre líneas** to read between the lines
lineal 1 *adj* (a) *(de la línea)* linear (b) *(aumento)* steady
　2 *nm (en supermercado)* shelf

linfa *nf* lymph

linfático, -a *adj* lymphatic

linfocito *nm* lymphocyte

linfoma *nm Med* lymphoma

lingotazo *nm Esp Fam* swig

lingote *nm* ingot

lingüista *nmf* linguist

lingüística *nf* linguistics *(singular)*

lingüístico, -a *adj* linguistic

linier [li'njer] *(pl* **liniers)** *nm* linesman

linimento *nm* liniment

lino *nm* (a) *(planta)* flax (b) *(tejido)* linen

linóleo *nm* linoleum

linotipia *nf* Linotype®

linotipista *nmf* linotypist

linotipo *nm* Linotype®

linterna *nf* (a) *(de pilas)* flashlight (b) *(farol)* lantern, lamp; **l. mágica** magic lantern

lío *nm* (a) *Fam (enredo)* mess; **esto de la declaración de hacienda es un l.** filling in your tax return is a real pain; **hacerse un l.** to get muddled up; **estoy hecho un l., no sé qué hacer** I'm all confused, I don't know what to do; **meterse en líos** to get into trouble (b) *Fam (alboroto)* racket, row; **armar un l.** to kick up a fuss (c) *Fam (amorío)* affair; **tiene un l. con alguien del trabajo** he's having an affair with someone from work; **tener un l. de faldas** to be having an affair (d) *(paquete)* bundle

liofilizado, -a *adj* freeze-dried

liofilizar [14] *vt* to freeze-dry

lioso, -a *adj Fam* (a) *(complicado) (asunto)* complicated; *(explicación, historia)* convoluted, involved (b) *(persona)* trouble-making

lípido *nm* lipid

liposoluble *adj* soluble in fat

liposoma *nm* liposome

liposucción *nf* liposuction

lipotimia *nf* fainting fit

liquen *nm* lichen

liquidación *nf* (a) *(pago)* settlement; *(de hipoteca)* redemption; **hacer la l. de una cuenta** to settle an account; *Fin* **l. de activos** asset stripping; **l. de bienes** liquidation of assets (b) *(rebaja)* **l. (de existencias)** clearance sale; **estar de l.** to be having a clearance sale (c) *(de empresa)* liquidation (d) *(finiquito)* layoff settlement

liquidador, -ora 1 *adj* liquidating
    2 *nm,f* liquidator

liquidar 1 *vt* (a) *(pagar) (deuda, préstamo)* to settle; *(hipoteca)* to redeem (b) *(rebajar)* to sell off; **l. existencias** to have a stock clearance sale (c) *(negocio, sociedad)* to liquidate, to wind up (d) *(malgastar)* to throw away (e) *Fam (acabar) (asunto)* to settle; **y con esto hemos liquidado el tema segundo** that's the second subject seen to *o* dealt with (f) *Fam (matar)* to liquidate
    2 liquidarse *vpr Fam (bebida, comida)* to polish off; *(dinero)* to blow; **se liquidó la botella él solito** he polished off the bottle by himself; **nos liquidamos el premio en dos semanas** we blew the prize money in two weeks

liquidez *nf Fin & Fís* liquidity

líquido, -a 1 *adj* (a) *(estado)* liquid; **el l. elemento** water (b) *Fin (neto)* net
    2 *nm* (a) *(sustancia)* liquid; **l. de frenos** brake fluid (b) *Fin* liquid assets (c) *Med* fluid; **l. amniótico** amniotic fluid

lira *nf* (a) *Mús* lyre (b) *(moneda)* lira

lírica *nf* lyric poetry

lírico, -a *adj* (a) *Lit* lyric, lyrical (b) *(musical)* musical

lirio *nm* iris

lirismo *nm* lyricism

lirón *nm Zool* dormouse; *Fig* **dormir como un l.** to sleep like a log

lis *nf* **(flor de) l.** iris

Lisboa *n* Lisbon

lisboeta 1 *adj* of/from Lisbon
    2 *nmf* person from Lisbon

lisiado, -a 1 *adj* crippled
    2 *nm,f* cripple

lisiar 1 *vt* to maim, to cripple
    2 lisiarse *vpr* to be maimed *o* crippled

liso, -a 1 *adj* (a) *(llano)* flat; *(sin asperezas)* smooth; *(pelo)* straight; *Esp* **los 400 metros lisos** the 400 meters; **lisa y llanamente** purely and simply; **hablando lisa y llanamente** to put it plainly (b) *(no estampado)* plain
    2 *nm,f Andes, CAm, Ven* cheeky person

lisonja *nf* flattering remark

lisonjear *vt* to flatter

lisonjero, -a *adj (persona, comentario)* flattering; *(perspectiva)* promising

lista *nf* (a) *(enumeración)* list; **pasar l.** to call the register; **l. de boda** wedding list; **l. de** *Esp* **la compra** *o Am* **las compras** shopping list; *Inform* **l. de correo** mailing list; **l. de correos** general delivery; *Av* **l. de embarque** passenger list; **l. de espera** waiting list; **l. de éxitos** *(musicales)* hit parade; **l. negra** blacklist; **l. de precios** price list (b) *(de tela, madera)* strip; *(de papel)* slip; *(de color)* stripe; **una camiseta a listas** a striped shirt

listado, -a 1 *adj* striped
    2 *nm Inform* listing

listar *vt Inform* to list

listillo, -a *nm,f Esp Fam Pey* a smart aleck

listín *nm Esp* **l. (de teléfonos)** (telephone) directory

listo, -a *adj* (a) *(inteligente, hábil)* clever, smart; *Fam* **dárselas de l.** to make oneself out to be clever; **no te hagas el l., que conozco tus intenciones** don't try and be clever, I know what you're up to; **pasarse de l.** to be too clever by half; **ser más l. que el hambre** to be nobody's fool
    (b) *(preparado)* ready; **¿estás l.?** are you ready?; **¡l.!** (that's me) ready!, finished!; **lo pones cinco minutos al fuego, y l.** you heat it for five minutes and that's it
    (c) *Fam (apañado)* **estás** *o* **vas l. (si crees que…)** you've got another think coming (if you think that…); **¡estamos listos!** we're in real trouble!, we've had it!

listón *nm (de madera)* lath; *Dep* bar; *Fig* **poner el l. muy alto** to set very high standards

lisura *nf Andes, CAm, Ven* rude remark

litera *nf* (a) *(cama)* bunk (bed); *(de barco)* berth; *(de tren)* berth (b) *(vehículo)* litter

literal *adj* literal

literario, -a *adj* literary

literato, -a *nm,f* writer, author

literatura *nf* literature

litigación *nf* litigation

litigante *adj & nmf* litigant

litigar [38] *vi* to go to law

litigio *nm Der* court case, law suit; *(disputa)* dispute; **en l.** in dispute

litigue *etc ver* **litigar**

litio *nm* lithium

litografía *nf* (a) *(arte)* lithography (b) *(grabado)* lithograph (c) *(taller)* lithographer's (workshop)

litografiar [32] *vt* to lithograph

litoral 1 *adj* coastal
    2 *nm* coast

litosfera *nf* lithosphere

litro *nm* liter

litrona *nf Esp Fam* = litre bottle of beer

Lituania *n* Lithuania

lituano, -a 1 *adj & nm,f* Lithuanian
   2 *nm (lengua)* Lithuanian

liturgia *nf* liturgy

litúrgico, -a *adj* liturgical

liviandad *nf* (**a**) *(levedad)* lightness (**b**) *(frivolidad)* flightiness, frivolousness

liviano, -a *adj* (**a**) *(ligero) (blusa)* thin; *(carga)* light (**b**) *(sin importancia)* slight (**c**) *(superficial)* frivolous

lividez *nf (palidez)* pallor

lívido, -a *adj* (**a**) *(pálido)* very pale, white as a sheet (**b**) *(amoratado)* livid

living ['liβin] *(pl* **livings**) *nm* living room

liza *nf (lucha)* battle; **en l.** in opposition

Ll, ll ['eʎe, 'eje] *nf (letra)* Ll, ll

llaga *nf Med* sore, ulcer; *Fig* open wound

llagar [38] **1** *vt* to bring out in sores
   2 llagarse *vpr* to become covered in sores

llama *nf* (**a**) *(de fuego, pasión)* flame; **en llamas** ablaze (**b**) *(animal)* llama

llamada *nf* (**a**) *(en general)* call; *(a la puerta)* knock; *(con timbre)* ring; **l. de atención** warning; **l. de socorro** distress signal (**b**) *(de teléfono)* (phone) call; **hacer una l.** to make a (phone) call; **tienes dos llamadas en el contestador** you have two messages on your answering machine; **l. a cobro revertido,** *Am* **l. por cobrar** collect call; **l. en espera** call waiting; **l. interurbana** long-distance; **l. local** local call; **l. urbana** local call (**c**) *(en un libro)* reference mark

llamado, -a 1 *adj* (**a**) *(con nombre)* **un naturalista l. Marcelino** a naturalist called *o* named Marcelino; **el l. "efecto invernadero"** what is known as the "greenhouse effect"; **Roma, también llamada la Ciudad Eterna** Rome, also known as the Eternal City (**b**) **l. a** *(destinado)* destined to
   2 *nm Am* (**a**) *(en general)* call; *(a la puerta)* knock; *(con timbre)* ring; **l. de atención** warning (**b**) *(de teléfono)* (phone) call; **hacer un l.** to make a (phone) call (**c**) *(apelación)* call, appeal; **hacer un l. a alguien para que haga algo** to call upon sb to do sth

llamador *nm (aldaba)* door knocker; *(timbre)* bell

llamamiento *nm* (**a**) *(apelación)* call, appeal; **un l. a la unidad/la compasión** a call for unity/compassion; **un l. a la calma** an appeal *o* a call for calm; **hacer un l. a alguien para que haga algo** to call upon sb to do sth (**b**) *Mil* call-up

llamar 1 *vt* (**a**) *(dirigirse a, hacer venir)* to call; *(con gestos)* to beckon; **l. (a) un taxi** *(en la calle)* to hail a cab; *(por teléfono)* to call for a taxi (**b**) *(por teléfono)* to call, to phone; **l. a los bomberos/al médico** to call the fire brigade/doctor; **te llamo mañana** I'll call you tomorrow; **te ha llamado Luis** Luis phoned (for you), there was a call from Luis for you (**c**) *(dar nombre, apelativo, apodo)* to call; **me llamó mentiroso** he called me a liar (**d**) *(convocar)* to summon, to call; *Mil* **l. (a filas)** to call up; **l. a la huelga** to call out on strike (**e**) *(atraer)* to attract
   2 *vi* (**a**) *(a la puerta) (con golpes)* to knock; *(con timbre)* to ring; **están llamando** there's somebody at the door (**b**) *(por teléfono)* to phone
   3 llamarse *vpr (tener por nombre, título)* to be called; **¿cómo te llamas?** what's your name?; **me llamo Patricia** my name's Patricia; **eso es lo que se llama buena suerte** that's what you call good luck

llamarada *nf* (**a**) *(de fuego, ira)* blaze (**b**) *(de rubor)* flush

llamativo, -a *adj (color)* bright, gaudy; *(ropa)* showy

llamear *vi* to burn, to blaze

llana *nf* (**a**) *Gram* word stressed on the last syllable (**b**) *Constr* trowel

llanear *vi* to roam the plains

llanero, -a 1 *adj* of the plainspeople
   2 *nm,f* plainsman, *f* plainswoman

llaneza *nf* naturalness, straightforwardness

llanito, -a *adj & nm,f Esp Fam* Gibraltarian

llano, -a 1 *adj* (**a**) *(campo, superficie)* flat (**b**) *(trato, persona)* natural, straightforward (**c**) *(pueblo, clase)* ordinary (**d**) *(lenguaje, expresión)* simple, plain (**e**) *Gram* stressed on the last syllable
   2 *nm (llanura)* plain; *Col, Ven* **los Llanos** = name of vast region of tropical plains, mainly in Venezuela and Colombia

llanta *nf* (**a**) *Aut* rim (**b**) *Am (cubierta)* tire; *(rueda)* wheel

llantera, llantina *nf Fam* blubbing

llanto *nm* crying

llanura *nf* plain

llave *nf* (**a**) *(de cerradura)* key; **bajo l.** under lock and key; **echar la l., cerrar con l.** to lock up; **l. en mano** *(vivienda)* ready for immediate occupation; **l. de contacto** ignition key; **l. maestra** master key (**b**) *(grifo)* faucet; **l. de paso** stopcock; **cerrar la l. de paso** to turn the water/gas off at the source (**c**) *(interruptor)* **l. de la luz** light switch (**d**) *(herramienta)* monkey wrench; **l. allen** Allen wrench; **l. inglesa** monkey wrench (**e**) *(de judo)* hold, lock (**f**) *(signo ortográfico)* brace

llavero *nm* keyring

llavín *nm* latchkey

llegada *nf* (**a**) *(acción)* arrival (**b**) *Dep* finish

llegar [38] **1** *vi* (**a**) *(a un sitio)* to arrive (**de** from); **l. a un hotel/una ciudad** to arrive at a hotel/in a city; **l. a casa** to get home; **¿falta mucho para l.** *o* **para que lleguemos?** is there far to go?; **llegaré pronto** I'll be there soon
   (**b**) *(un tiempo, la noche)* to come; **cuando llegue el momento te enterarás** you'll find out when the time comes; **ha llegado el invierno** winter has arrived
   (**c**) *(durar)* **l. a** *o* **hasta** to last until
   (**d**) *(alcanzar)* **l. a** to reach; **no llego al techo** I can't reach the ceiling; **l. hasta** to reach up to; **esta carretera sólo llega hasta Zihuatanejo** this road only goes as far as Zihuatanejo
   (**e**) *(ser suficiente)* to be enough (**para** for)
   (**f**) *(lograr)* **l. a (ser) algo** to get to be sth, to become sth; *Fig* **llegará lejos** she'll go far; **si llego a saberlo…** *(en el futuro)* if I happen to find out…; *(en el pasado)* if I had known…
   (**g**) *(al extremo de)* **llegó a decirme…** he went as far as to say to me…; **hemos llegado a pagar 8.000 euros** at times we've had to pay as much as 8,000 euros
   2 llegarse *vpr* **llegarse a** to go around to

llenar 1 *vt* (**a**) *(ocupar) (vaso, hoyo, habitación)* to fill (**de** with); *(pared, suelo)* to cover (**de** with); **l. el depósito** *(del coche)* to fill up the tank (**b**) *(colmar)* to fill (**de** with); **l. a alguien de alegría/tristeza** to fill sb with happiness/sadness; **este premio me llena de orgullo** this prize fills me with pride *o* makes me very proud (**c**) *(impreso, solicitud, quiniela)* to fill in *o* out (**d**) *(satisfacer)* to fulfill; **no le llena la relación con su novio** she finds her relationship with her boyfriend unfulfilling
   2 *vi (comida)* to be filling
   3 llenarse *vpr* (**a**) *(ocuparse)* to fill up; **la calle se llenó de gente** the street filled with people (**b**) *(saciarse)* **comieron hasta llenarse** they ate their fill; **me he llenado mucho con el arroz** this rice has really filled me up (**c**) *(cubrirse)* **llenarse de** to become covered in

llenazo *nm* full house

llenito, -a *adj Fam (regordete)* chubby

lleno, -a 1 *adj* (**a**) *(recipiente, habitación)* full (**de** of); *(suelo, mesa, pared)* covered (**de** *o* with); **l. hasta el borde** full to the brim; **el estadio estaba l. hasta los topes** *o* **hasta la bandera** the stadium was packed to the rafters; **l., por favor** *(en gasolinera)* fill her up, please (**b**) *(persona)* **estoy l.** I'm full (up)

2 *nm (en teatro, estadio)* full house; **se espera un l. total** a full house is expected

3 de lleno *loc adv* **le dio de l. en la cara** it hit him full in the face; **acertó de l.** he was right on target

llevadero, -a *adj* bearable

llevar 1 *vt* (**a**) *(de un lugar a otro)* to take; **l. algo/a alguien a** to take sth/sb to; **me llevó en coche** he drove me there

(**b**) *(acarrear)* to carry; **llevaban en hombros al entrenador** they were carrying the coach on their shoulders

(**c**) *(ropa, objeto personal)* to wear; **llevo gafas** I wear glasses; **no llevo dinero** I haven't got any money on me

(**d**) *(tener) (de alguna manera)* to have; **l. el pelo largo** to have long hair; **llevas las manos sucias** your hands are dirty

(**e**) *(ocuparse de) (problema, asunto)* to handle, to deal with; *(casa, negocio)* to look after, to run; **lleva la contabilidad** she keeps the books

(**f**) *(conducir)* **l. a alguien a algo** to lead sb to sth; **l. a alguien a hacer algo** to lead *o* cause sb to do sth

(**g**) *(mantener) (registro, cuenta, ritmo)* to keep; *(vida)* to lead; **l. el paso** to keep in step

(**h**) *(soportar)* to deal *o* cope with; **l. algo bien/mal** to deal *o* cope with sth well/badly; *Fam* **¿cómo lo llevas?** how are you getting on?

(**i**) *(tiempo)* **lleva tres semanas sin venir** she hasn't come for three weeks now, it's three weeks since she was last here; **me llevó un día hacer este guiso** it took me a day to make this dish

(**j**) *(sobrepasar)* **te llevo seis puntos** I'm six points ahead of you; **me lleva dos centímetros** he's two centimeters taller than me

(**k**) *(expresiones)* **lleva camino de ser famoso/rico** he's on the road to fame/riches; **l. las de perder** to be heading for defeat; **l. consigo** *(implicar)* to lead to, to bring about

2 *vi* (**a**) *(conducir)* **l. a** to lead to; **esta carretera lleva al norte** this road leads north (**b**) *(antes de participio) (tener, haber)* **llevo leída media novela** I'm halfway through the novel; **llevo dicho esto mismo docenas de veces** I've said the same thing time and again (**c**) *(antes de gerundio) (estar)* **l. mucho tiempo haciendo algo** to have been doing sth for a long time

3 llevarse *vpr* (**a**) *(tomar consigo)* to take; **alguien se ha llevado mi sombrero** someone has taken my hat

(**b**) *(conseguir)* to get; **se ha llevado el premio** she has carried off the prize; **yo me llevo siempre las culpas** I always get the blame

(**c**) *(recibir) (susto, sorpresa)* to get, to receive; **me llevé un disgusto** I was upset

(**d**) *(entenderse)* **llevarse bien/mal (con alguien)** to get on well/badly (with sb); **llevarse a matar con alguien** to be mortal enemies *o* at daggers drawn with sb

(**e**) *(estar de moda)* to be in (fashion); **este año se lleva el verde** green is in this year

(**f**) *Mat* **me llevo una** carry (the) one

llorar 1 *vi* (**a**) *(con lágrimas)* to cry; **me entraron ganas de l.** I felt like crying; **l. de rabia** to cry with anger *o* rage; **l. por alguien** to mourn sb; **l. a lágrima viva** to cry one's eyes out, to sob one's heart out (**b**) *Fam (quejarse)* to whine

2 *vt* **l. la muerte de alguien** to mourn sb's death

llorera *nf Fam* crying fit

llorica *Esp Fam Pey* **1** *adj* **ser l.** to be a crybaby

2 *nmf* crybaby

lloriquear *vi* to whine, to snivel

lloriqueo *nm* whining, sniveling

lloro *nm* crying, tears

llorón, -ona 1 *adj* **ser l.** to cry a lot

2 *nm,f* crybaby

lloroso, -a *adj* tearful

llover [41] **1** *v impersonal* to rain; **está lloviendo** it's raining;

Fig **está lloviendo a cántaros** *o* **a mares** it's pouring; **nunca llueve a gusto de todos** you can't please everyone; **llueve sobre mojado** it's just one thing after another; *Fig* **él, como quien oye l.** he wasn't paying the slightest bit of attention; *Fig* **ha llovido mucho desde entonces** a lot of water has passed *o* gone over the dam since then

2 *vi* **le llueven las ofertas** offers are raining down on him; **le llovieron las felicitaciones** everyone rushed to congratulate her; **el trabajo me cayó** *o* **llegó como llovido del cielo** the job fell into my lap

llovizna *nf* drizzle

lloviznar *v impersonal* to drizzle

llueva *ver* **llover**

lluvia *nf* (**a**) *(precipitación)* rain; **caía una l. torrencial** there was torrential rain; **la época de lluvias** the rainy season; **bajo la l.** in the rain; **l. ácida** acid rain; **l. de estrellas** shower of shooting stars; **l. radiactiva** (nuclear) fallout (**b**) *(de panfletos, regalos)* shower; *(de preguntas)* barrage

lluvioso, -a *adj* rainy

lo[1], -a *(mpl* **los**, *fpl* **las)** *pron personal (complemento directo) (cosa)* it, *pl* them; *(persona)* him, *f* her, *pl* them; *(usted)* you

lo[2] 1 *pron personal (neutro & predicado)* it; **su hermana es muy guapa pero él no lo es** his sister is very good-looking, but he isn't; **es muy bueno aunque no lo parezca** it's very good, even if it doesn't look it

2 *art (neutro)* **lo antiguo me gusta más que lo moderno** I like old things better than modern things; **lo mejor/peor** the best/worst part; **no me quiere ayudar, ¡con todo lo que yo he hecho por ella!** she doesn't want to help me, and after all I've done for her!; **no te imaginas lo grande que era** you can't imagine how big it was; **¿y lo de la fiesta?** what about the party, then?; **siento lo de ayer** I'm sorry about yesterday; **acepté lo que me ofrecieron** I accepted what they offered me

loa *nf* (**a**) *(alabanza)* praise (**b**) *Lit* eulogy

loable *adj* praiseworthy

loar *vt* to praise

lobato *nm* wolf cub

lobbista *nmf RP* lobbyist

lobby ['loβi] *(pl* **lobbies**) *nm* lobby

lobezno *nm* wolf cub

lobo, -a *nm,f* wolf; **l. de mar** *(marinero)* sea dog; **l. marino** *(foca)* seal

lobotomía *nf* lobotomy

lóbrego, -a *adj* gloomy, murky

lobulado, -a *adj* lobulate

lóbulo *nm* lobe; **l. de la oreja** ear lobe

lobuno, -a *adj* wolf-like

loca *nf Fam (homosexual)* queen

locación *nf Méx* location

local 1 *adj* local; **el equipo l.** the home team

2 *nm (establecimiento)* (business) premises *(plural)*; **l. comercial** business premises; **l. de ensayo** rehearsal space; **l. nocturno** nightspot

localidad *nf* (**a**) *(población)* place, town (**b**) *(asiento)* seat (**c**) *(entrada)* ticket; **no hay localidades** *(en letrero)* sold out

localismo *nm* (**a**) *(sentimiento)* parochialism (**b**) *Ling* localism

localista *adj* parochial

localización *nf (ubicación)* localization, tracking down; *Inform (de software)* localización *f*

localizado, -a *adj* localized

localizador, -ora *nm* (**a**) *Inform (de página Web)* URL (**b**) *Méx (buscapersonas)* pager

localizar [14] **1** *vt* (**a**) *(encontrar)* to locate, to track down (**b**) *(circunscribir)* to localize

2 localizarse *vpr* **la infección se localiza en el hígado** the infection is localized in the liver; **esta planta se localiza**

en los Alpes this plant is only found in the Alps

locatis *Esp Fam* **1** *adj inv* nutty
    2 *nmf inv* nutcase

locativo *nm* locative

loc. cit. (*abrev de* **loco citato**) loc cit

loción *nf* lotion; **l. bronceadora** suntan *o* sun lotion; **l. para después del afeitado** aftershave balm *o* lotion

loco, -a 1 *adj* (**a**) *(demente)* mad, crazy; **volver l. a alguien** to drive sb mad; **volverse l.** to go mad; **este niño me trae l.** this child is driving me mad; **l. de atar** *o* **remate** stark raving mad; **¡ni l.!** (absolutely) no way!; **¡no lo haría ni l.!** there's no way you'd get me doing that!

    (**b**) *(insensato)* mad, crazy; **no seas loca, es muy peligroso** don't be (so) stupid, it's very dangerous; **a lo l.** *(sin pensar)* hastily; *(temerariamente)* wildly

    (**c**) *(apasionado, entusiasmado)* mad, crazy; **estar l. de/por** to be mad with/about; **estar l. de contento/pasión** to be wild with joy/passion; **estar l. por alguien/algo** to be mad about sb/sth; **le vuelve l. el fútbol** he's mad about soccer, he's soccer-crazy

    (**d**) *(extraordinario) (interés, ilusión)* tremendous; *(suerte, precio)* extraordinary

    2 *nm,f también Fig (hombre)* lunatic, madman; *(mujer)* lunatic, madwoman; **un l. de atar** a raving lunatic; **hacerse el l.** to play dumb, to pretend not to understand

locomoción *nf (transporte)* transportation; *(de tren)* locomotion

locomotor, -ora *o* **-triz** *adj* locomotive

locomotora *nf* engine, locomotive

locoto *nm Andes* chilli

locuacidad *nf* loquacity, talkativeness

locuaz *adj* loquacious, talkative

locución *nf* phrase

locura *nf* (**a**) *(demencia)* madness (**b**) *(imprudencia)* **hacer locuras** to do stupid *o* crazy things; **temía que hiciera una l.** I was afraid he might do something desperate (**c**) *(exageración)* **estos precios son una l.** these prices are extortionate; **con l.** madly; **se quieren con l.** they're madly in love with each other (**d**) **una l.** *(mucho)* a fortune, a ridiculous amount; **gastar una l.** to spend a fortune

locutor, -ora *nm,f Rad & TV (de noticias)* news announcer; *(de continuación)* announcer; *(de programa de radio)* host, *f* hostess

locutorio *nm* (**a**) *(para visitas)* visiting room (**b**) *(telefónico)* = establishment containing a number of telephone booths for public use (**c**) *Rad* studio

lodazal *nm* quagmire

loden *nm* loden coat

lodo *nm también Fig* mud

logarítmico, -a *adj* logarithmic

logaritmo *nm* logarithm

logia *nf* (**a**) *(masónica)* lodge (**b**) *Arquit* loggia

lógica *nf* logic; **por l.** obviously; **tener l.** to make sense; **eso no tiene l.** that's absurd *o* ridiculous

lógico, -a *adj* logical; **es l. que se enfade** it stands to reason that he should get angry; **es l. que tras la enfermedad se sienta débil** it's only natural that she should feel weak after the illness; **como es l.,** ellos también están invitados naturally, they are also invited; **¿te gustaría acompañarnos? — ¡l.!** would you like to come with us? — of course I would!

logística *nf* logistics *(singular)*

logístico, -a *adj* logistic

logopeda *nmf* speech therapist

logopedia *nf* speech therapy

logos *nm inv* (**a**) *Filosofía* logos (**b**) *Rel* Logos, Word of God

logotipo *nm* logo

logrado, -a *adj (bien hecho)* accomplished

lograr *vt (objetivo)* to achieve; *(puesto, beca, divorcio)* to get, to obtain; *(resultado)* to obtain, to achieve; *(perfección)* to attain; *(victoria, premio)* to win; *(deseo, aspiración)* to fulfill; **¡lo logramos!** we did it!, we've done it!; **l. hacer algo** to manage to do sth; **l. que alguien haga algo** to manage to get sb to do sth; **no logro entender cómo lo hizo** I just can't see how he managed it

logro *nm* achievement

logroñés, -esa 1 *adj* of/from Logroño
    2 *nm,f* person from Logroño

Logroño *n* Logroño

LOGSE [lɒɣse] *nf* (*abrev de* **Ley Orgánica de Ordenación General del Sistema Educativo**) = Spanish Education Act

Loira *nm* **el L.** the (river) Loire

loísmo *nm* = incorrect use of "lo" as indirect object instead of "le"

lola *nf RP Fam* tit

loma *nf* hillock

lombarda *nf (verdura)* red cabbage

Lombardía *n* Lombardy

lombardo, -a *adj & nm,f (de Lombardía)* Lombard

lombriz *nf* **l. (de tierra)** worm, earthworm; **l. (intestinal)** worm, threadworm; **tener lombrices** to have worms

Lomé *n* Lomé

lomo *nm* (**a**) *(de animal)* back; **a lomos de** astride, riding (**b**) *(carne)* loin (**c**) *(de libro)* spine (**d**) *Fam (de persona)* loins, lower back (**e**) *(de cuchillo)* blunt edge

lona *nf* canvas; **una l.** a tarpaulin

loncha *nf* slice; *(de beicon)* rasher

lonchar *vi Méx* to have one's lunch

lonchería *nf Méx, Ven* snack bar

lonchero, -a *nm,f Méx, Ven* snack bar attendant

londinense 1 *adj* London; **las calles londinenses** the London streets, the streets of London
    2 *nmf* Londoner

Londres *n* London

loneta *nf* sailcloth

longaniza *nf* = type of spicy cold pork sausage

longevidad *nf* longevity

longevo, -a *adj* long-lived

longitud *nf* (**a**) *(dimensión)* length; *Fam (distancia)* distance; **tiene medio metro de l.** it's half a meter long; **l. de onda** wavelength (**b**) *Astron & Geog* longitude

longitudinal *adj* longitudinal, lengthwise

long play ['lɒmpleɪ] (*pl* **long plays**) *nm* LP, album

longui *nmf,* **longuis** *nmf inv Esp Fam* **hacerse el l.** to act dumb, to pretend not to understand

lonja *nf* (**a**) *(loncha)* slice (**b**) *(edificio)* exchange; *Esp* **l. de pescado** fish market

lontananza *nf* background; **en l.** in the distance

look [luk] (*pl* **looks**) *nm Fam* style

loor *nm* **fue recibido en l. de multitudes** he was welcomed by enraptured crowds

loquero *Fam nm* (**a**) *(manicomio)* loony bin, madhouse (**b**) *Am (alboroto)* commotion, uproar

lord (*pl* **lores**) *nm* lord

loro *nm* (**a**) *(animal)* parrot (**b**) *Fam (charlatán)* chatterbox (**c**) *Esp Fam (aparato de música)* sounds, = radio and/or cassette or CD player (**d**) *Esp Fam* **estar al l.** *(alerta)* to keep one's ears *o* eyes open; *(enterado)* to be well up (on what's happening); **si no estamos al l., no conseguiremos entradas** if we're not quick off the mark we won't get tickets; **¡al l. con Luis!** be careful with Luis!

los 1 *art ver* **el**
    2 *pron ver* **lo**[1]

losa nf (piedra) paving stone, flagstone; (de tumba) tombstone

loseta nf floor tile

lote nm (a) (parte) share (b) (conjunto) batch, lot; **un l. de libros** a set of books (c) Esp Fam **darse** o **pegarse el l. (con)** to neck (with)

lotería nf (a) (sorteo) lottery; **jugar a la l.** to play the lottery; **le tocó la l.** she won the lottery; también Irónico **con esa novia que tiene le ha tocado la l.** he's really hit the jackpot with that girlfriend of his; **es una l.** (es aleatorio) it's a lottery; **L. Nacional** = state-run lottery in which prizes are allocated to randomly chosen five-figure numbers; Esp **l. primitiva** weekly state-run lottery (b) (juego de mesa) lotto

lotero, -a nm,f seller of lottery tickets

loto 1 nf Esp Fam = weekly state-run lottery
2 nm (planta) lotus

loza nf (a) (material) earthenware; (porcelana) china (b) (objetos) crockery

lozanía nf (a) (de plantas) luxuriance (b) (de persona) youthful vigor

lozano, -a adj (a) (planta) lush, luxuriant (b) (persona) youthfully vigorous

LSD nm LSD

Luanda n Luanda

lubina nf sea bass

lubricación nf lubrication

lubricante, lubrificante 1 adj lubricating
2 nm lubricant

lubricar [59], **lubrificar** [59] vt to lubricate

lubricidad nf lewdness

lúbrico, -a adj lewd, salacious

lubrificante = lubricante

lubrificar = lubricar

lucense 1 adj of/from Lugo
2 nmf person from Lugo

lucero nm bright star; **l. del alba/de la tarde** morning/evening star; **como un l.** as bright as a button

lucha nf (combate, enfrentamiento) fight; (esfuerzo) struggle; **la l. contra el cáncer** the fight against cancer; **l. de clases** class struggle o war; **l. libre** all-in wrestling

luchador, -ora 1 adj ser muy l. to be a fighter o battler
2 nm,f Dep wrestler; (persona tenaz) fighter

luchar vi (combatir) to fight; (esforzarse) to struggle; **l. contra** to fight (against); **l. por** to fight for

lucidez nf lucidity, clarity

lucido, -a adj splendid

lúcido, -a adj lucid

luciérnaga nf glowworm

Lucifer nm Lucifer

lucimiento nm (de ceremonia) sparkle; (de actriz) brilliant performance

lucio nm pike

lucir [39] **1** vi (a) (brillar) to shine (b) (quedar bonito) to look good; **luce mucho en el salón** it looks really good in the lounge; **luce mucho decir que hablas cinco idiomas** being able to say that you speak five languages looks really good (c) (rendir) **no me lucían tantas horas de trabajo** I didn't have much to show for all those hours I worked; **dijo que estudió mucho para el examen — pues no le ha lucido** he said he studied very hard for the exam — well, it hasn't done him much good (d) Am (parecer) to look; **luce muy joven** she looks very young
2 vt (llevar) to wear, to sport; (exhibir) to show off, to sport
3 lucirse vpr (destacar) to shine (en at); **a la hora de cocinar, siempre se luce** he's a real star when he gets in the kitchen; Irónico **te has lucido** you've excelled yourself!

lucrarse vpr to make money (for oneself)

lucrativo, -a adj lucrative; **no l.** nonprofit-making

lucro nm profit, gain

luctuoso, -a adj sorrowful, mournful

lucubración nf (a) (reflexión) cogitation (b) (imaginación) brainwave, harebrained idea; **no son más que lucubraciones suyas** it's just a lot of nonsense he's dreamed up

lucubrar vt to cogitate about, to consider deeply

lúdico, -a adj of enjoyment, of pleasure; **actividades lúdicas** leisure activities

ludo nm RP = game similar to Parcheesi®

ludópata nmf = pathological gambling addict

ludopatía nf = pathological addiction to gambling

ludoteca nf toy library

luego 1 adv (a) (a continuación) then, next; **primero aquí y l. allí** first here and then there; **l. de** after; **l. que** as soon as (b) (más tarde) later; **os veré l.** I'll see you later; **¡hasta l.!** see you (later)!; **hazlo l.** do it later (c) Chile, Méx, Ven (pronto) soon; Méx Fam **l. l.** right away
2 conj (así que, por lo tanto) so, therefore; **pienso, l. existo** I think, therefore I am

lugar 1 nm (a) (sitio) place; (del crimen, accidente) scene; (para acampar, merendar) spot; **en algún l.** somewhere; **no lo veo por ningún l.** I can't see it anywhere; **vuelve a ponerlo todo en su l.** put everything back where it belongs; **yo en tu l.** if I were you; Fig **fuera de l.** out of place; **l. de encuentro** meeting place; **l. de trabajo** place of work
(b) (localidad) place, town; **las gentes del l.** the local people; **l. de nacimiento** place of birth
(c) (puesto) position; **en primer/segundo l.** in the first/second place, firstly/secondly
(d) (espacio libre) room, space; **aquí ya no hay l. para más gente** there's no room for anyone else here
(e) (expresiones) **dar l. a** to bring about, to cause; **sin l. a dudas** without doubt, undoubtedly; **tener l.** to take place; **l. común** platitude, commonplace
2 en lugar de loc prep instead of

lugareño, -a 1 adj village; **vino l.** local wine
2 nm,f villager

lugarteniente nm deputy

lúgubre adj gloomy, mournful

lujo nm (a) (fastuosidad) luxury; **a todo l.** with no expense spared; **de l.** luxury; **un hotel de l.** a luxury hotel; **hoy contamos con un invitado de l.** we have a really special guest today; **permitirse el l. de algo/de hacer algo** to be able to afford sth/to do sth; **l. asiático** undreamed-of opulence o luxury (b) (profusión) profusion; **con todo l. de detalles** in great detail

lujoso, -a adj luxurious

lujuria nf lust

lujurioso, -a 1 adj lecherous
2 nm,f lecher

lumbago nm lumbago

lumbar adj lumbar

lumbre nf fire; **dar l. a alguien** to give sb a light; **encender la l.** to light the fire

lumbrera nf Fam genius

luminaria nf (a) (luz) light; (en iglesia) altar lamp (b) esp Am (sabio) luminary (c) Am (persona importante) celebrity

lumínico, -a adj light; **energía lumínica** light energy

luminiscencia nf luminescence

luminosidad nf brightness

luminoso, -a adj (a) (con luz) bright; **fuente luminosa** light source (b) (idea) brilliant

luminotecnia nf lighting

luminotécnico, -a nm,f lighting specialist

lumpen nm el l. the underclass

luna nf (a) (astro) moon; **la L.** the Moon; **media l.** half-moon; Fig **estar en la l.** to be miles away; Fig **pedir la l.** to ask the impossible; **l. creciente** crescent moon *(when waxing)*; **l. llena** full moon; **l. menguante** crescent moon *(when waning)*; **l. nueva** new moon **(b)** *(cristal)* window (pane); *(espejo)* mirror **(c) l. de miel** *(de novios)* honeymoon; **las relaciones entre los dos países atraviesan una l. de miel** relations between the two countries are going through a honeymoon period

lunar 1 *adj* lunar
   2 *nm* **(a)** *(en la piel)* mole, beauty spot **(b)** *(en telas)* spot; **a lunares** spotted

lunático, -a 1 *adj* crazy
   2 *nm,f* lunatic

lunch [lantʃ] *(pl* **lunches)** *nm* buffet lunch

lunes *nm inv* Monday; *ver también* **sábado**

luneta *nf (de vehículo)* windshield; **l. trasera** rear windshield; **l. térmica** defogger

lunfardo *nm* = Buenos Aires slang

lupa *nf* magnifying glass

lupanar *nm Formal* brothel

lúpulo *nm* hops

Lusaka *n* Lusaka

lusitano, -a, luso, -a *adj & nm,f* **(a)** *(de Lusitania)* Lusitanian **(b)** *(de Portugal)* Portuguese

lustrabotas *nmf inv,* **lustrador, -ora** *nm,f Andes, RP (persona)* shoeshine

lustramuebles *nm inv CSur* furniture polish

lustrar *vt* to polish

lustre *nm* **(a)** *(brillo)* shine; **dar l. a** to polish **(b)** *(gloria)* glory

lustro *nm* five-year period

lustroso, -a *adj* shiny

luteranismo *nm Rel* Lutheranism

luterano, -a *adj & nm,f Rel* Lutheran

luto *nm* mourning; **estar de l.** to be in mourning

luxación *nf Med* dislocation

Luxemburgo *n* Luxembourg

luxemburgués, -esa 1 *adj* Luxembourg; **costumbres luxemburguesas** Luxembourg customs
   2 *nm,f* Luxembourger

Luxor *n* Luxor

luz *nf* **(a)** *(foco, energía, luminosidad)* light; *(destello)* flash (of light); **apagar la l.** to switch off the light; **estas farolas dan poca l.** these streetlights don't shine very brightly *o* aren't very bright; **a la l. de** in the light of; **a plena l. del día** in the full light of day; **arrojar l. sobre** to shed light on; **a todas luces** whichever way you look at it; **dar a l. (un niño)** to give birth (to a child); **dar l. verde** to give the green light *o* the go-ahead; **sacar a la l.** to bring to light; **l. natural** *(del sol)* natural light
   (b) *(electricidad)* electricity; **cortar la l.** to cut off the electricity supply; **encender** *o Esp* **dar la l.** to switch on the light; **se ha ido la l.** the lights have gone out; **pagar (el recibo de) la l.** to pay the electricity (bill)
   (c) **luces** *(de automóvil)* lights; **darle las luces a alguien** to flash (one's lights) at sb; **luces de emergencia** emergency lights; **poner las luces largas** *o* **de carretera** to put one's headlights on high beam; **luces cortas** *o* **de cruce** low beams; **luces de freno** brake lights; **luces de posición** sidelights; **luces de señalización** traffic lights; **luces de situación** sidelights; **luces traseras** taillights
   (d) *Hist* **las Luces** the Enlightenment
   (e) *(inteligencia)* **luces** intelligence; **de pocas luces** dim-witted

luzca *etc ver* **lucir**

lycra® *nf* Lycra®

Lyon *n* Lyons, Lyon

M

M, m ['eme] *nf* (**a**) *(letra)* M, m (**b**) *Fam* **lo mandé a la m…** I told him where to go…

m *(abrev de* **metro***)* m

maca *nf* (**a**) *(de fruta)* bruise (**b**) *(de objetos)* flaw

macabeo, -a *adj Fam* **ser un rollo m.** to be a real bore *o* drag

macabro, -a *adj* macabre

macaco, -a *nm,f (animal)* macaque

macana *Fam nf* (**a**) *CSur, Perú, Ven (disparate)* stupid thing; **decir macanas** to talk nonsense (**b**) *Andes, RP, Ven (fastidio)* pain, drag; **¡qué m.!** what a pain *o* drag!

macanudo, -a *adj Fam* (**a**) *Andes, RP (bueno)* great, terrific (**b**) *Andes, Ven (grande, fuerte)* **es un tipo m.** he's a great hulk of a man

macarra *Esp Fam* **1** *adj* loutish
   2 *nm* (**a**) *(de prostitutas)* pimp (**b**) *(matón)* lout

macarrón *nm* (**a**) **macarrones** *(pasta)* macaroni (**b**) *(dulce)* macaroon (**c**) *(tubo)* sheath *(of cable)*

macarrónico, -a *adj Fam* macaronic

Macedonia *n* Macedonia

macedonia *nf* **m. (de frutas)** fruit salad

macedonio, -a 1 *adj & nm,f* Macedonian
   2 *nm (lengua)* Macedonian

maceración *nf Culin* soaking, maceration

macerar *vt Culin* to soak, to macerate

maceta *nf* (**a**) *(tiesto)* flowerpot (**b**) *(herramienta)* mallet

macetero *nm* flowerpot holder

machaca *nmf Esp Fam* (**a**) *(pesado)* pain, bore (**b**) *(trabajador)* drudge

machacador, -ora *adj* crushing

machacadora *nf* crusher

machacar [59] **1** *vt* (**a**) *(desmenuzar)* to crush (**b**) *Esp Fam (estudiar)* to bone up on
   2 *vi Fam (insistir)* to go on and on (**sobre** about)

machacón, -ona *Fam* **1** *adj* tiresome
   2 *nm,f* pain, bore

machaconería *nf Fam* annoying insistence; **su m. me tiene harto** I'm fed up with the way she just won't let it drop

machada *nf* act of bravado

machamartillo: a machamartillo *loc adv* very firmly; **creer algo a m.** to be firm in one's belief of sth

machetazo *nm (golpe)* machete blow; *(herida)* machete wound

machete *nm* (**a**) *(arma)* machete (**b**) *Arg Fam (chuleta)* crib note

machetear *vt* to cut *o* strike (with a machete)

machihembrado *nm* tongue and groove

machismo *nm* male chauvinism, machismo

machista *adj & nmf* male chauvinist

macho 1 *adj* (**a**) *Biol* male; **un hipopótamo m.** a male hippopotamus (**b**) *Fam (hombre)* macho; *Fam* **es muy m.** he's a real man

2 *nm* (**a**) *Biol* male; **m. cabrío** billy goat; *Fig (hombre)* macho man, he-man (**b**) *Elec (enchufe)* (male) plug, jack plug; *(pata de enchufe)* pin (**c**) *Esp Fam (como apelativo)* **¡oye, m.!** hey, buddy!; **¡mira, m., cómo llueve!** Jesus, look at that rain!; **¡m., a ver si te callas!** just shut up will you buddy?

machote, -a 1 *adj Fam* brave
   2 *nm,f Fam (niño)* big boy, *f* big girl
   3 *nm CAm, Méx (modelo)* rough draft

macilento, -a *adj* wan

macizo, -a 1 *adj* solid; *Fam* **estar m.** *(hombre)* to be hunky; *(mujer)* to be gorgeous
   2 *nm* (**a**) *Geog* massif (**b**) *(de plantas)* flower bed; **m. de rosas** rose bed

macramé *nm* macramé

macro 1 *nf Inform* macro
   2 *nm Fot* macro

macro- *prefijo* macro-; **macrocárcel** super prison

macrobiótica *nf* macrobiotics

macrobiótico, -a *adj* macrobiotic

macrocefalia *nf Med* macrocephaly

macroconcierto *nm* big concert

macroeconomía *nf* macroeconomics

macroencuesta *nf* large-scale opinion poll

macrofestival *nm* = large open-air music festival

macroproceso *nm* super -trial *(of important case with many defendants)*

mácula *nf Formal* blemish

macuto *nm* backpack, knapsack

Madagascar *n* Madagascar

Madeira *n* Madeira

madeja *nf* hank, skein

madera *nf* (**a**) *(en árbol)* wood; *(en carpintería)* timber, lumber; **m. de pino** pinewood; **de m.** wooden; *Fam Fig* **tocar m.** to knock on wood; **m. contrachapada** plywood; **m. noble** fine wood (**b**) *(tabla)* piece of wood (**c**) *(cualidades)* **tener m. de algo** to have the makings of sth; **tener m. para algo** to have what it takes for sth (**d**) *Esp muy Fam (policía)* **la m.** the pigs

maderaje, maderamen *nm Constr* timbers

maderero, -a 1 *adj* timber, lumber; **industria maderera** timber *o* lumber industry
   2 *nm,f* timber merchant

madero *nm* (**a**) *(tabla)* (piece of) timber *o* lumber (**b**) *Esp muy Fam (agente de policía)* pig

madrás *nm inv (tejido)* madras

madrastra *nf* stepmother

madraza *nf Fam* = indulgent or doting mother

madrazo *nm Méx* hard blow

madre *nf* (**a**) *(mujer, hembra)* mother; **es m. de tres niños** she's a mother of three; **Alicia va a ser m.** Alicia's going to have a baby; **m. adoptiva** foster mother; **m. de alquiler** surrogate mother; **m. biológica** natural mother; **la m.**

patria the motherland; **m. política** mother-in-law; **m. soltera** single mother; *Rel* **m. superiora** mother superior

(**b**) *(cauce)* bed; **salirse de m.** *(río)* to burst its banks; *Fig (persona)* to go too far

(**c**) *(expresiones)* **¡m. mía!** Jesus!, Christ!; *Fam* **éramos ciento y la m.** there were hundreds of us there; *muy Fam* **¡la m. que te parió!** you bastard!; *Méx* **dar a alguien en la m.** to kick sb's head in; *Méx Fam* **me vale m.** I couldn't give a damn; *Fam Fig* **ser la m. del cordero** to be at the very root of the problem

madrear *vt Méx Fam* (**a**) *(golpear)* **m. a alguien** to knock the hell out of sb (**b**) *(estropear)* to bust, to jigger

madreperla *nf (ostra)* pearl oyster; *(nácar)* mother-of-pearl

madreselva *nf* honeysuckle

Madrid *n* Madrid

madrigal *nm Lit & Mús* madrigal

madriguera *nf (de animal) & Fig* den; *(de conejo)* burrow, rabbit hole

madrileño, -a 1 *adj* of/from Madrid
    2 *nm,f* person from Madrid

madrina *nf (de bautizo)* godmother; *(de boda)* ≃ matron of honor; *(de barco)* = woman who launches ship

madroño *nm (árbol)* strawberry tree; *(fruto)* strawberry-tree berry

madrugada *nf* (**a**) *(amanecer)* dawn; **de m.** at dawn (**b**) *(noche)* early morning; **las tres de la m.** three in the morning

madrugador, -ora 1 *adj* early-rising
    2 *nm,f* early riser

madrugar [38] *vi* (**a**) *(levantarse)* to get up early; *Prov* **no por mucho m. amanece más temprano** time must take its course; *Prov* **al que madruga, Dios le ayuda** the early bird catches the worm (**b**) *(ocurrir pronto)* **los goles madrugaron** it wasn't long before the goals started flowing

madrugón *nm Fam* early rising; **darse un m.** to get up pretty early

maduración *nf (de fruta)* ripening

madurar 1 *vt* (**a**) *(fruto)* to ripen (**b**) *(persona)* to mature (**c**) *(idea, proyecto)* to think through
    2 *vi* (**a**) *(fruto)* to ripen (**b**) *(persona)* to mature

madurez *nf* (**a**) *(de fruto)* ripeness (**b**) *(edad adulta)* adulthood (**c**) *(sensatez, juicio)* maturity

maduro, -a *adj* (**a**) *(fruto)* ripe; *Fig* **este poema aún no está m. para ser publicado** this poem isn't ready for publication yet (**b**) *(persona)* mature; **le gustan los hombres maduros** she likes mature *o* older men; **de edad madura** middle-aged

maestranza *nf Mil* arsenal

maestrazgo *nm Hist* = office and territory of the master of a military order

maestría *nf* (**a**) *(habilidad)* mastery, skill (**b**) *Am (título)* master's degree

maestro, -a 1 *adj* (**a**) *(excelente)* masterly (**b**) *(principal)* main; **llave maestra** passkey, master key
    2 *nm,f* (**a**) *(en colegio)* teacher; **m. de escuela** schoolmaster, *f* schoolmistress (**b**) *Méx (en universidad)* professor (**c**) *(en oficio)* master; **un m. de la cocina francesa** a master of French cuisine; **m. carpintero/albañil** master carpenter/builder (**d**) *(en música)* maestro; *(en ajedrez)* master (**e**) *(director)* **m. de ceremonias** master of ceremonies; **m. de obras** foreman (**f**) *Taurom* matador

mafia *nf* mafia; **la M.** the Mafia, the Mob

mafioso, -a 1 *adj* mafia; **organización mafiosa** mafia organization
    2 *nm,f* mafioso

magazine *nm* magazine

magdalena *nf* cupcake; **llorar como una m.** to cry one's eyes out

magenta *adj inv & nm* magenta

magia *nf* magic; **m. blanca/negra** white/black magic

magiar 1 *adj & nmf* Magyar
    2 *nm (lengua)* Magyar

mágico, -a *adj (palabras, alfombra, varita)* magic; *(momento, situación)* magical

magisterio *nm* (**a**) *(título)* teaching certificate (**b**) *(enseñanza)* teaching (**c**) *(profesión)* teaching profession

magistrado, -a *nm,f (juez)* judge

magistral *adj* (**a**) *(de maestro)* magisterial (**b**) *(excelente)* masterly

magistratura *nf Der* (**a**) *(oficio)* judgeship (**b**) *(jueces)* magistrature (**c**) *(tribunal)* tribunal; *Esp* **m. de trabajo** labor tribunal

magma *nm* magma

magnanimidad *nf* magnanimity

magnánimo, -a *adj* magnanimous

magnate *nm* magnate; **m. del petróleo/de la prensa** oil/press baron

magnesia *nf* magnesia

magnesio *nm Quím* magnesium

magnético, -a *adj también Fig* magnetic

magnetismo *nm también Fig* magnetism

magnetizar [14] *vt* to magnetize; *Fig* to mesmerize

magnetofónico, -a *adj (cinta)* magnetic

magnetófono *nm* tape recorder

magnetoscopio *nm* video recorder

magnicida *nmf* assassin *(of somebody important)*

magnicidio *nm* assassination *(of somebody important)*

magnificar [59] *vt (ensalzar)* to praise highly

magnificencia *nf* magnificence

magnífico, -a *adj* (**a**) *(muy bueno) (idea, invento, oportunidad)* wonderful, magnificent; **una habitación con magníficas vistas al mar** a room with a magnificent view of the sea; **tus amigos son una gente magnífica** your friends are wonderful; **llegaré a las ocho — ¡m.!** I'll be there at eight — splendid! (**b**) *(grandioso, espléndido)* great, fantastic; **¡con esa falda estás magnífica!** you look great *o* fantastic in that skirt!

magnitud *nf* magnitude

magno, -a *adj* great

magnolia *nf* magnolia

magnolio *nm* magnolia (tree)

mago, -a *nm,f (prestidigitador)* magician; *(en cuentos, leyendas)* wizard

magra *nf* slice

magrear *Esp muy Fam* **1** *vt* to fondle, to grope
    2 magrearse *vpr* to neck

Magreb *nm* **el M.** the Maghreb, = Morocco, Algeria and Tunisia

magrebí *(pl* **magrebíes** *o* **magrebís)** *adj & nmf* Maghrebi

magreo *nm Esp muy Fam* necking

magro, -a 1 *adj* (**a**) *(sin grasa)* lean (**b**) *(pobre)* poor
    2 *nm* lean meat

maguey *nm* maguey

magullado, -a *adj* bruised

magulladura *nf* bruise

magullar *vt* to bruise

maharajá [maraˈχa] *nm* maharaja

maharaní [maraˈni] *(pl* **maharaníes)** *nf* maharani

Mahoma *n* Mohammed

mahometano, -a *adj & nm,f* Muslim

mahonesa *nf* mayonnaise

maicena® *nf* cornstarch

mail [mail, meil] *(pl* **mails)** *nm Inform* e-mail message; **enviar un m. a alguien** to e-mail sb

mailing ['meilin] (*pl* **mailings**) *nm Com* bulk mailing; **hacer un m.** to do a bulk mailing

maillot [ma'jot] (*pl* **maillots**) *nm* (a) (*prenda femenina*) maillot (b) (*en ciclismo*) jersey; **m. amarillo** yellow jersey

maitines *nmpl Rel* matins

maître ['metre] *nm* maître d'

maíz *nm* (*planta*) (Indian) corn; (*utilizado en cocina*) corn; **m. tostado** = toasted, salted corn kernels

maizal *nm* cornfield

maizena® *nf* cornstarch

majadería *nf* idiocy

majadero, -a *nm,f* idiot

majar *vt* (*machacar*) to crush; (*moler*) to grind

majareta, *Esp* **majara** *Fam* **1** *adj* nutty
    2 *nmf* nutcase

majestad *nf* majesty; **Su M.** His/Her Majesty

majestuosidad *nf* majesty

majestuoso, -a *adj* majestic

majo, -a 1 *adj Esp Fam* (a) (*simpático*) nice (b) (*bonito*) pretty (c) (*como apelativo*) **¡oye, m., déjame ya!** look, leave me alone, will you?; **bueno, majos,…** right, guys,…
    2 *nm,f Arte & Hist* = lower-class native of 18th-19th century Madrid, characterized by colorful traditional dress and proud manner

majorette [majo'ret] *nf* majorette

mal 1 *adj ver* **malo**
    2 *nm* (a) (*maldad, perjuicio*) **el m.** evil; **un m. necesario** a necessary evil; **el m. menor** the lesser of two evils
    (b) (*daño*) harm, damage; **no te hará ningún m. salir un rato** it won't harm you *o* it won't do you any harm to go out for a while; **m. de ojo** evil eye
    (c) (*enfermedad*) illness; **m. de altura** *o* **montaña** altitude *o* mountain sickness; **el m. de las vacas locas** mad cow disease
    (d) (*expresiones*) *Prov* **a grandes males, grandes remedios** drastic situations demand drastic action; **del m., el menos** it's the lesser of two evils; *Prov* **m. de muchos, consuelo de todos** at least I'm not the only one; *Prov* **no hay m. que por bien no venga** every cloud has a silver lining
    3 *adv* (a) (*incorrectamente*) wrong; **hacer algo m.** to do sth wrong; **has escrito m. esta palabra** you've spelled that word wrong; **hiciste m. en decírselo** it was wrong of you to tell him; **portarse m.** to behave badly
    (b) (*inadecuadamente*) badly; **la conferencia/reunión salió m.** the talk/meeting went badly; **m. vestido** badly dressed; **oigo/veo m.** I can't hear/see very well; **esta puerta cierra m.** this door doesn't shut properly
    (c) (*expresa opinión desfavorable*) **estar m.** (*de salud*) to be *o* feel ill; (*de calidad*) to be bad; **está m. eso que has hecho** what you've done is wrong; **oler/saber m.** to smell/taste bad; **pasarlo m.** to have a bad time; **sentar m. a alguien** (*ropa*) not to suit sb; (*comida*) to disagree with sb; (*comentario, actitud*) to upset sb
    (d) (*difícilmente*) hardly; **m. puede saberlo si no se lo cuentas** he's hardly going to know it if you don't tell him
    (e) (*expresiones*) **ir de m. en peor** to go from bad to worse; **no estaría m. que…** it would be nice if…; **estar a m. con alguien** to have fallen out with sb; **tomar algo a m.** to take sth the wrong way; **m. que bien** somehow or other; **m. que te pese, las cosas están así** whether you like it or not, that's the way things are

malabar *adj* **juegos malabares** juggling

malabarismo *nm también Fig* juggling; **hacer malabarismos** to juggle

malabarista *nmf* juggler

malacostumbrado, -a *adj* spoiled

malacostumbrar *vt* to spoil

málaga *nm* (*vino*) Malaga (wine)

malagueño, -a 1 *adj* of/from Málaga
    2 *nm,f* person from Málaga

malaleche *nmf Esp muy Fam* (*persona*) mean son of a bitch

malandrín, -ina 1 *adj* wicked, evil
    2 *nm,f* scoundrel

malapata *nmf Esp Fam* (*persona*) clumsy oaf

malaquita *nf* malachite

malaria *nf* malaria

malasangre *nmf Fam* (*persona*) **ser un m.** to be a bit of a bastard

Malasia *n* Malaysia

malasio, -a *adj* Malaysian

malasombra *nmf Esp Fam* (*persona*) pest

Malaui *n* Malawi

malayo, -a 1 *adj & nm,f* Malay, Malayan
    2 *nm* (*lengua*) Malay, Malayan

malcomer *vi* to eat poorly

malcriado, -a 1 *adj* spoiled
    2 *nm,f* spoiled brat

malcriar [32] *vt* to spoil

maldad *nf* (a) (*cualidad*) evil (b) (*acción*) evil thing

maldecir [51] **1** *vt* to curse
    2 *vi* to curse; **m. de** to speak ill of

maldición *nf* curse

maldiga *etc ver* **maldecir**

maldijera *etc ver* **maldecir**

maldito, -a *adj* (a) (*condenado*) cursed, damned (b) *Fam (para enfatizar)* damned; **¡maldita sea!** damn it!

Maldivas *nfpl* **las (Islas) M.** the Maldives

maleable *adj también Fig* malleable

maleado, -a *adj* gone to the bad, led astray

maleante 1 *adj* wicked
    2 *nmf* crook

malear *vt* to corrupt

malecón *nm* (*muelle*) jetty

maledicencia *nf* (*difamación*) slander

maleducado, -a 1 *adj* rude
    2 *nm,f* rude person

maleficio *nm* curse

maléfico, -a *adj* evil

malenseñado, -a *adj CSur* rude, bad-mannered

malentendido *nm* misunderstanding

malestar *nm* (a) (*indisposición*) upset, discomfort; **sentir m. (general)** to feel unwell; **siento un m. en el estómago** I've got an upset stomach (b) (*inquietud*) uneasiness, unrest

maleta *nf* suitcase; **hacer** *o* **preparar la m.** to pack (one's bags)

maletero *nm Esp, Cuba,* **maletera** *nf Andes (de automóvil)* trunk

maletilla *nmf Taurom* apprentice bullfighter

maletín *nm* briefcase

malevolencia *nf* malevolence, wickedness

malévolo, -a *adj* malevolent, wicked

maleza *nf* (*arbustos*) undergrowth; (*malas hierbas*) weeds

malformación *nf Med* malformation

malgache *adj & nmf* Madagascan, Malagasy

malgastar *vt* (*dinero, tiempo*) to waste

malgenioso, -a *adj Chile, Méx* ill-tempered, irritable

malhablado, -a 1 *adj* foul-mouthed
    2 *nm,f* foul-mouthed person

malhechor, -ora *adj & nm,f* criminal

malherir [62] *vt* to injure seriously

malhumor *nm* bad mood

malhumorado, -a *adj* (*de mal carácter*) bad-tempered; (*enfadado*) in a bad mood

Malí, Mali n Mali

malicia nf (**a**) (mala intención) malice (**b**) (agudeza) sharpness, alertness

maliciarse vpr (**a**) (sospechar) to suspect (**b**) (malear) to go bad, to become spoiled

malicioso, -a adj (**a**) (malintencionado) malicious (**b**) (avispado) sharp, alert

malignidad nf malignance

maligno, -a adj malignant

malintencionado, -a 1 adj ill-intentioned
2 nm,f ill-intentioned person

malinterpretar vt to misinterpret, to misunderstand

malla nf (**a**) (tejido) mesh; **m. de alambre, m. metálica** wire mesh (**b**) (red) net; **las mallas** (en fútbol) the net (**c**) Ecuad, Perú, RP (traje de baño) swimsuit (**d**) Esp **mallas** (de gimnasia) leotard; (de ballet) tights

Mallorca n Majorca

mallorquín, -ina adj & nm,f Majorcan

malnacido, -a 1 adj undesirable, nasty
2 nm,f nasty type

malnutrición nf malnutrition

malnutrido, -a adj undernourished

malo, -a

> **mal** is used instead of **malo** before singular masculine nouns (e.g. **un mal ejemplo** a bad example). The comparative form of **malo** (= worse) is **peor**, the superlative forms (= the worst) are **el peor** (masculine) and **la peor** (feminine).

1 adj (**a**) (en general) bad; (calidad) poor, bad; **ser de mala calidad** to be poor quality; **lo m. es que...** the problem is (that)...; Am **mala palabra** swearword
(**b**) (travieso) naughty; (malicioso, malvado) wicked, evil; **¡no seas m. y obedece!** be good and do as I say!
(**c**) (enfermo) ill, sick; **estar/ponerse m.** to be/fall ill; Fig **poner m. a alguien** to drive sb mad
(**d**) (desagradable) bad; **mal tiempo** bad weather; **hace mal tiempo** the weather's bad
(**e**) (podrido, pasado) bad, spoiled; **estar/ponerse m.** to be o become spoiled
(**f**) (uso enfático) **ni un mal trozo de pan** not even a crust of bread; **no había ni un mal bar en el pueblo** there wasn't a single bar to be found in the village
2 nm,f Cine **el m.** the villain, the baddie
3 malas nfpl **ponerse a (las) malas con** to fall out with; **estar de malas** to be in a bad mood; **por las malas** by force

malogrado, -a adj (desaprovechado) wasted; **un actor/futbolista m.** (muerto) an actor/football player who died before fulfilling their promise; **la malograda princesa** the late princess

malograr 1 vt (desperdiciar) to waste
2 malograrse vpr (**a**) (fracasar) to fail (**b**) (morir) to die before one's time

maloliente adj smelly

malparado, -a adj **salir m. de algo** to come out of sth badly

malpensado, -a 1 adj (descreído) cynical; (calenturiento) dirty-minded
2 nm,f (descreído) cynic; **es un m.** he always thinks the worst of people

malquerencia nf dislike

malsano, -a adj unhealthy

malsonante adj rude

Malta n Malta

malta nm malt

malteada nf Am milk shake

malteado, -a adj malted

maltés, -esa adj & nm,f Maltese

maltraer [66] vt **llevar** o **traer a m.** to cause headaches

maltratado, -a adj (**a**) (persona) battered (**b**) (objeto) damaged

maltratador, -ora nm,f abuser, batterer

maltratar vt (**a**) (pegar, insultar) to ill-treat; **maltrató a su mujer durante cinco años** he mistreated his wife over a five-year period; **la novela fue maltratada por la crítica** the novel was mauled by the critics (**b**) (estropear) to damage

maltrato nm ill-treatment; **m. psicológico** psychological abuse

maltrecho, -a adj battered

malva 1 adj inv mauve
2 nf mallow; Fam Fig **criar malvas** to push up daisies
3 nm (color) mauve

malvado, -a 1 adj evil, wicked
2 nm,f villain, evil person

malvavisco nm marshmallow

malvender vt to sell at a loss

malversación nf **m. (de fondos)** embezzlement (of funds)

malversador, -ora nm,f embezzler

malversar vt to embezzle

Malvinas nfpl **las (islas) M.** the Falkland Islands, the Falklands

malviviente nmf CSur criminal

malvivir vi to live badly, to scrape together an existence

mama nf (**a**) (de mujer) breast; (de animal) udder (**b**) Fam (madre) mom, mommy

mamá nf Fam mom; Col, Méx Fam **m. grande** grandma

mamada nf (**a**) (de bebé) (breast-)feed, (breast-)feeding (**b**) Vulg blowjob

mamadera nf RP (baby's) bottle

mamado, -a adj muy Fam (**a**) Esp, RP (borracho) shit-faced, plastered (**b**) Esp (fácil) **estar m.** to be damn easy

mamar 1 vt (**a**) (leche) to suckle; Fig **lo mamó desde pequeño** (lo aprendió) he was immersed in it as a child (**b**) Esp muy Fam (beber) to knock back
2 vi to suckle; **dar de m.** to breast-feed
3 mamarse vpr Esp, RP muy Fam (emborracharse) to get plastered

mamario, -a adj Anat mammary

mamarrachada nf Fam stupid o idiotic thing

mamarracho nm Fam (**a**) (fantoche) sight, mess (**b**) (imbécil) idiot

mambo nm mambo

mameluco nm (**a**) Hist mameluke (**b**) Fam (torpe, necio) idiot (**c**) CSur (prenda) (con mangas) coveralls; (de peto) overalls

mamífero, -a 1 adj mammal
2 nm mammal

mamografía nf Med (**a**) (técnica) breast screening, Espec mammography (**b**) (imagen) breast scan

mamón, -ona 1 adj (**a**) (que mama) unweaned (**b**) muy Fam (insulto) **¡qué m. eres!** you jerk!
2 nm,f (**a**) (que mama) unweaned baby (**b**) muy Fam (insulto) jerk

mamotreto nm Fam (**a**) (libro) hefty volume (**b**) (objeto grande) unwieldy object

mampara nf screen

mamporro nm Fam (golpe) punch, clout; (al caer) bump

mampostería nf **muro de m.** drystone wall, = stones without mortar; **obra de m.** rubblework masonry

mamut (pl **mamuts**) nm mammoth

maná nm inv Rel manna; Fig **como m. caído del cielo** like manna from heaven

manada nf (rebaño) herd; (de lobos) pack; (de ovejas) flock; (de leones) pride; Fam (de gente) crowd

manager ['manajer] (pl **managers**) nmf manager

Managua n Managua

managüense 1 adj Managuan

2 nmf person from Managua

manantial nm (de agua) spring; Fig source

manar vi también Fig to flow (**de** from)

manatí (pl **manatíes** o **manatís**) nm manatee

manazas Fam**1** adj inv clumsy

2 nmf inv clumsy person

manceba nf Anticuado concubine

mancebo, -a nm,f (**a**) (mozo) young man, f girl (**b**) (en farmacia) assistant

mancha nf(**a**) (de suciedad) stain, spot; (de tinta) blot; (de color) spot, mark; **tienes una m. en la camisa** you've got a stain on your shirt; **una m. de petróleo** (en el mar) an oil slick (**b**) (en la piel) (por reacción) blotch; (de vejez) liver spot (**c**) Astron **m. solar** sunspot (**d**) (deshonra) blemish; **este suspenso supondrá una m. en su expediente** this fail grade will be a blot on his academic record

manchado, -a adj (sucio) dirty; (con manchas) stained; (emborronado) smudged

manchar1 vt (**a**) (ensuciar) to make dirty (**de** o **con** with); (con manchas) to stain (**de** o **con** with); (emborronar) to smudge (**de** o **con** with) (**b**) (deshonrar) to tarnish

2 vi to stain; **no toques la puerta, que la acaban de pintar y mancha** don't touch the door, it's just been painted and it's still wet

3 mancharse vpr (ensuciarse) to get dirty; **se ha manchado la pared** the wall has gotten dirty, there are stains on the wall; **me manché el vestido de grasa mientras cocinaba** I got grease stains on my dress while I was cooking; **el niño se ha manchado de barro los pantalones** the boy has gotten mud on his pants

manchego, -a1 adj of/from La Mancha

2 nm,f person from La Mancha

3 nm (queso) = hard yellow cheese made in La Mancha

mancillar vt Formal to tarnish, to sully

manco, -a adj (**a**) (sin una mano) one-handed; (sin un brazo) one-armed; Fig **no ser m. para** o **en** to be pretty good at (**b**) (incompleto) imperfect, defective

mancomunar1 vt to pool (together)

2 mancomunarse vpr to join together, to unite

mancomunidad nf association

mancuerna nf(**a**) (pesa) dumbbell (**b**) CAm, Chile, Col, Méx, Ven (botón) cuff link

mandado, -a1 nm,f (subordinado) underling; Fam **yo sólo soy un m.** I'm only doing what I was told (to do)

2 nm (recado) errand

mandamás (pl **mandamases**) nmf Fam head honcho

mandamiento nm (**a**) (orden) order, command (**b**) Der writ (**c**) Rel **los diez mandamientos** the Ten Commandments

mandanga nf Fam (**a**) **mandangas** (tonterías) nonsense (**b**) (hachís) dope, shit

mandar1 vt (**a**) (dar órdenes a) to order; **la profesora nos ha mandado deberes/una redacción** the teacher has set o given us some homework/an essay; **m. a alguien hacer algo** to order sb to do sth; **m. hacer algo** to have sth done; **¿quién te manda decirle nada?** who asked you to say anything to her?

(**b**) (enviar) to send; **m. algo a alguien** to send sb sth, to send sth to sb; **me mandó un correo electrónico** she sent me an e-mail, she e-mailed me

(**c**) (dirigir, gobernar) to lead, to be in charge of; (país) to rule

(**d**) Fam (lanzar) to send; **mandó la jabalina más allá de los 90 metros** he sent the javelin beyond the 90-meter mark

2 vi (**a**) (dirigir) to be in charge; (jefe de estado) to rule; **aquí mando yo** I'm in charge here (**b**) (dar órdenes) to order people around

mandarín nm (**a**) (título) mandarin (**b**) (dialecto) Mandarin

mandarina nf mandarin

mandarino nm mandarin tree

mandatario, -a nm,f representative, agent; **primer m.** (jefe de Estado) head of state

mandato nm (**a**) (orden, precepto) order, command; Der **m. judicial** warrant (**b**) (poderes de representación, disposición) mandate (**c**) (tiempo) (de político) term of office; (reinado) period of rule

mandíbula nf jaw; Fam **reír a m. batiente** to laugh one's head off

mandil nm apron

mandioca nf (**a**) (planta) cassava (**b**) (fécula) tapioca

mando nm (**a**) (poder) command, authority; **estar al m. (de)** to be in charge (of) (**b**) (jefe) **alto m.** high command; Mil **los mandos** the command; **mandos intermedios** middle management (**c**) (dispositivo) control; **m. automático/a distancia** automatic/remote control

mandolina nf mandolin

mandón, -ona Fam**1** adj bossy

2 nm,f bossy person

mandrágora nf mandrake

mandril nm (**a**) (animal) mandrill (**b**) (pieza) mandrel

manduca nf Esp Fam grub

manducar [59] vt & vi Fam to gobble

manecilla nf(**a**) (del reloj) hand (**b**) (cierre) clasp

manejable adj (persona, cosa) manageable; (herramienta) easy to use; (coche) maneuverable

manejar 1 vt (**a**) (máquina, mandos) to operate; (caballo, bicicleta) to handle; (arma) to wield (**b**) (datos) to handle; (conocimientos) to use, to marshal; **maneja varios lenguajes de programación** she can use several programming languages; **manejan información de primera mano** they use primary sources (**c**) (negocio) to manage, to run; (gente) to handle (**d**) (dominar) to boss around; **maneja a su novio a su antojo** she can twist her fiancé around her little finger (**e**) Am (vehículo) to drive

2 vi Am (en vehículo) to drive

3 manejarse vpr (desenvolverse) to manage, to get by; **no se maneja nada bien con las computadoras** he doesn't have much of an idea of how to use computers

manejo nm (**a**) (de máquina, mandos) operation; (de armas, herramientas) use; (de caballo, bicicleta) handling; **de fácil m.** user-friendly (**b**) (de datos) handling; (de conocimientos) marshaling; (de idiomas) command (**c**) (de negocio) management, running (**d**) (intriga) intrigue (**e**) Am (de automóvil) driving

manera nf(**a**) (forma) way, manner; **a m. de** (como) as, by way of; **a la m. de** in the style of, after the fashion of; **a mi m. de ver** the way I see it; **de cualquier m.** (sin cuidado) any old how; (de todos modos) anyway, in any case; **de esta m.** in this way; Esp **de mala m.** badly; **lo hice de la misma m. que ayer/tú** I did it the same way as yesterday/you; **de m. que** so (that); **de ninguna m., en m. alguna** (refuerza negación) by no means, under no circumstances; (respuesta exclamativa) no way!, certainly not!; **de todas maneras** anyway; **de una m. o de otra** one way or another; **en cierta m.** in a way; **no hay m.** there is no way, it's impossible; **¡contigo no hay m.!** you're impossible!; **¡qué m. de llover!** just look at that rain!; **m. de pensar** way of thinking; **m. de ser** way of being, nature

(**b**) **maneras** (modales) manners; **buenas/malas maneras** good/bad manners

manga nf (**a**) (de prenda) sleeve; **en mangas de camisa** in shirt sleeves; **un vestido sin mangas** a sleeveless dress; Fam **m. por hombro** topsy-turvy, higgledy-piggledy; Fig **sacarse algo de la m.** (improvisar) to make sth up on the spur of the moment; (idear) to come up with sth; Fig **ser de m. ancha,**

tener m. ancha to be over-indulgent; *Fig* tener *o* guardar algo en la m. to have sth up one's sleeve; m. corta/larga short/long sleeve; m. ranglan raglan sleeve (b) *(manguera)* hose (c) *(filtro)* muslin strainer (d) *(medidor de viento)* wind sock (e) *(de pastelería)* piping *o* forcing bag (f) *Dep* stage, round

manganeso *nm* manganese

mangante *Esp Fam* 1 *adj* (a) *(sinvergüenza)* good-for-nothing (b) *(ladrón)* thieving

   2 *nmf* (a) *(sinvergüenza)* good-for-nothing, layabout (b) *(ladrón)* thief

mangar [38] *vt Esp Fam* to pinch; m. algo a alguien to pinch sth from sb

manglar *nf* mangrove swamp

mango *nm* (a) *(asa)* handle (b) *(árbol)* mango tree; *(fruta)* mango (c) *RP Fam (dinero)* cash; no tener un m. not to have a dime, to be busted

mangonear *vi Fam* (a) *(entrometerse)* to meddle (b) *(mandar)* to push people around, to be bossy (c) *(manipular)* to fiddle around

mangoneo *nm Fam* (a) *(intromisión)* bossing *o* pushing around (b) *(manipulación)* fiddling

mangosta *nf* mongoose

manguera *nf* hose; *(de bombero)* fire hose

mangui *Esp Fam* 1 *adj (no fiable)* sneaky

   2 *nmf* (a) *(ladrón)* crook, thief (b) *(persona no fiable)* crook

manguito *nm* (a) *(para el frío)* muff (b) *(media manga)* protective sleeve, oversleeve (c) *(para nadar)* armband

maní *(pl* manises*) nm Andes, Carib, RP* peanut

manía *nf* (a) *(idea fija)* obsession; m. persecutoria persecution complex (b) *(mala costumbre)* bad habit (c) *(afición exagerada)* mania, craze (d) *Fam (ojeriza)* dislike; coger m. a alguien to take a dislike to sb; tener m. a alguien not to be able to stand sb (e) *Psi* mania

maniaco, -a, maníaco, -a 1 *adj* manic

   2 *nm,f* maniac; m. sexual sex maniac

maniacodepresivo, -a *adj & nm,f* manic-depressive

maniatar *vt* to tie the hands of

maniático, -a 1 *adj* fussy

   2 *nm,f* fussy person; es un m. del fútbol he's soccer crazy

manicomio *nm* psychiatric hospital, insane asylum

manicura *nf (técnica)* manicure; hacerle la m. a alguien to give sb a manicure

manicuro, -a *nm,f (persona)* manicurist

manido, -a *adj (tema)* hackneyed

manierismo *nm Arte* mannerism

manierista *adj & nmf Arte* mannerist

manifa *nf Esp Fam* demo

manifestación *nf* (a) *(de alegría, dolor)* show, display; *(de opinión)* declaration, expression; *(indicio)* sign (b) *(por la calle)* demonstration

manifestante *nmf* demonstrator

manifestar [3] 1 *vt* (a) *(alegría, dolor)* to show (b) *(opinión)* to express

   2 manifestarse *vpr* (a) *(por la calle)* to demonstrate (b) *(hacerse evidente)* to become clear *o* apparent

manifiesto, -a 1 *adj* clear, evident; poner de m. algo *(revelar)* to reveal sth; *(hacer patente)* to make sth clear; ponerse de m. *(descubrirse)* to become clear *o* obvious

   2 *nm* manifesto

manija *nf esp Am* handle

Manila *n* Manila

manilargo, -a *adj (generoso)* generous

manileño, -a *adj* of/from Manila

manilla *nf* (a) *(del reloj)* hand (b) *(tirador)* handle (c) *(grilletes)* manacle

manillar *nm* handlebars

maniobra *nf* (a) *(operación)* maneuver; hacer maniobras to maneuver (b) *Mil* maniobras maneuvers (c) *(treta)* trick

maniobrar *vi* to maneuver

manipulación *nf* (a) *(de objeto)* handling; m. de alimentos food handling (b) *(de persona, datos)* manipulation

manipulador, -ora 1 *adj (dominador)* manipulative

   2 *nm,f* (a) *(operario)* handler (b) *(dominador)* manipulator

manipular *vt* (a) *(manejar)* to handle (b) *(trastocar, dominar)* to manipulate

maniqueísmo *nm* (a) *(doctrina)* Manicheism (b) *(actitud)* seeing things in black and white

maniqueo, -a *adj & nm,f* Manichean

maniquí *(pl* maniquíes*)* 1 *nm* dummy

   2 *nmf (modelo)* model

manirroto, -a 1 *adj* extravagant

   2 *nm,f* spendthrift

manitas *Esp Fam* 1 *adj inv* handy; ser muy m. to be very good with one's hands

   2 *nmf inv* handy person; ser un m. (de plata) to be (very) good with one's hands; hacer m. to canoodle

manito *nm Méx Fam* pal, buddy

manivela *nf* crank

manjar *nm* manjares delicious food; ¡este queso es un m.! this cheese is delicious!

mano 1 *nf* (a) *(de persona)* hand; a m. *(sin máquina)* by hand; *(cerca)* at hand, handy; hecho a m. handmade; ¿tienes el encendedor a m.? have you got your lighter handy *o* at hand?; votación a m. alzada show of hands; a m. armada armed; dar *o* estrechar la m. a alguien to shake hands with sb; darse *o* estrecharse la m. to shake hands; lavarse las manos to wash one's hands; ¡manos arriba!, ¡arriba las manos! hands up!

   (b) *Zool (en general)* forefoot; *(de perro, gato)* (front) paw; *(de cerdo)* (front) trotter

   (c) *Econ* m. de obra labor, workers; m. de obra barata cheap labor costs; m. de obra especializada skilled labor *o* workers

   (d) *(de pintura)* coat

   (e) *(de mortero)* pestle

   (f) *(lado)* a m. derecha/izquierda on the right/left; gire a m. derecha turn right

   (g) *(partida de naipes)* game; ser m. to (be the) lead

   (h) *(serie, tanda)* series

   (i) *Dep (falta)* handball

   (j) *(expresiones)* a manos de at the hands of; alzar la m. contra alguien to raise one's hand to sb; bajo m. secretly; caer en manos de alguien to fall into sb's hands; cargar la m. to go over the top; *Esp* coger *o Am* agarrar a alguien con las manos en la masa to catch sb red-handed *o* in the act; con una m. delante y otra detrás without a penny to one's name, in the clothes one is standing up in; de primera m. *(vehículo)* brand new; *(noticias)* first-hand; de segunda m. secondhand; dejar de la m. to abandon; dejar algo en manos de alguien to leave sth in sb's hands; echar m. de algo to make use of sth, to resort to sth; echar/tender una m. to give/offer a hand; ensuciarse las manos to get one's hands dirty; escaparse de las manos a alguien *(oportunidad)* to slip through sb's hands; *(control, proyecto)* to get out of hand for sb; estar dejado de la m. de Dios *(lugar)* to be godforsaken; *(persona)* to be a total failure; ganar por la m. a alguien to beat sb to it; írsele la m. a alguien *(perder el control)* to lose control; *(exagerar)* to go too far; se me fue la m. con la sal I overdid the salt; ¡yo me lavo las manos! I wash my hands of it!; llevarse las manos a la cabeza *(gesticular)* to throw one's hands in the air (in horror); *Fig* to be horrified; m. a m. tête-à-tête; con m. dura *o* de hierro with a firm hand; m. sobre m. sitting around doing nothing; ¡manos a la obra! let's get down to it!; meter m.

a alguien *(investigar)* to get onto sb, to start to investigate sb; *(sobar sin consentimiento)* to grope sb; *(sobar con consentimiento)* to touch sb up; **meter m. a algo** to tackle sth; **meter la m. en algo** *(intervenir)* to poke one's nose in(to) sth, to meddle in sth; **pedir la m. de una mujer** to ask for a woman's hand (in marriage); **ponerse en manos de alguien** to put oneself in sb's hands; **ser la m. derecha de alguien** to be sb's right-hand man; **tener m. con alguien** *(influencia)* to have influence with sb; **tener buena m. para algo** to have a knack for sth; **tener las manos largas** to be fond of a fight; **tener m. izquierda con algo** to know how to deal with sth; **traerse entre manos algo** to be up to sth; **venir** *o* **llegar a las manos** to come to blows

  2 *nm Am salvo RP Fam* pal, buddy

manojo *nm* bunch; *Fig* **estar hecho** *o* **ser un m. de nervios** to be a bundle of nerves

manoletina *nf (a) Taurom* = pass with the cape in bullfighting invented by the Spanish bullfighter, Manolete **(b)** *(zapato)* = type of open, low-heeled shoe, often with a bow

manómetro *nm* pressure gauge

manopla *nf* mitten; **m. de cocina** oven glove

manoseado, -a *adj* shabby, worn

manosear *vt* **(a)** *(tocar)* to handle (roughly); *(papel, tela)* to rumple **(b)** *(persona)* to paw; *(sexualmente)* to grope

manoseo *nm* fingering, touching

manotazo *nm* slap

manotear *vi* to gesticulate

mansalva: a mansalva *loc adv (en abundancia)* in abundance

mansarda *nf* attic

mansedumbre *nf (tranquilidad)* calmness, gentleness; *(docilidad)* tameness

mansión *nf* mansion

manso, -a *adj (tranquilo)* calm; *(dócil)* docile; *(domesticado)* tame

manta 1 *nf* **(a)** *(abrigo)* blanket; *Fig* **liarse la m. a la cabeza** to take the plunge; *Fig* **tirar de la m.** to let the cat out of the bag; **m. eléctrica** electric blanket **(b)** *(pez)* manta ray **(c)** *Esp Fam* **a m.** *(muchísimo)* in abundance; **llovía a m.** it was pouring down; **han cosechado éxitos a m.** they have had loads of hits

  2 *nmf Esp Fam (persona)* **ser un m.** to be a waste of space

mantear *vt* to toss in a blanket

manteca *nf Esp (grasa)* fat; *RP, Ven (mantequilla)* butter; **m. de cacao** cocoa butter; **m. de cerdo** lard

mantecada *nf (magdalena)* = small rectangular sponge cake

mantecado *nm Esp* = very crumbly cookie made of flour, shortening and sugar

mantecoso, -a *adj* fatty, greasy

mantel *nm* tablecloth; **m. individual** place mat

mantelería *nf (set of)* table linen

manteleta *nf* shawl

mantener [65] **1** *vt* **(a)** *(conservar)* to keep; **m. algo en buen estado** to keep sth in good condition; **m. una promesa** to keep a promise; **m. la calma** to stay calm

  (b) *(aguantar)* *(con andamios, columnas)* to support; *(con la mano)* to hold; **mantén los brazos en alto** keep your arms in the air

  (c) *(sustentar)* to support; **con su sueldo mantiene a toda la familia** he has to support *o* keep his whole family with his wages

  (d) *(tener)* *(relaciones, conversación)* to have; **m. relaciones con alguien** to have a relationship with sb

  (e) *(defender)* *(convicción)* to stick to; *(candidatura)* to refuse to withdraw; **mantiene su inocencia** she maintains that she is innocent; **mantiene que no la vió** he maintains that he didn't see her

  2 mantenerse *vpr* **(a)** *(sustentarse)* to subsist, to support oneself **(b)** *(permanecer, continuar)* to remain; *(edificio)* to remain standing; **¡por favor, manténganse alejados!** please keep clear!; **mantenerse aparte** *(en discusión)* to stay out of it; **mantenerse en pie** to remain standing

mantengo *ver* **mantener**

mantenido, -a 1 *adj* sustained

  2 *nm,f (hombre)* gigolo; *(mujer)* kept woman

mantenimiento *nm* **(a)** *(conservación)* upkeep, maintenance; **clases de m.** *(gimnasia)* keep-fit classes **(b)** *(sustento)* sustenance

mantequera *nf* butter dish

mantequería *nf* **(a)** *(fábrica)* dairy, butter factory **(b)** *(tienda)* grocery store

mantequilla *nf* butter; **m. de cacahuete** peanut butter

mantilla *nf* **(a)** *(de mujer)* mantilla **(b)** *(de bebé)* shawl **(c)** **estar en mantillas** *(persona)* to be wet behind the ears; *(plan)* to be in its infancy

mantis *nf inv* mantis; **m. religiosa** praying mantis

manto *nm* **(a)** *(capa)* cloak; *Fig* mantle, layer **(b)** *Geol* mantle

mantón *nm* shawl; **m. de Manila** embroidered silk shawl

mantuviera *etc ver* **mantener**

manual 1 *adj* manual; *Educ* **trabajos manuales** *(clase)* craftwork, handicraft

  2 *nm* manual; **m. de conversación** phrase book; **m. de instrucciones** instruction manual; **m. de uso** *o* **del usuario** user's manual, instruction manual

manualidades *nfpl (objetos)* craftwork, handicrafts

manubrio *nm* **(a)** *(manivela)* crank **(b)** *Am (de bicicleta)* handlebars

manufactura *nf* **(a)** *(actividad)* manufacture **(b)** *Econ (producto)* manufacture, product **(c)** *(fábrica)* factory

manufacturado, -a *adj* manufactured

manufacturar *vt* to manufacture

manufacturero, -a *adj* manufacturing

manumisión *nf* liberation

manuscrito, -a 1 *adj* handwritten

  2 *nm* manuscript

manutención *nf* **(a)** *(sustento)* support, maintenance **(b)** *(alimento)* food

manzana *nf* **(a)** *(fruta)* apple; *Fig* **m. de la discordia** bone of contention; **m. podrida** bad apple **(b)** *(grupo de casas)* block (of houses)

manzanilla *nf* **(a)** *(planta)* camomile; *(infusión)* camomile tea **(b)** *(vino)* manzanilla (sherry) **(c)** *(aceituna)* manzanilla, = type of small olive

manzano *nm* apple tree

maña *nf* **(a)** *(destreza)* skill; *Prov* **más vale m. que fuerza** brain is better than brawn **(b)** *(astucia)* wits, guile; **darse m. para hacer algo** to contrive to do sth **(c)** *(engaño)* ruse, trick

mañana 1 *nf* morning; **(muy) de m.** (very) early in the morning; **a las dos de la m.** at two in the morning; *Esp* **por la m.**, *Am* **en la m.** in the morning

  2 *nm* **el m.** tomorrow, the future; **m. será otro día** tomorrow is another day

  3 *adv* tomorrow; **a partir de m.** starting tomorrow, as of tomorrow; **¡hasta m.!** see you tomorrow!; **m. por la m.** tomorrow morning; **pasado m.** the day after tomorrow

mañanero, -a *adj* **(a)** *(madrugador)* early rising **(b)** *(matutino)* morning; **paseo m.** morning walk

mañanitas *nfpl Méx* birthday song

maño, -a *adj & nm,f Esp Fam* Aragonese

mañoso, -a *adj Esp* skillful

maoísmo *nm* Maoism

maoísta *adj & nmf* Maoist

maorí *(pl* **maoríes***) adj & nmf* Maori

mapa *nm* map; *Fam Fig* **borrar algo del m.** to wipe sth off the map; *Fam Fig* **desaparecer del m.** to vanish into thin air; *Inform* **m. de bits** bit map; **m. de carreteras** road map; **m. físico** geographic map; **m. mudo** blank map; **m. político** political map; **m. del tiempo** weather map *o* chart; **m. topográfico** contour map

mapache *nm* raccoon

mapamundi *nm* world map

mapuche 1 *adj* Mapuche
  2 *nmf* Mapuche (Indian)
  3 *nm (lengua)* Mapuche

Maputo *n* Maputo

maqueta *nf* **(a)** *(reproducción a escala)* (scale) model; **m. de avión** model aircraft **(b)** *(de libro)* dummy **(c)** *(de disco)* demo (tape)

maquetación *nf Inform* page layout

maquetador, -ora *nm,f Inform* layout editor

maquetar *vt Inform* to do the layout of

maquetista *nmf Inform* layout editor

maqui *nmf inv* guerrilla

maquiavélico, -a *adj* Machiavellian

maquiavelismo *nm* Machiavellianism

maquiladora *nf* maquiladora, = bonded assembly plant set up by a foreign firm near the US border

maquilar *vt CAm, Méx (artículos electrónicos)* to assemble; *(ropa)* to make up

maquillador, -ora *nm,f* makeup artist

maquillaje *nm* **(a)** *(producto)* makeup **(b)** *(acción)* making-up

maquillar 1 *vt* **(a)** *(pintar)* to make up **(b)** *(manipular) (datos, cifras)* to massage
  2 maquillarse *vpr* to make oneself up; **se maquilla demasiado** she wears *o* uses too much makeup

máquina *nf* **(a)** *(aparato)* machine; **escribir a m.** to type; **escrito a m.** typewritten; **hecho a m.** machine-made; **lavar a m.** to machine wash; **pasar algo a m.** to type sth out *o* up; **a toda m.** at full tilt; *Fam Fig* **ser una m.** *(muy rápido, muy bueno)* to be a powerhouse; **m. de afeitar** electric razor; **m. de bebidas** drink vending machine; **m. de café** (espresso) coffee machine; **m. de coser** sewing machine; **m. de escribir** typewriter; **m. expendedora** vending machine; **m. de fotos** camera; **m. de marcianos** Space Invaders machine; **m. recreativa** arcade machine; **m. registradora** cash register; **m. de tabaco** cigarette machine; *Am* **m. tragamonedas,** *Esp* **m. tragaperras** slot machine **(b)** *(locomotora)* engine; **m. de vapor** steam engine **(c)** *(mecanismo)* mechanism **(d)** *Cuba (automóvil)* car

maquinación *nf* machination

maquinal *adj* mechanical

maquinar *vt* to machinate, to plot; **m. algo contra alguien** to plot sth against sb

maquinaria *nf* **(a)** *(aparatos)* machinery **(b)** *(mecanismo) (de reloj, aparato)* mechanism; *(de Estado, partido)* machinery

maquinilla *nf* **m. de afeitar** razor; **m. eléctrica** electric razor

maquinismo *nm* mechanization

maquinista *nmf (de tren)* engineer; *(de barco)* engineer

maquinizar [14] *vt* to mechanize

maquis *nmf inv* guerrilla

mar *nm o nf* **(a)** *también Fig* sea; **veranean en el m.** they spend their summer vacations at the seaside; **hacerse a la m.** to set sail, to put (out) to sea; **pasan meses en el m.** *(navegando)* they spend months at sea; **alta m.** high seas; **a mares** a lot; **llover a mares** to rain buckets; *Esp muy Fam* **me cago en la m.** goddamn it!; *Esp Fam Euf* **mecachis en la m.** shoot!; **m. abierto** the open sea; **m. adentro** out to sea; *también Fig* **m. de fondo** ground swell; **m. gruesa** rough *o* stormy sea; **m.**

rizada choppy sea; **el m. Báltico** the Baltic Sea; **el m. Cantábrico** the Cantabrian Sea; **el m. Caribe** the Caribbean Sea; **el m. Caspio** the Caspian Sea; **el m. Egeo** the Aegean Sea; **el m. Mediterráneo** the Mediterranean Sea; **el m. Muerto** the Dead Sea; **el m. del Norte** the North Sea; **el m. Negro** the Black Sea; **el m. Rojo** the Red Sea
  (b) *Fam* **la m. de** really, very; **es la m. de inteligente** she's really intelligent

marabunta *nf (de hormigas)* plague of ants; *(muchedumbre)* crowd

maraca *nf* maraca

maracuyá *nf* passion fruit

marajá *nm* maharaja; **vivir como un m.** to live in the lap of luxury

maraña *nf (de cabellos, hilos, normas)* tangle; *(de plantas)* thicket

marasmo *nm* **(a)** *Med* marasmus, wasting **(b)** *(de ánimo)* apathy; *(de negocio)* stagnation

maratón *nm también Fig* marathon

maratoniano, -a *adj* marathon; **un discurso m.** a marathon speech

maravilla *nf* marvel, wonder; **es una m.** it's wonderful; **a las mil maravillas, de m.** wonderfully; **decir maravillas de alguien/algo** to praise sb/sth to the skies; **hacer maravillas** to do *o* work wonders; **una m. de niño/coche/carretera** a wonderful *o* marvelous child/car/road; **venir de m.** to be just the thing *o* ticket

maravillar 1 *vt* to amaze
  2 maravillarse *vpr* to be amazed (**con** by)

maravilloso, -a *adj* marvelous, wonderful

marbellí *(pl* **marbellíes** *o* **marbellís) 1** *adj* of/from Marbella
  2 *nm,f* person from Marbella

marca *nf* **(a)** *(señal)* mark; *(de rueda, animal)* track; *(en ganado)* brand; *(en papel)* watermark; *(cicatriz)* mark, scar; **se le nota la m. del bañador** you can see her tan line, you can see where she's been wearing her swimsuit **(b)** *Com (de tabaco, café)* brand; *(de vehículo, máquina)* make; **unos vaqueros de m.** a pair of designer jeans; **m. comercial** trademark; **m. de fábrica** trademark; **m. registrada** registered trademark **(c)** *(etiqueta)* label **(d)** *Dep (tiempo)* time; *(plusmarca)* record **(e)** *Fam* **de m. mayor** *(muy grande)* enormous; *(excelente)* outstanding

marcado, -a 1 *adj (pronunciado)* marked
  2 *nm* **(a)** *(señalado)* marking **(b)** *(peinado)* set

marcador, -ora 1 *adj* marking
  2 *nm* **(a)** *(tablero)* scoreboard **(b)** *Dep (jugador) (defensor)* marker; *(goleador)* scorer **(c)** *(para libros)* bookmark **(d)** *Am (rotulador)* felt-tip pen; *Méx (fluorescente)* highlighter pen

marcaje *nm Dep* marking

marcapasos *nm inv* pacemaker

marcar [59] **1** *vt* **(a)** *(poner o dejar marca en)* to mark; **ese acontecimiento marcó su vida** her life was marked by that event; **m. el ritmo** to beat the rhythm **(b)** *(indicar)* to mark, to indicate; **la cruz marca el lugar donde está enterrado el tesoro** the cross marks *o* indicates (the spot) where the treasure is buried **(c)** *(número de teléfono)* to dial **(d)** *(sujeto: termómetro, contador)* to read; *(sujeto: reloj)* to say **(e)** *(poner precio a)* to price **(f)** *Dep (tanto)* to score; *(a un jugador)* to mark **(g)** *(cabello)* to set
  2 *vi* **(a)** *(dejar secuelas)* to leave a mark **(b)** *Dep (anotar un tanto)* to score
  3 marcarse *vpr* **(a)** *(ropa)* to show **(b)** *Esp Fam* **marcarse un detalle** to do something nice *o* kind; **marcarse un tanto** to earn a Brownie point

marcha *nf* **(a)** *(partida)* departure; **ha anunciado su m. de la empresa** she has announced that she will be leaving the company (**b**) *(transcurso)* course; *(progreso)* progress; **el tren detuvo su m.** the train stopped; *Esp* **a marchas forzadas** *(contrarreloj)* against the clock; **a toda m.** at top speed; **en m.** *(motor)* running; *(plan)* underway; **se bajó en m. del tren** he jumped off the train while it was moving; **poner en m.** *(empezar)* to start; *(dispositivo, alarma)* to activate; **hacer algo sobre la m.** to do sth as one goes along

(**c**) *(en automóvil)* gear; **cambiar de m.** to change gear; **meter la cuarta m.** to go into fourth gear; **m. atrás** reverse (gear); **dar m. atrás** to reverse; *Fig* to back out

(**d**) *Mil & Pol* march; **abrir la m.** to head the procession; **cerrar la m.** to bring up the rear

(**e**) *Mús* march; **m. fúnebre/nupcial** funeral/wedding march; **la M. Real** = the Spanish national anthem

(**f**) *Dep* walk

(**g**) *Esp Fam (animación)* liveliness, life; **hay mucha m.** there's a great atmosphere; **ir de m.** to go out on the town; **tener (mucha) m.** to be a (real) raver

marchamo *nm* (**a**) *(de aduana)* customs seal *o* stamp (**b**) *(marca distintiva)* seal

marchante, -a *nm,f* (art) dealer

marchar 1 *vi* (**a**) *(andar)* to walk (**b**) *(partir)* to leave, to go (**c**) *(funcionar)* to work; **hay algo aquí que no m.** something's not quite right here (**d**) *(desarrollarse)* to progress; **el negocio marcha** business is going well (**e**) **¡marchando!** *(en bar)* coming up!; **¡marchando dos cafés con leche!** two coffees with milk, coming up!

2 marcharse *vpr* to leave, to go; **se marchó de aquí cuando era muy pequeño** he left here when he was very young

marchitar 1 *vt también Fig* to wither

2 marchitarse *vpr (planta)* to fade, to wither; *(persona)* to languish, to fade away

marchito, -a *adj (planta)* faded; *(persona)* worn

marchoso, -a *Esp Fam* **1** *adj* lively

2 *nm,f* live wire

marcial *adj* martial

marcialidad *nf* martial nature

marcianitos *nmpl (juego)* Space Invaders

marciano, -a *adj & nm,f* Martian

marco *nm* (**a**) *(de cuadro)* frame; *(de puerta)* doorframe; **m. de ventana** window frame (**b**) *(ambiente, paisaje)* setting (**c**) *(ámbito)* framework; **acuerdo m.** general *o* framework agreement; **m. de referencia** frame of reference (**d**) *(moneda)* mark; *Antes* **m. alemán** Deutschmark, German mark (**e**) *Dep (portería)* goal mouth

marea *nf* (**a**) *(del mar)* tide; **m. alta/baja** high/low tide; **m. negra** oil slick; **m. viva** spring tide; **está subiendo/ bajando la m.** the tide is coming in/going out (**b**) *(multitud)* flood

mareado, -a *adj* (**a**) *(con náuseas)* sick, queasy; *(en coche, avión)* travel-sick; *(en barco)* seasick (**b**) *(aturdido)* dizzy (**c**) *Fam (fastidiado)* fed up to the back teeth

mareante *adj* infuriating, irritating

marear 1 *vt* (**a**) *(provocar náuseas)* to make sick; *(en coche, avión)* to make travel-sick; *(en barco)* to make seasick; **los viajes en barco me marean** I get seasick when I travel by boat (**b**) *(aturdir)* to make dizzy (**c**) *Fam (fastidiar)* to annoy; **me marea con sus quejas** she drives me up the wall with her complaining

2 *vi Fam (fastidiar)* to be a pain; **¡niño, deja de m.!** you naughty boy! stop annoying me!

3 marearse *vpr* (**a**) *(tener náuseas)* to get *o* become sick; *(en coche, avión)* to get travel-sick; *(en barco)* to get seasick (**b**) *(aturdirse)* to get dizzy (**c**) *(emborracharse)* to get drunk

marejada *nf* (**a**) *(mar agitada)* heavy sea (**b**) *(agitación)* wave of discontent

marejadilla *nf* slight swell

mare mágnum *nm inv* welter, plethora

maremoto *nm* tidal wave

marengo *adj* **gris m.** dark gray

mareo *nm* (**a**) *(náuseas)* sickness; *(en coche, avión)* travel sickness; *(en barco)* seasickness (**b**) *(aturdimiento)* dizziness, giddiness; **le dio un m.** he had a dizzy spell *o* turn, he felt dizzy (**c**) *Fam (fastidio)* drag, pain

marfil *nm* ivory

marfileño, -a *adj* ivory; **piel marfileña** ivory skin

marga *nf Geol* marl

margarina *nf* margarine

margarita 1 *nf* (**a**) *(flor)* daisy (**b**) *Imprenta* daisy wheel

2 *nm o nf (cóctel)* margarita

margen 1 *nm* (**a**) *(de camino)* side (**b**) *(de página)* margin (**c**) *Com* margin; **m. de beneficio** profit margin (**d**) *(límites)* leeway; **al m. de eso, hay otros factores** over and above this, there are other factors; **al m. de la ley** outside the law; **dejar al m.** to exclude; **estar al m. de** to have nothing to do with; **mantenerse al m. de** to keep out of; **m. de error** margin of error; **m. de seguridad** degree of certainty (**e**) *(ocasión)* **dar m. a alguien para hacer algo** to give sb the chance to do sth

2 *nf (de río)* bank

marginación *nf* exclusion; **m. social** social exclusion

marginado, -a 1 *adj* excluded

2 *nm,f* outcast

marginal *adj* (**a**) *(nota)* marginal; *(tema)* minor (**b**) *Arte & Pol* fringe; **grupo m.** fringe group

marginalidad *nf* **vivir en la m.** to live on the margins of society, to be a social outcast

marginalizar [14] *vt* to exclude

marginar *vt* (**a**) *(persona) (excluir)* to exclude, to make an outcast; *(dar de lado a)* to give the cold shoulder to (**b**) *(asunto, diferencias)* to set aside, to set to one side

maría *nf Fam* (**a**) *Esp,Ven (marihuana)* grass (**b**) *Esp (asignatura)* easy subject, Mickey Mouse course (**c**) *(mujer sencilla)* (typical) housewife (**d**) *Méx* = migrant from country to urban areas

mariachi *nm* (**a**) *(música)* mariachi (music) (**b**) *(orquesta)* mariachi band; *(músico)* mariachi (musician)

marianismo *nm* Marianism

mariano, -a *adj* Marian

marica *nm Fam* fag

maricón, -ona *muy Fam* **1** *adj* (**a**) *(homosexual)* faggy (**b**) *(insulto)* **¡qué tío más m.!** what a bastard!

2 *nm,f (insulto) (cobarde)* wimp; *(odioso)* bastard

3 *nm (homosexual)* fag

mariconada *nf Fam* (**a**) *(dicho, hecho)* **eso es una m.** that's really faggy (**b**) *(mala jugada)* dirty trick (**c**) *(tontería)* **no dice más que mariconadas** he talks a load of old nonsense

mariconear *vi Fam* to camp it up

mariconera *nf Fam* (man's) clutch bag

mariconería *nf Fam* (**a**) *(dicho, hecho)* **eso es una m.** that's really faggy (**b**) *(cualidad)* campness

maridaje *nm* union

marido *nm* husband

marihuana *nf* marijuana

marimacho *nm Fam (niña)* tomboy; *(mujer)* butch woman

marimandón, -ona *Esp Fam* **1** *adj* bossy

2 *nm,f* bossy person

marimba *nf (xilófon)* marimba

marimorena *nf* row; *Fig* **armar la m.** to kick up a row

marina *nf* (**a**) *Mil* **m. (de guerra)** navy; **m. mercante** merchant marine (**b**) *Arte* seascape

marinar *vt* to marinate

marine *nm Mil* marine

marinería *nf* (**a**) *(profesión)* sailoring (**b**) *(marineros)* crew, seamen

marinero, -a 1 *adj (de la marina, de los marineros)* sea; *(buque)* seaworthy; **un pueblo m.** *(nación)* a seafaring nation; *(población)* a fishing village; **vestido m.** sailor suit
2 *nm* sailor

marino, -a 1 *adj* sea, marine; **brisa marina** sea breeze
2 *nm* sailor

marioneta *nf* *(muñeco)* marionette, puppet; *Fig* puppet; **marionetas** *(teatro)* puppet show

mariposa *nf* (**a**) *(insecto)* butterfly (**b**) *(tuerca)* wing nut (**c**) *(candela, luz)* oil lamp (**d**) *(en natación)* **nadar a m.** to do the butterfly (stroke) (**e**) *Fam* **a otra cosa, m.** let's move on

mariposear *vi* (**a**) *(ser inconstante)* to flit about (**b**) *(galantear)* to flirt

mariposón *nm* *Fam* (**a**) *(afeminado)* fairy, pansy (**b**) *(ligón)* flirt, lounge lizard

mariquita 1 *nf (insecto)* ladybug
2 *nm* *Fam (homosexual)* fairy

marisabidilla *nf* *Esp Fam* know-it-all

mariscada *nf* seafood meal

mariscal *nm* marshal; **m. de campo** field marshal

mariscar [59] *vi* to gather shellfish

marisco *nm* seafood, shellfish

marisma *nf* salt marsh

marismeño, -a *adj* marshy

marisquería *nf* seafood restaurant

marista *adj & nm* Marist

marital *adj* marital

marítimo, -a *adj (del mar)* maritime; *(cercano al mar)* seaside; **pueblo m.** seaside town; **paseo m.** promenade

marketing ['marketin] *(pl* **marketings***) nm* marketing; **m. directo** direct marketing; **m. electrónico** e-marketing

marmita *nf* pot

marmitaco, marmitako *nm* = Basque stew containing tuna and potatoes

mármol *nm* marble

marmóreo, -a *adj* *Formal* marmoreal

marmota *nf* marmot; **dormir como una m.** to sleep like a log

maroma *nf* (**a**) *(cuerda)* rope (**b**) *Am salvo RP (acrobacia)* acrobatic stunt

maromo *nm* *Esp Fam* guy

maronita *adj & nmf* Maronite

marque *etc ver* **marcar**

marqués, -esa *nm,f* marquis, *f* marchioness

marquesina *nf* *(cubierta)* canopy; *(parada de autobús)* bus shelter

marquetería *nf* marquetry

marranada *nf* *Fam* (**a**) *(porquería)* filthy thing (**b**) *(mala jugada)* dirty trick

marrano, -a *nm,f* (**a**) *(animal)* pig (**b**) *Fam (sucio)* (filthy) pig (**c**) *Fam (sin escrúpulos)* swine

Marraquech *n* Marrakech

marras: de marras *loc adj* **el perrito de m.** that blasted dog (I was telling you about); **el problema de m.** the same old problem

marrón 1 *adj* brown; **m. claro** light brown, tan
2 *nm* (**a**) *(color)* brown (**b**) *Esp Fam (situación desagradable)* **¡qué m.!** what a pain!; **me ha tocado a mí comerme el m. de limpiar la casa tras la fiesta** I got lumbered with having to clean the house after the party; **pillar a alguien de m.** to catch sb in the act (**c**) **m. glacé** marron glacé

marroquí *(pl* **marroquíes***) adj & nmf* Moroccan

marroquinería *nf* (**a**) *(arte)* leatherwork (**b**) *(artículos)* leather goods

Marruecos *n* Morocco

marrullero, -a 1 *adj* sneaky, shrewd
2 *nm,f* cheat

Marsellesa *nf* Marseillaise

marsupial *adj & nm* marsupial

marta *nf* (pine) marten; **abrigo de m.** sable coat; **m. cebellina** sable

Marte *nm* Mars

martes *nm inv* Tuesday; **M. de Carnaval** Shrove Tuesday; **m. y trece** ≃ Friday the 13th; *ver también* **sábado**

martillar = **martillear**

martillazo *nm* hard hammer blow; **me di un m. en el dedo** I hit my finger with a hammer

martillear, martillar *vt* to hammer

martilleo *nm* hammering

martillo *nm* hammer; **m. neumático** jackhammer

martinete *nm* heron

martini *nm* martini

Martinica *n* Martinique

martín pescador *nm* kingfisher

mártir *nmf también Fig* martyr; *Fig* **hacerse el m.** to act the martyr

martirio *nm* *Rel* martyrdom; *(sufrimiento)* trial, torment

martirizar [14] *vt (torturar)* to martyr; *(hacer sufrir)* to torment, to torture

maruja *nf* *Esp Fam* (typical) housewife

marxismo *nm* Marxism

marxista *adj & nmf* Marxist

marzo *nm* March; *ver también* **septiembre**

mas *conj* but

más 1 *adv* (**a**) *(comparativo)* more; **Pepe es m. alto/ ambicioso** Pepe is taller/more ambitious; **tener m. hambre** to be hungrier *o* more hungry; **m. de/que** more than, **m.... que...** more... than...; **Juan es m. alto que tú** Juan is taller than you
(**b**) *(superlativo)* **el/la/lo m.** the most; **el m. listo/ ambicioso** the cleverest/most ambitious
(**c**) *(en frases negativas)* any more; **no necesito m. (trabajo)** I don't need any more (work)
(**d**) *(con pron interrogativos e indefinidos)* else; **¿qué/quién m.?** what/who else?; **nadie m. vino** nobody else came
(**e**) *(indica suma)* plus; **dos m. dos igual a cuatro** two plus two is four
(**f**) *(indica intensidad)* **¡qué día m. bonito!** what a lovely day!; **¡es m. tonto...!** he's so stupid!
(**g**) *(indica preferencia)* **m. vale que nos vayamos a casa** it would be better for us to go home
(**h**) *(expresiones)* **m. o menos** more or less; **¿qué m. da?** what difference does it make?; **de m.** *(en exceso)* too much; **me han cobrado 10 euros de m.** they've charged me 10 euros too much; **eso está de m.** that's not necessary; **ser de lo m. divertido** to be incredibly funny *o* amusing; **hoy está de lo m. amable** she's being really nice today; **el que m. y el que menos** everyone; **es m., m. aún** indeed, what is more; **lo que es m.** moreover; **sin m. (ni más)** just like that
2 *nm inv Mat* plus (sign); **tiene sus m. y sus menos** it has its good points and its bad points
3 más bien *loc adv* rather
4 por más que *loc adv* however much; **por m. que lo intente no lo conseguirá** however much *o* hard she tries, she'll never manage it

masa *nf* (**a**) *(en general)* mass; **m. atómica** atomic mass; **m. salarial** total wages bill (**b**) *(multitud)* throng; **en m.** en masse; **fabricación** *o* **producción en m.** mass production; **fuimos en m. a escuchar la conferencia** a large group of us went to listen to the lecture; **las masas** the masses (**c**) *(mezcla, pasta)* mixture; *Culin* dough (**d**) *Elec (tierra)* ground (**e**) *RP (pastelito)* cake

masacrar *vt* to massacre

masacre *nf* massacre

masaje *nm* massage

masajear *vt* to massage, to rub

masajista *nmf* masseur, *f* masseuse

mascar [59] *vt & vi* to chew

máscara *nf* mask; *(apariencia)* front, pretense; **m. antigás** gas mask; *Fig* **quitar la m. a alguien** to unmask sb; *Fig* **quitarse la m.** to reveal oneself

mascarada *nf (fiesta)* masquerade; *Fig (farsa)* farce

mascarilla *nf* (**a**) *(de protección)* mask; **m. de oxígeno** oxygen mask (**b**) *(cosmética)* face pack

mascarón *nm Arquit* grotesque head; **m. de proa** figurehead

mascota *nf* mascot

masculinidad *nf* masculinity

masculino, -a *adj* (**a**) *(género, órgano, población)* male; **un programa dirigido al público m.** a program aimed at male viewers; **los 100 metros masculinos** the men's 100 meters (**b**) *(varonil)* manly (**c**) *Gram* masculine

mascullar *vt* to mutter

masía *nf* = traditional Catalan or Aragonese farmhouse

masificación *nf* overcrowding (**de** in)

masificar [59] **1** *vt* to cause overcrowding in
2 masificarse *vpr* to become overcrowded

masilla *nf* putty

masita *nf RP* cake

masivo, -a *adj* mass; **despidos masivos** mass layoffs

masoca *nmf Fam* masochist

masón, -ona 1 *adj* masonic
2 *nm,f* mason, Freemason

masonería *nf* masonry, Freemasonry

masónico, -a *adj* Masonic

masoquismo *nm* masochism

masoquista 1 *adj* masochistic
2 *nmf* masochist

mass media, mass-media *nmpl* mass media

mastectomía *nf* mastectomy

máster *(pl másters)* *nm* Master's (degree)

masticar [59] *vt* to chew; *Fig* **hay que dárselo todo masticado** you need to spoon-feed him

mástil *nm* (**a**) *(de barco)* mast; *(de bandera, tienda)* pole (**b**) *(de instrumento musical)* neck

mastín *nm* mastiff

mastitis *nf inv Med* mastitis

mastodonte 1 *nm* mastodon
2 *nmf Fam* giant

mastodóntico, -a *adj Fam* mammoth, ginormous

mastuerzo *nm Fam* idiot

masturbación *nf* masturbation

masturbar 1 *vt* to masturbate
2 masturbarse *vpr* to masturbate

mata *nf* (**a**) *(arbusto)* bush, shrub; *(matojo)* tuft; **matas** scrub (**b**) *(de pelo)* mop (of hair)

matadero *nm* slaughterhouse, abattoir

matador, -ora 1 *adj Fam* (**a**) *(cansado)* killing, exhausting (**b**) *(feo, de mal gusto)* awful, horrendous
2 *nm Taurom* matador

matambre *nm Andes, RP* = flank steak rolled with boiled egg, olives and red pepper, which is cooked, then sliced and served cold

matamoscas *nm inv (pala)* flyswatter; *(espray)* fly spray

matanza *nf* (**a**) *(masacre)* slaughter (**b**) *Esp (del cerdo)* slaughtering

matar 1 *vt* (**a**) *(quitar la vida a)* to kill; **lo mataron a puñaladas** he was stabbed to death; *Fam Fig* **si se entera me mata** she'll kill me if she finds out; **¡me vas a m. a**

disgustos! you'll be the death of me!; **estar** *o* **llevarse a m. (con alguien)** to be at daggers drawn (with sb); *Fam* **matarlas callando** to be up to something on the quiet (**b**) *(animal) (para consumo)* to slaughter (**c**) *(apagar) (color)* to tone down; *(sed)* to slake, to quench; *(hambre)* to stave off; *(fuego)* to put out (**d**) *(redondear, limar)* to round (off)
2 matarse *vpr* (**a**) *(morir)* to die; **se mató en un accidente de coche** he was killed in a car accident (**b**) *(suicidarse)* to kill oneself (**c**) *(esforzarse)* **matarse trabajando,** *Esp* **matarse a trabajar** to work oneself to death; **matarse por hacer algo** to kill oneself in order to do sth

matarife *nm* butcher, (cattle) slaughterer

matarratas *nm inv* (**a**) *(veneno)* rat poison (**b**) *(bebida mala)* rotgut

matasanos *nmf inv Fam Pey* quack

matasellar *vt* to cancel, to postmark

matasellos *nm inv* postmark

matasuegras *nm inv* party blower

match [matʃ] *nm* match

mate 1 *adj* matte
2 *nm* (**a**) *Dep (en ajedrez)* mate, checkmate; *(en baloncesto)* dunk; *(en tenis)* smash (**b**) *CSur (infusión)* maté; **yerba m.** bitter maté tea

matear *vi CSur* to drink maté

matemático, -a 1 *adj* mathematical
2 *nm,f (científico)* mathematician
3 matemáticas *nfpl (ciencia)* mathematics *(singular)*; **matemáticas puras** pure mathematics

materia *nf* (**a**) *(sustancia, asunto)* matter; **en m. de** on the subject of, concerning; **la legislación en m. de medio ambiente** the legislation on the subject of *o* concerning the environment; **un especialista en m. de higiene** a hygiene expert; **entrar en m.** to get down to business; **m. grasa** fat content; **m. gris** gray matter; **m. orgánica** organic matter (**b**) *(material)* material; **m. prima** raw material (**c**) *(asignatura)* subject

material 1 *adj* (**a**) *(físico)* physical; *(daños, consecuencias)* material (**b**) *(real)* real, actual
2 *nm* (**a**) *(sustancia)* material; **m. de desecho** waste material (**b**) *(instrumentos)* equipment; **m. bélico** war material; **materiales de construcción** building materials; **m. escolar** school materials; **m. de guerra** war material; **m. de oficina** office stationery

materialismo *nm* materialism; **m. dialéctico/histórico** dialectical/historical materialism

materialista 1 *adj* materialistic
2 *nmf* materialist

materialización *nf* materialization

materializar [14] **1** *vt* (**a**) *(idea, proyecto)* to realize (**b**) *(hacer tangible)* to produce
2 materializarse *vpr* to materialize

maternal *adj* motherly, maternal

maternidad *nf* (**a**) *(cualidad)* motherhood (**b**) *(hospital)* maternity hospital

materno, -a *adj* maternal; **lengua materna** mother tongue

mates *nfpl Fam* math

matice *etc ver* **matizar**

matinal *adj* morning; **sesión m.** *(de cine)* morning showing

matiné *nf (en cine)* morning showing

matiz *nm* (**a**) *(de color, opinión)* shade; *(de sentido)* nuance, shade of meaning (**b**) *(diferencia)* subtle difference; **sin matices** *(apoyo)* unqualified, unconditional

matización *nf* clarification, explanation

matizar [14] *vt* (**a**) *(puntualizar)* to clarify, to explain (**b**) *(teñir)* to tinge (**de** with) (**c**) *Arte* to blend

matojo *nm (mata)* tuft; *(arbusto)* bush, shrub

matón, -ona *nm,f Fam* bully

matorral *nm* thicket

matraca *nf (instrumento)* rattle; *Fam* **dar la m.** to go on, to be a nuisance; *Fam* **ser una m.** to be a pain

matraz *nm* flask

matriarcado *nm* matriarchy

matriarcal *adj* matriarchal

matricidio *nm* matricide

matrícula *nf* (a) *(inscripción)* registration (b) *(documento)* registration document (c) *(de vehículo)* license plate (d) *Educ* **m. de honor** top marks

matriculación *nf (inscripción)* registration

matricular 1 *vt* to register
2 matricularse *vpr* to register

matrimonial *adj* marital; **vida m.** married life

matrimonio *nm* (a) *(boda)* marriage; **contraer m.** to get married; **m. civil** civil marriage; **m. de conveniencia** marriage of convenience (b) *(pareja)* married couple

matriz 1 *nf* (a) *Anat* womb (b) *(de talonario)* (check) stub (c) *(molde)* mold (d) *Mat & Inform* matrix
2 *adj (empresa)* parent; **casa m.** head office

matrona *nf* (a) *(madre)* matron (b) *(comadrona)* midwife

matusalén *nm Fam* very old person; **ser más viejo que M.** to be as old as Methuselah

matute: de matute *loc adv Fam (clandestinamente)* on the quiet

matutino, -a *adj* morning; **paseo m.** morning walk

maullar *vi* to meow

maullido *nm* meow, meowing

Mauricio *n* Mauritius

Mauritania *n* Mauritania

mauritano, -a *adj & nm,f* Mauritanian

máuser *(pl* **máuseres** *o* **máusers)** *nm* Mauser

mausoleo *nm* mausoleum

maxilar 1 *adj* maxillary, jaw; **hueso m.** jawbone, mandible
2 *nm* jaw

maxilofacial *adj Med* facial, *Espec* maxillofacial

máxima *nf* (a) *(sentencia, principio)* maxim (b) *(temperatura)* high, highest temperature

maximalismo *nm* maximalism

maximalista *adj & nmf* maximalist

máxime *adv* especially

maximizar [14] *vt* to maximize

máximo, -a 1 *adj (capacidad, cantidad, temperatura)* maximum; *(honor, galardón)* highest; **la máxima puntuación** *(posible)* the maximum score; *(entre varias)* the highest score
2 *nm* maximum; **al m.** to the utmost; **llegar al m.** to reach the limit; **como m.** *(a más tardar)* at the latest; *(como mucho)* at the most

maxisingle [maksi'singel] *nm* twelve inch (single)

maya 1 *adj* Mayan
2 *nmf* Maya, Mayan
3 *nm (lengua)* Maya

mayestático, -a *adj* majestic

mayo *nm* May; *ver también* **septiembre**

mayonesa *nf* mayonnaise

mayor 1 *adj* (a) *(comparativo) (en tamaño)* bigger (**que** than); *(en importancia)* greater (**que** than); *(en edad)* older (**que** than); *(en número)* higher (**que** than)
(b) *(superlativo)* **el/la m.**... *(en tamaño)* the biggest...; *(en importancia)* the greatest...; *(en edad)* the oldest...; *(en número)* the highest...; **la m. de las islas** the biggest island, the biggest of the islands
(c) *(adulto)* grown-up; **cuando sea m.** when I grow up; **ser m. de edad** to be an adult
(d) *(no joven)* older; *(anciano)* elderly; **una mujer m.** an older

woman; **ser muy m.** to be very old; **las personas mayores** *(los ancianos)* the elderly
(e) *(principal) (plaza, calle, palo)* main
(f) *Mús* **en do m.** in C major
(g) *Com* **al por m.** wholesale
2 *nmf* (a) **el/la m.** *(hijo, hermano)* the eldest; **mayores** *(adultos)* grown-ups; *(antepasados)* ancestors, forefathers; **es una película/revista para mayores** it's an adult movie/magazine (b) *Mil* major

mayoral *nm* (a) *(capataz)* foreman, overseer (b) *(pastor)* chief herdsman

mayorazgo *nm Hist* (a) *(institución)* primogeniture (b) *(bienes)* entailed estate (c) *(persona)* heir to an entailed estate

mayordomo *nm* butler

mayoreo *nm Am* wholesale

mayoría *nf* (a) *(mayor parte)* majority; **la m. de** most of; **la m. de los españoles** most Spaniards; **en su m.** in the main; **m. absoluta** absolute majority; **m. relativa** plurality; **m. silenciosa** silent majority (b) *(edad adulta)* **m. de edad** (age of) majority; **llegar a la m. de edad** to come of age

mayorista 1 *adj* wholesale
2 *nmf* wholesaler

mayoritario, -a *adj* majority; **decisión mayoritaria** majority decision

mayúscula *nf* capital letter, uppercase letter; **en mayúsculas** in capitals *o* capital letters, in upper case

mayúsculo, -a *adj* tremendous, enormous; **letra mayúscula** capital letter

maza *nf (arma)* mace; *(de bombo)* drumstick

mazacote *nm Fam* **la paella era un m.** the paella was a gooey mess

mazapán *nm* marzipan

mazazo *nm también Fig* heavy blow

mazmorra *nf* dungeon

mazo *nm* (a) *(martillo)* mallet (b) *(de mortero)* pestle (c) *(conjunto) (de cartas, papeles)* bundle; *(de billetes)* wad; *(de naipes)* balance (of the deck)

mazorca *nf* cob; **m. de maíz** corncob

mazurca *nf Mús* mazurka

MB *Inform (abrev de* **megabyte)** MB

MBA *nm (abrev de* **Master of Business Administration)** MBA

MCCA *(abrev de* **Mercado Común Centroamericano)** Central American Common Market

me *pron personal* (a) *(complemento directo)* me; **le gustaría verme** she'd like to see me (b) *(complemento indirecto)* (to) me; **me lo dio** he gave it to me; **me tiene miedo** he's afraid of me (c) *(reflexivo)* myself; **me visto** I get dressed

mea culpa *nm* mea culpa; **entonó el m.** he acknowledged he had made a mistake

meada *nf Fam (acción, orina)* piss; *(mancha)* piss stain; **echar una m.** to have a pee *o* piss

meadero *nm Fam (váter)* john

meandro *nm* meander

meapilas *nmf inv Fam Pey* holy Joe

mear *Fam* **1** *vt* to piss, to pee
2 *vi* to piss, to pee
3 mearse *vpr* to piss oneself; **mearse en la cama** to wet one's bed; *Fig* **mearse (de risa)** to hurt oneself laughing; *Fig* **yo con tu hermano me meo** I think your brother's a scream; *Fig* **estás meando fuera del tiesto** you've got hold of the wrong end of the stick

meca *nf* mecca; **La M.** Mecca

mecachis *interj Fam* **¡m.!** shoot!

mecánica *nf* (a) *(ciencia)* mechanics *(singular)*; **m. cuántica** quantum mechanics (b) *(funcionamiento)* mechanics

mecanicismo *nm* mechanism

mecánico, -a 1 *adj* mechanical

2 *nm,f (persona)* mechanic; **m. dentista** dental technician

mecanismo *nm* **(a)** *(de rueda, reloj)* mechanism **(b)** *(procedimiento)* mechanism; *Psi* **m. de defensa** defense mechanism

mecanización *nf* mechanization

mecanizado, -a *adj* mechanized

mecanizar [14] *vt* to mechanize

mecanografía *nf* typing; **m. al tacto** touch-typing

mecanografiar [32] *vt* to type

mecanógrafo, -a *nm,f* typist

mecapal *nm CAm, Méx* porter's leather harness

mecate *nm CAm, Méx, Ven* rope

mecedora *nf* rocking chair

mecenas *nmf inv* patron

mecenazgo *nm* patronage

mecer [40] **1** *vt* to rock

2 mecerse *vpr (en silla)* to rock; *(en columpio, hamaca)* to swing; *(árbol, rama)* to sway

mecha *nf* **(a)** *(de vela)* wick; *(de explosivos)* fuse; *Fam* **a toda m.** flat out; *Fam* **aguantar m.** to grin and bear it **(b)** *(de pelo)* streak

mechero *nm Esp* (cigarette) lighter

mechón *nm (de pelo)* lock; *(de lana)* tuft

medalla *nf* medal; **m. de oro/plata/bronce** gold/silver/bronze medal; *Fig* **ponerse medallas** to show off

medallero *nm* medals table

medallista *nmf* **(a)** *(oficio)* maker of medals **(b)** *Dep* medalist

medallón *nm* **(a)** *(joya)* medallion **(b)** *Culin (rodaja)* medaillon; **m. de pescado** *(empanado)* fish cake

médano *nm* **(a)** *(duna)* (sand) dune **(b)** *(banco de arena)* sandbank

media *nf* **(a)** *(prenda)* **medias** *(hasta la cintura)* panty hose; *(hasta medio muslo)* stockings; *Am (calcetines)* socks; *CSur Fam* **chupar las medias a alguien** to lick sb's boots; *Col* **medias veladas** panty hose **(b)** *Mat (promedio)* average; **m. aritmética/proporcional** arithmetic/proportional mean; **m. horaria** hourly average **(c)** *(hora)* **al dar la m.** on the half hour

mediación *nf* mediation; **por m. de** through

mediado, -a *adj (a media capacidad)* half-full; **mediada la película** halfway through the movie; **a mediados de abril/de año** in the middle of *o* halfway through April/the year

mediador, -ora 1 *adj* mediating

2 *nm,f* mediator

medialuna *nf* **(a)** *(símbolo musulmán)* crescent **(b)** *Am (bollo)* croissant

mediana *nf* **(a)** *(de autopista)* median (strip) **(b)** *Mat* median

medianamente *adv* acceptably, tolerably; **habla francés m. bien** he can get by in French; **sólo entendí m. lo que dijo** I only half understood what he said

medianía *nf* average *o* mediocre person

mediano, -a *adj* **(a)** *(de tamaño)* medium; *(de calidad)* average **(b)** *(mediocre)* average, ordinary

medianoche *nf* **(a)** *(hora)* midnight; **a m.** at midnight **(b)** *Esp* *(pl* **mediasnoches)** *(bollo)* = sandwich made with a small bun

mediante *prep* by means of; **lo levantaron m. una polea** it was lifted by means of a pulley system; **las obras se adjudicarán m. concurso público** the contract for the work will be put out to tender; **puede aplazar la compra m. 12 pagos mensuales** you can spread the purchase over 12 monthly payments

mediar *vi* **(a)** *(llegar a la mitad)* to be halfway through; **mediaba julio** it was mid-July **(b)** *(haber en medio)* **m. entre** to be between; **media un jardín/un kilómetro entre las dos casas** there is a garden/one kilometer between the two

houses; **medió una semana** a week passed by **(c)** *(intervenir)* to mediate **(en/entre** in/between); *(interceder)* to intercede **(en favor de** *o* **por** on behalf of *o* for) **(d)** *(ocurrir)* to intervene, to happen; **media la circunstancia de que...** it so happens that...

mediático, -a *adj* media

mediatizar [14] *vt* to determine

medicación *nf* medication

medicamento *nm* medicine

medicar [59] **1** *vt* to give medicine to

2 medicarse *vpr* to take medicine

medicina *nf* medicine; **m. alternativa** alternative medicine; **m. forense** forensic medicine; **m. homeopática** homeopathic medicine; **m. interna** internal medicine; **m. naturista** naturopathy, natural medicine; **m. preventiva** preventive medicine; **m. social** community medicine

medicinal *adj* medicinal

medición *nf* measurement

médico, -a 1 *adj* medical

2 *nm,f* doctor; **ir al m.** to go to the doctor; **m. de cabecera** *o* **familia** family doctor, general practitioner; **m. forense** specialist in forensic medicine; **m. de guardia** duty doctor; **m. interno (residente)** intern

medida 1 *nf* **(a)** *(dimensión, medición)* measurement; **¿qué medidas tiene el contenedor?** what are the measurements of the container?; **a (la) m.** *(mueble)* custom-built; *(ropa)* made-to-measure; **medidas** *(del cuerpo)* measurements; **tomar las medidas a alguien** to take sb's measurements; **m. de capacidad** measure *(liquid or dry)*

(b) *(disposición)* measure, step; **adoptar** *o* **tomar medidas** to take measures *o* steps; **m. preventiva** preventive measure; **medidas de seguridad** safety measures

(c) *(moderación)* moderation; **sin m.** without moderation

(d) *(grado)* extent, degree; **¿en qué m. nos afecta?** to what extent does it affect us?; **en cierta/gran m.** to some/a large extent; **en mayor/menor m.** to a greater/lesser extent; **en la m. de lo posible** as far as possible

2 a medida que *loc conj* as; **a m. que entraban** as they were coming in

mediería *nf RP* hosiery shop

medieval *adj* medieval

medievalismo *nm* medievalism

medievalista *nmf* medievalist

medievo *nm* Middle Ages

medio, -a 1 *adj* **(a)** *(mitad)* half; **media docena** half a dozen; **media hora** half an hour; **m. pueblo estaba allí** half the town was there; **a m. camino** *(en viaje)* halfway there; *(en trabajo)* halfway through; **a media luz** in the half-light; **un kilo y m.** one and a half kilos; **son las dos y media** it's half past two; **son y media** it's half past **(b)** *(intermedio) (estatura, tamaño)* medium; *(posición, punto)* middle; **a m. plazo** in the medium term; **de clase media** middle-class **(c)** *(de promedio)* *(temperatura, velocidad)* average; **el francés m.** your average Frenchman **(d)** *(corriente)* ordinary, average

2 *adv* half; **m. borracho** half drunk; **a m. hacer** half done

3 *nm* **(a)** *(mitad)* half

(b) *(centro)* middle, center; **en m. (de)** in the middle (of); **estar por (en) m.** to be in the way; **equivocarse de m. a m.** to be completely wrong; **meterse** *o* **ponerse de por m.** to get in the way; *Fig* to interfere; **quitar de en m. a alguien** to get rid of sb, to get sb out of the way

(c) *(sistema, manera)* means *(singular or plural)*, method; **por m. de** by means of, through; **por todos los medios** by all possible means; **los medios de comunicación** *o* **información** the media; **medios de producción** means of production; **medios de transporte** means *o* mode of transportation

(d) *(recursos)* **medios** means, resources

(**e**) *(elemento físico)* environment; **m. ambiente** environment
(**f**) *(ámbito)* **en medios bien informados** in well-informed circles

4 a medias *loc adv* **hacer algo a medias** to half-do sth; **pagar a medias** to go halves, to share the cost

medioambiental *adj* environmental

mediocampista *nmf Dep* midfielder

mediocre *adj* mediocre, average

mediocridad *nf* mediocrity

mediodía *nm* (**a**) *(hora)* midday, noon; **al m.** at noon *o* midday (**b**) *(sur)* south

medioevo *nm* Middle Ages

mediofondista *nmf Dep* middle-distance runner

medique *etc ver* **medicar**

medir [47] **1** *vt* (**a**) *(hacer mediciones)* to measure (**b**) *(sopesar)* to weigh up (**c**) *(palabras)* to weigh carefully (**d**) *(fuerzas)* **los dos equipos medirán sus fuerzas en la semifinal** the two sides will do battle in the semifinal

2 *vi* *(tener de medida)* **¿cuánto mides?** how tall are you?; **¿cuánto mide de largo?** how long *o* what length is it?; **mido 1,80** I'm 6 foot (tall); **mide diez metros** it's ten meters long; **mide 90-60-90** her vital statistics are 36-24-36

3 medirse *vpr* (**a**) *(tomarse medidas)* to measure oneself; **se midió la cintura** she measured her waist (**b**) *(moderarse)* to show restraint (**c**) *(enfrentarse)* **medirse con** to meet, to compete against

meditabundo, -a *adj* thoughtful, pensive

meditación *nf* meditation; **m. trascendental** transcendental meditation

meditar 1 *vi* to meditate (**sobre** on)

2 *vt* (**a**) *(considerar)* to meditate, to ponder (**b**) *(planear)* to plan, to think through

meditativo, -a *adj* pensive

mediterráneo, -a 1 *adj* Mediterranean

2 *nm* **el (mar) M.** the Mediterranean (Sea)

médium *nmf inv* medium

medrar *vi* (**a**) *(prosperar)* to prosper (**b**) *(enriquecerse)* to get rich (**c**) *(crecer)* to grow

medro *nm* **afán de m.** desire to get on in the world

medroso, -a 1 *adj* *(miedoso)* fearful

2 *nm,f* fearful person

médula *nf* (**a**) *Anat* (bone) marrow; **m. espinal** spinal cord (**b**) *(esencia)* core

medular *adj Anat* medullary, medullar

medusa *nf* jellyfish

mefistofélico, -a *adj* diabolical

megabit *(pl* **megabits)** *nm Inform* megabit

megabyte [meɣaˈβait] *nm Inform* megabyte

megafonía *nf* public-address system

megáfono *nm* megaphone

megahercio *nm* megahertz

megalito *nm* megalith

megalomanía *nf* megalomania

megalómano, -a *adj & nm,f* megalomaniac

megalópolis *nf inv* megalopolis

megatón *nm* megaton

meiga *nf* witch *(in Galicia)*

mejicanismo *nm* Mexicanism

mejicano, -a *adj & nm,f* Mexican

Méjico *n* Mexico

mejilla *nf* cheek; *Fig* **ofrecer** *o* **poner la otra m.** to turn the other cheek

mejillón *nm* mussel

mejor 1 *adj* (**a**) *(comparativo)* better (**que** than); **no hay nada m. que...** there's nothing better than...; **es m. que no vengas** it would be better if you didn't come; **será m. que**

te calles you'd better shut up, I suggest you shut up (**b**) *(superlativo)* **el/la m....** the best...; **el m. vino de todos/ del mundo** the best wine of all/in the world; **lo m. fue que...** the best thing was that...

2 *nmf* **el/la m. (de)** the best (in); **el m. de todos** the best of all

3 *adv* (**a**) *(comparativo)* better (**que** than); **ahora veo m.** I can see better now; **estar m.** *(no tan malo)* to feel better; *(recuperado)* to be better; **m. no se lo digas** it'd be better if you don't tell him; **m. dicho** (or) rather; **m. que m.** so much the better (**b**) *(superlativo)* best; **el que la conoce m.** the one who knows her best

4 a lo mejor *loc adv* maybe, perhaps; **a lo m. voy** I may go

mejora *nf* (**a**) *(progreso)* improvement (**b**) *(aumento)* increase

mejorable *adj* improvable

mejorana *nf* sweet marjoram

mejorar 1 *vt* *(hacer mejor)* to improve; *(enfermo)* to make better; **m. una oferta** to make a better offer

2 *vi* to improve, to get better

3 mejorarse *vpr* to improve, to get better; **¡que te mejores!** get well soon!

mejoría *nf* improvement

mejunje *nm Fam* concoction

melancolía *nf* melancholy

melancólico, -a *adj* melancholic

2 *nm,f* melancholic person

melanina *nf* melanin

melanoma *nm Med* melanoma

melaza *nf* molasses

melé *nf Esp Dep* scrum

melena *nf* (**a**) *(de persona)* long hair; **melenas** mop of hair (**b**) *(de león)* mane

melenudo, -a 1 *adj* with a mop of hair

2 *nm,f* person with a mop of hair

melifluo, -a *adj* honeyed, mellifluous

Melilla *n* Melilla

melillense 1 *adj* of/from Melilla

2 *nmf* person from Melilla

melindre *nm* (**a**) *Culin* = fried cake made from honey and sugar (**b**) **melindres** *(afectación)* affected scrupulousness

melindroso, -a 1 *adj* affectedly scrupulous

2 *nm,f* affectedly scrupulous person

melisa *nf* lemon balm

mella *nf* (**a**) *(muesca, hendidura)* nick; *Fig* **hacer m. en** *(ahorros, moral)* to make a dent in; *Fig* **hacer m. en alguien** to make an impression on sb (**b**) *(en dentadura)* gap

mellado, -a *adj* (**a**) *(dañado)* nicked (**b**) *(sin dientes)* gap-toothed

mellar *vt* (**a**) *(hacer mellas en)* to nick, to chip (**b**) *(menoscabar)* to damage

mellizo, -a *adj & nm,f* twin

melocotón *nm esp Esp* peach; **m. en almíbar** peaches in syrup

melocotonero *nm esp Esp* peach tree

melodía *nf* melody, tune; *(de teléfono)* ring tone

melódico, -a *adj* melodic

melodioso, -a *adj* melodious

melodrama *nm* melodrama

melodramático, -a *adj* melodramatic

melomanía *nf* love of music

melómano, -a *nm,f* music lover

melón *nm* (**a**) *(fruta)* melon (**b**) *Fam (idiota)* lemon, idiot

melonar *nm* melon field *o* patch

meloncillo *nm* = European variety of mongoose

melopea *nf Esp Fam* **agarrar** *o* **coger una m.** to get legless

melosidad *nf* *(dulzura)* sweetness; *(empalago)* sickliness

meloso, -a *adj (como la miel)* honey; *Fig (dulce)* sweet; *(empalagoso)* sickly

membrana *nf* membrane

membranoso, -a *adj* membranous

membresía *nf Am* membership

membrete *nm* letterhead

membrillo *nm* **(a)** *(fruto)* quince **(b)** *(dulce)* quince jelly

memez *nf Fam (cualidad)* stupidity; *(acción, dicho)* silly *o* stupid thing

memo, -a 1 *adj* stupid
   2 *nm,f* idiot, fool

memorable *adj* memorable

memorándum, memorando (*pl* **memorandos**) *nm* **(a)** *(cuaderno)* notebook **(b)** *(nota diplomática)* memorandum

memoria *nf* **(a)** *(capacidad de recordar)* memory; **tener buena/mala m., tener mucha/poca m.** to have a good/bad memory; **de m.** by heart; **hacer m.** to try to remember; **refrescar la m. a alguien** to refresh sb's memory; **traer a la m.** to call to mind; **si la m. no me engaña** *o* **falla** if I remember correctly; **venir a la m.** to come to mind
   (b) *(recuerdo)* remembrance, remembering; **ser de feliz/ingrata m.** to be a happy/an unhappy memory; **un monumento en m. del héroe nacional** a memorial to the national hero; **memorias** *(en literatura)* memoirs
   (c) *(disertación)* (academic) paper
   (d) *(informe)* **m. (anual)** (annual) report
   (e) *(lista)* list, record
   (f) *Inform* memory; **m. de acceso aleatorio/de sólo lectura** random-access/read-only memory; **m. expandida/extendida/programable** expanded/extended/programmable memory; **m. RAM/ROM** RAM/ROM

memorial *nm* petition, request

memorístico, -a *adj* memory; **ejercicio m.** memory exercise

memorización *nf* memorizing

memorizar [14] *vt* to memorize

ménage à trois [meˈnaʃaˈtrwa] *nm* ménage à trois

menaje *nm* household goods and furnishings; **m. de cocina** kitchenware

mención *nf* mention; **hacer m. de** to mention; **m. honorífica** honorable mention

mencionar *vt* to mention

menda *Esp Fam* **1** *pron Hum (el que habla)* yours truly
   2 *nmf (uno cualquiera)* **vino un m. y…** this guy came along and…

mendacidad *nf Formal* mendacity, untruthfulness

mendaz *adj Formal* mendacious, untruthful

mendicante *adj (orden religiosa)* mendicant

mendicidad *nf* begging

mendigar [38] **1** *vt* to beg for
   2 *vi* to beg

mendigo, -a *nm,f* beggar

mendrugo *nm* **(a)** *(de pan)* crust (of bread) **(b)** *Esp Fam (idiota)* fathead, idiot

menear 1 *vt* **(a)** *(mover)* to move; *(cabeza)* to shake; *(cola)* to wag; *(caderas)* to wiggle **(b)** *(activar)* to get moving
   2 menearse *vpr* **(a)** *(moverse)* to move (about); *(agitarse)* to shake; *(oscilar)* to sway **(b)** *(darse prisa, espabilarse)* to get a move on **(c)** *Esp Fam* **un susto de no te menees** a hell of a scare

meneo *nm* **(a)** *(movimiento)* movement; *(de cola)* wagging; *(de caderas)* wiggle; *Esp Fam* **dar un m. a algo** to knock sth; *Esp Fam* **dar un m. a alguien** to give sb a hiding

menester *nm* necessity; **haber m. de algo** to be in need of sth; **ser m. que alguien haga algo** to be necessary for sb to do sth; **menesteres** *(asuntos)* business, matters

menesteroso, -a *Formal* **1** *adj* needy, poor
   2 *nm,f* needy *o* poor person

menestra *nf* vegetable stew

mengano, -a *nm,f* so-and-so

mengua *nf (reducción)* reduction; **sin m. de** without detriment to

menguado, -a *adj* reduced, diminished

menguante *adj (luna)* waning; **en cuarto m.** on the wane

menguar [11] **1** *vi* **(a)** *(disminuir)* to decrease, to diminish; *(luna)* to wane **(b)** *(en labor de punto)* to decrease
   2 *vt* **(a)** *(disminuir)* to lessen, to diminish **(b)** *(en labor de punto)* to decrease

menhir *nm* menhir

meninge *nf Anat* meninx

meningitis *nf inv Med* meningitis

menisco *nm Anat* meniscus

menopausia *nf* menopause

menopáusico, -a *adj* menopausal

menor 1 *adj* **(a)** *(comparativo) (en tamaño)* smaller (**que** than); *(en edad)* younger (**que** than); *(en importancia)* less, lesser (**que** than); *(en número)* lower (**que** than)
   (b) *(superlativo)* **el/la m.…** *(en tamaño)* the smallest…; *(en edad)* the youngest…; *(en importancia)* the slightest…; *(en número)* the lowest…; **la m. de las islas** the smallest island, the smallest of the islands; **el m. ruido le molesta** the slightest noise disturbs him
   (c) *(intrascendente, secundario)* **un problema m.** a minor problem
   (d) **ser m. de edad** *(para votar, conducir)* to be under age; *Der* to be a minor; **aún es m. para salir solo** he's still a bit young to go out on his own
   (e) *Mús* **en do m.** in C minor
   (f) *Com* **al por m.** retail
   2 *nmf* **(a)** *(superlativo)* **el/la m.** *(hijo, hermano)* the youngest **(b)** *Der (niño)* minor

Menorca *n* Minorca

menorista *Chile, Méx* **1** *adj* retail
   2 *nmf* retailer

menorquín, -ina *adj & nm,f* Minorcan

menos 1 *adj inv* **(a)** *(comparativo) (cantidad)* less; *(número)* fewer; **m. aire** less air; **m. manzanas** fewer apples; **m.… que…** less/fewer… than…; **tiene m. experiencia que tú** she has less experience than you; **hace m. calor que ayer** it's not as hot as it was yesterday; **hay dos libros de m.** there are two books missing; **me han dado 10 euros de m.** they've given me 10 euros too little
   (b) *(superlativo) (cantidad)* the least; *(número)* the fewest; **el que compró m. acciones** the one who bought the fewest shares; **lo que m. tiempo llevó** the thing that took the least time; **la que m. nota sacó en el examen** the girl who did (the) worst *o* got the worst marks in the exam
   (c) *Fam (peor)* **éste es m. coche que el mío** that car isn't as good as mine
   2 *adv* **(a)** *(comparativo)* less; **m. de/que** less than; **son m. de las diez** it's not quite ten o'clock yet
   (b) *(superlativo)* **el/la/lo m.** the least; **el m. interesante/difícil** the least interesting/difficult; **él es el m. indicado para criticar** he's the last person who should be criticizing; **es lo m. que puedo hacer** it's the least I can do
   (c) *(expresa resta)* minus; **tres m. dos igual a uno** three minus two is one
   (d) *Esp, RP (con las horas)* to; **son las dos m. diez** it's ten to two; **son m. diez** it's ten to
   (e) *(expresiones)* **¡m. mal!** just as well!, thank God!; **es lo de m.** that's the least of it, that's of no importance; **hacer de m. a alguien** to snub sb; **lo m.** *(como mínimo)* at least; **nada m. (que)** no less (than); **ni mucho m.** nor anything like it; **no es para m.** not without (good) reason; **venir a m.** to go down in the world
   3 *nm inv Mat* minus (sign)

4 *prep (excepto)* except (for); **todo m. eso** anything but that

5 a menos que *loc conj* unless; **no iré a m. que me acompañes** I won't go unless you come with me

6 al menos *loc adv* at least

7 por lo menos *loc adv* at least

menoscabar *vt (fama, honra)* to damage; *(derechos, intereses, salud)* to harm; *(belleza, perfección)* to diminish

menoscabo *nm (de fama, honra)* damage; *(de derechos, intereses, salud)* harm; *(de belleza, perfección)* diminishing; **(ir) en m. de** (to be) to the detriment of

menospreciar *vt (despreciar)* to scorn, to despise; *(infravalorar)* to undervalue

menosprecio *nm* scorn, contempt

mensáfono *nm* pager

mensaje *nm* message; **te dejé un m. en el contestador** I left you a message on your answering machine; *Inform* **m. de alerta** alert message; *Inform* **m. por correo electrónico** e-mail message; **m. de texto** text message

mensajería *nf* (**a**) *(de paquetes, cartas)* courier service (**b**) *(por teléfono)* messaging; **m. de imágenes** picture messaging

mensajero, -a *nm,f (portador)* messenger; *(de mensajería)* courier

menstruación *nf* menstruation

menstrual *adj* menstrual

menstruar [4] *vi* to menstruate, to have a period

menstruo *nm* menstruation

mensual *adj* monthly; **5.000 pesos mensuales** 5,000 pesos a month

mensualidad *nf* (**a**) *(sueldo)* monthly salary (**b**) *(pago)* monthly payment *o* installment

menta *nf* mint

mentado, -a *adj* (**a**) *(mencionado)* above-mentioned, afore-mentioned (**b**) *(famoso)* famous

mental *adj* mental

mentalidad *nf* mentality

mentalización *nf* mental preparation

mentalizar [14] **1** *vt* to put into a frame of mind; **m. a alguien de algo** to make sb aware of sth

2 mentalizarse *vpr* to get into a frame of mind; **mentalizarse de que…** to get used to the idea that…

mentar [3] *vt* to mention; **mentarle la madre a alguien** to swear at sb

mente *nf* (**a**) *(pensamiento, intelecto)* mind; **tener en m. algo** to have sth in mind; **tener en m. hacer algo** to intend to do sth; **traer a la m.** to bring to mind (**b**) *(mentalidad)* mentality; **abierto de m.** open-minded; **cerrado de m.** set in one's ways *o* opinions; **tiene una m. muy abierta** she's very open-minded

mentecato, -a *nm,f* idiot

mentidero *nm* (**a**) *(lugar)* **es el m. del pueblo** it's where you get all the good village gossip (**b**) *(de personas)* **en los mentideros políticos/intelectuales** in political/intellectual circles

mentir [62] *vi* to lie; **no me mientas** don't lie to me; **miente más que habla** he's a born liar; **esas estadísticas mienten, porque no tienen en cuenta…** those statistics give a false picture *o* are misleading, because they don't take into account…; **llovía, miento, granizaba cuando nos preparábamos para salir** it was raining, I tell a lie, it was hailing as we were getting ready to leave

mentira *nf* lie; **es m.** it's not true, it's a lie; **aunque parezca m.** strange as it may seem; **parece m. que lo hayamos conseguido** I can hardly believe we've done it; **parece m. que te creas una cosa así** how can you possibly believe a thing like that?; **¡parece m., las cinco y todavía no ha llegado!** can you believe it, it's five o'clock and she's still hasn't arrived!; **de m.** pretend, false; **dinero de m.** pretend

money; **una m. como una casa** a whopping great lie; **m. piadosa** white lie

mentirijilla *nf Fam* fib; **de mentirijillas** *(en broma)* as a joke, in fun; *(falso)* pretend, make-believe

mentiroso, -a 1 *adj* lying; *(engañoso)* deceptive

2 *nm,f* liar

mentís *nm inv* denial; **dar un m. (a)** to issue a denial (of)

mentol *nm* menthol

mentolado, -a *adj* menthol, mentholated

mentón *nm* chin

mentor, -ora *nm,f* mentor

menú *nm* (**a**) *(lista)* menu; *(comida)* food; **m. del día** set meal (**b**) *Inform* menu; **m. desplegable** pull-down menu

menudear 1 *vi* to happen frequently

2 *vt* to repeat, to do repeatedly

menudencia *nf* trifle, insignificant thing

menudeo *nm Andes, Méx* retailing

menudillos *nmpl* giblets

menudo, -a 1 *adj* (**a**) *(pequeño)* small (**b**) *(insignificante)* trifling, insignificant (**c**) *(para enfatizar)* what a….!; **¡m. lío/gol!** what a mess/goal!

2 a menudo *loc adv* often

meñique *nm* **(dedo) m.** little finger, pinky

meódromo *nm Esp Fam* john

meollo *nm* core, heart; **el m. de la cuestión** the nub of the question, the heart of the matter

meón, -ona *nm,f Fam* **es un m.** he has a weak bladder

mequetrefe *nmf Fam* good-for-nothing

mercachifle *nmf Pey* (**a**) *(comerciante)* peddler (**b**) *(usurero)* money-grabber, shark

mercadear *vi* to trade, to do business

mercader *nmf* merchant, trader

mercadería *nf* merchandise, goods

mercadillo *nm* flea market

mercado *nm* market; **m. de abastos** wholesale food market; *Bolsa* **m. alcista** *o* **al alza** bull market; *Bolsa* **m. bajista** *o* **a la baja** bear market; **m. bursátil** stock market; *Bolsa* **m. de capitales** capital market; **el M. Común** Common Market; **m. de divisas** currency market; **m. exterior** foreign market; **m. financiero** financial market; *Bolsa* **m. de futuros** futures market; **m. inmobiliario** housing *o* property market; **m. interbancario** interbank market; **m. interior** domestic market; **m. laboral** labor market; **m. libre** free market; **m. monetario** money market; **m. negro** black market; **m. de trabajo** job market; **m. único** single market; **M. Único Europeo** European Single Market; *Bolsa* **m. de valores** securities market

mercadotecnia *nf* marketing

mercancía 1 *nf* merchandise, goods

2 mercancías *nm inv Ferroc* freight train

mercante 1 *adj* merchant

2 *nm (barco)* merchantman, merchant ship

mercantil *adj* mercantile, commercial

mercantilismo *nm* mercantilism; *Pey* commercialism

mercantilista *adj & mf* mercantilist

mercantilizar [14] *vt* to commercialize

merced *nf* favor; **m. a** thanks to; **a m. de algo/alguien** at the mercy of sth/sb

mercenario, -a *adj & nm,f* mercenary

mercería *nf* (**a**) *(género)* notions (**b**) *(tienda)* notions store

merchandising [mertʃanˈdaisin] *nm* merchandising

Mercosur *nm* *(abrev de* **Mercado Común del Sur***)* MERCOSUR

mercromina® *nf (para heridas)* Mercurochrome®

Mercurio *nm* Mercury

mercurio *nm* mercury

mercurocromo *nm* Mercurochrome®

merecedor, -ora *adj* m. de worthy of

merecer [46] **1** *vt* to deserve, to be worthy of; **la isla merece una visita** the island is worth a visit; **merece la pena detenernos un poco más en este punto** it's worth spending a bit more time on this point; **no merece la pena** it's not worth it; **no merece la pena que te enfades** it's not worth getting angry about, there's no point in getting angry about it

2 *vi* to be worthy; **en edad de m.** of marriageable age

3 merecerse *vpr* to deserve; **se merece ganar** she deserves to win; **se lo tiene bien merecido** it serves him right

merecido *nm* darle a alguien su m. to give sb his/her just deserts; **recibió su m.** he got his just deserts

merendar [3] **1** *vi* to have a late afternoon snack

2 *vt* to have as a late afternoon snack

3 merendarse *vpr Fam* **merendarse a alguien** to thrash sb

merendero *nm* = open-air café or bar (in the country or on the beach)

merendola *nf Esp Fam* splendid spread

merengue 1 *nm* (**a**) *Culin* meringue (**b**) *(baile)* merengue

2 *adj Esp Fam Dep* = relating to Real Madrid Football Club

meretriz *nf* prostitute

merezca *etc ver* **merecer**

Mérida *n* Merida

meridiano, -a 1 *adj* (**a**) *(hora)* midday (**b**) *(claro)* crystal-clear

2 *nm* meridian

meridional 1 *adj* southern

2 *nmf* southerner

merienda 1 *ver* **merendar**

2 *nf* late afternoon snack; *(en el campo)* picnic; *Esp* **fue una m. de negros** *(caos)* it was total chaos; *(masacre)* it was a massacre

merino, -a *adj* merino

mérito *nm* (**a**) *(cualidad)* merit; **hacer méritos para** to do everything possible to (**b**) *(valor)* value, worth; **tiene mucho m.** it's no mean achievement; **de m.** worthy, deserving

meritorio, -a 1 *adj* worthy, deserving

2 *nm,f* unpaid trainee *o* apprentice

merluza *nf* (**a**) *(pez, pescado)* hake (**b**) *Esp Fam (borrachera)* **agarrar una m.** to get sozzled

merluzo, -a *nm,f Esp Fam* idiot, fool

merma *nf* decrease, reduction

mermar 1 *vi* to diminish, to lessen

2 *vt* to reduce, to diminish

mermelada *nf* jam; **m. de frambuesa/fresa** raspberry/strawberry jam; **m. de naranja** marmalade

mero, -a 1 *adj* (**a**) *(simple)* mere; **una mera excusa** just an excuse (**b**) *CAm, Méx Fam* **me lo contó él m.** he told me himself *o* in person; **en el m. centro** right in the center; *Méx* **el m. m.** the big shot

2 *adv CAm, Méx Fam* (**a**) *(exactamente)* **aquí m.** right here; **ya m.** right now (**b**) *(casi)* nearly, almost; **m. me mato** I nearly *o* almost got killed

3 *nm (pez)* grouper

merodeador, -ora *nm,f* prowler, snooper

merodear *vi* to snoop, to prowl (**por** about)

mes *nm* (**a**) *(del año)* month; **al** *o* **por m.** a month; **viajo a Lima tres veces al** *o* **por m.** I go to Lima three times a month (**b**) *(salario)* monthly salary (**c**) *Fam (menstruación)* **está con el m.** it's her time of the month

mesa *nf* (**a**) *(mueble)* table; *(de oficina, despacho)* desk; **bendecir la m.** to say grace; **poner/quitar la m.** to set/clear the table; **sentarse a la m.** to sit down at the table; **¡a la m.!** dinner/lunch is ready!; **m. de billar** billiard table; **m.**

camilla = small round table under which a heater is placed; **m. de mezclas** mixing desk; **m. (de) nido** nest of tables; **m. de operaciones** operating table; **m. plegable** folding table (**b**) *(comité)* board, committee; *(en un debate)* panel; **m. directiva** executive board *o* committee; **m. electoral** = group supervising the voting in each ballot box; **m. redonda** *(coloquio)* round table

mesada *nf* (**a**) *Am (pago mensual)* monthly payment, monthly installment (**b**) *RP (para adolescentes)* allowance (**c**) *RP (encimera)* worktop

mesana *nf* (**a**) *(mástil)* mizenmast (**b**) *(vela)* mizensail

mesar 1 *vt* to tear

2 mesarse *vpr* **mesarse los cabellos** to pull *o* tear at one's hair

mescalina *nf* mescalin

mescolanza *nf Fam* hodgepodge, mishmash

mesero, -a *nm,f Col, Guat, Méx, Salv* waiter, *f* waitress

meseta *nf* plateau, tableland

mesetario, -a *adj* of/relating to the Castilian plateau *o* tableland

mesiánico, -a *adj* messianic

mesianismo *nm Rel* messianism; *Fig* blind faith in one person

mesías *nm inv también Fig* Messiah; **el M.** the Messiah

mesilla, *RP* **mesita** *nf* **m. (de noche)** bedside table

mesnada *nf* armed retinue

mesocracia *nf* = government by the middle classes

mesón *nm* (**a**) *Hist* inn (**b**) *(bar, restaurante)* = old, country-style restaurant and bar

mesonero, -a *nm,f Esp* innkeeper

Mesopotamia *n* Mesopotamia

mester *nm Anticuado* trade, craft

mestizaje *nm (de razas)* racial mix; *(de animales)* cross-breeding; *(de culturas)* mixing, cross-fertilization

mestizo, -a 1 *adj (persona)* of mixed race; *(animal, planta)* crossbred

2 *nm,f* person of mixed race

mesura *nf* (**a**) *(moderación)* moderation, restraint; **con m.** in moderation (**b**) *(cortesía)* courtesy, politeness (**c**) *(gravedad)* dignity, seriousness

mesurado, -a *adj* moderate, restrained

mesurarse *vpr* to restrain oneself

meta *nf* (**a**) *Dep (llegada)* finishing line; *(portería)* goal; **marcar en propia m.** to score an own goal; **m. volante** *(en ciclismo)* hot spot sprint (**b**) *(objetivo)* aim, goal; **fijarse una m.** to set oneself a target *o* goal

metabólico, -a *adj* metabolic

metabolismo *nm* metabolism

metabolizar [14] *vt* to metabolize

metacarpo *nm Anat* metacarpus

metacrilato *nm* methacrylate, = transparent resin used in furniture making

metadona *nf* methadone

metafísica *nf (disciplina)* metaphysics *(singular)*

metafísico, -a 1 *adj* metaphysical

2 *nm,f (filósofo)* metaphysicist

metáfora *nf* metaphor

metafórico, -a *adj* metaphorical

metal *nm* (**a**) *(material)* metal; **m. blanco** white metal; **m. pesado** heavy metal; **metales preciosos** precious metals (**b**) *Mús* brass

metalenguaje *nm Inform & Ling* metalanguage

metálico, -a 1 *adj (sonido, color)* metallic; *(objeto)* metal

2 *nm* **pagar en m.** to pay (in) cash

metalizado, -a *adj (pintura)* metallic

metalurgia *nf* metallurgy

metalúrgico, -a 1 *adj* metallurgical
  2 *nm,f* metallurgist
metamórfico, -a *adj* metamorphic
metamorfismo *nm* metamorphism
metamorfosis *nf inv también Fig* metamorphosis
metano *nm* methane
metanol *nm* methanol
metástasis *nf inv Med* metastasis
metatarso *nm Anat* metatarsus
metedura *nf* **m. de pata** blunder
meteórico, -a *adj también Fig* meteoric
meteorito *nm* meteorite
meteoro *nm* meteor
meteorología *nf* meteorology
meteorológico, -a *adj* meteorological
meteorólogo, -a *nm,f* meteorologist; *Rad & TV* weatherman, *f* weatherwoman
metepatas *nmf inv Fam* **es un m.** he's always putting his foot in it
meter 1 *vt* (**a**) *(introducir)* to put in; **m. algo/a alguien en algo** to put sth/sb in sth; **m. la llave en la cerradura** to get the key into the lock; **m. dinero en el banco** to put money in the bank; **he metido mis ahorros en esa empresa** I've put all my savings into this venture; **le metieron en la cárcel** they put him in prison; *Fam* **meterle ideas a alguien en la cabeza** to put ideas into sb's head; *Fam* **no consigo meterle en la cabeza (que…)** I can't get it into his head (that…)
  (**b**) *(hacer participar)* **m. a alguien en algo** to get sb into sth; **¡en buen lío nos has metido!** this is a fine mess you've gotten us into!
  (**c**) *(obligar a)* **m. a alguien a hacer algo** to make sb start doing sth
  (**d**) *(causar)* **m. prisa/miedo a alguien** to rush/scare sb; **m. ruido** to make a noise
  (**e**) *Fam (asestar)* to give; **le metió un puñetazo** he gave him a punch
  (**f**) *Fam (echar, soltar)* to give; **m. una bronca a alguien** to tell sb off; **me metió un rollo sobre la disciplina militar** he gave me this routine about military discipline
  (**g**) *(prenda, ropa)* to take in; **m. el bajo de una falda** to take up a skirt
  (**h**) *(en automóvil)* **m. la primera/la marcha atrás** to go into first gear/reverse
  (**i**) *(en deportes) (anotar)* to score; **nos metieron dos goles** they scored two goals against us
  (**j**) *Fam* **a todo m.** as quickly as possible
  2 meterse *vpr* (**a**) *(entrar)* to get in; **meterse en** to get into
  (**b**) *(en frase interrogativa) (estar)* to get to; **¿dónde se ha metido ese chico?** where has that boy got to?
  (**c**) *(dedicarse)* **meterse a** to become; **meterse a torero** to become a bullfighter
  (**d**) *(involucrarse)* to get involved (**en** in)
  (**e**) *(entrometerse)* to meddle, to interfere; **se mete en todo** he never minds his own business; **meterse por medio** to interfere
  (**f**) *(empezar)* **meterse a hacer algo** to get started on doing sth
  (**g**) **meterse con** *(incordiar)* to hassle; *(atacar)* to go for
  (**h**) *Fam (comer)* to wolf down
  (**i**) *Fam (drogas)* **meterse coca/LSD** to do coke/LSD
meterete, metete *Fam* **1** *adj* **ser m.** to be a busybody
  2 *nm,f* busybody
meticón, -ona *Fam* **1** *adj* **ser m.** to be a busybody
  2 *nm,f* busybody
meticulosidad *nf* meticulousness
meticuloso, -a *adj* meticulous
metido, -a *adj* (**a**) *(implicado)* **andar** *o* **estar m. en** to be

involved in (**b**) *(abundante)* **m. en años** elderly; **m. en carnes** plump
metódico, -a *adj* methodical
metodismo *nm* Methodism
metodista *adj & nmf* Methodist
método *nm* (**a**) *(sistema)* method; **no estoy de acuerdo con sus métodos de hacer las cosas** I don't agree with his way of doing things *o* his methods; **m. anticonceptivo** contraceptive method; **m. (de) Ogino** rhythm method (**b**) *Educ* method
metodología *nf* methodology
metodológico, -a *adj* methodological
metomentodo *Fam* **1** *adj inv* **ser m.** to be a busybody
  2 *nmf* busybody
metonimia *nf* metonymy
metraje *nm* length, running time
metralla *nf* shrapnel
metralleta *nf* submachine gun
métrica *nf Lit* metrics
métrico, -a *adj* (**a**) *(del metro)* metric; **sistema m. decimal** metric system (**b**) *Lit* metrical
metro *nm* (**a**) *(unidad) & Lit* meter; **m. cuadrado/cúbico** square/cubic meter; **metros por segundo** meters per second (**b**) *(transporte)* subway; **en m.** on the *o* by subway (**c**) *(cinta métrica)* tape measure
metrópoli *nf*, **metrópolis** *nf inv* (**a**) *(ciudad)* metropolis (**b**) *(nación)* home country
metropolitano, -a 1 *adj* metropolitan
  2 *nm (metro)* subway
mexicanismo [meçika'nismo] *nm* Mexicanism
mexicano, -a [meçi'kano] *adj & nm,f* Mexican
México ['meçiko] *n* Mexico
mezanine *nm CAm, Col, Méx* mezzanine
mezcla *nf* (**a**) *(unión, conjunto)* mixture; **una m. explosiva** *(de personalidades, factores)* an explosive combination; **una m. de tabacos** a blend of tobaccos (**b**) *(acción)* mixing (**c**) *Mús* mix
mezclador, -ora 1 *nm,f (persona)* mixer
  2 *nm (dispositivo)* mixer; **m. de imagen** switcher; **m. de sonido** mixer
mezclar 1 *vt* (**a**) *(combinar, unir)* to mix; **mezcló la pintura roja con la amarilla** she mixed the red and yellow paint together (**b**) *(confundir, desordenar)* to mix up (**c**) *(implicar)* **m. a alguien en** to get sb mixed up in; **no me mezcles en tus asuntos** don't involve me in your affairs
  2 mezclarse *vpr* (**a**) *(juntarse)* to mix (**con** with); **no me mezclo con gente como esa** I don't mix *o* associate with people like that (**b**) *(difuminarse)* **mezclarse entre** to disappear *o* blend into (**c**) *(implicarse)* **mezclarse en** to get mixed up in
mezclilla *nf* = cloth woven from mixed fibers
mezcolanza *nf Fam* mishmash, hodgepodge
mezquindad *nf* (**a**) *(cualidad)* meanness (**b**) *(acción)* mean action
mezquino¹, -a *adj* mean
mezquino² *nm Méx* wart
mezquita *nf* mosque
mezzanine *nm CAm, Col, Méx* mezzanine
mg *(abrev de* **miligramo**) mg
MHz *(abrev de* **megahercio**) MHz
mi¹ *nm Mús* E; *(en solfeo)* mi
mi² *(pl* **mis**) *adj posesivo* my; **mi casa** my house; **mis libros** my books
mí *pron personal (después de prep)* (**a**) *(en general)* me; **este trabajo no es para mí** this job isn't for me; **no se fía de mí** he doesn't trust me (**b**) *(reflexivo)* myself; **debo pensar más**

en mí (mismo) I should think more about myself (**c**) *(expresiones)* **¡a mí qué!** so what?, why should I care?; **para mí** *(yo creo)* as far as I'm concerned, in my opinion; **por mí** as far as I'm concerned; **por mí, no hay inconveniente** it's fine by me

mía *ver* **mío**

miaja *nf Fam* tiny bit

mialgia *nf Med* myalgia

miasma *nm* miasma

miau *nm* meow

mica *nf* mica

micción *nf Med (acción)* urination

micénico, -a *adj* Mycenaean

michelín *nm Fam* spare tire

mico *nm* (**a**) *(animal)* (long-tailed) monkey (**b**) *(expresiones)* **es un m.** *(pequeño)* he's a midget; *(feo)* he's an ugly devil; *Fig* **ser el último m.** to be the lowest of the low; **me volví m. para hacerlo** I had a devil of a job to do it

micología *nf* mycology

micosis *nf inv* mycosis

micra *nf* micron

micro 1 *nm Fam (abrev de **micrófono**)* mike
   2 *nm o nf Arg, Bol, Chile (microbús)* minibus

microbiano, -a *adj* microbial, microbic

microbio *nm* germ, microbe

microbiología *nf* microbiology

microbús *(pl* **microbuses***) nm* minibus

microcentro *nm RP* business district *(in a city center)*

microchip *(pl* **microchips***) nm* microchip

microcirugía *nf* microsurgery

microclima *nm* microclimate

microcomputador *nm,* **microcomputadora** *nf esp Am* microcomputer

microcosmo *nm,* **microcosmos** *nm inv* microcosm

microcrédito *nm Econ* microcredit

microeconomía *nf* microeconomics *(singular)*

microelectrónica *nf* microelectronics *(singular)*

microempresa *nf Com* very small company

microficha *nf* microfiche

microfilm *(pl* **microfilms***),* **microfilme** *nm* microfilm

micrófono *nm* microphone; **m. de solapa** clip-on microphone

microfotografía *nf* microphotography

microinformática *nf Inform* microcomputing

micrón *nm* micron

microonda 1 *nf* microwave
   2 microondas *nm inv* microwave (oven)

microordenador *nm Esp Inform* microcomputer

microorganismo *nm* microorganism

microprocesador *nm Inform* microprocessor

microscópico, -a *adj* microscopic

microscopio *nm* microscope; **m. electrónico** electron microscope

microsurco *nm* microgroove

mida *etc ver* **medir**

MIDI *nm Inform (abrev de **musical instrument digital interface**)* MIDI

midiera *etc ver* **medir**

miedica *Esp Fam* **1** *adj* yellow, chicken
   2 *nmf* scaredy-cat, coward

miedo *nm* fear; **dar m.** to be frightening; **me da m. conducir** I'm afraid *o* frightened of driving; **meter m. a** to frighten; **por m. a** for fear of; **tener m. a** *o* **de (hacer algo)** to be afraid of (doing sth); **le tiene m. a la oscuridad** he's scared *o* afraid of the dark; **tengo m. de que se estropee** I'm frightened it'll get damaged; *Esp Fam Fig* **de m.: la**

película estuvo de m. the movie was brilliant; **lo pasamos de m.** we had a fantastic time; *muy Fam* **estar cagado de m.** to be shit-scared; **morirse de m.** to die of fright, to be terrified; **m. cerval** terrible fear, terror; **m. escénico** stage fright

miedoso, -a 1 *adj* fearful
   2 *nm,f* fearful person

miel *nf* honey; **las mieles del éxito** the sweet smell of success; *Fig* **m. sobre hojuelas** all the better

miembro 1 *nm* (**a**) *(integrante)* member; **m. fundador** founder member; **m. de pleno derecho** full member (**b**) *(extremidad)* limb, member; **miembros superiores/inferiores** upper/lower limbs; **m. (viril)** penis
   2 *adj* **país/estado m.** member country/state

mienta (**a**) *ver* **mentar** (**b**) *ver* **mentir**

mientes *nfpl* mind; **parar m. (en algo)** to consider (sth); **traer a las m.** to bring to mind

mientras 1 *conj* (**a**) *(al tiempo que)* while; **leía m. comía** she was reading while eating (**b**) *(siempre que)* **m. viva** as long as I live; **m. pueda** as long as I can (**c**) *(hasta que)* **m. no se pruebe lo contrario** until proved otherwise (**d**) **m. (que)** *(por el contrario)* whereas, while
   2 *adv* **m. (tanto)** meanwhile, in the meantime

miércoles *nm inv* Wednesday; **M. de Ceniza** Ash Wednesday; *ver también* **sábado**

mierda *muy Fam* **1** *nf* (**a**) *(excremento)* shit (**b**) *(suciedad)* crap (**c**) *(cosa sin valor)* **es una m.** it's (a load of) crap; **de m.** *(malo)* shitty, crappy (**d**) *Esp (borrachera)* **agarrarse/tener una m.** to get/be shit-faced (**e**) *(expresiones)* **irse a la m.** *(proyecto)* to go down the tubes; **mandar a alguien a la m.** to tell sb to go to hell; **¡vete a la m.!** go to hell!
   2 *nmf* shithead
   3 *interj* **¡m.!** shit!

mies 1 *nf (cereal)* ripe corn
   2 mieses *nfpl (campo)* cornfields

miga *nf (de pan)* crumb; *Fam Fig* **tener m.** *(ser sustancioso)* to have a lot to it; *(ser complicado)* to have more to it than meets the eye; *Culin* **migas** fried breadcrumbs; *Fam* **hacer buenas/ malas migas** to get on well/badly; *Fam* **hacerse migas** *(cosa)* to be smashed to bits; *Fam* **hacer migas a alguien** *(desmoralizar)* to shatter sb

migaja *nf* (**a**) *(trozo)* bit; *(de pan)* crumb (**b**) *(pizca)* scrap; **migajas** *(restos)* leftovers

migra *nf Méx Fam Pey* **la m.** = US police Border Patrol

migración *nf* migration

migrante *nmf* migrant

migraña *nf* migraine

migrar *vi* to migrate

migratorio, -a *adj* migratory

mijo[1] *nm* millet

mijo[2]**, -a** *nm,f Am Fam (a un hijo)* honey; *(a un adulto)* dear; *(entre iguales)* pal, buddy

mil *núm* thousand; **dos m.** two thousand; **m. años/pesos** a thousand years/pesos; **m. cien** one thousand one hundred; *Fig* **m. y una/uno** a thousand and one; **m. y un detalles** a hundred and one details; **miles (de)** *(gran cantidad)* thousands (of); **tengo m. cosas que hacer** I've got loads of things to do; *ver también* **seis**

milagrero, -a *Fam* **1** *adj* (**a**) *(crédulo)* = who believes in miracles (**b**) *(milagroso)* miraculous, miracle-working
   2 *nm,f* = person who believes in miracles

milagro *nm* miracle; **fue un m. que nos encontráramos** it was a wonder *o* miracle we found each other; **se acordó de mi cumpleaños — ¡m.!** he remembered my birthday — wonders will never cease!; **de m.: me acordé de su cumpleaños de m.** by some miracle or other *o* amazingly enough, I remembered his birthday; **cupieron todos de m.**

it was a wonder o miracle that they all fitted in; *Fig* **hacer milagros** to work wonders

milagroso, -a *adj (aparición)* miraculous; *(remedio)* miracle; *(asombroso)* amazing

milamores *nf inv* valerian

milanés, -esa 1 *adj* of/from Milan
   2 *nmf* person from Milan

milanesa *nf* Wiener schnitzel, breaded veal cutlet

milano *nm* kite

milenario, -a 1 *adj (antiguo)* ancient
   2 *nm* millennium

milenio *nm* millennium

milésima *nf* thousandth; **m. de segundo** millisecond

milésimo, -a *núm* thousandth; **la milésima parte** a thousandth

milhojas *nm inv* Culin mille-feuille

mili *nf Esp Antes Fam* military service; **hacer la m.** to do one's military service

milibar *nm (unidad)* millibar

milicia *nf* (a) *(grupo armado)* militia (b) *(profesión)* military (profession)

miliciano, -a *nm,f* militiaman, *f* female soldier

milico *nm Andes, RP Fam Pey (soldado)* soldier; **los milicos tomaron el poder** the military took power

miligramo *nm* milligram

mililitro *nm* milliliter

milimetrado *adj* **papel m.** graph paper

milimétrico, -a *adj* millimetric

milímetro *nm* millimeter; *Fig* **al m.** down to the last detail

militancia *nf* militancy

militante *adj & nmf* militant

militar 1 *adj* military
   2 *nmf* soldier; **los militares** the military
   3 *vi* to be active (**en** in)

militarismo *nm* militarism

militarista *adj & nmf* militarist

militarización *nf* militarization

militarizar [14] *vt* to militarize

militroncho *nm Esp Antes Fam (soldado)* grunt

milla *nf* mile; **m. (marina)** nautical mile

millar *nm* thousand; **un m. de personas** a thousand people

millardo *nm* billion, thousand million

millón *núm* million; **dos millones** two million; **un m. de personas** a million people; **un m. de cosas que hacer** a million things to do; **un m. de gracias** thanks a million; **millones** *(dineral)* millions, a fortune

millonada *nf Fam* **una m.** a fortune, millions

millonario, -a 1 *adj* **es m.** he's a millionaire
   2 *nm,f* millionaire, *f* millionairess

millonésima *nf* millionth

millonésimo, -a *núm* millionth; **la millonésima parte** a millionth

milonga *nf* (a) *(baile)* = popular dance from Argentina and Uruguay (b) *(canción)* = popular song from Argentina and Uruguay

milrayas *nm inv* striped cloth

mimado, -a *adj* spoiled

mimar *vt* to spoil, to pamper

mimbre *nm* wicker; **de m.** wickerwork

mimético, -a *adj* mimetic

mimetismo *nm (de animal, planta)* mimetism

mimetizar [14] *vt* to copy, to imitate

mímica *nf* (a) *(mimo)* mime (b) *(lenguaje)* sign language

mímico, -a *adj* mime; **lenguaje m.** sign language

mimo 1 *nm* (a) *(zalamería)* mollycoddling (b) *(cariño)* show of

affection; **hacerle mimos a alguien** to kiss and cuddle sb (**c**) *Teatro* mime; **hacer m.** to perform mime
   2 *nmf Teatro (artista)* mime artist

mimosa *nf Bot* mimosa

mimoso, -a *adj* affectionate; *Fam* **el bebé está m.** the baby wants a cuddle

min *(abrev de* **minuto**) min

mina *nf* (a) *Geol & Mil* mine; **m. de carbón/oro** coal/gold mine (b) *(cosa rentable)* gold mine (c) *(de lápiz)* lead (d) *CSur Fam (chica)* chick

minar *vt* (a) *Mil* to mine (b) *(socavar)* to undermine; *(salud)* to damage

minarete *nm Arquit* minaret

mineral 1 *adj* mineral
   2 *nm* (a) *Geol* mineral (b) *Min* ore; **m. de hierro** iron ore

mineralizar [14] **1** *vt* to mineralize
   2 mineralizarse *vpr* to become mineralized

mineralogía *nf* minerology

minería *nf* (a) *(técnica)* mining (b) *(sector)* mining industry

minero, -a 1 *adj* mining; *(producción, riqueza)* mineral; **industria minera** mining industry
   2 *nm,f* miner

mineromedicinal *adj* **agua m.** mineral water

minestrone *nf* minestrone

mingitorio, -a 1 *adj* urinary
   2 *nm* urinal

mini *nm Esp Fam* **un m. de cerveza** a liter (glass) of beer

miniatura *nf* miniature; **el apartamento es una m.** the apartment is tiny; **en m.** in miniature

miniaturista *nmf* miniaturist

miniaturizar [14] *vt* to miniaturize

minibar *nm* minibar

minicadena *nf* MIDI system

minicine *nm* = movie theater with several small screens

MiniDisc® *nm inv* MiniDisc®

mini disk, mini disc *nm inv* minidisc

minifalda *nf* miniskirt

minifundio *nm* small holding

minifundismo *nm* = the system of land tenure characterized by the "minifundio"

minifundista *nmf* smallholder

minigolf *(pl* **minigolfs**) *nm* (a) *(lugar)* miniature golf course (b) *(juego)* miniature golf

mínima *nf* (a) *Meteo* low, lowest temperature (b) *(provocación)* **saltar a la m.** to blow up at the least thing

minimalismo *nm Mús* minimalism

minimalista *adj Mús* minimalist

minimizar [14] *vt* to play down

mínimo, -a 1 *adj* (a) *(lo más bajo posible o necesario)* minimum (b) *(lo más bajo temporalmente)* lowest (c) *(muy pequeño) (efecto, importancia)* minimal, very small; *(protesta, ruido)* slightest; **no tengo la más mínima idea** I haven't the slightest idea; **como m.** at the very least; **en lo más m.** in the slightest
   2 *nm (límite)* minimum; **estar bajo mínimos** to have almost run out; **m. común múltiplo** lowest common multiple; **m. personal** *(exento de impuestos)* (personal) tax allowance

minino, -a *nm,f Fam* pussy(cat)

minipímer® *(pl* **minipímers**) *nf* handheld mixer *(for whipping cream, mayonnaise)*

miniserie *nf* miniseries

ministerial *adj* ministerial

ministerio *nm* (a) *Pol (institución)* department; *(periodo)* time as minister; **durante el m. de Sánchez** while Sánchez was minister; **M. de Asuntos Exteriores** Ministry of Foreign Affairs, ≃ State Department; **M. de Economía** Ministry of

Economic Affairs, ≃ Treasury Department; **M. del Interior** Ministry of the Interior, ≃ Department of the Interior **(b)** *Der* **m. público, m. fiscal** public prosecutor **(c)** *Rel* ministry

ministrable *Pol/1 adj* likely to be appointed minister
    2 *nmf* potential minister

ministro, -a *nm,f* **(a)** *Pol* secretary; **primer m.** prime minister; **m. sin cartera** minister without portfolio; **M. de Asuntos Exteriores** Foreign Minister, ≃ Secretary of State; **M. del Interior** Minister of the Interior, ≃ Secretary of the Interior **(b)** *Rel* minister; **m. de Dios** minister of God

minoría *nf* minority; **m. de edad** (legal) minority; **minorías étnicas** ethnic minorities

minorista 1 *adj* retail
    2 *nmf* retailer

minoritario, -a *adj* minority; **partido/gobierno m.** minority party/government; **son un grupo m. dentro del partido** they are a minority within the party

mintiera *etc ver* **mentir**

minucia *nf* trifle, insignificant thing

minuciosidad *nf* meticulousness, attention to detail

minucioso, -a *adj* **(a)** *(meticuloso)* meticulous **(b)** *(detallado)* highly detailed

minué *nm* minuet

minuendo *nm* *Mat* figure from which another is to be subtracted, minuend

minúscula *nf* small letter, lowercase letter

minúsculo, -a *adj* **(a)** *(tamaño)* tiny, minute **(b)** *(letra)* small; *Imprenta* lowercase

minusvalía *nf* **(a)** *Fin* capital loss **(b)** *(física)* handicap, disability

minusválido, -a 1 *adj* disabled, handicapped
    2 *nm,f* disabled *o* handicapped person

minusvalorar *vt* to underestimate

minuta *nf (factura)* fee

minutero *nm* minute hand

minuto *nm* minute; **al m.** *(al momento)* a moment later; **vuelvo en un m.** I'll be back in a minute; **¿tienes un m.?** do you have a minute?; **vivo a cinco minutos de aquí** I live five minutes from here; **no tengo (ni) un m. libre** I don't have a minute free

Miño *nm* **el (río) M.** the Miño River

mío, -a 1 *adj posesivo* mine; **este libro es m.** this book is mine; **un amigo m.** a friend of mine; **no es asunto m.** it's none of my business
    2 *pron posesivo* **el m.** mine; **el m. es rojo** mine is red; *Fam* **esta es la mía** this is the chance I've been waiting for *o* my big chance; **lo m. es el teatro** *(lo que me va)* theater is my thing; *Fam* **los míos** *(mi familia)* my folks; *(mi bando)* my lot, my side

miocardio *nm Anat* myocardium

miope 1 *adj* shortsighted, nearsighted, *Espec* myopic; *Fig* **una política m.** a shortsighted policy
    2 *nmf* shortsighted *o* nearsighted person, *Espec* myopic person

miopía *nf* shortsightedness, nearsightedness, *Espec* myopia

MIR [mir] *Esp (abrev de* **médico interno residente) 1** *nm (examen)* = competitive national examination for placement in house officer's post
    2 *nmf (médico)* intern

mira *nf* **(a)** *(en instrumento, arma)* sight; **m. telescópica** telescopic sight **(b)** *(intención, propósito)* intention; **con miras a** with a view to, with the intention of; **poner la m.** *o* **las miras en algo** to set one's sights on sth

mirada *nf (acción de mirar)* look; *(rápida)* glance; *(de cariño, placer, admiración)* gaze; **apartar la m.** to look away; **dirigir** *o* **lanzar la m. a** to glance at; **echar una m. (a algo)** to glance *o* to have a quick look (at sth); **fulminar con la m. a alguien** to look daggers at sb; **levantar la m.** to look up

mirado, -a *adj* **(a)** *(prudente)* careful **(b)** **ser bien m.** *(bien considerado)* to be well regarded; **es mal m.** *(mal considerado)* he's not well regarded *o* thought of

mirador *nm* **(a)** *(balcón)* enclosed balcony **(b)** *(para ver un paisaje)* viewpoint

miramiento *nm* consideration; **sin miramientos** without the least consideration; **andarse con miramientos** to stand on ceremony

miranda: de miranda *loc adv Esp Fam* **estar de m.** to be loafing around *o* about

mirar 1 *vt* **(a)** *(dirigir la vista a)* to look at; *(observar)* to watch; *(fijamente)* to stare at; **m. algo de cerca/lejos** to look at sth closely/from a distance; **¡míralos!** look at them!; **m. algo por encima** to glance over sth, to have a quick look at sth; **m. a alguien bien/mal** to think highly/poorly of sb; **m. a alguien de arriba abajo** to look sb up and down; *Fig* **m. a alguien por encima del hombro** to look down on sb; *Fam* **de mírame y no me toques** very fragile
    (b) *(fijarse en)* **primero mira cómo lo hago yo** first, watch *o* see how I do it; **mira que no falte nada en las maletas** check to see nothing's missing from the suitcases
    (c) *(examinar)* to check, to look through; **le miraron todas las maletas** they searched all her luggage
    (d) *(considerar)* **mira bien lo que haces** be careful about what you do; **míralo desde este ángulo...** look at it this way...; **bien mirado..., mirándolo bien...** if you think about it...
    2 *vi* **(a)** *(dirigir la vista)* to look; *(observar)* to watch; *(fijamente)* to stare; **¡mira!** look (at that!); **mira, yo creo que...** look, I think (that)...; **mira que te avisé** I told you so; *Esp* **mira por dónde...** guess what?, would you believe it?; **¡mira que eres pesado/tonto!** you're being really tedious/silly!
    (b) *(buscar)* to check, to look; **he mirado en todas partes** I've looked everywhere
    (c) *(orientarse)* **m. a** to face
    (d) *(cuidar)* **m. por alguien/algo** to look after sb/sth; **m. por los demás** to look out for other people
    (e) *Fam (averiguar)* **m. a ver si** to see if *o* whether; **mira a ver si ha llegado la carta** (go and) see if the letter has arrived
    3 mirarse *vpr (uno mismo)* to look at oneself; *(uno al otro)* to look at each other

miríada *nf* myriad

mirilla *nf* **(a)** *(en puerta)* peephole **(b)** *(en arma)* sight

mirlo *nm* blackbird; *Fig* **ser un m. blanco** to be one in a million

mirón, -ona *Fam/1 adj (curioso)* nosy; *(con lascivia)* peeping
    2 *nm,f (espectador)* onlooker; *(curioso)* busybody; *(voyeur)* peeping Tom

mirra *nf* myrrh

mirto *nm* myrtle

misa *nf* Mass; **cantar/decir/oír m.** to sing/say/hear Mass; **ir a m.** to go to Mass *o* church; *Fam Fig* to be gospel; **lo que él dice va a m.** what he says goes; *Fam Fig* **no saber de la m. la media** not to know half the story; **m. cantada/de campaña** sung/open-air Mass; **m. de difuntos** requiem, Mass for the dead; **m. del gallo** midnight Mass *(on Christmas Eve)*; **m. solemne** High Mass

misal *nm* missal

misantropía *nf* misanthropy

misántropo, -a *nm,f* misanthrope, misanthropist

miscelánea *nf* miscellany

misceláneo, -a *adj* miscellaneous

miserable 1 *adj* **(a)** *(pobre)* poor; *(vivienda)* wretched, squalid **(b)** *(penoso, insuficiente)* miserable **(c)** *(vil)* contemptible, base **(d)** *(tacaño)* mean
    2 *nmf* **(a)** *(persona vil)* wretch, vile person **(b)** *(tacaño)* mean person, miser

miseria *nf* (**a**) *(pobreza)* poverty (**b**) *(desgracia)* misfortune (**c**) *(tacañería)* meanness (**d**) *(vileza)* baseness, wretchedness (**e**) *(poco dinero)* pittance; **le pagan una m.** they pay him next to nothing

misericordia *nf* compassion; **pedir m.** to beg for mercy; **para obras de m.** for charity

misericordioso, -a 1 *adj* compassionate, merciful
2 *nm,f Rel* **los misericordiosos** the merciful

mísero, -a *adj* (**a**) *(pobre, desdichado)* wretched, miserable; **ni un m....** not even a measly *o* miserable... (**b**) *(tacaño)* mean, stingy

misil *nm* missile; **m. de crucero** cruise missile; **m. teledirigido** guided missile

misión *nf* (**a**) *(delegación)* mission; *Rel* **misiones** (overseas) missions (**b**) *(cometido)* task, mission; **m. suicida** suicide mission (**c**) *(expedición científica)* expedition

misionero, -a *adj & nm,f Rel* missionary

Misisipí *nm* Mississippi; **el M.** the Mississippi

misiva *nf* missive

mismo, -a 1 *adj* (**a**) *(igual, no otro)* same; **del m. color/tipo que** the same color/type as; **son del m. pueblo** they're from the same village (**b**) *(para enfatizar)* **yo m.** I myself; **¿lo hiciste tú m.?** did you do it (by) yourself?; **en este m. sitio** in this very place; **delante de sus mismas narices** right in front of his nose; **por mí/ti m.** by myself/yourself; *Fam* **¡tú m.!** it's up to you!, suit yourself!
2 *pron* **el m.** the same; **el pueblo ya no era el m.** the town was no longer the same; **el m. que vi ayer** the same one I saw yesterday; **lo m.** the same (thing); **lo m. que** the same as; **da** *o* **es lo m.** it doesn't matter, it doesn't make any difference; **me da lo m.** I don't care; *Fig* **estar en las mismas** to be no further forward
3 *adv (para enfatizar)* **ahora/aquí m.** right now/here; **ayer m.** only yesterday; **llegarán mañana m.** they'll be arriving tomorrow, actually; **por eso m.** precisely for that reason

misoginia *nf* misogyny

misógino, -a 1 *adj* misogynistic
2 *nm,f* misogynist

miss *nf* beauty queen

míster *(pl* **místers)** *nm Fam Dep* **el m.** *(el entrenador)* the boss

misterio *nm* mystery; *Fam* **yo no le veo el m.** I don't see what's so hard to understand about it; **una novela de m.** a mystery

misterioso, -a *adj* mysterious

mística *nf (práctica)* mysticism

misticismo *nm* mysticism

místico, -a 1 *adj* mystical
2 *nm,f (persona)* mystic

mistificación *nf* mystification

mistificar [59] *vt* to mystify

Misuri *nm* Missouri; **el M.** the Missouri

mitad *nf* (**a**) *(parte)* half; **la m. de** half (of); **la m. del tiempo no está** half the time he's not in; **gana la m. que yo** he earns half as much as I do; **me costó la m. que a él** it cost me half what he paid, it cost me half as much as it cost him; **a m. de precio** at half price; **m. y m.** half-and-half; **está m. esperanzado m. triste** he's half hopeful, half downhearted (**b**) *(centro)* middle; **a m. de camino** halfway there; **a m. de (la) película** halfway through the movie; **en m. de** in the middle of; **(cortar algo) por la m.** (to cut sth) in half

mítico, -a *adj* mythical

mitificar [59] *vt* to mythologize

mitigador, -ora *adj* calming

mitigar [38] *vt (aplacar) (miseria, daño, efecto)* to alleviate, to reduce; *(ánimos)* to calm; *(sed)* to slake; *(hambre)* to take the edge off; *(choque, golpe)* to soften; *(dudas, sospechas)* to allay

mitin *nm* rally, meeting

mito *nm* (**a**) *(ficción, leyenda)* myth (**b**) *(personaje)* mythical figure

mitología *nf* mythology

mitológico, -a *adj* mythological

mitomanía *nf* mythomania

mitómano, -a *adj & nm,f* mythomaniac

mitón *nm* (fingerless) mitten

mitosis *nf Biol* mitosis

mitote *nm Méx Fam (alboroto)* commotion

mitra *nf* (**a**) *(tocado)* miter (**b**) *(cargo)* office of archbishop/bishop

mixtificar [59] *vt* to mystify

mixto, -a *adj* mixed; **comisión mixta** joint committee

mixtura *nf* mixture

mízcalo *nm* = edible variety of milk cap mushroom

ml *(abrev de* **mililitro)** ml

mm *(abrev de* **milímetro)** mm

MN *(abrev de* **moneda nacional)** national currency

mnemónico, -a *adj* mnemonic

mnemotecnia *nf* mnemonics *(singular)*

mnemotécnico, -a *adj* mnemonic

moaré *nm* moiré

mobiliario *nm* furniture; **m. urbano** street furniture

moca *nf* mocha

mocasín *nm* moccasin

mocedad *nf* youth

mocetón, -ona *nm,f Fam* strapping lad, *f* strapping lass

mochales *adj inv Esp Fam* **estar m.** to have a screw loose, to be a bit touched

moche: a troche y moche *loc adv* haphazardly

mochila *nf* backpack

mochilero, -a *nm,f* backpacker

mocho, -a 1 *adj (extremo, punta)* blunt; *(árbol)* lopped
2 *nm (fregona)* mop

mochuelo *nm* little owl; *Fam* **cargar con el m.** to be stuck with it

moción *nf* motion; *Pol* **m. de censura/confianza** motion of censure/confidence

moco *nm* (piece of) snot; *Med* mucus; **limpiarse los mocos** to wipe one's nose; **tener mocos** to have a runny nose; *Fam* **llorar a m. tendido** to cry one's eyes out; *Fam* **no ser m. de pavo** to be something not to be sneezed at, to be no mean feat; *Fam* **tirarse el m.** to brag

mocoso, -a 1 *adj* runny-nosed
2 *nm,f Fam* brat

moda *nf (uso, manera)* fashion; *(furor pasajero)* craze; **estar de m.** to be fashionable *o* in fashion; **el escritor/restaurante de m.** the most fashionable writer/restaurant at the moment; **estar pasado de m.** to be unfashionable *o* out of fashion; **pasar de m.** to go out of fashion; **ponerse de m.** to come into fashion; **un bar que se ha puesto muy de m.** a bar that has become very fashionable; **ir a la última m.** to wear the latest fashion

modal 1 *adj* modal
2 modales *nmpl* manners; **tener buenos/malos modales** to have good/bad manners

modalidad *nf* form, type; *Dep* discipline; *Com* **m. de pago** method of payment

modelado *nm* modeling

modelar *vt* (**a**) *Arte* to model; *Fig* to form, to shape (**b**) *Am (ropa)* to model

modélico, -a *adj* model, exemplary

modelismo *nm* modeling

modelo 1 *adj* model
2 *nmf (persona)* model
3 *nm* (**a**) *(arquetipo, diseño, representación)* model; **tengo una**

bicicleta último m. I have the latest model bicycle; **m. económico** economic model; **m. a escala** scale model; **m. matemático** mathematical model; **m. reducido** scale model (**b**) *(prenda de vestir)* number

módem *(pl* **modems**) *nm Inform* modem

moderación *nf* moderation

moderado, -a *adj & nm,f* moderate

moderador, -ora 1 *adj* moderating
2 *nm,f* chair, chairperson

moderar 1 *vt* (**a**) *(templar, atenuar)* to moderate; *(velocidad)* to reduce; **modere el consumo de alcohol** you should try to avoid drinking excessive amounts of alcohol; **modere su velocidad** *(en cartel)* reduce speed (**b**) *(debate)* to chair
2 moderarse *vpr* to restrain oneself; **moderarse en algo** to moderate sth

modernidad *nf* modernity

modernismo *nm* (**a**) *Lit* modernism (**b**) *Arte* Art Nouveau

modernista *adj & nmf* (**a**) *Lit* modernist (**b**) *Arte* Art Nouveau

modernización *nf* modernization

modernizar [14] **1** *vt* to modernize
2 modernizarse *vpr* to modernize

moderno, -a 1 *adj* modern
2 *nm,f Fam* trendy (person)

modestia *nf* modesty; **falsa m.** false modesty

modesto, -a 1 *adj* modest
2 *nm,f* modest person

módico, -a *adj* modest

modificación *nf* alteration

modificar [59] *vt* (**a**) *(variar)* to alter (**b**) *Gram* to modify

modismo *nm* idiom

modista *nmf* (**a**) *(diseñador)* fashion designer (**b**) *(que cose)* tailor, *f* dressmaker

modisto *nm* (**a**) *(diseñador)* fashion designer (**b**) *(sastre)* tailor

modo 1 *nm* (**a**) *(manera, forma)* way; **¿has visto el m. en que** *o* **el m. como te mira?** have you seen how *o* the way he's looking at you?; **no encuentro el m. de dejar el tabaco** whatever I do, I just can't seem to give up smoking; **a m. de** as, by way of; **al m. de** in the style of; **de ese m.** in that way; **de ningún m.** in no way; **de todos modos** in any case, anyway; **de un m. u otro** one way or another; **en cierto m.** in some ways; **m. de empleo** instructions for use; **de m. que** *(así que)* so; **¿de m. que no te gusta?** so, you don't like it (then)?
(**b**) **modos** *(modales)* manners; **buenos/malos modos** good/bad manners
(**c**) *Gram* mood; **m. adverbial** adverbial phrase
2 ni modo *loc adv Am salvo RP* no way, not a chance

modorra *nf Fam* drowsiness; **tener m.** to be *o* feel sleepy

modoso, -a *adj (recatado)* modest; *(formal)* well-behaved

modulación *nf* modulation; *Elec* **m. de frecuencia** frequency modulation

modulador, -ora 1 *adj* modulating
2 *nm* modulator

modular 1 *adj* modular
2 *vt* to modulate

módulo *nm* (**a**) *(pieza, unidad)* module (**b**) *(de muebles)* unit; **m. de cocina** kitchen unit

modus operandi *nm inv* modus operandi

modus vivendi *nm inv* way of life

mofa *nf* mockery; **hacer m. de** to mock

mofarse *vpr* to scoff; **m. de** to mock

mofeta *nf* skunk

moflete *nm* chubby cheek

mofletudo, -a *adj* chubby-cheeked

Mogadiscio *n* Mogadishu

mogol, -a 1 *adj* Mongolian
2 *nm,f (persona)* Mongol, Mongolian
3 *nm (lengua)* Mongol, Mongolian

mogollón *Esp Fam* **1** *nm* (**a**) **m. de** *(muchos)* tons of, loads of (**b**) *(lío)* row, commotion; **entraron/salieron a m.** everyone rushed in/out at once
2 *adv* loads

mogrebí *(pl* **mogrebíes** *o* **mogrebíes**) *adj & nmf* Maghrebi

mohair [mo'er] *nm* mohair

mohín *nm* grimace, face

mohíno, -a *adj* (**a**) *(triste)* sad, melancholy (**b**) *(enfadado)* sulky

moho *nm* (**a**) *(hongo)* mold (**b**) *(herrumbre)* rust

mohoso, -a *adj* (**a**) *(con hongo)* moldy (**b**) *(oxidado)* rusty

Moisés *n pr* Moses

moisés *nm inv* bassinet

mojado, -a *adj (empapado)* wet; *(húmedo)* damp; *Fig* **llover sobre m.** to be just too much

mojama *nf* dried salted tuna

mojar 1 *vt* to wet; *(humedecer)* to moisten; *(comida)* to dunk
2 mojarse *vpr* (**a**) *(con agua)* to get wet; **se ha mojado la ropa** the clothes have got wet; **no dejes que se moje la cámara** don't let the camera get wet (**b**) *Fam (comprometerse)* **yo prefiero no mojarme** I don't want to get involved; **no se moja por nadie** he wouldn't stick his neck out for anyone

mojigatería *nf* (**a**) *(beatería)* prudery (**b**) *(falsa humildad)* sanctimoniousness

mojigato, -a 1 *adj* (**a**) *(beato)* prudish (**b**) *(falsamente humilde)* sanctimonious
2 *nm,f* (**a**) *(beato)* prude (**b**) *(falsamente humilde)* sanctimonious person

mojito *nm* mojito, = cocktail containing rum, sugar, lemon juice and mint

mojón *nm (piedra)* milestone; *(poste)* milepost

moka *nf* mocha

molar¹ 1 *adj* **diente m.** molar
2 *nm* molar

molar² ** *vi Esp Fam* **¡cómo (me) mola esa moto/ese chico! that motorbike/that guy is really cool!

molcajete *nm Méx* mortar

Moldavia *n* Moldavia

moldavo, -a *adj & nm,f* Moldavian

molde *nm (objeto hueco)* mold; *(de hornear)* baking sheet

moldeado *nm* (**a**) *Esp (del pelo)* soft perm, body wave (**b**) *(de figura, cerámica)* molding

moldeador, -ora 1 *adj* molding
2 *nm Esp (del pelo)* soft perm

moldear *vt* (**a**) *(dar forma)* to mold (**b**) *(sacar un molde)* to cast (**c**) *(cabello)* to give a soft perm to

moldura *nf* molding

mole 1 *nf* hulk
2 *nm Méx* = thick, cooked chilli sauce

molécula *nf* molecule

molecular *adj* molecular

moler [41] *vt* (**a**) *(pulverizar)* to grind; *(trigo)* to mill; *(aceitunas)* to press (**b**) *(destrozar)* to beat; **lo molieron a palos** he was beaten to a pulp; **estas zapatillas me están moliendo los pies** these shoes are killing my feet (**c**) *Fam (cansar)* to wear out

molestar 1 *vt* (**a**) *(perturbar)* to bother; **perdone que le moleste...** I'm sorry to bother you...; **¿le molesta que fume?** do you mind if I smoke? (**b**) *(doler)* **me molesta la pierna** my leg is giving me a bit of trouble; **me molesta un poco la herida** my wound is rather uncomfortable *o* a bit sore (**c**) *(ofender)* to upset; **me molestó que no me saludaras** I was rather upset that you didn't say hello to me
2 *vi* **vámonos, aquí no hacemos más que m.** let's go,

we're in the way here; **deja ya de m. con tantas preguntas** stop being such a nuisance and asking all those questions; **no m.** *(en letrero)* do not disturb

3 molestarse *vpr* (a) *(incomodarse)* to bother; **no te molestes, yo lo haré** don't bother, I'll do it; **molestarse en hacer algo** to bother to do sth; **molestarse por alguien/algo** to put oneself out for sb/sth (b) *(ofenderse)* **molestarse (por algo)** to take offense (at sth)

molestia *nf* (a) *(incomodidad)* bother, trouble; **ocasionar** *o* **causar molestias a alguien** to cause sb trouble; **si no es demasiada m.** if it's not too much trouble; **perdone la m., pero…** sorry to bother you, but…; **tomarse la m. de hacer algo** to take the trouble to do sth (b) *(malestar)* discomfort

molesto, -a *adj* (a) **ser m.** *(costumbre, ruido)* to be annoying; *(humo, sensación)* to be unpleasant; *(visita)* to be inconvenient (b) **estar m.** *(ofendido)* to be upset; *(con malestar)* to be in discomfort; *(incómodo)* to be uncomfortable

molestoso, -a *Am salvo RP Fam* **1** *adj* annoying
2 *nm,f* nuisance

molicie *nf* (a) *(blandura)* softness (b) *(comodidad)* luxurious *o* easy living

molido, -a *adj* (a) *(pulverizado)* ground; *(trigo)* milled (b) *Fam (cansado)* worn out; **estar m. de** to be worn out from

molienda *nf (acción de moler)* grinding; *(de trigo)* milling

molinero, -a 1 *adj* milling
2 *nm,f* miller

molinete *nm* (a) *(ventilador)* exhaust fan (b) *(juguete)* toy windmill

molinillo *nm* grinder; **m. de café** coffee grinder; **m. de pimienta** pepper mill

molino *nm* mill; **m. de aceite** olive-oil mill; **m. de viento** windmill

molla *nf* (a) *(parte blanda)* flesh (b) *Esp* **mollas** *(gordura)* flab

molleja *nf* gizzard

mollera *nf Fam (cabeza)* nut; **ser duro de m.** *(estúpido)* to be thick in the head; *(testarudo)* to be pigheaded

molón, -ona *adj Esp Fam* (a) *(que gusta)* neat (b) *(elegante)* smart

molusco *nm* mollusk

momentáneo, -a *adj (de un momento)* momentary; *(pasajero)* temporary

momento *nm* (a) *(instante)* moment; **a cada m.** all the time; **al m.** straightaway; **de un m. a otro** any minute now; **de m., por el m.** for the time being *o* moment; **dentro de un m.** in a moment *o* minute; **desde el m. (en) que…** *(tiempo)* from the moment that…; **por momentos** by the minute; **en todo m.** at all times (b) *(periodo, ocasión)* time; **llegó un m. en que…** there came a time when…; **has venido en buen/mal m.** you've come at a good/bad time; **del m.** *(actual)* of the day

momia *nf* mummy

momificar [59] **1** *vt* to mummify
2 momificarse *vpr* to mummify

momio, -a *adj Chile Fam (carcamal)* square, untrendy

mona *nf Fam (borrachera)* **coger una m.** to get legless; **dormir la m.** to sleep it off

monacal *adj* monastic

Mónaco *n* Monaco

monada *nf Fam* (a) *(persona)* little beauty (b) *(cosa)* lovely thing (c) *(gracia)* antic

monaguillo *nm* altar boy

monarca *nm* monarch

monarquía *nf* monarchy; **m. absoluta/constitucional/parlamentaria** absolute/constitutional/parliamentary monarchy

monárquico, -a 1 *adj* monarchic
2 *nm,f* monarchist

monasterio *nm (de monjes)* monastery; *(de monjas)* convent

monástico, -a *adj* monastic

Moncloa *nf* **la M.** = residence of the Spanish premier which by extension refers to the Spanish government

monda *nf (piel)* peel; *Esp Fam* **ser la m.** *(extraordinario)* to be amazing; *(gracioso)* to be a scream

mondadientes *nm inv* toothpick

mondadura *nf (piel)* peel

mondar 1 *vt* to peel
2 mondarse *vpr Esp Fam* **mondarse (de risa)** to laugh one's head off

mondo, -a *adj (pelado, limpio)* bare; *(huesos)* picked clean; *Fam* **dejaron el pollo m. y lirondo** they picked the chicken clean; **la verdad monda y lironda** the plain unvarnished truth

mondongo *nm Méx, RP, Ven* tripe

moneda *nf* (a) *(pieza)* coin; **una m. de diez pesos** a ten peso coin; *Fig* **pagar a alguien con** *o* **en la misma m.** to pay sb back in kind; *Fig* **ser m. corriente** to be commonplace; **m. falsa** counterfeit coin (b) *Fin (divisa)* currency; **m. de curso legal** legal tender; **m. débil** weak currency; **m. extranjera** foreign currency; **m. fuerte** strong currency; **m. única** single currency

monedero *nm* purse; **m. electrónico** electronic purse

monegasco, -a *adj & nm,f* Monacan, Monegasque

monería *nf Fam (gracia)* antic; *(bobada)* foolish act

monetario, -a *adj* monetary

monetarismo *nm Econ* monetarism

monetarista *adj Econ* monetarist

mongol, -ola 1 *adj* Mongolian
2 *nm,f (persona)* Mongol, Mongolian
3 *nm (lengua)* Mongol, Mongolian

Mongolia *n* Mongolia

mongólico, -a 1 *adj* Down syndrome; **niño m.** child with Down syndrome
2 *nm,f* person with Down syndrome

mongolismo *nm* Down syndrome

monigote *nm* (a) *(muñeco)* rag *o* paper doll (b) *(dibujo)* doodle (c) *Pey (persona)* puppet

monitor, -ora 1 *nm,f (persona)* instructor; **m. de esquí** skiing instructor
2 *nm Inform & Mec* monitor; **m. en color** color monitor

monitorear *vt Am* to monitor

monitorio, -a *adj Formal* admonitory

monitorizar [14] *vt* to monitor

monja *nf* nun

monje *nm* monk

monjil *adj (de monje)* monk's; *(de monja)* nun's

mono, -a 1 *adj Fam* lovely
2 *nm,f (animal)* monkey; *Fam* **¿qué miras? ¿tengo monos en la cara?** what are you looking at? have I got two heads or something?; *Fam* **ser el último m.** to be bottom of the heap
3 *nm* (a) *(prenda) (con mangas)* coveralls; *(con peto)* overalls (b) *Ven (ropa deportiva)* tracksuit (c) *Esp Fam (síndrome de abstinencia)* withdrawal symptoms; **un ladrón estaba con el m.** a thief who was desperate for drugs; **tengo m. de playa** I'm dying to go to the beach

monocarril *adj & nm* monorail

monocolor *adj* monochrome

monocorde *adj* (a) *(monótono)* monotonous (b) *Mús* single-stringed

monóculo *nm* monocle

monocultivo *nm Agr* monoculture

monoesquí *(pl* **monoesquís** *o* **monoesquíes)** *nm* mono-ski

monofásico, -a *adj Elec* single-phase

monogamia *nf* monogamy

monógamo, -a 1 *adj* monogamous

   2 *nm,f* monogamous person

monografía *nf* monograph

monográfico, -a *adj* monographic

monokini *nm* monokini

monolingüe *adj* monolingual

monolítico, -a *adj* monolithic

monolito *nm* monolith

monologar [38] *vi* to give a monologue

monólogo *nm* monologue; *Teatro* soliloquy

monomando 1 *adj* **grifo m.** = faucet that combines hot and
cold water

   2 *nm* = faucet that combines hot and cold water

monomanía *nf* obsession

monomaníaco, -a, monomaniaco, -a *adj & nm,f*
obsessive

monoparental *adj* **familia m.** one-parent *o* single-parent
family

monopatín *nm Esp* skateboard

monoplano, -a 1 *adj* monoplane

   2 *nm* monoplane

monoplaza 1 *adj* single-seater; **avión m.** single-seater
airplane

   2 *nm* single-seater

monopolio *nm* monopoly

monopolización *nf* monopolization

monopolizador, -ora 1 *adj* monopolistic

   2 *nm,f* monopolist

monopolizar [14] *vt también Fig* to monopolize

monorraíl, *Am* **monorriel** *adj & nm* monorail

monosilábico, -a *adj* monosyllabic

monosílabo, -a 1 *adj* monosyllabic

   2 *nm* monosyllable; **responder con monosílabos** to reply
in monosyllables

monoteísmo *nm* monotheism

monoteísta 1 *adj* monotheistic

   2 *nmf* monotheist

monotipo *nm Imprenta* Monotype

monotonía *nf* (a) *(uniformidad)* monotony (b) *(entonación)*
monotone

monótono, -a *adj* monotonous

monovolumen *nm Aut* people mover

monóxido *nm Quím* monoxide; **m. de carbono** carbon
monoxide

Monrovia *n* Monrovia

monseñor *nm* Monsignor

monserga *nf Esp Fam* drivel

monstruo *nm* (a) *(ser fantástico)* monster (b) *(prodigio)* giant,
marvel

monstruosidad *nf* (a) *(anomalía)* freak (b) *(enormidad)*
hugeness (c) *(crueldad)* monstrosity, atrocity (d) *(fealdad)*
hideousness

monstruoso, -a *adj* (a) *(enorme)* huge, enormous (b)
(deforme) terribly deformed (c) *(cruel)* monstrous (d) *(feo)*
hideous

monta *nf* (a) *(suma)* total (b) *(importancia)* importance; **de
poca/mucha m.** of little/great importance (c) *(en caballo)*
ride, riding

montacargas *nm inv* freight elevator

montado *nm Esp (bocadillo)* = small piece of bread with a
savory topping

montador, -ora *nm,f* (a) *(obrero)* fitter (b) *Cine* editor

montaje *nm* (a) *(de máquina)* assembly (b) *Teatro* staging (c)
Fot montage (d) *Cine* editing (e) *(farsa)* put-up job

montante *nm* (a) *Arquit (de armazón)* upright; *(de ventana)*

mullion; *(de puerta)* jamb (b) *(ventanuco)* fanlight (c) *(importe)*
total; *Com* **montantes compensatorios** compensating
duties

montaña *nf* mountain; **pasaremos el verano en la m.**
we'll spend summer in the mountains; *Fam* **una m. de** *(un
montón de)* piles of; **tengo una m. de papeles sobre mi
mesa** I've got a mountain of papers on my desk; *Fig* **hacer
una m. de algo** to make a big thing of sth; *Fig* **hacer una
m. de un grano de arena** to make a mountain out of a
molehill; **Montañas Rocosas** Rocky Mountains; **m. rusa**
roller coaster

montañero, -a 1 *adj* mountaineering

   2 *nm,f* mountaineer

montañés, -esa 1 *adj* (a) *(de la montaña)* **pueblo m.**
mountain village (b) *Esp (cántabro)* of/from Cantabria

   2 *nm,f* (a) *(de la montaña)* **los montañeses** the people living
in the mountains (b) *Esp (cántabro)* person from Cantabria

montañismo *nm* mountaineering

montañoso, -a *adj* mountainous

montar 1 *vt* (a) *(ensamblar) (máquina, estantería)* to assemble;
(tienda de campaña, tenderete) to put up (b) *(encajar)* **m. algo en
algo** to fit sth into sth (c) *(organizar) (negocio, piso)* to set up;
m. una *o* **la casa** to set up home; *Fam* **me montó una
escena** *o* **escándalo** she made a scene in front of me (d)
(cabalgar) to ride (e) *(poner encima)* **m. a alguien en** to lift sb
onto (f) *Esp Culin (nata)* to whip; *(claras, yemas)* to beat (g)
Teatro to stage (h) *Cine* to edit

   2 *vi* (a) *(subir)* to get on; *(en vehículo)* to get in; **m. en** *(subir)* to
get onto; *(vehículo)* to get into; *(animal)* to mount (b) *(ir
montado)* to ride; **m. en bicicleta/a caballo** to ride a
bicycle/a horse (c) *(sumar)* **m. a** to come to, to total; **tanto
monta** it's all the same

   3 montarse *vpr* (a) *(subirse)* to get on; *(en vehículo)* to get in;
(en caballo) to mount; **montarse en** *(subirse)* to get onto;
(vehículo) to get into; *(caballo)* to mount; **nos montamos en
todas las atracciones** we went on all the rides (b) *Esp Fam*
montárselo to work it, to organize things

montaraz *adj* (a) *(del monte)* **un animal m.** a wild animal (b)
(tosco, rudo) savage, wild

Mont Blanc *nm* **el M.** Mont Blanc

monte *nm* (a) *(elevación)* mountain; **M. Sinaí** Mount Sinai;
m. de Venus mons veneris (b) *(terreno) (con arbustos)*
scrubland; *(bosque)* woodland; **echarse** *o* **tirarse al m.** to
take to the hills; *Fig* to go to extremes; *Prov* **no todo el m. es
orégano** life's not a bowl of cherries; **m. bajo** scrub (c) *Méx
(pasto)* pasture (d) *Esp* **m. de piedad** state pawnbroker

montenegrino, -a *adj & nm,f* Montenegran

montepío *nm* mutual aid society

montera *nf* bullfighter's hat

montés *(pl* **monteses)** *adj* wild

montevideano, -a 1 *adj* of/from Montevideo

   2 *nm,f* person from Montevideo

Montevideo *n* Montevideo

montículo *nm* hillock

montilla *nm* Montilla, = fortified sherry-type wine from
Montilla near Córdoba

monto *nm* total

montón *nm* (a) *(pila)* heap, pile; **a** *o* **en m.** everything
together *o* at once; *Fam* **del m.** ordinary, run-of-the-mill (b)
Fam **un m. de** a load of, loads of; **sabe un m. de
astronomía** he knows loads about astronomy; **me gusta
un m.** I'm mad about him; **me duele un m.** it hurts like
mad; **a montones** by the bucketload; **tiene dinero a
montones** she's got loads of money, she's loaded

Montreal *n* Montreal

montura *nf* (a) *(cabalgadura)* mount (b) *(arreos)* harness;
(silla) saddle (c) *(soporte) (de gafas)* frame; *(de joyas)* mounting

monumental *adj* (**a**) *(ciudad, lugar)* famous for its monuments (**b**) *(fracaso, éxito)* monumental

monumento *nm* (**a**) *(obra)* monument; **m. a los caídos** *(en guerra)* war memorial (**b**) *(mujer atractiva)* stunner

monzón *nm* monsoon

monzónico, -a *adj* monsoon; **lluvias monzónicas** monsoon rains

moña *nf* (**a**) *Esp Fam (borrachera)* **coger una m.** to get smashed (**b**) *(adorno)* ribbon

moñita *nf Urug* bow tie

moñito *nm Arg* bow tie

moño *nm* (**a**) *(de pelo)* bun *(of hair)*; **hacerse un m.** to put one's hair up in a bun; *Fig* **agarrarse del m.** *(pegarse)* to pull each other's hair out; *Esp Fam* **estar hasta el m. (de)** to be sick to death (of) (**b**) *Am (lazo)* bow (**c**) *Méx (pajarita)* bow tie

moquear *vi* to have a runny nose

moqueta *Esp,* **moquette** [mo'ket] *RP nf* wall-to-wall carpet

moquillo *nm (enfermedad de animal)* distemper

mor: por mor de *loc adv* on account of, for the sake of; **por m. de la verdad, debo decírselo** out of respect for the truth I have to tell him

mora *nf* (**a**) *(de la zarzamora)* blackberry (**b**) *(del moral)* mulberry

morada *nf* dwelling

morado, -a 1 *adj (color)* purple; *Esp Fam Fig* **pasarlas moradas** to have a bad time of it; *Esp Fam Fig* **las pasamos moradas para encontrar alojamiento** it was a nightmare finding somewhere to stay; *Esp Fam Fig* **ponerse m.** *(de comida)* to stuff oneself; **nos pusimos morados de cerveza** we drank gallons of beer; **me puse m. a bailar** I did nothing but dance

2 *nm* (**a**) *(color)* purple (**b**) *(moratón)* bruise

morador, -ora *nm,f* inhabitant

moradura *nf* bruise

moral 1 *adj* moral; **tienen el apoyo m. de todos nosotros** they have our moral support

2 *nf* (**a**) *(ética)* morals, morality; **m. estricta** strict morals (**b**) *(ánimo)* morale; **su victoria nos dio mucha m.** her win lifted our spirits *o* improved our morale; **estar bajo de m.** to be in poor spirits; **levantarle** *o* **subirle la m. a alguien** to lift sb's spirits, to cheer sb up

3 *nm (árbol)* mulberry tree

moraleja *nf* moral

moralidad *nf* morality

moralina *nf* moralizing

moralismo *nm* moralism

moralista *nmf* moralist

moralizar [14] *vi* to moralize

morapio *nm Esp Fam* cheap red wine

morar *vi* to dwell (**en** in)

moratón *nm* bruise

moratoria *nf* moratorium

morbidez *nf* delicacy

mórbido, -a *adj* (**a**) *(gen)* & *Med* morbid (**b**) *(delicado)* delicate

morbilidad *nf Med* morbidity

morbo *nm Fam* **el m. atrajo a la gente al lugar del accidente** people were attracted to the scene of the accident by a sense of morbid fascination; **los cementerios le dan mucho m.** he gets a morbid pleasure out of visiting cemeteries; **esa chica tiene mucho m.** there's something weirdly attractive about that girl

morbosidad *nf* **la m. de la historia atrajo a los espectadores** the morbidity of the story attracted the spectators; **abordaron la información del accidente con mucha m.** they reported the accident rather morbidly

morboso, -a 1 *adj (persona, interés)* morbid, ghoulish; *(escena, descripción)* gruesome

2 *nm,f* ghoul

morcilla *nf Culin* blood sausage; *Esp Fam* **¡que te/os den m.!** you can stuff it, then!

morcillo *nm* foreknuckle

morcón *nm* cured pork sausage

mordacidad *nf* sharpness, mordacity

mordaz *adj* caustic, biting

mordaza *nf* gag

mordedura *nf* bite

morder [41] **1** *vt* (**a**) *(con los dientes)* to bite (**b**) *(gastar)* to eat into (**c**) *Carib, Méx Fam (sobornar)* to buy off

2 *vi Fam* **salúdala, que no muerde** you can say hello to her, she doesn't bite; *Fam* **está que muerde** he's hopping mad

3 morderse *vpr* **morderse la lengua/las uñas** to bite one's tongue/nails

mordida *nf CAm, Méx Fam (soborno)* bribe

mordisco *nm* (**a**) *(con los dientes)* bite; **dar** *o* **pegar un m. a algo** to take a bite of sth; **¿me dejas darle un m.?** can I have a bite?; **a mordiscos** by biting (**b**) *(beneficio)* **un buen m.** a nice fat profit

mordisquear *vt* to nibble (at)

morena *nf (pez)* moray eel

moreno, -a 1 *adj* (**a**) *(pelo, piel)* dark; *(por el sol)* tanned; **ponerse m.** to get a tan (**b**) *(pan, azúcar)* brown

2 *nmf (por el pelo)* dark-haired person; *(por la piel)* dark-skinned person

morera *nf* white mulberry tree

morería *nf* Moorish quarter

moretón *nm* bruise

morfema *nm* morpheme

morfina *nf* morphine

morfinómano, -a 1 *adj* addicted to morphine

2 *nm,f* morphine addict

morfología *nf* morphology

morfológico, -a *adj* morphological

morganático, -a *adj* morganatic

morgue *nf* morgue

moribundo, -a 1 *adj* dying

2 *nm,f* dying person

morir [27] **1** *vi* (**a**) *(fallecer)* to die; **murió apuñalado** he was stabbed to death; **murió asesinado** he was murdered; **murió ahogado** he drowned (**b**) *(río, calle)* **este río muere en el lago** this river runs into the lake; **aquel camino muere en el bosque** that path peters out in the forest (**c**) *(fuego)* to die down; *(luz)* to go out; *(día)* to come to a close

2 morirse *vpr* (**a**) *(fallecer)* to die (**de** of); **se le ha muerto la madre** his mother has died; *Fam* **nadie se muere por hacer unas cuantas horas extras** a few hours of overtime never hurt anyone (**b**) *(sentir con fuerza)* **morirse de envidia/ira** to be burning with envy/rage; **morirse de risa** to die laughing; **me muero de ganas de ir a bailar** I'm dying to go dancing; **me muero de hambre/frío** I'm starving/freezing; **morirse por algo** to be dying for sth; **morirse por alguien** to be crazy about sb

morisco, -a 1 *adj* = referring to Moors in Spain baptized after the Reconquest

2 *nm,f* baptized Moor

mormón, -ona *adj* & *nm,f* Mormon

moro, -a 1 *adj* (**a**) *Hist* Moorish (**b**) *Esp muy Fam (machista)* sexist

2 *nm,f* (**a**) *Hist* Moor; **moros y cristianos** = traditional Spanish festival involving mock battle between Moors and Christians; *Fig* **no hay moros en la costa** the coast is clear (**b**) *Esp Fam Pey (árabe)* Arab, = pejorative term referring to a North African or Arab person

3 *nm Esp Fam (machista)* sexist man

morocho, -a *adj Andes, RP (moreno)* dark-haired

morosidad *nf* (**a**) *Com* defaulting, failure to pay on time (**b**) *(lentitud)* slowness

moroso, -a *Com* **1** *adj* defaulting

2 *nm,f* defaulter, bad debtor

morral *nm Mil* haversack; *(de cazador)* game bag

morralla *nf* (**a**) *Pey (personas)* scum; *(cosas)* junk (**b**) *(pescado)* small fry (**c**) *Méx (suelto)* loose change

morrazo *nf Fam* **darse** *o* **pegarse un m. contra algo** to thump *o* bump one's head against sth

morrear *Esp Fam* **1** *vi* to smooch

2 morrearse *vpr* to smooch

morreo *nm Esp Fam* smooch

morriña *nf Esp (por el país)* homesickness; *(por el pasado)* nostalgia

morro *nm* (**a**) *(hocico)* snout (**b**) *Esp (de avión)* nose; *(de coche)* front (**c**) *Esp Fam* **morros** *(labios)* lips; **estar de morros** to be in a bad mood; **romperle los morros a alguien** to smash sb's face in (**d**) *Esp Fam (caradura)* **¡qué m. tiene!** he's got a real nerve!

morrocotudo, -a *adj Fam* tremendous

morrón 1 *adj* **pimiento m.** red pepper

2 *nm Esp Fam* **darse un m.** to give oneself a real thump

morsa *nf* walrus

morse *nm* Morse (code)

mortadela *nf* mortadella

mortaja *nf* shroud

mortal 1 *adj (no inmortal)* mortal; *(caída, enfermedad)* fatal; *(aburrimiento, odio, enemigo)* deadly

2 *nmf* mortal

mortalidad *nf* mortality; **m. infantil** infant mortality

mortalmente *adv (enfermo, herido)* mortally, fatally

mortandad *nf* mortality

mortecino, -a *adj (luz, brillo)* faint; *(color, mirada)* dull

mortero *nm* (**a**) *(de cocina) (cuenco)* mortar; *(conjunto)* pestle and mortar (**b**) *(para construcción)* mortar (**c**) *(arma)* mortar

mortífero, -a *adj* deadly

mortificación *nf* mortification

mortificante *adj* mortifying

mortificar [59] **1** *vt* to mortify

2 mortificarse *vpr (torturarse)* to torment oneself

mortuorio, -a *adj* death; **cámara mortuoria** funerary chamber

moruno, -a *adj* Moorish; *Esp Culin* **pincho m.** = kebab of marinated pork

mosaico *nm* (**a**) *(artístico)* mosaic; **un m. de colores/ ideologías** a patchwork of colors/ideologies (**b**) *Am (baldosa)* tile

mosca 1 *nf* fly; *Fig* **aflojar** *o* **soltar la m.** to cough up, to fork out; *Fig* **cazar moscas** to twiddle one's thumbs; *Fam* **estar con** *o* **tener la m. detrás de la oreja** to be suspicious *o* distrustful; *Fam* **no se oía ni una m.** you could have heard a pin drop; *Fam* **por si las moscas** just in case; *Fam Fig* **¿qué m. te ha picado?** what's up with you?; *Fam Fig* **m. muerta** slyboots, hypocrite; **m. tse-tsé** tsetse fly

2 *adj inv Esp* **estar m.** *(con sospechas)* to smell a rat; *(enfadado)* to be in a mood

moscada *adj* **nuez m.** nutmeg

moscardón *nm* (**a**) *Zool* blowfly (**b**) *Fam (persona)* pest, creep

moscatel *nm* Muscatel, = dessert wine made from muscat grapes; **uvas de m.** muscat grapes

moscón *nm* (**a**) *Zool* flesh fly, bluebottle (**b**) *Fam (persona)* pest, creep

moscovita *adj & nmf* Muscovite

Moscú *n* Moscow

mosqueado, -a *adj Fam* (**a**) *(enfadado)* in a huff; **estar m. con alguien** to be in a huff with sb (**b**) *(con sospechas)* suspicious

mosquear *Fam* **1** *vt* (**a**) *(enfadar)* **m. a alguien** to tick sb off (**b**) *(hacer sospechar)* to make suspicious; **me mosquea que no haya llamado todavía** I'm a bit surprised he hasn't phoned yet

2 mosquearse *vpr (enfadarse)* to get in a huff

mosqueo *nm Fam* (**a**) *(enfado)* annoyance, anger (**b**) *(sospechas)* **tener/cogerse un m.** to be/get suspicious

mosquete *nm* musket

mosquetero *nm* musketeer

mosquetón *nm* short carbine

mosquitera *nf,* **mosquitero** *nm* mosquito net

mosquito *nm* mosquito

mosso d'esquadra *nm* = member of the Catalan police force

mostacho *nm* mustache

mostaza *nf* mustard

mosto *nm (residuo)* must; *(zumo de uva)* grape juice

mostrador *nm (en tienda)* counter; *(en bar)* bar; *(en aeropuerto)* desk; **m. de información/facturación** information/check-in desk

mostrar [63] **1** *vt* to show; **mostró su satisfacción por la concesión del premio** she expressed pleasure at having been awarded the prize

2 mostrarse *vpr* **se mostró muy amable con los invitados** he was very nice to the guests; **se mostró muy interesado** he expressed great interest; **se mostró reacia a colaborar** she was reluctant to cooperate; **se mostró conforme con el plan** he agreed to the plan

mostrenco, -a 1 *adj (sin dueño)* without an owner, unclaimed

2 *nm,f Fam (torpe)* thick *o* stupid person

mota *nf (de polvo)* speck; *(en una tela)* dot

mote *nm* nickname

moteado, -a *adj* speckled

motejar *vt (poner mote a)* to nickname; **m. a alguien de algo** to brand sb sth

motel *nm* motel

motero, -a *nm,f Fam* biker

motín *nm (del pueblo)* uprising, riot; *(de las tropas, en barco)* mutiny; *(en cárcel)* riot

motivación *nf* motivation

motivado, -a *adj (persona)* motivated

motivar *vt (impulsar)* to motivate; *(causar)* to cause

motivo *nm* (**a**) *(causa)* reason, cause; *(de crimen)* motive; **con m. de** *(por causa de)* because of; *(para celebrar)* on the occasion of; *(con el fin de)* in order to; **dar m. a** to give reason to; **no ser m. para** to be no reason to *o* for; **tener motivos para** to have reason to; **sin m.** for no reason; **m. de queja** ground *o* grounds for complaint (**b**) *Arte, Lit & Mús* motif

moto *nf* motorcycle, motorbike

motocicleta *nf* motorbike, motorcycle

motociclismo *nm* motorcycling

motociclista *nmf* motorcyclist

motociclo *nm* motorcycle

motocross *nm* motocross

motoesquí *(pl* **motoesquís** *o* **motoesquíes**) *nm* Snowbike®

motonáutica *nf* speedboat racing

motonáutico, -a *adj* speedboat; **competición motonáutica** speedboat race

motoneta *nf Am (motor)* scooter

motonetista *nmf Am* scooter rider

motor, -ora o **-triz 1** adj motor

  2 nm (**a**) (aparato) motor, engine; **m. de arranque** starter, starting motor; **m. de combustión interna** internal combustion engine; **m. diesel/de gasolina** diesel/fuel engine; **m. de dos/cuatro tiempos** two-/four-stroke engine; **m. eléctrico** electric motor; **m. de explosión** spark-ignition engine; **m. fuera borda** outboard motor; **m. de inyección/reacción** fuel-injection/jet engine (**b**) (fuerza) driving force; Dep **el m. del equipo** the team dynamo (**c**) (causa) instigator, cause (**d**) Inform **m. de búsqueda** search engine

motora nf motorboat

motorismo nm motorcycling

motorista nmf Esp motorcyclist

motorizado, -a adj motorized; Fam **estar m.** (tener coche) to have wheels

motorizar [14] **1** vt to motorize

  2 motorizarse vpr Fam to get oneself some wheels

motosierra nf power saw

motricidad nf motivity

motriz ver motor

motu propio, motu proprio adv (de) **m.** of one's own accord

mouse [maus] nm inv Am Inform mouse

mousse [mus] nf, Esp nm Culin mousse

movedizo, -a adj (**a**) (movible) movable, easily moved (**b**) (inestable) unsteady, unstable; **arenas movedizas** quicksand

mover [41] **1** vt (**a**) (en general) to move; (mecánicamente) to drive; **el fútbol profesional mueve mucho dinero** a lot of money changes hands in the world of professional soccer

  (**b**) (menear, agitar) (caja, sonajero) to shake; (bandera) to wave; **la vaca movía la cola** the cow was swishing its tail; **el perro movía la cola** the dog was wagging its tail; **m. la cabeza** (afirmativamente) to nod; (negativamente) to shake one's head

  (**c**) (impulsar) **m. a alguien a hacer algo** to prompt sb to do sth; **¿qué te movió a hacerlo?** what made you do it?, what prompted you to do it?; **m. a alguien a compasión** to excite sb's sympathy o pity (**d**) (hacer trámites con) to do something about

  2 moverse vpr (**a**) (en general) to move; (en la cama) to toss and turn (**b**) (darse prisa) to get a move on (**c**) Fam (hacer gestiones) to get things going o moving; **si te mueves puedes encontrar trabajo** if you make an effort you can get a job (**d**) (relacionarse) **moverse en/entre** to move in/among

movible adj movable

movida nf Esp, RP Fam (**a**) (lío, problema) problem; **mudarse es una m.** moving house is a real headache; **tener una m. con alguien** to have a bit of trouble with sb (**b**) (ambiente, actividad) scene; **no me va esa m.** it's not my scene; **la m. madrileña** = the Madrid cultural scene of the late 1970s and early 80s

movido, -a adj (**a**) (debate, torneo) lively; (jornada, viaje) hectic (**b**) Fot blurred, fuzzy

móvil 1 adj mobile, movable; **teléfono m.** cell phone

  2 nm (**a**) (motivo) motive (**b**) (teléfono) mobile (**c**) (juguete) mobile

movilidad nf mobility

movilización nf mobilization

movilizar [14] vt to mobilize

movimiento nm (**a**) (desplazamiento, corriente) movement; **m. obrero** working-class movement (**b**) Fís & Mec motion; **en m.** moving, in motion; **ponerse en m.** to start moving; **m. continuo/de rotación** perpetual/rotational motion; **m. sísmico** earth tremor (**c**) (actividad) activity; (de vehículos) traffic (**d**) (de personal, mercancías) turnover; (de cuenta bancaria) transaction; **m. de capital** cash flow (**e**) Mús (parte de la obra) movement; (velocidad del compás) tempo

moviola nf editing projector

moza nf (sirvienta) girl, maid

mozalbete nm young lad

Mozambique n Mozambique

mozambiqueño, -a adj & nm,f Mozambican

mozárabe 1 adj Mozarabic, = Christian in the time of Moorish Spain

  2 nmf (habitante) Mozarab, = Christian of Moorish Spain

  3 nm (lengua) Mozarabic

mozo, -a 1 adj (joven) young; (soltero) single, unmarried; **ser buen m.** to be a handsome young man

  2 nm,f (**a**) (niño) young boy, young lad; (niña) young girl, young lass (**b**) Andes, RP (camarero) waiter, f waitress

  3 nm (**a**) (trabajador) assistant (worker); **m. de cordel** o **de cuerda** porter; **m. de estación** (station) porter (**b**) Esp (recluta) draftee, conscript

mozzarella [motsaˈrela, moθaˈrela] nm mozzarella

MP3 nm (abrev de **MPEG-1 Audio Layer-3**) MP3

mu nm (mugido) moo; **no decir ni m.** not to say a word

muaré nm moiré

mucamo, -a nm,f Andes, RP servant

muchacha nf (sirvienta) maid

muchachada nf bunch of kids

muchacho, -a nm,f boy, f girl

muchedumbre nf (de gente) crowd, throng; (de cosas) great number, masses

mucho, -a 1 adj (**a**) (gran cantidad de) (singular) a lot of; (plural) many, a lot of; (en frases interrogativas y negativas) much, a lot of; **había mucha gente** there were a lot of people there; **no tengo m. tiempo** I haven't got much time; **hoy hace m. calor** it's very hot today; **tengo m. sueño** I'm very sleepy; **hace m. tiempo** a long time ago; **no nos quedan muchas entradas** we haven't got many o a lot of tickets left (**b**) (singular) (demasiado) **hay m. niño aquí** there are too many kids here; **mucha sal le estás echando** you're overdoing the salt a bit, you're adding a bit too much salt

  2 pron (singular) a lot; (plural) many, a lot; **tengo m. que contarte** I have a lot to tell you; **¿queda dinero? — no m.** is there any money left? — not much o not a lot; **muchos piensan igual** a lot of o many people think the same

  3 adv (**a**) (gran cantidad) a lot; **habla m.** he talks a lot; **me canso m.** I get really o very tired; **me gusta m.** I like it a lot o very much; **no me gusta m.** I don't like it much; (**no**) **m. más tarde** (not) much later

  (**b**) (largo tiempo) **hace m. que no vienes** I haven't seen you for a long time; **¿dura m. la obra?** is the play long?; **m. antes/después** long before/after

  (**c**) (a menudo) often; **¿vienes m. por aquí?** do you come here often?

  (**d**) (expresiones) **como m.** at the most; **con m.** by far, easily; **ni m. menos** far from it, by no means; **no está ni m. menos decidido** it is by no means decided; **por m. que** no matter how much, however much; **por m. que insistas** no matter how much you insist, however much you insist

mucosa nf mucous membrane

mucosidad nf mucus

mucoso, -a adj mucous

mucus nm inv mucus

muda nf (**a**) (de piel, plumas) molting (**b**) (ropa interior) change of underwear

mudable adj (persona) changeable; (carácter) fickle

mudanza nf (**a**) (cambio) change; (de carácter) changeability, fickleness; (de plumas, piel) molting (**b**) (de casa) move; **estar de m.** to be moving

mudar 1 vt (**a**) (cambiar) to change; (casa) to move; **cuando mude la voz** when his voice breaks (**b**) (piel, plumas) to molt

2 *vi (cambiar)* **m. de** *(opinión, color)* to change; *(domicilio)* to move

3 mudarse *vpr* **mudarse (de casa)** to move (house); **mudarse (de ropa)** to change

mudéjar *adj & nmf* Mudejar

mudez *nf* muteness, inability to speak

mudo, -a 1 *adj* **(a)** *(sin habla)* dumb **(b)** *(callado)* silent, mute; **se quedó m.** he was left speechless **(c)** *(sin sonido)* silent; **cine m.** silent cinema

2 *nm,f* dumb person, mute

mueble 1 *nm* piece of furniture; **los muebles** the furniture; **muebles antiguos** antique furniture; **muebles de baño** bathroom furniture; **m. bar** cocktail cabinet; **muebles de cocina** kitchen furniture; **m. de oficina** office furniture

2 *adj Der* **bienes muebles** personal property

mueca *nf (gesto)* face, expression; *(de dolor)* grimace; **hacer una m.** to make a face; **hizo una m. de dolor** she winced in pain, she grimaced with pain; **los niños hacían muecas a espaldas del profesor** the children were making faces behind the teacher's back

muela 1 *ver* **moler**

2 *nf* **(a)** *(diente)* back tooth, molar; **m. del juicio** wisdom tooth **(b)** *(de molino)* millstone; *(para afilar)* grindstone

muelle 1 *adj (vida)* easy, comfortable

2 *nm* **(a)** *(resorte)* spring **(b)** *(en puerto)* dock, quay; *(en el río)* wharf; *(de carga y descarga)* loading zone

muera *etc ver* **morir**

muerda *etc ver* **morder**

muérdago *nm* mistletoe

muerdo *nm Esp Fam* **(a)** *(mordisco)* bite **(b)** *(beso)* **se estaban dando un m.** they were necking

muermo *nm Esp Fam* **ser un m.** *(situación)* to be boring; *(persona)* to be a bore; **tener un m.** to be bored

muerte *nf* **(a)** *(fin de la vida)* death; **fallecer de m. natural** to die of natural causes; **fallecer de m. violenta** to die a violent death; **ha sido herido de m.** he has been fatally wounded; **a m.** *(lucha)* to the death; **la odio a m.** I hate her with all my heart, I absolutely loathe her; **un susto de m.** a terrible shock; *Fam* **de mala m.** third-rate, lousy; **m. cerebral** brain death; **m. súbita** *(en tenis)* tiebreak; **m. súbita infantil** *(en la cuna)* sudden infant death **(b)** *(homicidio)* murder; **se le acusa de la m. de varias mujeres** he has been accused of murdering *o* of the murder of several women

muerto, -a 1 *participio ver* **morir**

2 *adj* **(a)** *(sin vida)* dead; **estar m. de miedo/frío** to be scared/freezing to death; **estar m. de hambre** to be starving; *Fig* **estar m. de risa** *(objeto)* to be lying around doing nothing **(b)** *(color)* dull

3 *nm,f* dead person; *(cadáver)* corpse; **hubo dos muertos** two people died; **hacerse el m.** to pretend to be dead, to play dead; *Fig* **cargar con el m.** *(trabajo, tarea)* to be left holding the baby; *(culpa)* to get the blame; **hacer el m.** to float on one's back; **más m. que vivo de hambre/cansancio** half dead with hunger/exhaustion; **medio m.** *(cansado)* dead beat; **no tener donde caerse m.** not to have a penny to one's name

muesca *nf* **(a)** *(marca, concavidad)* notch, groove **(b)** *(corte)* nick

muesli *nm* muesli

muestra 1 *ver* **mostrar**

2 *nf* **(a)** *(cantidad representativa)* sample; **para m. (basta) un botón** one example is enough; **una m. representativa de la población** a cross section of the population; **m. gratuita** free sample **(b)** *(señal)* sign, show; *(prueba)* proof; *(de cariño, aprecio)* token; **dar muestras de** to show signs of **(c)** *(modelo)* model, pattern **(d)** *(exposición)* show, exhibition

muestrario *nm* collection of samples; *(libro)* pattern book

muestreo *nm* sampling; **m. aleatorio** random sampling

mueva *etc ver* **mover**

mugido *nm* **(a)** *(de vaca)* moo, mooing; **un m.** a moo; **el m. de las vacas** the mooing of the cows **(b)** *(de toro)* bellow, bellowing; **un m.** a bellow; **el m. de los toros** the bellowing of the bulls

mugir [24] *vi (vaca)* to moo; *(toro)* to bellow

mugre *nf* filth, muck

mugriento, -a *adj* filthy

muguete *nm* lily of the valley

mujer 1 *nf (en general)* woman; *(cónyuge)* wife; **m. de su casa** good housewife; **m. fatal** femme fatale; **m. de la limpieza** cleaning lady; **m. de negocios** businesswoman; **m. objeto** woman treated as a sex object; **m. policía** policewoman; **m. pública** prostitute

2 *interj Esp* **¿te acuerdas de Marisol?, ¡sí, m., nuestra compañera de clase!** do you remember Marisol? you know, she was at school with us!; **pero m., no te pongas así** oh, don't be like that!

mujeriego, -a 1 *adj* fond of the ladies

2 *nm* womanizer, ladies' man

mujeril *adj* female

mujerzuela *nf Pey* loose woman

muladar *nm* tip, pigpen

mulato, -a *adj & nm,f* mulatto

muleta *nf* **(a)** *(para andar)* crutch; *Fig* prop, support **(b)** *Taurom* muleta, = red cape hanging from a stick used to tease the bull

muletilla *nf (frase)* pet phrase; *(palabra)* pet word

Mulhacén *nm* **el M.** Mulhacén

mulillas *nfpl Taurom* = team of mules which drag out the dead bull at the end of a fight

mullido, -a *adj* soft, springy

mullir *vt* to soften; *(lana, almohada)* to fluff up

mulo, -a *nm,f* **(a)** *(animal)* mule **(b)** *Fam (persona)* brute, beast

multa *nf* fine; **poner una m. a alguien** to fine sb; **le pusieron cien euros de m.** he was fined a hundred euros

multar *vt* to fine

multicentro *nm* large shopping mall

multicine *nm* multiplex

multicolor *adj* multicolored

multicopista *nf Esp* duplicator, duplicating machine

multicultural *adj* multicultural

multidisciplinario, -a, multidisciplinar *adj* multidisciplinary

multiforme *adj* multiform, differently shaped

multigrado *adj* multigrade

multilateral *adj* multilateral

multimedia *adj inv Inform* multimedia

multimillonario, -a 1 *adj* **un negocio m.** a multimillion-dollar business

2 *nm,f* multimillionaire

multinacional *adj & nf* multinational

múltiple *adj (variado)* multiple; **múltiples** *(numerosos)* many, numerous

multiplicable *adj* multipliable

multiplicación *nf* multiplication

multiplicador, -ora 1 *adj* multiplying

2 *nm Mat* multiplier

multiplicar [59] **1** *vt (en general)* to multiply; *(efecto)* to magnify; *(riesgo, probabilidad)* to increase; **m. 4 por 5** to multiply 4 by 5; **4 multiplicado por 3 igual a 12** 4 multiplied by 3 is 12, 4 times 3 is 12

2 *vi* to multiply

3 multiplicarse *vpr* **(a)** *(reproducirse)* to multiply **(b)** *(incrementarse)* to increase rapidly; **se han multiplicado los robos en la zona** there has been a rapid rise in the number of burglaries in the area (**c**) (*desdoblarse*) to attend to lots of things at the same time

multiplicidad *nf* multiplicity

múltiplo *nm* multiple

multipropiedad *nf* time-sharing

multipuesto *adj inv Inform* multiterminal; **red m.** multiterminal network

multirracial *adj* multiracial

multirriesgo *adj* (*seguro*) all risks

multisalas *nm inv* (*cine*) multiplex

multitarea *adj inv & nf Inform* multitasking

multitud *nf* (*de personas*) crowd; **m. de cosas** a huge number of things

multitudinario, -a *adj* extremely crowded; **una manifestación multitudinaria** a massive demonstration

multiuso *adj inv* multipurpose

multiusuario *adj Inform* multiuser

mundanal *adj* worldly

mundano, -a *adj* (**a**) (*del mundo*) worldly, of the world (**b**) (*de la vida social*) (high) society

mundial 1 *adj* (*política, economía, guerra*) world; (*tratado, organización, fama*) worldwide

2 *nm* World Championships; (*en fútbol*) World Cup

mundialización *nf* globalization

mundillo *nm* world, circles; **el m. literario** the literary world, literary circles

mundo *nm* (**a**) (*la Tierra, el universo, civilización*) world; **es un actor conocido en todo el m.** he's a world-famous actor; **ha vendido miles de discos en todo el m.** she has sold thousands of records worldwide *o* all over the world; **seres de otro m.** creatures from another planet; **el Nuevo M.** the New World; **el otro m.** the next world, the hereafter; **el Tercer M.** the Third World; **desde que el m. es m.** since the dawn of time; **el m. es un pañuelo** it's a small world; **medio m.** half the world, a lot of people; **no es cosa** *o* **nada del otro m.** it's nothing special; **por nada del m.** not for (all) the world; **se le cayó el m. encima** his world fell apart; **todo el m.** everyone, everybody; **traer al m.** to give birth to; **venir al m.** to come into the world, to be born; **el m. del espectáculo** show business

(**b**) (*diferencia*) **hay un m. entre ellos** they're worlds apart

(**c**) (*experiencia*) **hombre/mujer de m.** man/woman of the world; **tener m.** to be worldly-wise, to know the ways of the world; **ver** *o* **correr m.** to see life

mundología *nf* worldly wisdom, experience of life

Munich *n* Munich

munición *nf* ammunition; **municiones** ammunition

municipal 1 *adj* city, municipal; (*elecciones*) local; (*instalaciones*) public; **las fiestas municipales** local *o* city festival

2 *nmf Esp* (*guardia*) (local) policeman, *f* policewoman

municipalidad *nf* (**a**) (*corporación*) local council (**b**) (*territorio*) city, municipality

municipalizar [14] *vt* to municipalize, to bring under municipal authority

municipio *nm* (**a**) (*corporación*) local council (**b**) (*edificio*) city hall, town hall (**c**) (*territorio*) city, municipality (**d**) (*habitantes*) **asistió todo el m.** the whole town *o* city was there

munificencia *nf* munificence

muniqués, -esa 1 *adj* of/from Munich

2 *nm,f* person from Munich

muñeca *nf* (**a**) *Anat* wrist (**b**) (*juguete*) doll; **m. de trapo** rag doll (**c**) *Fam* (*como apelativo*) darling, doll (**d**) *Andes, RP Fam* (*enchufe*) **tener m.** to have friends in high places

muñeco *nm* (**a**) (*juguete*) doll; (*marioneta*) puppet; (*peluche*) cuddly *o* stuffed toy; **m. de nieve** snowman; **m. de peluche** cuddly toy (**b**) *Pey* puppet

muñeira *nf* = popular Galician dance and music

muñequera *nf* wristband

muñón *nm* stump

mural 1 *adj* (*pintura*) mural; (*mapa*) wall

2 *nm* mural

muralista *nmf Arte* muralist

muralla *nf* wall

Murcia *n* Murcia

murciano, -a *adj & nm,f* Murcian

murciélago *nm* bat

murga *nf* (**a**) (*charanga*) band of street musicians (**b**) *Esp Fam* (*pesadez*) drag, pain; **dar la m.** to be a pain

muriera *etc ver* **morir**

murmullo *nm* (*de agua, viento, voces*) murmur, murmuring; (*de hojas*) rustle, rustling

murmuración *nf* backbiting, gossip

murmurador, -ora 1 *adj* backbiting, gossiping

2 *nm,f* backbiter, gossip

murmurar 1 *vt* to mutter; **se murmura que...** there are rumors that...

2 *vi* (**a**) (*susurrar*) (*persona*) to murmur, to whisper; (*agua, viento*) to murmur, to gurgle; (*hojas*) to rustle (**b**) (*criticar*) to gossip (**de** about); **se pasan el tiempo murmurando del jefe** they do nothing but gossip about the boss (**c**) (*rezongar, quejarse*) to grumble

muro *nm* wall; *Fig* **entre los dos hay un m. de silencio** there is a wall of silence between them; **el M. de Berlín** the Berlin Wall; **m. de contención** retaining wall; *Esp* **el M. de las Lamentaciones,** *Am* **el m. de los Lamentos** the Wailing Wall

mus *nm inv* = card game played in pairs with bidding and in which players communicate by signs

musa *nf* (**a**) (*inspiración*) muse (**b**) *Mitol* Muse

musaraña *nf Zool* shrew; *Fam* **mirar a las musarañas** to stare into space *o* thin air; *Fam* **pensar en las musarañas** to have one's head in the clouds

musculación *nf* bodybuilding

muscular *adj* muscular

musculatura *nf* muscles

músculo *nm* muscle

musculosa *nf RP* (*prenda*) undershirt (*sleeveless*)

musculoso, -a *adj* muscular

museístico, -a *adj* museum; **archivos museísticos** museum archives

muselina *nf* muslin

museo *nm* (*de ciencias, historia*) museum; (*de arte*) art gallery

museología *nf* museology

musgo *nm* moss

música *nf* music; *Fig* **irse con la m. a otra parte** to make oneself scarce; **m. ambiental** background music; **m. antigua** early music; **m. de baile** dance music; **m. de cámara** chamber music; *Fig* **m. celestial** hot air, empty words; **m. clásica** classical music; **m. étnica** world music; **m. de fondo** background music; **m. instrumental** instrumental music; **m. ligera** light music; **m. pop** pop music; **m. rock** rock music; **m. vocal** choral music

musical *adj & nm* musical

musicalidad *nf* musicality

music-hall ['musik'xol] (*pl* **music-halls**) *nm* vaudeville

músico, -a 1 *adj* musical

2 *nm,f* (*persona*) musician; **m. ambulante** street musician; **m. callejero** street musician

musicología *nf* musicology

musitar *vt* to mutter, to mumble

muslo *nm* (*de persona*) thigh; (*de pollo, pavo*) (*entero*) leg; (*parte inferior*) drumstick

mustela *nf* (**a**) (*comadreja*) weasel (**b**) (*pez*) dogfish

mustiar 1 *vt* to wither, to wilt
  2 mustiarse *vpr* to wither, to wilt
mustio, -a *adj* (**a**) *(flor, planta)* withered, wilted (**b**) *(persona)* down, gloomy
musulmán, -ana *adj & nm,f* Muslim, Moslem
mutable *adj* changeable, mutable
mutación *nf (cambio)* sudden change; *Biol* mutation
mutante *adj & nmf* mutant
mutar *vt* to mutate
mutilación *nf* mutilation
mutilado, -a 1 *adj* mutilated
  2 *nm,f* cripple; **m. de guerra** disabled war veteran
mutilar *vt (persona, texto)* to mutilate; *(estatua)* to vandalize
mutis *nm inv Teatro* exit; **hacer m.** *(en teatro)* to exit; *Fig (marcharse)* to leave, to go away
mutismo *nm* (**a**) *(mudez)* muteness, dumbness (**b**) *(silencio)* silence
mutua *nf* mutual benefit society
mutualidad *nf* (**a**) *(asociación)* mutual benefit society (**b**) *(reciprocidad)* mutuality

mutualista *nmf* member of a mutual benefit society
mutuo, -a *adj* mutual; **de m. acuerdo** by mutual *o* joint agreement; **el sentimiento es m.** the feeling is mutual; **se tienen una admiración mutua** they have a mutual admiration for each other, they both admire each other
muy *adv* (**a**) *(en alto grado)* very; **m. bueno/cerca** very good/ near; **es m. hombre** he's very manly, he's a real man; **m. de mañana** very early in the morning; **¡m. bien!** *(vale)* OK!, all right!; *(qué bien)* very good!, well done!; **eso es m. de ella** that's just like her; **eso es m. de los americanos** that's typically American; **¡el m. fresco!** the smart aleck!; **¡la m. tonta!** the silly idiot!; **Muy Sr. mío** dear Sir; **te cuidarás m. mucho de hacerlo** just make absolutely sure you don't do it (**b**) *(demasiado)* too; **no cabe ahí, es m. grande** it won't fit in there, it's too big
muyahidín *nm inv* mujahideen
muzzarella [musa'rela] *nm RP* mozzarella
Myanmar *n (Birmania)* Myanmar

N

N, n ['ene] *nf (letra)* N, n; **el 20 N** November 20, = the date of Franco's death

n° *(abrev de* **número***)* no

nabo *nm* (**a**) *(planta)* turnip (**b**) *muy Fam (pene)* tool

nácar *nm* mother-of-pearl

nacarado, -a *adj* mother-of-pearl; **piel nacarada** pearly skin

nacatamal *nm CAm* = steamed corn dumpling with savory filling, wrapped in a banana leaf

nacer [42] *vi* (**a**) *(venir al mundo) (niño, animal)* to be born; *(planta)* to sprout, to begin to grow; *(pájaro)* to hatch (out); **al n.** at birth; **¿dónde naciste? — nací en Brasil** where were you born? — I was born in Brazil; **n. de/en** to be born of/in; **n. de familia humilde** to be born into a poor family; **n. para algo** to be born for sth; **ha nacido cantante** she's a born singer; *Fig* **no he nacido ayer** I wasn't born yesterday; *Fig* **volver a n.** to have a lucky escape (**b**) *(surgir) (pelo)* to grow; *(río)* to rise, to have its source; *(sol, luna)* to rise; *(costumbre, duda)* to have its roots

nacido, -a **1** *adj* born

2 *nm,f* **los nacidos hoy** those born today; **recién n.** newborn baby; **ser un mal n.** to be a wicked *o* vile person

naciente *adj* (**a**) *(día)* dawning; *(sol)* rising (**b**) *(Gobierno, Estado)* new, fledgling; *(interés)* budding, growing

nacimiento *nm* (**a**) *(de niño, animal)* birth; *(de planta)* sprouting; *(de ave, reptil)* hatching; **de n.** from birth (**b**) *(de río)* source (**c**) *(origen)* origin, beginning (**d**) *(belén)* Nativity scene

nación *nf (pueblo)* nation; *(territorio)* country; **n. más favorecida** most favored nation; **Naciones Unidas** United Nations

nacional *adj (equipo, moneda, monumento)* national; *(vuelo)* domestic; *(mercado, noticias)* domestic, home; *Esp Hist* **las fuerzas nacionales** *(en la guerra civil)* the Nationalist forces

nacionalidad *nf* nationality; **doble n.** dual nationality

nacionalismo *nm* nationalism

nacionalista *adj & nmf* nationalist

nacionalización *nf (de banca, bienes)* nationalization; *(de persona)* naturalization

nacionalizar [14] **1** *vt* (**a**) *(banca, bienes)* to nationalize (**b**) *(persona)* to naturalize

2 **nacionalizarse** *vpr* to become naturalized; **nacionalizarse español** to become a Spanish citizen, to acquire Spanish nationality

nacionalsocialismo *nm* National Socialism

nacionalsocialista *adj & mf* National Socialist

nada **1** *pron* (**a**) *(en general) (en negativas)* anything; **no pasó n.** nothing happened; **no he leído n. de Lorca** I haven't read anything by Lorca; **n. me gustaría más que poder ayudarte** there's nothing I'd like more than to be able to help you; **no hay n. como un buen libro** there's nothing (quite) like a good book; **n. más** nothing else, nothing more; **no quiero n. más** I don't want anything else; **no dijo n. de**

n. he didn't say anything at all; **no es n.** it's nothing serious; **esto no es n.** that's nothing; **te he traído un regalito de n.** I've brought you a little something; **cuesta cinco millones, ¡ahí es n.!** it costs five million, a real bargain!; **casi n.** almost nothing; **como si n.** as if nothing was the matter, as if nothing had happened; **de n.** *(respuesta a "gracias")* don't mention it, you're welcome; **dentro de n.** any second now; **¡n. de eso!** absolutely not!

(**b**) *Esp (en tenis)* love

2 *adv* (**a**) *(en absoluto)* at all; **la película no me ha gustado n.** I didn't like the movie at all; **no es n. extraño** it's not at all strange; **la obra no es n. aburrida** the play isn't the slightest bit boring (**b**) *(poco)* a little, a bit; **no hace n. que salió** he left just a minute ago

3 *nf* **la n.** nothingness, the void

4 **nada más** *loc adv (+ infin)* as soon as; **n. más salir de casa…** no sooner had I left the house than…, as soon as I left the house…

5 **nada menos que** *loc adv (cosa)* no less than; *(persona)* none other than

nadador, -ora *nm,f* swimmer

nadar *vi (avanzar en el agua)* to swim; *(flotar)* to float; **no sé n.** I can't swim; **como si n.** *Fam* **n. contra corriente** to go against the tide; *Fig* **nadan en deudas** they're up to their necks in debt; *Fig* **n. entre dos aguas** to sit on the fence; *Fig* **n. en la abundancia** to be living in the lap of luxury

nadería *nf* trifle, little thing

nadie **1** *pron* nobody, no one; **n. lo sabe** nobody knows; **no se lo dije a n.** I didn't tell anybody; **no ha llamado n.** nobody phoned

2 *nm* **un don n.** a nobody

nado: a nado *loc adv* swimming

NAFTA *nf (abrev de* **North American Free Trade Agreement***)* NAFTA

nafta *nf* (**a**) *Quím* naphtha (**b**) *RP (gasolina)* gas, gasoline

naftalina *nf* naphthalene; **bolas de n.** mothballs

náhuatl **1** *adj* Nahuatl

2 *nmf (persona)* Nahuatl indian

3 *nm (idioma)* Nahuatl

naïf *(pl* **naïfs***) adj Arte* naive, primitivistic

nailon *nm* nylon

naipe *nm* (playing) card; **jugar a los naipes** to play cards

Nairobi *n* Nairobi

nalga *nf* buttock

nana *nf* (**a**) *(canción)* lullaby; *Fam* **más viejo que la n., del año de la n.** as old as the hills, ancient (**b**) *Fam (abuela)* grandma (**c**) *Col, Méx (niñera)* nanny; *(nodriza)* wet nurse

nanay *interj Fam* **¡n.!** no way!, not likely!

nanosegundo *nm* nanosecond

nanotecnología *nf* nanotechnology

nao *nf Literario* vessel

napa *nf* leather

napalm *nm* napalm

napia *nf Fam* schnoz

napoleónico, -a *adj* Napoleonic

napolitano, -a *adj & nm,f* Neapolitan

naranja 1 *adj inv* orange
 2 *nm (color)* orange
 3 *nf (fruto)* orange; *Fam* **¡naranjas de la china!** no way!; *Fam Fig* **media n.** other o better half

naranjada *nf* orange juice drink

naranjal *nm* orange grove

naranjo *nm* **(a)** *(árbol)* orange tree **(b)** *(madera)* orange (wood)

narcisismo *nm* narcissism

narcisista *nmf* narcissist

narciso *nm* **(a)** *Bot* daffodil **(b)** *(hombre)* narcissist

narco *Fam* **1** *nmf (persona)* drug trafficker
 2 *nm (tráfico)* drug trafficking

narcomanía *nf* narcotism

narcótico, -a 1 *adj* narcotic
 2 *nm (somnífero)* narcotic; *(droga)* drug

narcotizar [14] *vt* to drug

narcotraficante *nmf* drug trafficker

narcotráfico *nm* drug trafficking

nardo *nm (flor)* spikenard, nard

narices *interj* **¡n.!** no way!, not on your life!

narigudo, -a 1 *adj* big-nosed
 2 *nm,f* big-nosed person

nariz *nf* **(a)** *(órgano)* nose; **operarse (de) la n.** to have a nose job; **sangraba por la n.** her nose was bleeding; **sonarse la n.** to blow one's nose; **n. aguileña/chata/respingona** hooked/snub/turned-up nose
 (b) *(orificio)* nostril
 (c) *(olfato)* sense of smell
 (d) *(expresiones)* **me da en la n. que…** I've got a feeling that…; **darse de narices con o contra algo/alguien** to bump into sth/sb; **de narices** *(estupendo)* great, brilliant; **delante de las narices** in front of one's nose; **estar hasta las narices (de algo)** to be fed up to the back teeth (with sth); **en sus propias narices** to his/her face; *Esp* **me estás hinchando las narices** you're beginning to get up my nose; **meter las narices en algo** to poke o stick one's nose into sth; *Esp* **tenemos que ir por narices** we have to go whether we like it or not; **restregar algo a alguien en las narices** to rub sb's nose in sth; **romper las narices a alguien** to smash sb's face in; **romperse las narices** to fall flat on one's face; **¡porque me sale de las narices!** because I damn well want to!

narizotas *nmf inv Fam* big-nose

narración *nf* **(a)** *(cuento, relato)* narrative, story **(b)** *(acción)* narration

narrador, -ora *nm,f* narrator

narrar *vt (contar)* to recount, to tell

narrativa *nf* narrative

narrativo, -a *adj* narrative

NASA ['nasa] *nf (abrev de* **National Aeronautics and Space Administration)** NASA

nasal *adj* nasal

nasalizar [14] *vt* to nasalize

Nassau *n* Nassau

nata *nf* **(a)** *Esp (crema de leche)* cream; **n. batida** o **montada** whipped cream; **n. líquida** $\simeq$ half-and-half **(b)** *(en leche hervida)* skin

natación *nf* swimming

natal *adj (país, ciudad)* native; *(pueblo)* home

natalicio *nm (cumpleaños)* birthday

natalidad *nf (tasa o índice de)* **n.** birth rate

natillas *nfpl Esp* custard

natividad *nf* nativity; **la N.** Christmas

nativo, -a *adj & nm,f* native

nato, -a *adj (de nacimiento)* born; **un criminal n.** a born criminal

natura *nf* nature; **contra n.** against nature, unnatural; **una alianza contra n.** an unholy alliance

natural 1 *adj* **(a)** *(no artificial)* natural; *(flores, fruta, leche)* fresh; **al n.** *(en persona)* in the flesh; **es más guapa al n. que en la fotografía** she's prettier in real life than in the photograph; **ser n. en alguien** to be in sb's nature **(b)** *(lógico, normal)* natural, normal; **es lo más n. del mundo** it's the most natural thing in the world, it's perfectly natural; **es n. que se enfade** it's natural that he should be angry **(c)** *(nativo)* native; **ser n. de** to come from **(d)** *(ilegítimo) (hijo)* illegitimate **(e)** *(hábil y no hábil)* **mes/año n.** calendar month/year; **30 días naturales de vacaciones** 30 workdays' holiday
 2 *nmf (nativo)* native
 3 *nm (talante)* nature, disposition

naturaleza *nf* **(a)** *(en general)* nature; **aman a la n.** they love nature, they are nature lovers; **se desconoce la n. de la enfermedad** the nature of the illness is unknown; **una persona de n. nerviosa** a person of a nervous disposition, a person who is nervous by nature; **por n.** by nature; **la madre n.** Mother Nature; **la n. humana** human nature; **n. muerta** still life **(b)** *(complexión)* constitution

naturalidad *nf* naturalness; **con n.** naturally

naturalismo *nm Arte* naturalism

naturalista *nmf* naturalist

naturalización *nf* naturalization

naturalizado, -a *adj* naturalized

naturalizar [14] **1** *vt* to naturalize
 2 naturalizarse *vpr* to become naturalized; **naturalizarse español** to become a Spanish citizen, to acquire Spanish nationality

naturalmente *adv* **(a)** *(por naturaleza)* naturally **(b)** *(por supuesto)* of course

naturismo *nm (nudismo)* nudism

naturista *nmf (nudista)* nudist

naturópata *nmf* naturopath

naufragar [38] *vi* **(a)** *(barco)* to sink, to be wrecked; *(persona)* to be shipwrecked **(b)** *(fracasar)* to fail, to collapse

naufragio *nm* **(a)** *(de barco)* shipwreck **(b)** *(fracaso)* failure, collapse

náufrago, -a 1 *adj* shipwrecked
 2 *nm,f* shipwrecked person, castaway

náusea *nf* nausea, sickness; **me da náuseas** it makes me feel sick; *Fig* it makes me sick; **sentir o tener náuseas** to fall sick o nauseous; **náuseas del embarazo** morning sickness

nauseabundo, -a *adj* nauseating, sickening

náutica *nf* navigation, seamanship

náutico, -a 1 *adj (de la navegación)* nautical; *Dep* **deportes náuticos** water sports; **club n.** yacht club
 2 náuticos *nmpl (zapatos)* = lightweight lace-up shoes, made of colored leather

navaja *nf* **(a)** *(cuchillo) (pequeño)* penknife; *(más grande)* jackknife; **n. de afeitar** razor; **n. automática** switchblade **(b)** *(molusco)* razor clam, jackknife clam

navajazo *nm* stab, slash

navajero, -a *nm,f* = thug who carries a knife

naval *adj* naval

Navarra *n* Navarre

navarro, -a *adj & nm,f* Navarrese

nave *nf* **(a)** *(barco)* ship; *Fig* **quemar las naves** to burn one's bridges o boats **(b)** *(vehículo)* craft; **n. espacial** spaceship, spacecraft **(c)** *(de fábrica)* shop, plant; *(almacén)* warehouse; **n. industrial** = large building for industrial or commercial use **(d)** *(de iglesia)* **n. central** nave; **n. de crucero** transepts; **n. lateral** side aisle

navegable *adj* navigable

navegación *nf* navigation; **n. aérea/fluvial/marítima** air/river/sea navigation; **n. de altura** ocean navigation

navegador *nm Inform* browser

navegante 1 *adj (pueblo)* seafaring

    2 *nmf* navigator

navegar [38] *vi (barco)* to sail; *(avión)* to fly; **n. por Internet** to surf the Net

Navidad *nf* (**a**) *(día)* Christmas (Day) (**b**) *(periodo)* Christmas (time); **felices Navidades** Merry Christmas

navideño, -a *adj* Christmas; **adornos navideños** Christmas decorations

naviera *nf (compañía)* shipping company

naviero, -a 1 *adj* shipping

    2 *nm (armador)* shipowner

navío *nm* large ship

nazareno, -a 1 *adj & nm,f* Nazarene

    2 *nm* = penitent in Holy Week processions; **el N.** Jesus of Nazareth

nazca *etc ver* **nacer**

nazi *adj & nmf* Nazi

nazismo *nm* Nazism

NB *(abrev de* **nota bene***)* NB

neandertal, neanderthal *nm* neanderthal

neblina *nf* mist

neblinoso, -a *adj* misty

nebulosa *nf Astron* nebula

nebulosidad *nf (de nubes)* cloudiness; *(de niebla)* fogginess

nebuloso, -a *adj* (**a**) *(con nubes)* cloudy; *(de niebla)* foggy (**b**) *(poco claro)* vague

necedad *nf* (**a**) *(estupidez)* stupidity, foolishness (**b**) *(dicho, hecho)* stupid *o* foolish thing; **decir necedades** to talk nonsense

necesario, -a *adj* necessary; **me llevé la ropa necesaria para una semana** I took enough clothes for a week; **me eres muy necesaria** I really need you; **es n. hacerlo** it needs to be done; **hacer n. algo** to make sth necessary; **no es n. que lo hagas** you don't need to do it; **si fuera n.** if need be; **si es n.** if need be, if necessary

neceser *nm (bolsa)* toilet bag; *(maleta pequeña)* vanity case

necesidad *nf* (**a**) *(en general)* need; **tenemos una urgente n. de espacio** we are in urgent need of more space; **de (primera) n.** essential; **no hay n. de algo** there's no need for sth; **no hay n. de hacer algo** there's no need to do sth; **tener n. de algo** to need sth; **obedecer a la n. (de)** to arise from the need (to) (**b**) *(obligación)* necessity; **por n.** out of necessity; **una herida mortal de n.** a fatal wound (**c**) *(hambre)* hunger; *(pobreza)* poverty, need; **pasar necesidades** to suffer hardship (**d**) *Euf* **hacer sus necesidades** to answer a call of nature

necesitado, -a 1 *adj* needy; **n. de** in need of

    2 *nm,f* needy *o* poor person; **los necesitados** the poor

necesitar 1 *vt* to need; **necesito que me lo digas** I need you to tell me; **esta planta necesita que la rieguen** this plant needs watering; **se necesita camarero** *(en letrero)* waiter wanted; **se necesita ser ignorante para no saber eso** you'd have to be an ignoramus not to know that

    2 *vi* **n. de** to need, to have need of; **necesitamos de tu ayuda** we need your help

necio, -a 1 *adj* stupid, foolish

    2 *nm,f* idiot, fool

nécora *nf* small edible crab

necrófago, -a *adj* necrophagous

necrofilia *nf* necrophilia

necrológica *nf* obituary; **necrológicas** *(sección de periódico)* obituaries, obituary column

necrológico, -a *adj* **nota necrológica** obituary

necromancia *nf* necromancy

necrópolis *nf inv* necropolis

necrosis *nf inv* necrosis

néctar *nm* nectar

nectarina *nf* nectarine

neerlandés, -esa 1 *adj* Dutch

    2 *nm,f* Dutchman, *f* Dutchwoman

    3 *nm (idioma)* Dutch

nefando, -a *adj* abominable, odious

nefasto, -a *adj (funesto)* ill-fated; *(dañino)* bad, harmful; *(pésimo)* terrible, awful

nefrítico, -a *adj* renal, nephritic

nefritis *nf inv Med* nephritis

nefrología *nf* nephrology

negación *nf* (**a**) *(desmentido)* denial (**b**) *(negativa)* refusal (**c**) *(lo contrario)* antithesis, negation (**d**) *Gram* negative

negado, -a 1 *adj* useless, inept; **ser n. para algo** to be useless *o* no good at sth

    2 *nm,f* useless person, dead loss; **ser un n. para algo** to be useless *o* no good at sth

negar [43] **1** *vt* (**a**) *(rechazar)* to deny; **niega haber tenido nada que ver con el robo** he denies having had anything to do with the robbery; **no voy a n. que la idea me atrae** I won't deny that the idea appeals to me (**b**) *(denegar)* to refuse, to deny; **negarle algo a alguien** to refuse *o* deny sb sth; **nos negaron la entrada a la fiesta** they refused to let us into the party, they wouldn't let us into the party

    2 *vi* **n. con la cabeza** to shake one's head

    3 negarse *vpr* to refuse (**a** to); **me niego a creer que fuera él** I refuse to believe it was him; **negarse en redondo a hacer algo** to absolutely refuse to do sth

negativa *nf* (**a**) *(rechazo)* refusal (**b**) *(desmentido)* denial

negativo, -a 1 *adj* (**a**) *(en general)* negative; **el análisis ha dado n.** the test results were negative (**b**) *Mat* minus, negative; **signo n.** minus sign

    2 *nm Fot* negative

negligé [neɣliˈʒe] *nm* negligée

negligencia *nf* negligence

negligente *adj* negligent

negociable *adj* negotiable

negociación *nf* **el primer ministro participó en la n. del acuerdo** the prime minister was involved in negotiating the agreement; **negociaciones** negotiations; **n. colectiva** collective bargaining; **negociaciones de paz** peace negotiations; **n. salarial** pay bargaining

negociado *nm* department, section

negociador, -ora 1 *adj* negotiating

    2 *nm,f* negotiator

negociante *nmf (comerciante)* businessman, *f* businesswoman; *Fam Pey* con artist

negociar 1 *vi* (**a**) *(comerciar)* to do business; **n. con** to deal *o* trade with (**b**) *(discutir)* to negotiate

    2 *vt* to negotiate; **n. un acuerdo** to negotiate an agreement

negocio *nm* (**a**) *(empresa)* business; **¿cómo va el n.?** how's business?; **n. familiar** family business (**b**) **negocios** *(actividad)* business; **el mundo de los negocios** the business world; **se dedica a los negocios** he's in business; **estoy aquí por cuestiones de negocios** I'm here on business (**c**) *(transacción)* deal, (business) transaction; **(buen) n.** good deal, bargain; **hacer n.** to do well; *Fig* **¡mal n.!** that's a nasty business!; **n. redondo** great bargain, excellent deal; **n. sucio** shady deal, dirty business

negra *nf* (**a**) *Mús* quarter note (**b**) **tener la n.** to have bad luck; **se las va a ver negras para llegar a fin de mes** he'll have a hard job to get to the end of the month

negrero, -a 1 *adj (explotador)* tyrannical

    2 *nm,f* (**a**) *Hist* slave trader (**b**) *(explotador)* slave driver

negrita, negrilla *adj* (*letra*) **n.** bold (type), boldface; **en n.** in bold, in boldface

negro, -a 1 *adj* (**a**) (*color*) black (**b**) (*bronceado, moreno*) tanned; **estar n.** to have a deep tan (**c**) (*pan*) brown (**d**) (*suerte*) awful, rotten; (*porvenir*) black, gloomy; **llevo una tarde negra** I'm having a terrible afternoon; **pasarlas negras** to have a hard time; **ver(lo) todo n.** to be pessimistic (**e**) *Fam* (*furioso*) furious, fuming; **me pone n. que nunca me avisen de nada** it makes me mad that they never tell me anything (**f**) (*tabaco*) black, dark **n.** film noir

    2 *nm,f* black man, *f* black woman; *Fam Fig* **trabajar como un n.** to work like a slave

    3 *nm* (**a**) (*color*) black (**b**) (*tabaco*) black *o* dark tobacco

negroide *adj* negroid

negrura *nf* blackness

negruzco, -a *adj* blackish

negué *etc ver* **negar**

nemotecnia *nf* mnemonics (*singular*)

nemotécnico, -a *adj* mnemonic

nene, -a *nm,f* (**a**) *Fam* (*niño*) baby (**b**) (*apelativo cariñoso*) dear, darling

nenúfar *nm* water lily

neocapitalismo *nm* neocapitalism

neocelandés, -esa 1 *adj* New Zealand, of/from New Zealand; **un producto n.** a New Zealand product

    2 *nm,f* New Zealander

neoclasicismo *nm* neoclassicism

neoclásico, -a 1 *adj* neoclassical

    2 *nm,f* neoclassicist

neocolonialismo *nm* neocolonialism

neofascismo *nm* neofascism

neofascista *adj & nmf* neofascist

neófito, -a *nm,f* (**a**) *Rel* neophyte (**b**) (*aprendiz*) novice

neogótico, -a *adj* Neo-Gothic

neolatino, -a *adj* (*lengua*) Romance

neoliberal *adj & nmf* neoliberal

neoliberalismo *nm* neoliberalism

neolítico, -a 1 *adj* Neolithic

    2 *nm* Neolithic (period)

neologismo *nm* neologism

neón *nm* (**a**) *Quím* neon (**b**) (*luz de*) **n.** neon light

neonato, -a *adj* newborn

neonazi *adj & nmf* neo-Nazi

neoplasia *nf* tumor

neoplatónico, -a *adj* neo-Platonic

neopreno *nm* neoprene; **traje de n.** wet suit

neorrealismo *nm* neorealism

neoyorquino, -a 1 *adj* New York, of/from New York; **las calles neoyorquinas** the New York streets, the streets of New York

    2 *nm,f* New Yorker

neozelandés, -esa 1 *adj* New Zealand, of/from New Zealand; **un producto n.** a New Zealand product

    2 *nm,f* New Zealander

Nepal *n* Nepal

nepalés, -esa, nepalí (*pl* **nepalíes**) **1** *adj & nm,f* Nepalese

    2 *nm* (*lengua*) Nepalese

nepotismo *nm* nepotism

Neptuno *n* Neptune

nervadura *nf* (**a**) (*de construcción*) rib (**b**) (*de insecto*) nervure (**c**) (*de hoja*) vein

nervio *nm* (**a**) *Anat* nerve; **n. auditivo** auditory nerve; **n. ciático** sciatic nerve; **n. óptico** optic nerve (**b**) **nervios** (*estado mental*) nerves; **me ataca** *o* **crispa los nervios** it gets on my nerves; **me entraron los nervios** I got nervous; **estar de los nervios** to be in a nervous state; **perder los nervios** to lose one's cool *o* temper; **tener nervios** to be nervous; **tener nervios de acero** to have nerves of steel; **tener los nervios de punta** to be on edge; **poner los nervios de punta a alguien** to get on sb's nerves (**c**) (*en filete, carne*) sinew (**d**) *Bot* vein, rib (**e**) (*vigor*) energy, vigor (**f**) *Arquit* rib

nerviosismo *nm* nervousness, nerves

nervioso, -a *adj* (**a**) *Anat* (*sistema, enfermedad*) nervous; **centro/tejido n.** nerve center/tissue (**b**) (*inquieto*) nervous; **ponerse n.** to get nervous (**c**) (*muy activo*) high-strung (**d**) (*irritado*) worked-up, uptight; **poner n. a alguien** to get on sb's nerves; **ponerse n.** to get uptight *o* worked up

nervudo, -a *adj* sinewy

netamente *adv* clearly, distinctly

netiqueta *nf Inform* netiquette

neto, -a *adj* (**a**) (*peso, sueldo*) net (**b**) (*claro*) clear, clean; (*verdad*) simple, plain

neumático, -a 1 *adj* pneumatic

    2 *nm* tire; **n. de repuesto** spare tire

neumonía *nf* pneumonia

neura *Fam* **1** *adj* neurotic

    2 *nf* bug, mania; **le dio la n. de las maquetas** he caught the model-making bug

neuralgia *nf* neuralgia

neurálgico, -a *adj* (**a**) *Med* neuralgic (**b**) (*importante*) **centro n.** nerve center

neurastenia *nf* nervous exhaustion

neurasténico, -a *Med* **1** *adj* neurasthenic

    2 *nm,f* neurasthenic person

neuroanatomía *nf* neuroanatomy

neurobiología *nf* neurobiology

neurocirugía *nf* neurosurgery

neurocirujano, -a *nm,f* neurosurgeon, brain surgeon

neurofisiología *nf* neurophysiology

neurología *nf* neurology

neurológico, -a *adj* neurological

neurólogo, -a *nm,f* neurologist

neurona *nf* neuron, nerve cell

neuronal *adj* neural

neuropatía *nf* neuropathy

neuropsicología *nf* neuropsychology

neuropsiquiatría *nf* neuropsychiatry

neurosis *nf inv* neurosis

neurótico, -a *adj & nm,f* neurotic

neurotransmisor *nm* neurotransmitter

neutral *adj & nmf* neutral

neutralidad *nf* neutrality

neutralizable *adj* (*efecto, consecuencia*) remediable

neutralización *nf* neutralization

neutralizador, -ora *adj* neutralizing

neutralizar [14] **1** *vt* to neutralize

    2 neutralizarse *vpr* (*mutuamente*) to neutralize each other

neutrino *nm Fís* neutrino

neutro, -a 1 *adj* (**a**) (*color, actitud, voz*) neutral (**b**) *Biol & Gram* neuter

    2 *nm* (**a**) *Gram* neuter (**b**) *Am* (*marcha*) neutral

neutrón *nm* neutron

nevada *nf* snowfall

nevado, -a *adj* snowy

nevar [3] *v impersonal* to snow

nevera *nf* refrigerator, icebox

nevería *nf Carib, Méx* ice-cream parlor

nevisca *nf* snow flurry

neviscar [59] *v impersonal* to snow lightly

news ['nius] *nfpl Inform* newsgroup

newton ['niuton] (*pl* **newtons**) *nm Fís* newton

nexo nm link, connection

ni 1 conj **ni... ni...** neither... nor...; **ni mañana ni pasado** neither tomorrow nor the day after; **no... ni...** neither... nor..., not... or... (either); **no es alto ni bajo** he's neither tall nor short, he's not tall or short (either); **no es rojo ni verde ni azul** it's neither red nor green nor blue; **ni un/una...** not a single...; **no me quedaré ni un minuto más** I'm not staying a minute longer; **ni uno/una** not a single one; **no he aprobado ni una** I haven't passed a single one; **ni que** as if; **¡ni que yo fuera tonto!** as if I were that stupid!

2 adv not even; **ni siquiera** not even; **anda tan atareado que ni tiene tiempo para comer** he's so busy he doesn't even have time to eat

Niágara nm **las cataratas del N.** the Niagara Falls

Niamey n Niamey

Nicaragua n Nicaragua

nicaragüense adj & nmf Nicaraguan

nicho nm niche

Nicosia n Nicosia

nicotina nf nicotine

nidada nf (pollitos) brood; (huevos) clutch

nidal nm nest

nidificar [59] vi to (build a) nest

nido nm **(a)** (de animal) nest; Fig **irse del n.** to leave the nest **(b)** (lugar de reunión) **un n. de vicio/ladrones** a den of vice/thieves; **ese cuartel es un n. de conspiradores** that barracks is crawling with conspirators; Fig **ser un n. de víboras** to be a nest of vipers

niebla nf (densa) fog; (neblina) mist; **hay n.** it's foggy/misty; **hay n. densa** it's very foggy, there is thick o dense fog

niego etc ver **negar**

nieto, -a nm,f grandson, f granddaughter

nieva ver **nevar**

nieve nf **(a)** (precipitación) snow; **nieves** (nevada) snows, snowfall; **n. carbónica** dry ice; **nieves perpetuas** permanent snow; **n. en polvo** powder (snow) **(b)** Fam (cocaína) snow

NIF [nif] nm Esp (abrev de **número de identificación fiscal**) = identification number for tax purposes

Níger nm Niger

Nigeria n Nigeria

nigeriano, -a adj & nm,f Nigerian

nigromancia nf necromancy

nigromante nmf necromancer

nihilismo nm nihilism

nihilista 1 adj nihilistic

2 nmf nihilist

Nilo nm **el N.** the Nile (river)

nilón nm nylon

nimbo nm **(a)** (nube) nimbus **(b)** (de astro, santo) halo, nimbus

nimiedad nf **(a)** (cualidad) insignificance, triviality **(b)** (dicho, hecho) trifle

nimio, -a adj insignificant, trivial

ninfa nf nymph

ninfómana adj f & nf nymphomaniac

ninfomanía nf nymphomania

ninguno, -a

> **ningún** is used instead of **ninguno** before singular masculine nouns (e.g. **ningún hombre** no man).

1 adj no; **no se dio ninguna respuesta** no answer was given; **no tengo ningún interés en hacerlo** I've no interest in doing it, I'm not at all interested in doing it; **tengo ningún hijo/ninguna buena idea** I don't have any children/good ideas; **no lo veo por ninguna parte** I can't see it anywhere; **no tiene ninguna gracia** it's not funny; **en ningún momento** at no time; **no tengo ningunas**

ganas de ir I don't feel like going at all

2 pron (cosa) none, not any; (persona) nobody, no one; **n. funciona** none of them works; **no hay n.** there aren't any, there are none; **n. lo sabrá** no one o nobody will know; **n. de ellos** none of them; **n. de los dos** neither of them o the two; **no me gusta n. de los dos** I don't like either of them

niña nf (del ojo) pupil; Fig **la n. de los ojos** the apple of one's eye

niñato, -a nm,f Fam Pey **(a)** (inexperto) amateur, novice **(b)** (pijo) spoiled brat

niñera nf nanny

niñería nf **(a)** (cualidad) childishness **(b)** (tontería) silly o childish thing

niñez nf (infancia) childhood

niño, -a 1 adj young

2 nm,f **(a)** (crío) (varón) child, boy; (hembra) child, girl; (bebé) baby; **de n.** as a child; **desde n.** from childhood; **los niños** the children; **estar como un n. con zapatos nuevos** to be as pleased as punch; Fig **es culpa de la crisis — ¡qué crisis ni qué n. muerto!** it's the fault of the recession — don't talk to me about recessions!; **ser el n. bonito de alguien** to be sb's pet o blue-eyed boy; Pey **n. bien** rich kid; **el n. Jesús** the Baby Jesus; **n. probeta** test-tube baby; **n. prodigio** child prodigy; **n. de teta** o **pecho** tiny baby **(b)** (joven) young boy, f young girl

nipón, -ona adj & nm,f Japanese

níquel nm nickel

niquelar vt to nickel-plate

niqui nm Esp polo shirt

nirvana nm nirvana

níscalo nm = edible variety of milk cap mushroom

níspero nm medlar

nitidez nf (claridad) clarity; (de imagen, color) sharpness

nítido, -a adj (claro) clear; (imagen, color) sharp

nitrato nm nitrate; **n. de Chile** sodium nitrate

nítrico, -a adj nitric

nitrogenado, -a adj nitrogenous

nitrógeno nm nitrogen

nitroglicerina nf nitroglycerine

nitroso, -a adj nitrous

nivel nm **(a)** (altura) level, height; **al n. de** level with; **al n. del mar** at sea level; **la capital está a 250 metros sobre el n. del mar** the capital is 250 meters above sea level **(b)** (grado) level, standard; **no tiene un buen n. de inglés** his level of English is poor; **una reunión al más alto n.** a meeting at the highest level, a top-level meeting; **al mismo n. (que)** on a level o par (with); **a n. europeo** at a European level; **una campaña realizada a n. mundial** a worldwide campaign; **n. mental** level of intelligence; **n. de vida** standard of living **(c)** (instrumento) spirit level

nivelación nf **(a)** (allanamiento) leveling **(b)** (equilibrio) leveling out, evening out

nivelador, -ora adj leveling

niveladora nf bulldozer

nivelar vt **(a)** (allanar) to level **(b)** (equilibrar) to even out; Fin to balance

níveo, -a adj Formal snow-white

nixtamal nm CAm, Méx tortilla dough

no (pl **noes**) **1** adv **(a)** (negación) not; (en respuestas) no; (con sustantivos) non-; **no sé** I don't know; **no es fácil** it's not easy, it isn't easy; **no tiene dinero** he hasn't got any money; **no veo nada** I can't see anything; **todavía no** not yet; **¿has oído las noticias? — no** have you heard the news? — no(, I haven't); **¿aprobó? — no** did she pass? — no(, she didn't); **¿comen juntos? — no siempre** do they go for lunch together? — not always; **no fumadores** nonsmokers (**b**) *(expresa duda, extrañeza)* **¿no irás a venir?** you're not coming, are you?; **estamos de acuerdo, ¿no?** we're agreed then, are we?; **es español, ¿no?** he's Spanish, isn't he?

(**c**) *(expresiones)* **no ya... sino que...** not only... but (also)...; Fam **¡no es listo/guapo ni nada!** is he smart/good-looking or what?; **pues no** certainly not; **eso sí que no** certainly not; **¡que no!** I said no!

2 *nm* no

3 no bien *loc adv* as soon as

Nobel *nm (premio)* Nobel prize; *(galardonado)* Nobel prize winner

nobiliario, -a *adj* noble

noble *adj & nmf* noble; **los nobles** the nobility

nobleza *nf* nobility

nobuk *nm* nubuck

noche *nf (en oposición a día)* night; *(atardecer)* evening; **a las diez de la n.** at ten o'clock at night; **al caer** *o* **cuando cae la n.** at nightfall; **ayer (por la) n.** last night; **esta n.** *(próxima)* tonight; *(pasada)* last night; **hacer n. en** to stay the night in; **hacerse de n.** to get dark; **pasar la n. en claro** *o* **vela** to have a sleepless night; **de n.**, *Esp* **por la n.**, *Am* **en la n.** at night; **trabaja de n.** she works nights; **buenas noches** *(saludo)* good evening; *(despedida)* good night; **de la n. a la mañana** overnight; **ser la n. y el día** to be as different as night and day; **n. de bodas** wedding night; **n. de gala** gala evening; **N. de Reyes** Twelfth Night

Nochebuena *nf* Christmas Eve

nochero *nm* (**a**) *CSur (vigilante)* night watchman (**b**) *Col (mueble)* bedside table

Nochevieja *nf* New Year's Eve

noción *nf (concepto)* notion; **tener n. (de)** to have an idea (of); **perdió la n. del tiempo** he lost all track of time; **se busca guía con nociones de japonés** we are looking for a guide with a basic knowledge of Japanese; **tener nociones de** *(conocimiento básico)* to have a smattering of

nocividad *nf (cualidad de dañino)* harmfulness; *(de gas)* noxiousness

nocivo, -a *adj (dañino)* harmful; *(gas)* noxious

noctámbulo, -a 1 *adj* active at night; **animal n.** nocturnal animal

2 *nm,f (persona)* night owl

nocturnidad *nf* Der **con n.** under cover of darkness

nocturno, -a 1 *adj* (**a**) **tren/vuelo n.** night train/flight (**b**) *(animales, plantas)* nocturnal

2 *nm* Mús nocturne

nodo *nm* node

nodriza 1 *nf* wet nurse

2 *adj* **buque/avión n.** refueling ship/plane

nódulo *nm* nodule

nogal *nm* walnut

nómada 1 *adj* nomadic

2 *nmf* nomad

nomadismo *nm* nomadism

nomás *adv* (**a**) *Am* just; **así n.** just like that; **hasta allí n.** that far and no further; **¡pase n.!** come right in! (**b**) *Méx* **n. que** as soon as

nombrado, -a *adj* (**a**) *(citado)* mentioned (**b**) *(famoso)* famous, well-known

nombramiento *nm* appointment

nombrar *vt* (**a**) *(citar)* to mention (**b**) *(designar)* to appoint

nombre *nm* (**a**) *(apelativo)* name; **a n. de** *(carta)* addressed to; *(cheque)* made out to; **de n. Juan** called Juan, Juan by name; **en n. de** on behalf of; **llamar a las cosas por su n.** to call a spade a spade; **¿qué n. le vas a poner al perro?** what are you going to call the dog?; **le pusieron el n. de su abuelo** they named him for his grandfather; **no tener n.** to be unspeakable; **n. y apellidos** full name; **n. artístico/comer-**

cial stage/trade name; **n. de pila** first *o* Christian name; **n. de soltera** maiden name; *Inform* **n. de usuario** username

(**b**) *(fama)* reputation; **tener mucho n.** to be renowned *o* famous

(**c**) *Gram* noun; **n. abstracto/colectivo** abstract/collective noun; **n. común/propio** common/proper noun

nomenclatura *nf* nomenclature

nomeolvides *nm inv* (**a**) *(flor)* forget-me-not (**b**) *(pulsera)* identity bracelet

nómina *nf* (**a**) *(lista de empleados)* payroll; **estar en n.** to be on the staff (**b**) *(pago)* wage packet, wages (**c**) *(hoja de salario)* payslip

nominación *nf* nomination

nominado, -a *adj* nominated

nominal *adj* nominal

nominar *vt* to nominate

nominativo, -a 1 *adj* Com bearing a person's name, nominal

2 *nm* Gram nominative

non 1 *adj* odd, uneven

2 *nm* odd number

3 *adv* Fam **nones** *(no)* no way, absolutely not

nonagenario, -a *adj* ninety-year-old

2 *nm,f* person in his/her nineties

nonagésimo, -a *núm* ninetieth

nonato, -a *adj (bebé)* born by Cesarean section

nono, -a *núm* Formal ninth

non plus ultra *nm* **ser el n.** to be the best ever

noquear *vt* Dep to knock out

norcoreano, -a *adj & nm,f* North Korean

nordeste = **noreste**

nórdico, -a 1 *adj* (**a**) *(del norte)* northern, northerly (**b**) *(escandinavo)* Nordic

2 *nm,f* Nordic person

noreste, nordeste 1 *adj (posición, parte)* northeast, northeastern; *(dirección, viento)* northeasterly

2 *nm* northeast

noria *nf* (**a**) *(para agua)* waterwheel (**b**) *Esp (de feria)* Ferris wheel

norirlandés, -esa 1 *adj* Northern Irish

2 *nm,f* person from Northern Ireland

norma *nf (patrón, modelo)* standard; *(regla)* rule; **este producto no cumple la n. europea** this product does not meet European standards; **la n. es que llueva al final de la tarde** it usually *o* normally rains toward the end of the afternoon; **por n. (general)** as a rule; **tener por n. hacer algo** to make it a rule to do sth; **n. de conducta** *(principios)* standards (of behavior); *(pauta)* pattern of behavior

normal *adj* normal; **lleva una vida n.** she leads a fairly normal *o* ordinary life; **este hermano tuyo no es n.** there must be something wrong with that brother of yours; **es n. que estés cansado** it's hardly surprising that you're tired; **n. y corriente** run-of-the-mill; **es una persona n. y corriente** he's a perfectly ordinary person

normalidad *nf* normality

normalista *nmf* Bol, Méx (**a**) *(estudiante)* student teacher (**b**) *(profesor)* teaching graduate

normalización *nf* (**a**) *(vuelta a la normalidad)* normalization (**b**) *(regularización)* standardization

normalizar [14] **1** *vt* (**a**) *(volver normal)* to return to normal (**b**) *(estandarizar)* to standardize

2 normalizarse *vpr* to return to normal

normalmente *adv* usually, normally

Normandía *n* Normandy

normando, -a 1 *adj* (**a**) *(de Normandía)* of/from Normandy; **el paisaje n.** the Normandy countryside (**b**) *Hist (nórdico)* Norse; *(de Normandía)* Norman

2 *nm,f* (**a**) *(habitante de Normandía)* person from Normandy

(b) *Hist (nórdico)* Norseman, *f* Norsewoman; *(de Normandía)* Norman

normativa *nf* regulations

normativo, -a *adj* normative

noroeste 1 *adj (posición, parte)* northwest, northwestern; *(dirección, viento)* northwesterly

  2 *nm* northwest

norte 1 *adj (posición, parte)* north, northern; *(dirección)* northerly; **viento n.** north wind; **en la mitad n. del país** in the northern half of the country; **partieron con rumbo n.** they set off northwards

  2 *nm* **(a)** *Geog* north; **viento del n.** north wind; **ir hacia el n.** to go north(wards); **el n. de España** northern Spain, the north of Spain; **está al n. de Madrid** it's (to the) north of Madrid **(b)** *(objetivo)* goal, objective; **perder el n.** to lose one's bearings *o* way

norteafricano, -a *adj & nm,f* North African

norteamericano, -a *adj & nm,f* North American, American

norteño, -a 1 *adj* northern

  2 *nm,f* northerner

Noruega *n* Norway

noruego, -a 1 *adj & nm,f* Norwegian

  2 *nm (lengua)* Norwegian

norvietnamita *adj & mf* North Vietnamese

nos *pron personal* **(a)** *(complemento directo)* us; **le gustaría vernos** she'd like to see us; **n. atracaron en plena calle** we were attacked in the middle of the street **(b)** *(complemento indirecto)* (to) us; **n. lo dio** he gave it to us; **n. tiene miedo** he's afraid of us **(c)** *(reflexivo)* ourselves; **n. vestimos** we get dressed; **n. pusimos los abrigos y salimos** we put our coats on and left; **se n. olvidó** we forgot **(d)** *(recíproco)* each other; **n. enamoramos** we fell in love (with each other); **n. concedimos una segunda oportunidad** we gave ourselves a second chance

nosocomio *nm Am* hospital

nosotros, -as *pron personal*

Usually omitted in Spanish except for emphasis or contrast.

(a) *(sujeto)* we; **¿quién va primero? — n.** who's first? — we are; **ellos están invitados, n. no** they're invited, but we're not *o* but not us **(b)** *(predicado)* **somos n.** it's us; **sus hermanos somos n.** we are her brothers **(c)** *(después de prep & complemento)* us; **vente a comer con n.** come and eat with us; **lo arreglaremos entre n.** we'll sort it out among ourselves; **de n.** *(nuestro)* ours; **entre n.** between you and me, just between the two of us

nostalgia *nf (del pasado)* nostalgia; *(de país, amigos)* homesickness

nostálgico, -a 1 *adj (del pasado)* nostalgic; *(de país, amigos)* homesick

  2 *nm,f* nostalgic person

nota *nf* **(a)** *(apunte)* note; **tomar n. de algo** *(apuntar)* to note sth down; *(fijarse)* to take note of sth; **n. bene** nota bene, N.B.; **n. al margen** marginal note; **n. necrológica** obituary notice; **n. a pie de página** footnote; **notas de sociedad** society column

  (b) *Mús* note; *Fam Fig* **dar la n.** to make oneself conspicuous; *Fig* **forzar la n.** to go too far; *Fig* **de mala n.** of ill repute; *Fig* **n. discordante** discordant note; *Fig* **n. dominante** prevailing mood; **n. falsa** false note

  (c) *(calificación)* grade; **sacar** *o* **tener buenas notas** to get good marks; **las notas** *(de examen)* the (exam) results; **n. de corte** = minimum marks for entry into college

  (d) *(cuenta)* bill; *(en restaurante)* check; **n. de gastos** expenses claim

notable 1 *adj* remarkable, outstanding

  2 *nm* **(a)** *Educ* (pass with) credit **(b)** *(persona)* notable, distinguished person

notación *nm* notation

notar 1 *vt (advertir)* to notice; *(sentir)* to feel; **¿has notado algo extraño en su comportamiento?** have you noticed anything strange in her behavior?; **noto frío en los pies** my feet feel cold; **te noto cansado** you look tired to me; **hacer n. algo** to point sth out; **nótese que el acusado estaba bebido** note *o* observe that the accused was drunk

  2 notarse *vpr* **no se nota la herida** you can't see where the wound was; **se nota que le gusta** you can tell she likes it

notaría *nf* **(a)** *(profesión)* profession of notary **(b)** *(oficina)* notary's office

notariado *nm (profesión)* profession of notary

notarial *adj* notarial

notario, -a *nm,f* notary (public)

noticia *nf* news *(singular)*; **una n.** a piece of news; **su hijo le dio la n.** his son broke the news to him; **me enteré de la n. ayer** I heard the news yesterday; **tener noticias** to have news; **¿tienes noticias suyas?** have you heard from him?; **las noticias** the news; *Fam* **n. bomba** bombshell; **noticias de última hora** the latest news

noticiario, noticiero *nm Cine* newsreel; *Rad & TV* news bulletin

notición *nm Fam* bombshell

noticioso *nm Andes, RP* television news

notificación *nf* notification; **n. de despido** layoff notice

notificar [59] *vt* to notify, to inform

notoriedad *nf* **(a)** *(fama)* fame **(b)** *(evidencia)* obviousness

notorio, -a *adj* **(a)** *(evidente)* obvious **(b)** *(conocido)* widely known

novatada *nf* **(a)** *(broma)* practical joke *(on newcomer)* **(b)** *(error)* beginner's mistake; **pagar la n.** to learn the hard way

novato, -a 1 *adj* inexperienced

  2 *nm,f* novice, beginner

novecientos, -as *núm* nine hundred; *ver también* **seis**

novedad *nf* **(a)** *(cualidad) (de nuevo)* newness; *(de novedoso)* novelty; **el nuevo sistema operativo incluye muchas novedades** the new operating system incorporates many new features; **es igual que el model anterior con la n. de que utiliza energía solar** it is the same as the previous model except that it now uses solar power; **novedades** *(libros, discos)* new releases; *(moda)* latest fashion

  (b) *(cambio)* change; **desde que te fuiste ha habido muchas novedades en la oficina** there have been a lot of changes in the office since you left

  (c) *(noticia)* news *(singular)*; **sin n.** without incident; *Mil* all quiet

  (d) *(cosa nueva)* new thing; *(innovación)* innovation

novedoso, -a *adj* novel, new

novel *adj* new, first-time

novela *nf* novel; **n. de caballerías** tale of chivalry; **n. por entregas** serial; **n. histórica** historical novel; **n. policíaca** detective story; **n. rosa** romance, romantic novel

novelar *vt* to fictionalize, to make into a novel

novelería *nf* **(a)** *(ficciones)* fantasies **(b)** **novelerías** *(cosas novedosas)* novelties

novelero, -a 1 *adj* **(a)** *(fantasioso)* very imaginative **(b)** *(aficionado a las novelas)* fond of novels

  2 *nm,f* **(a)** *(fantasioso)* very imaginative person **(b)** *(aficionado a las novelas)* person fond of novels

novelesco, -a *adj* **(a)** *(de la novela)* fictional **(b)** *(fantástico)* fantastic, extraordinary

novelista *nmf* novelist

novelístico, -a *adj* novelistic

novelón *nm Fam* = hefty and badly written novel; *Fig* **¡menudo n.!** what a melodrama!

novena *nf Rel* novena

noveno, -a *núm* ninth; **la novena parte** a ninth

noventa *núm* ninety; **los (años) n.** the nineties; *ver también* **seis**

noviazgo *nm* engagement

noviciado *nm Rel* novitiate; *Fig (aprendizaje)* apprenticeship

novicio, -a *Rel & Fig nm,f* novice

noviembre *nm* November; *ver también* **septiembre**

novillada *nf Taurom* = bullfight with young bulls

novillero, -a *nm,f Taurom* apprentice bullfighter

novillo, -a *nm,f* young bull; *f* young cow; *Esp Fam* **hacer novillos** to play hooky

novio, -a *nm,f* (**a**) *(compañero)* boyfriend, *f* girlfriend; *(prometido)* fiancé, *f* fiancée (**b**) *(el día de la boda)* bridegroom, *f* bride; **los novios** the bride and groom

novísimo, -a *adj* brand-new, up-to-the-minute

Ntra. Sra. *(abrev de* **Nuestra Señora***)* Our Lady

ntro. *abrev de* **nuestro**

nubarrón *nm* storm cloud

nube *nf* (**a**) *(de lluvia, humo)* cloud; **como caído de las nubes** out of the blue; **estar en las nubes** to have one's head in the clouds; *Fam* **poner algo/a alguien por las nubes** to praise sth/sb to the skies; *Fam* **estar por las nubes** *(caro)* to be terribly expensive; **nubes de tormenta** storm clouds; *Fig* **n. de verano** short fit of anger (**b**) *(de personas, moscas)* swarm

núbil *adj Formal* nubile

nublado, -a *adj* (**a**) *(cielo)* cloudy, overcast (**b**) *(vista, entendimiento)* clouded

nublar 1 *vt también Fig* to cloud
2 nublarse *vpr* (**a**) *(cielo, vista)* to cloud over (**b**) *(turbarse, oscurecerse)* to become clouded

nubloso, -a *adj* cloudy

nubosidad *nf* cloudiness, clouds

nuboso, -a *adj* cloudy

nuca *nf* nape, back of the neck

nuclear *adj* nuclear

nuclearización *nf* (**a**) *Ind* introduction of nuclear power (**b**) *Mil* acquisition of nuclear weapons

nuclearizar [14] *vt* (**a**) *Ind* to introduce nuclear power into (**b**) *Mil* to acquire nuclear weapons for

nucleico *adj Bioquím* nucleic

núcleo *nm* (**a**) *(centro)* nucleus; *Fís* **n. atómico** atomic nucleus; **n. de población** population center (**b**) *(grupo)* core; **n. duro** *(de personas)* hard core

nudillo *nm* knuckle; **llamar con los nudillos** *(a la puerta)* to knock (on *o* at the door)

nudismo *nm* nudism

nudista *adj & nmf* nudist

nudo *nm* (**a**) *(lazo)* knot; **hacer un n.** to tie a knot; *Fig* **se le hizo un n. en la garganta** she got a lump in her throat; **n. corredizo** slipknot; **n. gordiano** Gordian knot (**b**) *(cruce)* junction; **n. de comunicaciones** communications center (**c**) *(vínculo)* tie, bond (**d**) *(punto principal)* crux, nub (**e**) *(en madera)* knot

nudoso, -a *adj* knotty, gnarled

nuera *nf* daughter-in-law

nuestro, -a 1 *adj posesivo* our; **n. coche** our car; **este libro es n.** this book is ours, this is our book; **un amigo n.** a friend of ours; **no es asunto n.** it's none of our business
2 *pron posesivo* **el n.** ours; **el n. es rojo** ours is red; *Fam* **esta es la nuestra** this is the chance we've been waiting for *o* our big chance; **lo n. es el teatro** *(lo que nos va)* theater is our thing; *Fam* **los nuestros** *(nuestra familia)* our folks; *(nuestro bando)* our lot, our side

nueva *nf Literario* (piece of) news; **buena n.** good news

Nueva Delhi *n* New Delhi

Nueva Hampshire *n* New Hampshire

Nueva Jersey *n* New Jersey

Nueva York *n* New York

Nueva Zelanda *n* New Zealand

nueve *núm* nine; *ver también* **seis**

nuevo, -a 1 *adj* (**a**) *(reciente)* new; *(hortaliza)* new, fresh; *(vino)* young; **estar/quedar como n.** to be as good as new; **ser n. en** to be new to; **N. México** New Mexico; **el N. Mundo** the New World; **el N. Testamento** the New Testament (**b**) **de n.** again
2 *nm,f* newcomer

nuez *nf* (**a**) *(de nogal)* walnut; **n. moscada** nutmeg (**b**) *Anat* Adam's apple

nulidad *nf* (**a**) *(no validez)* nullity (**b**) *(ineptitud)* incompetence (**c**) *Fam (persona)* nonentity; **ser una n.** to be useless

nulo, -a *adj* (**a**) *(sin validez)* null and void, invalid (**b**) *Fam (incapacitado)* useless (**para** at)

núm. *(abrev de* **número***)* No

numantino, -a *adj* brave, courageous

numen *nm Formal* inspiration, muse

numeración *nf* (**a**) *(acción)* numbering (**b**) *(sistema)* numerals, numbers; **n. arábiga** *o* **decimal** Arabic numerals; **n. binaria** binary numbers; **n. romana** Roman numerals

numerador *nm Mat* numerator

numeral *adj* numeral

numerar 1 *vt* to number
2 numerarse *vpr (personas)* to number off

numerario, -a *adj (profesor, catedrático)* tenured, permanent; *(miembro)* full

numérico, -a *adj* numerical

número *nm* (**a**) *(signo)* number; **mi n. de la suerte** my lucky number; **sin n.** *(muchos)* countless, innumerable; **en números rojos** in the red; **hacer números** to reckon up; **ser el n. uno** to be number one; *Quím* **n. atómico** atomic number; **n. binario** binary number; **n. cardinal** cardinal number; **n. complejo** complex number; **n. complementario** *(en lotería)* = complementary number; **n. entero** whole number, integer; **n. irracional** irrational number; **n. de fax** fax number; **n. fraccionario** fraction; **n. impar** odd number; *Aut* **n. de matrícula** license number; **n. ordinal** ordinal number; **n. par** even number; **n. primo** round number; **n. quebrado** fraction; **n. redondo** round number; **n. romano** Roman numeral; **n. de teléfono** (tele)phone number
(**b**) *(tamaño, talla)* size
(**c**) *(de publicación)* issue, number; **n. atrasado** back number; **n. extraordinario** special edition *o* issue
(**d**) *(de lotería)* ticket
(**e**) *Esp (de policía)* officer
(**f**) *(de espectáculo)* turn, number; *Fam* **montar el n.** to make *o* cause a scene

numeroso, -a *adj* numerous; **un grupo n.** a large group

numerus clausus *nm inv Educ* = restriction on number of students in college course

numismática *nf (estudio)* numismatics *(singular)*

numismático, -a 1 *adj* numismatic
2 *nm,f (persona)* numismatist

nunca *adv (en frases afirmativas)* never; *(en frases negativas)* ever; **no me cuentan n. nada** they never tell me anything; **casi n. viene** he almost never comes, he hardly ever comes; **¿no le has visto n.?** have you never seen her?, haven't you ever seen her?; **como n.** like never before; **más que n.** more than ever; **n. jamás** *o* **más** never more *o* again; **¡n. vi nada parecido!** I never saw anything like it!

nunciatura *nf Rel* (**a**) *(cargo)* nunciature (**b**) *(edificio)* nuncio's residence (**c**) *(tribunal de la Rota)* = ecclesiastical court in Spain

nuncio *nm Rel* nuncio; **n. apostólico** papal nuncio

nupcial *adj* wedding; **ceremonia/lecho n.** marriage ceremony/bed

nupcias *nfpl* wedding, nuptials; **contraer segundas n.** to remarry

nutria *nf* otter

nutrición *nf* nutrition

nutricionista *nmf* nutritionist

nutrido, -a *adj* (**a**) *(alimentado)* nourished, fed; **mal n.** undernourished (**b**) *(numeroso)* large

nutrir 1 *vt* (**a**) *(alimentar)* to nourish *o* feed (**con** *o* **de** with) (**b**) *(fomentar)* to feed, to nurture (**c**) *(suministrar)* to supply (**de** with)
    2 nutrirse *vpr* (**a**) *(alimentarse)* **nutrirse de** *o* **con** to feed on (**b**) *(proveerse)* **nutrirse de** *o* **con** to supply *o* provide oneself with

nutritivo, -a *adj* nutritious

nylon ['nailon] (*pl* **nylons**) *nm* nylon

Ñ

Ñ, ñ ['eɲe] *nf (letra)* Ñ, ñ, = 15th letter of the Spanish alphabet

ñacañaca *nm Esp Fam Hum* **hacer ñ.** to make out

ñame *nm CAm, CArib, Col* yam

ñandú (*pl* **ñandúes**) *nm* rhea

ñato, -a *adj Andes, RP* snub-nosed; **ser ñ.** to have a snub nose

ñoñería, ñoñez *nf* inanity

ñoño, -a *adj* (**a**) *(remilgado)* squeamish; *(quejica)* whining (**b**) *(soso)* dull, insipid

ñoqui *nm Culin* gnocchi

ñu *nm* gnu

O

O, o [o] *nf (letra)* O, o

o *conj*

> **u** is used instead of **o** in front of words beginning with **o** or **ho** (e.g. **mujer u hombre** woman or man).

or; **25 ó 26 invitados** 25 or 26 guests; **o.... o.** either... or; **o te comportas, o te quedarás sin cenar** either you behave yourself or you're not getting any dinner, unless you behave yourself, you won't get any dinner; **cansado o no, tendrás que ayudar** (whether you're) tired or not, you'll have to help; **o sea (que)** in other words

o/ *(abrev de* **orden**) order

oasis *nm inv también Fig* oasis; **un o. de tranquilidad** an oasis of calm

obcecación *nf* blindness, stubbornness

obcecado, -a *adj* (a) *(tozudo)* stubborn (b) *(obsesionado)* **o. por** *o* **con** blinded by

obcecar [59] **1** *vt* to blind

2 obcecarse *vpr* to become stubborn; **obcecarse en hacer algo** to stubbornly insist on doing sth

obedecer [46] **1** *vt* **o. a alguien** to obey sb; **obedece a tu madre** obey your mother, do as *o* what your mother tells you

2 *vi* (a) *(acatar)* to obey, to do as one is told; **hacerse o.** to command obedience (b) *(estar motivado)* **o. a** to be due to; **una actitud que sólo obedece al miedo** an attitude which is due entirely to fear (c) *(responder)* to respond; **las piernas no me obedecían** my legs wouldn't do what I wanted them to

obediencia *nf* obedience

obediente *adj* obedient

obelisco *nm* obelisk

obenque *nm Náut* shroud

obertura *nf* overture

obesidad *nf* obesity

obeso, -a 1 *adj* obese

2 *nm,f* obese person

óbice *nm Formal* **no ser ó. para** not to be an obstacle to

obispado *nm* bishopric

obispo *nm* bishop

óbito *nm Formal* decease, demise

obituario *nm* obituary

objeción *nf* objection; **poner objeciones a** to raise objections to; **tener objeciones** to have objections; **o. de conciencia** conscientious objection

objetar 1 *vt* to object to; **no tengo nada que o.** I have no objection

2 *vi Esp* to be a conscientious objector

objetivar *vt* to treat objectively

objetividad *nf* objectivity

objetivo, -a 1 *adj* objective

2 *nm* (a) *(finalidad)* objective, aim; *Com* **o. de producción** production target (b) *Mil* target (c) *Fot* lens

objeto *nm* (a) *(asunto, cosa)* object; **ser o. de** to be the object

of; **objetos perdidos** lost and found; **objetos de valor** valuables; **o. volador no identificado** unidentified flying object

(b) *(propósito)* purpose, object; **el o. de la visita** the purpose *o* object of the visit; **tener por o.** *(sujeto: plan)* to be aimed at; *(sujeto: persona)* to have as one's aim; **¿con qué o.?** to what end?; **sin o.** *(inútilmente)* to no purpose, pointlessly; **al** *o* **con o. de hacer algo** in order to do sth, with the aim of doing st

(c) *(blanco)* **fue o. de las burlas de sus compañeros** he was the butt of his classmates' jokes; **el artículo ha sido o. de duras críticas** the article has come in for some harsh criticism

objetor, -ora *nm,f* objector; **o. de conciencia** conscientious objector

oblación *nf Rel* oblation

oblea *nf* wafer

oblicuo, -a *adj* (a) *(inclinado)* oblique, slanting; *(mirada)* sidelong (b) *Mat* oblique

obligación *nf* (a) *(deber, imposición)* obligation, duty; **por o.** out of a sense of duty (b) *Fin* bond, security; **o. convertible** convertible bond; **o. del Estado** Treasury bond

obligacionista *nmf Fin* bondholder

obligado, -a *adj* obligatory, compulsory

obligar [38] **1** *vt* **o. a alguien a hacer algo/a que haga algo** to oblige *o* force sb to do sth, to make sb do sth; **yo no quería hacerlo, me obligaron** I didn't want to do it, they forced me to *o* they made me; **no lo compres, nadie te obliga** don't buy it, nobody is forcing you; **la obligué a que me contestase** I forced her to answer me, I made her answer me

2 obligarse *vpr* **obligarse a hacer algo** to undertake to do sth

obligatoriedad *nf* obligatory *o* compulsory nature

obligatorio, -a *adj* obligatory, compulsory

obligue *etc ver* **obligar**

obliterar *vt Med* to obliterate

oblongo, -a *adj* oblong

obnubilación *nf* bewilderment

obnubilar *vt* to bewilder, to daze

oboe 1 *nm (instrumento)* oboe

2 *nmf (persona)* oboist

óbolo *nm* small contribution

obra *nf* (a) *(trabajo, acción)* **una buena o.** a good deed; **es o. suya** it's his doing; **poner en o.** to put into effect; **por o. (y gracia) de** thanks to; **o. de caridad** *(institución)* charity; **obras sociales** community work

(b) *(creación artística)* work; *(de teatro)* play; *(de literatura)* book; *(de música)* work, opus; **la o. pictórica de Miguel Ángel** Michelangelo's paintings; **o. de arte** work of art; **obras completas** complete works; **o. de consulta** reference work; **o. maestra** masterpiece

(c) *(trabajo de construcción)* work; *(reforma doméstica, en hogar)* alteration; **obras** *(en carretera)* roadworks; **vamos a hacer o.**

o **obras en la cocina** we're going to make some alterations to our kitchen; **cerrado por obras** *(en letrero)* closed for refurbishment; **obras públicas** public works

(**d**) *(solar en construcción)* building site

obrador *nm* workshop

obrar 1 *vi* (**a**) *(actuar)* to act (**b**) *(causar efecto)* to work, to take effect; **el remedio obró como se esperaba** the remedy took effect *o* worked as anticipated (**c**) *(estar en poder)* **o. en manos de** *o* **en poder de** to be in the possession of

2 *vt* to work; **esta experiencia obró un cambio profundo en su persona** this experience brought about a profound change in him

obrero, -a 1 *adj* **clase obrera** working class; **movimiento o.** labor movement

2 *nm,f (en fábrica)* worker; *(en obra)* workman, laborer; *Esp* **o. cualificado**, *Am* **o. calificado** skilled worker; **o. de la construcción** construction worker

obscenidad *nf* obscenity

obsceno, -a *adj* obscene

obscurantismo = oscurantismo

obscurecer, obscuridad *etc* = oscurecer, oscuridad *etc*

obsequiar *vt Esp* **o. a alguien con algo**, *Am* **o. algo a alguien** to present sb with sth

obsequio *nm* gift, present; **o. de empresa** complimentary gift

obsequiosidad *nf* attentiveness, helpfulness

obsequioso, -a *adj* obliging, attentive

observación *nf* (**a**) *(examen, contemplación)* observation; **el paciente está en** *o* **bajo o.** the patient is under observation (**b**) *(comentario)* observation, remark; **hacer una o.** to make a comment *o* observation; **si se me permite una o.** if I might make an observation (**c**) *(nota)* note (**d**) *(cumplimiento)* observance; **Sanidad recomienda la o. de estas normas** the Department of Health recommends following these guidelines

observador, -ora 1 *adj* observant

2 *nm,f* observer

observancia *nf* observance

observar *vt* (**a**) *(contemplar)* to observe, to watch; **observaban todos sus movimientos mediante unos prismáticos** they observed *o* followed all his movements through binoculars (**b**) *(advertir)* to notice, to observe; **no se observan anomalías** no problems have been noted (**c**) *(acatar) (ley, normas)* to observe, to respect; *(conducta, costumbre)* to follow (**d**) *(comentar, señalar)* to remark, to observe; **"eso no es totalmente cierto", observó** "that's not entirely true," he remarked *o* pointed out

observatorio *nm* observatory

obsesión *nf* obsession

obsesionar 1 *vt* to obsess

2 obsesionarse *vpr* to be obsessed

obsesivo, -a *adj* obsessive

obseso, -a 1 *adj* obsessed

2 *nm,f* obsessed *o* obsessive person

obsolescencia *nf* obsolescence

obsoleto, -a *adj* obsolete

obstaculizar [14] *vt* to hinder, to hamper

obstáculo *nm* obstacle; **un o. para** an obstacle to; **poner obstáculos a algo/alguien** to hinder sth/sb

obstante *adv* **no o.** nevertheless, however

obstar *vi Formal* **eso no es obsta para que vengas si quieres** that isn't to say that you can't come if you want to

obstetra *nmf esp Am* obstetrician

obstetricia *nf* obstetrics *(singular)*

obstinación *nf (persistencia)* perseverance; *(terquedad)* obstinacy, stubbornness

obstinado, -a *adj (persistente)* persistent; *(terco)* obstinate, stubborn

obstinarse *vpr* to refuse to give way; **o. en** to persist in

obstrucción *nf también Fig* obstruction

obstruccionismo *nm* obstructionism, stonewalling

obstruccionista *adj & nmf* obstructionist

obstruir [34] **1** *vt* (**a**) *(bloquear)* to block, to obstruct (**b**) *(obstaculizar)* to obstruct, to impede

2 obstruirse *vpr* to get blocked (up)

obtención *nf* obtaining

obtener [65] *vt (beca, cargo, puntos)* to get; *(premio, victoria)* to win; *(ganancias)* to make; *(satisfacción)* to gain

obturación *nf* blockage, obstruction

obturador *nm Fot* shutter

obturar *vt* to block

obtuso, -a 1 *adj* (**a**) *(sin punta)* blunt (**b**) *(tonto)* obtuse, stupid

2 *nm,f* dimwit

obtuviera *etc ver* **obtener**

obús *(pl obuses) nm* (**a**) *(cañón)* howitzer (**b**) *(proyectil)* shell

obviamente *adv* obviously

obviar *vt* to avoid, to get around

obvio, -a *adj* obvious

oca *nf* (**a**) *(animal)* goose (**b**) *(juego)* **la o.** ≃ Chutes and Ladders®

ocarina *nf* ocarina

ocasión *nf* (**a**) *(oportunidad)* opportunity, chance; **una o. de oro** a golden opportunity; **en** *o* **a la primera o.** at the first opportunity; **tener o. de hacer algo** to have the chance to do sth; *Fam* **la o. la pintan calva** this is my/your/*etc* big chance (**b**) *(vez)* occasion; *(momento)* time, moment; **en dos ocasiones** on two occasions; **en alguna o.** sometimes; **en cierta o.** once; **en otra o.** some other time (**c**) *(motivo)* **con o. de** on the occasion of; **dar o. para algo/hacer algo** to give cause for sth/to do sth (**d**) *(ganga)* bargain; **artículos de o.** bargains; **automóviles de o.** secondhand *o* used cars

ocasional *adj* (**a**) *(accidental)* accidental (**b**) *(irregular)* occasional

ocasionar *vt* to cause

ocaso *nm (puesta del sol)* sunset; *(decadencia)* decline

occidental 1 *adj* western; **la España o.** western Spain

2 *nmf* westerner

occidentalismo *nm* western nature

occidentalizar [14] **1** *vt* to westernize

2 occidentalizarse *vpr* to become westernized

occidente *nm* west; **O.** *(bloque de países)* the West

occipital *adj* occipital

OCDE *nf (abrev de* **Organización para la Cooperación y el Desarrollo Económico**) OECD

Oceanía *n* Oceania *(including Australia and New Zealand)*

oceánico, -a *adj* (**a**) *(de un océano)* oceanic (**b**) *(de Oceanía)* Oceanian

océano *nm (mar)* ocean; *(inmensidad)* sea, host; **el o. Atlántico** the Atlantic Ocean; **el o. Glacial Ártico** the Arctic Ocean; **el o. Índico** the Indian Ocean; **el o. Pacífico** the Pacific Ocean

oceanografía *nf* oceanography

oceanográfico, -a *adj* oceanographical

oceanógrafo, -a *nm,f* oceanographer

ocelote *nm (mamífero)* ocelot

ochenta *núm* eighty; **los (años) o.** the eighties; *ver también* **seis**

ocho *núm* eight; **del sábado en o. días** the Saturday after next, a week on Saturday; *ver también* **seis**

ochocientos, -as *núm* eight hundred; *ver también* **seis**

ocio *nm (tiempo libre)* leisure; *(inactividad)* idleness; **en sus ratos de o. se dedica a leer** he spends his spare time reading

ociosidad *nf* idleness

ocioso, -a *adj* (**a**) *(inactivo)* idle (**b**) *(innecesario)* unnecessary; *(inútil)* pointless

oclusión *nf* blockage

oclusiva *nf Ling* occlusive

oclusivo, -a *adj Ling* occlusive

ocre 1 *nm* ocher
2 *adj inv* ocher

octaedro *nm* octahedron

octagonal *adj* octagonal

octágono, -a 1 *adj* octagonal
2 *nm* octagon

octanaje *nm* octane number *o* rating

octano *nm* octane

octava *nf Mús* octave

octavilla *nf* (**a**) *(de propaganda)* pamphlet, leaflet (**b**) *(tamaño)* octavo

octavo, -a 1 *núm* eighth; **la octava parte** an eighth
2 *nm* (**a**) *(parte)* eighth (**b**) *Dep* **octavos de final** round before the quarterfinal

octeto *nm* (**a**) *Mús* octet (**b**) *Inform* byte

octogenario, -a *adj & nm,f* octogenarian

octogésimo, -a *núm* eightieth

octogonal *adj* octagonal

octógono *nm* octagon

octosílabo, -a 1 *adj* octosyllabic
2 *nm* octosyllabic line

octubre *nm* October; *ver también* **septiembre**

óctuplo, -a *adj* octuple, eightfold

OCU ['oku] *nf* (*abrev de* **Organización de Consumidores y Usuarios**) = Spanish consumer organization

ocular *adj* eye; **testigo o.** eyewitness

oculista *nmf* ophthalmologist

ocultación *nf* concealment, hiding; *Der* **o. de pruebas** concealment, nondisclosure

ocultar 1 *vt* (**a**) *(esconder)* to hide; **o. algo a alguien** to hide sth from sb; **le ocultaron la verdad** they concealed the truth from him (**b**) *(delito)* to cover up
2 ocultarse *vpr* to hide

ocultismo *nm* occultism

ocultista *nmf* occultist

oculto, -a *adj* (**a**) *(escondido)* hidden (**b**) *(sobrenatural)* **lo o.** the occult

ocupa *nmf Fam* squatter

ocupación *nf* (**a**) *(de territorio)* occupation; **o. ilegal de viviendas** squatting (**b**) *(empleo)* job, occupation

ocupacional *adj* occupational

ocupado, -a *adj* (**a**) *(persona)* busy (**b**) *(teléfono)* busy; *(lavabo)* engaged (**c**) *(tiempo)* **tengo toda la tarde ocupada** I'm busy all afternoon (**d**) *(territorio)* occupied; *(plaza, asiento)* taken; **casa ocupada** *(ilegalmente)* squat

ocupante 1 *adj* occupying
2 *nmf* occupant; **o. ilegal de viviendas** squatter

ocupar 1 *vt* (**a**) *(invadir)* *(territorio, edificio)* to occupy; **han ocupado la casa** *(ilegalmente)* squatters have moved into the house
(**b**) *(llenar)* *(mente)* to occupy; **¿en qué ocupas tu tiempo libre?** how do you spend your spare time?; **los niños me ocupan mucho tiempo** the children take up a lot of my time; **este trabajo sólo te ocupará unas horas** this task will only take you a few hours
(**c**) *(superficie, espacio)* to take up; *(habitación, piso)* to live in; *(mesa)* to sit at; *(sillón)* to sit in
(**d**) *(cargo, puesto, cátedra)* to hold; **ocupa el primer puesto en las listas de éxitos** she's top of the charts
(**e**) *(dar trabajo a)* to find *o* provide work for

2 ocuparse *vpr* *(encargarse)* **ocúpate tú, yo no puedo** you do it, I can't; **ocuparse de** *(encargarse de)* to deal with; *(cuidar de)* to look after; **¿quién se ocupa de la compra/de cocinar en tu casa?** who does the shopping/cooking in your house?; **¡tú ocúpate de lo tuyo!** mind your own business!

ocurrencia *nf* (**a**) *(idea)* bright idea; **¡vaya o.!** the very idea!, what an idea! (**b**) *(dicho gracioso)* witty remark

ocurrente *adj* witty

ocurrir 1 *vi* *(suceder)* to happen; **nadie sabe lo que ocurrió** nobody knows what happened; **¿qué ocurre?** what's the matter?; **¿qué le ocurre a Juan?** what's up with Juan?; **¿te ocurre algo?** is anything the matter?; **lo que ocurre es que...** the thing is...
2 ocurrirse *vpr* *(venir a la cabeza)* **no se me ocurre ninguna solución** I can't think of a solution; **se me ha ocurrido una idea** I've got an idea; **¡ni se te ocurra!** don't even think about it!; **se me ocurre que...** it occurs to me that...; **¡se te ocurre cada cosa!** you do come out with some funny things!

oda *nf* ode

odalisca *nf* odalisque

odeón *nm* odeon

odiar *vt* to hate; **odio las lentejas** I hate *o* can't stand lentils; **odio levantarme pronto** I hate getting up early; **o. a muerte a alguien** to loathe sb

odio *nm* hatred; **tener o. a algo/alguien** to hate sth/sb

odioso, -a *adj* hateful, horrible

odisea *nf también Fig* odyssey

odontología *nf* dentistry

odontológico, -a *adj* dental

odontólogo, -a *nm,f* dentist, dental surgeon

odre *nm* *(de vino)* wineskin

OEA *nf* (*abrev de* **Organización de Estados Americanos**) OAS

oeste 1 *adj* *(posición, parte)* west, western; *(dirección, viento)* westerly; **viento o.** west wind; **tiempo nuboso en la mitad o. de la región** overcast in the western half of the region; **partieron con rumbo o.** they set off westward(s)
2 *nm* west; **viento del o.** west wind; **ir hacia el o.** to go west(wards); **está al o. de Madrid** it's (to the) west of Madrid; **el lejano o.** the Wild West

ofender 1 *vt* (**a**) *(injuriar)* to insult; **tus palabras me ofenden** I feel insulted (**b**) *(a la vista, al oído)* to offend
2 *vi* to cause offense
3 ofenderse *vpr* to take offense (**por** at)

ofendido, -a 1 *adj* offended
2 *nm,f* offended party

ofensa *nf* (**a**) *(acción)* offense; **una o. a la dignidad humana** an offense *o* insult to human dignity; **una o. a la buena educación** an affront to good manners (**b**) *(injuria)* slight, insult; **no lo tomes como una o. personal** don't take it as a personal insult *o* offense

ofensiva *nf* offensive; **pasar a la o.** to go on the offensive

ofensivo, -a *adj* offensive

ofensor, -ora *nm,f* offender

oferta *nf* (**a**) *(propuesta, ofrecimiento)* offer; **ofertas de trabajo** *o* **empleo** *(en anuncio)* situations vacant, job opportunities (**b**) *Econ (suministro)* supply; **la o. y la demanda** supply and demand; **o. monetaria** money supply (**c**) *(rebaja)* bargain, special offer; **de o.** bargain, on offer; **artículos de o.** sale goods, goods on offer; **estar de o.** to be on offer; **o. especial** special offer (**d**) *Fin (proposición)* bid, tender; *Com* **o. pública de adquisición** takeover bid

ofertar *vt* to offer

ofertorio *nm Rel* offertory

office ['ofis] *nm inv* scullery

offset (*pl* **offsets**) *nm Imprenta* offset

oficial¹ 1 *adj* official

2 *nm* (**a**) *Mil* officer; **o. de marina** naval officer (**b**) *(funcionario)* clerk

oficial², -ala *nm,f (obrero)* skilled worker, journeyman

oficialidad *nf* official nature

oficialismo *nm Am (Gobierno)* **el o.** the Government

oficialista *Am* **1** *adj* progovernment

2 *nm,f* government supporter

oficializar [14] *vt* to make official

oficiante *nmf Rel* officiant

oficiar 1 *vt (misa)* to celebrate; *(ceremonia)* to officiate at

2 *vi* (**a**) *(sacerdote)* to officiate (**b**) **o. de** *(actuar de)* to act as

oficina *nf* office; **o. de cambio** foreign-exchange bureau; **o. de correos** post office; **o. de empleo** unemployment office, job center; **o. de información** information office; **o. de objetos perdidos** lost-and-found office; **o. de prensa** press office; **o. de turismo** tourist office

oficinista *nmf* office worker

oficio *nm* (**a**) *(profesión manual)* trade; **de o.** by trade (**b**) *(trabajo)* job; **no tener o. ni beneficio** to have no trade (**c**) *Der* **de o.** *(abogado)* court-appointed, legal aid (**d**) *(documento)* official minute (**e**) *(experiencia)* **tener mucho o.** to be very experienced; **se llegó a un acuerdo gracias a los buenos oficios del ministro** an agreement was reached thanks to the good offices of the minister (**f**) *Rel (ceremonia)* service; **el Santo O.** the Holy Office, the Inquisition; **o. de difuntos** funeral service (**g**) *(función)* function, role

oficioso, -a *adj* unofficial

ofidio *nm (serpiente)* snake

ofimática *nf* office IT *o* automation

ofrecer [46] **1** *vt* (**a**) *(proporcionar, dar)* to offer; **ofrecerle algo a alguien** to offer sb sth; **¿puedo ofrecerle algo de beber?** may I offer you something to drink?; **¿cuánto te ofrecen por la casa?** how much are they offering you for the house?; **me ofrece la oportunidad** *o* **la ocasión de conocer la ciudad** it gives me the chance to get to know the city

(**b**) *(en subastas)* to bid; **¿qué ofrecen por esta mesa?** what am I bid for this table?

(**c**) *(tener, presentar) (imagen, dificultades)* to present; **la cocina ofrece un aspecto lamentable** the kitchen is a sorry sight

(**d**) *(oraciones, sacrificio)* to offer up

2 ofrecerse *vpr* (**a**) *(presentarse)* to offer, to volunteer; **varios se ofrecieron voluntarios** several people volunteered; **ofrecerse a** *o* **para hacer algo** to offer to do sth; **se ofrece diseñadora con mucha experiencia** *(en letrero, anuncio)* highly experienced designer seeks employment (**b**) *Formal (desear)* **¿qué se le ofrece?** what can I do for you?

ofrecimiento *nm* offer

ofrenda *nf Rel* offering; *(por gratitud, amor)* gift

ofrendar *vt* to offer up

ofrezca *etc ver* **ofrecer**

oftalmología *nf* ophthalmology

oftalmólogo, -a *nm,f* ophthalmologist

ofuscación *nf* blindness, confusion

ofuscar [59] **1** *vt* (**a**) *(deslumbrar)* to dazzle (**b**) *(turbar)* to blind

2 ofuscarse *vpr* to be blinded (**con** *o* **por** by)

ogro *nm también Fig* ogre

oh *interj* **¡oh!** oh!

ohmio *nm* ohm

oídas: de oídas *loc adv* by hearsay

oído *nm* (**a**) *(órgano)* ear; **decir algo al o. a alguien** to whisper sth in sb's ear; **me zumban los oídos** my ears are burning; **o. interno** inner ear (**b**) *(sentido)* (sense of) hearing; **ser duro de o.** to be hard of hearing; **tener o., tener buen o.**

to have a good ear; **tocar de o.** to play by ear (**c**) *(expresiones)* **abrir los oídos** to pay close attention; **entrar por un o. y salir por el otro** to go in one ear and out the other; **hacer oídos sordos** to turn a deaf ear; *Fig* **lastimar los oídos** to offend one's ears; **si llega a oídos de ella…** if she gets to hear about this…; **ser todo oídos** to be all ears

OIEA *nm (abrev de* **Organismo Internacional para la Energía Atómica**) IAEA

oigo *ver* **oír**

oír [44] **1** *vt* (**a**) *(sonidos, voces)* to hear; **los oí hablando** *o* **hablar** *o* **que hablaban** I heard them talking; **¡lo que hay que o.!, ¡se oye cada cosa!** whatever next!; **como quien oye llover** without paying the least attention; **¡como lo oyes!** absolutely!, just like I'm telling you!; *Fam* **¡me va a o.!** I'm going to give him a piece of my mind! (**b**) *(escuchar)* to listen to; **voy a o. las noticias** I'm going to listen to the news

2 *vi* to hear; **¡oiga, por favor!** excuse me!; **¡oye!** hey!; **o., ver y callar** hear no evil, see no evil, speak no evil

OIT *nf (abrev de* **Organización Internacional del Trabajo**) ILO

ojal *nm* buttonhole

ojalá *interj* **¡o.!** I hope so!; **¡o. lo haga!** I hope she does it!; **¡o. fuera viernes!** I wish it was Friday!

ojeada *nf* glance, look; **echar una o. a algo/alguien** to take a quick glance at sth/sb, to take a quick look at sth/sb

ojear *vt* to have a look at

ojeras *nfpl* bags under the eyes

ojeriza *nf Fam* dislike; **tener o. a alguien** to have it in for sb

ojeroso, -a *adj* with bags under the eyes, haggard

ojete *nm* (**a**) *(bordado)* eyelet (**b**) *muy Fam (ano)* asshole

ojiva *nf* (**a**) *Arquit* ogive (**b**) *Mil* warhead

ojo 1 *nm* (**a**) *Anat* eye; **mírame a los ojos cuando te hablo** look at me when I'm speaking to you; *también Fig* **poner los ojos en blanco** to roll one's eyes; *Fig* **ojos de carnero (degollado)** pleading eyes; *Esp* **o. de cristal** glass eye; **o. de gallo** *(callo)* corn; **o. morado** black eye; **ojos rasgados** almond eyes; **ojos saltones** bulging eyes; *Am* **o. de vidrio** glass eye; **o. a la virulé,** *Esp* **o. a la funerala** shiner

(**b**) *(agujero) (de aguja)* eye; *(de puente)* span; **o. de buey** *(ventana)* porthole; **o. de la cerradura** keyhole; **el o. del huracán** the eye of the storm; *Fig* **el ministro está en el o. del huracán** the minister is at the center of the controversy; **o. de pez** *Fot* fish-eye lens

(**c**) *(expresiones)* **a o. (de buen cubero)** roughly, approximately; **a ojos vistas** visibly; **abrir los ojos a alguien** to open sb's eyes; **en un abrir y cerrar de ojos** in the twinkling of an eye; **andar con (mucho) o.** to be (very) careful; **cerrar los ojos ante algo** *(ignorar)* to close one's eyes to sth; **costar un o. de la cara** to cost an arm and a leg; *Fam* **¡dichosos los ojos (que te ven)!** long time no see!; **echar el o. a algo** to have one's eye on sth; **estar o. alerta** *o* **avizor** to be on the lookout; **mirar algo con buenos/malos ojos** to look favorably/unfavorably on sth; **no pegar o.** not to get a wink of sleep; **no quitar los ojos de encima a alguien** not to take one's eyes off sb; **tener ojos de lince** to have eyes like a hawk; **poner los ojos en alguien** to set one's sights on sb; **ser todo ojos** to be all eyes; **tener (buen) o.** to have a good eye; **tener o. clínico para algo** to be a good judge of sth; **sólo tiene ojos para él** she only has eyes for him; *Prov* **o. por o., diente por diente** an eye for an eye, a tooth for a tooth; *Prov* **ojos que no ven, corazón que no siente** what the eye doesn't see, the heart doesn't grieve over

2 *interj* **¡o.!** be careful!, watch out!

ojota *nf Andes (sandalia)* sandal; *RP (chancleta)* thong

OK, okey [o'kei] *interj* OK, okay

okapi *nm* okapi

okupa *nmf Esp Fam* squatter

ola *nf* wave; **una o. de atentados terroristas** a wave *o* spate of terrorist attacks; **una o. de visitantes** a flood of tourists; **la nueva o.** the New Wave; **o. de calor** heatwave; **o. de delincuencia** crime wave; **o. de frío** cold spell; **la ola (mexicana)** the Mexican wave

ole, olé *interj* **¡o.!** bravo!

oleada *nf* (**a**) *(del mar)* swell (**b**) *(de protestas, atentados)* wave

oleaginoso, -a *adj* oleaginous

oleaje *nm* waves

óleo *nm* oil (painting); **al ó.** in oils

oleoducto *nm* oil pipeline

oleoso, -a *adj* oily

oler [45] **1** *vt* to smell; **desde aquí huelo el tabaco** I can smell the cigarette smoke from here
   2 *vi* (**a**) *(despedir olor)* to smell (**a** of); **¡qué mal huele aquí!** it smells awful here!; **este guisado huele que alimenta** this stew smells delicious; **o. a rayos** to stink (to high heaven) (**b**) *(parecer)* **o. a** to smack of
   3 **olerse** *vpr (persona)* **olerse algo** to sense sth; **ya me olía yo algo así** I suspected as much

olfatear *vt* (**a**) *(olisquear)* to sniff (**b**) *(barruntar)* to smell, to sense; **o. en** *(indagar)* to pry into

olfativo, -a *adj* olfactory

olfato *nm* (**a**) *(sentido)* sense of smell (**b**) *(sagacidad)* nose, instinct; **tener o. para algo** to be a good judge of sth

oligarca *nmf* oligarch

oligarquía *nf* oligarchy

oligárquico, -a *adj* oligarchic

oligoelemento *nm* trace element

oligofrenia *nf* mental handicap

oligofrénico, -a 1 *adj* mentally handicapped
   2 *nm,f* mentally handicapped person

oligopolio *nm Econ* oligopoly

olimpiada, olimpíada *nf* Olympiad, Olympic Games; **las Olimpiadas** the Olympics

olímpicamente *adv Fam* **paso o. de ayudarlos** I'm damned if I'm going to help them

olímpico, -a *adj Dep* Olympic

olimpismo *nm* Olympic movement

Olimpo *nm* **el O.** (Mount) Olympus

olisquear *vt* to sniff (at)

oliva *nf* olive

oliváceo, -a *adj* olive

olivar *nm* olive grove

olivarero, -a 1 *adj* olive; **el sector o.** the olive growing industry
   2 *nm,f* olive grower

olivo *nm* olive tree

olla *nf* (**a**) *(cacerola)* pot; **o. exprés** *o* **a presión** pressure cooker; *Fig* **o. de grillos** bedlam, madhouse; *Culin* **o. podrida** stew (**b**) *Fam (cabeza)* noggin

olmeda *nf* elm grove

olmo *nm* elm (tree)

olor *nm* smell (**a** of); **tener o. a** to smell of; **los niños acudieron al o. de la comida** the children were drawn to the smell of cooking; *Fam* **en o. de multitudes** enjoying popular acclaim; **o. corporal** body odor

oloroso, -a 1 *adj* fragrant
   2 *nm* oloroso (sherry)

OLP *nf* *(abrev de* **Organización para la Liberación de Palestina**) PLO

olvidadizo, -a *adj* forgetful

olvidar 1 *vt* (**a**) *(hecho, dato, persona)* to forget (**b**) *(dejarse)* to leave; **olvidé las llaves en la oficina** I left my keys at the office
   2 **olvidarse** *vpr* (**a**) *(en general)* to forget; **olvidarse de**

algo/hacer algo to forget sth/to do sth; **me olvidé de su cumpleaños** I forgot her birthday; **olvídate de lo ocurrido** forget what happened; **se me olvidaba decirte que...** I almost forgot to tell you that... (**b**) *(dejarse)* to leave; **me he olvidado el paraguas en el tren** I've left my umbrella on the train

olvido *nm* (**a**) *(de un nombre, hecho)* **caer en el o.** to fall into oblivion (**b**) *(descuido)* oversight

Omán *n* Oman

ombligo *nm Anat* navel; **se cree el o. del mundo** he thinks the world revolves around him; *Fig* **mirarse el o.** to contemplate one's navel

ombudsman *nm inv* ombudsman

OMC *nf* *(abrev de* **Organización Mundial del Comercio**) WTO

omelet *(pl* **omelets**), **omelette** [ome'let] *nm Am* omelet

ominoso, -a *adj* abominable

omisión *nf* omission

omiso, -a *adj* **hacer caso o. de algo** to ignore sth, to pay no attention to sth

omitir *vt* to omit

ómnibus *nm inv Cuba, Urug (urbano)* bus; *Andes, Cuba, Urug (interurbano, internacional)* bus

omnipotencia *nf* omnipotence

omnipotente *adj* omnipotent

omnipresencia *nf* omnipresence

omnipresente *adj* omnipresent

omnisciente *adj* omniscient

omnívoro, -a 1 *adj* omnivorous
   2 *nm,f* omnivore

omoplato, omóplato *nm* shoulder blade

OMS [oms] *nf* *(abrev de* **Organización Mundial de la Salud**) WHO

onagra *nf* evening primrose

onanismo *nm* onanism

ONCE ['onθe] *nf* *(abrev de* **Organización Nacional de Ciegos Españoles**) = Spanish association for the blind, famous for its national lottery

once 1 *núm* eleven; *ver también* **seis**
   2 *nm Andes* **onces** *(por la mañana)* midmorning snack; *(por la tarde)* midafternoon snack

onceavo, -a *núm (fracción)* eleventh; **la onceava parte** an eleventh

oncogén *nm* oncogene

oncología *nf* oncology

oncólogo, -a *nm,f* oncologist

onda *nf* (**a**) *Fís & Rad* wave; **o. corta** short wave; **o. eléctrica** Hertzian wave; **o. expansiva** shock wave; **o. hertziana** Hertzian wave; **o. larga** long wave; **o. luminosa** light wave; **o. media** medium wave; **o. sísmica** seismic wave; **o. sonora** sound wave (**b**) *(en pelo, agua)* wave (**c**) *(expresiones) Fam* **estar en la o.** to be hip; *Fam* **estamos en la misma o.** we're on the same wavelength; *Fam* **me da mala o.** I've got bad vibes about him/her/it; *Fam* **tus primos tienen muy buena o.** your cousins are really cool

ondeante *adj* rippling

ondear *vi (bandera)* to flutter, to fly

ondulación *nf* (**a**) *(acción)* rippling (**b**) *(onda)* ripple; *(del pelo)* wave

ondulado, -a *adj* wavy

ondulante *adj* undulating

ondular 1 *vi (agua)* to ripple; *(terreno)* to undulate
   2 *vt (pelo)* to wave

ondulatorio, -a *adj* wave-like

oneroso, -a *adj* (**a**) *(pesado)* burdensome, onerous (**b**) *(caro)* costly, expensive

ONG *nf inv (abrev de* **Organización no Gubernamental)** NGO

ónice *nm o nf* onyx

onírico, -a *adj* dreamlike; **experiencia onírica** dreamlike experience

ónix *nm o nf* onyx

onomástica *nf Esp* name day

onomástico, -a 1 *adj* onomastic; **índice o.** name index
2 *nm Am (cumpleaños)* birthday; *(santo)* name day

onomatopeya *nf* onomatopoeia

onomatopéyico, -a *adj* onomatopoeic

Ontario *nm* **el lago O.** Lake Ontario

ontología *nf* ontology

ONU ['onu] *nf (abrev de* **Organización de las Naciones Unidas)** UN

onubense 1 *adj* of/from Huelva
2 *nmf* person from Huelva

ONUDI [o'nuði] *nf (abrev de* **Organización de las Naciones Unidas para el Desarrollo Industrial)** UNIDO

onza *nf* **(a)** *(unidad de peso)* ounce **(b)** *(de chocolate)* square **(c)** *(guepardo)* cheetah

op. *(abrev de* **opus)** op.

OPA ['opa] *nf (abrev de* **oferta pública de adquisición)** takeover bid; **O. hostil** hostile takeover bid

opacidad *nf también Fig* opacity

opaco, -a *adj* opaque

opalescente *adj* opalescent

opalina *nf* opaline

opalino, -a *adj* opaline

ópalo *nm* opal

opar *vt (empresa) (intentar adquirir)* to launch a takeover bid for; *(adquirir)* to take over

opción *nf* **(a)** *(elección)* option; **no hay o.** there is no alternative; *Fin* **opciones sobre acciones** stock options **(b)** *(derecho)* right; **dar o. a** to give the right to; **tener o. a** *(empleo, cargo)* to be eligible for

opcional *adj* optional

open *nm inv Dep* Open (tournament)

OPEP [o'pep] *nf (abrev de* **Organización de Países Exportadores de Petróleo)** OPEC

ópera *nf* opera; **ó. bufa** comic opera, opera buffa; **ó. prima** *(novela, película)* first work; **ó. rock** rock opera

operación *nf* **(a)** *(en general)* operation; **o. quirúrgica** (surgical) operation; **o. retorno/salida** = police operation to assist traffic at the end/beginning of popular vacation periods **(b)** *Com* transaction

operacional *adj* operational

operador, -ora 1 *nm,f* **(a)** *Inform & Tel* operator **(b)** *(de la cámara)* cameraman; *(del proyector)* projectionist
2 *nm* **(a)** **o. turístico** tour operator **(b)** *Mat* operator

operar 1 *vt* **(a)** *(enfermo)* **o. a alguien (de algo)** to operate on sb (for sth); **el médico que la operó** the surgeon who operated on her; **le operaron del hígado** they've operated on his liver; **me han operado de apendicitis** I had my appendix out; **casi me tienen que o. de urgencia** I almost needed an emergency operation **(b)** *(cambio)* to bring about, to produce
2 *vi* to operate
3 **operarse** *vpr* **(a)** *(enfermo)* to be operated on, to have an operation; **o. del estómago** to have a stomach operation; **se ha operado de un tumor** he's had an operation to remove a tumor **(b)** *(cambio)* to occur, to come about

operario, -a *nm,f* worker

operatividad *nf* preparedness

operativo, -a *adj* operative

opereta *nf* operetta

operístico, -a *adj* operatic

opiáceo, -a *adj & nm* opiate

opinar 1 *vt* to believe, to think
2 *vi* to give one's opinion; **o. de algo/alguien, o. sobre algo/alguien** to think about sth/sb; **o. bien de alguien** to think highly of sb

opinión *nf* opinion; **en mi o. no deberíamos ir** in my opinion, we shouldn't go; **¿cuál es tu o. al respecto?** what's your opinion *o* view on this matter?; **he cambiado de o.** I've changed my mind; **expresar** *o* **dar una o.** to give an opinion; **reservarse la o.** to reserve judgment; **tener buena/mala o. de alguien** to have a high/low opinion of sb; **la o. pública** public opinion

opio *nm* opium

opíparo, -a *adj* sumptuous

opondré *etc ver* **oponer**

oponente *nmf* opponent

oponer [50] **1** *vt* **(a)** *(resistencia)* to put up **(b)** *(argumento, razón)* to put forward, to give
2 **oponerse** *vpr* to be opposed; **oponerse a algo** to be opposed to sth; **todos se opusieron al plan** everybody was opposed to the plan; **me opongo a que vengan ellos también** I'm opposed to having them come along too

Oporto *n* Oporto

oporto *nm* port (wine)

oportunidad *nf* **(a)** *(ocasión)* opportunity, chance; **aprovechar la o.** to seize the opportunity; **a la primera o. que tenga se lo digo** I'll tell her just as soon as I get the chance *o* at the earliest opportunity; **me dio una segunda o.** he gave me a second chance; **es una o. única** it's a unique opportunity **(b)** **oportunidades** *(en tienda)* bargains

oportunismo *nm* opportunism

oportunista 1 *adj* opportunistic; *Med* **una infección o.** an opportunistic infection
2 *nmf* opportunist

oportuno, -a *adj* **(a)** *(pertinente)* appropriate; **me pareció o. callarme** I thought it was best to say nothing **(b)** *(propicio)* timely; **el momento o.** the right time; **en el momento menos o.** at the very worst time *o* moment; **su llegada fue muy oportuna** she arrived at an opportune moment; *Irónico* **¡él siempre tan o.!** you can always trust him to do the wrong thing!

oposición *nf* **(a)** *(en general)* opposition; **los partidos de la o.** the opposition parties **(b)** *(resistencia)* resistance **(c)** *(examen)* = competitive public examination for employment in the civil service, education, legal system etc; **o. a profesor** = public examination to obtain a state teaching post; **preparar oposiciones** to be studying for a public examination

opositar *vi* = to take a public entrance examination

opositor, -ora *nm,f* **(a)** *(a un cargo)* = candidate in a public entrance examination **(b)** *(oponente)* opponent

opresión *nf* **(a)** *(represión)* oppression **(b)** *(molestia, ahogo)* **sentía una o. en el pecho** he felt a tightness in his chest

opresivo, -a *adj* oppressive

opresor, -ora 1 *adj* oppressive
2 *nm,f* oppressor

oprimido, -a *adj* oppressed

oprimir *vt* **(a)** *(ejercer presión sobre) (botón)* to press; *(garganta, brazo)* to squeeze **(b)** *(apretar)* to pinch, to be too tight for; **la corbata le oprimía el cuello** his tie felt too tight **(c)** *(políticamente)* to oppress **(d)** *(angustiar)* to weigh down on, to burden

oprobio *nm* shame, disgrace

optar *vi* **(a)** *(escoger)* **o. (por algo)** to choose (sth); **o. por hacer algo** to choose to do sth; **o. entre** to choose between **(b)** *(aspirar)* **o. a** to aim for, to go for; **optan al puesto siete candidatos** there are seven candidates for the job

optativa *nf Educ* elective

optativo, -a *adj* elective

óptica *nf* (a) *Fís* optics (b) *(tienda)* optician, optician's (c) *(punto de vista)* point of view

óptico, -a 1 *adj* optic

2 *nm,f (persona)* optician

optimismo *nm* optimism

optimista 1 *adj* optimistic

2 *nmf* optimist

optimización *nf* optimization

optimizar [14] *vt* to optimize

óptimo, -a *adj* optimum

optometría *nf* optometry

opuesto, -a 1 *participio ver* **oponer**

2 *adj* (a) *(contrario)* opposed, contrary (**a** to); **los dos hermanos son opuestos en todo** the two brothers are completely different; **opiniones opuestas** contrary *o* opposing opinions (b) *(del otro lado)* opposite

opulencia *nf (riqueza)* opulence; *(abundancia)* abundance; **vivir en la o.** to live in luxury; **nadar en la o.** to be filthy rich

opulento, -a *adj* (a) *(rico)* opulent (b) *(abundante)* abundant

opus *nm inv Mús* opus; **el O. Dei** the Opus Dei, = traditionalist religious organization, whose members include many professional people and public figures

opúsculo *nm* short work

opusiera *etc ver* **oponer**

OPV *nf (abrev de* **Oferta Pública de Venta (de acciones))** public offering

oquedad *nf (cavidad)* hole; *(en pared)* recess

ora *conj* o.... o.... now... now...

oración *nf* (a) *(rezo)* prayer; **o. fúnebre** memorial speech (b) *Gram* sentence; **o. principal/subordinada** main/subordinate clause

oráculo *nm* (a) *(mensaje, divinidad)* oracle (b) *(persona)* fount of wisdom

orador, -ora *nm,f* speaker

oral 1 *adj* oral

2 *nm (examen)* oral exam

órale *interj Méx Fam* **¡ó.!** come on!

orangután *nm* orangutan

orar *vi* to pray

oratoria *nf* oratory

oratorio, -a 1 *adj* oratorical

2 *nm* (a) *(lugar)* oratory (b) *Mús* oratorio

orbe *nm* world, globe

órbita *nf* (a) *Astron* orbit; **entrar/poner en ó.** to go/put into orbit (b) *(de ojo)* eye socket; **casi se le salen los ojos de las órbitas** his eyes nearly popped out of his head (c) *(ámbito)* sphere, realm

orca *nf* killer whale

órdago *nm* = all-or-nothing stake in the game of "mus"; *Fig* **de ó.** magnificent

orden 1 *nm* (a) *(en secuencia, funcionamiento)* order; **en o.** *(bien colocado)* tidy, in its place; *(como debe ser)* in order; **en** *o* **por o. alfabético/cronológico** in alphabetical/chronological order; **llamar al o. a alguien** to call sb to order; **poner en o. algo** to tidy sth up; **por o.** in order; **sin o. ni concierto** in a haphazard way; **las fuerzas del o.** the forces of law and order; **o. del día** agenda; **el o. establecido** the established order; **o. público** law and order

(b) *(tipo)* type, order; **problemas de o. económico** economic problems; **del o. de** around, approximately, of *o* in the order of; **en otro o. de cosas** on the other hand

2 *nf* (a) *(mandato)* order; *Mil* **¡a la o.!, ¡a sus órdenes!** (yes) sir!; **dar órdenes** to give orders; **estar a la o. del día** to be the order of the day; **hasta nueva o.** until further notice; **por o. de** by order of; **o. de busca y captura** warrant for search

and arrest; *Com* **o. de compra** purchase order; *Der* **o. de desahucio** *o* **desalojo** eviction order; *Com* **o. de pago** payment order; *Der* **o. de registro** search warrant

(b) *(organización)* order; **o. de caballería** order of knighthood; **o. militar** military order

(c) *Am (pedido)* order; **¿ya les tomaron la o.?** have you ordered yet?

ordenación *nf* (a) *(organización)* ordering, arranging; *(disposición)* order, arrangement; *(de recursos, edificios)* planning; **o. territorial** administrative structure (b) *Rel* ordination

ordenada *nf Mat* ordinate

ordenadamente *adv (desfilar, salir)* in an orderly fashion *o* manner; *(colocar)* neatly

ordenado, -a *adj* (a) *(lugar, persona)* tidy (b) *(sacerdote)* ordained

ordenador *nm Esp Inform* computer; **pasar algo a o.** to type sth up on a word processor *o* computer; **o. central** mainframe computer; **o. personal** personal computer; **o. portátil** laptop computer; **o. de sobremesa** desktop computer

ordenamiento *nm* legislation, regulations

ordenanza 1 *nm* (a) *(de oficina)* messenger (b) *Mil* orderly

2 *nf* ordinance, law; **ordenanzas municipales** bylaws

ordenar 1 *vt* (a) *(poner en orden) (alfabéticamente, numéricamente)* to arrange, to put in order; *(habitación, papeles)* to tidy (up) (b) *(mandar)* to order (c) *Rel* to ordain (d) *Am (en restaurante)* to order

2 ordenarse *vpr Rel* to be ordained

ordeñadora *nf* milking machine

ordeñar *vt* to milk

ordeño *nm Esp* milking

ordinal 1 *adj* ordinal

2 *nm (número)* ordinal (number)

ordinariez *nf* commonness, coarseness; **decir/hacer una o.** to say/do something rude; **¡qué o.!** how vulgar!

ordinario, -a 1 *adj* (a) *(común)* ordinary, usual; **de o.** usually (b) *(vulgar)* common, coarse (c) *(no selecto)* unexceptional (d) *(correo)* ≃ second class; *(tribunal)* of first instance

2 *nm,f* common *o* coarse person

orear 1 *vt* to air

2 orearse *vpr (ventilarse)* to air

orégano *nm* oregano

Oregón *n* Oregon

oreja *nf* (a) *Anat* ear; **tenía una sonrisa de o. a o.** he was grinning from ear to ear; *Fam* **agachar** *o* **bajar las orejas** *(en discusión)* to back down; **calentarle a alguien las orejas** to box sb's ears; **con las orejas gachas** with one's tail between one's legs; *Fig* **tirar a alguien de las orejas** to give sb a good telling-off; **verle las orejas al lobo** to see what's coming; **orejas de soplillo** stick-out ears (b) *(de sillón)* wing

orejera *nf (en gorra)* earflap; **orejeras** earmuffs

orejón, -ona 1 *adj* big-eared

2 *nm (dulce)* dried apricot/peach

orejudo, -a *adj* big-eared

orensano, -a 1 *adj* of/from Orense

2 *nm,f* person from Orense

orfanato, *Méx* **orfanatorio** *nm* orphanage

orfandad *nf* orphanhood

orfebre *nmf (de plata)* silversmith; *(de oro)* goldsmith

orfebrería *nf* (a) *(objetos) (de plata)* silver work; *(de oro)* gold work (b) *(oficio) (de plata)* silversmithing; *(de oro)* goldsmithing

orfelinato *nm* orphanage

orfeón *nm* choral group *o* society

organdí *(pl* **organdíes)** *nm* organdie

orgánico, -a *adj* organic

organigrama *nm (de organización)* organization chart; *(esquema)* flow chart

organillero, -a *nm,f* organ-grinder

organillo *nm* barrel organ

organismo *nm* (**a**) *Biol* organism (**b**) *Anat* body (**c**) *(entidad)* organization, body

organista *nmf* organist

organización *nf* organization; **o. de ayuda humanitaria** humanitarian aid organization; **o. benéfica** charity, charitable organization; **O. de las Naciones Unidas** United Nations Organization; **las organizaciones sindicales** the labor unions

organizado, -a *adj* organized

organizador, -ora 1 *adj* organizing
   2 *nm,f* organizer

organizar [14] **1** *vt* to organize
   2 organizarse *vpr* (**a**) *(persona)* to organize oneself (**b**) *Esp (pelea, lío)* to break out, to happen suddenly

organizativo, -a *adj* organizing

órgano *nm* (**a**) *Anat* organ; **órganos reproductores** reproductive organs; **órganos sensoriales** sensory organs; **ó. vital** vital organ (**b**) *Mús* organ; **ó. electrónico** electronic organ (**c**) *(organización)* organ; **ó. ejecutivo** executive

orgasmo *nm* orgasm

orgía *nf* orgy

orgiástico, -a *adj* orgiastic

orgullo *nm* (**a**) *(actitud negativa, amor propio)* pride; **no aguanto su o.** I can't bear his haughtiness *o* arrogance (**b**) *(satisfacción)* pride; **es el o. de la familia** he's the pride of the family; **me llena de o. poder inaugurar este centro** it fills me with pride *o* I am very proud to be able to open this center; **tuve el o. de conocerlo** I'm proud to say I knew him; **no caber en sí de o.** to be bursting with pride

orgulloso, -a 1 *adj* proud
   2 *nm,f* proud person

orientación *nf* (**a**) *(dirección) (acción)* guiding; *(rumbo)* direction; **sentido de la o.** sense of direction (**b**) *(posicionamiento) (acción)* positioning; *(lugar)* position (**c**) *(información)* guidance; **o. profesional** careers advice *o* guidance (**d**) *(tendencia)* tendency, leaning; **o. sexual** sexual orientation

orientador, -ora 1 *adj* guiding, directing
   2 *nm,f* guide; **o. psicológico** (psychological) counselor

oriental 1 *adj* (**a**) *(del este)* eastern; *(del Lejano Oriente)* oriental (**b**) *Am (uruguayo)* Uruguayan
   2 *nmf* (**a**) *(del Lejano Oriente)* oriental (**b**) *Am (uruguayo)* Uruguayan

orientalismo *nm* orientalism

orientalista *nmf* orientalist

orientar 1 *vt* (**a**) *(dirigir)* to direct; **mi ventana está orientada hacia el sur** my window faces south *o* is south-facing (**b**) *(aconsejar)* to give advice *o* guidance to (**c**) *(medidas, fondos)* **o. hacia** to direct toward *o* at
   2 orientarse *vpr* (**a**) *(dirigirse) (foco)* **orientarse a** to point toward *o* at (**b**) *(encontrar el camino)* to get one's bearings, to find one's way around (**c**) *(encaminarse)* **orientarse hacia** to be aiming at

orientativo, -a *adj* illustrative, guiding

oriente *nm* east; **el O.** the East, the Orient; **O. Medio/ Próximo** Middle/Near East; **Lejano** *o* **Extremo O.** Far East

orificio *nm* hole; *Mec* opening

origen *nm* (**a**) *(principio)* origin; **en su o.** originally; **dar o. a** to give rise to; **tener su o. en** *(lugar)* to have one's origins in, to originate in (**b**) *(ascendencia)* origins, birth; **los aceites de o. español** oils of Spanish origin, Spanish oils; **Alicia es colombiana de o.** Alicia is Colombian by birth; **de o. humilde** of humble origin (**c**) *(causa)* cause; **el o. del problema** the cause *o* source of the problem

original 1 *adj* (**a**) *(nuevo, primero)* original (**b**) *(raro)* eccentric, different
   2 *nm* original

originalidad *nf* (**a**) *(novedad)* originality (**b**) *(extravagancia)* eccentricity

originar 1 *vt* to cause
   2 originarse *vpr* *(acontecimiento)* to (first) start; *(costumbre, leyenda)* to originate

originario, -a *adj* (**a**) *(inicial, primitivo)* original (**b**) *(procedente)* **ser o. de** to come from (originally)

orilla *nf* (**a**) *(ribera) (de río)* bank; *(de mar)* shore; **a orillas de** *(río)* on the banks of; **a orillas del mar** by the sea; *Fig* **fue aclamado en las dos orillas del Atlántico** he was acclaimed on both sides of the Atlantic (**b**) *(borde)* edge (**c**) *(acera)* sidewalk

orillar *vt* (**a**) *(dificultad, obstáculo)* to skirt around (**b**) *(tela)* to edge

orín *nm* *(herrumbre)* rust; **orines** *(orina)* urine

orina *nf* urine

orinal *nm* chamber pot

orinar 1 *vi & vt* to urinate
   2 orinarse *vpr* to wet oneself; **orinarse en la cama** to wet the bed

Orinoco *nm* **el O.** the Orinoco

oriundo, -a 1 *adj* **o. de** native of
   2 *nm,f* *Dep* = non-Spanish soccer player whose mother or father is Spanish

orla *nf* (**a**) *(adorno)* (decorative) trimming (**b**) *Esp (fotografía)* graduation photograph

orlar *vt* to decorate with trimmings

ornamentación *nf* ornamentation

ornamental *adj* *(de adorno)* ornamental; *Fig (inútil)* merely decorative

ornamentar *vt* to decorate, to adorn

ornamento *nm* *(objeto)* ornament; *Rel* **ornamentos** vestments

ornar *vt* to decorate, to adorn

ornato *nm* decoration

ornitología *nf* ornithology

ornitológico, -a *adj* ornithological

ornitólogo, -a *nm,f* ornithologist

ornitorrinco *nm* duck-billed platypus

oro *nm* (**a**) *(metal)* gold; **de o.** gold; **o. en barras** bullion; **o. negro** oil, black gold; **o. en polvo** gold dust (**b**) **oros** *(naipes)* = suit in Spanish deck of cards, with the symbol of a gold coin (**c**) *(expresiones)* **guardar algo como o.** *Esp* **en paño** *o Am* **en polvo** to treasure sth; **no lo haría ni por todo el o. del mundo** I wouldn't do it for all the tea in China; **hacerse de o.** to make one's fortune; **no es o. todo lo que reluce** all that glitters is not gold; **pedir el o. y el moro** to ask the earth; **prometer el o. y el moro** to promise the earth

orogénesis *nf inv* orogenesis

orografía *nf* (**a**) *Geog* orography (**b**) *(relieve)* terrain

orondo, -a *adj Fam* (**a**) *(gordo)* plump (**b**) *(satisfecho)* self-satisfied, smug

oropel *nm* glitter, glitz

oropéndola *nf* golden oriole

orquesta *nf* (**a**) *(músicos)* orchestra; **o. de baile** dance band; **o. de cámara/sinfónica** chamber/symphony orchestra (**b**) *(lugar)* orchestra pit

orquestación *nf* orchestration

orquestar *vt también Fig* to orchestrate

orquestina *nf* dance band

orquídea *nf* orchid

ortiga *nf* (stinging) nettle

ortodoncia *nf* orthodontics *(singular)*; **hacerse la o.** to have orthodontic work done

ortodoxia *nf* orthodoxy

ortodoxo, -a 1 *adj* orthodox
  2 *nm,f Rel* member of the Orthodox Church

ortografía *nf* spelling

ortográfico, -a *adj* spelling; **reglas ortográficas** spelling rules

ortopedia *nf* orthopedics *(singular)*

ortopédico, -a *adj (zapato, corsé)* orthopedic; **pierna ortopédica** artificial leg

ortopedista *nmf* orthopedist

oruga *nf* (**a**) *(insecto)* caterpillar (**b**) *(vehículo)* Caterpillar® tractor

orujo *nm* = strong spirit made from grape pressings

orzuelo *nm* sty

os *pron personal Esp* (**a**) *(complemento directo)* you; **me gustaría veros** I'd like to see you (**b**) *(complemento indirecto)* (to) you; **os lo dio** he gave it to you; **os tengo miedo** I'm afraid of you (**c**) *(reflexivo)* yourselves; **os vestís** you get dressed (**d**) *(recíproco)* each other; **os enamorasteis** you fell in love (with each other)

Osa *nf Astron* **O. Mayor** Great Bear; **O. Menor** Little Bear

osadía *nf* (**a**) *(valor)* boldness, daring (**b**) *(descaro)* audacity, cheek

osado, -a *adj* (**a**) *(valeroso)* daring, bold (**b**) *(descarado)* impudent, cheeky

osamenta *nf* skeleton

osar *vi* to dare

osario *nm* ossuary

Oscar, Óscar *nm inv Cine* Oscar

oscense 1 *adj* of/from Huesca
  2 *nmf* person from Huesca

oscilación *nf* (**a**) *(movimiento) (de péndulo)* swinging; *Fís* oscillation (**b**) *(variación)* fluctuation

oscilador *nm* oscillator

oscilar *vi* (**a**) *(moverse) (péndulo)* to swing; *Fís* to oscillate (**b**) *(variar)* to fluctuate; **el precio oscila entre los mil y los dos mil euros** the price can be anything between one and two thousand euros

oscilatorio, -a *adj* swinging; *Fís* oscillating

ósculo *nm Formal* kiss

oscurantismo, obscurantismo *nm* obscurantism

oscurecer, obscurecer [46] **1** *vt* (**a**) *(privar de luz)* to darken (**b**) *(mente)* to confuse, to cloud (**c**) *(deslucir)* to overshadow
  2 *v impersonal (anochecer)* to get dark
  3 oscurecerse *vpr* to grow dark

oscurecimiento, obscurecimiento *nm* darkening

oscuridad, obscuridad *nf* (**a**) *(falta de luz)* darkness; **en la o.** in the dark (**b**) *(falta de claridad, fama)* obscurity

oscuro, -a, obscuro, -a 1 *adj* (**a**) *(sin luz)* dark; **¡qué o. está este cuarto!** this room is very dark! (**b**) *(color, traje, piel, pelo)* dark (**c**) *(nublado)* overcast (**d**) *(poco claro, poco conocido)* obscure (**e**) *(incierto)* uncertain, unclear; **tiene un origen o.** she's of uncertain origin (**f**) *(intenciones, asunto)* shady
  2 a oscuras *loc adv* **nos quedamos a oscuras** we were left in the dark; *Fig* **en este tema estoy a oscuras** I'm ignorant about this subject

óseo, -a *adj* bone; **médula ósea** bone marrow; **esqueleto ó.** bony skeleton

osezno *nm* bear cub

osificarse [59] *vpr* to ossify

Oslo *n* Oslo

osmosis, ósmosis *nf inv Fís & Fig* osmosis

oso, -a *nm,f* bear, *f* she-bear; **hacer el o.** to act the fool; *Esp Fam* **¡anda la osa!** well I never!, upon my word!; **o. de felpa** *o* **peluche** teddy bear; **o. hormiguero** anteater; **o. panda** panda; **o. polar** polar bear

osobuco *nm Culin* osso bucco

ostensible *adj* evident, clear

ostentación *nf* ostentation, show; **hacer o. de algo** to show sth off, to parade sth

ostentador, -ora *nm,f* show-off, ostentatious person

ostentar *vt* (**a**) *(poseer)* to hold, to have (**b**) *(exhibir)* to show off, to parade (**c**) *(cargo)* to hold, to occupy

ostentoso, -a *adj* ostentatious

osteoartritis *nf inv Med* osteoarthritis

osteópata *nmf* osteopath

osteopatía *nf (terapia)* osteopathy

osteoplastia *nf* osteoplasty

osteoporosis *nf inv* osteoporosis

ostra 1 *nf* oyster; *Fam* **aburrirse como una o.** to be bored stiff
  2 *interj Esp Fam* **¡ostras!** good grief!

ostracismo *nm* ostracism; **o. político** political wilderness

OTAN ['otan] *nf (abrev de* **Organización del Tratado del Atlántico Norte***)* NATO

otear *vt* to survey, to scan

otero *nm* hillock

OTI ['oti] *nf (abrev de* **Organización de Televisiones Iberoamericanas***)* = association of all Spanish-speaking television networks; **el festival de la O.** = televised song competition across the Spanish-speaking world

otitis *nf inv* inflammation of the ear

otomano, -a *adj & nm,f* Ottoman

otoñal *adj* fall, autumn, autumnal; **viento o.** autumn wind

otoño *nm* fall, autumn; **en o.** in the fall

otorgamiento *nm (de favor, petición)* granting; *(de premio, beca)* award; *Der (de documento)* execution

otorgar [38] *vt (favor, petición)* to grant; *(honor, título)* to confer; *(premio, beca)* to award, to present; *Der* to execute

otorrino, -a *nm,f Fam* ear, nose and throat specialist

otorrinolaringología *nf* ear, nose and throat medicine

otorrinolaringólogo, -a *nm,f* ear, nose and throat specialist

otro, -a 1 *adj* (**a**) *(distinto)* another; **otros/otras** other; **o. chico** another boy; **el o. chico** the other boy; **(los) otros chicos** (the) other boys; **no hacer otra cosa que llorar** to do nothing but cry; **el o. día** *(pasado)* the other day; **fue otra persona** it was somebody else; **el o. extremo** the far end; **el o. lado de la calle** the opposite side of the street (**b**) *(nuevo)* another; **estamos ante o. Dalí** this is another Dali; **otros tres goles** another three goals; **yo hubiera hecho o. tanto** I would have done just the same
  2 *pron* another (one); **otros/otras** others; **dame o.** give me another (one); **el o.** the other one; **(los) otros** (the) others; **yo no lo hice, fue o.** it wasn't me, it was somebody else; **o. habría abandonado, pero no él** anyone else would have given up, but not him; **¡o. que tal!** there's another one!; **¡otra!** *(en conciertos)* encore!, more!; **¡hasta otra!** see you again!

otrora *adv Formal* formerly

otrosí *adv Formal* besides, moreover

Ottawa [o'tawa] *n* Ottawa

OUA *nf Antes (abrev de* **Organización para la Unidad Africana***)* OAU

ouija ['wiχa] *nf (mesa)* ouija board

output ['autput] *(pl* **outputs***) nm Inform* output

ovación *nf* ovation

ovacionar *vt* to give an ovation to, to applaud

oval *adj* oval

ovalado, -a *adj* oval

óvalo *nm* oval

ovárico *adj* ovarian

ovario *nm* ovary

oveja *nf* sheep, ewe; **o. descarriada** lost sheep; **o. negra** black sheep

ovejero, -a *nm,f* shepherd, shepherdess *f*

overbooking [oβer'βukin] (*pl* **overbookings**) *nm* overbooking

overol *nm Am (de peto)* overalls; *(completo)* overalls

ovetense 1 *adj* of/from Oviedo

   2 *nmf* person from Oviedo

Oviedo *n* Oviedo

ovillar 1 *vt* to roll *o* wind into a ball

   2 ovillarse *vpr* to curl up into a ball

ovillo *nm* ball *(of wool etc)*; **hacerse un o.** to curl up into a ball

ovino, -a *adj* sheep; **productos ovinos** sheep products

ovíparo, -a *adj* oviparous

ovni *nm (abrev de* **objeto volador no identificado**) UFO

ovoide *adj* ovoid

ovulación *nf* ovulation

ovular 1 *adj* ovular

   2 *vi* to ovulate

óvulo *nm* ovum

oxidación *nf* rusting

oxidado, -a *adj* rusty

oxidante 1 *adj* oxidizing

   2 *nm* oxidizing agent

oxidar 1 *vt* to rust; *Quím* to oxidize

   2 oxidarse *vpr también Fig* to get rusty

óxido *nm* (a) *Quím* oxide (b) *(herrumbre)* rust

oxigenación *nf* oxygenation

oxigenado, -a *adj* (a) *Quím* oxygenated (b) *(cabello)* peroxide; **una rubia oxigenada** a peroxide blonde

oxigenar 1 *vt Quím* to oxygenate

   2 oxigenarse *vpr* (a) *(airearse)* to get a breath of fresh air (b) *(cabello)* to bleach

oxígeno *nm* oxygen

oye *ver* **oír**

oyente *nmf* (a) *(de programa)* listener (b) *(alumno)* auditing student

oyera *etc ver* **oír**

ozono *nm* ozone

ozonosfera *nf* ozonosphere

P

P, p [pe] *nf (letra)* P, p

p. *(abrev, pabilo)* p

p.a. (**a**) *(abrev de* **por ausencia**) pp (**b**) *(abrev de* **por autorización**) pp

pabellón *nm* (**a**) *(edificio)* pavilion (**b**) *(parte de un edificio)* block, section; *(en hospital)* ward (**c**) *(en parques, jardines)* summerhouse (**d**) *(tienda de campaña)* bell tent (**e**) *(dosel)* canopy (**f**) *(bandera)* flag (**g**) **p. auditivo** outer ear

pábilo, pabilo *nm* wick

pábulo *nm* **dar p. a** to feed, to encourage

PAC [pak] *nf (abrev de* **política agrícola común**) CAP

pacato, -a 1 *adj* (**a**) *(mojigato)* prudish (**b**) *(tímido)* shy
2 *nm,f (mojigato)* prude

pacense 1 *adj* of/from Badajoz
2 *nmf* person from Badajoz

paceño, -a 1 *adj* of/from La Paz
2 *nm,f* person from La Paz

pacer [42] *vi* to graze

pachá *nm* pasha; *Fam* **vivir como un p.** to live like a lord

pachanga *nf Fam* rowdy celebration

pachanguero, -a *adj Esp Fam (música)* catchy; *Am (alegre)* lively, party-loving

pacharán *nm* = liqueur made from brandy and sloes

pachorra *nf Fam* calmness

pachucho, -a *adj Fam* off-color

pachulí *(pl* **pachulíes)** *nm* patchouli

paciencia *nf* patience; **¡p., que todo se arreglará!** be patient, it'll all get sorted out!; **¡qué p. hay que tener contigo!** you'd try the patience of a saint!; **¡este niño va a acabar con mi p.!** I'm losing my patience with this child!; **armarse de p.** to summon up one's patience; **perder la p.** to lose one's patience; **tener más p. que un santo** to have the patience of a saint; **tener p.** to be patient

paciente *adj & nmf* patient

pacienzudo, -a *adj* patient

pacificación *nf* pacification

pacificador, -ora 1 *adj* pacifying; **las fuerzas pacificadoras de la ONU** the UN peacekeeping forces
2 *nm,f* pacifier, peacemaker

pacificar [59] **1** *vt* (**a**) *(país)* to pacify (**b**) *(ánimos)* to calm
2 **pacificarse** *vpr (persona)* to calm down

Pacífico 1 *nm* **el P.** the Pacific
2 *adj* **el océano P.** the Pacific Ocean

pacífico, -a *adj (vida, relaciones)* peaceful; *(persona)* peaceable

pacifismo *nm* pacifism

pacifista *adj & nmf* pacifist

pack [pak] *(pl* **packs)** *nm* pack; **un p. de seis** a six-pack

paco, -a *nm,f Andes, Pan Fam* cop

pacotilla: de pacotilla *loc adj* trashy, third-rate

pactar 1 *vt* to agree to; **p. un acuerdo** to reach an agreement
2 *vi* to strike a deal (**con** with)

pacto *nm* agreement, pact; **hacer/romper un p.** to make/ break an agreement; **p. electoral** electoral pact; **p. social** social contract

padecer [46] **1** *vt (sufrimiento)* to endure, to undergo; *(hambre, injusticia)* to suffer; *(enfermedad)* to suffer from; **p. inundaciones/un terremoto** to be hit by floods/an earthquake
2 *vi* to suffer; **p. del corazón/riñón** to suffer from a heart/ kidney complaint; **padeció mucho por sus hijos** she suffered a lot for the sake of her children

padecimiento *nm* suffering

pádel *nm Dep* paddle tennis

padezca *etc ver* **padecer**

padrastro *nm* (**a**) *(pariente)* stepfather (**b**) *(pellejo)* hangnail

padrazo *nm Fam* adoring father

padre 1 *nm* (**a**) *(hombre)* father; *Fam* **de p. y muy señor mío** incredible, tremendous; *Esp Fam* **hacer p. a alguien** to make sb a happy man; **p. de familia** head of the family; **p. político** father-in-law (**b**) **padres** *(hombre y mujer)* parents; *(antepasados)* ancestors, forefathers (**c**) *Rel* father; **Santo P.** Holy Father, Pope; **p. espiritual** confessor; **Padres de la Iglesia** Fathers of the Christian Church
2 *adj inv Fam* (**a**) *Esp* incredible, tremendous; **se armó el lío p.** there was a terrible *o* huge fuss; **fue el cachondeo p.** it was a great laugh (**b**) *Méx* great; **está muy p.** it's really great *o* fantastic

padrenuestro *nm* Lord's Prayer; **saberse algo como el p.** to know sth by heart, to have sth down pat

padrino *nm* (**a**) *(de bautismo)* godfather; *(de boda)* best man; **padrinos** *(padrino y madrina)* godparents (**b**) *(en duelos, torneos)* second (**c**) *(protector)* patron

padrísimo, -a *adj Méx Fam* fantastic, great

padrón *nm (censo)* census; *(para votar)* electoral roll *o* register

padrote *nm Méx Fam* pimp

paella *nf* paella

paellera *nf* = large frying pan for cooking paella

paf *interj* bang!, crash!

pág. *(abrev de* **página**) p

paga *nf (salario)* salary, wages; *(de niño)* allowance; **p. extra** *o* **extraordinaria** = additional payment of a month's salary or wages made to Spanish workers in June and December

pagadero, -a *adj* payable; **p. a 90 días/a la entrega** payable within 90 days/on delivery

pagado, -a *adj* paid; **p. de sí mismo** pleased with oneself

pagador, -ora 1 *adj* paying; **ser buen/mal p.** to be a reliable/unreliable payer
2 *nm,f (de obreros)* paymaster

paganismo *nm* paganism

pagano, -a *adj & nm,f* pagan, heathen

pagar [38] **1** *vt (empleado, persona)* to pay; *(factura, gastos, delito)* to pay for; *(deuda)* to pay off, to settle; *(ayuda, favor)* to repay; **pagó dos millones por la casa** she paid two million for the house; **yo pago la cena** I'll pay for dinner; **su padre**

le paga los estudios his father is supporting him through college; **no iría aunque me lo pagaras** I wouldn't go (even) if you paid me; **¡que Dios se lo pague!** God bless you!; *Fam Fig* **me las pagarás** you'll pay for this

2 *vi* (**a**) *(con dinero)* to pay (**b**) *Am Fam (compensar)* to be worth it; **no paga** it's not worth it

pagaré *nm Com* promissory note, IOU; **p. del Tesoro** Treasury note

pagel *nm* sea bream

página *nf* page; **las páginas amarillas** the Yellow Pages; **p. central** centerfold; *Inform* **p. inicial** *o* **de inicio** home page; *Inform* **p. personal** personal home page; *Inform* **p. web** Web page

paginación *nf* pagination

paginar *vt Inform* to paginate

pago 1 *nm (de dinero)* payment; *Fig* reward, payment; **en p. de** *o* **a** *(en recompensa por)* as a reward for; *(a cambio de)* in return for; **p. anticipado** *o* **por adelantado** advance payment; **p. al contado** *(en un plazo)* single payment; *(en metálico)* cash payment; **p. a plazos** payment by installments; **p. en efectivo** cash payment; **p. inicial** down payment; **p. en metálico** cash payment

2 pagos *nmpl (lugar)* **por estos pagos** around here; **¿qué hacías tú por aquellos pagos?** what were you doing around there *o* in those parts?

pagoda *nf* pagoda

pague *etc ver* **pagar**

paila *nf* (**a**) *Andes, CAm, Carib (sartén)* frying pan (**b**) *Chile (huevos fritos)* fried eggs

paipái, paipay *nm Esp* = rigid circular fan with handle

país *nm* country; **el p. votó "no" en el referéndum** the country *o* nation voted "no" in the referendum; **en un p. muy lejano…** in a distant *o* far-off land…; **los Países Bajos** the Netherlands; **los países bálticos** the Baltic States; **países desarrollados** developed countries; **P. de Gales** Wales; **p. natal** native country, homeland; **p. satélite** satellite state; **países subdesarrollados** underdeveloped countries; **el P. Valenciano** the autonomous region of Valencia; **el P. Vasco** the Basque Country; **países en vías de desarrollo** developing countries

paisaje *nm (pintura, terreno)* landscape; *(vista panorámica)* scenery, view

paisajismo *nm* landscape painting

paisajista 1 *adj* landscape; **pintor p.** landscape painter

2 *nmf* landscape painter

paisajístico, -a *adj* landscape; **belleza paisajística** natural beauty

paisanaje *nm* civilians

paisano, -a 1 *adj (del mismo país)* from the same country

2 *nm,f* (**a**) *(del mismo país) (hombre)* compatriot, fellow countryman; *(mujer)* compatriot, fellow countrywoman (**b**) *(campesino)* country person, peasant

3 *nm (civil)* civilian; **de p.** *(militar)* in civilian clothes; *(policía)* in plain clothes

paja *nf* (**a**) *(hierba, caña)* straw; *Fig (relleno)* waffle (**b**) *muy Fam (masturbación)* jerkoff; **hacerse una** *o Am* **la p.** to jerk off

pajar *nm* straw loft

pájara *nf Pey* crafty *o* sly woman

pajarera *nf* aviary

pajarería *nf* pet store *o* shop

pajarita *nf* (**a**) *(de papel)* paper bird (**b**) *Esp (corbata)* bow tie

pájaro *nm* (**a**) *(ave)* bird; *Fig* **matar dos pájaros de un tiro** to kill two birds with one stone; *Fig* **tener pájaros en la cabeza** to be scatterbrained *o* empty-headed; *Prov* **más vale p. en mano que ciento volando** a bird in the hand is worth two in the bush; **p. bobo** penguin; **p. carpintero**

woodpecker; **p. de mal agüero** bird of ill omen (**b**) *(persona)* crafty devil, sly old fox

pajarraco *nm Pey* (**a**) *(pájaro)* big ugly bird (**b**) *(persona)* unpleasant person

paje *nm* page

pajita, pajilla *nf* (drinking) straw

pajizo, -a *adj (color, pelo)* straw-colored

pajolero, -a *adj Esp muy Fam* damn, blessed; **no tengo ni pajolera idea** I haven't the faintest goddamn idea

Pakistán *n* Pakistan

pakistaní (*pl* **pakistaníes**) *adj & nmf* Pakistani

pala *nf* (**a**) *(herramienta)* spade; *(para recoger)* shovel; *Culin* slice; **p. mecánica** *o* **excavadora** excavator, digger (**b**) *(de frontón, ping-pong)* paddle, bat; **jugar a las palas** *(en la playa)* to play beach tennis (**c**) *(de remo, hélice)* blade (**d**) *(diente)* (upper) front tooth

palabra *nf* (**a**) *(en general)* word; **de p.** by word of mouth, verbally; **dejar a alguien con la p. en la boca** to cut sb off in midsentence; **en cuatro** *o* **dos palabras** in a few words; **en una p.** in a word; **no dijo p.** he didn't say a word; **medir las palabras** to weigh one's words (carefully); **no habla ni (media) p. de español** she doesn't speak a word of Spanish; **p. por p.** word for word; **ser palabras mayores** to be an important matter; **sin mediar p.** without a single word; *Inform* **p. clave** keyword; **p. divina** *o* **de Dios** word of God

(**b**) *(juramento, promesa)* word; **dar su p.** to give one's word; **estar bajo p.** *(en juicio)* to be under oath; **faltó a su p.** he went back on his word, he broke *o* didn't keep his word; **mantuvo su p.** she kept her word; **tienes mi p.** you have my word; **tomar la p. a alguien** to hold sb to their word

(**c**) *(habla)* speech

(**d**) *(derecho de hablar)* **dar la p. a alguien** to give the floor to sb; **tomar la p.** to take the floor

palabrería *nf Fam* hot air

palabrota *nf* swearword, rude word; **decir palabrotas** to swear

palacete *nm* mansion, small palace

palaciego, -a *adj* palace, court; **lujo p.** palatial luxury; **intrigas palaciegas** court intrigues

palacio *nm* palace; **p. de congresos** conference center; **p. de deportes** sports hall; **p. de exposiciones** exhibition center; **P. de Justicia** Law Courts; **p. real** royal palace

palada *nf* (**a**) *(con pala)* spadeful, shovelful (**b**) *(con remo)* stroke

paladar 1 *nm (en la boca)* palate; *Fig (gusto)* palate, taste; **su arte no se ajusta al p. europeo** his art doesn't appeal to European taste

2 *nf o nm Cuba* = small restaurant in a private house

paladear *vt* to savor

paladín *nm Hist* paladin, heroic knight; *Fig (adalid)* champion, defender

palanca *nf* (**a**) *(barra, mando)* lever; *Aut* **p. de cambio** gearshift, stick shift; **p. de mando** joystick (**b**) *(trampolín)* diving board (**c**) *Am Fam* **tener p.** *(contactos)* to have friends in high places

palangana *nf (para fregar)* dishpan; *(para lavarse)* washbowl

palangre *nm* fishing line with hooks

palanqueta *nf* jimmy, crowbar

palatal *adj* palatal

palatino, -a *adj* (**a**) *(de paladar)* palatine (**b**) *(de palacio)* palace, court; **oficio p.** position at court

palco *nm* box *(at theater)*

palé *nm* pallet

palenque *nm* (**a**) *(estacada)* fence, palisade (**b**) *(recinto)* arena; **salir al p.** to enter the fray (**c**) *Méx (para peleas de gallos)* cockpit, cockfighting arena (**d**) *Andes, RP (para animales)* hitching post

palentino, -a 1 *adj* of/from Palencia
   2 *nm,f* person from Palencia
paleocristiano, -a *adj* early Christian
paleografía *nf* paleography
paleográfico, -a *adj* paleographic
paleógrafo, -a *nm,f* paleographer
paleolítico, -a 1 *adj* paleolithic
   2 *nm* Paleolithic period
paleontología *nf* paleontology
paleontólogo, -a *nm,f* paleontologist
Palermo *n* Palermo
Palestina *n* Palestine
palestino, -a *adj & nm,f* Palestinian
palestra *nf* arena; *Fig* **salir** *o* **saltar a la p.** to enter the fray
paleta *nf* (**a**) *(pala pequeña)* small shovel, small spade; *(de albañil)* trowel; *(de pintor)* palette; *(en máquina)* blade, vane; *(para servir)* fish slice; *Inform* **p. de herramientas** toolbox (**b**) *Andes, CAm, Méx (pirulí)* lollipop; *Bol, Col, Perú (polo)* Popsicle®
paletada *nf* *(con paleta)* shovelful, spadeful; *(de yeso)* trowelful
paletilla *nf Culin* shoulder
paleto, -a *Esp Pey* **1** *adj* coarse, uncouth
   2 *nm,f* hick, country bumpkin, yokel
paliar [32] *vt* (**a**) *(atenuar)* to ease, to relieve (**b**) *(disculpar)* to excuse, to justify
paliativo, -a 1 *adj* palliative
   2 *nm* (**a**) *(excusa)* excuse, mitigation; **sin paliativos** unmitigated (**b**) *Med* palliative
palidecer [46] *vi (ponerse pálido)* to go *o* turn pale; *Fig (perder importancia)* to pale, to fade
palidez *nf* paleness
pálido, -a *adj* pale; **ponerse p.** to turn *o* go pale; *Fig* **ser un p. reflejo** *o* **una pálida imagen de** to be a pale reflection of; **el premio es un p. reconocimiento de su trabajo** the prize is meager reward for her work
palier *nm Aut* bearing
palillero *nm* toothpick holder
palillo *nm* (**a**) *(mondadientes)* toothpick; *(para tapa)* cocktail stick (**b**) *(baqueta)* drumstick (**c**) *(para comida china)* chopstick (**d**) *(persona delgada)* matchstick
palio *nm* canopy
palique *nm Esp Fam* chat; **estar de p.** to have a chat
palisandro *nm* rosewood
palito *nm Culin* **p. (de pescado)** fish stick
paliza 1 *nf* (**a**) *(golpes, derrota)* beating (**b**) *(esfuerzo)* hard grind (**c**) *Fam (rollo)* drag; **dar la p. (a alguien)** to go on and on (to sb)
   2 *nmf inv Fam* **ser un p.** *o* **palizas** to be a pain in the neck
palma *nf* (**a**) *(de mano)* palm; **conocer algo como la p. de la mano** to know sth like the back of one's hand (**b**) *(palmera)* palm (tree); *(hoja de palmera)* palm leaf; *Fig* **llevarse la p.** to be the best; *Irónico* **él, es tonto, pero su hermano se lleva la p.** he's stupid but his brother takes the cake; **llevar** *o* **traer en palmas a alguien** to pamper sb (**c**) **palmas** *(aplausos)* clapping, applause; **batir** *o* **dar palmas** to clap (one's hands)
palmada *nf* (**a**) *(suave)* pat; *(más fuerte)* slap; **dar palmadas en la espalda a alguien** to pat sb on the back (**b**) *(aplauso)* clap; **palmadas** clapping
palmar¹ 1 *adj* of the palm *(of the hand)*
   2 *nm* palm grove
palmar² ** *Fam* **1 *vi* to kick the bucket
   2 *vt* **palmarla** to kick the bucket
palmarés *nm inv* (**a**) *(historial)* record (**b**) *(lista)* list *o* roll of winners
palmario, -a *adj* obvious, clear
palmatoria *nf* candlestick

palmear 1 *vt* (**a**) *(aplaudir)* to applaud (**b**) *(espalda, hombro)* to slap, to pat
   2 *vi* to clap, to applaud
palmeño, -a 1 *adj* of/from Las Palmas
   2 *nm,f* person from Las Palmas
palmera *nf* (**a**) *(árbol)* palm (tree); *(datilera)* date palm (**b**) *(pastel)* = flat, heart-shaped pastry
palmeral *nm* palm grove
palmesano, -a 1 *adj* of/from Palma (Mallorca)
   2 *nm,f* person from Palma (Mallorca)
palmípedo, -a 1 *adj* web-footed
   2 palmípedas *nfpl* waterfowl *(plural)*
palmito *nm* (**a**) *(árbol)* palmetto, fan palm (**b**) *Culin* palm heart (**c**) *Fam (buena planta)* good looks; **lucir el p.** to show off one's good looks
palmo *nm* handspan; **p. a p.** bit by bit, inch by inch; *Fam* **dejar a alguien con un p. de narices** to bring sb down to earth with a bump
palmotear *vi* to clap
palmoteo *nm* clapping
palo *nm* (**a**) *(trozo de madera)* stick; **los palos de la tienda de campaña** the tent poles; *Fam* **a p. seco** *(sin nada más)* without anything else, on its own; *(bebida)* neat; *Fig* **dar palos de ciego** *(criticar)* to lash out (wildly); *(no saber qué hacer)* to grope around in the dark; *Prov* **de tal p. tal astilla** he's/she's a chip off the old block
   (**b**) *(de golf)* club; *(de escoba)* handle; *(de portería) (lateral)* post; *(larguero)* bar; **estrellaron tres disparos en los palos** they hit the woodwork three times
   (**c**) *(mástil)* mast; **p. mayor** mainmast
   (**d**) *(de baraja)* suit
   (**e**) *(madera)* **de p.** wooden
   (**f**) *Bot* tree; **p. santo** lignum vitae
   (**g**) *(golpe)* blow *(with a stick)*; *(mala crítica)* bad review; **se ha llevado muchos palos últimamente** he's had to put up with a lot recently; **liarse a palos (con alguien)** to come to blows (with sb); **moler a alguien a palos** to thrash sb
   (**h**) *Fam (problema)* **me da p. hacerlo/decirlo** I hate having to do/say it; **¡qué p., me han suspendido!** what a drag, I've failed!; **da mucho p. ponerse a estudiar en verano** it's a pain *o* drag having to start studying during the summer
   (**i**) *Col, Méx, Pan, Ven Fam (como intensificador)* **p. de hombre** great man; **p. de agua** *(aguacero)* downpour, deluge of rain
paloma *nf* dove, pigeon; **p. mensajera** carrier *o* homing pigeon; **p. torcaz** ringdove, wood pigeon
palomar *nm (pequeño)* dovecote; *(grande)* pigeon shed
palometa *nf* pomfret
palomilla *nf* (**a**) *(insecto)* grain moth (**b**) *(rosca)* wing nut, butterfly nut (**c**) *(soporte)* bracket
palomino *nm (ave)* young dove *o* pigeon
palomitas *nfpl* **p. (de maíz)** popcorn
palomo *nm* male dove *o* pigeon
palote *nm (trazo)* downstroke
palpable *adj (tocable)* touchable, palpable; *(evidente)* obvious, clear
palpación *nf* palpation
palpar 1 *vt* (**a**) *(tocar)* to feel, to touch; *Med* to palpate (**b**) *(percibir)* to feel
   2 *vi* to feel around
palpitación *nf (de corazón)* beating; *(con fuerza)* throbbing; **una p.** *(de corazón)* a beat; *(con fuerza)* a throb; *Med* **palpitaciones** palpitations
palpitante *adj* (**a**) *(que palpita)* beating; *(con fuerza)* throbbing (**b**) *(interesante) (discusión, competición)* lively; *(interés, deseo, cuestión)* burning
palpitar *vi* (**a**) *(latir)* to beat; *(con fuerza)* to throb (**b**) *(sentimiento)* to be evident

pálpito *nm* feeling, hunch

palta *nf Andes, RP* avocado

palúdico, -a *adj Med* malarial

paludismo *nm Med* malaria

palurdo, -a *Pey* **1** *adj* coarse, uncouth
  2 *nm,f* hick, country bumpkin, yokel

pamela *nf* sun hat

pampa *nf* **la p.** the pampas *(plural)*

pampero, -a 1 *adj* of/from the pampas
  2 *nm,f* inhabitant of the pampas

pamplina *nf Fam* trifle, unimportant thing; **¡no me vengas con pamplinas!** don't try that nonsense with me!

Pamplona *n* Pamplona

pamplonés, -esa 1 *adj* of/from Pamplona
  2 *nm,f* person from Pamplona

pamplonica *adj & nmf* = **pamplonés**

pan *nm* (**a**) *(alimento)* bread; **un p.** a loaf of bread; **p. de barra** French bread; *Esp* **p. Bimbo®** sliced bread; **p. francés** French bread; **p. de centeno** rye bread; **p. integral** whole wheat bread; **p. de molde** sliced bread; **p. moreno** *o* **negro** *(integral)* brown bread; *(con centeno)* black *o* rye bread; **p. de oro** gold leaf *o* foil; **p. rallado** breadcrumbs
  (**b**) *(expresiones)* **a p. y agua** on bread and water; *Fig* on the breadline; *Fam* **contigo, p. y cebolla** I'll go through thick and thin with you; **ganarse el p.** to earn a living; **llamar al p. p. y al vino vino** to call a spade a spade; *Fam* **ser más bueno que el p.** to be kindness itself; *Fam* **estar más bueno que el p.** to be gorgeous; *Fam* **ser p. comido** to be a piece of cake, to be as easy as pie; *Fam* **ser el p. nuestro de cada día** to be commonplace, to be an everyday occurence; *Prov* **a falta de p. buenas son tortas** you have to make the most of what you've got

pana *nf* corduroy; **pantalones/camisa de p.** corduroy pants/shirt

panacea *nf también Fig* panacea

panadería *nf* bakery, baker's

panadero, -a *nm,f* baker

panal *nm* honeycomb

Panamá *n* Panama

panamá *nm* panama (hat)

panameño, -a *adj & nm,f* Panamanian

Panamericana *nf* **la P.** the Pan-American Highway

panamericanismo *nm* Pan-Americanism

pancarta *nf* placard, banner

panceta *nf* bacon

panchitos *nmpl Esp Fam* salted peanuts

pancho, -a *adj Fam* calm, unruffled; **estar/quedarse tan p.** to be/remain perfectly calm

páncreas *nm inv* pancreas

pancreático, -a *adj* pancreatic

panda 1 *adj* **oso p.** panda
  2 *nm* panda
  3 *nf Esp (de amigos)* crowd, gang; *(de gamberros, delincuentes)* gang

pandemia *nf Med* pandemic

pandemónium *nm* pandemonium

pandereta *nf* tambourine

pandero *nm* (**a**) *(instrumento)* tambourine (**b**) *Esp Fam (culo)* butt

pandilla *nf* gang

pandillero, -a *nm,f* member of a gang

pandorga *nf Par (cometa)* kite

panecillo *nm Esp* bread roll

panegírico, -a 1 *adj* panegyrical, eulogistic
  2 *nm* panegyric, eulogy

panel *nm* (**a**) *(pared, biombo)* screen (**b**) *(tablero)* board; **p. de**

información *(en estación)* arrival/departure board (**c**) *(de personas)* panel

panera *nf (para servir pan)* breadbasket; *(para guardar pan)* bread box

pánfilo, -a *Fam* **1** *adj* simple, foolish
  2 *nm,f* fool, simpleton

panfletario, -a *adj* propagandist

panfleto *nm* polemical pamphlet

pánico *nm* panic; **ser presa del p.** to be panic-stricken; **tenerle p. a** to be terrified of

panificación *nf* bread making

panificadora *nf* (large) bakery

panocha *nf* (**a**) *(de maíz)* ear, cob (**b**) *Méx Vulg (vulva)* cunt

panoplia *nf* (**a**) *(armas)* mounted display of weapons (**b**) *(conjunto, gama)* range, gamut

panorama *nm* (**a**) *(vista)* panorama (**b**) *(situación)* overall state; *(perspectiva)* outlook

panorámica *nf* panorama

panorámico, -a *adj* panoramic

panqueque *nm Am* pancake

pantagruélico, -a *adj* gargantuan, enormous

pantaleta *nf*, **pantaletas** *nfpl CAm, Carib, Méx (bragas)* panties

pantalla *nf* (**a**) *(de cine, televisión, ordenador)* screen; **la pequeña p.** the small screen, television; **la p. grande** the big screen; **mostrar en p.** to show on the screen; **una estrella de la p.** a TV/movie star; **p. (acústica)** baffle; **p. de cristal líquido** liquid crystal display; **p. gigante** big screen; **p. plana** flat screen; **p. de radar** radar screen; **p. táctil** touch screen (**b**) *(de lámpara)* lampshade (**c**) *(de chimenea)* fireguard (**d**) *(encubridor)* front; **esta empresa les sirve de p. para sus actividades ilegales** this company serves as a front for their illegal activities

pantalón *nm*, **pantalones** *nmpl* pants, trousers; **unos pantalones** a pair of pants *o* trousers; *Fam Fig* **bajarse los pantalones** to climb down; *Fam Fig* **llevar los pantalones** to wear the pants *o* trousers; **p. de campana** bell-bottoms; **pantalones de chándal** tracksuit bottoms *o* pants; **p. corto** short pants *o* trousers, shorts; **pantalones de esquí** ski pants; **p. largo** (long) pants *o* trousers; **p. de montar** jodhpurs; **p. de pana** cords; **p. de pinzas** pleated pants *o* trousers; **p. (de) pitillo** drainpipe pants *o* trousers; **p. tejano** jeans; **p. vaquero** jeans

pantaloncillos *nmpl Col, Ven (calzoncillos)* shorts

pantanal *nm* marsh, bog

pantano *nm* (**a**) *(ciénaga)* marsh; *(laguna)* swamp (**b**) *(embalse)* reservoir

pantanoso, -a *adj* (**a**) *(cenagoso)* marshy, boggy (**b**) *(difícil)* tricky

panteísmo *nm* pantheism

panteísta 1 *adj* pantheistic
  2 *nmf* pantheist

panteón *nm (sepultura)* mausoleum, vault; *Am salvo RP (cementerio)* cemetery

pantera *nf* panther; **p. negra** black panther

panti *nm* panty hose

pantimedias *nfpl Méx* panty hose

pantocrátor *nm Arte* Christ Pantocrator

pantomima *nf* mime; *Fig* pantomime, acting

pantorrilla *nf* calf

pants *nmpl Méx (pantalón)* tracksuit bottoms *o* pants; *(traje)* tracksuit, jogging suit

pantufla *nf* slipper

panty *(pl* **pantis)** *nm* panty hose

panza *nf* belly

panzada *nf* (**a**) *(en el agua)* belly flop (**b**) *Fam (hartura)* bellyful;

darse una p. (de algo) to stuff oneself (with sth)

pañal *nm* diaper; *Fam Fig* **estar en pañales** *(en sus inicios)* to be in its infancy; *(sin conocimientos)* not to have a clue; *Fam Fig* **dejar a alguien en pañales** to leave sb standing *o* behind

pañería *nf (producto)* drapery; *(tienda)* dry goods store

paño *nm* (a) *(tela)* cloth, material (b) *(trapo)* cloth; *(para polvo)* duster; *(de cocina)* dish towel; *Chile* **p. de loza** dish towel (c) *(lienzo)* panel, length (d) *(expresiones)* **conocer el p.** to know the score; **ser el p. de lágrimas de alguien** to be a shoulder to cry on for sb; **en paños menores** in one's underthings; **paños calientes** half-measures

pañol *nm Náut* storeroom

pañolada *nf* = waving of handkerchiefs by crowd at sporting events to signal approval or disapproval

pañoleta *nf* shawl, wrap

pañuelo *nm (de nariz)* handkerchief; *(para el cuello)* scarf; *(para la cabeza)* headscarf; **p. de papel** paper handkerchief, tissue; *Fam* **¡el mundo es un p.!** it's a small world!

Papa *nm* Pope

papa *nf esp Am* potato; *Fam* **no saber ni p.** not to have a clue; **papas fritas** *(de sartén)* (French) fries; *(de bolsa)* (potato) chips

papá *nm Fam* dad; **P. Noel** Santa (Claus), Kriss Kringle

papachar *vt Méx* to cuddle, to pamper

papacho *nm Méx* hug, cuddle

papada *nf (de persona)* double chin; *(de animal)* dewlap

papado *nm* papacy

papagayo *nm* parrot; **como un p.** parrot-like

papal *adj* papal

papalote *nm CAm, Méx (cometa)* kite

papamoscas *nm inv* flycatcher

papanatas *nmf inv Fam* sucker

paparazzi [papa'ratsi] *nmf inv* paparazzi

paparruchas *nfpl Fam* nonsense

papaya *nf (fruta)* papaya, pawpaw

papear *Esp, Ven Fam* **1** *vt* to eat, to gobble

2 *vi* to eat

papel *nm* (a) *(material)* paper; *(hoja)* sheet of paper; *(trozo)* piece of paper; **un p. en blanco** a blank sheet of paper; *Fig* **ser p. mojado** to be worthless; *Fig* **perder los papeles** to lose control; **p. de aluminio** tin *o* aluminum foil; **p. de barba** untrimmed paper; **p. biblia** bible paper; **p. de calco** *o* **de calcar** *(transparente)* tracing paper; *(entintado)* carbon paper; **p. carbón** carbon paper; **p. de carta** notepaper; **p. cebolla** onionskin; **p. celofán** Cellophane®; **p. de cocina** paper towel; *Inform* **p. continuo** continuous paper; **p. cuadriculado** graph paper; **p. de embalar** *o* **envolver** wrapping paper; **p. de estaño** tin *o* aluminum foil; **p. de estraza** brown paper; **p. de fumar** cigarette paper; **p. higiénico** toilet paper; **p. de lija** sandpaper; **p. milimetrado** graph paper; **p. de periódico** newspaper, newsprint; **p. pintado** wallpaper; **p. de regalo** wrapping paper, gift-wrapping (paper); **p. secante** blotting paper; **p. de seda** tissue paper; **p. sellado** *o* **timbrado** stamp, stamped paper; **p. vegetal** tracing paper

(b) *(en película, teatro) & Fig* role, part; **desempeñar** *o* **hacer el p. de** to play the role *o* part of; **hacer buen/mal p.** to do well/badly; **p. principal/secundario** main/minor part

(c) *Fin* paper; **p. de pagos** = special stamps for making certain payments to the state; **p. del Estado** government bonds; **p. moneda** paper money, banknotes

(d) *(documento)* **los sin papeles** undocumented immigrants

papela *nf Esp Fam (documentación)* ID card

papeleo *nm* paperwork, red tape

papelera *nf* (a) *(cesto)* wastepaper basket; *(en la calle)* garbage can (b) *(fábrica)* paper mill

papelería *nf* stationer's

papelero, -a 1 *adj* paper; **industria papelera** paper industry

2 *nm CSur* wastepaper basket

papeleta *nf* (a) *(boleto)* ticket, slip (of paper); *(de votación)* ballot paper (b) *Educ* = slip of paper with college exam results (c) *(problema)* **¡menuda p.!** that's a nasty one!

papelina *nf Fam* = sachet of paper containing drugs

papelón *nm Fam* spectacle; **hacer un p.** to make a fool of oneself, to be left looking ridiculous

papeo *nm Fam* grub

paperas *nfpl* mumps

papi *nm Fam* daddy, pop

papila *nf Anat* papilla; **p. gustativa** taste bud

papilar *adj* papillary

papilla *nf* (a) *(para niños)* puree; *Fam* **echar** *o* **arrojar hasta la primera p.** to be as sick as a dog; *Fam* **hecho p.** *(cansado)* shattered, exhausted; *(roto)* smashed to bits, ruined (b) *Med* barium meal

papiloma *nm* papilloma

papiro *nm* papyrus

papiroflexia *nf* origami

papirotazo *nm* flick *(of finger)*

papista *nmf* papist; *Fam* **ser más p. que el Papa** to be more Catholic than the Pope

papo *nm Fam (moflete)* jowls; *Fig (descaro)* **tener mucho p.** to have a lot of cheek

páprika *nf* paprika

papú *(pl* **papúes)** *adj & nmf* Papuan

Papúa-Nueva Guinea *n* Papua New Guinea

paquebote *nm* packet boat

paquete *nm* (a) *(de libros, regalos)* package, parcel; **p. bomba** mail bomb; **p. postal** package, parcel

(b) *(de cigarrillos, folios)* pack; *(de azúcar, arroz)* bag; **p. de tabaco** cigarette pack

(c) *(maleta, bulto)* bag

(d) *(conjunto)* package; **p. de acciones** shareholding; **p. de medidas** group of measures; **p. turístico** package vacation

(e) *Inform* package

(f) *(en motocicleta)* passenger; **ir de p.** to ride on the passenger seat

(g) *Esp Fam (genitales masculinos)* bulge

(h) *Fam (cosa fastidiosa)* **me ha tocado el p. de hacer…** I've been lumbered with doing…

(i) *Fam* **meter un p. a alguien** *(castigar)* to come down on sb like a ton of bricks

paquetería *nf* (a) *(mercancía)* small goods; **empresa de p.** parcel delivery company (b) *(negocio)* small goods store (c) *RP Fam (elegancia)* smartness, elegance

paquidermo *nm* pachyderm

Paquistán *n* Pakistan

paquistaní *(pl* **paquistaníes)** *adj & nmf* Pakistani

par 1 *adj* (a) *(número)* even (b) *(igual)* equal

2 *nm* (a) *(dos cosas o personas)* pair; **a** *o* **en pares** in pairs, two by two (b) *(número indeterminado)* couple; **un p. de copas** a couple of *o* a few drinks; **un p. de veces** a couple of times, a few times (c) *(en golf)* par; **dos bajo/sobre p.** two under/over par (d) *(noble)* peer (e) *(expresiones)* **sin p.** without equal, matchless; **de una belleza sin p.** incomparably beautiful; **(abierto) de p. en p.** *(puerta, ventana)* wide open

3 a la par *loc adv* (a) *(simultáneamente)* at the same time (b) *(a igual nivel)* at the same level (c) *Fin* at par

para *prep* (a) *(finalidad)* for; **es p. ti** it's for you; **una mesa p. el salón** a table for the living room; **esta agua no es buena p. beber** this water isn't fit for drinking *o* to drink; **te lo repetiré p. que te enteres** I'll repeat it so you understand; **¿p. qué?** what for?

(b) *(motivación)* (in order) to; **p. conseguir sus propósitos** in order to achieve his aims; **lo he hecho p. agradarte** I did it to please you

　(**c**) *(dirección)* toward; **ir p. casa** to head (for) home; **salir p. el aeropuerto** to leave for the airport

　(**d**) *(tiempo)* for; **tiene que estar acabado p. mañana** it has to be finished by *o* for tomorrow; *Am* **salvo** *RP* **diez p. las once** ten to eleven

　(**e**) *(comparación)* **está muy delgado p. lo que come** he's very thin considering how much he eats; **p. ser verano hace mucho frío** considering it's summer, it's very cold

　(**f**) *(después de adj y antes de infin)* *(inminencia, propósito)* to; **la comida está lista p. servir** the meal is ready to be served; **el atleta está preparado p. ganar** the athlete is ready to win

　(**g**) *(expresiones)* **p. con** toward; **es buena p. con los demás** she is kind toward other people; **p. mí/ti/**etc *(en mi/tu opinión)* as far as you're concerned; **p. mí que no van a venir** it looks to me like they're not coming

parabién *nm Formal* congratulations

parábola *nf* (**a**) *(alegoría)* parable (**b**) *Mat* parabola

parabólica *nf* satellite dish

parabólico, -a *adj* parabolic

parabrisas *nm inv* windshield

paracaídas *nm inv* parachute

paracaidismo *nm* parachuting, parachute jumping

paracaidista *nmf* parachutist; *Mil* paratrooper

paracas *nmpl Fam Mil (paracaidistas)* troopers

paracetamol *nm* acetaminophen

parachispas *nm inv* fireguard

parachoques *nm inv (de automóvil)* fender; *(de tren)* buffer

parada *nf* (**a**) *(detención)* stop, stopping (**b**) *Dep* save (**c**) *(de autobús)* (bus) stop; *(de taxis)* taxi stand; *(de metro)* (subway) station; **p. discrecional** flag stop (**d**) *Mil* parade

paradero *nm* (**a**) *(de persona)* whereabouts; **están en p. desconocido** their present whereabouts are unknown (**b**) *Chile, Col, Méx, Perú (de autobús)* bus stop

paradigma *nm* paradigm, example

paradigmático, -a *adj* paradigmatic

paradisiaco, -a, paradisíaco, -a *adj* heavenly

parado, -a 1 *adj* (**a**) *(inmóvil)* *(vehículo)* stationary, standing; *(persona)* still, motionless; *(fábrica, proyecto)* at a standstill (**b**) *Esp (pasivo)* lacking in initiative; **ser muy p.** to lack initiative (**c**) *Esp (sin empleo)* unemployed, out of work (**d**) *Am (en pie)* standing; **caer p.** to land on one's feet (**e**) **salir bien/mal p. de algo** to come off well/badly out of sth

　2 *nm,f Esp (desempleado)* unemployed person; **los parados** the unemployed; **los parados de larga duración** the long-term unemployed

paradoja *nf* paradox

paradójico, -a *adj* paradoxical, ironical

parador *nm* (**a**) *(mesón)* roadside inn (**b**) *Esp (hotel)* **p. (nacional)** = state-owned luxury hotel, often in a building of historic or artistic importance

parafarmacia *nf* alternative medicines *o* health remedies

parafernalia *nf* paraphernalia

parafina *nf* paraffin wax

parafrasear *vt* to paraphrase

paráfrasis *nf inv* paraphrase

paragolpes *nm inv RP (en vehículo)* fender

paraguas *nm inv* umbrella

Paraguay *nm* (**el**) **P.** Paraguay

paraguaya *nf (fruta)* = fruit similar to peach

paraguayo, -a *adj & nm,f* Paraguayan

paragüero *nm* umbrella stand

paraíso *nm* (**a**) *Rel* Paradise; *Fig* paradise; **p. fiscal** tax haven; **p. terrenal** earthly paradise (**b**) *Teatro* **asientos de p.** upper balcony

paraje *nm* spot, place

paralela *nf Mat* parallel (line); *Dep* **paralelas** parallel bars

paralelismo *nm* (**a**) *Mat* parallelism (**b**) *(semejanza)* similarity, parallels

paralelo, -a 1 *adj* parallel (**a** to); **la cordillera corre paralela al mar** the mountain range runs parallel to the sea; **los dos políticos han seguido caminos paralelos** the two politicians have followed similar paths; *Dep* **barras paralelas** parallel bars

　2 *nm* (**a**) *Geog* parallel (**b**) *(comparación)* comparison; **trazar un p. con** to draw a comparison *o* parallel with (**c**) *Elec* **estar en p.** to be in parallel

paralelogramo *nm* parallelogram

paralímpico, -a *adj Dep* **juegos paralímpicos** Paralympic games, Paralympics

parálisis *nf inv* paralysis; **p. cerebral** cerebral palsy; **p. infantil** polio

paralítico, -a *adj & nm,f* paralytic

paralización *nf (física)* paralysis; *Fig* halting

paralizar [14] **1** *vt* to paralyze

　2 paralizarse *vpr (producción, proyecto)* to come to a standstill

Paramaribo *n* Paramaribo

paramento *nm* (**a**) *(adorno)* adornment (**b**) *Constr* facing *(of a wall)*

parámetro *nm* parameter

paramilitar *adj* paramilitary

páramo *nm* moor; **los páramos** the moors, the moorland

parangón *nm* paragon; **sin p.** unparalleled; **tener p. con** to be comparable with

paraninfo *nm* assembly hall, auditorium

paranoia *nf* paranoia

paranoico, -a 1 *adj* paranoiac; *Fam* **estar p.** to be going up the wall

　2 *nm,f* paranoiac

paranormal *adj* paranormal

paraolímpico, -a *adj Dep* **juegos paraolímpicos** Paralympic games, Paralympics

parapente *nm (actividad) (desde montaña)* paragliding; *(a remolque de lancha motora)* parasailing

parapetarse *vpr también Fig* to take refuge (**tras** behind)

parapeto *nm (antepecho)* parapet; *(barandilla)* banister; *(barricada)* barricade

paraplejía, paraplejia *nf Med* paraplegia

parapléjico, -a *adj & nm,f Med* paraplegic

parapsicología *nf* parapsychology

parapsicológico, -a *adj* parapsychological

parapsicólogo, -a *nm,f* parapsychologist

parar 1 *vi* (**a**) *(detenerse, interrumpirse)* to stop; **¿paramos a** *o* **para comer algo?** shall we stop and *o* to have something to eat?; **p. de hacer algo** to stop doing sth; **no para de molestarme** he keeps annoying me; **¡para ya!** stop it!; **¡para ya de hacer ruido!** stop that noise!; *Fam* **no p.** to be always on the go; **¡no para quieto un momento!** he won't stay still for a single moment!; **sin p.** nonstop

　(**b**) *(alojarse)* to stay; **paro poco en** *o* **por casa** I'm not at home much

　(**c**) *(recaer)* **p. en manos de alguien** to come into the possession of sb

　(**d**) *(acabar)* to end up; **¿en qué parará este lío?** where will it all end?; **ir a p. a** to end up in; **¿dónde habrán ido a p. mis gafas?** where can my glasses have got to?

　(**e**) *Am (hacer huelga)* to go on strike

　2 *vt* (**a**) *(detener, interrumpir)* to stop; *(golpe)* to parry (**b**) *Am (levantar)* to raise

　3 pararse *vpr* (**a**) *(detenerse)* to stop; **pararse a hacer algo** to stop to do sth (**b**) *Am (ponerse de pie)* to stand up

pararrayos *nm inv* lightning rod

parasitario, -a *adj* parasitic

parasitismo *nm* parasitism

parásito, -a 1 *adj Biol* parasitic
2 *nm Biol & Fig* parasite; *Tel* **parásitos** *(interferencias)* static

parasitología *nf* parasitology

parasol *nm (sombrilla)* parasol; *(en automóvil)* sun shield *o* visor

parcela *nf* plot (of land)

parcelación *nf* parceling out, division into plots

parcelar *vt* to parcel out, to divide into plots

parcelario, -a *adj* of *o* relating to plots of land

parche *nm* **(a)** *(de tela, goma)* patch **(b)** *(emplasto)* poultice **(c)** *(chapuza)* botched job; *(para salir del paso)* makeshift solution

parchear *vt* to patch up

parchís *nm inv* ≃ Parcheesi®

parcial 1 *adj* **(a)** *(no total)* partial **(b)** *(no ecuánime)* biased
2 *nm (examen)* final exam

parcialidad *nf* **(a)** *(tendenciosidad)* bias, partiality **(b)** *(bando)* faction

parco, -a *adj* **(a)** *(moderado)* sparing **(en** in) **(b)** *(escaso)* meager; *(cena)* frugal; *(explicación)* brief, concise

pardiez *interj Anticuado o Hum* **¡p.!** good gracious!

pardillo, -a 1 *adj Esp Fam* **(a)** *(ingenuo)* naive **(b)** *(palurdo)* **ser p.** to be a hick
2 *nm,f Esp Fam* **(a)** *(ingenuo)* naive person **(b)** *(palurdo)* hick
3 *nm (pájaro)* linnet

pardo, -a 1 *adj* grayish-brown, dull brown
2 *nm* grayish-brown, dull brown

pareado 1 *adj* **chalet p.** semidetached house
2 *nm* **(a)** *(verso)* couplet **(b)** *(vivienda)* semidetached house

parear *vt* to pair

parecer [46] **1** *nm* **(a)** *(opinión)* opinion; **cambiar de p.** to change one's mind **(b)** *(apariencia)* **de buen p.** good-looking
2 *vi* **(a)** *(+ sustantivo)* to look like; **parece un palacio** it looks like a palace; **parecía un sueño** it was like a dream
(b) *(+ adjetivo)* to look, to seem; **pareces cansado** you look *o* seem tired; **es alemán, pero no lo parece** he's German, but he doesn't look it; **¡pareces bobo!** are you stupid, or what?
(c) *(expresa opinión)* **me parece que…** I think *o* it seems to me that…; **me parece que sí/no** I think/don't think so; **¿qué te parece mi vestido?** what do you think of my dress?; **¿qué te parece la idea? — me parece bien/mal** what do you think of the idea? — it seems OK to me/I don't think much of it
(d) *(tener aspecto de)* **parece que va a llover** it looks like it's going to rain; **parece que le gusta** it looks as if *o* it seems that she likes it; **eso parece** so it seems; **al p.** apparently
4 parecerse *vpr* to be alike **(en** in); **parecerse a alguien** *(físicamente)* to look like sb; *(en carácter)* to be like sb; **no tenemos yate ni nada que se le parezca** we haven't got a yacht or anything (like that)

parecido, -a 1 *adj* similar; **p. a** similar to, like; **bien p.** *(atractivo)* good-looking
2 *nm* resemblance **(con/entre** to/between); **cualquier p. es pura coincidencia** any similarity is purely coincidental; **p. de familia** family resemblance

pared *nf* **(a)** *(de construcción)* wall; **entre cuatro paredes** cooped up at home; **las paredes oyen** walls have ears; **si las paredes hablasen…** if the walls could talk…; *Fig* **subirse por las paredes** to hit the roof, to go up the wall; **está que se sube por las paredes** she's in an absolute rage, she's fit to be tied; *Fam* **intenté convencerle, pero como si hablara a la p.** I tried to persuade him, but it was like talking to a brick wall; *Fig* **me pusieron contra la p.** they had me up

against the wall; **p. maestra** main wall; **p. medianera** party wall
(b) *(de montaña)* side
(c) *Dep* one-two; **hacer la p.** to play a one-two

paredón *nm (muro)* (thick) wall; *(de fusilamiento)* (execution) wall

pareja *nf* **(a)** *(par)* pair; **por parejas** in pairs; **formar parejas** to get into pairs **(b)** *(de novios)* couple; **vivir en p.** to live together; **p. de hecho** unmarried couple **(c)** *(miembro del par)* *(persona)* partner; *(guante, zapato)* other one; **la p. de este calcetín** the other sock of this pair

parejo, -a *adj* similar **(a** to)

parentela *nf* relations, family

parenteral *adj* **por vía p.** by injection

parentesco *nm* relationship

paréntesis *nm inv* **(a)** *(signo)* parenthesis; **entre p.** in parentheses **(b)** *(intercalación)* digression **(c)** *(interrupción)* break; **hacer un p.** to have a break

pareo *nm* wraparound skirt

parezca *etc ver* **parecer**

pargo *nm* porgy

paria *nmf* pariah

parida *nf Esp Fam* **decir paridas** to talk garbage

paridad *nf* **(a)** *(semejanza)* similarity; *(igualdad)* evenness **(b)** *Fin & Inform* parity; **p. de cambio** parity of exchange

parienta *nf Esp Fam* **la p.** *(cónyuge)* my old lady

pariente *nm,f* *(familiar)* relation, relative; **p. cercano** *o* **próximo** close relative; **parientes más cercanos** *(en impreso)* next of kin; **p. lejano** distant relative

parietal *nm Anat* parietal

parihuela *nf (camilla)* stretcher

paripé *nm Esp Fam* **hacer el p.** to put on an act, to pretend

parir *vi* to give birth; *Esp Fam* **poner algo/a alguien a p.** to badmouth sth/sb
2 *vt* to give birth to

París *n* Paris

parisiense *adj & nmf*, **parisino, -a** *adj & nm,f* Parisian

paritario, -a *adj* joint

paritorio *nm* delivery room

parka *nf (abrigo)* parka

parking ['parkin] *(pl* **parkings***)* *nm* parking lot

párkinson *nm Med* Parkinson's disease

parlamentar *vi* to negotiate

parlamentario, -a 1 *adj* parliamentary
2 *nm,f* member of parliament

parlamentarismo *nm* parliamentary system

parlamento *nm* **(a)** *Pol* parliament; **P. Europeo** European Parliament **(b)** *Teatro* speech

parlanchín, -ina 1 *adj* talkative
2 *nm,f* chatterbox

parlante 1 *adj* talking
2 *nm Am (altavoz)* speaker

parlotear *vi Fam* to chatter

parloteo *nm Fam* chatter

parmesano, -a 1 *adj* **queso p.** Parmesan cheese
2 *nm (queso)* Parmesan (cheese)

parnaso *nm Formal* Parnassus

parné *nm Esp Fam* loot

paro *nm* **(a)** *Esp (desempleo)* unemployment; **estar en (el) p.** to be unemployed; **quedarse en p.** to be left unemployed; **p. cíclico/encubierto/estructural** cyclical/hidden/structural unemployment **(b)** *Esp (subsidio)* unemployment benefit, dole money **(c)** *(cesación)* *(acción)* shutdown; *(estado)* stoppage; **p. biológico** = temporary halt to fishing at sea to preserve fish stocks; **p. cardiaco** cardiac arrest; **p. laboral** labor action; **p. técnico** *(de máquina)* down time **(d)** *esp Am (huelga)* strike; *Am* **hacer p.** to strike

parodia *nf (de texto, estilo)* parody; *(de película)* spoof; **hacer una p. de alguien** to do a takeoff of sb

parodiar *vt (texto, estilo)* to parody; *(película)* to spoof; *(persona)* to do a takeoff of

parón *nm* sudden stoppage

paroxismo *nm* paroxysm

paroxítono, -a *adj* paroxytone, word where the penultimate syllable is stressed

parpadeante *adj (luz)* flickering

parpadear *vi (ojos)* to blink; *(luz)* to flicker

parpadeo *nm (de ojos)* blinking; *(de luz)* flickering

párpado *nm* eyelid

parque *nm* (a) *(terreno)* park; **p. acuático** water park; **p. de atracciones** amusement park; *Esp* **p. de bomberos** fire station; **p. comercial** shopping mall; **p. empresarial** business park; **p. eólico** wind farm; **p. infantil** playground; **p. nacional** national park; **p. natural** nature reserve; **p. tecnológico** science park; **p. temático** theme park; **p. zoológico** zoo (b) *(vehículos)* fleet; **el p. automovilístico español** the Spanish vehicle fleet; **p. móvil** fleet (c) *(para bebés)* playpen

parqué *nm (suelo)* parquet (floor)

parqueadero *nm Col, Ecuad, Pan,Ven* parking lot

parquear *Bol, Carib, Col* **1** *vt* to park

2 parquearse *vpr* to park

parquedad *nf* moderation; **con p.** sparingly

parquet [par'ke] (*pl* **parquets**) *nm (suelo)* parquet (floor)

parquímetro *nm* parking meter

parra *nf* grapevine; *Fam Fig* **subirse a la p.** to get above oneself

parrafada *nf* earful, dull monologue; **soltar una p.** to go on (and on)

párrafo *nm* paragraph

parral *nm* (a) *(emparrado)* vine arbor (b) *(terreno)* vineyard

parranda *nf Fam (juerga)* **irse de p.** to go out on the town

parrandear *vi Fam* to go out on the town

parricida *nmf* parricide

parricidio *nm* parricide

parrilla *nf* (a) *(utensilio)* grill; **a la p.** grilled (b) *(restaurante)* grill room, grill (c) *Dep* **p. (de salida)** (starting) grid (d) *Am (baca)* roof rack

parrillada *nf* mixed grill

parrillero, -a **1** *adj RP (salchicha)* grilling, barbecue

2 *nm,f* (a) *(en parrillada)* cook, barbecue cook (b) *Ven (en moto)* passenger

párroco *nm* parish priest

parroquia *nf* (a) *(iglesia)* parish church (b) *(jurisdicción)* parish (c) *(fieles)* parishioners, parish (d) *(clientela)* clientele

parroquial *adj* parish; **iglesia p.** parish church

parroquiano, -a *nm,f* (a) *(feligrés)* parishioner (b) *(cliente)* customer, regular

parsimonia *nf* deliberation, calmness; **con p.** unhurriedly

parsimonioso, -a *adj* unhurried, deliberate

parte 1 *nm* report; **dar p. (a alguien de algo)** to report (sth to sb); **p. de accidente** *(para aseguradora)* (accident) claim form; **p. facultativo** *o* **médico** medical report; **p. meteorológico** weather report

2 *nf* (a) *(porción, cantidad)* part; **la mayor p. de la gente** most people; **la tercera p. de** a third of; **repartir algo a partes iguales** to share sth out equally; **en p.** to a certain extent, partly; **por mi/tu p.** for my/your part; **por partes** bit by bit

(b) *(lugar)* part; **en alguna p.** somewhere; **en otra p.** elsewhere, somewhere else; **no lo veo por ninguna p.** I can't find it anywhere; **¿de qué p. de España es?** what part of Spain is he from?, whereabouts in Spain is he from?; *Fig* **en todas partes cuecen habas** it's the same the whole world over

(c) *(bando, lado)* side; *Der* party; **estar/ponerse de p. de alguien** to be on/to take sb's side; **por p. de padre/madre** on one's father's/mother's side; **por una p.... por otra...** on the one hand... on the other (hand)...; **por otra p.** *(además)* what is more, besides; **tener a alguien de p. de uno** to have sb on one's side

(d) *Méx (repuesto)* (spare) part, spare

(e) **partes** *(genitales)* private parts

(f) **formar p. de** to be part of; **tomar p. en algo** to take part in sth

(g) **de p. de** on behalf of, for; **¿de p. de (quién)?** *(contestando al teléfono)* who is calling, please?

parteluz *nm Arquit* mullion

partenaire [parte'ner] *nmf (pareja artística)* partner

partenogénesis *nf inv* parthenogenesis

partera *nf* midwife

parterre *nm Esp* flower bed

partición *nf (reparto)* sharing out; *(de territorio)* partitioning

participación *nf* (a) *(colaboración, intervención)* participation; **hubo mucha p.** *(en actividad)* many people took part; *(en elecciones)* there was a high turnout (b) *Fin (acción, cuota)* share; *(inversión)* interest; **p. en los beneficios** profit-sharing; **p. mayoritaria** majority interest; **p. minoritaria** minority interest (c) *(de lotería)* = ticket representing a share in a lottery number (d) *(comunicación)* notice

participante 1 *adj* participating

2 *nmf* participant

participar 1 *vi* (a) *(colaborar, intervenir)* to take part, to participate (**en** in); *Fin* to have a share (**en** in); **participaron diez corredores/equipos** ten runners/teams took part *o* participated; **todo el mundo participó con entusiasmo en la limpieza del río** everyone joined in enthusiastically in cleaning up the river (b) *(recibir)* to receive a share (**de** of) (c) *(compartir)* **p. de** to share

2 *vt* **p. algo a alguien** to notify sb of sth

participativo, -a *adj* **es muy p. en clase** he participates a lot in class

partícipe 1 *adj* involved (**de** in); **hacer p. de algo a alguien** *(notificar)* to notify sb of sth; *(compartir)* to share sth with sb

2 *nmf* participant

participio *nm* participle

partícula *nf* particle

particular 1 *adj* (a) *(especial)* particular; **tiene su sabor p.** it has its own particular taste; **en casos particulares puede hacerse una excepción** we can make an exception in special cases; **en p.** in particular; **eso no tiene nada de p.** that's nothing special *o* unusual; **lo que tiene de p. es...** the unusual thing about it is... (b) *(privado)* private; **dar clases particulares** to teach private classes; **domicilio p.** home address; **la casa tiene jardín p.** the house has its own yard

2 *nmf (persona)* member of the public

3 *nm (asunto)* matter; **sin otro p., se despide atentamente** *(en carta)* sincerely yours

particularidad *nf* (a) *(rasgo)* distinctive characteristic, peculiarity (b) *(cualidad)* **la p. de su petición** the unusual nature of his request

particularizar [14] **1** *vt (caracterizar)* to characterize

2 *vi* (a) *(detallar)* to go into details (b) *(personalizar)* **p. en alguien** to single sb out

3 particularizarse *vpr (caracterizarse)* **particularizarse por** to be characterized by

partida *nf* (a) *(marcha)* departure (b) *(en juego)* game; **echar una p.** to have a game (c) *(documento)* certificate; **p. de bautismo/defunción** baptismal/death certificate; **p. de matrimonio/nacimiento** marriage/birth certificate (d) *Com (mercancía)* consignment; *(entrada)* item, entry

partidario, -a 1 *adj* **ser p. de** to be in favor of; **es p. de medidas más radicales** he is in favor of *o* he supports more radical measures; **yo sería p. de invitarles a ellos también** I think we should invite them as well

2 *nm,f* supporter; **los partidarios de la paz** those in favor of peace

partidismo *nm* partisanship, bias

partidista *adj* partisan, biased

partido *nm* (**a**) *(político)* party (**b**) *(deportivo)* game; **p. amistoso** friendly; **un p. de baloncesto/fútbol** a game of basketball/soccer (**c**) *(futuro cónyuge)* match; **buen/mal p.** good/bad match (**d**) **sacar p. de, sacarle p. a** to make the most of; **tomar p. por** to side with (**e**) *Esp* **p. judicial** = area under the jurisdiction of a court of first instance

partir 1 *vt* (**a**) *(dividir)* to divide, to split (**en** into) (**b**) *(romper)* to break open; *(cascar)* to crack; *(tronco, loncha)* to cut; **le partieron el brazo** they broke his arm; **le partieron la ceja/el labio** they split *o* cut her eyebrow/lip; **párteme un pedazo de pan** break me off a piece of bread; *Fam* **partirle la cara a alguien** to smash sb's face in

2 *vi* (**a**) *(marchar)* to leave, to set off (**b**) *(empezar)* **p. de** to start from; **p. de cero** to start from scratch; **partimos de la base de que todos saben leer** we are assuming that everyone can read

3 partirse *vpr* (**a**) *(romperse)* to split; **el vaso se partió al caer al suelo** the glass smashed when it hit the floor; **partirse en dos** to split *o* break in two (**b**) *(rajarse)* to crack (**c**) *Fam (de risa)* **partirse (de risa)** to crack up (with laughter); **¡yo me parto con su tío!** his uncle really kills me!; *muy Fam* **partirse el culo** to kill oneself laughing

4 a partir de *loc prep* from; **a p. de mañana** from tomorrow; **a p. de aquí** from here on

partisano, -a *adj & nm,f* partisan

partitivo, -a 1 *adj* partitive

2 *nm* partitive

partitura *nf* score

parto *nm* birth; **estar de p.** to be in labor; **p. natural** natural childbirth; **p. prematuro** premature birth

parturienta *nf* woman in labor

parvulario *nm* nursery school, kindergarten

párvulo, -a *nm,f* preschooler

pasa *nf (fruta)* raisin; **p. de Corinto** currant; **p. de Esmirna** sultana

pasable *adj* passable

pasacalles *nm inv* street procession *(during town festival)*

pasada *nf* (**a**) *(con el trapo)* wipe; **dar una segunda p. a** *(con la brocha)* to apply a second coat to (**b**) *(a texto)* **dar una p. a** to read through (**c**) **de p.** *(sin detalles)* in passing; *(de paso)* on the way; **decir algo de p.** to say sth in passing; **vete a comprar el pan y de p. tráeme el periódico** go and buy the bread and get me the paper while you are at it (**d**) *Esp Fam (exageración)* **lo que le hiciste a Sara fue una p.** what you did to Sara was a bit much, you went too far doing that to Sara; **ese sitio es una p. de bonito** that's a really lovely spot (**e**) *Fam* **mala p.** dirty trick

pasadizo *nm* passage

pasado, -a 1 *adj* (**a**) *(terminado)* past; **p. un año** a year later; **lo p., p. está** let bygones be bygones (**b**) *(último)* last; **el año p.** last year (**c**) *(podrido)* off, bad (**d**) *(muy hecho) (filete, carne)* well done

2 *nm (tiempo)* past; *Gram* past (tense)

pasador *nm* (**a**) *(cerrojo)* bolt (**b**) *Méx (horquilla)* hairpin, bobby pin

pasaje *nm* (**a**) *esp Am (billete)* ticket (**b**) **el p.** *(pasajeros)* the passengers (**c**) *(calle)* passage (**d**) *(fragmento)* passage

pasajero, -a 1 *adj* passing; **una molestia pasajera** a passing discomfort; **es algo p.** it's someting temporary, it'll pass

2 *nm,f* passenger; **"pasajeros, al tren"** "all aboard"; **p. en lista de espera** standby passenger; **p. en tránsito** transfer passenger

pasamanería *nf (adornos)* decorative fringe

pasamanos *nm inv (de escalera interior)* banister; *(de escalera exterior)* handrail

pasamontañas *nm inv* balaclava (helmet)

pasante *nmf* (**a**) *(de abogado)* trainee clerk (**b**) *Am (ayudante en prácticas)* assistant

pasantía *nf Com* (**a**) *(función)* assistantship (**b**) *(tiempo)* probationary period, apprenticeship

pasaporte *nm* passport

pasapuré *nm*, **pasapurés** *nm inv* = hand-operated food mill

pasar 1 *vt* (**a**) *(dar, transmitir)* to pass; *(noticia, aviso)* to pass on; **¿me pasas la sal?** would you pass me the salt?; **le paso (con él)** *(al teléfono)* I'll put you through (to him); **p. algo por** *(filtrar)* to pass sth through

(**b**) *(cruzar)* to cross; **p. la calle** to cross the road; **pasé el río a nado** I swam across the river

(**c**) *(rebasar, sobrepasar)* to go through; *(vehículo)* to overtake; **p. un semáforo en rojo** to go through a red light

(**d**) *(llevar adentro)* to show in; **el criado nos pasó al salón** the butler showed us into the living room

(**e**) *(trasladar)* **p. algo a** to move sth to

(**f**) *(contagiar)* **p. algo a alguien** to give sth to sb, to infect sb with sth; **me has pasado la tos** you've given me your cough

(**g**) *(consentir)* **p. algo a alguien** to let sb get away with sth

(**h**) *(emplear) (tiempo)* to spend; **pasó dos años en Roma** he spent two years in Rome; **¿dónde vas a p. las vacaciones?** where are you going on vacation?, where are you going to spend your vacation?

(**i**) *(experimentar)* to go through, to experience; **p. frío/miedo** to be cold/scared; **pasarlo bien** to enjoy oneself, to have a good time; **pasarlo mal** to have a hard time of it; *Fam* **pasarlas canutas** to have a rough time

(**j**) *(sobrepasar)* **ya ha pasado los veinticinco** he's over twenty-five now; **mi hijo me pasa ya dos centímetros** my son is already two centimeters taller than me

(**k**) *Cine* to show

2 *vi* (**a**) *(ir, moverse)* to pass, to go; **pasó por mi lado** he passed by my side; **el autobús pasa por mi casa** the bus goes past *o* passes in front of my house; **el Manzanares pasa por Madrid** the Manzanares goes *o* passes through Madrid; **he pasado por tu calle** I went down your street; **p. de... a...** to go *o* pass from... to...; **p. de largo** to go by

(**b**) *(entrar)* to go/come in; **pasen por aquí, por favor** come this way, please; **¡pase!** come in!

(**c**) *(poder entrar)* to go (**por** through); **por ahí no pasa** it won't go through there

(**d**) *(ir un momento)* to pop in; **pasaré por mi oficina/por tu casa** I'll pop into my office/around to your place

(**e**) *(suceder)* to happen; **¿qué pasa aquí?** what's going on here?; **¿qué pasa?** what's the matter?; **¿qué le pasa?** what's wrong with him?, what's the matter with him?; **pase lo que pase** whatever happens, come what may

(**f**) *(terminarse)* to be over; **ya ha pasado lo peor** the worst is over now; **pasó la Navidad** Christmas is over

(**g**) *(transcurrir)* to go by; **pasaron tres meses** three months went by

(**h**) *(cambiar) (acción)* **p. a** to move on to; **pasemos a otra cosa** let's move on to something else

(**i**) *(conformarse)* **p. (con/sin algo)** to make do (with/without sth); **tendrá que p. sin coche** she'll have to make do without a car

(**j**) *(servir)* to be all right, to be usable; **puede p.** it'll do

(**k**) *Fam (prescindir)* **p. de algo/alguien** to want nothing to do with sth/sb; **paso de política** I'm not into politics; **paso**

olímpicamente de hacerlo I'm damned if I'm going to do it
(**l**) *(tolerar)* **p. por algo** to put up with sth

3 pasarse *vpr* (**a**) *(cesar)* to pass; **siéntate hasta que se te pase** sit down until you feel better

(**b**) *(emplear) (tiempo)* to spend, to pass; **se pasaron el día hablando** they spent all day talking

(**c**) *(desaprovecharse)* to slip by; **se me pasó la oportunidad** I missed my chance

(**d**) *(estropearse) (comida)* to spoil; *(flores)* to fade

(**e**) *(cambiar de bando)* **pasarse a** to go over to

(**f**) *(omitir)* to leave out; **te has pasado una página** you've left a page out

(**g**) *(olvidarse)* **pasársele a alguien** to slip sb's mind; **se me pasó decírtelo** I forgot to mention it to you

(**h**) *(no fijarse)* **pasársele a alguien** to escape sb's attention; **no se le pasa nada** he never misses a thing

(**i**) *(excederse)* **pasarse de generoso/bueno** to be far too generous/kind

(**j**) *Fam (propasarse)* to go too far, to go over the top; **te has pasado diciéndole eso** what you said went too far *o* was over the top

(**k**) *(divertirse)* **¿qué tal te lo estás pasando?** how are you enjoying yourself?; **pasárselo bien/mal** to have a good/bad time

(**l**) *(ir un momento)* to pop in; **me pasaré por mi oficina/por tu casa** I'll pop into my office/around to your place

pasarela *nf* (**a**) *(puente)* footbridge; *(para desembarcar)* gangway (**b**) *(en desfile de moda)* runway

pasatiempo *nm (hobby)* pastime, hobby; *Prensa* **pasatiempos** crossword and puzzles section

pascua *nf* (**a**) *(de los cristianos)* Easter; *Fam* **hacer la p. a alguien** *(ser pesado)* to pester sb; *(poner en apuros)* to land sb into trouble; **Pascuas** *(Navidad)* Christmas *(singular)*; **¡felices Pascuas!** Merry Christmas!; **de Pascuas a Ramos** once in a blue moon (**b**) *(de los judíos)* Passover

pascual *adj* Easter; **cordero p.** Paschal lamb

pase *nm* (**a**) *(permiso)* pass (**b**) *(cambio de lugar)* **aprobaron su p. al departamento de contabilidad** they approved her transfer to the accounts department (**c**) *Dep & Taurom* pass (**d**) *Esp (proyección)* showing, screening (**e**) *(desfile)* parade; **p. de modelos** fashion parade, (**f**) *Esp Fam* **eso tiene un p.** you can live with that

paseante *nmf* person out for a stroll

pasear 1 *vi* to go for a walk; **p. a caballo** to go horse riding

2 *vt* **p. a alguien** to take sb for a walk; *Fig* to show sb off, to parade sb; **p. al perro** to walk the dog

3 pasearse *vpr* (**a**) *(caminar)* to go for a walk (**b**) *(ganar con facilidad)* **Colombia se paseó en la final** the final was a walkover for Colombia

paseíllo *nm Taurom* = parade of bullfighters when they come out into the ring before the bullfight starts

paseo *nm* (**a**) *(acción) (a pie)* walk; *(en coche)* drive; *(a caballo)* ride; *(en barca)* row; **dar un p.** *(a pie)* to go for a walk (**b**) *(lugar)* avenue; **p. marítimo** promenade (**c**) *Fam* **mandar** *o* **enviar a alguien a p.** to send sb packing

pasillo *nm* corridor; **hacer (el) p.** to form a corridor *(for people to walk down)*; **p. aéreo** air corridor; **p. deslizante** *o* **rodante** moving sidewalk

pasión *nf* passion; **hacer las cosas con p.** to do things passionately; **siente** *o* **tiene gran p. por los trenes** he really loves *o* adores trains; **siente** *o* **tiene gran p. por Isabel** he's passionately in love with Isabel; *Rel* **la P.** the Passion

pasional *adj* passionate

pasionaria *nf* passion flower

pasividad *nf* passivity

pasivo, -a 1 *adj* (**a**) *(gen) & Gram* passive (**b**) *(población)* inactive

2 *nm Fin* liabilities; **p. corriente** current liabilities

pasma *nf Esp muy Fam* **la p.** the cops, the pigs

pasmado, -a 1 *adj* (**a**) *(asombrado)* astonished, astounded (**b**) *(atontado)* stunned

2 *nm,f* halfwit

pasmar 1 *vt* to astound

2 pasmarse *vpr* to be astounded

pasmarote *nmf Fam* halfwit, dumbo

pasmo *nm* (**a**) *(asombro)* astonishment (**b**) *(de frío)* chill; **te va a dar un p.** you'll catch your death

pasmoso, -a *adj* astonishing

paso *nm* (**a**) *(acción de pasar)* passing; **el p. del tiempo** the passage of time; **con el p. de los años** as the years go by; **el Ebro, a su p. por Zaragoza** the Ebro, as it flows through Zaragoza; **su p. fugaz por la universidad** his brief spell at college; *también Fig* **abrir p. a alguien** to make way for sb; **abrirse p. entre la multitud** to make *o* force one's way through the crowd; **ceder el p. (a alguien)** to let (sb) past; *Aut* to yield (to sb); **ceda el p.** *(en letrero)* yield; **de p.** *(de pasada)* in passing; *(aprovechando)* while I'm/you're/etc at it; **prohibido el p.** *(en letrero)* no entry; **p. del ecuador** = (celebration marking) halfway stage in a college course

(**b**) *(con el pie)* step; *(huella)* footprint; **dar un p. adelante** *o* **al frente** to step forward, to take a step forward

(**c**) *(forma de andar)* walk; *(ritmo)* pace; **a p. ligero** at a brisk pace; **marcar el p.** to keep time; **a este p. no acabaremos nunca** at this rate we'll never finish

(**d**) *(etapa, acontecimiento)* step; *(progreso)* step forward, advance; **dar los pasos necesarios** to take the necessary steps; **p. a p.** step by step

(**e**) *(cruce)* crossing; **p. de cebra** = pedestrian crossing marked with black and white lines; **p. elevado** overpass; **p. fronterizo** border crossing (point); **p. a nivel** grade crossing; **p. peatonal** *o* **de peatones** pedestrian crossing; **p. subterráneo** underpass

(**f**) *Geog (en montaña)* pass; *(en el mar)* strait

(**g**) *(mal momento)* **(mal) p.** difficult situation

(**h**) *(expresiones)* **a cada p.** every other minute; **está a dos** *o* **cuatro pasos** it's just down the road; **avanzar a pasos agigantados** to come on by leaps and bounds; **disminuir a pasos agigantados** to decrease at an alarming rate; **a p. de tortuga** at a snail's pace; **dar un p. en falso** to make a false move *o* a mistake; **estar de p.** to be passing through; **salirle al p. a alguien** to come up to sb; **salir del p.** to get out of trouble

pasodoble *nm* paso doble

pasota *Esp Fam* **1** *adj* apathetic; **actitud p.** couldn't-care-less attitude

2 *nmf* **es un p.** he couldn't care less about anything

pasotismo *nm Esp Fam* couldn't-care-less attitude

pasquín *nm* lampoon

pasta *nf* (**a**) *(masa)* paste; *(de papel)* pulp; **p. dentífrica** *o* **de dientes** toothpaste; **p. de hojaldre** puff pastry; **p. quebrada** crumbly pastry (**b**) *(espaguetis, macarrones)* pasta; **pastas alimenticias** pasta *(pastelito)* shortcake cookie (**d**) *Esp Fam (dinero)* dough; **costar/ganar una p. gansa** to cost/earn a bundle *o* fortune; **aflojar** *o* **soltar la p.** to cough up the money (**e**) *(encuadernación)* **de p. dura/blanda** hardback/paperback (**f**) *Fam* **ser de buena p.** to be good-natured

pastar *vi* to graze

pastel 1 *adj inv (color)* pastel; **colores p.** pastel colors

2 *nm* (**a**) *Culin (dulce)* cake; *(salado)* pie; **p. de bodas** wedding cake; **p. de cumpleaños** birthday cake; **p. de manzana** apple pie (**b**) *Arte* pastel; **pintar al p.** to draw in pastels (**c**) *(expresiones)* **descubrir el p.** to let the cat out of the bag; **repartirse el p.** to share things out

pastelería *nf* (**a**) *(establecimiento)* cake store, patisserie (**b**) *(repostería)* pastries

pastelero, -a 1 *adj* pastry; **crema pastelera** confectioner's custard; **la industria pastelera** the cake and cookie manufacturing industry

2 *nm,f (cocinero)* pastry cook; *(vendedor)* owner of a patisserie

pasteurización, pasterización *nf* pasteurization

pasteurizado, -a, pasterizado, -a *adj* pasteurized

pasteurizar, pasterizar [14] *vt* to pasteurize

pastiche *nm* pastiche

pastilla *nf* (a) *Med* pill, tablet; **p. para la tos** cough drop (b) *(de jabón, chocolate)* bar; **p. (de caldo)** (bouillon) cube (c) *Aut* shoe *(of brakes)* (d) *Elec* microchip (e) *Esp Fam* **ir a toda p.** *(vehículo)* to go at top speed; *(persona)* to go at the double

pastizal *nm* pasture

pasto *nm* (a) *(hierba)* fodder (b) *(sitio)* pasture (c) *Am (césped)* lawn, grass (d) *(expresiones)* **a todo p.** in abundance; **ser p. de las llamas** to go up in flames

pastón *nm Esp Fam* **vale un p.** it costs a fortune

pastor, -ora 1 *nm,f (de ganado)* shepherd, *f* shepherdess

2 *nm* (a) *(sacerdote)* minister; **p. protestante** Protestant minister (b) *(perro)* **p. alemán** German shepherd, Alsatian

pastoral *adj* pastoral

pastorear *vt* to put out to pasture

pastoreo *nm* shepherding

pastoril *adj* pastoral, shepherd; **novela p.** pastoral novel

pastoso, -a *adj* (a) *(blando)* pasty; *(arroz)* sticky (b) *(seco)* dry; **tener la boca pastosa** to have a furry tongue

pata 1 *nf* (a) *(pierna de animal)* leg; **las patas delanteras** the forelegs; **las patas traseras** the hindlegs; *Culin* **p. negra** = type of top-quality cured ham

(b) *(pie de animal)* foot; *(de perro, gato)* paw; *(de vaca, caballo)* hoof

(c) *Fam (de persona)* leg; **a p.** on foot; **ir a la p. coja** to hop; **a cuatro patas** on all fours; **p. de palo** wooden leg

(d) *(de mueble)* leg; *(de gafas)* arm

(e) *(expresiones) Fam* **estirar la p.** to kick the bucket; **meter la p.** to put one's foot in it; *también Fig* **poner algo patas arriba** to turn sth upside down; **tener mala p.** to be unlucky; **p. de gallo** *(tejido)* houndstooth check material; **patas de gallo** *(arrugas)* crow's feet

2 patas *nfpl Chile Fam (poca vergüenza)* cheek

patada *nf* kick; *(en el suelo)* stamp; **había turistas a patadas** there were loads of tourists; **dar una p. a** to kick; **me da cien patadas (que…)** it makes me mad (that…); **dar la p. a alguien** to kick sb out; *Fig* **en dos patadas** *(en seguida)* in two shakes; **sentar como una p. (en el estómago)** to be like a kick in the teeth; **tratar a alguien a patadas** to treat sb like dirt

patagón, -ona *adj & nm,f* Patagonian

Patagonia *n* **la P.** Patagonia

patalear *vi (en el aire)* to kick about; *(en el suelo)* to stamp one's feet

pataleo *nm (en el aire)* kicking, thrashing around *o* about; *(en el suelo)* stamping; **derecho al p.** right to complain

pataleta *nf* tantrum

patán 1 *adj* uncivilized, uncouth

2 *nm* bumpkin

patata *nf Esp* potato; *Fam* **no entendí ni p.** I didn't understand a word of it; *Fam* **¡(di) p.!** *(en foto)* say cheese!; *Fam Fig* **esta impresora es una p.** this printer's a dud; **patatas bravas** = sautéed potatoes served with spicy tomato sauce; *Fig* **p. caliente** hot potato; **patatas fritas** *(de sartén)* (French) fries; *(de bolsa)* (potato) chips

patatero, -a *Esp* **1** *adj Fam* **un rollo p.** *(mentira)* a ridiculous spiel; **la película fue un rollo p.** the movie was unbelievably boring

2 *nm,f* potato farmer

patatín: que si patatín, que si patatán *loc adv Fam*

estuvimos hablando que si p., que si patatán we talked about this, that and the next thing

patatús *(pl patatuses) nm Fam* funny turn

paté *nm* paté

patear 1 *vt (dar un puntapié a)* to kick; *(pisotear)* to stamp on

2 *vi* (a) *(patalear)* to stamp one's feet (b) *Fam (andar)* to tramp (c) *Am (cocear)* to kick

3 patearse *vpr Fam (recorrer)* to tramp; **se pateó toda la ciudad** he tramped *o* traipsed all over town

patena *nf* paten; *Esp* **limpio** *o* **blanco como una p.** as clean as a new pin

patentado, -a *adj* patent, patented

patentar *vt* to patent

patente 1 *adj (descontento, indignación)* obvious; *(demostración, prueba)* clear; **su dolor era p.** he was clearly in pain

2 *nf* (a) *(de invento)* patent; **tener la p. de algo** to hold the patent on *o* for sth (b) *(certificado)* **p. de navegación** certificate of registration (c) *CSur (de auto)* license number

pateo *nm Fam* stamping

patera *nf (embarcación)* small boat, dinghy

paternal *adj* fatherly, paternal; *Fig* paternal

paternalismo *nm* paternalism

paternalista *adj* paternalistic

paternidad *nf* fatherhood; *Der* paternity

paterno, -a *adj* paternal

patético, -a *adj* pathetic, moving

patetismo *nm* pathos

patíbulo *nm* scaffold, gallows

patidifuso, -a *adj Fam* stunned

patilla *nf* (a) *(de pelo)* sideboard, sideburn (b) *(de gafas)* arm

patín *nm* (a) *(de hielo)* ice skate; *(de ruedas paralelas)* roller skate; **patines en línea** Rollerblades® (b) *(patinete)* scooter (c) *Esp (embarcación)* pedal paddleboat

pátina *nf* patina

patinador, -ora *nm,f* skater

patinaje *nm* skating; **p. artístico** figure skating; **p. sobre hielo** ice-skating; **p. sobre ruedas** roller-skating; *(con patines en línea)* Rollerblading®

patinar *vi* (a) *(sobre hielo)* to skate; *(sobre ruedas)* to roller-skate; *(con patines en línea)* to Rollerblade® (b) *(resbalar) (coche)* to skid; *(persona)* to slip; *Esp Fam* **le patinan las neuronas** he's going a bit funny in the head (c) *Fam (equivocarse)* to put one's foot in it

patinazo *nm* (a) *(de vehículo)* skid; *(de persona)* slip (b) *Fam (equivocación)* blunder; **tener un p.** to make a blunder

patinete *nm* scooter

patio *nm (de casa)* courtyard; *(de escuela)* playground; *(de cuartel)* parade ground; *Esp Fam* **¡cómo está el p.!** what a fine state of affairs!; *Esp* **p. de butacas** orchestra seats; **p. interior** *(en edificio)* light shaft

patita *nf Fam Fig* **poner a alguien de patitas en la calle** to kick sb out

patitieso, -a *adj* (a) *(de frío)* frozen stiff (b) *(de sorpresa)* stunned

patito *nm* **el p. feo** the ugly duckling

patizambo, -a *adj* knock-kneed

pato, -a *nm,f* duck; *Fig* **pagar el p.** to pick up the tab

patochada *nf Fam* piece of nonsense, idiocy; **la última p. del Gobierno** the government's latest clumsy action

patógeno, -a *adj* infectious

patología *nf* pathology

patológico, -a *adj* pathological

patoso, -a *adj Esp Fam* clumsy

patraña *nf* absurd story

patria *nf* native country, fatherland; **p. chica** hometown; *Der* **p. potestad** parental authority

patriarca *nm* patriarch

patriarcado *nm* patriarchy

patriarcal *adj* patriarchal

patricio, -a *adj & nm,f* patrician

patrimonial *adj* hereditary

patrimonio *nm* (a) *(bienes) (de empresa)* assets; *(propios)* estate, assets; **el p. de la empresa asciende a mil millones de dólares** the company has net assets of one billion dollars; **p. personal** personal estate (b) *(nacional)* heritage; **los ríos son p. de todos** rivers are a heritage shared by all; **es p. (mundial) de la humanidad** it's a World Heritage site; **p. histórico-artístico** artistic *o* cultural heritage

patrio, -a *adj* native; **el suelo p.** one's native soil

patriota 1 *adj* patriotic

   2 *nmf* patriot

patrioterismo *nm Pey* jingoism, chauvinism

patriotero, -a *adj Pey* jingoistic, chauvinistic

patriótico, -a *adj* patriotic

patriotismo *nm* patriotism

patrocinador, -ora 1 *adj* sponsoring

   2 *nm,f* sponsor

patrocinar *vt* to sponsor

patrocinio *nm* sponsorship

patrón, -ona 1 *nm,f* (a) *(de obreros)* boss; *(de criados)* master, *f* mistress (b) *Esp (de pensión)* landlord, *f* landlady (c) *(santo)* patron saint (d) *(de barco)* skipper

   2 *nm* (a) *(medida)* standard; *Econ* **p. oro** gold standard (b) *(en costura)* pattern; *Fig* **estar cortados por el mismo p.** to be cast in the same mold

patronal 1 *adj* (a) *(empresarial)* management; **organización p.** employers' organization (b) *Rel* **fiestas patronales** = celebrations for the feast day of a town's patron saint

   2 *nf (organización)* employers' organization; **la p. y los sindicatos** management and unions

patronato *nm (dirección)* board of trustees; *(con fines benéficos)* trust

patronazgo *nm* patronage

patronímico, -a *adj* patronymic

patronista *nmf* pattern cutter

patrono, -a *nm,f* (a) *(de empresa) (encargado)* boss; *(empresario)* employer (b) *(santo)* patron saint

patrulla *nf* patrol; **estar de p.** to be on patrol; **p. urbana** vigilante group

patrullar *vt & vi* to patrol

patrullero, -a 1 *adj* patrol; **barco p.** patrol boat

   2 *nm,f (barco)* patrol boat

patuco *nm Esp* bootee

paulatino, -a *adj* gradual

pauperización *nf* impoverishment

paupérrimo, -a *adj* very poor, impoverished

pausa *nf* pause, break; *Mús* rest; **con p.** unhurriedly; **hacer una p.** *(al hablar)* to pause; *(en actividad)* to take a break; *TV* **p. publicitaria** commercial break

pausado, -a *adj* deliberate, slow

pauta *nf* (a) *(modelo)* standard, model; **seguir una p.** to follow an example (b) *(en un papel)* guideline

pautado, -a *adj (papel)* lined, ruled

pava *nf* (a) *Esp Fam (colilla)* butt (b) *CAm (flequillo)* bangs (c) *Chile, Perú (broma)* coarse *o* tasteless joke (d) *Arg (hervidor)* kettle

pavimentación *nf (de una carretera)* road surfacing; *(de la acera)* paving; *(de un suelo)* flooring

pavimentar *vt (carretera)* to surface; *(acera)* to pave; *(suelo)* to floor

pavimento *nm (de carretera)* road surface; *(de acera)* paving; *(de suelo)* flooring

pavisoso, -a *adj* dull, insipid

pavo, -a 1 *adj Fam Pey* wet, drippy

   2 *nm,f* (a) *(ave)* turkey; **p. real** peacock, *f* peahen (b) *Fam Pey (persona)* drip

pavonearse *vpr Pey* to boast, to brag (**de** about)

pavoneo *nm Pey* showing off, boasting

pavor *nm* terror

pavoroso, -a *adj* terrifying

paya *nf Chile,* **payada** *nf CSur* = improvised folksong

payasada *nf* (a) *(graciosa)* piece of clowning; **hacer payasadas** to clown around (b) *(grotesca)* ludicrous thing to say/do

payaso, -a 1 *adj* clownish

   2 *nm,f* clown

payés, -esa *nm,f* = peasant farmer from Catalonia or the Balearic Islands

payo, -a *adj & nm,f Esp* non-Gypsy

paz *nf (en general)* peace; *(tranquilidad)* peacefulness; **dejar a alguien en p.** to leave sb alone *o* in peace; **estar** *o* **quedar en p.** to be quits; **firmar la p.** to sign a peace treaty; **hacer las paces** to make (it) up; **poner p. entre** to reconcile, to make peace between; **que en p. descanse** may he/she rest in peace; **y en p.** and that's that; **p. interior** inner peace

pazguato, -a *Fam* **1** *adj (simple)* simple; *(mojigato)* prudish

   2 *nm,f (simple)* simpleton; *(mojigato)* prude

pazo *nm* = Galician mansion, belonging to noble family

PC *nm (abrev de* **personal computer***)* PC

PCE *nm (abrev de* **Partido Comunista de España***)* Spanish Communist Party

PCUS [pe'kus] *nm Hist (abrev de* **Partido Comunista de la Unión Soviética***)* Soviet Communist Party

PD *(abrev de* **posdata***)* PS

pe *nf Fam Fig* **de pe a pa** from beginning to end

peaje *nm* toll

peana *nf* pedestal

peatón *nm* pedestrian

peatonal *adj* pedestrian; **calle p.** pedestrian street

peca *nf* freckle

pecado *nm* sin; **p. mortal** mortal sin; **p. original** original sin; **pecados capitales** deadly sins; *también Fig* **ser un p.** to be a sin *o* crime

pecador, -ora 1 *adj* sinful

   2 *nm,f* sinner

pecaminoso, -a *adj* sinful

pecar [59] *vi* (a) *Rel* to sin (b) *(pasarse)* **p. de confiado/ generoso** to be overconfident/too generous

pecera *nf (acuario)* fish tank; *(redonda)* fishbowl

pechar 1 *vt* (a) *CSur Fam (pedir)* to scrounge, to bum (b) *Andes, RP (empujar)* to push, to shove

   2 *vi* **p. con** to bear, to shoulder

pechera *nf (de camisa)* shirt front; *(de blusa, vestido)* bust

pecho *nm* (a) *(tórax)* chest; *(de mujer)* bosom (b) *(mama)* breast; **dar el p. a** to breast-feed (c) *(interior)* heart (d) *Am (en natación)* breaststroke; **los 100 metros p.** the 100 meters breaststroke (e) *(expresiones)* **a lo hecho, p.** it's no use crying over spilled milk; **a p. descubierto** without protection *o* any form of defense; *Fam* **echarse** *o* **meterse algo entre p. y espalda** *(comida)* to put o tuck sth away; *(bebida)* to put sth away, to down sth; **tomarse algo a p.** to take sth to heart

pechuga *nf* (a) *(de ave)* breast *(meat)* (b) *Fam (de mujer)* bosom, bust

pechugona *adj Fam* busty, buxom

pecíolo, peciolo *nm Bot* stalk

pécora *nf* **ser una mala p.** to be a bitch *o* harpy

pecoso, -a *adj* freckly

pectoral 1 *adj* (a) *Anat* pectoral, chest; **músculos**

pectorales pectorals (**b**) *Med* cough; **jarabe p.** cough syrup
2 *nm* (**a**) *Anat* pectoral (**b**) *Med* cough mixture *o* medicine
pecuario, -a *adj* livestock; **actividad pecuaria** livestock raising
peculiar *adj* (**a**) *(característico)* typical, characteristic (**b**) *(raro, curioso)* peculiar
peculiaridad *nf* (**a**) *(cualidad)* uniqueness (**b**) *(detalle)* particular feature *o* characteristic
pecuniario, -a *adj* pecuniary
pedagogía *nf* education, pedagogy
pedagógico, -a *adj* educational
pedagogo, -a *nm,f* *(especialista)* educationist; *(profesor)* teacher, educator
pedal *nm* (**a**) *(de bicicleta, coche, piano)* pedal; **p. de embrague** clutch pedal; **p. del freno** brake pedal (**b**) *Esp Fam (borrachera)* **agarrarse un p.** to get plastered
pedalada *nf* pedal, pedaling
pedalear *vi* to pedal
pedante 1 *adj* pretentious
2 *nmf* pretentious person
pedantería *nf (cualidad)* pretentiousness; *(dicho, hecho)* piece of pretentiousness
pedazo *nm* (**a**) *(trozo)* piece, bit; **hacer pedazos algo** to break sth to bits; *Fig* to destroy sth; **saltar en (mil) pedazos** to be smashed to pieces; *Fig* **ser un p. de pan** to be an angel, to be a real sweetie (**b**) *Fam (para enfatizar)* **un p. de libro/casa** a thumping great book/house; **p. de alcornoque** *o* **de animal** *o* **de bruto** stupid oaf *o* brute
pederasta *nm* (**a**) *Der (contra menores)* child molester (**b**) *(homosexual)* (active) homosexual
pederastia *nf* (**a**) *Der (contra menores)* child molesting (**b**) *(sodomía)* sodomy
pedernal *nm* flint
pedestal *nm* pedestal, stand; **poner/tener a alguien en un p.** to put sb on a pedestal
pedestre *adj* (**a**) *(a pie)* on foot (**b**) *(corriente)* pedestrian, prosaic
pediatra *nmf* pediatrician
pediatría *nf* pediatrics *(singular)*
pediátrico, -a *adj* pediatric
pedicuro, -a *nm,f* podiatrist, chiropodist
pedida *nf Esp* ≃ engagement party, = family ceremony in which the groom-to-be asks his future wife's parents for their daughter's hand in marriage
pedido *nm* (**a**) *Com (de producto)* order; **hacer un p.** to place an order (**b**) *Am (petición)* request; **a p. de** at the request of
pedigrí *(pl* **pedigríes)** *nm* pedigree
pedigüeño, -a 1 *adj* demanding, clamoring
2 *nm,f (que pide)* demanding person; *(mendigo)* beggar
pedir [47] **1** *vt* (**a**) *(solicitar)* to ask for; **p. algo a alguien** to ask sb for sth; **p. a alguien que haga algo** to ask sb to do sth; **p. a alguien (en matrimonio)** to ask for sb's hand (in marriage); **p. (prestado) algo a alguien** to borrow sth from sb; **pide un millón por la moto** he's asking a million for the motorbike (**b**) *(en bares, restaurantes)* to order; **¿qué has pedido de postre?** what have you ordered for dessert? (**c**) *(exigir)* to demand (**d**) *(requerir)* to call for, to need
2 *vi* (**a**) *(mendigar)* to beg (**b**) *(en bares, restaurantes)* to order (**c**) *(rezar)* **p. por el alma de alguien** to pray for sb's soul
3 **pedirse** *vpr (escoger)* **¿qué pastel te pides tú?** which cake do you want?; **¡me pido prímer para subir al columpio!** *(uso infantil)* dibs on first go on the swing!
pedo 1 *nm* (**a**) *(ventosidad)* fart; **tirarse un p.** to fart (**b**) *Fam (borrachera)* **agarrarse un p.** to get plastered (**c**) *RP Fam* **al p.** *(inútilmente)* for nothing; **de p.** *(de casualidad)* by chance
2 *adj inv Esp, Méx Fam* **estar p.** to be smashed
pedofilia *nf* pedophilia

pedófilo, -a *nm,f* pedophile
pedorrear *vi Fam* to fart a lot
pedorreta *nf Fam* raspberry *(sound)*
pedorro, -a *nm,f Fam* (**a**) *(que se tira pedos)* person who farts a lot (**b**) *(tonto, pesado)* pain, bore
pedrada *nf* (**a**) *(acción)* throw of a stone (**b**) *(golpe)* blow *o* hit with a stone; **a pedradas** by stoning
pedrea *nf* (**a**) *Esp (en lotería)* = group of smaller prizes in the Spanish national lottery (**b**) *(lucha)* stone fight
pedregal *nm* stony ground
pedregoso, -a *adj* stony
pedrera *nf* stone quarry
pedrería *nf* precious stones
pedrisco *nm* hail
pedrusco *nm* rough stone
peeling ['pilin] *(pl* **peelings)** *nm* face mask *o* pack
pega *nf* (**a**) *Esp (obstáculo)* difficulty, hitch; **poner pegas (a)** to find problems (with) (**b**) **de p.** false, fake
pegadizo, -a *adj* (**a**) *(música)* catchy (**b**) *(contagioso)* catching
pegado *nm (parche)* plaster
pegajoso, -a *adj* (**a**) *(material, calor)* sticky (**b**) *Fam (persona)* clingy, clinging (**c**) *Méx (música)* catchy
pegamento *nm* glue
pegar [38] **1** *vt* (**a**) *(adherir)* to stick; *(con pegamento)* to glue; *(póster, cartel)* to fix, to put up (**b**) *(arrimar)* **p. algo a** *o* **contra algo** to put *o* place sth against sth (**c**) *(golpear)* to hit; **pega a su mujer/a sus hijos** he beats his wife/children (**d**) *(propinar)* *(bofetada, paliza)* to give; **p. un golpe a alguien** to hit sb; **p. un tiro a alguien** to shoot sb (**e**) *(contagiar)* **p. algo a alguien** to give sb sth, to pass sth on to sb (**f**) *(corresponder a, ir bien a)* to suit, to go with; **no le pega ese vestido** that dress doesn't suit her; **no le pega ese novio** that boyfriend isn't right for her (**g**) *Inform* to paste
2 *vi* (**a**) *(adherir)* to stick (**b**) *(golpear)* to hit (**c**) *(armonizar)* to go together, to match; **p. con** to go with (**d**) *(sol)* to beat down
3 **pegarse** *vpr* (**a**) *(adherirse)* to stick
(**b**) *(agredirse)* to fight, to hit one another
(**c**) *(golpearse)* **pegarse (un golpe) con** *o* **contra algo** to bump into sth; **me pegué (un golpe) en la pierna/la cabeza** I hit *o* bumped my leg/head
(**d**) *(contagiarse)* *(enfermedad)* to be transmitted, to be passed on; *(canción)* to be catchy; **se me pegó su acento** I picked up his accent
(**e**) *(engancharse)* **pegarse a alguien** to stick to sb
(**f**) *(darse)* *(baño, desayuno)* to have; **nos pegamos un viaje de diez horas** we had a ten-hour journey; **me pegué un buen susto** I got a real fright
(**g**) *Esp Fam Fig* **pegársela a alguien** to have sb on, to deceive sb; *(cónyuge)* to cheat on sb; **se la pega a su mujer con la vecina** he's cheating on his wife with the woman next door
pegatina *nf Esp* sticker
pego *nm Esp Fam Fig* **dar el p.** to look like the real thing
pegote *nm Fam* (**a**) *(masa pegajosa)* sticky mess (**b**) *(chapucería)* botch (**c**) *Esp (mentira)* **tirarse pegotes** to tell tall stories, to boast
pegotear *CSur Fam* **1** *vt* to make sticky
2 **pegotearse** *vpr* to get oneself all sticky
pegue *etc ver* **pegar**
peinado *nm (estilo, tipo)* hairstyle; *(más elaborado)* hairdo
peinador, -ora 1 *nm,f Am (peluquero)* hairdresser
2 *nm* (**a**) *(ropa)* dressing gown (**b**) *Bol, Chile, Cuba (tocador)* dressing table
peinar 1 *vt también Fig* to comb
2 **peinarse** *vpr* to comb one's hair
peine *nm* comb; *Fam Fig* **enterarse de** *o* **saber lo que vale un p.** to find out what's what *o* a thing or two

peineta *nf* decorative comb worn in hair

p.ej. (*abrev de* **por ejemplo**) e.g.

pejiguera *nf Esp Fam* drag, pain

Pekín *n* Beijing, Peking

pekinés, -esa = **pequinés**

pela *nf Esp Antes Fam* peseta; **no tengo pelas** I'm broke

peladilla *nf* sugared almond

pelado, -a 1 *adj* (**a**) (*cabeza*) shorn (**b**) (*piel, cara*) peeling; (*fruta*) peeled (**c**) (*habitación, monte, árbol*) bare (**d**) (*número*) exact, round; **saqué un aprobado p.** I passed, but only just (**e**) *Fam* (*sin dinero*) broke
   2 *nm,f CAm, Méx Fam* (*persona humilde*) common person

peladura *nf* peeling

pelagatos *nmf inv Fam Pey* nobody

pelaje *nm* (*de gato, oso, conejo*) fur; (*de perro, caballo*) coat

pelambre *nm* mane *o* mop of hair

pelambrera *nf* long thick hair

pelandusca *nf Fam Pey* tart, slut

pelapatatas *Esp,* **pelapapas** *Am nm inv* potato peeler

pelar 1 *vt* (**a**) (*persona*) to cut the hair of (**b**) (*fruta, patatas*) to peel; (*guisantes, marisco*) to shell (**c**) (*aves*) to pluck; (*conejos*) to skin; **p. la pava** (*novios*) to flirt, to have a lovey-dovey conversation (**d**) *Fam* (*dejar sin dinero*) to fleece (**e**) *Fam* **hace un frío que pela** it's freezing cold
   2 pelarse *vpr* (**a**) (*cortarse el pelo*) to have one's hair cut (**b**) (*piel, espalda*) to peel (**c**) **pelarse de frío** to be frozen stiff, to be freezing cold

peldaño *nm* (*escalón*) step; (*de escalera de mano*) rung

pelea *nf* (**a**) (*a golpes*) fight; **peleas callejeras** street fighting (**b**) (*riña*) row, quarrel

peleado, -a *adj* (**a**) (*combate, campaña electoral*) hard-fought (**b**) (*personas*) **están peleados** they've fallen out

pelear 1 *vi* (**a**) (*a golpes*) to fight (**b**) (*a gritos*) to have a quarrel *o* row (**c**) (*esforzarse*) to struggle
   2 pelearse *vpr* (**a**) (*a golpes*) to fight (**b**) (*a gritos*) to have a quarrel *o* row (**c**) (*enfadarse*) to fall out; **se ha peleado con su hermano** he's fallen out with his brother

pelele *nm* (**a**) *Fam Pey* (*persona*) puppet (**b**) (*muñeco*) straw doll (**c**) *Esp* (*prenda de bebé*) romper, jumpsuit

peleón, -ona *adj* (**a**) (*persona*) aggressive (**b**) (*vino*) rough

peletería *nf* (**a**) (*tienda*) fur shop *o* store, furrier's (**b**) (*oficio*) furriery (**c**) (*pieles*) furs; **artículos de p.** furs

peletero, -a *nm,f* furrier

peliagudo, -a *adj* tricky

pelícano, pelicano *nm* pelican

película *nf* (**a**) (*de cine*) movie; **echar** *o* **poner una p.** to show a movie; *Fig* **de p.** amazing; **una casa/unas vacaciones de p.** a dream house/vacation; **p. muda** silent movie; **p. del Oeste** Western; **p. de terror** horror movie (**b**) *Fot* **p. virgen** blank film (**c**) (*capa*) film (**d**) *Fam* (*historia increíble*) (tall) story; **montarse una p.** to dream up an incredible story

peliculero, -a *nm,f Fam* teller of tall stories

peliculón *nm Fam* (*película buena*) fantastic *o* great movie

peligrar *vi* to be in danger

peligro *nm* danger; **correr p. (de)** to be in danger (of); **estar/poner en p.** to be/put at risk; **en p. de extinción** (*especie, animal*) endangered; **fuera de p.** out of danger; **¡p. de muerte!** (*en letrero*) danger!; **p. de incendio** (*en letrero*) fire hazard; **ser un p.** to be dangerous *o* a menace

peligrosidad *nf* danger

peligroso, -a *adj* dangerous

pelillo *nm Esp* **¡pelillos a la mar!** let bygones be bygones

pelín *nm Esp Fam* **un p.** a tiny bit

pelirrojo, -a 1 *adj* ginger, red-headed
   2 *nm,f* redhead

pella *nf Esp Fam* **hacer pellas** to play hooky

pellejo *nm* (**a**) *Fam* (*piel, vida*) skin; **estar/ponerse en el p. de otro** to be/put oneself in someone else's shoes; **salvar el p.** to save one's skin (**b**) (*padrastro*) hangnail

pelliza *nf* fur jacket

pellizcar [59] *vt* (**a**) (*persona*) to pinch (**b**) (*pan*) to pick at

pellizco *nm* pinch; *Fig* **un buen p.** (*de dinero*) a tidy sum

pelma *adj & nmf Esp* = **pelmazo**

pelmazo, -a *Fam* **1** *adj* annoying, tiresome
   2 *nm,f* bore, pain

pelo *nm* (**a**) (*cabello*) hair; **la bañera estaba llena de pelos** the bathtub was full of hair
   (**b**) (*de oso, conejo, gato*) fur; (*de perro, caballo*) coat
   (**c**) (*de melocotón*) down
   (**d**) (*de una tela*) nap
   (**e**) *Fam* (*pizca, poquito*) **échame un p. más de ginebra** could I have a smidgin *o* tad more gin?; **pasarse un p.** to go a bit too far; **no me gusta (ni) un p. ese tipo** I don't like that guy at all
   (**f**) (*expresiones*) **se le va a caer el p.** he'll be in big trouble; **con pelos y señales** with all the details; **de medio p.** second-rate; **no estudias nada y así te luce el p. en los exámenes** you never study and it shows in your exam results; **montar a caballo a p.** to ride bareback; **presentarse a un examen a p.** to go to an exam unprepared; **no tener un p. de tonto** to be nobody's fool; **no tener pelos en la lengua** not to mince one's words; **no verle el p. a alguien** not to see hide nor hair of sb; **poner a alguien los pelos de punta** to make sb's hair stand on end; **por los pelos, por un p.** by the skin of one's teeth, only just; **ser un hombre de p. en pecho** to be a real man; **soltarse el p.** to let one's hair down; **tomar el p. a alguien** to pull sb's leg; **venir al p. a alguien** to be just right for sb; *también Fig* **a contra p.** against the grain

pelón, -ona *adj Fam* (**a**) (*sin pelo*) bald (**b**) *Méx* (*difícil*) tricky

pelota¹ *nf* (**a**) (*bola*) ball; **jugar a la p.** to play ball; *Fig* **devolver la p. a alguien** to put the ball back into sb's court; *Esp Fam* **hacer la p. (a alguien)** to suck up (to sb); **p. de goma** rubber ball; **p. de tenis** tennis ball; **p. vasca** pelota (**b**) *Am* (*béisbol*) baseball (**c**) *muy Fam* (*testículo*) **pelotas** balls; **en pelotas** buck-naked, butt-naked

pelota² *Esp Fam Pey* **1** *adj* (*adulador*) **ser p.** to be a creep
   2 *nmf* (*persona*) creep, yes-man

pelotari *nmf* pelota player

pelotazo *nm* (**a**) (*con pelota*) kick *o* throw of a ball (**b**) *Esp Fam* (*enriquecimiento*) **la cultura del p.** = ruthless obsession with money and power

pelotear *vi* (*en tenis*) to practice

peloteo *nm* (**a**) (*en tenis*) practice (**b**) *Esp Fam* (*adulación*) fawning (**con** on)

pelotera *nf Fam* scrap, fight

pelotero, -a 1 *adj Esp Fam Pey* fawning
   2 *nm,f* (**a**) *Esp Fam Pey* (*adulador*) creep, yes-man (**b**) *Am* (*jugador de béisbol*) baseball player

pelotilla *nf Fam* (**a**) *Esp* **hacer la p. a alguien** to suck up to sb (**b**) (*de suciedad*) = ball of grime rubbed from skin

pelotillero, -a *Esp Fam Pey* **1** *adj* **es muy p.** he's always sucking up to people
   2 *nm,f* creep, yes-man

pelotón *nm* (*de soldados*) squad; (*de gente*) crowd; *Dep* pack; **p. de ejecución** firing squad

pelotudo, -a *adj RP Fam* damn stupid

peluca *nf* wig

peluche *nm* (**a**) (*material*) plush (**b**) (*muñeco*) cuddly toy; **osito de p.** teddy bear

peludo, -a *adj* hairy

peluquería *nf* (**a**) (*establecimiento*) hairdresser's (**b**) (*oficio*) hairdressing

peluquero, -a *nm,f* hairdresser

peluquín *nm* toupee

pelusa *nf* (**a**) *(de tela)* fluff (**b**) *(vello)* down (**c**) *(de polvo)* ball of fluff (**d**) *Esp (celos)* **tener p. de** to be jealous of

pélvico, -a *adj* pelvic

pelvis *nf inv* pelvis

PEMEX ['pemeks] *nmpl (abrev de* **Petróleos Mexicanos**) = Mexican state oil company

pena *nf* (**a**) *(lástima)* shame, pity; **da p. no poder hacer nada** it's a shame *o* pity we can't do anything; **el pobre me da p.** I feel sorry for the poor fellow; **¡qué p.!** what a shame *o* pity!

(**b**) *(tristeza)* sadness, sorrow; **sentía una gran p.** I felt terribly sad

(**c**) *(desgracia)* problem, trouble

(**d**) *(dificultad)* struggle; **a duras penas** with great difficulty

(**e**) *(castigo)* punishment; **le cayó** *o* **le impusieron una p. de treinta años** he was sentenced to *o* given thirty years; **so** *o* **bajo p. de** under penalty of; **p. capital** *o* **de muerte** death penalty

(**f**) *Carib, CAm, Col, Méx (vergüenza)* embarrassment; **me da p.** I'm embarrassed about it

(**g**) *(expresiones) Esp* **de p.** *(muy malo)* atrocious, appalling; **dibuja/cocina de p.** he can't draw/cook to save his life; **hecho una p.** in a real mess, in a terrible state; **(no) valer** *o* **merecer la p.** (not) to be worthwhile *o* worth it; **una película que merece la p.** a movie that's worth seeing; **sin p. ni gloria** without distinction

penacho *nm* (**a**) *(de pájaro)* crest (**b**) *(adorno)* plume

penado, -a *nm,f* convict

penal 1 *adj* criminal

2 *nm* prison

penalidad *nf* suffering, hardship

penalista *nmf (abogado)* criminal lawyer

penalización *nf* (**a**) *(acción)* penalization (**b**) *(sanción)* penalty

penalizar [14] *vt (gen) & Dep* to penalize

penalti, penalty *nm Dep* penalty; **parar un p.** to save a penalty; *Esp Fam* **casarse de p.** to have a shotgun wedding

penar 1 *vt (castigar)* to punish

2 *vi (sufrir)* to suffer

penca *nf (de cactus)* fleshy leaf

pendejada *nf Am muy Fam (acto)* goddamn stupid thing; *(dicho)* goddamn stupid remark

pendejear *vi Méx Fam* to mess around *o* about

pendejo, -a *nm,f* (**a**) *Méx Fam (cobarde)* coward (**b**) *Am muy Fam (tonto)* jerk

pendenciero, -a 1 *adj* who always gets into a fight

2 *nm,f* = person who is always getting into fights

pender *vi* (**a**) *(colgar)* to hang (**de** from); *Fig* **p. de un hilo** to be hanging by a thread (**b**) *(amenaza)* **p. sobre** to hang over (**c**) *(sentencia)* to be pending

pendiente 1 *adj* (**a**) *(por resolver)* pending; *(deuda)* outstanding; **estar p. de** *(atento a)* to keep an eye on; *(a la espera de)* to be waiting for; *Fig* **estar p. de un hilo** to be hanging by a thread (**b**) *(asignatura)* failed

2 *nm Esp* earring

3 *nf* slope; **el terreno está en p.** the ground slopes *o* is on a slope; **una p. del 25 por ciento** a gradient of 1 in 4, a 1 in 4 gradient

pendón¹ *nm (estandarte)* banner

pendón², -ona *nm,f Esp Fam (golfa)* floozy; *(vago)* layabout, good-for-nothing

pendonear *vi Fam* to hang out

pendular *adj (movimiento)* swinging, swaying

péndulo *nm* pendulum

pene *nm* penis

penene *nmf* = untenured teacher

penetración *nf* (**a**) *(introducción)* penetration; *Com* **p. de mercado** market penetration (**b**) *(sagacidad)* astuteness, sharpness

penetrante *adj* (**a**) *(intenso) (dolor)* acute; *(olor)* sharp; *(frío)* biting; *(mirada)* penetrating; *(voz, sonido)* piercing (**b**) *(sagaz)* sharp, penetrating

penetrar 1 *vi* **p. en** *(internarse en)* to enter; *(filtrarse por)* to get into, to penetrate; *(perforar)* to pierce; *(llegar a conocer)* to get to the bottom of

2 *vt* (**a**) *(introducirse en) (sujeto: arma, sonido)* to pierce, to penetrate; *(sujeto: humedad, líquido)* to permeate; *(sujeto: emoción, sentimiento)* to pierce (**b**) *(secreto, misterio)* to get to the bottom of (**c**) *(sexualmente)* to penetrate

peneuvista *Esp* **1** *adj* of/relating to the Basque nationalist party PNV

2 *nmf* member/supporter of the Basque nationalist party PNV

penicilina *nf* penicillin

península *nf* peninsula; **la p. Ibérica** the Iberian peninsula

peninsular 1 *adj* peninsular

2 *nmf* peninsular Spaniard

penique *nm* penny; **peniques** pence

penitencia *nf* penance; **hacer p.** to do penance

penitenciaría *nf* prison, penitentiary

penitenciario, -a *adj* prison; **régimen p.** prison regime

penitente *nmf* penitent

penoso, -a *adj* (**a**) *(trabajoso)* laborious (**b**) *(lamentable)* distressing; *(aspecto, espectáculo)* sorry (**c**) *Am salvo RP (embarazoso)* embarrassing

pensado, -a *adj* **mal p.** twisted, evil-minded; **en el día/momento menos p.** when you least expect it; **un mal p.** a twisted person; **bien p.** on reflection

pensador, -ora *nm,f* thinker

pensamiento *nm* (**a**) *(facultad)* thought; *(mente)* mind; *(idea)* idea, thought; **leer el p. a alguien** to read sb's mind *o* thoughts (**b**) *Bot* pansy

pensar [3] **1** *vi* to think; **p. en algo/en alguien/en hacer algo** to think about sth/about sb/about doing sth; **piensa en un número/buen regalo** think of a number/good present; **dar que p. a alguien** to give sb food for thought; **no pienses mal...** don't get the wrong idea...; **p. mal de alguien** to think badly *o* ill of sb

2 *vt* (**a**) *(reflexionar sobre)* to think about *o* over; **ahora que lo pienso,...** come to think of it,..., now that I think about it...; **cuando menos lo pienses, te llamarán** they'll call you when you least expect it (**b**) *(opinar, creer)* to think; **p. algo de alguien/algo** to think sth of sb/sth; **pienso que no vendrá** I don't think she'll come (**c**) *(idear)* to think up (**d**) *(tener la intención de)* **p. hacer algo** to intend to do sth; **no pienso decírtelo** I have no intention of telling you; **¿qué piensas hacer?** what are you going to do?, what are you thinking of doing?; **¡ni pensarlo!** no way!, not a chance!

3 pensarse *vpr* **pensarse algo** to think about sth, to think sth over; **me ofrecieron el trabajo y no me lo pensé (dos veces)** they offered me the job and I had no hesitation in accepting it

pensativo, -a *adj* pensive, thoughtful

pensil, pénsil *nm* delightful garden

Pensilvania *n* Pennsylvania

pensión *nf* (**a**) *(dinero)* pension; **p. alimenticia** *o* **alimentaria** maintenance; **p. de jubilación/de viudedad** retirement/widow's pension (**b**) *(de huéspedes)* guest house; **media p.** *(en hotel)* half board, = breakfast and one other meal included at hotel or guesthouse; **estar a media p.** *(en colegio)* to have school dinners; **p. completa** full board, = all meals included at hotel or guesthouse

pensionado *nm Esp* boarding school

pensionista *nmf* (a) *(jubilado)* pensioner (b) *(en una pensión)* guest, lodger (c) *Esp (en un colegio)* boarder

pentaedro *nm* pentahedron

pentagonal *adj* pentagonal

pentágono *nm* pentagon; **el P.** *(edificio)* the Pentagon

pentagrama *nm Mús* stave

pentámetro *nm (en poesía)* pentameter

pentatlón *nm* pentathlon

Pentecostés *nm* (a) *(cristiano)* Whitsunday, Pentecost (b) *(judío)* Pentecost

pentotal *nm* Pentothal®

penúltimo, -a *adj & nm,f* penultimate, last but one

penumbra *nf* semidarkness, half-light; **en p.** in semidarkness

penuria *nf* (a) *(pobreza)* penury, poverty (b) *(escasez)* paucity, dearth

peña *nf* (a) *(roca)* crag, rock; *(monte)* cliff (b) *(club)* club; *(quinielística)* syndicate; *Esp (grupo de amigos)* crowd

peñasco *nm* large crag *o* rock

peñazo *nm Esp Fam* bore

peñón *nm* rock; **el P. (de Gibraltar)** the Rock (of Gibraltar)

peón *nm* (a) *(obrero)* unskilled laborer; **p. caminero** road worker (b) *(en ajedrez)* pawn (c) *(peonza)* (spinning) top

peonada *nf* (a) *(día de trabajo)* day's work (b) *(sueldo)* day's wages (c) *(obreros)* gang of laborers

peonza *nf* (spinning) top

peor 1 *adj* (a) *(comparativo)* worse **(que** than); **he visto cosas peores** I've seen worse (b) *(superlativo)* **el/la p....** the worst...; **lo p. fue que...** the worst thing was that...

2 *pron* **el/la p. (de)** the worst (in); **el p. de todos** the worst of all; **en el p. de los casos** at worst, if the worst comes to the worst

3 *adv* (a) *(comparativo)* worse **(que** than); **ahora veo p.** I see worse now; **¿qué tal las vacaciones? — p. imposible** how were your holidays? — they couldn't have been worse; **estoy p.** *(de salud)* I feel worse; **p. para ti/él/***etc.* that's your/his/*etc* problem; **p. que p.** so much the worse (b) *(superlativo)* worst; **el que lo hizo p.** the one who did it (the) worst

pepinazo *nm Fam* (a) *(explosión)* explosion, blast (b) *Dep (disparo)* powerful shot, screamer; *(pase)* powerful pass

pepinillo *nm* gherkin

pepino *nm* cucumber; *Fam* **me importa un p.** I couldn't care less, I don't give a damn

pepita *nf* (a) *(de fruta)* pip (b) *(de oro)* nugget

pepito *nm Esp* (a) *(de carne)* grilled meat sandwich (b) *(dulce)* = long, cream-filled cake made of dough similar to doughnut

pepitoria *nf* = fricassee made with egg yolk

pepona *nf* large cardboard doll

péptico, -a *adj* peptic

peque¹ *nmf (diminutivo de* **pequeño**) *Fam (niño)* kid

peque² *etc ver* **pecar**

pequeñez *nf (cualidad)* smallness; *(cosa insignificante)* trifle

pequeño, -a 1 *adj* small, little; *(hermano)* little; *(posibilidad)* slight; *(ingresos, cifras)* low; **la casa se nos ha quedado pequeña** the house is too small for us now; **pequeña empresa** small business; **la pequeña pantalla** the small screen

2 *nm,f (niño)* little one; **de p.** as a child; **el p., la pequeña** *(benjamín)* the youngest, the baby

pequeñoburgués, -esa 1 *adj* petit bourgeois

2 *nm,f* petit bourgeois, *f* petite bourgeoise

pequinés, -esa, pekinés, -esa 1 *adj & nm,f* Pekinese

2 *nm (perro)* Pekinese

PER [per] *nm (abrev de* **Plan de Empleo Rural**) = Spanish government project to support rural employment

pera 1 *nf* (a) *(fruta)* pear (b) *(de goma)* (rubber) bulb (c) *(interruptor)* = light switch on cord (d) *(expresiones)* **partir peras** to fall out; **pedir peras al olmo** to ask (for) the impossible; *Esp Fam* **ser la p.** to be the limit

2 *adj inv Esp Fam* grand, highfalutin; **niño p.** spoiled brat

peral *nm* pear tree

peralte *nm (de carretera)* banking

perborato *nm* perborate

perca *nf* perch

percal *nm* percale; **conocer el p.** to know the score *o* what's what

percance *nm* mishap

per cápita *adj & adv* per capita

percatarse *vpr* **p. (de algo)** to notice (sth)

percebe *nm* (a) *(marisco)* goose barnacle (b) *Fam (persona)* fool

percepción *nf* (a) *(por los sentidos, la inteligencia)* perception; **p. extrasensorial** extrasensory perception (b) *(cobro)* receipt, collection

perceptible *adj* (a) *(por los sentidos)* noticeable, perceptible (b) *(que se puede cobrar)* receivable, payable

perceptivo, -a *adj* sensory

percha *nf* (a) *(de armario)* (coat-)hanger; *(de pared)* coat hook; *(de pie)* coatstand, hat stand (b) *(para pájaros)* perch (c) *Fam* **ser una buena p.** to have a good figure

perchero *nm (de pared)* coat rack; *(de pie)* coatstand, hat stand

percibir *vt* (a) *(con los sentidos)* to perceive, to notice; *(por los oídos)* to hear (b) *(cobrar)* to receive, to get

percusión *nf* percussion

percusionista *nmf* percussionist

percutor, percusor *nm* hammer, firing pin

perdedor, -ora 1 *adj* losing

2 *nm,f* loser

perder [64] **1** *vt* (a) *(dinero, objeto, amigo)* to lose (b) *(desperdiciar) (tiempo)* to waste; *(oportunidad)* to miss; **no pierdas el tiempo con *o* en tonterías** don't waste your time on nonsense like that; **no hay tiempo que p.** there's no time to lose (c) *(tren, vuelo)* to miss (d) *(tener un escape de) (agua)* to lose, to leak; **ese camión va perdiendo aceite** this truck is losing *o* leaking oil (e) *(perjudicar)* to be the ruin of; **le pierde su pasión por el juego** his passion for gambling is ruining him

2 *vi* (a) *(salir derrotado)* to lose; **no te pelees con él, que llevas las de p.** don't get into a fight with him, you're bound to lose (b) *(empeorar)* to go downhill (c) *(tener un escape) (de agua, aceite)* to leak (d) **echar algo a p.** to spoil sth; **echarse a p.** *(alimento)* to spoil

3 perderse *vpr* (a) *(extraviarse)* to get lost; **me he perdido** I'm lost; **se me ha perdido el reloj** I've lost my watch (b) *(desaparecer)* to disappear; *Fam* **¡piérdete!** get lost! (c) *(desperdiciarse)* to be wasted (d) *(desaprovechar)* **perderse algo** to miss out on sth; **¡no te lo pierdas!** don't miss it! (e) *(por los vicios)* to be beyond salvation (f) **perderse por** *(anhelar)* to be mad about

perdición *nf* ruin, undoing

pérdida *nf* (a) *(de objeto, persona, peso)* loss; **en caso de p., entregar en ...** in the event of loss, deliver to...; *Esp* **no tiene p.** you can't miss it; **p. del conocimiento** loss of consciousness (b) *(de tiempo, dinero)* waste (c) *(escape)* leak (d) *Fin* **pérdidas** losses (e) **pérdidas (materiales)** *(daños)* damage

perdidamente *adv* hopelessly

perdido, -a 1 *adj* (a) *(extraviado)* lost; *(animal, bala)* stray; *Fig* **¡estamos perdidos!** we're done for!, we're lost! (b) *Esp (sucio)* filthy; **ponerse p. de pintura/barro** to get (oneself) covered in paint/mud (c) *(tiempo)* wasted; *(ocasión)* missed (d) *Fam (de remate)* complete, utter; **es idiota p.** he's a complete idiot

2 *nm,f* reprobate

perdigón nm pellet

perdigonada nf (a) (tiro) shot (b) (herida) gunshot wound

perdiguero nm gundog

perdiz nf partridge; **fueron felices y comieron perdices** they all lived happily ever after

perdón nm pardon, forgiveness; **con p.** if you'll forgive the expression; **no tener p.** to be unforgivable; **pedir p.** to apologize; **¡p.!** (lo siento) sorry!; **p., ¿me deja pasar?** excuse me, can I get past?

perdonar 1 vt (a) (ofensa, falta) to forgive; **perdonarle algo a alguien** to forgive sb for sth; **perdone que le moleste** sorry to bother you; **perdona la pregunta, ¿estás casada?** forgive o pardon my asking, but are you married?; **perdone, ¿me deja salir?** excuse me, can I get past? (b) (eximir de) (deuda, condena) **p. algo a alguien** to let sb off sth; **perdonarle la vida a alguien** to spare sb their life (c) (desperdiciar) **no p. algo** not to miss sth
2 vi **los años no perdonan** the years take their toll; **un delantero que no perdona** a forward who never misses

perdonavidas nmf inv Fam bully

perdurable adj (a) (que dura siempre) eternal (b) (que dura mucho) long-lasting

perdurar vi (a) (durar mucho) to endure, to last (b) (persistir) to persist

perecedero, -a adj (a) (productos) perishable (b) (naturaleza) transitory

perecer [46] vi to perish, to die

peregrina nf (vieira) scallop

peregrinación nf, **peregrinaje** nm Rel pilgrimage; Fig (a un lugar) trek

peregrinar vi Rel to make a pilgrimage; Fig (a un lugar) to trail, to trek

peregrino, -a 1 adj (a) (ave) migratory (b) (idea, argumento) strange, bizarre
2 nm,f (persona) pilgrim

perejil nm parsley

perenne adj (a) Bot perennial (b) (recuerdo) enduring (c) (continuo) constant

perentorio, -a adj urgent, pressing; (gesto, tono) peremptory; **plazo p.** fixed time limit

perestroika nf perestroika

pereza nf idleness; **me da p. ir a pie** I can't worry about walking; **no lo hice por p.** I couldn't worry about doing it; **sacudirse la p.** to wake oneself up; **sentir p.** to feel lazy

perezoso, -a 1 adj (a) (vago) lazy (b) (lento) slow, sluggish
2 nm,f (vago) lazy person, idler
3 nm (animal) sloth

perfección nf perfection; **es de una gran p.** it's exceptionally good; **a la p.** perfectly

perfeccionamiento nm (a) (acabado) perfecting (b) (mejoramiento) improvement

perfeccionar vt (a) (redondear) to perfect (b) (mejorar) to improve

perfeccionismo nm perfectionism

perfeccionista adj & nmf perfectionist

perfectamente adv (a) (sobradamente) perfectly (b) (muy bien) fine; **¿cómo estás? — estoy p.** how are you? — I'm fine (c) (de acuerdo) **¡p.!** fine!, great!

perfectivo, -a adj perfective

perfecto, -a adj **1** adj (a) (impecable, inmejorable) perfect (b) (total) absolute, complete; **es un p. idiota** he's an absolute o complete idiot; **es un p. desconocido** he's a complete unknown
2 interj **¡p.!** (de acuerdo) fine!, great!

perfidia nf perfidy, treachery

pérfido, -a 1 adj perfidious, treacherous
2 nm,f treacherous person

perfil nm (a) (contorno) outline, shape (b) (de cara, cuerpo) profile; **de p.** in profile (c) (psicológico, de candidato) profile

perfilar 1 vt to outline
2 **perfilarse** vpr (a) (destacarse) to be outlined (b) (concretarse) to shape up

perforación nf (a) (acción) drilling, boring (b) Med perforation (c) (taladro, hueco) borehole

perforador, -ora adj drilling

perforadora nf (a) (herramienta) drill (b) (para papel) paper punch

perforar 1 vt (agujerear) to cut a hole/holes in; (con taladro) to drill a hole/holes in; **la bala le perforó el pulmón** the bullet pierced his lung
2 **perforarse** vpr **perforarse las orejas** to have o get one's ears pierced

perfumar 1 vt to perfume
2 **perfumarse** vpr to put perfume on

perfume nm perfume

perfumería nf (a) (tienda, arte) perfumery (b) (productos) perfumes

pergamino nm parchment

pergeñar vt (plan, idea) to rough out; (comida) to whip up

pérgola nf pergola

pericardio nm Anat pericardium

pericia nf skill

pericial adj expert

perico nm (a) (pájaro) parakeet (b) Esp, RP, Ven Fam (cocaína) snow (c) Col (café con leche) coffee with milk

periferia nf (contorno) periphery; (alrededores) outskirts

periférico, -a 1 adj peripheral; **barrio p.** outlying district
2 nm Inform peripheral

perifollo 1 nm (planta) chervil
2 **perifollos** nmpl Fam frills (and fripperies)

perífrasis nf inv wordy explanation; Gram **p. verbal** compound verb

perifrástico, -a adj long-winded

perilla nf (a) (barba) goatee; **venir de p. o perillas** to be just the right thing (b) Am (de aparato) knob

perímetro nm perimeter

periodicidad nf (regularidad, frecuencia) frequency; Mec periodicity

periódico, -a 1 adj (a) (regular) regular, periodic (b) Mat recurrent
2 nm newspaper; **p. dominical** o **del domingo** Sunday paper

periodismo nm journalism; **p. de investigación** investigative journalism

periodista nmf journalist

periodístico, -a adj journalistic

periodo, período nm period; Dep half; **p. de gestación** gestation period; **p. glacial** ice age; **p. de incubación** incubation period; **p. interglacial** interglacial age; **p. de prácticas** trial period; **p. de prueba** trial period; **p. de transición** transition period

peripatético, -a 1 adj (a) Filosofía Peripatetic (b) Fam (ridículo) ludicrous
2 nm,f Peripatetic

peripecia nf incident, adventure; **sus peripecias en la selva** his adventures in the jungle

periplo nm journey, voyage

peripuesto, -a adj Fam dolled-up

periquete nm Fam **en un p.** in a jiffy

periquito 1 nm parakeet
2 adj Esp Fam Dep = of/relating to the Español Football Club

periscopio nm periscope

perista nmf Fam fence, = receiver of stolen goods

peritaje *nm (trabajo)* expert work; *(informe)* expert's report

peritar *vt (casa)* to value; *(daños)* to assess the value of

perito *nm* (**a**) *(experto)* expert; **p. agrónomo** agronomist (**b**) *(ingeniero técnico)* technician

perjudicado, -a 1 *adj* affected; *Der* **la parte perjudicada** the injured party
2 *nm,f* **los perjudicados por la inundación** those affected by the flood; *Der* **el p.** the injured party

perjudicar [59] *vt* to damage, to harm

perjudicial *adj* harmful (**para** to)

perjuicio *nm* harm, damage; **causar perjuicios (a)** to do harm *o* damage (to); **ir en p. de** to be detrimental to; **la reforma educativa favorece a algunas asignaturas en p. de otras** the education reform favors some subjects at the expense of others; **lo haré, sin p. de que proteste** I'll do it, but I retain the right to make a complaint about it

perjurar *vi* (**a**) *(jurar mucho)* **juró y perjuró que no había sido él** he swore fervently that he hadn't done it (**b**) *(jurar en falso)* to commit perjury

perjurio *nm* perjury

perjuro, -a 1 *adj* perjured
2 *nm,f* perjurer

perla *nf* pearl; *Fig (maravilla)* gem, treasure; *Fig* **de perlas** great, fine; **me viene de perlas** it's just the right thing

perlado, -a *adj (de gotas)* beaded

permanecer [46] *vi* (**a**) *(en un lugar)* to stay (**b**) *(en un estado)* to remain, to stay; **p. en silencio** to remain silent; **permanezcan en sus asientos** please remain seated

permanencia *nf* (**a**) *(en un lugar)* staying, continued stay (**b**) *(en un estado)* continuation

permanente 1 *adj* permanent; *(comisión)* standing
2 *nf* perm; **hacerse la p.** to have a perm

permeabilidad *nf* permeability

permeable *adj* permeable

permisible *adj* permissible, acceptable

permisividad *nf* permissiveness

permisivo, -a *adj* permissive

permiso *nm* (**a**) *(autorización)* permission; **pedir p. para hacer algo** to ask permission to do sth (**b**) *(fórmula de cortesía)* **con p.** if I may, if you'll excuse me; **con p., ¿puedo pasar?** may I come in? (**c**) *(documento)* license, permit; **p. de armas** gun license; **p. de conducción** *o* **de conducir** driver's license; **p. de residencia** residence permit; **p. de trabajo** work permit (**d**) *(vacaciones)* leave (of absence); **estar de p.** to be on leave; **le concedieron un p. carcelario de tres días** he was allowed out of prison for three days; **p. por maternidad** maternity leave

permitido, -a *adj* permitted, allowed

permitir 1 *vt* (**a**) *(autorizar)* to allow, to permit; **p. a alguien hacer algo** to allow sb to do sth; **¿me permite?** may I?; **¡no te permito que me hables así!** I won't have you talking to me like that!; **si el tiempo lo permite** weather permitting; **no se permite fumar** *(en letrero)* no smoking (**b**) *(hacer posible)* to allow, to enable; **el cable permite enviar información a mayor velocidad** cable allows *o* enables information to be sent faster
2 permitirse *vpr* (**a**) *(uno mismo)* to allow oneself; **de vez en cuando se permite un cigarrillo** he allows himself a cigarette from time to time; **me permito recordarte que...** let me remind you that... (**b**) *(económicamente)* **no puedo permitírmelo** I can't afford it

permuta *nf* exchange

permutable *adj* exchangeable

permutación *nf* (**a**) *(permuta)* exchange (**b**) *Mat* permutation

permutar *vt* to exchange, to swap

pernera *nf* pant *o* trouser leg

pernicioso, -a *adj* damaging, harmful

pernil *nm* leg of ham

perno *nm* bolt

pernoctar *vi* to stay overnight

pero 1 *conj* (**a**) *(adversativo)* but; **el reloj es viejo, p. funciona bien** the watch is old but it keeps good time (**b**) *(enfático)* **p. ¿qué es todo este ruido?** what on earth is all this noise about?; **¡p. si eso lo sabe todo el mundo!** come on, everyone knows that!
2 *nm* snag, fault; **poner peros a todo** to find fault with everything

perogrullada *nf Fam* truism

Perogrullo *nm* **una verdad de P.** a truism

perol *nm* casserole (dish)

peroné *nm* fibula

peronismo *nm Pol* Peronism

peronista *adj & nmf Pol* Peronist

perorar *vi Fam Pey* to speechify

perorata *nf* long-winded speech

peróxido *nm* peroxide

perpendicular 1 *adj* perpendicular; **ser p. a algo** to be at right angles to sth
2 *nf* perpendicular (line)

perpetrar *vt* to perpetrate, to commit

perpetuar [4] **1** *vt* to perpetuate
2 perpetuarse *vpr* to last, to endure

perpetuidad *nf* perpetuity; **a p.** in perpetuity; **presidente a p.** president for life; **condenado a p.** condemned to life imprisonment

perpetuo, -a *adj* (**a**) *(para siempre)* perpetual (**b**) *(vitalicio)* lifelong; *Der* **cadena perpetua** life imprisonment

perplejidad *nf* perplexity, bewilderment

perplejo, -a *adj* perplexed, bewildered

perra *nf* (**a**) *(animal)* bitch (**b**) *Esp Fam (rabieta)* tantrum; **coger una p.** to throw a tantrum (**c**) *Esp Fam (dinero)* penny; **estoy sin una p.** I'm flat broke; **no tiene una p. gorda** *o* **chica** he hasn't got a dime; **no vale una p. gorda** *o* **chica** it isn't worth a dime

perrera *nf* (**a**) *(lugar)* kennels (**b**) *(vehículo)* dogcatcher's van

perrería *nf Fam* **hacer perrerías a alguien** to play dirty tricks on sb

perrero, -a *nm,f (persona)* dogcatcher

perrito *nm* **p. (caliente)** hot dog

perro, -a 1 *adj Fam* wretched, lousy; **¡qué vida más perra!** life's a bitch!
2 *nm* (**a**) *(animal)* dog; **andar como el p. y el gato** to fight like cats and dogs; *Fam* **de perros** *(tiempo, humor)* lousy; **hace un día de perros** the weather's foul today, it's lousy weather today; **ser p. viejo** to be an old hand; *Prov* **p. ladrador poco mordedor** his/her bark is worse than his/her bite; *Prov* **muerto el p., se acabó la rabia** deal with a problem at its source; **p. callejero** stray dog; **p. de caza** hunting dog; **p. faldero** lapdog; *Fig* lackey; **p. guardián** guard dog, watchdog; **p. lazarillo** Seeing Eye® dog; **p. lobo** German Shepherd, Alsatian; **p. pastor** sheepdog; **p. policía** police dog; **p. salchicha** sausage dog
(**b**) *Fam (persona)* swine, dog

perruno, -a *adj* canine

persa 1 *adj & nmf* Persian
2 *nm (idioma)* Persian, Farsi

persecución *nf* (**a**) *(seguimiento)* pursuit (**b**) *(acoso)* persecution

per sécula seculorum *adv* for ever and ever

persecutorio, -a *adj* **complejo p.** persecution complex

perseguir [61] *vt* (**a**) *(seguir, tratar de obtener)* to pursue; **con esta medida, el gobierno persigue la contención de la inflación** the government's purpose in taking this measure is to curb inflation (**b**) *(acosar)* to persecute; **lo persiguieron por sus ideas** he was persecuted for his beliefs; **le persigue la mala suerte** he's dogged by bad luck; **los fantasmas de la niñez la persiguen** she is tormented by the ghosts of her childhood

perseverancia *nf* perseverance

perseverante *adj* persistent

perseverar *vi* to persevere (**en** with), to persist (**en** in)

Persia *n* Persia

persiana *nf* blind

persignarse *vpr Rel* to cross oneself

persigo *etc ver* **perseguir**

persiguiera *etc ver* **perseguir**

persistencia *nf* persistence

persistente *adj* persistent

persistir *vi* to persist (**en** in)

persona *nf* (**a**) *(individuo)* person; **vinieron varias personas** several people came; **cien personas** a hundred people; **en p.** in person; **por p.** per head; **ser buena p.** to be a good person *o* type; **p. mayor** adult, grown-up; **p. non grata** persona non grata (**b**) *Der* party; **p. física** private individual; **p. jurídica** legal entity *o* person (**c**) *Gram* person; **la segunda p. del singular** the second person singular

personaje *nm* (**a**) *(en novela, teatro)* character; **p. central** central character (**b**) *(persona importante)* important person, celebrity; **¡menudo p.!** *(persona despreciable)* what an unpleasant individual!

personal 1 *adj (privado, íntimo)* personal; **una opinión/ pregunta p.** a personal opinion/question; **p. e intransferible** nontransferable

2 *nm* (**a**) *(trabajadores)* staff, personnel; **p. de a bordo** *(en avión)* cabin crew; **p. docente** teaching staff; **p. mínimo** skeleton staff; **p. en plantilla** in-house staff; **p. sanitario** health workers; **p. de tierra** ground crew (**b**) *Esp Fam* **el p.** *(la gente)* people *(plural)*

3 *nf (en baloncesto)* personal foul

personalidad *nf* (**a**) *(características)* personality (**b**) *(identidad)* identity (**c**) *(persona importante)* important person, celebrity (**d**) *Der* legal personality *o* status

personalismo *nm* (**a**) *(parcialidad)* favoritism (**b**) *(egocentrismo)* self-centeredness

personalizado, -a *adj* personalized

personalizar [14] *vi* (**a**) *(nombrar)* to name names (**b**) *(aludir)* to get personal

personalmente *adv* personally; **me encargaré yo p.** I'll deal with it myself *o* personally; **a mí, p., no me importa** it doesn't matter to me personally; **les afecta p.** it affects them personally

personarse *vpr* to turn up

personero, -a *nm,f Am* representative

personificación *nf* personification

personificar [59] *vt* to personify

perspectiva *nf* (**a**) *(punto de vista)* perspective; **en p.** *(dibujo)* in perspective (**b**) *(paisaje)* view (**c**) *(futuro)* prospect; **en p.** in prospect

perspicacia *nf* insight, perceptiveness

perspicaz *adj* sharp, perceptive

persuadir 1 *vt* to persuade; **p. a alguien para que haga algo** to persuade sb to do sth

2 persuadirse *vpr* to convince oneself; **persuadirse de algo** to become convinced of sth

persuasión *nf* persuasion

persuasiva *nf* persuasive power

persuasivo, -a *adj* persuasive

pertenecer [46] *vi* **p. a** *(ser propiedad de)* to belong to; *(corresponder a)* to be up to, to be a matter for; **este libro pertenece a la biblioteca de mi tío** this book is part of my

uncle's library; **el león pertenece a la categoría de los felinos** the lion belongs to the cat family

perteneciente *adj* **p. a** belonging to

pertenencia *nf* (**a**) *(propiedad)* ownership (**b**) *(afiliación)* membership; **pertenencias** *(efectos personales)* belongings

pértiga *nf* (**a**) *(vara)* pole (**b**) *Dep* (**salto con**) **p.** pole vault

pertinaz *adj* (**a**) *(terco)* stubborn (**b**) *(persistente)* persistent

pertinencia *nf* (**a**) *(adecuación)* appropriateness (**b**) *(relevancia)* relevance

pertinente *adj* (**a**) *(adecuado)* appropriate; **se tomarán las medidas pertinentes** the appropriate measures will be taken; **si lo consideras p., llámale** telephone him if you think it's necessary (**b**) *(relativo)* relevant, pertinent; **ya he enviado todos los documentos pertinentes a la beca** I have already sent off all the forms relating to the grant

pertrechar 1 *vt Mil* to supply with food and ammunition; *(equipar)* to equip

2 pertrecharse *vpr* **pertrecharse de** to equip oneself with

pertrechos *nmpl* (**a**) *Mil* supplies and ammunition (**b**) *(utensilios)* gear

perturbación *nf* (**a**) *(desconcierto)* disquiet, unease (**b**) *(disturbio)* disturbance; **p. del orden público** breach of the peace (**c**) *Med* mental imbalance (**d**) *Meteo* **p. atmosférica** atmospheric disturbance

perturbado, -a 1 *adj* (**a**) *Med* disturbed, mentally unbalanced (**b**) *(desconcertado)* perturbed

2 *nm,f Med* mentally unbalanced person

perturbador, -ora 1 *adj* unsettling

2 *nm,f* troublemaker

perturbar *vt* (**a**) *(trastornar)* to disrupt (**b**) *(inquietar)* to disturb, to unsettle (**c**) *(enloquecer)* to perturb

Perú *nm* (**el**) **P.** Peru

peruano, -a *adj & nm,f* Peruvian

perversidad *nf* wickedness

perversión *nf* perversion

perverso, -a *adj* depraved

pervertido, -a *nm,f* pervert

pervertidor, -ora 1 *adj* pernicious, corrupting

2 *nm,f* reprobate, corrupter

pervertir [62] **1** *vt* to corrupt

2 pervertirse *vpr* to become corrupt, to be corrupted

pervivir *vi* to survive

pesa *nf* (**a**) *(balanza, contrapeso)* weight (**b**) *Dep* **pesas** weights; *Fam* **hacer pesas** to do weight training; **levantamiento de pesas** weight lifting

pesabebés *nm inv* baby-weighing scales

pesacartas *nm inv* letter-weighing scales

pesadez *nf* (**a**) *(peso)* weight (**b**) *(sensación)* heaviness (**c**) *(molestia, fastidio)* drag, pain (**d**) *(aburrimiento)* bore

pesadilla *nf también Fig* nightmare

pesado, -a 1 *adj* (**a**) *(que pesa)* heavy (**b**) *(calor)* oppressive (**c**) *(sueño)* deep (**d**) *(lento)* ponderous, sluggish (**e**) *(tarea, trabajo)* difficult, tough (**f**) *(aburrido)* boring (**g**) *(molesto)* annoying, tiresome; **¡qué pesada eres!** you're so annoying!; **ponerse p.** to be a pain

2 *nm,f* bore, pain

pesadumbre *nf* grief, sorrow

pésame *nm* sympathy, condolences; **dar el p.** to offer one's condolences

pesar 1 *nm* (**a**) *(tristeza)* grief (**b**) *(arrepentimiento)* remorse

2 *vt* (**a**) *(en balanza)* to weigh (**b**) *(examinar)* to weigh up

3 *vi* (**a**) *(tener peso)* to weigh; **¿cuánto pesa?** how much *o* what does it weigh? (**b**) *(ser pesado)* to be heavy; **pesa mucho** it's very heavy (**c**) *(importar)* to play an important part; **en su decisión pesaron muchas razones** a number of reasons influenced her decision (**d**) *(entristecer)* **no me pesa haber**

dejado ese trabajo I have no regrets about leaving that job, I'm not at all sorry I left that job; **me pesa tener que decirte esto** I'm sorry to have to tell you this

4 pesarse *vpr* to weigh oneself

5 a pesar de *loc prep* in spite of, despite; **a p. de las críticas** in spite of *o* despite all the criticism; **a p. mío** against my will; **muy a nuestro p., hubo que invitarles** we had to invite them, even though we really didn't want to; **a p. de que** in spite of the fact that; **a p. de todo** in spite of *o* despite everything

6 pese a *loc prep* in spite of, despite; **pese a no conocerla…** in spite of *o* despite the fact that I didn't know her…; **pese a que…** in spite of *o* despite the fact that…

pesaroso, -a *adj* (a) *(arrepentido)* remorseful (b) *(afligido)* sad

pesca *nf* (a) *(acción)* fishing; **ir de p.** to go fishing; **p. de altura** deep-sea fishing; **p. de arrastre** trawling; **p. de bajura** coastal fishing; **p. con caña** angling; **p. submarina** underwater fishing (b) *(captura)* catch (c) *Fam* **y toda la p.** and all the rest of it; **vinieron Luis, su hermano y toda la p.** Luis, his brother and the rest of the crew all came

pescadería *nf* fish shop *o* store

pescadero, -a *nm,f* fish seller

pescadilla *nf* whiting; *Esp Fam Fig* **ser como la p. que se muerde la cola** to be a vicious circle

pescado *nm* fish; **p. azul/blanco** blue/white fish

pescador, -ora *nm,f* fisherman, *f* fisherwoman; **p. de perlas** pearl diver

pescante *nm* (a) *(de carruaje)* driver's seat (b) *Náut* davit

pescar [59] **1** *vt* (a) *(peces)* to catch (b) *Fam (contraer) (enfermedad)* to catch (c) *Fam (atrapar)* to catch; **lo pescaron intentando entrar sin pagar** he got caught trying to get in without paying (d) *Fam (conseguir)* to land, to get oneself; **pescó un buen marido** she landed herself a good husband (e) *Fam (entender)* to pick up, to understand; **¿has pescado el chiste?** did you get the joke?

2 *vi* to fish, to go fishing

pescuezo *nm* neck; *Fam* **retorcer el p. a alguien** to wring sb's neck

pese *ver* **pesar**

pesebre *nm* (a) *(para los animales)* manger (b) *(belén)* crib, Nativity scene

pesero *nm Méx* collective taxi *(with a fixed rate and that travels a fixed route)*

peseta *nf Antes (unidad)* peseta; **pesetas** *(dinero)* money; *Esp Fam Fig* **mirar la p.** to watch one's money

pesetero, -a *Esp Fam Pey* **1** *adj* money-grubbing

2 *nm,f* money-grubber

pesificación *nf RP* pesification

pesimismo *nm* pessimism

pesimista 1 *adj* pessimistic

2 *nmf* pessimist

pésimo, -a *adj* terrible, awful

peso *nm* (a) *(en general)* weight; **tiene un kilo de p.** it weighs a kilo; **de p.** *(razones)* weighty, sound; *(persona)* influential; *Fig* **caer por su propio p.** to be self-evident; *Fig* **pagar algo a p. de oro** to pay a fortune for sth; **p. atómico** atomic weight; **p. bruto** gross weight; *Fís* **p. específico** specific gravity; **p. ligero** lightweight; **p. medio** middleweight; **p. molecular** molecular weight; **p. mosca** flyweight; **p. muerto** dead weight; **p. neto** net weight; **p. pesado** heavyweight

(b) *(fuerza, influencia)* weight; **su palabra tiene mucho p.** his word carries a lot of weight

(c) *(carga, preocupación)* burden; **el p. de la culpabilidad** the burden of guilt; **quitarse un p. de encima** to take a weight off one's mind

(d) *(balanza)* scales

(e) *Dep* shot; **lanzamiento de p.** shot put

(f) *(moneda)* peso

pespunte *nm* backstitch

pespuntear *vt* to backstitch

pesque *etc ver* **pescar**

pesquería *nf (sitio)* fishery, fishing ground

pesquero, -a 1 *adj* fishing

2 *nm* fishing boat

pesquisa *nf* investigation, inquiry

pestaña *nf* (a) *(de párpado)* eyelash; *Fam Fig* **quemarse las pestañas** to burn the midnight oil (b) *(de recortable)* flap (c) *Mec* flange

pestañear *vi* to blink; **sin p.** *(con serenidad)* without batting an eyelid; *(con atención)* without losing concentration once

pestañeo *nm* blinking

peste *nf* (a) *(enfermedad)* plague; **p. bubónica** bubonic plague; **la p. negra** the Black Death; **p. porcina** hog cholera (b) *(mal olor)* stink, stench (c) *Fam (molestia)* pest (d) *(expresiones)* **decir** *o* **echar pestes de alguien** to bad-mouth sb; **echar pestes** to curse, to swear

pesticida 1 *adj* pesticidal

2 *nm* pesticide

pestilencia *nf* stench

pestilente *adj* foul-smelling

pestillo *nm (cerrojo)* bolt; *(mecanismo, en verjas)* latch; **correr** *o* **echar el p.** to shoot the bolt

pestiño *nm (dulce)* honey-dipped fritter

pesto *nm (salsa)* pesto (sauce)

petaca *nf* (a) *(para cigarrillos)* cigarette case; *(para tabaco)* tobacco pouch (b) *(para bebidas)* hip flask (c) *Méx (maleta)* suitcase (d) *Fam* **hacer la p.** *(como broma)* to make an apple-pie bed

petaco *nm Fam* pinball machine

pétalo *nm* petal

petanca *nf* = game similar to lawn bowling played in parks, on beach etc

petardo 1 *nm* (a) *(cohete)* firecracker (b) *Fam (aburrimiento)* bore; **¡qué p. de película!** what a boring movie! (c) *Esp Fam (porro)* joint

2 *nmf Fam (persona fea)* horror, ugly person

petate *nm* kit bag; *CAm, Méx Fam Fig* **doblar el p.** to kick the bucket; *Fam Fig* **liar el p.** *Esp (marcharse)* to pack one's bags and go; *CAm, Méx (morir)* to kick the bucket

petatearse *vpr CAm, Méx Fam* to kick the bucket

petenera *nf* = Andalusian popular song; *Esp Fam* **salir por peteneras** to go off on a tangent

petición *nf* (a) *(acción)* request; **a p. de** at the request of; **p. de mano** proposal (of marriage) (b) *Der (escrito)* petition

peticionar *vt Am* to petition

petimetre *nm* fop, dandy, dude

petirrojo *nm* robin

petiso, -a *adj Andes, RP Fam* short

peto *nm* (a) *(de prenda)* bib (b) *(de armadura)* breastplate (c) *Dep* breast guard

pétreo, -a *adj (de piedra)* stone; *(como piedra)* stony

petrificar [59] *vt también Fig* to petrify

petrodólar *nm* petrodollar

petróleo *nm* oil, petroleum; **p. crudo** crude oil

petrolera *nf* oil company

petrolero, -a 1 *adj* oil; **compañía petrolera** oil company

2 *nm* oil tanker

petrolífero, -a *adj* oil; **pozo p.** oil well

petroquímica *nf* petrochemistry

petroquímico, -a *adj* petrochemical

petulancia *nf* arrogance

petulante 1 *adj* opinionated, arrogant
2 *nmf* opinionated person

petunia *nf* petunia

peúco *nm* bootee

peyorativo, -a *adj* pejorative

pez 1 *nm (animal)* fish; *Fig* **estar como p. en el agua** to be in one's element; *Esp Fam* **estar p. (en algo)** to have no idea (about sth); **p. de colores** goldfish; *Fam* **me río yo de los peces de colores** I couldn't care less; **p. espada** swordfish; *Fam* **p. gordo** big shot; **p. martillo** hammerhead shark; **p. de río** freshwater fish; **p. volador** flying fish
2 *nf (sustancia)* pitch, tar

pezón *nm* **(a)** *(de teta)* nipple **(b)** *(de planta)* stalk

pezuña *nf* **(a)** *(de animal)* hoof **(b)** *Fam (mano)* paw

pH *nm* pH

phishing ['fiʃin] *nm Inform* phishing

Phnom Penh [nom'pen] *n* Phnom Penh

pi *nf Mat* pi

piadoso, -a *adj* **(a)** *(compasivo)* kindhearted **(b)** *(religioso)* pious

Piamonte *nm* **(el) P.** Piedmont

pianista *nmf* pianist

piano 1 *nm* piano; **p. bar** piano bar; **p. de cola** grand piano; **p. de media cola** baby grand; **p. vertical** upright piano
2 *adv Mús* piano

pianola *nf* pianola

piar [32] *vi* to cheep, to tweet

piara *nf* herd

PIB *nm (abrev de* **producto** *Esp* **interior** *o Am* **interno bruto)** GDP

pibe, -a *nm,f Arg Fam (niño)* kid, boy; *(niña)* kid, girl

PIC [pik] *nm inv Esp (abrev de* **punto de información cultural)** = computer terminal for accessing cultural information

pica *nf* **(a)** *(lanza)* pike; *Fig* **poner una p. en Flandes** to do the impossible **(b)** *Taurom* goad, picador's spear **(c)** *Fam (revisor de tren)* ticket inspector **(d) picas** *(palo de baraja)* spades

picada *nf* **(a)** *(de mosquito, serpiente)* bite; *(de avispa, escorpión, ortiga)* sting **(b)** *Am Av* **hacer una p.** to dive; *Fig* **caer en p.** to plummet

picadero *nm* **(a)** *(de caballos)* riding school **(b)** *Fam (de soltero)* bachelor pad

picadillo *nm (de carne)* mince; *(de verdura)* chopped vegetables; *Fam* **hacer p. a alguien** to beat sb to a pulp

picado, -a *adj* **(a)** *(marcado) (piel)* pockmarked; *(fruta)* bruised **(b)** *(agujereado)* perforated; **p. de polilla** moth-eaten **(c)** *(triturado) (alimento)* chopped; *(tabaco)* cut; *Esp, RP* **carne picada** ground beef **(d)** *(vino)* sour **(e)** *(diente)* decayed **(f)** *(mar)* choppy **(g)** *Fam (enfadado)* annoyed **(h)** *Esp Av* **hacer un p.** to dive; *Fig* **caer en p.** to plummet

picador, -ora *nm,f* **(a)** *Taurom* picador **(b)** *(domador)* (horse) trainer **(c)** *(minero)* face worker

picadora *nf Esp, RP* mincer

picadura *nf* **(a)** *(de mosquito, serpiente)* bite; *(de avispa, ortiga, escorpión)* sting **(b)** *(de viruela)* pockmark **(c)** *(de diente)* decay **(d)** *(tabaco)* (cut) tobacco

picaflor *nm Am* **(a)** *(ave)* hummingbird **(b)** *(persona)* flirt

picajoso, -a *adj Fam* touchy

picana *nf Am* goad

picante 1 *adj* **(a)** *(comida)* spicy, hot **(b)** *(chiste, comedia)* saucy
2 *nm (comida)* spicy food; *(sabor)* spiciness

picantería *nf Andes* cheap restaurant

picapica *nm* **(polvos de) p.** = powder which causes sneezing and itching

picapleitos *nmf inv Pey* bad lawyer

picaporte *nm* **(a)** *(mecanismo)* latch **(b)** *(aldaba)* door knocker

picar [59] **1** *vt* **(a)** *(sujeto: mosquito, serpiente)* to bite; *(sujeto: avispa, escorpión, ortiga)* to sting; **me picó una avispa** I was stung by a wasp
(b) *(sujeto: ave)* to peck; **la gaviota me picó (en) una mano** the seagull pecked my hand
(c) *(triturar) (verdura)* to chop, *Esp, RP (carne)* to mince
(d) *(piedra, hielo)* to break up
(e) *(pared)* to chip the plaster off
(f) *(aperitivo)* **p. unas aceitunas** to have a few olives as an aperitif
(g) *Esp Fam (enojar)* to annoy
(h) *(estimular) (persona, caballo)* to spur on; **aquello me picó la curiosidad** that aroused my curiosity
(i) *(perforar) (billete, ficha)* to punch
(j) *Fam (mecanografiar)* to type (up)
(k) *Taurom* to goad
(l) *Am (botar) (balón, pelota)* to bounce
2 *vi* **(a)** *(escocer) (parte del cuerpo, herida, prenda)* to itch; **me pican los ojos** my eyes are stinging **(b)** *(alimento)* to be spicy o hot **(c)** *(pez)* to bite; *Fig (dejarse engañar)* to take the bait **(d)** *(ave)* to peck **(e)** *(tomar un aperitivo)* to nibble; **¿te pongo unas aceitunas para p.?** would you like some olives as an aperitif? **(f)** *(sol)* to burn **(g)** *Am (balón, pelota)* to bounce; **la pelota picó fuera** the ball went out **(h)** **p. (muy) alto** to have great ambitions
3 picarse *vpr* **(a)** *(mar)* to get choppy **(b)** *(diente)* to rot **(c)** *(vino)* to turn sour **(d)** *(ropa)* to become moth-eaten **(e)** *(oxidarse)* to go rusty **(f)** *Fam (enfadarse)* to get annoyed o cross **(g)** *Fam (inyectarse droga)* to shoot up

picardía *nf* **(a)** *(astucia)* sharpness, craftiness **(b)** *(travesura)* naughty trick, mischief **(c)** *(atrevimiento)* brazenness

picardías *nm inv (prenda femenina)* negligee

picaresca *nf* **(a)** *Lit* picaresque literature **(b)** *(modo de vida)* roguery

picaresco, -a *adj* mischievous, roguish

pícaro, -a *nm,f* **(a)** *(astuto)* sly person, rogue **(b)** *(travieso)* rascal **(c)** *(atrevido)* brazen person

picarón, -ona *Fam* **1** *adj* roguish, mischievous
2 *nm,f* rogue, rascal

picatoste *nm* crouton

picazón *nf* **(a)** *(en el cuerpo)* itch **(b)** *Fam (inquietud)* uneasiness

picha *nf Esp Vulg* prick; *Fig* **hacerse la p. un lío** to get in a total goddamn muddle

pichi *nm Esp* sweater

pichichi *nm Esp Dep* top scorer

pichincha *nf RP Fam* snip, bargain

pichón *nm* **(a)** *(ave)* young pigeon **(b)** *Fam (apelativo cariñoso)* darling, sweetheart

pichula *nf Chile, Perú Vulg* prick, cock

picnic *(pl* **picnics)** *nm* picnic

pico *nm* **(a)** *(de ave)* beak
(b) *Fam (boca)* mouth; **¡cierra el p.!** shut your trap!; **darle al p.** to talk a lot; **irse del p.** to shoot one's mouth off; **ser o tener un p. de oro** to be a smooth talker, to have the gift of the gab
(c) *(punta, saliente)* corner
(d) *(herramienta)* pick, pickax
(e) *(cumbre)* peak
(f) *(cantidad indeterminada)* **cincuenta y p.** fifty-odd, fifty-something; **pesa diez kilos y p.** it weighs just over ten kilos; **llegó a las cinco y p.** he got there just after five; **le costó un p.** *(cantidad elevada)* it cost her a fortune
(g) *Fam (inyección de heroína)* fix; **meterse un p.** to give oneself a fix
(h) *Chile Vulg (pene)* cock, knob

picor *nm* itch; **tengo un p. en la espalda** my back itches, I've got an itchy back

picoso, -a *adj Méx* spicy, hot

picota *nf* (**a**) *(de ajusticiados)* pillory; *Fig* **poner a alguien en la p.** to pillory sb (**b**) *(cereza)* cherry

picotazo *nm* peck

picotear *vt* (**a**) *(ave)* to peck (**b**) *(comer)* to pick at

pictograma *nm* pictogram

pictórico, -a *adj* pictorial

picudo, -a *adj* pointed

pida *etc ver* **pedir**

pidiera *etc ver* **pedir**

pie *nm* (**a**) *(de persona)* foot; **a p.** on foot; **prefiero ir a p.** I'd rather walk *o* go on foot; **estar de** *o* **en p.** to be on one's feet *o* standing; **ponerse de** *o* **en p.** to stand up; **llevamos dos horas de p.** we've been on our feet for two hours; *Fig* **de pies a cabeza** from head to toe; **perder/no hacer p.** to go/to be out of one's depth; **p. de atleta** athlete's foot; **pies de cerdo** (pig's) trotters; **pies planos** flat feet
(**b**) *(de lámpara, micrófono)* stand; *(de copa)* stem; *(de montaña, árbol)* foot; **p. de foto** caption; *Inform* **p. de página** footer
(**c**) *Teatro* cue
(**d**) *(expresiones)* **al p. de la letra** to the letter, word for word; **al p. del cañón** ready for action; **andar con pies de plomo** to tread carefully; **a pies juntillas** unquestioningly; **a sus pies** at your service; **buscar (los) tres** *o* **cinco pies al gato** to overcomplicate matters; **con buen p.** on the right footing; **dar p. a alguien para que haga algo** to give sb cause to do sth; **el ciudadano de a p.** the man in the street; **en p. de igualdad** on an equal footing; **en p. de guerra** on a war footing; **levantarse con el p. izquierdo** to get out of bed on the wrong side; **no dar p. con bola** to get everything wrong; **no tener ni pies ni cabeza** to make no sense at all; **no tenerse de** *o* **en p.** *(por cansancio)* not to be able to stand up a minute longer; *Fig (por ser absurdo)* not to stand up; **pararle los pies a alguien** to put sb in their place; **poner pies en polvorosa** to make a run for it; *Esp* **saber de qué p. cojea alguien** to know sb's weaknesses; *Fig* **seguir en p.** *(propuesta)* to be still valid; **tener un p. en la tumba** to have one foot in the grave

piedad *nf* (**a**) *(compasión)* pity; **tener p. de** to take pity on (**b**) *(religiosidad)* piety (**c**) *Arte* Pietà

piedra *nf* (**a**) *(material, roca)* stone; **una casa/un muro de p.** a stone house/wall; **poner la primera p.** *(inaugurar)* to lay the foundation stone; *Fig* to lay the foundations; **dejar a alguien de p.** to stun sb; **no dejar p. sobre p.** to leave no stone standing; *Fam* **menos da una p.** it's better than nothing; **quedarse de p.** to be thunderstruck; *Fig* **tirar la p. y esconder la mano** to play the innocent; *también Fig* **p. angular** cornerstone; **p. pómez/preciosa** pumice/precious stone (**b**) *(de mechero)* flint (**c**) *(en vejiga, riñón, vesícula)* stone; **una p. en la vesícula** a gallstone

piel *nf* (**a**) *(epidermis)* skin; *Fig* **dejarse la p.** to sweat blood; *Fig* **jugarse la p.** to risk one's neck; *Fig* **ser de la p. del diablo** to be a little devil (**b**) *(pelo)* fur; **abrigo de p.** fur coat (**c**) *Esp, Méx (cuero)* leather; **cazadora/guantes de p.** leather jacket/gloves; **p. sintética** imitation leather (**d**) *(cáscara) (de cítricos)* peel; *(de manzana, plátano)* skin, peel

pienso 1 *ver* **pensar**
2 *nm* fodder

piercing ['pirsin] *(pl* **piercings)** *nm* body piercing; **hacerse un p. en el ombligo** to have one's navel pierced

pierda *etc ver* **perder**

pierna *nf* leg; **cruzar las piernas** to cross one's legs; **dormir a p. suelta** to sleep like a log; **estirar las piernas** to stretch one's legs; *Fam* **salir por piernas** to go haring off, to take to one's heels; **p. de cordero** *(plato)* gigot, leg of lamb; **p. ortopédica** artificial leg

pieza *nf* (**a**) *(pedazo, parte)* piece; *(de mecanismo)* part; **una p.**

de ajedrez a chess piece; **una p. de fruta** a piece of fruit; **un dos piezas** a two-piece suit; **dejar/quedarse de una p.** to leave/be thunderstruck; **p. de coleccionista** collector's item; **p. de museo** museum piece, exhibit; **p. de recambio** *o* **repuesto** spare part, extra (**b**) *(de pesca)* catch; *(de caza)* kill (**c**) *Irónico (persona)* **ser una buena p.** to be a fine one (**d**) *(habitación)* room (**e**) *(obra) (dramática)* play; *Mús* piece

pifia *nf Fam* blunder

pifiar *vt Fam* **pifiarla** to put one's foot in it

pigmentación *nf* pigmentation

pigmento *nm* pigment

pigmeo, -a *nm,f* pygmy

pija *nf esp RP Vulg (pene)* prick, cock

pijada *nf Esp Fam* (**a**) *(dicho)* **decir pijadas** to talk bull (**b**) *(cosa insignificante)* **discutieron por una p.** they fell out over something really daft

pijama *nm* pajamas

pijo, -a *Esp* **1** *adj Fam* posh
2 *nm,f Fam (persona)* rich kid
3 *nm muy Fam (pene)* prick, cock

pijotero, -a *adj Esp Fam* annoying, irritating

pila *nf* (**a**) *(generador)* battery; **funciona a** *o* **con pilas** it works *o* runs off batteries; *Fam Fig* **ponerse las pilas** to get moving *o* cracking; **p. alcalina** alkaline battery; **p. atómica** atomic pile; **p. recargable** rechargeable battery; **p. solar** solar cell (**b**) *(montón)* pile; **tiene una p. de deudas** he's up to his neck in debt (**c**) *(fregadero)* sink; **p. bautismal** (baptismal) font (**d**) *Arquit* pile

pilar *nm también Fig* pillar

pilastra *nf* pilaster

píldora *nf* *(pastilla)* pill; **la p.** *(anticonceptivo)* the pill; *Fam* **dorar la p.** to sugar the pill; **p. anticonceptiva** contraceptive pill

pileta *nf RP* swimming pool

pilila *nf Fam* peter

pillaje *nm* pillage

pillar 1 *vt* (**a**) *(coger, tomar, atrapar)* to catch; *Fam* **p. una pulmonía/un taxi** to catch pneumonia/a taxi (**b**) *(atropellar)* to knock down (**c**) *(chiste, explicación)* to get; **no lo pillo** I don't get it
2 *vi Esp (hallarse)* **me pilla lejos** it's out of the way for me; **me pilla de camino** it's on my way
3 pillarse *vpr* **pillarse los dedos** to catch one's fingers; *Fig* to get burned

pillastre *nmf Fam* rogue, crafty person

pillín, -ina *nm,f Fam* little scamp, rascal

pillo, -a 1 *adj* (**a**) *(travieso)* mischievous (**b**) *(astuto)* crafty
2 *nm,f* (**a**) *(pícaro)* rascal (**b**) *(astuto)* crafty person

pilón *nm* (**a**) *(pila) (para lavar)* basin; *(para animales)* trough (**b**) *(torre eléctrica)* pylon (**c**) *(pilar grande)* post (**d**) *Méx (regalo)* **si compra una docena lleva uno de p.** if you buy a dozen you get one thrown in for free (**e**) *RP,Ven Fam (gran cantidad)* **un p.** *o* **pilones de libros** stacks of books

pilotar *vt (avión)* to fly, to pilot; *(coche)* to drive; *(barco)* to steer

piloto 1 *nmf (de avión, barco)* pilot; *(de coche)* driver; **p. comercial** airline pilot; **p. de pruebas** test pilot
2 *nm (luz) (de coche)* taillight; *(de aparato)* pilot light; **p. automático** automatic pilot
3 *adj inv* pilot; **piso p.** show apartment; *TV* **programa p.** pilot (program); **proyecto p.** pilot project

piltra *nf Esp Fam* pit, bed

piltrafa *nf (de comida)* scrap; *Fam (persona débil)* wreck; *Fam (cosa inservible)* piece of junk; **estar hecho una p.** *(persona, coche)* to be a wreck; *(chaqueta, zapatos)* to be worn out

pimentón *nm* paprika

pimienta *nf* pepper; **p. blanca/negra** white/black pepper

pimiento *nm (fruto)* pepper, capsicum; *(planta)* pimiento, pepper plant; **p. morrón** sweet pepper; **p. verde** green pepper

pimpante *adj Fam* (**a**) *(satisfecho)* well-pleased (**b**) *(garboso)* swish, smart

pimpinela *nf* pimpernel

pimplar *Esp Fam* **1** *vi* to booze

2 pimplarse *vpr* **pimplarse una botella** to down one bottle

pimpollo *nm* (**a**) *(de rama, planta)* shoot; *(de flor)* bud (**b**) *Fam (persona atractiva)* gorgeous person

pin *(pl* **pins)** *nm* pin, (lapel) badge

pinacoteca *nf* art gallery

pináculo *nm* (**a**) *(de edificio)* pinnacle (**b**) *(juego de naipes)* pinochle

pinar *nm* pine wood *o* grove

pinaza *nf* pine needles

pincel *nm (para pintar)* paintbrush; *(para maquillar)* brush

pincelada *nf* brushstroke; *Fig* **a grandes pinceladas** in broad terms

pinchadiscos *nmf inv Esp* disc jockey

pinchar 1 *vt* (**a**) *(punzar)* to prick; *(rueda)* to puncture; *(globo, balón)* to burst (**b**) *(con chinchetas, alfileres)* **p. algo en la pared** to pin sth to the wall (**c**) *(inyectar)* **p. a alguien** to give sb an injection *o* a jab (**d**) *Fam (teléfono)* to tap (**e**) *Fam (irritar)* to wind up (**f**) *(incitar)* **p. a alguien para que haga algo** to prod sb into doing sth (**g**) *Esp Fam* **p. discos** to DJ

2 *vi* (**a**) *(rueda)* to get a puncture; **pinchó a cinco kilómetros de la meta** he got a puncture *o* flat tire five kilometers from the finish (**b**) *(barba)* to be prickly (**c**) *Fam (fracasar)* to be a flop; **pinchó con su última película** his latest movie has been a flop (**d**) *(expresiones)* **ni pincha ni corta** she cuts no ice; **p. en hueso** to go wide of the mark, to misfire

3 pincharse *vpr* (**a**) *(punzarse) (persona)* to prick oneself; *(rueda)* to get a puncture (**b**) *(irritarse)* to get annoyed (**c**) *(inyectarse)* **pincharse (algo)** *(medicamento)* to inject oneself (with sth); *Fam (droga)* to shoot up (with sth)

pinchazo *nm* (**a**) *(punzada)* prick (**b**) *(marca)* needle mark (**c**) *(de neumático, balón)* puncture, flat

pinche 1 *nmf* kitchen boy, *f* maid

2 *adj Méx Fam* damn

pinchito *nm Esp (tapa)* bar snack, aperitif

pincho *nm* (**a**) *(punta)* (sharp) point (**b**) *(espina) (de planta)* prickle, thorn (**c**) *(varilla)* pointed stick (**d**) *Esp (tapa)* bar snack, aperitif; **p. moruno** shish kebab

pindonguear *vi Esp Fam* to loaf around

pinga *nf Andes, Carib, Méx muy Fam* prick

pingajo *nm Esp Fam* rag

pingo *nm* (**a**) *Esp Fam (pingajo)* rag (**b**) *(mamarracho)* **ir hecho un p.** to look a state, to be dressed in rags (**c**) *Fam (persona despreciable)* stinker, dog

pingonear *vi Fam* to loaf around

ping-pong [pim'pon] *nm* ping-pong, table tennis

pingüe *adj* plentiful; **pingües beneficios** fat profit

pingüino *nm* penguin

pinitos *nmpl Fam* **hacer sus p. en fotografía** to dabble in photography; **desde sus primeros p. como cantante ha mejorado muchísimo** she's improved enormously since she first started out as a singer

pino *nm* pine; *Esp Fam* **en el quinto p.** way out in the sticks; *Esp* **hacer el p.** to do a handstand

pinsapo *nm* Spanish fir

pinta *nf* (**a**) *(lunar)* spot (**b**) *(aspecto)* appearance; **tener p. de algo** to look *o* seem sth; **tiene buena p.** it looks good (**c**) *(unidad de medida)* pint (**d**) *Méx (pintada)* graffiti (**e**) *Méx* **irse de p.** *(hacer novillos)* to play hooky

pintada *nf* (**a**) *(en pared)* graffiti (**b**) *(ave)* guinea fowl

pintado, -a *adj* (**a**) *(objeto)* **recién p.** *(en letrero)* wet paint (**b**) *(maquillado)* made-up; **le gusta ir muy pintada** she likes to wear a lot of makeup (**c**) *(moteado)* speckled (**d**) *(expresiones)* **es capaz de timar al más p.** there's nobody he couldn't take in; **eso le puede pasar al más p.** it could happen to anyone *o* to the best of us; **venir que ni p.** to be just the thing

pintalabios *nm inv* lipstick

pintamonas *nmf inv Esp Fam Pey* dauber

pintar 1 *vt* (**a**) *(cuadro, pared)* to paint; **p. algo de verde/azul** to paint sth green/blue (**b**) *(dibujar)* to draw; *(con lápices de colores)* to color; **pintó una casa** she drew a house (**c**) *(describir)* to paint, to describe; **me pintó la escena con pelos y señales** he painted the scene in graphic detail

2 *vi* (**a**) *(con pintura)* to paint (**b**) *Fam (significar, importar)* to count; **aquí no pinto nada** there's no place for me here; **¿qué pinto yo en este asunto?** where do I come in?

3 pintarse *vpr* (**a**) *(maquillarse)* to make oneself up; **pintarse las uñas** to paint one's nails (**b**) *Fam* **pintárselas solo para algo** to be a past master at sth

pintarrajear *vt Fam* to daub

pinto, -a *adj* speckled, spotted

pintor, -ora *nm,f* painter; **p. de brocha gorda** painter and decorator; *Pey* dauber

pintoresco, -a *adj (bonito)* picturesque; *Fig (extravagante)* colorful

pintura *nf* (**a**) *(técnica, cuadro)* painting; **la p. renacentista** Renaissance painting; *Fig* **no poder ver a alguien ni en p.** not to be able to stand the sight of sb; **p. a la acuarela** watercolor; **p. al fresco** fresco; **p. mural** mural painting; **p. al óleo** oil painting; **p. rupestre** cave painting (**b**) *(materia líquida)* paint; **p. plástica** emulsion (paint) (**c**) *(lápiz)* color(ed) pencil; *(de cera)* crayon

pinza *nf* (**a**) *(de tender ropa)* clothespin; *(para el pelo)* bobby pin; **p.** *o* **pinzas** *(instrumento)* tweezers; *Fam Fig* **coger algo con pinzas** to handle sth with great care (**b**) *(de animal)* pincer, claw (**c**) *(en ropa) (cosida)* dart; *(en pantalones)* pleat

piña *nf* (**a**) *(fruta)* pineapple; **p. colada** piña colada (**b**) *(del pino)* pinecone (**c**) *(de gente)* close-knit group; **formar una p.** to rally around (**d**) *Fam (golpe)* knock, bash; **darse una p.** to have a crash

piñata *nf* = suspended pot full of candy which blindfolded children try to break open with sticks at parties

piñón *nm* (**a**) *(fruto)* pine nut *o* kernel; **estar a partir un p. con alguien** to be hand in glove with sb (**b**) *(rueda dentada)* pinion; **ser de p. fijo** to be fixed *o* rigid

pío¹ *interj* cheep; **¡p., p.!** cheep, cheep!; *Fig* **no decir ni p.** not to make a peep

pío², -a *adj* pious

piojo *nm* louse

piojoso, -a 1 *adj (con piojos)* lousy, covered in lice; *Fig (sucio)* flea-bitten, filthy

2 *nm,f (con piojos)* louse-ridden person; *Fig (sucio)* scuzzball

piola *adj RP Fam* (**a**) *(persona)* nice (**b**) *(lugar)* cozy

piolet *(pl* **piolets)** *nm* ice ax

pionero, -a *nm,f* pioneer

piorrea *nf* pyorrhea

pipa *nf* (**a**) *(para fumar)* pipe; **fumar en p.** to smoke a pipe (**b**) *(pepita)* seed, pip; **pipas (de girasol)** sunflower seeds *(sold as a snack)* (**c**) *(tonel)* barrel (**d**) **pasarlo** *o* **pasárselo p.** to have a whale of a time

pipermín *nm* peppermint liqueur

pipeta *nf* pipette

pipí *nm Fam* pee; **hacer p.** to have a pee

pipiolo *nm Fam* (**a**) *(muchacho)* youngster (**b**) *(principiante)* novice, beginner

pique 1 *ver* **picar**

2 *nm* (**a**) *(enfado)* grudge; **tener un p. con alguien** to have a grudge against sb (**b**) *(rivalidad)* rivalry (**c**) **irse a p.** *(barco)* to sink; *(negocio)* to go under; *(plan)* to fail (**d**) *Am (de pelota)* bounce

piqué *nm* piqué

piquera *nf Méx (antro)* dive, seedy bar

piqueta *nf (herramienta)* pickax; *(en tienda de campaña)* tent peg

piquete *nm* (**a**) *(herramienta)* peg, stake (**b**) *(grupo)* **p. de ejecución** firing squad; **p. (de huelga)** picket (**c**) *Méx Fam (picadura, pinchazo) (de aguja)* prick; *(de insecto)* sting; *(dolor)* stabbing pain

pira *nf* pyre

pirado, -a *Fam* **1** *adj* crazy
2 *nm,f* loony

piragua *nf* canoe

piragüismo *nm* canoeing

piramidal *adj* pyramid-shaped, pyramidal

pirámide *nf* pyramid

piraña *nf* piranha

pirarse *vpr Esp, RP Fam* to clear off; **¡nos piramos!** we're off!; **¿ya te piras?** you off, then?

pirata **1** *adj* (**a**) *(barco, ataque)* pirate (**b**) *(radio, edición, vídeo)* pirate; *(casete, grabación)* bootleg (**c**) *Am (profesional, servicio)* cowboy
2 *nmf* (**a**) *(del mar)* pirate; **p. del aire** hijacker; **p. informático** cracker, hacker (**b**) *Am (mal profesional)* cowboy

piratear **1** *vi* (**a**) *(asaltar barcos)* to be involved in piracy (**b**) *Inform* to hack
2 *vt* (**a**) *(propiedad intelectual)* to pirate (**b**) *Inform* to hack into

pirateo *nm Fam (de programa informático, de vídeos)* piracy

piratería *nf* piracy; **p. aérea** hijacking; **p. informática** *(copias ilegales)* software piracy; *(acceso no autorizado)* hacking; **p. musical** music piracy

pirenaico, -a *adj* Pyrenean

pírex *nm* Pyrex®

pirindolo *nm Fam* decorative knob

Pirineos *nmpl* **los P.** the Pyrenees

piripi *adj Fam* tipsy

pirita *nf* pyrite

piro *nm Esp Fam* **darse el p.** to split

pirograbado *nm (técnica)* pokerwork

piromanía *nf* pyromania

pirómano, -a **1** *adj* pyromaniacal
2 *nm,f* pyromaniac

piropear *vt Fam* = to make flirtatious comments to, to give a wolf whistle at

piropo *nm Fam* flirtatious remark

pirotecnia *nf* pyrotechnics *(singular)*

pirotécnico, -a **1** *adj* firework; **un montaje p.** a firework display
2 *nm,f* firework specialist

pirrar *Fam* **1** *vt* **me pirran las albóndigas** I just adore *o* love meatballs
2 **pirrarse** *vpr* **p. por algo/alguien** to be dead keen on sth/sb

pírrico, -a *adj* Pyrrhic

pirueta *nf* pirouette; *Fig* **hacer piruetas** *(esfuerzo)* to perform miracles

piruja *nf Col, Méx muy Fam (prostituta)* whore, hooker

pirula *nf Esp Fam* (**a**) *(jugarreta)* dirty trick (**b**) *(escándalo)* **montar una p.** to make *o* cause a scene (**c**) *(maniobra ilegal)* **hacer una p.** to break the traffic regulations

piruleta *nf Esp* lollipop

pirulí *(pl* **pirulís** *o* **pirulíes**) *nm* lollipop

pis *nm Fam* pee; **hacer p.** to have a pee; **hacerse p.** *(tener ganas)* to be dying *o* bursting for a pee

Pisa *n* Pisa

pisada *nf* (**a**) *(acción)* footstep; **seguir las pisadas de alguien** to follow in sb's footsteps (**b**) *(huella)* footprint

pisadura *nf* footprint

pisapapeles *nm inv* paperweight

pisar **1** *vt* (**a**) *(con el pie)* to tread on; **p. el freno** to put one's foot on the brake; **prohibido p. el césped** *(en cartel)* keep off the grass; *Fig* **nunca he pisado su casa** I've never set foot in her house (**b**) *(despreciar)* to trample on (**c**) *(anticiparse)* **p. un contrato a alguien** to beat sb to a contract; **p. una idea a alguien** to think of something before sb; **el periódico rival les pisó la noticia** the rival paper stole *o* pinched the story from them, the rival paper got in first with the news
2 *vi* to tread, to step; **pisa con cuidado** tread carefully; *Fig* **venir pisando fuerte** to be on the road to success

pisciano, -a *Am* **1** *adj* Pisces; **ser p.** to be (a) Pisces
2 *nm,f* Pisces, Piscean

piscícola *adj* piscicultural

piscicultor, -ora *nm,f* fish farmer

piscicultura *nf* fish farming

piscifactoría *nf* fish farm

piscina *nf* swimming pool; **p. cubierta/descubierta** indoor/outdoor swimming pool

Piscis **1** *nm (zodiaco)* Pisces; *Esp* **ser P.** to be (a) Pisces
2 *nmf Esp (persona)* Pisces

piscolabis *nm inv Esp Fam* snack

piso *nm* (**a**) *(planta) (de edificio)* floor; *(de autobús)* deck; **primer p.** second floor; **un autobús de dos pisos** a double-decker bus (**b**) *(suelo) (de habitación)* floor; *(de carretera)* surface (**c**) *(capa)* layer; **un sandwich de dos pisos** a double-decker sandwich (**d**) *Esp (apartamento)* apartment; **p. franco** safe house; **p. piloto** show apartment; **pisos tutelados** supported accommodation

pisotear *vt* (**a**) *(con el pie)* to trample on (**b**) *(humillar)* to scorn (**c**) *(desobedecer)* to trample over

pisotón *nm* stamp *(of the foot)*; **darle un p. a alguien** to stamp on sb's foot

pista *nf* (**a**) *(carretera)* unsurfaced road; **p. forestal** forest track; **p. de tierra** dirt road *o* track (**b**) *(superficie, terreno) (de tenis, squash)* court; *(de atletismo, ciclismo)* track; **p. de aterrizaje** runway; **p. de baile** dance floor; **p. de cemento** *(en tenis)* hard court; **p. de esquí** ski slope; **p. de hielo** ice rink; **p. de hierba** *(en tenis)* grass court; **p. de patinaje** skating rink; **p. de tierra batida** *(en tenis)* clay court (**c**) *(indicio)* clue; **te daré una p.** I'll give you a clue (**d**) *(rastro)* trail, track; **estar sobre la p.** to be on the trail *o* track; **seguir la p. a alguien** to be on sb's trail (**e**) *(en grabación)* track

pistacho *nm* pistachio

pistilo *nm* pistil

pisto *nm* ratatouille; *Esp Fam* **darse p.** to be bigheaded

pistola *nf* (**a**) *(arma) (con cilindro)* gun; *(sin cilindro)* pistol; **p. de agua** water pistol (**b**) *(pulverizador)* spray gun; **pintar a p.** to spray-paint (**c**) *(herramienta)* gun (**d**) *(de pan)* French bread

pistolera *nf* (**a**) *(funda)* holster (**b**) *Fam* **pistoleras** *(celulitis)* saddlebags

pistolero, -a *nm,f (persona)* gunman

pistoletazo *nm* pistol shot; **p. de salida** shot from the starter's gun

pistón *nm* (**a**) *Mec* piston (**b**) *Mús (corneta)* cornet; *(llave)* key (**c**) *(de arma)* percussion cap

pita *nf* agave

pitada *nf* (**a**) *(silbidos)* whistling (**b**) *Am Fam (de cigarrillo)* drag, puff

pitagorín, -ina *nm,f Fam* brain

pitanza *nf* (**a**) *(ración de comida)* daily rations (**b**) *Fam (alimento)* grub

pitar 1 vt (**a**) (arbitrar) (partido) to referee; (falta) to blow for (**b**) (abuchear) **p. a alguien** to whistle at sb in disapproval (**c**) Am Fam (cigarrillo) to puff (on)

2 vi (**a**) (tocar el pito) to blow a whistle; (del coche) to toot one's horn (**b**) (funcionar) (cosa) to work; (persona) to get on (**c**) Esp Fam **salir/irse pitando** to rush out/off; **venir pitando** to come rushing

pitido nm (con pito) whistle; (de aparato electrónico) beep, bleep; **los pitidos de los coches** the honking of car horns

pitillera nf cigarette case

pitillo nm (**a**) (cigarrillo) cigarette (**b**) Col (paja) (drinking) straw

pito nm (**a**) (silbato) whistle (**b**) (claxon) horn (**c**) Fam (cigarrillo) fag (**d**) Fam (pene) peter (**e**) esp Méx Vulg (pene) cock (**f**) (expresiones) **entre pitos y flautas** what with one thing and another; (**no**) **me importa un p.** I couldn't give a damn; **por pitos o por flautas** for one reason or another; **tomar a alguien por el p. del sereno** not to take sb seriously

pitón 1 nm (**a**) (cuerno) horn (**b**) (pitorro) spout

2 nf (serpiente) python

pitonisa nf fortune-teller

pitorrearse vpr Esp Fam **p. de alguien** to make fun of sb

pitorreo nm Esp making fun, joking; **tomarse algo a p.** to treat sth as a joke

pitorro nm spout

pitote nm (jaleo) row, fuss; **armar un p.** to kick up a row o fuss

pitufo, -a nm,f (**a**) Fam (persona pequeña) shorty; (niño) rug rat, ankle biter (**b**) **los pitufos®** the Smurfs®

pituitaria nf pituitary gland

pívot (pl **pivots**) nmf (en baloncesto) pivot

pivotar vi Dep to pivot

pivote nmf (**a**) (eje) pivot (**b**) Dep pivot

píxel nm pixel

pizarra nf (**a**) (roca, material) slate (**b**) (encerado) chalkboard

pizarrón nm Am (en aula) chalkboard

pizca nf Fam (poco) tiny bit; (de sal) pinch; **ni p.** not one bit

pizpireta adj Fam (niña, mujer) spirited, zippy

pizza ['pitsa] nf pizza

pizzería [pitse'ria] nf pizzeria, pizza parlor

placa nf (**a**) (lámina) plate; Med **p. dental** dental plaque; **p. de hielo** black ice, icy patch; **p. solar** solar panel; **p. de vitrocerámica** (de cocina) ceramic burner (**b**) (inscripción) plaque; (de policía) badge (**c**) Aut **p. (de matrícula)** license plate (**d**) Geol plate (**e**) Inform board; **p. lógica** logic board; **p. madre** motherboard

placaje nm Dep tackle

placar [59] vt Dep to tackle

placebo nm placebo

placenta nf placenta

placentero, -a adj pleasant

placer [48] **1** nm pleasure; **un viaje de p.** a pleasure trip; **ha sido un p. (conocerle)** it has been a pleasure meeting you; **es un p. ayudarte** it's a pleasure to help you

2 vt to please; **nos place comunicarle que…** we are pleased to inform you that…; **si me place** if I want to, if I feel like it

plácet (pl **plácets**) nm Formal (aprobación) approval; **dar el p. a un embajador** to accept an ambassador's credentials

placidez nf (de persona) placidness; (de día, vida, conversación) peacefulness

plácido, -a adj (persona) placid; (día, vida, conversación) peaceful

plafón nm Arquit soffit

plaga nf (**a**) (de insectos) plague; **p. de langostas** plague of locusts (**b**) (de gente) swarm (**c**) (epidemia) plague; **una de las plagas modernas** one of the plagues of modern society

plagado, -a adj (de insectos) infested (**de** with); **p. de dificultades** beset o plagued with difficulties; **la ciudad está plagada de turistas** the city is overrun with tourists

plagar [38] vt **p. de** (propaganda) to swamp with; (moscas) to infest with

plagiar vt (**a**) (copiar) to plagiarize (**b**) CAm, Col, Perú, Ven (secuestrar) to kidnap

plagiario, -a nm,f CAm, Col, Perú, Ven kidnapper

plagio nm (**a**) (copia) plagiarism (**b**) CAm, Col, Perú, Ven (secuestro) kidnapping

plaguicida 1 adj pesticidal

2 nm pesticide

plan nm (**a**) (proyecto, programa) plan; **hacer planes** to plan; **p. de adelgazamiento** diet; **p. de emergencia** contingency plan; **p. de estudios** syllabus; **p. de pensiones** pension plan (**b**) Fam (ligue) date (**c**) Fam (modo, forma) **a todo p.** in the greatest luxury, with no expense spared; **lo dijo en p. serio** he was serious about it; **si te pones en ese p.…** if you're going to be like that about it…; **se puso en p. violento** he got o became violent; **no es p.** it's just not on; **¡vaya p. de vida!** what a life!

plana nf (**a**) (página) page; **en primera p.** on the front page (**b**) (llanura) plain (**c**) Mil **p. mayor** staff

plancha nf (**a**) (para planchar) iron; **pasar la p. a algo** to give sth a quick ironing; **odio la p.** I hate ironing; **esas camisas necesitan una p.** those shirts need ironing; **p. de vapor** steam iron (**b**) (para cocinar) grill; **a la p.** grilled (**c**) (placa) plate; (de madera) sheet (**d**) Fam (metedura de pata) boo-boo, blunder (**e**) (en fútbol) dangerous tackle (with cleats showing) (**f**) Imprenta plate (**g**) (al nadar) **hacer la p.** to float on one's back

planchado nm ironing

planchar vt to iron

planchazo nm Fam boo-boo, blunder

plancton nm plankton

planeador nm glider

planeadora nf (lancha) speedboat

planear 1 vt to plan

2 vi (**a**) (hacer planes) to plan (**b**) (en el aire) to glide

planeta nm planet

planetario, -a 1 adj (**a**) (de un planeta) planetary (**b**) (mundial) world; **a nivel p.** on a global scale

2 nm planetarium

planicie nf plain

planificación nf planning; **p. familiar** family planning

planificar [59] vt to plan

planilla nf Am (formulario) form; (nómina) payroll

planisferio nm planisphere

planning ['planin] (pl **plannings**) nm scheduling

plano, -a 1 adj flat

2 nm (**a**) (diseño, mapa) plan; (de ciudad) map; **p. de calles** street map (**b**) (nivel, aspecto) level (**c**) (en pintura) **primer p.** foreground; **segundo p.** background (**d**) Cine shot; **primer p.** closeup; también Fig **en segundo p.** in the background; **p. general** pan shot (**e**) Mat plane

3 **de plano** loc adv (golpear) right, directly; (negar, rechazar) flatly; Fam **cantar de p.** to make a full confession

planta nf (**a**) (vegetal) plant; **p. de interior** house plant (**b**) (fábrica) plant; **p. depuradora** purification plant; **p. desalinizadora** desalination plant; **p. de envase** o **envasadora** packaging plant; **p. de montaje** assembly plant (**c**) (piso) floor; **p. baja** first floor; **primera p.** second floor (**d**) (del pie) sole (**e**) (expresiones) **de nueva p.** brand new; **tener buena p.** to be good-looking

plantación nf (**a**) (terreno) plantation; **p. de azúcar** sugar plantation (**b**) (acción) planting

plantado, -a adj (**a**) (planta, árbol) planted; **un terreno p. de trigo** a field planted with wheat (**b**) (expresiones) Fam dejar p. a alguien *(no acudir)* to stand sb up; **ser bien p.** to be good-looking

plantar 1 *vt* (a) *(sembrar)* to plant (**de** with) (**b**) *(fijar) (tienda de campaña)* to pitch; *(poste)* to put in (**c**) *Fam (beso)* to plant; *(bofetada)* to deal, to land (**d**) *Fam (decir con brusquedad)* **le plantó cuatro frescas** she gave him a piece of her mind (**e**) *Fam (dejar plantado)* **p. a alguien** *(no acudir)* to stand sb up; *(novio)* to ditch sb, to dump sb (**f**) *Fam (construcción, mueble, objeto)* to plunk; **plantó los pies en el sofá** she plunked her feet on the sofa

2 plantarse *vpr* (a) *(ponerse, colocarse)* to plant oneself (**b**) *(en un sitio con rapidez)* **plantarse en** to get to, to make it to; **nos podemos p. ahí en quince minutos** we'll be able to get there in fifteen minutes (**c**) *(en una actitud)* **plantarse en algo** to stick to sth, to insist on sth; **se ha plantado y dice que no quiere venir** he's standing firm *o* digging his heels in and refusing to come (**d**) *(en naipes)* to stick

plante *nm* (a) *(para protestar)* protest (**b**) *(plantón)* **dar** *o* **hacer un p. a alguien** to stand sb up

planteamiento *nm* (a) *(exposición)* raising, posing (**b**) *(enfoque)* approach

plantear 1 *vt* (a) *(exponer) (problema)* to pose; *(posibilidad, dificultad, duda)* to raise; **me planteó sus preocupaciones** he put his concerns to me, he raised his concerns with me (**b**) *(proponer) (solución, posibilidad)* to propose; **plantean una solución radical al cambio climático** they are proposing a radical solution to climate change

2 plantearse *vpr* **plantearse algo** to consider sth, to think about sth; **nunca me había planteado esa posibilidad** I had never considered that possibility

plantel *nm* (a) *(criadero)* nursery bed (**b**) *(de gente)* team

planteo *nm Am (propuesta)* idea

plantígrado, -a *adj & nm Zool* plantigrade

plantilla *nf* (a) *(de empresa)* staff; **estar en p.** to be on the staff (**b**) *(para zapatos)* insole (**c**) *(patrón)* pattern, template

plantío *nm* plot (of land)

plantón *nm Fam* **dar un p. a alguien** to stand sb up

plañidero, -a *adj* plaintive, whining

plañido *nm* moan

plañir 1 *vt* to bewail

2 *vi* to moan, to wail

plaqueta *nf Biol* platelet

plasma *nm* plasma

plasmar 1 *vt* (a) *(reflejar) (sentimientos)* to give expression to; *(realidad)* to reflect (**b**) *(modelar)* to shape, to mold

2 plasmarse *vpr* to emerge, to take shape

plasta 1 *adj Esp Fam* **ser p.** to be a pain; **un tío p.** a real bore, a pain in the neck

2 *nmf Esp Fam (pesado)* pain, drag

3 *nf* (a) *(cosa blanda)* mess (**b**) *Fam (cosa mal hecha)* botch-up

plastelina® *nf* Plasticine®

plástica *nf* plastic art

plasticidad *nf* (a) *(moldeabilidad)* plasticity (**b**) *(expresividad)* expressiveness

plástico, -a 1 *adj* (a) *(moldeable)* plastic (**b**) *(expresivo)* expressive

2 *nm* (a) *(material)* plastic (**b**) *Fam (tarjetas de crédito)* plastic (money)

plastificar [59] *vt (carné, tarjeta)* to cover in plastic

plastilina® *nf* Plasticine®

plata *nf* (a) *(metal)* silver; *Fam* **hablar en p.** to speak bluntly; **p. de ley** sterling silver; **p. maciza** solid silver (**b**) *(objetos de plata)* silverware (**c**) *Am (dinero)* money

plataforma *nf* (a) *(superficie elevada, estrado)* platform; **p. de lanzamiento** launch pad; **p. petrolífera** oil rig (**b**) *(punto de partida)* launching pad (**c**) *Pol* platform, program (**d**) *Geol* shelf; **p. continental** continental shelf

platanal, platanar *nm* banana plantation

platanera *nf*, **platanero** *nm* banana tree

plátano *nm* (a) *(fruta)* banana (**b**) *(árbol de sombra)* plane tree

platea *nf* orchestra

plateado, -a *adj* (a) *(con plata)* silver-plated (**b**) *(color)* silvery

plateresco, -a *adj* plateresque

platería *nf* (a) *(arte, oficio)* silversmithing (**b**) *(tienda)* jeweler's

platero, -a *nm,f* silversmith

plática *nf* (a) *CAm, Méx (charla)* talk, chat (**b**) *Rel* sermon

platicador, -ora *adj CAm, Méx* conversational

platicar [59] **1** *vi CAm, Méx* to talk, to chat

2 *vt* to tell

platija *nf (pez)* plaice

platillo *nm* (a) *(plato pequeño)* small plate; *(de taza)* saucer; **p. volador,** *Esp* **p. volante** flying saucer (**b**) *(de una balanza)* pan (**c**) *Mús* **platillos** cymbals

platina *nf* (a) *(de casete)* cassette deck (**b**) *(de microscopio)* slide

platino *nm (metal)* platinum; *Aut & Mec* **platinos** contact points

plato *nm* (a) *(recipiente)* plate, dish; **lavar los platos** to wash the dishes; *Fig* **pagar los platos rotos** to carry the can; *Fig* **parece que no ha roto un p. en su vida** he looks as if butter wouldn't melt in his mouth; **p. hondo** *o* **sopero** soup dish *o* plate; **p. llano** plate; **p. de postre** dessert plate

(**b**) *(parte de una comida)* course; **primer p.** first course, appetizer; **de primer p.** for appetizer; **segundo p.** second course, main course; **p. fuerte** *(en una comida)* main course; *Fig* main part; **su actuación es el p. fuerte de la noche** her performance is the night's main event; **p. principal** main course

(**c**) *(comida)* dish; **p. combinado** = single-course meal which usually consists of meat or fish accompanied by French fries and vegetables; **p. del día** dish of the day; **p. precocinado** precooked meal; **p. preparado** ready-made meal; **p. típico** typical dish

(**d**) *(de tocadiscos, microondas)* turntable

(**e**) *(de bicicleta)* chain wheel

(**f**) *Dep* clay pigeon

plató *nm* set

platónico, -a *adj* platonic

platudo, -a *adj Am Fam* loaded, rolling in it

plausibilidad *nf* (a) *(admisibilidad)* acceptability (**b**) *(posibilidad)* plausibility

plausible *adj* (a) *(admisible)* acceptable (**b**) *(posible)* plausible

playa *nf* (a) *(en el mar)* beach; **ir a la p. de vacaciones** to go on vacation to the seaside (**b**) *Am* **p. de estacionamiento** *(en ciudad)* parking lot

play-back ['pleiβak] *(pl* play-backs*) nm* **hacer p.** to mime (the lyrics)

playboy [plei'βoi] *(pl* playboys*) nm* playboy

playera *nf* (a) *(zapato) (para la playa)* canvas shoe; *(de deporte)* tennis shoe (**b**) *Méx (camiseta)* T-shirt

playero, -a *adj* beach; **toalla playera** beach towel

plaza *nf* (a) *(en una población)* square; **la p. del pueblo** the town *o* village square; **p. mayor** main square (**b**) *(sitio)* place; **tenemos plazas limitadas** there are a limited number of places available; **p. de aparcamiento** parking space; **p. de garaje** parking space *(in a private garage)* (**c**) *(asiento)* seat; **un vehículo de dos plazas** a two-seater vehicle (**d**) *(puesto de trabajo)* position, job; **está buscando una p. de médico** she's looking for a position as a doctor; **p. vacante** vacancy (**e**) *(mercado)* market, marketplace (**f**) *Taurom* **p. (de toros)** bullring (**g**) *Com (zona)* area (**h**) *(fortificación)* **p. fuerte** stronghold

plazo *nm* (a) *(de tiempo)* period (of time); **en el p. de un mes** within a month; **mañana termina el p. de inscripción** the deadline for registration is tomorrow; **tenemos de p. hasta**

el domingo we have until Sunday; **a corto/medio/largo p.** in the short/medium/long term; **una solución a corto/ largo p.** a short-/long-term solution; **en breve p.** within a short time; Com **p. de entrega** delivery time (**b**) (de dinero) installment; **comprar a plazos** to buy on an installment plan; **pagar a plazos** to pay in installments; **p. mensual** monthly installment

plazoleta, plazuela nf small square

pleamar nf high tide

plebe 1 nf **la p.** the plebs
  2 nmf Méx Fam (niño) kid

plebeyo, -a adj (**a**) Hist plebeian (**b**) (vulgar) common

plebiscito nm plebiscite

plegable adj collapsible, foldaway; (silla) folding

plegar [43] **1** vt (papel) to fold; (mesita, hamaca) to fold away
  2 plegarse vpr **plegarse a algo** to give in o yield to sth

plegaria nf prayer

pleitear vi Der to litigate, to conduct a lawsuit

pleitesía nf homage; **rendir p. a alguien** to pay homage to sb

pleito nm (**a**) Der (litigio) legal action, lawsuit; (disputa) dispute; **poner un p. (a alguien)** to take legal action (against sb) (**b**) Am (discusión) argument

plenario, -a adj plenary

plenilunio nm full moon

plenipotenciario, -a 1 adj plenipotentiary
  2 nm,f envoy

plenitud nf (**a**) (apogeo) completeness, fullness; **en la p. de** at the height of (**b**) (abundancia) abundance

pleno, -a 1 adj (**a**) (completo) full, complete; **en p. uso de sus facultades** in full command of his faculties; **en plena forma** on top form; **la reunión en p.** the meeting as a whole, everyone at the meeting; **miembro de p. derecho** full member; **p. empleo** full employment; **plenos poderes** plenary powers (**b**) (para enfatizar) **en p. día** in broad daylight; **en p. invierno** in the middle of winter; **en plena naturaleza** in the middle of the country(side); **en plena guerra** in the middle of the war; **le dio en plena cara** he hit him right in the face
  2 nm (**a**) (reunión) plenary meeting (**b**) Esp (en las quinielas) full claim (14 correct forecasts); **p. al quince** full claim (14 correct forecasts plus bonus)

pletina nf cassette deck

pletórico, -a adj **p. de felicidad** radiant with happiness; **p. de salud** bursting with health

pleura nf pleural membrane

pleuresía nf Med pleurisy

plexiglás® nm inv Plexiglas®

pléyade nf (conjunto) cluster

pliego 1 ver **plegar**
  2 nm (**a**) (de papel, de cartulina) sheet (**b**) (carta, documento) sealed document o letter; **p. de condiciones** specifications; **p. de descargos** list of rebuttals (**c**) Imprenta signature

pliegue nm (**a**) (gen) & Geol fold (**b**) (en un plisado) pleat

plinto nm Dep vaulting box

plisado nm pleating

plisar vt to pleat

plomada nf plumb line

plomería nf Méx, RP,Ven plumber's

plomero nm Méx, RP,Ven plumber

plomizo, -a adj (color, cielo) leaden

plomo nm (**a**) (metal) lead; **sin p.** (gasolina) unleaded; Fig **caer a p.** to fall o drop like a stone (**b**) (pieza de metal) lead weight (**c**) (fusible) fuse (**d**) Fam (pelmazo) bore, drag

plóter (pl **ploters**), **plotter** (pl **plotters**) nm Inform plotter

pluma 1 nf (**a**) (de ave) feather; **un sombrero de plumas** a feathered hat (**b**) (para escribir) (fountain) pen; (de ave) quill

(pen); Carib, Méx (bolígrafo) (ballpoint) pen; **p. estilográfica** fountain pen (**c**) Fig (estilo de escribir) style; (escritor) writer (**d**) Carib, Col, Méx (grifo) faucet (**e**) Fam **tener p.** (persona) to be camp
  2 adj inv Dep featherweight; **peso p.** featherweight

plumaje nm (**a**) (de ave) plumage (**b**) (adorno) plume

plumazo nm stroke of the pen; **de un p.** (al tachar) with a stroke of one's pen; Fig (al hacer algo) in one fell swoop, at a stroke

plúmbeo, -a adj tedious, heavy

plum-cake [plun'keik] nm Esp fruitcake

plumero nm feather duster; Fam Fig **se le ve el p.** you can see through him

plumier (pl **plumiers**) nm pencil box

plumífero nm (anorak) feather-lined anorak

plumilla nf, **plumin** nm nib

plumón nm (**a**) (de ave) down (**b**) Méx (para escribir) felt-tip pen

plural 1 adj (**a**) (múltiple) pluralistic (**b**) Gram plural
  2 nm Gram plural

pluralidad nf diversity

pluralismo nm pluralism

pluralizar [14] vi to generalize

pluricelular adj multicellular

pluriempleado, -a1 adj **estar p.** to have more than one job
  2 nm,f = person with more than one job

pluriempleo nm **hacer p.** to have more than one job

pluripartidismo nm multiparty system

pluripartidista adj (democracia, sistema) multiparty

plurivalente adj polyvalent

plus nm bonus; **p. de peligrosidad** hazardous-duty pay; **p. de productividad** productivity bonus

pluscuamperfecto adj & nm pluperfect

plusmarca nf record

plusmarquista nmf record-holder

plusvalía nf Econ appreciation, added value

plutocracia nf plutocracy

Plutón n Pluto

plutonio nm plutonium

pluvial adj rain; **régimen p.** annual rainfall pattern

pluviómetro nm rain gauge

pluviosidad nf rainfall

pluvioso, -a adj Formal rainy

PM nf (abrev de **policía militar**) MP

p.m. (abrev de **post meridiem**) pm

PNB nm (abrev de **producto nacional bruto**) GNP

PNN nmf (abrev de **profesor no numerario**) Esp Antes = college lecturer who does not have tenure

PNV nm (abrev de **Partido Nacionalista Vasco**) = Basque nationalist party to the right of the political spectrum

p.o., p/o (abrev de **por orden**) pp

población nf (**a**) (ciudad) town, city; (pueblo) village (**b**) (personas, animales) population; **p. activa/flotante** work-ing/transient population (**c**) (acción de poblar) settlement, populating

poblado, -a 1 adj (**a**) (habitado) inhabited; **una zona muy poblada** a densely populated area (**b**) (lleno) full; (barba, cejas) bushy
  2 nm settlement

poblador, -ora nm,f (habitante) inhabitant; (colono) settler

poblano, -a1 adj of/from Puebla
  2 nm,f person from Puebla

poblar [63] **1** vt (**a**) (establecerse en) to settle, to colonize (**b**) (habitar) to inhabit; **pueblan esa laguna muchas espe-cies** the lagoon is home to a great variety of species (**c**) (llenar) **p. (de)** (plantas, árboles) to plant (with); (peces) to stock (with)

2 poblarse *vpr* to fill up (**de** with); **la zona se pobló de aves tropicales** the area was colonized by tropical birds

pobre 1 *adj* (**a**) *(necesitado)* poor; *Fam* **más p. que las ratas** as poor as a church mouse (**b**) *(desdichado)* poor; **¡p. hombre!** poor man!; **¡p. de mí!** poor me!; **p. de aquél que se atreva a comerse mi ración** woe betide anyone who dares to eat my portion (**c**) *(mediocre, defectuoso)* poor (**d**) *(escaso)* poor; **una dieta p. en proteínas** a diet with a low protein content; **esta región es p. en recursos naturales** this region lacks natural resources

2 *nmf* (**a**) *(sin dinero, infeliz)* poor person; **los pobres** the poor, poor people; **¡el p.!** poor thing!; **la p. está siempre luchando por dar de comer a sus hijos** the poor woman is forever struggling to keep her children fed (**b**) *(mendigo)* beggar

pobreza *nf* poverty; **p. de** lack *o* scarcity of; **p. de espíritu** weakness of character

pocha *nf (judía)* haricot bean

pocho, -a *adj* (**a**) *(persona)* off-color (**b**) *(fruta)* over-ripe (**c**) *Méx Fam (americanizado)* Americanized

pocholada *nf Esp Fam* **una p. de niño/vestido** a cute little child/dress

pocholo, -a *adj Esp Fam* cute

pocilga *nf también Fig* pigpen

pocillo *nm RP* small cup

pócima *nf* (**a**) *(poción)* potion (**b**) *(bebida de mal sabor)* concoction

poción *nf* potion

poco, -a 1 *adj (singular)* little, not much; *(plural)* few, not many; **poca agua** not much water; **de poca importancia** of little importance; **hay pocos árboles** there aren't many trees; **pocas personas lo saben** few *o* not many people know it; **tenemos p. tiempo** we don't have much time; **hace p. tiempo** not long ago; **dame unos pocos días** give me a few days; **esto ocurre pocas veces** this rarely happens, this doesn't happen often; **poca sal me parece que le estás echando** I don't think you're putting enough salt in, I think you're putting too little salt in

2 *pron (singular)* little, not much; *(plural)* few, not many; **hay p. que decir** there isn't much to say, there's very little to say; **queda p.** there's not much left; **tengo muy pocos** I don't have very many, I have very few; **pocos hay que sepan tanto** not many people know so much; **éramos pocos** there weren't very many of us, there were only a few of us; **un p. a** bit; **¿me das un p.?** can I have a bit?; **un p. de** a bit of; **un p. de sentido común** a bit of common sense; **unos pocos** a few

3 *adv* (**a**) *(escasamente) (tras verbo)* not much; *(+ adjetivo)* not very; **este niño come p.** this boy doesn't eat much; **es p. común** it's not very common; **es un p. triste** it's a bit sad (**b**) *(brevemente)* **tardaré muy p.** I won't be long; **al p. de...** shortly after...; **dentro de p.** soon, in a short time; **hace p. a** little while ago, not long ago (**c**) *(no a menudo)* not often; **voy p. por allí** I don't go there very often; **voy muy p. por allí** I seldom go there (**d**) *(expresiones)* **p. a p.** *(progresivamente)* little by little, bit by bit; **¡p. a p.!** *(despacio)* steady on!, slow down!; **p. más o menos** more or less; **por p.** almost, nearly; **tener en p. a alguien** not to think much of sb

poda *nf* (**a**) *(acción)* pruning (**b**) *(tiempo)* pruning time

podadera *nf* garden shears

podar *vt* to prune

podenco *nm* hound

poder [49] **1** *nm* (**a**) *(mando, competencia)* power; **estar en/ hacerse con el p.** to be in/to seize power; **p. adquisitivo** purchasing power; **p. calorífico** calorific value; **p. de convicción** persuasive powers; **tener p. de convocatoria** to be a crowd-puller; **el p. ejecutivo/legislativo/judicial** *(personas)* the executive/legislature/judiciary; **poderes fácti-**

cos the church, military and press; **poderes públicos** public authorities

(**b**) *(posesión)* **estar en p. de alguien** to be in sb's hands

(**c**) *(autorización)* power, authorization; **dar poderes a alguien para que haga algo** to authorize sb to do sth; **por poderes** by proxy; **p. notarial** power of attorney

2 *vi* (**a**) *(tener facultad)* can, to be able to; **no puedo decírtelo** I can't tell you, I'm unable to tell you

(**b**) *(tener permiso)* can, may; **no puedo salir por la noche** I'm not allowed to *o* I can't go out at night; **¿puedo fumar aquí?** may I smoke here?; **¿se puede?** may I come in?

(**c**) *(ser capaz moralmente)* can; **no podemos portarnos así con él** we can't treat him like that

(**d**) *(tener posibilidad, ser posible)* may, can; **puede estallar la guerra** war could *o* may break out; **podías haber ido en tren** you could have gone by train; **¡podría habernos invitado!** *(expresa enfado)* she could *o* might have invited us!

(**e**) *(tener fuerza)* **p. con** *(enfermedad, rival)* to be able to overcome; *(tarea, problema)* to be able to cope with; **no p. con algo/alguien** *(no soportar)* not to be able to stand sth/ sb; **no puedo con la hipocresía** I can't stand hypocrisy; **no p. más** *(estar cansado)* to be too tired to carry on; *(estar harto de comer)* to be full (up); *(estar enfadado)* to have had enough

(**f**) *(expresiones)* **a** *o* **hasta más no p.** as much as can be; **es avaro a más no p.** he's as miserly as can be

3 *v impersonal (ser posible)* may; **puede que llueva** it may *o* might rain; **¿vendrás mañana? — puede** will you come tomorrow? — I may do; **puede ser** perhaps, maybe

4 *vt (ser más fuerte que)* to be stronger than; **tú eres más alto, pero yo te puedo** you may be taller than me, but I could still beat you up

poderío *nm* (**a**) *(poder, fuerza)* power (**b**) *(riqueza)* riches

poderoso, -a 1 *adj* powerful

2 *nm,f* powerful person; **los poderosos** the powerful

podio, pódium *nm* podium

podología *nf* podiatry, chiropody

podólogo, -a *nm,f* podiatrist, chiropodist

podré *etc ver* **poder**

podredumbre *nf (putrefacción)* putrefaction; *Fig (inmorali- dad)* corruption

podría *etc ver* **poder**

podrido, -a 1 *participio ver* **pudrir**

2 *adj* rotten

poema *nm* poem; **ser todo un p.** to be pathetic

poesía *nf* (**a**) *(género literario)* poetry (**b**) *(poema)* poem

poeta *nmf* poet

poética *nf* poetics *(singular)*

poético, -a *adj* poetic

poetisa *nf* female poet

póker *nm* (**a**) *(juego)* poker (**b**) *(jugada)* four of a kind

polaco, -a 1 *adj* (**a**) Polish (**b**) *Esp Fam Pey (catalán)* = pejorative term for a Catalan

2 *nm,f* (**a**) Pole (**b**) *Esp Fam Pey (catalán)* = pejorative term for a Catalan

3 *nm (lengua)* Polish

polaina *nf* leggings

polar *adj* polar

polaridad *nf* polarity

polarizar [14] **1** *vt* (**a**) *(miradas, atención, esfuerzo)* to concentrate (**b**) *Fís* to polarize

2 polarizarse *vpr (vida política, opinión pública)* to become polarized

polaroid® *nf inv* Polaroid®

polca *nf* polka

polea *nf* pulley

polémica *nf* controversy

polémico, -a *adj* controversial
polemista *nmf* polemicist
polemizar [14] *vi* to argue, to debate
polen *nm* pollen
polenta *nf* polenta
poleo *nm (planta)* pennyroyal; *(infusión)* pennyroyal tea
poli *Fam* **1** *nmf* cop
   2 *nf* cops
poliamida *nf* polyamide
polichinela *nm* (a) *(personaje)* Punchinello (b) *(títere)* puppet, marionette
policía 1 *nmf* policeman, *f* policewoman
   2 *nf* **la p.** the police; **viene la p.** the police are coming; **p. antidisturbios** riot police; **p. militar/secreta** military/ secret police; **p. de tráfico** traffic police
policiaco, -a, policíaco, -a *adj* **película/novela policiaca** detective movie/novel
policial *adj* police; **investigación p.** police investigation *o* inquiry
policlínica *nf* private hospital
policromado, -a *adj Arte* polychrome
policromía *nf Arte* polychromy
policromo, -a, polícromo, -a *adj* polychromatic
polideportivo, -a 1 *adj* multisport; *(gimnasio)* multiuse
   2 *nm* sports center
poliedro *nm* polyhedron
poliéster *nm inv* polyester
polietileno *nm* polyethylene
polifacético, -a *adj (persona)* multifaceted; *(actor)* versatile
polifonía *nf* polyphony
polifónico, -a *adj* polyphonic
poligamia *nf* polygamy
polígamo, -a 1 *adj* polygamous
   2 *nm,f* polygamist
políglota *adj & nmf* polyglot
poligonal *adj* polygonal
polígono *nm* (a) *Mat* polygon (b) *(terreno)* **p. industrial** industrial park; **p. residencial** housing development; **p. de tiro** firing range
polilla *nf* moth
polímero *nm* polymer
Polinesia *n* Polynesia
polinesio, -a *adj & nm,f* Polynesian
polinización *nf* pollination
polinizar [14] *vt* to pollinate
polinomio *nm* polynomial
polio *nf* polio
poliomielitis *nf inv* poliomyelitis
polipiel *nf* artificial skin
pólipo *nm* polyp
Polisario *nm* **el (Frente) P.** Polisario, = Western Sahara liberation front
polisemia *nf* polysemy
polisílabo, -a 1 *adj* polysyllabic
   2 *nm* polysyllable
politburó *nm* politburo
politécnico, -a *adj* polytechnic; **universidad politécnica** technical college
politeísta *adj* polytheistic
política *nf* (a) *(arte de gobernar)* politics *(singular)*; **hablar de p.** to discuss politics, to talk (about) politics (b) *(modo de gobernar, táctica)* policy; **P. Agrícola Común** Common Agricultural Policy; **p. exterior/monetaria** foreign/monetary policy
politicastro *nm Pey* bad politician
político, -a 1 *adj* (a) *(de gobierno)* political (b) *(prudente)*

tactful (c) *(pariente)* **hermano p.** brother-in-law; **familia política** in-laws
   2 *nm* politician
politiqueo *nm* politicking
politización *nf* politicization
politizar [14] **1** *vt* to politicize
   2 politizarse *vpr* to become politicized
poliuretano *nm* polyurethane
polivalencia *nf* polyvalency
polivalente *adj (vacuna, suero)* polyvalent; *(edificio, sala)* multipurpose
póliza *nf* (a) *(de seguros)* (insurance) policy (b) *(sello)* = stamp on a document showing that a certain tax has been paid
polizón *nm* stowaway
polizonte *nm Fam* cop
polla *nf Esp Vulg* cock, prick; **¡una p.!** *(no)* no fucking way!
pollera *nf CSur* skirt
pollería *nf* poultry store
pollino *nm* donkey
pollito *nm* chick
pollo, -a 1 *nm,f* (a) *(animal)* chick; **polla de agua** *(ave)* moorhen (b) *Méx Fam (inmigrante)* = illegal immigrant who is smuggled from Mexico into the US
   2 *nm* (a) *Culin* chicken; **p. al ajillo** chicken fried with garlic; **p. asado** roast chicken; **p. frito** fried chicken (b) *Anticuado o Hum (joven)* young shaver
polluelo *nm* chick
polo *nm* (a) *(de la tierra)* pole; *Fig* **p. de atracción** *o* **atención** center of attraction; **p. geográfico** terrestrial pole; **p. magnético** magnetic pole; **p. Norte/Sur** North/South Pole (b) *Elec* terminal; **p. negativo/positivo** negative/positive terminal; *Fig* **ser polos opuestos** to be poles apart; *Fig* **ser el p. opuesto de** to be the complete opposite of (c) *(helado)* Popsicle® (d) *(jersey)* polo shirt (e) *Dep* polo; *Am* **p. acuático** water polo
pololear *vi Chile Fam* to go out (together)
pololeo *nm Chile Fam* small job
pololo, -a *nm,f Chile Fam* boyfriend, *f* girlfriend
Polonia *n* Poland
polonio *nm Quím* polonium
poltrón, -ona *adj* lazy
poltrona *nf* easy chair
polución *nf* (a) *(contaminación)* pollution (b) *(eyaculación)* **p. nocturna** wet dream
polucionar *vt* to pollute
polvareda *nf* dust cloud; *Fig* **levantar una gran p.** to cause a commotion
polvera *nf* (powder) compact
polvo *nm* (a) *(en el aire)* dust; **limpiar** *o* **quitar el p.** to do the dusting (b) *(de un producto)* powder; **en p.** powdered; **polvos** *(maquillaje)* powder; **polvos (de) picapica** itching powder; **polvos de talco** talcum powder (c) *muy Fam (coito)* screw; **echar un p.** to have a screw; **¡qué p. tiene!** what a babe! (d) *(expresiones) Fam* **estar hecho p.** *(cansado)* to be dead beat; *(deprimido)* to be shattered; *Fam* **hacer p. algo** to smash sth; *Fam* **morder el p.** to be humiliated; *Fam* **hacer morder el p. a alguien** to make sb eat dirt
pólvora *nf (sustancia explosiva)* gunpowder; **correr como la p.** to spread like wildfire; *Fam* **no ha inventado la p.** he's not the most intelligent person in the world
polvoriento, -a *adj (superficie)* dusty; *(sustancia)* powdery
polvorín *nm* munitions dump; *Fig* powder keg
polvorón *nm* = very crumbly shortbread cookie
pomada *nf* ointment
pomelo *nm* (a) *(fruto)* grapefruit (b) *(árbol)* grapefruit tree
pómez *adj* **piedra p.** pumice stone

pomo *nm* (**a**) *(de puerta, mueble)* knob; *(de espada)* pommel (**b**) *Am (de pasta)* tube (**c**) *RP (de agua)* spray bottle (**d**) *Méx (pote)* jar

pompa *nf* (**a**) *(suntuosidad)* pomp (**b**) *(ostentación)* show, ostentation (**c**) **p. (de jabón)** (soap) bubble (**d**) **pompas fúnebres** *(servicio)* undertaker's; *(ceremonia)* funeral

Pompeya *n* Pompeii

pompis *nm inv Fam* behind, bottom

pompón *nm* pom-pom

pomposidad *nf* (**a**) *(suntuosidad)* splendor, pomp; *(ostentación)* showiness (**b**) *(en el lenguaje)* pomposity

pomposo, -a *adj* (**a**) *(suntuoso)* sumptuous, magnificent; *(ostentoso)* showy (**b**) *(lenguaje)* pompous

pómulo *nm* (**a**) *(hueso)* cheekbone (**b**) *(mejilla)* cheek

pon *ver* **poner**

ponchadura *nf CAm, Carib, Méx* blowout, puncture, flat

ponchar *CAm, Carib, Méx* **1** *vt (rueda)* to puncture
  2 poncharse *vpr (rueda)* to blow

ponche *nm* (**a**) *(en fiesta)* punch (**b**) *(con leche y huevo)* eggnog

ponchera *nf* punch bowl

poncho *nm* poncho, blanket *(for wearing)*

ponderable *adj* (**a**) *(en peso)* weighable (**b**) *(en ponderación)* worthy of consideration

ponderación *nf* (**a**) *(alabanza)* praise (**b**) *(moderación)* deliberation, considered nature (**c**) *(en estadística)* weighting

ponderado, -a *adj* (**a**) *(moderado)* considered (**b**) *(en estadística)* weighted

ponderar *vt* (**a**) *(alabar)* to praise (**b**) *(considerar)* to consider, to weigh up (**c**) *(en estadística)* to weight

pondré *etc ver* **poner**

ponedero *nm* nesting box

ponedor, -ora **1** *adj* egg-laying
  2 *nm (ponedero)* nesting box

ponencia *nf (conferencia)* lecture, paper; *(informe)* report

ponente *nmf (en congreso)* speaker; *(relator)* reporter, rapporteur

poner [50] **1** *vt* (**a**) *(situar, agregar, meter)* to put; *(colocar)* to place, to put
  (**b**) *(ropa, zapatos, maquillaje)* **p. algo a alguien** to put sth on sb
  (**c**) *(asignar) (tarea, examen)* to give, to set; *(precio)* to fix, to settle; *(multa)* to give; **le pusieron Mario** they called him Mario; **le pusieron un cinco en el examen** he got five out of ten in the exam
  (**d**) *(conectar) (televisión, radio)* to switch *o* put on; *(despertador)* to set; *(instalación, gas)* to put in; *(música, disco)* to put on
  (**e**) *(servir)* **¿qué le pongo?** what can I get you?, what would you like?; **póngame una cerveza, por favor** I'd like *o* I'll have a beer, please
  (**f**) *(comunicar) (telegrama, fax)* to send; *(conferencia)* to make; *Esp* **¿me pones con él?** can you put me through to him?
  (**g**) *Cine, Teatro & TV* to show; **¿qué ponen en la tele?** what's on the TV?
  (**h**) *(montar)* to set up; **ha puesto una tienda** she has opened a shop *o* store; **p. la mesa** to lay the table
  (**i**) *(decorar)* to do up; **han puesto su casa con mucho lujo** they've done up their house in real style
  (**j**) *(contribuir, invertir)* to put in; **p. dinero en el negocio** to put money into the business; **p. algo de mi/tu/***etc.* **parte** to do my/your/*etc* bit; **p. mucho empeño en (hacer) algo** to put a lot of effort into (doing) sth
  (**k**) *(hacer estar de cierta manera)* **p. a alguien en un aprieto/de mal humor** to put sb in a difficult position/in a bad mood; **le has puesto colorado/nervioso** you've made him blush/feel nervous; **p. cara de tonto/inocente** to put on a stupid/an innocent face
  (**l**) *(calificar)* **p. a alguien de algo** to call sb sth; **p. bien**

algo/a alguien to praise sth/sb; **p. mal algo/a alguien** to criticize sth/sb
  (**m**) *(oponer)* **p. obstáculos a algo** to hinder sth; **p. pegas a algo** to raise objections to sth
  (**n**) *(suponer)* to suppose; **pongamos que sucedió así** (let's) suppose that's what happened; **pon que necesitemos cinco días** suppose we need five days; **poniendo que todo salga bien** assuming everything goes according to plan
  (**o**) *Esp (decir)* to say; **¿qué pone ahí?** what does it say?
  (**p**) *(huevo)* to lay
  2 *vi (ave)* to lay (eggs)
  3 ponerse *vpr* (**a**) *(colocarse)* to put oneself; **ponte en la ventana** stand by the window; **ponerse de pie** to stand up; **ponte en mi lugar** put yourself in my position
  (**b**) *(ropa, gafas, maquillaje)* to put on; **¿qué te vas a p.?** what are you going to wear?
  (**c**) *(iniciar)* **ponerse a hacer algo** to start doing sth
  (**d**) *(volverse de cierta manera)* to go, to become; **se puso rojo de ira** he went red with anger; **se puso colorado** he blushed; **se puso muy guapa** she looked lovely; **¡cómo te pones por una nadería!** there's no need to react like that!; **¡no te pongas así!** *(no te enfades)* don't be like that!; *(no te pongas triste)* don't get upset!, don't be sad!
  (**e**) *(de salud)* **ponerse malo** *o* **enfermo** to fall ill; **ponerse bien** to get better
  (**f**) *(llenarse)* **ponerse de algo** to get covered in sth; **se puso de barro hasta las rodillas** he got covered in mud up to his knees
  (**g**) *(sol, luna)* to set
  (**h**) *Esp (al teléfono)* **ahora se pone** she's just coming, I'll put her on in a moment
  (**i**) *Esp (llegar)* **ponerse en** to get to
  (**j**) *Am Fam (parecer)* **se me pone que...** it seems to me that...

poney ['poni] *nm* pony

pongo *ver* **poner**

poni *nm* pony

poniente *nm (occidente)* West; *(viento)* west wind

pontevedrés, -esa **1** *adj* of/from Pontevedra
  2 *nm,f* person from Pontevedra

pontificado *nm* papacy

pontifical *adj* papal

pontificar [59] *vi* to pontificate

pontífice *nm (obispo)* bishop; *(Papa)* Pope; **el Sumo P.** the Supreme Pontiff, the Pope

pontificio, -a *adj (de los obispos)* episcopal; *(del Papa)* papal

pontón *nm* pontoon

ponzoña *nf (veneno)* venom, poison; *Fig* venom

ponzoñoso, -a *adj (venenoso)* venomous, poisonous; *Fig* venomous

pop 1 *adj* pop
  2 *nm (música)* pop (music)

popa *nf* stern

pope *nm* (**a**) *Rel* = priest of the Orthodox church (**b**) *Fam (pez gordo)* big shot

popelín *nm,* **popelina** *nf* poplin

popote *nm Méx* (drinking) straw

populachero, -a *adj Pey* (**a**) *(fiesta)* common, popular (**b**) *(discurso)* populist

populacho *nm Pey* mob, masses

popular *adj* (**a**) *(del pueblo) (creencia, movimiento, revuelta)* popular; *(arte, música)* folk; *(lenguaje)* colloquial; **la voluntad p.** the will of the people (**b**) *(famoso aceptado)* popular; **hacerse p.** to catch on

popularidad *nf* popularity

popularización *nf* popularization

popularizar [14] **1** *vt* to popularize

2 popularizarse *vpr* to become popular

popularmente *adv* **p. conocido como...** more commonly known as...

populismo *nm* populism

populista *adj & nmf* populist

populoso, -a *adj* populous, crowded

popurrí *nm* potpourri

póquer *nm* (**a**) *(juego)* poker (**b**) *(jugada)* four of a kind

poquito *nm* **un p.** a little bit

por *prep* (**a**) *(causa)* because of; **se enfadó p. tu comportamiento** she got angry because of your behavior; **lo hizo p. amor** he did it out of *o* for love; **p. mí no te preocupes** don't worry about me; **¿p. qué?** why?; **¿p. qué lo dijo?** why did she say it?; **¿p. qué no vienes?** why don't you come?; *Fam* **¿p.?** why?

(**b**) *(finalidad)* (+ *infinitivo*) (in order) to; (+ *sustantivo o pronombre*) for; **lo hizo p. complacerte** he did it to please you; **lo hice p. ella** I did it for her

(**c**) *(medio, modo, agente)* by; **p. mensajero/fax/teléfono** by courier/fax/telephone; **estuvimos hablando p. teléfono** we were talking on the phone; **p. escrito** in writing; **lo cogieron p. el brazo** they took him by the arm; **el récord fue batido p. el atleta** the record was broken by the athlete

(**d**) *(tiempo concreto)* **p. la mañana/tarde** in the morning/afternoon; **p. la noche** at night; **ayer salimos p. la noche** we went out last night; **p. unos días** for a few days

(**e**) *(tiempo aproximado)* **creo que la boda será p. abril** I think the wedding will be some time in April

(**f**) *(lugar)* **¿p. dónde vive?** whereabouts does he live?; **vive p. las afueras** he lives somewhere on the outskirts; **había papeles p. el suelo** there were papers all over the floor; **p. delante parece muy bonita** it looks very nice from the front; **está escrito p. detrás** there's writing on the back; **sólo quedaba sitio p. detrás** there was only room at the back

(**g**) *(a través de)* through; **vamos p. aquí/allí** let's go this/that way; **iba paseando p. el bosque/la calle** she was walking through the forest/along the street; **pasar p. la aduana** to go through customs

(**h**) *(a cambio de, en lugar de)* for; **lo ha comprado p. poco dinero** she bought it for very little; **cambió el coche p. la moto** he exchanged his car for a motorbike; **él lo hará p. mí** he'll do it for me

(**i**) *(distribución)* per; **80 céntimos p. unidad** 80 cents each; **mil unidades p. semana** a thousand units a *o* per week; **uno p. uno** one by one; **20 kms p. hora** 20 km an *o* per hour

(**j**) *Mat* **dos p. dos igual a cuatro** two times two is four

(**k**) *(en busca de)* for; **baja p. tabaco** go down to the stores for some cigarettes, go down to get some cigarettes; **a p.** for; **vino a p. las entradas** she came for the tickets

(**l**) *(concesión)* **p. más** *o* **mucho que lo intentes no lo conseguirás** however hard you try *o* try as you might, you'll never manage it; **no me cae bien, p. (muy) simpático que te parezca** you may think he's nice, but I don't like him

(**m**) **p. mí/nosotros** as far as I'm/we're concerned

porcelana *nf* (**a**) *(material)* porcelain, china (**b**) *(objeto)* piece of porcelain *o* china

porcentaje *nm* percentage

porcentual *adj* percentage; **seis puntos porcentuales** six percentage points

porche *nm* *(entrada)* porch; *(soportal)* arcade

porcino, -a *adj* pig; **ganado p.** pigs

porción *nf* portion, piece

pordiosero, -a 1 *adj* begging

2 *nm,f* beggar

porfía *nf* (**a**) *(disputa)* dispute; **a p.** determinedly (**b**) *(insistencia)* persistence; *(tozudez)* stubbornness

porfiado, -a *adj* *(insistente)* persistent; *(tozudo)* stubborn

porfiar [32] *vi* (**a**) *(disputar)* to argue obstinately (**b**) *(empeñarse)* **p. en** to be insistent on

pormenor *nm* detail

pormenorizar [14] **1** *vt* to describe in detail

2 *vi* to go into detail

porno *adj* *Fam* porn, porno; **p. duro** hard-core porn

pornografía *nf* pornography

pornográfico, -a *adj* pornographic

poro *nm* (**a**) *(en la piel)* pore (**b**) *Chile, Méx (verdura)* leek

poroso, -a *adj* porous

poroto *nm* *Andes, RP* kidney bean; *Chile* **p. verde** green bean

porque *conj* (**a**) *(debido a que)* because; **¡p. sí/no!** just because!; **lo hice p. sí** I did it because I felt like it; **¡p. lo digas tú!** says who?; **lo vais a hacer p. lo digo yo** you are going to do it because I say so; **p. haga mal tiempo no vamos a quedarnos en casa** we're not going to stay at home just because the weather's bad (**b**) *(para que)* so that, in order that; **reza p. no nos descubran** pray that they don't find us out

porqué *nm* reason; **el p. de** the reason for

porquería *nf* (**a**) *(suciedad)* filth (**b**) *(cosa de mala calidad)* garbage; **es una p. de libro** the book is garbage (**c**) **porquerías** *(comida)* garbage

porqueriza *nf* pigpen

porquero, -a *nm,f* swineherd

porra 1 *nf* (**a**) *(palo)* club; *(de policía)* nightstick (**b**) *Culin* = deep-fried pastry stick (**c**) *Esp Fam (para apuesta)* sweepstake (among friends or work colleagues) (**d**) *Méx Dep (hinchas)* fans (**e**) *(expresiones)* *Fam* **mandar a alguien a la p.** to tell sb to go to hell; **¿por qué/dónde porras...?** why/where the blazes...?; **¡una p.!** no way! not likely!

2 *interj* *Fam* **¡porras!** hell!, damn it!

porrada *nf* *Fam* **una p. (de)** heaps *o* tons (of)

porrazo *nm* *(golpe)* blow; *(caída)* bump

porreta *Fam* **1** *nmf (fumador de porros)* pothead

2 *nf* (**a**) *(nariz)* hooter (**b**) **en p.** *(desnudo)* in the altogether

porrillo: a porrillo *loc adv* *Fam* by the bucket

porrista 1 *nmf Méx (hincha)* fan, supporter

2 *nf Col, Méx (animadora)* cheerleader

porro *nm* (**a**) *Fam (de droga)* joint (**b**) *Am (verdura)* leek

porrón *nm* (**a**) *(vasija)* = glass wine jar used for drinking wine from its long spout (**b**) *Esp Fam* **un p. de** loads of

portaaviones *nm inv* aircraft carrier

portada *nf* (**a**) *(de libro)* title page; *(de revista)* (front) cover; *(de periódico)* front page (**b**) *(de disco)* sleeve (**c**) *Arquit* façade

portadocumentos *nm inv Andes, RP* document wallet

portador, -ora 1 *adj* carrying, bearing

2 *nm,f* carrier, bearer; *Com* **al p.** to the bearer

portaequipajes *nm inv (maletero)* trunk; *(baca)* roof *o* luggage rack

portaestandarte *nm* standard-bearer

portafolio *nm*, **portafolios** *nm inv (carpeta)* file; *(maletín)* attaché case

portal *nm* (**a**) *(entrada)* entrance hall; *(puerta)* main door; **viven en aquel p.** they live at that number (**b**) *(belén)* crib, Nativity scene (**c**) *Inform (página web)* portal

portalámparas *nm inv* socket

portaligas *nm inv Am* garter belt

portalón *nm* = large doors or gate giving access to interior courtyard from street

portamaletas *nm inv* trunk

portaminas *nm inv* mechanical pencil

portamonedas *nm inv* purse

portaobjeto *nm,* **portaobjetos** *nm inv* slide; *(de microscopio)* glass slide

portapapeles *nm inv Inform* clipboard

portar 1 *vt* to carry

  2 portarse *vpr* to behave; **portarse bien** to behave (well); **pórtate bien** behave (yourself)!; *Fam* **se ha portado bien conmigo** she has treated me well; **portarse mal** to misbehave; **se portó muy mal con su hermano** he treated his brother very badly

portátil 1 *adj* portable

  2 *nm (ordenador)* laptop

portaviones *nm inv* aircraft carrier

portavoz 1 *nmf (persona)* spokesman, *f* spokeswoman

  2 *nm (periódico)* voice

portazo *nm* **dar un p.** to slam the door; **la puerta se cerró de un p.** the door slammed shut

porte *nm* **(a)** *(gasto de transporte)* carriage, transportation costs; *Com* **portes debidos** freight collect; *Com* **portes pagados** freight paid **(b)** *(transporte)* carriage, transport; **una empresa de portes y mudanzas** a moving firm **(c)** *(aspecto)* bearing, demeanor

porteador, -ora 1 *adj* bearing, carrying

  2 *nm,f* porter

portento *nm* wonder, marvel

portentoso, -a *adj* wonderful, amazing

porteño, -a 1 *adj (bonaerense)* of/from Buenos Aires

  2 *nm,f (bonaerense)* person from Buenos Aires

portería *nf* **(a)** *(de casa, colegio)* super(intendent)'s office; *(de hotel, ministerio)* porter's office *o* lodge **(b)** *Dep* goal, goal mouth

portero, -a *nm,f* **(a)** *(de casa, colegio)* super(intendent); *(de hotel, ministerio) (en recepción)* porter; *(a la puerta)* doorman; **p. automático** *o* **eléctrico** entry-phone **(b)** *Dep* goalkeeper

portezuela *nf (de coche)* door

pórtico *nm* **(a)** *(fachada)* portico **(b)** *(arcada)* arcade

portilla *nf Náut* porthole

portillo *nm* **(a)** *(abertura)* opening, gap **(b)** *(puerta pequeña)* wicket gate

portón *nm* large door *o* entrance

portorriqueño, -a *adj & nm,f* Puerto Rican

portuario, -a *adj* **(a)** *(del puerto)* port; **ciudad portuaria** port **(b)** *(de los muelles)* dock; **trabajador p.** longshoreman; **la zona portuaria** the docks (area)

Portugal *n* Portugal

portugués, -esa 1 *adj & nm,f* Portuguese

  2 *nm (lengua)* Portuguese

porvenir *nm* future

pos: en pos de *loc prep (detrás de)* behind; *(en busca de)* after

posada *nf* **(a)** *(fonda)* inn **(b)** *(hospedaje)* lodging, accommodation

posaderas *nfpl Fam* backside, bottom

posadero, -a *nm,f* innkeeper

posar 1 *vt (dejar, poner) (objeto)* to put *o* lay down; *(mano, mirada)* to rest

  2 *vi* to pose

  3 posarse *vpr* **(a)** *(insecto, polvo)* to settle **(b)** *(pájaro)* to perch; *(nave, helicóptero)* to come down

posavasos *nm inv* coaster

posdata *nf* postscript

pose *nf* pose

poseedor, -ora 1 *adj (propietario)* owning, possessing; *(de cargo, acciones, récord)* holding

  2 *nm,f (propietario)* owner; *(de cargo, acciones, récord)* holder

poseer [37] *vt* **(a)** *(ser dueño de) (propiedades)* to own; *(puesto, marca)* to hold; **no poseo la llave del archivo** I don't have the key to the archive **(b)** *(sexualmente)* to have

poseído, -a 1 *adj* **p. por** possessed by

  2 *nm,f* possessed person

posesión *nf* possession; **tomar p. de un cargo** to take up a position *o* post

posesivo, -a 1 *adj* possessive

  2 *nm Gram* possessive

poseso, -a 1 *adj* possessed

  2 *nm,f* possessed person; **gritar como un p.** to scream like one possessed

poseyera *etc ver* **poseer**

posgrado *nm* postgraduate; **estudios de p.** postgraduate studies

posgraduado, -a *adj & nm,f* postgraduate

posguerra *nf* postwar period

posibilidad *nf* possibility, chance; **cabe la p. de que...** there is a chance that...; **posibilidades económicas** financial means *o* resources

posibilitar *vt* to make possible

posible 1 *adj* possible; **es p. que llueva** it could rain; **dentro de lo p., en lo p.** as far as possible; **de ser p.** if possible; **hacer p.** to make possible; **hacer (todo) lo p.** to do everything possible; **lo antes p.** as soon as possible; **¿cómo es p. que no me lo hayas dicho antes?** how could you possibly not have told me before?; **¡será p.!** I can't believe this!; **¡no es p.!** surely not!

  2 posibles *nmpl* (financial) means

posición *nf* **(a)** *(lugar, postura)* position; **tomaron las posiciones enemigas** they took the enemy positions; **quedó en quinta p.** he was fifth; **p. fetal** fetal position **(b)** *(situación)* position; **no estoy en p. de opinar** I'm not in a position to comment **(c)** *(categoría) (social)* status; *(económica)* situation

posicionamiento *nm* position; **su p. con respecto a algo** his position on sth

posicionarse *vpr* to take a position *o* stance

positivar *vt Fot (negativos)* to print

positivismo *nm* **(a)** *(realismo)* pragmatism **(b)** *Filosofía* positivism

positivista *adj & nmf Filosofía* positivist

positivo, -a 1 *adj* positive; **el test dio p.** the test was positive; *Fin* **saldo p.** credit balance

  2 *nm Fot* print

posmodernidad *nf* postmodernism

posmoderno, -a *adj & nm,f* postmodernist

poso *nm* sediment; *Fig (resto, huella)* trace; **posos del café** coffee grounds

posología *nf* dosage

posparto 1 *adj* postnatal

  2 *nm* postnatal period

posponer [50] *vt* **(a)** *(relegar)* to put behind, to relegate **(b)** *(aplazar)* to postpone

pospuesto, -a *participio ver* **posponer**

pospusiera *etc ver* **posponer**

posta 1 *nf* **(a)** *Chile, Perú (médica)* clinic **(b)** *Am* **postas** *(carrera)* relay (race)

  2 a posta *loc adv* on purpose

postal 1 *adj* postal

  2 *nf* postcard

postdata *nf* postscript

poste *nm* post, pole; *Dep* post; *Fam* **¡no te quedes ahí como un p.!** don't just stand there!; **p. de alta tensión** electricity pylon; **p. kilométrico** kilometer marker, $\simeq$ milepost; *Am* **p. restante** general delivery; **p. telegráfico** telegraph pole

póster *(pl pósters o posters)* *nm* poster

postergación *nf (aplazamiento)* postponement

postergar [38] *vt* **(a)** *(aplazar)* to postpone **(b)** *(relegar)* to put behind, to relegate

posteridad *nf* **(a)** *(generación futura)* posterity; **quedar para la p.** to be left to posterity **(b)** *(futuro)* future

posterior *adj* (**a**) *(en el espacio)* rear, back; **p. a** behind; **la piscina está en la parte p. del hotel** the swimming pool is at the back *o* rear of the hotel (**b**) *(en el tiempo)* subsequent, later; **p. a** subsequent to, after; **fue un descubrimiento p. al de la penicilina** it was a discovery made after that of penicillin

posteriori: a posteriori *loc adv* with hindsight; **habrá que juzgarlo a p.** we'll have to judge it after the event

posterioridad *nf* **con p.** later, subsequently

postgrado *nm* postgraduate; **estudios de p.** postgraduate studies

postgraduado, -a *adj & nm,f* postgraduate

postguerra *nf* postwar period

postigo *nm* (**a**) *(contraventana)* shutter (**b**) *(puerta)* wicket gate

postilla *nf* scab

postimpresionismo *nm Arte* Postimpressionism

postín *nm* showiness, boastfulness; **darse p.** to show off; **de p.** posh

postindustrial *adj* postindustrial

post-it® *nm inv* Post-it®

postizo, -a 1 *adj* (**a**) *(falso)* false (**b**) *(añadido)* detachable
  2 *nm* hairpiece

post mórtem *adj* **1** postmortem
  2 *nm* postmortem (examination)

postoperatorio, -a 1 *adj* postoperative
  2 *nm (periodo)* postoperative period

postor, -ora *nm,f* bidder; **mejor p.** highest bidder

postparto 1 *adj* postnatal
  2 *nm* postnatal period

postración *nf* prostration

postrado, -a *adj* prostrate; **p. por el dolor** prostrate with grief

postrar 1 *vt* to weaken, to (make) prostrate
  2 postrarse *vpr* to prostrate oneself

postre 1 *nm* dessert; **de p.** for dessert; *Fig* **para p.** to cap it all
  2 a la postre *loc adv* in the end

postrero, -a *adj* last, final

---
postrer is used instead of **postrero** before singular masculine nouns (e.g. **el postrer día** the last day).

---

postrimerías *nfpl* final stages; **en las p. del siglo XIX** at the end *o* close of the 19th century

postulado *nm* postulate

postulante, -a *nm,f (en colecta)* collector; *Rel* postulant

postular 1 *vt* (**a**) *(ideas)* to call for (**b**) *Am (candidato)* to nominate
  2 *vi* (**a**) *(en colecta)* to collect (**b**) *CSur (para trabajo)* to apply
  3 postularse *vpr CSur* (**a**) *(para cargo)* to stand, to run (**b**) *(para trabajo)* to apply

póstumo, -a *adj* posthumous

postura *nf* (**a**) *(posición)* position, posture (**b**) *(actitud)* attitude, stance (**c**) *(en subasta)* bid

posventa, postventa *adj inv Com* after-sales; **servicio p.** after-sales service

pota *nf Fam (vómito)* puke; **echar la p.** to puke (up)

potabilización *nf* purification

potabilizadora 1 *adj* water-treatment; **planta p.** water-treatment plant, waterworks *(singular)*
  2 *nf* water-treatment plant, waterworks *(singular)*

potabilizar [14] *vt* to purify

potable *adj* (**a**) *(bebible)* drinkable; **agua p.** drinking water (**b**) *Fam (aceptable)* acceptable, passable

potaje *nm (guiso)* vegetable stew; *(caldo)* vegetable stock; *Fam (brebaje)* potion, brew

potar *vi Fam* to puke (up)

potasa *nf* potash

potásico, -a *adj Quím* **cloruro p.** potassium chloride

potasio *nm* potassium

pote *nm* pot

potencia *nf* (**a**) *(capacidad, fuerza, poder)* power; **tiene mucha p.** it's very powerful; **las grandes potencias** the major (world) powers (**b**) *(posibilidad)* **en p.** potentially; **una campeona en p.** a potential champion (**c**) *Mat* **a la tercera/cuarta p.** to the third/fourth power

potenciación *nf* increase; **ayudar a la p. de** to promote, to encourage

potenciador *nm* enhancer

potencial 1 *adj* potential
  2 *nm* (**a**) *(fuerza)* power (**b**) *(posibilidades)* potential (**c**) *Gram* conditional (**d**) *Elec* (electric) potential

potenciar *vt* (**a**) *(fomentar)* to encourage, to promote (**b**) *(reforzar)* to boost, to strengthen

potentado, -a *nm,f* potentate

potente *adj* powerful

potestad *nf* authority, power

potingue *nm Fam (cosmético)* potion

potito *nm* = jar of baby food

potra *nf* (**a**) *(yegua joven)* filly (**b**) *Fam (suerte)* luck; **tener p.** to be lucky

potranco, -a *nm,f* = horse under three years of age

potrero *nm Am* field, pasture

potro *nm* (**a**) *(caballo joven)* colt (**b**) *Dep* vaulting horse (**c**) *(aparato de tormento)* rack

poza *nf (de río)* pool, deep section of small river

pozo *nm (de agua)* well; *(de mina)* shaft; **p. negro** cesspool; **p. de petróleo** oil well; **ser un p. de sabiduría** to be a fountain of knowledge; *Fig* **un p. sin fondo** a bottomless pit

PP *nm (abrev de* **Partido Popular***)* = Spanish political party to the right of the political spectrum

p.p. (**a**) *(abrev de* **por poder***)* pp (**b**) *(abrev de* **porte pagado***)* c/p

práctica *nf* (**a**) *(ejercicio, destreza)* practice; *(de un deporte)* playing; **llevar algo a la p., poner algo en p.** to put sth into practice; **en la p.** in practice; **prácticas de tiro** target practice (**b**) *(clase no teórica)* practical (**c**) **prácticas** *(laborales)* training

practicable *adj* (**a**) *(realizable)* practicable (**b**) *(transitable)* passable

prácticamente *adv (casi)* practically

practicante 1 *adj* practicing
  2 *nmf* (**a**) *(de deporte)* practitioner; *(de religión)* practicing member of a Church (**b**) *Med* medical assistant

practicar [59] **1** *vt* (**a**) *(ejercitar) (idioma, profesión, religión)* to practice; *(deporte)* to play; **es creyente pero no practica su religión** he's a believer, but he doesn't practice his religion (**b**) *(realizar)* to carry out, to perform; **le practicaron la autopsia** they carried out *or* performed an autopsy on him; **tuvieron que p. un hueco en la pared para poder salir** they had to make a hole in the wall to get out
  2 *vi* to practice; **es católico pero no practica** he's a Catholic, but not a practicing one

practicidad *nf CSur* **me fascina la p. de esta herramienta** I'm fascinated by how useful *o* handy this tool is; **por su p.** because it is very practical

práctico, -a 1 *adj* (**a**) *(objeto, conocimientos, persona)* practical; *(útil)* handy, useful; **un curso p. de fotografía** a practical photography course; **es muy p. vivir cerca del centro** it's very handy *o* convenient living near the center (**b**) *(casi)* **la práctica desaparición de la variedad silvestre** the virtual extinction of the wild variety (**c**) *RP (experimentado)* **estar p.** to be experienced
  2 *nm Náut* pilot

pradera *nf* large meadow, prairie

prado *nm* meadow; **el (Museo del) P.** the Prado (Museum)

Praga *n* Prague

pragmática *nf* (a) *Hist (edicto)* royal edict (b) *Ling* pragmatics *(singular)*

pragmático, -a 1 *adj* pragmatic

  2 *nm,f (persona)* pragmatist

pragmatismo *nm* pragmatism

praguense 1 *adj* of/from Prague

  2 *nmf* person from Prague

praliné *nm* praline

praxis *nf inv* practice; *Filosofía* praxis

preacuerdo *nm* draft agreement

preámbulo *nm* (a) *(introducción) (de libro)* foreword, preface; *(de congreso, conferencia)* introduction, preamble (b) *(rodeo)* digression

preaviso *nm* prior notice

prebenda *nf* (a) *Rel* prebend (b) *(privilegio)* sinecure

preboste *nm* provost

precalentamiento *nm Dep* warm-up

precalentar [3] *vt* (a) *Culin* to preheat (b) *Dep* to warm up

precampaña *nf Pol* preliminaries to election

precariedad *nf* precariousness

precario, -a *adj* precarious

precaución *nf* (a) *(prudencia)* caution, care (b) *(medida)* precaution; **tomar precauciones** to take precautions

precaver 1 *vt* to guard against

  2 precaverse *vpr* to take precautions; **precaverse de** *o* **contra** to guard (oneself) against

precavido, -a *adj* (a) *(prevenido)* prudent; **es muy p.** he always comes prepared (b) *(cauteloso)* wary

precedente 1 *adj* previous, preceding

  2 *nm* precedent; **sentar p.** to set a precedent; **sin precedentes** unprecedented

preceder *vt* to go before, to precede

preceptiva *nf* rules

preceptivo, -a *adj* obligatory, compulsory

precepto *nm* precept; *Rel* **fiestas de p.** days of obligation

preceptor, -ora *nm,f* (private) tutor

preces *nfpl Formal* prayers

preciado, -a *adj* valuable, prized

preciar 1 *vt* to appreciate

  2 preciarse *vpr* to have self-respect; **preciarse de** to pride oneself on

precintado *nm* sealing

precintadora *nf* sealing machine

precintar *vt* to seal

precinto *nm* seal

precio *nm* (a) *(en dinero)* price; **¿qué p. tiene esta corbata?** how much is this tie?; **está muy bien de p.** it's very reasonably priced; *Fig* **la merluza está a p. de oro** hake has become ridiculously expensive; *Fig* **no tener p.** to be priceless; **p. al contado** cash price; **p. de compra** purchase price; **p. de costo,** *Esp* **p. de coste** cost price; **p. de fábrica** factory price; **p. indicativo** guide price; **p. de mercado** market price; **p. prohibitivo** prohibitively high price; **p. de saldo** bargain price; **p. de salida** starting price; **p. de venta (al público)** retail price *(b) (sacrificio)* price; **pagaron un p. muy alto por la victoria** they paid a very high price for victory, victory cost them dearly; **a cualquier p.** at any price

preciosidad *nf* (a) *(cosa, persona)* **ser una p.** to be lovely *o* beautiful (b) *(valor)* value

precioso, -a *adj* (a) *(valioso)* precious (b) *(bonito)* lovely, beautiful

precipicio *nm* precipice

precipitación *nf* (a) *(apresuramiento)* haste (b) *Meteo*

precipitaciones *(lluvia)* rain; **precipitaciones en forma de nieve** snow (c) *Quím* precipitation

precipitado, -a 1 *adj* hasty

  2 *nm Quím* precipitate

precipitar 1 *vt* (a) *(arrojar)* to throw *o* hurl down (b) *(acelerar)* to hasten, to speed up (c) *Quím* to precipitate

  2 precipitarse *vpr* (a) *(caer)* to plunge (down) (b) *(acelerarse) (acontecimientos)* to speed up (c) *(apresurarse)* to rush **(hacia** towards) (d) *(obrar irreflexivamente)* to act rashly

precisamente *adv* (a) *(con precisión)* precisely (b) *(justamente)* **¡p.!** exactly!, precisely!; **p. por eso** for that very reason; **p. tú lo sugeriste** in fact it was you who suggested it

precisar *vt* (a) *(determinar)* to fix, to set; *(aclarar)* to specify exactly (b) *(necesitar)* to need, to require

precisión *nf* accuracy, precision; **instrumento de p.** precision instrument

preciso, -a *adj* (a) *(determinado, conciso)* precise (b) *(necesario)* **ser p. (para algo/hacer algo)** to be necessary (for sth/to do sth); **es p. que vengas** you must come

preclaro, -a *adj Formal* illustrious, eminent

precocidad *nf* precociousness

precocinado, -a *adj* precooked

precolombino, -a *adj* pre-Columbian

preconcebido, -a *adj (idea)* preconceived; *(plan)* drawn up in advance

preconcebir [47] *vt* to draw up in advance

preconizar [14] *vt* to recommend, to advise

precoz *adj* (a) *(persona)* precocious (b) *(lluvias, frutos)* early

precursor, -ora *nm,f* precursor

predador, -ora 1 *adj* predatory

  2 *nm* predator

predatorio, -a *adj (animal, instinto)* predatory

predecesor, -ora *nm,f* predecessor

predecible *adj* predictable

predecir [51] *vt* to predict

predestinación *nf* predestination

predestinado, -a *adj* predestined **(a** to)

predestinar *vt* to predestine

predeterminación *nf* predetermination

predeterminado, -a *adj* predetermined

predeterminar *vt* to predetermine

prédica *nf* sermon

predicado *nm Gram* predicate

predicador, -ora *nm,f* preacher

predicar [59] **1** *vt* to preach

  2 *vi* to preach; **es como p. en el desierto** it's like talking to a brick wall

predicción *nf* prediction

predice *ver* **predecir**

predicho, -a *participio ver* **predecir**

predigo *ver* **predecir**

predijera *etc ver* **predecir**

predilección *nf* preference **(por** for)

predilecto, -a *adj* favorite

predio *nm* (a) *(finca)* estate, property (b) *Am (edificio)* building

predisponer [50] *vt* to predispose **(a** to)

predisposición *nf* (a) *(aptitud)* **p. para** aptitude for (b) *(tendencia)* **p. a** predisposition to

predispuesto, -a 1 *participio ver* **predisponer**

  2 *adj* predisposed **(a** to)

predominancia *nf* predominance

predominante *adj (que prevalece)* predominant; *(viento, actitudes)* prevailing

predominar *vi* to predominate, to prevail **(sobre** over)

predominio *nm* preponderance, predominance

preeminencia *nf* preeminence

preeminente *adj* preeminent

preescolar 1 *adj* preschool, nursery; **educación p.** nursery education

  2 *nm* nursery school, kindergarten

preestablecido, -a *adj* preestablished

preestreno *nm* preview

preexistente *adj* preexisting

prefabricado, -a *adj* prefabricated

prefabricar [59] *vt* to prefabricate

prefacio *nm* preface

prefecto *nm* prefect

prefectura *nf* prefecture; **p. de tráfico** traffic division

preferencia *nf* preference; **con** *o* **de p.** preferably; *Aut* **tener p.** to have right of way; **tener p. por** to have a preference for

preferente, preferencial *adj* preferential

preferentemente *adv* preferably

preferible *adj* preferable (**a** to)

preferido, -a *adj* favorite

preferir [62] *vt* to prefer; **¿qué prefieres, vino o cerveza?** what would you prefer, wine or beer?; **prefiere no salir** she'd prefer not to go out, she'd rather not go out; **p. algo (a algo)** to prefer sth (to sth); **prefiero que me digan las cosas a la cara** I prefer people to say things to my face, I'd rather people said things to my face

prefigurar *vt* to prefigure

prefijar *vt* to fix in advance

prefijo *nm* (**a**) *Gram* prefix (**b**) *(telefónico)* area code

prefiriera *etc ver* **preferir**

pregón *nm* (**a**) *(bando)* proclamation, announcement (**b**) *(discurso)* speech

pregonar *vt* (**a**) *(bando)* to proclaim, to announce (**b**) *(secreto)* to spread about

pregonero, -a *nm,f* *(de pueblo)* town crier; *Fig (bocazas)* blabbermouth

pregunta *nf* question; **hacer una p.** to ask a question; **p. retórica** rhetorical question

preguntar 1 *vt* to ask; **p. algo a alguien** to ask sb sth; **a mí no me lo preguntes** don't ask me; **si no es mucho p., ¿cuántos años tiene?** if you don't mind my asking, how old are you?

  2 *vi* to ask; **p. por** to ask about *o* after; **preguntan por tí** they're asking for you

  3 preguntarse *vpr* to wonder; **preguntarse si** to wonder whether

prehistoria *nf* prehistory

prehistórico, -a *adj* prehistoric

preimpresión *nf Inform* pre-press

preindustrial *adj* preindustrial

prejubilación *nf* = voluntary layoff before entitlement to early retirement, with agreed benefits and/or additional payments, partly funded by the government

prejubilar 1 *vt* **p. a alguien** to give someone early retirement *(through a "prejubilación" agreement)*

  2 prejubilarse *vpr* to take early retirement *(through a "prejubilación" agreement)*

prejuicio *nm* prejudice

prejuicioso, -a, prejuiciado, -a *Am adj* prejudiced

prejuzgar [38] *vt & vi* to prejudge

prelado *nm Rel* prelate

preliminar 1 *adj* preliminary

  2 *nm* preliminary

preludiar *vt (iniciar)* to initiate, to begin; **un fuerte viento preludiaba el invierno** a strong wind signaled the beginning *o* onset of winter

preludio *nm (gen) & Mús* prelude

premamá *adj inv (ropa)* maternity

prematrimonial *adj* premarital; **relaciones prematrimoniales** premarital sex

prematuro, -a 1 *adj* premature

  2 *nm,f* premature baby

premeditación *nf* premeditation; *Der & Fig* **con p. y alevosía** with malice aforethought

premeditado, -a *adj* premeditated

premeditar *vt* to think out in advance

premenstrual *adj* premenstrual

premiación *nf Am (en escuela, club)* prize-awarding; *(de cine, música)* awards ceremony

premiado, -a 1 *adj (vencedor) (número)* winning; *(película, escritor)* prize-winning

  2 *nm,f* winner, prizewinner

premiar *vt* (**a**) *(recompensar)* to reward (**b**) *(dar un premio a)* to give a prize to

premier *nm* (British) prime minister

premio *nm* (**a**) *(en competición, sorteo)* prize; *(recompensa)* reward; **como p. a** as a reward for; **p. de consolación** consolation prize; **p. gordo** first prize; **p. en metálico** cash prize, prize money; **P. Nobel** *(galardón)* Nobel Prize (**b**) *(ganador)* prizewinner; **el P. Nobel** the Nobel Prize winner

premisa *nf* premise

premolar *adj & nm* premolar

premonición *nf* premonition

premonitorio, -a *adj* warning

premura *nf* (**a**) *(urgencia)* urgency (**b**) *(escasez)* lack, shortage

prenatal *adj* prenatal, antenatal

prenda *nf* (**a**) *(de vestir)* garment, article of clothing; **p. interior** undergarment; **p. íntima** undergarment, piece of underwear (**b**) *(garantía)* pledge; **dejar algo en p.** to leave sth as a pledge (**c**) *(en juego)* forfeit (**d**) *(virtud)* talent, gift (**e**) *(apelativo cariñoso)* darling, treasure (**f**) *(expresiones)* *Fam* **no me duelen prendas reconocer que estaba equivocado** I don't mind admitting I was wrong; *Fam* **no soltar p.** not to say a word

prendado, -a *adj* **quedar p. de** to be captivated by

prendar 1 *vt* to enchant

  2 prendarse *vpr* **prendarse de** to fall in love with

prendedor *nm* brooch

prender 1 *vt* (**a**) *(arrestar)* to arrest, to apprehend (**b**) *(sujetar)* to fasten (**c**) *(encender) esp Am (luz, interruptor)* to light; **p. fuego a algo** to set fire to sth, to set sth on fire (**d**) *(agarrar)* to grip

  2 *vi* (**a**) *(arder)* to catch (fire) (**b**) *(planta)* to take root (**c**) *(opinión)* to spread; **una idea que ha prendido entre el público** an idea that has caught on among the public

  3 prenderse *vpr (arder)* to catch fire

prensa *nf* (**a**) *(periódicos, periodistas)* press; **compro la p. todos los días** I buy the newspapers every day; *Fig* **tener buena/mala p.** to have a good/bad press; **la p. amarilla** the gutter press, the tabloids; **p. del corazón** gossip magazines; **la p. escrita** the press (**b**) *(imprenta)* printing press; **entrar en p.** to go to press (**c**) *(máquina)* press

prensar *vt* to press

prenupcial *adj* premarital

preñada *nf* pregnant woman

preñado, -a *adj* (**a**) *(hembra)* pregnant (**b**) *(lleno)* **p. de** full of

preñar *vt* (**a**) *(hembra)* to make pregnant (**b**) *(llenar)* **p. de** to fill with

preñez *nf* pregnancy

preocupación *nf* concern, worry

preocupado, -a *adj* worried, concerned (**por** about)

preocupante *adj* worrying

preocupar 1 *vt* (**a**) *(inquietar)* to worry; **me preocupa no saber nada de él** I'm worried I haven't heard from him (**b**) *(importar)* to bother; **sólo le preocupa su apariencia**

externa he's only bothered about his appearance

2 preocuparse *vpr* (**a**) *(inquietarse)* to worry (**por** about), to be worried (**por** about); **no te preocupes** don't worry; **no te preocupes por ella** don't worry about her (**b**) *(encargarse)* **preocuparse de algo** to take care of sth; **preocuparse de hacer algo** to see to it that sth is done; **preocuparse de que...** to make sure that...

preolímpico, -a *adj Dep* in the preliminaries to the Olympics; **torneo p.** Olympic qualifying competition

prepa = **preparatoria**

prepago *nm* pay-as-you-go; **tarjeta de p.** *(para móvil)* top-up card

preparación *nf* (**a**) *(disposición, elaboración)* preparation (**b**) *(conocimientos)* training (**c**) *(para microscopio)* specimen

preparado, -a 1 *adj* (**a**) *(dispuesto)* ready; *(de antemano)* prepared; **preparados, listos, ¡ya!** ready, steady, go! (**b**) *(capacitado)* competent, talented (**para** in)

2 *nm (medicamento)* preparation

preparador, -ora *nm,f Dep (entrenador)* trainer

preparar 1 *vt* (**a**) *(disponer, elaborar)* to prepare; *(trampa)* to set, to lay; *(maletas)* to pack; **voy a p. la cena/el arroz** I'm going to get dinner ready/cook the rice; **le hemos preparado una sorpresa** we've got a surprise for him (**b**) *(examen)* to prepare for (**c**) *Dep* to train

2 prepararse *vpr* to prepare oneself, to get ready (**para algo** for sth); **¡prepárate!** *(disponte)* get ready!; **prepararse para hacer algo** to prepare o get ready to do sth; **prepárate para oír una buena/mala noticia** are you ready for some good/bad news?

preparativo, -a 1 *adj* preparatory, preliminary

2 *nmpl* preparations

preparatoria, *Fam* **prepa** *nf Méx* ≃ senior high school studies, = three-year course of studies for students aged 14-17

preparatorio, -a *adj* preparatory

preponderancia *nf* preponderance; **tener p. (sobre)** to predominate (over)

preponderante *adj* prevailing

preponderar *vi* to prevail

preposición *nf* preposition

preposicional *adj* prepositional

prepotencia *nf* (**a**) *(arrogancia)* arrogance (**b**) *(poder)* dominance, power

prepotente *adj* (**a**) *(arrogante)* domineering, overbearing (**b**) *(poderoso)* very powerful

prepucio *nm* foreskin

prerrequisito *nm* prerequisite

prerrogativa *nf* prerogative

prerrománico *nm* early medieval architecture *(of 5th to 11th centuries)*

presa *nf* (**a**) *(captura)* catch; *(de cazador)* catch; *(de animal)* prey; **hacer p. en alguien** to seize o grip sb; **ser p. de** to be prey to; **ser p. del pánico** to be panic-stricken (**b**) *(dique)* dam

presagiar *vt (prever)* to foretell, to foresee; *(tormenta, problemas)* to warn of

presagio *nm* (**a**) *(premonición)* premonition (**b**) *(señal)* omen

presbiterianismo *nm* Presbyterianism

presbiteriano, -a *adj & nm,f* Presbyterian

presbiterio *nm* presbytery

presbítero *nm Rel* priest

prescindir *vi* **p. de** *(renunciar a)* to do without; *(omitir)* to dispense with

prescribir 1 *vt* to prescribe

2 *vi Der (plazo, deuda)* to expire, to lapse

prescripción *nf* prescription; **por p. facultativa** on medical advice, on doctor's orders

prescrito, -a *participio ver* **prescribir**

preselección *nf* short list, short-listing

preseleccionar *vt* to shortlist; *Dep* to name on the team o squad

presencia *nf (asistencia, aspecto)* presence; **en p. de** in the presence of; **buena p.** good looks; **mucha/poca p.** great/little presence; **p. de ánimo** presence of mind

presencial *adj* **testigo p.** eyewitness

presenciar *vt (asistir)* to be present at; *(ser testigo de)* to witness

presentable *adj* presentable

presentación *nf* (**a**) *(aspecto exterior)* presentation (**b**) *(entrega)* presentation; **mañana concluye el plazo de p. de candidaturas** tomorrow is the last day for submitting applications (**c**) *(entre personas)* introduction (**d**) *(ante público)* *(de libro, disco)* launch; **p. en sociedad** coming out, debut

presentador, -ora *nm,f (de programa)* host/hostess

presentar 1 *vt* (**a**) *(en general)* to present; *(dimisión)* to tender; *(tesis, pruebas, propuesta)* to hand in, to submit; *(recurso, denuncia)* to lodge; *(solicitud)* to make; *(moción)* to propose

(**b**) *(ofrecer) (disculpas, excusas)* to make; *(respetos)* to pay

(**c**) *(persona)* to introduce; **me presentó a sus amigos** she introduced me to her friends; **me parece que no nos han presentado** I don't think we've been introduced; **Juan, te presento a Carmen** Juan, this is Carmen; **permítame que le presente a nuestra directora** allow me to introduce you to our manager, I'd like you to meet our manager

(**d**) *(tener) (aspecto)* to have, to show; **presenta difícil solución** it's going to be difficult to solve

(**e**) *(proponer)* **p. a alguien para** to propose sb for, to put sb forward for

2 presentarse *vpr* (**a**) *(personarse)* to turn up, to appear; *(en juzgado, comisaría)* to report (**en** to); **presentarse a un examen** to take an exam (**b**) *(darse a conocer)* to introduce oneself (**c**) *(para un cargo)* to stand, to run (**a** for) (**d**) *(futuro)* to appear, to look (**e**) *(problema, situación)* to arise, to come up

presente 1 *adj* (**a**) *(asistente, que está delante)* present; **siempre está p. en mí su recuerdo** her memory is always present in my mind; **aquí p.** here present; **hacer p. algo a alguien** to notify sb of sth; **tener p.** *(recordar)* to remember; *(tener en cuenta)* to bear in mind; **¡p.!** present!; **Carlos Muñoz — ¡p.!** *(al pasar lista)* Carlos Muñoz — present! (**b**) *(en curso)* current; **del p. mes** of this month

2 *nmf (en un lugar)* **los (aquí) presentes** all those present

3 *nm* (**a**) *(gen) & Gram* present; **hasta el p.** up to now; **p. histórico** historical present (**b**) *(regalo)* gift, present (**c**) *(corriente)* **el p.** *(mes)* the current month; *(año)* the current year (**d**) **mejorando lo p.** present company excepted

4 *nf (escrito)* **por la p. le informo...** I hereby inform you...

presentimiento *nm* presentiment, feeling

presentir [62] *vt* to foresee; **p. que algo va a pasar** to have a feeling that something is going to happen; **p. lo peor** to fear the worst

preservación *nf* preservation

preservante *nm Am* preservative

preservar 1 *vt* to protect

2 preservarse *vpr* **preservarse de** to protect oneself o shelter from

preservativo, -a 1 *adj* protective

2 *nm* (**a**) *(anticonceptivo)* condom; **p. femenino** female condom (**b**) *Am (en producto)* preservative

presidencia *nf (de nación)* presidency; *(de asamblea, empresa)* chairmanship; *Méx* **p. municipal** city o town council

presidencialismo *nm Pol* presidential system

presidencialista 1 *adj Pol* presidential

2 *nmf* supporter of the presidential system

presidente, -a *nm,f (de nación)* president; *(de asamblea, jurado)* chairman, *f* chairwoman; *(de empresa)* president, chairman, *f* chairwoman; **p. (del Gobierno)** prime minister

presidiario, -a *nm,f* convict
presidio *nm* prison
presidir *vt* (**a**) *(ser presidente de)* to preside over; *(reunión)* to chair (**b**) *(predominar sobre)* to dominate
presienta *etc ver* **presentir**
presintiera *etc ver* **presentir**
presintonía *nf (de radio)* preset station selector
presión *nf* pressure; **a p.** under pressure; **hacer p.** *(fuerza)* to press; *(coacción, influencia)* to pressure; **p. arterial** blood pressure; **p. atmosférica** atmospheric pressure; *Econ* **p. fiscal** tax burden; **p. de los neumáticos** tire pressure; **p. sanguínea** blood pressure
presionar *vt* (**a**) *(apretar)* to press (**b**) *(coaccionar)* to pressurize, to put pressure on
preso, -a 1 *adj* imprisoned
2 *nm,f* prisoner; **p. político** political prisoner; **p. preventivo** remand prisoner
prestación *nf* (**a**) *(de servicio) (acción)* provision; *(resultado)* service; **p. social** welfare, social security benefit; **p. social sustitutoria** = community service done as alternative to military service (**b**) *(de dinero)* lending (**c**) **prestaciones** *(de coche)* performance features
prestado, -a *adj* on loan; **dar p. algo** to lend sth; **pedir/ tomar p. algo** to borrow sth; **de p.** *(con cosas prestadas)* with borrowed things; *(de modo precario)* on borrowed time
prestamista *nmf* moneylender
préstamo *nm* (**a**) *(acción) (de prestar)* lending; *(de pedir prestado)* borrowing (**b**) *(cantidad)* loan; **p. bancario** bank loan
prestancia *nf* excellence, distinction
prestar 1 *vt* (**a**) *(dejar) (dinero, cosa)* to lend, to loan; **¿me prestas mil pesos? ¿could you lend me a thousand pesos?; ¿me prestas tu pluma?** can I borrow your pen? (**b**) *(dar) (ayuda)* to give, to offer; *(servicio)* to offer, to provide; *(atención)* to pay (**c**) *(declaración, juramento)* to make
2 prestarse *vpr* (**a**) *(ser apto)* **prestarse (para)** to be suitable (for), to lend itself (to); **el lugar se presta para descansar** this is a good place to rest (**b**) **prestarse a** *(ofrecerse a)* to offer to; **se prestó a ayudarme enseguida** she immediately offered to help me (**c**) **prestarse a** *(acceder a)* to consent to; **no sé cómo se ha prestado a participar en esa película** I don't know how he consented to take part in that movie (**d**) **prestarse a** *(dar motivo a)* to be open to; **sus palabras se prestan a muchas interpretaciones** her words are open to various interpretations
presteza *nf* promptness, speed
prestidigitación *nf* conjuring
prestidigitador, -ora *nm,f* conjuror
prestigiado, -a *adj Chile, Méx* prestigious
prestigio *nm* prestige
prestigioso, -a *adj* prestigious
presto, -a *adj* **1** (**a**) *(dispuesto)* ready (**a** to) (**b**) *(rápido)* prompt
2 *adv Mús* presto
presumible *adj* probable, likely
presumido, -a 1 *adj* vain
2 *nm,f* vain person
presumir 1 *vt* *(suponer)* to presume, to assume; **presumo que no tardarán en llegar** I presume *o* suppose they'll be here soon
2 *vi* (**a**) *(jactarse)* to show off; **presume de artista** he likes to think he's an artist, he fancies himself as an artist; **presume de guapa** she thinks she's pretty (**b**) *(ser vanidoso)* to be conceited *o* vain
presunción *nf* (**a**) *(suposición)* presumption; *Der* **p. de inocencia** presumption of innocence (**b**) *(vanidad)* conceit, vanity

presunto, -a *adj (supuesto)* presumed, supposed; *(criminal)* alleged, suspected
presuntuoso, -a 1 *adj (vanidoso)* conceited; *(pretencioso)* pretentious
2 *nm,f* conceited person
presuponer [50] *vt* to presuppose
presuposición *nf* assumption
presupuestar *vt (hacer un presupuesto para)* to give an estimate for; *Fin* to budget for
presupuestario, -a *adj* budgetary
presupuesto, -a 1 *participio ver* **presuponer**
2 *nm* (**a**) *(dinero disponible)* budget; *(cálculo de costes)* estimate; *Econ* **Presupuestos Generales del Estado** Spanish national budget (**b**) *(suposición)* assumption
presurizar [14] *vt* to pressurize
presuroso, -a *adj* in a hurry
prêt-à-porter [pretapor'te] **1** *adj (ropa, moda)* ready-made, ready-to-wear
2 *nm* ready-to-wear clothing
pretencioso, -a 1 *adj (persona)* pretentious; *(cosa)* showy
2 *nm,f* pretentious person
pretender *vt* (**a**) *(intentar)* **p. hacer algo** to try to do sth (**b**) *(aspirar a)* **p. hacer algo** to aspire *o* want to do sth; **p. que alguien haga algo** to want sb to do sth; **¿qué pretendes decir?** what do you mean? (**c**) *(afirmar)* to claim (**d**) *(solicitar)* to apply for (**e**) *(cortejar)* to court
pretendido, -a *adj* supposed
pretendiente 1 *nmf* (**a**) *(aspirante)* candidate (**a** for) (**b**) *(a un trono)* pretender (**a** to)
2 *nm (a noviazgo, matrimonio)* suitor
pretensión *nf* (**a**) *(intención)* aim, intention (**b**) *(aspiración)* aspiration (**c**) *(supuesto derecho)* claim (**a** *o* **sobre** to) (**d**) *(afirmación)* claim (**e**) **pretensiones** *(exigencias)* demands
pretérito, -a 1 *adj* past
2 *nm Gram* preterite, past; **p. imperfecto** imperfect; **p. indefinido** simple past; **p. perfecto** (present) perfect; **p. pluscuamperfecto** pluperfect
pretextar *vt* to use as a pretext, to claim
pretexto *nm* pretext, excuse
pretil *nm* parapet
Pretoria *n* Pretoria
preuniversitario, -a *adj* precollege
prevalecer [46] *vi* to prevail (**sobre** over)
prevaleciente *adj* prevailing, prevalent
prevaler [69] **1** *vi* to prevail (**sobre** over)
2 prevalerse *vpr* to take advantage (**de** of)
prevaricación *nf Der* breach of trust
prevaricar [59] *vi Der* to betray one's trust
prevención *nf* (**a**) *(acción)* prevention; *(medida)* precaution; **en p. de** as a precaution against (**b**) *(prejuicio)* prejudice
prevengo *ver* **prevenir**
prevenido, -a *adj* (**a**) *(previsor)* **ser p.** to be cautious (**b**) *(avisado, dispuesto)* **estar p.** to be prepared
prevenir [69] **1** *vt* (**a**) *(evitar)* to prevent; *Prov* **más vale p. que curar** prevention is better than cure (**b**) *(avisar)* to warn; **te prevengo de que la carretera es muy mala** be warned that the road is very bad (**c**) *(prever)* to foresee, to anticipate (**d**) *(predisponer)* **p. a alguien contra algo/alguien** to prejudice sb against sth/sb
2 prevenirse *vpr* *(tomar precauciones)* to take precautions; **prevenirse contra algo** to take precautions against sth
preventivo, -a *adj (medicina, prisión)* preventive; *(medida)* precautionary
prever [70] **1** *vt* (**a**) *(anticipar)* to foresee, to anticipate; **una reacción que los médicos no habían previsto** a reaction the doctors hadn't foreseen; **se prevé una fuerte oposición popular a la ley** strong popular opposition to the law is

anticipated o expected (**b**) *(planear)* to plan; **prevén vender un millón de unidades** they plan to sell a million units; **tenía previsto ir al cine esta tarde** I was planning to go to the movies this evening (**c**) *(predecir)* *(catástrofe, acontecimiento)* to forecast, to predict

   2 *vi* **como era de p.** as was to be expected

previamente *adv* previously

previera *etc ver* **prever**

previniera *etc ver* **prevenir**

previo, -a 1 *adj* prior; **p. pago de multa** on payment of a fine

   2 *nm Cine* prescoring, playback

previó *ver* **prever**

previsible *adj* foreseeable

previsión *nf* (**a**) *(predicción)* forecast; **las previsiones son muy malas** the outlook is gloomy (**b**) *(visión de futuro)* foresight (**c**) *(precaución)* **en p. de** as a precaution against (**d**) *Andes, RP* **p. social** social security

previsional *adj Andes, RP* **gastos previsionales** social security spending

previsor, -ora *adj* prudent, farsighted

previsto, -a 1 *participio ver* **prever**

   2 *adj (conjeturado)* predicted; *(planeado)* forecast, expected, planned

PRI [pri] *nm (abrev de* **Partido Revolucionario Institucional**) = Mexican political party, the governing party from 1929 to 2000

prieto, -a *adj* (**a**) *(ceñido)* tight; **íbamos muy prietos en el coche** we were really squashed together in the car (**b**) *Cuba, Méx Fam (moreno)* dark-skinned

prima *nf* (**a**) *(paga extra)* bonus (**b**) *(de seguro)* premium; **p. de riesgo** risk premium (**c**) *(subvención)* subsidy

primacía *nf* primacy

primado *nm Rel* primate

primar 1 *vi* to have priority (**sobre** over)

   2 *vt* to give a bonus to

primario, -a *adj* primary; *Fig* primitive

primate *nm (simio)* primate

primavera *nf* (**a**) *(estación)* spring; **en p.** in (the) spring (**b**) *(juventud)* springtime (**c**) *(año)* **tiene diez primaveras** she is ten years old, she has seen ten summers

primaveral *adj* spring; **día p.** spring day

primer *ver* **primero**

primera *nf* (**a**) *Aut* first (gear); **meter (la) p.** to go into first (gear) (**b**) *Av & Ferroc* first class; **viajar en p.** to travel first class (**c**) *Dep* first division; **subir a p.** to go up into the first division (**d**) *(expresiones)* **de p.** first-class, excellent

primeriza *nf (madre)* first-time mother

primerizo, -a 1 *adj* (**a**) *(principiante)* novice (**b**) *(embarazada)* first-time

   2 *nm,f (principiante)* beginner

primero, -a

> **primer** is used instead of **primero** before singular masculine nouns (e.g. **el primer hombre** the first man).

1 *núm* (**a**) *(en orden)* first; **a primera hora de la mañana** first thing in the morning; **primeros auxilios** first aid; **la Primera Guerra Mundial** the First World War; **primera piedra** foundation stone; **el primer piso** the second floor; **primera plana** front page (**b**) *(en importancia)* main, basic; **lo p.** the most important o main thing; **lo p. es lo p.** first things first; **primer ministro** prime minister

   2 *nm,f* (**a**) *(en orden)* **el p.** the first one; **llegó el p.** he came first; **es el p. de la clase** he's top of the class (**b**) *(mencionado antes)* **el p.** the former; **vinieron Pedro y Juan, el p. con...** Pedro and Juan arrived, the former with...

   3 *adv* (**a**) *(en primer lugar)* first (**b**) *(antes)* **p.... que...**

rather... than...; **p. morir que traicionarle** I'd rather die than betray him

   4 *nm* (**a**) *(piso)* second floor (**b**) *(curso escolar)* ≃ first grade (**c**) **el p. de mayo** the first of May; **a primeros** *(de mes, año)* at the beginning; **a primeros de junio** at the beginning of June, in early June

primicia *nf* scoop, exclusive

primigenio, -a *adj* original, primitive

primitiva *nf Esp (lotería)* = weekly state-run lottery

primitivo, -a *adj* (**a**) *(arcaico, rudimentario)* primitive (**b**) *(original)* original (**c**) **lotería primitiva** = weekly state-run lottery

primo, -a 1 *adj Mat (número)* prime

   2 *nm,f* (**a**) *(pariente)* cousin; **p. carnal** o **hermano** first cousin; **p. segundo** second cousin (**b**) *Fam (tonto)* sucker; **hacer el p.** to be taken for a ride

primogénito, -a *adj & nm,f* first-born

primor *nm* (**a**) *(persona)* treasure, marvel; *(cosa, trabajo)* fine thing; **hecho un p.** spick and span (**b**) *(esmero)* **con p.** with skill

primordial *adj* fundamental

primoroso, -a *adj* (**a**) *(delicado)* exquisite, fine (**b**) *(hábil)* skillful

princesa *nf* princess

principado *nm* principality

principal 1 *adj* main, principal; **lo p. es...** the main thing is...; **puerta p.** front door

   2 *nm (planta)* second floor

príncipe *nm* prince; **p. azul** Prince Charming; **p. consorte** prince consort; **p. heredero** crown prince

principesco, -a *adj* princely

principiante, -a 1 *adj* novice, inexperienced

   2 *nm,f* novice, beginner

principio *nm* (**a**) *(comienzo)* beginning, start; **el p. del fin** the beginning of the end; **del p. al fin, desde el p. hasta el fin** from beginning to end, from start to finish; **a principios de** at the beginning of; **al p.** at first, in the beginning; **en p. quedamos en hacer una reunión el jueves** provisionally o unless you hear otherwise, we've arranged to meet on Thursday; **en un p.** at first

   (**b**) *(fundamento, ley)* principle; **en p.** in principle; **por p.** on principle

   (**c**) *(origen)* origin, source

   (**d**) *(elemento)* element; **p. activo** active ingredient

   (**e**) **principios** *(reglas de conducta)* principles; *(nociones)* rudiments, first principles

pringado, -a *nm,f Esp Fam (desgraciado)* loser; *(iluso)* mug, sucker

pringar [38] **1** *vt* (**a**) *(ensuciar)* to make greasy (**b**) *(mojar)* to dip (**c**) *Fam (comprometer)* to involve

   2 *vi Fam* to get stuck in

   3 pringarse *vpr* (**a**) *(ensuciarse)* to get covered in grease (**b**) *Fam (en asunto sucio)* to get one's hands dirty

pringoso, -a *adj (grasiento)* greasy; *(pegajoso)* sticky

pringue 1 *ver* **pringar**

   2 *nm (suciedad)* muck, dirt; *(grasa)* grease

prión *nm* prion

prior *nm Rel* prior

priora *nf Rel* prioress

priorato *nm* (**a**) *Rel* priorate (**b**) *(vino)* = wine from El Priorato in Tarragona

priori: a priori *loc adv* in advance, a priori

prioridad *nf* priority; *Aut* right of way

prioritario, -a *adj* priority; **objetivo p.** key objective o aim; **ser p.** to be a priority

priorizar [14] *vt* to give priority to

prisa *nf* hurry, haste; **con las prisas me olvidé de llamarte**

in the rush I forgot to call you; **a toda p.** very quickly; **correr p.** to be urgent; **darse p.** to hurry (up); **de p.** quickly; **de p. y corriendo** in a slapdash way; **ir con p.** to be in a hurry; **meter p. a alguien** to hurry o rush sb; **tener p.** to be in a hurry; *Prov* **la p. es mala consejera** more haste, less speed

prisión *nf* (a) *(cárcel)* prison (b) *(encarcelamiento)* imprisonment

prisionero, -a *nm,f* prisoner; **hacer p. a alguien** to take sb prisoner; **p. de guerra** prisoner of war

prisma *nm* (a) *Fís & Geom* prism (b) *(perspectiva)* viewpoint, perspective

prismático, -a 1 *adj* prismatic
2 prismáticos *nmpl* binoculars

priva *nf Esp Fam (bebida)* booze

privacidad *nf* privacy

privación *nf* deprivation; **p. de libertad** loss of freedom; **pasar privaciones** to suffer hardship

privado, -a *adj* (a) *(no público)* private; **en p.** in private (b) **p. de cariño** emotionally deprived

privar 1 *vt* (a) **p. a alguien/algo de** *(dejar sin)* to deprive sb/ sth of (b) **p. a alguien de hacer algo** *(prohibir)* to forbid sb to do sth
2 *vi Fam* (a) *(gustar)* **le privan los pasteles** he adores cakes (b) *(estar de moda)* to be in (fashion) (c) *(beber)* to booze
3 privarse *vpr* **privarse de** to go without

privativo, -a *adj* exclusive

privatización *nf* privatization

privatizar [14] *vt* to privatize

privilegiado, -a 1 *adj* (a) *(favorecido)* privileged (b) *(excepcional)* exceptional
2 *nm,f* (a) *(afortunado)* privileged person (b) *(muy dotado)* very gifted person

privilegiar *vt (persona)* to favor; *(intereses)* to put first

privilegio *nm* privilege

pro 1 *prep* for, supporting; **una asociación p. derechos humanos** a human rights organization
2 *nm* advantage; **los pros y los contras** the pros and cons
3 en pro de *loc prep* for, in support of

proa *nf Náut* prow, bows; *Av* nose

probabilidad *nf* (gen) & *Mat* probability; *(oportunidad)* likelihood, chance

probable *adj* probable, likely; **es p. que llueva** it'll probably rain; **es p. que no diga nada** he probably won't say anything

probador *nm* fitting room

probar [63] **1** *vt* (a) *(demostrar, indicar)* to prove; **eso prueba que tenía razón** that proves I was right (b) *(experimentar)* to try; **lo hemos probado todo** we've tried everything (c) *(ropa)* to try on; **p. una camisa** to try on a shirt (d) *(degustar)* to taste, to try (e) *(comprobar)* to test, to check
2 *vi* **p. a hacer algo** to try to do sth; **por p. no se pierde nada** there is no harm in trying
3 probarse *vpr (ropa)* to try on

probeta 1 *adj* **bebé** o **niño p.** test-tube baby
2 *nf* test tube

probidad *nf Formal* integrity

problema *nm* problem; **el p. del terrorismo** the terrorist problem, the problem of terrorism; **los niños no causan más que problemas** children cause nothing but trouble o problems; **el p. es que no nos queda tiempo** the problem o thing is that we don't have any time left

problemática *nf* problems

problemático, -a *adj* problematic

probo, -a *adj Formal* honest

procacidad *nf (desvergüenza)* obscenity; *(acto)* indecent act

procaz *adj* indecent, obscene

procedencia *nf* (a) *(origen)* origin (b) *(punto de partida)* point of departure; **con p. de** (arriving) from (c) *(pertinencia)* properness, appropriateness

procedente *adj* (a) *(originario)* **p. de** *(proveniente de)* originating in; *(avión, tren)* (arriving) from (b) *(oportuno)* appropriate; *Der* fitting, right and proper

proceder 1 *nm* conduct, behavior
2 *vi* (a) *(originarse)* **p. de** to come from; **esta costumbre procede del siglo XIX** this custom dates back to the 19th century (b) *(actuar)* to act (**con** with) (c) *(empezar)* to proceed (**a** with); **procedemos a leer el nombre de los ganadores** we will now read out the names of the winners (d) *(ser oportuno)* to be appropriate

procedimiento *nm* (a) *(método)* procedure, method (b) *Der* proceedings

prócer *nm Formal* great person

procesado, -a *nm,f Der* accused, defendant

procesador *nm Inform* processor; **p. de textos** word processor

procesal *adj (costas, alegaciones)* legal; *(derecho)* procedural

procesamiento *nm* (a) *Der* prosecution (b) *Inform* processing; **p. automático de datos** automatic data processing; **p. de textos** word processing

procesar *vt* (a) *Der* to prosecute (b) *Inform* to process

procesión *nf Rel & Fig* procession; **la p. va por dentro** he/ she is putting on a brave face

procesionaria *nf* processionary moth

proceso *nm* (a) *(fenómeno, operación)* process; **el p. creativo** the creative process; **el paciente está en un p. de recuperación** the patient is in the process of recovering (b) *Der (juicio)* trial; *(causa)* lawsuit; **abrir un p. contra** to bring an action against (c) *Inform (procesamiento)* processing

proclama *nf* proclamation

proclamación *nf* (a) *(anuncio)* notification (b) *(acto, ceremonia)* proclamation

proclamar 1 *vt* (a) *(nombrar)* to proclaim (b) *(aclamar)* to acclaim (c) *(anunciar)* to declare
2 proclamarse *vpr* (a) *(nombrarse)* to proclaim oneself (b) *(conseguir un título)* **proclamarse campeón** to become champion

proclive *adj* **p. a** prone to

procreación *nf* procreation

procrear 1 *vi* to procreate
2 *vt* to generate, to bear

procurador, -ora *nm,f Der* attorney; *Hist* **p. en Cortes** Member of Spanish Parliament *(in 19th century or under Franco)*

procurar 1 *vt* (a) *(intentar)* **p. hacer algo** to try to do sth; **procura llegar puntual** try to arrive on time; **p. que...** to make sure that...; **procuraré que no les falte nada** I'll make sure they have everything they need (b) *(proporcionar)* to get, to secure; **nos procurarán todos los medios necesarios** they will provide us with everything we need
2 procurarse *vpr* to get, to obtain; **se procuró un trabajo en el extranjero** she got herself a job abroad

Prode *nm Arg* = gambling game involving betting on the results of soccer matches

prodigalidad *nf* (a) *(derroche)* prodigality (b) *(abundancia)* profusion

prodigar [38] **1** *vt* **p. algo a alguien** to lavish sth on sb
2 prodigarse *vpr* (a) *(exhibirse)* to appear a lot in public (b) *(excederse)* **prodigarse en** to be lavish with

prodigio 1 *adj* **niño p.** child prodigy
2 *nm (suceso)* miracle; *(persona)* wonder, prodigy

prodigioso, -a *adj* (a) *(sobrenatural)* miraculous (b) *(extraordinario)* wonderful, marvelous

pródigo, -a 1 *adj* (a) *(derrochador)* extravagant; **el hijo p.** *(en la Biblia)* the prodigal son (b) *(generoso)* generous, lavish
2 *nm,f* spendthrift

producción *nf* (a) *(gen)* & *Cine* production; *Ind* **p. en serie** mass production (b) *(productos)* products

producir [18] **1** *vt* (**a**) *(producto, sonido)* to produce (**b**) *(ocasionar)* to cause, to give rise to; **tu actuación me produce tristeza** your conduct makes me very sad (**c**) *(interés, fruto)* to yield, to bear; **este negocio produce grandes pérdidas** this business is making huge losses (**d**) *Cine & TV* to produce

2 producirse *vpr (ocurrir)* to take place; **el accidente se produjo a las nueve de la mañana** the accident took place o occurred at nine o'clock in the morning; **se produjeron varios heridos** there were several casualties

productividad *nf* productivity

productivo, -a *adj (trabajador, método)* productive; *(inversión, negocio)* profitable

producto *nm* (**a**) *(bien, objeto)* product; **productos (agrícolas)** produce; **p. acabado** finished product; **p. alimenticio** foodstuff; **productos de belleza** cosmetics; **p. final** end product; *Econ* **p.** *Esp* **interior** o *Am* **interno bruto** gross domestic product; **productos lácteos** dairy produce; **p. manufacturado** manufactured product; *Econ* **p. nacional bruto** gross national product; **p. químico** chemical (**b**) *(resultado)* result, product; **el accidente fue p. de un despiste del conductor** the accident resulted from a lapse of attention on the part of the driver (**c**) *Mat* product

productor, -ora 1 *adj* producing; **país p. de petróleo** oil-producing country

2 *nm,f Cine (persona)* producer

productora *nf (de cine, televisión)* production company

proeza *nf* exploit, deed

profanación *nf* desecration

profanar *vt* to desecrate

profano, -a 1 *adj* (**a**) *(no sagrado)* profane, secular (**b**) *(ignorante)* ignorant, uninitiated

2 *nm,f (hombre)* layman, layperson; *(mujer)* laywoman, layperson

profe *nmf Fam (de colegio)* teacher; *(de universidad)* lecturer

profecía *nf (predicción)* prophecy

proferir [5] *vt (palabras, sonidos)* to utter; *(insultos)* to hurl

profesar 1 *vt* (**a**) *(religión)* to follow; *(arte, oficio)* to practice (**b**) *(admiración, amistad)* to profess

2 *vi Rel* to take one's vows

profesión *nf* (**a**) *(empleo, ocupación)* profession; *(en formularios)* occupation; **de p.** by profession; **ser de la p.** to be in the same profession; **p. liberal** liberal profession (**b**) *(declaración)* declaration, avowal; *Rel* **p. de fe** profession o declaration of faith

profesional *adj & nmf* professional

profesionalidad *nf*, **profesionalismo** *nm* professionalism

profesionalización *nf* professionalization

profesionalizar [14] *vt* to professionalize

profesionista *nmf Méx* professional

profeso, -a 1 *adj* professed

2 *nm,f* professed monk, *f* professed nun

profesor, -ora *nm,f (en colegio)* teacher; *(de universidad)* professor; *(de autoescuela, esquí)* instructor; **p. agregado** lecturer; **p. asociado** associate professor; **p. ayudante** assistant professor; **p. particular** (private) tutor; **p. titular** professor *(with tenure)*

profesorado *nm* (**a**) *(plantilla)* faculty, teaching staff; *(profesión)* teachers, teaching profession (**b**) *(cargo)* post of teacher; *(en universidad)* lectureship

profeta *nm* prophet

profético, -a *adj* prophetic

profetisa *nf* prophetess

profetizar [14] *vt* to prophesy

profiláctico, -a 1 *adj* prophylactic

2 *nm* prophylactic, condom

profilaxis *nf inv* prophylaxis

prófugo, -a 1 *adj* fugitive

2 *nm,f* fugitive; **p. de la justicia** fugitive from justice

3 *nm Mil* = person evading military service

profundidad *nf también Fig* depth; **tiene dos metros de p.** it's two meters deep

profundizar [14] **1** *vt (hoyo, conocimientos)* to deepen

2 *vi (en excavación)* to dig deeper; *(en estudio, conocimientos)* to go into depth; **p. en** *(tema)* to study in depth

profundo, -a *adj* (**a**) *(hoyo, río, raíces, herida)* deep; **es un lago muy poco p.** it's a very shallow lake; *Fig* **la España profunda** = backward, traditional Spain (**b**) *(libro, sentimiento)* profound, deep; *(sueño)* deep; *(dolor, alegría)* intense

profusión *nf* profusion

profuso, -a *adj* profuse

progenie *nf Formal* (**a**) *(familia)* lineage (**b**) *(descendencia)* offspring

progenitor, -ora *nm,f* father, *f* mother; **progenitores** parents

progesterona *nf* progesterone

programa *nm* (**a**) *(de proyecto, espectáculo)* program; **p. electoral** platform; **p. espacial** space program; **p. de fiestas** program of events *(during annual town festival)*; **p. de intercambio** exchange (program) (**b**) *(de actividades)* schedule, program; *(de curso, asignatura)* syllabus (**c**) *(de televisión, radio)* program; **p. concurso** quiz (show); **p. de entrevistas** talk show; **p. de humor** comedy show (**d**) *Inform* program; **p. informático** computer program (**e**) *(de lavadora, lavavajillas)* cycle; **p. de lavado** wash cycle

programación *nf* (**a**) *Inform* programming (**b**) *TV* scheduling; **la p. del lunes** Monday's programs

programador, -ora 1 *nm,f (persona)* programmer

2 *nm (aparato)* programmer

programar *vt* (**a**) *(actividades, proyecto)* to plan (**b**) *TV* to schedule; *Cine* to put on (**c**) *Mec* to program; *Inform* to program

progre *Fam* **1** *adj* liberal, permissive

2 *nmf* progressive

progresar *vi* to progress, to make progress; **p. en** to make progress in

progresión *nf* progression, advance; **p. aritmética/geométrica** arithmetic/geometric progression

progresismo *nm* progressivism

progresista *adj & nmf* progressive

progresivo, -a *adj* progressive

progreso *nm* progress; **hacer progresos** to make progress

prohibición *nf* ban, banning

prohibido, -a *adj* prohibited, banned; **un libro p.** a banned book; **la fruta prohibida** the forbidden fruit; **está p. fumar aquí** this is a no-smoking area; **p. aparcar/fumar** *(en letrero)* no parking/smoking, parking/smoking prohibited; **p. fijar carteles** *(en letrero)* post no bills; **prohibida la entrada** *(en letrero)* no entry

prohibir *vt* (**a**) *(impedir, proscribir)* to forbid; **p. a alguien hacer algo** to forbid sb to do sth; **tengo prohibido el alcohol** I've been told I mustn't touch alcohol; **se prohíbe el paso** *(en letrero)* no entry (**b**) *(por ley) (de antemano)* to prohibit; *(a posteriori)* to ban; **a partir de ahora está prohibido fumar en los lugares públicos** smoking in public places has now been banned; **está prohibida la venta de alcohol a menores** *(en letrero)* it is illegal to sell alcoholic drinks to anyone under the age of 18; **se prohíbe la entrada a menores de 18 años** *(en letrero)* over 18s only

prohibitivo, -a *adj* prohibitive

prohijar *vt* to adopt

prohombre *nm Formal* great man

prójimo *nm* fellow human being, neighbor

prole *nf* offspring

prolegómenos *nmpl (de una obra)* preface

proletariado *nm* proletariat

proletario, -a *adj & nm,f* proletarian

proliferación *nf* proliferation; **p. nuclear** proliferation (of nuclear arms)

proliferar *vi* to proliferate

prolífico, -a *adj* prolific

prolijidad *nf* (a) *(extensión)* long-windedness (b) *RP (pulcritud)* tidiness, neatness

prolijo, -a *adj* (a) *(extenso)* long-winded (b) *(esmerado)* meticulous; *(detallado)* exhaustive (c) *RP (pulcro)* tidy, neat

prologar *vt* to preface

prólogo *nm (de libro)* preface, foreword; *(de obra de teatro)* prologue; *Fig* prelude; **como p. a** as a prelude to

prolongación *nf* extension

prolongado, -a *adj (largo)* long; *(en el tiempo)* lengthy

prolongar [38] *vt (alargar)* to extend; *(espera, visita, conversación)* to prolong; *(cuerda, tubo)* to lengthen

promediar *vt Mat* to average out

promedio *nm* average

promesa *nf* (a) *(compromiso)* promise (b) *(persona)* promising talent

prometedor, -ora *adj* promising

prometer 1 *vt* to promise; **(te) lo prometo** I promise; **te prometo que no miento** I promise you I'm not lying; **p. el cargo** to be sworn in

2 *vi (tener futuro)* to be promising; **el programa de fiestas promete** the program for the celebrations looks promising

3 **prometerse** *vpr* (a) *(novios)* to get engaged (b) *Fam (esperar)* **se las promete muy felices** he thinks he's got it made

prometido, -a 1 *nm,f* fiancé, *f* fiancée

2 *adj* (a) *(para casarse)* engaged (b) *(asegurado)* **lo p.** what has been promised, promise; **cumplir lo p.** to keep one's promise; **lo p. es deuda** a promise is a promise

prominencia *nf* (a) *(abultamiento)* protuberance (b) *(elevación)* rise (c) *(importancia)* prominence

prominente *adj* (a) *(abultado)* protruding (b) *(elevado, ilustre)* prominent

promiscuidad *nf* promiscuity

promiscuo, -a *adj* promiscuous

promoción *nf* (a) *(ascenso) & Dep* promotion; *Com* **p. de ventas** sales promotion (b) *(curso)* class, year

promocional *adj* promotional

promocionar 1 *vt* to promote

2 **promocionarse** *vpr* to put oneself forward, to promote oneself

promontorio *nm* promontory

promotor, -ora 1 *adj* promoting

2 *nm,f (organizador)* organizer; *Com* **p. inmobiliario** real estate developer

promover [41] *vt* (a) *(iniciar)* to initiate, to bring about; *(impulsar)* to promote (b) *(ocasionar)* to cause (c) *(ascender)* **p. a alguien a** to promote sb to

promulgación *nf (de ley)* passing

promulgar [38] *vt (ley)* to pass

pronombre *nm Gram* pronoun; **p. demostrativo** demonstrative pronoun; **p. indefinido** indefinite pronoun; **p. interrogativo** interrogative pronoun; **p. personal** personal pronoun; **p. posesivo** possessive pronoun; **p. relativo** relative pronoun

pronominal *Gram* **1** *adj* pronominal

2 *nm* pronominal verb

pronosticar [59] *vt* to predict, to forecast

pronóstico *nm* (a) *(predicción)* forecast; **p. meteorológico** o

del tiempo weather forecast (b) *Med* prognosis; **de p. leve** suffering from a mild condition; **de p. grave** in a serious condition; **de p. reservado** under observation

prontitud *nf* promptness

pronto, -a 1 *adj (rápido)* quick, fast; *(respuesta)* prompt, early; *(curación, tramitación)* speedy

2 *adv* (a) *(dentro de poco)* soon; **p. se acabará el año** the year will soon be over; **¡hasta p.!** see you soon!; **tan p. como** as soon as; **lo más p. posible** as soon as possible (b) *Esp (temprano)* early; **salimos p.** we left early (c) *(rápidamente)* quickly

3 *nm Fam* sudden impulse; **le dio un p. y se fue** something got into him and he left

4 **de pronto** *loc adv* suddenly

5 **por lo pronto** *loc adv (de momento)* for the time being; *(para empezar)* to start with

pronunciación *nf* pronunciation

pronunciado, -a *adj (facciones)* pronounced; *(curva)* sharp; *(pendiente, cuesta)* steep

pronunciamiento *nm* (a) *(golpe)* (military) coup (b) *Der* pronouncement

pronunciar 1 *vt* (a) *(palabra, sílaba)* to pronounce; *(discurso)* to deliver, to make; **no pronunció palabra en toda la reunión** she didn't utter a word during the whole meeting (b) *(acentuar, realzar)* to accentuate (c) *Der* to pronounce, to pass

2 **pronunciarse** *vpr* (a) *(definirse)* to state an opinion (**sobre** on); **el presidente se pronunció a favor del proyecto** the president declared that he was in favor of the project (b) *(sublevarse)* to stage a coup

propagación *nf* (a) *(extensión, divulgación)* spreading (b) *(de especies, ondas)* propagation

propaganda *nf* (a) *(publicidad)* advertising (b) *(prospectos)* publicity leaflets; *(por correo)* junk mail; **repartir p.** to distribute advertising leaflets; *(en la calle)* to hand out advertising leaflets; **p. electoral** *(folletos)* election literature; *(anuncios, emisiones)* election campaign advertising (c) *(política, religiosa)* propaganda

propagandista *nmf* propagandist

propagandístico, -a *adj* (a) *(publicitario)* advertising; **campaña propagandística** advertising campaign (b) *Pol* propaganda; **actividad propagandística** propaganda activity

propagar [38] **1** *vt (extender)* to spread; *(especies)* to propagate

2 **propagarse** *vpr* (a) *(extenderse)* to spread (b) *(especies, ondas)* to propagate

propalar *vt* to divulge

propano *nm* propane

propasarse *vpr* to go too far (**con** with); **p. con alguien** *(sexualmente)* to take liberties with sb

propensión *nf* propensity, tendency

propenso, -a *adj* **p. a algo/a hacer algo** prone to sth/to doing sth

propiamente *adv (adecuadamente)* properly; *(verdaderamente)* really, strictly; **p. dicho** strictly speaking

propiciar *vt (favorecer)* to be conducive to

propiciatorio, -a *adj* propitiatory

propicio, -a *adj* (a) *(favorable)* propitious, favorable (b) *(adecuado)* suitable, appropriate

propiedad *nf* (a) *(derecho)* ownership; *(bienes)* property; **tener algo en p.** to own sth; **p. ajena** other people's property; **p. horizontal** joint ownership *(in a block of flats)*; **p. industrial** patent rights; **p. intelectual** copyright; **p. privada** private property; **p. pública** public ownership (b) *(facultad)* property (c) *(exactitud)* accuracy; **expresarse** o **hablar con p.** to express oneself precisely, to use words properly

(**c**) *(comprobación)* test; **de p.** *(producto comprado)* on approval; **p. de alcoholemia** breath test; **p. del embarazo** pregnancy test; **la p. de fuego** the acid test; **p. de resistencia** endurance test (**d**) *(examen académico)* test; **p. de acceso** entrance examination; **p. de aptitud** aptitude test (**e**) *(trance)* ordeal, trial (**f**) *Dep* event; **p. de saltos** *(de equitación)* show jumping (**g**) *Imprenta* proof

3 a prueba *loc adv (trabajador)* on trial; *(producto comprado)* on approval; **a p. de balas** bulletproof; **fe a toda p.** *o* **a p. de bombas** unshakable faith; **poner a p.** to (put to the) test

prurito *nm Med* itch, itching; *Fig* urge

Prusia *n Hist* Prussia

prusiano, -a *adj & nm,f Hist* Prussian

PS *(abrev de* **post scríptum)** PS

pseudo- *prefijo* pseudo-

pseudociencia *nf* pseudoscience

pseudónimo *nm* pseudonym

psicoanálisis *nm inv* psychoanalysis

psicoanalista *nmf* psychoanalyst

psicoanalítico, -a *adj* psychoanalytic(al)

psicoanalizar [14] *vt* to psychoanalyze

psicodélico, -a *adj* psychedelic

psicodrama *nm* psychodrama

psicofármaco *nm* psychotropic *o* psychoactive drug

psicología *nf también Fig* psychology

psicológico, -a *adj* psychological

psicólogo, -a *nm,f* psychologist

psicometría *nf* psychometrics *(singular)*

psicométrico, -a *adj* psychometric

psicomotor, -ora *adj* psychomotor

psicomotricidad *nf* psychomotricity

psicópata *nmf* psychopath

psicopatía *nf* psychopathy, psychopathic personality

psicosis *nf inv* psychosis; **p. maniaco-depresiva** manic-depressive psychosis

psicosomático, -a *adj* psychosomatic

psicotécnico, -a 1 *adj* psychotechnical

2 *nm,f* psychotechnician

3 *nm (prueba)* psychotechnical test

psicoterapeuta 1 *nmf* psychotherapist

2 *adj* psychotherapeutic

psicoterapia *nf* psychotherapy

psicótico, -a *adj & nm,f* psychotic

psicotrópico, -a *adj* psychotropic, psychoactive

psique *nf* psyche

psiquiatra *nmf* psychiatrist

psiquiatría *nf* psychiatry

psiquiátrico, -a 1 *adj* psychiatric

2 *nm* psychiatric *o* mental hospital

psíquico, -a *adj* psychic

psiquis *nf inv* psyche

PSOE [pe'soe, soe] *nm (abrev de* **Partido Socialista Obrero Español)** = Spanish political party to the centre-left of the political spectrum

psoriasis *nf inv* psoriasis

pta. *(pl* **ptas.)** *Antes (abrev de* **peseta)** pta

pterodáctilo *nm* pterodactyl

púa *nf* (**a**) *(de planta)* thorn; *(de erizo)* barb, quill; *(de peine)* spine, tooth; *(de tenedor)* prong (**b**) *Mús* plectrum

pub [paβ, paf] *(pl* **pubs)** *nm* bar *(open late, usually with music)*

púber *adj Formal* adolescent

púbero, -a *nm,f Formal* adolescent

pubertad *nf* puberty

púbico, -a, pubiano, -a *adj* pubic

pubis *nm inv* pubes

publicación *nf* publication

publicar [59] *vt* (**a**) *(libro, revista)* to publish (**b**) *(difundir)* to publicize; *(noticia)* to make known, to make public; *(aviso)* to issue; *(ley)* = to bring a law into effect by publishing it in the official government gazette

publicidad *nf* (**a**) *(difusión)* publicity; **dar p. a algo** to publicize sth (**b**) *Com* advertising; *TV* ads, commercials; **p. directa** direct mailing; **p. subliminal** subliminal advertising (**c**) *(folletos)* advertising material

publicista *nmf* advertising agent

publicitario, -a 1 *adj* advertising; **pausa publicitaria** commercial break

2 *nm,f* advertising agent

público, -a 1 *adj* (**a**) *(transporte, servicio)* public; **en p.** in public; **hacer algo p.** to make sth public; **personaje p.** public figure (**b**) *(del Estado)* public; **el sector p.** the public sector (**c**) *(conocido)* public; **ser p.** to be common knowledge

2 *nm* (**a**) *(en espectáculo)* audience; *(en encuentro deportivo)* crowd; **para todos los públicos** *o CSur* **para todo p.** (suitable) for all ages; *(película)* ≃ G; **muy poco p. asistió al encuentro** very few people attended the game (**b**) *(comunidad)* public; **el gran p.** the (general) public; **abierto al p.** open to the public

publirreportaje *nm (anuncio de televisión)* promotional movie; *(en revista)* advertising spread

pucha *interj Andes, RP (lamento, enojo)* shoot!; *(sorpresa)* wow!

pucherazo *nm Pol* electoral fraud

puchero *nm* (**a**) *(perola)* cooking pot (**b**) *(comida)* stew (**c**) *(gesto)* pout; **hacer pucheros** to pout

pucho *nm Andes, RP (colilla)* cigarette butt

pudding ['puðin] *(pl* **puddings)** *nm* (plum) pudding

pudendo, -a *adj* **partes pudendas** private parts

pudibundez *nf* prudishness

pudibundo, -a *adj* prudish

púdico, -a *adj* modest, demure

pudiente 1 *adj* wealthy, well-off

2 *nmf* wealthy person

pudiera *etc ver* **poder**

pudin *(pl* **púdines), pudín** *(pl* **pudines)** *nm* (plum) pudding

pudor *nm* (**a**) *(recato)* shyness; *(vergüenza)* (sense of) shame (**b**) *(modestia)* modesty

pudoroso, -a *adj* (**a**) *(recatado)* modest, demure (**b**) *(modesto)* modest, shy

pudridero *nm* garbage dump

pudrir 1 *vt* to rot

2 pudrirse *vpr* (**a**) *(descomponerse)* to rot; *Fam* **pudrirse en la cárcel** *(preso)* to rot in jail (**b**) *Fam* **¡ahí te pudras!** to hell with you!

pueblerino, -a 1 *adj Pey* rustic, provincial

2 *nm,f (habitante)* villager; *Pey (paleto)* yokel

pueblo 1 *ver* **poblar**

2 *nm* (**a**) *(población) (pequeña)* village; *(grande)* town; *Pey* **ser de p.** to be a country bumpkin *o* a hick; *Perú* **p. joven** *o Am* **p. nuevo** shantytown (**b**) *(nación, ciudadanos)* people; **el p. español** the Spanish people (**c**) *(proletariado)* **el p.** the (common) people

puedo *etc ver* **poder**

puente *nm* (**a**) *(construcción)* bridge; *Fig* **tender un p.** to offer a compromise; **p. colgante** suspension bridge; **p. levadizo** drawbridge; **p. peatonal** footbridge (**b**) *(días festivos)* ≃ long weekend *(consisting of a public holiday, the weekend and the day in between)*; **hacer p.** = to take an extra day off to join a public holiday with the weekend (**c**) **p. aéreo** *(civil)* air shuttle; *(militar)* airlift (**d**) *(en barco)* gun deck; **p. de mando** bridge (**e**) *Fam* **hacer un p.** *(para arrancar un coche)* to hot-wire a car (**f**) *(en dientes)* bridge

puentear *vt Elec (circuito)* to bridge; *(para arrancar un coche)* to hot-wire

puenting *nm* bungee jumping; **hacer p.** to go bungee jumping

puerco, -a 1 *adj* dirty, filthy

2 *nm,f* (**a**) *(animal)* pig, *f* sow (**b**) *Fam (persona)* pig, swine

3 *nm Méx (carne)* pork

puercoespín *nm* porcupine

puericultor, -ora *nm,f* nursery nurse

puericultura *nf* child care

pueril *adj* childish

puerilidad *nf* childishness

puerperio *nm* puerperium

puerro *nm* leek

puerta *nf* (**a**) *(de habitación, vehículo, armario)* door; *(de jardín, ciudad, aeropuerto)* gate; **te acompañaré hasta la p.** I'll see you out; **te espero en la** *o* **a la p. del cine** I'll wait for you outside the entrance to the movie theater; **de p. en p.** from door-to-door; **p. blindada** reinforced door; **p. corrediza** sliding door; **p. de embarque** *(en aeropuerto)* departure gate; **p. giratoria** revolving door; **p. principal** *(en casa)* front door; *(en hotel, museo, hospital)* main door *o* entrance; **p. trasera** *(en casa)* back door; *(en hotel, museo, hospital)* rear entrance; **p. vidriera** glass door

(**b**) *(posibilidad)* gateway, opening

(**c**) *Dep* goal, goal mouth

(**d**) *(expresiones)* **a las puertas de** on the verge of; **a p. cerrada** *(reunión)* behind closed doors; *(juicio)* in camera; *Esp* **coger la p. y marcharse** to up and go; **dar a alguien con la p. en las narices** to slam the door in sb's face; *Fam* **dar p. a alguien** to give sb the boot, to send sb packing; **estar en puertas** to be knocking on the door, to be imminent

puerto *nm* (**a**) *(de mar)* port; **llegar a p.** to come into port; *Fig* to make it in the end; **p. deportivo** marina; **p. franco** *o* **libre** free port; **p. pesquero** fishing port (**b**) *(de montaña)* pass; **subir/bajar un p.** to go up/down a mountain pass (**c**) *Inform* port; **p. paralelo/serie** parallel/serial port (**d**) *(refugio)* haven

Puerto España *n* Port of Spain

Puerto Príncipe *n* Port-au-Prince

Puerto Rico *n* Puerto Rico

puertorriqueño, -a *adj & nm,f* Puerto Rican

pues *conj* (**a**) *(dado que)* since, as (**b**) *(por lo tanto)* therefore, so; **creo, p., que…** so, I think that… (**c**) *(así que)* so; **querías verlo, p. ahí está** you wanted to see it, so here it is (**d**) *(enfático)* **¡p. ya está!** well, that's it!; **¡p. claro!** but of course!; **¡p. vaya amigo que tienes!** some friend he is!

puesta *nf* (**a**) *(acción) (de un motor)* tuning; **p. al día** updating; **p. en escena** staging, production; **p. de largo** debut (in society); **p. en marcha** *(de máquina)* starting, start-up; *(de acuerdo, proyecto)* implementation; **p. en órbita** putting into orbit; **p. a punto** *(de una técnica)* perfecting (**b**) *(de ave)* laying (**c**) **p. de sol** sunset

puesto, -a 1 *participio ver* **poner**

2 *adj* **iba sólo con lo p.** all she had with her were the clothes on her back; **ir muy p.** *(arreglado)* to be all dressed up; *Fam* **estar muy p. en algo** to be well up on sth

3 *nm* (**a**) *(empleo)* post, position; **escalar puestos** to work one's way up (**b**) *(en fila, clasificación)* place (**c**) *(tenderete)* stall, stand (**d**) *Mil* post; **p. de mando/vigilancia** command/sentry post; **p. de policía** police station; **p. de socorro** first-aid post

4 puesto que *loc conj* since, as

puf *(pl* **pufs)** *nm* pouf, pouffe

pufo *nm Fam* swindle

púgil *nm* boxer

pugilato *nm (pelea)* fistfight; *(disputa)* battle

pugilístico, -a *adj* boxing; **combate p.** boxing match

pugna *nf* fight, battle

pugnar *vi* (**a**) *(luchar)* to fight (**b**) *(esforzarse)* to struggle (**por** for), to fight (**por** for)

puja *nf* (**a**) *(en subasta) (acción)* bidding; *(cantidad)* bid (**b**) *(lucha)* struggle

pujante *adj* vigorous

pujanza *nf* vigor, strength

pujar 1 *vi* (**a**) *(en subasta)* to bid higher (**b**) *(luchar)* to struggle

2 *vt* to bid

pulcritud *nf* neatness, tidiness

pulcro, -a *adj* neat, tidy

pulga *nf (insecto)* flea; *Fig* **tener malas pulgas** to be bad-tempered

pulgada *nf* inch

pulgar *nm (dedo)* thumb

pulgón *nm* plant louse, aphid

pulgoso, -a *adj* flea-ridden

pulido, -a 1 *adj* polished, clean

2 *nm* **durante el p. del suelo** while polishing the floor

pulidor, -ora *adj* polishing

pulidora *nf* polisher

pulimentar *vt* to polish

pulimento *nm* polish, polishing

pulir 1 *vt* to polish; **necesito p. mi alemán** I've got to brush up my German

2 pulirse *vpr Fam (gastarse)* to blow, to throw away; **se pulió el sueldo en una semana** he blew his wages in a week; **nos pulimos una botella de whisky** we polished off *o* put away a bottle of whiskey

pulla *nf* gibe

pulmón *nm* lung; **a pleno p.** *(gritar)* at the top of one's voice; *(respirar)* deeply; **tener buenos pulmones** *(vozarrón)* to have a powerful voice; *Fig* **el p. de la ciudad** *(parque)* the lungs of the city; **Silva es el p. del equipo** Silva is the backbone of the team; **p. de acero** *o* **artificial** iron lung

pulmonar *adj* pulmonary, lung; **enfermedad p.** lung disease

pulmonía *nf* pneumonia

pulóver *nm* pullover

pulpa *nf (de fruta)* flesh; *(de papel)* pulp

púlpito *nm* pulpit

pulpo *nm* (**a**) *(animal)* octopus (**b**) *Fam Pey (hombre)* **es un p.** he can't keep his hands off women (**c**) *(correa elástica)* spider strap

pulque *nm CAm, Méx* pulque, = fermented agave cactus juice

pulsación *nf* (**a**) *(del corazón)* beat, beating (**b**) *(en máquina de escribir)* keystroke, tap; *(en piano)* touch; **pulsaciones por minuto** keystrokes per minute

pulsador *nm* button, push button

pulsar *vt* (**a**) *(botón, timbre)* to press; *(teclas de ordenador)* to press, to strike; *(teclas de piano)* to play; *(cuerdas de guitarra)* to pluck (**b**) *(opinión pública)* to sound out

púlsar *nm Astron* pulsar

pulsera *nf* bracelet

pulso *nm* (**a**) *(latido)* pulse; **tomar el p. a alguien** to take sb's pulse; *Fig* **tomar el p. a algo/alguien** to sound sth/sb out (**b**) *(firmeza)* **tener buen p.** to have a steady hand; **a p.** unaided (**c**) *(lucha)* **echar un p. (con alguien)** to arm-wrestle (with sb) (**d**) *(situación conflictiva)* battle of wills; **las negociaciones se han convertido en un p. entre patronal y sindicatos** the negotiations have turned into a battle of wills between management and the unions

pulular *vi* to swarm

pulverización *nf (de sólido)* pulverization; *(de líquido)* spraying

pulverizador *nm* spray

pulverizar [14] *vt* (**a**) *(líquido)* to spray (**b**) *(sólido)* to reduce to dust; *Mec* to pulverize (**c**) *(aniquilar)* to pulverize

pum *interj* ¡**p.!** bang!

puma *nm* puma

pumba *interj* ¡**p.!** wham!, bang!

puna *nf Andes* (**a**) *Geog* Andean plateau (**b**) *(mal de altura)* altitude sickness

punción *nf* puncture

pundonor *nm* pride

punible *adj* punishable

punición *nf* punishment

púnico, -a *adj* Punic

punitivo, -a *adj* punitive

punk [pank] *(pl* **punks**) *adj, nm & nmf* punk

punki *adj & nmf* punk

punta *nf* (**a**) *(extremo) (de cuchillo, lápiz, aguja)* point; *(de pan, pelo, nariz)* end; *(de dedo, cuerno, flecha)* tip; *(de sábana, pañuelo)* corner; **este zapato me aprieta en la p.** this shoe's squashing the ends of my toes; **recorrimos Chile de p. a p.** we traveled from one end of Chile to the other; **en la otra p. de la ciudad** on the other side of town; **en la otra p. de la mesa** at the other end of the table; **sacar p. a un lápiz** to sharpen a pencil

(**b**) *(pizca)* touch, bit; *(de sal)* pinch

(**c**) *(clavo)* small nail

(**d**) *Geog* point, headland

(**e**) *(expresiones)* **a p. de pistola** at gunpoint; *Am* **a p. de** *(a fuerza de)* by dint of; *Fam* **a p. pala** by the dozen *o* bucket; **estar de p. con alguien** to be on edge with sb; **ir de p. en blanco** to be dressed up to the nines; *Fam Fig* **sacarle p. a algo** to read too much into sth; *Fig* **la p. del iceberg** the tip of the iceberg; *Fig* **tener algo en la p. de la lengua** to have sth on the tip of one's tongue

puntada *nf* (**a**) *(en costura)* stitch (**b**) *RP (dolor)* stabbing pain (**c**) *Méx (broma)* witticism

puntal *nm* (**a**) *(madero)* prop; *Fig (apoyo)* mainstay (**b**) *Andes, CAm, Méx (aperitivo)* snack

puntapié *nm* kick; **echar a alguien a puntapiés** to kick sb out; *Fig* **tratar a alguien a puntapiés** to be nasty to sb

punteado, -a 1 *adj (línea)* dotted

2 *nm Mús* plucking

puntear *vt Mús* to pluck

punteo *nm* guitar solo

puntera *nf (de zapato)* toecap; *(de calcetín)* toe

puntería *nf* (**a**) *(destreza)* marksmanship; **tener p.** to be a good shot (**b**) *(orientación para apuntar)* aim

puntero, -a 1 *adj* leading

2 *nm,f CSur Dep* winger

3 *nm* (**a**) *(para señalar)* pointer (**b**) *Andes, RP, Méx (líder)* leader

puntiagudo, -a *adj* pointed

puntilla 1 *nf* (**a**) *(encaje)* point lace (**b**) *Fig* **dar la p.** to give the coup de grâce; **aquello fue la p.** that was what did it

2 de puntillas, *Am* **en puntillas** *loc adv* on tiptoe

puntillismo *nm Arte* pointillism

puntillo *nm* pride

puntilloso, -a *adj* (**a**) *(susceptible)* touchy (**b**) *(meticuloso)* punctilious

punto 1 *nm* (**a**) *(marca)* spot, dot; *(en geometría)* point; **recorte por la línea de puntos** cut along the dotted line

(**b**) *(signo ortográfico) (al final de frase)* period; *(sobre i, j, en dirección de correo electrónico)* dot; **dos puntos** colon; *Fig* **poner los puntos sobre las íes** to dot the i's and cross the t's; *Fam* **y p.** and that's that; **p. y aparte** period, new paragraph; **p. y coma** semicolon; **p. final** period; *Fig* **poner p. final a algo** to bring sth to a close; **p. y seguido** period *(no new paragraph)*; **puntos suspensivos** dots, suspension points

(**c**) *(unidad)* point; **ganar/perder por seis puntos** to win/lose by six points

(**d**) *(asunto)* point; **p. débil/fuerte** weak/strong point; **puntos a tratar** matters to be discussed; **p. de vista** point of view, viewpoint

(**e**) *(lugar)* spot, place; **este es el p. exacto donde ocurrió todo** this is the exact spot where it all happened; **p. de apoyo** *(en palanca)* fulcrum; *Fig* backup, support; **p. cardinal** point of the compass, *Espec* cardinal point; **p. de contacto** point of contact; **p. de encuentro** meeting point; **p. negro** *(grano)* blackhead; *(en carretera)* accident hot spot; *Com* **p. de venta** point of sale; *(tienda)* retail outlet

(**f**) *(momento)* point, moment; *(estado, fase)* point, stage; **llegar a un p. en que...** to reach the stage where...; **estando las cosas en este p.** things being as they are; **p. culminante** high point; **p. de ebullición/fusión** boiling/melting point; **p. de inflexión** turning point; **p. de partida** starting point

(**g**) *Aut* **p. muerto** neutral; *Fig* deadlock; **estar en un p. muerto** to be deadlocked

(**h**) *(puntada)* stitch; **p. de cruz** cross-stitch

(**i**) *(estilo de tejer)* knitting; **hacer p.** to knit; **un jersey de p.** a knitted sweater; **p. de ganchillo** crochet

(**j**) *(expresiones)* **al p.** at once, there and then; **en p.** exactly, on the dot; **a las seis en p.** at six o'clock on the dot, at six o'clock sharp; **estar en su p.** to be just right; **de todo p.** *(completamente)* absolutely; **hasta tal p. que** to such an extent that; **hasta cierto p.** to some extent, up to a point

(**k**) *Esp Fam (borrachera ligera)* **cogerse/tener un p.** to get/be merry

(**l**) *Fam (reacción, estado de ánimo)* **le dan unos puntos muy raros** he can be really weird sometimes; **le dio el p. generoso** he had a fit of generosity

2 a punto *loc adv* **estar a p.** to be ready; **estar a p. de hacer algo** to be on the point of doing sth; **a p. de** *(echarse a)* **llorar** near to tears; **llegar a p. (para hacer algo)** to arrive just in time (to do sth); **poner a p.** *(motor)* to tune; *Fig* to fine-tune; **batir a p. de nieve** to beat until stiff

puntocom *nf (empresa)* dotcom

puntuable *adj* **p. para** that counts toward

puntuación *nf* (**a**) *(calificación)* mark; *(en concursos, competiciones)* score (**b**) *(ortográfica)* punctuation

puntual *adj* (**a**) *(en el tiempo)* punctual (**b**) *(exacto, detallado)* detailed (**c**) *(aislado)* isolated, singular

puntualidad *nf* (**a**) *(en el tiempo)* punctuality (**b**) *(exactitud)* exactness

puntualización *nf* clarification

puntualizar [14] *vt (aclarar)* to specify, to clarify

puntualmente *adv (en el momento justo)* punctually, promptly

puntuar [4] **1** *vt* (**a**) *(calificar)* to grade, to mark (**b**) *(escrito)* to punctuate

2 *vi* (**a**) *(calificar)* to grade, to mark (**b**) *(entrar en el cómputo)* to count (**para** towards)

punzada *nf* (**a**) *(pinchazo)* prick (**b**) *(dolor intenso)* stabbing pain; *(de remordimiento)* pang, twinge

punzante *adj* (**a**) *(que pincha)* sharp (**b**) *(intenso)* sharp, stabbing (**c**) *(mordaz)* caustic

punzar [14] *vt* (**a**) *(pinchar)* to prick (**b**) *(sujeto: dolor)* to stab; *(sujeto: actitud)* to wound

punzón *nm (herramienta)* punch

puñado *nm* handful; *Fig* **a puñados** by the handful

puñal *nm* dagger

puñalada *nf (acción)* stab; *(herida)* stab wound; *Fig* **coser a puñaladas** to stab repeatedly; *Fig* **p. trapera** stab in the back

puñeta 1 *nf* (**a**) *Fam (tontería)* **hacer la p.** to be a pain; **mandar a alguien a hacer puñetas** to tell sb to get lost (**b**) *(bocamanga)* border

2 *interj Fam* ¡**p.!,** ¡**puñetas!** damn it!

puñetazo *nm* punch; **darle un p. a alguien** to punch sb; **dio un p. en la mesa** he thumped his fist on the table

puñetería *nf Esp Fam* pigheadedness

puñetero, -a *Esp Fam* **1** *adj* (**a**) *(persona)* damn (**b**) *(cosa)* tricky, awkward
2 *nm,f* pain

puño *nm* (**a**) *(mano cerrada)* fist; **son verdades como puños** it's as clear as daylight; **de su p. y letra** in his/her own handwriting; **meter** *o* **tener a alguien en un p.** to have sb under one's thumb (**b**) *(de manga)* cuff (**c**) *(empuñadura) (de espada)* hilt; *(de paraguas)* handle

pupa *nf* (**a**) *(erupción)* blister (**b**) *Fam (daño)* pain; **hacerse p.** to hurt oneself (**c**) *(crisálida)* pupa

pupila *nf* pupil

pupilo, -a *nm,f* (**a**) *(discípulo)* pupil (**b**) *(huérfano)* ward

pupitre *nm* desk

pupusa *nf CAm* corn dumpling

purasangre *nm inv* thoroughbred

puré *nm Culin* thick soup; **p. de patatas** mashed potatoes; *Fam* **estar hecho p.** to be beat

pureta *Fam* **1** *adj* fogyish
2 *nmf* old fogy

pureza *nf* purity

purga *nf* (**a**) *Med* purgative (**b**) *(depuración)* purge

purgaciones *nfpl Med* gonorrhea

purgante *adj & nm* purgative

purgar [38] **1** *vt también Fig* to purge
2 purgarse *vpr* to take a purge

purgatorio *nm* purgatory

purgue *etc ver* **purgar**

purificación *nf* purification

purificador *nm Am (de agua)* purifier

purificar [59] *vt (agua, sangre, aire)* to purify; *(mineral, metal)* to refine

purista **1** *adj* purist; **una corriente p.** a purist tendency
2 *nmf* purist

puritanismo *nm* puritanism

puritano, -a *adj & nm,f* puritan

puro, -a **1** *adj* (**a**) *(limpio, sin mezcla)* pure; *(oro)* solid; **pura lana virgen** pure wool (**b**) *(cielo, atmósfera)* clear (**c**) *(conducta, persona)* decent, honorable (**d**) *(mero)* sheer; *(verdad)* plain; **por pura casualidad** by pure chance; **fue una pura coincidencia** it was pure coincidence; **me quedé dormido de p. cansancio** I fell asleep from sheer exhaustion; *Fam* **y ésta es la realidad pura y dura** and that is the harsh reality of the matter
2 *nm* (**a**) *(cigarro)* cigar; **p. habano** Havana cigar (**b**) *Esp Fam* **meterle un p. a alguien** *(regañina)* to read the riot act to sb; *(castigo)* to throw the book at sb

púrpura **1** *adj inv* purple
2 *nm (color)* purple

purpúreo, -a *adj* purple

purpurina *nf* purpurin

purulencia *nf* purulence

purulento, -a *adj* purulent

pus *nm* pus

puse *ver* **poner**

pusiera *etc ver* **poner**

pusilánime *adj* cowardly

pústula *nf* pustule

puta *nf muy Fam* whore

putada *nf muy Fam* **hacerle una p. a alguien** to be a mean bastard to sb; **¡qué p.!** what a real bitch!

putativo, -a *adj* putative

puteada *nf RP muy Fam (insulto)* swear word

puteado, -a *adj muy Fam* **está p. en el trabajo** he's being screwed around at work; **está p. porque no tiene dinero** he's screwed because he's short of money; **tengo la espalda puteada** my back is screwed

putear *muy Fam* **1** *vt* (**a**) *(fastidiar)* **p. a alguien** to screw sb around (**b**) *Am (insultar)* **p. a alguien** to call sb for everything
2 *vi* (**a**) *(salir con prostitutas)* to go whoring (**b**) *Am (decir malas palabras)* to swear like a trooper

puteo *muy Fam nm* (**a**) *(fastidio)* **es un p.** it's a pain in the ass (**b**) *(con prostitutas)* **ir de p.** to go whoring

putero *nm muy Fam* whoremaster

puticlub *(pl* puticlubs*) nm Fam* cathouse

puto, -a **1** *adj* (**a**) *Vulg (maldito)* fucking; *Esp muy Fam* **no tengo ni puta idea** I don't have a goddamn clue (**b**) *muy Fam (difícil)* goddamn difficult (**c**) *muy Fam* **de puta madre** *(estupendo)* goddamn brilliant; **nos lo pasamos de puta madre** we had a goddamn marvelous time
2 *nm Fam* rent boy

putón *nm muy Fam* **un p. (verbenero)** a cheap slut

putrefacción *nf* rotting, putrefaction

putrefacto, -a *adj* rotting

pútrido, -a *adj* putrid

puya *nf* (**a**) *(punta de vara)* goad (**b**) *Fam (palabras)* gibe, dig

puyazo *nm* (**a**) *(golpe)* jab *(with goad)* (**b**) *Fam (palabras)* taunt

puzzle ['puθle], **puzle** *nm* jigsaw puzzle

PVC *nm (abrev de* **cloruro de polivinilo***)* PVC

PVP *nm (abrev de* **precio de venta al público***)* retail price

PYME ['pime] *nf (abrev de* **Pequeña y Mediana Empresa***)* SME

pyrex® *nm* Pyrex®

pza. *(abrev de* **plaza***)* Sq

Q

Qatar *n* Qatar

qatarí (*pl* **qataríes**) *adj & nmf* Qatari

q.e.p.d. (*abrev de* **que en paz descanse**) RIP

quark (*pl* **quarks**) *nm Fís* quark

quásar *nm Astron* quasar

que 1 *pron relativo* (**a**) *(sujeto) (persona)* who, that; *(cosa)* that, which; **la mujer q. me saluda** the woman (who *o* that is) waving to me; **el q. me lo compró** the one who bought it from me; **la moto q. me gusta** the motorbike (that) I like; **el hombre, q. decía llamarse Simón, era bastante sospechoso** the man, who said he was called Simón, seemed rather suspicious; **el q. más y el q. menos** every last one of us, all of us without exception

(**b**) *(complemento directo) (se puede omitir en inglés) (persona)* who, whom; *(cosa)* that, which; **el hombre q. conociste ayer** the man (who *o* whom) you met yesterday; **la persona/el lugar q. estás buscando** the person/the place you're looking for; **ese libro es el q. me quiero comprar** that book is the one (that *o* which) I want to buy

(**c**) *(complemento indirecto) (se puede omitir en inglés)* **al q., a la q., a los/las q.** (to) who, (to) whom; **ese es el chico al q. presté dinero** that's the boy I lent some money to

(**d**) *(complemento circunstancial)* **la playa a la q. fui** the beach where I went, the beach I went to; **la mujer con la q. hablas** the woman (who) you are talking to; **la mesa en la que escribes** the table on which you are writing, the table you are writing on

(**e**) *(complemento de tiempo)* (**en**) **q.** when; **el día (en) q. me fui** the day (when) I left

2 *conj* (**a**) *(con oraciones de sujeto)* that; **es importante q. me escuches** it's important that you listen to me; **q. haya pérdidas no es un problema insuperable** the fact that we've suffered losses isn't an insurmountable problem

(**b**) *(con oraciones de complemento directo)* that; **me ha confesado q. me quiere** he has told me that he loves me

(**c**) *(comparativo)* than; **es más rápido q. tú** he's quicker than you; **antes morir q. vivir la guerra** I'd rather die than live through a war

(**d**) *(expresa causa)* **hemos de esperar, q. todavía no es la hora** we'll have to wait, as it isn't time yet

(**e**) *(expresa consecuencia)* that; **tanto me lo pidió q. se lo di** he asked me for it so insistently that I gave it to him

(**f**) *(expresa finalidad)* so (that); **ven aquí q. te vea** come over here so (that) I can see you

(**g**) *(expresa deseo)* that; **quiero q. lo hagas** I want you to do it; **espero q. te diviertas** I hope (that) you have fun

(**h**) *(en oraciones exclamativas)* **¡q. te diviertas!** have fun!; **¡q. te doy un bofetón!** do that again and I'll slap you!; **¿no vas a venir? — ¡q. sí!** aren't you coming? — of course I am!; **¿pero de verdad no quieres venir? — ¡q. no!** but do you really not want to come? – definitely not!; **¡q. me dejes!** just leave me alone!

(**i**) *(en oraciones interrogativas)* **¿q. quiere venir? pues que venga** so she wants to come? then let her

(**j**) *(para explicar)* **es q....** the thing is that…, it's just that…

(**k**) *(expresa hipótesis)* if; **q. no quieres hacerlo, pues no pasa nada** it doesn't matter if you don't want to do it

(**l**) *(expresa disyunción)* or; **quieras q. no, harás lo que yo mando** you'll do what I tell you, whether you like it or not

(**m**) *(expresa reiteración)* **estuvieron charla q. te charla toda la mañana** they were chatting away all morning

qué 1 *adj (interrogativo) (en general)* what; *(al elegir, al concretar)* which; **¿q. hora es?** what's the time?; **¿q. coche prefieres?** which car do you prefer?; **¿a q. distancia?** how far away?

2 *pron (interrogativo)* what; **¿q. te dijo?** what did he tell you?; **no sé q. hacer** I don't know what to do; **¿q.?** *(¿cómo dices?)* sorry? pardon?; **¿y q.?** so what?

3 *adv* (**a**) *(exclamativo)* how; **¡q. horror!** how awful!; **¡q. tonto eres!** how stupid you are!, you're so stupid!; **¡q. casa más bonita!** what a lovely house! (**b**) *(expresa gran cantidad)* **¡q. de…!** what a lot of…!; **¡q. de gente hay aquí!** what a lot of people there are here!, there are so many people here! (**c**) *(expresiones)* **¿q. tal?** how are things?, how are you doing?; **¿q. tal la fiesta/película?** how was the party/movie?; **¿por q.?** why?; *Am* **¿q. tan…?** how…?; **q. tanto?** *(¿cuánto?)* how much?

Quebec *nm* (**el**) **Q.** Quebec

quebequés, -esa 1 *adj* Quebecois

2 *nm,f* Quebecois, Quebecker

quebrada *nf* (**a**) *(desfiladero)* gorge (**b**) *Am (arroyo)* stream

quebradero *nm* **q. de cabeza** headache, problem

quebradizo, -a *adj* (**a**) *(frágil)* fragile, brittle (**b**) *(débil)* frail (**c**) *(voz)* wavering, faltering

quebrado, -a 1 *adj* (**a**) *(terreno)* rough, uneven; *(perfil)* rugged (**b**) *(fraccionario)* **número q.** fraction (**c**) *Lit* broken (**d**) *Méx (pelo)* curly

2 *nm (fracción)* fraction

quebradura *nf* (**a**) *(grieta)* crack, fissure (**b**) *Med* rupture

quebrantado, -a *adj* frail

quebrantahuesos *nm inv* bearded vulture, lammergeier

quebrantamiento *nm* (**a**) *(incumplimiento)* breaking (**b**) *(rotura)* cracking; *Fig (de moral, resistencia)* breaking (**c**) *(debilitamiento)* weakening

quebrantar 1 *vt* (**a**) *(incumplir) (promesa, ley)* to break; *(obligación)* to fail in (**b**) *(romper)* to crack; *Fig (moral, resistencia)* to break (**c**) *(debilitar)* to weaken

2 quebrantarse *vpr* (**a**) *(romperse)* to crack (**b**) *(debilitarse)* to decline, to deteriorate

quebranto *nm* (**a**) *(pérdida)* loss (**b**) *(debilitamiento)* weakening, debilitation (**c**) *(pena)* grief

quebrar [3] **1** *vt* (**a**) *(romper)* to break; *Fig (esperanzas, ilusiones)* to destroy, to shatter (**b**) *(debilitar)* to weaken

2 *vi* (**a**) *Fin (empresa)* to go bankrupt (**b**) *Méx (torcer)* to turn

3 quebrarse *vpr* (**a**) *(romperse)* to break; *Méx Fam Fig* **quebrarse la cabeza** to rack *o* cudgel one's brains (**b**) *(voz)* to break, to falter (**c**) *Am (darse por vencido)* to give in, to throw in the towel

quechua 1 *adj* Quechuan
  2 *nmf (persona)* Quechua
  3 *nm (idioma)* Quechua

queda *nf* **toque de q.** curfew

quedada *nf Fam* **(a)** *(tomadura de pelo)* wind-up **(b)** *(por Internet)* meetup

quedar 1 *vi* **(a)** *(haber aún, faltar)* to be left, to remain; **¿queda azúcar?** is there any sugar left?; **nos quedan 100 pesos** we have 100 pesos left; **¿cuánto queda para León?** how much further is it to León?; **quedan dos vueltas para que termine la carrera** there are two laps to go until the end of the race; **q. por hacer** to remain to be done; **queda por fregar el suelo** the floor has still to be cleaned
  (b) *(permanecer)* to remain, to stay; **el viaje quedó en proyecto** the trip never got beyond the planning stage; **¡esto no puede** *o* **no va a q. así!** I'm not going to let it rest at this!
  (c) *(mostrarse)* **q. bien/mal (con alguien)** to make a good/bad impression (on sb); **no me hagas q. mal** don't show me up; **le gusta q. bien con todo el mundo** he likes to keep everyone happy; **q. como un idiota** to look stupid, to end up looking stupid
  (d) *(llegar a ser, resultar)* **el trabajo ha quedado perfecto** the job turned out perfectly; **el cuadro queda muy bien ahí** the picture looks great there
  (e) *(llegar)* **q. en** to end in; **q. en quinto lugar, q. el quinto** to come fifth; **q. en nada** to come to nothing
  (f) *(sentar)* to look; **te queda un poco corto el traje** your suit is a bit too short; **q. bien/mal a alguien** to look good/bad on sb; **q. bien/mal con algo** to go well/badly with sth
  (g) *(citarse)* **q. (con alguien)** to arrange to meet (sb); **hemos quedado el lunes** we've arranged to meet on Monday; **he quedado con Juan esta noche** I've arranged to meet Juan this evening; **¿cuándo/dónde quedamos?** when/where shall we meet?
  (h) *(acordar)* **q. en algo/en hacer algo** to agree on sth/to do sth; **q. en que...** to agree that...; **¿en qué quedamos?** what's it to be, then?
  (i) *Fam (estar situado)* to be; **queda por las afueras** it's somewhere on the outskirts; **¿por dónde queda?** whereabouts is it?
  2 *v impersonal* **por mí que no quede** don't let me be the one to stop you; **que no quede por falta de dinero** we don't want it to fall through for lack of money
  3 quedarse *vpr* **(a)** *(permanecer)* to stay, to remain **(b)** *(terminar en un estado)* **quedarse ciego/sordo** to go blind/deaf; **quedarse triste** to be *o* feel sad; **quedarse sin dinero** to be left penniless **(c)** *(comprar, elegir)* to take; **me quedo éste** I'll take this one **(d) quedarse con** *(retener, guardarse)* to keep **(e) quedarse con** *(preferir)* to go for, to prefer **(f)** *Fam (morir)* to kick the bucket **(g)** *Esp Fam* **quedarse con alguien** *(burlarse de)* to needle sb; **te estás quedando conmigo** you're having me on!

quedo, -a 1 *adj* quiet, soft
  2 *adv* quietly, softly

quehacer *nm* task; **quehaceres domésticos** housework

queimada *nf* = punch made from spirits and sugar, which is set alight to burn off some of the alcohol before being drunk

queja *nf* **(a)** *(protesta)* complaint; **presentar una q.** *(formalmente)* to make *o* lodge a complaint; **tener q. de algo/alguien** to have a complaint about sth/sb **(b)** *(lamento)* moan, groan

quejarse *vpr* **(a)** *(protestar)* to complain **(de** about); *(refunfuñar)* to moan **(de** about); **siempre está quejándose del frío que hace en este país** he's always complaining about how cold it is in this country; **no sé de qué te quejas** I don't know what you're complaining about; *Fam* **q. de vicio** to complain about nothing **(b)** *(expresar dolor, pena)* to moan,

to groan; **últimamente se queja mucho de la espalda** recently she's been complaining a lot that her back hurts

quejica, quejicoso, -a *Fam Pey* **1** *adj* whining
  2 *nmf* whiner

quejido *nm* cry, moan

quejoso, -a 1 *adj* **estar q. de** *o* **por** to be unhappy *o* dissatisfied with
  2 *nm,f* **(a)** *Méx, RP Fam Pey (quejica)* whiner **(b)** *Méx Der (demandante)* plaintiff

quejumbroso, -a *adj* whining

quema *nf* burning

quemado, -a *adj* **(a)** *(por fuego)* burned; *(por agua hirviendo)* scalded; *(por electricidad)* burned-out **(b)** *Am (bronceado)* tanned **(c)** *Fam* **estar q.** *(agotado)* to be burned-out; *(harto)* to be fed up

quemador *nm* burner

quemadura, *Méx* **quemada** *nf (por fuego)* burn; *(por agua hirviendo)* scald; **hacerse una q.** to burn/scald oneself; **quemaduras de tercer grado** third-degree burns

quemar 1 *vt* **(a)** *(con fuego, calor, sol)* to burn; *(con líquido hirviendo)* to scald; **quemaron una bandera americana** they set fire to an American flag **(b)** *(plantas)* **la helada quemó las plantas** the frost killed the plants; **el sol quemó las plantas** the plants withered in the sun **(c)** *(malgastar) (ahorros)* to go through, to fritter away **(d)** *Fam (desgastar)* to burn out
  2 *vi* **(a)** *(estar caliente)* to be (scalding) hot; **ten cuidado que la sopa quema** be careful, the soup's (scalding) hot **(b)** *Fam (desgastar)* **la política quema** politics burns you out
  3 quemarse *vpr* **(a)** *(por fuego)* to burn down; *(por agua hirviendo)* to get scalded; *(por calor)* to burn; *(por electricidad)* to burn out; **se ha quemado la lasaña** the lasagne's burned **(b)** *(por el sol)* to get (sun)burned **(c)** *Fam (desgastarse)* to burn out; *Esp (hartarse)* to get fed up

quemarropa: a quemarropa *loc adv* point-blank

quemazón *nf (ardor)* burning (sensation); *(picor)* itch

quena *nf* Andean flute

quepa *etc ver* **caber**

quepis *nm inv* kepi

quepo *ver* **caber**

queque *nm Andes, CAm, Méx* sponge (cake)

queratina *nf* keratin

querella *nf* **(a)** *Der (acusación)* charge **(b)** *(discordia)* dispute

querellante *adj & nmf Der* plaintiff

querellarse *vpr Der* to bring an action **(contra** against)

querencia *nf* homing instinct

querer [53] **1** *vt* **(a)** *(desear)* to want; **quiero una bicicleta** I want a bicycle; **¿quieren ustedes algo más?** would you like anything else?; **haz lo que quieras** do what you want *o* like, do as you please *o* like; **q. que alguien haga algo** to want sb to do sth; **quiero que lo hagas tú** I want you to do it; **queremos que las cosas le vayan bien** we want things to go well for you; **quisiera hacerlo, pero...** I'd like to do it, but...; **¡qué quieres que haga!** what am I supposed to do?; **qué quieres que te diga, a mí me parece caro** to be honest, it seems expensive to me, what can I say? it seems expensive to me
  (b) *(amar)* to love; **te quiero** I love you
  (c) *(en preguntas) (con amabilidad)* **¿querrías explicarme qué ha pasado aquí?** would you mind explaining what happened here?; **¿quiere decirle a su amigo que pase?** could you tell your friend to come in, please?
  (d) *(pedir)* **q. algo (por)** to want sth (for); **¿cuánto quieres por el coche?** how much do you want for the car?
  (e) *Irónico (dar motivos para)* **tú lo que quieres es que te pegue** you're asking for a smack; **¿quieres que te atropelle el tren o qué?** do you want to get run over by a train or something?

(f) *(expresiones)* **como quien no quiere la cosa** as if it were nothing; *Prov* **quien bien te quiere te hará llorar** you have to be cruel to be kind

2 *vi* to want; **ven cuando quieras** come whenever you like *o* want; **no me voy porque no quiero** I'm not going because I don't want to; **queriendo** on purpose; **sin q.** accidentally; **q. decir** to mean; **¿qué quieres decir con eso?** what do you mean by that?; **q. es poder** where there's a will there's a way

3 *v impersonal (haber atisbos)* **parece que quiere llover** it looks like rain

5 *nm (amor)* love

4 quererse *vpr (dos personas)* to love each other

querido, -a 1 *adj* dear

2 *nm,f (amante)* lover; *(apelativo afectuoso)* darling

queroseno, *Am* **querosén,** *Am* **querosene** *nm* kerosene

querré *etc ver* **querer**

querubín *nm* cherub

quesadilla *nf CAm, Méx* = filled fried tortilla

quesera *nf* cheese dish

quesería *nf* cheese shop *o* store

quesero, -a 1 *adj* cheese; **la industria quesera** the cheese-making industry

2 *nm,f (persona)* cheesemaker

quesito *nm* cheese portion *o* triangle

queso *nm* cheese; **q. azul** blue cheese; **q. de bola** Dutch cheese; **q. fresco** cottage cheese; **q. gruyère** Gruyère (cheese); **q. manchego** = hard yellow cheese made in La Mancha; **q. parmesano** Parmesan (cheese); **q. en porciones** cheese portions *o* triangles; **q. rallado** grated cheese; **q. roquefort** Roquefort (cheese)

quetzal *nm* quetzal

quevedos *nmpl* pince-nez

quia *interj Fam* **¡q.!** huh!, ha!

quiche [kiʃ] *nf* quiche

quicio *nm (de puerta)* (door)jamb *(on hinge side)*; *Fig* **estar fuera de q.** to be out of kilter; *Fig* **sacar de q. a alguien** to drive sb mad; *Fig* **sacar las cosas de q.** to blow things (up) out of all proportion

quid *(pl* **quids)** *nm* crux; **el q. de la cuestión** the crux of the matter

quiebra 1 *ver* **quebrar**

2 *nf* **(a)** *(ruina)* bankruptcy; *(en Bolsa)* crash; *Der* **q. fraudulenta** fraudulent bankruptcy; **ir a la q.** to go bankrupt **(b)** *(pérdida)* collapse; **q. moral** moral bankruptcy

quiebro *nm* **(a)** *(ademán)* swerve **(b)** *Mús* trill

quien *pron* **(a)** *(relativo) (sujeto)* who; *(complemento)* who, *Formal* whom; **fue mi hermano q. me lo explicó** it was my brother who explained it to me; **era Pepe a q. vi/de q. no me fiaba** it was Pepe (whom) I saw/didn't trust **(b)** *(indefinido)* **gane q. gane, va a ser un partido memorable** whoever wins, it will be an unforgettable game; **quienes quieran verlo que se acerquen** whoever wants to see it will have to come closer; **q. no sabe nada de esto es tu madre** one person who knows nothing about it is your mother; **hay q. lo niega** there are those who deny it; **al billar no hay q. le gane** he's unbeatable at billiards; **q. más q. menos** everyone

quién *pron* **(a)** *(interrogativo) (sujeto)* who; *(complemento)* who, *Formal* whom; **¿q. es ese hombre?** who's that man?; **no sé q. viene** I don't know who is coming; **¿a quiénes has invitado?** who *o* whom have you invited?; **¿de q. es?** whose is it?; **¿q. es?** *(en la puerta)* who is it?; *(al teléfono)* who's calling? **(b)** *(exclamativo)* **¡q. pudiera verlo!** if only I could see!

quienquiera *(pl* **quienesquiera)** *pron* whoever; **q. que venga** whoever comes

quiera *etc ver* **querer**

quieto, -a *adj* **(a)** *(parado)* still; **¡estate q.!** keep still!; **¡q. ahí!** don't move!; **¡las manos quietas!** keep your hands to yourself! **(b)** *(tranquilo)* quiet; **desde que se fue el director el trabajo está q.** things have been a lot quieter at work since the boss left

quietud *nf* **(a)** *(inmovilidad)* stillness **(b)** *(tranquilidad)* quietness

quif *nm* hashish

quihubo *interj CAm, Col, Méx, Ven Fam* **¿q.?** how are you doing?

quijada *nf* jaw

quijotada *nf* quixotic deed

quijote *nm* do-gooder

quijotesco, -a *adj* quixotic

quijotismo *nm* quixotism

quilate *nm* carat

quilla *nf* **(a)** *Náut* keel **(b)** *(de ave)* breastbone

quilo *nm* kilo, kilogram

quimbambas *nfpl Fam* **en las q.** way out in the sticks

quimera *nf* fantasy

quimérico, -a *adj* fanciful, unrealistic

química *nf* chemistry

químico, -a 1 *adj* chemical

2 *nm,f (científico)* chemist

quimioterapia *nf* chemotherapy

quimono *nm* kimono

quina *nf (extracto)* quinine; **árbol de la q.** cinchona; **ser más malo que la q.** to be truly horrible; **tragar q.** to grin and bear it

quincalla *nf* trinket

quincallería *nf (chatarra)* trinkets

quince *núm* fifteen; **q. días** a fortnight; *ver también* **seis**

quinceañero, -a 1 *adj* teenage

2 *nm,f* teenager

quinceavo, -a *núm (fracción)* fifteenth; **la quinceava parte** a fifteenth

quincena *nf* fortnight

quincenal *adj* fortnightly

quincuagésimo, -a *núm* fiftieth

quinesioterapia, quinesiterapia *nf* kinesitherapy

quiniela *nf* **(a)** *Esp (boleto)* pools coupon; **quinielas** *(apuestas)* sports lottery; **hacer una q.** to play the sports lottery; **echar una q.** to hand in one's sports lottery ticket; **q. hípica** = gambling pool based on the results of horse races **(b)** *Méx, RP (juego de azar)* lottery

quinielista *nmf Esp* = person who plays the sports lottery

quinielístico, -a *adj Esp* **peña quinielística** = group who combine to play the "quinielas"

quinientos, -as *núm* five hundred; *ver también* **seis**

quinina *nf* quinine

quino *nm (árbol)* cinchona

quinqué *nm* oil lamp

quinquenal *adj* five-year; **plan q.** five-year plan

quinquenio *nm* **(a)** *(periodo)* five-year period **(b)** *(paga)* = five-yearly increment of salary

quinqui *nmf Esp Fam (macarra)* lout

quinta *nf* **(a)** *(finca)* country house **(b)** *Aut* fifth (gear) **(c)** *Mil* call-up time; **entrar en quintas** to be called up; *Fig* **es de mi q.** *(tiene mi edad)* he's my age

quintacolumnista *nmf* fifth columnist

quintaesencia *nf inv* quintessence

quintal *nm* = weight measure equivalent to 46 kilos; **q. métrico** 100 kilos; *Fig* **pesar un q.** to weigh a ton

quinteto *nm* quintet

quintillizo, -a *adj & nm,f* quintuplet

quinto, -a 1 *núm* fifth; **la quinta parte** a fifth
2 *nm* (**a**) *(parte)* fifth (**b**) *Mil* = person who has been chosen (by lots) to do military service (**c**) *(de cerveza)* small bottle of beer *(0.2 liter)*

quintuplicar [59] **1** *vt* to increase fivefold
2 quintuplicarse *vpr* to increase fivefold

quíntuplo, -a, quíntuple 1 *adj* quintuple
2 *nm* quintuple

quiosco *nm (tenderete)* kiosk; *(de periódicos)* newspaper stand *o* kiosk; **q. de música** bandstand

quiosquero, -a *nm,f* = person selling newspapers, drinks etc from a kiosk

quiquiriquí (*pl* **quiquiriquíes** *o* **quiquiriquís**) **1** *nm* crowing
2 *interj* cock-a-doodle-do

quirófano *nm* operating room

quiromancia *nf* palmistry, chiromancy

quiromántico, -a 1 *adj* chiromantic
2 *nm,f* palmist

quiromasaje *nm* (manual) massage

quiromasajista *nmf* masseur, *f* masseuse

quiropráctico, -a 1 *adj* chiropractic
2 *nm,f* chiropractor

quirúrgico, -a *adj* surgical

quisiera *etc ver* **querer**

quisque, quisqui *nm* **cada** *o* **todo q.** every man jack, everyone

quisquilla *nf* prawn

quisquilloso, -a 1 *adj* (**a**) *(detallista)* persnickety (**b**) *(susceptible)* touchy, oversensitive
2 *nm,f* (**a**) *(detallista)* nit-picker (**b**) *(susceptible)* touchy person

quiste *nm* cyst; **q. ovárico** ovarian cyst

quitaesmalte *nm* nail-polish remover

quitamanchas *nm inv* stain remover

quitamiedos *nm inv (en carretera)* crash barrier; *(para evitar caída)* railing

quitanieves *nm inv* snowplow

quitapenas *nm inv Fam (licor)* pick-me-up

quitar 1 *vt* (**a**) *(en general)* to remove; *(ropa, zapatos)* to take off; *Esp* **q. la mesa** to clear the table; **quitarle algo a alguien** to take sth away from sb; **quita tus cosas de en medio** clear your things up (out of the way); **de quita y pon** removable; *(capucha)* detachable
(**b**) *(dolor, ansiedad)* to take away, to relieve; *(sed)* to quench; **el aperitivo me ha quitado el hambre** I don't feel hungry after that snack
(**c**) *(tiempo)* to take up; **me quitan mucho tiempo los niños** the children take up a lot of my time
(**d**) *(robar)* to take, to steal; **me han quitado la cartera** someone has taken *o* stolen my wallet
(**e**) *(impedir)* **esto no quita que sea un vago** that doesn't change the fact that he's a layabout; **que me mude de ciudad no quita que nos sigamos viendo** just because I'm moving to another city doesn't mean we won't still be able to see each other
(**f**) *(exceptuar)* **quitando el queso, me gusta todo** apart from cheese, I like everything
(**g**) *(desconectar)* to switch off
2 quitarse *vpr* (**a**) *(apartarse)* to get out of the way; **¡quítate de en medio!** get out of the way! (**b**) *(ropa)* to take off (**c**) *(sujeto: mancha)* to come out (**d**) *(expresiones)* **quitarse la vida** to kill oneself; **quitarse a alguien de encima** *o* **de en medio** to get rid of sb

quitasol *nm* sunshade, parasol

quite *nm Dep* parry; **estar al q.** to be on hand to help; *Fam (alerta)* to keep one's ears/eyes open

quiteño, -a 1 *adj* of/from Quito
2 *nm,f* person from Quito

Quito *n* Quito

quizá, quizás *adv* perhaps; **q. llueva mañana** it might rain tomorrow; **q. no lo creas** you may not believe it; **q. sí** maybe; **q. no** maybe not

quórum *nm inv* quorum; **hay q.** we have a quorum; **no hay q.** we don't have a quorum

R

R, r [*Esp* 'erre, *Am* 'ere] *nf (letra)* R, r
rabadilla *nf* coccyx
rabanillo *nm* wild radish
rábano *nm* radish; *Fam* **me importa un r.** I couldn't care less, I don't give a damn
Rabat *n* Rabat
rabel *nm* rebec
rabia *nf* (**a**) *(ira)* rage; **me da r.** it makes me mad; **me da r. no haber podido ayudarles** it's so annoying *o* frustrating not having been able to help them; **¡qué r.!** how annoying!; **"¡déjame!", dijo con r.** "leave me alone," she said angrily; **¿dónde dejo esto? — donde más r. te dé** where shall I put this? — wherever you like; **compra el que más r. te dé** buy whichever one you like *o* fancy (**b**) *(antipatía)* **tenerle r. a alguien** not to be able to stand sb (**c**) *(enfermedad)* rabies *(singular)*
rabiar *vi* (**a**) *(sufrir)* to writhe in pain (**b**) *(enfadarse)* to be furious; **estar a r. (con alguien)** to be furious (with sb); **hacer r. a alguien** to make sb furious (**c**) *(desear)* **r. por algo/hacer algo** to be dying for sth/to do sth; **me gusta a r.** I'm crazy about it
rabicorto, -a *adj* short-tailed
rabieta *nf Fam* tantrum
rabilargo, -a *adj* long-tailed
rabillo *nm* (**a**) *(de fruta, hoja)* stalk (**b**) *(del ojo)* corner; **mirar algo con el r. del ojo** to look at sth out of the corner of one's eye
rabino *nm* rabbi
rabiosamente *adv* (**a**) *(mucho)* terribly (**b**) *(con enfado)* furiously, in a rage
rabioso, -a *adj* (**a**) *(furioso)* furious (**b**) *(excesivo)* terrible; *Fig* **de rabiosa actualidad** *(libro, emisión)* extremely topical (**c**) *(enfermo de rabia)* rabid (**d**) *(chillón)* loud, gaudy
rabo *nm* (**a**) *(de animal)* tail; **r. de buey** oxtail; **irse** *o* **salir con el r. entre las piernas** to go off with one's tail between one's legs (**b**) *(de hoja, fruto)* stem (**c**) *muy Fam (pene)* prick, cock
rabona *nf RP Fam* **hacerse la r.** to play hooky
racanear *Fam* **1** *vt* to be stingy with
   2 *vi* (**a**) *(ser tacaño)* to be stingy (**b**) *(holgazanear)* to loaf about
racaneo *nm,* **racanería** *nf Fam* stinginess
rácano, -a *Fam* **1** *adj* (**a**) *(tacaño)* mean, stingy (**b**) *(gandul)* idle, lazy
   2 *nm,f* (**a**) *(tacaño)* mean devil (**b**) *(gandul)* lazybones
RACE ['rraθe] *nm (abrev de* **Real Automóvil Club de España**) ≃ AAA, = Spanish automobile association
racha *nf* (**a**) *(época)* spell; *(serie)* string; **buena/mala r.** good/bad patch; **una r. de buena suerte** a run of good luck; **una mala r. de resultados económicos** a string of poor financial results; **rompieron una r. de seis derrotas consecutivas** they ended a run of six consecutive defeats; **a rachas** in fits and starts (**b**) *(ráfaga)* gust (of wind)
racheado, -a *adj* gusty, squally
racial *adj* racial

racimo *nm (de uvas)* bunch
raciocinio *nm* (**a**) *(razón)* (power of) reason (**b**) *(razonamiento)* reasoning
ración *nf* (**a**) *(porción)* portion (**b**) *(en bar, restaurante)* = portion of a dish served as a substantial snack
racionado, -a *adj* rationed
racional *adj* rational
racionalidad *nf* rationality
racionalismo *nm* rationalism
racionalización *nf* rationalization
racionalizar [14] *vt* to rationalize
racionamiento *nm* rationing
racionar *vt* to ration
racismo *nm* racism
racista *adj & nmf* racist
rada *nf* roadstead, inlet
radar *nm* radar
radiación *nf* radiation; **r. solar** solar radiation; **r. de baja intensidad** low-level radiation
radiactividad *nf* radioactivity
radiactivo, -a *adj* radioactive
radiado, -a *adj* (**a**) *(mensaje)* radioed; **programa r.** radio program (**b**) *(radial)* radiate
radiador *nm* radiator
radial *adj* (**a**) *Tec & Mat (del radio)* radial (**b**) *Am (programa, cadena)* radio
radiante *adj también Fig* radiant; **estar r. de felicidad** to be beaming with joy
radiar [32] *vt* (**a**) *(irradiar)* to radiate (**b**) *Fís* to irradiate; *Med* to give X-ray treatment to (**c**) *(por radio)* to broadcast
radicación *nf (establecimiento)* settling
radical 1 *adj & nmf* radical
   2 *nm* (**a**) *Gram & Mat* root (**b**) *Quím* radical
radicalismo *nm* (**a**) *(intransigencia)* inflexibility, unwillingness to compromise (**b**) *Pol* radicalism
radicalización *nf* radicalization
radicalizar [14] **1** *vt* to harden, to make more radical
   2 radicalizarse *vpr* to become more radical *o* extreme
radicalmente *adv* radically
radicar [59] **1** *vi* (**a**) *(consistir)* **r. en** to lie in (**b**) *(estar situado)* to be (situated) (**en** in)
   2 radicarse *vpr (establecerse)* to settle (**en** in)
radio 1 *nm* (**a**) *Anat & Geom* radius; **en un r. de** within a radius of; **r. de acción** range; *Fig* sphere of influence (**b**) *(de rueda)* spoke (**c**) *Quím* radium (**d**) *Am salvo CSur (transistor)* radio
   2 *nf* (**a**) *(medio)* radio; **oír algo por la r.** to hear sth on the radio; **r. digital** digital radio; **r. pirata** pirate radio (**b**) *Esp, CSur (transistor)* radio; **r. despertador** clock radio
radioactividad *nf* radioactivity
radioactivo, -a *adj* radioactive
radioaficionado, -a *nm,f* radio ham

radiobaliza *nf* radio beacon

radiocasete *nm* radio cassette (player)

radiocomunicación *nf* radio communication

radiocontrol *nm* remote control

radiodespertador *nm* clock radio

radiodifusión *nf* broadcasting

radiodifusora *nf Am* radio station, radio transmitter

radioemisor, -ora *adj* radio broadcasting

radioemisora *nf* radio station, radio transmitter

radioenlace *nm* radio link

radioescucha *nmf inv* listener

radiofaro *nm* radio beacon

radiofonía *nf* radio *(technology)*

radiofónico, -a *adj* radio; **programa r.** radio program

radiofórmula *nf Esp* = radio station which only plays hits and formulaic pop music

radiofrecuencia *nf* radio frequency

radiograbador *nm*, **radiograbadora** *nf CSur* radio cassette (player)

radiografía *nf (fotografía)* X-ray

radiografiar [32] *vt* to X-ray

radiología *nf* radiology

radiológico, -a *adj* X-ray, radiological; **examen r.** X-ray examination

radiólogo, -a *nm,f* radiologist

radiomensaje *nm RP (buscapersonas)* pager

radiomensajería *nf* radio messages

radionovela *nf* radio soap opera

radiooperador, -ora *nm,f* radio operator

radiorreceptor *nm* radio (receiver)

radiorreloj *nm* clock radio

radioscopia *nf* radioscopy

radiotaxi *nm (aparato de radio)* = taxi driver's two-way radio; *(taxi)* taxi *(fitted with two-way radio)*

radioteléfono *nm* radiotelephone

radiotelegrafía *nf* radiotelegraphy

radiotelegrafista *nmf* wireless operator

radiotelescopio *nm* radio telescope

radiotelevisión *nf* empresa de r. broadcasting company

radioterapeuta *nmf* radiotherapist

radioterapia *nf* radiotherapy

radiotransmisión *nf* broadcasting

radiotransmisor *nm* radio transmitter

radioyente *nmf* listener

radique *etc ver* **radicar**

RAE ['rrae] *nf (abrev de Real Academia Española)* = institution that sets lexical and syntactical standards for Spanish

raer [54] *vt* to scrape (off)

ráfaga *nf (de aire, viento)* gust; *(de disparos)* burst; *(de luces)* flash

rafia *nf* raffia

rafting *nm Dep* rafting

raglán *adj* **manga r.** raglan sleeve

ragout [rra'vu] *(pl ragouts)*, **ragú** *nm* ragout

raído, -a *adj (desgastado)* threadbare; *(por los bordes)* frayed

raigambre *nf (a) (tradición)* tradition; **de r.** traditional **(b)** *(origen)* roots

raíl, rail *nm* rail

raíz *(pl raíces)* **1** *nf (a) (de planta, pelo, muela)* root; *(causa)* root cause, origin; **arrancar algo de r.** to root sth out completely; **cortar algo de r.** to nip sth in the bud; **echar raíces** to put down roots **(b)** *(origen)* origin; **de raíces humildes** of humble origins; **la costumbre tiene su r. en la España del siglo XV** the custom has its roots *o* origin in 15th-century Spain **(c)** *Mat* root; **r. cuadrada/cúbica** square/cube root

2 a raíz de *loc prep* as a result of, following; **se produjo un gran escándalo a r. de sus declaraciones** his statements caused outrage

raja *nf (a) (porción)* slice **(b)** *(grieta)* crack

rajá *(pl rajaes)* *nm* raja

rajado, -a *nm,f Fam (a) (cobarde)* chicken **(b)** ¡**eres un r.!** *(siempre te echas atrás)* you're always pulling out at the last minute!; *(nunca te unes)* you never join in anything!

rajar 1 *vt (a) (partir)* to crack; *Esp (melón)* to slice **(b)** *Fam (apuñalar)* to slash, to cut up

2 *vi Esp Fam (hablar)* to chatter on

3 rajarse *vpr (a) (partirse)* to crack **(b)** *Fam (echarse atrás)* to back *o* pull out **(c)** *Andes, Carib, RP Fam (huir)* to hightail it **(d)** *Chile, Col Fam (suspender)* to fail, to flunk

rajatabla: a rajatabla *loc adv* to the letter, strictly

ralea *nf Pey* breed, ilk

ralentí *nm* neutral; **al r.** *Aut* ticking over; *Cine* in slow motion

ralentización *nf* slowing down

ralentizar [14] **1** *vt* to slow down

2 ralentizarse *vpr* to slow down

rallado, -a 1 *adj* grated; **pan r.** breadcrumbs

2 *nm* grating

rallador *nm* grater

ralladura *nf* grating; **r. de limón** grated lemon rind

rallar *vt* to grate

rally ['rrali] *(pl rallys)* *nm* rally

ralo, -a *adj (pelo, barba)* sparse, thin; *(dientes)* with gaps between them

RAM [rram] *nf (abrev de random access memory)* RAM

rama *nf* branch; **la r. materna de mi familia** my mother's side of the family; **en r.** raw; *Fam* **andarse por las ramas** to beat about the bush; *Fig* **ir de r. en r.** to jump from one thing to another

ramadán *nm* Ramadan

ramaje *nm* branches

ramal *nm (de carretera, ferrocarril)* branch

ramalazo *nm (a) Fam (hecho que delata)* giveaway sign; **tener r.** *(ser afeminado)* to be limp-wristed **(b)** *(ataque)* fit

rambla *nf (a) (avenida)* avenue, boulevard **(b)** *(río)* watercourse

ramera *nf* whore, hooker

ramificación *nf (a) (acción de dividirse)* branching **(b)** *(rama)* branch **(c)** *(consecuencia)* ramification

ramificarse [59] *vpr* to branch out

ramillete *nm (de flores)* bunch, bouquet; *(de personas)* handful

ramo *nm (a) (de flores)* bunch, bouquet **(b)** *(rama)* branch; **el r. de la construcción** the building industry

rampa *nf (a) (para subir y bajar)* ramp; **r. de lanzamiento** launch pad **(b)** *(cuesta)* steep incline **(c)** *(calambre)* cramp

ramplón, -ona *adj* vulgar, coarse

ramplonería *nf* vulgarity, coarseness

rana *nf* frog; *Fam* **te devolverá el libro cuando las ranas críen pelo** you'll be waiting till the cows come home for him to give you that book back; *Fam* **salir r.** to be a major disappointment

ranchera *nf (a) (canción)* = popular Mexican song **(b)** *(automóvil)* station wagon

ranchería *nf Col, Méx, RP, Ven (a) (en el campo)* = group of labourers' dwellings **(b)** *(en la ciudad)* shantytown

ranchero, -a *nm,f* rancher

rancho *nm (a) (comida)* mess **(b)** *(granja del Oeste)* ranch **(c)** *CSur, Ven (en la ciudad)* shack, shanty **(d)** *Méx (pequeña finca)* = small farmhouse and outbuildings

rancio, -a *adj (a) (pasado) (mantequilla, aceite)* rancid; *(pan)* stale **(b)** *(antiguo)* ancient **(c)** *(añejo)* **vino r.** mellow wine **(d)** *(persona)* sour, unpleasant

ranglan *adj* **manga r.** raglan sleeve

rango *nm* (**a**) *(social)* standing (**b**) *(jerárquico)* rank; **de alto r.** high-ranking

Rangún *n* Rangoon

ranking ['rrankin] *(pl* **rankings)** *nm* ranking

ranúnculo *nm* buttercup

ranura *nf (para monedas)* slot; *(debajo de la puerta, ventana)* gap; *(surco)* groove

rap *nm Mús* rap

rapacidad *nf* rapacity, greed

rapado, -a *adj* shaven

rapapolvo *nm Esp Fam* dressing-down; **dar** *o* **echar un r. a alguien** to dress sb down

rapar 1 *vt (barba, bigote)* to shave off; *(cabeza)* to shave; *(persona)* to shave the hair of

 2 raparse *vpr* to shave one's head

rapaz[1] 1 *adj* (**a**) *(que roba)* rapacious, greedy (**b**) *Zool* **ave r.** bird of prey

 2 *nf Zool* bird of prey

rapaz[2], -aza *nm,f Fam (muchacho)* lad, *f* lass

rape *nm* (**a**) *(pez)* monkfish (**b**) **cortar el pelo al r. a alguien** to crop sb's hair

rapé *nm* snuff

rapear *vi* to rap

rápel *(pl* **rapels)** *nm Dep* rapelling; **hacer r.** to rappel

rapero, -a *nm,f* rapper

rápidamente *adv* quickly

rapidez *nf* speed; **con r.** quickly

rápido, -a 1 *adj (veloz)* quick, fast; *(coche)* fast; *(beneficio, decisión)* quick; **ser r. de reflejos** to have quick reflexes

 2 *adv* quickly; **más r.** quicker; **¡ven, r.!** come, quick!; **¡hazlo/termina r.!** hurry up!; **si vamos r. puede que lleguemos a tiempo** if we're quick *o* if we hurry we may get there on time

 3 *nm* (**a**) *(tren)* express train (**b**) *(de río)* **rápidos** rapids

rapiña *nf* (**a**) *(robo)* robbery with violence (**b**) **ave de r.** bird of prey

rapiñar *vt* to steal

raposo, -a *nm,f* fox, *f* vixen

rappel *(pl* **rappels** *o* **rappeles)** *nm Dep* rapelling; **hacer r.** to rappel

rapsodia *nf* rhapsody

raptar *vt* to abduct, to kidnap

rapto *nm* (**a**) *(secuestro)* abduction, kidnapping (**b**) *(ataque)* fit

raptor, -ora *nm,f* abductor, kidnapper

raqueta *nf* (**a**) *(para jugar) (al tenis)* racquet; *(al ping pong)* bat, paddle (**b**) *(para la nieve)* snowshoe

raquianestesia *nf Med* epidural (anesthetic)

raquídeo, -a *adj Anat* **bulbo r.** medulla oblongata

raquis *nm inv* vertebral column

raquítico, -a 1 *adj* (**a**) *(pequeño)* scrawny (**b**) *(escaso)* miserable (**c**) *Med* rachitic

 2 *nm,f Med* rickets sufferer

raquitismo *nm Med* rickets

rara avis *nf inv* **ser una r.** to be rather unusual

raramente *adv* rarely, seldom

rareza *nf* (**a**) *(de persona, cosa)* rarity (**b**) *(de visita)* infrequency (**c**) *(extravagancia)* idiosyncrasy, eccentricity

raro, -a *adj* (**a**) *(extraño)* strange; **¡qué r.!** how odd *o* strange!; **es r. que no nos lo haya dicho** it's odd *o* funny that she didn't tell us (**b**) *(excepcional)* unusual, rare; *(visita)* infrequent; **rara vez** rarely; **es r. el día que viene a comer** she very rarely comes around for lunch; **r. es el que no fuma** very few of them don't smoke (**c**) *(extravagante)* odd, eccentric (**d**) *(escaso)* rare

ras: a ras de *loc prep* level with; **a r. de tierra** at ground level; **volar a r. de tierra** to fly low

rasante 1 *adj (vuelo)* low-level; *(tiro)* grazing

 2 *nf (de carretera)* **cambio de r.** brow of a hill; *(en letrero)* blind hill

rasar *vt* to skim, to graze

rasca *nf Esp Fam (frío)* freezing cold; **hace r.** it's goddamn freezing

rascacielos *nm inv* skyscraper

rascador *nm* (**a**) *(herramienta)* scraper (**b**) *(para las cerillas)* striking surface

rascar [59] **1** *vt* (**a**) *(con uñas, clavo)* to scratch (**b**) *(con espátula)* to scrape (off); *(con cepillo)* to scrub (**c**) *(instrumento)* to scrape away at

 2 *vi* to be rough

 3 rascarse *vpr* to scratch oneself; *Fam Fig* **rascarse el bolsillo** to fork out; *Fam Fig* **rascarse la barriga** to twiddle one's thumbs, to laze around; *RP muy Fam* **se pasa todo el día rascándose las bolas** he doesn't do shit all day

RASD [rrasð] *nf (abrev de* **República Árabe Saharaui Democrática)** Democratic Arab Republic of the Western Sahara

rasera *nf* fish slice

rasero *nm* strickle; **medir por el mismo r.** to treat alike

rasgado, -a *adj* **ojos rasgados** almond(-shaped) eyes

rasgadura *nf* (**a**) *(en tela)* rip, tear (**b**) *(acción)* ripping, tearing

rasgar [38] **1** *vt* to tear; **r. un sobre** to tear open an envelope

 2 rasgarse *vpr* to tear; *Fig* **rasgarse las vestiduras** to kick up a fuss

rasgo *nm* (**a**) *(característica)* trait, characteristic; *(del rostro)* feature (**b**) *(acto elogiable)* act (**c**) *(trazo)* flourish, stroke (**d**) *(expresiones)* **a grandes rasgos** in general terms; **explicar algo a grandes rasgos** to outline sth

rasgón *nm* tear

rasgue *etc ver* **rasgar**

rasguear *vt (guitarra)* to strum

rasguñar 1 *vt* to scratch

 2 rasguñarse *vpr* to scratch; **se rasguñó la rodilla** she scraped *o* grazed her knee

rasguño *nm* scratch; **sin un r.** without a scratch

raso, -a 1 *adj* (**a**) *(terreno)* flat (**b**) *(cucharada)* level (**c**) *(cielo)* clear (**d**) *(a poca altura)* low (**e**) *Mil* **soldado r.** private

 2 *nm (tela)* satin

 3 al raso *loc adv* in the open air

raspa *nf (espina)* bone; *(espina dorsal)* backbone

raspadita *nf Arg*, **raspadito** *nm Am* scratch card

raspado *nm* (**a**) *Med* scrape (**b**) *(de pieles)* scraping (**c**) *Méx (refresco)* = drink of flavored crushed ice

raspador *nm* scraper

raspadura *nf (señal)* scratch

raspar 1 *vt* (**a**) *(rascar)* to scrape (off) (**b**) *(rasguñar)* to graze, to scrape; **se raspó el codo** she grazed *o* scraped her elbow

 2 *vi* to be rough

raspón, rasponazo *nm* graze, scrape

rasposo, -a *adj* rough

rasque *etc ver* **rascar**

rasta *adj Fam (rastafari)* Rasta; **pelo** *o* **peinado r.** dreadlocks

rastafari *adj & nmf* Rastafarian

rasterizar [14] *vt Inform* to rasterize

rastras: a rastras *loc adv también Fig* **llevar algo/a alguien a r.** to drag sth/sb along; **trajeron el piano a r.** they dragged the piano in; **tuvo que llevarlo a r. al colegio** she had to drag him kicking and screaming to school; **llegaron casi a r.** *(agotados)* they were on their last legs when they arrived

rastreador, -ora 1 *adj* tracker; **perro r.** tracker dog

 2 *nm,f* tracker

rastrear *vt* (**a**) *(bosque, zona)* to search, to comb (**b**) *(persona, información)* to track

rastreo *nm (de una zona)* searching, combing

rastrero, -a *adj (despreciable)* despicable

rastrillar *vt* to rake (over)

rastrillo *nm* (a) *(instrumento)* rake (b) *(mercado)* flea market; *(benéfico)* rummage sale (c) *Méx (para afeitarse)* razor

rastro *nm* (a) *(pista)* trail; **seguir el r. de alguien** to trail sb; **perder el r. de alguien** to lose track of sb (b) *(vestigio)* trace; **sin dejar r.** without trace; **no hay** *o* **queda ni r. de él** there's no sign of him; **cuando llegamos no había ni r. de cerveza** when we got there there wasn't a drop of beer left (c) *(mercado)* flea market

rastrojo *nm* stubble

rasurador *nm*, **rasuradora** *nf Méx* shaver, electric razor

rasurar 1 *vt* to shave

    2 rasurarse *vpr* to shave

rata 1 *adj Fam* stingy, mean

    2 *nmf Fam* stingy person

    3 *nf* rat; **r. de agua** water rat; *Fam* **r. de sacristía** fanatical churchgoer

rataplán *nm* rat-a-tat

ratear *vt & vi* to pilfer, to steal

ratería *nf Fam* pilfering, stealing

ratero, -a *nm,f* petty thief

raticida *nm* rat poison

ratificación *nf* ratification

ratificar [59] **1** *vt* to ratify

    2 ratificarse en *vpr* to stand by, to stick to

ratio *nf* ratio

rato *nm* while; **estuvimos hablando mucho r.** we were talking for quite a while; **a cada r. viene a hacerme preguntas** he keeps coming and asking me questions (all the time); **un buen r.** *(momento agradable)* a good time; *(mucho tiempo)* a good while, quite some time; **¡hasta otro r.!** see you soon!; **al poco r. (de)** shortly after; **con esto hay para r.** that should keep us going for a while; **pasar el r.** to kill time, to pass the time; **pasar un mal r.** to have a hard time of it; **ratos libres** spare time; **a ratos** at times; **a ratos perdidos** at odd moments; **tenemos lluvia para r.** the rain will be with us for some time; **va para r.** it will take some (considerable) time; *Esp Fam* **un r. (largo)** *(mucho)* really, terribly

ratón *nm* (a) *(animal)* mouse; **r. de biblioteca** bookworm (b) *Esp Inform* mouse

ratoncito *nm* **el r. Pérez** ≃ the tooth fairy

ratonera *nf* (a) *(para ratas) (guarida)* mousehole; *(tampa)* mousetrap (b) *(peligro)* trap

raudal *nm* (a) *(de agua)* torrent (b) *Fig* **a raudales** in abundance, by the bucket

raudo, -a *adj* fleet, swift

ravioli *nm* (piece of) ravioli; **raviolis** ravioli

raya 1 *ver* **raer**

    2 *nf* (a) *(línea)* line; *(en tejido)* stripe; **a rayas** striped; **una camisa a** *o* **de rayas** a striped shirt (b) *Esp, Andes, RP (del pelo)* part; **hacerse la r.** to part one's hair; **se peina con la r. en el medio** she has a center part (c) *(de pantalón)* crease (d) *(límite)* **mantener** *o* **tener a r. a alguien** to keep sb in line; **pasarse de la r.** to overstep the mark; **poner a r.** to check, to hold back (e) *(señal) (en disco, pintura)* scratch (f) *(pez)* ray (g) *(guión)* dash

rayado, -a 1 *adj* (a) *(a rayas) (tela)* striped; *(papel)* ruled (b) *(disco, superficie)* scratched (c) *CSur Fam (loco)* **estar r.** to be a head case

    2 *nm (rayas)* stripes

rayano, -a *adj* **r. en** bordering on

rayar 1 *vt* (a) *(disco, superficie)* to scratch (b) *(papel)* to rule lines on

    2 *vi* (a) *(aproximarse)* **r. en algo** to border on sth; **raya en los**

cuarenta he's pushing forty (b) *(alba)* to break

    3 rayarse *vpr* (a) *(disco, superficie)* to get scratched; *Fig* **parece que te has rayado** you're like a broken record (b) *CSur Fam (volverse loco)* to go crazy

rayo 1 *ver* **raer**

    2 *nm* (a) *(de luz)* ray; *Fig* **un r. de esperanza** a beacon of hope; **r. solar** sunbeam (b) *Fís* beam, ray; **rayos infrarrojos** infrared rays; **r. láser** laser beam; **rayos ultravioleta/uva** ultraviolet/UVA rays; **rayos X** X-rays (c) *Meteo* bolt of lightning; **rayos** lightning; *Fig* **caer como un r.** to be a bombshell; *Esp Fam* **oler a rayos** to stink to high heaven; *Esp Fam* **sabe a rayos** *(comida)* it tastes foul; *Fam* **¡que le parta un r.!** he can go to hell!, to hell with him! (d) *(persona)* **ser un r.** to be like greased lightning; **pasar como un r.** to flash by

    3 *interj* **¡rayos (y centellas)!** heavens above!

rayón *nm* rayon

rayuela *nf (juego)* hopscotch

raza *nf* (a) *(humana)* race; **r. humana** human race; **la r. blanca** whites, white people (b) *(animal)* breed; **de (pura) r.** *(caballo)* thoroughbred; *(perro)* pedigree

razón *nf* (a) *(motivo, argumento)* reason; **la r. de la huelga/de que estén en huelga** the reason for the strike/why they are on strike; **atender a razones** to listen to reason; **por razones de salud/seguridad** for health/safety reasons; **y con r.** and quite rightly so; **¡con r. no quería venir!** no wonder he didn't want to come!; **r. de más para quedarse/protestar** all the more reason to stay/protest; **r. de ser** raison d'être; *Pol* **r. de Estado** reasons of state; *Com* **r. social** trade name *(of company)*

    (b) *(acierto, verdad)* **dar la r. a alguien** to say that sb is right; **tener r. (en** *o* **al hacer algo)** to be right (to do sth); **no tener r.** to be wrong

    (c) *(juicio)* reason; **entrar en r.** to see reason; **perder la r.** to lose one's reason *o* mind

    (d) *(información)* **se vende piso: r. aquí** apartment for sale: inquire within; **dar r. de** to give an account of

    (e) *Mat* ratio; **a r. de** at a rate of

    (f) *Col, Méx, Ven (recado)* message; **dejar r.** to leave a message

razonable *adj* reasonable

razonado, -a *adj* reasoned

razonamiento *nm* reasoning

razonar 1 *vt (argumentar)* to reason out

    2 *vi (pensar)* to reason

RDA *nf (abrev de* **República Democrática Alemana**) *Antes* GDR

RDSI *nf Inform & Tel (abrev de* **Red Digital de Servicios Integrados**) ISDN

re *nm Mús* D; *(en solfeo)* re

reabrir 1 *vt* to reopen

    2 reabrirse *vpr* to reopen

reabsorber 1 *vt* to reabsorb

    2 reabsorberse *vpr* to be reabsorbed

reacción *nf* (a) *(de persona)* reaction; **tuvo una r. rara/buena** she reacted strangely/well (b) *Fís, Med & Quím* reaction; **avión/motor a r.** jet plane/engine; **r. en cadena** chain reaction; **r. nuclear** nuclear reaction

reaccionar *vi* to react

reaccionario, -a *adj & nm,f* reactionary

reacio, -a *adj* reluctant; **r. a algo** resistant to sth; **ser r. a hacer algo** to be reluctant to do sth

reactivación *nf* recovery

reactivar *vt* to revive; **r. la economía** to jump-start the economy

reactivo, -a 1 *adj* reactive

    2 *nm Quím* reagent

reactor *nm* (a) *(propulsor)* reactor (b) *(avión)* jet (plane) (c) *(nuclear)* reactor

readaptación *nf* readjustment

readaptar 1 *vt* to adapt

  2 readaptarse *vpr* to readjust

readmisión *nf* readmission

readmitir *vt* to accept *o* take back

reafirmar 1 *vt* to confirm; **r. a alguien en algo** to confirm sb in sth

  2 reafirmarse *vpr* to assert oneself; **reafirmarse en algo** to become confirmed in sth

reagrupar *vt (reunir)* to regroup; *(reorganizar)* to reorganize

reajustar *vt* (**a**) *(corregir)* to rearrange (**b**) *(precios, impuestos)* to make changes to, to adjust; *(sector)* to streamline

reajuste *nm* (**a**) *(cambio)* readjustment; **r. ministerial** cabinet reshuffle (**b**) *Econ (de precios, impuestos)* increase; *(de sector)* streamlining; *(de salarios)* reduction; **r. de plantilla** staff redeployment

real 1 *adj* (**a**) *(verdadero)* real (**b**) *(de la realeza)* royal

  2 *nm (moneda) (de Brasil)* real; *Antes (de España)* = old Spanish coin worth one quarter of a peseta; *Fig* **no tener un r.** not to have a penny to one's name; *Fig* **no valer un r.** to be worthless

realce 1 *ver* **realzar**

  2 *nm* (**a**) *(esplendor)* glamor; **dar r. a algo/alguien** to enhance sth/sb (**b**) *(en arquitectura, escultura)* relief

realeza *nf* (**a**) *(monarcas)* royalty (**b**) *(grandeza)* magnificence

realidad *nf* (**a**) *(mundo real)* reality; **r. virtual** virtual reality (**b**) *(verdad)* truth; **en r.** actually, in fact; **hacerse r.** to come true

realismo *nm* realism; *Lit* **r. mágico** magic(al) realism

realista 1 *adj* realistic

  2 *nmf Arte* realist

reality show [rre'aliti'ʃou] *nm* **los r. shows** reality TV

realizable *adj* (**a**) *(factible)* feasible (**b**) *Fin* realizable

realización *nf* (**a**) *(ejecución)* carrying-out; *(de proyecto, medidas)* implementation; *(de sueños, deseos)* fulfillment; **r. de beneficios** profit-taking (**b**) *(obra)* achievement (**c**) *Cine (película)* production; *(actividad)* direction

realizado, -a *adj* (**a**) *(hecho)* carried out, performed (**b**) *(satisfecho)* fulfilled; **sentirse r.** to feel fulfilled

realizador, -ora *nm,f Cine & TV* director

realizar [14] **1** *vt* (**a**) *(ejecutar) (esfuerzo, viaje, inversión)* to make; *(operación, experimento, trabajo)* to perform; *(encargo)* to carry out; *(plan, reformas)* to implement; *(desfile)* to go on (**b**) *(hacer real)* to fulfill, to realize; **realizó su sueño** he fulfilled his dream (**c**) *Cine* to direct (**d**) *Fin (beneficios)* to realize

  2 realizarse *vpr* (**a**) *(en un trabajo, actividad)* to find fulfillment; **quiere buscar trabajo fuera de casa para realizarse** she wants to get a more fulfilling job outside of the home (**b**) *(hacerse real) (sueño, predicción, deseo)* to come true; *(esperanza, ambición)* to be fulfilled (**c**) *(ejecutarse)* to be carried out

realmente *adv* (**a**) *(en verdad)* in fact, actually (**b**) *(muy)* really, very

realojar *vt* to rehouse

realquilado, -a 1 *adj* sublet

  2 *nm,f* subtenant

realquilar *vt* to sublet

realzar [14] *vt (destacar)* to enhance

reanimación *nf* (**a**) *(física, moral)* recovery (**b**) *Med* resuscitation

reanimar 1 *vt* (**a**) *(físicamente)* to revive (**b**) *(moralmente)* to cheer up (**c**) *Med* to resuscitate

  2 reanimarse *vpr* to revive

reanudación *nf (de conversación, actividad)* resumption; *(de amistad)* renewal

reanudar 1 *vt (conversación, actividad)* to resume; *(amistad)* to renew

  2 reanudarse *vpr (conversación, actividad)* to resume; *(amistad)* to be renewed

reaparecer [46] *vi* to reappear

reaparición *nf (de enfermedad, persona)* reappearance; *(de artista)* comeback

reapertura *nf* reopening

rearmar *vt* to rearm

rearme *nm* rearmament

reasegurar *vt* to reinsure

reaseguro *nm* reinsurance

reavivar *vt* to revive

rebaba *nf* jagged edge

rebaja *nf* (**a**) *(acción)* reduction (**b**) *(descuento)* discount; **hacer una r. a alguien** to give sb a discount; **estar de rebajas** to have a sale on; **grandes rebajas** *(en letrero)* massive reductions; **las rebajas** the sales

rebajado, -a *adj* (**a**) *(precio)* reduced (**b**) *(humillado)* humiliated (**c**) *(diluido)* diluted (**con** with)

rebajar 1 *vt* (**a**) *(precio)* to reduce; **te rebajo 10 euros** I'll knock 10 euros off for you (**b**) *(persona)* to humiliate (**c**) *(intensidad)* to tone down (**d**) *(altura)* to lower (**e**) *(diluir)* to dilute

  2 rebajarse *vpr (persona)* to humble oneself; **rebajarse a hacer algo** to lower oneself *o* stoop to do sth

rebanada *nf* slice

rebanar *vt (pan)* to slice; *(dedo, cabeza)* to cut off

rebañar *vt* to scrape clean

rebaño *nm (de ovejas)* flock; *(de vacas)* herd

rebasar *vt* (**a**) *(sobrepasar)* to exceed, to surpass; **el agua rebasó el borde de la bañera** the bath overflowed (**b**) *CAm, Méx (adelantar)* to pass, to overtake

  2 *vi CAm, Méx (adelantar)* to overtake

rebatible *adj* refutable

rebatir *vt* to refute

rebato *nm* alarm; **tocar a r.** to sound the alarm

rebeca *nf* cardigan

rebeco *nm* chamois

rebelarse *vpr* to rebel

rebelde 1 *adj* (**a**) *(sublevado)* rebel; **ejército r.** rebel army (**b**) *(desobediente)* rebellious; **ese niño es muy r.** that child is very disobedient (**c**) *(difícil de dominar) (pelo)* unmanageable; *(tos)* persistent; *(pasiones)* unruly (**d**) *Der* defaulting

  2 *nmf* (**a**) *(sublevado, desobediente)* rebel (**b**) *Der* defaulter

rebeldía *nf* (**a**) *(cualidad)* rebelliousness (**b**) *(acción)* (act of) rebellion (**c**) *Der* default; **declarar a alguien en r.** to declare sb in default

rebelión *nf* rebellion

rebenque *nm RP (látigo)* (riding) crop, whip

reblandecer [46] **1** *vt* to soften

  2 reblandecerse *vpr* to get soft

reblandecimiento *nm* softening

rebobinado *nm* rewinding

rebobinar *vt* to rewind

reboce *etc ver* **rebozar**

reborde *nm* edge

rebosadero *nm (desagüe)* overflow

rebosante *adj (recipiente)* brimming, overflowing (**de** with); *(persona)* brimming (**de** with)

rebosar 1 *vt* to overflow with, to brim with

  2 *vi (recipiente)* to overflow; **estar (lleno) a r.** to be full to overflowing; **r. de** *(persona)* to brim with

rebotado, -a *adj* (**a**) *(cura)* who has given up the cloth *o* left the priesthood (**b**) *Fam (enfadado)* pissed

rebotar 1 *vi* to bounce (**en** off), to rebound (**en** off)

  2 rebotarse *vpr Esp Fam (irritarse)* to get pissed

rebote *nm* (**a**) *(bote)* bounce, bouncing; *Fig* **de r.** by chance, indirectly (**b**) *Dep* rebound; **de r.** on the rebound (**c**) *Esp Fam (enfado)* **coger** *o* **pillarse un r.** to get pissed

rebozado, -a *adj Culin* coated in batter *o* breadcrumbs; *Fig* **r. de** *o* **en** *(barro)* covered in

rebozar [14] *vt Culin* to coat in batter *o* breadcrumbs; *Fig* **r. de** *o* **en** *(barro)* to cover in

rebozo *nm Am* wrap, shawl; *Fig* **sin r.** *(con franqueza)* frankly

rebrotar *vi Bot* to sprout; *(fenómeno)* to reappear

rebufo *nm (de vehículo)* slipstream; **ir a r. de algo/alguien** to travel along in the wake of sth/sb

rebuscado, -a *adj (lenguaje)* obscure, recherché; **una explicación rebuscada** a roundabout explanation

rebuscamiento *nm (de lenguaje)* obscurity; *(de explicación)* roundabout nature

rebuscar [59] *vt* to search (around in)

rebuznar *vi* to bray

rebuzno *nm* bray, braying

recabar *vt (pedir)* to ask for; *(conseguir)* to manage to get

recadero, -a *nm,f (de mensajes)* messenger; *(de encargos)* errand boy, *f* errand girl

recado *nm* (**a**) *(mensaje)* message (**b**) *(encargo)* errand; **hacer recados** to run errands

recaer [13] *vi* (**a**) *(enfermo)* to have a relapse (**b**) *(ir a parar)* **r. sobre** to fall on (**c**) *(reincidir)* **r. en** to relapse into

recaída *nf* relapse

recaiga *etc ver* **recaer**

recalar *vi Náut* to put in (**en** at); *Fam (aparecer, pasar por)* to drop *o* look in (**en** *o* **por** at)

recalcar [59] *vt* to stress, to emphasize

recalcitrante *adj (persona, mancha, actitud)* stubborn

recalentamiento *nm* overheating

recalentar [3] **1** *vt* (**a**) *(volver a calentar)* to warm up (**b**) *(calentar demasiado)* to overheat

2 recalentarse *vpr* to overheat

recalificar [59] *vt* to reclassify *(land as rural or urban)*

recámara *nf* (**a**) *(habitación)* dressing room (**b**) *(de arma de fuego)* chamber (**c**) *CAm, Col, Méx (dormitorio)* bedroom

recamarera *nf CAm, Col, Méx* maid

recambiar *vt* to replace

recambio *nm (repuesto)* spare; *(para pluma, cuaderno)* refill; **de r.** spare

recapacitar *vi* to reflect, to think

recapitalización *nf* recapitalization

recapitulación *nf* recap, recapitulation

recapitular *vt* to recapitulate, to summarize

recarga *nf (de teléfono móvil)* top-up

recargable *adj (batería, pila)* rechargeable; *(encendedor)* refillable

recargado, -a *adj (estilo)* overelaborate, affected

recargar [38] *vt* (**a**) *(volver a cargar) (encendedor, recipiente)* to refill; *(batería, pila)* to recharge; *(fusil, camión)* to reload; *(teléfono móvil)* to top up (**b**) *(cargar demasiado)* to overload (**c**) *(adornar en exceso)* to overelaborate (**d**) *(cantidad)* **r. 100 euros a alguien** to charge sb 100 euros extra (**e**) *(poner en exceso)* **r. algo de algo** to put too much of sth in sth

recargo *nm* extra charge, surcharge

recatado, -a *adj (pudoroso)* modest, demure

recatarse *vpr* **r. de hacer algo** to shy away from doing sth; **sin r.** openly

recato *nm* (**a**) *(pudor)* modesty, demureness (**b**) *(reserva)* **sin r.** openly, without reserve (**c**) *(cautela)* prudence, caution

recauchutado *nm* remold, retread

recauchutaje *nm Am* (**a**) *(lugar)* tire center (**b**) *(acción)* remolding, retreading

recauchutar *vt* to remold, to retread

recaudación *nf* (**a**) *(acción)* collection, collecting; **r. de**

impuestos tax collection (**b**) *(cantidad)* takings; *Dep* gate; *Teatro* box-office takings

recaudador, -ora *nm,f* **r. (de impuestos)** tax collector

recaudar *vt* to collect

recaudo *nm* (**a**) **a buen r.** in safekeeping; **poner a buen r.** to put in a safe place (**b**) *Chile, Guat, Méx (condimentos)* spices and condiments

recayera *etc ver* **recaer**

rece *etc ver* **rezar**

recelar 1 *vt* (**a**) *(sospechar)* to suspect (**b**) *(temer)* to fear

2 *vi* to be mistrustful; **r. de** to mistrust

recelo *nm* mistrust, suspicion

receloso, -a *adj* mistrustful, suspicious

recensión *nf* review, writeup

recepción *nf* (**a**) *(de hotel, sonido)* reception (**b**) *(de carta, paquete)* receipt

recepcionar *vt Am* to receive

recepcionista *nmf* receptionist

receptáculo *nm* receptacle

receptividad *nf* receptiveness

receptivo, -a *adj* receptive

receptor, -ora 1 *adj* receiving

2 *nm,f (persona)* recipient; **r. de órgano** organ recipient

3 *nm (aparato)* receiver

recesión *nf* recession

recesivo, -a *adj* (**a**) *Econ* recessionary (**b**) *Biol* recessive

receso *nm (en juicio)* adjournment; *(parlamentario)* recess

receta *nf* (**a**) *Culin & Fig* recipe (**b**) *Med* prescription

recetar *vt* to prescribe

recetario *nm* (**a**) *Med* prescription pad (**b**) *Culin* recipe book

rechazar [14] *vt* (**a**) *(no aceptar)* to reject; *(oferta)* to turn down; **el gobierno rechazó las acusaciones de corrupción** the government rejected *o* denied the accusations of corruption (**b**) *(repeler) (a una persona)* to push away; *Mil* to drive back, to repel (**c**) *Med (órgano)* to reject (**d**) *Dep* to clear; **el portero rechazó la pelota y la mandó fuera** the goalkeeper tipped the ball out of play

rechazo *nm* (**a**) *(no aceptación)* rejection; *(hacia una ley, un político)* disapproval; **mostró su r.** he made his disapproval clear; **r. a hacer algo** refusal to do sth (**b**) *(negación)* denial (**c**) *Med (de órgano)* rejection

rechifla *nf* (**a**) *(abucheo)* booing, hissing (**b**) *(burla)* derision, mockery

rechinar *vi* (**a**) *(puerta)* to creak; *(dientes)* to grind; *(frenos, ruedas)* to screech; *(metal)* to clank (**b**) *(dando dentera)* to grate

rechistar *vi* to answer back; **sin r.** without a word of protest

rechoncho, -a *adj Fam* tubby, chubby

rechupete: de rechupete *Fam* **1** *loc adj* **estar de r.** *(comida)* to be yummy

2 *loc adv* **pasarlo de r.** to have a brilliant *o* great time

recibí *nm (en documentos)* received

recibidor *nm* entrance hall

recibimiento *nm* reception, welcome

recibir 1 *vt* (**a**) *(tomar, aceptar)* to receive; *(clase, instrucción)* to have; **recibió un golpe en la cabeza** he was hit on the head, he took a blow to the head; **estoy recibiendo clases de piano** I'm having *o* taking piano classes; *Formal* **reciba mi más cordial** *o* **sincera felicitación** please accept my sincere congratulations (**b**) *(persona, visita)* to receive; **lo recibieron con un cálido aplauso** he was received with a warm round of applause (**c**) *(ir a buscar)* to meet (**d**) *(captar) (ondas de radio, televisión)* to get; **aquí no recibimos la CNN** we don't get CNN here

2 *vi (atender visitas) (médico, dentista)* to hold surgery; *(rey, papa, ministro)* to receive visitors

3 recibirse *vpr Am (graduarse)* to graduate, to qualify (**de** as)

recibo nm (**a**) (de compra) receipt; Fam (del gas, de la luz) bill; **al r. de tu carta…** on receipt of your letter…; **acusar r. de** to acknowledge receipt of (**b**) **ser de r.: no sería de r. ocultarle la situación** it wouldn't be right not to tell her the situation; **no es de r. que nos traten así** it's not on for them to treat us like that

reciclable adj recyclable

reciclado, -a adj recycled

reciclaje nm (**a**) (de residuos) recycling (**b**) (de personas) retraining

reciclar vt (**a**) (residuos) to recycle (**b**) (personas) to retrain

recidiva nf reappearance (of illness)

reciedumbre nf strength

recién adv (**a**) (con participio) recently, newly; **los r. casados** the newlyweds; **los r. llegados** the newcomers; **el r. nacido** the newborn baby; **r. hecho/pintado** freshly made/painted (**b**) Am (hace poco) (only) just; **r. me llamaron** they (only) just called me (**c**) Am (sólo) only; **r. el martes lo sabremos** we'll only know it on Tuesday, we won't know it until Tuesday

reciente adj (**a**) (acontecimiento) recent (**b**) (pintura, pan) fresh

recientemente adv (**a**) (hace poco) recently (**b**) (en los últimos tiempos) recently, of late

recinto nm (zona cercada) enclosure; (área) place, area; (alrededor de edificios) grounds; **r. ferial** fairground (of trade fair)

recio, -a adj (**a**) (persona) robust (**b**) (voz) gravelly (**c**) (objeto) solid (**d**) (material, tela) tough, strong (**e**) (lluvia, viento) harsh

recipiente nm container, receptacle

reciprocidad nf reciprocity; **en r. a** in return for

recíproco, -a adj mutual, reciprocal

recital nm (**a**) (de música clásica) recital; (de rock) concert (**b**) (de lectura) reading; **r. de poesía** poetry reading

recitar vt to recite

reclamación nf (**a**) (petición) claim, demand (**b**) (queja) complaint

reclamante 1 adj claiming
2 nmf claimant

reclamar 1 vt (**a**) (pedir, exigir) to demand, to ask for; **le he reclamado todo el dinero que me debe** I've demanded that he return to me all the money he owes me; **la multitud reclamaba que cantara otra canción** the crowd clamored for her to sing another song (**b**) (necesitar) to demand, to require; **el negocio reclama toda mi atención** the business requires o demands all my attention (**c**) (llamar) to ask for; **te reclaman en la oficina** they're asking for you at the office
2 vi (protestar) to protest (**contra** against); (quejarse) to complain (**contra** about)

reclame nm Am advertisement

reclamo nm (**a**) (para atraer) inducement; **r. publicitario** advertising gimmick; **r. de ventas** loss leader (**b**) (para cazar) decoy, lure (**c**) (de ave) call (**d**) Am (queja) complaint; (reivindicación) claim

reclinable adj reclining

reclinar 1 vt to lean (**sobre** on)
2 reclinarse vpr to lean back (**sobre** against)

reclinatorio nm prie-dieu, prayer stool

recluir [34] **1** vt to shut o lock away, to imprison
2 recluirse vpr to shut oneself away

reclusión nf (**a**) (encarcelamiento) imprisonment (**b**) (encierro) seclusion

recluso, -a nm,f (preso) prisoner

recluta nmf (obligatorio) draftee, conscript; (voluntario) recruit

reclutamiento nm (**a**) (de soldados) (obligatorio) draft, conscription; (voluntario) recruitment (**b**) (de trabajadores) recruitment

reclutar vt (**a**) (soldados) (obligatoriamente) to draft, to conscript; (voluntariamente) to recruit (**b**) (trabajadores) to recruit

recobrar 1 vt (recuperar) to recover; (conocimiento) to regain; (tiempo perdido) to make up for
2 recobrarse vpr to recover (**de** from)

recochinearse vpr Fam **r. de alguien** to laugh at sb

recochineo nm Fam crowing, gloating; **decir algo con r.** to say sth to really rub it in

recodo nm bend

recogedor nm dustpan

recogemigas nm inv crumb scoop

recogepelotas nmf inv ball boy, f ball girl

recoger [52] **1** vt (**a**) (levantar) to pick up; **recogí los papeles del suelo** I picked the papers up off the ground (**b**) (reunir) to collect, to gather (**c**) (ordenar, limpiar) (mesa) to clear; (habitación, cosas) to tidy o clear up (**d**) (ir a buscar) to pick up, to fetch; **iré a r. a los niños a la escuela** I'll pick the children up from school (**e**) (acoger) (mendigo, huérfano, animal) to take in (**f**) (cosechar) to gather, to harvest; (fruta) to pick (**g**) (acortar) (prenda) to take up, to shorten (**h**) (mostrar) (sujeto: foto, película) to show; (sujeto: novela) to depict; **la exposición recoge su obra más reciente** the exhibition brings together his latest works
2 recogerse vpr (**a**) (a dormir, meditar) to retire; **aquí la gente se recoge pronto** people go to bed early here (**b**) **recogerse el pelo** to put one's hair up

recogida nf (**a**) (acción) collection; **hacer una r. de firmas** to collect signatures; **r. de basuras** garbage collection; **r. de equipajes** baggage reclaim (**b**) (cosecha) harvest, gathering; (de fruta) picking

recogido, -a adj (**a**) (vida) quiet, withdrawn; (lugar) secluded (**b**) (cabello) tied back

recogimiento nm (**a**) (concentración) concentration, absorption (**b**) (retiro) withdrawal, seclusion

recoja etc ver **recoger**

recolección nf (**a**) (cosecha) harvest, gathering (**b**) (recogida) collection

recolectar vt (**a**) (cosechar) to harvest, to gather; (fruta) to pick (**b**) (reunir) to collect

recolector, -ora 1 adj harvesting
2 nm,f (de cosecha) harvester; (de fruta) picker; Am **r. de basura** garbage collector, refuse collector

recoleto, -a adj quiet, secluded

recombinante adj Biol recombinant

recomendable adj recommendable; **no es r.** it's not a good idea; **esa zona no es r.** it's not a very nice area; **va con gente poco r.** he keeps bad company

recomendación nf (**a**) (consejo) recommendation; **por r. de alguien** on sb's advice o recommendation (**b**) (referencia) **(carta de) r.** letter of recommendation

recomendado, -a 1 nm,f Pey **es un r. del jefe** the boss got him the job
2 adj Am (carta, paquete) registered

recomendar [3] vt (**a**) (aconsejar) to recommend; **r. a alguien que haga algo** to recommend that sb do sth, to advise sb to do sth; **se recomienda precaución** caution is advised; **no recomendada para menores de 18** (película) not suitable for persons under 18 (**b**) (trabajador, restaurante) to recommend

recomenzar [17] vt to begin o start again, to recommence

recompensa nf reward; **en r. por** in return for

recompensar vt (**a**) (premiar) to reward (**b**) (compensar) **r. a alguien algo** to compensate o reward sb for sth

recomponer [50] vt to repair, to mend

recompra nf (de acciones) buyback

recompuesto, -a participio ver **recomponer**

reconcentrar 1 vt (**a**) (reunir) to bring together (**b**) (concentrar) **r. algo en** to center o concentrate sth on (**c**) (hacer denso) to thicken

2 reconcentrarse *vpr* to concentrate (**en** on), to be absorbed (**en** in)

reconciliación *nf* reconciliation

reconciliar 1 *vt* to reconcile

2 reconciliarse *vpr* to be reconciled

reconcomerse *vpr* to get worked up

reconcomio *nm* grudge, resentment

recóndito, -a *adj* hidden, secret; **en lo más r. de mi corazón** in the depths of my heart

reconducir [18] *vt* (*desviar*) to redirect; (*devolver*) to return

reconfortante *adj* (**a**) (*anímicamente*) comforting (**b**) (*físicamente*) revitalizing

reconfortar *vt* (**a**) (*anímicamente*) to comfort (**b**) (*físicamente*) to revitalize

reconocer [19] **1** *vt* (**a**) (*identificar*) to recognize; **no te reconocía** I didn't recognize you; **el buen vino se reconoce por el color** you can tell a good wine by its color (**b**) (*admitir*) to admit; **reconozco que estaba equivocada** I accept *o* admit that I was mistaken; **hay que r. que lo hace muy bien** you have to admit that she's very good at it (**c**) (*examinar*) to examine (**d**) (*terreno*) to survey (**e**) *Der* (*hijo, derecho, partido*) to recognize

2 reconocerse *vpr* (**a**) (*identificarse mutuamente*) to recognize each other (**b**) (*confesarse*) **reconocerse culpable** to admit one's guilt

reconocible *adj* recognizable

reconocido, -a *adj* (**a**) (*admitido*) recognized, acknowledged (**b**) (*agradecido*) grateful

reconocimiento *nm* (**a**) (*identificación, admisión*) recognition; *Inform & Ling* **r. del habla** speech recognition; *Inform* **r. óptico de caracteres** optical character recognition (**b**) (*agradecimiento*) gratitude (**c**) *Med* examination (**d**) *Mil* reconnaissance

reconquista *nf* reconquest, recapture; *Hist* **la R.** = the Reconquest of Spain, when the Christian Kings retook the country from the Muslims

reconquistar *vt* (*territorio, ciudad*) to recapture, to reconquer; (*título, amor*) to regain, to win back

reconsiderar *vt* to reconsider

reconstituir [34] **1** *vt* (**a**) (*rehacer*) to reconstitute (**b**) (*reproducir*) to reconstruct

2 reconstituirse *vpr* (*país, organización*) to rebuild itself

reconstituyente *adj & nm* tonic

reconstrucción *nf* (**a**) (*de edificios, país*) rebuilding (**b**) (*de sucesos*) reconstruction

reconstruir [34] *vt* (**a**) (*edificio, país*) to rebuild (**b**) (*suceso*) to reconstruct

reconvención *nf* reprimand, reproach

reconvenir [69] *vt* to reprimand, to reproach

reconversión *nf* restructuring; **r. industrial** rationalization of industry

reconvertir [62] *vt* (*reestructurar*) to restructure; (*industria*) to rationalize

recopa *nf* (*soccer*) Cup-Winners' Cup

recopilación *nf* (**a**) (*acción*) collecting, gathering (**b**) (*libro*) collection, anthology; (*disco*) compilation; (*de leyes*) code

recopilar *vt* (**a**) (*recoger*) to collect, to gather (**b**) (*escritos, leyes*) to compile

recopilatorio, -a 1 *adj* **un disco r.** a compilation (record)

2 *nm* compilation

recórcholis *interj Fam* **¡r.!** (*sorpresa*) good heavens!; (*enfado*) for heaven's sake!

récord (*pl* **récords**) *nm* record; **batir un r.** to break a record; **establecer un r.** to set a new record; **tener el r.** to hold the record; **en un tiempo r.** in record time; **r. mundial** *o* **del mundo** world record; **r. personal** (*en deportes*) personal best

recordar [63] **1** *vt* (**a**) (*acordarse de*) to remember (**b**) (*traer a la memoria*) to remind; **me recuerda a un amigo mío** he reminds me of a friend of mine; **recuérdame que cierre el gas** remind me to turn the gas off; **tienes que ir al dentista esta tarde — ¡no me lo recuerdes!** you have to go to the dentist this afternoon — don't remind me!

2 *vi* to remember; **ese pintor recuerda a Picasso** that painter is reminiscent of Picasso; **si mal no recuerdo** as far as I can remember

recordatorio *nm* (**a**) (*aviso*) reminder (**b**) (*estampa*) = card given to commemorate sb's first communion, a death etc

recordman *nm inv Dep* record holder

recorrer *vt* (**a**) (*atravesar*) (*lugar, país*) to travel through *o* across, to cross; (*ciudad*) to go around; **recorrieron la sabana en un camión** they drove around the savanna in a truck; **recorrió la región a pie** he walked around the region (**b**) (*distancia*) to cover (**c**) (*con la mirada*) to look over; **lo recorrió de arriba a abajo con la mirada** she looked him up and down

recorrida *nf Am* (*ruta, itinerario*) route; (*viaje*) journey

recorrido *nm* (**a**) (*trayecto*) route, path; *Fig* **hacer un r. (mental) por algo** (*narración*) to run over sth (in one's head) (**b**) (*viaje*) journey

recortable 1 *adj* cutout

2 *nm* cutout (figure)

recortado, -a *adj* (**a**) (*cortado*) cut (**b**) (*borde*) jagged

recortar 1 *vt* (**a**) (*cortar*) (*lo que sobra*) to cut off *o* away; (*figuras*) to cut out (**b**) (*pelo, flequillo*) to trim (**c**) (*gastos*) to cut (down)

2 recortarse *vpr* (*perfil*) to stand out (**en** against), to be outlined (**en** against)

recorte *nm* (**a**) (*pieza cortada*) cut, trimming; (*de periódico, revista*) clipping; **r. de prensa** press clipping (**b**) (*reducción*) cut, cutback; **r. presupuestario/salarial** budget/salary cut (**c**) (*cartulina*) cutout (**d**) *Dep* swerve, sidestep

recostar [63] **1** *vt* to lean (back)

2 recostarse *vpr* (*tumbarse*) to lie down; **recostarse en** (*apoyarse*) to lean on *o* against

recoveco *nm* (**a**) (*rincón*) nook, hidden corner (**b**) (*complicación*) **sin recovecos** uncomplicated (**c**) (*lo más oculto*) **los recovecos del alma** the innermost recesses of the soul

recrear 1 *vt* (**a**) (*volver a crear*) to re-create (**b**) (*entretener*) to amuse, to entertain

2 recrearse *vpr* (**a**) (*entretenerse*) to amuse oneself, to entertain oneself (**b**) (*regodearse*) to take delight *o* pleasure

recreativo, -a *adj* recreational

recreo *nm* (**a**) (*entretenimiento*) recreation, amusement (**b**) *Educ* (*en primaria*) playtime; (*en secundaria*) break

recriminación *nf* reproach, recrimination

recriminar 1 *vt* to reproach

2 recriminarse *vpr* (*mutuamente*) to reproach each other

recriminatorio, -a *adj* reproachful

recrudecer [46] **1** *vi* to get worse

2 recrudecerse *vpr* to get worse

recrudecimiento *nm* (*de crisis*) worsening; (*de criminalidad*) upsurge (**de** in)

recta *nf* straight line; *también Fig* **la r. final** the home straight

rectal *adj* rectal

rectangular *adj* (**a**) (*de forma*) rectangular (**b**) *Mat* right-angled

rectángulo *nm* rectangle

rectificable *adj* rectifiable

rectificación *nf* (*de error*) rectification; (*en periódico*) correction

rectificar [59] *vt* (**a**) (*error*) to rectify, to correct (**b**) (*conducta, actitud*) to improve (**c**) (*ajustar*) to put right

rectilíneo, -a *adj Mat* rectilinear; **una carretera rectilínea** a straight road

rectitud *nf (de línea)* straightness; *(de conducta)* rectitude, uprightness

recto, -a 1 *adj* (**a**) *(sin curvas, vertical)* straight; *(ángulo)* right (**b**) *(íntegro)* upright, honorable (**c**) *(justo, verdadero)* true, correct (**d**) *(literal)* literal, true (**e**) *Mat* **un ángulo r.** a right angle

2 *nm Anat* rectum

3 *adv* straight on *o* ahead; **todo r.** straight on *o* ahead

rector, -ora 1 *adj* governing, guiding

2 *nm,f* (**a**) *(de universidad)* president (**b**) *(dirigente)* leader, head

3 *nm Rel* rector

rectorado *nm* (**a**) *(cargo)* presidency (**b**) *(lugar)* president's office

rectoría *nf* (**a**) *(cargo)* rectorate, rectorship (**b**) *(casa)* rectory

recua *nf* (**a**) *(de animales)* pack, drove (**b**) *Fam (de personas)* crowd

recuadro *nm* box

recubierto, -a *participio ver* **recubrir**

recubrimiento *nm* covering, coating

recubrir *vt (cubrir)* to cover; *(con pintura, barniz)* to coat

recuento *nm (por primera vez)* count; *(otra vez)* recount

recuerdo 1 *ver* **recordar**

2 *nm* (**a**) *(rememoración)* memory; **quedar en el r. (de)** to be remembered (by); **traer recuerdos a alguien de algo** to bring back memories of sth to sb; **tengo muy buen/mal r. de ese viaje** I have very fond/bad memories of that trip (**b**) *(objeto) (de viaje)* souvenir; *(de persona)* keepsake (**c**) **recuerdos** *(saludos)* regards; **dar recuerdos a alguien (de parte de alguien)** to give one's regards to sb (on sb's behalf); **dale recuerdos de mi parte** give her my regards

recuesto *etc ver* **recostar**

recular *vi* (**a**) *(retroceder)* to go *o* move back (**b**) *(ceder)* to back down

recuperable *adj (información, objeto)* recoverable, retrievable; **esta clase es r.** you can catch *o* make this class up later

recuperación *nf* (**a**) *(de lo perdido, la salud, la economía)* recovery; *(de espacios naturales)* reclamation (**b**) *(fisioterapia)* physiotherapy (**c**) *Educ (examen)* retake; **(clase de) r.** = extra class for pupils or students who have to retake their exams

recuperar 1 *vt (lo perdido, la salud)* to recover; *(espacios naturales)* to reclaim; *(horas de trabajo)* to make up; *(conocimiento)* to regain; *(examen)* to retake; **r. el tiempo perdido** to make up for lost time; **recuperó la salud** she got better, she recovered; **recuperó la libertad tras diez años en la cárcel** he regained his freedom after ten years in prison

2 recuperarse *vpr* (**a**) *(enfermo)* to recuperate, to recover (**b**) *(de una crisis)* to recover; *(negocio)* to pick up; **recuperarse de algo** to get over sth; **tardé en recuperarme del susto** it took me a while to recover from *o* get over the shock

recurrencia *nf* recurrence

recurrente 1 *adj* (**a**) *Der* appellant (**b**) *(repetido)* recurrent

2 *nmf Der* appellant

recurrir *vi* (**a**) *(buscar ayuda)* **r. a alguien** to turn to sb; **r. a algo** to resort to sth (**b**) *Der* to appeal

recurso *nm* (**a**) *(medio)* resort; **como último r.** as a last resort; **es un hombre de recursos** he's very resourceful (**b**) *Der* appeal; **presentar r. (ante)** to appeal (against); **r. de alzada** appeal (against an official decision); **r. de apelación** appeal; **r. de casación** High Court appeal (**c**) *(bien, riqueza)* resource; **recursos humanos** human resources; **recursos naturales** natural resources; *Fin* **recursos propios** equity

recusar *vt* (**a**) *Der* to challenge (**b**) *(rechazar)* to reject, to refuse

red *nf* (**a**) *(malla)* net; *(para cabello)* hairnet; *Fig* **caer en las redes de alguien** to fall into sb's trap; *también Fig* **echar** *o* **tender las redes** to cast one's net; **r. de arrastre** dragnet; **r. de deriva** drift net (**b**) *(sistema)* network, system; *(de*

electricidad, agua) source *(singular)*; **conectar algo a la r.** to connect sth to the source; **r. ferroviaria** rail network; **r. viaria** road network *o* system (**c**) *(organización) (de espionaje)* ring; *(de tiendas, hoteles)* chain (**d**) *Inform* network; **la Red** *(Internet)* the Net; **r. local/neuronal** local (area)/neural network

redacción *nf* (**a**) *(acción)* writing; *(de periódico)* editing (**b**) *(estilo)* wording (**c**) *(equipo de redactores)* editorial team *o* staff (**d**) *(oficina)* editorial office (**e**) *Educ* essay

redactar *vt* to write; **r. un contrato/un tratado** to draw up a contract/a treaty

redactor, -ora *nm,f Prensa (escritor)* writer; *(editor)* editor; **r. jefe** editor-in-chief

redada *nf (de policía) (en un solo lugar)* raid; *(en varios lugares)* roundup

redaños *nmpl (valor)* spirit; **no tener r. para hacer algo** not to have the courage to do sth

redecilla *nf (de pelo)* hairnet

rededor: en rededor *loc adv* around

redefinir *vt* to redefine

redención *nf* redemption

redentor, -ora *nm,f (persona)* redeemer; *Rel* **el R.** the Redeemer

redicho, -a *adj Fam* affected, pretentious

rediez *interj Fam* **¡r.!** good grief!, my goodness!

redil *nm* fold, pen; *Fig* **volver al r.** to return to the fold

redimible *adj* redeemable

redimir 1 *vt Rel & Fin* to redeem (**de** from)

2 redimirse *vpr* to redeem oneself

redistribución *nf* redistribution

redistribuir [34] *vt* to redistribute

rédito *nm* interest, yield

redoblar 1 *vt (aumentar)* to redouble

2 *vi (tambor)* to roll

redoble *nm* roll, drumroll

redomado, -a *adj (mentiroso, jugador)* inveterate

redonda *nf* (**a**) *Mús* whole note (**b**) **a la r.** around; **en quince kilómetros a la r.** within a fifteen-kilometer radius

redondeado, -a *adj* rounded

redondear *vt* (**a**) *(hacer redondo)* to round, to make round (**b**) *(negocio, acuerdo)* to round off (**c**) *(cifra, precio)* to round up/down

redondel *nm* (**a**) *(círculo)* circle, ring (**b**) *Taurom* bullring

redondeo *nm (de cifra, precio) (al alza)* rounding up; *(a la baja)* rounding down

redondo, -a 1 *adj* (**a**) *(circular, esférico)* round; **girar en r.** to turn around; *Fig* **caerse r.** to collapse in a heap (**b**) *(perfecto)* excellent; **fue una compra redonda** it was an excellent buy; **salir r.** to go like a dream, to turn out perfectly (**c**) *(rotundo)* categorical; **se negó en r. a escucharnos** she refused point-blank to listen to us (**d**) *(cantidad)* round; **cien euros redondos** a round hundred euros

2 *nm Culin* topside

reducción *nf* (**a**) *(disminución)* reduction; **r. al absurdo** reductio ad absurdum; **r. fiscal** tax cut; **r. de precios** price cut (**b**) *(sometimiento) (de rebelión)* suppression; *(de ejército)* defeat

reducido, -a *adj* (**a**) *(pequeño)* small (**b**) *(limitado)* limited (**c**) *(estrecho)* narrow

reducir [18] **1** *vt* (**a**) *(disminuir)* to reduce; *(gastos, costes, impuestos, plantilla)* to cut; **reduzca la velocidad** *(en letrero)* reduce speed now; **nos han reducido el sueldo** our salary has been cut; **r. algo a algo** to reduce sth to sth; **r. algo al absurdo** to make a nonsense of sth (**b**) *(someter) (país, ciudad)* to suppress, to subdue; *(sublevados, atracadores)* to bring under control (**c**) *Mat (convertir)* to convert (**d**) *Med* to set

2 *vi (en el automóvil)* **r. (de marcha** *o* **velocidad)** to change down

3 reducirse a *vpr* (**a**) *(limitarse a)* to be reduced to (**b**) *(equivaler a)* to boil *o* come down to; **todo se reduce a una cuestión de dinero** it all boils *o* comes down to money

reducto *nm* (**a**) *(fortificación)* redoubt (**b**) *(refugio)* stronghold, bastion

reductor, -ora 1 *adj* reducing
    2 *nm* reducer

redujera *etc ver* **reducir**

redundancia *nf* redundancy, superfluousness

redundante *adj* redundant, superfluous

redundar *vi* **r. en algo** to have an effect on sth; **redunda en beneficio nuestro** it is to our advantage

reduplicar [59] *vt* to redouble

reduzco *ver* **reducir**

reedición *nf (nueva edición)* new edition; *(reimpresión)* reprint

reedificación *nf* rebuilding

reedificar [59] *vt* to rebuild

reeditar *vt (publicar nueva edición de)* to bring out a new edition of; *(reimprimir)* to reprint

reeducar [59] *vt* to reeducate

reelección *nf* reelection

reelegir [55] *vt* to reelect

reembolsable *adj (gastos)* reimbursable; *(fianza)* refundable; *(deuda)* repayable

reembolsar 1 *vt (gastos)* to reimburse; *(fianza)* to refund; *(deuda)* to repay
    2 reembolsarse *vpr* to be reimbursed

reembolso *nm (de gastos)* reimbursement; *(de fianza, dinero)* refund; *(de deuda)* repayment; **contra r.** cash on delivery

reemplazar [14] *vt (gen) & Inform* to replace

reemplazo *nm* (**a**) *(gen) & Inform* replacement (**b**) *Mil* call-up, draft; **soldados de r.** conscripts

reemprender *vt* to start again

reencarnación *nf* reincarnation

reencarnar 1 *vt* to reincarnate
    2 reencarnarse *vpr* to be reincarnated (**en** as)

reencontrar [63] **1** *vt* to find again
    2 reencontrarse *vpr (varias personas)* to meet again

reencuentro *nm* reunion

reengancharse *vpr Mil* to reenlist

reenviar [32] *vt* (**a**) *(devolver)* to return, to send back (**b**) *(reexpedir)* to forward, to send on

reenvío *nm* (**a**) *(devolución)* return, sending back (**b**) *(reexpedición)* forwarding

reestrenar *vt Cine* to rerun; *Teatro* to revive

reestreno *nm* (**a**) *Cine* rerun, rerelease; **cine de r.** second-run movie theater; **reestrenos, películas de r.** *(en cartelera)* rereleases (**b**) *Teatro* revival

reestructuración *nf* restructuring

reestructurar *vt* to restructure

reexpedir [47] *vt* to forward, to send on

reexportación *nf* reexportation

reexportar *vt* to reexport

refacción *nf* (**a**) *Andes, CAm, RP, Ven (reforma)* refurbishment; *(reparación)* restoration (**b**) *Méx (recambio)* spare part

refaccionar *vt Andes, CAm, Ven (reformar)* to refurbish; *(reparar)* to restore

refajo *nm* underskirt, slip

refanfinflar *vt Esp Fam Hum* **me la refanfinfla** I don't care two hoots

refectorio *nm* refectory

referencia *nf* reference; **con r. a** with reference to; **hacer r. a** to make reference to, to refer to; **referencias** *(información)* information; *(para puesto de trabajo)* references

referéndum *(pl* **referendos** *o* **referéndums)** *nm* referendum

referente *adj* **r. a** concerning, relating to

referí *nmf Am* referee

referir [62] **1** *vt* (**a**) *(narrar)* to tell, to recount (**b**) *(remitir)* **r. a alguien a** to refer sb to (**c**) *(relacionar)* **r. algo a** to relate sth to (**d**) *Com (convertir)* **r. algo a** to convert sth into
    2 referirse a *vpr* (**a**) *(estar relacionado con)* to refer to; **por o en lo que se refiere a…** as far as… is concerned (**b**) *(aludir, mencionar)* **¿a qué te refieres?** what do you mean?; **¿te referías a ella?** were you referring to her?, did you mean her?; **no me refiero a ti, sino a ella** I don't mean you, I mean her; **se refirió brevemente al problema de la vivienda** he briefly mentioned the housing problem

refilón: de refilón *loc adv (de lado)* sideways; *(de pasada)* briefly; **mirar algo de r.** to look at sth out of the corner of one's eye

refinado, -a 1 *adj* refined
    2 *nm* refining

refinamiento *nm* refinement

refinanciación *nf* refinancing

refinanciar *vt* to refinance

refinar *vt* to refine

refinería *nf* refinery; **r. de petróleo** oil refinery

refiriera *etc ver* **referir**

reflectar *vt* to reflect

reflector *nm* (**a**) *Elec* spotlight; *Mil* searchlight (**b**) *(telescopio)* reflector

reflejar 1 *vt* (**a**) *(onda, rayo)* to reflect; **no me veo reflejado en esa descripción** I don't see myself in that description (**b**) *(sentimiento, duda)* to show; **esa pregunta refleja su ignorancia** that question shows *o* demonstrates his ignorance; **su rostro reflejaba el cansancio** his face looked tired
    2 reflejarse *vpr también Fig* to be reflected (**en** in)

reflejo, -a 1 *adj* (**a**) *(onda, rayo)* reflected (**b**) *(movimiento, dolor)* reflex; **acto r.** reflex action
    2 *nm* (**a**) *(imagen, manifestación)* reflection (**b**) *(destello)* glint, gleam (**c**) *Anat* reflex; **tener buenos reflejos** to have good *o* quick reflexes; **r. condicional** *o* **condicionado** conditioned reflex *o* response (**d**) *(de peluquería)* **reflejos** highlights; **hacerse** *o* **darse reflejos** to have highlights put in one's hair

réflex *Fot* **1** *adj inv* reflex, SLR
    2 *nf inv (cámara)* reflex *o* SLR camera

reflexión *nf* reflection; **sin previa r.** without thinking; **periodo de r.** *(en ventas)* cooling-off period

reflexionar *vi* to reflect (**sobre** on), to think (**sobre** about)

reflexivo, -a *adj* (**a**) *(que piensa)* reflective, thoughtful (**b**) *Gram* reflexive

reflexología *nf* reflexology

reflexoterapia *nf* reflexology

reflorecimiento *nm* resurgence, rebirth; **r. de la economía** economic recovery

refluir [34] *vi* to flow back *o* out

reflujo *nm* ebb (tide)

refocilarse *vpr* **r. haciendo algo** to take delight in doing sth; **r. en la desgracia ajena** to gloat over others' misfortune

reforestación *nf* reforestation

reforestar *vt* to reforest

reforma *nf* (**a**) *(modificación)* reform; **r. agraria** land reform, agrarian reform (**b**) *(en local, casa)* alterations; **hacer reformas en casa** to do up the house (**c**) *Rel* **la R.** the Reformation

reformado, -a *adj* (**a**) *(modificado)* altered (**b**) *(rehecho)* reformed

reformar 1 *vt* (**a**) *(cambiar)* to reform (**b**) *(local, casa)* to renovate, to do up
    2 reformarse *vpr* to mend one's ways

reformatorio *nm* reformatory

reformismo *nm* reformism

reformista *adj & nmf* reformist

reformular *vt* to reformulate, to put another way

reforzado, -a *adj* reinforced

reforzar [31] *vt* to reinforce

refracción *nf* refraction

refractar *vt* to refract

refractario, -a *adj* (a) *(material)* refractory, heat-resistant (b) *(opuesto)* **r. a** averse to (c) *(inmune)* **r. a** immune to

refrán *nm* proverb, saying

refranero *nm* collection of proverbs *o* sayings

refregar [43] *vt* (a) *(frotar)* to scrub (b) *(restregar)* **r. algo a alguien** to rub sb's nose in sth

refreír [56] *vt* (a) *(volver a freír)* to refry (b) *(freír en exceso)* to overfry

refrenar 1 *vt* to curb, to restrain

   2 refrenarse *vpr* to hold back, to restrain oneself

refrendar *vt* (a) *(confirmar)* to confirm; *(aprobar)* to approve (b) *(legalizar)* to endorse, to countersign

refrescante *adj* refreshing

refrescar [59] **1** *vt* (a) *(enfriar)* to refresh; *(bebidas)* to chill (b) *(conocimientos)* to brush up; **r. la memoria a alguien** to refresh sb's memory

   2 *vi (bebida)* to be refreshing

   3 *v impersonal* to cool down

   4 refrescarse *vpr* (a) *(tomar aire fresco)* to get a breath of fresh air (b) *(mojarse con agua fría)* to splash water on oneself

refresco *nm* (a) *(bebida)* soft drink; **refrescos** refreshments (b) *Mil* **de r.** new, fresh

refresquería *nf CAm, Carib, Méx* = store which sells soft drinks

refría *etc ver* **refreír**

refriega 1 *ver* **refregar**

   2 *nf* scuffle; *Mil* fracas, skirmish

refriera *etc ver* **refreír**

refrigeración *nf* (a) *(aire acondicionado)* air-conditioning (b) *(de alimentos)* refrigeration (c) *(de máquinas, motores)* cooling; **(sistema de) r.** cooling system

refrigerado, -a *adj* (a) *(local)* air-conditioned (b) *(alimentos)* refrigerated (c) *(líquido, gas)* cooled

refrigerador *nm* (a) *(frigorífico)* refrigerator, icebox (b) *(de máquinas, motores)* cooling system

refrigerante *adj* (a) *(para alimentos)* refrigerating (b) *(para motores)* cooling

refrigerar *vt* (a) *(local)* to air-condition (b) *(alimentos)* to refrigerate (c) *(máquina, motor)* to cool

refrigerio *nm* refreshments

refrito, -a 1 *participio ver* **refreír**

   2 *adj (demasiado frito)* overfried; *(frito de nuevo)* refried

   3 *nm* (a) *Culin* = sauce made from fried tomato and onion (b) *(cosa rehecha)* rehash

refuerce *etc ver* **reforzar**

refuerzo *nm* reinforcement; *Mil* **refuerzos** reinforcements

refugiado, -a *adj & nm, f* refugee

refugiar 1 *vt* to give refuge to

   2 refugiarse *vpr* to take refuge; **refugiarse de algo** to shelter from sth

refugio *nm* (a) *(lugar)* shelter, refuge; **r. antiaéreo** air-raid shelter; **r. atómico** nuclear bunker; **r. de montaña** *(muy básico)* mountain shelter; *(albergue)* mountain refuge; **r. subterráneo** bunker, underground shelter (b) *(amparo, consuelo)* refuge, comfort (c) *Aut* traffic island

refulgencia *nf* brilliance

refulgente *adj* brilliant

refulgir [24] *vi* to shine brightly

refundir *vt* (a) *(material)* to recast (b) *Lit* to adapt (c) *(unir)* to bring together

refunfuñar *vi* to grumble

refunfuñón, -ona 1 *adj* grumpy

   2 *nm,f* grumbler

refutable *adj* refutable

refutación *nf* refutation

refutar *vt* to refute

regadera *nf* (a) *(para regar)* watering can; *Esp Fig* **estar como una r.** to be as mad as a hatter (b) *Col, Méx, Ven (ducha)* shower

regadío *nm* irrigated land; **de r.** irrigated, irrigable

regalado, -a *adj* (a) *(muy barato)* dirt cheap; **te lo doy r.** I'm giving it away to you (b) *(agradable) (vida)* comfortable, easy (c) *Am Fam (muy fácil)* dead easy

regalar 1 *vt* (a) *(dar) (de regalo)* to give (as a present); *(gratis)* to give away; **¿qué le regalarás para Navidad?** what are you going to give *o* get her for Christmas?; **me regalaron un reloj para mi cumpleaños** I got a watch for my birthday; **si lo quieres, te lo regalo** if you'd like it, you can have it for free *o* I'll give it to you; **si compras dos, te regalan una** if you buy two, you get one free (b) *(agasajar)* **r. a alguien con algo** to shower sb with sth (c) *Am salvo RP (prestar)* to lend

   2 regalarse con *vpr* to treat oneself to

regalía *nf* royal prerogative

regaliz *nm* liquorice

regalo *nm* (a) *(obsequio)* present, gift; **r. de cumpleaños** birthday present; **por ese precio, es un auténtico r.** at that price, it's a real giveaway; **de r.** *(gratuito)* free; **compras tres y te dan uno de r.** if you buy three, you get one free (b) *(placer)* joy, delight (c) *(en rifa)* prize

regalón, -ona *adj CSur Fam (niño)* spoiled

regalonear *vt CSur Fam* to spoil

regañadientes: a regañadientes *loc adv Fam* unwillingly, reluctantly

regañar 1 *vt (reprender)* to tell off

   2 *vi Esp (pelearse)* to fall out, to argue

regañina *nf* (a) *(reprimenda)* telling off, dressing down (b) *Esp (enfado)* argument, row

regaño *nm* telling off

regañón, -ona 1 *adj* **es muy r.** he's always telling people off for nothing

   2 *nm,f* **es un r.** he's always telling people off for nothing

regar [43] *vt* (a) *(con agua) (planta, campo)* to water; *(calle)* to hose down; **regaron la comida con un buen vino tinto** they washed down the meal with a good red wine (b) *(sujeto: río)* to flow through; **el río que riega la región** the river which flows through the region (c) *(sujeto: vasos sanguíneos)* to supply with blood; **esta arteria riega de sangre los pulmones** this artery supplies blood to the lungs (d) *(desparramar)* to sprinkle, to scatter

regata *nf* (a) *Náut* regatta, boat race (b) *(reguera)* irrigation channel

regate *nm* (a) *Dep* swerve, sidestep (b) *(evasiva)* dodge

regatear 1 *vt* (a) *(escatimar)* to be sparing with; **no ha regateado esfuerzos** he has spared no effort (b) *Dep* to beat, to dribble past (c) *(precio)* to haggle over

   2 *vi* (a) *(negociar el precio)* to barter, to haggle (b) *Náut* to race

regateo *nm* bartering, haggling

regatista *nmf Dep* participant in a regatta *o* boat race

regato *nm* brook, rivulet

regazo *nm* lap

regencia *nf* (a) *(reinado)* regency (b) *(administración)* running, management

regeneración *nf (recuperación, restablecimiento)* regeneration; *(de delincuente, degenerado)* reform

regeneracionismo *nm* political reform movement

regenerar 1 *vt (recuperar, restablecer)* to regenerate; *(delincuente, degenerado)* to reform

2 regenerarse *(recuperarse, restablecerse)* to regenerate; *(delincuente, degenerado)* to reform

regenerativo, -a *adj* regenerative

regenta *nf* wife of the regent

regentar *vt (país)* to run, to govern; *(negocio)* to run, to manage; *(puesto)* to hold *(temporally)*

regente 1 *adj* regent

2 *nmf* **(a)** *(de un país)* regent **(b)** *(administrador) (de tienda)* manager; *(de colegio)* principal **(c)** *Méx (alcalde)* mayor, *f* mayoress

reggae ['rrivi, 'rrevi] *nm* reggae

regicida *nmf* regicide *(person)*

regicidio *nm* regicide *(crime)*

regidor, -ora *nm,f* **(a)** *Teatro* stage manager; *Cine & TV* assistant director **(b)** *(concejal)* councilor

régimen *(pl* **regímenes)** *nm* **(a)** *(sistema político)* regime; **r. parlamentario** parliamentary system **(b)** *(normativa)* rules; **alojarse en un hotel en r. de pensión completa** to stay at a hotel with all meals included; **una cárcel en r. abierto** an open prison; **estar en r. abierto** *(preso)* to be allowed to leave the prison during the day **(c)** *(dieta)* diet; **estar/ ponerse a r.** to be/go on a diet **(d)** *(rutina)* pattern; **r. de lluvias** pattern of rainfall; **r. de vida** lifestyle **(e)** *Ling* government

regimiento *nm Mil & Fig* regiment

regio, -a *adj* **(a)** *(real)* royal **(b)** *Andes, RP* great, fabulous

regiomontano, -a 1 *adj* of/from Monterrey

2 *nm,f* person from Monterrey

región *nf* region; *Mil* district

regional *adj* regional

regionalismo *nm* regionalism

regionalista *adj & nmf* regionalist

regionalizar [14] *vt* to regionalize

regir [55] **1** *vt* **(a)** *(gobernar)* to rule, to govern; *(administrar)* to run, to manage **(b)** *(sujeto: ley, norma)* to govern; **las leyes que rigen los intercambios comerciales** the laws governing trade **(c)** *Ling* to govern

2 *vi* **(a)** *(ley)* to be in force, to apply **(b)** *Fam (persona)* **ya no rige** he has gone a bit gaga

3 regirse por *vpr* to trust in, to be guided by

registrado, -a *adj* **(a)** *(grabado, anotado)* recorded **(b)** *(patentado, inscrito)* registered

registrador, -ora 1 *adj* registering

2 *nm,f* registrar

registradora *nf Am* cash register

registrar 1 *vt* **(a)** *(zona, piso, persona)* to search; *Fam* **a mí, que me registren** it wasn't me, don't look at me **(b)** *(datos, hechos)* to register, to record; **la empresa ha registrado un aumento de las ventas** the company has recorded an increase in sales, the company's sales have gone up **(c)** *(grabar)* to record **(d)** *Am (certificar)* to register

2 registrarse *v impersonal* **(a)** *(suceder)* to occur, to happen **(b)** *(observarse)* to be recorded; **se registró una inflación superior a la prevista** the inflation figures were higher than predicted

registro *nm* **(a)** *(oficina)* registry (office); **r. civil** registry (office); **r. de comercio** *o* **mercantil** business registry office; **r. de la propiedad** land recorder's office; **r. de la propiedad industrial/intelectual** trademark/copyright registry office **(b)** *(inscripción)* registration; **llevar el r. de algo** to keep a record of sth **(c)** *(libro)* register; **r. parroquial** parish register **(d)** *(inspección)* search, searching; **efectuaron un r. domiciliario** they searched his/her/etc home **(e)** *(de libro)* bookmark **(f)** *Inform* record **(g)** *Ling & Mús* register

regla *nf* **(a)** *(para medir)* ruler, rule; **r. de cálculo** slide rule **(b)** *(norma)* rule; **por r. general** as a rule, generally; **salirse de la r.** to overstep the mark *o* line; **en r.** in order; **r. de oro** golden rule; **r. ortográficas** spelling rules **(c)** *Mat* operation; **r. de tres** rule of three; *Fam Fig* **por la misma r. de tres...** by the same token... **(d)** *Fam (menstruación)* period **(e)** *(modelo)* example, model

reglaje *nm (de motor)* tuning

reglamentación *nf (acción)* regulation; *(reglas)* rules, regulations

reglamentar *vt* to regulate

reglamentario, -a *adj (legal)* lawful; *Der* statutory; **arma reglamentaria** regulation weapon

reglamento *nm (normas)* regulations, rules; **balón de r.** regulation soccer ball

reglar *vt* to regulate

regocijar 1 *vt* to delight

2 regocijarse *vpr* to rejoice (**de** *o* **con** in)

regocijo *nm* joy, delight

regodearse *vpr* to take pleasure *o* delight (**en** *o* **con** in)

regodeo *nm (deleite)* delight, pleasure; *(malicioso)* (cruel) delight *o* pleasure

regordete *adj* chubby, tubby

regrabable *adj Inform* rewritable

regresar 1 *vi (yendo)* to go back, to return; *(viniendo)* to come back, to return; **¿cuándo regresará?** when will she be back?; **regresó a su casa después de dos meses en el extranjero** she returned home after two months abroad

2 *vt Am salvo RP (devolver)* to give back

3 regresarse *vpr Am salvo RP (volver)* to come back

regresión *nf* **(a)** *(de economía, exportaciones)* drop, decline **(b)** *(de epidemia)* regression

regresivo, -a *adj* regressive

regreso *nm* **(a)** *(a un lugar)* return; **estar de r.** to be back **(b)** *Am salvo RP (de dinero, producto)* return

regué *etc ver* **regar**

regüeldo *nm* belch

reguero *nm* **(a)** *(rastro) (de sangre, agua)* trickle; *(de harina, arena)* trail; **correr como un r. de pólvora** to spread like wildfire **(b)** *(canal)* irrigation ditch

regulable *adj* adjustable, variable

regulación *nf (de actividad, economía)* regulation; *(de nacimientos, tráfico)* control; *(de mecanismo)* adjustment; **r. de empleo** streamlining, redundancies

regulador, -ora *adj* regulating, regulatory

regular 1 *adj* **(a)** *(uniforme)* regular; **de un modo r.** regularly **(b)** *(mediocre)* average, fair **(c)** *(normal)* normal, usual; *(de tamaño)* medium; **por lo r.** as a rule, generally

2 *nm Mil* regular

3 *adv (no muy bien)* so-so; **lleva unos días r., tiene un poco de fiebre** she's been so-so the last few days, she's got a bit of a temperature; **¿qué tal el concierto? — r.** how was the concert? — nothing special

4 *vt (actividad, economía, tráfico)* to control, to regulate; *(mecanismo)* to adjust; **la normativa regula estos casos** the regulations govern these cases

regularidad *nf* regularity; **con r.** regularly

regularización *nf* regularization

regularizar [14] **1** *vt* **(a)** *(devolver a la normalidad)* to get back to normal **(b)** *(legalizar)* to regularize

2 regularizarse *vpr* **(a)** *(volver a la normalidad)* to return to normal **(b)** *(legalizarse)* to become legitimate

regurgitar *vt & vi* to regurgitate

regusto *nm (sabor)* aftertaste; *(semejanza, aire)* flavor, hint

rehabilitación *nf* **(a)** *(de enfermo, de delincuente)* rehabilitation; *(en un puesto)* reinstatement **(b)** *(de local, edificio)* refurbishment

rehabilitar *vt* **(a)** *(enfermo, delincuente)* to rehabilitate; *(en un puesto)* to reinstate **(b)** *(local, edificio)* to refurbish

rehacer [33] **1** vt (**a**) *(volver a hacer)* to redo, to do again (**b**) *(reconstruir)* to rebuild
    2 rehacerse vpr *(recuperarse)* to recuperate, to recover

rehecho, -a *participio ver* **rehacer**

rehén nm hostage

rehíce etc ver **rehacer**

rehiciera etc ver **rehacer**

rehogar [38] vt = to fry over a low heat

rehuir [34] vt to avoid

rehusar vt & vi to refuse

rehuya etc ver **rehuir**

rehuyera etc ver **rehuir**

Reikiavik n Reykjavik

reimplantar vt (**a**) *(reintroducir)* to reintroduce (**b**) *Med* to implant again

reimportación nf reimporting

reimpresión nf *(tirada)* reprint; *(acción)* reprinting

reimprimir vt to reprint

reina nf *(en general)* queen; *(apelativo)* love, darling; **ven aquí, mi r.** come here, princess

reinado nm *también Fig* reign

reinante adj (**a**) *(monarquía, persona)* reigning, ruling (**b**) *(viento, ambiente)* prevailing

reinar vi (**a**) *(gobernar)* to reign (**b**) *(caos, confusión, pánico)* to reign; **el silencio reinó en la sala durante varios minutos** the hall fell completely silent for several minutes; **en esta casa reina la alegría** everyone is always happy in this house

reincidencia nf *(en un vicio)* relapse; *(en un delito)* recidivism

reincidente adj & nmf recidivist

reincidir vi **r. en** *(falta, error)* to relapse into, to fall back into; *(delito)* to repeat

reincorporación nf return (**a** to)

reincorporar 1 vt to reincorporate
    2 reincorporarse a vpr to rejoin, to go back to

reineta nf (**manzana**) **r.** = type of apple with tart flavor, used for cooking and eating

reingresar vi to return (**en** to)

reinicializar [14] vt *Inform (ordenador)* to reboot; *(impresora)* to reset

reino nm *Biol & Pol* kingdom; *(ámbito)* realm; **el r. animal** the animal kingdom; **el r. de los cielos** the kingdom of Heaven

Reino Unido nm **el R.** the United Kingdom

reinserción nf **r. (social)** rehabilitation o reintegration (into society); **la r. (laboral) de los desempleados de larga duración** getting the long-term unemployed back to work

reinsertar vt (**a**) *(en sociedad)* to reintegrate, to rehabilitate (**b**) *(en ranura)* to reinsert

reinstalación nf (**a**) *(en lugar)* reinstallation (**b**) *(en puesto)* reinstatement

reinstalar vt (**a**) *(en lugar)* to reinstall (**b**) *(en puesto)* to reinstate

reinstaurar vt to reestablish

reintegración nf (**a**) *(a puesto)* reinstatement (**b**) *(de dinero)* repayment, reimbursement

reintegrar 1 vt (**a**) *(a un puesto)* to reinstate (**b**) *(dinero)* to repay, to reimburse
    2 reintegrarse vpr to return (**a** to)

reintegro nm (**a**) *(de dinero)* repayment, reimbursement; *Com* withdrawal (**b**) *(en lotería)* = refund of one's stake as prize

reinversión nf reinvestment

reinvertir [62] vt to reinvest

reír [56] **1** vi to laugh
    2 vt to laugh at; **no le rías las gracias** don't laugh at his antics
    3 reírse vpr to laugh (**de** at); **reírse por lo bajo** to snicker,

to snigger; **¡me río yo de los sistemas de seguridad!** I laugh at security systems!, security systems are no obstacle to me!

reiteración nf reiteration, repetition

reiterar 1 vt to reiterate, to repeat
    2 reiterarse en vpr to reaffirm

reiterativo, -a adj repetitive, repetitious

reivindicación nf claim, demand; **r. salarial** pay claim; **estamos a la espera de la r. del atentado** no one has yet claimed responsibility for the attack

reivindicar [59] vt (**a**) *(derechos, salario)* to claim, to demand (**b**) *(atentado)* to claim responsibility for (**c**) *(herencia, territorio)* to lay claim to (**d**) *(memoria)* to defend
    2 reivindicarse vpr *Am* (**a**) *(recuperarse)* to vindicate oneself (**b**) *(responsabilizarse de)* to claim responsibility for

reivindicativo, -a adj **jornada reivindicativa** day of protest; **plataforma reivindicativa** pressure group

reja nf *(barrotes)* bars; *(en el suelo)* grating; *(en ventana)* grille; **poner una r. en la ventana** to put bars on the window; **estar entre rejas** to be behind bars

rejilla nf (**a**) *(enrejado)* grid, grating; *(de ventana)* grille; *(de cocina)* grill *(on stove)*; *(de horno)* gridiron (**b**) *(en sillas, muebles)* wickerwork; **silla de r.** chair with a wickerwork seat (**c**) *(para equipaje)* luggage rack

rejón nm *Taurom* = type of pike used by mounted bullfighter

rejoneador, -ora nm,f *Taurom* = bullfighter on horseback who uses the "rejón"

rejoneo nm *Taurom* = use of the "rejón"

rejuntarse vpr *Fam (pareja)* to shack up together; **r. con alguien** to move in with sb

rejuvenecedor, -ora adj *(efecto)* rejuvenating

rejuvenecer [46] **1** vt & vi to rejuvenate
    2 rejuvenecerse vpr to be rejuvenated

rejuvenecimiento nm rejuvenation

relación nf (**a**) *(nexo)* relation, connection; **con r. a, en r. con** in relation to, with regard to; **guardar r. con algo** to be related to sth; **no guardar r. con algo** to bear no relation to sth; **r. calidad-precio** value for money
    (**b**) *(comunicación, trato)* relations, relationship; **mantener relaciones con alguien** to keep in touch with sb; **relaciones comerciales** *(vínculos)* business links; *(comercio)* trade; **relaciones diplomáticas** diplomatic relations; **relaciones laborales** industrial relations; **relaciones públicas** public relations, PR
    (**c**) *(lista)* list
    (**d**) *(descripción)* account
    (**e**) *(informe)* report
    (**f**) **relaciones** *(noviazgo)* relationship; **llevan cinco años de relaciones** they've been going out together for five years; **relaciones prematrimoniales** premarital sex; **relaciones sexuales** sexual relations
    (**g**) **relaciones** *(contactos)* contacts, connections
    (**h**) *Mat* ratio; **una r. 5:1** a ratio of 5 to 1

relacionar 1 vt (**a**) *(vincular)* to relate, to connect; **estar bien relacionado** to be well-connected (**b**) *(enumerar)* to list, to enumerate
    2 relacionarse vpr *(alternar)* to mix (**con** with)

relajación nf, **relajamiento** nm relaxation; **r. de la moral** lowering of moral standards

relajado, -a adj *(tranquilo)* relaxed

relajamiento = **relajación**

relajante 1 adj relaxing
    2 nm relaxant

relajar 1 vt to relax
    2 relajarse vpr to relax

relajo nm *Am Fam (alboroto)* **se armó un r.** there was an almighty row; **esta mesa es un r.** this table is a complete mess

relamer 1 *vt* to lick repeatedly

2 relamerse *vpr* (**a**) *(persona)* to lick one's lips; **relamerse de gusto** to smack one's lips; **se relamía de gusto al pensar en…** he savored the thought of… (**b**) *(animal)* to lick its chops

relamido, -a *adj* prim and proper

relámpago *nm (descarga)* flash of lightning; *(destello)* flash; **hubo muchos relámpagos** there was a lot of lightning; *Fig* **pasar como un r.** to pass by as quick as lightning, to flash past

relampaguear 1 *v impersonal* **relampagueó** lightning flashed

2 *vi* to flash

relampagueo *nm Meteo* lightning; *(destello)* flashing

relanzamiento *nm* relaunch

relanzar [14] *vt* to relaunch

relatar *vt (suceso)* to relate, to recount; *(historia)* to tell

relativamente *adv* relatively

relatividad *nf* relativity

relativismo *nm* relativism

relativizar [14] *vt* to play down

relativo, -a *adj* (**a**) *(no absoluto)* relative (**b**) *(relacionado, tocante)* relating; **en lo r. a…** regarding… (**c**) *(escaso)* limited

relato *nm (exposición)* account, report; *(cuento)* tale, story

relax *nm inv* (**a**) *(relajación)* relaxation (**b**) *(sección de periódico)* personal services section

relé *nm Elec* relay

releer [37] *vt* to reread

relegación *nf* relegation

relegar [38] *vt* to relegate (**a** to); **r. algo al olvido** to banish sth from one's mind

relente *nm* (night) dew

relevancia *nf* importance

relevante *adj* outstanding, important

relevar *vt* (**a**) *(sustituir)* to relieve, to take over from (**b**) *(destituir)* to dismiss (**de** from), to relieve (**de** of) (**c**) *(eximir)* to free (**de** from) (**d**) *Dep (en partidos)* to substitute; *(en relevos)* to take over from

relevo *nm* (**a**) *(sustitución, cambio)* change; **tomar el r.** to take over; **el r. de la guardia** the changing of the guard (**b**) *(sustituto, grupo)* relief (**c**) *Dep (acción)* relay; *(carrera)* **relevos** relay (race)

releyera *etc ver* **releer**

relicario *nm Rel* reliquary; *(estuche)* locket

relieve *nm* (**a**) *Geog* terrain; **un r. muy accidentado** very rugged terrain (**b**) *Arte* **alto r.** high relief; **bajo r.** bas-relief; **en r.** in relief (**c**) *(elevación)* **la pieza tiene un centímetro de r.** the part protrudes by a centimeter (**d**) *(importancia)* importance; **para dar r. al acontecimiento,…** to lend importance to the event…; **poner de r.** to underline (the importance of), to highlight

religión *nf* religion

religiosamente *adv también Fig* religiously

religiosidad *nf también Fig* religiousness

religioso, -a 1 *adj* religious

2 *nm,f (monje)* monk; *(monja)* nun; *(cura)* priest *(of a religious order)*

relinchar *vi* to neigh, to whinny

relincho *nm* neigh, neighing

reliquia *nf (restos)* relic; *(familiar)* heirloom; **este ordenador es una r.** this computer is a museum piece

rellano *nm* (**a**) *(de escalera)* landing (**b**) *(de terreno)* shelf

rellenar *vt* (**a**) *(volver a llenar)* to refill (**b**) *(documento, formulario)* to fill in *o* out (**c**) *(pollo, cojín)* to stuff; *(tarta, pastel)* to fill

relleno, -a 1 *adj* (**a**) *(lleno)* stuffed; *(tarta, pastel)* filled (**b**) *(gordo)* plump

2 *nm (de pollo, almohadón)* stuffing; *(de pastel)* filling; **páginas de r.** padding

reloj *nm (de pared, en torre)* clock; *(de pulsera)* watch; *Dep* **(carrera) contra r.** time trial; **hacer algo contra r.** to do sth against the clock; *Fig* **funcionar como un r.** to go like clockwork; *Fam* **es un r.** *(es puntual)* you can set your watch by him; **r. analógico** analog watch; **r. de arena** hourglass; **r. biológico** body clock, biological clock; **r. de bolsillo** pocket watch; **r. de cuco** cuckoo clock; **r. despertador** alarm clock; **r. digital** digital watch; *Inform* **r. interno** internal clock; **r. de pared** grandfather clock; **r. de pulsera** watch, wristwatch; **r. de sol** sun dial

relojería *nf* (**a**) *(tienda)* watchmaker's (**b**) *(arte)* watchmaking

relojero, -a *nm,f* watchmaker

reluciente *adj* shining, gleaming

relucir [39] *vi también Fig* to shine; **sacar algo a r.** to bring sth up, to mention sth

relumbrar *vi* to shine brightly

relumbrón *nm* (**a**) *(golpe de luz)* flash (**b**) *(oropel)* tinsel; *Fig* **un trabajo de r.** a job that's not as important as it sounds

reluzca *etc ver* **relucir**

remachar *vt* (**a**) *(machacar)* to rivet (**b**) *(recalcar)* to drive home, to stress

remache *nm* (**a**) *(acción)* riveting (**b**) *(clavo)* rivet

remake [rri'meik] *nm* remake

remanente *nm* (**a**) *(de géneros)* surplus stock; *(de productos agrícolas)* surplus (**b**) *(en cuenta bancaria)* balance (**c**) *(de beneficios)* net profit

remangar [38] **1** *vt* to roll up

2 remangarse *vpr (mangas, camisa)* to roll up one's sleeves; **remangarse los pantalones** to roll up one's pants legs

remanguillé *nf Fam* **a la r.** any old how; **la casa estaba a la r.** the house was in an awful mess

remanso *nm* still pool; **r. de paz** oasis of peace

remar *vi* to row

remarcar [59] *vt (recalcar)* to underline, to stress

rematadamente *adv* absolutely, utterly

rematado, -a *adj* utter, complete

rematar 1 *vt* (**a**) *(acabar)* to finish (**b**) *(matar)* to finish off; *Fig* **para r.** *(para colmo)* to cap *o* crown it all (**c**) *Dep* to shoot (**d**) *(liquidar, vender)* to sell off cheaply (**e**) *(costura)* to finish off (**f**) *(adjudicar en subasta)* to knock down

2 *vi Dep* to shoot; **r. de cabeza** to head at goal

remate 1 *nm* (**a**) *(fin, colofón)* end; **para r.** *(colmo)* to cap it all (**b**) *(costura)* overstitch (**c**) *Arquit* top (**d**) *Dep (con el pie)* shot; **r. de cabeza** header (at goal); **r. a puerta** *(con el pie)* shot at goal

2 de remate *loc adj* totally, completely

remedar *vt (imitar)* to imitate; *(por burla)* to ape, to mimic

remediar *vt (daño)* to remedy, to put right; *(problema)* to solve; *(crisis, situación)* to resolve; *(peligro)* to avoid, to prevent; **al fin se remedió su situación** her situation was finally resolved; **si puedes remediarlo, no vayas ese día** don't go on that day if you can help it; **ya no se puede r.** there's nothing to be done about it, it can't be helped; **no lo puedo r.** I can't help it

remedio *nm* (**a**) *(solución)* solution, remedy; **no hay** *o* **queda más r. que…** there's nothing for it but…; **poner r. a algo** to do sth about sth; **¡qué r.!** there's no alternative!, what else can I/we *etc* do?; **no tener más r. (que)** to have no alternative *o* choice (but); **no tiene r.** *(persona)* he's a hopeless case; *(problema)* nothing can be done about it; **sin r.** *(sin cura, solución)* hopeless; *(ineludiblemente)* inevitably; **es peor el r. que la enfermedad** the solution is worse than the problem (**b**) *(consuelo)* comfort, consolation; **el mejor r. contra la depresión es el trabajo** the best cure for depression is work (**c**) *(medicamento)* remedy, cure; **un r. contra el sida** a cure for AIDS; **r. casero** home remedy

remedo *nm (imitación)* imitation; *(por burla)* parody

rememorar *vt* to remember, to recall

remendado, -a *adj (con parches)* patched; *(zurcido)* darned, mended

remendar [3] *vt (con parches)* to patch, to mend; *(zurcir)* to darn, to mend

remendón, -ona *adj* **zapatero r.** cobbler

remera *nf RP (prenda)* T-shirt

remero, -a *nm,f (persona)* rower

remesa *nf (de productos)* shipment, consignment; *(de dinero)* remittance

remeter *vt* to tuck in

remiendo 1 *ver* **remendar**
  2 *nm* (**a**) *(parche)* mend, darn (**b**) *Fam (apaño)* patching up, makeshift mending

remilgado, -a *adj* (**a**) *(afectado)* affected (**b**) *(escrupuloso)* squeamish; *(con comida)* fussy, finicky

remilgo *nm* (**a**) *(afectación)* affectation (**b**) *(escrúpulos)* squeamishness; *(con comida)* fussiness; **hacerle remilgos a algo** to turn one's nose up at sth

reminiscencia *nf* reminiscence; **tener reminiscencias de** to be reminiscent of

remise *nm RP* taxi *(in private car without meter)*

remisero, -a *nm,f RP* taxi driver *(of private car without meter)*

remisión *nf* (**a**) *(envío)* sending (**b**) *(en texto)* cross-reference, reference (**c**) *(perdón)* remission, forgiveness; **sin r.** without hope of a reprieve

remiso, -a *adj (reacio)* reluctant; **ser r. a hacer algo** to be reluctant to do sth

remite *nm* = sender's name and address

remitente *nmf* sender

remitir 1 *vt* (**a**) *(enviar)* to send; **r. algo a** to refer sth to (**b**) *(perdonar)* to forgive, to remit
  2 *vi* (**a**) *(en texto)* to refer (**a** to) (**b**) *(disminuir) (tormenta, viento)* to subside; *(fiebre, temperatura)* to go down; *(enfermedad)* to go into remission; *(lluvia, calor)* to ease off
  3 remitirse a *vpr* (**a**) *(atenerse a)* to comply with, to abide by (**b**) *(referirse a)* to refer to

remo *nm* (**a**) *(pala)* oar (**b**) *(deporte)* rowing

remodelación *nf (modificación)* redesign; *(conversión)* conversion; *(de Gobierno)* reshuffle

remodelar *vt (modificar)* to redesign; *(gobierno)* to reshuffle; **r. algo para convertirlo en** to convert sth into

remojar *vt* (**a**) *(mojar)* to soak (**b**) *Fam (celebrar bebiendo)* to celebrate with a drink

remojo *nm* **poner en** *o* **a r.** to leave to soak; **estar en r.** to be soaking

remojón *nm (en la piscina, el mar)* dip; *(bajo la lluvia)* soaking, drenching; **darse un r.** to go for a dip

remolacha *nf (planta)* beet; **r. azucarera** (sugar) beet

remolachero, -a 1 *adj* beet; **el sector r.** the beet sector
  2 *nm,f* beet grower

remolcador, -ora 1 *adj (vehículo)* **camión r.** tow truck; *(barco)* **lancha remolcadora** tug, tugboat
  2 *nm (camión)* tow truck; *(barco)* tug, tugboat

remolcar [59] *vt (coche)* to tow; *(barco)* to tug

remolino *nm* (**a**) *(de agua)* eddy, whirlpool; *(de viento)* whirlwind; *(de humo)* cloud, swirl (**b**) *(de gente)* throng, mass (**c**) *(de ideas)* confusion (**d**) *(de pelo)* cowlick

remolón, -ona 1 *adj* lazy
  2 *nm,f* **hacerse el r.** to shirk, to be lazy

remolonear *vi Fam (perder el tiempo)* to shirk, to be lazy; *(en la cama)* to laze about in bed

remolque *nm* (**a**) *(acción)* towing; **ir a r. de** to be towed along by; *Fig* to follow along behind, to be led by (**b**) *(vehículo)* trailer

remontada *nf Fam Dep* comeback; **la r. del equipo en la liga** the team's climb back up the league table

remontar 1 *vt (pendiente, río)* to go up; *(obstáculo)* to get over, to overcome; *(puestos)* to pull back, to catch up; **r. el vuelo** to soar
  2 remontarse *vpr* (**a**) *(ave, avión)* to soar, to climb high (**b**) *(gastos)* **remontarse a** to amount *o* come to (**c**) *(en el tiempo)* **remontarse a** *(hecho)* to go *o* date back to; *(persona)* to go back to

remonte *nm* ski lift

rémora *nf* (**a**) *(pez)* remora (**b**) *(impedimento)* hindrance

remorder [41] *vt* **me remuerde (la conciencia) haberle mentido** I feel guilty *o* bad about lying to him

remordimiento *nm* remorse; **tener remordimientos (de conciencia) por algo** to feel remorse about sth

remotamente *adv* remotely; **no se parecen ni r.** they don't look even remotely like each other

remoto, -a *adj (gen) & Inform* remote; **no tengo ni la más remota idea** I haven't got the faintest idea

remover [41] **1** *vt* (**a**) *(agitar) (sopa, café)* to stir; *(ensalada)* to toss; *(tierra)* to turn over, to dig up (**b**) *(recuerdos, pasado)* to stir up, to rake up (**c**) *Am (despedir)* to dismiss, to fire
  2 removerse *vpr (moverse)* to fidget; *(en la cama)* to toss and turn

remozar [14] *vt (edificio, fachada)* to renovate; *(equipo)* to give a new look to

remplazar [14] *vt (gen) & Inform* to replace

remplazo *nm* (**a**) *(gen) & Inform* replacement (**b**) *Mil* call-up, draft; **soldados de r.** conscripts

remuerda *etc ver* **remorder**

remuevo *etc ver* **remover**

remuneración *nf* remuneration

remunerado, -a *adj* paid; **bien r.** well-paid; **mal r.** badly paid; **no r.** unpaid

remunerar *vt* (**a**) *(pagar)* to remunerate (**b**) *(recompensar)* to reward

renacentista 1 *adj* Renaissance; **pintor r.** Renaissance painter
  2 *nmf (artista)* Renaissance artist

renacer [42] *vi* (**a**) *(flores, hojas)* to grow again (**b**) *(sentimiento, interés)* to return, to revive; **sentirse r.** to feel reborn, to feel one has a new lease of life

Renacimiento *nm* **el R.** the Renaissance

renacimiento *nm* (**a**) *(de flores, hojas)* budding (**b**) *(de sentimiento, interés)* revival, return; **r. espiritual** spiritual rebirth

renacuajo 1 *nm (animal)* tadpole
  2 *nmf Fam (niño)* small fry

renal *adj* renal, kidney; **infección r.** kidney infection

renazca *etc ver* **renacer**

rencilla *nf* (long-standing) quarrel, feud

rencor *nm* resentment, bitterness; **espero que no me guardes r.** I hope you don't feel bitter toward me; **me guarda r. por lo que le hice** he bears me a grudge because of what I did to him

rencoroso, -a 1 *adj* resentful, bitter
  2 *nm,f* resentful *o* bitter person

rendición *nf* surrender; **r. incondicional** unconditional surrender

rendido, -a *adj* (**a**) *(agotado)* exhausted, worn-out (**b**) *(sumiso)* submissive; *(admirador)* servile, devoted

rendija *nf* crack, gap

rendimiento *nm* (**a**) *(de inversión, negocio)* yield, return; *(de trabajador, fábrica)* productivity; *(de tierra, cosecha)* performance, yield; **r. bruto** gross yield; **r. del capital** capital yield (**b**) *(de motor)* performance

rendir [47] **1** *vt* (**a**) *(entregar, dar) (arma, alma)* to surrender; **r. cuentas a alguien de algo** to give an account of sth to sb (**b**) *(ofrecer) (pleitesía)* to pay; **r. culto a** to worship; **r. homenaje**

o **tributo a alguien** to pay tribute to sb (**c**) *(rentar)* to yield (**d**) *(vencer)* to defeat, to subdue (**e**) *(cansar)* to wear out, to tire out

2 *vi* (**a**) *(máquina)* to perform well; *(negocio)* to be profitable; *(fábrica, trabajador)* to be productive; **este atleta ya no rinde como antes** this athlete isn't as good as he used to be (**b**) *(dar de sí)* **esta pintura rinde mucho** a little of this paint goes a long way; **me rinde mucho el tiempo** I get a lot done (in the time)

3 rendirse *vpr* (**a**) *(entregarse)* to give oneself up, to surrender (**b**) *(ceder, abandonar)* to submit, to give in; **¡me rindo!** *(en adivinanza)* I give in *o* up!; **rendirse a la evidencia** to bow to the evidence

renegado, -a *adj & nm,f* renegade

renegar [43] *vi* (**a**) *(repudiar)* **r. de** *Rel* to renounce; *(familia)* to disown (**b**) *Fam (gruñir)* to grumble

renegociar *vt* to renegotiate

renegrido, -a *adj* grimy, blackened

renegué *ver* **renegar**

Renfe ['rrenfe] *nf (abrev de* **Red Nacional de los Ferro-carriles Españoles**) = Spanish state railway company

renglón *nm* line; *Fig* **a r. seguido** in the same breath, straight after; **escribir a alguien unos renglones** to drop sb a line

reniego *etc ver* **renegar**

reno *nm* reindeer

renombrado, -a *adj* renowned, famous

renombrar *vt Inform* to rename

renombre *nm* renown, fame; **de r.** famous

renovable *adj* renewable

renovación *nf (de carné, contrato)* renewal; *(de mobiliario, local)* renovation

renovado, -a *adj (carné, contrato)* renewed; **con renovados bríos** with renewed energy

renovador, -ora 1 *adj* innovative; *Pol* reformist

2 *nm,f* innovator; *Pol* reformer

renovar [41] **1** *vt* (**a**) *(cambiar) (mobiliario, local)* to renovate; *(personal, plantilla)* to make changes to, to shake out; **r. el vestuario** to buy new clothes, to update one's wardrobe; **la empresa ha renovado su imagen** the company has brought its image up to date (**b**) *(rehacer) (carné, contrato, ataques)* to renew (**c**) *(restaurar)* to restore (**d**) *(transformar)* to revitalize; *Pol* to reform

2 renovarse *vpr* **¡renovarse o morir!** adapt or die!

renqueante *adj* limping, hobbling

renquear *vi (cojear)* to limp, to hobble; *(tener problemas)* to struggle along

renqueo *nm, Am* **renquera** *nf* limp

renta *nf* (**a**) *(ingresos)* income; **vivir de las rentas** to live off one's (private) income; **r. del capital** capital yield; **r. fija** fixed income; **r. per cápita** *o* **por habitante** per capita income; **r. del trabajo** wage income; **r. variable/vitalicia** variable/life annuity (**b**) *(alquiler)* rent (**c**) *(beneficios)* return (**d**) *(intereses)* interest (**e**) *(deuda pública)* national *o* public debt

rentabilidad *nf* profitability

rentabilizar [14] *vt* to make profitable

rentable *adj* profitable

rentar 1 *vt* (**a**) *(rendir)* to produce, to yield (**b**) *Méx (alquilar)* to rent; **se renta** *(en letrero)* for rent

2 *vi* to be profitable

rentista *nmf* = person of independent means

renuencia *nf* reluctance, unwillingness

renuente *adj* reluctant (**a** to), unwilling (**a** to)

renuevo *etc ver* **renovar**

renuncia *nf* (**a**) *(abandono)* giving up (**b**) *(dimisión)* resignation; **presentó su r.** he handed in his (letter of) resignation

renunciar *vi* (**a**) **r. a algo** *(abandonar, prescindir de)* to give sth up; **r. al tabaco** to give up *o* stop smoking; **r. a la violencia** to

renounce the use of violence (**b**) *(dimitir)* to resign; **renunció a su cargo de secretario** he resigned his position as secretary (**c**) *(rechazar)* **r. a algo** *(premio, oferta)* to turn sth down; **r. a hacer algo** to refuse to do sth; **renunció a recibir ayuda del extranjero** he refused to accept help from abroad

renuncio *nm* (**a**) *(en naipes)* revoke (**b**) *(mentira)* lie; **pillar a alguien en (un) r.** to catch sb lying

reñido, -a *adj* (**a**) *(enfadado)* on bad terms *o* at odds (**con** with); **están reñidos** they've fallen out (**b**) *(disputado)* fierce, hard-fought; **unas elecciones muy reñidas** a keenly contested election (**c**) *(incompatible)* **estar r. con** to be at odds with, to be incompatible with

reñir [47] **1** *vt (regañar)* to tell off

2 *vi (enfadarse)* to argue, to squabble; **r. con** to fall out with

reo *nmf (culpado)* offender, culprit; *(acusado)* accused, defendant

reoca *nf Fam* **ser la r.** *(gracioso)* to be a scream; *(el colmo)* to be the limit

reojo: de reojo *loc adv* **mirar algo/a alguien de r.** to look at sth/sb out of the corner of one's eye

reordenación *nf* restructuring, reorganization

reordenar *vt* to restructure

reorganización *nf (reestructuración)* reorganization; *(del gobierno)* reshuffle

reorganizar [14] *vt (reestructurar)* to reorganize; *(gobierno)* to reshuffle

reorientar 1 *vt (carrera, empresa, vida)* to give a new direction to; *(energías, interés)* to refocus (**hacia** on), to redirect (**hacia** toward)

2 reorientarse *(carrera, empresa, vida)* to take a new direction; *(energías, interés)* to refocus (**hacia** on), to be redirected (**hacia** towards)

repanchigarse, repanchingarse [38] *vpr Fam* to sprawl out

repanocha *nf Fam* **ser la r.** *(gracioso)* to be a scream; *(el colmo)* to be the limit

repantigarse, repantingarse [38] *vpr Fam* to sprawl out

reparación *nf* (**a**) *(arreglo)* repair; **necesita varias reparaciones** it needs several things repairing; **en r.** under repair (**b**) *(compensación)* reparation, redress

reparador, -ora *adj (descanso, sueño)* refreshing

reparar 1 *vt (coche, aparato)* to repair, to fix; *(error, daño)* to make amends for; *(fuerzas)* to make up for, to restore

2 *vi (advertir)* **r. en algo** to notice sth; **no r. en gastos** to spare no expense

reparo *nm* (**a**) *(objeción)* objection; **poner reparos a algo** to raise objections to sth (**b**) *(apuro)* **con reparos** with hesitation *o* reservations; **me da r.** I feel awkward about it; **no tener reparos en hacer algo** to have no qualms *o* scruples about doing sth; **sin reparos** without reservation, with no holds barred

repartición *nf (reparto)* sharing out

repartidor, -ora 1 *adj* delivery; **camión r.** delivery truck

2 *nm,f (de butano, carbón)* deliveryman, *f* deliverywoman; *(de leche)* milkman, *f* milkwoman; *(de periódicos)* paperboy, *f* papergirl; **es r. de publicidad** *(en la calle)* he hands out advertising leaflets; *(en buzones)* he distributes advertising leaflets

repartir 1 *vt* (**a**) *(dividir)* to share out, to divide; **repartió los terrenos entre sus hijos** she divided the land among her children; **la riqueza está mal repartida** there is an uneven distribution of wealth (**b**) *(entregar) (leche, periódicos, correo)* to deliver; *(naipes)* to deal (out); **repartimos a domicilio** we do home deliveries; *Fam* **repartió puñetazos a diestro y siniestro** he lashed out with his fists in every direction (**c**) *(esparcir) (pintura, mantequilla)* to spread (**d**) *(asignar) (trabajo, órdenes)* to give out, to allocate; *(papeles)* to assign

2 repartirse *vpr* (**a**) *(dividirse)* to divide up, to share out; **se repartieron el botín** they divided up *o* shared out the loot (**b**) *(distribuirse)* to spread out

reparto *nm* (**a**) *(división)* division; **hacer el r. de algo** to divide sth up, to share out; *Esp Fin* **r. de beneficios** profit sharing; **el r. de la riqueza** the distribution of wealth; **r. del trabajo** work sharing; *Am Fin* **r. de utilidades** profit sharing (**b**) *(entrega)* *(de leche, periódicos, correo)* delivery; *(de naipes)* dealing; **el camión del r.** the delivery van; **se dedica al r. de publicidad** he distributes advertising leaflets; **r. a domicilio** home delivery (**c**) *(asignación)* giving out, allocation; **r. de premios** prize-awarding (**d**) *Cine & Teatro* cast; **actor de r.** supporting actor

repasador *nm RP (trapo)* dish towel

repasar *vt* (**a**) *(revisar)* to go over, to check; **hay que r. las cuentas para detectar el error** we'll have to go through all the accounts to find the mistake; **hoy repasaremos la segunda lección** we'll go over lesson two again today (**b**) *(estudiar)* to review (**c**) *(zurcir)* to darn, to mend

repaso *nm* (**a**) *(revisión)* check; **hacer un r. de algo** to check sth over (**b**) *(estudio)* review; **dar un r. a algo** to review sth (**c**) *(de ropa)* **dar un r. a algo** to darn *o* mend sth; **necesita un r.** it needs darning *o* mending (**d**) *Fam* **dar un r. a alguien** *(regañar)* to give sb a telling off; *(apabullar)* to thrash sb

repatear *vt Fam* **me repatea que...** it really annoys me that...; **ese tipo me repatea** I can't stand that guy

repatriación *nf* repatriation

repatriar [32] **1** *vt* to repatriate
 2 repatriarse *vpr* to return home

repecho *nm* steep slope

repeinado, -a *adj* dolled up

repelencia *nf* repulsion

repelente 1 *adj* (**a**) *(desagradable, repugnante)* repulsive (**b**) *(de insectos)* repellent
 2 *nm* insect repellent

repeler *vt* (**a**) *(rechazar)* to repel (**b**) *(repugnar)* to repulse, to disgust

repelús *nm* **me da r.** it gives me the shivers

repeluzno *nm* shiver

repente 1 *nm (arrebato)* fit
 2 de repente *loc adv* suddenly

repentinamente *adv* suddenly

repentino, -a *adj* sudden

repera *nf Fam* **ser la r.** to be the limit

repercusión *nf* (**a**) *(consecuencia)* repercussion (**b**) *(resonancia)* echoes

repercutir *vi* (**a**) *(afectar)* to have repercussions (**en** on) (**b**) *(resonar)* to resound, to echo

repertorio *nm* (**a**) *(obras)* repertoire (**b**) *(serie)* selection

repesca *nf* (**a**) *Educ* retake (**b**) *Dep* repechage

repescar [59] *vt* (**a**) *Educ* to allow a retake (**b**) *Dep* to allow into the repechage

repetición *nf (de acción, dicho)* repetition; *(de una jugada)* instant replay

repetido, -a *adj* (**a**) *(reiterado)* repeated; **repetidas veces** time and time again (**b**) *(duplicado)* **tengo este libro r.** I've got two copies of this book

repetidor, -ora 1 *adj* repeating the year
 2 *nm,f Educ* = student repeating a year
 3 *nm (de radio, televisión)* repeater

repetir [47] **1** *vt (hacer, decir de nuevo)* to repeat; *(ataque)* to renew; *(en comida)* to have seconds of; **repíteme tu apellido** could you repeat your surname?, could you tell me your surname again?; **te lo he repetido mil veces** I've told you a thousand times; *Educ* **repitió tercero** he repeated his third year
 2 *vi* (**a**) *(alumno)* to repeat a year (**b**) *(sabor, alimento)* **r. (a**

alguien) to repeat (on sb); **el ajo repite mucho** garlic really repeats on you (**c**) *(comensal)* to have seconds
 3 repetirse *vpr* (**a**) *(fenómeno)* to recur; **este fenómeno se repite cada verano** this phenomenon recurs *o* is repeated every summer (**b**) *(persona)* to repeat oneself

repetitivo, -a *adj* repetitive

repicar [59] **1** *vt (campanas)* to ring; *(tambor)* to beat
 2 *vi (campanas)* to ring; *(tambor)* to sound

repipi 1 *adj* (irritatingly) precocious
 2 *nmf* precocious brat

repique 1 *ver* **repicar**
 2 *nm* peal, ringing

repiquetear *vi (campanas)* to ring out; *(tambor)* to beat; *(timbre)* to ring; *(lluvia, dedos)* to drum

repiqueteo *nm (de campanas)* pealing; *(de tambor)* beating; *(de timbre)* ringing; *(de lluvia, dedos)* drumming

repisa *nf* (**a**) *(estante)* shelf; *(sobre chimenea)* mantelpiece (**b**) *Arquit* bracket

repitiera *etc ver* **repetir**

repito *etc ver* **repetir**

replantar *vt* to replant

replanteamiento *nm* restatement, reconsideration

replantear 1 *vt* (**a**) *(situación, problema)* to restate (**b**) *(cuestión) (de nuevo)* to raise again; *(parafrasear)* to rephrase
 2 replantearse *vpr* to reconsider

replegar [43] **1** *vt (ocultar)* to retract
 2 replegarse *vpr (retirarse)* to withdraw, to retreat

repleto, -a *adj (habitación, autobús)* packed (**de** with); **estoy r.** *(de comida)* I'm full (up)

réplica *nf* (**a**) *(respuesta)* reply (**b**) *(copia)* replica

replicación *nf Biol* replication

replicar [59] **1** *vt (responder)* to answer; *(objetar)* to answer back, to retort
 2 *vi (objetar)* to answer back

repliego *etc ver* **replegar**

repliegue *nm* (**a**) *(retirada)* withdrawal, retreat (**b**) *(pliegue)* fold

repoblación *nf (con gente)* repopulation; *(con peces)* restocking; **r. forestal** reafforestation

repoblar [63] *vt (con gente)* to repopulate; *(con peces)* to restock; *(con árboles)* to replant, to reforest

repollo *nm* cabbage

reponer [50] **1** *vt* (**a**) *(existencias, trabajador)* to replace (**b**) *Cine* to reshow; *Teatro* to revive; *TV* to rerun (**c**) *(replicar)* **r. que** to reply that
 2 reponerse *vpr* to recover (**de** from)

repóquer *nm* **un r. de ases** five aces *(when playing with two decks)*

reportaje *nm Rad & TV* report; *Prensa* article; **r. gráfico** illustrated article

reportar 1 *vt* (**a**) *(traer)* to bring; **no le ha reportado más que problemas** it has caused him nothing but problems (**b**) *Andes, CAm, Méx, Ven (informar)* to report (**c**) *CAm, Méx (a la policía)* to report
 2 reportarse *vpr* (**a**) *(reprimirse)* to control oneself (**b**) *CAm, Méx, Ven (presentarse)* to report (**a** to)

reporte *nm Am* report

reportear *Chile, Méx* **1** *vt* to report on, to cover
 2 *vi* to work as a reporter

reportero, -a *nm,f* reporter; **r. gráfico** press photographer

reposabrazos *nm inv* armrest

reposacabezas *nm inv* headrest

reposado, -a *adj* relaxed, calm

reposamuñecas *nf* wrist rest

reposapiés *nm inv* footrest

reposar *vi* (**a**) *(descansar) (persona)* to (have a) rest (**b**) *(sedimentarse) (líquido, masa)* to stand (**c**) *(yacer) (restos)* to lie

reposera *nf RP (silla)* beach recliner

reposición *nf* (**a**) *Cine* reshowing; *Teatro* revival; *TV* rerun (**b**) *(de existencias, pieza)* replacement

reposo *nm (descanso)* rest; **en r.** *(cuerpo, persona)* at rest; *(máquina)* not in use; *Culin* standing

repostar 1 *vi (coche)* to fill up; *(avión)* to refuel

2 *vt* (**a**) *(gasolina)* to fill up with (**b**) *(provisiones)* to stock up on

repostería *nf* (**a**) *(establecimiento)* confectioner's (shop) (**b**) *(oficio, productos)* confectionery

repostero, -a 1 *nm,f (persona)* confectioner

2 *nm Andes (armario)* larder, pantry

reprender *vt (a niños)* to tell off; *(a empleados)* to reprimand

reprensible *adj* reprehensible

reprensión *nf (a niños)* telling-off; *(a empleados)* reprimand

represa *nf* dam

represalia *nf* reprisal; **tomar represalias** to retaliate, to take reprisals

representación *nf* (**a**) *(gen) & Com* representation; **en r. de** on behalf of; *Com* **tener la r. de** to act as a representative for; *Pol* **r. proporcional** proportional representation (**b**) *Teatro* performance

representante 1 *adj* representative

2 *nmf* (**a**) *(gen) & Com* representative (**b**) *(de artista)* agent

representar *vt* (**a**) *(simbolizar, ejemplificar)* to represent; **este cuadro representa la Última Cena** this painting depicts the Last Supper (**b**) *(actuar en nombre de alguien)* to represent; **representa a varios artistas** she acts as an agent for several artists (**c**) *(aparentar)* to look; **representa unos 40 años** she looks about 40 (**d**) *(significar)* to mean; **representa el 50 por ciento del consumo interno** it accounts for 50 percent of domestic consumption; **representa mucho para él** it means a lot to him (**e**) *Teatro (función)* to perform; *(papel)* to play

representatividad *nf* representativeness

representativo, -a *adj* (**a**) *(simbolizador)* **ser r. de algo** to represent sth; **un grupo r. de la población general** a group that represents the population as a whole (**b**) *(característico, relevante)* **r. (de)** representative (of); **este cuadro es poco r. de su estilo** this painting is not very representative of his style

represión *nf* repression

represivo, -a *adj* repressive

represor, -ora 1 *adj* repressive

2 *nm,f* oppressor

reprimenda *nf* reprimand

reprimido, -a 1 *adj* repressed

2 *nm,f* repressed person

reprimir 1 *vt* (**a**) *(llanto, risa)* to suppress (**b**) *(minorías, disidentes)* to repress

2 reprimirse *vpr* **reprimirse (de hacer algo)** to restrain oneself (from doing sth)

reprís, reprise *(pl* **reprises***) nm* acceleration

reprobable *adj* reprehensible

reprobación *nf* reproof, censure

reprobar [63] *vt* (**a**) *(desaprobar)* to censure, to condemn (**b**) *Am (estudiante, examen)* to fail

reprobatorio, -a *adj* reproving

réprobo, -a 1 *adj* damned

2 *nm,f* lost soul

reprochar *vt* **r. algo a alguien** to reproach sb for sth

2 reprocharse *vpr* **reprocharse algo (uno mismo)** to reproach oneself for sth

reproche *nm* reproach; **hacer un r. a alguien** to reproach sb

reproducción *nf* reproduction; **tratamiento de r. asistida** fertility treatment; **r. sexual** sexual reproduction

reproducir [18] **1** *vt (copiar, repetir)* to reproduce; *(gestos)* to copy, to imitate; **reprodujo su declaración por escrito** he put his statement into writing; **la novela reproduce fielmente la atmósfera del periodo** the novel faithfully recreates the atmosphere of the period

2 reproducirse *vpr* (**a**) *(volver a suceder)* to recur; **anoche se reprodujeron los choques armados en la frontera** last night there were renewed armed clashes on the border (**b**) *(procrear)* to reproduce

reproductor, -ora 1 *adj* reproductive

2 *nm* player; **r. de discos compactos** compact disc player

reprografía *nf* reprographics; **(servicio de) r.** copying service

repruebo *etc ver* **reprobar**

reptar *vi* to crawl

reptil *nm* reptile

república *nf* republic; **r. bananera** banana republic

República Centroafricana *nf* Central African Republic

República Checa *nf* Czech Republic

República Dominicana *nf* Dominican Republic

republicanismo *nm* republicanism

republicano, -a *adj & nm,f* republican

repudiar *vt* (**a**) *(condenar)* to condemn (**b**) *(rechazar)* to disown

repudio *nm* (**a**) *(condena)* condemnation (**b**) *(rechazo)* disowning

repueblo *etc ver* **repoblar**

repuesto, -a 1 *participio ver* **reponer**

2 *adj* recovered (**de** from)

3 *nm (provisión extra)* reserve; *Aut* spare part; **de r.** spare, in reserve; **la rueda de r.** the spare wheel

repugnancia *nf* disgust

repugnante *adj* disgusting

repugnar 1 *vt* **me repugna ese olor/su actitud** I find that smell/her attitude disgusting; **me repugna hacerlo** I'm loath to do it

2 *vi* to be disgusting

repujado, -a 1 *adj* embossed

2 *nm* embossed work

repujar *vt* to emboss

repulsa *nf (censura)* condemnation

repulsión *nf* repulsion

repulsivo, -a *adj* repulsive

repuntar *vi Fin (valor)* to rally, to recover

repunte *nm (de valores, precios)* rally, recovery; **un r. de la inflación** a slight rise in inflation

repusiera *etc ver* **reponer**

reputación *nf* reputation; **tener mucha r.** to be very famous

reputado, -a *adj* highly reputed

reputar *vt* to consider

requemado, -a *adj* burned

requemar 1 *vt (quemar)* to burn; *(planta, tierra)* to scorch

2 requemarse *vpr* to get burned, to burn

requerimiento *nm* (**a**) *(demanda)* entreaty; **a r. de** on the request of (**b**) *Der (intimación)* writ, injunction; *(aviso)* summons *(singular)*

requerir [62] **1** *vt* (**a**) *(necesitar)* to require (**b**) *(ordenar)* to demand (**c**) *(pedir)* **r. a alguien (para) que haga algo** to ask sb to do sth (**d**) *Der* to order

2 requerirse *vpr (ser necesario)* to be required *o* necessary

requesón *nm* = ricotta-type cheese

requete- *prefijo Fam* **requetebién** wonderfully *o* marvellously well; **requetegrande** absolutely enormous

requiebro *nm* flirtatious remark

réquiem *(pl* **requiems***) nm* requiem

requiero *etc ver* **requerir**

requisa *nf* (**a**) *(requisición) Mil* requisition; *(en aduana)* seizure (**b**) *(inspección)* inspection

requisar *vt Mil* to requisition; *(en aduana)* to seize

requisito *nm* requirement; **cumplir los requisitos** to fulfill all the requirements; **r. previo** prerequisite

res *nf* (**a**) *(animal)* beast, animal (**b**) *Am* **reses** *(ganado vacuno)* cattle

resabiado, -a *adj* **estar r.** to be hardened; **un caballo r.** a vicious horse

resabio *nm* (**a**) *(sabor)* nasty aftertaste (**b**) *(vicio)* persistent bad habit

resaca *nf* (**a**) *(de borrachera)* hangover (**b**) *(de las olas)* undertow

resacoso, -a *adj Fam* **estar r.** to be hungover

resalado, -a *adj Fam* charming

resaltar 1 *vi* (**a**) *(destacar)* to stand out (**b**) *(en edificios) (balcón)* to stick out; *(decoración)* to stand out

2 *vt (destacar)* to highlight

resarcimiento *nm* compensation

resarcir [72] **1** *vt* **r. a alguien (de)** to compensate sb (for)

2 resarcirse *vpr (daño, pérdida)* to be compensated (**de** for); **se resarció de la derrota del mes pasado** he gained revenge for his defeat the previous month

resbalada *nf Am Fam* slip

resbaladizo, -a *adj también Fig* slippery

resbalar 1 *vi* (**a**) *(caer)* to slip (**con** *o* **en** on) (**b**) *(deslizarse)* to slide; **le resbalaban las lágrimas por el rostro** tears ran *o* trickled down her cheeks (**c**) *(estar resbaladizo)* to be slippery

2 *vt Fam (no preocupar a)* **le resbala todo lo que le digo** everything I say to him goes in one ear and out the other; **¡me resbala lo que diga de mí!** I couldn't care less what she says about me!

3 resbalarse *vpr* to slip (over); **me resbalé y me caí** I slipped and fell; **se resbaló con una piel de plátano** he slipped on a banana skin

resbalón *nm también Fig* slip; **dar** *o* **pegar un r.** to slip

resbaloso, -a *adj* slippery

rescatar *vt* (**a**) *(liberar, salvar)* to rescue; *(pagando rescate)* to ransom (**b**) *(recuperar) (herencia)* to recover

rescate *nm* (**a**) *(liberación, salvación)* rescue (**b**) *(dinero)* ransom (**c**) *(recuperación)* recovery

rescindir *vt* to rescind

rescisión *nf* cancellation

rescoldo *nm (en fuego)* ember; *(resto)* lingering feeling, flicker

resecar [59] **1** *vt* (**a**) *(piel)* to dry out (**b**) *(tierra)* to parch

2 resecarse *vpr* (**a**) *(piel)* to dry out (**b**) *(tierra)* to become parched

reseco, -a *adj* (**a**) *(piel, garganta, pan)* very dry (**b**) *(tierra)* parched (**c**) *(flaco)* emaciated

resentido, -a 1 *adj* bitter, resentful; **estar r. con alguien** to be really upset with sb

2 *nm, f* bitter *o* resentful person

resentimiento *nm* resentment, bitterness

resentirse [62] *vpr* (**a**) *(debilitarse)* to be weakened; *(salud)* to deteriorate (**b**) *(sentir molestias)* **r. de** to be suffering from (**c**) *(ofenderse)* to be offended

reseña *nf (de libro, concierto)* review; *(de partido, conferencia)* report

reseñar *vt* (**a**) *(criticar) (libro, concierto)* to review; *(partido, conferencia)* to report on (**b**) *(describir)* to describe

reseque *etc ver* **resecar**

reserva 1 *nf* (**a**) *(de hotel, avión)* reservation, booking; **he hecho la r. de las entradas** I've booked the tickets; **r. anticipada** advance booking; **r. de grupo** block booking

(**b**) *(provisión)* reserves; **tener algo de r.** to keep sth in reserve; **reservas** *(energía acumulada)* energy reserves; *(recursos)* resources; *Econ* **reservas de divisas** foreign currency; **reservas monetarias** monetary reserves; **reservas de oro** gold reserves

(**c**) *(objeción, cautela)* reservation; **sin reservas** without reservation

(**d**) *(discreción)* discretion

(**e**) *(de indígenas)* reservation

(**f**) *(de animales)* reserve; **r. natural** nature reserve

(**g**) *Mil* reserves; **pasar a la r.** to become a reservist

2 *nmf Dep* reserve, substitute

3 *nm (vino)* vintage (wine)

reservación *nf Méx* reservation

reservado, -a 1 *adj* (**a**) *(mesa)* reserved (**b**) *(tema, asunto)* confidential (**c**) *(persona)* reserved

2 *nm (en restaurante)* private room; *Ferroc* reserved compartment

reservar 1 *vt* (**a**) *(billete, habitación)* to book, to reserve (**b**) *(guardar, apartar)* to set aside; **reservan la primera fila para los críticos** the front row is reserved for the critics; **¿me puedes r. un sitio a tu lado?** could you save a seat for me next to you?; **reservó la buena noticia para el final** she saved the good news till last (**c**) *(callar) (opinión, comentarios)* to reserve

2 reservarse *vpr* (**a**) *(esperar)* **reservarse para** to save oneself for; **me estoy reservando para el postre** I'm saving myself for the dessert (**b**) *(guardar para sí) (secreto)* to keep to oneself; *(dinero, derecho)* to retain (for oneself); **me reservo mi opinión sobre este asunto** I'm reserving judgment on this matter

reservista *Mil* **1** *adj* reserve; **militar r.** officer in the reserves

2 *nmf* reservist

resfriado, -a 1 *adj* **estar r.** to have a cold

2 *nm* cold

resfriarse [32] *vpr* to catch a cold

resfrío *nm Andes, RP* cold

resguardar 1 *vt* to protect; **la sombrilla nos resguarda del sol** the parasol shades us from the sun

2 *vi* **r. de** to protect against

3 resguardarse *vpr (en un portal)* to shelter (**de** from); *(con abrigo, paraguas)* to protect oneself (**de** against); **se resguardaron de la lluvia debajo de un árbol** they sheltered from the rain under a tree

resguardo *nm* (**a**) *(documento)* receipt (**b**) *(protección)* protection; **al r. de** safe from

residencia *nf* (**a**) *(establecimiento) (de oficiales)* residence; **r. (de ancianos)** retirement home; **r. (de estudiantes)** dormitory (**b**) *(hotel)* boardinghouse (**c**) *(hospital)* hospital (**d**) *(permiso para extranjeros)* residence permit (**e**) *(periodo de formación)* residency (**f**) *(estancia)* stay (**g**) *(localidad, domicilio)* residence

residencial *adj* residential; **barrio r.** *(lujoso)* residential area

residente *adj & nmf* resident

residir *vi* (**a**) *(vivir)* to reside (**b**) *(radicar)* to lie (**en** in), to reside (**en** in)

residual *adj* residual; **aguas residuales** sewage

residuo *nm* (**a**) *(material inservible)* waste; *Quím* residue; **residuos industriales** industrial waste; **residuos nucleares** nuclear waste; **residuos radiactivos** radioactive waste (**b**) *(restos)* leftovers

resiento *etc ver* **resentirse**

resignación *nf* resignation

resignarse *vpr* **r. (a hacer algo)** to resign oneself (to doing sth)

resina *nf* resin

resinoso, -a *adj* resinous

resintiera *etc ver* **resentirse**

resistencia *nf* (**a**) *(gen) & Elec & Pol* resistance; **ofrecer r.** to put up resistance; **r. pasiva** passive resistance (**b**) *(de puente, cimientos)* strength (**c**) *(para correr, hacer deporte)* stamina

resistente *adj (fuerte)* tough, strong; **r. al calor** heat-resistant

resistir 1 *vt* (**a**) *(dolor, peso, críticas)* to withstand; **resiste muy mal el calor** he can't take the heat (**b**) *(tentación, impulso, deseo)* to resist (**c**) *(tolerar)* to tolerate, to stand; **no lo resisto más, me voy** I can't stand it any longer, I'm off

2 *vi* (**a**) *(ejército, ciudad)* **r. (a algo/a alguien)** to resist (sth/sb) (**b**) *(persona)* to keep going; **ese corredor resiste mucho** that runner has a lot of stamina; **el tocadiscos aún resiste** the record player's still going strong; **r. a algo** to stand up to sth, to withstand sth (**c**) *(mesa, dique)* to take the strain; **r. a algo** to withstand sth (**d**) *(mostrarse firme) (ante tentaciones)* to resist (it); **r. a algo** to resist sth

3 resistirse *vpr* **resistirse (a algo)** to resist (sth); **por más que empujo esta puerta se resiste** however hard I push, this door refuses to give way; **resistirse a hacer algo** to refuse to do sth; **me resisto a creerlo** I refuse to believe it; **no hay hombre que se le resista** no man can resist her; **se le resisten las matemáticas** she just can't get the hang of math

resma *nf* ream

resol *nm* (sun's) glare; **hace r.** it's cloudy but very bright

resollar [63] *vi (jadear)* to pant; *(respirar)* to breathe

resolución *nf* (**a**) *(solución) (de una crisis)* resolution; *(de un crimen)* solution (**b**) *(firmeza)* determination (**c**) *(decisión)* decision; *Der* ruling; **tomar una r.** to take a decision (**d**) *(de Naciones Unidas)* resolution

resoluto, -a *adj* resolute

resolver [41] **1** *vt* (**a**) *(solucionar) (duda, crisis)* to resolve; *(problema, caso)* to solve (**b**) *(decidir)* **r. hacer algo** to decide to do sth (**c**) *(partido, disputa, conflicto)* to settle; **una canasta en el último segundo resolvió el partido a favor del equipo visitante** a basket in the last second of the game secured victory for the visitors

2 resolverse *vpr* (**a**) *(solucionarse) (duda, crisis)* to be resolved; *(problema, caso)* to be solved; **el secuestro se resolvió con la liberación de los rehenes** the hijacking was resolved *o* brought to an end with the release of the hostages (**b**) *(decidirse)* **resolverse a hacer algo** to decide to do sth (**c**) *(terminar)* **el huracán se resolvió en una tormenta tropical** the hurricane ended up as a tropical storm

resonancia *nf* (**a**) *(gen)* & *Fís* resonance; *Med* **r. magnética** magnetic resonance (**b**) *(importancia)* repercussions

resonante *adj (que suena, retumba)* resounding; *Fís* resonant

resonar [63] *vi* to resound, to echo

resoplar *vi (de cansancio)* to pant; *(de enfado)* to snort

resoplido *nm (por cansancio)* pant; *(por enfado)* snort

resorte *nm* (**a**) *(muelle)* spring (**b**) *(medio)* means; **tocar todos los resortes** to pull out all the stops (**c**) *Méx (elástico)* elastic

respaldar 1 *vt* to back, to support; **varios intelectuales respaldan la candidatura del escritor** several intellectuals are backing *o* supporting the writer as a candidate; **el descubrimiento respalda su teoría** the discovery backs up *o* supports his theory

2 respaldarse *vpr (apoyarse)* **respaldarse en** to fall back on

respaldo *nm* (**a**) *(de asiento)* back (**b**) *(apoyo)* backing, support

respectar *v impersonal* **por** *o* **en lo que respecta a alguien/a algo** as far as sb/sth is concerned

respectivamente *adv* respectively

respectivo, -a *adj* respective; **en lo r. a** with regard to

respecto *nm* **1 al respecto, a ese respecto** *loc adv* in this respect; **no sé nada al r.** I don't know anything about it

2 (con) respecto a, respecto de *loc prep* regarding

respetabilidad *nf* respectability

respetable 1 *adj (venerable)* respectable

2 *nm Fam (público)* **el r.** the audience

respetar *vt* (**a**) *(persona, costumbre)* to respect; *(la palabra)* to

honor; **hay que r. a los ancianos** you should show respect for the elderly; **no respeta las señales de tráfico** he takes no notice of traffic signs; **hacerse r.** to make oneself respected (**b**) *(no destruir)* to spare; **respeten las plantas** *(en letrero)* keep off the flower beds

respeto *nm* (**a**) respect (**a** *o* **por** for); **el r. a los derechos humanos** respect for human rights; **trata a sus profesores con mucho r.** he shows a great deal of respect toward his teachers, he is very respectful toward his teachers; **es una falta de r.** it shows a lack of respect; **faltar al r. a alguien** to be disrespectful to sb; **dentro de la iglesia hay que guardar r.** you must be respectful inside the church; **por r.** out of consideration for; **presentar uno sus respetos a alguien** to pay one's respects to sb (**b**) *(miedo)* **tener r. a las alturas** to be afraid of heights

respetuoso, -a *adj* respectful (**con** of)

respingar [38] *vi (protestar)* to make a fuss, to complain

respingo *nm* (**a**) *(movimiento)* start, jump; **dar un r.** to start (**b**) *(contestación)* shrug (of annoyance)

respingón, -ona *adj (nariz)* snub; *(trasero)* pert

respiración *nf* breathing; *Med* respiration; **r. artificial** *o* **asistida** artificial respiration; **r. boca a boca** mouth-to-mouth resuscitation, the kiss of life; *Fig* **quedarse sin r.** *(asombrado)* to be stunned

respiradero *nm (hueco)* vent; *(conducto)* ventilation shaft

respirador *nm* **r. (artificial)** *(máquina)* respirator, ventilator

respirar 1 *vt* (**a**) *(aire)* to breathe; *Fig* **en esa casa se respira el amor por la música** a love of music pervades that house (**b**) *(bondad)* to exude

2 *vi* (**a**) *(aire)* to breathe (**b**) *(sentir alivio)* to breathe again; *Fig* **no dejar r. a alguien** not to allow sb a moment's peace (**c**) *(relajarse)* to have a breather; **sin r.** *(sin descanso)* without a break; **después de tanto trabajo necesito r.** I need a breather after all that work

respiratorio, -a *adj* respiratory

respiro *nm* (**a**) *(descanso)* rest (**b**) *(alivio)* relief, respite

resplandecer [46] *vi* (**a**) *(brillar)* to shine (**b**) *(destacar)* to shine, to stand out; **r. de algo** to shine with sth

resplandeciente *adj (brillante)* shining; *(sonrisa)* beaming; *(época)* glittering; *(vestimenta, color)* resplendent

resplandor *nm* (**a**) *(luz)* brightness; *(de fuego)* glow (**b**) *(brillo)* gleam

responder 1 *vt (contestar)* to answer; *(con insolencia)* to answer back

2 *vi* (**a**) *(contestar)* **r. (a algo)** to answer (sth); **responde al nombre de Toby** he answers to the name of Toby (**b**) *(reaccionar)* to respond (**a** to) (**c**) *(responsabilizarse)* **r. de algo/por alguien** to answer for sth/for sb; **¡no respondo de mis actos!** I can't be responsible for what I might do! (**d**) *(replicar)* to answer back (**e**) *(corresponder)* **r. a** to correspond to; **las medidas responden a la crisis** the measures are in keeping with the nature of the crisis

respondón, -ona 1 *adj* insolent

2 *nm,f* insolent person

responsabilidad *nf* responsibility; *Der* liability; **puesto de r.** responsible position; **tener la r. de algo** to be responsible for sth; *Der* **r. civil/penal** civil/criminal liability; **r. limitada** limited liability

responsabilizar [14] **1** *vt* **r. a alguien (de algo)** to hold sb responsible (for sth)

2 responsabilizarse *vpr* to accept responsibility (**de** for)

responsable 1 *adj* responsible; **r. de** responsible for; **hacerse r. de** *(responsabilizarse de)* to take responsibility for; *(atentado, secuestro)* to claim responsibility for

2 *nmf* (**a**) *(culpable, autor)* person responsible; **los responsables** those responsible; **tú eres el r. de…** you're responsible for… (**b**) *(encargado)* person in charge; **soy el r.**

de la sección de ventas I'm in charge of the sales department

responso *nm* prayer for the dead

respuesta *nf* (**a**) *(contestación)* answer, reply; *(en exámenes)* answer; **en r. a** in reply to; **r. afirmativa** affirmative (**b**) *(reacción)* response

resquebrajadura *nf* crack

resquebrajamiento *nm* (**a**) *(grieta)* crack (**b**) *(cuarteamiento)* cracking

resquebrajar 1 *vt* to crack
   2 resquebrajarse *vpr* *(piedra, loza, plástico)* to crack; *(madera)* to split; *Fig* **se está resquebrajando la sociedad** society is beginning to fall apart

resquemor *nm* resentment, bitterness

resquicio *nm* (**a**) *(abertura)* chink; *(grieta)* crack (**b**) *(pizca)* glimmer

resta *nf Mat* subtraction

restablecer [46] **1** *vt* to reestablish, to restore
   2 restablecerse *vpr* (**a**) *(curarse)* to recover (**de** from) (**b**) *(reinstaurarse)* to be reestablished

restablecimiento *nm* (**a**) *(reinstauración)* restoration, reestablishment (**b**) *(cura)* recovery

restallar *vt & vi* *(látigo)* to crack; *(lengua)* to click

restallido *nm* *(de látigo)* crack

restante *adj* remaining; **lo r.** the rest

restañar *vt* *(herida)* to staunch

restar 1 *vt* (**a**) *Mat* to subtract; **r. una cantidad de otra** to subtract one figure from another (**b**) *(disminuir)* **r. importancia a algo** to play down the importance of sth; **r. méritos a alguien/a algo** to detract from sb/sth
   2 *vi* *(faltar)* to be left; **sólo restan tres días** only three days are left; **sólo me resta agradecerles su ayuda** all that remains is for me to thank you for your help

restauración *nf* restoration

restaurador, -ora *nm,f* restorer

restaurante, *Am* **restaurant,** *Am* **restaurán** *nm* restaurant

restaurar *vt* to restore

restitución *nf* return

restituir [34] **1** *vt* (**a**) *(devolver)* *(objeto)* to return; *(salud)* to restore (**b**) *(restaurar)* to restore
   2 restituirse *vpr* *(regresar)* **restituirse a** to return to

resto *nm* (**a**) **el r.** the rest; *Mat* the remainder; **el r. se fue a bailar** the rest (of them) went dancing; **me da igual lo que opine el r.** I don't care what the rest of them think *o* what the others think; *Fig* **echar el r.** to do one's utmost (**b**) **restos** *(sobras)* leftovers; *(cadáver)* remains; *(ruinas)* ruins; **restos mortales** mortal remains (**c**) *(en tenis)* return (of serve); **al r., Jiménez** Jiménez to return

restorán *nm RP* restaurant

restregar [43] **1** *vt* *(frotar)* to rub hard; *(para limpiar)* to scrub
   2 restregarse *vpr* *(frotarse)* to rub

restregón *nm* scrub; **dar un r. a alguien** to give sb a scrub

restricción *nf* restriction; **han impuesto restricciones a la importación de vehículos extranjeros** restrictions have been placed on the importing of foreign vehicles; **no hay restricciones de edad** there's no age limit; **restricciones de agua** water rationing; **restricciones eléctricas** power cuts; **esta opción permite navegar por Internet sin restricciones horarias** this option allows you unmetered access to the Net 24 hours a day

restrictivo, -a *adj* restrictive

restringido, -a *adj* limited, restricted

restringir [24] *vt* to limit, to restrict

resucitar 1 *vt* *(persona)* to bring back to life; *(costumbre)* to resurrect, to revive
   2 *vi* *(persona)* to rise from the dead

resuello 1 *ver* **resollar**
   2 *nm* *(jadeo)* pant, panting; **quedarse sin r.** to be out of breath

resuelto, -a 1 *participio ver* **resolver**
   2 *adj* (**a**) *(solucionado)* solved (**b**) *(decidido)* determined; **estar r. a hacer algo** to be determined to do sth

resuelvo *etc ver* **resolver**

resueno *etc ver* **resonar**

resultado *nm* result; **dar r.** to work (out), to have the desired effect; **dar buenos resultados** to work well

resultante *adj & nf* resultant

resultar 1 *vi* (**a**) *(salir)* to (turn out to) be; **¿cómo resultó?** how did it turn out?; **resultó un éxito** it was a success; **r. en** *(dar como resultado)* to result in; **r. herido/muerto** to be injured/killed; **resultó ileso** he was uninjured; **nuestro equipo resultó vencedor** our team came out on top (**b**) *(originarse)* **r. de** to come of, to result from (**c**) *(ser)* to be; **resulta sorprendente** it's surprising; **r. útil** to be useful; **me resultó imposible terminar antes** I was unable to finish earlier; **me resulta muy simpática** I find her very nice; **este tema me está resultando ya aburrido** this topic is beginning to bore me; **resultó ser mentira** it turned out to be a lie
   2 *v impersonal* *(suceder)* **r. que** to turn out that; **al final resultó que tenía razón** in the end it turned out that she was right; **ahora resulta que no quiere alquilarlo** now it seems that he doesn't want to rent it

resultas: de resultas de *loc prep* as a result of

resultón, -ona *adj Fam* attractive

resumen *nm* summary; **en r.** in short

resumir 1 *vt* *(abreviar)* to summarize; *(discurso)* to sum up
   2 resumirse *vpr* **se resume en pocas palabras** it can be summed up in a few words

resurgimiento *nm* resurgence

resurgir [24] *vi* **el equipo ha resurgido tras una mala racha** the team has bounced back *o* returned to form after a bad time; **el movimiento pacifista resurgió con fuerza en aquella década** the pacifist movement experienced a major resurgence during that decade; **la empresa ha resurgido de sus cenizas** the company has risen from the ashes

resurrección *nf* resurrection

retablo *nm* altarpiece

retaco *nm Fam* shorty, midget

retacón, -ona *adj RP Fam* short and fat

retaguardia *nf* *(tropa)* rearguard; *(territorio)* rear

retahíla *nf* string, series

retal *nm* remnant

retama *nf* broom

retar *vt* to challenge (**a** to)

retardado, -a *adj* delayed

retardar *vt* *(retrasar)* to delay; *(frenar)* to hold up, to slow down

retardo *nm* delay

retazo *nm* *(de tela)* remnant; *(de discurso, recuerdo)* fragment

retén *nm* reserve

retención *nf* (**a**) *(en comisaría)* detention (**b**) *(en el sueldo)* deduction; **r. fiscal** tax (**c**) *(de tráfico)* holdup, delay (**d**) *Med* retention

retener [65] *vt* (**a**) *(detener)* to hold back; *(en comisaría)* to detain; **no me retuvo mucho tiempo** he didn't keep me long; **r. el tráfico** to hold up the traffic (**b**) *(contener)* *(impulso, ira)* to hold back, to restrain; *(aliento)* to hold (**c**) *(conservar)* to retain (**d**) *(memorizar)* to remember (**e**) *(deducir del sueldo)* to deduct; **el fisco me retiene el 20 por ciento del sueldo** 20 percent of my salary goes for tax

retengo *ver* **retener**

retentiva *nf* memory

reticencia *nf* (**a**) *(resistencia)* unwillingness (**b**) *(insinuación)* insinuation, innuendo

reticente *adj* (**a**) *(reacio)* unwilling, reluctant (**b**) *(con insinuaciones)* full of insinuation

retícula *nf* reticle

reticular *adj Anat* reticular

retículo *nm* reticle

retiene *ver* **retener**

retina *nf* retina

retintín *nm* (**a**) *(ironía)* sarcastic tone; **con r.** sarcastically (**b**) *(tintineo)* ringing

retirada *nf* (**a**) *Mil* retreat; **batirse en r.** to beat a retreat; **cubrir la r.** to cover the retreat (**b**) *(de fondos, moneda, carné, producto)* withdrawal; **han ordenado la r. del mercado del producto** they have ordered the product to be withdrawn from *o* taken off the market (**c**) *(de competición, actividad)* withdrawal; **ha anunciado su r. de los terrenos de juego** he has announced his retirement from the game

retirado, -a 1 *adj* (**a**) *(jubilado)* retired (**b**) *(solitario, alejado)* isolated, secluded

2 *nm,f (jubilado)* retired person, retiree

retirar 1 *vt* (**a**) *(quitar, sacar)* to remove; *(dinero, moneda, carné)* to withdraw; *(nieve)* to clear; *(mano)* to withdraw; **me ha retirado el saludo** he's not speaking to me (**b**) *(jubilar)* (a *deportista)* to force to retire; *(a empleado)* to retire; **una lesión lo retiró de la alta competición** an injury forced him to retire from top-flight competition (**c**) *(recoger, llevarse)* to pick up, to collect; **puede pasar a r. sus fotos el jueves** you can pick your photos up *o* collect your photos on Thursday (**d**) *(retractarse de)* to take back; **¡retira eso que *o* lo que dijiste!** take that back!, take back what you said!

2 retirarse *vpr* (**a**) *(jubilarse)* to retire (**b**) *(de competición, elecciones)* to withdraw; *(de reunión)* to leave; *(irse a dormir)* to retire (for the evening) (**c**) *(de campo de batalla)* to retreat (**d**) *(apartarse)* to move away; **retírate, que no dejas pasar** move out of the way, people can't get past

retiro *nm* (**a**) *(jubilación)* retirement; *(pensión)* pension (**b**) *(refugio, ejercicio)* retreat

reto *nm* challenge

retocado *nm Inform* **r. de imagen** image retouching

retocar [59] *vt (prenda de vestir)* to alter; **r. la pintura** to touch up the paintwork

retoce *etc ver* **retozar**

retomar *vt* to take up again

retoñar *vi* (**a**) *(planta)* to sprout, to shoot (**b**) *(situación, problema)* to reappear

retoño *nm* (**a**) *Bot* sprout, shoot (**b**) *(hijo)* **mis retoños** my offspring

retoque 1 *ver* **retocar**

2 *nm (toque)* touching-up; *(de prenda de vestir)* alteration; **dar los últimos retoques a algo** to put the finishing touches to sth

retorcer [15] **1** *vt* (**a**) *(torcer) (brazo, alambre)* to twist; *(ropa, cuello)* to wring (**b**) *(tergiversar)* to twist

2 retorcerse *vpr (de risa)* to double up (**de** with); *(de dolor)* to writhe about (**de** in)

retorcido, -a *adj* (**a**) *(torcido) (brazo, alambre)* twisted; *(ropa)* wrung out (**b**) *(rebuscado)* complicated, involved (**c**) *(malintencionado)* twisted, warped

retórica *nf Lit & Fig* rhetoric

retórico, -a 1 *adj* rhetorical

2 *nm,f (persona)* rhetorician

retornable *adj* returnable; **no r.** nonreturnable

retornar *vt & vi* to return

retorno *nm (gen) & Inform* return; **r. automático** soft return; **r. de carro** carriage return; **r. manual** hard return

retortero *nm Fam* **andar al r.** to be extremely busy; **traer a alguien al r.** to keep sb on the go

retortijón *nm* stomach cramp

retozar [14] *vi (niños, cachorros)* to gambol, to frolic; *(amantes)* to romp around *o* about

retozón, -ona *adj* playful

retractación *nf* retraction

retractarse *vpr (de una promesa)* to go back on one's word; *(de una opinión)* to take back what one has said; **r. de** *(lo dicho)* to retract, to take back

retráctil *adj (antena, brazo mecánico)* retractable; *(uña)* retractile

retraer [66] **1** *vt* (**a**) *(encoger)* to retract (**b**) *(disuadir)* **r. a alguien de hacer algo** to persuade sb not to do sth

2 retraerse *vpr* (**a**) *(encogerse)* to retract (**b**) *(aislarse, retroceder)* to withdraw, to retreat; **se retrae cuando hay extraños** he becomes very withdrawn in the company of strangers

retraído, -a *adj* withdrawn, retiring

retraimiento *nm* shyness, reserve

retranca *nf* **hacer algo con r.** to have an ulterior motive in doing sth

retransmisión *nf* broadcast; **r. en directo/diferido** live/recorded broadcast

retransmitir *vt* to broadcast

retrasado, -a 1 *adj* (**a**) *(país, industria)* backward; *(reloj)* slow; *(tren)* late, delayed; **número r.** *(de periódico, revista)* back number *o* issue (**b**) *(en el pago, los estudios)* behind; **vamos muy retrasados en el proyecto** we're a long way behind (schedule) with the project (**c**) *Med* retarded, backward

2 *nm,f* **r. (mental)** mentally retarded person; *Fig (tonto)* retard

retrasar 1 *vt* (**a**) *(aplazar)* to postpone; **retrasaron la fecha de la reunión** the meeting was postponed, they put back the date of the meeting (**b**) *(demorar)* to delay, to hold up (**c**) *(hacer más lento)* to slow down, to hold up (**d**) *(en el pago, los estudios)* to set back (**e**) *(reloj)* to put back; **habrá que r. los relojes una hora** the clocks will have to be put back an hour (**f**) *Dep (balón)* to pass back

2 *vi (reloj)* to be slow

3 retrasarse *vpr* (**a**) *(llegar tarde)* to be late; **el vuelo se ha retrasado una hora** the flight is an hour late (**b**) *(quedarse atrás)* to fall behind; **se retrasaron un mes en la entrega** they were a month late with the delivery (**c**) *(aplazarse)* to be put off (**d**) *(reloj)* to lose time; **mi reloj se retrasa cinco minutos al día** my watch loses five minutes a day

retraso *nm* (**a**) *(demora)* delay; **perdón por el r.** I'm sorry about the delay; **el vuelo ha sufrido un pequeño r.** the flight has been slightly delayed; **llegar con (15 minutos de) r.** to be (15 minutes) late; **los trenes circulan hoy con (una hora de) r.** trains are running (an hour) late today (**b**) *(por sobrepasar un límite)* **el proyecto lleva dos semanas de r.** the project is two weeks behind schedule; **llevo en mi trabajo un r. de 20 páginas** I'm 20 pages behind with my work (**c**) *(subdesarrollo)* backwardness; **llevar (siglos de) r.** to be (centuries) behind; *Med* **r. mental** mental deficiency; **tener un r. mental** to be mentally retarded

retratar 1 *vt* (**a**) *(fotografiar)* to photograph (**b**) *(dibujar)* to do a portrait of (**c**) *(describir)* to portray

2 retratarse *vpr (describirse)* to describe oneself

retratista *nmf Arte* portraitist; *Fot* (portrait) photographer

retrato *nm* (**a**) *(dibujo)* portrait; *(fotografía)* portrait (photograph); **ser el vivo r. de alguien** to be the spitting image of sb; **r. robot** Identikit® picture (**b**) *(descripción)* portrayal

retreta *nf Mil* retreat

retrete *nm (taza)* toilet; *(habitación)* bathroom, toilet

retribución *nf* payment; **en r. por sus servicios** as payment for your services

retribuir [34] *vt* (**a**) *(pagar)* to pay; *(recompensar)* to reward (**b**) *Am (favor, obsequio)* to return, to repay

retributivo, -a *adj* **la política retributiva** pay policy; **un premio r.** a cash prize

retro *adj* (**a**) *(estilo, moda)* retro (**b**) *Pol* reactionary

retroactividad *nf (de ley)* retroactivity; *(del pago)* backdating

retroactivo, -a *adj* *(ley)* retrospective, retroactive; *(pago)* backdated; **con efecto** *o* **con carácter r.** retroactively

retroalimentación *nf* feedback

retroceder *vi (moverse)* to go back; *(ante obstáculo)* to back down; **tuvo que r. para salir del garaje** he had to back out of the garage; **la lluvia de piedras obligó a r. a la policía** the shower of stones forced the police to move back; **retrocedió dos puestos en la clasificación** he dropped *o* fell two places in the table; **no retrocederé ante nada** there's no stopping me now

retroceso *nm* (**a**) *(movimiento hacia atrás, regresión)* backward movement; *(de fusil, cañón)* recoil; *(en negociaciones)* setback; *(en la economía)* recession (**b**) *(en enfermedad)* deterioration

retrógrado, -a *adj Pey* backward-looking, hidebound; *Pol* reactionary

retropropulsión *nf* jet propulsion

retroproyector *nm* overhead projector

retrospección *nf* retrospection

retrospectiva *nf* retrospective

retrospectivo, -a *adj* retrospective; **echar una mirada retrospectiva a** to look back over

retrotraer [66] **1** *vt (relato)* to set in the past
2 retrotraerse *vpr (al pasado)* to cast one's mind back, to go back

retrovisor *nm* rearview mirror; **r. lateral** side mirror

retuerzo *ver* **retorcer**

retumbante *adj* resounding

retumbar *vi (resonar)* to resound; *(hacer ruido)* to thunder, to boom; *Fam* **me retumban los oídos** my ears are ringing

retuviera *etc ver* **retener**

reuma, reúma *nm o nf* rheumatism

reumático, -a *adj & nm,f* rheumatic

reumatismo *nm* rheumatism

reumatología *nf* rheumatology

reumatólogo, -a *nm,f* rheumatologist

reunificación *nf* reunification

reunificar [59] **1** *vt* to reunify
2 reunificarse *vpr* to reunify

reunión *nf* (**a**) *(encuentro, asistentes)* meeting; **r. del consejo** board meeting (**b**) *(recogida)* gathering, collection

reunir **1** *vt* (**a**) *(público, tendencias)* to bring together (**b**) *(objetos, información)* to collect, to bring together; *(fondos)* to raise; **reunió una gran fortuna** he amassed a large fortune (**c**) *(requisitos, condiciones)* to meet, to fulfill; *(cualidades)* to possess, to combine; **el plan reúne todas las condiciones para ser aceptado** the plan meets *o* fulfills all the criteria for acceptance; **no reúne los requisitos necesarios para el puesto** he doesn't meet the requirements for the post (**d**) *(volver a unir)* to put back together
2 reunirse *vpr (congregarse, juntarse)* to meet; **reunirse con alguien** to meet sb

reutilizable *adj* reusable

reutilizar [14] *vt* to reuse

revalida *nf* (**a**) *(confirmación)* **pasó la r. del título** he successfully defended the title (**b**) *Am (de estudios, título)* recognition

revalidar *vt* (**a**) *Esp (en deportes)* to successfully defend (**b**) *Am (estudios, diploma)* to validate

revalorización *nf* (**a**) *(aumento del valor)* appreciation; *(de moneda)* revaluation; **r. de activos** appreciation of assets (**b**) *(restitución del valor)* favorable reassessment

revalorizar [14] **1** *vt* (**a**) *(aumentar el valor de)* to increase the value of; *(moneda)* to revalue (**b**) *(restituir el valor de)* to reassess in a favorable light
2 revalorizarse *vpr* (**a**) *(aumentar de valor)* to appreciate; *(moneda)* to be revalued (**b**) *(recuperar valor)* to be reassessed favorably

revancha *nf (venganza)* revenge; **tomarse la r.** to take revenge

revanchismo *nm* vengefulness

revelación *nf* revelation

revelado *nm Fot* developing

revelador, -ora **1** *adj (aclarador)* revealing
2 *nm Fot* developer

revelar **1** *vt* (**a**) *(descubrir)* to reveal; **se negó a r. la localización de la bomba** he refused to reveal *o* disclose the whereabouts of the bomb (**b**) *(manifestar)* to show (**c**) *Fot* to develop
2 revelarse *vpr* (**a**) *(descubrirse)* **revelarse como...** to show oneself to be... (**b**) *(resultar)* **sus esfuerzos se han revelado inútiles** their efforts proved useless

revendedor, -ora *nm,f* ticket scalper

revender *vt (productos, bienes)* to resell; *(entradas)* to scalp

revenirse [69] *vpr* (**a**) *(ponerse correoso)* to go soggy (**b**) *(avinagrarse)* to turn sour

reventa *nf (de productos, bienes)* resale; *(de entradas)* scalping

reventado, -a *adj Fam (cansado)* whacked-out

reventador *nm (boicoteador)* heckler

reventar [3] **1** *vt* (**a**) *(explotar)* to burst (**b**) *(echar abajo)* to break down; *(con explosivos)* to blow up (**c**) *(hacer fracasar)* to ruin, to spoil; *(boicotear)* to disrupt; *Com* **r. los precios** to make massive price cuts (**d**) *Fam (cansar mucho)* to shatter (**e**) *Fam (fastidiar)* to annoy; **me revienta que...** it really bugs me that...
2 *vi* (**a**) *(explotar)* to burst; *Fig* **si no se lo digo, reviento** I'd have exploded if I hadn't said anything to him; *Fam Fig* **por mí, como si revienta** he can drop dead as far as I'm concerned (**b**) *(estar lleno)* **r. de** to be bursting with; **la sala estaba (llena) a r.** the room was bursting at the seams (**c**) *(desear mucho)* **r. por hacer algo** to be bursting to do sth (**d**) *Fam (perder los nervios)* to explode
3 reventarse *vpr* (**a**) *(rueda, tuberías)* to burst (**b**) *Fam (cansarse)* to get whacked-out, to tire oneself to death

reventón *nm* (**a**) *(pinchazo)* blowout, puncture, flat (**b**) *(estallido)* burst

reverberación *nf (de sonido)* reverberation; *(de luz, calor)* reflection

reverberar *vi (sonido)* to reverberate; *(luz, calor)* to reflect

reverdecer [46] *vi* (**a**) *(campos)* to become green again (**b**) *(interés, sentimientos)* to revive

reverencia *nf* (**a**) *(respeto)* reverence (**b**) *(saludo) (inclinación)* bow; *(flexión de piernas)* curtsy (**c**) *(tratamiento)* **su r.** Your/His Reverence

reverenciar *vt* to revere

reverendísimo, -a *adj* Right Reverend

reverendo, -a *adj & nm* reverend

reverente *adj* reverent

reversa *nf Méx* reverse

reversibilidad *nf* reversibility

reversible *adj* reversible

reverso *nm (parte de atrás)* back, other side; *(de moneda, medalla)* reverse; **ser el r. de la medalla** to be the other side of the coin

reverter [64] *vi* to overflow

revertir [62] **1** *vi* (**a**) *(resultar)* **r. en** to result in; **r. en**

beneficio/perjuicio de to be to the advantage/detriment of (**b**) *(volver)* **r. a** to revert to

2 *vt Am (invertir)* to reverse

revés *(pl* **reveses)** *nm* (**a**) *(parte opuesta) (de papel, mano)* back; *(de tela)* other side, wrong side; **al r.** *(en dirección o sentido equivocado)* the wrong way around; *(en forma opuesta, invertido)* the other way around; **no estoy triste, al r. estoy contentísima** I'm not sad, on the contrary, I'm very happy; **lo hizo al r. de como le dije** he did the opposite of what I told him to; **al** *o* **del r.** *(lo de detrás, delante)* the wrong way around, backward; *(lo de dentro, fuera)* inside out; *(lo de arriba, abajo)* upside down; **volver algo del r.** to turn sth around (**b**) *(contratiempo)* setback, blow (**c**) *(bofetada)* slap (**d**) *Dep* backhand

revestimiento *nm (por fuera)* covering; *(por dentro)* lining

revestir [47] **1** *vt* (**a**) *(recubrir)* to cover; *(con pintura)* to coat; *(con forro)* to line (**b**) *(poseer) (solemnidad, gravedad)* to take on, to have

2 revestirse *vpr* **revestirse de** *(actitud)* to arm oneself with

reviento *etc ver* **reventar**

revierta *etc ver* **revertir**

revirtiera *etc ver* **revertir**

revisación *nf RP* (**a**) *(médica, odontológica)* examination (**b**) *(registro)* search

revisar *vt* (**a**) *(repasar)* to go over again (**b**) *(examinar)* to check; *(cuentas)* to audit; **revíseme los frenos** could you check my brakes?; **me tengo que r. la vista** I have to get my eyes tested; **le revisaron el equipaje** they searched her luggage (**c**) *(modificar)* to revise (**d**) *Am (registrar)* to search

revisión *nf* (**a**) *(repaso)* review (**b**) *(examen)* check; *(de vehículo)* service; **r. de cuentas** audit; **r. médica** checkup (**c**) *(modificación)* review (**d**) *CAm, Méx (registro)* search

revisionismo *nm* revisionism

revisionista *nmf* revisionist

revisor, -ora *nm,f (en tren, autobús)* conductor

revista 1 *ver* **revestir**

2 *nf* (**a**) *(publicación)* magazine; *(académica)* journal; **r. del corazón** gossip magazine (**b**) *(espectáculo teatral)* revue (**c**) *(inspección)* **pasar r. a** *Mil* to inspect, to review; *(examinar)* to examine

revistero *nm (mueble)* magazine rack

revistiera *etc ver* **revestir**

revitalizar [14] *vt* to revitalize

revival [rri'βaiβal] *(pl* **revivals)** *nm* revival

revivificar [59] *vt* to revive

revivir **1** *vi también Fig* to revive

2 *vt (recordar)* to revive memories of; *(resucitar)* to revive, to rekindle

revocable *adj* revocable

revocación *nf* revocation

revocar [59] *vt* (**a**) *(orden, decisión)* to revoke (**b**) *Constr* to plaster

revolcar [67] **1** *vt* to throw to the ground, to upend

2 revolcarse *vpr* (**a**) *(por el suelo)* to roll around *o* about (**b**) *Fam (amantes)* to roll around *o* about *(kissing and canoodling)*

revolcón *nm* (**a**) *(caída)* tumble, fall (**b**) *Fam (juegos amorosos)* **darse un r.** to roll around *o* about *(kissing and canoodling)*

revolotear *vi* (**a**) *(pájaro, mariposa)* to flutter (around) (**b**) *(persona)* to flit around *o* about

revoloteo *nm* (**a**) *(de pájaro, mariposa)* fluttering (around) (**b**) *(de persona)* flitting around *o* about

revoltijo, revoltillo *nm* jumble

revoltoso, -a 1 *adj (rebelde)* rebellious; *(travieso)* naughty

2 *nm,f (alborotador)* troublemaker; *(sedicioso)* rebel; *(travieso)* rascal

revolución *nf* revolution; **la R. Industrial** the Industrial Revolution

revolucionar *vt* (**a**) *(agitar) (crear conflicto en)* to cause uproar in; *(crear excitación en)* to cause a stir in; **¡no revoluciones a los niños!** don't get the children all excited! (**b**) *(transformar)* to revolutionize

revolucionario, -a *adj & nm,f* revolutionary

revolver [41] **1** *vt* (**a**) *(mezclar) (líquido)* to stir; *(ensalada)* to toss; *(objetos)* to mix (**b**) *(desorganizar)* to turn upside down, to mess up; *(cajones)* to turn out (**c**) *(irritar)* to upset; **me revuelve el estómago** *o* **las tripas** it makes my stomach turn

2 *vi* **r. en** *(armario, pasado)* to rummage around in

3 revolverse *vpr* (**a**) *(moverse) (en un sillón)* to shift around *o* about; *(en la cama)* to toss and turn; **revolverse contra alguien** to turn on sb (**b**) *(el mar)* to become rough; *(el tiempo)* to turn stormy

revólver *nm* revolver

revoque *etc ver* **revocar**

revuelco *etc ver* **revolcar**

revuelo *nm (agitación)* commotion; **armar** *o* **causar un gran r.** to cause a stir

revuelque *etc ver* **revolcar**

revuelta *nf* (**a**) *(disturbio)* riot, revolt (**b**) *(curva)* bend

revuelto, -a 1 *participio ver* **revolver**

2 *adj* (**a**) *(desordenado) (habitación)* upside down, in a mess; *(época)* troubled, turbulent; *(pelo)* disheveled (**b**) *(mezclado)* mixed up; **viven todos revueltos** they live on top of one another; **huevos revueltos** scrambled eggs (**c**) *(clima)* unsettled; *(aguas)* choppy, rough

3 *nm Culin* scrambled eggs; **r. de espárragos** = scrambled egg with asparagus

revuelvo *etc ver* **revolver**

revulsión *nf* revulsion

revulsivo *nm* (**a**) *(fármaco)* counterirritant, *Espec* revulsive (**b**) *(estímulo)* jump-start, stimulus

rey *nm* king; **los Reyes** the King and Queen; **hablando del r. de Roma** talk *o* speak of the devil; **(Día de) Reyes** Epiphany *(6 January, day on which children receive presents)*; **los Reyes Católicos** the Spanish Catholic monarchs Ferdinand V and Isabella; **los Reyes Magos** the Three Kings, the Three Wise Men; **¿qué les vas a pedir a los Reyes (Magos)?** ≃ what are you going to ask Santa Claus for?; **el rey de la selva** the king of the jungle

reyerta *nf* fight, brawl

rezagado, -a 1 *adj* **ir r.** to lag behind

2 *nm,f* straggler

rezagarse [38] *vpr* to lag *o* fall behind

rezar [14] **1** *vt* (**a**) *(oración)* to say; **r. el rosario** to say *o* to recite the rosary (**b**) *(decir)* to read, to say; **el cartel reza: "prohibido el paso"** the sign says "no entry"; **como reza el artículo segundo de la ley** as stated in article two of the law

2 *vi* (**a**) *(orar)* to pray (**a** to); **r. por alguien/algo** to pray for sb/sth (**b**) *Fam (tener que ver)* **esto no reza conmigo** that has nothing to do with me

rezo *nm* (**a**) *(acción)* praying (**b**) *(oración)* prayer

rezongar [38] *vi* to grumble, to moan

rezumar 1 *vt* to ooze

2 *vi* to ooze *o* seep out

RFA *nf Antes (abrev de* **República Federal de Alemania)** FRG

Rh *nf (abrev de* **Rhesus)** Rh; **Rh positivo/negativo** rhesus positive/negative

rhesus *nm* rhesus monkey

Rhin *nm* **el R.** the Rhine

ría 1 *ver* **reír**

2 *nf* ria, = long narrow sea inlet

riachuelo *nm* brook, stream

Riad n Riyadh

riada nf también Fig flood

ribazo nm (terreno inclinado) slope; (del río) sloping bank

ribeiro nm = wine from the province of Orense, Spain

ribera nf (del río) bank; (del mar) shore; **la r. del Ebro** the banks of the Ebro

ribereño, -a 1 adj (de río) riverside; (de mar) coastal
2 nm,f = person who lives by a river

ribete nm (**a**) (cinta) edging, trimming (**b**) **ribetes** (rasgos) touches, nuances; **tener ribetes de poeta/orador** to be something of a poet/an orator

ribeteado, -a adj edged, trimmed

ribetear vt to edge, to trim

ribonucleico adj Biol **ácido r.** ribonucleic acid

ricachón, -ona nm,f Pey filthy o stinking rich person

ricamente adv **tan r.** quite happily

rice etc ver **rizar**

ricino nm (planta) castor oil plant

rico, -a 1 adj (**a**) (adinerado) (persona) rich (**b**) (abundante) (región) rich (**en** in); **una dieta rica en proteínas** a protein-rich diet, a diet rich in protein (**c**) (fértil) (suelo) fertile, rich (**d**) (sabroso) (comida) delicious; **¡qué r.!** this is delicious! (**e**) (simpático) (niño, perrito) cute (**f**) Am salvo RP (agradable) lovely
2 nm,f (**a**) (adinerado) rich person; **los ricos** the rich; **los nuevos ricos** the nouveaux riches (**b**) Fam (apelativo) **¡oye r.!** hey, sunshine!; **¿por qué no te callas, r.?** shut up, you!

rictus nm inv (de dolor) wince; (de ironía) smirk; (de desprecio) sneer; **un r. de amargura** a bitter expression

ricura nf Fam (**a**) (persona) delight, lovely person; **¡qué r. de niño!** what a lovely o charming child! (**b**) (guiso) **¡qué r. de sopa!** what delicious soup!

ridiculez nf (**a**) (payasada) silly thing, nonsense (**b**) (nimiedad) trifle; **cuesta una r.** it costs next to nothing

ridiculizar [14] vt to ridicule

ridículo, -a 1 adj (**a**) (situación, persona, ropa) ridiculous; **estás r. con esos pantalones** you look ridiculous in those pants; **acéptalo, ¡no seas r.!** take it, don't be ridiculous o silly! (**b**) (precio, suma) laughable, derisory
2 nm ridicule; **hacer el r.** to make a fool of oneself; **poner** o **dejar en r. a alguien** to make sb look stupid; **quedar en r.** to look like a fool; **no tiene sentido del r.** he doesn't get embarrassed easily

ríe ver **reír**

riego 1 ver **regar**
2 nm (de campo) irrigation; (de jardín) watering; **r. sanguíneo** (blood) circulation

riegue etc ver **regar**

riel nm (**a**) (de vía) rail (**b**) (de cortina) (curtain) rod

rienda nf (de caballería) rein; Fig **aflojar las riendas** to ease up; Fig **comer a r. suelta** to eat one's fill; Fig **dar r. suelta a** to give free rein to; Fig **llevar** o **tener las riendas** to hold the reins, to be in control

riera etc ver **reír**

riesgo nm risk; **a todo r.** (seguro, póliza) comprehensive; **correr (el) r. de** to run the risk of; **a r. de** at the risk of; **un r. calculado** a calculated risk

rifa nf raffle

rifar 1 vt to raffle
2 rifarse vpr (disputarse) to fight over, to contest

rifirrafe nm Fam skirmish, flare-up

rifle nm rifle

Riga n Riga

rige ver **regir**

rigidez nf (**a**) (de objeto, material) rigidity (**b**) (de pierna, brazo) stiffness (**c**) (del rostro) stoniness (**d**) (severidad) strictness, harshness

rígido, -a adj (**a**) (objeto, material) rigid (**b**) (pierna, brazo) stiff (**c**) (rostro) stony (**d**) (severo) (normas) harsh; (carácter) inflexible

rigiera etc ver **regir**

rigor nm (**a**) (severidad) strictness; **con r.** strictly (**b**) (exactitud) accuracy, rigor; **no tiene ningún r. científico** it's totally lacking in scientific rigor; **en r.** strictly (speaking) (**c**) (inclemencia) harshness (**d**) (rigidez) **r. mortis** rigor mortis (**e**) **de r.: nos cayó la bronca de r.** we got the inevitable telling-off; **es de r. en esas ocasiones** it's de rigueur on such occasions

rigurosidad nf (**a**) (severidad) strictness (**b**) (exactitud) accuracy, rigor (**c**) (inclemencia) harshness

riguroso, -a adj (**a**) (severo) strict (**b**) (exacto) rigorous, disciplined (**c**) (inclemente) harsh

rijo etc ver **regir**

rijoso, -a adj (**a**) (pendenciero) always getting into fights (**b**) (lujurioso) lustful

rima nf rhyme

rimar vt & vi to rhyme

rimbombancia nf (**a**) (de estilo, frases) pomposity (**b**) (de desfile, fiesta) razzmatazz

rimbombante adj (**a**) (estilo, frases) pompous (**b**) (desfile, fiesta) spectacular

rímel nm mascara

Rin nm **el R.** the Rhine

rincón nm (**a**) (de habitación) corner (inside) (**b**) (lugar apartado) corner; **vive en un r. apartado del mundo** she lives in a remote spot; **recorrimos todos los rincones de la ciudad** we explored every nook and cranny of the city (**c**) (lugar pequeño) corner; **te he dejado un r. para que guardes tus cosas** I've given you a corner to keep your things in

rinconada nf corner

rinconera nf corner piece

rindiera, rindo etc ver **rendir**

ring [rrin] (pl **rings**) nm (boxing) ring

rinitis nf inv Med rhinitis

rinoceronte nm rhinoceros, rhino

riña 1 ver **reñir**
2 nf (disputa) quarrel; (pelea) fight

riñera etc ver **reñir**

riñón nm kidney; Fig **costar/valer un r.** to cost/be worth a fortune; Fam Fig **tener el r. bien cubierto** to be well-heeled; **riñones** (región lumbar) lower back; **r. artificial** kidney machine

riñonada nf (región lumbar) lower back

riñonera nf (pequeño bolso) fanny pack

río 1 ver **reír**
2 nm (**a**) (corriente de agua, de lava) river; **ir r. arriba/abajo** to go upstream/downstream; **¡de perdidos, al r.!** in for a penny, in for a pound; Prov **a r. revuelto, ganancia de pescadores** it's an ill wind that blows nobody any good; Prov **cuando el r. suena, agua lleva** there's no smoke without fire; **el R. Bravo** the Rio Grande; **R. de Janeiro** Rio de Janeiro; **R. de la Plata** Plate River (**b**) (gran cantidad) (de cartas) flood; (de insultos) stream; **un r. de gente** a mass of people; **se han escrito ríos de tinta sobre el tema** people have written reams on the subject

rioja nm Rioja (wine)

riojano, -a adj & nm,f Riojan

rioplatense adj of/from the Plate River region nmf person from the Plate River region

R.I.P [rrip] (abrev de requiescat in pace) RIP

ripio nm (**a**) Lit = word or phrase included to complete a rhyme; Fig **no perder r.** to be all ears (**b**) Andes, RP gravel

riqueza nf (**a**) (fortuna) wealth (**b**) (abundancia) richness

risa nf laugh; **tiene una r. muy contagiosa** she has a very infectious laugh; **se me escapó la r.** I burst out laughing; **se oían risas** laughter could be heard; **provocó las risas del público** it made the audience laugh; **me da r.** I find it funny; **¡qué r.!** how funny!; *Fam Fig* **morirse** *o* **partirse de r.** to die laughing, to split one's sides (laughing); **fue una r. verle imitar a los profesores** it was hilarious *o* a scream watching him take off the teachers; **no es cosa de r.** it's no laughing matter; **tomar algo a r.** to take sth as a joke

risco *nm* cliff, crag

risible *adj* laughable

risotada *nf* guffaw; **soltar una r.** to let out a guffaw, to guffaw

ristra *nf también Fig* string; **r. de ajos** string of garlic

ristre *nm* **en r.** at the ready

risueño, -a *adj* (a) *(alegre)* smiling (b) *(próspero)* sunny, promising

rítmico, -a *adj* rhythmic

ritmo *nm* (a) *(compás, repetición)* rhythm, beat; *(cardíaco)* beat; **esa canción tiene mucho r.** that song's got a very strong beat *o* rhythm; **llevaba el r. con los pies** she was tapping the rhythm *o* keeping time with her feet (b) *(velocidad)* pace; **acelerar el r.** to speed up; **la economía está creciendo a un buen r.** the economy is growing at a healthy pace *o* rate

rito *nm* (a) *Rel* rite (b) *(costumbre)* ritual

ritual *adj & nm* ritual

rival *adj & nmf* rival

rivalidad *nf* rivalry

rivalizar [14] *vi* to compete (**con/por** with/for)

rivera *nf* brook, stream

rizado, -a 1 *adj* (a) *(pelo)* curly (b) *(mar)* choppy
  2 *nm (en peluquería)* **hacerse un r.** to have one's hair curled

rizar [14] **1** *vt* (a) *(pelo)* to curl (b) *(mar)* to ripple
  2 rizarse *vpr* (a) *(pelo)* to curl (b) *(mar)* to get choppy

rizo, -a 1 *adj* (a) *(pelo)* curly (b) *(mar)* choppy
  2 *nm* (a) *(de pelo)* curl (b) *(del agua)* ripple (c) *(de avión)* loop; **rizar el r.** to loop the loop; *Fig (complicar)* to overcomplicate (things); *Fig* **para rizar el r. hizo un doble salto mortal** as if all that wasn't impressive enough, he performed a double somersault (d) *(tela)* toweling, terry (cloth)

RNE *nf (abrev de* **Radio Nacional de España**) = Spanish national radio station

roast-beef [rros'βif] *(pl* **roast-beefs**) *nm* roast beef

róbalo, robalo *nm* sea bass

robar *vt* (a) *(objeto)* to steal; *(casa)* to burgle; **me han robado la moto** my motorbike's been stolen; **r. a alguien** to rob sb; **r. el corazón a alguien** to steal sb's heart; **la contabilidad me roba mucho tiempo** doing the accounts takes up a lot of my time (b) *(en naipes)* to draw (c) *(cobrar caro)* to rob; **en esa tienda te roban** the prices in that store are daylight robbery (d) *(encuentro)* **nos robaron el partido** we were robbed

roble *nm* (a) *(árbol, madera)* oak (b) *(persona)* strong person

robledal, robledo *nm* oak wood *o* grove

robo *nm* (a) *(atraco, hurto)* robbery, theft; *(en casa)* burglary; **r. a mano armada** armed robbery; **ser un r.** *(precios)* to be daylight robbery (b) *(cosa robada)* stolen goods

robot *(pl* **robots**) *nm (gen) & Inform* robot; **actuar como un r.** to behave like a machine *o* robot; **r. de cocina** food processor

robótica *nf* robotics *(singular)*

robotización *nf* automation

robotizar [14] *vt* to automate

robustecer [46] **1** *vt* to strengthen
  2 robustecerse *vpr* to get stronger

robustez *nf* robustness

robusto, -a *adj* robust

roca *nf* rock

rocalla *nf* rubble

rocambolesco, -a *adj* fantastic, incredible; **nos sucedió una aventura rocambolesca** the most incredible series of things happened to us

roce 1 *ver* **rozar**
  2 *nm* (a) *(contacto)* rubbing; *Fís* friction; **el r. de la seda contra su piel** the feel of the silk against her skin; **el r. de su mano en la mejilla** the touch of his hand on her cheek; **el r. del viento en la piedra** the weathering effect of the wind on the stone; **me ha salido una ampolla del r. del zapato** I've got a blister from my shoe rubbing against my foot
  (b) *(rasguño) (en piel)* graze; *(en madera, zapato)* scuff mark; *(en metal)* scratch; **el pantalón tiene roces en las rodillas** the pants are worn at the knees; **la pared está llena de roces** the wall has had the paint scraped off it in several places
  (c) *(trato)* close contact
  (d) *(desavenencia)* brush, quarrel; **tener un r. con alguien** to have a brush with sb

rociada *nf* (a) *(rocío)* dew (b) *(aspersión)* sprinkling (c) *(de insultos, perdigones)* shower

rociador *nm* **r. contra incendios** sprinkler

rociar [32] **1** *vt* (a) *(arrojar gotas)* to sprinkle; *(con espray)* to spray (b) *(arrojar cosas)* **r. algo/alguien (de)** to shower sth/sb (with)
  2 *v impersonal (caer rocío)* **roció anoche** a dew fell last night

rociero, -a *nm,f* = participant in the "Rocío" pilgrimage to Almonte, Huelva

rocín *nm* nag

rocío *nm* dew

rock *nm inv* rock; **r. duro** hard rock; **r. and roll** rock and roll

rocker *(pl* **rockers**) *nmf Fam* rocker

rockero, -a, roquero, -a 1 *adj* rock; **grupo r.** rock band
  2 *nm,f* (a) *(músico)* rock musician (b) *(fan)* rock fan

rococó *adj inv & nm* rococo

rocoso, -a *adj* rocky

roda *nf Náut* stem

rodaballo *nm* turbot

rodada *nf* tire track

rodado, -a *adj* (a) *(por carretera)* road; **tráfico r.** road traffic (b) *(piedra)* rounded (c) *(expresiones)* **estar muy r.** *(persona)* to be very experienced; **venir r. para** to be the perfect opportunity to

rodaja *nf* slice; **en rodajas** sliced

rodaje *nm* (a) *(filmación)* shooting (b) *(de motor)* breaking in (c) *(experiencia)* experience

rodamiento *nm* bearing

Ródano *nm* **el R.** the Rhône (River)

rodante *adj* rolling

rodapié *nm* baseboard

rodar [63] **1** *vi* (a) *(deslizar)* to roll (b) *(circular)* to travel, to go; **rodaban a más de 180 km/h** they were doing more than 180 km/h (c) *(girar)* to turn (d) *(caer)* to tumble (**por** down); **rodó escaleras abajo** he tumbled down the stairs (e) *(ir de un lado a otro)* to go around; **ha rodado por todo el mundo** he's been all over the world (f) *Cine* to shoot; **¡silencio, se rueda!** we're rolling!
  2 *vt* (a) *Cine* to shoot (b) *(automóvil)* to break in

Rodas *n* Rhodes

rodear 1 *vt* (a) *(poner o ponerse alrededor)* to surround; **le rodeó el cuello con los brazos** she put her arms around his neck; **¡ríndete, estás rodeado!** surrender, we have you *o* you're surrounded!; **vive rodeado de libros** he's always surrounded by books (b) *(estar alrededor de)* to surround; **el misterio que rodea la investigación** the mystery surrounding the investigation; **todos los que la rodean hablan muy bien de ella** everyone around her speaks very highly of her (c) *(dar la vuelta a)* to go around (d) *(eludir)* to skirt around

2 rodearse *vpr* **r. de** to surround oneself with

rodeo *nm* (**a**) *(camino largo)* detour; **dar un r.** to make a detour (**b**) *(evasiva)* **rodeos** evasiveness; **andar** *o* **ir con rodeos** to beat around *o* about the bush; **hablar sin rodeos** to come straight to the point (**c**) *(espectáculo)* rodeo (**d**) *(reunión de ganado)* rounding up

rodete *nm* round pad

rodilla *nf* knee; **estaba de rodillas** he was on his knees; *Fig* **te lo pido de rodillas** I'm begging you; **doblar** *o* **hincar la r.** *(arrodillarse)* to go down on one knee; *Fig* to bow (down), to humble oneself; **ponerse de rodillas** to kneel (down)

rodillera *nf* (**a**) *(protección)* knee pad (**b**) *(remiendo)* knee patch

rodillo *nm* (**a**) *(para amasar)* rolling pin (**b**) *(en máquina)* roller (**c**) *(para pintar)* (paint) roller

rododendro *nm* rhododendron

rodrigón *nm* stake, prop

rodríguez *nm inv Fam* = man who stays at home working while his family goes away on vacation; **estar** *o* **quedarse de r.** to be left at home while one's family is away on vacation

roedor, -ora 1 *adj Zool* rodent; **animal r.** rodent

2 *nm* rodent

roedura *nf* (**a**) *(acción)* gnawing (**b**) *(señal)* gnaw mark

roer [57] *vt* (**a**) *(con dientes)* to gnaw (at) (**b**) *(desgastar)* to eat away (at) (**c**) *(atormentar)* to nag *o* gnaw (at) (**d**) *Fig* **ser duro de r.** to be a tough nut to crack

rogar [16] *vt* *(implorar)* to beg; *(pedir)* to ask; **r. a alguien que haga algo** to beg/ask sb to do sth; **te lo ruego, no se lo cuentes a ella** don't tell her, I beg you; **le ruego (que) me perdone** I beg your pardon; **ruego a Dios que…** I pray to God that…; **hacerse (de) r.** to play hard to get; **se ruega silencio** *(en letrero)* silence, please

rogativa *nf* rogation

rogatoria *nf Der* = request made by a court of one country to that of another country

rogué *etc ver* **rogar**

rojez *nf* (**a**) *(cualidad)* redness (**b**) *(en la piel)* (red) blotch

rojizo, -a *adj* reddish

rojo, -a 1 *adj* red; **ponerse r.** *(semáforo)* to turn red; *(ruborizarse)* to blush

2 *nm,f Pol* red

3 *nm (color)* red; **al r. vivo** *(incandescente)* red hot; *Fig* heated

rol *(pl* **roles)** *nm* (**a**) *(papel)* role; **juegos de r.** *(técnica terapéutica, de enseñanza)* role-play; *(juegos de fantasía)* fantasy role-playing games (**b**) *Náut* muster

rollito *nm Culin* **r. de primavera** spring roll

rollizo, -a *adj* chubby, plump

rollo *nm* (**a**) *(cilindro)* roll; **r. de papel higiénico** toilet roll; *Culin* **r. de primavera** spring roll

(**b**) *(cine (de película)* reel

(**c**) *Fam (pesadez, aburrimiento)* drag, bore; **¡qué r.!** what a bore *o* drag!; **un r. de discurso/tío** an incredibly boring speech/guy; **el r. de costumbre** the same old story; **¡corta el r. ya!** shut up, you're boring me to death!; **soltar el r.** to go on and on; **tener mucho r.** to chatter on

(**d**) *Fam (embuste)* tall story; **meter un r. a alguien** *(engañar)* to put one over on sb; **r. patatero** *(mentira)* ridiculous spiel

(**e**) *Fam (tema, historia)* stuff; **el r. ese de la clonación** all that stuff about cloning, all that cloning business

(**f**) *Esp Fam (ambiente, tipo de vida)* scene; **el r. de la droga/ de las discotecas** the drug/nightclub scene; **no me va ese r.** it's not my scene, I'm not into all that

(**g**) *Esp Fam (relación)* relationship; **tener un r. (con)** to have a fling (with); **tener buen/mal r. (con alguien)** to get on/ not to get on (with sb)

(**h**) *Ven (para el pelo)* roller, curler

ROM [rrom] *nf (abrev de* **read-only memory**) ROM

Roma *n* Rome; *Prov* **todos los caminos llevan a R.** all roads lead to Rome

romance 1 *adj* Romance

2 *nm* (**a**) *Ling* Romance language (**b**) *Lit* romance (**c**) *(idilio)* romance

romancero *nm Lit* collection of romances

romaní 1 *adj & nmf* Romany

2 *nm (lengua)* Romany

románico, -a 1 *adj* (**a**) *Arquit & Arte* Romanesque (**b**) *Ling* Romance

2 *nm* **el (estilo) r.** the Romanesque (style)

romanización *nf* Romanization

romanizar [14] *vt* to Romanize

romano, -a 1 *adj* Roman; *Rel* Roman Catholic

2 *nm,f* Roman

romanticismo *nm* (**a**) *Arte, Hist & Lit* Romanticism (**b**) *(sentimentalismo)* romanticism

romántico, -a *adj & nm,f* (**a**) *Arte, Hist & Lit* Romantic (**b**) *(sentimental)* romantic

romanza *nf Mús* ballad

rombo *nm (figura)* rhombus; *Imprenta* lozenge

romboide *nm Geom* rhomboid

romeo *nm* sweetheart

romería *nf* (**a**) *(peregrinación)* pilgrimage (**b**) *(fiesta)* = open-air festivities to celebrate a religious event (**c**) *(mucha gente)* throng, crowd

romero, -a 1 *nm,f (peregrino)* pilgrim

2 *nm (arbusto, condimento)* rosemary

romo, -a *adj* (**a**) *(sin filo)* blunt (**b**) *(de nariz)* snub-nosed

rompecabezas *nm inv* (**a**) *(juego)* jigsaw (puzzle) (**b**) *Fam (problema)* puzzle

rompecorazones *nmf inv Fam* heartbreaker

rompehielos *nm inv* ice-breaker

rompehuelgas *nmf inv Am* scab

rompeolas *nm inv* breakwater

romper 1 *vt* (**a**) *(partir, fragmentar)* to break; *(hacer añicos)* to smash; *(rasgar)* to tear; **r. algo en pedazos** to break/smash/ tear sth to pieces (**b**) *(estropear)* to break (**c**) *(desgastar)* to wear out (**d**) *(interrumpir)* *(monotonía, silencio, hábito)* to break; *(hilo del discurso)* to break off; *(tradición)* to put an end to, to stop (**e**) *(terminar)* to break off

2 *vi* (**a**) *(terminar una relación)* **r. (con alguien)** to break up *o* split up (with sb); **r. con la tradición** to break with tradition; **rompió con el partido** she broke with the party (**b**) *(empezar)* *(día)* to break; *(hostilidades)* to break out; **al r. el alba** *o* **día** at daybreak; **r. a hacer algo** to suddenly start doing sth; **r. a llorar** to burst into tears; **r. a reír** to burst out laughing (**c**) *(olas)* to break (**d**) *Fam* **una mujer de rompe y rasga** a woman who knows what she wants *o* knows her own mind

3 romperse *vpr* (**a**) *(partirse)* to break; *(rasgarse)* to tear; **se rompió en mil pedazos** it smashed to pieces; **se ha roto una pierna** he has broken a leg (**b**) *(estropearse)* to break; **se ha roto la tele** the TV is broken (**c**) *(desgastarse)* to wear out

rompevientos *nm RP* (**a**) *(jersey)* turtleneck (**b**) *(anorak)* Windbreaker®

rompiente *nm* reef, shoal

rompimiento *nm (rotura)* breaking; *(de relaciones)* breaking-off

ron *nm* rum

roncar [59] *vi* to snore

roncha *nf* lump *(on skin)*

ronco, -a *adj (persona, voz)* hoarse; *(sonido)* harsh

ronda *nf* (**a**) *(de vigilancia)* patrol; **salir de r.** to go out on patrol (**b**) *(de visitas)* **hacer la r.** to do one's rounds; **salir de r.** *(músico)* to go (out) serenading (**c**) *(de conversaciones, en el juego)* round; *Fam* **pagar una r.** *(de bebidas)* to buy a round

(d) *(avenida)* avenue; **r. de circunvalación** beltway (e) *Dep (carrera ciclista)* tour; **la r. francesa** the Tour de France

rondalla *nf* group of minstrels

rondar 1 *vt* (a) *(vigilar)* to patrol (b) *(parecer próximo)* **me está rondando un resfriado** I've got a cold coming on; **le ronda el sueño** he's about to drop off (c) *(cortejar)* to court (d) *(edad, cifra)* to be around; **ronda los cuarenta años** he's about forty
   2 *vi (merodear)* to wander **(por** around); **me ronda una idea por la cabeza** I've been turning over an idea in my head

rondín *nm Andes* (a) *(vigilante)* watchman, guard (b) *(armónica)* harmonica, mouth organ

rondón *nm Fam* **entrar de r.** to barge in

ronque *etc ver* **roncar**

ronquear *vi* to be hoarse

ronquera *nf* hoarseness

ronquido *nm* snore, snoring

ronroneante *adj* purring

ronronear *vi* to purr

ronroneo *nm* purr, purring

roña 1 *adj Fam (tacaño)* stingy, tight
   2 *nmf Fam (tacaño)* stingy person
   3 *nf* (a) *(suciedad)* filth, dirt (b) *Fam (tacañería)* stinginess (c) *(enfermedad)* mange (d) *Méx (juego)* catch

roñería *nf Fam* stinginess

roñica *Fam* **1** *adj* stingy, tight
   2 *nmf* stingy person

roñoso, -a 1 *adj* (a) *(sucio)* dirty (b) *Fam (tacaño)* mean, tight-fisted
   2 *nm,f Fam* mean person, skinflint

ropa *nf* clothes; **ligero de r.** scantily clad; *Fig* **nadar y guardar la r.** to cover one's back; **r. de abrigo** warm clothes; **r. blanca** linen; **r. de cama** bed linen; **r. deportiva** sportswear; **r. de diseño** designer clothes; **r. hecha** ready-to-wear clothes; **r. para el hogar** linen and curtains; **r. interior** underwear; **r. interior femenina** lingerie; **r. de invierno** winter clothing; **r. de sport** casual clothes; **r. sucia** *(para lavar)* laundry, washing; **r. de trabajo** working clothes; **r. usada** secondhand *o* old clothes

ropaje *nm* robes

ropero *nm* (a) *(armario)* wardrobe; *(habitación)* walk-in wardrobe (b) *(guardarropa)* cloakroom

roque 1 *adj Fam* **estar r.** to be out for the count; **quedarse r.** to drop *o* nod off
   2 *nm (en ajedrez)* castle, rook

roquefort [rroke'for] *nm* Roquefort (cheese)

roquero, -a = **rockero**

rorcual *nm* rorqual, finback

rorro *nm Fam* baby

rosa 1 *adj* (a) *(color)* pink; *Fig* **verlo todo de color (de) r.** to see everything through rose-colored glasses (b) *(del corazón)* **la prensa r.** gossip magazines; **una novela r.** a romance, a romantic novel
   2 *nm (color)* pink
   3 *nf (flor)* rose; **estar (fresco) como una r.** to be as fresh as a daisy; **r. de los vientos** compass rose

rosáceo, -a *adj* pinkish

rosado, -a 1 *adj* pink
   2 *nm (vino)* rosé

rosal *nm (arbusto)* rose bush

rosaleda *nf* rose garden

rosario *nm* (a) *Rel* rosary; **rezar el r.** to say one's rosary (b) *(serie)* string; **un r. de desgracias** a string of disasters (c) *Fam* **acabar como el r. de la aurora** to finish up badly

rosbif *(pl* **rosbifs)** *nm* roast beef

rosca *nf* (a) *(de tornillo)* thread (b) *(forma) (de anillo)* ring; *(espiral)* coil (c) *Culin* = ring-shaped bread roll; *Méx* sponge cake (d) *(expresiones)* **nunca se come una r.** he never gets

off with anyone; **hacerle la r. a alguien** to suck up to sb; **pasarse de r.** *(persona)* to go over the top

rosco *nm* = ring-shaped bread roll; *Esp Fam Fig* **nunca se come un r.** he never gets off with anyone

roscón *nm* = ring-shaped bread roll; **r. de Reyes** = ring-shaped pastry eaten on January 6

roseta *nf* (a) *(rubor)* flush (b) *(de regadera)* nozzle (c) **rosetas** *(palomitas)* popcorn

rosetón *nm* (a) *Arquit (ventana)* rose window (b) *(adorno)* ceiling rose

rosquete *adj Perú Fam Pey* queer

rosquilla *nf* ring donut; *Fam* **venderse como rosquillas** to sell like hot cakes

rosticería *nf Chile, Méx* = store selling roast chicken

rostizar [14] *vt Méx* to spit-roast

rostro *nm* face; *Fam Fig* **tener (mucho) r.** to have a (lot of) nerve

rotación *nf* (a) *(giro)* rotation (b) *(alternancia)* = list of people rotating on assignments; **r. de cultivos** crop rotation; **por r.** in turn

rotar *vi* (a) *(girar)* to rotate, to turn (b) *(alternar)* to rotate

rotativa *nf* rotary press

rotativo, -a 1 *adj* rotary, revolving
   2 *nm* newspaper

rotatorio, -a *adj* rotary, revolving

rotisería *nf CSur* delicatessen

roto, -a 1 *participio ver* **romper**
   2 *adj* (a) *(partido, rasgado)* broken; *(tela, papel)* torn (b) *(estropeado)* broken (c) *(deshecho) (vida)* destroyed; *(corazón)* broken (d) *Fam (exhausto)* tuckered out
   3 *nm,f Chile (trabajador)* worker
   4 *nm (en tela)* tear, rip

rotonda *nf* (a) *Aut* traffic circle (b) *(plaza)* circus (c) *(edificio)* rotunda

rotoso, -a *adj Andes, RP* ragged, in tatters

rotring® ['rrotrin] *nm* Rotring® pen

Rotterdam *n* Rotterdam

rótula *nf* kneecap

rotulación *nf* lettering

rotulador *nm* felt-tip pen; **r. fluorescente** highlighter (pen)

rotular *vt* (a) *(con rotulador)* to highlight (b) *(carta, artículo)* to head with fancy lettering (c) *(mapa, gráfico)* to label

rotulista *nmf* sign painter

rótulo *nm* (a) *(letrero)* sign (b) *(encabezamiento)* headline, title

rotundidad *nf* firmness, categorical nature; **con r.** categorically

rotundo, -a *adj* (a) *(negativa, persona)* categorical (b) *(lenguaje, estilo)* emphatic, forceful (c) *(completo)* total; **r. fracaso** total *o* complete failure

rotura *nf (en general)* break; *(de hueso)* fracture; *(en tela)* rip, hole

roturar *vt* to plow

roulotte [rru'lot] *nf* trailer

royalty [rro'jalti] *(pl* **royalties)** *nm* royalty

royera *etc ver* **roer**

rozadura *nf* (a) *(señal)* scratch, scrape (b) *(herida)* graze

rozagante *adj Esp* **estar r.** *(satisfecho)* to be extremely pleased; *(con buen aspecto)* to look lovely

rozamiento *nm (fricción)* rubbing; *Fís* friction

rozar [14] **1** *vt* (a) *(tocar, frotar)* to rub; *(suavemente)* to brush; **me roza el zapato en la parte de atrás** my shoe is rubbing my heel (b) *(pasar cerca de)* to skim, to shave; **la bala lo pasó rozando** the bullet missed him by a hair's breadth (c) *(estar cerca de)* to border on; **roza los cuarenta** he's almost forty; **su talento roza lo divino** he is touched by genius
   2 *vi* **r. con** *(tocar)* to brush against

3 rozarse *vpr* (a) *(uso recíproco) (tocarse)* to touch; *(pasar cerca)* to brush past each other (b) *(rasguñarse)* to graze; **me rocé la mano con la pared** I grazed my hand on the wall

RR HH *(abrev de* **recursos humanos**) HR

Rte. *(abrev de* **remitente**) sender

RTVE *nf (abrev de* **Radiotelevisión Española**) = Spanish state broadcasting company

rúa *nf* street

ruana *nf Andes* poncho

Ruanda *n* Rwanda

ruandés, -esa *adj & nm,f* Rwandan

rubeola, rubéola *nf* German measles

rubí *(pl* **rubíes** *o* **rubís**) *nm* ruby

rubia *nf Fam Antes (moneda)* peseta

rubiales *Esp Fam* **1** *adj inv* blond(e), fair-haired
2 *nmf inv* blond *o* fair-haired man, *f* blonde

rubicundo, -a *adj* ruddy

rubio, -a 1 *adj* (a) *(pelo, persona)* blond(e), fair; **r. platino** platinum blonde (b) *(tabaco)* **tabaco r.** Virginia tobacco *(as opposed to black tobacco)* (c) *(cerveza)* **cerveza rubia** lager
2 *nm,f (persona)* blond(e), fair-haired person; **rubia de bote** peroxide blonde; **rubia** *Esp* **platino** *o Am* **platinada** platinum blonde
3 *nm (tabaco)* Virginia tobacco *(as opposed to black tobacco)*

rublo *nm* ruble

rubor *nm* (a) *(vergüenza)* embarrassment; **causar r.** to embarrass (b) *(sonrojo)* blush (c) *Am (colorete)* blusher

ruborizado, -a *adj* flushed

ruborizar [14] **1** *vt* to make blush
2 ruborizarse *vpr* to blush

ruboroso, -a *adj* blushing

rúbrica *nf* (a) *(de firma)* flourish (b) *(título)* title (c) *(conclusión)* final flourish; **poner r. a algo** to conclude sth, to bring sth to a close *o* conclusion

rubricar [59] *vt* (a) *(firmar)* to sign with a flourish (b) *(confirmar)* to confirm (c) *(concluir)* to complete

rubro *nm Am* (a) *(apartado)* heading; *(en contabilidad)* item (b) *(campo)* area, field; **empresas líderes en su r.** companies which are leaders in their field

rucio, -a 1 *adj* (a) *(gris)* gray (b) *Chile Fam* blond(e)
2 *nm* ass, donkey

rudeza *nf* (a) *(tosquedad)* roughness (b) *(grosería, descortesía)* coarseness (c) *(dureza, rigurosidad)* harshness

rudimentario, -a *adj* rudimentary

rudimentos *nmpl* rudiments

rudo, -a *adj* (a) *(tosco, basto)* rough (b) *(brusco)* sharp, brusque; *(grosero)* rude, coarse (c) *(riguroso, duro)* harsh

rueca *nf* distaff

rueda *nf* (a) *(pieza)* wheel; *Fig* **ir sobre ruedas** to go smoothly; *Andes* **r. de Chicago** Ferris wheel; **r. delantera** front wheel; **r. dentada** cogwheel; *Fig* **la r. de la fortuna** *(de hechos)* the wheel of fortune; *Méx (noria)* Ferris wheel; *Chile, Urug* **r. gigante** Ferris wheel; **r. de molino** millstone; *Fig* **comulgar con ruedas de molino** to be very gullible; **r. de repuesto** *o* **recambio** spare wheel; **r. trasera** rear wheel (b) *(corro)* circle; **r. de prensa** press conference; **r. de reconocimiento** identification parade (c) *(rodaja)* slice

ruedo 1 *ver* **rodar**
2 *nm Taurom* bullring; *Fig* **echarse al r.** to enter the fray

ruego 1 *ver* **rogar**
2 *nm* request; **ruegos y preguntas** any other business

rufián *nm* villain

rufianesca *nf* **la r.** the underworld

rufianesco, -a *adj* villainous

rugby ['rruɣbi], *CSur* ['rraɣbi] *nm* rugby

rugido *nm (de animales, mar, viento)* roar; *(de persona)* bellow; *(de tripas)* rumble

rugir [24] *vi (animal, mar, viento)* to roar; *(persona)* to bellow; *(tripas)* to rumble

rugosidad *nf* (a) *(cualidad)* roughness (b) *(arruga) (de piel)* wrinkle; *(de tejido)* crinkle

rugoso, -a *adj* (a) *(áspero)* rough (b) *(con arrugas) (piel)* wrinkled; *(tejido)* crinkled

ruibarbo *nm* rhubarb

ruido *nm* (a) *(sonido)* noise; **desde aquí se escuchan los ruidos de la fiesta** you can hear the noise of the party from here; **esta lavadora hace mucho r.** this washing machine is very noisy; **¡no hagas r.!** be quiet!; **r. de fondo** background noise; **mucho r. y pocas nueces** much ado about nothing (b) *(alboroto)* row; **hacer** *o* **meter r.** to cause a stir

ruidoso, -a *adj* (a) *(que hace ruido)* noisy (b) *(escandaloso)* controversial, sensational

ruin *adj* (a) *(vil)* low, contemptible (b) *(avaro)* mean

ruina *nf* (a) *(quiebra)* ruin; **dejar en** *o* **llevar a la r. a alguien** to ruin sb; **estar en la r.** to be ruined; **su negocio es una r.** his business is swallowing up his money (b) *(destrucción)* destruction; **amenazar r.** *(edificio)* to be about to collapse; **el alcohol será su r.** drink will be the ruin *o* ruination of him (c) **ruinas** *(de una construcción)* ruins (d) *(persona)* wreck; **estar hecho una r.** to be a wreck

ruindad *nf* (a) *(cualidad)* meanness, baseness (b) *(acto)* vile deed

ruinoso, -a *adj* (a) *(poco rentable)* ruinous (b) *(edificio)* ramshackle

ruiseñor *nm* nightingale

ruja *etc ver* **rugir**

rular *vi Fam* to go, to work; **esta tele no rula** this TV is busted

rulero *nm RP (para el pelo)* roller, curler

ruleta *nf* roulette; **r. rusa** Russian roulette

ruletear *vi CAm, Méx Fam* to drive a taxi

ruletero *nm CAm, Méx Fam (de taxi)* taxi driver

rulo *nm* (a) *(para el pelo)* roller, curler (b) *(rizo)* curl

rulot *(pl* **rulots** *o* **rulotes**) *nf* trailer

Rumanía, Rumania *n* Romania

rumano, -a 1 *adj & nm,f* Romanian
2 *nm (lengua)* Romanian

rumba *nf* rumba

rumbo *nm (en navegación)* course; **ir con r. a** to be heading for; **cambió el r. de su vida** it changed the course of her life; **caminar sin r. (fijo)** to wander aimlessly; *Fig* **corregir el r.** to correct one's course; *Fig* **habrá que corregir el r. de la empresa** we will have to change the company's direction; **mantener el r.** to maintain one's course; **poner r. a** to set course for; **perder el r.** *(barco)* to go off course; *Fig (persona)* to lose one's way; **el r. de los acontecimientos** the course of events; *Fig* **tomar otro r.** to take a different tack; **no me gusta el r. que están tomando las negociaciones** I don't like the direction *o* turn the negotiations have taken

rumboso, -a *adj Fam* generous

rumiante *adj & nm* ruminant

rumiar 1 *vt (masticar)* to chew; *(pensar)* to ruminate, to chew over
2 *vi (masticar)* to ruminate, to chew the cud

rumor *nm* (a) *(ruido sordo)* murmur; **un r. de voces** the sound of voices (b) *(chisme)* rumor; **corre un r.** there's a rumor going around; **corre el r. de que va a dimitir** it is rumored that he's going to resign

rumorearse *v impersonal* **se rumorea que...** it is rumored that...

runrún *nm* (a) *(ruido)* hum, humming (b) *(chisme)* rumor

runrunear *vi* to hum

runrunearse *v impersonal* **se runrunea que...** it is rumored that...

runruneo *nm* *(ruido)* hum, humming

rupestre *adj* cave; **arte r.** cave paintings

rupia *nf* rupee

ruptura *nf* *(rotura)* break; *(de relaciones, conversaciones)* breaking-off; *(de pareja)* breakup; *(de contrato)* breach

rural *adj* rural

Rusia *n* Russia

ruso, -a 1 *adj & nm,f* Russian
  2 *nm (lengua)* Russian

rústica *nf* **en r.** *(encuadernación)* paperback

rústico, -a *adj* **(a)** *(del campo)* country; **casa rústica** country cottage **(b)** *(tosco)* rough, coarse

ruta *nf* route; **en r. (hacia)** en route (to); **en r.** *(en carretera)* on the road; **la seguridad en r.** safety on the roads, road safety; **r. marítima** sea *o* shipping lane; **r. de vuelo** flight path; **r. marítima** sea lane; **r. turística** scenic route

rutenio *nm* *Quím* ruthenium

rutilante *adj* shining

rutilar *vi* to shine brightly

rutina *nf* *(gen) & Inform* routine; **de r.** routine; **por r.** as a matter of course; **la r. diaria** the daily grind

rutinario, -a *adj* routine

Rvda. *(abrev de* **Reverenda***)* Rev *(Mother etc)*

Rvdo. *(abrev de* **Reverendo***)* Rev *(Father etc)*

S

S, s ['ese] *nf (letra)* S, s

S. (**a**) *(abrev de* **San**) St (**b**) *(abrev de* **Sur**) S

s.[1] (**a**) *(abrev de* **san**) St (**b**) *(abrev de* **siglo**) C (**c**) *(abrev de* **segundo**) s

s.[2], **sig.** *(abrev de* **siguiente**) following

S.A. *nf (abrev de* **sociedad anónima**) ≃ Inc

sábado *nm* Saturday; **¿qué día es hoy? — (es) s.** what day is it (today)? — (it's) Saturday; **cada s., todos los sábados** every Saturday; **cada dos sábados, un s. sí y otro no** every other Saturday; **caer en s.** to be on a Saturday; **te llamo el s.** I'll call you on Saturday; **el próximo s., el s. que viene** next Saturday; **el s. pasado** last Saturday; **el s. por la mañana/tarde/noche** Saturday morning/afternoon/night; **en s.** on Saturdays; **nací en s.** I was born on a Saturday; **este s.** *(pasado)* last Saturday; *(próximo)* this (coming) Saturday; **¿trabajas los sábados?** do you work (on) Saturdays?; **trabajar un s.** to work on a Saturday; **un s. cualquiera** on any Saturday

sabana *nf* savanna

sábana *nf* sheet; **s. bajera/encimera** bottom/top sheet; *Fig* **se le pegan las sábanas** she's not good at getting up; *Fig* **se me han pegado las sábanas** I slept late, I overslept

sabandija *nf* (**a**) *(animal)* creepy-crawly, bug (**b**) *Pey (persona)* worm

sabañón *nm* chilblain

sabático, -a *adj (de descanso)* sabbatical; **año s.** sabbatical year

sabedor, -ora *adj* **ser s. de** to be aware of

sabelotodo *nmf inv Fam* know-it-all

saber [58] **1** *nm* knowledge; *Prov* **el s. no ocupa lugar** you can never know too much

2 *vt* (**a**) *(conocer)* to know; **ya lo sé** I know; **de haberlo sabido (antes)** *o* **si lo llego a s., me quedo en casa** if I'd known, I'd have stayed at home; **hacer s. algo a alguien** to inform sb of sth, to tell sb sth; **para que lo sepas, somos amigos** we're friends, for your information

(**b**) *(ser capaz de)* **s. hacer algo** to know how to do sth, to be able to do sth; **no sé nadar** I can't swim, I don't know how to swim; **sabe hablar inglés/montar en bici** she can speak English/ride a bike

(**c**) *(enterarse de)* to learn, to find out; **lo supe ayer** I found out yesterday; **¿sabes algo de Juan?, ¿qué sabes de Juan?** have you had any news from *o* heard from Juan?

(**d**) *(entender de)* to know about; **sabe mucha física** he knows a lot about physics

(**e**) *(expresiones)* **no s. dónde meterse** not to know where to put oneself; **no sabe lo que se hace** he doesn't know what he's doing; **no sabe lo que tiene** he doesn't realize just how lucky he is; **no sé qué decir** I don't know what to say; **¡qué sé yo!** how should I know!

3 *vi* (**a**) *(tener sabor)* to taste (**a** of); **s. bien/mal** to taste good/bad; *Fam Fig* **s. a cuernos** *o* **rayos** to taste disgusting *o* revolting; *Fig* **le supo mal** *(le enfadó)* it upset *o* annoyed him;

Fig **me sabe mal mentirle** I feel bad about lying to him (**b**) *(entender)* **s. de algo** to know about sth; **ése sí que sabe** he's a canny one (**c**) *(tener noticia)* **s. de alguien** to hear from sb; **s. de algo** to learn of sth (**d**) *(parecer)* **eso me sabe a disculpa** that sounds like an excuse to me (**e**) *(expresiones)* **a s.** *(es decir)* namely; **¡quién sabe!, ¡vete a s.!** who knows!; **que yo sepa** as far as I know; **no sabe por dónde se anda** he doesn't have a clue

4 saberse *vpr* **saberse algo** to know sth; **saberse algo al dedillo** to know sth inside out; *Fig* **sabérselas todas** to know all the tricks; **llegar a saberse** to come to light

sabido, -a *adj* **como es (bien) s.** as everyone knows

sabiduría *nf* (**a**) *(conocimientos)* knowledge, learning; **la s. popular** popular wisdom (**b**) *(prudencia)* wisdom

sabiendas: a sabiendas *loc adv* knowingly; **utilizaron una sustancia tóxica a s.** they knowingly used a toxic substance; **presentó la propuesta a s. de que sería derrotada** she presented the bill knowing full well that it would be defeated

sabihondo, -a = sabiondo

sabina *nf (arbusto)* savin

sabio, -a 1 *adj* (**a**) *(sensato, inteligente)* wise (**b**) *(docto)* learned (**c**) *(amaestrado)* trained

2 *nm,f* (**a**) *(sensato, inteligente)* wise person (**b**) *(docto)* learned person

sabiondo, -a, sabihondo, -a *nm,f Fam* know-it-all

sablazo *nm* (**a**) *Fam (de dinero)* scrounging; **dar** *o* **pegar un s. a alguien** to scrounge money off sb (**b**) *(golpe)* blow with a saber (**c**) *(herida)* saber wound

sable *nm* saber

sableador, -ora *nm,f Fam* scrounger

sablear *vi Fam* to scrounge money

sablista *nmf Fam* scrounger

sabor *nm* (**a**) *(gusto)* taste, flavor; **un s. dulce** a sweet taste; **con s. a limón** lemon-flavored; **tener s. a algo** to taste of sth; *Fig* **dejó mal s. (de boca)** it left a nasty taste in my mouth; *Fig* **dejó buen s. (de boca)** it left me with a warm feeling inside (**b**) *(de obra)* flavor

saborear *vt también Fig* to savor

sabotaje *nm* sabotage

saboteador, -ora *nm,f* saboteur

sabotear *vt* to sabotage

sabré *etc ver* **saber**

sabroso, -a *adj* (**a**) *(gustoso)* tasty (**b**) *(substancioso) (cantidad)* tidy, considerable (**c**) *(comentario) (gracioso)* juicy, tasty (**d**) *Carib, Col, Méx (grato)* pleasant, nice; *(entretenido)* entertaining (**e**) *Carib, Col, Méx (contagioso) (ritmo)* catchy; *(risa)* contagious

sabrosón, -ona *adj Carib, Col, Méx Fam* (**a**) *(gustoso)* tasty (**b**) *(grato)* pleasant, nice; *(entretenido)* entertaining (**c**) *(contagioso) (ritmo)* catchy; *(risa)* contagious

sabueso *nm* (**a**) *(perro)* bloodhound (**b**) *Fig (detective)* sleuth, detective

saca *nf* sack

sacacorchos *nm inv* corkscrew

sacacuartos, sacadineros 1 *nm inv Fam (oferta, producto)* rip-off; **este coche es un s.** this car is a drain on our finances

2 *nmf inv (persona)* scrounger

sacamuelas *nm inv Fam* dentist

sacapuntas *nm inv* pencil sharpener

sacar [59] **1** *vt* (**a**) *(poner fuera, hacer salir)* to take out; *(pistola, navaja)* to draw; *(lengua)* to stick out; **s. algo de** to take sth out of; **sacó la mano/la cabeza por la ventanilla** he stuck his hand/head out of the window; **nos sacaron algo de comer** they gave us something to eat

(**b**) *(quitar)* to remove (**de** from); **el dentista me sacó una muela** I had a tooth out at the dentist's

(**c**) *(obtener) (carné, entradas, buenas notas)* to get; **¿qué sacaste en el examen de inglés?** what did you get for *o* in your English exam?; **s. dinero del banco** to get *o* take some money out of the bank; **la sidra se saca de las manzanas** cider is made from apples; **¿y qué sacamos con reñirle?** what do we gain by telling him off?, what's the point in telling him off?

(**d**) *(realizar) (foto)* to take; *(fotocopia)* to make; **siempre me sacan fatal en las fotos** I always look terrible in photos

(**e**) *(al mercado) (nuevo producto, modelo)* to bring out; *(disco)* to release

(**f**) *(resolver, encontrar)* to work out, to do; **s. la cuenta/la solución** to work out the total/the answer; **s. una conclusión** to come to a conclusion

(**g**) *(deducir)* to gather, to understand; **lo leí tres veces, pero no saqué nada en claro** *o* **limpio** I read it three times, but I couldn't make much sense of it

(**h**) *(sonsacar)* **s. algo a alguien** to get sth out of sb

(**i**) *(librar, salvar)* **s. a alguien de algo** to get sb out of sth

(**j**) *(manifestar)* **s. a relucir algo** to bring sth up

(**k**) *Esp (prenda) (de ancho)* to let out; *(de largo)* to let down

(**l**) *Am (camisa, zapatos)* to take off; **sácale la ropa al niño** get the child undressed

(**m**) *(aventajar en)* **sacó tres minutos a su rival** he was three minutes ahead of his rival

(**n**) **s. adelante** *(hijos)* to bring up; *(negocio)* to keep going

(**o**) *Dep (con la mano)* to throw in; *(con la raqueta)* to serve

2 *vi Dep* to put the ball into play; *(con la raqueta)* to serve; **s. de banda/de esquina/de puerta** to take a throw-in/corner/goal kick

3 sacarse *vpr* (**a**) *(poner fuera)* **sacarse algo (de)** to take sth out (of); *Fam Fig* **sacarse algo de la manga** to make sth up (on the spur of the moment) (**b**) *(carné, título)* to get (**c**) *Am (ropa, lentes)* to take off

sacárido *nm Quím* saccharide

sacarina *nf* saccharine

sacarosa *nf* sucrose

sacerdocio *nm* priesthood; *Fig* vocation

sacerdotal *adj* priestly

sacerdote, -isa 1 *nm,f (pagano)* priest, *f* priestess

2 *nm (cristiano)* priest; **mujer s.** woman priest

saciar 1 *vt (sed)* to quench; *(hambre)* to satisfy, to sate; *(curiosidad)* to satisfy; *(ambición)* to fulfill

2 saciarse *vpr (de comida, bebida)* to have had one's fill; *(de conocimientos, poder)* to be satisfied

saciedad *nf* **comió hasta la s.** she ate until she couldn't have any more; **repetir algo hasta la s.** to repeat sth over and over

saco 1 *nm* (**a**) *(bolsa)* sack, bag; **s. de arena** sandbag; **s. de dormir** sleeping bag (**b**) *Am (abrigo)* coat; *(chaqueta)* jacket (**c**) *(expresiones)* **caer en s. roto** to fall on deaf ears; **espero que no eches es s. roto mis consejos** I hope you take good note of my advice; **ser (como) un s. sin fondo** to be (like) a bottomless pit

2 a saco *loc adv* **entrar a s. en** *(saquear)* to sack, to pillage; **los asaltantes entraron a s. en el palacio presidencial** the attackers stormed the presidential palace; *Fam* **el periodista entró a s. con las preguntas** the journalist didn't beat about the bush with his questions

sacralizar [14] *vt* to consecrate

sacramental *adj* sacramental

sacramentar *vt* to administer the last rites to

sacramento *nm* sacrament

sacrificar [59] **1** *vt* (**a**) *(renunciar a)* to sacrifice, to give up (**b**) *(matar) (para consumo)* to slaughter; *(por enfermedad)* to put to sleep, to put down; *(a los dioses)* to sacrifice (**a** to)

2 sacrificarse *vpr* **sacrificarse (para hacer algo)** to make sacrifices (in order to do sth); **sacrificarse por alguien** to make sacrifices for sb

sacrificio *nm también Fig* sacrifice

sacrilegio *nm también Fig* sacrilege

sacrílego, -a 1 *adj* sacrilegious

2 *nm,f* sacrilegious person

sacristán, -ana *nm,f* sacristan, sexton

sacristía *nf* sacristy

sacro, -a 1 *adj* (**a**) *(sagrado)* holy, sacred (**b**) *Anat* sacral

2 *nm Anat* sacrum

sacrosanto, -a *adj* sacrosanct

sacudida *nf* (**a**) *(movimiento)* shake; *(de la cabeza)* toss; *(de tren, coche)* jolt (**b**) *(terremoto)* tremor (**c**) *(conmoción)* shock; **s. eléctrica** electric shock

sacudidor *nm* carpet beater

sacudir 1 *vt* (**a**) *(agitar)* to shake (**b**) *(golpear) (alfombra)* to beat; *Fam (persona)* to smack, to give a hiding to (**c**) *(conmover)* to shake, to shock

2 sacudirse *vpr (persona)* to get rid of; *(responsabilidad, tarea)* to get out of

S.A. de C.V. *nf Méx (abrev de* **sociedad anónima de capital variable**) = limited liability corporation with variable capital

sádico, -a 1 *adj* sadistic

2 *nm,f* sadist

sadismo *nm* sadism

sadomasoquismo *nm* sadomasochism

sadomasoquista 1 *adj* sadomasochistic

2 *nmf* sadomasochist

saeta *nf* (**a**) *(flecha)* arrow (**b**) *(de reloj)* hand; *(de brújula)* needle (**c**) *Mús* = flamenco-style song sung on religious occasions

safari *nm* (**a**) *(expedición)* safari; **ir de s.** to go on safari; **s. fotográfico** = vacation/trip photographing African wildlife (**b**) *(zoológico)* wild animal park, safari park

saga *nf* saga

sagacidad *nf* astuteness

sagaz *adj* astute, shrewd

sagitariano, -a *Am* **1** *adj* Sagittarian; **ser s.** to be (a) Sagittarian *o* Sagittarius

2 *nm,f* Sagittarian, Sagittarius

sagitario 1 *nm (zodiaco)* Sagittarius; *Esp* **ser s.** to be (a) Sagittarius

2 *nmf Esp (persona)* Sagittarian, Sagittarius

sagrado, -a *adj (libro, lugar)* holy, sacred; *(deber, vida)* sacred

sagrario *nm* (**a**) *(parte del templo)* shrine (**b**) *(tabernáculo)* tabernacle

Sáhara ['saxara], **Sahara** [sa'ara] *nm* **el (desierto del) S.** the Sahara (Desert)

saharaui *adj & nmf* Saharan

sahariana *nf (prenda)* safari jacket

sahariano, -a [saxa'rjano, -a, saa'rjano, -a] *adj & nm,f* Saharan

SAI ['sai] *nm Inform (abrev de* **sistema de alimentación**

ininterrumpida) uninterrupted power supply, UPS

sainete *nm Teatro* = short, popular comic play

sajar *vt* to cut open

sajón, -ona *adj & nm,f* Saxon

Sajonia *nf* Saxony

sake *nm* sake

sal 1 *nf* (**a**) *Culin & Quím* salt; **s. común** *o* **de cocina** cooking salt; **s. gema** rock salt; *Esp* **s. gorda** coarse salt; **s. marina** sea salt; **s. de mesa** table salt (**b**) *(gracia)* wit; **es la s. de la vida** it's one of the little things that makes life worth living (**c**) *(garbo)* charm (**d**) *CAm, Carib, Méx (desgracia)* misfortune, bad luck; **echar la s. a alguien** to put a jinx on sb

2 sales *nfpl* (**a**) *(para reanimar)* smelling salts (**b**) *(para baño)* **sales (de baño)** bath salts

sala *nf* (**a**) *(habitación) (de una casa)* lounge, living room; *(de hospital)* ward; **s. de bingo** bingo hall; **s. de calderas** boiler room; **s. de espera** waiting room; **s. de estar** lounge, living room; **s. de juntas** boardroom; **s. de lectura** reading room; **s. de máquinas** engine room; **s. de operaciones** operating room; **s. de partos** delivery room; **s. de profesores** staff room

(**b**) *(local) (de conferencias, conciertos)* hall; *(de cine, teatro)* auditorium; **un cine de ocho salas** an eight-screen movie theater complex *o* multiplex; **s. de embarque** departure lounge; **s. de fiestas** discotheque; **s. de subastas** auction room; **s. de tránsito** transfer lounge; **s. VIP** VIP lounge; **s. X** X-rated movie theater

(**c**) *Der (lugar)* court(room); *(magistrados)* bench

salacot (*pl* **salacots** *o* **salacotes**) *nm* pith helmet

saladero *nm* salting room

saladillo, -a *adj* salted

salado, -a *adj* (**a**) *(con sal)* salted; *(con demasiada sal)* salty; **estar s.** to be (too) salty; **agua s.** saltwater (**b**) *(opuesto a lo dulce)* savory (**c**) *Esp (gracioso)* amusing; *(encantador)* charming (**d**) *CAm, Carib, Méx (desgraciado)* unlucky

salamandra *nf (animal)* salamander

salamanquesa, *Andes* **salamanqueja** *nf* Moorish gecko

salame 1 *nm CSur (carne)* salami

2 *nmf RP Fam (tonto)* idiot

salami *nm* salami

salar *vt* (**a**) *(para conservar)* to salt (**b**) *(para cocinar)* to add salt to (**c**) *CAm, Carib, Méx (echar a perder)* to spoil, to ruin; *(causar mala suerte)* to bring bad luck to

salarial *adj* wage; **congelación s.** pay freeze; **incremento s.** pay raise

salario *nm* salary, wages; *(semanal)* wage; **s. base** *o* **básico** basic wage; **s. bruto/neto** gross/net wage; **s. mínimo (interprofesional)** minimum wage

salaz *adj* salacious

salazón 1 *nf (acción)* salting

2 salazones *nfpl (carne)* salted meat; *(pescado)* salted fish

salchicha *nf* sausage

salchichón *nm* = cured pork sausage similar to salami

salchichonería *nf Méx* delicatessen

saldar 1 *vt* (**a**) *(pagar) (cuenta)* to close; *(deuda)* to settle; *(asunto)* to settle (**b**) *Com* to sell off

2 saldarse *vpr (acabar)* **saldarse con** to produce; **la pelea se saldó con once heridos** eleven people were injured in the brawl

saldo *nm* (**a**) *(de cuenta)* balance; **s. acreedor/deudor** credit/debit balance; **s. medio** average (bank) balance; **s. negativo** overdraft; **la iniciativa tuvo un s. positivo** on balance, the outcome of the initiative was positive (**b**) *(de deudas)* settlement (**c**) *(restos de mercancías)* remnant; **saldos** *(rebajas)* sale; **de s.** bargain

saldré *etc ver* **salir**

saledizo *nm Arquit* overhang

salero *nm* (**a**) *(recipiente)* saltcellar, salt shaker (**b**) *Fam (gracia, donaire)* **baila con s.** she dances with great verve; **tiene mucho s. al hablar** she's a lively and entertaining conversationalist; **cuenta chistes con s.** she's good at telling jokes

saleroso, -a *adj Fam (gracioso)* witty, funny; *(garboso)* charming

salesiano, -a *adj & nm,f Rel* Salesian

salga *etc ver* **salir**

sálico, -a *adj Hist* **ley sálica** Salic law

salida *nf* (**a**) *(partida)* departure; **va a efectuar su s.** it's about to depart

(**b**) *Dep* start; **dar la s. a una carrera** to start a race; **s. nula** false start

(**c**) *(lugar)* exit, way out; **¿dónde está la s.?** where's the way out?; **s. de emergencia** emergency exit; **s. de humos** air vent; **s. de incendios** fire exit

(**d**) *(viaje)* trip

(**e**) *(aparición) (de revista, nuevo modelo)* appearance; **a la s. del sol** at sunrise; **esta llave regula la s. del agua** this faucet controls the flow of water; *Fin* **s. a bolsa** *(de empresa)* flotation

(**f**) *(momento)* **quedamos a la s. del trabajo** we agreed to meet after work; **te espero a la s. del cine** I'll meet you after the movie

(**g**) *Com (producción)* output; *(posibilidades)* market; **este producto no tiene s.** there's no market for this product

(**h**) *Inform* output

(**i**) *(solución)* way out; **si no hay otra s.** if there's no alternative

(**j**) *(ocurrencia)* witty remark; **tener salidas** to be witty; **s. de tono** out-of-place remark

(**k**) **salidas** *(laborales)* openings, opportunities; **carreras con salidas** college *o* university courses with good job prospects

salido, -a 1 *adj* (**a**) *(saliente)* projecting, sticking out; *(ojos)* bulging; **dientes salidos** buck teeth (**b**) *(animal)* on heat (**c**) *muy Fam (persona)* horny

2 *nm,f muy Fam (persona)* horny rascal

saliente 1 *adj* (**a**) *(destacable)* salient, important (**b**) *(presidente, ministro)* outgoing

2 *nm* projection

salina *nf* (**a**) *Min* salt mine (**b**) *(en el mar)* **salinas** saltworks *(singular)*

salinidad *nf* salinity

salino, -a *adj* saline

salir [60] **1** *vi* (**a**) *(ir fuera)* to go out; *(venir fuera)* to come out; **s. de** to go/come out of; **¿salimos al jardín?** shall we go out into the garden?; **¡sal aquí fuera!** come out here!

(**b**) *(ser novios)* to go out (**con** with); **están saliendo** they are going out (together)

(**c**) *(marcharse)* **s. (para)** to leave (for); **s. de viaje** to go away (on a trip); **cuando salimos de Quito** when we left Quito

(**d**) *(desembocar) (calle)* **s. a** to open out onto

(**e**) *(separarse) (tapón, anillo)* **s. (de algo)** to come off (sth)

(**f**) *(resultar)* to turn out; **ha salido muy estudioso** he has turned out to be very studious; **¿qué salió en la votación?** what was the result of the vote?; **s. elegida actriz del año** to be voted actress of the year; **s. premiado** to be awarded a prize; **s. bien/mal** to turn out well/badly; **s. ganando/perdiendo** to come off well/badly; **me ha salido mal** *(examen, entrevista)* it didn't go very well; *(plato, dibujo)* it didn't turn out very well; *(cuenta)* I got the wrong result; **¿qué tal te ha salido?** how did it go?

(**g**) *(proceder)* **s. de** to come from; **el vino sale de la uva** wine comes from grapes

(**h**) *(a divertirse)* to go out; **salen mucho a cenar** they eat out a lot (**i**) *(surgir) (luna, estrellas, planta)* to come out; *(sol)* to rise; *(dientes)* to come through; **le ha salido un sarpullido en la espalda** her back has come out in a rash

(**j**) *(aparecer) (publicación, producto, traumas)* to come out; *(moda, ley)* to come in; *(en imagen, prensa, televisión)* to appear; **¡qué bien sales en la foto!** you look great in the photo!; **ha salido en los periódicos/en la tele** it's been in the papers/on TV; *Cine & Teatro* **s. de** to appear as

(**k**) *(en sorteo)* to come up

(**l**) *(presentarse) (ocasión, oportunidad)* to turn up, to come along; *(problema, contratiempo)* to arise

(**m**) *(costar)* to work out (**a** *o* **por** at); **s. caro** *(de dinero)* to be expensive; *(por las consecuencias)* to be costly

(**n**) *(decir u obrar inesperadamente)* **nunca se sabe por dónde va a s.** you never know what she's going to do/come out with next

(**o**) *(parecerse)* **s. a alguien** to turn out like sb, to take after sb

(**p**) *(en juegos)* to lead; **te toca s. a ti** it's your lead

(**q**) *(desaparecer)* to come out; **la mancha de vino no sale** the wine stain won't come out

(**r**) *(librarse)* **s. de un apuro** to get out of a tight spot; **no sé si podremos s. de esta** I don't know how we're going to get out of this one

(**s**) *Inform* **s. (de)** to quit, to exit

(**t**) *Fam* **porque me sale/no me sale de las narices** because I damn well feel like it/damn well can't be bothered

(**u**) **s. adelante** *(persona, empresa)* to get by; *(proyecto, propuesta, ley)* to be successful

2 salirse *vpr* (**a**) *(marcharse)* **salirse (de)** to leave; **me salí del agua porque tenía frío** I came out of the water because I was cold (**b**) *(filtrarse) (líquido, gas)* to leak, to escape (**por** through); *(humo, aroma)* to come out (**por** through) (**c**) *(rebosar)* to overflow; *(leche)* to boil over; **el río se salió del cauce** the river broke its banks (**d**) *(desviarse)* **salirse (de)** to come off; **el coche se salió de la carretera** the car came off *o* left the road (**e**) *(escaparse)* **salirse de** *(límites)* to go beyond; **salirse del tema** to digress (**f**) **salirse con la suya** to get one's own way

salitre *nm* saltpeter

salitroso, -a *adj* containing saltpeter

saliva *nf* saliva; *Fam Fig* **gastar s. (en balde)** to waste one's breath; *Fig* **tragar s.** to bite one's tongue

salivación *nf* salivation

salivajo = **salivazo**

salival *adj* salivary

salivar 1 *adj* salivary

2 *vi* to salivate

salivazo, salivajo *nm* spit; **echar un s.** to spit

salmantino, -a 1 *adj* of/from Salamanca

2 *nm,f* person from Salamanca

salmo *nm* psalm

salmodia *nf Rel* singing of psalms; *Fig (letanía)* drone

salmodiar *vt* to sing in a monotone

salmón 1 *adj & nm inv (color)* salmon (pink)

2 *nm (pez)* salmon

salmonella [salmo'nela] *nf* salmonella *(bacterium)*

salmonelosis *nf inv* salmonella *(illness)*

salmonete *nm* red mullet

salmuera *nf* brine

salobre *adj* salty

salobridad *nf* saltiness

salomón *nm* sage, wise person

salomónico, -a *adj* equitable, even-handed

salón *nm* (**a**) *(en vivienda)* sitting room (**b**) *(para reuniones, ceremonias)* hall; **s. de actos** assembly hall; **s. de baile** dance hall; **s. de sesiones** meeting room (**c**) *(mobiliario)* sitting room suite (**d**) *(establecimiento)* **s. de belleza/masaje** beauty/

massage parlor; **s. de peluquería** hairdressing salon; **s. recreativo** game arcade; **s. de té** tearoom (**e**) *(feria)* show, exhibition; **s. del automóvil** auto show (**f**) *Fig* **revolucionario de s.** armchair revolutionary; **intelectual de s.** pseudointellectual

salpicadera *nf Méx (protección)* fender

salpicadero *nm Esp* dashboard

salpicadura *nf (acción)* splashing, spattering; *(mancha)* spot, spatter

salpicar [59] *vt* (**a**) *(con líquido)* to splash, to spatter; *(en reputación)* **el escándalo salpicó al presidente** the president was tainted by the scandal (**b**) *(diseminar)* to pepper (**de** with)

salpicón *nm Culin* = cold dish of chopped fish or meat, seasoned with pepper, salt, vinegar and onion

salpimentar [3] *vt* to season (with salt and pepper)

salsa *nf* (**a**) *Culin* sauce; *(de carne)* gravy; *Fig* **en su (propia) s.** in one's element; **s. agridulce** sweet-and-sour sauce; **s. bearnesa** bearnaise sauce; **s. bechamel** *o* **besamel** bechamel *o* white sauce; **s. mahonesa** *o* **mayonesa** mayonnaise; **s. rosa** ≃ Thousand Island dressing; **s. tártara** tartar sauce; **s. de tomate** tomato sauce (**b**) *(interés)* spice; **ser la s. de la vida** to make life worth living (**c**) *Mús* salsa

salsera *nf* gravy boat

saltador, -ora 1 *adj* jumping

2 *nm,f Dep* jumper; **s. de altura** high jumper; **s. de esquí** ski jumper; **s. de longitud** long jumper

saltamontes *nm inv* grasshopper

saltar 1 *vt* (**a**) *(obstáculo)* to jump (over) (**b**) *(omitir)* to skip, to miss out

2 *vi* (**a**) *(brincar, lanzarse)* to jump; **saltó de** *o* **desde una ventana** she jumped out of *o* from a window; **s. sobre alguien** *(abalanzarse)* to set upon sb; **s. a la cuerda** *o Esp* **a la comba** to skip; **s. de un tema a otro** to jump (around) from one subject to another

(**b**) *(levantarse)* to jump up; **s. de la silla** to jump out of one's seat

(**c**) *(salir disparado) (objeto)* to jump, to shoot; *(aceite)* to spurt; *(corcho, válvula)* to pop out; *(chispas)* to fly

(**d**) *(agua, cascada)* **s. por** to gush down, to pour down

(**e**) *(alarma)* to go off; **hacer s.** to set off

(**f**) *(explotar)* to explode, to blow up; **el automóvil saltó por los aires** the car was blown into the air; **han saltado los plomos** the fuses have blown

(**g**) *(romperse)* to break

(**h**) *(reaccionar bruscamente)* to explode; **s. a la mínima** to be quick to lose one's temper

(**i**) *(decir inesperadamente)* **"de eso nada", saltó ella** "no way," she blurted out; **s. con** to suddenly come out with

(**j**) *(expresiones)* **salta a la vista que...** it's patently obvious that...; **estar a la que salta** to be always on the lookout

3 saltarse *vpr* (**a**) *(omitir)* to skip, to miss out (**b**) *(salir despedido)* to pop off; **se le saltaban las lágrimas** tears were welling up in her eyes (**c**) *(no respetar) (cola, semáforo)* to jump; *(ley, normas)* to break

saltarín, -ina 1 *adj* fidgety

2 *nm,f* fidget

salteado, -a *adj* (**a**) *Culin* sautéed (**b**) *(espaciado)* unevenly spaced; **en días salteados** every other day; **se sentaron en pupitres salteados** they sat at alternate desks

salteador, -ora *nm,f* **s. de caminos** highway robber

saltear *vt* (**a**) *(asaltar)* to rob (**b**) *Culin* to sauté

saltimbanqui *nmf* acrobat

salto *nm* (**a**) *(gen) & Dep* jump; *(grande)* leap; *(al agua)* dive; **dar** *o* **pegar un s.** to jump; *(grande)* to leap; **triple s.** triple jump; **s. de altura** high jump; **s. de esquí** ski jump; **s. de longitud** long jump; **s. mortal** somersault; **s. en para-**

caídas parachute jump; **s. con pértiga** pole vault (**b**) *(diferencia, omisión)* gap (**c**) *(progreso)* leap forward; **un s. hacia atrás** a major step backward (**d**) *(despeñadero)* precipice; **s. de agua** waterfall (**e**) **s. de cama** *(prenda)* negligée (**f**) *(expresiones)* **vivir a s. de mata** to live from one day to the next; **dar saltos de alegría** *o* **contento** to jump with joy

saltón, -ona *adj (ojos)* bulging; *(dientes)* sticking out

salubre *adj* healthy

salubridad *nf* healthiness

salud 1 *nf* health; **estar bien/mal de s.** to be well/unwell; **beber** *o* **brindar a la s. de alguien** to drink to sb's health; **curarse en s.** to cover one's back; **rebosar de s.** to glow with health; **tiene una s. de hierro** she has an iron constitution; **s. mental** mental health; **s. pública** public health

2 *interj* **¡s.!** *(para brindar)* cheers!; *(después de estornudar)* bless you!; **¡s., camaradas!** greetings, comrades!

saludable *adj* (**a**) *(sano)* healthy (**b**) *(provechoso)* beneficial

saludar 1 *vt* to greet; *Mil* to salute; **ni siquiera nos saludó** he didn't even say hello (to us); **me saludó con la mano** he waved to me (in greeting); **saluda a Ana de mi parte** give my regards to Ana; **le saluda atentamente** yours faithfully; **siempre que vamos a Lima pasamos a saludarlos** whenever we go to Lima we drop in to say hello

2 saludarse *vpr (recíproco)* to greet one another; **ni siquiera se saludan** they don't even acknowledge each other

saludo *nm* greeting; *Mil* salute; **Ana te manda saludos** *(en carta)* Ana sends you her regards; *(al teléfono)* Ana says hello; **dale saludos de mi parte** give her my regards; **un s. afectuoso** *(en cartas)* yours sincerely

salutación *nf* greeting

salva *nf Mil* salvo; *Fig* **una s. de aplausos** a round of applause

salvación *nf* (**a**) *(remedio, solución)* **no tener s.** to be beyond hope; **las lluvias fueron la s. de los agricultores** the rains were the farmers' salvation (**b**) *(rescate)* rescue (**c**) *Rel* salvation

salvado *nm* bran

Salvador *nm* (**a**) *Rel* **el S.** the Saviour (**b**) *Geog* **El S.** El Salvador

salvador, -ora 1 *adj* saving
2 *nm,f (persona)* savior

salvadoreño, -a *adj & nm,f* Salvadoran

salvaguarda = **salvaguardia**

salvaguardar *vt* to safeguard

salvaguardia, salvaguarda *nf* (**a**) *(defensa)* safeguard (**b**) *(salvoconducto)* safe-conduct, pass

salvajada *nf* atrocity

salvaje 1 *adj* (**a**) *(animal, terreno)* wild; **el s. oeste** the Wild West (**b**) *(pueblo, tribu)* savage (**c**) *(cruel, brutal)* brutal, savage (**d**) *(incontrolado)* **acampada s.** unauthorized camping; **una huelga s.** an unofficial strike, a wildcat strike

2 *nmf* (**a**) *(primitivo)* savage (**b**) *(bruto)* brute; **unos salvajes prendieron fuego a un inmigrante** some inhuman brutes set fire to an immigrant

salvajismo *nm* savagery

salvamanteles *nm inv (plano)* table mat; *(con pies)* trivet

salvamento *nm* rescue, saving; **equipo de s.** rescue team

salvapantallas *nm inv Inform* screensaver

salvar 1 *vt* (**a**) *(librar de peligro)* to save; **nos salvó del peligro** he saved us from danger (**b**) *(rescatar)* to rescue (**c**) *(superar)* *(dificultad)* to overcome; *(obstáculo)* to go over *o* around (**d**) *(recorrer)* to cover (**e**) *(exceptuar)* **salvando algunos detalles** except for a few details; **salvando las distancias** allowing for the obvious differences

2 salvarse *vpr* (**a**) *(librarse)* to escape; **se salvó de morir ahogado** he escaped drowning; **sálvese quien pueda** every man for himself (**b**) *(exceptuarse)* **sus amigos son inaguantables, ella es la única que se salva** her friends are unbearable, she's the only one who's O.K. (**c**) *Rel* to be saved

salvavidas 1 *adj inv* **bote s.** lifeboat; **chaleco s.** lifejacket
2 *nm (chaleco)* lifejacket; *(flotador)* lifebelt

salve¹ *interj* hail!

salve² *nf* = prayer or hymn to the Virgin Mary

salvedad *nf* exception; **con la s. de** with the exception of

salvia *nf* sage

salvo, -a 1 *adj* **sano y s.** safe and sound
2 *prep* except; **todos, s. los enfermos** everyone except (for) the sick; **s. ella, nadie más conocía el camino** apart from her, nobody else knew the way, nobody knew the way except for her; **s. que** unless; **s. error u omisión** errors and omissions excepted
3 *nm* **estar a s.** to be safe; **poner algo a s.** to put sth in a safe place; **ponerse a s.** to reach safety

salvoconducto *nm* safe-conduct, pass

samaritano, -a *adj & nm,f* Samaritan

samba *nf* samba

sambenito *nm* **poner** *o* **colgar a alguien el s. de borracho** to brand sb a drunk

Samoa Occidental *n* Western Samoa

samovar *nm* samovar

sámpler *(pl* **sámplers)** *nm Mús* sampler

samurái, samuray *nm* samurai

san *adj* Saint; **San Bernardo** *(perro)* Saint Bernard; **s. José** Saint Joseph

Sana *n* Sanaa

sanador, -ora *nm,f* healer

sanar 1 *vt (persona)* to cure; *(herida)* to heal
2 *vi (persona)* to get better; *(herida)* to heal

sanatorio *nm* sanatorium

sanción *nf* (**a**) *(castigo, multa)* punishment; *Econ* sanction (**b**) *(aprobación)* approval

sancionar *vt* (**a**) *(castigar, multar)* to punish; *Econ* to impose sanctions on (**b**) *(aprobar)* to approve, to sanction

sancocho *nm Andes* = stew of beef, chicken or fish, vegetables and green bananas

sanctasanctórum *nm inv también Fig* sanctum

sandalia *nf* sandal

sándalo *nm* sandalwood

sandez *nf* silly thing; **decir sandeces** to talk nonsense

sandía *nf* watermelon

sandinismo *nm* Sandinista movement

sandinista *adj & nmf* Sandinista

sánduche, sánguche *nm Am* (**a**) *(con pan de molde) (sin tostar)* sandwich; *(tostado)* toasted sandwich (**b**) *(con pan de barra)* sandwich *(made with French bread)*

sandunguero, -a *adj* witty, charming

sándwich ['sanwitʃ, 'sanwis] *(pl* **sándwiches)** *nm (sin tostar)* sandwich; *(tostado)* toasted sandwich

sandwichera [sanwi'tʃera] *nf* toasted sandwich maker

saneado, -a *adj Fin (bienes)* written off, written down; *(economía)* sound, healthy; *(cuenta)* regularized

saneamiento *nm* (**a**) *(limpieza)* disinfection; *(fontanería)* plumbing; *(de río)* cleanup; **artículos de s.** bathroom furniture (**b**) *Fin (bienes)* write-off, write-down; *(de moneda)* stabilization; *(de economía)* putting back on a sound footing

sanear *vt* (**a**) *(higienizar) (tierras)* to drain; *(edificio)* to disinfect (**b**) *Fin (bienes)* to write off *o* down; *(moneda)* to stabilize; *(economía)* to put back on a sound footing

sanfermines *nmpl* = festival held in Pamplona in July during which bulls are run through the streets of the town

sangrado *nm Imprenta* indentation

sangrante *adj (herida)* bleeding; *(situación, injusticia)* shameful, outrageous

sangrar 1 *vi* to bleed

  2 *vt* (**a**) *(sacar sangre a)* to bleed (**b**) *(árbol)* to tap (**c**) *Fam (robar)* to bleed dry (**d**) *Imprenta* to indent

sangre *nf* (**a**) *(líquido)* blood; **me he hecho s. en el dedo** I've cut my finger; **te está saliendo s.** you're bleeding; *Zool* **de s. caliente** warm-blooded; *Zool* **de s. fría** cold-blooded; **ha corrido mucha s. en este conflicto** there has been a lot of bloodshed in this conflict; **un baño de s.** a bloodbath; **evitar un derramamiento de s.** to avoid bloodshed

  (**b**) *(expresiones) Fam Fig* **chuparle a alguien la s.** to bleed sb dry; *Fam Fig* **encender** *o* **quemar la s. a alguien** to make sb's blood boil; *Fig* **llevar algo en la s.** to have sth in one's blood; *Fig* **no llegó la s. al río** it didn't get too nasty; *Fig* **no tiene s. en las venas** he's got no life in him; *Fig* **sudar s.** to sweat blood; *Fam* **hacerse mala s.** to get worked up; **tener mala s.** to be malicious; **s. azul** blue blood; **s. fría** sangfroid; **a s. fría** in cold blood

sangría *nf* (**a**) *(bebida)* sangria (**b**) *(matanza)* bloodbath (**c**) *(ruina)* drain (**d**) *Med* bloodletting

sangriento, -a *adj* (**a**) *(ensangrentado, cruento)* bloody (**b**) *(despiadado, hiriente)* cruel

sangrón, -ona *adj CAm, Col, Méx Fam (persona)* nasty

sánguche = sanduche

sanguijuela *nf también Fig* leech

sanguinario, -a *adj* bloodthirsty

sanguíneo, -a *adj* blood; **presión sanguínea** blood pressure

sanguinolento, -a *adj (que echa sangre)* bleeding; *(bañado en sangre)* bloody; *(manchado de sangre)* bloodstained; *(ojos)* bloodshot

sanidad *nf* (**a**) *(salubridad)* health, healthiness (**b**) *(ministerio)* health department; **s. (pública)** public health service; **s. privada** private health care

sanitario, -a 1 *adj* health; **personal s.** health-care workers

  2 *nm,f (persona)* health officer

  3 *nm (retrete)* toilet, bathroom; **sanitarios** *(bañera, lavabo, retrete)* bathroom furniture

sanjacobo *nm Culin* = two slices of steak or ham with a slice of cheese in between, fried in breadcrumbs

San José *n* San José

San Marino *n* San Marino

sano, -a *adj* (**a**) *(saludable)* healthy; **un ejercicio/clima muy s.** a very healthy exercise/climate; **hacer vida sana** to have a healthy lifestyle; **s. y salvo** safe and sound (**b**) *(positivo) (ambiente, educación)* wholesome (**c**) *(entero)* intact, undamaged; **no quedó ni un vaso s.** not a glass was left unbroken *o* undamaged (**d**) **cortar por lo s.** to make a clean break

San Salvador *n* San Salvador

sansalvadoreño, -a 1 *adj* of/from San Salvador

  2 *nm,f* person from San Salvador

sánscrito, -a *adj & nm* Sanskrit

sanseacabó *interj Fam* **¡s.!** that's an end to it!

sansón *nm* very strong man

Santander *n* Santander

santanderino, -a 1 *adj* of/from Santander

  2 *nm,f* person from Santander

santería *nf* (**a**) *(beatería)* sanctimoniousness (**b**) *(religión)* santeria, = Afro-Cuban religion (**c**) *Am (tienda)* = store selling religious mementos such as statues of saints

santero, -a *adj* pious

Santiago (de Chile) *n* Santiago

Santiago de Compostela *n* Santiago de Compostela

Santiago de Cuba *n* Santiago de Cuba

santiaguero, -a 1 *adj* of/from Santiago de Cuba

  2 *nm,f* person from Santiago de Cuba

santiagués, -esa 1 *adj* of/from Santiago de Compostela

  2 *nm,f* person from Santiago de Compostela

santiaguino, -a 1 *adj* of/from Santiago (de Chile)

  2 *nm,f* person from Santiago (de Chile)

santiamén *nm Fam* **en un s.** in a flash

santidad *nf* (**a**) *(cualidad)* saintliness, holiness (**b**) **Su S.** His Holiness

santificación *nf* sanctification

santificar [59] *vt Rel* (**a**) *(consagrar)* to sanctify (**b**) *(respetar) (días festivos)* to keep holy; *(padres)* to honor

santiguar [11] **1** *vt* to make the sign of the cross over

  2 santiguarse *vpr* to cross oneself

santo, -a 1 *adj* (**a**) *(sagrado)* holy; **el S. Padre** the Holy Father; **la Santa Sede** the Holy See (**b**) *(virtuoso)* saintly (**c**) *Fam (dichoso)* damn; **todo el s. día** all day long; **el teléfono lleva sonando toda la santa mañana** the damn phone hasn't stopped ringing all morning

  2 *nm,f Rel & Fig* saint

  3 *nm* (**a**) *(onomástica)* saint's day; **el día de Todos los Santos** All Saints' Day (**b**) *(ilustración)* illustration (**c**) *(contraseña)* **s. y seña** password (**d**) *(expresiones)* **¿a s. de qué?** why on earth?, for what earthly reason?; **desnudar a un s. para vestir a otro** to rob Peter to pay Paul; **se le fue el s. al cielo** he completely forgot; **llegar y besar el s.** to get it at the first attempt; **no es s. de mi devoción** he's not my cup of tea; **quedarse para vestir santos** to be left on the shelf

Santo Domingo *n* Santo Domingo

santón *nm* (**a**) *Rel* holy man (**b**) *(persona influyente)* guru

santoral *nm* (**a**) *(libro)* = book containing lives of saints (**b**) *(onomásticas)* = list of saints' days

Santo Tomé *n* São Tomé

Santo Tomé y Príncipe *n* Sao Tomé and Príncipe

santuario *nm (templo)* shrine; *(de animales)* sanctuary

santurrón, -ona 1 *adj* excessively pious

  2 *nm,f* excessively pious person

santurronería *nf* sanctimoniousness

saña *nf* viciousness, malice; **con s.** viciously, maliciously

sañudo, -a *adj* vicious, malicious

Sao Paulo *n* São Paulo

sapiencia *nf Formal* knowledge

sapo *nm* toad; *Fig* **echar sapos y culebras** to rant and rave

saque 1 *ver* **sacar**

  2 *nm* (**a**) *(en fútbol)* **s. de banda** throw-in; **s. inicial** *o* **de centro** kickoff; **s. de esquina** corner kick; **s. de puerta** *o* **meta** goal kick; **s. de honor** = ceremonial kickoff by celebrity (**b**) *(en rugby)* **s. de banda** line-out (**c**) *(en tenis, voleibol)* serve; **tener buen s.** to have a good serve (**d**) *(apetito)* **tener buen s.** to have a hearty appetite

saqueador, -ora 1 *adj* looting, plundering

  2 *nm,f* looter

saquear *vt* (**a**) *(ciudad, población)* to sack (**b**) *(tienda)* to loot; *Fam (nevera, armario)* to raid

saqueo *nm (de ciudad)* sacking; *(de tienda)* looting

S.A.R. (*abrev de* **Su Alteza Real**) HRH

Sarajevo *n* Sarajevo

sarampión *nm* measles

sarao *nm* (**a**) *(fiesta)* party (**b**) *Fam (jaleo)* row, rumpus

sarasa *nm Fam Pey* queer, fag

sarcasmo *nm* sarcasm

sarcástico, -a 1 *adj* sarcastic

  2 *nm,f* sarcastic person

sarcófago *nm* sarcophagus

sarcoma *nm* sarcoma

sardana *nf* = traditional Catalan dance and music

sardina *nf* sardine; **como sardinas en lata** like sardines

sardinel *nm Col, Perú (bordillo)* curb

sardinero, -a *adj* sardine; **barco s.** sardine fishing boat

sardo, -a 1 *adj & nm,f* Sardinian

   2 *nm (lengua)* Sardinian

sardónico, -a *adj* sardonic

Sargazos *nmpl* **el mar de los S.** the Sargasso Sea

sargento 1 *nmf* (**a**) *Mil* sergeant (**b**) *Fam Pey (mandón)* dictator, little Hitler

   2 *nm (herramienta)* small clamp

sari *nm* sari

sarmiento *nm* vine shoot

sarna *nf Med* scabies; *(en animales)* mange; *Prov* **s. con gusto no pica** I'm/he's *etc* more than happy to put up with it

sarnoso, -a 1 *adj (perro)* mangy

   2 *nm,f (persona)* scabies sufferer

sarpullido *nm* rash

sarraceno, -a *adj & nm,f* Saracen

sarrio *nm* chamois

sarro *nm* (**a**) *(de dientes)* tartar (**b**) *(poso)* sediment

sarta *nf también Fig* string; **una s. de insultos/mentiras** a string of insults/lies

sartén *nf, Am nm o nf* frying pan, frypan; *Fam Fig* **tener la s. por el mango** to call the shots

sastre, -tra *nm,f* tailor

sastrería *nf (oficio)* tailoring; *(taller)* tailor's (store); *Cine & Teatro* wardrobe (department)

Satanás *nm* Satan

satánico, -a *adj* satanic

satanismo *nm* Satanism

satélite 1 *adj inv* satellite; **las ciudades s. de Madrid** the towns around Madrid; **estado s.** satellite (country)

   2 *nm* satellite; **s. artificial** satellite; **s. espía/meteorológico** spy/weather satellite

satén *nm (de seda)* satin; *(de algodón)* sateen

satinado, -a 1 *adj (papel)* glossy; *(tela)* shiny, satiny; *(pintura)* satin

   2 *nm (de papel)* glossy finish; *(de tela)* shiny *o* satiny finish; *(de pintura)* satin finish

satinar *vt* to make glossy

sátira *nf* satire

satírico, -a 1 *adj* satirical

   2 *nm,f* satirist

satirizar [14] *vt* to satirize

sátiro *nm* (**a**) *Mitol* satyr (**b**) *(lujurioso)* lecher

satisfacción *nf* (**a**) *(agrado)* satisfaction; **me dio mucha s.** I found it very satisfying; **espero que todo sea de su s.** *o* **esté a su s.** I hope everything is to your satisfaction (**b**) *(gusto)* satisfaction; **darle a alguien la s. de hacer algo** to give sb the satisfaction of doing sth; **darse la s. de hacer algo** to allow oneself the pleasure of doing sth (**c**) *(orgullo)* **nos mostró sus trofeos con s.** he took great pleasure in showing us his trophies; **sentir una gran s. personal** to feel a sense of fulfillment *o* satisfaction

satisfacer [33] **1** *vt* (**a**) *(persona, curiosidad, hambre)* to satisfy; *(sueño)* to fulfill; **su explicación no nos satisfizo** we weren't satisfied with his explanation (**b**) *(gustar, agradar)* to please; **me satisface anunciar...** I am pleased to announce... (**c**) *(deuda, pago)* to pay, to settle (**d**) *(ofensa, daño)* to redress (**e**) *(duda, pregunta)* to answer (**f**) *(cumplir)* *(requisitos, exigencias)* to meet

   2 satisfacerse *vpr* to be satisfied; **no se satisfacen con nada** nothing seems to satisfy them

satisfactorio, -a *adj (suficientemente bueno)* satisfactory; *(gratificante)* rewarding, satisfying

satisfecho, -a 1 *participio ver* **satisfacer**

   2 *adj* satisfied; **s. de sí mismo** self-satisfied; **darse por s.** to be satisfied; **dejar s. a alguien** to satisfy sb

sátrapa *nm* (**a**) *(rico)* **vivir como un s.** to live like a lord (**b**) *(dictador)* dictator, little Hitler

saturación *nf* saturation; *Fig* **hasta la s.** ad nauseam

saturado, -a *adj* saturated (**de** with); *Fig* **estar s. de trabajo** to have all the work one can manage

saturar 1 *vt* to saturate

   2 saturarse *vpr* to become saturated (**de** with)

saturnal *adj* Saturnian

saturnismo *nm Med* lead poisoning

Saturno *nm* Saturn

sauce *nm* willow; **s. llorón** weeping willow

saúco *nm* elder

saudí (*pl* **saudíes**), **saudita** *adj & nmf* Saudi

sauna *nf* sauna

saurio *nm* lizard, saurian

savia *nf (de planta)* sap; *(vitalidad)* vitality; *Fig* **s. nueva** new blood

saxo 1 *nm (instrumento)* sax; **s. alto** alto sax; **s. tenor** tenor sax

   2 *nmf (persona)* sax player, saxophonist

saxofón, saxófono 1 *nm (instrumento)* saxophone

   2 *nmf (persona)* sax player, saxophonist

saxofonista *nmf* sax player, saxophonist

saxófono = **saxofón**

saya *nf Anticuado* petticoat

sayal *nm Anticuado* sackcloth

sayo *nm Anticuado* smock

sazón *nf* (**a**) *(madurez)* ripeness; **en s.** ripe (**b**) *(sabor)* seasoning, flavoring (**c**) **a la s.** then, at that time

sazonado, -a *adj* seasoned

sazonar *vt* to season

scooter [es'kuter] (*pl* **scooters**) *nm* (motor) scooter

scout [es'kaut] (*pl* **scouts**) **1** *adj* **un grupo s.** a Scout troop

   2 *nmf* (Boy) Scout, *f* Girl Guide

script [es'kript] (*pl* **scripts**) **1** *nm* script

   2 *nf* script girl

SE (*abrev de* **Su Excelencia**) HE

se *pron personal* (**a**) *(reflexivo) (de personas) (singular)* himself, *f* herself; *(plural)* themselves; *(usted mismo)* yourself; *(ustedes mismos)* yourselves; *(de cosas, animales) (singular)* itself; *(plural)* themselves; **se está lavando, está lavándose** she is washing (herself); **se lavó los dientes** she cleaned her teeth; **espero que se diviertan** I hope you enjoy yourselves; **el perro se lame** the dog is licking itself; **se lame la herida** it's licking its wound; **se levantaron y se fueron** they got up and left

   (**b**) *(reflexivo impersonal)* oneself; **hay que afeitarse todos los días** one has to shave every day, you have to shave every day

   (**c**) *(recíproco)* each other, one another; **se aman** they love each other; **se escriben cartas** they write to each other

   (**d**) *(impersonal)* **en esta sociedad ya no se respeta a los ancianos** in our society old people are no longer respected; **se ha suspendido la reunión** the meeting has been canceled; **se dice que...** it is said that..., people say that...; **se prohíbe fumar** *(en cartel)* no smoking; **se habla español** *(en cartel)* Spanish spoken

   (**e**) *(como complemento indirecto) (de personas) (singular)* (to) him, *f* (to) her; *(plural)* (to) them; *(de cosas, animales) (singular)* (to) it; *(plural)* (to) them; *(usted, ustedes)* (to) you; **se lo dio** he gave it to him/her/*etc*; **se lo dije, pero no me hizo caso** I told her, but she didn't listen; **si usted quiere, yo se lo arreglo en un minuto** if you like, I'll sort it out for you in a minute

sé (**a**) *ver* **saber** (**b**) *ver* **ser**

sebáceo, -a *adj* sebaceous

sebo *nm (grasa sólida)* fat; *(para jabón, velas)* tallow

seborrea *nf* seborrhea

seboso, -a *adj* fatty

secadero *nm* drying room

secado *nm* drying

secador *nm* (**a**) *(aparato)* dryer; **s. (de pelo)** hair dryer (**b**) *CAm (trapo)* dish towel

secadora *nf* (**a**) *(de ropa)* clothes dryer, tumble dryer (**b**) *Méx (de pelo)* hair dryer

secamanos *nm inv* hand dryer

secano *nm* unirrigated *o* dry land; **cultivos de s.** = crops suitable for unirrigated land

secante1 *adj* (**a**) *(secador)* drying (**b**) **papel s.** blotting paper (**c**) *Mat* secant; **línea s.** secant
　2 *nf Mat* secant

secar [59] **1** *vt* (**a**) *(quitar humedad a)* to dry; **el sol secó los campos** the sun dried out the fields (**b**) *(enjugar)* to wipe away; *(con fregona)* to mop up
　2 secarse *vpr (planta, pozo)* to dry up; *(vajilla, suelo, ropa)* to dry; **nos secamos al sol** we dried off in the sunshine; **me sequé las manos en la toalla** I dried my hands with the towel

secarropas *nf inv RP* tumble dryer

sección *nf* (**a**) *(departamento)* department; **s. de caballeros** *(en tienda)* menswear department (**b**) *Geom* section

seccional *nf RP* (**a**) *(policial)* police district, police precinct (**b**) *(gremial)* section

seccionar *vt* (**a**) *(cortar)* to cut; *Mec* to section (**b**) *(dividir)* to divide (up)

secesión *nf* secession

secesionismo *nm* secessionism

secesionista *adj* secessionist

seco, -a 1 *adj* (**a**) *(en general)* dry; *(plantas, flores)* withered; *(higos, pasas)* dried; **tiene la piel seca/el cabello s.** she has dry skin/hair (**b**) *(persona, actitud)* brusque; **estuvo muy s. con su madre** he was very short with his mother; **me contestó con un no s.** she answered me with a curt "no" (**c**) *(flaco)* thin, lean (**d**) *(ruido)* dull; *(tos)* dry; *(voz)* sharp; **un golpe s.** a rap (**e**) *Fam (sediento)* thirsty; **estar s.** to be thirsty (**f**) *(expresiones)* **dejar a alguien s.** *(matar)* to kill sb stone dead; *(pasmar)* to stun sb; **parar en s.** to stop dead
　2 a secas *loc adv* just, simply; **llámame Juan a secas** just call me Juan; **no comas pan a secas** don't eat just bread

secoya *nf* sequoia

secreción *nf* secretion

secretar *vt* to secrete

secretaría *nf* (**a**) *(cargo administrativo)* post of secretary (**b**) *(oficina administrativa)* secretary's office (**c**) *(organismo)* secretariat; **S. de Estado** *(en España)* = government department under the control of an undersecretary; *(en Latinoamérica)* ministry; *(en Estados Unidos)* State Department

secretariado *nm* (**a**) *Educ* secretarial skills; **estudia s.** she's doing a secretarial course (**b**) *(cargo)* post of secretary (**c**) *(oficina, lugar)* secretary's office (**d**) *(organismo)* secretariat

secretario, -a *nm,f* secretary; **s. de dirección** secretary to the director; **s. de Estado** *(en España)* undersecretary; *(en Latinoamérica)* secretary; *(en Estados Unidos)* Secretary of State; **s. general** General Secretary; **s. personal** personal assistant

secretear *vi Fam* to whisper, to talk secretively

secreter *nm* bureau, writing desk

secretismo *nm* (excessive) secrecy

secreto, -a 1 *adj (reservado)* secret; *(confidencial)* confidential
　2 *nm* (**a**) *(en general)* secret; **no es ningún s. que el país atraviesa una crisis** it's no secret that the country is going through a crisis; **guardar un s.** to keep a secret; **mantener algo en s.** to keep sth secret; **s. bancario** banking confidentiality; **s. de confesión** secrecy of the confessional; **s. de**

Estado state *o* official secret; **s. profesional** professional secret; *Der* **decretar el s. sumarial** = to deny public access to information relating to a judicial investigation; **s. a voces** open secret (**b**) *(sigilo)* secrecy; **en s.** in secret

secta *nf* sect

sectario, -a 1 *adj* sectarian
　2 *nm,f* (**a**) *(miembro de secta)* sect member (**b**) *(fanático)* fanatic

sectarismo *nm* sectarianism

sector *nm* (**a**) *(división)* section; *Econ* sector; **el s. automovilístico** the auto industry; **s. cuaternario** leisure industries *o* sector; **s. primario/secundario** primary/secondary sector; **s. privado/público** private/public sector; **s. servicios** *o* **terciario** services industries *o* sector (**b**) *(zona)* sector, area

sectorial *adj* sectorial

secuaz *nmf Pey* minion

secuela *nf* consequence; **dejar secuelas a alguien** to leave sb suffering from the aftereffects

secuencia *nf* sequence; *Inform* **s. de arranque** boot sequence

secuenciador *nm Mús & Inform* sequencer

secuencial *adj* sequential

secuenciar *vt* to arrange in sequence

secuestrador, -ora *nm,f* kidnapper

secuestrar *vt* (**a**) *(raptar)* to kidnap (**b**) *(avión, barco)* to hijack (**c**) *(embargar)* to seize

secuestro *nm* (**a**) *(rapto)* kidnapping (**b**) *(de avión, barco)* hijack (**c**) *(de bienes)* seizure, confiscation

secular *adj* (**a**) *(seglar)* secular, lay; **clero s.** secular clergy (**b**) *(centenario)* centuries-old, age-old

secularización *nf* secularization

secularizar [14] *vt* to secularize

secundar *vt* to support, to back (up); **s. una propuesta** to second a proposal

secundario, -a *adj* secondary; **actor s.** supporting actor

secuoya *nf* sequoia

sed 1 *ver* **ser**
　2 *nf* thirst; **las palomitas dan s.** popcorn makes you thirsty; **tener s.** to be thirsty; *Fig* **s. de** thirst for; **s. de conocimientos** thirst for knowledge; **tener s. de venganza** to be thirsty for revenge

seda *nf* silk; **ir como una** *o* **la s.** to go smoothly; **s. artificial** rayon, artificial silk; **s. cruda** raw silk; **s. dental** dental floss; **s. natural** pure silk

sedación *nf Med* sedation; *(con música)* soothing, calming

sedal *nm* fishing line

sedán *nm* sedan

sedante 1 *adj Med* sedative; *(música)* soothing
　2 *nm* sedative

sedar *vt Med* to sedate; *(sujeto: música)* to soothe, to calm

sede *nf* (**a**) *(de organización, empresa)* headquarters; *(de Gobierno)* seat; *(de acontecimiento)* venue (**de** for); **s. social** head office (**b**) *Rel* see; **la Santa S.** the Holy See

sedentario, -a *adj* sedentary

sedentarismo *nm* **el s. avanza** people are adopting an increasingly sedentary lifestyle

sedente *adj* seated

sedición *nf* sedition

sedicioso, -a 1 *adj* seditious
　2 *nm,f* rebel

sediento, -a *adj (de agua)* thirsty; *Fig* **s. de** *(deseoso)* hungry for

sedimentación *nf* sedimentation

sedimentar 1 *vt* to deposit
　2 sedimentarse *vpr* to settle

sedimentario, -a *adj* sedimentary

sedimento nm (poso) sediment

sedoso, -a adj silky

seducción nf (a) (cualidad) seductiveness (b) (atracción) attraction, charm; (sexual) seduction

seducir [18] vt (a) (atraer) to attract, to charm; (sexualmente) to seduce (b) (persuadir) **s. a alguien para que haga algo** to charm sb into doing sth

seductor, -ora 1 adj (a) (atractivo) attractive, charming; (sexualmente) seductive (b) (persuasivo) persuasive, charming **2** nm,f seducer

sedujera etc ver **seducir**

seduzca etc ver **seducir**

sefardí (pl sefardíes), **sefardita 1** adj Sephardic **2** nmf (persona) Sephardi **3** nm (lengua) Sephardi

segada nf (en fútbol) scything tackle

segador, -ora nm,f (agricultor) reaper

segadora nf (máquina) reaping machine

segar [43] vt (a) Agr to reap (b) (cortar) to cut off (c) (acabar con) **la epidemia segó la vida de cientos de personas** the epidemic claimed the lives of hundreds of people

seglar 1 adj secular, lay **2** nm lay person

segmentación nf division

segmentar vt to cut o divide into pieces

segmento nm (a) Mat & Zool segment (b) (trozo) piece

segoviano, -a 1 adj of/from Segovia **2** nm,f person from Segovia

segregación nf (a) (separación, discriminación) segregation; **s. racial** racial segregation (b) (secreción) secretion

segregacionismo nm policy of racial segregation

segregacionista adj segregationist; **política s.** policy of racial segregation

segregar [38] vt (a) (separar, discriminar) to segregate (b) (secretar) to secrete

segué etc ver **segar**

segueta nf fretsaw

seguidamente adv next, immediately afterward

seguidilla nf (a) Lit = poem containing four or seven verses used in popular songs (b) (cante flamenco) = mournful flamenco song

seguido, -a 1 adj (a) (consecutivo) consecutive; **diez años seguidos** ten years in a row; **llamó a la puerta cinco veces seguidas** she knocked at the door five times (b) (sin interrupción) continuous; **llevan reunidos cuatro horas seguidas** they've been in the meeting for four hours without a break; **ha nevado durante dos semanas seguidas** it's been snowing for two weeks solid (c) (inmediatamente después) **s. de** followed by; **sopa, seguida de carne o pescado** soup, followed by meat or fish **2** adv (a) (sin interrupción) continuously (b) (en línea recta) straight on; **todo s.** straight on o ahead (c) Am (a menudo) often **3 en seguida** loc adv straight away, at once; **en seguida nos vamos** we're going right away

seguidor, -ora nm,f follower

seguimiento nm (de noticia) following; (de clientes) follow-up; **efectuar un s. de una epidemia** to monitor the course of an epidemic

seguir [61] **1** vt (a) (ir detrás de) to follow; **tú ve delante, que yo te sigo** you go ahead, I'll follow o I'll go behind; **s. algo de cerca** (desarrollo, resultados) to follow o monitor sth closely (b) (perseguir) to follow; **me parece que nos siguen** I think we're being followed (c) (reanudar) to continue, to resume (d) (cursar) **sigue un curso de italiano** he's doing an Italian course **2** vi (a) (sucederse) **s. a algo** to follow sth; **la lluvia siguió a**

los truenos the thunder was followed by rain (b) (continuar) to continue, to go on; **¡sigue, no te pares!** go o carry on, don't stop!; **aquí se baja él, yo sigo** (al taxista) he's getting out here, I'm going on; **sigo trabajando en la fábrica** I'm still working at the factory; **debes s. haciéndolo** you should keep on o carry on doing it; **sigo pensando que está mal** I still think it's wrong; **sigue enferma/en el hospital** she's still ill/in hospital; **¿qué tal sigue la familia?** how's the family getting on?

3 seguirse v impersonal to follow; **seguirse de algo** to follow o be deduced from sth; **de esto se sigue que estás equivocado** it therefore follows that you are wrong

según 1 prep (a) (de acuerdo con) according to; **s. su opinión, ha sido un éxito** in her opinion o according to her, it was a success; **s. yo/tú**/etc in my/your/etc opinion (b) (dependiendo de) depending on; **s. la hora que sea** depending on the time **2** adv (a) (como) (just) as; **todo permanecía s. lo recordaba** everything was just as she remembered it; **actuó s. se le recomendó** he did as he had been advised (b) (a medida que) as; **entrarás en forma s. vayas entrenando** you'll get fit as you train (c) (dependiendo) **¿te gusta la música? — s.** do you like music? — it depends; **lo intentaré s. esté de tiempo** I'll try to do it, depending on how much time I have; **s. que** depending on whether; **s. qué** certain; **s. qué días la clase es muy aburrida** some days the class is really boring

segunda nf (a) Aut second (gear); **meter (la) s.** to go into second (gear) (b) Av & Ferroc second class; **viajar en s.** to travel second class (c) Dep second division; **bajar a s.** to be relegated to the second division (d) (expresiones) **con segundas (intenciones)** with ulterior motives; **¿me lo dices con segundas?** are you telling me this for any particular reason?

segundero nm second hand

segundo, -a 1 núm second; **segunda clase** (en tren, avión) second class; **la Segunda Guerra Mundial** the Second World War; **segunda lengua** second language; **de segunda mano** secondhand; **segunda oportunidad** second chance; **segunda parte** part two; **segunda vivienda** second home; **s. violín** second violin **2** nm,f (a) (en orden) **el s.** the second one; **llegó el s.** he came second (b) (mencionado antes) latter; **vinieron Pedro y Juan, el s. con...** Pedro and Juan arrived, the latter with... (c) (ayudante) number two; Náut **s. de abordo** first mate **3** nm (en general) second; (piso) third floor

segundón, -ona nm,f second son; Fig **ser el eterno s.** to be one of life's eternal bridesmaids

seguramente adv probably; **s. iré, pero aún no lo sé** the chances are I'll go, but I'm not sure yet

seguridad nf (a) (ausencia de peligro) safety; **de s.** (cinturón, cierre) safety; **s. en el trabajo** safety at work o in the workplace; **s. vial** road safety (b) (protección) security; **s. ciudadana** public safety; **S. Social** Social Security (c) (guardias) security (d) (estabilidad, firmeza) security; **una inversión que ofrece s.** a safe o secure investment (e) (certidumbre) certainty; **con s.** for sure, definitely; **con toda s.** with absolute certainty; **tener la s. de que** to be certain that (f) (confianza) confidence; **habla con mucha s.** she speaks very confidently; **s. en sí mismo** self-confidence; **mostrar una falsa s.** to put on a show of confidence

seguro, -a 1 adj (a) (sin peligro) safe; **¿es éste un lugar s.?** is it safe here?; **sobre s.** safely, without risk; **es una inversión segura** it's a safe investment; **prefiero ir sobre s.** I'd rather play (it) safe (b) (protegido, estable) secure; **un trabajo s.** a secure job (c) (fiable) reliable (d) (indudable, cierto) definite, certain; **su nombramiento es s.** he's certain to be given the post; **ya sabemos la fecha segura de su llegada** we've now got a definite date for his arrival; **lo puedes dar por s.**

you can be sure of it; **tener por s. que** to be sure that (**e**) *(confiado)* sure; **estar s. de algo** to be sure about sth

2 *nm* (**a**) *(contrato)* insurance; **s. de accidentes** accident insurance; **s. del coche** car insurance; **s. de desempleo** unemployment benefit; **s. de enfermedad** health insurance; **s. de hogar** home insurance; **s. de incendios** fire insurance; **s. de invalidez** *o* **incapacidad** disability insurance; **s. médico** medical insurance; **s. a todo riesgo/a terceros** comprehensive/third party insurance; **s. de vida** life insurance

(**b**) *Fam* **el s.** *(la seguridad social)* ≃ Medicaid; **ese tratamiento no lo cubre el s.** ≃ you can't get that treatment on Medicaid

(**c**) *(dispositivo)* safety device; *(de armas)* safety catch

(**d**) *CAm, Méx (imperdible)* safety pin

3 *adv* for sure, definitely; **s. que vendrá** she's bound to come

seis 1 *núm adj inv* (**a**) *(para contar)* six; **tiene s. años** she's six (years old) (**b**) *(para ordenar)* (number) six; **la página s.** page six

2 *núm pron* (**a**) *(en fechas)* sixth; **el s. de agosto** the sixth of August (**b**) *(en direcciones)* **calle Mayor (número) s.** number six calle Mayor (**c**) *(en horas)* **las s.** six o'clock; **son las s.** it's six o'clock (**d**) *(referido a grupos)* **invité a diez y sólo vinieron s.** I invited ten and only six came along; **somos s.** there are six of us; **de s. en s.** in sixes; **los s.** the six of them (**e**) *(en temperaturas)* **estamos a s. bajo cero** the temperature is six below zero (**f**) *(en puntuaciones)* **empatar a s.** to tie, to six to six; **s. a cero** six to nothing (**g**) *(en naipes)* six; **el s. de diamantes** the six of diamonds; **echar** *o* **tirar un s.** to play a six

3 *núm nm (número)* six; **el s.** number six; **doscientos s.** two hundred and six; **treinta y s.** thirty-six

seiscientos, -as *núm* six hundred; *ver también* **seis**

seísmo *nm* earthquake

selección *nf* (**a**) *(en general)* selection; *(de personal)* recruitment; **test de s. múltiple** multiple-choice test; **s. natural** natural selection (**b**) *(equipo)* team; **s. nacional** national team

seleccionado *nm Dep* **el s. cubano** the Cuban (national) team

seleccionador, -ora 1 *adj* (**a**) *Dep* selecting (**b**) *(de personal)* recruiting

2 *nm,f* (**a**) *Dep* selector, coach (**b**) *(de personal)* recruiter

seleccionar *vt* to pick, to select

selectividad *nf* (**a**) *(selección)* selectivity (**b**) *Esp (examen)* college entrance examination

selectivo, -a *adj* selective

selecto, -a *adj* select

selector, -ora 1 *adj* selecting

2 *nm* selector (button)

selenio *nm* selenium

selenita 1 *nf* selenite

2 *nmf (habitante)* moon dweller

self-service [self'serβis] *nm inv* self-service restaurant

sellado, -a 1 *adj (documento)* sealed; *(pasaporte, carta)* stamped

2 *nm (de documento)* sealing; *(de pasaporte, carta)* stamping

sellar *vt* (**a**) *(timbrar)* to stamp (**b**) *(lacrar)* to seal (**c**) *(pacto, labios)* to seal

sello *nm* (**a**) *(de correos)* stamp; **s. postal** *o* **de correos** postage stamp (**b**) *(tampón)* rubber stamp; *(marca)* stamp (**c**) *(lacre)* seal (**d**) *(sortija)* signet ring (**e**) *(carácter)* hallmark; **ese libro lleva el s. de su autor** this book is unmistakably the author's work (**f**) *(compañía)* **s. discográfico** record label; **s. editorial** imprint; **s. independiente** independent record label (**g**) *Andes,Ven (de moneda)* reverse; **cara o s.** heads or tails

Seltz, seltz *nm (agua de)* **S.** seltzer (water)

selva *nf (jungla)* jungle; *(bosque)* forest; *Fig* **una s. de libros** mountains of books; **s. tropical** tropical rain forest; **s. virgen** virgin forest

Selva Negra *nf* **la S.** the Black Forest

selvático, -a *adj* woodland; **zona selvática** woodland area

semáforo *nm* traffic lights; **s. sonoro** pedestrian crossing *(with audible signal)*

semana *nf* week; **entre s.** during the week; **fin de s.** weekend; **la s. próxima** *o* **que viene** next week; **dos veces por s.** twice a week, twice weekly; **me deben tres semanas de alquiler** they owe me three weeks' rent; **s. laboral** work week; **S. Santa** Easter; *Rel* Holy Week

semanal *adj* weekly

semanalmente *adv* every week, once a week; **se publica s.** it's published weekly

semanario, -a 1 *adj* weekly

2 *nm (publicación semanal)* weekly

semántica *nf* semantics *(singular)*

semántico, -a *adj* semantic

semblante *nm* countenance, face

semblanza *nf* portrait, profile

sembrado, -a 1 *adj* (**a**) *(plantado)* sown (**b**) *(lleno)* **s. de** scattered *o* plagued with

2 *nm* sown field

sembrador, -ora 1 *adj* sowing

2 *nm,f (persona)* sower

sembradora *nf (máquina)* seed drill

sembrar [3] *vt* (**a**) *(plantar)* to sow (**b**) *(llenar)* to scatter, to strew (**c**) *(confusión, pánico)* to sow

semejante 1 *adj* (**a**) *(parecido)* similar (**a** to); **son de una edad s.** they are (of) a similar age (**b**) *(tal)* such; **jamás aceptaría s. invitación** I would never accept such an invitation; **una propuesta de s. talante** a proposal of this nature, such a proposal; **¡cómo pudo decir s. tontería!** how could he say something so stupid!

2 *nm* fellow (human) being

semejanza *nf* similarity

semejar 1 *vt* to resemble

2 semejarse *vpr* to be alike, to resemble each other; **semejarse a algo/alguien** to resemble sth/sb

semen *nm* semen

semental 1 *adj* stud; **toro s.** stud bull

2 *nm* stud; *(caballo)* stallion

sementera *nf (tierra)* sown land

semestral *adj* half-yearly, six-monthly

semestre *nm* period of six months; *Univ* semester; **cada s.** every six months

semiautomático, -a *adj* semiautomatic

semicircular *adj* semicircular

semicírculo *nm* semicircle

semicircunferencia *nf* semicircumference

semiconductor *nm* semiconductor

semiconsciente *adj* semiconscious

semiconsonante *nf* semiconsonant

semicorchea *nf Mús* sixteenth note

semiderruido, -a *adj* crumbling

semidesconocido, -a 1 *adj* almost unknown

2 *nm,f* **es un s.** he is almost unknown

semidesértico, -a *adj* semidesert; **un clima s.** a semi-desert climate

semidesierto, -a 1 *adj (calle, playa)* almost deserted; *(sala, oficina)* almost empty

2 *nm Geog* semidesert

semidesnatado, -a *adj* semiskimmed, = milk with some cream removed

semidesnudo, -a *adj* half-naked

semidiós, -osa *nm,f* demigod, *f* demigoddess

semienterrado, -a *adj* half-buried

semiesférico, -a *adj* semispherical

semifinal *nf* semifinal

semifinalista 1 *adj* semifinalist; **equipo s.** semifinalist
  2 *nmf* semifinalist

semifusa *nf Mús* sixty-fourth note

semilla *nf también Fig* seed

semillero *nm* (a) *(para plantar)* seedbed (b) *(para guardar)* seed box

seminario *nm* (a) *(escuela para sacerdotes)* seminary (b) *Educ (curso, conferencia)* seminar; *(departamento)* department, school

seminarista *nm* seminarist

seminuevo, -a *adj* almost new

semioculto, -a *adj* partially hidden

semiología *nf Ling & Med* semiology

semiólogo, -a *nm,f Ling & Med* semiologist

semiótica *nf Ling & Med* semiotics *(singular)*

semipesado, -a *Dep* **1** *adj* light heavyweight; **peso s.** light heavyweight
  2 *nm* light heavyweight

semiprecioso, -a *adj* semiprecious

semiseco, -a *adj* medium-dry

semisótano *nm* = level of building partially below ground level

semita 1 *adj* Semitic
  2 *nmf* Semite

semítico, -a *adj* Semitic

semitismo *nm* Semitism

semitono *nm Mús* semitone

semitransparente *adj* translucent

semivocal *nf Ling* semivowel

sémola *nf* semolina

sempiterno, -a *adj Formal* eternal

Sena *nm* **el S.** the Seine (river)

senado *nm* senate

senador, -ora *nm,f* senator

senatorial *adj* (a) *(del senado)* senate; **comité s.** senate committee (b) *(de senador)* senatorial

sencillamente *adv* simply

sencillez *nf* (a) *(facilidad)* simplicity (b) *(modestia)* unaffectedness, naturalness (c) *(discreción)* plainness

sencillo, -a 1 *adj* (a) *(fácil, sin lujo, llano)* simple (b) *(campechano)* natural, unaffected (c) *(billete)* one-way (d) *(no múltiple)* single; **habitación sencilla** single room
  2 *nm* (a) *(disco)* single (b) *Andes, CAm, Méx Fam (cambio)* loose change

senda *nf* path

senderismo *nm* hiking, trekking

senderista *nmf* hill walker, hiker

sendero *nm* path

sendos, -as *adj pl* **llegaron con s. paquetes** they each arrived with a package

senectud *nf* old age

Senegal *nm* **(el) S.** Senegal

senegalés, -esa *adj & nm,f* Senegalese

senil *adj* senile

senilidad *nf* senility

sénior (*pl* **séniors**) *adj & nm* senior

seno *nm* (a) *(pecho)* breast; **senos** breasts, bosom (b) *(amparo, cobijo)* refuge, shelter; **acogieron en su s. a los refugiados** they gave shelter to *o* took in the refugees (c) *(útero)* **s. (materno)** womb (d) *(de una organización)* heart; **en el s. de** within (e) *(concavidad)* hollow (f) *Mat* sine (g) *Anat (de la nariz)* sinus

sensación *nf* (a) *(percepción)* feeling, sensation; **una s. de dolor** a painful sensation; **tengo la s. de que estoy perdiendo el tiempo** I get the feeling I'm wasting my time (b) *(efecto)* sensation; **causar s.** to cause a sensation; **causar**

una gran s. a alguien to make a great impression on sb (c) *(premonición)* feeling; **tener la s. de que** to have a feeling that

sensacional *adj* sensational

sensacionalismo *nm* sensationalism

sensacionalista *adj* sensationalist

sensatez *nf* wisdom, common sense

sensato, -a *adj* sensible

sensibilidad *nf* (a) *(percepción)* feeling; **no tiene s. en los brazos** she has no feeling in her arms (b) *(emotividad)* sensitivity; **tener la s. a flor de piel** to be easily hurt, to be very sensitive (c) *(inclinación)* feeling; **s. artística/musical** feeling for art/music (d) *(de instrumento, película)* sensitivity; **un termómetro de gran s.** a very sensitive thermometer

sensibilización *nf* (a) *(concienciación)* increased awareness (b) *Fot* sensitization

sensibilizar [14] *vt* (a) *(concienciar)* to raise the awareness of (b) *Fot* to sensitize

sensible *adj* (a) *(en general)* sensitive (b) *(evidente)* noticeable; **pérdidas sensibles** significant losses; **mostrar una s. mejoría** to show a noticeable improvement

sensiblería *nf Pey* mushiness

sensiblero, -a *adj Pey* mushy, sloppy

sensitivo, -a *adj* (a) *(de los sentidos)* sensory (b) *(receptible)* sensitive

sensor *nm* sensor

sensorial *adj* sensory

sensual *adj* sensual

sensualidad *nf* sensuality

sentada *nf* (a) *(protesta)* sit-in (b) *Fam* **hacer algo de una s.** to do sth at one sitting *o* in one go

sentado, -a *adj* (a) *(en asiento)* seated; **estar s.** to be sitting down (b) *(establecido)* **dar algo por s.** to take sth for granted, to assume sth; **dejar s. que…** to make it clear that…

sentar [3] **1** *vt* (a) *(en asiento)* to seat, to sit (b) *(establecer)* **s. las bases para** to lay the foundations of; **s. precedente** to set a precedent
  2 *vi* (a) *(comida)* **s. bien/mal a alguien** to agree/disagree with sb; **algunos consideran que una copita de vino sienta bien** some people think a glass of wine is good for you (b) *(ropa, color)* to suit; **no le sienta bien** it doesn't suit her (c) *(vacaciones, medicamento)* **s. bien a alguien** to do sb good (d) *(comentario, consejo)* **le sentó mal** it upset her; **le sentó bien** she appreciated it
  3 sentarse *vpr* to sit down; **sentarse a hacer algo** to sit down and do sth; **siéntate** take a seat; **siéntate donde quieras** sit wherever you like

sentencia *nf* (a) *Der* sentence; **visto para s.** ready for judgment; **una s. benévola** a light sentence (b) *(proverbio, máxima)* maxim

sentenciar *vt* (a) *Der* to sentence (**a alguien a algo** sb to sth) (b) *(condenar, juzgar)* to condemn

sentencioso, -a *adj* sententious

sentido, -a 1 *adj* (a) *(profundo)* heartfelt (b) *(sensible)* **ser muy s.** to be very sensitive
  2 *nm* (a) *(capacidad para percibir)* sense; **sexto s.** sixth sense; **s. común** common sense; **s. del deber** sense of duty; **s. del humor** sense of humor; **s. del oído** sense of hearing; **s. del olfato** sense of smell; **s. de la orientación** sense of direction; **s. del ridículo** sense of the ridiculous (b) *(conocimiento)* consciousness; **perder/recobrar el s.** to lose/regain consciousness; **sin s.** unconscious (c) *(significado)* meaning, sense; **el s. de la vida** the meaning of life; **doble s.** double meaning; **tener s.** to make sense; **sin s.** *(ilógico)* meaningless; *(inútil, irrelevante)* pointless; **un sin s.** nonsense (d) *(dirección)* direction; **de s. único** one-way

sentimental 1 *adj* sentimental
  2 *nmf* **es un s.** he's very sentimental

sentimentalismo *nm* sentimentality

sentimentaloide *adj* mushy, sloppy

sentimiento *nm* (**a**) *(en general)* feeling; **s. de culpabilidad/pena** feeling of guilt/sorrow; **le acompaño en el s.** my deepest sympathy (**b**) **sentimientos** feelings; **dejarse llevar por los sentimientos** to get carried away; **¡no tienes sentimientos!** you have no feelings!

sentir [62] **1** *vt* (**a**) *(percibir, notar)* to feel; **sentimos mucha alegría/pena al enterarnos** we were very happy/sad when we found out (**b**) *(lamentar)* to regret, to be sorry about; **sentimos mucho la muerte de su amigo** we deeply regret the death of your friend; **siento que no puedas venir** I'm sorry you can't come; **siento haberle hecho esperar** sorry to keep you waiting; **lo siento (mucho)** I'm (really) sorry (**c**) *(oír)* to hear (**d**) *Am (olor, gusto)* **siento mal olor** there's a bad smell; **por el resfrío, no le siente gusto a la comida** she can't taste the food because of her cold

2 *vi* to feel; **sin s.** without noticing

3 *nm* feelings, sentiments

4 sentirse *vpr* (**a**) *(notarse, considerarse)* to feel; **¿te sientes mal/ bien?** are you feeling ill/all right?; **me siento mareada** I feel sick; **se siente superior** he feels superior (**b**) *Am (ofenderse)* to take offense

senyera *nf* Catalan national flag

seña 1 *nf (gesto, indicio, contraseña)* sign, signal; **hacer señas (a alguien)** to signal (to sb); **hablar por señas** to talk in sign language

2 señas *nfpl* (**a**) *(dirección)* address; **señas personales** (personal) description (**b**) *(indicio)* signs; **dar señas de algo** to show signs of sth (**c**) *(detalle)* details; **para o por más señas** to be precise

señal *nf* (**a**) *(gesto, sonido, acción)* signal; *(tono de teléfono)* tone; **cuando dé la s. empujamos todos a la vez** when I give the signal, everyone push together; **hacerle una s. a alguien para que haga algo** to signal to sb to do sth; **s. de alarma** alarm signal; **s. de salida** starting signal; **s. de socorro** distress signal

(**b**) *(indicio, símbolo)* sign; **esto es s. de que están interesados** this is a sign that *o* this shows they're interested; **dar señales de vida** to show signs of life; **en s. de** as a mark *o* sign of; **s. de la cruz** sign of the Cross; **señales de humo** smoke signals; **s. de peligro** danger sign; **s. de tráfico** road sign

(**c**) *(marca, huella)* mark; **hice o puse una s. en las cajas** I marked *o* put a mark on the boxes

(**d**) *(cicatriz)* scar, mark

(**e**) *(fianza)* deposit

señalado, -a *adj* (**a**) *(importante) (fecha)* special; *(personaje)* distinguished (**b**) *(con cicatrices)* scarred, marked

señalar 1 *vt* (**a**) *(marcar, denotar)* to mark; *(hora, temperatura)* to indicate, to say (**b**) *(indicar)* to point out; **nos señaló con el dedo** he pointed at us; **no quiero s. a nadie, pero...** I don't want to point the finger at anyone, but... (**c**) *(fijar)* to set, to fix; **señaló su valor en 1.000 dólares** he set *o* fixed its value at $1,000

2 señalarse *vpr (destacar)* to stand out

señalero *nm* Urug turn signal

señalización *nf* (**a**) *(conjunto de señales)* signs (**b**) *(colocación de señales)* signposting

señalizador *nm* Chile turn signal

señalizar [14] *vt* to signpost

señera *nf* Catalan flag

señor, -ora 1 *adj* (**a**) *(refinado)* noble, refined (**b**) *Fam (gran)* real; *(excelente)* wonderful, splendid; **tienen una señora casa** that's some house they've got

2 *nm* (**a**) *(tratamiento) (antes de nombre, cargo)* Mr; *(al dirigir la palabra)* Sir; **el s. López** Mr. López; **¡s. presidente!** Mr. President!; **el s. director les atenderá enseguida** the manager will see you shortly; **los señores Ruiz** Mr. and Mrs. Ruiz; **¿qué desea el s.?** what would you like, Sir?; **¡oiga s., se le ha caído esto!** excuse me! you dropped this; **señores, debo comunicarles algo** gentlemen, there's something I have to tell you; **Muy s. mío** *(en cartas)* Dear Sir (**b**) *(hombre)* man (**c**) *(caballero)* gentleman (**d**) *(noble)* lord; **s. feudal** feudal lord; **s. de la guerra** warlord (**e**) *(amo)* master (**f**) *Rel* **el S.** the Lord

señora *nf* (**a**) *(tratamiento) (antes de nombre, cargo)* Mrs; *(al dirigir la palabra)* Madam; **la s. López** Mrs. López; **¡s. presidenta!** Madam President!; **¿qué desea la s.?** what would you like, Madam?; **¡señoras y señores!** Ladies and Gentlemen!; **Estimada s.** *(en cartas)* Dear Madam; **¿es usted s. o señorita?** are you a Mrs. or a Miss? (**b**) *(mujer)* lady; **s. de compañía** female companion (**c**) *(dama)* lady (**d**) *(dueña)* owner (**e**) *(ama)* mistress (**f**) *(esposa)* wife; **el señor Ruiz y s.** Mr. and Mrs. Ruiz; **mi s. esposa** my (good) wife (**g**) *Rel* **Nuestra S.** Our Lady

señorear *vt (dominar)* to control, to rule

señoría *nf* lordship, *f* ladyship; **su s.** *(en general)* his lordship; *(a un noble)* Your Lordship; *(a un parlamentario)* the Right Honorable gentleman/lady; *(a un juez)* your Honor

señorial *adj* (**a**) *(majestuoso)* stately (**b**) *(del señorío)* lordly

señorío *nm* (**a**) *(dominio)* dominion, rule (**b**) *(distinción)* nobility

señorita *nf* (**a**) *(soltera, tratamiento)* Miss (**b**) *(joven)* young lady (**c**) *(maestra)* **la s.** miss, the teacher (**d**) *Anticuado (hija del amo)* mistress

señorito, -a 1 *adj* Fam Pey *(refinado)* lordly

2 *nm* (**a**) *Anticuado (hijo del amo)* master (**b**) *Fam Pey (niñato)* rich kid

señuelo *nm* (**a**) *(reclamo)* decoy (**b**) *(trampa)* bait, lure

seo *nf (catedral)* cathedral

sepa *etc ver* **saber**

sépalo *nm* Bot sepal

separación *nf* (**a**) *(en general)* separation; **se reunieron tras una s. de tres meses** they were reunited after being apart for three months; **hay demasiada s. entre las plantas** the plants are too far apart (**b**) *(espacio)* space, distance (**c**) *(matrimonial)* separation; *Der* **s. de bienes** separate estates (in matrimony)

separado, -a 1 *adj* (**a**) *(en general)* separate; **está muy s. de la pared** it's too far away from the wall; **por s.** separately (**b**) *(del cónyuge)* separated

2 *nm,f* separated person

separador, -ora 1 *adj* separating

2 *nm,f* separator

3 *nm* (**a**) *Tec* separator (**b**) *Med* retractor

separar 1 *vt* (**a**) *(desunir, alejar)* to separate (**de** from); **las hojas se han pegado y no las puedo s.** the pages have stuck together and I can't separate them *o* get them apart; **son muchas las cosas que nos separan** there are many differences between us (**b**) *(apartar)* to move away (**de** from); **separa un poco las sillas** move the chairs apart a bit (**c**) *(reservar)* to put aside (**d**) *(destituir)* **s. de** to remove *o* dismiss from

2 separarse *vpr* (**a**) *(apartarse)* to move apart; **separarse de** to move away from; **no se separen del grupo** don't leave the group, stay together with the group; **no se separaba de mí** he didn't leave my side (**b**) *(ir por distinto lugar)* to separate, to part company (**c**) *(matrimonio)* to separate (**de** from) (**d**) *(desprenderse)* to come away *o* off

separata *nf* pullout supplement

separatismo *nm* separatism

separatista *adj & nmf* separatist

separo *nm Méx* cell

sepelio *nm* burial

sepia 1 *adj & nm inv (color)* sepia
2 *nf (molusco)* cuttlefish

septentrional 1 *adj* northern
2 *nmf* northerner

septicemia *nf Med* septicemia

séptico, -a *adj* septic

septiembre, setiembre *nm* September; **el 1 de s.** September 1; **uno de los septiembres más lluviosos de la última década** one of the rainiest Septembers in the last decade; **a principios/mediados/finales de s.** at the beginning/in the middle/at the end of September; **el pasado/próximo (mes de) s.** last/next September; **en s.** in September; **en pleno s.** in mid-September; **este (mes de) s.** *(pasado)* (this) last September; *(próximo)* next September, this coming September; **para s.** by September

séptimo, -a, sétimo, -a *núm* seventh; **la séptima parte** a seventh

septuagenario, -a *adj & nm,f* septuagenarian

septuagésimo, -a *núm* seventieth

septuplicar [59] **1** *vt* to multiply by seven
2 septuplicarse *vpr* to increase sevenfold

sepulcral *adj* **(a)** *(del sepulcro)* **arte s.** funerary art **(b)** *(profundo) (voz, silencio)* lugubrious, gloomy; *(frío)* deathly

sepulcro *nm* tomb

sepultar *vt* to bury

sepultura *nf* **(a)** *(enterramiento)* burial **(b)** *(fosa)* grave

sepulturero, -a *nm,f* gravedigger

seque *etc ver* **secar**

sequedad *nf* **(a)** *(falta de humedad)* dryness **(b)** *(antipatía)* abruptness, brusqueness

sequía *nf* drought

séquito *nm (comitiva)* retinue, entourage

ser [2] **1** *vi* **(a)** *(en general)* to be; **fue aquí** it was here; **lo importante es decidirse** the important thing is to reach a decision; **s. de** *(estar hecho de)* to be made of; *(provenir de)* to be from; *(ser propiedad de)* to belong to; *(formar parte de)* to be a member of; **¿de dónde eres?** where are you from?; **los juguetes son de mi hijo** the toys are my son's
(b) *(con precios, horas, números)* to be; **¿cuánto es?** how much is it?; **son 300 pesos** that'll be 300 pesos; **¿qué (día) es hoy?** what day is it today?, what's today?; **mañana será 15 de julio** tomorrow (it) will be July 15; **¿qué hora es?** what time is it?, what's the time?; **son las tres (de la tarde)** it's three o'clock (in the afternoon), it's three (pm)
(c) *(servir, ser adecuado)* **s. para** to be for; **este trapo es para (limpiar) las ventanas** this cloth is for (cleaning) the windows; **este libro es para niños** this book is (meant) for children
(d) *(uso partitivo)* **s. de los que...** to be one of those (people) who...; **ése es de los que están en huelga** he is one of those on strike
2 *v copulativo* **(a)** *(en general)* to be; **es alto/gracioso** he is tall/funny; **es azul/difícil** it's blue/difficult; **es un amigo/el dueño** he is a friend/the owner **(b)** *(empleo, dedicación)* to be; **soy abogado/actriz** I'm a lawyer/an actress; **son estudiantes** they're students
3 *v impersonal* **(a)** *(expresa tiempo)* to be; **es muy tarde** it's rather late; **era de noche/de día** it was night/day **(b)** *(expresa necesidad, posibilidad)* **es de desear que...** it is to be hoped that...; **es de suponer que aparecerá** presumably, he'll turn up **(c)** *(expresa motivo)* **es que no vine porque estaba enfermo** the reason I didn't come is that I was ill **(d)** *(expresiones)* **a no s. que** unless; **como sea** one way or another, somehow or other; **de no s. por** had it not been for; **érase una vez, érase que se era** once upon a time; **no es para menos** not without reason; **o sea** that is (to say), I mean; **por si fuera poco** as if that wasn't enough; *Am*

siendo que... seeing that *o* as..., given that...
4 *v aux (para formar la voz pasiva)* to be; **fue visto por un testigo** he was seen by a witness
5 *nm (ente)* being; **s. humano** human being; **los seres vivos** living things

serafín *nm* seraph

Serbia *n* Serbia

serbio, -a *adj & nm,f* Serbian

serbocroata 1 *adj & nmf* Serbo-Croat
2 *nm (idioma)* Serbo-Croat

serenar 1 *vt (calmar)* to calm
2 serenarse *vpr (calmarse)* to calm down; *(tiempo)* to clear up; *(viento)* to die down; *(aguas)* to grow calm

serenata *nf Mús* serenade

serenidad *nf* **(a)** *(tranquilidad)* calm **(b)** *(quietud)* tranquility

sereno, -a 1 *adj* **(a)** *(sobrio)* sober **(b)** *(tranquilo)* calm
2 *nm* **(a)** *Antes (vigilante)* night watchman **(b)** *(humedad)* night dew

serial *nm* serial

sericultura *nf* sericulture

serie *nf* **(a)** *(sucesión, conjunto)* series (singular); *(de sellos, monedas)* set; *(de mentiras)* string; **me dijo una s. de cosas** he told me a number of things **(b)** *TV* series (singular) **(c)** *(producción)* run, batch; **este coche es de la primera s. que se fabricó** this car is from the first batch that was produced; **fabricación en s.** mass production; **con ABS de s.** with ABS as standard; *Fig* **ser un fuera de s.** to be unique, to be one of a kind **(d)** *Elec* **en s.** in series

seriedad *nf* **(a)** *(gravedad, importancia)* seriousness; **viste con demasiada s.** he dresses too formally **(b)** *(responsabilidad)* sense of responsibility; *(formalidad)* reliability; **¡qué falta de s.!** what an irresponsible way to behave!

serigrafía *nf* silk screen printing

serio, -a 1 *adj* **(a)** *(grave, importante)* serious; **estar s.** to look serious; **es una enfermedad muy seria** it's a very serious illness **(b)** *(responsable)* responsible; *(cumplidor, formal)* reliable; **no son gente seria** they are very unreliable; **lo que no es s. es que ahora digan que necesitan dos meses más** what's really unacceptable is that now they're saying they need another two months
2 en serio *loc adv* seriously; **en s., me ha tocado la lotería** seriously, I've won the lottery; **tomarse algo/a alguien en s.** to take sth/sb seriously; **lo digo en s.** I'm serious

sermón *nm también Fig* sermon

sermoneador, -ora *adj* sermonizing

sermonear *vt* to give a lecture *o* telling-off to

seropositivo, -a *Med* **1** *adj* HIV-positive
2 *nm,f* HIV-positive person

serotonina *nf Bioquím* serotonin

serpentear *vi* **(a)** *(río, camino)* to wind, to snake **(b)** *(culebra)* to wriggle

serpentina *nf* streamer

serpiente *nf (culebra)* snake; *Lit* serpent; **s. de cascabel** rattlesnake; **s. pitón** python

serrallo *nm* seraglio

serranía *nf* mountainous region

serrano, -a 1 *adj* **(a)** *(de la sierra)* mountain, highland; **aire/pueblo s.** mountain air/village **(b)** *(jamón)* cured **(c)** *Fam (expresiones)* **¡vaya cuerpo s.!** what a great bod!; **¡vaya cuerpo s. tengo!** I feel like death warmed up!
2 *nm,f Am* person from the mountains

serrar [3] *vt* to saw (up)

serrería *nf* sawmill

serrín *nm* sawdust

serrucho *nm* handsaw

servicentro *nm CAm, CSur* service station

servicial *adj* attentive, helpful

servicio *nm* (**a**) *(prestación, asistencia, sistema)* service; **hubo que recurrir a los servicios de un abogado** we had to use the services of a lawyer; **s. discrecional** private service; **s. de asistencia** help desk; **s. a domicilio** home delivery service; **s. de habitaciones** room service; **s. de inteligencia** intelligence service; **s. militar** military service; **servicios mínimos** skeleton service; **s. de paquetería** parcel service; **s. posventa** after-sales service; **s. público** public service; **s. secreto** secret service; **los servicios sociales** the social services

(**b**) *(funcionamiento)* service; **entrar en s.** to come into service; **estar fuera de s.** *(máquina)* to be out of order

(**c**) *(turno)* duty; **estar de s.** to be on duty

(**d**) *(servidumbre)* servants; **s. doméstico** domestic help

(**e**) *Esp (WC)* toilet, bathroom; **¿dónde están los servicios?** where's the bathroom?

(**f**) *Econ* **servicios** *(sector terciario)* services; **una empresa de servicios** a services company

(**g**) *Dep* serve, service

(**h**) *(juego)* **s. de mesa** dinner service; **s. de té** tea set

servidor, -ora 1 *nm,f* (**a**) *(criado)* servant (**b**) *(en cartas)* **su seguro s.** yours faithfully (**c**) *(yo)* yours truly, me; **¿quién es el último? — s.** who's last? — I am

2 *nm Inform* server; **s. de ficheros** *o* **archivos** file server

servidumbre *nf* (**a**) *(criados)* servants (**b**) *(dependencia)* servitude

servil *adj* servile

servilismo *nm* subservience

servilleta *nf* napkin

servilletero *nm* napkin ring

servir [47] **1** *vt* to serve; **¿te sirvo más patatas?** would you like some more potatoes?; **¿me sirve un poco más, por favor?** could I have a bit more, please?; **¿en qué puedo servirle?** what can I do for you?; **la polémica está servida** the gloves are off

2 *vi* (**a**) *(prestar servicio)* to serve; **s. en el Ejército** to serve in the Army (**b**) *(valer, ser útil)* **esta batidora ya no sirve/aún sirve** this mixer is no good anymore/can still be used; **no sirve para estudiar** he's no good at studying; **de nada sirve que se lo digas** it's no use telling him; **s. de algo** to serve as sth (**c**) *(como criado)* to be in service

3 servirse *vpr* (**a**) *(aprovecharse)* **servirse de** *(medio, objeto)* to make use of; *(persona)* to use (**b**) *(comida, bebida)* to help oneself; **que cada uno se sirva lo que prefiera** help yourselves to whatever you like (**c**) *Formal* **sírvase llamar cuando quiera** please call whenever you wish

servoasistido, -a *adj Aut* servo; **dirección servoasistida** power steering

servodirección *nf* power steering

servofreno *nm* servo brake

sésamo *nm* sesame

sesear *vi Gram* = to pronounce "c" and "z" as "s", as in Andalusian and Latin American dialects

sesenta *núm* sixty; **los (años) s.** the sixties; *ver también* **seis**

sesentón, -ona *nm,f Fam* person in their sixties

seseo *nm Gram* = pronunciation of "c" and "z" as an "s"

sesera *nf Fam* (**a**) *(cabeza)* nut (**b**) *(inteligencia)* brains

sesgado, -a *adj* biased, partial; **información sesgada** biased information

sesgar [38] *vt* to cut on the bias

sesgo *nm* (**a**) *(oblicuidad)* slant; **al s.** *(en general)* on a slant; *(costura)* on the bias (**b**) *(rumbo)* course, path

sesgue *etc ver* **sesgar**

sesión *nf* (**a**) *(reunión)* meeting, session; *Der* sitting, session; **abrir la s.** to open the meeting; **s. informativa** *(para presentar algo)* briefing; **s. plenaria** *(de congreso)* plenary (session); *(de organización)* plenary assembly (**b**) *(proyección, representación)* show, performance; **s. continua** continuous performance; **s. doble** double bill; **s. matinal** matinee; **s. de noche** evening showing; **s. de tarde** afternoon matinée (**c**) *(periodo)* session

seso *nm* (**a**) *(cerebro)* brain; *Culin* **sesos** brains (**b**) *(sensatez)* brains, sense (**c**) *(expresiones)* **calentarse** *o* **devanarse los sesos** to cudgel one's brains; **sorber el s.** *o* **los sesos a alguien** to brainwash sb; *Fam* **tener poco s.** not to be very bright

sestear *vi* to have a nap

sesudo, -a *adj* (**a**) *(inteligente)* brainy (**b**) *(sensato)* wise, sensible

set (*pl* **sets**) *nm (gen)* & *Dep* set

seta *nf Esp* mushroom; **s. venenosa** poisonous mushroom

setecientos, -as *núm* seven hundred; *ver también* **seis**

setenta *núm* seventy; **los (años) s.** the seventies; *ver también* **seis**

setiembre = **septiembre**

sétimo, -a = **séptimo**

seto *nm* fence; **s. vivo** hedge

setter ['seter] (*pl* **setters**) *nm* setter

seudo *adj* pseudo

seudónimo *nm* pseudonym

Seúl *n* Seoul

s.e.u.o. *(abrev de* **salvo error u omisión**) E & OE

severidad *nf* (**a**) *(de castigo, clima)* severity, harshness; *(de enfermedad)* severity, seriousness (**b**) *(de persona)* strictness

severo, -a *adj* (**a**) *(castigo, clima)* severe, harsh; *(enfermedad)* serious (**b**) *(persona)* strict

Sevilla *n* Seville

sevillana *nf* = Andalusian dance and song

sevillano, -a *adj* & *nm,f* Sevillian

sexagenario, -a *adj* & *nm,f* sexagenarian

sexagésimo, -a *núm* sixtieth; **s. primero** sixty-first

sex-appeal [seksa'pil] *nm inv* sex appeal

sexi *adj Fam* sexy

sexismo *nm* sexism

sexista *adj* & *nmf* sexist

sexo *nm* (**a**) *(en general)* sex; **el bello s., el s. débil** the fair sex; **un organismo de s. masculino** a male organism; **s. oral** oral sex; **s. seguro** *o* **sin riesgo** safe sex (**b**) *(genitales)* genitals

sexología *nf* sexology

sexólogo, -a *nm,f* sexologist

sex-shop [sek'ʃop] (*pl* **sex-shops**) *nm* sex shop

sex-symbol (*pl* **sex-symbols**) *nm* sex symbol

sextante *nm* sextant

sexteto *nm* (**a**) *Mús* sextet (**b**) *Lit* sestina

sexto, -a *núm* sixth; **la sexta parte** a sixth; **s. sentido** sixth sense

sextuplicar [59] **1** *vt* to multiply by six

2 sextuplicarse *vpr* to increase sixfold

séxtuplo, -a 1 *adj* sixfold

2 *nm* sextuple

sexuado, -a *adj* sexed

sexual *adj* sexual; **educación/vida s.** sex education/life

sexualidad *nf* sexuality

sexy *adj Fam* sexy

Seychelles [sei'ʃels] *nfpl* **las (islas) S.** the Seychelles

SGAE *nf* (*abrev de* **Sociedad General de Autores de España**) = society that safeguards the interests of Spanish authors, musicians etc

sha [sa, ʃa] *nm* shah

shakesperiano, -a [ʃespi'rjano] *adj* Shakespearian

shareware ['ʃerwer] *nm Inform* shareware

sheriff ['ʃerif] (*pl* **sheriffs**) *nm* sheriff

sherpa ['serpa, 'ʃerpa] *nm* sherpa

shiatsu ['ʃiatsu] *nm* shiatsu

shock [ʃok] (*pl* **shocks**) *nm* shock

shopping ['ʃopin] (*pl* **shoppings**) *nm RP* (shopping) mall

shorts [ʃorts] *nmpl*, *Am* **short** [ʃor, ʃort] (*pl* **shores**) *nm* shorts

show [ʃou, tʃou] (*pl* **shows**) *nm* show; *Fig* **montar un s.** to cause a scene

si¹ (*pl* **sis**) *nm Mús* B; (*en solfeo*) ti

si² 1 *conj* (a) (*condicional*) if; **si no te das prisa perderás el tren** if you don't hurry up you'll miss the train; **si viene él yo me voy** if he comes, then I'm going; **si hubieses venido te habrías divertido** if you had come, you would have enjoyed yourself (b) (*en oraciones interrogativas indirectas*) if, whether; **ignoro si lo sabe** I don't know if *o* whether she knows (c) (*expresa protesta*) but; **¡si te dije que no lo hicieras!** but I told you not to do it!

  2 si no *loc adv* if not, otherwise

sí (*pl* **síes**) 1 *adv* (a) (*afirmación*) yes; **¿vendrás? — sí** will you come? — yes, I will; **¿aún te duele? — sí** does it still hurt? — yes, it does; **claro que sí** of course; **yo digo que sí, que se lo digamos** I say we tell her; **creo que sí** I think so; **¿están de acuerdo? — algunos sí** do they agree? — some do; **un día sí y uno no** every other day

  (b) (*uso enfático*) **sí que** really, certainly; **sí que me gusta** I certainly do *o* really like it; **éste sí que me gusta** this one I DO like

  (c) (*expresiones*) **no creo que puedas hacerlo — ¡a que sí!** I don't think you can do it — I bet I can!; **van a subir la gasolina — ¡pues sí que…!** gas prices are going up — what a pain!; **pero no me negarás que la obra es divertida — eso sí** but you can't deny that the play's entertaining — that's true; **¿sí?** (*incredulidad*) really?; (*¿de acuerdo?*) all right?

  2 *pron personal* (a) (*reflexivo*) (*de personas*) (*singular*) himself, *f* herself, (*plural*) themselves; (*usted*) yourself, *pl* yourselves; (*de cosas, animales*) itself, *pl* themselves; **lo quiere todo para sí (misma)** she wants everything for herself; **se acercó la silla hacia sí** he drew the chair nearer (himself); **de (por) sí** (*cosa*) in itself (b) (*reflexivo impersonal*) oneself; **cuando uno piensa en sí mismo** when one thinks about oneself, when you think about yourself

  3 *nm* consent; **dar el sí** to give one's consent

Siam *n* Siam

siamés, -esa 1 *adj* Siamese; **hermanos siameses** Siamese twins

  2 *nm,f* (a) (*de Siam*) Siamese person, Thai (b) (*gemelo*) Siamese twin

  3 *nm* (*gato*) Siamese

sibarita 1 *adj* sybaritic

  2 *nmf* sybarite, epicure

sibaritismo *nm* sybaritism, epicureanism

Siberia *n* Siberia

siberiano, -a *adj & nm,f* Siberian

sibila *nf Mitol* sibyl

sibilante *adj* sibilant

sibilino, -a *adj* (*incomprensible*) mysterious, cryptic

sic *adv* sic

sicario *nm* hired assassin

Sicilia *n* Sicily

siciliano, -a *adj & nm,f* Sicilian

sicoanálisis *nm inv* psychoanalysis

sicoanalista *nmf* psychoanalyst

sicoanalítico, -a *adj* psychoanalytic(al)

sicoanalizar [14] *vt* to psychoanalyze

sicodélico, -a *adj* psychedelic

sicodrama *nm* psychodrama

sicofármaco *nm* psychotropic *o* psychoactive drug

sicología *nf también Fig* psychology

sicológico, -a *adj* psychological

sicólogo, -a *nm,f* psychologist

sicometría *nf* psychometrics (*singular*)

sicomoro, sicómoro *nm* (*planta*) sycamore

sicomotricidad *nf* psychomotricity

sicópata *nmf* psychopath

sicopatía *nf* psychopathy, psychopathic personality

sicosis *nf inv* psychosis

sicosomático, -a *adj* psychosomatic

sicotécnico, -a 1 *adj* psychotechnical

  2 *nm,f* psychotechnician

  3 *nm* (*prueba*) psychotechnical test

sicoterapia *nf* psychotherapy

sicotrópico, -a *adj* psychotropic, psychoactive

sida *nm* (*abrev de* **síndrome de inmunodeficiencia adquirida**) AIDS

sidecar [siðe'kar] *nm* sidecar

sideral *adj* sidereal

siderurgia *nf* iron and steel industry

siderúrgico, -a *adj Ind* iron and steel; **el sector s.** the iron and steel industry

sidoso, -a *Fam Pey* 1 *adj* suffering from AIDS

  2 *nm,f* AIDS sufferer

sidra *nf* hard cider

sidrería *nf* hard-cider bar

siega 1 *ver* **segar**

  2 *nf* (a) (*acción*) reaping, harvesting (b) (*época*) harvest (time)

siembra 1 *ver* **sembrar**

  2 *nf* (a) (*acción*) sowing (b) (*época*) sowing time

siempre 1 *adv* (a) (*todo el tiempo*) always; **tú s. quejándote** you're always complaining; **somos amigos de s.** we've always been friends; **como s.** as usual; **lo de s.** the usual; **hemos quedado en el bar de s.** we've arranged to meet at the usual bar; **hasta s.** farewell; **para s., para s. jamás** for ever and ever (b) (*en cualquier caso*) always; **s. es mejor estar preparado** it's always better to be prepared; **si no hay autobuses s. podemos ir a pie** if there aren't any buses, we can always walk (c) *Am* (*todavía*) still; **s. viven allí** they still live there, they're still living there

  2 **siempre y cuando** *loc conj* provided that, as long as

  3 **siempre que** *loc conj* (*cada vez que*) whenever; (*siempre y cuando*) provided that, as long as

siempreviva *nf* everlasting flower

sien *nf* temple

siento *etc* (a) *ver* **sentar** (b) *ver* **sentir**

sierpe *nf Anticuado* serpent

sierra 1 *ver* **serrar**

  2 *nf* (a) (*herramienta*) saw; **s. eléctrica** power saw; **s. mecánica** chain saw (b) (*cordillera*) mountain range (c) (*región montañosa*) mountains; **se van a la s. los fines de semana** they go to the mountains at the weekend

Sierra Leona *n* Sierra Leone

siervo, -a *nm,f* (a) (*esclavo*) serf (b) *Rel* servant

siesta *nf* siesta, nap; **dormir** *o* **echarse la s.** to have an afternoon nap

siete 1 *núm* seven; **las s. y media** = card game, related to blackjack, in which players aim to get seven and a half points; *ver también* **seis**

  2 *nm* (*roto*) tear (*right-angled in shape*)

  3 *nf RP Fam* **de la gran s.** amazing, incredible; **¡la gran s.!** shoot!

sietemesino, -a 1 *adj* premature (*by two months*)

  2 *nm,f* premature baby (*by two months*)

sífilis *nf inv* syphilis

sifilítico, -a *adj & nm,f Med* syphilitic

sifón *nm* (**a**) *(agua carbónica)* soda (water) (**b**) *(de WC)* trap (**c**) *(tubo)* siphon

SIG [siχ] *nm Inform* *(abrev de* **sistema de información geográfica**) GIS

sigilo *nm (secreto)* secrecy; *(al robar, escapar)* stealth

sigiloso, -a *adj (discreto)* secretive; *(al robar, escapar)* stealthy

sigla *nf* letter *(in an acronym);* **siglas (de)** *(acrónimo)* acronym (for)

siglo *nm* (**a**) *(cien años)* century; **el s. XX** the 20th century; **el s. de las Luces** the Age of Enlightenment (**b**) *(mucho tiempo)* **hace siglos que no la veo** I haven't seen her for ages; **por los siglos de los siglos** for ever and ever

signatario, -a *adj & nm,f* signatory

signatura *nf* (**a**) *(en biblioteca)* catalog number (**b**) *(firma)* signature

significación *nf* (**a**) *(importancia)* significance (**b**) *(significado)* meaning

significado, -a 1 *adj* important
  2 *nm* (**a**) *(sentido)* meaning (**b**) *Ling* signifier

significante *nm Ling* signifier

significar [59] **1** *vt* (**a**) *(querer decir)* to mean; **la luz roja significa que está en funcionamiento** the red light means (that) it's working (**b**) *(suponer, causar)* to mean; **eso significaría una subida de los precios** that would mean a price rise (**c**) *(expresar)* to express
  2 *vi (tener importancia)* **no significa nada para mí** it means nothing to me
  3 significarse *vpr* **significarse por** to become known for; **se significó como pacifista** he showed himself to be a pacifist

significativo, -a *adj* significant

signo *nm* (**a**) *(señal)* sign; **el acuerdo nace bajo el s. del fracaso** the agreement is doomed to failure (**b**) *(matemático)* sign; **s. de división** division sign; **s. más** plus sign; **s. menos** minus sign; **s. de multiplicar** multiplication sign (**c**) *(en la escritura)* mark; **s. de admiración** exclamation point; **s. de interrogación** question mark (**d**) *(del zodiaco)* (star) sign; **¿de qué s. eres?** what (star) sign are you?

sigo *etc ver* **seguir**

siguiente 1 *adj* (**a**) *(en el tiempo, espacio)* next; **me llamó al día s.** she called me the next *o* following day; **eso está explicado en el capítulo s.** that is explained in the next chapter; **el día s. a la catástrofe** the day after the disaster (**b**) *(a continuación)* following; **me contó la s. historia** he told me the following story; **lo s.** the following
  2 *nmf* **el s.** the next one; **¡el s.!** next, please!

siguiera *etc ver* **seguir**

sij *(pl* **sijs)** *adj & nmf* Sikh

sílaba *nf* syllable

silabear 1 *vt* to spell out syllable by syllable
  2 *vi* to read syllable by syllable

silábico, -a *adj* syllabic

silbante *adj (respiración)* whistling

silbar 1 *vt* (**a**) *(melodía)* to whistle; *(como piropo)* to whistle at (**b**) *(abuchear)* to whistle at
  2 *vi* (**a**) *(con melodía)* to whistle (**b**) *(abuchear)* (**c**) *(oídos)* to ring

silbato *nm* whistle

silbido *nm* (**a**) *(sonido)* whistle; **el s. del viento** the whistling of the wind (**b**) *(para abuchear, de serpiente)* whistle; **los silbidos del público eran ensordecedores** the whistling of the crowd was deafening; **su actuación fue recibida con silbidos y abucheos** her performance was greeted with booing and hissing

silenciador *nm (de arma)* silencer; *(de vehículo)* muffler

silenciar *vt* to hush up, to keep quiet

silencio *nm* (**a**) *(en general)* silence; **el s. reinaba en la habitación** there was complete *o* absolute silence in the room; **¡s.!** silence!, quiet!; **¡s. en la sala!** silence in court!; **en s.** in silence; **guardar s. (sobre algo)** to keep silent (about sth); **guardaron un minuto de s.** they held a minute's silence; **romper el s.** to break the silence; **s. administrativo** = lack of official response to a request, claim, etc. within a given period, signifying refusal or tacit assent, depending on circumstances (**b**) *Mús* rest

silencioso, -a *adj* silent, quiet

sílex *nm inv* flint

sílfide *nf* sylph; **está hecha una s.** she's really slim

silicato *nm* silicate

sílice *nf* silica

silicio *nm* silicon

silicona *nf* silicone

silicosis *nf inv* silicosis

silla *nf* chair; **s. eléctrica** electric chair; **s. giratoria** swivel chair; **s. de manos** sedan chair; **s. (de montar)** saddle; *Esp* **s. de niño** pushchair; **s. de pista** courtside seat; **s. plegable** folding chair; **s. de la reina** = seat made by two people joining hands; **s. de ruedas** wheelchair

sillar *nm Arquit* ashlar

sillería *nf (sillas)* set of chairs; **la s. del coro** the choir stalls

sillín *nm* saddle, seat

sillita *nf (de niño)* pushchair

sillón *nm* armchair

silo *nm* silo

silogismo *nm* syllogism

silueta *nf* (**a**) *(cuerpo)* figure (**b**) *(contorno)* outline (**c**) *(dibujo)* silhouette

silvestre *adj* wild

silvicultura *nf* forestry

SIM *nm Tel* *(abrev de* **subscriber identity module**) SIM; **tarjeta SIM** SIM card

sima *nf* chasm

simbiosis *nf inv* symbiosis

simbiótico, -a *adj* symbiotic

simbólico, -a *adj* symbolic

simbolismo *nm* symbolism

simbolista *adj & nmf* symbolist

simbolizar [14] *vt* to symbolize

símbolo *nm* symbol; **s. del euro** euro sign *o* symbol; **s. fálico** phallic symbol; **s. sexual** sex symbol

simbología *nf* system of symbols

simetría *nf* symmetry

simétrico, -a *adj* symmetrical

simiente *nf* seed

simiesco, -a *adj* simian, ape-like

símil *nm* (**a**) *(paralelismo)* similarity, resemblance (**b**) *Lit* simile

similar *adj* similar (**a** to)

similitud *nf* similarity

simio, -a *nm,f* simian, ape

simpatía *nf* (**a**) *(cordialidad)* friendliness (**b**) *(cariño)* affection; **tomar** *o Esp* **coger s. a alguien** to take a liking to sb; **ganarse la s. de** to win the affection of; **inspirar s.** to inspire affection; **tener s. a, sentir s. por** to like (**c**) **simpatías** *(apoyo)* support (**d**) *Med* sympathy

simpático, -a *adj* (**a**) *(persona) (agradable)* nice, likeable; *(abierto, cordial)* friendly; **estuvo muy s. conmigo** he was very friendly to me; **hacerse el s.** to be all friendly (**b**) *(anécdota, comedia)* amusing, entertaining (**c**) *Anat* sympathetic

simpatizante 1 *adj* sympathizing
  2 *nmf* sympathizer

simpatizar [14] *vi (persona)* to hit it off (**con** with), to get on (**con** with); *(cosa)* to sympathize (**con** with); **simpatiza con**

la ideología comunista she has communist sympathies

simple 1 *adj* (**a**) *(sin componentes)* simple (**b**) *(sencillo, tonto)* simple (**c**) *(fácil)* simple, easy; **es muy s., metes la moneda y ya está** it's quite simple, all you have to do is insert the coin (**d**) *(mero)* mere; **por s. estupidez** through sheer stupidity; **nos basta con su s. palabra** his word is enough for us by itself; **no le pedí más que un s. favor** all I asked him for was a favor (**e**) *Mat* prime

2 *nmf (persona)* simpleton

simplemente *adv* simply; **su actuación fue, s., vergonzosa** his behavior was, quite simply, disgraceful; **es s. genial** it's simply *o* just brilliant; **s. quería que supieras que lo siento** I just wanted you to know that I'm sorry; **s. por eso ya se merecería un ascenso** for that alone he would deserve promotion

simpleza *nf* (**a**) *(de persona)* simple-mindedness (**b**) *(tontería)* trifle

simplicidad *nf* simplicity

simplificación *nf* simplification

simplificar [59] **1** *vt* to simplify

2 simplificarse *vpr* to be simplified

simplismo *nm* oversimplification

simplista 1 *adj* simplistic

2 *nmf* naïve person

simplón, -ona 1 *adj* simple, simpleminded

2 *nm,f* simpleminded person

simposio, simposium *nm* symposium

simulación *nf* pretense, simulation; **s. por ordenador** computer simulation

simulacro *nm* simulation; **s. de combate** mock battle; **s. de incendio** fire drill

simulado, -a *adj* (**a**) *(fingido)* feigned; **su tristeza era simulada** he was only pretending to be sad (**b**) *(de prueba)* simulated

simulador *nm* simulator; **s. de vuelo** flight simulator

simular *vt* (**a**) *(aparentar)* to feign; **s. una enfermedad** to pretend to have an illness; **simuló que no me había visto** he pretended not to have seen me (**b**) *(copiar, emular)* to simulate

simultanear *vt* to do at the same time (**con** as)

simultaneidad *nf* simultaneousness

simultáneo, -a *adj* simultaneous

sin 1 *prep* without; **buscan gente s. experiencia previa** they are looking for people with no *o* without previous experience; **s. alcohol** alcohol-free; **ha escrito cinco libros s. (contar) las novelas** he has written five books, not counting his novels; **está s. hacer** it hasn't been done yet; **estamos s. vino** we're out of wine; **muchos se quedaron s. casa** a lot of people were left homeless, a lot of people lost their homes; **lleva tres noches s. dormir** she hasn't slept for three nights; **s. que** without; **s. que nadie se enterara** without anyone noticing; **s. más (ni más)** just like that

2 sin embargo *loc conj* however

sinagoga *nf* synagogue

Sinaí *nm* **el monte S.** Mount Sinai; **el S., la península del S.** the Sinai Peninsula

sinapsis *nf inv Fisiol* synapse

sincerarse *vpr* to open one's heart (**con alguien** to sb)

sinceridad *nf* sincerity; **con toda s.** in all honesty *o* sincerity

sincero, -a *adj* sincere; **para serte s.,…** to be honest *o* frank,…

síncopa *nf* (**a**) *(en palabra)* syncope (**b**) *Mús* syncopation

sincopado, -a *adj* syncopated

sincopar *vt* to syncopate

síncope *nm* blackout; *Fam Fig* **le dio un s.** he had a fit

sincretismo *nm* syncretism

sincronía *nf* (**a**) *(simultaneidad)* simultaneity (**b**) *Ling* synchrony

sincrónico, -a *adj* (**a**) *(simultáneo)* simultaneous (**b**) *(coordinado)* synchronous (**c**) *Ling* synchronic

sincronismo *nm* (**a**) *(simultaneidad)* simultaneity (**b**) *Fís* tuning

sincronización *nf* synchronization

sincronizar [14] *vt* (**a**) *(coordinar)* to synchronize; **sincronizaron los relojes** they synchronized their watches (**b**) *Fís* to tune

síncrono, -a *adj Inform* synchronous

sindicación *nf* labor union membership

sindicado, -a *adj* **estar s.** to belong to a (labor) union, to be unionized

sindical *adj* (labor) union; **organización s.** labor union organization

sindicalismo *nm* unionism

sindicalista *nmf* union member

sindicar [59] **1** *vt* to unionize

2 sindicarse *vpr* to join a union

sindicato *nm* union, labor union; **s. amarillo** yellow union, = conservative trade union that leans towards the employers' interests; **s. obrero** blue-collar union; *Esp* **s. vertical** = workers' and employers' union during the Franco period

síndico *nm* (**a**) *(representante)* community representative (**b**) *(administrador)* (official) receiver (**c**) *Fin* trustee; **s. de la Bolsa** = Chairman of the Spanish Stock Exchange Commission

síndrome *nm* syndrome; **s. de abstinencia** withdrawal symptoms; **s. de Down** Down's syndrome; **s. de Estocolmo** Stockholm syndrome; **s. de inmunodeficiencia adquirida** acquired immune deficiency syndrome; **s. de la muerte súbita infantil** sudden infant death syndrome; **s. premenstrual** premenstrual syndrome

sinecura *nf* sinecure

sine die 1 *adj* **un aplazamiento s.** an indefinite postponement

2 *adv* indefinitely

sinergia *nf* synergy

sinestesia *nf* synesthesia

sinfín *nm* vast number; **un s. de problemas** no end of problems

sinfonía *nf* symphony

sinfónico, -a *adj* symphonic

Singapur *n* Singapore

singladura *nf Náut (distancia)* day's run; *Fig (dirección)* course

single ['singel] *nm* single

singular 1 *adj* (**a**) *(raro)* peculiar, odd (**b**) *(único)* unique; **s. batalla** single combat (**c**) *Gram* singular

2 *nm Gram* singular; **en s.** in the singular

singularidad *nf* (**a**) *(rareza, peculiaridad)* peculiarity; **una de las singularidades de esta especie** one of the special characteristics of this species (**b**) *(exclusividad)* uniqueness

singularizar [14] **1** *vt* to distinguish, to single out

2 singularizarse *vpr* to stand out, to be conspicuous

siniestra *nf Anticuado* left hand

siniestrado, -a 1 *adj (coche, avión)* crashed, smashed up; *(edificio)* ruined, destroyed

2 *nm,f* victim

siniestralidad *nf* accident rate

siniestro, -a 1 *adj* (**a**) *(malo)* sinister (**b**) *(desgraciado)* disastrous

2 *nm (daño, catástrofe)* disaster; *(accidente de coche)* accident, crash; *(incendio)* fire; *(atentado)* terrorist attack; **s. total** total wreck

sinnúmero *nm* **un s. de** countless

sino[1] *nm* fate, destiny

sino[2] *conj* (**a**) *(para contraponer)* but; **no lo hizo él, s. ella** he didn't do it, she did; **no sólo es listo, s. también trabajador** he's not only clever but also hardworking (**b**) *(para exceptuar)* except, but; **¿quién s. tú lo haría?** who else but you would do it?; **no quiero s. que se haga justicia** I only want justice to be done

sínodo *nm* synod

sinonimia *nf* synonymy

sinónimo, -a 1 *adj* synonymous
2 *nm* synonym

sinopsis *nf inv* synopsis

sinóptico, -a *adj* synoptic; **cuadro s.** tree diagram

sinovial *adj* synovial

sinrazón *nf* injustice

sinsabores *nmpl* trouble, upsetting experiences; **ese trabajo me causó muchos s.** the job gave me a lot of headaches

sinsentido *nm* **decir un s.** to say something stupid

sintáctico, -a *adj* syntactic

sintagma *nm* **s. nominal/verbal** noun/verb phrase

sintaxis *nf inv* syntax

síntesis *nf inv* synthesis; **en s.** in short; **esta obra hace una s. de sus ideas sobre el tema** this work draws together his ideas on the subject; *Inform & Ling* **s. del habla** speech synthesis

sintético, -a *adj* (**a**) *(artificial)* synthetic (**b**) *(conciso)* concise

sintetizador, -ora 1 *adj* synthesizing
2 *nm* synthesizer

sintetizar [14] *vt* (**a**) *(resumir)* to summarize; *(reunir)* to draw together (**b**) *(fabricar artificialmente)* to synthesize

sintiera *etc ver* **sentir**

sintoísmo *nm* Shintoism

sintoísta *adj & nmf* Shintoist

síntoma *nm* symptom

sintomático, -a *adj* symptomatic

sintomatología *nf* symptoms

sintonía *nf* (**a**) *(música)* theme song (**b**) *(conexión)* tuning (**c**) *(compenetración)* harmony

sintonización *nf* (**a**) *(conexión)* tuning (**b**) *(compenetración)* harmonization

sintonizador *nm* tuner, tuning dial

sintonizar [14] **1** *vt (conectar)* to tune in to
2 *vi* (**a**) *(conectar)* to tune in (**con** to) (**b**) *(compenetrarse)* **s. en algo (con alguien)** to be on the same wavelength (as sb) about sth

sinuosidad *nf* bend, wind

sinuoso, -a *adj* (**a**) *(camino)* winding (**b**) *(movimiento)* sinuous (**c**) *(disimulado)* devious

sinusitis *nf inv* sinusitis

sinvergüenza 1 *adj* (**a**) *(canalla)* shameless (**b**) *(fresco, descarado)* cheeky
2 *nmf* (**a**) *(canalla)* rogue (**b**) *(fresco, descarado)* cheeky person

sionismo *nm* Zionism

sionista *adj & nmf* Zionist

sioux ['siuks] *o* ['sius] *adj inv & nmf inv* Sioux

siquiatra *nmf* psychiatrist

siquiatría *nf* psychiatry

siquiátrico, -a 1 *adj* psychiatric
2 *nm* psychiatric *o* mental hospital

síquico, -a *adj* psychic

siquiera 1 *conj (aunque)* even if; **ven s. por pocos días** do come, even if it's only for a few days
2 *adv (por lo menos)* at least; **dime s. tu nombre** (you could) at least tell me your name; **ni (tan) s.** not even; **ni (tan) s. me hablaron** they didn't even speak to me

sirena *nf* (**a**) *Mitol* mermaid, siren (**b**) *(señal)* siren

Siria *n* Syria

sirimiri *nm* drizzle

sirio, -a *adj & nm,f* Syrian

sirlero, -a *nm,f Fam* = thug who carries a knife

siroco *nm* sirocco; *Fam* **le ha dado el s.** she's had a brainstorm

sirope *nm* golden syrup; **s. de fresa/chocolate** *(para helado)* strawberry/chocolate sauce

sirviente, -a *nm,f* servant

sirviera *etc ver* **servir**

sirvo *etc ver* **servir**

sisa *nf* (**a**) *(de manga)* armhole (**b**) *(de dinero)* pilfering

sisal *nm* sisal

sisar *vt & vi Esp* to pilfer

sisear *vt & vi* to hiss

siseo *nm* hiss, hissing

sísmico, -a *adj* seismic; **zona sísmica** earthquake zone

sismo *nm* earthquake

sismógrafo *nm* seismograph

sismología *nf* seismology

sisón, -ona 1 *adj* pilfering
2 *nm,f (ladrón)* pilferer, petty thief
3 *nm (ave)* little bustard

sistema *nm* (**a**) *(conjunto ordenado)* system; **por s.** systematically; **s. circulatorio** circulatory system; **s. decimal** decimal system; **s. fiscal** *o* **impositivo** tax system; **s. inmunológico** immune system; **s. internacional de unidades** SI system; **s. métrico (decimal)** metric (decimal) system; **s. monetario europeo** European Monetary System; **s. montañoso** mountain chain *o* range; **s. nervioso** nervous system; **s. periódico de los elementos** periodic table of elements; **s. de seguridad** security system; **s. solar** solar system
(**b**) *(método, orden)* method
(**c**) *(político)* **el s.** the establishment
(**d**) *Inform* system; **s. experto/operativo** expert/operating system

Sistema Ibérico *nm* **el S.** the Iberian mountain chain

sistemático, -a *adj* systematic

sistematización *nf* systematization

sistematizar [14] *vt* to systematize

sistémico, -a *adj* systemic

sístole *nf* systole

sitar *nm* sitar

sitiado, -a *adj* besieged

sitiador, -a 1 *adj* besieging
2 *nm,f* besieger

sitial *nm Formal* seat of honor

sitiar *vt* (**a**) *(cercar)* to besiege (**b**) *(acorralar)* to surround

sitio *nm* (**a**) *(lugar)* place; **cambiar de s. (con alguien)** to change places (with sb); **en cualquier s.** anywhere; **en ningún s.** nowhere; **en otro s.** elsewhere; **en todos los sitios** everywhere; **no queda ni un s. (libre)** *(en cine, teatro)* there isn't a single free seat; *Fig* **poner a alguien en su s.** to put sb in their place; *Inform* **s. web** web site (**b**) *(espacio)* room, space; **hacer s. a alguien** to make room for sb; **ocupa mucho s.** it takes up a lot of room *o* space; **no queda más s.** there's no more room (**c**) *(cerco)* siege (**d**) *Méx (de taxis)* taxi stand

sito, -a *adj* located

situación *nf* (**a**) *(circunstancias)* situation; *(legal, social)* status; **s. económica** economic situation; **s. límite** extreme *o* critical situation (**b**) *(estado, condición)* state, condition; **estar en s. de hacer algo** *(en general)* to be in a position to do sth; *(sujeto: enfermo, borracho)* to be in a fit state to do sth (**c**) *(ubicación)* location

situado, -a *adj* (**a**) *(ubicado)* located; **estar bien s.** *(casa)* to be conveniently located; *Fig* to be well-placed (**b**) *(acomodado)* comfortably off

situar [4] **1** *vt* (**a**) *(colocar)* to place, to put; *(edificio, ciudad)* to site, to locate; **situó la acción de la novela en la Edad Media** he set the novel in the Middle Ages; **me suena pero no lo sitúo** he sounds familiar, but I can't place him (**b**) *(en clasificación)* **su victoria les sitúa en el primer puesto** their win moves them up to first place; **la nueva obra lo sitúa entre los artistas más importantes de su generación** his latest work places him among the most important artists of his generation

2 situarse *vpr* (**a**) *(colocarse)* to take up position (**b**) *(ubicarse)* to be located; **está cerca de la plaza, ¿te sitúas?** it's near the square, do you know where I mean? (**c**) *(desarrollarse) (acción)* to be set (**d**) *(acomodarse, establecerse)* to get oneself established (**e**) *(en clasificación)* to be placed; **se sitúa entre los mejores** he's (ranked) among the best

siútico, -a *adj Chile Fam* stuck-up

skateboard [es'keidβor] (*pl* **skateboards**) *nm* (**a**) *(tabla)* skateboard (**b**) *(deporte)* skateboarding

skay [es'kai] *nm* Leatherette®

sketch [es'ketʃ] (*pl* **sketches**) *nm Cine & Teatro* sketch

skin head [es'kinχeð] (*pl* **skin heads**) *nmf* skinhead

S.L. *nf* (*abrev de* **sociedad limitada**) ≃ Inc

slalom [es'lalom] (*pl* **slaloms**) *nm Dep* slalom; **s. gigante** giant slalom

slip [es'lip] (*pl* **slips**) *nm* briefs

SM (*abrev de* **Su Majestad**) HM

smash [es'maʃ] (*pl* **smashes**) *nm Dep* smash

SME *nm* (*abrev de* **Sistema Monetario Europeo**) EMS

SMI *nm* (**a**) (*abrev de* **sistema monetario internacional**) IMS (**b**) (*abrev de* **salario mínimo interprofesional**) minimum wage

SMS *nm Tel* (*abrev de* **short message service**) SMS; **un mensaje SMS** an SMS

s/n (*abrev de* **sin número**) = abbreviation used in addresses after the street name, where the building has no number

snob (*pl* **snobs**) **1** *adj* trying to be trendy
2 *nmf* person who wants to be trendy

snobismo *nm* desire to be trendy

snowboard [es'nouβor] (*pl* **snowboards**) *nm* (**a**) *(tabla)* snowboard (**b**) *(deporte)* snowboarding

so 1 *prep* under; **so pretexto de** under the pretext of
2 *adv* **¡so tonto!** you idiot!
3 *interj* **¡so, caballo!** whoa!

soba *nf Fam (paliza)* hiding; **dar una s. a alguien** to give sb a good hiding

sobaco *nm* armpit

sobado, -a *adj* (**a**) *(cuello, puños)* worn, shabby; *(libro)* dog-eared (**b**) *(argumento, tema)* well-worn, hackneyed

sobao *nm Culin* = small, flat, square sponge cake

sobaquera *nf* armhole

sobaquina *nf Fam* body odor, BO

sobar 1 *vt* (**a**) *(tocar)* to finger, to paw; *Fam (persona)* to touch up, to fondle (**b**) *(ablandar)* to soften
2 *vi Esp Fam* to catch some z's

soberanamente *adv* (**a**) *(independientemente)* independently, free from outside interference (**b**) *(enormemente)* incredibly, unbelievably

soberanía *nf* sovereignty

soberano, -a 1 *adj* (**a**) *(independiente)* sovereign (**b**) *(grande) (paliza)* thorough; *(belleza, calidad)* supreme, unrivaled; **decir/hacer una soberana tontería** to say/do something unbelievably stupid
2 *nm,f* sovereign

soberbia *nf* (**a**) *(arrogancia)* pride, arrogance (**b**) *(magnificencia)* grandeur, splendor

soberbio, -a 1 *adj* (**a**) *(arrogante)* proud, arrogant (**b**) *(magnífico)* superb, magnificent
2 *nm,f (persona)* arrogant o proud person

sobón, -ona *adj & nm,f Fam* groper

sobornable *adj* bribable

sobornar *vt* to bribe

soborno *nm* (**a**) *(acción)* bribery (**b**) *(dinero, regalo)* bribe

sobra 1 *nf* excess, surplus; **de s.** *(en exceso)* more than enough; *(de más)* superfluous; **aquí estoy de s., me voy** I'm off, it's obvious I'm not wanted here; **lo sabemos de s.** we know it only too well
2 sobras *nfpl* (**a**) *(de comida)* leftovers (**b**) *(de tela)* remnants

sobradamente *adv* **s. conocido** extremely well-known; **como es s. conocido…** as I/we *etc* know all too well…

sobrado, -a *adj* (**a**) *(de sobra)* more than enough, plenty of (**b**) *(de dinero)* well-off; **estar s. de dinero** to have more than enough money

sobrante 1 *adj* remaining
2 *nm* surplus

sobrar *vi* (**a**) *(quedar, restar)* to be left over, to be spare; **nos sobró comida** we had some food left over (**b**) *(haber de más)* to be more than enough; **parece que van a s. bocadillos** it looks like there are going to be too many sandwiches (**c**) *(estar de más)* to be superfluous; **lo que dices sobra** that goes without saying; *Fig* **aquí sobra alguien** someone here is not welcome

sobrasada *nf* = Mallorcan spicy pork sausage that can be spread

sobre¹ *nm* (**a**) *(para cartas)* envelope (**b**) *(para alimentos, medicamentos)* sachet, packet (**c**) *Am (bolsa)* clutch bag (**d**) *Fam (cama)* sack; **irse al s.** to hit the sack

sobre² *prep* (**a**) *(encima de)* on (top of); **fui apilando las tejas una s. otra** I piled the tiles up one on top of the other; **el libro está s. la mesa** the book is on (top of) the table; **varios policías saltaron s. él** several policemen fell upon him; **una cruz roja s. fondo blanco** a red cross o against a white background
(**b**) *(por encima de)* over, above; **el pato vuela s. el lago** the duck is flying over the lake; **a 3.000 metros s. el nivel del mar** 3,000 meters above sea level
(**c**) *(acerca de)* about, on; **un libro s. el amor** a book about o on love; **una conferencia s. el desarme** a conference on disarmament
(**d**) *(aproximadamente)* about; **llegarán s. las diez** they'll arrive at about ten o'clock
(**e**) *(superioridad)* **su opinión está s. las de los demás** his opinion is more important than that of the others; **tiene muchas ventajas s. el antiguo modelo** it has a lot of advantages over the old model
(**f**) *(acumulación)* upon; **nos contó mentira s. mentira** he told us lie upon lie o one lie after another
(**g**) *(cerca de)* upon; **la desgracia estaba ya s. nosotros** the disaster was already upon us

sobreabundancia *nf* excess

sobreabundante *adj* excessive

sobreabundar *vi* to abound

sobreactuar [4] *vi* to overact

sobrealimentación *nf* overfeeding

sobrealimentar *vt* to overfeed

sobreañadido *nm* unnecessary addition

sobreañadir *vt* to add on top of

sobrecalentamiento *nm* overheating

sobrecalentar [3] *vt* to overheat

sobrecarga *nf* (**a**) *(exceso de carga)* excess weight (**b**) *(saturación)* overload

sobrecargado, -a adj overloaded

sobrecargar [38] vt (con peso, trabajo) to overload; (decoración) to overdo

sobrecargo nm (**a**) Náut supercargo; Av flight attendant (**b**) Com surcharge

sobrecogedor, -ora adj frightening, startling

sobrecoger [52] **1** vt to frighten, to startle
   2 sobrecogerse vpr to be frightened, to be startled

sobrecoste, sobrecosto nm extra costs

sobrecubierta nf (**a**) (de libro) book jacket (**b**) (de barco) upper deck

sobredosis nf inv overdose

sobreentender, sobrentender [64] **1** vt to understand, to deduce
   2 sobreentenderse vpr to be inferred o implied

sobreentendido, -a adj implied, implicit

sobreesdrújula = sobresdrújula

sobreesdrújulo, -a = sobresdrújulo

sobreexcitar = sobrexcitar

sobreexponer = sobrexponer

sobreexposición = sobrexposición

sobrefusión nf supercooling

sobregiro nm Com overdraft

sobrehilar vt to whipstitch

sobrehumano, -a adj superhuman

sobreimpresión nf superimposing

sobreimprimir vt to superimpose

sobrellevar vt to bear, to endure

sobremanera adv exceedingly

sobremesa nf **quedarse de s.** to stay at the table (talking, playing cards etc); **la programación de s.** afternoon TV (programs)

sobrenadar vi to float

sobrenatural adj supernatural; **poderes sobrenaturales** supernatural powers

sobrenombre nm nickname

sobrentender = sobreentender

sobrepasar vt (**a**) (exceder) to exceed (**b**) (aventajar) **s. a alguien** to overtake sb

sobrepelliz nf surplice

sobrepeso nm excess weight

sobreponer [50] **1** vt (**a**) (poner encima) to put on top (**b**) (anteponer) **s. algo a algo** to put sth before sth
   2 sobreponerse vpr **sobreponerse a algo** to overcome sth

sobreposición nf superimposing

sobreproducción nf Econ overproduction

sobreproteger [52] vt to overprotect

sobrepuesto, -a 1 participio ver **sobreponer**
   2 adj superimposed

sobrepujar vt to outdo, to surpass

sobresaliente 1 adj (destacado) outstanding
   2 nm (nota) excellent, ≃ A

sobresalir [60] vi (**a**) (en tamaño) to jut out, to stick out; **el tejado sobresale varios metros** the roof juts out several meters; **la enagua le sobresale por debajo de la falda** her petticoat is showing beneath her skirt (**b**) (en importancia) to stand out; **sobresale por su inteligencia** he is outstandingly intelligent

sobresaltar 1 vt to startle
   2 sobresaltarse vpr to be startled, to start

sobresalto nm start, fright; **dar un s. a alguien** to make sb start, to give sb a fright

sobresaturar vt to supersaturate

sobrescribir vt to overwrite

sobrescrito, -a participio ver **sobrescribir**

sobresdrújula, sobreesdrújula nf = word stressed on the fourth-to-last syllable

sobresdrújulo, -a, sobreesdrújulo, -a adj = stressed on the fourth-to-last syllable

sobreseer [37] vt Der to discontinue, to stay

sobreseimiento nm Der stay

sobrestimar vt to overestimate

sobresueldo nm extra money on the side

sobretasa nf surcharge

sobretodo nm overcoat

sobrevalorado, -a adj (artista, obra) overrated; (casa, acciones) overvalued

sobrevalorar 1 vt (artista, obra) to overrate; (casa, acciones) to overvalue
   2 sobrevalorarse vpr to have too high an opinion of oneself

sobrevenir [69] vi to happen, to ensue; **sobrevino la guerra** the war intervened

sobreviviente 1 adj surviving
   2 nmf survivor

sobrevivir vi to survive; **s. a alguien** to outlive sb

sobrevolar [63] vt to fly over

sobrexcitar, sobreexcitar vt to overexcite
   2 sobrexcitarse vpr to get overexcited

sobrexponer, sobreexponer [50] vt to overexpose

sobrexposición, sobreexposición nf overexposure

sobriedad nf (**a**) (moderación) restraint, moderation; (sencillez) simplicity, sobriety (**b**) (no embriaguez) soberness

sobrino, -a nm, f nephew, f niece

sobrio, -a adj (**a**) (moderado) restrained; (no excesivo) simple; **s. en** moderate in (**b**) (austero, no borracho) sober

SOC nm (abrev de **Sindicato de Obreros del Campo**) Spanish farm workers' union

socaire nm Náut lee; Fig **al s. de** under the protection of

socarrado, -a adj burned, scorched

socarrar 1 vt (quemar) to burn, to scorch
   2 socarrarse vpr to burn

socarrón, -ona adj ironic

socarronería nf irony, ironic humor

socavar vt (excavar por debajo) to dig under; Fig (debilitar) to undermine

socavón nm (**a**) (hoyo) hollow; (en la carretera) pothole (**b**) Min gallery

sociabilidad nf sociability

sociable adj sociable

social adj (**a**) (clase, organización, vida) social (**b**) Com **capital s.** equity capital; **sede s.** head office

socialdemocracia nf social democracy

socialdemócrata 1 adj social democratic
   2 nmf social democrat

socialismo nm socialism

socialista adj & nmf socialist

socialización nf Econ nationalization

socializar [14] vt Econ to nationalize

socialmente adv socially

sociedad nf (**a**) (de seres vivos) society; **las hormigas viven en s.** ants are social creatures; **entrar** o **presentarse en s.** to come out, to make one's debut; **alta s.** high society; **notas de s.** society column; **la s. civil** civilian society; **s. de consumo** consumer society; **la s. de la información** the information society; **la s. del ocio** the leisure society

   (**b**) Com (empresa) company; **s. anónima** incorporated company; **s. de cartera** portfolio company; **s. colectiva** general partnership; **s. comanditaria** o **en comandita** general and limited partnership; **s. industrial** industrial society; **s. mercantil** trading company; **s. (de responsa-**

bilidad) limitada private limited company

(**c**) *(asociación)* **s. deportiva** sports club; **s. gastronómica** dining club, gourmet club; **s. literaria** literary society; *Hist* **S. de Naciones** League of Nations

socio, -a *nm,f* (**a**) *Com* partner; **hacerse s. de una empresa** to become a partner in a company; **s. capitalista** *o* **comanditario** silent partner; **s. comercial** trading partner; **s. fundador** founding partner; **s. mayoritario** majority shareholder (**b**) *(miembro)* member; **hacerse s. de un club** to join a club; **s. honorario** *o* **de honor** honorary member; **s. de número** full member; **s. vitalicio** life member (**c**) *Fam (amigo)* buddy

sociocultural *adj* sociocultural

socioeconomía *nf* socioeconomics *(singular)*

socioeconómico, -a *adj* socioeconomic

sociolingüística *nf* sociolinguistics *(singular)*

sociolingüístico, -a *adj* sociolinguistic

sociología *nf* sociology

sociológico, -a *adj* sociological

sociólogo, -a *nm,f* sociologist

sociopolítico, -a *adj* sociopolitical

socorrer *vt* to help

socorrido, -a *adj (útil)* useful, handy

socorrismo *nm* first aid; *(en la playa)* lifesaving

socorrista *nmf* first-aid worker; *(en la playa)* lifeguard

socorro 1 *nm* help, aid

2 *interj* ¡**s.!** help!

soda *nf (bebida)* soda water

sódico, -a *adj* sodium; **cloruro s.** sodium chloride

sodio *nm* sodium

sodomía *nf* sodomy

sodomita *adj & nmf* sodomite

sodomizar [14] *vt* to sodomize

soez *adj* vulgar, dirty

sofá *nm* sofa; **s. cama** *o* **nido** sofa bed

Sofía *n* Sofia

sofisma *nm* sophism

sofisticación *nf* sophistication

sofisticado, -a *adj* sophisticated

soflama *nf Pey* harangue

sofocado, -a *adj* (**a**) *(por cansancio)* gasping for breath; *(por calor)* suffocating (**b**) *(por vergüenza)* mortified (**c**) *(por irritación)* hot under the collar

sofocante *adj* suffocating, stifling

sofocar [59] **1** *vt* (**a**) *(ahogar)* to suffocate, to stifle (**b**) *(incendio)* to put out, to smother (**c**) *(rebelión)* to suppress, to quell (**d**) *(avergonzar)* to mortify

2 sofocarse *vpr* (**a**) *(ahogarse)* to suffocate (**b**) *(avergonzarse)* to go red as a beet (**c**) *(irritarse)* to get hot under the collar (**por** about)

sofoco *nm* (**a**) *(ahogo)* breathlessness; *(sonrojo, bochorno)* hot flush (**b**) *(vergüenza)* mortification (**c**) *(disgusto)* **llevarse un s.** to have a fit

sofocón *nm Fam* **llevarse un s.** to get hot under the collar

sofoque *etc ver* **sofocar**

sofreír [56] *vt* to fry lightly over a low heat

sofría, sofriera *etc ver* **sofreír**

sofrito, -a 1 *participio ver* **sofreír**

2 *nm* = lightly fried onions and garlic, used as a base for sauces, stews etc

sofrología *nf* relaxation therapy

software ['sofwer] *nm Inform* software; **paquete de s.** software package; **s. integrado** integrated software; **s. de dominio público** public domain software

soga *nf* rope; *(para ahorcar)* noose; *Fig* **estar con la s. al cuello** to be in dire straits; *Fig* **mentar la s. en casa del**

ahorcado to really put one's foot in it *(by mentioning a sensitive subject)*

sois *ver* **ser**

soja *nf (planta, fruto)* soybean, soya bean; *(proteína)* soy

sojuzgar [38] *vt* to subjugate

sol *nm* (**a**) *(astro)* sun; **de s. a s.** from dawn to dusk; **s. naciente/poniente** rising/setting sun

(**b**) *(rayos, luz)* sunshine, sun; **estar/ponerse al s.** to be in/move into the sun; **entraba el s. por la ventana** sunlight was coming in through the window; **¡cómo pega o pica el s.!** the sun's really hot!; **hace s.** it's sunny; **hace un s. de justicia** it's blazing hot; **tomar el s.** to sunbathe; *Fam* **siempre se arrima al s. que más calienta** he sides with whoever is most beneficial for him at the time; *Fam* **no dejar a alguien ni a s. ni a sombra** to follow sb around wherever they go

(**c**) *(ángel, ricura)* darling, angel; **tu hermana es un s.** your sister's an angel

(**d**) *Mús* G; *(en solfeo)* so

(**e**) *(moneda)* sol; *Méx* **¿águila o s.?** heads or tails?

(**f**) *Taurom* = seats in the sun, the cheapest in the bullring

(**g**) **s. y sombra** *(bebida)* mixture of brandy and anisette

solamente *adv* only, just; **vino s. él** only he came

solana *nf* (**a**) *(lugar)* sunny spot (**b**) *(galería)* sun lounge

solano *nm* east wind

solapa *nf* (**a**) *(de prenda)* lapel (**b**) *(de libro, sobre)* flap

solapado, -a *adj* underhand, devious

solapamiento *nm* overlapping

solapar *vt* to cover up

solar 1 *adj* solar

2 *nm* undeveloped plot (of land)

solariego, -a *adj* ancestral

solario, solárium *(pl* **solariums***)* *nm* solarium

solaz *nm* (**a**) *(entretenimiento)* amusement, entertainment (**b**) *(descanso)* rest

solazar [14] **1** *vt* to amuse, to entertain

2 solazarse *vpr* to enjoy oneself

soldada *nf* pay

soldado *nm* soldier; **el s. desconocido** the Unknown Soldier; **s. de infantería** foot soldier; **s. de plomo** tin soldier; **s. de primera** private first class; **s. raso** private

soldador, -ora 1 *nm,f (persona)* welder

2 *nm (aparato)* soldering iron

soldadura *nf* (**a**) *(acción) (con material adicional)* soldering; *(sin material adicional)* welding (**b**) *(juntura) (con material adicional)* soldered joint; *(sin material adicional)* weld

soldar [63] *vt (con material adicional)* to solder; *(sin material adicional)* to weld

soleá *(pl* **soleares***)* *nf* = type of flamenco song and dance

soleado, -a *adj* sunny

solear *vt* to put in the sun

solecismo *nm* solecism

soledad *nf* loneliness; **vive en completa s.** he lives in complete solitude

solemne *adj* (**a**) *(con pompa, importante)* formal, solemn; *(serio)* solemn; **una promesa s.** a solemn promise (**b**) *(enorme)* utter, complete; **hacer/decir una s. tontería** to do/say something incredibly stupid

solemnidad *nf* (**a**) *(suntuosidad)* pomp, solemnity (**b**) *(acto)* ceremony

solemnizar [14] *vt* to celebrate, to commemorate

soler [41] *vi* (**a**) *(en presente)* **s. hacer algo** to do sth usually; **solemos comer fuera los viernes** we usually eat out on Fridays; **aquí suele llover mucho** it usually rains a lot here; **como se suele hacer en estos casos** as is customary in such cases; **este restaurante suele ser bueno** this restaurant is usually good (**b**) *(en pasado)* **solía ir a la playa**

cada día I used to go to the beach every day; **solíamos vernos más** we used to see more of each other

solera nf (a) (tradición) tradition (b) **vino de s.** (añejo) vintage wine (c) Chile (de acera) curb

solfa nf (a) Mús (tonic) sol-fa (b) Fam (paliza) thrashing (c) Fam **poner algo en s.** to make fun of sth

solfeo nm Mús music reading; **estudia primero de s.** he's in his first year of music theory; **saber s.** to be able to read music

solicitado, -a adj **estar muy s.** to be very popular, to be much sought after

solicitante 1 adj applying
2 nmf applicant

solicitar vt (a) (pedir) (información, permiso) to request; (empleo, préstamo) to apply for; **s. algo a** o **de alguien** to request sth of sb; **me han solicitado que lo haga** they've requested that I do it (b) (persona) to ask for; **le solicita el director de ventas** the sales manager wants to see you

solícito, -a adj solicitous, obliging

solicitud nf (a) (petición) (de información, permiso) request; (de empleo, préstamo) application (b) (documento) application form (c) (atención) attentiveness

solidaridad nf solidarity

solidario, -a adj (a) (actitud) supportive (**con** of); **un gesto s.** a gesture of solidarity; **contamos con el apoyo s. de nuestros compañeros en otras fábricas** we have the support of our fellow workers in other factories; **ser s. con alguien** to show solidarity with sb; **nos hacemos solidarios de vuestra causa** we join with you in your cause (b) (obligación, compromiso) mutually binding

solidarizarse [14] vpr to make common cause, to show one's solidarity

solidez nf (física) solidity; (moral) firmness

solidificación nf solidification

solidificar [59] **1** vt to solidify
2 solidificarse vpr to solidify

sólido, -a 1 adj (a) (en general) solid; (cimientos, fundamento) firm (b) (argumento, conocimiento, idea) sound (c) (color) fast
2 nm solid

soliloquio nm soliloquy

solista 1 adj solo
2 nmf soloist

solitaria nf (tenia) tapeworm

solitario, -a 1 adj (a) (persona, vida) solitary (b) (lugar) lonely, deserted
2 nm,f (persona) loner
3 nm (a) (diamante) solitaire (b) (juego) solitaire

soliviantar 1 vt (a) (excitar, incitar) to stir up (b) (indignar) to exasperate
2 soliviantarse vpr to be infuriated

solla nf plaice

sollozar [14] vi to sob

sollozo nm sob

solo, -a 1 adj (a) (sin nadie) alone; **me gusta estar s.** I like being alone o on my own o by myself; **¿vives s.?** do you live alone o on your own o by yourself ?; **lo hice yo s.** I did it on my own o by myself; Fam Fig **estar más s. que la una** to be all on one's own; **a solas** alone, by oneself (b) (solitario) lonely; **sentirse s.** to feel lonely (c) (sin nada más) on its own; (café) black; (whisky) neat (d) (único) single; **no me han comprado ni un s. regalo** they didn't buy me a single present; **ni una sola gota** not a (single) drop; **dame una sola razón** give me one reason (e) (mero, simple) very, mere; **la sola idea de suspender me deprime** the very o mere idea of failing depresses me
2 nm Mús solo

sólo adv only, just; **no s.... sino (también)...** not only... but (also)...; **con s., s. con** just by; **s. que...** only...

solomillo nm sirloin

solsticio nm solstice

soltar [63] **1** vt (a) (desasir) to let go of; **¡suéltame!** let me go!, let go of me! (b) (dejar ir) (preso, animales, freno) to release; **no suelta ni un** Esp **duro** o Am **centavo** you can't get a penny out of her; Fam **si yo pillo un trabajo así, no lo suelto** if I got a job like that I wouldn't let go of it o I'd make sure I hung on to it (c) (desenrollar) (cable, cuerda) to let o pay out (d) (risotada, grito, suspiro) to give; **s. una patada a alguien** to give sb a kick, to kick sb; **s. un puñetazo a alguien** to punch sb (e) (decir bruscamente) to come out with (f) (desprender) (calor, olor, gas) to give off; **estas hamburguesas sueltan mucha grasa** a lot of fat comes out of these burgers when you fry them (g) (laxar) **s. el vientre** to loosen one's bowels
2 soltarse vpr (a) (desasirse) to break free (b) (desatarse) **se soltó el moño** she let her bun down (c) (desprenderse) to come off (d) (perder timidez) to let go; **soltarse en algo** (adquirir habilidad) to get the hang of sth

soltería nf (de hombre) bachelorhood; (de mujer) spinsterhood

soltero, -a 1 adj single, unmarried
2 nm,f bachelor, f single woman

solterón, -ona 1 adj unmarried
2 nm,f old bachelor, f spinster, f old maid

soltura nf (a) (fluidez) fluency (b) (facilidad, desenvoltura) assurance; **con s.** fluently

solubilidad nf solubility

soluble adj (a) (que se disuelve) soluble (b) (que se soluciona) solvable

solución nf (a) (de situación, problema) solution; **este problema no tiene s.** there's no solution to this problem; Fam **este niño no tiene s.** this child is impossible; **s. de continuidad** interruption; **sin s. de continuidad** uninterrupted (b) (disolución) solution; **s. acuosa** aqueous solution; **s. salina** saline solution

solucionar vt (problema) to solve; (disputa) to resolve

solvencia nf (a) (económica) solvency (b) (capacidad) reliability

solventar vt (a) (pagar) to settle (b) (resolver) to resolve

solvente adj (a) (económicamente) solvent (b) (fuentes) reliable

somalí (pl **somalíes**) **1** adj & nmf Somali
2 nm (lengua) Somali

Somalia n Somalia

somanta nf Fam (paliza) hiding; **s. de palos** beating, thrashing

somático, -a adj somatic

somatizar [14] vt Med to convert into physical symptoms

sombra nf (a) (proyección) (fenómeno) shadow; (zona) shade; **a la s.** in the shade; Fam (en la cárcel) in the slammer; **dar s. a** to cast a shadow over; Fig **hacer s. a alguien** to overshadow sb; Fam Fig **no se fía ni de su propia s.** he wouldn't trust his own mother; **reírse de su propia s.** to make a joke of everything, to laugh at everything; Fig **ser la s. de alguien** to be sb's shadow; Fam Fig **tener mala s.** to be nasty o a swine; **sombras chinescas** (marionetas) shadow puppets; **hacer sombras chinescas** (con las manos) to make shadow pictures; **s. de ojos** eyeshadow
(b) (en pintura) shade
(c) (anonimato) background; **permanecer en la s.** to stay out of the limelight
(d) (imperfección) stain, blemish
(e) (atisbo, apariencia) trace, touch; **no tener ni s. de** not to have the slightest bit of
(f) (suerte) **buena/mala s.** good/bad luck
(g) Taurom = most expensive seats in bullring, located in the shade
(h) (oscuridad, inquietud) darkness
(i) (ignorancia) gaps in one's knowledge

sombreado *nm* shading

sombrear *vt (dibujo)* to shade

sombrerería *nf* (**a**) *(fábrica)* hat factory (**b**) *(tienda)* hat store *o* shop

sombrero *nm* (**a**) *(prenda)* hat; *Fig* **pasar el s.** to pass round the hat; *Fig* **quitarse el s. (ante)** to take one's hat off (to); **s. de copa** top hat; **s. hongo** derby (**b**) *(de setas)* cap

sombrilla *nf* (**a**) *(quitasol)* sunshade, parasol (**b**) *Col (paraguas)* umbrella

sombrío, -a *adj* (**a**) *(oscuro)* gloomy, dark (**b**) *(triste, lúgubre)* somber, gloomy

somero, -a *adj* superficial

someter 1 *vt* (**a**) *(dominar, subyugar)* to subdue (**b**) *(presentar)* **s. algo a la aprobación de alguien** to submit sth for sb's approval; **s. algo a votación** to put sth to the vote (**c**) *(subordinar)* **someto mi decisión a los resultados de la encuesta** my decision will depend on the results of the poll; **sometió su opinión a la de la mayoría** she went along with the opinion of the majority (**d**) *(a interrogatorio, presiones)* **s. a alguien a algo** to subject sb to sth; **s. a alguien a una operación** to operate on sb

2 someterse *vpr* (**a**) *(rendirse)* to surrender (**b**) *(conformarse)* **someterse a algo** to yield *o* bow to sth (**c**) *(a interrogatorio, pruebas)* to undergo; **someterse a una operación** to have an operation; **se sometió voluntariamente al experimento** he participated voluntarily in the experiment

sometimiento *nm* (**a**) *(en general)* submission; **evitar el s. a los rayos del sol** *(en frasco, envoltorio)* keep out of direct sunlight (**b**) *(dominio)* subjugation

somier *nm (de muelles)* bedsprings; *(de tablas)* slats *(of bed)*

somnífero, -a 1 *adj* somniferous

2 *nm* sleeping pill

somnolencia *nf* sleepiness, drowsiness

somnoliento, -a *adj* drowsy, sleepy

somontano, -a *adj* mountainside

somos *ver* ser

son 1 *ver* ser

2 *nm* (**a**) *(sonido)* sound; *Fig* **bailar al s. que le tocan** to toe the line (**b**) *(canción y baile)* = Cuban song and dance of African origin

3 en son de *loc prep* **en s. de paz** in peace; **lo dijo en s. de burla** he said it as a taunt

sonado, -a *adj* (**a**) *(renombrado)* famous (**b**) *Fam (loco)* crazy (**c**) *(boxeador)* punch-drunk

sonajero *nm* rattle

sonambulismo *nm* sleepwalking

sonámbulo, -a 1 *adj* sleepwalking; **es s.** he walks in his sleep

2 *nm,f* sleepwalker

sonante *adj* **dinero contante y s.** hard cash

sonar¹ *nm* *Náut* sonar

sonar² [63] **1** *vi* (**a**) *(producir sonido) (timbre, teléfono, alarma)* to ring; **sonó un disparo** a shot rang out; **sonaba a lo lejos una sirena** you could hear (the sound of) a siren in the distance; **suena a falso/chiste** it sounds false/like a joke; **(así** *o* **tal) como suena** literally, in so many words (**b**) *(ser conocido, familiar)* **me suena** it rings a bell; **esa cara me suena** I know that face, I've seen that face somewhere before; **no me suena su nombre** I don't remember hearing her name before (**c**) *(pronunciarse)* to be pronounced; **la letra "h" no suena** the "h" is silent (**d**) *(mencionarse, citarse)* to be mentioned; **su nombre suena como futuro ministro** his name is being mentioned as a future minister

2 sonarse *vpr* **sonarse (la nariz)** to blow one's nose

sonata *nf* sonata

sonda *nf* (**a**) *Med & Mec* probe; **s. espacial** space probe; **s. gástrica** stomach pump (**b**) *Náut* sounding line (**c**) *Min* drill, bore

sondar *vt* (**a**) *Med* to sound, to probe (**b**) *Náut* to sound (**c**) *Min (terreno)* to test; *(roca)* to drill

sondear *vt* (**a**) *(indagar)* to sound out (**b**) *Min (terreno)* to test; *(roca)* to drill

sondeo *nm* (**a**) *(encuesta)* (opinion) poll (**b**) *Min* drilling, boring (**c**) *Náut* sounding

soneto *nm* sonnet

sonido *nm* sound; **s. vocálico** vowel sound

soniquete *nm* *(sonido)* monotonous noise; *Fam* **el s. de siempre** the same old story

sonora *nf* *Gram* voiced consonant

sonoridad *nf* (**a**) *(armonía)* sonority (**b**) *(acústica)* acoustics (**c**) *(resonancia)* resonance

sonorización *nf* soundtrack recording

sonorizar [14] *vt* (**a**) *(con amplificadores)* to fit with a public-address system (**b**) *Cine (poner sonido a)* to record the sound track for (**c**) *Gram* to voice

sonoro, -a *adj* (**a**) *(del sonido)* sound; *(película)* talking; **ondas sonoras** sound waves (**b**) *(ruidoso, resonante, vibrante)* resonant (**c**) *Gram* voiced

sonotone® *nm* hearing aid

sonreír [56] **1** *vi* (**a**) *(reír levemente)* to smile; **me sonrió** she smiled at me (**b**) *(ser favorable) (suerte)* to smile on

2 sonreírse *vpr* to smile

sonriente *adj* smiling; **estás muy s. hoy** you're looking very cheerful today

sonriera *etc ver* sonreír

sonrisa *nf* smile

sonrojar 1 *vt* to cause to blush

2 sonrojarse *vpr* to blush

sonrojo *nm* blush, blushing

sonrosado, -a *adj* rosy

sonrosar *vt* to color pink

sonsacar [59] *vt* **s. algo a alguien** to extract sth from sb

sonso, -a *adj* *Am Fam* silly

sonsonete *nm* (**a**) *(ruido)* tapping (**b**) *(entonación)* monotonous intonation (**c**) *(cantinela)* old tune (**d**) *(sarcasmo)* hint of sarcasm

soñador, -ora 1 *adj* dreamy

2 *nm,f* dreamer

soñar [63] *también Fig* **1** *vt* to dream; **soñé que podía volar** I dreamed (that) I could fly; *Fam* **¡ni soñarlo!, ¡ni lo sueñes!** not on your life!

2 *vi* to dream (**con** *o* about); **anoche soñé con ella** I dreamed about her last night; **sueña con que le ofrezcan el puesto** she dreams of being offered the job; **s. con los angelitos** to have sweet dreams; **s. despierto** to daydream

soñarrera *nf* *Fam* **tener una s.** to feel drowsy

soñolencia *nf* sleepiness, drowsiness

soñoliento, -a *adj* sleepy, drowsy

sopa *nf* (**a**) *(guiso)* soup; **s. de ajo** garlic soup; *Am* **s. inglesa** trifle; **s. instantánea** instant soup; **s. juliana** vegetable soup; **s. de letras** *(alimento)* alphabet soup; *(pasatiempo)* word-search; **s. de sobre** packaged soup; **s. de verduras** vegetable soup (**b**) *(de pan)* sop, piece of soaked bread; **hacer sopas (en)** to dip bread (into) (**c**) *(expresiones)* *Esp Fam* **andar a la s. boba** to scrounge; *Esp* **dar s. con hondas a alguien** to run rings around sb; **últimamente ese cantante está hasta en la s.** that singer has been everywhere you look, recently; **me lo encuentro hasta en la s.** I bump into him wherever I go; **estar como una s.** to be sopping wet

sopapo *nm* slap

sopera *nf (recipiente)* soup tureen

sopero, -a *adj* soup; **plato s.** soup plate

sopesar *vt (pros y contras)* to weigh up

sopetón: de sopetón *loc adv* suddenly, abruptly

soplado nm (del vidrio) glassblowing

soplagaitas nmf inv Fam (estúpido, pesado) jerk

soplamocos nm inv Fam box on the ears

soplar 1 vt (a) (vela, fuego) to blow out (b) (ceniza, polvo) to blow off (c) (globo) to blow up (d) (vidrio) to blow (e) Fam (en examen) to prompt; **me sopló las respuestas** he whispered the answers to me (f) Fam (denunciar) **le sopló a la policía la hora del atraco** he informed the police of the time of the robbery (g) Esp Fam (hurtar) to pinch; **s. algo a alguien** to pinch sth off sb

2 vi (a) (echar aire) to blow (b) Esp Fam (beber) to booze (c) Fam (en examen) **le expulsaron por s.** he was thrown out for whispering the answers

3 soplarse vpr (a) Esp Fam (comida) to gobble up; (bebida) to knock back (b) Méx Fam (aguantar) to put up with

soplete nm blowtorch

soplido nm blow, puff

soplillo nm (a) (para fuego) fan, blower (b) Fam **orejas de s.** jug ears

soplo nm (a) (soplido) blow, puff (b) (instante) breath, moment (c) Med murmur (d) Fam (chivatazo) tip-off; **dar el s.** to squeal

soplón, -ona nmf Fam (criminal) rat; (escolar) tattletale

soponcio nm Fam fainting fit; **le dio un s.** she passed out

sopor nm drowsiness

soporífero, -a adj también Fig soporific

soportable adj bearable, endurable

soportal nm (pórtico) porch; **soportales** arcade

soportar 1 vt (a) (sostener) to support (b) (resistir, tolerar) to stand; **¡no lo soporto!** I can't stand him/it!; **no sé cómo soportas que te hablen así** I don't know how you put up with them talking to you like that; **no soporta que le griten** he can't bear being shouted at (c) (sobrellevar) to endure, to bear; **el niño soportó el castigo sin inmutarse** the child took his punishment bravely

2 soportarse vpr (mutuamente) to stand one another

soporte nm (a) (apoyo) support; **s. publicitario** publicity medium (b) Inform medium; **s. físico/lógico** hardware/software

soprano nmf soprano

sor nf Rel sister

sorber vt (a) (beber) to sip; (haciendo ruido) to slurp (b) (absorber) to soak up, to absorb (c) (atraer) to draw o suck in (d) (escuchar atentamente) to drink in

sorbete nm sherbet; CAm (helado) ice cream

sorbetería nf CAm ice-cream parlor

sorbo nm (a) (acción) gulp, swallow; (pequeño) sip; **beber a sorbos** to sip (b) (trago) mouthful; (pequeño) sip (c) (cantidad pequeña) drop

sorda nf Gram voiceless consonant

sordera nf deafness

sordidez nf (a) (miseria) squalor (b) (obscenidad, perversión) sordidness

sórdido, -a adj (a) (miserable) squalid (b) (obsceno, perverso) sordid

sordina nf (a) Mús (en instrumentos de viento, cuerda) mute; (en pianos) damper; Fig **con s.** (hablar) under one's breath (b) (de reloj) muffle

sordo, -a 1 adj (a) (que no oye) deaf; Fig **permanecer s. a** o **ante algo** to be deaf to sth; **estar más s. que una tapia** to be stone deaf (b) (pasos) quiet, muffled (c) (ruido, dolor) dull (d) Gram voiceless, unvoiced

2 nm,f (persona) deaf person; **los sordos** the deaf; **hacerse el s.** to turn a deaf ear

sordomudo, -a 1 adj deaf and dumb

2 nm,f deaf mute

sorgo nm sorghum

soriano, -a 1 adj of/from Soria

2 nm,f person from Soria

soriasis nf inv psoriasis

sorna nf **con s.** ironically, mockingly

soroche nm Andes, Arg altitude sickness

sorprendente adj surprising

sorprender 1 vt (a) (asombrar) to surprise; **me sorprende verte por aquí** I'm surprised to see you here; **no me sorprende que se haya marchado** I'm not surprised she's left (b) (atrapar, pillar) to catch; **nos sorprendió la tormenta** we got caught in the storm; **s. a alguien (haciendo algo)** to catch sb (doing sth)

2 sorprenderse vpr to be surprised (**de** by o at)

sorprendido, -a adj surprised

sorpresa nf surprise; **¡qué s.!** what a surprise!; **¡qué s. verte por aquí!** what a surprise, seeing you here!; **dar una s. a alguien** to surprise sb; **llevarse una s.** to get a surprise; **de** o **por s.** unexpectedly; **pillar a alguien por s.** to catch sb by surprise

sorpresivo, -a adj unexpected

sortear 1 vt (a) (rifar) to raffle; (echar a suertes) to draw lots for; **van a s. un viaje** there will be a prize draw for a vacation (b) (esquivar) (obstáculos) to negotiate; (preguntas) to avoid, to sidestep; **sortearon todas las dificultades que encontraron** they got o worked around all the difficulties they came up against

2 sortearse vpr **se sortearon quién iría primero** they drew lots to decide who would go first; **se sorteará un viaje al Caribe** there will be a draw for a Caribbean vacation

sorteo nm (lotería) draw; (rifa) raffle; **haremos un s. con los premios** we'll raffle the prizes

sortija nf ring; **s. de diamantes** diamond ring

sortilegio nm (a) (hechizo) spell (b) (atractivo) charm, magic

SOS nm SOS

sosa nf soda; **s. cáustica** caustic soda

sosaina 1 adj (sin gracia) dull, insipid

2 nmf dull person, bore

sosegado, -a adj calm

sosegar [43] **1** vt to calm

2 sosegarse vpr to calm down

soseras nmf inv Fam dull person, bore

sosería nf lack of sparkle

sosia nm inv double, look-alike

sosiego 1 ver **sosegar**

2 nm calm

soslayar vt to avoid

soslayo: de soslayo loc adv (oblicuamente) sideways, obliquely; **mirar a alguien de s.** to look at sb out of the corner of one's eye

soso, -a 1 adj (a) (sin sal) bland, tasteless (b) (sin gracia) dull, insipid

2 nm,f dull person, bore

sospecha nf suspicion; **despertar sospechas** to arouse suspicion; **tengo la s. de que...** I have a suspicion that..., I suspect that...; **tengo fundadas sospechas de que miente** I have reason to suspect that he's lying

sospechar 1 vt (creer, suponer) to suspect; **sospecho que no lo terminará** I doubt whether she'll finish it

2 vi **s. de** to suspect

sospechoso, -a 1 adj suspicious

2 nm,f suspect

sostén nm (a) (apoyo) support (b) (sustento) main support; (alimento) sustenance (c) (sujetador) bra, brassiere

sostener [65] **1** vt (a) (sujetar) to support, to hold up; **sostenme esto, por favor** hold this for me, please (b) (defender) (idea, opinión, tesis) to defend; (promesa, palabra) to stand by, to keep; **s. que...** to maintain that... (c) (mantener, *costear)* to support (**d**) *(tener) (conversación)* to hold, to have; **s. correspondencia con alguien** to correspond with sb (**e**) *(aguantar)* **el corredor no podía s. aquel ritmo de carrera** the athlete couldn't keep up with the pace of the race; **era una situación imposible de s.** the situation was untenable

2 sostenerse *vpr* (**a**) **sostenerse (en pie)** *(persona)* to stay on one's feet; *(edificio, estructura)* to stay up; **es muy pequeño y aún le cuesta sostenerse de pie/sentado** he's only little and he still has difficulty standing up/sitting up (**b**) *(sustentarse)* **la organización se sostiene a base de donaciones** the organization depends on donations for its survival

sostenible *adj (objeto, desarrollo)* sustainable; *(idea, argumento)* tenable

sostenido, -a 1 *adj* (**a**) *(persistente)* sustained (**b**) *Mús* sharp
　　2 *nm Mús* sharp

sostiene, sostuviera *etc ver* **sostener**

sota *nf* jack

sotabanco *nm (ático)* attic

sotabarba *nf* double chin

sotana *nf* cassock

sótano *nm* basement, cellar

sotavento *nm* leeward

soterrado, -a *adj (enterrado)* buried; *(oculto)* hidden

soterrar [3] *vt (enterrar)* to bury; *(ocultar)* to hide

sotobosque *nm* undergrowth

sotto voce [soto'βotʃe] *adv* sotto voce

soufflé [su'fle] *nm* soufflé

soul *nm Mús* soul (music)

souvenir [suβe'nir] *(pl* **souvenirs**) *nm* souvenir

soviet *(pl* **soviets**) *nm* soviet; *Antes* **el s. supremo** the Supreme Soviet

soviético, -a 1 *adj (de la URSS)* Soviet
　　2 *nm,f* Soviet

soy *ver* **ser**

SP *(abrev de* **servicio público**) = sign indicating public transportation vehicle

spaghetti [espa'yeti] *nm o nmpl* spaghetti

spanglish [es'panglis] *nm* Spanglish

spaniel [es'paniel] *(pl* **spaniels**) *nm* spaniel

sparring [es'parrin] *(pl* **sparrings**) *nm Dep* sparring partner

speed [es'piθ] *nm (droga)* speed

sport [es'por]: **de sport** *loc adj* **chaqueta de s.** sports jacket; **ropa de s.** casual clothes

spot [es'pot] *(pl* **spots**) *nm (TV)* advert; **un s. publicitario** a (television) commercial

spray [es'prai] *nm* spray

sprint [es'prin] *(pl* **sprints**) *nm* sprint

sprinter [es'printer] *(pl* **sprinters**) *nmf* sprinter

squash [es'kwas] *nm inv Dep* squash

Sr. *(abrev de* **señor**) Mr.

Sra. *(abrev de* **señora**) Mrs.

Sres. *(abrev de* **señores**) Messrs

Sri Lanka *n* Sri Lanka

Srta. *(abrev de* **señorita**) Miss

SS *(abrev de* **Su Santidad**) HH

SS. MM. *(abrev de* **Sus Majestades**) their Royal Highnesses

Sta. *(abrev de* **santa**) St

stand [es'tan] *(pl* **stands**) *nm* stall, stand

standing [es'tandin] *(pl* **standings**) *nm* standing, social status; **un apartamento de alto s.** a luxury apartment; **una compañía de alto s.** a top company

starter [es'tarter] *(pl* **starters**) *nm* choke

statu quo [es'tatu'kwo] *nm inv* status quo

step [es'tep] *(pl* **steps**) *nm* step (aerobics)

stick [es'tik] *(pl* **sticks**) *nm Dep* hockey stick

Sto. *(abrev de* **santo**) St

stock [es'tok] *(pl* **stocks**) *nm Com* stock

stop [es'top] *(pl* **stops**) *nm* (**a**) *Aut* stop sign (**b**) *(en telegrama)* stop

strip-tease [es'triptis] *nm inv* striptease

su *(pl* **sus**) *adj posesivo (de él)* his; *(de ella)* her; *(de cosa, animal)* its; *(de uno)* one's; *(de ellos, ellas)* their; *(de usted, ustedes)* your; **su libro** his/her/your/their book; **sus libros** his/her/your/their books; **su hocico** its snout

suahili [swa'xili], **suajili** *nm (lengua)* Swahili

suave 1 *adj* (**a**) *(al tacto)* soft (**b**) *(liso, no brusco)* smooth; **este coche tiene la dirección muy s.** this car has very smooth steering (**c**) *(sabor, olor, color)* delicate; **este curry está bastante s.** this curry is quite mild (**d**) *(apacible) (persona, carácter)* gentle; *(clima)* mild (**e**) *(fácil, lento) (cuesta, tarea, ritmo)* gentle (**f**) *Méx Fam (agradable)* pleasant
　　2 *adv Méx Fam (de acuerdo)* all right, fine

suavemente *adv (acariciar)* gently; *(hablar)* softly

suavidad *nf* (**a**) *(de tacto)* softness (**b**) *(lisura, falta de brusquedad)* smoothness (**c**) *(de sabor, olor, color)* delicacy (**d**) *(de carácter)* gentleness (**e**) *(de clima)* mildness (**f**) *(de cuesta, tarea, ritmo)* gentleness

suavizante 1 *adj (para ropa, cabello)* conditioning; *(para piel)* moisturizing
　　2 *nm* conditioner; **s. para la ropa** fabric conditioner *o* softener

suavizar [14] *vt* (**a**) *(poner blando)* to soften; *(hacer liso)* to smooth; *(ropa, cabello)* to condition (**b**) *(hacer dócil)* to temper (**c**) *(dificultad, tarea)* to ease; *(conducción)* to make smoother; *(clima)* to make milder (**d**) *(sabor, olor, color)* to tone down

Suazilandia *n* Swaziland

subacuático, -a *adj* subaquatic

subafluente *nm* minor tributary

subalimentación *nf* undernourishment

subalimentar *vt* to undernourish

subalquilar *vt* to sublet

subalterno, -a 1 *adj (subordinado)* auxiliary
　　2 *nm,f (empleado)* subordinate
　　3 *nm Taurom* assistant to bullfighter

subarrendar [3] *vt* to sublet

subarrendatario, -a *nm,f* subtenant

subarriendo *nm* (**a**) *(acción)* subtenancy (**b**) *(contrato)* sublease (agreement)

subasta *nf* (**a**) *(venta pública)* auction; **sacar algo a s.** to put sth up for auction (**b**) *(contrata pública)* tender; **sacar algo a s.** to put sth out to tender

subastador, -ora *nm,f* auctioneer

subastar *vt* to auction

subcampeón, -ona *nm,f* runner-up

subcampeonato *nm* second place, runner-up's position

subclase *nf* subclass

subcomandante *nmf* = military rank below that of commander

subcomisión *nf* subcommittee

subcomité *nm* subcommittee

subconjunto *nm Mat* subset

subconsciencia *nf* subconscious

subconsciente *adj & nm* subconscious

subcontinente *nm* subcontinent

subcontratación *nf* subcontracting

subcontratar *vt* to subcontract

subcontrato *nm* subcontract

subcultura *nf* subculture

subcutáneo, -a *adj* subcutaneous

subdelegación *nf* subdelegation
subdelegado, -a *nm,f* subdelegate
subdesarrollado, -a *adj* underdeveloped
subdesarrollo *nm* underdevelopment
subdirección *nf (puesto)* post of assistant manager
subdirector, -ora *nm,f* assistant manager
subdirectorio *nm Inform* subdirectory
súbdito, -a *nm,f* (**a**) *(de monarca)* subject (**b**) *(ciudadano)* citizen, national
subdividir 1 *vt* to subdivide
2 subdividirse *vpr* to be subdivided (**en** into)
subdivisión *nf* subdivision
subemplear *vt* to underemploy
subempleo *nm* underemployment
subespecie *nf* subspecies
subestimar 1 *vt* to underestimate; *(infravalorar)* to underrate
2 subestimarse *vpr* to underrate oneself
subfusil *nm* automatic rifle
subgénero *nm* subgenus
subgrupo *nm* subgroup
subibaja *nm* seesaw
subida *nf* (**a**) *(cuesta)* hill (**b**) *(ascensión)* ascent, climb (**c**) *(aumento)* increase, rise; **se espera una s. de las temperaturas** temperatures are expected to rise; **s. de precios** price increase; **s. de sueldo** pay raise
subido, -a *adj* (**a**) *(intenso)* strong, intense (**b**) *Fam (en cantidad)* **tiene el guapo s.** he really fancies himself; **está de un imbécil s.** he has been acting like an idiot recently (**c**) *Fam (atrevido)* risqué; **s. de tono** *(impertinente)* impertinent
subidón *nm Fam (de drogas)* high
subíndice *nm* subscript
subinspector, -ora *nm,f* deputy inspector
subir 1 *vt* (**a**) *(ascender) (calle, escaleras)* to go/come up; *(pendiente, montaña)* to go up; **subió las escaleras a toda velocidad** she ran up *o* climbed the stairs as fast as she could (**b**) *(poner arriba)* to lift up; *(llevar arriba)* to take/bring up; **ayúdame a s. la caja** *(a lo alto)* help me get the box up; *(al piso de arriba)* help me carry the box upstairs (**c**) *(aumentar) (precio, peso)* to put up, to increase; *(volumen)* to turn up; *(voz)* to raise (**d**) *(montar)* **s. algo/a alguien a** to lift sth/sb onto (**e**) *(alzar) (mano, bandera, voz)* to raise; *(persiana)* to roll up; *(ventanilla)* to wind up (**f**) *Mús* to raise the pitch of
2 *vi* (**a**) *(a piso, azotea)* to go/come up; *(a montaña, cima)* to climb; **s. en ascensor** to go/come up in the elevator; **s. por la escalera** to go/come up the stairs (**b**) *(aumentar) (precio, temperatura)* to go up, to rise; *(cauce, marea)* to rise; **s. de categoría** *(mejorar)* to improve; *(ser ascendido)* to be promoted (**c**) *(montar) (en avión, barco)* to get on; *(en coche)* to get in; **sube al coche** get into the car (**d**) *(cuenta, importe)* **s. a** to come *o* amount to (**e**) *Culin (crecer)* to rise
3 subirse *vpr* (**a**) *(ascender)* **subirse a** *(árbol)* to climb up; *(mesa)* to climb onto; *(piso)* to go/come up to; *Fig* **subirse por las paredes** to hit the roof (**b**) *(montarse)* **subirse a** *(tren, avión)* to get on, to board; *(caballo, bicicleta)* to mount, to get on; *(coche)* to get into; **el taxi paró y me subí** the taxi stopped and I got in (**c**) *(alzarse)* **subirse las mangas** to roll one's sleeves up; **subirse los pantalones/calcetines** to pull one's pants/socks up; **subirse la cremallera** to do one's zipper up (**d**) **subirse (a la cabeza)** *(alcohol, éxito)* to go to one's head
súbito, -a *adj* sudden; **de s.** suddenly
subjefe, -a *nm,f* deputy manager
subjetividad *nf* subjectivity
subjetivismo *nm* subjectivism
subjetivo, -a *adj* subjective
sub júdice [suβ'juðiθe] *adj Der* sub judice
subjuntivo, -a *adj & nm* subjunctive

sublevación *nf,* **sublevamiento** *nm* uprising
sublevar 1 *vt* (**a**) *(amotinar)* to stir up (**b**) *(indignar)* to infuriate
2 sublevarse *vpr (amotinarse)* to rise up, to rebel
sublimación *nf* (**a**) *(exaltación)* exaltation (**b**) *Psi & Quím* sublimation
sublimar *vt* (**a**) *(exaltar)* to exalt (**b**) *Psi & Quím* to sublimate
sublime *adj* sublime
sublimidad *nf* sublimity
subliminal *adj* subliminal
submarinismo *nm* scuba diving
submarinista *nmf* scuba diver
submarino, -a 1 *adj* underwater; **fotografía submarina** underwater photography
2 *nm* submarine
submúltiplo, -a *adj & nm* submultiple
submundo *nm* world, scene; **el s. de las drogas** the drugs world *o* scene
subnormal 1 *adj* (**a**) *(retrasado)* mentally retarded (**b**) *Pey (insulto)* moronic
2 *nmf* (**a**) *(retrasado)* mentally retarded person (**b**) *Pey (insulto)* moron, cretin
subnormalidad *nf* **una campaña de prevención de la s.** a campaign aimed at preventing children from being born with a mental handicap; **la actitud de la sociedad ante la s.** society's attitude to the mentally retarded
suboficial *nmf Mil* noncommissioned officer
suborden *nm Biol* suborder
subordinación *nf (gen) & Gram* subordination
subordinado, -a *adj & nm,f* subordinate
subordinante *adj Gram* subordinating
subordinar 1 *vt (gen) & Gram* to subordinate
2 subordinarse *vpr* to be subordinate (**a** to)
subproducto *nm* by-product
subrayado, -a 1 *adj* underlined
2 *nm* underlining
subrayar *vt también Fig* to underline
subrepticio, -a *adj* surreptitious
subrogación *nf* subrogation
subrogar [38] *vt* to subrogate
subsahariano, -a *adj* sub-Saharan
subsanable *adj* (**a**) *(solucionable)* solvable (**b**) *(corregible)* rectifiable
subsanación *nf (de errores)* correction
subsanar *vt* (**a**) *(solucionar)* to resolve (**b**) *(corregir)* to correct (**c**) *(disculpar)* to excuse
subscribir, subscripción, *etc* = suscribir, suscripción, *etc*
subsecretaría *nf* (**a**) *(oficina)* undersecretary's office (**b**) *(cargo)* undersecretaryship
subsecretario, -a *nm,f* (**a**) *(de secretario)* assistant secretary (**b**) *(de ministro)* undersecretary
subsidiar *vt* to subsidize
subsidiariedad *nf* subsidiarity
subsidiario, -a *adj* (**a**) *(empresa, compañía)* subsidiary (**b**) *Der* ancillary (**c**) *(de subvención)* paid for by the state
subsidio *nm* benefit, allowance; **s. de desempleo** unemployment benefit; **s. de invalidez** disability pay
subsiguiente *adj* subsequent
subsistema *nm* subsystem
subsistencia *nf* (**a**) *(vida)* subsistence (**b**) *(conservación)* continued existence (**c**) **subsistencias** *(provisiones)* provisions
subsistente *adj* surviving
subsistir *vi* (**a**) *(vivir)* to live, to exist (**b**) *(sobrevivir)* to survive
substancia, substancial, *etc* = sustancia, sustancial, *etc*
substantivar, substantivo, -a, *etc* = sustantivar, sustantivo, -a, *etc*

substitución, substituir, *etc* = sustitución, sustituir, *etc*

substracción, substraer, *etc* = sustracción, sustraer, *etc*

substrato *nm* substratum

subsuelo *nm* subsoil

subte *nm RP* metro, subway

subteniente *nm* sublieutenant

subterfugio *nm* subterfuge; **sin subterfugios** without subterfuge

subterráneo, -a 1 *adj* subterranean, underground
  2 *nm* underground tunnel

subtipo *nm Biol* subtype

subtitular *vt (gen) & Cine* to subtitle

subtítulo *nm (gen) & Cine* subtitle

subtotal *nm* subtotal

subtropical *adj* subtropical

suburbano, -a 1 *adj* suburban
  2 *nm (tren)* suburban train

suburbial *adj* **barrio s.** poor suburb

suburbio *nm* poor suburb

subvalorar *vt* to undervalue, to underrate

subvención *nf (para un proyecto)* grant; *(para proteger precios, una industria)* subsidy; **la orquesta recibe una s. del ayuntamiento** the orchestra receives financial support from the city council

subvencionar *vt (precios, industria)* to subsidize; *(proyecto, actividad cultural, estudios)* to provide financial support for

subversión *nf* subversion

subversivo, -a *adj* subversive

subvertir [62] *vt* to subvert

subyacente *adj* underlying

subyacer [71] *vi (ocultarse)* **s. bajo algo** to underlie sth

subyugado, -a *adj* (**a**) *(sometido)* subjugated (**b**) *(cautivado)* **s. por** captivated by

subyugador, -ora, subyugante *adj* (**a**) *(dominador)* conquering (**b**) *(atrayente)* captivating

subyugar [38] *vt* (**a**) *(someter)* to subjugate (**b**) *(atraer)* to captivate

succión *nf* suction

succionar *vt (sujeto: raíces)* to suck up; *(sujeto: bebé)* to absorb, to suck

sucedáneo, -a 1 *adj* ersatz, substitute
  2 *nm (sustituto)* substitute; *Fig* **ser un s. de** *(mala copia)* to be an apology for

suceder 1 *v impersonal (ocurrir)* to happen; **suceda lo que suceda** whatever happens
  2 *vt (sustituir)* to succeed (**en** in)
  3 *vi (venir después)* **s. a** to come after, to follow; **a la guerra sucedieron años muy tristes** the war was followed by years of misery

sucesión *nf* (**a**) *(serie)* succession (**b**) *(cambio) (de monarca)* succession; *(de cargo importante)* changeover (**c**) *(descendencia)* **morir sin s.** to die without issue

sucesivamente *adv* successively; **y así s.** and so on

sucesivo, -a *adj* (**a**) *(consecutivo)* successive, consecutive (**b**) *(siguiente)* **en días sucesivos les informaremos** we'll let you know over the next few days; **en lo s.** in future

suceso *nm* (**a**) *(acontecimiento)* event (**b**) *(hecho delictivo)* crime; *(incidente)* incident; **sección de sucesos** *(en prensa)* = section of newspaper dealing with accidents, crimes, disasters etc

sucesor, -ora 1 *adj* succeeding
  2 *nm,f* successor

suciedad *nf* (**a**) *(cualidad)* dirtiness (**b**) *(porquería)* dirt, filth

sucinto, -a *adj* (**a**) *(conciso)* succinct (**b**) *(pequeño, corto)* skimpy

sucio, -a 1 *adj* (**a**) *(sin limpieza)* dirty; **estar s.** to be dirty; **tiene muy sucia la cocina** his kitchen is very dirty; **la ropa sucia** the dirty clothes; **el blanco es un color muy s.** white is a color that gets dirty easily; **en s.** *(escribir)* in rough (**b**) *(conciencia)* bad, guilty
  2 *adv* **jugar s.** to play dirty

sucre *nm (moneda)* sucre

suculento, -a *adj* tasty

sucumbir *vi* (**a**) *(rendirse, ceder)* to succumb (**a** to) (**b**) *(fallecer)* to die

sucursal *nf* branch

sudaca *adj & nmf Fam* = term used to refer to Latin American people, which can sometimes be pejorative

sudadera *nf* (**a**) *(prenda)* sweatshirt (**b**) *(sudor)* sweat

Sudáfrica *n* South Africa

sudafricano, -a *adj & nm,f* South African

Sudamérica *n* South America

sudamericano, -a *adj & nm,f* South American

Sudán *n* Sudan

sudanés, -esa *adj & nm,f* Sudanese

sudar 1 *vi (transpirar)* to sweat; *(pared)* to run with condensation; *Fam* **sudaban a chorros** they were running with sweat; *Fam* **s. la gota gorda** to sweat buckets; *Fig (trabajar duro)* to sweat blood
  2 *vt* (**a**) *(empapar)* to make sweaty (**b**) *Fam (trabajar duro por)* to work hard for

sudario *nm* shroud

sudeste 1 *adj (posición, parte)* southeast, southeastern; *(dirección, viento)* southeasterly
  2 *nm* southeast

sudista *Hist* **1** *adj* Southern *(in US Civil War)*
  2 *nmf* Southerner *(in US Civil War)*

sudoeste 1 *adj (posición, parte)* southwest, southwestern; *(dirección, viento)* southwesterly
  2 *nm* southwest

sudor *nm (transpiración)* sweat; *(de pared)* condensation; **con el s. de mi frente** by the sweat of my brow; *Fig* **me costó muchos sudores conseguirlo** I had a real struggle to get it; *Fig* **me entran sudores fríos de pensarlo** *(me entra miedo)* it makes me break out in a cold sweat *o* it sends a shiver down my spine just to think of it

sudoración *nf* sweating, perspiration

sudoriento, -a *adj* sweaty

sudoríparo, -a *adj* sweat; **glándula sudorípara** sweat gland

sudoroso, -a *adj* sweaty

Suecia *n* Sweden

sueco, -a 1 *adj* Swedish
  2 *nm,f (persona)* Swede; *Fig* **hacerse el s.** to play dumb, to pretend not to understand
  3 *nm (lengua)* Swedish

suegro, -a *nm,f* father-in-law, *f* mother-in-law

suela *nf* sole; *Fig* **no llegarle a alguien a la s. del zapato** not to hold a candle to sb

sueldo 1 *ver* **soldar**
  2 *nm* salary, wages; *(semanal)* wage; **a s.** *(empleado)* salaried; *(asesino)* hired; **me han subido el s.** they've given me a pay raise; **s. base** basic salary; *(semanal)* basic wage; **s. mínimo** minimum wage; **s. neto** take-home pay

suelo 1 *ver* **soler**
  2 *nm* (**a**) *(pavimento) (en interiores)* floor; *(en el exterior)* ground; **venir** *o* **venirse al s.** *(caer)* to fall down, to collapse; *Fig (fracasar)* to fail (**b**) *(terreno, territorio)* soil; *(para edificar)* land; **en s. colombiano** on Colombian soil; **s. urbanizable** land suitable for development (**c**) *(expresiones)* **arrastrarse por el s.** to grovel, to humble oneself; **besar el s.** to fall flat on one's face; **estar por los suelos** *(persona, precio)* to be at rock

bottom; *(producto)* to be dirt cheap; **poner** *o* **tirar por los suelos** to run down, to criticize

suelta *nf (liberación)* release

suelto, -a 1 *ver* **soltar**

2 *adj* (**a**) *(en general)* loose; *(cordones)* undone; **¿tienes tres euros sueltos?** have you got three euros in loose change?; **andar s.** *(en libertad)* to be free; *(en fuga)* to be at large; *(con diarrea)* to have diarrhea (**b**) *(separado)* separate; *(desparejado)* odd; **no los vendemos sueltos** we don't sell them separately (**c**) *(arroz)* fluffy (**d**) *(lenguaje, estilo)* fluent, fluid (**e**) *(desenvuelto)* comfortable, at ease

3 *nm (calderilla)* loose change

sueno *etc ver* **sonar**

sueño 1 *ver* **soñar**

2 *nm* (**a**) *(ganas de dormir)* sleepiness; *(por medicamento)* drowsiness; **¡qué s.!** I'm really sleepy!; **(estoy que) me caigo** *o* **me muero de s.** I'm falling asleep on my feet; **tener s.** to be sleepy; **tienes cara de s.** you look sleepy (**b**) *(estado)* sleep; *Esp* **coger el s.** to get to sleep; **conciliar el s.** to get to sleep; **descabezar un s.** to have a nap; *Fam* **no pierdas el s. por él/ello** don't lose any sleep over him/it; **no me quita el s.** I'm not losing any sleep over it; *Fig* **s. eterno** eternal rest; **s. pesado/ligero** heavy/light sleep (**c**) *(imagen mental, objetivo, quimera)* dream; *Fam* **esta casa es un s.** this house is a dream; **en sueños** in a dream; *Fig* **ni en sueños** no way, under no circumstances; **un s. hecho realidad** a dream come true

suero *nm* (**a**) *Med* serum; **s. artificial** saline solution (**b**) *(de la leche)* whey

suerte *nf* (**a**) *(fortuna)* luck; **estar de s.** to be in luck; **por s.** luckily; **probar s.** to try one's luck; **¡qué s.!** that was lucky!; **¡qué s. que traje el paraguas!** how lucky that I brought my umbrella!; **tener (buena) s.** to be lucky; **tener mala s.** to be unlucky; **tener la s. de espaldas** to be having a run of bad luck (**b**) *(azar)* chance; **echar** *o* **tirar algo** *Esp* **a suertes** *o Am* **a la s.** to draw lots for sth; **tocar** *o* **caer en s. a alguien** to fall to sb's lot; **la s. está echada** the die is cast (**c**) *(destino)* fate; **tentar a la s.** to tempt fate (**d**) *(clase)* **toda s. de** all manner of; **ser una s. de** to be a kind *o* sort of (**e**) **de s. que** in such a way that

suertudo, -a *nm,f Fam* lucky devil

suéter *nm* sweater

Suez *n* Suez

sufí *(pl* **sufíes) 1** *adj* Sufic

2 *nmf* Sufi

suficiencia *nf* (**a**) *(capacidad)* proficiency (**b**) *(idoneidad)* suitability; *(de medidas, esfuerzos)* adequacy (**c**) *(presunción)* smugness, self-importance (**d**) *Esp Educ (examen)* = retake of secondary school end-of-year examination at end of June

suficiente 1 *adj* (**a**) *(bastante)* enough; *(medidas, esfuerzos)* adequate; **no llevo (dinero) s.** I don't have enough (money) on me; **no tienes la estatura s.** you're not tall enough (**b**) *(presuntuoso)* smug, full of oneself

2 *nm (nota)* pass

suficientemente *adv* enough, sufficiently

sufijo *nm* suffix

suflé *nm* soufflé

sufragar [38] **1** *vt (gastos)* to defray

2 *vi Am (votar)* to vote

sufragio *nm* suffrage; **s. directo/indirecto** direct/indirect suffrage; **s. restringido/universal** restricted/universal suffrage

sufragismo *nm Hist* suffragette movement

sufragista *Hist* **1** *adj* suffragette; **movimiento s.** suffragette movement

2 *nmf* suffragette

sufrido, -a *adj* (**a**) *(resignado)* patient, uncomplaining; *(durante mucho tiempo)* long-suffering (**b**) *(resistente) (tela)* hard-

wearing; *(color)* that does not show the dirt

sufridor, -ora *adj* easily worried

sufrimiento *nm* suffering

sufrir 1 *vt* (**a**) *(padecer)* to suffer; *(accidente)* to have; **no sufrió daños** it wasn't damaged; **sufrió una agresión** he was the victim of an attack (**b**) *(soportar)* to bear, to stand; **tengo que s. sus manías** I have to put up with his idiosyncrasies (**c**) *(experimentar)* to undergo, to experience; **la Bolsa sufrió una caída** the stock market fell; **la empresa ha sufrido pérdidas** the company has reported *o* made losses

2 *vi (padecer)* to suffer; **s. de** *(enfermedad)* to suffer from; **s. del estómago** to have a stomach complaint

sugerencia *nf* suggestion

sugerente *adj* evocative

sugerir [62] *vt* (**a**) *(proponer)* to suggest; **¿qué sugieres que hagamos?** what do you suggest we do?; **sugirió que diéramos una vuelta** he suggested we (should) go for a walk (**b**) *(evocar)* to evoke; **¿qué te sugiere este poema?** what does this poem remind you of?

sugestión *nf* suggestion

sugestionable *adj* impressionable

sugestionar 1 *vt* to influence

2 sugestionarse *vpr* (**a**) *(obsesionarse)* to become obsessed (**b**) *Psi* to use autosuggestion

sugestivo, -a *adj* attractive

sugiero *etc ver* **sugerir**

sugiriera *etc ver* **sugerir**

suiche *nm Col,Ven* switch

suicida 1 *adj* suicidal

2 *nmf (por naturaleza)* suicidal person; *(suicidado)* person who has committed suicide

suicidarse *vpr* to commit suicide

suicidio *nm* suicide

sui géneris *adj inv* unusual, individual

suite [suit] *nf (gen) & Mús* suite; **s. nupcial** bridal suite

Suiza *n* Switzerland

suizo, -a 1 *adj & nm,f* Swiss

2 *nm Esp (bollo)* = type of sugared bun

sujeción *nf* (**a**) *(atadura)* fastening (**b**) *(sometimiento)* subjection

sujetador *nm Esp* bra, brassiere

sujetalibros *nm inv* bookend

sujetapapeles *nm inv* paper clip

sujetar 1 *vt* (**a**) *(agarrar) (para mantener en su sitio)* to hold in place; *(sobre una superficie, con un peso)* to hold down; *(para que no se caiga)* to hold up; **sujeta la cuerda al poste** tie the rope to the post; **s. con clavos/cola** to fasten with nails/glue; **sujeta los papeles con un clip** fasten the papers together with a paper clip; **intentó escapar, pero la sujetaron firmemente** she tried to escape, but they kept a firm grip on her; **si no lo llegan a s., la mata** if they hadn't held him back, he would have killed her (**b**) *(sostener)* to hold

2 sujetarse *vpr* (**a**) *(agarrarse)* **sujétate bien o te caerás** hold on tight or you'll fall; **sujetarse a** to hold on to, to cling to; **se sujeta el pelo con una horquilla** she keeps her hair in place with a hairclip (**b**) *(aguantarse)* to keep in place (**c**) *(someterse)* **sujetarse a** to keep *o* stick to

sujeto, -a 1 *adj* (**a**) *(agarrado)* fastened; **las cuerdas están bien sujetas** the ropes are secure *o* are firmly fastened (**b**) *(expuesto)* subject (**a** to); **este proyecto está s. a modificaciones** this plan is subject to modification

2 *nm* (**a**) *(de acción, frase)* subject (**b**) *(individuo)* individual; **un s. sospechoso** a suspicious individual; *Econ* **s. pasivo** taxpayer

sulfamida *nf Med* sulfonamide

sulfatarse *vpr (pilas)* to leak

sulfato *nm* sulfate; **s. de cobre** copper sulfate

sulfurar 1 *vt* (**a**) *(encolerizar)* to infuriate (**b**) *Quím* to sulfurate
2 sulfurarse *vpr (encolerizarse)* to get mad
sulfúrico, -a *adj* sulfuric
sulfuro *nm* sulfide
sulfuroso, -a *adj Quím* sulfurous
sultán, -ana *nm,f* sultan, *f* sultana
suma *nf* (**a**) *Mat (acción)* addition; *(resultado)* total (**b**) *(conjunto) (de conocimientos, datos)* total, sum; *(de dinero)* sum (**c**) *(resumen)* **en s.** in short
sumamente *adv* extremely
sumando *nm Mat* = amount to be added, addend
sumar 1 *vt* (**a**) *(varias cantidades)* to add together; **tres y cinco suman ocho** three and five are *o* make eight; **súmale diez** add ten (**b**) *(añadir)* to add; **súmale a eso todas las mentiras que nos ha dicho** to that we also have to add all the lies he's told us; **suma y sigue** *(en contabilidad)* carried forward; *Fam Fig* here we go again! (**c**) *(costar)* to come to
2 sumarse *vpr* to join (**a** in); **sumarse a la opinión de alguien** to adhere to sb's opinion
sumarial *adj* pertaining to an indictment
sumario, -a 1 *adj* (**a**) *(conciso)* brief (**b**) *Der* summary
2 *nm* (**a**) *Der* indictment (**b**) *(resumen)* summary
sumarísimo, -a *adj Der* swift, expeditious
Sumatra *n* Sumatra
sumergible 1 *adj* waterproof
2 *nm* submarine
sumergir [24] **1** *vt (hundir)* to submerge; *(con fuerza)* to plunge; *(bañar)* to dip; **s. en el caos** to plunge into chaos; **el libro sumerge al lector en otra época** the book immerses the reader in another age
2 sumergirse *vpr* (**a**) *(hundirse)* to submerge; *(con fuerza)* to plunge; **el coche se sumergió en el río** the car sank to the bottom of the river (**b**) *(abstraerse)* to immerse oneself (**en** in); **se sumergió en sus pensamientos** he immersed himself in his thoughts
sumerio, -a *adj & nm,f* Sumerian
sumidero *nm* drain
sumiller *(pl* **sumillers)** *nm* sommelier, wine waiter
suministrador, -ora *nm,f* supplier
suministrar *vt* to supply; **s. algo a alguien** to supply sb with sth
suministro *nm (productos)* supply; *(acción)* supplying
sumir 1 *vt* **s. a alguien en** to plunge sb into
2 sumirse en *vpr* (**a**) *(depresión, sueño)* to sink into (**b**) *(estudio, tema)* to immerse oneself in
sumisión *nf* (**a**) *(obediencia) (acción)* submission; *(cualidad)* submissiveness (**b**) *(rendición)* surrender
sumiso, -a *adj* submissive
súmmum *nm* **el s. de** the height of; **esto es el s.** this is wonderful *o* magnificent
sumo, -a *adj* **1** (**a**) *(supremo)* highest, supreme (**b**) *(gran)* extreme, great; **a lo s.** at most
2 *nm (lucha japonesa)* sumo (wrestling)
sunnita 1 *adj* Sunni
2 *nmf* Sunni Muslim, Sunnite
suntuario, -a *adj* luxury; **unas vacaciones suntuarias** a luxury vacation
suntuosidad *nf* sumptuousness, magnificence
suntuoso, -a *adj* sumptuous, magnificent
supe *ver* **saber**
supeditación *nf* subordination
supeditar 1 *vt* to subordinate (**a** to); **estar supeditado a** to be dependent on
2 supeditarse *vpr* **supeditarse a** to submit to
super- *prefijo Fam (muy)* really; **es supermajo** he's lovely *o* really nice; **superfácil** really *o* incredibly easy

súper 1 *adj Fam* great, super
2 *adv Fam* **pasarlo s.** to have a great time
3 *nm Fam* supermarket
4 *nf* **(gasolina) s.** regular
superable *adj* surmountable
superabundancia *nf* excess
superabundante *adj* excessive
superabundar *vi* to abound
superación *nf* overcoming; **afán de s.** drive to improve
superar 1 *vt* (**a**) *(sobrepasar)* to beat; **queremos s. los resultados del año pasado** we want to improve on *o* beat last year's results; **me superó por dos décimas de segundo** she beat me by two-tenths of a second; **s. algo/a alguien en algo** to beat sth/sb for sth; **nos superan en número** they outnumber us; **me supera en altura/ inteligencia** he's taller/cleverer than me
(**b**) *(adelantar)* to overtake, to pass
(**c**) *(época, técnica)* **estar superado** to have been superseded
(**d**) *(resolver)* to overcome; **s. un examen** to get through an exam; **tener algo superado** to have got over sth
2 superarse *vpr* (**a**) *(mejorar)* to better oneself; **se supera día a día** he goes from strength to strength (**b**) *(lucirse)* to excel oneself
superávit *nm inv* surplus; **s. presupuestario** budget surplus
supercarburante *nm* high-grade fuel
superchería *nf* (**a**) *(engaño)* fraud, hoax (**b**) *(superstición)* superstition
superconductor *nm* superconductor
supercopa *nf (en Europa)* European Supercup; *(en España)* = cup contested by the soccer league champions and the winner of the cup at the end of the season
superdotado, -a 1 *adj* extremely gifted
2 *nm,f* extremely gifted person
superego *nm Psi* superego
superestrella *nf* superstar
superestructura *nf* superstructure
superficial *adj también Fig* superficial
superficialidad *nf* superficiality
superficie *nf* (**a**) *(parte exterior)* surface; **salir a la s.** to come to the surface, to surface (**b**) *(área)* area; **tiene una s. de 2.500 metros cuadrados** it covers 2,500 square meters; **s. comercial/de venta** floor space
superfino, -a *adj* superfine
superfluo, -a *adj* superfluous; *(gasto)* unnecessary
supergigante *nm Dep* super giant slalom, Super G
superhéroe *nm* superhero
superhombre *nm* superman
superíndice *nm* superscript
superintendente *nmf* superintendent
superior¹ 1 *adj* (**a**) *(de arriba)* top; **la parte s. (de algo)** the top (of sth); **la mitad s.** the top *o* upper half (**b**) *(mayor)* higher (**a** than); **ser s. en número, ser numéricamente s.** to have a numerical advantage (**c**) *(mejor)* superior (**a** to); **es s. a la media** it's above average (**d**) *(excelente)* excellent (**e**) *Fam* **es s. a mí** *o* **a mis fuerzas** *(insoportable)* it's too much for me (**f**) *Anat & Geog* upper (**g**) *Educ* higher
2 *nm (jefe)* superior
superior², -ora *Rel* **1** *adj* superior
2 *nm,f* superior, *f* mother superior
superioridad *nf también Fig* superiority
superlativo, -a 1 *adj* (**a**) *(belleza, inteligencia)* exceptional (**b**) *Gram* superlative
2 *nm Gram* superlative
supermán *nm* superman
supermercado *nm* supermarket
superministro, -a *nm,f* = powerful government minister in charge of more than one department

supernova *nf* supernova

supernumerario, -a 1 *adj* (**a**) *(que está de más)* supernumerary, extra (**b**) *(funcionario)* on temporary leave
  2 *nm,f* supernumerary

superpetrolero *nm* supertanker

superpoblación *nf* overpopulation

superpoblado, -a *adj* overpopulated

superponer [50] *vt (poner encima)* to put on top (**a** of)

superposición *nf* superimposing

superpotencia *nf* superpower

superproducción *nf* (**a**) *Econ* overproduction (**b**) *Cine* big-budget movie

superpuesto, -a 1 *participio ver* **superponer**
  2 *adj* superimposed

supersónico, -a *adj* supersonic

superstición *nf* superstition

supersticioso, -a *adj* superstitious

supervalorar *vt (artista, obra)* to overrate; *(casa, acciones)* to overvalue

superventas *nm inv* best seller

supervisar *vt* to supervise

supervisión *nf* supervision

supervisor, -ora 1 *adj* supervisory
  2 *nm,f* supervisor

supervivencia *nf* survival

superviviente 1 *adj* surviving
  2 *nmf* survivor

supiera *etc ver* **saber**

supino, -a 1 *adj* (**a**) *(tendido)* supine (**b**) *(excesivo)* utter; **estupidez supina** crass stupidity
  2 *nm Gram* supine

suplantación *nf* s. **(de personalidad)** impersonation

suplantador, -ora *nm,f* impostor

suplantar *vt* to take the place of

suplementario, -a *adj* supplementary, extra

suplemento *nm* (**a**) *(añadido) & Prensa* supplement; **s. a color** color supplement; **s. dominical** Sunday supplement (**b**) *(complemento)* attachment

suplencia *nf* hacer una s. *(profesor)* to do substitute teaching; *(médico)* to do a locum tenens

suplente 1 *adj* stand-in; **profesor s.** substitute teacher
  2 *nmf (sustituto)* substitute, stand-in; *Teatro* understudy; *Dep* substitute

supletorio, -a 1 *adj* additional, extra
  2 *nm Tel* extension (phone)

súplica *nf* (**a**) *(ruego)* plea, entreaty (**b**) *Der* petition

suplicar [59] *vt* (**a**) *(rogar)* **s. algo (a alguien)** to plead for sth (with sb); **s. a alguien que haga algo** to beg sb to do sth (**b**) *Der* to appeal to

suplicatorio *nm Der (a tribunal superior)* = request by lower court for assistance from a higher court; *(a órgano legislativo)* = request by court for the parliamentary immunity of the accused to be waived

suplicio *nm también Fig* torture; **es un s.** it's torture; **¡qué s.!** what a life!

suplique *etc ver* **suplicar**

suplir *vt* (**a**) *(sustituir)* to replace (**con** with) (**b**) *(compensar)* **s. algo (con)** to compensate for sth (with)

supo *ver* **saber**

suponer [50] **1** *vt* (**a**) *(creer, presuponer)* to suppose; **supongo que ya habrán llegado** I suppose *o* expect (that) they'll have arrived by now; **supongo que sí/no** I suppose *o* expect so/not; **supongamos que me niego** supposing I refuse; **es de s. que se disculparán** I would expect them to apologize; **suponiendo que...** supposing *o* assuming that... (**b**) *(implicar)* to involve, to entail (**c**) *(significar)* to mean (**d**)

(conjeturar) to imagine; **lo suponía** I guessed as much; **te suponía mayor** I thought you were older
  2 *vi* to be important
  3 *nm* **ser un s.** to be conjecture
  4 suponerse *vpr* **se supone que habíamos quedado a las ocho** we were supposed *o* meant to meet at eight; **se supone que todos tenemos los mismos derechos** we're all supposed to have the same rights

suposición *nf* assumption

supositorio *nm* suppository

supranacional *adj* supranational

suprarrenal *adj* suprarenal

supremacía *nf* supremacy

supremo, -a 1 *adj también Fig* supreme
  2 *nm Der* **el (Tribunal) S.** $\simeq$ the Supreme Court

supresión *nf* (**a**) *(de ley, impuesto, derecho)* abolition; *(de sanciones, restricciones)* lifting (**b**) *(de palabras, texto)* deletion (**c**) *(de puestos de trabajo, proyectos)* axing

suprimir *vt* (**a**) *(ley, impuesto, derecho)* to abolish; *(sanciones, restricciones)* to lift; **hay que s. todo lo superfluo** we have to get rid of everything that's superfluous (**b**) *(palabras, texto)* to delete; **suprime los detalles y ve al grano** forget the details and get to the point (**c**) *(puestos de trabajo, proyectos)* to ax

supuesto, -a 1 *participio ver* **suponer**
  2 *adj* supposed; *(culpable, asesino)* alleged; *(nombre)* false; **dar algo por s.** to take sth for granted
  3 *nm* assumption; **en el s. de que...** assuming...
  4 por supuesto *loc adv* of course

supuración *nf* suppuration

supurar *vi* to suppurate, to fester

supusiera *etc ver* **suponer**

sur 1 *adj (posición, parte)* south, southern; *(dirección, viento)* southerly; **tiempo soleado en la mitad s. del país** it will be sunny in the southern half of the country; **partieron con rumbo s.** they headed south
  2 *nm* south; **viento del s.** south wind; **ir hacia el s.** to go south(wards); **está al s. de Madrid** it's (to the) south of Madrid

Suramérica *n* South America

suramericano, -a *adj & nm,f* South American

surcar [59] *vt (tierra)* to plow; *(aire, agua)* to cut *o* slice through

surco *nm* (**a**) *(zanja)* furrow (**b**) *(señal) (de disco)* groove; *(de rueda)* rut (**c**) *(arruga)* line, wrinkle

surcoreano, -a 1 *adj* South Korean
  2 *nm,f* South Korean

sureño, -a 1 *adj* southern; *(viento)* southerly
  2 *nm,f* southerner

sureste 1 *adj (posición, parte)* southeast, southeastern; *(dirección, viento)* southeasterly
  2 *nm* southeast

surf, surfing *nm* surfing

surfear *vt & vi Fam Inform* to surf

surfista *nmf* surfer

surgir [24] *vi* (**a**) *(brotar)* to spring forth (**b**) *(aparecer)* to appear; **surgió de detrás de las cortinas** he emerged from behind the curtains (**c**) *(producirse)* to arise; **se lo preguntaré si surge la ocasión** I'll ask her if the opportunity arises; **nos surgieron varios problemas** we ran into a number of problems; **me surge una duda** I have one doubt

Surinam *n* Surinam

suroeste 1 *adj (posición, parte)* southwest, southwestern; *(dirección, viento)* southwesterly
  2 *nm* southwest

surque *etc ver* **surcar**

surrealismo *nm* surrealism

surrealista *adj & nmf* surrealist

surtido, -a 1 *adj* (a) *(bien aprovisionado)* well-stocked (b) *(variado)* assorted

2 *nm* (a) *(gama)* range (b) *(caja surtida)* assortment

surtidor *nm (de gasolina)* pump; *(de un chorro)* spout

surtir 1 *vt (proveer)* to supply (**de** with)

2 *vi (brotar)* to spout, to spurt (**de** from)

3 surtirse *vpr (proveerse)* **surtirse de** to stock up on

susceptibilidad *nf* oversensitivity

susceptible *adj* (a) *(sensible)* oversensitive (b) *(posible)* **s. de** liable to

suscitar *vt (discusión)* to give rise to; *(dificultades)* to cause, to create; *(interés, simpatía, sospechas)* to arouse; *(dudas)* to raise

suscribir, subscribir 1 *vt* (a) *(firmar)* to sign (b) *(ratificar)* to endorse (c) *Com (acciones)* to subscribe for

2 suscribirse *vpr* (a) *Prensa* to subscribe (**a** to) (b) *Com* **suscribirse a** to take out an option on

suscripción, subscripción *nf* subscription

suscriptor, -ora, subscriptor, -ora *nm,f* subscriber

suscrito, -a 1 *participio ver* **suscribir**

2 *adj* **estar s. a** to subscribe to

susodicho, -a *adj* above-mentioned

suspender 1 *vt* (a) *(colgar)* to hang (up); **lo suspendieron de una cuerda/de un clavo** they hung it from a rope/nail (b) *Esp (examen, asignatura)* to fail; **me suspendieron la Historia** I failed History (c) *(interrumpir)* to suspend; *(reunión, sesión)* to adjourn; **el partido se suspendió a causa de la lluvia** the game was postponed *o* called off because of the rain (d) *(sancionar) (trabajador)* to suspend; *Am (alumno)* to suspend; **s. a alguien de empleo y sueldo** to suspend sb without pay

2 *vi Esp (alumno)* to fail

suspense *nm* suspense

suspensión *nf* (a) *(gen)* & *Aut* suspension; **en s.** in suspension; **s. de empleo** suspension on full pay; **s. de pagos** temporary receivership, ≃ Chapter 11 (b) *(interrupción)* postponement; *(de reunión, sesión)* adjournment

suspenso, -a *adj* **1** (a) *(colgado)* **s. de** hanging from (b) *Esp (no aprobado)* **estar s.** to have failed

2 *nm* (a) *Esp (nota)* **sacar un s.** to fail (b) **en s.** *(interrumpido)* pending (c) *Am (suspense)* suspense

suspensorio *nm* jockstrap

suspicacia *nf* suspicion

suspicaz *adj* suspicious

suspirar *vi* (a) *(dar suspiros)* to sigh; **s. de** to sigh with (b) *(desear)* **s. por algo/por hacer algo** to long for sth/to do sth

suspiro *nm (aspiración)* sigh; **dar un s.** to heave a sigh (b) *(instante)* **en un s.** in no time at all

sustancia, substancia *nf* (a) *(materia)* substance; **s. gris** gray matter; **s. química** chemical (b) *(esencia)* essence; **sin s.** lacking in substance; **este artículo no tiene mucha s.** this article lacks substance (c) *(de alimento)* nutritional value

sustancial, substancial *adj* substantial, significant

sustanciar, substanciar *vt* (a) *(resumir)* to summarize (b) *Der* to substantiate

sustancioso, -a, substancioso, -a *adj* substantial

sustantivación, substantivación *nf Gram* nominalization, use as a noun

sustantivar, substantivar *vt Gram* to nominalize, to use as a noun

sustantivo, -a, substantivo, -a 1 *adj Formal (fundamental)* substantial, significant

2 *nm Gram* noun

sustentación *nf* support

sustentar 1 *vt* (a) *(sostener)* to support; **sustenta a toda la familia con su salario** he supports his entire family on his salary (b) *(defender) (argumento, teoría)* to defend

2 sustentarse *vpr* (a) *(sostenerse)* to support oneself (b)

(apoyarse) **su ilusión se sustenta en vanas promesas** her hopes are based *o* founded on empty promises

sustento *nm* (a) *(alimento)* sustenance; *(mantenimiento)* livelihood; **ganarse el s.** to earn one's living (b) *(apoyo)* support

sustitución, substitución *nf* (a) *(cambio)* replacement; **aprobaron la s. del sistema informático por uno más moderno** they approved the relacement of the computer system by a more up-to-date one; **entró al terreno de juego en s. del defensa francés** he went onto the field as a replacement for the French defender; **trabajar haciendo sustituciones** to temp *(for sb ill or on leave)* (b) *Der* subrogation

sustituible, substituible *adj* replaceable

sustituir, substituir [34] *vt* to replace (**por** with); *(temporalmente)* to substitute for; **sustituyó a su secretaria** he replaced his secretary, he got a new secretary; **tuve que sustituirle durante su enfermedad** I had to stand in *o* substitute for him while he was ill; **la sustituyó como presidenta de la empresa** he took her place as president of the company

sustitutivo, -a, substitutivo, -a *adj* & *nm* substitute (**de** for)

sustituto, -a substituto, -a *nm,f* substitute, replacement

susto *nm* fright; **dar** *o* **pegar un s. a alguien** to give sb a fright; **darse** *o* **pegarse un s.** to get a fright; *Fam Fig* **darse un s. mortal** *o* **de muerte** to be scared to death; **no ganar para sustos** to have no end of troubles

sustracción, substracción *nf* (a) *(robo)* theft (b) *Mat* subtraction

sustraendo, substraendo *nm Mat* subtrahend, = amount to be subtracted

sustraer substraer [66] **1** *vt* (a) *(robar)* to steal (b) *Mat* to subtract

2 sustraerse *vpr* **sustraerse a** *o* **de** *(obligación, problema)* to avoid

sustrato *nm* substratum

susurrador, -ora, susurrante *adj* whispering

susurrar *vt* & *vi* to whisper

susurro *nm (palabras)* whisper; *(de agua, viento)* murmur

sutil *adj (en general)* subtle; *(velo, tejido)* delicate, thin; *(brisa)* gentle; *(hilo, línea)* fine

sutileza *nf (en general)* subtlety; *(de velo, tejido)* delicacy, thinness; *(de brisa)* gentleness; *(de hilo, línea)* fineness

sutura *nf* suture

suturar *vt* to stitch

Suva *n* Suva

suyo, -a 1 *adj posesivo (de él)* his; *(de ella)* hers; *(de uno)* one's (own); *(de ellos, ellas)* theirs; *(de usted, ustedes)* yours; **este libro es s.** this book is his/hers/etc; **un amigo s.** a friend of his/hers/etc; **no es asunto s.** it's none of his/her/etc business; *Fam Fig* **es muy s.** he's a law unto himself

2 *pron posesivo* (a) **el s.** *(de él)* his; *(de ella)* hers; *(de cosa, animal)* its (own); *(de uno)* one's own; *(de ellos, ellas)* theirs; *(de usted, ustedes)* yours (b) *(expresiones)* **de s.** in itself; **hacer de las suyas** to be up to his/her/etc usual tricks; **hacer s.** to make one's own; *Fam* **esta es la suya** this is the chance he's been waiting for *o* his big chance; **lo s. es el teatro** theater is his/her *etc* thing; **lo s. sería volver** the proper thing to do would be to go back; *Fam* **los suyos** *(su familia)* his/her/etc folks; *(su bando)* his/her/etc lot *o* side

svástica [es'βastika] *nf* swastika

SWAPO ['swapo] *nm (abrev de* **South West African People's Organization**) SWAPO

swing [swin] *(pl* **swings**) *nm Mús* & *Dep* swing

Sydney *n* Sydney

T

T, t [te] *nf (letra)* T, t

t (a) *(abrev de* **tonelada**) t (b) *(abrev de* **tomo**) vol

taba *nf* **jugar a las tabas** to play at fivestones *(similar to jacks)*

tabacalero, -a *adj* tobacco; **la industria tabacalera** the tobacco industry

tabaco 1 *nm* (a) *(planta)* tobacco plant (b) *(picadura)* tobacco; **t. de liar** rolling tobacco; **t. negro/rubio** dark/Virginia tobacco; **t. de pipa** pipe tobacco (c) *(cigarrillos)* cigarettes
   2 *adj inv (color)* light brown

tábano *nm* horsefly

tabaquera *nf (caja)* tobacco tin

tabaquería *nf Am* cigar store

tabaquismo *nm* = addiction to tobacco, and its damaging effects on one's health

tabardo *nm (de soldado)* greatcoat

tabarra *nf Fam* **dar la t.** to be a pest, to act up; **dar la t. con algo** to go on and on about sth

tabasco *nm* Tabasco® (sauce)

taberna *nf (bar)* bar *(old-fashioned in style)*; *(antiguo)* tavern, inn

tabernáculo *nm* tabernacle

tabernario, -a *adj* coarse

tabernero, -a *nm,f (propietario)* landlord, *f* landlady; *(encargado)* bartender, barman, *f* barmaid

tabicar [59] *vt* to wall up

tabique *nm* (a) *(pared)* partition (wall) (b) *Anat* **t. nasal** nasal septum (c) *Méx (ladrillo)* brick

tabla 1 *nf* (a) *(de madera)* plank; **t. de planchar** ironing board; *Dep* **t. de saltos** *(trampolín)* diving board
   (b) *(pliegue)* pleat
   (c) *(lista, gráfico)* table; **t. de conversión** *(para medidas)* conversion table; **t. de materias** table of contents; **t. de multiplicación** multiplication table; **t. periódica (de los elementos)** periodic table (of elements)
   (d) *Culin* **t. de cocina** chopping board; **t. de patés** selection of pâtés; **t. de quesos** cheeseboard
   (e) *(de surf, vela)* board; **t. de surf** surfboard
   (f) *Arte* panel
   (g) *(expresiones)* **ser una t. de salvación** to be a last resort *o* hope; **hacer t. rasa** to wipe the slate clean
   2 tablas *nfpl* (a) *(en ajedrez)* **quedar en** *o* **hacer tablas** to end in stalemate; **quedamos/el debate quedó en tablas** *(en enfrentamiento)* we reached a stalemate, the debate ended in a stalemate (b) *Teatro* stage, boards; **tener (muchas) tablas** to be an experienced actor; *Fig* to be an old hand (c) *Taurom* fence surrounding bullring

tablado *nm (de teatro)* stage; *(de baile)* dance floor; *(plataforma)* platform

tablao *nm (local)* = club where flamenco dancing and singing is performed

tableado, -a *adj (falda)* pleated

tablero *nm* (a) *(tabla)* board; **t. de ajedrez** chessboard; **t. de dibujo** drawing board (b) *(en baloncesto)* backboard (c) **t. (de mandos)** *(de avión)* instrument panel; *(de coche)* dashboard

tableta *nf* (a) *Med* tablet (b) *(de chocolate)* bar

tablilla *nf* (a) *Med (para entablillar)* splint (b) *Méx (de chocolate)* bar

tabloide *nm* tabloid

tablón *nm (tabla)* plank; *(viga)* beam; **t. de anuncios** bulletin board

tabú *(pl* **tabúes** *o* **tabús**) *adj & nm* taboo

tabulación *nf* tab settings

tabulador *nm (tecla)* tabulator, tab (key)

tabular *vt & vi* to tabulate

taburete *nm* stool

TAC [tak] *Med nf (abrev de* **tomografía axial computerizada**) *(sistema)* CAT; *(escáner)* CAT scan

tacada *nf (en billar) (golpe)* stroke; *(carambolas)* break

tacañería *nf* miserliness

tacaño, -a 1 *adj* miserly
   2 *nm,f* miserly person

tacataca, tacatá *nm (baby)* walker

tacha *nf* (a) *(defecto)* flaw, fault; **sin t.** faultless (b) *(clavo)* tack

tachadura *nf* crossing out

tachar *vt* (a) *(lo escrito)* to cross out (b) *(acusar)* **t. a alguien de mentiroso/cobarde** to accuse sb of being a liar/coward

tacho *nm Andes, RP (metálico, de hojalata)* tin; *(de plástico)* container; *(papelera)* wastebasket

tachón *nm* (a) *(tachadura)* crossing out (b) *(clavo)* stud

tachonado, -a *adj (salpicado)* studded **(de** with)

tachonar *vt* (a) *(poner clavos)* to decorate with studs (b) *(salpicar)* to stud

tachuela *nf* tack

tácito, -a *adj (acuerdo)* tacit; *(norma, regla)* unwritten

taciturno, -a *adj* taciturn

taco *nm* (a) *(tarugo)* plug; *(para tornillo)* plastic anchor *(to secure screw in wall)* (b) *(cuña)* wedge (c) *Esp Fam (palabrota)* swearword; **decir tacos** to swear (d) *Esp Fam (confusión)* mess, muddle; **armarse un t. (con algo)** to get into a muddle (over sth) (e) *(de billar)* cue (f) *(de billetes de banco)* wad; *(de billetes de autobús, metro)* book; *(de hojas)* pile, stack (g) *(de jamón, queso)* cube (h) *Esp Fam* **tacos** *(años)* years (of age) (i) *Culin* taco, = filled tortilla (j) *Andes, RP (tacón)* heel; **tacos altos** high heels

tacógrafo *nm* tachograph

tacón *nm* heel; **de t. (alto)** high-heeled; **t. de aguja** stiletto heel

taconazo *nm* stamp (of the heel); **dar un t.** to stamp one's foot

taconear *vi* (a) *(bailarín)* to stamp one's feet (b) *Mil* to click one's heels

taconeo *nm (de bailarín)* foot-stamping

táctica *nf también Fig* tactics

táctico, -a *adj* tactical

táctil *adj* tactile

tacto nm (**a**) (sentido) sense of touch (**b**) (textura) feel; **áspero/ suave al t.** rough/soft to the touch (**c**) (delicadeza) tact; **con t.** tactfully; **tener t.** to be tactful (**d**) Med manual examination

TAE ['tae] nf Fin (abrev de **tasa anual equivalente**) APR, Annual Percentage Rate

taekwondo [tae'kwondo] nm tae kwon do

tafetán nm taffeta

tafilete nm morocco leather

tagalo, -a 1 adj & nm,f Tagalog
   2 nm (lengua) Tagalog

tahona nf bakery

tahúr, -ura nm,f cardsharp

tai-chi nm tai chi

taifa nf Hist = independent Muslim kingdom in Iberian peninsula

taiga nf taiga

tailandés, -esa 1 adj & nm,f Thai
   2 nm (lengua) Thai

Tailandia n Thailand

taimado, -a 1 adj crafty
   2 nm,f crafty person

Taipei n Taipei

Taiwán [tai'wan] n Taiwan

taiwanés, -esa [taiwa'nes, -esa] adj & nm,f Taiwanese

tajada nf (**a**) (rodaja) slice (**b**) (parte) share; **sacar t. de algo** to get something out of sth (**c**) Esp Fam (borrachera) **agarrarse una t. (como un piano)** to get plastered o legless

tajadera nf (**a**) (tabla) chopping board (**b**) (cuchillo) chopping knife

tajante adj (respuesta, rechazo) categorical; (tono) emphatic

tajar vt (cortar) to cut o slice up; (en dos) to slice in two

Tajo nm **el (río) T.** the (River) Tagus

tajo nm (**a**) (corte) deep cut (**b**) Esp (trabajo) workplace, work (**c**) (de carnicero) chopping block (**d**) (acantilado) precipice

tal 1 adj (**a**) (semejante, tan grande) such; **¡jamás se vio cosa t.!** you've never seen such a thing!; **lo dijo con t. seguridad que...** he said it with such conviction that...; **su miedo era t. o t. era su miedo que...** so great o such was her fear that..., she was so afraid that...; **en t. caso** in such a case; **dijo cosas tales como...** he said things like...
   (**b**) (sin especificar) such and such; **a t. hora** at such and such a time
   (**c**) (desconocido) **te ha llamado un t. Pérez** a Mr. Pérez called for you; **hay un t. Jiménez que te puede ayudar** there's someone called Mr. Jiménez who can help you
   2 pron (**a**) (alguna cosa) such a thing (**b**) (expresiones) **que si t. que si cual** this, that and the other; **ser t. para cual** to be two of a kind; **t. y cual, t. y t.** this and that; **y t.** (etcétera) and so on
   3 adv **¿qué t....?** how...?; **¿qué t. (estás)?** how's it going?, how are you doing?; **¿qué t. el viaje?** how was the journey?; **déjalo t. cual** leave it just as it is; **t. (y) como** just as o like; Fam **t. que** (como por ejemplo) like
   4 tal vez loc adv perhaps, maybe
   5 con tal de loc conj as long as, provided; **con t. de volver pronto...** as long as we're back early...; **con t. (de) que** as long as, provided

tala nf felling

taladradora nf (para pared, madera) drill; (para papel) paper punch

taladrar vt to drill; **este ruido te taladra los tímpanos** the noise is ear-piercing

taladro nm (**a**) (taladradora) drill (**b**) (agujero) drill hole

tálamo nm (**a**) Formal (cama) marriage bed (**b**) Anat & Bot thalamus

talante nm (**a**) (humor) mood; **estar de buen t.** to be in a good mood (**b**) (carácter) character, disposition

talar vt to fell

talasoterapia nf thalassotherapy

talco nm talc; **polvos de t.** talcum powder

talega nf sack

talego nm Esp Fam (cárcel) slammer, pen

talento nm (**a**) (don natural) talent (**b**) (inteligencia) intelligence

talentoso, -a, talentudo, -a adj talented

Talgo ['talgo] nm (abrev de **tren articulado ligero Goicoechea Oriol**) = Spanish intercity high-speed train

talibán adj & nmf Taliban

talidomida nf thalidomide

talión nm **la ley del t.** an eye for an eye and a tooth for a tooth

talismán nm talisman

talla nf (**a**) (medida) size; **¿qué t. usas?** what size are you?; **no es de mi t.** it's not my size (**b**) (estatura) height; **es de mi t.** she's as tall as me (**c**) (capacidad) stature; **dar la t.** to be up to it; **no dio la t. como representante del colegio** he wasn't up to the task of representing his school (**d**) Arte (en madera) carving; (en piedra) sculpture (**e**) (de piedra preciosa) cutting

tallado, -a 1 adj (madera) carved; (piedra preciosa) cut
   2 nm (de madera, piedra) carving; (de piedra preciosa) cutting

tallar vt (**a**) (esculpir) (madera, piedra) to carve; (piedra preciosa) to cut (**b**) (medir) to measure (the height of) (**c**) Méx (limpiar) to scrub; (masajear) to rub

tallarines nmpl (chinos) noodles; (italianos) tagliatelle

talle nm (**a**) (cintura) waist (**b**) (figura, cuerpo) figure (**c**) (medida) measurement

taller nm (**a**) (lugar de trabajo) workshop; (de artista) studio; **t. de artesanía** craft studio (**b**) Aut garage; **t. de chapa y pintura** body shop; **t. mecánico** o **de reparaciones** garage, repair shop (**c**) (cursillo, seminario) workshop

Tallin n Tallin

tallista nmf (de madera) wood carver; (de piedra) stone carver

tallo nm (de planta, flor) stem; (brote) sprout, shoot

talludito, -a adj **estar** o **ser t.** to be getting on (a bit)

talludo, -a adj (**a**) (planta) thick-stemmed (**b**) (persona) tall

Talmud nm **el T.** the Talmud

talón nm (**a**) (de pie) heel; Fig **t. de Aquiles** Achilles' heel; **pisarle a alguien los talones** to be hot on sb's heels (**b**) (cheque) check; (matriz) stub; **t. devuelto/en blanco** bounced/blank check; **t. sin fondos** bad check

talonario nm (de cheques) checkbook; (de recibos) receipt book

talonera nf heelpiece

talud nm bank, slope; **t. continental** continental slope

talvez adv Am perhaps, maybe; **¿vienes? — t.** are you coming? — perhaps o maybe; **t. vaya** I may go

tamal nm tamale

tamaño, -a 1 adj such; **¡cómo pudo decir tamaña estupidez!** how could he say such a stupid thing!
   2 nm size; **son del mismo t.** they're the same size; **de gran t.** large; **del t. de** as large as, the size of; **de t. familiar** family(-size); **de t. natural** life-size; **t. carné** o **carnet** passport-size

tamarindo nm (**a**) (fruta) tamarind (**b**) Méx Fam (policía de tránsito) traffic cop

tambaleante adj (**a**) (inestable) (mesa) wobbly, unsteady; (persona) staggering (**b**) (gobierno, economía) unstable, shaky

tambalearse vpr (**a**) (bambolearse) (persona) to stagger, to totter; (mueble) to wobble, to be unsteady; (tren) to sway (**b**) (gobierno, sistema) to totter

tambaleo nm (de tren) rocking motion; (de mueble) wobble; (de persona) staggering

también adv also, too; **yo t.** me too; **yo t. vivo en Chile, yo vivo en Chile t.** I live in Chile too o as well; **dormí muy bien — yo t.** I slept very well — me too o so did I; **t. a mí me gusta** I like it too, I also like it; **sabes cantar y bailar, pero**

no tocar el piano — sí, t. you can sing and dance, but you can't play the piano — yes, I can do that too; *Fam* **le eché un broncazo increíble — ¡tú t.!** I gave him a real telling off — was that really necessary?

tambor 1 *nm* (**a**) *Mús & Mec* drum; *(de pistola)* cylinder (**b**) *Anat* eardrum

2 *nmf (tamborilero)* drummer

tamboril *nm* small drum

tamborilear *vi Mús & Fig* to drum

tamborileo *nm* drumming

tamborilero, -a *nm,f* drummer

Támesis *nm* **el (río) T.** the Thames (River)

tamice *etc ver* **tamizar**

tamil 1 *adj & nmf* Tamil

2 *nm (lengua)* Tamil

tamiz *nm* (**a**) *(cedazo)* sieve (**b**) *(selección)* **la prueba es un t. para eliminar a los peores** the test is designed to weed out the weaker candidates

tamizar [14] *vt* (**a**) *(cribar)* to sieve (**b**) *(seleccionar)* to screen

tampoco *adv* neither, not… either; **ella no va y tú t.** she's not going and neither are you *o* and you aren't either; **yo no voy — yo t.** I'm not going — neither am I *o* me neither; **yo t. lo veo** I can't see it either; **no me gusta éste ni ése t.** I don't like this one or this one either; **¡t. nos íbamos a presentar sin un regalo!** we were hardly going to turn up without a present!; **t. es que me importe mucho** it's not as if it matters much to me; **t. vendría mal descansar un poco** it wouldn't be a bad idea to have a little rest, a little rest wouldn't come amiss

tampón *nm* (**a**) *(sello)* stamp; *(almohadilla)* inkpad (**b**) *(para la menstruación)* tampon; **t. contraceptivo** contraceptive sponge

tam-tam *nm inv* tom tom

tan *adv* (**a**) *(mucho)* so; **t. grande/deprisa (que…)** so big/quickly (that…); **¡qué película t. larga!** what a long movie!; **t. es así que…** so much so that…; **de t. amable que es, se hace inaguantable** she's so kind it can get unbearable (**b**) *(en comparaciones)* **t.… como…** as… as… (**c**) **t. sólo** only

tanatorio *nm* = building where relatives and friends of a dead person can stand vigil over the deceased in a private room on the night before the burial

tanda *nf* (**a**) *(grupo, lote)* group, batch (**b**) *(serie)* series

tándem *nm* (**a**) *(bicicleta)* tandem (**b**) *(pareja)* duo, pair

tanga *nm* tanga

tangana *nf Fam Dep* fistfight, free-for-all

Tanganica *nm* **el lago T.** Lake Tanganyika

tangar *vt Fam* to rip off

tangencial *adj* tangential

tangente 1 *adj* tangential

2 *nf* tangent; **irse** *o* **salirse por la t.** to go off at a tangent

Tánger *n* Tangiers

tangible *adj* tangible

tango *nm* tango

tanguero, -a 1 *adj* **ser muy t.** to love the tango

2 *nm,f (aficionado)* tango enthusiast

tanguista *nmf* tango singer

tanino *nm* tannin

tanque *nm* (**a**) *Mil* tank (**b**) *(vehículo cisterna)* tanker (**c**) *(depósito)* tank (**d**) *Esp (de cerveza)* beer mug

tanqueta *nf* armored car

tanteador *nm (marcador)* scoreboard

tantear 1 *vt* (**a**) *(probar, sondear)* to test (out); *(toro, contrincante)* to size up; *Fig* **t. el terreno** to see how the land lies, to test the waters (**b**) *(sopesar)* *(peso, precio, cantidad)* to try to guess; *(problema, posibilidades, ventajas)* to weigh up

2 *vi (andar a tientas)* to feel one's way

tanteo *nm* (**a**) *(prueba, sondeo)* testing out; *(de posibilidades, ventajas)* weighing up; *(de contrincante, puntos débiles)* sizing up (**b**) *(cálculo aproximado)* rough calculation, estimate; **a t.** roughly (**c**) *(puntuación)* score (**d**) *Der* first option *(on a purchase)*

tanto, -a 1 *adj* (**a**) *(gran cantidad)* so much; **tantos** so many; **t. dinero** so much money, such a lot of money; **tanta gente** so many people; **tiene t. entusiasmo/tantos amigos que…** she has so much enthusiasm/so many friends that… (**b**) *(cantidad indeterminada)* so much; **tantos** so many; **nos daban tantos pesos al día** they used to give us so many pesos per day; **cuarenta y tantos** forty-something, forty-odd; **nos conocimos en el sesenta y tantos** we met sometime in the sixties (**c**) *(en comparaciones)* **t.… como** as much… as; **tantos… como** as many… as

2 *pron* (**a**) *(gran cantidad)* so much; **tantos** so many; **¿cómo puedes tener tantos?** how can you have so many? (**b**) *(cantidad indeterminada)* so much; **tantos** so many; **a tantos de agosto** on such and such a date in August (**c**) *(igual cantidad)* as much; **tantos** as many; **había mucha gente aquí, pero allí no había tanta** there were a lot of people here, but there weren't as many there; **otro t.** as much again, the same again; **otro t. les ocurrió a los demás** the same thing happened to the rest of them (**d**) *(expresiones)* **ser uno de tantos** to be nothing special; **¡y t.!** most certainly!, you bet! (**e**) *Fam* **las tantas** very late

3 *nm* (**a**) *(punto)* point; *(gol)* goal; **marcar un t.** to score; **apuntarse un t. (a favor)** to earn oneself a point in one's favor (**b**) *(cantidad indeterminada)* **un t.** so much, a certain amount; **t. por ciento** percentage (**c**) **estar al t. (de)** to be up to date (with); **mantener a alguien al t. de algo** *(informado)* to keep sb up to date on *o* informed about sth

4 *adv* (**a**) *(mucho)* **t. (que…)** *(cantidad)* so much (that…); *(tiempo)* so long (that…); **no bebas t.** don't drink so much; **de eso hace t. que ya no me acordaba** it's been so long since that happened that I don't even remember; **t. (es así) que…** so much so that…; **t. mejor/peor** so much the better/worse (**b**) *(en comparaciones)* **t. como** as much as; **t. hombres como mujeres** both men and women; **t. si estoy como si no** whether I'm there or not

5 en tanto que *loc prep* as; **en t. que director** as director

6 entre tanto *loc adv* meanwhile

7 por (lo) tanto *loc adv* therefore, so

Tanzania *n* Tanzania

tanzano, -a *adj & nm,f* Tanzanian

tañer *vt (instrumento)* to strum; *(campana)* to ring

tañido *nm (de instrumento)* strumming; *(de campana)* ringing

taoísmo *nm* Taoism

taoísta *adj & nmf* Taoist

tapa *nf* (**a**) *(para cerrar)* lid; *(de frasco)* top; *Andes, RP (de botella, bolígrafo)* top; *Fam* **levantarse la t. de los sesos** to blow one's brains out; **t. del objetivo** *(de cámara)* lens cap (**b**) *Culin* snack, tapa (**c**) *(portada) (de libro)* cover; *(de disco)* sleeve (**d**) *(de zapato)* heel plate (**e**) *(trozo de carne)* topside

tapabarro *nm Andes* mudguard

tapacubos *nm inv* hubcap

tapadera *nf* (**a**) *(tapa)* lid (**b**) *(para encubrir)* front

tapadillo: de tapadillo *loc adv* on the sly

tapado *nm CSur (abrigo)* overcoat

tapar 1 *vt* (**a**) *(cerrar) (ataúd, cofre)* to close (the lid of); *(olla, caja)* to put the lid on; *(botella)* to put the top on (**b**) *(ocultar, cubrir)* to cover; *(no dejar ver)* to block out; **quítate, que me tapas la tele** could you move out of the way? — I can't see the TV with you in the way; **me tapó los ojos** *(con las manos)* he put his hands over my eyes; *(con venda)* he blindfolded me (**c**) *(abrigar)* to cover up; *(en la cama)* to tuck in; **lo tapó con una manta** she put a blanket over him to keep him warm (**d**) *(encubrir)* to cover up (**e**) *Am (taponar)* to block

2 taparse *vpr* (**a**) *(cubrirse)* to cover (up); **se tapó la boca con la mano** she put her hand over her mouth (**b**) *(abrigarse) (con ropa)* to wrap up; *(en la cama)* to tuck oneself in; **me tapé con una manta** I pulled a blanket over me (**c**) *Am (taponarse)* to get blocked (up)

taparrabos *nm inv* (**a**) *(de hombre primitivo)* loincloth (**b**) *(tanga)* tanga briefs

tapear *vi Esp Fam* to have some tapas

tapeo *nm Esp Fam* **ir de t.** to go out for some tapas; **bar de t.** tapas bar

tapete *nm (paño)* runner; *(en mesa de billar, para cartas)* baize; *Am (alfombra)* carpet; *Fig* **estar sobre el t.** to be up for discussion; *Fig* **poner algo sobre el t.** to put sth up for discussion; **t. verde** *(mesa de juego)* card table

tapia *nf* (stone) wall; *Fam* **estar sordo como una t.** to be (as) deaf as a post

tapiar *vt* (**a**) *(obstruir)* to brick up (**b**) *(cercar)* to wall in

tapice *etc ver* **tapizar**

tapicería *nf* (**a**) *(tela)* upholstery (**b**) *(tienda) (para muebles)* upholsterer's; *(para cortinas)* draper's (**c**) *(tapices)* tapestries (**d**) *(oficio) (de muebles)* upholstery; *(de tapices)* tapestry making

tapicero, -a *nm,f* (**a**) *(de muebles)* upholsterer (**b**) *(de tapices)* tapestry maker

tapioca *nf* tapioca

tapir *nm* tapir

tapiz *nm (para la pared)* tapestry

tapizado, -a 1 *adj (sillón)* upholstered (**en** *o* **con** with); *(pared)* lined (**en** *o* **con** with)

2 *nm* (**a**) *(de mueble)* upholstery (**b**) *(de pared)* tapestries

tapizar [14] *vt (mueble)* to upholster

tapón *nm* (**a**) *(para tapar) (botellas, frascos)* stopper; *(de corcho)* cork; *(de metal, plástico)* cap, top; *(de bañera, lavabo)* plug; **t. de rosca** screw-top (**b**) *(atasco)* traffic jam (**c**) *(en el oído) (de cerumen)* wax in the ear; *(de algodón, goma)* earplug (**d**) *Fam (persona baja)* shorty (**e**) *(en baloncesto)* block; **poner un t.** to block a shot (**f**) *Am (plomo)* fuse

taponamiento *nm* (**a**) *Med* tamponage (**b**) *Mec* plugging

taponar 1 *vt* (**a**) *(cerrar) (botella)* to put the top on; *(lavadero)* to put the plug in; *(salida)* to block; *(tubería)* to stop up (**b**) *Med* to tampon

2 taponarse *vpr* to get blocked

tapujo *nm* subterfuge; **hacer algo con/sin tapujos** to do sth deceitfully/openly

taquear 1 *vt Col, Ven Fam (atiborrar)* **no taquees ese armario** don't stuff too many things into that cupboard

2 *vi* (**a**) *Am Fam (jugar)* to play billiards, to play *o* shoot pool (**b**) *Méx (comer)* to eat tacos

3 taquearse *vpr Col, Ven Fam (de comida)* to stuff oneself

taquería *nf Méx (quiosco)* taco stall; *(restaurante)* taco restaurant

taquicardia *nf* tachycardia

taquigrafía *nf* shorthand, stenography

taquigrafiar [32] *vt* to write (down) in shorthand

taquígrafo, -a *nm,f* shorthand writer, stenographer

taquilla *nf* (**a**) *(ventanilla)* ticket office; *(de cine, teatro)* box office (**b**) *(armario)* locker (**c**) *(recaudación)* takings (**d**) *(casillero)* set of pigeonholes

taquillero, -a 1 *adj* **es un espectáculo t.** the show is a box-office hit

2 *nm,f* ticket clerk

taquimecanografía *nf* shorthand and typing

taquimecanógrafo, -a *nm,f* shorthand typist

taquímetro *nm (en topografía)* tachometer

tara *nf* (**a**) *(defecto)* defect; **artículos con t.** seconds (**b**) *(peso)* tare

taracea *nf* inlay

tarado, -a 1 *adj* (**a**) *(defectuoso)* defective (**b**) *(tonto)* thick

2 *nm,f* idiot

tarambana *nmf Fam* ne'er-do-well

tarántula *nf* tarantula

tarar *vt* to tare

tararear *vt* to hum, to sing

tarareo *nm* humming, singing

tardanza *nf* lateness

tardar 1 *vi* (**a**) *(llevar tiempo)* to take; **tardó un año en hacerlo** she took a year to do it; **tardó en darse cuenta** it took him awhile *o* he took awhile to realize; **¿cuánto tardarás (en hacerlo)?** how long will you be (doing it)?, how long will it take you (to do it)? (**b**) *(retrasarse)* to be late; *(ser lento)* to be slow; **t. en hacer algo** to take a long time to do sth; **no tardará en llegar** he won't be long (in coming); **ahora vuelvo, no tardo** I'll be back in a minute, I won't be long; **no tardaron en hacerlo** they were quick to do it; **a más t.** at the latest; **sin t.** promptly

2 tardarse *vpr Méx* **no me tardaré** I won't be long

tarde 1 *nf (hasta las cinco)* afternoon; *(después de las cinco)* evening; **por la t.** *(hasta las cinco)* in the afternoon; *(después de las cinco)* in the evening; **buenas tardes** *(hasta las cinco)* good afternoon; *(después de las cinco)* good evening; **de t. en t.** from time to time; **muy de t. en t.** very occasionally

2 *adv* late; **(demasiado) t.** too late; **ya es t. para eso** it's too late for that now; **llegar t.** to be late; **se está haciendo t.** it's getting late; **corre, no se te vaya a hacer t.** hurry or you'll be late; **como muy t. el miércoles** by Wednesday at the latest; **t. o temprano** sooner or later; **más vale t. que nunca** better late than never

tardíamente *adv* belatedly

tardío, -a *adj (que ocurre tarde)* late; *(que ocurre demasiado tarde)* belated

tardo, -a *adj* (**a**) *(lento)* slow (**b**) *(torpe)* dull; **t. de oído** hard of hearing

tardón, -ona *nm,f* (**a**) *(impuntual)* person who is always late (**b**) *(lento)* slowpoke

tarea *nf (trabajo)* task; *Educ* homework; **tareas domésticas** household chores, housework

tarifa *nf* (**a**) *(precio)* charge; *(de servicio telefónico, postal)* rate; *(en transportes)* fare; *(de médico, abogado)* fee; **t. reducida** cheap rate; *Inform* **t. plana** flat rate (**b**) *Com (arancel)* tariff

tarifar 1 *vt* to price

2 *vi Fam (pelear)* to have a row

tarima *nf* platform

tarjeta *nf (gen) & Inform* card; *Dep* **t. amarilla/roja** yellow/red card; **t. de compra** store card, charge card; **t. de crédito** credit card; **t. de débito** debit card; **t. de embarque** boarding pass; **t. inteligente** smart card; **t. multiviaje** travel pass; **t. postal** postcard; **t. sanitaria** = national health insurance card; *Inform* **t. de sonido** sound card; **t. de visita** visiting *o* calling card

tarjetero *nm* credit-card wallet

tarot *nm* tarot

tarraconense 1 *adj* of/from Tarragona

2 *nmf* person from Tarragona

tarrina *nf (envase)* tub; *Culin* terrine

tarro *nm* (**a**) *(recipiente)* jar (**b**) *Esp Fam (cabeza)* nut

tarso *nm* tarsus

tarta *nf (pastel)* cake; *(plana, con base de pasta dura)* tart; *(plana, con base de bizcocho)* flan; **t. de cumpleaños** birthday cake; **t. de manzana** apple tart

tartaja *Fam* **1** *adj* **ser t.** to have a stammer *o* stutter

2 *nmf* **ser un t.** to have a stammer *o* stutter

tartajear *vi Fam* to stammer, to stutter

tartajeo *nm Fam* stammer, stutter

tartaleta *nf* tartlet

tartamudear *vi* to stammer, to stutter

tartamudeo *nm* stammer, stutter

tartamudez *nf* stammer, stutter

tartamudo, -a 1 *adj* stammering, stuttering
  2 *nm,f* stammerer, stutterer

tartán *nm inv* tartan

tartana *nf* (**a**) *(carruaje)* trap (**b**) *Fam (coche viejo)* jalopy

tártaro, -a 1 *adj* (**a**) *(pueblo)* Tartar (**b**) *Culin* **salsa tártara** tartar sauce
  2 *nm,f* Tartar

tartera *nf* (fiambrera) lunch box

tarugo *nm* (**a**) *Fam (necio)* blockhead (**b**) *(de madera)* block of wood (**c**) *(de pan)* chunk (of stale bread)

tarumba *adj Fam* crazy

Tarzán *n pr* Tarzan

tasa *nf* (**a**) *(índice)* rate; **t. de cambio** exchange rate; **t. de crecimiento** growth rate; **t. de desempleo** (level of) unemployment; **una t. de desempleo del 10 por ciento** 10 percent unemployment; **t. de interés** interest rate; **t. de mortalidad/natalidad** death/birth rate; **t. de paro** (level of) unemployment (**b**) *(impuesto)* tax; **tasas de aeropuerto** airport tax (**c**) *Educ* fee (**d**) *(tasación)* valuation

tasación *nf* valuation

tasador, -ora 1 *adj* evaluating
  2 *nm,f* valuer

tasar *vt* (**a**) *(valorar)* to value (**b**) *(fijar precio)* to fix a price for

tasca *nf* cheap bar; **ir de tascas** to go around a few bars

Tasmania *n* Tasmania

tasquear *vi* to go around a few bars

tasqueo *nm* barhopping

tata 1 *nf Esp (niñera)* nanny
  2 *nm Am Fam (papá)* dad, pop

tatami *nm Dep* tatami, judo/karate mat

tatarabuelo, -a *nm,f* great-great-grandfather, *f* great-great-grandmother

tataranieto, -a *nm,f* great-great-grandson, *f* great-great-granddaughter

tate *interj* **¡t.!** *(¡cuidado!)* watch out!; *(¡ya comprendo!)* I see!

tato, -a *Fam nm,f (hermano)* big brother, *f* big sister

tatuador, -ora *nm,f* tattooist

tatuaje *nm* (**a**) *(dibujo)* tattoo (**b**) *(acción)* tattooing

tatuar [4] **1** *vt* to tattoo
  2 *vi* to make a tattoo
  3 tatuarse *vpr* to have a tattoo done

taumaturgia *nf* miracle-working

taumaturgo, -a *nm,f* miracle worker

taurino, -a *adj* bullfighting; **temporada taurina** bullfighting season

tauro 1 *nm (zodiaco)* Taurus; *Esp* **ser t.** to be (a) Taurus
  2 *nmf Esp (persona)* Taurean

tauromaquia *nf* bullfighting

tautología *nf* tautology

tautológico, -a *adj* tautological

taxativo, -a *adj (órdenes)* strict

taxi *nm* taxi, cab

taxidermia *nf* taxidermy

taxidermista *nmf* taxidermist

taxiflet *(pl* **taxiflets** *o* **taxifletes)** *nm RP (vehículo)* moving truck

taximetrero, -a, *nm,f,* **taximetrista** *nmf RP* taxi driver

taxímetro *nm* taximeter

taxista *nmf* taxi driver

taxonomía *nf* taxonomy

taxonómico, -a *adj* taxonomic

taxonomista *nmf* taxonomist

Tayikistán *n* Tajikistan

tayiko, -a 1 *adj & nm,f* Tajik
  2 *nm (lengua)* Tajik

taza *nf* (**a**) *(para beber)* cup; **t. de café/té** cup of coffee/tea (**b**) *(de retrete)* bowl

tazón *nm* bowl

TC *nm* *(abrev de* **Tribunal Constitucional)** constitutional court

te *pron personal* (**a**) *(complemento directo)* you; **le gustaría verte** she'd like to see you (**b**) *(complemento indirecto)* (to) you; **te lo dio** he gave it to you, he gave you it; **te tiene miedo** he's afraid of you (**c**) *(reflexivo)* yourself; **¡vístete!** get dressed! (**d**) *(valor impersonal)* **si te dejas pisar, estás perdido** if you let people walk all over you, you've had it

té *nm* tea; **té con limón** lemon tea

tea *nf (antorcha)* torch

teatral *adj* (**a**) *(de teatro)* theater; **grupo t.** drama group; **temporada t.** theater season (**b**) *(exagerado)* theatrical

teatralidad *nf también Fig* theatricality

teatralizar [14] *vt* to exaggerate

teatrero, -a *adj Fam (persona)* **¡no seas tan t.!** don't be such a drama queen!

teatro *nm* (**a**) *(espectáculo, edificio)* theater; **t. experimental** fringe theater; **t. lírico** opera and light opera; **t. de variedades** variety, vaudeville (**b**) *(fingimiento)* playacting; **hacer t.** to playact

tebeo *nm Esp* (children's) comic; *Fam* **estar más visto que el t.** to be old hat

teca *nf* teak

techado *nm* roof; **bajo t.** under cover

techar *vt* to roof

techo *nm* (**a**) *(tejado)* roof; *(dentro de casa)* ceiling; **bajo t.** under cover; **dormir bajo t.** to sleep with a roof over one's head *o* indoors; *Fig* **quedarse sin t.** to become homeless; **los sin t.** the homeless; **t. solar** *(en coche)* sunroof (**b**) *(límite)* ceiling; **tocar t.** *(inflación, precios)* to level off and start to drop; **la crisis ha tocado t.** the worst of the recession is behind us

techumbre *nf* roof

tecla *nf Inform & Mús* key; *(botón)* button; **t. de borrado/control/función/mayúsculas/retorno** delete/control/function/shift/return key; **pulsar** *o* **tocar una t.** to press *o* strike a key; **tocar muchas teclas** *(contactar)* to pull lots of strings; *(abarcar mucho)* to have too many things on the go at once

tecladista *nmf Am* keyboard player

teclado *nm Inform & Mús* keyboard; **t. expandido** expanded *o* enhanced keyboard; **t. numérico** (numeric) keypad

teclear 1 *vt (en ordenador)* to type; *(en piano)* to play; **teclee su número secreto** enter your PIN number
  2 *vi (en ordenador)* to type; *(en piano)* to play

tecleo *nm (en piano)* playing; *(en máquina de escribir)* clattering

teclista *nmf* keyboard player

técnica *nf* (**a**) *(procedimiento)* technique (**b**) *(tecnología)* technology

tecnicismo *nm* (**a**) *(cualidad)* technical nature (**b**) *(término)* technical term

técnico, -a 1 *adj* technical
  2 *nm,f* (**a**) *(mecánico)* technician (**b**) *(experto)* expert

tecnicolor® *nm* Technicolor®

tecnificación *nf* application of technology

tecnificar [59] *vt* to apply technology to

tecno *nm inv* techno (music)

tecnocracia *nf* technocracy

tecnócrata 1 *adj* technocratic
  2 *nmf* technocrat

tecnología *nf* technology; **t. punta** state-of-the-art technology

tecnológico, -a *adj* technological

tecnólogo, -a *nm,f* technologist

tecolote *nm CAm, Méx* owl

tectónica *nf* tectonics *(singular)*

tectónico, -a *adj* tectonic

tedéum *nm inv* Te Deum

tedio *nm* boredom, tedium

tedioso, -a *adj* tedious

teflón® *nm* Teflon®

Tegucigalpa *n* Tegucigalpa

tegucigalpeño, -a 1 *adj* of/from Tegucigalpa
  2 *nm,f* person from Tegucigalpa

tegumento *nm Biol* integument

Teherán *n* Teheran

Teide *nm* **el T.** (Mount) Teide

teína *nf* caffeine *(contained in tea)*

teísmo *nm* theism

teja *nf (de tejado)* tile; **color t.** brick red

tejado *nm* roof

tejano, -a 1 *adj* **(a)** *(de Texas)* Texan **(b)** *(tela)* denim
  2 *nm,f (persona)* Texan

tejanos *nmpl (pantalones)* jeans

tejar 1 *nm* brickworks *(singular)*
  2 *vt & vi* to tile

Tejas *n* Texas

tejedor, -ora 1 *adj* weaving
  2 *nm,f* weaver

tejeduría *nf* **(a)** *(arte)* weaving **(b)** *(taller)* weaver's

tejemaneje *nm Fam* **(a)** *(maquinación)* intrigue **(b)** *(ajetreo)* to-do, fuss

tejer 1 *vt* **(a)** *(hilos, mimbre)* to weave **(b)** *(labor de punto)* to knit **(c)** *(telaraña)* to spin **(d)** *(labrar) (porvenir)* to carve out; *(ruina)* to bring about **(e)** *(tramar)* **t. un plan** to forge a plot
  2 *vi (hacer punto)* to knit

tejido *nm* **(a)** *(tela)* fabric, material; *Ind* textile; **el t. social** the fabric of society **(b)** *Anat* tissue; **t. adiposo** fatty tissue, *Espec* adipose tissue; **t. blando** soft tissue **(c)** *Am (labor de lana)* knitting

tejo *nm* **(a)** *(juego)* hopscotch **(b)** *Bot* yew **(c)** *Esp Fam Fig* **tirar los tejos a alguien** to make a pass at sb

tejón *nm* badger

tel. *(abrev de* **teléfono***)* tel.

tela *nf* **(a)** *(tejido)* fabric, material; *(retal)* piece of material; **t. de araña** cobweb; **t. asfáltica** asphalt roofing/flooring; **t. metálica** wire netting **(b)** *Arte (lienzo)* canvas **(c)** *Fam (dinero)* dough **(d)** *Fam (cosa complicada)* **el examen era t.** the exam was really tricky; **tener (mucha) t.** *(ser difícil)* to be (very) tricky; **hay t. (para rato)** *(trabajo)* there's no shortage of things to do; **¡t. marinera!** that's too much! **(e)** **poner en t. de juicio** to call into question

telar *nm* **(a)** *(máquina)* loom **(b)** *Teatro* gridiron **(c)** **telares** *(fábrica)* textiles mill

telaraña *nf* spider's web, cobweb

tele *nf Fam* TV

teleadicto, -a *nm,f* TV addict

teleapuntador *nm* Teleprompter®

telearrastre *nm* ski tow

teleaudiencia *nf Am* TV audience, viewers

telebanca *nf* telephone banking

telebasura *nf Fam* junk TV

telecabina *nf* cable car

telecomedia *nf* sitcom

telecompra *nf* teleshopping, home shopping

telecomunicación *nf (medio)* telecommunication; **telecomunicaciones** telecommunications

telecontrol *nm* remote control

telediario *nm Esp* television news

teledifusión *nf* broadcasting

teledirigido, -a *adj* remote-controlled

teledirigir [24] *vt* to operate by remote control

teléf. *(abrev de* **teléfono***)* tel.

telefax *nm inv* fax

teleférico *nm* cable car

telefilme *(pl* **telefilmes***)*, **telefilm** *(pl* **telefilms***) nm* TV movie

telefonazo *nm Fam* buzz; **dar un t. a alguien** to give sb a buzz

telefonear *vi* to phone

telefonema *nm Am* telephone call

telefonía *nf* telephony; **sistema de t. móvil** cell-phone system

Telefónica *nf* = main Spanish telephone company, formerly a state-owned monopoly

telefónico, -a *adj* telephone; **llamada telefónica** telephone call

telefonillo *nm (portero automático)* entryphone

telefonista *nmf* telephone switchboard operator

teléfono *nm* **(a)** *(aparato, sistema)* telephone, phone; **coger el t.** to answer *o* pick up the phone; **hablar por t.** to be on the phone; **t. celular** cellular *o* cell phone; **t. fijo** land line; **t. inalámbrico** cordless phone; **t. modular** *o* **inteligente** cell phone; **t. móvil** cell phone; **t. público** public phone; **t. rojo** hot line; **t. sin manos** phone with hands-free facility **(b)** *(número)* telephone number; **t. gratuito** toll-free number

telefotografía *nf* telephotography

telegénico, -a *adj* telegenic

telegrafía *nf* telegraphy

telegrafiar [32] *vt & vi* to telegraph

telegráfico, -a *adj también Fig* telegraphic

telegrafista *nmf* telegrapher, telegraphist

telégrafo *nm (medio, aparato)* telegraph; **telégrafos** *(oficina)* telegraph office

telegrama *nm* telegram

telejuego *nm* television game show

telele *nm Fam* **le dio un t.** *(desmayo)* he passed out, he fainted; *(enfado, susto)* he had a fit

telemando *nm* remote control

telemarketing *nm* telesales, telemarketing

telemática *nf* electronic communications technology

telemático, -a *adj Inform* telematic

telémetro *nm* telemeter

telenovela *nf* television soap opera

teleobjetivo *nm* telephoto lens

telepatía *nf* telepathy

telepático, -a *adj* telepathic

teleplatea *nf CSur* TV audience, viewers

telequinesia *nf* telekinesis

telerruta *nf* = telephone service giving traffic information

telescópico, -a *adj* telescopic

telescopio *nm* telescope

teleserie *nf* TV series

telesilla *nm* chairlift

telespectador, -ora *nm,f* viewer

telesquí *(pl* **telesquíes** *o* **telesquís***) nm* ski tow

teletexto *nm* teletext

teletienda *nf* home shopping program

teletipo *nm* **(a)** *(aparato)* teleprinter **(b)** *(texto)* Teletype®

teletrabajador, -ora *nm,f* teleworker

teletrabajo *nm* teleworking

televendedor, -ora *nm,f* telesales assistant

televenta *nf* (**a**) *(por teléfono)* telesales (**b**) *(por televisión)* home shopping

televidente *nmf* viewer

televisado, -a *adj* televised

televisar *vt* to televise

televisión *nf* television; **t. en blanco y negro/en color** black and white/color television; **t. por cable** cable television; **t. digital** digital television; **t. interactiva** interactive television; **t. privada/pública** privately owned/public television; **t. vía satélite** satellite television

televisivo, -a *adj* television; **concurso t.** television game show

televisor *nm* television (set)

télex *nm inv* telex; **mandar por t.** to telex

telón *nm* *(de escenario)* *(delante)* curtain; *(detrás)* backcloth; *Fig* **t. de acero** Iron Curtain; *Fig* **t. de fondo** backdrop

telonero, -a 1 *adj* **grupo t.** support (band)
 2 *nm,f* *(cantante)* supporting artist; *(grupo)* support (band)

telúrico, -a *adj* telluric

tema *nm* (**a**) *(asunto)* subject; **cambiar de t.** to change the subject; **temas de actualidad** current affairs; **t. de conversación** talking point, topic of conversation (**b**) *Educ (lección)* topic (**c**) *Mús* theme; *(canción)* track, song

temario *nm* (**a**) *(de una asignatura)* syllabus; *(de oposiciones)* = list of topics for public examination (**b**) *(de reunión, congreso)* agenda

temática *nf* subject matter

temático, -a *adj* thematic; **parque t.** theme park

tembladera *nf* trembling fit

temblar [3] *vi* (**a**) *(persona)* *(de miedo)* to tremble (**de** with); *(de frío)* to shiver (**de** with); **le temblaba la voz de la emoción** her voice was trembling with emotion; *Fig* **tiemblo por lo que pueda pasarle** I shudder to think what could happen to him; **t. como un flan** to shake like jelly (**b**) *(suelo, máquina)* to shudder, to shake

tembleque *nm* trembling fit; **le dio** *o* **entró un t.** he got the shakes

temblequear *vi* (**a**) *(persona)* to tremble; *(de frío)* to shiver (**b**) *(suelo, máquina)* to shudder, to shake

temblón, -ona *adj* shaky, trembling

temblor *nm* shaking, trembling; **t. de tierra** earth tremor

tembloroso, -a *adj* trembling, shaky

temer 1 *vt* (**a**) *(tener miedo de)* to fear, to be afraid of; **yo no te temo** I'm not afraid of you; **temo herir sus sentimientos** I'm afraid of hurting her feelings; *Fam* **cuando se pone a hablar le temo** my heart sinks whenever he opens his mouth (**b**) *(sospechar)* to fear
 2 *vi* to be afraid; **no temas** don't worry; **le teme mucho al fuego** she's very afraid of fire; **t. por** to fear for
 3 temerse *vpr* **temerse que…** to be afraid that…, to fear that…; **me temo que no vendrá** I'm afraid she won't come; **temerse lo peor** to fear the worst

temerario, -a *adj* rash, reckless; **conducción temeraria** reckless driving

temeridad *nf* (**a**) *(cualidad)* recklessness (**b**) *(acción)* folly, reckless act

temeroso, -a *adj* *(receloso)* fearful

temible *adj* fearsome

temor *nm* fear (**a** *o* **de** of); **por t. a** *o* **de** for fear of

témpano *nm* **t. (de hielo)** ice floe

témpera *nf* *Arte* tempera

temperado, -a *adj* temperate

temperamental *adj* (**a**) *(cambiante)* temperamental (**b**) *(impulsivo)* impulsive

temperamento *nm* temperament

temperancia *nf* temperance

temperar *vt* *(moderar)* to temper

temperatura *nf* temperature; **se espera un aumento/descenso de las temperaturas** temperatures are expected to rise/fall; **tomar la t. a alguien** to take sb's temperature; **t. ambiental** *o* **ambiente** room temperature; **t. máxima/mínima** highest/lowest temperature

tempestad *nf* storm; *Fig* **levantar una t. de protestas** to raise a storm of protest; *Fig* **una t. en un vaso de agua** a tempest in a teapot; **t. de nieve** snowstorm

tempestuoso, -a *adj también Fig* stormy

templado, -a *adj* (**a**) *(agua, comida)* lukewarm (**b**) *Geog (clima, zona)* temperate (**c**) *(nervios)* steady (**d**) *(persona, carácter)* calm, composed

templanza *nf* (**a**) *(serenidad)* composure (**b**) *(moderación)* moderation (**c**) *(benignidad)* *(del clima)* mildness

templar 1 *vt* (**a**) *(entibiar)* *(lo frío)* to warm (up); *(lo caliente)* to cool down (**b**) *(calmar)* *(nervios, ánimos)* to calm; *(ira, pasiones)* to restrain; *(voz)* to soften (**c**) *Mec (metal)* to temper (**d**) *Mús* to tune (**e**) *(tensar)* to tighten (up)
 2 *vi* *(entibiarse)* to get milder
 3 templarse *vpr* (**a**) *(calentarse)* to warm up (**b**) *Chile (enamorarse)* to fall in love

templario *nm* Templar

temple *nm* (**a**) *(serenidad)* composure; **estar de buen/mal t.** to be in a good/bad mood (**b**) *Mec* tempering (**c**) *(pintura)* *(témpera)* tempera; *(para paredes)* distemper

templete *nm* pavilion

templo *nm* (**a**) *(edificio)* *(no cristiano)* temple; *(católico, protestante)* church; *(judío)* synagogue; *(musulmán)* mosque (**b**) *(lugar mitificado)* temple

tempo *nm* tempo

temporada *nf* (**a**) *(periodo concreto)* season; *(de exámenes)* period; **de t.** *(fruta, trabajo)* seasonal; **los kiwis están fuera de t.** kiwis are out of season; **t. alta/baja** high/low season; **t. de caza** hunting season; **t. media** midseason; **t. turística** tourist *o* vacation season (**b**) *(periodo indefinido)* (period of) time; **pasé una t. en el extranjero** I spent some time abroad; **tras una t. como profesor, se puso a traducir** after a stint *o* spell of teaching, he went into translating; **por temporadas** off and on

temporal 1 *adj* (**a**) *(no permanente)* temporary (**b**) *(del tiempo)* time; **el factor t.** the time factor (**c**) *Anat & Rel* temporal
 2 *nm* (**a**) *(tormenta)* storm (**b**) *Anat* temporal bone

temporalidad *nf* *(transitoriedad)* temporary nature

temporalmente, *Am* **temporariamente** *adv* temporarily

temporario, -a *adj Am* temporary

témporas *nfpl Rel* ember days

temporero, -a 1 *adj* seasonal
 2 *nm,f* seasonal worker

temporizador *nm* timer

tempranero, -a *adj (persona)* early-rising

temprano, -a *adj & adv* early

ten *ver* **tener**

tenacidad *nf* tenacity

tenacillas *nfpl (para rizar el pelo)* curling iron

tenaz *adj* (**a**) *(perseverante)* tenacious (**b**) *(persistente)* stubborn

tenaza *nf*, **tenazas** *nfpl* (**a**) *(herramienta)* pliers (**b**) *(pinzas)* tongs (**c**) *Zool* pincer

tendal *nm* awning

tendedero *nm* (**a**) *(armazón)* clotheshorse; *(cuerda)* clothesline (**b**) *(lugar)* drying place

tendencia *nf* (**a**) *(inclinación)* tendency; **tener t. a hacer algo** to have a tendency to do sth; **t. a la depresión** tendency to get depressed (**b**) *(corriente)* trend; **las últimas tendencias de la moda** the latest fashion trends

tendenciosidad *nf* tendentiousness

tendencioso, -a *adj* tendentious

tendente *adj* **t. a** intended *o* designed to; **medidas tendentes a mejorar la economía** measures (intended *o* designed) to improve the economy

tender [64] **1** *vt* **(a)** *(ropa)* to hang out **(b)** *(tumbar)* to lay (out); **lo tendieron en una camilla** they laid him out on a stretcher **(c)** *(extender, colocar) (manta)* to stretch (out); *(mantel)* to spread; *Am (mesa)* to set, to lay; *Am (cama)* to make **(d)** *(entre dos puntos) (cable, vía)* to lay; *(puente)* to build; *(cuerda)* to stretch **(e)** *(dar) (cosa)* to hand; *(mano)* to hold out, to offer; **t. la mano a alguien** *(extender la mano)* to hold out one's hand to sb, to offer sb one's hand **(f)** *(trampa, emboscada)* to lay

  2 *vi* **t. a hacer algo** to tend to do something; **t. a la depresión** to be prone to depression; **un azul que tiende a violeta** a blue which is almost violet

  3 tenderse *vpr* to stretch out, to lie down

tenderete *nm (puesto)* stall

tendero, -a *nm,f* shopkeeper

tendido, -a 1 *adj* **(a)** *(extendido, tumbado)* stretched out **(b)** *(colgado) (ropa)* on the line

  2 *nm* **(a)** *(instalación) (de puente)* construction; *(de cable)* laying; **t. eléctrico** power lines **(b)** *Taurom* front rows; **saludar al t.** *(monarca, personaje público)* to wave to the crowd

tendinitis *nf inv* tendinitis

tendón *nm* tendon

tendré *etc ver* **tener**

tenebrismo *nm* tenebrism

tenebroso, -a *adj (oscuro)* dark, gloomy; *(siniestro) (asunto, personaje)* shady, sinister

tenedor[1] *nm (utensilio)* fork

tenedor[2]**, -ora** *nm,f (poseedor)* holder; **t. de acciones** stockholder, shareholder; **t. de libros** bookkeeper

teneduría *nf Com* **t. (de libros)** bookkeeping

tenencia *nf* **(a)** *(posesión)* possession; **t. ilícita de armas** illegal possession of arms **(b)** *Méx (impuesto)* road tax

tener [65] *vt* **(a)** *(poseer, experimentar)* to have; **tengo un hermano** I have *o* I've got a brother; **t. fiebre** to have a temperature; **tuvieron una pelea** they had a fight; **t. un niño** to have a baby; **¡que tengan buen viaje!** have a good journey!; **tengo las vacaciones en agosto** my vacation is in August

  (b) *(medida, años, sensación, cualidad)* to be; **tiene 3 metros de ancho** it's 3 meters wide; **¿cuántos años tienes?** how old are you?; **tiene diez años** she's ten (years old); *Am* **tengo tres años aquí** I've been here for three years; **t. hambre/miedo** to be hungry/afraid; **t. mal humor** to be bad-tempered; **le tiene lástima** he feels sorry for her

  (c) *(recibir) (mensaje, regalo, visita, sensación)* to get; **tuve un verdadero desengaño** I was really disappointed; **tendrá una sorpresa** he'll get a surprise

  (d) *(sujetar)* to hold; **tenlo por el asa** hold it by the handle

  (e) *(tomar)* **ten el libro que me pediste** here's the book you asked me for; **¡aquí tienes!, ¡ten!** here you are!

  (f) *(valorar)* **me tienen por tonto** they think I'm stupid; **t. a alguien en mucho** to think the world of sb

  (g) *(expresiones)* **no las tiene todas consigo** he is not too sure about it; **t. a bien hacer algo** to be kind enough to do sth; **t. que ver con algo/alguien** *(existir relación)* to have something to do with sth/sb; *(existir semejanza)* to be in the same league as sth/sb

  2 *v aux* **(a)** *(antes de participio) (haber)* **teníamos pensado ir al teatro** we had thought of going to the theater **(b)** *(antes de adj) (hacer estar)* **me tuvo despierto** it kept me awake; **eso la tiene despistada** that has confused her **(c)** **t. que:** *(expresa obligación)* **t. que hacer algo** to have to do sth; **tiene que ser así** it has to be this way; **tenías que haber visto cómo corría** you should have seen him run **(d)** **t. que:** *(expresa*

propósito) **tenemos que ir a cenar un día** we ought to *o* should go for dinner sometime

  3 tenerse *vpr* **(a)** *(sostenerse)* **tenerse de pie** to stand upright **(b)** *(considerarse)* **se tiene por listo** he thinks he's clever

tengo *ver* **tener**

tenia *nf* tapeworm

teniente 1 *nm* **(a)** *Mil* lieutenant; **t. coronel/general** lieutenant colonel/general **(b)** *(sustituto)* deputy; **t. (de) alcalde** deputy mayor

  2 *adj Fam (sordo)* **estar t.** to be a bit deaf

tenis *nm inv* tennis; **t. de mesa** table tennis

tenista *nmf* tennis player

tenístico, -a *adj* tennis; **campeonato t.** tennis championship

Tenochtitlán *n* Tenochtitlan *(Aztec capital)*

tenor[1] *nm* **(a)** *Mús* tenor **(b)** *(estilo)* tone; **a este t.** *(de la misma manera)* in the same vein

  2 a tenor de *loc prep* judging by

tenorio *nm* ladies' man, Casanova

tensado *nm* tightening

tensar *vt (cable, cuerda)* to tauten; *(arco)* to draw

tensión *nf* **(a)** *(estado emocional)* tension; **estar en t.** to be tense; **hubo muchas tensiones entre ellos** there was a lot of tension between them; **t. nerviosa** nervous tension; **t. premenstrual** premenstrual tension, PMT **(b)** *(de cuerda, cable)* tension; **en t.** tensed; **puso sus músculos en t.** he tensed his muscles **(c)** *Med* **t. (arterial)** blood pressure; **tener la t. (arterial) alta/baja** to have high/low blood pressure; **tener una subida/bajada de t.** to suffer a rise/drop in blood pressure **(d)** *Elec* voltage; **alta t.** high voltage

tenso, -a *adj (cuerda, cable)* taut; *(músculo, persona, situación)* tense

tensor, -ora 1 *adj* tightening

  2 *nm* **(a)** *(dispositivo)* turnbuckle **(b)** *Anat* tensor

tentación *nf* temptation; **caer en la t.** to give in to temptation; **tener la t. de** to be tempted to

tentáculo *nm* tentacle

tentador, -ora *adj* tempting

tentar [3] *vt* **(a)** *(palpar)* to feel **(b)** *(atraer, incitar)* to tempt

tentativa *nf* attempt; **t. de asesinato** attempted murder; **t. de suicidio** suicide attempt

tentempié *nm* snack

tentetieso *nm* Weeble®, tumbler (doll)

tenue *adj* **(a)** *(tela, hilo, lluvia)* fine **(b)** *(luz, sonido, dolor)* faint **(c)** *(relación)* tenuous

teñido, -a 1 *adj (pelo, tela)* dyed

  2 *nm* dyeing

teñir [47] **1** *vt* **(a)** *(ropa, pelo)* **t. algo (de rojo/verde)** to dye sth (red/green) **(b)** *(matizar)* to tinge sth **(de** with)

  2 teñirse *vpr* **teñirse (el pelo)** to dye one's hair

teocracia *nf* theocracy

teocrático, -a *adj* theocratic

teodolito *nm* theodolite

teologal *adj* theological

teología *nf* theology; **t. de la liberación** liberation theology

teológico, -a *adj* theological

teólogo, -a *nm,f* theologian

teorema *nm* theorem

teoría *nf* theory; **en t.** in theory; **t. del caos** chaos theory; **t. del conocimiento** epistemology; **t. cuántica** quantum theory; **la t. de la evolución** the theory of evolution; **t. de la información** information theory; **t. monetaria** monetary theory; **la t. de la relatividad** the theory of relativity

teóricamente *adv* theoretically

teórico, -a 1 *adj* theoretical

  2 *nm,f (persona)* theorist

teorizador, -ora *adj* theorizing

teorizar [14] *vi* to theorize

tequila *nmf* tequila

terapeuta *nmf (médico)* doctor; *(fisioterapeuta)* physiotherapist

terapéutica *nf* therapeutics *(singular)*

terapéutico, -a *adj* therapeutic

terapia *nf* therapy; **t. de electrochoque** shock therapy; **t. genética** gene therapy; **t. hormonal sustitutiva** hormone replacement therapy; **t. de grupo** group therapy; **t. ocupacional** occupational therapy

tercer *ver* tercero

tercera *nf Aut* third (gear)

tercerización *nf Am Com* outsourcing

tercerizar [14] *vt Am Com* to outsource

tercermundismo *nm (de países pobres)* underdevelopment; *(de servicios, sistema)* backwardness

tercermundista *adj* third-world; **un país t.** a third-world country; **¡este servicio es t.!** this service is appalling *o* a disgrace!

tercero, -a

> **tercer** is used instead of **tercero** before masculine singular nouns (e.g. **el tercer piso** the third floor).

1 *núm* third; *Esp* **a la tercera va la vencida** third time lucky; **la tercera edad** senior citizens; **durante la tercera edad** in old age; **el Tercer Mundo** the Third World

2 *nm* (**a**) *(piso)* third floor (**b**) *(curso escolar)* = third year of primary school, ≃ third grade (**c**) *(mediador, parte interesada)* third party

terceto *nm* (**a**) *(estrofa)* tercet (**b**) *Mús* trio

terciado, -a *adj (mediano)* medium-sized

terciar 1 *vt* (**a**) *(poner en diagonal)* to place diagonally; *(sombrero)* to tilt (**b**) *(dividir)* to divide into three

2 *vi* (**a**) *(mediar)* to mediate (**en** in) (**b**) *(participar)* to intervene, to take part

3 terciarse *vpr* to arise; **si se tercia** if the opportunity arises

terciario, -a 1 *adj* tertiary

2 *nm Geol* **el T.** the Tertiary (era)

tercio *nm* (**a**) *(tercera parte)* third (**b**) *Mil* regiment; **t. de la guardia civil** Civil Guard division (**c**) *Taurom* stage *(of bullfight)* (**d**) *(de cerveza)* bottle of beer *(0.33 liter)*

terciopelo *nm* velvet

terco, -a 1 *adj* stubborn; **t. como una mula** as stubborn as a mule

2 *nm,f* stubborn person; **ser un t.** to be stubborn

tergal® *nm* = type of synthetic fiber containing polyester

tergiversación *nf* distortion

tergiversador, -ora 1 *adj* distorting

2 *nm,f* person who distorts the facts

tergiversar *vt* to distort, to twist

termal *adj* thermal; **fuente de aguas termales** hot spring

termas *nfpl (baños)* hot baths, spa

termes *nm inv* termite

térmico, -a *adj* (**a**) *(de la temperatura)* temperature; **descenso t.** drop in temperature (**b**) *(aislante)* thermal

terminación *nf* (**a**) *(finalización)* completion (**b**) *(parte final)* end (**c**) *Gram* ending

terminal 1 *adj* (**a**) *(del fin)* final; *(del extremo)* end (**b**) *(enfermedad)* terminal; **es un enfermo t.** he's terminally ill

2 *nm Elec & Inform* terminal; **t. videotexto** videotext terminal

3 *nf (de aeropuerto)* terminal; *(de autobuses)* terminus

terminante *adj (categórico)* categorical; *(prueba)* conclusive

terminantemente *adv* categorically; **está t. prohibido** it is strictly forbidden

terminar 1 *vt* to finish; **terminamos el viaje en San Francisco** we ended our journey in San Francisco

2 *vi* (**a**) *(acabar)* to end, to finish; *(tren)* to stop, to terminate; **¿cómo termina la historia?** how does the story end *o* finish?; **t. con** *(pobreza, corrupción)* to put an end to; **t. de hacer algo** to finish doing sth; **t. en** *(objeto)* to end in (**b**) *(reñir)* to finish, to split up; **¡hemos terminado!** it's over! (**c**) *(ir a parar)* **terminó de camarero/en la cárcel** he ended up as a waiter/in jail; **t. por hacer algo** to end up doing sth (**d**) *(llegar a)* **no termino de entenderlo** I still can't quite understand it

3 terminarse *vpr* (**a**) *(finalizar)* to finish (**b**) *(agotarse) (repuestos, víveres)* to run out; **se nos ha terminado el azúcar** we've run out of sugar, the sugar has run out (**c**) *(acabar) (comida, revista)* to finish off; **me terminé la novela en una noche** I finished off the novel in one night

término *nm* (**a**) *(fin, extremo)* end; **dar t. a algo** to bring sth to a close; **llegó a su t.** it came to an end; **llevar algo a buen t.** to bring sth to a successful conclusion; **poner t. a algo** to put a stop to sth

(**b**) *(territorio)* **t. municipal** = area under the jurisdiction of a city council

(**c**) *(plazo)* period; **en el t. de un mes** within (the space of) a month

(**d**) *(lugar, posición)* place; *Arte & Fot* **en primer t.** in the foreground; **quedar** *o* **permanecer en un segundo t.** *(pasar inadvertido)* to remain in the background; **en último t.** in the background; *Fig (si es necesario)* as a last resort; *(en resumidas cuentas)* in the final analysis

(**e**) *(elemento)* point; **t. medio** *(media)* average; *(compromiso)* compromise, happy medium; **por t. medio** on average

(**f**) *(palabra)* term; **lo dijo, aunque no con** *o* **en esos términos** that's what he said, although he didn't put it quite the same way; **en términos generales** generally speaking; **los términos del contrato** the terms of the contract

(**g**) *(relaciones)* **estar en buenos/malos términos (con)** to be on good/bad terms (with)

terminología *nf* terminology

terminológico, -a *adj* terminological

termita *nf* termite

termitero *nm* termite mound *o* nest

termo *nm* thermos

termoaislante *adj* heat insulating

termodinámica *nf* thermodynamics *(singular)*

termodinámico, -a *adj* thermodynamic

termoeléctrico, -a *adj* thermoelectric

termografía *nf* thermography

termometría *nf* thermometry

termométrico, -a *adj* thermometric

termómetro *nm* thermometer; **t. centígrado/clínico** centigrade/clinical thermometer; **poner el t. a alguien** to take sb's temperature

termonuclear *adj* thermonuclear

termorregulador *nm* thermostat

termostato *nm* thermostat

termoterapia *nf* heat treatment

terna *nf Pol* = short list of three candidates

ternario, -a *adj* ternary

ternasco *nm* suckling lamb

ternera *nf (carne)* veal

ternero, -a *nm,f (animal)* calf

ternilla *nf* (**a**) *Culin* gristle (**b**) *Anat* cartilage

terno *nm* (**a**) *(trío)* trio (**b**) *(traje)* three-piece suit

ternura *nf* tenderness

terquedad *nf* stubbornness

terracota *nf* terracotta

terrado *nm* terrace roof

terral *nm Am* dust cloud

Terranova *n* Newfoundland

terraplén *nm* steep embankment

terráqueo, -a *adj* Earth; **globo t.** *(Tierra)* Earth; *(representación)* globe

terrario, terrarium *nm* terrarium

terrateniente *nmf* landowner

terraza *nf* (a) *(balcón)* balcony (b) *(de café)* terrace, patio (c) *(azotea)* terrace roof (d) *(bancal)* terrace

terrazo *nm* terrazzo, = polished composite floor covering made from stone chips

terremoto *nm* earthquake; *Fam* **este niño es un t.** this boy is a menace

terrenal *adj* earthly

terreno, -a 1 *adj* earthly

2 *nm* (a) *(suelo)* land; *(por su relieve)* terrain; *(por su composición, utilidad agrícola)* soil; **t. montañoso/abrupto** mountainous/rugged terrain; **t. arenoso/volcánico** sandy/volcanic soil; **t. irregular** uneven ground

(b) *(solar)* plot (of land); **t. edificable** land suitable for development

(c) *(en deportes)* **t. (de juego)** field

(d) *(ámbito)* field; **en el t. de la música/medicina** in the field of music/medicine

(e) *(expresiones)* **ceder t.** to give ground; **estar** *o* **encontrarse en su propio t.** to be on home ground; **ganar t. (a alguien)** to gain ground (on sb); **perder t.** to lose ground; **preparar** *o* **trabajar el t. (para)** to pave the way (for); **reconocer** *o* **tantear el t.** to see how the land lies; **saber el t. que se pisa** to know what one is about; **ser t. abonado (para algo)** to be fertile ground (for sth); **estudiar algo sobre el t.** to study something in the field

térreo, -a *adj* earthy

terrestre 1 *adj* (a) *(del planeta)* terrestrial (b) *(de la tierra)* land; **animales terrestres** land animals

2 *nmf* terrestrial, Earth dweller

terrible *adj* (a) *(tremendo)* terrible (b) *(aterrador)* terrifying

terrícola *nmf* earthling

terrier *(pl* terriers*) nm* terrier; **t. escocés** Scottish terrier, Scottie

territorial *adj* territorial

territorialidad *nf Der* territoriality

territorio *nm* territory; **fuera del t. brasileño** outside of Brazilian territory; **por todo el t. nacional** across the country, nationwide; **los territorios ocupados** *(de Palestina)* the occupied territories

terrón *nm (de tierra)* clod of earth; **t. de azúcar** sugar lump

terror *nm* terror; **de t.** *(cine)* horror; **le da t.** it terrifies her; **me da t. pensar en las vacaciones con los niños** I shudder to think what the vacation with the children will be like; **esa banda de delincuentes es el t. del pueblo** this gang of criminals is terrorizing the village

terrorífico, -a *adj* terrifying

terrorismo *nm* terrorism

terrorista *adj & nmf* terrorist

terroso, -a *adj* (a) *(parecido a la tierra)* earthy (b) *(con tierra)* muddy

terruño *nm* (a) *(terreno)* plot of land (b) *(patria)* homeland

tersar *vt* to make smooth

terso, -a *adj* (a) *(piel, superficie)* smooth (b) *(aguas, mar)* clear (c) *(estilo, lenguaje)* polished

tersura *nf* (a) *(de piel, superficie)* smoothness (b) *(de aguas, mar)* clarity (c) *(de estilo, lenguaje)* polish

tertulia *nf* = regular informal social gathering where issues of common interest are discussed; *Fam* **estar de t.** to sit (there) chatting; **t. literaria** literary circle

tertuliano, -a *nm,f Rad* panelist

Tesalónica *n* Thessalonica

tesauro *nm* thesaurus

tesela *nf* tessera

tesina *nf* (undergraduate) thesis

tesis *nf inv* thesis

tesitura *nf* (a) *(situación)* circumstances, situation (b) *Mús* tessitura, pitch

tesón *nm* (a) *(tenacidad)* tenacity, perseverance (b) *(firmeza)* firmness

tesorería *nf* (a) *(cargo)* treasurership (b) *(oficina)* treasurer's office (c) *Com* liquid capital

tesorero, -a *nm,f* treasurer

tesoro *nm* (a) *(botín)* treasure; **el cofre del t.** the treasure chest (b) *(hacienda pública)* treasury, exchequer; *Econ* **el T.** the Treasury (c) *(persona valiosa)* gem, treasure (d) *(apelativo)* darling

test [tes] *o* [test] *(pl* tests*) nm* test; **hacer un t.** to do *o* take a test; **hacer un t. a alguien** to give sb a test; **tipo t.** *(examen, pregunta)* multiple-choice; **t. de embarazo** pregnancy test; **t. de inteligencia** intelligence test

testa *nf* head

testado, -a *adj (persona)* testate; *(herencia)* testamentary

testaferro *nm* front man

testamentaría *nf* (a) *(documentos)* documentation *(of a will)* (b) *(bienes)* estate, inheritance

testamentario, -a 1 *adj* testamentary

2 *nm,f* executor

testamento *nm* will; **hacer t.** to write one's will; **Antiguo/Nuevo T.** Old/New Testament

testar *vi* to make a will

testarudez *nf* stubbornness

testarudo, -a 1 *adj* stubborn

2 *nm,f* stubborn person

testear *vt CSur* to test

testicular *adj* testicular

testículo *nm* testicle

testificación *nf* testimony; **es la t. de su talento** it is proof of her talent

testificar [59] **1** *vt Der* to testify; *(ser muestra de)* to testify to

2 *vi Der* to testify, to give evidence

testigo 1 *nmf (persona)* witness; **ser t. de algo** to witness sth; **tú eres t. de que estuve allí** you are my witness that I was there; **un castillo que ha sido t. de innumerables batallas** a castle that has witnessed countless battles; **poner por t. a alguien** to cite sb as a witness; **t. de cargo/descargo** witness for the prosecution/defense; **t. de Jehová** Jehovah's Witness; **t. ocular** *o* **presencial** eyewitness

2 *nm Dep* baton

testimonial *adj* (a) *(documento, prueba)* testimonial (b) *(simbólico)* token, symbolic

testimoniar *vt* to testify to, to bear witness to

testimonio *nm* (a) *Der* testimony; **falso t.** perjury, false evidence (b) *(prueba)* proof; **como t. de** as proof of; **dar t. de** to prove

testosterona *nf* testosterone

testuz *nm o nf* (a) *(frente)* brow (b) *(nuca)* nape

teta 1 *nf* (a) *Fam (de mujer)* tit; **dar la t.** to breastfeed; **de t.** nursing (b) *(de animal)* teat

2 *adv Esp Fam* **pasarlo t.** to have a swell time

tétanos *nm inv* tetanus

tetera *nf* teapot

tetería *nf* tearoom

tetilla *nf* (a) *(de hombre, animal)* nipple (b) *(de biberón)* teat

tetina *nf* teat

tetona *adj f Fam* busty, top-heavy; **es muy t.** she has big boobs

tetrabrik® (*pl* **tetrabriks**) *nm* carton

tetracampeón, -ona 1 *adj* **el equipo t.** the four-times winners *o* champions

2 *nm,f* four-times winner *o* champion

tetraedro *nm* tetrahedron

tetralogía *nf Lit* tetralogy

tetraplejía *nf* quadriplegia

tetrapléjico, -a *adj & nm,f* quadriplegic

tétrico, -a *adj* gloomy

teutón, -ona *Hist* **1** *adj* Teutonic

2 *nm,f* Teuton

teutónico, -a *adj Hist* Teutonic

Texas ['teχas] *n* Texas

textil *adj & nm* textile

texto *nm* (**a**) *(palabras, libro)* text (**b**) *(pasaje)* passage

textual *adj* (**a**) *(del texto)* textual (**b**) *(exacto)* exact; **dijo, palabras textuales, que era horroroso** her exact words were "it was terrible"

textualmente *adv* literally, word for word

textura *nf* texture

tez *nf* complexion

thriller ['triler, 'θriler] (*pl* **thrillers**) *nm* thriller

ti *pron personal (después de prep)* (**a**) *(en general)* you; **siempre pienso en ti** I'm always thinking about you; **me acordaré de ti** I'll remember you (**b**) *(reflexivo)* yourself; **sólo piensas en ti (mismo)** you only think about yourself (**c**) *(en frases)* **¡a ti qué!** so what?, why should you care?; **para ti** *(tú crees)* as far as you're concerned, in your opinion; **si por ti no hay inconveniente, lo hacemos mañana** if it's fine by you we can do it tomorrow

tianguis *nm inv CAm, Méx* open-air market

tiara *nf* tiara

tiarrón, -ona *nm,f Fam* hulk

Tibet *nm* **el T.** Tibet

tibetano, -a *adj & nm,f* Tibetan

tibia *nf* shinbone, tibia

tibieza *nf* (**a**) *(de líquido)* tepidness, lukewarmness (**b**) *(de reacción, posición)* lukewarmness

tibio, -a *adj* (**a**) *(líquido)* tepid, lukewarm (**b**) *(reacción, posición)* lukewarm (**c**) *(expresiones) Fam* **poner t. a alguien** *(por la espalda)* to dump on sb; *(delante)* to tear into sb; **ponerse t. de algo** *(comer)* to stuff one's face with sth; *(beber)* to down bucketfuls of sth

tiburón *nm* (**a**) *(pez)* shark (**b**) *Fin* raider

tic (*pl* **tics**) *nm* tic

ticket ['tike] *o* ['tiket] (*pl* **tickets**) *nm* (**a**) *(billete)* ticket (**b**) *(recibo)* **t. (de compra)** receipt

tictac *nm* ticktock

tiemblo *etc ver* **temblar**

tiempo *nm* (**a**) *(en general)* time; **al poco t.** soon afterward; **a t. (de hacer algo)** in time (to do sth); **a un t., al mismo t.** at the same time; **cada cierto t.** every so often; **con el t.** in time; **con t.** with plenty of time to spare, in good time; **dar t. al t.** to give things time; **del t.** *(fruta)* of the season; *(bebida)* at room temperature; **de un t. a esta parte** recently, for a while now; **en mis tiempos** in my day *o* time; **estar a t. de** to have time to; **tener t. de** to have time to; **fuera de t.** at the wrong moment; **ganar t.** to save time; **hace mucho t. que no lo veo** I haven't seen him for ages; **hacer t.** to pass the time; **matar** *o* **engañar el t.** to kill time; **perder el t.** to waste time; **en tiempos de Maricastaña** donkey's years ago; **a t. completo** full-time; **a t. parcial** part-time; **t. de cocción** cooking time; **t. de exposición** *(en cámara)* shutter speed; **t. libre** spare time; *Dep* **t. muerto** time out; *Inform* **t. real** real time; **t. de respuesta** response time

(**b**) *(periodo largo)* long time; **hace t. que** it is a long time since; **hace t. que no vive aquí** he hasn't lived here for some time; **tomarse uno su t.** to take one's time

(**c**) *(edad)* age; **¿qué t. tiene?** how old is he?

(**d**) *(movimiento)* movement; **motor de cuatro tiempos** four-stroke engine

(**e**) *(clima)* weather; **hizo buen/mal t.** the weather was good/bad; **si el t. lo permite** *o* **no lo impide** weather permitting; **hace un t. de perros** it's a foul day; **poner a** *o* **al mal t. buena cara** to put a brave face on things

(**f**) *Dep* half

(**g**) *Gram* tense; **t. simple/compuesto** simple/composite tense

(**h**) *Mús (compás)* time; *(ritmo)* tempo

tienda *nf* (**a**) *(establecimiento)* store, shop; **ir de tiendas** to go shopping; **t. de antigüedades** antique store; **t. de artículos de regalo** gift shop; *Méx* **t. de departamentos** department store; **t. de deportes** sports store; **t. libre de impuestos** duty-free shop *o* store; **t. de muebles** furniture store; **t. de ropa** clothes store; **t. virtual** online store *o* retailer (**b**) *(para acampar)* **t. (de campaña)** tent

tiendo *ver* **tender**

tiene *ver* **tener**

tienta 1 *nf Taurom* trial *(of the bulls)*

2 a tientas *loc adv* blindly; **buscar algo a tientas** to grope around *o* about for sth; **andar a tientas** to grope along

tiento 1 *ver* **tentar**

2 *nm* (**a**) *(cuidado)* care; *(tacto)* tact (**b**) **dar un t. a algo** *(probar)* to try sth (**c**) *(de ciego)* white stick (**d**) *(de equilibrista)* balancing pole

tierno, -a 1 *adj* (**a**) *(blando, cariñoso)* tender (**b**) *(del día)* fresh

2 *nm Am* baby

tierra *nf* (**a**) *(terrenos, continentes)* land; **en tierras mexicanas/del rey** on Mexican soil/the King's land; **por estas tierras** around these parts, down this way; **t. adentro** inland; **t. firme** *(por oposición al mar)* dry land; **t. de nadie** no-man's-land; **t. prometida** Promised Land; **T. del Fuego** Tierra del Fuego; **T. Santa** the Holy Land; **t. virgen** virgin land

(**b**) *(en agricultura)* land; **cultivar la t.** to farm the land

(**c**) *(materia inorgánica)* earth; *(para nutrir plantas)* soil; **se me ha metido t. en los zapatos** I've got some dirt in my shoes; **un camino de t.** a dirt track; **t. batida** *(en tenis)* clay

(**d**) *(suelo)* ground; **bajo t.** underground; **caer a t.** to fall to the ground; **tomar t.** to land

(**e**) *(lugar de origen) (país)* homeland, native land; *(región)* home *o* native region; **vino/queso de la t.** local wine/cheese; **t. natal** homeland, native land

(**f**) *Elec* **(toma de) t.** ground

(**g**) *(expresiones)* **besar la t.** to fall flat on one's face; **echar por t. algo** to ruin sth; **echar t. a un asunto** to hush up an affair; **poner t. por medio** to make oneself scarce; **quedarse en t.** to miss the boat/train/plane/*etc*; *Fam* **¡t., trágame!** I wish the earth would swallow me up!

(**h**) *Am (polvo)* dust

(**i**) **la T.** *(planeta)* the Earth

tierral *nm Am* dust cloud

tieso, -a *adj* (**a**) *(rígido)* stiff; *Fig* **dejar t. a alguien** to kill sb; **quedarse t.** *(de frío)* to freeze (**b**) *(erguido)* erect (**c**) *Fam (engreído)* haughty (**d**) *Fam (distante)* distant

tiesto *nm* flowerpot

tifoideo, -a *adj* typhoid; **fiebres tifoideas** typhoid fever

tifón *nm* typhoon

tifosi *nmpl Dep* = Italian soccer fans

tifus *nm inv* typhus

tigre *nm* (**a**) *(animal)* tiger; **los tigres económicos del sudeste asiático** the tiger economies of Southeast Asia; *Fam Fig* **oler a t.** to stink (**b**) *Esp Fam (WC)* john (**c**) *Am (jaguar)* jaguar

tigresa *nf* tigress

TIJ [tiχ] *nm* (*abrev de* **Tribunal Internacional de Justicia**) ICJ, International Court of Justice

tijera *nf* (*en general*) scissors; (*de jardinero, esquilador*) shears; **unas tijeras** (a pair of) scissors/shears; **de t.** (*escalera, silla*) folding; **tijeras de podar** pruning shears

tijereta *nf* (**a**) (*insecto*) earwig (**b**) *Dep* (overhead) bicycle *o* scissors kick

tijeretazo *nm* snip

tijeretear *vt* to snip

tila *nf* (**a**) (*flor*) lime blossom (**b**) (*infusión*) lime blossom tea

tildar *vt* **t. a alguien de algo** to brand *o* call sb sth

tilde *nf* (*acento gráfico*) accent

tilín *nm* tinkle, tinkling; *Fam* **me hace t.** I like the look of him/her/it; *Fam* **no me hizo mucho t.** he/she/it didn't do much for me

tilo *nm* (**a**) (*árbol*) linden *o* lime tree (**b**) (*madera*) lime

timador, -ora *nm,f* con artist, confidence trickster, swindler

timar *vt* (**a**) (*estafar*) **t. a alguien** to swindle sb; **t. algo a alguien** to swindle sb out of sth (**b**) (*engañar*) to cheat, to con; **te han timado** you've been done *o* had

timba *nf* card game (*in gambling den*)

timbal *nm* *Mús* (*de orquesta*) kettledrum, timbal; (*tamboril*) small drum

timbrado, -a *adj* (**a**) (*sellado*) stamped (**b**) (*sonido*) clear

timbrar **1** *vt* (*documento*) to stamp
2 *vi Andes, CAm, Méx* to ring

timbrazo *nm* loud ring

timbre *nm* (**a**) (*aparato*) bell; **tocar el t.** to ring the bell; **t. de alarma** alarm (bell) (**b**) (*de voz, sonido*) timbre; **el t. de su voz** the sound of her voice (**c**) (*sello*) (*de documentos*) (official) stamp; (*de impuestos*) seal; *CAm, Méx* (*de correos*) stamp

timidez *nf* shyness

tímido, -a **1** *adj* shy
2 *nm,f* shy person

timo *nm* (**a**) (*estafa*) swindle; *Fam* **¡eso es el t. de la estampita!** it's a complete rip-off! (**b**) *Fam* (*engaño*) trick (**c**) *Anat* thymus

timón *nm* (**a**) *Av & Náut* rudder (**b**) (*gobierno*) helm; **llevar el t. de** to be at the helm of (**c**) *Andes, Cuba* (*de vehículo*) steering wheel

timonear *vi* to steer

timonel, timonero *nm Náut* helmsman

timorato, -a *adj* (**a**) (*mojigato*) prudish (**b**) (*tímido*) fearful

tímpano *nm* (**a**) *Anat* eardrum (**b**) *Mús* (*tamboril*) small drum; (*de cuerda*) hammer dulcimer (**c**) *Arquit* tympanum

tina *nf* (**a**) (*tinaja*) pitcher (**b**) (*gran cuba*) vat (**c**) *CAm, Col, Méx* (*bañera*) bathtub

tinaja *nf* (large) pitcher

tinción *nf* dyeing

tinerfeño, -a **1** *adj* of/from Tenerife
2 *nm,f* person from Tenerife

tinglado *nm* (**a**) (*cobertizo*) shed (**b**) (*armazón*) platform (**c**) (*lío*) fuss; (*maquinación*) plot

tinieblas *nfpl* darkness; *Fig* **estar en t. sobre algo** to be in the dark about sth

tino *nm* (**a**) (*puntería*) good aim (**b**) (*habilidad*) skill (**c**) (*juicio*) sense, good judgment; (*prudencia*) moderation

tinta *nf* ink; **andarse con medias tintas** to be wishy-washy; **cargar** *o* **recargar las tintas** to exaggerate; **se han escrito ríos de t. sobre el tema** people have written reams on the subject; **saberlo de buena t.** to have it on good authority; **sudar t.** to sweat blood; **t. china** Indian ink; **t. indeleble** marking ink; **t. invisible** *o* **simpática** invisible ink

tintar *vt* to dye

tinte *nm* (**a**) (*sustancia*) dye (**b**) (*operación*) dyeing (**c**) (*tintorería*) dry cleaner's (**d**) (*rasgo*) overtone; **una novela de tintes autobiográficos** a novel with autobiographical overtones *o* elements

tintero *nm* (*frasco*) inkpot; (*en la mesa*) inkwell; **dejarse algo en el t.** to leave sth unsaid

tintinear *vi* to jingle, to tinkle

tintineo *nm* tinkle, tinkling

tinto, -a **1** *adj* (**a**) (*vino*) red (**b**) (*teñido*) dyed (**c**) (*manchado*) stained
2 *nm* (*vino*) red wine

tintorera *nf* porbeagle, mackerel shark

tintorería *nf* dry cleaner's

tintorero, -a *nm,f* dry cleaner

tintorro *nm Fam* cheap red wine

tintura *nf* (**a**) *Quím* tincture; **t. de yodo** (tincture of) iodine (**b**) (*tinte*) dye; (*proceso*) dyeing

tiña *nf Med* ringworm

tiñera *etc ver* **teñir**

tiño *ver* **teñir**

tiñoso, -a *adj* (**a**) *Med* suffering from ringworm (**b**) *Fam* (*miserable*) grotty

tío, -a *nm,f* (**a**) (*familiar*) uncle, *f* aunt; **t. abuelo** great uncle, *f* great aunt; **t. carnal** uncle, *f* aunt (*blood relative*); *Fig* **el t. Sam** Uncle Sam (**b**) *Esp Fam* (*hombre*) guy; (*mujer*) woman; (*mujer joven*) girl; **t. bueno** hunk; **tía buena** gorgeous woman (**c**) *Esp Fam* (*apelativo*) (*hombre*) pal; (*mujer*) **¡tía, déjame en paz!** leave me alone, will you?; **¡tía, qué guapa estás!** wow, you look fantastic! (**d**) *Fam* **no hay tu tía, no puedo abrir el cajón** this drawer just refuses to open; **por más que se lo pido, no hay tu tía** I've asked him and asked him, but he's not having any of it

tiovivo *nm* merry-go-round, carousel

tiparraco, -a = **tipejo**

tipazo *nm Fam* (*de mujer*) great figure; (*de hombre*) good build

tipear *vt & vi Am* to type

tipejo, -a, tiparraco, -a *nm,f Fam Pey* individual, character

típico, -a *adj* (*característico*) typical (**de** of); (*traje, restaurante*) traditional; **es un plato t. de Francia** this is a typical French dish; **es un rasgo t. de los orientales** it is a characteristic feature of orientals; **es t. de** *o* **en él llegar tarde** it's typical of him to arrive late; **¿y qué hicisteis? — pues lo t.** so what did you do? — all the usual *o* typical things

tipificación *nf* (**a**) (*gen*) *& Der* classification (**b**) (*normalización*) standardization (**c**) (*paradigma, representación*) epitome

tipificar [59] *vt* (**a**) (*gen*) *& Der* to classify (**b**) (*normalizar*) to standardize (**c**) (*representar*) to epitomize, to typify

tipismo *nm* local color

tiple **1** *nmf* (*cantante*) soprano
2 *nm* (**a**) (*voz*) soprano (**b**) (*guitarra*) treble guitar

tipo, -a **1** *nm,f Fam* (*hombre*) guy; (*mujer*) woman; (*mujer joven*) girl
2 *nm* (**a**) (*clase*) type, sort; **no es mi t.** he's not my type; **todo t. de** all sorts of; **personas de todo t.** all sorts of people; **no me gustan las películas de ese t.** I don't like those sorts of movies *o* movies like that
(**b**) (*cuerpo*) (*de mujer*) figure; (*de hombre*) build; **tiene muy buen t.** she has a very good body; *Fam* **jugarse el t.** to risk one's neck; *Fam* **aguantar** *o* **mantener el t.** to keep one's cool, not to lose one's head
(**c**) *Econ* rate; **t. de cambio** exchange rate; **t. de descuento** base rate; **t. impositivo** tax bracket; **t. de interés** interest rate; **t. (de interés) hipotecario** mortgage rate
(**d**) *Imprenta* type

tipografía *nf* (**a**) (*procedimiento*) printing (**b**) (*taller*) printing works (*singular*)

tipográfico, -a *adj* typographical, printing; **industria tipográfica** printing industry

tipógrafo, -a *nm,f* printer
tipología *nf* typology
típula *nf* daddy longlegs
tíquet (*pl* **tíquets**) *nm* (**a**) (*billete*) ticket (**b**) (*recibo*) **t. (de compra)** receipt
tiquismiquis 1 *adj inv* (*maniático*) persnickety
    2 *nmf inv* (*maniático*) fussbudget
    3 *nmpl* (**a**) (*riñas*) squabbles (**b**) (*bagatelas*) trifles
tira 1 *nf* (**a**) (*banda cortada*) strip (**b**) (*tirante*) strap (**c**) (*de viñetas*) **t. (cómica)** comic *o* cartoon strip (**d**) *Fam* **me gustó la t.** I really loved it; **la t. de** loads of; **¿tienes juguetes? — ¡la t.!** have you got any toys? — loads (of them)!; **hace la t. que no viene por aquí** it's ages since she's been here
    2 *nm* **hubo un t. y afloja entre las dos partes** there was a lot of hard bargaining between the two sides
tirabeque *nm* snow pea
tirabuzón *nm* (**a**) (*rizo*) curl (**b**) (*sacacorchos*) corkscrew
tirachinas *nm inv* slingshot
tirada *nf* (**a**) (*lanzamiento*) throw (**b**) *Imprenta* (*número de ejemplares*) print run; (*reimpresión*) reprint (**c**) (*sucesión*) series (**d**) *Fam* (*distancia*) **hay una buena t. hasta allí** it's a fair way *o* quite a stretch; **de** *o* **en una t.** in one go
tiradero *nm Méx* garbage dump
tirado, -a *Fam* **1** *adj* (**a**) (*barato*) dirt cheap (**b**) (*fácil*) simple, easy as pie; **estar t.** to be a cinch (**c**) (*débil, cansado*) worn-out (**d**) (*miserable*) seedy (**e**) (*abandonado, plantado*) **dejar t. a alguien** to leave sb in the lurch
    2 *nm,f* (*persona*) wretch
tirador, -ora 1 *nm,f* (*persona*) marksman, *f* markswoman
    2 *nm* (**a**) (*mango*) handle (**b**) (*de campanilla*) bell rope
tiragomas *nm inv* slingshot
tiralíneas *nm inv* ruling pen, = pen used with bottled ink for drawing geometrical figures, plans etc
Tirana *n* Tirana
tiranía *nf* tyranny
tiránico, -a *adj* tyrannical
tiranizar [14] *vt* to tyrannize
tirano, -a 1 *adj* tyrannical
    2 *nm,f* tyrant
tiranosaurio *nm* tyrannosaurus
tirante 1 *adj* (**a**) (*cuerda, goma*) taut; **me noto la piel t.** my skin feels stretched (**b**) (*situación, relaciones*) tense; **estar t. con alguien** to be tense with sb
    2 *nm* (**a**) (*de tela*) strap; **un sostén sin tirantes** a strapless bra; **tirantes** (*para pantalones*) suspenders (**b**) *Arquit* brace
tirantez *nf también Fig* tension
tirar 1 *vt* (**a**) (*lanzar*) to throw; **t. algo a algo/alguien** (*para que lo agarre*) to throw sth to sth/sb; (*para hacer daño*) to throw sth at sth/sb; **tírame una manzana** throw me an apple
    (**b**) (*dejar caer*) (*objeto*) to drop; (*líquido*) to spill
    (**c**) (*derribar*) (*botella, lámpara*) to knock over; (*muro, edificio*) to knock down
    (**d**) (*desechar*) to throw away; **t. algo a la basura** to throw sth away; **eso es t. el dinero** that's a complete waste of money
    (**e**) (*disparar*) (*bala, misil*) to fire; (*bomba*) to drop; (*petardo, cohete*) to let off; (*dardo, flecha*) to shoot; **t. una foto** to take a picture
    (**f**) (*jugar*) (*carta*) to play; (*dado*) to throw
    (**g**) *Dep* (*falta, penalti*) to take; (*balón*) to pass; **t. a gol** to shoot, to have a shot at goal
    (**h**) (*imprimir*) to print
    (**i**) *Fam* (*suspender*) to fail, to flunk
    2 *vi* (**a**) (*estirar, arrastrar*) **t. (de algo)** to pull (sth); **la chaqueta me tira de atrás** the jacket's a bit tight at the back
    (**b**) (*disparar*) to shoot; **t. a matar** to shoot to kill
    (**c**) *Fam* (*atraer*) to have a pull; **me tira la vida del campo** I

feel drawn toward life in the country; **t. de algo** to attract sth
    (**d**) (*cigarrillo, chimenea*) to draw
    (**e**) *Fam* (*funcionar*) to go, to work
    (**f**) (*dirigirse*) to go, to head; **tira por esa calle** go up *o* take that street
    (**g**) (*jugar*) to (have one's) go
    (**h**) *Dep* (*con el pie*) to kick; (*con la mano*) to throw; (*a meta, canasta*) to shoot
    (**i**) *Fam* **ir tirando** (*apañárselas*) to get by; **voy tirando** I'm OK, I've been worse
    (**j**) (*durar*) to last
    (**k**) (*parecerse*) **tira a gris** it's grayish; **tira a su abuela** she takes after her grandmother; **tirando a** approaching, not far from
    (**l**) *Fam* (*hacer uso*) **t. de algo** to use sth; **hubo que t. de los ahorros** we had to draw on our savings
    (**m**) (*tender*) **t. para algo** (*persona*) to have the makings of sth; **este programa tira a (ser) hortera** this program is a bit on the tacky side; **el tiempo tira a mejorar** the weather looks as if it's getting better
    3 tirarse *vpr* (**a**) (*lanzarse*) (*al agua*) to dive (**a** into); (*al aire*) to jump (**a** into); **tirarse sobre alguien** to jump on top of sb; **tirarse de** to jump from; (*para bajar*) to jump down from; (*para matarse*) to throw oneself from (**b**) (*tumbarse*) to stretch out; **tirarse en el suelo** to stretch out on the ground (**c**) *Fam* (*pasar tiempo*) to spend; **se tiraba todo el día viendo la tele** she'd be in front of the TV all day long, she'd spend the whole day in front of the TV (**d**) *muy Fam* (*sexualmente*) **tirarse a alguien** to lay sb
tirita *nf* Band-Aid®
tiritar *vi* to shiver (**de** with)
tiritona, tiritera *nf* **le dio una t.** he had a fit of shivering
tiro *nm* (**a**) (*disparo*) shot; **le dieron un t. en el brazo** he was shot in the arm; **lo mataron de un t.** he was shot dead; **pegar un t. a alguien** to shoot sb; **pegarse un t.** to shoot oneself; **t. de gracia** coup de grâce; *Dep* **t. libre** (*en fútbol*) free kick; (*en baloncesto*) free throw; *Fam* **ni a tiros: este cajón no se abre ni a tiros** this drawer just refuses to open; **esta cuenta no me sale ni a tiros** however hard I try I don't seem to be able to get this sum right; **me salió el t. por la culata** it backfired on me; **no van por ahí los tiros** you're a bit wide of the mark there; *Fam* **sentar como un t. (a alguien)** to go down badly (with sb)
    (**b**) (*acción*) shooting; **t. con arco** archery; **t. al blanco** (*deporte*) target shooting; (*lugar*) shooting range; **t. al plato** clay-pigeon shooting
    (**c**) (*huella, marca*) bullet mark; (*herida*) gunshot wound
    (**d**) (*alcance*) range; **a t. de** within range of; **a t. de piedra** a stone's throw away; **ponerse/estar a t.** (*de arma*) to come/be within range; *Fig* (*de persona*) to come/be within one's reach; **si se me pone a t. no dejaré escapar la ocasión** if the chance comes up, I won't miss it
    (**e**) (*de chimenea, horno*) draw
    (**f**) (*de pantalón*) = distance between crotch and waist; **vestirse** *o* **ponerse de tiros largos** to dress up to the nines
    (**g**) (*de caballos*) team
tiroideo, -a *adj* thyroid; **glándula tiroidea** thyroid (gland)
tiroides *nm inv* thyroid (gland)
tirolés, -esa 1 *adj* Tyrolean; **sombrero t.** Tyrolean hat
    2 *nm,f* Tyrolean
tirón *nm* (**a**) (*estirón*) pull; **de un t.** in one go; **un t. de orejas** (*como reprimenda*) a slap on the wrist (**b**) (*robo*) bag snatching
tironear *vt* to tug (at)
tirotear 1 *vt* to fire at
    2 *vi* to shoot
    3 tirotearse *vpr* to fire at each other
tiroteo *nm* (*tiros*) shooting; (*intercambio de disparos*) shootout
Tirreno *nm* **el (mar) T.** the Tyrrhenian Sea

tirria *nf Fam* **le tengo t.** I can't stand him

tisana *nf* herbal tea

tísico, -a *adj & nm,f Med* consumptive

tisis *nf inv Med* (pulmonary) tuberculosis

tisú *nm (tela)* lamé

titán *nm* giant

titánico, -a *adj* titanic

titanio *nm* titanium

títere *nm también Fig* puppet; **no dejar t. con cabeza** *(destrozar)* to destroy everything in sight; *(criticar)* to spare nobody; **títeres** *(guiñol)* puppet show

titi *nf Esp muy Fam (chica)* broad

tití *(pl* **titíes** *o* **titís)** *nm (mono)* titi, = small monkey common in Central and South America

Titicaca *nm* **el lago T.** Lake Titicaca

titilar *vi* **(a)** *(temblar)* to tremble **(b)** *(estrella, luz)* to flicker

titiritar *vi* to shiver **(de** with)

titiritero, -a *nm,f* **(a)** *(de títeres)* puppeteer **(b)** *(acróbata)* acrobat

titubeante *adj (actitud)* hesitant; *(voz)* hesitant, faltering

titubear *vi (dudar)* to hesitate; *(al hablar)* to falter, to hesitate

titubeo *nm (duda, al hablar)* hesitation, hesitancy; **tras muchos titubeos** after much hesitation

titulación *nf (académica)* qualifications

titulado, -a **1** *adj (diplomado)* qualified; *(licenciado)* graduate; **abogado t.** law graduate; **t. en** with a diploma *o* qualification/degree in

    2 *nm,f (diplomado)* holder of a diploma *o* qualification; *(licenciado)* graduate

titular 1 *adj (profesor)* tenured; **el equipo t.** the first team

    2 *nmf (poseedor)* holder; *(profesor)* tenured professor; **t. de una tarjeta de crédito/cuenta corriente** credit card/checking account holder

    3 *nm Prensa* headline; **con grandes titulares** splashed across the front page

    4 *vt (libro, cuadro)* to call, to title

    5 titularse *vpr* **(a)** *(llamarse)* to be titled *o* called; **¿cómo se titula la película?** what's the title of the movie?, what's the movie called? **(b)** *(licenciarse)* to graduate **(en** in); *(diplomarse)* to obtain a diploma *o* qualification **(en** in); **se tituló por la universidad de Cuernavaca** she graduated from *o* earned her degree at Cuernavaca University

titularidad *nf Dep* **perder la t.** to lose one's first-team place

título 1 *nm* **(a)** *(de obra)* title; *Cine* **títulos de crédito** credits; **t. nobiliario** title **(b)** *(licenciatura)* degree; *(diploma)* diploma; **tiene muchos títulos** she has a lot of qualifications; **t. universitario** college *o* university degree **(c)** *(de derecho, obligación) (documento)* deed; **t. de propiedad** title deed **(d)** *Fin* security; **t. de acción** stock certificate

    2 a título *loc prep* **a t. individual** on an individual basis; **a t. de amigo** as a friend

tiza *nf* chalk; **una t.** a piece of chalk

tiznadura *nf* **(a)** *(acción)* blackening, dirtying **(b)** *(mancha)* black mark

tiznar 1 *vt* to blacken

    2 tiznarse *vpr* to be blackened

tizne *nm o nf* soot

tizón *nm* burning stick *o* log

tizona *nf* sword

tlapalería *nf Méx* hardware store

TLC *nm (abrev de* **Tratado de Libre Comercio)** NAFTA, North American Free Trade Agreement

TNT *nm (abrev de* **trinitrotolueno)** TNT

toalla *nf* **(a)** *(para secarse)* towel; *Fig* **arrojar** *o* **tirar la t.** to throw in the towel; **t. de baño** bath towel; *Am* **t. femenina** *o* **sanitaria** sanitary napkin **(b)** *(tejido)* toweling

toallero *nm* towel bar

toallita *nf* **(a)** *(para la cara)* washcloth, facecloth **(b)** *(refrescante)* towelette **(c)** *(para bebés)* baby *o* wet wipe

toallón *nm RP (de baño)* bath towel; *(de playa)* beach towel

toba *nf Fam (papirotazo)* flick

tobera *nf (de horno)* air inlet; *(de propulsor)* nozzle

tobillera *nf* ankle support

tobillo *nm* ankle

tobogán *nm* **(a)** *(rampa)* slide; *(en parque de atracciones)* = spiral slide around a tower; *(en piscina)* chute, flume **(b)** *(trineo)* toboggan; *(pista)* toboggan run

toca *nf* wimple

tocadiscos *nm inv* record player

tocado, -a 1 *adj* **(a)** *Fam (loco)* **t. (del ala)** soft in the head **(b)** *(fruta)* bad, rotten

    2 *nm* **(a)** *(prenda)* headgear **(b)** *(peinado)* hairdo

tocador *nm* **(a)** *(mueble)* dressing table **(b)** *(habitación) (en lugar público)* powder room; *(en casa)* boudoir

tocamientos *nmpl* **(a)** *Der* sexual assault **(b)** *Euf (masturbación)* touching oneself

tocante *adj* **(en lo) t. a** regarding

tocar [59] **1** *vt* **(a)** *(entrar en contacto con)* to touch; *(palpar)* to feel **(b)** *(hacer sonar) (instrumento, canción)* to play; *(bombo)* to bang; *(sirena, alarma)* to sound; *(campana, timbre)* to ring; **el reloj tocó las doce** the clock struck twelve **(c)** *(abordar) (tema)* to touch on; **no toques ese tema** don't mention that subject **(d)** *(concernir)* **por lo que a mí me toca/a eso le toca** as far as I'm/that's concerned; **t. a alguien de cerca** to concern sb closely **(e)** *(conmover)* to touch

    2 *vi* **(a)** *(entrar en contacto)* to touch

    (b) *(estar próximo)* **t. con** *(pared, mueble)* to be touching; *(país, jardín)* to border (on)

    (c) *(llamar)* **t. a la puerta/ventana** to knock on the door/window

    (d) *(en un reparto)* **le tocó la mitad** he got half of it; **tocamos a dos trozos cada uno** there's enough for two slices each; **tocamos a mil cada uno** *(nos deben)* we're due a thousand each; *(debemos)* it's a thousand each; **te toca a ti hacerlo** *(turno)* it's your turn to do it; *(responsabilidad)* it's up to you to do it; **a mí me toca fregar la cocina** I've got to mop the kitchen

    (e) *(caer en suerte)* **me ha tocado la lotería** I've won the lottery; **le ha tocado sufrir mucho** he has had to suffer a lot **(f)** *(llegar el momento)* **hoy toca limpiar** it's cleaning day today; **ahora toca divertirse** now it's time to have some fun

    3 tocarse *vpr* **(a)** *(reflexivo) (palparse)* to touch **(b)** *(dos objetos, personas) (estar en contacto)* to touch

tocata 1 *nm Fam (tocadiscos)* record player

    2 *nf Mús* toccata

tocateja: a tocateja *loc adv* in cash

tocayo, -a *nm,f* namesake; **somos tocayos** we have the same (first) name

tocho 1 *adj Fam (grande)* huge

    2 *nm* **(a)** *Fam (cosa grande)* massive *o* huge great thing; *(libro)* massive tome **(b)** *(hierro)* iron ingot

tocinería *nf* pork butcher's

tocinero, -a *nm,f* pork butcher

tocino *nm* **(a)** *(para cocinar)* pork *o* bacon fat; **t. entreverado** = pork fat containing streaks of meat **(b)** *Méx (beicon)* bacon **(c)** **t. de cielo** = dessert made of syrup and eggs

tocología *nf* obstetrics

tocólogo, -a *nm,f* obstetrician

tocomocho *nm* = confidence trick involving the sale of a lottery ticket, claimed to be a certain winner, for a large amount of money

tocón *nm* stump

todavía *adv* **(a)** *(con afirmación)* still; *(con negación)* yet, still; **están t. aquí** they are still here; **¿pero vive t.?** but is she still alive?; **t. no** not yet; **t. no lo he recibido** I still haven't got it, I haven't got it yet (**b**) *(con más énfasis)* still; **he hecho todo lo que me ha pedido y t. no está contento** I've done everything he asked and he still isn't happy (**c**) *(incluso)* even; **t. más** even more; **¡t. querrá más!** I hope he's not going to ask for more!

todo, -a 1 *adj* (**a**) *(en general)* all; **t. el día** all day; **t. el libro** the whole book, all (of) the book; **t. el mundo** everybody (**b**) *(cada, cualquier)* every; **todos los días/lunes** every day/Monday; **t. español** every Spaniard, all Spaniards (**c**) *(para enfatizar)* **es t. un hombre** he's every inch a man; **ya es toda una mujer** she's a grown woman now; **fue t. un éxito** it was a great success

2 *pron* (**a**) *(singular)* everything; *(plural)* all of them; **lo vendió t.** he sold everything, he sold it all; **de t.** everything (you can think of)

(**b**) **todos** *(todas las personas)* everybody; *(todas las cosas)* all of them; **vinieron todos** everybody *o* they all came; **están todos rotos** they're all broken, all of them are broken

(**c**) *(expresiones)* **ante t.** *(sobre todo)* above all; *(en primer lugar)* first of all; **con t.** despite everything; **del t.** completely; **no estoy del t. contento** I'm not entirely happy; **no lo hace mal del t.** she doesn't do it at all badly; **después de t.** after all; **estar en t.** to think of everything; **de todas todas** without a shadow of a doubt; **sobre t.** above all; **t. lo más** at the most; **me invitó a cenar y t.** she even asked me to dinner

3 *nm* whole; **jugarse el t. por el t.** to stake everything

todopoderoso, -a *adj* almighty; **el T.** the Almighty

todoterreno *nm* (**a**) *(vehículo)* four-wheel drive, all-terrain vehicle, ATV (**b**) *(persona)* versatile person

toffee ['tofe] *nm* coffee-flavored toffee

tofu *nm* tofu

toga *nf* (**a**) *(romana)* toga (**b**) *(de académico)* gown; *(de magistrado)* robes (**c**) *(en el pelo)* **hacerse la t.** = to wrap one's wet hair around one's head and cover it with a towel to dry, in order to straighten out curls

togado, -a *adj* robed

Togo *n* Togo

toilette [twa'let] **1** *nm CSur* toilet, lavatory

2 *nf Anticuado* **hacer la t.** to perform one's toilet(te)

toisón *nm* **t. de oro** *(insignia)* golden fleece

tojo *nm* gorse

Tokio *n* Tokyo

toldo *nm (de tienda)* awning; *(de playa)* sunshade

toledano, -a 1 *adj* of/from Toledo

2 *nm,f* person from Toledo

Toledo *n* Toledo

tolerable *adj* (**a**) *(aguantable)* tolerable (**b**) *(perdonable)* acceptable

tolerado, -a *adj (película)* suitable for all ages

tolerancia *nf* tolerance

tolerante 1 *adj* tolerant

2 *nmf* tolerant person

tolerar *vt* (**a**) *(consentir aceptar)* to tolerate; **t. que alguien haga algo** to tolerate sb doing sth; **no tolero esa actitud** I won't tolerate that sort of attitude; **¡cómo toleras que te hable así!** how can you let him talk to you like that! (**b**) *(aguantar) (altas temperaturas)* to stand, to tolerate; *(medicinas)* to tolerate; **esta planta tolera muy bien la sequedad** this plant survives very well in dry conditions

tolva *nf* hopper

toma 1 *nf* (**a**) *(acción de tomar)* **t. de decisiones** decision-making; **t. de posesión** *(de gobierno, presidente)* investiture; *(de cargo)* undertaking (**b**) *(de biberón, papilla)* feed (**c**) *(de medicamento)* dose (**d**) *(de ciudad)* capture (**e**) *(de agua, aire)* inlet; *Elec* **t. de corriente** socket; *Elec* **t. de tierra** ground (**f**)

Cine (plano) take; **t. de exteriores** location shot

2 *nm Fam* **t. y daca** give and take

tomacorriente *nm Am* socket

tomadura *nf* **t. de pelo** hoax

tomahawk [toma'χauk] (*pl* **tomahawks**) *nm* tomahawk

tomar 1 *vt* (**a**) *(agarrar, obtener, recibir)* to take

(**b**) *(comida, bebida)* to have; **¿qué quieres t.?** *(beber)* what would you like (to drink)?; *Esp (comer)* what would you like (to eat)?

(**c**) *(trasporte) (autobús, tren)* to catch; *(taxi, ascensor)* to take

(**d**) *(adquirir) (actitud, costumbre)* to adopt; **tomarle manía/cariño a algo/alguien** to take a dislike/a liking to sth/sb

(**e**) *(apuntar) (datos, información)* to take down

(**f**) *(exponerse a)* **t. el sol** to sunbathe; **t. el aire** *o* **el fresco** to go out for a breath of fresh air

(**g**) *(considerar, confundir)* **t. a alguien por algo/alguien** to take sb for sth/sb

(**h**) *(expresiones) Fam* **tomarla con alguien** to have it in for sb; **¡toma ésa!** *(expresa venganza)* that'll teach you!, chew on that!

2 *vi* (**a**) *(encaminarse)* to go, to head (**b**) *Am (beber alcohol)* to drink (**c**) *toma (al dar algo)* here you are

3 tomarse *vpr* (**a**) *(comida, bebida)* to have; *(tiempo, medicina)* to take (**b**) *(interpretar)* to take; **tomarse algo bien/a mal/en serio** to take sth well/badly/seriously

4 *interj Fam* **¡t.!** *(expresa sorpresa)* good grief!; **¡t. ya!, ¡qué golazo!** wow, what a goal!

tomate *nm* (**a**) *(fruto)* tomato; **ponerse como un t.** to go as red as a beet; **t. frito** = unconcentrated puree made by frying peeled tomatoes; **t. ketchup** tomato ketchup (**b**) *Fam (de calcetín)* hole (**c**) *Fam (jaleo)* uproar, commotion

tomatera *nf* tomato plant

tomavistas *nm inv* cine camera

tómbola *nf* = type of raffle with non-monetary prizes

tomillo *nm* thyme

tomo *nm* (**a**) *(volumen)* volume (**b**) *(libro)* tome

tomografía *nf* tomography

ton: sin ton ni son *loc adv* for no apparent reason

tonada *nf* (**a**) *(melodía)* tune (**b**) *Am (acento)* (regional) accent

tonadilla *nf* ditty

tonadillero, -a *nm,f* ditty singer/writer

tonal *adj* tonal

tonalidad *nf* (**a**) *Mús* key (**b**) *(de color)* tone

tonel *nm* *(recipiente)* barrel; **estar/ponerse como un t.** to be/become (like) an elephant *o* a whale

tonelada *nf* tonne; **t. métrica** metric ton, tonne; **pesar una t.** to weigh a ton

tonelaje *nm* tonnage

tóner (*pl* **tóner** *o* **tóners**) *nm* toner

Tonga *n* Tonga

tongada *nf* layer

tongo *nm (engaño)* **en la pelea hubo t.** the fight was fixed

tónica *nf* (**a**) *(tendencia)* trend (**b**) *Mús* tonic (**c**) *(bebida)* tonic water

tónico, -a 1 *adj* (**a**) *(reconstituyente)* revitalizing (**b**) *Gram & Mús* tonic

2 *nm* (**a**) *(reconstituyente)* tonic (**b**) *(cosmético)* skin toner

tonificación *nf* invigoration

tonificante, tonificador, -ora *adj* invigorating

tonificar [59] *vt* to invigorate

tonillo *nm Pey (retintín)* sarcastic tone of voice

tono *nm* (**a**) *(de sonido, palabras)* tone; **¡no me hables en ese t.!** don't speak to me in that tone (of voice)!; **subir el t., subir de t.** *(volumen, ruido)* to get *o* grow louder; *(situación)* to get angrier and angrier; **t. de voz** tone of voice; **t. de llamada** *(de teléfono)* dial tone

(**b**) *(de color)* shade, tone; **t. de piel** complexion

(c) *(de músculo)* tone; **t. muscular** muscle tone

(d) *Mús (tonalidad)* key; *(altura)* pitch; *(intervalo)* tone, step; **t. mayor** major key; **t. menor** minor key

(e) *(expresiones)* **estar a t. con algo** to suit sth; *Fam* **darse t.** to give oneself airs; **fuera de t.** out of place; **ponerse a t.** *(emborracharse)* to get in the mood

tonsura *nf* tonsure

tonsurado *nm (sacerdote)* priest

tontaina *Fam* **1** *adj* daft

2 *nmf* crazy idiot

tontear *vi* **(a)** *(hacer el tonto)* to fool about **(b)** *(coquetear)* **t. (con alguien)** to flirt (with sb)

tontería, *Am* **tontera** *nf* **(a)** *(estupidez)* stupid thing; **decir una t.** to say something stupid, to talk nonsense; **decir tonterías** to talk nonsense; **hacer una t.** to do something foolish; **hizo la t. de decírselo** he was stupid enough to tell her **(b)** *(cosa sin importancia o valor)* trifle; **¿qué te ha pasado? — nada, una t.** what happened to you? — oh, it's nothing serious; **por hacer cuatro tonterías me ha cobrado 100 euros** he charged me 100 euros for doing next to nothing

tonto, -a 1 *adj* **(a)** *(persona) (estúpido)* stupid; *(menos fuerte)* silly; **pero ¿seré t.? otra vez me he vuelto a confundir** I must be stupid or something, I've gone and got it wrong again; **nos toman por tontos** they think we're idiots; **¿estás t.? para qué me pegas?** don't be stupid! what are you hitting me for?; **ponerse t.** *(pesado, insistente)* to be difficult; *(arrogante)* to get awkward; **t. de remate** crazy as a loon **(b)** *(retrasado)* dim, backward **(c)** *(sin sentido) (risa)* mindless; *(esfuerzo)* pointless; **a lo t.** *(sin notarlo)* without realizing it

2 *nm,f* idiot; **el t. del pueblo** the village idiot; **hacer el t.** *(juguetear)* to mess around; *(no actuar con inteligencia)* to be stupid o foolish; **hacerse el t.** to act innocent; **a tontas y a locas** without thinking

tontorrón, -ona 1 *adj* daft

2 *nm,f* crazy idiot

toña *nf Fam (borrachera)* **cogerse una t.** to get smashed

top *(pl* **tops)** *nm (prenda)* cropped top

topacio *nm* topaz

topadora *nf RP* bulldozer

topar 1 *vi* **(a)** *(chocar)* to bump into each other **(b)** *(encontrarse)* **t. con alguien** to bump into sb; **t. con algo** to come across sth

2 toparse *vpr* **toparse con** *(persona)* to bump into; *(cosa)* to come across

tope 1 *adj inv* **(a)** *(máximo)* top, maximum; **fecha t.** deadline **(b)** *Esp Fam (genial)* fab

2 *adv Fam (muy)* mega, really

3 *nm* **(a)** *(pieza)* block; *(para puerta)* doorstop **(b)** *Ferroc* buffer **(c)** *(límite máximo)* limit; *(de plazo)* deadline **(d)** *Méx (para velocidad)* speed bump **(e)** *(freno)* **poner t. a** to rein in, to curtail **(f)** *(expresiones)* **a t.** *(de velocidad, intensidad)* flat out; *(lleno)* packed; **abrir el grifo a t.** to turn the faucet on full; **estar hasta los topes** to be bursting at the seams

topera *nf* molehill

topetazo *nm* bump; **darse un t.** *(en la cabeza)* to bump oneself on the head

topetear *vi* to butt

tópico, -a 1 *adj* **(a)** *Med* topical **(b)** *(manido)* clichéd

2 *nm* cliché

topless ['toples] *nm inv* topless sunbathing; **en t.** topless; **hacer t.** to go topless

topo *nm* **(a)** *Zool & Fig* mole **(b)** *Esp (lunar en tela)* polka dot; **una falda de topos** a polka-dot skirt

topografía *nf* topography

topográfico, -a *adj* topographical

topógrafo, -a *nm,f* topographer

topología *nf* topology

toponimia *nf* **(a)** *(nombres)* place names **(b)** *(ciencia)* toponymy

topónimo *nm* place name

toque 1 *ver* **tocar**

2 *nm* **(a)** *(golpe)* knock; **dio unos toques en la puerta** she knocked on the door **(b)** *(detalle)* touch; **dar los últimos toques a algo** to put the finishing touches to sth **(c)** *(aviso)* warning; **dar un t. a alguien** *(llamar)* to call sb; *(llamar la atención)* to prod sb, to warn sb; **t. de atención** warning **(d)** *(sonido) (de campana)* chime; *(de tambor)* beat; *(de sirena)* blast; **t. de diana** reveille; **t. de difuntos** death knell; **t. de queda** curfew

toquetear 1 *vt (manosear) (cosa)* to fiddle with; *(persona)* to fondle

2 *vi Fam (sobar)* to fiddle about

toqueteo *nm (de cosa)* fiddling; *(a persona)* fondling

toquilla *nf* shawl

tora *nf (libro)* Torah

torácico, -a *adj* thoracic

tórax *nm inv* thorax

torbellino *nm* **(a)** *(remolino) (de aire)* whirlwind; *(de agua)* whirlpool; *(de polvo)* dustcloud **(b)** *(de actividad, emociones)* whirlwind **(c)** *(persona inquieta)* whirlwind

torcaz *adj* **paloma t.** ringdove, wood pigeon

torcedura *nf* **(a)** *(torsión)* twist **(b)** *(esguince)* sprain

torcer [15] **1** *vt* **(a)** *(retorcer) (cuerda, cuerpo)* to twist; *(doblar) (aguja, alambre)* to bend; **t. el gesto** to make a face **(b)** *(girar)* to turn; **torció la cabeza** she turned her head **(c)** *(persona)* to corrupt

2 *vi (girar)* to turn; **el camino tuerce a la izquierda** the road turns to the left

3 torcerse *vpr* **(a)** *(retorcerse) (cuerda, cuerpo)* to twist; *(doblarse) (aguja, alambre)* to bend; **me tuerzo al andar/ escribir** I can't walk/write in a straight line; **se ha torcido el cuadro** the painting's not straight **(b)** *(lastimarse)* **torcerse el tobillo** to twist one's ankle **(c)** *(ir mal) (esperanzas, negocios, día)* to go wrong; *(persona)* to go astray

torcido, -a *adj (enroscado)* twisted; *(doblado)* bent; *(cuadro, corbata)* crooked

tordo, -a 1 *adj* dappled

2 *nm,f (caballo)* dapple (horse)

3 *nm (pájaro)* thrush

toreador, -ora *nm,f* bullfighter

torear 1 *vt* **(a)** *(lidiar)* to fight (bulls) **(b)** *(eludir)* to dodge **(c)** *(burlarse de)* **t. a alguien** to mess sb about

2 *vi (lidiar)* to fight bulls

toreo *nm* bullfighting

torera *nf* **(a)** *(prenda)* bolero (jacket) **(b)** **saltarse algo a la t.** to flout sth

torero, -a *nm,f (persona)* bullfighter

toril *nm* bullpen *(in bullring)*

tormenta *nf* storm; *Fig* **esperar a que pase la t.** to wait until things have calmed down; *Fig* **fue una t. en un vaso de agua** it was a tempest in a teapot; **t. de arena** sandstorm; **t. eléctrica** electric storm; **t. de ideas** brainstorming session; **t. de nieve** snowstorm

tormento *nm (dolor físico)* torment, agony; *(angustia)* torment, anguish; **el t. de un amor no correspondido** the torment o anguish of unrequited love; **ser un t.** *(persona)* to be a torment; *(cosa)* to be torture

tormentoso, -a *adj (cielo, día, relación)* stormy; *(época)* troubled, turbulent

tornadizo, -a *adj* fickle

tornado *nm* tornado

tornar 1 *vt* **(a)** *(convertir)* **t. algo en algo** to turn sth into sth **(b)** *(devolver)* to return

2 *vi* **(a)** *(regresar)* to return **(b)** *(volver a hacer)* **t. a hacer algo** to do sth again

3 tornarse *vpr* (**a**) *(volverse)* to become (**b**) *(convertirse)* **tornarse en** to turn into

tornas *nfpl* **volver las t.** to turn the tables; **las t. han cambiado** the shoe is on the other foot

tornasol *nm* (**a**) *(girasol)* sunflower (**b**) *(reflejo)* sheen (**c**) *Quím* **papel de t.** litmus paper

tornasolado, -a *adj* iridescent

torneado, -a 1 *adj* (**a**) *(madera)* turned (**b**) *(brazos, piernas)* shapely
2 *nm (de madera)* turning

tornear *vt* to turn

torneo *nm* tournament, tourney

tornero, -a *nm,f (con madera)* lathe operator

tornillo *nm* (**a**) *(con punta)* screw; *(con tuerca)* bolt (**b**) *(expresiones)* **apretar los tornillos a alguien** to put the screws on sb; *Fam* **le falta un t.** he has a screw loose

torniquete *nm* (**a**) *Med* tourniquet (**b**) *(en entrada)* turnstile

torno 1 *nm* (**a**) *(de dentista)* drill (**b**) *(de alfarero)* (potter's) wheel (**c**) *(de carpintero)* lathe (**d**) *(para pesos)* winch
2 en torno a *loc prep (alrededor de)* around, round; *(aproximadamente)* around, about; **la familia se reunía en t. al televisor** the family gathered around *o* round the television; **girar en t. a** *(tema)* to revolve around; **el debate giró en t. al tema del euro** the debate revolved around the subject of the euro; **el misterio que gira en t. a su muerte** the mystery surrounding her death; **ocurrió en t. a finales de siglo** it happened somewhere around the turn of the century

toro *nm* bull; **los toros** *(lidia)* bullfighting; **t. de lidia** fighting bull; *Fig* **agarrar** *o Esp* **coger el t. por los cuernos** to take the bull by the horns; *Fig* **ver los toros desde la barrera** to watch from the wings; **ir a los toros** to go to a bullfight; *Fig* **nos va a pillar el t.** we're going to be late

toronja *nf* grapefruit

toronjil *nm* lemon balm

Toronto *n* Toronto

torpe *adj* (**a**) *(sin destreza, sin tacto)* clumsy; **sus movimientos son torpes** her movements are clumsy; **t. con las manos** *(que rompe las cosas)* ham-handed, ham-fisted; *(que deja caer las cosas)* butterfingered; **es muy t. conduciendo** he's a terrible driver (**b**) *(sin inteligencia)* slow, dim-witted

torpedear *vt* to torpedo

torpedero *nm* torpedo boat

torpedo *nm* (**a**) *(proyectil)* torpedo (**b**) *(pez)* electric ray

torpeza *nf* (**a**) *(falta de destreza, tacto)* clumsiness; **fue una t. hacerlo/decirlo** it was a clumsy thing to do/say (**b**) *(falta de inteligencia)* slowness

torpor *nm* torpor, sluggishness

torrar 1 *vt* to roast
2 torrarse *vpr Fam* to be roasting

torre *nf* (**a**) *(construcción)* tower; *(de apartamentos)* high-rise (apartment) block; **una t. de quince pisos** a fifteen-story block; **la T. de Babel** the Tower of Babel; **t. de control** control tower; **t. del homenaje** keep; *Fig* **t. de marfil** ivory tower; **t. de perforación** oil derrick; **t. de refrigeración** cooling tower; **t. del reloj** clock tower (**b**) *(en ajedrez)* rook, castle (**c**) *Mil* turret (**d**) *Elec* pylon (**e**) *Inform* tower (computer)

torrefacto, -a *adj* high-roast; **café t.** strongly roasted coffee

torrencial *adj* torrential

torrente *nm* torrent; **un t. de** *(gente, palabras)* a stream *o* flood of; *(dinero, energía)* masses of

torrentera *nf* channel *(made by flowing water)*

torreón *nm* large fortified tower

torreta *nf* (**a**) *Mil* turret (**b**) *Elec* pylon

torrezno *nm* = chunk of fried bacon

tórrido, -a *adj* torrid

torrija *nf* = French toast topped with cinnamon and sugar or treacle, typically eaten at Easter

torsión *nf* (**a**) *(del cuerpo, brazo)* twist, twisting (**b**) *Mec* torsion

torso *nm* torso

torta *nf* (**a**) *Culin Esp (de harina)* = flat, round plain cake; *CSur, Ven (dulce)* cake; *Andes, CAm, Carib, RP (salada)* pie; *Méx (tortilla)* flat omelet, frittata; *Méx (sandwich)* filled roll; *Fig* **nos costó la t. un pan** it cost us an arm and a leg (**b**) *Fam (bofetada)* slap (in the face); **dar** *o* **pegar una t. a alguien** to slap sb (in the face) (**c**) *Fam (golpe, accidente)* thump; **darse** *o* **pegarse una t.** *(al caer)* to bang oneself; *(con el coche)* to have a crash (**d**) *Fam* **ni t.** not a thing

tortazo *nm Fam* (**a**) *(bofetón)* slap (in the face); **dar** *o* **pegar un t. a alguien** to slap sb (in the face); **liarse a tortazos** to come to blows (**b**) *(golpe, accidente)* thump, wallop; **darse** *o* **pegarse un t.** to give oneself a real thump *o* wallop; *(con el coche)* to have a crash

tortería *nf Méx* sandwich shop, luncheonette

tortícolis *nf inv* = crick in the neck

tortilla *nf* (**a**) *(de huevo)* omelet; *Fig* **dar la vuelta a la t.** to turn everything upside down; **t. (a la) española** Spanish *o* potato omelet; *Esp* **t. (a la) francesa** French *o* plain omelet (**b**) *(de maíz)* tortilla, = thin corn pancake

tortillera *nf muy Fam* dyke, lezzy

tortillería *nf Am* = store selling (corn) tortillas

tortita *nf* small pancake

tórtola *nf* turtledove

tortolito, -a *nm,f* (**a**) *(inexperto)* novice (**b**) *Fam (enamorado)* lovebird

tortuga *nf* *(terrestre)* turtle, tortoise; *(marina)* turtle; *(fluvial)* terrapin; *Fig* **ser una t.** *(ser lento)* to be a snail

tortuosidad *nf* (**a**) *(sinuosidad)* tortuousness (**b**) *(perversidad)* deviousness

tortuoso, -a *adj* (**a**) *(sinuoso)* tortuous, winding (**b**) *(perverso)* devious

tortura *nf* torture

torturador, -ora 1 *adj* torturing
2 *nm,f* torturer

torturar 1 *vt* to torture
2 torturarse *vpr* to torture oneself

torunda *nf (de algodón)* swab

torvo, -a *adj* fierce

torzamos *ver* torcer

tos *nf* cough; **t. ferina** whooping cough

Toscana *nf* **(la) T.** Tuscany

toscano, -a *adj & nm,f* Tuscan

tosco, -a *adj* (**a**) *(primitivo)* crude (**b**) *(persona, modales)* rough

toser *vi* to cough

tosferina *nf* whooping cough

tosquedad *nf* (**a**) *(de objeto)* crudeness (**b**) *(de persona, modales)* roughness

tostada *nf* piece of toast; **tostadas** toast

tostadero *nm (de café)* roaster

tostado, -a *adj* (**a**) *(pan)* toasted; *(almendras, café)* roasted (**b**) *(color)* brownish (**c**) *(piel)* tanned

tostador *nm* toaster

tostar [63] **1** *vt* (**a**) *(dorar, calentar) (pan)* to toast; *(café, almendras)* to roast; *(carne)* to brown (**b**) *(broncear)* to tan
2 tostarse *vpr* to get brown; **tostarse al sol** to sunbathe

tostón *nm* (**a**) *Fam (aburrimiento)* bore, drag; **dar el t. a alguien** to pester sb, to go on and on at sb (**b**) *Fam (persona)* pain (**c**) *(de pan)* crouton (**d**) *(cochinillo)* roast sucking pig

total 1 *adj* (**a**) *(completo) (cifra, coste)* total; *(confianza, ruptura)* total, complete (**b**) *Fam (fantástico)* fab
2 *nm* (**a**) *(suma)* total; **me da un t. de 580 libras** I make it 580 (**b**) *(totalidad, conjunto)* whole; **el t. del grupo** the whole group; **nos costó 200 dólares en t.** it cost us 200 dollars in

total *o* all; **en t. fuimos más de treinta personas** in total there were more than thirty of us

3 *adv (en resumen)* basically, in a word; *(en realidad)* anyway; **t. que me marché** so anyway, I left; **t., ¿qué más da?** what difference does it make anyway?

totalidad *nf* whole; **en su t.** as a whole

totalitario, -a *adj & nm,f* totalitarian

totalitarismo *nm* totalitarianism

totalizar [14] *vt* to obtain, to score

totalmente *adv* totally, completely

tótem (*pl* **tótems** *o* **tótemes**) *nm* totem

totémico, -a *adj* totemic

totogol *nm Col, CRica* = gambling game involving betting on the results of soccer games

totuma *nf Am* calabash, gourd

Tour [tur] *nm* **el T. (de Francia)** the Tour (de France)

tour [tur] (*pl* **tours**) *nm* tour; **t. de force** tour de force; **t. operador** tour operator

tournedós [turne'ðo] *nm inv* tournedos

tournée [tur'ne] *nf* tour; **estar de t.** to be on tour

toxicidad *nf* toxicity

tóxico, -a 1 *adj* toxic, poisonous

2 *nm* poison

toxicología *nf* toxicology

toxicológico, -a *adj* toxicological

toxicomanía *nf* drug addiction

toxicómano, -a 1 *adj* addicted to drugs

2 *nm,f* drug addict

toxina *nf* toxin

tozudez *nf* stubbornness, obstinacy

tozudo, -a 1 *adj* stubborn

2 *nm,f* stubborn person

TPI *nm* (*abrev de* **Tribunal Penal Internacional**) ICC

traba *nf* (**a**) *(obstáculo)* obstacle; **poner trabas (a alguien)** to put obstacles in the way (of sb) (**b**) *(para coche)* chock (**c**) *(de mesa)* crosspiece

trabado, -a *adj* (**a**) *(unido) (salsa)* smooth; *(discurso)* coherent (**b**) *(atascado)* jammed (**c**) *Gram* ending in a consonant

trabajado, -a *adj* (**a**) *(obra)* well-crafted (**b**) *(músculo)* developed

trabajador, -ora 1 *adj* hardworking

2 *nm,f* worker; **t. por cuenta propia** self-employed person; **t. cualificado** skilled worker; **t. manual** blue-collar worker

trabajar 1 *vi* (**a**) *(en empleo, tarea)* to work; **¿de qué trabaja?** what does she do (for a living)?; **t. de/en** to work as/in; **t. en una empresa** to work for a firm; **ponerse a t.** to get to work (**b**) *Cine & Teatro* to act; **¡qué bien trabajan todos!** the acting is really good!

2 *vt* (**a**) *(hierro, barro, tierra)* to work; *(masa)* to knead (**b**) *(vender) (producto, género, marca)* to sell, to stock (**c**) *(mejorar)* to work on *o* at

3 trabajarse *vpr Fam* **trabajarse a alguien (para que haga algo)** to work on sb (to get them to do sth)

trabajo *nm* (**a**) *(tarea, actividad)* work; **una casa tan grande da mucho t.** a big house like that is a lot of work; **hacer un buen t.** to do a good job; *Fam Fig* **ser un t. de chinos** to be a finicky job; **t. de campo** fieldwork; **t. en** *o* **de equipo** teamwork; **t. físico** physical effort; **t. intelectual** mental effort; **t. manual** manual labor; **trabajos forzados** *o* **forzosos** hard labor; **t. de oficina** office work; **t. social** social work; **t. sucio** dirty work; **t. temporal** temporary work

(**b**) *(empleo)* job; **buscar/encontrar t.** to look for/find work *o* a job; **no tener t.** to be out of work

(**c**) *(lugar)* work; **en el t.** at work; **ir al t.** to go to work

(**d**) *(escrito) (por estudiante)* essay

(**e**) *Econ & Pol* labor

(**f**) *(esfuerzo)* effort; **costar mucho t.** to take a lot of effort; **tomarse el t. de hacer algo** to go to *o* take the trouble of doing sth

trabajoso, -a *adj* (**a**) *(difícil)* hard, difficult (**b**) *(molesto)* tiresome

trabalenguas *nm inv* tongue twister

trabar 1 *vt* (**a**) *(sujetar)* to fasten; *(a preso)* to shackle (**b**) *(unir)* to join (**c**) *(iniciar) (conversación, amistad)* to strike up (**d**) *(obstaculizar)* to obstruct, to hinder (**e**) *(espesar)* to thicken

2 trabarse *vpr* (**a**) *(enredarse)* to get tangled (**b**) *(espesarse)* to thicken (**c**) *(al hablar)* to get one's tongue tied in knots; **se le trabó la lengua** he tripped over his tongue

trabazón *nf* (**a**) *(unión)* assembly (**b**) *(conexión)* link, connection

trabilla *nf* *(de pantalón)* belt loop

trabucar [59] **1** *vt* to mix up

2 trabucarse *vpr (liarse)* to get things mixed up; *(al hablar)* to get one's tongue tied in knots

trabuco *nm* *(arma de fuego)* blunderbuss

traca *nf* string of firecrackers

tracción *nf* traction; **vehículo de t. animal** vehicle drawn by an animal; **t. delantera/trasera** front-wheel/rearwheel drive; **t. a las cuatro ruedas** four-wheel drive

trace *etc ver* **trazar**

tracoma *nm* trachoma

tracto *nm* tract; **t. digestivo** digestive tract

tractor *nm* tractor

tractorista *nmf* tractor driver

tradición *nf* tradition; **se hace por t.** it's done *o* people do it out of tradition

tradicional *adj* traditional

tradicionalismo *nm* traditionalism; *Pol* conservatism

tradicionalista *adj & nmf* traditionalist

tradicionalmente *adv* traditionally

traducción *nf* translation; **t. automática/simultánea** machine/simultaneous translation; **t. directa/inversa** translation into/out of one's own language

traducir [18] **1** *vt* (**a**) *(a otro idioma)* to translate; **t. algo del alemán al castellano** to translate sth from German into Spanish (**b**) *(expresar)* to express; **una actitud corporal que traduce aplomo y seguridad** a posture that conveys composure and self-confidence

2 *vi* to translate (**de/a** from/into)

3 traducirse *vpr* (**a**) *(a otro idioma)* **traducirse (por)** to be translated (by *o* as) (**b**) **traducirse en** *(ocasionar)* to translate into; **la subida de la inflación se traduce en una pérdida de poder adquisitivo** the rise in inflation translates into a loss of purchasing power

traductor, -ora 1 *adj* translating

2 *nm,f* translator; **t. jurado** = translator qualified to work in court

traer [68] **1** *vt* (**a**) *(de un lugar a otro)* to bring; **trae a tus amigos** bring your friends (along) (**b**) *(llevar encima)* to carry; **¿qué traes ahí?** what have you got there? (**c**) *(contener)* to have; **trae un artículo interesante** it has an interesting article in it; **¿qué trae ese sobre?** what's in that envelope? (**d**) *(llevar puesto)* to wear (**e**) *(provocar) (ruina, pobreza, suerte)* to bring; *(consecuencias)* to carry, to have; **t. consigo** *(implicar)* to mean, to lead to (**f**) *Fam (en un estado concreto)* **t. a alguien loco** *o* **de cabeza** to be driving sb mad

2 traerse *vpr* (**a**) *(llevar con uno)* to bring (along); **se trajo un cuaderno/a unos amigos** she brought (along) a notebook/some friends (**b**) *Fam (tramar)* **me pregunto qué se traerán (entre manos) esos dos** I wonder what those two are up to (**c**) *Fam* **traérselas** *(trabajo, asunto, persona)* to be a real handful

tráfago *nm* drudgery

traficante *nmf (de drogas, armas)* trafficker

traficar [59] *vi* to traffic (**en/con** in)

tráfico *nm* (**a**) *(de vehículos)* traffic; **t. aéreo** air traffic; **t. fluvial** river traffic; **t. rodado** road traffic (**b**) *(comercio)* traffic; **t. de armas** arms trafficking; **t. de drogas** drug trafficking; **el t. de esclavos** the slave trade; **t. de influencias** political corruption, graft

tragaderas *nfpl Fam* **tener (buenas) t.** *(ser crédulo)* to fall for anything; *(ser tolerante)* to be able to stomach anything

tragaldabas *nmf inv Fam* human garbage can

tragaluz *nm* skylight

tragamonedas *nf inv Am Fam* slot machine

tragaperras *nf inv Fam* slot machine, one-armed bandit

tragar [38] **1** *vt* (**a**) *(ingerir, creer)* to swallow (**b**) *(absorber)* to swallow up (**c**) *Fam (soportar)* to put up with; **no la puedo t.** *o* **no la trago** I can't stand her (**d**) *Fam (consumir mucho)* to devour, to guzzle; **¡cómo traga gasolina este coche!** this car is a real gas guzzler!
  2 *vi* (**a**) *(ingerir)* to swallow (**b**) *Fam (acceder)* to give in
  3 tragarse *vpr* (**a**) *(ingerir, creerse)* to swallow; *Fig* **se tuvo que t. sus propias palabras** he had to swallow his words; **se tragó el cuento** he swallowed the story (**b**) *(disimular) (orgullo)* to swallow; *(lágrimas)* to choke back (**c**) *Fam (soportarse)* **no se tragan** they can't stand each other

tragedia *nf* tragedy

trágico, -a 1 *adj* tragic
  2 *nm,f* tragedian

tragicomedia *nf* tragicomedy

tragicómico, -a *adj* tragicomic

trago *nm* (**a**) *(de líquido)* mouthful; **de un t.** in one gulp (**b**) *Fam (copa)* drink; **echar** *o* **tomar un t.** to have a quick drink (**c**) *Am Fam* **el t.** *(la bebida)* the booze (**d**) *Fam (disgusto)* **ser un t. para alguien** to be tough on sb; **pasar un mal t.** to have a tough time of it

tragón, -ona *Fam* **1** *adj* greedy
  2 *nm,f* **ser un t.** to be greedy

trague *etc ver* **tragar**

traición *nf* (**a**) *(infidelidad)* betrayal; **a t.** treacherously (**b**) *Der* treason; **alta t.** high treason

traicionar *vt (amigo, ideal, país)* to betray; *(ser descubierto por)* to give away; **su acento lo traicionó** his accent gave him away

traicionero, -a 1 *adj* (**a**) *(desleal)* treacherous; *Der* treasonous (**b**) *(peligroso, dañino)* treacherous, dangerous
  2 *nm,f* traitor

traído, -a *adj* worn-out; **t. y llevado** well-worn, hackneyed

traidor, -ora 1 *adj* (**a**) *(desleal)* treacherous; *Der* treasonous (**b**) *(peligroso, dañino)* treacherous, dangerous
  2 *nm,f* traitor

traigo *etc ver* **traer**

tráiler ['trailer] *(pl* **tráilers**) *nm* (**a**) *Cine* preview, trailer (**b**) *(remolque)* trailer; *(camión)* semitrailer (**c**) *Méx (casa rodante)* trailer

trainera *nf* = small boat, for fishing or rowing in races

traje 1 *ver* **traer**
  2 *nm* (**a**) *(con chaqueta)* suit; *(de una pieza)* dress; **t. de baño** swimsuit, bathing suit; **t. de buceo** wet suit; **t. de chaqueta** woman's two-piece suit; **t. espacial** space suit; **t. de etiqueta** evening dress; **t. de gala** dress suit; **llevar t. de gala** to wear formal dress; **t. de luces** matador's outfit; **t. de noche** evening dress; **t. de novia** wedding dress; **t. pantalón** pantsuit; **t. de submarinismo** wet suit
  (**b**) *(regional, disfraz)* costume; **t. de época** period dress; **t. típico** *(de un país)* national dress
  (**c**) *(ropa)* clothes; **t. de diario** everyday clothes; **t. de paisano** *(de militar)* civilian clothes; *(de policía)* plainclothes

trajeado, -a *adj* (**a**) *(con chaqueta)* wearing a jacket (**b**) *Fam (arreglado)* spruced up

trajear 1 *vt* to dress in a suit
  2 trajearse *vpr* to wear a suit

trajera *etc ver* **traer**

trajín *nm* (**a**) *Fam (ajetreo)* bustle (**b**) *(transporte)* transportation, haulage

trajinar 1 *vi Fam* to bustle about
  2 *vt* to transport
  3 trajinarse *vpr muy Fam* **trajinarse a alguien** *(sexualmente)* to bone sb

tralla *nf* (**a**) *(látigo)* whip (**b**) *Fam* **dar t. a** *(criticar)* to slate

trallazo *nm* (**a**) *(chasquido)* lash, crack (**b**) *Fam Dep (disparo)* screamer, powerful shot

trama *nf* (**a**) *(historia)* plot (**b**) *(confabulación)* plot, intrigue (**c**) *(de hilos)* weft

tramar *vt* (**a**) *(hilo)* to weave (**b**) *(planear)* to plot; *(complot)* to hatch; **estar tramando algo** to be up to something

tramitación *nf (acción)* processing; **está en t.** it is being processed

tramitar *vt (sujeto: autoridades) (pasaporte, solicitud)* to process; *(sujeto: solicitante)* to be in the process of applying for; **me están tramitando la renovación de la licencia** my application for a new license is being processed

trámite *nm (gestión)* formal step; **de t.** routine, formal; **trámites** *(proceso)* procedure; *(papeleo)* paperwork

tramo *nm* (**a**) *(espacio)* section, stretch (**b**) *(de escalera)* flight (of stairs) (**c**) *(de tarifa)* rate; *(de edad)* bracket; **t. impositivo** tax bracket

tramontana *nf* north wind

tramoya *nf* (**a**) *Teatro* stage machinery (**b**) *(enredo)* intrigue

tramoyista *nmf* (**a**) *Teatro* stagehand (**b**) *(tramposo)* schemer

trampa *nf* (**a**) *(para cazar)* trap (**b**) *(trampilla)* trapdoor (**c**) *(engaño)* trick; **caer en la t.** to fall into the trap; **tender una t. (a alguien)** to set *o* lay a trap (for sb); **hacer trampas** to cheat (**d**) *(deuda)* debt

trampear *vi Fam* (**a**) *(estafar)* to swindle money (**b**) *(ir tirando)* to struggle along

trampero, -a *nm,f* trapper

trampilla *nf (puerta)* trapdoor

trampolín *nm* (**a**) *(de piscina)* diving board; *(de esquí)* ski jump; *(en gimnasia)* springboard (**b**) *(medio, impulso)* springboard

trampolinista *nmf* diver

tramposo, -a 1 *adj* cheating
  2 *nm,f* cheat

tranca *nf* (**a**) *(de puerta)* bar; **poner una t. en la puerta** to bar the door (**b**) *(arma)* cudgel, stick (**c**) *Fam (borrachera)* **coger una t.** to get plastered (**d**) *Fam* **a trancas y barrancas** with great difficulty

trancar [59] *vt (puerta)* to bar

trancazo *nm* (**a**) *(golpe)* blow (with a stick) (**b**) *Fam (gripe)* bout of the flu

trance *nm* (**a**) *(situación crítica)* difficult situation; **pasar por un mal t.** to go through a bad time; **a todo t.** at all costs (**b**) *(estado hipnótico)* trance; **estar en t.** to be in a trance

tranco *nm* stride

tranquilamente *adv* (**a**) *(con calma)* calmly (**b**) *(con frescura)* coolly; **me lo dijo tan t.** he told me without batting a eyelid (**c**) *(sin dificultad)* easily; **cuesta t. dos millones** it costs at least two million, it easily costs two million

tranquilidad *nf* (**a**) *(sosiego) (de lugar, música, vida)* calm, peacefulness; *(de ambiente, tono de voz)* quietness, calmness; *(de mar)* calmness (**b**) *(falta de preocupaciones)* peace of mind; **para mayor t.** to be on the safe side; **para tu t.** to put your mind at rest (**c**) *(de conciencia)* clearness (**d**) *(despreocupación)* calm

tranquilizador, -ora *adj* calming

tranquilizante 1 *adj* (**a**) *(música, color)* soothing (**b**) *Med* tranquilizing
  2 *nm Med* tranquilizer

tranquilizar [14] **1** *vt* (**a**) *(calmar)* to calm (down) (**b**) *(dar confianza a)* to reassure

  2 tranquilizarse *vpr* (**a**) *(calmarse)* to calm down (**b**) *(ganar confianza)* to feel reassured

tranquillo *nm Esp Fam* **cogerle el t. a algo** to get the hang of sth

tranquilo, -a *adj* (**a**) *(sosegado) (lugar, música, vida)* quiet, peaceful; *(ambiente, tono de voz)* quiet, calm; *(mar)* calm; *(viento)* gentle; **¡(tú) t.!** don't you worry! (**b**) *(sin preocupaciones)* relaxed, calm; **no estoy t. hasta que no llega a casa** I can't relax until she gets home; **dejar a alguien t.** to leave sb alone (**c**) *(sin culpabilidad) (mente)* untroubled; *(conciencia)* clear; **tengo la conciencia tranquila** my conscience is clear (**d**) *(despreocupado)* casual, laid-back; **quedarse tan t.** not to bat an eyelid

transacción *nf Com* transaction

transalpino, -a, trasalpino, -a *adj* transalpine

transandino, -a, trasandino, -a *adj* trans-Andean

transar *vi Am (transigir)* to compromise, to give in; *(negociar)* to come to an arrangement, to reach a compromise

transatlántico, -a, trasatlántico, -a 1 *adj* transatlantic

  2 *nm Náut* (ocean) liner

transbordador, trasbordador *nm* (**a**) *Náut* ferry (**b**) *Av* **t. (espacial)** space shuttle

transbordar, trasbordar *vi* to change *(trains)*

transbordo, trasbordo *nm* **hacer t.** to change *(trains)*

transcendencia, transcendental, *etc* = **trascendencia, trascendental**, *etc*

transcontinental *adj* transcontinental

transcribir, trascribir *vt* to transcribe

transcripción, trascripción *nf* transcription

transcriptor, -ora trascriptor, -ora 1 *nm,f (persona)* transcriber

  2 *nm (aparato)* transcriber

transcrito, -a, trascrito, -a *adj* transcribed

transcurrir, trascurrir *vi* (**a**) *(tiempo)* to pass, to go by (**b**) *(ocurrir)* to take place, to happen; **t. sin incidentes** to go off without incident

transcurso, trascurso *nm* (**a**) *(paso de tiempo)* passing (**b**) *(periodo de tiempo)* **en el t. de** in the course of

transeúnte 1 *adj* passing

  2 *nmf* (**a**) *(paseante)* passerby (**b**) *(residente temporal)* temporary resident

transexual *adj & nmf* transsexual

transferencia, trasferencia *nf* transfer; **t. electrónica de fondos** electronic transfer of funds

transferible, trasferible *adj* (**a**) *(en general)* transferable (**b**) *(deportista)* transfer-listed; **ser t.** to be on the transfer list

transferir, trasferir [62] *vt* to transfer

transfiguración, trasfiguración *nf* transfiguration

transfigurar, trasfigurar 1 *vt* to transfigure

  2 transfigurarse *vpr* to become transfigured

transformación, trasformación *nf* transformation

transformador, -ora, trasformador, -ora 1 *adj* transforming

  2 *nm Elec* transformer

transformar, trasformar 1 *vt* (**a**) *(convertir)* **t. algo (en)** to convert sth (into); **un convento transformado en hotel** a convent converted into a hotel; **las penas lo han transformado en un alcohólico** his troubles have turned him into an alcoholic (**b**) *(cambiar radicalmente)* **t. algo/a alguien (en)** to transform sth/sb (into)

  2 transformarse *vpr* (**a**) *(convertirse)* **transformarse en algo** to be converted into sth; **el pañuelo se transformó en una paloma** the handkerchief turned into a dove; **la zona se ha transformado en un campo de batalla** the area has

become a battleground (**b**) *(cambiar radicalmente)* to be transformed; **en un año la jovencita se había transformado** in just one year the young girl had undergone a transformation

transformismo, trasformismo *nm* evolution

transformista, trasformista 1 *adj* evolutionary

  2 *nmf* (**a**) *(seguidor)* evolutionist (**b**) *(artista) (que cambia de trajes)* quick-change artist

  3 *nm (travestido)* drag artist

transfronterizo, -a *adj* cross-border

tránsfuga, trásfuga *nmf Pol* defector

transfuguismo, trasfuguismo *nm Pol* defection *(to another party)*

transfusión, trasfusión *nf* transfusion; **t. sanguínea** blood transfusion

transfusor, trasfusor *nm (aparato)* transfuser

transgénico, -a 1 *adj* genetically modified, GM

  2 transgénicos *nmpl* GM foods

transgredir, trasgredir *vt* to transgress

transgresión, trasgresión *nf* transgression

transgresor, -ora, trasgresor, -ora *nm,f* transgressor

transiberiano *nm* Trans-Siberian Railroad

transición *nf* transition; **periodo de t.** transition period; **t. democrática** transition to democracy

transido, -a *adj* stricken (**de** with); **t. de pena** grief-stricken

transigencia *nf* (**a**) *(espíritu negociador)* willingness to compromise (**b**) *(tolerancia)* tolerance

transigente *adj* (**a**) *(que cede)* willing to compromise (**b**) *(tolerante)* tolerant

transigir [24] *vi* (**a**) *(ceder)* to compromise (**en** on) (**b**) *(ser tolerante)* to be tolerant

transistor *nm* transistor

transitable *adj (franqueable)* passable; *(no cerrado al tráfico)* open to traffic

transitar *vi* to go (along)

transitivo, -a *adj* transitive

tránsito *nm* (**a**) *(circulación)* movement; *(de coches)* traffic; **t. rodado** road traffic; **pasajeros en t. hacia Roma** *(en aeropuerto)* passengers with connecting flights to Rome (**b**) *(transporte)* transit

transitoriedad *nf* temporary nature; **la t. de la vida** the transience of life

transitorio, -a *adj (temporal)* transitory; *(residencia)* temporary; *(régimen, medida)* transitional, interim

translación = **traslación**

translúcido, -a, translucirse = **traslúcido, traslucirse**

transmediterráneo, -a, trasmediterráneo, -a *adj* transmediterranean

transmigración *nf* transmigration

transmigrar *vi* to transmigrate

transmisible, trasmisible *adj* (**a**) *(enfermedad)* transmittable (**b**) *(título, posesiones)* transferrable

transmisión, trasmisión *nf* (**a**) *(gen) & Aut* transmission; *(de saludos, noticias)* passing on; **t. del pensamiento** telepathy (**b**) *Rad & TV (programa)* broadcast; *(servicio)* broadcasting (**c**) *(de herencia, poderes)* transference

transmisor, -ora, trasmisor, -ora 1 *adj* transmitting

  2 *nm* transmitter

transmitir, trasmitir 1 *vt* (**a**) *(sonido, onda)* to transmit; *(saludos, noticias)* to pass on (**b**) *Rad & TV* to broadcast (**c**) *(ceder)* to transfer

  2 transmitirse *vpr* to be transmitted

transmutación, trasmutación *nf* transmutation

transmutar, trasmutar *vt* to transmute

transnacional, trasnacional *adj* transnational

transoceánico, -a *adj* transoceanic

transparencia, trasparencia *nf* transparency

transparentarse, trasparentarse *vpr* (a) *(ser transparente) (tela)* to be see-through; *(cristal, líquido)* to be transparent (b) *(verse)* to show through; **se transparentan sus intenciones/sentimientos** her intentions/feelings are obvious

transparente, trasparente *adj (cristal, líquido)* transparent; *(tela)* see-through

transpiración, traspiración *nf* perspiration; *Bot* transpiration

transpirar, traspirar 1 *vi (sudar)* to perspire; *Bot* to transpire
    2 *vt (exudar)* to exude

transpirenaico, -a, traspirenaico, -a *adj* trans-Pyrenean

transplantar = trasplantar

transplante = trasplante

transponer, trasponer [50] **1** *vt* (a) *(cambiar)* to switch (b) *(desaparecer detrás de)* to disappear behind
    2 transponerse *vpr* (a) *(adormecerse)* to doze off (b) *(ocultarse)* to disappear; *(sol)* to set

transportable *adj* portable

transportador *nm* (a) *(para transportar)* **t. aéreo** cableway; **t. de cinta** conveyor belt (b) *(para medir ángulos)* protractor

transportar 1 *vt* (a) *(trasladar) (mercancías, pasajeros)* to transport; **transportaba una maleta en cada mano** he was carrying a suitcase in each hand; **esta música me transporta a la infancia** this music takes me back to my childhood (b) *(embelesar)* to captivate
    2 transportarse *vpr (embelesarse)* to go into raptures

transporte *nm* transportation, transport; **t. aéreo** air freight; **t. por carretera** road transportation; **t. colectivo** mass transit; **t. de mercancías** freight transportation; **t. público** mass transit

transportista *nmf Com* carrier

transposición, trasposición *nf* transposition

transpuesto, -a, traspuesto *adj (dormido)* dozing; **quedarse t.** to doze off

transubstanciación *nf Rel* transubstantiation

transvasar, trasvasar *vt* (a) *(líquido)* to decant (b) *(agua de río)* to transfer

transvase, trasvase *nm* (a) *(de líquido)* decanting (b) *(entre ríos)* transfer

transversal, trasversal 1 *adj* transverse
    2 *nf Mat* transversal

transversalmente, trasversalmente *adv* crosswise

tranvía *nm* streetcar

trapecio *nm* (a) *Geom* trapezoid (b) *(de gimnasia)* trapeze (c) *Anat (músculo)* trapezius

trapecista *nmf* trapeze artist

trapense *adj & nmf* Trappist

trapero, -a *nm,f* junkman

trapezoide *nm Anat & Geom* trapezium

trapichear *vi Fam* to be crooked

trapicheo *nm Fam* (a) *(negocio sucio)* fiddle (b) *(tejemaneje)* scheme; **estoy harto de sus trapicheos** I'm sick of his scheming

trapillo: de trapillo *loc adv Fam* **vestir de t.** to wear any old thing

trapío *nm Formal* (a) *(garbo)* elegance (b) *Taurom* good bearing

trapisonda *nf Fam* (a) *(riña)* row, commotion (b) *(enredo)* scheme

trapisondear *vi Fam* (a) *(reñir)* to kick up a row (b) *(liar, enredar)* to scheme

trapisondista *nmf Fam* (a) *(camorrista)* troublemaker (b) *(liante)* schemer

trapo 1 *nm* (a) *(trozo de tela)* rag (b) *(gamuza, bayeta)* cloth; *Fam Fig* **sacar los trapos sucios (a relucir)** to wash one's dirty linen in public; *Fam* **poner a alguien como un t.** to tear sb to pieces; **t. de cocina** dish towel; **t. del polvo** dustcloth, dish towel (c) *Taurom* cape (d) *Fam* **a todo t.** at full pelt
    2 trapos *nmpl Fam (ropa)* clothes

trapón *nm Méx (trapo)* dishcloth

tráquea *nf* windpipe, trachea

traqueotomía *nf Med* tracheotomy

traquetear 1 *vt* to shake
    2 *vi (hacer ruido)* to rattle

traqueteo *nm (ruido)* rattling

tras *prep* (a) *(detrás de)* behind (b) *(después de, en pos de)* after; **uno t. otro** one after the other; **andar t. algo** to be after sth

trasalpino, -a = transalpino

trasandino, -a = transandino

trasatlántico, -a = transatlántico

trasbordador, trasbordar, *etc* = transbordador, transbordar, *etc*

trascendencia, transcendencia *nf* importance, significance; **esta decisión tendrá una gran t.** this decision will be of major significance

trascendental, transcendental *adj* (a) *(importante)* momentous (b) *(filosófico, elevado)* transcendental; *Fam* **ponerse t.** to wax philosophical

trascendente, transcendente *adj* momentous

trascender, transcender [64] *vi* (a) *(extenderse)* to spread (**a** across) (b) *(filtrarse)* to be leaked (c) *(sobrepasar)* **t. de** to transcend, to go beyond

trascribir, trascripción, *etc* = transcribir, transcripción, *etc*

trascurrir = transcurrir

trascurso = transcurso

trasegar [43] *vt* (a) *(desordenar)* to rummage about among (b) *(transvasar)* to decant

trasera *nf* rear

trasero, -a 1 *adj* back, rear
    2 *nm* backside

trasferencia, trasferir, *etc* = transferencia, transferir, *etc*

trasfiguración = transfiguración

trasfigurar = transfigurar

trasfondo *nm (contexto)* background; *(de palabras, intenciones)* undertone

trasformar, trasformación, *etc* = transformar, transformación, *etc*

trásfuga = tránsfuga

trasfuguismo = transfuguismo

trasfusión = transfusión

trasfusor = transfusor

trasgredir, trasgresión, *etc* = transgredir, transgresión, *etc*

trashumancia *nf* seasonal migration *(of livestock)*

trashumante *adj* seasonally migratory

trashumar *vi* to migrate seasonally

trasiego 1 *ver* trasegar
    2 *nm* (a) *(movimiento)* comings and goings (b) *(transvase)* decanting

trasiegue *etc ver* trasegar

traslación, translación *nf Astron* passage

trasladar 1 *vt* (a) *(desplazar) (objeto)* to move; *(detenido, sede)* to transfer, to move; **trasladaron su cuartel general a Túnez** they transferred *o* moved their headquarters to Tunis;

fue trasladada al hospital en una ambulancia she was taken to hospital in an ambulance (**b**) *(empleado)* to transfer (**c**) *(reunión, fecha)* to postpone, to move back (**d**) *(petición, información)* to refer, to pass on (**e**) *(reproducir)* **t. algo al papel** to transfer sth onto paper (**f**) *(traducir)* to translate

2 **trasladarse** *vpr* (**a**) *(desplazarse)* to go; **las batallas comerciales se han trasladado a Internet** the battle for sales has moved over *o* shifted to the Internet (**b**) *(mudarse)* to move; **me traslado de casa** I'm moving house

traslado *nm* (**a**) *(de casa, empresa)* move; **el t. de los muebles** the moving of the furniture (**b**) *(de trabajo)* transfer (**c**) *(de personas)* movement

traslúcido, -a, translúcido *adj* translucent

traslucirse, translucirse [39] *vpr* to show through, to be obvious

trasluz *nm* reflected light; **al t.** against the light

trasmano: a trasmano *loc adv (fuera de alcance)* out of reach; *(lejos)* out of the way

trasmediterráneo, -a = transmediterráneo

trasmisible, trasmisión, *etc* = transmisible, transmisión, *etc*

trasmutación = transmutación

trasmutar = transmutar

trasnacional = transnacional

trasnochado, -a *adj Fam* **estar t.** to be old hat

trasnochador, -ora 1 *adj* given to staying up late

2 *nm,f* night owl

trasnochar *vi* to stay up late, to go to bed late

traspapelar 1 *vt (papeles, documentos)* to mislay, to misplace

2 **traspapelarse** *vpr* to get mislaid *o* misplaced

transparencia, trasparentarse, *etc* = transparencia, transparentarse, *etc*

traspasable *adj (camino)* passable; *(río)* crossable

traspasar *vt* (**a**) *(atravesar)* to go through, to pierce; **t. la puerta** to go through the doorway; **t. una valla saltando** to jump over a fence; **la tinta traspasó el papel** the ink soaked through the paper (**b**) *(transferir) (jugador)* to transfer; *(negocio)* to sell (as a going concern); **se traspasa (negocio)** *(en cartel)* (business) for sale (**c**) *(desplazar)* to move (**d**) *(exceder)* to go beyond

traspaso *nm* (**a**) *(transferencia) (de jugador)* transfer; *(de negocio)* sale (as a going concern); **t. de competencias** devolution; **t. de poderes** transfer of power (**b**) *(precio) (de jugador)* transfer fee; *(de negocio)* takeover fee

traspié *nm* (**a**) *(resbalón)* trip, stumble; **dar un t.** to trip up (**b**) *(error)* blunder, slip; **dar un t.** to slip up, to make a mistake

traspiración = transpiración

traspirar = transpirar

traspirenaico, -a = transpirenaico

trasplantar, transplantar *vt* to transplant

trasplante, transplante *nm* transplant; **t. de corazón** heart transplant; **t. de órganos** organ transplant

trasponer = transponer

trasportín *nm (rejilla)* rear rack *(on bike)*; *(caja)* = container carried on rear rack

trasposición = transposición

traspuesto, -a = transpuesto

trasquilado, -a *adj Fig* **salir t.** to come off badly

trasquilar *vt* (**a**) *(esquilar)* to shear (**b**) *Fam* **me trasquilaron (el pelo)** they gave me a terrible haircut

trasquilón *nm Fam* **hacerle un t. a alguien** *(cortar el pelo)* to give sb a terrible haircut

trastabillar *vi* to stagger

trastada *nf Fam (travesura)* prank

trastazo *nm* bump, bang; **darse** *o* **pegarse un t.** to bang *o* bump oneself

traste *nm* (**a**) *Mús* fret (**b**) *Am salvo RP (utensilio de cocina)* cooking utensil; **fregar los trastes** to wash the dishes (**c**) **dar al t. con algo** to ruin sth; **irse al t.** to fall through

trasteado *nm Mús* frets

trastear *vi* (**a**) *(mudar trastos)* to move things around (**b**) *(hacer travesuras)* to play pranks

trastero 1 *adj* **cuarto t.** lumber room

2 *nm* lumber room

trastienda *nf* backroom

trasto *nm* (**a**) *(utensilio inútil)* piece of junk; **trastos** junk (**b**) *Fam (persona traviesa)* menace, nuisance (**c**) *Fam (persona inútil)* **t. (viejo)** dead loss (**d**) *Fam* **trastos** *(pertenencias, equipo)* things, stuff; **tirarse los trastos a la cabeza** to have a flaming row

trastocar [67] **1** *vt* (**a**) *(cambiar)* to turn upside down (**b**) *(enloquecer)* **t. a alguien** to drive sb mad, to unbalance sb's mind

2 **trastocarse** *vpr (enloquecer)* to go mad

trastornable *adj* oversensitive

trastornado, -a *adj* disturbed, unbalanced

trastornar 1 *vt* (**a**) *(volver loco)* to drive mad (**b**) *(inquietar)* to worry, to trouble (**c**) *(alterar)* to turn upside down; *(planes)* to disrupt, to upset (**d**) *(estómago)* to upset

2 **trastornarse** *vpr (volverse loco)* to go mad

trastorno *nm* (**a**) *(mental)* disorder; *(digestivo)* upset; **t. de la personalidad** personality disorder (**b**) *(alteración)* **causar trastornos** *o* **un t.** *(huelga, nevada)* to cause trouble *o* disruption; *(guerra)* to cause upheaval

trastrocar [67] **1** *vt* (**a**) *(en orden)* to mix up (**b**) *(en sentido)* to change

2 **trastrocarse** *vpr* (**a**) *(en orden)* to get mixed up (**b**) *(en sentido)* to change

trasvasar = transvasar

trasvase = transvase

trasversal = transversal

trasversalmente = transversalmente

trata *nf* slave trade; **t. de blancas** white slave trade

tratable *adj* easygoing, friendly

tratadista *nmf* treatise writer, essayist

tratado *nm* (**a**) *(convenio)* treaty; **T. de Libre Comercio** *(entre EE.UU., Canadá y México)* NAFTA Treaty; **t. de paz** peace treaty (**b**) *(escrito)* treatise

tratamiento *nm* (**a**) *(hacia persona, de tema)* treatment (**b**) *(título)* title, form of address; **apear el t. a alguien** to address sb more informally (**c**) *Med* treatment; **estoy en t.** I'm receiving treatment (**d**) *(agua, sustancia, alimento)* treatment (**e**) *Inform* processing; **t. de datos/textos** data/ word processing

tratante *nmf* dealer; **t. de vinos** wine merchant

tratar 1 *vt* (**a**) *(comportarse con) (persona, objeto)* to treat; **¿qué tal te trataron?** how were you treated? (**b**) *(tener relación con)* to have dealings *o* contact with; **la traté muy poco** I didn't have much to do with her (**c**) *(dirigirse a)* **t. a alguien de usted/tú** = to address sb using the "usted" form/ the "tú" form; **t. a alguien de cretino/tonto** to call sb a cretin/an idiot (**d**) *(tema, asunto)* to treat; **eso lo tienes que t. con el jefe** that's something you'll have to discuss with the boss (**e**) *(paciente, enfermedad)* to treat (**f**) *(agua, sustancia, alimento)* to treat (**g**) *Inform (datos, información)* to process

2 *vi* (**a**) *(versar)* **t. de** *o* **sobre** to be about; **¿de qué trata el documental?** what's the documentary about *o* on? (**b**) *(intentar)* **t. de hacer algo** to try to do sth (**c**) *(tener relación)* **t. con alguien** to mix with sb, to have dealings with sb (**d**) *(comerciar)* to deal (**en** in)

3 **tratarse** *vpr* (**a**) *(relacionarse)* **tratarse con** to mix with, to have dealings with; **no se trata con su padre** he has no contact with his father (**b**) *(versar)* **tratarse de** to be about;

¿de qué se trata? what's it about? (**c**) *(ser cuestión de, ser el caso de)* **tratarse de** to be a question *o* matter of; **necesito hablar contigo — ¿de qué se trata?** I need to talk to you — what about?

tratativas *nfpl CSur* negotiation

trato *nm* (**a**) *(comportamiento, conducta)* treatment; **de t. agradable** pleasant; **malos tratos** battering *(of child, wife)* (**b**) *(relación)* dealings; **tener t. con** to associate with, to be friendly with; **no querer tratos con alguien** to want (to have) nothing to do with sb (**c**) *(acuerdo)* deal; **cerrar** *o* **hacer un t.** to do *o* make a deal; **¡t. hecho!** it's a deal! (**d**) *(tratamiento)* title, term of address

trauma *nm* trauma

traumático, -a *adj* traumatic

traumatismo *nm* traumatism

traumatizante *adj* traumatic

traumatizar [14] **1** *vt* to traumatize
   2 traumatizarse *vpr* to be devastated

traumatología *nf* traumatology

traumatólogo, -a *nm,f* traumatologist

travellers ['traβelers] *nmpl* traveler's checks

travelling ['traβelin] (*pl* **travellings**) *nm Cine* traveling shot

través 1 a través de *loc prep* (**a**) *(lugar, medio)* through; **a t. del cristal** through the glass; **lo supe a t. de ella** I learned of it through *o* from her; **la difusión de la cultura a t. de los libros** the spreading *o* diffusion of culture through books (**b**) *(tiempo)* over; **a t. de los años** over the years; **costumbres transmitidas a t. de generaciones** customs passed on *o* handed down over generations
   2 de través *loc adv* *(transversalmente)* crosswise, crossways; *(de lado)* crosswise, sideways; **mirar de t.** to give a sidelong glance

travesaño *nm* (**a**) *Arquit* crosspiece (**b**) *Dep* crossbar

travesero, -a *adj* **flauta travesera** flute

travesía *nf* (**a**) *(viaje) (por mar)* voyage, crossing; *(por aire)* flight (**b**) *(calle) (entre otras dos)* cross street, connecting street; *(en pueblo)* = main road through a town

travestí (*pl* **travestíes** *o* **travestís**), **travesti** *nmf* (**a**) *(que se viste de mujer)* transvestite, cross-dresser (**b**) *(artista)* drag artist

travestirse [47] *vpr* to cross-dress

travestismo *nm* transvestism

travesura *nf* prank, mischief

traviesa *nf* (**a**) *Ferroc* tie *(on track)* (**b**) *Constr* crossbeam, tie beam

travieso, -a *adj* mischievous

trayecto *nm* (**a**) *(distancia)* distance; *(ruta)* route; **todas las estaciones del t.** all the stations along the way; **el avión que cubría el t. París-Bonn** the plane that used to fly the Paris-Bonn route; **final de t.** end of the line (**b**) *(viaje)* journey, trip; **se puede realizar el t. en una hora** the journey *o* trip can be done in an hour

trayectoria *nf* (**a**) *(recorrido)* trajectory (**b**) *(evolución)* path, development

traza *nf* (**a**) *(aspecto)* appearance, looks (**b**) *(boceto, plano)* plan, design (**c**) *(habilidad)* **tener buena/mala t. (para algo)** to be good/no good (at sth)

trazado, -a 1 *adj* designed, laid out
   2 *nm* (**a**) *(trazo)* outline, sketching (**b**) *(diseño)* plan, design (**c**) *(recorrido)* route

trazar [14] *vt* (**a**) *(línea)* to draw, to trace; *(plano, mapa)* to draw; *(ruta)* to plot (**b**) *(indicar, describir)* **t. las líneas generales del proyecto** to give an outline of the project; **t. un paralelismo entre dos cosas** to draw a parallel between two things (**c**) *(plan, estrategia)* to draw up; *(objetivo)* to set

trazo *nm* (**a**) *(de dibujo, rostro)* line (**b**) *(de letra)* stroke

trébol *nm* (**a**) *(planta)* clover (**b**) **tréboles** *(naipes)* clubs

trece *núm* thirteen; **mantenerse** *o* **seguir en sus t.** to stick to one's guns; *ver también* **seis**

treceavo, -a *núm (fracción)* thirteenth; **la treceava parte** a thirteenth

trecho *nm* *(espacio)* distance; *(tiempo)* time, while; **de t. en t.** every so often

tregua *nf* *(en guerra)* truce; *(respiro)* respite; **no dar t.** to give no respite

treinta *núm* thirty; **los (años) t.** the thirties; *ver también* **seis**

treintañero, -a *adj & nm,f Fam* thirtysomething

treintavo, -a *núm (fracción)* thirtieth; **la treintava parte** a thirtieth

treintena *nf* thirty; **andará por la t.** he must be about thirty; **una t. de...** *(unos treinta)* about thirty...; *(treinta)* thirty...

trekking ['trekin] *nm* hiking

tremebundo, -a *adj* terrifying

tremenda *nf* **tomar** *o* **tomarse algo a la t.** to take sth hard

tremendismo *nm* (**a**) *(exageración)* alarmism (**b**) *Lit* = gloomy Spanish postwar realism

tremendista *adj & nmf (exagerado)* alarmist

tremendo, -a *adj* (**a**) *(enorme)* tremendous, enormous (**b**) *(enfadado)* **ponerse t.** to get very angry

trementina *nf* turpentine

tremolar *vi Formal* to wave, to flutter

tremolina *nf* row, uproar

trémolo *nm Mús* tremolo

trémulo, -a *adj (voz)* trembling; *(luz)* flickering

tren *nm* (**a**) *(ferrocarril)* train; **ir en t.** to go by rail *o* train; **el t. en Suiza funciona muy bien** the railroads in Switzerland are very efficient; **t. de alta velocidad** high-speed train; **t. de carga** freight train; **t. de cercanías** local train, suburban train; **t. correo** mail train; **t. directo** through train; **t. de largo recorrido** long-distance train; **t. de mercancías** freight train; **t. nocturno** overnight train
   (**b**) *Mec* line; **t. de aterrizaje** undercarriage, landing gear; **t. de lavado** car wash
   (**c**) *(estilo) Fam* **vivir a todo t.** to live in style; **t. de vida** lifestyle
   (**d**) *(expresiones) Fam* **estar como (para parar) un t.** to be really gorgeous; *Fig* **perder el t.** to miss the boat; *Fig* **subirse al t. del progreso** to keep pace with progress

trena *nf Fam* slammer, pen

trenca *nf* duffle coat

trence *etc ver* **trenzar**

trencilla *nm Fam Dep* ref

trencito *nm Urug Fam (chuleta)* crib

trenza *nf* (**a**) *(de pelo)* braid, plait; *(de fibras)* braid (**b**) *Culin* = sweet bun made of plaited dough

trenzado, -a 1 *adj* braided, plaited
   2 *nm* (**a**) *(peinado)* plait, braid (**b**) *(en danza)* entrechat

trenzar [14] *vt* (**a**) *(pelo)* to braid, to plait (**b**) *(fibras)* to braid

trepa *nmf Esp Fam Pey* social climber

trepador, -ora 1 *adj* **planta trepadora** climbing plant
   2 *nm,f Fam* social climber

trepanación *nf* trepanation

trepanar *vt* to trepan

trepar 1 *vt* to climb
   2 *vi* (**a**) *(subir)* to climb (**b**) *Fam (medrar)* to be a social climber

trepidación *nf* shaking, vibration

trepidante *adj* (**a**) *(rápido, vivo)* frenetic (**b**) *(que tiembla)* shaking, vibrating

trepidar *vi* to shake, to vibrate

tres 1 *núm* three; *Fam* **de t. al cuarto** cheap, third-rate; *Fam* **no ver t. en un burro** to be as blind as a bat; **t. cuartos de lo mismo** the same thing; *Fam* **no le convencimos ni a la de**

t. there was no way we could convince him; *ver también* **seis**

  2 *nm inv* **t. cuartos** *(abrigo)* three-quarter-length coat

  3 *nm* **t. en raya** tic-tac-toe

trescientos, -as *núm* three hundred; *ver también* **seis**

tresillo *nm* (**a**) *(sofá)* three-piece suite (**b**) *(juego de naipes)* ombre, = card game (**c**) *Mús* triplet

treta *nf (engaño)* trick

tri- *prefijo* tri-

tríada *nf* triad

trial *nm Dep* trial; **t. indoor** indoor trial

triangular *adj* triangular

triángulo *nm* (**a**) *Mat & Mús* triangle; **t. equilátero/ rectángulo** equilateral/right-angled triangle; **t. escaleno/ isósceles** scalene/isosceles triangle (**b**) *Fam* **t. amoroso** love triangle

triatlón *nm Dep* triathlon

tribal *adj* tribal

tribalismo *nm* tribalism

tribu *nf* tribe; **t. urbana** = identifiable social group, such as punks or yuppies, made up of young people living in urban areas

tribulación *nf* tribulation

tribuna *nf* (**a**) *(estrado)* rostrum, platform; *(del jurado)* jury box (**b**) *Dep (localidad)* stand; *(graderío)* grandstand; **t. de prensa** press box (**c**) *Prensa* **t. libre** open forum

tribunal *nm* (**a**) *(de justicia)* court; **llevar a alguien/acudir a los tribunales** to take sb/go to court; **T. de Apelación** Court of Appeal; **T. Constitucional** Constitutional Court; **T. de Cuentas** *(español)* ≃ National Audit Office; *(europeo)* Court of Audit; **T. Europeo de Derechos Humanos** European Court of Human Rights; **T. Internacional de Justicia** International Court of Justice; **T. de Justicia Europeo** European Court of Justice; **T. Penal Internacional** International Criminal Court; **el T. Supremo** ≃ the Supreme Court; **T. Tutelar de Menores** Juvenile Court (**b**) *(de examen)* board of examiners; *(de concurso)* panel

tributable *adj* taxable

tributación *nf* (**a**) *(impuesto)* tax (**b**) *(sistema)* taxation

tributar 1 *vt (homenaje)* to pay; **t. respeto** *o* **admiración a** to have respect *o* admiration for

  2 *vi (pagar impuestos)* to pay taxes

tributario, -a 1 *adj* tax; **sistema t.** tax system; **derecho t.** tax law

  2 *nm,f* taxpayer

tributo *nm* (**a**) *(impuesto)* tax (**b**) *(homenaje)* tribute

tricampeón, -ona *nm,f* three-times champion

tricéfalo, -a *adj* three-headed

tricentenario *nm* tricentenary

tríceps *nm inv* triceps

triciclo *nm* tricycle

tricolor 1 *adj* tricolor, three-colored

  2 *nf* tricolor

tricornio *nm* three-cornered hat

tricot *nm inv* knitting

tricota *nf RP (cerrado)* sweater; *(abierto)* knitted jacket, cardigan

tricotar *vt & vi* to knit

tricotosa *nf* knitting machine

tridente *nm* trident

tridimensional *adj* three-dimensional

trienal *adj* triennial, three-yearly

trienio *nm* (**a**) *(tres años)* three years (**b**) *(paga)* three-yearly salary increase

trifásico, -a *adj* (**a**) *Elec* three-phase (**b**) *(de tres fases)* three-part

trifulca *nf Fam* row, squabble

trigal *nm* wheat field

trigésimo, -a *núm* thirtieth

trigo *nm* wheat

trigonometría *nf* trigonometry

trigueño, -a *adj (tez)* olive; *(cabello)* corn-colored

triguero, -a *adj (del trigo)* wheat; **espárrago t.** wild asparagus

trilateral *adj* trilateral

trilero, -a *nm,f Fam* = person who runs a game where people bet on which is the correct card, shell etc out of three

trilingüe *adj* trilingual

trilita *nf* trinitrotoluene, TNT

trilla *nf* (**a**) *(acción)* threshing (**b**) *(tiempo)* threshing time *o* season

trillado, -a *adj* well-worn, trite

trillador, -ora 1 *adj* threshing

  2 *nm,f (persona)* thresher

trilladora *nf (máquina)* threshing machine

trillar *vt* to thresh

trillizo, -a *nm,f* triplet

trilogía *nf* trilogy

trimestral *adj* three-monthly, quarterly; **exámenes/notas trimestrales** end-of-term exams/grades

trimestralmente *adv* quarterly, every three months

trimestre *nm* three months, quarter; *Educ* term

trimotor 1 *adj* three-engined

  2 *nm* three-engined airplane

trinar *vi* to chirp, to warble; *Fam Fig* **está que trina** he's fuming

trinca *nf* trio

trincar [59] *vt Fam* to grab; **han trincado al ladrón** they've caught the thief

trincha *nf* strap

trinchante *nm* (**a**) *(cuchillo)* carving knife (**b**) *(tenedor)* meat fork

trinchar *vt* to carve

trinchera *nf Mil* trench

trineo *nm (pequeño)* sleigh; *(grande)* sledge

Trinidad *nf* **la (Santísima) T.** the (Holy) Trinity

Trinidad y Tobago *n* Trinidad and Tobago

trinitario, -a *adj & nm,f Rel* Trinitarian

trinitrotolueno *nm* trinitrotoluene

trino *nm (de pájaros)* chirp; *Mús* trill

trinque *etc ver* **trincar**

trinquete *nm Náut* foremast

trío *nm (en general)* trio; *(de naipes)* three of a kind

tripa *nf* (**a**) *(vientre)* stomach; **me duele la t.** I've got a stomachache; *Fam* **echar las tripas** to throw up, to puke; *Fam* **hacer de tripas corazón** to pluck up one's courage; *Fam* **¿qué t. se te ha roto?** what's up with you, then?, what's bugging you?; *Fam* **revolverle las tripas a alguien** to turn sb's stomach (**b**) *Esp Fam (barriga)* gut, belly; **está echando t.** he's getting a potbelly *o* a bit of a gut (**c**) *Fam* **tripas** *(interior)* insides; **quiero ver las tripas de la máquina** I want to see the workings of the machine

tripartito, -a *adj* tripartite

tripi *nm Fam (de LSD)* tab

triple 1 *adj* triple

  2 *nm* (**a**) **el t.** three times as much; **el t. de gente** three times as many people (**b**) *Elec* three-way adapter

triplicado *nm* second copy, triplicate; **por t.** in triplicate

triplicar [59] **1** *vt* to triple, to treble

  2 triplicarse *vpr* to triple, to treble

trípode *nm* tripod

Trípoli *n* Tripoli

tripón, -ona *nm,f Esp Fam* paunchy *o* potbellied person

tríptico *nm* (**a**) *Arte* triptych (**b**) *(folleto)* leaflet *(folded twice to form three parts)*

triptongo *nm Gram* triphthong

tripudo, -a *nm,f Esp Fam* paunchy o potbellied person

tripulación *nf* crew

tripulante *nmf* crew member

tripular *vt* to man

triquina *nf* trichina

triquinosis *nf inv* trichinosis

triquiñuela *nf Fam (truco)* trick

triquitraque *nm (apagado)* creaking; *(fuerte)* rattling

tris: en un tris *loc adv* **estar en un t. de** to be within a whisker of

trisílabo, -a *Gram* **1** *adj* trisyllabic
    2 *nm,f* three-syllable word

triste *adj* (**a**) *(persona)* sad; **no te pongas t.** don't be sad (**b**) *(que entristece) (noticia, suceso)* sad; *(día, tiempo, paisaje)* gloomy, dreary; *(color, vestido, luz)* dull, dreary; **es t. que...** it's sad o a shame that...; **ofrecen un t. espectáculo** they present a sorry spectacle (**c**) *(insignificante)* **un t. sueldo** a miserable salary; **es un t. consuelo** it's small consolation, it's cold comfort; **ni un t....** not a single...; **no tengo ni una t. radio** I haven't even got a radio (**d**) *(humilde)* poor; **un t. viejo** a poor old man

tristemente *adv* sadly

tristeza *nf (de persona)* sadness; *(de día, tiempo, paisaje)* gloominess, dreariness; *(de color, vestido, luz)* dullness

tristón, -ona *adj* rather sad o miserable

tritón *nm* newt

trituración *nf* crushing, grinding

triturador *nm (de basura)* waste disposal unit; *(de papeles)* shredder; *(de ajos)* garlic press

trituradora *nf* crushing machine, grinder

triturar *vt* (**a**) *(moler, desmenuzar)* to crush, to grind; *(papel)* to shred (**b**) *(mascar)* to chew

triunfador, -ora **1** *adj* winning, victorious
    2 *nm,f* winner

triunfal *adj* triumphant

triunfalismo *nm* triumphalism

triunfalista *adj* triumphalist

triunfante *adj* victorious; **salir t.** to win, to emerge triumphant o victorious

triunfar *vi* (**a**) *(vencer)* to win, to triumph (**b**) *(tener éxito)* to succeed, to be successful

triunfo *nm* (**a**) *(victoria)* triumph; *(en encuentro, elecciones)* victory, win; *Fam* **le costó un t. hacerlo** it was a great effort for him to do it (**b**) *(en juegos de naipes)* trump; **sin t.** no trump

triunvirato *nm* triumvirate

trivial *adj* trivial

trivialidad *nf* triviality

trivializar [14] *vt* to trivialize

trizas *nfpl* **hacer t. algo** *(hacer añicos)* to smash sth to pieces; *(desgarrar)* to tear sth to shreds; *Fig* **hacer t. a alguien** to tear o pull sb to pieces; *Fig* **estar hecho t.** *(persona)* to be shattered

trocar [67] **1** *vt* (**a**) *(transformar)* **t. algo (en algo)** to change sth (into sth) (**b**) *(intercambiar)* to swap, to exchange (**c**) *(malinterpretar)* to mix up
    2 trocarse *vpr (transformarse)* **trocarse (en)** to change (into)

trocear *vt* to cut up (into pieces)

trocha *nf (camino)* path; *Am Ferroc* gauge

troche: a troche y moche *loc adv* **repartir puñetazos a t. y moche** to dish out punches left and right

trofeo *nm* trophy

troglodita **1** *adj* (**a**) *(cavernícola)* cave dwelling (**b**) *Fam (bárbaro, tosco)* rough, brutish

    2 *nmf* (**a**) *(cavernícola)* cave dweller (**b**) *Fam (bárbaro, tosco)* brute

troika *nf* troika

trola *nf Fam* fib, lie

trolebús *(pl* **trolebuses***) nm* trolleybus

trolero, -a *Fam* **1** *adj* fibbing, lying
    2 *nm,f* fibber, liar

tromba *nf* waterspout; *Fig* **entrar en t.** to burst in; **t. de agua** heavy downpour

trombo *nm* thrombus

trombón *nm Mús (instrumento)* trombone; *(músico)* trombonist; **t. de pistones** o **de llaves** valve trombone; **t. de varas** slide trombone

trombosis *nf inv* thrombosis; **t. coronaria** coronary thrombosis

tromba 1 *nf* (**a**) *Mús* horn (**b**) *(de elefante)* trunk; *(de oso hormiguero)* snout; *(de insecto)* proboscis (**c**) *Anat* tube; **t. de Eustaquio/de Falopio** Eustachian/Fallopian tube (**d**) *(músico)* horn player (**e**) *Fam (borrachera)* **coger** o **pillar una t.** to get plastered
    2 *adj Fam (borracho)* plastered

trompada *nf Fam* thump, punch

trompazo *nm* bang; **darse** o **pegarse un t. con** to bang into

trompeta 1 *nf* trumpet
    2 *nmf* trumpeter

trompetilla *nf* ear trumpet

trompetista *nmf* trumpeter, trumpet player

trompicar *vi* to stumble

trompicón *nm (tropezón)* stumble; **a trompicones** in fits and starts

trompo *nm* (**a**) *(peonza)* spinning top (**b**) *(giro)* spin

trona *nf* high chair

tronada *nf* thunderstorm

tronado, -a *adj Fam (loco)* crazy

tronar [63] **1** *v impersonal* to thunder; **está tronando** it's thundering
    2 *vt Méx* (**a**) *(hacer estallar) (cohetes)* to let off (**b**) *Fam (destruir, acabar con)* to get rid of, to do away with (**c**) *Fam (suspender)* to fail
    3 *vi Méx* (**a**) *(estallar)* to explode (**b**) *Fam (en relación)* to split up, to break up (**con**) with

troncal *adj* **carretera t.** trunk road; **asignatura t.** compulsory o core subject

tronchante *adj Fam* hilarious

tronchar 1 *vt (partir)* to snap
    2 troncharse *vpr Fam* **troncharse (de risa)** to split one's sides laughing

troncho *nm (de lechuga)* heart

tronco¹ *nm* (**a**) *Anat & Bot* trunk; *(talado y sin ramas)* log; *Fam* **dormir como un t.** to sleep like a log (**b**) *Culin* **t. (de Navidad)** yule log (**c**) *Univ* **t. común** compulsory subjects

tronco², **-a 1** *nm,f Fam* (**a**) *Esp (como apelativo)* pal (**b**) *Am (persona torpe)* klutz
    2 *adj Am (estúpido)* thick; *(torpe)* clumsy, klutzy

tronera *nf* (**a**) *Arquit & Hist* embrasure (**b**) *(en billar)* pocket

tronío *nm Fam* (**a**) *(despilfarro)* **comportarse/vivir con mucho t.** to throw one's money around (**b**) *(gracia)* style; **tener mucho t.** to have style

trono *nm* throne

tropa *nf* (**a**) *Mil (no oficiales)* rank and file; *(ejército)* troops; **tropas de asalto** assault troops, storm troops; **tropas de choque** shock troops; **tropas mecanizadas** mechanized troops; **tropas de refresco** fresh troops (**b**) *Fam (multitud)* troop, flock

tropecientos, -as *adj inv Fam* hundreds (and hundreds) of, umpteen

tropel nm (**a**) (de personas) mob, crowd; **en t.** in a mad rush, en masse (**b**) (de cosas) mass, heap

tropelía nf outrage

tropezar [17] **1** vi (**a**) (con los pies) to trip o stumble (**con** on); **tropecé con el bordillo y me caí** I tripped on the curb and fell over (**b**) (por casualidad) **t. con alguien** to bump o run into sb (**c**) (enfrentarse) **t. con** (problema, obstáculo) to come up against
2 tropezarse vpr Fam (dos personas) to bump into each other, to come across one another; **tropezarse con alguien** to bump into sb

tropezón nm (**a**) (con los pies) trip, stumble; **dar un t.** to trip up, to stumble; **a tropezones** (hablar) haltingly; (moverse) in fits and starts (**b**) (desacierto) slipup, blunder (**c**) Culin **tropezones** = finely chopped ham, boiled egg etc added as a garnish to soups or other dishes

tropical adj tropical

trópico nm tropic

tropiece etc ver **tropezar**

tropiezo nm (**a**) (con los pies) trip, stumble; **dar un t.** to trip up, to stumble (**b**) (contratiempo) setback; **tener un t.** to suffer a setback; **realizamos la gira sin ningún t.** we finished the tour without a hitch (**c**) (equivocación) slipup, mistake; (desliz sexual) indiscretion; **los tropiezos de la vida que me han ayudado a crecer** the mistakes in life that have helped me to grow as a person

tropismo nm tropism

tropo nm figure of speech, trope

troposfera nf troposphere

troqué ver **trocar**

troquel nm (**a**) (molde) mold, die (**b**) (cuchilla) cutter

troquelado nm (acuñado) (de moneda) minting, mintage; (de medalla) die-casting

troquelar vt (**a**) (acuñar) (moneda) to mint; (medalla) to cast (**b**) (recortar) to cut

troquemos ver **trocar**

trotamundos nmf inv globe-trotter

trotar vi to trot; Fam (andar mucho) to dash o run around

trote nm (**a**) (de caballo) trot; **al t.** at a trot (**b**) Fam (actividad) **no estar para (estos) trotes** not to be up to it o to that kind of thing; **le he dado un buen t. a esta chaqueta** I've got good wear out of this jacket

trotskismo [tros'kismo] nm Trotskyism

trotskista [tros'kista] adj & nmf Trotskyite

troupe [trup] nf troupe

trova nf Lit lyric

trovador nm troubadour

Troya n Troy

troyano, -a adj & nm,f Trojan

trozar vt Am (carne) to cut up; (res, tronco) to butcher, to cut up

trozo nm (pedazo) piece; (de obra) extract; (de película) snippet; **hacer algo a trozos** to do sth bit by bit; **cortar algo en trozos** to cut sth into pieces

trucado, -a adj **una baraja/fotografía trucada** a trick deck/photograph; **dados trucados** (cargados) loaded dice; **el contador del gas estaba t.** the gas meter had been tampered with

trucaje nm trick effect; **t. fotográfico** trick photography

trucar [59] vt to doctor; **t. el motor** to soup up the engine

trucha nf (pez) trout; **t. arcoiris** rainbow trout; **t. asalmonada** salmon trout; Culin **t. a la navarra** = fried trout stuffed with ham

truchero, -a adj **río t.** trout river

truco nm (**a**) (trampa, engaño) trick; **un t. de magia** a magic trick; **la baraja no tiene t.** it's a perfectly normal deck of cards (**b**) (habilidad, técnica) knack; **el t. está en saber no dejarlo demasiado tiempo en el horno** the secret is not to leave it

in the oven for too long; **pillarle el t. (a algo)** to get the knack (of sth); **tiene t.** there's a knack to it; **no tiene t.** there's nothing to it; **t. publicitario** advertising gimmick

truculencia nf horror, terror

truculento, -a adj horrifying, terrifying

truena ver **tronar**

trueno nm (**a**) Meteo clap of thunder; **truenos** thunder (**b**) (ruido) thunder, boom

trueque 1 ver **trocar**
2 nm (intercambio) exchange, swap; Com & Hist barter

trufa nf (hongo, bombón) truffle

trufar vt Culin to stuff with truffles

truhán, -ana 1 adj crooked
2 nm,f rogue, crook

trullo nm Fam slammer, pen

truncado, -a adj (**a**) (frustrado) (vida, carrera) cut short; (planes, ilusiones) ruined (**b**) Mat truncated

truncar [59] vt (frustrar) (vida, carrera) to cut short; (planes, ilusiones) to spoil, to ruin

truque etc ver **trucar**

trusa nf (**a**) Carib (traje de baño) swimsuit (**b**) Perú (short) briefs (**c**) RP (faja) girdle

trust [trus] o [trust] (pl **trusts**) nm trust, cartel

TS nm (abrev de **Tribunal Supremo**) = Spanish Supreme Court

tsé-tsé adj inv **mosca t.** tsetse fly

tsunami nm tsunami

tu (pl **tus**) adj posesivo your; **tu casa** your house; **tus libros** your books

tú pron personal

Usually omitted in Spanish except for emphasis or contrast.

you; **tú te llamas Sara** your name is Sara; **es más alta que tú** she's taller than you; **hablar** o **tratar de tú a alguien** = to address sb as "tú", i.e. informally

tuareg adj inv & mf inv Tuareg

tuba nf tuba

tuberculina nf tuberculin

tubérculo nm tuber, root vegetable

tuberculosis nf inv tuberculosis

tuberculoso, -a 1 adj (**a**) Med tuberculous (**b**) Bot tuberous
2 nm,f tuberculosis sufferer

tubería nf (**a**) (cañerías) pipes, pipework (**b**) (tubo) pipe

tubo nm (**a**) (tubería) pipe; **t. del desagüe** drainpipe; **t. de escape** exhaust (pipe) (**b**) (cilindro, recipiente) tube; **t. de ensayo** test tube; **t. fluorescente** fluorescent tube; **t. de rayos catódicos** cathode ray tube (**c**) Anat tract; **t. digestivo** digestive tract, alimentary canal (**d**) Fam **por un t.: comimos por un t.** we ate a hell of a lot; **tiene dinero por un t.** he's got loads of money (**e**) Esp Fam (de cerveza) = tall glass of beer (**f**) RP, Ven (de teléfono) receiver (**g**) Chile (para el pelo) roller, curler

tubolux, tuboluz nm RP fluorescent tube

tubular 1 adj tubular
2 nm bicycle tire

tucán nm toucan

tuerca nf nut; **apretar las tuercas a alguien** to tighten the screws on sb

tuerce ver **torcer**

tuerto, -a 1 adj (sin un ojo) one-eyed; (ciego de un ojo) blind in one eye
2 nm,f (sin un ojo) one-eyed person; (ciego de un ojo) person who is blind in one eye

tuerzo ver **torcer**

tueste nm **t. natural** medium roast; **t. torrefacto** strong roast

tuesto etc ver **tostar**

tuétano *nm* (**a**) *Anat* (bone) marrow (**b**) *(meollo)* crux, heart; **hasta el t.** *o* **los tuétanos** to the core; **mojado hasta los tuétanos** soaked through, soaked to the skin

tufarada *nf* waft

tufillo *nm* whiff

tufo *nm* (**a**) *Fam (mal olor)* stench, foul smell (**b**) *(emanación)* vapor

tugurio *nm* hovel

tul *nm* tulle

tulipa *nf* (**a**) *(tulipán)* tulip (**b**) *(de lámpara)* tulip-shaped lampshade

tulipán *nm* tulip

tullido, -a 1 *adj* paralyzed, crippled
   2 *nm,f* cripple, disabled person

tullir *vt* to paralyze, to cripple

tumba *nf* grave, tomb; *Fam* **a t. abierta** at breakneck speed; *Fam* **ser (como) una t.** to be as silent as the grave

tumbado *nm Ecuad* ceiling

tumbar 1 *vt* (**a**) *(derribar)* to knock over *o* down; *Fam Fig* **tiene un olor que tumba** it stinks to high heaven (**b**) *(reclinar)* **t. al paciente** lie the patient down (**c**) *Fam (suspender)* to fail
   2 tumbarse *vpr* (**a**) *(acostarse)* to lie down (**b**) *(repantigarse)* to lounge, to stretch out

tumbo *nm* jolt, jerk; **dar tumbos** *o* **un t.** *(coche)* to jolt, to jerk; *Fig* **ir dando tumbos** *(persona)* to have a lot of ups and downs

tumbona *nf* (beach) recliner

tumefacción *nf* swelling

tumefacto, -a *adj* swollen

tumescencia *nf* swelling

tumor *nm* tumor; **t. cerebral** brain tumor

tumoración *nf* lump, swelling

túmulo *nm* (**a**) *(sepulcro)* tomb (**b**) *(montecillo)* burial mound (**c**) *(catafalco)* catafalque

tumulto *nm* (**a**) *(disturbio)* riot, disturbance (**b**) *(alboroto)* uproar, tumult

tumultuoso, -a *adj* (**a**) *(conflictivo)* tumultuous, riotous (**b**) *(turbulento)* rough, stormy

tuna *nf* (**a**) *(agrupación)* = group of student minstrels (**b**) *Am (planta)* prickly pear

tunante, -a *nm,f* crook, scoundrel

tunco *nm CAm, Méx* pig

tunda *nf Fam* (**a**) *(paliza)* beating, thrashing (**b**) *(esfuerzo)* drag, exhausting job

tundra *nf* tundra

tunecino, -a *adj & nm,f* Tunisian

túnel *nm* tunnel; *Fig* **salir del t.** to turn the corner; *Dep* **hacerle el t. a alguien** to nutmeg sb; **t. aerodinámico** wind tunnel; **T. del Canal de la Mancha** Channel Tunnel; *Aut* **t. de lavado** car wash

Túnez *n* (**a**) *(capital)* Tunis (**b**) *(país)* Tunisia

tungsteno *nm* tungsten

túnica *nf* tunic

tuno, -a *nm,f* (**a**) *(tunante)* rogue, scoundrel (**b**) *(músico)* student minstrel

tuntún *nm* **al (buen) t.** without thinking

tupamaro, -a *nm,f Pol* Tupamaro, = member of a Uruguayan Marxist urban guerrilla group of the 1960s and 70s

tupé *nm* (**a**) *(cabello)* prominent forelock (**b**) *Fam (atrevimiento)* cheek, nerve

tupido, -a *adj* thick, dense

tupí-guaraní 1 *adj & nmf* Tupí-Guaranian
   2 *nm (lengua)* Tupí-Guaraní

tupir *vt* to pack tightly

tupperware® [ˈtaperˈwer] *nm* Tupperware®

turba *nf* (**a**) *(combustible)* peat, turf (**b**) *(muchedumbre)* mob

turbación *nf* (**a**) *(desconcierto)* upset, disturbance (**b**) *(vergüenza)* embarrassment

turbador, -ora *adj* (**a**) *(desconcertante)* disconcerting, troubling (**b**) *(emocionante)* upsetting, disturbing

turbante *nm* turban

turbar 1 *vt* (**a**) *(alterar)* to disturb (**b**) *(emocionar)* to upset (**c**) *(desconcertar)* to trouble, to disconcert
   2 turbarse *vpr (emocionarse)* to get upset

turbera *nf* peat bog

turbiedad *nf* (**a**) *(de líquido)* cloudiness (**b**) *(de negocios)* shadiness

turbina *nf* turbine

turbio, -a *adj* (**a**) *(líquido)* cloudy (**b**) *(vista)* blurred (**c**) *(negocio)* shady (**d**) *(época, periodo)* turbulent, troubled

turbión *nm* downpour

turbo *nm* turbocharger; **poner el t.** to put one's foot down (on the accelerator)

turbodiesel *adj* **motor t.** turbocharged diesel engine

turbohélice *nf* turboprop

turbopropulsor *nm* turboprop

turborreactor *nm* turbojet (engine)

turbulencia *nf* (**a**) *(de fluido)* turbulence (**b**) *(alboroto)* uproar, clamor

turbulento, -a *adj* (**a**) *(situación, aguas)* turbulent (**b**) *(persona)* unruly, rebellious

turco, -a 1 *adj* Turkish
   2 *nm,f (persona)* Turk
   3 *nm (lengua)* Turkish

turcochipriota 1 *adj* Turkish-Cypriot
   2 *nmf* Turkish Cypriot

turgente *adj (forma, muslos)* well-rounded

turismo *nm* (**a**) *(actividad)* tourism; **hacer t. (por)** to go touring (around); **t. de aventura** adventure vacations; **t. ecológico** ecotourism; **t. rural** rural tourism, country vacations; **casas de t. rural** country vacation properties (**b**) *Aut* private car

turista *nmf* tourist

turístico, -a *adj* tourist; **atracción turística** tourist attraction

Turkmenistán *n* Turkmenistan

turmalina *nf* tourmaline

túrmix® *nf inv* blender, liquidizer

turnarse *vpr* to take turns (**con** with)

turnedó *nm* tournedos

turno *nm* (**a**) *(tanda)* turn, go; **cuando le llegue el t. hará como todos** when it's his turn he'll do the same as everyone else; **hacer algo por turnos** to take turns to do sth (**b**) *(de trabajo)* shift; **trabajar por turnos** to work shifts; **t. de día/noche** day/night shift; **tiene el t. de noche** he's on the night shift, he's on nights; **de t.** on duty; **el médico de t.** the doctor on duty; **el gracioso de t.** the inevitable smart alec

turolense 1 *adj* of/from Teruel
   2 *nmf* person from Teruel

turón *nm* polecat

turquesa 1 *nf (mineral)* turquoise
   2 *adj inv (color)* turquoise
   3 *nm (color)* turquoise

Turquía *n* Turkey

turrón *nm* = Christmas sweet similar to marzipan or nougat, made with almonds and honey

turulato, -a *adj Fam* flabbergasted, dumbfounded

tururú *interj Fam* ¡**t.**! get away!, you must be joking!

tute *nm* (**a**) *(juego)* = card game similar to whist (**b**) *Fam (trabajo intenso)* hard slog; **darse** *o* **pegarse un (buen) t.** *(trabajar)* to slog away

tutear 1 *vt* = to address as "tú", i.e. informally
   2 tutearse *vpr* = to address each other as "tú", i.e. informally

tutela *nf* (**a**) *Der* guardianship (**b**) *(cargo)* responsibility (**de** for); **bajo la t. de** under the protection of

tutelaje *nm Der* guardianship

tutelar 1 *adj* (**a**) *Der* tutelary (**b**) *(protector)* protecting
2 *vt* to act as guardian to

tuteo *nm* = use of "tú" form of address, as opposed to formal "usted" form

tutiplén: a tutiplén *loc adv Fam* galore, a-go-go; **tenía abrigos y zapatos a t.** she had coats and shoes galore; **repartió mamporros a t.** he clouted people left and right

tutor, -ora *nm,f* (**a**) *Der* guardian (**b**) *(profesor) (privado)* tutor; *(en colegio, instituto)* class teacher

tutoría *nf* (**a**) *Der* guardianship (**b**) *(clase)* ≃ form class

tutorial *nm Inform* tutorial

tutti frutti, tuttifrutti *nm* tutti-frutti

tutú *nm* tutu

tuviera *etc ver* **tener**

tuyo, -a 1 *adj posesivo* yours; **este libro es t.** this book is yours; **un amigo t.** a friend of yours; **no es asunto t.** it's none of your business
2 *pron posesivo* **el t.** yours; **el t. es rojo** yours is red; *Fam* **esta es la tuya** this is the chance you've been waiting for *o* your big chance; **lo t. es el teatro** *(lo que haces bien)* theater is your thing; *Fam* **los tuyos** *(tu familia)* your folks; *(tu bando)* your lot, your side

TV *nf* (*abrev de* **televisión**) TV

TV3 [teβe'tres] *nf* (*abrev de* **Televisión de Cataluña**) = Catalan television channel

TVE *nf* (*abrev de* **Televisión Española**) = Spanish state television network

TVG *nf* (*abrev de* **Televisión de Galicia**) = Galician television channel

twist [twist] *nm inv* twist *(dance)*

U

U, u [u] *nf (letra)* U, u

u *conj* or; *ver también* **o**

UA *nf (abrev de* **Unión Africana**) AU

ubérrimo, -a *adj Formal (tierra)* extremely fertile; *(vegetación)* luxuriant, abundant

ubicación *nf* position, location

ubicado, -a *adj (edificio)* located, situated

ubicar [59] **1** *vt* (**a**) *(situar) (edificio)* to locate (**b**) *Am (colocar) (mueble, persona)* to put, to place (**c**) *Am (encontrar)* to find, to locate; **¿cómo te ubico?** where can I get hold of *o* contact you? (**d**) *Am (identificar)* **¿González?, no lo ubico** González? I can't quite place him
2 ubicarse *vpr (edificio)* to be situated, to be located (**b**) *Am (persona)* to get one's bearings

ubicuidad *nf* ubiquity; **tiene el don de la u.** he seems to be everywhere at once

ubicuo, -a *adj* ubiquitous

ubique *etc ver* **ubicar**

ubre *nf* udder

UCI ['uθi] *nf (abrev de* **unidad de cuidados intensivos**) ICU, intensive care unit

Ucrania *n* the Ukraine

ucraniano, -a *adj & nm,f* Ukrainian

Ud. *abrev de* **usted**

UDC *nf (abrev de* **universal decimal classification**) UDC

Uds. *abrev de* **ustedes**

UE *nf (abrev de* **Unión Europea**) EU

UEFA ['uefa] *nf (abrev de* **Union of European Football Associations**) UEFA

UEM [uem] *nf (abrev de* **unión económica y monetaria**) EMU

UEO *nf (abrev de* **Unión Europea Occidental**) WEU

uf *interj* **¡uf!** *(expresa cansancio, calor)* phew!; *(expresa fastidio)* tut!; *(expresa repugnancia)* ugh!

ufanarse *vpr* **u. de** to boast about

ufano, -a *adj* (**a**) *(satisfecho)* proud, pleased (**b**) *(engreído)* boastful, conceited (**c**) *(lozano)* luxuriant, lush

ufología *nf* ufology

ufólogo, -a *nm,f* ufologist

Uganda *n* Uganda

ugandés, -esa *adj & nm,f* Ugandan

ugetista 1 *adj* = of or belonging to the "UGT"
2 *nmf* = member of the "UGT"

UGT *nf (abrev de* **Unión General de los Trabajadores**) = major socialist labor union in Spain

UHF *nf (abrev de* **ultra high frequency**) UHF

UHT *adj (abrev de* **ultra heat treated**) UHT

ujier *nm* usher

ukelele *nm* ukulele

úlcera *nf Med* ulcer; **ú. de estómago** stomach ulcer; **ú. perforada** perforated ulcer

ulceración *nf* ulceration

ulcerar 1 *vt* to ulcerate
2 ulcerarse *vpr Med* to ulcerate

ulceroso, -a *adj* ulcerous

Ulster *nm* (**el**) U. Ulster

ulterior *adj* (**a**) *(en el tiempo)* subsequent (**b**) *(en el espacio)* further

ulteriormente *adv* subsequently

ultimación *nf* conclusion, completion

últimamente *adv* recently, of late

ultimar *vt* (**a**) *(terminar)* to conclude, to complete (**b**) *Am (matar)* to kill

ultimátum (*pl* **ultimátums** *o* **ultimatos**) *nm* ultimatum

último, -a 1 *adj* (**a**) *(en una serie, en el tiempo)* last; **hizo un ú. intento** he made one last *o* final attempt; **en una situación así es lo ú. que haría** it's the last thing I'd do in a situation like that; **por ú.** lastly, finally; **ser lo ú.** *(lo final)* to come last; *(el último recurso)* to be a last resort; *(el colmo)* to be the last straw; **última voluntad** last wish(es)
(**b**) *(más reciente)* latest, most recent; **las últimas noticias son inquietantes** the latest news is very worrying; **la ú. vez que lo vi** the last time I saw him; *Fam* **ser lo ú. en...** to be the latest thing in...
(**c**) *(más remoto)* furthest, most remote
(**d**) *(más bajo)* bottom; *(más alto)* top; *(de más atrás)* back
2 *nm,f* (**a**) *(en fila, carrera)* **el ú.** the last (one); **el ú. de la fila** the last person in the line; **llegar el ú.** to come last (**b**) *(en comparaciones, enumeraciones)* **este ú.** the latter (**c**) *(expresiones)* **a últimos de mes** at the end of the month; **estar en las últimas** *(muriéndose)* to be on one's deathbed; *(sin dinero)* to be down to one's last penny; *(sin provisiones)* to be down to one's last provisions; *Fam* **ir a la última** to wear the latest fashion

ultra *adj & nmf Pol* extremist

ultracongelado, -a *adj* deep-frozen; **ultracongelados** deep-frozen food

ultraconservador, -ora *adj & nm,f* ultraconservative

ultracorrección *nf* hypercorrection

ultraderecha *nf* far right

ultraderechista 1 *adj* far right
2 *nmf* extreme right-winger

ultraísmo *nm* = Spanish and Latin American literary movement of the early 20th century

ultraizquierda *nf* far left

ultraizquierdista 1 *adj* far left
2 *nmf* extreme left-winger

ultrajante *adj* insulting, offensive

ultrajar *vt* to insult, to offend

ultraje *nm* insult

ultraligero *nm* microlight

ultramar *nm* overseas; **territorios de u.** overseas territories

ultramarino, -a *adj* overseas; **posesiones ultramarinas** overseas territories

ultramarinos *nmpl* (**a**) *(comestibles)* groceries (**b**) *(tienda)* grocery store

ultramicroscopio *nm* ultramicroscope

ultramoderno, -a *adj* ultramodern

ultramontano, -a 1 *adj* (**a**) *Rel* ultramontane (**b**) *(reaccionario)* reactionary

2 *nm,f* (**a**) *Rel* ultramontane (**b**) *(reaccionario)* reactionary

ultranza *nf* **a u.** *(con decisión)* to the death; *(acérrimamente)* out-and-out

ultrasecreto, -a *adj* top-secret

ultrasonido *nm* ultrasound

ultratumba *nf* **de u.** from beyond the grave

ultravioleta *adj inv* ultraviolet

ulular *vi* (**a**) *(viento, lobo)* to howl (**b**) *(búho)* to hoot

umbilical *adj* **cordón u.** umbilical cord

umbral *nm* (**a**) *(de puerta, periodo)* threshold (**b**) *(nivel básico)* threshold; **el u. de la pobreza** the poverty line

umbrío, -a *adj* shady

un, una *art*

---

un is used instead of **una** before feminine nouns which begin with a stressed **a** or **ha** (e.g. **un águila** an eagle; **un hacha** an ax).

(**a**) *(singular)* a; *(ante sonido vocálico)* an; **un hombre/coche** a man/car; **una mujer/mesa** a woman/table; **una hora** an hour (**b**) *(plural)* some; **había unos coches mal aparcados** there were some badly parked cars; **había unos doce muchachos** there were about *o* some twelve boys there

unánime *adj* unanimous

unanimidad *nf* unanimity; **por u.** unanimously

unción *nf* unction

uncir [72] *vt* to yoke

UNCTAD [un'tað] *nf* (*abrev de* **United Nations Conference on Trade and Development**) UNCTAD

undécimo, -a *núm* eleventh

underground [ander'vraun] *adj inv* underground

UNED [u'neð] *nf* (*abrev de* **Universidad Nacional de Educación a Distancia**) = Spanish university offering televised and distance learning courses

Unesco [u'nesko] *nf* (*abrev de* **United Nations Educational, Scientific and Cultural Organization**) UNESCO

ungimiento *nm* unction

ungir [24] *vt* to put ointment on; *Rel* to anoint

ungüento *nm* ointment

únicamente *adv* only, solely

unicameral *adj* single-chamber

Unicef [uni'θef] *nm* (*abrev de* **United Nations Children's Fund**) UNICEF

unicelular *adj* single-cell, unicellular

unicidad *nf* uniqueness

único, -a *adj* (**a**) *(solo)* only; **hijo ú.** only child, only son; **hija única** only child, only daughter; **es lo ú. que quiero** it's all I want; **lo ú. es que...** the (only) thing is..., it's just that...; **única y exclusivamente** only, exclusively (**b**) *(excepcional)* unique; **eres ú.** you're one of a kind (**c**) *(precio, función, moneda)* single

unicornio *nm* unicorn; **u. marino** narwhal

unidad *nf* (**a**) *(cohesión, acuerdo)* unity; **la fundación fracasó por falta de u.** the foundation failed for lack of unity; **necesitamos u. de acción** we need unity of action, we need to act as one

(**b**) *(elemento, medida)* unit; **un euro la u.** one euro each; **quiero comprar seis unidades** I'd like to buy six; **u. de medida** unit of measurement

(**c**) *(sección)* unit; *Inform* **u. de CD-ROM** CD-ROM drive; *Inform* **u. central de proceso** central processing unit; *Mil* **u. de combate** combat unit; **u. de cuidados intensivos** intensive care (unit); *Inform* **u. de disco** disk drive; *TV* **u.**

---

móvil mobile unit; **u. de vigilancia intensiva** intensive care (unit)

unidimensional *adj* one-dimensional

unidireccional *adj* unidirectional, one-way

unido, -a *adj* *(junto, reunido)* united; *(familia, amigos)* close

unifamiliar *adj* **vivienda u.** house *(detached, semidetached or terraced)*

unificación *nf* (**a**) *(unión)* unification (**b**) *(uniformización)* standardization

unificador, -ora *adj* (**a**) *(que une)* unifying (**b**) *(que uniformiza)* standardizing

unificar [59] *vt* (**a**) *(unir)* to unite, to join; *(países)* to unify (**b**) *(uniformar)* to standardize

uniformado, -a *adj* (**a**) *(igual, normalizado)* standardized (**b**) *(policía, soldado)* uniformed

uniformar *vt* (**a**) *(igualar, normalizar)* to standardize (**b**) *(poner uniforme a)* to put into uniform

uniforme 1 *adj* *(movimiento, temperatura, criterios)* uniform; *(superficie)* even

2 *nm* uniform; **de u.** in uniform; **u. escolar** school uniform; **u. de gala** dress uniform

uniformidad *nf* *(de movimiento, temperatura, criterios)* uniformity; *(de superficie)* evenness

uniformización *nf* *(normalización)* standardization

uniformizar [14] *vt* *(normalizar)* to standardize

unilateral *adj* unilateral

unión *nf* (**a**) *(asociación)* union; **en u. con** *o* **de** together with; **u. aduanera** customs union; **U. Africana** African Union; **la U. Europea** the European Union; **u. de hecho** unmarried couple; *Antes* **U. Soviética** Soviet Union

(**b**) *(acción)* joining, union; **un compuesto es el resultado de la u. de dos palabras** a compound is the result of the joining of two words; **la u. de las dos empresas** the union *o* merger of the two companies

(**c**) *Mec* join, joint

(**d**) *(cohesión)* **hay que potenciar la u. entre los ciudadanos** we have to encourage a sense of solidarity among the people; **la u. hace la fuerza** unity is strength

unionismo *nm* *Pol* unionism

unionista *adj & nmf* *Pol* unionist

unipersonal *adj* = designed for one person; **verbo u.** impersonal verb

unir 1 *vt* (**a**) *(juntar)* *(pedazos, habitaciones)* to join; *(empresas, estados, facciones)* to unite; **unió los dos palos con una cuerda** he joined *o* tied the two sticks together with a piece of string

(**b**) *(relacionar)* *(personas)* **les une una fuerte amistad** they are very close friends, they share a very close friendship; **les une su pasión por la música** they share a passion for music; **u. a dos personas en matrimonio** to join two people in matrimony

(**c**) *(comunicar)* *(ciudades, terminales, aparatos)* to connect, to link

(**d**) *(combinar)* to combine; **en su obra une belleza y técnica** her work combines beauty with technique; **u. algo a algo** to add sth to sth

2 unirse *vpr* *(personas, empresas, grupos)* to join together; *(factores, circunstancias)* to come together; **se unieron para derrocar al gobierno** they joined together *o* joined forces to bring down the government; **unirse en matrimonio** to join in wedlock *o* matrimony; **unirse a algo** to join sth; **a la falta de interés se unió el mal tiempo** the lack of interest was compounded by the bad weather

unisex *adj inv* unisex

unisexual *adj* unisexual

unísono *nm* **al u.** in unison

UNITA [u'nita] *nf* (*abrev de* **Unión Nacional para la Inde-**

pendencia **Total de Angola**) UNITA
unitario, -a *adj (unido, único)* single; *(de una unidad)* unitary; **precio u.** unit price
unitarismo *nm Rel* Unitarianism
universal *adj* **(a)** *(total)* universal **(b)** *(mundial)* world; **historia u.** world history; *Filosofía* **universales** universals
universalidad *nf* universality
universalismo *nm* universalism
universalizar [14] **1** *vt* to make widespread
   2 universalizarse *vpr (costumbre, uso)* to become widespread
universiada *nf Dep* **la U.** the World Student Games
universidad *nf* university; **u. a distancia** = distance learning college *o* university
universitario, -a 1 *adj* university; **estudiante u.** university student
   2 *nm,f* **(a)** *(estudiante)* university student **(b)** *(profesor)* university professor **(c)** *(licenciado)* university graduate
universo *nm* **(a)** *Astron* universe **(b)** *(mundo)* world
unívoco, -a *adj* univocal, unambiguous
UNIX ['unɪks] *nm Inform* UNIX
unjo *etc ver* **ungir**
uno, -a

> **un** is used instead of **uno** before singular masculine nouns (e.g. **un perro** a dog; **un coche** a car).

1 *adj* **(a)** *(numeral)* one; **un hombre, un voto** one man, one vote; **una hora y media** an hour and a half, one and a half hours; **treinta y un días** thirty-one days **(c)** *(indefinido)* one; **un día volveré** one *o* some day I'll return
   2 *pron* **(a)** *(indefinido, numeral)* one; **coge u.** take one; **u. de ellos** one of them; **unos… otros…** some… others…; **u. a otro, unos a otros** each other, one another; **u. y otro** both; **unos y otros** all of them; **unos cuantos** a few
   (b) *(cierta persona)* someone, somebody; **hablé con u. que te conoce** I spoke to someone who knows you; **me lo han contado unos** certain people told me so
   (c) *(yo)* one; **u. ya no está para estos trotes** one isn't really up to this sort of thing anymore
   (d) *(expresiones)* **a una** together; **todos a una** *(a la vez)* everyone at once; **de u. en u., u. a u., u. por u.** one by one; **juntar varias cosas en una** to combine several things into one; **lo u. por lo otro** it all evens out in the end; **más de u.** many people; *(unánimemente)* as one; **una de dos** it's either one thing or the other; **una de las suyas** one of his/her/their tricks *o* pranks; **u. de tantos** one of many; **una y no más** once was enough, once bitten, twice shy
   3 *nm (número)* (number) one; **el u.** number one; **la fila u.** row one; **la una** *(hora)* one o'clock; *ver también* **seis**
untar 1 *vt* **(a)** *(piel, cara)* to smear **(con** *o* **de** with); **u. el paté en el pan** to spread the pâté on the bread **(b)** *Fam (sobornar)* to grease the palm of, to bribe
   2 untarse *vpr* **(a)** *(embadurnarse)* **untarse la piel/cara (con** *o* **de)** to smear one's skin/face (with) **(b)** *Fam (enriquecerse)* to line one's pockets
unto *nm (grasa)* grease
untuosidad *nf* greasiness, oiliness
untuoso, -a *adj* greasy, oily
untura *nf* **(a)** *(ungüento)* ointment **(b)** *(grasa)* grease
uña *nf* **(a)** *(de mano)* fingernail, nail; **hacerse las uñas** to do one's nails; **comerse** *o* **morderse las uñas** to bite one's nails; *Fig* **con uñas y dientes** *(agarrarse)* doggedly; *(defender)* fiercely; *Fig* **ser u. y carne** to be as thick as thieves **(b)** *(de pie)* toenail **(c)** *(garra)* claw; **enseñar** *o* **sacar las uñas** to get one's claws out **(d)** *(casco)* hoof **(e)** *Méx (para instrumento musical)* plectrum
uñero *nm* **(a)** *(inflamación)* whitlow **(b)** *(uña encarnada)* ingrown nail

uperisación, uperización *nf* UHT treatment
uperisar, uperizar [14] *vt* to give UHT treatment
Urales *nmpl* **los U.** the Urals
uralita® *nf Constr* = material made of asbestos and cement, usually corrugated and used mainly for roofing
uranio *nm* uranium
Urano *nm* Uranus
urbanidad *nf* politeness, courtesy
urbanismo *nm* town planning
urbanista *nmf* town planner
urbanístico, -a *adj* town-planning; **plan u.** urban development plan
urbanita *nmf* city dweller
urbanización *nf* **(a)** *(zona residencial)* (private) housing project **(b)** *(acción)* urbanization
urbanizador, -ora 1 *adj* developing
   2 *nm,f* developer
urbanizar [14] *vt* to develop, to urbanize
urbano, -a *adj* urban, city; **autobús u.** city bus; **guardia u.** local policeman, *f* local policewoman
urbe *nf* large city
urdimbre *nf* **(a)** *(de hilos)* warp **(b)** *(plan)* plot
urdir *vt* **(a)** *(plan)* to plot, to forge **(b)** *(hilos)* to warp
urdu, urdú *nm (lengua)* Urdu
urea *nf* urea
uremia *nf* uremia
uréter *nm* ureter
uretra *nf* urethra
urgencia *nf* **(a)** *(cualidad)* urgency; **con u.** urgently; **necesitan con u. alimentos y medicinas** they urgently need food and medicine; **en caso de u.** in case of emergency **(b)** *(necesidad)* urgent need **(c)** *(en hospital) (caso)* emergency (case); **urgencias (médicas)** emergency room
urgente *adj* **(a)** *(apremiante)* urgent **(b)** *(correo)* express
urgir [24] *v impersonal* to be urgently necessary; **me urge hacerlo** I urgently need to do it
úrico, -a *adj* uric
urinario, -a 1 *adj* urinary
   2 *nm* urinal, comfort station
URL *nm Inform (abrev de* **uniform resource locator**) URL
urna *nf* **(a)** *(caja de cristal)* glass case; *(para votar)* ballot box; **acudir a las urnas** to go to the polls **(b)** *(vasija)* urn; **u. cineraria** urn *(for somebody's ashes)*
uro *nm* aurochs, urus
urogallo *nm* capercaillie
urogenital *adj* urogenital
urología *nf* urology
urólogo, -a *nm,f* urologist
urraca *nf* magpie
URSS [urs] *nf Antes (abrev de* **Unión de Repúblicas Socialistas Soviéticas**) USSR
ursulina *nf* **(a)** *Rel* Ursuline (nun) **(b)** *(mujer recatada)* prudish woman
urticaria *nf* nettle rash, hives, urticaria
Uruguay *nm* **(el) U.** Uruguay
uruguayo, -a *adj & nm,f* Uruguayan
usado, -a *adj* **(a)** *(utilizado)* used; **muy u.** widely used **(b)** *(gastado)* worn-out, worn **(c)** *(de segunda mano)* secondhand
usanza *nf* custom, usage; **a la vieja** *o* **antigua u.** in the old way *o* style
usar 1 *vt* **(a)** *(aparato, herramienta, término)* to use; **¿sabes usar esta máquina?** do you know how to use this machine?; **de u. y tirar** *(producto)* disposable; **sin u.** unused **(b)** *(ropa, lentes, maquillaje)* to wear; **estos guantes están sin u.** these gloves haven't been worn
   2 *vi* **u. de** to use, to make use of

3 usarse *vpr* (**a**) *(aparato, herramienta, término)* to be used; **ya casi no se usan las máquinas de escribir** people hardly use typewriters anymore (**b**) *(ropa, lentes)* to be worn; **ya no se usan esos zapatos** those shoes are no longer worn *o* in fashion

usía *nmf Anticuado* Your Lordship, *f* Your Ladyship

usina *nf Andes, RP* plant; **u. eléctrica** power station, power plant

uso *nm* (**a**) *(utilización)* use; **hacer u. de** *(utilizar)* to make use of, to use; *(de prerrogativa, derecho)* to exercise; **de u. externo** *(medicamento)* for external use only; **fuera de u.** out of use, obsolete; **tener el u. de la palabra** to have the floor; **u. de razón** power of reason (**b**) *(costumbre)* custom; **al u.** fashionable; **al u. andaluz** in the Andalusian style (**c**) *Ling* usage (**d**) *(desgaste)* wear and tear

usted *pron personal (tratamiento de respeto)* you; **ustedes** you *(plural)*; **contesten ustedes a las preguntas** please answer the questions; **de u./ustedes** yours; **me gustaría hablar con u.** I'd like to talk to you; **hablar** *o* **tratar de u. a alguien** = to address sb as "usted", i.e. formally

usual *adj* usual; **lo u. es hacerlo así** people usually do it this way; **no es u. verlo por aquí** it's unusual to see him here

usuario, -a *nm,f* user

usufructo *nm Der* usufruct, use

usufructuar [4] *vt Der* to have the usufruct *o* use of

usufructuario, -a *adj & nm,f Der* usufructuary

usura *nf* usury

usurero, -a *nm,f* usurer

usurpación *nf* usurpation

usurpador, -ora 1 *adj* usurping
  2 *nm,f* usurper

usurpar *vt* to usurp

utensilio *nm (instrumento)* tool, implement; **utensilios de cocina** cooking utensils; **utensilios de pesca** fishing tackle

uterino, -a *adj* uterine

útero *nm* womb, uterus

útil 1 *adj* useful; **este hallazgo podría ser muy ú. en el tratamiento del cáncer** this discovery may be useful in the treatment of cancer; **es ú. para cargar maletas** it comes in handy for carrying suitcases
  2 útiles *nmpl (herramientas)* tools; *Agr* implements; *Am* **útiles escolares** school writing materials; **útiles de pesca** fishing tackle

utilería *nf (útiles)* equipment; *Cine & Teatro* props

utilidad 1 *nf* (**a**) *(cualidad)* usefulness (**b**) *Inform* utility (program)
  2 utilidades *nfpl Am Fin* profits

utilitario, -a 1 *adj* (**a**) *(persona)* utilitarian (**b**) *(vehículo)* runabout, utility
  2 *nm Aut* runabout car, utility car

utilitarismo *nm* utilitarianism

utilización *nf* use; **el tratamiento de las aguas residuales para su posterior u.** the treatment of waste water for subsequent use; **de fácil u.** easy to use; **una interfaz de fácil u.** a user-friendly interface

utilizar [14] *vt* to use

utillaje *nm* tools

utopía *nf* utopia

utópico, -a *adj* utopian

uva *nf* grape; **de uvas a peras** once in a blue moon; **estar de mala u.** to be in a bad mood; **tener mala u.** to be a bad sort, to be an unpleasant person; **uvas de la suerte** = grapes eaten for good luck as midnight chimes on New Year's Eve; **nos van a dar las uvas** we're going to be here forever!, this is taking forever!

UVI ['uβi] *nf (abrev de* **unidad de vigilancia intensiva**) ICU, intensive care unit

úvula *nf* uvula

uxoricida *Formal* **1** *adj* uxoricidal, wife murdering
  2 *nm* uxoricide, wife murderer

Uzbekistán *n* Uzbekistan

uzbeko, -a *adj & nm,f* Uzbek

V

V, v [*Esp* 'uβe, *Am* be'korta] *nf (letra)* V, v; **v doble** W

v. (*abrev de* **véase**) v., vide

va *ver* **ir**

vaca *nf* (**a**) *(animal)* cow; *Fam* **estar como una v.** *(gordo)* to be as fat as an elephant; **v. lechera** dairy cow; **v. marina** manatee; **v. sagrada** sacred cow; *Fam* **vacas flacas** lean years; *Fam* **vacas gordas** years of plenty; **la enfermedad** *o* **el mal de las vacas locas** mad cow disease (**b**) *(carne)* beef

vacacional *adj* vacation; **periodo v.** vacation period

vacaciones *nfpl* vacation, holiday; **tomar** *o Esp* **coger (las) v.** to take one's vacation; **estar/irse de v.** to be/go on vacation; **diez días de v.** ten days' vacation; **v. pagadas** paid vacation; **v. de verano** summer vacation

vacacionista *nmf Am* vacationer

vacante 1 *adj* vacant

2 *nf* vacancy

vaciado *nm* (**a**) *(de recipiente)* emptying (**b**) *(de escultura)* casting, molding

vaciar [32] **1** *vt* (**a**) *(recipiente)* to empty (**de** of); *(líquido)* to pour; **v. el agua de la botella** to pour the water out of the bottle; **vacía las bolsas de la compra** take the shopping out of the bags (**b**) *(dejar hueco)* to hollow (out) (**c**) *Arte* to cast, to mold

2 vaciarse *vpr* to empty; **en verano se vacía la ciudad** the city empties out in summer

vaciedad *nf (tontería)* trifle

vacilación *nf* (**a**) *(duda)* hesitation; *(al elegir)* indecision (**b**) *(oscilación)* swaying; *(de la luz)* flickering

vacilante *adj* (**a**) *(dudoso, indeciso)* hesitant; *(al elegir)* indecisive (**b**) *(luz)* flickering; *(pulso)* irregular; *(paso)* swaying, unsteady

vacilar 1 *vi* (**a**) *(dudar)* to hesitate; *(al elegir)* to be indecisive (**b**) *(voz, principios, régimen)* to falter (**c**) *(fluctuar)* *(luz)* to flicker; *(pulso)* to be irregular (**d**) *(tambalearse)* to wobble, to sway (**e**) *Fam (chulear)* to swank, to show off (**f**) *Esp, Carib, Méx Fam (bromear)* **está vacilando** he's pulling your leg *o* kidding

2 *vt Esp, Carib, Méx Fam* **v. a alguien** *(tomar el pelo)* to pull sb's leg

vacile *nm Esp, Carib, Méx Fam (tomadura de pelo)* joke; **estar de v.** *(de broma)* to be kidding *o* joking

vacilón, -ona *Fam* **1** *adj* (**a**) *(fanfarrón)* swanky (**b**) *Esp, Carib, Méx (bromista)* jokey, teasing

2 *nm,f* (**a**) *(fanfarrón)* show-off (**b**) *Esp, Carib, Méx (bromista)* tease

3 *nm CAm, Carib, Méx (fiesta)* party

vacío, -a 1 *adj (recipiente, palabras, vida)* empty; **la ciudad estaba vacía** the city was empty *o* deserted; **v. de** *(contenido)* devoid of

2 *nm* (**a**) *Fís* vacuum; **envasar al v.** to vacuum-pack (**b**) *(abismo, carencia)* void; **su muerte ha dejado un gran v.** his death has left a big gap; **v. legal** legal vacuum; *Pol* **v. de poder** power vacuum (**c**) *(espacio libre)* **se lanzó al v.** she threw herself into the void; **caer en el v.** *(palabras)* to fall on deaf

ears; **hacer el v. a alguien** to refuse to speak to sb; **tener un v. en el estómago** to feel hungry

vacuidad *nf (trivialidad)* shallowness, vacuity

vacuna *nf* vaccine

vacunación *nf* vaccination

vacunar 1 *vt* to vaccinate

2 vacunarse *vpr* to get vaccinated

vacuno, -a 1 *adj* bovine

2 *nm* cattle; **carne de v.** beef

vacuo, -a *adj (trivial)* shallow, vacuous

vadeable *adj* fordable

vadear *vt (río)* to ford; *(dificultad)* to overcome

vademécum (*pl* **vademécums**) *nm* vade mecum, handbook

vade retro *interj Hum & Formal (márchate)* get thee gone!

vado *nm* (**a**) *(en acera)* lowered curb; **v. permanente** *(en letrero)* keep clear at all times (**b**) *(de río)* ford

Vaduz *n* Vaduz

vagabundear *vi* (**a**) *(ser un vagabundo)* to lead a vagrant's life (**b**) *(vagar)* **v. (por)** to wander, to roam

vagabundeo *nm* vagrant's life

vagabundo, -a 1 *adj (persona)* vagrant; *(perro)* stray

2 *nm,f* tramp, vagrant, bum

vagamente *adv* vaguely

vagancia *nf* (**a**) *(holgazanería)* laziness, idleness (**b**) *(vagabundeo)* vagrancy

vagar [38] *vi* **v. (por)** to wander, to roam

vagido *nm* = cry of a newborn baby

vagina *nf* vagina

vaginal *adj* vaginal

vago, -a 1 *adj* (**a**) *(perezoso)* lazy, idle (**b**) *(impreciso)* vague

2 *nm,f* lazy person, idler

vagón *nm (de pasajeros)* car; *(de mercancías)* freight car; **v. cisterna** tanker, tank car; **v. delantero** front car; **v. mercancías** freight car, delivery van; **v. de primera** first-class car; **v. restaurante** dining car, restaurant car; **v. de segunda** second-class car

vagoneta 1 *nf* wagon

2 *adj RP Fam* lazy

vaguada *nf* valley floor

vague *etc ver* **vagar**

vaguear *vi* to laze around

vaguedad *nf* (**a**) *(cualidad)* vagueness (**b**) *(dicho)* vague remark

vaguería *nf Fam (holgazanería)* laziness, idleness

vaharada *nf (de olor)* whiff

vahído *nm* blackout, fainting fit; **me dio un v.** I fainted

vaho *nm* (**a**) *(vapor)* steam; *Med* **hacer vahos** to inhale (medicinal vapors) (**b**) *(aliento)* breath

vaina *nf* (**a**) *(en planta)* pod (**b**) *(de espada)* scabbard (**c**) *Col, Perú, Ven muy Fam (problema, molestia)* pain; **¡déjate de vainas!** stop messing around!; **cualquier v.** *(cosa)* anything

vainica *nf* hemstitch

vainilla *nf* vanilla

vainita *nf Carib* green bean

vaivén *nm* (**a**) *(balanceo) (de barco)* swaying, rocking; *(de péndulo, columpio)* swinging (**b**) *(altibajo)* ups and downs

vajilla *nf* crockery; **una v.** a dinner service

valdepeñas *nm inv* Valdepeñas, = Spanish wine from the La Mancha region, usually red

valdré *etc ver* **valer**

vale 1 *nm* (**a**) *(bono)* coupon, voucher; **v. de comida** luncheon voucher; *Fin* **v. de compra** credit note; **v. de regalo** gift token (**b**) *(entrada gratuita)* free ticket (**c**) *(comprobante)* receipt (**d**) *(pagaré)* IOU (**e**) *Méx, Ven Fam (compañero)* pal, buddy
  2 *interj Esp* **¡v.!** okay!, all right!; **¿v.?** okay?, all right?; **¡v. (ya)!** that's enough!

valedero, -a *adj* valid

valedor, -ora *nm,f* protector

Valencia *n* Valencia

valencia *nf Quím* valence

valenciano, -a 1 *adj & nm,f* Valencian
  2 *nm (idioma)* Valencian

valentía *nf* (**a**) *(valor)* bravery (**b**) *(hazaña)* act of bravery

valentón, -ona *nm,f* **hacerse el v.** to boast of one's bravery

valentonada *nf* boast, brag

valer [69] **1** *vt* (**a**) *(costar) (precio)* to cost; *(tener un valor de)* to be worth; **¿cuánto vale?** how much does it cost?, how much is it?; **este cuadro vale mucho dinero** this painting is worth a lot of money
  (**b**) *(suponer)* to earn; **su generosidad le valió el afecto de todos** her generosity earned her everyone's affection; **esta victoria puede valerles el campeonato** this win may be enough for them to take the championship; **aquello nos valió muchos disgustos** that cost us a lot of trouble
  (**c**) *(merecer)* to deserve; **esta noticia bien vale una celebración** this news deserves a celebration
  (**d**) *(en exclamaciones)* **¡válgame Dios!** good God *o* heavens!
  2 *vi* (**a**) *(tener valor, merecer aprecio) (persona, obra)* to be good; **la obra vale poco/no vale (nada)** the play isn't worth much/is no good at all; **hacer v. algo** *(derechos, autoridad)* to assert sth; **hacerse v.** to show one's worth
  (**b**) *(servir)* **eso aún vale** you can still use that; **v. para algo** *(objeto)* to be for sth; *(persona)* to be good at sth; **¿para qué vale?** what's it for?; **v. a alguien** to be of use to sb
  (**c**) *(ser válido) (documento, norma)* to be valid; *(respuesta)* to be correct; *(en juegos)* to be allowed
  (**d**) *(equivaler)* **v. por** to be worth
  (**e**) *Esp (ser la talla)* **v. a alguien** to fit sb
  (**f**) *Méx Fam (no importar)* **lo que él piense me vale** I couldn't care less what he thinks
  (**g**) *(expresiones)* **más vale tarde que nunca** better late than never; **más vale que te calles/vayas** it would be better if you shut up/left
  3 *nm* worth, value
  4 valerse *vpr* (**a**) *(servirse)* **valerse de algo/alguien** to use sth/sb (**b**) *(desenvolverse)* **valerse (por sí mismo)** to manage on one's own (**c**) *Méx (estar permitido)* to be allowed; **no se vale mentir** lying's not allowed

valeriana *nf* valerian, allheal

valeroso, -a *adj* brave, courageous

valgo *ver* **valer**

valía *nf* value, worth

validación *nf (de documento, billete)* validation

validar *vt (documento, billete)* to validate; *(resultado)* to (officially) confirm

validez *nf* validity; **este proyecto confirma la v. científica de su enfoque** this project confirms the scientific validity of his approach; **dar v. a** to validate; **tener v.** to be valid

valido, -a *nm,f Hist* royal adviser, éminence grise

válido, -a *adj* valid

valiente 1 *adj* (**a**) *(valeroso)* brave (**b**) *Irónico (menudo)* **¡en v. lío te has metido!** you've got yourself into some mess *o* into a fine mess!
  2 *nmf (valeroso)* brave person

valija *nf* (**a**) *(maleta)* case, suitcase; **v. diplomática** diplomatic pouch (**b**) *(de correos)* mailbag

valioso, -a *adj* (**a**) *(de valor)* valuable (**b**) *(intento, esfuerzo)* worthy

valium® *(pl* **valiums)** *nm* Valium®

valla *nf* (**a**) *(cerca)* fence; **poner una v. alrededor de un terreno** to fence off a piece of land; **v. electrificada** electric fence; **v. publicitaria** billboard (**b**) *Dep* hurdle; **los 110 metros vallas** the 110 meters hurdles

vallado *nm* fence

Valladolid *n* Valladolid

vallar *vt* to put a fence around

valle *nm* valley; **v. de lágrimas** vale of tears

vallisoletano, -a *adj* **1** of/from Valladolid
  2 *nm,f* person from Valladolid

valón, -ona *adj & nm,f* Walloon

valor *nm* (**a**) *(precio, utilidad, mérito)* value; **de v.** valuable; **joyas por v. de…** jewels worth…; **sin v.** worthless; **tener v.** *(ser valioso)* to be valuable; *(ser válido)* to be valid; **tiene v. sentimental** it is of sentimental value; **sin el sello oficial carece de** *o* **no tiene v.** it is not valid without the official seal; **v. adquisitivo** purchasing power; *Econ* **v. añadido,** *Am* **v. agregado** added value; **v. comercial** commercial value; **v. nominal** face *o* nominal value; **v. nutritivo** nutritional value
  (**b**) *Mat & Mús* value
  (**c**) *(importancia)* importance; **su opinión es de enorme v. para nosotros** her opinion is of great value *o* importance to us; **dar v. a** to give *o* attach importance to; **quitar v. a algo** to take away from sth, to diminish the importance of sth
  (**d**) *(valentía)* bravery, courage; **armarse de v.** to pluck up one's courage
  (**e**) *(desvergüenza)* cheek, nerve; **tener el v. de hacer algo** to have the cheek *o* nerve to do sth
  (**f**) *Fam (personaje)* **un joven v.** a young prospect
  (**g**) **valores** *(principios)* values
  (**h**) *Fin* **valores** securities; **valores en cartera** investment portfolio

valoración *nf* (**a**) *(de propiedad, obra)* valuation; *(de pérdidas, daños)* assessment, estimation (**b**) *(de mérito, cualidad, ventajas)* evaluation, assessment

valorar *vt* (**a**) *(tasar) (propiedad, obra)* to value; *(pérdidas, daños)* to assess, to estimate; **la casa está valorada en 25 millones** the house is valued at 25 million (**b**) *(evaluar)* to evaluate, to assess; **su actuación ha sido valorada muy positivamente** her performance has been judged very favorably; **el peor valorado entre todos los candidatos** the least favored among the candidates (**c**) *(apreciar)* to value; **valoran mucho los conocimientos de inglés** they value a knowledge of English very highly

valorización *nf (revalorización)* appreciation, increase in value

valorizar [14] **1** *vt* to increase the value of
  2 valorizarse *vpr* to increase in value

valquiria *nf* Valkyrie

vals *nm* waltz

valuar [4] *vt* to value

valva *nf Bot & Zool* valve

válvula *nf* valve; *Fig* **v. de escape** means of letting off steam; **v. de seguridad** safety valve

vamos 1 *ver* **ir**
  2 *adv (introduce inciso, matiz o conclusión)* **tendrás que hacer**

la compra tú, v., si no es mucha molestia you'll have to do the shopping yourself, if it's not too much trouble, of course; **se trata de un amigo, v., de un conocido** he's a friend, well, more of an acquaintance, really; **v., que al final la fiesta fue un desastre** anyway, the party was a disaster in the end

vampiresa *nf Fam* vamp, femme fatale

vampirismo *nm* vampirism

vampiro *nm* (**a**) *(personaje)* vampire (**b**) *(murciélago)* vampire bat

vanagloria *nf* boastfulness

vanagloriarse *vpr* to boast (**de** about), to show off (**de** about)

Vancouver *n* Vancouver

vandálico, -a *adj (salvaje)* vandalistic; **un acto v.** an act of vandalism

vandalismo *nm* vandalism

vándalo, -a 1 *nm,f Hist* Vandal
   2 *nm (salvaje)* vandal

vanguardia *nf* (**a**) *Mil* vanguard; *Fig* **ir a la v. de** to be at the forefront of (**b**) *(cultural)* avant-garde, vanguard

vanguardismo *nm* avant-garde

vanguardista 1 *adj* avant-garde
   2 *nmf* member of the avant-garde

vanidad *nf* (**a**) *(orgullo)* vanity (**b**) *(inutilidad)* futility

vanidoso, -a 1 *adj* vain, conceited
   2 *nm,f* vain person

vano, -a 1 *adj* (**a**) *(inútil, infundado)* vain; **en v.** in vain (**b**) *(vacío, superficial) (palabras)* shallow, superficial; *(persona)* vain, conceited
   2 *nm Arquit (de puerta)* doorway

Vanuatú *n* Vanuatu

vapor *nm (emanación)* vapor; *(de agua)* steam; *Culin* **al v.** steamed; **barco de v.** steamer, steamship; **máquina de v.** steam engine; *Fís & Quím* **v. de agua** water vapor

vaporización *nf* (**a**) *(pulverización)* spraying (**b**) *Fís* vaporization

vaporizador *nm* (**a**) *(pulverizador)* spray (**b**) *(para evaporar)* vaporizer

vaporizar [14] **1** *vt* (**a**) *Fís* to vaporize (**b**) *(pulverizar)* to spray
   2 vaporizarse *vpr Fís* to evaporate, to vaporize

vaporoso, -a *adj* (**a**) *(tela, vestido)* diaphanous, sheer (**b**) *(con vapor) (ducha, baño)* steamy; *(cielo)* hazy, misty

vapulear *vt* (**a**) *(golpear)* to beat, to thrash; *(zarandear)* to shake around *o* about (**b**) *(criticar)* to criticize; **v. los derechos de alguien** to trample on sb's rights

vapuleo *nm* (**a**) *(golpes)* beating; *(zarandeo)* shaking around *o* about (**b**) *(crítica)* criticizing; *(falta de respeto)* contemptuous treatment, abuse

vaquería *nf* dairy

vaquero, -a 1 *adj (tela)* denim; **falda/camisa vaquera** denim skirt/shirt; **tela vaquera** denim; **pantalón v.** jeans, denims
   2 *nm,f (persona)* cowboy, *f* cowgirl; **una película de vaqueros** a Western, a cowboy movie
   3 *nm (pantalón)* jeans; **unos vaqueros** (a pair of) jeans

vaquilla *nf (vaca)* heifer; *(toro)* young bull

vara *nf* (**a**) *(rama, palo)* stick (**b**) *(pértiga)* pole (**c**) *(fabricada)* rod (**d**) *(tallo)* stem, stalk (**e**) *(de trombón)* slide (**f**) *(insignia)* staff

varadero *nm* dry dock

varado, -a *adj Náut (encallado)* aground, stranded; *(en el dique seco)* in dry dock

varapalo *nm (paliza)* hiding

varar 1 *vi Náut* to run aground
   2 vararse *vpr Am (averiarse)* to break down

varear *vt (golpear)* to beat (with a pole); **v. las aceitunas** = to knock the branches of olive trees with a pole to bring down the ripe olives

variabilidad *nf* changeability, variability

variable 1 *adj* changeable, variable
   2 *nf Mat* variable

variación *nf (cambio)* variation; *(del tiempo)* change; **v. magnética** magnetic declination

variado, -a *adj (diverso)* varied; *(galletas, bombones)* assorted

variante 1 *adj* variant
   2 *nf* (**a**) *(variación)* variation; *(versión)* version; **v. ortográfica** variant spelling (**b**) *Aut* bypass (**c**) *(en quiniela)* tie or away win (**d**) **variantes** mixed pickles

varianza *nf (en estadística)* variance

variar [32] **1** *vt* (**a**) *(modificar)* to alter, to change; **v. el rumbo** to change course (**b**) *(dar variedad a)* to vary; **me gusta v. el camino al trabajo** I like to vary my route to work
   2 *vi* (**a**) *(cambiar)* to change; **las circunstancias varían a lo largo del año** the circumstances change over the year; **v. (de)** to change; *también Irónico* **para v.** (just) for a change (**b**) *(ser diferente)* to vary, to differ (**de** from); **las causas varían de un país a otro** the causes vary from one country to another

varicela *nf* chicken pox

varicoso, -a *adj* varicose

variedad *nf* (**a**) *(diversidad)* variety (**b**) *Teatro* **variedades** variety

varilla *nf (barra delgada)* rod; *(de abanico, paraguas)* spoke, rib; *(de gafas)* arm

varillaje *nm (de abanico, paraguas)* spokes, ribbing; *(de gafas)* arms

variopinto, -a *adj* diverse

varios, -as 1 *adj (variados)* several; **pantalones de v. colores** pants in several *o* different colors; **hay varias maneras de hacerlo** there are several *o* various ways of doing it; **los motivos son v.** there are various reasons
   2 *pron pl* several; **delante de v. de sus compañeros** in front of several of his colleagues; **el accidente lo vimos v.** quite a few of us saw the accident

varita *nf* wand; **v. mágica** magic wand

variz *nf* varicose vein

varón *nm (hombre)* male, man; *(chico)* boy

varonil *adj (masculino)* masculine, male; *(viril)* manly, virile

Varsovia *n* Warsaw

varsoviano, -a 1 *adj* of/from Warsaw
   2 *nm,f* person from Warsaw

vasallaje *nm Hist* (**a**) *(servidumbre)* servitude (**b**) *(impuesto)* liege money

vasallo, -a *nm,f* (**a**) *(siervo)* vassal (**b**) *(súbdito)* subject

vasco, -a 1 *adj & nm,f* Basque
   2 *nm (lengua)* Basque

vascofrancés, -esa 1 *adj* of/from the French Basque provinces
   2 *nm* French Basque

Vascongadas *nfpl* **las V.** the Basque provinces of Spain

vascongado, -a *adj & nm,f* Basque

vascuence *nm (lengua)* Basque

vascular *adj* vascular

vasectomía *nf* vasectomy

vaselina *nf* Vaseline®

vasija *nf (de barro)* earthenware vessel

vaso *nm* (**a**) *(recipiente, contenido)* glass; **un v. de vino** a glass of wine; **un v. de plástico** a plastic cup; **se bebió un v. entero** he drank a whole glass; *Fig* **ahogarse en un v. de agua** to make a mountain out of a molehill; **vasos comunicantes** communicating vessels (**b**) *Anat* vessel; **vasos capilares** capillaries; **vasos sanguíneos** blood vessels (**c**) *Bot* vein

vasoconstricción *nf Med* vasoconstriction

vasoconstrictor *adj Med* vasoconstrictor

vasodilatador *adj Med* vasodilator

vástago *nm* (a) *(descendiente)* offspring (b) *(brote)* shoot (c) *(varilla)* rod

vastedad *nf* vastness

vasto, -a *adj* vast

vate *nm Formal* bard

váter *nm* toilet

Vaticano *n* **el V.** the Vatican

vaticinar *vt* to prophesy, to predict

vaticinio *nm* prophecy, prediction

vatio *nm* watt

vaya 1 *ver* **ir**

  2 *interj* (a) *(expresa sorpresa)* **¡v.!** well!; **¡v.! ¡tú por aquí!** fancy seeing you here!; **¡v., v.! no me esperaba eso de ti** well, I certainly didn't expect that from you!

  (b) *(expresa admiración)* **¡v. moto!** what a motorbike!; **¡v. si me gusta!** you bet I like it!; *Irónico* **¡v. (un) amigo!** some friend he is!

  (c) *(expresa contrariedad, disgusto)* **¡v.!** oh no!; **¡v., me equivoqué otra vez!** oh, no, I've got it wrong again!; **¡v. con la dichosa cuestecita!** so much for this being a little hill!, some little hill this is!; **¡v. por Dios!** *o Esp* **¡v., hombre! para una vez que compro gambas, me las dan pasadas** can you believe it *o* honestly, the one time I buy some shrimps, they're spoiled!

  3 *adv (bueno, bien)* not bad, OK

VB *(abrev de* **visto bueno***) (en ejercicios escolares)* = abbreviation equivalent to a check on a piece of schoolwork

Vd. *(abrev de* **usted***)* you

Vda. *(abrev de* **viuda***)* widow

Vds. *abrev de* **ustedes**

ve¹ *ver* **ir**

ve² *nf (letra) Am* **ve corta** v *(to distinguish from b)*

véase *ver* **ver**

vecinal *adj* (a) *(relaciones, trato)* neighborly (b) *(camino, impuestos)* local

vecindad *nf* (a) *(vecindario)* neighborhood (b) *(cualidad)* neighborliness (c) *(alrededores)* vicinity (d) *Méx* = communal dwelling where poor families each live in a single room with shared bathroom and kitchen

vecindario *nm (de barrio)* neighborhood; *(de población)* community, inhabitants

vecino, -a 1 *adj (cercano)* neighboring; **v. a** next to

  2 *nm,f* (a) *(de la misma casa, calle)* neighbor; *(de un barrio)* resident; **los vecinos de arriba** my/our/*etc* upstairs neighbors; **los vecinos de al lado** next-door neighbors (b) *(de una localidad)* inhabitant

vector *nm* vector

vectorial *adj* vectorial

veda *nf* (a) *(prohibición)* ban *(on hunting and fishing)*; **levantar la v.** to open the season (b) *(periodo)* off-season

vedado, -a 1 *adj* prohibited

  2 *nm* reserve

vedar *vt* to prohibit

vedette [be'ðet] *nf* star

vedismo *nm* Vedaism

vega *nf* fertile plain

vegetación 1 *nf* vegetation

  2 vegetaciones *nfpl Med* adenoids

vegetal 1 *adj* (a) *Biol* vegetable, plant; **aceite v.** vegetable oil; **el mundo v.** the plant kingdom (b) *Culin* **sandwich v.** salad sandwich

  2 *nm* vegetable

vegetar *vi* (a) *(planta)* to grow (b) *Fam (holgazanear)* to vegetate

vegetarianismo *nm* vegetarianism

vegetariano, -a *adj & nm,f* vegetarian

vegetativo, -a *adj* vegetative

vehemencia *nf* (a) *(pasión, entusiasmo)* vehemence (b) *(irreflexión)* impulsiveness, impetuosity

vehemente *adj* (a) *(apasionado, entusiasta)* vehement (b) *(irreflexivo)* impulsive, impetuous

vehicular *adj* **lengua v.** teaching language

vehículo *nm* (a) *(medio de transporte)* vehicle; **v. pesado** heavy truck (b) *(medio de propagación) (de enfermedad)* carrier; *(de ideas)* vehicle

veinte *núm* twenty; **los (años) v.** the twenties; *ver también* **seis**

veinteañero, -a 1 *adj* = in one's (early) twenties

  2 *nm,f* = person in their (early) twenties

veinteavo, -a *núm (fracción)* twentieth; **la veinteava parte** a twentieth

veintena *nf* twenty; **andará por la v.** he must be about twenty; **una v. de...** *(unos veinte)* about twenty...; *(veinte)* twenty...

veinticinco *núm* twenty-five; *ver también* **seis**

veinticuatro *núm* twenty-four; *ver también* **seis**

veintidós *núm* twenty-two; *ver también* **seis**

veintinueve *núm* twenty-nine; *ver también* **seis**

veintiocho *núm* twenty-eight; *ver también* **seis**

veintiséis *núm* twenty-six; *ver también* **seis**

veintisiete *núm* twenty-seven; *ver también* **seis**

veintitantos, -as *núm Fam* twenty-odd

veintitrés *núm* twenty-three; *ver también* **seis**

veintiuno, -a *núm* twenty-one; *ver también* **seis**

---

veintiún is used instead of **veintiuno** before masculine nouns (e.g. **veintiún hombres** twenty-one men).

---

vejación *nf*, **vejamen** *nm* humiliation

vejar *vt* to humiliate

vejatorio, -a *adj* humiliating

vejestorio *nm* (a) *Fam Pey* old codger (b) *Am (cosa)* old thing *o* relic

vejete *nm Fam* old guy

vejez *nf* old age; **¡a la v. viruelas!** fancy that at his/her age!

vejiga *nf* bladder; **v. de la bilis** gall bladder

vela 1 *nf* (a) *(para dar luz)* candle; *Fam Fig* **estar a dos velas** not to have two pennies to rub together; *Fam Fig* **quedarse a dos velas** to be left none the wiser; *Fam Fig* **¿quién te ha dado v. en este entierro?** who asked you to butt in? (b) *(de barco)* sail; **a toda v.** under full sail; **v. mayor** mainsail (c) *Dep* sailing; **hacer v.** to go sailing; **v. deportiva** sailing (d) *(vigilia)* vigil; **pasar la noche en v.** *(adrede)* to stay awake all night; *(desvelado)* to have a sleepless night

  2 velas *nfpl Fam (mocos)* snot

velada *nf* evening

veladamente *adv* covertly; **le acusó v. de ser el culpable** she hinted he was the guilty one

velado, -a *adj* (a) *(oculto)* veiled, hidden (b) *Fot* damaged by exposure to sunlight

velador *nm* (a) *(mesa)* pedestal table (b) *Andes, Méx (mesilla de noche)* bedside table (c) *Méx, RP (lámpara)* bedside lamp

veladora *nf* (a) *Méx (vela)* candle (b) *Méx, RP (lámpara)* bedside lamp

velamen *nm* sails

velar¹ *adj Anat & Ling* velar

velar² **1** *vi* (a) *(cuidar)* **v. por** to look after, to watch over (b) *(no dormir)* to stay awake

  2 *vt* (a) *(de noche) (muerto)* to keep a vigil over; *(enfermo)* to sit up with (b) *(ocultar)* to mask, to veil (c) *Fot* to damage by exposure to sunlight

  3 velarse *vpr Fot* to be damaged by exposure to sunlight

velatorio *nm* (a) *(acto)* wake, vigil (b) *(lugar)* = room where vigil is held over a dead person's remains on the night before burial

velcro® *nm* Velcro®

veleidad *nf* (**a**) *(inconstancia)* fickleness, capriciousness (**b**) *(antojo, capricho)* whim, caprice

veleidoso, -a *adj* (**a**) *(inconstante)* fickle (**b**) *(caprichoso)* capricious

velero *nm* sailing boat *o* ship

veleta 1 *nf* weather vane

    2 *nmf* capricious person

velista *nmf* yachtsman, *f* yachtswoman

vello *nm* (**a**) *(pelusilla)* down (**b**) *(pelo)* hair

vellocino *nm* fleece; **el v. de oro** the Golden Fleece

vellón *nm* *(lana)* fleece

vellosidad *nf* *(presencia de pelo)* hairiness; *(más fino)* downiness

velloso, -a *adj* *(con pelo)* hairy; *(más fino)* downy

velludo, -a *adj* hairy

velo *nm* (**a**) *(prenda)* veil; *Fam* **correr** *o* **echar un (tupido) v. sobre algo** to draw a veil over sth (**b**) **v. del paladar** soft palate

velocidad *nf* (**a**) *(rapidez)* speed, *Espec* velocity; **¿a qué v. van?** what speed are they going at?, how fast are they going?; **a toda v.** *(en vehículo)* at full speed; **lo tuvimos que hacer a toda v.** we had to do it as fast as we could; **de alta v.** high-speed; **con la v. de un rayo** as quick as lightning; **v. de crucero** cruising speed; **la v. de la luz** the speed of light; **v. máxima** top speed; *Inform* **v. de proceso** processing speed; **la v. del sonido** the speed of sound; *Inform* **v. de transmisión** *(en módem)* baud rate; **v. de vuelo** airspeed (**b**) *Aut (marcha)* gear; **cambiar de v.** to change gear

velocímetro *nm* speedometer

velocípedo *nm* velocipede

velocista *nmf* sprinter

velódromo *nm* cycle track, velodrome

velomotor *nm* moped

velorio *nm* wake

veloz *adj* fast, quick

velozmente *adv* quickly, rapidly

ven *ver* **venir**

vena *nf* (**a**) *(gen) & Anat & Min* vein (**b**) *(inspiración)* inspiration; *Fam* **estar en v., tener la v.** to be on form; *Fam* **le dio la v. de hacerlo** she took it into her head to do it (**c**) *(don)* vein, streak; **tener v. de pintor** to have a gift for painting

venado *nm* *(animal)* deer; *(carne)* venison

venal *adj* (**a**) *(sobornable)* venal, corrupt (**b**) *(vendible)* for sale, salable

vencedor, -ora 1 *adj* winning, victorious

    2 *nm,f* winner

vencejo *nm* *(pájaro)* swift

vencer [40] **1** *vt* (**a**) *(derrotar) (rival)* to beat; *(enemigo)* to defeat; **consiguió v. al cáncer** he won his battle against cancer (**b**) *(superar) (miedo, obstáculo)* to overcome; *(tentación)* to resist; **venció al cansancio/sueño** she overcame her exhaustion/sleepiness; **lo venció el cansancio** he was overcome by tiredness (**c**) *(aventajar)* **v. a alguien a** *o* **en algo** to outdo sb at sth

    2 *vi* (**a**) *(equipo, partido)* to win; *(ejército)* to be victorious; **dejarse v. por el desánimo/la apatía** to let oneself be discouraged/to give in *o* succumb to apathy (**b**) *(caducar) (garantía, contrato)* to expire; *(deuda, pago)* to fall due, to mature; *(bono)* to mature; *Am (medicamento)* to reach *o* pass its expiry date; **el plazo para entregar las solicitudes vence el 15 de mayo** the closing date *o* the deadline for sending in applications is May 15 (**c**) *(prevalecer)* to prevail

    3 vencerse *vpr* (**a**) *(estante)* to give way, to collapse (**b**) *Am (medicamento)* to pass its expiry date

vencido, -a 1 *adj* (**a**) *(derrotado)* defeated; **darse por v.** to

give up (**b**) *(caducado) (garantía, contrato, plazo)* expired; *(pago, deuda)* due, payable; *(bono)* mature; *Am (medicamento)* past its expiry date

    2 *nm,f (en guerra)* conquered *o* defeated person; *(en deportes, concursos)* loser

vencimiento *nm* (**a**) *(término) (de garantía, contrato, plazo)* expiry; *(de pago, deuda)* falling due; *(de bono)* maturing (**b**) *(inclinación)* giving way, collapse

venda *nf* bandage; *Fig* **tener una v. en** *o* **delante de los ojos** to be blind

vendaje *nm* bandaging

vendar *vt* to bandage; **v. los ojos a alguien** to blindfold sb

vendaval *nm* gale

vendedor, -ora 1 *adj* selling

    2 *nm,f (en general)* seller; *(en tienda)* salesclerk; *(de coches, seguros)* salesman, *f* saleswoman; **v. ambulante** peddler, hawker; **v. a domicilio** door-to-door salesman

vender 1 *vt* to sell; **v. algo a** *o* **por** to sell sth for; **venden naranjas a 2 euros el kilo** they're selling oranges for 2 euros a kilo; **es capaz de v. a su madre** he'd sell his own mother; **es capaz de v. su alma al diablo por triunfar** he'd sell his soul to the Devil if that's what it took to be successful

    2 *vi (producto, autor)* to sell

    3 venderse *vpr* (**a**) *(ser vendido)* to be sold *o* on sale; **se vende** *(en letrero)* for sale (**b**) *(dejarse sobornar)* to sell oneself, to be bribed

vendetta *nf* vendetta

vendido, -a *adj* sold; *Fig* **estar** *o* **ir v.** not to stand a chance

vendimia *nf* grape harvest

vendimiador, -ora *nm,f* grape picker

vendimiar 1 *vt* to harvest *(grapes)*

    2 *vi* to pick grapes

vendré *etc ver* **venir**

Venecia *n* Venice

veneciano, -a *adj & nm,f* Venetian

veneno *nm* (**a**) *(sustancia tóxica)* poison; *(de serpiente, insecto)* venom (**b**) *(mala intención)* venom

venenoso, -a *adj* (**a**) *(tóxico)* poisonous (**b**) *(malintencionado)* venomous

venerable *adj* venerable

veneración *nf* veneration, worship

venerador, -ora 1 *adj* venerational

    2 *nm,f* venerator

venerar *vt* to venerate, to worship

venéreo, -a *adj* venereal

venezolano, -a *adj & nm,f* Venezuelan

Venezuela *n* Venezuela

venga *interj Esp Fam* **¡v.!** come on!

vengador, -ora 1 *adj* avenging

    2 *nm,f* avenger

venganza *nf* vengeance, revenge

vengar [38] **1** *vt* to avenge

    2 vengarse *vpr* to take revenge (**de** on), to avenge oneself (**de** on)

vengativo, -a *adj* vengeful, vindictive

vengo *ver* **venir**

vengue *etc ver* **vengar**

venia *nf* (**a**) *(permiso)* permission; **con la v.** *(tomando la palabra)* by your leave (**b**) *(perdón)* pardon

venial *adj* petty, venial

venialidad *nf* veniality, pettiness

venida *nf* (**a**) *(llegada)* arrival (**b**) *(regreso)* return

venidero, -a *adj* future

venir [69] **1** *vi* (**a**) *(en general)* to come; **v. a/de hacer algo** to come to do sth/from doing sth; **v. de algo** *(proceder, derivarse)* to come from sth; **v. a alguien con algo** to come to sb with sth; **no me vengas con exigencias** don't come to me making demands; **el año que viene** next year

(**b**) *(llegar)* to arrive; **vino a las doce** he arrived at twelve o'clock

(**c**) *(hallarse)* to be; **su foto viene en primera página** his photo is o appears on the front page; **el texto viene en inglés** the text is in English; **vienen en todos los tamaños** they come in every size; **las anchoas vienen en lata** anchovies come in cans

(**d**) *(acometer, sobrevenir)* **me viene sueño** I'm getting sleepy; **le vinieron ganas de reír** he was seized by a desire to laugh; **le vino una tremenda desgracia** he suffered a great misfortune

(**e**) *(ropa, calzado)* **v. a alguien** to fit sb; **¿qué tal te viene?** does it fit all right?; **el abrigo le viene pequeño** the coat is too small for her

(**f**) *(convenir)* **v. bien/mal a alguien** to suit/not to suit sb

(**g**) *(aproximarse)* **viene a costar un millón** it costs almost a million

(**h**) *(indica resultado)* **esto viene a significar...** this means...; **v. a parar en** to end in; **v. a ser** to amount to

(**i**) *(expresiones)* **¿a qué viene esto?** what do you mean by that?, what's that in aid of?; **v. a menos** *(negocio)* to go downhill; *(persona)* to go down in the world

2 *v aux* (**a**) *(antes de gerundio)* *(haber estado)* **v. haciendo algo** to have been doing sth; **las peleas vienen sucediéndose desde hace tiempo** fighting has been going on for some time (**b**) *(antes de participio)* *(estar)* **los cambios vienen motivados por la presión de la oposición** the changes have resulted from pressure on the part of the opposition

3 venirse *vpr* (**a**) *(venir)* to come; **venirse (de)** *(volver)* to come back o return (from); **¿te vienes?** are you coming? (**b**) **venirse abajo** *(techo, estante)* to collapse; *(ilusiones)* to be dashed

venoso, -a *adj* venous

venta *nf* (**a**) *(acción)* sale; **de v. en...** on sale at...; **estar en v.** to be for sale; **poner a la v.** *(casa)* to put up for sale; *(producto)* to put on sale; **v. ambulante** street vending; **v. por catálogo** mail-order selling; **v. al contado** cash sale; **v. por correo** o **por correspondencia** mail-order selling; **v. a crédito** credit sale; **v. directa** direct selling; **v. a domicilio** door-to-door selling; **v. al por mayor** wholesale; **v. al por menor** retail; **v. a plazos** sale by installments; **v. pública** public auction (**b**) *(cantidad)* sales; **han aumentado/caído las ventas** sales have risen/fallen (**c**) *(posada)* country inn

ventaja *nf* (**a**) *(hecho favorable)* advantage; **tiene la v. de que es más manejable** it has the advantage of being easier to handle; **ventajas fiscales** tax breaks (**b**) *(en competición)* lead; **dar v. a alguien** to give sb a start; **le dieron 2 metros de v.** they gave him a 2-meter start; **llevar v. a alguien** to have a lead over sb (**c**) *(en tenis)* advantage

ventajista *adj & nmf* opportunist

ventajoso, -a *adj* advantageous

ventana *nf* (**a**) *(de edificio)* window; *Fig* **echar** o **tirar algo por la v.** to let sth go to waste; **v. de socorro** emergency exit (window) (**b**) *(de nariz)* nostril (**c**) *Inform* window; **v. activa** active window; **v. de diálogo** dialog box

ventanal *nm* large window

ventanilla *nf* (**a**) *(de vehículo, sobre)* window (**b**) *(taquilla)* counter

ventarrón *nm Fam* strong o blustery wind

ventear 1 *v impersonal* to be very windy

2 *vi* to sniff the air

ventero, -a *nm,f* innkeeper

ventilación *nf* ventilation

ventilador *nm* ventilator, fan

ventilar 1 *vt* (**a**) *(airear)* *(habitación)* to air, to ventilate; *(ropa,*

colchón) to air (**b**) *Fam (resolver) (asunto)* to clear up (**c**) *Fam (discutir)* to air; **le encanta v. sus problemas en público** she loves to air her problems in public (**d**) *(difundir) (secreto)* to spread, to make public

2 ventilarse *vpr* (**a**) *(airearse)* to air; **voy a salir a ventilarme un poco** I'm going to pop out for a breath of fresh air (**b**) *Fam (terminarse) (botella)* to knock back, to polish off; **se ventiló el pastel en un periquete** he wolfed down the cake in next to no time (**c**) *Fam (asesinar)* to rub out

ventisca *nf* blizzard

ventiscar [59], **ventisquear** *v impersonal* to blow a blizzard

ventisquero *nm (nieve amontonada)* snowdrift

ventolera *nf* (**a**) *(viento)* gust of wind (**b**) *Fam (idea extravagante)* wild idea; **le ha dado la v. de hacerlo** she has taken it into her head to do it

ventosa *nf (gen) & Zool* sucker

ventosear *vi* to break wind

ventosidad *nf* wind, flatulence

ventoso, -a *adj* windy

ventresca *nf* belly *(of fish)*

ventricular *adj* ventricular

ventrículo *nm* ventricle

ventrílocuo, -a *nm,f* ventriloquist

ventriloquía *nf* ventriloquism

ventura *nf* (**a**) *(felicidad)* happiness, contentment (**b**) *(suerte)* luck; **por v.** luckily; **a la (buena) v.** *(al azar)* at random, haphazardly; *(sin nada previsto)* without planning o a fixed plan

venturoso, -a *adj* happy, fortunate

Venus *nm Astron* Venus

venza *etc ver* **vencer**

veo-veo *nm* I spy

ver [70] **1** *vt* (**a**) *(en general)* to see; *(mirar)* to look at; *(televisión, partido de fútbol)* to watch; **¿ves algo?** can you see anything?; **he estado viendo tu trabajo** I've been looking at your work; **ya ves que estás de mal humor** I can see you're in a bad mood; **¿ves lo que quiero decir?** do you see what I mean?; **ir a v. lo que pasa** to go and see what's going on; **es una manera de v. las cosas** that's one way of looking at it; **yo no lo veo tan mal** I don't think it's that bad

(**b**) *(expresiones)* **eso habrá que verlo** that remains to be seen; **¡hay que v. qué lista es!** you wouldn't believe how clever she is!; *Fam* **no puedo verlo (ni en pintura)** I can't stand him; **si no lo veo, no lo creo** I would never have believed this was possible; **pero ahora, si te he visto, no me acuerdo** but now he/she etc doesn't want anything to do with me; **v. venir a alguien** to see what sb is up to

2 *vi* (**a**) *(en general)* to see (**b**) *(expresiones)* **dejarse v. (por un sitio)** to show one's face (somewhere); **v. para creer** seeing is believing; **eso está por v.** that remains to be seen; **ni visto ni oído** in the twinkling of an eye; **ya veremos** we'll see

3 *nm* **estar de buen v.** to be good-looking

4 a ver *loc adv (veamos)* let's see; **¿a v.?** *(mirando con interés)* let me see, let's have a look; **¡a v.!** *(¡pues claro!)* what do you expect?; *(al empezar algo)* right!

5 verse *vpr* (**a**) *(reflexivo) (mirarse, imaginarse)* to see oneself; **verse en el espejo** to see oneself in the mirror; **ya me veo haciéndolo yo solo** I can see myself doing it on my own (**b**) *(pasivo, impersonal) (percibirse)* **desde aquí se ve el mar** you can see the sea from here (**c**) *(recíproco) (encontrarse)* to meet, to see each other; **hace mucho que no nos vemos** we haven't seen each other for a long time (**d**) *(expresiones)* **vérselas y deseárselas para hacer algo** to have a real struggle doing sth; **por lo que se ve** apparently; **véase** *(en textos)* see

vera *nf* (**a**) *(orilla) (de río, lago)* bank; *(de camino)* edge, side (**b**) *(lado)* side; **a la v. de** next to

veracidad *nf* truthfulness

veraneante 1 *adj* vacationing
  2 *nmf* (summer) vacationer
veranear *vi* **v. en** to spend one's summer vacation in
veraneo *nm* summer vacation; **irse de v.** to go on (one's summer) vacation, to vacation
veraniego, -a *adj* summer; **ropa veraniega** summer clothing
veranillo *nm* Indian summer
verano *nm* (a) *(estación)* summer; **en v.** in (the) summer (b) *Am (estación seca)* dry season
veras 1 *nfpl* truth; **lo dijo entre bromas y v.** she was only half-joking
  2 de veras *loc adv (verdaderamente)* really; *(en serio)* seriously; **de v., yo no quería hacerte daño** I really didn't want to hurt you; **esta vez va de v.** this time it's serious *o* for real
veraz *adj* truthful
verbal *adj* verbal
verbalizar [14] *vt* to verbalize
verbena *nf* (a) *(fiesta)* street party (b) *(planta)* verbena
verbenero, -a *adj* street-party; **ambiente v.** festive atmosphere
verbigracia *adv Formal* for example, for instance
verbo *nm* (a) *Gram* verb; **v. auxiliar** auxiliary (verb); **v. copulativo** copula, copulative verb; **v. impersonal** impersonal verb; **v. intransitivo** intransitive verb; **v. reflexivo** reflexive verb; **v. transitivo** transitive verb (b) *(lenguaje)* language
verborrea *nf* verbal diarrhea, verbosity
verbosidad *nf* verbosity
verboso, -a *adj* verbose
verdad 1 *nf* (a) *(en general)* truth; **decir la v.** to tell the truth; **a decir v.** to tell the truth; **¿es v.?** is that true *o* right?; **eso no es v.** that isn't true *o* so; **en v.** truly, honestly; **la v., no me importa** to tell the truth *o* to be honest, I don't care; **la v. es que no lo sé** to be honest, I don't know, I don't really know; *Fam* **una v. como un puño** an undeniable fact; *Fig* **cantar las verdades** to speak one's mind; *Fig* **cantarle** *o* **decirle a alguien cuatro verdades** to tell sb a few home truths
  (b) *(buscando confirmación)* **no te gusta, ¿v.?** you don't like it, do you?; **está bueno, ¿v.?** it's good, isn't it?
  (c) *(principio aceptado)* fact
  2 de verdad *loc adv (en serio)* seriously; *(realmente)* really; *(auténtico)* real
verdaderamente *adv* (a) *(de verdad)* really; **v., no sé cómo lo soportas** I really *o* honestly don't know how you put up with him (b) *(muy)* truly, really; **una historia v. increíble** a truly amazing story
verdadero, -a *adj* (a) *(cierto, real)* true, real (b) *(sin falsificar)* real (c) *(enfático)* real; **fue un v. lío** it was a real mess
verde 1 *adj* (a) *(en general)* green; **v. botella** bottle green; **v. oliva** olive (green); **v. esmeralda** emerald (green); *Fam* **poner v. a alguien** to run sb down (b) *(poco maduro) (fruta)* unripe, green; *Fam (persona)* green, wet behind the ears; *(proyecto, plan)* in its early stages (c) *(ecologista)* Green, green (d) *(obsceno)* blue, dirty (e) *Esp Antes Fam* **billete v.** = 1,000 peseta note
  2 *nm (color)* green
  3 *nmpl* **los Verdes** *(partido)* the Greens
verdear *vi* (a) *(parecer verde)* to look green (b) *(plantas)* to turn *o* go green
verdecer [46] *vi* to turn *o* go green
verdinegro, -a *adj* very dark green
verdor *nm* (a) *(color)* greenness (b) *(madurez)* lushness
verdoso, -a *adj* greenish
verdugo *nm* (a) *(de preso)* executioner; *(que ahorca)* hangman (b) *(tirano)* tyrant (c) *(pasamontañas)* balaclava helmet

verdulera *nf Fam Pey (ordinaria)* fishwife
verdulería *nf* fruit and vegetable store
verdulero, -a *nm,f (tendero)* fruit and vegetable grocer
verdura *nf* (a) *(comestible)* vegetables, greens (b) *(color verde)* greenness
verdusco, -a *adj* dirty green
vereda *nf* (a) *(senda)* path; *Fam* **hacer entrar** *o* **meter a alguien en v.** to bring sb into line (b) *CSur, Perú (acera)* sidewalk
veredicto *nm* verdict
verga *nf* (a) *Zool* penis (b) *esp Am muy Fam (de hombre)* cock (c) *Náut* yard
vergel *nm* lush, fertile place
vergonzante *adj* shameful
vergonzoso, -a 1 *adj* (a) *(deshonroso)* shameful (b) *(tímido)* bashful
  2 *nm,f* bashful person
vergüenza 1 *nf* (a) *(deshonra)* shame; **me da v. confesar que...** I'm ashamed to admit that...; **sentir v.** to feel ashamed (b) *(bochorno)* embarrassment; **me da v. decírtelo** I'm embarrassed to tell you; **¡qué v.!** how embarrassing!; **sentir v.** to feel embarrassed; **sentir v. ajena** to feel embarrassed for sb; **¿quién quiere el de la v.?** who wants the last one? (c) *(timidez)* bashfulness; **perder la v.** to lose one's inhibitions; **tener poca v.** to be shameless (d) *(escándalo)* disgrace; **¡es una v.!** it's disgraceful!; **¡qué v.!** what a disgrace!
  2 vergüenzas *nfpl (genitales)* private parts, privates
vericueto *nm (camino difícil)* rough track; *Fig* **vericuetos** ins and outs
verídico, -a *adj* (a) *(cierto)* true, truthful (b) *(verosímil)* true-to-life, real
verificable *adj* verifiable
verificación *nf* check, checking
verificador, -ora 1 *adj (confirmador)* checking; *(examinador)* testing, inspecting
  2 *nm,f* tester, inspector
verificar [59] **1** *vt* (a) *(verdad, autenticidad)* to check, to verify (b) *(funcionamiento, buen estado)* to check, to test (c) *(fecha, cita)* to confirm (d) *(llevar a cabo)* to carry out
  2 verificarse *vpr* (a) *(tener lugar)* to take place (b) *(resultar cierto) (predicción)* to come true; *(comprobarse)* to be verified
verja *nf* (a) *(puerta)* iron gate (b) *(valla)* railings (c) *(enrejado)* grille
vermú *(pl* **vermús)**, **vermut** *(pl* **vermuts)** *nm (bebida)* vermouth
vernáculo, -a *adj* vernacular
verónica *nf* (a) *Taurom* = pass in which the matador swings his cape away from the bull (b) *(planta)* veronica
verosímil *adj* (a) *(creíble)* believable, credible (b) *(probable)* likely, probable
verosimilitud *nf* (a) *(credibilidad)* credibility (b) *(probabilidad)* likeliness
verraco *nm* boar
verruga *nf* wart
verrugoso, -a *adj* warty
versado, -a *adj* versed (**en** in)
versal *nf* capital (letter)
versalita *nf* small capital
Versalles *n* Versailles
versallesco, -a *adj Fam (cortés)* gallant, chivalrous
versar *vi* **v. sobre** to be about, to deal with
versátil *adj* (a) *(voluble)* changeable, fickle (b) *(polifacético)* versatile
versatilidad *nf* (a) *(volubilidad)* changeability, fickleness (b) *(adaptabilidad)* versatility

versículo *nm* verse

versificación *nf* versification

versificar [59] **1** *vi* to write (in) verse
2 *vt* to put into verse

versión *nf* (**a**) *(en general)* version; *(en música pop)* cover version; *Cine* **v. original** original (version) (**b**) *(traducción)* translation, version

versionar *vt Fam (en música pop)* to cover

verso *nm* (**a**) *(género)* verse; **en v.** in verse; **v. blanco/libre** blank/free verse (**b**) *(unidad rítmica)* line *(of poetry)*

versus *prep Formal* versus

vértebra *nf* vertebra

vertebrado, -a 1 *adj* vertebrate
2 vertebrados *nmpl* vertebrates

vertebral *adj* vertebral

vertebrar *vt* to form the backbone of

vertedero *nm* (**a**) *(de basuras)* garbage dump (**b**) *(de pantano)* drain, spillway

verter [64] **1** *vt* (**a**) *(derramar)* to spill (**b**) *(vaciar) (líquido)* to pour (out); *(recipiente)* to empty; *(basura, residuos)* to dump; **los ríos vierten sus aguas en el mar** rivers flow into the sea (**c**) *(traducir)* to translate (**a** into) (**d**) *(expresar) (acusación, crítica)* to make; **v. insultos sobre alguien** to shower sb with insults
2 *vi* **v. a** *o* **en** to flow into
3 verterse *vpr (derramarse)* to spill

vertical 1 *adj* (**a**) *Mat* vertical; *(derecho)* upright; **el respaldo estaba casi v.** the back was almost vertical; **poner en posición v.** to place in an upright position (**b**) *(formato, orientación)* portrait
2 *nm Astron* vertical circle
3 *nf Mat* vertical (line)

verticalidad *nf* verticality, vertical position

verticalmente *adv* vertically

vértice *nm (en general)* vertex; *(de cono)* apex; **v. geodésico** triangulation pillar

vertido *nm* (**a**) *(residuo)* waste; **vertidos radiactivos** radioactive waste (**b**) *(acción)* dumping; **v. de residuos** waste dumping

vertiente *nf* (**a**) *(pendiente)* slope (**b**) *(aspecto)* side, aspect

vertiginosamente *adv* with dizzying speed

vertiginosidad *nf* dizziness

vertiginoso, -a *adj* (**a**) *(mareante)* dizzy (**b**) *(raudo)* giddy

vértigo *nm* (**a**) *(enfermedad)* vertigo; *(mareo)* dizziness; **treparme da v.** climbing makes me dizzy; **sólo de pensarlo me da v.** just thinking about it makes me feel dizzy; *Fig* **de v.** *(velocidad, altura)* giddy; *(cifras)* mind-boggling (**b**) *(apresuramiento)* mad rush, hectic pace

vesícula *nf (ampolla)* blister; **v. biliar** gall bladder

vesicular *adj* vesicular

vespa® *nf* Vespa®, motor scooter

vespertino, -a 1 *adj* evening; **diario v.** evening (news)paper
2 *nm (periódico)* evening (news)paper

vespino® *nm* moped

vestal *nf* vestal (virgin)

vestíbulo *nm (de casa)* (entrance) hall; *(de hotel, oficina)* lobby, foyer

vestido, -a 1 *adj* dressed; **iba v. con ropa de trabajo** he was dressed in *o* wearing his work clothes; **ir v. de** *(blanco, negro)* to be dressed in; *(marinero, príncipe)* to be dressed as
2 *nm* (**a**) *(indumentaria)* clothes; **el v. a través de los siglos** clothing *o* costume through the ages (**b**) *(prenda femenina)* dress; **v. de novia** wedding dress; **v. premamá** maternity dress

vestidor *nm* (**a**) *(en casa)* dressing room (**b**) *CAm, Méx (en club)* locker room

vestiduras *nfpl* clothes; *Rel* vestments

vestigio *nm (de otras épocas, civilizaciones)* vestige; *(de vida)* trace

vestimenta *nf* clothes, wardrobe

vestir [47] **1** *vt* (**a**) *(poner ropa a)* to dress; **viste al niño y vámonos** dress the child *o* get the child dressed and let's go; **v. a alguien de algo** *(disfrazar)* to dress sb up as sth (**b**) *(llevar puesto)* to wear; **viste unos tejanos negros** he's wearing black jeans (**c**) *Literario (encubrir)* **v. algo de** to disguise sth with
2 *vi* (**a**) *(ser elegante) (ropa)* to be smart; **de v.** dressy (**b**) *(llevar ropa)* to dress; **siempre viste muy bien** she always dresses very well (**c**) *(estar bien visto)* to be the done thing
3 vestirse *vpr* (**a**) *(ponerse ropa)* to get dressed, to dress; **vestirse de algo** *(disfrazarse)* to dress up as sth; **se vistió de luto/de blanco** she dressed in *o* wore mourning/white (**b**) *(adquirir ropa)* **vestirse en** to buy one's clothes at (**c**) *Literario (cubrirse)* **vestirse de** to be covered in

vestuario *nm* (**a**) *(vestimenta)* clothes, wardrobe; *Teatro* costumes (**b**) *(guardarropa)* cloakroom (**c**) *(para cambiarse) (en deportes)* locker room; *(en teatro)* dressing room

Vesubio *nm* **el V.** (Mount) Vesuvius

veta *nf* (**a**) *(de mineral)* seam (**b**) *(en madera)* knot; *(en mármol)* vein

vetar *vt* to veto

veteado, -a *adj* grained

vetear *vt* to grain

veteranía *nf* seniority, age

veterano, -a *adj & nm,f* veteran

veterinaria *nf (ciencia)* veterinary science

veterinario, -a 1 *adj* veterinary
2 *nm,f (persona)* vet, veterinarian

veto *nm* veto; **poner v. a algo** to veto sth

vetusto, -a *adj Formal* ancient, very old

vez *nf* (**a**) *(en general)* time; **una v.** once; **¿te acuerdas de una v. (en) que fuimos a pescar?** do you remember that time we went fishing?; **dos veces** twice; **tres veces** three times; **¿has estado allí alguna v.?** have you ever been there?; **a mi/tu/***etc* **v.** in my/your/*etc* turn; **a la v. (que)** at the same time (as); **alguna que otra v.** occasionally; **a veces, algunas veces** sometimes, at times; **cada v. (que)** every time; **cada v. más** more and more; **resulta cada v. más difícil** it's getting harder and harder; **cada v. menos** less and less; **cada v. la veo más feliz** she seems happier and happier; **de una v.** in one go; **de una v. para siempre** *o* **por todas** once and for all; **de v. en cuando** from time to time, now and again; **vete de una v.** just go, for heaven's sake; **en v. de** instead of; **érase una v.** once upon a time; **hacer las veces de** to act as; **muchas veces** often, a lot; **otra v.** again; **pocas veces, rara v.** rarely, seldom; **por última/enésima v.** for the last/umpteenth time; **tal v.** perhaps, maybe; **una v. más** once again; **una v. que** once, after; **una y otra v.** time and again
(**b**) *(turno)* turn; **¿quién lleva** *o* **da la v.?** who's the last in the line?; **voy a pedir la v.** I'm going to ask who's last

v.g., v.gr. *(abrev de* **verbigracia***)* e.g.

VHF *nf (abrev de* **very high frequency***)* VHF

VHS *nm (abrev de* **video home system***)* VHS

vía 1 *nf* (**a**) *(medio de transporte)* route; **por v. aérea** *(en general)* by air; *(correo)* (by) airmail; **por v. marítima** by sea; **por v. terrestre** overland, by land; *Fam* **solucionar/conseguir algo por la v. rápida** to solve/get sth as quickly as possible; **v. de comunicación** communication route; **v. fluvial** waterway
(**b**) *(calzada, calle)* road; **v. pública** public thoroughfare; **Vía Láctea** Milky Way
(**c**) *Ferroc (raíl)* rails, track; *(andén)* platform; **v. estrecha** narrow gauge; **v. férrea** *(ruta)* railway line; **v. muerta** siding

(d) *Anat* tract; **por v. oral** orally

(e) *(proceso)* **estar en vías de** to be in the process of; **país en vías de desarrollo** developing country; **una especie en vías de extinción** an endangered species

(f) *(opción)* channel, path; **por v. oficial/judicial** through official channels/the courts

(g) *(camino)* **dar v. libre** *(dejar paso)* to yield; *(dar libertad de acción)* to give a free rein; **tener v. libre** *(proyecto)* to have received the go-ahead; **tener v. libre para hacer algo** to have carte blanche to do sth

(h) *(en barco)* **v. de agua** leakage, hole (below the water line)

(i) *Der* procedure

2 *prep* via; **volar v. Bangkok** to fly via Bangkok

3 vía crucis *nm inv Rel* Stations of the Cross, Way of the Cross

viabilidad *nf* viability

viabilizar [14] *vt* to make viable

viable *adj* viable

viaducto *nm* viaduct

Viagra® *nm o nf* Viagra®

viajante *nmf* traveling salesperson

viajar *vi* (a) *(trasladarse, irse)* to travel (**en** by) (b) *(circular)* to run

viaje *nm* (a) *(en general)* journey, trip; *(en barco)* voyage; **¡buen v.!** have a good journey *o* trip!; **fue un v. agotador** it was an exhausting journey; **estar/ir de v.** to be/go away (on a trip); **hay once días de v.** it's an eleven-day journey; **en sus viajes al extranjero** on his journeys *o* travels abroad; **los viajes de Colón** the voyages of Columbus; **viajes espaciales** space travel; **v. de Estado** state visit; **v. de estudios** *(en colegio, universidad)* class trip; **v. de ida** outward journey; **v. de ida y vuelta** round trip; **v. marítimo** sea voyage; **v. de negocios** business trip; **v. de novios** honeymoon; **v. oficial** official visit; **v. organizado** organized trip; **v. de placer** pleasure trip; **v. relámpago** lightning trip *o* visit; **v. de vuelta** return journey

(b) *(recorrido)* trip; **di varios viajes para trasladar los muebles** it took me a good few trips to move all the furniture

(c) *Fam (alucinación)* trip

(d) *Fam (golpe)* bang, bump

viajero, -a 1 *adj (persona)* traveling; *(ave)* migratory

2 *nm,f (en general)* traveler; *(en transporte público)* passenger

vial 1 *adj* road; **seguridad v.** road safety

2 *nm (frasco)* vial

vialidad *nf* **departamento de v.** roads and highways department

vianda *nf* (a) *(comida)* food (b) *Méx, RP (tentempié)* packed lunch; *(fiambrera)* lunch box

viandante *nmf* (a) *(peatón)* pedestrian (b) *(transeúnte)* passerby

viario, -a *adj* road; **red viaria** road network

viático *nm* (a) *(dieta)* expenses allowance (b) *Rel* last rites, viaticum

víbora *nf (animal)* adder, viper; *(persona)* viper

viborear *vi Méx Fam* to bitch, to backbite

vibración *nf* vibration

vibrador, -ora 1 *adj* vibrating

2 *nm* vibrator

vibráfono *nm* vibraphone

vibrante *adj* (a) *(aparato)* vibrating (b) *(música, espectáculo)* vibrant (c) *Ling* rolled, trilled

vibrar *vi* (a) *(onda, aparato)* to vibrate (b) *(voz, edificio)* to shake (c) *(público)* to be thrilled; **el teatro entero vibraba con la música** the whole theater was thrilled by the music; **el concierto hizo v. al público** the concert had an electrifying effect on the audience

vibrátil *adj* vibratile

vibratorio, -a *adj* vibratory

vicaría *nf* (a) *(cargo)* vicarship, vicariate (b) *(residencia)* vicarage (c) *Fam* **pasar por la v.** *(casarse)* to tie the knot

vicario *nm* vicar

vicealmirante *nm* vice admiral

vicecanciller *nmf* vice-chancellor

vicecónsul *nm* vice-consul

vicepresidencia *nf (de país, asociación)* vice-presidency; *(de comité, empresa)* vice-chairmanship, vice-presidency

vicepresidente, -a *nm,f (de país, asociación)* vice-president; *(de comité, empresa)* vice-chairman, vice-president; **v. (del Gobierno)** deputy prime minister

vicerrector, -ora *nm,f* = deputy to the vice-chancellor of a university

vicesecretario, -a *nm,f* assistant secretary

viceversa *adv* vice versa

vichy [bi'tʃi] *(pl* **vichys**) *nm (tejido)* gingham

vichyssoise [bitʃi'swas] *nf Culin* vichyssoise

viciado, -a *adj (aire) (maloliente)* stuffy; *(contaminado)* polluted

viciar 1 *vt* (a) *(enviciar)* **v. a alguien** to get sb into a bad habit; *(pervertir)* to corrupt sb (b) *(falsear)* to falsify; *(tergiversar)* to distort, to twist

2 viciarse *vpr* (a) *(enviciarse)* to get into a bad habit; *(pervertirse)* to become *o* get corrupted; **es muy fácil viciarse con estos bombones** it's very easy to get addicted to these chocolates (b) *(aire)* to get stuffy (c) *(deformarse)* to warp

vicio *nm* (a) *(libertinaje, actividad inmoral)* vice (b) *(mala costumbre)* bad habit, vice; **quejarse** *o* **llorar de v.** to complain for no (good) reason; *Fam* **para mí, viajar es un v.** I'm addicted to traveling; **vicios posturales** bad postural habits (c) *(defecto, error)* defect; **tiene un v. al andar** he walks in a strange way; **v. de dicción** incorrect use of language (d) *Fam* **de v.** *(fenomenal)* brilliant; **esta tarta está de v.** this cake is yummy *o* scrumptious; **nos lo pasamos de v.** we had a great *o* fantastic time

vicioso, -a 1 *adj* depraved

2 *nm,f* (a) *(depravado)* depraved person (b) *(enviciado)* addict; *Fam* **es un v. de las novelas policíacas** he's addicted to detective novels

vicisitudes *nfpl* vicissitudes, ups and downs

víctima *nf (por mala suerte o negligencia)* victim; *(en accidente, guerra)* casualty; **v. propiciatoria** scapegoat

victimar *vt Am* to kill, to murder

victimario, -a *nm,f Am* killer, murderer

Victoria *n* **el lago V.** Lake Victoria

victoria *nf* victory; **adjudicarse la v.** to win a victory; **cantar v.** to claim victory; *Dep* **v. local** home win; **v. moral** moral victory; **v. pírrica** Pyrrhic victory; *Dep* **v. visitante** away win

victoriano, -a *adj* Victorian

victorioso, -a *adj* victorious

vicuña *nf* vicuña

vid *nf* vine

vid. *(abrev de* **véase**) v., vide

vida *nf* (a) *(existencia)* life; **en v. de** during the life *o* lifetime of; **estar con v.** to be alive; **perder la v.** to lose one's life; **quitar la v. a alguien** to kill sb; **¿qué es de tu v.?** how's life?; **v. amorosa** love life; **v. campestre** country life; **la v. estudiantil** student life; **v. eterna** eternal life; **v. de familia** family life; **v. laboral** working life; **v. matrimonial** married life; **v. privada** private life; **v. sana** clean living; **v. sentimental** love life; **v. sexual** sex life; **v. social** social life; **v. útil** shelf life

(b) *(expresiones)* **amargarse la v.** to make one's life a misery; **buscarse la v.** to try to earn one's own living; **dar la v. por** to give one's life for; **de toda la v.** *(amigo)* lifelong; **le conozco de toda la v.** I've known him all my life; **de por v.** for life; **una mujer de v. alegre** a loose woman; **en mi/tu/***etc* **v.** never (in my/your/*etc* life); **estar entre la v. y la muerte** to be at death's door; **ganarse la v.** to earn a living; **pasar a mejor v.** to pass away; **pasarse la v. haciendo algo** to spend one's life doing sth; **se pasa la v. quejándose** he does nothing but complain all the time; **su v. es el teatro** the theater is her life; **¡así es la v.!** that's life!, such is life!; **darse** *o* **pegarse la gran v., darse** *o* **pegarse la v. padre** to live the life of Riley; **enterrarse en v.** to forsake the world; **la v. y milagros de alguien** sb's life story; **llevar una v. de perros** to lead a dog's life; **¡mi v.!, ¡v. mía!** my darling!; **tener siete vidas (como los gatos)** to have nine lives; **la otra v.** the next life

vidente *nmf* clairvoyant

vídeo, *Am* **video** *nm (aparato, sistema)* video; *(cinta)* video(tape); *(videoclip)* (pop) video; **en v.** on video; **grabar en v.** to videotape, to record on video; **cámara de v.** *(profesional)* video camera; *(de aficionado)* camcorder; **v. comunitario** = system enabling one video to be shown simultaneously on different television sets in one block of apartments; **v. doméstico** home video; **v. interactivo** interactive video

videoaficionado, -a *nm,f* = person who makes amateur videos

videocámara *nf* camcorder

videocasete *nm* video, videocassette

videocinta *nf* video, videotape

videoclip *(pl* **videoclips)** *nm* (pop) video

videoclub *(pl* **videoclubs** *o* **videoclubes)** *nm* video (rental) store *o* shop

videoconferencia *nf* videoconference

videoconsola *nf* game console

videodisco *nm* videodisc

videoedición *nf* video editing

videojuego *nm* video game

videoportero *nm* video intercom entry system

videoteca *nf* video library

videoteléfono *nm* videophone

videoterminal *nm* video terminal

videotexto *nm,* **videotex** *nm inv (por señal de televisión)* teletext; *(por línea telefónica)* videotex, viewdata

vidorra *nf Fam* **pegarse una gran v.** to live the life of Riley

vidriado, -a 1 *adj* glazed

  2 *nm* **(a)** *(técnica)* glazing **(b)** *(material)* glaze

vidriar *vt* to glaze

vidriera *nf* **(a)** *(ventana)* glass window; *(en catedrales)* stained glass window **(b)** *Am (escaparate)* store *o* shop window

vidriero, -a *nm,f* **(a)** *(que fabrica cristales)* glass merchant *o* manufacturer **(b)** *(que coloca cristales)* glazier

vidrio *nm* **(a)** *(material)* glass; **v. de seguridad** safety glass **(b)** *(de ventana)* window (pane); *Am (de anteojos)* lens; *Am (de vehículo)* window; **pagar los vidrios rotos** to take the rap

vidrioso, -a *adj* **(a)** *(quebradizo)* brittle **(b)** *(tema, asunto)* thorny, delicate **(c)** *(ojos)* glazed

vieira *nf* scallop

viejo, -a 1 *adj* **(a)** *(persona, aparato)* old; **está muy v. para su edad** he looks very old for his age; **hacerse v.** to get *o* grow old; **esa ropa te hace más v.** those clothes make you look older **(b)** *(antiguo)* old; **un v. conocido** an old acquaintance

  2 *nm,f* **(a)** *(anciano)* old man, *f* old lady; **los viejos** the elderly; **los viejos del pueblo** the old people in the village; **llegar a v.** to live to be an old man; **v. verde** dirty old man **(b)** *Fam (padre, madre)* old man, *f* old girl; **mis viejos** my folks **(c)** *Am Fam (amigo)* pal, buddy **(d)** *Am* **V. de Pascua** Santa Claus

3 *nf Col, Méx,Ven Fam (mujer, chica)* woman

Viena *n* Vienna

viene *ver* **venir**

vienés, -esa *adj & nm,f* Viennese

viento *nm* **(a)** *(aire)* wind; **hace v.** it's windy; **vientos alisios** trade winds; **v. de cara** headwind; **v. de costado** crosswind; **v. fuerte** high winds; **v. de lado** crosswind; **v. del norte** north *o* northerly wind **(b)** *(cuerda)* guy (rope) **(c)** *Mús* wind; **la sección de v.** the wind section **(d)** *Náut (rumbo)* course, bearing **(e)** *(expresiones)* **a los cuatro vientos** from the rooftops; **contra v. y marea** in spite of everything; **despedir** *o* **echar a alguien con v. fresco** to send sb packing; **v. en popa** splendidly, very nicely

vientre *nm* **(a)** *(de persona)* stomach, belly; **hacer de v.** to have a bowel movement; **bajo v.** lower abdomen **(b)** *(de vasija)* belly, rounded part

viera *etc ver* **ver**

viernes *nm inv* Friday; **V. Santo** Good Friday; *ver también* **sábado**

vierto *etc ver* **verter**

viese *etc ver* **ver**

Vietnam *n* Vietnam

vietnamita *adj & nmf* Vietnamese

viga *nf (de madera)* beam, rafter; *(de metal)* girder; **v. maestra** main beam

vigencia *nf (de ley)* validity; *(de costumbre)* use

vigente *adj (ley)* in force; *(costumbre)* in use

vigésimo, -a *núm* twentieth

vigía 1 *nmf* lookout

  2 *nf (atalaya)* watchtower

vigilancia *nf* **(a)** *(cuidado)* vigilance **(b)** *(seguridad)* security; **tras la fuga aumentaron la v.** after the escape security was increased

vigilante 1 *adj* vigilant

  2 *nmf* guard; **v. nocturno** night watchman

vigilar 1 *vt (preso, banco)* to guard; *(niño, bolso)* to keep an eye on; *(enfermo)* to watch over; *(proceso)* to oversee; **vigila que nadie toque esto** make sure no one touches this; **me vigilan desde hace días** they've been watching me for days

  2 *vi* to keep watch; **v. por algo** to (keep a) watch over sth

vigilia *nf* **(a)** *(vela)* wakefulness; *(periodo)* period of wakefulness **(b)** *(insomnio)* sleeplessness **(c)** *(víspera)* vigil

vigor *nm* **(a)** *(fuerza)* vigor **(b)** *(vigencia)* **en v.** in force; **entrar en v.** to come into force, to take effect

vigorizador, -ora, vigorizante *adj (medicamento)* fortifying; *(actividad)* invigorating

vigorizar [14] *vt* to invigorate

vigoroso, -a *adj (robusto)* vigorous; *(colorido)* strong

vigués, -esa 1 *adj* of/from Vigo

  2 *nm,f* person from Vigo

VIH *nm (abrev de* **virus de la inmunodeficiencia humana)** HIV

vihuela *nf* vihuela, = guitar-like musical instrument

vikingo, -a *adj & nm,f* Viking

vil *adj* vile, despicable; *Hum* **el v. metal** filthy lucre

vileza *nf* **(a)** *(acción)* vile *o* despicable act **(b)** *(cualidad)* vileness

vilipendiar *vt* **(a)** *(ofender)* to vilify, to revile **(b)** *(despreciar)* to despise; *(humillar)* to humiliate

vilipendio *nm* **(a)** *(ofensa)* vilification **(b)** *(desprecio)* scorn, contempt; *(humillación)* humiliation

vilipendioso, -a *adj* **(a)** *(ofensivo)* vilifying **(b)** *(despreciativo)* scornful, contemptuous; *(humillante)* humiliating

villa *nf* **(a)** *(población)* small town; **v. olímpica** Olympic village **(b)** *(casa)* villa, country house **(c)** *Arg, Bol* **v. miseria** shantytown

Villadiego *nm Fam* **tomar** *o Esp* **coger las de V.** to take to one's heels

villancico *nm (navideño)* Christmas carol

villanía *nf* vile *o* despicable act, villainy

villano, -a 1 *adj* villainous

    2 *nm,f* villain

villorrio *nm Pey* one-horse town, backwater

Vilna *n* Vilnius

vilo *nm* **en v.** *(suspendido)* in the air, suspended; *(inquieto)* on tenterhooks; **tener a alguien en v.** to keep sb in suspense

vinagre *nm* vinegar; **v. de malta** malt vinegar; **v. de vino** wine vinegar

vinagrera *nf (vasija)* vinegar bottle; **vinagreras** *(para aceite y vinagre)* cruet set

vinagreta *nf* vinaigrette, French dressing

vinajera *nf* cruet, = vessel holding wine or water in Catholic mass

vinatero, -a *nm,f* vintner, wine merchant

vinculación *nf* link, connection

vinculante *adj Der* binding

vincular 1 *vt* **(a)** *(enlazar)* to link; *(por obligación)* to tie, to bind **(b)** *Der* to entail

    2 vincularse *vpr (enlazarse)* **vincularse con** *o* **a** to form links with

vínculo *nm* **(a)** *(lazo) (entre hechos, países)* link; *(personal, familiar)* tie, bond **(b)** *Der* entail

vindicación *nf* **(a)** *(venganza)* vengeance, revenge **(b)** *(defensa, rehabilitación)* vindication

vindicar [59] *vt* **(a)** *(vengar)* to avenge, to revenge **(b)** *(defender, rehabilitar)* to vindicate **(c)** *(reivindicar)* to claim

vindicatorio, -a, vindicativo, -a *adj (reivindicativo)* in defense (**de** of)

vinería *nf Am* wine store *o* shop

vinícola *adj (país, región)* wine-producing; **industria v.** wine industry

vinicultor, -ora *nm,f* wine producer

vinicultura *nf* wine producing

viniera *etc ver* **venir**

vinilo *nm* vinyl

vino 1 *ver* **venir**

    2 *nm* wine; **v. blanco/tinto** white/red wine; **v. de la casa** house wine; **v. clarete** light red wine; **v. dulce/seco** sweet/dry wine; **v. espumoso** sparkling wine; **v. generoso** full-bodied wine; **v. de mesa** table wine; **v. peleón** cheap wine; **v. rosado** rosé

viña *nf* vineyard

viñador, -ora *nm,f (productor)* wine grower; *(dueño)* vineyard owner; *(trabajador)* vineyard worker

viñedo *nm* (large) vineyard

viñeta *nf* **(a)** *(de tebeo)* (individual) cartoon **(b)** *(de libro)* vignette

vio *ver* **ver**

viola 1 *nf* viola

    2 *nmf* viola player

violáceo, -a *adj & nm* violet

violación *nf* **(a)** *(de ley, derechos)* violation, infringement **(b)** *(de persona)* rape **(c) v. de domicilio** unlawful entry

violador, -ora *adj & nm,f* rapist

violar *vt* **(a)** *(ley, derechos)* to violate, to infringe **(b)** *(persona)* to rape

violencia *nf* **(a)** *(agresividad)* violence; **v. doméstica** domestic violence **(b)** *(de viento, pasiones)* force **(c)** *(incomodidad)* awkwardness

violentar 1 *vt* **(a)** *(incomodar)* **v. a alguien** to make sb feel awkward **(b)** *(forzar) (cerradura)* to force; *(domicilio)* to break into

    2 violentarse *vpr (incomodarse)* to feel awkward

violento, -a *adj* **(a)** *(persona, deporte, acción)* violent; *(pasión, tempestad)* intense; **muerte violenta** violent death **(b)** *(incómodo)* awkward; **me resulta v. hablar con ella** I feel awkward talking to her

violeta 1 *nf (flor)* violet

    2 *adj inv & nm (color)* violet

violetera *nf* violet seller

violín 1 *nm* violin

    2 *nmf* violinist

violinista *nmf* violinist

violón 1 *nm* double bass

    2 *nmf* double bass player

violonchelista, violoncelista *nmf* cellist

violonchelo, violoncelo 1 *nm* cello

    2 *nmf* cellist

VIP [bip] *nmf (abrev de* **very important person***)* VIP

viperino, -a *adj* venomous

virada *nf* **(a)** *(vuelta)* turn **(b)** *Náut* tack

viraje *nm* **(a)** *(giro) Aut* turn; *Náut* tack **(b)** *(curva)* bend, curve **(c)** *Fot* toning **(d)** *(cambio)* change of direction

viral *adj* viral

virar 1 *vt* **(a)** *(girar) Náut* to tack, to put about **(b)** *Fot* to tone

    2 *vi (girar)* to turn (around); **v. en redondo** to turn around; *Fig (persona)* to do an about-face *o* a volte-face *o* a U-turn; *(ideas, política)* to change radically

virgen 1 *adj (en general)* virgin; *(cinta)* blank; *(película)* unused

    2 *nmf (persona)* virgin

    3 *nf Arte* Madonna; *Rel* **la V.** the Virgin (Mary)

virginal *adj (puro)* virginal

Virginia *n* Virginia; **V. Occidental** West Virginia

virginiano, -a *Am* **1** *adj* Virgo; **ser v.** to be (a) Virgo

    2 *nm,f* Virgo

virginidad *nf* virginity

virgo 1 *nm* **(a)** *(virginidad)* virginity; *(himen)* hymen **(b)** *(zodiaco)* Virgo; *Esp* **ser V.** to be (a) Virgo

    2 *nmf Esp (persona)* Virgo

virguería *nf Fam* gem; **hacer virguerías** to do wonders

vírico, -a *adj* viral

viril *adj* virile, manly

virilidad *nf* virility

virola *nf (de bastón, paraguas)* ferrule

virolento, -a *adj* pockmarked

virología *nf* virology

virólogo, -a *nm,f* virologist

virreina *nf* vicereine

virreinato, virreino *nm* viceroyalty

virrey *nm* viceroy

virtual *adj* **(a)** *(posible)* possible, potential **(b)** *(casi real)* virtual

virtualidad *nf* potential

virtud 1 *nf* **(a)** *(cualidad)* virtue; **la principal v. de este método es que...** the principal virtue of this method is that...; **v. cardinal/teologal** cardinal/theological virtue **(b)** *(poder, facultad)* power; **tener la v. de** to have the power *o* ability to

    2 en virtud de by virtue of; **en v. del tratado de París, cedieron varios territorios** under the Paris treaty they ceded several territories

virtuosismo *nm* virtuosity

virtuoso, -a 1 *adj (honrado)* virtuous

    2 *nm,f (genio)* virtuoso

viruela *nf* **(a)** *(enfermedad)* smallpox **(b)** *(pústula)* pockmark; **picado de viruelas** pockmarked

virulé *nf Fam* **a la v.** *(torcido)* skew-gee; **un ojo a la v.** a shiner, a black eye

virulencia *nf también Fig* virulence

virulento, -a *adj también Fig* virulent

virus *nm inv* virus; **v. informático** computer virus; **v. del sida** AIDS virus

viruta *nf* shaving

vis *nf* (**a**) **v. a v.** face-to-face meeting (**b**) **v. cómica** sense of humor

visado *nm, Am* **visa** *nf* visa; **v. de entrada** entry visa; **v. de salida** exit visa; **v. de tránsito** transit visa

visar *vt (pasaporte)* to put a visa in

víscera *nf* internal organ; **vísceras** entrails

visceral *adj también Fig* visceral; **un sentimiento/una reacción v.** a gut feeling/reaction

viscosa *nf (tejido)* viscose

viscosidad *nf* (**a**) *(cualidad)* viscosity (**b**) *(substancia)* slime

viscoso, -a *adj (denso)* viscous; *(baboso)* slimy

visera *nf* (**a**) *(de gorra)* peak (**b**) *(de casco, suelta)* visor (**c**) *(de automóvil)* sun visor

visibilidad *nf* visibility

visible *adj* visible; **estar v.** *(presentable)* to be decent *o* presentable

visigodo, -a 1 *adj* Visigothic

2 *nm,f* Visigoth

visigótico, -a *adj* Visigothic

visillo *nm* sheer curtain, lace curtain

visión *nf* (**a**) *(sentido, lo que se ve)* sight (**b**) *(alucinación, lucidez)* vision; **ver visiones** to be seeing things; **tener v. de futuro** to be forward-looking (**c**) *(punto de vista)* (point of) view; **una v. clara de la situación** a clear view *o* appreciation of the situation

visionar *vt Cine* to view *(during production or before release)*

visionario, -a *adj & nm,f* visionary

visir *nm* vizier

visita *nf* (**a**) *(acción) (en general)* visit; *(breve)* call; **estar de v.** to be visiting *o* on a visit; **hacer una v. a alguien** to visit sb, to pay sb a visit; **hacer una v. a un museo** to visit *o* go to a museum; **hacer una v. turística de la ciudad** to do some sightseeing in the city; **ir de v.** to go visiting; *Med* **pasar v.** to see one's patients; **v. de cortesía** *o* **cumplido** courtesy visit *o* call; **v. guiada** guided tour; **visitas médicas** doctor's rounds; **v. relámpago** flying visit (**b**) *(visitante)* visitor; **tener v.** *o* **visitas** to have visitors (**c**) *(a página web)* hit

visitador, -ora 1 *adj* fond of visiting

2 *nm,f* (**a**) *(de laboratorio)* medical sales representative (**b**) *(visitante)* visitor

visitante 1 *adj Dep* visiting, away

2 *nmf* visitor

visitar *vt (en general)* to visit; **el médico visitó al paciente** the doctor called on *o* visited the patient

vislumbrar 1 *vt* (**a**) *(entrever)* to make out, to discern (**b**) *(adivinar)* to have an inkling of

2 vislumbrarse *vpr* (**a**) *(entreverse)* to be barely visible (**b**) *(adivinarse)* to become a little clearer

vislumbre *nf también Fig* glimmer

viso *nm* (**a**) *(aspecto)* **tener visos de** to seem; **tiene visos de verdad** it seems pretty true; **tiene visos de hacerse realidad** it could become a reality (**b**) *(reflejo) (de tejido)* sheen; *(de metal)* glint (**c**) *(de prenda)* lining

visón *nm* mink; **abrigo de v.** mink coat

visor *nm* (**a**) *Fot* viewfinder (**b**) *(de arma)* sight (**c**) *(en fichero)* file tab

víspera *nf* (**a**) *(día antes)* day before, eve; **en vísperas de** on the eve of (**b**) *Rel* **vísperas** evensong, vespers

vista 1 *adj ver* **visto**

2 *nf* (**a**) *(sentido)* sight, eyesight; *(ojos)* eyes; **tiene buena/mala v., está bien/mal de la v.** she has good/poor eyesight; **perder la v.** to lose one's sight, to go blind; **corto**

de v. shortsighted; **v. cansada** eyestrain

(**b**) *(observación)* watching

(**c**) *(mirada)* gaze; **dirigió la v. hacia la pantalla** she turned her eyes *o* gaze to the screen; **fijar la v. en** to fix one's eyes on, to stare at; **a primera** *o* **simple v.** *(aparentemente)* at first sight, on the face of it

(**d**) *(panorama)* view; **una habitación con vistas** a room with a view; **con vistas al mar** with a sea view; **v. frontal** front view; **v. lateral** side view; **v. panorámica** bird's-eye view

(**e**) *Der* hearing

(**f**) *Com* **a la v.** at sight

(**g**) *(expresiones)* **a v. de pájaro** seen from above; **conocer a alguien de v.** to know sb by sight; **hacer la v. gorda** to turn a blind eye; **¡hasta la v.!** see you!; **no perder de v. a algo/alguien** *(vigilar)* not to let sth/sb out of one's sight; *(tener en cuenta)* not to lose sight of sth/sb, not to forget about sth/sb; **perder de v.** *(dejar de ver)* to lose sight of; *(perder contacto)* to lose touch with; **saltar a la v.** to be blindingly obvious; **tener v.** to have vision *o* foresight; **volver la v. atrás** to look back

3 a la vista *loc adj* **estar a la v.** *(visible)* to be visible; *(muy cerca)* to be staring one in the face

4 a la vista de *loc prep (delante de)* in full view of; *(en vista de)* in view of

5 con vistas a *loc prep (con la intención de)* with a view to

6 en vista de *loc prep* in view of, considering; **en v. de que** since, seeing as

vistazo *nm* glance, quick look; **echar** *o* **dar un v. a** to have a quick look at

viste *ver* **ver**

vistiera *etc ver* **vestir**

visto, -a 1 *participio ver* **ver**

2 *ver* **vestir**

3 *adj* **estar muy v.** to be old hat; **ese modelo está muy v.** that model's really old *o* ancient; **estar bien/mal v.** to be considered good/frowned upon; **está v. que hoy no tendremos tranquilidad** it's quite clear that *o* obviously we're not going to get any peace today; **es lo nunca v.** you've never seen anything like it; **fue v. y no v.** it happened just like that, it was over in a flash

4 *nm* **v. bueno** *(en documento)* approved; **el v. bueno** *(aprobación)* the go-ahead; **dar el v. bueno (a algo)** to give (sth) the go-ahead

5 visto que *loc conj* seeing as, given that

6 por lo visto *loc adv* apparently; **por lo v. no han aceptado la idea** apparently they haven't accepted the idea, they don't seem *o* appear to have accepted the idea

vistosidad *nf* brightness, colorfulness

vistoso, -a *adj* eye-catching

Vístula *nm* **el V.** the Vistula

visual 1 *adj* visual

2 *nf* line of sight

visualización *nf* (**a**) *(en general)* visualization (**b**) *Inform* display

visualizador *nm Inform* viewer

visualizar [14] *vt* (**a**) *(en general)* to visualize (**b**) *Inform* to display

vital *adj* (**a**) *(de la vida, esencial)* vital; **ciclo v.** life cycle (**b**) *(persona)* full of life, vivacious

vitalicio, -a 1 *adj* for life, life; **renta vitalicia** life annuity

2 *nm* (**a**) *(pensión)* life annuity (**b**) *(seguro)* life insurance policy

vitalidad *nf* vitality

vitalismo *nm* vitality

vitalista *adj* dynamic

vitalizar [14] *vt* to vitalize

vitamina *nf* vitamin

vitaminado, -a *adj* with added vitamins, vitamin-enriched

vitamínico, -a *adj* vitamin; **complejo v.** vitamin complex

vitícola *adj (región, industria)* grape-producing

viticultor, -ora *nm,f* grape grower, viticulturist

viticultura *nf* grape growing, viticulture

vitivinícola *adj (región)* wine-producing; **producción v.** wine production

vítor *nm* cheer; **los vítores de la multitud** the cheers *or* cheering of the crowd

vitorear *vt* to cheer

Vitoria *n* Vitoria

vitoriano, -a *adj* **1** of/from Vitoria

2 *nmf* person from Vitoria

vitral *nm* stained-glass window

vítreo, -a *adj* vitreous

vitrificar [59] *vt* to vitrify

vitrina *nf (en casa)* display cabinet; *(en tienda)* showcase, glass case; *Am (escaparate)* store *o* shop window

vitriolo *nm* vitriol

vitrocerámica *nf* **cocina (de) v.** ceramic burner

vituallas *nfpl* provisions

vituperar *vt* to criticize harshly, to condemn

vituperio *nm* harsh criticism, condemnation

viudedad *nf* **(a)** *(viudez) (de mujer)* widowhood; *(de hombre)* widowerhood **(b)** **(pensión de) v.** widow's/widower's pension

viudez *nf (de mujer)* widowhood; *(de hombre)* widowerhood

viudo, -a **1** *adj* widowed

2 *nm,f* widower, *f* widow

viva 1 *nm* cheer

2 *interj* ¡v.! hurray!; ¡v. el rey! long live the King!

vivac *(pl vivacs) nm* bivouac; **hacer v.** to bivouac

vivacidad *nf* liveliness

vivalavirgen *nmf inv* = person with a devil-may-care attitude

vivales *nmf inv* crafty person

vivamente *adv* **(a)** *(relatar, describir)* vividly **(b)** *(afectar, emocionar)* deeply

vivaque *nm* bivouac

vivaquear *vi* to bivouac

vivaracho, -a *adj* lively, vivacious

vivaz *adj* **(a)** *(despierto)* alert, sharp **(b)** *Bot* perennial

vivencia *nf* experience

víveres *nmpl* provisions, food (supplies)

vivero *nm* **(a)** *(de plantas)* nursery **(b)** *(de peces)* fish farm; *(de moluscos)* bed **(c)** **v. (de empresas)** business incubator

viveza *nf* **(a)** *(de colorido, descripción)* vividness **(b)** *(de persona, discusión, ojos)* liveliness; *(de ingenio, inteligencia)* sharpness

vivido, -a *adj* real-life, true

vívido, -a *adj* vivid

vividor, -ora *nm,f* parasite, scrounger

vivienda *nf* **(a)** *(casa)* home; **primera/segunda v.** first/second home; **la carestía de las viviendas en la capital** the high cost of housing in the capital; **v. de protección oficial** = low-cost home subsidized by the government; **v. de renta limitada** public-housing property with fixed maximum rent **(b)** *(alojamiento)* housing; **plan de v.** housing plan

viviente *adj* living

vivificante *adj (que da vida)* life-giving; *(que reanima)* revitalizing

vivificar [59] *vt (dar vida)* to give life to; *(reanimar)* to revitalize

vivíparo, -a *adj* viviparous

vivir 1 *vi* **(a)** *(existir, residir, subsistir)* to live; **vivió noventa años** she lived for ninety years; **alcanzar** *o* **dar para v.** *(sujeto: sueldo, pensión)* to be enough to live on; **v. de** to live on *o* off; **v. para algo/alguien** to live for sth/sb; **v. bien**

(económicamente) to be well-off; *(en armonía)* to be happy; **no dejar v. a alguien** not to give sb any peace; **¿quién vive?** who goes there?; **v. para ver** who'd have thought it? **(b)** *(estar vivo)* to be alive; **todavía vive** he's still alive

2 *vt (experimentar)* to live through; **he vivido momentos difíciles** I've gone through *o* had some difficult times

vivisección *nf* vivisection

vivito, -a *adj Fam* **v. y coleando** alive and kicking

vivo, -a 1 *adj* **(a)** *(ser, lengua)* living; **un animal v.** a live animal; **estar v.** *(persona, costumbre, recuerdo)* to be alive; **v. o muerto** dead or alive **(b)** *(dolor, deseo, olor)* intense; *(luz, color, tono)* bright; **un v. interés por algo** a lively interest in sth **(c)** *(gestos, ojos, descripción)* lively, vivid; **es el v. retrato de su padre** he's the spitting image of his father **(d)** *(ingenio, niño)* quick, sharp; *(ciudad)* lively **(e)** *(genio)* quick, hot

2 *nm,f* **los vivos** the living

3 *nm* **en v.** *(en directo)* live; *(sin anestesia)* without anesthetic

vizcaíno, -a *adj & nm,f* Biscayan

Vizcaya *n* Vizcaya; **Golfo de V.** Bay of Biscay

vizconde, -esa *nm,f* viscount, *f* viscountess

V.O. *nf (abrev de* **versión original***)* original language version; **V.O. subtitulada** subtitled version

vocablo *nm* word, term

vocabulario *nm* **(a)** *(riqueza léxica)* vocabulary **(b)** *(diccionario)* dictionary

vocación *nf* vocation, calling

vocacional 1 *adj* vocational

2 *nf Méx Fam* technical college

vocal 1 *adj* vocal

2 *nmf* member

3 *nf* vowel

vocálico, -a *adj* **sonido v.** vowel sound

vocalista *nmf* vocalist

vocalización *nf* vocalization

vocalizar [14] *vi* to enunciate clearly

vocativo *nm* vocative

vocear 1 *vt* **(a)** *(gritar)* to shout out, to call out **(b)** *(llamar)* to shout to, to call to **(c)** *(vitorear)* to cheer **(d)** *(pregonar) (mercancía)* to hawk; *(secreto)* to publicize

2 *vi (gritar)* to shout

vocerío *nm* shouting

vocero, -a *nm,f (portavoz)* spokesperson

vociferante *adj* shouting

vociferar *vi* to shout

vocinglero, -a 1 *adj* **(a)** *(que grita mucho)* screaming, shrieking **(b)** *(que dice necedades)* loudmouthed

2 *nm,f* **(a)** *(persona gritona)* screamer, shrieker **(b)** *(persona que dice necedades)* loudmouth

vodevil *nm* variety (show), vaudeville

vodka ['boðka] *nm o nf* vodka

vol. *(abrev de* **volumen***)* vol

voladizo *nm* ledge

volado, -a *adj Fam (ido)* **estar v.** to be out of it

volador, -ora 1 *adj* flying

2 *nm* **(a)** *(pez)* flying fish **(b)** *(calamar)* = type of squid **(c)** *(cohete)* rocket

voladura *nf (en guerras, atentados)* blowing-up; *(de edificio en ruinas)* demolition *(with explosives)*; *Min* blasting

volandas: en volandas *loc adv* **levantar a alguien en v.** to lift sb off the ground; **la multitud le llevó en v.** the crowd carried him on their shoulders

volantazo *nm* **dar un v.** to slew one's car around, to swerve

volante 1 *adj* flying

2 *nm* **(a)** *(para conducir)* (steering) wheel; **estar** *o* **ir al v.** to be at the wheel **(b)** *(automovilismo)* auto racing **(c)** *(de tela)* frill, flounce **(d)** *Esp (del médico)* (referral) note **(e)** *(en bádminton)* shuttlecock **(f)** *Am (de propaganda)* leaflet

volantín *nm Carib, Chile* kite

volapié *nm Taurom* = method of killing the bull

volar [63] **1** *vi* (**a**) *(en el aire)* to fly; *(papeles)* to blow away; **hubo una pelea y empezaron a v. sillas y botellas** there was a fight and the chairs and bottles started to fly; **v. a** *(una altura)* to fly at; *(un lugar)* to fly to; **echar(se) a v.** to fly away *o* off; **salir volando** *(pájaro, insecto)* to fly off; *(papeles, sombrero, ceniza)* to blow away; **v. por los aires** *(estallar)* to be blown into the air (**b**) *Fam (desaparecer)* to disappear, to vanish (**c**) *(correr)* to fly (off), to rush (off); **v. a hacer algo** to rush off to do sth; **hacer algo volando** to do sth at top speed; **me voy volando** I must fly *o* dash (**d**) *(días, años)* to fly by

     2 *vt* (**a**) *(hacer estallar) (en guerras, atentados)* to blow up; *(caja fuerte, puerta)* to blow open; *(edificio en ruinas)* to demolish *(with explosives); Min* to blast (**b**) *Am Fam (robar)* to swipe

     3 volarse *vpr (papeles)* to be blown away

volatería *nf* birds, fowl

volátil *adj Quím & Fig* volatile

volatilidad *nf* volatility

volatilización *nf* volatilization

volatilizar [14] **1** *vt* to volatilize

     2 volatilizarse *vpr* (**a**) *Fís* to volatilize, to evaporate (**b**) *Fam (desaparecer)* to vanish into thin air

volatinero, -a *nm,f* acrobat

volcado *nm Inform* **v. de pantalla** screen dump; **v. de pantalla en impresora** hard copy

volcán *nm* volcano

volcánico, -a *adj* volcanic

volcar [67] **1** *vt* (**a**) *(tirar)* to knock over; *(carretilla)* to tip up (**b**) *(vaciar)* to empty out

     2 *vi (coche, camión)* to overturn; *(barco)* to capsize

     3 volcarse *vpr* (**a**) *(caerse)* to fall over (**b**) *(esforzarse)* to bend over backward (**con/en** for/in)

volea *nf* volley

volear *Dep* **1** *vt* to volley

     2 *vi* to volley

voleibol *nm* volleyball

voleo *nm* volley; **a** *o* **al v.** randomly, any old how; **sembrar a v.** to sow seed by hand

volframio *nm* wolfram

volitivo, -a *adj* voluntary

volován *nm* vol-au-vent

volqué *etc ver* **volcar**

volquete *nm* dump truck

voltaico, -a *adj* voltaic

voltaje *nm* voltage

volteador, -ora *nm,f* acrobat

voltear 1 *vt* (**a**) *(heno, crepe, torero)* to toss; *(tortilla)* to turn over; *(mesa, silla)* to turn upside down (**b**) *Am (derribar)* to knock over (**c**) *Am salvo RP (dar la vuelta)* to turn over; *(cabeza, espalda)* to turn

     2 *vi* (**a**) *Méx (doblar la esquina)* to turn (**b**) *Méx (volcar) (auto)* to overturn (**c**) *Andes (girar) (persona)* to turn (around)

     3 voltearse *vpr* (**a**) *Am salvo RP (volverse)* to turn around (**b**) *Méx (vehículo)* to overturn

voltereta *nf (en el suelo)* handspring; *(en el aire)* somersault; **dar una v.** to do a somersault; **v. lateral** cartwheel

voltímetro *nm* voltmeter

voltio *nm* (**a**) *(electricidad)* volt (**b**) *Fam (paseo)* walk, stroll; **dar un v.** to go for a walk

volubilidad *nf* changeability, fickleness

voluble *adj* (**a**) *(persona)* changeable, fickle (**b**) *Bot* climbing

volumen *nm* (**a**) *(de sonido)* volume; **subir/bajar el v.** to turn up/down the volume; **sube el v. que no te oímos** speak up, please, we can't hear you; **a todo v.** at full volume (**b**) *Com & Fin* volume; **v. de contratación** *(en Bolsa)* trading volume; **v. de negocio** *o* **ventas** turnover (**c**) *(espacio ocupado)* size, bulk;

ocupa poco v. it doesn't take up a lot of space; **el sofá tiene un v. excesivo para la habitación** the sofa is too big for the room (**d**) *(libro)* volume

voluminoso, -a *adj* bulky

voluntad *nf* (**a**) *(determinación)* will, willpower; **tiene mucha/poca (fuerza de) v.** she has a very strong/weak will; **v. de hierro** iron will

     (**b**) *(deseo)* will; **no existe la v. política de resolver el problema** there isn't the political will to solve the problem; **contra la v. de alguien** against sb's will; **por causas ajenas a mi v.** for reasons beyond my control; **por v. propia** of one's own free will; **última v.** last will and testament

     (**c**) *(intención)* intention; **buena v.** goodwill; **mala v.** ill will

     (**d**) *(albedrío)* free will; **a v.** *(cuanto se quiere)* as much as one likes; **¿qué le debo? — la v.** what do I owe you? — whatever you think fit

voluntariado *nm (actividad)* voluntary work; *(voluntarios)* volunteers

voluntariedad *nf* (**a**) *(intencionalidad)* volition (**b**) *(no obligatoriedad)* voluntary nature

voluntario, -a 1 *adj* voluntary

     2 *nm,f* volunteer

voluntarioso, -a *adj* willing

voluntarismo *nm* will to succeed

voluptuosidad *nf* voluptuousness

voluptuoso, -a *adj* voluptuous

voluta *nf* spiral

volver [41] **1** *vt* (**a**) *(dar la vuelta a)* to turn around; *(lo de arriba abajo)* to turn over; *(lo de dentro fuera)* to turn inside out; **al v. la esquina** when we turned the corner (**b**) *(cabeza, ojos)* to turn (**c**) *(convertir en)* **eso le volvió un delincuente** that made him a criminal, that turned him a criminal; **la lejía volvió blanca la camisa** the bleach turned the shirt white

     2 *vi* (**a**) *(ir de vuelta)* to go back, to return; *(venir de vuelta)* to come back, to return; **yo allí no vuelvo** I'm not going back there; **vuelve, no te vayas** come back, don't go; **al v. pasé por el supermercado** I stopped off at the supermarket on the *o* my way back; **aún no ha vuelto del trabajo** she isn't back *o* hasn't got back from work yet; **v. en sí** to come to, to regain consciousness (**b**) *(reanudar)* **v. a la tarea** to return to one's work; *(hacer otra vez)* **v. a hacer algo** to do sth again; *Fig* **v. a nacer** to be reborn

     3 volverse *vpr* (**a**) *(darse la vuelta, girar la cabeza)* to turn around (**b**) *(ir de vuelta)* to go back, to return; *(venir de vuelta)* to come back, to return (**c**) *(convertirse en)* to become; **volverse loco/pálido** to go mad/pale (**d**) **volverse atrás** *(de una afirmación, promesa)* to go back on one's word; *(de una decisión)* to change one's mind, to back out; **volverse (en) contra (de) alguien** to turn against sb

vomitar 1 *vt* to vomit, to bring up

     2 *vi* to vomit, to be sick; *Fig* **me dan** *o* **entran ganas de v.** it makes me want to throw up

vomitera *nf* acute vomiting

vomitivo, -a 1 *adj* (**a**) *Med* emetic (**b**) *Fam (asqueroso)* sick-making

     2 *nm* emetic

vómito *nm* (**a**) *(acción)* vomiting (**b**) *(substancia)* vomit

vomitona *nf Fam* **me dio una v.** I threw up

voracidad *nf* voraciousness

vorágine *nf* confusion, whirl

voraz *adj* (**a**) *(persona, apetito)* voracious (**b**) *(fuego, enfermedad)* raging

vórtice *nm* (**a**) *(de agua)* whirlpool, vortex (**b**) *(de aire)* whirlwind

vos *pron personal Am* you

V.O.S.E. *nf (abrev de* **versión original subtitulada en**

español) = original language version subtitled in Spanish

voseo *nm* = practice of using the "vos" pronoun

vosotros, -as *pron personal*

> Usually omitted in Spanish except for emphasis or contrast.

Esp you *(plural)*; **v. bailáis muy bien** you dance very well; **son más fuertes que v.** they're stronger than you

votación *nf* vote, voting; **decidir algo por v.** to put sth to the vote; **v. a mano alzada** show of hands

votante *nmf* voter

votar 1 *vt* (a) *(partido, candidato)* to vote for; *(ley)* to vote on; **¿qué has votado, sí o no?** how did you vote, yes or no? (b) *(aprobar)* to pass, to approve *(by vote)*

2 *vi* to vote; **v. a favor de/en contra de alguien** to vote for/against sb; **v. por** *(emitir un voto por)* to vote for; *Fig (estar a favor de)* to be in favor of; **yo voto por ir a la playa** I'm for going to the beach; **v. por que…** to vote (that)…; **v. en blanco** to return a blank ballot paper

voto *nm* (a) *(en elección)* vote; **tres votos a favor/en contra** three votes in favor/against; **pide el v. para el partido reformista** she's asking people to vote for the reformist party; **v. afirmativo** vote in favor; **v. en contra** unmarked ballot; **v. de calidad** casting vote; **v. de castigo** vote against one's own party; **v. de censura** vote of no confidence; **v. de confianza** vote of confidence; **v. por correspondencia** *o* **correo** postal vote; **v. a favor** vote in favor; **v. nulo** spoiled ballot; **v. secreto** secret ballot; **v. útil** tactical voting

(b) *(derecho a votar)* **tener v.** to have a vote

(c) *Rel* vow; **hacer v. de** to vow to; **v. de castidad/pobreza/silencio** vow of chastity/poverty/silence

(d) *(ruego)* prayer, plea; **hacer votos por** to pray for; **votos de felicidad** best wishes

vox populi *nf* **ser v. que…** to be common knowledge that…

voy *ver* **ir**

voyeur [bwaˈjer] *(pl* **voyeurs)** *nmf* voyeur

voyeurismo [bwajeˈrismo] *nm* voyeurism

voyeurístico, -a [bwajeˈristiko, -a] *adj* voyeuristic

voz *nf* (a) *(sonido, habla, tono)* voice; **a media v.** in a low voice, under one's breath; **a v. en grito** at the top of one's voice; **aclarar** *o* **aclararse la v.** to clear one's throat; **alzar** *o* **levantar la v. a alguien** to raise one's voice to sb; **de viva v.** by word of mouth; **en v. alta** aloud; **en v. baja** softly, in a low voice; **mudó la v.** his voice broke; **tener la v. tomada** to be hoarse; **la v. de la conciencia** the voice of conscience; *Cine* **v. en off** voice-over

(b) *(grito)* shout; **decir algo a voces** to shout sth; **dar voces** to shout; **dar la v. de alerta** to raise the alarm; **v. de mando** order, command

(c) *(derecho a expresarse)* say, voice; **la v. de la experiencia/del pueblo** the voice of experience/of the people; **no tener ni v. ni voto** to have no say in the matter

(d) *(rumor)* rumor; **corre la v. de que va a dimitir** people are saying that she's going to resign; **¡corre la v.!** pass it on!

(e) *(cantante)* voice; **una de las mejores voces del país** one of the best voices in the country

(f) *(vocablo)* word

(g) *Gram* voice; **v. activa/pasiva** active/passive voice

(h) *(expresiones)* **pedir algo a voces** to be crying out for sth; **llevar la v. cantante** to be the boss

vozarrón *nm* loud voice

VPO *nf (abrev de* **vivienda de protección oficial)** = low-cost home subsidized by the government

vudú *nm* voodoo

vuelapluma: a vuelapluma *loc adv* **escribir algo a v.** to dash sth off

vuelco 1 *ver* **volcar**

2 *nm* upset; **dar un v.** *(coche)* to overturn; *(relaciones, vida)* to

change completely; *(empresa)* to go to ruin; **me dio un v. el corazón** my heart missed *o* skipped a beat

vuelo 1 *ver* **volar**

2 *nm* (a) *(gen)* & *Av* flight; **alzar** *o* **emprender** *o* **levantar el v.** *(despegar)* to take flight, to fly off; *Fig (irse de casa)* to fly the nest; **coger algo al v.** *(en el aire)* to catch sth in flight; *Fig (rápido)* to catch on to sth very quickly; **remontar el v.** to soar; **de altos vuelos, de mucho v.** of great importance; **no se oía el v. de una mosca** you could have heard a pin drop; **v. chárter** charter flight; **v. sin escalas** direct flight; **v. espacial** space flight; **v. libre** hang gliding; **v. sin motor** gliding; **vuelos nacionales** domestic flights; **v. de reconocimiento** reconnaissance flight; **v. regular** scheduled flight

(b) *(de vestido)* fullness; **una falda de v.** a full skirt

(c) *Arquit* projection

vuelque *etc ver* **volcar**

vuelta *nf* (a) *(giro)* turn; *(acción)* turning; **dar una v.** to turn around; **dar una v. a algo, dar vueltas a algo** *(girándolo)* to turn sth around; *(recorriéndolo)* to go around sth; **darse la v.** to turn around; *Mil* **media v.** about-turn; *Aut* U-turn; *Arg* **v. al mundo** *(noria)* Ferris wheel; *Taurom* **v. al ruedo** bullfighter's lap of honor

(b) *(parte opuesta)* back, other side; **dar la v. a** *(colchón, tortilla, disco, naipe)* to turn over; *también Fig* **a la v. de la esquina** around the corner; **a la v. de la página** over the page

(c) *(regreso, devolución)* return; **a la v.** *(volviendo)* on the way back; *(al llegar)* on one's return; **estar de v.** to be back

(d) *(paseo)* **dar una v.** *(a pie)* to go for a walk; *(en vehículo)* to go for a drive *o* spin; **dar vueltas** *(en vehículo)* to drive around and around

(e) *Dep* lap; **v. (ciclista)** tour; **v. de honor** lap of honor

(f) *(ronda, turno)* *(de elecciones, competición deportiva)* round; *Dep* **la primera/segunda v.** the first/second round

(g) *(dinero sobrante)* change

(h) *(cambio, avatar)* change; **dar la** *o* **una v.** to turn around completely

(i) *(de pantalón)* cuff; *(de manga)* cuff

(j) *(en labor de punto)* row

(k) *(expresiones)* **a la v. de** *(tras)* at the end of; **a v. de correo** by return mail; *Fam* **dar la v. a la tortilla** to turn the tables; *Fam* **darle cien vueltas a alguien** to run rings around sb; **dar una/dos/***etc* **vueltas de campana** *(vehículo)* to turn over once/twice/*etc*; **darle vueltas a algo** to turn sth over in one's mind; **estar de v. de algo** to be blasé about sth; **estar de v. de todo** to have seen it all before; **la cabeza me da vueltas** my head's spinning; **no tiene v. de hoja** there are no two ways about it; *Fam* **poner a alguien de v. y media** *(criticar)* to call sb all the names under the sun; *(regañar)* to give sb a good telling-off; **sin v. de hoja** irrevocable

vuelto, -a 1 *participio ver* **volver**

2 *adj* turned

3 *nm Am* change

vuelvo *etc ver* **volver**

vuestro, -a *Esp* **1** *adj posesivo* your; **v. libro/amigo** your book/friend; **este libro es v.** this book is yours; **un amigo v.** a friend of yours; **no es asunto v.** it's none of your business

2 *pron posesivo* **el v.** yours; **los vuestros están en la mesa** yours are on the table; *Fam* **ésta es la vuestra** this is the chance you've been waiting for *o* your big chance; **lo v. es el teatro** *(lo que hacéis bien)* theater is your thing; *Fam* **los vuestros** *(vuestra familia)* your folks; *(vuestro bando)* your lot, your side

vulcanología *nf* vulcanology

vulcanólogo, -a *nm,f* vulcanologist

vulgar *adj* (a) *(no refinado)* vulgar (b) *(corriente, común)* ordinary, common (c) *(no técnico)* nontechnical, lay

vulgaridad *nf* (**a**) *(grosería)* vulgarity; **hacer/decir una v.** to do/say something vulgar (**b**) *(banalidad)* banality

vulgarismo *nm Gram* vulgarism

vulgarización *nf* popularization

vulgarizar [14] **1** *vt* to popularize

2 vulgarizarse *vpr* to become popular *o* common

vulgo *nm* **el v.** *(plebe)* the masses, the common people; *(no expertos)* the lay public

vulnerabilidad *nf* vulnerability

vulnerable *adj* vulnerable

vulneración *nf* (**a**) *(de prestigio, reputación)* harming, damaging; *(de intimidad)* invasion (**b**) *(de ley, pacto)* violation, infringement

vulnerar *vt* (**a**) *(prestigio, reputación)* to harm, to damage; *(intimidad)* to invade (**b**) *(ley, pacto)* to violate, to break

vulva *nf* vulva

W

W, w [uβe'ðoβle] *nf (letra)* W, w

walkie-talkie [*Esp* 'walki'talki, *Am* 'woki'toki] (*pl* **walkie-talkies**) *nm* walkie-talkie

walkiria [bal'kiria] *nf* Valkyrie

walkman® ['walman] (*pl* **walkmans**) *nm* Walkman®

WAP [wap] *nm Inform (abrev de* **Wireless Application Protocol**) WAP

Washington ['wasinton] *n* Washington

wáter [*Esp* 'bater, *Am* 'water] *nm* toilet

waterpolista [waterpo'lista] *nmf* water-polo player

waterpolo [water'polo] *nm* water polo

watio ['batio] *nm* watt

WC [*Esp* uβe'θe, *Am* doβleβe'se] *nm (abrev de* **water closet**) WC *(room)*

web [weβ] *Inform* **1** *nm o nf (página Web)* web site **2** *nf (World Wide Web)* **la Web** the Web

weblog ['weβloɣ] (*pl* **weblogs**) *n Inform* weblog

Wellington ['welinton] *n* Wellington

western ['wester] (*pl* **westerns**) *nm Cine* Western

whiskería [wiske'ria] *nf* = bar where hostesses chat with clients

whisky ['wiski] (*pl* **whiskys**) *nm* whiskey; **w. escocés** Scotch whiskey; **w. de malta** malt whiskey

windsurf ['winsurf], **windsurfing** ['winsurfin] *nm* windsurfing

windsurfista [winsur'fista] *nmf* windsurfer

wireless ['waiales] *adj Inform (tecnología, red)* wireless

WWW (*abrev de* **World Wide Web**) WWW

X

X, x ['ekis] **1** *nf (letra)* X, x
  2 *nmf* **la señora X** Mrs. X
xenofobia *nf* xenophobia
xenófobo, -a 1 *adj* xenophobic
  2 *nm,f* xenophobe
xenón *nm Quím* xenon
xerocopia *nf* photocopy
xerografía *nf* photocopying

xerografiar [32] *vt* to photocopy
xilofón *nm* xylophone
xilofonista *nmf* xylophone player
xilófono *nm* xylophone
xilografía *nf* (**a**) *(técnica)* woodcut printing (**b**) *(impresión)* woodcut
Xunta [ʃunta] *nf* = autonomous government of the Spanish region of Galicia

Y

Y, y [iˈvrjeɣa] *nf (letra)* Y, y

y *conj*

> **e** is used instead of **y** before words beginning with **i** or **hi** (e.g. **Pérez e hijos** Perez and Sons).

(**a**) *(en general)* and; **un ordenador y una impresora** a computer and a printer; **horas y horas de espera** hours and hours of waiting (**b**) *(en preguntas)* what about; **¿y tu mujer?** what about your wife?

ya 1 *adv* (**a**) *(en el pasado)* already; **ya me lo habías contado** you had already told me; **¿llamaron o han llamado ya?** have they called yet?; **¿habrán llegado ya?** will they have arrived yet *o* by now?; **ya en 1926** as long ago as 1926

(**b**) *(ahora)* now; **bueno, yo ya me voy** right, I'm off now; **¡ya voy!** I'm coming!

(**c**) *(en frases negativas)* **ya no me duele** it doesn't hurt anymore, it no longer hurts; **ya no es así** it's no longer like that

(**d**) *(inmediatamente)* at once; **hay que hacer algo ya** something has to be done now *o* at once

(**e**) *(en el futuro)* **ya te llamaré** I'll call you sometime; **¡ya te agarraré yo a ti!** I'll get you sooner or later!; **ya hablaremos** we'll talk later; **ya verás** you'll (soon) see

(**f**) *(refuerza al verbo)* **ya entiendo/lo sé** I understand/know

2 *conj* (**a**) *(distributiva)* **ya (sea) por... ya (sea) por...** whether for... or... (**b**) *(adversativa)* **ya no... sino...**, **no ya... sino...** not only... but... (**c**) *(consecutiva)* **ya que** since; **ya que has venido, ayúdame con esto** since you're here, give me a hand with this

3 *interj* **¡ya!** *(expresa asentimiento)* right!; *(expresa comprensión)* yes!; *Irónico* **¡ya, ya!** sure!, yes, of course!

yac *(pl* **yacs)** *nm* yak

yacaré *nm* cayman

yacente, yaciente *adj (tumbado)* lying; *Arte* recumbent, reclining

yacer [71] *vi* (**a**) *(estar tumbado, enterrado)* to lie; **aquí yace...** here lies... (**b**) *(tener relaciones sexuales)* to lie together

yaciente = yacente

yacimiento *nm (minero)* bed, deposit; *(arqueológico)* site; **y. de petróleo** oil field

yago *ver* yacer

yak *(pl* **yaks)** *nm* yak

Yakarta *n* Jakarta

yanqui 1 *adj* (**a**) *Hist* Yankee (**b**) *Fam (estadounidense)* American; **un político y.** an American politician

2 *nmf* (**a**) *Hist* Yankee (**b**) *Fam (estadounidense)* Yank

yantar *Anticuado* **1** *nm* fare, food

2 *vt* to eat

Yaoundé [jaunˈde] *n* Yaoundé

yarda *nf* yard

yate *nm* yacht

yayo, -a *nm,f Fam* grandad, *f* grandma

yazco *ver* yacer

yazgo *ver* yacer

yedra *nf* ivy

yegua *nf* mare

yeguada *nf* herd of horses; **tiene una gran y.** he's got a lot of horses

yeísmo *nm* = pronunciation of Spanish "ll" as "y", widespread in practice, though regarded as incorrect by purists

yeísta *nmf* = person who pronounces Spanish "ll" as "y"

yelmo *nm* helmet

yema *nf* (**a**) *(de huevo)* yolk (**b**) *(de planta)* bud, shoot (**c**) *(de dedo)* fingertip (**d**) *Culin* = sweet made from sugar and egg yolk

Yemen *nm* (**el**) **Y.** Yemen

yemení *(pl* yemeníes**), yemenita** *adj & nmf* Yemeni

yen *nm* yen

yerba = hierba

yerbatero *nm Andes, Carib (curandero)* healer; *(vendedor de hierbas)* herbalist

Yereván *n* Yerevan

yergo *etc ver* erguir

yermar *vt* to leave unsown *o* fallow

yermo, -a 1 *adj* (**a**) *(estéril)* barren (**b**) *(despoblado)* uninhabited

2 *nm* wasteland

yerno *nm* son-in-law

yerro 1 *ver* errar

2 *nm* mistake, error

yerto, -a *adj* rigid, stiff

yesca *nf* tinder

yesería *nf (fábrica)* gypsum kiln

yesero, -a 1 *adj* plaster; **producción yesera** plaster production

2 *nm,f* (**a**) *(fabricante)* plaster manufacturer (**b**) *(obrero)* plasterer

yeso *nm* (**a**) *Geol* gypsum (**b**) *Constr* plaster (**c**) *Arte* gesso (**d**) *esp Am (vendaje)* plaster

yesquero *nm RP* cigarette lighter

yeta *nf RP Fam* **tener y.** to be jinxed

yeti *nm* yeti

yeyé *adj inv Fam* **música/ropa y.** sixties music/clothes

Yibuti *n* Djibouti

yiddish *nm* Yiddish

yihad [jiˈχað] *nf* jihad

yiu-yitsu *nm* jujitsu

yo

> Usually omitted as a personal pronoun in Spanish except for emphasis or contrast.

1 *pron personal* (**a**) *(sujeto)* I; **yo me llamo Luis** I'm called Luis (**b**) *(predicado)* **soy yo** it's me (**c**) **yo de ti/él/***etc* if I were you/him/etc; *Fam* **yo que tú/él/***etc* if I were you/him/etc

2 *nm Psi* **el yo** the ego

yodado, -a *adj* iodized

yodo *nm* iodine
yoduro *nm* iodide
yoga *nm* yoga
yogui *nmf* yogi
yogur (*pl* **yogures**), **yogurt** (*pl* **yogurts**) *nm* yogurt
yogurtera *nf* yogurt maker
yonqui *nmf Fam* junkie
yóquey *nm* jockey
yoyó *nm* yo-yo
yubarta *nf* humpback whale
yuca *nf* (**a**) *Bot* yucca (**b**) *Culin* cassava, manioc
Yucatán *n* (**el**) **Y.** (the) Yucatan
yudo *nm* judo
yudoka *nmf* judo player, judoist, judoka
yugo *nm también Fig* yoke
Yugoslavia *n* Yugoslavia

yugoslavo, -a 1 *adj* Yugoslavian
2 *nm,f* Yugoslav
yugular *adj & nf* jugular
yunque *nm* anvil
yunta *nf (de bueyes, vacas)* yoke, team
yupi *interj Fam* ¡**y.**! yippee!
yuppie ['jupi] (*pl* **yuppies**), **yupi** *nmf* yuppie
yute *nm* jute
yuxtaponer [50] **1** *vt* to juxtapose
2 yuxtaponerse *vpr* to be juxtaposed (**a** with)
yuxtaposición *nf* juxtaposition
yuxtapuesto, -a *participio ver* **yuxtaponer**
yuyería *nf RP* herbalist's
yuyo *nm* (**a**) *CSur (mala hierba)* weed; *(medicinal)* medicinal herb (**b**) *Andes (silvestre)* wild herb

Z

Z, z ['θeta] *nf (letra)* Z, z

zafacón *nm RDom (para basura)* trash can

zafado, -a *Am Fam* **1** *adj* nuts, crazy
2 *nm,f* nutcase

zafarrancho *nm* (**a**) *Náut* clearing of the decks; *Mil* **z. de combate** call to action stations (**b**) *(destrozo)* mess (**c**) *(riña)* row, fracas

zafarse *vpr* to get out of it, to escape; **z. de** *(persona)* to get rid of; *(obligación)* to get out of

zafiedad *nf* roughness, uncouthness

zafio, -a *adj* rough, uncouth

zafiro *nm* sapphire

zaga *nf Dep* defense; **a la z.** behind, at the back; *Fam* **no irle a la z. a alguien** to be every bit *o* just as good as sb

zagal, -ala *nm,f* (**a**) *(muchacho)* adolescent, teenager (**b**) *(pastor)* shepherd, *f* shepherdess

zaguán *nm* (entrance) hall

zaguero, -a *nm,f Dep* defender; *(en rugby)* fullback

zaherir *vt* (**a**) *(herir)* to hurt (**b**) *(burlarse de)* to mock (**c**) *(criticar)* to pillory

zahorí *(pl* **zahoríes)** *nmf* (**a**) *(de agua)* water diviner (**b**) *(clarividente)* mindreader

zaino, -a *adj* (**a**) *(caballo)* chestnut (**b**) *(res)* black

Zaire *n Antes* Zaire

zaireño, -a *adj & nm,f* Zairean

zalamería *nf* flattery, fawning

zalamero, -a **1** *adj* flattering, fawning
2 *nm,f* flatterer

zamarra *nf* sheepskin jacket

Zambia *n* Zambia

zambo, -a **1** *adj* knock-kneed
2 *nm,f Am* = person who has one Black and one Indian parent

zambomba **1** *nf Mús* type of rustic drum
2 *interj Fam* **¡z.!** wow!

zambombazo *nm* (**a**) *(ruido)* bang (**b**) *Dep* cracker of a shot, rocket

zambra *nf* (**a**) *(fiesta morisca)* Moorish festival (**b**) *(baile gitano)* = Andalusian Gypsy dance

zambullida *nf* dive; **darse una z.** *(baño)* to go for a dip

zambullir **1** *vt* to dip, to submerge
2 **zambullirse** *vpr (agua)* to dive (**en** into); *(actividad)* to immerse oneself (**en** in)

zamorano, -a **1** *adj* of/from Zamora
2 *nm,f* person from Zamora

zampabollos *nmf inv Fam* human garbage can

zampar *Fam* **1** *vt Am* (**a**) *(meter)* to shove, to stick (**b**) *(decir)* to say (right out)
2 *vi* to gobble
3 **zamparse** *vpr* to wolf down

zampoña *nf* panpipes

zanahoria *nf* carrot

zanca *nf (de ave)* leg, shank

zancada *nf* stride

zancadilla *nf* trip; **poner una** *o* **la z. a alguien** *(hacer tropezar)* to trip sb up; *Fig* to put a spoke in sb's wheel

zancadillear *vt* **z. a alguien** to trip sb up; *Fig* to put a spoke in sb's wheel

zanco *nm* stilt

zancuda *nf* wader

zancudo, -a **1** *adj* long-legged
2 *nm Am* mosquito

zanganear *vi Fam* to laze about

zángano, -a **1** *nm,f Fam (persona)* lazy oaf, idler
2 *nm (abeja)* drone

zanja *nf* ditch

zanjar *vt (poner fin a)* to put an end to; *(resolver)* to settle, to resolve

zapa *nf* **les acusó de hacer labor de z.** he accused them of undermining him

zapador *nm Mil* sapper

zapallito *nm CSur (planta)* zucchini

zapallo *nm Andes, RP (calabaza)* pumpkin; **z. (italiano)** zucchini

zapapico *nm* pickax

zapata *nf* (**a**) *(cuña)* wedge (**b**) *(de freno)* shoe

zapatazo *nm* stamp (of the foot)

zapateado *nm* = type of flamenco music and dance

zapatear *vi* to stamp one's feet

zapatería *nf* (**a**) *(oficio)* shoemaking (**b**) *(taller)* shoemaker's (**c**) *(tienda)* shoe store *o* shop

zapatero, -a **1** *adj* **industria zapatera** shoemaking industry
2 *nm,f* (**a**) *(fabricante)* shoemaker (**b**) *(reparador)* **z. de viejo** *o* **remendón** cobbler; *Fig* **¡z. a tus zapatos!** mind your own business! (**c**) *(vendedor)* shoe seller (**d**) *(insecto)* water strider, pond skater

zapatilla *nf* (**a**) *(de baile)* shoe, pump; *(de estar en casa)* slipper; *(de deporte)* sports shoe, sneaker; **zapatillas de lona** canvas shoes (**b**) *Méx (de tacón)* high-heeled shoe (**c**) *(de grifo)* washer

zapatillazo *nm* whack *(with a slipper)*

zapatismo *nm* (**a**) *Pol* Zapatism (**b**) *Hist* = movement led by the Mexican revolutionary Emiliano Zapata

zapatista **1** *adj Pol & Hist* Zapatista
2 *nmf Pol* Zapatista, = member of the Zapatista Front, a mainly indigenous insurrectionist group in the Southern Mexican state of Chiapas; *Hist* Zapatista, = follower or supporter of the Mexican revolutionary Emiliano Zapata (1879-1919)

zapato *nm* shoe; **ponerse los zapatos** to put one's shoes on; *Fig* **saber dónde le aprieta el z. a alguien** to know how to deal with sb; **z. de cordones** lace-up (shoe); **zapatos de plataforma** platform shoes; **z. de salón** pump

zape *interj Fam (sorpresa)* ¡z.! wow!

zapear *vi Fam* to channel-hop

zapeo *nm Fam* channel surfing, channel-hopping

zapping ['θapin] *nm inv Fam* channel surfing, channel-hopping; **hacer z.** to channel-hop

zar *nm* czar, czar

zarabanda *nf* (a) *(danza)* saraband (b) *(jaleo)* commotion, uproar

Zaragoza *n* Saragossa, Zaragoza

zaragozano, -a 1 *adj* of/from Saragossa
2 *nm,f* person from Saragossa

zarajo *nm* = lamb intestines, rolled around two crossed sticks and fried

zarandajas *nfpl Fam* nonsense, trifles

zarandeado, -a *adj* eventful, turbulent

zarandear *vt (cosa)* to shake; *(persona)* to jostle, to knock around *o* about

zarandeo *nm* (a) *(sacudida)* shake, shaking (b) *(empujón)* pushing *o* knocking around *o* about

zarcillo *nm* earring

zarco, -a *adj* light blue

zarina *nf* czarina, tsarina

zarismo *nm* **el fin del z.** the end of the Czars *o* Tsars

zarista *adj & nmf* Czarist, Tsarist

zarpa *nf* (a) *(de animal) (uña)* claw; *(mano)* paw (b) *Fam (de persona)* paw, hand

zarpar *vi* to weigh anchor, to set sail

zarpazo *nm* clawing

zarrapastroso, -a *Fam* **1** *adj* scruffy, shabby
2 *nm,f* scruff

zarza *nf* bramble, blackberry bush

zarzal *nm* bramble patch

zarzamora *nf* blackberry

zarzaparrilla *nf* sarsaparilla

zarzuela *nf* (a) *Mús* zarzuela, = Spanish light opera (b) *Culin* = fish and/or seafood stew

zas *interj* ¡z.! wham!, bang!

zascandil *nm Fam* fidget, restless person

zascandilear *vi Fam* to fiddle around *o* about

zen *adj inv & nm* Zen

zenit *nm también Fig* zenith

zepelín *nm* zeppelin

zeta *nm Esp Fam* **(coche) z.** *(de policía)* police patrol car

zigoto *nm* zygote

zigurat *(pl* **zigurats)** *nm* ziggurat

zigzag *(pl* **zigzags** *o* **zigzagues)** *nm* zigzag

zigzagueante *adj* **una carretera z.** a winding road

zigzaguear *vi* to zigzag

zigzagueo *nm (de carretera, sendero)* twisting and turning

Zimbabue *n* Zimbabwe

zinc *nm* zinc

zíngaro, -a *adj & nm,f* Gypsy

zíper *nm CAm, Méx* zipper

zipizape *nm Fam* squabble, set-to

zloty *nm (moneda)* zloty

zócalo *nm* (a) *(de pared)* baseboard (b) *(de edificio, pedestal)* plinth (c) *(pedestal)* pedestal (d) *Méx* main square

zoco *nm* souk, Arabian market

zodiac® *(pl* **zodiacs)** *nf* Zodiac boat, = rubber dinghy with outboard motor

zodiacal *adj* zodiacal

zodiaco, zodíaco *nm* zodiac

zombi, zombie 1 *adj Fam (atontado)* zonked
2 *nmf también Fig* zombie

zona *nf* (a) *(espacio)* zone, area; **¿vives por la z.?** *(por aquí)* do you live around here?; **ésta es la z. de copas de la ciudad** this is the center of the city's nightlife; **z. azul** *(de estacionamiento)* restricted parking zone; **z. de carga y descarga** loading zone; **z. catastrófica** disaster area; **z. comercial** shopping area; **z. erógena** erogenous zone; **z. de exclusión** exclusion zone; **z. euro** euro zone; *Com* **z. franca** free-trade zone; **z. de guerra** war zone; **z. de libre comercio** free-trade zone; **z. peatonal** pedestrian mall; **z. protegida** *(natural)* conservation area; **z. residencial** residential area; **z. verde** *(grande)* park, green area; *(pequeña)* lawn (b) *(en baloncesto)* key

zonal *adj* **plano z.** map of the area

zoo *nm* zoo

zoofilia *nf* bestiality

zoología *nf* zoology

zoológico, -a 1 *adj* zoological
2 *nm* zoo

zoólogo, -a *nm,f* zoologist

zoom [θum] *(pl* **zooms)** *nm Fot* zoom

zooplancton *nm* zooplankton

zopenco, -a *Fam* **1** *adj* idiotic, daft
2 *nm,f* idiot, nitwit

zopilote *nm CAm, Méx* black vulture

zoquete 1 *adj Fam* thick, dense
2 *nm CSur (calcetín)* ankle sock
3 *nmf Fam (tonto)* blockhead, idiot

zorra *nf Esp Fam Pey (ramera)* slut

zorro, -a 1 *adj* foxy, crafty; *Esp muy Fam* **no tengo ni zorra (idea)** I haven't got a goddamn clue
2 *nm,f también Fig* fox; **z. azul/ártico** blue/arctic fox
3 *nm (piel)* fox (fur)
4 zorros *nmpl (utensilio)* feather duster; *Fam* **estar hecho unos zorros** *(cansado, maltrecho)* to be tuckered out, to be done in; *(enfurecido)* to be fuming

zorzal *nm (ave)* thrush

zozobra *nf* (a) *(inquietud)* anxiety, worry (b) *(naufragio) (de barco)* sinking; *(de empresa, planes)* ruin, end

zozobrar *vi* (a) *(naufragar)* to be shipwrecked (b) *(fracasar)* to fall through

zueco *nm* clog

zulo *nm* hiding place

zulú *(pl* **zulúes)** *adj & nmf* Zulu

zumaque *nm (planta)* sumac; **z. venenoso** poison sumac, poison ivy

zumbado, -a *Fam* **1** *adj* screwy
2 *nm,f* nut, crackpot

zumbador *nm* buzzer

zumbar 1 *vi (producir ruido) (insecto)* to buzz; *(máquina)* to whirr, to hum; **me zumban los oídos** my ears are buzzing; *Fig* **pasar zumbando** to shoot past; *Fig* **venir zumbando** to come running; *Fig* **salir zumbando** to dash off
2 *vt Fam (golpear)* to beat, to thump

zumbido *nm (de insecto)* buzz, buzzing; *(de máquina)* whirr, whirring

zumbón, -ona *Fam* **1** *adj* funny, joking
2 *nm,f* joker, tease

zumo *nm Esp* juice; **z. de frutas** fruit juice; **z. de naranja** orange juice

zurcido *nm* (a) *(acción)* darning (b) *(remiendo)* darn

zurcidor, -ora *nm,f* darner, mender

zurcir [72] *vt* to darn; *Fam* **¡anda y que te zurzan!** scram!, get lost!

zurda *nf* (a) *(mano)* left hand (b) *(pierna)* left foot

zurdazo *nm* left-footed kick

zurdo, -a 1 *adj (mano, pierna)* left; *(persona)* left-handed
2 *nm,f (persona)* left-handed person

Zurich ['θurik] *n* Zurich

zurito *nm Esp* = little glass of wine

zurra *nf Fam* beating, hiding

zurrar *vt Fam (pegar)* to beat, to thrash

zurrón *nm* shepherd's shoulder bag

zurullo *nm Fam (excremento)* turd

zurzo *ver* **zurcir**

zutano, -a *nm,f (hombre)* so-and-so, what's-his-name; *(mujer)* so-and-so, what's-her-name

Supplement
Suplemento

Spanish Verbs	(3)-(17)
Verbos irregulares ingleses	(18)-(20)
Spanish Communication Guide	(21)-(45)
Guía de comunicación en inglés	(47)-(72)

Spanish Verbs

This guide to Spanish verbs opens with the three regular conjugations (verbs ending in -ar", "-er" and "-ir"), followed by the two most common auxiliary verbs: **haber**, which is used to form the perfect tenses, and **ser**, which is used to form the passive. These five verbs are given in full.

These are followed by a list of Spanish irregular verbs, numbered 3–72. A number refers you to these tables after irregular verbs in the main part of the dictionary.

The first person of each tense is always shown, even if it is regular. Of the other forms, only those which are irregular are given. An *etc* after a form indicates that the other forms of that tense use the same irregular stem, e.g. the future of **decir** is **yo diré** *etc*, i.e.: **yo diré, tú dirás, él dirá, nosotros diremos, vosotros diréis, ellos dirán**.

When the first person of a tense is the only irregular form, then it is not followed by *etc*, e.g. the present indicative of **placer** is **yo plazco** (irregular), but the other forms (**tú places, él place, nosotros placemos, vosotros placéis, ellos placen**) are regular and are thus not shown.

For the imperative, only the **tú** form is shown. The **vosotros** form is derived from the infinitive by replacing the final "-r" with a "-d". The other forms of the imperative (**usted, nosotros, ustedes**) are the same as the present subjunctive.

In Latin America the **vosotros** forms are rarely used, and the **ustedes** forms are used instead, even in informal contexts. In the imperative, the plural form is therefore not the "-d" form but instead the same as the third person plural of the present subjunctive, e.g. the plural imperatives of **ser** and **decir** are **sean** and **digan**.

INDICATIVE Present	Imperfect	Preterite	Future	CONDITIONAL Present
Regular "-ar": amar				
yo amo	yo amaba	yo amé	yo amaré	yo amaría
tú amas	tú amabas	tú amaste	tú amarás	tú amarías
él ama	él amaba	él amó	él amará	él amaría
nosotros amamos	nosotros amábamos	nosotros amamos	nosotros amaremos	nosotros amaríamos
vosotros amáis	vosotros amabais	vosotros amasteis	vosotros amaréis	vosotros amaríais
ellos aman	ellos amaban	ellos amaron	ellos amarán	ellos amarían
Regular "-er": temer				
yo temo	yo temía	yo temí	yo temeré	yo temería
tú temes	tú temías	tú temiste	tú temerás	tú temerías
él teme	él temía	él temió	él temerá	él temería
nosotros tememos	nosotros temíamos	nosotros temimos	nosotros temeremos	nosotros temeríamos
vosotros teméis	vosotros temíais	vosotros temisteis	vosotros temeréis	vosotros temeríais
ellos temen	ellos temían	ellos temieron	ellos temerán	ellos temerían
Regular "-ir": partir				
yo parto	yo partía	yo partí	yo partiré	yo partiría
tú partes	tú partías	tú partiste	tú partirás	tú partirías
él parte	él partía	él partió	él partirá	él partiría
nosotros partimos	nosotros partíamos	nosotros partimos	nosotros partiremos	nosotros partiríamos
vosotros partís	vosotros partíais	vosotros partisteis	vosotros partiréis	vosotros partiríais
ellos parten	ellos partían	ellos partieron	ellos partirán	ellos partirían
[1] haber				
yo he	yo había	yo hube	yo habré	yo habría
tú has	tú habías	tú hubiste	tú habrás	tú habrías
él ha	él había	él hubo	él habrá	él habría
nosotros hemos	nosotros habíamos	nosotros hubimos	nosotros habremos	nosotros habríamos
vosotros habéis	vosotros habíais	vosotros hubisteis	vosotros habréis	vosotros habríais
ellos han	ellos habían	ellos hubieron	ellos habrán	ellos habrían
[2] ser				
yo soy	yo era	yo fui	yo seré	yo sería
tú eres	tú eras	tú fuiste	tú serás	tú serías
él es	él era	él fue	él será	él sería
nosotros somos	nosotros éramos	nosotros fuimos	nosotros seremos	nosotros seríamos
vosotros sois	vosotros erais	vosotros fuisteis	vosotros seréis	vosotros seríais
ellos son	ellos eran	ellos fueron	ellos serán	ellos serían
[3] acertar				
yo acierto	yo acertaba	yo acerté	yo acertaré	yo acertaría
tú aciertas				
él acierta				
ellos aciertan				
[4] actuar				
yo actúo	yo actuaba	yo actué	yo actuaré	yo actuaría
tú actúas				
él actúa				
ellos actúan				
[5] adquirir				
yo adquiero	yo adquiría	yo adquirí	yo adquiriré	yo adquiriría
tú adquieres				
él adquiere				
ellos adquieren				
[6] agorar				
yo agüero	yo agoraba	yo agoré	yo agoraré	yo agoraría
tú agüeras				
él agüera				
ellos agüeran				

SUBJUNCTIVE		IMPERATIVE	PARTICIPLE	
Present	Imperfect		Present	Past

yo ame	yo amara *or* amase		amando	amado
tú ames	tú amaras *or* amases	ama (tú)		
él ame	él amara *or* amase	ame (usted)		
nosotros amemos	nosotros amáramos *or* amásemos	amemos (nosotros)		
vosotros améis	vosotros amarais *or* amaseis	amad (vosotros)		
		amen (ustedes)		
ellos amen	ellos amaran *or* amasen			

yo tema	yo temiera *or* temiese		temiendo	temido
tú temas	tú temieras *or* temiese	teme (tú)		
él tema	él temiera *or* temiese	tema (usted)		
nosotros temamos	nosotros temiéramos *or* temiésemos	temamos (nosotros)		
vosotros temáis	vosotros temierais *or* temieseis	temed (vosotros)		
		teman (ustedes)		
ellos teman	ellos temieran *or* temiesen			

yo parta	yo partiera *or* partiese		partiendo	partido
tú partas	tú partieras *or* partieses	parte (tú)		
él parta	él partiera *or* partiese	parta (usted)		
nosotros partamos	nosotros partiéramos *or* partiésemos	partamos (nosotros)		
vosotros partáis	vosotros partierais *or* partieseis	partid (vosotros)		
		partan (ustedes)		
ellos partan	ellos partieran *or* partiesen			

yo haya	yo hubiera *or* hubiese		habiendo	habido
tú hayas	tú hubieras *or* hubieses	he (tú)		
él haya	él hubiera *or* hubiese	haya (usted)		
nosotros hayamos	nosotros hubiéramos *or* hubiésemos	hayamos (nosotros)		
vosotros hayáis	vosotros hubierais *or* hubieseis	habed (vosotros)		
		hayan (ustedes)		
ellos hayan	ellos hubieran *or* hubiesen			

yo sea	yo fuera *or* fuese		siendo	sido
tú seas	tú fueras *or* fueses	sé (tú)		
él sea	él fuera *or* fuese	sea (usted)		
nosotros seamos	nosotros fuéramos *or* fuésemos	seamos (nosotros)		
vosotros seáis	vosotros fuerais *or* fueseis	sed (vosotros)		
		sean (ustedes)		
ellos sean	ellos fueran *or* fuesen			

yo acierte	yo acertara *or* acertase	acierta (tú)	acertando	acertado
tú aciertes				
él acierte				
ellos acierten				

yo actúe	yo actuara *or* actuase	actúa (tú)	actuando	actuado
tú actúes				
él actúe				
ellos actúen				

yo adquiera	yo adquiriera *or* adquiriese	adquiere (tú)	adquiriendo	adquirido
tú adquieras				
él adquiera				
ellos adquieran				

yo agüere	yo agorara *or* agorase	agüera (tú)	agorando	agorado
tú agüeres				
él agüere				
ellos agüeren				

	INDICATIVE Present	Imperfect	Preterite	Future	CONDITIONAL Present
[7]	**andar** yo ando	yo andaba	yo anduve tú anduviste él anduvo nosotros anduvimos vosotros anduvisteis ellos anduvieron	yo andaré	yo andaría
[8]	**argüir** yo arguyo tú arguyes él arguye ellos arguyen	yo argüía	yo argüí él arguyó ellos arguyeron	yo argüiré	yo argüiría
[9]	**asir** yo asgo	yo asía	yo así	yo asiré	yo asiría
[10]	**avergonzar** yo avergüenzo tú avergüenzas él avergüenza ellos avergüenzan	yo avergonzaba	yo avergoncé	yo avergonzaré	yo avergonzaría
[11]	**averiguar** yo averiguo	yo averiguaba	yo averigüé	yo averiguaré	yo averiguaría
[12]	**caber** yo quepo	yo cabía	yo cupe tú cupiste él cupo nosotros cupimos vosotros cupisteis ellos cupieron	yo cabré *etc*	yo cabría *etc*
[13]	**caer** yo caigo	yo caía	yo caí tú caíste él cayó nosotros caímos vosotros caísteis ellos cayeron	yo caeré	yo caería
[14]	**cazar** yo cazo	yo cazaba	yo cacé	yo cazaré	yo cazaría
[15]	**cocer** yo cuezo tú cueces él cuece ellos cuecen	yo cocía	yo cocí	yo coceré	yo cocería
[16]	**colgar** yo cuelgo tú cuelgas él cuelga ellos cuelgan	yo colgaba	yo colgué	yo colgaré	yo colgaría
[17]	**comenzar** yo comienzo tú comienzas él comienza ellos comienzan	yo comenzaba	yo comencé	yo comenzaré	yo comenzaría

| SUBJUNCTIVE | | IMPERATIVE | PARTICIPLE | |
Present	Imperfect		Present	Past
yo ande	yo anduviera *or* anduviese *etc*	anda (tú)	andando	andado
yo arguya *etc*	yo arguyera *or* arguyese *etc*	arguye (tú)	arguyendo	argüido
yo asga *etc*	yo asiera *or* asiese	ase (tú)	asiendo	asido
yo avergüence tú avergüences él avergüence nosotros avergoncemos vosotros avergoncéis ellos avergüencen	yo avergonzara *or* avergonzase	avergüenza (tú)	avergonzando	avergonzado
yo averigüe *etc*	yo averiguara *or* averiguase	averigua (tú)	averiguando	averiguado
yo quepa *etc*	yo cupiera *or* cupiese *etc*	cabe (tú)	cabiendo	cabido
yo caiga *etc*	yo cayera *or* cayese *etc*	cae (tú)	cayendo	caído
yo cace *etc*	yo cazara *or* cazase	caza (tú)	cazando	cazado
yo cueza tú cuezas él cueza nosotros cozamos vosotros cozáis ellos cuezan	yo cociera *or* cociese	cuece (tú)	cociendo	cocido
yo cuelgue tú cuelgues él cuelgue nosotros colguemos vosotros colguéis ellos cuelguen	yo colgara *or* colgase	cuelga (tú)	colgando	colgado
yo comience tú comiences él comience nosotros comencemos vosotros comencéis ellos comiencen	yo comenzara *or* comenzase	comienza (tú)	comenzando	comenzado

		INDICATIVE Present	Imperfect	Preterite	Future	CONDITIONAL Present
[18]	**conducir** yo conduzco	yo conducía	yo conduje tú condujiste él condujo nosotros condujimos vosotros condujisteis ellos condujeron	yo conduciré	yo conduciría
[19]	**conocer** yo conozco	yo conocía	yo conocí	yo conoceré	yo conocería
[20]	**dar** yo doy	yo daba	yo di tú diste él dio nosotros dimos vosotros disteis ellos dieron	yo daré	yo daría
[21]	**decir** yo digo tú dices él dice ellos dicen	yo decía	yo dije tú dijiste él dijo nosotros dijimos vosotros dijisteis ellos dijeron	yo diré *etc*	yo diría *etc*
[22]	**delinquir** yo delinco	yo delinquía	yo delinquí	yo delinquiré	yo delinquiría
[23]	**desosar** yo deshueso tú deshuesas él deshuesa ellos deshuesan	yo desosaba	yo desosé	yo desosaré	yo desosaría
[24]	**dirigir** yo dirijo	yo dirigía	yo dirigí	yo dirigiré	yo dirigiría
[25]	**discernir** yo discierno tú disciernes él discierne ellos disciernen	yo discernía	yo discerní	yo discerniré	yo discerniría
[26]	**distinguir** yo distingo	yo distinguía	yo distinguí	yo distinguiré	yo distinguiría
[27]	**dormir** yo duermo tú duermes él duerme ellos duermen	yo dormía	yo dormí él durmió ellos durmieron	yo dormiré	yo dormiría
[28]	**erguir** yo irgo *or* yergo tú irgues *or* yergues él irgue *or* yergue nosotros erguimos vosotros erguís ellos irguen *or* yerguen	yo erguía	yo erguí él irguió ellos irguieron	yo erguiré	yo erguiría

SUBJUNCTIVE Present	Imperfect	IMPERATIVE	PARTICIPLE Present	Past
yo conduzca *etc*	yo condujera *or* condujese *etc*	conduce (tú)	conduciendo	conducido
yo conozca *etc*	yo conociera *or* conociese	conoce (tú)	conociendo	conocido
yo dé él dé	yo diera *or* diese *etc*	da (tú)	dando	dado
yo diga *etc*	yo dijera *or* dijese *etc*	di (tú)	diciendo	dicho
yo delinca *etc*	yo delinquiera *or* delinquiese	delinque (tú)	delinquiendo	delinquido
yo deshuese tú deshueses él deshuese ellos deshuesen	yo desosara *or* desosase	deshuesa (tú)	desosando	desosado
yo dirija *etc*	yo dirigiera *or* dirigiese	dirige (tú)	dirigiendo	dirigido
yo discierna tú disciernas él discierna ellos disciernan	yo discerniera *or* discerniese	discierne (tú)	discerniendo	discernido
yo distinga *etc*	yo distinguiera *or* distinguiese	distingue (tú)	distinguiendo	distinguido
yo duerma tú duermas él duerma nosotros durmamos vosotros durmáis ellos duerman	yo durmiera *or* durmiese *etc*	duerme (tú)	durmiendo	dormido
yo irga *or* yerga tú irgas *or* yergas él irga *or* yerga nosotros irgamos vosotros irgáis ellos irgan *or* yergan	yo irguiera *or* irguiese	irgue *or* yergue (tú)	irguiendo	erguido

	INDICATIVE Present	Imperfect	Preterite	Future	CONDITIONAL Present
[29]	**errar** yo yerro tú yerras él yerra ellos yerran	yo erraba	yo erré	yo erraré	yo erraría
[30]	**estar** yo estoy tú estás él está ellos están	yo estaba	yo estuve tú estuviste él estuvo nosotros estuvimos vosotros estuvisteis ellos estuvieron	yo estaré	yo estaría
[31]	**forzar** yo fuerzo tú fuerzas él fuerza ellos fuerzan	yo forzaba	yo forcé	yo forzaré	yo forzaría
[32]	**guiar** yo guío tú guías él guía ellos guían	yo guiaba	yo guié	yo guiaré	yo guiaría
[33]	**hacer** yo hago	yo hacía	yo hice tú hiciste él hizo nosotros hicimos vosotros hicisteis ellos hicieron	yo haré *etc*	yo haría *etc*
[34]	**huir** yo huyo tú huyes él huye ellos huyen	yo huía	yo huí él huyó ellos huyeron	yo huiré	yo huiría
[35]	**ir** yo voy tú vas él va nosotros vamos vosotros vais ellos van	yo iba *etc*	yo fui tú fuiste él fue nosotros fuimos vosotros fuisteis ellos fueron	yo iré	yo iría
[36]	**jugar** yo juego tú juegas él juega ellos juegan	yo jugaba	yo jugué	yo jugaré	yo jugaría
[37]	**leer** yo leo	yo leía	yo leí tú leíste él leyó nosotros leímos vosotros leísteis ellos leyeron	yo leeré	yo leería

SUBJUNCTIVE		IMPERATIVE	PARTICIPLE	
Present	Imperfect		Present	Past
yo yerre tú yerres él yerre ellos yerren	yo errara *or* errase	yerra (tú)	errando	errado
yo esté tú estés él esté ellos estén	yo estuviera *or* estuviese *etc*	está (tú)	estando	estado
yo fuerce tú fuerces él fuerce nosotros forcemos vosotros forcéis ellos fuercen	yo forzara *or* forzase	fuerza (tú)	forzando	forzado
yo guíe tú guíes él guíe ellos guíen	yo guiara *or* guiase	guía (tú)	guiando	guiado
yo haga *etc*	yo hiciera *or* hiciese *etc*	haz (tú)	haciendo	hecho
yo huya *etc*	yo huyera *or* huyese *etc*	huye (tú)	huyendo	huido
yo vaya *etc*	yo fuera *or* fuese *etc*	ve (tú)	yendo	ido
yo juegue tú juegues él juegue nosotros juguemos vosotros juguéis ellos jueguen	yo jugara *or* jugase	juega (tú)	jugando	jugado
yo lea	yo leyera *or* leyese *etc*	lee (tú)	leyendo	leído

	INDICATIVE Present	Imperfect	Preterite	Future	CONDITIONAL Present
[38]	**llegar** yo llego	yo llegaba	yo llegué	yo llegaré	yo llegaría
[39]	**lucir** yo luzco	yo lucía	yo lucí	yo luciré	yo luciría
[40]	**mecer** yo mezo	yo mecía	yo mecí	yo meceré	yo mecería
[41]	**mover** yo muevo tú mueves él mueve ellos mueven	yo movía	yo moví	yo moveré	yo movería
[42]	**nacer** yo nazco	yo nacía	yo nací	yo naceré	yo nacería
[43]	**negar** yo niego tú niegas él niega ellos niegan	yo negaba	yo negué	yo negaré	yo negaría
[44]	**oír** yo oigo tú oyes él oye ellos oyen	yo oía	yo oí él oyó ellos oyeron	yo oiré	yo oiría
[45]	**oler** yo huelo tú hueles él huele ellos huelen	yo olía	yo olí	yo oleré	yo olería
[46]	**parecer** yo parezco	yo parecía	yo parecí	yo pareceré	yo parecería
[47]	**pedir** yo pido tú pides él pide ellos piden	yo pedía	yo pedí él pidió ellos pidieron	yo pediré	yo pediría
[48]	**placer** yo plazco	yo placía	yo plací él plació or plugo ellos placieron or pluguieron	yo placeré	yo placería
[49]	**poder** yo puedo tú puedes él puede ellos pueden	yo podía	yo pude tú pudiste él pudo nosotros pudimos vosotros pudisteis ellos pudieron	yo podré *etc*	yo podría *etc*

SUBJUNCTIVE Present	Imperfect	IMPERATIVE	PARTICIPLE Present	Past
yo llegue *etc*	yo llegara *or* llegase	llega (tú)	llegando	llegado
yo luzca *etc*	yo luciera *or* luciese	luce (tú)	luciendo	lucido
yo meza *etc*	yo meciera *or* meciese	mece (tú)	meciendo	mecido
yo mueva tú muevas él mueva ellos muevan	yo moviera *or* moviese	mueve (tú)	moviendo	movido
yo nazca *etc*	yo naciera *or* naciese	nace (tú)	naciendo	nacido
yo niegue tú niegues él niegue nosotros neguemos vosotros neguéis ellos nieguen	yo negara *or* negase	niega (tú)	negando	negado
yo oiga *etc*	yo oyera *or* oyese *etc*	oye (tú)	oyendo	oído
yo huela tú huelas él huela ellos huelan	yo oliera *or* oliese	huele (tú)	oliendo	olido
yo parezca *etc*	yo pareciera *or* pareciese	parece (tú)	pareciendo	parecido
yo pida *etc*	yo pidiera *or* pidiese *etc*	pide (tú)	pidiendo	pedido
yo plazca tú plazcas él plazca *or* plegue nosotros plazcamos vosotros plazcáis ellos plazcan	yo placiera *or* placiese él placiera *or* placiese, pluguiera *or* pluguiese ellos placieran *or* placiesen	place (tú)	placiendo	placido
yo pueda tú puedas él pueda ellos puedan	yo pudiera *or* pudiese *etc*	puede (tú)	pudiendo	podido

	INDICATIVE Present	Imperfect	Preterite	Future	CONDITIONAL Present
[50]	**poner**				
	yo pongo	yo ponía	yo puse	yo pondré *etc*	yo pondría *etc*
			tú pusiste		
			él puso		
			nosotros pusimos		
			vosotros pusisteis		
			ellos pusieron		
[51]	**predecir**				
	yo predigo	yo predecía	yo predije	yo prediciré	yo prediciría
				or prediré *etc*	*or* prediría *etc*
	tú predices		tú predijiste		
	él predice		él predijo		
			nosotros predijimos		
			vosotros predijisteis		
	ellos predicen		ellos predijeron		
[52]	**proteger**				
	yo protejo	yo protegía	yo protegí	yo protegeré	yo protegería
[53]	**querer**				
	yo quiero	yo quería	yo quise	yo querré *etc*	yo querría *etc*
	tú quieres		tú quisiste		
	él quiere		él quiso		
			nosotros quisimos		
			vosotros quisisteis		
	ellos quieren		ellos quisieron		
[54]	**raer**				
	yo rao, raigo	yo raía	yo raí	yo raeré	yo raería
	or rayo				
			tú raíste		
			él rayó		
			nosotros raímos		
			vosotros raísteis		
			ellos rayeron		
[55]	**regir**				
	yo rijo	yo regía	yo regí	yo regiré	yo regiría
	tú riges				
	él rige		él rigió		
	ellos rigen		ellos rigieron		
[56]	**reír**				
	yo río	yo reía	yo reí	yo reiré	yo reiría
	tú ríes				
	él ríe		él rió		
	ellos ríen		ellos rieron		
[57]	**roer**				
	yo roo, roigo *or*	yo roía	yo roí	yo roeré	yo roería
	royo				
			él royó		
			ellos royeron		
[58]	**saber**				
	yo sé	yo sabía	yo supe	yo sabré *etc*	yo sabría *etc*
			tú supiste		
			él supo		
			nosotros supimos		
			vosotros supisteis		
			ellos supieron		
[59]	**sacar**				
	yo saco	yo sacaba	yo saqué	yo sacaré	yo sacaría

SUBJUNCTIVE Present	Imperfect	IMPERATIVE	PARTICIPLE Present	Past
yo ponga *etc*	yo pusiera *or* pusiese *etc*	pon (tú)	poniendo	puesto
yo prediga *etc*	yo predijera *or* predijese *etc*	predice (tú)	prediciendo	predicho
yo proteja *etc*	yo protegiera *or* protegiese	protege (tú)	protegiendo	protegido
yo quiera tú quieras él quiera ellos quieran	yo quisiera *or* quisiese *etc*	quiere (tú)	queriendo	querido
yo raa, raiga *or* raya *etc*	yo rayera *or* rayese *etc*	rae (tú)	rayendo	raído
yo rija *etc*	yo rigiera *or* rigiese *etc*	rige (tú)	rigiendo	regido
yo ría tú rías él ría nosotros riamos vosotros riáis ellos rían	yo riera *or* riese *etc*	ríe (tú)	riendo	reído
yo roa, roiga *or* roya *etc*	yo royera *or* royese *etc*	roe (tú)	royendo	roído
yo sepa *etc*	yo supiera *or* supiese *etc*	sabe (tú)	sabiendo	sabido
yo saque *etc*	yo sacara *or* sacase	saca (tú)	sacando	sacado

	INDICATIVE Present	Imperfect	Preterite	Future	CONDITIONAL Present
[60]	**salir**				
	yo salgo	yo salía	yo salí	yo saldré *etc*	yo saldría *etc*
[61]	**seguir**				
	yo sigo	yo seguía	yo seguí	yo seguiré	yo seguiría
	tú sigues				
	él sigue		él siguió		
	ellos siguen		ellos siguieron		
[62]	**sentir**				
	yo siento	yo sentía	yo sentí	yo sentiré	yo sentiría
	tú sientes				
	él siente		él sintió		
	ellos sienten		ellos sintieron		
[63]	**sonar**				
	yo sueno	yo sonaba	yo soné	yo sonaré	yo sonaría
	tú suenas				
	él suena				
	ellos suenan				
[64]	**tender**				
	yo tiendo	yo tendía	yo tendí	yo tenderé	yo tendería
	tú tiendes				
	él tiende				
	ellos tienden				
[65]	**tener**				
	yo tengo	yo tenía	yo tuve	yo tendré *etc*	yo tendría *etc*
	tú tienes		tú tuviste		
	él tiene		él tuvo		
			nosotros tuvimos		
			vosotros tuvisteis		
	ellos tienen		ellos tuvieron		
[66]	**traer**				
	yo traigo	yo traía	yo traje	yo traeré	yo traería
			tú trajiste		
			él trajo		
			nosotros trajimos		
			vosotros trajisteis		
			ellos trajeron		
[67]	**trocar**				
	yo trueco	yo trocaba	yo troqué	yo trocaré	yo trocaría
	tú truecas				
	él trueca				
	ellos truecan				
[68]	**valer**				
	yo valgo	yo valía	yo valí	yo valdré *etc*	yo valdría *etc*
[69]	**venir**				
	yo vengo	yo venía	yo vine	yo vendré *etc*	yo vendría *etc*
	tú vienes		tú viniste		
	él viene		él vino		
			nosotros vinimos		
			vosotros vinisteis		
	ellos vienen		ellos vinieron		
[70]	**ver**				
	yo veo	yo veía *etc*	yo vi	yo veré	yo vería
[71]	**yacer**				
	yo yazco, yazgo	yo yacía	yo yací	yo yaceré	yo yacería
	or yago				
[72]	**zurcir**				
	yo zurzo	yo zurcía	yo zurcí	yo zurciré	yo zurciría

SUBJUNCTIVE Present	Imperfect	IMPERATIVE	PARTICIPLE Present	Past
yo salga *etc*	yo saliera *or* saliese	sal (tú)	saliendo	salido
yo siga *etc*	yo siguiera *or* siguiese *etc*	sigue (tú)	siguiendo	seguido
yo sienta tú sientas él sienta nosotros sintamos vosotros sintáis ellos sientan	yo sintiera *or* sintiese *etc*	siente (tú)	sintiendo	sentido
yo suene tú suenes él suene ellos suenen	yo sonara *or* sonase	suena (tú)	sonando	sonado
yo tienda tú tiendas él tienda ellos tiendan	yo tendiera *or* tendiese	tiende (tú)	tendiendo	tendido
yo tenga *etc*	yo tuviera *or* tuviese *etc*	ten (tú)	teniendo	tenido
yo traiga *etc*	yo trajera *or* trajese *etc*	trae (tú)	trayendo	traído
yo trueque tú trueques él trueque ellos truequen	yo trocara *or* trocase	troca (tú)	trocando	trocado
yo valga *etc*	yo valiera *or* valiese	vale (tú)	valiendo	valido
yo venga *etc*	yo viniera *or* viniese *etc*	ven (tú)	viniendo	venido
yo vea *etc*	yo viera *or* viese	ve (tú)	viendo	visto
yo yazca, yazga *or* yaga *etc*	yo yaciera *or* yaciese	yace *or* yaz (tú)	yaciendo	yacido
yo zurza *etc*	yo zurciera *or* zurciese	zurce (tú)	zurciendo	zurcido

Verbos irregulares ingleses

Infinitivo	Pretérito	Participio
arise	arose	arisen
awake	awoke, awaked	awoken, awoke, awaked
be	were/was	been
bear	bore	borne, born
beat	beat	beaten
become	became	become
begin	began	begun
bend	bent	bent
beseech	besought, beseeched	besought, beseeched
bet	bet, betted	bet, betted
bid	bade, bid	bidden, bid
bind	bound	bound
bite	bit	bitten
bleed	bled	bled
blow	blew	blown
break	broke	broken
breed	bred	bred
bring	brought	brought
build	built	built
burn	burnt, burned	burnt, burned
burst	burst	burst
bust	bust, busted	bust, busted
buy	bought	bought
cast	cast	cast
catch	caught	caught
chide	chided, chid	chided, chidden
choose	chose	chosen
cleave	cleaved, cleft, clove	cleaved, cleft, cloven
cling	clung	clung
clothe	clad, clothed	clad, clothed
come	came	come
cost	cost	cost
creep	crept	crept
cut	cut	cut
deal	dealt	dealt
dig	dug	dug
dive	dived, dove	dived
do	did	done
draw	drew	drawn
drink	drank	drunk
drive	drove	driven
dwell	dwelt	dwelt
eat	ate	eaten
fall	fell	fallen
feed	fed	fed
feel	felt	felt
fight	fought	fought
find	found	found
flee	fled	fled
fling	flung	flung
fly	flew	flown
forget	forgot	forgotten
forgive	forgave	forgiven
forsake	forsook	forsaken
freeze	froze	frozen
get	got	got, gotten

Infinitivo	Pretérito	Participio
gild	gilded, gilt	gilded, gilt
gird	girded, girt	girded, girt
give	gave	given
go	went	gone
grind	ground	ground
grow	grew	grown
hang	hung/hanged	hung/hanged
have	had	had
hear	heard	heard
hew	hewed	hewn, hewed
hide	hid	hidden
hit	hit	hit
hold	held	held
hurt	hurt	hurt
keep	kept	kept
kneel	knelt	knelt
knit	knitted, knit	knitted, knit
know	knew	known
lay	laid	laid
lead	led	led
leap	leapt, leaped	leapt, leaped
leave	left	left
lend	lent	lent
let	let	let
lie	lay	lain
light	lit	lit
lose	lost	lost
make	made	made
mean	meant	meant
meet	met	met
mow	mowed	moved, mown
pay	paid	paid
plead	pled	pled
prove	proved	proved, proven
put	put	put
quit	quit, quitted	quit, quitted
read	read	read
rend	rent	rent
rid	rid	rid
ride	rode	ridden
ring	rang	rung
rise	rose	risen
run	ran	run
saw	sawed	sawn, sawed
say	said	said
see	saw	seen
seek	sought	sought
sell	sold	sold
send	sent	sent
set	set	set
sew	sewed	sewn
shake	shook	shaken
shear	sheared	shorn, sheared
shed	shed	shed
shine	shone	shone
shit	shit, shat	shit, shat
shoe	shod	shod
shoot	shot	shot
show	showed	shown
shrink	shrank, shrunk	shrunk, shrunken
shut	shut	shut
sing	sang	sung

Infinitivo	Pretérito	Participio
sink	sank	sunk
sit	sat	sat
slay	slew	slain
sleep	slept	slept
slide	slid	slid
sling	slung	slung
slink	slinked, slunk	slinked, slunk
slit	slit	slit
smell	smelled, smelt	smelled, smelt
smite	smote	smitten
sneak	sneaked, snuck	sneaked, snuck
sow	sowed	sown, sowed
speak	spoke	spoken
speed	sped, speeded	sped, speeded
spend	spent	spent
spin	spun	spun
spit	spat, spit	spat, spit
split	split	split
spoil	spoilt, spoiled	spoilt, spoiled
spread	spread	spread
spring	sprang, sprung	sprung
stand	stood	stood
stave in	staved in, stove in	staved in, stove in
steal	stole	stolen
stick	stuck	stuck
sting	stung	stung
stink	stank, stunk	stunk
strew	strewed	strewed, strewn
stride	strode	stridden
strike	struck	struck
string	strung	strung
strive	strove	striven
swear	swore	sworn
sweep	swept	swept
swell	swelled	swollen, swelled
swim	swam	swum
swing	swung	swung
take	took	taken
teach	taught	taught
tear	tore	torn
tell	told	told
think	thought	thought
thrive	thrived, throve	thrived
throw	threw	thrown
thrust	thrust	thrust
tread	treaded, trod	trodden
wake	waked, woke	woken
wear	wore	worn
weave	wove, weaved	woven, weaved
weep	wept	wept
wet	wet, wetted	wet, wetted
win	won	won
wind	wound	wound
wring	wrung	wrung
write	wrote	written

Spanish Communication Guide

Letters   (23)

Arranging a meeting   (27)

Applying for a job   (28)

Writing an advertisement   (38)

Telephone   (39)

E-mail   (42)

Text messaging   (44)

Letters

Layout of a letter in Spanish

▪ The date

There are various ways of writing the date in a letter in Spanish. The full form is generally used in formal correspondence, while a shortened form is preferred for documents such as business letters and memos, which need to be clear and concise.

In official or legal correspondence, for example to government departments, the date appears after the place of origin in the bottom left-hand corner of the page, preceded by the preposition a.

> **Barcelona, a 4 de mayo de 2006**
> *Barcelona, 4th May 2006*

In all other cases the date should appear in the top right-hand corner of the page, under the printed letterhead if there is one, in which case there is no need to include the town or city.

> **20 de enero de 2006**
> *January 20, 2006*

Abbreviated forms using slashes or dashes may also be used. It is more common to use numerals for months than their written abbreviations. The year can be written in full or abbreviated.

> **México, D.F., 14/03/06**
> *Mexico City, 03/14/06*

> **Madrid, 5-sept.-2006**
> *Madrid, Sept 5, 2006*

In letters to friends or family the date is usually written in full, without the place.

> **27 de junio de 2006**
> *June 27, 2006*

▪ The sender

The name of the sender or **remitente** usually appears in the printed letterhead on business correspondence. When writing a business letter the sender's details normally go in the top left-hand corner or in the center at the top of the page. However, this information could also be shown at the bottom of the page together with the addresses of other branches of a company. In private letters to friends and family the address is omitted.

> *NEWSITEMS, S.R.L*
> *Avda. Rivadavia 3657 2°E*
> *C1204AAB Buenos Aires*
> *Tel. 4418 2507*
> *Fax. 4418 2508*
>
> *email: newsitems@ciudad.com.ar*

■ The recipient

The name and address of the person the letter is sent to appear lower down than the sender's details, on the left, with the job title if appropriate.

A la atención del Sr. Pérez (Director de Ventas)
For the attention of Mr. Pérez (Sales Manager)

This form is not normally used in memos or informal communications.

A/A: Jaime López
FAO: Jaime López

■ Addresses

In Spanish addresses you will often find no word for "street", only the actual name of the street, unless it is called, for example, "Avenida" or "Paseo". You can also see the abbreviation C/ for "Calle". The words for "Avenue", "Road" or "Square" may be abbreviated to **Avda. (avenida), Ctra. (carretera), Pza. (plaza)** respectively. The house number comes after the street name, and the zip code precedes the name of the city.

Gran Vía, 13
28005 Madrid

Some countries use different names to refer to "street". In Perú "Jirón" is often used, and in Colombia a street can be referred to as "Carrera", followed by a number, which is the number of the street.

Carrera 3, 17

In some Latin American countries, street names may actually be numbers and are then written as follows:

Calle 13 n° 683

You will often see a number followed by superscript ^{a} or $^\circ$, given after the house number. This indicates which floor of a building the apartment is situated on. For example, the third floor (fourth in US terms) in the following example:

Gran Vía 13 3^a

If a third number is given, this refers to the door number:

Gran Vía 13 3°, 1^a

In some Latin American countries, this information is often given in full:

Insurgentes 28, 3er. piso, despacho (*or* oficina) 305

or sometimes the floor number is omitted:

Insurgentes 28, despacho 305
     or
Insurgentes 28-305

> The Web sites of the various postal services in Spanish-speaking countries are a useful source of information regarding addresses and zip codes in particular. Here are some useful addresses:
> Spain: www.correos.es
> Mexico: http://www.sepomex.gob.mx
> Argentina: www.correoargentino.com.ar

■ Starting a letter

If you do not know the name of the person you are writing to, start the letter with **Estimado Sr.:** or, more formally, **Distinguido Sr.:** *Dear Sir,;* if you do know it you begin with **Estimada Sra. Olmedillo:** *Dear Mrs. Olmedillo,*.

To a friend or relative you would write **Querido Javier:** *Dear Javier,* **Queridos papis:** *Dear Mom and Dad,* or even use the superlative **Queridísima María:** *Dearest María,*.

These introductory phrases are always followed by a colon and a single line space.

▪ Ending a letter

The way you end a letter should match the level of formality or informality used at the start. The most common ways of ending a formal letter are:

> **Le/Les saluda atentamente,**
>
> **Muy atentamente,** or
>
> **Atentamente,.**

These all translate as: *Yours truly,*

or, if the recipient's name is known: *Sincerely yours,*.

Reciba un cordial saludo, or **Cordialmente** *(With kind) regards,* or *Best wishes,* are used if a relationship has already been established.

Ways of ending a letter to a friend or relative are:

> **Un abrazo,**
> *Love,*
>
> **Un fuerte abrazo,** *or* **Con cariño,**
> *Lots of love,*
>
> **Recuerdos** *or* **Saludos a la tía Teresa,**
> *Regards to Aunt Teresa,*
>
> **Saluda de mi parte a tu mujer,**
> *Give my regards to your wife,*

You can end more affectionately by saying:

> **Con todo mi cariño,**
> *With all my love,*
>
> **Tu nieto que te quiere,**
> *Your loving grandson,*
>
> **Besos,**
> *Lots of love,*

▪ Sample layout of a business letter

> *PLÁSTICOS ONFALOS, S.L*
> *Dpto. contabilidad*
> *Avda. de la Luz, 45*
> *19005 Guadalajara*
> *Tel: 949 458 67 48 Fax: 949 458 67 40*
> *Email: admin@pl-onfalos.es*
>
> *Atn.: Sr. D. Agustín Rodríguez*
> *CAJA DE INDUSTRIALES*
> *Romero, 257*
> *19004 Guadalajara*
>
> *2 de diciembre de 2006*
>
> *Estimado Sr. Rodríguez:*
> *Nos es grato poner en su conocimiento que a partir de primeros de septiembre*
> *nos trasladaremos a nuestras nuevas oficinas, cuya dirección es la que figura en*
> *el membrete de la presente.*
> *Le rogamos que a partir de dicha fecha se sirva dirigirnos toda la correspondencia*
> *a la referida dirección.*
> *Agradeciendo de antemano su colaboración, le saluda atentamente.*
> *Ángela Fernández*
> *Dpto. Administración*

The date may also appear higher up on the right-hand side, in between the sender's and recipient's details.

▪ Addressing an envelope

The recipient's address goes on the lower right-hand side of the envelope, as in the example below:

Sr. Juan María Albizu
Director General
ILUMINACIÓN ALBIZU, S.L.
C/ Del Puerto, 28
48010 BILBAO

In private correspondence the sender's name and address go on the back of the envelope. Before the name you write **Rte. :** the abbreviation of **remitente** (*sender*).

In Spain zip codes always consist of five numbers and go before the name of the town or city. The first two numbers indicate the **provincia**, or province, in alphabetical order. Thus the province of Álava would be 01 and Zaragoza 50. If the city is not the provincial capital, the capital city is shown either in brackets or in upper case.

37008 SALAMANCA
46730 Gandía (Valencia)

In Mexico, the 5-digit zip code goes on the left, followed by the city, a comma, and then the abbreviated name of the state (e.g: **Mexico DF (DF)**, Jalisco **(JAL)**, Chiapas **(CHIS)**, etc). When known, the corresponding city district ("Colonia") should be included:

Facultad Latinoamericana de Ciencias Sociales
Carretera al Ajusco Km.13,
Colonia Héroes de Padierna
Apartado 20-021,
Delegación Álvaro Obregón
01000 México, DF
México

In Argentina, the zip code is made up of three parts — a letter, 4 digits, and three letters. The 4-digit number represents the former national postal code, the initial letter stands for the province (Buenos Aires, Córdoba, etc), and the three last letters help to identify the exact location of the address in question in the corresponding block. The postal code is followed by the name of the town or city.

Héctor Raúl Sampedro
Calle 13 n° 683
B7620BAM Balcarce
Argentina

Arranging a meeting

Formal meetings and appointments

In order to make an appointment you will often need to speak to someone else on the telephone first:

> **Buenas tardes. Desearía concertar una cita con el Señor Rodríguez lo antes posible.**
> *Hello, I'd like to arrange a meeting with Mr. Rodríguez as soon as possible, please.*

> **Hola, buenos días. ¿Podría darme una cita con la Doctora Casas para esta tarde?**
> *Hello, would it be possible to make an appointment with Dr. Casas for this afternoon?*

> **¿A qué hora le iría mejor? ¿Le parece bien a las cuatro?**
> *What time would suit you? Is four o'clock convenient?*

Sometimes you may be speaking directly to the person you wish to meet:

> **Buenas tardes. Soy Gerardo González. ¿Cuándo podríamos reunirnos para hablar del proyecto?**
> *Hello, my name is Gerardo González. When could we meet to talk about the project?*

Business appointments are often arranged by e-mail. In this case, the tone of the message will obviously be more formal:

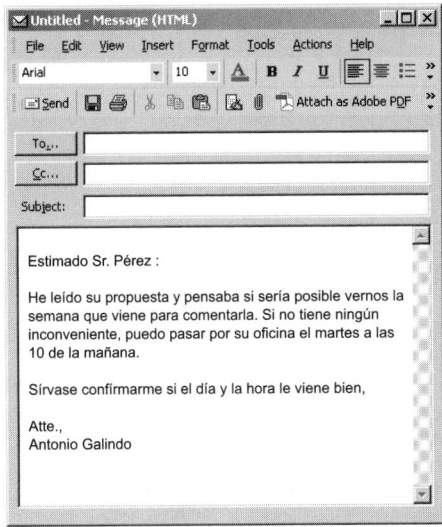

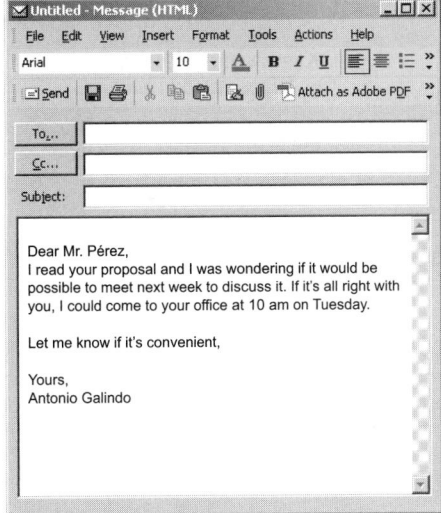

Here are some more phrases you can use when fixing the date, time and place of a meeting, or when confirming or cancelling a meeting:

> **¿Tiene algún momento libre para que nos reunamos esta semana?**
> *Are you free any time this week when we can meet up?*

> **¿Sería posible reunirnos sobre las seis de la tarde?**
> *Would it be possible to meet around six?*

> **¿Dónde será la reunión?**
> *Where will we have the meeting?*

¿Prefiere que nos veamos en un restaurante?
Would you rather we met in a restaurant?

Buenos días. Llamaba para confirmar nuestra cita del próximo martes.
Hello, I'm ringing to confirm our appointment next Tuesday.

> *Desafortunadamente no podré asistir a la entrevista que acordamos para el próximo viernes.*
> *Unfortunately I won't be able to attend the interview we arranged for next Friday.*
>
> This more formal type of expression would be used in a letter.

Meeting friends

Between friends the language used when arranging a meeting is more direct:

¿Vas a hacer algo esta noche?
Are you doing anything tonight?

¿Nos vemos a las siete?
How about if we meet at seven?

¿Puede ser el viernes?
Is Friday OK?

¿Voy yo a tu casa o vienes tú a la mía?
Shall I go around to yours or do you want to come to my place?

OK, nos vemos el jueves.
OK, I'll see you on Thursday.

Applying for a job

General points

Letters to potential employers should be printed on good quality A4-size paper [8.27"x11.69"], with your signature added by hand. Try to obtain as much information as possible about the company you are applying to, as well as the name of the person to whom the letter should be addressed. It is always better to avoid standard letters in favor of a personalized approach, which will create a better impression.

> It is not usual to mention salary aspirations, either in a letter or a job interview, unless specifically requested to do so.

▪ The CV

A CV should be clear, concise and honest and must be capable of being adapted to all the different businesses that you contact. If you are looking for a first job, you should give more space to the section on education and training and mention any work experience in companies, holiday jobs and voluntary work. Your educational qualifications and work experience should be shown in chronological order, with the most recent first.

Only mention hobbies if they add something personal to your profile or if they are particularly relevant to the job. Do not include references on your CV.

IGNACIO MENÉNDEZ BRAVO

DATOS PERSONALES
Nacido el 7/1/82
Lugar: Puebla
Estado civil: soltero
Nacionalidad: mexicana

DIRECCIÓN ACTUAL
Paseo del Río 14
C.P. 71010 Puebla
Tel.: 01 (2) 434 55 21
imenendez@uni3.com

Formación

2004 – 2005	Maestría en Mercadotecnia Internacional (Programa All-America impartido por la CONCAMIN, Confederación de Cámaras Industriales de México)
2002 – 2004	Diplomado en Estudios Empresariales, Universidad de Guadalajara
1998 – 2000	Bachillerato Instituto Ignacio Zaragoza

Experiencia profesional

enero – agosto 2002	CIES S.L., Puebla Coordinador comercial: preparación de ofertas y promociones, seguimiento de pedidos
octubre – diciembre 2005	Arco S.A., Polígono Industrial Malpica, Puebla Prácticas en el departamento de mercadotecnia: seguimiento de clientes y proveedores
julio – septiembre 2005	Vendedor en Electrodomésticos Torres, Puebla

Idiomas
Inglés: hablado y escrito
Francés: nivel medio

Formación complementaria

septiembre 2004	Curso de Gestión Económica Financiera (Cepyme)
julio – agosto 2002	Diploma de instructor de tiempo libre, EPAJ (Escuela Poblana de Actividades pata Jóvenes), Tehuacán
agosto 95 – junio 96	Curso académico en Inglaterra

CURRÍCULUM VITAE

DATOS PERSONALES

Nombre y apellidos	Jill Farmer
Lugar y fecha de nacimiento	Boston, 17 de junio de 1964
Nacionalidad	estadounidense
Estado civil	soltera
Domicilio	Bolívar 134, Caracas
Teléfono	(02) 551.63.60
Correo electrónico	jfarmer@inicia.ve

FORMACIÓN ACADÉMICA

1990	MBA, Harvard Business School
1986	MS (equivalente a maestría) en Economía y Gestión, Universidad de Boston
1982	High school diploma (equivalente a bachillerato superior)

EXPERIENCIA LABORAL

Desde 1998

ACT Venezolana S.A., Caracas
Dirección Corporativa Adjunta al Consejero Delegado
· Diseño de estrategias comerciales
· Diversificación y desarrollo de los mercados existentes
· Apertura de 3 nuevos mercados (Francia, Italia, Grecia)
· Mejora de objetivos entre 80 y 120%

1990-1998

ICN Europa, Amsterdam
Directora Comercial
· Responsable de la política comercial
· Selección y dirección de un equipo de 25 personas
· Definición de objetivos comerciales
· Captación de inversiones

1984-1989

ENSA Tecnología Química, Madrid
Responsable de ventas
· Seguimiento y apoyo de tareas comerciales
· Apertura de nuevas cuentas
· Coordinación de un equipo de 6 personas

IDIOMAS
Inglés: lengua materna
Español: bilingüe
Francés: nociones

Replying to a job advertisement

■ How to structure a letter of application

When you send your CV in response to a job advertisement, it is normally accompanied by a letter mentioning the source and date of the advertisement, as well as the job title and any reference number. Here are some examples of introductory sentences and a sample letter:

Me dirijo a Uds. para expresar mi interés por la oferta aparecida en su página web con la referencia 102-TES, en la que solicitan un Adjunto al departamento de Tesorería de una importante empresa de cosmética.
I am writing to express my interest in the vacancy advertised on your Web site, reference 102-TES, for an assistant in the finance department of a large cosmetics firm.

Con referencia al anuncio aparecido en El Independiente del 4 de agosto, quisiera ser considerada para el puesto arriba mencionado.
I am writing to apply for the above post, as advertised in El Independiente of August 4.

> The last example shown here would be used when the job title and reference number, usually underlined, have been inserted at the beginning of the letter.

Javier Pérez Cruz
Oriente 117, Núm. 22
México DF, CP08500

7 de febrero de 2006

Estimados Sres.:

En documento adjunto, les envío mi CV actualizado en respuesta a su anuncio aparecido en la edición del domingo, 05/02/06, por el que solicitan un Asistente para su departamento de Recursos Humanos, oferta con la referencia A-RRHH. Quedo a su disposición para cualquier aclaración o comentario al respecto en los teléfonos que figuran en mi CV, que les recuerdo a continuación: 55596787 / Celular 85581563.

Les saluda attentemente,
Javier Pérez Cruz

Javier Pérez Cruz
Oriente 117, Núm. 22
México DF, CP08500

February 7, 2006

Dear Sirs,

I am enclosing my CV in reply to your advertisement of 2/5/06 for an assistant in your Personnel Department, reference A-RRHH.

Should you need any further information I can be contacted on the telephone numbers which appear on my CV: 55596787 / Cell 85581563.

Yours truly,
Javier Pérez Cruz

You may like to draw attention to any aspects of your CV which demonstrate how you fulfill the requirements of the job, or highlight particular strengths or achievements which could be of interest to the employer in question:

Tal y como solicitan, poseo una titulación académica en Ciencias Exactas, además de un posgrado en Cálculo Infinitesimal, que según deduzco de sus requisitos, resultaría muy adecuado para el puesto que ofrecen.
As mentioned in the job description, I have a college degree in mathematics, as well as a postgraduate qualification in calculus, which I believe would be ideally suited to the post you are advertising.

Tengo una amplia y contrastada experiencia en los departamentos de Contabilidad y Administración de grandes empresas, tanto nacionales como internacionales.
I have extensive and varied experience in the accounting and administrative departments of large companies, both Spanish* and international.

*or Canadian, Colombian, etc, depending on where the letter is written.

Además de haber seguido algunos cursos de especialización en gestión de proyectos, he ocupado puestos de responsabilidad como coordinador de equipos de hasta 10 personas.
In addition to completing specialist training courses in project management, I have held positions of responsibility, supervising teams of up to 10 people.

In Spanish, **una carrera** refers to the college course studied, rather than the idea of a professional career. For example **tus exámenes de fin de carrera** would be your finals, while **hacer la carrera de Derecho** is to study for a law degree.

Don't be afraid of talking about your personal qualities:

Soy una persona muy trabajadora, capaz de mantener la calma bajo presión.
I am hardworking and able to stay calm under pressure.

Trabajo bien en equipo y me relaciono bien con la gente.
I am a team player with an ability to get on well with people.

Explain the reason why you are applying for the position:

Mi capacidad de comunicación en entornos altamente profesionales, sumada a mi interés por orientar mi trayectoria hacia el sector de las relaciones públicas, me han animado a escribirles.
My ability to communicate in specialized professional contexts, together with my interest in establishing a career in the field of public relations, are what prompted me to write.

Try to appear motivated and available for interview:

Mi disponibilidad para incorporarme a la empresa es inmediata, ya que el pasado mes de junio finalicé mis estudios de licenciatura.
I am available for immediate employment, having completed my degree in June.

▪ Speculative applications

A speculative application is one possible way of obtaining a job, but such letters are difficult to write, since your request for work does not correspond to any official advertisement. For this reason it is important to write a letter that "gets you noticed." The main aim of a speculative letter of application is to secure an offer of an interview.

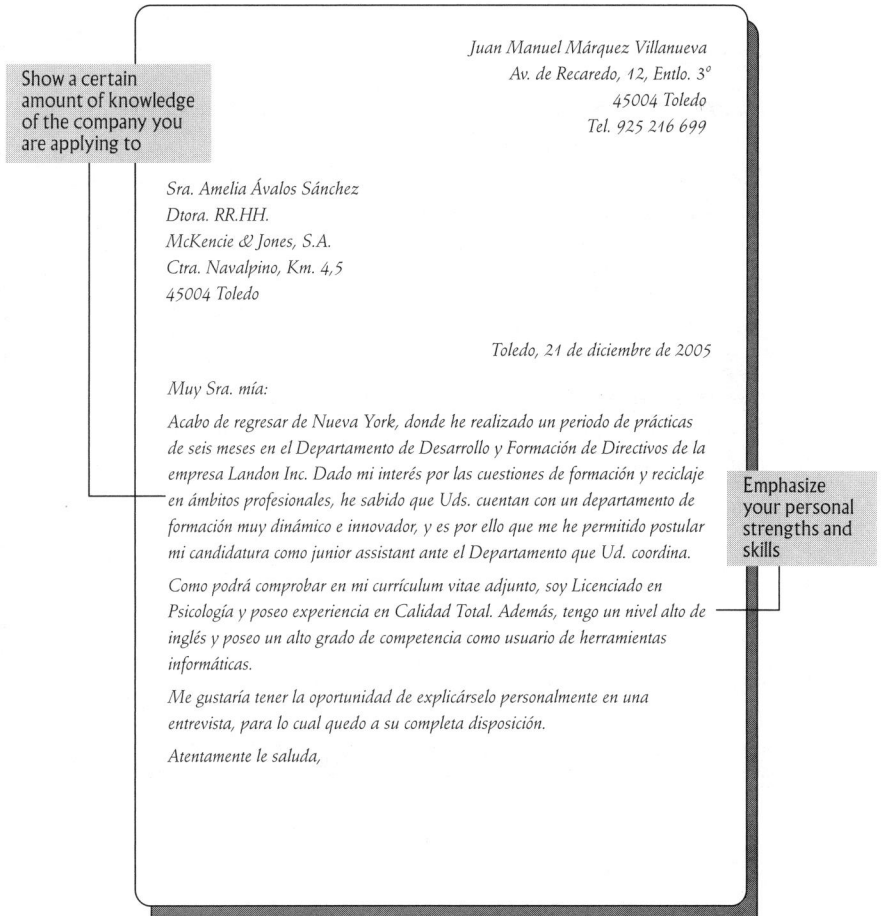

Show a certain amount of knowledge of the company you are applying to

Juan Manuel Márquez Villanueva
Av. de Recaredo, 12, Entlo. 3º
45004 Toledo
Tel. 925 216 699

Sra. Amelia Ávalos Sánchez
Dtora. RR.HH.
McKencie & Jones, S.A.
Ctra. Navalpino, Km. 4,5
45004 Toledo

Toledo, 21 de diciembre de 2005

Muy Sra. mía:

Acabo de regresar de Nueva York, donde he realizado un periodo de prácticas de seis meses en el Departamento de Desarrollo y Formación de Directivos de la empresa Landon Inc. Dado mi interés por las cuestiones de formación y reciclaje en ámbitos profesionales, he sabido que Uds. cuentan con un departamento de formación muy dinámico e innovador, y es por ello que me he permitido postular mi candidatura como junior assistant ante el Departamento que Ud. coordina.

Emphasize your personal strengths and skills

Como podrá comprobar en mi currículum vitae adjunto, soy Licenciado en Psicología y poseo experiencia en Calidad Total. Además, tengo un nivel alto de inglés y poseo un alto grado de competencia como usuario de herramientas informáticas.

Me gustaría tener la oportunidad de explicárselo personalmente en una entrevista, para lo cual quedo a su completa disposición.

Atentamente le saluda,

Juan Manuel Márquez Villanueva
Av. de Recaredo, 12, Entlo. 3°
45004 Toledo
Tél. 925 216 699

Mrs. Amelia Avalos Sánchez
Head of Personnel
McKencie & Jones S.A.
Ctra. Navalpino, Km. 4,5
45004 Toledo

Toledo, December 21, 2005

Dear Mrs Avalos,

I have just returned from New York, where I completed a six-month work experience in the Management Development and Training Department of Landon Inc. Given my interest in training and professional development issues, I learned that your company have a particularly dynamic and innovative training department. It is for this reason that I should like to be considered for a junior assistant post in your department.

As you will see from the enclosed CV, I have a degree in psychology and experience in Total Quality management. I am also proficient in English and possess excellent computer skills.
I would like the opportunity to discuss this personally in an interview and look forward to hearing from you,

Sincerely yours,

■ Asking for work experience

If you are applying for work experience, it's probable that you don't have much professional experience on which to base your request for work. You can, nevertheless, concentrate on the qualities that you think you have that make you suitable for the type of work in question.

Estimado Sr. Suarez:

Los estudios que estoy cursando actualmente en la Escuela de Negocios de Guadalajara tratan principalmente sobre técnicas de venta y los aspectos logísticos de la distribución de bienes de consumo. Estoy en el segundo curso y tengo que hacer unas prácticas de tres meses en una empresa.

Me han recomendado su compañía por el enfoque dinámico y creativo que ofrece sobre estos dos campos y me gustaría unirme a uno de sus grupos de representantes durante el período prácticas.

Como sabe, tras éste tendré que realizar un informe, lo que podría ser de interés para sus departamentos puesto que ofrecería una visión fresca, aunque inexperta, de parte de sus actividades.

Espero que considere seriamente mi solicitud.

Atentamente,

Dear Mr. Suarez,

The course I am currently taking at the Guadalajara Business School deals principally with marketing techniques and the logistical aspects of consumer goods distribution. I am in my second year and have to do three months' work experience in-house.

Your company has been highly recommended to me for its dynamic and creative approach in these two fields and I would like to join one of your teams of reps during the period of my work experience.

As you know, this work experience must be followed by a report, which might be of interest to your departments in that it would offer a fresh, although inexperienced, look at a part of your activities.

I hope that you will give my request serious consideration.

Sincerely yours,

■ Asking for a reference

It is recommended that you include in a letter of application the names and details of two references, a work experience supervisor or a previous employer, who can vouch for your skills and qualities.

> Do obtain the agreement of references before you put their names forward to potential employers.

Marina Gómez Calvo
Avenida García Lorca, 32, Ático 1º
39006 Santander

Sr. Ildefonso García-Prieto
Director de Comunicación y Relaciones Externas
Centro de Estudios para el Desarrollo del Medio Rural
C/ Nicolás Salmerón, 52
39009 Santander

Santander, 5 de octubre de 2005

Estimado Sr. García-Prieto:

Durante el primer semestre del presente año tuve la oportunidad de realizar en su departamento mi práctica como estudiante de la Facultad de Comunicación y Relaciones Públicas con la que su institución tiene acuerdo de colaboración. Acabados mis estudios en junio, me encuentro en situación de búsqueda de empleo.

El motivo de mi carta es preguntarle si podría dar su nombre como superior responsable del trabajo que desempeñé para la Fundación para dar referencias mías en las entrevistas de trabajo que estoy realizando. Espero que esto no le cause ningún inconveniente.

Agradecida por su atención, aprovecho para agradecerle una vez más la buena acogida que me dispensaron y lo mucho que aprendí y disfruté en esos seis meses.

Reciba mi más cordial saludo,

Marina Gómez Calvo
Avenida García Lorca, 32, Ático 1º
39006 Santander

Mr. Ildefonso García-Prieto
Head of Communication and External Relations
Center for Rural Development Studies
C/ Nicolás Salmerón, 52
39009 Santander

Santander, October 5, 2005

Dear Mr. García-Prieto,

As a student in the Faculty of Communication and Public Relations, with which your Center has a cooperation agreement, I had the opportunity of doing my work experience in your department during the first six months of this year. Having completed my studies in June I am now seeking employment.

The reason I am writing is to ask if I could give your name, as my supervising officer while I was working for the Center, as a reference for any job interviews I attend. I hope this will be all right with you.

Thanking you for your cooperation, I'd like to take the opportunity to thank you again for looking after me so well and for all that I learned during a really enjoyable six months.

Sincerely yours ,

Writing an advertisement

Advertisements offering or requesting goods or services are found in some newspapers or in shops. Free newspapers that specialize in them are often available at newsstands, in the subway in big cities, at the entrance to supermarkets, etc.

The advertisements are written in a telegraphic style, often with abbreviations or omitted articles and prepositions, and must give the advertiser's details clearly.

▪ Offers of goods or services

In the interests of clarity the abbreviations in the first advertisement below have been translated in full.

> **CTRA. REGIONAL - PZA. JALISCO. Amplio piso en finca rehabilitada. Gran salón-com. ext. con balcón. Tres hab., cocina, galería, mucho sol, tranquilidad. Oportunidad por zona.**
> **320.000 pesos. 56829811**
> CARRETERA REGIONAL- PLAZA JALISCO. Spacious apartment in newly renovated building. Large living-dining room, with balcony, facing the street. Three rooms, kitchen, veranda, very sunny, quiet. Bargain for the area.
> 320,000 pesos. 56829811

> **Renault Scénic seminuevo, modelo 5 puertas, aire acondicionado, radio-CD, pocos kilómetros, se vende. Tel. 972 456 883**
> For sale: Renault Scenic, nearly new, 5-door, air-conditioning, radio-CD player, low mileage. Tel. 972 456 883

> **Estudiante de medicina cuida niños, noches a partir de 20h.**
> **Tel: 541 928 335**
> Medical student available for babysitting. Evenings from 8 p.m. Tel: 541 928 335

> **Se vende refrigerador, en buen estado, con congelador.**
> **2,000 pesos ó 200 dólares, a negociar. Tel: 028 536 475 (mañanas)**
> For sale: fridge, in good condition, with freezer compartment. 2,000 pesos or $200. Tel: 02 18 53 64 75 (mornings)

▪ Requests for goods or services

Here are some examples of advertisements:

> Estudiante español cambiaría horas de conversación en italiano por horas de conversación en español, con vistas a una beca Erasmus en Padua. Tel: 054 367 788
> *Spanish student seeks conversation exchange with Italian speaker with view to ERASMUS scholarship in Padua. Tel: 054 367 788*

Compro juegos de Playstation 2 a buen precio (200 pesos). Contactar a: tauro66@hotmail.com
Playstation 2 games bought, good prices (200 pesos). E-mail: tauro66@hotmail.com

Se busca: programador en plataforma Linux, que tenga conocimientos de SQL y C++. Interesados mandar correo con currículum, así como sueldo al que se aspira a: Las Huertas, 213-215, 46001 Valencia
Linux programmer required, knowledge of SQL and C++. Write with CV and salary expected to: Las Huertas, 213-215, 46001 Valencia

Profesor nativo se ofrece para clases particulares de inglés. Clases de conversación. Preparación exámenes First/Proficiency. Descuentos para grupos. Llamar tardes a partir de 17h. Tel. 91 348 75 69
Native speaker offers private English lessons. Conversation classes. Preparation for First/Proficiency exams. Group discounts. Telephone after 5 pm: 91 348 75 69

Telephone

Making and answering telephone calls

▪ Making a call

If you call someone you know at home you can use the following phrases:

Hola or Aló, ¿está Pilar?
Hello, is Pilar there?

Hola, soy Carmen. ¿Puedo hablar con Juan, por favor?
Hi, this is Carmen. Can I speak to Juan, please?

Hola, ¿hablo con Rodrigo?
Hello, is that Rodrigo?

Hola, soy yo, cariño.
Hello, it's me, dear.

Business calls use more formal expressions:

Disculpe, ¿puede ponerme con la extensión 333?
Could I have extension 333, please?

Buenas tardes, ¿es el departamento de contabilidad?
Good afternoon, is that the accounts department?

▪ Answering

These are typical ways of answering the telephone in different situations:

¿Bueno? *(Méx) or* ¿Aló? *or* ¿Dígame? *or* ¿Hola?
Hello?

Despacho del Sr. Álvarez. ¿Con quién hablo?
Mr. Álvarez's office. Who's calling, please?

Oficina de turismo. ¿En qué puedo ayudarle?
Tourist office. How can I help you?

To answer someone who wants to speak to someone else, use the following expressions:

Sí, un momento. ¿De parte de quién?
Just a moment. Who's calling, please?

No cuelgue. Enseguida se lo paso.
Hold on. I'll just get him for you.

¿Con quién quiere hablar?
Who do you want to speak to?

> Marta no se encuentra en este momento. ¿Quién la llama?
> *Marta's not here. Who's calling, please?'*

If you are answering the phone and someone is not available, you can say:

> Lo siento, hoy no está. ¿Quiere dejarle un mensaje?
> *I'm sorry, she's not in today. Would you like to leave a message?*

> Sí, está, pero ahora no puede venir.
> *Yes, he's here, but he can't come to the phone at the moment.*

> En estos momentos está ocupado. ¿Podría volver a llamar más tarde?
> *He's a bit busy at the moment. Could you call back later?*

The caller might then say:

> ¿Cuándo va a regresar?
> *When will he be back?*

> ¿Puede decirle que he llamado, por favor?
> *Can you tell her I called, please?*

> ¿Podría decirle que me llame? Tiene mi teléfono.
> *Could you ask him to call me? He has my phone number.*

Problems during a telephone call

You could have a bad line, be unable to get through or be speaking to someone you can't understand very well. In this case you could use one of the following phrases:

> No le oigo bien, hay interferencias.
> *I can't hear you properly, there's a lot of noise on the line.*

> Las líneas estaban saturadas.
> *All the lines were engaged.*

> Por favor, ¿puede repetir la primera parte del número?
> *Could you repeat the first part of the number, please?*

> ¿Puede deletrearme el nombre?
> *Can you spell that name, please?*

■ If it's the wrong number

If you are answering :

> Creo que se ha equivocado de número.
> *I think you've got the wrong number.*

> ¿Está seguro que ha marcado bien?
> *Are you sure you dialed the right number?*

If you are the caller:

> Disculpe, me he equivocado de número.
> *Sorry, wrong number.*

Finishing a telephone conversation

These are expressions you might use if you have to cut short a telephone call :

> Tengo que dejarte. Hay una llamada por la otra línea.
> *I have to go. There's a call on the other line.*

> Tengo que colgar, que están llamando a la puerta.
> *Look, I'll have to hang up now. There's someone at the door.*

You can use these phrases if you're talking to a friend:

> OK, te llamo mañana. Chao.
> *OK, I'll call you tomorrow. Bye.*

Nos vemos.
See you.

Hasta pronto.
See you soon.

In a more formal context it would be:

Hasta luego.
Goodbye.

Cellular phones

New expressions have come into use with the advent of cellular phones. The following could be useful:

No te encontraba. ¿Tenías el móvil desconectado/apagado?
I couldn't get hold of you. Did you have your cell phone switched off?

Si se corta, te llamo más tarde, ¿OK?
If we get cut off, I'll call you later, OK?

Si no contesto, déjame un mensaje en el buzón de voz.
If I don't answer, leave a message on my voice mail.

Voy a entrar en el metro y no tengo cobertura, llámame en 15 minutos.
I'm going into the subway and there's no signal. Call me in 15 minutes.

Envíame un mensaje con tu número de (teléfono) celular.
Text me your cell (phone) number.

No me queda mucha batería.
I haven't got much battery left.

Answering machines

▪ Recorded greetings

These usually follow a fairly standard format:

Ha llamado al 93.123.44.55. En este momento no podemos atenderle. Si quiere, puede dejar un mensaje/su número de teléfono al oír la señal y nos pondremos en contacto con usted.
Hello, you have reached the number 93.123.44.55. We are unable to take your call at the moment. If you wish, you may leave a message/your telephone number after the beep and we will contact you.

Aló. Ahora no estamos en casa, pero si dejas un mensaje, te llamaremos en cuanto podamos.
Hello, this is Eva and José. We're not at home right now, but if you leave a message, we'll call you as soon as we can.

▪ Leaving a message

This is an example of a message relating to a business telephone call:

Me llamo Luis Martín y llamo por el anuncio del periódico. Mi número de teléfono es el 907.123.45.67 y pueden llamarme a cualquier hora del día. Gracias.
Hello. My name is Luis Martín and I'm calling about the advertisement in the newspaper. My telephone number is 907.123.45.67 and I can be reached any time of day. Thank you.

And here is a message for a friend:

Hola, éste es un mensaje para Jorge. Llevo llamándote todo el día, ¿dónde te metes? Llámame cuando llegues. Chao.
Hello, this is a message for Jorge. I've been calling you all day. What are you up to? Call me when you get in. Bye.

E-mail

Starting and ending e-mails

Symbols common in e-mail addresses such as: **G_perez-menescal@terra.es** are **@** (arroba) *[at]*, **_** (guión bajo) *[underscore]*, **-** (guión) *[hyphen]*, **.** (punto) *[dot]*.

The header of a message consists of a series of sections:

> **De:** *From:* refers to the address of the sender, while

> **Para:** or **A:** *To:* refers to the address of the person the e-mail is sent to,

> **Cc:** (con copia) *Cc: [courtesy copy]* refers to the addresses of other recipients.

> **Cco:** (con copia oculta) *Bcc: [blind courtesy copy]* refers to the addresses of other recipients when they are not told who else has been sent the e-mail.

> **Asunto:** *Subject:*, which is optional, says what the message is about.

> **Adjuntar archivo:** *Attach:* refers to a file sent as an attachment to the e-mail.

It's not always necessary to start an e-mail with a standard greeting. The following are commonly used in messages between friends:

> **Hola, Pablo:**
> *Hi Pablo,*

> **¿Qué tal, Isabel?**
> *How's things, Isabel?*

To business colleagues greetings are more formal:

> **Estimado Sr. Hernández:**
> *Dear Mr. Hernández,*

> **Sra. Martín:**
> *Dear Mrs. Martín,*

To end an e-mail you can use:

> **Cordialmente**
> *Best wishes,*

> **Saludos**
> *Regards,*

> **Abrazos** *or*

> **Un beso**
> *Love,*

> **Nos vemos** *or* **Hasta pronto**
> *See you soon,*

Writing an e-mail message

Probably because of the immediacy of the communication, the language used in e-mails can be much more direct than in a letter.

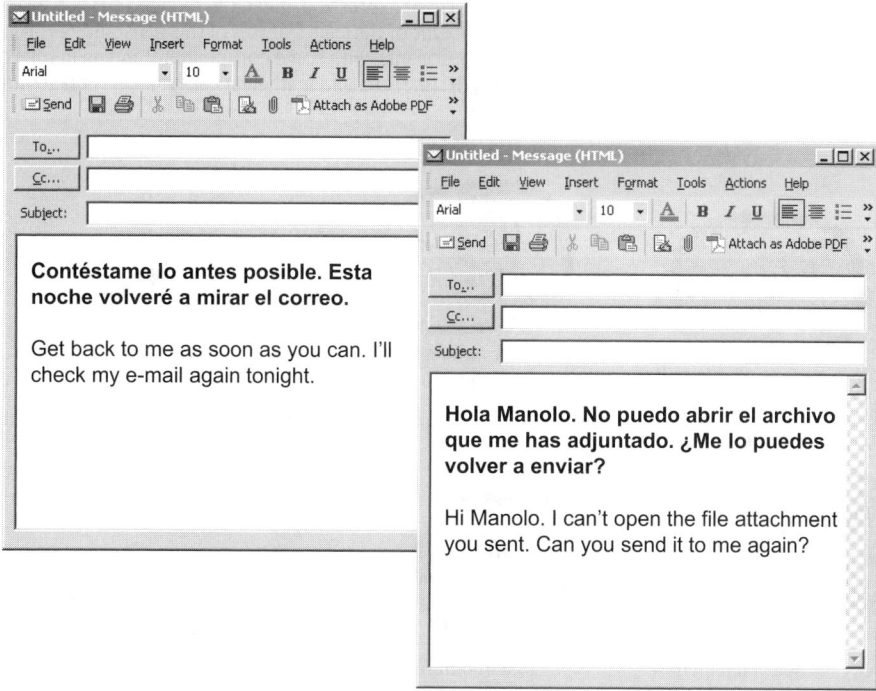

Here is an example of an e-mail from one friend to another, suggesting they meet:

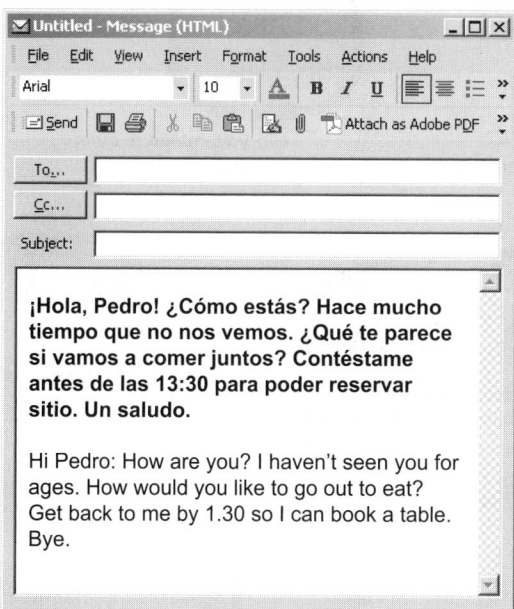

Text messaging

Cell phones have brought with them a whole new form of expression, given the reduced space available for text messages and the time it takes to write them. One of the main features of this constantly evolving shorthand is the elimination of many vowels and consonants, with some consonants standing in for vowels: Q (que or cu), T (te), K (ca, cu or que), S (se), M (me) etc. and mathematical symbols representing some words. Here are some typical examples:

K H?
HRU?
¿qué tal?
how are you?

tas OK?
RUOK?
¿estás bien?
are you OK?

NV
CU
Nos vemos
see you

hsta mñn
CU2MORO
hasta mañana
see you tomorrow

a q ora?
wot time?
¿a qué hora?
what time?

ablamos + tard
TLK2UL8R
hablamos más tarde
talk to you later

qirsir?
DUWAN2G?
¿quieres ir?
do you want to go?

yo tb tq
ILUVU2
yo también te quiero
I love you too

slmos ste find?
wnt 2 go out @ wknd?
¿salimos este fin de semana?
shall we go out this weekend?

yaman
llámame
call me

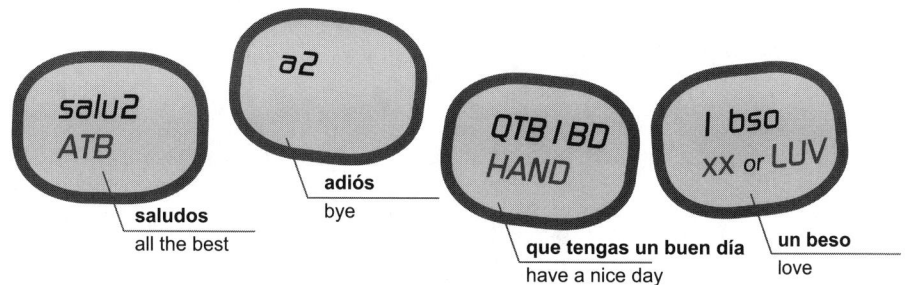

salu2
ATB
saludos
all the best

a2
adiós
bye

QTB I BD
HAND
que tengas un buen día
have a nice day

I bso
XX or LUV
un beso
love

Here are some examples of longer messages:

m e kambiao l numero
d mvl. apuntad l nuevo:
672 345 124
got nu mob no:
672 345 124

Me he cambiado el número de móvil.
Apunta el nuevo: 672 345 124
I've changed my cell number. Make a
note of the new one: 672 345 124

doy l fiesta n kasa l
vierns a las 10, t apuntas?
party @ mine Fri @ 10 u
up 4 it?

Doy una fiesta en casa el viernes a
las 10, ¿vas a venir?
I'm having a party at home this Friday
at 10, are you up for it ?

Guía de comunicación en inglés

1. La correspondencia por carta   (49)

2. Concertar una cita   (53)

3. Búsqueda de empleo   (55)

4. Redactar un anuncio   (64)

5. El teléfono   (66)

6. El correo electrónico   (69)

7. El mensaje de texto o SMS   (71)

La correspondencia por carta
Presentación de una carta destinada a un amigo o conocido

En una carta personal, la dirección del remitente (sin su nombre) se escribe en la parte superior derecha del papel. La fecha se pone justo debajo.

La fecha puede escribirse completa:

September 29 2006,
July 12th 2006,
January 3rd 2006,
April 19th 2006.

O bien abreviada:

Sept-29-06,
09/29/06,
09.29.06.

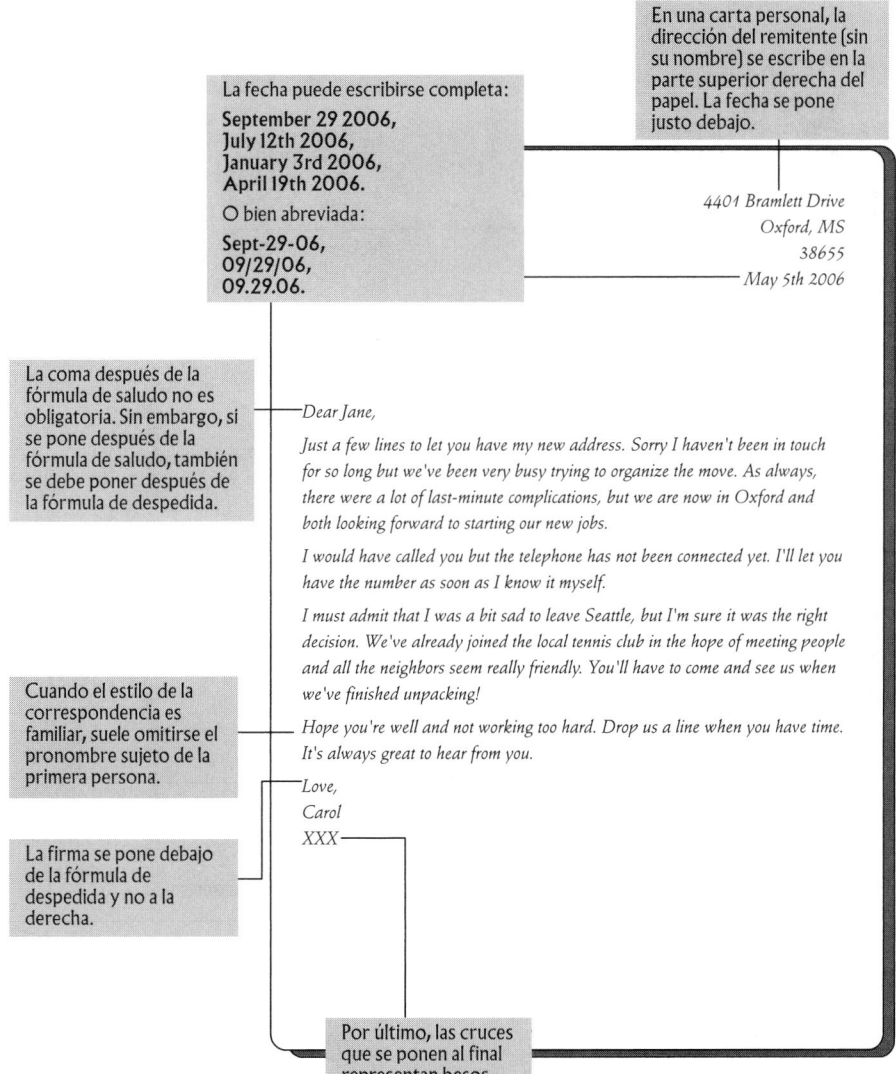

4401 Bramlett Drive
Oxford, MS
38655
May 5th 2006

La coma después de la fórmula de saludo no es obligatoria. Sin embargo, si se pone después de la fórmula de saludo, también se debe poner después de la fórmula de despedida.

Dear Jane,

Just a few lines to let you have my new address. Sorry I haven't been in touch for so long but we've been very busy trying to organize the move. As always, there were a lot of last-minute complications, but we are now in Oxford and both looking forward to starting our new jobs.

I would have called you but the telephone has not been connected yet. I'll let you have the number as soon as I know it myself.

I must admit that I was a bit sad to leave Seattle, but I'm sure it was the right decision. We've already joined the local tennis club in the hope of meeting people and all the neighbors seem really friendly. You'll have to come and see us when we've finished unpacking!

Cuando el estilo de la correspondencia es familiar, suele omitirse el pronombre sujeto de la primera persona.

Hope you're well and not working too hard. Drop us a line when you have time. It's always great to hear from you.

Love,
Carol
XXX

La firma se pone debajo de la fórmula de despedida y no a la derecha.

Por último, las cruces que se ponen al final representan besos.

No es necesario mencionar el nombre del lugar desde donde se escribe. Después del número del día puede añadirse 'th', 'st' o 'rd', aunque esto está cada vez más en desuso. En Estados Unidos, los nombres y la dirección del remitente ya no aparecen en la correspondencia personal.

Presentación de una carta formal o comercial

En la correspondencia más formal, el nombre y la dirección del remitente se escriben en la parte superior derecha del papel (salvo cuando se trata de un papel con membrete, en cuyo caso se escribe en el centro).

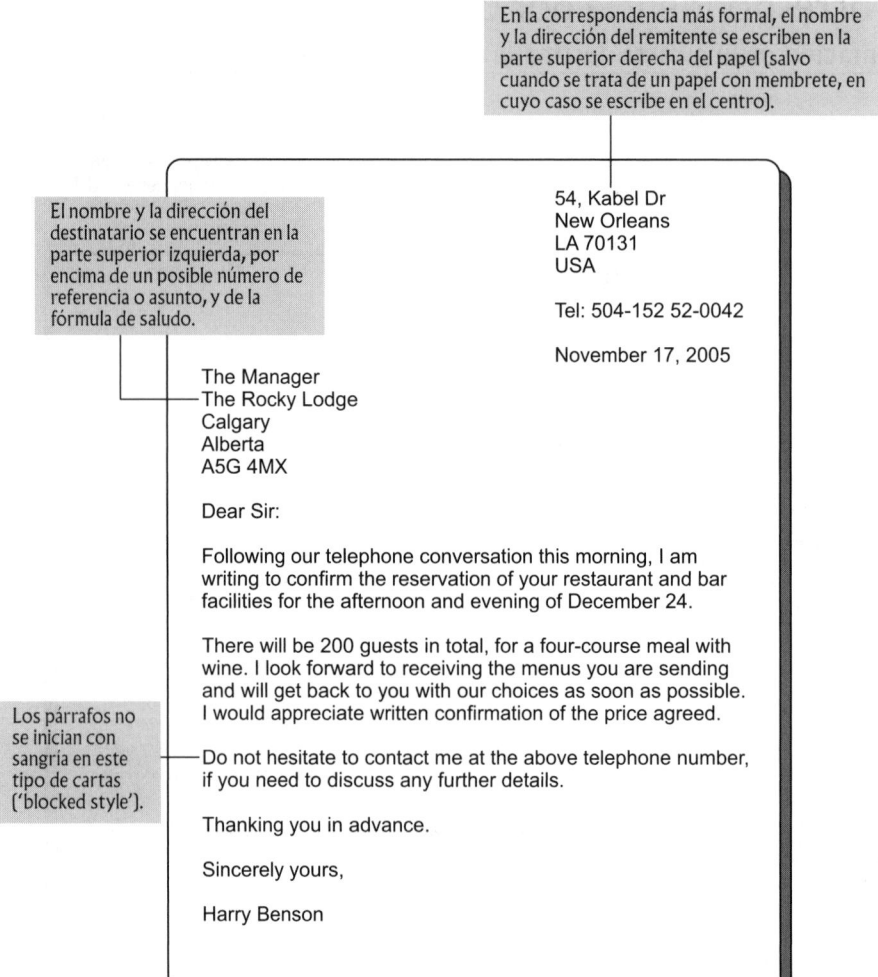

El nombre y la dirección del destinatario se encuentran en la parte superior izquierda, por encima de un posible número de referencia o asunto, y de la fórmula de saludo.

54, Kabel Dr
New Orleans
LA 70131
USA

Tel: 504-152 52-0042

November 17, 2005

The Manager
The Rocky Lodge
Calgary
Alberta
A5G 4MX

Dear Sir:

Following our telephone conversation this morning, I am writing to confirm the reservation of your restaurant and bar facilities for the afternoon and evening of December 24.

There will be 200 guests in total, for a four-course meal with wine. I look forward to receiving the menus you are sending and will get back to you with our choices as soon as possible. I would appreciate written confirmation of the price agreed.

Los párrafos no se inician con sangría en este tipo de cartas ('blocked style').

Do not hesitate to contact me at the above telephone number, if you need to discuss any further details.

Thanking you in advance.

Sincerely yours,

Harry Benson

En el cuerpo de la carta, las fechas nunca van precedidas de 'of' o 'the'. Aún así se pronuncia 'July the seventh' o 'the seventh of July'.

Fórmulas de saludo y fórmulas de despedida

■ Carta destinada a una persona conocida o amiga

Fórmulas de saludo   Fórmulas de despedida

Dear David   *Love*
Dear Lily   *With love*
Dear Mom and Dad   *Love from both of us*
Dear Uncle Toby   *Love to all*

Si queremos emplear un tono más afectuoso, utilizaremos alguna de las siguientes fórmulas:

My dearest Jill   *Lots of love*
My dear Patrick   *All my love*
With all our love

Las siguientes expresiones son más neutrales:

Yours
Best wishes

■ Carta formal o de negocios

Si conocemos el nombre de nuestro destinatario, podemos emplear:

Dear Mr. Jones   *Sincerely*
Dear Mrs. Clarke   *Yours truly*
Dear Ms. Fletcher

> Con frecuencia se prefiere la abreviatura **Ms** con respecto a **Mrs** o a **Miss** ya que así se evita la referencia al estado civil de nuestra corresponsal.

Las fórmulas siguientes se emplean cuando ya existe una cierta familiaridad con la otra persona:

Dear Dr. Martin   *With best wishes*
With kind regards

Si nos dirigimos a alguien cuyo nombre desconocemos:

Dear Sir   *Sincerely yours*
Dear Madam

Finalmente, si nos dirigimos a alguien cuyo nombre desconocemos y además no sabemos si es hombre o mujer:

Dear Sir or Madam   *Sincerely yours*
Dear Sir/Madam
Dear Sirs

Presentación de un sobre

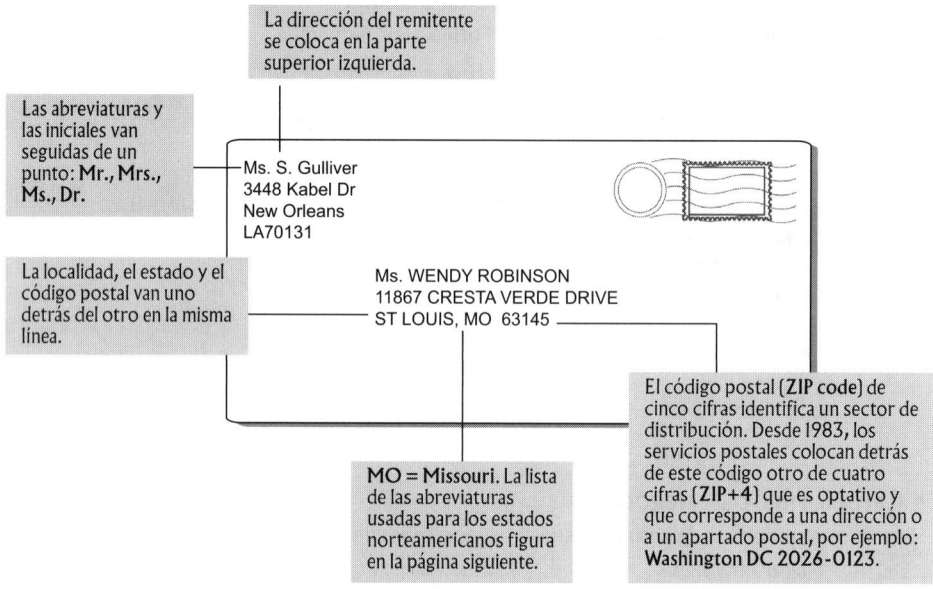

La dirección del remitente se coloca en la parte superior izquierda.

Las abreviaturas y las iniciales van seguidas de un punto: **Mr., Mrs., Ms., Dr.**

Ms. S. Gulliver
3448 Kabel Dr
New Orleans
LA70131

La localidad, el estado y el código postal van uno detrás del otro en la misma línea.

Ms. WENDY ROBINSON
11867 CRESTA VERDE DRIVE
ST LOUIS, MO 63145

MO = Missouri. La lista de las abreviaturas usadas para los estados norteamericanos figura en la página siguiente.

El código postal (**ZIP code**) de cinco cifras identifica un sector de distribución. Desde 1983, los servicios postales colocan detrás de este código otro de cuatro cifras (**ZIP+4**) que es optativo y que corresponde a una dirección o a un apartado postal, por ejemplo: **Washington DC 2026-0123**.

Abreviaturas utilizadas en los sobres

Dr (Doctor)
Doctor

Prof (Professor)
Profesor

Ave (Avenue)
Avenida

Blvd (Boulevard)
Bulevar

Rd (Road)
Calle

St (Street)
Calle

En la actualidad, las abreviaturas de los títulos, las calles y las iniciales no van seguidas de punto.

■ Abreviaturas de los estados de EE.UU.

AK	Alaska	MT	Montana
AL	Alabama	NC	North Carolina
AR	Arkansas	ND	North Dakota
AZ	Arizona	NE	Nebraska
CA	California	NH	New Hampshire
CO	Colorado	NJ	New Jersey
CT	Connecticut	NM	New Mexico
DC	District of Columbia	NV	Nevada
DE	Delaware	NY	New York
FL	Florida	OH	Ohio
GA	Georgia	OK	Oklahoma
HI	Hawaii	OR	Oregon
IA	Iowa	PA	Pennsylvania
ID	Idaho	RI	Rhode Island
IL	Illinois	SC	South Carolina
IN	Indiana	SD	South Dakota
KS	Kansas	TN	Tennessee
KY	Kentucky	TX	Texas
LA	Louisiana	UT	Utah
MA	Massachusetts	VA	Virginia
MD	Maryland	VT	Vermont
ME	Maine	WA	Washington
MI	Michigan	WI	Wisconsin
MN	Minnesota	WY	Wyoming
MO	Missouri		
MS	Mississippi		

Concertar una cita

Concertar un encuentro por teléfono

El teléfono es el medio más utilizado para ponerse de acuerdo con alguien para hacer algo. Además del día, la hora y el lugar del encuentro, por lo general se hacen sugerencias sobre lo que se va a hacer. He aquí algunas expresiones útiles:

> **What about ten o'clock?**
> *¿Qué tal a las diez?*

> **Why don't we meet next weekend?**
> *¿Nos vemos el fin de semana que viene?*

> **Let's have a coffee before we go home.**
> *Vamos a tomar un café antes de volver a casa.*

> **I suggest we meet up after the show.**
> *¿Porqué no nos vemos después del espectáculo?*

Shall we just stay in and watch TV?
¿Y si nos quedamos en casa viendo la tele?

Can we meet soon?
¿Podemos vernos pronto?

Are you busy on Friday evening?
¿Estás ocupada el viernes por la noche?

Quedar por e-mail

Aunque es habitual organizar citas de negocios por e-mail y el estilo todavía sigue siendo algo formal, este medio nos permite expresarnos de manera más directa:

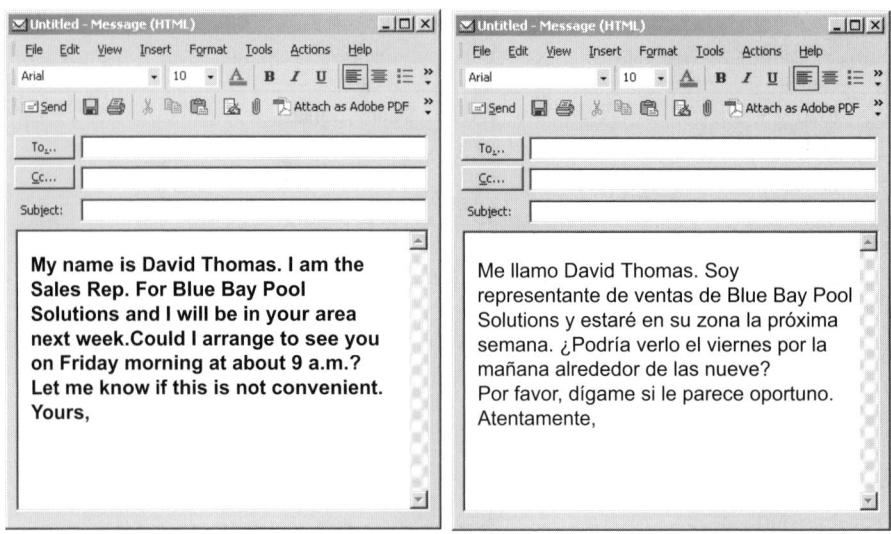

En caso de que sea una cita entre amigos, el estilo es más informal aún:

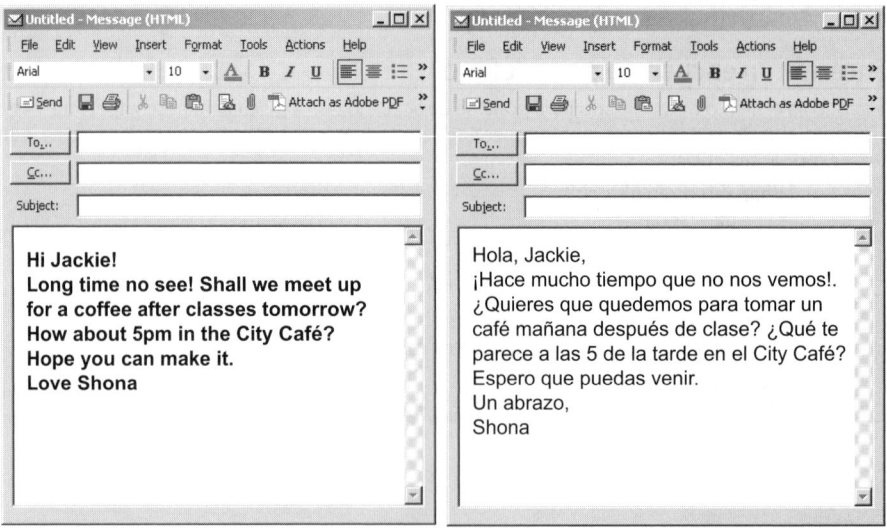

Nótese el uso de las abreviaturas latinas **'a.m.'** y **'p.m.'** para expresar la hora antes del mediodía y después del mediodía ('ante meridian', 'post meridian').

Búsqueda de empleo

Cartas de presentación

Para solicitar un puesto de trabajo en prácticas, responder a una oferta de trabajo o presentarnos de manera espontánea en una empresa hay que tener en cuenta varios elementos fundamentales. A continuación, encontraremos algunas expresiones que nos orientarán en cada momento. En primer lugar, debemos precisar el puesto para el que nos presentamos:

> **I am writing to inquire as to whether you would be interested in offering me a short period of work experience in your company.**
> *Les escribo para saber si estarían interesados en ofrecerme un trabajo en prácticas o una pasantía en su empresa durante un periodo de tiempo corto.*

> **I would like to inquire as to whether there are any openings for junior sales administrators in your company.**
> *Me gustaría saber si existe alguna vacante en su empresa para subdirectores de ventas.*

> **I would like to apply for the position of computer programmer, as advertised on your Web site.**
> *Quisiera presentarme al puesto de programador informático, que aparece anunciado en su página web.*

> **I am writing to apply for the above post, as advertised in the *Times* of August 4, 2006.**
> *Escribo en solicitud del puesto antes mencionado, anunciado en el periódico Times de fecha 4 de agosto de 2006.*

A continuación se deben incluir algunos ejemplos de nuestra experiencia personal para demostrar que tenemos el perfil adecuado para el puesto:

> **I contributed to the development of our accounting software.**
> *Colaboré en la creación de nuestros programas de contabilidad.*

> **I coordinated the changeover from one operating system to another.**
> *Coordiné el cambio de un sistema operativo al otro.*

> **I developed new designs for a range of table linen.**
> *Creé nuevos diseños para una línea de mantelerías.*

> **I gained experience in several major aspects of marketing.**
> *He adquirido experiencia en varios aspectos importantes de marketing.*

> **I presented our new products at the annual sales fair.**
> *Presenté nuestros nuevos productos en la exposición anual de ventas.*

> **I have supervised a team of freelancers on several projects.**
> *He sido supervisor de un equipo de colaboradores externos en diferentes proyectos.*

Después podemos referirnos a nuestras cualidades personales:

I see myself as systematic and methodical in my approach to work.
Me considero una persona que trabaja de forma sistemática y metódica.

I am an impartial and tolerant person, with an ability to get on well with people from all walks of life.
Soy una persona imparcial y tolerante, con capacidad de llevarme bien con personas de diferentes estilos de vida.

I am hardworking and commercially minded, and able to stay calm under pressure.
Trabajo mucho y tengo espíritu comercial. También soy capaz de mantener la calma, bajo presión.

My last job required me to be sensitive and tactful, and I feel that my personality proved to be suited to this type of work.
Mi último trabajo me exigía sensibilidad y tacto, y creo que mi personalidad demostró ser adecuada a este tipo de trabajo.

Del mismo modo, explicaremos por qué nos interesa obtener el puesto:

I am keen to find a post with more responsibility where I can use my programming skills.
Tengo intención de encontrar un puesto de mayor responsabilidad en el que pueda aplicar mis conocimientos de programación.

I have been doing temporary work, and now wish to find a more permanent full-time position.
Llevo tiempo realizando trabajos temporales y ahora quisiera encontrar un puesto con mayor estabilidad laboral y a tiempo completo.

I would now like to further my career.
Me gustaría darle un nuevo empuje a mi carrera.

Debemos mostrarnos motivados y disponibles para una entrevista:

I would be pleased to come for an interview at your convenience.
Estaría encantado de asistir a una entrevista cuando lo consideren oportuno.

I would be delighted to meet you to discuss the position further. I am available on Monday and Wednesday afternoons.
Estaría encantado de reunirme con ustedes para comentar más detalles sobre el puesto. Estoy disponible los lunes y miércoles por la tarde.

Please do not hesitate to contact me if you need more detailed information.
Por favor no duden en llamarme si necesitan más información.

Solicitar un trabajo en prácticas

Si buscamos un trabajo en prácticas, debemos concentrarnos en las cualidades requeridas para este tipo de trabajo y subrayar que creemos tener el perfil adecuado, a pesar de que no tengamos mucha experiencia laboral.

---

215 Lower Beresford Street
Boston, MA 02458

Ms. F Osborne
Grandley Commercial Finance
45-47 Monument Plaza
Dayton, OH 45418

January 4, 2006

Dear Ms. Osborne,

I am a student, currently in my final year of a Business Studies degree.

I am writing to inquire as to whether you have any openings for three months' work experience in your department during the period July to September this year.

Throughout my course of study, I have concentrated particularly on overseas markets, imports and exports, and business English, and so I hope that while learning from your business activities, I may also be able to help out with some of the simpler tasks in the office.

I am reliable and punctual, and am looking forward to getting an insight into the world of work.

Please do not hesitate to contact me if you require any more information. I am available for interview on Wednesday and Friday afternoons. In the meantime, I look forward to hearing from you.

Yours sincerely,
Jane Parkinson

4 de enero de 2006

Estimada Sra. Osborne:

En la actualidad, estoy cursando el ultimo año de licenciatura en Administración de Empresas.

Les escribo para saber si en su departamento cuentan con vacantes para una práctica profesional de tres meses, en el período de julio a septiembre de este año.

Durante mis estudios me he concentrado particularmente en mercados americanos, importaciones y exportaciones, e inglés comercial, así que espero que mientras aprendo de su actividad empresarial, pueda colaborar en alguna de las tareas más sencillas de la oficina.

Soy una persona confiable y puntual, y mi intención es conocer el mundo laboral desde dentro.

No dude en llamarme si necesita más información. Estoy disponible para una entrevista los miércoles y viernes por la tarde. Mientras tanto, quedo a la espera de sus noticias.

Attentamente,
Jane Parkinson

Presentarse de forma espontánea

Si no respondemos a una demanda de trabajo en concreto, sino que sólo nos presentamos a la empresa por si acaso surge alguna oportunidad, debemos tratar de obtener la máxima información sobre el puesto que nos podría interesar y preguntar si está disponible. Si ya tenemos un contacto con la empresa en cuestión, podemos mencionarlo en nuestra carta y adjuntar nuestro currículum.

2246 Cambleton Drive
Milwauke, WI 53216

Mr. D. Thomson
Personnel Manager
Fraser's Department Store
20-24 West Moore Street
Waukesha, WI 53216

July 4, 2005

Dear Mr. Thomson,

Thank you very much for taking the time last Wednesday to speak to me about the possibility of a training position with your company.

Your advice has strongly encouraged me to pursue a career in this field, and your company's core activities closely match my own interests.I would therefore like to apply for a Trainee Manager placement. Please find attached a CV which highlights my professional experience and qualities which I feel make me suited to this position.

I have a strong interest in and knowledge of staff management, and have gained extensive experience in handling heavy workloads and meeting deadlines. I pride myself on being well-organised and a self-starter, and have excellent communication skills. I am extremely motivated to develop my career with Frasers' department stores, and so would very much appreciate the opportunity to discuss further mysuitability for a traineeship.

Please feel free to contact me, either by e-mail: fobrien@quickserve.com, or by leaving a message on 545-6123.

I look forward to speaking to you soon.

Yours sincerely,
Ms. Fiona O'Brien

Asunto: Puesto de gerente en prácticas o Pasantía en puesto de gerente
Estimado Sr. Thomson:

Muchas gracias por el tiempo que me dedicó el pasado miércoles para hablar de la posibilidad de un puesto en prácticas en su empresa.

Sus consejos me han animado mucho a emprender una trayectoria profesional en este campo, y las actividades principales a las que se dedica su empresa coinciden con mis propios intereses. Por ello me gustaría presentarme como candidato para un puesto de gerente en practicas. Adjunto le envío mi currículum, en el que se subraya la información más destacada en relación con mi experiencia profesional, así como las cualidades que considero me hacen adecuada para este puesto.

Tengo un gran interés en la gestión de personal y tengo bastante conocimiento del mismo. También he adquirido suficiente experiencia para hacer frente a un grand volumen de trabajo y cumplir los plazos establecidos.

Puedo afirmar que soy una persona organizada y autosuficiente y cuento con excelentes aptitudes de comunicación. Por otro lado, sería para mí una gran satisfacción poder desarrollar mi carrera en los grandes almacenes Fraser's, de manera que estaría muy agradecida de tener la oportunidad de hablar con más detenimiento sobre la adecuación de mi perfil profesional para el puesto en prácticas.

No dude en ponerse en contacto conmigo, por correo electrónico (fobrien@quickserve.com), o dejando un mensaje en el contestador del 01625 456123.

Con la confianza de que pronto pueda hablar con usted, me despido muy atentamente,

Fiona O'Brien

Responder a una oferta de trabajo

Si respondemos a un anuncio específico, debemos indicar dónde lo hemos visto, así como el puesto que nos interesa:

> **I am responding to your advertisement for a graphic designer, which appeared in the** *Sentinel* **on October 22, 2005**
> *En respuesta a su anuncio aparecido en el Sentinel del 22 de octubre de 2005, quisiera manifestarle mi interés por el puesto de diseñador gráfico.*

He aquí un modelo de respuesta a una oferta:

Subject: application for post of desktop publishing manager
Dear Mrs. Williams,

I am writing in response to your advertisement in the January edition of
"Publishing News," and am enclosing my CV for your review.

I have gained valuable experience in book design using various types of
publishing software, and have written technical specifications and super-
vised page design and layout for both dictionary text and illustrated
books. In my current position at Isis Press, I have initiated monitoring
systems that enable pre-press controllers to work more easily with authors
and other editors. I am currently attending an evening class on the use of
QuarkXPress for the advanced user, and am now looking for a post which
would give me an opportunity to use my new skills. I look forward to
having the opportunity to discuss the position further with you. I shall be
in Denver for a week at the end of January, and would be available for
interview anytime between the 24th and the 31st.

Yours sincerely,
Katie Mitchell

Asunto: Solicitud del puesto de director de autoedición

Estimada Sra. Williams:

Les escribo en respuesta a su anuncio aparecido en el ejemplar de enero de
"Publishing News" y les adjunto mi currículum para su consideración.

Tengo bastante experiencia en el área del diseño de libros y he utilizado varios
programas de software de edición. También he escrito especificaciones
técnicas y he sido supervisora del diseño y la maquetación de algunas páginas, tanto para diccionarios como para libros ilustrados. En mi actual trabajo
de Isis Press, he puesto en marcha unos sistemas de control que permiten a los
encargados de primpresión trabajar con más facilidad con autores y con otros
editores. En la actualidad estoy asistiendo a un curso nocturno de QuarkX-
Press avanzado y busco un puesto que me dé la oportunidad de poner en
práctica mis nuevos conocimientos. Confío en tener la oportunidad de hablar
más detenidamente de este puesto con usted. Estaré en Denver durante una
semana a finales de enero y podría asistir a una entrevista en cualquier
momento entre los días 24 y 31.

Muy atentamente,
Katie Mitchell

Modelos de currículum

JESSICA O'GARA
725 Boulder Henry Dr.,
Blacksburg, VA 24060
(540) 961-6666
jogara@vt.edu

OBJECTIVE
Product Designer/Manager

EXPERIENCE
Computer Consultant and Systems Designer, Systems Go Inc, Blacksburg, VA, 1999-present
Troubleshoot hardware and software problems
Design and test new operating systems
Head up large team of consultants

Assistant Systems Consultant, Benson Inc, Redmond, WA, 1995-1999
Created Web pages and customized computer systems for clients in the Redmond area

Intern, JCN Corp., Redmond, WA, June-August 1995
Worked as software design engineer intern.

EDUCATION
Bachelor of Science Degree in Computer Science, May 1995
Virginia Polytechnic Institute & State University (Virginia Tech), Blacksburg, VA

COMPUTER SKILLS
Languages and Software : B, CC, Java, HTML, Excel, Word
Operating Systems : Unix, Windows, Mac OS

ACTIVITIES
Society of Manufacturing Engineers
Aircraft Owners and Pilots Association

Claudia Quiroga Ramos
CURRICULUM VITAE

PERSONAL DETAILS

CURRENT ADDRESS:	10 Poniente 1909
	Colonia Santiago C.P. 72130
	Puebla, Pue.
	México
TELEPHONE:	01 (2) 234 55 21
E-MAIL:	qr@yahoo.com
DATE OF BIRTH:	3rd May 1983
PLACE OF BIRTH:	Puebla
NATIONALITY:	Mexican
MARITAL STATUS:	Single

ACADEMIC RECORD

2001 - 2006	Universidad de las Américas, Puebla, Mexico
	Degree in International Relations
1998 - 2001	High School leaving certificate,
	Instituto Salvador Allende, Puebla
1995 - 1998	Secondary,
	Instituto Salvador Allende, Puebla
1989 - 1995	Primary,
	Escuela Primaria Oficial "2 de Abril", Puebla

EXTRACURRICULAR ACTIVITIES

2001	Participant in the 5th International Congress of the Americas
	Universidad de Las Américas, Puebla
IDIOMAS	Spanish
	English
PASATIEMPOS	Swimming
	Reading
	Listening to music

Pedir una referencia

Es recomendable incluir en la carta de presentación los nombres y direcciones de dos personas que puedan proporcionar referencias sobre tus habilidades y/o desempeño en puestos anteriores.

> Obten siempre el permiso de estas personas antes de proporcionar sus nombres en tu solicitud.

Alberto de Benito
c/ Juana de Vega, 8
15003 A Coruña

Dr. Mary Neuberger
Macpherson's Frozen Foods
24 Lowport Street
Urbana, IL 61801

February 6, 2006

Dear Dr. Neuberger,

I am writing to you to ask if I could give your name as a reference in future job applications.

My degree course ends in June and I am currently preparing to submit applications to a number of companies. As you were my immediate superior during my three-month placement with the company, it would be very helpful for me if you would be willing to provide a reference to potential employers.

I hope it will be possible to use your name as a reference , as several of the companies I am interested in are outside Spain. It would therefore be particularly useful to have a reference who could provide information on how I coped with the demands of working in a foreign country, and in a second language. However, do let me know if this would in any way be inconvenient.

Thanking you in advance, and with fond memories of my time in the US!

Yours sincerely,

Alberto de Benito
c/ Juana de Vega, 8
15003 A Coruña

Dr. Mary Neuberger
Macpherson's Frozen Foods
24 Lowport Street
Urbana, IL 61801

Febrero 6, 2006

Estimada Dra. Neuberger,

Le escribo para preguntarle si podría incluir su nombre en mis solicitudes de trabajo para posibles referencias.

Acabaré mis estudios en junio y actualmente estoy preparando solicitudes para enviar a diversas compañías. Dado que usted fue mi superior directo durante los tres meses de prácticas que realicé en su compañía, sería muy útil para mí si estuviese dispuesto a proporcionar referencias ante alguna posibilidad de empleo.

Espero que sea posible dar su nombre en mis solicitudes, ya que varias de las compañías que me interesan están fuera de España. Por ello, sería especialmente útil tener referencias de alguien que pudiese proporcionar información sobre cómo hice frente a las dificultades de trabajar en otro país y con un idioma extranjero. Por favor, dígame si esto pudiera causarle cualquier tipo de inconveniente.

Guardo un recuerdo entrañable de mi estancia en los Estados Unidos.

Agradeciéndole de antemano, le saluda atentamente,

Redactar un anuncio

Un anuncio para un periódico o revista debe redactarse de la forma más breve posible, por lo que podemos omitir artículos, preposiciones y algunas formas verbales, y se suele redactar en tercera persona. No hay que olvidar incluir un número de teléfono de contacto:

Experienced, mature babysitter seeks 4-5 hours' work per week.
Niñera responsable con experiencia busca trabajo de 4-5 horas a la semana.

Cleaner required light housework two days a week. Good rates offered.
Se busca empleada doméstica para labores menores dos días a la semana. Buen salario.

Maths undergraduate offers help with revision. Friendly approach. $18/hour.
Estudiante de matemáticas ofrece clases de apoyo. Buen ambiente de aprendizaje. $18/hora.

Spanish student studying for MBA at Harvard offers private Spanish tuition. Competitive rates. Grammar and spoken language covered. Preparation for exams. Phone Daniel on...
Estudiante universitario español en Harvard ofrece clases particulares de español. Precios asequibles. Gramática y expresión oral, preparación para exámenes. Llamar a Daniel al ...

Si se está buscando u ofreciendo alojamiento y se quiere poner un anuncio, es recomendable indicar la zona en la que se busca, así como todos los detalles que puedan ser de interés, como el precio a pagar y el número de teléfono de contacto, o si buscamos compartir con algún tipo concreto de persona, o que sea no fumador, etc.

To rent
Room in friendly shared house in downtown area.
Central heating, access to shared kitchen and living area.
Rent $350 per calendar month.
Call 992 6755
Nonsmokers only

Se alquila
Habitación en casa compartida en zona centro. Ambiente agradable. Calefacción central, cocina y sala de estar compartida. Alquiler: 350 dólares/mes. 992 6755
Sólo para no fumadores

For rent
Beautiful family house set in breathtaking Vermont countryside.
Four bedrooms, two reception rooms, two bathrooms, farmhouse kitchen, utility room. Large garden.
$850 per month
Fenwick Lettings 867-7895

RENTO[1]
Hermosa casa de campo familiar, situada en la impresionante zona de Vermont. Cuatro recámaras[1], dos salas, dos baños, cocina rústica, lavadero. Amplio jardín.
850 dólares/mes.
Inmobiliaria Fenwick 867-7895

[1] Mexican

El teléfono

Responder al teléfono

Hello
¿Hola o Aló? o Bueno? (Méx)

Mary Stephens? – Speaking. This is he/she.
¿Mary Stephens? – Soy yo

Pasar una llamada

I'll just get him/her for you
En un momento le paso con él/ella.

Can I ask/say who's calling?
¿Me podría decir su nombre?

Who's calling, please?
Perdone, ¿con quién hablo?

Just one moment. I'll put you through.
Un momento, por favor. En seguida le paso.

Hang/Hold on. I'll try to connect you.
No cuelgue. Intentaré pasarle la llamada.

Si no es posible pasar la llamada

I'm sorry. She's not here today. Can I take a message? / Would you like to leave a message?
Lo siento, pero hoy no se encuentra aquí. ¿Quiere dejar un mensaje?

I'm afraid he's not at his desk at the moment. Can I get him to call you back?
En estos momentos no se encuentra en su despacho. ¿Quiere que le diga que le llame?

I'm afraid she's on another call. Would you like to hold?
Lo siento, pero en este momento está hablando por otra línea. ¿Puede mantenerse a la espera?

Dejar un mensaje

Can I leave a message?
¿Le puedo dejar un mensaje?

Could you give him a message?
¿Le podría dar un mensaje?

Would you ask her to call me? She has my number.
¿Le puede decir que me llame? Ella tiene mi número.

Could you tell her I called?
¿Le puede decir que he llamado?

Would you ask her to call me on 555-7846?
¿Le puede decir que me llame al 555-7846?

En caso de interferencias durante la llamada

Puede suceder que haya interferencias en la línea o que no se entienda bien al interlocutor. Se pueden usar las frases siguientes:

I'm sorry, I didn't catch that. This is a really bad line.
Lo siento, no le entiendo. Hay problemas con la línea.

Could you say that again?
¿Puede repetir eso, por favor?

Could you spell that for me?
¿Me lo podría deletrear?

Was that 'M' for 'Mark' and 'N' for 'Nick?
¿Ha dicho M de Mark y N de Nick?

I'm sorry. Could you repeat the first part of the number again, please?
Perdón. ¿Puede repetir la primera parte del número otra vez, por favor?

Si el número está equivocado

Al llamar:

I'm sorry. Wrong number.
Perdón. Me he equivocado de número.

I'm terribly sorry. I think I must have the wrong number.
Perdone. Creo que tengo un número equivocado.

Al responder:

I'm sorry. I think you must have the wrong number.
Lo siento. Creo que tiene el número equivocado.

Are you sure you've got the right number? There's no one here by that name.
¿Seguro que tiene el número correcto? Aquí no hay nadie con ese nombre.

Acabar la llamada

Thanks for calling.
Gracias por su llamada.

Speak to you soon.
Nos hablamos pronto.

I have to go. Someone's trying to get through on the other line.
Tengo que colgar. Hay alguien que intenta comunicarse por la otra línea.

Can I call you back? Someone's at the door.
¿Te puedo llamar más tarde? Están llamando a la puerta.

El teléfono móvil

Existen algunas frases que se usan mucho más al hablar por el móvil que por el fijo.

I'm on my cell phone.
Llamo desde el móvil o celular (Méx).

I'm sorry. You're breaking up.
Perdona. Te estás quedando sin señal.

I'm sorry, the reception is really bad.
Lo siento, la señal es muy mala.

If we get cut off, I'll call you back.
Si se corta te vuelvo a llamar.

Can you text me the number?
¿Me puedes mandar el número en un mensaje?

I called her three times, but I keep getting her voice mail.
La he llamado tres veces, pero siempre me sale el buzón de voz.

El contestador automático

Al hacer una llamada, en muchas ocasiones nos saldrá un contestador automático, con mensajes como estos:

Hello. This is 148-3397. I'm afraid there's no one here to take your call right now but please leave your name and number and we'll get back to you as soon as possible. Thanks for calling.
Hola. Has llamado al 148-3397. En estos momentos no hay nadie en casa para atender la llamada. Por favor, deja tu nombre y número de teléfono y te llamaremos en cuanto podamos. Gracias por llamar.

This is the cell-phone messaging service of Indigo. Richard Stubbs is not available to take your call at the moment. Please try later or leave a message after the tone.
Éste es el servicio de buzón de voz de Indigo. En este momento Richard Stubbs no puede atender su llamada. Por favor llame más tarde o deje un mensaje después de la señal.

Como respuesta, podemos dejar un mensaje grabado:

Hello. This is Andrew Taylor calling. It's 9:30 on Monday morning. I'll phone back later.
Hola. Soy Andrew Taylor. Son las nueve y media de la mañana del lunes. Llamaré más tarde.

Hello. This is a message for Patrick Blanco. Could you call Claire Stevenson on 347-6998? Thank you.
Hola. Este mensaje es para Patrick Blanco. ¿Puedes llamar a Claire Stevenson al 347-6998? Gracias.

I'd like to make an appointment to see the dentist. It's Penny Worth speaking. My number is 844-6579.
Quisiera pedir cita con el dentista. Soy Penny Worth. Mi número de teléfono es el 844-6579.

Jade, it's Alison here. I need to speak to you urgently. In case you haven't got my mobile number, it's 219-2561.
Jade, soy Alison. Tengo que hablar contigo urgentemente. Por si no tienes mi número de móvil o celular, es el 219-2561.

Cuando se da un número de teléfono en inglés, se pronuncia cada cifra por separado.

El correo electrónico

Un lenguaje escrito espontáneo

Con excepción de los saludos, en el correo electrónico nos expresamos de forma muy parecida a cuando hablamos:

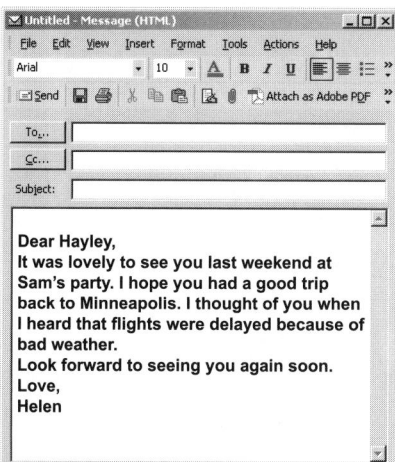

Dear Hayley,
It was lovely to see you last weekend at Sam's party. I hope you had a good trip back to Minneapolis. I thought of you when I heard that flights were delayed because of bad weather.
Look forward to seeing you again soon.
Love,
Helen

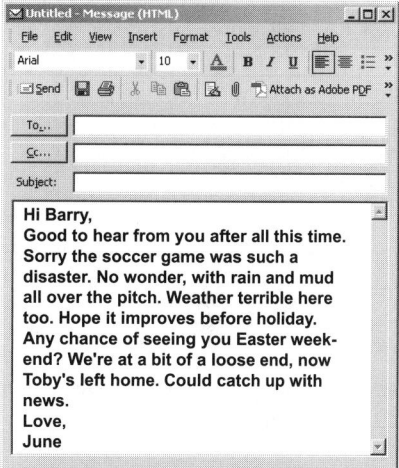

Hi Barry,
Good to hear from you after all this time. Sorry the soccer game was such a disaster. No wonder, with rain and mud all over the pitch. Weather terrible here too. Hope it improves before holiday.
Any chance of seeing you Easter week-end? We're at a bit of a loose end, now Toby's left home. Could catch up with news.
Love,
June

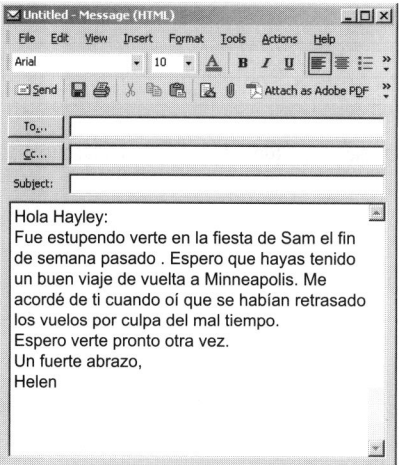

Hola Hayley:
Fue estupendo verte en la fiesta de Sam el fin de semana pasado . Espero que hayas tenido un buen viaje de vuelta a Minneapolis. Me acordé de ti cuando oí que se habían retrasado los vuelos por culpa del mal tiempo.
Espero verte pronto otra vez.
Un fuerte abrazo,
Helen

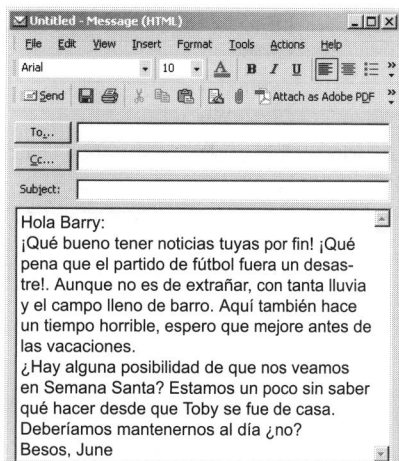

Hola Barry:
¡Qué bueno tener noticias tuyas por fin! ¡Qué pena que el partido de fútbol fuera un desas-tre!. Aunque no es de extrañar, con tanta lluvia y el campo lleno de barro. Aquí también hace un tiempo horrible, espero que mejore antes de las vacaciones.
¿Hay alguna posibilidad de que nos veamos en Semana Santa? Estamos un poco sin saber qué hacer desde que Toby se fue de casa. Deberíamos mantenernos al día ¿no?
Besos, June

El encabezamiento

El encabezamiento de un e-mail se compone de una serie de secciones:

To (Para) debe contener la dirección electrónica del destinatario.

Cc ('courtesy copy') y **Bcc** ('blind courtesy copy') sirven para enviar copias del e-mail. **Bcc** está reservado para copias en las cuales no queremos que aparezca el nombre del destinatario.

La sección **Subject** está destinada al asunto de nuestro mensaje.

Fórmulas de saludo

No son indispensables, aunque las siguientes suelen ser las más habituales:

Hi Jenny
Hola Jenny:

Jenny,
Jenny:

Hi there,
Hola:

Si el estilo es más formal, se recomienda utilizar **Dear** (seguido por un nombre):

Dear Jenny,
Estimada Jenny:

Para finalizar un e-mail informal se puede usar:

See you soon,
Hasta pronto,

Take care,
Un abrazo,

Love,
Besos,

Lots of love,
Muchos besos,

Las formulas **Take care** y **See you soon** tienen un uso muy parecido, aunque **Take care** tiene un tono más afectuoso.

En un e-mail más formal, puede decirse (de menos a más formal):

All the best,
Saludos cordiales,

Best wishes,
Cordialmente,

Kind regards,
Atentamente,

Abreviaturas empleadas en el correo electrónico

En los e-mails se recurre con frecuencia al uso de las abreviaturas y contracciones. A continuación aparecen algunas de las que se pueden encontrar con más frecuencia:

AFAIK (as far as I know)
En lo que a mí respecta

BTW (by the way)
A propósito

FAQ (frequently asked questions)
Preguntas más frecuentes

FYI (for your information)
Para su información

HTH (hope this helps)
Espero que esto sirva de ayuda

IMHO (in my humble opinion)
En mi modesta opinión

Msg (message)
Mensaje

TNX (thanks)
Gracias

WRT (with regard to)
En lo que se refiere a

Una **FAQ** es una página web que contiene las preguntas más frecuentes en relación con un tema concreto. La expresión **IMHO**, que puede parecer muy formal es algo irónica y simplemente significa: pienso que...

El mensaje de texto o SMS

La clave principal para escribir un mensaje de texto es la concisión.

La mayor parte de las abreviaturas utilizadas para el correo electrónico también sirven para acortar los mensajes de texto. Muchas veces se trata de pronunciar las letras por separado, con lo que se obtiene un sonido similar a la palabra que queremos escribir; otras veces se escriben sólo las iniciales de las palabras que componen la frase o simplemente se eliminan las vocales:

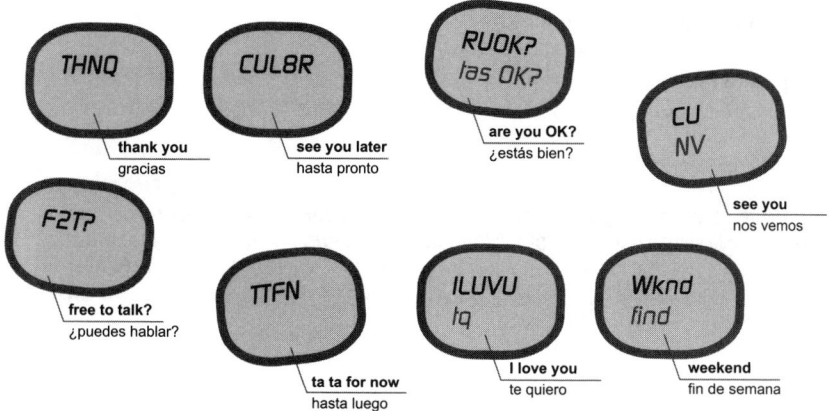

THNQ
thank you
gracias

CUL8R
see you later
hasta pronto

RUOK?
 las OK?
are you OK?
¿estás bien?

CU
NV
see you
nos vemos

F2T?
free to talk?
¿puedes hablar?

TTFN
ta ta for now
hasta luego

ILUVU
tq
I love you
te quiero

Wknd
find
weekend
fin de semana

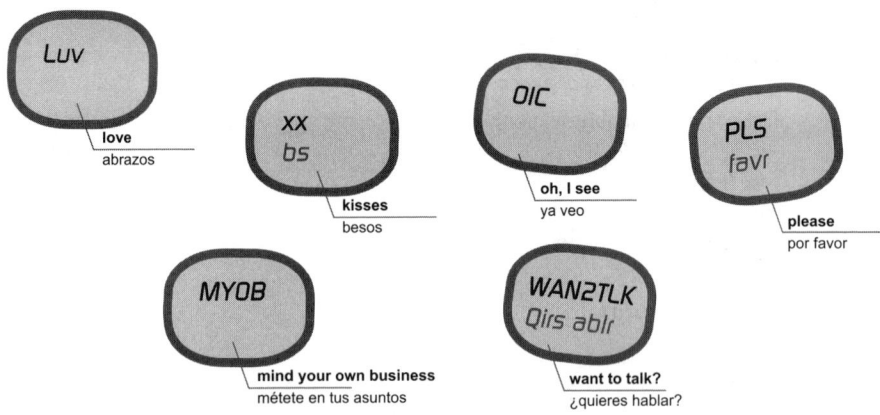

Hay algunas letras del alfabeto y algunas cifras que se utilizan mucho en los mensajes de texto por su parecido con la pronunciación de algunas palabras inglesas, sobre todo: **U** (you), **R** (are), **C** (see, sea), **2** (to, two, too) y **4** (for, four).

Todo lo anterior nos puede servir para fijar una cita con alguien:

> **Guess what? I passed. Luv Jo**
> *Adivina. Aprobé. Besos Jo*

> **CU 2nite. Jim's 7ish. Ang**
> *Nos vemos esta noche en casa de Jim a las 7. Ang*

> **CU 2mrw 11am. Outside pool. Roy**
> *Te veo mañana a las 11 fuera de la piscina. Roy*

> **Mon eve OK? XXX Al**
> *Lunes por la tarde ¿ok? Besos. Al*

Además de las fórmulas que se han visto, también se usan numerosas abreviaturas, como para los días de la semana, por ejemplo: *Mon, Tues, Wed, Thur, Fri, Sat* y *Sun* o la expresión *asap*, es decir *as soon as possible*, que se traduce en español como 'cuanto antes'. Al final de un mensaje se puede escribir **Luv** para **Love**, o **XXX** para **Kisses**, que significa 'Te mando un abrazo/Besos'.

A

A, a [eɪ] *n* (**a**) *(letter)* A, a *f*; **to get from A to B** ir de un lugar a otro; **from A to Z** de principio a fin; **A bomb** bomba *f* atómica; **an A-Z of gardening** una guía completa de jardinería (**b**) *Sch (grade)* sobresaliente *m*; **to get an A** *(in exam, essay)* sacar un sobresaliente (**c**) *Mus* la *m*

a [ə, *stressed* eɪ] *indefinite art*

Antes de vocal o "h" muda se usa **an** [ən, *stressed* æn].

(**a**) *(in general)* un, una; **a man** un hombre; **a woman** una mujer; **an hour** una hora; **he has a red nose** tiene la nariz roja; **I haven't got a car** no tengo coche; **he is an Englishman/a father/a lawyer** es inglés/padre/abogado (**b**) *(expressing prices, rates)* **30 cents a kilo** 30 centavos el kilo; **three times a week/a year** tres veces a la semana/al año; **50 miles an hour** 50 millas por hora (**c**) *(a certain)* **a Mr. Watkins phoned** llamó un tal Sr. Watkins

AA [eɪ'eɪ] *n (abbr* **Alcoholics Anonymous)** AA, alcohólicos *mpl* anónimos

AAA [eɪeɪ'eɪ, trɪpəl'eɪ] *n (abbr* **American Automobile Association)** = asociación automovilística estadounidense

aardvark ['ɑːdvɑːk] *n* cerdo *m* hormiguero

AB [eɪ'biː] *n Univ (abbr* **artium baccalaureus)** *(qualification)* = licenciatura en letras; *(person)* = licenciado en letras

aback [ə'bæk] *adv* **to be taken a. (by)** quedarse desconcertado(a) (por)

abacus ['æbəkəs] (*pl* **abaci** ['æbəsaɪ] *or* **abacuses** ['æbəkəsɪz]) *n* ábaco *m*

abandon [ə'bændən] **1** *n* **with reckless a.** como loco(a)
2 *vt (give up, leave)* abandonar; *(match)* suspender; **to a. ship** abandonar el barco

abandonment [ə'bændənmənt] *n (of idea, project)* abandono *m*

abase [ə'beɪs] *vt* **to a. oneself** humillarse, degradarse

abashed [ə'bæʃt] *adj* **to be a.** estar avergonzado(a) *or* abochornado(a) *or Am salvo RP* apenado(a)

abate [ə'beɪt] *vi (storm, wind)* amainar; *(pain)* remitir; *(noise)* disminuir

abatement [ə'beɪtmənt] *n Formal (of storm)* amaine *m*; *(of pain)* remisión *f*; *(of noise)* disminución *f*

abattoir ['æbətwɑː(r)] *n* matadero *m*

abbess ['æbes] *n* abadesa *f*

abbey ['æbɪ] *n* abadía *f*

abbot ['æbət] *n* abad *m*

abbreviate [ə'briːvɪeɪt] *vt* abreviar

abbreviation [əbriːvɪ'eɪʃən] *n* abreviatura *f*

ABC [eɪbiː'siː] *n* (**a**) *(alphabet)* abecedario *m*; **an A. of gardening** una guía básica de jardinería (**b**) *(abbr* **American Broadcasting Corporation)** cadena *f* ABC *(de radio y televisión)*

abdicate ['æbdɪkeɪt] **1** *vt (throne)* abdicar; *(responsibility)* desatender, abandonar
2 *vi (monarch)* abdicar

abdication [æbdɪ'keɪʃən] *n (of throne)* abdicación *f*; *(of responsibilities)* descuido *m*, abandono *m*

abdomen ['æbdəmən] *n Anat & Zool* abdomen *m*

abdominal [əb'dɒmɪnəl] *adj Anat* abdominal

abduct [əb'dʌkt] *vt* raptar, secuestrar

abduction [əb'dʌkʃən] *n* rapto *m*, secuestro *m*

abductor [əb'dʌktə(r)] *n (of person)* secuestrador(ora) *m,f*, raptor(ora) *m,f*

aberration [æbə'reɪʃən] *n* anomalía *f*, aberración *f*; **mental a.** desvarío *m*, despiste *m*

abet [ə'bet] (*pt & pp* **abetted)** *vt Law* **to aid and a. sb** ser cómplice de alguien

abetting [ə'betɪŋ] *n Law* **to be accused of aiding and a. sb** ser acusado(a) de complicidad con alguien

abeyance [ə'beɪəns] *n* **to fall into a.** *(law, custom)* caer en desuso

abhor [əb'hɔː(r)] (*pt & pp* **abhorred)** *vt* aborrecer

abhorrence [əb'hɒrəns] *n* aversión *f* (**of** hacia *or* por), aborrecimiento *m* (**of** hacia *or* por)

abhorrent [əb'hɒrənt] *adj* aborrecible, repugnante; **it is a. to me** me resulta repugnante

abide [ə'baɪd] *vt (tolerate)* soportar; **I can't a. him** no lo soporto

▶**abide by** *vt insep (promise)* cumplir; *(rule, decision)* acatar, atenerse a

abiding [ə'baɪdɪŋ] *adj (interest, impression)* duradero(a); **my a. memory of Spain is...** mi recuerdo más destacado de España es...

ability [ə'bɪlɪtɪ] *n* (**a**) *(talent, skill)* aptitud *f*, habilidad *f*; **he did it to the best of his a.** lo hizo lo mejor que supo (**b**) *(capability)* capacidad *f*; **we now have the a. to record all calls** ahora podemos grabar todas las llamadas

abject ['æbdʒekt] *adj (very bad)* deplorable; **to look a.** *(unhappy)* tener un aspecto lamentable; **an a. apology** una disculpa degradante; **a. poverty** pobreza *f* extrema

ablaze [ə'bleɪz] *adj* **to be a.** estar ardiendo *or* en llamas; **to set sth a.** prender fuego a algo; *Fig* **her eyes were a. with passion** sus ojos ardían de pasión

able ['eɪbəl] *adj* (**a**) **to be a. to do sth** *(have the capability)* ser capaz de hacer algo, poder hacer algo; *(manage)* conseguir *or* poder hacer algo; **I was a. to speak to him myself** conseguí *or* pude hablar con él; **she was a. to see exactly what was happening** pudo ver exactamente lo que estaba sucediendo (**b**) *(competent) (person)* capaz; *(piece of work, performance)* logrado(a), conseguido(a)

able-bodied ['eɪbəl'bɒdɪd] *adj* sano(a); *Naut* **a. seaman** marinero *m* de primera

abnormal [æb'nɔːməl] *adj* anormal, anómalo(a)

abnormality [æbnɔː'mælɪtɪ] *n* anormalidad *f*, anomalía *f*

aboard [ə'bɔːd] **1** *adv* a bordo; **to go a.** subir a bordo
2 *prep (ship, airplane)* a bordo de; *(bus, train)* en; **a. ship** a bordo (del barco)

abode [ə'bəʊd] *n* vivienda *f*

abolish [ə'bɒlɪʃ] *vt (law, custom)* abolir

abolition [æbə'lɪʃən] *n (of law, custom)* abolición *f*

abominable [əˈbɒmɪnəbəl] *adj* espantoso(a), abominable; **the a. snowman** el abominable hombre de las nieves

abomination [əbɒmɪˈneɪʃən] *n (thing, action)* abominación *f*, horror *m*; *(disgust)* repugnancia *f*, aversión *f*

aboriginal [æbəˈrɪdʒənəl] **1** *adj* (**a**) *(inhabitant)* aborigen, indígena (**b**) *(in Australia)* aborigen

   2 *n* = **Aborigine**

Aborigine [æbəˈrɪdʒɪnɪ] *n* aborigen *mf (de Australia)*

abort [əˈbɔːt] **1** *vt* (**a**) *Med* **the fetus was aborted in the 14th week of pregnancy** se provocó un aborto en la 14ª semana de embarazo (**b**) *(project)* interrumpir, suspender; *Comptr* cancelar

   2 *vi* abortar

abortion [əˈbɔːʃən] *n* aborto *m (provocado)*; **to have an a.** abortar, tener un aborto

abortive [əˈbɔːtɪv] *adj (attempt, plan)* fallido(a), malogrado(a)

abound [əˈbaʊnd] *vi* abundar (**in** *or* **with** en)

about [əˈbaʊt] **1** *prep* (**a**) *(regarding)* sobre, acerca de; **a book a. France** un libro sobre Francia; **the good/bad thing a....** lo bueno/malo de...; **to talk/argue a. sth** hablar/discutir de *or* sobre algo; **we must do something a. this problem** tenemos que hacer algo con este problema *or* para solucionar este problema (**b**) *(in various parts of)* por; **to walk a. the town** caminar por la ciudad

   2 *adv* (**a**) *(in different directions, places)* **to run a.** correr de aquí para allá; **to walk a.** caminar *or* pasear por ahí; **there were books lying all a.** había libros por todas partes

   (**b**) *(in the general area)* **is Jack a.?** ¿está Jack por ahí?; **there was nobody a.** no había nadie (por allí)

   (**c**) *(approximately)* más o menos; **a. thirty** unos treinta; **at a. one o'clock** alrededor de la una, a eso de la una; **a. a week** una semana más o menos; **she's a. as tall as you** es más o menos como tú de alta; **I've just a. finished** estoy a punto de acabar; **that's a. enough** con eso basta; **a. time!** ¡ya era hora!

   (**d**) *(on the point of)* **to be a. to do sth** estar a punto de hacer algo; **I'm not a. to...** *(have no intention of)* no tengo la más mínima intención de...

about-face [əˈbaʊtˈfeɪs] *n (radical change)* giro *m* radical *or* de 180 grados

above [əˈbʌv] **1** *prep* (**a**) *(physically)* por encima de; **a. sea level** sobre el nivel del mar; **the Ebro a. Zaragoza** el Ebro, antes de llegar a Zaragoza

   (**b**) *(with numbers)* **a. twenty** por encima de veinte; **a. \$100** más de 100 dólares; **the temperature didn't rise a. 10°C** la temperatura no pasó de *or* superó los 10 grados

   (**c**) *(in importance, rank)* **a. all** por encima de todo, sobre todo; **he is a. me** está por encima de mí

   (**d**) *(not subject to)* **to be a. suspicion** estar libre de sospecha; **she thinks she's a. criticism** cree que está por encima de las críticas

   (**e**) *(superior to)* **he thinks he's a. all that** cree que hacer eso sería humillarse; **he's not a. telling the occasional lie** incluso él miente de vez en cuando

   2 *adv* (**a**) *(in general)* **the tenants (of the apartment) a.** los inquilinos de arriba; **to have a view from a.** ver desde arriba; **imposed from a.** impuesto(a) desde arriba (**b**) *(in book, document)* **the paragraph a.** el párrafo anterior; **as noted a.,...** como se dice más arriba,... (**c**) *(with numbers)* **women aged eighteen and a.** las mujeres a partir de los dieciocho años

aboveboard [əˈbʌvbɔːd] *adj (honest)* honrado(a), sincero(a)

above-mentioned [əbʌvˈmenʃənd], **above-named** [əbʌvˈneɪmd] **1** *adj* arriba mencionado(a), susodicho(a)

   2 *n* **the a.** *(person)* el arriba mencionado, la arriba mencionada

abrasion [əˈbreɪʒən] *n (on skin)* abrasión *f*

abrasive [əˈbreɪsɪv] **1** *n (substance)* abrasivo *m*

   2 *adj (surface, substance)* abrasivo(a); *(person, manner)* acre, corrosivo(a)

abreast [əˈbrest] *adv* **three/four a.** en fila de a tres/cuatro, de tres/cuatro en fondo; **to come a. of** situarse a la altura de; **to keep a. of sth** mantenerse al tanto de algo

abridge [əˈbrɪdʒ] *vt (book)* resumir; *(speech)* resumir, abreviar

abridged [əˈbrɪdʒd] *adj* abreviado(a)

abroad [əˈbrɔːd] *adv* en el extranjero, fuera del país; **to be/live a.** estar/vivir en el extranjero; **to go a.** ir al extranjero; **to get a.** *(news)* difundirse

abrupt [əˈbrʌpt] *adj* (**a**) *(sudden)* brusco(a), repentino(a); **the evening came to an a. end** la velada terminó bruscamente (**b**) *(curt)* brusco(a), abrupto(a)

abruptly [əˈbrʌptlɪ] *adv* (**a**) *(suddenly)* bruscamente, repentinamente (**b**) *(curtly)* bruscamente

ABS [eɪbiːˈes] *n Aut (abbr* **antilock braking system***)* ABS *m*

abscess [ˈæbses] *n (abscess* absceso *m*; *(in mouth)* flemón *m*

abscond [əbˈskɒnd] *vi Formal* darse a la fuga, huir

abseil [ˈæbseɪl] *vi* hacer rappel; **to a. down sth** bajar algo haciendo rappel

abseiling [ˈæbseɪlɪŋ] *n* rappel *m*; **to go a.** ir a hacer rappel

absence [ˈæbsəns] *n (of person, thing)* ausencia *f*; *(of evidence, information)* ausencia *f*, falta *f* (**of** de); **in the a. of...** a falta de...; *Law* **sentenced in one's a.** juzgado(a) en rebeldía; *Prov* **a. makes the heart grow fonder** la ausencia aviva el cariño

absent 1 *adj* [ˈæbsənt] *(pupil, expression)* ausente; *Mil* **a. without leave** ausente sin permiso

   2 *vt* [æbˈsent] **to a. oneself (from)** ausentarse (de)

absentee [æbsənˈtiː] *n* ausente *mf*; **a. landlord** *(propietario(a) m,f)* ausentista *mf or Esp* absentista *mf*

absenteeism [æbsənˈtiːɪzəm] *n* ausentismo *m*, *Esp* absentismo *m*

absentminded [æbsəntˈmaɪndɪd] *adj* distraído(a), despistado(a)

absentmindedness [æbsəntˈmaɪndɪdnɪs] *n* distracción *f*, despiste *m*

absinthe [ˈæbsɪnθ] *n* absenta *f*, ajenjo *m*

absolute [ˈæbsəluːt] *adj* (**a**) *(in general)* absoluto(a); **a. majority** mayoría *f* absoluta (**b**) *(emphatic)* absoluto(a), auténtico(a); **he's an a. fool!** ¡es un completo idiota!; **a. garbage!** ¡no son más que tonterías!; **it's an a. disgrace!** ¡es una auténtica vergüenza!

absolutely [æbsəˈluːtlɪ] *adv* (**a**) *(in general)* absolutamente; **you're a. right** tienes toda la razón; **do you support him? — a.** ¿lo apoyas? — completamente; **a. not!** ¡en absoluto!; **it is a. forbidden** está terminantemente prohibido

absolution [æbsəˈluːʃən] *n Rel* absolución *f*

absolutism [æbsəˈluːtɪzəm] *n Hist* absolutismo *m*

absolve [əbˈzɒlv] *vt (person)* absolver (**from** *or* **of** de)

absorb [əbˈzɔːb] *vt (liquid)* absorber; *(information, ideas)* asimilar; **paperwork absorbs too much of my time** paso demasiado tiempo ocupado en papeleos; **to be absorbed in sth** estar absorto(a) en algo

absorbency [əbˈzɔːbənsɪ] *n* absorbencia *f*

absorbent [əbˈzɔːbənt] *adj* absorbente; **a. cotton** algodón *m* hidrófilo

absorbing [əbˈzɔːbɪŋ] *adj (book, work)* absorbente

abstain [əbˈsteɪn] *vi* (**a**) *(not act, vote)* abstenerse (**from** de) (**b**) *(not drink alcohol)* no beber alcohol, *Am* no tomar

abstainer [əbˈsteɪnə(r)] *n* (**a**) *(person not voting)* abstencionista *mf* (**b**) *(teetotaler)* abstemio(a) *m,f*

abstemious [əbˈstiːmɪəs] *adj* frugal, mesurado(a)

abstention [əbˈstenʃən] *n* abstención *f*

abstinence [ˈæbstɪnəns] *n* abstinencia *f*

abstract 1 *n* [ˈæbstrækt] (**a**) **in the a.** en abstracto (**b**) *(of article)* resumen *m*

   2 *adj* [ˈæbstrækt] abstracto(a)

   3 *vt* [æbˈstrækt] *Formal (remove)* extraer (**from** de); *(steal)* sustraer (**from** de)

abstraction [æbˈstrækʃən] n abstracción f

abstruse [əbˈstruːs] adj abstruso(a), impenetrable

absurd [əbˈsɜːd] adj absurdo(a)

absurdity [əbˈsɜːdɪtɪ] n irracionalidad f

abundance [əˈbʌndəns] n abundancia f; **in a.** en abundancia

abundant [əˈbʌndənt] adj abundante (**in** en)

abundantly [əˈbʌndəntlɪ] adv en abundancia; **it is a. clear that...** está clarísimo que...

abuse 1 n [əˈbjuːs] (**a**) (of power) abuso m, mal uso m (**b**) (insults) insultos mpl, improperios mpl; **term of a.** insulto m, término m ofensivo; **to shower a. on sb** despotricar contra alguien (**c**) (cruelty) malos tratos mpl; (**sexual**) **a.** abuso m (sexual)
2 vt [əˈbjuːz] (**a**) (misuse) abusar de (**b**) (insult) insultar (**c**) (ill-treat) (physically) maltratar; (sexually) abusar de

abuser [əˈbjuːzə(r)] n (**a**) (misuser) (**alcohol**) **a.** alcohólico(a) m,f; (**drug**) **a.** drogodependiente mf (**b**) (of child) pederasta m

abusive [əˈbjuːsɪv] adj (person) grosero(a); (language) injurioso(a)

abusively [əˈbjuːsɪvlɪ] adv (**a**) (insultingly) de manera insultante or ofensiva (**b**) (to behave, treat sb) abusivamente

abysmal [əˈbɪzməl] adj (stupidity, ignorance) profundo(a); (performance, quality) pésimo(a)

abyss [əˈbɪs] n also Fig abismo m

AC [ˈeɪˈsiː] n (**a**) Elec (abbr **alternating current**) corriente f alterna (**b**) (abbr **air-conditioning**) aire m acondicionado

a/c (abbr **account**) cuenta f

academic [ækəˈdemɪk] **1** n (university teacher) profesor(ora) m,f de universidad
2 adj (**a**) (of school, university) académico(a) (**b**) (intellectual) académico(a), intelectual (**c**) **it's entirely a. now** ya carece por completo de relevancia

academy [əˈkædəmɪ] n academia f; **a. of music** conservatorio m

accede [ækˈsiːd] vi Formal (**a**) (agree) **to a. to** acceder a (**b**) (monarch) **to a. to the throne** acceder al trono

accelerate [əkˈseləreɪt] **1** vt (rate, progress) acelerar
2 vi (car, driver) acelerar; (rate, growth) acelerarse

acceleration [əkseləˈreɪʃən] n aceleración f; **a. lane** carril m de aceleración

accelerator [əkˈseləreɪtə(r)] n (gen) & Comptr acelerador m

accent [ˈæksənt] n (when speaking) acento m; (in writing) acento m, tilde f; **to put the a. on sth** (emphasize) hacer hincapié en algo

accentuate [ækˈsentʃʊeɪt] vt acentuar

accept [əkˈsept] vt (**a**) (invitation, apology, defeat) aceptar; (reasons) aceptar, admitir; (blame) admitir; **the machine won't a. foreign coins** la máquina no funciona con or no admite monedas extranjeras; **to a. responsibility for sth** asumir la responsabilidad de algo; **it is generally accepted that...** en general, se acepta or se admite que... (**b**) (into university) admitir

acceptable [əkˈseptəbəl] adj aceptable, admisible; **to be a. to sb** (suit) venirle bien a alguien; Comptr **A. Use Policy** = código de conducta definido por un proveedor de acceso a Internet

acceptance [əkˈseptəns] n (of invitation, apology, defeat) aceptación f; **to find a.** tener aceptación; **a. speech** discurso m de agradecimiento (al recibir un premio)

access [ˈækses] **1** n acceso m; **to gain a. to sth** acceder a algo; **a. road** (vía f de) acceso m; Comptr **a. code** código m de acceso; Comptr **a. provider** proveedor m de acceso (a Internet); Comptr **a. time** tiempo m de acceso
2 vt Comptr (data) acceder a

accessible [əkˈsesəbəl] adj (place, person, explanation) accesible; **the beach is easily a. by car** se puede acceder fácilmente a la playa en coche

accession [əkˈseʃən] n (to power, throne) acceso m; (library book) adquisición f

accessorize [əkˈsesəraɪz] vt complementar

accessory [əkˈsesərɪ] n (**a**) (for car, camera) accesorio m; **accessories** (handbag, gloves etc) complementos mpl (**b**) Law **a. (to a crime)** cómplice mf (de un delito)

accident [ˈæksɪdənt] n accidente m; **by a.** (by chance) por casualidad; (unintentionally) sin querer; **to have an a.** tener or sufrir un accidente; **that was no a.** eso no fue casualidad; **car** or **road a.** accidente de coche or de tráfico; **a. insurance** seguro m de accidentes

accidental [æksɪˈdentəl] adj accidental, casual; Law **a. death** muerte f accidental

accidentally [æksɪˈdentəlɪ] adv (unintentionally) sin querer, accidentalmente; (by chance) por casualidad

accident-prone [ˈæksɪdəntprəʊn] adj propenso(a) a tener accidentes

acclaim [əˈkleɪm] **1** n alabanza f, elogios mpl
2 vt alabar, elogiar

acclamation [ækləˈmeɪʃən] n aclamación f

acclimate = **acclimatize**

acclimatization [əklaɪmətaɪˈzeɪʃən], **acclimation** [æklɪˈmeɪʃən] n aclimatación f

acclimatize [əˈklaɪmətaɪz], **acclimate** [ˈæklɪmeɪt] vi aclimatarse (**to** a)

accolade [ˈækəleɪd] n (praise) elogio m; (prize) galardón m

accommodate [əˈkɒmədeɪt] vt (**a**) (provide room for) alojar, acomodar; **the hotel can a. three hundred people** el hotel puede albergar or alojar a trescientas personas (**b**) (satisfy) complacer; (point of view) tener en cuenta

accommodating [əˈkɒmədeɪtɪŋ] adj (helpful) servicial; (easy to please) flexible

accommodation [əkɒməˈdeɪʃən] n (**a**) (lodging) alojamiento m; **there is a. in this hotel for fifty people** este hotel alberga a cincuenta personas (**b**) Formal (agreement) **to come to an a.** llegar a un acuerdo satisfactorio (**c**) **accommodations** (lodging) alojamiento m

accompaniment [əˈkʌmpənɪmənt] n acompañamiento m

accompany [əˈkʌmpənɪ] vt acompañar

accompanying [əˈkʌmpənɪɪŋ] adj **the a. documents** los documentos adjuntos

accomplice [əˈkʌmplɪs] n cómplice mf

accomplish [əˈkʌmplɪʃ] vt (task) realizar; (aim) cumplir, alcanzar; **we didn't a. much** no logramos or conseguimos gran cosa

accomplished [əˈkʌmplɪʃt] adj (performer) hábil; (performance) logrado(a), conseguido(a)

accord [əˈkɔːd] **1** n (agreement, pact) acuerdo m; **in a. with** de acuerdo con, acorde con; **with one a.** unánimemente, al unísono; **of one's own a.** de motu propio
2 vt conceder (**to** a)

▸**accord with** vt insep ser acorde con, estar de acuerdo con

accordance [əˈkɔːdəns] n **in a. with** de acuerdo con

accordingly [əˈkɔːdɪŋlɪ] adv (**a**) (appropriately) como corresponde; **to act a.** actuar en consecuencia (**b**) (therefore) así pues, por consiguiente

according to [əˈkɔːdɪŋtuː] prep (**a**) (depending on) **a. whether one is rich or poor** dependiendo de si se es rico o pobre, según se sea rico o pobre (**b**) (in conformity with) **a. instructions** según las instrucciones; **everything went a. plan** todo fue de acuerdo con lo planeado (**c**) (citing a source) según

accordion [əˈkɔːdɪən] n acordeón m

accost [əˈkɒst] vt (person) abordar

account [əˈkaʊnt] n (**a**) (at bank) cuenta f; **to open an a.** abrir una cuenta; Com **accounts department** departamento m de contabilidad; **a. number** número m de cuenta (**b**) *(reckoning)* **to keep (an) a. of sth** llevar la cuenta de algo; **to take sth into a., to take a. of sth** tener *or* tomar algo en cuenta; **to call sb to a.** pedir cuentas a alguien; **the terrorists will be brought to a.** los terroristas tendrán que responder de sus acciones

(**c**) *(importance)* **of no a.** sin importancia

(**d**) **on a. of** *(because of)* a causa de; **on no a., not on any a.** bajo ningún concepto; **on one's own a.** por cuenta propia; **don't do it on my a.!** ¡no lo hagas por mí!

(**e**) *(report)* relato *m*, descripción *f*; *Fig* **to give a good a. of oneself** *(in fight, contest)* salir airoso(a), lucirse; **by all accounts** a decir de todos

▸**account for** *vt insep* (**a**) *(explain, justify)* explicar; **I can't a. for it** no puedo dar cuenta de ello; **five people have still not been accounted for** todavía no se conoce la suerte de cinco personas; **there's no accounting for taste** sobre gustos no hay nada escrito (**b**) *(constitute)* constituir

accountability [əkaʊntə'bɪlɪtɪ] *n* responsabilidad *f*

accountable [ə'kaʊntəbəl] *adj* **to be a. (to sb/for sth)** ser responsable (ante alguien/de algo); **to hold sb a.** considerar a alguien responsable

accountancy [ə'kaʊntənsɪ] *n* contabilidad *f*

accountant [ə'kaʊntənt] *n Esp* contable *mf*, *Am* contador(ora) *m,f*

accounting [ə'kaʊntɪŋ] *n* contabilidad *f*; **a. period** periodo *m* contable

accredit [ə'kredɪt] *vt* acreditar

accreditation [əkredɪ'teɪʃən] *n* (**a**) *(credentials)* *(for ambassador, envoy)* credencial *f*, acreditación *f* (**b**) *(recognition)* *(for school, course)* reconocimiento *m*, homologación *f*

accrual [ə'kruəl] *n Fin (of interest, debt)* acumulación *f*

accrue [ə'kru:] *vi Fin (interest)* acumularse; **to a. to sb** *(interest, benefits)* ir a parar a alguien

accumulate [ə'kju:mjʊleɪt] **1** *vt* acumular
2 *vi* acumularse

accumulation [əkju:mjʊ'leɪʃən] *n* acumulación *f*

accuracy ['ækjʊrəsɪ] *n (of calculation, report, measurement)* exactitud *f*, precisión *f*; *(of translation, portrayal)* fidelidad *f*; *(of firearm, shot)* precisión *f*

accurate ['ækjʊrət] *adj (calculation, report, measurement)* exacto(a), preciso(a); *(translation, portrayal)* fiel; *(firearm, shot)* certero(a)

accurately ['ækjʊrətlɪ] *adv (calculate)* exactamente; *(measure, aim, report)* con exactitud, con precisión; *(translate, portray)* fielmente

accusation [ækjʊ'zeɪʃən] *n* acusación *f*

accusative [ə'kju:zətɪv] **1** *n* acusativo *m*
2 *vi* acusativo(a)

accuse [ə'kju:z] *vt* acusar; **to a. sb of sth/of doing sth** acusar a alguien de algo/de hacer algo

accused [ə'kju:zd] *n Law* **the a.** el/la acusado(a)

accuser [ə'kju:zə(r)] *n* acusador(ora) *m,f*

accusing [ə'kju:zɪŋ] *adj (look, stare)* acusador(ora)

accustom [ə'kʌstəm] *vt* acostumbrar; **to be accustomed to sth/to doing sth** estar acostumbrado(a) a algo/a hacer algo; **to get** *or* **grow accustomed to sth/to doing sth** acostumbrarse a algo/a hacer algo

AC/DC ['eɪsi:'di:si:] *n Elec (abbr* **alternating current/ direct current**) corriente *f* alterna/continua

ace [eɪs] **1** *n* (**a**) *(in cards)* as *m*; **a. of spades** as de picas; *Fig* **to have an a. up one's sleeve** tener un as en la manga; **she came within an a. of winning** *(very near to)* estuvo a punto *or* en un tris de ganar (**b**) *(tennis)* ace *m* (**c**) *Fam (expert)* as *m*; **a flying a.** un as del vuelo
2 *adj Fam (very good)* genial, *Esp* guay, *Am* salvo *RP* chévere, *Méx* padre, *RP* bárbaro(a)

acerbic [ə'sɜ:bɪk] *adj (wit, remark)* acre, mordaz

acetate ['æsɪteɪt] *n Chem* acetato *m*

acetic acid [æ'si:tɪk'æsɪd] *n* ácido *m* acético

ache [eɪk] **1** *n* dolor *m*; **aches and pains** achaques *mpl*
2 *vi* doler; **my head aches** me duele la cabeza; **I a. all over** me duele todo; *Fig* **to be aching to do sth** estar deseando hacer algo

achieve [ə'tʃi:v] *vt* conseguir, lograr

achievement [ə'tʃi:vmənt] *n (action)* realización *f*, consecución *f*; *(thing achieved)* logro *m*

achiever [ə'tʃi:və(r)] *n* triunfador(ora) *m,f*

aching ['eɪkɪŋ] *adj (head, limbs)* dolorido(a); **with an a. heart** con gran dolor

achoo [ə'tʃu:] *exclam* ¡achís!

acid ['æsɪd] **1** *n* (**a**) *(chemical)* ácido *m* (**b**) *Fam (LSD)* ácido *m*; **a. house** *(music)* acid house *m*
2 *adj* (**a**) *(chemical, taste)* ácido(a); **a. rain** lluvia *f* ácida; *Fig* **a. test** prueba *f* de fuego (**b**) *(tone, remark)* sarcástico(a)

acidic [ə'sɪdɪk] *adj* ácido(a)

acidity [ə'sɪdɪtɪ] *n (of chemical, taste)* acidez *f*; *(of tone, remark)* sarcasmo *m*

acknowledge [ək'nɒlɪdʒ] *vt (mistake, debt, truth)* reconocer, admitir; **to a. (receipt of) a letter** acusar recibo de una carta; **to a. defeat** admitir una derrota; **she didn't a. me** *or* **my presence** no me saludó

acknowledged [ək'nɒlɪdʒd] *adj (expert, authority)* de reconocido prestigio

acknowledg(e)ment [ək'nɒlɪdʒmənt] *n (of mistake, debt, truth)* reconocimiento *m*; *(of letter)* acuse *m* de recibo; **in a. of** en reconocimiento a; **acknowledgments** *(in book)* menciones *fpl*, agradecimientos *mpl*

ACLU [eɪsi:el'ju:] *n (abbr* **American Civil Liberties Union**) = organización americana para la defensa de las libertades civiles

acne ['æknɪ] *n* acné *m*

acolyte ['ækəlaɪt] *n* acólito *m*

acorn ['eɪkɔ:n] *n* bellota *f*

acoustic [ə'ku:stɪk] *adj* acústico(a); **a. guitar** guitarra *f* acústica

acoustics [ə'ku:stɪks] *npl* acústica *f*

acquaint [ə'kweɪnt] *vt* (**a**) *(with person)* **to be acquainted with sb** conocer a alguien; **to become** *or* **get acquainted** entablar relación (**b**) *(with facts, situation)* **to be acquainted with sth** conocer algo, estar al corriente de algo; **to a. sb with sth** poner al corriente de algo a alguien; **to a. oneself with sth** familiarizarse con algo

acquaintance [ə'kweɪntəns] *n* (**a**) *(person)* conocido(a) *m,f* (**b**) *(familiarity)* *(with person)* relación *f*; *(with facts)* conocimiento *m* (**with** de); **to make sb's a.** conocer a alguien

acquiesce [ækwɪ'es] *vi* acceder (**in** a)

acquiescence [ækwɪ'esəns] *n* aquiescencia *f*, consentimiento *m*

acquiescent [ækwɪ'esənt] *adj* aquiescente

acquire [ə'kwaɪə(r)] *vt* adquirir; **to a. a taste for sth** aprender a disfrutar de algo

acquired [ə'kwaɪəd] *adj (characteristic, habit)* adquirido(a); **it's an a. taste** es un placer adquirido con el tiempo; **a. immune deficiency syndrome** síndrome *m* de inmunodeficiencia adquirida

acquisition [ækwɪ'zɪʃən] *n* adquisición *f*

acquisitive [ə'kwɪzɪtɪv] *adj (person)* consumista

acquit [ə'kwɪt] *(pt & pp* **acquitted**) *vt* (**a**) *Law* absolver, declarar inocente (**b**) **to a. oneself well/badly** salir bien/mal parado(a)

acquittal [ə'kwɪtəl] *n Law* absolución *f*

acre ['eɪkə(r)] *n* acre *m*, = 4047 m^2; *Fam* **acres of space** *(lots)* un montón *or Méx* un chorro *or RP* una pila de espacio

acrid ['ækrɪd] *adj* acre

acrimonious [ækrɪ'məʊnɪəs] *adj (discussion, debate)* agrio(a); *(words, remark)* mordaz, acre

acrimony ['ækrɪmənɪ] *n* acritud *f*, acrimonia *f*

acrobat ['ækrəbæt] *n* acróbata *mf*

acrobatic [ækrə'bætɪk] *adj* acrobático(a)

acrobatics [ækrə'bætɪks] **1** *n* acrobacias *fpl*
   2 *npl Fig* **mental a.** gimnasia *f* mental

acronym ['ækrənɪm] *n* siglas *fpl*, acrónimo *m*

across [ə'krɒs] *prep* **1** **(a)** *(from one side to the other of)* a través de; **to go a. sth** cruzar algo; **he ran a. the road** cruzó corriendo la calle; **to run a. the road** cruzar la calle corriendo; **we drove a. the desert** cruzamos el desierto en coche; **she swam a. the river** cruzó el río a nado; **the bridge a. the river** el puente que cruza el río; **she threw it a. the room** lo tiró al otro lado de la habitación
   (b) *(on the other side of)* al otro lado de; **a. the street/border** al otro lado de la calle/frontera; **I saw him a. the room** lo vi en el otro extremo de la sala
   (c) *(throughout)* **a. the country** por todo el país; **changes have been introduced a. the syllabus** se han introducido cambios en todo el programa
   2 *adv* **(a)** *(from one side to the other)* de un lado a otro; **to run/swim a.** cruzar corriendo/a nado **(b)** *(with distance)* **it's 10 inches/2 miles a.** tiene 10 pulgadas/2 millas de ancho **(c)** **a. from me/my house** enfrente **(d)** *(in crosswords)* **8 a.** 8 horizontal

across-the-board [ə'krɒsðə'bɔːd] *adj* generalizado(a); **an a. increase** *(in salary)* un aumento lineal

acrylic [ə'krɪlɪk] **1** *n* acrílico *m*
   2 *adj* acrílico(a)

act [ækt] **1** *n* **(a)** *(thing done)* acto *m*; **to catch sb in the a.** pillar *or* atrapar a alguien in fraganti; **to catch sb in the a. of doing sth** pillar a alguien haciendo algo; **to be in the a. of doing sth** estar haciendo algo (precisamente); *Fam* **to get in on the a.** *(get involved)* apuntarse, *Am* anotarse; **an a. of war** una acción de guerra; *Law* **a. of God** caso *m* fortuito **(b)** *(in play)* acto *m*; *(in cabaret, circus)* número *m*; *Fig* **to put on an a.** hacer teatro; *Fig* **it's all an a.** es puro teatro *or* pura farsa; *Fig* **to get one's a. together** organizarse, ponerse las pilas **(c)** *Law* **a. (of Congress)** ley *f*
   2 *vt* **(a)** *(of actor)* interpretar; *Fig* **he was acting the part of the caring husband** estaba interpretando *or* haciendo el papel del marido solícito **(b)** *(behave like)* **to a. the fool** *or* **the goat** hacer el tonto; *Fam* **a. your age!** ¡no seas infantil!
   3 *vi* **(a)** *(take action)* actuar; **to a. for sb** *(lawyer)* representar a alguien; **to a. as secretary/chairperson** actuar *or* hacer de secretario(a)/presidente(a); **to a. as a warning/an incentive** servir de advertencia/incentivo **(b)** *(behave)* actuar, comportarse; **to a. stupid** hacerse el tonto **(c)** *(actor)* actuar

▶**act out** *vt sep (fantasy)* realizar; *(scene)* representar

▶**act up** *vi (child, car, injury)* dar guerra

acting ['æktɪŋ] **1** *n (performance)* interpretación *f*, actuación *f*; *(profession)* interpretación *f*, profesión *f* de actor/actriz
   2 *adj (temporary)* en funciones

action ['ækʃən] *n* **(a)** *(individual act)* acto *m*, acción *f*; **to be responsible for one's actions** ser responsable de los propios actos; *Prov* **actions speak louder than words** hechos son amores y no buenas razones
   (b) *(activity)* acción *f*; **to take a.** actuar; **in a.** en acción; **to go into a.** ponerse en acción; **to be out of a.** *(machine)* no funcionar; *(person)* estar fuera de combate; **to put a plan into a.** poner en marcha un plan; *Fam* **they were looking for some a.** *(excitement)* estaban buscando acción, *RP* querían un poco de agite; *Fam* **to want a piece of the a.** querer un trozo del pastel; *Com* **a. plan** plan *m* de acción
   (c) *Mil* (acción *f* de) combate *m*; **to see a.** entrar en combate; **missing in a.** desaparecido(a) en combate; **a. stations** *(positions)* puestos *mpl* de combate; *Fam Fig* **a. stations!** *(get ready!)* ¡a sus puestos *or* Col, *RP* marcas!
   (d) *(of movie, novel)* acción *f*
   (e) *Law* demanda *f*; **to bring an a. against sb** poner una demanda a alguien, demandar a alguien

actionable ['ækʃənəbəl] *adj Law* susceptible de procesamiento

action-packed ['ækʃənpækt] *adj (movie, novel)* lleno(a) de acción

activate ['æktɪveɪt] *vt (alarm, mechanism)* activar

active ['æktɪv] *adj* **(a)** *(person, imagination, life)* activo(a); *(interest, dislike)* profundo(a); *(volcano)* activo(a); **to take an a. part in sth** participar activamente en algo; *Mil* **on a. duty** *or* **service** en servicio activo **(b)** *Gram* activo(a) **(c)** *Comptr* **a. window** ventana *f* activa

actively ['æktɪvlɪ] *adv* activamente; **I a. dislike him** me desagrada profundamente

activist ['æktɪvɪst] *n Pol* activista *mf*

activity [æk'tɪvɪtɪ] *n* actividad *f*; **a. vacation** = vacaciones organizadas en las que se practica algún deporte o actividad similar

actor ['æktə(r)] *n* actor *m*

actress ['æktrɪs] *n* actriz *f*

actual ['æktʃʊəl] *adj (real)* real; **her a. words were…** lo que dijo exactamente fue…; **an a. example** un ejemplo real; **in a. fact** de hecho, en realidad; **although the garden is big, the a. house is small** aunque el jardín es grande, la casa en sí es pequeña

actually ['æktʃʊəlɪ] *adv* **(a)** *(really)* en realidad; **what a. happened?** ¿qué ocurrió en realidad?; **what she a. means is…** lo que quiere decir en realidad es…; **he a. believed me!** ¡me creyó y todo! **(b)** *(in fact)* **a., I rather like it** la verdad es que me gusta; **a., it WAS the right number** de hecho, sí que era el número correcto; **I'm not sure, a.** pues… no estoy seguro

actuary ['æktʃʊərɪ] *n* actuario(a) *m,f* de seguros

acumen ['ækjʊmən] *n* perspicacia *f*, sagacidad *f*; **business a.** perspicacia para los negocios

acupuncture ['ækjʊpʌŋktʃə(r)] *n* acupuntura *f*

acupuncturist ['ækjʊpʌŋktʃərɪst] *n* acupuntor(ora) *m,f*

acute [ə'kjuːt] *adj (pain, mind, eyesight) Gram & Math* agudo(a); *(hearing, sense of smell)* muy fino(a); *(problem, shortage)* acuciante; *(remorse, embarrassment)* intenso(a)

acutely [ə'kjuːtlɪ] *adv (painful, embarrassing)* extremadamente; **to be a. aware of sth** ser plenamente consciente de algo

AD [eɪ'diː] *adv (abbr **Anno Domini**)* d. J.C., d.C.

ad [æd] *n Fam (advertisement)* anuncio *m*

Adam ['ædəm] *pr n Fam* **I wouldn't know him from A.** no lo conozco de nada *or RP* para nada; **A.'s apple** nuez *f*, bocado *m* de Adán

adamant ['ædəmənt] *adj* inflexible; **she is a. that she saw him** insiste en que lo vio

adamantly ['ædəməntlɪ] *adv* rotundamente, categóricamente

adapt [ə'dæpt] **1** *vt* adaptar **(for** a); **to a. oneself to sth** adaptarse a algo
   2 *vi* adaptarse

adaptable [ə'dæptəbəl] *adj (instrument, person)* adaptable; **she's very a.** se adapta a todo

adaptation [ædæp'teɪʃən] *n* adaptación *f*

adapter, adaptor [ə'dæptə(r)] *n (for different socket)* adaptador *m*

ADC [eɪdiː'siː] *n Mil (abbr **aide-de-camp**)* ayudante *m* de campo, edecán *m*

add [æd] *vt* añadir **(to** a); *Math* sumar

▶**add up 1** *vt sep (figures)* sumar
   2 *vi (give correct total)* cuadrar; *(make sense)* encajar

▶**add up to** *vt insep* **it adds up to $126** suma un total de 126 dólares; **it all adds up to an enjoyable day out** todo esto da como resultado una agradable excursión; **it doesn't a. up to much** no viene a ser gran cosa

added ['ædɪd] *adj* (**a**) *(additional)* adicional; **with a. vitamins** con vitaminas añadidas (**b**) *(in addition)* **a. to that,...** además de eso,...

adder ['ædə(r)] *n* víbora *f*

addict ['ædɪkt] *n* adicto(a) *m,f*; (**drug**) **a.** drogadicto(a) *m,f*, toxicómano(a) *m,f*; **heroin a.** heroinómano(a) *m,f*; **TV a.** teleadicto(a) *m,f*

addicted [ə'dɪktɪd] *adj* **to be a. to sth** ser adicto(a) a algo; **to become** *or* **get a. to sth** hacerse *or* volverse adicto(a) a algo

addiction [ə'dɪkʃən] *n* adicción *f*

addictive [ə'dɪktɪv] *adj also Fig* adictivo(a)

Addis Ababa ['ædɪs'æbəbə] *n* Addis Abeba

addition [ə'dɪʃən] *n* (**a**) *Math* suma *f* (**b**) *(action)* incorporación *f*, adición *f*; *(thing added)* incorporación *f*, añadido *m*; **in a. (to)** además (de); **an a. to the family** un nuevo miembro en la familia

additional [ə'dɪʃənəl] *adj* adicional

additionally [ə'dɪʃənəlɪ] *adv* (**a**) *(further, more)* adicionalmente, de forma *or* manera adicional (**b**) *(moreover)* además

additive ['ædɪtɪv] *n* aditivo *m*

addled ['ædəld] *adj (mind)* embarullado(a), abotargado(a)

add-on ['ædɒn] *(pl* **add-ons**) *n Comptr* extra *m*

address [ə'dres] **1** *n* (**a**) *(of person, letter)* dirección *f*, domicilio *m*; **a. book** agenda *f* de direcciones (**b**) *(speech)* alocución *f*, discurso *m*; **form of a.** *(when speaking to sb)* tratamiento *m*

2 *vt* (**a**) *(letter, remarks, criticism)* dirigir (**to** a) (**b**) *(speak to) (person, crowd)* dirigirse a; **he addressed her as "Your Majesty"** le dio el tratamiento de "Su Majestad" (**c**) *(question, problem)* abordar; **to a. oneself to sth** abordar algo

addressee [ædre'si:] *n* destinatario(a) *m,f*

adenoids ['ædɪnɔɪdz] *npl Anat* vegetaciones *fpl* (adenoideas)

adept [ə'dept] *adj* **she is a. at getting her own way** siempre consigue lo que quiere; **he had always been a. at persuading people to support him** siempre se le había dado muy bien conseguir el apoyo de la gente

adequate ['ædɪkwət] *adj (enough)* suficiente; *(satisfactory)* adecuado(a), apropiado(a)

adhere [əd'hɪə(r)] *vi* (**a**) *(stick)* adherirse (**to** a) (**b**) **to a. to** *(rule)* cumplir, observar; *(belief, plan)* atenerse a

adherence [əd'hɪərəns] *n* (**to** *rule)* cumplimiento *m*, observancia *f* (**to** de); *(to belief, plan)* adhesión *f*, apoyo *m* (**to** a)

adherent [əd'hɪərənt] *n* adepto(a) *m,f*

adhesion [əd'hi:ʒən] *n* (**a**) *(stickiness)* adherencia *f* (**b**) *(to belief, plan)* adhesión *f*, apoyo *m* (**to** a)

adhesive [əd'hi:sɪv] **1** *n* adhesivo *m*

2 *adj* adhesivo(a), adherente; **a. tape** cinta *f* adhesiva

ad hoc ['æd'hɒk] *adj* improvisado(a); **on an a. basis** improvisadamente; **a. committee** comisión *f* especial

ad infinitum ['ædɪnfɪ'naɪtəm] *adv* hasta el infinito

adjacent [ə'dʒeɪsənt] *adj* adyacente, contiguo(a); **to be a. to** estar al lado de

adjectival [ædʒek'taɪvəl] *adj* adjetival; **an a. use** un uso adjetival

adjective ['ædʒɪktɪv] *n* adjetivo *m*

adjoin [ə'dʒɔɪn] *vt (of building, land)* lindar con

adjoining [ə'dʒɔɪnɪŋ] *adj (building, room)* contiguo(a)

adjourn [ə'dʒɜ:n] **1** *vt (meeting, trial)* aplazar, posponer

2 *vi* **the trial/meeting adjourned** se levantó la sesión *(tras juicio/reunión)*; **to a. to another room** pasar a otra habitación

adjournment [ə'dʒɜ:nmənt] *n (of meeting, trial)* aplazamiento *m*

adjudge [ə'dʒʌdʒ] *vt* **to a. sb guilty** declarar a alguien culpable; **to a. sb the winner** proclamar a alguien ganador

adjudicate [ə'dʒu:dɪkeɪt] *vt* juzgar

adjudication [ədʒu:dɪ'keɪʃən] *n* fallo *m*

adjudicator [ə'dʒu:dɪkeɪtə(r)] *n (of dispute)* árbitro *m*; *(of contest)* juez *mf*

adjunct ['ædʒʌŋkt] *n* apéndice *m*

adjust [ə'dʒʌst] **1** *vt (machine, mechanism)* ajustar, regular; *(method)* ajustar, adaptar; **to a. one's tie** ajustarse la corbata; **to a. oneself to sth** adaptarse a algo

2 *vi (person)* adaptarse (**to** a)

adjustable [ə'dʒʌstəbəl] *adj* ajustable, regulable; **a. wrench** llave *f* inglesa

adjustment [ə'dʒʌstmənt] *n* ajuste *m*; **to make an a. to sth** hacer un ajuste a algo, ajustar algo

ad-lib ['æd'lɪb] **1** *adv* improvisadamente

2 *vi (pt & pp* **ad-libbed**) improvisar

adman ['ædmæn] *n Fam* publicista *m*, publicitario *m*

admin ['ædmɪn] *n Fam (work)* papeleo *m*

administer [əd'mɪnɪstə(r)] *vt* (**a**) *(estate, funds)* administrar, dirigir (**b**) *(give) (punishment)* aplicar; *(blow)* propinar; *(medication)* administrar

administrate [əd'mɪnɪstreɪt] *vt (business, institution)* administrar, dirigir

administration [ədmɪnɪ'streɪʃən] *n* (**a**) *(act, activity)* administración *f* (**b**) *(government)* gobierno *m*, administración *f*

administrative [əd'mɪnɪstrətɪv] *adj* administrativo(a)

administrator [əd'mɪnɪstreɪtə(r)] *n* administrador(ora) *m,f*

admirable ['ædmərəbəl] *adj* admirable

admiral ['ædmərəl] *n* almirante *m*

admiration [ædmə'reɪʃən] *n* admiración *f*

admire [əd'maɪə(r)] *vt* admirar

admirer [əd'maɪərə(r)] *n* admirador(ora) *m,f*

admiring [əd'maɪrɪŋ] *adj (look, glance)* de admiración

admissible [əd'mɪsɪbəl] *adj* admisible

admission [əd'mɪʃən] *n* (**a**) *(entry) (to school, hospital)* ingreso *m* (**to** en); *(to museum, exhibition)* visita *f* (**to** a), entrada *f* (**to** a); *(price)* entrada *f*; **a. free** entrada gratuita; **no a. to unaccompanied children** *(sign)* prohibida la entrada a menores no acompañados (**b**) *(acknowledgment) (of guilt, mistake)* confesión *f*; **by his own a.** según él mismo admite

admit [əd'mɪt] *(pt & pp* **admitted**, *continuous* **admitting**) **1** *vt* (**a**) *(allow to enter)* admitir, dejar pasar; **he was admitted to a hospital** ingresó en un hospital; **children not admitted** *(sign)* prohibida la entrada a niños; **admits one** *(on ticket)* individual (**b**) *(acknowledge) (fact, mistake)* admitir; *(crime, guilt)* confesar; **I must a. that...** tengo que reconocer *or* debo confesar que...; **to a. defeat** darse por vencido(a)

2 *vi* **to a. to** *(mistake)* admitir; *(crime)* confesar; **to a. to doing sth** admitir haber hecho algo

admittance [əd'mɪtəns] *n (entry)* acceso *m*, admisión *f*; **to gain a.** ser admitido(a); **to refuse sb a.** no dejar entrar a alguien; **no a.** *(sign)* prohibido el paso

admittedly [əd'mɪtɪdlɪ] *adv* es cierto que; **a., it was dark when I saw him** es cierto que estaba oscuro cuando lo vi; **an a. serious case** un caso sin duda serio

admonish [əd'mɒnɪʃ] *vt (reprimand)* reprender (**for** por)

admonition [ædmə'nɪʃən] *n Formal* admonición *f*

ad nauseam [æd'nɔ:sɪæm] *adv* hasta la saciedad

ado [ə'du:] *n* **without further a.** sin más dilación; **much a. about nothing** mucho ruido y pocas nueces

adobe [ə'dəʊbɪ] *n (clay)* adobe *m*

adolescence [ædə'lesəns] *n* adolescencia *f*

adolescent [ædə'lesənt] *n* adolescente *mf*

adopt [ə'dɒpt] *vt (child, approach, measure)* adoptar; *(candidate)* nombrar

adopted [ə'dɒptɪd] *adj (country)* adoptivo(a), de adopción; **a. daughter** hija *f* adoptiva; **a. son** hijo *m* adoptivo

adoption [ə'dɒpʃən] n adopción f
adorable [ə'dɔːrəbəl] adj encantador(ora)
adoration [ædə'reɪʃən] n adoración f
adore [ə'dɔː(r)] vt (person) adorar; **I adored her last movie** me encantó su última película
adoringly [ə'dɔːrɪŋlɪ] adv apasionadamente, fervorosamente
adorn [ə'dɔːn] vt adornar
adornment [ə'dɔːnmənt] n adorno m, ornamento m
ADP [eɪdiː'piː] n Comptr (abbr **automatic data processing**) proceso m or procesamiento m automático de datos
adrenalin(e) [ə'drenəlɪn] n adrenalina f
Adriatic [eɪdrɪ'ætɪk] n **the A. (Sea)** el (mar) Adriático
adrift [ə'drɪft] adv to be a. (boat) ir a la deriva; Fig **to go a.** (plan) irse a pique or al garete
adroit [ə'drɔɪt] adj diestro(a), hábil
ADSL [eɪdiːes'el] n (abbr **asymmetric digital subscriber line**) ADSL m
adulation [ædjʊ'leɪʃən] n adulación f
adult ['ædʌlt, ə'dʌlt] **1** n adulto(a) m,f
2 adj (person, animal) adulto(a); (attitude) adulto(a), maduro(a); (movie) para adultos; **a. education** educación f de or para adultos
adulterate [ə'dʌltəreɪt] vt adulterar
adulteration [ədʌltə'reɪʃən] n adulteración f
adulterer [ə'dʌltərə(r)] n adúltero(a) m,f
adulteress [ə'dʌltərəs] n adúltera f
adulterous [ə'dʌltərəs] adj adúltero(a)
adultery [ə'dʌltərɪ] n adulterio m; **to commit a.** cometer adulterio
adulthood ['ædʌlthʊd] n edad f adulta
advance [əd'vɑːns] **1** n (**a**) (forward movement) avance m; (progress) avance m, progreso m; **to make advances to sb** (sexual) insinuarse a alguien; (in business) hacer una propuesta inicial a alguien; **in a.** (pay) por adelantado; (give notice) con antelación; **thanking you in a.** (in letter) le doy las gracias de antemano; **six weeks in a.** con seis semanas de antelación; **a. booking** reserva f (anticipada); **a. notice** aviso m previo; **a. warning** advertencia f previa (**b**) (loan) anticipo m, adelanto m
2 vt (**a**) (move forward) (chesspiece, troops) avanzar, adelantar; (science, knowledge) hacer avanzar, adelantar (**b**) (idea, opinion) presentar (**c**) (loan) anticipar, adelantar
3 vi (move forward, make progress) avanzar; **the troops advanced on the city** las tropas avanzaron hacia la ciudad
advanced [əd'vɑːnst] adj (child, student) avanzado(a), aventajado(a); (country) avanzado(a); **she's very a. for her age** está muy adelantada para su edad
advantage [əd'vɑːntɪdʒ] n ventaja f; **to have an a. over** tener ventaja sobre; **to take a. of** aprovecharse de; **to turn sth to one's a.** sacar provecho de algo; **it would be to your a.** te conviene; **a. Sampras** (in tennis) ventaja de or para Sampras
advantageous [ædvən'teɪdʒəs] adj ventajoso(a)
advent ['ædvənt] n (arrival) llegada f, advenimiento m; Rel **A.** Adviento m
adventure [əd'ventʃə(r)] n aventura f; Comptr **a. game** juego m de aventuras; **a. playground** parque m infantil; **a. story** historia f de aventuras
adventurer [əd'ventʃərə(r)] n (**a**) (person fond of adventure) aventurero(a) m,f (**b**) (dishonest person) sinvergüenza mf
adventurous [əd'ventʃərəs] adj (plan, choice) aventurado(a), arriesgado(a); (person) aventurero(a)
adverb ['ædvɜːb] n adverbio m
adverbial [əd'vɜːbɪəl] adj adverbial; **an a. use** un uso adverbial
adversarial [ædvə'seərɪəl] adj Law de adversarios, = basado en el enfrentamiento de dos partes
adversary ['ædvəsərɪ] n adversario(a) m,f

adverse ['ædvɜːs] adj adverso(a), desfavorable
adversely ['ædvɜːslɪ] adv desfavorablemente, negativamente; **to be a. affected by sth** resultar perjudicado(a) por algo
adversity [əd'vɜːsɪtɪ] n adversidad f; **in a.** en la adversidad
advertise ['ædvətaɪz] **1** vt (**a**) (product, job) anunciar (**b**) (call attention to) **he didn't want to a. his presence** no quería llamar la atención
2 vi poner un anuncio; **to a. for sth/sb** poner un anuncio pidiendo algo/a alguien
advertisement [əd'vɜːtɪsmənt] n (on TV, in newspaper) anuncio m; Fig **you're not a good a. for your school** no le haces buena publicidad a tu colegio
advertiser ['ædvətaɪzə(r)] n anunciante mf
advertising ['ædvətaɪzɪŋ] n publicidad f; **a. agency** agencia f de publicidad; **a. campaign** campaña f publicitaria
advice [əd'vaɪs] n consejo m; **a piece of a.** un consejo; **that's good a.** es un buen consejo; **to give sb a.** aconsejar a alguien; **to ask sb's a.** pedir consejo a alguien; **to take sb's a.** seguir el consejo de alguien; **a. column** (in newspaper) consultorio m sentimental
advisable [əd'vaɪzəbəl] adj aconsejable, recomendable
advise [əd'vaɪz] **1** vt (**a**) (give advice to) aconsejar; **to a. sb to do sth** aconsejar a alguien hacer or que haga algo; **to a. sb against doing sth** aconsejar a alguien que no haga algo; **you'd be well advised to take an umbrella** más vale que lleves un paraguas (**b**) (inform) **to a. sb that...** informar a alguien de que...; **to a. sb of sth** informar a alguien de algo (**c**) (give professional guidance) asesorar (**on** sobre)
2 vi **to a. with sb** consultar con alguien
adviser, advisor [əd'vaɪzə(r)] n consejero(a) m,f; (professional) asesor(ora) m,f
advisory [əd'vaɪzərɪ] adj asesor(ora); **in an a. capacity** en calidad de asesor(ora)
advocate 1 n ['ædvəkət] (of cause, doctrine) defensor(ora) m,f
2 vt ['ædvəkeɪt] (policy, plan) abogar por, defender
AEC [eiiː'siː] n (abbr **Atomic Energy Commission**) = comisión americana para la energía nuclear
Aegean [ɪ'dʒiːən] n **the A. (Sea)** el (mar) Egeo
aegis = **egis**
aeon = **eon**
aerate ['eəreɪt] vt (blood) oxigenar
aerial ['eərɪəl] **1** n (of radio, TV) antena f
2 adj aéreo(a); **a. photography** fotografía f aérea
aerobic [eə'rəʊbɪk] adj (exercise) aeróbico(a)
aerobics [eə'rəʊbɪks] n aerobic m, aeróbic m
aerobridge ['eərəʊbrɪdʒ] n Av finger m
aerodynamic [eərəʊdaɪ'næmɪk] adj aerodinámico(a)
aerogram(me) ['eərəgræm] n aerograma m
aeronautic(al) [eərə'nɔːtɪk(əl)] adj aeronáutico(a)
aerosol ['eərəsɒl] n aerosol m; **a. spray** aerosol m
aerospace ['eərəspeɪs] adj aeroespacial
aesthetic = **esthetic**
afar [ə'fɑː(r)] adv Literary **from a.** desde lejos
AFC [eɪef'siː] n (abbr **American Football Conference**) = una de las conferencias que forman la liga nacional de la NFL
affable ['æfəbəl] adj afable, amable
affably ['æfəblɪ] adv afablemente, amablemente
affair [ə'feə(r)] n (**a**) (matter, concern) asunto m; **that's my a.** eso es asunto mío; **she put her affairs in order** puso sus asuntos en orden; **in the present state of affairs** tal y como están las cosas; **foreign affairs** asuntos exteriores; **current affairs** (temas mpl de) actualidad f; **affairs of state** asuntos de Estado (**b**) (sexual) aventura f, lío m; **to have an a. with sb** tener una aventura con alguien (**c**) (event) acontecimiento m; **the wedding was a quiet a.** fue una boda discreta
affect[1] [ə'fekt] vt (**a**) (have effect on) (person, organ, health)

afectar; *(decision)* afectar a, influir en (**b**) *(move emotionally)* afectar; **to be deeply affected by sth** estar muy afectado(a) por algo

affect² *vt (indifference, interest)* afectar, fingir; **to a. an accent** poner un acento

affectation [æfek'teɪʃən] *n* afectación *f*, amaneramiento *m*

affected [ə'fektɪd] *adj (unnatural, pretended)* afectado(a), artificial

affection [ə'fekʃən] *n* afecto *m*, cariño *m*

affectionate [ə'fekʃənət] *adj* afectuoso(a), cariñoso(a)

affidavit [æfɪ'deɪvɪt] *n Law* declaración *f* jurada

affiliate 1 *n* [ə'fɪliət] filial *f*
2 *vt* [ə'fɪlieɪt] afiliar (**to** *or* **with** a); **affiliated company** (empresa *f*) filial *f*

affiliated [ə'fɪlieɪtɪd] *adj (member, organization)* afiliado(a); **a. company** (empresa *f*) filial *f*

affiliation [əfɪlɪ'eɪʃən] *n (link, connection)* conexión *f*; *(political, religious)* filiación *f*

affinity [ə'fɪnɪtɪ] *n* (**a**) *(liking, attraction)* afinidad *f* (**with/between** con/entre); **she felt an a. for such places** sentía atracción por ese tipo de lugares (**b**) *(relationship, connection)* afinidad *f* (**between/with** entre/con)

affirm [ə'fɜːm] *vt* afirmar

affirmation [æfə'meɪʃən] *n* afirmación *f*

affirmative [ə'fɜːmətɪv] **1** *n* **to answer in the a.** responder afirmativamente
2 *adj (answer)* afirmativo(a); **a. action** discriminación *f* positiva

affix 1 *n* ['æfɪks] *Ling* afijo *m*
2 *vt* [ə'fɪks] *(notice, poster)* pegar (**to** a)

afflict [ə'flɪkt] *vt* afligir; **to be afflicted with sth** padecer algo

affliction [ə'flɪkʃən] *n (suffering)* padecimiento *m*; *(misfortune)* desgracia *f*

affluent ['æflʊənt] *adj* opulento(a), acomodado(a); **the a. society** la sociedad opulenta

afford [ə'fɔːd] *vt* (**a**) *(financially)* permitirse; **to be able to a. sth** poder permitirse algo; **I can't a. it** no me lo puedo permitir (**b**) *(nonfinancial use)* **I can a. to wait** puedo esperar; **can you a. the time?** ¿tienes tiempo?; **I can't a. not to** no puedo permitirme no hacerlo; **we can't a. another mistake** no podemos permitirnos cometer otro error (**c**) *Formal (give)* proporcionar

affordable [ə'fɔːdəbəl] *adj (price, purchase)* asequible

affray [ə'freɪ] *n* altercado *m*, reyerta *f*

affront [ə'frʌnt] **1** *n* afrenta *f*, ofensa *f*
2 *vt* afrentar, ofender; **to be/feel affronted** estar/sentirse ofendido(a)

Afghan ['æfgæn] **1** *n* (**a**) *(person)* afgano(a) *m,f* (**b**) *(dog)* (galgo *m*) afgano *m*
2 *adj* afgano(a); **A. hound** galgo *m* afgano

Afghanistan [æf'gænɪstɑːn] *n* Afganistán

aficionado [əfɪsɪə'nɑːdəʊ] *(pl* **aficionados**) *n* aficionado(a) *m,f*

afield [ə'fiːld] *adv* **to go further a.** ir más allá; **to look further a.** buscar más

AFL-CIO [eɪef'elsiaɪ'əʊ] *n (abbr* **American Federation of Labor and Congress of Industrial Organizations**) = federación de sindicatos

afloat [ə'fləʊt] *adv* a flote; **to stay a.** *(boat, company)* mantenerse a flote

afoot [ə'fʊt] *adv* **there's something a.** se está tramando algo

aforementioned [ə'fɔːmenʃənd], **aforesaid** [ə'fɔːsed] *adj Formal* susodicho(a), mencionado(a)

afraid [ə'freɪd] *adj* (**a**) *(scared)* **to be a.** tener miedo; **I'm a. of him** me da miedo; **I'm a. of dogs** tengo miedo a los perros; **I'm a. of making a mistake** tengo miedo de equivocarme;

that's exactly what I was a. of! ¡eso es precisamente lo que me temía!; **I was a. there would be an accident** temía que ocurriera un accidente (**b**) *(sorry)* **I'm a. so/not** me temo que sí/no; **I'm a. she's out** me temo que ha salido; **I'm a. I can't help you** lo siento, no puedo ayudarle

afresh [ə'freʃ] *adv* de nuevo, otra vez; **to start a.** empezar de nuevo

Africa ['æfrɪkə] *n* África

African ['æfrɪkən] **1** *n* africano(a) *m,f*
2 *adj* africano(a); **A. Union** Unión *f* Africana

African-American ['æfrɪkənə'merɪkən] *n & adj* afroamericano(a) *m,f*

Afrikaans [æfrɪ'kɑːnz] *n* afrikaans *m*

Afro ['æfrəʊ] **1** *n* peinado *m* (a lo) afro
2 *adj* afro

Afro-American ['æfrəʊə'merɪkən] *n & adj* afroamericano(a) *m,f*

Afro-Caribbean ['æfrəʊkærɪ'bɪən] *n & adj* afrocaribeño(a) *m,f*

aft [ɑːft] *adv Naut* a popa

after ['ɑːftə(r)] **1** *prep* (**a**) *(with time)* después de; **a. today** a partir de hoy; **a. dinner** después de cenar; **the day a. tomorrow** pasado mañana; **it's a. five** son más de las cinco; **it's twenty a. six** son las seis y veinte; **a. all** *(all things considered)* después de todo; *(despite everything)* a pesar de todo
(**b**) *(with motion)* **to run a. sb** correr tras (de) alguien; **close the door a. you** cierra la puerta al salir
(**c**) *(looking for)* **to be a. sb** buscar a alguien, andar detrás de alguien; **the police are a. him** la policía lo busca; **I think she's a. a raise** me parece que anda detrás de *or* va buscando un aumento de sueldo
(**d**) *(expressing order)* **a. you!** *(you first)* ¡después de usted!; **am I a. you (in line** *or* **in the queue)?** ¿voy detrás de usted (en la cola)?; **the first crossing a. the traffic lights** el primer cruce después del semáforo; **a. her, he is the best** después de ella, el mejor es él
(**e**) *(expressing repetition)* **day a. day** un día tras otro; **time a. time** una y otra vez; **year a. year** año tras año; **one a. the other** uno tras otro; **page a. page of statistics** páginas y más páginas de estadísticas
(**f**) *(in honor of)* **to name sth/sb a. sb** ponerle a algo/alguien el nombre de alguien
2 *adv* después; **soon/long a.** poco/mucho después; **the day/the week a.** el día/la semana siguiente
3 *conj* después de que; **I came a. he left** llegué cuando él ya se había ido; **a. doing sth** después de hacer algo

afterbirth ['ɑːftəbɜːθ] *n* placenta *f*, secundinas *fpl*

aftercare ['ɑːftəkeə(r)] *n (after operation)* atención *f* posoperatoria; *(of convalescent, delinquent)* seguimiento *m*

after-dinner ['ɑːftədɪnə(r)] *adj (speaker, speech)* de sobremesa

aftereffects ['ɑːftərəfekts] *npl (of accident, crisis)* secuelas *fpl*; *(of drug)* efectos *mpl* secundarios

afterglow ['ɑːftəgləʊ] *n (of sunset)* luz *f* del crepúsculo; *(of pleasant feeling)* regusto *m* placentero

after-hours ['æftər'aʊəz] *adv (after closing time)* después de cerrar; *(after work)* después del trabajo

afterlife ['ɑːftəlaɪf] *n* otra vida *f*, vida *f* de ultratumba

aftermath ['ɑːftəmæθ] *n (period)* periodo *m* posterior; *(result)* secuelas *fpl*, consecuencias *fpl*

afternoon [ɑːftə'nuːn] *n* tarde *f*; **in the a.** por la tarde; **at two o'clock in the a.** a las dos de la tarde; **good a.!** ¡buenas tardes!; **a. tea** *(meal)* merienda *f*

after-sales service ['ɑːftəseɪlz'sɜːvɪs] *n Com* servicio *m* posventa

after-school ['ɑːftəskuːl] *adj (activities)* extraescolar *(después de las clases)*

aftershave ['ɑːftəʃeɪv] *n (as perfume)* colonia *f*; **a. balm** *or* **lotion** *(to protect skin)* loción *f* para después del afeitado *or* Méx rasurado

aftersun ['ɑːftəsʌn] *adj* **a. cream/lotion** crema *f*/loción *f* para después del sol

aftertaste ['ɑːftəteɪst] *n also Fig* regusto *m*; **it leaves an unpleasant a.** deja mal sabor de boca

after-tax ['ɑːftətæks] *adj (profits, salary)* después de impuestos

afterthought ['ɑːftəθɔːt] *n* idea *f* tardía; **it was an a.** se me ocurrió después

afterward(s) ['ɑːftəwəd(z)] *adv* después

again [ə'gen] *adv* **(a)** *(in general)* de nuevo, otra vez; **to begin a.** volver a empezar; **he never came back a.** no volvió nunca más; **once a.** una vez más; **don't do it a.!** ¡no lo vuelvas a hacer!; **not you a.!** ¡otra vez tú!; **a. and a.** una y otra vez; **now and a.** de vez en cuando; **half as much a.** la mitad más; **what did you say a.?** ¿qué?, ¿cómo has dicho? **(b)** *(besides)* además, **(then) a.** *(on the other hand)* por otra parte; **a., I may have imagined it** en fin, *Esp* puede que me lo haya imaginado *or Am* tal vez me lo imaginé

against [ə'genst] *prep* **(a)** *(in opposition to)* contra, en contra de; **to be a. sth/sb** estar en contra de algo/alguien; **to have something a. sth/sb** tener algo en contra de algo/alguien; **to have nothing a. sth/sb** no tener nada en contra de algo/alguien; **it was a. my principles** iba (en) contra (de) mis principios; **a. the law** ilegal; **a. my will** en contra de mi voluntad

(**b**) *(as protection from)* contra; **to warn sb a. sth/sb** poner a alguien en guardia contra algo/alguien

(**c**) *(in contact with)* contra; **to lean a. sth** apoyarse en *or Am* contra algo; **she put the ladder a. the wall** apoyó la escalera contra la pared

(**d**) *(in comparison with)* frente; **the pound rose/fell a. the dollar** la libra subió/bajó frente al dólar; **inflation was 4.1 percent, as a. 3.2 percent last year** hubo una inflación del 4,1 por ciento frente a un 3,2 por ciento del año pasado; **a. the light** a contraluz

age [eɪdʒ] *(continuous* **aging** *or* **ageing)* **1** *n* **(a)** *(of person)* edad *f*; **to be twenty years of a.** tener veinte años; **what a. is she?, what's her a.?** ¿qué edad tiene?, ¿cuántos años tiene?; **he doesn't look his a.** no aparenta la edad que tiene; **at a. twenty, at the a. of twenty** a los veinte años; **people of all ages** gente de todas las edades; **the fifteen-to-twenty a. bracket** *or* **group** la franja de edad comprendida entre los quince y los veinte años; **a. of consent** edad núbil; **a. limit** límite *m* de edad

(**b**) *(old)* **a.** vejez *f*

(**c**) *(adulthood)* **to come of a.** alcanzar la mayoría de edad; **to be under a.** ser menor *(para beber, tener relaciones sexuales, etc.)*

(**d**) *(era)* época *f*, edad *f*; **through the ages** a lo largo del tiempo

(**e**) *Fam (long time)* **it's ages since I saw him** hace siglos que no lo veo; **I've been waiting (for) ages** llevo esperando una eternidad

2 *vt & vi* envejecer

aged *adj* **(a)** [eɪdʒd] *(of the age of)* **a. twenty** de veinte años (de edad) **(b)** ['eɪdʒɪd] *(old)* anciano(a)

ageing = **aging**

ageism, agism ['eɪdʒɪzəm] *n* discriminación *f* por motivos de edad

ageist, agist ['eɪdʒɪst] *adj* discriminatorio(a) por motivos de edad

agency ['eɪdʒənsɪ] *n* **(a)** *Com* agencia *f*; **advertising/travel a.** agencia de publicidad/viajes **(b)** **through the a. of** mediante la intervención de

agenda [ə'dʒendə] *n (of meeting)* orden *m* del día, programa *m*; *Fig* **to be on top of the a.** ser un asunto prioritario; *Fig* **what**

is his real a.? ¿cuáles son sus verdaderas intenciones?

agent ['eɪdʒənt] *n* **(a)** *(representative)* agente *mf*, representante *mf* **(b)** **(secret) a.** agente *mf* secreto(a) **(c)** *(instrument)* **to be the a. of** ser la causa de

age-old ['eɪdʒəʊld] *adj (custom, problem)* antiguo(a)

aggravate ['ægrəveɪt] *vt* **(a)** *(worsen)* agravar; *Law* **aggravated assault** agresión con agravantes **(b)** *Fam (annoy)* fastidiar, molestar, *RP* hinchar

aggravating ['ægrəveɪtɪŋ] *adj* **(a)** *Law* agravante **(b)** *Fam (annoying)* molesto(a), *RP* hinchón(ona); **it's very a.** fastidia un montón

aggravation [ægrə'veɪʃən] *n* **(a)** *(worsening)* agravamiento *m*, empeoramiento *m* **(b)** *Fam (annoyance)* fastidio *m*, molestia *f*

aggregate ['ægrɪgət] **1** *n* conglomerado *m*

2 *adj* total, conjunto(a)

aggression [ə'greʃən] *n (violence)* agresividad *f*; **an act of a.** una agresión

aggressive [ə'gresɪv] *adj (violent)* agresivo(a); *(vigorous, dynamic)* enérgico(a), agresivo(a)

aggressively [ə'gresɪvlɪ] *adv (violently)* agresivamente; *(vigorously)* enérgicamente, agresivamente

aggressiveness [ə'gresɪvnɪs] *n (hostility)* agresividad *f*; *(vigor)* acometividad *f*, agresividad *f*

aggressor [ə'gresə(r)] *n* agresor(ora) *m,f*

aggrieved [ə'griːvd] *adj* agraviado(a), ofendido(a); **to be a.** estar ofendido(a)

aghast [ə'gɑːst] *adj* horrorizado(a), espantado(a)

agile ['ædʒaɪl] *adj* ágil

agility [ə'dʒɪlɪtɪ] *n* agilidad *f*

aging, ageing ['eɪdʒɪŋ] **1** *n (of person, wine)* envejecimiento *m*; **a. process** proceso *m* de envejecimiento

2 *adj (old)* viejo(a); **the problem of America's a. population** el problema del envejecimiento de la población americana

agism, agist = **ageism, ageist**

agitate ['ædʒɪteɪt] **1** *vt (liquid)* revolver, agitar; *(person)* inquietar, agitar

2 *vi* **to a. for/against sth** hacer campaña a favor de/en contra de algo

agitated ['ædʒɪteɪtɪd] *adj* inquieto(a), agitado(a); **to be a.** estar inquieto(a) *or* agitado(a)

agitation [ædʒɪ'teɪʃən] *n* **(a)** *(of person)* inquietud *f*, agitación *f* **(b)** *(campaign)* campaña *f*

agitator ['ædʒɪteɪtə(r)] *n Pol* agitador(ora) *m,f*, activista *mf*

aglow [ə'gləʊ] *adj* **to be a. with** *(with color)* estar encendido(a) de; *(with pleasure, excitement)* estar rebosante de

agnostic [æg'nɒstɪk] *n & adj* agnóstico(a) *m,f*

agnosticism [æg'nɒstɪsɪzəm] *n* agnosticismo *m*

ago [ə'gəʊ] *adv* **ten years a.** hace diez años; **a little while a., a short time a.** hace un rato; **long a.** hace mucho (tiempo); **not long a.** no hace mucho (tiempo); **as long a. as 1840** ya en 1840; **how long a. was that?** ¿hace cuánto tiempo fue (eso)?

agog [ə'gɒg] *adj* **to be a. at sth** estar entusiasmado(a) *or* emocionado(a) con algo

agonize ['ægənaɪz] *vi* angustiarse, agobiarse (**over** por *or* con)

agonizing ['ægənaɪzɪŋ] *adj (pain, death)* atroz; *(silence, wait)* angustioso(a); *(decision, dilemma)* peliagudo(a)

agony ['ægənɪ] *n (physical pain)* dolor *m* intenso; *(anguish)* angustia *f*, agonía *f*; **to be in a.** morirse de dolor; **it's a. walking in these shoes** andar con estos zapatos es un martirio

agoraphobia [ægərə'fəʊbɪə] *n* agorafobia *f*

agoraphobic [ægərə'fəʊbɪk] *n & adj* agorafóbico(a) *m,f*

agrarian [ə'greərɪən] *adj* agrario(a)

agree [ə'griː] **1** *vt* **(a)** *(reach agreement on) (price, conditions)* acordar, pactar; **(are we) agreed?** ¿(estamos) de acuerdo?

(**b**) *(concur)* **to a. (that)...** estar de acuerdo en que...; **it is generally agreed that...** se suele admitir que... (**c**) *(consent)* **to a. to do sth** acordar hacer algo; **we agreed to meet at six** quedamos a las seis; **he agreed to pay** estuvo de acuerdo en pagar él; **we'll have to a. to differ on that** tendremos que aceptar las discrepancias en cuanto a eso

2 *vi* (**a**) *(be of same opinion, concur)* estar de acuerdo (**about/with** en cuanto a/con); **I quite** *or* **entirely a.** estoy completamente de acuerdo; **I'm afraid I can't a.** lo siento, pero no puedo estar conforme; **I couldn't a. more!** ¡estoy completamente de acuerdo!; **at least we a. about that** al menos estamos de acuerdo en eso; **I don't a. with all this violence on television** no me parece bien toda esa violencia que aparece en televisión (**b**) *(match) (statements, facts, opinions)* coincidir, concordar (**with** con); *Gram* concordar (**c**) *(accept)* acceder, consentir

▸**agree on** *vt insep (be in agreement on)* estar de acuerdo en; *(reach agreement on)* ponerse de acuerdo en

▸**agree to** *vt insep* acceder a, aceptar; **he'll never a. to that** nunca accederá a eso; **to a. to a condition/a proposal** aceptar una condición/una propuesta

▸**agree with** *vt insep (of food, climate)* sentar bien a

agreeable [ə'griːəbəl] *adj* (**a**) *(pleasant)* agradable; *(person)* simpático(a) (**b**) *(acceptable)* **if that is a. to you** si le parece bien

agreed [ə'griːd] *adj (price, time)* fijado(a)

agreement [ə'griːmənt] *n* (**a**) *(contract, assent)* acuerdo *m*; **to come to an a.** llegar a un acuerdo; **by mutual a.** de mutuo acuerdo; **the proposal met with unanimous a.** la propuesta recibió un apoyo unánime; **to be in a. with sth/sb** estar de acuerdo con algo/alguien (**b**) *(of facts, account)* **to be in a. (with)** concordar (con), coincidir (con) (**c**) *Gram* concordancia *f*

agribusiness ['ægrɪbɪznɪs] *n* industria *f* agropecuaria, agroindustria *f*

agricultural [ægrɪ'kʌltʃərəl] *adj* agrícola; **a. college** escuela *f* de agricultura; **a. laborer** trabajador(ora) *m,f* agrícola

agriculture ['ægrɪkʌltʃə(r)] *n* agricultura *f*

agronomy [ə'grɒnəmɪ] *n* agronomía *f*

aground [ə'graʊnd] *adv* **to run a.** *(ship)* varar, encallar; *(project, government)* encallar

ahead [ə'hed] *adv* (**a**) *(forward)* adelante; *(in front)* delante, *Am* adelante; **to go on a.** adelantarse; **to send sb (on) a.** enviar a alguien por delante, *Am* mandar a alguien adelante; **a. of** delante de; **the road a. was clear** no había nadie en la carretera delante *or Am* adelante de nosotros/él/ellos/*etc.*

(**b**) *(winning)* **to be a. (of)** *(in race, opinion poll)* ir por delante (de); *(in match)* ir ganando (a); **Mexico is two goals a.** México gana por dos goles; **to get a.** *(in career)* triunfar; **to get a. of sb** adelantar a alguien

(**c**) *(in time)* **to plan a.** hacer planes con antelación *or* por adelantado; **in the years a.** en los años venideros; **a. of time** antes de tiempo; **he was a. of his time** se adelantó a su tiempo; **how far a. should one book?** ¿con cuánta antelación hace falta reservar?; **the project is a. of schedule** el proyecto va adelantado *or* va por delante del calendario previsto

ahem [ə'hem] *exclam* ¡ejem!

ahoy [ə'hɔɪ] *exclam* **a. there!** ¡ha del barco!; **ship a.!** ¡barco a la vista!

AI ['eɪaɪ] *n* (**a**) *Comptr (abbr* **artificial intelligence**) inteligencia *f* artificial (**b**) *Biol (abbr* **artificial insemination**) inseminación *f* artificial (**c**) *Pol (abbr* **Amnesty International**) AI *f*, Amnistía *f* Internacional

aid [eɪd] **1** *n* (**a**) *(help, for disaster relief)* ayuda *f*; **with the a. of** con la ayuda de; **to go to sb's a.** acudir en ayuda de alguien; **in a. of** *(fundraising event)* a beneficio de; **a. worker** cooperante *mf* (**b**) *(device)* ayuda *f*; **teaching aids** material *m* didáctico *or* docente

2 *vt (growth, development)* ayudar a, contribuir a; *(person)* ayudar; *Law* **to a. and abet sb** ser cómplice de alguien

aide [eɪd] *n* asistente *mf*

aide-de-camp ['eɪddə'kɒŋ] *(pl* **aides-de-camp***) n Mil* ayudante *mf* de campo, edecán *m*

aide-mémoire ['eɪdmem'wɑː(r)] *(pl* **aides-mémoire** ['eɪdzmem'wɑː(r)]*) n* recordatorio *m*

AIDS [eɪdz] *n (abbr* **Acquired Immunodeficiency Syndrome**) sida *m*; **A. sufferer** enfermo(a) *m,f* de sida; **A. clinic** clínica *f* para enfermos de sida; **A. virus** virus *m* del sida

AIDS-related ['eɪdzrɪleɪtɪd] *adj* asociado(a) al sida; **A. complex** CAS *m*, complejo *m* asociado al sida

ailing ['eɪlɪŋ] *adj (person)* enfermo(a); *(company, economy)* enfermizo(a), débil

ailment ['eɪlmənt] *n* achaque *m*

aim [eɪm] **1** *n* (**a**) *(at target)* puntería *f*; **to take a. at** apuntar a; **her a. was good** tenía buena puntería (**b**) *(goal)* objetivo *m*, propósito *m*; **with the a. of doing sth** con el propósito de hacer algo

2 *vt (blow, remark, TV program)* dirigir (**at** a); *(gun, camera)* apuntar (**at** hacia *or* a); **to be aimed at sb** *(remarks, TV program)* estar dirigido(a) a alguien

3 *vi* **to a. at sth/sb** *(with gun)* apuntar a *or* hacia algo/alguien; **to a. to do sth** *(intend)* tener la intención de hacer algo

aimless ['eɪmlɪs] *adj (existence)* sin objetivos; *(remark)* vago(a)

ain't [eɪnt] *Fam* (**a**) = **is not, am not, are not** (**b**) = **has not, have not**

air [eə(r)] **1** *n* (**a**) *(in general)* aire *m*; **by a.** en avión; **to be on the a.** *(person, program)* estar en el aire; **to throw sth (up) in the a.** lanzar algo al aire; **our plans are up in the a.** *(undecided)* nuestros planes están en el aire; **there's a feeling of hope in the a.** hay (un) ambiente de esperanza; *Aut* **a. bag** airbag *m*; **a. base** base *f* aérea; **a. bed** colchón *m* hinchable; **a. filter** filtro *m* del aire; **the A. Force** las Fuerzas Aéreas; **a. freight** transporte *m* aéreo; **a. freshener** ambientador *m*; **a. hostess** azafata *f* de vuelo, *Am* aeromoza *f*; **a. marshal** teniente *m* general de las fuerzas aéreas; **a. pollution** contaminación *f* atmosférica, polución *f* ambiental; **a. pressure** presión *f* atmosférica; **a. raid** ataque *m* aéreo; **a. rifle** escopeta *f* de aire comprimido; **a. show** demostración *f* *or* exhibición *f* aérea; **a. steward** auxiliar *m* de vuelo; **a. stewardess** auxiliar *f* de vuelo, azafata *f* de vuelo, *Am* aeromoza *f*; **a. terminal** terminal *f* de vuelo; **a. traffic control** control *m* (del tráfico) aéreo; **a. traffic controller** controlador(ora) *m,f* aéreo(a)

(**b**) *(melody)* melodía *f*, aire *m*

(**c**) *(look)* aire *m*; **he has the a. of somebody who has traveled** tiene aire de haber viajado mucho; **to give oneself airs, to put on airs** darse aires, darse tono

2 *vt (room, opinions, grievances)* ventilar, airear; *(clothing, bedding)* airear, orear

airborne ['eəbɔːn] *adj (aircraft)* en vuelo; *(seeds, particles)* transportado(a) por el viento; *(troops)* aerotransportado(a); **to be a.** *(aircraft)* estar volando

airbrush ['eəbrʌʃ] **1** *n* aerógrafo *m*

2 *vt (photograph)* retocar (con aerógrafo)

air-conditioned ['eəkən'dɪʃənd] *adj* climatizado(a), con aire acondicionado; **to be a.** *(room)* tener aire acondicionado

air-conditioning ['eəkən'dɪʃənɪŋ] *n* aire *m* acondicionado

air-cooled ['eəkuːld] *adj* con refrigeración de aire

aircraft ['eəkrɑːft] *(pl* **aircraft***) n (airplane)* avión *m*; *(any flying vehicle)* aeronave *f*; **a. carrier** portaaviones *m inv*

aircrew ['eəkruː] *n Av* tripulación *f*

airfare ['eəfeə(r)] *n (precio m del) Esp* billete *m or Am* boleto *m or Am* pasaje *m*

airfield ['eəfiːld] *n* campo *m* de aviación

airhead ['eəhed] *n Fam* cabeza *mf* de chorlito, simple *mf*

airing ['eərɪŋ] *n* **to give sth an a.** *(room, opinions, grievances)* ventilar *or* airear algo; *(clothing)* airear *or* orear algo

air-kiss ['eəkɪs] *vi* besar al aire

airless ['eəlɪs] *adj (evening, atmosphere)* cargado(a); **an a. room** una habitación en la que falta el aire

airlift ['eəlɪft] **1** *n* puente *m* aéreo
   2 *vt (supplies, troops)* transportar mediante un puente aéreo

airline ['eəlaɪn] *n* línea *f* aérea; **a. pilot** piloto *mf* comercial

airlock ['eəlɒk] *n* (**a**) *(in submarine, spacecraft)* compartimento *m* estanco, esclusa *f* de aire (**b**) *(in pipe)* burbuja *f* de aire

airmail ['eəmeɪl] **1** *n* correo *m* aéreo; **a. letter** carta *f* por vía aérea
   2 *adv* **to send sth a.** enviar algo por vía aérea
   3 *vt (letter)* mandar por vía aérea

airplane ['eəpleɪn] *n* avión *m*

airport ['eəpɔ:t] *n* aeropuerto *m*

air-sea rescue ['eəsi:'reskju:] *n* rescate *m* marítimo desde el aire

airship ['eəʃɪp] *n* dirigible *m*

airsick ['eəsɪk] *adj* **to be a.** marearse *(en un avión)*

airspace ['eəspeɪs] *n* espacio *m* aéreo

airstrip ['eəstrɪp] *n* pista *f* de aterrizaje

airtight ['eətaɪt] *adj* hermético(a)

airtime ['eətaɪm] *n Rad & TV* tiempo *m* de emisión

air-to-surface ['eətə'sɜːfɪs] *adj (missile)* aire-superficie

airwaves ['eəweɪvz] *npl* **his voice came over the a.** su voz llegó a través de las ondas

airway ['eəweɪ] *n* (**a**) *(of body)* vía *f* respiratoria (**b**) *(for airplane)* ruta *f* aérea

airworthy ['eəwɜːðɪ] *adj Av* **to be a.** estar en condiciones de volar

airy ['eərɪ] *adj* (**a**) *(room, house)* aireado(a) y espacioso(a) (**b**) *(person, attitude)* ligero(a), despreocupado(a)

aisle [aɪl] *n (in church)* nave *f* lateral; *(in plane, bus, theater)* pasillo *m*; *Fam* **to have them rolling in the aisles** *(comedian)* hacer que se caigan por los suelos *or RP* se revuelquen por el piso de risa; **a. seat** *(in plane)* asiento *m* de pasillo

ajar [ə'dʒɑ:(r)] *adj & adv* entornado(a)

aka [eɪkeɪ'eɪ] *adv (abbr* **also known as***)* alias

akimbo [ə'kɪmbəʊ] *adj* **with arms a.** con los brazos en jarras

akin [ə'kɪn] *adj* **a. to** parecido(a) a

alabaster ['æləbæstə(r)] *n* alabastro *m*

alacrity [ə'lækrɪtɪ] *n* presteza *f*

à la mode [ælə'məʊd] *adj (dessert)* con helado

alarm [ə'lɑ:m] **1** *n* alarma *f*; **to raise** *or* **give the a.** dar la alarma; **there's no cause for a.** no hay motivo de alarma; **a. clock** (reloj *m*) despertador *m*; **a. signal** señal *f* de alarma
   2 *vt* alarmar; **to be alarmed at sth** estar alarmado(a) por algo

alarming [ə'lɑ:mɪŋ] *adj* alarmante

alarmist [ə'lɑ:mɪst] *n & adj* alarmista *mf*

alas [ə'læs] **1** *exclam* ¡ay de mí!
   2 *adv* desgraciadamente

Albania [æl'beɪnɪə] *n* Albania

Albanian [æl'beɪnɪən] **1** *n* (**a**) *(person)* albanés(esa) *m,f* (**b**) *(language)* albanés *m*
   2 *adj* albanés(esa)

albatross ['ælbətrɒs] *n* albatros *m inv*

albeit [ɔ:l'bi:ɪt] *conj* aunque; **a brilliant, a. uneven, novel** una novela brillante, aunque desigual

albino [æl'bi:nəʊ] *(pl* **albinos***)* *n* albino(a) *m,f*

album ['ælbəm] *n (for photos, stamps, record)* álbum *m*

albumen ['ælbjʊmɪn] *n* (**a**) *(in egg)* albumen *m* (**b**) *(in blood)* albúmina *f*

alchemist ['ælkəmɪst] *n* alquimista *mf*

alchemy ['ælkəmɪ] *n* alquimia *f*

alcohol ['ælkəhɒl] *n* alcohol *m*

alcoholic [ælkə'hɒlɪk] **1** *n (person)* alcohólico(a) *m,f*
   2 *adj* alcohólico(a)

alcoholism ['ælkəhɒlɪzəm] *n* alcoholismo *m*

alcove ['ælkəʊv] *n* hueco *m*

alder ['ɔ:ldə(r)] *n (tree)* aliso *m*

ale [eɪl] *n* = cerveza inglesa de malta

alert [ə'lɜːt] **1** *n* alerta *f*; **to be on the a.** estar alerta
   2 *adj (mind)* lúcido(a); **to be a.** *(watchful)* estar alerta *or* vigilante; *(lively)* ser despierto(a) *or* espabilado(a); **to be a. to sth** *(aware of)* ser consciente de algo
   3 *vt* alertar; **he alerted them to the danger** los alertó del peligro

alertness [ə'lɜːtnɪs] *n (watchfulness)* actitud *f* vigilante; *(liveliness)* vivacidad *f*

Aleutian Islands [æl'u:ʃən'aɪləndz] *npl* **the A.** las (Islas) Aleutianas

Alexandria [ælɪg'zɑːndrɪə] *n* Alejandría

alfalfa [æl'fælfə] *n* alfalfa *f*

alfresco [æl'freskəʊ] *adj & adv* al aire libre

algae ['ældʒi:] *npl* algas *fpl*

algebra ['ældʒɪbrə] *n* álgebra *f*

Algeria [æl'dʒɪərɪə] *n* Argelia

Algerian [æl'dʒɪərɪən] *n & adj* argelino(a) *m,f*

Algiers [æl'dʒɪəz] *n* Argel

algorithm ['ælgərɪðəm] *n Comptr* algoritmo *m*

alias ['eɪlɪəs] **1** *n* alias *m inv*
   2 *adv* alias

alibi ['ælɪbaɪ] *n Law* coartada *f*

alien ['eɪlɪən] **1** *n* (**a**) *Formal (foreigner)* extranjero(a) *m,f* (**b**) *(from outer space)* extraterrestre *mf*, alienígena *mf*
   2 *adj* (**a**) *(strange)* extraño(a); **it was a. to her nature** era ajeno a su carácter (**b**) *(from outer space)* extraterrestre, alienígena

alienate ['eɪlɪəneɪt] *vt (supporters, readers)* alejar, provocar el distanciamiento de

alienated ['eɪlɪəneɪtɪd] *adj* **they feel a. from society** se sienten marginados de la sociedad

alight[1] [ə'laɪt] *adj (burning)* **to be a.** estar ardiendo *or* en llamas; **to set sth a.** prender fuego a algo

alight[2] *vi* (**a**) *Formal (from train, car)* apearse *(at* en*)* (**b**) *(bird, glance)* posarse *(on* sobre *or* en*)*

align [ə'laɪn] *vt* alinear; **to a. oneself with/against sb** alinearse con/contra alguien

alignment [ə'laɪnmənt] *n* alineamiento *m*, alineación *f*; **out of a.** desalineado(a), no alineado(a); **in a.** alineado(a)

alike [ə'laɪk] **1** *adj* igual; **to look a.** parecerse; **they are all a.!** ¡todos son iguales!
   2 *adv (treat, dress, think)* igual; **old and young a.** jovenes y viejos por igual

alimentary canal [ælɪ'mentərɪkə'næl] *n Anat* tracto *m* alimentario, tubo *m* digestivo

alimony ['ælɪmənɪ] *n Law* pensión *f* (matrimonial) compensatoria

alive [ə'laɪv] *adj* (**a**) *(living)* vivo(a); **to be a.** estar vivo(a); **to keep sb a.** mantener vivo(a) a alguien; **to keep a memory a.** mantener un recuerdo vivo; **to stay a.** sobrevivir; **to be burnt/buried a.** ser quemado(a)/enterrado(a) vivo(a); **to be a. and well** *(still living)* estar a salvo; **the oldest man a.** el hombre más viejo del mundo (**b**) *(aware)* **to be a. to sth** ser consciente de algo, darse cuenta de algo (**c**) *(full of vitality)* **I've never felt so a.** nunca me he sentido tan lleno de vida; **he came a. when someone mentioned food** revivió cuando alguien nombró la comida (**d**) *(teeming)* **to be a. with sth** ser un hervidero de algo

alkali ['ælkəlaɪ] *n* álcali *m*, base *f*

alkaline ['ælkəlaɪn] *adj* alcalino(a)

all [ɔ:l] **1** *adj* (**a**) *(every one of)* todos(as); **a. men** todos los hombres; **a. the others** todos los demás; **a. four of them** los cuatro; **a. the books** todos los libros; **they are a. smokers** todos fuman, todos son fumadores; **at a. hours** a todas horas, continuamente

(**b**) *(the whole of)* todo(a); **a. the wine** todo el vino; **a. day** todo el día; **a. week** toda la semana; **she has lived here a. her life** ha vivido aquí toda la *or* su vida; **a. the time** todo el tiempo; **he leaves the door open a. the time** siempre se deja la puerta abierta; **is that a. the money you're taking?** ¿no te llevas más que ese dinero?

(**c**) *(for emphasis)* **she helped me in a. sorts of ways** me ayudó de mil maneras; **what's a. that noise?** ¿qué es ese escándalo?; **in a. honesty** para ser francos; *Fam* **and a. that** y todo eso; **it's not a. that easy** no es tan fácil; **for a. her apparent calm, she was actually very nervous** a pesar de su aparente tranquilidad, estaba realmente muy nerviosa; **you, of a. people, should understand** tú deberías comprenderlo mejor que nadie; **of a. the times to phone!** ¡vaya un momento para llamar!

2 *pron* (**a**) *(everyone)* todos(as) *m,fpl*; **a. of them say that…**, **they a. say that…** todos dicen que…; **a. of us** todos (nosotros); **we a. love him** todos lo queremos; **a. together** todos juntos

(**b**) *(everything)* *(replacing uncountable noun)* todo(a) *m,f*; *(replacing plural noun)* todos(as) *m,fpl*; **I want a. of it** lo quiero todo; **a. of them are blue, they are a. blue** todos son azules; **I did a. I could** hice todo lo que pude; **it was a. I could do not to laugh** apenas pude aguantar la risa; **best/worst of a.,…** y lo que es mejor/peor,…; **I like this one best of a.** este es el que más me gusta; **most of a.** ante todo; **when I was busiest of a.** cuando estaba más ocupado; **that's a.** eso es todo; **is that a.?** ¿nada más?, ¿es eso todo?; **a. I said was "good morning"** sólo dije "buenos días"; **when all's said and done** a fin de cuentas; **for a. I know** por lo que yo sé; **it's a. the same to me** me da lo mismo; **thirty men in a.** treinta hombres en total; **a. in a.** en resumen, en suma; **it cost $260, a. in** costó 260 dólares con todo incluido; *Ironic* **it cost a. of $2** costó la increíble suma de 2 dólares

3 *adv* (**a**) *(entirely)* totalmente, completamente; **he was left a. alone** lo dejaron (completamente) solo(a); **he did it a. on his own** lo hizo él solo; **to be (dressed) a. in black** ir (vestido(a)) todo de negro; **to be a. for sth** ser partidario(a) de algo; **to be a. ears** ser todo oídos; **he's not a. bad** no es del todo malo; **a. around the room** por toda la habitación; **a. over (the place)** por todas partes; **a. too soon** demasiado pronto; **a. at once** *(suddenly)* de repente; *(at the same time)* a la vez; **a. along** desde el principio; **a. but** *(almost)* casi; **it's a. yours** es todo tuyo; *Fam* **to be a. in** *(exhausted)* estar hecho(a) polvo *or* una piltrafa, *Méx* estar camotes

(**b**) *(with comparatives)* **a. the better/worse** tanto mejor/peor; **the noise made it a. the harder to hear them** con el ruido era aún más difícil oírlos

(**c**) *(in games)* **two a.** *(in soccer)* empate *m* a dos; **four (games) a.** *(in tennis)* empate a cuatro juegos; **fifteen a.** *(in tennis)* quince iguales

4 *n* **to give one's a.** darlo todo

Allah ['ælə] *n* Alá *m*

all-American [ɔ:lə'merɪkən] *adj* típico(a) americano(a), típico(a) estadounidense

all-around ['ɔ:lərəʊnd], **all-round** ['ɔ:l'raʊnd] *adj* *(education, improvement)* general; **an a. athlete** un/una atleta completo(a)

allay [ə'leɪ] *vt* *(doubts, suspicions)* despejar; *(fear, pain)* apaciguar, aplacar

all-clear ['ɔ:l'klɪə(r)] *n* *(after air raid)* señal *f* de que pasó el peligro; *(for project)* luz *f* verde

all-day ['ɔ:l'deɪ] *adj* de todo el día

allegation [ælɪ'geɪʃən] *n* acusación *f*

allege [ə'ledʒ] *vt* alegar; **it is alleged that…** se dice que…

alleged [ə'ledʒd] *adj* presunto(a)

allegedly [ə'ledʒɪdlɪ] *adv* presuntamente

allegiance [ə'li:dʒəns] *n* lealtad *f*

allegory ['ælɪgərɪ] *n* alegoría *f*

all-embracing [ɔ:lɪm'breɪsɪŋ] *adj* general, global

allergen ['ælədʒən] *n* alergeno *m*

allergic [ə'lɜ:dʒɪk] *adj* alérgico(a) (**to** a)

allergy ['ælədʒɪ] *n* alergia *f*; **to have an a. to sth** tener alergia a algo

alleviate [ə'li:vɪeɪt] *vt* *(pain, symptoms)* aliviar

alley ['ælɪ] *n* callejón *m*, callejuela *f*; *Fig* **that's right up my a.** eso es lo mío, *Esp* eso es lo que me va; **a. cat** gato *m* callejero

alleyway ['ælɪweɪ] *n* callejón *m*, callejuela *f*

alliance [ə'laɪəns] *n* alianza *f*; **to enter into an a. (with)** formar una alianza (con), aliarse (con)

allied ['ælaɪd] *adj* *(countries)* aliado(a); *(issues, phenomena)* afín, asociado(a)

alligator ['ælɪgeɪtə(r)] *n* caimán *m*; **a. shoes/handbag** zapatos *mpl*/bolso *m* de cocodrilo

all-important ['ɔ:lɪm'pɔ:tənt] *adj* fundamental, esencial

all-inclusive ['ɔ:lɪn'klu:sɪv] *adj* *(price, vacation)* con todo incluido

all-in-one ['ɔ:lɪn'wʌn] *adj* *(garment)* de una pieza

alliteration [əlɪtə'reɪʃən] *n* aliteración *f*

all-night ['ɔ:lnaɪt] *adj* *(party, session)* de toda la noche

all-nighter ['ɔ:l'naɪtə(r)] *n* **the party was an a.** la fiesta duró toda la noche

allocate ['æləkeɪt] *vt* asignar (**to** a)

allocation [ælə'keɪʃən] *n* asignación *f*

allot [ə'lɒt] *(pt & pp* **allotted***)* *vt* asignar; **in the allotted time** en el tiempo asignado

allotment [ə'lɒtmənt] *n* *(of time, money)* asignación *f*

all-out ['ɔ:'laʊt] **1** *adj* *(effort)* supremo(a); *(opposition, resistance)* total; *(war)* sin cuartel; *(attack)* frontal; **an a. strike** una huelga general

2 *adv* **to go a. to do sth** poner toda la carne en el asador para hacer algo

allow [ə'laʊ] *vt* (**a**) *(permit)* permitir; **to a. sb to do sth** permitir a alguien hacer *or* que haga algo, dejar a alguien hacer algo; **smoking is not allowed** se prohíbe *or* no se permite fumar; **they'll never a. you to do it** nunca te dejarán hacerlo; **a. me!** *(offering help)* ¡permítame!; **I am allowed to do it** tengo permiso para hacerlo; **to a. oneself to be deceived/persuaded** dejarse engañar/convencer (**b**) *(allocate, grant)* dar, conceder; **a. an hour to get to the airport** deja una hora para llegar al aeropuerto

▶**allow for** *vt insep* tener en cuenta; **add another hour to a. for delays** añade una hora más por si hay retraso

allowable [ə'laʊəbəl] *adj* *(error, delay)* permisible

allowance [ə'laʊəns] *n* (**a**) *(government grant)* subsidio *m*; *(from parents)* asignación *f*; *(pocket money)* paga *f*; **travel a.** gastos *mpl* de viaje, dietas *fpl* (**b**) **to make a. for sth** *(take into account)* tener algo en cuenta; **I'm tired of making allowances for his inexperience** estoy harto de hacer concesiones *or* de disculparle por su falta de experiencia

alloy ['ælɔɪ] *n* aleación *f*

all-powerful ['ɔ:l'paʊəfʊl] *adj* todopoderoso(a)

all-purpose ['ɔ:l'pɜ:pəs] *adj* multiuso; **a. cleaner/adhesive** limpiador *m*/adhesivo *m* multiuso

all right, alright [ɔ:l'raɪt] **1** *adj* *(well)* **to be a.** estar bien; **are you a.?** ¿estás bien?; **he was in a car crash but he's a.** tuvo un accidente, pero no le pasó nada; **it's a.** *(acceptable)* no está mal; *(not a problem)* está bien; **to be a. for money** tener dinero suficiente; **she's a. at dancing/at French** no se le da mal el baile/el francés

2 adv (yes) vale; **is it a. if I smoke?** ¿puedo fumar?; **a., let's get started** venga, vamos a empezar

all-round = **all-around**

all-singing, all-dancing [ɔːlˈsɪŋɪŋɔːlˈdɑːnsɪŋ] adj Hum **(a)** (versatile) multiusos inv, todoterreno **(b)** (extravagant) **the conference was an a. affair** el congreso resultó una celebración por todo lo alto

allspice [ˈɔːlspaɪs] n pimienta f inglesa

all-star [ˈɔːlstɑː(r)] adj **an a. cast** un reparto de primeras figuras, un reparto estelar

all-terrain [ˈɔːltərem] adj **a. vehicle** todoterreno m

all-time [ˈɔːlˈtaɪm] adj (record) sin precedentes; (favorite) de todos los tiempos; **a. high/low** máximo m/mínimo m histórico

allude [əˈluːd] vi aludir (**to** a)

allure [əˈlʊə(r)] n atractivo m, encanto m

allusion [əˈluːʒən] n alusión f; **to make an a. (to)** hacer (una) alusión (a)

allusive [əˈluːsɪv] adj alusivo(a)

all-weather [ˈɔːlˈweðə(r)] adj para cualquier tiempo

ally 1 n [ˈælaɪ] aliado(a) m,f
2 vt [əˈlaɪ] **to a. oneself with...** aliarse con...

alma mater [ˈælməˈmɑːtə(r)] n alma mater f

almanac [ˈælmənæk] n (calendar) almanaque m

almighty [ɔːlˈmaɪtɪ] **1** n **the A.** el Todopoderoso
2 adj Fam (fuss, row) de mil demonios, RP de la gran siete

almond [ˈɑːmənd] n almendra f; **a. tree** almendro m

almost [ˈɔːlməʊst] adv casi; **it's a. six o'clock** son casi las seis; **we're a. there** (in journey) casi hemos llegado; (in task) casi hemos acabado

alms [ɑːmz] npl limosna f

aloft [əˈlɒft] adv por el aire, en vilo; **to hold sth a.** levantar algo en el aire

alone [əˈləʊn] adj & adv solo(a); **to be a.** estar solo(a); **to leave sth/sb a.** dejar algo/a alguien en paz; **I did it a.** lo hice yo solo; **to go it a.** ir por libre; **we are not a. in thinking that...** no somos los únicos que pensamos que...; **you a. can help me** tú eres el/la único(a) que me puede ayudar; **my salary a. isn't enough** con mi sueldo sólo no es suficiente; **let a....** mucho menos...; **I can't afford a bicycle, let a. a car!** no puedo comprarme una bicicleta, mucho menos un coche or Am carro or RP auto

along [əˈlɒŋ] **1** prep a lo largo de; **to walk a. the shore/a street** caminar por la costa/una calle; **somewhere a. the way** en algún punto (del camino)
2 adv **to move a.** avanzar; **he'll be a. in ten minutes** vendrá en diez minutos; **to bring sth/sb a.** traerse algo/a alguien (consigo); **he knew all a.** lo sabía todo el tiempo, lo sabía desde el principio; **a. with** (as well as) además de, junto con

alongside [əˈlɒŋˈsaɪd] prep (next to) junto a; (together with) junto con; Naut **to come a. the quay** arrimarse de costado al muelle

aloof [əˈluːf] **1** adj (person, manner) distante
2 adv al margen; **to remain a. (from)** mantenerse al margen (de)

aloofness [əˈluːfnɪs] n actitud f distante

aloud [əˈlaʊd] adv en alto, en voz alta; **I was thinking a.** estaba pensando en voz alta

alpha [ˈælfə] n alfa f; Phys **a. rays** radiación f or rayos mpl alfa

alphabet [ˈælfəbet] n alfabeto m

alphabetical [ælfəˈbetɪkl] adj alfabético(a); **in a. order** en orden alfabético

alphabetically [ælfəˈbetɪklɪ] adv alfabéticamente

alpine [ˈælpaɪn] adj alpino(a)

Alps [ælps] npl **the A.** los Alpes

al-Qaeda [ælˈkaɪdə] n Al-Qaeda n

already [ɔːlˈredɪ] adv ya; **I a. saw it, I've a. seen it** ya lo he visto, Am ya lo vi

alright = **all right**

Alsatian [ælˈseɪʃən] **1** n (dog) pastor m alemán; (person from Alsace) alsaciano(a) m,f
2 adj (from Alsace) alsaciano(a)

also [ˈɔːlsəʊ] adv también, además; **not only... but a....** no sólo..., sino también...

also-ran [ˈɔːlsəʊræn] n (in horse race) = caballo no clasificado entre los tres primeros; Fig (person) **he is just an a.** sólo es uno más or uno del montón

alt [ɔːlt] n Comptr **a. key** tecla f alt

altar [ˈɔːltə(r)] n altar m; **a. boy** monaguillo m

alter [ˈɔːltə(r)] **1** vt (person, design, plan) cambiar, alterar; (garment) arreglar; **he altered his opinion** cambió de opinión; **that doesn't a. the fact that...** eso no cambia el hecho de que...
2 vi cambiar, alterarse

alteration [ɔːltəˈreɪʃən] n (to design, plan) cambio m, alteración f; (to timetable) alteración f; (to garment) arreglo m

altercation [ɔːltəˈkeɪʃən] n altercado m

alter ego [ˈæltəˈriːɡəʊ] (pl **alter egos**) n álter ego m

alternate 1 adj [ɔːlˈtɜːnət] alterno(a); **on a. days** en días alternos, cada dos días
2 vt [ˈɔːltəneɪt] alternar
3 vi alternar (**with** con)

alternately [ɔːlˈtɜːnətlɪ] adv alternativamente

alternating [ˈɔːltəneɪtɪŋ] adj alterno(a); Elec **a. current** corriente f alterna

alternative [ɔːlˈtɜːnətɪv] **1** n (choice) alternativa f; **there is no a.** no hay alternativa; **she had no a. but to obey** no tenía más remedio que obedecer
2 adj (plan, route, music, comedy) alternativo(a); **an a. proposal** una alternativa; **a. energy** energía f alternativa; **a. medicine** medicina f alternativa

alternatively [ɔːlˈtɜːnətɪvlɪ] adv (on the other hand) si no; **a., we could go to the beach** si no, podríamos ir a la playa

alternator [ˈɔːltəneɪtə(r)] n Elec alternador m

although [ɔːlˈðəʊ] conj aunque

altitude [ˈæltɪtjuːd] n altitud f; **a. sickness** mal m de altura, Andes soroche m

alto [ˈæltəʊ] Mus **1** n (pl **altos**) contralto m,f
2 adj contralto; **a. saxophone** saxo m alto

altogether [ɔːltəˈɡeðə(r)] **1** adv **(a)** (entirely) completamente, enteramente; **I was not a. pleased** no estaba del todo contento **(b)** (in total) en total **(c)** (on the whole) en general
2 n Fam **in the a.** (naked) como Dios lo/la trajo al mundo, en cueros, Chile pilucho(a), Col en bola

altruism [ˈæltrɔɪzəm] n altruismo m

altruist [ˈæltrɔɪst] n altruista mf

altruistic [æltrɔˈɪstɪk] adj altruista

aluminum [əˈluːmɪnəm] n aluminio m; **a. foil** papel m de aluminio

alumna [əˈlʌmnə] (pl **alumnae** [əˈlʌmniː]) n antigua alumna f

alumnus [əˈlʌmnəs] (pl **alumni** [əˈlʌmnaɪ]) n antiguo alumno m

always [ˈɔːlweɪz] adv siempre; **I can a. try** siempre puedo intentarlo

always-on [ˈɔːlweɪzˈɒn] adj Comptr permanente

AM [ˈeɪˈem] n Rad (abbr **amplitude modulation**) AM f

am [æm] 1st person singular of **be**

a.m. [ˈeɪˈem] adv (abbr **ante meridiem**) a.m., de la mañana; **five a.m.** las cinco de la mañana

amalgam [əˈmælɡəm] n amalgama f

amalgamate [əˈmælgəmeɪt] **1** vt (metals, ideas) amalgamar; (companies) fusionar
2 vi (companies) unirse, fusionarse

amass [əˈmæs] vt (wealth) amasar; (objects, information, evidence) acumular, reunir

amateur [ˈæmətə(r)] **1** n (nonprofessional) aficionado(a) m,f
2 adj (painter, musician) aficionado(a); (work, performance) de aficionado; **it was a rather a. job** fue un trabajo chapucero or de aficionados

amateurish [æməˈtɜːrɪʃ] adj Pej chapucero(a)

amateurism [ˈæmətərɪzəm] n (**a**) Sport amateurismo m (**b**) Pej (of work, performance) chapucería f

amaze [əˈmeɪz] vt asombrar, pasmar; **to be amazed at** or **by sth** quedarse atónito(a) or pasmado(a) ante algo

amazement [əˈmeɪzmənt] n asombro m, estupefacción f; **she watched in a.** miró asombrada

amazing [əˈmeɪzɪŋ] adj (**a**) (surprising) asombroso(a), extraordinario(a); **it's a. that no one was hurt** es increíble que nadie resultara herido (**b**) (excellent) genial, extraordinario(a)

Amazon [ˈæməzən] n (**a**) **the A.** (river) el Amazonas; (region) la Amazonia (**b**) (female warrior) amazona f

ambassador [æmˈbæsədə(r)] n embajador(ora) m,f

amber [ˈæmbə(r)] **1** n ámbar m
2 adj ambarino(a)

ambiance = ambience

ambidextrous [æmbɪˈdekstrəs] adj ambidextro(a), ambidiestro(a)

ambience, ambiance [ˈæmbɪəns] n ambiente m

ambient [ˈæmbɪənt] adj (temperature) ambiente, ambiental; (noise, lighting) ambiental

ambiguity [æmbɪˈgjuːɪtɪ] n ambigüedad f

ambiguous [æmˈbɪgjʊəs] adj ambiguo(a)

ambition [æmˈbɪʃən] n ambición f

ambitious [æmˈbɪʃəs] adj ambicioso(a)

ambivalent [æmˈbɪvələnt] adj ambivalente

amble [ˈæmbəl] vi (person) deambular

ambulance [ˈæmbjʊləns] n ambulancia f; **a. man/woman** hombre m/mujer f de la ambulancia

ambush [ˈæmbʊʃ] **1** n also Fig emboscada f
2 vt also Fig tender una emboscada a

ameba, amebic = amoeba, amoebic

amen [ˈɑːmen] exclam Rel amén

amenable [əˈmiːnəbəl] adj receptivo(a); **to be a. to reason** atender a razones; **to prove a. to a suggestion** acoger bien una sugerencia

amend [əˈmend] vt (text, law) enmendar, modificar; (plans, schedule) modificar; (error) corregir

amendment [əˈmendmənt] n (to text, law) enmienda f (**to** a), modificación f (**to** de); (to plans, schedule) modificación f; (of error) corrección f

amends [əˈmendz] npl **to make a. (for sth)** compensar (algo); **to make a. to sb for sth** resarcir a alguien por or de algo

amenity [əˈmiːnɪtɪ] n (facility, service) servicio m; **amenities** comodidades fpl, servicios mpl

America [əˈmerɪkə] n (United States) Estados Unidos, América; (continent) América

American [əˈmerɪkən] **1** n (from USA) estadounidense mf, americano(a) m,f
2 adj (of USA) estadounidense, americano(a); (of continent) americano(a); **A. eagle** (bald eagle) pigargo m cabeciblanco, águila f cabeciblanca; (symbol of USA) águila f americana; **A. English** inglés m americano; **A. Indian** amerindio(a) m,f

Americanization [əmerɪkənaɪˈzeɪʃen] n americanización f

amethyst [ˈæmɪθɪst] n amatista f

amiable [ˈeɪmɪəbəl] adj afable, amable

amicable [ˈæmɪkəbəl] adj (relationship, agreement) amistoso(a), amigable

amid [əˈmɪd], **amidst** [əˈmɪdst] prep entre, en medio de

amino acid [əˈmiːnəʊˈæsɪd] n aminoácido m

amiss [əˈmɪs] **1** adj **there's something a.** algo va mal
2 adv **to take sth a.** tomarse algo a mal; **a cup of coffee wouldn't go a.** no vendría mal un café

ammeter [ˈæmiːtə(r)] n Elec amperímetro m

ammonia [əˈməʊnɪə] n amoniaco m

ammunition [æmjʊˈnɪʃən] n (for guns) munición f; Fig (in debate, argument) argumentos mpl

amnesia [æmˈniːzɪə] n Med amnesia f

amnesty [ˈæmnɪstɪ] n amnistía f

amniotic [æmnɪˈɒtɪk] adj amniótico(a); **a. fluid** líquido m amniótico

amoeba, ameba [əˈmiːbə] n ameba f

amoebic, amebic [əˈmiːbɪk] adj amebiano(a); **a. dysentery** disentería f amebiana

amok [əˈmɒk], **amuck** [əˈmʌk] adv **the demonstrators ran a. through the town** los manifestantes se descontrolaron y recorrieron la ciudad destrozando todo a su paso; **a gunman ran a.** un hombre perturbado disparó indiscriminadamente contra la multitud

among [əˈmʌŋ], **amongst** [əˈmʌŋst] prep entre; **we are a. friends** estamos entre amigos; **a. the best** entre los mejores; **a. other things** entre otras cosas; **they quarrel a. themselves** se pelean entre ellos; **the money was divided a. them** se repartió el dinero entre ellos

amoral [eɪˈmɒrəl] adj amoral

amorphous [əˈmɔːfəs] adj amorfo(a)

amortization [əmɔːtaɪˈzeɪʃən] n Fin (of debt, asset) amortización f

amount [əˈmaʊnt] n cantidad f; **a certain a. of discomfort** una cierta incomodidad; **no a. of money could persuade her to do it** no lo haría ni por todo el oro del mundo

▶**amount to** vt insep (**a**) (add up to) ascender a; **her debts a. to $700** sus deudas ascienden a 700 dólares (**b**) (mean) **it amounts to the same thing** viene a ser lo mismo, equivale a lo mismo; **he'll never a. to much** nunca llegará a nada

amp [æmp] n (**a**) Elec (unit) amperio m; **a 13-a. fuse** un fusible de 13 amperios (**b**) (amplifier) amplificador m

ampere [ˈæmpeə(r)] n Elec amperio m

ampersand [ˈæmpəsænd] n Typ signo m et, ampersand m

amphetamine [æmˈfetəmɪn] n anfetamina f

amphibian [æmˈfɪbɪən] **1** n anfibio m
2 adj anfibio(a)

amphibious [æmˈfɪbɪəs] adj (animal, vehicle) anfibio(a)

amphitheater [ˈæmfɪθɪətə(r)] n anfiteatro m

ample [ˈæmpəl] adj (large) (garment) amplio(a); (bosom, proportions) abundante; (plentiful) sobrado(a), abundante; **this will be a.** esto será más que suficiente; **to have a. time/opportunity to do sth** tener tiempo/ocasiones de sobra para hacer algo

amplification [æmplɪfɪˈkeɪʃən] n (of sound) amplificación f; (of remark) ampliación f

amplifier [ˈæmplɪfaɪə(r)] n amplificador m

amplify [ˈæmplɪfaɪ] vt (essay, remarks) ampliar; (current, volume) amplificar

amplitude [ˈæmplɪtjuːd] n Phys (of wave, signal) amplitud f; Rad **a. modulation** modulación f de la amplitud

amputate [ˈæmpjʊteɪt] vt amputar

amputation [æmpjʊˈteɪʃən] n amputación f

amputee [æmpjʊˈtiː] n amputado(a) m,f

Amsterdam [æmstəˈdæm] n Amsterdam

Amtrak [ˈæmtræk] n = compañía ferroviaria estadounidense

amuck = amok

amulet ['æmjʊlet] n amuleto m

amuse [ə'mju:z] vt (a) (make laugh) divertir (b) (occupy) distraer; **to a. oneself by doing sth** divertirse haciendo algo; **to keep sb amused** entretener a or distraer a alguien

amusement [ə'mju:zmənt] n (a) (enjoyment) diversión f; **much to everyone's a.** para regocijo or diversión de todos (b) (pastime) distracción f, entretenimiento m; **a. park** parque m de atracciones

amusing [ə'mju:zɪŋ] adj divertido(a)

an see **a**

anabolic steroid [ænə'bɒlik'stɪərɔid] n (esteroide m) anabolizante m

anachronism [ə'nækrənizəm] n anacronismo m

anaconda [ænə'kɒndə] n anaconda f

anaemia, anaemic = anemia, anemic

anagram ['ænəgræm] n anagrama m

anal ['einəl] adj Anat anal

analgesic [ænəl'dʒi:zik] 1 n analgésico m
   2 adj analgésico(a)

analog, analogue ['ænəlɒg] 1 n equivalente m
   2 adj analógico(a); **a. clock** reloj m analógico

analogous [ə'næləgəs] adj análogo(a) (**to** a)

analogy [ə'nælədʒi] n analogía f; **to draw an a. between two things** establecer una analogía entre dos cosas

analysis [ə'næləsis] (pl **analyzes** [ə'næləsi:z]) n análisis m inv; Psy psicoanálisis m inv; **in the final a.** a fin de cuentas

analyst ['ænəlist] n analista mf; Psy psicoanalista mf

analytic(al) [ænə'litik(əl)] adj analítico(a)

analyze ['ænəlaiz] vt analizar; Psy psicoanalizar

anarchic [ə'nɑ:kik] adj anárquico(a)

anarchist ['ænəkist] n anarquista mf

anarchistic [ænə'kistik] adj anarquista

anarchy ['ænəki] n anarquía f

anathema [ə'næθəmə] n (a) Rel anatema m (b) (repellent) **the very idea was a. to her** la sola idea le resultaba repugnante

anatomical [ænə'tɒmikəl] adj anatómico(a)

anatomically [ænə'tɒmikli] adv anatómicamente

anatomy [ə'nætəmi] n anatomía f

ANC [eien'si:] n (abbr **African National Congress**) ANC m, Congreso m Nacional Africano

ancestor ['ænsestə(r)] n ancestro m, antepasado(a) m,f

ancestral [æn'sestrəl] adj de los antepasados; **a. home** casa f solariega

ancestry ['ænsestri] n (descent) linaje m, abolengo m

anchor ['æŋkə(r)] 1 n (a) Naut ancla f; **at a.** fondeado(a), anclado(a); **to drop a.** echar el ancla, fondear; **to weigh a.** levar anclas (b) (in radio, TV program) presentador(ora) m,f, locutor(ora) m,f; Fig (of team) eje m
   2 vt (a) Naut anclar (b) (fix securely) sujetar, anclar (**to** a) (c) (radio, TV program) presentar
   3 vi Naut fondear, anclar

anchorman ['æŋkəmən] n (in radio, TV program) presentador m, locutor m

anchorperson ['æŋkəpɜ:sən] n (in radio, TV program) presentador(ora) m,f, locutor(ora) m,f

anchorwoman ['æŋkəwʊmən] n (in radio, TV program) presentadora f, locutora f

anchovy [æn'tʃəʊvi, 'æntʃəvi] n anchoa f

ancient ['einʃənt] 1 n **the ancients** los antiguos
   2 adj antiguo(a); Fam (car, clothes) vetusto(a); **you're forty? that's a.!** ¿cuarenta años? ¡estás hecho un carroza!; **a. history** historia f antigua; **A. Rome** la antigua Roma

ancillary [æn'siləri] adj (staff, workers) auxiliar

and [ænd, unstressed ənd, ən] conj (a) (in general) y; (before **i**, **hi**) e; **she can read a. write** sabe leer y escribir; **father a. son** padre e hijo; **my father a. brother** mi padre y mi hermano;

chicken a. (French) fries pollo con patatas fritas; **go a. look for it** ve a buscarlo; **come a. see me** ven a verme; **try a. help me** intenta ayudarme; **wait a. see** espera a ver; **nice a. warm** bien calentito(a); **do that again a. I'll hit you!** como lo vuelvas a hacer, te pego
   (b) (in numbers) **two hundred a. two** doscientos dos; **four a. a half** cuatro y medio; **an hour a. twenty minutes** una hora y veinte minutos; **four a. five make nine** cuatro y cinco, nueve
   (c) (expressing repetition) **hours a. hours** horas y horas; **better a. better** cada vez mejor; **she talked a. talked** no paraba de hablar
   (d) **a. so on a. so forth** etcétera, etcétera

Andalusia [ændə'lu:siə] n Andalucía

Andalusian [ændə'lu:siən] n & adj andaluz(uza) m,f

Andean ['ændiən] adj andino(a)

Andes ['ændi:z] npl **the A.** los Andes

Andorra [æn'dɔ:rə] n Andorra

Andorran [æn'dɔ:rən] n & adj andorrano(a) m,f

anecdotal [ænik'dəʊtəl] adj anecdótico(a)

anecdote ['ænikdəʊt] n anécdota f

anemia, anaemia [ə'ni:miə] n anemia f

anemic, anaemic [ə'ni:mik] adj Med anémico(a); Fig (weak) pobre

anemone [ə'neməni] n (flower) anémona f; **sea a.** anémona f de mar

anesthetic [ænəs'θetik] n anestesia f, anestésico m; **under a.** bajo (los efectos de la) anestesia; **local/general a.** anestesia local/general

anesthetist [ə'ni:sθətist] n anestesista mf

anesthetize [ə'ni:sθətaiz] vt Med anestesiar

anew [ə'nju:] adv de nuevo

angel ['eindʒəl] n ángel m; Fam **you're an a.!** ¡eres un ángel or un sol!; Culin **a. food cake** = bizcocho ligero elaborado con claras de huevo

Angeleno [ændʒə'li:nəʊ] (pl **Angelenos**) n = habitante o nativo de Los Angeles

angelfish ['eindʒəlfiʃ] n (a) (saltwater fish) chiribico m (b) (freshwater fish) escalar m (c) (shark) angelote m

angelic [æn'dʒelik] adj angelical

Angelus ['ændʒələs] n ángelus m

anger ['æŋgə(r)] 1 n ira f, esp Esp enfado m, esp Am enojo m; **a fit of a.** un ataque de ira; **to speak in a.** hablar con ira
   2 vt esp Esp enfadar, esp Am enojar
   3 vi **to be slow to a.** tardar en esp Esp enfadarse or esp Am enojarse; **to be quick to a.** esp Esp enfadarse or esp Am enojarse con facilidad

angina [æn'dʒainə] n Med angina f (de pecho)

angle ['æŋgəl] 1 n (a) Math ángulo m (b) (viewpoint) ángulo m, punto m de vista; **seen from this a.** visto(a) desde este ángulo (c) **a. bracket** (for shelving) escuadra f (en ángulo); Typ paréntesis m angular
   2 vi (a) (fish) pescar con caña (b) Fam **to a. for an invitation** andar a la caza or Chile, RP la pesca de una invitación

angler ['æŋglə(r)] n (person) pescador(ora) m,f (con caña); **a. fish** rape m

Anglican ['æŋglikən] n & adj Rel anglicano(a) m,f

Anglicanism ['æŋglikənizəm] n Rel anglicanismo m

anglicize ['æŋglisaiz] vt anglicanizar

angling ['æŋgliŋ] n pesca f con caña

Anglo-American ['æŋgləʊə'merikən] adj angloamericano(a)

Anglo-Irish ['æŋgləʊ'airiʃ] 1 adj angloirlandés(esa)
   2 npl **the A.** los angloirlandeses

anglophile ['æŋgləfail] n anglófilo(a) m,f

anglophobe ['æŋgləfəʊb] n anglófobo(a) m,f

Anglo-Saxon ['æŋgləʊ'sæksən] n & adj anglosajón(ona) m,f

Angola [æŋˈgəʊlə] n Angola

Angolan [ænˈgəʊlən] n & adj angoleño(a) m,f

angora [æŋˈgɔːrə] n (textile) angora f; **a. goat** cabra f de angora; **a. sweater** jersey m de angora; **a. rabbit** conejo m de angora; **a. wool** lana f de angora

angrily [ˈæŋgrɪlɪ] adv airadamente, con esp Esp enfado or esp Am enojo

angry [ˈæŋgrɪ] adj (person) esp Esp enfadado(a), esp Am enojado(a); (voice, letter) airado(a); **to be a.** estar esp Esp enfadado(a) or esp Am enojado(a); **to get a.** esp Esp enfadarse, esp Am enojarse; **to make sb a.** (hacer) esp Esp enfadar or esp Am enojar a alguien, hacer que alguien se esp Esp enfade or esp Am enoje

angst [æŋgst] n angustia f

anguish [ˈæŋgwɪʃ] n angustia f

anguished [ˈæŋgwɪʃt] adj (look, cry) angustiado(a)

angular [ˈæŋgjʊlə(r)] adj (face, shape) anguloso(a)

animal [ˈænɪməl] n (creature) animal m; **the a. kingdom** el reino animal; **a. rights** derechos mpl de los animales; **he's an a.** (uncivilized person) es un animal, es un bestia

animate 1 adj [ˈænɪmɪt] animado(a)

     2 vt [ˈænɪmeɪt] animar

animated [ˈænɪmeɪtɪd] adj (expression, discussion) animado(a); **to be a.** estar animado(a); **to become a.** animarse; **a. cartoon** dibujos mpl animados

animation [ænɪˈmeɪʃən] n animación f

animator [ˈænɪmeɪtə(r)] n Cin animador(ora) m,f

animism [ˈænɪmɪzəm] n Rel animismo m

animosity [ænɪˈmɒsɪtɪ] n animosidad f

aniseed [ˈænɪsiːd] n anís m

Ankara [ˈæŋkərə] n Ankara

ankle [ˈæŋkəl] n tobillo m; **a. boots** botines mpl; **a. socks** calcetines mpl cortos, CSur zoquetes mpl, Col medias fpl tobilleras

ankle-deep [ˈæŋkəlˈdiːp] adj hasta los tobillos; **she was a. in mud** estaba metida en barro hasta los tobillos

ankle-length [ˈæŋkəlleŋθ] adj **a. sock** calcetín m corto or tobillero

anklet [ˈæŋklət] n (ankle bracelet) pulsera f para el tobillo

annals [ˈænəlz] npl anales mpl

annex 1 vt [æˈneks] (territory) anexionar, anexar

     2 n [ˈæneks] (of building) edificio m anejo; (of document) anexo m

annexation [ænekˈseɪʃən] n anexión f

annihilate [əˈnaɪəleɪt] vt aniquilar

annihilation [ənaɪəˈleɪʃən] n aniquilación f

anniversary [ænɪˈvɜːsərɪ] n aniversario m; **wedding a.** aniversario de boda

anno Domini [ˈænəʊˈdɒmɪnaɪ] adv después de Cristo

annotate [ˈænəteɪt] vt anotar

annotation [ænəˈteɪʃən] n anotación f

announce [əˈnaʊns] vt anunciar; **"I think they're all wrong,"** she **announced** "creo que están todos equivocados", declaró or anunció

announcement [əˈnaʊnsmənt] n (of news) anuncio m; (formal statement) declaración f, anuncio m

announcer [əˈnaʊnsə(r)] n (on radio, TV program) presentador(ora) m,f

annoy [əˈnɔɪ] vt fastidiar, molestar, esp Am enojar; **to get annoyed** molestarse, esp Esp enfadarse, esp Am enojarse; **to be annoyed with sb** estar molesto(a) or esp Esp enfadado(a) or esp Am enojado(a) con alguien

annoyance [əˈnɔɪəns] n (feeling) esp Esp enfado m; esp Am enojo m; (annoying thing) molestia f, fastidio m

annoying [əˈnɔɪɪŋ] adj molesto(a), irritante; **he has an a. habit of interrupting me** tiene la mala or molesta

costumbre de interrumpirme; **how a.!** ¡qué fastidio!

annoyingly [əˈnɔɪɪŋlɪ] adv irritantemente

annual [ˈænjʊəl] **1** n (a) (plant) planta f anual (b) (book) anuario m; (for children) = libro grueso de historietas o de una serie televisiva que se publica cada año

     2 adj anual; **a. general meeting** asamblea for junta f general anual; Com **a. turnover** volumen m de negocio anual

annually [ˈænjʊəlɪ] adv anualmente

annuity [əˈnjuːɪtɪ] n anualidad f

annul [əˈnʌl] (pt & pp **annulled**) vt Law (contract, marriage) anular

annulment [əˈnʌlmənt] n anulación f

anode [ˈænəʊd] n Elec ánodo m

anodyne [ˈænəʊdaɪn] adj (bland) anodino(a), insulso(a)

anoint [əˈnɔɪnt] vt ungir (**with** con)

anomalous [əˈnɒmələs] adj anómalo(a)

anomaly [əˈnɒməlɪ] n anomalía f

anon[1] [əˈnɒn] adv Literary (soon) pronto

anon[2] n (abbr **anonymous**) anón., anónimo(a)

anonymity [ænəˈnɪmɪtɪ] n anonimato m

anonymous [əˈnɒnɪməs] adj (gift, donor) anónimo(a); **to remain a.** permanecer en el anonimato; **a. letter** carta f anónima, anónimo m

anorak [ˈænəræk] n anorak m

anorexia [ænəˈreksɪə] n Med anorexia f; **a. nervosa** anorexia nerviosa

anorexic [ænəˈreksɪk] adj Med anoréxico(a)

another [əˈnʌðə(r)] **1** adj otro(a); **a. cup of tea** otra taza de té; **it lasted for a. fifty years** duró otros cincuenta años or cincuenta años más; **don't say a. word** ni una palabra más; **that's quite a. matter** eso es algo (totalmente) distinto; **a. time, perhaps** (declining invitation) quizá en otra ocasión; **let's do it a. way** vamos a hacerlo de otra manera

     2 pron (a) (in general) otro(a) m,f; **give me a.** dame otro; **one or a. of us will be there** alguno de nosotros estará allí; **what with one thing and a., I forgot** entre unas cosas y otras, se me olvidó (b) (reciprocal) **they saw one a.** se vieron; **we always help one a.** siempre nos ayudamos el uno al otro

ANSI [ˈænsɪ] n (abbr **American National Standards Institute**) = instituto que crea estándares de calidad en el ámbito tecnológico

answer [ˈɑːnsə(r)] **1** n (to question, letter) respuesta f, contestación f; (to problem) solución f; **I knocked but there was no a.** llamé a la puerta, pero no hubo respuesta; **there's no a.** (on telephone) no contestan; **he has an a. to everything** tiene respuesta para todo; Formal **in a. to your letter** en respuesta a su carta

     2 vt (person, question, letter) responder, contestar; **to a. the telephone** contestar or Esp coger el teléfono; **to a. the door** abrir la puerta; **to a. a description/need** responder a una descripción/una necesidad

     3 vi (person) responder, contestar

▸**answer back** vi (be impertinent) replicar, contestar; **don't a. back!** ¡no me repliques!

▸**answer for** vt insep responder de, ser responsable de; **he has a lot to a. for** tiene mucho que explicar

▸**answer to** vt insep (a) (be accountable to) **to a. to sb (for sth)** ser responsable ante alguien (de algo), responder ante alguien (de algo) (b) (correspond to) (description) responder a (c) **the dog answers to the name of Rover** el perro responde al nombre de Rover

answerable [ˈɑːnsərəbl] adj **to be a. to sb** ser responsable ante alguien, responder ante alguien

answering machine [ˈɑːnsərɪŋməʃiːn] n contestador m (automático)

ant [ænt] n hormiga f

antagonism [ænˈtægənɪzəm] n antagonismo m

antagonist [æn'tægənɪst] *n* antagonista *mf*

antagonize [æn'tægənaɪz] *vt* enfurecer, enfadar

Antarctica [æn'tɑːktɪkə] *n* la Antártida

ante ['æntɪ] *n* **to up the a.** *Fam (in gambling, conflict)* elevar la apuesta

anteater ['æntiːtə(r)] *n* oso *m* hormiguero

antecedents [æntɪ'siːdənts] *npl* antecedentes *mpl*

antelope ['æntɪləʊp] *(pl* **antelopes** *or* **antelope)** *n* antílope *m*

antenatal [æntɪ'neɪtəl] *adj* prenatal; **a. clinic** clínica *f* de obstetricia *or* de preparación para el parto

antenna [æn'tenə] *n* **(a)** *(pl* **antennae** [æn'teniː]) *(of insect, snail)* antena *f* **(b)** *(pl* **antennas)** *(of radio, TV)* antena *f*

anteroom ['æntɪruːm] *n* antesala *f*

anthem ['ænθəm] *n* himno *m*; **national a.** himno nacional

anthill ['ænthɪl] *n* hormiguero *m*

anthology [æn'θɒlədʒɪ] *n* antología *f*

anthracite ['ænθrəsaɪt] *n* antracita *f*

anthrax ['ænθræks] *n Med* carbunco *m*, ántrax *m inv*

anthropological ['ænθrəpə'lɒdʒɪkəl] *adj* antropológico(a)

anthropologist [ænθrə'pɒlədʒɪst] *n* antropólogo(a) *m,f*

anthropology [ænθrə'pɒlədʒɪ] *n* antropología *f*

anti- ['æntɪ] *prefix* anti-; **a.-American** antiamericano(a)

antiabortion ['æntɪə'bɔːʃən] *adj* antiabortista

antiaircraft ['æntɪ'eəkrɑːft] *adj (gun, defenses)* antiaéreo(a)

antibacterial [æntɪbæk'tiːrɪəl] *adj* antibacteriano(a)

antibiotic [æntɪbaɪ'ɒtɪk] *n* antibiótico *m*

antibody ['æntɪbɒdɪ] *n Med* anticuerpo *m*

Antichrist ['æntɪkraɪst] *n* Anticristo *m*

anticipate [æn'tɪsɪpeɪt] *vt* **(a)** *(expect)* esperar; *(foresee)* prever; **as anticipated, there was trouble** como se preveía, hubo problemas **(b)** *(foreshadow)* anticipar, anunciar **(c)** *(do or say before)* adelantarse a

anticipation [æntɪsɪ'peɪʃən] *n* **(a)** *(foresight)* previsión *f*; **in a. of trouble** en previsión de posibles problemas; *Formal* **thanking you in a.** *(in letter)* le doy las gracias de antemano; **to show great a.** *(tennis player, soccer player)* tener mucha visión de juego **(b)** *(eagerness)* ilusión *f*, expectación *f*

anticlimax [æntɪ'klaɪmæks] *n* gran decepción *f*

antics ['æntɪks] *npl* payasadas *fpl*; **he's been up to his usual a.** ha estado haciendo las payasadas de costumbre

anticyclone [æntɪ'saɪkləʊn] *n Met* anticiclón *m*

antidepressant [æntɪdɪ'presənt] **1** *n* antidepresivo *m*
2 *adj* antidepresivo(a)

antidote ['æntɪdəʊt] *n also Fig* antídoto *m* **(to** contra)

antidumping ['æntɪ'dʌmpɪŋ] *adj (laws, legislation)* anti-dumping

antiestablishment ['æntɪɪs'tæblɪʃmənt] *adj* en contra del orden establecido

antifreeze ['æntɪfriːz] *n* anticongelante *m*

antiglare ['æntɪ'gleə(r)] *adj* **(a)** *(mirror, finish)* antirreflector(ora), antirreflejante **(b)** *Comptr* **a. filter** filtro *m* de pantalla

antiglobalization ['æntɪgləʊbəlaɪ'zeɪʃən] *n* antiglobalización *f*

Antigua and Barbuda [æn'tiːgənbɑː'bjuːdə] *n* Antigua y Barbuda

antihistamine [æntɪ'hɪstəmiːn] **1** *n* antihistamina *f*
2 *adj* antihistamínico(a); **a. drug** antihistamínico *m*

anti-inflammatory [æntɪɪn'flæmətərɪ] **1** *n* antiinflamatorio *m*
2 *adj* antiinflamatorio(a); **a. drug** antiinflamatorio *m*

antipathy [æn'tɪpəθɪ] *n* antipatía *f*

antiperspirant [æntɪ'pɜːspɪrənt] *n* antitranspirante *m*

antipodean [æntɪpə'diːən] **1** *n Hum (Australian)* australiano(a) *m,f*
2 *adj* **(a)** *Geog* antípoda, de las antípodas **(b)** *Hum* australiano(a)

antiquarian [æntɪ'kweərɪən] **1** *n (dealer)* anticuario(a) *m,f*; *(collector)* coleccionista *mf* de antigüedades
2 *adj (book)* antiguo(a); **a. bookshop** librería *f* de viejo

antiquated ['æntɪkweɪtɪd] *adj* anticuado(a)

antique [æn'tiːk] **1** *n* antigüedad *f*; **a. dealer** anticuario(a) *m,f*; **a. shop** tienda *f* de antigüedades
2 *adj* antiguo(a); **a. furniture** muebles *mpl* antiguos

antiquity [æn'tɪkwɪtɪ] *n* antigüedad *f*

antiracist [æntɪ'reɪsɪst] *adj* antirracista

anti-Semitic [æntɪsɪ'mɪtɪk] *adj (person)* antisemita; *(beliefs, remarks)* antisemítico(a)

antiseptic [æntɪ'septɪk] **1** *n Med* antiséptico *m*
2 *adj* **(a)** *(antibacterial)* antiséptico(a) **(b)** *Fig (lacking character or warmth)* aséptico(a)

antisocial [æntɪ'səʊʃəl] *adj* **(a)** *(disruptive)* incívico(a), antisocial **(b)** *(unsociable)* insociable

antiterrorist ['æntɪ'terərɪst] *adj* antiterrorista

antithesis [æn'tɪθɪsɪs] *(pl* **antitheses** [æn'tɪθɪsiːz]) *n* antítesis *f inv*

antivirus ['æntɪvaɪrəs] *adj* antivirus; *Comptr* **a. program** programa *m* antivirus

antler ['æntlə(r)] *n* cuerno *m*; **antlers** cornamenta *f*

antonym ['æntənɪm] *n* antónimo *m*

Antwerp ['æntwɜːp] *n* Amberes

anus ['eɪnəs] *n* ano *m*

anvil ['ænvɪl] *n* yunque *m*

anxiety [æŋ'zaɪətɪ] *n* **(a)** *(worry, concern)* preocupación *f*; *(anguish, impatience)* ansiedad *f*; **her behavior has been the cause of great a.** su comportamiento ha causado gran preocupación **(b)** *(eagerness)* ansia *f*, afán *m*; **in her a. not to offend...** en su afán por no ofender...

anxious ['æŋkʃəs] *adj* **(a)** *(worried)* preocupado(a); *(anguished, impatient)* ansioso(a); **to be a. (for)** estar preocupado(a) (por); **I am a. about his health** me preocupa su salud; **he was a. that all his work might come to nothing** temía que todo su trabajo quedara en nada **(b)** *(worrying)* **an a. moment** un momento de preocupación; **it was an a. time for us** en esos momentos estábamos muy preocupados **(c)** *(eager)* **to be a. to do sth** estar ansioso(a) por hacer algo

anxiously ['æŋkʃəslɪ] *adv* **(a)** *(worriedly)* con preocupación **(b)** *(with anguish, impatience)* ansiosamente

anxiousness ['æŋkʃəsnɪs] *n (worry, concern)* preocupación *f*; *(anguish, impatience)* ansiedad *f*; **in her a. not to offend...** en su afán por no ofender...

any ['enɪ] **1** *pron* **(a)** *(some)* **have you got a.?** *(with plural nouns)* ¿tienes alguno(a)?; *(with uncountable nouns)* ¿tienes algo?; **I fancy some cookies, have you got a.?** me apetecen unas galletas, ¿tienes?; **are there a. left?** ¿queda alguno(a)?; **is there a. left?** ¿queda algo?; **is there a. more?** ¿hay más?; **can a. of them speak English?** ¿alguno (de ellos) habla inglés?
(b) *(in negatives)* ninguno(a) *m,f*; **I haven't got a.** no tengo; **there was nothing in a. of the boxes** no había nada en ninguna de las cajas; **few, if a., can read** pocos, o ninguno, saben leer
(c) *(no particular one)* cualquiera; *(before noun)* cualquier; **a. of us** cualquiera de nosotros; **take a. of the bottles** toma *or Esp* coge cualquier botella *or* una botella cualquiera
(d) *(every one)* **keep a. you find** quédate con todos los que encuentres
2 *adj* **(a)** *(some)* **have you a. milk/sugar?** ¿tienes leche/azúcar?; **have you a. apples/cigarettes?** ¿tienes manzanas/cigarrillos?; **is there a. hope?** ¿hay alguna esperanza?
(b) *(in negatives)* ninguno(a); *(before masculine singular noun)* ningún; **he hasn't got a. money** no tiene dinero; **I didn't get a. of your letters** no recibí ninguna de tus cartas; **without a. help** sin ninguna ayuda

(c) *(no particular) (before noun)* cualquier; *(after noun)* cualquiera; **come a. day** ven cualquier día, ven un día cualquiera; **a. doctor will tell you the same** cualquier médico te diría lo mismo; **a. minute now** de un momento a otro; **I don't want just a. (old) wine** no quiero un vino cualquiera

(d) *(every)* **a. pupil who forgets his books will be punished** los alumnos que olviden sus libros serán castigados; **I'll take a. books you don't want** me quedaré con todos los libros que no quieras; **at a. rate, in a. case** en cualquier caso

3 *adv* **(a)** *(with comparative)* **I'm not a. better** no me encuentro mejor; **the weather couldn't be a. worse** el tiempo no podía ser peor; **have you a. more milk?** ¿tienes más leche?; **we don't see them a. longer** ya no los vemos; **I don't like her a. more than you do** a mí no me gusta más que a ti; **is that a. easier?** ¿es así más fácil? **(b)** *Fam* **that didn't help us a.** eso no nos ayudó para nada

anybody ['enɪbɒdɪ], **anyone** ['enɪwʌn] *pron* **(a)** *(indeterminate)* alguien; **would a. like some more cake?** ¿quiere alguien más pastel?; **does a. mind if I close the window?** ¿les importa que cierre la ventana?; **she'll know if a. does** si alguien lo sabe es ella

(b) *(in negatives)* nadie; **there isn't a. here** aquí no hay nadie; **there was hardly a.** no había apenas nadie, apenas había nadie

(c) *(no matter who)* cualquiera; **a. will tell you so** cualquiera te lo dirá; **bring along a. you like** trae a quien quieras; **a. but her would have refused** cualquiera menos ella se habría negado; **I don't want just a.!** ¡no quiero a cualquiera!

(d) *(person with status)* **he'll never be a.** nunca será nadie

anyhow ['enɪhaʊ] *adv* **(a)** *(however)* de todas maneras *or* formas, de todos modos; **a., let's get back to what we were saying** bueno, volvamos a lo que estábamos diciendo **(b)** *Fam (carelessly)* a la buena de Dios, de cualquier manera; **I don't want it done just a.** no quiero que se haga de cualquier manera

anymore, any more [enɪ'mɔ:(r)] *adv* **(a)** *(any longer)* **they don't live here a.** ya no viven aquí; **I won't do it a.** no lo haré nunca más, no lo volveré a hacer **(b)** *(now)* ahora; **every time I start the bike a., I remember to check the gas** ahora cuando pongo en marcha la moto, siempre me acuerdo de comprobar la gasolina

anyone = **anybody**

anyplace = **anywhere**

anything ['enɪθɪŋ] **1** *pron* **(a)** *(indeterminate)* algo; **is there a. I can do (to help)?** ¿puedo ayudarte en algo?; **have you a. to write with?** ¿tienes con qué escribir?; **will there be a. else?** *(in shop)* ¿algo más?; **have you a. smaller?** ¿tendría algo más pequeño?; **if a. should happen to me** si me ocurriera algo; **do you notice a. strange about him?** ¿le notas algo raro?; **is (there) a. the matter?** ¿ocurre algo?

(b) *(in negatives)* nada; **he doesn't do a.** no hace nada; **hardly a.** apenas nada

(c) *(no matter what)* cualquier cosa; **he eats a.** come cualquier cosa; **a. you want** lo que quieras; **I love a. French** me gusta todo lo francés; **he would do a. for me** haría cualquier cosa por mí; **he was a. but friendly** fue de todo menos amable; **are you angry? — a. but** ¿estás *esp Esp* enfadado *or esp Am* enojado? — ni mucho menos

2 *adv* **is it a. like the last one?** ¿se parece en algo al anterior?; **it didn't cost a. like $500** no costó 500 dólares, ni muchísimo menos; **the food wasn't a. like as bad as they said** la comida no fue en absoluto tan mala como decían; *Fam* **as funny as a.** divertidísimo(a); *Fam* **to work like a.** trabajar como loco(a); *Fam* **it's not that you were wrong or a.** no es que estuvieras equivocado ni nada parecido

anytime ['enɪtaɪm] *adv (whenever)* **come a. you like** ven cuando quieras

anyway ['enɪweɪ] *adv (however)* de todas maneras *or* formas, de todos modos; **a., let's get back to what we were saying** bueno, volvamos a lo que estábamos diciendo

anywhere ['enɪweə(r)], **anyplace** ['enɪpleɪs] *adv* **(a)** *(in questions)* **can you see it a.?** ¿lo ves por alguna parte?; **have you found a. to live?** ¿has encontrado un lugar *or* algún sitio para vivir?; **did you go a. yesterday?** ¿fuiste a alguna parte ayer?

(b) *(in negatives)* **I can't find it a.** no lo encuentro por ningún sitio; **we never go a. interesting** nunca vamos a ningún sitio interesante; **he isn't a. near as clever as her** no es ni mucho menos tan listo como ella

(c) *(no matter where)* en cualquier lugar, en cualquier sitio; **put it a.** ponlo en cualquier sitio; **I'd know him a.** lo reconocería en cualquier parte; **it's miles from a.** está en un lugar muy aislado; **a. else** en cualquier otro lugar

aorta [eɪ'ɔ:tə] *n Anat* aorta *f*

apart [ə'pɑ:t] *adv* **(a)** *(at a distance)* alejado(a), separado(a); **to stand a.** estar separado(a)

(b) *(separated)* **the two towns are 10 miles a.** las dos ciudades están a 10 millas una de la otra; **boys and girls were kept a.** los chicos y las chicas estaban separados; **they're never a.** no se separan nunca; **with one's legs a.** con las piernas abiertas *or* separadas; **they were born two years a.** nacieron con dos años de diferencia; **they've lived a. since 1987** viven separados desde 1987; **it is difficult to tell them a.** es difícil distinguirlos

(c) *(to pieces)* **to take sth a.** desmontar algo; **to come a.** destrozarse

(d) **a. from** *(excepting)* aparte de; **quite a. from the fact that...** independientemente del hecho de que...; **joking a.** bromas aparte

apartheid [ə'pɑ:taɪt] *n* apartheid *m*

apartment [ə'pɑ:tmənt] *n* apartamento *m*, *Esp* piso *m*, *Arg* departamento *m*; **a. building** bloque *m* de pisos

apathetic [æpə'θetɪk] *adj* apático(a) **(about** respecto a)

apathy ['æpəθɪ] *n* apatía *f*

ape [eɪp] **1** *n (animal)* simio *m*; *Fam* **to go a. (over)** *(lose one's temper)* ponerse hecho(a) una furia (por); *(enthuse)* ponerse como loco(a) (por *or* con), *Esp* despendolarse (por *or* con)

2 *vt (imitate)* imitar, remedar

aperitif [əperɪ'ti:f] *n* aperitivo *m (bebida)*

aperture ['æpətjʊə(r)] *n (opening)* abertura *f*; *(of camera)* (apertura *f* del) diafragma *m*

APEX ['eɪpeks] *adj* **A. ticket** billete *m or Am* boleto *m or Am* pasaje *m* (con tarifa) APEX

apex ['eɪpeks] *n (of triangle)* vértice *m*; *(of career)* cima *f*, cumbre *f*

aphasia [ə'feɪzɪə] *n Med* afasia *f*

aphid ['eɪfɪd] *n* pulgón *m*

aphorism ['æfərɪzəm] *n* aforismo *m*

aphrodisiac [æfrəʊ'dɪzɪæk] **1** *n* afrodisíaco *m*

2 *adj* afrodisíaco(a)

apiece [ə'pi:s] *adv* cada uno(a); **they cost $3 a.** cuestan 3 dólares cada uno, están a 3 dólares

aplenty [ə'plentɪ] *adv* en abundancia; **there was wine a.** corría el vino a raudales

aplomb [ə'plɒm] *n* aplomo *m*

apocalypse [ə'pɒkəlɪps] *n* apocalipsis *m inv*

apocalyptic [əpɒkə'lɪptɪk] *adj* apocalíptico(a)

apolitical [eɪpə'lɪtɪkəl] *adj* apolítico(a)

apologetic [əpɒlə'dʒetɪk] *adj (tone, smile)* de disculpa; **she was quite a. about it** lo sentía mucho

apologist [ə'pɒlədʒɪst] *n Formal* apologista *mf*, defensor(ora) *m,f* **(for** de)

apologize [ə'pɒlədʒaɪz] *vi* disculparse (**to sb/for sth** ante alguien/por algo); **I had to a. for you** tuve que pedir disculpas por ti; **there's no need to a.** no hay por qué disculparse

apology [ə'pɒlədʒi] *n* disculpa *f*; **to make/offer an a.** disculparse; **I owe you an a.** te debo una disculpa; **please accept my apologies** le ruego (que) acepte mis disculpas; *Pej* **an a. for a dinner** una birria de cena

apoplectic [æpə'plektɪk] *adj* (**a**) *(angry)* **to be a. (with rage)** estar hecho(a) una furia (**b**) *Med* **to be a.** tener apoplejía

apoplexy ['æpəpleksi] *n Med* apoplejía *f*

apostle [ə'pɒsəl] *n* apóstol *m*

apostolic(al) [æpɒs'tɒlɪk(əl)] *adj* apostólico(a)

apostrophe [ə'pɒstrəfi] *n* apóstrofo *m*

appall, appal [ə'pɔːl] *(pt & pp* **appalled**) *vt* horrorizar, espantar; **he was appalled at** *or* **by...** le horrorizaba...

appalling [ə'pɔːlɪŋ] *adj* espantoso(a), horroroso(a)

apparatus [æpə'reɪtəs] *n (in laboratory, gym)* aparatos *mpl*; **a piece of a.** un aparato

apparel [ə'pærəl] *n* (**a**) *(clothes)* indumentaria *f*, ropa *f* (**b**) *Literary (garb)* atuendo *m*, atavío *m*

apparent [ə'pærənt] *adj* (**a**) *(obvious)* evidente; **to become a.** hacerse patente *or* evidente (**b**) *(seeming)* aparente

apparently [ə'pærəntli] *adv* al parecer; **a. easy/innocent** aparentemente fácil/inocente; **a. not** parece que no

apparition [æpə'rɪʃən] *n* aparición *f*

appeal [ə'piːl] **1** *n* (**a**) *(call)* llamamiento *m*; **to make an a. for sth** hacer un llamamiento para solicitar algo; **an a. for calm** un llamamiento a la calma; **charity a.** = campaña de recaudación de fondos para fines benéficos (**b**) *Law* apelación *f*; **to lodge an a.** presentar una apelación; **A. Court, Court of A.** tribunal *m* de apelación (**c**) *(attraction)* atractivo *m*; **to have** *or* **hold little a. for sb** no atraer mucho a alguien; **to have great a.** ser muy atractivo(a); **their music has a wide a.** su música gusta a gente muy diversa

   2 *vt Law* **to a. a decision** entablar recurso de apelación contra una decisión

   3 *vi* (**a**) *(make a plea)* **to a. (to sb) for help/money** solicitar ayuda/dinero (a alguien); **to a. to sb's generosity** apelar a la generosidad de alguien (**b**) *(attract)* **to a. to sb** atraer a alguien; **it doesn't a. to me** no me atrae (**c**) *Law* apelar, recurrir; **to a. against a decision** entablar recurso de apelación contra una decisión

appealing [ə'piːlɪŋ] *adj* atractivo(a), atrayente

appear [ə'pɪə(r)] *vi* (**a**) *(come into view)* aparecer; *(publication, movie)* salir, aparecer; **where did you a. from?** ¿de dónde has salido?; **to a. from nowhere** aparecer de repente; **to a. on TV** salir en televisión (**b**) *Law* **to a. before a court** comparecer ante un tribunal; **to a. for sb** *(counsel)* representar a alguien (**c**) *(look, seem)* parecer; **to a. to be lost** parecer perdido(a); **there appears to be a mistake** parece que hay un error; **so it would a.** eso parece

appearance [ə'pɪərəns] *n* (**a**) *(arrival)* aparición *f*; **to put in an a.** hacer acto de presencia (**b**) *(of actor)* aparición *f* (**c**) *(of publication)* publicación *f* (**d**) *Law (in court)* comparecencia *f* (**e**) *(looks, demeanor)* apariencia *f*, aspecto *m*; **you should not judge by appearances** no se debe juzgar por las apariencias; **it has all the appearances of a conspiracy** tiene todo el aspecto de ser una conspiración; **appearances can be deceptive** las apariencias engañan; **to keep up appearances** guardar las apariencias

appease [ə'piːz] *vt (anger)* aplacar, apaciguar; *(person)* calmar, apaciguar; *Pol* contemporizar con

appeasement [ə'piːzmənt] *n (of person, anger)* apaciguamiento *m*; *Pol* contemporización *f*

append [ə'pend] *vt (list, document)* adjuntar; *(one's signature)* añadir

appendage [ə'pendɪdʒ] *n* apéndice *m*; **she was tired of being treated as his a.** estaba harta de que se la tratara como si fuera un mero apéndice de él

appendicitis [əpendɪ'saɪtɪs] *n* apendicitis *f inv*

appendix [ə'pendɪks] *(pl* **appendixes** *or* **appendices** [ə'pendɪsiːz]) *n* (**a**) *Anat* apéndice *m*; **to have one's a. (taken) out** operarse de apendicitis (**b**) *(of book)* apéndice *m*

appetite ['æpɪtaɪt] *n* (**a**) *(for food)* apetito *m*; **to have a good a.** tener buen apetito; **to spoil sb's a.** quitarle el apetito a alguien; **to give sb an a.** abrirle el apetito a alguien (**b**) *(for knowledge, sex)* afán *m*, apetito *m* (**for** de)

appetizer ['æpɪtaɪzə(r)] *n also Fig* aperitivo *m*

appetizing ['æpɪtaɪzɪŋ] *adj* apetitoso(a)

applaud [ə'plɔːd] *vt & vi* aplaudir

applause [ə'plɔːz] *n (clapping)* aplauso *m*, ovación *f*; *(approval)* aplauso *m*, aprobación *f*

apple ['æpəl] *n* manzana *f*; **she was the a. of his eye** *(his favorite)* era la niña de sus ojos; **a. core** corazón *m* de manzana; **a. juice** *Esp* zumo *m* *or* *Am* jugo *m* de manzana; **a. pie** pastel *m* de manzana; **as American as a. pie** típicamente americano(a); **a. tart** tarta *f* de manzana; **a. tree** manzano *m*

applecart ['æpəlkɑːt] *n* **to upset the a.** *(spoil plan)* estropearlo todo

apple-pie ['æpəlpaɪ] *adj* **in a. order** en perfecto orden

applesauce ['æpəlsɔːs] *n* compota *f* de manzanas

appliance [ə'plaɪəns] *n* (**electrical** *or* **domestic**) **a.** electrodoméstico *m*

applicable [ə'plɪkəbəl] *adj* válido(a) (**to** para), aplicable (**to** a); **delete where not a.** *(on form)* táchese lo que no proceda

applicant ['æplɪkənt] *n (for job)* solicitante *mf*

application [æplɪ'keɪʃən] *n* (**a**) *(for job, patent)* solicitud *f*; **to make an a. for sth** solicitar algo; **a. form** *(for job)* impreso *m* de solicitud (**b**) *(of paint, theory)* aplicación *f* (**c**) *(effort)* aplicación *f*, entrega *f* (**d**) *Comptr* aplicación *f*

applied [ə'plaɪd] *adj (maths, physics)* aplicado(a)

apply [ə'plaɪ] **1** *vt* (**a**) *(put on)* aplicar; **to a. pressure to** ejercer presión sobre, presionar (**b**) *(use) (system, theory)* aplicar; **to a. one's mind to sth** concentrarse en algo; **to a. oneself to one's work** aplicarse en el trabajo

   2 *vi* (**a**) *(for job, grant)* **to a. (to sb) for sth** solicitar algo (a alguien) (**b**) *(law, rule)* **rule 26b applies in all other cases** la norma 26b se aplicará en todos los demás casos; **this clause no longer applies** esta cláusula ya no está en vigor; **that applies to you too!** ¡esto es válido *or* vale para ti también!

appoint [ə'pɔɪnt] *vt (person, committee)* nombrar, designar; **to a. sb to a post** designar a alguien para un cargo

appointed [ə'pɔɪntɪd] *adj Formal (agreed) (place, hour)* fijado(a)

appointment [ə'pɔɪntmənt] *n* (**a**) *(meeting)* cita *f*; **to make an a. with sb** concertar una cita con alguien; **she didn't keep the a.** faltó a la cita; **I've made/got an a. with the doctor** he pedido/tengo hora con el médico; **by a. only** con cita previa (**b**) *(to job, committee)* nombramiento *m*, designación *f*; **to make an a.** hacer un nombramiento

apportion [ə'pɔːʃən] *vt (food, praise)* distribuir, repartir; **to a. blame** repartir la culpa

appraisal [ə'preɪzəl] *n (of standards, personnel)* evaluación *f*, valoración *f*

appraise [ə'preɪz] *vt (performance, situation)* evaluar, valorar; **to a. the value of sth** tasar algo

appreciable [ə'priːʃəbəl] *adj (change, difference)* apreciable

appreciate [ə'priːʃɪeɪt] **1** *vt* (**a**) *(be grateful for)* agradecer; **I a. your helping me** te agradezco tu ayuda; **I would a. it if you didn't shout** te agradecería que no gritaras (**b**) *(grasp, understand)* darse cuenta de; **I fully a. (the fact) that...** me doy perfecta cuenta de que...; **we a. the risks** somos conscientes de los riesgos (**c**) *(value)* apreciar

2 *vi (goods, investment)* revalorizarse, aumentar de valor

appreciation [əpriːʃɪ'eɪʃən] *n* (**a**) *(gratitude)* gratitud *f*, agradecimiento *m*; **in a. of** en agradecimiento por (**b**) *(understanding)* apreciación *f*, percepción *f*; **she has no a. of what is involved** no se da cuenta de lo que implica (**c**) *(review, assessment) (of movie, author's work)* reseña *f*, crítica *f*; **a musical/wine a. society** una asociación de amigos de la música/del vino (**d**) *(valuing) (of music, art)* valorización *f* (**e**) *Fin* **a. of assets** revalorización *f* de activos

appreciative [ə'priːʃɪətɪv] *adj (person, response, audience)* agradecido(a); *(review)* elogioso(a); **to be a. of sb's help/efforts** sentirse muy agradecido(a) por la ayuda/los esfuerzos de alguien

apprehend [æprɪ'hend] *vt* (**a**) *(arrest)* detener, aprehender (**b**) *Formal (understand)* aprehender, comprender

apprehension [æprɪ'henʃən] *n* (**a**) *(fear)* aprensión *f* (**b**) *Law (arrest)* detención *f*, aprehensión *f*

apprehensive [æprɪ'hensɪv] *adj (look, smile)* temeroso(a), receloso(a); **to be a. about (doing) sth** tener miedo de (hacer) algo

apprentice [ə'prentɪs] **1** *n* aprendiz(iza) *m,f*
2 *vt* **he was apprenticed to a tailor** estaba de aprendiz con un sastre

apprenticeship [ə'prentɪʃɪp] *n also Fig* aprendizaje *m*; **to serve one's a.** hacer el aprendizaje

approach [ə'prəʊtʃ] **1** *n* (**a**) *(coming) (of person, season)* llegada *f*; *(of night)* caída *f*; **to make an a. to sb** *(proposal)* hacer una propuesta inicial a alguien (**b**) *(method)* enfoque *m*, planteamiento *m* (**c**) *(route of access)* acceso *m*; **the approaches to a town** los accesos a una ciudad; *Aut* **a. road** (vía *f* de) acceso *m* (**d**) **a. (shot)** *(in golf, tennis)* golpe *m* de aproximación
2 *vt* (**a**) *(get nearer to)* acercarse a, aproximarse a; **I'm approaching forty-five** tengo casi cuarenta y cinco años (**b**) *(go up to)* acercarse a, aproximarse a; **she approached several organizations** acudió *or* se dirigió a varias organizaciones; **to be easy/difficult to a.** ser/no ser accesible (**c**) *(tackle)* abordar, enfocar
3 *vi* acercarse, aproximarse

approachable [ə'prəʊtʃəbəl] *adj (person)* accesible

approaching [ə'prəʊtʃɪŋ] *adj (holiday, season)* próximo(a); **the a. car** el coche que viene de frente

appropriate¹ [ə'prəʊprɪət] *adj (suitable)* apropiado(a), adecuado(a); *(moment)* oportuno(a), adecuado(a)

appropriate² [ə'prəʊprɪeɪt] *vt* (**a**) *(take, steal)* apropiarse de (**b**) *(set aside) (money, funds)* destinar, asignar

appropriately [ə'prəʊprɪətlɪ] *adv (suitably)* apropiadamente, adecuadamente; *(properly)* con propiedad

appropriation [əprəʊprɪ'eɪʃən] *n (of funds)* apropiación *f*

approval [ə'pruːvəl] *n* aprobación *f*; **he gave/withheld his a.** dio/no dio su aprobación; *Com* **on a.** a prueba; **a. rating** *(of product, politician)* índice *m* de aceptación *or* popularidad

approve [ə'pruːv] *vt* aprobar

▶**approve of** *vt insep* aprobar; **she doesn't a. of them smoking** no aprueba que fumen; **I don't a. of your friends** no me gustan tus amigos

approving [ə'pruːvɪŋ] *adj* de aprobación

approx [ə'prɒks] *adv (abbr* **approximately)** aprox., aproximadamente

approximate 1 *adj* [ə'prɒksɪmɪt] aproximado(a)
2 *vi* [ə'prɒksɪmeɪt] **to a. to** aproximarse a

approximately [ə'prɒksɪmətlɪ] *adv* aproximadamente

approximation [əprɒksɪ'meɪʃən] *n* aproximación *f*

APR [eɪpiː'ɑː] *n Fin (abbr* **annual percentage rate)** TAE *m or f*

Apr *(abbr* **April)** abril *m*

apricot ['eɪprɪkɒt] *n (fruit) Esp* albaricoque *m*, *Andes, RP* damasco *m*, *Méx* chabacano *m*; **a. tree** *Esp* albaricoquero *m*, *Andes, RP* damasco *m*, *Méx* chabacano *m*

April ['eɪprɪl] *n* abril *m*; **A. showers** lluvias *fpl* de abril; **A. Fools' Day** ≃ día *m* de los (Santos) Inocentes *(uno de abril)*; *see also* **May**

apron ['eɪprən] *n* (**a**) *(clothing)* delantal *m*; *Fam* **he's still tied to his mother's a. strings** *(dependent on her)* sigue pegado a las faldas de su madre (**b**) *Av* área *f* de estacionamiento

apt¹ [æpt] *adj* (**a**) *(word, description)* apropiado(a), acertado(a) (**b**) *(likely)* **to be a. to do sth** ser propenso(a) a hacer algo

apt² *(abbr* **apartment)** apto.

aptitude ['æptɪtjuːd] *n* aptitud *f*; **to have an a. for** tener aptitudes para; **a. test** prueba *f* de aptitud

aptly ['æptlɪ] *adv* acertadamente

aquamarine [ækwəmə'riːn] **1** *n (gem)* aguamarina *f*
2 *adj (color)* azul verdoso(a)

aquarium [ə'kweərɪəm] *(pl* **aquariums** *or* **aquaria** [ə'kweərɪə]) *n* acuario *m*

Aquarius [ə'kweərɪəs] *n (sign of zodiac)* acuario *m*; **to be (an) A.** ser acuario

aquatic [ə'kwætɪk] *adj* acuático(a)

aqueduct ['ækwɪdʌkt] *n* acueducto *m*

aquiline ['ækwɪlaɪn] *adj* aguileño(a), aquilino(a)

Arab ['ærəb] *n & adj* árabe *mf*

Arabia [ə'reɪbɪə] *n* Arabia

Arabian [ə'reɪbɪən] *adj* árabe; **the A. Sea** el Mar de Arabia *or* de Omán

Arabic ['ærəbɪk] **1** *n (language)* árabe *m*
2 *adj* árabe; **A. numerals** números *mpl* arábigos

arable ['ærəbəl] *adj* cultivable, arable

arachnid [ə'ræknɪd] *n Zool* arácnido *m*

Aragon ['ærəgən] *n* Aragón

Aragonese [ærəgə'niːz] *n & adj* aragonés(esa) *m,f*

arbiter ['ɑːbɪtə(r)] *n (of taste, fashion)* árbitro *m*

arbitrary ['ɑːbɪtrərɪ] *adj* arbitrario(a)

arbitrate ['ɑːbɪtreɪt] **1** *vt* arbitrar
2 *vi* arbitrar (**between** entre)

arbitration [ɑːbɪ'treɪʃən] *n* arbitraje *m*; **the dispute went to a.** el conflicto se llevó ante un árbitro

arbitrator ['ɑːbɪtreɪtə(r)] *n (in dispute)* árbitro *m*

arc [ɑːk] *n* arco *m*; **a. lamp** lámpara *f* de arco (voltaico)

arcade [ɑː'keɪd] *n* (**a**) *(for shopping)* galería *f* comercial (**b**) *Archit* galería *f*

arch¹ [ɑːtʃ] **1** *n* (**a**) *Archit* arco *m* (**b**) *(of foot)* puente *m*; **to have fallen arches** tener los pies planos
2 *vt* **to a. one's back** arquear la espalda

arch² *adj* **a. enemy** mayor enemigo(a) *m,f*; **a. traitor** gran traidor(ora) *m,f*

arch³ *adj (mischievous)* pícaro(a)

archaeological, archeological [ɑːkɪə'lɒdʒɪkəl] *adj* arqueológico(a)

archaeologist, archeologist [ɑːkɪ'ɒlədʒɪst] *n* arqueólogo(a) *m,f*

archaeology, archeology [ɑːkɪ'ɒlədʒɪ] *adj* arqueología *f*

archaic [ɑː'keɪɪk] *adj* arcaico(a)

archangel ['ɑːkeɪndʒəl] *n* arcángel *m*

archbishop [ɑːtʃ'bɪʃəp] *n* arzobispo *m*

archduke [ɑːtʃ'djuːk] *n* archiduque *m*

archeological, archeologist *etc* = **archaeological, archaeologist** *etc*

archer ['ɑːtʃə(r)] *n* arquero(a) *m,f*

archery ['ɑːtʃərɪ] *n* tiro *m* con arco

archetypal [ɑːkɪ'taɪpəl] *adj* arquetípico(a), típico(a)

archetype ['ɑːkɪtaɪp] *n* arquetipo *m*, modelo *m*

archipelago [ɑːkɪ'peləgəʊ] *(pl* **archipelagos** *or* **archipelagoes)** *n* archipiélago *m*

architect ['ɑːkɪtekt] *n (of building)* arquitecto(a) *m,f*; *Fig (of scheme)* artífice *mf*

architecturally [ɑːkɪˈtektʃərəlɪ] *adv* arquitectónicamente

architecture ['ɑːkɪtektʃə(r)] *n* arquitectura *f*

archive ['ɑːkaɪv] *n (gen) & Comptr* archivo *m*

archives ['ɑːkaɪvz] *npl* archivos *mpl*

archway ['ɑːtʃweɪ] *n (passage)* arcada *f*; *(entrance)* arco *m*

arctic ['ɑːktɪk] **1** *n* the A. el Ártico
2 *adj* **(a)** *(climate)* ártico(a); **the A. Circle** el Círculo Polar Ártico; **the A. Ocean** el Océano Glacial Ártico **(b)** *Fam (very cold)* gélido(a), glacial

ardent ['ɑːdənt] *adj (desire, love)* ardiente; *(admirer, believer)* ferviente

ardently ['ɑːdəntlɪ] *adv (to desire, love)* apasionadamente; *(to admire, believe)* fervientemente

ardor ['ɑːdə(r)] *n* ardor *m*, fervor *m*

arduous ['ɑːdjʊəs] *adj* arduo(a)

are [ɑː(r)] *plural and 2nd person singular of* **be**

area ['eərɪə] *n* **(a)** *(surface)* área *f* **(b)** *(region)* área *f*, zona *f*; *(of town, city)* zona *f*, barrio *m*; *(of knowledge)* área *f*, ámbito *m*; **the London a.** la región londinense; **an a. of agreement** un área de acuerdo; *Tel* **a. code** prefijo *m*; *Com* **a. manager** jefe(a) *m,f* de zona

arena [əˈriːnə] *n* **(a)** *(stadium)* estadio *m* **(b)** *(area of activity) (economic, international)* ruedo *m*; **to enter the a.** salir al ruedo, saltar a la palestra

aren't [ɑːnt] **(a)** = **are not (b)** **a. I?** = **am I not?**

Argentina [ɑːdʒənˈtiːnə] *n* Argentina

Argentine ['ɑːdʒəntaɪn] **1** *n (person)* argentino(a) *m,f*; *Old-fashioned* **the A.** *(country)* (la) Argentina
2 *adj* argentino(a)

Argentinian [ɑːdʒənˈtɪnɪən] *n & adj* argentino(a) *m,f*

argon ['ɑːɡɒn] *n Chem* argón *m*

arguable ['ɑːɡjʊəbəl] *adj* **(a)** *(questionable)* discutible; **it is a. whether it would have made any difference** cabe dudar que las cosas hubiesen sido distintas **(b)** *(conceivable)* **it is a. that...** se podría afirmar que...

arguably ['ɑːɡjʊəblɪ] *adv* **it's a. the city's best restaurant** es, probablemente, el mejor restaurante de la ciudad

argue ['ɑːɡjuː] **1** *vt (case, position)* argumentar; **to a. that...** aducir *or* argumentar que...
2 *vi (quarrel)* discutir; **to a. about sth** discutir sobre algo; **to a. for** *(defend)* abogar por; **to a. against** *(oppose)* oponerse a

argument ['ɑːɡjʊmənt] *n* **(a)** *(quarrel)* discusión *f*, pelea *f*; **to have an a. (about sth)** discutir (por algo); **to get into an a.** meterse en una discusión; **and I don't want any arguments!** ¡y punto! **(b)** *(reason)* argumento *m*; **an a. for/against doing sth** un argumento a favor de/en contra de hacer algo; **suppose for a.'s sake that...** pongamos por caso que...

argumentative [ɑːɡjʊˈmentətɪv] *adj* discutidor(ora), peleón(ona)

aria ['ɑːrɪə] *n Mus* aria *f*

arid ['ærɪd] *adj* árido(a)

Aries ['eəriːz] *n (sign of zodiac)* aries *m*; **to be (an) A.** ser aries

arise [əˈraɪz] *(pt* **arose** [əˈrəʊz], *pp* **arisen** [əˈrɪzən]) *vi (problem, situation)* surgir; **the question has not yet arisen** todavía no se ha presentado la cuestión; **should the need a.** si surgiera la necesidad; **a storm arose** se formó una tormenta

aristocracy [ærɪsˈtɒkrəsɪ] *n* aristocracia *f*

aristocrat [əˈrɪstəkræt, ˈærɪstəkræt] *n* aristócrata *mf*

aristocratic [ərɪstəˈkrætɪk, ærɪstəˈkrætɪk] *adj* aristocrático(a)

arithmetic [əˈrɪθmətɪk] *n (calculations)* cálculos *mpl*, aritmética *f*; *(subject)* aritmética *f*

arithmetical [ærɪθˈmetɪkəl] *adj* aritmético(a)

ark [ɑːk] *n* arca *f*

arm [ɑːm] **1** *n* **(a)** *(of person, chair)* brazo *m*; *(of garment)* manga *f*; **to carry sth/sb in one's arms** llevar algo/a alguien en brazos; **he took my a.** me tomó *or* cogió del brazo; **to walk a. in a.** caminar *or* ir del brazo; **to receive sb with open arms** *(warmly welcome)* recibir a alguien con los brazos abiertos; *Fig* **to keep sb at arm's length** mantenerse a una distancia prudencial de alguien; **a. wrestling** los pulsos, *Am* la pulseada **(b)** **arms** *(weapons)* armas *fpl*; **arms race** carrera *f* armamentística **(c)** *(in heraldry)* **(coat of) arms** escudo *m* de armas
2 *vt (person, country)* armar; **to a. oneself with the facts** armarse de datos

armadillo [ɑːməˈdɪləʊ] *(pl* **armadillos)** *n* armadillo *m*

Armageddon [ɑːməˈɡedən] *n* apocalipsis *m inv*

armaments ['ɑːməmənts] *npl* armamento *m*

armband ['ɑːmbænd] *n (at funeral, for swimming)* brazalete *m*

armchair ['ɑːmtʃeə(r)] *n* sillón *m*; **an a. strategist** un estratega de salón

armed [ɑːmd] *adj* armado(a); **to be a.** estar armado(a); **a. forces** fuerzas *fpl* armadas; **a. robbery** atraco *m* a mano armada

Armenia [ɑːˈmiːnɪə] *n* Armenia

Armenian [ɑːˈmiːnɪən] *n & adj* armenio(a) *m,f*

armful ['ɑːmfʊl] *n* brazada *f*; **an a. of papers** un montón de papeles (en los brazos)

armhole ['ɑːmhəʊl] *n* sisa *f*

armistice ['ɑːmɪstɪs] *n* armisticio *m*; **A. Day** = día en que se conmemora el final de la primera Guerra Mundial

armor ['ɑːmə(r)] *n* **(a)** *(of knight)* armadura *f*; **suit of a.** armadura *f* **(b)** *Mil (of tank)* blindaje *m*; *(tanks)* división *f* acorazada

armored ['ɑːməd] *n* **a. car** carro *m* de combate

armory ['ɑːmərɪ] *n* arsenal *m*

armpit ['ɑːmpɪt] *n* axila *f*, sobaco *m*

armrest ['ɑːmrest] *n* reposabrazos *m inv*

arm-twisting ['ɑːmtwɪstɪŋ] *n Fam* **it took a bit of a., but I got him to agree** tuve que apretarle las clavijas un poco, pero logré que cediese

arm-wrestle ['ɑːmresəl] *vi* **to a. with sb** echar un pulso con alguien

army ['ɑːmɪ] *n* ejército *m*; **to be in the a.** ser militar; *Fig* **an a. of workers/assistants** un ejército de obreros/ayudantes

aroma [əˈrəʊmə] *n* aroma *m*

aromatic [ærəʊˈmætɪk] *adj* aromático(a)

arose [əˈrəʊz] *pt of* **arise**

around [əˈraʊnd] **1** *prep* **(a)** *(indicating position)* alrededor de; **a. the table** en torno a la mesa; **there were hills all a. the town** la ciudad estaba rodeada de colinas; **a. here** por aquí (cerca) **(b)** *(indicating circular motion)* **to go a. an obstacle** rodear un obstáculo; **to go a. the corner** doblar la esquina; **it's just a. the corner** está a la vuelta de la esquina, *RP* queda a la vuelta; *Fig* **to drive** *or* **send sb a. the bend** volver loco(a) a alguien **(c)** *(to all parts of)* **to look a. the room** mirar por toda la habitación; **to travel a. the world** viajar por todo el mundo; **to walk a. the town/the streets** caminar por la ciudad/las calles **(d)** *(approximately)* **a. about** alrededor de, aproximadamente; **a. about midday** a eso de mediodía
2 *adv* **(a)** *(surrounding)* alrededor; **a garden with a fence a.** un jardín rodeado por una valla; **there were open fields all a.** estábamos rodeados de campo por todas partes; **for miles a.** en millas a la redonda
(b) *(in different directions)* **to walk a.** pasear (por ahí); **there were books lying all a.** había libros por todas partes
(c) *(in the general area)* **is Jack a.?** *(there)* ¿está Jack por ahí?; *(here)* ¿está Jack por aquí?; **there was nobody a.** no había nadie; **there's never a policeman a. when you need one** nunca hay un policía a mano cuando lo necesitas

(d) *(approximately)* **a. thirty** unos treinta; **a. ten years** diez años; **at a. one o'clock** alrededor de la una

around-the-clock [ə'raʊndðə'klɒk] **1** *adj* continuo(a), 24 horas al día

2 *adv* (durante) las 24 horas del día

arousal [ə'raʊzəl] *n* excitación *f*

arouse [ə'raʊz] *vt (sleeping person)* despertar; *(emotion, desire)* despertar, provocar; *(suspicion)* levantar, despertar; *(sexually)* excitar

arr *Rail (abbr* **arrival)** llegada *f*

arraign [ə'reɪn] *vt Law* hacer comparecer, citar

arraignment [ə'reɪnmənt] *n Law* acusación *f*

arrange [ə'reɪndʒ] **1** *vt* **(a)** *(put in order) (books, furniture)* ordenar, colocar; *(hair, flowers)* arreglar **(b)** *(organize) (wedding, meeting)* organizar; *(time, date)* fijar; *(accommodation)* buscar; **to a. to do sth** quedar en hacer algo; **to a. to meet** quedar; **to a. what to do** planear qué hacer; **it was arranged that...** se quedó en que...; **an arranged marriage** un matrimonio concertado

2 *vi* **to a. for sth to be done** disponer que se haga algo

arrangement [ə'reɪndʒmənt] *n* **(a)** *(order, placing)* disposición *f* **(b)** *(plan, preparations)* **to make arrangements** hacer los preparativos **(c)** *(agreement)* acuerdo *m*; **to come to an a. (with sb)** llegar a un acuerdo (con alguien); **by a.** con cita previa **(d)** *Mus* arreglo *m*

array [ə'reɪ] *n (collection)* muestrario *m*

arrears [ə'rɪəz] *npl* atrasos *mpl*; **to be in a. with the rent** ir atrasado(a) en el pago del alquiler *or Méx* de la renta; **I am paid monthly in a.** me pagan al final de cada mes

arrest [ə'rest] **1** *n* detención *f*, arresto *m*; **to be under a.** estar detenido(a); **to make an a.** realizar *or* practicar una detención

2 *vt (person, development)* detener; **my attention was arrested by...** me llamó poderosamente la atención...

arresting [ə'restɪŋ] *adj (expression, look)* llamativo(a)

arrival [ə'raɪvəl] *n* llegada *f*; **on a.** al llegar; **a new a.** *(at work, in club)* un/una recién llegado(a); *(baby)* un/una recién nacido(a)

arrive [ə'raɪv] *vi* **(a)** *(at place)* llegar; **to a. at a decision/ solution** llegar a una decisión/solución **(b)** *Fam (attain success)* triunfar

arrogance ['ærəgəns] *n* arrogancia *f*

arrogant ['ærəgənt] *adj* arrogante

arrow ['ærəʊ] *n* flecha *f*; *Comptr* **a. key** tecla *f* de dirección *or* de movimiento del cursor

arrowhead ['ærəʊhed] *n* punta *f* de flecha

arrowroot ['ærəʊruːt] *n Culin* arrurruz *m*

arsenal ['ɑːsənəl] *n* arsenal *m*

arsenic ['ɑːsənɪk] *n Chem* arsénico *m*

arson ['ɑːsən] *n* incendio *m* provocado

arsonist ['ɑːsənɪst] *n* incendiario(a) *m,f*, pirómano(a) *m,f*

art [ɑːt] *n* **(a)** *(in general)* arte *m*; **the arts** las artes; **arts and crafts** artes *fpl* y oficios; **a. exhibition** exposición *f* (artística); **a. form** manifestación *f* artística; **a. gallery** *(for sale)* galería *f* de arte; *(for exhibition)* museo *m*; **a. school** escuela *f* de bellas artes **(b)** *Univ* **arts** letras *fpl* **(c)** *(technique)* arte *m*; **there's an a. to making omelets** hacer tortillas tiene su arte; **the a. of war/conversation** el arte de la guerra/la conversación

artefact, artifact ['ɑːtɪfækt] *n* objeto *m*

arteriosclerosis [ɑː'tɪərɪəʊsklə'rəʊsɪs] *n Med* arteriosclerosis *f inv*

artery ['ɑːtərɪ] *n* arteria *f*

artful ['ɑːtfʊl] *adj (person)* astuto(a), artero(a); *(solution)* astuto(a), hábil

arthritic [ɑː'θrɪtɪk] *adj* artrítico(a)

arthritis [ɑː'θraɪtɪs] *n* artritis *f inv*

arthropod ['ɑːθrəpɒd] *n Zool* artrópodo *m*

arthrosis [ɑː'θrəʊsɪs] *n Med* artrosis *f inv*

artichoke ['ɑːtɪtʃəʊk] *n* **(globe) a.** alcachofa *f*, *Am* alcaucil *m*

article ['ɑːtɪkəl] **1** *n* artículo *m*; **a. of clothing** prenda *f* de vestir; *Gram* **definite/indefinite a.** artículo *m* determinado/indeterminado

2 *vt Law* **to be articled to a firm of solicitors** trabajar en prácticas *or* hacer una pasantía en un bufete de abogados

articulate¹ [ɑː'tɪkjʊlət] *adj (person)* elocuente; *(description, account)* claro(a), comprensible

articulate² [ɑː'tɪkjʊleɪt] *vt (word)* articular; *(idea, feeling)* formular, expresar

articulately [ɑː'tɪkjʊlətlɪ] *adv (to speak, explain)* claramente

articulation [ɑːtɪkjʊ'leɪʃən] *n (of words)* articulación *f*; *(of ideas, feelings)* formulación *f*

artifice ['ɑːtɪfɪs] *n* artificio *m*

artificial [ɑːtɪ'fɪʃəl] *adj (conditions, light, distinction)* artificial; *(limb, hair)* postizo(a), artificial; *(smile)* afectado(a), artificial; **a. insemination** inseminación *f* artificial; *Comptr* **a. intelligence** inteligencia *f* artificial; **a. respiration** respiración *f* artificial

artificially [ɑːtɪ'fɪʃəlɪ] *adv* artificialmente

artillery [ɑː'tɪlərɪ] *n* artillería *f*

artisan [ɑːtɪ'zæn] *n* artesano(a) *m,f*

artist ['ɑːtɪst] *n* artista *mf*

artistic [ɑː'tɪstɪk] *adj* artístico(a); **she is very a.** tiene mucha sensibilidad artística

artistry ['ɑːtɪstrɪ] *n* arte *m*, destreza *f*

artless ['ɑːtlɪs] *adj (simple)* inocente, ingenuo(a); *(clumsy)* torpe

artsy = **arty**

artwork ['ɑːtwɜːk] *n (in book, magazine)* ilustraciones *fpl*

arty ['ɑːtɪ], **artsy** ['ɑːtsɪ] *adj Fam (person)* = que se interesa por las artes

Aryan ['eərɪən] *n & adj* ario(a) *m,f*

as [əz, *stressed* æz] **1** *prep* como; **to work as a team** trabajar en equipo; **to regard sb as a friend** considerar a alguien un amigo; **to treat sb as a stranger** tratar a alguien como a un extraño; **to act/serve as a protection against sth** actuar/ servir de protección contra algo; **she used it as a bandage** lo utilizó a modo de venda; **as a woman, I think that...** como mujer, creo que...

2 *adv* **(a)** *(with manner)* (tal y) como; **we arrived at eight o'clock, as requested** llegamos a las ocho, tal y como se nos había pedido; **we did exactly as we had been told** hicimos exactamente lo que nos habían dicho; **B as in Birmingham** B de Birmingham

(b) *(in comparisons)* **as... as...** tan... como...; **not as** *or* **so... as...** no tan... como...; **as tall as me** tan alto(a) como yo; **as white as a sheet** blanco(a) como la nieve; **twice as big** el doble de grande; **I pushed/tried as hard as I could** empujé/lo intenté con todas mis fuerzas; **as many as you want** todos los que quieras; **as much as you want** todo lo que quieras; **as recently as last week** hace tan sólo una semana; **as soon as possible** cuanto antes

(c) *(phrases)* **she looked as if** *or* **though she was upset** parecía (como si estuviera) disgustada; **it isn't as if** *or* **though I haven't tried** no será porque no lo he intentado, no es que no lo haya intentado; **it looks as if...** parece que...; **as for the cost/the food,...** en *or* por lo que se refiere al coste/a la comida,...; **as well** también

3 *conj* **(a)** *(with time) (when)* cuando; *(whilst)* mientras; **he went out as I came in** salió cuando yo entraba; **she talked to me as I worked** me hablaba mientras trabajaba; **as you get older...** a medida que te haces mayor...; **as necessary** según sea necesario; **as always** como siempre

(b) *(because)* como; **as he has now left,...** como se ha ido,..., ahora que se ha ido,...

(c) *(concessive)* **late as it was,...** aunque era tarde,...; **try as she might,...** por mucho que lo intentara,...; **unlikely as it might seem,...** por improbable que parezca,...; **stupid as he is, even he saw the mistake** hasta él, que es tan estúpido, se dio cuenta del error

(d) *(with manner)* como; **as I was saying,...** como iba diciendo,...; **do as you like** haz lo que quieras; **as often happens,...** como suele suceder,...; **it's hard enough as it is without this happening!** ¡ya es lo bastante duro como para que ahora pase esto!; **it's far enough as it is!** ¡ya está suficientemente lejos así!

(e) *(in addition)* **I'm well, as are the children** estoy bien y los niños también

ASAP [eɪeseɪˈpi:] *adv* (*abbr* **as soon as possible**) cuanto antes, lo antes posible

asbestos [æsˈbestəs] *n* amianto *m*, asbesto *m*

asbestosis [æsbesˈtəʊsɪs] *n Med* asbestosis *f inv*

ascend [əˈsend] **1** *vt* (*mountain*) ascender, subir; (*throne*) ascender a, subir a
  2 *vi* ascender

ascendancy, ascendency [əˈsendənsɪ] *n* dominio *m*, ascendiente *m*

ascendant, ascendent [əˈsendənt] *n* **to be in the a.** ir en ascenso

Ascension [əˈsenʃən] *n Rel* Ascensión *f*; **A. Island** Ascensión

ascent [əˈsent] *n* (*of mountain*) ascenso *m*, subida *f*; **her a. to power** su ascenso al poder

ascertain [æsəˈteɪn] *vt* (*establish*) precisar, determinar; (*find out*) averiguar

ascetic [əˈsetɪk] **1** *n* asceta *mf*
  2 *adj* ascético(a)

ASCII [ˈæskɪ] *n Comptr* (*abbr* **American Standard Code for Information Interchange**) ASCII *m*

ascribe [əˈskraɪb] *vt* atribuir

ASEAN [ˈæzɪæn] *n* (*abbr* **Association of Southeast Asian Nations**) ASEAN *f*

aseptic [eɪˈseptɪk] *adj* aséptico(a)

asexual [eɪˈseksjʊəl] *adj* asexual

ash¹ [æʃ] *n* (*tree*) fresno *m*

ash² *n* (*from fire, cigarette*) ceniza *f*; *Rel* **Ash Wednesday** Miércoles *m inv* de Ceniza

ashamed [əˈʃeɪmd] *adj* avergonzado(a), *Am salvo RP* apenado(a); **to be a. (of)** estar avergonzado(a) *or Am salvo RP* apenado(a) (de); **to feel a.** sentir vergüenza *or Am salvo RP* pena; **I'm a. of you!** ¡me das vergüenza *or Am salvo RP* pena!; **I am a. to say that...** me avergüenza *or Am salvo RP* apena decir que...; **there is nothing to be a. of** no hay de qué avergonzarse *or Am salvo RP* apenarse; **you ought to be a. of yourself!** ¡debería darte vergüenza *or Am salvo RP* pena!

ashcan [ˈæʃkæn] *n* cubo *m* de la basura

ashen [ˈæʃən] *adj* pálido(a)

ashore [əˈʃɔ:(r)] *adv* en tierra; **to go a.** desembarcar

ashtray [ˈæʃtreɪ] *n* cenicero *m*

Asia [ˈeɪʒə] *n* Asia; **A. Minor** Asia Menor

Asian [ˈeɪʒən] **1** *n* asiático(a) *m,f*
  2 *adj* asiático(a); **A.-American** americano(a) de origen asiático

Asiatic [eɪsɪˈætɪk] *n & adj* asiático(a) *m,f*

aside [əˈsaɪd] **1** *adv* aparte, a un lado; **a. from** aparte de; **to put** *or* **set sth a.** apartar *or* reservar algo; **stand a. please!** ¡apártense, por favor!; **to take sb a.** llevarse a alguien aparte; **politics a.,...** dejando a un lado la política,...
  2 *n Theat* aparte *m*

asinine [ˈæsɪnaɪn] *adj* cretino(a), majadero(a)

ask [ɑ:sk] **1** *vt* **(a)** (*inquire about*) preguntar; **to a. sb sth** preguntar algo a alguien; **to a. (sb) a question** hacer una pregunta (a alguien); **to a. sb the time** preguntar la hora a alguien; **to a. sb the way** preguntar a alguien el camino; **don't a. me!** ¿a mí me lo vas a preguntar?

(b) (*request*) pedir; **to a. sb for sth** pedir algo a alguien; **to a. to do sth** *Esp* pedir hacer algo, *Am* pedir para hacer algo; **to a. sb to do sth** pedir a alguien que haga algo; **to a. a favor of sb, to a. sb a favor** pedir un favor a alguien; **if it isn't asking too much** si no es mucho pedir; **to a. sb's permission to do sth** pedir permiso a alguien para hacer algo

(c) (*invite*) invitar, convidar; **to a. sb to lunch** invitar a alguien a comer

  2 *vi* **(a)** (*inquire*) preguntar (**about** por) **(b)** (*request*) **to a. for sth** pedir algo; **you only have to a.!** ¡no tienes más que pedirlo!; *Fam* **he was asking for it!** (*deserved it*) ¡se lo estaba buscando!

▸**ask after** *vt insep* preguntar por

askance [əˈskæns] *adv* **to look a. at sb** mirar a alguien con recelo

askew [əˈskju:] *adv* **her dress was a.** llevaba el vestido torcido

asking [ˈɑːskɪŋ] *n* **it's yours for the a.** si lo pides, es tuyo; **a. price** precio *m* de salida

ASL [eɪes'el] *n* (*abbr* **American Sign Language**) = lenguaje de signos para sordos

asleep [əˈsli:p] *adj* **to be a.** estar dormido(a) *or* durmiendo; **to be fast** *or* **sound a.** estar profundamente dormido(a); **to fall a.** quedarse dormido(a), dormirse

asocial [eɪˈsəʊʃəl] *adj* asocial

asparagus [əˈspærəgəs] *n* (*plant*) esparraguera *f*; (*vegetable*) espárragos *mpl*

aspect [ˈæspekt] *n* **(a)** (*of problem, subject*) aspecto *m* **(b)** (*of building*) orientación *f*

asperity [æˈsperɪtɪ] *n* aspereza *f*

aspersions [əsˈpɜːʃənz] *npl* **to cast a. on sth** poner en duda algo

asphalt [ˈæsfælt] *n* asfalto *m*

asphyxia [æsˈfɪksɪə] *n Med* asfixia *f*

asphyxiate [æsˈfɪksɪeɪt] **1** *vt* asfixiar
  2 *vi* asfixiarse

asphyxiation [æsfɪksɪˈeɪʃən] *n* asfixia *f*

aspic [ˈæspɪk] *n Culin* gelatina *f*; *Fig* **it was as if the house had been preserved in a.** parecía que hubieran conservado la casa en alcanfor

aspirant [ˈæspɪrənt] *n* aspirante *mf*

aspirate [ˈæspərət] *adj Ling* aspirado(a)

aspiration [æspɪˈreɪʃən] *n* (*ambition*) aspiración *f*

aspire [əˈspaɪə(r)] *vi* **to a. to do sth** aspirar a hacer algo

aspirin [ˈæsprɪn] *n* aspirina *f*

aspiring [əˈspaɪərɪŋ] *adj* **to be an a. actor** aspirar a ser actor

ass¹ [æs] *n* **(a)** (*animal*) burro *m*, asno *m* **(b)** *Fam* (*idiot*) burro(a) *m,f*, tonto(a) *m,f*; **to make an a. of oneself** quedar como un tonto

ass² *n Vulg* culo *m*

assail [əˈseɪl] *vt* (*attack*) asaltar, agredir (**with** con); **to a. sb with questions** asediar a alguien a preguntas; **assailed by doubt** asaltado(a) por la duda

assailant [əˈseɪlənt] *n* asaltante *mf*, agresor(ora) *m,f*

assassin [əˈsæsɪn] *n* asesino(a) *m,f*

assassinate [əˈsæsɪneɪt] *vt* asesinar

assassination [əsæsɪˈneɪʃən] *n* asesinato *m*

assault [əˈsɔːlt] **1** *n* ataque *m* (**on** a), asalto *m* (**on** a); *Law* agresión *f*; **a. and battery** agresión *f* con resultado de lesiones; *Mil* **a. course** pista *f* de entrenamiento; **a. rifle** rifle *m* de asalto
  2 *vt* atacar, asaltar; *Law* agredir; **to be sexually assaulted** ser objeto de una agresión sexual

assemble [əˈsembl] **1** *vt* (*people*) reunir, congregar; (*facts,* *objects)* reunir, juntar; *(machine, furniture)* montar, ensamblar

2 *vi (people)* reunirse, congregarse

assembly [ə'semblɪ] *n* (**a**) *(gathering)* reunión *f*; *Sch* = reunión de todos los profesores y los alumnos al principio de la jornada escolar; **a. hall** *(in school)* salón *m* de actos (**b**) *Pol (legislature)* asamblea *f* legislativa (**c**) *(of machine, furniture)* montaje *m*, ensamblaje *m*; **a. instructions** instrucciones *fpl* de montaje; *Ind* **a. line** cadena *f* de montaje

assent [ə'sent] **1** *n* asentimiento *m*, consentimiento *m*; **she gave/withheld her a.** dio/no dio su consentimiento

2 *vi* dar el consentimiento (**to** a)

assert [ə'sɜːt] *vt (one's rights, point of view, authority)* afirmar, hacer valer; **to a. oneself** mostrarse firme, imponerse; **to a. that...** afirmar que...

assertion [ə'sɜːʃən] *n (of right)* afirmación *f*; *(statement)* afirmación *f*, aseveración *f*

assertive [ə'sɜːtɪv] *adj* **a course aimed at teaching women to be more a.** un curso para potenciar la afirmación personal de las mujeres

assertiveness [ə'sɜːtɪvnəs] *n* afirmación *f* personal, autoafirmación *f*; **a. training** cursos *mpl* de afirmación personal

assess [ə'ses] *vt* (**a**) *(estimate) (value)* tasar, valorar; *(damage)* evaluar, valorar; **to a. sb's income** *(for tax purposes)* evaluar la renta de alguien (**b**) *(analyze)* evaluar

assessment [ə'sesmənt] *n* (**a**) *(estimate) (of value)* tasación *f*, valoración *f*; *(of damage)* evaluación *f*, valoración *f*; *(for insurance or tax purposes)* tasación *f* (**b**) *(analysis)* evaluación *f*

assessor [ə'sesə(r)] *n Fin* tasador(ora) *m,f*

asset ['æset] *n* ventaja *f*, beneficio *m*; **she is a great a. to the firm** es una valiosa aportación a la empresa; *Fin* **assets** activos *mpl*; *Fin* **a. stripper** liquidador(ora) *m,f* de activos; *Fin* **a. stripping** liquidación *f* (especulativa) de activos

asshole ['æʃhəʊl] *n Vulg* (**a**) *(anus)* ojete *m* (**b**) *(unpleasant person)* hijo(a) *m,f* de puta, cabrón(ona) *m,f*

assiduous [ə'sɪdjʊəs] *adj* perseverante

assign [ə'saɪn] *vt (task, funds)* asignar (**to** a); *(importance)* atribuir; **to a. sb to do sth** asignar a alguien la tarea de hacer algo

assignation [æsɪg'neɪʃən] *n Formal (meeting)* cita *f*

assignee [æsaɪ'niː] *n Law* sucesor(ora) *m,f*, concesionario(a) *m,f*

assignment [ə'saɪnmənt] *n* (**a**) *(allocation)* asignación *f* (**b**) *(task) Sch* tarea *f*, trabajo *m*; *Journ* encargo *m*, trabajo *m*; *Mil* misión *f*

assignor [ə'saɪnə(r)] *n Law* cesionario(a) *m,f*

assimilate [ə'sɪmɪleɪt] **1** *vt (food, ideas)* asimilar

2 *vi (immigrants)* integrarse

assimilation [əsɪmɪ'leɪʃən] *n (of food, ideas)* asimilación *f*; *(of immigrants)* integración *f*

assist [ə'sɪst] **1** *vt (person)* ayudar; *(process, development)* colaborar en, contribuir a; **to a. sb in doing** *or* **to do sth** ayudar a alguien a hacer algo; **assisted suicide** suicidio *m* asistido

2 *vi* prestar ayuda; **to a. in sth** colaborar en algo

assistance [ə'sɪstəns] *n* ayuda *f*, asistencia *f*; **to come to sb's a.** acudir en ayuda de alguien; **can I be of any a.?** ¿puedo ayudar en algo?

assistant [ə'sɪstənt] *n* ayudante *mf*; **(shop) a.** dependiente(a) *m,f*; **a. manager** subdirector(ora) *m,f*; **a. professor** profesor(ora) *m,f* adjunto(a)

associate 1 *n* [ə'səʊsɪət] *(in business)* socio(a) *m,f*; *(in crime)* cómplice *mf*

2 *adj (company)* asociado(a); **a. professor** profesor(ora) *m,f* adjunto(a) *or* titular

3 *vt* [ə'səʊsɪeɪt] (**a**) *(mentally)* asociar (**b**) **to be associated with** estar asociado(a) *or* relacionado(a) con

4 *vi* **to a. with sb** frecuentar a *or* tratar con alguien

associated [ə'səʊsɪeɪtɪd] *adj* asociado(a)

association [əsəʊsɪ'eɪʃən] *n* asociación *f*; **the name has unfortunate associations for her** ese nombre le trae malos recuerdos, ese nombre tiene connotaciones desagradables para ella; **in a. with...** conjuntamente con...; **to form an a.** crear una asociación

assonance ['æsənəns] *n* asonancia *f*

assorted [ə'sɔːtɪd] *adj (colors, flavors)* diverso(a); *(biscuits, sweets)* surtido(a)

assortment [ə'sɔːtmənt] *n (of colors, reasons)* diversidad *f*; *(of biscuits, sweets)* surtido *m*

assuage [ə'sweɪdʒ] *vt Formal (anger, person)* apaciguar; *(hunger, thirst)* aplacar

assume [ə'sjuːm] *vt* (**a**) *(suppose)* suponer; **I a. so/not** supongo que sí/no; **he was assumed to be rich** se suponía que era rico; **let us a. that...** supongamos que... (**b**) *(take over) (duty, power)* asumir; *(name)* adoptar; **to a. responsibility for sth** asumir la responsabilidad de algo; **an assumed name** un nombre falso (**c**) *(take on) (appearance, shape)* adquirir, adoptar

assumption [ə'sʌmpʃən] *n* (**a**) *(supposition)* suposición *f*; **to work on the a. that...** trabajar sobre la base de que... (**b**) *(of power, responsibility)* asunción *f* (**c**) *Rel* **the A.** la Asunción

assurance [ə'ʃʊərəns] *n* (**a**) *(guarantee)* garantía *f*; **to give sb one's a.** dar garantías a alguien (**b**) *(confidence)* seguridad *f*; **to answer with a.** responder con seguridad

assure [ə'ʃʊə(r)] *vt* asegurar; **to a. sb of sth** asegurar algo a alguien

assured [ə'ʃʊəd] *adj (certain, confident)* seguro(a); **to be a. of sth** tener algo asegurado(a); **he gave a very a. performance** se mostró muy seguro en su actuación

assuredly [ə'ʃʊərɪdlɪ] *adv (undoubtedly)* sin duda

asterisk ['æstərɪsk] *n* asterisco *m*

asteroid ['æstərɔɪd] *n* asteroide *m*

asthma ['æsmə] *n* asma *f*

asthmatic [æs'mætɪk] *n & adj* asmático(a) *m,f*

astonish [ə'stɒnɪʃ] *vt* asombrar; **to be astonished at** *or* **by** quedarse asombrado(a) por; **I am astonished that...** me asombra que...

astonished [ə'stɒnɪʃt] *adj (look, reaction)* de asombro, asombrado(a)

astonishing [ə'stɒnɪʃɪŋ] *adj* asombroso(a); **I find it a. that...** me parece asombroso que...

astonishingly [ə'stɒnɪʃɪŋlɪ] *adv* asombrosamente

astonishment [ə'stɒnɪʃmənt] *n* asombro *m*; **to my a.** para mi asombro

astound [ə'staʊnd] *vt* dejar atónito(a), pasmar

astounded [ə'staʊndɪd] *adj* atónito(a), pasmado(a); **I was a.** me quedé atónito(a) *or* pasmado(a)

astounding [ə'staʊndɪŋ] *adj* pasmoso(a), asombroso(a)

astoundingly [ə'staʊndɪŋlɪ] *adv* increíblemente, asombrosamente

astral ['æstrəl] *adj* astral

astray [ə'streɪ] *adv* **to go a.** *(become lost)* perderse, extraviarse; **to lead sb a.** descarriar a alguien

astride [ə'straɪd] *prep* **to sit a. sth** sentarse a horcajadas sobre algo

astringent [ə'strɪndʒənt] *n & adj* astringente *m*

astrologer [ə'strɒlədʒə(r)] *n* astrólogo(a) *m,f*

astrological [æstrə'lɒdʒɪkəl] *adj* astrológico(a); **a. chart** carta *f* astral

astrology [ə'strɒlədʒɪ] *n* astrología *f*

astronaut ['æstrənɔːt] *n* astronauta *mf*

astronomer [ə'strɒnəmə(r)] *n* astrónomo(a) *m,f*

astronomic(al) [æstrə'nɒmɪk(əl)] *adj* astronómico(a)

astronomically [æstrə'nɒmɪklɪ] *adv Fam (to increase)* astronómicamente, desorbitadamente; **it's a. expensive** tiene un precio astronómico

astronomy [ə'strɒnəmɪ] *n* astronomía *f*

astrophysics [æstrəʊ'fɪzɪks] *npl* astrofísica *f*

Astroturf® ['æstrəʊtɜːf] *n Sport* (césped *m* de) hierba *f* artificial

Asturian [æ'stʊərɪən] *n & adj* asturiano(a) *m,f*

Asturias [æ'stʊərɪəs] *n* Asturias

astute [ə'stjuːt] *adj* astuto(a), sagaz

astutely [ə'stjuːtlɪ] *adv* astutamente, con sagacidad

astuteness [ə'stjuːtnɪs] *n (of person)* astucia *f*, sagacidad *f*

asunder [ə'sʌndə(r)] *adv Literary* **to tear sth a.** hacer pedazos algo

asylum [ə'saɪləm] *n* asilo *m*; **to seek a.** buscar asilo; **(mental) a.** manicomio *m*; **political a.** asilo político; **a. seeker** solicitante *mf* de asilo

asymmetric(al) [eɪsɪ'metrɪk(əl)] *adj* asimétrico(a)

asymmetry [eɪ'sɪmɪtrɪ] *n* asimetría *f*

at [æt, *unstressed* ət] **1** *prep* (**a**) *(with place)* en; **at the top/bottom** (en la parte de) arriba/abajo; **at the university/the station** en la universidad/la estación; **at the side** al lado; **at John's (house)** en casa de John; **at home** en casa

(**b**) *(with time)* **at six o'clock** a las seis; **at night** *Esp* por la noche, *Am* en la noche; **at Christmas** en Navidad; **at a good time** en un momento oportuno; **at the beginning/end** al principio/final; **at (the age of) twenty** a los veinte años

(**c**) *(with price, speed)* a; **at 60 mph** a 60 millas por hora; **at 50 cents a pound** a 50 centavos la libra

(**d**) *(with direction)* a; **to throw a stone at sb** tirarle una piedra a alguien; **to look at sth/sb** mirar algo/a alguien

(**e**) *(with cause)* **to be angry at sb** estar *esp Esp* enfadado(a) *or esp Am* enojado(a) con alguien; **to be surprised at sth** sorprenderse de algo

(**f**) *(with activity)* **to be at work/play** estar trabajando/jugando; **she's been at it all weekend** *(working)* ha pasado todo el fin de semana trabajando; **while you're at it, could you buy some sugar?** ya que vas, ¿podrías comprar azúcar?; **I am good at languages** tengo facilidad para los idiomas, *Esp* los idiomas se me dan bien; **he's bad at sport** no tiene habilidad para los deportes, *Esp* se le dan mal los deportes

2 *(at all)* *adv* **do you know him at all?** ¿lo conoces de algo?; **anything at all** cualquier cosa; **nothing at all** nada en absoluto; **not at all** *(not in the slightest)* en absoluto; *(when thanked)* de nada

atavistic [ætə'vɪstɪk] *adj* atávico(a)

ate [eɪt] *pt of* **eat**

atheism ['eɪθɪɪzəm] *n* ateísmo *m*

atheist ['eɪθɪɪst] *n* ateo(a) *m,f*

Athenian [ə'θiːnɪən] *n & adj* ateniense *mf*

Athens ['æθənz] *n* Atenas

athlete ['æθliːt] *n* atleta *mf*; *Med* **a.'s foot** pie *m* de atleta

athletic [æθ'letɪk] *adj* atlético(a)

athletics [æθ'letɪks] *npl* deportes *mpl*

Atlantic [ət'læntɪk] **1** *n* **the A.** el (océano) Atlántico

2 *adj* atlántico(a); **the A. Ocean** el océano Atlántico

atlas ['ætləs] *n* atlas *m inv*

ATM [eɪtiː'em] *n Fin (abbr* **automated** *or* **automatic teller machine)** cajero *m* automático

atmosphere ['ætməsfɪə(r)] *n (of planet)* atmósfera *f*; *(feeling, mood)* ambiente *m*

atmospheric [ætməs'ferɪk] *adj (pressure)* atmosférico(a); *Fig* **the music was very a.** la música te ponía la carne de gallina

atoll ['ætɒl] *n Geog* atolón *m*

atom ['ætəm] *n* átomo *m*; **a. bomb** bomba *f* atómica

atomic [ə'tɒmɪk] *adj* atómico(a); **a. bomb** bomba *f* atómica;

a. energy energía *f* atómica *or* nuclear; **a. warfare** guerra *f* nuclear

atomizer ['ætəmaɪzə(r)] *n* atomizador *m*

atone for [ə'təʊn] *vt insep (sin, crime)* expiar; *(mistake)* subsanar

atonement [ə'təʊnmənt] *n (for sin, crime)* expiación *f*; *(for mistake, behavior)* subsanación *f*

atrocious [ə'trəʊʃəs] *adj (crime, behavior)* atroz, cruel; *(mistake, decision, weather, meal)* atroz, terrible

atrociously [ə'trəʊʃəslɪ] *adv* (**a**) *(cruelly)* atrozmente, despiadadamente (**b**) *Fam (very badly)* de pena; **a. bad** malísimo(a), pésimo(a)

atrocity [ə'trɒsɪtɪ] *n* atrocidad *f*

atrophy ['ætrəfɪ] *vi* atrofiarse

attach [ə'tætʃ] *vt (label, check)* sujetar, fijar (**to** a); *(document)* adjuntar (**to** a); *(blame, responsibility, importance)* atribuir (**to** a); **to a. oneself to sb** pegarse a alguien; **to be very attached to sth/sb** tenerle mucho cariño a algo/alguien

attaché [ə'tæʃeɪ] *n* agregado(a) *m,f*; **military a.** agregado(a) militar; **a. case** maletín *m*

attachment [ə'tætʃmənt] *n* (**a**) *(device)* accesorio *m* (**b**) *(secondment)* **to be on a. to a department** estar destinado(a) a un departamento (**c**) *(fondness)* cariño *m*; **to form an a. to sb** tomar cariño a alguien

attack [ə'tæk] **1** *n* ataque *m*; **to be under a.** estar siendo atacado(a); **to come under a.** ser atacado(a); **to launch an a. on sb** lanzar un ataque contra alguien; **an a. of nerves** un ataque de nervios; **I had an a. of doubt** me asaltaron las dudas; **an a. of fever** un acceso de fiebre

2 *vt* atacar; *(problem)* acometer, abordar; **he was attacked in the street** lo asaltaron en la calle

attacker [ə'tækə(r)] *n (assailant, sportsperson)* atacante *mf*

attain [ə'teɪn] *vt (ambition, age)* alcanzar; *(rank)* llegar a

attainable [ə'teɪnəbəl] *adj (goal, ambition)* alcanzable

attainment [ə'teɪnmənt] *n (of goal, ambition)* consecución *f*, logro *m*

attempt [ə'tempt] **1** *n (effort)* intento *m*, tentativa *f*; **to make an a. at doing sth** *or* **to do sth** intentar hacer algo; **they made no a. to help** no trataron de ayudar; **to make an a. on sb's life** atentar contra la vida de alguien; **at the first a.** al primer intento

2 *vt (task)* intentar; **to a. to do sth** tratar de *or* intentar hacer algo; **to a. a smile** intentar sonreír; *Law* **attempted murder/robbery** intento *m* de asesinato/robo

attend [ə'tend] **1** *vt* (**a**) *(meeting, school)* asistir a, acudir a (**b**) *(patient)* atender; **we were attended by three waiters** nos atendieron tres camareros

2 *vi (be present)* asistir

▸**attend to** *vt insep (matter, problem)* ocuparse de; *(patient)* atender, asistir; *(customer)* atender

attendance [ə'tendəns] *n (presence, people present)* asistencia *f*; **there was a good/poor a.** acudió mucha/poca gente; **a. roll** lista *f* de asistencia

attendant [ə'tendənt] *n (in museum)* vigilante *mf*; *(in car park, cloakroom)* encargado(a) *m,f*

attention [ə'tenʃən] *n* (**a**) *(in general)* atención *f*; **to pay a. to sth/sb** prestar atención a algo/alguien; **to pay a. to detail** fijarse en los detalles; **to give sth/sb one's full a.** atender bien algo/a alguien; **to attract** *or* **catch sb's a.** llamar la atención de alguien; **to draw a. to oneself** llamar la atención; **your a. please, ladies and gentlemen** atención, señoras y señores; **for the a. of** a la atención de; *Med* **a. deficit disorder** trastorno *m* por déficit de atención (**b**) *(repairs)* **the engine needs some a.** hay que revisar el motor (**c**) *Mil* **a.!** ¡firmes!; **to stand at** *or* **to a.** ponerse firme, cuadrarse

attentive [ə'tentɪv] *adj (paying attention, considerate)* atento(a); **to be a. to sb** estar pendiente de alguien

attentively [ə'tentɪvlɪ] *adv* atentamente

attest [ə'test] **1** *vt (affirm, prove)* atestiguar
2 *vi* **to a. to** dar testimonio de

attic ['ætɪk] *n (storage space)* desván *m; (room)* ático *m*

attire [ə'taɪə(r)] *n* atuendo *m*, atavío *m*

attitude ['ætɪtjuːd] *n* (**a**) *(opinion, behavior)* actitud *f;* **what's your a. to abortion?** ¿cuál es tu actitud *or* postura ante el aborto?; **to take the a. that...** adoptar la actitud de que...; **I don't like your a.** no me gusta tu actitud; *Com* **a. survey** = estudio de la actitud del personal en materia laboral (**b**) *(pose)* postura *f;* **to strike an a.** adoptar una pose

attn *Com (abbr* **attention** *or* **for the attention of**) a la atención de

attorney [ə'tɜːnɪ] *n* (**a**) abogado(a) *m,f* (**b**) **A. General** *(in United States)* ≃ ministro(a) *m,f* de Justicia

attract [ə'trækt] *vt* atraer; **to a. sb's attention** llamar la atención de alguien; **to be attracted to sth/sb** sentirse atraído(a) por algo/alguien

attraction [ə'trækʃən] *n* (**a**) *(power)* atracción *f;* **the prospect holds little a. for me** la perspectiva no me atrae mucho (**b**) *(attractive aspect)* atractivo *m*

attractive [ə'træktɪv] *adj (person, offer, prospect)* atractivo(a)

attributable [ə'trɪbjʊtəbəl] *adj* atribuible

attribute 1 *n* ['ætrɪbjuːt] atributo *m*
2 *vt* [ə'trɪbjuːt] atribuir (**to** a)

attributive [ə'trɪbjʊtɪv] *adj* atributivo(a); **an a. use** un uso atributivo

attrition [ə'trɪʃən] *n* desgaste *m;* **war of a.** guerra *f* de desgaste

attuned [ə'tjuːnd] *adj* **he's a. to their way of thinking** sintoniza muy bien con su manera de pensar

ATV [eɪtiː'viː] *n (abbr* **all-terrain vehicle**) todoterreno *m*

atypical [eɪ'tɪpɪkəl] *adj* atípico(a)

AU [eɪ'juː] *n (abbr* **African Union**) UA *f*

auburn ['ɔːbən] *adj (hair)* (color) caoba

auction ['ɔːkʃən] **1** *n* subasta *f;* **to put sth up for a.** sacar algo a subasta; **a. room** sala *f* de subastas
2 *vt* subastar

▶**auction off** *vt sep* liquidar mediante subasta, subastar

auctioneer [ɔːkʃə'nɪə(r)] *n* subastador(ora) *m,f*

audacious [ɔː'deɪʃəs] *adj* audaz

audacity [ɔː'dæsɪtɪ] *n* audacia *f*

audible ['ɔːdɪbəl] *adj* audible

audibly ['ɔːdɪblɪ] *adv* de manera audible

audience ['ɔːdɪəns] *n* (**a**) *(spectators)* público *m; TV & Rad* audiencia *f;* **a. participation** participación *f* del público (**b**) *(meeting with monarch, Pope)* audiencia *f;* **to grant sb an a.** conceder una audiencia a alguien

audio ['ɔːdɪəʊ] *adj* **a. book** audiolibro *m;* **a. cassette** cinta *f* de audio; **a. equipment** equipo *m* de sonido

audiotypist ['ɔːdɪəʊtaɪpɪst] *n* mecanógrafo(a) *m,f* con dictáfono

audiovisual [ɔːdɪəʊ'vɪzjʊəl] *adj* audiovisual

audit ['ɔːdɪt] **1** *n Fin* auditoría *f*
2 *vt* (**a**) *Fin* auditar (**b**) *(class, lecture)* asistir de oyente a

audition [ɔː'dɪʃən] *Theat* **1** *n* prueba *f*, audición *f;* **to hold auditions for a play** realizar pruebas a actores para una obra de teatro
2 *vt (of director)* hacer una prueba a
3 *vi (actor)* hacer una prueba

auditor ['ɔːdɪtə(r)] *n Fin* auditor(ora) *m,f*

auditorium [ɔːdɪ'tɔːrɪəm] *(pl* **auditoriums** *or* **auditoria** [ɔːdɪ'tɔːrɪə]) *n* auditorio *m*

auditory ['ɔːdɪtrɪ] *adj* auditivo(a)

Aug *(abbr* **August**) agosto *m*

augment [ɔːg'ment] *vt* incrementar, aumentar

augur ['ɔːgə(r)] *vi* **to a. well/badly** ser un buen/mal augurio

August ['ɔːgəst] *n* agosto *m; see also* **May**

august [ɔː'gʌst] *adj Literary (distinguished)* augusto(a)

aunt [ɑːnt] *n* tía *f*

auntie, aunty ['ɑːntɪ] *n Fam* tita *f*

AUP [eɪjuː'piː] *n Comptr (abbr* **Acceptable Use Policy**) = código de conducta definido por un proveedor de acceso a Internet

au pair [əʊ'peə(r)] *n* au pair *f*

aura ['ɔːrə] *n* aura *f*

aural ['ɔːrəl] *adj* auditivo(a)

aurora [ə'rɔːrə] *(pl* **auroras** *or* **aurorae** [ə'rɔːriː]) *n Astron* aurora *f;* **a. australis** aurora *f* austral; **a. borealis** aurora *f* boreal

auspices ['ɔːspɪsɪz] *npl* **under the a. of** bajo los auspicios de

auspicious [ɔː'spɪʃəs] *adj* prometedor(a), halagüeño(a)

auspiciously [ɔː'spɪʃəslɪ] *adv* de manera halagüeña

Aussie ['ɒzɪ] *n & adj Fam* australiano(a) *m,f*

austere [ɒ'stɪə(r)] *adj* austero(a)

austerity [ɒ'sterɪtɪ] *n* austeridad *f*

Australasia [ɒstrə'leɪʒə] *n* Australasia

Australasian [ɒstrə'leɪʒən] *adj* de Australasia

Australia [ɒ'streɪlɪə] *n* Australia

Australian [ɒ'streɪlɪən] *n & adj* australiano(a) *m,f*

Austria ['ɒstrɪə] *n* Austria

Austrian ['ɒstrɪən] *n & adj* austriaco(a) *m,f*

autarchy ['ɔːtɑːkɪ] *n* autarquía *f*

authentic [ɔː'θentɪk] *adj* auténtico(a)

authenticate [ɔː'θentɪkeɪt] *vt* autentificar, autenticar

authenticity [ɔːθen'tɪsɪtɪ] *n* autenticidad *f*

author ['ɔːθə(r)] *n (by profession)* escritor(ora) *m,f; (of a book)* autor(a) *m,f*

authoritarian [ɔːθɒrɪ'teərɪən] *n & adj* autoritario(a) *m,f*

authoritative [ɔː'θɒrɪtətɪv] *adj* (**a**) *(manner, voice, person)* autoritario(a) (**b**) *(study, source)* autorizado(a)

authoritatively [ɔː'θɒrɪtətɪvlɪ] *adv (reliably)* con autoridad, con dominio

authority [ɔː'θɒrɪtɪ] *n* (**a**) *(power)* autoridad *f;* **the authorities** las autoridades; **I'd like to speak to someone in a.** quisiera hablar con el responsable; **to have an air of a.** mostrar seguridad *or* aplomo (**b**) *(authorization)* autorización *f;* **to give sb a. to do sth** autorizar a alguien a hacer algo; **he did it on his own a.** lo hizo bajo su responsabilidad (**c**) *(expert)* autoridad *f;* **to be an a. on sth** ser una autoridad en algo; **to have it on good a.** saberlo de buena tinta

authorization [ɔːθəraɪ'zeɪʃən] *n* autorización *f*

authorize ['ɔːθəraɪz] *vt* autorizar; **to a. sb to do sth** autorizar a alguien a hacer algo

authorized ['ɔːθəraɪzd] *adj* **a. dealer** distribuidor *m* autorizado

autism ['ɔːtɪzəm] *n* autismo *m*

autistic [ɔː'tɪstɪk] *adj* autista

auto ['ɔːtəʊ] *(pl* **autos**) *n* automóvil *m, Esp* coche *m, Am* carro *m, RP* auto *m*

auto- ['ɔːtəʊ] *prefix* auto-

autobiographic(al) [ɔːtəʊbaɪə'græfɪk(əl)] *adj* autobiográfico(a)

autobiography [ɔːtəʊbaɪ'ɒgrəfɪ] *n* autobiografía *f*

autocracy [ɔː'tɒkrəsɪ] *n* autocracia *f*

autocrat ['ɔːtəkræt] *n* autócrata *mf*

autocratic [ɔːtə'krætɪk] *adj* autocrático(a)

autodialer ['ɔːtəʊdaɪələ(r)] *n* (dispositivo *m* de) marcación *f* automática

autofocus ['ɔːtəʊfəʊkəs] *n* autofocus *m*, autofoco *m*

autograph ['ɔ:təgrɑ:f] **1** n autógrafo m; **a. album** álbum m de autógrafos
2 vt autografiar, firmar

automat ['ɔ:təmæt] n = restaurante en el que la comida se obtiene de máquinas expendedoras

automata pl of **automaton**

automate ['ɔ:təmeɪt] vt automatizar

automated teller machine ['ɔ:təmeɪtɪd'telərməʃi:n], **automatic teller machine** [ɔ:tə'mætɪk'telərməʃi:n] n cajero m automático

automatic [ɔ:tə'mætɪk] **1** n (car) Esp coche m or Am carro m or RP auto m (con cambio) automático; (pistol) pistola f automática; (washing machine) lavadora f (automática)
2 adj automático(a); Comptr **a. data processing** proceso m or procesamiento m automático de datos; Av **a. pilot** piloto m automático; Fig **to be on a. pilot** tener puesto el piloto automático

automatically [ɔ:tə'mætɪklɪ] adv automáticamente

automation [ɔ:tə'meɪʃən] n automatización f

automaton [ɔ:'tɒmətən] (pl **automata** [ɔ:'tɒmətə]) n autómata m

automobile ['ɔ:təməubi:l] n automóvil m, Esp coche m, Am carro m, RP auto m; **the a. industry** la industria automovilística or del automóvil

autonomous [ɔ:'tɒnəməs] adj autónomo(a)

autonomy [ɔ:'tɒnəmɪ] n autonomía f

autopsy ['ɔ:tɒpsɪ] n autopsia f

auto-save ['ɔ:təuseɪv] Comptr **1** n autoguardado m
2 vt guardar automáticamente

autumn ['ɔ:təm] n otoño m; **in (the) a.** en otoño

autumnal [ɔ:'tʌmnəl] adj otoñal

auxiliary [ɔ:g'zɪl(ɪ)ərɪ] **1** n (**a**) (person) auxiliar mf (**b**) **a. (verb)** (verbo m) auxiliar m
2 adj auxiliar

avail [ə'veɪl] **1** n **of no a.** (not useful) inútil; **to no a.** (in vain) en vano
2 vt **to a. oneself of sth** aprovechar algo

availability [əveɪlə'bɪlɪtɪ] n disponibilidad f

available [ə'veɪləbəl] adj (information, services, products) disponible; (person) disponible, libre; **to be a.** (person) estar disponible or libre; **tickets are still a.** todavía quedan entradas or Am boletos; **money is a. for...** hay dinero para...

avalanche ['ævəlɑ:ntʃ] n also Fig avalancha f

avant-garde [ævɒŋ'gɑ:d] adj vanguardista

avarice ['ævərɪs] n avaricia f

Ave (abbr **Avenue**) Avda., avenida f

avenge [ə'vendʒ] vt (person, crime) vengar; **to a. oneself on sb** vengarse de alguien

avenger [ə'vendʒə(r)] n vengador(ora) m,f

avenue ['ævɪnju:] n avenida f; Fig **an a. to success/fame** un camino hacia el éxito/la fama

aver [ə'vɜ:(r)] (pt & pp **averred**) vt Formal aseverar

average ['ævərɪdʒ] **1** n promedio m, media f; **on a.** de media, como promedio; **above/below a.** por encima/debajo del promedio or de la media
2 adj (**a**) (mean, typical) medio(a); **the a. Englishman** el inglés medio (**b**) (unexceptional) regular
3 vt alcanzar una media or un promedio de; **to a. eight hours work a day** trabajar un promedio de ocho horas diarias

▶**average out** vi **my expenses a. out at $400 per month** tengo una media de gastos de 400 dólares al mes

averse [ə'vɜ:s] adj reacio(a) (**to** a); **to be a. to sth** ser reacio a algo; **he is not a. to the occasional glass of wine** no le hace ascos a un vino de vez en cuando

aversion [ə'vɜ:ʃən] n (feeling) aversión f; **to have an a. to sth/sb** sentir aversión por algo/alguien; **a. therapy** terapia f de aversión

avert [ə'vɜ:t] vt (**a**) (turn away) (eyes, thoughts) apartar, desviar (**b**) (prevent) (misfortune, accident) evitar, impedir

aviary ['eɪvɪərɪ] n pajarera f

aviation [eɪvɪ'eɪʃən] n aviación f

avid ['ævɪd] adj ávido(a) (**for** de)

avidly ['ævɪdlɪ] adv ávidamente

avocado [ævə'kɑ:dəu] (pl **avocados**) n aguacate m, Andes, CSur palta f

avoid [ə'vɔɪd] vt (person, thing) evitar; (punishment, danger, question) evitar, eludir; **to a. doing sth** evitar hacer algo; **to a. sth/sb like the plague** huir de algo/alguien como de la peste

avoidable [ə'vɔɪdəbəl] adj evitable

avowed [ə'vaud] adj declarado(a)

AWACS ['eɪwæks] n Mil (abbr **Airborne Warning and Control System**) AWACS m, = sistema de control y alarma aéreo

await [ə'weɪt] vt esperar, Esp aguardar; **a nasty surprise awaited her** le esperaba una desagradable sorpresa; Law **to be awaiting trial** estar en espera de juicio

awake [ə'weɪk] **1** adj **to be a.** estar despierto(a); **he lay a. for hours** permaneció despierto en la cama durante horas; **the coffee kept her a.** el café la mantuvo despierta; Fig **he was a. to the danger** era consciente del peligro
2 vt (pt awaked or awoke [ə'wəuk], pp awaked or awoke or awoken [ə'wəukən]) despertar
3 vi despertarse

awaken [ə'weɪkən] **1** vt despertar
2 vi despertarse

awakening [ə'weɪkənɪŋ] n despertar m

award [ə'wɔ:d] **1** n (prize) premio m; Law indemnización f
2 vt (prize, contract, damages) otorgar, conceder

award-winner [ə'wɔ:dwɪnə(r)] n (person) galardonado(a) m,f; (movie, book) obra f galardonada or premiada

award-winning [ə'wɔ:dwɪnɪŋ] adj premiado(a)

aware [ə'weə(r)] adj **to be a. of** ser consciente de; **to be a. that...** ser consciente de que...; **not that I am a. of** no, que yo sepa; **as far as I'm a.** por lo que yo sé; **to become a. of** darse cuenta de; **environmentally a.** preocupado(a) por los temas del medio ambiente

awareness [ə'weənɪs] n conciencia f (**of** de)

awash [ə'wɒʃ] adj **to be a. (with)** estar inundado(a) (de)

away [ə'weɪ] adv (**a**) (with distance) **a long way a.**, **far a.** muy lejos; **it's 10 miles a.** está a 10 millas; **to keep a. from sth/sb** mantenerse alejado(a) de algo/alguien; **to go a.** marcharse, irse; **go a.!** ¡vete!; **to put sth a.** recoger or guardar algo; **to take sth a. from sb** quitarle algo a alguien; **to stand a. from sth** mantenerse alejado(a) de algo; **to turn a.** apartar or desviar la mirada (**b**) (not at school, work) **to be a.** estar fuera (**c**) (in time) **right a.** inmediatamente; **Christmas is only two weeks a.** sólo quedan dos semanas para la Navidad

awe [ɔ:] n sobrecogimiento m, temor m; **to be in a. of sth/sb** estar intimidado(a) ante algo/alguien

awe-inspiring ['ɔ:ɪnspaɪərɪŋ] adj sobrecogedor(ora)

awesome ['ɔ:səm] adj (incredible) sobrecogedor(ora); Fam (wonderful) alucinante, Andes, RP macanudo(a), Méx padrísimo(a)

awestruck ['ɔ:strʌk] adj sobrecogido(a), impresionado(a)

awful ['ɔ:ful] adj (day, death, weather) horrible, espantoso(a); Fam **an a. lot** muchísimo, un montón; **an a. lot of people** un montón de gente, Am salvo RP harta gente

awfully ['ɔ:flɪ] adv (**a**) (very badly) fatal, espantosamente (**b**) (very) tremendamente; Fam **I'm a. sorry/glad** lo siento/me alegro muchísimo; **she's an a. good player** es una jugadora buenísima

awhile [ə'waɪl] adv **wait a.** espera un poco

awkward ['ɔ:kwəd] adj (**a**) (clumsy) torpe (**b**) (inconvenient) *(moment, time)* inoportuno(a); *(silence, situation)* incómodo(a), embarazoso(a); *(location, person)* difícil; *Fam* **he's an a. customer** es un tipo difícil

awl [ɔːl] *n* lezna *f*

awning ['ɔːnɪŋ] *n (of shop, over window)* toldo *m*

awoke [ə'wəʊk] *pt, pp of* **awake**

awoken [ə'wəʊkən] *pp of* **awake**

AWOL ['eɪwɒl] *adj Mil (abbr* **absent without leave)** **to be A.** estar ausente sin permiso; *Fig* **to go A.** desaparecer así como así

awry [ə'raɪ] *adv* **to go a.** salir mal

ax, axe [æks] **1** *n* hacha *f*; *Fig* **to have an a. to grind** tratar de barrer para dentro; *Fam* **two hospitals have been given the a.** van a cerrar dos hospitales

2 *vt Fam (jobs, project)* suprimir; *(spending, costs)* recortar

axiom ['æksɪəm] *n* axioma *m*

axiomatic [æksɪə'mætɪk] *adj* axiomático(a), incontrovertible

axis ['æksɪs] *(pl* **axes** ['æksiːz]) *n Math* eje *m*; *Hist* **the A. powers** las potencias del Eje

axle ['æksəl] *n* eje *m*

azalea [ə'zeɪlɪə] *n* azalea *f*

Azerbaijan [æzəbaɪ'dʒɑːn] *n* Azerbaiyán

Azerbaijani [æzəbaɪ'dʒɑːnɪ], **Azeri** [ə'zeərɪ] *n & adj* azerbaiyano(a) *m,f*

Azores [ə'zɔːz] *npl* **the A.** las Azores

Aztec ['æztek] *n & adj* azteca *mf*

azure ['eɪʒə(r)] *n & adj* azul *m* celeste, celeste *m*

B

B, b [biː] *n* (**a**) *(letter)* B, b *f*; **B-movie** película *f* de serie B (**b**) *Mus* si *m* (**c**) *Sch (grade)* notable *m*; **to get a B** sacar un notable

b *(abbr* **born**) nacido(a)

BA [biːˈeɪ] *n Univ (abbr* **Bachelor of Arts**) *(qualification)* licenciatura *f* en Filosofía y Letras; *(person)* licenciado(a) *m,f* en Filosofía y Letras

baa [bɑː] **1** *n* balido *m*
   2 *vi (pt & pp* **baaed** *or* **baa'd** [bɑːd]) balar

babble [ˈbæbəl] **1** *n (of voices)* parloteo *m*
   2 *vi* (**a**) *(baby)* balbucear; *(adult)* farfullar; **to b. away** *or* **on (about sth)** parlotear (sobre algo) (**b**) *(water)* murmurar

babbling [ˈbæblɪŋ] *adj (stream)* murmurante, susurrante

babe [beɪb] *n* (**a**) *Literary (child)* bebé *m, Andes* guagua *mf, RP* nene(a) *m,f*; **a b. in arms** un niño de pecho (**b**) *Fam (woman)* nena *f*, bombón *m*

baboon [bəˈbuːn] *n* babuino *m*, papión *m*

baby [ˈbeɪbɪ] **1** *n* (**a**) *(infant)* bebé *m, Andes* guagua *mf, RP* nene(a) *m,f*; **b. brother** hermanito *m*; **b. sister** hermanita *f*; **b. boom** explosión *f* de la natalidad; **b. carriage** cochecito *m* de niño; **b. doll** *(toy)* muñeca *f*; **b. grand** *(piano)* piano *m* de media cola; **b. snatcher** *(woman)* ladrona *f* de bebés; **b. talk** habla *f* infantil; **b. wipes** toallitas *fpl* húmedas (**b**) *(idioms)* **we have to avoid throwing the b. out with the bathwater** tenemos que evitar dañar lo bueno al eliminar lo malo; **to leave sb holding the b.** endilgar el muerto a alguien
   2 *vt* mimar, tratar como a un bebé

baby-face(d) [ˈbeɪbɪfeɪs(t)] *adj* con cara de niño

Babygro® [ˈbeɪbɪɡrəʊ] *(pl* **Babygros**) *n* pelele *m*

babyhood [ˈbeɪbɪhʊd] *n* primera infancia *f*

babyish [ˈbeɪbɪʃ] *adj Pej* infantil

Babylon [ˈbæbɪlən] *n* Babilonia

babysit [ˈbeɪbɪsɪt] *(pt & pp* **babysat** [ˈbeɪbɪsæt]) cuidar a niños, hacer de *Esp* canguro *or Am* babysitter; **to b. for sb** cuidar a los niños de alguien

babysitter [ˈbeɪbɪsɪtə(r)] *n Esp* canguro *mf, Am* babysitter *mf*

baby-walker [ˈbeɪbɪwɔːkə(r)] *n* andador *m*, tacataca *m*

baccalaureate [bækəˈlɔːrɪət] *n (at school)* bachillerato *m*

bachelor [ˈbætʃələ(r)] *n* soltero *m*; **b. apartment** apartamento *m or Esp* piso *m or Am* departamento *m* de soltero; *Univ* **B. of Arts** *(qualification)* licenciatura *f* en Filosofía y Letras; *(person)* licenciado(a) *m,f* en Filosofía y Letras; **b. party** despedida *f* de soltero; *Univ* **B. of Science** *(qualification)* licenciatura *f* en Ciencias; *(person)* licenciado(a) *m,f* en Ciencias

bacillus [bəˈsɪləs] *(pl* **bacilli** [bəˈsɪlaɪ]) *n Biol* bacilo *m*

back [bæk] **1** *n* (**a**) *(of person)* espalda *f*; *(of animal)* lomo *m*; *also Fig* **to turn one's b. on sb** volver la espalda a alguien; **to sit/ stand with one's b. to sth/sb** dar la espalda a algo/alguien; **b. pain** dolor *m* de espalda; **to have b. problems** tener problemas de espalda

   (**b**) *(of page, hand, book)* dorso *m*; *(of chair)* respaldo *m*; *(of house, car)* parte *f* trasera *or* de atrás; *(of room)* fondo *m*; **at the b. of the book** al final del libro; **the b. of the neck** la nuca, el cogote; **at the b. (of)** *(behind)* en la parte de atrás (de), detrás

(de); *(to the rear of)* al fondo (de); **in b. of** *(behind)* en la parte de atrás (de), detrás (de); *(to the rear of)* al fondo (de); **in b.** *(of car)* atrás, en el asiento trasero; **to have sth at the b. of one's mind** tener algo en la cabeza; **he knows London like the b. of his hand** conoce Londres como la palma de la mano; *Fam* **in the b. of beyond** en el quinto pino, *Chile* en la punta del cerro, *Col* en la Patagonia, *RP* donde el diablo perdió el poncho

   (**c**) *(in soccer, rugby)* **right/left b.** defensa *mf*

   (**d**) *(idioms)* **to do sth behind sb's b.** hacer algo a espaldas de alguien; **to be glad to see the b. of sb** alegrarse de perder a alguien de vista; **to have one's b. to the wall** estar contra las cuerdas; **put your b. into it!** ¡ponte a hacerlo en serio!; **to break the b. of the work** hacer la parte más dura del trabajo; *Fam* **the boss was on my b. all day** el jefe estaba todo el día encima de mí; *Fam* **get off my b.!** ¡déjame en paz!, ¡deja de fastidiarme!; *Fam* **to put** *or* **get sb's b. up** hinchar las narices a alguien

   2 *adj* (**a**) *(in space) (part, wheel)* trasero(a), de atrás; *Fig* **to put sth on the b. burner** dejar algo para más tarde, aparcar algo; **b. door** puerta *f* trasera *or* de atrás; *Fig* **he got it through the b. door** lo consiguió de manera poco ortodoxa; **the b. page** *(of newspaper)* la contraportada; **b. road** carretera *f* secundaria; **b. room** cuarto *m* del fondo, habitación *f* trasera; *Fig* **to take a b. seat** quedarse en segundo plano

   (**b**) *(in time)* **b. number** número *m* atrasado; **b. pay** atrasos *mpl*, salario *m* atrasado; **b. rent** alquiler *m or Am* renta *f* pendiente de pago, atrasos *mpl*

   3 *adv* (**a**) *(in space)* atrás; **stand b.!** ¡atrás!; **to step b.** dar un paso atrás; **3 miles b.** 3 millas atrás

   (**b**) *(in return, retaliation)* **to get one's own b. (on sb)** tomarse la revancha (contra alguien), desquitarse (de alguien); **to get b. at sb** vengarse de alguien; **to call sb b.** llamar más tarde a alguien; **if you kick me I'll kick you b.** si me pegas una patada, te la devolveré

   (**c**) *(to original starting point)* **to come/go b.** volver, *Am salvo RP* regresarse; **when will she be b.?** ¿cuándo estará de vuelta?; **b. in Britain** en Gran Bretaña; **a few pages b.** unas cuantas páginas atrás

   (**d**) *(in time)* **a few years b.** hace unos cuantos años; **b. when...** cuando..., en el tiempo en que...; **b. in 1982** allá por 1982; **as far b. as 1914** ya en 1914

   4 *vt* (**a**) *(support)* respaldar, apoyar; *(financially)* financiar, dar respaldo financiero a (**b**) *(bet on)* apostar por (**c**) *(move backward)* mover hacia atrás; **to b. one's car into the garage** entrar en el garaje (dando) marcha atrás; **he backed his car into a lamppost** dio marcha atrás y chocó contra una farola

   5 *vi (move backward)* retroceder, ir hacia atrás; *(car, driver)* recular, dar marcha atrás

▸ **back away** *vi* alejarse (retrocediendo) (**from** de)

▸ **back down** *vi* echarse atrás

▸ **back off** *vi (move back)* echarse atrás; *Fig* **b. off!** *(leave me alone)* ¡déjame en paz!

▶**back on to** *vt insep* dar por la parte de atrás a; **the house backs on to the park** la parte trasera de la casa da al parque

▶**back out** *vi* (a) *(move backward)* salir de espaldas; *(in car)* salir marcha atrás (b) *(withdraw)* echarse atrás; **to b. out of an agreement** retirarse de un acuerdo

▶**back up 1** *vt sep* (a) *(support)* respaldar (b) *Comptr (file)* hacer una copia de seguridad de

 2 *vi* (a) *(move backward)* retroceder; *(in car)* ir marcha atrás (b) *Comptr* hacer copias de seguridad

backache ['bækeɪk] *n* dolor *m* de espalda

backbiting ['bækbaɪtɪŋ] *n Fam* chismorreo *m*, murmuración *f*, *RP* chusmerío *m*

backbone ['bækbəʊn] *n* columna *f* vertebral, espina *f* dorsal; *Fig* **he's got no b.** no tiene agallas

backbreaking ['bækbreɪkɪŋ] *adj (work)* extenuante, agotador(ora)

backchat ['bæktʃæt] *n Fam* impertinencias *fpl*, insolencias *fpl*

backdate ['bækdeɪt] *vt* **the increase will be backdated to 1 July** el aumento tendrá efecto retroactivo a partir del uno de julio

backdrop ['bækdrɒp] *n Theat* telón *m* de fondo; *Fig* **against a b. of continuing violence** con la violencia como constante telón de fondo

-backed [bækt] *suffix* (a) *(with back)* **a high-b. chair** una silla de respaldo alto; **a broad-b. man** un hombre ancho de hombros *or* de espaldas anchas (b) *(supported by)* **US-b. rebels** rebeldes apoyados por Estados Unidos

backer ['bækə(r)] *n (of political party)* partidario(a) *m,f; Fin* fuente *f* de financiación, apoyo *m* económico

backfire [bæk'faɪə(r)] *vi (car)* petardear; *Fig* **it backfired on them** les salió el tiro por la culata

backflip ['bækflɪp] *n* voltereta *f* hacia atrás

backgammon ['bækgæmən] *n* backgammon *m*

background ['bækgraʊnd] *n* (a) *(in scene, painting, view)* fondo *m*; **in the b.** al fondo, en el fondo; **to stay in the b.** quedarse en segundo plano; **to push sb into the b.** relegar a alguien a un segundo plano; **b. music** música *f* de fondo; **b. noise** ruido *m* de fondo

 (b) *(social)* origen *m*, extracción *f*; *(educational)* formación *f*; *(professional)* experiencia *f*; **he comes from a disadvantaged b.** procede de un entorno desfavorecido; **we need someone with a b. in computers** necesitamos a alguien con conocimientos de informática

 (c) *(circumstances)* antecedentes *mpl*; **against a b. of unrest** en un contexto de disturbios; **give me some b.** *(information)* ponme en contexto; **b. information** información *f*, antecedentes *mpl*

backhand ['bækhænd] *n (in tennis)* revés *m*

backhanded [bæk'hændɪd] *adj* equívoco(a), ambiguo(a); **a b. compliment** un cumplido con doble sentido

backing ['bækɪŋ] *n (support)* apoyo *m*, respaldo *m*; **financial b.** respaldo *m* financiero; **b. vocals** coros *mpl*

backlash ['bæklæʃ] *n (reaction)* reacción *f* violenta

backlit ['bæklɪt] *adj Comptr* retroiluminado(a)

backlog ['bæklɒg] *n* acumulación *f*; **to clear a b.** ponerse al día con el trabajo; **a b. of work** trabajo *m* atrasado *or* acumulado

backpack ['bækpæk] **1** *n* mochila *f*

 2 *vi* viajar con la mochila al hombro; **she backpacked around Europe** recorrió Europa con la mochila al hombro

backpacker ['bækpækə(r)] *n* mochilero(a) *m,f*

back-pedal ['bæk'pedəl] *vi (change mind)* dar marcha atrás, echarse atrás

backrest ['bækrest] *n* respaldo *m*

back-seat driver ['bæksiːt'draɪvə(r)] *n Fam* = pasajero que molesta constantemente al conductor con sus consejos

backside [bæk'saɪd] *n Fam* trasero *m*

backslapping ['bækslæpɪŋ] *n (self-congratulation)* felicitaciones *fpl* efusivas

backslash ['bækslæʃ] *n Comptr* barra *f* invertida

backsliding ['bækslaɪdɪŋ] *n Fam* recaída *f*, reincidencia *f*

backspace ['bækspeɪs] *n Comptr* (tecla *f* de) retroceso *m*

backstage [bæk'steɪdʒ] *adv also Fig* entre bastidores; **to go b. after the performance** ir a los camerinos después de la representación

backstairs [bæk'steəz] *n* escalera *f* de servicio

backstitch ['bækstɪtʃ] *n (in sewing)* pespunte *m*

backstreet ['bækstriːt] *n* callejuela *f*; **the backstreets** *(of city)* las zonas deprimidas; **b. abortion** aborto *m* clandestino

backstroke ['bækstrəʊk] *n (in swimming)* espalda *f*; **to do** *or* **swim (the) b.** nadar a espalda

backtalk ['bæktɔːk] *n Fam* impertinencias *fpl*, insolencias *fpl*

back-to-back [bæktə'bæk] **1** *adj (in time)* **b. meetings** reuniones *fpl* seguidas

 2 *adv* (a) *(physically)* espalda con espalda (b) *(consecutively)* sucesivamente; **to watch two films b.** ver dos películas seguidas

backtrack ['bæktræk] *vi* (a) *(retrace one's steps)* volver atrás, retroceder; **we backtracked to the main road** recorrimos el camino de vuelta hasta la carretera principal (b) *(renege)* retractarse, volverse atrás; **to b. on a promise** incumplir una promesa; **to b. on a decision** retractarse de una decisión

backup ['bækʌp] *n* (a) *(support)* apoyo *m*, respaldo *m*; **to call for b.** pedir refuerzos; **the expedition had no technical b.** la expedición no contaba con medios técnicos; **b. system** sistema *m* de apoyo; **b. team** equipo *m* técnico (b) *Comptr* **b. copy/file** copia *f* de seguridad; **b. disk** disquete *m* con la copia de seguridad (c) *Aut* caravana *f*

backward ['bækwəd] **1** *adj* (a) *(direction)* hacia atrás; **she left without a b. glance** partió sin mirar atrás; *Fig* **a b. step** un paso atrás (b) *(retarded) (child, country)* atrasado(a)

 2 *adv* hacia atrás; **to walk b. and forward** caminar de un lado para otro; *Fig* **a step b.** un paso atrás; *Fig* **to bend** *or* **lean over b. to help** hacer todo lo posible por ayudar; *Fig* **to know sth b.** conocer algo de pe a pa

backwardness ['bækwədnɪs] *n (of child, country)* atraso *m*

backwards ['bækwədz] *adv* = **backward**

backwash ['bækwɒʃ] *n (of boat)* estela *f*; *Fig* repercusiones *fpl*

backwater ['bækwɔːtə(r)] *n* (a) *(of river)* remanso *m*, aguas *fpl* estancadas (b) *(isolated place)* zona *f* estancada, lugar *m* atrasado; **Jibrovia is a cultural b.** Jibrovia está muy atrasado culturalmente

backyard ['bækjɑːd] *n* jardín *m* trasero

bacon ['beɪkən] *n* panceta *f*, *Méx* tocino *m*, *Esp* bacon *m*, *Esp* beicon *m*; *Fam* **to save sb's b.** salvarle el pellejo a alguien; *Fam* **to bring home the b.** *(succeed)* triunfar; *(earn wages)* ganar el pan

bacteria [bæk'tɪərɪə] *npl* bacterias *fpl*

bacterial [bæk'tɪərɪəl] *adj* bacteriano(a)

bacteriological [bæktɪərɪə'lɒdʒɪkəl] *adj* bacteriológico(a)

bacteriology [bæktɪərɪ'ɒlədʒɪ] *n* bacteriología *f*

bad [bæd] *(comparative* **worse** [wɜːs], *superlative* **worst** [wɜːst])

 1 *adj* (a) *(of poor quality)* malo(a); **it's not b.** *(fair)* no está mal; *(good)* no está nada mal; **he's b. at English** se le da mal el inglés; **I'm really b. at cooking** soy un desastre cocinando; **things are going from b. to worse** las cosas van de mal en peor; **it was a b. time to leave** era un mal momento para irse; **to have a b. time** pasarlo mal; **b. check** cheque *m* sin fondos; *Fin* **b. debt** deuda *f* incobrable; **in b. faith** de mala fe; **b. feeling** animadversión *f*; **it was a b. idea to invite them** no fue una buena idea invitarles; **to give sth up as a b. job** dejar algo por imposible; **to be a b. loser** ser un mal perdedor; **b. luck** mala suerte *f*

 (b) *(unpleasant)* malo(a); **b. blood** *(mutual resentment)* mala sangre *f*; **there's b. blood between them** existe una gran hostilidad entre ellos; **to get into sb's b. books** entrar en la lista negra de alguien; **b. manners** mala educación *f*, malos modales *mpl*; **it's b. manners to…** es de mala educación…; **to be in a b. mood** estar de mal humor; *Fig* **she's b. news** no te traerá más que problemas

(**c**) *(unfortunate)* **it's (really) too b.!, that's too b.!** ¡es una (verdadera) pena!; **to have a b. effect on sth** perjudicar algo; **he'll come to a b. end** terminará mal

(**d**) *(not healthy)* enfermo(a); **he's got a b. back/heart** está mal de la espalda/del corazón; **smoking/alcohol is b. for you** fumar/el alcohol es perjudicial para la salud; **to be in a b. way** estar muy mal

(**e**) *(wicked)* *(person, behavior)* malo(a); **to use b. language** decir palabrotas; **b. word** palabrota *f*

(**f**) *(serious)* *(mistake, illness, accident)* grave; *(pain, headache)* fuerte

(**g**) *(rotten)* malo(a), podrido(a); **to be b.** estar malo(a) or podrido(a); **to go b.** estropearse, echarse a perder; *Fig* **a b. apple** una manzana podrida

(**h**) *(guilty)* **to feel b. about sth** sentirse mal por algo

2 *adv (badly)* **he treats me b.** me trata muy mal; *Fam* **he's got it b. (for her)** *(he's in love)* está enamoradísimo (de ella)

baddie, baddy ['bædɪ] *n Fam (in movie)* **the b.** el malo (de la película); **the goodies and the baddies** *(in conflict, war)* los buenos y los malos

bade [bæd, beɪd] *pt of* **bid**

badge [bædʒ] *n (bearing coat of arms, logo) also Fig* insignia *f*; *(round, made of metal)* chapa *f*; *(pin)* pin *m*

badger ['bædʒə(r)] **1** *n (animal)* tejón *m*

2 *vt* acosar, importunar; **to b. sb into doing sth** dar la lata a alguien para que haga algo; **she's always badgering me with questions** siempre me está acosando con preguntas

bad-looking [bæd'lʊkɪŋ] *adj* **he's not b.** es bastante guapo

badly ['bædlɪ] *adv (comparative* **worse** [wɜːs], *superlative* **worst** [wɜːst]) (**a**) *(not well)* mal; **to do b.** hacerlo mal; **he didn't do b.** *(in contest)* le fue (bastante) bien; **he took it very b.** se lo tomó muy mal; **we are b. off for money/ time** nos falta dinero/tiempo; **to get on b. (with sb)** llevarse mal (con alguien); **b. dressed** mal vestido(a) (**b**) *(seriously)* gravemente; **to be b. beaten** recibir una buena paliza; **b. damaged** gravemente dañado(a) (**c**) *(greatly)* mucho; **to want sth b.** desear algo mucho; **to be b. in need of sth** necesitar algo urgentemente

bad-mannered [bæd'mænəd] *adj* maleducado(a)

badminton ['bædmɪntən] *n* bádminton *m*

bad-mouth ['bædmaʊθ] *vt Fam* hablar mal de

badness ['bædnɪs] *n* (**a**) *(poor quality)* mala calidad *f* (**b**) *(wickedness)* maldad *f*

bad-tempered [bæd'tempəd] *adj (remark)* malhumorado(a); **to be b.** *(person) (by nature)* tener mal carácter; *(temporarily)* estar de mal humor; **he made a b. apology** se excusó malhumorado

BA Ed [beɪ'ed] *n Univ (abbr* **Bachelor of Arts in Education**) *(qualification)* licenciatura *f* en ciencias de la educación; *(person)* licenciado(a) *m,f* en ciencias de la educación

baffle ['bæfəl] *vt* (**a**) *(confuse)* desconcertar; **to be baffled** estar desconcertado(a) or atónito(a); **I'm baffled as to why she did it** no logro entender por qué lo hizo (**b**) *(foil) (plot, attempt)* frustrar

baffling ['bæfəlɪŋ] *adj* desconcertante, incomprensible

bag [bæg] **1** *n* (**a**) *(of paper, plastic)* bolsa *f*; *(handbag)* bolso *m*, *Andes, RP* cartera *f*, *Méx* bolsa *f*; **to have bags under one's eyes** tener ojeras; *Fam* **to be a b. of bones** estar esquelético(a) or *Esp* en los huesos; *Fig* **to be left holding the b.** pagar los platos rotos; *Fig* **it's in the b.** *(deal, victory)* lo tenemos en el bote; *Fig* **he let the secret out of the b.** descubrió el secreto; **b. snatcher** tironero(a) *m,f* (**b**) *Fam* **bags of** *(lots)* un montón de; **there's bags of room** hay muchísimo sitio

2 *vt (pt & pp* **bagged**) (**a**) *(put in bag)* guardar en una bolsa, embolsar (**b**) *(in hunting)* cobrar

bagel ['beɪgəl] *n* = tipo de rosca de pan compacto de origen judío

baggage ['bægɪdʒ] *n* equipaje *m*; **b. allowance** equipaje *m* permitido; **b. handler** mozo(a) *m,f* de equipajes; **b. reclaim** recogida *f* de equipajes; **b. room** consigna *f*

baggy ['bægɪ] *adj (garment)* suelto(a), holgado(a)

Baghdad [bæg'dæd] *n* Bagdad

bagpipes ['bægpaɪps] *npl* gaita *f*

baguette [bæ'get] *n* barra *f* de pan

bah [bɑː] *exclam* ¡bah!

Bahamas [bə'hɑːməz] *npl* **the B.** las Bahamas

Bahrain [bɑː'reɪn] *n* Bahrein

Bahraini [bɑː'reɪnɪ] *n & adj* bahreiní *mf*

bail [beɪl] *n Law (guarantee)* fianza *f*; **on b.** bajo fianza; **to release sb on b.** poner a alguien en libertad bajo fianza; **to grant b.** conceder la libertad bajo fianza; **to post b. for sb** pagar la fianza de alguien

▸**bail out** *vt sep Law* **to b. sb out** pagar la fianza de alguien; *Fig* **your parents won't always be there to b. you out!** ¡tus padres no van a estar siempre ahí para sacarte las castañas del fuego!; **to b. a company out** sacar a una empresa del apuro

bailiff ['beɪlɪf] *n Law* alguacil *mf*

bait [beɪt] **1** *n (for fish)* cebo *m*; *Fig* cebo *m*, anzuelo *m*; *Fig* **to rise to the b.** morder el anzuelo; *Fig* **to swallow** or **take the b.** morder el anzuelo, picar

2 *vt* (**a**) *(torment)* hostigar, atormentar (**b**) *(attach bait to)* cebar

baize [beɪz] *n* tapete *m*

bake [beɪk] **1** *vt (bread, cake)* cocer (al horno), hornear; *(potatoes)* asar

2 *vi (food)* cocerse

baked [beɪkt] *adj* **b. beans** alubias *fpl* con tomate or *Méx* jitomate; **b. potato** = patata asada con piel que se suele comer con un relleno

baker ['beɪkə(r)] *n* panadero(a) *m,f*; **b.'s (shop)** panadería *f*; **b.'s dozen** docena *f* de fraile *(trece)*

bakery ['beɪkərɪ] *n* panadería *f*

baking ['beɪkɪŋ] **1** *n* **to do the b.** *(bread)* cocer el pan; *(cakes)* hacer pasteles; **b. pan** molde *m* para hornear; **b. powder** levadura *f* (en polvo); **b. sheet** or **tray** placa *f* or bandeja *f* de hornear; **b. soda** bicarbonato *m* sódico

2 *adj Fam* **it's b. (hot)** hace un calor achicharrante or *RP* calcinante; **I'm b. (hot)** ¡me estoy asando!, ¡estoy asado(a)!

balaclava [bælə'klɑːvə] *n* pasamontañas *m inv*

balance ['bæləns] **1** *n* (**a**) *(equilibrium)* equilibrio *m*; **to keep/ lose one's b.** mantener/perder el equilibrio; **to throw sb off b.** hacer que alguien pierda el equilibrio; *Fig* **to catch sb off b.** *Esp* pillar or *Esp* coger or *Am* agarrar a alguien desprevenido(a); **the b. of power** el equilibrio de fuerzas; **on b.** en conjunto; **to strike a b.** establecer un equilibrio (**b**) *(of bank account)* saldo *m*; *Econ* **b. of trade/payments** balanza *f* comercial/de pagos; **b. sheet** balance *m* (**c**) *(for weighing)* balanza *f*; *Fig* **to hang** or **be in the b.** *(decision, result)* estar en el aire

2 *vt (object)* poner en equilibrio; **she balanced the basket on her head** se puso la cesta en equilibrio sobre la cabeza; **he sought to b. the claims of the two parties** trató de equilibrar las reivindicaciones de ambos bandos; *Fin* **to b. the books** hacer que cuadren las cuentas

3 *vi* (**a**) *(physically)* estar or mantenerse en equilibrio (**b**) *Fin* cuadrar; **she couldn't get the accounts to b.** no consiguió que le cuadraran las cuentas

balanced ['bælənst] *adj (unbiased)* objetivo(a), imparcial; **b. diet** dieta *f* equilibrada

balancing act ['bælənsɪŋ'ækt] *n* **to do a political b.** hacer malabarismos en política

balcony ['bælkənɪ] *n (small)* balcón *m; (larger)* terraza *f; (in theater)* anfiteatro *m*

bald [bɔːld] *adj* **(a)** *(person)* calvo(a); *(tire)* desgastado(a); **to go b.** quedarse calvo(a); *Fam* **as b. as a coot** con la cabeza monda y lironda; **b. eagle** águila *f* calva; **b. patch** calva *f*, claro *m* **(b)** *(truth)* simple, llano(a); **the report contained a b. statement of the facts** el informe *or Am* reporte contenía una mera descripción de los hechos

balderdash ['bɔːldədæʃ] *n Fam* bobadas *fpl*, tonterías *fpl*; **b.!** ¡bobadas!; **to talk b.** decir bobadas

bald-faced ['bɔːldfeɪst] *adj* descarado(a)

bald-headed ['bɔːld'hedɪd] *adj* calvo(a)

balding ['bɔːldɪŋ] *adj* medio calvo(a)

baldly ['bɔːldlɪ] *adv* francamente, llanamente

baldness ['bɔːldnɪs] *n* **(a)** *(of person)* calvicie *f* **(b)** *(of statement, demand)* franqueza *f*

bale [beɪl] *n (of cloth)* fardo *m*, bala *f; (of hay)* paca *f*, bala *f*

►**bale out** *vi (pilot)* tirarse *or* lanzarse en paracaídas; *(from difficult situation)* desentenderse, lavarse las manos

Balearic [bælɪ'ærɪk] **1** *n* **the Balearics** las (Islas) Baleares
2 *adj* **the B. Islands** las (Islas) Baleares

baleful ['beɪlfʊl] *adj* maligno(a); **she gave me a b. stare** me lanzó una mirada asesina

Bali ['bɑːlɪ] *n* Bali

Balinese [bælɪ'niːz] *adj* balinés(esa)

balk, baulk [bɔːk] **1** *vt (frustrate, defeat)* frustrar, hacer fracasar
2 *vi* **to b. at sth** *(person)* mostrarse reticente *or* echarse atrás ante algo; **he balked at paying such a price** se mostraba reticente a pagar un precio tan alto

Balkan ['bɔːlkən] **1** *npl* **the Balkans** los Balcanes
2 *adj* balcánico(a), de los Balcanes

ball¹ [bɔːl] *n* **(a)** *(for tennis, golf)* pelota *f; (of clay, of dough, for billiards)* bola *f; (for rugby, basketball, soccer)* balón *m*, pelota *f;* **to roll sth (up) into a b.** hacer una bola con algo; **a b. of wool** un ovillo de lana; **b. bearing** rodamiento *m or* cojinete *m* de bolas; **b. boy/girl** *(in tennis)* recogepelotas *mf inv*; **b. game** *(in general)* juego *m* de pelota; *(baseball game)* partido *m* de béisbol; *Fig* **that's a whole new b. game** esa es una historia completamente diferente
(b) *(of foot)* **to stand on the balls of one's feet** estar de puntillas
(c) b. cock *or* **valve** *(in plumbing)* flotador *m*
(d) *Vulg* **balls** *(testicles)* huevos *mpl*, cojones *mpl; (nonsense) Esp* gilipolleces *fpl, Am* pendejadas *fpl, RP* boludeces *fpl; (courage)* huevos *mpl*, cojones *mpl; Fig* **to have sb by the balls** tener a alguien cogido *or* agarrado por los huevos
(e) *(idioms)* **to be on the b.** *(alert)* estar despierto(a); *(knowledgeable)* estar muy enterado(a); **to start the b. rolling** poner las cosas en marcha; **the b. is in your court** te toca dar el siguiente paso; **to play b.** *(co-operate)* cooperar

►**ball up** *vt sep very Fam* **he balled up the accounts** armó un cacao *or RP* despelote con las cuentas

ball² *n (party)* baile *m; Fam* **to have a b.** pasárselo en grande; **b. dress** *or* **gown** traje *m* de fiesta

ballad ['bæləd] *n* balada *f*

ball-and-socket joint [bɔːlənd'sɒkɪt'dʒɔɪnt] *n* **(a)** *Tech* junta *f* articulada **(b)** *Med* enartrosis *f inv*

ballast ['bæləst] *n* **(a)** *Naut* lastre *m* **(b)** *Rail* balasto *m*

ballerina [bælə'riːnə] *n* bailarina *f*; **prima b.** primera bailarina *f*

ballet ['bæleɪ] *n* ballet *m*; **b. dancer** bailarín(ina) *m,f*; **b. shoe** zapatilla *f* de ballet

ballistic [bə'lɪstɪk] *adj (missile)* balístico(a); *Fam Fig* **to go b.** ponerse hecho(a) una furia

ballistics [bə'lɪstɪks] *n* balística *f*

balloon [bə'luːn] **1** *n* **(a)** *(for party, travel)* globo *m; Fam Fig* **when the b. goes up** cuando se arme la gorda **(b)** *(in cartoon)* bocadillo *m*
2 *vi (swell)* hincharse como un globo

ballooning [bə'luːnɪŋ] *n* **to go b.** montar en globo

balloonist [bə'luːnɪst] *n* piloto *mf* de aerostación

ballot ['bælət] **1** *n (process)* votación *f; (paper)* voto *m*; **to hold a b.** celebrar una votación; **to put sth to a b.** someter algo a votación; **b. box** urna *f*; **this matter should be decided at the b. box** este asunto habrá que decidirlo en las urnas; **b. paper** papeleta *f* (de voto), *Chile, Méx* voto *m, Col* tarjetón *m, RP* boleta *f*
2 *vt Pol* consultar por votación

ballpark ['bɔːlpɑːk] **1** *n* campo *m* de béisbol
2 *adj* **a b. figure** una cifra aproximada

ballpoint ['bɔːlpɔɪnt] *n* **b. (pen)** bolígrafo *m, Carib, Méx* pluma *f, Col, Ecuad* esferográfico *m, CSur* lapicera *f*

ballroom ['bɔːlruːm] *n* salón *m* de baile; **b. dancing** baile *m* de salón

ballsy ['bɔːlzɪ] *n very Fam* con (muchos) huevos

ball-up ['bɔːlʌp] *n very Fam* **he made a total b. of the timetable** armó un cacao *or RP* despelote con el horario

ballyhoo [bælɪ'huː] *n Fam* alboroto *m, Esp* escandalera *f, RP* batifondo *m*

balm [bɑːm] *n* bálsamo *m*

balmy ['bɑːmɪ] *adj (weather)* cálido(a), suave

baloney [bə'ləʊnɪ] *n Fam (nonsense)* tonterías *fpl*, bobadas *fpl*

balsa ['bɔːlsə] *n* **b. (wood)** madera *f* de balsa

balsam ['bɔːlsəm] *n* bálsamo *m*

Baltic ['bɔːltɪk] **1** *n* **the B.** el (mar) Báltico
2 *adj* báltico(a); **the B. Sea** el mar Báltico

balustrade [bælə'streɪd] *n* balaustrada *f*

bamboo [bæm'buː] *n* bambú *m*; **b. shoots** brotes *mpl* de bambú

bamboozle [bæm'buːzəl] *vt Fam (confuse)* embarullar; *(trick)* engatusar

ban [bæn] **1** *n* prohibición *f*; **to impose a b. on sth** prohibir algo
2 *vt (pt & pp banned)* prohibir; **to b. sb from doing sth** prohibir a alguien hacer algo

banal [bə'næl] *adj* banal

banality [bə'nælɪtɪ] *n* banalidad *f*

banana [bə'nɑːnə] *n* plátano *m, CAm, Col* banano *m, RP* banana *f, Ven* cambur *m; Fam* **to be bananas** *(mad)* estar como una cabra *or Méx* destrompado(a) *or RP* de la nuca; *Fam* **to go bananas** *(angry)* ponerse hecho(a) un basilisco, *CSur* rayarse; *Fam* **b. republic** república *f* bananera; **b. skin** *(of fruit)* piel *f* de plátano *or CAm, Col* banano *or RP* banana *or Ven* cambur; *Fig* **trampa** *f* potencial; **b. split** banana split *m*; **b. tree** platanero *m, Am* bananero *m*

band¹ [bænd] *n* **(a)** *(of metal, cloth)* banda *f*, tira *f; (of color)* raya *f*, franja *f; (on hat)* cinta *f; (on cigar)* vitola *f; (to identify bird)* anilla *f* **(b)** *Rad* banda *f* **(c)** *(of age, ability)* franja *f*, banda *f*

band² *n (of friends)* pandilla *f*, grupo *m; (of robbers)* banda *f; (of pop musicians)* grupo *m; (jazz, brass)* banda *f*

►**band together** *vi* unirse

bandage ['bændɪdʒ] **1** *n (fabric)* venda *f; (on wound, broken arm)* vendaje *m*, venda *f*
2 *vt* vendar; **the nurse bandaged his arm** la enfermera le vendó el brazo

►**bandage up** *vt sep* vendar

Band-Aid® ['bændeɪd] *n Esp* tirita® *f, Am* curita *f*

bandit ['bændɪt] *n* bandolero *m*, bandido *m*

bandleader ['bændliːdə(r)] *n* líder *mf (de un grupo musical)*

bandmaster ['bændmɑːstə(r)] *n Mus* director *m (de una banda)*

bandsman ['bændzmən] *n Mus* músico *m (de banda)*

bandstand ['bændstænd] *n* quiosco *m* de música

bandwagon ['bændwægən] *n Fam* **to jump on the b.** subirse al carro

bandwidth ['bændwɪdθ] *n Comptr* ancho *m* de banda

bandy[1] ['bændɪ] *adj (legs)* arqueado(a) *(hacia afuera)*

bandy[2] *vt (words, insults)* intercambiar, cambiar; **his name is being bandied about** se está barajando su nombre

bandy-legged [bændɪ'leg(ɪ)d] *adj* estevado(a)

bane [beɪn] *n* cruz *f*, perdición *f*; **he's the b. of my life** es mi cruz, es mi ruina

bang [bæŋ] **1** *n* **(a)** *(noise)* golpe *m*; *(explosion)* explosión *f*; **the door shut with a b.** la puerta se cerró de un portazo **(b)** *(blow)* golpe *m*; **to get a b. on the head** darse un golpe en la cabeza

2 *adv* **(a) to go b.** explotar ruidosamente; *Fam* **b. went my hopes of a quiet weekend** adiós a mi esperado fin de semana tranquilo **(b)** *Fam (exactly)* **b. in the middle** justo en medio; **b. on time** justo a tiempo

3 *exclam (sound of gun)* ¡pum!; *(explosion)* ¡bum!

4 *vt (hit)* golpear; **to b. one's head** golpearse la cabeza

5 *vi (door, window)* batir, dar golpes; **the door banged shut** la puerta se cerró de un portazo; **to b. at** *or* **on the door** aporrear la puerta; **to b. into sth** chocar con algo

▸**bang around, bang about** *vi (make noise) (person)* armar jaleo

Bangkok [bæŋ'kɒk] *n* Bangkok

Bangladesh [bæŋglə'deʃ] *n* Bangladesh

Bangladeshi [bæŋglə'deʃi] *n & adj* bangladesí *mf*

bangle ['bæŋgəl] *n* brazalete *m*, pulsera *f*

bangs [bæŋz] *npl* flequillo *m*, *Am* cerquillo *m (corto)*

banish ['bænɪʃ] *vt (exile)* desterrar; **he banished all thought of her from his mind** se la quitó de la cabeza

banishment ['bænɪʃmənt] *n* destierro *m*

banister ['bænɪstə(r)] *n* barandilla *f*

banjo ['bændʒəʊ] *(pl* **banjos)** *n* banjo *m*

bank[1] [bæŋk] **1** *n* **(a)** *(of river)* orilla *f*; *(of earth)* terraplén *m* **(b)** *(of clouds, fog)* banco *m* **(c)** *(of lights, switches)* batería *f*; **banks of seats** gradas *fpl* con asientos

2 *vt* flanquear; **the road is banked by trees** la carretera se halla flanqueada por dos filas de árboles

3 *vi* **(a)** *(clouds, mist)* formar bancos; *(snow)* acumularse **(b)** *(plane)* ladearse, escorarse

bank[2] **1** *n* **(a)** *(financial institution)* banco *m*; **b. account** cuenta *f* bancaria; **b. balance** saldo *m* bancario, haberes *mpl* bancarios; **b. charges** comisión *f* bancaria, gastos *mpl* bancarios; **b. loan** préstamo *m* or crédito *m* bancario; *Fin* **b. rate** tipo *m* or *Am* tasa *f* de interés básico; **b. robber** atracador(ora) *m,f* or ladrón(ona) *m,f* de bancos; **b. statement** extracto *m* or balance *m* de cuenta; **b. teller** empleado(a) *m,f* de banca; **b. vice-president** director(ora) *m,f* de banco

(b) *(in gambling)* banca *f*

(c) *(store)* **blood/data b.** banco de sangre/datos

2 *vt (funds)* ingresar (en un banco)

3 *vi* **to b. with** tener una cuenta en

▸**bank on** *vt insep (outcome, success)* contar con

bankable ['bæŋkəbəl] *adj (actor, actress)* taquillero(a), de éxito

bankbook ['bæŋkbʊk] *n* cartilla *f*, libreta *f*

banker ['bæŋkə(r)] *n Fin* banquero *m*

banking ['bæŋkɪŋ] *n (occupation)* banca *f*, sector *m* bancario; *(activity)* operaciones *fpl* bancarias; **b. hours** horario *m* de los bancos

banknote ['bæŋknəʊt] *n* billete *m (de banco)*

bankroll ['bæŋkrəʊl] *vt (finance)* financiar

bankrupt ['bæŋkrʌpt] **1** *n Fin* quebrado(a) *m,f*

2 *adj* en quiebra, en bancarrota; **to be b.** estar en quiebra; **to**

go b. quebrar, ir a la quiebra; *Fig* **to be morally b.** estar en quiebra moral

3 *vt Law* conducir a la quiebra; *Fam (make poor)* arruinar, dejar en la ruina

bankruptcy ['bæŋkrʌptsɪ] *n Law* quiebra *f*, bancarrota *f*; *Fam (poverty)* ruina *f*

banner ['bænə(r)] *n (flag)* bandera *f*; *(of trade union, political party)* pancarta *f*; **b. headlines** *(in newspaper)* grandes titulares *mpl*

bannister = **banister**

banns [bænz] *npl* amonestaciones *fpl*; **to publish the b.** correr las amonestaciones

banquet ['bæŋkwɪt] *n* banquete *m*

bantam ['bæntəm] *n* gallina *f* de Bantam

bantamweight ['bæntəmweɪt] *n (in boxing)* peso *m* gallo

banter ['bæntə(r)] **1** *n* bromas *fpl*, chanzas *fpl*

2 *vi* bromear

baptism ['bæptɪzəm] *n* bautismo *m*; *Fig* **a b. of fire** un bautismo de fuego

baptismal [bæp'tɪzməl] *adj* **b. certificate** partida *f* de bautismo; **b. font** pila *f* bautismal

Baptist ['bæptɪst] *n* baptista *mf*, bautista *mf*

baptize ['bæptaɪz] *vt* bautizar

bar [bɑ:(r)] **1** *n* **(a)** *(of metal)* barra *f*; *(of soap)* pastilla *f*; *(on window)* barrote *m*; **to be behind bars** estar entre rejas; **chocolate b.** chocolatina *f*; **gold bars** lingotes *mpl* de oro, oro *m* en barras; **b. chart** gráfico *m* de barras; **b. of chocolate** tableta de chocolate; *Comptr* **b. code** código *m* de barras **(b)** *(obstacle)* barrera *f*; **to be a b. to sth** constituir una barrera para algo; **to impose a b. on sth** prohibir algo **(c)** *Law* **the B.** la abogacía; **the prisoner at the b.** el/la acusado(a) **(d)** *(selling alcohol)* bar *m*; *(counter)* barra *f*; **b. snack** aperitivo *m*, tentempié *m* **(e)** *Mus* compás *m*

2 *vt (pt & pp* **barred) (a)** *(obstruct)* obstruir; **to b. the door against sb** atrancar la puerta para impedir el paso a alguien; **to b. sb's way** obstruir el camino *or* impedir el paso a alguien **(b)** *(ban)* **to b. sb from a place** prohibir la entrada de alguien a un lugar; **to b. sb from doing sth** prohibir a alguien hacer algo

3 *prep* salvo, excepto; **b. none** sin excepción

barb [bɑ:b] *n* **(a)** *(on hook)* lengüeta *f* **(b)** *(remark)* dardo *m*

Barbadian [bɑ:'beɪdɪən] **1** *n* = habitante *o* nativo de Barbados

2 *adj* de Barbados

Barbados [bɑ:'beɪdɒs] *n* Barbados

barbarian [bɑ:'beərɪən] *n & adj* bárbaro(a) *m,f*

barbaric [bɑ:'bærɪk] *adj* salvaje

barbarism ['bɑ:bərɪzəm] *n* barbarie *f*

barbarity [bɑ:'bærɪtɪ] *n (act)* barbaridad *f*; *(cruelty)* barbarie *f*

barbarous ['bɑ:bərəs] *adj (act, behavior)* bárbaro(a)

barbecue, barbeque ['bɑ:bɪkju:] **1** *n* barbacoa *f*, *Andes, RP* asado *m*; **to have a b.** hacer una barbacoa *or Andes, RP* un asado; **b. sauce** salsa *f* para barbacoa

2 *vt* asar en la barbacoa

barbed [bɑ:bd] *adj* **(a)** *(hook)* con lengüeta(s); **b. wire** alambre *m* de espino *or* de púas **(b)** *(remark, comment)* afilado(a), mordaz

barber ['bɑ:bə(r)] *n* barbero *m*; **to go to the b.'s** ir a la peluquería

barbershop ['bɑ:bəʃɒp] *n* barbería *f*; **b. quartet** cuarteto *m* de voces masculinas

barbiturate [bɑ:'bɪtjʊreɪt] *n* barbitúrico *m*

Barcelona [bɑːsə'ləʊnə] *n* Barcelona

bard [bɑ:d] *n* bardo *m*, trovador *m*; **the B.** = Shakespeare

bare [beə(r)] **1** *adj* **(a)** *(not covered)* desnudo(a); **to strip a house b.** *(thieves)* llevarse absolutamente todo de una casa; **to fight with one's b. hands** luchar sin armas; **in one's b. feet** descalzo(a); **to lay sth b.** poner algo de manifiesto, descubrir algo (**b**) *(just sufficient)* **the b. minimum** lo imprescindible, lo indispensable; **the b. bones of the case are…** lo esencial del caso es…; **the b. necessities (of life)** lo indispensable (para vivir); **a b. pass** *(in exam)* un aprobado raspado *or* por los pelos; **a b. majority** una mayoría por los pelos

  2 *vt* descubrir; **to b. one's head** descubrirse (la cabeza); **to b. one's teeth** enseñar los dientes; **he bared his heart** *or* **soul to me** me abrió su corazón *or* alma

bareback ['beəbæk] **1** *adj* **b. rider** jinete *m*/amazona *f* que monta a pelo

  2 *adv* **to ride b.** montar a pelo

barefaced ['beəfeɪst] *adj* descarado(a)

barefoot ['beəfʊt], **barefooted** [beə'fʊtɪd] *adj & adv* descalzo(a)

bareheaded [beə'hedɪd] *adj & adv* sin sombrero

barelegged [beə'leg(ɪ)d] *adj & adv* con las piernas desnudas

barely ['beəlɪ] *adv* (**a**) *(scarcely)* apenas (**b**) *(sparsely)* **b. furnished** amueblado(a) con lo indispensable

barf [bɑːf] *vi Fam* echar la papa, potar

bargain ['bɑːgɪn] **1** *n* (**a**) *(agreement)* pacto *m*, trato *m*; **to make** *or* **strike a b.** hacer un pacto; **you haven't kept your side** *or* **part of the b.** no has cumplido tu parte del trato; **he drives a hard b.** es bueno regateando; **into the b.** *(what's more)* encima, además (**b**) *(good buy)* ganga *f*, chollo *m*; **b. basement** sección *f* de oportunidades; **b. hunter** buscador(ora) *m,f* de gangas; **b. price** precio *m* de saldo

  2 *vi* negociar

▸**bargain away** *vt sep (rights, privileges)* malvender, malbaratar

▸**bargain for** *vt insep* **I hadn't bargained for that** no contaba con eso; **he got more than he bargained for** recibió más de lo que esperaba

▸**bargain on** *vt insep* **I didn't b. on that** no contaba con eso

barge [bɑːdʒ] *n (boat)* gabarra *f*; *(for parties, river cruises)* = barco para fiestas o pequeñas travesías turísticas

▸**barge in** *vi (enter)* irrumpir

barhop ['bɑːhɒp] *vi* ir de copas *or* de bares

baritone ['bærɪtəʊn] *n* barítono *m*

barium ['beərɪəm] *n Chem* bario *m*; *Med* **b. meal** (papilla *f* de) sulfato *m* de bario

bark[1] [bɑːk] **1** *n (of tree)* corteza *f*

  2 *vt* **to b. one's shins** arañarse *or* rasguñarse las espinillas

bark[2] **1** *n (of dog)* ladrido *m*; *Fig* **his b. is worse than his bite** perro ladrador, poco mordedor, *RP* perro que ladra no muerde

  2 *vt (order)* gritar

  3 *vi* ladrar; *(person)* gritar; *Fam* **you're barking up the wrong tree** estás aviado *or* muy equivocado

barkeep(er) ['bɑːkiːp(ər)] *n* camarero(a) *m,f*, *Am* mesero(a) *m,f*, *RP* mozo(a) *m,f*

barley ['bɑːlɪ] *n* cebada *f*; **b. sugar** azúcar *m or f* cande

barman ['bɑːmən] *n* camarero *m*, *Am* mesero *m*, *RP* mozo *m*

barn [bɑːn] *n* granero *m*, pajar *m*; **b. dance** baile *m* campestre; **b. owl** lechuza *f*

barnacle ['bɑːnəkəl] *n* bálano *m*, bellota *f* de mar

barnstorming ['bɑːnstɔːmɪŋ] *adj (speech, performance)* apoteósico(a)

barnyard ['bɑːnjɑːd] *n* corral *m*

barometer [bə'rɒmɪtə(r)] *n* barómetro *m*

baron ['bærən] *n* barón *m*; **press/oil b.** *(tycoon)* magnate *m* de la prensa/del petróleo

baroness ['bærənes] *n* baronesa *f*

baronet ['bærənet] *n* baronet *m (título inglés)*

baroque [bə'rɒk] **1** *n* barroco *m*

  2 *adj* barroco(a)

barracks ['bærəks] *npl* cuartel *m*

barracuda [bærə'kjuːdə] *n* barracuda *f*

barrage ['bærɑːʒ] *n* (**a**) *(dam)* presa *f* (**b**) *Mil (of artillery fire)* batería *f* de fuego; *Fig (of questions, complaints)* lluvia *f*

  2 *vt* **to b. sb with questions** acribillar a alguien a preguntas

barrel ['bærəl] *n* (**a**) *(container)* barril *m*, tonel *m*; *(of oil)* barril *m*; *Fam* **to have sb over a b.** tener a alguien en un puño; *Fam* **the party wasn't exactly a b. of fun** *or* **laughs** la fiesta no fue la más divertida del mundo; **b. organ** organillo *m* (**b**) *(of gun)* cañón *m*

barren ['bærən] *adj (land, woman)* yermo(a); *(landscape)* árido(a)

barrenness ['bærənnɪs] *n* aridez *f*, esterilidad *f*

barrette [bə'ret] *n* pasador *m*

barricade ['bærɪkeɪd] **1** *n* barricada *f*

  2 *vt (door, street)* poner barricadas en; **she had barricaded herself into the room** se había atrincherado en su habitación

barrier ['bærɪə(r)] *n also Fig* barrera *f*; **the Great B. Reef** la Gran Barrera de Coral

barring ['bɑːrɪŋ] *prep* salvo, excepto; **b. accidents** salvo imprevistos; **b. a miracle** a menos que ocurra un milagro

barrow ['bærəʊ] *n (wheelbarrow)* carretilla *f*

bartender ['bɑːtendə(r)] *n* camarero *m*, *Am* mesero *m*, *RP* mozo *m*

barter ['bɑːtə(r)] **1** *n* trueque *m*

  2 *vt* trocar, cambiar (**for** por)

  3 *vi* hacer trueques, practicar el trueque

basalt ['bæsɔːlt] *n* basalto *m*

base [beɪs] **1** *n* (**a**) *(bottom)* base *f*; **b. pay** salario *m or* sueldo *m* mínimo; **b. rate** *(interest rate)* tipo *m or Am* tasa *f* de interés básico; **b. salary** salario *m or* sueldo *m* mínimo (**b**) *(for explorers, military forces)* base *f*; **b. camp** campamento *m* base (**c**) *(in baseball)* base *f*; *Fig* **she didn't get past first b.** no llegó a superar la primera etapa

  2 *adj* (**a**) *Formal (motive, conduct)* vil, bajo(a) (**b**) **b. metals** metales *mpl* comunes *or* no preciosos

  3 *vt* basar (**on** en); **to be based on** estar basado(a) en, basarse en; **to be based in Boston** *(job, operation)* desarrollarse en Boston; *(troops, company)* estar radicado(a) en Boston

baseball ['beɪsbɔːl] *n* béisbol *m*; **b. cap** gorra *f* de visera

baseboard ['beɪsbɔːd] *n (along base of wall)* zócalo *m*, rodapié *m*

Basel ['bɑːzəl] *n* Basilea

baseless ['beɪslɪs] *adj* infundado(a), sin fundamento; **to be b.** carecer de fundamento

baseline ['beɪslaɪn] *n (in tennis)* línea *f* de saque *or* de fondo

basement ['beɪsmənt] *n* sótano *m*; **b. apartment** *(apartamento m or Esp* piso *m or Am* departamento *m* del) sótano *m*

bash [bæʃ] *Fam* **1** *n* (**a**) *(blow)* porrazo *m*, castaña *f* (**b**) *(party)* fiesta *f*

  2 *vt* golpear; **to b. one's head** darse una castaña en la cabeza

bashful ['bæʃfʊl] *adj* tímido(a)

bashfulness ['bæʃfʊlnɪs] *n* timidez *f*

-bashing ['bæʃɪŋ] *suffix Fam* **union-b.** ataque *m* a los sindicatos

BASIC ['beɪsɪk] *n Comptr (abbr* **Beginners' All-purpose Symbolic Instruction Code)** *(lenguaje m)* BASIC *m*

basic ['beɪsɪk] **1** *n* **the basics** *(fundamental aspects)* lo esencial; *(of language, science)* los fundamentos; **let's get down to basics** centrémonos en lo esencial

  2 *adj* básico(a); **I get the b. idea** me hago una idea; **to be b. to sth** ser básico(a) para algo; **b. pay** sueldo *m* base

basically ['beɪsɪklɪ] *adv* básicamente, fundamentalmente

basil ['bæzɪl] *n* albahaca *f*

basilica [bə'zɪlɪkə] *n* basílica *f*

basin ['beɪsən] *n* (**a**) *(for cooking)* recipiente *m*, bol *m*; *(for* *washing hands)* lavabo *m*, *Am* lavamanos *m inv*; *(plastic, for dish washing)* barreño *m*, palangana *f* **(b)** *Geog* cuenca *f*

basis ['beɪsɪs] *(pl* **bases** ['beɪsiːz]) *n* base *f*; **on a weekly b.** semanalmente; **on a monthly b.** mensualmente; **on an informal b.** informalmente; **the accusations have no b. in fact** las acusaciones no se basan en los hechos; **on the b. of…** según…

bask [bɑːsk] *vi* **to b. in the sun** estar tumbado(a) al sol; **to b. in sb's favor** gozar del favor de alguien

basket ['bɑːskɪt] *n* cesta *f*; *(in basketball)* canasta *f*; **wastepaper b.** papelera *f*; *Fam* **to be a b. case** *(person)* estar loco(a) de remate, estar *Esp* majareta *or Méx* zafado(a)

basketball ['bɑːskɪtbɔːl] *n* baloncesto *m*, *Am* básquetbol *m*

basketful ['bɑːskɪtfʊl] *n* cesta *f*

Basle [bɑːl] *n* Basilea

Basque [bɑːsk] **1** *n* **(a)** *(person)* vasco(a) *m,f* **(b)** *(language)* vasco *m*, vascuence *m*
  2 *adj* vasco(a); **the B. Country** el País Vasco, Euskadi

bas-relief [bɑːrɪ'liːf] *n Art* bajorrelieve *m*

bass[1] [bæs] *n (seawater)* lubina *f*, róbalo *m*; *(freshwater)* perca *f*

bass[2] [beɪs] *Mus* **1** *n (voice, singer, guitar)* bajo *m*; *(on amplifier)* graves *mpl*; *(double-bass)* contrabajo *m*; **b. player** bajista *m,f*
  2 *adj* bajo(a); **b. clef** clave *f* de fa; **b. drum** bombo *m*; **b. guitar** bajo *m*

basset ['bæsɪt] *n* **b. (hound)** basset *m*

bassist ['beɪsɪst] *n Mus* bajista *mf*

bassoon [bə'suːn] *n* fagot *m*

bastard ['bɑːstəd] **1** *n* **(a)** *(illegitimate child)* hijo(a) *m,f* ilegítimo(a), (hijo(a) *m,f)* bastardo(a) *m,f* **(b)** *very Fam (unpleasant person)* hijo(a) *m,f* de puta, cabrón(ona) *m,f*; **you lucky b.!** ¡qué suerte (tienes), desgraciado(a) *or* cabrón!; **a b. of a job** un trabajo muy jodido
  2 *adj (child)* bastardo(a)

baste [beɪst] *vt* **(a)** *(meat)* regar con grasa **(b)** *(sew)* hilvanar

bastion ['bæstɪən] *n also Fig* bastión *m*, baluarte *m*

bat[1] [bæt] *n (animal)* murciélago *m*; *Fam* **like a b. out of hell** como alma que lleva el diablo

bat[2] **1** *n (for baseball, cricket)* bate *m*; *(for table tennis)* pala *f*
  2 *vt (pt & pp* **batted**) **he didn't b. an eyelid** ni se inmutó
  3 *vi (in baseball, cricket)* batear

batch [bætʃ] *n (of goods, material)* lote *m*, partida *f*; *(of recruits)* tanda *f*; *(of bread)* hornada *f*; *Comptr* **b. file** fichero *m* por lotes; *Comptr* **b. processing** proceso *m* por lotes

bated ['beɪtɪd] *adj* **with b. breath** con el alma en vilo

bath [bɑːθ] **1** *n (action)* baño *m*; *(bathtub)* bañera *f*, *Am* tina *f*; **to take** *or* **have a b.** tomar *or* darse un baño, bañarse; **to give sb a b.** bañar a alguien; **b. mat** alfombrilla *f* de baño; **b. salts** sales *fpl* de baño; **b. towel** toalla *f* de baño
  2 *vt* bañar
  3 *vi* bañarse

bathe [beɪð] **1** *vt (wound)* lavar; **she was bathed in sweat** estaba empapada en *or* de sudor
  2 *vi* bañarse

bather ['beɪðə(r)] *n* bañista *mf*

bathing ['beɪðɪŋ] *n* **b. is prohibited** *(sign)* prohibido bañarse; **b. cap** gorro *m* de baño; **b. suit** bañador *m*, traje *m* de baño, *Col* vestido *m* de baño, *RP* malla *f*; **b. trunks** bañador *m* (de hombre)

bathos ['beɪθ ɒs] *n* = paso de lo sublime a lo común

bathrobe ['bɑːθrəʊb] *n* albornoz *m*

bathroom ['bɑːθruːm] *n* **(a)** *(with bath)* cuarto *m* de baño; **b. scales** báscula *f* de baño; **b. suite** = conjunto de bañera, lavabo e inodoro **(b)** *(toilet)* baño *m*, *Esp* servicio *m*, *CSur* toilette *m*; **to go to the b.** ir al baño *or Esp* servicio

bathtub ['bɑːθtʌb] *n* bañera *f*, *Am* tina *f*

batik [bə'tiːk] *n* batik *m*

baton ['bætən] *n (in relay race)* testigo *m*; *(of conductor)* batuta *f*;

(of policeman) porra *f*; **b. charge** carga *f* con porras

battalion [bə'tæljən] *n* batallón *m*

▶**batten down** ['bætən] *vt insep* **to b. down the hatches** *(on ship)* cerrar las escotillas; *Fig (before crisis)* atarse *or* apretarse los machos

batter[1] ['bætə(r)] *n (in baseball)* bateador(ora) *m,f*

batter[2] *n (to coat food for frying)* pasta *f* para rebozar

batter[3] *vt (beat) (door)* aporrear; *(person)* pegar, maltratar

battered ['bætəd] *adj* **(a)** *(person)* maltratado(a) **(b)** *(furniture)* desvencijado(a); *(hat)* ajado(a); *(car)* abollado(a)

battering ram ['bætərɪŋ'ræm] *n* ariete *m*

battery ['bætərɪ] *n* **(a)** *(of radio, clock)* pila *f*; *(of car, video camera)* batería *f*; **to be b. operated** *or* **powered** funcionar a *or* con pilas; **b. charger** cargador *m* de pilas/baterías **(b)** *Mil* batería *f*; *Fig* **a b. of criticism** un aluvión de críticas; *Psy* **a b. of tests** una batería de pruebas

battle ['bætəl] **1** *n also Fig* batalla *f*; **to fight a b.** librar una batalla; **to do b. with sb** librar una batalla contra alguien; **a b. of wits** un duelo de ingenio; **that's half the b.** ya está recorrido medio camino; **b. cry** grito *m* de guerra; **b. royal** batalla campal
  2 *vi* batallar, luchar

battle-ax, battle-axe ['bætəlæks] *n (weapon)* hacha *f* de guerra; *Fam Pej (woman)* arpía *f*, bruja *f*

battlefield ['bætəlfiːld], **battleground** ['bætəlgraʊnd] *n also Fig* campo *m* de batalla

battle-hardened ['bætəl'hɑːdənd] *adj* curtido(a)

battlements ['bætəlmənts] *npl* almenas *fpl*

battle-scarred ['bætəl'skɑːd] *adj (place)* minado(a) por la guerra *or* la batalla

battleship ['bætəlʃɪp] *n* acorazado *m*

batty ['bætɪ] *adj Fam* pirado(a), chiflado(a); **to be b.** *(person)* estar chiflado(a) *or* pirado(a); *(idea)* ser peregrino(a)

bauble ['bɔːbəl] *n (cheap ornament)* chuchería *f*; *(Christmas decoration)* bola *f* de Navidad

baud [bɔːd] *n Comptr* baudio *m*; **b. rate** velocidad *f* de transmisión

baulk = balk

bauxite ['bɔːksaɪt] *n* bauxita *f*

Bavaria [bə'veərɪə] *n* Baviera

Bavarian [bə'veərɪən] *n & adj* bávaro(a) *m,f*

bawdy ['bɔːdɪ] *adj (remark, humor)* picante, verde

bawl [bɔːl] **1** *vt* gritar, proferir; **to b. an order** gritar una orden
  2 *vi* **(a)** *(shout)* gritar, vociferar **(b)** *(cry) (baby, child)* berrear

▶**bawl out** *vt sep* **(a)** **to b. out an order** gritar una orden **(b)** *Fam (reprimand)* **to b. sb out** reñir *or* regañar a alguien

bay[1] [beɪ] *n (shrub)* laurel *m*; **b. leaf** (hoja *f* de) laurel *m*

bay[2] **1** *n* **(a)** *(on coastline)* bahía *f*; **the Bay of Bengal** el Golfo de Bengala; **the Bay of Biscay** el Golfo de Vizcaya **(b)** *Archit* entrante *m*, hueco *m*; **b. window** ventana *f* salediza **(c)** **to keep** *or* **hold sth/sb at b.** tener a raya algo/a alguien
  2 *vi (dog, wolf)* aullar

bayonet ['beɪənɪt] **1** *n* bayoneta *f*
  2 *vt* **to b. sb to death** matar a alguien a bayonetazos

bazaar [bə'zɑː(r)] *n (in Middle East)* bazar *m*; *(for charity)* mercadillo *m*

bazooka [bə'zuːkə] *n* bazuca *m*, bazooka *m*

BBC [biːbiː'siː] *n (abbr* **British Broadcasting Corporation)** BBC *f*

BB gun ['biːbiː'gʌn] *n* escopeta *f* de aire comprimido

BBQ ['bɑːbɪkjuː] *n Fam (abbr* **barbecue)** barbacoa *f*, *Andes, RP* asado *m*; **B. sauce** salsa *f* (para) barbacoa

BC [biː'siː] *adv (abbr* **before Christ)** a.C.

BCE [biːsiː'iː] *adv (abbr* **before the Common Era)** ≃ a.C.

BCG [biːsiː'dʒiː] *n Med (abbr* **bacillus Calmette-Guérin)** B.C.G. *m*, = vacuna contra la tuberculosis

be [biː]

En el inglés hablado, y en el escrito en estilo coloquial, el verbo **be** se contrae de forma que **I am** se transforma en **I'm, he/she/it is** se transforman en **he's/she's/it's** y **you/we/they are** se transforman en **you're/we're/they're**. Las formas negativas **is not, are not, was not** y **were not** se transforman en **isn't, aren't, wasn't** y **weren't**.

(*present* **I am, you/we/they are** [aː(r)], **he/she/it is** [ɪz], *pt* **were** [wɜː(r)], *1st and 3rd person singular* **was** [wɒz], *pp* **been** [biːn]) **1** *vi* (**a**) *(indicating permanent quality, condition)* ser; **sugar is sweet** el azúcar es dulce; **it's two meters wide** tiene dos metros de ancho; **three and two are five** tres y dos (son) cinco; **she is English** es inglesa; **he is clever** es inteligente; **I'm a doctor** soy médico

(**b**) *(indicating temporary state)* estar; **to be wet/dry** estar seco(a)/mojado(a); **the bottle is empty/full** la botella está vacía/llena; **to be cold/hot** *(of person)* tener frío/calor; *(of thing)* estar frío(a)/caliente; **it's cold/hot** *(weather)* hace frío/calor; **to be hungry/thirsty** tener hambre/sed; **to be right** tener razón; **to be wrong** estar equivocado(a); **to be twenty (years old)** tener veinte años

(**c**) *(with time, date)* ser; **it's six o'clock** son las seis (en punto); **when is the concert?** ¿cuándo es el concierto?; **today is the tenth** hoy estamos a (día) diez; **what day is it today?** ¿qué día es hoy?; **it's a year since I saw her** hace un año que no la veo

(**d**) *(with location)* estar; **where is the station?** ¿dónde está la estación?; **is this where you work?** ¿es aquí donde trabajas?; **to be at home** estar en casa; **where was I?** *(after disgression)* ¿por dónde iba?

(**e**) *(with cost)* ser, costar; **how much are the shoes?** ¿cuánto son *or* cuestan los zapatos?; **how much is it?** ¿cuánto es?; **how much is a pound of beef?** ¿a cuánto está la libra de ternera?

(**f**) *(with health)* estar; **how are you?** ¿cómo estás?; **I'm fine** estoy bien; **he's better** está mejor

(**g**) *(with imperatives)* **be good!** ¡sé bueno!; **be still!** ¡estate quieto!; **don't be stupid!** ¡no seas tonto!; **let's be reasonable** seamos razonables

(**h**) *(with question tags)* **she's beautiful, isn't she?** es guapa, ¿verdad?; **they're big, aren't they?** son grandes, ¿verdad?; **you aren't from around here, are you?** tú no eres de aquí, ¿no?

(**i**) *(as past participle of* go*)* **I have been to London** he estado en Londres

2 *v aux* (**a**) *(in continuous tenses)* estar; **to be doing sth** estar haciendo algo; **she is/was laughing** se está/estaba riendo; **I'm leaving tomorrow** me voy mañana; **I've been waiting for hours** llevo horas esperando

(**b**) *(in passives)* ser; **six employees were made redundant** fueron despedidos seis empleados; **they have been seen in Chicago** han sido vistos *or* se les ha visto en Chicago; **he was killed** lo mataron; **she is respected by all** todos la respetan

(**c**) *(followed by infinitive)* **the house is to be sold** la casa se va a vender; **he was never to see them again** nunca volvería a verlos; **you are not to mention this to anyone** no debes decir esto a nadie

beach [biːtʃ] **1** *n* playa *f*; **b. ball** balón *m or* pelota *f* de playa; **b. hut** caseta *f*; **b. recliner** tumbona *f*

2 *vt (boat, ship)* varar

beachcomber ['biːtʃkəʊmə(r)] *n* raquero(a) *m,f*

beachhead ['biːtʃhed] *n Mil* cabeza *f* de playa

beacon ['biːkən] *n (for plane, ship)* baliza *f*; *(lighthouse)* faro *m*; *(bonfire)* fuego *m*, hoguera *f*; *Fig* **a b. of hope** un rayo de esperanza

---

bead [biːd] *n (of glass)* cuenta *f*; *(of dew, sweat)* gota *f*, perla *f*; **a string of beads** unas cuentas ensartadas

beady ['biːdɪ] *adj* **he had his b. eyes on it** lo miraba intensamente

beady-eyed ['biːdɪ'aɪd] *adj (observant)* atento(a), vigilante

beagle ['biːgəl] *n* beagle *m*

beak [biːk] *n (of bird)* pico *m*; *Fam (nose)* napias *fpl*

beaker ['biːkə(r)] *n* vaso *m (generalmente de plástico)*

be-all and end-all ['biːɔːləˈnendɔːl] *n Fam* **the b.** lo más importante del mundo

beam [biːm] **1** *n* (**a**) *(in building)* viga *f*; *(in gymnastics)* barra *f* de equilibrio (**b**) *(of light)* rayo *m*; *Phys* haz *m* (**c**) *(idioms) Fam* **you're way off the b.** te equivocas de medio a medio; *Fam* **broad in the b.** *(person)* ancho(a) de caderas

2 *vt (program)* emitir; *(information)* mandar, enviar

3 *vi (shine) (sun, moon)* brillar; **to b. with pride/pleasure** sonreír con orgullo/de placer

bean [biːn] *n* (**a**) *(vegetable) Esp* alubia *f*, *Esp* judía *f*, *Am salvo RP* frijol *m*, *Andes, RP* poroto *m*; *(of coffee)* grano *m*; **(green) b.** *Esp* judía *f* verde, *Esp, Carib, Col* habichuela *f*, *Bol, RP* chaucha *f*, *Andes, RP* poroto *m* verde, *Méx, CAm* ejote *m*, *Ven* vainita *f*; **b. curd** tofu *m* (**b**) *Fam* **to be full of beans** *(energy)* estar lleno(a) de vitalidad

beanbag ['biːnbæg] *n (for juggling)* bola *f* de malabares; *(for sitting on)* puf *m* relleno de bolitas

beanie ['biːnɪ] *n* **b. (hat)** casquete *m*

beanpole ['biːnpəʊl] *n* (**a**) *(stick)* guía *f*, rodrigón *m* (**b**) *Fam (tall, thin person)* larguirucho(a) *m,f*, espagueti *m*

beansprouts ['biːnspraʊts] *npl* brotes *mpl* de soja

beanstalk ['biːnstɔːk] *n* tallo *m* de *Esp* judía *or Am salvo RP* frijol *or Andes, RP* poroto

bear¹ [beə(r)] *n (animal)* oso(a) *m,f*; **b. cub** osezno *m*; **to give sb a b. hug** dar un fuerte abrazo a alguien; *Fin* **b. market** mercado *m* a la baja

bear² (*pt* **bore** [bɔː(r)], *pp* **borne** *or* **born** [bɔːn]) **1** *vt* (**a**) *(carry)* llevar; *(bring)* traer, portar; *(weight, load)* soportar; **to b. sth away** llevarse algo; **to b. sth in mind** tener algo presente *or* en cuenta; **it bears no relation to...** no tiene nada que ver con...; **we will b. the costs** nos haremos cargo de los costos *or Esp* costes; **to b. the responsibility for sth** cargar con la responsabilidad de algo

(**b**) *(endure)* soportar, aguantar; **I can't b. him** no puedo soportarlo, no lo soporto; **I could b. it no longer** no podía aguantar más; **it doesn't b. thinking about** no quiero ni pensarlo

(**c**) *(produce)* **she bore him three children** le dio tres hijos; **to b. interest** *(investment)* devengar intereses; **to b. fruit** *(tree)* dar fruto, fructificar; *(effort, plan)* dar fruto(s), ser fructífero(a)

2 *vi (move)* **to b. (to the) right/left** echarse hacia la derecha/izquierda

▶**bear down (up)on** *vt insep* abalanzarse sobre

▶**bear out** *vt sep (theory)* corroborar, confirmar

▶**bear up** *vi* resistir; **b. up!** ¡ánimo!

▶**bear with** *vt insep* tener paciencia con; **if you could b. with me a minute...** si no le importa esperar un momento...

bearable ['beərəbəl] *adj* soportable

bear-baiting ['beəbeɪtɪŋ] *n Hist* = espectáculo que consiste en atar a un oso y atacarle con perros y pinchos

beard [bɪəd] *n* barba *f*; **to grow/have a b.** dejarse/tener barba

bearded ['bɪədɪd] *adj* con barba

bearer ['beərə(r)] *n (of news, check)* portador(ora) *m,f*; *(of passport)* titular *mf*

bearing ['beərɪŋ] *n* (**a**) *(of person)* porte *m* (**b**) *(in mechanism, engine)* cojinete *m*, rodamiento *m* (**c**) *(orientation)* **to find** *or* **get one's bearings** orientarse; **to lose one's bearings**

desorientarse (**d**) *(relevance)* relación *f* (**on** con); **it has no b. on the matter** es ajeno al asunto

beast [bi:st] *n* (**a**) *(animal)* bestia *f*, animal *m*; **b. of burden** bestia de carga (**b**) *Fam (unpleasant person)* bestia *mf*; **a b. of a job** un trabajo de chinos *or Am* negros

beastly ['bi:stlɪ] *adj Fam (smell, taste)* horroroso(a); **to be b. to sb** portarse como un canalla con alguien; **what b. weather!** ¡qué tiempo tan horrible!

beat [bi:t] **1** *n* (**a**) *(of heart)* latido *m*; *(in music) (rhythm)* ritmo *m*; *(in bar)* tiempo *m* (**b**) *(of policeman)* ronda *f*; **on the b.** de ronda

2 *adj Fam (exhausted)* **to be dead b.** estar hecho(a) polvo

3 *vt (pt* **beat**, *pp* **beaten** ['bi:tən]) (**a**) *(hit) (person)* golpear (repetidamente); *(eggs)* batir; **to b. a drum** tocar el tambor; **to b. the retreat** batirse en retirada; **to b. a path through the crowd** abrirse camino entre la multitud; *Fam* **b. it!** ¡largo!, ¡esfúmate!, *RP* ¡bórrate!; **the bird b. its wings** el pájaro batió las alas

(**b**) *(defeat)* ganar; **we b. them easily** les ganamos sin dificultad; **that will take some beating** eso va a ser difícil de mejorar; **I got up early to b. the traffic** me levanté temprano para adelantarme a la hora *Esp* punta *or Am* pico; **he b. me to it** se me adelantó; **you can't b. a good book** no hay nada mejor que un buen libro; *Prov* **if you can't b. them, join them** si no puedes vencer al enemigo, únete a él; *Fam* **that beats everything!** ¡es lo mejor que he oído en mi vida!; *Fam* **it beats me why he did it** no tengo ni idea de por qué lo hizo

4 *vi* (**a**) *(heart)* latir (**b**) **to b. around** *or* **about the bush** andarse por las ramas

▸**beat back** *vt sep* rechazar

▸**beat down 1** *vt sep (price)* conseguir una rebaja en; **I beat him down to $40 for the dress** conseguí que me dejara el vestido en 40 dólares

2 *vi (rain)* caer con fuerza; *(sun)* caer a plomo

▸**beat off** *vt sep* rechazar

▸**beat out** *vt sep (fire, flames)* apagar

▸**beat up** *vt sep (assault)* dar una paliza a

beaten ['bi:tən] **1** *adj* **b. earth** tierra *f* batida; *Fig* **off the b. track** retirado(a)

2 *pp of* **beat**

beaten-up ['bi:tənʌp] *adj Fam (vehicle)* desvencijado(a), destartalado(a)

beater ['bi:tə(r)] *n* (**a**) *(in hunting)* ojeador(ora) *m,f* (**b**) *(in cookery)* batidora *f*, batidor *m*

beatification [bi:ætɪfɪ'keɪʃən] *n Rel* beatificación *f*

beating ['bi:tɪŋ] *n (assault, defeat)* paliza *f*; **to give sb a b.** dar una paliza a alguien

beatitude [bi:'ætɪtju:d] *n Rel* beatitud *f*; **the Beatitudes** *(in the Bible)* las Bienaventuranzas

beat-up ['bi:tʌp] *adj Fam (car)* desvencijado(a)

beaut [bju:t] *n Fam* **what a b.!** ¡qué preciosidad *or Am* preciosura!

beautician [bju:'tɪʃən] *n* esteticista *mf*

beautiful ['bju:tɪfʊl] *adj (woman)* bonita, *esp Esp* guapa; *(child, animal)* bonito(a), precioso(a); *(music, dress, landscape)* hermoso(a), precioso(a); *(smell, taste)* delicioso(a)

beautifully ['bju:tɪfʊlɪ] *adv* de maravilla

beautify ['bju:tɪfaɪ] *vt* embellecer

▸**beauty** ['bju:tɪ] *n (attribute, person)* belleza *f*; *(object)* preciosidad *f*; **that's the b. of it** eso es lo mejor; **b. contest** concurso *m* de belleza; **b. parlor** salón *m* de belleza; **b. queen** miss *f*; **b. salon** salón *m* de belleza; *Hum* **b. sleep** dosis *f inv* de sueño; **I need my b. sleep** necesito dormir para estar como una rosa; **b. spot** *(on face)* lunar *m*; *(in country)* paraje *m* de gran belleza

beaver ['bi:və(r)] *n* (**a**) *(animal)* castor *m* (**b**) *Vulg (woman's*

genitals) Esp coño *m*, *Esp* conejo *m*, *Andes, RP* concha *f*, *Méx* panocha *f*

▸**beaver away** *vi* afanarse, aplicarse (**at** en)

bebop ['bi:bɒp] *n Mus* bebop *m*

becalmed [bɪ'kɑ:md] *adj* **the ship lay b.** el barco estaba al pairo

became [bɪ'keɪm] *pt of* **become**

because [bɪ'kɒz] *conj* porque; **why? — just b.** ¿por qué? — porque sí; **b. of** debido a, a causa de

beck [bek] *n* **to be at sb's b. and call** estar a (la entera) disposición de alguien

beckon ['bekən] **1** *vt* **to b. sb in** hacer a alguien una seña para que entre

2 *vi* (**a**) *(signal)* **to b. to sb** hacer una seña a alguien (**b**) *(attract, call)* **I can't stay, work beckons** no puedo quedarme, el trabajo me reclama; **the beach beckoned** la playa era una gran tentación; **fame beckoned** la fama llamó a mi/su, *etc.* puerta

become [bɪ'kʌm] *(pt* **became** [bɪ'keɪm], *pp* **become**) **1** *vi* (**a**) *(a teacher, a doctor)* hacerse; *(boring, jealous, suspicious)* volverse; *(old, difficult, stronger)* hacerse; *(happy, sad, thin)* ponerse; **to b. angry** *esp Esp* enfadarse, *esp Am* enojarse; **to b. interested** interesarse; **to b. king** convertirse en rey; **to b. known** saberse (**b**) **what will b. of him?** ¿qué va a ser de él?; **I don't know what has b. of her** no sé qué ha sido de ella

2 *vt Formal (of clothes, color)* sentar bien a; **such behavior doesn't b. you** ese comportamiento no es propio *or* digno de ti

becoming [bɪ'kʌmɪŋ] *adj (behavior)* apropiado(a); **green looks very b. on her** le sienta muy bien el verde

bed [bed] **1** *n* (**a**) *(for sleeping)* cama *f*; **to be in b.** estar en la cama; **to go to b.** irse a la cama, ir a acostarse; **to put a child to b.** acostar a un niño; **to go to b. with sb** irse a la cama con alguien; *Fam* **to have got out of b. on the wrong side** haberse levantado con el pie izquierdo; **b. and breakfast** *(hotel)* = hostal familiar en el que el desayuno está incluido en el precio de la habitación; *(service)* habitación *f* y desayuno; **b. linen** ropa *f* de cama (**b**) *(of river)* lecho *m*, cauce *m* (**c**) *(of flowers)* macizo *m* (**d**) *Geol* estrato *m* (**e**) *(of rice, lettuce)* base *f*, lecho *m*

2 *vt (pt & pp* **bedded**) *Old-fashioned* acostarse con

▸**bed down** *vi* **to b. down (for the night)** acostarse

bedazzle [bɪ'dæzəl] *vt (impress)* deslumbrar, impresionar

bedbug ['bedbʌg] *n* chinche *f*

bedclothes ['bedkləʊðz] *npl* ropa *f* de cama

bedding ['bedɪŋ] *n (sheets, blankets)* ropa *f* de cama

bedevil [bɪ'devəl] *vt* **to be bedeviled by problems** tener muchos problemas; **to be bedeviled by bad luck** tener la negra, estar maldito(a)

bedfellow ['bedfeləʊ] *n* **they make strange bedfellows** forman una extraña pareja

bedlam ['bedləm] *n* jaleo *m*, alboroto *m*

Bedouin ['beduɪn] *n & adj* beduino(a) *m,f*

bedpan ['bedpæn] *n* cuña *f*

bedpost ['bedpəʊst] *n* pilar *f* de la cama

bedraggled [bɪ'drægəld] *adj* desaliñado(a) y empapado(a)

bedridden ['bedrɪdən] *adj* **to be b.** estar postrado(a) en la cama

bedrock ['bedrɒk] *n Geol* lecho *m* rocoso; *Fig (of beliefs, faith)* base *f*, fondo *m*

bedroll ['bedrəʊl] *n* petate *m*

bedroom ['bedru:m] *n (in house)* dormitorio *m*, habitación *f*, *CAm, Col, Méx* recámara *f*; *(in hotel)* habitación *f*, *Am* cuarto *m*, *CAm, Col, Méx* recámara *f*

-bedroomed ['bedru:md] *suffix* **two/three-b. house** casa de dos/tres dormitorios

bedside ['bedsaɪd] *n* **at sb's b.** al lado de la cama de alguien;

b. lamp lamparita *f* de noche; **b. manner** *(of doctor)* actitud *f* ante el paciente; **b. table** mesilla *f* or mesita *f* (de noche), *Andes* velador *m*, *Méx* buró *m*, *RP* mesa *f* de luz

bedsock ['bedsɒk] *n* calcetín *m* para dormir

bedsore ['bedsɔː(r)] *n* úlcera *f* de decúbito

bedspread ['bedspred] *n* colcha *f*

bedsprings ['bedsprɪŋz] *npl* somier *m* (de muelles)

bedstead ['bedsted] *n* (armazón *m* or *f* de la) cama *f*

bedtime ['bedtaɪm] *n* it's b.! ¡es hora de irse a la cama!; **what's your usual b.?** ¿a qué hora te sueles acostar?; **it's past my b.** ya debería estar acostado; **b. story** cuento *m* (contado antes de acostarse)

bed-wetting ['bedwetɪŋ] *n* eneuresis *f inv*

bee [biː] *n* abeja *f*; *Fam* **to have a b. in one's bonnet about sth** estar obsesionado(a) con algo

beech [biːtʃ] *n* haya *f*

beechnut ['biːtʃnʌt] *n* hayuco *m*

beef [biːf] 1 *n* **(a)** *(meat)* (carne *f* de) vaca *f* or *Am* res *f*; **b. stew** guiso *m* de vaca **(b)** *Fam (strength)* **to have plenty of b.** ser fornido(a), *Esp* estar cachas; **give it some b.!** ¡un poco más de esfuerzo! **(c)** *Fam (complaint)* queja *f*
2 *vi Fam (complain)* quejarse (**about** de)

▸**beef up** *vt sep Fam (text, resources)* ampliar

beefburger ['biːfbɜːgə(r)] *n* hamburguesa *f*

Beefeater ['biːfiːtə(r)] *n* = guardia de la Torre de Londres

beefsteak ['biːfsteɪk] *n* filete *m*, bistec *m*, *RP* bife *m*

beefy ['biːfɪ] *adj Fam (muscular)* fornido(a), *Esp* muy cachas

beehive ['biːhaɪv] *n* colmena *f*

beekeeper ['biːkiːpə(r)] *n* apicultor(ora) *m,f*, colmenero(a) *m,f*

beeline ['biːlaɪn] *n Fam* **to make a b. for sth** ir directamente hacia algo

been [biːn] *pp of* **be**

beep [biːp] 1 *n (sound)* pitido *m*
2 *vt (page)* llamar *(a un busca)*
3 *vi* pitar

beeper ['biːpə(r)] *n (pager)* buscapersonas *m inv*, *Esp* busca *m*, *Méx* localizador *m*, *RP* radiomensaje *m*

beer [bɪə(r)] *n* cerveza *f*; **to go for a b.** ir a tomar una cerveza; **b. garden** terraza *f* (interior) de un bar; **b. glass** jarra *f* de cerveza

beery ['bɪərɪ] *adj (smell, breath, taste)* a cerveza

beeswax ['biːzwæks] *n* cera *f* (de abeja)

beet [biːt] *n* **(a)** *(sugar beet)* remolacha *f* (azucarera) **(b)** *(beetroot)* remolacha *f*, *Méx* betabel *m*

beetle ['biːtəl] *n* escarabajo *m*

befall [bɪ'fɔːl] *(pt* befell [bɪ'fel], *pp* befallen [bɪ'fɔːlən]*) vi Literary* sobrevenir

befit [bɪ'fɪt] *(pt & pp* befitted*) vt* ser digno(a) de

befitting [bɪ'fɪtɪŋ] *adj* digno(a)

before [bɪ'fɔː(r)] 1 *prep* **(a)** *(with time)* antes de; **b. Christmas** antes de Navidad; **I got here b. you** he llegado antes que tú; **the day b. the battle** la víspera de la batalla; **b. that,...** antes (de eso),... **(b)** *(with place)* ante, delante de; **b. my very eyes** ante mis propios ojos; **to appear b. the judge** comparecer ante el juez **(c)** *(in importance)* **she puts her family b. everything else** su familia es lo primero para ella
2 *adv* **(a)** *(with time)* antes; **two days b.** dos días antes; **the day/year b.** el día/año anterior; **I have seen him b.** lo he visto antes; **I've told you b.** ya te lo he dicho (otras veces); **(b)** *(in space)* **this page and the one b.** esta página y la anterior
3 *conj* antes de que; **come and see me b. you leave** ven a verme antes de marcharte; **b. I forget, will you...** antes de que se me olvide, ¿podrías...?; **give it to her b. she cries** dáselo antes de que empiece a llorar

beforehand [bɪ'fɔːhænd] *adv (in advance)* de antemano; **two**

hours b. con dos horas de antelación, dos horas antes; **I must tell you b. that...** debo prevenirte de que...

befriend [bɪ'frend] *vt* hacerse amigo(a) de

befuddled [bɪ'fʌdəld] *adj (confused)* aturdido(a); **to be b. (with)** estar aturdido(a) (por)

beg [beg] *(pt & pp* begged*)* 1 *vt* **to b. sb to do sth** rogar *or* suplicar a alguien que haga algo; **to b. a favor of sb** pedir un favor a alguien; **to b. forgiveness** pedir *or* implorar perdón; **I b. your pardon** *(I apologize)* perdón; *(what did you say?)* ¿cómo dice?; **I b. to differ** me temo que no comparto tu opinión; **this begs the question why** esto nos lleva a preguntarnos el porqué
2 *vi* **to b. for sth** *(money, food)* mendigar algo; *(help, a chance)* pedir *or* rogar algo; **to b. for mercy** implorar clemencia; **these jobs are going begging** estos trabajos los hay a patadas; **b. bowl** platillo *m* de las limosnas

began [bɪ'gæn] *pt of* **begin**

beggar ['begə(r)] 1 *n* mendigo(a) *m,f*; *Prov* **beggars can't be choosers** a buen hambre no hay pan duro
2 *vt* **to b. description** *(be impossible to describe)* resultar indescriptible; *(sth bad)* no tener nombre; **to b. belief** ser difícil de creer

begin [bɪ'gɪn] *(pt* began [bɪ'gæn], *pp* begun [bɪ'gʌn]*)* 1 *vt* empezar, comenzar; **to b. a new job** empezar en un trabajo nuevo; **to b. to do sth, to b. doing sth** empezar *or* comenzar a hacer algo; **I couldn't (even) b. to describe** no sé ni cómo empezar a describir
2 *vi* empezar, comenzar; **to b. by doing sth** empezar por hacer algo; **to b. again** comenzar de nuevo; **to b. with,...** para empezar,...

beginner [bɪ'gɪnə(r)] *n* principiante *mf*

beginning [bɪ'gɪnɪŋ] *n* principio *m*, comienzo *m*; **in** *or* **at the b.** al principio; **at the b. of the year/month** a principios de año/mes; **from the b.** desde el principio; **from b. to end** de principio a fin; **the b. of the end** el principio del fin; **the first beginnings of civilization** los orígenes de la civilización; **the problem has its beginnings in...** el problema tiene su origen en...

begonia [bɪ'gəʊnɪə] *n* begonia *f*

begrudge [bɪ'grʌdʒ] *vt* **(a)** *(resent)* **I b. spending so much money** me duele gastar tanto **(b)** *(envy)* **I don't b. him his success** no le envidio su éxito

beguile [bɪ'gaɪl] *vt* **(a)** *(enchant)* seducir **(b)** *(deceive)* engañar; **to b. sb into doing sth** engatusar a alguien para que haga algo; **to b. sb with promises** encandilar a alguien con promesas

beguiling [bɪ'gaɪlɪŋ] *adj* seductor(ora)

begun [bɪ'gʌn] *pp of* **begin**

behalf [bɪ'hɑːf] *n* **in** *or* **on b. of sb, in** *or* **on sb's b.** en nombre de alguien; **don't worry on my b.** no te preocupes por mí

behave [bɪ'heɪv] *vi (person)* portarse, comportarse; *(car, machine)* funcionar; **to b. (well)** portarse bien; **to b. badly** portarse mal; **what a way to b.!** ¡menudo comportamiento!; **b. (yourself)!** ¡compórtate como es debido!

behavior [bɪ'heɪvjə(r)] *n* comportamiento *m*, conducta *f*; **to be on one's best b.** (com)portarse muy bien

behavioral [bɪ'heɪvjərəl] *adj* del comportamiento, de la conducta

behaviorism [bɪ'heɪvjərɪzəm] *n Psy* conductismo *m*

behead [bɪ'hed] *vt* decapitar

beheld [bɪ'held] *pt & pp of* **behold**

behest [bɪ'hest] *n* **at sb's b., at the b. of sb** por orden *or* a instancias de alguien

behind [bɪ'haɪnd] 1 *prep* detrás de, tras; **to be b. sb** *(situated)* estar detrás de alguien; *(support)* respaldar a alguien; **to follow close b. sb** seguir de cerca a alguien; **look b. you** mira detrás de ti; **to be b. schedule** ir atrasado(a); **to put sth b. one**

dejar algo atrás; **let's put it all b. us** olvidemos todo esto; **she's ten minutes b. the leaders** *(in race)* está a diez minutos de la cabeza de la carrera; **to be b. the times** no andar con los tiempos; **the reasons b. sth** los motivos de algo; **what's b. all this?** ¿qué hay detrás de todo esto?

2 *adv* atrás; **from b.** *(attack)* por la espalda; **to stay** or **remain b.** quedarse; **to leave sth b.** dejarse algo; **to be b. with one's work/with the rent** estar atrasado(a) en el trabajo/en el pago del alquiler; **they are only three points b.** *(in contest)* están a sólo tres puntos

3 *n Fam (buttocks)* trasero *m*

behindhand [bɪ'haɪndhænd] *adv* **to be b. with one's work/with the rent** estar atrasado(a) en el trabajo/en el pago del alquiler

behind-the-scenes [bɪ'haɪndðə'siːnz] *adj* entre bastidores, oculto(a); **a b. look at politics/the world of newspapers** una mirada a la cara desconocida or oculta de la política/del mundo de la prensa

behold [bɪ'həʊld] *(pt & pp* **beheld** [bɪ'held]) *vt Literary* contemplar

beholden [bɪ'həʊldən] *adj Formal* **to be b. to sb** estar en deuda con alguien

beholder [bɪ'həʊldə(r)] *n Prov* **beauty is in the eye of the b.** sobre gustos no hay nada escrito

beige [beɪʒ] *n & adj* beige *m inv, Esp* beis *m inv*

Beijing [beɪ'ʒɪŋ] *n* Pekín

being ['biːɪŋ] *n* **(a)** *(creature)* ser *m* **(b)** *(existence)* **to come into b.** nacer; **the company is no longer in b.** la empresa ya no existe; **with all my b.** con todo mi corazón

Beirut [beɪ'ruːt] *n* Beirut

belabor [bɪ'leɪbə(r)] *vt* apalear; **to b. sb with insults** poner verde a alguien

Belarus [belə'ruːs] *n* Bielorrusia

belated [bɪ'leɪtɪd] *adj* tardío(a); **wishing you a b. happy birthday** deseándote, con retraso or *Am* demora, un feliz cumpleaños

belch [beltʃ] **1** *n (burp)* eructo *m*
2 *vt (smoke, flames)* escupir
3 *vi (person)* eructar

beleaguered [bɪ'liːgəd] *adj (city, army)* sitiado(a), asediado(a); *(government)* acosado(a); *(person)* atormentado(a)

Belfast [bel'fɑːst] *n* Belfast

belfry ['belfrɪ] *n* campanario *m*

Belgian ['beldʒən] *n & adj* belga *mf*

Belgium ['beldʒəm] *n* Bélgica

Belgrade [bel'greɪd] *n* Belgrado

belie [bɪ'laɪ] *vt* contradecir

belief [bɪ'liːf] *n* **(a)** *(conviction)* creencia *f*; **in the b. that…** en el convencimiento de que…; **it is my b. that…** estoy convencido(a) de que…; **it is beyond b.** es imposible de creer **(b)** *(confidence)* confianza *f*, fe *f*; **to have b. in oneself** tener confianza en uno(a) mismo(a)

believable [bɪ'liːvəbəl] *adj* verosímil

believe [bɪ'liːv] **1** *vt* creer; **I b. (that) I am right** creo no equivocarme; **I b. him to be alive** creo que está vivo; **she is believed to be here** se cree que está aquí; **I don't b. a word of it** no me creo (ni) una palabra; **I could scarcely b. my eyes** no podía creer lo que veían mis ojos; **I don't b. it!** ¡no me lo puedo creer!; **I can well b. it** no me extrañaría nada
2 *vi* **(a)** *(have faith)* creer; **to b. in God** creer en Dios; **to b. in sb** *(have confidence)* creer en alguien, tener fe en alguien; **to b. in oneself** tener confianza en uno(a) mismo(a) **(b)** *(be in favor)* **to b. in sth** ser partidario(a) de algo; **I don't b. in making promises** no soy partidario de las promesas **(c)** *(think, suppose)* creer; **I b. not** creo que no; **I b. so** así lo creo, creo que sí

believer [bɪ'liːvə(r)] *n* **(a)** *(religious person)* creyente *mf* **(b)**

(supporter) **to be a b. in sth** ser partidario(a) de algo

belittle [bɪ'lɪtəl] *vt* menospreciar, restar importancia a; **to b. oneself** restarse importancia

Belize [be'liːz] *n* Belice

bell [bel] *n* *(of church)* campana *f*; *(handbell)* campanilla *f*; *(on door, bicycle)* timbre *m*; *(on cat, hat)* cascabel *m*; **to ring the b.** *(on door)* llamar al timbre; *Fig* **a model with bells and whistles** un modelo de lo más completo; **b. jar** campana de vidrio or *Esp* cristal; **b. pepper** pimiento *m* (morrón); **b. ringer** campanero(a) *m,f*; **b. tower** (torre *f* del) campanario *m*

belladonna [belə'dɒnə] *n* *(plant)* belladona *f*; *(poison)* atropina *f*

bell-bottoms ['belbɒtəmz] *npl* pantalones *mpl* de campana; **a pair of b.** unos pantalones de campana

bellboy ['belbɔɪ] *n Fam* botones *m inv*

belle [bel] *n* bella *f*, belleza *f*

bellhop ['belhɒp] *n Fam* botones *m inv*

bellicose ['belɪkəʊs] *adj* belicoso(a)

belligerence [be'lɪdʒərəns] *n* beligerancia *f*

belligerent [be'lɪdʒərənt] **1** *n* contendiente *m*
2 *adj* beligerante

bellow ['beləʊ] **1** *n* bramido *m*
2 *vi* bramar

bellows ['beləʊz] *npl* fuelle *m*; **a pair of b.** un fuelle

belly ['belɪ] *n* vientre *m*, barriga *f*, *Chile* guata *f*; **to have a full/an empty b.** tener la barriga llena/vacía; **b. dance** danza *f* del vientre; **b. laugh** sonora carcajada *f*

bellyache ['belɪeɪk] *Fam* **1** *n* dolor *m* de barriga
2 *vi (complain)* rezongar or quejarse or *Méx* repelar (**about** de)

bellybutton ['belɪbʌtən] *n Fam* ombligo *m*

belly-flop ['belɪflɒp] **1** *n* **to do a b.** darse un panzazo or tripazo
2 *vi (pt & pp* **belly-flopped**) darse un panzazo or tripazo

bellyful ['belɪfʊl] *n Fam* **I've had a b. of his complaints!** ¡estoy hasta el gorro de sus quejas!

belong [bɪ'lɒŋ] *vi* **(a)** *(be property of)* pertenecer a; **that book belongs to me** este libro me pertenece **(b)** **to b. to** *(be member of) (club)* pertenecer a, ser socio(a) de; *(party)* pertenecer a, estar afiliado(a) a **(c)** *(have a proper place)* ir; **to put sth back where it belongs** devolver algo a su sitio; **the saucepans don't b. in that cupboard** las ollas no van en esa alacena; **I feel I b. here** aquí me siento (como) en casa; **to feel that one doesn't b.** sentirse un(a) extraño(a)

belonging [bɪ'lɒŋɪŋ] *n* **to have a sense of b.** sentirse (como) en casa

belongings [bɪ'lɒŋɪŋz] *npl* pertenencias *fpl*; **personal b.** efectos *mpl* personales

Belorussian [beləʊ'rʌʃən] *n & adj* bielorruso(a) *m,f*

beloved 1 [bɪ'lʌvɪd] *Literary* amado(a) *m,f*
2 *adj* [bɪ'lʌvd] amado(a), querido(a)

below [bɪ'ləʊ] **1** *prep* debajo de, bajo, *Am* abajo de; **b. the knee** por debajo de la rodilla; **10 degrees b. zero** 10 (grados) bajo cero; **b. sea level** por debajo del nivel del mar; **b. the surface** bajo la superficie
2 *adv* abajo; **see b.** *(on document)* ver más abajo or adelante; **on the floor b.** en el piso de abajo; **it's 10 degrees b.** hace 10 grados bajo cero

belt [belt] **1** *n* **(a)** *(for pants)* cinturón *m*, correa *f*; *Fig* **to tighten one's b.** apretarse el cinturón; *Fig* **now that I've got some experience under my b.** ahora que tengo algo de experiencia a mis espaldas; **to hit sb below the b.** *(in boxing)* dar un golpe bajo a alguien; *Fig* **that was a bit below the b.!** *(remark, criticism)* ¡eso ha sido un golpe bajo! **(b)** *(of machine)* correa *f* **(c)** *(of land)* franja *f*, cinturón *m* **(d)** *Fam (blow)* golpetazo *m*; **to give sb a b.** dar a alguien un golpetazo
2 *vt (hit)* dar un golpetazo a; *(with belt)* dar correazos a; *(ball)* pegar un cañonazo a

3 *vi Fam (move quickly)* **to b. along** ir a toda pastilla *or RP* máquina; **she belted down the stairs** bajó las escaleras a toda pastilla *or RP* máquina

▶**belt out** *vt sep Fam (sing loudly)* cantar a grito pelado

beltway ['beltweɪ] *n* carretera *f* de circunvalación, ronda *f* (de circunvalación)

bemoan [bɪ'məʊn] *vt* lamentar, lamentarse de

bemused [bɪ'mju:zd] *adj* perplejo(a), desconcertado(a); **to be b.** estar perplejo(a) *or* desconcertado(a)

bench [bentʃ] *n (seat, work table)* banco *m; Parl* escaños *mpl*; **to be on the b.** *(in football)* estar en el banquillo

benchmark ['bentʃmɑ:k] *n (for comparison)* punto *m* de referencia

bend [bend] **1** *n* (a) *(of road, river)* curva *f; (of pipe, arm)* codo *m; Fam* **to be around the b.** estar *Esp* majara *or Am* zafado(a) *or RP* piantado(a); *Fam* **to drive sb around the b.** sacar a alguien de sus casillas, poner a alguien a cien (b) **the bends** *(decompression sickness)* enfermedad *f* de los buzos; *Med* aeroembolismo *m*

  2 *vt (pt & pp bent* [bent]*)* doblar; **to b. one's arm/back** doblar el brazo/la espalda; **do not b.** *(on envelope)* no doblar; **on bended knee** de rodillas; **to b. the rules** ser flexible en la interpretación de las reglas

  3 *vi (road, river)* hacer una curva, girar; **to b. under the strain of sth** ceder bajo la presión de algo

▶**bend down** *vi* agacharse

▶**bend over** *vi* agacharse; **to b. over backward for sb/to do sth** desvivirse por alguien/por hacer algo

bender ['bendə(r)] *n Fam* **to go on a b.** irse de juerga *or* de copas

beneath [bɪ'ni:θ] **1** *prep* (a) *(physically)* debajo de, bajo (b) *(unworthy of)* **to marry b. one** casarse con alguien de clase social inferior; **she thinks it's b. her to work** cree que trabajar supondría rebajarse; **b. contempt** (completamente) despreciable

  2 *adv* abajo; **from b.** desde abajo

Benedictine [benɪ'dɪktɪn] *n & adj Rel* benedictino(a) *m,f*

benediction [benɪ'dɪkʃən] *n Rel* bendición *f*

benefactor ['benɪfæktə(r)] *n* benefactor *m*

benefactress ['benɪfæktrɪs] *n* benefactora *f*

beneficent [bɪ'nefɪsənt] *adj* benéfico(a)

beneficial [benɪ'fɪʃəl] *adj* beneficioso(a) (**to** para)

beneficiary [benɪ'fɪʃərɪ] *n* beneficiario(a) *m,f*

benefit ['benɪfɪt] **1** *n* (a) *(advantages)* beneficio *m*, provecho *m; (individual advantage)* ventaja *f;* **to have the b. of sth** contar con algo; **to derive b. from** sacar provecho de; **for sb's b.,** for the b. of sb en atención a alguien; **that remark was for your b.** ese comentario iba dirigido a ti; **to give sb the b. of the doubt** dar a alguien el beneficio de la duda (b) *(charity event)* acto *m* benéfico; **b. match** *(in soccer)* partido *m* de homenaje (c) *(state payment)* prestación *f*, subsidio *m;* **to receive benefits** cobrar un subsidio; **social security benefits** prestaciones *fpl* sociales

  2 *vt* beneficiar, favorecer

  3 *vi* **to b. by** *or* **from** beneficiarse de, sacar provecho de

Benelux ['benɪlʌks] *n* (el) Benelux; **the B. countries** los países del Benelux

benevolence [bɪ'nevələns] *n* benevolencia *f*

benevolent [bɪ'nevələnt] *adj* benévolo(a); **b. society** cofradía *f* benéfica

Bengal [beŋ'gɔ:l] *n* Bengala

Bengali [beŋ'gɔ:lɪ] **1** *n* (a) *(person)* bengalí *mf* (b) *(language)* bengalí *m*

  2 *adj* bengalí

benign [bɪ'naɪn] *adj (attitude, look)* bondadoso(a); *(climate, tumor)* benigno(a)

Benin [be'ni:n] *n* Benín

bent [bent] **1** *n (inclination)* inclinación *f;* **to have a natural b. for music** tener una inclinación natural por la música

  2 *adj* (a) *(curved)* torcido(a), curvado(a) (b) **to be b. on (doing) sth** *(determined)* estar empeñado(a) en hacer algo

  3 *pt & pp of* **bend**

benzene ['benzi:n] *n Chem* benceno *m*

benzin(e) ['benzi:n] *n Chem* bencina *f*

bequeath [bɪ'kwi:ð] *vt Formal* legar

bequest [bɪ'kwest] *n Law* legado *m*

berate [bɪ'reɪt] *vt Formal* reconvenir, reñir

Berber ['bɜ:bə(r)] *n & adj* bereber *mf*

bereaved [bɪ'ri:vd] **1** *npl* **the b.** la familia del (de la) difunto(a)

  2 *adj* privado(a) de un ser querido

bereavement [bɪ'ri:vmənt] *n* pérdida *f* (de un ser querido); **b. counseling** = atención psicológica prestada a personas que sufren por la pérdida de un ser querido

bereft [bɪ'reft] *adj* **to be b. of** estar privado(a) de

beret ['bereɪ] *n* boina *f*

bergamot ['bɜ:gəmɒt] *n* bergamota *f*

Berlin [bɜ:'lɪn] *n* Berlín; **the B. Wall** el Muro de Berlín

Berliner [bɜ:'lɪnə(r)] *n* berlinés(esa) *m,f*

Bermuda [bə'mju:də] *n* (las) Bermudas; **B. shorts** bermudas *fpl*

Bern(e) [bɜ:n] *n* Berna

berry ['berɪ] *n* baya *f*

berserk [bə'zɜ:k] *adj Fam* **to go b.** volverse loco(a)

berth [bɜ:θ] **1** *n* (a) *(on train, ship)* litera *f* (b) *(in harbor)* amarradero *m; Fig* **to give sb a wide b.** evitar a alguien

  2 *vt & vi Naut* atracar

beseech [bɪ'si:tʃ] *(pt & pp besought* [bɪ'sɔ:t] *or* **beseeched**) *vt Literary* implorar, suplicar

beseeching [bɪ'si:tʃɪŋ] *adj* suplicante, implorante

beset [bɪ'set] *(pt & pp beset) vt* acosar; **b. with dangers/difficulties** plagado(a) de peligros/dificultades; **she was b. by doubts** le asaltaron las dudas

beside [bɪ'saɪd] *prep* (a) *(next to)* al lado de; **seated b. me** sentado(a) a mi lado; **a house b. the lake** una casa a la orilla del *or* junto al lago; **that's b. the point** eso no viene al caso; **he was b. himself with joy** no cabía en sí de gozo; **he was b. himself with anger** estaba fuera de sí (de ira) (b) *(compared to)* al lado de; **b. him, everyone else appears slow** a su lado todos parecen lentos

besides [bɪ'saɪdz] **1** *prep* (a) *(apart from)* además de, aparte de (b) *(in addition to)* además de; **...b. which, she was unwell** ...además de lo cual, no se encontraba bien

  2 *adv* además; **many more b.** muchos(as) otros(as)

besiege [bɪ'si:dʒ] *vt (castle, town)* asediar, sitiar; *Fig* **to b. sb with complaints/requests** asediar a alguien con quejas/peticiones

besmirch [bɪ'smɜ:tʃ] *vt Literary (face)* manchar; *(reputation)* mancillar

besotted [bɪ'sɒtɪd] *adj* **to be b. with sth/sb** estar embobado(a) con algo/alguien

besought [bɪ'sɔ:t] *pt & pp of* **beseech**

bespatter [bɪ'spætə(r)] *vt* salpicar (**with** de)

bespectacled [bɪ'spektəkəld] *adj* con gafas

bespoke [bɪ'spəʊk] *adj (made to measure)* a medida; **b. tailor** sastre *m (que hace trajes a medida)*

best [best] *(superlative of good, well)* **1** *n* **the b.** el/la/lo mejor; **at b.** en el mejor de los casos; **the b. of it is...** lo mejor del caso es que...; **it's hard enough at** *or* **in the b. of times** incluso en el mejor de los casos ya resulta bastante difícil; **she did her b.** hizo todo lo que pudo; **I'll want to look my b.** tendré que arreglarme lo mejor posible; **he was at his b.** estaba en plena forma; **to bring out the b. in sb** poner de manifiesto lo mejor de alguien; **to get the b. of the**

bargain salir ganando en un trato; **to get the b. out of sth** sacar el máximo provecho de algo; **we will have to make the b. of it** nos las tendremos que arreglar *or Esp* apañar; **we are the b. of friends** somos muy buenos amigos; **I am in the b. of health** estoy pletórico(a) de salud; **to the b. of my belief** *or* **knowledge** por lo que yo sé; **I will do it to the b. of my ability** lo haré lo mejor que pueda; **he can sing with the b. of them** canta como el mejor; **to hope for the b.** esperar que todo vaya bien; **to have** *or* **get the b. of both worlds** salir ganando por partida doble; *Fam* **all the b.!** ¡te deseo lo mejor!; *(at end of letter)* un saludo, *RP* cariños

2 *adj* **my b. dress** mi mejor vestido; **she is b. at French** *(of group of people)* es la que mejor habla francés; *(French is her best subject)* lo que mejor se le da es el francés; **to put one's b. foot forward** dar lo mejor de sí mismo(a); **it took the b. part of a year** llevó casi todo un año; **to know what is b. for sb** saber lo que le conviene a alguien; **it is b. to…** lo mejor es…; *Com* **b. before…** consumir preferentemente antes de…; **b. man** *(at wedding)* padrino *m*; **may the b. man win** *(in contest)* que gane el mejor

3 *adv* mejor; **I like fish b.** lo que más me gusta es el pescado; **I comforted her as b. I could** la consolé lo mejor que pude; **you know b.** tú sabrás; **do as you think b.** haz lo que te parezca mejor; **the b. dressed man** el hombre mejor vestido; **she came off b.** ella fue la que salió mejor parada; **b. seller** *(book)* éxito *m* de ventas, bestseller *m*

4 *vt (in contest, argument)* superar

best-case scenario [ˈbestˈkeɪsɪˈnɑːrɪəʊ] *n* **the b.** lo mejor que podría pasar

bestial [ˈbestɪəl] *adj* brutal, bestial

bestiality [bestɪˈælɪtɪ] *n* **(a)** *(cruelty)* brutalidad *f*, bestialidad *f* **(b)** *(sexual practice)* bestialismo *m*, zoofilia *f*

bestow [bɪˈstəʊ] *vt (title)* conceder (**on** a); *(honor)* conferir (**on** a)

best-selling [bestˈselɪŋ] *adj* **b. novel/author** novela *f*/escritor(ora) *m,f* de éxito

bet [bet] **1** *n* **(a)** *(gamble)* apuesta *f*; **to make** *or* **place a b.** hacer una apuesta **(b)** *(guess, option)* **my b. is that he'll come** personalmente, creo que vendrá; **your best b. would be to…** lo mejor que puedes hacer es…; **it's a safe b.** es casi seguro

2 *vt (pt & pp* **bet** *or* **betted)** **(a)** *(gamble)* apostar; **I'll b. you $10** te apuesto 10 dólares **(b)** *Fam (expressing conviction)* **I b. you don't!** ¡a que no!; **I b. you she'll win** te apuesto *or* qué te apuestas a que gana ella; **I b. you anything he won't do it** te apuesto lo que quieras a que no lo consigue

3 *vi* **(a)** *(gamble)* **to b. on a horse** apostar a un caballo **(b)** *Fam (expressing conviction)* **I wouldn't b. on it!** yo no me apostaría nada; **you b.!** ¡ya lo creo!, ¡por supuesto!; **John says he's sorry — I b. he does!** John dice que lo siente — ¡ya lo creo! *or Esp* ¡hombre, claro!

beta [ˈbiːtə] *n* **(a)** *(Greek letter)* beta *f* **(b)** *Phys* **b. rays** rayos *mpl* beta **(c)** *Comptr* **b. testing** pruebas *fpl* beta; **b. version** versión *f* beta

betel [ˈbiːtəl] *n* betel *m*; **b. nut** areca *f*

Bethlehem [ˈbeθlɪhem] *n* Belén

betide [bɪˈtaɪd] *vt Literary* **woe b. him/you** pobre de él/ti

betray [bɪˈtreɪ] *vt* **(a)** *(person, country)* traicionar; **to b. sb's trust** abusar de la confianza de alguien **(b)** *(secret, fact)* revelar; **his tone betrayed a lack of conviction** su tono revelaba falta de convicción

betrayal [bɪˈtreɪəl] *n* **(a)** *(of person, country)* traición *f*; **a b. of trust** un abuso de confianza **(b)** *(of secret, fact)* muestra *f*, indicio *m*; **her expression gave no b. of her true feelings** su expresión no permitía adivinar sus verdaderos sentimientos

betrothal [bɪˈtrəʊðəl] *n Literary* compromiso *m*

betrothed [bɪˈtrəʊðd] *n & adj Formal* prometido(a) *m,f*

better [ˈbetə(r)] *(comparative of* **good, well)** **1** *n* **I expected b. of you** esperaba más de ti; **you should respect your (elders and) betters** deberías guardar respeto a tus mayores; **to change for the b.** cambiar para mejor; **to get the b. of sb** poder con alguien; **his shyness got the b. of him** pudo más su timidez; **the sooner/faster the b.** cuanto antes/más rapido, mejor

2 *adj* mejor; **to be b.** *(feel well again)* estar mejor; **to get b.** mejorar; **he's b. at tennis than his brother** juega al tenis mejor que su hermano; **she's b. at chemistry than he is** se le da mejor la química que a él; **it would be b. for you to go** más vale que te vayas; **that's b.** ¡así está mejor!; **b. luck next time!** ¡a ver si hay más suerte la próxima vez!; **it took the b. part of a week** llevó casi toda una semana; **to have seen b. days** haber visto mejores tiempos

3 *adv* mejor; **I am feeling b.** me siento mejor; **to get to know sb b.** ir conociendo mejor a alguien; **b. and b.** cada vez mejor; **so much the b., all the b.** tanto mejor; **for b. or worse** para bien o para mal; **you had b. not stay** más vale que no te quedes; **to think b. of it** cambiar de idea, pensárselo mejor; **to think b. of sb (for doing sth)** tener mejor concepto de alguien (por haber hecho algo); **to be b. off** estar mejor; *(financially)* tener más dinero

4 *vt (improve)* superar; *(surpass)* mejorar; **she wants to b. herself** quiere mejorar su situación

betterment [ˈbetəmənt] *n* mejora *f*

betting [ˈbetɪŋ] *n* juego *m*, apuestas *fpl*; *Fam Fig* **the b. is that…** lo más probable es que…

bettor [ˈbetə(r)] *n* apostante *mf*

between [bɪˈtwiːn] **1** *prep* entre; **b. eight and nine o'clock** entre (las) ocho y (las) nueve; **b. New York and Philadelphia** entre Nueva York y Philadelphia; **you must choose b. them** tienes que elegir entre ellos; **we bought it b. us** lo compramos entre todos; **this is strictly b. you and me** esto debe quedar entre tú y yo

2 *adv* **(in) b.** en medio; **the trees in b.** los árboles que están en medio

bevel [ˈbevəl] **1** *n (on wood, glass)* bisel *m*

2 *vt (wood, glass)* biselar

beverage [ˈbevərɪdʒ] *n* bebida *f*

bevy [ˈbevɪ] *n (group)* nube *f*, grupo *m*

bewail [bɪˈweɪl] *vt* lamentar

beware [bɪˈweə(r)] *vi* tener cuidado (**of** con); **b.!** ¡cuidado!; **b. of the dog** *(sign)* cuidado con el perro

bewilder [bɪˈwɪldə(r)] *vt* desconcertar

bewildered [bɪˈwɪldəd] *adj* desconcertado(a); **I was b. by their lack of interest** me dejó atónito su falta de interés

bewildering [bɪˈwɪldərɪŋ] *adj* desconcertante

bewilderment [bɪˈwɪldəmənt] *n* desconcierto *m*

bewitch [bɪˈwɪtʃ] *vt (fascinate)* embrujar, cautivar

bewitching [bɪˈwɪtʃɪŋ] *adj (smile, beauty)* cautivador(ora)

beyond [bɪˈjɒnd] **1** *prep* **(a)** *(in space)* más allá de; **the house is b. the church** la casa está pasada la iglesia

(b) *(in time)* **b. a certain date** después de *or* pasada una fecha determinada

(c) *(exceeding)* **he lived b. his means** vivió por encima de sus posibilidades; **it's b. me (how they can do it)** no comprendo cómo lo hacen; **due to circumstances b. our control** por circunstancias ajenas a nuestra voluntad; **I am b. caring** ya me trae sin cuidado; **it's b. doubt/question (that…)** es indudable/incuestionable (que…); **it's b. a joke** esto ya pasa de castaño oscuro; **to be b. belief** ser difícil de creer; **b. reach** inalcanzable; **b. repair** irreparable

(d) *(except)* aparte de, además de; **I have nothing to say b. observing that…** únicamente quisiera hacer notar que…

2 *adv* más allá

3 *n* **the b.** el más allá

B-girl ['biːgɜːl] *n* chica *f* de alterne

bhangra ['bæŋgrə] *n Mus* bhangra *m*

Bhutan [buːˈtɑːn] *n* Bután

bias ['baɪəs] **1** *n* (**a**) *(prejudice)* prejuicio *m*; *(inclination)* inclinación *f*; **to have a b. toward** sentir inclinación por; **to have a b. against** tener prejuicios contra, estar predispuesto(a) en contra de (**b**) *(in sewing)* bies *m*, sesgo *m*

2 *vt* (*pt & pp* **biased** *or* **biassed**) influir en; **to b. sb against/for sth** predisponer a alguien en contra/a favor de algo

bias(s)ed ['baɪəst] *adj* parcial; *(opinion)* parcial, sesgado(a); **you're b. in her favor** estás predispuesto a favor de ella

biathlon [baɪˈæθlɒn] *n* biatlón *m*

bib [bɪb] *n (for baby)* babero *m*; *(of apron, dungarees)* peto *m*

bible ['baɪbəl] *n* biblia *f*; **the B.** la Biblia; *Fig* **this dictionary is his b.** este diccionario es su Biblia; **the B. Belt** = zona integrista protestante en el sur de los Estados Unidos; *Fam Pej* **B. thumper** proselitista *mf* fanático(a)

biblical ['bɪblɪkəl] *adj* bíblico(a); *Hum* **to know sb in the b. sense** haberse llevado al huerto a alguien

bibliography [bɪblɪˈɒgrəfɪ] *n* bibliografía *f*

bibliophile ['bɪblɪəfaɪl] *n* bibliófilo(a) *m,f*

bicameral [baɪˈkæmərəl] *adj Pol* bicameral

bicarbonate [baɪˈkɑːbəneɪt] *n* bicarbonato *m*; **b. of soda** bicarbonato sódico

bicentennial [baɪsenˈtenɪəl], **bicentenary** [baɪsenˈtiːnərɪ] **1** *n* bicentenario *m*

2 *adj* bicentenario(a)

biceps ['baɪseps] *npl Anat* bíceps *m inv*

bicker ['bɪkə(r)] *vi* reñir, pelearse

bickering ['bɪkərɪŋ] *n* riñas *fpl*, peleas *fpl*

bicultural [baɪˈkʌltʃərəl] *adj* con dos culturas

bicycle ['baɪsɪkəl] *n* bicicleta *f*; **to ride a b.** montar en bicicleta; **b. clips** = pinzas que ciñen los pantalones a las pantorrillas para montar en bicicleta; **b. kick** *(in soccer)* tijereta *f*, chilena *f*; **b. path** *(through park, town)* carril *m* para bicicletas; *(through countryside)* sendero *m* para bicicletas; **b. rack** *(on pavement)* soporte *m* para estacionar bicicletas; *(on car)* baca *f* para bicicletas

bid¹ [bɪd] **1** *n* (**a**) *(offer)* oferta *f*; *(at auction)* puja *f*; *St Exch* **b. price** precio *m* comprador (**b**) *(attempt)* tentativa *f*, intento *m*; **a rescue/suicide b.** un intento de rescate/suicidio; **to make a b. for power** intentar conseguir el poder

2 *vt* (*pt & pp* **bid**) *(offer)* ofrecer; *(at auction)* pujar (**for** por); **what am I bid for this table?** ¿qué ofrecen por esta mesa?

3 *vi (at auction)* pujar (**for** por)

bid² (*pt* **bade** [bæd, beɪd] *or* **bid**, *pp* **bidden** ['bɪdən] *or* **bid**) *vt Literary* (**a**) *(greet)* **to b. sb welcome** dar la bienvenida a alguien; **to b. sb goodbye** despedir a alguien (**b**) *(order)* **to b. sb be silent** ordenar callar a alguien

bidder ['bɪdə(r)] *n* postor(ora) *m,f*; **the highest b.** el mejor postor

bidding¹ ['bɪdɪŋ] *n (at auction)* puja *f*; **to start the b. at $5,000** comenzar la puja con 5.000 dólares

bidding² *n Literary (command)* **to do sb's b.** llevar a cabo las órdenes de alguien

bide [baɪd] *vt* **to b. one's time** esperar el momento oportuno

bidet ['biːdeɪ] *n* bidé *m*

biennial [baɪˈenɪəl] **1** *n Bot* planta *f* bienal

2 *adj* bienal

bier [bɪə(r)] *n (for carrying coffin)* andas *fpl*

biff [bɪf] *Fam* **1** *n* mamporro *m*

2 *vt* dar un mamporro a

bifocal [baɪˈfəʊkəl] **1** *n* **bifocals** gafas *fpl or Am* anteojos *fpl* (con lentes) bifocales; **a pair of bifocals** unas gafas *or Am* unos anteojos bifocales

2 *adj* bifocal

big [bɪg] **1** *adj* (**a**) *(tall, large)* grande; *(before singular nouns)* gran; **a b. problem** un problema grande, un gran problema; **to grow big(ger)** crecer; **my b. brother** mi hermano mayor; **he's a b. eater** come un montón; **a b. hand for our guest!** ¡un gran aplauso para nuestro invitado!; *Fam* **the Big Apple** *(New York)* Nueva York; **the Big Bang theory** la teoría del big bang; **b. business** grandes negocios *mpl*; *Fam* **the Big Easy** *(New Orleans)* Nueva Orleans; **b. game** *(in hunting)* caza *f* mayor; **the b. screen** la pantalla grande; **to be a b. spender** gastar mucho; **b. toe** dedo *m* gordo del pie; **b. top** *(of circus)* carpa *f*; **b. wheel** *(at fair) Esp* noria *f*, *Andes* rueda *f* de Chicago, *Arg* vuelta *f* al mundo, *Chile, Urug* rueda *f* gigante, *Méx* rueda *f* de la fortuna

(**b**) *(idioms)* **it's her b. day tomorrow** mañana es el gran día para ella; **to have b. ideas** tener grandes ideas; *Fam* **hey, what's the b. idea?** ¡eh!, ¿qué está pasando aquí?; **to earn b. money** *or Fam* **bucks** ganar millones; **I've got b. plans for you** tengo grandes planes para ti; **she's into computers in a b. way** le van mucho los ordenadores; *Ironic* **that's b. of you!** ¡qué generoso(a)!; **he's getting too b. for his britches** está empezando a darse humos, se lo tiene muy creído; **the boss is very b. on punctuality** el jefe le da mucha importancia a la puntualidad; **it was b. last year** *(music, fashion)* hizo furor el año pasado; *Fam* **to have a b. mouth** *(be indiscreet)* ser un/una bocazas; *Fam* **the b. guns** *(important people)* los pesos pesados; **a b. name** una gran figura; *Fam* **b. shot** pez *m* gordo; **to make** *or* **hit the b. time** conseguir el éxito

2 *adv* **he always talks b.** se le va siempre la fuerza por la boca; **to think b.** pensar a lo grande; **to make it b.** triunfar

bigamist ['bɪgəmɪst] *n* bígamo(a) *m,f*

bigamous ['bɪgəməs] *adj* bígamo(a)

bigamy ['bɪgəmɪ] *n* bigamia *f*

big-boned ['bɪgˈbəʊnd] *adj* huesudo(a)

biggie, biggy ['bɪgɪ] *n Fam* **I think this storm's going to be a b.** me parece que ésta va a ser una tormenta de las gordas

bighead ['bɪghed] *n Fam* creído(a) *m,f*

bigheaded [bɪgˈhedɪd] *adj* creído(a), engreído(a); **we don't want him getting b.** no queremos que se vuelva un creído

bighearted [bɪgˈhɑːtɪd] *adj* **to be b.** tener gran corazón

bigmouth ['bɪgmaʊθ] *n Fam* bocazas *mf inv*, *Am* bocón(ona), *m,f*

bigot ['bɪgət] *n* fanático(a) *m,f*, intolerante *mf*

bigoted ['bɪgətɪd] *adj* fanático(a), intolerante

bigotry ['bɪgətrɪ] *n* fanatismo *m*, intolerancia *f*

bigwig ['bɪgwɪg] *n Fam* pez *m* gordo

bike [baɪk] *n Fam (bicycle)* bici *f*; *(motorcycle)* moto *f*; **b. shed** cobertizo *m* para bicicletas

biker ['baɪkə(r)] *n Fam* motero(a) *m,f*

bikeway ['baɪkweɪ] *n* carril-bici *m*

bikini [bɪˈkiːnɪ] *n* biquini *m*; **to have one's b. line done** depilarse las ingles; **b. bottom** parte *f* de abajo del biquini; **b. top** parte *f* de arriba del biquini

bilateral [baɪˈlætərəl] *adj* bilateral

bilberry ['bɪlbərɪ] *n* arándano *m*

bile [baɪl] *n also Fig* bilis *f inv*, hiel *f*

bilge [bɪldʒ] *n Fam (nonsense)* tonterías *fpl*, *Esp* chorradas *fpl*, *Am* pendejadas *fpl*; **to talk (a lot of) b.** no decir más que tonterías *or Esp* chorradas *or Am* pendejadas

bilingual [baɪˈlɪŋgwəl] *adj* bilingüe

bilingualism [baɪˈlɪŋgwəlɪzəm] *n* bilingüismo *m*

bilious ['bɪlɪəs] *adj* (**a**) *Med* bilioso(a); **b. attack** cólico *m* bilioso; **b. yellow/green** amarillo/verde nauseabundo (**b**) *(bad-tempered)* bilioso(a), atrabiliario(a)

bill¹ [bɪl] **1** *n (of bird)* pico *m*

2 *vi Fam (lovers)* **to b. and coo** hacerse mimos *or* arrumacos

bill² **1** *n* (**a**) *(in restaurant)* cuenta *f*; *(for goods, services)* factura *f*;

Fin **b. of exchange** letra *f* de cambio (**b**) *(banknote)* billete *m* (**c**) *(notice)* cartel *m*; **(stick) no bills** *(sign)* prohibido fijar carteles; *Theat* **to head** *or* **top the b.** estar en cabecera de cartel (**d**) *(list)* **b. of fare** menú *m*, carta *f*; **the doctor gave me a clean b. of health** el médico me dio el visto bueno; *Fam* **to fit the b.** venir como anillo al dedo (**e**) *Pol (proposed law)* proyecto *m* de ley; *Pol* **the B. of Rights** = las diez primeras enmiendas a la constitución estadounidense, relacionadas con la garantía de las libertades individuales

2 *vt* (**a**) *(give invoice to)* pasar (la) factura a (**b**) *(publicize)* anunciar; **it was billed as the debate of the decade** fue anunciado como el debate del decenio

billboard ['bɪlbɔːd] *n* valla *f* publicitaria

billet ['bɪlɪt] **1** *n Mil* acantonamiento *m*
2 *vt* acantonar

billfold ['bɪlfəʊld] *n* cartera *f*, billetera *f*

billiard ['bɪljəd] *n* **billiards** billar *m*; **to play billiards** jugar al billar; **b. ball/table** bola *f*/mesa *f* de billar

billion ['bɪljən] *n* mil millones *mpl*, millardo *m*; *Fam* **I've got billions of things to do!** tengo miles de cosas que hacer

billionaire [bɪljə'neə(r)] *n* multimillonario(a) *m,f*

billow ['bɪləʊ] **1** *n (of smoke)* nube *f*
2 *vi* ondear

billowy ['bɪləʊɪ] *adj (dress, sail)* ondeante; *(clouds)* ondulante

billposter ['bɪlpeʊstə(r)] *n* **billposters will be prosecuted** *(sign)* prohibido fijar carteles (responsable la empresa anunciadora)

billy goat ['bɪlɪɡəʊt] *n* macho *m* cabrío

bimbo ['bɪmbəʊ] *(pl* **bimbos)** *n Fam Pej* = mujer atractiva y de pocas luces

bin [bɪn] *n (for coal)* carbonera *f*; *(for grain)* granero *m*

binary ['baɪnərɪ] *adj Math & Comptr* binario(a); **b. code** código *m* binario; **b. number** número *m* binario

bind [baɪnd] **1** *n Fam* **to be in a b.** estar en un apuro
2 *vt (pt & pp* **bound** [baʊnd]) (**a**) *(tie)* atar; **to b. sb hand and foot** atar a alguien de pies y manos; *Fig* **they are bound together by ties of friendship** les unen lazos *or* vínculos de amistad (**b**) *(bandage)* vendar (**c**) *(book)* encuadernar (**d**) *(cause to stick)* unir, ligar; **b. the mixture with egg** ligar la mezcla con huevo (**e**) *(oblige)* **she bound me to secrecy** me hizo prometer que guardaría el secreto; **you are bound to report any change in your income** tienes obligación de notificar cualquier cambio en tus ingresos; **to be bound by an oath** estar obligado(a) por un juramento

▸**bind over** *vt sep Law* **to b. sb over** obligar judicialmente a alguien

▸**bind up** *vt sep* (**a**) *(cut, wound)* vendar (**b**) **to be bound up with sth** *(involved)* estar íntimamente relacionado(a) con algo

binder ['baɪndə(r)] *n* (**a**) *(for papers)* carpeta *f* (**b**) *(bookbinder)* encuadernador(ora) *m,f* (**c**) *(farm machinery)* empacadora *f*

binding ['baɪndɪŋ] **1** *n* cubierta *f*, tapa *f*
2 *adj* vinculante

binge [bɪndʒ] *Fam* **1** *n (drinking spree)* borrachera *f*; **to go on a b.** ir de juerga *or Esp* marcha; **to go on a shopping b.** ir de compras y traerse media tienda; **a chocolate b.** un atracón de chocolate
2 *vi* **to b. on sth** darse un atracón de algo

bingo ['bɪŋɡəʊ] **1** *n* bingo *m*; **b. hall** (sala *f* de) bingo *m*
2 *exclam* ¡ole!, ¡bravo!

binocular [bɪ'nɒkjʊlə(r)] *adj* binocular; **b. vision** visión *f* binocular

binoculars [bɪ'nɒkjʊləz] *npl* prismáticos *mpl*

biochemic(al) [baɪəʊ'kemɪk(əl)] *adj* bioquímico(a)

biochemist [baɪəʊ'kemɪst] *n* bioquímico(a) *m,f*

biochemistry [baɪəʊ'kemɪstrɪ] *n* bioquímica *f*

biodegradable [baɪəʊdɪ'ɡreɪdəbəl] *adj* biodegradable

biodiversity [baɪəʊdaɪ'vɜːsɪtɪ] *n* biodiversidad *f*

biographer [baɪ'ɒɡrəfə(r)] *n* biógrafo(a) *m,f*

biographic(al) [baɪə'ɡræfɪk(əl)] *adj* biográfico(a)

biography [baɪ'ɒɡrəfɪ] *n* biografía *f*

biological [baɪə'lɒdʒɪkəl] *adj* biológico(a); **b. clock** reloj *m* biológico; **b. warfare** guerra *f* bacteriológica; **b. washing powder** detergente *m* de *or* con acción biológica; **b. weapon** arma *f* biológica

biologist [baɪ'ɒlədʒɪst] *n* biólogo(a) *m,f*

biology [baɪ'ɒlədʒɪ] *n* biología *f*

biopsy ['baɪɒpsɪ] *n Med* biopsia *f*

biorhythm ['baɪəʊrɪðəm] *n* biorritmo *m*

biosphere ['baɪəsfɪə(r)] *n* biosfera *f*

biotech ['baɪəʊtek] **1** *n* biotecnología *f*
2 *adj (industry, company)* de biotecnología

biotechnology [baɪəʊtek'nɒlədʒɪ] *n* biotecnología *f*

bioterrorism ['baɪəʊ'terərɪzəm] *n* bioterrorismo *m*

bipartisan [baɪ'pɑːtɪzæn] *adj Pol* bipartito(a)

biped ['baɪped] *n & adj* bípedo(a) *m,f*

biplane ['baɪpleɪn] *n* biplano *m*

birch [bɜːtʃ] **1** *n* abedul *m*
2 *vt (beat)* azotar

bird [bɜːd] *n* (**a**) *(in general)* pájaro *m*; *(as opposed to mammals, reptiles etc)* ave *f*; **b. of paradise** ave del paraíso; **b. of prey** (ave) rapaz *f*, ave de presa; **b. sanctuary** refugio *m* de aves; **b. table** comedero *m* de pájaros

(**b**) *(idioms) Fam* **a little b. told me** me lo ha dicho un pajarito; **the b. has flown** el pájaro ha volado; *Prov* **a b. in the hand is worth two in the bush** más vale pájaro en mano que ciento volando; *Prov* **birds of a feather flock together** Dios los cría y ellos se juntan; **to give** *or* **flip sb the b.** *(gesture at)* = hacerle un gesto grosero a alguien con el dedo corazón hacia arriba, ≃ hacerle un corte de mangas a alguien; **to kill two birds with one stone** matar dos pájaros de un tiro; *Euph* **to tell sb about the birds and the bees** explicar a alguien de dónde vienen los niños

birdbath ['bɜːdbɑːθ] *n* = especie de pila con agua que se coloca en el jardín para que los pájaros se refresquen

birdbrained ['bɜːdbreɪnd] *adj Fam* **to be b.** ser un majadero; **a b. idea** una majadería

birdcage ['bɜːdkeɪdʒ] *n* jaula *f*

birder ['bɜːdə(r)] *n* aficionado(a) *m,f* a la observación de aves

birdie ['bɜːdɪ] *n* (**a**) *Fam (bird)* pajarito *m* (**b**) *(in golf)* uno *m* bajo par, menos uno *m*

birdseed ['bɜːdsiːd] *n* alpiste *m*

bird's-eye view ['bɜːdzaɪ'vjuː] *n* **to have a b.** *(place)* tener una vista panorámica *(desde arriba)*; *(of situation)* tener una visión de conjunto

bird-watcher ['bɜːdwɒtʃə(r)] *n* aficionado(a) *m,f* a la observación de aves

bird-watching ['bɜːdwɒtʃɪŋ] *n* observación *f* de aves

Birmingham ['bɜːmɪŋəm] *n* Birmingham

birth [bɜːθ] *n also Fig* nacimiento *m*; *(delivery)* parto *m*; **to give b. (to sb)** dar a luz (a alguien); **at b.** al nacer; **from b.** de nacimiento; **Irish by b.** irlandés(esa) de nacimiento; **b. certificate** partida *f* de nacimiento; **b. control** control de natalidad; **b. control methods** métodos *mpl* anticonceptivos; *Fig* **b. pangs** dolores *mpl* del parto; **b. rate** índice *m* de natalidad

birthday ['bɜːθdeɪ] *n* cumpleaños *m inv*; *Fam* **she was in her b. suit** estaba como su madre la trajo al mundo; **b. card** tarjeta *f* de felicitación de cumpleaños; **b. present** regalo *m* de cumpleaños

birthmark ['bɜːθmɑːk] *n* antojo *m*, mancha *f (en la piel)*

birthplace ['bɜːθpleɪs] *n* lugar *m* de nacimiento

birthright ['bɜːθraɪt] *n* derecho *m* natural

birthstone ['bɜːθstəʊn] *n* piedra *f* de nacimiento

Biscay ['bɪskeɪ] *n* **the Bay of B.** el Golfo de Vizcaya

biscuit ['bɪskɪt] *n (muffin)* tortita *f*, bollo *m*

bisect [baɪ'sekt] *vt Math* bisecar; *(town, area)* dividir por la mitad

bisexual [baɪ'seksjʊəl] *n & adj* bisexual *mf*

bisexuality [baɪseksjʊ'ælɪtɪ] *n* bisexualidad *f*

bishop ['bɪʃəp] *n* obispo *m*; *(in chess)* alfil *m*

bishopric ['bɪʃəprɪk] *n* obispado *m*

bison ['baɪsən] *n* bisonte *m*

bisque [bɪsk] *n Culin* crema *f* de mariscos, bisqué *m*; **lobster b.** crema *f* de langosta

bistro ['biːstrəʊ] *(pl* **bistros***) n* restaurante *m* pequeño

bit¹ [bɪt] *n* (**a**) *(in horseriding)* bocado *m*; *Fig* **to have the b. between one's teeth** haber tomado *or Esp* cogido carrerilla (**b**) *(for drill)* broca *f*

bit² *n* (**a**) *(piece)* trozo *m*; **a b. of news** una noticia; **with a b. of luck** con un poco de suerte; **I have done my b.** yo he cumplido con mi parte

(**b**) *(component part)* **to take sth to bits** desarmar *or* desmontar algo; **to tear/smash sth to bits** hacer añicos algo; **he has eaten every b.** se ha comido hasta el último bocado; **bits and pieces** *(personal belongings)* cosas *fpl*, trastos *mpl*

(**c**) *(expressing degree)* **a b. late/heavy/tired** un poco tarde/pesado(a)/cansado(a); **we had a b. of difficulty in finding him** nos costó un poco encontrarlo; **he's a b. of an idiot** es un imbécil; **b. by b.** poco a poco; **not a b. of it!** ¡en absoluto!; **wait a b.!** ¡espera un poco!; **it takes a b. of getting used to** lleva algo de tiempo acostumbrarse; **a good b. older** bastante más viejo(a); **a little b. worried/tired** algo preocupado(a)/cansado(a); **I'm every b. as good as him** no tengo nada que envidiarle; *Fam* **that's a b. much!** ¡eso es pasarse!; **b. part** *(in play, movie)* papel *m* secundario

(**d**) *Comptr* bit *m*

(**e**) *Fam (coin)* moneda *f*; **two bits** 25 centavos

bit³ *pt of* **bite**

bitch [bɪtʃ] **1** *n* (**a**) *(female dog)* perra *f* (**b**) *very Fam Pej (unpleasant woman)* bruja *f*, zorra *f*; **I've had a b. of a day** he tenido un día bien jodido; **life's a b.!** ¡qué vida más perra!

2 *vi Fam (complain)* quejarse, *Esp* dar la tabarra; **he's always bitching about his colleagues** siempre está poniendo a parir *or RP* sacándole el cuero a sus compañeros

bitchy ['bɪtʃɪ] *adj Fam* malicioso(a), *Esp* puñetero(a)

bite [baɪt] **1** *n* (**a**) *(of person, dog)* mordisco *m*; *(of insect)* picadura *f*; *(of snake)* mordedura *f*, picadura *f* (**b**) *(mouthful)* bocado *m*; **he took a b. out of the apple** dio un bocado a la manzana; **I haven't had a b. to eat all day** no he probado bocado en todo el día (**c**) *(sharpness, fierceness) (of speech, article)* chispa *f*; **this mustard has a bit of a b.** esta mostaza está fuertecilla

2 *vt (pt* **bit** [bɪt], *pp* **bitten** ['bɪtən]) (**a**) *(of person, dog)* morder; *(of insect, snake)* picar; **the dog bit him in the leg** el perro le mordió en la pierna; **to b. one's nails** morderse las uñas (**b**) *(idioms)* **to b. one's tongue** *(stay silent)* morderse la lengua; *Fam* **to b. the bullet** agarrar el toro por los cuernos *or RP* las astas; *Fam* **to b. the dust** *(scheme, plan)* irse a pique *or* al garete *or RP* al cuerno; **to b. the hand that feeds you** morder la mano que nos da de comer; *Prov* **once bitten twice shy** gato escaldado del agua fría huye, *RP* el que se quemó con leche, ve una vaca y llora

3 *vi* (**a**) *(person, dog)* morder; *(insect, snake)* picar; **to b. into sth** dar un mordisco a algo; *Fig* **the cost bit into our savings** los gastos supusieron una merma de nuestros ahorros (**b**) *Fig (be felt) (cuts)* hacerse notar (**c**) *Fam (be bad)* ser una mierda

▶**bite off** *vt sep* arrancar de un mordisco; *Fig* **to b. off more than one can chew** querer abarcar demasiado; *Fam Fig* **there's no need to b. my head off** ¡no hace falta que me contestes así!

bite-sized ['baɪtsaɪzd], **bitesize** ['baɪtsaɪz] *adj* del tamaño de un bocado

biting ['baɪtɪŋ] *adj (wind, satire)* penetrante

bitmap ['bɪtmæp] *Comptr* **1** *adj* en mapa de bits
2 *n* mapa *m* de bits

bit-mapped ['bɪtmæpt] *adj Comptr* en mapa de bits

bitten ['bɪtən] *pp of* **bite**

bitter ['bɪtə(r)] *adj* (**a**) *(taste)* amargo(a); *Fig* **it was a b. pill to swallow** costó mucho tragar (con) aquello (**b**) *(wind, opposition)* recio(a); *(struggle)* encarnizado(a); *(tears)* de amargura; **to go on/resist to the b. end** seguir/resistir hasta el final (**c**) *(resentful) (person)* amargado(a), resentido(a); *(argument, words)* agrio(a); *(experience, memories, disappointment)* amargo(a); **to be b. about sth** estar resentido(a) por algo

bitterly ['bɪtəlɪ] *adv* (**a**) *(extremely)* enormemente, terriblemente; **we were b. disappointed** nos llevamos una decepción tremenda; **I b. regretted telling them** me arrepentí enormemente de habérselo dicho; **it was b. cold** hacía un frío horrible (**b**) *(resentfully)* **to complain b.** quejarse amargamente

bitterness ['bɪtənɪs] *n* (**a**) *(taste)* amargor *m* (**b**) *(resentment)* amargura *f*, amargor *m*

bittersweet ['bɪtəswiːt] *adj (taste)* agridulce; *Fig* **b. memories** recuerdos *mpl* entre dulces y amargos

bitty ['bɪtɪ] *adj Fam (small)* **a little b. town** una ciudad chiquitita

bitumen ['bɪtjʊmɪn] *n* betún *m*

bivouac ['bɪvʊæk] **1** *n* vivac *m*, vivaque *m*
2 *vi (pt & pp* **bivouacked***)* vivaquear

biweekly [baɪ'wiːklɪ] **1** *adj (fortnightly)* quincenal; *(twice weekly)* bisemanal
2 *adv (fortnightly)* quincenalmente; *(twice weekly)* dos veces por semana

biz [bɪz] *n Fam* negocio *m*

bizarre [bɪ'zɑː(r)] *adj* extraño(a), raro(a)

blab [blæb] *(pt & pp* **blabbed***) Fam* **1** *vt* soltar
2 *vi (chatter)* parlotear, *Esp* largar, *Méx* platicar, *RP* chusmear; **someone has blabbed to the newspapers** alguien se lo ha soplado a los periódicos

blabber ['blæbə(r)] *vi Fam* parlotear, *Esp* largar, *Méx* platicar, *RP* chusmear

blabbermouth ['blæbəmaʊθ] *n Fam* cotorra *f*, bocazas *mf inv*, *Am* bocón(ona) *m,f*

black [blæk] **1** *n* (**a**) *(color)* negro *m* (**b**) *(person)* negro(a) *m,f* (**c**) *(idioms)* **to be in the b.** *(financially)* tener saldo positivo; **it says here in b. and white…** aquí *Esp* pone *or Am* dice claramente que…; **to see everything in b. and white** tener una actitud maniquea

2 *adj* (**a**) *(color)* negro(a); **a b. man** un negro; **a b. woman** una negra; **b. and blue** *(bruised)* amoratado(a); **b. belt** *(in martial arts)* cinturón *m* negro; *Av* **b. box** caja *f* negra; **b. coffee** café *m* solo; **b. currant** *(berry)* grosella *f* negra; *(bush)* grosellero *m* (negro); **b. eye** ojo *m* morado; *Astron* **b. hole** agujero *m* negro; **b. humor** humor *m* negro; **b. ice** placas *fpl* de hielo; **b. pepper** pimienta *f* negra; **b. pudding** morcilla *f*; *Fig* **b. sheep** oveja *f* negra; **b. tie** *Esp* pajarita *f* negra, *Chile* humita *f* negra, *Col* corbatín *m* negro, *Méx* corbata *f* de moño negra, *RP* moñito *m* negro, *Ven* corbata *f* de lazo negra; *(on invitation)* se ruega ir de etiqueta

(**b**) *(evil, unfavorable)* **to give sb a b. look** lanzar a alguien una mirada asesina; **the future is looking b.** el futuro se presenta muy negro; **it's a b. day for Britain** es un día negro *or* aciago para Gran Bretaña; **b. magic** magia *f* negra; **that earned him a b. mark** aquello supuso un borrón en su historial

(**c**) *(unofficial)* **b. economy** economía *f* sumergida; **b.**

market mercado *m* negro; **b. marketeer** estraperlista *mf*
(**d**) *(in proper names)* **the B. Death** la peste negra; **the B. Forest** la Selva Negra; **B. Forest gateau** = tarta de chocolate y guindas; **B. Maria** *(police van)* coche *m* celular; **B. Muslims** musulmanes *mpl* negros, negros *mpl* musulmanes; **the B. Sea** el Mar Negro

   3 *vt (blacken)* ennegrecer, pintar de negro

▸**black out 1** *vt sep* (**a**) *(censor) (piece of writing)* borrar, tachar; *(person in photo)* suprimir (**b**) *(city)* dejar a oscuras (**c**) *TV* **job action has blacked out this evening's programs** la huelga ha obligado a suspender los programas de esta noche

   2 *vi (faint)* desmayarse

black-and-white [blækən'waɪt] *adj (movie, TV, illustration)* en blanco y negro

blackball ['blækbɔːl] *vt* vetar, votar en contra de

blackberry ['blækbərɪ] *n (bush)* zarzamora *f; (berry)* mora *f*

blackbird ['blækbɜːd] *n* mirlo *m*

blackboard ['blækbɔːd] *n* pizarra *f*, encerado *m*, *Am* pizarrón *m*

blacken ['blækən] *vt* ennegrecer; *Fig (reputation)* manchar; **clouds blackened the sky** las nubes oscurecían el cielo

blackguard ['blægɑːd] *n Old-fashioned* villano *m*, bellaco *m*

blackhead ['blækhed] *n* punto *m* negro, barrillo *m*

blackjack ['blækdʒæk] *n* (**a**) *(truncheon)* porra *f* (**b**) *(card game)* veintiuna *f*

blacklist ['blæklɪst] **1** *n* lista *f* negra

   2 *vt* poner en la lista negra

blackmail ['blækmeɪl] **1** *n* chantaje *m*

   2 *vt* hacer chantaje a, chantajear

blackness ['blæknɪs] *n (dirtiness)* negrura *f; (darkness)* oscuridad *f*

blackout ['blækaʊt] *n* (**a**) *(during air-raid)* apagón *m; Fig* **to impose a news b.** prohibir la cobertura informativa (**b**) *(fainting fit)* desmayo *m*

blacksmith ['blæksmɪθ] *n* herrero *m*

blacktop ['blæktɒp] *n* (**a**) *(substance)* asfalto *m* (**b**) *(road)* carretera *f*

bladder ['blædə(r)] *n* vejiga *f*

blade [bleɪd] *n (of knife, sword)* hoja *f; (of propeller, oar)* pala *f; (of grass)* brizna *f*, hoja *f*

blah [blɑː] *n Fam (meaningless remarks, nonsense)* sandeces *fpl*, *Esp* chorradas *fpl*, *Am* pendejadas *fpl*, *RP* pavadas *fpl;* **b., b., b.** *(to avoid repetition)* y tal y cual, patatín patatán

blame [bleɪm] **1** *n* culpa *f;* **to put the b. (for sth) on sb** culpar a alguien (de algo), echar la culpa a alguien (de algo); **to take the b. (for sth)** asumir la culpa (de algo)

   2 *vt* culpar, echar la culpa a; **to b. sb for sth, to b. sth on sb** echar la culpa a alguien de algo; **to be to b.** tener la culpa; **I b. myself for what happened** lo que pasó fue culpa mía; **I don't b. you for wanting to leave** no me extraña que quieras marcharte; **she has nobody to b. but herself** ella, y sólo ella, tiene la culpa

blameless ['bleɪmlɪs] *adj (person)* inocente; *(conduct, life)* intachable

blameworthy ['bleɪmwɜːðɪ] *adj (person)* culpable; *(conduct)* reprobable

blanch [blɑːntʃ] **1** *vt Culin* escaldar

   2 *vi (go pale)* palidecer, ponerse pálido(a)

blancmange [blə'mɒnʒ] *n* = budín dulce de aspecto gelatinoso a base de leche y maicena

bland [blænd] *adj* soso(a), insulso(a); **b. assurances** promesas *fpl* tibias

blandishments ['blændɪʃmənts] *npl Formal* halagos *mpl*, lisonjas *fpl*

blandly ['blændlɪ] *adv (reply, smile)* tibiamente, con tibieza

blank [blæŋk] **1** *n* (**a**) *(space)* espacio *m* en blanco; **my mind is a b.** no recuerdo absolutamente nada; *Fig* **to draw a b.**

(inquiry) no sacar nada en claro *or* en limpio (**b**) *(rifle cartridge)* cartucho *m* de fogueo; **to fire blanks** disparar tiros de fogueo

   2 *adj (paper, screen)* en blanco; *(face, look)* vacío(a), inexpresivo(a); **he looked b. when I mentioned your name** no dio muestras de reconocer tu nombre cuando lo mencioné; **my mind went b.** se me quedó la mente en blanco; **b. cassette** cinta *f* virgen; **b. check** cheque *m* en blanco; *Fig* **to give sb a b. check to do sth** dar carta blanca a alguien para hacer algo; **b. verse** *(in poetry)* verso *m* blanco, verso *m* suelto

▸**blank out** *vt sep (erase)* borrar

blanket ['blæŋkɪt] **1** *n* manta *f*, *Am* cobija *f*, *Am* frazada *f; (of fog, cloud)* manto *m*

   2 *adj (agreement, ban)* general, total; **the government imposed a b. ban on demonstrations** el gobierno prohibió todas las manifestaciones; **b. term** término *m* general

blankly ['blæŋklɪ] *adv (without expression)* inexpresivamente; *(without understanding)* sin comprender; **she stared b. into the distance** tenía la mirada perdida en la distancia

blare ['bleə(r)] **1** *n* estruendo *m*

   2 *vi (radio, music)* retumbar

blarney ['blɑːnɪ] *n Fam* coba *f*, labia *f*

blasé [blɑː'zeɪ] *adj* **she was very b. about the accident** no le dio mayor importancia al accidente

blaspheme [blæs'fiːm] *vi* blasfemar

blasphemer [blæs'fiːmə(r)] *n* blasfemo(a) *m,f*

blasphemous ['blæsfəməs] *adj* blasfemo(a)

blasphemy ['blæsfəmɪ] *n* blasfemia *f*

blast [blɑːst] **1** *n* (**a**) *(of wind)* ráfaga *f; (of heat)* bocanada *f; (of whistle, horn)* pitido *m;* **at full b.** *(machines)* a toda máquina; *Fam* **the radio was on full b.** la radio estaba a todo volumen; **b. furnace** alto horno *m* (**b**) *(explosion)* explosión *f; (shock wave)* onda *f* expansiva; *Fam* **meeting him was a real b. from the past!** encontrarme con él fue como volver de repente al pasado (**c**) *Fam (good time)* pasada *f;* **it was a b.** lo pasamos genial, *Esp* fue una pasada; **we had a b.** lo pasamos bomba

   2 *vt* (**a**) *(hole, tunnel)* abrir (con la ayuda de explosivos); **the building had been blasted by a bomb** una bomba había volado el edificio; *Fam* **to b. sb's head off** volarle la cabeza a alguien; *Fam* **to b. sb's hopes** dar al traste con las esperanzas de alguien (**b**) *Fam (criticize)* machacar, atacar

▸**blast off** *vi (space rocket)* despegar

blastoff ['blɑːstɒf] *n (of space rocket)* lanzamiento *m*

blatant ['bleɪtənt] *adj* descarado(a), manifiesto(a); **a b. lie** una mentira evidente

blatantly ['bleɪtəntlɪ] *adv* descaradamente, ostensiblemente; **b. obvious** más que evidente

blather ['blæðə(r)] *vi Fam* desbarrar, decir *Esp* paridas *or Am* pendejadas *or RP* pavadas

blaze [bleɪz] **1** *n* (**a**) *(fire) (in hearth)* fuego *m*, hoguera *f; (uncontrolled)* fuego *m*, incendio *m* (**b**) *(of color, light)* explosión *f;* **in a b. of anger** en un ataque de ira; **in a b. of publicity** acompañado(a) de una gran campaña publicitaria; **to go out in a b. of glory** marcharse de forma apoteósica (**c**) *Fam* **what the blazes does he want?** ¿qué diantre(s) quiere?

   2 *vt Fig* **to b. a trail** abrir nuevos caminos

   3 *vi (fire)* arder; *(sun)* abrasar; *(light)* estar encendido(a) *or Am* prendido(a); **to b. with anger** estar encendido(a) de ira

blazer ['bleɪzə(r)] *n* chaqueta *f*, americana *f*

blazing ['bleɪzɪŋ] *adj (building)* en llamas; *Fig* **a b. row** una discusión violenta

bleach [bliːtʃ] **1** *n* lejía *f*, *Arg* lavandina *f*, *CAm, Chile, Méx, Ven* cloro *m*, *Urug* jane *f*

   2 *vt (cloth)* desteñir; **hair bleached by the sun** cabellos descoloridos por el sol

bleak [bliːk] *adj (landscape, mountain)* desolado(a); *(weather)* miserable; *(outlook)* desolador(ora)

bleary ['blɪərɪ] *adj (eyes)* enrojecido(a)

bleary-eyed [blɪərɪ'aɪd] *adj* **to be b.** tener los ojos enrojecidos

bleat [bliːt] **1** *n (of lamb)* balido *m*
2 *vi (lamb)* balar; *Pej (complain)* lamentarse (**about** de)

bleed [bliːd] *(pt & pp* **bled** [bled]*)* **1** *vt Med* sangrar; *(radiator)* purgar; *Fig* **to b. sb dry** chupar la sangre a alguien
2 *vi* sangrar; **his nose is bleeding** le sangra la nariz; **to b. to death** morir desangrado(a)

bleeding ['bliːdɪŋ] **1** *n* hemorragia *f*; **has the b. stopped?** ¿me/te/le *etc* ha dejado de salir sangre?
2 *adj (wound)* sangrante

bleep [bliːp] **1** *n* pitido *m*
2 *vi* pitar

blemish ['blemɪʃ] **1** *n (mark)* mancha *f*, marca *f*; *(on reputation)* mancha *f*, mácula *f*
2 *vt Fig (spoil)* manchar, perjudicar

blench [blentʃ] *vi (flinch)* inmutarse

blend [blend] **1** *n* mezcla *f*
2 *vt (styles, ideas)* conjugar (**with** con); *Culin* mezclar; **b. the eggs and butter together** mezclar los huevos y la mantequilla; **blended tea/tobacco** mezcla *f* de tés/tabacos
3 *vi (mix together)* mezclarse

▶**blend in** *vi (with surroundings)* armonizar (**with** con)

▶**blend into** *vt insep (surroundings)* confundirse con; **to b. into the background** *(go unnoticed)* pasar desapercibido(a)

blender ['blendə(r)] *n Esp* batidora *f*, *Am* licuadora *f*

bless [bles] *(pt & pp* **blessed** [blest]*)* *vt (say blessing for)* bendecir; **God b. you!** ¡(que) Dios te bendiga!; **b. you!** *(when someone sneezes)* ¡salud!, *Esp* ¡jesús!; **he is blessed with quick wits** tiene la suerte de ser muy espabilado; **they have been blessed with two fine children** han tenido dos hermosos hijos

blessed ['blesɪd] *adj (a) (holy)* sagrado(a), santo(a); **the B. Sacrament** el Santísimo Sacramento *(b) Fam (for emphasis)* dichoso(a); **a b. nuisance** una pesadez; **I can't see a b. thing!** ¡no veo un pimiento!

blessing ['blesɪŋ] *n (a) (religious)* bendición *f*; *Fig* **she gave her son/the plan her b.** bendijo a su hijo/el plan *(b) (benefit, advantage)* bendición *f*, bondad *f*; **it turned out to be a b. in disguise** a pesar de lo que parecía al principio, resultó ser una bendición; **it was a mixed b.** tuvo sus cosas malas y sus cosas buenas; **to count one's blessings** dar gracias (a Dios) por lo que se tiene

blew [bluː] *pt of* **blow²**

blight [blaɪt] **1** *n (crop disease)* mildiu *m*; *Fig* plaga *f*; **potato b.** mildiu *m* de la patata; **to cast a b. on sth** enturbiar algo
2 *vt Fig* menoscabar, socavar; **to b. sb's hopes** truncar las esperanzas de alguien

blind¹ [blaɪnd] **1** *npl* **the b.** los ciegos; *Fig* **it's like the b. leading the b.** es como un ciego guiando a otro ciego; **b. school** escuela *f* para ciegos
2 *adj* ciego(a); **to be b.** ser *or* estar ciego(a); **to go b.** quedarse ciego(a); **to be b. to sth** no ver algo; **a b. man** un ciego; **a b. woman** una ciega; **to be b. in one eye** ser tuerto(a); **to be as b. as a bat** ser cegato(a) perdido(a); **to turn a b. eye (to sth)** hacer la vista gorda (con algo); **to be b. with fury** estar ciego(a) de ira; **b. alley** callejón *m* sin salida; **b. date** cita *f* a ciegas; **b. man's buff** la gallinita ciega; **b. spot** *(for driver)* ángulo *m* muerto
3 *adv* **to be b. drunk** estar borracho(a) perdido(a)
4 *vt (deprive of sight, dazzle)* cegar; *Fig* **love blinded her to his faults** el amor le impedía ver sus defectos

blind² *n* persiana *f*

blinders ['blaɪndəz] *npl (for horse)* anteojeras *fpl*

blindfold ['blaɪndfəʊld] **1** *n* venda *f*
2 *vt* vendar los ojos a

blinding ['blaɪndɪŋ] *adj (light)* cegador(ora), *Fig (intensity)* violento(a)

blindly ['blaɪndlɪ] *adv (to obey, follow)* ciegamente

blindness ['blaɪndnɪs] *n also Fig* ceguera *f*

blink [blɪŋk] **1** *n (a) (of eyes)* parpadeo *m*, pestañeo *m (b) Fam* **the TV is on the b. again** ya se ha vuelto a escacharrar la tele
2 *vt* **to b. one's eyes** parpadear, pestañear
3 *vi (person)* parpadear, pestañear; *(lights)* parpadear

blinkered ['blɪŋkəd] *adj (approach, attitude)* estrecho(a) de miras, cerrado(a)

blinkers ['blɪŋkəz] *npl (a) (for horse)* anteojeras *fpl*; *Fig* **to be wearing b.** ser estrecho(a) de miras *(b) Fam (indicators)* intermitentes *mpl*

blinking ['blɪŋkɪŋ] **1** *adj (light)* intermitente
2 *adv (for emphasis)* **it's b. cold/expensive** hace un frío/es caro de narices

blip [blɪp] *n (on radar screen)* parpadeo *m*; *Fam (temporary problem)* pequeño problema *m*

bliss [blɪs] *n* éxtasis *m inv*; **breakfast in bed, what b.!** el desayuno en la cama, ¡qué maravilla!

blissful ['blɪsfʊl] *adj* maravilloso(a), feliz; **to be in b. ignorance** ser felizmente ignorante

blissfully ['blɪsfʊlɪ] *adv* felizmente; **b. happy** completamente feliz; **b. ignorant** felizmente ignorante

blister ['blɪstə(r)] **1** *n (on feet, skin)* ampolla *f*; *(on paint)* burbuja *f*
2 *vt (feet, skin)* levantar ampollas en, ampollar; *(paint)* hacer que salgan burbujas en
3 *vi (feet, skin)* ampollarse; *(paint)* hacer burbujas

blistering ['blɪstərɪŋ] *adj (sun, heat)* abrasador(ora), achicharrante; *(criticism, attack)* feroz, despiadado(a)

blithe ['blaɪð] *adj* alegre

blithely ['blaɪðlɪ] *adv* alegremente

blithering ['blɪðərɪŋ] *adj* **a b. idiot** un verdadero idiota

blitz [blɪts] *n (air bombardment)* bombardeo *m*, ataque *m* aéreo; *Hist* **The B.** = bombardeo alemán de ciudades británicas en 1940-41; *Fam Fig* **let's have a b. on that paperwork** vamos a quitarnos de encima estos papeles

blizzard ['blɪzəd] *n* ventisca *f*, tormenta *f* de nieve

bloated ['bləʊtɪd] *adj (stomach, budget)* hinchado(a); *(ego)* exagerado(a)

blob [blɒb] *n (of cream, jam)* cuajarón *m*; *(of paint)* goterón *m*; *(of ink)* gota *f*

bloc [blɒk] *n Pol* bloque *m*

block [blɒk] **1** *n (a) (of ice, wood, stone)* bloque *m*; *(of butcher, for execution)* tajo *m*; *Fam* **I'll knock your b. off!** ¡te rompo la crisma!; **b. and tackle** *(for lifting)* polipasto *m*, sistema *m* de poleas; **b. capitals** *(letters fpl)* mayúsculas *fpl*; **b. diagram** *(flowchart)* diagrama *m* (de flujo *or* bloques) *(b) (building)* bloque *m*; *(group of buildings)* manzana *f*, *Am* cuadra *f (c) (of shares)* paquete *m*; *(of seats, tickets)* grupo *m*, conjunto *m*; *Comptr* **a b. of text** un bloque de texto; **b. booking** reserva *f* de grupo; **b. vote** voto *m* por delegación
2 *vt (a) (pipe, road, proposal)* bloquear; *(toilet, sink)* atascar; *(exit, stairs)* obstruir; **to b. sb's way** cerrar el paso a alguien; **to b. sb's view** no dejar ver a alguien; *Fin* **to b. a check** anular un cheque *(b) Comptr* **to b. text** marcar un bloque de texto

▶**block off** *vt sep (road, exit)* cortar, bloquear

▶**block out** *vt sep (light)* impedir el paso de; *(memory)* enterrar; **she wears ear plugs to b. out the music** se pone tapones en los oídos para no oír la música

▶**block up** *vt sep (door, window)* atrancar; *(hole, entrance)* tapar; **to have a blocked-up nose** tener la nariz taponada

blockade [blɒ'keɪd] **1** *n* bloqueo *m*, embargo *m*
2 *vt* bloquear

blockage ['blɒkɪdʒ] *n* obstrucción *f*

blockbuster ['blɒkbʌstə(r)] *n (success)* bombazo *m*, gran éxito *m*

blockhead ['blɒkhed] *n Fam* zoquete *m*, *Esp* tarugo *m*

blog [blɒg] *n Comptr (abbr* **weblog**) blog *m*, bitácora *f*

blogger ['blɒgə(r)] *n* blogger *mf*, bitacorero(a) *m,f*

blonde [blɒnd] **1** *n (woman)* rubia *f*, *Méx* güera *f*, *CAm* chela *f*, *Carib* catira *f*, *Col* mona *f*
2 *adj* rubio(a), *Méx* güero(a), *CAm* chele(a), *Carib* catire(a), *Col* mono(a)

blood [blʌd] **1** *n* **(a)** sangre *f*; **to give b.** donar sangre; **b. bank** banco *m* de sangre; **b. cell** glóbulo *m*; **b. clot** coágulo *m*; **b. count** recuento *m* de células sanguíneas, hemograma *m*; **b. donor** donante *mf* de sangre; **b. group** grupo *m* sanguíneo; **b. poisoning** septicemia *f*; **b. pressure** tensión *f* (arterial), presión *f* sanguínea; **to have high/low b. pressure** tener la tensión alta/baja; **they are b. relations** les unen lazos de sangre; **b. sausage** morcilla *f*; **b. sports** deportes *mpl* cinegéticos; **b. sugar** (nivel *m* de) azúcar *m or f* en la sangre; **b. test** análisis *m inv* de sangre; **b. transfusion** transfusión *f* sanguínea; **b. vessel** vaso *m* sanguíneo
(b) *(idioms)* **to have b. on one's hands** tener las manos manchadas de sangre; **it makes my b. boil when…** me hierve la sangre cuando…; **it makes my b. run cold** me hiela la sangre; **in cold b.** a sangre fría; **he's after your b.** te tiene ojeriza; **to have sth in one's b.** llevar algo en la sangre; **it's like trying to get b. out of a stone** *or* **turnip** es como intentar sacar agua de una piedra; *Prov* **b. is thicker than water** la sangre tira
2 *vt (initiate) (soldier, politician)* dar el bautismo de fuego a

bloodbath ['blʌdbɑ:θ] *n* baño *m* de sangre

bloodcurdling ['blʌdkɜ:dlɪŋ] *adj* aterrador(ora), horripilante

bloodhound ['blʌdhaʊnd] *n* sabueso *m*

bloodless ['blʌdlɪs] *adj* **(a)** *(without bloodshed)* incruento(a), sin derramamiento de sangre; **b. coup** *(in country)* golpe *m* incruento; *Fig (in company, political party)* golpe *m* de mano
(b) *(pale)* pálido(a)

bloodletting ['blʌdletɪŋ] *n* **(a)** *Med* sangría *f* **(b)** *(slaughter)* sangría *f*, matanza *f*; *(internal feuding)* luchas *fpl* intestinas

bloodshed ['blʌdʃed] *n* derramamiento *m* de sangre

bloodshot ['blʌdʃɒt] *adj (eyes)* inyectado(a) de sangre

bloodstain ['blʌdsteɪn] *n* mancha *f* de sangre

bloodstained ['blʌdsteɪnd] *adj* manchado(a) de sangre

bloodstream ['blʌdstri:m] *n* torrente *m or* flujo *m* sanguíneo

bloodsucker ['blʌdsʌkə(r)] *n (mosquito, leech)* chupador(ora) *m,f* de sangre; *Fam (person)* sanguijuela *f*, parásito(a) *m,f*

bloodthirsty ['blʌdθɜ:stɪ] *adj* sanguinario(a)

bloody ['blʌdɪ] *adj (bleeding)* sanguinolento(a), sangriento(a); *(bloodstained)* ensangrentado(a); *(battle, revolution)* sangriento(a); *Fig* **to give sb a b. nose** poner a alguien en su sitio

bloom [blu:m] **1** *n* flor *f*; **in (full) b.** en flor, florecido(a); *Fig* en su apogeo; **in the b. of youth** en la flor de la edad
2 *vi (garden, flower, talent)* florecer; *Fig* **to b. with health** estar rebosante de salud

bloomer ['blu:mə(r)] *n Fam (mistake)* metedura *f* de pata

bloomers ['blu:məz] *npl* pololos *mpl*

blooming ['blu:mɪŋ] *adj (healthy)* **b. (with health)** rebosante de salud

blooper ['blu:pə(r)] *n Fam Hum* metedura *f* de pata

blossom ['blɒsəm] **1** *n* flor *f*; **to be in b.** estar en flor
2 *vi also Fig* florecer; *Fig* **to b. into sth** transformarse en algo

blot [blɒt] **1** *n (of ink)* borrón *m*, mancha *f*; *Fig* tacha *f*, mácula *f*
2 *vt (pt & pp* **blotted**) **(a)** *(stain)* emborronar, manchar **(b)** *(with blotting paper)* secar

▶**blot out** *vt sep (sun, light)* impedir el paso de; *(memory)* enterrar

blotch [blɒtʃ] *n (on skin)* mancha *f*, enrojecimiento *m*

blotchy ['blɒtʃɪ] *adj (skin)* con manchas

blotter ['blɒtə(r)] *n (blotting pad)* secante *m* (de rodillo)

blotting paper ['blɒtɪŋpeɪpə(r)] *n* papel *m* secante

blouse [blaʊz] *n* blusa *f*

blow¹ [bləʊ] *n* **(a)** *(hit)* golpe *m*; **to come to blows (over sth)** llegar a las manos (por algo); *Fig* **to strike a b. for sth** romper una lanza por algo; *Fig* **to soften the b.** para suavizar el golpe **(b)** *(setback)* duro golpe *m*; **this news was a b. to us** la noticia fue un duro golpe para nosotros

blow² (*pt* **blew** [blu:], *pp* **blown** [bləʊn]) **1** *vt* **(a)** *(of wind)* **the wind blew down the fence** el viento derribó la valla; **the wind blew the door open** el viento abrió la puerta
(b) *(of person) (flute, whistle, horn)* tocar; **to b. glass** soplar vidrio; **to b. the dust off sth** soplar el polvo que hay en algo; **to b. sb a kiss** lanzar un beso a alguien; **to b. one's nose** sonarse la nariz; *Fig* **to b. one's own trumpet** echarse flores, *RP* batirse el parche; *Fig* **to b. the whistle on sth/sb** dar la alarma sobre algo/ alguien
(c) *Elec* **the hairdryer has blown a fuse** se ha fundido el fusible (del enchufe) del secador; *Fig* **to b. a fuse** *(person)* ponerse hecho(a) una furia; *CSur* rayarse; *Fam Fig* **the Grand Canyon blew my mind** el Gran Cañón me dejó patidifuso
(d) *Fam (chance, opportunity)* echar a perder, *Esp* mandar al garete; **that's blown it!** ¡lo ha estropeado todo!
(e) *Fam (money)* fundir, *RP* fumar; **he blew all his savings on a vacation** se fundió *or RP* fumó todos sus ahorros en unas vacaciones
2 *vi* **(a)** *(wind, person)* soplar; **the fence blew down** el viento derribó la valla; **my papers blew out of the window** mis papeles salieron volando por la ventana; **the door blew open/shut** el viento abrió/cerró la puerta; **to b. on one's fingers** calentarse los dedos soplando; *Fig* **he's always blowing hot and cold** está cambiando constantemente de opinión **(b)** *Elec (fuse)* fundirse

▶**blow away 1** *vt sep* **the wind blew the newspaper away** el viento se llevó el periódico; *Fam* **to b. sb away** *(shoot dead)* pegar un tiro a alguien; *Fam Fig* **his latest movie blew me away** su última película me dejó alucinado
2 *vi (paper, hat)* salir volando

▶**blow off 1** *vt sep* **the wind blew her hat off** el viento le quitó el sombrero; *Fam* **to b. sb's head off** *(with gun)* volarle la cabeza a alguien
2 *vi (hat)* salir volando

▶**blow out** *vt sep (extinguish)* apagar

▶**blow over** *vi (storm)* amainar; *(scandal)* calmarse

▶**blow up 1** *vt sep* **(a)** *(inflate) (balloon, tire)* inflar, hinchar **(b)** *(explode)* explosionar, (hacer) explotar **(c)** *Phot (enlarge)* ampliar; *Fig* **it had been blown up out of all proportion** se sacaron las cosas de quicio
2 *vi (bomb)* explotar, hacer explosión; *Fig (lose one's temper)* explotar, ponerse hecho(a) una furia

blow-by-blow ['bləʊbaɪ'bləʊ] *adj (account)* detallado(a), con todo lujo de detalles

blow-dry ['bləʊdraɪ] **1** *n* secado *m*
2 *vt* secar con secador de mano

blowgun ['bləʊgʌn] *n* cerbatana *f*

blowhole ['bləʊhəʊl] *n (of whale)* espiráculo *m*

blowjob ['bləʊdʒɒb] *n Vulg* chupada *f*, *Esp* mamada *f*; **to give sb a b.** chupársela *or Esp* comérsela a alguien

blown [bləʊn] *pp of* **blow²**

blowout ['bləʊaʊt] *n* **(a)** *(of tire)* reventón *m*, *Am* ponchadura *f* **(b)** *Fam (big meal)* comilona *f*, *Esp* cuchipanda *f*

blowpipe ['bləʊpaɪp] *n (weapon)* cerbatana *f*

blowtorch ['bləʊtɔ:tʃ] *n* soplete *m*

blowzy, blowsy ['blaʊzɪ] *adj (woman)* desaseada y gorda

blubber ['blʌbə(r)] **1** n (fat) grasa f

2 vi Fam (cry) lloriquear

bludgeon ['blʌdʒən] vt apalear; Fig **to b. sb into doing sth** forzar a alguien a que haga algo

blue [blu:] **1** n (**a**) (color) azul m; Fig **out of the b.** inesperadamente (**b**) **the blues** (music) el blues; Fam **to have the blues** (be depressed) estar muy depre

2 adj (**a**) (color) azul; **b. with cold** amoratado(a) de frío; Fam **she can complain until she's b. in the face** puede quejarse todo lo que quiera; **once in a b. moon** de uvas a peras, RP cada muerte de obispo; Fam **to scream b. murder** poner el grito en el cielo; **b. blood** sangre f azul; **b. cheese** queso m azul; **b. tit** herrerillo m; **b. whale** ballena f azul (**b**) Fam (sad) **to feel b.** estar depre or triste (**c**) Fam (obscene) (joke) verde; **to tell b. stories** contar chistes verdes; **a b. movie** una película porno

bluebell ['blu:bel] n campanilla f

blueberry ['blu:bərɪ] n arándano m

bluebird ['blu:bɜ:d] n azulejo m

bluebottle ['blu:bɒtəl] n moscarda f, mosca f azul

blue-chip ['blu:tʃɪp] adj Fin (shares, company) de gran liquidez, puntero(a)

blue-collar ['blu:ˈkɒlə(r)] adj **b. worker** trabajador(ora) m,f manual

blue-eyed ['blu:aɪd] adj de ojos azules

blueprint ['blu:prɪnt] n Archit & Ind cianotipo m, plano m; Fig (plan) proyecto m

blue-sky ['blu:skaɪ] adj (**a**) (research) puramente teórico(a) or especulativo(a) (**b**) (stocks, shares) fraudulento(a)

bluff¹ [blʌf] **1** n (pretense) farol m; **to call sb's b.** (at cards) ver a alguien un farol; (in negotiation) retar a alguien a que cumpla sus amenazas

2 vi (pretend) fingir, simular; (in cards) tirarse un farol

bluff² n (cliff) despeñadero m

bluff³ adj (manner) abrupto(a)

blunder ['blʌndə(r)] **1** n metedura f or Am metida f de pata; (more serious) error m

2 vi (**a**) (make mistake) meter la pata; (more seriously) cometer un error (**b**) (move clumsily) **to b. along** avanzar dando tumbos; **to b. into sth/sb** tropezar con algo/alguien

blunderbuss ['blʌndəbʌs] n trabuco m

blunt [blʌnt] **1** adj (**a**) (blade) romo(a), desafilado(a); (pencil) desafilado(a) (**b**) (manner, statement, person) franco(a); (refusal) contundente; **to be b.,...** para ser francos,...

2 vt (**a**) (blade, pencil) desafilar (**b**) (dull) (anger, enthusiasm) atenuar, templar

bluntly ['blʌntlɪ] adv (frankly) sin rodeos, claramente

bluntness ['blʌntnɪs] n (**a**) (of blade) embotadura f (**b**) (of manner, statement, person) franqueza f, llaneza f

blur [blɜ:(r)] **1** n (vague shape) imagen f borrosa; (unclear memory) vago recuerdo m; **to go by in a b.** (time) pasar sin sentir or en un suspiro

2 vt (pt & pp **blurred**) desdibujar

3 vi also Fig desdibujarse

blurb [blɜ:b] n Fam (on book jacket) notas y citas fpl promocionales

blurred [blɜ:d] adj borroso(a)

▶**blurt out** [blɜ:t] vt sep soltar

blush [blʌʃ] **1** n (**a**) (flush) rubor m, sonrojo m; **to spare sb's blushes** salvar a alguien del bochorno (**b**) (rouge) colorete m

2 vi ruborizarse, sonrojarse; **I b. to admit it** me da vergüenza or Am pena confesarlo

blusher ['blʌʃə(r)] n (rouge) colorete m

bluster ['blʌstə(r)] **1** n (protests, threats) bravuconadas fpl, fanfarronadas fpl

2 vi (protest, threaten) echar bravatas

blustery ['blʌstərɪ] adj (wind) tempestuoso(a); **a b. day** un día de vientos tempestuosos

Blvd (abbr **Boulevard**) bulevar

BO [bi:ˈəʊ] n Fam (abbr **body odor**) sobaquina f, olor m a sudor

boa ['bəʊə] n **b. (constrictor)** boa f (constrictor); **feather b.** boa m

boar ['bɔ:(r)] n (male pig) verraco m; (wild pig) jabalí m

board [bɔ:d] **1** n (**a**) (of wood) tabla f, tablón m; (for notices) tablón m; (for chess, checkers) tablero m; (blackboard) pizarra f, encerado m, Am pizarrón m; **to go by the b.** (be abandoned, ignored) irse a pique; **across the b.** de manera global or general; **b. game** juego m de mesa (**b**) (group of people) **b. (of directors)** consejo m de administración; **b. of inquiry** comisión f investigadora; Educ **b. of examiners** tribunal m (de examinadores); **b. meeting** reunión f del consejo, junta f; **b. of trade** cámara f de comercio (**c**) (meals) **half b.** media pensión f; **full b.** pensión f completa; **b. and room** alojamiento m y comida (**d**) Naut **on b.** a bordo; **to go on b.** subir a bordo

2 vt (ship, plane) embarcar en; (train, bus) subir a, montar en

3 vi (**a**) (lodge) alojarse (**with** en casa de); (at school) estar interno(a) (**b**) Av **flight 123 is now boarding** el vuelo 123 está en estos momentos procediendo al embarque

▶**board up** vt sep (house, window) cubrir con tablas, entablar

boarder ['bɔ:də(r)] n (lodger) huésped mf; (at school) interno(a) m,f

boarding ['bɔ:dɪŋ] n (**a**) Av **b. card** or **pass** tarjeta f de embarque (**b**) **b. school** internado m

boardinghouse ['bɔ:dɪŋhaʊs] n pensión f

boardroom ['bɔ:dru:m] n sala f de juntas

boardwalk ['bɔ:dwɔ:k] n paseo m marítimo entarimado

boast [bəʊst] **1** n jactancia f, alarde m

2 vt **the school boasts a fine library** el colegio posee una excelente biblioteca

3 vi alardear (**about** de); **it's nothing to b. about!** ¡no es como para estar orgulloso!

boastful ['bəʊstfʊl] adj jactancioso(a), presuntuoso(a)

boasting ['bəʊstɪŋ] n jactancia f, alardeo m

boat [bəʊt] n (in general) barco m; (small) barca f, bote m; (large) buque m; **I came by b.** vine en barco; Fig **we're all in the same b.** estamos todos en el mismo barco; **b. train** = ferrocarril que enlaza con una línea marítima

boatbuilder ['bəʊtbɪldə(r)] n constructor(ora) m,f de barcos

boater ['bəʊtə(r)] n (straw hat) canotier m

boathouse ['bəʊthaʊs] n cobertizo m para barcas

boating ['bəʊtɪŋ] n paseo m en barca; **to go b.** ir a pasear en barca

boat-load ['bəʊtləʊd] n (of cargo, tourists) cargamento m; Fig **by the b.** a espuertas

boatswain ['bəʊsən] n Naut contramaestre m

boatyard ['bəʊtja:d] n astillero m

bob [bɒb] **1** n (**a**) (curtsey) ligera genuflexión f (a modo de saludo) (**b**) (hairstyle) corte m estilo paje (**c**) (bobsleigh) bobsleigh m, bob m

2 vt (pt & pp **bobbed**) (**a**) **to b. one's head** hacer un gesto con la cabeza (**b**) **to have one's hair bobbed** cortarse el pelo a lo paje

3 vi **to b. up and down** moverse arriba y abajo; **to b. around** (on water) mecerse

bobbin ['bɒbɪn] n (on machine) canilla f, bobina f; (for thread) carrete m, bobina f

bobble ['bɒbəl] n (on hat) borla f

bobby ['bɒbɪ] n **b. pin** horquilla f

bobsled ['bɒbsled], **bobsleigh** ['bɒbsleɪ] n bobsleigh m, bob m

bod [bɒd] n Fam (body) cuerpo m; **he's got a nice b.** tiene un cuerpazo

bode [bəʊd] vi **this bodes well/ill for the future** es un buen/mal presagio para el futuro

bodice ['bɒdɪs] n (a) *(part of dress)* cuerpo m (b) *(undergarment)* corpiño m

bodily ['bɒdɪlɪ] **1** adj corporal; **b. functions** funciones fpl fisiológicas; **b. needs** necesidades fpl físicas

2 adv en volandas; **he was carried b. to the door** lo llevaron en volandas hasta la puerta

body ['bɒdɪ] n (a) *(of person, animal)* cuerpo m; *(dead)* cadáver m; *Fig* **to have enough to keep b. and soul together** tener lo justo para vivir; *Fam* **over my dead b.!** ¡por encima de mi cadáver!; **b. bag** bolsa f para cadáveres; *Fig* **a b. blow** *(severe setback)* un duro golpe; **b. clock** reloj m biológico; *Mil* **b. count** *(of casualties)* número m de bajas; **b. fascism** dictadura m del cuerpo; **b. language** lenguaje m corporal; **b. lotion** loción f corporal; **b. odor** olor m corporal; **b. piercing** perforaciones fpl en el cuerpo, "piercing" m; **b. warmer** chaleco m acolchado

(b) *(of hair, wine)* cuerpo m

(c) *(group)* grupo m, conjunto m; *(organization)* entidad f; **public b.** organismo m público; **a large b. of people** un nutrido grupo de gente; **a b. of evidence** un conjunto de pruebas; **the b. politic** el Estado, la nación; **b. of water** masa f de agua

(d) *(main part) (of car)* carrocería f; *(of letter, argument)* núcleo m; **b. shop** taller m de carrocería

(e) *(garment)* body m; **b. stocking** *(leotard)* malla f; *(women's undergarment)* body m

bodybuilder ['bɒdɪbɪldə(r)] n culturista mf

bodybuilding ['bɒdɪbɪldɪŋ] n culturismo m

bodyguard ['bɒdɪgɑːd] n *(person)* guardaespaldas mf inv, escolta mf; *(group)* escolta f

bodywork ['bɒdɪwɜːk] n *(of car)* carrocería f

Boer ['bəʊə(r)] n bóer mf; **the B. War** la guerra de los bóers

bog [bɒg] n *(marsh)* pantano m, ciénaga f

▶**bog down** vt sep **to get bogged down** *(in mud, details)* quedarse atascado(a)

bogey ['bəʊgɪ] n *(cause of fear)* pesadilla f

bogeyman, bogyman ['bəʊgɪmæn] n **the b.** el coco, el hombre del saco

boggle ['bɒgəl] vi *Fam* **he boggled at the thought of her reaction** le horripilaba pensar cómo reaccionaría ella; **she boggled at paying such a price** se quedó pasmada de tener que pagar un precio tan alto; **the mind boggles!** no me lo puedo ni imaginar

Bogota [bɒgə'tɑː] n Bogotá

bogus ['bəʊgəs] adj falso(a); *Fam* **he's completely b.** es un farsante

Bohemian [bəʊ'hiːmɪən] n & adj also Fig bohemio(a) m,f

boil[1] [bɔɪl] n *Med* forúnculo m, pústula f

boil[2] **1** n **to come to the b.** empezar or romper a hervir; **to bring sth to the b.** hacer que algo hierva

2 vt hervir, cocer; **to b. the kettle** poner el agua a hervir; **a boiled egg** un huevo cocido

3 vi hervir; **the kettle's boiling** el agua está hirviendo; **the kettle boiled dry** el hervidor se quedó sin agua; *Fig* **to b. with rage** enfurecerse

▶**boil down to** vt insep *Fam* **it all boils down to...** todo se reduce a...

▶**boil over** vi *(milk, soup)* salirse, rebosar; *Fig (situation)* estallar

▶**boil up** vt insep *(milk, water)* (poner a) hervir

boiler ['bɔɪlə(r)] n caldera f; **b. room** *(sala f de)* calderas fpl

boilermaker ['bɔɪləmeɪkə(r)] n calderero m

boiling ['bɔɪlɪŋ] **1** adj hirviente; *Fam* **I'm b.!** ¡me estoy asando!; **b. point** punto m de ebullición; *Fig* **the situation has reached b. point** la situación está al rojo vivo

2 adv **it's b. hot** hace un calor abrasador

boisterous ['bɔɪstərəs] adj *(person)* alborotador(ora), bullicioso(a)

bold [bəʊld] adj (a) *(brave)* audaz (b) *(shameless)* fresco(a); **to be as b. as brass** ser un(a) caradura, *Esp* tener más cara que espalda (c) *(striking)* marcado(a), acentuado(a); *Typ* **b. type** negrita f

boldly ['bəʊldlɪ] adv *(bravely)* audazmente, con audacia

boldness ['bəʊldnɪs] n audacia f

Bolivia [bə'lɪvɪə] n Bolivia

Bolivian [bə'lɪvɪən] n & adj boliviano(a) m,f

bollard ['bɒləd] n *Naut* bolardo m, noray m

Bolshevik ['bɒlʃəvɪk] n & adj bolchevique mf

Bolshevism ['bɒlʃəvɪzəm] n bolchevismo m

bolster ['bəʊlstə(r)] **1** n almohada f cilíndrica

2 vt *(confidence, pride)* reforzar, fortalecer

bolt [bəʊlt] **1** n (a) *(on door)* cerrojo m, pestillo m; *(metal fastening)* perno m; *Fam* **he has shot his b.** ha quemado sus últimos cartuchos (b) *(dash)* **she made a b. for the door** se precipitó hacia la puerta (c) *(of lightning)* rayo m; *Fig* **to come like a b. from the blue** ocurrir de sopetón, pillar or *Am* agarrar a todo el mundo por sorpresa

2 adv **b. upright** erguido(a)

3 vt (a) *(lock)* **to b. the door/window** cerrar la puerta/ventana con pestillo (b) *(attach with bolts)* atornillar (c) *(eat)* engullir

4 vi *(horse)* salir de estampida; *(person)* salir huyendo

▶**bolt down** vt insep *(eat quickly)* **to b. sth down** engullir or zamparse algo

bomb [bɒm] **1** n bomba f; **to drop/plant a b.** arrojar/colocar una bomba; **b. disposal expert** *(experto m)* artificiero m; **b. scare** amenaza f de bomba

2 vt bombardear

3 vi *Fam (fail)* fracasar (estrepitosamente)

bombard [bɒm'bɑːd] vt bombardear; *Fig* **to b. sb with questions** bombardear a alguien con preguntas

bombardment [bɒm'bɑːdmənt] n bombardeo m

bombast ['bɒmbæst] n ampulosidad f, altisonancia f

bombastic [bɒm'bæstɪk] adj ampuloso(a), altisonante

bomber ['bɒmə(r)] n *(aircraft)* bombardero m; *(person)* terrorista mf *(que coloca bombas)*; **b. jacket** cazadora f or *CSur* campera f or *Méx* chamarra f de aviador

bombing ['bɒmɪŋ] n *(aerial)* bombardeo m; *(by terrorist)* atentado m con bomba

bombshell ['bɒmʃel] n obús m; *Fig* **to drop a b.** dejar caer una bomba; *Fam* **a blonde b.** una rubia explosiva

bombsight ['bɒmsaɪt] n visor m de bombardeo

bombsite ['bɒmsaɪt] n lugar m arrasado por un bombardeo

bona fide ['bəʊnə'faɪdɪ] adj auténtico(a), genuino(a)

bonanza [bə'nænzə] n filón m; **a b. year** un año de grandes beneficios or de bonanza

bonbon ['bɒnbɒn] n caramelo m

bond [bɒnd] **1** n (a) *(between materials)* unión f; *(between people)* vínculo m; **to feel a b. with sb** sentir un vínculo de unión con alguien; *Literary* **bonds** *(ropes, chains)* ataduras fpl (b) *Fin* bono m (c) *Law* fianza f; *Formal* **my word is my b.** siempre cumplo mi palabra (d) *Com* **to be in b.** estar en depósito aduanero

2 vt (a) *(stick)* pegar, adherir (b) *Fig (unite)* **to b. together** unir

3 vi (a) *(stick)* pegar, adherirse (b) *Fig (form attachment)* unirse **(with** a)

bondage ['bɒndɪdʒ] n (a) *(slavery)* esclavitud f, servidumbre f (b) *(sexual practice)* bondage m, = práctica sexual en la que se ata a uno de los participantes

bonding ['bɒndɪŋ] n *(lazos mpl de)* unión f; *Hum* **they're doing a bit of male b.** están haciendo cosas de hombres

bone [bəʊn] **1** n (a) *(of person, animal)* hueso m; *(of fish)* espina f; **b. china** porcelana f fina; **b. meal** harina f de hueso (b) *(idioms)* **to work one's fingers to the b.** matarse trabajando *or Esp* a trabajar; **to be b. idle** *or* **lazy** ser más vago(a) que la chaqueta de un guardia; **I feel it in my bones** tengo una corazonada; **b. of contention** manzana *f* de la discordia; *Fam* **to have a b. to pick with sb** tener que arreglar *or* ajustar cuentas con alguien; **he made no bones about it** no trató de disimularlo; **close to the b.** *(tactless, risqué)* fuera de tono

2 *vt* **(a)** *(fillet) (chicken)* deshuesar; *(fish)* quitar las espinas a **(b)** *Vulg (have sex with) Esp* follarse *or* tirarse a, *Am* cogerse a, *Méx* chingarse a

▶**bone up on** *vt insep Fam* empollarse

bone-dry ['bəʊn'draɪ] *adj* completamente seco(a)

bonehead ['bəʊnhed] *Fam* **1** *n* estúpido(a) *m,f*, *Esp* berzotas *mf inv*

2 *adj* estúpido(a)

bonfire ['bɒnfaɪə(r)] *n* hoguera *f*, fogata *f*

bongo ['bɒŋgəʊ] *n Mus* **b. drums, bongos** bongos *mpl*, bongós *mpl*

bonhomie ['bɒnɒmi:] *n* camaradería *f*

bonk [bɒŋk] *vt Fam (hit)* pegar

Bonn [bɒn] *n* Bonn

bonnet ['bɒnɪt] *n (hat)* cofia *f*, papalina *f*

bonny ['bɒnɪ] *adj Scot* bonito(a), precioso(a)

bonsai ['bɒnsaɪ] *n* bonsai *m*

bonus ['bəʊnəs] *n* **(a)** *(for productivity, seniority)* plus *m*; *(in insurance, for investment)* prima *f*; **Christmas b.** aguinaldo *m (dinero)*; **b. number** *(in lottery)* ≃ (número *m*) complementario *m*; **b. scheme** sistema *m* de primas **(b)** *(advantage)* ventaja *f* adicional

bony ['bəʊnɪ] *adj (person, limb)* huesudo(a); *(fish)* con muchas espinas

boo [bu:] **1** *n (pl* **boos)** abucheo *m*

2 *vt* abuchear

3 *exclam (of audience, crowd)* ¡buu!; *(to frighten sb)* ¡uuh!; **he wouldn't say b. to a goose** es muy tímido, *Esp* es un cortado

boob [bu:b] *Fam n* **(a)** **boobs** *(breasts)* tetas *fpl*; **b. tube** = top ajustado sin mangas ni tirantes **(b)** *(person)* lelo(a) *m,f*, bobalicón(ona) *m,f*; **b. tube** *(television)* caja *f* tonta

boo-boo ['bu:bu:] *n Fam* **(a)** *(blunder)* metedura *for Am* metida *f* de pata; **to make a b.** meter la pata **(b)** *(injury)* pupa *f*

booby ['bu:bɪ] *n* **b. prize** premio *m* para el farolillo rojo; **b. trap** *(explosive device)* bomba *f* trampa *or* camuflada; *(practical joke)* trampa *f*

booby-trap ['bu:bɪtræp] *vt (pt & pp* **booby-trapped)** *(with explosive device)* colocar una bomba trampa en; *(as practical joke)* colocar una trampa en

booger ['bu:gə(r)] *n (nasal mucus)* moco *m*

boogeyman ['bu:gɪmæn] *n* **the b.** el coco, el hombre del saco

boo-hoo ['bu:'hu:] *exclam* ¡buaaah!

book [bʊk] *n* **1** **(a)** *(in general)* libro *m*; *(of stamps)* librillo *m*; *(of matches)* caja *f* (de solapa); *(of tickets)* talonario *m*; *Fin* **the books** *(of company)* la contabilidad; **b. certificate** vale *m* para comprar libros; **b. club** círculo *m* de lectores; **b. review** reseña *f* literaria

(b) *(idioms)* **physics is a closed b. to me** la física es un misterio para mí; **in my b....** a mi modo de ver...; **to be in sb's good/bad books** estar a buenas/malas con alguien, *RP* estar en buenos/malos términos con alguien; **to bring sb to b. for sth** obligar a alguien a rendir cuentas por algo; **by** *or* **according to the b.** según las normas; **to throw the b. at sb** castigar a alguien con la máxima severidad

2 *vt* **(a)** *(reserve)* reservar; *(performer)* contratar; **to b. sb on a flight** reservarle (plaza en) un vuelo a alguien; **to be fully booked** *(theater, flight)* estar completo(a); *(person)* tener la agenda completa **(b)** *(record details of) (police suspect)* fichar; *(traffic offender)* multar

▶**book in 1** *vt sep* **to b. sb in** hacer una reserva para alguien

2 *vi (take a room)* coger una habitación

▶**book up** *vt sep* **the hotel is fully booked up** el hotel está al completo; **I'm booked up for this evening** ya he quedado para esta noche

bookable ['bʊkəbəl] *adj (seat, flight)* que se puede reservar con antelación

bookbinder ['bʊkbaɪndə(r)] *n* encuadernador(ora) *m,f*

bookbinding ['bʊkbaɪndɪŋ] *n* encuadernación *f*

bookcase ['bʊkkeɪs] *n* librería *f*, estantería *f*

bookend ['bʊkend] *n* sujetalibros *m inv*

bookie ['bʊkɪ] *n Fam (in betting)* corredor(ora) *m,f* de apuestas

booking ['bʊkɪŋ] *n* **(a)** *(reservation)* reserva *f*; **to make a b.** hacer una reserva; **b. office** taquilla *f*, *Am* boletería *f* **(b)** *(in soccer)* amonestación *f*; **to receive a b.** ser amonestado(a)

bookish ['bʊkɪʃ] *adj (person)* estudioso(a); *Pej (approach, style)* académico(a), sesudo(a)

bookkeeping ['bʊkki:pɪŋ] *n Fin* contabilidad *f*

booklet ['bʊklɪt] *n* folleto *m*

bookmaker ['bʊkmeɪkə(r)] *n (in betting)* corredor(ora) *m,f* de apuestas

bookmark ['bʊkmɑ:k] **1** *n* **(a)** *(for book)* marcapáginas *m* **(b)** *Comptr* marcador *m*

2 *vt Comptr (Web page)* añadir a la lista de marcadores

bookseller ['bʊksɛlə(r)] *n* librero(a) *m,f*

bookshelf ['bʊkʃelf] *n (single shelf)* estante *m*; **bookshelves** *(set of shelves)* estantería *f*

bookshop ['bʊkʃɒp] *n* librería *f*

bookstall ['bʊkstɔ:l] *n (in street)* puesto *m* de libros

bookstand ['bʊkstænd] *n* **(a)** *(in bookstore, library)* expositor *m* de libros **(b)** *(for supporting book)* atril *m* (de pie) **(c)** *(in railway station)* quiosco *m* de prensa

bookstore [bʊkstɔ:(r)] *n* librería *f*

bookworm ['bʊkwɜ:m] *n Fam (avid reader)* ratón *m* de biblioteca

boom[1] [bu:m] *n* **(a)** *Naut (barrier)* barrera *f*; *(for sail)* botavara *f* **(b)** *Cin & TV* jirafa *f*

boom[2] **1** *n (economic)* auge *m*, boom *m*; **b. town** ciudad *f* en auge

2 *vi (business, trade)* estar en auge, dispararse

boom[3] **1** *n (sound)* estruendo *m*, retumbo *m*

2 *vi (thunder, gun)* retumbar

boomerang ['bu:məræŋ] *n* bumerán *m*

booming ['bu:mɪŋ] *adj (voice)* estruendoso(a), atronador(ora)

boon [bu:n] *n* bendición *f*

boor ['bʊə(r)] *n* grosero(a) *m,f*, cafre *mf*

boorish ['bʊərɪʃ] *adj (person, behavior)* grosero(a), ordinario(a)

boost [bu:st] **1** *n (of rocket)* propulsión *f*; *(of economy)* impulso *m*; **to give sth/sb a b.** dar un impulso a algo/alguien

2 *vt* **(a)** *(rocket)* propulsar; *Tel (signal)* amplificar; *(economy, production)* impulsar, estimular; *(hopes, morale)* levantar **(b)** *Fam (steal)* afanar, *Esp* sisar

booster ['bu:stə(r)] *n* **(a)** **b. (rocket)** *(cohete m)* propulsor *m* **(b)** *Elec* elevador *m* de tensión **(c)** *Med* revacunación *f* **(d)** *Fam (supporter)* **he's a great b. for his home town** le entusiasma ir cantando las maravillas de su ciudad natal

boot [bu:t] **1** *n* **(a)** *(footwear)* bota *f*; *(ankle-length)* botín *m*; *Mil* **b. camp** campamento *m* de reclutas **(b)** *(idioms) Fam* **to give sb the b.** poner a alguien de patitas en la calle; *Fam* **to get the b.** ser despedido(a); **to b.** además, por añadidura

2 *vt* **(a)** *Fam (kick)* dar una patada a; **to b. sb out** poner a alguien en la calle **(b)** *Comptr* arrancar

3 *vi Comptr* **to b. (up)** arrancar

bootee ['bu:ti:] *n (child's shoe)* patuco *m*

booth [bu:ð] *n (at fair)* barraca *f* (de feria); *(for telephone, in voting)* cabina *f*; *(in restaurant)* mesa *f (rodeada de asientos corridos fijados al suelo)*

bootlace ['buːtleɪs] n cordón m

bootleg ['buːtleg] adj (alcohol) de contrabando; (recording, cassette) pirata

bootlicker ['buːtlɪkə(r)] n Fam lameculos mf inv, Esp pelota mf, Méx arrastrado(a) m,f, RP chupamedias mf inv

bootstrap ['buːtstræp] n (a) trabilla f, tirante m; Fig **he pulled himself up by his bootstraps** logró salir adelante por su propio esfuerzo (b) Comptr arranque m; **b. routine** secuencia f de arranque

booty ['buːtɪ] n (loot) botín m

booze [buːz] Fam **1** n bebida f, Esp priva f, RP chupi m
2 vi empinar el codo, RP chupar

boozer ['buːzə(r)] n Fam (person) bebedor(ora) m,f, esponja f, Am tomador(ora) m,f

boozy ['buːzɪ] adj Fam (voice, breath) de borracho(a)

bop [bɒp] Fam **1** n (blow) golpecito m
2 vt (pt & pp **bopped**) (hit) dar un golpecito a

boracic [bəˈræsɪk] adj Chem bórico(a)

border ['bɔːdə(r)] **1** n (a) (edge) borde m; (on clothes) ribete m; (in garden) arriate m (b) (frontier) frontera f; **b. guard** guardia m fronterizo; **b. town** ciudad f fronteriza
2 vt bordear; (country) limitar con

▸**border on** vt insep (of country) limitar con; **to b. on insanity/the ridiculous** bordear la locura/lo ridículo

borderland ['bɔːdəlænd] n frontera f, zona f fronteriza

borderline ['bɔːdəlaɪn] n frontera f, divisoria f; **a b. case** un caso dudoso

bore[1] [bɔː(r)] **1** n (person) pelma mf, pelmazo(a) m,f; (thing) fastidio m, lata f; **what a b.!** ¡qué lata or pesadez!
2 vt aburrir

bore[2] **1** n (caliber) calibre m
2 vt (with drill) perforar, taladrar; **to b. a hole in sth** taladrar algo
3 vi **to b. for water/minerals** hacer perforaciones or prospecciones en búsqueda or Esp busca de agua/minerales

bore[3] pt of **bear**[2]

bored [bɔːd] adj aburrido(a); **to be b.** estar aburrido(a); Fam **I was b. stiff** or **to tears** me aburrí como una ostra or RP un perro

boredom ['bɔːdəm] n aburrimiento m

boric ['bɒrɪk] adj Chem bórico(a)

boring ['bɔːrɪŋ] adj aburrido(a); **to be b.** ser aburrido(a)

born [bɔːn] **1** adj **he's a b. storyteller/leader** es un narrador/líder nato
2 (pp of **bear**[2] used to form passive) **to be b.** nacer; **I was b. in Miami/in 1975** nací en Miami/en 1975; Fam **I wasn't b. yesterday** no me chupo el dedo

-born [bɔːn] suffix **she's English-b.** es inglesa de nacimiento, nació en Inglaterra

born-again Christian ['bɔːnəgenˈkrɪstʃən] n Rel = cristiano convertido a un culto evangélico

borne [bɔːn] pp of **bear**[2]

Borneo ['bɔːnɪəʊ] n Borneo

borrow ['bɒrəʊ] **1** vt **can I b. your book?** ¿me prestas or Esp dejas tu libro?; **I borrowed his bicycle without him knowing** le tomé la bicicleta prestada sin que lo supiera; **to b. a book from the library** tomar prestado un libro de la biblioteca; **to b. money from the bank** pedir un crédito al banco; **to be living on borrowed time** (ill person, government) tener los días contados
2 vi **she's always borrowing from other people** siempre está pidiendo cosas prestadas a los demás

borrower ['bɒrəʊə(r)] n (from bank) prestatario(a) m,f; (from library) usuario(a) m,f

bosh [bɒʃ] Fam **1** n tonterías fpl, Am pendejadas fpl, RP pavadas fpl
2 exclam ¡pamplinas!

Bosnia(-Herzegovina) ['bɒznɪə(hɜːtsəgəˈviːnə)] n Bosnia (-Herzegovina)

Bosnian ['bɒznɪən] **1** n bosnio(a) m,f
2 adj bosnio(a); **B. Croat** croata mf de Bosnia; **B. Muslim** musulmán(ana) m,f de Bosnia; **B. Serb** serbio(a) m,f de Bosnia

bosom ['bʊzəm] **1** n (of woman) pecho m; Fig seno m; Fig **in the b. of one's family** en el seno de la familia
2 adj **b. friend** amigo(a) m,f del alma

Bosphorus ['bɒsfərəs] n **the B.** el Bósforo

boss[1] [bɒs] n (on shield) tachón m

boss[2] Fam **1** n (at work) jefe(a) m,f; **he's his own b.** trabaja por cuenta propia; Fig **to show sb who's b.** enseñar a alguien quién manda
2 vt **to b. sb around** or **about** dar órdenes a alguien (a diestro y siniestro)

bossy ['bɒsɪ] adj mandón(ona)

bosun ['bəʊsən] n Naut contramaestre m

botanic(al) [bəˈtænɪk(əl)] adj botánico(a); **b. garden(s)** jardín m botánico

botanist ['bɒtənɪst] n botánico(a) m,f

botany ['bɒtənɪ] n botánica f

botch [bɒtʃ] Fam **1** n chapuza f; **to make a b. of a job/an interview** hacer una chapuza de trabajo/entrevista
2 vt **to b. a job/an interview** hacer una chapuza de trabajo/entrevista

botched [bɒtʃt] adj chapucero(a); **a b. job** una chapuza

both [bəʊθ] **1** pron ambos(as), los/las dos; **b. (of them) are dead** los dos or ambos están muertos; **b. of us agree** los dos estamos de acuerdo
2 adj ambos(as), los/las dos; **b. (the) brothers** ambos hermanos, los dos hermanos; **to hold sth in b. hands** sostener algo con las dos manos; **b. my brothers** mis dos hermanos; **on b. sides** a ambos lados; **to look b. ways** mirar a uno y otro lado; **you can't have it b. ways** o una cosa o la otra, no puedes tenerlo todo
3 adv **b. you and I** tanto tú como yo; **she is b. intelligent and beautiful** es inteligente y, además, guapa

bother ['bɒðə(r)] **1** n (trouble) problemas mpl, dificultades fpl; (inconvenience) molestia f; **to go to the b. of doing sth** tomarse la molestia de hacer algo
2 vt (a) (annoy) molestar; **my back's still bothering me** todavía me molesta la espalda; **I hate to b. you but…** siento tener que molestarte pero… (b) (care about) **to be bothered about sth** estar preocupado(a) por algo; Fam **I can't be bothered** no tengo ganas, paso; Fam **I'm not bothered** me da igual
3 vi (care) preocuparse (**about** por); **he didn't even b. to apologize** ni siquiera se molestó en pedir disculpas; **don't b.!** no te molestes

bothersome ['bɒðəsəm] adj incordiante

Botox ['bəʊtɒks] n Botox m

Botswana [bɒtˈswɑːnə] n Botsuana

bottle ['bɒtəl] **1** n (container) botella f; (of medicine) frasco m; (for baby) biberón m; **bring your own b.** trae una botella de algo; Fam **to take to** or **hit the b.** darse a la bebida; **b. green** verde m botella; **b. opener** abrebotellas m inv; **b. party** fiesta f (a la que cada invitado lleva una botella)
2 vt embotellar

▸**bottle up** vt sep (emotions, anger) reprimir, contener

bottled ['bɒtəld] adj embotellado(a); **b. water** agua f embotellada

bottle-feed ['bɒtəlfiːd] (pt & pp **bottle-fed**) vt dar el biberón a

bottleneck ['bɒtəlnek] n (in road, traffic) embotellamiento m, estrechamiento m; (in production) atasco m

bottom ['bɒtəm] **1** n (a) (lowest part) (of well, corridor, sea) fondo m; (of stairs, mountain, page) pie m; (of list) final m; **it's**

in the b. of the cup está en el fondo de la taza; **at the b. of** *(well, sea)* en el fondo de; *(stairs, mountain, page)* al pie de; **from the b. of one's heart** de todo corazón; **he's at the b. of the class** es el último de la clase; **to touch b.** *(boat)* tocar fondo

(**b**) *(underside) (of cup, box)* parte f de abajo; *(of shoe)* suela f; *(of ship)* casco m; **there's a sticker on the b. of the box** hay una etiqueta en la parte de abajo de la caja

(**c**) *Fam (buttocks)* trasero m, culo m

(**d**) *(idioms)* **to be at the b. of sth** *(be the cause of)* ser el motivo de algo; **to get to the b. of sth** llegar hasta el fondo de algo; **at b.** *(fundamentally)* en el fondo; **the b. has fallen out of the market** la demanda ha caído en *Esp* picado *or Am* picada; *Fam* **bottoms up!** ¡salud!

2 *adj* inferior; **the b. layer/drawer** la capa/el cajón de abajo del todo; **b. floor** planta f baja; *Fam* **you can bet your b. dollar that...** puedes apostar lo que quieras a que...; **in b. gear** en primera (velocidad); **the b. line** *(financially)* el saldo final; **the b. line is that he is unsuited to the job** la realidad es que no resulta adecuado para el trabajo

▸**bottom out** *vi (recession, unemployment)* tocar fondo

bottomless ['bɒtəmlɪs] *adj (abyss)* sin fondo; *(reserve)* inagotable; *Fig* **a b. pit** *(costly project)* un pozo *or Am* barril sin fondo

bottommost ['bɒtəmməʊst] *adj* de más abajo; **the b. layers of society** los estratos más bajos de la sociedad

botulism ['bɒtjʊlɪzəm] *n* botulismo m

boudoir ['buːdwɑː(r)] *n* tocador m

bouffant ['buːfɒn] *adj* ahuecado(a)

bough [baʊ] *n* rama f

bought [bɔːt] *pt & pp of* **buy**

bouillon ['buːjɒn] *n Culin* caldo m; **b. cube** pastilla f *or* cubito m de caldo (concentrado)

boulder ['bəʊldə(r)] *n* roca f (redondeada)

boulevard ['buːləvɑːd] *n* bulevar m

bounce [baʊns] **1** *n* (**a**) *(of ball)* rebote m, bote m (**b**) *(energy)* vitalidad f

2 *vt* botar; *Fig* **to b. an idea off sb** preguntar a alguien su opinión acerca de una idea

3 *vi* (**a**) *(ball)* botar, rebotar; **to b. off the wall** *(ball)* rebotar en la pared; *Fig* **criticism bounces off him** las críticas le resbalan; **to b. into/out of a room** *(person)* entrar a/salir de una habitación dando brincos de alegría (**b**) *Fam (check)* ser rechazado

▸**bounce back** *vi (after illness, disappointment)* recuperarse, reponerse

bouncer ['baʊnsə(r)] *n Fam (doorman)* gorila m, matón m

bouncing ['baʊnsɪŋ] *adj (baby)* robusto(a)

bouncy ['baʊnsɪ] *adj* (**a**) *(ball)* que bota bien; *(mattress)* elástico(a) (**b**) *(lively)* **to be b.** *(person)* tener mucha vitalidad

bound¹ [baʊnd] **1** *n (leap)* salto m; **at one b.** de un salto

2 *vi (leap)* saltar

bound² *adj* (**a**) *(destined)* **b. for** con destino a; **where are you b. for?** ¿hacia dónde se dirige? (**b**) *(certain)* **he's b. to come** seguro que viene; **it was b. to happen** tenía que suceder

bound³ *pt & pp of* **bind**

-bound [baʊnd] *suffix (heading toward)* **a south-b. train** un tren (que va) hacia el sur

boundary ['baʊndərɪ] *n* frontera f, límite m

bounder ['baʊndə(r)] *n Old-fashioned Fam* sinvergüenza m

boundless ['baʊndlɪs] *adj* ilimitado(a)

bounds [baʊndz] *npl (limit)* límites mpl; **to be out of b.** estar vedado(a); **it is (not) beyond the b. of possibility** (no) es del todo imposible; **to know no b.** *(anger, ambition, grief)* no conocer límites

bountiful ['baʊntɪfʊl] *adj* abundante, copioso(a)

bounty ['baʊntɪ] *n* (**a**) *(reward)* recompensa f; **b. hunter**

cazarrecompensas mf inv (**b**) *(generosity)* generosidad f, exuberancia f

bouquet [buːˈkeɪ] *n* (**a**) *(of flowers)* ramo m (**b**) *(of wine)* buqué m

bourbon ['bɜːbən] *n (whiskey)* whisky m americano, bourbon m

bourgeois ['bʊəʒwɑː] *adj* burgués(esa)

bourgeoisie [bʊəʒwɑːˈziː] *n* burguesía f

bout [baʊt] *n* (**a**) *(of illness)* ataque m; *(of work, activity)* periodo m (**b**) *(boxing match)* combate m

boutique [buːˈtiːk] *n* boutique f

bovine ['bəʊvaɪn] *adj* bovino(a)

bow¹ [bəʊ] *n* (**a**) *(weapon, for violin)* arco m (**b**) *(in hair, on dress)* lazo m; **b. tie** *Esp* pajarita f, *Arg* moñito m, *CAm, Carib, Col* corbatín m, *Chile* humita f, *Méx* corbata f de moño, *Urug* moñita f, *Ven* corbata f de lacito

bow² [baʊ] *n (of ship)* proa f

bow³ **1** *n (with head)* reverencia f; **to take a b.** salir a saludar

2 *vt* **to b. one's head** inclinar la cabeza

3 *vi* (**a**) *(as greeting, sign of respect)* inclinar la cabeza; **to b. down** inclinarse; *Fig* **to b. down before sb** inclinarse ante alguien (**b**) *(yield)* **to b. to sth/sb** rendirse ante algo/alguien

▸**bow out** *vi (resign)* retirarse, hacer mutis (por el foro)

bowdlerize ['baʊdləraɪz] *vt (text, account)* expurgar, censurar

bowed [baʊd] *adj* **with b. head** con la cabeza inclinada; **b. with age** encorvado(a) por la edad

bowel ['baʊəl] *n* intestino m; **bowels** entrañas fpl; *Literary* **the bowels of the earth** las entrañas de la Tierra; **b. complaint** afección f intestinal

bower ['baʊə(r)] *n* rincón m umbrío

bowl [bəʊl] *n* (**a**) *(dish)* cuenco m, bol m; **a b. of soup, please** un plato de sopa, por favor; **soup b.** plato m sopero; **salad b.** ensaladera f; **fruit b.** frutero m (**b**) *(of toilet)* taza f

▸**bowl along** *vi (car, bicycle)* rodar

▸**bowl over** *vt sep (knock down)* derribar; *Fig* **she was bowled over by the news** la noticia la dejó pasmada

bowlegged [bəʊˈlegɪd] *adj* con las piernas arqueadas, estevado(a)

bowler ['bəʊlə(r)] *n (hat)* sombrero m hongo, bombín m

bowlful ['bəʊlfʊl] *n* cuenco m, bol m

bowling ['bəʊlɪŋ] *n* (**a**) *(on grass)* **to go b.** ir a jugar a las bochas; **b. green** cancha f de bochas (inglesas) (**b**) *(in bowling alley)* (juego m de) bolos mpl; **b. alley** pista f de bolos; *(building)* bolera f

box [bɒks] **1** *n* (**a**) *(container)* caja f; **b. number 12** *(postal)* apartado m de correos número 12; **b. camera** cámara f de cajón (**b**) *(printed, drawn)* recuadro m; **check the b.** ponga una cruz en la casilla (**c**) *(in theater)* palco m

2 *vt* (**a**) *(place in box)* guardar en una caja (**b**) *(hit)* **to b. sb's ears** abofetear a alguien

3 *vi (fight)* boxear

boxcar ['bɒkskɑː(r)] *n* vagón m de mercancías, furgón m (de mercancías)

boxer ['bɒksə(r)] *n* (**a**) *(fighter)* boxeador m; **b. shorts, boxers** *(underwear)* calzoncillos mpl, bóxers mpl (**b**) *(dog)* bóxer m

boxing ['bɒksɪŋ] *n* boxeo m, *CAm, Méx* box m; **b. glove** guante m de boxeo; **b. match** combate m de boxeo; **b. ring** ring m

box-office ['bɒksɒfɪs] *n* taquilla f, *Am* boletería f; **a b. success** un éxito de taquilla *or Am* boletería

boy [bɔɪ] *n* chico m; *(baby)* niño m; **one of the boys** uno del grupo, un amigo; *Fam* **oh b.!** ¡vaya!; *Fam* **boys will be boys** son como niños; **Boy Scout** boy scout m, escultista m; **b. band** = grupo de música formado por chicos jóvenes

boycott ['bɔɪkɒt] **1** *n* boicot m

2 *vt* boicotear

boyfriend ['bɔɪfrend] *n* novio m

boyhood ['bɔɪhʊd] *n* niñez *f*

boyish ['bɔɪɪʃ] *adj* (**a**) *(of man) (looks, grin)* infantil (**b**) *(of woman) (looks, behavior)* varonil

bozo ['bəʊzəʊ] *(pl* **bozos)** *n Fam* zoquete *m*, tarugo *m*

bps [biːpiːˈes] *n Comptr (abbr* **bits per second)** bps

bra [brɑː] *n* sostén *m, Esp* sujetador *m, Carib, Col, Méx* brasier *m, RP* corpiño *m*

brace [breɪs] **1** *n* (**a**) *(on teeth)* aparato *m* (corrector) (**b**) *(pair) (of birds, pistols)* par *m* (**c**) **b. and bit** *(tool)* berbiquí *m*
  2 *vt* (**a**) *(reinforce)* reforzar (**b**) **to b. oneself (for)** prepararse *or Chile, Méx, Ven* alistarse (para)

bracelet ['breɪslɪt] *n* pulsera *f*

bracing ['breɪsɪŋ] *adj (wind, weather)* vigorizante

bracken ['brækən] *n* helechos *mpl*

bracket ['brækɪt] **1** *n* (**a**) *(for shelves)* escuadra *f*, soporte *m* (**b**) *(in writing)* paréntesis *m inv;* **in brackets** entre paréntesis (**c**) *(group)* banda *f*, grupo *m;* **age/income b.** banda de edad/de renta; **tax b.** banda impositiva
  2 *vt* (**a**) *(word, phrase)* poner entre paréntesis (**b**) *(classify)* asociar; **bracketed together** asociado(a)

brackish ['brækɪʃ] *adj (water)* ligeramente salobre *or* salado(a)

brag [bræg] *(pt & pp* **bragged)** *vi* jactarse (**about** de)

braggart ['brægət] *n* fanfarrón(ona) *m,f*

braid [breɪd] **1** *n (of hair)* trenza *f; (of thread)* galón *m*
  2 *vt (hair, thread)* trenzar

Braille [breɪl] *n* braille *m*

brain [breɪn] **1** *n* cerebro *m;* **brains** *(as food)* sesos *mpl; Fam* **to have brains** tener cerebro; *Fam* **she's the brains of the business** ella es el cerebro del negocio; *Fam* **to have money/sex on the b.** estar obsesionado(a) con el dinero/sexo; *Med* **to suffer b. damage** sufrir una lesión cerebral; *Med* **b. death** muerte *f* cerebral; **the b. drain** la fuga de cerebros; **b. surgeon** neurocirujano(a) *m,f; Med* **b. tumor** tumor *m* cerebral; *Fam* **b. wave** *(brilliant idea)* idea *f* genial
  2 *vt Fam (hit)* descalabrar

brainchild ['breɪntʃaɪld] *n (idea, project)* idea *f*

brain-dead ['breɪnded] *adj* (**a**) *Med* clínicamente muerto(a) (**b**) *Pej* subnormal

brainless ['breɪnlɪs] *adj* insensato(a)

brainpower ['breɪnpaʊə(r)] *n* capacidad *f* intelectual, intelecto *m*

brainstorm ['breɪnstɔːm] *n Fam (brilliant idea)* idea *f* genial

brainstorming ['breɪnstɔːmɪŋ] *n* **b. session** tormenta *f* de ideas, sesión *f* de reflexión creativa

brainwash ['breɪnwɒʃ] *vt* lavar el cerebro a; **to b. sb into doing sth** lavar el cerebro a alguien para que haga algo

brainy ['breɪnɪ] *adj Fam* **to be b.** tener mucho coco

braise [breɪz] *vt* estofar, *Andes, Méx* ahogar

brake [breɪk] **1** *n* freno *m;* **to apply the b.** *or* **brakes** frenar; *Fig* **to put the brakes on a project** frenar un proyecto; **b. fluid** líquido *m* de frenos; **b. lights** luces *mpl* de freno; **b. pedal** (pedal *m* del) freno *m*
  2 *vi* frenar

braking distance ['breɪkɪŋ'dɪstəns] *n* distancia *f* de frenado *or* de seguridad

bramble ['bræmbəl] *n (plant)* zarza *f*

bran [bræn] *n* salvado *m*

branch [brɑːntʃ] **1** *n* (**a**) *(of tree, family, subject)* rama *f; (of river)* afluente *m; (of road, railway)* ramal *m*, derivación *f;* **b. line** *(railway)* línea *f* secundaria, ramal *m* (**b**) *(of bank)* sucursal *f; (of shop)* establecimiento *m*
  2 *vi* bifurcarse

▶**branch off** *vi (discussion)* desviarse

▶**branch out** *vi* ampliar horizontes, diversificarse; **the company has branched out into electronics** la compañía ha ampliado su oferta a productos de electrónica

brand [brænd] **1** *n* (**a**) *Com (of product)* marca *f; Fig* **she has** her own **b. of humor** tiene un humor muy suyo; **b. image** imagen *f* de marca; **b. leader** marca *f* líder (en el mercado); **b. loyalty** fidelidad *f* a la marca; **b. name** marca *f* de fábrica, nombre *m* comercial; **b. recognition** reconocimiento *m* de marca (**b**) *(on cattle)* hierro *m*
  2 *vt (cattle)* marcar con el hierro; *Fig* **the image was branded on her memory** la imagen se le quedó grabada en la memoria; *Fig* **to b. sb (as) a liar/coward** tildar a alguien de mentiroso(a)/cobarde

brandish ['brændɪʃ] *vt* blandir

brand-new ['brænd'njuː] *adj* flamante, completamente nuevo(a)

brandy ['brændɪ] *n (cognac)* brandy *m*, coñac *m, RP* cognac *m; (more generally)* aguardiente *m;* **cherry/plum b.** aguardiente de cerezas/ciruelas

brash [bræʃ] *adj (person)* demasiado seguro(a) de sí mismo(a) y chillón(ona)

brass [brɑːs] *n* (**a**) *(metal)* latón *m; Fam* **the top b.** *(in army)* la plana mayor, los peces gordos; **to get down to b. tacks** ir al grano; **b. knuckles** puño *m* americano (**b**) *Mus (brass instruments)* metales *mpl;* **b. band** banda *f*

brassière ['bræzɪə(r)] *n* sostén *m, Esp* sujetador *m, Carib, Col, Méx* brasier *m, RP* corpiño *m*

brassy ['brɑːsɪ] *adj Fam (woman)* demasiado segura de sí misma y chillona

brat [bræt] *n Pej* niñato(a) *m,f; Fam* **b. pack** camada *f or* hornada *f* de jóvenes promesas

Bratislava [brætɪ'slɑːvə] *n* Bratislava

bravado [brə'vɑːdəʊ] *n* fanfarronería *f*, bravuconería *f*

brave [breɪv] **1** *n (Native American)* guerrero *m* indio
  2 *adj* valiente, valeroso(a); **a b. effort** un intento encomiable; **to put a b. face on it** poner al mal tiempo buena cara
  3 *vt (danger, weather)* encarar, afrontar

bravely ['breɪvlɪ] *adv* valientemente, valerosamente

bravery ['breɪvərɪ] *n* valentía *f*, valor *m*

bravo [brɑː'vəʊ] *exclam* ¡bravo!

bravura [brə'vjʊərə] *n (spirit, zest)* brío *m*, entrega *f; Mus* virtuosismo *m;* **a b. performance** *Mus* una virtuosa interpretación; *Fig* una brillante actuación

brawl [brɔːl] **1** *n* trifulca *f*, refriega *f*
  2 *vi* pelearse

brawn [brɔːn] *n Fam (strength)* fuerza *f*, músculo *m;* **he's got more b. than brains** tiene más músculo que seso

brawny ['brɔːnɪ] *adj* musculoso(a)

bray [breɪ] **1** *n (of donkey)* rebuzno *m; (laugh)* risotada *f*
  2 *vi (donkey)* rebuznar; *(laugh)* carcajearse

brazen ['breɪzən] *adj* descarado(a)

▶**brazen out** *vt sep* **to b. it out** echarle mucha cara al asunto

brazier ['breɪzɪə(r)] *n* brasero *m*

Brazil [brə'zɪl] *n* Brasil

brazil [brə'zɪl] *n* **b. (nut)** coquito *m* del Brasil

Brazilian [brə'zɪlɪən] *n & adj* brasileño(a) *m,f*

breach [briːtʃ] **1** *n* (**a**) *(in wall)* brecha *f; Fig* **to step into the b.** *(in emergency)* echar un cable, cubrir el vacío (**b**) *(of agreement, rules)* violación *f*, incumplimiento *m; (of trust)* abuso *m;* **b. of discipline** incumplimiento *m* de las normas; *Law* **b. of the peace** alteración *f* del orden público (**c**) *(in friendship)* ruptura *f*
  2 *vt* (**a**) *(defenses)* atravesar, abrir brecha en (**b**) *(contract, agreement)* violar, incumplir

bread [bred] *n* (**a**) *(food)* pan *m;* **a loaf of b.** un pan; **b. and butter** pan con mantequilla; *Fig* **the customers are our b. and butter** lo que nos da de comer son los clientes; *Fig* **he knows which side his b. is buttered on** él sabe lo que le conviene; **b. box** panera *f;* **b. knife** cuchillo *m* del pan (**b**) *Fam (money) Esp* pasta *f, Esp, RP* guita *f, Am* plata *f, Méx* lana *f*

bread-and-butter [bredən'bʌtə(r)] *adj Fam* **b. issues** asuntos *mpl* básicos

breadbasket [ˈbredbɑːskɪt] n cesta f del pan

breadboard [ˈbredbɔːd] n tabla f de cortar el pan

breadcrumb [ˈbredkrʌm] n miga f; **breadcrumbs** (in recipe) pan m rallado; **fried in breadcrumbs** empanado(a)

breadline [ˈbredlaɪn] n **on the b.** en la pobreza

breadstick [ˈbredstɪk] n colín m

breadth [bredθ] n (width) ancho m, anchura f; (of outlook, understanding) amplitud f

breadwinner [ˈbredwɪnə(r)] n **the b.** el que gana el pan

break [breɪk] **1** n **(a)** (fracture) (in bone) fractura f, rotura f; (in wall, fence) abertura f, hueco m; (in clouds) claro m; (in electric circuit) corte m; **at b. of day** al despuntar el día; Elec **b. switch** interruptor m

(b) (interval, pause) descanso m, pausa f; (vacation) vacaciones fpl; **(commercial) b.** (on TV, radio) pausa f publicitaria, anuncios mpl; **to work/talk without a b.** trabajar/hablar sin pausa or sin descanso; **a b. in the weather** un periodo de buen tiempo; Fam **give me a b.!** (leave me alone) ¡déjame en paz!; (I don't believe you) ¡no digas tonterías!

(c) Fam (escape) fuga f; **to make a b. for it** intentar escaparse

(d) Fam (chance) oportunidad f, Am chance f; **to give sb a b.** (give opportunity) dar una oportunidad or Am (un) chance a alguien; **a lucky b.** golpe m de suerte; **big b.** gran oportunidad f

2 vt (pt **broke** [brəʊk], pp **broken** [ˈbrəʊkən]) **(a)** (in general) romper; **she broke the roll in two** partió el panecillo en dos; **to b. one's arm/leg** romperse or partirse un brazo/una pierna; **to b. sth into pieces** romper algo en pedazos; **to b. the sound barrier** superar la barrera del sonido; Fig **to b. cover** salir del escondite; Fig **to b. the ice** romper el hielo; **to b. one's journey** interrumpir el viaje; **to b. ranks** romper filas; Fig **b. a leg!** (good luck!) ¡buena suerte!

(b) (soften) **the undergrowth broke his fall** la maleza amortiguó su caída

(c) (destroy) (person, health, resistance) acabar con, arruinar; (strike) reventar; **to b. sb's heart** romper el corazón a alguien; **to b. sb's spirit** minar la moral a alguien; **to b. the bank** hacer saltar la banca; Fig **it won't b. the bank** no vamos a arruinarnos por eso; **to b. sb's serve** (in tennis) romper el servicio a alguien

(d) (agreement, promise) romper; (law, rules) violar

(e) (story) descubrir, revelar (**to** a); **to b. the news of sth to sb** dar la noticia de algo a alguien

3 vi **(a)** (glass, machine, bone) romperse; (person's health) sucumbir; (weather) abrirse; **to b. in two** romperse or partirse en dos; **the sea broke against the rocks** el mar rompía contra las rocas; **day was beginning to b.** despuntaba el día **(b)** (news, story) saltar, estallar **(c)** (voice) (at puberty) cambiar; **her voice broke with emotion** se quedó con la voz quebrada por la emoción

▸**break away** vi **(a)** (escape) escapar (**from** de) **(b)** (from party, country) separarse (**from** de)

▸**break down 1** vt sep **(a)** (destroy) (resistance) vencer **(b)** (analyze) (argument) dividir; (figures) desglosar

2 vi (car, machine) estropearse, averiarse; (talks) romperse; (argument) fallar, desmoronarse; (person under pressure) derrumbarse; **to b. down in tears** romper a llorar

▸**break even** vi cubrir gastos, no tener pérdidas

▸**break in 1** vt sep (horse, new shoes) domar; (new recruit) amoldar

2 vi (burglar) forzar la entrada (a una casa o edificio)

▸**break into** vt insep **(a)** (of burglar) (house) entrar en **(b)** (begin suddenly) **to b. into laughter/a song/a run** echarse a reír/cantar/correr

▸**break loose** vi soltarse

▸**break off 1** vt sep **(a)** (detach) (twig, handle) partir, desprender **(b)** (terminate) (relations, engagement) romper

2 vi **(a)** (become detached) partirse, desprenderse **(b)** (stop talking) interrumpirse; **to b. off to do sth** parar para hacer algo

▸**break open 1** vt sep (lock, safe) forzar; (door) (kick down) echar abajo

2 vi romperse, partirse

▸**break out** vi **(a)** (escape) escaparse (**of** de) **(b)** (disease, argument) desatarse; (war) estallar; **he broke out in a sweat** le entraron sudores; **she broke out in a rash** le salió un sarpullido

▸**break through 1** vt insep (wall, barrier) atravesar; Fig (sb's reserve, shyness) superar

2 vi (sun) salir

▸**break up 1** vt sep **(a)** (machine, company) desmantelar **(b)** (fight, quarrel) poner fin a

2 vi **(a)** (disintegrate) hacerse pedazos **(b)** (end) (meeting, school term) terminar; (marriage, relationship) romperse, terminar; (couple) separarse; **to b. up with sb** romper con alguien

▸**break with** vt insep romper con

breakable [ˈbreɪkəbəl] **1** n **breakables** objetos mpl frágiles

2 adj frágil, rompible

breakage [ˈbreɪkɪdʒ] n **all breakages must be paid for** (sign) el cliente deberá abonar cualquier artículo que resulte roto

breakaway [ˈbreɪkəweɪ] adj **a b. group** un grupo escindido (del principal)

breakdance [ˈbreɪkdɑːns] **1** n breakdance m

2 vi hacer breakdance, bailar breakdance

breakdown [ˈbreɪkdaʊn] n **(a)** (failure) (of car, machine, computer) avería f; (of talks) ruptura f; (of communication) Esp fallo m, Am falla f; **(nervous) b.** depresión f or crisis f inv nerviosa; **he had a b.** (nervous) le dio una depresión **(b)** (analysis) (of figures, costs) desglose m

breaker [ˈbreɪkə(r)] n (wave) ola f grande

break-even point [breɪkˈiːvənpɔɪnt] n Fin punto m de equilibrio, umbral m de rentabilidad

breakfast [ˈbrekfəst] **1** n desayuno m; **to have b.** desayunar; **to have sth for b.** desayunar algo; **b. cereal** cereales mpl (de desayuno)

2 vi **to b. (on sth)** desayunar (algo)

break-in [ˈbreɪkɪn] n (burglary) robo m (en el interior de una casa o edificio)

breaking [ˈbreɪkɪŋ] n **(a)** Law **b. and entering** allanamiento m de morada **(b)** **b. point** (of person, patience) límite m

breakneck [ˈbreɪknek] adj **at b. speed** a una velocidad de vértigo

breakout [ˈbreɪkaʊt] n (from prison) evasión f

breakthrough [ˈbreɪkθruː] n (major advance) avance m, adelanto m; **to make a b.** (in talks) dar un gran paso adelante

breakup [ˈbreɪkʌp] n (of relationship) ruptura f; (of country, organization) desintegración f, desmembración f

breakwater [ˈbreɪkwɔːtə(r)] n rompeolas m inv

bream [briːm] n (freshwater) brema f; **(sea) b.** besugo m

breast [brest] n (of woman) pecho m, seno m; Literary (of man, woman) pecho m; (of chicken) pechuga f; **to make a clean b. of it** confesarlo todo; **b. cancer** cáncer m de mama; **b. pocket** bolsillo m or CAm, Méx, Perú bolsa f superior

breastbone [ˈbrestbəʊn] n esternón m

breastfed [ˈbrestfed] adj amamantado(a)

breastfeed [ˈbrestfiːd] (pt & pp **breastfed** [ˈbrestfed]) **1** vt dar el pecho a, amamantar

2 vi dar el pecho

breastfeeding [ˈbrestfiːdɪŋ] n lactancia f materna

breastplate [ˈbrestpleɪt] n (of armor) peto m (de armadura)

breaststroke [ˈbres(t)strəʊk] n braza f; **to do** or **swim (the) b.** Esp nadar a braza, Am nadar pecho

breath [breθ] n respiración f; **take a deep b.** inspirar profundamente; **to pause for b.** pararse para tomar aliento;

bad b. mal aliento *m*; **in the same b.** a la vez, al mismo tiempo; **they are not to be mentioned in the same b.** no tienen punto de comparación; **in the next b.** al momento siguiente; *also Fig* **to hold one's b.** contener la respiración; *Fam* **don't hold your b.!** ¡ya puedes esperar sentado(a)!; **to waste one's b.** malgastar saliva; **out of b.** sin aliento, sin respiración; **to get one's b. back** recuperar la respiración; **under one's b.** en voz baja, en un susurro; *Fig* **to take sb's b. away** quitar la respiración a alguien; **a b. of wind** una brisa; **to go out for a b. of fresh air** salir a tomar el aire; *Fig* **she's a real b. of fresh air** es una verdadera bocanada de aire fresco; **b. test** prueba *f* de alcoholemia

breathalyze ['breθəlaɪz] *vt (driver)* hacer la prueba de la alcoholemia a

Breathalyzer® ['breθəlaɪzə(r)] *n* alcoholímetro *m*

breathe [briːð] **1** *vt* **(a)** *(inhale)* respirar, inspirar; *(exhale)* espirar, exhalar; **he breathed alcohol over her** le echó el aliento (con olor) a alcohol **(b)** *(idioms)* **to b. a sigh of relief** dar un suspiro de alivio; *Literary* **to b. one's last** exhalar el último suspiro; **don't b. a word (of it)!** ¡no digas una palabra!; **to b. fire** *(in anger)* echar chispas; **to b. new life into sth** *(project, scheme)* dar vida a algo

2 *vi* respirar; *Fig* **to b. easily again** volver a respirar tranquilo(a); *Fig* **to b. down sb's neck** pisar los talones a alguien

▸**breathe in** *vt & vi* inspirar, aspirar

▸**breathe out** *vi* espirar

breather ['briːðə(r)] *n Fam (rest)* respiro *m*; **to take a b.** tomarse un respiro

breathing ['briːðɪŋ] *n* respiración *f*; **b. apparatus** respirador *m*; *Fig* **b. space** respiro *m*

breathless ['breθlɪs] *adj (person)* jadeante; *(calm, silence)* completo(a)

breathtaking ['breθteɪkɪŋ] *adj* impresionante, asombroso(a)

breathy ['breθɪ] *adj* **to have a b. voice** tener la voz jadeante

bred [bred] *pt & pp of* **breed**

breech [briːtʃ] *n* **(a)** *Med* **b. delivery** *or* **birth** parto *m* de nalgas **(b)** *(of gun)* recámara *f*

breeches ['brɪtʃɪz] *npl* (pantalones *mpl*) bombachos *mpl*; **a pair of b.** unos (pantalones) bombachos

breed [briːd] **1** *n (of animal) also Fig* raza *f*; *Fig* **a dying b.** una especie en extinción

2 *vt (pt & pp* **bred** [bred]) *(animals)* criar; *Fig (discontent)* crear, producir

3 *vi* reproducirse

breeder ['briːdə(r)] *n (of animals)* criador(ora) *m,f*; *Phys* **b. reactor** reactor *m* nuclear reproductor

breeding ['briːdɪŋ] *n* **(a)** *(of animals)* cría *f*; **b. ground** criadero *m*; *Fig (of discontent, revolution)* caldo *m* de cultivo **(b)** *(of person)* **(good) b.** (buena) educación *f*; **to lack b.** no tener educación

breeze [briːz] **1** *n* brisa *f*; *Fam* **it was a b.** fue coser y cantar

2 *vi* **to b. in/out** *(casually)* entrar/salir despreocupadamente

breezy ['briːzɪ] *adj* **(a)** *(weather)* **it's b.** hace aire **(b)** *(person, attitude)* despreocupado(a)

brethren ['breðrɪn] *npl Rel* hermanos *mpl*

Breton ['bretɒn] *n & adj* bretón(ona) *m,f*

breviary ['briːvɪərɪ] *n Rel* breviario *m*

brevity ['brevɪtɪ] *n* brevedad *f*

brew [bruː] **1** *n (beer)* cerveza *f*; *Fam (drink of beer)* birra *f*; *(tea)* té *m*; *(strange mixture)* brebaje *m*

2 *vt (beer)* elaborar, fabricar; *(tea)* preparar

3 *vi (beer)* fermentar; *(tea)* hacerse; **there's a storm brewing** se está preparando una tormenta; *Fig* **there's trouble brewing** se está fraguando *or* cociendo algo

brewer ['bruːə(r)] *n (firm)* fabricante *mf* de cerveza

brewery ['broərɪ] *n* fábrica *f* de cerveza

briar ['braɪə(r)] *n (plant)* brezo *m*; *(pipe)* pipa *f* (de madera) de brezo; **b. rose** escaramujo *m*

bribe [braɪb] **1** *n* soborno *m*, *Andes, CSur* coima *f*, *CAm, Méx* mordida *f*

2 *vt* sobornar; **to b. sb into doing sth** sobornar a alguien para que haga algo

bribery ['braɪbərɪ] *n* soborno *m*

bric-a-brac ['brɪkəbræk] *n* baratijas *fpl*, chucherías *fpl*

brick [brɪk] *n* ladrillo *m*; *Fig* **to drop a b.** meter la pata; **b. wall** muro *m* de ladrillo(s); **you're banging your head against a b. wall** te estás esforzando para nada

▸**brick up** *vt sep* tapiar

bricklayer ['brɪkleɪə(r)] *n* albañil *m*

brick-red ['brɪk'red] *adj* (de) color teja

brickwork ['brɪkwɜːk] *n* albañilería *f*

bridal ['braɪdəl] *adj* nupcial; **b. dress** *or* **gown** traje *m* de novia; **b. suite** suite *f* nupcial

bride [braɪd] *n* novia *f*; **the b. and groom** los novios

bridegroom ['braɪdgruːm] *n* novio *m*

bridesmaid ['braɪdzmeɪd] *n* dama *f* de honor

bride-to-be ['braɪdtə'biː] *n* futura esposa *f*

bridge¹ [brɪdʒ] **1** *n (over river, on ship, of violin, on teeth)* puente *m*; *(of nose)* caballete *m*; *Fig* **we'll cross that b. when we come to it** no adelantemos acontecimientos; *Fig* **a b. building effort** un esfuerzo por tender un puente; *Fin* **b. loan** crédito *m* de puente

2 *vt (river)* tender un puente sobre; **to b. a gap** llenar un vacío; **to b. the gap between rich and poor** acortar la distancia entre ricos y pobres

bridge² *n (cardgame)* bridge *m*

bridgehead ['brɪdʒhed] *n Mil* cabeza *f* de puente

bridle ['braɪdəl] **1** *n* brida *f*; **b. path** camino *m* de herradura

2 *vt* embridar, poner la brida a

3 *vi (with anger)* indignarse (**at** por)

brief [briːf] **1** *n* **(a)** *Law* escrito *m*; *(instructions)* misión *f*; *Fig* **that goes beyond our b.** eso no entra en el ámbito de nuestras competencias **(b)** **in b.** *(briefly)* en suma

2 *adj* breve; **a very b. pair of shorts** unos pantalones muy cortos; **to be b.** *(when talking)* ser breve; **to be b...., in b....** en pocas palabras...

3 *vt (inform)* informar

briefcase ['briːfkeɪs] *n* maletín *m*, portafolios *m inv*

briefing ['briːfɪŋ] *n (meeting)* sesión *f* informativa; *(information)* información *f*; *(written)* informe *m*

briefly ['briːflɪ] *adv* brevemente; **(put) b....** en pocas palabras...

briefs [briːfs] *npl (underwear) (woman's) Esp* bragas *fpl*, *Andes, Méx, RP* calzones *mpl*, *Ecuad* follones *mpl*, *RP* bombacha *f*; *(man's)* calzoncillos *mpl*, *Chile* fundillos *mpl*, *Col* pantaloncillos *mpl*, *Méx* calzones *mpl*

brier = **briar**

brigade [brɪ'geɪd] *n* brigada *f*

brigadier [brɪgə'dɪə(r)] *n* **b. general** general *m* de brigada

brigand ['brɪgənd] *n Literary* malhechor *m*, bandido *m*

bright [braɪt] **1** *adj* **(a)** *(sun, light, eyes)* brillante; *(day)* claro(a), luminoso(a); *(color)* vivo(a); **b. red** rojo *m* vivo; **to go b. red** *(blush)* ruborizarse **(b)** *(optimistic) (future, situation)* prometedor(ora); **it was the only b. spot in the day** fue el único momento bueno del día; **to look on the b. side (of things)** fijarse en el lado bueno (de las cosas) **(c)** *(cheerful)* jovial **(d)** *(clever) (person)* inteligente; *(idea, suggestion)* excelente, brillante; **he's b. at physics** se le da bien la física

2 *adv* **b. and early** tempranito

brighten ['braɪtən] **1** *vt* **(a)** *(room)* alegrar, avivar **(b)** *(mood)* alegrar, animar

2 *vi (weather, sky)* aclararse; *(face, eyes, mood)* alegrarse, animarse; *(prospects)* mejorar

▸**brighten up 1** *vt sep (room, mood)* alegrar
2 *vi (person, face)* animarse; *(weather, sky)* despejarse
bright-eyed ['braɪtaɪd] *adj* con los ojos brillantes; *Fig (enthusiasm)* vivo(a); *Fam* **b. and bushy-tailed** alegre y contento(a)
brightly ['braɪtlɪ] *adv (shine)* radiantemente; *(say, smile)* alegremente; **b. colored** de vivos colores
brightness ['braɪtnɪs] *n* **(a)** *(of light, sun)* luminosidad *f*, brillo *m*; *(of color)* viveza *f*; **b. (control)** *(on TV)* (mando *m* del) brillo *m* **(b)** *(cleverness)* inteligencia *f*
brilliance ['brɪljəns] *n* **(a)** *(of light, color)* resplandor *m* **(b)** *(of person, idea)* genialidad *f*
brilliant ['brɪljənt] *adj* **(a)** *(light, sun, smile)* radiante, resplandeciente **(b)** *(person)* genial; *(future, career)* brillante
brilliantly ['brɪljəntlɪ] *adv* **(a)** *(to shine)* radiantemente; **b. lit** muy iluminado(a); **b. colored** de vivos colores **(b)** *(acted, played)* magníficamente
brim [brɪm] **1** *n (of cup, glass)* borde *m*; *(of hat)* ala *f*
2 *vi (pt & pp* **brimmed)** *(with liquid, enthusiasm)* **to be brimming with** rebosar de; **her eyes brimmed with tears** tenía los ojos anegados de lágrimas
▸**brim over** *vi* rebosar, desbordarse; *Fig* **to be brimming over with health/ideas** estar rebosante de salud/ideas
brimful ['brɪmfʊl] *adj* hasta el borde; *Fig* **b. of health/ideas** pletórico(a) de salud/ideas
brimstone ['brɪmstəʊn] *n Literary* azufre *m*; **fire and b.** fuego *m* del infierno
brine [braɪn] *n (for preserving)* salmuera *f*
bring [brɪŋ] *(pt & pp* **brought** [brɔːt]) *vt* **(a)** *(take)* traer; **to b. sth to sb's attention** llamar la atención de alguien sobre algo; **what brings you to London?** ¿qué os trae por Londres?; **that brings us to my final point...** esto nos lleva al último punto...; **to b. sth out of a box** sacar algo de una caja; **to b. a child into the world** traer al mundo a un niño; *Law* **to b. an action against sb** interponer una demanda *or* entablar un pleito contra alguien
(b) *(lead to, cause)* traer; **it has brought me great happiness** me ha causado gran alegría; **to b. sb (good) luck/bad luck** traer (buena) suerte/mala suerte a alguien; **the announcement brought an angry reaction** el anuncio produjo una reacción airada; **to b. new hope to sb** infundir nuevas esperanzas a alguien; **to b. tears to sb's eyes** hacer llorar a alguien
(c) *(cause to come to a particular condition)* **to b. sth into disrepute** perjudicar la reputación de *or* desprestigiar algo; **to b. sth into question** poner en duda algo; **to b. sth to the boil** hacer que algo hierva; **to b. sth to an end** poner fin a algo; **to b. sth to light** sacar algo a la luz; **to b. sth to mind** traer a la memoria algo; **to b. oneself to do sth** resolverse a hacer algo; **I couldn't b. myself to tell her** no pude decírselo
(d) *(be sold for)* **the house won't b. very much** la casa no reportará mucho dinero
▸**bring about** *vt sep (cause)* provocar, ocasionar
▸**bring along** *vt sep* traer
▸**bring around** *vt sep* **(a)** *(revive)* hacer volver en sí, reanimar **(b)** *(persuade)* convencer; **she brought him around to her point of view** le convenció **(c)** *(direct)* **he brought the conversation around to the subject of...** sacó a colación el tema de...
▸**bring back** *vt sep* **(a)** *(purchase)* devolver; *(person)* traer de vuelta; **to b. sb back to life/health** devolver la vida/la salud a alguien **(b)** *(occasion)* recordar; **to b. back memories of sth to sb** traer a alguien recuerdos de algo **(c)** *(law, punishment)* reinstaurar
▸**bring down** *vt sep* **(a)** *(from shelf, attic)* bajar **(b)** *(cause to fall) (soldier, plane)* derribar; *(government)* derrocar; *Fam* **her**

performance brought the house down su actuación enfervorizó al público **(c)** *(price, temperature)* bajar
▸**bring forward** *vt sep* **(a)** *(proposal, plan)* presentar **(b)** *(advance time of)* adelantar **(c)** *Fin* pasar a cuenta nueva; **brought forward** saldo *m* anterior
▸**bring in** *vt sep* **(a)** *(expert, consultant)* contratar los servicios de; **the police brought him in for questioning** la policía lo llevó a comisaría para interrogarlo **(b)** *(earn) (of person)* ganar; *(of sale, investment)* generar **(c)** *Pol (law, bill)* introducir **(d)** *Law (verdict)* pronunciar
▸**bring off** *vt sep (accomplish)* conseguir
▸**bring on** *vt sep* provocar; **you've brought it on yourself** tú te lo has buscado
▸**bring out** *vt sep* **(a)** *(new product)* sacar **(b)** *(provoke, elicit)* **to b. out the best/the worst in sb** sacar lo mejor/peor de alguien; **strawberries b. her out in a rash** las fresas *or CSur* frutillas le provocan un sarpullido; **to b. sb out of his/her shell** sacar a alguien de su concha
▸**bring round** = **bring around**
▸**bring to** *vt sep (revive)* hacer volver en sí, reanimar
▸**bring together** *vt sep* reunir
▸**bring up** *vt sep* **(a)** *(subject)* sacar a colación **(b)** *(child)* educar; **I was brought up in Spain** fui criado en España; **they're very well/badly brought up** están muy bien/mal educados **(c)** *(vomit)* vomitar
brink [brɪŋk] *n also Fig* borde *m*; **on the b. of** al borde de; *Fig* **to be on the b. of doing sth** estar a punto de hacer algo
brink(s)manship ['brɪŋk(s)mənʃɪp] *n (in politics, diplomacy)* = política consistente en arriesgarse hasta el límite para obtener concesiones de la parte contraria
brisk [brɪsk] *adj* **(a)** *(weather, wind)* fresco(a), vigorizante **(b)** *(person, manner)* enérgico(a); **to be b. with sb** *(rude)* ser brusco(a) con alguien **(c)** *(rapid)* rápido(a); **at a b. pace** a paso ligero; **business is b.** el negocio va muy bien
briskly ['brɪsklɪ] *adv* **(a)** *(efficiently)* enérgicamente; *(dismissively)* bruscamente **(b)** *(rapidly)* rápidamente
bristle ['brɪsəl] **1** *n (of animal, brush)* cerda *f*; *(on face)* pelo *m* de la barba; *(of plant)* pelo *m*
2 *vi* **(a)** *(animal's fur)* erizarse; *Fig* **to b. (with anger)** enfurecerse **(b)** *(be full)* **the room was bristling with security men** la habitación estaba repleta de agentes de seguridad; **the situation was bristling with difficulties** la situación estaba erizada de dificultades
Brit [brɪt] *n Fam* británico(a) *m,f*
Britain ['brɪtən] *n* Gran Bretaña
British ['brɪtɪʃ] **1** *npl* **the B.** los británicos
2 *adj* británico(a); **the B. Isles** las Islas Británicas; **B. Broadcasting Corporation** = nombre completo de la BBC; **B. Summer Time** = hora oficial de verano en Gran Bretaña
Briton ['brɪtən] *n* británico(a) *m,f*; *Hist* britano(a) *m,f*
Brittany ['brɪtənɪ] *n* Bretaña
brittle ['brɪtəl] *adj* **(a)** *(glass, bones)* frágil; *(paper, branches)* quebradizo(a) **(b)** *(irritable)* **to be b.** *(permanent quality)* ser susceptible; *(temporarily)* estar susceptible
broach [brəʊtʃ] *vt (subject, question)* sacar a colación, abordar
broad¹ [brɔːd] *adj (wide)* ancho(a); *(smile, sense)* amplio(a); *(accent)* marcado(a); *(humor)* basto(a); *(mind)* abierto(a); **in b. daylight** en pleno día; **to be in b. agreement** estar de acuerdo en líneas generales; **b. bean** haba *f*; **a b. hint** una clara indirecta; **b. outline** líneas *fpl* generales
broad² *n Fam* tipa *f*, *Esp* tía *f*
broadband ['brɔːdbænd] **1** *n Tel* banda *f* ancha
2 *adj Comptr* de banda ancha
broad-brush ['brɔːd'brʌʃ] *adj* a grandes rasgos
broadcast ['brɔːdkɑːst] **1** *n (program)* emisión *f*

2 *vt* (*pt & pp* **broadcast**) transmitir, emitir; *Fam* **don't b. it!** ¡no lo pregones!

3 *vi (station)* emitir

broadcaster ['brɔːdkɑːstə(r)] *n (person)* presentador(ora) *m,f*

broadcasting ['brɔːdkɑːstɪŋ] *n (programs)* emisiones *fpl*, programas *mpl*; **he works in b.** trabaja en la televisión/radio; **b. station** emisora *f*

broaden ['brɔːdən] **1** *vt (road)* ensanchar; **to b. sb's horizons** ampliar los horizontes de alguien

2 *vi* **to b. (out)** ensancharse, ampliarse

broadly ['brɔːdlɪ] *adv (generally)* en general; **to smile b.** esbozar una amplia sonrisa; **b. speaking** en términos generales

broad-minded [brɔːd'maɪndɪd] *adj* tolerante, de mentalidad abierta

broad-mindedness [brɔːd'maɪndɪdnɪs] *n* tolerancia *f*, mentalidad *f* abierta

broad-shouldered [brɔːd'ʃəʊldəd] *adj* ancho(a) de espaldas

broadside ['brɔːdsaɪd] **1** *n also Fig* **to fire a b.** soltar una andanada

2 *adv* **b. (on)** lateralmente, de lado

brocade [brə'keɪd] *n (cloth)* brocado *m*

broccoli ['brɒkəlɪ] *n* brécol *m*, brócoli *m*

brochure ['brəʊʃə(r)] *n* folleto *m*

brogue¹ [brəʊg] *n (shoe)* zapato *m* de vestir *(de cuero calado)*

brogue² *n (accent)* acento *m (especialmente el irlandés)*

broil [brɔɪl] *vt (grill)* asar a la parrilla

broke [brəʊk] **1** *adj Fam* **to be b.** *(penniless)* estar sin un centavo *or Méx* sin un peso *or Esp* sin blanca; **to go for b.** jugarse el todo por el todo

2 *pt of* **break**

broken ['brəʊkən] **1** *adj (object, bone, promise)* roto(a); *(ground, surface)* accidentado(a); *Fig (person, heart)* destrozado(a); **in a b. voice** con la voz quebrada; **to speak b. English** chapurrear inglés; **b. home** hogar *m* deshecho *or* roto

2 *pp of* **break**

broken-hearted [brəʊkən'hɑːtɪd] *adj* **to be b.** estar desolado(a) *or* desconsolado(a)

broker ['brəʊkə(r)] *n Fin* agente *mf*, corredor(ora) *m,f*

bromide ['brəʊmaɪd] *n Chem* bromuro *m*; *Fig* fórmula *f* caduca

bronchial ['brɒŋkɪəl] *adj Anat* bronquial; **the b. tubes** los bronquios

bronchitic [brɒŋ'kɪtɪk] *adj Med* bronquítico(a)

bronchitis [brɒŋ'kaɪtɪs] *n* bronquitis *f inv*

bronze [brɒnz] **1** *n* bronce *m*; **to win a b.** ganar una medalla de bronce; **the B. Age** la Edad del Bronce

2 *adj (material)* de bronce; *(color)* color (de) bronce

bronzed [brɒnzd] *adj (tanned)* bronceado(a)

brooch [brəʊtʃ] *n* broche *m*

brood [bruːd] **1** *n (of baby birds)* nidada *f*; *Hum (of children)* prole *f*, progenie *f*

2 *vi (hen)* empollar; *Fig* **to b. over one's mistakes** rumiar los propios errores

broody ['bruːdɪ] *adj (hen)* clueca

brook¹ [brʊk] *n (stream)* arroyo *m*, riachuelo *m*

brook² *vt Formal (tolerate)* tolerar, consentir; **he will b. no opposition** no admitirá oposición

broom [bruːm] *n* (**a**) *(plant)* retama *f*, escoba *f* (**b**) *(for cleaning)* escoba *f*; *Fig* **a new b.** = jefe recién llegado que quiere cambiar radicalmente las cosas

broomstick ['bruːmstɪk] *n* palo *m* de escoba

Bros *npl Com (abbr* **Brothers**) Riley B. Hnos. Riley

broth [brɒθ] *n (soup) (thin)* sopa *f*, caldo *m*; *(thick)* potaje *m*, sopa *f*

brothel ['brɒθəl] *n* burdel *m*

brother ['brʌðə(r)] *n* hermano *m*

brotherhood ['brʌðəhʊd] *n (feeling)* fraternidad *f*; *Rel* hermandad *f*; **the b. of man** la humanidad

brother-in-law ['brʌðərɪnlɔː] *(pl* **brothers-in-law**) *n* cuñado *m*

brought [brɔːt] *pt & pp of* **bring**

brow [braʊ] *n* (**a**) *(forehead)* frente *f*; *(eyebrow)* ceja *f* (**b**) *(of hill)* cima *f*, cumbre *f*

browbeat ['braʊbiːt] *(pt* **browbeat**, *pp* **browbeaten** ['braʊbiːtən]) *vt* intimidar; **to b. sb into doing sth** intimidar a alguien para que haga algo

brown [braʊn] **1** *n* marrón *m*, *Am* color *m* café

2 *adj* marrón, *Am* café; *(hair, eyes)* castaño(a); *(skin)* moreno(a); **b. bread** pan *m* integral; **b. paper** papel *m* de estraza; **b. rice** arroz *m* integral; **b. sugar** azúcar *m or f* moreno(a)

3 *vt (in cooking)* dorar

4 *vi (in cooking)* dorarse

Brownie ['braʊnɪ] *(member of girls' organization)* escultista *f*; *Fig* **to win** *or* **get b. points** anotarse tantos *or RP* porotos

brownie ['braʊnɪ] *n (cake)* bizcocho *m* de chocolate y nueces

brown-nose ['braʊnnəʊz] *very Fam vt* lamer el culo a

brownout ['braʊnaʊt] *n* apagón *m* momentáneo

browse [braʊz] **1** *n* **to have a b.** echar una ojeada

2 *vi* (**a**) *(in bookshop, magazine)* echar una ojeada; **to b. through sth** *(book, magazine)* hojear algo (**b**) *(animal)* pacer

3 *vt Comptr* **to b. the Web** navegar por la Web

browser ['braʊzə(r)] *n Comptr* navegador *m*

bruise [bruːz] **1** *n (on body)* cardenal *m*, moradura *f*; *(on fruit)* maca *f*, magulladura *f*

2 *vt (person, sb's arm)* magullar; *(feelings)* herir; **to b. one's arm** hacerse un cardenal en el brazo

3 *vi* **to b. easily** *(fruit)* macarse con facilidad; **he bruises easily** le salen cardenales con facilidad

bruiser ['bruːzə(r)] *n Fam* matón *m*

bruising ['bruːzɪŋ] **1** *n (bruises)* moratones *mpl*, moraduras *fpl*

2 *adj (encounter, impact)* duro(a), violento(a)

brunch [brʌntʃ] *n Fam* desayuno-comida *m*, *RP* brunch *m*

Brunei [bruː'naɪ] *n* Brunei

brunette [bruː'net] *n* morena *f*

brunt [brʌnt] *n* **she bore the b. of the criticism** recibió la mayor parte de las críticas; **the north of the city bore the b. of the attack** el norte de la ciudad fue la parte más afectada por el ataque

bruschetta [brʊs'ketə] *n* = tostada con tomate, albahaca y aceite de oliva

brush [brʌʃ] **1** *n* (**a**) *(for clothes, hair)* cepillo *m*; *(for sweeping)* cepillo *m*, escoba *f*; *(for painting pictures)* pincel *m*; *(for house-painting, shaving)* brocha *f* (**b**) *(action) (to hair, teeth, horse)* cepillado *m*; **to give one's hair a b.** cepillarse el pelo; **to give the floor a b.** barrer el suelo (**c**) *(light touch)* roce *m*; *Fam* **to have a b. with the law** tener un problemilla con la ley (**d**) *(of fox)* cola *f* (**e**) *(undergrowth)* maleza *f*

2 *vt* (**a**) *(clean)* cepillar; *(floor)* barrer; **to b. one's hair** cepillarse el pelo; **to b. one's teeth** lavarse *or* cepillarse los dientes (**b**) *(touch lightly)* rozar

3 *vi* **to b. against sth/sb** rozar algo/a alguien; **to b. past sth/sb** pasar rozando algo/a alguien

▶**brush aside** *vt sep (objection, criticism)* no hacer caso a; *(opponent)* deshacerse de

▶**brush off** *vt sep* (**a**) *(dust, dirt)* sacudir (**b**) *Fam (dismiss)* no hacer caso a, *Esp* pasar de

▶**brush up** *vt sep* (**a**) *(leaves, crumbs)* barrer (**b**) *Fam (subject, language)* **to b. up (on)** pulir, dar un repaso a

brushed [brʌʃt] *adj (cotton, nylon)* afelpado(a)

brush-off ['brʌʃɒf] n Fam **to give sb the b.** no hacer ni caso a alguien

brushwood ['brʌʃwʊd] n (a) (as fuel) leña f, broza f (b) (undergrowth) maleza f, broza f

brushwork ['brʌʃwɜːk] n Art pincelada f, técnica f del pincel

brusque [bruːsk] adj brusco(a)

brusquely ['bruːsklɪ] adv bruscamente

Brussels ['brʌsəlz] n Bruselas; **b. sprouts** coles fpl de Bruselas

brutal ['bruːtəl] adj brutal

brutality [bruː'tælɪtɪ] n brutalidad f

brutalize ['bruːtəlaɪz] vt (make cruel or insensitive) embrutecer; (ill-treat) tratar con brutalidad

brutally ['bruːtəlɪ] adv brutalmente

brute [bruːt] **1** n bestia mf
  2 adj **b. force** or **strength** fuerza f bruta

brutish ['bruːtɪʃ] adj brutal

BS [biː'es], **BSc** [biːes'siː] n Univ (abbr **Bachelor of Science**) (qualification) licenciatura f en Ciencias; (person) licenciado(a) m,f en Ciencias

BSE [biːes'iː] n (abbr **bovine spongiform encephalopathy**) encefalopatía f espongiforme bovina (enfermedad de las vacas locas)

bubble ['bʌbəl] **1** n (of air) burbuja f; (of soap) pompa f; **to blow bubbles** hacer pompas de jabón; Fig **the b. has burst** la buena racha ha terminado; **b. bath** (liquid) espuma f de baño; (bath) baño m de espuma; **b. gum** chicle m; Comptr **b. jet (printer)** impresora f de inyección; Com **b. pack** blister m
  2 vi (form bubbles) burbujear, borbotar

▸**bubble over** vi (soup, milk) salirse, desbordarse; Fig **to b. over with joy** rebosar alegría

bubblegum ['bʌbəlɡʌm] n chicle m

bubbly ['bʌblɪ] **1** n Fam (champagne) champán m
  2 adj (a) (liquid) espumoso(a) (b) (personality) alegre, jovial

bubonic plague [bjuː'bɒnɪk'pleɪɡ] n peste f bubónica

buccaneer [bʌkə'nɪə(r)] n bucanero m

Bucharest ['bʊkərest] n Bucarest

buck [bʌk] **1** n (a) (deer) ciervo m (macho); (rabbit) conejo m (macho) (b) Fam (dollar) dólar m; **to make a fast** or **quick b.** hacer dinero fácil (c) Fam (responsibility) **to pass the b.** escurrir el bulto; **the b. stops here** aquí recae la responsabilidad última
  2 vt **to b. the odds** desafiar las leyes de la probabilidad; **to b. the system** oponerse al sistema; **to b. a trend** invertir una tendencia
  3 vi (horse) corcovear

▸**buck up** Fam **1** vt sep (encourage) animar, entonar; **to b. up one's ideas** espabilarse
  2 vi (cheer up) animarse; (hurry) espabilarse, aligerar

bucket ['bʌkɪt] **1** n balde m, Esp cubo m; Fam **to cry** or **weep buckets** llorar a mares; Fam **b. shop** (for shares) = agencia de cambio y bolsa fraudulenta
  2 vi Fam **it's bucketing (down)** está lloviendo a cántaros or RP a baldes

buckle ['bʌkəl] **1** n hebilla f
  2 vt (a) (fasten) abrochar (b) (deform) combar
  3 vi (deform) combarse; (knees) doblarse; **he buckled at the knees** se le doblaron las rodillas

▸**buckle down** vi poner manos a la obra; **to b. down to a task** ponerse a hacer una tarea

buckshot ['bʌkʃɒt] n perdigones mpl

buckskin ['bʌkskɪn] n piel f (de ciervo o cabra)

buckteeth [bʌk'tiːθ] npl dientes mpl de conejo

bucktoothed [bʌk'tuːθt] adj con dientes de conejo

buckwheat ['bʌkwiːt] n alforfón m

bucolic [bjuː'kɒlɪk] adj Literary bucólico(a)

bud [bʌd] **1** n (of leaf, branch) brote m; (of flower) capullo m
  2 vi (pt & pp **budded**) brotar, salir

Budapest ['bʊdəpest] n Budapest

Buddha ['bʊdə] pr n Buda m

Buddhist ['bʊdɪst] n & adj budista mf

budding ['bʌdɪŋ] adj (genius, actor) en ciernes, incipiente

buddy ['bʌdɪ] n Fam (friend) Esp colega mf, Am compadre, Am hermano(a), Méx cuate

budge [bʌdʒ] **1** vt (move) mover; **I couldn't b. him** (change his mind) no conseguí hacerle cambiar de opinión
  2 vi (move) moverse; (yield) ceder

budgerigar ['bʌdʒərɪɡɑː(r)] n periquito m (australiano)

budget ['bʌdʒɪt] **1** n presupuesto m; **to go over b.** salirse del presupuesto; **we are within b.** no nos hemos salido del presupuesto; **b. deficit** déficit m presupuestario; **b. surplus** superávit m presupuestario
  2 vt (time, money) calcular
  3 vi **to b. for** (include in budget) contemplar en el presupuesto; Fig contar con

budgetary ['bʌdʒɪtərɪ] adj Fin presupuestario(a)

Buenos Aires ['bwenəʊ'saɪrɪz] n Buenos Aires

buff [bʌf] **1** n (a) (color) marrón m claro; Fam **in the b.** (naked) en cueros (b) (enthusiast) **film b.** cinéfilo(a) m,f; **opera b.** entendido(a) m,f en ópera
  2 adj marrón claro
  3 vt (polish) sacar brillo a

buffalo ['bʌfələʊ] (pl **buffalo** or **buffaloes**) n búfalo m

buffer ['bʌfə(r)] n (a) (barrier) **to act as a b.** hacer de amortiguador; **b. state** estado m barrera; **b. zone** zona f de protección (b) Comptr buffer m

buffet[1] ['bʌfɪt] vt (of wind) zarandear, azotar; Fig **he was buffeted by the crowds** le arrolló or zarandeó la multitud; Fig **to be buffeted by events** verse sacudido(a) por el remolino de los acontecimientos

buffet[2] ['bʊfeɪ] n (a) (sideboard) mostrador m de comidas, bufé m (b) (meal) bufé m; **b. lunch** (almuerzo m tipo) bufé m

buffeting ['bʌfɪtɪŋ] n **to take a b.** (ship) ser zarandeado(a); Fig (person) recibir muchos golpes

buffoon [bə'fuːn] n payaso m, bufón m

bug [bʌg] **1** n (a) (insect) bicho m, insecto m (b) Fam (illness) infección f; **there's a b. going around** hay un virus rondando por ahí; Fig **the travel b.** el gusanillo de viajar (c) Comptr error m (d) (listening device) micrófono m oculto
  2 vt (pt & pp **bugged**) (a) (telephone) pinchar, intervenir; (room) poner micrófonos en (b) Fam (annoy) molestar, fastidiar; **stop bugging me about it!** ¡deja de darme la lata con eso!

▸**bug off** vi Fam (leave) largarse, Esp pirarse

bugbear ['bʌgbeə(r)] n Fam tormento m, pesadilla f

bug-eyed ['bʌgaɪd] adj con ojos saltones

bug-free [bʌg'friː] adj Comptr sin errores

bugger ['bʌgə(r)] vt sodomizar

buggery ['bʌgərɪ] n Law sodomía f

bugging device ['bʌgɪŋdɪ'vaɪs] n (in room) micrófono m oculto; (in telephone line) aparato m de escucha telefónica

buggy ['bʌgɪ] n (carriage) calesa f

bugle ['bjuːgəl] n corneta f, clarín m

bugler ['bjuːglə(r)] n corneta m, clarín m

build [bɪld] **1** n complexión f, constitución f
  2 vt (pt & pp **built** [bɪlt]) construir; **to be built (out) of sth** estar hecho(a) de algo; **to b. sth into sth** incorporar algo en algo; **they have built their hopes on it** han basado sus esperanzas en ello

▸**build on** vt sep (a) (add) añadir (b) (use as foundation) **she built on their achievements** siguió avanzando a partir de sus logros

▸**build up 1** vt sep (a) (hopes, expectations) alimentar; (resources) aumentar (b) (reputation) crear; **to b. up speed** tomar or Esp coger velocidad; **to b. up an immunity (to**

sth) hacerse inmune (a algo) **(c)** *(hype)* **the press built her up as a future champion** la prensa construyó su imagen de futura campeona

2 *vi (clouds)* formarse; *(tension, pressure)* incrementarse, aumentar

builder ['bɪldə(r)] *n (worker)* albañil *m; (small businessman)* contratista *mf* de obras

building ['bɪldɪŋ] *n* **(a)** *(structure)* edificio *m* **(b)** *(trade)* construcción *f;* **b. block** *(toy)* pieza *f* (de construcción); *Fig* unidad *f* básica; **b. site** obra *f*

buildup ['bɪldʌp] *n (of tension, forces)* incremento *m,* aumento *m; (before election, public event)* periodo *m* previo; **after all the b....** después de toda la expectación creada...

built [bɪlt] *pt & pp of* **build**

built-in ['bɪl'tɪn] *adj (cupboard)* empotrado(a); *(included)* incorporado(a); *Fig (safeguard, obsolescence)* inherente; **his height gives him a b. advantage** su altura le proporciona una ventaja de entrada

built-up ['bɪl'tʌp] *adj (area)* urbanizado(a)

bulb [bʌlb] *n (of plant)* bulbo *m; (lightbulb) Esp* bombilla *f, Andes, Méx* foco *m, CAm, Carib* bombillo *m, RP* lamparita *f*

bulbous ['bʌlbəs] *adj* bulboso(a)

Bulgaria [bʌl'geərɪə] *n* Bulgaria

Bulgarian [bʌl'geərɪən] **1** *n* **(a)** *(person)* búlgaro(a) *m,f* **(b)** *(language)* búlgaro *m*

2 *adj* búlgaro(a)

bulge [bʌldʒ] **1** *n* bulto *m,* abultamiento *m*

2 *vi* **(a)** *(be full of)* estar repleto(a) (**with** de) **(b)** *(swell)* abombarse; *Fig* **her eyes bulged at the sight of all the food** al ver tanta comida parecía que se le iban a salir los ojos de las órbitas

bulimia [bu:'lɪmɪə] *n Med* bulimia *f*

bulk [bʌlk] **1** *n* **(a)** *(mass)* masa *f,* volumen *m;* **the b. (of sth)** *(most)* el grueso (de algo) **(b)** *Com* **in b.** a granel; **to buy/sell in b.** comprar/vender al por mayor; **b. mail** envío *m* (postal) masivo; **b. purchase** compra *f* al por mayor

2 *vt* **to b. sth out** abultar algo

3 *vi* **to b. large** *(problem)* tener relieve

bulkhead ['bʌlkhed] *n Naut* mamparo *m*

bulky ['bʌlkɪ] *adj (thing)* grande, voluminoso(a); *(person)* corpulento(a)

bull¹ [bʊl] *n* **(a)** *(animal)* toro *m;* **b. elephant** elefante *m* (macho); *Fin* **b. market** mercado *m* al alza **(b)** *Fam (nonsense)* **to talk b.** decir sandeces **(c)** *(idioms)* **to take the b. by the horns** agarrar *or Esp* coger el toro por los cuernos; **like a b. in a china shop** como un elefante en una cacharrería

bull² *n Rel* bula *f*

bulldog ['bʊldɒg] *n* bulldog *m*

bulldoze ['bʊldəʊz] *vt (flatten) (area, land)* allanar, nivelar; *(building)* demoler, derribar; *Fig* **to b. sb into doing sth** forzar *or* obligar a alguien a hacer algo

bulldozer ['bʊldəʊzə(r)] *n* bulldozer *m*

bullet ['bʊlɪt] *n* bala *f,* proyectil *m;* **b. hole** agujero *m* de bala; **b. wound** herida *f* de bala

bulletin ['bʊlɪtɪn] *n* boletín *m; (gen) & Comptr* **b. board** tablón *m* de anuncios

bulletproof ['bʊlɪtpru:f] *adj* antibalas *inv;* **b. vest** chaleco *m* antibalas

bullfight ['bʊlfaɪt] *n* corrida *f* de toros

bullfighter ['bʊlfaɪtə(r)] *n* torero *m*

bullfighting ['bʊlfaɪtɪŋ] *n* toreo *m*

bullfinch ['bʊlfɪntʃ] *n* camachuelo *m*

bullfrog ['bʊlfrɒg] *n* rana *f* toro

bullhorn ['bʊlhɔːn] *n* megáfono *m*

bullion ['bʊljən] *n* **gold/silver b.** oro *m*/plata *f* en lingotes *or* barras

bullish ['bʊlɪʃ] *adj Fin (market)* al alza; *Fam (person)* optimista

bullock ['bʊlək] *n* buey *m*

bullring ['bʊlrɪŋ] *n (building)* plaza *f* de toros; *(arena)* ruedo *m*

bullrush ['bʊlrʌʃ] *n* junco *m*

bull's-eye ['bʊlzaɪ] *n* diana *f,* blanco *m; also Fig* **to hit the b.** dar en el blanco *or* clavo

bullshit ['bʊlʃɪt] *Vulg* **1** *n (nonsense) Esp* gilipolleces *fpl, Am* pendejadas *fpl, RP* boludeces *fpl*

2 *exclam* ¡y un huevo!

3 *vt (pt & pp* **bullshitted)** **to b. sb** vacilar a alguien; **she bullshitted her way into the job** consiguió el puesto engañando a todo el mundo

4 *vi (talk nonsense)* decir *Esp* gilipolleces *or Am* pendejadas *or RP* boludeces

bully ['bʊlɪ] **1** *n* matón(ona) *m,f; (at school) Esp* abusón(ona) *m,f, Am* abusador(ora) *m,f*

2 *exclam Ironic* **b. for you!** ¡toma ya!

3 *vt* intimidar; **to b. sb into doing sth** intimidar a alguien para que haga algo

bullyboy ['bʊlɪbɔɪ] *n* matón *m;* **b. tactics** tácticas *fpl* de intimidación

bullying ['bʊlɪɪŋ] **1** *n* intimidación *f*

2 *adj* intimidatorio(a), amenazador(ora)

bulrush ['bʊlrʌʃ] *n (soft rush)* junco *m*

bulwark ['bʊlwɜːk] *n also Fig* bastión *m* (**against** contra)

bum [bʌm] *Fam* **1** *n (tramp)* vagabundo(a) *m,f*

2 *adj (of poor quality)* malo(a), *Esp* cutre, *RP* berreta; **she got a b. deal** la trataron a patadas

3 *vt (pt & pp* **bummed)** **to b. sth from** *or* **off sb** *Esp* gorronear *or Méx* gorrear *or RP* garronear algo a alguien

▶**bum around** *vi Fam (be idle)* holgazanear, gandulear; *(travel)* vagabundear

bumblebee ['bʌmbəlbi:] *n* abejorro *m*

bumbling ['bʌmbəlɪŋ] *adj* **b. fool** *or* **idiot** tonto(a) *m,f,* inútil *mf*

bummer ['bʌmə(r)] *n Fam (annoying thing)* lata *f, RP* embole *m, Ven* lava *f;* **what a b.!** ¡qué lata!

bump [bʌmp] **1** *n* **(a)** *(jolt)* golpe *m,* sacudida *f; Fig* **to come back down to earth with a b.** volver a la dura realidad; **b. start** *(for car)* = método de arranque de un coche empujándolo mientras se mete la marcha conforme se pone en movimiento **(b)** *(lump)* chichón *m*

2 *vt* **to b. one's head against sth** golpearse en la cabeza con algo

▶**bump into** *vt insep (collide with)* chocar con; *Fam (meet by chance)* encontrarse con, toparse con

▶**bump off** *vt sep Fam (kill)* liquidar, cargarse a

▶**bump up** *vt sep Fam (price)* subir

bumper ['bʌmpə(r)] **1** *n* **b. car** *(at fairground)* auto *m or* coche *m* de choque, *Méx* carrito *m* chocón, *RP* autito *m* chocador

2 *adj* abundante, excepcional; **b. crop** cosecha *f* excepcional

bumpkin ['bʌmpkɪn] *n* **(country) b.** palurdo(a) *m,f, Esp* paleto(a) *m,f*

bump-start ['bʌmpstɑːt] *vt* **to b. a car** arrancar un coche empujando

bumptious ['bʌmpʃəs] *adj* presuntuoso(a), engreído(a)

bumpy ['bʌmpɪ] *adj (road)* lleno(a) de baches, accidentado(a); *(journey)* incómodo(a), agitado(a); *Fam Fig* **to have a b. ride** encontrar muchos obstáculos

bun [bʌn] *n* **(a)** *(food)* bollo *m* **(b)** *(hair)* moño *m*

bunch [bʌntʃ] *n (of flowers)* ramo *m,* ramillete *m; (of bananas, grapes)* racimo *m; (of keys)* manojo *m; (of friends)* pandilla *f; (of people)* grupo *m;* **to wear one's hair in bunches** peinarse con *or* llevar coletas; **to have a whole b. of things to do** tener un montón de cosas que hacer; **the best** *or* **the pick of the b.** el mejor de todo el lote

▶**bunch together** *vi (people)* apiñarse

bundle ['bʌndəl] **1** *n (of papers)* manojo *m; (of banknotes)* fajo

m; *(of straw)* haz *m*, gavilla *f*; *(of clothes)* fardo *m*, hato *m*; *Fam* **she's a b. of nerves** es un manojo de nervios; *Fam Ironic* **he's a real b. of laughs** es un tipo aburridísimo, *Esp* es un muermo de tío, *RP* es un tipo embolante
  2 *vt* **to b. sb out of the door** sacar a alguien a empujones por la puerta; **to b. sb into a car** meter a alguien a empujones en un coche

▶**bundle off** *vt sep (send)* despachar

▶**bundle up** *vt sep (dress warmly)* arropar, envolver

bung [bʌŋ] **1** *n (of barrel)* tapón *m*
  2 *vt (pipe, hole)* atascar, taponar

▶**bung up** *vt sep Fam (pipe, hole)* atascar, taponar; **my nose is bunged up** tengo la nariz taponada

bungalow ['bʌŋgələʊ] *n* bungalow *m*

bungee jumping ['bʌndʒiː'dʒʌmpɪŋ] *n* puenting *m*

bunghole ['bʌŋhəʊl] *n* agujero *m* de barril

bungle ['bʌŋgəl] **1** *vt (job, task)* echar a perder, hacer mal; **they bungled their attempt to escape** su intento de fuga les salió mal
  2 *vi* hacer chapuzas

bunion ['bʌnjən] *n (on foot)* juanete *m*

bunk [bʌŋk] *n (bed)* litera *f*

bunker ['bʌŋkə(r)] *n* **(a)** *(for coal)* carbonera *f* **(b)** *Mil* búnker *m*; **nuclear b.** refugio *m* antinuclear

bunkum ['bʌŋkəm] *n Fam* palabrería *f*, tonterías *fpl*

bunny ['bʌnɪ] *n Fam* **b. (rabbit)** conejito *m*

Bunsen burner ['bʌnsən'bɜːnə(r)] *n* mechero *m* Bunsen

bunting ['bʌntɪŋ] *n (decorations)* banderines *mpl*

buoy [buːɪ] *n* boya *f*

▶**buoy up** *vt sep (person)* animar, alentar; *(prices)* mantener al alza

buoyancy ['bɔɪənsɪ] *n* **(a)** *(in water)* flotabilidad *f*; *Fig (of market)* estabilidad *f*, optimismo *m*

buoyant ['bɔɪənt] *adj (in water)* flotante; *Fig (economy, prices)* boyante; *Fig (person, mood)* optimista, vital

burble ['bɜːbəl] **1** *vt (say)* farfullar
  2 *vi (stream)* borbotar; *(person)* mascullar

burden ['bɜːdən] **1** *n also Fig* carga *f*; *Law* **b. of proof** obligación *f* de probar
  2 *vt* cargar, sobrecargar (**with** con *or* de)

burdensome ['bɜːdənsəm] *adj* pesado(a), molesto(a)

bureau ['bjʊərəʊ] *(pl* **bureaux** ['bjʊərəʊz]*) n* **(a)** *(office)* oficina *f*, departamento *m* **(b)** *(government department)* departamento *m*

bureaucracy [bjʊə'rɒkrəsɪ] *n* burocracia *f*

bureaucrat ['bjʊərəkræt] *n* burócrata *mf*

bureaucratic [bjʊərə'krætɪk] *adj* burocrático(a)

burgeon ['bɜːdʒən] *vi (trade, relationship)* florecer; **a burgeoning talent** un talento incipiente

burger ['bɜːgə(r)] *n Fam (hamburger)* hamburguesa *f*

burglar ['bɜːglə(r)] *n* ladrón(ona) *m,f*; **b. alarm** alarma *f* antirrobo

burglarize ['bɜːgləraɪz] *vt* robar, desvalijar

burglar-proof ['bɜːgləpruːf] *adj* a prueba de ladrones

burglary ['bɜːglərɪ] *n* robo *m (en una casa o edificio)*

burgle ['bɜːgəl] *vt* robar, desvalijar

burgundy ['bɜːgəndɪ] *adj (color)* (color) burdeos

burial ['berɪəl] *n* entierro *m*; **b. ground** cementerio *m*

Burkina Faso [bɜː'kiːnə'fæsəʊ] *n* Burkina Faso

burlap ['bɜːlæp] *n* arpillera *f*

burlesque [bɜː'lesk] **1** *n* parodia *f*
  2 *adj* burlesco(a), paródico(a)

burly ['bɜːlɪ] *adj* fornido(a), corpulento(a)

Burma ['bɜːmə] *n* Birmania

Burmese [bɜː'miːz] **1** *npl (people)* **the B.** los birmanos
  2 *n (language)* birmano *m*
  3 *adj* birmano(a)

burn¹ [bɜːn] **1** *n* quemadura *f*

2 *vt (pt & pp* **burned** *or* **burnt** [bɜːnt]*)* **(a)** *(fuel, building)* quemar; **the stove burns wood/coal** la cocina funciona con leña/carbón; **to b. one's hand/finger** quemarse la mano/el dedo; **to b. a hole in sth** hacer un agujero a algo quemándolo
  (b) *Comptr (CD-ROM)* estampar
  (c) *(idioms)* **to have money to b.** *(rich person)* tener dinero de sobra; **she's just got paid and she's got money to b.** le acaban de pagar y tiene dinero para gastar; **to b. one's bridges** quemar las naves; **to b. the candle at both ends** darse demasiado trote; **to b. the midnight oil** quedarse hasta muy tarde *(estudiando o trabajando)*, *Andes* trasnocharse
  3 *vi (fire, fuel, building)* arder; *(light)* estar encendido(a); *Fig (with desire, anger, enthusiasm)* arder (**with** de); **the fire is burning low** el fuego está bajo

▶**burn down 1** *vt sep* incendiar, quemar
  2 *vi* quemarse

▶**burn out 1** *vt sep* **to b. itself out** *(fire)* consumirse, agotarse; *Fig* **to b. oneself out** *(become exhausted)* agotarse
  2 *vi (fire)* consumirse; *Fig (person)* quemarse

▶**burn up 1** *vt sep (energy)* quemar, consumir
  2 *vi (rocket)* entrar en combustión

burn² *n Scot (stream)* arroyo *m*

burner ['bɜːnə(r)] *n* quemador *m*

burning ['bɜːnɪŋ] *adj (on fire)* en llamas; *(heat, sun, passion)* abrasador(ora); *(ambition)* irrefrenable; **to be b. hot** abrasar; **a b. issue** un asunto candente

burnish ['bɜːnɪʃ] *vt (polish)* bruñir

burn-out ['bɜːnaʊt] *n* **(a)** **I had a b.** *(engine)* se me quemó; **what caused the b.?** *(in electrical system)* ¿por qué se fundió? **(b)** *Fam (exhaustion)* agotamiento *m*

burnt [bɜːnt] **1** *adj* quemado(a); **to be b.** estar quemado(a)
  2 *pt & pp of* **burn¹**

burnt-out ['bɜːnt'aʊt] *adj (building)* calcinado(a), carbonizado(a); *(fuse)* fundido(a)

burp [bɜːp] **1** *n* eructo *m*
  2 *vi* eructar

burr¹ [bɜː(r)] *n (of plant)* erizo *m*

burr² *n* **to speak with a b.** hablar arrastrando la "r"

burrow ['bʌrəʊ] **1** *n (of animal)* madriguera *f*
  2 *vi (animal)* cavar; *Fig* **he burrowed around in his desk** rebuscó en su escritorio

bursar ['bɜːsə(r)] *n Univ* tesorero(a) *m,f*

burst [bɜːst] **1** *n (of applause)* salva *f*; *(of activity, enthusiasm)* arranque *m*; **a b. of gunfire** una ráfaga de disparos; **a b. of laughter** una carcajada; **a b. of speed** un acelerón
  2 *vt (pt & pp* **burst***) (balloon, tire)* reventar; **to b. its banks** *(river)* desbordarse
  3 *vi (balloon, tire, pipe)* reventar; *Fig* **to be bursting with pride/joy** reventar de orgullo/alegría; *Fig* **to be bursting to do sth** morirse de ganas de hacer algo; *Fig* **to be bursting at the seams** *(room, bus)* estar hasta los topes; *Fam* **I'm bursting for the bathroom** (estoy que) me meo

▶**burst into** *vt insep* **(a)** *(enter)* irrumpir en **(b)** *(suddenly start)* **to b. into flames** inflamarse; **to b. into song** ponerse a cantar; **to b. into laughter/tears** echarse a reír/llorar

▶**burst open** *vi (door, suitcase)* abrirse de golpe; *(plastic bag)* reventar

▶**burst out** *vi* **to b. out laughing** soltar una carcajada; **to b. out crying** echarse a llorar

Burundi [bə'rʊndɪ] *n* Burundi

bury ['berɪ] *vt (body, treasure)* enterrar; *(of avalanche, mudslide)* sepultar; **she buried the knife in his back** le clavó el cuchillo en la espalda; *Fig* **to b. oneself in the country** retirarse al campo; **to b. one's face in one's hands** esconder la cara en las manos; *Fig* **to b. the hatchet** *(end quarrel)* enterrar el hacha de guerra

bus [bʌs] **1** *n* (**a**) autobús *m*, *Andes* buseta *f*, *Bol*, *RP* colectivo *m*, *CAm*, *Méx* camión *m*, *CAm*, *Carib* guagua *f*, *Urug* ómnibus *m*, *Ven* microbusete *m*; **by b.** en autobús; **b. conductor** cobrador(ora) *m,f* de autobús; **b. driver** conductor(ora) *m,f* de autobús; **b. lane** carril *m* bus; **b. route** línea *f* de autobús; **b. shelter** marquesina *f*; **b. station** estación *f* de autobuses, *CAm*, *Méx* central *f* camionera; **b. stop** parada *f* de autobús (**b**) *Comptr* bus *m*
2 *vt* (*pt* & *pp* **bused** *or* **bussed**) llevar *or* transportar en autobús

bush [bʊʃ] *n* (*plant*) arbusto *m*, mata *f*; **the b.** (*in Africa, Australia*) el monte; *Fam* **b. telegraph** *Esp* radio *f* macuto, *Cuba, CRica, Pan* radio *f* bemba

bushed [bʊʃt] *adj Fam* (*exhausted*) **to be b.** estar molido(a) *or* derrengado(a)

bushel [ˈbʊʃəl] *n* = medida de áridos (= *35,23 litros*); *Fig* **don't hide your light under a b.** no ocultes tus buenas cualidades

bushfire [ˈbʊʃfaɪə(r)] *n* incendio *m* de matorral

Bushman [ˈbʊʃmən] *n* bosquimano(a) *m,f*

bushy [ˈbʊʃɪ] *adj* espeso(a)

busily [ˈbɪzɪlɪ] *adv* activamente, diligentemente

business [ˈbɪznɪs] *n* (**a**) (*task, concern*) asunto *m*; **it's none of your b.** no es asunto tuyo; **it's not my b. to…** no me corresponde a mí…; **mind your own b.** métete en tus asuntos; **to make it one's b. to do sth** proponerse algo; **I was just going about my b.** yo simplemente iba a lo mío; **to get down to b.** ir a lo esencial, ir a lo importante; **to mean b.** ir en serio; **it's a sad** *or* **sorry b.** es un asunto lamentable *or* triste; **I'm sick of the whole b.** estoy harto de todo este asunto; *Fam* **he was working like nobody's b.** estaba trabajando de lo lindo
(**b**) (*individual company*) empresa *f*; (*commercial activity*) negocios *mpl*; **to be in b.** dedicarse a los negocios; **to be in the computing b.** (*person*) trabajar en el sector de la informática; **I'm not in the b. of making concessions** no estoy por hacer concesiones; **to go into b. (with)** montar un negocio (con); **to go out of b.** quebrar; **to go to London on b.** ir a Londres en viaje de negocios; **how's b.?** ¿cómo van los negocios?; **it's good/bad for b.** es bueno/malo para los negocios; **to talk b.** hablar de negocios; **to do b. (with)** hacer negocios (con); *Fig* **he's a man you can do b. with** es un hombre con el que se puede tratar; *Fin* **b. account** cuenta *f* comercial; **b. card** tarjeta *f* de visita; **b. center** (*in hotel*) centro *m* de negocios; (*city*) centro *m* comercial; *Av* **b. class** clase *f* preferente; **b. college** facultad *f* de ciencias empresariales; **b. hours** (*of company*) horario *m* de trabajo; (*of shop*) horario *m* comercial; **b. incubator** vivero *m* (de empresas); **b. lunch** comida *f* de trabajo; **b. management** gestión *f* *or* administración *f* de empresas; **b. manager** administrador(ora) *m,f* de empresa; **b. park** parque *m* empresarial; **b. plan** plan *m* económico; **b. school** escuela *f* de negocios; **b. studies** empresariales *fpl*; **b. suit** traje *m* de calle; **b. trip** viaje *m* de negocios

businesslike [ˈbɪznɪslaɪk] *adj* eficiente

businessman [ˈbɪznɪsmæn] *n* (*executive, manager*) hombre *m* de negocios, ejecutivo *m*; (*owner of business*) empresario *m*; **to be a good b.** tener cabeza para los negocios

businesswoman [ˈbɪznɪswʊmən] *n* (*executive, manager*) mujer *f* de negocios, ejecutiva *f*; (*owner of business*) empresaria *f*; **to be a good b.** tener cabeza para los negocios

busload [ˈbʌsləʊd] *n* **a b. of workers** un autobús repleto de trabajadores

busman [ˈbʌsmən] *n Fam* **a b.'s holiday** = tiempo libre que se ocupa con una actividad similar a la del trabajo habitual

bust¹ [bʌst] *n* (**a**) (*of woman*) busto *m*; **b. measurement** medida *f* de busto (**b**) (*statue*) busto *m*

bust² *Fam* **1** *n* (**a**) (*police raid*) redada *f*; **drug(s) b.** operación *or* redada antidroga (**b**) (*failure*) quiebra *f*

2 *adj* (*broken*) **to be b.** estar estropeado(a) *or Esp* escacharrado(a); **to go b.** (*bankrupt*) quebrar
3 *vt* (*pt* & *pp* **bust** *or* **busted**) (**a**) (*break*) estropear, *Esp* escacharrar (**b**) (*arrest*) trincar, empapelar
▸**bust out** *vi Fam* (*escape*) fugarse, largarse
▸**bust up** *vt sep Fam* (*disrupt*) (*event*) reventar; (*friendship, relationship*) romper

buster [ˈbʌstə(r)] *n Fam* (*term of address*) *Esp* tío *m*, *Esp* tronco *m*, *Méx* cuate *m*, *RP* boludo *m*; **who are you looking at, b.?** ¿tú qué miras, *Esp* tronco *or Méx* cuate *or RP* boludo?

bustle [ˈbʌsəl] **1** *n* (*activity*) bullicio *m*, trajín *m*
2 *vi* **to b. (about)** trajinar

busty [ˈbʌstɪ] *adj Fam* pechugona, tetona

busy [ˈbɪzɪ] **1** *adj* (**a**) (*person*) ocupado(a); (*day, week*) ajetreado(a); **to be b.** (*person*) estar ocupado(a); (*day, week*) ser ajetreado(a); **to be b. doing sth** estar haciendo algo; **the train was very b.** el tren iba muy lleno; **a b. road** una carretera con mucho tráfico (**b**) (*telephone line*) ocupado(a); **the line is b.** (el teléfono) da ocupado, *Esp* (el teléfono) está comunicando
2 *vt* **to b. oneself with sth** entretenerse con algo

busybody [ˈbɪzɪbɒdɪ] *n Fam* metomentodo *mf*, entrometido(a) *m,f*

but [bʌt] **1** *prep* (*except*) salvo, excepto; **any day b. tomorrow** cualquier día salvo mañana; **it's nothing b. prejudice** no son más que prejuicios; **she is anything b. stupid** es todo menos tonta; **b. for** de no ser por, si no es por
2 *adv Formal* **he is b. a child** no es más que un niño; **had I b. known!** ¡si lo hubiera sabido!; **one can b. try** al menos, se debe intentar
3 *conj* (**a**) (*in general*) pero; **small b. strong** pequeño, pero fuerte; **I told her to do it b. she refused** le dije que lo hiciera, pero se negó; **b. I tell you I saw it!** ¡te aseguro que lo vi!; **what could I do b. invite him?** ¿qué otra cosa podía hacer más que invitarlo? (**b**) (*direct contrast*) sino; **not once b. twice** no una vez sino dos
4 *n* **no buts!** ¡no hay peros que valgan!

butane [ˈbjuːteɪn] *n* butano *m*

butch [bʊtʃ] *adj Fam* **she looks rather b.** tiene pinta de marimacho

butcher [ˈbʊtʃə(r)] **1** *n also Fig* carnicero(a) *m,f*; **the b.'s** (*shop*) la carnicería
2 *vt also Fig* matar

butchery [ˈbʊtʃərɪ] *n* carnicería *f*; *Fig* carnicería *f*, matanza *f*

butler [ˈbʌtlə(r)] *n* mayordomo *m*

butt [bʌt] **1** *n* (**a**) (*of rifle*) culata *f*; (*of cigarette*) colilla *f*; **to be the b. of a joke** ser el blanco de una broma (**b**) *Fam* (*buttocks*) trasero *m*
2 *vt* (*hit with head*) dar *or* arrear un cabezazo a
▸**butt in** *vi* (*interrupt*) inmiscuirse, entrometerse

butter [ˈbʌtə(r)] **1** *n* mantequilla *f*, *RP* manteca *f*; *Fig* **she looks as if b. wouldn't melt in her mouth** parece incapaz de matar una mosca, *Esp* parece como si no hubiera roto un plato en su vida; **b. bean** = tipo de judía *f* blanca; **b. dish** mantequera *f*; **b. knife** cuchillo *m* de mantequilla *or RP* manteca
2 *vt* untar de mantequilla *or RP* manteca
▸**butter up** *vt sep Fam* (*flatter*) hacer la rosca a

buttercup [ˈbʌtəkʌp] *n* ranúnculo *m*, botón *m* de oro

butterfingers [ˈbʌtəfɪŋɡəz] *n Fam* (*clumsy person*) torpe *mf*, manazas *mf inv*

butterfly [ˈbʌtəflaɪ] *n* mariposa *f*; *Fig* **I had butterflies (in my stomach)** me temblaban las rodillas; **b. (stroke)** (*in swimming*) (estilo *m*) mariposa *f*; **to do** *or* **swim (the) b.** nadar a mariposa

buttermilk [ˈbʌtəmɪlk] *n* (*by-product from butter making*) suero *m* (de leche); (*curdled milk*) leche *f* cuajada *or* batida (*para beber*)

butterscotch ['bʌtəskɒtʃ] *n* = dulce de mantequilla y azúcar

butt-naked ['bʌt'neɪkɪd] *adj Fam* en pelotas, en cueros

buttock ['bʌtək] *n* nalga *f*

button ['bʌtən] **1** *n* (a) *(on shirt, machine)* botón *m*; **b. mushroom** champiñón *m (pequeño)* (b) *(badge)* chapa *f*
  2 *vt (shirt)* abotonar; **to b. one's shirt** abotonarse la camisa; *Fam* **b. it!** ¡cierra el pico!

▸**button up** *vt sep (shirt, dress)* abotonar; **to b. up one's shirt** abotonarse la camisa

buttonhole ['bʌtənhəʊl] **1** *n* ojal *m*
  2 *vt (detain)* agarrar

buttress ['bʌtrɪs] **1** *n Archit* contrafuerte *m*; *Fig* apoyo *m*, pilar *m*
  2 *vt Fig (support)* respaldar

buxom ['bʌksəm] *adj (full-bosomed)* de amplios senos; *(plump)* de carnes generosas

buy [baɪ] **1** *n* compra *f*; **a good/bad b.** una buena/mala compra
  2 *vt (pt & pp* **bought** [bɔːt]) (a) *(purchase)* comprar; **to b. sb sth, to b. sth for sb** comprar algo a *or* para alguien; **to b. sth from sb** comprarle algo a alguien (b) *(idioms)* **to b. time** ganar tiempo; *Fam* **he bought the farm** *(has died)* estiró la pata, *Esp* la ha palmado; *Fam* **she won't b. that** *(won't believe)* no se lo tragará

▸**buy in** *vt sep (supplies)* aprovisionarse de

▸**buy into** *vt insep (company, scheme)* adquirir una parte *or* acciones de

▸**buy off** *vt sep Fam (opponent)* comprar

▸**buy out** *vt sep Com* comprar la parte de

▸**buy up** *vt sep* acaparar, comprar la totalidad de

buyer ['baɪə(r)] *n* comprador(ora) *m,f*; **b.'s market** mercado *m* favorable al comprador

buy-out ['baɪaʊt] *n Com* adquisición *f* (de todas las acciones)

buzz [bʌz] **1** *n* (a) *(noise) (of conversation)* rumor *m*; *(of machine, insects)* zumbido *m*; **b. saw** sierra *f* circular; *Fam* **b. word** palabra *f* de moda (b) *Fam (phone call)* **to give sb a b.** dar a alguien un toque *or* un telefonazo, *Méx* echar un fonazo a alguien (c) *Fam (thrill)* **to get a b. out of sth** entusiasmarse con algo
  2 *vt Fam (on intercom)* llamar por el portero electrónico; *(on pager)* llamar a través del buscapersonas *or Esp* busca *or Méx* localizador *or RP* radiomensaje
  3 *vi (make noise)* zumbar; *Fig* **the whole town was buzzing with excitement** toda la ciudad hervía de animación; *Fam* **my head was buzzing with ideas** las ideas me bullían en la cabeza; **my ears were buzzing** me zumbaban los oídos

buzzard ['bʌzəd] *n (hawk)* ratonero *m* común; *(vulture)* buitre *m*

buzzer ['bʌzə(r)] *n (electric bell)* timbre *m*

buzzing ['bʌzɪŋ] *n* zumbido *m*

b & w *Phot & Cin (abbr* **black and white**) b/n, blanco y negro

by¹ [baɪ] **1** *prep* (a) *(expressing agent)* por; **he was arrested by the police** fue detenido por la policía; **made by hand** hecho(a) a mano; **a play by Shakespeare** una obra de Shakespeare
  (b) *(close to)* junto a; **by the fire** junto al fuego; **by the side of the road** al borde de la carretera

  (c) *(via)* por; **to go by the same route** ir por la misma ruta; **by land/sea** por tierra/mar
  (d) *(with manner, means)* **by rail** en tren; **by car/plane** en coche/avión; **to pay by credit card** pagar con tarjeta de crédito; **he had two children by his first wife** tuvo dos hijos de su primera esposa; **to take sb by the hand/arm** tomar *or Esp* coger a alguien de la mano/del brazo; **to know sb by sight** conocer a alguien de vista; **to earn one's living by teaching** ganarse la vida enseñando; **to go by appearances** fiarse de las apariencias; **to call sb by their first name** llamar a alguien por su nombre (de pila); **what do you mean by that?** ¿qué quieres decir con eso?
  (e) *(past)* **he walked right by me without stopping** pasó por mi lado sin detenerse; **we drove by the school on the way here** pasamos delante del colegio camino de aquí
  (f) *(at or before)* **he should be here by now** debería estar ya aquí; **by then it was too late** para entonces ya era demasiado tarde; **by tomorrow** para mañana; **by 1980 they were all dead** en 1980 ya estaban todos muertos
  (g) *(during)* **by day** de día; **by night** de noche, por la noche
  (h) *(with measurements, quantities, numbers)* **to divide by three** dividir entre tres; **to multiply by three** multiplicar por tres; **to sell sth by weight** vender algo al peso; **three inches by two** tres por dos pulgadas, tres pulgadas por dos; **one by one** uno(a) a uno(a); **to increase by 50 percent** aumentar en un 50 por ciento
  (i) *(with reflexive pronouns) see* **myself, himself, yourself** *etc*
  (j) *(as a result of)* **by chance/mistake** por casualidad/error
  2 *adv* (a) **by and by** *(gradually)* poco a poco; *(soon)* dentro de poco; **by and large** en general, por lo general; **by the way,…** a propósito,… (b) *(past)* **to pass by** *(person)* pasar; *(time)* transcurrir, pasar; **to drive by** pasar sin detenerse *(en coche)*

bye, by² [baɪ] *exclam Fam* ¡adiós!, ¡hasta luego!, *Am* ¡bye!, *Am* ¡chau!

bye-bye, by-by ['baɪ'baɪ] *exclam Fam* ¡adiós!, ¡hasta luego!, *Am* ¡bye!, *Am* ¡chau!

byelaw, bylaw ['baɪlɔː] *n* byelaws *(of company, association)* estatutos *mpl*

bygone ['baɪgɒn] **1** *n* **let bygones be bygones** lo pasado, pasado está, *Am* lo pasado, pisado
  2 *adj* pasado(a), pretérito(a); **in b. days** en otros tiempos

bylaw = **byelaw**

byline ['baɪlaɪn] *n Journ* pie *m* de autor

BYOB *(abbr* **bring your own bottle**) = en invitaciones a una fiesta o en restaurantes, siglas que invitan a llevar bebidas

bypass ['baɪpɑːs] **1** *n* (a) *(road)* (carretera *f* de) circunvalación *f* (b) *(heart operation)* by-pass *m*
  2 *vt (of road)* circunvalar; *Fig (difficulty)* evitar, esquivar

by-product ['baɪprɒdʌkt] *n (of industrial process)* subproducto *m*; *Fig* consecuencia *f*

bystander ['baɪstændə(r)] *n* espectador(ora) *m,f*, transeúnte *mf*

byte [baɪt] *n Comptr* byte *m*

byway ['baɪweɪ] *n* carretera *f* secundaria

byword ['baɪwɜːd] *n* **to be a b. for…** ser sinónimo de…

Byzantine [bɪ'zæntaɪn] *n & adj Hist also Fig* bizantino(a) *m,f*

C

C, c [si:] *n* (**a**) *(letter)* C, c *f* (**b**) *Mus* do *m* (**c**) *Sch (grade)* aprobado *m*; **to get a C** *(in exam, essay)* sacar un aprobado

C (**a**) *(abbr* **celsius** *or* **centigrade**) C, centígrado (**b**) *(abbr* **century**) s., siglo; **C.16** s. XVI

c, ca *(abbr* **circa**) hacia

cab [kæb] *n* (**a**) *(taxi)* taxi *m*; **c. driver** taxista *mf*; **c. line** parada *f* de taxis (**b**) *(of truck)* cabina *f*

cabaret ['kæbəreɪ] *n* cabaret *m*; **c. artist** *(female)* cabaretera *f*; *(male or female)* artista *mf* de variedades

cabbage ['kæbɪdʒ] *n* col *f*, repollo *m*; **red c.** lombarda *f*; **c. white** *(butterfly)* mariposa *f* de la col

cabbie, cabby ['kæbɪ] *n Fam* taxista *mf*, *RP* tachero(a) *mf*

cabin ['kæbɪn] *n (hut)* cabaña *f*; *(of ship)* camarote *m*; *(of plane)* cabina *f*; **c. boy** *(on ship)* grumete *m*; **c. crew** *(on plane)* personal *m* de a bordo, auxiliares *mfpl* de vuelo

cabinet ['kæbɪnɪt] *n* (**a**) *(piece of furniture)* armario *m*; *(with glass front)* vitrina *f* (**b**) *Pol* Consejo *m* de Ministros; **c. meeting** (reunión *f* del) Consejo *m* de Ministros; **c. member** miembro *mf* del Gabinete

cabinetmaker ['kæbɪnɪtmeɪkə(r)] *n* ebanista *mf*

cable ['keɪbəl] **1** *n (electrical)* cable *m*; *Tel* cable(grama) *m*; **c. car** teleférico *m*, funicular *m*; *Comptr* **c. modem** módem *m* cable; **c. television** televisión *f* por cable

2 *vt (message)* cablegrafiar

cabling ['keɪbəlɪŋ] *n* cables *mpl*

caboodle [kə'bu:dəl] *n Fam* **the whole (kit and) c.** todo, *Esp* toda la pesca

caboose [kə'bu:s] *n* furgón *m* de equipajes

cacao [kə'kɑːəʊ] *n (plant)* cacao *m*

cache [kæʃ] *n* (**a**) *(of drugs, arms)* alijo *m* (**b**) *Comptr* (memoria *f*) caché *f*

cackle ['kækəl] **1** *n* (**a**) *(of hen)* cacareo *m*, cloqueo *m* (**b**) *Fam (talking)* parloteo *m*; *(laughter)* carcajeo *m*; **cut the c.!** ¡corta el rollo!

2 *vi* (**a**) *(hen)* cacarear, cloquear (**b**) *Fam (laugh)* carcajearse

cacophonous [kə'kɒfənəs] *adj* cacofónico(a)

cactus ['kæktəs] *(pl* **cacti** ['kæktaɪ]) *n* cactus *m inv*

CAD [si:eɪ'di:] *n Comptr (abbr* **computer-aided** *or -* **assisted design**) CAD *m*, diseño *m* asistido por *Esp* ordenador *or Am* computadora

cadaver [kə'dævə(r)] *n* cadáver *m*

cadaverous [kə'dævərəs] *adj* cadavérico(a)

CAD/CAM ['kæd'kæm] *n Comptr (abbr* **computer-aided design/computer-assisted manufacture**) CAD/CAM *m*

caddy[1] ['kædɪ] *n (in golf)* caddie *mf*, ayudante *mf*

caddy[2] ['kædɪ] *n (tea) c.* caja *f* para el té

cadence ['keɪdəns] *n* cadencia *f*

cadet [kə'det] *n Mil* cadete *m*; **c. corps** = organismo que, en algunas escuelas, enseña disciplina militar

cadge [kædʒ] *vt Fam* gorrear, *Esp, Méx* gorronear, *RP* garronear (**from** *or* **off** a); **can I c. a lift from you?** ¿me puedes llevar *or CAm, Méx, Perú* dar aventón?

cadmium ['kædmɪəm] *n Chem* cadmio *m*

caecum = cecum

Caesar ['si:zə(r)] *pr n* César; **C. salad** ensalada *f* César, = ensalada de lechuga, huevo pasado por agua, ajo, queso y picatostes

caesarean = cesarian

café, cafe ['kæfeɪ] *n* café *m*, cafetería *f*

cafeteria [kæfɪ'tɪərɪə] *n* cafetería *f*, cantina *f*

caffeine ['kæfi:n] *n* cafeína *f*

caffeine-free ['kæfi:n'fri:] *adj* sin cafeína

cage [keɪdʒ] **1** *n (for bird or animal, of lift)* jaula *f*
2 *vt* enjaular; **to feel caged in** sentirse enjaulado(a)

cagey ['keɪdʒɪ] *adj* **to be c. (about sth)** *(cautious)* ir *or Esp* andar con tiento (con algo); *(evasive)* salirse por la tangente (en cuanto a algo)

cahoots [kə'hu:ts] *npl Fam* **to be in c. (with sb)** estar conchabado(a) (con alguien), *RP* estar metido(a) (con alguien)

CAI [si:eɪ'aɪ] *n Comptr (abbr* **computer-aided** *or* **-assisted instruction**) enseñanza *f* asistida por *Esp* ordenador *or Am* computadora

cairn ['keən] *n* hito *m* de piedras

Cairo ['kaɪrəʊ] *n* El Cairo

cajole [kə'dʒəʊl] *vt* engatusar; **to c. sb into doing sth** engatusar a alguien para que haga algo

cake [keɪk] **1** *n* (**a**) *(food)* pastel *m*, tarta *f*; *(small)* pastel *m*; **a birthday c.** una tarta de cumpleaños; **a wedding c.** un pastel de boda; **c. shop** pastelería *f* (**b**) *(of soap)* pastilla *f* (**c**) *(idioms)* **it's a piece of c.** está tirado, es facilísimo; *Fam* **that really takes the c.!** ¡esto es el colmo!; *Prov* **you can't have your c. and eat it** no se puede estar en misa y repicando

2 **her shoes were caked with mud** tenía los zapatos llenos de barro seco

CAL [kæl] *n Comptr (abbr* **computer-aided** *or* **-assisted learning**) enseñanza *f* asistida por *Esp* ordenador *or Am* computadora

calamity [kə'læmɪtɪ] *n* calamidad *f*

calcium ['kælsɪəm] *n Chem* calcio *m*

calculate ['kælkjʊleɪt] **1** *vt* calcular; **his remark was calculated to shock** pretendió impresionar con el comentario

2 *vi* **to c. on (doing) sth** contar con (hacer) algo

calculated ['kælkjʊleɪtɪd] *adj (intentional)* deliberado(a); **a c. risk** un riesgo calculado

calculating ['kælkjʊleɪtɪŋ] *adj (scheming)* calculador(ora)

calculation [kælkjʊ'leɪʃən] *n* cálculo *m*; **to upset sb's calculations** desbaratar los cálculos de alguien

calculator ['kælkjʊleɪtə(r)] *n (electronic)* calculadora *f*

calculus ['kælkjʊləs] *(pl* **calculuses** *or* **calculi** ['kælkjʊlaɪ, 'kælkjʊli:]) *n Math* cálculo *m* (infinitesimal)

calendar ['kælɪndə(r)] *n* calendario *m*; **c. month/year** mes *m*/año *m* natural, *Am* mes *m*/año *m* calendario

calf[1] [kɑːf] *(pl* **calves** [kɑːvz]) *n (animal)* becerro(a) *m,f*, ternero(a) *m,f*; **the cow is with c.** la vaca está preñada; *Fig* **to kill the fatted c.** tirar la casa por la ventana

calf² (*pl* **calves** [kɑːvz]) *n* (*of leg*) pantorrilla *f*

calfskin ['kɑːfskɪn] *n* piel *f* de becerro

caliber ['kælɪbə(r)] *n* (*of firearm*) calibre *m*; (*of person*) calibre *m*, categoría *f*

calibrate ['kælɪbreɪt] *vt* (*instrument*) calibrar

calibration [kælɪ'breɪʃən] *n* (*of instrument*) calibrado *m*, calibración *f*

calico ['kælɪkəʊ] (*pl* **calicoes**) *n* percal *m*, calicó *m*

California [kælɪ'fɔːnɪə] *n* California

Californian [kælɪ'fɔːnɪən] *n & adj* californiano(a) *m,f*

calipers ['kælɪpəz] *npl* (**a**) (*for legs*) aparato *m* ortopédico (**b**) (*measuring device*) calibrador *m*, calibre *m*

calisthenics [kælɪs'θenɪks] *n* gimnasia *f* sueca, calistenia *f*

call [kɔːl] **1** *n* (**a**) (*shout*) (*of person*) llamada *f*, grito *m*, *Am* llamado *m*; (*of bird*) reclamo *m*

(**b**) (*appeal*) llamamiento *m*, llamada *f*, *Am* llamado *m*; **a c. for unity/compassion** un llamamiento a la unidad/la compasión; **a c. to arms** una llamada *or Am* un llamado a (tomar) las armas

(**c**) (*on phone*) llamada *f*, *Am* llamado *m*; **to give sb a c.** llamar a alguien; **to make a c.** hacer una llamada *or Am* un llamado; **to return sb's c.** devolverle la llamada *or Am* el llamado a alguien; **c. box** teléfono *m* de emergencia; **c. center** centro *m* de atención telefónica; **c. girl** prostituta *f* (*que concierta sus citas por teléfono*); **c. waiting** llamada *f or Am* llamado *m* en espera

(**d**) (*visit*) visita *f*; **to pay a c. on sb** hacer una visita a alguien

(**e**) (*demand*) demanda *f*; **there are a lot of calls on my time** estoy muy solicitado; **there's not much c. for it** no tiene mucha demanda, no hay mucha demanda de ello; **there's no c. for rudeness!** ¡no hace falta ser grosero!; **to be on c.** (*doctor*) estar de guardia

(**f**) (*at airport*) aviso *m*, llamada *f*, *Am* llamado *m*

2 *vt* (**a**) (*summon*) (*person*) llamar; (*meeting, strike*) convocar; **he called me over to show me something** me llamó para enseñarme una cosa; **to c. sb's attention to sth** llamar la atención de alguien sobre algo

(**b**) (*on phone*) llamar, telefonear, *Am* hablar

(**c**) (*name*) llamar; **she is called Teresa** se llama Teresa; **to c. sb names** insultar a alguien; **to c. sb a liar/a thief** llamar a alguien mentiroso(a)/ladrón; **we'll c. it $10** dejémoslo en *or* digamos 10 dólares; **do you c. that clean?** ¿llamas limpio a esto?; *Ironic* **c. yourself a computer expert!** ¡vaya un experto en informática (estás hecho)!; **let's c. it a day** ya está bien por hoy

(**d**) **to c. sb's name** llamar a alguien por su nombre

3 *vi* (**a**) (*to attract sb's attention*) llamar; **to c. for help** pedir ayuda; **he called to his companions** llamó a sus compañeros

(**b**) (*on phone*) llamar, *Am* hablar; **did anyone c. while I was out?** ¿me llamó alguien mientras no estaba?; **(may I ask) who's calling?** ¿de parte de quién?

(**c**) (*demand*) **to c. for sth** exigir algo

(**d**) (*visit*) **to c. at** pasarse por, hacer una visita a; **this train will c. at Memphis and New Orleans** este tren efectúa parada en Memphis y New Orleans

▸**call back 1** *vt sep* (**a**) (*summon again*) hacer volver; **as I was leaving he called me back** me llamó cuando ya me iba (**b**) (*on phone*) volver a llamar; **could you c. me back later?** ¿podría llamarme *or Am* hablarme más tarde?

2 *vi* (*on phone*) volver a llamar *or Am* hablar

▸**call for** *vt insep* (*require*) requerir, necesitar; **this calls for a celebration!** ¡esto hay que celebrarlo!; **that wasn't called for!** ¡eso no era necesario!, ¡no había necesidad de eso!

▸**call in 1** *vt sep* (*doctor, police*) llamar

2 *vi* (*visit*) **to c. in on sb** ir a *or* pasarse por casa de alguien; **he**

called in sick llamó diciendo que estaba enfermo

▸**call off** *vt sep* (**a**) (*cancel*) suspender (**b**) (*dogs*) hacer retroceder

▸**call on** *vt insep* (**a**) (*request*) **to c. on sb to do sth** instar a alguien a que haga algo (**b**) (*visit*) visitar

▸**call out 1** *vt sep* (**a**) (*troops*) convocar; (*doctor*) llamar; **the workers were called out on strike** se convocó a los trabajadores a la huelga (**b**) (*shout*) gritar

2 *vi* (*shout out*) gritar

▸**call up** *vt sep* (**a**) (*reinforcements*) pedir (**b**) (*on phone*) llamar, *Am* hablar (**c**) *Mil* (*draft*) llamar a filas, reclutar

caller [kɔːlə(r)] *n* (*visitor*) visita *f*; (*on phone*) persona *f* que llama; **c. ID** identificador *m* de llamada

calligraphy [kə'lɪgrəfɪ] *n* caligrafía *f*

calling ['kɔːlɪŋ] *n* (*vocation*) vocación *f*; **c. card** tarjeta *f* de visita

callous ['kæləs] *adj* cruel, desalmado(a)

call-up ['kɔːlʌp] *n Mil* llamada *f or Am* llamado *m* a filas, reclutamiento *m*; **to get one's c. papers** recibir la orden de reclutamiento, ser llamado(a) a filas

callus ['kæləs] *n* callo *m*, callosidad *f*

calm [kɑːm] **1** *n* calma *f*, tranquilidad *f*; *also Fig* **the c. before the storm** la calma que precede a la tormenta

2 *adj* (*person, sea, water*) tranquilo(a); (*weather*) apacible; **to stay c.** mantener la calma; **to become** *or* **grow calmer** calmarse

3 *vt* calmar, tranquilizar

▸**calm down 1** *vt sep* (*person*) calmar, tranquilizar

2 *vi* (*person*) calmarse, tranquilizarse; (*situation*) calmarse

calming ['kɑːmɪŋ] *adj* (*influence, effect*) tranquilizador(ora), tranquilizante; **her words had a c. effect on him** sus palabras consiguieron tranquilizarlo

calmly ['kɑːmlɪ] *adv* serenamente, tranquilamente

calorie ['kælərɪ] *n* caloría *f*

calorific [kælə'rɪfɪk] *adj* calorífico(a)

calumny ['kæləmnɪ] *n* calumnia *f*

calve [kɑːv] *vi* (*cow*) parir

calves *pl of* **calf**

calypso [kə'lɪpsəʊ] (*pl* **calypsos**) *n Mus* calipso *m*

CAM [siːeɪ'em] *n Comptr* (*abbr* **computer-aided** *or* **-assisted manufacturing**) CAM *f*, fabricación *f* asistida por *Esp* ordenador *or Am* computadora

Cambodia [kæm'bəʊdɪə] *n* Camboya

Cambodian [kæm'bəʊdɪən] *n & adj* camboyano(a) *m,f*

camcorder ['kæmkɔːdə(r)] *n* videocámara *f* (*portátil*)

came [keɪm] *pt of* **come**

camel ['kæməl] *n* camello *m*; **c. driver** camellero(a) *m,f*

camel hair ['kæməlheə(r)], **camel's hair** ['kæməlzheə(r)] *n* pelo *m* de camello; **c. coat** abrigo *m* de pelo de camello

camellia [kə'miːlɪə] *n* camelia *f*

cameo ['kæmɪəʊ] (*pl* **cameos**) *n* (**a**) **c. (brooch)** camafeo *m* (**b**) *Cin* aparición *f* breve (*de un actor famoso*)

camera ['kæmərə] *n* (**a**) (*photographic*) cámara *f* (fotográfica); *TV & Cin* cámara *f*; *TV* **off c.** fuera de imagen; *TV* **on c.** delante de la cámara; *TV* **c. crew** equipo *m* de filmación (**b**) *Law* **in c.** a puerta cerrada

cameraman ['kæmərəmən] *n* cámara *m*, operador *m*

camera-shy ['kæmrəʃaɪ] *adj* **she's extremely c.** le da muchísima vergüenza *or Am* pena que le hagan fotos/que le filmen

camerawoman ['kæmərəwʊmən] *n* cámara *f*, operadora *f*

camerawork ['kæmərəwɜːk] *n* fotografía *f*

Cameroon [kæmə'ruːn] *n* Camerún

camisole ['kæmɪsəʊl] *n* combinación *f*

camomile = **chamomile**

camouflage ['kæməflɑːʒ] **1** *n also Fig* camuflaje *m*

2 *vt also Fig* camuflar

camp¹ [kæmp] **1** *n (place)* campamento *m*; **(summer) c.** colonia *f*, campamento *m* de verano; **c. bed** cama *f* plegable, catre *m*; **c. site** lugar *m* de acampada; *(commercial)* camping *m*
2 *vi* **to c. (out)** acampar

camp² *adj Fam* (**a**) *(behavior, manner)* amariposado(a), amanerado(a) (**b**) *(style, taste)* hortera

campaign [kæm'peɪn] **1** *n* campaña *f*
2 *vi* **to c. for/against** hacer campaña a favor de/en contra de

campaigner [kæm'peɪnə(r)] *n* defensor(ora) *m,f*; **to be a c. for/against sth** hacer campaña a favor de/en contra de algo

camper ['kæmpə(r)] *n* (**a**) *(person)* campista *mf* (**b**) *(vehicle)* **c. (van)** autocaravana *f*

campfire ['kæmpfaɪə(r)] *n* fuego *m or* hoguera *f* (de campamento)

campground ['kæmpgraʊnd] *n* camping *m*

camphor ['kæmfə(r)] *n* alcanfor *m*

camping ['kæmpɪŋ] *n* acampada *f*; *(on commercial camp site)* camping *m*; **to go c.** ir de acampada; *(on commercial camp site)* ir de camping; **c. site** lugar *m* de acampada; *(commercial)* camping *m*

campus ['kæmpəs] *n* campus *m inv*

camshaft ['kæmʃɑːft] *n Tech* árbol *m* de levas

can¹ [kæn] **1** *n* (**a**) *(container)* lata *f*, *Am* tarro *m*; *Fig* **to open a c. of worms** sacar a la luz un asunto espinoso; **c. opener** abrelatas *m inv* (**b**) *Fam (toilet)* baño *m*, *Esp* tigre *m* (**c**) *Fam (prison)* cárcel *f*, *Esp* chirona *f*, *Andes, RP* cana *f*, *Méx* bote *m*
2 *vt (pt & pp canned)* (**a**) *(fruit, meat)* enlatar; *Fig* **canned laughter** *(on radio, TV)* risas *fpl* grabadas (**b**) *Fam* **c. it!** *(keep quiet)* ¡cállate la boca!

can² [*stressed* kæn, *unstressed* kən] *modal aux v*

El verbo **can** carece de infinitivo, de gerundio y de participio. En infinitivo o en participio, se empleará la forma correspondiente de **be able to**, por ejemplo **he wanted to be able to speak English**; **she has always been able to swim**. En el inglés hablado, y en el escrito en estilo coloquial, la forma negativa **cannot** se transforma en **can't**.

(**a**) *(be able to)* poder; **I c. go** puedo ir; **c. you help me?** ¿puedes ayudarme?; **we cannot possibly do it** no podemos hacerlo de ninguna manera; **I will come as soon as I c.** iré lo antes posible; **he will do what he c.** hará lo que pueda; **it can't be done** es imposible, no se puede hacer; **we c. but try** habrá que intentarlo

(**b**) *(know how to)* saber; **I c. swim** sé nadar; **she c. play the violin** sabe tocar el violín

(**c**) *(indicating possibility)* poder; **adult animals c. grow to 6 feet** los ejemplares adultos pueden alcanzar los 6 pies; **you can't be serious!** ¡no lo dirás en serio!; **what can he want now?** ¿pero qué es lo que quiere ahora?

(**d**) *(indicating permission)* poder; **c. I ask you something?** ¿te puedo hacer una pregunta?; **you can't smoke in here** aquí está prohibido fumar

(**e**) *(with see, hear etc: not translated)* **I c. see them** los veo; **I c. see you don't believe me** ya veo que no me crees; **how c. you tell?** ¿cómo lo sabes?

Canada ['kænədə] *n* (el) Canadá

Canadian [kə'neɪdɪən] *n & adj* canadiense *mf*

canal [kə'næl] *n* canal *m*

canapé ['kænəpeɪ] *n* canapé *m*

Canary [kə'neərɪ] *n* **the C. Islands, the Canaries** las (Islas) Canarias

canary [kə'neərɪ] *n* canario *m*; **c. yellow** amarillo *m* canario

cancel ['kænsəl] **1** *vt (game, trip)* suspender; *(flight, train)* suspender, cancelar; *(order, subscription)* anular
2 *vi* **they were supposed to be playing tonight, but they've canceled** iban a tocar hoy, pero lo han suspendido
▶**cancel out** *vt sep* **to c. each other out** neutralizarse, contrarrestarse

cancellation [kænsə'leɪʃən] *n (of game, trip, flight)* suspensión *f*; *(of order, subscription)* anulación *f*; **c. fee** tarifa *f* de cancelación de reserva

Cancer ['kænsə(r)] *n (sign of zodiac)* Cáncer *m*; **to be (a) C.** ser Cáncer; *Geog* **the Tropic of C.** el Trópico de Cáncer

cancer ['kænsə(r)] *n (disease)* cáncer *m*; **lung/skin c.** cáncer de pulmón/de piel; **c. research** investigación *f* del cáncer

cancerous ['kænsərəs] *adj Med* canceroso(a)

candelabra [kændɪ'lɑːbrə] *(pl* **candelabras** *or* **candelabra**) *n* candelabro *m*

candid ['kændɪd] *adj* sincero(a), franco(a)

candidacy ['kændɪdəsɪ], **candidature** ['kændɪdətʃə(r)] *n* candidatura *f*

candidate ['kændɪdeɪt] *n* (**a**) *(for job, in election)* candidato(a) *m,f*; **to run as a c.** presentarse como candidato (**b**) *(in exam)* examinando(a) *m,f*, candidato(a) *m,f*

candidature = **candidacy**

candidly ['kændɪdlɪ] *adv* sinceramente, francamente

candied ['kændɪd] *adj* escarchado(a), confitado(a), *Col, Méx* cristalizado(a), *RP* abrillantado(a); **c. peel** piel *f* de naranja/limón escarchada

candle ['kændəl] *n* (**a**) vela *f* (**b**) *(idioms)* **he can't hold a c. to you** no te llega ni a la suela del zapato; **it's not worth the c.** no vale *or Esp* merece la pena

candlelight ['kændəllaɪt] *n* luz *f* de las velas; **by c.** a la luz de las velas

candlelit [kændəllɪt] *adj (room)* iluminado(a) con velas; **a c. dinner** una cena a la luz de las velas

candlestick ['kændəlstɪk] *n* palmatoria *f*

candor ['kændə(r)] *n* sinceridad *f*, franqueza *f*

candy ['kændɪ] *n (sweet)* caramelo *m*; *(sweets)* dulces *mpl*, golosinas *fpl*; **c. bar** barra *f* de chocolate, chocolatina *f*; **c. store** confitería *f*

cane [keɪn] **1** *n (of sugar, bamboo)* caña *f*; *(walking stick)* bastón *m*; *(for punishment)* vara *f*, palmeta *f*; **to get the c.** ser castigado(a) con la vara; **c. furniture** muebles *mpl* de mimbre; **c. sugar** azúcar *m or f* de caña
2 *vt (beat)* pegar con la vara

canine ['keɪnaɪn] **1** *n (dog)* can *m*; *(tooth)* colmillo *m*, canino *m*
2 *adj* canino(a); **c. tooth** colmillo *m*, (diente *m*) canino *m*

canister ['kænɪstə(r)] *n (for tear gas, smoke)* bote *m*; *(for movie, oil)* lata *f*

canker ['kæŋkə(r)] *n Med* ulceración *f*; *Bot* cancro *m*; *Fig* cáncer *m*

cannabis ['kænəbɪs] *n* hachís *m*, cannabis *m*

cannery ['kænərɪ] *n* fábrica *f* de conservas

cannibal ['kænɪbəl] *n* caníbal *mf*

cannibalism ['kænɪbəlɪzəm] *n* canibalismo *m*

cannibalize ['kænɪbəlaɪz] *vt (machinery, car)* desguazar *(para aprovechar las piezas)*

cannon ['kænən] *n* cañón *m*; **c. fodder** carne *f* de cañón

cannonball ['kænənbɔːl] *n* bala *f* de cañón

cannot ['kænɒt] = **can not**

canny ['kænɪ] *adj* astuto(a)

canoe [kə'nuː] *n* canoa *f*; *Sport* piragua *f*

canoeing [kə'nuːɪŋ] *n* piragüismo *m*; **to go c.** ir a hacer piragüismo

canoeist [kə'nuːɪst] *n* piragüista *mf*

canon ['kænən] *n Rel* (**a**) *(religious decree)* canon *m*; *Fig* **canons of good taste** cánones del buen gusto; **c. law** derecho *m* canónico (**b**) *(priest)* canónigo *m*

canonize ['kænənaɪz] *vt Rel* canonizar

canoodle [kə'nuːdəl] *vi Hum* besuquearse, *Esp* darse el lote

canopy ['kænəpɪ] *n (above bed)* dosel *m*; *(outside shop)* toldo *m*; *(of tree)* copa *f*; **forest c.** fronda *f*, copas *fpl* de los árboles

cant [kænt] *n* hipocresías *fpl*, falsedades *fpl*

can't [kɑːnt] = **can not**

Cantabria [kænˈtæbriə] n Cantabria

Cantabrian [kænˈtæbriən] **1** n (person) cántabro(a) m,f
  2 adj cántabro(a); **the C. Mountains** la Cordillera Cantábrica; **the C. Sea** el (Mar) Cantábrico

cantaloup(e) [ˈkæntəluːp] n **c. (melon)** melón m francés

cantankerous [kænˈtæŋkərəs] adj cascarrabias inv, refunfuñón(ona)

canteen [kænˈtiːn] n **(a)** (restaurant) cantina f, cafetería f **(b)** (water bottle) cantimplora f

canter [ˈkæntə(r)] **1** n (on horse) medio galope m
  2 vi (horse) ir a medio galope; Fig **to c. through an exam** pasar un examen con facilidad

cantilever bridge [ˈkæntɪliːvəbrɪdʒ] n puente m voladizo

Cantonese [kæntəˈniːz] **1** n **(a)** (person) cantonés(esa) m,f **(b)** (language) cantonés m
  2 adj cantonés(esa)

canvas [ˈkænvəs] n **(a)** (cloth) lona f; **under c.** (in tent) en una tienda de campaña or Am carpa; Naut a vela; **c. shoes** zapatillas fpl de lona **(b)** Art lienzo m

canvass [ˈkænvəs] **1** vt **(a)** Pol **to c. a street/an area** visitar las casas de una calle/zona haciendo campaña electoral **(b)** Com (consumers, customers) encuestar; Fig **to c. opinion** hacer un sondeo de opinión informal
  2 vi **(a)** Pol = hacer campaña electoral hablando directamente con los electores por las casas o en la calle **(b)** Com **to c. for customers** tratar de captar clientes

canvasser [ˈkænvəsə(r)] n Pol = persona que va de casa en casa tratando de captar votos para un partido

canyon [ˈkænjən] n cañón m

cap [kæp] **1** n **(a)** (headgear) (without peak) gorro m; (with peak) gorra f; Fig **to go c. in hand to sb** acudir a alguien con actitud humilde **(b)** (cover) (of bottle) tapón m; (for tooth) funda f **(c)** (for toy gun) fulminante m
  2 vt (pt & pp capped) **(a)** (cover) **to be capped with** estar cubierto(a) de or por **(b)** (surpass, do better than) superar; **that caps the lot!** ¡es el colmo!; **to c. it all, . . .** para colmo, . . .

capability [keɪpəˈbɪlɪti] n capacidad f (**to do sth** para hacer algo); **it is beyond our capabilities** no entra dentro de nuestras posibilidades

capable [ˈkeɪpəbəl] adj (competent) capaz, competente; **to be c. of doing sth** (be able to do) ser capaz de hacer algo

capacious [kəˈpeɪʃəs] adj espacioso(a)

capacitor [kəˈpæsɪtə(r)] n Elec condensador m

capacity [kəˈpæsɪti] n **(a)** (of container, bus, theater) capacidad f; **a c. crowd** (in hall, stadium) un lleno (absoluto) **(b)** (aptitude) **to have a c. for sth** tener capacidad para algo; **beyond/within my c.** fuera de/dentro de mis posibilidades **(c)** (role) **in my c. as. . .** en mi calidad de. . .

cape[1] [keɪp] n (cloak) capa f

cape[2] n Geog cabo m; **the C. of Good Hope** el Cabo de Buena Esperanza; **C. Town** Ciudad del Cabo, El Cabo

caper[1] [ˈkeɪpə(r)] n Culin alcaparra f

caper[2] **1** n **capers** correrías fpl, peripecias fpl; **what a c.!** (fuss) ¡qué lío or Esp follón!
  2 vi **to c. (about)** retozar

Cape Verde [keɪpˈvɜːd] n Cabo Verde

capful [ˈkæpfʊl] n (of liquid) tapón m (lleno)

capillary [kəˈpɪləri] n & adj capilar m

capital [ˈkæpɪtəl] **1** n **(a)** (letter) mayúscula f **(b)** (city) capital f **(c)** Fin capital m; Fig **to make c. out of sth** sacar partido de algo; **c. assets** activo m fijo, bienes mpl de capital; **c. expenditure** inversión f en activo fijo; **c. gains tax** impuesto m sobre las plusvalías; **c. goods** bienes mpl de equipo or de producción; **c. investment** inversión f (de capital); **c. stock** capital m escriturado
  2 adj **(a)** (letter) mayúscula; **c. T** T mayúscula; Fam **he's**

arrogant with a c. A es terriblemente arrogante, Esp es un arrogante de tomo y lomo, RP es rearrogante **(b)** **c. city** capital f **(c)** Law **c. crime** or **offense** delito m capital; **c. punishment** pena f capital or de muerte **(d)** (important) capital; **of c. importance** de capital importancia

capitalism [ˈkæpɪtəlɪzəm] n capitalismo m

capitalist [ˈkæpɪtəlɪst] n & adj capitalista mf

capitalization [kæpɪtəlaɪˈzeɪʃən] n Fin capitalización f

capitalize [ˈkæpɪtəlaɪz] vt **(a)** Fin capitalizar **(b)** (word, letter) escribir con mayúscula

▸**capitalize on** vt insep aprovechar, aprovecharse de

Capitol [ˈkæpɪtəl] n Pol **the C.** el Capitolio; **C. Hill** el Capitolio

capitulate [kəˈpɪtjʊleɪt] vi capitular

capon [ˈkeɪpən] n Culin capón m

capper [ˈkæpə(r)] n Fam **that was the c.** aquello fue el colmo

caprice [kəˈpriːs] n capricho m

capricious [kəˈprɪʃəs] adj caprichoso(a)

Capricorn [ˈkæprɪkɔːn] n (sign of zodiac) Capricornio m; **to be (a) C.** ser Capricornio; Geog **the Tropic of C.** el Trópico de Capricornio

capsicum [ˈkæpsɪkəm] n pimiento m

capsize [kæpˈsaɪz] vt & vi volcar

capstan [ˈkæpstən] n Naut cabrestante m

capsule [ˈkæpsjuːl] n cápsula f; **(space) c.** cápsula espacial

Capt Mil (abbr **Captain**) Capitán m

captain [ˈkæptɪn] **1** n (in army, air force, of team) capitán(ana) m,f; (in police) comisario(a) m,f
  2 vt Sport capitanear

captaincy [ˈkæptɪnsɪ] n capitanía f

caption [ˈkæpʃən] n (under picture) pie m de foto; (under cartoon) texto m

captivate [ˈkæptɪveɪt] vt cautivar, embelesar

captivating [ˈkæptɪveɪtɪŋ] adj (smile, manner) cautivador(ora)

captive [ˈkæptɪv] **1** n cautivo(a) m,f, prisionero(a) m,f
  2 adj cautivo(a); **he was taken c.** fue hecho prisionero; **he knew he had a c. audience** sabía que su público no tenía elección; **c. market** mercado m cautivo

captivity [kæpˈtɪvɪti] n cautividad f; **in c.** en cautividad

captor [ˈkæptə(r)] n captor(ora) m,f

capture [ˈkæptʃə(r)] **1** vt (person) capturar; (town) tomar; (in chess, checkers) comer; Fig (mood) reflejar
  2 n (of person) captura f; (of town) toma f

CAR [siːeɪˈɑː(r)] n (abbr **Central African Republic**) República f Centroafricana

car [kɑː(r)] n **(a)** (automobile) coche m, Am carro m, CSur auto m; **by c.** en coche or Am carro or CSur auto; **c. bomb** coche m bomba; **c. crash** accidente m de coche; **c. door** puerta f (del coche); **c. industry** industria f automovilística; **c. phone** teléfono m de coche; **c. pool** parque m móvil; **c. radio** radio f (del coche); **c. rental** alquiler m de coches, Méx renta f de carros; **c. sickness** mareo m (en el coche); **he suffers from c. sickness** se marea en el coche or Am carro or CSur auto **(b)** (train carriage) vagón m, coche m

Caracas [kəˈrækəs] n Caracas

carafe [kəˈræf] n jarra f

caramel [ˈkærəməl] n caramelo m

carat [ˈkærət] n (of gold) quilate m; **18-c. gold** oro m de 18 quilates

caravan [ˈkærəvæn] n (in desert) caravana f

caraway [ˈkærəweɪ] n (plant) alcaravea f; **c. seeds** carvis mpl

carbohydrate [kɑːbəʊˈhaɪdreɪt] n hidrato m de carbono, carbohidrato m

carbolic [kɑːˈbɒlɪk] adj Chem **c. acid** fenol m, ácido m fénico or carbólico; **c. soap** jabón m (desinfectante) de brea

carbon [ˈkɑːbən] n Chem carbono m; **c. copy** copia f en papel carbón; *Fig* calco *m*, copia *f* exacta; **c. dioxide** dióxido *m* de carbono; **c. monoxide** monóxido *m* de carbono; **c. paper** papel *m* carbón *or* de calco

carbonated [ˈkɑːbəneɪtɪd] *adj* carbónico(a), con gas; **c. water** agua *f* con gas

carbonize [ˈkɑːbənaɪz] *vt* convertir en carbono

carbuncle [ˈkɑːbʌŋkəl] *n Med* forúnculo *m*

carburetor [ˈkɑːbjʊretə(r)] *n* carburador *m*

carcass [ˈkɑːkəs] *n (of animal)* restos *mpl*, cadáver *m*; *(at butcher's)* canal *m*

carcinogen [kɑːˈsɪnədʒen] *n Med* agente *m* cancerígeno

carcinogenic [kɑːsɪnəʊˈdʒenɪk] *adj Med* cancerígeno(a), carcinógeno(a)

carcinoma [kɑːsɪˈnəʊmə] *n Med* carcinoma *m*

card [kɑːd] *n* **(a)** *(for game)* carta *f*, naipe *m*; **to play cards** jugar a las cartas; **c. game** juego *m* de cartas *or* naipes; **c. table** mesa *f* de juego (para las cartas); **c. trick** truco *m or* juego *m* de cartas

  (b) *(with printed information)* tarjeta *f*; *(for identification)* carné *m*, carnet *m*, *CSur, Méx* credencial *m*; *(postcard)* (tarjeta) postal *f*; **birthday c.** tarjeta de felicitación de cumpleaños; **Christmas c.** crismas *m inv*; **c. index** *or* **file** fichero *m* de tarjetas

  (c) *(thin cardboard)* cartulina *f*

  (d) *(idioms)* **play your cards right and you could get promoted** si juegas bien tus cartas, puedes conseguir un ascenso; **to put one's cards on the table** poner las cartas sobre la mesa; **to have a c. up one's sleeve** tener un as en la manga; **it is in the cards that...** es más que probable que...

cardamom [ˈkɑːdəməm] *n* cardamomo *m*

cardboard [ˈkɑːdbɔːd] *n* cartón *m*; **c. box** caja *f* de cartón; **c. city** = lugar donde duermen los vagabundos

card-carrying [ˈkɑːdkærɪŋ] *adj* **c. member** miembro *m or* socio(a) *m,f* (de pleno derecho)

cardiac [ˈkɑːdɪæk] *adj* cardíaco(a); **c. arrest** paro *m* cardíaco

cardigan [ˈkɑːdɪgən] *n* rebeca *f*, cárdigan *m*

cardinal [ˈkɑːdɪnəl] **1** *n* **(a)** *Rel* cardenal *m* **(b)** *(bird)* cardenal *m*
  2 *adj (importance, significance)* capital, cardinal; **c. number** número *m* cardinal; **c. sins** pecados *mpl* capitales; **c. virtues** virtudes *fpl* cardinales

cardiogram [ˈkɑːdɪəgræm] *n* cardiograma *m*

cardiograph [ˈkɑːdɪəʊgræf] *n* cardiógrafo *m*

cardiologist [kɑːdɪˈɒlədʒɪst] *n* cardiólogo(a) *m,f*

cardiology [kɑːdɪˈɒlədʒɪ] *n* cardiología *f*

cardiovascular [kɑːdɪəʊˈvæskjʊlə(r)] *adj* cardiovascular

cardsharp(er) [ˈkɑːdʃɑːp(ər)] *n* tahúr *m*, fullero(a) *m,f*

care [keə(r)] **1** *n* **(a)** *(worry)* preocupación *f*, inquietud *f*; **she doesn't have a c. in the world** no tiene ni una sola preocupación
  (b) *(attention)* cuidado *m*, atención *f*; **medical c.** asistencia *f* médica; **to do sth with great c.** hacer algo con mucho cuidado; **to take c. to do sth** procurar hacer algo; **to take c. of** *(look after)* cuidar de; *(deal with)* ocuparse de; **to take c. of oneself** cuidarse; **it will take c. of itself** se resolverá por sí solo
  (c) *(looking after, maintenance)* cuidado *m*; **to be in** *or* **under sb's c.** estar al cuidado de alguien; **write to me c. of Mrs. Wallace** escríbeme a la dirección de la Sra Wallace
  2 *vt* **(a)** *(mind)* **I don't c. what he says** no me importa lo que diga; **I don't c. whether he likes it or not** me da lo mismo que le guste o no **(b)** *(like)* **would you c. to come with me?** ¿te gustaría venir conmigo?
  3 *vi (be concerned)* preocuparse (**about** por); **no-one seems to c.** no parece importarle a nadie, nadie parece preocuparse; **that's all he cares about** eso es lo único que le preocupa; **who cares?** ¿qué más da?; **I could be dead for all they c.**

por ellos, como si me muero, *Am* por ellos, podría morirme; **I don't c.!** ¡me da igual!, ¡no me importa!

▶**care for** *vt insep* **(a)** *(look after)* cuidar; **well cared for** bien cuidado(a) **(b)** *(like)* **I don't c. for this music** no me gusta esta música; **would you c. for some tea?** ¿quiere un té?, ¿le *Esp* apetece *or Carib, Col, Méx* provoca *or Méx* antoja un té?

career [kəˈrɪə(r)] **1** *n (working life, profession)* carrera *f*; **c. diplomat** diplomático(a) *m,f* de carrera; **it was a good c. move** fue bueno para mi/tu/*etc.* carrera; **c. officer** asesor(ora) *m,f* de orientación profesional; **a job with c. prospects** un trabajo con buenas perspectivas profesionales; **c. service** servicio *m* de orientación profesional
  2 *vi* **to c. (along)** ir a toda velocidad

careerist [kəˈrɪərɪst] *n Pej* arribista *mf*

carefree [ˈkeəfriː] *adj* despreocupado(a)

careful [ˈkeəfʊl] *adj* **(a)** *(taking care)* cuidadoso(a); *(prudent)* cauto(a), precavido(a); **(be) c.!** ¡(ten) cuidado!; **to be c. to do sth** tener cuidado de *or* procurar hacer algo; **she was c. not to mention this** tuvo cuidado de *or* procuró no mencionar esto; **be c. not to drop it** procura que no se te caiga; **be c. what you say** cuidado con lo que dices; **you can't be too c. these days** en estos tiempos que corren toda precaución es poca **(b)** *(thorough) (work, inspection)* cuidadoso(a); **after c. consideration** tras mucho reflexionar

carefully [ˈkeəfʊlɪ] *adv (taking care, thoroughly)* cuidadosamente; *(to think, choose)* con cuidado; *(to drive)* con precaución; **to listen c.** escuchar atentamente

caregiver [ˈkeəgɪvə(r)] *n* **he's his grandmother's c.** se encarga de cuidar de su abuela

careless [ˈkeəlɪs] *adj (negligent)* descuidado(a); **he's c. about his appearance** descuida mucho su aspecto; **a c. mistake** un descuido; **a c. remark** una observación inoportuna

carelessly [ˈkeəlɪslɪ] *adv (negligently)* descuidadamente

carelessness [ˈkeəlɪsnɪs] *n* descuido *m*, negligencia *f*

caress [kəˈres] **1** *n* caricia *f*
  2 *vt* acariciar

caret [ˈkærət] *n Typ & Comptr* signo *m* de intercalación

careworn [ˈkeəwɔːn] *adj* agobiado(a); **to be c.** estar agobiado(a)

cargo [ˈkɑːgəʊ] *n (pl* **cargos***)* cargamento *m*; **c. boat** *or* **ship** barco *m* de carga, carguero *m*; **c. plane** avión *m* de carga

Caribbean [kərˈɪbɪən] **1** *n* **the C.** *(region, sea)* el Caribe
  2 *adj* **the C. islands** las Antillas; **the C. Sea** el (mar) Caribe

caribou [ˈkærɪbuː] *n* caribú *m*

caricature [ˈkærɪkətjə(r)] **1** *n* caricatura *f*
  2 *vt (distort)* caricaturizar

caricaturist [kærɪkəˈtjuːrɪst] *n* caricaturista *mf*

caries [ˈkeəriːz] *n Med* caries *f inv*

caring [ˈkeərɪŋ] *adj (society)* solícito(a), afectuoso(a)

carjack [ˈkɑːdʒæk] *vt Fam* **they were carjacked** se los llevaron secuestrados en el coche *or Am* carro *or CSur* auto

carjacking [ˈkɑːdʒækɪŋ] *n Fam* secuestro *m* de un coche *or Am* carro *or CSur* auto

carload [ˈkɑːləʊd] *n* **(a)** *(in car)* **we got them home in three carloads** los llevamos a casa en tres viajes **(b)** *(by rail)* vagón *m* (lleno)

carnage [ˈkɑːnɪdʒ] *n* matanza *f*

carnal [ˈkɑːnəl] *adj* carnal

carnation [kɑːˈneɪʃən] *n* clavel *m*

carnival [ˈkɑːnɪvəl] *n (funfair)* feria *f*; *(traditional festival)* carnaval *m*

carnivore [ˈkɑːnɪvɔː(r)] *n* carnívoro *m*

carnivorous [kɑːˈnɪvərəs] *adj* carnívoro(a)

carob [ˈkærəb] *n (substance)* extracto *m* de algarroba *(sucedáneo de chocolate)*

carol [ˈkærəl] *n* **(Christmas) c.** villancico *m*

carouse [kəˈraʊz] *vi* estar de parranda

carousel [kærə'sel] n (**a**) (at fair) tiovivo m (**b**) (at airport) cinta f transportadora de equipajes (**c**) (for slides) carro m

carp[1] [kɑːp] (pl **carp**) n (fish) carpa f

carp[2] vi quejarse (sin motivo) (**at** de)

Carpathians [kɑː'peɪθɪənz] npl **the C.** los Cárpatos

carpenter ['kɑːpɪntə(r)] n carpintero(a) m,f

carpentry ['kɑːpɪntrɪ] n carpintería f

carpet ['kɑːpɪt] **1** n (**a**) (rug) alfombra f; (wall-to-wall) Esp moqueta f, Am alfombra f; Fig **a c. of flowers** una alfombra de flores; **c. slippers** zapatillas fpl de (andar por) casa; **c. sweeper** cepillo m mecánico (para alfombras) (**b**) (idiom) **c. bombing** bombardeo m de saturación
2 vt (floor) Esp enmoquetar, Am alfombrar

carport ['kɑːpɔːt] n Aut plaza f de estacionamiento or Esp aparcamiento techado (al lado de una casa)

carriage ['kærɪdʒ] n (**a**) (vehicle) carruaje m, coche m (**b**) (of typewriter) carro m (**c**) Com (transport) transporte m, porte m (**d**) (bearing) (of person) porte m

carrier ['kærɪə(r)] n (**a**) (of disease, infection) portador(ora) m,f (**b**) Com (company) transportista m; (airline) línea f aérea (**c**) (container) (on bicycle) portaequipaje m, transportín m

carrion ['kærɪən] n carroña f

carrot ['kærət] n zanahoria f; Fig **to hold out a c.** mostrar un señuelo; **to use the c. and stick approach** prometer premios si se trabaja bien y amenazar con castigos si no

carry ['kærɪ] **1** vt (**a**) (transport, convey) llevar, CAm andar; (goods, passengers) transportar; (have on one's person) (gun, money) llevar (encima), Méx cargar; **to c. sth away** or **off** llevarse algo; **to be carrying a child** (be pregnant) estar embarazada; **to c. oneself well** tener buen porte
(**b**) (involve) **to c. a fine/a penalty** conllevar una multa/un castigo; **to c. weight/authority** tener peso/autoridad
(**c**) (take, lead, extend) **to c. sth too far** llevar algo demasiado lejos; **to c. an argument to its logical conclusion** llevar un argumento hasta las últimas consecuencias
(**d**) (capture, win) **he carried all before him** arrolló, tuvo un éxito arrollador; **his argument carried the day** su argumentación consiguió la victoria
(**e**) Pol **the bill was carried** se aprobó el proyecto de ley
(**f**) Com (keep in stock) tener (en almacén)
(**g**) (contain) **to c. an advertisement/article** (newspaper) publicar un anuncio/artículo
2 vi (sound) oírse; **her voice carries well** tiene una voz potente

▶**carry away** vt sep (make excited, over-enthusiastic) **to get carried away (by sth)** emocionarse (por or con algo), entusiasmarse (por or con algo)

▶**carry forward** vt sep Fin pasar a nueva columna; **carried forward** suma y sigue

▶**carry off** vt sep (**a**) (take away) llevarse; **to c. off a prize** (win) llevarse un premio (**b**) (do successfully) **she carried it off (well)** salió airosa

▶**carry on 1** vt sep (tradition) seguir; (business, trade) dirigir, gestionar; (correspondence, conversation) mantener
2 vi (**a**) (continue) continuar, seguir; **to c. on doing sth** seguir haciendo algo; **c. on!** ¡sigue!, ¡adelante! (**b**) Fam (behave badly) hacer trastadas; **I don't like the way she carries on** no me gusta su forma de comportarse (**c**) Fam (have an affair) tener un lío or Méx una movida or RP un asunto (**with** con)

▶**carry out** vt sep llevar a cabo

carryall ['kærɔːl] n balsa f (de viaje o de deporte)

carry-out ['kærɪaʊt] n (food) = comida preparada para llevar; (restaurant) = restaurante donde se vende comida para llevar

carsick ['kɑːsɪk] adj **to be c.** estar mareado(a) (en el coche); **to get c.** marearse (en el coche)

cart [kɑːt] **1** n (drawn by horse) carro m, carreta f; (in supermarket) carrito m; Fig **to put the c. before the horse** empezar la casa por el tejado
2 vt Fam (carry) cargar con

▶**cart off** vt sep Fam **to c. sb off** llevarse a alguien (a la fuerza)

carte blanche ['kɑːt'blɑːʃ] n **to give sb c. (to do sth)** dar a alguien carta blanca (para hacer algo)

cartel [kɑː'tel] n Econ cartel m, cártel m

carthorse ['kɑːthɔːs] n caballo m de tiro

cartilage ['kɑːtɪlɪdʒ] n cartílago m

cartographer [kɑː'tɒgrəfə(r)] n cartógrafo(a) m,f

cartography [kɑː'tɒgrəfɪ] n cartografía f

carton ['kɑːtən] n (for yoghurt, cream) envase m; (for milk) cartón m, tetrabrik® m; **a c. of cigarettes** un cartón de cigarrillos

cartoon [kɑː'tuːn] n (in newspaper) chiste m, viñeta f; (animated movie) dibujos mpl animados; **c. strip** tira f cómica

cartoonist [kɑː'tuːnɪst] n dibujante mf de humor or de chistes

cartridge ['kɑːtrɪdʒ] n (**a**) (for firearm, of movie) cartucho m; (for pen) recambio m; **c. belt** canana f, cartuchera f (**b**) **c. paper** papel m de dibujo

cartwheel ['kɑːtwiːl] n (wheel) rueda f de carro; **to turn cartwheels** hacer la voltereta lateral

carve [kɑːv] vt (wood, stone) tallar, esculpir; (meat) trinchar

▶**carve out** vt sep **to c. out a career for oneself** forjarse una carrera

▶**carve up** vt sep (territory) repartir, dividir

carving ['kɑːvɪŋ] n (**a**) Art talla f (**b**) **c. knife** (for meat) cuchillo m de trinchar

carwash ['kɑːwɒʃ] n lavado m de coches

cascade [kæs'keɪd] **1** n cascada f
2 vi (water) caer formando una cascada

case[1] [keɪs] n (**a**) (instance, situation) & Med caso m; **a c. in point** un buen ejemplo, un caso claro; **in c. of emergency/ accident** en caso de urgencia/accidente; **in c. he isn't there** en caso de que no esté allí; **just in c.** por si acaso; **in any c.** en cualquier caso; **in that c.** en ese caso; **as the c. may be** según el caso; Med **c. history** historial m médico, ficha f; **c. study** estudio m de caso (real)
(**b**) Law causa f; **to bring a c. for sth against sb** entablar un pleito por algo contra alguien; **the c. for the defense** la defensa; **the c. for the prosecution** la acusación; Fig **the c. for sth** los argumentos a favor de algo; Fig **to have a good c.** estar respaldado(a) por buenos argumentos; **c. law** jurisprudencia f

case[2] n (**a**) (container) (for spectacles) funda f; (for jewelry) estuche m; **a cigarette c.** una pitillera; (packing) **c.** cajón m; (display or glass) **c.** vitrina f; **a c. of wine** una caja de vino (**b**) (suitcase) maleta f, RP valija f; (briefcase) maletín m, cartera f (**c**) Typ **lower/upper c.** caja f baja/alta

casement ['keɪsmənt] n (window) ventana f (batiente)

casette = **cassette**

casework ['keɪswɜːk] n asistencia f social en casos individuales

caseworker ['keɪswɜːkə(r)] n asistente mf social

cash [kæʃ] **1** n (coins, banknotes) (dinero m en) efectivo m; Fam (money in general) dinero m, Am plata f; **to pay (in) c.** pagar en efectivo; **c. on delivery** entrega f contra reembolso; **c. and carry** (shop) almacén m (de venta) al por mayor; **c. in hand** al contado; **c. box** caja f (para el dinero); **c. card** tarjeta f (del cajero automático); Fam **c. cow** fuente f de ingresos, mina f; **c. crop** cultivo m comercial; **c. dispenser** cajero automático m; Fin **c. flow** flujo m de caja, cash-flow m; **c. machine** cajero m automático; **c. price** precio m al contado; **c. register** caja f registradora
2 vt (check, postal order) hacer efectivo(a)

▶**cash in on** vt insep Fam aprovechar, sacar provecho de

cashbook ['kæʃbʊk] n libro m de caja

cashew [ˈkæʃuː] *n* **c. (nut)** anacardo *m*

cashier¹ [kæˈʃɪə(r)] *n* cajero(a) *m,f*; **c.'s check** talón *m* bancario

cashier² *vt Mil* destituir

cashmere [ˈkæʃmɪə(r)] *n* cachemir *m*

casing [ˈkeɪsɪŋ] *n Tech (of machine)* cubierta *f*, carcasa *f*; *(of tire)* cubierta *f*; *(of wire, shaft)* revestimiento *m*; *(of sausage)* piel *f*

casino [kəˈsiːnəʊ] *(pl* **casinos)** *n* casino *m*

cask [kɑːsk] *n* tonel *m*, barril *m*

casket [ˈkɑːskɪt] *n* **(a)** *(for jewelry)* estuche *m* **(b)** *(coffin)* ataúd *m*

Caspian [ˈkæspɪən] *adj* **the C. Sea** el mar Caspio

cassava [kəˈsɑːvə] *n* mandioca *f*

casserole [ˈkæsərəʊl] *n (cooking vessel)* cazuela *f*, cacerola *f*; *(food)* guiso *m*

cassette, casette [kæˈset] *n (audio, video)* cinta *f*, casete *f*; **c. player** casete *m*, magnetófono *m*; **c. recorder** casete *m*, magnetófono *m*

cassock [ˈkæsək] *n* sotana *f*

cast [kɑːst] **1** *n* **(a)** *(of play, movie)* reparto *m* **(b)** *(reproduction)* reproducción *f*; *(mold)* molde *m*; *Med* **(plaster) c.** escayola *f*, *esp Am* yeso *m*; *Fig* **c. of mind** mentalidad *f* **(c)** **c. iron** hierro *m* fundido *or* colado

2 *vt (pt & pp* **cast) (a)** *(throw) (stone)* tirar, lanzar; *(shadow)* proyectar, hacer; *(net, line)* lanzar; **to c. one's eyes over sth** echar una ojeada a algo; **to c. doubt on sth** poner en duda algo; *Fig* **to c. light on sth** arrojar luz sobre algo; **to c. one's mind back to sth** remontarse a algo; **to c. its skin** *(reptile)* mudar de piel *or* camisa; **to c. a spell over sb** hechizar a alguien **(b) to c. one's vote** emitir el voto, votar **(c)** *Theat & Cin* **to c. a movie/play** seleccionar a los actores para una película u obra; **she was c. in the role of** *or* **as Desdemona** la eligieron para el papel de Desdémona **(d)** *(metal, statue)* fundir

▸**cast around, cast about** *vi* **to c. around** *or* **about for sth** buscar algo

▸**cast aside** *vt sep (idea, prejudice)* abandonar

▸**cast away** *vt sep* **to be cast away** ser un/una náufrago(a)

▸**cast down** *vt sep* **to be cast down** estar deprimido(a), estar abatido(a)

▸**cast off 1** *vt sep (clothes, chains)* deshacerse de
2 *vi* **(a)** *Naut* soltar amarras **(b)** *(in knitting)* rematar una vuelta

▸**cast on** *vi (in knitting)* engarzar una vuelta

castanets [kæstəˈnets] *npl* castañuelas *fpl*

castaway [ˈkɑːstəweɪ] *n* náufrago(a) *m,f*

caste [kɑːst] *n (social rank)* casta *f*

castigate [ˈkæstɪgeɪt] *vt Formal (criticize)* reprender

Castile [kæˈstiːl] *n* Castilla

Castilian [kæsˈtɪlɪən] **1** *n* **(a)** *(person)* castellano(a) *m,f* **(b)** *(language)* castellano *m*
2 *adj* castellano(a)

casting [ˈkɑːstɪŋ] **1** *n Theat & Cin* reparto *m*; **he denied having got the part on the c. couch** negó haberse acostado con alguien para obtener el papel
2 *adj* **c. vote** voto *m* de calidad

cast-iron [kɑːstˈaɪən] *n* **c. alibi/guarantee** coartada *f*/ garantía *f* irrefutable

castle [ˈkɑːsəl] **1** *n (building)* castillo *m*; *(in chess)* torre *f*; *Fig* **to build castles in the air** construir castillos en el aire
2 *vi (in chess)* enrocarse

cast-off [ˈkɑːstɒf] **1** *n (garment)* prenda *f* vieja *or* usada; *Fam (person)* persona *f* rechazada
2 *adj* **c. clothing** ropa *f* vieja *or* usada

castor [ˈkɑːstə(r)] *n (on furniture)* ruedecita *f*

castor oil [ˈkɑːstərˈɔɪl] *n* aceite *m* de ricino

castrate [kæsˈtreɪt] *vt* castrar

castration [kæsˈtreɪʃən] *n* castración *f*

casual [ˈkæʒjʊəl] *adj* **(a)** *(remark, glance)* de pasada, casual **(b)** *(relaxed, informal)* informal; **c. clothes** ropa *f* informal *or* de sport **(c)** *(unconcerned)* despreocupado(a); *(careless)* descuidado(a); **c. sex** relaciones *fpl* sexuales ocasionales **(d)** *(employment, worker)* eventual

casually [ˈkæʒjʊəlɪ] *adv* **she remarked quite c. that...** comentó de pasada que...; **he treated the issue rather c.** se tomó el asunto bastante a la ligera; **to dress c.** vestirse de manera informal, vestirse de sport

casualty [ˈkæʒjʊəltɪ] *n (in accident, earthquake)* víctima *f*; *(in war)* baja *f*

CAT [kæt] *n Med (abbr* **Computerized Axial Tomography)** TAC *f*; **C. scan** escáner *m* (TAC)

cat [kæt] *n* **(a)** *(animal)* gato(a) *m,f*; **the big cats** los grandes felinos; **c. burglar** ladrón(ona) *m,f (que entra en las casas escalando)*; **c. flap** gatera *f*; **c. litter** arena *f* para gatos
(b) *(idioms)* **to fight like c. and dog** *Esp* llevarse como el perro y el gato, *Am* pelear como perro y gato; **to play a c.-and-mouse game with sb** jugar al ratón y al gato con alguien; *Fam* **to be like a c. on a hot tin roof** estar histérico(a); **to let the c. out of the bag** revelar el secreto, *Esp* descubrir el pastel; **to set the c. among the pigeons** sembrar la discordia; *Fam* **there isn't enough room to swing a c.** no se puede uno ni mover; *Fam* **he thinks he's the c.'s whiskers** *or* **pajamas** se lo tiene muy creído, se cree el no va más *or RP* el súmum, *Méx* se cree que es la única Coca-Cola en el desierto

cataclysm [ˈkætəklɪzəm] *n* cataclismo *m*

Catalan [ˈkætəlæn] **1** *n* **(a)** *(person)* catalán(ana) *m,f* **(b)** *(language)* catalán *m*
2 *adj* catalán(ana)

catalog, catalogue [ˈkætəlɒg] **1** *n* catálogo *m*
2 *vt* catalogar

Catalonia [kætəˈləʊnɪə] *n* Cataluña

catalyst [ˈkætəlɪst] *n also Fig* catalizador *m*

catamaran [kætəməˈræn] *n* catamarán *m*

catapult [ˈkætəpʌlt] **1** *n (medieval siege weapon, on aircraft carrier)* catapulta *f*
2 *vt* **to be catapulted into the air** salir despedido(a) por los aires; **to c. sb to stardom** lanzar *or* catapultar a alguien al estrellato

cataract [ˈkætərækt] *n (in river) & Med* catarata *f*

catarrh [kəˈtɑː(r)] *n* catarro *m*

catastrophe [kəˈtæstrəfɪ] *n* catástrofe *f*

catastrophic [kætəˈstrɒfɪk] *adj* catastrófico(a)

catatonic [kætəˈtɒnɪk] *adj Med* catatónico(a)

catcall [ˈkætkɔːl] *n* silbido *m*

catch [kætʃ] **1** *n* **(a)** *(of ball)* parada *f (sin que la pelota toque el suelo)*; **to play c.** *(ball game)* jugar a (que no caiga) la pelota; *(chasing game)* jugar al corre-corre-que-te-pillo, *RP* jugar a la mancha **(b)** *(in fishing)* pesca *f*, captura *f* **(c)** *(fastening) (on door, window)* cierre *m* **(d)** *(disadvantage)* **what's the c.?** ¿cuál es la pega?; **it's a c.-22 situation** es como la pescadilla que se muerde la cola

2 *vt (pt & pp* **caught** [kɔːt]) **(a)** *(thrown object, falling object)* atrapar, *Esp* coger, *Am* agarrar; *(fish)* pescar; *(prey, thief)* atrapar, capturar; **c. (it)!** *(when throwing something)* ¡agárralo!, *Esp* ¡cógelo!; **to c. sb doing sth** pillar a alguien haciendo algo; **you won't c. me doing that again** no pienso volver a hacerlo; **my bedroom catches the sun** a mi dormitorio le da el sol; **you look as if you've caught the sun** parece que te ha pegado el sol
(b) *(bus, train)* tomar, *Esp* coger; *(program, movie)* ver, alcanzar a ver
(c) *(hear)* oír, alcanzar a oír
(d) *(manage to find) Esp* pillar, *Esp* coger, *Am* agarrar; **you've**

caught me at a bad time me *Esp* pillas *or Am* agarras en un mal momento; **I'll c. you later!** luego te veo

(e) *(trap, entangle)* **I caught my dress on a nail** me enganché el vestido en un clavo; **don't c. your fingers in the door!** no te *Esp* pilles *or Am* agarres los dedos con la puerta; **to c. sb's attention** *or* **eye** llamar la atención de alguien

(f) *(illness)* agarrar, *Esp* coger, *Am* pescar; **to c. a cold** resfriarse, *Esp* coger *or Méx* pescar un resfriado, *Andes, RP* agarrarse *or* pescarse un resfrío; **I caught this cold from you** tú me pegaste este *Esp* resfriado *or Andes, RP* resfrío; **you'll c. your death (of cold) out there!** ¡vas a agarrar *or Esp* coger un resfriado de muerte ahí fuera!, *Andes, RP* ¡te vas a agarrar un resfrío mortal ahí afuera!

(g) *(of blow, missile)* **he caught me (a blow) on the chest** me dio un golpe en el pecho; **the stone caught her on the arm** la piedra le dio en el brazo; *Fam* **you'll c. it!** *(get into trouble)* ¡te la vas a *Esp* cargar *or Esp* ganar *or Méx, RP* ligar!

(h) **to c. fire** *or* **light** prenderse

3 *vi* (a) *(fire)* prender (b) *(in door)* quedarse pillado(a); *(on a nail)* quedarse enganchado(a); **my skirt caught on a nail** se me enganchó la falda en un clavo (c) *(person)* **to c. at sth** tratar de agarrar *or Esp* coger algo

▸**catch on** *vi* (a) *(fashion)* cuajar (b) *Fam (understand)* darse cuenta (**to** de), enterarse (**to** de)

▸**catch out** *vt sep* **to c. sb out** *(discover, trick) Esp* pillar *or Am* agarrar a alguien

▸**catch up 1** *vi (close gap, get closer)* **to c. up with sb** alcanzar a alguien; **to c. up with one's work** ponerse al día en el trabajo; **his past has caught up with him** ha salido a relucir su pasado

2 *vt sep* (a) **to c. sb up** alcanzar a alguien (b) **to get caught up in sth** *(become entangled)* verse envuelto(a) *or* enredarse en algo

catchall ['kætʃɔːl] *adj Fam* **a c. term** un término que vale para todo *or* muy general

catching ['kætʃɪŋ] *adj (disease, habit)* contagioso(a)

catchment area ['kætʃmənt'eərɪə] *n (of school)* área *f* de cobertura

catchphrase ['kætʃfreɪz] *n* coletilla *f*, latiguillo *m*

catchup ['kætʃʌp] *n* **(tomato) c.** ketchup *m*

catchy ['kætʃɪ] *adj (tune, slogan)* pegadizo(a)

catechism ['kætəkɪzəm] *n* catecismo *m*

categorical [kætɪ'gɒrɪkəl] *adj (denial, refusal)* categórico(a)

categorize ['kætɪgəraɪz] *vt* clasificar (**as** como)

category ['kætɪgərɪ] *n* categoría *f*

cater ['keɪtə(r)] *vi* **1** (a) *(provide food) (at weddings)* dar *or* organizar banquetes; *(for company, airline)* dar servicio de comidas *or* catering; **we c. for groups of up to fifty** *(in restaurant)* servimos a grupos de hasta cincuenta personas; **parties catered for** *(sign in restaurant)* se organizan banquetes (b) **to c. for** *(needs, requirements)* tener en cuenta; **to c. for all tastes** atender a todos los gustos

2 *(party, event)* dar el servicio de comida y bebida de, hacer el catering de

caterer ['keɪtərə(r)] *n (company)* empresa *f* de hostelería; *(person)* hostelero(a) *m,f*

catering ['keɪtərɪŋ] *n (trade)* hostelería *f*; **to do the c.** *(at party)* dar el servicio de comida y bebida; **c. school** escuela *f* de hostelería

caterpillar ['kætəpɪlə(r)] *n* oruga *f*; **c. track** *(on tank, tractor)* oruga *f*

catfish ['kætfɪʃ] *n* siluro *m*

cathartic [kə'θɑːtɪk] *adj* catártico(a)

cathedral [kə'θiːdrəl] *n* catedral *f*; **c. town/city** ciudad *f* catedralicia

catheter ['kæθɪtə(r)] *n Med* catéter *m*

cathode ['kæθəʊd] *n Elec* cátodo *m*; **c. ray tube** tubo *m* de rayos catódicos

Catholic ['kæθlɪk] *n & adj Rel* católico(a) *m,f*

catholic ['kæθlɪk] *adj (wide-ranging)* ecléctico(a)

Catholicism [kə'θɒlɪsɪzəm] *n* catolicismo *m*

catkin ['kætkɪn] *n (on bush, tree)* amento *m*, candelilla *f*

catnap ['kætnæp] *n Fam* siestecilla *f*, *Am* siestita *f*

catsup ['kætsʌp] *n* **(tomato) c.** ketchup *m*

cattail ['kætteɪl] *n* espadaña *f (planta)*

cattle ['kætəl] *npl* ganado *m* (vacuno); **c. breeding** cría *f* de ganado vacuno; **c. grid** paso *m* canadiense, reja *f (que impide el paso del ganado)*; **c. market** feria *f* de ganado; **c. truck** vagón *m* de ganado

catty ['kætɪ] *adj Fam* avieso(a), malintencionado(a)

CATV [siːeɪtiː'viː] *n (abbr* **community antenna television)** *(cable TV)* televisión *f* por cable; *(via shared aerial)* antena *f* (colectiva) comunitaria

catwalk ['kætwɔːk] *n* pasarela *f*

Caucasian [kɔː'keɪʒən] **1** *n (white person)* blanco(a) *m,f*

2 *adj (in ethnology)* caucásico(a)

Caucasus ['kɔːkəsəs] *n* **the C. (Mountains)** el Cáucaso

caucus ['kɔːkəs] *n* = congreso de los dos principales partidos de Estados Unidos

caught [kɔːt] *pt & pp of* **catch**

cauldron ['kɔːldrən] *n* caldero *m*

cauliflower ['kɒlɪflaʊə(r)] *n* coliflor *f*; **c. cheese** = coliflor con besamel de queso; **c. ear** *(swollen ear)* oreja *f* hinchada por los golpes

cause [kɔːz] **1** *n* (a) *(origin)* causa *f*; **c. and effect** causa y efecto (b) *(reason)* motivo *m*, razón *f*; **to have good c. for doing sth** tener un buen motivo para hacer algo; **his condition is giving c. for concern** su estado es preocupante (c) *(purpose, mission)* causa *f*; **to make common c.** hacer causa común; **it's all in a good c.** es por una buena causa

2 *vt* causar, provocar; **to c. trouble** crear problemas; **to c. sb to do sth** hacer que alguien haga algo

causeway ['kɔːzweɪ] *n* paso *m* elevado *(sobre agua)*

caustic ['kɔːstɪk] *adj also Fig (humor, joke)* cáustico(a); **c. soda** sosa *f* cáustica

cauterize ['kɔːtəraɪz] *vt Med* cauterizar

caution ['kɔːʃən] **1** *n* (a) *(prudence)* precaución *f*, cautela *f*; **to exercise c.** actuar con precaución; **to throw c. to the wind(s)** olvidarse de la prudencia (b) *(warning)* advertencia *f*; *Law & Sport* **to be given a c.** recibir una advertencia

2 *vt* (a) *(warn)* advertir; **to c. sb against sth** prevenir a alguien contra algo (b) *Law (on arrest)* leer los derechos a; *(instead of prosecuting)* amonestar

cautionary ['kɔːʃənrɪ] *adj* **a c. tale** un cuento ejemplar

cautious ['kɔːʃəs] *adj* cauto(a), prudente

cautiously ['kɔːʃəslɪ] *adv* cautelosamente, con prudencia

cautiousness ['kɔːʃəsnɪs] *n* cautela *f*, prudencia *f*

cavalier [kævə'lɪə(r)] *adj* demasiado despreocupado(a); **to be c. about sth** tomarse algo a la ligera

cavalry ['kævəlrɪ] *n* caballería *f*

cave [keɪv] *n* cueva *f*, caverna *f*; **c. dweller** cavernícola *mf*; **c. paintings** pinturas *fpl* rupestres

▸**cave in** *vi (ground, structure)* hundirse, ceder; *Fig (stop resisting)* rendirse, darse por vencido(a)

caveat ['kævɪæt] *n* (a) *Law* = demanda de notificación previa ante un tribunal (b) *Formal (warning)* salvedad *f*, reserva *f*; **with the c. that...** con la salvedad de que...

caveman ['keɪvmæn] *n* cavernícola *m*

cavern ['kævən] *n* caverna *f*

cavernous ['kævənəs] *adj (room, pit)* cavernoso(a)

caviar(e) ['kævɪɑː(r)] *n* caviar *m*

cavil ['kævɪl] *vi Literary* poner reparos (**at** a)

cavity ['kævɪtɪ] *n (hole)* cavidad *f; (of tooth)* caries *f inv*

cavort [kə'vɔːt] *vi* retozar, brincar

caw [kɔː] **1** *n (of bird)* graznido *m*
2 *vi* graznar

cayenne [keɪ'en] *n* **c. (pepper)** cayena *f*

CB [siː'biː] *n Rad (abbr* **Citizens' Band**) banda *f* ciudadana *or* de radioaficionados

cc [siː'siː] *n (abbr* **cubic centimeter(s)**) c.c., centímetros *mpl* cúbicos

CCTV [siːsiːtiː'viː] *n (abbr* **closed-circuit television**) circuito *m* cerrado de televisión

CD [siː'diː] *n* (**a**) *(abbr* **compact disk**) CD *m*, (disco *m*) compacto *m*; **CD burner** estampadora *f* de CD; **CD player** (lector *m or* reproductor *m* de) CD *m*; **CD writer** grabadora *f* de CD (**b**) *(abbr* **Corps Diplomatique**) CD *m*, cuerpo *m* diplomático

CDI [siːdiː'aɪ] *n Comptr (abbr* **compact disk interactive**) CDI *m*

CD-R [siːdiː'ɑ(r)] *n Comptr (abbr* **compact disk recordable**) CD-R *m*

Cdr *Mil (abbr* **Commander**) Comandante *m*

Cdre *Naut (abbr* **Commodore**) Comodoro *m*

CD-ROM [siːdiː'rɒm] *n Comptr (abbr* **compact disk-read only memory**) CD-ROM *m*; **C. drive** unidad *f* de CD-ROM

CD-RW *n (abbr* **compact disk rewritable**) CD-RW *m*

CDT [siːdiː'tiː] *n (abbr* **Central Daylight Time**) = hora en el huso horario del centro de los Estados Unidos y Canadá

cease [siːs] **1** *vt* abandonar, suspender; **c. fire!** ¡alto el fuego!
2 *vi* cesar; **to c. doing sth** *or* **to do sth** dejar de hacer algo; **it never ceases to amaze me (that...)** no deja de sorprenderme (que...)

cease-fire [siːsfaɪə(r)] *n* alto *m* el fuego, tregua *f*

ceaseless ['siːslɪs] *adj* incesante

ceaselessly ['siːslɪslɪ] *adv* incesantemente, sin parar

cecum, caecum ['siːkəm] *(pl* **ceca, caeca** ['siːkə]) *n* (intestino *m*) ciego *m*

cedar ['siːdə(r)] *n (tree, wood)* cedro *m*

cede [siːd] *vt Law (territory, property)* ceder

cedilla [sɪ'dɪlə] *n* cedilla *f*

ceiling ['siːlɪŋ] *n (of room)* techo *m*; *Fig* **to hit the c.** *(lose one's temper)* ponerse hecho(a) una furia; *Fig* **to reach a c.** tocar techo; **c. price** precio *m* máximo autorizado

celebrant ['selɪbrənt] *n Rel* celebrante *mf*

celebrate ['selɪbreɪt] **1** *vt* celebrar; *Rel* **to c. mass** decir misa
2 *vi* **let's c.!** ¡vamos a celebrarlo!

celebrated ['selɪbreɪtɪd] *adj* célebre

celebration [selɪ'breɪʃən] *n* celebración *f*; **celebrations** *(of anniversary, victory)* actos *mpl* conmemorativos; **in c.** en celebración; **this calls for a c.!** ¡esto hay que celebrarlo!

celebrity [sɪ'lebrɪtɪ] *n* (**a**) *(person)* celebridad *f* (**b**) *(fame)* celebridad *f*, fama *f*

celery ['selərɪ] *n* apio *m*

celestial [sɪ'lestɪəl] *adj* celeste

celibacy ['selɪbəsɪ] *n* celibato *m*

celibate ['selɪbət] *adj* célibe

cell [sel] *n* (**a**) *(in prison, monastery)* celda *f* (**b**) *Elec* pila *f* (**c**) *Biol & Pol* célula *f* (**d**) **c. phone** teléfono *m* móvil *or Am* celular

cellar ['selə(r)] *n (basement)* sótano *m*; *(for wine)* bodega *f*

cellist ['tʃelɪst] *n* violonchelista *mf*

cello ['tʃeləʊ] *(pl* **cellos**) *n* violonchelo *m*

cellular ['seljʊlə(r)] *adj* celular; **c. phone** teléfono *m* móvil *or Am* celular

cellulite ['seljʊlaɪt] *n* celulitis *f inv*

celluloid® ['seljʊlɔɪd] *n* celuloide *m*

cellulose ['seljʊləʊs] *n* celulosa *f*

Celsius ['selsɪəs] *adj* centígrado(a); **10 degrees C.** 10 grados centígrados

Celt [kelt] *n* celta *mf*

Celtic ['keltɪk] *adj* celta, céltico(a)

cement [sɪ'ment] **1** *n* cemento *m*; **c. mixer** hormigonera *f*
2 *vt (glue together)* encolar, pegar; *(cover with cement)* cubrir de cemento; *Fig (friendship)* consolidar

cemetery ['semətrɪ] *n* cementerio *m*

cenotaph ['senətæf] *n* cenotafio *m*

censor ['sensə(r)] **1** *n* censor(ora) *m,f*
2 *vt* censurar

censorious [sen'sɔːrɪəs] *adj (person)* censurador(ora); *(look)* reprobatorio(a); **to be c. of** censurar

censorship ['sensəʃɪp] *n* censura *f*

censure ['senʃə(r)] **1** *n* censura *f*, crítica *f*; *Pol* **vote of c.** moción *f* de censura
2 *vt* censurar, criticar

census ['sensəs] *n* censo *m*; **to take a c. of** censar

cent [sent] *n* centavo *m*; *Fam* **I haven't got a c.** no tengo ni un centavo *or Esp* duro *or Méx* peso

centaur ['sentɔː(r)] *n* centauro *m*

centenarian [sentɪ'neərɪən] *n* centenario(a) *m,f*

centennial [sen'tenɪəl], **centenary** [sen'tiːnərɪ] **1** *n* centenario *m*
2 *adj* centenario(a)

center ['sentə(r)] **1** *n* (**a**) *(of object, shape, town)* centro *m*; **in the c.** en el centro; **c. of gravity** centro de gravedad (**b**) *(in politics)* centro *m*; **left of c.** de izquierdas; **right of c.** de derechas (**c**) *(location, focus)* centro *m*; *(of unrest)* foco *m*; **c. of attraction** foco *or* centro de atracción (**d**) *(in football)* central *mf*; **c. back** *(in soccer)* defensa *mf* central, central *mf*; **c. forward** *(in soccer)* delantero *mf* centro; **c. half** *(in soccer)* medio *mf* centro
2 *vt (attention, interest)* centrar (**on** en)

centerfold ['sentəfəʊld] *n (in magazine)* póster *m* central

centerline ['sentəlaɪn] *n (of tennis court, road)* línea *f* central; *(of geometrical figure)* eje *m*

centerpiece ['sentəpiːs] *n (on table)* centro *m* de mesa; *(main element)* núcleo *m*, eje *m*

centigrade ['sentɪgreɪd] *adj* centígrado(a); **10 degrees c.** 10 grados centígrados

centigram ['sentɪgræm] *n* centigramo *m*

centiliter ['sentɪliːtə(r)] *n* centilitro *m*

centimeter ['sentɪmiːtə(r)] *n* centímetro *m*

centipede ['sentɪpiːd] *n* ciempiés *m inv*

central ['sentrəl] *adj* central; *(in convenient location)* céntrico(a); *(in importance)* central, primordial; **it is c. to our plans** es el eje sobre el que giran nuestros planes; **c. Manhattan** el centro de Manhattan; **our hotel is quite c.** nuestro hotel es bastante céntrico; **C. African Republic** República Centroafricana; **C. America** Centroamérica, América Central; **C. American** centroamericano(a); **c. bank** banco *m* central; **c. character** *(in book, movie)* personaje *m* central, protagonista *mf*; **C. Europe** Europa Central; **C. European** centroeuropeo(a); **c. government** gobierno *m* central; **c. heating** calefacción *f* central; **c. nervous system** sistema *m* nervioso central; *Comptr* **c. processing unit** unidad *f* central de proceso; **C. Standard Time** = hora oficial en el centro de los Estados Unidos

centralism ['sentrəlɪzəm] *n Pol* centralismo *m*

centralization [sentrəlaɪ'zeɪʃən] *n* centralización *f*

centralize ['sentrəlaɪz] *vt* centralizar

centrally ['sentrəlɪ] *adv* **c. controlled** de control *or Am* monitoreo centralizado; **c. funded** de financiación *or Am* financiamiento central; **the apartment is c. heated** el piso tiene calefacción central

centrifugal [sentrɪ'fjʊgəl] *adj* centrífugo(a)

century ['sentʃərɪ] n (**a**) (a hundred years) siglo m; **the 19th c.** el siglo XIX (**b**) (in cricket) = cien (o más de cien) carreras

CEO [si:i:'əʊ] (pl **CEOs**) n Com (abbr **chief executive officer**) director(ora) m,f gerente, consejero(a) m,f delegado(a)

ceramic [sə'ræmɪk] **1** n cerámica f
   2 adj de cerámica

ceramics [sə'ræmɪks] n (art) cerámica f

cereal ['sɪərɪəl] n cereal m; (**breakfast**) **c.** cereales mpl (de desayuno)

cerebellum [serɪ'beləm] (pl **cerebella** [serɪ'belə]) n Anat cerebelo m

cerebra pl of **cerebrum**

cerebral ['serɪbrəl] adj (intellectual) & Anat cerebral; Med **c. palsy** parálisis f inv cerebral

cerebrum ['serɪbrəm] (pl **cerebrums** or **cerebra** ['serɪbrə]) n Anat cerebro m

ceremonial [serɪ'məʊnɪəl] **1** n ceremonial m; **ceremonials** ceremoniales mpl
   2 adj ceremonial

ceremonious [serɪ'məʊnɪəs] adj ceremonioso(a)

ceremoniously [serɪ'məʊnɪəslɪ] adv ceremoniosamente

ceremony ['serɪmənɪ] n ceremonia f; **the marriage c.** la ceremonia nupcial; **with/without c.** con/sin ceremonia; Fig **he was sacked without c.** lo despidieron sin ningún miramiento; **there's no need to stand on c.** no hace falta cumplir con formalidades

certain ['sɜːtən] adj (**a**) (sure) seguro(a); **to be c. of sth** estar seguro(a) de algo; **to make c. of sth** asegurarse de algo; **for c.** con certeza; **he is c. to come** vendrá con toda seguridad (**b**) (particular) cierto(a), determinado(a); **for c. reasons** por ciertos motivos; **a c. person** cierta persona; **a c. Richard Sanders** un tal Richard Sanders

certainly ['sɜːtənlɪ] adv (definitely) por supuesto; **c. not!** ¡ni hablar!; **she's c. very clever, but...** sin duda es muy lista, pero...

certainty ['sɜːtəntɪ] n certeza f, certidumbre f; **she said it with some c.** lo dijo con certidumbre; **there is no c. that we will win** no es seguro que ganemos; **to know sth for a c.** saber algo a ciencia cierta

certifiable ['sɜːtɪfaɪəbəl] adj Fam (mad) **to be c.** estar como para que lo/la encierren

certificate [sə'tɪfɪkət] n certificado m; (in education) título m; **marriage/death c.** certificado or partida f de matrimonio/defunción

certified ['sɜːtɪfaɪd] adj (qualified) diplomado(a); (document) certificado(a); **c. letter** carta f certificada; **c. mail** correo m certificado; **c. public accountant** Esp censor(ora) m,f jurado(a) de cuentas, Am contador(ora) m,f público(a)

certify ['sɜːtɪfaɪ] vt (confirm) certificar; **to c. that sth is true** dar fe de que algo es verdad; **this is to c. that...** por la presente certifico que...; **to c. sb insane** declarar demente a alguien

certitude ['sɜːtɪtju:d] n certidumbre f

cervical ['sɜːvɪkəl] adj Anat cervical; **c. cancer** cáncer m cervical; **c. smear** frotis m inv cervical, citología f (cervical)

cervix ['sɜːvɪks] (pl **cervices** ['sɜːvɪsi:z]) n Anat cuello m del útero

cesarean, caesarian [sɪ'zeərɪən] n **c. (section)** (operación f de) cesárea f

cessation [se'seɪʃən] n cese m

cesspit ['sespɪt], **cesspool** ['sespu:l] n pozo m negro; Fig sentina f, cloaca f

CET [si:i:'ti:] n (abbr **Central European Time**) = hora de Europa central

Ceylon [sɪ'lɒn] n Formerly Ceilán

cf [si:'ef] (abbr **confer, compare**) cf., cfr., compárese

CFC [si:ef'si:] n Chem (abbr **chlorofluorocarbon**) CFC m, clorofluorocarbono m

CFO [si:ef'əʊ] n (abbr **chief financial officer**) director(ora) m,f financiero(a)

CGI [si:dʒi:'aɪ] n (abbr **computer-generated images**) imágenes fpl generadas por Esp ordenador or Am computadora

Chad [tʃæd] n Chad

chafe [tʃeɪf] **1** vt (rub) rozar, hacer rozadura en
   2 vi (rub) rozar, hacer rozadura; Fig **to c. at** or **against sth** (resent) sentirse irritado(a) por algo

chaff [tʃɑːf] **1** n granzas fpl, barcia f; Fig **to separate the wheat from the c.** separar el grano de la paja
   2 vt (tease) tomar el pelo a

chaffinch ['tʃæfɪntʃ] n pinzón m

chagrin ['ʃægrɪn] n disgusto m, desazón f; **much to my/her c.** muy a mi/su pesar

chain [tʃeɪn] **1** n cadena f; (of mountains) cadena f montañosa, cordillera f; **in chains** encadenado(a); Fig **a c. of events** una concatenación de sucesos; **c. gang** cadena f de presidiarios; **c. letter** = carta en la que se pide al destinatario que envíe copias de la misma a otras personas; **c. mail** cota f de malla; **c. reaction** reacción f en cadena; **c. saw** motosierra f, sierra f mecánica; **c. store** cadena f de tiendas
   2 vt encadenar; **to c. sth to sth** encadenar algo a algo
► **chain up** vt sep encadenar

chain-smoke ['tʃeɪnsməʊk] vi fumar un cigarrillo tras otro

chain-smoker ['tʃeɪn'sməʊkə(r)] n fumador(ora) m,f empedernido(a)

chair [tʃeə(r)] **1** n (**a**) (seat) silla f; (armchair) sillón m (**b**) (chairperson) presidente(a) m,f (**c**) Univ (of professor) cátedra f
   2 vt (meeting) presidir

chairlift ['tʃeəlɪft] n telesilla m

chairman ['tʃeəmən] n presidente m

chairmanship ['tʃeəmənʃɪp] n presidencia f

chairperson ['tʃeəpɜːsən] n presidente(a) m,f

chairwoman ['tʃeəwʊmən] n presidenta f

chalet ['ʃæleɪ] n chalé m

chalice ['tʃælɪs] n Rel cáliz m

chalk [tʃɔːk] **1** n (mineral) creta f; (for blackboard) tiza f, Méx gis m
   2 vt (mark) trazar or marcar con tiza; (write) escribir con tiza
► **chalk up** vt sep (victory) apuntarse

chalkboard ['tʃɔːkbɔːd] n pizarra f, encerado m, Am pizarrón m

chalky ['tʃɔːkɪ] adj (soil) calizo(a)

challenge ['tʃælɪndʒ] **1** n (exacting task, to duel) desafío m, reto m; (competition) competición f, Am competencia f; **to issue/accept a c.** lanzar/aceptar un desafío; **to enjoy a c.** disfrutar con las tareas difíciles; **the job presents a real c.** el trabajo constituye un auténtico reto; **leadership c.** asalto m al liderato or a la presidencia
   2 vt (**a**) (to a contest, fight) desafiar, retar; **to c. sb to do sth** desafiar or retar a alguien a hacer algo; **you need a job that will c. you** necesitas un trabajo que represente un reto para ti (**b**) (statement, authority) cuestionar, poner en duda; **she challenged his right to decide** puso en duda que él tuviera derecho a decidir (**c**) Mil dar el alto a

challenger ['tʃælɪndʒə(r)] n aspirante mf

challenging ['tʃælɪndʒɪŋ] adj (job) estimulante

chamber ['tʃeɪmbə(r)] n (**a**) (hall) sala f; Pol **Lower/Upper C.** cámara f alta/baja; **C. of Commerce** cámara f de comercio; **c. music** música f de cámara; **c. pot** orinal m, Am bacinica f (**b**) (of heart) cavidad f (cardíaca); (of revolver) recámara f (**c**) Law **chambers** (of barrister, judge) despacho m

chambermaid ['tʃeɪmbəmeɪd] n camarera f (de hotel)

chamberpot ['tʃeɪmbəpɒt] n orinal m, Am bacinica f

chameleon [kə'mi:lɪən] n camaleón m

chamois (*pl* **chamois**) *n* (**a**) ['ʃæmwɑː] (*deer*) rebeco *m*, gamuza *f* (**b**) ['ʃæmɪ] **c. (leather)** (*material*) ante *m*; (*cloth*) gamuza *f*

chamomile ['kæməmaɪl] *n* manzanilla *f*, camomila *f*; **c. tea** (*infusión f de*) manzanilla *f*

champ¹ [tʃæmp] *n Fam* campeón(ona) *m,f*

champ² *vi* **to c. at the bit** (*person*) hervir de impaciencia

champagne [ʃæm'peɪn] *n* champán *m*

champion ['tʃæmpɪən] **1** *n* (**a**) (*in sport*) campeón(ona) *m,f*; **world/European c.** campeón(ona) mundial/de Europa (**b**) (*of cause*) abanderado(a) *m,f*, defensor(ora) *m,f*
     2 *vt* defender, abanderar

championship ['tʃæmpɪənʃɪp] *n* campeonato *m*

chance [tʃɑːns] **1** *n* (**a**) (*luck*) casualidad *f*, suerte *f*; **by c.** por casualidad; **to leave nothing to c.** no dejar nada a la improvisación
     (**b**) (*opportunity*) oportunidad *f*, *Am* chance *f*; **to give sb a c.** darle una oportunidad a alguien; **now's your c.!** ¡ésta es la tuya!, ¡ésta es tu oportunidad!; **it's your last c.** es tu última oportunidad; **when I get the c.** en cuanto tenga ocasión *or* oportunidad
     (**c**) (*likelihood*) posibilidad *f* (**of** de); **to have** *or* **stand a c.** tener posibilidades; **there's no c. of that happening** es imposible que suceda
     (**d**) (*risk*) riesgo *m*; **to take a c.** correr el riesgo; **it's a c. we'll have to take** es un riesgo que habrá que correr; **I'm taking no chances** no pienso correr riesgos
     2 *adj* **a c. discovery/meeting** un descubrimiento/encuentro casual
     3 *vt* **to c. doing sth** arriesgarse a hacer algo
     4 *vi* (*happen*) **to c. to do sth** hacer algo por casualidad

▶**chance on, chance upon** *vt insep* encontrar por casualidad

chancellor ['tʃɑːnsələ(r)] *n* (**a**) (*of university*) rector(ora) *m,f* (**b**) (*of Austria, Germany*) canciller *m*

chancy ['tʃɑːnsɪ] *adj Fam* (*risky*) arriesgado(a)

chandelier [ʃændə'lɪə(r)] *n* araña *f* (lámpara)

change [tʃeɪndʒ] **1** *n* (**a**) (*alteration*) cambio *m*; **a c. for the better/worse** un cambio a mejor/peor; **a c. of address** un cambio de domicilio; **a c. of clothes** una muda; **to have a c. of heart** cambiar de parecer; **for a c.** para variar; **that makes a c.** es toda una novedad; **the c. (of life)** (*menopause*) la menopausia (**b**) (*money*) cambio *m*, *Am* vuelto *m*, *Andes, CAm, Méx* sencillo *m*, *Carib, Col* devuelta *f*; **small** *or* **loose c.** (*dinero m*) suelto *m*; **have you got c. for a $10 bill?** ¿tienes cambio *or Am* vuelto de 10 dólares?; **keep the c.** quédese con el cambio *or Am* vuelto
     2 *vt* (**a**) (*transform*) cambiar; **to c. sth into sth** transformar algo en algo; **to c. one's ways** cambiar de comportamiento; **to c. one's mind/the subject** cambiar de opinión/de tema
     (**b**) (*exchange*) cambiar (**for** por); **to c. one thing for another** cambiar una cosa por otra; **to c. hands** (*money, car*) cambiar de manos; **to c. trains** hacer transbordo; **to c. places with sb** (*in room*) cambiar el sitio con alguien; (*in job*) ponerse en el lugar de alguien; *Fig* **I wouldn't like to c. places with him** no me gustaría estar en su lugar
     (**c**) (*money*) cambiar; **to c. dollars into francs** cambiar dólares por francos
     (**d**) **to get changed** cambiarse (de ropa)
     3 *vi* (**a**) (*alter*) cambiar; **to c. for the better/worse** cambiar a mejor/peor; **to c. into** (*become*) transformarse en (**b**) (*put on other clothes*) cambiarse (**c**) (*passenger*) hacer transbordo

▶**change over** *vi* cambiarse; **to c. over from sth to sth** cambiar de algo a algo; **to c. over from dictatorship to democracy** pasar de la dictadura a la democracia; **to c. over to another channel** cambiar de canal

changeable ['tʃeɪndʒəbəl] *adj* (*person, weather*) variable

changeless ['tʃeɪndʒlɪs] *adj* invariable

changeover ['tʃeɪndʒəʊvə(r)] *n* transición *f* (**to** a)

changing ['tʃeɪndʒɪŋ] *adj* cambiante

changing room ['tʃeɪndʒɪŋ'ruːm] *n* (**a**) (*for sport, in theater*) vestuario *m*, vestuarios *mpl* (**b**) (*in shop*) probador *m*

channel ['tʃænəl] **1** *n* canal *m*; **c. of communication** canal *m* de comunicación; **all inquiries must go through the proper channels** todas las consultas han de seguir los trámites *or* cauces apropiados; **the (English) C.** el Canal de la Mancha; **the C. Islands** las Islas del Canal de la Mancha; **the C. Tunnel** el Eurotúnel
     2 *vt* canalizar

channel-surf ['tʃænəlsɜːf], **channel-hop** ['tʃænəlhɒp] *vi Fam* zapear, hacer zapping

chant [tʃɑːnt] **1** *n* (**a**) (*of demonstrators, crowd*) consigna *f*; (*at sports matches*) canción *f* (coreada) (**b**) *Rel* canto *m*
     2 *vt & vi* corear

chaos ['keɪɒs] *n* caos *m inv*; **there has been c. on the roads today** hoy el tráfico en las carreteras ha sido infernal; **c. theory** teoría *f* del caos

chaotic [keɪ'ɒtɪk] *adj* caótico(a)

chap [tʃæp] *n Fam* (*man*) tipo *m*, *Esp* tío *m*; **a good c.** un buen tipo

chapel ['tʃæpəl] *n* capilla *f*

chaperone ['ʃæpərəʊn] **1** *n* señora *f* de compañía, *Esp* carabina *f*, *Am* chaperona *f*
     2 *vt* **to c. sb** acompañar a alguien como carabina

chaplain ['tʃæplɪn] *n Rel* capellán *m*

chaplaincy ['tʃæplɪnsɪ] *n* capellanía *f*

chapped [tʃæpt] *adj* (*lips*) cortado(a); (*skin*) agrietado(a)

chapter ['tʃæptə(r)] *n* capítulo *m*; **c. eight** capítulo ocho; **the holiday was a c. of accidents** las vacaciones consistieron en una sucesión de accidentes; *Fig* **to quote c. and verse for sth** dar pelos y señales en relación con algo; *Fin* **c. 11** (*part of bankruptcy laws*) = sección de la ley de quiebras que regula el proceso de declaración oficial de bancarrota

char [tʃɑː(r)] (*pt & pp* **charred**) *vt* (*burn*) carbonizar, quemar

character ['kærɪktə(r)] *n* (**a**) (*in novel, play*) personaje *m*; **c. actor** = actor especializado en personajes poco convencionales; **c. sketch** descripción *f* de un personaje, semblanza *f*
     (**b**) (*personality*) carácter *m*; **to be in/out of c.** ser/no ser típico de él/ella, *etc.*; **to have/lack c.** tener/no tener carácter; **a person of good c.** una persona íntegra; **c. assassination** campaña *f* de desprestigio; **c. witness** = testigo que declara en favor del buen carácter del acusado
     (**c**) (*person*) personaje *m*; **he's quite a c.!** es todo un personaje
     (**d**) (*letter*) carácter *m*; *Comptr* **c. set** juego *m* de caracteres

characteristic [kærɪktə'rɪstɪk] **1** *n* característica *f*
     2 *adj* característico(a)

characterization [kærɪktəraɪ'zeɪʃən] *n* caracterización *f*

characterize ['kærɪktəraɪz] *vt* caracterizar; **I would hardly c. him as naive!** ¡yo no lo definiría como ingenuo, ni mucho menos!

characterless ['kærɪktəlɪs] *adj* anodino(a), sin carácter

charade [ʃə'rɑːd] *n* (*farce*) farsa *f*; **charades** (*party game*) charada *f*

charcoal ['tʃɑːkəʊl] *n* carbón *m* vegetal; **c. drawing** dibujo *m* al carboncillo; **c. gray** gris *m* marengo

charge [tʃɑːdʒ] **1** *n* (**a**) (*cost*) precio *m*, tarifa *f*; **free of c.** gratis; **c. account** cuenta *f* de crédito; **c. card** tarjeta *f* de compra (**b**) *Law* cargo *m*; **on a c. of...** acusado(a) de...; **to bring a c. against sb** presentar cargos contra alguien (**c**) (*responsibility*) **to take c. (of)** hacerse cargo (de); **to be in c.** estar a cargo, ser el/la encargado(a) (**d**) (*of explosive*) carga *f*
     2 *vt* (**a**) (*price*) cobrar; **c. it to my account** cárguelo a mi cuenta (**b**) *Law* acusar; **to c. sb with a crime** acusar a alguien de un delito (**c**) *Mil* (*attack*) cargar contra, atacar (**d**)

Elec cargar; *Fig* **a highly charged atmosphere** un ambiente muy tenso

3 *vi (rush)* cargar; **he charged in** entró apresuradamente

chargé d'affaires [ˈʃɑːʒeɪdæˈfeəz] *(pl* **chargés d'affaires)** *n* encargado(a) *m,f* de negocios

chariot [ˈtʃærɪət] *n (in battles)* carro *m (de caballos); (in ancient Rome)* cuadriga *f*

charisma [kæˈrɪzmə] *n* carisma *m*

charismatic [kærɪzˈmætɪk] *adj* carismático(a)

charitable [ˈtʃærɪtəbəl] *adj (person, action)* caritativo(a); *(organization, work)* benéfico(a), de caridad; **it would be c. to call him misguided** decir que va *or Esp* anda descaminado sería demasiado generoso

charitably [ˈtʃærɪtəblɪ] *adv (kindly)* con generosidad; **he spoke very c. of his former opponent** habló con mucha generosidad de su antiguo rival

charity [ˈtʃærɪtɪ] *n* (a) *(quality)* caridad *f; Prov* **c. begins at home** *Esp* la caridad bien entendida empieza por uno mismo, *Am* la caridad empieza por casa (b) *(organization)* entidad *f* benéfica; **all proceeds will go to c.** toda la recaudación se dedicará a obras de beneficencia

charlatan [ˈʃɑːlətən] *n* charlatán(ana) *m,f,* embaucador(ora) *m,f*

charm [tʃɑːm] **1** *n* (a) *(attractiveness)* encanto *m* (b) *(spell)* hechizo *m;* **to be under a c.** estar hechizado(a); **it worked like a c.** funcionó a las mil maravillas (c) *(talisman)* **a lucky c.** un amuleto (de la suerte)

2 *vt* hechizar, encantar; **she charmed the money out of him** me cameló para sacarle dinero; **to lead a charmed life** tener buena estrella

charmer [ˈtʃɑːmə(r)] *n* **to be a real c.** ser todo cumplidos, ser todo gentileza

charming [ˈtʃɑːmɪŋ] *adj* encantador(ora)

charred [tʃɑːd] *adj* carbonizado(a)

chart [tʃɑːt] **1** *n (graph)* gráfico *m; (map)* carta *f;* **the charts** *(pop music)* las listas (de éxitos)

2 *vt (on map)* hacer un mapa de; *Fig* **the book charts the rise of fascism** el libro describe el auge del fascismo

charter [ˈtʃɑːtə(r)] **1** *n (of town)* fuero *m; (of university, organization)* estatutos *mpl;* **the UN c.** la carta de las Naciones Unidas; **c. flight** vuelo *m* chárter; **c. member** miembro *mf* fundador(ora); **c. plane** avión *m* chárter

2 *vt (plane, ship)* fletar

chary [ˈtʃeərɪ] *adj (cautious)* cauteloso(a); **to be c. of doing sth** mostrarse reacio(a) a la hora de hacer algo

chase [tʃeɪs] **1** *n (pursuit)* persecución *f;* **to give c. to sb** perseguir a alguien

2 *vt (pursue)* perseguir

3 *vi* **to c. after sb** perseguir a alguien

▸**chase up** *vt sep (person)* localizar; *(report, information)* hacerse con

chaser [ˈtʃeɪsə(r)] *n (drink)* = vasito de licor que se bebe después de la cerveza

chasm [ˈkæzəm] *n also Fig* abismo *m*

chassis [ˈʃæsɪ] *(pl* **chassis** [ˈʃæsɪz]) *n (of car)* chasis *m inv*

chaste [tʃeɪst] *adj* casto(a)

chasten [ˈtʃeɪsən] *vt* aleccionar

chastise [tʃæsˈtaɪz] *vt (tell off)* reprender

chastisement [tʃæsˈtaɪzmənt] *n* castigo *m*

chastity [ˈtʃæstɪtɪ] *n* castidad *f;* **c. belt** cinturón *m* de castidad

chat [tʃæt] **1** *n* (a) *(informal conversation)* charla *f, CAm, Méx* plática *f;* **to have a c.** charlar (b) *Comptr* charla *f,* chat *m;* **c. room** sala *f* de conversación

2 *vi (pt & pp* **chatted)** (a) *(talk informally)* charlar, *CAm, Méx* platicar (**to** *or* **with** con) (b) *Comptr* charlar, chatear (**to** *or* **with** con)

chattel [ˈtʃætəl] *n Law* **goods and chattels** bienes *mpl* (muebles)

chatter [ˈtʃætə(r)] **1** *n* cháchara *f*

2 *vi* parlotear; **my teeth were chattering (with cold/fear)** me rechinaban *or* castañeteaban los dientes (de frío/miedo)

chatterbox [ˈtʃætəbɒks] *n Fam* cotorra *f*

chatty [ˈtʃætɪ] *adj (person)* hablador(ora); *(letter)* desenfadado(a)

chauffeur [ˈʃəʊfə(r)] **1** *n Esp* chófer *m, Am* chofer *m*

2 *vt* **we were chauffeured to the airport** el chófer nos llevó al aeropuerto

chauffeur-driven [ˈʃəʊfəˈdrɪvən] *adj* con *Esp* chófer *or Am* chofer

chauvinism [ˈʃəʊvɪnɪzəm] *n (sexism)* machismo *m; (nationalism)* chovinismo *m*

chauvinist [ˈʃəʊvɪnɪst] *n (sexist)* machista *m; (nationalist)* chovinista *mf*

cheap [tʃiːp] **1** *n* **to do sth on the c.** hacer algo en plan barato *or* mirando el dinero

2 *adj* (a) *(inexpensive)* barato(a); **c. rate** tarifa *f* reducida (b) *(of little value)* **I feel c.** ¡qué bajo he caído!; **c. and nasty** de chichinabo, de chicha y nabo; **a c. joke/remark** *(tasteless)* un chiste/comentario de mal gusto; **that was a c. shot** eso ha sido un golpe bajo (c) *(stingy)* mezquino(a)

3 *adv Fam* **it was going c.** estaba tirado(a) de precio

cheapen [ˈtʃiːpən] *vt* **to c. oneself** rebajarse

cheaply [ˈtʃiːplɪ] *adv* barato; **to live c.** vivir con poco dinero

cheapo [ˈtʃiːpəʊ] *adj Fam (of low quality)* barato(a), *Esp* cutre, *RP* berreta

cheapskate [ˈtʃiːpskeɪt] *n Fam* roñica *mf*

cheat [tʃiːt] **1** *n (dishonest person)* tramposo(a) *m,f; (deception, trick)* trampa *f;* **that's a c.** eso es trampa; **c. sheet** *Esp, Ven* chuleta *f, Arg* machete *m, Col, Méx* acordeón *m, Perú* comprimido *m, Urug* trencito *m*

2 *vt* engañar; **he cheated her out of the money** le estafó todo el dinero

3 *vi (in game)* hacer trampa; *(in exam)* copiar

▸**cheat on** *vt insep (be unfaithful to)* engañar

cheating [ˈtʃiːtɪŋ] *n (in game)* trampas *fpl; (in exam)* copieteo *m;* **that's c.!** ¡eso es trampa!

Chechen [ˈtʃetʃen] *n & adj* checheno(a) *m,f*

Chechnya, Chechenia [ˈtʃetʃnɪə] *n* Chechenia

check¹ [tʃek] **1** *n* (a) *(inspection)* control *m,* inspección *f;* **to keep a c. on sth/sb** llevar un control de algo/alguien; **the police ran a c. on her** la policía investigó sus antecedentes (b) *(restraint)* **to keep sth/sb in c.** mantener algo/a alguien a raya *or* bajo control; *Pol* **checks and balances** control *m* mutuo (c) *(in chess)* jaque *m;* **to put sb in c.** poner en jaque a alguien (d) *(bank check)* cheque *m,* talón *m; (in restaurant)* cuenta *f;* **to make out** *or* **write a c. (to sb)** extender un cheque *or* talón (a alguien); **a c. for $50** un cheque de 50 dólares

2 *vt* (a) *(verify, examine) (information)* comprobar, *Guat, Méx* checar; *(passport, ticket)* revisar; **to c. that...** comprobar que... (b) *(restrain) (inflation, enemy advance)* frenar; *(emotion, impulse)* contener, reprimir; **to c. oneself** contenerse

3 *vi (verify)* comprobar, *Guat, Méx* checar; **to c. on sth** comprobar algo; **to c. on sb** controlar *or* vigilar a alguien; **to c. with sb** preguntar a alguien

check² *n (pattern)* cuadros *mpl;* **a jacket in broad c.** una chaqueta a cuadros grandes

▸**check in 1** *vi (at hotel)* registrarse; *(at airport)* facturar

2 *vt sep (baggage)* facturar, *Am* despachar

▸**check out 1** *vt sep (investigate) (person)* investigar; *(information)* comprobar, verificar, *Am* chequear, *Méx* checar; *Fam (look at)* mirar, echar un ojo a

2 *vi (leave hotel)* dejar el hotel

▸**check up** *vi* asegurarse, cerciorarse; **to c. up on sb** hacer averiguaciones sobre alguien

checkbook ['tʃekbʊk] *n* talonario *m* (de cheques); **c. journalism** periodismo *m* de exclusivas (a golpe de talonario)

checkerboard ['tʃekəbɔ:d] *n* tablero *m* de damas *or* de ajedrez

checkered ['tʃekəd] *adj (pattern)* a cuadros; *Fig* **she's had a somewhat c. career** su trayectoria ha estado llena de altibajos

checkers ['tʃekəz] *npl* damas *fpl*

check-in ['tʃekɪn] *n Av* facturación *f*; **c. (desk)** mostrador *m* de facturación; **c. time** = hora a la que hay que facturar

checking account ['tʃekɪŋə'kaʊnt] *n* cuenta *f* corriente

checklist ['tʃeklɪst] *n* lista *f* de comprobaciones *or* de control

checkmate ['tʃekmeɪt] **1** *n (in chess)* jaque *m* mate
2 *vt (in chess)* dar jaque mate a; *Fig (opponent)* poner fuera de combate

checkout ['tʃekaʊt] *n (in supermarket)* (mostrador *m* de) caja *f*

checkpoint ['tʃekpɔɪnt] *n* control *m*

checkroom ['tʃekru:m] *n (for luggage)* consigna *f*

checkup ['tʃekʌp] *n Med* revisión *f* (médica), chequeo *m* (médico)

cheek [tʃi:k] *n* **(a)** *(of face)* mejilla *f*; **to dance c. to c.** bailar muy agarrados; **c. by jowl (with sb)** hombro con hombro (con alguien); *Fig* **to turn the other c.** poner la otra mejilla **(b)** *(buttock)* nalga *f* **(c)** *Fam (impudence)* cara *f*; **he's got a c.!** ¡qué cara tiene!, *Esp* ¡vaya morro!

cheekbone ['tʃi:kbəʊn] *n* pómulo *m*

cheeky ['tʃi:kɪ] *adj Fam* descarado(a)

cheep [tʃi:p] *vi (birds)* piar

cheer [tʃɪə(r)] **1** *n* **(a)** *(shout) (of crowd)* ovación *f*; *(of single person)* grito *m* de entusiasmo; **three cheers for Lidia!** ¡tres hurras por Lidia! **(b)** *Fam* **cheers!** *(when drinking)* ¡salud! **(c)** *Literary (mood)* **to be of good c.** estar de buen humor
2 *vt (applaud)* aclamar, vitorear; *(make happier)* animar
3 *vi (shout)* lanzar vítores, gritar de entusiasmo

▶**cheer on** *vt sep (support)* animar, vitorear

▶**cheer up 1** *vt sep (person)* animar; *(room)* alegrar
2 *vi* animarse; **c. up!** ¡anímate!

cheerful ['tʃɪəfʊl] *adj* alegre

cheerfully ['tʃɪəfʊlɪ] *adv* alegremente; *Fam* **I could c. strangle him!** ¡lo estrangularía con sumo gusto!

cheerily ['tʃɪərɪlɪ] *adv* jovialmente

cheerleader ['tʃɪəli:də(r)] *n* animadora *f*

cheerless ['tʃɪəlɪs] *adj* triste, sombrío(a)

cheery ['tʃɪərɪ] *adj* jovial, alegre

cheese [tʃi:z] *n* queso *m*; *Fam* **(say) c.!** *(for photograph)* ¡sonríe!, *Esp* ¡(di) patata!, *Méx* ¡(di) rojo!, *RP* ¡decí (whisky)!; **c. sandwich/omelet** sandwich *m*/tortilla *f* de queso

cheeseboard ['tʃi:zbɔ:d] *n (selection)* tabla *f* de quesos

cheeseburger ['tʃi:zbɜ:gə(r)] *n* hamburguesa *f* de *or* con queso

cheesecake ['tʃi:zkeɪk] *n* tarta *f* de queso

cheesy ['tʃi:zɪ] *n Fam Pej (inferior)* de tres al cuarto, *Esp* cutre

cheetah ['tʃi:tə] *n* guepardo *m*

chef [ʃef] *n* chef *m*, jefe(a) *m,f* de cocina

chemical ['kemɪkəl] **1** *n* producto *m* químico
2 *adj* químico(a); **c. warfare** guerra *f* química; **c. weapons** armas *fpl* químicas

chemist ['kemɪst] *n (scientist)* químico(a) *m,f*

chemistry ['kemɪstrɪ] *n* química *f*; *Fig* **there was a certain c. between them** entre ambos había una cierta química

chemotherapy ['ki:məʊ'θerəpɪ] *n Med* quimioterapia *f*

cherish ['tʃerɪʃ] *vt (person)* querer, tener mucho cariño a; *(possessions)* apreciar; *(hopes, illusion)* albergar; *(memory)* atesorar

cherry ['tʃerɪ] *n (fruit)* cereza *f*; **c. orchard** cerezal *m*; **c. tree** cerezo *m*

cherub ['tʃerəb] *(pl* **cherubs** *or* **cherubim** ['tʃerəbɪm]) *n* querubín *m*

chess [tʃes] *n* ajedrez *m*; **a game of c.** una partida de ajedrez; **c. player** ajedrecista *mf*, jugador(ora) *m,f* de ajedrez

chessboard ['tʃesbɔ:d] *n* tablero *m* de ajedrez

chessman ['tʃesmæn], **chesspiece** ['tʃespi:s] *n* pieza *f* (de ajedrez)

chest [tʃest] *n* **(a)** *(of person)* pecho *m*; *Fig* **I needed to get it off my c.** necesitaba desahogarme **(b)** *(box)* baúl *m*; **c. of drawers** cómoda *f*

chestnut ['tʃesnʌt] **1** *n (nut)* castaña *f*; *(tree, wood)* castaño *m*; **horse c. (tree)** castaño de Indias; *Fam* **an old c.** un chiste viejísimo
2 *adj (hair, horse)* castaño(a)

chew [tʃu:] *vt* masticar; **to c. one's nails** morderse las uñas

▶**chew over** *vt sep Fam* rumiar

chewing gum ['tʃu:ɪŋ'gʌm] *n* chicle *m*

chewy ['tʃu:ɪ] *adj (meat, bread)* correoso(a); *(sweet)* gomoso(a), correoso(a)

chic [ʃi:k] *adj* chic, elegante

Chicago [ʃɪ'kɑ:gəʊ] *n* Chicago

Chicana [tʃɪ'kɑ:nə] *n* chicana *f*

Chicano [tʃɪ'kɑ:nəʊ] *n* chicano *m*

chick [tʃɪk] *n* **(a)** *(young bird)* polluelo *m*; *(young chicken)* pollito *m* **(b)** *Fam (woman)* nena *f*, *Arg* piba *f*, *Méx* chava *f*

chicken ['tʃɪkɪn] **1** *n* **(a)** *(bird)* gallina *f*; *(meat)* pollo *m*; *Prov* **don't count your chickens before they are hatched** no cantes victoria antes de tiempo; **c. feed** *(food)* grano *m*; *Fam Fig (insignificant sum)* calderilla *f*; **c. pox** varicela *f* **(b)** *Fam (coward)* gallina *mf*, *Esp* miedica *mf*
2 *adj Fam (cowardly) (action)* cobarde; **to be c.** ser un/una gallina

▶**chicken out** *vi Fam* amilanarse, acoquinarse, *Méx* ciscarse, *RP* achicarse; **to c. out of (doing) sth** amilanarse ante (la idea de hacer) algo

chickpea ['tʃɪkpi:] *n* garbanzo *m*

chicory ['tʃɪkərɪ] *n* achicoria *f*

chide [tʃaɪd] *(pt* **chided** *or* **chid** [tʃɪd], *pp* **chided** *or* **chidden** ['tʃɪdən]) *vt Literary* reprender, regañar

chief [tʃi:f] **1** *n (of tribe)* jefe(a) *m,f*; *Fam* **the c.** *(boss)* el/la jefe(a)
2 *adj (most important)* principal; *Com* **c. executive officer** consejero(a) *m,f* delegado(a), director(ora) *m,f* gerente; *Com* **c. financial officer** director(ora) *m,f* financiero(a); *Law* **c. justice** = presidente del Tribunal Supremo

chiefly ['tʃi:flɪ] *adv* principalmente

chieftain ['tʃi:ftən] *n (of clan)* jefe *m* (del clan)

chiffon ['ʃɪfɒn] *n* gasa *f*; **c. scarf** fular *m*

chihuahua [tʃɪ'wɑ:wə] *n (perro m)* chihuahua *m*

chilblain ['tʃɪlbleɪn] *n* sabañón *m*

child [tʃaɪld] *(pl* **children** ['tʃɪldrən]) *n* niño(a) *m,f*; *(son)* hijo *m*; *(daughter)* hija *f*; **they have three children** tienen tres hijos; **it's c.'s play** es un juego de niños; **children's literature** literatura *f* infantil; **c. abuse** = malos tratos y/o agresión sexual a menores; **c. care** cuidado *m* de menores *or* niños; **c. labor** trabajo *m* de menores; **c. poverty** pobreza *f* infantil

child-bearing ['tʃaɪldbeərɪŋ] *n* maternidad *f*; **of c. age** en edad de tener hijos

childbirth ['tʃaɪldbɜ:θ] *n* parto *m*; **to die in c.** morir al dar a luz, morir en el parto

child-friendly ['tʃaɪld'frendlɪ] *adj* **a c. restaurant** un restaurante en el que están bienvenidos los niños

childhood ['tʃaɪldhʊd] *n* infancia *f*

childish ['tʃaɪldɪʃ] *adj Pej* pueril, infantil

childless ['tʃaɪldlɪs] *adj* **to be c.** no tener hijos; **a c. couple** una pareja sin hijos

childlike ['tʃaɪldlaɪk] *adj (innocence)* infantil; *(appearance)* aniñado(a)

childproof ['tʃaɪldpruːf] *adj* **c. bottle** = botella que los niños no pueden abrir; **c. lock** *(in car)* cierre *m* de seguridad a prueba de niños

children *pl of* **child**

Chile ['tʃɪlɪ] *n* Chile

Chilean ['tʃɪlɪən] *n & adj* chileno(a) *m,f*

chill [tʃɪl] **1** *n* **(a)** *Med (cold)* resfriado *m*; **to catch a c.** resfriarse, agarrar *or Esp* coger un resfriado **(b)** *(cold temperature)* **there's a c. in the air** hace bastante fresco; **to take the c. off sth** templar algo; *Fig* **c. of fear** escalofrío *m* de temor

2 *adj* frío(a)

3 *vt (wine, food)* poner a enfriar; **serve chilled** *(on product)* sírvase frío; **chilled to the bone** helado(a) de frío

▸**chill out** *vi Fam* relajarse, estar tranqui

chilli ['tʃɪlɪ] *n* **c. (pepper)** chile *m, Esp* guindilla *f, Andes, RP* ají *m*; **c. (con carne)** = guiso picante de carne picada y alubias rojas; **c. powder** guindilla *or* chile en polvo

chilling ['tʃɪlɪŋ] *adj (frightening)* escalofriante

chilly ['tʃɪlɪ] *adj* **(a)** *(cold)* frío(a); **it's a bit c. out** hace bastante fresco fuera **(b)** *(unfriendly)* frío(a)

chime [tʃaɪm] **1** *n (of bells)* carillón *m; (of clock)* campanada *f*

2 *vt* **the clock chimed nine o'clock** el reloj dio las nueve

3 *vi (clock)* dar la hora; *(bells)* repicar

▸**chime in** *vi Fam (in conversation)* meter baza *or Méx, RP* la cuchara; **they all chimed in at once** se pusieron todos a hablar a la vez

chimney ['tʃɪmnɪ] *n* chimenea *f; Fam* **to smoke like a c.** *(person)* fumar como un carretero *or Méx* un chacuaco *or RP* un escuerzo; **c. pot** (cañón *m* exterior de) chimenea *f*; **c. sweep** deshollinador(ora) *m,f*

chimpanzee [tʃɪmpæn'ziː], *Fam* **chimp** [tʃɪmp] *n* chimpancé *m*

chin [tʃɪn] *n* mentón *m*, barbilla *f; Fig* **to keep one's chin up** mantener los ánimos; *Fam* **to have a c. wag** charlar, *CAm, Méx* platicar

China ['tʃaɪnə] *n* China

china ['tʃaɪnə] *n* porcelana *f*; **c. clay** caolín *m*

Chinese [tʃaɪ'niːz] **1** *n* **(a)** *(person)* chino(a) *m,f* **(b)** *(language)* chino *m*

2 *npl* **the C.** los chinos

3 *adj* chino(a)

chink¹ [tʃɪŋk] *n (gap)* resquicio *m; Fig* **to find a c. in sb's armor** encontrar el punto flaco de alguien

chink² **1** *n (sound)* tintineo *m*

2 *vt (glasses)* entrechocar

3 *vi* tintinear

chintz [tʃɪnts] *n (textile)* cretona *f* satinada

chip [tʃɪp] **1** *n* **(a)** *(of wood)* viruta *f; (of marble)* lasca *f; (out of plate, cup)* mella *f*, desportilladura *f*; **chocolate chips** trozos *mpl* de chocolate **(b)** *(food)* **(potato) chips** *(crisps) Esp* patatas *fpl or Am* papas *fpl* fritas *(de bolsa)* **(c)** *(in card games)* ficha *f* **(d)** *Comptr* chip *m*, pastilla *f* **(e)** *(idioms)* **he's a c. off the old block** de tal palo, tal astilla; **to have a c. on one's shoulder (about sth)** tener complejo (por algo); *Fam* **when the chips are down** en los momentos difíciles

2 *vt (pt & pp* **chipped)** **(a)** *(cut at)* tallar; *(damage) (knife)* mellar; *(plate)* mellar, desportillar; *(furniture)* astillar; **to c. one's tooth** mellarse un diente **(b)** *(in soccer) (ball)* picar; *(in golf)* dar un golpe corto con la cucharilla a

3 *vi (plate, cup)* mellarse, desportillarse

▸**chip in** *vi Fam (in collection of money)* poner algo (de dinero); **to c. in with a suggestion** *(in discussion)* aportar alguna sugerencia

chipboard ['tʃɪpbɔːd] *n* aglomerado *m*

chipmunk ['tʃɪpmʌŋk] *n* ardilla *f* listada

chippy, chippie ['tʃɪpɪ] *adj (aggressive)* irritable

chiropodist [kɪ'rɒpədɪst] *n* podólogo(a) *m,f, Am* podiatra *mf*

chiropody [kɪ'rɒpədɪ] *n* podología *f*

chirp [tʃɜːp], **chirrup** ['tʃɪrəp] **1** *n (of birds)* trino *m; (of grasshopper)* chirrido *m*

2 *vi (bird)* trinar; *(grasshopper)* chirriar

chirpy ['tʃɜːpɪ] *adj* alegre, jovial

chirrup = **chirp**

chisel ['tʃɪzəl] **1** *n (for wood)* formón *m; (for stone)* cincel *m*

2 *vt* **(a)** *(in woodwork, sculpture)* tallar **(b)** *Fam (cheat)* **to c. sb out of his money** estafar a alguien

chit [tʃɪt] *n (note)* nota *f*

chitchat ['tʃɪtʃæt] *n Fam* charla *f*, cháchara *f, CAm, Méx* plática *f*

chivalrous ['ʃɪvəlrəs] *adj* caballeroso(a)

chivalry ['ʃɪvəlrɪ] *n (courteous behavior)* caballerosidad *f; Hist* caballería *f*

chives [tʃaɪvz] *npl* cebollinos *mpl*

chloride ['klɔːraɪd] *n Chem* cloruro *m*

chlorinate ['klɔːrɪneɪt] *vt* clorar

chlorine ['klɔːriːn] *n Chem* cloro *m*

chloroform ['klɒrəfɔːm] *n Chem* cloroformo *m*

chlorophyl(l) ['klɒrəfɪl] *n Biol* clorofila *f*

chock [tʃɒk] *n (for wheel of car, plane)* calzo *m*

chockablock ['tʃɒkə'blɒk] *adj Fam* abarrotado(a) (**with** de)

chocolate ['tʃɒklət] **1** *n* chocolate *m*; **a c.** *(sweet)* un bombón; **bar of c.** tableta *f* de chocolate; **hot** *or* **drinking c.** chocolate a la taza *or* caliente

2 *adj (made of chocolate)* de chocolate; **c. (colored)** marrón oscuro, color chocolate

choice [tʃɔɪs] **1** *n* **(a)** *(act, thing chosen)* elección *f*; **to make** *or* **take one's c.** elegir, escoger; **by c.** por (propia) elección **(b)** *(alternative)* alternativa *f*, opción *f*; **you have no c. in the matter** no tienes otra opción; **we had no c. but to do it** no tuvimos más remedio que hacerlo **(c)** *(selection)* selección *f*, surtido *m*; **there isn't much c.** no hay mucho donde elegir; **available in a wide c. of colors** disponible en una amplia gama de colores

2 *adj* **(a)** *(well chosen)* escogido(a); **she used some c. language** *(offensive)* soltó unas cuantas lindezas **(b)** *(food, wine)* selecto(a)

choir ['kwaɪə(r)] *n* coro *m*

choirboy ['kwaɪəbɔɪ] *n* niño *m* de coro

choke [tʃəʊk] **1** *n Aut* estrangulador *m*, estárter *m*

2 *vt* **(a)** *(strangle)* ahogar, estrangular **(b)** *(block) (sink)* atascar; **the roads were choked with traffic** las carreteras estaban atascadas *or* colapsadas de tráfico

3 *vi* ahogarse; **she choked on a fish bone** se atragantó con una espina; **to c. with anger** ponerse rojo(a) de ira

▸**choke back** *vt sep (tears, words, anger)* contener

choked ['tʃəʊkt] *adj Fam (emotional)* conmovido(a), emocionado(a); **I was really c. at the wedding** me emocioné mucho en la boda

cholera ['kɒlərə] *n* cólera *m*

cholesterol [kɒ'lestərɒl] *n* colesterol *m*

chomp [tʃɒmp] *vt & vi* masticar, mascar

choose [tʃuːz] *(pt* **chose** [tʃəʊz], *pp* **chosen** ['tʃəʊzən]) **1** *vt* elegir, escoger; **to c. to do sth** decidir hacer algo; **there's not much to c. between them** no es fácil escoger entre los dos

2 *vi* elegir, escoger; **I'll do as I c.** haré lo que me parezca

choosy ['tʃuːzɪ] *adj Fam* exigente (**about** con)

chop [tʃɒp] **1** *n* **(a)** *(with ax)* hachazo *m* **(b)** *(of lamb, pork)* chuleta *f*

2 *vt (pt & pp* **chopped)** *(wood)* cortar; *(meat)* trocear; *(vegetables)* picar

▶**chop down** *vt sep (tree)* derribar, talar

▶**chop off** *vt sep* cortar; **to c. sb's head off** cortale a alguien la cabeza

chopper ['tʃɒpə(r)] *n* (**a**) *(for meat)* tajadera *f* (**b**) *Fam (helicopter)* helicóptero *m*

chopping ['tʃɒpɪŋ] *n* **c. block** *(butcher's)* tajo *m*, tajadera *f*; **c. board** tabla *f* (para cortar)

choppy ['tʃɒpɪ] *adj (sea, lake)* picado(a); **to be c.** estar picado(a)

chopsticks ['tʃɒpstɪks] *npl* palillos *mpl*

choral ['kɔːrəl] *adj Mus* coral; **c. society** orfeón *m*, coral *f*

chord [kɔːd] *n* (**a**) *Mus* acorde *m*, *Fig* **her speech struck a c. with the electorate** su discurso caló hondo en el electorado (**b**) *Math (of arc)* cuerda *f*

chore [tʃɔː(r)] *n* **to do the chores** hacer las tareas; **what a c.!** ¡vaya lata!

choreograph ['kɒrɪəgræf] *vt* coreografiar

choreography [kɒrɪ'ɒgrəfɪ] *n* coreografía *f*

chorister ['kɒrɪstə(r)] *n* orfeonista *mf*, miembro *mf* de un coro

chortle ['tʃɔːtəl] **1** *n* risa *f* placentera
 2 *vi* reírse con placer

chorus ['kɔːrəs] **1** *n* *(of song)* estribillo *m*; *(group of singers, actors)* coro *m*; **in c.** a coro; **a c. of protest** un coro de protestas; **c. girl** corista *f*
 2 *vt* corear, decir a coro

chose [tʃəʊz] *pt of* **choose**

chosen ['tʃəʊzən] **1** *adj* escogido(a); **the c. few** los elegidos
 2 *pp of* **choose**

Christ [kraɪst] *n* Cristo; *Fam* **C. (Almighty)!** ¡Dios!

christen ['krɪsən] *vt* bautizar

christening ['krɪsənɪŋ] *n* bautizo *m*

Christian ['krɪstʃən] **1** *n* cristiano(a) *m,f*
 2 *adj* cristiano(a); **C. name** nombre *m* de pila

Christianity [krɪstɪ'ænɪtɪ] *n* cristianismo *m*

Christmas ['krɪsməs] *n* Navidad *f*, Navidades *fpl*; **at C.** en Navidad; **Merry** or **Happy C.!** ¡Feliz Navidad!; **C. cake** = pastel de Navidad a base de frutas; **C. card** tarjeta *f* de Navidad, *Esp* crismas *m*; **C. carol** villancico *m*; **C. Day** día *m* de Navidad; **C. dinner** comida *f* de Navidad; **C. Eve** Nochebuena *f*; **C. present** regalo *m* de Navidad; **C. pudding** = pudín con pasas y otras frutas típico de Navidad; **C. tree** árbol *m* de Navidad

chrome [krəʊm] *adj* cromado(a)

chromium ['krəʊmɪəm] **1** *n* *Chem* cromo *m*
 2 *adj* de cromo

chromosome ['krəʊməsəʊm] *n* *Biol* cromosoma *m*

chronic ['krɒnɪk] *adj (invalid, ill-health)* crónico(a); **c. unemployment** desempleo *m* crónico, *Esp* paro *m* estructural, *Am* desocupación *f* crónica

chronicle ['krɒnɪkəl] **1** *n* crónica *f*
 2 *vt* relatar, dar cuenta de

chronicler ['krɒnɪklə(r)] *n* cronista *mf*

chronological [krɒnə'lɒdʒɪkəl] *adj* cronológico(a)

chronology [krə'nɒlədʒɪ] *n* cronología *f*

chrysalis ['krɪsəlɪs] *n* *Zool* pupa *f*, crisálida *f*

chrysanthemum [krɪ'sænθəməm] *n* crisantemo *m*

chubby ['tʃʌbɪ] *adj* rechoncho(a); **c.-cheeked** mofletudo(a)

chuck [tʃʌk] *vt Fam* (**a**) *(throw)* tirar, *Am* botar (**b**) *(finish relationship with)* cortar con, *Andes, CAm, Carib* botar a

▶**chuck away** *vt sep Fam* tirar (a la basura), *Am* botar; *Fig (opportunity)* desperdiciar

▶**chuck out** *vt sep Fam (throw away)* tirar, *Am* botar; *(eject from bar, house)* echar

chuckle ['tʃʌkəl] **1** *n* risita *f*
 2 *vi* reírse por lo bajo

chug [tʃʌg] *(pt & pp* **chugged)** *vi* **the train chugged up the hill** el tren resollaba cuesta arriba; *Fam* **he's still chugging along in the same job** sigue tirando con el mismo trabajo

chum [tʃʌm] *n Fam* amiguete(a) *m,f*

chummy ['tʃʌmɪ] *adj Fam* **to be c. with sb** ir de amiguete(a) con alguien

chump [tʃʌmp] *n Fam (foolish person)* zoquete *mf*

chunk [tʃʌŋk] *n* trozo *m*

chunky ['tʃʌŋkɪ] *adj Fam (person)* fortachón(ona), *Esp* cuadrado(a)

church [tʃɜːtʃ] *n* iglesia *f*; **to go to c.** ir a misa

churchgoer ['tʃɜːtʃgəʊə(r)] *n* **to be a c.** ser cristiano(a) practicante

churchyard ['tʃɜːtʃjɑːd] *n* *(burial ground)* cementerio *m*, camposanto *m* *(de iglesia)*

churlish ['tʃɜːlɪʃ] *adj* grosero(a)

churn [tʃɜːn] **1** *n* *(for making butter)* mantequera *f*
 2 *vt (butter)* batir; **the propeller churned up the water** la hélice agitaba el agua
 3 *vi* **my stomach's churning** *(because of nervousness)* tengo un nudo en el estómago

▶**churn out** *vt sep Fam* **he churns out four novels a year** escribe como una máquina cuatro novelas al año

chute [ʃuːt] *n* (**a**) *(for parcels, coal)* rampa *f*; **(garbage) c.** colector *m* de basuras (**b**) *(in swimming pool, playground)* tobogán *m*; **chutes and ladders** ≃ el juego de la oca (**c**) *Fam (parachute)* paracaídas *m inv*

chutney ['tʃʌtnɪ] *n* = salsa agridulce y picante a base de fruta

chutzpah ['hʊtspə] *n Fam* descaro *m*, frescura *f*

CIA [siːaɪ'eɪ] *n (abbr* **Central Intelligence Agency)** CIA *f*, Agencia *f* Central de Inteligencia

ciabatta [tʃə'bɑːtə] *n* ciabatta *f*

cicada [sɪ'kɑːdə] *n (insect)* cigarra *f*, chicharra *f*

cider ['saɪdə(r)] *n* sidra *f*; **c. apple** manzana *f* sidrera; **c. vinegar** vinagre *m* de sidra

cigar [sɪ'gɑː(r)] *n (cigarro m)* puro *m*; **c. butt** colilla *f* de puro; **c. store** ≃ estanco *m*

cigarette, cigaret [sɪgə'ret] *n* cigarrillo *m*; **c. ash** ceniza *f* (de cigarrillo); **c. butt** colilla *f*, *Am* pucho *m*; **c. case** pitillera *f*; **c. end** colilla *f*, *Am* pucho *m*; **c. holder** boquilla *f*; **c. lighter** encendedor *m*, *Esp* mechero *m*; **c. machine** máquina *f* (expendedora) de tabaco; **c. packet** paquete *m* de cigarrillos *or* tabaco, *RP* atado *m*; **c. paper** papel *m* de fumar, *Andes* mortaja *f*

cilantro [sɪ'læntrəʊ] *n* cilantro *m*

C-in-C [siːɪn'siː] *n Mil (abbr* **Commander in Chief)** comandante *m* en jefe

cinch [sɪntʃ] *n Fam* **it's a c.** es pan comido

cinder ['sɪndə(r)] *n* **cinders** cenizas *fpl*; **burned to a c.** completamente carbonizado(a)

Cinderella [sɪndə'relə] *n* Cenicienta *f*

cinema ['sɪnəmə] *n* cine *m*

cinematography [sɪnəmə'tɒgrəfɪ] *n* fotografía *f*

cinnamon ['sɪnəmən] *n* canela *f*

cipher ['saɪfə(r)] *n (code)* clave *f*, cifra *f*; *Fig* **he's a mere c.** es un don nadie

circa ['sɜːkə] *prep* hacia, circa

circle ['sɜːkəl] **1** *n* (**a**) *(shape)* círculo *m*; **to sit in a c.** sentarse en círculo; *Fig* **we're going around in circles** estamos dándole vueltas a lo mismo (**b**) *(movement)* **to come full c.** volver al punto de partida (**c**) *(in theater)* anfiteatro *m* (**d**) *(group)* círculo *m*; **c. of friends** círculo de amistades; **in certain circles** en determinados círculos
 2 *vt* (**a**) *(go around)* girar en torno de (**b**) *(surround)* rodear
 3 *vi (plane, birds)* volar en círculo, hacer círculos

circuit ['sɜːkɪt] *n* (**a**) *(electric)* circuito *m*; **c. breaker** cortacircuitos *m inv* (**b**) *(in motor racing)* circuito *m*

circuitous [sə'kjuːɪtəs] *adj (reasoning)* enrevesado(a); **we got**

there by a c. route dimos muchos rodeos para llegar

circular ['sɜːkjʊlə(r)] **1** n (letter, advertisement) circular f
2 adj (movement, argument) circular

circulate ['sɜːkjʊleɪt] **1** vt hacer circular
2 vi circular; (at party) alternar

circulation [sɜːkjʊ'leɪʃən] n (of air, blood, money) circulación f; (of newspaper) tirada f; **for internal c. only** (on document) para uso interno solamente; Med **to have poor c.** tener mala circulación; Fig **to be out of c.** (person) estar fuera de la circulación

circumcise ['sɜːkəmsaɪz] vt circuncidar

circumcision [sɜːkəm'sɪʒən] n circuncisión f; **female c.** ablación f del clítoris

circumference [sə'kʌmfərəns] n circunferencia f

circumflex ['sɜːkəmfleks] n acento m circunflejo

circumlocution [sɜːkəmlə'kjuːʃən] n circunloquio m

circumnavigate [sɜːkəm'nævɪgeɪt] vt circunnavegar

circumscribe ['sɜːkəmskraɪb] vt (limit) restringir, circunscribir

circumspect ['sɜːkəmspekt] adj circunspecto(a), Esp comedido(a)

circumstance ['sɜːkəmstəns] n (situation) circunstancia f; **in** or **under the circumstances** dadas las circunstancias; **in** or **under no circumstances** en ningún caso; **due to circumstances beyond our control** debido a circunstancias ajenas a nuestra voluntad

circumstantial [sɜːkəm'stænʃəl] adj **c. evidence** prueba f indiciaria

circumvent [sɜːkəm'vent] vt eludir

circus ['sɜːkəs] n circo m

cirrhosis [sɪ'rəʊsɪs] n Med cirrosis f inv; **c. of the liver** cirrosis hepática

CIS [siːaɪ'es] n (abbr **Commonwealth of Independent States**) CEI f

cistern ['sɪstən] n cisterna f

citadel ['sɪtədəl] n ciudadela f

citation [saɪ'teɪʃən] n (a) (from author) cita f (b) Mil mención f (de honor)

cite [saɪt] vt (quote) citar

citizen ['sɪtɪzən] n ciudadano(a) m,f; **citizens' band (radio)** (radio f de) banda f ciudadana or de radioaficionados

citizenship ['sɪtɪzənʃɪp] n ciudadanía f

citric acid ['sɪtrɪk'æsɪd] n ácido m cítrico

citrus ['sɪtrəs] n **c. fruit** cítrico m

city ['sɪtɪ] n ciudad f; **c. center** centro m urbano; **c. council** ayuntamiento m; **c. dweller** habitante mf de ciudad, urbanita mf; Journ **c. editor** redactor(ora) m,f de local; **c. hall** ayuntamiento m; **c. manager** administrador(ora) m,f municipal; **c. planner** urbanista mf

civic ['sɪvɪk] adj cívico(a); **to do one's c. duty** cumplir con la obligación de uno como ciudadano; **c. center** centro m cívico

civil ['sɪvəl] adj (a) (of society) civil; **c. aviation** aviación f civil; **c. defense** protección f civil; **c. disobedience** desobediencia f civil; **c. engineering** ingeniería f civil; **c. law** derecho m civil; **c. marriage** matrimonio m civil; **c. rights** derechos mpl civiles; **c. servant** funcionario(a) m,f; **the c. service** la administración (pública), el funcionariado; **c. war** guerra f civil; Hist **the (American) Civil War** la guerra civil or de secesión americana; **to have a c. wedding** casarse por lo civil (b) (polite) cortés

civilian [sɪ'vɪljən] n & adj civil mf

civility [sɪ'vɪlɪtɪ] n cortesía f

civilization [sɪvɪlaɪ'zeɪʃən] n civilización f

civilize ['sɪvɪlaɪz] vt civilizar

civilized ['sɪvɪlaɪzd] adj civilizado(a)

cl (abbr **centiliter**) cl, centilitro m

clad [klæd] **1** adj ataviado(a) (**in** de)
2 pt & pp of **clothe**

claim [kleɪm] **1** n (a) (for damages, compensation) reclamación f (**for** de); **wage c.** reivindicación f salarial; **to make** or **put in a c.** hacer or presentar una reclamación; **to make a c. on the insurance** dar parte al seguro; **I have many claims on my time** estoy muy ocupado; **he has a c. to the throne of France** tiene derechos sobre el trono de Francia; **his only c. to fame** su único título de gloria (b) (assertion) afirmación f; **she makes no c. to originality** no pretende ser original
2 vt (a) (as a right) reclamar; **to c. compensation/damages (from sb)** reclamar (a alguien) una compensación/daños y perjuicios; **to c. responsibility for sth** atribuirse la responsabilidad de algo (b) (assert) **to c. that...** afirmar que...; **he claims to be an expert** asegura ser un experto (c) (baggage) recoger; (lost property) reclamar; **the epidemic claimed thousands of lives** la epidemia segó miles de vidas

claimant ['kleɪmənt] n (to throne) aspirante mf, pretendiente mf; (for social security) solicitante mf; (for insurance) reclamante mf

clairvoyant [kleə'vɔɪənt] **1** n vidente mf
2 adj **to be c.** ser clarividente

clam [klæm] n almeja f

▶**clam up** (pt & pp **clammed**) vi Fam meterse uno en su concha, retraerse

clamber ['klæmbə(r)] vi trepar (**up** or **over** por)

clammy ['klæmɪ] adj (weather) húmedo(a); **his hands were c.** tenía las manos húmedas y frías

clamor ['klæmə(r)] **1** n (noise) griterío m, clamor m; (demands) demandas fpl (**for** de); **a c. of protest** una oleada de protestas
2 vi (make noise) clamar; **to c. for sth** (demand) clamar por algo

clamorous ['klæmərəs] adj (crowd) vociferante; (protest, complaint) vehemente

clamp [klæmp] **1** n (of vice) mordaza f, abrazadera f
2 vt sujetar (**to** a); (car) poner un cepo a

▶**clamp down on** vt insep Fam (people) tomar medidas contundentes contra; (tax evasion, violence) poner coto a

clampdown ['klæmpdaʊn] n medidas fpl contundentes (**on** contra)

clan [klæn] n clan m

clandestine [klæn'destɪn] adj clandestino(a)

clang [klæŋ] **1** n ruido m metálico, estrépito m
2 vi (bell) repicar; **the gate clanged shut** la verja se cerró con gran estrépito

clank ['klæŋk] **1** n sonido m metálico
2 vi **the chains clanked** las cadenas produjeron un sonido metálico

clap [klæp] **1** n (a) (with hands) **to give sb a c.** aplaudir a alguien (b) (noise) **a c. of thunder** el estampido de un trueno (c) very Fam (venereal disease) **the c.** la gonorrea
2 vt (pt & pp **clapped**) (a) (applaud) aplaudir; **to c. one's hands** dar palmadas; **to c. sb on the back** dar a alguien una palmada en la espalda (b) (put) **he clapped his hat on** se encasquetó el sombrero; Fam **to c. sb in prison** Esp enchironar a alguien, meter Méx en el bote or RP en cana a alguien; Fam **to c. eyes on sth/sb** ver algo/a alguien
3 vi (applaud) aplaudir

clapper ['klæpə(r)] n (of bell) badajo m

clapping ['klæpɪŋ] n (applause) aplausos mpl

claptrap ['klæptræp] n Fam majaderías fpl, Am huevadas fpl, Am pendejadas fpl

claret ['klærət] n burdeos m inv (tinto)

clarification [klærɪfɪ'keɪʃən] n aclaración f

clarify ['klærɪfaɪ] vt aclarar

clarinet [klærɪ'net] n clarinete m

clarinet(t)ist [klærɪ'netɪst] *n Mus* clarinetista *mf*

clarity ['klærɪtɪ] *n* claridad *f*

clash [klæʃ] **1** *n (of opinions)* discrepancia *f; (between people)* enfrentamiento *m,* choque *m;* **there have been clashes in the streets** ha habido enfrentamientos callejeros

2 *vi* **(a)** *(come into conflict)* enfrentarse **(with** con *or* a) **(b)** *(evidence, explanations)* contradecirse; **the wallpaper clashes with the carpet** el papel no pega con la moqueta **(c)** *(events)* **to c. with** coincidir con **(d)** *(metal objects)* entrechocar

clasp [klɑːsp] **1** *n (on necklace, handbag)* broche *m,* cierre *m;* **c. knife** navaja *f*

2 *vt (grip)* agarrar; *(embrace)* estrechar; **to c. sb's hand** agarrar a alguien de la mano

class [klɑːs] **1** *n (in school, category, social group)* clase *f;* **to be in a c. of one's own** constituir una clase aparte; *Fam* **to have a lot of c.** tener mucha clase; **c. struggle** lucha *f* de clases

2 *vt (classify)* clasificar **(as** como)

classic ['klæsɪk] **1** *adj* clásico(a); **a c. example** un ejemplo típico

2 *n* **(a)** *(book)* clásico *m* **(b)** *Sch Univ* **classics** (lenguas *fpl*) clásicas *fpl*

classical ['klæsɪkəl] *adj* clásico(a); **c. music** música *f* clásica

classification [klæsɪfɪ'keɪʃən] *n* clasificación *f*

classified ['klæsɪfaɪd] **1** *adj* **(a)** *(secret)* reservado(a) **(b) c. advertisements** *(in newspaper)* anuncios *mpl* por palabras

2 *n* **the classifieds** *(in newspaper)* los anuncios por palabras

classify ['klæsɪfaɪ] *vt* clasificar

classmate ['klɑːsmeɪt] *n* compañero(a) *m,f* de clase

classroom ['klɑːsruːm] *n* aula *f,* clase *f*

classy ['klɑːsɪ] *adj Fam* con clase, elegante

clatter ['klætə(r)] **1** *n* ruido *m,* estrépito *m*

2 *vi* **he clattered up the stairs** subió las escaleras con estrépito; **to c. about** *(person)* trastear, trapalear

clause [klɔːz] *n (of contract)* cláusula *f; (of sentence)* oración *f* (simple), cláusula *f*

claustrophobia [klɔːstrə'fəʊbɪə] *n* claustrofobia *f*

claustrophobic [klɔːstrə'fəʊbɪk] *adj* claustrofóbico(a)

clavichord ['klævɪkɔːd] *n Mus* clavicordio *m*

clavicle ['klævɪkəl] *n Anat* clavícula *f*

claw [klɔː] **1** *n (of animal, bird)* garra *f; (of crab, lobster)* pinza *f;* **c. hammer** martillo *m* de carpintero *or* de oreja

2 *vt (scratch)* arañar; *Fig* **to c. one's way to the top** lograr abrirse paso hasta la cima del éxito

▸**claw back** *vt (money)* recobrar, recuperar

clay [kleɪ] *n* arcilla *f; Sport* **c. court** *(for tennis)* pista *f* de tierra batida; **c. pigeon** plato *m;* **c. pigeon shooting** tiro *m* al plato

clean [kliːn] **1** *adj* **(a)** *(not dirty)* limpio(a); **he keeps his flat very c.** tiene su piso muy limpio; **a c. piece of paper** una hoja (de papel) en blanco; **a c. game** un juego limpio; **c. living** vida *f* sana; **to have a c. driver's license** no tener puntos de penalización en *Esp* el carné de conducir *or Am* la licencia para conducir **(b)** *(not obscene) (humor, joke)* sano(a); *(language)* correcto(a), sin tacos; **good c. fun** diversión *f* sana **(c)** *(clear) (shape, outline)* nítido(a); **to make a c. break with** *(separate completely)* romper radicalmente con

2 *adv* **(a)** *(completely)* **to cut c. through sth** hacer un corte a través de algo; *Fam* **I c. forgot** me olvidé completamente **(b)** *Fam* **to come c. (about sth)** decir la verdad *or* sincerarse (acerca de algo)

3 *vt* limpiar; **to c. one's teeth/hands** limpiarse los dientes/las manos

▸**clean out** *vt sep* **(a)** *(cupboard, room)* limpiar de arriba abajo **(b)** *Fam (rob)* desplumar; *(leave without money)* dejar *Esp* sin blanca *or Am* sin un centavo

▸**clean up 1** *vt sep* limpiar

2 *vi* **(a)** *(tidy up)* ordenar; *(wash oneself)* lavarse **(b)** *Fam (win money)* arrasar, ganar un pastón

clean-cut ['kliːn'kʌt] *adj (features)* nítido(a)

cleaner ['kliːnə(r)] *n (person)* limpiador(ora) *m,f; (substance)* producto *m* de limpieza; *Fam* **to take sb to the c.'s** *(cheat)* desplumar a alguien

cleaning ['kliːnɪŋ] *n* limpieza *f;* **c. lady** mujer *f or* señora *f* de la limpieza

cleanliness ['klenlɪnɪs] *n (of place)* limpieza *f; (of person)* higiene *f*

clean-living ['kliːn'lɪvɪŋ] *adj* sano(a), sin vicios

cleanly ['kliːnlɪ] *adv* limpiamente

cleanse [klenz] *vt* limpiar

cleanser ['klenzə(r)] *n* loción *f* limpiadora

clean-shaven ['kliːn'ʃeɪvən] *adj (man, face)* (bien) afeitado(a); **to be c.** *(just shaved)* estar bien afeitado(a); *(not having a beard)* no tener barba ni bigote

cleansing ['klenzɪŋ] *adj* limpiador(ora); **c. lotion** loción *f* limpiadora; **c. solution** *(for contact lenses)* solución *f* limpiadora

cleanup ['kliːnʌp] *n* limpieza *f*

clear [klɪə(r)] **1** *adj* **(a)** *(liquid, image, explanation)* claro(a); *(sky, road)* despejado(a); **all c.!** ¡no hay peligro!; **to be c.** *(image, explanation)* ser claro(a); *(sky, road)* estar despejado(a); **to have a c. conscience** tener la conciencia tranquila; **as c. as a bell** *(voice, sound)* perfectamente audible; **a c. profit** un beneficio neto; **a c. winner** un claro vencedor

(b) *(obvious)* claro(a); **to make it c. to sb that...** dejar bien claro a alguien que...; **it is c. that...** es evidente *or* está claro que...; **to make oneself c.** expresarse con claridad *or* claramente; **I wasn't c. what she meant** no me quedó claro lo que quería decir

(c) *(free)* **c. of** *(not touching)* despegado(a) de; *(at safe distance)* alejado(a) de; **when the plane is c. of the ground** cuando el avión haya despegado; **they are six points c. of their nearest rivals** les sacan seis puntos a sus inmediatos perseguidores

2 *adv* **to steer c. of sth/sb** evitar algo/a alguien; **stand c. of the doors!** ¡apártense de las puertas!

3 *vt* **(a)** *(road, area)* despejar; **to c. one's throat** carraspear; **to c. the table** recoger la mesa; **to c. a debt** saldar una deuda; **the police cleared the square of demonstrators** la policía despejó la plaza de manifestantes; *Fig* **to c. the decks** ponerse al día y finalizar los asuntos pendientes; *also Fig* **to c. the way (for sth)** abrir el camino (a algo); *Fig* **to c. the air** disipar los malentendidos

(b) *(exonerate)* eximir; *Law* absolver; **to c. sb of blame** eximir de culpa a alguien; **they campaigned to c. his name** hicieron una campaña para limpiar su nombre

(c) *(jump over)* **to c. a fence** sortear una valla

(d) *(authorize)* autorizar; *(plan, proposals)* aprobar; **we've been cleared for take-off** nos han dado permiso para el despegue *or Am* decolaje; **I'll need to c. it with the boss** necesito el visto bueno del jefe

4 *vi* **(a)** *(weather, sky)* despejarse **(b)** *(check)* **the check hasn't cleared yet** el cheque no ha sido compensado todavía

5 *n* **to be in the c.** *(not under suspicion)* estar fuera de sospecha; *(out of danger)* estar fuera de peligro

▸**clear away** *vt sep* quitar (de en medio)

▸**clear out 1** *vt sep (empty)* limpiar, ordenar

2 *vi Fam (leave)* largarse

▸**clear up 1** *vt sep* **(a)** *(room)* ordenar **(b)** *(doubt, misunderstanding, problem)* aclarar

2 *vi (weather)* despejarse

clearance ['klɪərəns] *n* **(a)** *Com* **reduced for c.** rebajado(a) por liquidación (de existencias); **c. sale** liquidación *f* (de existencias) **(b)** *(authorization)* autorización *f;* **to get c. to do sth** obtener autorización para hacer algo

clear-cut ['klɪə'kʌt] *adj* claro(a), inequívoco(a)

clear-headed ['klɪə'hedɪd] *adj* lúcido(a)

clearing ['klɪərɪŋ] *n (in forest)* claro *m*

clearinghouse ['klɪərɪŋhaʊs] *n Fin* cámara *f* de compensación

clearing-out ['klɪərɪŋaʊt] *n* **I need to give my desk a c.** tengo que limpiar *or* ordenar mi escritorio

clearly ['klɪəlɪ] *adv* **(a)** *(to see, explain, write)* claramente, con claridad **(b)** *(obviously)* claramente; **he is c. wrong** está claramente equivocado; **c.!** ¡sin duda!; **c. not!** ¡en absoluto!

clearness ['klɪənɪs] *n* claridad *f*

clear-sighted [klɪə'saɪtɪd] *adj (perceptive)* lúcido(a), clarividente

cleat [kli:t] *n (on shoe)* taco *m*

cleavage ['kli:vɪdʒ] *n* escote *m*

cleave [kli:v] *(pt* **cleaved** *or* **cleft** [kleft] *or* **clove** [kləʊv], *pp* **cleaved** *or* **cleft** *or* **cloven** [kləʊvən]) *vt Literary* hendir, partir en dos

▸**cleave to** *(pt & pp* **cleaved)** *vt insep Formal* aferrarse a

cleaver ['kli:və(r)] *n* cuchillo *m* de carnicero, tajadera *f*

clef [klef] *n Mus* clave *f*

cleft [kleft] **1** *n* grieta *f*, hendidura *f*
2 *adj* hendido(a); **to have a c. palate** tener fisura de paladar
3 *pt & pp of* **cleave**

clemency ['klemənsɪ] *n* clemencia *f*

clench [klentʃ] *vt (teeth, fist)* apretar

clergy ['klɜːdʒɪ] *n* clero *m*

clergyman ['klɜːdʒɪmən] *n* clérigo *m*

clergywoman ['klɜːdʒɪwʊmən] *n* mujer *f* sacerdote

cleric ['klerɪk] *n Rel* clérigo *m*

clerical ['klerɪkəl] *adj* **(a)** *(administrative)* **c. assistant** auxiliar *mf* administrativo(a); **c. work** trabajo *m* de oficina **(b)** *Rel* clerical

clerk [klɑːrk] *n (in office)* oficinista *mf*; *(in court)* oficial(ala) *m,f*, secretario(a) *m,f*; *(in store)* dependiente(a) *m,f*

clever ['klevə(r)] *adj (person, animal)* listo(a); *(plan, idea)* ingenioso(a); **she's very c. at mathematics** se le dan muy bien las matemáticas; **to be c. with one's hands** ser muy habilidoso(a), *Esp* ser un(a) manitas; *Fam* **she's too c. by half** se pasa de lista

cleverly ['klevəlɪ] *adv (intelligently)* inteligentemente; *(ingeniously)* ingeniosamente

cleverness ['klevənɪs] *n (of person, plan)* inteligencia *f*

cliché ['kli:ʃeɪ] *n* tópico *m*

clichéd ['kli:ʃeɪd] *adj* tópico(a); **a c. comment** *or* **remark** un tópico, un lugar común

click ['klɪk] **1** *n (sound) (of button)* clic *m*; *(of fingers, tongue)* chasquido *m*
2 *vt* **to c. one's heels** dar un taconazo; **to c. one's tongue** chasquear la lengua
3 *vi* **(a)** *(make a sound)* hacer clic **(b)** *Fam (idioms)* **suddenly it clicked** *(became obvious to me)* de pronto caí en la cuenta; **they clicked at once** *(got on)* se entendieron desde el primer momento

clickable image ['klɪkəbəl'ɪmɪdʒ] *n Comptr* imagen *f* interactiva

client ['klaɪənt] *n* cliente(a) *m,f*; **c. state** estado *m* satélite

clientele [kli:ɒn'tel] *n* clientela *f*

client-server database ['klaɪəntsɜːvə'deɪtəbeɪs] *n Comptr* base *f* de datos cliente/servidor

cliff [klɪf] *n* acantilado *m*

cliff-hanger ['klɪfhæŋə(r)] *n* **the movie was a real c.** la película tenía mucho *Esp* suspense *or Am* suspenso

climactic [klaɪ'mæktɪk] *adj* culminante

climate ['klaɪmət] *n* clima *m*

climatic [klaɪ'mætɪk] *adj* climático(a)

climax ['klaɪmæks] **1** *n (peak)* clímax *m inv*, momento *m* culminante; *(sexual)* orgasmo *m*
2 *vi* culminar

climb [klaɪm] **1** *n (up hill)* ascensión *f*, subida *f*; *(of mountaineer)* escalada *f*; **it's quite a c.** hay una buena subida
2 *vt (tree)* subir a, trepar a; *(mountain)* escalar
3 *vi (road, prices)* subir; **to c. over a wall** trepar por un muro

▸**climb down 1** *vt insep (descend)* bajar por
2 *vi* **(a)** *(descend)* descender, bajar **(b)** *Fig (in argument, conflict)* echarse atrás, dar marcha atrás

climber ['klaɪmə(r)] *n* **(a)** *(mountain climber)* alpinista *mf*, *Am* andinista *mf*; *(rock climber)* escalador(ora) *m,f* **(b)** *(plant)* (planta *f*) trepadora *f*

climbing ['klaɪmɪŋ] **1** *n (mountain climbing)* alpinismo *m*, *Am* andinismo *m*; *(rock climbing)* escalada *f*
2 *adj (plant)* trepador(ora)

clinch [klɪntʃ] **1** *n (of lovers, fighters)* abrazo *m*; **they were in a c.** estaban abrazados
2 *vt (settle) (deal)* cerrar; *(argument)* zanjar; **that clinches it!** ¡eso lo resuelve del todo!

cling [klɪŋ] *(pt & pp* **clung** [klʌŋ]) *vi* **to c. to** *(rope, person)* aferrarse a; *Fig* **to c. to an opinion** aferrarse a una idea

clingy ['klɪŋɪ] *adj* **(a)** *(child)* mimoso(a), pegajoso(a); *(boyfriend, girlfriend)* pegajoso(a), empalagoso(a) **(b)** *(clothes)* ceñido(a), ajustado(a)

clinic ['klɪnɪk] *n* clínica *f*

clinical ['klɪnɪkəl] *adj* **(a)** *Med* clínico(a) **(b)** *(unemotional)* aséptico(a)

clink[1] [klɪŋk] **1** *n (sound)* tintineo *m*
2 *vt* hacer tintinear; **to c. glasses (with sb)** brindar (con alguien)
3 *vi (glasses)* tintinear

clink[2] *n Fam (prison) Esp* trena *f*, *Esp* trullo *m*, *Andes, RP* cana *f*, *Méx* bote *m*

clip[1] [klɪp] **1** *n (for paper)* clip *m*, sujetapapeles *m inv*
2 *vt (pt & pp* **clipped)** *(attach)* sujetar (con un clip)
3 *vi* **the two pieces c. together** las dos piezas se acoplan

clip[2] **1** *n (of movie)* fragmento *m*; *(of program)* avance *m*
2 *(pt & pp* **clipped)** *vt (hair)* cortar; *(hedge)* podar; *(ticket)* picar; *Fig* **to c. sb's wings** cortar las alas a alguien

clipboard ['klɪpbɔːd] *n* carpeta *f* con sujetapapeles

clip-on ['klɪpɒn] *adj* **c. bow tie** *Esp* pajarita *f (de broche)*, *Méx* corbata *f* de moño *(de broche)*, *RP* moñito *m (de broche)*; **c. earrings** pendientes *mpl or Am* aretes *mpl* de clip; **c. microphone** micrófono *m* de solapa; **c. sunglasses** suplemento *m* (de sol), = gafas de sol para ponerse sobre las gafas graduadas

clipped [klɪpt] *adj (accent, tone)* entrecortado(a)

clipper ['klɪpə(r)] *n (ship)* clíper *m*

clippers ['klɪpəz] *npl (for hair)* maquinilla *f (para cortar el pelo)*; *(for nails)* cortaúñas *m inv*; *(for hedge)* podadera *f*, tijeras *fpl* de podar

clipping ['klɪpɪŋ] *n (from newspaper)* recorte *m*

clique [kli:k] *n* camarilla *f*, círculo *m*

cliquey ['kli:kɪ] *adj* exclusivista

clitoris ['klɪtərɪs] *n* clítoris *m inv*

cloak [kləʊk] **1** *n* capa *f*; *Fig* **under the c. of darkness** bajo el manto de la oscuridad
2 *vt Fig* **cloaked in secrecy** rodeado(a) de secreto

cloak-and-dagger [kləʊkən'dægə(r)] *adj (movie, book)* de intriga; **a c. affair** un asunto lleno de intrigas

cloakroom ['kləʊkru:m] *n (for coats, bags)* guardarropa *m*

clobber *vt Fam (hit)* sacudir; *(defeat)* dar una paliza a

clock [klɒk] **1** *n* **(a)** *(for telling the time)* reloj *m (grande o de pared)*; **to work round the c.** trabajar día y noche; **a race against the c.** una carrera contrarreloj; **to put the c. forward/back** adelantar/atrasar el reloj; *Fig* **to turn the c. back** retroceder en el tiempo; **c. radio** radio *f* despertador **(b)** *Fam (odometer)* ≃ cuentakilómetros *m inv*

2 vt *(measure speed of)* medir la velocidad de; *(reach speed of)* alcanzar

▶**clock in, clock on** vi *(at work)* fichar (a la entrada), *Am* marcar tarjeta (a la entrada)

▶**clock off, clock out** vi *(at work)* fichar (a la salida), *Am* marcar tarjeta (a la salida)

▶**clock on** = **clock in**

▶**clock out** = **clock off**

▶**clock up** vt sep *(votes, profits)* registrar; **this car has clocked up 10,000 miles** este coche or *Am* carro or *CSur* auto marca 10.000 millas

clockmaker ['klɒkmeɪkə(r)] n relojero(a) m,f

clockwise ['klɒkwaɪz] adv en el sentido de las agujas del reloj

clockwork ['klɒkwɜ:k] **1** n **to go like c.** marchar a la perfección
2 adj *(toy)* mecánico(a)

clod [klɒd] n **(a)** *(of earth)* terrón m **(b)** *Fam (stupid person)* lelo(a) m,f, *Esp* memo(a) m,f

clog [klɒg] **1** n *(shoe)* zueco m
2 vt bloquear, atascar
3 vi *(pt & pp* **clogged***)* bloquearse, atascarse

▶**clog up 1** vt bloquear, atascar
2 vi bloquearse, atascarse

cloister ['klɔɪstə(r)] n claustro m

cloistered ['klɔɪstəd] adj **to lead a c. life** no tener mucha relación con el mundo exterior

clone [kləʊn] **1** n clon m
2 vt *Biol* clonar

cloning ['kləʊnɪŋ] n *Biol* clonación f

close¹ [kləʊs] **1** adj **(a)** *(in distance, time, relationship)* cercano(a), próximo(a); *(contact, links, cooperation)* estrecho(a); **to be c.** estar cerca de; **to be c. to tears/victory** estar a punto de llorar/vencer; **to be c. to sb** *(friends)* tener mucha confianza con alguien; *(relatives)* estar muy unido(a) a alguien; **in c. proximity to** muy cerca de; **to be in c. contact with sb** tener mucho contacto con alguien; **a c. friend** un(a) amigo(a) íntimo; **a c. relative** un pariente cercano or próximo; **c. combat** combate m cuerpo a cuerpo; **that was a c. call** or **shave** ha faltado un pelo; **at c. quarters** de cerca; **he was shot at c. range** le dispararon or *Am* balearon a quemarropa
(b) *(inspection, attention)* cuidadoso(a); *(observer)* atento(a); **to keep a c. watch on sth/sb** vigilar de cerca algo/a alguien
(c) *(weather)* bochornoso(a); *(room)* cargado(a)
(d) *(contest, election, race)* reñido(a)
2 adv *(near)* cerca; **to hold sb c.** abrazar a alguien fuerte; **c. to** cerca de; **he lives c. to here** vive cerca de aquí; **to come c. to death** estar a punto de morir; **c. at hand** a mano; **to follow c. behind sb** seguir de cerca a alguien; **to be c. to fifty** estar cerca de los cincuenta

close² [kləʊz] **1** n *(end)* final m; **to draw to a c.** tocar or llegar a su fin; **to bring sth to a c.** poner término a or dar por terminado(a) algo
2 vt **(a)** *(door, eyes, shop)* cerrar; *Fig* **to c. ranks (around sb)** cerrar filas (en torno a alguien) **(b)** *(meeting, debate)* terminar; *(conference, Olympics)* clausurar; *(account)* cancelar; **to c. a deal** cerrar un trato
3 vi *(shop, door, business)* cerrar

▶**close down 1** vt sep *(production, operations)* cesar; *(business, factory)* cerrar (definitivamente)
2 vi *(business)* cerrar (definitivamente)

▶**close in** vi **to c. in on sb** ir cercando a alguien

▶**close up 1** vi **(a)** *(wound, hole)* cerrarse **(b)** *(shopkeeper)* cerrar
2 vt sep *(hole, shop)* cerrar

close-cropped ['kləʊs'krɒpt] adj *(hair)* al rape

closed [kləʊzd] adj cerrado(a); **c. circuit television** circuito m cerrado de televisión; **behind c. doors** a puerta cerrada; *Ind*

c. shop = centro de trabajo que emplea exclusivamente a trabajadores sindicados

close-fitting [kləʊs'fɪtɪŋ] adj ajustado(a)

close-knit [kləʊs'nɪt] adj *(community, group)* muy unido(a)

closely ['kləʊsli] adv **(a)** *(to examine, watch)* de cerca; **to listen c.** escuchar atentamente; **to c. resemble sb** parecerse mucho a alguien; **c. related/connected** íntimamente relacionado(a)/conectado(a); **c. contested** muy reñido(a) **(b)** *(populated)* densamente; **c. packed** apiñado(a)

closeness ['kləʊsnɪs] n *(physical nearness)* proximidad f, cercanía f; *(of relationship, contact)* intimidad f

close-set ['kləʊs'set] adj **to have c. eyes** tener los ojos muy juntos

closet ['klɒzɪt] **1** n *(small room)* habitación f pequeña; *Fig* **to come out of the c.** salir del armario
2 adj **c. gay** homosexual m no declarado; **she's a c. Julio Iglesias fan** le encanta Julio Iglesias, pero nunca lo confesaría
3 vt **to be closeted with sb** *(in meeting)* estar encerrado(a) con alguien

close-up ['kləʊsʌp] n primer plano m; **in c.** en primer plano

closing ['kləʊzɪŋ] n *(shutting)* cierre m; **c. date** fecha f límite; **c. prices** cotizaciones fpl al cierre; **c. speech/ceremony** discurso m/ceremonia f de clausura; **c. time** hora f de cierre

closure ['kləʊʒə(r)] n *(of company, shop)* cierre m; **the bereaved families need some sort of c.** *(feeling of completion)* los familiares de las víctimas necesitan llegar a un desenlace satisfactorio

clot [klɒt] **1** n *(of blood)* coágulo m
2 vi *(pt & pp* **clotted***)* *(blood)* coagularse

cloth [klɒθ] n **(a)** *(material)* tela f, tejido m; **a man of the c.** un ministro de Dios **(b)** *(individual piece)* trapo m

clothe [kləʊð] *(pt & pp* **clad** [klæd] or **clothed***)* vt vestir

clothes [kləʊðz] npl ropa f; **to put one's c. on** vestirse, ponerse la ropa; **to take one's c. off** quitarse or *Am* sacarse la ropa, desvestirse; **c. brush** cepillo m para la ropa

clotheshorse [kləʊðzhɔ:s] n tendedero m (plegable)

clothesline [kləʊðzlaɪn] n cuerda f de tender la ropa

clothespin [kləʊðzpɪn] n pinza f de la ropa

clothing ['kləʊðɪŋ] n *(clothes)* ropa f; **an article of c.** una prenda de vestir; **the c. industry** la industria del vestido

cloud [klaʊd] **1** n nube f; **to be under a c.** *(in disgrace)* haber caído en desgracia; **to have one's head in the clouds** estar en Babia; *Fam* **she is on c. nine** está más contenta que un chico con zapatos nuevos or *Esp* que unas castañuelas
2 vt **(a)** *(mirror)* empañar **(b)** *(obscure)* **the news clouded their happiness** las noticias enturbiaron su alegría; **to c. the issue** embrollar las cosas

▶**cloud over** vi *(sky)* nublarse

cloudburst ['klaʊdbɜ:st] n chaparrón m

cloudless ['klaʊdlɪs] adj despejado(a)

cloudy ['klaʊdɪ] adj **(a)** *(sky, day)* nublado(a) **(b)** *(liquid)* turbio(a)

clout [klaʊt] **1** n **(a)** *Fam (blow)* tortazo m, sopapo m; **to give sb a c.** dar a alguien un tortazo or sopapo **(b)** *(power, influence)* poder m, influencia f; **to have a lot of c.** ser muy influyente
2 vt *Fam (hit)* sacudir, *Esp* atizar, *RP* mandar

clove¹ [kləʊv] n *(of garlic)* diente m

clove² n *(spice)* clavo m

clove³ pt of **cleave**

cloven ['kləʊvən] **1** adj **c. hoof** pata f hendida
2 pp of **cleave**

clover ['kləʊvə(r)] n *(plant)* trébol m; *Fig* **to be in c.** vivir a cuerpo de rey

clown [klaʊn] **1** n *(in circus)* payaso m; **to act the c.** hacer el payaso
2 vi **to c. around** or **about** hacer el payaso

cloying ['klɔɪɪŋ] adj *(taste, smell)* empalagoso(a)

club [klʌb] **1** n **(a)** (society) club m; Fam Fig **join the c.!** ¡ya eres uno más!; **soccer/tennis c.** club de fútbol/tenis; **c. sandwich** sándwich m club; **c. soda** soda f **(b)** (nightclub) discoteca f, sala f (de fiestas) **(c)** (weapon) palo m, garrote m **(d)** (in golf) palo m **(e)** (in cards) **clubs** tréboles mpl; **ace of clubs** as m de tréboles

2 vt (pt & pp **clubbed**) (hit) apalear

►**club together** vi **to c. together (to buy sth)** poner dinero a escote (para comprar algo)

clubbing [ˈklʌbɪŋ] n **to go c.** ir de discotecas

clubhouse [ˈklʌbhaʊs] n = en unas instalaciones de golf, edificio en el que se encuentran los vestuarios y el bar

cluck [klʌk] **1** n cacareo m

2 vi cacarear

clue [kluː] n (in crime, mystery) pista f; (in crossword) definición f, pregunta f; **to give sb a c.** dar una pista a alguien; **he hasn't got a c.** no tiene ni idea

►**clue in** vt sep Fam **to be clued in (on sth)** estar muy puesto(a) (en algo)

clueless [ˈkluːlɪs] adj Fam **he's c. (about)** es un Esp negado or Méx desmadre or RP queso (para)

clump [klʌmp] **1** n **(a)** (of bushes) mata f; (of people) grupo m **(b)** (sound) **the c. of her footsteps** el ruido de sus pisotones

2 vi **to c. about** andar dando pisotones

clumsiness [ˈklʌmzɪnɪs] n torpeza f

clumsy [ˈklʌmzɪ] adj (person, movement) torpe

clung [klʌŋ] pt & pp of **cling**

clunk [klʌŋk] **1** n estrépito m

2 vi golpear estrepitosamente

cluster [ˈklʌstə(r)] **1** n (of flowers) ramo m; (of grapes) racimo m; (of people, islands, houses) grupo m; **c. bomb** bomba f de dispersión or fragmentación

2 vi **to c. around sth/sb** apiñarse en torno a algo/alguien

clutch[1] [klʌtʃ] **1** n **(a)** Aut embrague m; **to let the c. in** pisar el embrague, embragar; **to let the c. out** soltar el embrague, desembragar; **c. pedal** (pedal m de) embrague m **(b)** (grasp) **she had fallen into his clutches** ella había caído en sus garras **(c)** (critical situation) **to come through in the c.** tener éxito a la hora de la verdad

2 vt agarrar

3 vi **to c. at sth** agarrarse a algo; Fig **to c. at straws** agarrarse a un clavo ardiendo

clutch[2] n (of eggs) nidada f

clutter [ˈklʌtə(r)] **1** n desbarajuste m; **in a c.** revuelto(a)

2 vt **to be cluttered (up) with sth** estar abarrotado(a) de algo

cluttered [ˈclʌtəd] adj revuelto(a)

cm (abbr **centimeter(s)**) cm, centímetro m

C-note [ˈsiːnəʊt] n Fam billete m de cien dólares

CO [siːˈəʊ] (pl **COs**) n Mil (abbr **Commanding Officer**) oficial m al mando

Co, co [kəʊ] n Com (abbr **company**) cía, compañía f

c/o [siːˈəʊ] (abbr **care of**) en el domicilio de

coach [kəʊtʃ] **1** n **(a)** (bus) autobús m, Esp autocar m; (horse-drawn carriage) coche m de caballos, diligencia f; (section of train) vagón m; **c. class** (on plane) clase f turista; **c. party** grupo m de viajeros en autobús **(b)** (of athlete, team) entrenador(ora) m,f

2 vt (athlete, team) entrenar; **to c. sb for an exam** ayudar a alguien a preparar un examen

coachbuilder [ˈkəʊtʃbɪldə(r)] n Aut carrocero(a) m,f

coachload [ˈkəʊtʃləʊd] n **a c. of tourists** un autobús (lleno) de turistas

coagulant [kəʊˈægjʊlənt] n Med coagulante m

coagulate [kəʊˈægjʊleɪt] vi coagularse

coal [kəʊl] n **(a)** carbón m; **a lump of c.** un trozo de carbón; **c. bunker** carbonera f; **c. dealer** carbonero(a) m,f; **c. mine**

mina f de carbón; **c. miner** minero(a) m,f (del carbón); **c. mining** minería f del carbón; **c. tar** alquitrán m mineral **(b)** (idioms) **to carry coals to Newcastle** ir a vendimiar y llevar uvas de postre; **to haul sb over the coals** echar una regañina or Esp una bronca a alguien

coalesce [kəʊəˈles] vi (views, interests) fundirse; (movements, groups) coaligarse

coalfield [ˈkəʊlfiːld] n yacimiento m de carbón; (large region) cuenca f carbonífera

coalition [kəʊəˈlɪʃən] n coalición f; **to form a c.** formar una coalición

coalman [ˈkəʊlmæn] n carbonero m

coarse [kɔːs] adj **(a)** (person, language) grosero(a), basto(a) **(b)** (surface, texture) áspero(a); **to have c. hair** tener el pelo basto

coarsely [ˈkɔːslɪ] adv **(a)** (vulgarly) groseramente **(b)** (roughly) **c. chopped** cortado(a) en trozos grandes; **c. ground** molido(a) grueso(a)

coarseness [ˈkɔːsnɪs] n **(a)** (of person, language) grosería f **(b)** (of surface, texture) aspereza f

coast [kəʊst] **1** n costa f; Fig **the c. is clear** no hay moros en la costa; **C. Guard** guardacostas mf inv

2 vi (in car) rodar en punto muerto; (on bicycle) rodar sin pedalear; Fig **she coasted through her exams** pasó sus exámenes con toda facilidad

coastal [ˈkəʊstəl] adj costero(a)

coaster [ˈkəʊstə(r)] n **(a)** (ship) buque m de cabotaje **(b)** (for glass) posavasos m inv

coastline [ˈkəʊstlaɪn] n costa f, litoral m

coast-to-coast [ˈkəʊsttəˈkəʊst] adj de costa a costa

coat [kəʊt] **1** n **(a)** (overcoat) abrigo m; (jacket) chaqueta f, Méx chamarra f, RP campera f; **c. hanger** percha f; **c. hook** colgador m **(b)** (of dog, horse) pelaje m **(c)** (of snow, paint) capa f **(d)** (in heraldry) **c. of arms** escudo m de armas

2 vt cubrir (**with** de); **coated with mud** cubierto(a) de barro, embarrado(a); **hazelnuts coated with chocolate** avellanas recubiertas de chocolate

coating [ˈkəʊtɪŋ] n (of paint, dust) capa f

coattails [ˈkəʊteɪlz] npl frac m; Fig **on sb's c.** a la sombra de alguien

coauthor [kəʊˈɔːθə(r)] **1** n coautor(ora) m,f

2 vt **to c. a book with sb** escribir un libro conjuntamente con alguien

coax [kəʊks] vt persuadir; **to c. sb into doing sth** persuadir a alguien para que haga algo; **to c. sth out of sb** sonsacar algo a alguien

cob [kɒb] n **(a)** (horse) jaca f **(b)** (of corn) mazorca f

cobalt [ˈkəʊbɔːlt] n Chem cobalto m; **c. blue** azul m cobalto

cobble [ˈkɒbəl] **1** n adoquín m

2 vt adoquinar

►**cobble together** vt sep (make hastily) improvisar, Esp apañar

cobbled [ˈkɒbəld] adj (path, street) adoquinado(a)

cobbler [ˈkɒblə(r)] n zapatero m (remendón)

COBOL, Cobol [ˈkəʊbɒl] n Comptr (abbr **Common Business Oriented Language**) (lenguaje m) COBOL m

cobra [ˈkəʊbrə] n cobra f

cobweb [ˈkɒbweb] n telaraña f; Fig **to brush the cobwebs off sth** desempolvar algo

cocaine [kəˈkeɪn] n cocaína f

coccyx [ˈkɒksɪks] n coxis m

cock [kɒk] **1** n **(a)** (male fowl) gallo m **(b)** Vulg (penis) Esp polla f, esp Am verga f, Chile pico m, Méx pito m, RP pija f

2 vt (gun) montar, amartillar; **to c. a snook at sb** hacer burla a alguien; **to c. its ears** (horse, dog) aguzar las orejas

cockade [kɒˈkeɪd] n escarapela f

cock-a-doodle-doo [ˈkɒkəduːdəlˈduː] exclam ¡quiquiriquí!

cock-a-hoop ['kɒkə'huːp] *adj* **he was c. about the result** estaba encantado con el resultado

cock-and-bull story ['kɒkən'bʊlstɔːrɪ] *n Fam* cuento *m* chino

cockatoo [kɒkə'tuː] (*pl* **cockatoos**) *n* cacatúa *f*

cockcrow ['kɒkkrəʊ] *n Literary* **at c.** al amanecer

cocked [kɒkt] *adj* **to knock sb into a c. hat** (*outclass*) dar mil *or* cien vueltas a alguien

cockerel ['kɒkərəl] *n* gallo *m* joven

cocker spaniel ['kɒkə'spænjəl] *n* cocker *mf*

cockeyed ['kɒkaɪd] *adj Fam* (*decision, plan*) disparatado(a)

cockfight ['kɒkfaɪt] *n* pelea *f* de gallos

cockiness ['kɒkɪnɪs] *n* descaro *m*, engreimiento *m*, *Esp* chulería *f*

cockle ['kɒkəl] *n* (**a**) (*shellfish*) berberecho *m* (**b**) *Fam* **it warmed the cockles of his heart** le alegró el corazón

Cockney ['kɒknɪ] **1** *n* (*person*) = habitante de los barrios obreros del este de Londres; (*dialect*) = habla de los barrios obreros del este de Londres
2 *adj* = de los barrios obreros del este de Londres

cockpit ['kɒkpɪt] *n* (*of passenger plane*) cabina *f*; (*of fighter plane*) carlinga *f*

cockroach ['kɒkrəʊtʃ] *n* cucaracha *f*

cocksure ['kɒk'ʃʊə(r)] *adj* (*person, manner*) arrogante

cocktail ['kɒkteɪl] *n also Fig* cóctel *m*; **c. bar** coctelería *f*, bar *m* de cócteles; **c. dress** vestido *m* de noche; **c. lounge** bar *m* (*de hotel*); **c. party** cóctel *m*; **c. shaker** coctelera *f*; **c. stick** palillo *m*

cocky ['kɒkɪ] *adj Fam* gallito(a), engreído(a), *Esp* chulo(a)

cocoa ['kəʊkəʊ] *n* (*powder, drink*) cacao *m*; **c. bean** semilla *f* or grano *m* de cacao; **c. butter** crema *f* de cacao

coconut ['kəʊkənʌt] *n* (*fruit*) coco *m*; **c. milk** leche *f* de coco; **c. palm** cocotero *m*

cocoon [kə'kuːn] **1** *n* capullo *m*
2 *vt* **to be cocooned from the outside world** estar sobreprotegido(a) del mundo exterior

COD [siːəʊ'diː] *Com* (*abbr* **cash on delivery**) entrega *f* contra reembolso

cod [kɒd] *n* bacalao *m*; **c. liver oil** aceite *m* de hígado de bacalao

coddle ['kɒdəl] *vt* (*child*) mimar

code [kəʊd] **1** *n* (**a**) (*cipher*) código *m*, clave *f*; **in c.** cifrado(a); **c. book** libro *m* de códigos; **c. name** nombre *m* en clave; **c. number** prefijo *m*; **c. word** contraseña *f* (**b**) (*rules*) código *m*; **c. of conduct** código de conducta; **c. of practice** código de conducta
2 *vt* (*message*) codificar, cifrar

codeine ['kəʊdiːn] *n* codeína *f*

codify ['kəʊdɪfaɪ] *vt* codificar

co-ed [kəʊ'ed] **1** *n* (**a**) (*school*) colegio *m* mixto (**b**) (*female student*) alumna *f* de escuela mixta
2 *adj* mixto(a)

coeducation ['kəʊedjʊ'keɪʃən] *n* educación *f* or enseñanza *f* mixta

coeducational ['kəʊedjʊ'keɪʃənəl] *adj* (*school*) mixto(a)

coefficient [kəʊɪ'fɪʃənt] *n Math* coeficiente *m*

coerce [kəʊ'ɜːs] *vt* coaccionar; **to c. sb into doing sth** coaccionar a alguien para que haga algo

coercion [kəʊ'ɜːʃən] *n* coacción *f*

coexist ['kəʊɪg'zɪst] *vi* convivir, coexistir

coexistence ['kəʊɪg'zɪstəns] *n* convivencia *f*, coexistencia *f*

coffee ['kɒfɪ] *n* café *m*; **two coffees, please!** ¡dos cafés, por favor!; **black c.** café *Esp* solo *or Am* negro; **white c.** café con leche; **c. bar** café, cafetería *f*; **c. bean** grano *m* de café; **c. break** descanso *m* para el café; **c. cup** taza *f* de café; **c. grinder** molinillo *m* de café; **c. grounds** posos *mpl* del café;

c. machine cafetera *f*; **c. pot** cafetera *f*; **c. table** mesita *f* baja, mesa *f* de centro

coffee-table ['kɒfɪteɪbəl] *adj* **c. book** libro *m* de lujo para adornar

coffer ['kɒfə(r)] *n* (*chest*) cofre *m*; *Fig* **the company's coffers** las arcas de la empresa

coffin ['kɒfɪn] *n* ataúd *m*, féretro *m*

cog [kɒg] *n* diente *m* (*en engranaje*); *Fig* **I'm only a c. in the machinery** no soy más que una pieza del engranaje

cogent ['kəʊdʒənt] *adj* poderoso(a), convincente

cogitate ['kɒdʒɪteɪt] *Formal vi* meditar, reflexionar

cognac ['kɒnjæk] *n* coñá *m*, coñac *m*

cognition [kɒg'nɪʃən] *n* cognición *f*, conocimiento *m*

cognoscenti [kɒgnə'sentiː] *npl* entendidos *mpl*

coherence [kəʊ'hɪərəns] *n* coherencia *f*

coherent [kəʊ'hɪərənt] *adj* coherente

cohesion [kəʊ'hiːʒən] *n* cohesión *f*

cohesive [kəʊ'hiːsɪv] *adj* cohesivo(a)

coiffure [kwɑː'fjʊə(r)] *n* peinado *m*

coil [kɔɪl] **1** *n* (**a**) (*of rope, wire*) rollo *m*; (*electrical*) bobina *f* (**b**) (*single loop*) bucle *m*, vuelta *f*; **the snake's coils** los anillos de la serpiente
2 *vt* enrollar (**around** alrededor de)
▶ **coil up** *vi* (*snake*) enrollarse, enroscarse

coin [kɔɪn] **1** *n* moneda *f*; *Fig* **the other side of the c.** la otra cara de la moneda
2 *vt* **to c. money** acuñar moneda; **to c. a phrase…** por así decirlo…, valga la expresión…

coinage ['kɔɪnɪdʒ] *n* (**a**) (*coins*) monedas *fpl* (**b**) (*phrase*) **a recent c.** una expresión de nuevo cuño

coincide [kəʊɪn'saɪd] *vi* coincidir (**with** con)

coincidence [kəʊ'ɪnsɪdəns] *n* coincidencia *f*; **what a c.!** ¡qué coincidencia!

coincidental [kəʊɪnsɪ'dentəl] *adj* casual, accidental

coin-operated ['kɔɪnɒpəreɪtɪd] *adj* **c. machine** máquina *f* de monedas

coitus ['kɔɪtəs] *n Formal* coito *m*; **c. interruptus** coitus *m inv* interruptus

coke [kəʊk] *n* (**a**) (*fuel*) coque *m* (**b**) *Fam* (*cocaine*) coca *f*

Col *Mil* (*abbr* **Colonel**) coronel *m*

col (*abbr* **column**) col., columna *f*

colander ['kɒləndə(r)] *n* (*sieve*) escurridor *m*

cold [kəʊld] **1** *n* (**a**) (*low temperature*) frío *m*; **he doesn't seem to feel the c.** parece que no siente el frío; *Fig* **to be left out in the c.** ser dejado(a) de lado (**b**) (*illness*) catarro *m*, *Esp, Méx* resfriado *m*, *Andes, RP* resfrío *m*; **to have a c.** estar acatarrado(a), tener un *Esp, Méx* resfriado *or Andes, RP* resfrío; **to catch a c.** agarrar *or Esp* coger *or Méx* pescar un resfriado, *Andes, RP* agarrarse *or* pescarse un resfrío
2 *adj* (**a**) (*in temperature*) frío(a); **to be c.** (*person*) tener frío; (*thing*) estar frío(a); **it's c.** hace frío; **to get c.** enfriarse; **to be in a c. sweat** tener sudores fríos; **c. calling** (*in marketing*) contacto *m* en frío *or* sin previo aviso; **c. cream** crema *f* de belleza; **c. cuts** fiambres *mpl* y embutidos; *Met* **c. front** frente *m* frío; **c. meats** fiambres *mpl* y embutidos; **c. sore** herpes *m inv* labial, *Esp* calentura *f*, *Méx* fuego *m*; **c. start** (*of car*) arranque *m* en frío; **c. storage** conservación *f* en cámara frigorífica; **c. war** guerra *f* fría
(**b**) (*person, manner, welcome*) frío(a)
(**c**) (*idioms*) *Fam* **it leaves me c.** (*doesn't interest or impress me*) ni me va ni me viene, *Esp* me deja frío(a); **in c. blood** a sangre fría; **that's c. comfort** eso no es un consuelo; **to get c. feet** echarse atrás; **to give sb the c. shoulder** dar de lado a alguien

3 *adv* **to do sth c.** *(without preparation)* hacer algo en frío; *Fam* **to be out c.** *(unconscious)* estar inconsciente

cold-blooded ['kəʊld'blʌdɪd] *adj (animal)* de sangre fría; *Fig (act)* desalmado(a); **to be c.** *(animal)* tener la sangre fría; *(person) Fig* ser desalmado(a); **c. murder** asesinato *m* a sangre fría

cold-hearted ['kəʊld'hɑːtɪd] *adj (person, decision)* insensible

coldly ['kəʊldlɪ] *adv* fríamente, con frialdad

coldness ['kəʊldnɪs] *n (of weather, manner)* frialdad *f*

cold-shoulder ['kəʊld'ʃəʊldə(r)] *vt* dar de lado a, dar la espalda a

coleslaw ['kəʊlslɔː] *n* = ensalada de repollo, zanahoria y cebolla con mayonesa

colic ['kɒlɪk] *n* cólico *m*

collaborate [kə'læbəreɪt] *vi also Pej* colaborar (**with** con)

collaboration [kəlæbə'reɪʃən] *n also Pej* colaboración *f*

collaborator [kə'læbəreɪtə(r)] *n* colaborador(ora) *m,f*; *Pej (with the enemy)* colaboracionista *mf*

collage ['kɒlɑːʒ] *n (artwork)* collage *m*

collagen ['kɒlədʒən] *n* colágeno *m*

collapse [kə'læps] **1** *n (of building)* hundimiento *m*, desplome *m*; *(of prices)* caída *f*, desplome *m*; *(of government)* caída *f*, hundimiento *m*; *(of business)* hundimiento *m*
   2 *vi (person)* desplomarse; *(building, prices, resistance)* desplomarse, hundirse; *(government)* caer, hundirse; *(business)* hundirse

collapsible [kə'læpsəbəl] *adj (table, bed)* plegable

collar ['kɒlə(r)] **1** *n (of shirt)* cuello *m*; *(for dog)* collar *m*
   2 *vt Fam (seize)* cazar, agarrar

collarbone ['kɒləbəʊn] *n* clavícula *f*

collate [kɒ'leɪt] *vt* cotejar

collateral [kə'lætərəl] **1** *n Fin* garantía *f* (prendaria)
   2 *adj Mil* **c. damage** bajas *fpl* civiles *(en un bombardeo)*

colleague ['kɒliːg] *n* colega *mf*, compañero(a) *m,f*

collect [kə'lekt] **1** *vt* **(a)** *(as pastime) (stamps, books)* coleccionar **(b)** *(gather) (supporters, belongings)* reunir, juntar; *(data, news)* recoger, reunir; *(taxes)* recaudar; **I'll c. you at midday** te recogeré al mediodía **(c)** *(compose)* **she collected her thoughts** puso en orden sus ideas; **to c. oneself** concentrarse
   2 *vi (people)* reunirse; *(things)* acumularse
   3 *adj* **c. call** llamada *f* or *Am* llamado *m* a cobro revertido
   4 *adv* **to call sb c.** llamar or *Am* hablar a alguien a cobro revertido

collected [kə'lektɪd] *adj* **(a)** *(calm)* sereno(a), entero(a) **(b)** **the c. works of...** las obras completas de...

collection [kə'lekʃən] *n* **(a)** *(group) (of stamps, paintings)* colección *f*; *(of poems, essays)* recopilación *f*; *(of objects)* montón *m*; *(of people)* grupo *m* **(b)** *(act of collecting) (of money)* colecta *f*; *(of garbage)* recogida *f*; *(of taxes)* recaudación *f*; **to make a c.** *(for charity)* hacer una colecta; **c. plate** *(in church)* platillo *m* para las limosnas

collective [kə'lektɪv] **1** *n (group)* colectivo *m*; *(farm)* granja *f* cooperativa *f*
   2 *adj* colectivo(a); **c. bargaining** negociación *f* colectiva; *Gram* **c. noun** sustantivo *m* colectivo

collectively [kə'lektɪvlɪ] *adv* colectivamente; **they are c. known as...** se los/las conoce como...

collectivize [kə'lektɪvaɪz] *vt* colectivizar

collector [kə'lektə(r)] *n* **(a)** *(of paintings, stamps)* coleccionista *mf*; **c.'s item** pieza *f* de coleccionista **(b)** **c. of taxes** recaudador(ora) *m,f* de impuestos

college ['kɒlɪdʒ] *n* **(a)** *(for adult or further education)* escuela *f*; *(for vocational training)* instituto *m*; *(university)* universidad *f*; **to be at c.** *(be a student)* estar en la universidad

collide [kə'laɪd] *vi* colisionar, chocar (**with** con or contra)

collie ['kɒlɪ] *n (dog)* collie *m*

colliery ['kɒlɪərɪ] *n (coal mine)* mina *f* de carbón

collision [kə'lɪʒən] *n* colisión *f*, choque *m*; *Fig* **they are on a c. course** terminarán enfrentándose

colloquial [kə'ləʊkwɪəl] *adj* coloquial

colloquialism [kə'ləʊkwɪəlɪzəm] *n* voz *f* or término *m* coloquial

collude [kə'luːd] *vi* conspirar, confabularse

collusion [kə'luːʒən] *n* connivencia *f*; **to be in c. with sb** estar en connivencia con alguien

collywobbles ['kɒlɪwɒbəlz] *npl Fam* **to have the c.** *(be nervous)* tener canguelo

Colombia [kə'lʌmbɪə] *n* Colombia

Colombian [kə'lʌmbɪən] *n & adj* colombiano(a) *m,f*

colon ['kəʊlən] *n* **(a)** *Anat* colon *m* **(b)** *(punctuation mark)* dos puntos *mpl*

colonel ['kɜːnəl] *n* coronel *m*

colonial [kə'ləʊnɪəl] *adj* colonial

colonialism [kə'ləʊnɪəlɪzəm] *n* colonialismo *m*

colonist ['kɒlənɪst] *n* colonizador(ora) *m,f*, colono *m*

colonize ['kɒlənaɪz] *vt* colonizar

colonnade [kɒlə'neɪd] *n Archit* columnata *f*

colony ['kɒlənɪ] *n* colonia *f*

color ['kʌlə(r)] **1** *n* **(a)** color *m*; **what c. is it?** ¿de qué color es?; **c. bar** *(racial discrimination)* discriminación *f* racial; **c. code** código *m* de colores; **c. scheme** combinación *f* de colores; **c. supplement** *(of newspaper)* suplemento *m* en color **(b)** *(idioms)* **to be off c.** *(person) Esp* estar pocho(a), *Am* estar de capa caída; **to give c. to a story** dar colorido a una historia; **let's see the c. of your money** veamos primero el dinero; **to pass with flying colors** aprobar con todos los honores; **to show oneself in one's true colors** quitarse la máscara; **she nailed her colors to the mast** manifestó públicamente su postura
   2 *vt (change color of)* colorear; *Fig (judgment, view)* influir en; **to c. one's hair** teñirse el pelo; **to c. sth blue** pintar or colorear algo de azul
   3 *vi (blush)* ruborizarse

▸**color in** *vt sep* colorear

color-blind ['kʌləblaɪnd] *adj* daltónico(a)

color-blindness ['kʌləblaɪndnɪs] *n* daltonismo *m*

color-coded ['kʌlə'kəʊdɪd] *adj* **the wires are c.** los cables están coloreados de acuerdo con un código

colored ['kʌləd] *adj* **(a)** *(illustration)* en color; **brightly c.** de colores vivos; *Fig* **a highly c. narrative** una narrativa llena de colorido **(b)** *(person)* de color

colorful ['kʌləfʊl] *adj* **(a)** *(having bright colors)* de colores vivos **(b)** *(interesting, exciting)* lleno(a) de colorido; **a c. character** un personaje pintoresco **(c)** *(vivid) (language, description)* expresivo(a), vívido(a)

coloring ['kʌlərɪŋ] *n* **(a)** *(in food)* colorante *m* **(b)** *(complexion)* tez *f*; **to have dark/fair c.** ser de tez morena/clara **(c)** **c. book** libro *m* para colorear

colorless ['kʌlələs] *adj* **(a)** *(clear)* incoloro(a) **(b)** *Fig (dull)* insulso(a), inexpresivo(a)

colossal [kə'lɒsəl] *adj* colosal

colt [kəʊlt] *n (horse)* potro *m*

column ['kɒləm] *n (of building, troops, in newspaper)* columna *f*; **the story got a lot of c. inches** *(good coverage)* la prensa se hizo amplio eco de la noticia

columnist ['kɒləmɪst] *n (for newspaper, magazine)* columnista *mf*

coma ['kəʊmə] *n* coma *m*; **to go into/be in a c.** entrar en/ estar en coma

comatose ['kəʊmətəʊs] *adj Med* comatoso(a); *Fam (exhausted)* hecho(a) polvo

comb [kəʊm] **1** *n* **(a)** *(for hair)* peine *m*; **to run a c. through one's hair, to give one's hair a c.** peinarse **(b)** *(of cock)* cresta *f*

2 vt (**a**) (hair) peinar; **to c. one's hair** peinarse (**b**) (search) (area, town) peinar, rastrear minuciosamente

combat ['kɒmbæt] **1** n combate m; **c. fatigue** fatiga f de combate; **c. jacket** guerrera f; **c. zone** área f de combate

2 vt (disease, prejudice, crime) combatir

combatant ['kɒmbətənt] n & adj combatiente mf

combination [kɒmbɪ'neɪʃən] n combinación f; **a c. of circumstances** un cúmulo de circunstancias; **c. lock** cierre m de combinación; **c. skin** piel f mixta

combine 1 n ['kɒmbaɪn] (**a**) **c. (harvester)** cosechadora f (**b**) Econ grupo m empresarial

2 vt [kəm'baɪn] combinar; **to c. business with pleasure** combinar los negocios con el placer

3 vi (people) unirse; (merge) unirse, combinarse; (chemical elements) combinarse

combined [kəm'baɪnd] adj conjunto(a); **our c. efforts** todos nuestros esfuerzos

combustible [kəm'bʌstɪbəl] adj combustible

combustion [kəm'bʌstʃən] n combustión f; **c. chamber** cámara f de combustión

come [kʌm] (pt **came** [keɪm], pp **come**) vi (**a**) (in general) venir (**from** de); (arrive) venir, llegar; **to c. from France** ser francés(esa); **to c. from Nashville** ser de Nashville; **here c. the children** ya llegan or ahí vienen los niños; **c. here!** ¡ven aquí!; **I'll c. and help** iré a ayudar; **coming!** ¡ya voy!; **she always comes to me for help** siempre acude a mí en busca de ayuda; **to c. first/last** (in race, competition) llegar or terminar primero/último; **my name comes before hers on the list** mi nombre está or va antes que el de ella en la lista; **the mud came up to our knees** el barro nos llegaba a las rodillas; Fig **she has c. a long way since then** ha progresado mucho desde entonces; Fam **I don't know whether I'm coming or going!** ¡no sé dónde tengo la cabeza!; Fam **c., c.!** ¡bueno, bueno!; ¡venga ya!; **she won't let anything c. between her and her work** no permite que nada interfiera con su trabajo; **that's surprising coming from him** viniendo de él, es sorprendente; **now that I c. to think of it** ahora que lo pienso; **c. away from there, it's dangerous** quítate de ahí, que es peligroso; **the rain came pouring down** se puso a llover a cántaros; **to c. for sth/sb** venir en busca de algo/alguien; **she came running toward us** vino corriendo hacia nosotros

(**b**) (in time) venir; **in the days/years to c.** en días/años venideros; **to take things as they c.** tomarse las cosas como vienen; **what comes next?** ¿qué viene a continuación?; **she will be ten c. January** cumple diez años en enero; **c. what may** suceda lo que suceda; **it came as a relief to me** fue un gran alivio para mí; Fam **he had it coming (to him)** si lo estaba buscando

(**c**) (be available) **it comes in three sizes** viene en tres tallas; **work of that quality doesn't c. cheap** un trabajo de esa calidad no sale barato; Fam **he's as tough as they c.** es duro como el que más; **it's as good as they c.** es de lo mejor que hay

(**d**) (become) **to c. loose** aflojarse; **to c. true** cumplirse, hacerse realidad; **to c. of age** hacerse mayor de edad; **how did the door c. to be open?** ¿cómo es que estaba la puerta abierta?

(**e**) very Fam (have orgasm) Esp correrse, Am venirse, RP irse

▸**come about** vi ocurrir, suceder; **how did it c. about that…?** ¿cómo fue que…?

▸**come across 1** vt insep (find) encontrar, encontrarse con

2 vi (make an impression) **to c. across well/badly** quedar bien/mal, dar buena/mala impresión; **she comes across as a bit arrogant** da la impresión de que es un poco arrogante

▸**come after** vt insep (chase) perseguir

▸**come along** vi (**a**) (as exhortation) **c. along!** ¡vamos!, Esp ¡venga! (**b**) (project, work) marchar, progresar; **how's the**

project coming along? ¿qué tal marcha el proyecto?; **his Spanish is coming along well** su español va mejorando

▸**come around** vi (**a**) (visit) **c. around and see me one day** pásate a verme un día (**b**) (regain consciousness) volver en sí (**c**) (accept) **to c. around to sb's way of thinking** terminar aceptando la opinión de alguien

▸**come at** vt insep (attack) atacar, Esp ir a por; **he came at me with a knife** me atacó or Esp fue a por mí con un cuchillo

▸**come away** vi (become detached) soltarse

▸**come back** vi volver, regresar, Col, Méx regresarse; **to c. back to what I was saying,…** volviendo a lo que decía antes,…; **it's all coming back to me** ahora me acuerdo de todo

▸**come by 1** vt insep (acquire) conseguir; **how did she c. by all that money?** ¿de dónde sacó todo ese dinero?

2 vi (visit) pasarse; **I'll c. by tomorrow** me pasaré mañana (por tu casa)

▸**come down** vi (**a**) (descend) bajar; (rain) caer; Fig **to c. down in the world** venir a menos; **to c. down with the flu** Esp coger or Am agarrarse la gripe (**b**) (decrease) (temperature, prices) bajar, descender (**c**) (decide) **to c. down in favor of** decantarse a favor de

▸**come down on** vt insep (reprimand) regañar

▸**come down to** vt insep (be a matter of) reducirse a, tratarse de

▸**come forward** vi presentarse

▸**come in** vi (**a**) (person) entrar; (tide) subir; **c. in!** ¡adelante!; **to c. in first/second** llegar en primer/segundo lugar (**b**) (have a role) entrar; Fam **that's where you c. in** ahí es cuando entras tú; **to c. in handy** or **useful** resultar útil, venir bien

▸**come in for** vt insep **to c. in for praise/criticism** recibir alabanzas/críticas

▸**come into** vt insep (**a**) (room, city) entrar en; **to c. into the world** venir al mundo; **to c. into existence** nacer, surgir; **to c. into force** or **effect** (law, ruling) entrar en vigor; **luck didn't c. into it** la suerte no tuvo nada que ver (**b**) (inherit) heredar

▸**come of** vi (result from) **no good will c. of it** no saldrá nada bueno de esto; **that's what comes of being too ambitious** eso es lo que pasa por ser demasiado ambicioso

▸**come off 1** vt insep (**a**) (fall from) (horse, bicycle) caerse de (**b**) **c. off it!** ¡anda ya!

2 vi (**a**) (be removed) (button) caerse; (paint) levantarse (**b**) (succeed) (plan) salir; **to c. off well/badly** (in contest) quedar bien/mal

▸**come on** vi (**a**) (as exhortation) **c. on!** ¡vamos!, Esp ¡venga! (**b**) (make progress) progresar; **I feel a cold coming on** me estoy resfriando or acatarrando

▸**come on to** vt insep Fam (flirt with) intentar seducir a, Esp tirar los tejos a, Méx echarle los perros a, RP cargar a

▸**come out** vi (**a**) (person, sun, magazine) salir; (movie) estrenarse; **the truth will c. out in the end** al final se sabrá la verdad; **to c. out of an affair well/badly** salir bien/mal parado(a) de un asunto; **the photos have c. out well** las fotos han salido bien; **to c. out on strike** declararse en huelga; **she came out in a rash** le salió un sarpullido; **to c. out in favor of/against sth** declararse a favor de/en contra de algo; **to c. out with an opinion** expresar una opinión (**b**) (tooth, screw, hair) caerse; (stain) salir, quitarse (**c**) (as gay or lesbian) declararse homosexual

▸**come over 1** vt insep (affect) sobrevenir; **a strange feeling came over me** me sobrevino una extraña sensación; **what's come over you?** ¿qué te ha pasado?

2 vi (**a**) (make impression) **to c. over well/badly** quedar bien/mal (**b**) (visit) pasarse; **I'll c. over tomorrow** me pasaré mañana (por tu casa)

▸**come round** = **come around**

▶**come through 1** vi (message, news) llegar

  2 vt insep (survive) (war, crisis, illness) sobrevivir a

▶**come to 1** vt insep (**a**) (amount to) sumar, alcanzar; **how much does it c. to?** ¿a cuánto asciende?; **the scheme never came to anything** el plan se quedó en nada (**b**) (reach) **to c. to a crossroads** llegar a un cruce; **to c. to the end (of sth)** llegar al final (de algo); **to c. to the point** ir al grano; **what is the world coming to?** ¿adónde vamos a ir a parar?; **when it comes to…** en cuestión de…; **if it comes to that, you're not exactly a genius either** si se trata de eso, tú tampoco eres exactamente un genio

  2 vi (regain consciousness) volver en sí

▶**come together** vi (gather) reunirse

▶**come up 1** vt insep (stairs, hill) subir

  2 vi (**a**) (sun) salir; (opportunity, problem) surgir, presentarse; **to c. up against opposition/a problem** enfrentarse con la oposición/un problema; **there are some interesting movies coming up on television** van a poner algunas películas interesantes en la televisión; **I'll let you know if anything comes up** te avisaré si surge algo; **the case comes up for trial tomorrow** el caso se verá mañana (**b**) **to c. up with** (funding, solution) encontrar; (idea, theory) formular

▶**come upon** vt insep (find) (person, object) encontrar, encontrarse con

▶**come up to** vt insep (**a**) (approach) acercarse a; **a man came up to me and started talking** un hombre se me acercó y comenzó a hablarme; **we're coming up to Christmas** se acerca la Navidad (**b**) (equal) estar a la altura de; **the movie didn't c. up to my expectations** la película no fue tan buena como yo esperaba

comeback ['kʌmbæk] n (of sportsperson) vuelta f a la competición or Am competencia; (of actor) regreso m; **to make a c.** (fashion) volver; (actor) volver a actuar; (sportsperson) volver a la competición or Am competencia

comedian [kə'miːdɪən] n humorista mf

comedienne [kəmiːdɪ'en] n humorista f

comedown ['kʌmdaʊn] n Fam degradación f

comedy ['kɒmɪdɪ] n (play, movie) comedia f; (TV series) serie f cómica or de humor; (humorous entertainment) humor m, humorismo m; **c. show** (on TV) programa m de humor

come-hither ['kʌm'hɪðə(r)] adj Fam **c. look** mirada f seductora

come-on ['kʌmɒn] n Fam **to give sb the c.** (sexually) intentar seducir a, Esp tirar los tejos a alguien, Méx echarle los perros a alguien, RP cargar a alguien

comer ['kʌmə(r)] n **open to all comers** abierto(a) para todo el mundo

comet ['kɒmɪt] n cometa m

comeuppance [kʌm'ʌpəns] n Fam **he'll get his c.** ya tendrá su merecido

comfort ['kʌmfət] **1** n (**a**) (ease) comodidad f; **to live in c.** vivir confortablemente; **in the c. of one's own home** en el calor del hogar; **home comforts** las comodidades del hogar; **the bullets were too close for c.** las balas pasaban peligrosamente cerca; **c. station** servicio m, Esp aseos mpl, Am baños mpl, Am lavatorios mpl (**b**) (consolation) consuelo m; **if it's any c.,…** si te sirve de consuelo,…; **to take c. from** or **in sth** consolarse con algo

  2 vt (console) consolar, confortar

comfortable ['kʌmfətəbəl] adj (**a**) (bed, chair) cómodo(a); **to be c.** (person) estar cómodo(a); **the patient is c.** el paciente no sufre demasiados dolores; **to make oneself c.** ponerse cómodo(a); **to feel c.** sentirse a gusto, sentirse cómodo(a); **I wouldn't feel c. accepting that money** no me sentiría bien si aceptara ese dinero (**b**) (majority, income) holgado(a); **to be in c. circumstances** estar en una situación holgada or desahogada

comfortably ['kʌmftəblɪ] adv (**a**) (to sit) cómodamente (**b**) (without difficulty) holgadamente, cómodamente; **to be c. off** estar en una situación holgada or desahogada; **to live c.** vivir sin apuros; **to win c.** ganar holgadamente

comforter ['kʌmfətə(r)] n (**a**) (quilt) edredón m (**b**) (baby's pacifier) chupete m

comforting ['kʌmfətɪŋ] adj (news, thought) reconfortante

comfy ['kʌmfɪ] adj Fam (person, place) cómodo(a)

comic ['kɒmɪk] **1** n (**a**) (performer) cómico(a) m,f, humorista mf (**b**) **c. (book)** (for children) Esp tebeo m, Am revista f de historietas; (for adults) cómic m

  2 adj cómico(a); **c. opera** ópera f cómica; **to provide some c. relief** aliviar la tristeza con un toque de humor; **c. strip** tira f cómica

comical ['kɒmɪkəl] adj cómico(a)

coming ['kʌmɪŋ] **1** n (**a**) (of person) venida f, llegada f; (of night) caída f; **comings and goings** idas fpl y venidas (**b**) **c. of age** (reaching adulthood) mayoría f de edad; **the c. of age of the Icelandic cinema** la mayoría de edad del cine m islandés (**c**) **c. out** (in society) debut m, presentación f

  2 adj (year, week) próximo(a)

comma ['kɒmə] n coma f

command [kə'mɑːnd] **1** n (**a**) (order) orden f; Comptr comando m, instrucción f; **to do sth at sb's c.** hacer algo por orden de alguien (**b**) (authority, control) (of army, expedition) mando m; **to be in c. (of)** estar al mando (de); **to be in c. of a situation** dominar una situación; **to be at sb's c.** estar a las órdenes de alguien; **he has many resources at his c.** tiene muchos recursos a su disposición; **she has a good c. of English** tiene un buen dominio del inglés; **c. economy** economía f dirigida; Comptr **c. language** lenguaje m de comandos or de mando

  2 vt (**a**) (order) mandar, ordenar; **to c. sb to do sth** mandar a alguien que haga algo (**b**) (ship, regiment) estar al mando de, mandar (**c**) (have at one's disposal) disponer de; **with all the skill he could c.** con toda la habilidad de que disponía (**d**) (inspire) (respect, admiration) infundir, inspirar; (attention) obtener; **to c. a high price** alcanzar un precio elevado

commandant ['kɒmǝndænt] n Mil comandante mf

commandeer [kɒmǝn'dɪǝ(r)] vt (requisition) requisar

commander [kǝ'mɑːndǝ(r)] n Mil comandante mf

commander-in-chief [kǝ'mɑːndǝrɪn'tʃiːf] (pl **commanders-in-chief**) n Mil comandante mf en jefe

commanding [kǝ'mɑːndɪŋ] adj (tone, appearance) autoritario(a); (position) dominante; (lead) abrumador(ora); Mil **c. officer** oficial m al mando

commandment [kǝ'mɑːndmǝnt] n Rel mandamiento m

commando [kǝ'mɑːndǝʊ] (pl **commandos** or **commandoes**) n Mil (soldier) comando m

commemorate [kǝ'memǝreɪt] vt conmemorar

commemoration [kǝmemǝ'reɪʃǝn] n conmemoración f; **in c. of** en conmemoración de

commemorative [kǝ'memǝrǝtɪv] adj conmemorativo(a)

commence [kǝ'mens] Formal **1** vt comenzar; **to c. doing sth** comenzar a hacer algo

  2 vi comenzar

commencement [kǝ'mensmǝnt] n (**a**) comienzo m, inicio m (**b**) Univ ceremonia f de licenciatura

commend [kǝ'mend] vt (**a**) (praise) encomiar, elogiar; **to c. sb for bravery** elogiar la valentía de alguien; **highly commended** accésit (**b**) (recommend) **the train journey has little to c. it** el viaje en tren tiene poco de recomendable (**c**) (entrust) encomendar (**to** a)

commendable [kǝ'mendǝbǝl] adj encomiable

commendably [kǝ'mendǝblɪ] adv **his speech was c. brief** su discurso fue de una brevedad digna de encomio

commendation [kɒmen'deɪʃǝn] n **to receive a c.** recibir una mención; **worthy of c.** digno(a) de encomio *or* mención

commensurate [kəˈmensərət] *adj Formal* acorde (**with** con), proporcional (**with** a); **you will receive a salary c. with the position** percibirá un salario adecuado a su puesto

comment [ˈkɒment] **1** *n* comentario *m*; **to make a c. on sth** hacer un comentario acerca de algo; **no c.** sin comentarios

2 *vt* **to c. that…** comentar que…; **"how interesting," he commented** "qué interesante", comentó

3 *vi* hacer comentarios; **to c. on sth** comentar algo

commentary [ˈkɒməntərɪ] *n* (**a**) *(on TV, radio)* comentarios *mpl* (**b**) *(on text)* comentario *m*

commentate [ˈkɒmənteɪt] *vi (for TV, radio)* hacer de comentarista; **to c. on a match** ser el comentarista de un partido

commentator [ˈkɒmənteɪtə(r)] *n (on TV, radio)* comentarista *mf*

commerce [ˈkɒmɜːs] *n* comercio *m*

commercial [kəˈmɜːʃəl] **1** *adj also Pej* comercial; **c. artist** diseñador(ora) *m,f* gráfico(a) de publicidad; *Fin* **c. bank** banco *m* comercial; *TV & Rad* **c. break** pausa *f* publicitaria; **c. law** derecho *m* mercantil; **c. traveler** viajante *mf* de comercio; **c. value** valor *m* comercial; **c. vehicle** vehículo *m* de transporte de mercancías

2 *n (TV, radio advertisement)* anuncio *m* (publicitario)

commercialism [kəˈmɜːʃəlɪzəm] *n Pej* comercialidad *f*

commercialization [kəmɜːʃəlaɪˈzeɪʃən] *n* comercialización *f*

commercialize [kəˈmɜːʃəlaɪz] *vt* comercializar

commercially [kəˈmɜːʃəlɪ] *adv* comercialmente

commie [ˈkɒmɪ] *n & adj Fam Pej (communist)* rojo(a) *m,f*

commiserate [kəˈmɪzəreɪt] *vi* **he commiserated with me** me dijo cuánto lo sentía

commiseration [kəmɪzəˈreɪʃən] *n* **he offered his commiserations** dijo cuánto lo sentía; **(you have) my commiserations** te compadezco, cuánto lo siento

commission [kəˈmɪʃən] **1** *n* (**a**) *Com (payment)* comisión *f*; **to charge c.** cobrar comisión (**b**) *(order)* encargo *m* (**c**) *(investigating body)* comisión *f*, comité *m* (**d**) **out of/in c.** *(ship)* fuera de/en servicio (**e**) *Mil* nombramiento *m*

2 *vt* (**a**) *(order) (person)* encargar; **to c. sb to do sth** encargar a alguien hacer algo (**b**) *Mil* **to be commissioned** ser nombrado(a)

commissioner [kəˈmɪʃənə(r)] *n* comisario(a) *m,f*; **c. of baseball** comisionado(a) *m,f* de béisbol; **c. of police** comisario(a) *m,f* de policía

commit [kəˈmɪt] *vt* (**a**) *(error, crime)* cometer; **to c. suicide** suicidarse (**b**) *(promise)* **to c. oneself** comprometerse; **to c. oneself to (doing) sth** comprometerse a (hacer) algo (**c**) *(entrust)* confiar, encomendar; **to c. sth to writing** *or* **paper** poner algo por escrito; **to c. sth to memory** memorizar algo (**d**) *(confine)* **to c. sb to prison** encarcelar a alguien; **he was committed** *(to mental institution)* fue ingresado en un psiquiátrico (**e**) *Law* **to c. sb for trial** enviar a alguien a un tribunal superior para ser juzgado(a)

commitment [kəˈmɪtmənt] *n (obligation, loyalty)* compromiso *m*; **to make a c. (to sth/sb)** comprometerse (con algo/alguien); **she lacks c.** no se compromete lo suficiente; **family commitments** compromisos familiares

committal [kəˈmɪtəl] *n (to mental hospital, prison)* reclusión *f* (**to** en), ingreso *m* (**to** en); *Law* **c. proceedings** auto *m* de prisión, orden *f* de encarcelamiento

committed [kəˈmɪtɪd] *adj* comprometido(a); **to be c. to an idea** estar comprometido(a) con una idea

committee [kəˈmɪtɪ] *n* comité *m*, comisión *f*; **to sit** *or* **be on a c.** ser miembro de un comité; **c. meeting** reunión *f* del comité; **c. member** miembro *mf* del comité

commode [kəˈməʊd] *n* (**a**) *(chest of drawers)* cómoda *f* (**b**) *(toilet)* silla *f* (de) servicio, silla *f* con inodoro

commodious [kəˈməʊdɪəs] *adj* amplio(a), espacioso(a)

commodity [kəˈmɒdɪtɪ] *n Econ & Fin* producto *m* básico; *Fig* **a rare c.** un bien muy escaso; **c. market** mercado *m* de productos básicos

commodore [ˈkɒmədɔː(r)] *n Naut* comodoro *m*

common [ˈkɒmən] **1** *n* (**a**) **to have sth in c. (with sb)** tener algo en común (con alguien) (**b**) *(land)* = campo municipal para uso del común, ≃ ejido *m*

2 *adj* (**a**) *(frequent)* común, frecuente; **in c. use** de uso corriente

(**b**) *(shared)* común; **it is by c. consent the best** está considerado por todos como el mejor; *also Fig* **c. denominator** denominador *m* común; *also Fig* **c. factor** factor *m* común; **the c. good** el bien común; *Fig* **c. ground** puntos *mpl* en común; **it's c. knowledge** es de(l) dominio público; *Sch* **c. room** *(for pupils)* sala *f* de alumnos; *(for teachers)* sala *f* de profesores

(**c**) *(average, ordinary)* común, corriente; **the c. cold** el *Esp,* *Méx* resfriado *or Andes, RP* resfrío común; **the c. man** el ciudadano medio; **the c. people** la gente corriente; **c. sense** sentido *m* común; *St Exch* **c. stock** acciones *fpl* ordinarias

(**d**) *(vulgar)* ordinario(a)

commoner [ˈkɒmənə(r)] *n* plebeyo(a) *m,f*

common-law [ˈkɒmənlɔː] *adj* **c. marriage** matrimonio *m* *or* unión *f* de hecho; **c. husband/wife** esposo *m*/esposa *f* de hecho

commonly [ˈkɒmənlɪ] *adv* comúnmente

commonplace [ˈkɒmənpleɪs] **1** *n* tópico *m*, lugar *m* común

2 *adj* común, habitual

Commonwealth [ˈkɒmənwelθ] *n* **the C. of Massachusetts/Pennsylvania** el Estado de Massachusetts/Pensilvania

commotion [kəˈməʊʃən] *n* alboroto *m*, tumulto *m*; **to cause a c.** causar un alboroto

communal [ˈkɒmjʊnəl] *adj* comunal

communally [ˈkɒmjʊnəlɪ] *adv* en comunidad; **c. owned** de propiedad comunitaria

commune 1 *n* [ˈkɒmjuːn] *(collective)* comuna *f*

2 *vi* [kəˈmjuːn] estar en comunión (**with** con)

communicable [kəˈmjuːnɪkəbəl] *adj (disease)* contagioso(a)

communicant [kəˈmjuːnɪkənt] *n Rel* comulgante *mf*

communicate [kəˈmjuːnɪkeɪt] **1** *vt (information, idea)* comunicar (**to** a)

2 *vi* (**a**) *(person)* comunicarse (**with** con) (**b**) *(rooms)* comunicarse

communication [kəmjuːnɪˈkeɪʃən] *n* comunicación *f*; **to be in c. (with sb)** estar en contacto (con alguien); **radio c.** comunicación *f* por radio; **communications technology** tecnología *f* de las telecomunicaciones

communicative [kəˈmjuːnɪkətɪv] *adj* comunicativo(a)

communion [kəˈmjuːnjən] *n Rel* comunión *f*; **to take C.** comulgar

communism [ˈkɒmjʊnɪzəm] *n* comunismo *m*

communist [ˈkɒmjʊnɪst] *n & adj* comunista *mf*

community [kəˈmjuːnɪtɪ] *n* comunidad *f*; **the Asian c.** la comunidad asiática; **the business c.** el sector empresarial, los empresarios; **c. care** asistencia *f* social domiciliaria; **c. center** ≃ centro *m* cívico *or* social; **c. college** = centro docente que ofrece cursos de enseñanza superior de dos años de duración; **c. property** *(of couple)* propiedad *f* en común; **c. service** servicios *mpl* a la comunidad *(impuestos como pena sustitutiva de cárcel)*; **c. spirit** espíritu *m* comunitario

commute [kəˈmjuːt] **1** *vt Law* conmutar

2 *vi* **to c. (to work)** viajar diariamente al lugar de trabajo

commuter [kəˈmjuːtə(r)] *n* = persona que viaja diariamente al trabajo; **c. lane** carril *m* VAO, carril *m* para vehículos de alta ocupación; **c. train** = tren de cercanías que las personas utilizan para desplazarse diariamente al lugar de trabajo

Comoros ['kɒmərɒs] *n* the C. (Islands) las (Islas) Comores

compact 1 *n* ['kɒmpækt] (a) *(for powder)* polvera *f* (b) *(treaty)* pacto *m* (c) *(car)* utilitario *m*

2 *adj* [kəm'pækt] compacto(a); **c. disc** *or* **disk** (disco *m*) compacto *m*; **c. disc** *or* **disk player** reproductor *m* de discos compactos

3 *vt* [kɒm'pækt] *(scrap metal)* compactar, comprimir

companion [kəm'pænjən] *n* (a) *(friend)* compañero(a) *m,f;* **a drinking/traveling c.** un(a) compañero(a) de borrachera/viaje (b) *(guidebook)* guía *f*

companionable [kəm'pænjənəbəl] *adj* sociable

companionship [kəm'pænjənʃɪp] *n* compañía *f*

company ['kʌmpənɪ] *n* (a) *(companionship)* compañía *f;* **in sb's c.** en compañía de alguien; **to keep sb c.** hacer compañía a alguien; **to be good c.** ser buena compañía; **to part c. (with sb)** separarse (de alguien); **to get into bad c.** mezclarse con malas compañías; **you shouldn't pick your nose in c.** no se debe uno meter el dedo en la nariz delante de (la) gente; **we're expecting c.** *(guests)* tenemos invitados; *Prov* **two's c., three's a crowd** dos es compañía, tres es multitud

(b) *Com* empresa *f,* compañía *f;* **c. car** coche *m or Am* carro *m or RP* auto *m* de empresa; **c. policy** política *f* de empresa; *Com* **c. secretary** jefe(a) *m,f* de administración

(c) *(army unit, theater group)* compañía *f*

(d) *Naut* **the ship's c.** la tripulación (del barco)

comparable ['kɒmpərəbəl] *adj* comparable

comparative [kəm'pærətɪv] **1** *n Gram* comparativo *m*

2 *adj (cost, comfort, wealth)* relativo(a); *(study, research)* comparado(a)

compare [kəm'peə(r)] **1** *n Literary* **beyond c.** incomparable

2 *vt* comparar (**with** *or* **to** con); **compared with** *or* **to...** comparado(a) con...; *Fig* **to c. notes (with sb)** intercambiar pareceres *or* opiniones (con alguien)

3 *vi* compararse (**with** con *or* a); **to c. favorably with sth** resultar ser mejor que algo

comparison [kəm'pærɪsən] *n* comparación *f;* **in** *or* **by c.** en comparación; **there is no c.** no hay punto de comparación; **to draw** *or* **make a c. between** establecer un paralelismo entre

compartment [kəm'pɑːtmənt] *n* compartimento *m*

compass ['kʌmpəs] *n* (a) *(for finding direction)* brújula *f* (b) *Math* **compasses** compás *m;* **a pair of compasses** un compás (c) *(range)* ámbito *m,* alcance *m*

compassion [kəm'pæʃən] *n* compasión *f*

compassionate [kəm'pæʃənət] *adj (person, attitude)* compasivo(a); **to be c. toward sb** ser compasivo(a) con alguien; **on c. grounds** por compasión; **c. leave** = permiso por enfermedad grave o muerte de un familiar

compatibility [kəmpætə'bɪlɪtɪ] *n* compatibilidad *f*

compatible [kəm'pætəbəl] *adj* compatible (**with** con)

compatriot [kəm'pætrɪət] *n* compatriota *mf*

compel [kəm'pel] *(pt & pp* **compelled)** *vt* obligar; **to c. sb to do sth** obligar a alguien a hacer algo; **to c. admiration/respect** inspirar admiración/respeto

compelling [kəm'pelɪŋ] *adj (movie, performance)* absorbente; *(argument)* poderoso(a), convincente; *(urgency)* apremiante

compensate ['kɒmpenseɪt] **1** *vt* compensar, indemnizar (**for** por)

2 *vi* **to c. for sth** compensar algo

compensation [kɒmpen'seɪʃən] *n (reparation)* compensación *f; (money)* indemnización *f*

compensatory [kɒmpen'seɪtərɪ] *adj* compensatorio(a)

compete [kəm'piːt] *vi* competir (**with** con *or* contra); **to c. for a prize** competir por un premio

competence ['kɒmpɪtəns] *n* (a) *(ability)* competencia *f,* cualidades *fpl* (b) *Law* competencia *f*

competent ['kɒmpɪtənt] *adj* competente

competition [kɒmpɪ'tɪʃən] *n* (a) *(contest)* concurso *m; (in sport)* competición *f, Am* competencia *f* (b) *(rivalry)* competencia *f;* **to be in c. with sb** competir con alguien; **the c.** *(rivals)* la competencia

competitive [kəm'petɪtɪv] *adj* competitivo(a); **c. sports** deportes *mpl* de competición *or Am* competencia; *Com* **c. tendering** adjudicación *f* por concurso público

competitiveness [kəm'petɪtɪvnɪs] *n* competitividad *f*

competitor [kəm'petɪtə(r)] *n* competidor(ora) *m,f*

compilation [kɒmpɪ'leɪʃən] *n* recopilación *f,* compilación *f*

compile [kəm'paɪl] *vt* recopilar, compilar

compiler [kəm'paɪlə(r)] *n* (a) *(of book, information)* recopilador(ora) *m,f,* compilador(ora) *m,f; (of dictionary)* redactor(ora) *m,f* (b) *Comptr* compilador *m*

complacency [kəm'pleɪsənsɪ], **complacence** [kəm'pleɪsəns] *n* autocomplacencia *f*

complacent [kəm'pleɪsənt] *adj* autocomplaciente; **to be c. about sth** ser demasiado relajado(a) respecto a algo

complain [kəm'pleɪn] *vi* quejarse (**about** de); **to c. of** *(symptoms)* estar aquejado(a) de; **she complained that he had cheated** se quejó de que él había hecho trampa; **I can't c. about the service** no tengo queja alguna del servicio; **how are things? — I can't c.** ¿cómo van las cosas? — no me puedo quejar

complainant [kəm'pleɪnənt] *n Law* reclamante *mf*

complaint [kəm'pleɪnt] *n* (a) *(grievance)* queja *f;* **to have cause** *or* **grounds for c.** tener motivos de queja; **to lodge** *or* **make a c. (against sb)** presentar una queja (contra alguien) (b) *(illness)* afección *f,* problema *m;* **she suffers from a skin c.** tiene un problema de piel

complement 1 *n* ['kɒmplɪmənt] (a) *Gram* complemento *m* (b) *Naut* **the full c.** la dotación, la tripulación; *Fig* **I still have my full c. of teeth** todavía conservo toda mi dentadura

2 *vt* complementar

complementary [kɒmplɪ'mentərɪ] *adj* complementario(a); **c. medicine** medicina *f* alternativa

complete [kəm'pliːt] **1** *adj* (a) *(lacking nothing)* completo(a); **the c. works of...** las obras completas de... (b) *(finished)* terminado(a), acabado(a); **the work is now c.** el trabajo ya está terminado (c) *(total, thorough)* total, absoluto(a); **a c. turnaround in the situation** un vuelco total de la situación; **it came as a c. surprise** fue una sorpresa absoluta; **she is a c. fool** es tonta de remate; **he's a c. stranger** es un completo desconocido

2 *vt* completar, terminar; **to c. a form** rellenar un impreso

completely [kəm'pliːtlɪ] *adv* completamente, totalmente

completeness [kəm'pliːtnɪs] *n* (a) *(wholeness)* **they added a final volume to the series for c.** añadieron un último volumen para redondear la colección (b) *(thoroughness)* **the c. of their victory/defeat** lo categórico de su victoria/derrota

completion [kəm'pliːʃən] *n* finalización *f,* terminación *f;* **on c.** al terminar; **to be nearing c.** estar próximo a concluir

complex ['kɒmpleks] **1** *n (of buildings, psychological)* complejo *m;* **to have a c. about one's weight** tener complejo de gordo(a)

2 *adj* complejo(a)

complexion [kəm'plekʃən] *n* tez *f;* **to have a dark/fair c.** tener la tez oscura/clara; *Fig* **that puts a different c. on it** eso le da otro color

complexity [kəm'pleksɪtɪ] *n* complejidad *f*

compliance [kəm'plaɪəns] *n* cumplimiento *m* (**with** de); **in c. with your wishes** en cumplimiento de sus deseos

compliant [kəm'plaɪənt] *adj* dócil, sumiso(a)

complicate ['kɒmplɪkeɪt] *vt* complicar; **the issue is complicated by the fact that...** el asunto se complica aún más debido al hecho de que...

complicated ['kɒmplɪkeɪtɪd] *adj* complicado(a)

complication [kɒmplɪ'keɪʃən] *n* complicación *f*; **complications** *(in patient's condition)* complicaciones

complicity [kəm'plɪsɪtɪ] *n* complicidad *f*

compliment ['kɒmplɪmənt] **1** *n* cumplido *m*; **to pay sb a c.** hacer un cumplido a alguien; **to return the c.** *also Ironic* devolver el cumplido; **with compliments** con mis mejores deseos; **to send one's compliments to sb** enviar saludos *or CAm, Col, Ecuad* saludes a alguien
    2 *vt* **to c. sb on sth** felicitar a alguien por algo

complimentary [kɒmplɪ'mentərɪ] *adj* (**a**) *(praising)* elogioso(a) (**b**) *(free)* de regalo, gratuito(a); **c. ticket** invitación *f*

comply [kəm'plaɪ] *vi* **to c. with** *(rule)* cumplir, ajustarse a; *(order)* cumplir; *(request)* someterse a

component [kəm'pəʊnənt] **1** *n* pieza *f*
    2 *adj* **c. part** pieza *f*

compose [kəm'pəʊz] *vt* (**a**) *(music, poetry)* componer (**b**) *(constitute)* **to be composed of** estar compuesto(a) de (**c**) *(calm)* **to c. oneself** serenarse

composed [kəm'pəʊzd] *adj* sereno(a)

composer [kəm'pəʊzə(r)] *n Mus* compositor(ora) *m,f*

composite ['kɒmpəzɪt] *adj* compuesto(a)

composition [kɒmpə'zɪʃən] *n (piece of music, act of composing)* composición *f*; *(essay)* redacción *f*

compositor [kəm'pɒzɪtə(r)] *n Typ* cajista *mf*

compos mentis ['kɒmpəs'mentɪs] *adj Law* en pleno uso de sus facultades mentales

compost ['kɒmpɒst] *n* compost *m*, mantillo *m*; **c. heap** *or* **pile** montón *m* de compost *or* mantillo

composure [kəm'pəʊʒə(r)] *n* compostura *f*; **to lose/ recover one's c.** perder/recobrar la compostura

compound¹ *n* ['kɒmpaʊnd] *Chem & Gram* compuesto *m*
    2 *adj* compuesto(a); *Math* **c. fraction** fracción *f* mixta; *Med* **c. fracture** fractura *f* abierta; *Fin* **c. interest** interés *m* compuesto
    3 *vt* [kəm'paʊnd] *(problem)* complicar, empeorar

compound² ['kɒmpaʊnd] *n (enclosure)* recinto *m*

comprehend [kɒmprɪ'hend] *vt* comprender

comprehensible [kɒmprɪ'hensəbəl] *adj* comprensible

comprehension [kɒmprɪ'henʃən] *n* comprensión *f*; **it is beyond my c.** me resulta incomprensible

comprehensive [kɒmprɪ'hensɪv] *adj (answer, study, view)* detallado(a), completo(a); *(defeat, victory)* rotundo(a); *Fin* **c. insurance** seguro *m* a todo riesgo

compress 1 *n* ['kɒmpres] *Med* compresa *f*, apósito *m*
    2 *vt* [kəm'pres] *(gas)* comprimir; *(text)* condensar

compression [kəm'preʃən] *n* compresión *f*

compressor [kəm'presə(r)] *n* compresor *m*

comprise [kəm'praɪz] *vt (include)* comprender, incluir; **to be comprised of** constar de

compromise ['kɒmprəmaɪz] **1** *n* solución *f* negociada *or* intermedia; **to reach a c.** alcanzar una solución intermedia
    2 *vt* poner en peligro; **to c. oneself** ponerse en una situación comprometida; **he compromised his principles** traicionó sus principios
    3 *vi* transigir, hacer concesiones

compromising ['kɒmprəmaɪzɪŋ] *adj* comprometedor(ora)

compulsion [kəm'pʌlʃən] *n (urge)* impulso *m*; *(obligation)* obligación *f*; **under c.** bajo coacción; **to be under no c. to do sth** no estar obligado(a) a hacer algo

compulsive [kəm'pʌlsɪv] *adj* compulsivo(a); **it's c. viewing** hay que verlo

compulsory [kəm'pʌlsərɪ] *adj* obligatorio(a)

compunction [kəm'pʌŋkʃən] *n* reparo *m*; **without c.** sin reparos

computation [kɒmpjʊ'teɪʃən] *n* cálculo *m*

computational [kɒmpjʊ'teɪʃənəl] *adj* computacional

compute [kəm'pju:t] *vt* calcular

computer [kəm'pju:tə(r)] *n Esp* ordenador *m*, *Am* computadora *f*, *Am* computador *m*; **c. crime** delitos *mpl* informáticos; **c. game** juego *m* de *Esp* ordenador *or Am* computadora; **c. literacy** conocimientos *mpl* de informática; **c. literate** con conocimientos de informática; **c. printout** listado *m*, copia *f* impresa; **c. program** programa *m* informático; **c. programmer** programador(ora) *m,f*; **c. programming** programación *f* (de *Esp* ordenadores *or Am* computadoras); **c. rage** = comportamiento agresivo por ordenador; **c. science** informática *f*; **c. scientist** informático(a) *m,f*; **c. simulation** simulación *f* por *Esp* ordenador *or Am* computadora; **c. virus** virus *m inv* informático

computer-aided [kəm'pju:təreɪdɪd], **computer-assisted** [kəm'pju:tərə'sɪstɪd] *adj* **c. design** diseño *m* asistido por *Esp* ordenador *or Am* computadora; **c. instruction** *or* **learning** enseñanza *f* asistida por *Esp* ordenador *or Am* computadora; **c. manufacturing** fabricación *f* asistida por *Esp* ordenador *or Am* computadora

computerization [kəmpju:təraɪ'zeɪʃən] *n* informatización *f*, *Am* computarización *f*, *Am* computadorización *f*

computerize [kəm'pju:təraɪz] *vt* informatizar, *Am* computarizar, *Am* computadorizar

computing [kəm'pju:tɪŋ] *n* informática *f*, *Am* computación *f*

comrade ['kɒmreɪd] *n* camarada *mf*, compañero(a) *m,f*

comradeship ['kɒmrədʃɪp] *n* camaradería *f*

con¹ [kɒn] *Fam* **1** *n (swindle)* timo *m*, *Andes, RP* truchada *f*; **what a c.!** ¡menudo timo!, *Andes, RP* ¡qué truchada!; **c. artist** *or* **man** timador *m*, *Andes, RP* cagador *m*
    2 *vt (pt & pp* **conned)** *(swindle)* timar, *RP* cagar; **to c. sth out of sb, to c. sb out of sth** timarle *or* estafarle algo a alguien; **to c. sb into doing sth** embaucar a alguien para que haga algo

con² *n Fam (prisoner)* recluso(a) *m,f*, preso(a) *m,f*

con³ *n (disadvantage)* **the pros and cons** los pros y los contras

concave ['kɒnkeɪv] *adj* cóncavo(a)

conceal [kən'si:l] *vt (object)* ocultar, esconder (**from** de); *(fact)* ocultar (**from** a); **to c. oneself** esconderse, ocultarse

concealed [kən'si:ld] *adj (lighting)* indirecto(a); *(driveway, entrance)* oculto(a)

concede [kən'si:d] **1** *vt* (**a**) *(admit)* reconocer, admitir; **to c. defeat** admitir la derrota; **she was forced to c. that he was right** se vio obligada a reconocer que él tenía razón (**b**) *(grant, allow)* conceder (**c**) *Sport* **to c. a goal** encajar un gol
    2 *vi* ceder

conceit [kən'si:t] *n (vanity)* engreimiento *m*, presuntuosidad *f*

conceited [kən'si:tɪd] *adj* engreído(a), presuntuoso(a)

conceivable [kən'si:vəbəl] *adj* concebible, posible; **it is c. that…** es posible que…

conceivably [kən'si:vəblɪ] *adv* posiblemente; **she could c. have done it** es posible que lo haya hecho ella

conceive [kən'si:v] **1** *vt* concebir
    2 *vi* **to c. of** imaginar, concebir

concentrate ['kɒnsəntreɪt] **1** *vt* concentrar; **the threat helped to c. their minds** la amenaza les hizo aplicarse
    2 *vi* concentrarse (**on** en)
    3 *n* concentrado *m*

concentration [kɒnsən'treɪʃən] *n* concentración *f*; **c. camp** campo *m* de concentración; **c. span** capacidad *f* de concentración

concentric [kɒn'sentrɪk] *adj Math* concéntrico(a)

concept ['kɒnsept] *n* concepto *m*

conception [kən'sepʃən] *n* (**a**) *(of child, idea)* concepción *f* (**b**) *(understanding)* idea *f*; **to have no c. of sth** no tener ni idea de algo

conceptual [kən'septjʊəl] *adj* conceptual

conceptualize [kən'septjʊəlaız] *vt* formarse un concepto de

concern [kən'sɜːn] **1** *n* (**a**) *(interest)* interés *m*; **it's no c. of mine/yours** no es de mi/tu incumbencia; **of public c.** de interés público (**b**) *(worry, compassion)* preocupación *f*; **to give cause for c.** dar motivos de preocupación; **there is no cause for c.** no hay motivo de preocupación; **to show c.** mostrar preocupación (**c**) *(company)* empresa *f*
    2 *vt* (**a**) *(affect)* concernir, incumbir; **to c. oneself with** *or* **about sth** preocuparse de algo; **as far as I'm concerned...** por lo que a mí respecta...; **to whom it may c.** a quien pueda interesar (**b**) *(worry)* preocupar (**c**) *(be about)* concernir, atañer; **it concerns your request for a transfer** tiene que ver con tu petición de traslado

concerned [kən'sɜːnd] *adj (worried)* preocupado(a) (**about** por)

concerning [kən'sɜːnɪŋ] *prep* en relación con *or* a

concert ['kɒnsət] *n* (**a**) *(musical)* concierto *m*; **in c.** en concierto; **c. hall** sala *f* de conciertos; **c. pianist** concertista *mf* de piano (**b**) *(cooperation)* **in c. with** en colaboración con

concerted [kən'sɜːtɪd] *adj* conjunto(a), concertado(a)

concertgoer ['kɒnsətgəʊə(r)] *n* **a crowd of concertgoers** una multitud de asistentes al concierto

concertina [kɒnsə'tiːnə] *n (musical instrument)* concertina *f*

concerto [kən'tʃɜːtəʊ] *(pl* **concertos***)* *n Mus* concierto *m*; **piano/violin c.** concierto para piano/violín

concession [kən'seʃən] *n* (**a**) *(compromise)* concesión *f*; **to make concessions** hacer concesiones (**b**) *(discount)* descuento *m* (**c**) *(within store)* concesión *f*; **c. stand** puesto *m* de refrescos

concessionary [kən'seʃənərɪ] *adj* con descuento

conciliate [kən'sɪlɪeɪt] *vt (appease)* apaciguar; *(reconcile)* conciliar

conciliation [kənsɪlɪ'eɪʃən] *n* arbitraje *m*, conciliación *f*; **the dispute went to c.** se recurrió al arbitraje para dirimir el conflicto

conciliatory [kən'sɪlɪətərɪ] *adj* conciliador(ora)

concise [kən'saɪs] *adj* conciso(a)

conclude [kən'kluːd] **1** *vt* (**a**) *(finish)* concluir; **to c. a treaty** firmar un tratado (**b**) *(deduce)* **to c. that...** concluir que...
    2 *vi (finish)* concluir

concluding [kən'kluːdɪŋ] *adj* final

conclusion [kən'kluːʒən] *n* (**a**) *(inference)* conclusión *f*; **to draw a c.** sacar una conclusión; **to come to** *or* **reach a c.** llegar a una conclusión; **to jump to conclusions** sacar conclusiones precipitadas (**b**) *(end)* conclusión *f*; **in c.** en conclusión, concluyendo

conclusive [kən'kluːsɪv] *adj* concluyente

conclusively [kən'kluːsɪvlɪ] *adv* de manera concluyente

concoct [kən'kɒkt] *vt (dish)* preparar, confeccionar; *(plan, excuse)* tramar, fraguar

concoction [kən'kɒkʃən] *n* poción *f*, brebaje *m*

concord ['kɒŋkɔːd] *n* armonía *f*, concordia *f*

concordance [kən'kɔːdəns] *n (agreement)* consonancia *f*, acuerdo *m*; **to be in c. with...** estar en consonancia con...

concourse ['kɒnkɔːs] *n (in airport, railway station)* vestíbulo *m*

concrete ['kɒnkriːt] **1** *n* hormigón *m*, *Am* concreto *m*; **c. jungle** jungla *f* de(l) asfalto; **c. mixer** hormigonera *f*
    2 *adj (definite)* concreto(a); *Gram* **c. noun** sustantivo *m* concreto

concubine ['kɒŋkjʊbaɪn] *n* concubina *f*

concur [kən'kɜː(r)] *(pt & pp* **concurred***)* *vi (agree)* coincidir, estar de acuerdo (**with** con)

concurrent [kən'kʌrənt] *adj* simultáneo(a)

concurrently [kən'kʌrəntlɪ] *adv* simultáneamente

concuss [kən'kʌs] *vt* conmocionar

concussed [kən'kʌst] *adj* conmocionado(a)

concussion [kən'kʌʃən] *n* conmoción *f* cerebral

condemn [kən'dem] *vt* (**a**) *Law (sentence)* condenar (**to** a); **to c. sb to death** condenar a alguien a muerte (**b**) *(censure)* condenar (**c**) *(building)* declarar en ruina

condemnation [kɒndem'neɪʃən] *n* condena *f*

condensation [kɒnden'seɪʃən] *n (on glass)* vaho *m*; *(on walls)* condensación *f*, vapor *m* condensado

condense [kən'dens] **1** *vt* (**a**) *(gas, liquid)* condensar; **condensed milk** leche *f* condensada (**b**) *(text)* condensar
    2 *vi* condensarse

condenser [kən'densə(r)] *n Tech* condensador *m*

condescend [kɒndɪ'send] *vi* **to c. toward sb** tratar a alguien con aires de superioridad; **to c. to do sth** dignarse a *or* tener a bien hacer algo

condescending [kɒndɪ'sendɪŋ] *adj* altivo(a)

condescension [kɒndɪ'senʃən] *n* altivez *f*

condiment ['kɒndɪmənt] *n* condimento *m*

condition [kən'dɪʃən] **1** *n* (**a**) *(state)* condiciones *fpl*, estado *m*; **in good/bad c.** en buen/mal estado; **you're in no c. to drive!** no estás en condiciones de conducir *or Am* manejar; **to be out of c.** *(person)* no estar en forma
    (**b**) **conditions** *(circumstances)* circunstancias *fpl*; **working conditions** condiciones *fpl* laborales; **driving conditions** estado *m* de las carreteras; *Law* **conditions of employment** términos *mpl* del contrato
    (**c**) *(requirement)* condición *f*; **on (the) c. that...** con la condición *or* a condición de que...; **on no c.** bajo ningún concepto; **on one c.** con una condición
    (**d**) *Med* enfermedad *f*, afección *f*; **heart c.** afección cardíaca
    2 *vt* (**a**) *(influence)* condicionar; **we have been conditioned to believe that...** nos han programado para creer que...; *Psy* **a conditioned reflex** un reflejo condicionado (**b**) *(hair)* suavizar

conditional [kən'dɪʃənəl] **1** *n Gram* condicional *m*, potencial *m*
    2 *adj* condicional; **to be c. on sth** depender de algo, tener algo como condición; *Law* **c. discharge** remisión *f* condicional de la pena

conditionally [kən'dɪʃənəlɪ] *adv (accept, grant)* condicionalmente

conditioner [kən'dɪʃənə(r)] *n (for hair)* suavizante *m*

conditioning [kən'dɪʃənɪŋ] *n (psychological)* condicionamiento *m*

condo ['kɒndəʊ] *(pl* **condos***)* *n (apartment)* apartamento *m*, *Esp* piso *m*, *Arg* departamento *m (en propiedad)*; *(building)* = bloque de pisos poseídos por diferentes propietarios

condolences [kən'dəʊlənsɪz] *npl* pésame *m*; **to offer sb one's c.** dar el pésame a alguien

condom ['kɒndəm] *n* preservativo *m*, condón *m*

condominium [kɒndə'mɪnɪəm] *n (apartment)* apartamento *m*, *Esp* piso *m*, *Arg* departamento *m (en propiedad)*; *(building)* = bloque de pisos poseídos por diferentes propietarios

condone [kən'dəʊn] *vt* justificar; **I cannot c. such behavior** no puedo justificar ese tipo de comportamiento

condor ['kɒndɔː(r)] *n* cóndor *m*

conducive [kən'djuːsɪv] *adj* **to be c. to** ser favorable para, facilitar; **these conditions are not c. to economic growth** estas condiciones no son favorables para el crecimiento de la economía

conduct 1 *n* ['kɒndʌkt] *(behavior)* conducta *f*
    2 *vt* [kən'dʌkt] (**a**) *(business, operations)* gestionar, hacer; *(campaign, experiment)* realizar, hacer; *Mus (orchestra)* dirigir; **to c. oneself** comportarse, conducirse (**b**) *(guide)* **we were conducted around the factory** nos llevaron por toda la fábrica; **a conducted tour** una visita guiada (**c**) *(heat, electricity)* conducir
    3 *vi Mus* dirigir

conduction [kən'dʌkʃən] *n Phys* conducción *f*

conductivity [kɒndʌk'tɪvɪtɪ] n Phys conductividad f

conductor [kən'dʌktə(r)] n (**a**) (of orchestra) director(ora) m,f de orquesta (**b**) (of heat, electricity) conductor m

conduit ['kɒndjʊɪt] n conducto m

cone [kəʊn] n (shape) cono m; (of pine) piña f; (for ice cream) cucurucho m; (for traffic) cono m (de tráfico)

cone-shaped ['kəʊnʃeɪpt] adj cónico(a)

confab ['kɒnfæb] n Fam (discussion) deliberación f; **to have a c. about sth** deliberar sobre algo

confectioner [kən'fekʃənə(r)] n pastelero(a) m,f; Culin **c.'s custard** crema f pastelera; **c.'s (shop)** pastelería f; **c.'s sugar** azúcar m Esp, Méx glas or Esp de lustre or Chile flor or Col pulverizado or RP impalpable

confectionery [kən'fekʃənərɪ] n dulces mpl

confederacy [kən'fedərəsɪ] n confederación f, liga f; Hist **the C.** la Confederación

confederate [kən'fedərət] **1** n compinche mf, cómplice mf; Hist **C.** confederado(a) m,f
2 adj confederado(a)

confederation [kənfedə'reɪʃən] n confederación f

confer [kən'fɜː(r)] (pt & pp **conferred**) **1** vt (title, rank, powers) conferir, otorgar (**on** a); (degree, diploma) conceder, otorgar (**on** a)
2 vi (discuss) deliberar (**with** con)

conference ['kɒnfərəns] n (**a**) (congress) congreso m (**b**) (meeting) reunión f; **to be in (a) c.** estar reunido(a) (**c**) Sport conferencia f

confess [kən'fes] **1** vt confesar, admitir; Rel confesar; **to c. that...** confesar que...
2 vi confesar; Rel confesarse; **to c. to sth** confesarse culpable de algo, confesar algo

confession [kən'feʃən] n confesión f; Rel **to go to c.** confesarse

confessional [kən'feʃənəl] n Rel confesionario m, confesonario m

confessor [kən'fesə(r)] n Rel confesor m

confetti [kən'fetɪ] n confeti m

confidant [kɒnfɪ'dænt] n confidente m

confide [kən'faɪd] **1** vt confiar; **to c. sth to sb** confiarle algo a alguien
2 vi **to c. in sb** confiarse a or confesarse con alguien

confidence ['kɒnfɪdəns] n (**a**) (trust) confianza f; **to have c. in sb** fiarse de alguien, tener confianza en alguien; **to have every c. that...** estar completamente seguro(a) de que...; **to take sb into one's c.** confiarse a alguien; **c. trick** timo m, estafa f (**b**) (self-assurance) confianza f (en uno/una mismo(a)); **she's full of c.** tiene mucha confianza en sí misma (**c**) (secret) **to exchange confidences** intercambiar confidencias; **in c.** confidencialmente

confident ['kɒnfɪdənt] adj seguro(a) de sí mismo(a); **to be c. that...** estar seguro(a) de que...

confidential [kɒnfɪ'denʃəl] adj (secret) confidencial, secreto(a)

confidentiality [kɒnfɪdenʃɪ'ælɪtɪ] n confidencialidad f

confidentially [kɒnfɪ'denʃəlɪ] adv confidencialmente

confidently ['kɒnfɪdəntlɪ] adv con seguridad

configuration [kənfɪg(j)ʊ'reɪʃən] n configuración f

configure [kən'fɪg(j)ə(r)] vt configurar

confine [kən'faɪn] vt (**a**) (imprison) confinar, recluir; **to be confined to bed** tener que guardar cama; **to be confined to barracks** quedarse arrestado(a) en el cuartel; **in a confined space** en un espacio limitado (**b**) (limit) **to c. oneself to sth** limitarse a algo

confinement [kən'faɪnmənt] n (**a**) (in prison) reclusión f, encierro m (**b**) Old-fashioned Med (birth) parto m

confines ['kɒnfaɪnz] npl límites mpl; **within the c. of the home** en el ámbito del hogar

confirm [kən'fɜːm] vt confirmar

confirmation [kɒnfə'meɪʃən] n (gen) & Rel confirmación f

confirmed [kən'fɜːmd] adj (smoker, liar) empedernido(a)

confiscate ['kɒnfɪskeɪt] vt confiscar

confiscation [kɒnfɪs'keɪʃən] n confiscación f

conflagration [kɒnflə'greɪʃən] n Formal incendio m

conflict 1 n ['kɒnflɪkt] conflicto m; **to come into c. with** entrar en conflicto con; **a c. of interests** un conflicto de intereses
2 vi [kən'flɪkt] (evidence, reports) chocar (**with** con)

conflicting [kən'flɪktɪŋ] adj (opinions) encontrado(a); (reports, evidence) contradictorio(a)

confluence ['kɒnfluəns] n confluencia f

conform [kən'fɔːm] vi (**a**) (be in keeping with) (laws, standards) ajustarse (**to** a); (expectations) ajustarse, responder (**with** a) (**b**) (behave normally) ser conformista, actuar como todo el mundo

conformism [kən'fɔːmɪzəm] n conformismo m

conformist [kən'fɔːmɪst] n & adj conformista mf

conformity [kən'fɔːmɪtɪ] n conformidad f; **in c. with...** de conformidad con...

confound [kən'faʊnd] vt (**a**) (frustrate) frustrar (**b**) (surprise) desconcertar, sorprender (**c**) Fam **c. it/him!** ¡maldita sea!

confront [kən'frʌnt] vt (face up to, meet face to face) enfrentarse a, hacer frente a; **to be confronted by a problem** enfrentarse a un problema; **to c. sb (about sth)** hablar cara a cara con alguien (acerca de algo); **to c. sb with the facts** enfrentar a alguien a los hechos

confrontation [kɒnfrʌn'teɪʃən] n confrontación f

confuse [kən'fjuːz] vt (bewilder) desconcertar, confundir; (mix up) confundir

confused [kən'fjuːzd] adj (person) confundido(a), desorientado(a); (mind, ideas, situation) confuso(a); **to get c.** desorientarse

confusing [kən'fjuːzɪŋ] adj confuso(a); **Mexican history is very c.** la historia de México es muy complicada

confusingly [kən'fjuːzɪŋlɪ] adv confusamente; **c., both twins do exactly the same courses at the university** para mayor confusión, ambos gemelos cursan la misma carrera universitaria

confusion [kən'fjuːʒən] n (of person) desconcierto m; (disorder) confusión f; **to throw sth into c.** (country, party) sumir a algo en el desconcierto; (plans) trastocar algo por completo

congeal [kən'dʒiːl] vi (blood) coagularse

congenial [kən'dʒiːnɪəl] adj (person) simpático(a); (atmosphere) agradable

congenital [kən'dʒenɪtəl] adj congénito(a); Fig **c. liar** mentiroso(a) m,f patológico(a)

conger ['kɒŋgə(r)] n **c. (eel)** congrio m

congested [kən'dʒestɪd] adj (street, lungs) congestionado(a)

congestion [kən'dʒestʃən] n (of traffic, lungs) congestión f

conglomerate [kən'glɒmərət] n (**a**) Com conglomerado m de empresas (**b**) Geol conglomerado m

Congo ['kɒŋgəʊ] n **the C.** (country) el Congo

Congolese ['kɒŋgəliːz] n & adj congoleño(a) m,f

congrats [kən'græts] exclam Fam **c.!** ¡felicidades!, ¡enhorabuena!

congratulate [kən'grætjʊleɪt] vt felicitar; **to c. oneself on (having done) sth** felicitarse por (haber hecho) algo

congratulations [kəngrætjʊ'leɪʃənz] npl enhorabuena f, felicitaciones fpl; **to give** or **offer one's c. to sb** dar la enhorabuena a alguien; **c.!** ¡felicidades!

congratulatory [kən'grætjʊleɪtərɪ] adj de felicitación

congregate ['kɒŋgrɪgeɪt] vi congregarse

congregation [kɒŋgrɪ'geɪʃən] n (of church) fieles mpl, feligreses mpl

congress ['kɒŋgres] *n (conference)* congreso *m; Pol* **C.** el Congreso *(de los Estados Unidos)*

congressional [kən'greʃənəl] *adj Pol (leaders, report, committee)* del Congreso; *(election)* al Congreso; **c. elections** ≃ elecciones *fpl* legislativas

Congressman ['kɒŋgresmæn] *n Pol* congresista *m, Am* congresal *m*

Congresswoman ['kɒŋgreswʊmən] *n Pol* congresista *f, Am* congresal *f*

conical ['kɒnɪkəl] *adj* cónico(a)

conifer ['kɒnɪfə(r)] *n* conífera *f*

coniferous [kə'nɪfərəs] *adj* conífero(a)

conjecture [kən'dʒektʃə(r)] **1** *n* conjetura *f*; **it's sheer c.** no son más que conjeturas

2 *vt* conjeturar

3 *vi* hacer conjeturas

conjugal ['kɒndʒʊgəl] *adj* conyugal

conjugate ['kɒndʒʊgeɪt] *Gram* **1** *vt* conjugar

2 *vi* conjugarse

conjugation [kɒndʒʊ'geɪʃən] *n Gram* conjugación *f*

conjunction [kən'dʒʌŋkʃən] *n* conjunción *f*; **in c. with** junto con

conjunctivitis [kəndʒʌŋktɪ'vaɪtɪs] *n Med* conjuntivitis *f inv*

conjure ['kʌndʒə(r)] *vi (do magic)* hacer juegos de manos

▸**conjure up** *vt sep* **(a)** *(produce)* hacer aparecer; **she conjured up a meal** preparó una comida prácticamente con nada **(b)** *(call to mind)* evocar

conjurer, conjuror ['kʌndʒərə(r)] *n* mago(a) *m,f*, prestidigitador(ora) *m,f*

conjuring ['kʌndʒərɪŋ] *n* magia *f*, prestidigitación *f*; **c. trick** juego *m* de manos

conjuror = **conjurer**

▸**conk out** [kɒŋk] *vi Fam* **(a)** *(stop working) (car, TV) Esp* escacharrarse, *Am* descomponerse, *Méx* desconchinflarse **(b)** *(fall asleep)* quedarse frito/a *or Esp* roque *or Méx* súpito(a)

conman ['kɒnmæn] *n* timador *m*

connect [kə'nekt] **1** *vt* **(a)** *(pipes, wires, circuits)* conectar **(to** con *or* a), empalmar **(to** con *or* a) **(b)** *(relate) (person, problem)* relacionar **(with** con), vincular **(with** con *or* a); **to be connected with...** estar relacionado(a) con...; **are they connected?** ¿existe algún vínculo *or* alguna relación entre ellos?; **the two issues are not connected** los dos asuntos no están relacionados; **to be well connected** *(socially)* estar bien relacionado(a) **(c)** *Tel* poner, pasar; **could you c. me with Lost Property, please?** ¿me pasa *or Esp* pone con el departamento de objetos perdidos, por favor?

2 *vi* **(a)** *(wires, roads, pipes)* conectarse, empalmarse; **the living room connects with the kitchen** el salón da a la cocina **(b)** *(train, plane)* enlazar **(with** con) **(c)** *(blow)* dar en el blanco

▸**connect up** *vt sep (pipes, wires)* conectar

connection [kə'nekʃən] *n* **(a)** *(link, association)* conexión *f*, vínculo *m*; **to make a c. between X and Y** relacionar X con Y; **that was when I made the c.** entonces lo relacioné; **in c. with** en relación con; **in this c.** a este respecto **(b)** *(acquaintance)* contacto *m*; **she has important connections** está bien relacionada **(c)** *(of pipes, wires)* conexión *f*, empalme *m* **(d)** *(train, plane)* enlace *m*; **I missed my c.** he perdido el enlace

connivance [kə'naɪvəns] *n* connivencia *f*; **to be in c. with sb** estar en connivencia con alguien

connive [kə'naɪv] *vi* **(a)** *(conspire)* **to c. with** confabularse con **(b)** *(contribute)* **to c. at** contribuir a

conniving [kə'naɪvɪŋ] *adj* confabulador(ora)

connoisseur [kɒnɪ'sɜ:(r)] *n* entendido(a) *m,f* **(of** en)

connotation [kɒnə'teɪʃən] *n* connotación *f*

connote [kə'nəʊt] *vt (imply)* tener connotaciones de, connotar

conquer ['kɒŋkə(r)] *vt (country, sb's heart)* conquistar; *(difficulty, one's shyness, fears)* vencer

conquering ['kɒŋkərɪŋ] *adj* vencedor(ora)

conqueror ['kɒŋkərə(r)] *n* conquistador(ora) *m,f*

conquest ['kɒŋkwest] *n* conquista *f*; **to make a c. of sb** conquistar a alguien

conscience ['kɒnʃəns] *n* conciencia *f*; **to have a clear c.** tener la conciencia tranquila; **to have a guilty c.** tener sentimiento de culpa; **she had three deaths on her c.** sobre su conciencia pesaban tres muertes; **in all c.** en conciencia

conscientious [kɒnʃɪ'enʃəs] *adj* concienzudo(a); **she's c. about wiping her feet before entering the house** nunca deja de limpiarse los zapatos antes de entrar en casa; **c. objector** objetor(ora) *m,f* de conciencia

conscious ['kɒnʃəs] *adj* **(a)** *(awake)* **to be c.** estar consciente; **to become c.** volver en sí, recobrar la con(s)ciencia **(b)** *(aware)* **to be c. of** ser consciente de; **to become c. of** cobrar conciencia de, darse cuenta de; **to be c. that...** ser consciente de que...; *Psy* **the c. mind** la con(s)ciencia, el consciente **(c)** *(intentional)* consciente, deliberado(a); **to make a c. effort to do sth** hacer un esfuerzo consciente para hacer algo; **to make a c. decision to do sth** tomar conscientemente la decisión de hacer algo

-**conscious** ['kɒnʃəs] *suffix* **fashion-c.** que sigue la moda; **health-c.** preocupado(a) por la salud

consciousness ['kɒnʃəsnɪs] *n* **(a)** *Med* con(s)ciencia *f*; **to lose c.** quedar inconsciente; **to regain c.** volver en sí **(b)** *(awareness)* conciencia *f*, concienciación *f*; **to raise sb's c. of sth** concienciar a alguien de algo; **c. raising** concienciación *f*

conscript 1 *n* ['kɒnskrɪpt] recluta *mf* (forzoso)

2 *vt* [kən'skrɪpt] reclutar *(forzosamente)*

conscription [kən'skrɪpʃən] *n* reclutamiento *m* obligatorio

consecrate ['kɒnsɪkreɪt] *vt Rel & Fig* consagrar **(to** a)

consecration [kɒnsɪ'kreɪʃən] *n* consagración *f*

consecutive [kən'sekjʊtɪv] *adj* consecutivo(a); **on three c. days** tres días consecutivos

consensual [kən'sensjʊəl] *adj* **(a)** *(approach, politics)* consensuado(a) **(b)** *(sexual activity)* consentido(a) **(c)** *Law (contract)* consensual

consensus [kən'sensəs] *n* consenso *m*; **to reach a c.** alcanzar un consenso

consent [kən'sent] **1** *n* consentimiento *m*

2 *vi* **to c. to (do) sth** consentir (en hacer) algo; *Law* **consenting adult** mayor *mf* de edad (que actúa de motu proprio)

consequence ['kɒnsɪkwəns] *n* **(a)** *(result)* consecuencia *f*; **as a c.** como consecuencia; **in c.** en consecuencia; **to take the consequences** asumir las consecuencias **(b)** *(importance)* **of little c.** de poca relevancia; **of no c.** irrelevante

consequent ['kɒnsɪkwənt] *adj* consiguiente; **c. upon sth** resultante de algo

consequential [kɒnsɪ'kwenʃəl] *adj Formal* **(a)** *(resultant)* consiguiente, resultante **(b)** *(significant)* trascendente, relevante

conservation [kɒnsə'veɪʃən] *n (of the environment)* conservación *f or* protección *f* del medio ambiente; *(of energy, resources)* conservación *f*; **c. area** *(of town, city)* zona *f* arquitectónica protegida; *(nature reserve)* zona *f* protegida

conservationist [kɒnsə'veɪʃənɪst] *n* ecologista *mf*

conservative [kən'sɜ:vətɪv] **1** *n* conservador(ora) *m,f*

2 *adj* conservador(ora); **a c. estimate** un cálculo prudente *or* por lo bajo

conservatively [kən'sɜ:vətɪvlɪ] *adv* **(a)** *(to dress)* de forma conservadora, con un estilo conservador **(b)** *(cautiously)* **it was c. estimated at $5,000** se calculó en 5.000 dólares como mínimo

conservator [kən'sɜ:vətə(r)] *n* conservador(ora) *m,f*

conservatory [kən'sɜːvətrɪ] n (**a**) (room) = habitación adicional acristalada (**b**) Mus conservatorio m

conserve 1 vt [kən'sɜːv] (monument) conservar, preservar; (water, energy) reservar

   2 n ['kɒnsɜːv] (jam) compota f

consider [kən'sɪdə(r)] vt (**a**) (think over) considerar; **to c. doing sth** considerar hacer algo; **to c. whether to do sth** contemplar la posibilidad de hacer algo; **the jury retired to c. its verdict** el jurado se retiró a deliberar; **to c. sb for a job** tener en cuenta a alguien para un puesto (**b**) (take into account) tener en cuenta; **all things considered** mirándolo bien (**c**) (regard) considerar; **c. it done** considéralo hecho; **to c. oneself happy** considerarse feliz

considerable [kən'sɪdərəbəl] adj considerable; **with c. difficulty** con grandes dificultades

considerate [kən'sɪdərət] adj considerado(a) (**toward** or **to** con)

considerately [kən'sɪdərətlɪ] adv con consideración

consideration [kənsɪdə'reɪʃən] n (**a**) (deliberation) **different possibilities are under c.** se están estudiando varias posibilidades; **after due c.** tras las debidas deliberaciones; **to give a proposal some c.** considerar una propuesta; **to take sth into c.** tomar algo en consideración (**b**) (factor) factor m; **for a small c.** (payment) a cambio de una pequeña retribución (**c**) (respect) consideración f; **show some c.!** ¡ten un poco de consideración!; **out of c. for** por consideración hacia

considering [kən'sɪdərɪŋ] **1** prep considerando, teniendo en cuenta

   2 conj considerando que, teniendo en cuenta que; **c. (that) he is so young** teniendo en cuenta su juventud

   3 adv **it's not so bad, c.** no está tan mal, después de todo

consign [kən'saɪn] vt (**a**) (entrust) confiar (**to** a) (**b**) (send) consignar (**to** a), enviar (**to** a)

consignment [kən'saɪnmənt] n (of goods) envío m

▸**consist of** [kən'sɪst] vt insep consistir en

consistency [kən'sɪstənsɪ] n (**a**) (of substance, liquid) consistencia f (**b**) (of actions, arguments) coherencia f, congruencia f; **to lack c.** ser incongruente (**c**) (of performance, work) regularidad f, constancia f

consistent [kən'sɪstənt] adj (reasoning, behavior) coherente, congruente; (quality, standard) invariable, constante; (refusal, failure) constante, continuo(a); **c. with** coherente con, consecuente con

consistently [kən'sɪstəntlɪ] adv (play, perform) con regularidad; (fail, deny, oppose) constantemente

consolation [kɒnsə'leɪʃən] n consuelo m; **that's one c.** es un consuelo; **if it's any c.** si te sirve de consuelo; **c. prize** premio m de consolación

console[1] ['kɒnsəʊl] n (control panel) consola f

console[2] [kən'səʊl] vt consolar

consolidate [kən'sɒlɪdeɪt] **1** vt consolidar

   2 vi consolidarse

consolidated [kən'sɒlɪdeɪtɪd] adj consolidado(a); Fin **c. accounts** cuentas fpl consolidadas

consolidation [kənsɒlɪ'deɪʃən] n consolidación f

consonant ['kɒnsənənt] **1** n consonante f

   2 adj Formal **c. with** en consonancia con

consort ['kɒnsɔːt] n (spouse of monarch) consorte mf

▸**consort with** [kən'sɔːt] vt insep asociarse con

consortium [kən'sɔːtɪəm] (pl **consortiums** or **consortia** [kən'sɔːtɪə]) n Com consorcio m

conspicuous [kən'spɪkjʊəs] adj (person) visible; (color) llamativo(a); (bravery, intelligence) notable; **to look c.** resaltar, llamar la atención; **to make oneself c.** hacerse notar; **in a c. position** en un lugar bien visible; **to be c. by one's/its absence** brillar por su ausencia; **c. consumption** ostentación f en el consumo

conspiracy [kən'spɪrəsɪ] n conspiración f, conjura f; **c. theory** = teoría que sostiene la existencia de una conspiración, generalmente imaginaria

conspirator [kən'spɪrətə(r)] n conspirador(ora) m,f

conspiratorial [kənspɪrə'tɔːrɪəl] adj conspirador(ora), de conspiración

conspire [kən'spaɪə(r)] vi (person) conspirar (**against/with** contra/con); (events) obrar; **to c. with sb to do sth** conspirar con alguien para hacer algo; **circumstances conspired against me** las circunstancias obraban en mi contra

constant ['kɒnstənt] **1** adj (**a**) (unchanging) (price, temperature) constante; (friend) leal (**b**) (unceasing) (attention, questions) continuo(a), constante; **a c. stream of insults** una sarta de insultos

   2 n constante f

constellation [kɒnstə'leɪʃən] n constelación f

consternation [kɒnstə'neɪʃən] n consternación f

constipated ['kɒnstɪpeɪtɪd] adj estreñido(a)

constipation [kɒnstɪ'peɪʃən] n estreñimiento m

constituency [kən'stɪtjʊənsɪ] n Pol circunscripción f electoral

constituent [kən'stɪtjʊənt] **1** n (**a**) Pol elector(ora) m,f (**b**) (part) elemento m (constitutivo)

   2 adj constitutivo(a)

constitute ['kɒnstɪtjuːt] vt constituir

constitution [kɒnstɪ'tjuːʃən] n (of state, organization) constitución f; **to have a strong c.** ser de constitución robusta

constitutional [kɒnstɪ'tjuːʃənəl] **1** n (walk) paseo m

   2 adj (reform, decision) constitucional; **c. law** derecho m constitucional; **c. monarchy** monarquía f constitucional

constitutionally [kɒnstɪ'tjuːʃənəlɪ] adv constitucionalmente

constrain [kən'streɪn] vt restringir, constreñir; **to feel constrained to do sth** sentirse obligado(a) a hacer algo

constraint [kən'streɪnt] n (restriction) limitación f, restricción f; **to place constraints (up)on sb/sth** imponer restricciones a alguien/algo; **to do sth under c.** hacer algo bajo coacción; **to speak without c.** hablar abiertamente; **financial constraints** restricciones económicas

constrict [kən'strɪkt] vt (blood vessel) constreñir, contraer; (person, economy) constreñir

constriction [kən'strɪkʃən] n (of person, economy) constricción f; **c. of the blood vessels** vasoconstricción f

construct 1 n ['kɒnstrʌkt] (idea) concepto m

   2 vt [kən'strʌkt] (build) construir

construction [kən'strʌkʃən] n (**a**) (act of building, thing built) construcción f; **under c.** en construcción; **the c. industry** (el sector de) la construcción; **c. site** obra f; **c. workers** obreros mpl de la construcción (**b**) (interpretation) **to put a favorable/ unfavorable c. on sb's words** darle un sentido bueno/malo a las palabras de alguien

constructive [kən'strʌktɪv] adj (comment, proposal) constructivo(a)

construe [kən'struː] vt (interpret) interpretar

consul ['kɒnsəl] n cónsul mf

consular ['kɒnsjʊlə(r)] adj consular

consulate ['kɒnsjʊlət] n consulado m

consult [kən'sʌlt] **1** vt consultar

   2 vi consultar (**with sb/about sth** con alguien/sobre algo)

consultancy [kən'sʌltənsɪ] n (**a**) (of medical specialist) = plaza de especialista hospitalario(a) (**b**) Com asesoría f, consultoría f

consultant [kən'sʌltənt] n (**a**) (medical specialist) médico(a) m,f especialista (en hospital) (**b**) Com asesor(ora) m,f, consultor(ora) m,f

consultation [kɒnsəl'teɪʃən] n consulta f; **to hold a c.**

(with) consultar (con); **in c. with sb** con la asesoría de alguien

consultative [kən'sʌltətɪv] *adj* consultivo(a)

consumables [kən'sju:məbəlz] *npl* bienes *mpl* consumibles; *Comptr* consumibles *mpl*

consume [kən'sju:m] *vt (food, fuel)* consumir; **to be consumed with jealousy/desire** estar consumido(a) por los celos/el deseo

consumer [kən'sju:mə(r)] *n (of product)* consumidor(ora) *m,f*; **the c. society** la sociedad de consumo; **c. durables** bienes *mpl* de consumo duraderos; **c. goods** bienes *mpl* de consumo; *Econ* **c. price index** índice *m* de precios al consumo, IPC *m*; **c. protection** protección *f* del consumidor

consumerism [kən'sju:mərɪzəm] *n* consumismo *m*

consummate 1 *adj* ['kɒnsjʊmət] *(skilled)* consumado(a)
   2 *vt* ['kɒnsəmeɪt] *(marriage, relationship)* consumar

consumption [kən'sʌmpʃən] *n* **(a)** *(of goods, resources)* consumo *m*; **unfit for human c.** no apto(a) para el consumo humano **(b)** *Old-fashioned (tuberculosis)* tisis *f inv*

contact ['kɒntækt] **1** *n* contacto *m*; **to be in/come into c. with** estar/ponerse en contacto con; **to make c. with sb** contactar con alguien, ponerse en contacto con alguien; **to lose c. with sb** perder el contacto con alguien; **he has lots of contacts** tiene muchos contactos; **c. lens** lente *f* de contacto, *Esp* lentilla *f*, *Méx* pupilente *f*; **c. lenses, contacts** lentillas *fpl*; **c. sport** deporte *m* de contacto
   2 *vt* contactar con, ponerse en contacto con

contactable [kən'tæktəbəl] *adj* localizable

contagious [kən'teɪdʒəs] *adj (disease, laughter)* contagioso(a)

contain [kən'teɪn] *vt* **(a)** *(hold, include)* contener **(b)** *(control)* contener; **I could scarcely c. my indignation** apenas podía contener la indignación; **to c. oneself** contenerse

container [kən'teɪnə(r)] *n (for storage)* recipiente *m*; *(for transport)* contenedor *m*; **c. lorry** camión *m* de transporte de contenedores; **c. ship** buque *m* de transporte de contenedores; **c. terminal** terminal *f* de contenedores

contaminate [kən'tæmɪneɪt] *vt also Fig* contaminar

contamination [kəntæmɪ'neɪʃən] *n* contaminación *f*

contd *(abbr* **continued)** cont., continúa, sigue; **c. on page 14** sigue en la página 14

contemplate ['kɒntempleɪt] *vt (look at, consider)* contemplar; **to c. doing sth** contemplar (la posibilidad de) hacer algo

contemplation [kɒntem'pleɪʃən] *n* contemplación *f*

contemplative [kən'templətɪv] *adj* contemplativo(a)

contemporary [kən'tempərərɪ] *n & adj* contemporáneo(a) *m,f*

contempt [kən'tempt] *n* desprecio *m*, menosprecio *m*; **to hold sb/sth in c.** sentir desprecio por alguien/algo; *Law* **c. of court** desacato *m* (al tribunal)

contemptible [kən'temptəbəl] *adj* despreciable

contemptuous [kən'temptjʊəs] *adj* despreciativo(a); **to be c. of** mostrar desprecio hacia

contend [kən'tend] **1** *vt* **to c. that...** afirmar que..., alegar que...
   2 *vi* **(a)** *(struggle)* enfrentarse **(with** a *or* con); **the difficulties I have to c. with** las dificultades a las que me tengo que enfrentar **(b)** *(compete)* **to c. for sth** disputarse algo, competir por algo

contender [kən'tendə(r)] *n* contendiente *mf*

content[1] ['kɒntent] *n* contenido *m*; **contents** *(of pockets, drawer, house)* contenido *m*; *(in book)* índice *m*; **high protein/fiber c.** alto contenido en proteínas/fibra; **contents page** *(of book)* página *f* de índice

content[2] [kən'tent] **1** *adj* **to be c. with sth** estar satisfecho(a) con *or* de algo
   2 *vt* **to c. oneself with (doing) sth** contentarse con (hacer) algo

contented [kən'tentɪd] *adj (person, smile)* satisfecho(a) **(with** con *or* de); **to be c. (with)** estar satisfecho(a) (con *or* de)

contention [kən'tenʃən] *n* **(a)** *(dispute)* disputa *f*; **to be in c. (for sth)** tener posibilidades (de ganar algo) **(b)** *(opinion)* argumento *m*; **my c. is that...** sostengo que...

contentious [kən'tenʃəs] *adj (issue, views)* polémico(a); *(person)* que siempre se mete en discusiones

contentment [kən'tentmənt] *n* satisfacción *f*

contest 1 *n* ['kɒntest] *(competition)* concurso *m*; *(in boxing)* combate *m*; **leadership c.** carrera *f or* lucha *f* por el liderazgo
   2 *vt* [kən'test] *(right, decision)* impugnar, rebatir; **to c. a seat** disputar un escaño; *Pol* **a fiercely contested election** unas elecciones muy reñidas

contestant [kən'testənt] *n (in competition, game)* concursante *mf*; *(in sporting competition)* competidor(ora) *m,f*; *(in election)* candidato(a) *m,f*

context ['kɒntekst] *n* contexto *m*; **in/out of c.** en/fuera de contexto; **to quote sth out of c.** citar algo fuera de contexto; **to put sth into c.** poner algo en contexto

contextual [kən'tekstjʊəl] *adj* contextual, relativo(a) al contexto

contextualize [kɒn'tekstjʊəlaɪz] *vt* contextualizar

continent[1] ['kɒntɪmənt] *n (landmass)* continente *m*

continent[2] *adj Med & Formal* continente

continental [kɒntɪ'nentəl] *adj* continental; **c. drift** deriva *f* continental; **c. shelf** plataforma *f* continental

contingency [kən'tɪndʒənsɪ] *n* contingencia *f*, eventualidad *f*; **to allow for contingencies** tomar precauciones ante cualquier eventualidad; *Law* **c. fee** honorarios *mpl* condicionales; **c. fund** fondo *m* de emergencia; **c. plan** plan *m* de emergencia

contingent [kən'tɪndʒənt] **1** *n* contingente *m*
   2 *adj* contingente; **to be c. on sth** depender de algo

continual [kən'tɪnjʊəl] *adj* continuo(a)

continuation [kəntɪnjʊ'eɪʃən] *n (of story, situation)* continuación *f*; *(of road)* continuación *f*, prolongación *f*

continue [kən'tɪnju:] **1** *vt* continuar, seguir; *(after interruption)* reanudar; **to c. doing** *or* **to do sth** continuar *or* seguir haciendo algo; **to be continued** continuará; **continued on page 30** sigue en la página 30
   2 *vi* continuar, seguir; **he continued on his way** siguió su camino; **the situation cannot c.** esto no puede continuar así

continuity [kɒntɪ'nju:ɪtɪ] *n* continuidad *f*; *Cin* **c. girl** script *f*, anotadora *f*

continuous [kən'tɪnjʊəs] *adj* continuo(a); *Sch & Univ* **c. assessment** evaluación *f* continua; *Comptr* **c. paper** *or* **stationery** papel *m* continuo; *Cin* **c. performance** sesión *f* continua

contort [kən'tɔ:t] *vt* contorsionar

contortion [kən'tɔ:ʃən] *n* contorsión *f*

contour ['kɒntʊə(r)] *n* contorno *m*, perfil *m*; **c. (line)** *(on map)* curva *f* de nivel; **c. map** mapa *m* topográfico

contraband ['kɒntrəbænd] *n* contrabando *m*; **c. goods** mercancía *f* de contrabando

contraception [kɒntrə'sepʃən] *n* anticoncepción *f*

contraceptive [kɒntrə'septɪv] **1** *n* anticonceptivo *m*
   2 *adj* **c. method** método *m* anticonceptivo; **c. pill** píldora *f* anticonceptiva

contract 1 *n* ['kɒntrækt] contrato *m*; **to break one's c.** incumplir el contrato; **to be under c.** estar contratado(a); **to enter into a c.** firmar un contrato; **to take out a c. on sb** *(hire assassin)* contratar a un asesino para matar a alguien; **c. killer** asesino(a) *m,f* a sueldo
   2 *vt* [kən'trækt] *(illness)* contraer; **to c. debts** contraer deudas; **to c. to do sth** firmar un contrato para hacer algo; **to c. sb to do sth** contratar a alguien para hacer algo
   3 *vi (shrink)* contraerse

▶**contract out** _Com vt sep_ **the cleaning service was contracted out** el servicio de limpieza lo lleva una contrata

contraction [kən'trækʃən] _n_ contracción _f_; **contractions have begun** _(before childbirth)_ han empezado las contracciones

contractor [kən'træktə(r)] _n_ contratista _mf_

contractual [kən'træktjʊəl] _adj (agreement, obligations)_ contractual

contractually [kən'træktjʊəlɪ] _adv_ contractualmente

contradict [kɒntrə'dɪkt] _vt (disagree with)_ contradecir; _(deny)_ desmentir; **to c. oneself** contradecirse

contradiction [kɒntrə'dɪkʃən] _n_ contradicción _f_; **it's a c. in terms** es una contradicción en sí misma

contradictory [kɒntrə'dɪktərɪ] _adj_ contradictorio(a)

contralto [kən'træltəʊ] _(pl_ **contraltos)** _n Mus_ contralto _f_

contraption [kən'træpʃən] _n Fam_ cachivache _m_, artilugio _m_

contrary ['kɒntrərɪ] **1** _n_ **the c.** lo contrario; **on the c.** por el _or_ al contrario; **unless you hear to the c.** salvo que te digan lo contrario _or_ otra cosa
2 _adj_ **(a)** _(opposite)_ contrario(a); **c. to** contrario(a) a; **c. to my expectations** al contrario de lo que esperaba; **c. to popular belief,...** en contra de lo que vulgarmente se cree,... **(b)** [kən'treərɪ] _(awkward)_ puñetero(a), difícil

contrast 1 _n_ ['kɒntrɑːst] contraste _m_; **in c. with** _or_ **to** en contraste con
2 _vt_ [kən'trɑːst] **to c. sth with sth** contrastar _or_ comparar algo con algo _or_ algo y algo
3 _vi_ contrastar **(with** con)

contravene [kɒntrə'viːn] _vt_ contravenir

contravention [kɒntrə'venʃən] _n (of law)_ contravención _f_; **in c. of...** contraviniendo...

contribute [kən'trɪbjuːt] **1** _vt_ contribuir con, aportar; **to c. an article to a newspaper** escribir una colaboración para un periódico
2 _vi_ contribuir

contribution [kɒntrɪ'bjuːʃən] _n_ contribución _f_, aportación _f_; _(to charity)_ donación _f_; **social security contributions** cotizaciones _fpl_ a la seguridad social

contributor [kən'trɪbjʊtə(r)] _n (to charity)_ donante _mf_; _(to newspaper)_ colaborador(ora) _m,f_

contributory [kən'trɪbjʊtərɪ] _adj (cause, factor)_ coadyuvante; _Law_ **c. negligence** imprudencia _f or_ negligencia _f_ (culposa), culpa _f_ concurrente

contrite [kən'traɪt] _adj_ arrepentido(a); **to be c.** estar arrepentido(a)

contrition [kən'trɪʃən] _n_ arrepentimiento _m_, contrición _f_

contrivance [kən'traɪvəns] _n (device)_ aparato _m_; _(scheme, plan)_ estratagema _f_

contrive [kən'traɪv] _vt (device, scheme)_ idear, inventar; **to c. to do sth** arreglárselas _or_ ingeniárselas para hacer algo

contrived [kən'traɪvd] _adj (words, compliment)_ estudiado(a), forzado(a); _(ending, plot)_ artificioso(a)

control [kən'trəʊl] **1** _n_ **(a)** _(power, restriction)_ control _m_; **to take c.** ponerse al mando, tomar el control; **to have c. over** controlar; **to be in c. of** _(in charge of)_ estar al cargo de; **to be back in c.** _(of situation)_ volver a controlar la situación; **to get out of c.** descontrolarse; **under c.** bajo control; **to bring a fire under c.** controlar un incendio; **due to circumstances beyond our c.** debido a circunstancias ajenas a nuestra voluntad; **to lose/regain c.** perder/recuperar el control; **he lost c. of himself** perdió el control; **c. group** grupo _m_ de control; **c. room** sala _f_ de control; **c. tower** _(at airport)_ torre _f_ de control
(b) _(of device)_ mando _m_; **volume/brightness c.** mando del volumen/brillo; **the controls** los mandos; **to be at the controls** estar a los mandos; **c. panel** tablero _m_ de mandos
(c) _(experiment)_ prueba _f_ de control; **c. group** grupo _m_ de control

2 _vt (pt & pp_ **controlled)** _(business, production, expenditure)_ controlar, regular; _(child, pupils)_ controlar, dominar; _(disease)_ controlar; _(vehicle)_ manejar, controlar; **to c. oneself** controlarse, dominarse; **to c. the traffic** dirigir el tráfico; **she was unable to c. her anger** fue incapaz de dominar su ira

controllable [kən'trəʊləbəl] _adj_ controlable; **it's no longer c.** está fuera de control

controlled [kən'trəʊld] _adj (person)_ controlado(a), contenido(a); _(experiment)_ controlado(a); **c. explosion** explosión _f_ controlada

controlling interest [kɒn'trəʊlɪŋ'ɪntrest] _n Fin_ control _m_ accionarial, participación _f_ mayoritaria

controversial [kɒntrə'vɜːʃəl] _adj_ polémico(a), controvertido(a)

controversy ['kɒntrəvɜːsɪ, kən'trɒvəsɪ] _n_ polémica _f_, controversia _f_

conundrum [kə'nʌndrəm] _n_ enigma _m_

conurbation [kɒnɜː'beɪʃən] _n_ conurbación _f_

convalesce [kɒnvə'les] _vi_ convalecer

convalescence [kɒnvə'lesəns] _n_ convalecencia _f_

convalescent [kɒnvə'lesənt] _n (patient)_ convaleciente _mf_; **c. home** clínica _f_ de reposo

convection [kən'vekʃən] _n_ convección _f_; **c. heater** calentador _m_ de aire

convene [kən'viːn] **1** _vt (meeting)_ convocar
2 _vi (committee)_ reunirse

convenience [kən'viːnɪəns] _n_ conveniencia _f_; **at your c.** a su conveniencia, como mejor le convenga; _Formal_ **at your earliest c.** en cuanto le sea posible; **c. food** comida _f_ preparada

convenient [kən'viːnɪənt] _adj_ **(a)** _(suitable) (arrangement, method)_ conveniente, adecuado(a); _(time, place)_ oportuno(a); **if it is c. for you** si te viene bien **(b)** _(handy) (place)_ bien situado(a); **c. for** próximo(a) a

convent ['kɒnvənt] _n Rel_ convento _m_; **c. school** colegio _m_ de monjas

convention [kən'venʃən] _n_ **(a)** _(conference)_ congreso _m_ **(b)** _(agreement)_ convención _f_, convenio _m_ **(c)** _(established practice)_ convencionalismo _m_, convención _f_; **to go against c.** ir contra las convenciones; **the c. is that...** según la costumbre,...

conventional [kən'venʃənəl] _adj_ convencional; **the c. wisdom is that...** la sabiduría popular dice que...; **c. warfare** guerra _f_ convencional

converge [kən'vɜːdʒ] _vi_ converger, convergir **(on** con)

conversant [kən'vɜːsənt] _adj_ **to be c. with sth** estar familiarizado(a) con algo

conversation [kɒnvə'seɪʃən] _n_ conversación _f_, _CAm, Méx_ plática _f_; **to have a c. (with sb)** mantener una conversación (con alguien); **to make c. (with)** dar conversación (a); **c. piece** tema _m_ de conversación; **c. stopper** _or_ **killer** comentario _m_ que corta la conversación

conversational [kɒnvə'seɪʃənəl] _adj (tone, style)_ coloquial; _Comptr (mode)_ conversacional

conversationalist [kɒnvə'seɪʃənəlɪst] _n_ conversador(ora) _m,f_; **to be a good c.** ser buen conversador

conversationally [kɒnvə'seɪʃənəlɪ] _adv_ **he mentioned, quite c., that he had got a new job** como quien no quiere la cosa, mencionó que tenía un empleo nuevo

converse[1] [kən'vɜːs] _vi (talk)_ conversar **(about** sobre)

converse[2] ['kɒnvɜːs] _n (opposite)_ **the c.** lo contrario, lo opuesto

conversion [kən'vɜːʃən] _n_ **(a)** _Rel & Fig_ conversión _f_ **(b)** _(alteration)_ conversión _f_, transformación _f_; **c. table** _(for measurements)_ tabla _f_ de conversión _or_ de equivalencias **(c)** _(in football)_ transformación _f_

convert 1 _n_ ['kɒnvɜːt] _Rel & Fig_ converso(a) _m,f_ **(to** a)

2 vt [kən'vɜːt] (**a**) Rel & Fig convertir (**b**) (alter, adapt) transformar, convertir (**into** en) (**c**) (in rugby) **to c. a try** transformar un ensayo, realizar la transformación

3 vi Rel & Fig convertirse (**to** a)

convertible [kən'vɜːtəbəl] **1** adj (settee) convertible; (car) descapotable, Am convertible; **c. currency** moneda f convertible; **c. top** capota f

2 n (car) descapotable m, Am convertible m

convex ['kɒnveks] adj convexo(a)

convey [kən'veɪ] vt (**a**) (communicate) transmitir (**b**) (transport) transportar

conveyancing [kən'veɪənsɪŋ] n Law (escrituración f de) traspaso m de propiedad

conveyor belt [kən'veɪə'belt] n cinta f transportadora

convict 1 n ['kɒnvɪkt] convicto(a) m,f

2 [kən'vɪkt] vt **to c. sb (of a crime)** declarar a alguien culpable (de un delito), condenar a alguien (por un delito)

conviction [kən'vɪkʃən] n (**a**) Law condena f; **to have no previous convictions** no tener condenas anteriores (**b**) (belief) convicción f; **her voice lacked c.** le faltaba convicción en la voz; **to carry c.** ser convincente

convince [kən'vɪns] vt convencer; **to c. sb to do sth** convencer a alguien para hacer or para que haga algo; **to c. sb of sth** convencer a alguien de algo

convincing [kən'vɪnsɪŋ] adj convincente

convincingly [kən'vɪnsɪŋlɪ] adv convincentemente

convivial [kən'vɪvɪəl] adj (person) sociable; (atmosphere) agradable

convoluted ['kɒnvəluːtɪd] adj (argument, explanation) intrincado(a), enrevesado(a)

convoy ['kɒnvɔɪ] n (of ships, trucks) convoy m

convulse [kən'vʌls] vt convulsionar; **to be convulsed with laughter/pain** retorcerse de risa/dolor

convulsions [kən'vʌlʃənz] npl Med convulsiones fpl; **to be in c.** (laughter) desternillarse de risa

coo [kuː] vi (dove) arrullar; **the neighbors came to c. over the baby** los vecinos vinieron a hacer monerías al niño

cook [kʊk] **1** n cocinero(a) m,f; Prov **too many cooks spoil the broth** = es difícil obtener un buen resultado cuando hay demasiadas personas trabajando en lo mismo

2 vt (prepare) (meal, dish, dinner) preparar; (boil, bake, fry) guisar, cocinar; Fam **to c. the books** falsificar las cuentas

3 vi (person) cocinar; (food) cocinarse, hacerse; Fam **what's cooking?** (what's happening?) ¿qué se cuece por aquí?, Am ¿qué andan tramando por acá?

▸**cook up** vt insep (food) preparar, cocinar; Fam Fig **to c. up an excuse/a story** inventarse una excusa/un cuento

cookbook ['kʊkbʊk] n libro m de cocina

cookie, cooky ['kʊkɪ] n (**a**) (small cake) galleta f; Fam Fig **that's the way the c. crumbles!** ¡qué se le va a hacer!; **c. cutter** molde m de galletas; **c. sheet** bandeja f de hornear (**b**) Fam (person) **a smart c.** un(a) espabilado(a), Méx un(a) listo(a), RP un(a) avivado(a); **a tough c.** un(a) tío(a) duro(a) de pelar

cooking ['kʊkɪŋ] n cocina f; **to do the c.** cocinar; **c. apple** manzana f para asar; **c. time** tiempo m de cocción; **c. utensils** utensilios mpl de cocina

cookout ['kʊkaʊt] n comida f al aire libre

cool [kuːl] **1** n (**a**) (coldness) fresco m; **in the c. of the evening** al fresco de la tarde (**b**) (calm) **to keep/lose one's c.** mantener/perder la calma

2 adj (**a**) (wind, weather) (cold) fresco(a); (lukewarm) tibio(a); **it's c.** hace fresco (**b**) (person) sereno(a); (unfriendly) frío(a); **keep c.!** (stay calm) ¡mantén la calma!; **to keep a c. head** mantener la cabeza fría; **he's a c. customer!** ¡qué sangre fría tiene!; **as c. as a cucumber** imperturbable, impasible, RP fresco(a) como una lechuga; Fam **he lost a c.**

thousand (money) perdió nada menos que mil dólares (**c**) Fam (fashionable) genial, Esp guay, Méx padre, RP copado(a) (**d**) Fam (excellent) genial, Esp guay, Andes, RP macanudo(a), Méx padre

3 adv Fam **to play it c.** aparentar calma; **play it c.!** ¡tómatelo con calma!

4 vt (make cold) enfriar; (make less warm) (air, one's feet) refrescar; (food, drink) enfriar (un poco); Fam **c. it!** ¡tranquilo!, Esp ¡tranqui!; Fam **to c. one's heels** esperar, hacer antesala

5 vi (become cold) enfriarse; (become less warm) (air) refrescarse; (food, drink) enfriarse (un poco); **his anger soon cooled** pronto se le pasó el esp Esp enfado or esp Am enojo

▸**cool down 1** vt sep **this will c. you down** (cold drink) esto te refrescará

2 vi (**a**) (weather) refrescar; (liquid) enfriarse (un poco) (**b**) (become calm) calmarse, tranquilizarse

▸**cool off** vi (**a**) **he had a shower to c. off** se dio una ducha para refrescarse (**b**) (affection, enthusiasm) enfriarse; (angry person) calmarse, tranquilizarse

coolant ['kuːlənt] n (for engine, reactor) refrigerante m

cool-headed ['kuːl'hedɪd] adj **to be c.** tener la cabeza fría, tener serenidad

cooling ['kuːlɪŋ] adj refrescante; **c. tower** torre f de refrigeración

cooling-off ['kuːlɪŋ'ɒf] adj **c. period** Ind (before strike) fase f de relexion; Fin (after sale) periodo f de reflexion

coop [kuːp] n (for chickens) corral m

▸**coop up** vt sep encerrar

co-op ['kəʊɒp] n cooperativa f

cooperate [kəʊ'ɒpəreɪt] vi cooperar (**with** con)

cooperation [kəʊɒpə'reɪʃən] n cooperación f

cooperative [kəʊ'ɒpərətɪv] **1** n cooperativa f

2 adj cooperativo(a)

co-opt [kəʊ'ɒpt] vt **to c. sb onto a committee** nombrar a alguien miembro de una comisión; **to c. sb to do sth** elegir a alguien para que haga algo

coordinate 1 n [kəʊ'ɔːdɪnət] (**a**) Math coordenada f (**b**) **coordinates** (clothes) conjuntos mpl

2 vt [kəʊ'ɔːdɪneɪt] (campaign, efforts) coordinar

coordination [kəʊɔːdɪ'neɪʃən] n coordinación f

coordinator [kəʊ'ɔːdɪneɪtə(r)] n coordinador(ora) m,f

co-owner ['kəʊ'əʊnə(r)] n copropietario(a) m,f

cop [kɒp] Fam **1** n (policeman) poli mf; **to play cops and robbers** jugar a policías y ladrones

2 vt **to c. a plea** = declararse culpable de un delito menor para evitar ser acusado de otro más grave

▸**cop out** vi Fam zafarse, Esp escaquearse, RP zafar; **he copped out of telling her** se zafó or Esp escaqueó de decírselo, RP zafó de decírselo

copartner [kəʊ'pɑːtnə(r)] n socio(a) m,f

cope [kəʊp] vi arreglárselas; **to c. with** hacer frente a, poder con; **he can't c. with his job** su trabajo es demasiado para él; **I just can't c.!** ¡es demasiado para mí!, ¡no puedo con ello!

Copenhagen [kəʊpən'hɑːgən] n Copenhague

copier ['kɒpɪə(r)] n (photocopying machine) fotocopiadora f

copilot ['kəʊpaɪlət] n copiloto mf

copious ['kəʊpɪəs] adj abundante, copioso(a)

cop-out ['kɒpaʊt] n Fam **to be a c.** ser una forma de zafarse or Esp escaquearse or RP zafar

copper ['kɒpə(r)] **1** n (**a**) (metal) cobre m (**b**) Fam **coppers** (coins) calderilla f, Méx morralla f, RP chirolas fpl (sólo monedas de uno y dos peniques) (**c**) Fam (policeman) poli m

2 adj **c.(-colored)** cobrizo(a)

copperplate ['kɒpəpleɪt] n (writing) letra f de caligrafía

coppice ['kɒpɪs] n arboleda f, soto m

coproduction [kəʊprə'dʌkʃən] n Cin coproducción f

copse [kɒps] *n* arboleda *f*, soto *m*

copulate ['kɒpjʊleɪt] *vi* copular

copulation [kɒpjʊ'leɪʃən] *n* cópula *f*

copy ['kɒpɪ] **1** *n* (**a**) *(reproduction)* copia *f* (**b**) *(of letter, document)* copia *f* (**c**) *(of book, newspaper)* ejemplar *m* (**d**) *Journ advertising* c. textos *mpl* publicitarios; **the story made good c.** la noticia dio mucho de sí; **c. editor** corrector(ora) *m,f* de estilo

2 *vt & vi* copiar; *Comptr* **to c. and paste** copiar y pegar

copybook ['kɒpɪbʊk] *n* cuaderno *m* de caligrafía; **a c. example** un ejemplo perfecto

copycat ['kɒpɪkæt] **1** *n Fam* copión(ona) *m,f*

2 *adj* **c. crime** = delito inspirado en otro similar

copyreader ['kɒpɪriːdə(r)] *n* corrector(ora) *m,f* de estilo

copyright ['kɒpɪraɪt] **1** *n* derechos *mpl* de autor, propiedad *f* intelectual; **this book is out of c.** los derechos de autor sobre este libro han vencido

2 *adj* = protegido(a) por las leyes de la propiedad intelectual

copywriter ['kɒpɪraɪtə(r)] *n* redactor(ora) *m,f* de publicidad

coquette [kɒ'ket] *n* (mujer *f*) coqueta *f*

coral ['kɒrəl] *n* coral *m*; **c. island** isla *f* coralina; **c. reef** arrecife *m* de coral; **the C. Sea** el Mar del Coral

cord [kɔːd] *n* (**a**) *(string)* cuerda *f*, cordel *m*; *(for curtains, pajamas)* cordón *m* (**b**) *Elec* cable *m*, cordón *m* (**c**) *(corduroy)* pana *f*; **a c. jacket/skirt** una chaqueta *or Méx* chamarra *or RP* campera/falda *or RP* pollera de pana; **cords** pantalones *mpl* de pana

cordial ['kɔːdɪəl] **1** *n (drink)* refresco *m*

2 *adj* (**a**) *(friendly)* cordial (**b**) *(deeply felt)* profundo(a)

cordless ['kɔːdlɪs] *adj* **c. kettle** = hervidor eléctrico con soporte independiente enchufado a la red; **c. phone** teléfono *m* inalámbrico

cordon ['kɔːdən] *n* cordón *m*

▶**cordon off** *vt sep* acordonar

corduroy ['kɔːdərɔɪ] *n* pana *f*; **a c. jacket/skirt** una chaqueta *or Méx* chamarra *or RP* campera/falda *or RP* pollera de pana; **c. pants** pantalones *mpl* de pana

core [kɔː(r)] **1** *n (of apple)* corazón *m*; *(of earth, nuclear reactor)* núcleo *m*; **a hard c. of support** un núcleo sólido de apoyo; **he's rotten to the c.** está corrompido hasta la médula; *Sch* **c. curriculum** asignaturas *fpl* troncales

2 *vt (apple)* quitar el corazón a

Corfu [kɔː'fuː] *n* Corfú

coriander [kɒrɪ'ændə(r)] *n* cilantro *m*

cork [kɔːk] **1** *n (material)* corcho *m*; *(stopper)* (tapón *m* de) corcho *m*

2 *vt (bottle)* encorchar

corked [kɔːkt] *adj (wine)* agrio(a) *(por entrada de aire al descomponerse el corcho)*

corkscrew ['kɔːkskruː] *n* sacacorchos *m inv*

cormorant ['kɔːmərənt] *n* cormorán *m*

corn¹ [kɔːn] *n* maíz *m*, *Andes, RP* choclo *m*; **c. on the cob** mazorca *f* de maíz *or Andes, RP* choclo, *Méx* elote *m*; **c. bread** pan *m* de maíz *or Andes, RP* choclo; **c. oil** aceite *m* de maíz

corn² *n Med* callo *m*; **c. plaster** parche *m* para callos

cornea ['kɔːnɪə] *n Anat* córnea *f*

corned beef ['kɔːnd'biːf] *adj* = fiambre de carne de vaca prensado y enlatado

corner ['kɔːnə(r)] **1** *n* (**a**) *(of page, screen, street)* esquina *f*; *(of room)* rincón *m*; *also Fig* **it's just around the c.** está a la vuelta de la esquina; **to turn the c.** doblar la esquina; *(economy, company)* empezar a mejorar; **c. store** = tienda pequeña de barrio que vende productos alimenticios, de limpieza, golosinas, *etc.*; **from the four corners of the earth** desde todos los rincones de la tierra; **out of the c. of one's eye** con el rabillo del ojo (**b**) *(bend in road)* curva *f* (cerrada); *Fig* **to cut corners** hacer las cosas chapucera-

mente (**c**) *(in soccer)* **c. (kick)** saque *m* de esquina, córner *m*

2 *vt* (**a**) *(enemy)* acorralar, arrinconar (**b**) *(market)* monopolizar, acaparar

3 *vi (car)* girar, torcer

cornerstone ['kɔːnəstəʊn] *n also Fig* piedra *f* angular

cornet [kɔː'net] *n (musical instrument)* corneta *f*

cornflakes ['kɔːnfleɪks] *npl* copos *mpl* de maíz

cornflower ['kɔːnflaʊə(r)] *n (plant)* aciano *m*; **c. blue** azul *m* violáceo

cornice ['kɔːnɪs] *n* cornisa *f*

Cornish ['kɔːnɪʃ] **1** *npl (people)* **the C.** la gente de Cornualles

2 *n (language)* córnico *m*

3 *adj* de Cornualles

cornmeal ['kɔːnmiːl] *n* harina *f* de maíz *or Andes, RP* choclo

cornstarch ['kɔːnstɑːtʃ] *n* harina *f* de maíz *or Andes, RP* choclo, maicena® *f*

Cornwall ['kɔːnwəl] *n* Cornualles

corny ['kɔːnɪ] *adj Fam (joke)* viejo(a), trillado(a); *(sentimental) (movie, novel)* sensiblero(a), cursi

corollary [kə'rɒlərɪ] *n* corolario *m*

coronary ['kɒrənərɪ] **1** *n* **he had a c.** le dio un infarto (de miocardio)

2 *adj Med* coronario(a); **c. thrombosis** trombosis *f* coronaria

coronation [kɒrə'neɪʃən] *n* coronación *f*

coroner ['kɒrənə(r)] *n Law* = persona que preside una investigación sobre un caso de muerte sospechosa

corporal¹ ['kɔːpərəl] *adj* corporal; **c. punishment** castigo *m* corporal

corporal² *n Mil* cabo *mf*

corporate ['kɔːpərət] *adj Com* de empresa, corporativo(a); **c. culture** cultura *f* empresarial; **c. image** imagen *f* corporativa *or* de empresa; **c. (income) tax** impuesto *m* de sociedades

corporation [kɔːpə'reɪʃən] *n Com* sociedad *f* anónima

corporatism ['kɔːpərətɪzəm] *n Pol* corporativismo *m*

corps [kɔː(r)] *(pl* **corps** [kɔːz]) *n Mil* cuerpo *m*; **medical c.** cuerpo *m* médico

corpse [kɔːps] *n* cadáver *m*

corpulent ['kɔːpjʊlənt] *adj* obeso(a)

corpuscle ['kɔːpʌsəl] *n Anat* glóbulo *m*

corral [kɒ'rɑːl] *n (for cattle, horses)* corral *m*, cercado *m*

correct [kə'rekt] **1** *adj* (**a**) *(exact) (amount, change)* exacto(a); *(information, use, spelling)* correcto(a); **do you have the c. time?** ¿sabes qué hora es exactamente?; **he is c.** tiene razón; **that is c.** (eso es) correcto; **to prove c.** resultar (ser) correcto(a) (**b**) *(person, behavior)* correcto(a)

2 *vt* corregir; **to c. a misunderstanding** corregir un malentendido; **c. me if I'm wrong, but...** corríjame si me equivoco, pero...; **I stand corrected** reconozco mi error

correction [kə'rekʃən] *n* corrección *f*; **c. fluid** líquido *m* corrector

correctness [kə'rektnɪs] *n* corrección *f*

correlate ['kɒrɪleɪt] **1** *vt* relacionar (**with** con)

2 *vi* presentar una correlación (**with** con)

correlation [kɒrɪ'leɪʃən] *n* correlación *f*

correspond [kɒrɪ'spɒnd] *vi* (**a**) *(be in accordance, be equivalent)* corresponder (**with** *or* **to** con *or* a), corresponderse (**with** *or* **to** con) (**b**) *(write letters)* mantener correspondencia (**with** con)

correspondence [kɒrɪ'spɒndəns] *n* (**a**) *(relationship)* correspondencia *f*, relación *f* (**between** entre) (**b**) *(letter writing)* correspondencia *f*; **to be in c. with sb** mantener correspondencia con alguien; **c. course** curso *m* por correspondencia

correspondent [kɒrɪ'spɒndənt] *n (of newspaper)* corresponsal *mf*; **our Middle East c.** nuestro corresponsal en Oriente Medio

corresponding [kɒrɪ'spɒndɪŋ] *adj* correspondiente

corridor ['kɒrɪdɔ:(r)] *n* pasillo *m*; *Fig* **the corridors of power** las altas esferas

corroborate [kə'rɒbəreɪt] *vt* corroborar

corroboration [kərɒbə'reɪʃən] *n* corroboración *f*

corrode [kə'rəʊd] **1** *vt also Fig* corroer
  2 *vi (metal)* corroerse

corrosion [kə'rəʊʒən] *n* corrosión *f*

corrosive [kə'rəʊsɪv] *n & adj* corrosivo(a) *m*

corrugated ['kɒrʊgeɪtɪd] *adj* ondulado(a); **c. iron** chapa *f* ondulada

corrupt [kə'rʌpt] **1** *adj (dishonest)* corrupto(a)
  2 *vt* corromper; *Comptr* introducir errores en; **to c. sb's morals** pervertir a alguien

corruptible [kə'rʌptəbəl] *adj* corruptible

corruption [kə'rʌpʃən] *n* corrupción *f*

corruptly [kə'rʌptlɪ] *adv* corruptamente, de forma deshonesta

corset ['kɔ:sɪt] *n* corsé *m*

Corsica ['kɔ:sɪkə] *n* Córcega

Corsican ['kɔ:sɪkən] *n & adj* corso(a) *m,f*

cortege [kɔ:'teʒ] *n* cortejo *m* (fúnebre)

cortex ['kɔ:teks] (*pl* **cortices** ['kɔ:tɪsi:z]) *n* corteza *f*

cortisone ['kɔ:tɪzəʊn] *n* cortisona *f*

cos[1] [kɒz] *n Math (abbr* **cosine**) cos

cos[2] *conj Fam (because)* porque

cos[3] [kɒs] *n* **c. (lettuce)** lechuga *f* romana

cosily ['kəʊzɪlɪ] *adv (furnished, decorated)* acogedoramente

cosmetic [kɒz'metɪk] **1** *n* cosmético *m*; **cosmetics** cosméticos *mpl*, maquillaje *m*
  2 *adj* cosmético(a); **c. surgery** cirugía *f* estética

cosmic ['kɒzmɪk] *adj* cósmico(a)

cosmology [kɒz'mɒlədʒɪ] *n* cosmología *f*

cosmonaut ['kɒzmənɔ:t] *n* cosmonauta *mf*

cosmopolitan [kɒzmə'pɒlɪtən] *adj* cosmopolita

cosmos ['kɒzmɒs] *n* cosmos *m inv*

cosset ['kɒsɪt] *vt* mimar

cost [kɒst] **1** *n* (a) *(price)* costo *m*, *Esp* coste *m*; *Law* **costs** costas *fpl*; **at little c.** a bajo precio; **at great c.** *(financial)* por un precio alto; *Fig* a un alto precio; *Fig* **at the c. of…** a costa de…; *Econ* **c. of living** costo *m or Esp* coste *m* de la vida; *Com* **c. of production** coste *m* de producción; *Fin* **c. accounting** contabilidad *f* de costes; *Com* **at c. (price)** a precio de costo *or Esp* coste (b) *(idioms)* **to count the c. of sth** ver las consecuencias de algo; **at all costs** a toda costa, a cualquier precio; **as I found out to my c.** como pude comprobar para mi desgracia
  2 *vt* (a) *(pt & pp* **cost***)* costar; **how much does it c.?** ¿cuánto cuesta?; **it costs $25** cuesta 25 dólares; **whatever it costs** cueste lo que cueste; *Fam* **to c. a fortune** *or* **the earth** costar una fortuna *or* un ojo de la cara; **the attempt c. him his life** el intento le costó la vida (b) *(pt & pp* **costed***) Com (budget)* presupuestar, calcular el coste de

costar ['kəʊstɑ:(r)] **1** *n (in movie)* coprotagonista *mf*
  2 *vt (pt & pp* **costarred***) **costarring…** coprotagonizada por…
  3 *vi* ser el coprotagonista

Costa Rica ['kɒstə'ri:kə] *n* Costa Rica

Costa Rican ['kɒstə'ri:kən] *n & adj* costarricense *mf*

cost-benefit ['kɒst'benɪfɪt] *adj Econ* **c. analysis** análisis *m inv* de costo-beneficio *or Esp* coste-beneficio

cost-conscious ['kɒst'kɒnʃəs] *adj* **to be c.** ser consciente de los costos *or Esp* costes

cost-cutting ['kɒst'kʌtɪŋ] **1** *n* reducción *f* de costos *or Esp* costes
  2 *adj (drive, campaign)* de reducción de costos *or Esp* costes

cost-effective [kɒstɪ'fektɪv] *adj* rentable

costing ['kɒstɪŋ] *n Com* cálculo *m* de costos *or Esp* costes

costly ['kɒstlɪ] *adj* caro(a); **a c. error** *or* **mistake** un error muy caro

costume ['kɒstjʊm] *n* traje *m*; **(swimming) c.** traje *m* de baño, *Esp* bañador *m*, *RP* malla *f*; **national c.** traje *m* típico; **c. jewelry** bisutería *f*

cosy = cozy

cot [kɒt] *n (folding bed)* catre *m*, cama *f* plegable

coterie ['kəʊtərɪ:] *n* camarilla *f*

cottage ['kɒtɪdʒ] *n* casa *f* de campo, chalé *m*; **c. cheese** queso *m* fresco; **c. industry** industria *f* artesanal; **c. pie** = pastel de carne picada y puré *Esp* patata *or Am* papa

cotton ['kɒtən] *n* algodón *m*, *Am* cotón *m*; **a c. shirt** una camisa de algodón; **c. bud** bastoncillo *m* (de algodón); **c. candy** algodón dulce

▸**cotton to** *vt insep Fam (take a liking to)* **I didn't c. to to her at first** al principio no me cayó bien

couch [kaʊtʃ] **1** *n* sofá *m*; *Fam* **to be on the c.** *(in psychoanalysis)* estar yendo al psicoanalista; *Fam* **c. potato** = persona que se pasa el día apoltronada viendo la tele
  2 *vt (express)* expresar, formular

cougar ['ku:gə(r)] *n* puma *m*

cough [kɒf] **1** *n* tos *f*; **to have a c.** tener tos; **c. drop** pastilla *f* para la tos; **c. syrup** jarabe *m* para la tos
  2 *vi* toser

▸**cough up 1** *vt sep* (a) *(phlegm, blood)* toser (b) *Fam (money)* poner, *Esp* apoquinar, *RP* garpar
  2 *vi Fam (pay up)* poner dinero, *Esp* apoquinar, *RP* garpar

could [kʊd] *modal aux v*

En el inglés hablado, y en el escrito en estilo coloquial, la forma negativa **could not** se transforma en **couldn't**.

(a) *(was able to: past of* **can***)* **I c. swim well at that age** a esa edad nadaba muy bien; **I c. hear them talking** los oía hablar; **I c. have tried harder** podía haberme esforzado más; **he couldn't have been kinder** fue de lo más amable; **how COULD you!** ¡cómo has podido!; **I c. have hit him!** *(I was so angry)* ¡me dieron ganas de pegarle!; **you c. have warned me!** ¡me podías haber avisado!, ¡haberme avisado!
  (b) *(in requests)* **c. you get me some water?** ¿me puedes traer un poco de agua?; **c. you be quiet please?** ¿te podrías callar, por favor?; **c. I borrow your newspaper?** ¿me prestas el periódico?
  (c) *(in conditional, suggestions)* **(it) c. be** podría ser; **if I had more money, I c. buy a new car** si tuviera más dinero podría comprarme un coche nuevo; **we c. always telephone** siempre podríamos llamar *or Am* hablar por teléfono; **you c. go to the beach** podrías ir a la playa

couldn't ['kʊdənt] = **could not**

couldn't-care-less ['kʊdəntkeə'les] *adj* **c. attitude** actitud *f* pasota

council ['kaʊnsəl] *n* (a) *(organization)* consejo *m*; **C. of Economic Advisers** Consejo *m* de Asesores Económicos (b) *(local government) (of town)* ayuntamiento *m*; *(of region, county)* autoridades *fpl* regionales, ≃ diputación *f* provincial

councilor ['kaʊnsɪlə(r)] *n Pol* concejal(ala) *m,f*

counsel ['kaʊnsəl] **1** *n* (a) *(advice)* consejo *m*; **he's someone who keeps his own c.** siempre se reserva su opinión (b) *Law* **c. for the defense** abogado(a) *m,f* defensor(ora); **c. for the prosecution** fiscal *mf*
  2 *vt (pt & pp* **counseled***) (advise)* aconsejar; *(give psychological help to)* proporcionar apoyo psicológico a; **to c. sb to do sth** aconsejar a alguien que haga algo

counseling ['kaʊnsəlɪŋ] *n* apoyo *m* psicológico, orientación *f* psicológica

counselor ['kaʊnsələ(r)] *n* (a) *(adviser)* consejero(a) *m,f* asesor(ora) *m,f; (therapist)* orientador(ora) *m,f* psicológico(a) (**b**) *Law* abogado(a) *m,f*

count¹ [kaʊnt] *n (nobleman)* conde *m*

count² 1 *n* (**a**) *(calculation)* cuenta *f*, recuento *m*; **at the last c.** según las cifras más recientes; **to keep/lose c.** llevar/perder la cuenta (**b**) *(in boxing)* cuenta *f* (hasta diez); **to be out for the c.** *(boxer)* estar fuera de combate; *Fig (fast asleep)* estar roque (**c**) *Law* cargo *m*, acusación *f*; **guilty on both counts** culpable de los dos cargos; *Fig* **on a number of counts** en una serie de puntos

2 *vt* (**a**) *(enumerate)* contar; **to c. sheep** *(in order to fall asleep)* contar ovejitas; **counting the dog there were four of us** éramos cuatro, contando al perro (**b**) *(consider)* considerar; **I c. him as a friend** lo considero un amigo; **c. yourself lucky you weren't killed** considérate afortunado(a) por haber salido con vida

3 *vi* (**a**) *(count)* contar; **to c. (up) to ten** contar hasta diez (**b**) *(be valid)* contar, valer; **that one doesn't c.** ese no cuenta; **it counts as one of my worst vacations** fue una de mis peores vacaciones (**c**) *(be important)* contar; **every vote counts** todos los votos cuentan *or* son importantes

count against *vt insep* ir en contra de, perjudicar

count down *vi* hacer la cuenta atrás; *Fig* **the whole nation is counting down to the elections** toda la nación espera *or Esp* aguarda con interés el día de las elecciones

count in *vt sep* **c. me in!** ¡cuenta conmigo!

count on *vt insep* contar con; **to c. on sb to do sth** contar con que alguien haga algo

count out *vt sep* (**a**) *(money)* contar (**b**) *(exclude)* dejar fuera, excluir; **c. me out!** ¡no cuentes conmigo! (**c**) *(in boxing)* **to be counted out** quedar fuera de combate (tras la cuenta hasta diez)

count up *vt sep* contar, hacer la cuenta de

countable [ˈkaʊntəbəl] *adj* contable

countdown [ˈkaʊntdaʊn] *n* cuenta *f* atrás

countenance [ˈkaʊntɪnəns] *Formal* 1 *n* (**a**) *(face)* semblante *m* (**b**) *(support)* **to give c. to sth** dar respaldo a algo

2 *vt* respaldar

counter¹ [ˈkaʊntə(r)] *n* (**a**) *(in shop)* mostrador *m*; *(in bank)* ventanilla *f*; **it's available over the c.** *(medicines)* se vende sin receta (médica); **under the c.** bajo cuerda (**b**) *(token)* ficha *f* (**c**) *(counting device)* contador *m*

counter² 1 *adv* **c. to** en contra de; **to run c. to** estar en contra de

2 *vt (argument, assertion)* responder a; **to c. that...** replicar que...

3 *vi* **to c. by doing sth** reaccionar haciendo algo

counteract [kaʊntəˈrækt] *vt* contrarrestar

counterattack [ˈkaʊntərətæk] 1 *n* contraataque *m*

2 *vt & vi* contraatacar

counterbalance [kaʊntəˈbæləns] 1 *n* contrapeso *m*; *Fig* **to act as a c. (to sth)** contrarrestar (algo)

2 *vt* contrarrestar

counterbid [ˈkaʊntəbɪd] *n Fin (during takeover)* contraoferta *f*

counterblast [ˈkaʊntəblɑːst] *n* dura réplica *f*

counterclockwise [ˈkaʊntəˈklɒkwaɪz] 1 *adj* **in a c. direction** en sentido opuesto al de las agujas del reloj

2 *adv* en sentido opuesto al de las agujas del reloj

counterculture [ˈkaʊntəkʌltʃə(r)] *n* contracultura *f*

counterespionage [kaʊntərˈespɪənɑːʒ] *n* contraespionaje *m*

counterfeit [ˈkaʊntəfɪt] 1 *n* falsificación *f*

2 *adj* falso(a)

3 *vt* falsificar

counterfoil [ˈkaʊntəfɔɪl] *n* matriz *f*

counterintelligence [ˈkaʊntərɪnˈtelɪdʒəns] *n* contraespionaje *m*

countermand [ˈkaʊntəmɑːnd] *vt* revocar

countermeasure [ˈkaʊntəmeʒə(r)] *n* medida *f* en sentido contrario

counteroffensive [ˈkaʊntərəˈfensɪv] *n* contraofensiva *f*

counteroffer [ˈkaʊntərˈɒfə(r)] *n* contraoferta *f*

counterpane [ˈkaʊntəpeɪn] *n* colcha *f*

counterpart [ˈkaʊntəpɑːt] *n* homólogo(a) *m,f*

counterpoint [ˈkaʊntəpɔɪnt] *n Mus* contrapunto *m*

counterproductive [ˈkaʊntəprəˈdʌktɪv] *adj* contraproducente

counterproposal [ˈkaʊntəprəˈpəʊzəl] *n* contrapropuesta *f*

counterrevolution [ˈkaʊntərevəˈluːʃən] *n* contrarrevolución *f*

counterrevolutionary [kaʊntərevəˈluːʃənərɪ] *n & adj* contrarrevolucionario(a) *m,f*

countersign [ˈkaʊntəsaɪn] *vt* refrendar

counterterrorism [kaʊntəˈterərɪzəm] *n* contraterrorismo *m*

counterweight [ˈkaʊntəweɪt] *n* contrapeso *m*; **to act as a c. (to sth)** servir de contrapeso (a algo), contrarrestar (algo)

countess [ˈkaʊntɪs] *n* condesa *f*

countless [ˈkaʊntlɪs] *adj* innumerables, incontables; **on c. occasions** en innumerables ocasiones

country [ˈkʌntrɪ] *n* (**a**) *(state, people)* país *m* (**b**) *(as opposed to town)* campo *m*; **in the c.** en el campo; **c. club** club *m* de campo; **c. life** vida *f* campestre; **c.-and-western music** música *f* country

countryman [ˈkʌntrɪmən] *n* paisano *m*; **a fellow c.** un compatriota

countryside [ˈkʌntrɪsaɪd] *n* campo *m*

countrywoman [ˈkʌntrɪwʊmən] *n* paisana *f*; **a fellow c.** una compatriota

county [ˈkaʊntɪ] *n* condado *m*; **c. fair** feria *f* rural anual; **the c. line** el límite del condado; **c. seat** capital *f* de condado

coup [kuː] *n (surprising achievement)* golpe *m* de efecto; *Pol* **c. (d'état)** golpe *m* de Estado

couple [ˈkʌpəl] 1 *n* (**a**) *(of things)* par *m*; **a c. of** un par de (**b**) *(people)* pareja *f*

2 *vt* (**a**) *(associate)* relacionar, asociar (**b**) *(combine)* conjugar, combinar; **coupled with** junto con

couplet [ˈkʌplɪt] *n (in poem)* pareado *m*

coupon [ˈkuːpɒn] *n* cupón *m*, vale *m*

courage [ˈkʌrɪdʒ] *n* valor *m*, coraje *m*; **to have the c. to do sth** tener valor para hacer algo; **he didn't have the c. of his convictions** no tuvo coraje para defender sus convicciones

courageous [kəˈreɪdʒəs] *adj* valiente

courageously [kəˈreɪdʒəslɪ] *adv* valientemente

courier [ˈkʊrɪə(r)] *n (messenger)* mensajero(a) *m,f; (in tourism)* guía *mf; (drug smuggler)* correo *m*, enlace *m*

course [kɔːs] *n* (**a**) *(of river, illness)* curso *m; (of time, events)* transcurso *m*, curso *m*; **to be on c.** *(ship)* seguir el rumbo; **to be on c. for** *(likely to achieve)* ir camino de; **to be off c.** haber perdido el rumbo; *also Fig* **to change c.** cambiar de rumbo; **in the c. of time** con el tiempo; **a c. of action** una táctica (a seguir); **to be in the c. of doing sth** estar haciendo algo; **in the normal c. of events** normalmente; **to let things take** *or* **run their c.** dejar que las cosas sigan su curso

(**b**) **of c.** *(clearly, unsurprisingly)* naturalmente; *(expressing agreement)* **of c. you can come!** ¡pues claro que puedes venir!; **of c. not!** ¡por supuesto que no!

(**c**) *Educ (as part of degree)* curso *m*; **to take a c. in sth** hacer un curso de algo; **(degree) c.** carrera *f*; **a c. of lectures** un ciclo de conferencias

(**d**) *Med* **c. of treatment** tratamiento *m*

(**e**) *(of meal)* plato *m*; **first c.** primer plato; **main c.** plato principal

(f) *(for race)* circuito *m*; *(for golf) Esp* campo *m*, *Am* cancha *f*; *(for show-jumping)* recorrido *m*

2 *vi (liquid)* correr

court [kɔːt] **1** *n* **(a)** *Law* tribunal *m*; **to go to c.** ir a los tribunales *or* a juicio; **to take sb to c.** llevar a alguien a juicio *or* a los tribunales; **to settle a case out of c.** arreglar una disputa sin acudir a los tribunales; **c. of appeals** tribunal *m* de apelación; **c. of inquiry** comisión *f* de investigación; **c. of law** tribunal *m*; **c. appearance** *(of defendant)* comparecencia *f* en un juicio; *Mil* **c. martial** consejo *m* de guerra; **c. order** orden *f* judicial

(b) *(for tennis, basketball, squash)* pista *f*, cancha *f*

(c) *(royal)* corte *f*; *Fig* **she held c. in the hotel bar, surrounded by a posse of journalists** entretuvo a un grupo de periodistas en el bar del hotel

2 *vt* **(a)** *Old-fashioned (woo)* cortejar **(b)** *(seek) (sb's friendship, favor)* intentar ganarse; *(failure)* exponerse a; *(death)* jugar con

3 *vi Old-fashioned* **to be courting** *(couple)* cortejarse

courteous ['kɜːtɪəs] *adj* cortés

courteously ['kɜːtɪəslɪ] *adv* cortésmente

courtesy ['kɜːtəsɪ] *n* cortesía *f*; **do me the c. of listening** ten la cortesía de escucharme; **by c. of...** por cortesía de...; **to exchange courtesies** intercambiar cumplidos; **c. call** visita *f* de cortesía; **c. car** coche *m* gratuito *(cortesía de la empresa)*

courthouse ['kɔːthaʊs] *n* palacio *m* de justicia

courtier ['kɔːtɪə(r)] *n* cortesano(a) *m,f*

court-martial ['kɔːt'mɑːʃəl] *(pt & pp* **court-martialed)** *vt* hacer un consejo de guerra a

courtroom ['kɔːtruːm] *n Law* sala *f* de juicios

courtship ['kɔːtʃɪp] *n (of people, animals)* cortejo *m*

courtyard ['kɔːtjɑːd] *n* patio *m*

cousin ['kʌzən] *n* primo(a) *m,f*; **first c.** primo(a) hermano(a); **second c.** primo(a) segundo(a)

cove [kəʊv] *n (small bay)* cala *f*, ensenada *f*

covenant ['kʌvənənt] *Law n (agreement)* pacto *m*, convenio *m*

Coventry ['kʌvəntrɪ, 'kɒvəntrɪ] *n* **to send sb to C.** hacer el vacío a alguien

cover ['kʌvə(r)] **1** *n* **(a)** *(lid)* tapa *f*

(b) *(soft covering)* funda *f*; **covers** *(blankets)* mantas *fpl*

(c) *(of book)* tapa *f*; *(of magazine)* portada *f*; **front c.** portada *f*; **back c.** contraportada *f*, *Perú, RP* contratapa *f*; **to read a book from c. to c.** leerse un libro de principio a fin; **c. story** tema *m* de portada

(d) *(shelter)* protección *f*; **to break c.** ponerse al descubierto; **to take c.** ponerse a cubierto; **under c. of darkness** al amparo de la oscuridad

(e) *(disguise, front)* tapadera *f*; **my c. has been blown** me han desenmascarado; **c. story** tapadera *f*

(f) *Fin (in insurance)* cobertura *f*; **full c.** cobertura máxima

(g) *(song)* **c. (version)** versión *f (de una canción original)*

(h) *(in restaurant)* **c. charge** cubierto *m*

(i) **c. letter** *(for job application)* carta *f* de presentación

2 *vt* **(a)** *(person, object)* cubrir; *(with a lid)* tapar; **to c. one's eyes** taparse los ojos; **to c. a wall with paint** recubrir de pintura una pared; **to c. oneself with glory** cubrirse de gloria; **to c. one's costs** cubrir gastos; **to c. a song** *(musician)* hacer una versión de una canción

(b) *(hide) (one's embarrassment, confusion)* ocultar; **to c. one's tracks** no dejar rastro

(c) *(travel over)* cubrir, recorrer; **we covered 100 miles** cubrimos *or* recorrimos 100 millas; *Fig* **to c. a lot of ground** abarcar mucho

(d) *(include, deal with)* cubrir; **to c. a story** *(journalist)* cubrir una noticia

(e) *(protect) Fin (with insurance)* asegurar; *Fig* **to c. oneself** *(take precautions)* cubrirse las espaldas

▶**cover for** *vt insep (replace)* reemplazar *or* sustituir

temporalmente; *(provide excuses for)* excusar

▶**cover up 1** *vt sep* **(a)** *(conceal)* ocultar **(b)** *(cover)* cubrir, tapar

2 *vi (conceal the truth)* encubrir **(for sb** a alguien)

coverage ['kʌvərɪdʒ] *n* **(a)** *(on TV, in newspapers)* cobertura *f* informativa **(b)** *(in insurance)* cobertura *f*

coveralls ['kʌvərɔːlz] *npl* mono *m* (de trabajo), *Am* overol *m*

covering ['kʌvərɪŋ] *n (on furniture)* funda *f*; *(of snow, dust, chocolate)* capa *f*

coverlet ['kʌvəlɪt] *n* colcha *f*

covert ['kʌvət] *adj* encubierto(a)

cover-up ['kʌvərʌp] *n* encubrimiento *m*

covet ['kʌvɪt] *vt* codiciar

covetous ['kʌvɪtəs] *adj* codicioso(a); **to be c. of** codiciar

cow¹ [kaʊ] *n* **(a)** *(animal)* vaca *f*; *(female elephant, whale)* hembra *f*; **till the cows come home** hasta que las ranas críen pelo **(b)** *Pej very Fam (woman)* bruja *f*, pécora *f*

cow² *vt* acobardar, intimidar; **to c. sb into submission** reducir a alguien a la obediencia; **to look cowed** parecer intimidado(a)

coward ['kaʊəd] *n* cobarde *mf*

cowardice ['kaʊədɪs], **cowardliness** ['kaʊədlɪnəs] *n* cobardía *f*

cowardly ['kaʊədlɪ] *adj* cobarde

cowboy ['kaʊbɔɪ] *n* vaquero *m*; **to play cowboys and Indians** jugar a indios y vaqueros

cower ['kaʊə(r)] *vi* acoquinarse, amilanarse

cowhide ['kaʊhaɪd] *n* cuero *m*

cowl [kaʊl] *n (monk's hood)* capucha *f*; *(on chimney)* sombrerete *m*

coworker [kəʊ'wɜːkə(r)] *n* compañero(a) *m,f* de trabajo

cowshed ['kaʊʃed] *n* establo *m*

cox [kɒks] **1** *n (in rowing)* timonel *mf*

2 *vt* llevar el timón de

3 *vi* hacer de timonel

coy [kɔɪ] *adj (shy)* timorato(a); **to be c. about sth** mostrarse evasivo(a) en relación con algo

coyness ['kɔɪnɪs] *n (shyness)* timidez *f*; *(evasiveness)* evasión *f*

coyote [kɔɪ'jəʊtɪ] *n* coyote *m*

cozy ['kəʊzɪ] *adj* acogedor(ora); **it's c. here** se está bien aquí, **to feel c.** sentirse a gusto; **a c. relationship** una relación demasiado estrecha *or* amistosa

CPA [siː'piː'eɪ] *n (abbr* **certified public accountant)** *Esp* censor(ora) *m,f* jurado(a) de cuentas, *Am* contador(ora) *m,f* público(a)

CPI [siː'piː'aɪ] *n Econ (abbr* **consumer price index)** IPC *m* Índice *m* de Precios al Consumo

Cpl *Mil (abbr* **Corporal)** cabo *m*

CPR [siː'piː'ɑː(r)] *n Med (abbr* **cardiopulmonary resuscitation)** masaje *m* cardiaco

CPU [siː'piː'juː] *n Comptr (abbr* **central processing unit)** CPU *f*, unidad *f* central de proceso

Cr *(abbr* **Crescent)** = calle en forma de media luna

crab [kræb] *n* **(a)** *(crustacean)* cangrejo *m*, *Am* jaiba *f* **(b)** *Fam (pubic louse)* ladilla *f* **(c)** **c. apple** *(fruit)* manzana *f* silvestre; *(tree)* manzano *m* silvestre

crabbed ['kræbɪd] *adj* **c. writing** letra *f* apretada y difícil de leer

crabby ['kræbɪ] *adj Fam (bad-tempered)* gruñón(ona)

crack [kræk] **1** *n* **(a)** *(in glass, porcelain)* raja *f*; *(in wood, wall, ground, ice)* grieta *f*; **the door was open a c.** la puerta estaba entreabierta; *Fig* **cracks have started to appear in his alibi** su coartada está empezando a hacer agua; **to get up at the c. of dawn** levantarse al amanecer **(b)** *(sound)* chasquido *m*; *Fig* **to have a c. at sth** intentar algo **(c)** *(blow)* **a c. on the head** un porrazo en la cabeza **(d)** *Fam (joke, insult)* chiste *m* **(e)** *(drug)* crack *m*

2 *adj Fam* de primera; **c. troops** tropas *fpl* de élite

3 *vt* (**a**) *(fracture) (cup, glass)* rajar; *(skin, wood, ground, wall)* agrietar (**b**) *(make sound with) (whip)* chasquear; *(fingers)* hacer crujir (**c**) *Fam (hit)* **to c. sb over the head** dar a alguien un porrazo en la cabeza; **he cracked his head against the wall** se dio con la cabeza contra la pared (**d**) *(solve) (problem)* resolver; *(code)* descifrar (**e**) *(break open) (safe)* forzar; *(nut, egg)* cascar (**f**) **to c. a joke** soltar un chiste

4 *vi* (**a**) *(cup, glass)* rajarse; *(skin, wood, ground, wall)* agrietarse (**b**) *(voice) (with emotion)* fallar (**c**) *(person) (under pressure)* venirse abajo, derrumbarse; **his nerve cracked** perdió los nervios (**d**) *(make sound)* crujir; *(whip)* chasquear; *Fam Fig* **get cracking!** ¡manos a la obra!

▸**crack down** *vi* **to c. down on sth** adoptar medidas severas contra algo

▸**crack up** *Fam* **1** *vt sep* **it's not all it's cracked up to be** no es tan bueno como lo pintan

2 *vi* (**a**) *(laugh)* partirse *or* morirse *or Esp* troncharse *or Méx* atacarse *or RP* descostillarse de risa (**b**) *(go mad)* (empezar a) desvariar

crackbrained ['krækbreɪnd] *adj Fam (plan)* descabellado(a)

crackdown ['krækdaʊn] *n* medidas *fpl* severas; **a c. on drugs/tax evasion** medidas severas contra las drogas/la evasión fiscal

cracked [krækt] *adj Fam (crazy)* **to be c.** estar chiflado(a) *or Esp* majara

cracker ['krækə(r)] *n* (**a**) *(biscuit)* galleta *f* salada, cracker *f* (**b**) *(firework)* petardo *m* (**c**) *Comptr* cracker

crackle ['krækəl] **1** *n* *(of twigs)* crujido *m*; *(of fire)* crepitación *m*
2 *vi (twigs)* crujir; *(fire)* crepitar

crackling ['kræklɪŋ] *n (pork skin)* cortezas *fpl* de cerdo, *Am* chicharrones *mpl*

crackpot ['krækpɒt] *Fam* **1** *n (person)* pirado(a) *m,f*, *Méx* zafado(a) *m,f*
2 *adj (plan)* descabellado(a)

crack-up ['krækʌp] *n Fam (of person)* hundimiento *m*, derrumbe *m*

cradle ['kreɪdəl] **1** *n* (**a**) *(of child, civilization)* cuna *f*; **from the c. to the grave** de la cuna a la sepultura (**b**) *(for cleaning windows)* andamio *m* colgante
2 *vt* acunar

craft[1] [krɑːft] **1** *n* (**a**) *(trade)* oficio *m*; *(skill)* arte *m* (**b**) *(cunning)* maña *f*, astucia *f*
2 *vt (fashion)* elaborar

craft[2] *(pl* **craft***) n (boat)* embarcación *f*

craftily ['krɑːftɪlɪ] *adv* muy ladinamente; **c. worded** muy hábilmente *or* astutamente expresado

craftiness ['krɑːftɪnɪs] *n* astucia *f*, maña *f*

craftsman ['krɑːftsmən] *n* artesano *m*

craftsmanship ['krɑːftsmənʃɪp] *n* destreza *f*, maestría *f*

crafty ['krɑːftɪ] *adj* ladino(a)

crag [kræg] *n* peñasco *m*, risco *m*

craggy ['krægɪ] *adj (rocky)* escarpado(a); *(features)* marcado(a)

cram [kræm] *(pt & pp* **crammed***)* **1** *vt (things)* embutir (**into** en); *(people)* apiñar (**into** en); **he crammed the clothes into the suitcase** llenó la maleta *or RP* valija de ropa hasta los topes; **to be crammed with sth** estar repleto(a) de algo; **they crammed as much sightseeing as possible into their three days** no pararon de ver monumentos y sitios en los tres días que tenían
2 *vi* (**a**) apiñarse; **we all crammed into the taxi** nos embutimos todos en el taxi (**b**) *Fam (study)* matarse estudiando, *Esp* empollar, *RP* tragar

cram-full [kræm'fʊl] *adj Fam* atestado(a), abarrotado(a)

cramp [kræmp] **1** *n* calambre *m*; **to have (a) c.** tener calambres
2 *vt (restrict)* limitar, coartar; *Fam* **to c. sb's style** ser un estorbo para *or* coartar a alguien

cramped [kræmpt] *adj (room)* estrecho(a); **to be c. for space** tener muy poco espacio

crampon ['kræmpɒn] *n* crampón *m*

cranberry ['krænbərɪ] *n* arándano *m* agrio

crane [kreɪn] **1** *n* (**a**) *(for lifting)* grúa *f* (**b**) *(bird)* grulla *f*; **c. fly** *(insect)* típula *f*
2 *vt* **to c. one's neck** estirar el cuello
3 *vi* **to c. forward** inclinarse hacia delante (estirando el cuello)

cranium ['kreɪnɪəm] *(pl* **crania** ['kreɪnɪə]*) n Anat* cráneo *m*

crank[1] [kræŋk] *n (gear mechanism)* cigüeñal *m*; **c. handle** manivela *f*

crank[2] *n Fam (eccentric)* rarito(a) *m,f*, maniático(a) *m,f*

crankshaft ['kræŋkʃɑːft] *n Aut* cigüeñal *m*

cranky ['kræŋkɪ] *adj Fam (eccentric)* rarito(a), maniático(a)

crap [kræp] *very Fam n* (**a**) *(excrement)* mierda *f*; **to have** *or* **take a c.** cagar, *Esp* echar una cagada, *Col, RP* embarrarla, *Méx* chingarla (**b**) *(worthless things)* mierdas *fpl*, porquerías *fpl*; *(nonsense) Esp* gilipolleces *fpl*, *Esp* paridas *fpl*, *Col, Méx* pendejadas *fpl*, *RP* pelotudeces *fpl*; *(disgusting substance)* porquería *f*, mierda *f*

crash [kræʃ] **1** *n* (**a**) *(noise)* estruendo *m* (**b**) *(accident)* choque *m*, colisión *f*; **car/train/plane c.** accidente *m* de coche *or Am* carro *or CSur* auto/tren/avión; *Aut* **c. barrier** quitamiedos *m inv*; *Aut* **c. helmet** casco *m* (protector); *Av* **c. landing** aterrizaje *m* forzoso *or* de emergencia (**c**) *(financial)* quiebra *f* (financiera), crac *m*
2 *adj* **c. course** curso *m* intensivo; **c. diet** dieta *f* drástica
3 *vt* (**a**) *(plane)* estrellar; **she crashed the car** se estrelló con el coche *or Am* carro *or CSur* auto (**b**) *Fam* **to c. a party** colarse en una fiesta
4 *vi* (**a**) *(make noise) (waves)* romper; **the bookcase crashed to the ground** la estantería cayó con estruendo (**b**) *(cars)* chocar; **to c. into** estrellarse contra (**c**) *(business, economy)* quebrar (**d**) *Comptr* bloquearse, colgarse (**e**) *Fam (sleep)* dormir, *Esp* sobar; **he lets me use his place as a c. pad** me deja dormir *or Esp* sobar en su casa

▸**crash out 1** *vi* **he was crashed out on the sofa** estaba frito *or Esp* sopa en el sofá
2 *vi Fam (go to sleep)* quedarse frito(a) *or Esp* sopa

crashing ['kræʃɪŋ] *adj* **a c. bore** un tostón

crash-land ['kræʃ'lænd] *vi* realizar un aterrizaje forzoso

crass [kræs] *adj* zafio(a); **c. ignorance/stupidity** ignorancia/estupidez supina

crate [kreɪt] *n (box)* caja *f*

crater ['kreɪtə(r)] *n* cráter *m*

cravat [krə'væt] *n* pañuelo *m*, fular *m*

crave [kreɪv] **1** *vt (affection, a cigarette)* ansiar
2 *vi* **to be craving for** *(affection, a cigarette)* ansiar

craving ['kreɪvɪŋ] *n (in general)* ansia *f* (**for** de); *(of pregnant woman)* antojo *m*; **to have a c. for sth** desear vehementemente *or* ansiar algo

crawl [krɔːl] **1** *n* (**a**) *(slow pace)* paso *m* lento; **the traffic was moving at a c.** el tráfico avanzaba lentamente (**b**) *(swimming stroke)* (estilo *m*) crol *m*; **to do** *or* **swim (the) c.** nadar a crol
2 *vi* (**a**) *(person)* arrastrarse; *(baby)* gatear; *(car)* avanzar lentamente (**b**) *Fam (be infested)* **the apartment was crawling with cockroaches** el piso estaba infestado de cucarachas; **it makes my skin c.** me pone la carne de gallina (**c**) *Fam (be obsequious)* **to c. to sb** arrastrarse ante alguien

crayfish ['kreɪfɪʃ] *n* cangrejo *m* de río

crayon ['kreɪɒn] **1** *n (wax)* (barra *f* de) cera *f*; *(pastel)* (barra *f* de) pastel *m*; *(pencil)* lápiz *m* de color
2 *vt* pintar

craze [kreɪz] *n* locura *f*, moda *f* (**for** de)

crazed [kreɪzd] *adj (look, person)* demente, delirante

crazily ['kreızılı] *adv (to behave)* alocadamente

craziness ['kreızınıs] *n* locura *f*

crazy ['kreızı] *adj (person)* loco(a); **to be c.** estar loco(a); **to go c.** volverse loco(a); **to drive sb c.** volver loco(a) a alguien; **she's c. about motorbikes** las motos la vuelven loca; **to be c. about sb** estar loco(a) por alguien; **like c.** *(to run, work)* como un loco

creak [kri:k] **1** *n (of hinge)* chirrido *m; (of timber, shoes)* chirrido, crujido *m*
   2 *vi (hinge)* chirriar, rechinar; *(timber, shoes)* crujir

creaky ['kri:kı] *adj (chair)* que cruje; *Fig* **the dialogue is a bit c.** los diálogos chirrían un poco

cream [kri:m] **1** *n* **(a)** *(of milk) Esp* nata *f, Am* crema *f* (de leche); **c. of tomato/chicken soup** crema *f* de tomate *or Méx* jitomate/pollo; **c. cake** pastel *m* de *Esp* nata *or Am* crema; **c. cheese** queso *m* blanco para untar **(b)** *Fig* **the c.** *(best part)* la flor y nata **(c)** *(lotion)* crema *f;* **face/hand c.** crema facial/de manos **(d)** *(color)* (color *m*) crema *m*
   2 *adj* **c.(-colored)** (color) crema
   3 *vt Culin (beat)* batir

▶**cream off** *vt sep* seleccionar, quedarse con

creamy ['kri:mı] *adj (in texture)* cremoso(a)

crease [kri:s] **1** *n (in skin, crumpled fabric)* arruga *f; (in ironed pants)* raya *f*
   2 *vt* arrugar; **to c. one's brow** fruncir el ceño
   3 *vi (become creased)* arrugarse

create [krı'eıt] *vt* crear; **to c. a sensation** causar sensación

creation [krı'eıʃən] *n* creación *f*

creative [krı'eıtıv] *adj* creativo(a); **the c. process** el proceso creativo; *Fin* **c. accounting** maquillaje *m* de cuentas, artificios *mpl* contables; **c. writing** creación *f* literaria

creatively [krı'eıtıvlı] *adv* creativamente, de forma creativa

creativity [krıə'tıvıtı] *n* creatividad *f*

creator [krı'eıtə(r)] *n* creador(ora) *m,f; Rel* **the C.** el Creador

creature ['kri:tʃə(r)] *n (living being, animal)* criatura *f;* **he's a c. of habit** es un animal de costumbres; **the chairman is a c. of the government** *(instrument)* el presidente es un títere del Gobierno; **c. comforts** (pequeños) placeres *mpl* de la vida

credence ['kri:dəns] *n* **to give c. to sth** dar crédito a algo

credentials [krı'denʃəlz] *npl (of ambassador)* credenciales *fpl; Fig* **he quickly established his c.** pronto demostró su valía

credibility [kredı'bılıtı] *n* credibilidad *f;* **c. gap** vacío *m or* falta *f* de credibilidad

credible ['kredıbəl] *adj* creíble

credibly ['kredəblı] *adv* de forma creíble

credit ['kredıt] **1** *n* **(a)** *Fin* crédito *m;* **to be in c.** tener saldo positivo; **to give sb c.** conceder un crédito a alguien; **to buy/sell on c.** comprar/vender a crédito; **c. card** tarjeta *f* de crédito; *Econ* **c. control** control *m* crediticio *or* de crédito; **c. limit** límite *m* de descubierto *or* de crédito; **c. rating** clasificación *f or* grado *m* de solvencia; *Econ* **c. squeeze** restricción *f* de crédito; **c. terms** condiciones *fpl* de crédito; **c. transfer** transferencia *f* bancaria
   (b) *(belief)* crédito *m;* **to give c. to sth** dar crédito a algo; **to gain c.** *(theory)* ganar aceptación
   (c) *(recognition)* reconocimiento *m;* **you'll have to give her c. for that** se lo tendrás que reconocer; **to take the c. for sth** apuntarse el mérito de algo; **c. where c.'s due** las cosas como son; **to her c., she refused** se negó, lo cual dice mucho en su favor; **it does you c.** puedes estar orgulloso de ello; **you're a c. to the school** eres motivo de orgullo para la escuela
   (d) *(of movie)* **credits** títulos *mpl* de crédito
   2 *vt* **(a)** *(money)* abonar; **to c. money to sb's account** abonar dinero en la cuenta de alguien **(b)** *(attribute)* **to c. sb with sth** atribuir algo a alguien; **I credited you with more sense** te consideraba más sensato

creditable ['kredıtəbəl] *adj (praiseworthy)* encomiable, digno(a) de encomio

creditor ['kredıtə(r)] *n Fin* acreedor(ora) *m,f*

creditworthy ['kredıtwɜ:ðı] *adj* solvente

credulity [krı'dju:lıtı] *n* credulidad *f*

credulous ['kredjʊləs] *adj* crédulo(a)

creed [kri:d] *n also Fig* credo *m*

creep [kri:p] **1** *Fam* **(a)** *(unpleasant person)* asqueroso(a) *m,f* **(b)** **he/it gives me the creeps** *(makes me uneasy)* me pone la piel de gallina; **I always get the creeps when I'm alone in the house** *(get frightened)* siempre que me quedo solo(a) en casa me entra el *Esp* canguelo *or Arg* cuiqui *or Col* culillo *or Méx* mello
   2 *vi (pt & pp* **crept** [krept]) *(animal, person)* moverse sigilosamente, deslizarse; *(plants)* trepar; **to c. in** colarse; **to c. out** escapar (sigilosamente); **a mistake has crept into our calculations** se nos ha colado un error en los cálculos; **old age has crept up on me** los años se me han echado encima; *Fam* **it makes my flesh c.** me pone la carne de gallina

creeper ['kri:pə(r)] *n (plant)* enredadera *f; (in wild)* liana *f*

creeping ['kri:pıŋ] *adj (gradual)* paulatino(a); **c. privatization** privatización *f* gradual subrepticia

creepy ['kri:pı] *adj Fam* **(a)** *(unpleasant)* repugnante, repelente **(b)** *(frightening)* espeluznante

creepy-crawly ['kri:pı'krɔ:lı] *n Fam* bicho *m*, bicharraco *m*

cremate [krı'meıt] *vt* incinerar

cremation [krı'meıʃən] *n* incineración *f*, cremación *f*

crematory ['kremətərı], **crematorium** [kremə'tɔ:rıəm] *(pl* **crematoriums, crematoria** [kremə'tɔ:rıə]) *n* crematorio *m*

crème [krem] *n* **c. caramel** flan *m;* **the c. de la c.** *(the best)* la flor y nata; **c. fraîche** *Esp* nata *f or Am* crema *f* fresca fermentada

creole ['kri:əʊl] *Ling* **1** *n* criollo *m*
   2 *adj* criollo(a)

creosote ['krıəsəʊt] *n* creosota *f*

crepe, crêpe *n* **(a)** [kreıp] *(textile)* crepé *m*, crespón *m;* **c. paper** papel *m* crespón *or* pinocho; **c.(-rubber) soles** zapatos *mpl* de suela de goma *or* de crepé **(b)** [krep] *(pancake)* crepe *f*

crept [krept] *pt & pp of* **creep**

crescendo [krı'ʃendəʊ] *(pl* **crescendos**) *n Mus & Fig* crescendo *m;* **to rise to a c.** *(music, complaints)* alcanzar el punto culminante

crescent ['kresənt] **1** *n (shape)* medialuna *f*
   2 *adj* **c.(-shaped)** en forma de medialuna; **c. moon** cuarto *m* creciente

cress [kres] *n* berro *m*

crest [krest] *n (of bird, wave)* cresta *f; (of helmet)* penacho *m; (of hill)* cima *f; (coat of arms)* escudo *m; Fig* **on the c. of a wave** en la cresta de la ola

crestfallen ['krestfɔ:lən] *adj* abatido(a)

Cretan ['kri:tən] *n & adj* cretense *mf*

Crete [kri:t] *n* Creta

cretin ['kretın] *n Fam* cretino(a) *m,f*

cretinous ['kretınəs] *adj* estúpido(a), cretino(a)

Creutzfeldt-Jakob disease ['krɔıtsfelt'jɑ:kɒbdı'zi:z] *n* enfermedad *f* de Creutzfeld(t)-Jakob

crevice ['krevıs] *n* grieta *f*

crew [kru:] **1** *n (of ship, plane)* tripulación *f; (of ambulance)* personal *m* de ambulancia; *Fam (gang, group)* pandilla *f, Méx* bola *f, RP* barra *f;* **c. cut** *(hairstyle)* rapado *m*, corte *m* al cero; **c. neck** cuello *m* redondo
   2 *vt (ship)* tripular

crib [krıb] **1** *n* **(a)** *(cradle)* cuna *f; (Nativity scene)* belén *m*, pesebre *m;* **c. death** (síndrome *m* de la) muerte *f* súbita infantil (**b**) *Fam (at school) (translation)* traducción *f (que permite entender el original); (in exam) Esp, Ven* chuleta *f, Arg* machete *m, Col, Méx* acordeón *m, Perú* comprimido *m, Urug* trencito *m*

  2 *vt (pt & pp* **cribbed**) *Fam (at school)* copiar

crick [krɪk] **1** *n (in neck)* tortícolis *f inv;* **to have a c. in one's neck** tener tortícolis

  2 *vt* **to c. one's neck** hacerse daño en el cuello

cricket¹ ['krɪkɪt] *n (insect)* grillo *m*

cricket² *n (sport)* críquet *m;* **c. ball** pelota *f* de críquet; **c. bat** bate *m* de críquet; **c. pitch** campo *m* de críquet

crime [kraɪm] *n (serious criminal act)* crimen *m; (less serious)* delito *m;* **c. is on the increase** está aumentando la delincuencia; **to commit a c.** cometer un delito, delinquir; *Fig* **it's a c.** *(outrageous)* es un crimen; **c. wave** ola *f* de delincuencia; **c. writer** *(of detective novels)* escritor(ora) *m,f* de novela negra

Crimea [kraɪ'mɪə] *n* Crimea

Crimean [kraɪ'mɪən] *adj* de Crimea

criminal ['krɪmɪnəl] **1** *n (in general)* delincuente *mf; (serious)* criminal *mf*

  2 *adj* delictivo(a), criminal; *Fig* **a c. waste of money** un despilfarro disparatado; **c. court** juzgado *m* de lo penal; **c. damage** daños *mpl* criminales; **c. law** derecho *m* penal; **c. lawyer** abogado(a) *m,f* criminalista, penalista *mf;* **c. offense** delito *m* (penal); **to instigate c. proceedings against sb** demandar a alguien ante un juzgado de lo penal; **c. record** antecedentes *mpl* penales

criminality [krɪmɪ'nælɪtɪ] *n (in general)* delincuencia *f; (serious)* criminalidad *f*

criminalize ['krɪmɪnəlaɪz] *vt* penalizar

criminally ['krɪmɪnəlɪ] *adv* **the c. insane** los (delincuentes) psicópatas; **he was c. negligent** cometió un delito de negligencia

criminology [krɪmɪ'nɒlədʒɪ] *n* criminología *f*

crimp [krɪmp] **1** *vt* (**a**) *(hair)* rizar (con tenacillas) (**b**) *Fam (hinder)* obstaculizar

  2 *n Fam* **to put a c. in sth** obstacularizar algo

crimson ['krɪmzən] *n & adj* carmesí *m*

cringe [krɪndʒ] *vi* (**a**) *(show fear)* encogerse (**b**) *(be embarrassed)* tener vergüenza ajena, abochornarse; **it makes me c.** me produce vergüenza ajena

cringing ['krɪndʒɪŋ] *adj (afraid)* atemorizado(a); *(servile)* servil

crinkle ['krɪŋkəl] **1** *vt (paper)* arrugar; **to c. one's nose** arrugar la nariz

  2 *vi* arrugarse

crinkly ['krɪŋklɪ] *adj (skin, paper)* arrugado(a)

cripple ['krɪpəl] **1** *n* inválido(a) *m,f*

  2 *vt* (**a**) *(person)* dejar inválido(a), lisiar (**b**) *(industry, system)* deteriorar, arruinar

crippling ['krɪplɪŋ] *adj* (**a**) *(illness)* incapacitante (**b**) *(taxes, strike)* pernicioso(a)

crisis ['kraɪsɪs] *(pl* **crises** ['kraɪsiːz]) *n* crisis *f inv;* **in c.** en crisis; **to go through a c.** atravesar una crisis; **c. management** gestión *f* de crisis

crisp [krɪsp] **1** *n* **burned to a c.** achicharrado(a)

  2 *adj (apple, lettuce)* fresco(a); *(pastry, bacon)* crujiente; *(air, breeze)* fresco(a); *(style)* conciso(a); *(tone)* seco(a)

crisply ['krɪsplɪ] *adv (say)* secamente

crispy ['krɪspɪ] *adj (bacon, pastry)* crujiente

crisscross ['krɪskrɒs] **1** *vt* entrecruzar

  2 *vi* entrecruzarse

criterion [kraɪ'tɪərɪən] *(pl* **criteria** [kraɪ'tɪərɪə]) *n* criterio *m*

critic ['krɪtɪk] *n* crítico(a) *m,f*

critical ['krɪtɪkəl] *adj* (**a**) *(negative)* crítico(a); **to be c. of** criticar (**b**) *(essay, study)* crítico(a); **it was a c. success** fue un éxito de crítica *or* entre la crítica (**c**) *(decisive)* crítico(a),

decisivo(a); **she was in a c. condition** *(patient)* se encontraba en estado crítico

criticism ['krɪtɪsɪzəm] *n* crítica *f*

criticize ['krɪtɪsaɪz] *vt* criticar; **to c. sb for (doing) sth** criticar a alguien por (hacer) algo

critique [krɪ'tiːk] *n* crítica *f*

croak [krəʊk] **1** *n (of frog)* croar *m; (of raven)* graznido *m; (of person)* gruñido *m*

  2 *vi* (**a**) *(frog)* croar; *(raven)* graznar; *(person)* gruñir (**b**) *very Fam (die)* palmar, espicharla

Croat ['krəʊæt], **Croatian** [krəʊ'eɪʃən] **1** *n* (**a**) *(person)* croata *mf* (**b**) *(language)* croata *m*

  2 *adj* croata

Croatia [krəʊ'eɪʃə] *n* Croacia

Croatian = Croat

crochet ['krəʊʃeɪ] **1** *n* ganchillo *m, Col, CSur* crochet *m, Méx* gancho *m;* **c. hook** aguja *f* de ganchillo *or Col, CSur* crochet *or Méx* gancho *m*

  2 *vt* **to c. sth** hacer algo a ganchillo *or Col, CSur* crochet *or Méx* gancho

  3 *vi* hacer ganchillo *or Col, CSur* crochet *or Méx* gancho

crock [krɒk] *n* (**a**) *(pot)* vasija *f* de barro (**b**) *Fam* **old c.** *(person)* viejo(a) *m,f* chocho(a); *(car)* cacharro *m, Esp* tartana *f* (**c**) *Fam* **it's a c.** no sirve para nada

crockery ['krɒkərɪ] *n* vajilla *f*

crocodile ['krɒkədaɪl] *n* cocodrilo *m;* **c. tears** lágrimas *fpl* de cocodrilo

crocus ['krəʊkəs] *n* azafrán *m*

croissant ['krwæsɒŋ] *n* croissant *m*

crone [krəʊn] *n Pej* **old c.** bruja *f*

crony ['krəʊnɪ] *n* amigote *m*, amiguete(a) *m,f*

cronyism ['krəʊnɪɪzəm] *n Pej* amiguismo *m*, enchufismo *m*

crook [krʊk] **1** *n* (**a**) *(criminal)* granuja *mf*, bribón(ona) *m,f* (**b**) *(shepherd's staff)* cayado *m; (bishop's)* báculo *m* (**c**) *(curve)* recodo *m;* **to hold sth in the c. of one's arm** llevar algo en brazos *or* en el brazo

  2 *vt (finger, arm)* doblar

crooked ['krʊkɪd] *adj* (**a**) *(not straight)* torcido(a); *(lane, path)* tortuoso(a) (**b**) *(dishonest, illegal) (deal)* sucio(a); *(policeman, politician)* corrupto(a)

croon [kruːn] *vt & vi* canturrear

crop [krɒp] **1** *n* (**a**) *(of fruit, vegetables)* cosecha *f; Fig* **this year's c. of movies** la cosecha de películas de este año; **c. circle** = franja aplastada y circular de terreno cultivado, que aparece por causas supuestamente paranormales (**b**) *(handle of whip)* (**riding**) **c.** fusta *f* (**c**) *(of bird)* buche *m*

  2 *vt (pt & pp* **cropped**) (**a**) *(cut) (hair)* cortar; *(photograph)* recortar (**b**) *(of cattle) (grass)* pacer

▸**crop up** *vi (arise)* surgir

cropper ['krɒpə(r)] *n Fam* **to come a c.** *(fall)* darse un porrazo *or Esp* batacazo *or Méx* madrazo; *(fail)* pinchar

croquet ['krəʊkeɪ] *n (game)* croquet *m*

croquette [krɒ'ket] *n Culin* croqueta *f*

cross [krɒs] **1** *n* (**a**) *(sign, shape)* cruz *f;* **to make the sign of the c.** *(blessing self)* santiguarse; *(blessing others)* dar la bendición

  (**b**) *(hybrid) (of animals)* cruce *m*, híbrido *m, Am* cruza *f; Fig* **to be a c. between A and B** ser una mezcla de A y B

  (**c**) *(in soccer)* centro *m; (in boxing)* (golpe *m*) directo *m*

  (**d**) **c. section** sección *f* transversal; **a c. section of the population** una muestra representativa de la población

  (**e**) *also Fig* **c. fire** fuego *m* cruzado; **they were caught in the c. fire** el fuego cruzado los pilló *or Esp* cogió *or Am* agarró en medio

  2 *adj (annoyed) esp Esp* enfadado(a), *esp Am* enojado(a); **to be c.** estar *esp Esp* enfadado(a) *or esp Am* enojado(a); **to get c.** *esp Esp* enfadarse, *esp Am* enojarse

3 *vt* *(river, road)* cruzar, atravesar; **to c. sb's path** cruzarse en el camino de alguien; **it crossed my mind (that…)** se me ocurrió (que…); *Fig* **we'll c. that bridge when we come to it** *Esp* no nos adelantemos acontecimientos, *Am* no nos adelantamos a los acontecimientos

(**b**) *(place across)* cruzar; **to c. one's legs/arms** cruzar las piernas/los brazos; *Fig* **to keep one's fingers crossed** cruzar los dedos; **to c. one's eyes** poner los ojos bizcos; *Fig* **to c. swords (with)** verse las caras *or* habérselas (con); *Fig* **we must have got our wires crossed** parece que no nos hemos entendido bien

(**c**) *(oppose)* oponerse a, contrariar

(**d**) *(animals, plants)* cruzar (**with** con)

(**e**) *Rel* **to c. oneself** santiguarse; *Fam* **c. my heart!** ¡te lo juro!

4 *vi* (**a**) *(roads, lines)* cruzarse; **our letters crossed in the mail** nuestras cartas se cruzaron en el correo (**b**) *(go across)* cruzar

▸**cross off, cross out** *vt sep* tachar

crossbar ['krɒsbɑ:(r)] *n* *(on bike)* barra *f (de la bicicleta)*; *(of goalposts)* larguero *m*

crossbow ['krɒsbəʊ] *n* ballesta *f*

crossbreed ['krɒsbri:d] *n* híbrido *m*, cruce *m*, *Am* cruza *f*

cross-Channel ['krɒs'tʃænəl] *adj* **c. ferry** = transbordador que cruza el Canal de la Mancha; **c. trade** = comercio entre Gran Bretaña y el resto de Europa

cross-check ['krɒs'tʃek] **1** *n* comprobación *f*, verificación *f*
2 *vt* comprobar, contrastar

cross-country ['krɒs'kʌntrɪ] *adj* *(vehicle)* todoterreno; **c. runner** corredor(ora) *m,f* de cross; **c. running** campo *m* a través, cross *m*; **c. skiing** esquí *m* de fondo

cross-examination ['krɒsɪgzæmɪ'neɪʃən] *n* interrogatorio *m*

cross-examine ['krɒsɪg'zæmɪn] *vt* interrogar

cross-eyed ['krɒsaɪd] *adj* bizco(a)

cross-fertilization ['krɒsfɜ:tɪlaɪ'zeɪʃən] *n* (**a**) *(between plants)* polinización *f* cruzada (**b**) *(cultural)* mestizaje *m* (cultural); *(of ideas)* intercambio *m*

cross-fertilize [krɒs'fɜ:tɪlaɪz] *n* (**a**) *(plants)* polinizar con fecundación cruzada (**b**) *Fig* favorecer el mestizaje (cultural) entre

crossing ['krɒsɪŋ] *n* (**a**) *(of sea)* travesía *f* (**b**) *(in street)* paso *m* de peatones

cross-legged ['krɒs'leg(ɪ)d] *adv* **to sit c.** sentarse con las piernas cruzadas

cross-over ['krɒsəʊvə(r)] **1** *n* *(of career)* salto *m*, cambio *m*
2 *adj Mus (style)* híbrido(a), de fusión

cross-party ['krɒs'pɑ:tɪ] *adj* interpartidista

cross-platform [krɒs'plætfɔ:m] *adj Comptr* multiplataforma *inv*

cross-purposes ['krɒs'pɜ:pəsɪz] *npl* **they were at c. with each other** sin darse cuenta, estaban hablando de cosas distintas

cross-reference ['krɒs'refərəns] *n* referencia *f*, remisión *f*

crossroads ['krɒsrəʊdz] *n also Fig* encrucijada *f*

crosswalk ['krɒswɔ:k] *n* paso *m* de peatones

crosswind ['krɒswɪnd] *n* viento *m* lateral

crossword ['krɒswɜ:d] *n* **c. (puzzle)** crucigrama *m*

crotch [krɒtʃ] *n* *(of pants, person)* entrepierna *f*

crotchety ['krɒtʃətɪ] *adj (grumpy)* gruñón(ona)

crouch [kraʊtʃ] *vi (animal)* agazaparse; *(person)* agacharse

croupier ['kru:pɪə(r)] *n* crupier *m*

crouton ['kru:tɒn] *n* picatoste *m*, = dado de pan frito

crow [krəʊ] **1** *n* *(bird)* corneja *f*; **as the c. flies** en línea recta; **c.'s feet** *(facial lines)* patas *fpl* de gallo; **c.'s nest** *(on ship)* cofa *f*
2 *vi* (**a**) *(cock)* cacarear (**b**) *(show off)* pavonearse (**about** de)

crowbar ['krəʊbɑ:(r)] *n* palanqueta *f*

crowd [kraʊd] **1** *n* (**a**) *(large number of people)* muchedumbre *f*, multitud *f*; *(at soccer match)* público *m*; *Fig* **to stand out from the c.** destacar, sobresalir; *Fig* **to follow the c.** dejarse llevar por la masa; **to be a c. puller** atraer a las masas; **c. scene** *(in movie)* escena *f* de masas (**b**) *Fam (group)* pandilla *f*, *Méx* bola *f*, *RP* barra *f*; **the usual c. were there** estaba la gente de siempre, estaban los de siempre
2 *vt* atestar, abarrotar
3 *vi* **to c. (together)** apiñarse, amontonarse; **to c. around sb** apiñarse en torno de alguien

crowded ['kraʊdɪd] *adj (room, bus)* abarrotado(a), atestado(a); **to be c.** estar abarrotado(a) *or* atestado(a)

crown [kraʊn] **1** *n* (**a**) *(of monarch)* corona *f*; **the C.** la Corona; **the c. jewels** las joyas de la corona; **c. prince** príncipe *m* heredero (**b**) *(top) (of head)* coronilla *f*; *(of hat)* copa *f*; *(of hill)* cima *f*; *(on tooth)* corona *f*
2 *vt also Fig* coronar; **to c. sb king** coronar rey a alguien; **to c. a tooth** ponerle una corona a una muela; *Fam Fig* **I'll c. you!** *(hit on the head)* ¡te voy a dar una!, *Esp* ¡te voy a sacudir!

crowning ['kraʊnɪŋ] *adj (achievement)* supremo(a); **c. glory** gloria *f* suprema

crucial ['kru:ʃəl] *adj (very important)* crucial

crucible ['kru:sɪbəl] *n* crisol *m*

crucifix ['kru:sɪfɪks] *n* crucifijo *m*

crucifixion [kru:sɪ'fɪkʃən] *n* crucifixión *f*

crucify ['kru:sɪfaɪ] *vt also Fig* crucificar

crude [kru:d] *adj* (**a**) *(unsophisticated, unrefined)* burdo(a); **c. (oil)** *(petróleo m)* crudo *m* (**b**) *(rude, vulgar)* ordinario(a), grosero(a)

cruel ['kruəl] *adj* cruel (**to** con); **you have to be c. to be kind** quien bien te quiere te hará llorar

cruelty ['kruəltɪ] *n* crueldad *f*

cruet ['kru:ɪt] *n Culin* **c. (stand** *or* **set)** vinagreras *fpl*

cruise [kru:z] **1** *n* *(on ship)* crucero *m*; **to go on a c.** ir de crucero; **c. missile** misil *m* de crucero
2 *vi* *(ship)* navegar tranquilamente; *(passengers)* hacer un crucero; *(car, plane)* ir a velocidad de crucero; *Fam (look for sexual partner)* tratar de ligar, *Esp* buscar ligue; **it was cruising at 25 knots** *(ship)* navegaba a 25 nudos; **cruising speed** *(of ship, plane)* velocidad *f* de crucero

cruiser ['kru:zə(r)] *n* *(ship)* **(battle) c.** crucero *m* (de guerra); **(cabin) c.** yate *m*

crumb [krʌm] *n* *(of bread)* miga *f*; **my only c. of comfort is…** lo único que me consuela es…; *Fig* **he was left with the crumbs** no le dejaron más que las migajas

crumble ['krʌmbəl] **1** *n* *(dessert)* = postre al horno a base de compota con masa quebrada dulce por encima
2 *vt (bread)* desmigajar
3 *vi (stone)* desmenuzarse; *(bread)* desmigajarse; *Fig (empire, resistance)* desmoronarse, venirse abajo

crumbly ['krʌmblɪ] *adj* **it's very c.** se desmenuza muy fácilmente

crumpet ['krʌmpɪt] *n (teacake)* = torta pequeña que se come con mantequilla

crumple ['krʌmpəl] **1** *vt (material, dress)* arrugar
2 *vi* arrugarse; *Fig (person)* desplomarse; *(resistance)* sucumbir

crunch [krʌntʃ] **1** *n (sound)* crujido *m*; *Fig* **when it comes to the c.** a la hora de la verdad
2 *vt (with teeth)* ronzar, machacar con los dientes
3 *vi* crujir

crunchy ['krʌntʃɪ] *adj* crujiente

crusade [kru:'seɪd] **1** *n also Fig* cruzada *f*
2 *vi* **to c. for/against** emprender una cruzada a favor de/en contra de

crusader [kru:'seɪdə(r)] *n Hist* cruzado *m*; *Fig* paladín *m*

crush [krʌʃ] **1** *n* (**a**) *(crowd)* muchedumbre *f*, aglomeración *f* (**b**) *(drink)* **orange c.** naranjada *f* (**c**) *Fam (infatuation)* **to**

have a c. on sb estar embobado(a) con alguien, *Esp* estar colado(a) por *or* encaprichado(a) de alguien

2 *vt (person, thing)* estrujar, aplastar; *(grapes, garlic)* prensar, aplastar; *Fig (opponent, revolt)* aplastar, destrozar; **to c. sb's hopes** tirar abajo las esperanzas de alguien

3 *vi* **we crushed into the car** nos estrujamos para entrar en el coche

crushing ['krʌʃɪŋ] *adj (blow, defeat)* demoledor(ora), aplastante

crust [krʌst] *n (of bread, pie, the earth)* corteza *f*

crustacean [krʌs'teɪʃən] *n* crustáceo *m*

crusty ['krʌstɪ] *adj (bread, roll)* crujiente

crutch [krʌtʃ] *n* **(a)** *(for walking)* muleta *f*; *Fig (support)* apoyo *m*, sostén *m*; **to be on crutches** ir con muletas **(b)** *(of pants, person)* entrepierna *f*

crux [krʌks] *n* **the c. of the matter** el quid de la cuestión

cry [kraɪ] **1** *n* **(a)** *(call) (of person, animal)* grito *m*; *(in demonstration)* consigna *f*; **to give a c.** dar un grito; **a c. of pain** un grito de dolor; *Fig* **a c. for help** una petición de ayuda; **it's a far c. from what was promised** no tiene nada que ver con lo que se prometió **(b)** *(weeping)* **to have a good c.** llorar abundantemente

2 *vt (pt & pp* **cried** [kraɪd]) **(a)** *(exclaim)* exclamar **(b)** *(weep)* **she cried herself to sleep** lloró hasta quedarse dormida

3 *vi* **(a)** *(weep)* llorar; **to c. over sth** llorar por algo; *Prov* **there's no point in crying over spilled milk** a lo hecho, pecho **(b)** *(shout, call)* gritar; **to c. for help** gritar pidiendo ayuda

▸**cry off** *vi* volverse atrás

▸**cry out1** *vt sep* **(a)** *(shout) (name, warning)* gritar **(b)** *(weep)* **to c. one's eyes** *or* **heart out** llorar a lágrima viva

2 *vi (shout)* gritar; *Fam* **for crying out loud!** ¡por el amor de Dios!; *Fam* **that wall is crying out for a coat of paint** esa pared está pidiendo a gritos una mano de pintura

crybaby ['kraɪbeɪbɪ] *n Fam* llorica *mf*

crying ['kraɪɪŋ] **1** *n (weeping)* llanto *m*

2 *adj (need)* acuciante; **it's a c. shame that...** es una auténtica vergüenza que...

crypt [krɪpt] *n* cripta *f*

cryptic ['krɪptɪk] *adj* críptico(a)

crystal ['krɪstəl] **1** *n (glass, mineral)* cristal *m*; **salt/sugar crystals** cristales *mpl* de sal/azúcar

2 *adj* **(a)** *(clear)* transparente, claro(a) **(b)** *(made of glass)* de cristal; **c. ball** bola *f* de vidrio *or Esp* cristal **(c)** **c. gazing** clarividencia *f*

crystal-clear ['krɪstəl'klɪə(r)] *adj (water)* cristalino(a); *(explanation)* clarísimo(a), más claro(a) que el agua

crystallize, crystalize ['krɪstəlaɪz] **1** *vt Chem* cristalizar; **crystallized fruits** frutas *fpl* escarchadas *or Col, Méx* cristalizadas *or RP* abrillantadas

2 *vi Chem & Fig* cristalizar

CST [si:es'ti:] *n (abbr* **Central Standard Time)** = hora oficial en el centro de los Estados Unidos

cub [kʌb] *n (of fox, lion)* cachorro *m*; *(of bear)* osezno *m*; *(of wolf)* lobezno *m*, lobato *m*; **C. (Scout)** lobato *m*, niño *m* explorador

Cuba ['kju:bə] *n* Cuba

Cuban ['kju:bən] *n & adj* cubano(a) *m,f*

cubbyhole ['kʌbɪhəʊl] *n (cupboard)* armario *m* empotrado; *(room)* cuartito *m*

cube [kju:b] **1** *n (shape)* cubo *m*; *(of sugar)* terrón *m*; *Math* **c. root** raíz *f* cúbica

2 *vt Math* elevar al cubo

cubic ['kju:bɪk] *adj* cúbico(a); **c. capacity** capacidad *f*, volumen *m*; **c. meter** metro *m* cúbico

cubicle ['kju:bɪkəl] *n (in hospital, dormitory)* cubículo *m*; *(in swimming pool)* cabina *f*, vestuario *m*; *(in rest room)* cubículo *m*

cubism ['kju:bɪzəm] *n Art* cubismo *m*

cuckold ['kʌkəld] **1** *n* cornudo *m*

2 *vt* poner los cuernos a

cuckoo ['kʊku:] **1** *n (pl* **cuckoos)** cuco *m*; **c. clock** reloj *m* de cuco, *RP* reloj *m* cucú

2 *adj Fam (mad)* **to be c.** estar pirado(a), *Méx* estar zafado(a)

cucumber ['kju:kʌmbə(r)] *n* pepino *m*

cud [kʌd] *n* **to chew the c.** rumiar

cuddle ['kʌdəl] **1** *n* abrazo *m*; **to give sb a c.** dar un abrazo a alguien

2 *vt* abrazar

3 *vi* arrimarse; **to c. up to sb** arrimarse a alguien

cuddly ['kʌdlɪ] *adj Fam (child, animal)* tierno(a); **a c. toy** un muñeco de peluche

cudgel ['kʌdʒəl] **1** *n* porra *f*, palo *m*; *Fig* **to take up the cudgels on sb's behalf** salir en defensa de alguien, *Am* quebrar una lanza por alguien

2 *vt (pt & pp* **cudgeled)** **to c. one's brains** estrujarse el cerebro

cue[1] *n (of actor)* entrada *f*; **to miss one's c.** no oír la entrada; *Fig* **to take one's c. from sb** tomar ejemplo de alguien; **c. card** *(for public speaker)* chuleta *f (en la que están anotados los puntos más importantes)*

cue[2] *n (in billiards, pool)* taco *m*; **c. ball** bola *f* jugadora

cuff[1] [kʌf] *n (of shirt)* puño *m*; *(of pants)* vuelta *f*; **cuffs** *(handcuffs)* esposas *fpl*; *Fam* **off the c.** improvisadamente; **c. links** gemelos *mpl*

cuff[2] *n (blow)* cachete *m*, cate *m*

2 *vt (hit)* dar un sopapo *or Am* una cachetada a

cuisine [kwɪ'zi:n] *n* cocina *f*

cul-de-sac ['kʌldəsæk] *n* callejón *m* sin salida

culinary ['kʌlɪnərɪ] *adj* culinario(a)

cull [kʌl] **1** *n (of seals, deer)* sacrificio *m*

2 *vt* **(a)** *(animals)* sacrificar **(b)** *(select)* extraer, recoger **(from** de)

culminate ['kʌlmɪneɪt] *vi* **to c. in** culminar en

culmination [kʌlmɪ'neɪʃən] *n* culminación *f*

culottes [kju:'lɒts] *npl* falda *f or Am* pollera *f* pantalón; **a pair of c.** una falda *or Am* pollera pantalón

culpable ['kʌlpəbəl] *adj* culpable

culprit ['kʌlprɪt] *n* culpable *mf*

cult [kʌlt] *n* culto *m*; **he became a c. figure** se convirtió en objeto de culto; **c. movie/novel** película *f*/novela *f* de culto

cultivate ['kʌltɪveɪt] *vt also Fig* cultivar

cultivated ['kʌltɪveɪtɪd] *adj* **(a)** *(land, plant)* cultivado(a) **(b)** *(educated)* culto(a)

cultivation [kʌltɪ'veɪʃən] *n* cultivo *m*

cultivator ['kʌltɪveɪtə(r)] *n (machine)* cultivadora *f*; *(person)* cultivador(ora) *m,f*

cultural ['kʌltʃərəl] *adj* cultural

culturally ['kʌltʃərəlɪ] *adv* culturalmente

culture ['kʌltʃə(r)] *n* **(a)** *(artistic activity, refinement)* cultura *f*; *Hum* **c. vulture** devorador(ora) *m,f* de cultura **(b)** *(society)* cultura *f*; **c. shock** choque *m* cultural **(c)** *Biol* cultivo *m*

cultured ['kʌltʃəd] *adj (educated)* culto(a)

cumbersome ['kʌmbəsəm] *adj* engorroso(a)

cumin ['kʌmɪn] *n* comino *m*

cumulative ['kju:mjʊlətɪv] *adj* acumulativo(a)

cunning ['kʌnɪŋ] **1** *n* astucia *f*

2 *adj (devious)* astuto(a), artero(a); *(ingenious)* ingenioso(a)

cunningly ['kʌnɪŋlɪ] *adv (deviously)* astutamente; *(ingeniously)* ingeniosamente

cunt [kʌnt] *n Vulg (vagina)* coño *m*, *Col* cuca *f*, *Méx* paloma *f*, *Andes, RP* concha *f*; *(as insult)* hijo(a) *m,f* de puta, cabrón(ona) *m,f*

cup [kʌp] **1** *n* **(a)** *(for drinking)* taza *f*; *(measurement)* taza *f*, vaso *m*; **c. of coffee/tea** (taza *f* de) café *m*/té *m*; *Fam Fig* **it's not**

my c. of tea no es santo de mi devoción, *Esp* no me va mucho; *Fam Fig* **it's not everyone's c. of tea** no (le) gusta a todo el mundo (**b**) *(trophy)* copa *f*; **c. final** final *f* de la copa (**c**) *(of bra)* copa *f*

2 *vt (pt & pp* **cupped)** **to c. one's hands around one's mouth** poner las manos en la boca a modo de bocina

cupboard ['kʌbəd] *n* armario *m*; *Fam* **it was just c. love** era un amor interesado; **c. space** armarios *mpl*

cupcake ['kʌpkeɪk] *n* ≃ magdalena *f*

Cupid ['kju:pɪd] *n* Cupido *m*

curable ['kjʊərəbəl] *adj* curable

curate ['kjʊərət] *n Rel* coadjutor *m*

curator [kjʊə'reɪtə(r)] *n* conservador(ora) *m,f* (de museos)

curb [kɜ:b] **1** *n* (**a**) *(limit)* **to put a c. on sth** poner freno a algo (**b**) *(at roadside)* bordillo *m* (de la acera), *Chile* solera *f*, *Col, Perú* sardinel *m*, *CSur, Cuba* cordón *m* (de la vereda), *Méx* borde *m* (de la banqueta)

2 *vt (spending)* reducir; *(emotions)* refrenar

curbside [kɜ:b] *n* borde *m* de la acera *or CSur* vereda *or Méx* banqueta

curbstone ['kɜ:bstəʊn] *n* adoquín *m* (del bordillo)

curd [kɜ:d] *n* **c., curds** cuajada *f*; **c. cheese** queso *m* blanco

curdle ['kɜ:dəl] **1** *vt* cortar; *Fam Fig* **to have a face that would c. milk** tener la cara avinagrada

2 *vi* cortarse

cure ['kjʊə(r)] **1** *n* cura *f*; **there is no known c.** no se conoce ninguna cura; **beyond c.** incurable

2 *vt* (**a**) *(person) (of illness)* curar, sanar; *Fig (of bad habit)* quitar, curar; **to c. sb of sth** curar a alguien de algo (**b**) *(preserve) (by salting, drying)* curar; *(hides)* curtir

cure-all ['kjʊərɔ:l] *n* panacea *f*

curfew ['kɜ:fju:] *n* toque *m* de queda

curio ['kjʊərɪəʊ] *(pl* **curios)** *n* curiosidad *f*, rareza *f*

curiosity [kjʊərɪ'ɒsɪtɪ] *n* curiosidad *f*; *Prov* **c. killed the cat** mejor no te metas donde no te llaman

curious ['kjʊərɪəs] *adj (inquisitive, strange)* curioso(a); **to be c. to see/know** tener curiosidad por ver/saber

curl [kɜ:l] **1** *n (of hair)* rizo *m*, *Andes, RP* rulo *m*; *(of smoke)* voluta *f*

2 *vt (hair)* rizar; **to c. one's lip** hacer un gesto de desprecio; **to c. oneself into a ball** enroscarse, hacerse un ovillo

3 *vi (hair)* rizarse; *(paper)* abarquillarse; *(smoke)* formar volutas

▶**curl up** *vi* (**a**) *(settle down) (in bed, on sofa)* acurrucarse (**b**) *(hedgehog, person)* enroscarse, hacerse un ovillo (**c**) *(leaves)* rizarse; *(paper)* abarquillarse

curler ['kɜ:lə(r)] *n (for hair)* rulo *m*, *Chile* tubo *m*, *RP* rulero *m*, *Ven* rollo *m*

curlew ['kɜ:lju:] *n* zarapito *m*

curling ['kɜ:lɪŋ] *n* (**a**) *(sport)* curling *m*, = deporte consistente en el deslizamiento sobre hielo de piedras pulidas lo más cerca posible de una meta (**b**) **c. tongs** tenacillas *fpl*

curly ['kɜ:lɪ] *adj (hair)* rizado(a), crespo(a), *Méx* quebrado(a), *Chile, RP* enrulado(a)

currant ['kʌrənt] *n (dried grape)* pasa *f* (de Corinto)

currency ['kʌrənsɪ] *n* (**a**) *Fin* moneda *f*; **to buy c.** comprar divisas; **foreign c.** divisas *fpl*; **c. market** mercado *m* de divisas (**b**) *Fig* **to give c. to a rumor** extender un rumor; **to gain c.** *(idea, belief)* extenderse

current ['kʌrənt] **1** *n (of water, electricity, opinion)* corriente *f*; *Fig* **to swim against the c.** ir a *or* nadar contra corriente

2 *adj (existing, present)* actual; *(common)* corriente; **to be c.** ser corriente; **in c. use** de uso corriente; **c. affairs** (temas *mpl* de) actualidad *f*; **c. issue** *(of magazine)* (último) número *m*

currently ['kʌrəntlɪ] *adv* actualmente, en este momento

curriculum [kə'rɪkjʊləm] *(pl* **curriculums** *or* **curricula** [kə'rɪkjʊlə]) *n Sch* programa *m*, plan *m* de estudios; **c. vitae** currículum *m* (vitae)

curry¹ ['kʌrɪ] *Culin* **1** *n* curry *m*; **c. powder** curry *m (especia)*

2 *vt* **curried chicken/lamb** pollo *m*/cordero *m* al curry

curry² *vt* **to c. favor with sb** ganarse el favor de alguien con zalamerías

curse [kɜ:s] **1** *n (jinx, affliction)* maldición *f*; *(swearword)* maldición *f*, juramento *m*; **to put a c. on sb** echar una maldición a alguien; **a c. on…!** ¡maldito(a) sea…!

2 *vt* maldecir; **he is cursed with a violent temper** tiene la desgracia de tener mal genio

3 *vi* maldecir

cursor ['kɜ:sə(r)] *n Comptr* cursor *m*; **c. keys** (teclas *fpl* de) flechas *fpl*, teclas *fpl* (de desplazamiento) del cursor

cursory ['kɜ:sərɪ] *adj (glance, examination)* somero(a)

curt [kɜ:t] *adj* brusco(a), seco(a)

curtail [kɜ:'teɪl] *vt (shorten)* acortar; *(limit)* restringir, limitar

curtain ['kɜ:tən] *n (for window)* cortina *f*; *(in theater)* telón *m*; **to draw the curtains** *(open)* descorrer las cortinas; *(close)* correr *or* echar las cortinas; *Fam* **it's curtains for him** es su final; *Theat* **c. call** saludo *m*; **c. raiser** *Theat* número *m* introductorio; *Fig* prólogo *m*; **c. rod** barra *f* para las cortinas; **c. ring** anilla *f* de cortina

▶**curtain off** *vt sep* separar con una cortina

curts(e)y ['kɜ:tsɪ] **1** *n* reverencia *f*

2 *vi* hacer una reverencia

curvaceous [kɜ:'veɪʃəs] *adj* escultural

curvature ['kɜ:vətʃə(r)] *n* curvatura *f*; *Med* **c. of the spine** desviación *f* de la columna vertebral

curve [kɜ:v] **1** *n* curva *f*; **c. (ball)** *(in baseball)* bola *f* con mucho efecto

2 *vi (surface)* curvarse; *(road, river)* hacer una curva

curved [kɜ:vd] *adj* curvo(a), curvado(a)

cushion ['kʊʃən] **1** *n (on chair)* cojín *m*, almohadón *m*; *(of air)* colchón *m*; *(on billiard table)* banda *f*; *Fig* amortiguador *m* (**against** para)

2 *vt (blow, impact)* amortiguar; **to c. sb against sth** proteger a alguien de algo

cushy ['kʊʃɪ] *adj Fam* fácil; **a c. number** una ganga, *Esp* un chollo, *Méx* pan *m* comido

custard ['kʌstəd] *n* natillas *fpl*; **c. pie** *(in slapstick comedy)* pastel *m or Esp* tarta *f* de crema; **c. powder** polvos *mpl* para hacer natillas

custodial [kʌ'stəʊdɪəl] *adj* **c. parent** progenitor que tiene custodia

custodian [kʌs'təʊdɪən] *n (of building, library)* conservador(ora) *m,f*; *(of principles, morals)* guardián(ana) *m,f*

custody ['kʌstədɪ] *n (of children)* custodia *f*; **to have c. of sb** tener la custodia de alguien; **in safe c.** bien custodiado(a); **to take sb into c.** detener a alguien

custom ['kʌstəm] *n (tradition, practice)* costumbre *f*; **it was his c. to rise early** tenía la costumbre de levantarse temprano

customary ['kʌstəmərɪ] *adj* acostumbrado(a), de costumbre; **it is c. to…** es costumbre…

custom-built ['kʌstəmbɪlt] *adj* hecho(a) de encargo

customer ['kʌstəmə(r)] *n (in shop, of business)* cliente(a) *m,f*; *Fam* **an awkward c.** un tipo quisquilloso; *Com* **c. base** clientela *f* fija, clientes *mpl* fijos; *Com* **c. care** atención *f* al cliente; *Com* **c. loyalty** fidelidad *f* del cliente; *Com* **c. services (department)** (departamento *m* de) atención *f* al cliente

customize ['kʌstəmaɪz] *vt* adaptar al gusto del cliente

custom-made ['kʌstəm'meɪd] *adj (equipment)* personalizado(a); *(clothes)* hecho(a) a medida; *(musical instrument)* de encargo

customs ['kʌstəmz] *npl* aduana *f*; **to go through c.** pasar la aduana; **c. declaration** declaración *f* en la aduana; **c. duties** derechos *mpl* de aduana; **c. officer** empleado(a) *m,f* de aduanas

cut [kʌt] **1** n (**a**) (in flesh, wood, cloth) corte m; **a c. of meat** una pieza de carne; **the c. and thrust of debate** el duelo del debate; Fig **to make cuts to** (text, movie) cortar; (budget) recortar; Fam **to be a c. above sb/sth** ser mejor que or estar por encima de alguien/algo (**b**) (reduction) (in wages, prices) recorte m (**c**) (portion, share) **a c. of the profits** una tajada de los beneficios (**d**) (style) (of clothes, hair) corte m

2 adj Fig **c. and dried** (situation) claro(a), nítido(a); (solution, result) preestablecido(a); **c. flowers** flores fpl cortadas; **c. glass** vidrio m or Esp cristal m tallado

3 vt (pt & pp **cut**) (**a**) (in general) cortar; (in slices) rebanar; (wages, prices) recortar; **to c. one's finger** hacerse un corte en un dedo; **to c. one's nails** cortarse las uñas; **to have one's hair cut** (ir a) cortarse el pelo; **to c. sb's hair** cortarle el pelo a alguien; also Fig **to c. one's throat** cortarse el cuello; **to c. sth in two** or **in half** cortar algo en dos or por la mitad; **to c. sth to pieces** cortar algo en pedazos; Fig (criticize) poner algo por los suelos; Comptr **to c. and paste sth** cortar y pegar algo; **to c. oneself loose** soltarse; **to c. the cards/deck** cortar la baraja; **to c. a disc** (make recording) grabar un disco

(**b**) (idioms) **to c. one's losses** cortar por lo sano; **to c. one's teeth on sth** iniciarse con or en algo; **to c. sb dead** (ignore) no hacer ni caso a alguien; **to c. a deal (with sb)** hacer un trato (con alguien); **it's cutting it** or **things (a bit) fine** eso es ir muy justo; **to c. sb short** cortar a alguien; **to c. a speech/a visit short** abreviar un discurso/una visita; **to c. a long story short…** en resumidas cuentas…

4 vi cortar; Cin **cut!** ¡corten!; **that's an argument that cuts both ways** es un arma de doble filo; Comptr **to c. and paste** cortar y pegar; Fam **to c. and run** escabullirse, escaquearse

▸**cut across** vt insep (take short cut) atajar por; **this issue cuts across party lines** este tema está por encima de las diferencias entre partidos

▸**cut back 1** vt sep (bush, tree) podar; (costs, production) recortar

2 vi **to c. back on expenses** recortar gastos; **to c. back on smoking/drinking** fumar/beber or Am tomar menos

▸**cut down 1** vt sep (tree) talar, cortar; (speech, text) reducir; (spending, time) recortar, reducir; **they were cut down by machine-gun fire** se abatió una ráfaga de ametralladora; Fig **to c. sb down to size** bajarle los humos a alguien

2 vi **to c. down on sth** reducir algo; **he has cut down on smoking** fuma menos

▸**cut in** vi (interrupt conversation) interrumpir; **a van cut in in front of me** una camioneta me cerró el paso; **to c. in line** colarse

▸**cut into** vt insep (with knife) cortar; **the rope was cutting into his wrists** la cuerda se le hincaba en las muñecas; **the work was cutting into her free time** el trabajo estaba interfiriendo en su tiempo libre

▸**cut off** vt sep (**a**) (remove) cortar; **to c. off sb's head** cortarle la cabeza a alguien; Fig **to c. off one's nose to spite one's face** tirar piedras contra el propio tejado (**b**) (disconnect) cortar; **I've been cut off** (of electricity, water etc) me han cortado la luz/el agua/etc.; (during phone conversation) se ha cortado la comunicación (**c**) (isolate) aislar; **to be cut off (from)** quedar aislado(a) (de)

▸**cut out 1** vt sep (**a**) (picture) recortar; (tumor) extirpar; (from text, movie) eliminar; **to c. out cigarettes** dejar de fumar (**b**) (idioms) **to c. sb out of a deal** excluir a alguien de un trato; **to c. sb out of one's will** desheredar a alguien; **to be cut out for sth** (suited) estar hecho(a) para algo; Fam **I've really got my work cut out** lo tengo verdaderamente difícil, me las estoy viendo negras; Fam **c. it out!** ¡basta ya!

2 vi (engine) calarse

▸**cut up** vt sep (**a**) (meat, vegetables) cortar, trocear; (paper) recortar (**b**) Fam **to be very cut up (about sth)** (upset) estar

muy afectado(a) (por algo) (**c**) US (misbehave) hacer el ganso

cutback ['kʌtbæk] n reducción f, recorte m

cute [kjuːt] adj bonito(a), mono(a)

cuticle ['kjuːtɪkəl] n cutícula f

cutlery ['kʌtlərɪ] n cubiertos mpl, cubertería f

cutlet ['kʌtlɪt] n (of meat) chuleta f

cutoff ['kʌtɒf] n **c. date** fecha f tope; **c. point** límite m, tope m

cutout ['kʌtaʊt] n (**a**) (shape) figura f recortada (**b**) Elec cortacircuitos m inv

cut-rate ['kʌtreɪt] adj (goods) rebajado(a)

cutter ['kʌtə(r)] n (ship) cúter m

cutthroat ['kʌtθrəʊt] **1** n matón m, asesino(a) m,f

2 adj **c. competition** competencia f salvaje or sin escrúpulos

cutting ['kʌtɪŋ] **1** n (**a**) (of plant) esqueje m (**b**) (railroad) **c.** desmonte m (para el ferrocarril)

2 adj (wind) cortante; (remark) hiriente, cortante; **c. edge** filo m cortante; Fig **to be at the c. edge of** estar a la vanguardia de

cuttlefish ['kʌtəlfɪʃ] n sepia f, jibia f

CV [siːˈviː] n (abbr **curriculum vitae**) CV m, currículum m vitae

cwt (abbr **hundredweight**) (**a**) (metric) 50 kg (**b**) (100 lb) = 45,36 kg

cyanide ['saɪənaɪd] n Chem cianuro m

cybercafe ['saɪbəkæfe] n Comptr cibercafé m

cyberculture ['saɪbəkʌltʃə(r)] n Comptr cibercultura f

cybernaut ['saɪbənɔːt] n Comptr cibernauta mf

cybernetics [saəbəˈnetɪks] n Comptr cibernética f

cyberpunk ['saɪbəpʌŋk] n Comptr (science fiction) ciberpunk m

cybersex ['saɪbəseks] n Comptr cibersexo m

cyberspace ['saɪbəspeɪs] n Comptr ciberespacio m

cyberterrorism ['saɪbətərərɪzəm] n Comptr ciberterrorismo m

cyborg ['saɪbɔːg] n Comptr ciborg m

cyclamen ['sɪkləmən] n ciclamen m, pamporcino m

cycle ['saɪkəl] **1** n (**a**) (pattern) ciclo m (**b**) (bicycle) bicicleta f; **c. path** sendero m para bicicletas (por parque, ciudad, campo); **c. racing** carreras fpl ciclistas

2 vi ir en bicicleta

cyclic(al) ['sɪklɪk(əl)] adj cíclico(a)

cycling ['saɪklɪŋ] n ciclismo m; **to go on a c. vacation** hacer cicloturismo; **c. path** pista f de ciclismo

cyclist ['saɪklɪst] n ciclista mf

cyclo-cross ['saɪkləkrɒs] n ciclocross m

cyclone ['saɪkləʊn] n Met ciclón m

cygnet ['sɪgnɪt] n cisne m joven

cylinder ['sɪlɪndə(r)] n (shape, in engine) cilindro m; (gas container) bombona f; **c. block** bloque m (de cilindros); **c. head** culata f

cylindrical [sɪˈlɪndrɪkəl] adj cilíndrico(a)

cymbal ['sɪmbəl] n (musical instrument) platillo m

cynic ['sɪnɪk] n (skeptic) descreído(a) m,f, suspicaz mf; **you're such a c.** ¡siempre estás pensando en lo peor!

cynical ['sɪnɪkəl] adj (**a**) (skeptical) descreído(a), suspicaz; **you're so c.!** ¡cómo puedes pensar siempre en lo peor! (**b**) (unscrupulous) desaprensivo(a)

cypress ['saɪprəs] n ciprés m

Cypriot ['sɪprɪət] n & adj chipriota mf

Cyprus ['saɪprəs] n Chipre

cyst [sɪst] n Med quiste m

cystitis [sɪsˈtaɪtɪs] n Med cistitis f inv

czar [zɑː(r)] n zar m

Czech [tʃek] **1** n (**a**) (person) checo(a) m,f (**b**) (language) checo m

2 adj checo(a); **C. Republic** República f Checa

Czechoslovakia [tʃekəʊsləˈvækɪə] n Formerly Checoslovaquia

D

D, d [diː] n **(a)** *(letter)* D, d f **(b)** *Mus* re m **(c)** *Sch* **to get a D** *(in exam, essay) (pass)* sacar un aprobado or suficiente bajo; *(fail)* *Esp* suspender, *Am* reprobar

D *Pol (abbr* **Democratic** or **Democrat***)* demócrata mf

DA [diːˈeɪ] n *Law (abbr* **district attorney***)* fiscal mf *(del distrito)*

dab [dæb] **1** n *(of paint, glue, perfume)* pizca f, toque m

2 vt *(pt & pp* **dabbed***) (paint, glue, perfume)* aplicar, poner; **she dabbed her eyes with a handkerchief** se secó los ojos delicadamente con un pañuelo

dabble [ˈdæbəl] vi **he dabbles in politics** se entretiene con la política

dabbler [ˈdæblə(r)] n *(dilettante)* aficionado(a) m,f, diletante mf

dachshund [ˈdækshʊnd] n dachshund m, perro m salchicha

dad [dæd] n *Fam (said by child)* papá m; *(said by adult)* padre m, *Am* papá m

daddy [ˈdædɪ] n *Fam* papi m, papaíto m; *Fam* **d. longlegs** *(crane fly)* típula f; *(harvestman)* segador m

daffodil [ˈdæfədɪl] n narciso m

daft [dɑːft] adj *(person, idea)* tonto(a), *Am* sonso(a), *Am* zonzo(a); **to be d. about sb/sth** estar loco por alguien/algo

dagger [ˈdægə(r)] n **(a)** daga f, puñal m **(b)** *(idioms)* **to be at daggers drawn (with sb)** estar a matar (con alguien); **to look** or **shoot daggers at sb** fulminar a alguien con la mirada

dago [ˈdeɪgəʊ] *(pl* **dagos***)* n *very Fam* = término ofensivo para referirse a españoles, italianos, portugueses o latinoamericanos

dahlia [ˈdeɪlɪə] n dalia f

daily [ˈdeɪlɪ] **1** n *(newspaper)* diario m, periódico m

2 adj diario(a); **on a d. basis** a diario; **our d. bread** el pan nuestro de cada día; *Fam* **the d. grind** la rutina diaria; **d. paper** diario m, periódico m

3 adv diariamente; **twice d.** dos veces al día

dainty [ˈdeɪntɪ] adj *(movement)* grácil; *(porcelain, lace)* delicado(a), fino(a)

dairy [ˈdeərɪ] n *(shop)* lechería f; *(factory)* central f lechera; **d. cow** vaca f lechera; **d. farm** vaquería f; **d. farming** industria f lechera; **d. produce** productos mpl lácteos

dais [ˈdeɪɪs] n tarima f

daisy [ˈdeɪzɪ] n *(flower)* margarita f; *Fam* **he's pushing up the daisies** *(dead)* está criando malvas; **d. chain** guirnalda f de margaritas

daisywheel [ˈdeɪzɪwiːl] n *(on printer)* margarita f

dale [deɪl] n valle m

dalliance [ˈdælɪəns] n *Formal* flirteo m, coqueteo m

dally [ˈdælɪ] vi *(dawdle)* perder el tiempo; **to d. over a decision** demorarse en tomar una decisión; **to d. with sb** coquetear con alguien

Dalmatian [dælˈmeɪʃən] n *(dog)* dálmata m

dam [dæm] **1** n *(of lake)* dique m, presa f

2 vt *(pt & pp* **dammed***) (valley)* construir una presa en; *(river, lake)* embalsar

▸**dam up** vt insep *(one's feelings)* reprimir

damage [ˈdæmɪdʒ] **1** n *(to machine, building)* daños mpl; *(to health, reputation)* perjuicio m, daño m; **to do** or **cause d. to sth** ocasionar daños a algo, perjudicar a algo; *Law* **damages** daños mpl y perjuicios; **the d. is done** el daño ya está hecho; **d. limitation** limitación f de daños

2 vt *(machine, building)* dañar; *(health, reputation)* perjudicar, dañar

damaging [ˈdæmɪdʒɪŋ] adj perjudicial

Damascus [dəˈmæskəs] n Damasco

damask [ˈdæməsk] n *(cloth)* damasco m

dame [deɪm] n *Fam (woman)* tipa f, *Esp* gachí f, *CSur* mina f, *Méx* vieja f

dammit [ˈdæmɪt] exclam *Fam* **d.!** ¡maldita sea!

damn [dæm] **1** n *Fam* **I don't give a d.** me importa un bledo; **it's not worth a d.** no vale un pimiento; **d.!** ¡maldita sea!

2 adj *Fam* maldito(a); **you d. fool!** ¡maldito idiota!; **it's a d. nuisance!** ¡qué fastidio!

3 adv *Fam* **d. good** genial, buenísimo(a); **you know d. well what I mean!** ¡sabes de sobra lo que quiero decir!

4 vt **(a)** *(criticize severely)* vapulear, criticar duramente **(b)** *Fam* **d. the expense/the consequences!** ¡a la porra con los gastos/las consecuencias!; *Fam* **well I'll be damned!** ¡que me aspen!, ¡madre mía!

5 exclam *Fam* ¡maldita sea!

damnation [dæmˈneɪʃən] n *Rel* condenación f; *Fam* **d.!** ¡maldición!

damned [dæmd] **1** adj *Fam* maldito(a); **you d. fool!** ¡maldito idiota!

2 adv *Fam* **d. good** genial, buenísimo(a)

3 n **the d.** los condenados

damnedest [ˈdæmdəst] *Fam* **1** n **to do one's d. (to do sth)** hacer todo lo posible (por hacer algo)

2 adj **it was the d. thing!** ¡fue de lo más raro!, ¡fue una cosa rarísima!

damn-fool [ˈdæmfuːl] adj *Fam* estúpido(a), ridículo(a)

damning [ˈdæmɪŋ] adj *(admission, revelation)* condenatorio(a)

damp [dæmp] **1** n humedad f

2 adj húmedo(a)

3 vt *(make wet)* humedecer; **to d. sb's spirits** desanimar a alguien; **to d. down a fire** sofocar un fuego

dampen [ˈdæmpən] vt *(make wet)* humedecer; *Fig* **to d. sb's spirits** desanimar a alguien

damper [ˈdæmpə(r)] n *Mus* apagador m; *Fig* **to put a d. on sth** ensombrecer algo

damp-proof [ˈdæmppruːf] vt aislar de la humedad

damsel [ˈdæmzəl] n *Literary* doncella f, damisela f; *Hum* **a d. in distress** una doncella en apuros

damson [ˈdæmzən] n *(fruit)* ciruela f damascena; *(tree)* ciruelo m damasceno

dance [dɑːns] **1** n baile m; *Fam* **to lead sb a (merry) d.** traer a alguien al retortero or a mal traer; **d. band** orquesta f de baile; **d. floor** pista f de baile; **d. hall** salón m de baile; **d. music** música f de baile or de discoteca

2 *vt* bailar; **to d. attendance on sb** atender servilmente a alguien

3 *vi* bailar; **they danced down the road** bajaron la calle dando brincos

dancer ['dɑːnsə(r)] *n* bailarín(ina) *m,f*

dancing ['dɑːnsɪŋ] *n* baile *m*; **d. shoes** zapatos *mpl* de baile

dandelion ['dændɪlaɪən] *n* diente *m* de león

dander ['dændə(r)] *n Fam* **to get sb's d. up** *(annoy)* sacar de quicio a alguien

dandruff ['dændrəf] *n* caspa *f*

dandy ['dændɪ] **1** *n (person)* petimetre *m*, dandi *m*

2 *adj Fam* genial; **everything's just (fine and) d.** está todo perfecto

Dane [deɪn] *n* danés(esa) *m,f*

danger ['deɪndʒə(r)] *n* peligro *m*; **in/out of d.** en/fuera de peligro; **to be in d. of doing sth** correr el peligro de hacer algo; **there is no d. that...** no hay peligro de que...; **to be on the d. list** *(patient)* estar muy grave; **to be off the d. list** *(patient)* estar fuera de peligro; **d. pay** prima *f* or plus *m* de peligrosidad; *Fig* **d. sign** señal *f* de peligro

dangerous ['deɪndʒərəs] *adj* peligroso(a)

dangerously ['deɪndʒərəslɪ] *adv* peligrosamente; **they came d. close to losing** estuvieron en un tris de caer derrotados

dangle ['dæŋgəl] **1** *vt* balancear, hacer oscilar; *Fig* **the company dangled a bonus in front of its workers** la empresa ofreció una paga extra a sus trabajadores como incentivo

2 *vi* colgar; *Fig* **to keep sb dangling** tener a alguien pendiente

Danish ['deɪnɪʃ] **1** *n (language)* danés *m*

2 *adj* danés(esa); **D. pastry** = pastel dulce de hojaldre

dank [dæŋk] *adj (place, atmosphere)* frío(a) y húmedo(a)

Danube ['dænjuːb] *n* **the D.** el Danubio

dapper ['dæpə(r)] *adj* pulcro(a), atildado(a)

dappled ['dæpəld] *adj* **the d. light on the forest floor** el lecho del bosque, salpicado de luces y sombras

dare ['deə(r)] **1** *n* reto *m*, desafío *m*; **he would do anything for a d.** es capaz de hacer cualquier cosa si le desafían a ello

2 *vt* **(a) to d. to do sth** atreverse a hacer algo **(b) to d. sb to do sth** retar a alguien a que haga algo; **I d. you to tell her!** ¿a que no se lo dices?, ¿a que no eres capaz de decírselo?

3 *modal aux v* **to d. do sth** atreverse a hacer algo; **I d. not** or **daren't ask him** no me atrevo a preguntarle; **don't you d. tell her!** ¡ni se te ocurra decírselo!; **how d. you!** ¡cómo te atreves!; **I d. say** probablemente

daredevil ['deədevəl] *n & adj* temerario(a) *m,f*

daring ['deərɪŋ] **1** *n* atrevimiento *m*, osadía *f*

2 *adj (courageous)* audaz, atrevido(a); *(provocative)* atrevido(a)

daringly ['deərɪŋlɪ] *adv (courageously)* con audacia or atravemiento; *(provocatively)* con atrevimiento

dark [dɑːk] **1** *n* **(a)** *(darkness)* oscuridad *f*; **before/after d.** antes/después del anochecer; **in the d.** en la oscuridad **(b)** *(idioms)* **to be in the d. (about sth)** *Esp* estar en albis (sobre algo), *Am* no tener idea (sobre algo); **to keep sb in the d. (about sth)** mantener a alguien en la ignorancia (acerca de algo)

2 *adj* **(a)** *(not light)* oscuro(a); *(skin, hair)* oscuro(a), moreno(a); **it's d. by six o'clock** a las seis ya es de noche; **it's getting d.** está oscureciendo or anocheciendo; **d. glasses** gafas *fpl* oscuras; *Fig* **to be a d. horse** *(in competition)* ser quien puede dar la campanada; *(in politics)* ser el/la candidato(a) sorpresa; *(secretive person)* ser un enigma **(b)** *Fig (thought, period)* sombrío(a), oscuro(a); *(look)* siniestro(a); *Hist* **the D. Ages** la Edad Media *(antes del año mil)*; *Fig* **to be in the D. Ages** estar en la prehistoria

darken ['dɑːkən] **1** *vt (sky, color)* oscurecer; **never d. my door**

again! ¡no vuelvas a pisar el umbral de mi casa!

2 *vi (sky, color)* oscurecerse; *(thoughts)* ensombrecerse

darkish ['dɑːkɪʃ] *adj* tirando a oscuro(a); **d. hair** pelo tirando a moreno

darkly ['dɑːklɪ] *adv (say, hint)* con tono sombrío

darkness ['dɑːknɪs] *n* oscuridad *f*; **in d.** a oscuras, en tinieblas

darkroom ['dɑːkruːm] *n Phot* cuarto *m* oscuro

dark-skinned ['dɑːkˈskɪnd] *adj* moreno(a)

darling ['dɑːlɪŋ] **1** *n* encanto *m*; **d.!** ¡querido(a)!; **be a d. and...** sé bueno(a) y...; **she's the d. of the press** es la niña mimada de la prensa

2 *adj* encantador(ora)

darn[1] [dɑːn] *vt (mend)* zurcir

darn[2] *Fam* **1** *adj* maldito(a); **it's a d. nuisance!** ¡es un verdadero fastidio!

2 *exclam* **d. (it)!** ¡caramba!

darning needle ['dɑːnɪŋˈniːdəl] *n* aguja *f* de zurcir

dart [dɑːt] **1** *n* **(a)** *(missile)* dardo *m*; **darts** *(game)* dardos *mpl* **(b)** *(movement)* **to make a d. for sth** salir disparado(a) hacia algo

2 *vt* **to d. a glance at sb** lanzar una mirada a alguien

3 *vi (move quickly)* precipitarse; **to d. in/out** entrar/salir precipitadamente

dartboard ['dɑːtbɔːd] *n* diana *f*

dash [dæʃ] **1** *n* **(a)** *(of liquid)* chorrito *m*; *Fig (of humor, color)* toque *m*, pizca *f* **(b)** *(hyphen, in Morse)* raya *f* **(c)** *(run)* carrera *f*; **to make a d. for it** echar a correr **(d)** *(style)* dinamismo *m*, brío *m*; **to cut a d.** causar sensación

2 *vt* **(a)** *(throw)* arrojar; **to d. sth to the ground** arrojar algo al suelo **(b)** *(destroy)* **to d. sb's hopes** truncar las esperanzas de alguien; *Fam* **d. (it)!** ¡caramba!

3 *vi (move quickly)* correr, ir apresuradamente; **to d. in/out** entrar/salir apresuradamente; **to d. around** or **about** correr de acá para allá; *Fam* **I must d.** tengo que salir pitando

▶**dash off 1** *vt sep* **to d. off a letter** escribir a toda prisa or *Am* a todo apuro una carta

2 *vi (leave)* salir corriendo

dashboard ['dæʃbɔːd] *n* tablero *m* de mandos, *Esp* salpicadero *m*

dashing ['dæʃɪŋ] *adj (person)* imponente; *(appearance)* deslumbrante

DAT [diːeɪˈtiː] *n (abbr* **digital audio tape)** cinta *f* digital de audio, DAT

data ['deɪtə] *n* datos *mpl*; **an item** or **a piece of d.** un dato; **d. bank** banco *m* de datos; *Comptr* **d. processing** proceso *m* or procesamiento *m* de datos; *Comptr* **d. protection** protección *f* de datos

database ['deɪtəbeɪs] *n Comptr* base *f* de datos

date[1] [deɪt] *n (fruit)* dátil *m*; **d. palm** palmera *f* datilera

date[2] **1** *n* **(a)** *(day)* fecha *f*; **d. of birth** fecha de nacimiento; **what's the d. (today)?** ¿a qué (fecha) estamos hoy?, ¿qué fecha es hoy?, *Am* ¿a cómo estamos?; **to fix a d. for sth** fijar una fecha para algo; **to have a d. with sb** haber quedado or tener una cita con alguien; **to d.** hasta la fecha; **up to d.** al día; **out of d.** anticuado(a), pasado(a) de moda; **d. stamp** sello *m* con la fecha **(b)** *(with girlfriend, boyfriend)* cita *f*; **d. rape** = violación por una persona a la que se ha conocido de forma circunstancial o en una cita **(c)** *(girlfriend, boyfriend)* pareja *f*

2 *vt* **(a)** *(letter, ticket)* fechar; **that dates you** eso demuestra lo viejo que eres **(b)** *(go out with)* salir con

3 *vi* **(a) to d. from** or **back to** *(custom, practice)* remontarse a; *(building)* datar de **(b)** *(go out of fashion)* pasar de moda

dateline ['deɪtlaɪn] *n* meridiano *m* de cambio de fecha; *Journ* **d. Tel Aviv** fechado(a) en Tel Aviv

date-stamp ['deɪtstæmp] *vt (book, letter)* fechar, poner fecha a

dating agency ['deɪtɪŋˈeɪdʒənsɪ] *n* agencia *f* de contactos

dative ['deɪtɪv] *n Gram* dativo *m*

daub [dɔːb] *vt (with mud, paint)* embadurnar (**with** de)

daughter ['dɔːtə(r)] *n* hija *f*

daughter-in-law ['dɔːtərɪnlɔː] (*pl* **daughters-in-law**) *n* nuera *f*

daunt [dɔːnt] *vt* intimidar, acobardar; *Formal* **nothing daunted** sin dejarse arredrar

daunting [dɔːntɪŋ] *adj* desalentador(ora), desmoralizante; **a d. task** una tarea ingente

dauntless ['dɔːntlɪs] *adj* impávido(a), imperturbable

dawdle ['dɔːdəl] *vi* perder el tiempo

dawdler ['dɔːdlə(r)] *n* lento(a) *m,f*

dawn [dɔːn] **1** *n* amanecer *m*, alba *f*; *Fig (of life, civilization)* albores *mpl*, despertar *m*; **at d.** al alba; **from d. to dusk** de sol a sol; **the d. chorus** el canto de los pájaros al amanecer; **d. raid** *(by soldiers, police)* incursión *f* de madrugada; *St Exch* = compra masiva de acciones al comienzo de la sesión

2 *vi* amanecer; *Fig (life, civilization)* despertar; **the day dawned bright and clear** el día amaneció claro y despejado

▸**dawn on** *vt insep* **the truth finally dawned on him** finalmente vio la verdad; **it dawned on me that…** caí en la cuenta de que…

day [deɪ] *n* **(a)** *(period of daylight, 24 hours)* día *m*; *(period of work)* jornada *f*; **once/twice a d.** una vez/dos veces al día; **the d. before yesterday** anteayer; **the d. after tomorrow** pasado mañana; **all d.** todo el día; **d. after d.** día tras día; **from d. to d.** de un día para otro; **one d., one of these days** un día (de estos); **any d. now** cualquier día de estos; **the other d.** el otro día; **every other d.** cada dos días, un día sí y otro no; **a year ago to the d.** hace exactamente un año; **from d. one** desde el primer día; **to take a d. off** tomarse un día libre; **to be paid by the d.** cobrar por día trabajado; **to work d. and night** trabajar día y noche; *Fam* **he's sixty if he's a d.** tiene como mínimo sesenta años; **d. care** *(for children)* servicio *m* de guardería (infantil); *(for elderly people)* = servicio de atención domiciliaria a los ancianos; **d. care center** *(for children)* guardería *f* (infantil); **d. nursery** guardería *f*; **d. school** colegio *m* sin internado; **d. shift** *(in factory)* turno *m* de día; **d. student** alumno(a) *m,f* externo(a); **d. trip** excursión *f* (de un día)

(b) *(era)* **in my d.** en mis tiempos; **in this d. and age** en los tiempos que corren; **Communism has had its d.** el auge del comunismo ya es historia; **in the days of…** en tiempos de…; **these days** hoy (en) día; **in those days** en aquellos tiempos; **those were the days!** ¡aquellos sí que eran buenos tiempos!; **in days to come** más adelante, en el futuro; **he ended his days in poverty** terminó sus días en la pobreza

(c) *(idioms)* **it's all in a day's work** son los gajes del oficio; *Fam* **let's call it a d.** dejémoslo por hoy; *Fam* **that'll be the d.!** ¡no lo verán tus ojos!, ¡cuando las ranas críen pelo!; *Fam* **to make sb's d.** alegrarle el día a alguien; **to name the d.** *(of wedding)* fijar la fecha de la boda; **to carry** *or* **win the d.** *(bring victory)* conseguir la victoria

daybook ['deɪbʊk] *n Fin* diario *m* de entradas y salidas

daybreak ['deɪbreɪk] *n* amanecer *m*, alba *f*; **at d.** al alba

daydream ['deɪdriːm] **1** *n* fantasía *f*

2 *vi* fantasear, soñar despierto(a); **to d. about sth** fantasear sobre algo

daydreamer ['deɪdriːmə(r)] *n* soñador(ora) *m,f*

daylight ['deɪlaɪt] *n* (luz *f* del) día *m*; **it was still d.** todavía era de día; **d. hours** horas *fpl* de luz; *Fig* **it's d. robbery!** ¡es un atraco a mano armada!; **d. saving time** horario *m* oficial de verano

daytime ['deɪtaɪm] *n* día *m*; **in the d.** durante el día; **d. TV** programación *f* diurna *or* de día

day-to-day ['deɪtə'deɪ] *adj* diario(a), cotidiano(a); **on a d. basis** día a día

day-tripper ['deɪ'trɪpə(r)] *n* dominguero(a) *m,f*

daze [deɪz] **1** *n* aturdimiento *m*; **to be in a d.** estar aturdido(a) **2** *vt* aturdir

dazed [deɪzd] *adj* aturdido(a)

dazzle ['dæzəl] *vt also Fig* deslumbrar

dazzling ['dæzlɪŋ] *adj also Fig* deslumbrante

DC [diː'siː] *n* **(a)** *Elec (abbr* **direct current***)* corriente *f* continua **(b)** *(abbr* **District of Columbia***)* DC, Distrito de Columbia

deacon ['diːkən] *n Rel* diácono *m*

deaconess [diːkən'es] *n Rel* diaconisa *f*

dead [ded] **1** *adj* **(a)** *(not alive)* muerto(a); **a d. man** un muerto; **a d. woman** una muerta; **to be d.** estar muerto(a); *Fig* **to be d. to the world** dormir como un tronco; *Fam* **over my d. body!** ¡por encima de mi cadáver!; *Fam* **I wouldn't be seen d. in that dress!** ¡no me pondría ese vestido ni borracha!; *Fam* **as d. as a doornail** *or* **a dodo** muerto(a) y bien muerto(a); *Fig* **d. and buried** finiquitado(a); **half d. with fright** medio muerto(a) de miedo; **d. or alive** vivo(a) o muerto(a); *Fam* **if dad finds out, you're d.** si papá se entera, te mata; **the D. Sea** el Mar Muerto

(b) *(numb)* dormido(a); **my leg went d.** se me durmió la pierna

(c) *(lacking energy) (voice, eyes)* apagado(a); *(battery)* gastado(a), agotado(a); **the phone** *or* **line is d.** no hay línea; **this place is d. in winter** este lugar está muerto en invierno; **d. ball situation** *(in football, soccer, basketball etc)* jugada *f* a balón parado; *also Fig* **d. end** callejón *m* sin salida; *Fig* **he's a d. weight** es un peso muerto

(d) *(absolute)* **d. calm** calma *f* chicha; **d. heat** *(in race)* empate *m*; *Fam* **it/he was a d. loss** resultó ser un desastre total; *Fam* **to be a d. ringer for sb** ser idéntico(a) a alguien

2 *adv* **(a)** *(completely)* **to be d. set against sth** oponerse rotundamente a algo; **to stop d.** pararse en seco; *Fam* **to be d. wrong** equivocarse de medio a medio; *Fam* **d. beat** *or* **tired** hecho(a) polvo, molido(a); **d. slow** *(sign)* muy despacio

(b) *Fam (very)* tela de; **d. easy** facilísimo(a), chupado(a)

(c) *(exactly)* **d. on six o'clock** a las seis en punto

3 *n* **in the d. of the night** a altas horas de la noche; **in the d. of winter** en pleno invierno

4 *npl* **the d.** los muertos; **to rise from the d.** resucitar (de entre los muertos)

deadbeat ['dedbiːt] *n Fam (lazy person)* vago(a) *m,f*, holgazán(ana) *m,f*

deaden ['dedən] *vt (blow, sound, pain)* amortiguar, atenuar; **to become deadened to sth** volverse insensible a algo

dead-end ['dedend] *adj* **d. street** *(cul-de-sac)* callejón *m*

deadline ['dedlaɪn] *n (day)* fecha *f* tope; *(time)* plazo *m*; **to meet a d.** cumplir un plazo; **to work to a d.** trabajar con un plazo

deadlock ['dedlɒk] **1** *n* punto *m* muerto; **to reach (a) d.** llegar a un punto muerto

2 *vt* **to be deadlocked** *(talks, negotiations)* estar en un punto muerto

deadly ['dedlɪ] **1** *adj* **(a)** *(poison, blow, enemy)* mortal, mortífero(a); *(weapon)* mortífero(a); *(pallor)* cadavérico(a); *(silence)* sepulcral; **d. nightshade** *(plant)* belladona *f* **(b)** *Fam (boring)* aburridísimo(a)

2 *adv (very)* **d. accurate** tremendamente exacto(a); **d. boring** mortalmente aburrido(a); **to be d. serious about sth** decir algo completamente en serio

deadpan ['dedpæn] *adj (expression)* inexpresivo(a); *(humor)* socarrón(ona)

deadwood ['dedwʊd] *n* **there is too much d. in this office** en esta oficina sobra mucha gente *or* hay mucha gente que está de más

deaf [def] **1** *adj* sordo(a); **to be d.** ser/estar sordo(a); **d. and**

dumb sordomudo(a); **to go d.** quedarse sordo(a); **to be d. in one ear** ser sordo(a) de un oído; **as d. as a post** sordo(a) como una tapia; **to turn a d. ear to sb** hacer caso omiso de alguien; **the appeal fell on d. ears** la apelación cayó en saco roto; **d. mute** sordomudo(a) *m,f*

2 *npl* **the d.** los sordos

deafen ['defən] *vt* ensordecer

deafening ['defənɪŋ] *adj* ensordecedor(ora)

deafness ['defnəs] *n* sordera *f*

deal¹ [diːl] *n (wood)* madera *f* de conífera, madera *f* blanda

deal² **1** *n* (**a**) *(agreement)* acuerdo *m*; *(in business)* trato *m*; **to do a d.** hacer un trato; **it's a d.!** ¡trato hecho!; **to get a good/ bad d.** recibir un buen/mal trato; *Ironic Fam* **big d.!** ¡vaya cosa!; *Fam* **it's no big d.** ¡no es nada!, ¡no es para tanto!; *Fam* **what's the d.?** *(what happened?)* ¿qué pasó?, ¿qué ha pasado? (**b**) *(amount)* **a good** *or* **great d.** *(a lot)* mucho; **not a great d.** no mucho; **to have a great d. to do** tener mucho que hacer; **a good** *or* **great d. of my time** gran parte de mi tiempo (**c**) *(in cards)* **your d.** te toca repartir *or* dar

2 *vt (pt & pp dealt [delt])* (**a**) *(cards)* repartir, dar (**b**) **to d. sb/ sth a blow** dar un golpe a alguien/algo

3 *vi* **to d. in leather/shares** comerciar con pieles/acciones; **to d. in drugs** traficar con drogas

▸**deal out** *vt sep (cards, justice)* repartir

▸**deal with** *vt insep* (**a**) *(be about) (subject)* tratar (**b**) *(handle) (complaint, problem)* ocuparse de; **I know how to d. with him** sé cómo tratarlo; **I'll d. with you later** ya hablaremos tú y yo después

dealer ['diːlə(r)] *n* (**a**) *(in cardgame)* = jugador que reparte (**b**) *Com* comerciante *mf*; *(in drugs)* traficante *mf*; **art d.** marchante *mf* de arte

dealership ['diːləʃɪp] *n (showroom)* concesionario *m*; *(franchise)* concesión *f*

dealings ['diːlɪŋz] *npl* tratos *mpl*; **to have d. with sb** estar en tratos con alguien

dealt [delt] *pt & pp of* **deal**

dean [diːn] *n Rel* deán *m*; *Univ* decano(a) *m,f*; *US* **D.'s List** = lista de los alumnos considerados más sobresalientes por el decano de una universidad

dear [dɪə(r)] **1** *adj* (**a**) *(loved)* querido(a); **to hold sth/sb d.** apreciar mucho algo/a alguien; **a d. friend** un amigo muy querido; **my dearest wish is that…** mi mayor deseo es que…; **a place d. to the hearts of…** un lugar muy querido para…; *Fam* **to run for d. life** correr desesperadamente

(**b**) *(in letter)* **D. Sir** Muy Sr. mío; **D. Madam** Muy Sra. mía; **D. Sir or Madam, D. Sir/Madam** *(when sex of addressee is unknown)* Muy Sres. míos; **D. Mr. Thomas** Estimado Sr. Thomas; **D. Andrew** Querido Andrew; **My dearest Gertrude** Queridísima Gertrude

(**c**) *(expensive)* caro(a)

(**d**) *(exclamation)* **oh d.!** ¡vaya!

2 *n* **poor d.** pobrecito(a); **my d.** cariño mío, mi amor; **be a d. and…** sé bueno y…; *Fam* **an old d.** una viejecita

3 *adv (to buy, sell)* caro; *Fig* **it cost me d.** me costó muy caro

dearly ['dɪəlɪ] *adv (very much)* **I love him d.** lo quiero muchísimo; **I would d. love to know** me encantaría saberlo; *Fig* **she paid d. for her mistake** pagó muy caro su error

dearth [dɜːθ] *n* escasez *f* (**of** de)

death [deθ] *n* (**a**) muerte *f*; **to put sb to d.** ejecutar a alguien; **a fight to the d.** una lucha a muerte; **d. to traitors!** ¡muerte a *or* mueran los traidores!; **d. camp** campo *m* de exterminio; **d. certificate** certificado *m or* partida *f* de defunción; **d. mask** mascarilla *f*; **d. penalty** pena *f* de muerte; **d. rate** tasa *f* de mortalidad; **d. row** galería *f* de los condenados a muerte; **d. sentence** pena *f* de muerte; **d. squad** escuadrón *m* de la muerte; **d. throes** últimos estertores *mpl*, agonía *f*; **d. toll**

número *m or* saldo *m* de víctimas mortales; **d. warrant** orden *f* de ejecución

(**b**) *(idioms)* **to be sick to d. of sth** estar hasta la coronilla de algo; **to be scared to d.** estar muerto(a) de miedo; **those children will be the d. of her!** esos niños la van a matar (a disgustos); **you'll catch your d. (of cold)!** ¡vas a agarrar *or Esp* coger un resfriado de muerte!; **to be at d.'s door** estar a las puertas de la muerte; **to sound the d. knell for sth** asestar el golpe de gracia a algo; **to look like d. warmed over** tener una pinta horrorosa

deathbed ['deθbed] *n* lecho *m* de muerte

deathblow ['deθbləʊ] *n Fig* golpe *m* mortal; **to deal a d. to sth** asestarle un golpe mortal a algo

deathly ['deθlɪ] *adj (pallor)* cadavérico(a); *(silence)* sepulcral

deathtrap ['deθtræp] *n* **this house/this car is a d.** esta casa/este coche *or Am* carro *or RP* auto es un auténtico peligro

deathwatch beetle ['deθwɒtʃ'biːtəl] *n* carcoma *f*

debacle [deɪ'bɑːkl] *n* desastre *m*, debacle *f*

debar [diː'bɑː(r)] *(pt & pp debarred) vt (from club, bar)* prohibir la entrada (**from** en); **to d. sb from doing sth** prohibirle a alguien hacer algo

debase [dɪ'beɪs] *vt (person, reputation)* degradar; **to d. oneself** degradarse

debasement [dɪ'beɪsmənt] *n* degradación *f*

debatable [dɪ'beɪtəbəl] *adj* discutible

debate [dɪ'beɪt] **1** *n* debate *m*; **after much d.** tras mucho debatir

2 *vt (issue)* debatir, discutir; **he debated whether to go** se debatía entre ir y no ir

3 *vi* debatir

debating society [dɪ'beɪtɪŋsə'saɪətɪ] *n* = asociación que organiza debates en una universidad o instituto

debauched [dɪ'bɔːtʃt] *adj* depravado(a), degenerado(a)

debauchery [dɪ'bɔːtʃərɪ] *n* libertinaje *m*, depravación *f*

debilitate [dɪ'bɪlɪteɪt] *vt* debilitar

debilitating [dɪ'bɪlɪteɪtɪŋ] *adj* debilitador(ora), debilitante

debility [dɪ'bɪlɪtɪ] *n* debilidad *f*

debit ['debɪt] *Fin* **1** *n* cargo *m*, adeudo *m*; *Fig* **on the d. side** en el lado negativo

2 *vt* cargar, adeudar; **to d. sb with an amount** cargar una cantidad negativa a alguien

debonair [debə'neə(r)] *adj* gallardo(a)

debrief [diː'briːf] *vt* **to d. sb on a mission** pedir a alguien que rinda cuentas sobre una misión

debriefing [diː'briːfɪŋ] *n* interrogatorio *m (tras una misión)*

debris [də'briː] *n (of building)* escombros *mpl*; *(of plane, car)* restos *mpl*

debt [det] *n* deuda *f*; **to be in d.** estar endeudado(a); *Fig* **I shall always be in your d.** siempre estaré en deuda contigo; **to owe sb a d. of gratitude** tener una deuda de gratitud con alguien; **d. collector** cobrador(ora) *m,f* de morosos

debtor ['detə(r)] *n* deudor(ora) *m,f*

debt-ridden ['detrɪdən] *adj* agobiado(a) *or* abrumado(a) por las deudas

debug [dɪ'bʌg] *(pt & pp debugged) vt Comptr (program)* depurar, eliminar errores en

debunk [diː'bʌŋk] *vt Fam (theory, myth)* echar por tierra

debut ['deɪbjuː] *n* debut *m*; **to make one's d.** debutar

Dec *(abbr December)* diciembre *m*

decade ['dekeɪd] *n* decenio *m*, década *f*

decadence ['dekədəns] *n* decadencia *f*

decadent ['dekədənt] *adj* decadente

decaffeinated [diː'kæfɪneɪtɪd] *adj* descafeinado(a)

decal ['diːkæl] *n* calcomanía *f*

decant [dɪ'kænt] *vt (wine)* decantar

decanter [dɪˈkæntə(r)] *n* licorera *f*

decapitate [dɪˈkæpɪteɪt] *vt* decapitar

decathlon [dɪˈkæθlɒn] *n* decatlón *m*

decay [dɪˈkeɪ] **1** *n* (**a**) *(of wood)* putrefacción *f*, descomposición *f*; *(of teeth)* caries *f inv* (**b**) *(decline)* declive *m*, decadencia *f*; *(of building)* ruina *f*
2 *vi* (**a**) *(timber)* pudrirse; *(teeth)* picarse, cariarse (**b**) *(decline)* declinar

decease [dɪˈsiːs] *n Formal* fallecimiento *m*

deceased [dɪˈsiːst] **1** *adj* difunto(a)
2 *n* the d. el/la difunto(a)

deceit [dɪˈsiːt] *n* engaño *m*

deceitful [dɪˈsiːtfʊl] *adj (person)* falso(a); *(behavior)* engañoso(a); to be d. ser un(a) falso(a)

deceitfully [dɪˈsiːtfʊlɪ] *adv* to obtain sth d. conseguir algo con engaños

deceive [dɪˈsiːv] *vt* engañar; to be deceived by appearances dejarse engañar por las apariencias; to d. oneself engañarse; to d. sb into thinking sth hacer creer algo a alguien; I thought my eyes were deceiving me no creía lo que veían mis ojos

decelerate [diːˈseləreɪt] *vi* decelerar, desacelerar

deceleration [diːseləˈreɪʃən] *vi* deceleración *f*, desaceleración *f*; d. lane carril *m* de deceleración *or* de salida

December [dɪˈsembə(r)] *n* diciembre *m*; *see also* **May**

decency [ˈdiːsənsɪ] *n (of dress, behavior)* decencia *f*, decoro *m*; common d. (mínima) decencia *f*; he didn't even have the d. to tell us first ni siquiera tuvo la delicadeza de decírnoslo primero

decent [ˈdiːsənt] *adj* (**a**) *(respectable)* decente, decoroso(a) (**b**) *(of acceptable quality, size)* decente (**c**) *Fam (kind)* a d. guy un buen tipo; it's very d. of you es muy amable de tu parte

decently [ˈdiːsəntlɪ] *adv* (**a**) *(respectably, to an acceptable degree)* decentemente; they pay quite d. pagan un sueldo bastante decente (**b**) *Fam (kindly)* con amabilidad

decentralization [diːsentrəlaɪˈzeɪʃən] *n* descentralización *f*

decentralize [diːˈsentrəlaɪz] *vt* descentralizar

deception [dɪˈsepʃən] *n* engaño *m*

deceptive [dɪˈseptɪv] *adj* engañoso(a)

deceptively [dɪˈseptɪvlɪ] *adv* engañosamente; it looks d. easy a primera vista parece muy fácil

decibel [ˈdesɪbel] *n* decibelio *m*

decide [dɪˈsaɪd] **1** *vt* decidir; to d. to do sth decidir hacer algo; it was decided to wait for her reply se decidió esperar su respuesta; that was what decided me eso fue lo que me hizo decidirme; that decides the matter eso zanja la cuestión
2 *vi* decidir; to d. against doing sth decidir no hacer algo; to d. in favor of doing sth decidir hacer algo

decided [dɪˈsaɪdɪd] *adj (person)* decidido(a), resuelto(a); *(opinion)* tajante; *(difference, preference, improvement)* claro(a), marcado(a)

decidedly [dɪˈsaɪdɪdlɪ] *adv* (**a**) *(to answer, say)* categóricamente (**b**) *(very)* decididamente; he was d. unhelpful no ayudó en lo más mínimo

deciding [dɪˈsaɪdɪŋ] *adj* decisivo(a)

deciduous [dɪˈsɪdjʊəs] *adj* de hoja caduca, caducifolio(a)

decimal [ˈdesɪməl] **1** *n* número *m* decimal
2 *adj* decimal; d. point coma *f* (decimal); correct to five d. places correcto hasta la quinta cifra decimal

decimalization [desɪməlaɪˈzeɪʃən] *n* conversión *f* al sistema decimal

decimate [ˈdesɪmeɪt] *vt* diezmar

decipher [dɪˈsaɪfə(r)] *vt* descifrar

decision [dɪˈsɪʒən] *n* decisión *f*; to come to *or* arrive at *or* reach a d. llegar a una decisión; to make *or* take a d. tomar una decisión; to act/speak with d. actuar/hablar con decisión

decision-making [dɪˈsɪʒənmeɪkɪŋ] *n* toma *f* de decisiones

decisive [dɪˈsaɪsɪv] *adj* decisivo(a)

deck 1 *n* [dek] (**a**) *(of ship)* cubierta *f*; on d. en cubierta; d. chair tumbona *f*, hamaca *f* (**b**) top/bottom d. *(of bus)* piso *m* de arriba/abajo (**c**) cassette *or* tape d. pletina *f* (**d**) d. of cards baraja *f*
2 *vt* to d. oneself out in sth engalanarse con algo

declaim [dɪˈkleɪm] **1** *vt* proclamar, pregonar
2 *vi* pregonar

declamatory [dɪˈklæmətərɪ] *adj (style, tone)* declamatorio(a)

declaration [dekləˈreɪʃən] *n* declaración *f*; *Hist* the D. of Independence la declaración de independencia de los Estados Unidos

declare [dɪˈkleə(r)] **1** *vt* declarar; to d. war (on) declarar la guerra (a); to d. sb guilty/innocent declarar a alguien culpable/inocente; have you anything to d.? *(at customs)* ¿(tiene) algo que declarar?
2 *vi* to d. for/against sth declararse a favor de/en contra de algo; *Old-fashioned* I do d.! ¡demontre!

declassified [diːˈklæsɪfaɪd] *adj* desclasificado(a)

declassify [diːˈklæsɪfaɪ] *vt* desclasificar

declension [dɪˈklenʃən] *n Gram* declinación *f*

decline [dɪˈklaɪn] **1** *n (of person, empire)* declive *m*; *(decrease, reduction)* descenso *m*, disminución *f*; to go into d. decaer, debilitarse; to be on the d. estar en declive
2 *vt* (**a**) *(offer, invitation)* declinar; to d. to do sth declinar hacer algo (**b**) *Gram* declinar
3 *vi* (**a**) *(refuse)* rehusar (**b**) *(health, influence)* declinar; to d. in importance perder importancia

declining [dɪˈklaɪnɪŋ] *adj (decreasing)* decreciente; *(deteriorating)* en declive, en decadencia

decode [diːˈkəʊd] *vt* descodificar, descifrar

decompose [diːkəmˈpəʊz] *vi* descomponerse

decomposition [diːkɒmpəˈzɪʃən] *n* descomposición *f*

decompress [diːkəmˈpres] *vt Comptr (file)* descomprimir

decompression [diːkəmˈpreʃən] *n* descompresión *f*; d. chamber cámara *f* de descompresión; d. sickness aeroembolismo *m*

decongestant [diːkənˈdʒestənt] *n Med* descongestionante *m*

deconstruct [diːkənˈstrʌkt] *vt Lit* deconstruir

deconstruction [diːkənˈstrʌkʃən] *n Lit* teoría *f* desconstructiva, desconstruccionismo *m*

decontaminate [diːkənˈtæmɪneɪt] *vt* descontaminar

decontamination [diːkəntæmɪˈneɪʃən] *n* descontaminación *f*

decor [ˈdeɪkɔː(r)] *n* decoración *f*

decorate [ˈdekəreɪt] *vt* (**a**) *(cake, room) (with decorations)* decorar, adornar (with con) (**b**) *(room) (with paint)* pintar; *(with wallpaper)* empapelar (**c**) *(with medal)* condecorar

decoration [dekəˈreɪʃən] *n* (**a**) *(on cake, for party)* decoración *f*; decorations adornos *mpl* (**b**) *(of room) (with paint)* pintado *m*; *(with wallpaper)* empapelado *m* (**c**) *(medal)* condecoración *f*

decorative [ˈdekərətɪv] *adj* decorativo(a)

decorator [ˈdekəreɪtə(r)] *n* (painter and) d. pintor(ora) *m,f* (que también empapela)

decorous [ˈdekərəs] *adj Formal* decoroso(a)

decorum [dɪˈkɔːrəm] *n* decoro *m*

decoy [ˈdiːkɔɪ] **1** *n also Fig* señuelo *m*
2 *vt* [dɪˈkɔɪ] atraer con un señuelo; to d. sb into doing sth lograr que alguien haga algo utilizando un señuelo

decrease 1 *n* [ˈdiːkriːs] reducción *f* (in de); disminución *f* (in de); to be on the d. estar disminuyendo, decrecer
2 *vt* [dɪˈkriːs] disminuir, reducir
3 *vi* disminuir, reducirse

decreasing [dɪ'kriːsɪŋ] *adj* decreciente

decree [dɪ'kriː] **1** *n* decreto *m*; **to issue a d.** promulgar un decreto; *Law* **d. nisi** sentencia *f* provisional de divorcio
2 *vt* decretar

decrepit [dɪ'krepɪt] *adj (person)* decrépito(a); *(thing)* ruinoso(a)

decrepitude [dɪ'krepɪtjuːd] *n Formal (of person)* decrepitud *f*; *(of thing)* ruina *f*, deterioro *m*

decriminalization [diːkrɪmɪnəlaɪ'zeɪʃən] *n* despenalización *f*

decriminalize [diː'krɪmɪnəlaɪz] *vt* despenalizar

decry [dɪ'kraɪ] *vt* censurar, condenar

dedicate ['dedɪkeɪt] *vt* dedicar; **to d. oneself to (doing) sth** consagrarse a (hacer) algo; **she dedicated her life to helping the poor** consagró *or* dedicó su vida a ayudar a los pobres

dedicated ['dedɪkeɪtɪd] *adj* (**a**) *(committed)* entregado(a), dedicado(a); **to be d. to sth** estar consagrado(a) a algo (**b**) *Comptr* dedicado(a), especializado(a); **d. word processor** procesador *m* de textos *(ordenador)*

dedication [dedɪ'keɪʃən] *n* (**a**) *(of book)* dedicatoria *f* (**b**) *(devotion)* dedicación *f*, entrega *f*

deduce [dɪ'djuːs] *vt* deducir (**from** de)

deducible [dɪ'djuːsɪbəl] *adj* deducible (**from** de)

deduct [dɪ'dʌkt] *vt* **to d. sth from sth** descontar *or* deducir algo de algo

deductible [dɪ'dʌktɪbəl] *adj* deducible; *Fin* **d. for tax purposes** desgravable

deduction [dɪ'dʌkʃən] *n* (**a**) *(subtraction)* deducción *f*; **after deductions** después de (hacer las) deducciones (**b**) *(conclusion)* deducción *f*; **by a process of d.** por deducción

deed [diːd] *n* (**a**) *(action)* acción *f*, obra *f*; **to do one's good d. for the day** hacer la buena acción *or* obra del día (**b**) *Law (document)* escritura *f*, título *m* de propiedad

deejay ['diːdʒeɪ] *n Fam* pinchadiscos *mf inv*

deem [diːm] *vt Formal* considerar, estimar

de-emphasize [diː'emfəsaɪz] *vt (need, claim, feature)* quitar énfasis *or* importancia a

deep [diːp] **1** *n Literary* **the d.** las profundidades del mar
2 *adj* (**a**) *(water, sleep, thinker)* profundo(a); **to be 10 feet d.** tener 10 pies de profundidad; **take a d. breath** respire hondo; *Fig* **to be in d. water** estar en un lío; **d. in debt** endeudado(a) hasta el cuello; **d. in thought** ensimismado(a); **in deepest sympathy** *(on card)* con mi más sincero pésame; **d. end** *(of swimming pool)* parte *f* profunda; *Fig* **to go off the d. end (at sb)** ponerse hecho(a) un basilisco (con alguien); *Fig* **she was thrown in at the d. end** le hicieron empezar de golpe, sin preparación; **d. fryer** freidora *f*; **the D. South** *(of USA)* la América profunda de los estados del sur
(**b**) *(color)* intenso(a); *(sound, voice)* grave
3 *adv* profundamente; **to walk d. into the forest** internarse en el bosque; **to look d. into sb's eyes** mirar a alguien fijamente a los ojos; **to work d. into the night** trabajar hasta bien entrada la noche; **d. down he's very kind** en el fondo, es muy amable; **mistrust between the two families runs d.** la desconfianza entre las dos familias está profundamente arraigada; **the crowd lining the road was four d.** la gente se agolpaba en cuatro filas a lo largo de la calle

deep-dish ['diːpdɪʃ] *adj Culin* **d. pie** = pastel que se cuece en un recipiente hondo y que sólo tiene una costra por encima

deepen ['diːpən] **1** *vt (well, ditch)* profundizar, ahondar; *(sorrow, interest)* acentuar, agudizar; **to d. one's understanding of sth** ahondar en el conocimiento de algo
2 *vi* (**a**) *(river, silence, mystery)* hacerse más profundo(a); *(conviction, belief)* afianzarse; *(sorrow, interest)* acentuarse, agudizarse (**b**) *(color)* intensificarse; *(sound, voice)* hacerse más grave

Deepfreeze® ['diːp'friːz] *n* congelador *m*

deep-fried ['diːpfraɪd] *adj* frito(a) (en aceite abundante)

deep-fry ['diːp'fraɪ] *vt* freír (en aceite abundante)

deepness = **depth**

deep-rooted ['diːpruːtɪd] *adj (prejudice, fear)* muy arraigado(a)

deep-sea ['diːp'siː] *adj* **d. diver** buceador(ora) *m,f or* buzo *m* de profundidad; **d. fishing** pesca *f* de altura

deep-seated ['diːp'siːtɪd] *adj* muy arraigado(a)

deep-vein ['diːp'veɪn] *adj* **d. thrombosis** trombosis *f* venosa profunda

deer ['dɪə(r)] *(pl* **deer**) *n* ciervo *m*, venado *m*

deerstalker ['dɪəstɔːkə(r)] *n (hat)* gorro *m* de cazador (con orejeras)

deface [dɪ'feɪs] *vt* dañar, deteriorar

de facto [deɪ'fæktəʊ] *adj & adv* de hecho

defamation [defə'meɪʃən] *n* difamación *f*

defamatory [dɪ'fæmətərɪ] *adj (article, remark)* difamatorio(a)

defame [dɪ'feɪm] *vt* difamar

default [dɪ'fɔːlt] **1** *n Law & Sport (failure to appear)* incomparecencia *f*; **to win sth by d.** ganar algo por incomparecencia (del contrario); *Fig* **he became the boss by d.** a falta de otra persona, él terminó por convertirse en el jefe; *Comptr* **d. drive** unidad *f* (de disco) por defecto *or* omisión; *Comptr* **d. settings** valores *mpl or* configuración *f* por defecto *or* omisión
2 *vi Law* **to d. on payments** *(of debt, alimony)* incumplir los pagos

defaulter [dɪ'fɔːltə(r)] *n (on fine, payment)* moroso(a) *m,f*

defeat [dɪ'fiːt] **1** *n* derrota *f*; **to admit d.** admitir la derrota; **to suffer (a) d.** sufrir una derrota
2 *vt (army, government, opponent)* derrotar, vencer; *(proposal, bill, motion)* rechazar; **that rather defeats the object of the exercise** eso se contradice con la finalidad de la operación

defeatism [dɪ'fiːtɪzəm] *n* derrotismo *m*

defeatist [dɪ'fiːtɪst] *n & adj* derrotista *mf*

defecate ['defəkeɪt] *vi Formal* defecar

defect 1 *n* ['diːfekt] defecto *m*
2 *vi* [dɪ'fekt] desertar (**from** de); **to d. to another party** pasarse a otro partido

defection [dɪ'fekʃən] *n* deserción *f*; *(to another party)* cambio *m* de partido

defective [dɪ'fektɪv] *adj (machine)* defectuoso(a); *(reasoning)* erróneo(a)

defector [dɪ'fektə(r)] *n* desertor(ora) *m,f*; *(to another party)* tránsfuga *mf*

defend [dɪ'fend] **1** *vt* defender (**from** de)
2 *vi* defender

defendant [dɪ'fendənt] *n Law* acusado(a) *m,f*

defender [dɪ'fendə(r)] *n (of country, belief)* defensor(ora) *m,f*; *(Sport)* defensa *mf*

defending [dɪ'fendɪŋ] *adj* **the d. champion** el defensor del título, el actual campeón

defense [dɪ'fens] *n (of country, in sport, in court case)* defensa *f*; *Univ (of thesis)* lectura *f*; **defenses** *(of country)* defensas *fpl*; **to come to sb's d.** salir en defensa de alguien; **the Department of Defense** el Ministerio de Defensa; *Law* **d. counsel** abogado(a) *m,f* defensor(ora); **d. mechanism** mecanismo *m* de defensa; **d. spending** gasto *m* de defensa; *Law* **d. witness** testigo *mf* de descargo

defenseless [dɪ'fenslɪs] *adj* indefenso(a)

defensible [dɪ'fensəbəl] *adj* justificable, defendible

defensive [dɪ'fensɪv] **1** *n* **on the d.** a la defensiva
2 *adj* defensivo(a); **to get d.** ponerse a la defensiva

defensively [dɪ'fensɪvlɪ] *adv (gen) & Sport* a la defensiva; **she answered d.** respondió en actitud defensiva

defer [dɪˈfɜː(r)] (*pt & pp* **deferred**) **1** *vt* (*delay, postpone*) aplazar, posponer

2 *vi* **to d. to** (*person, knowledge*) ceder ante, deferir a

deference [ˈdefərəns] *n* deferencia *f*; **in** *or* **out of d. to...** por deferencia hacia...

deferential [defəˈrenʃəl] *adj* deferente; **to be d. to sb** mostrar deferencia hacia alguien

deferment [dɪˈfɜːmənt] *n* aplazamiento *m*

deferred [dɪˈfɜːd] *adj* aplazado(a)

defiance [dɪˈfaɪəns] *n* desafío *m*; **a gesture of d.** un gesto desafiante; **in d. of the law/my instructions** desafiando la ley/mis instrucciones

defiant [dɪˈfaɪənt] *adj* (*look, gesture, remark*) desafiante; (*person*) insolente

deficiency [dɪˈfɪʃənsɪ] *n* (**a**) (*lack*) (*of resources*) escasez *f*; (*of vitamins, minerals*) carencia *f*, deficiencia *f* (**b**) (*flaw, defect*) deficiencia *f*, defecto *m*

deficient [dɪˈfɪʃənt] *adj* (*unsatisfactory*) deficiente; **he is d. in vitamin C** le falta *or Esp* anda bajo de vitamina C

deficit [ˈdefɪsɪt] *n Fin* déficit *m*

defile [dɪˈfaɪl] *vt* (*memory*) manchar, mancillar; (*sacred place, tomb*) profanar

definable [dɪˈfaɪnəbəl] *adj* definible

define [dɪˈfaɪn] *vt* (**a**) (*give meaning of*) definir (**b**) (*delimit, identify*) delimitar, distinguir

defining [dɪˈfaɪnɪŋ] *adj* (**a**) (*decisive*) decisivo(a) (**b**) (*distinctive*) definidor(ora), distintivo(a)

definite [ˈdefɪnɪt] *adj* (**a**) (*precise*) (*plan, date, answer, decision*) claro(a), definitivo(a); (*views*) concluyente (**b**) (*noticeable*) (*change, advantage, improvement*) claro(a), indudable (**c**) (*sure, certain*) seguro(a); **are you d. about it?** ¿estás seguro (de ello)?, ¿lo tienes claro?; **it's not d. yet** todavía no está claro (**d**) *Gram* **d. article** artículo *m* determinado

definitely [ˈdefɪnɪtlɪ] *adv* (**a**) (*certainly*) con certeza; **I'll d. be there** seguro que estaré allí; **are you going? — d.!** ¿vas a ir? — ¡claro!; **d. not!** ¡desde luego que no! (**b**) (*noticeably*) (*improved, superior*) claramente, sin duda

definition [defɪˈnɪʃən] *n* (**a**) (*of word*) definición *f*; **by d.** por definición (**b**) (*of TV, binoculars*) definición *f*

definitive [dɪˈfɪnɪtɪv] *adj* definitivo(a)

definitively [dɪˈfɪnɪtɪvlɪ] *adv* definitivamente

deflate [diːˈfleɪt] **1** *vt* (**a**) (*ball, tire*) deshinchar, desinflar (**b**) (*economy*) producir una deflación en (**c**) (*person*) desanimar; **to d. sb's ego** bajarle los humos a alguien

2 *vi* (**a**) (*ball, tire*) deshincharse, desinflarse (**b**) (*economy*) sufrir una deflación

deflated [diːˈfleɪtɪd] *adj* (**a**) (*ball, tire*) deshinchado(a) (**b**) (*person*) desanimado(a)

deflation [diːˈfleɪʃən] *n* deflación *f*

deflationary [diːˈfleɪʃənərɪ] *adj* deflacionario(a)

deflect [dɪˈflekt] **1** *vt* (*ball, bullet, sound*) desviar; *Fig* (*person*) distraer, desviar (**from** de); **to d. criticism** distraer la atención de los críticos

2 *vi* (*projectile, light*) desviarse

deflection [dɪˈflekʃən] *n* desviación *f*

defogger [diːˈfɒɡə(r)] *n Aut* luneta *f* térmica, dispositivo *m* antivaho

deforestation [diːfɒrɪsˈteɪʃən] *n* de(s)forestación *f*

deform [dɪˈfɔːm] *vt* deformar

deformation [diːfɔːˈmeɪʃən] *n* deformación *f*

deformity [dɪˈfɔːmɪtɪ] *n* deformidad *f*; (*in baby, unborn child*) malformación *f* congénita

defraud [dɪˈfrɔːd] *vt* defraudar, estafar; **to d. sb of sth** defraudar algo a alguien

defray [dɪˈfreɪ] *vt Formal* sufragar

defrost [diːˈfrɒst] **1** *vt* descongelar

2 *vi* descongelarse

deft [deft] *adj* diestro(a), hábil

defunct [dɪˈfʌŋkt] *adj* (*person*) difunto(a); (*company, scheme*) ya desaparecido(a)

defuse [diːˈfjuːz] *vt* (*bomb*) desactivar; *Fig* (*situation*) calmar, apaciguar

defy [dɪˈfaɪ] *vt* desafiar; **to d. description** ser indescriptible; **to d. sb to do sth** desafiar a alguien a hacer *or* a que haga algo

degenerate 1 *n* [dɪˈdʒenərət] (*person*) degenerado(a) *m,f*

2 *adj* degenerado(a)

3 *vi* [dɪˈdʒenəreɪt] degenerar (**into** en)

degeneration [dɪdʒenəˈreɪʃən] *n* degeneración *f*

degenerative [dɪˈdʒenərətɪv] *adj* degenerativo(a)

degradation [deɡrəˈdeɪʃən] *n* degradación *f*

degrade [dɪˈɡreɪd] *vt* rebajar, degradar; **I won't d. myself by answering that** no me rebajaré a contestar a eso

degrading [dɪˈɡreɪdɪŋ] *adj* degradante

degree [dɪˈɡriː] *n* (**a**) (*extent*) grado *m*; **a d. of risk** un cierto riesgo, un elemento de riesgo; **to a d.** hasta cierto punto; **to such a d. that...** hasta tal punto que...; **by degrees** gradualmente (**b**) (*of temperature, in geometry*) grado *m*; **it's 25 degrees** (*of temperature*) hace 25 grados (**c**) (*at university*) (*title*) título *m* universitario, licenciatura *f*; (*course*) carrera *f*; **postgraduate d.** título *m*/curso *m* de posgrado; **to take a d.** hacer *or* estudiar una carrera; **to have a d. in physics** ser licenciado(a) en Física

dehumanize [diːˈhjuːmənaɪz] *vt* deshumanizar

dehumidifier [diːhjuːˈmɪdɪfaɪə(r)] *n* deshumidificador *m*

dehydrate [diːhaɪˈdreɪt] **1** *vt* deshidratar

2 *vi* (*person*) deshidratarse

dehydrated [diːhaɪˈdreɪtɪd] *adj* deshidratado(a); **to be d.** estar deshidratado(a); **to become d.** deshidratarse

dehydration [diːhaɪˈdreɪʃən] *n* deshidratación *f*

deicer [diːˈaɪsə(r)] *n* (*for car*) descongelador *m* de parabrisas; (*on plane*) dispositivo *m* de descongelación

deification [deɪɪfɪˈkeɪʃən] *n* deificación *f*, divinización *f*

deify [ˈdeɪɪfaɪ] *vt* deificar, divinizar

deign [deɪn] *vt* **to d. to do sth** dignarse a hacer algo

deindustrialization [diːɪndʌstrɪəlaɪˈzeɪʃən] *n* desindustrialización *f*

deity [ˈdeɪɪtɪ] *n* deidad *f*, divinidad *f*

dejected [dɪˈdʒektɪd] *adj* abatido(a); **to be d.** estar abatido(a)

dejectedly [dɪˈdʒektɪdlɪ] *adv* con abatimiento

dejection [dɪˈdʒekʃən] *n* abatimiento *m*, desencanto *m*

delay [dɪˈleɪ] **1** *n* retraso *m*, *Am* demora *f*; **without d.** sin (mayor) demora; **an hour's d.** un retraso *or Am* una demora de una hora; **all flights are subject to d.** todos los vuelos llevan retraso *or Am* demora

2 *vt* (*project, decision, act*) retrasar; (*traffic*) retener, demorar; **to be delayed** (*train*) llevar retraso; (*person*) llegar tarde, retrasarse, *Am* demorarse; **I don't want to d. you** no te quiero entretener; **delaying tactics** tácticas *fpl* dilatorias

3 *vi* retrasarse, demorarse; **don't d.!** ¡no deje pasar más tiempo!

delayed-action [dɪˈleɪdˈækʃən] *adj* (*drug, fuse*) de efecto retardado

delectable [dɪˈlektəbəl] *adj* delicioso(a)

delectation [dɪlekˈteɪʃən] *n Formal or Hum* deleite *m*; **for your d.** para mayor deleite suyo

delegate 1 *n* [ˈdelɪɡət] delegado(a) *m,f*

2 *vt* [ˈdelɪɡeɪt] (*power, responsibility*) delegar (**to** en); **to d. sb to do sth** delegar en alguien para hacer algo

3 *vi* delegar responsabilidades

delegation [delɪˈɡeɪʃən] *n* delegación *f*

delete [dɪˈliːt] *vt* borrar; **d. where inapplicable** táchese lo que no corresponda

deleterious [delɪˈtɪərɪəs] *adj Formal* nocivo(a), deletéreo(a)

deletion [dɪˈliːʃən] *n Comptr* supresión *f*, borrado *m*

deli ['delɪ] n Fam (shop) = tienda de productos de alimentación de calidad

deliberate 1 adj [dɪ'lɪbərət] (**a**) (intentional) deliberado(a), intencionado(a); **it wasn't d.** fue sin querer (**b**) (unhurried) pausado(a)
2 vi [dɪ'lɪbəreɪt] (think) reflexionar (**on** sobre); (discuss) deliberar (**on** sobre)

deliberately [dɪ'lɪbərətlɪ] adv (**a**) (intentionally) a propósito, deliberadamente (**b**) (unhurriedly) pausadamente

deliberation [dɪlɪbə'reɪʃən] n (**a**) (thought) reflexión f; (discussion) deliberación f (**b**) (unhurriedness) pausa f; **to do sth with d.** hacer algo pausadamente

delicacy ['delɪkəsɪ] n (**a**) (of situation) dificultad f (**b**) (tact) delicadeza f, tacto m (**c**) (food) exquisitez f

delicate ['delɪkət] adj (glass, situation, flavor) delicado(a); (health) frágil, delicado(a)

delicately ['delɪkətlɪ] adv (**a**) (finely) **d. carved** primorosamente tallado(a) (**b**) (tactfully) con delicadeza

delicatessen [delɪkə'tesən] n (shop) = tienda de productos de alimentación de calidad

delicious [dɪ'lɪʃəs] adj delicioso(a)

deliciously [dɪ'lɪʃəslɪ] adv deliciosamente

delight [dɪ'laɪt] **1** n (pleasure) gusto m, placer m; **to my/her d.** para mi/su deleite; **he took d. in her failure** se alegró de su fracaso; **to take d. in doing sth** disfrutar haciendo algo; **the car is a d. to drive** Esp conducir or Am manejar ese coche or Am carro or RP auto es una delicia; **the delights of Las Vegas** los encantos de Las Vegas
2 vt deleitar, encantar
3 vi **to d. in doing sth** disfrutar haciendo algo

delighted [dɪ'laɪtɪd] adj encantado(a); **to be d. (with sth)** estar encantado(a) (con algo); **I'm d. to see you** me alegro mucho de verte

delightful [dɪ'laɪtfʊl] adj (person, smile) encantador(ora); (meal, evening) delicioso(a)

delightfully [dɪ'laɪtfʊlɪ] adv (to sing, write) maravillosamente

delimit [di:'lɪmɪt] vt delimitar

delineate [dɪ'lɪnɪeɪt] vt (plan, proposal) detallar, especificar

delineation [dɪlɪnɪ'eɪʃən] n Formal descripción f

delinquency [dɪ'lɪŋkwənsɪ] n delincuencia f

delinquent [dɪ'lɪŋkwənt] n & adj delincuente mf

delirious [dɪ'lɪrɪəs] adj also Fig delirante; **to be d.** delirar; **to be d. about sth** estar como loco(a) con algo

deliriously [dɪ'lɪrɪəslɪ] adv **to be d. happy** estar loco(a) de alegría

delirium [dɪ'lɪrɪəm] n also Fig delirio m; Med **d. tremens** delírium m tremens

deliver [dɪ'lɪvə(r)] **1** vt (letter, package) entregar (**to** a); (blow) propinar; (speech, verdict) pronunciar; **to d. a service** prestar un servicio; Fig **to d. the goods** cumplir (con lo esperado); **to d. a child** traer al mundo a un niño
2 vi repartir; **we d.** repartimos a domicilio; Fig **their proposal is impressive, but can they d.?** la propuesta es impresionante, pero ¿podrán llevarla a la práctica?

deliverance [dɪ'lɪvərəns] n Formal liberación f

delivery [dɪ'lɪvərɪ] n (**a**) (of letter, package) entrega f; **to take d. of sth** recibir algo; **d. date** fecha f de entrega; **d. man** repartidor m; **d. van** furgoneta f de reparto (**b**) (of child) parto m (**c**) (style of speaking) discurso m, oratoria f

delta ['deltə] n (Greek letter) delta f; (rivermouth) delta m; **d. wing** (of plane) Av ala f supercrítica

delude [dɪ'lu:d] vt engañar; **to d. oneself** engañarse

deluded [dɪ'lu:dɪd] adj (mistaken, foolish) engañado(a)

deluge ['delju:dʒ] **1** n (of water) diluvio m; Fig (of letters, questions) avalancha f, lluvia f
2 vt inundar (**with** de)

delusion [dɪ'lu:ʒən] n engaño m, ilusión f; **to be under a d.**

estar engañado(a); **delusions of grandeur** delirios mpl de grandeza

deluxe [dɪ'lʌks] adj de lujo

delve [delv] vi rebuscar; **to d. into a bag** rebuscar en una bolsa; **to d. into the past** hurgar en el pasado

demagogue, demagog ['deməgɒg] n demagogo(a) m,f

demand [dɪ'mɑ:nd] **1** n (**a**) (request) exigencia f; **to make demands on sb** exigir mucho de alguien (**b**) (for goods) demanda f (**for** de); **to be in d.** estar muy solicitado(a)
2 vt (**a**) (request) exigir (**b**) (require) requerir, exigir

demanding [dɪ'mɑ:ndɪŋ] adj (person) exigente; **to be d.** (job) exigir mucho (esfuerzo); **he's a d. child** (trying) es un niño que da mucho trabajo

demarcate ['di:mɑ:keɪt] vt Formal delimitar, demarcar

demarcation [di:mɑ:'keɪʃən] n demarcación f; Ind **d. dispute** = enfrentamiento entre grupos sindicales sobre la delimitación de las tareas que sus miembros deben realizar en el trabajo; **d. line** línea f de demarcación

demean [dɪ'mi:n] vt **to d. oneself** rebajarse

demeanor [dɪ'mi:nə(r)] n comportamiento m, conducta f

demented [dɪ'mentɪd] adj demente; **to be d. with grief** estar trastornado(a) por el dolor

dementia [dɪ'menʃə] n demencia f

demerara sugar [demə'reərə'ʃugə(r)] n azúcar m moreno de caña (procedente de las Antillas)

demerit [di:'merɪt] n (**a**) Formal (fault, flaw) demérito m, deficiencia f (**b**) Sch & Mil falta f (en el historial)

demigod ['demɪgɒd] n semidiós m

demilitarize [di:'mɪlɪtəraɪz] vt desmilitarizar

demise [dɪ'maɪz] n desaparición f, extinción f

demo ['deməʊ] (pl demos) n Fam (**a**) (protest) mani f (**b**) (musical) maqueta f (**c**) Comptr demo f; **d. version** versión f demo or de demostración

demobilization [di:məʊbɪlaɪ'zeɪʃən] n (of troops) licencia f (absoluta), desmovilización f

demobilize [di:'məʊbɪlaɪz] vt (troops) licenciar, desmovilizar

democracy [dɪ'mɒkrəsɪ] n democracia f

Democrat ['deməkræt] n Pol (politician, voter) demócrata m,f; **the Democrats** (party) los demócratas, el partido demócrata

democrat ['deməkræt] n demócrata mf

democratic [demə'krætɪk] adj democrático(a)

democratically [demə'krætɪklɪ] adv democráticamente

demographic [demə'græfɪk] adj demográfico(a)

demolish [dɪ'mɒlɪʃ] vt (building) demoler, derribar; Fig (theory) desbaratar; (opponent) aplastar

demolition [demə'lɪʃən] n demolición f, derribo m; **d. squad** equipo m de demolición

demon ['di:mən] n demonio m; Fam **he's a d. tennis player** es un fiera jugando al tenis

demonic [dɪ'mɒnɪk] adj demoníaco(a)

demonstrable [dɪ'mɒnstrəbəl] adj demostrable

demonstrate ['demənstreɪt] **1** vt (fact, theory) demostrar; **to d. how sth works** hacer una demostración de cómo funciona algo
2 vi (politically) manifestarse

demonstration [demən'streɪʃən] n (**a**) (of fact, theory, skills) demostración f (**b**) (political) manifestación f

demonstrative [dɪ'mɒnstrətɪv] adj (**a**) (person) efusivo(a), extravertido(a) (**b**) Gram demostrativo(a)

demonstrator ['demənstreɪtə(r)] n (political) manifestante mf

demoralization [dɪmɒrəlaɪ'zeɪʃən] n desmoralización f

demoralize [dɪ'mɒrəlaɪz] vt desmoralizar

demoralizing [dɪ'mɒrəlaɪzɪŋ] adj desmoralizador(ora)

demote [dɪ'məʊt] vt degradar, relegar (a un puesto más bajo); **two teams were demoted** dos equipos fueron descendidos de categoría

demotion [dɪˈməʊʃən] *n (of person)* degradación *f*; *Sport* descenso *m* de categoría

demur [dɪˈmɜː(r)] *(pt & pp* **demurred***)* *vi* objetar; **to d. at a suggestion** poner objeciones a una sugerencia

demure [dɪˈmjʊə(r)] *adj* recatado(a)

demutualize [diːˈmjuːtʃʊəlaɪz] *vi Fin* desmutualizarse

demystify [diːˈmɪstɪfaɪ] *vt* aclarar, clarificar

den [den] *n* (**a**) *(of animal)* guarida *f*; *Fig* **a d. of thieves** una cueva de ladrones; **a d. of iniquity** un antro de depravación (**b**) *(room)* cuarto *m* privado, madriguera *f*

denationalize [diːˈnæʃənəlaɪz] *vt* privatizar, desnacionalizar

denature [diːˈneɪtʃə(r)] *vt* desnaturalizar

deniable [dɪˈnaɪəbəl] *adj* refutable, negable

denial [dɪˈnaɪəl] *n* (**a**) *(of right, request)* denegación *f* (**b**) *(of accusation, guilt)* negación *f*; *Psy* **to be in d.** atravesar una fase de negación *or* rechazo

denigrate [ˈdenɪɡreɪt] *vt* denigrar

denim [ˈdenɪm] *n* tela *f* vaquera; **denims** *(jeans)* vaqueros *mpl*, *Andes,Ven* bluyíns *nmpl*, *Méx* pantalones *mpl* de mezclilla; **d. skirt/shirt** falda *f*/camisa *f* vaquera

Denmark [ˈdenmɑːk] *n* Dinamarca

denomination [dɪnɒmɪˈneɪʃən] *n* (**a**) *(religious)* confesión *f* (**b**) *Fin* valor *m* (nominal)

denominator [dɪˈnɒmɪneɪtə(r)] *n Math* denominador *m*

denote [dɪˈnəʊt] *vt* denotar

denouement [deɪˈnuːmɒŋ] *n* desenlace *m*

denounce [dɪˈnaʊns] *vt* (**a**) *(inform against)* denunciar (**b**) *(criticize publicly)* denunciar, condenar

dense [dens] *adj* (**a**) *(smoke, fog)* denso(a); *(jungle)* tupido(a); *(crowd)* nutrido(a) (**b**) *Fam (stupid)* corto(a)

densely [ˈdenslɪ] *adv* densamente; **d. packed** muy apretado(a); **d. populated** densamente poblado(a)

density [ˈdensɪtɪ] *n* densidad *f*

dent [dent] **1** *n* abolladura *f*; *Fig* **the wedding made a d. in his savings** la boda le costó una buena parte de sus ahorros **2** *vt (car, bumper)* abollar; *Fig (confidence, pride)* minar

dental [ˈdentəl] *adj* dental; **d. appointment** cita *f* con el dentista; **d. assistant** enfermera *f* de dentista; **d. floss** hilo *m* (de seda) dental; **d. hygiene** higiene *f* dental; **d. hygienist** higienista *mf* dental; **d. surgeon** cirujano(a) *m,f* dentista

dentist [ˈdentɪst] *n* dentista *mf*; **to go to the d.** ir al dentista

dentistry [ˈdentɪstrɪ] *n (subject)* odontología *f*

dentures [ˈdentʃəz] *npl* (**set of**) **d.** dentadura *f* postiza

denude [dɪˈnjuːd] *vt* **to be denuded of** estar desprovisto(a) de

denunciation [dɪnʌnsɪˈeɪʃən] *n* (**a**) *(accusation)* denuncia *f* (**b**) *(criticism)* denuncia *f*, condena *f*

Denver boot [ˈdenvəˈbuːt] *n Aut Fam* cepo *m*

deny [dɪˈnaɪ] *vt* (**a**) *(right, request)* denegar; **to d. sb his rights** denegar *or* negar a alguien sus derechos; **to d. oneself sth** privarse de algo (**b**) *(accusation, fact)* negar; *(rumor)* desmentir; **to d. doing sth, d. having done sth** negar haber hecho algo; **there's no denying that…** es innegable que…; **to d. all knowledge of sth** negar tener conocimiento de algo

deodorant [diːˈəʊdərənt] *n* desodorante *m*

deodorize [diːˈəʊdəraɪz] *vt* desodorizar, eliminar el mal olor de

dep *Rail (abbr* **departure***)* salida *f*

depart [dɪˈpɑːt] *vi (leave)* salir (**from** de); **to d. from** *(tradition, subject, truth)* desviarse de; **the Atlanta train will d. from platform 6** el tren con destino a Atlanta efectuará su salida por la vía 6

department [dɪˈpɑːtmənt] *n (in company, shop)* departamento *m*; *(in college)* cátedra *f*, departamento *m*; *(of government)* ministerio *m*; **that's not my d.** eso no es de mi competencia; **d. store** grandes almacenes *mpl*

departmental [diːpɑːtˈmentəl] *adj* de departamento; **d. head** jefe(a) *m,f* de departamento

departure [dɪˈpɑːtʃə(r)] *n (from place)* salida *f*; *(from tradition, subject, truth)* desviación *f*; **d. lounge** *(in airport)* sala *f* de embarque; **d. time** hora *f* de salida

depend [dɪˈpend] *vi* depender (**on** de); **that/it depends** depende; **to d. on sb** *(be dependent on)* depender de alguien; *(count on)* confiar en alguien; **it depends on how much money I have** depende de cuánto dinero tenga; *Ironic* **you can d. on him to be late** puedes estar seguro de que llegará tarde

dependable [dɪˈpendəbəl] *adj (person)* formal; *(friend)* leal; *(car)* fiable, *Am* confiable

dependence [dɪˈpendəns] *n (reliance)* dependencia *f*; *(trust)* confianza *f*

dependency [dɪˈpendənsɪ] *n (territory)* dependencia *f*

dependent [dɪˈpendənt] **1** *n* **his/her dependents** las personas a su cargo **2** *adj* dependiente; **to be d. on** depender de

depending [dɪˈpendɪŋ] *adv* **d. on** dependiendo de

depersonalize [diːˈpɜːsənəlaɪz] *vt* despersonalizar, deshumanizar

depict [dɪˈpɪkt] *vt (of painting)* retratar, plasmar; *(of book, piece of writing)* describir

depiction [dɪˈpɪkʃən] *n (picture)* representación *f*; *(description)* descripción *f*

depilatory [dɪˈpɪlətərɪ] *adj* depilatorio(a)

deplete [dɪˈpliːt] *vt* mermar

depletion [dɪˈpliːʃən] *n* merma *f*

deplorable [dɪˈplɔːrəbəl] *adj* deplorable

deplore [dɪˈplɔː(r)] *vt* deplorar

deploy [dɪˈplɔɪ] *vt* desplegar

deployment [dɪˈplɔɪmənt] *n* despliegue *m*

depoliticize [diːpəˈlɪtɪsaɪz] *vt* despolitizar

depopulate [diːˈpɒpjʊleɪt] *vt* despoblar

depopulation [diːpɒpjʊˈleɪʃən] *n* despoblación *f*

deport [dɪˈpɔːt] *vt* deportar

deportation [diːpɔːˈteɪʃən] *n* deportación *f*

deportee [diːpɔːˈtiː] *n* deportado(a) *m,f*

deportment [dɪˈpɔːtmənt] *n* porte *m*

depose [dɪˈpəʊz] *vt* deponer

deposit [dɪˈpɒzɪt] **1** *n* (**a**) *(in bank)* depósito *m*; *Fin* imposición *f*; **to make a d.** hacer *or* realizar un depósito *or Esp* ingreso (**b**) *(returnable)* señal *f*, fianza *f*; *(first payment)* entrega *f* inicial, *Esp* entrada *f*; **to put down a d. (on sth)** pagar la entrega inicial *or Esp* entrada (de algo) (**c**) *(of minerals)* yacimiento *m*; *(in wine)* poso *m* **2** *vt* depositar; *(in bank account) Esp* ingresar, *Am* depositar

deposition [diːpəˈzɪʃən] *n Law* declaración *f*

depositor [dɪˈpɒzɪtə(r)] *n Fin* depositante *mf*

depot [ˈdiːpəʊ] *n Mil* depósito *m*; *Com* almacén *m*; *(train or bus station)* estación *f* de autobuses, *CAm, Méx* central *f* camionera

depravation [deprəˈveɪʃən] *n* depravación *f*

depraved [dɪˈpreɪvd] *adj* depravado(a)

depravity [dɪˈprævɪtɪ] *n* depravación *f*

deprecate [ˈdeprɪkeɪt] *vt* censurar; **to d. sb's efforts** restar importancia *or* mérito a los esfuerzos de alguien

deprecatory [ˈdeprɪkeɪtərɪ] *adj* de desaprobación; **to be d. about sth/sb** mostrar desaprobación por algo/alguien

depreciate [dɪˈpriːʃɪeɪt] *vi (value, currency)* depreciarse

depreciation [dɪpriːʃɪˈeɪʃən] *n (of value, currency)* depreciación *f*

depress [dɪˈpres] *vt (person, economy)* deprimir; *(prices)* hacer bajar

depressed [dɪˈprest] *adj (person, economy)* deprimido(a); **to**

be d. estar deprimido(a); **to make sb d.** deprimir a alguien

depressing [dɪ'presɪŋ] *adj* deprimente

depressingly [dɪ'presɪŋlɪ] *adv* **d. slow** de una lentitud deprimente

depression [dɪ'preʃən] *n* (**a**) *(of person, economy)* depresión *f* (**b**) *Met* depresión *f* atmosférica, zona *f* de bajas presiones

deprivation [deprɪ'veɪʃən] *n* privación *f*

deprive [dɪ'praɪv] *vt* **to d. sb of sth** privar a alguien de algo

deprived [dɪ'praɪvd] *adj (background, area)* desfavorecido(a)

dept *(abbr* **department**) dpto., departamento *m*

depth [depθ], **deepness** ['diːpnɪs] *n (of water, hole, sleep, feeling)* profundidad *f*; **in d.** *(investigate, discuss)* a fondo, en profundidad; *Fig* **she was out of her d. in her new job/in the competition** el nuevo trabajo/el campeonato le venía grande; **in the depths of winter** en pleno invierno; **the depths of despair** la más absoluta desesperación; *Mil* **d. charge** carga *f* de profundidad

deputation [depjʊ'teɪʃən] *n* delegación *f*

depute [dɪ'pjuːt] *vt* delegar

deputize ['depjʊtaɪz] *vi* **to d. for sb** suplir a alguien

deputy ['depjʊtɪ] *n* (**a**) *(substitute)* sustituto(a) *m,f*; *(second-in-command)* asistente *mf*, lugarteniente *mf*; **d. prime minister** vicepresidente(a) *m,f* del Gobierno (**b**) *(political representative)* diputado (a) *m,f* (**c**) *(policeman)* **d. (sheriff)** ayudante *mf* del sheriff

derail [diː'reɪl] **1** *vt* **to be derailed** *(train)* descarrilar; *Fig (project, plan)* fracasar
2 *vi (train)* descarrilar

derailment [dɪ'reɪlmənt] *n* descarrilamiento *m*

deranged [dɪ'reɪndʒd] *adj* perturbado(a); **to be d.** estar perturbado(a)

derby *n* (**a**) ['dɑːbɪ] *(soccer match)* derby *m* (**b**) ['dɜːrbɪ] *(hat)* bombín *m*, sombrero *m* hongo

deregulate [diː'regjʊleɪt] *vt Com & Econ* liberalizar

deregulation [diːregjʊ'leɪʃən] *n Com & Econ* liberalización *f*

derelict ['derəlɪkt] *adj* ruinoso(a), en ruinas

dereliction [derɪ'lɪkʃən] *n* ruina *f*; **d. of duty** incumplimiento *m* del deber

deride [dɪ'raɪd] *vt* ridiculizar, burlarse de

derision [dɪ'rɪʒən] *n* burla *f*, escarnio *m*; **to be an object of d.** ser objeto de burla

derisive [dɪ'raɪsɪv] *adj* burlón(ona)

derisively [dɪ'raɪsɪvlɪ] *adv (to say, speak)* con sorna, con burla

derisory [dɪ'raɪsərɪ] *adj* irrisorio(a)

derivation [derɪ'veɪʃən] *n* origen *m*

derivative [dɪ'rɪvətɪv] **1** *n* derivado *m*
2 *adj* poco original

derive [dɪ'raɪv] **1** *vt (pleasure, satisfaction)* encontrar (**from** en); *(benefit, profit)* obtener (**from** de); **to be derived from** *(name, behavior)* derivar *or* provenir de
2 *vi* **to d. from** derivar *or* provenir de

dermatitis [dɜːmə'taɪtɪs] *n Med* dermatitis *f inv*

dermatology [dɜːmə'tɒlədʒɪ] *n Med* dermatología *f*

derogatory [dɪ'rɒgətərɪ] *adj* despectivo(a)

derrick ['derɪk] *n (in oil industry)* torre *f* de perforación

desalination [diːsælɪ'neɪʃən] *n* desalinización *f*, desalación *f*

descend [dɪ'send] **1** *vt* (**a**) *(hill, stairs)* descender por, bajar (**b**) *(be related to)* **to be descended from sb** descender de alguien
2 *vi* (**a**) *(come down)* descender; **darkness descended** cayó la noche; **in descending order** en orden descendente; **a mood of despair descended upon the country** el país quedó sumido en un sentimiento de desesperación; **every summer tourists d. on the town** todos los veranos los turistas invaden la ciudad; *Fig* **to d. to sb's level** rebajarse al nivel de alguien (**b**) **to d. from sb** *(be related to)* descender de alguien

descendant [dɪ'sendənt] *n* descendiente *m*

descent [dɪ'sent] *n* (**a**) *(way down)* descenso *m* (**b**) *(ancestry)* ascendencia *f*

describe [dɪs'kraɪb] *vt* (**a**) *(depict verbally)* describir; **she describes herself as an artist** se define a sí misma como artista (**b**) *Formal (draw) (circle, line)* describir, trazar

description [dɪs'krɪpʃən] *n* descripción *f*; **to give a d. (of)** dar *or* hacer una descripción (de); **to answer** *or* **fit the d.** responder a la descripción; **beyond d.** indescriptible; **birds of all descriptions** todo tipo de aves

descriptive [dɪs'krɪptɪv] *adj* descriptivo(a)

desecrate ['desɪkreɪt] *vt* profanar

desecration [desɪ'kreɪʃən] *n* profanación *f*

desegregate [diː'segrɪgeɪt] *vt* terminar con la segregación racial en

desensitize [diː'sensɪtaɪz] *vt (emotionally)* insensibilizar

desert¹ ['dezət] *n* desierto *m*; **d. island** isla *f* desierta

desert² [dɪ'zɜːt] **1** *vt (place, family)* abandonar; *Fig* **his courage deserted him** el valor le abandonó
2 *vi (from army)* desertar

deserted [dɪ'zɜːtɪd] *adj* desierto(a)

deserter [dɪ'zɜːtə(r)] *n (soldier)* desertor(ora) *m,f*

desertification [dɪzɜːtɪfɪ'keɪʃən] *n* desertización *f*

desertion [dɪ'zɜːʃən] *n Law* abandono *m* del hogar; *Mil* deserción *f*

deserts [dɪ'zɜːts] *npl* **he got his just d.** recibió su merecido

deserve [dɪ'zɜːv] *vt* merecer, merecerse, *Am* ameritar; **to d. (to do) sth** merecer (hacer) algo; **she got what she deserved** recibió su merecido

deserving [dɪ'zɜːvɪŋ] *adj* **to be d. of sth** ser digno(a) *or* merecedor(ora) de algo; **a d. case** un caso merecedor de ayuda

design [dɪ'zaɪn] **1** *n* (**a**) *(decorative pattern)* dibujo *m*, motivo *m* (**b**) *(style) (of car, furniture, clothes)* modelo *m*, diseño *m*; **our latest d.** nuestro último diseño (**c**) *(drawing, subject)* diseño *m* (**d**) *(intention)* propósito *m*; **by d.** a propósito; **to have designs on sb/sth** tener las miras puestas en alguien/algo
2 *vt (building, vehicle, clothes)* diseñar; **the book is designed for children** el libro está pensado *or* concebido para los niños; **his remarks were designed to shock** sus comentarios pretendían escandalizar

designate ['dezɪgneɪt] **1** *vt (person)* designar; **to d. sb to do sth** designar a alguien para hacer algo; **he designated her as his successor** la nombró su sucesora; **this area has been designated a national park** esta zona ha sido declarada parque nacional
2 *adj* designado(a), nombrado(a)

designation [dezɪg'neɪʃən] *n* (**a**) *(appointment)* nombramiento *m* (**b**) *(title)* denominación *f*

designer [dɪ'zaɪnə(r)] *n* diseñador(ora) *m,f*; **(set) d.** *Theat* escenógrafo(a) *m,f*; *Cin* decorador(ora) *m,f*; **d. clothes/drugs** ropa *f*/drogas *fpl* de diseño; *Hum* **d. stubble** barba *f* de tres días

desirability [dɪzaɪərə'bɪlɪtɪ] *n (of outcome)* conveniencia *f*; *(of person)* atractivo *m*

desirable [dɪ'zaɪərəbəl] *adj (attractive)* apetecible; *(sexually)* deseable; *(appropriate)* deseable; **a knowledge of French is d.** *(in job advert)* se valorarán los conocimientos de francés; **d. residence** *(in advert)* propiedad *f* impecable

desire [dɪ'zaɪə(r)] **1** *n* deseo *m*; **I feel no d. to go** no me *Esp* apetece *or Carib, Col, Méx* provoca nada ir, *CSur* no tengo nada de ganas de ir
2 *vt* desear; **to d. (to do) sth** desear (hacer) algo; **it leaves a lot to be desired** deja mucho que desear

desirous [dɪ'zaɪərəs] *adj Formal* deseoso(a) (**of** de)

desist [dɪ'sɪst] *vi Formal* desistir (**from** de)

desk [desk] *n (in school)* pupitre *m*; *(in office)* mesa *f*, escritorio *m*; *(in hotel)* mostrador *m*; **the foreign/sports d.** *(of news-*

paper) la sección de noticias internacionales/de información deportiva; **d. diary** agenda *f*; **a d. job** un trabajo de oficina; **d. lamp** lámpara *f* de mesa *or* de escritorio

desk-bound ['deskbaʊnd] *adj* **a d. job** un trabajo de oficina

de-skilling [diː'skɪlɪŋ] *n* = pérdida de la aportación humana en un trabajo como resultado de la introducción de una nueva tecnología

desktop ['desktɒp] *n Comptr* **d. computer** *Esp* ordenador *m or Am* computadora *f* de sobremesa; **d. publishing** autoedición *f*

desolate ['desələt] *adj (place)* desolado(a); *(person, look)* desolado(a), afligido(a); *(future, prospect)* desolador(ora)

desolation [desə'leɪʃən] *n (of landscape, person, defeated country)* desolación *f*

despair [dɪs'peə(r)] **1** *n* desesperación *f*; **to be in d.** estar desesperado(a); **to drive sb to d.** llevar a alguien a la desesperación

   2 *vi* desesperarse; **to d. of doing sth** perder la esperanza de hacer algo; **I d. of you** contigo me desespero, no sé qué voy a hacer contigo

despairing [dɪs'peərɪŋ] *adj* de desesperación

desperate ['despərət] *adj (person, situation)* desesperado(a); **to be d.** *(person)* estar desesperado(a); **to be d. to do sth** morirse de ganas de hacer algo; **to be d. for sth, to be in d. need of sth** necesitar algo desesperadamente

desperately ['despərətlɪ] *adv (to fight, plead)* desesperadamente; *(in love)* perdidamente; **d. ill** gravísimamente enfermo(a); **to be d. sorry about sth** lamentar algo muchísimo

desperation [despə'reɪʃən] *n* desesperación *f*; **in d.** presa de la desesperación; **she did it in d.** lo hizo por desesperación *or* a la desesperada

despicable [dɪ'spɪkbəəl] *adj* despreciable

despise [dɪ'spaɪz] *vt* despreciar

despite [dɪs'paɪt] *prep* a pesar de, pese a

despondency [dɪs'pɒndənsɪ] *n* desánimo *m*, abatimiento *m*

despondent [dɪ'spɒndənt] *adj* desanimado(a), abatido(a); **to be d.** estar desanimado(a) *or* abatido(a); **to become d.** desanimarse, abatirse

despondently [dɪ'spɒndəntlɪ] *adv* con desánimo, con aire abatido

despot ['despɒt] *n* déspota *mf*

despotic [dɪs'pɒtɪk] *adj* despótico(a)

despotism ['despətɪzəm] *n* despotismo *m*

dessert [dɪ'zɜːt] *n* postre *m*; **d. wine** vino *m* dulce

dessertspoon [dɪ'zɜːtspuːn] *n* cuchara *f or Ven* cucharilla *f* de postre; *(as measurement)* cucharada *f* de (las de) postre

destabilization [diːsteɪbɪlaɪ'zeɪʃən] *n* desestabilización *f*

destabilize [diː'steɪbəlaɪz] *vt* desestabilizar

destination [destɪ'neɪʃən] *n* (lugar *m* de) destino *m*; *Comptr* **d. disk** disco *m* de destino; *Comptr* **d. drive** unidad *f* (de disco) de destino

destine ['destɪn] *vt* destinar

destined ['destɪnd] *adj (a) (meant)* destinado(a); **to be d. to do sth** estar destinado a hacer algo *(b) (of plane, ship)* **d. for** con destino *or* rumbo a

destiny ['destɪnɪ] *n* destino *m*, sino *m*

destitute ['destɪtjuːt] *adj (needy)* indigente; **to be utterly d.** estar en la miseria

destitution [destɪ'tjuːʃən] *n* indigencia *f*

destroy [dɪs'trɔɪ] *vt (a) (damage, ruin)* destruir; *(health, career, reputation)* acabar con, destruir *(b) (kill) (sick or unwanted animal)* sacrificar; *(vermin)* acabar con, destruir

destroyer [dɪs'trɔɪə(r)] *n (ship)* destructor *m*

destruction [dɪs'trʌkʃən] *n (action)* destrucción *f*; *(damage)* destrozos *mpl*

destructive [dɪs'trʌktɪv] *adj* destructivo(a); **d. criticism** crítica *f* destructiva

destructiveness [dɪ'strʌktɪvnɪs] *n (of bomb, weapon)* capacidad *f* destructora *or* destructiva; *(of person)* tendencia *f* destructiva *or* destructora

desultory ['desəltərɪ] *adj (attempt, manner)* sin convicción, desganado(a); **to have a d. conversation** mantener a desgana una conversación *or CAm, Méx* plática

detach [dɪ'tætʃ] *vt* separar (**from** de); **to d. oneself from sth** distanciarse de algo

detachable [dɪ'tætʃəbəl] *adj (cover, handle)* extraíble; *(accessories)* desmontable; *(hood)* de quita y pon

detached [dɪ'tætʃt] *adj (a) (separate)* separado(a); **to become** *or* **get d. from sth** alejarse *or* separarse de algo; **to become d. from reality** perder el contacto con la realidad; **d. house** casa *f or* chalé *m* individual; *Med* **d. retina** desprendimiento *m* de retina *(b)* **to be d.** *(objective)* ser imparcial; *(cold, distant)* ser despegado(a) *or* distante

detachment [dɪ'tætʃmənt] *n (a) (military unit)* destacamento *m (b) (objectivity)* imparcialidad *f*; **with an air of d.** con (aire de) despego *or* desapego

detail [dɪ'teɪl] **1** *n (a) (item of information)* detalle *m*; **to pay attention to detail(s)** prestar atención a los pequeños detalles; **to go into d.(s)** entrar en detalles; **in d.** en *or* con detalle; **details** *(information)* detalles *mpl*; *(address and phone number)* datos *mpl*; **minor details** detalles sin importancia *(b) Mil (group of soldiers)* piquete *m*, cuadrilla *f*

   2 *vt (a) (describe)* detallar *(b) Mil* **to d. sb to do sth** encomendar a alguien hacer algo

detailed ['diːteɪld] *adj (account, description)* detallado(a)

detain [dɪ'teɪn] *vt (suspect)* detener; **such details need not d. us** no deberíamos entretenernos en estos detalles

detainee [diːteɪ'niː] *n* prisionero(a) *m,f or* preso(a) *m,f* político(a)

detect [dɪ'tekt] *vt (of person)* percibir; *(of machine)* detectar; *(source of a problem)* identificar, hallar

detectable [dɪ'tektəbəl] *adj (by person)* perceptible; *(by machine, device)* detectable

detection [dɪ'tekʃən] *n (of mines, planes)* detección *f*; *(by detective)* investigación *f*; **to escape d.** no ser detectado(a)

detective [dɪ'tektɪv] *n* detective *mf*; **d. story** relato *m* detectivesco; **d. work** investigación *f*

detector [dɪ'tektə(r)] *n (device)* detector *m*

détente, detente [deɪ'tɒnt] *n* distensión *f (entre países)*

detention [dɪ'tenʃən] *n (a) Law* detención *f*, arresto *m*; **in d.** bajo arresto; **d. center** *or* **home** centro *m* de internamiento *or* reclusión de menores *(b) Sch* **to get d.** = ser castigado a quedarse en el colegio después de terminadas las clases

deter [dɪ'tɜː(r)] *(pt & pp* **deterred)** *vt* disuadir (**from** de); **to d. sb from doing sth** disuadir a alguien de que haga algo

detergent [dɪ'tɜːdʒənt] *n* detergente *m*

deteriorate [dɪ'tɪərɪəreɪt] *vi (situation, health, relations)* deteriorarse; *(weather)* empeorar

deterioration [dɪtɪərɪə'reɪʃən] *n (of situation, health, relations)* deterioro *m*; *(of weather)* empeoramiento *m*

determination [dɪtɜːmɪ'neɪʃən] *n (resoluteness)* decisión *f*, determinación *f*

determine [dɪ'tɜːmɪn] *vt (a) (decide)* decidir, resolver; **to d. to do sth** tomar la determinación de hacer algo *(b) (cause, date)* determinar

determined [dɪ'tɜːmɪnd] *adj* decidido(a), resuelto(a); **to be d. to do sth** estar decidido(a) a hacer algo

determining [dɪ'tɜːmɪnɪŋ] *adj (factor, influence)* determinante, decisivo(a)

deterrent [dɪ'terənt] **1** *n* elemento *m* de disuasión; **to act as a d.** tener un efecto disuasorio

   2 *adj (effect)* disuasivo(a), disuasorio(a)

detest [dɪ'test] *vt* detestar

dethrone [di:'θrəʊn] *vt* destronar

detonate ['detəneɪt] **1** *vt (bomb, explosive)* explosionar, hacer explotar
  2 *vi* detonar, explotar

detonation [detə'neɪʃən] *n* detonación *f*

detonator ['detəneɪtə(r)] *n* detonador *m*

detour ['di:tʊə(r)] *n* desvío *m*; *(diversion of traffic)* desviación *f*; **to make a d.** dar un rodeo

detoxification [di:tɒksɪfɪ'keɪʃən], *Fam* **detox** ['di:tɒks] *n* desintoxicación *f*; **d. center/program** centro *m*/programa *m* de desintoxicación

detoxify [di:'tɒksɪfaɪ] *vt (person)* desintoxicar; *(substance)* purificar, eliminar la toxicidad de

▸**detract from** [dɪ'trækt] *vt insep* disminuir, mermar; *(achievement, contribution)* restar importancia *or* valor a; **the oil refinery detracts from the beauty of the place** la refinería de petróleo resta belleza al lugar

detraction [dɪ'trækʃən] *n* detracción *f*

detractor [dɪ'træktə(r)] *n* detractor(ora) *m,f*

detriment ['detrɪmənt] *n* **to the d. of...** en detrimento de...; **without d. to...** sin perjuicio para...

detrimental [detrɪ'mentəl] *adj* perjudicial (**to** para); **to have a d. effect on** perjudicar

detritus [dɪ'traɪtəs] *n* detrito *m*

deuce [dju:s] *n (in tennis)* deuce *m*, cuarenta *m* iguales

Deutschmark ['dɔɪtʃmɑːk] *n Formerly* marco *m* alemán

devaluation [di:væljʊ'eɪʃən] *n* devaluación *f*

devalue [di:'vælju:] *vt* **(a)** *(currency)* devaluar **(b)** *(person, achievements, efforts)* restar mérito a

devastate ['devəsteɪt] *vt (crops, village)* devastar; *Fam* **I was devastated by the news** la noticia me dejó consternado *or* desolado

devastating ['devəsteɪtɪŋ] *adj (storm, bombardment)* devastador(ora); *(news)* desolador(ora); *(argument, criticism)* demoledor(ora); *(charm, beauty)* arrollador(ora)

devastatingly ['devəsteɪtɪŋlɪ] *adv* **d. effective** de efectos devastadores; **d. beautiful/handsome** de una belleza arrolladora

devastation [devəs'teɪʃən] *n* devastación *f*

develop [dɪ'veləp] **1** *vt* **(a)** *(theory, argument, design)* desarrollar; *(skills)* perfeccionar **(b)** *(region)* desarrollar; *(site)* urbanizar; **developed countries** países *mpl* desarrollados **(c)** *(acquire) (infection)* contraer; *(habit)* adquirir; **to d. a liking for sth** tomar afición a algo; **to d. a taste for sth** agarrarle *or Esp* cogerle el gusto a algo **(d)** *Phot* revelar
  2 *vi* **(a)** *(body, faculties, region, trade)* desarrollarse; **to d. into sth** transformarse *or* convertirse en algo **(b)** *(become apparent)* surgir

developer [dɪ'veləpə(r)] *n* **(a)** *(builders)* promotor(ora) *m,f* inmobiliario(a) **(b)** *Phot* revelador *m*, líquido *m* de revelado

developing [dɪ'veləpɪŋ] *adj (region, country)* en (vías de) desarrollo; *(crisis)* creciente

development [dɪ'veləpmənt] *n* **(a)** *(growth, expansion)* desarrollo *m*; **d. aid** ayuda *f* al desarrollo; *Econ* **d. potential** potencial *m* de explotación **(b)** *(progress, change)* cambio *m*, variación *f*; **recent developments in the industry** la evolución reciente de la industria; **there have been some interesting developments** se han dado novedades interesantes; **to await further developments** esperar a ver cómo se desarrolla la situación; **the latest developments in medical research** los últimos avances de la investigación médica

developmental [dɪveləp'mentəl] *adj* de desarrollo

deviance ['di:vɪəns] *n* desviación *f*

deviant ['di:vɪənt] *adj* desviado(a), anómalo(a)

deviate ['di:vɪeɪt] *vi* desviarse (**from** de)

deviation [di:vɪ'eɪʃən] *n* desviación *f* (**from** de)

device [dɪ'vaɪs] *n* **(a)** *(for measuring, processing, cutting)* aparato *m*; *(for safety, security)* dispositivo *m*; **an explosive d.** un artefacto explosivo **(b)** *(method, scheme)* estratagema *f*; **to leave sb to his own devices** dejar a alguien que se las arregle solo(a)

devil ['devəl] *n* **(a)** diablo *m*, demonio *m*; **the D.** el diablo *or* demonio; **poor d.!** ¡pobre diablo!; **you little d.!** *(to child)* ¡granujilla!; **you lucky d.!** ¡qué suerte tienes!; *Culin* **d.'s food cake** pastel *m* de chocolate
  (b) *Fam (for emphasis)* **what the d. are you doing?** ¿qué diablos *or* demonios estás haciendo?; **how the d....?** ¿cómo diablos *or* demonios...?; **we had a d. of a job moving it** sudamos tinta para moverlo
  (c) *(idioms)* **he's a bit of a d.** *(daring, reckless)* no se corta un pelo; *Fam* **go on, be a d.!** ¡venga pues, date el gusto!; **to be (caught) between the d. and the deep blue sea** estar entre la espada y la pared; **talk of the d....** hablando del rey de Roma...; *Prov* **better the d. you know (than the d. you don't)** más vale lo malo conocido (que lo bueno por conocer); **(to play) d.'s advocate** (hacer de) abogado *m* del diablo

devilish ['devəlɪʃ] *adj* diabólico(a)

devil-may-care ['devəlmeɪ'keə(r)] *adj* despreocupado(a)

devious ['di:vɪəs] *adj (person, mind)* retorcido(a); *(route)* sinuoso(a); **that's a bit d. of you!** ¡qué maquiavélico eres!

deviously ['di:vɪəslɪ] *adv* maquiavélicamente

devise [dɪ'vaɪz] *vt* idear

devoid [dɪ'vɔɪd] *adj* desprovisto(a) (**of** de)

devolution [di:və'lu:ʃən] *n Pol* transferencia *f* de poder político, traspaso *m* de competencias; **they want d.** quieren la autonomía (política)

devolve [dɪ'vɒlv] **1** *vt (functions, powers)* transferir, traspasar
  2 *vi* recaer (**on** en)

devote [dɪ'vəʊt] *vt (time, money)* dedicar (**to** a); **to d. oneself to** consagrarse a

devoted [dɪ'vəʊtɪd] *adj (father)* muy afectuoso(a); *(admirer)* devoto(a), ferviente; **they are d. to each other** están muy unidos; **after years of d. service** tras años de abnegada dedicación

devotee [devəʊ'ti:] *n (of person, idea)* adepto(a) *m,f*; *(of sport, music)* fanático(a) *m,f*, entusiasta *mf*

devotion [dɪ'vəʊʃən] *n (to friend, family)* devoción *f*; *(to cause, leader of party)* dedicación *f*, entrega *f*; *(to god, saint)* devoción *f*; **devotions** *(prayers)* oraciones *fpl*

devour [dɪ'vaʊə(r)] *vt also Fig* devorar

devout [dɪ'vaʊt] *adj (person)* devoto(a); *(wish)* sincero(a)

dew [dju:] *n* rocío *m*

dewy-eyed [dju:ɪ'aɪd] *adj (loving)* cándido(a), inocente, sentimental; *(naive)* ingenuo(a), candoroso(a)

dexterity [deks'terɪtɪ] *n (mental, physical)* destreza *f*

dext(e)rous ['dekstrəs] *adj* diestro(a), hábil

DG [di:'dʒi:] *n (abbr* **director-general**) director(ora) *m,f* general

DHTML [di:eɪtʃti:em'el] *n Comptr (abbr* **Dynamic Hypertext Transfer Protocol**) DHTML *m*

diabetes [daɪə'bi:ti:z] *n* diabetes *f inv*

diabetic [daɪə'betɪk] **1** *n* diabético(a) *m,f*; **d. chocolate** chocolate *m* para diabéticos
  2 *adj* diabético(a)

diabolic [daɪə'bɒlɪk] *adj* diabólico(a), demoníaco(a)

diabolical [daɪə'bɒlɪkəl] *adj (evil)* diabólico(a), demoníaco(a)

diadem ['daɪədem] *n* diadema *f*

diagnose ['daɪəgnəʊz] *vt also Fig* diagnosticar

diagnosis [daɪəg'nəʊsɪs] *(pl* **diagnoses** [daɪəg'nəʊsi:z]) *n Med & Fig* diagnóstico *m*; **to make** *or* **give a d.** emitir un diagnóstico

diagnostic [daɪəg'nɒstɪk] **1** *adj* diagnóstico(a)

2 *n (symptom)* síntoma *m*, indicador *m*

diagonal [daɪˈægənəl] *n & adj* diagonal *f*

diagram [ˈdaɪəgræm] *n* diagrama *m*

dial [ˈdaɪəl] **1** *n (of clock)* esfera *f; (of radio)* dial *m; (of phone)* disco *m;* **d. tone** tono *m (de marcar)*
    2 *vt (pt & pp* **dialed)** *(phone number)* marcar, *Andes, CSur* discar

dialect [ˈdaɪəlekt] *n* dialecto *m*

dialectic(al) [daɪəˈlektɪk(əl)] *adj* dialéctico(a)

dialectics [daɪəˈlektɪks] *n* dialéctica *f*

dialogue, dialog [ˈdaɪəlɒg] *n* diálogo *m; Pol* **to enter into a d.** establecer un diálogo; *Comptr* **d. box** cuadro *m* de diálogo

dial-up [ˈdaɪlʌp] *n Comptr* conexión *f* telefónica *or; Spec* por línea conmutada

dialysis [daɪˈælɪsɪs] *n Med* diálisis *f inv*

diameter [daɪˈæmɪtə(r)] *n* diámetro *m;* **the wheel is 60 inches in d.** la rueda tiene 60 pulgadas de diámetro

diametrically [daɪəˈmetrɪklɪ] *adv* **to be d. opposed to** ser diametralmente opuesto(a) a

diamond [ˈdaɪəmənd] *n* **(a)** *(gem)* diamante *m; (shape)* rombo *m;* **diamonds** *(in cards)* diamantes *mpl;* **d. jubilee** (celebración *m* del) sexagésimo *m* aniversario; **d. necklace** collar *m* de diamantes; **d. ring** sortija *f* de diamantes **(b)** *(in baseball)* diamante *m*

diamondback [ˈdaɪəməndbæk] *n* **(a)** *(snake)* serpiente *f* de cascabel *(con manchas en forma de diamante)* **(b)** *(turtle)* tortuga *f* diamante

diaper [ˈdaɪəpə(r)] *n* pañal *m*

diaphanous [daɪˈæfənəs] *adj* diáfano(a)

diaphragm [ˈdaɪəfræm] *n* diafragma *m*

diarist [ˈdaɪərɪst] *n* escritor(ora) *m,f* de diarios

diarrhea [daɪəˈrɪə] *n* diarrea *f*

diary [ˈdaɪərɪ] *n (as record)* diario *m; (for appointments)* agenda *f;* **to keep a d.** llevar un diario

diatribe [ˈdaɪətraɪb] *n* diatriba *f* **(against** contra *or* en contra de)

dice [daɪs] **1** *n (pl* **dice)** *(in game)* dado *m;* **to shoot d.** jugar a los dados; *Fam* **no d.!** ¡no ha habido suerte!
    2 *vt (meat, potatoes)* cortar en dados
    3 *vi* **to d. with death** jugarse la piel *or Am* la vida

dicey [ˈdaɪsɪ] *adj Fam* arriesgado(a)

dichotomy [daɪˈkɒtəmɪ] *n* dicotomía *f*

dick [dɪk] *n* **(a)** *Fam (detective)* sabueso(a) *m,f* **(b)** *Vulg (penis) Esp* polla *f, esp Am* verga *f, Méx* pito *m, RP* pija *f*

dickens [dɪkɪnz] *n* **what the d.?** ¿qué diablos?

dickey bird, dicky bird [ˈdɪkɪbɜːd] *n (in children's language)* pío pío *m*, pajarito *m*

dictate 1 *n* [ˈdɪkteɪt] **she followed the dictates of her conscience** siguió los dictados de su conciencia
    2 *vt* [dɪkˈteɪt] **(a)** *(letter, passage)* dictar **(b)** *(determine) (choice)* imponer, dictar; *(conditions)* imponer; **circumstances d. that we postpone the meeting** las circunstancias obligan a aplazar la reunión
    3 *vi* **(a)** *(dictate text)* dictar **(b)** *(give orders)* **to d. to sb** dar órdenes a alguien; **I won't be dictated to!** ¡no voy a permitir que me den órdenes!

dictation [dɪkˈteɪʃən] *n* dictado *m;* **to take d.** escribir al dictado; *Sch* **to do d.** hacer un dictado

dictator [dɪkˈteɪtə(r)] *n* dictador(ora) *m,f*

dictatorial [dɪktəˈtɔːrɪəl] *adj* dictatorial

dictatorship [dɪkˈteɪtəʃɪp] *n* dictadura *f*

diction [ˈdɪkʃən] *n* dicción *f*

dictionary [ˈdɪkʃənərɪ] *n* diccionario *m*

dictum [ˈdɪktəm] *(pl* **dicta** [ˈdɪktə] *or* **dictums)** *n Formal* **(a)** *(statement)* sentencia *f*, aforismo *m; (maxim)* máxima *f* **(b)** *Law* dictamen *m*

did [dɪd] *pt of* **do**

didactic [dɪˈdæktɪk] *adj* didáctico(a)

diddle [ˈdɪdəl] *vt Fam* tangar, timar; **they diddled him out of the money** le engatusaron para sacarle el dinero

didn't [ˈdɪdənt] = **did not**

die¹ [daɪ] *n* **(a)** *(pl* **dice** [daɪs]) *(in game)* dado *m; Fig* **the d. is cast** la suerte está echada **(b)** *(pl* **dies** [daɪz]) *(mold for casting or stamping)* cuño *m*, troquel *m*

die²1 *vi* morir; **she is dying** se está muriendo; **to d. from** *or* **of one's wounds** morir de las heridas recibidas; **to d. hard** *(habit, rumor)* ser difícil de eliminar; *Fam* **never say d.!** ¡nunca te des por vencido!; *Fam* **I nearly died (laughing/of shame)** casi me muero (de risa/de vergüenza *or CAm, Carib, Col, Méx* de pena); *Fam* **to be dying to do sth** morirse de ganas de hacer algo; *Fam* **I'm dying for a cigarette** me muero de ganas de fumar un cigarrillo; **the engine died on me** se me estropeó el motor; **their love died** su amor se extinguió
    2 *vt* **to d. a natural/violent death** morir de muerte natural/violenta; *Fig* **his proposal died the death** su propuesta no llegó a cuajar

▸**die away** *vi (sound, voice)* desvanecerse

▸**die down** *vi (fire)* remitir; *(wind)* calmarse; *(sound)* atenuarse; *(excitement, scandal)* apaciguarse

▸**die off** *vi* **the few remaining veterans were dying off** iban muriendo los pocos veteranos que quedaban

▸**die out** *vi (family, species)* extinguirse, desaparecer

die-hard [ˈdaɪhɑːd] *n & adj* intransigente *mf*

diesel [ˈdiːzəl] **1** *n (fuel)* gasoil *m*, gasóleo *m; (railroad engine)* locomotora *f* diesel; *(car)* coche *m or Am* carro *m or RP* auto *m* (de motor) diesel
    2 *adj (engine, train)* diesel; **d. oil** *or* **fuel** gasoil *m*, gasóleo *m*

diet [ˈdaɪət] **1** *n (habitual food)* dieta *f; (restricted food)* dieta *f*, régimen *m;* **to be/go on a d.** estar/ponerse a dieta *or* régimen
    2 *vi* hacer dieta *or* régimen
    3 *adj (low-calorie)* light, bajo(a) en calorías

dietary [ˈdaɪətərɪ] *adj* dietético(a); **d. fiber** fibra *f* alimenticia

dietician [daɪəˈtɪʃən] *n* especialista *mf* en dietética, *Am* dietista *mf*

differ [ˈdɪfə(r)] *vi* **(a)** *(be different)* ser distinto(a) *or* diferente **(from** de); **to d. in size/color** diferenciarse por el tamaño/color **(b)** *(disagree)* discrepar **(with sb/about sth** de alguien/en algo); **I beg to d.** me veo obligado a discrepar; **to agree to d.** reconocer mutuamente las discrepancias

difference [ˈdɪfərəns] *n* **(a)** *(disparity)* diferencia *f* **(between** entre); **that doesn't make any d.** eso no cambia nada; **it makes no d. (to me)** (me) da igual *or* lo mismo; **that makes all the d.** eso cambia mucho las cosas; **a car with a d.** un coche distinto a los demás; **to pay the d.** pagar la diferencia; **a d. of opinion** una diferencia de opiniones **(b)** *(disagreement)* diferencia *f*, discrepancia *f;* **we have to settle our differences** tenemos que resolver nuestras diferencias

different [ˈdɪfərənt] *adj* **(a)** *(not the same)* diferente, distinto(a); **that's quite a d. matter** eso es una cuestión aparte; **she feels a d. person** se siente otra (persona); **he just wants to be d.** sólo busca ser diferente **(b)** *(various)* diferente, distinto(a); **I spoke to d. people about it** he hablado de ello con varias personas

differential [dɪfəˈrenʃəl] **1** *n* diferencial *m;* **wage** *or* **pay differentials** diferencias *fpl* salariales
    2 *adj* diferencial; *Math* **d. calculus** cálculo *m* diferencial; *Aut* **d. gear** diferencial *m*

differentiate [dɪfəˈrenʃɪeɪt] **1** *vt* diferenciar, distinguir **(from** de)
    2 *vi* diferenciar, distinguir **(between** entre)

differently [ˈdɪfərəntlɪ] *adv* de forma diferente; *Euph* **d. abled** discapacitado(a)

difficult ['dɪfɪkəlt] *adj (task, problem)* difícil; **he's d. to get on with** no es fácil llevarse bien con él; **you're just being d.** no estás siendo razonable; **to make life d. for sb** complicarle la vida a alguien; **to make things d. for sb** poner las cosas difíciles a alguien

difficulty ['dɪfɪkəltɪ] *n* (a) *(trouble)* dificultad *f*; **to have d. in doing sth** tener dificultad en hacer algo; **to be in d.** *or* **difficulties** estar en dificultades; **with d.** con dificultad (b) *(obstacle, problem)* dificultad *f*, problema *m*; **to make difficulties (for sb)** crear dificultades (a alguien)

diffidence ['dɪfɪdəns] *n* pudor *m*, retraimiento *m*

diffident ['dɪfɪdənt] *adj* pudoroso(a), retraído(a)

diffuse 1 *adj* [dɪ'fjuːs] *(light)* difuso(a); *(literary style)* difuso(a), prolijo(a); *(sense of unease)* vago(a), difuso(a)
  2 *vt* [dɪ'fjuːz] difundir
  3 *vi* difundirse

dig [dɪg] **1** *n* (a) *(in archeology)* excavación *f* (b) *(poke)* golpe *m*; **a d. in the ribs** *(with elbow)* un codazo en las costillas (c) *(remark)* pulla *f*; **to get a d. in at sb, to have a d. at sb** lanzar una pulla a alguien
  2 *vt (pt & pp* **dug** [dʌg]) (a) *(hole, grave)* cavar; *(garden)* cavar en; *(well)* excavar; **the dog dug a hole by the tree** el perro escarbó *or* hizo un agujero junto al árbol; *Fig* **she is digging her own grave** está cavando su propia tumba (b) *(thrust)* **to d. sth into sth** clavar algo en algo (c) *Fam (like)* **she really digs that kind of music** ese tipo de música le gusta un montón
  3 *vi* (a) *(person)* cavar (**for** en búsqueda *or Esp* busca de); *(animal)* escarbar; *(in archeology)* excavar (b) *Fam (understand)* **you d.?** ¿lo pillas?

▶**dig in 1** *vt sep* **to d. one's heels in** emperrarse; **to d. oneself in** *(soldiers)* atrincherarse
  2 *vi* (a) *Fam (start eating)* ponerse a comer; **d. in!** ¡a comer! (b) *(soldiers)* atrincherarse

▶**dig out** *vt sep* (a) *(bullet, splinter)* extraer; *(person) (from ruins, snow drift)* rescatar (b) *Fam (find) (information)* encontrar; *(object)* rescatar

▶**dig up** *vt sep* (a) *(plant)* arrancar, desarraigar; *(treasure, body)* desenterrar; *(road)* levantar (b) *Fam (find) (information)* desenterrar, sacar a la luz; *(person)* sacar

digest 1 *n* ['daɪdʒest] *(summary)* resumen *m*
  2 *vt* [dɪ'dʒest] *also Fig* digerir

digestible [dɪ'dʒestəbəl] *adj* digerible; **to be easily d.** digerirse fácilmente

digestion [dɪ'dʒestʃən] *n* digestión *f*

digestive [dɪ'dʒestɪv] *adj* digestivo(a); **d. system** aparato *m* digestivo; **d. tract** tubo *m* digestivo

digger ['dɪgə(r)] *n* excavadora *f*

digicam ['dɪdʒɪkæm] *n* cámara *f* digital

digit ['dɪdʒɪt] *n (finger)* dedo *m*; *Math* dígito *m*

digital ['dɪdʒɪtəl] *adj (watch, computer)* digital; **d. audio tape** cinta *f* digital (de audio); **d. camera** cámara *f* digital; **d. radio** radio *f* digital; **d. recording** grabación *f* digital; **d. television** televisión *f* digital

digitization [dɪdʒɪtaɪ'zeɪʃən] *n Comptr* digitalización *f*

digitize ['dɪdʒɪtaɪz] *vt & vi Comptr* digitalizar, escanear

dignified ['dɪgnɪfaɪd] *adj* solemne

dignify ['dɪgnɪfaɪ] *vt* dignificar

dignitary ['dɪgnɪtərɪ] *n Formal* dignatario(a) *m,f*

dignity ['dɪgnɪtɪ] *n* dignidad *f*; **she considered it beneath her d. to respond** le pareció que responder supondría una degradación

digress [daɪ'gres] *vi* divagar; **..., but I d.** ..., pero me estoy alejando del tema

digression [daɪ'greʃən] *n* digresión *f*

dike [daɪk] *n* (a) *(barrier)* dique *m* (b) *very Fam (lesbian)* tortillera *f*

dilapidated [dɪ'læpɪdeɪtɪd] *adj (building)* derruido(a); *(car)* destartalado(a); **to be d.** estar derruido(a)/destartalado(a)

dilapidation [dɪlæpɪ'deɪʃən] *n (of building, car)* ruina *f*, grave deterioro *m*

dilate [daɪ'leɪt] **1** *vt* dilatar
  2 *vi* dilatarse

dilation [daɪ'leɪʃən] *n* dilatación *f*

dilatory ['dɪlətərɪ] *adj Formal* dilatorio(a); **to be d. in doing sth** hacer algo con dilación

dilemma [daɪ'lemə] *n* dilema *m*, disyuntiva *f*; **to be in a d.** estar en un dilema

dilettante [dɪlɪ'tɑːntɪ] *n* diletante *mf*

diligence ['dɪlɪdʒəns] *n* diligencia *f*

diligent ['dɪlɪdʒənt] *adj* diligente

diligently ['dɪlɪdʒəntlɪ] *adv* con diligencia, diligentemente

dill [dɪl] *n* eneldo *m*

dillydally ['dɪlɪdælɪ] *vi Fam (loiter)* entretenerse; *(hesitate)* titubear, vacilar

dilute [daɪ'luːt] **1** *adj* diluido(a)
  2 *vt (wine, acid)* diluir; *Fig (policy, proposal)* debilitar, restar eficacia a; **d. to taste** diluir al gusto de cada uno

dilution [daɪ'luːʃən] *n Fig (of policy, proposal)* debilitamiento *m*

dim [dɪm] **1** *adj* (a) *(light, outline)* tenue; *(memory)* vago(a); *(eyesight)* débil; *(chance, hope)* remoto(a), lejano(a); **to take a d. view of sth** desaprobar algo (b) *Fam (stupid)* tonto(a), corto(a) de alcances, *Am* sonso(a), *Am* zonzo(a)
  2 *vt (pt & pp* **dimmed**) *(light)* atenuar
  3 *vi (light)* atenuarse

dime [daɪm] *n* = moneda de diez centavos; *Fam* **it's not worth a d.** no vale un centavo *or Esp* un duro; *Fam* **they're a d. a dozen** los hay a patadas; **d. store** (tienda *f* de) baratillo *m*, *Esp* (tienda *f* de) todo a cien *m*

dimension [daɪ'menʃən] *n* dimensión *f*

diminish [dɪ'mɪnɪʃ] **1** *vt* disminuir; *Law* **diminished responsibility** responsabilidad *f* atenuada
  2 *vi* disminuir

diminishing [dɪ'mɪnɪʃɪŋ] *adj* decreciente; **law of d. returns** ley *f* de los rendimientos decrecientes

diminution [dɪmɪ'njuːʃən] *n Formal* disminución *f*; **there has been no d. in his powers as a novelist** sus grandes facultades como novelista no se han visto mermadas

diminutive [dɪ'mɪnjʊtɪv] **1** *n Gram* diminutivo *m*
  2 *adj* diminuto(a), minúsculo(a)

dimly ['dɪmlɪ] *adv (remember)* vagamente; *(see)* con dificultad; **d. lit** en penumbra, con luz tenue

dimmer ['dɪmə(r)] *n* (a) *(for lamp)* **d. (switch)** potenciómetro *m*, regulador *m or* modulador *m* de (potencia de) luz (b) *US Aut* **dimmers** *(headlights)* luces *fpl* cortas or de cruce; *(parking lights)* luces *fpl* de estacionamiento

dimple ['dɪmpəl] *n* hoyuelo *m*

dimwit ['dɪmwɪt] *n Fam* estúpido(a) *m,f*, idiota *mf*

din [dɪn] *n (of traffic, machinery)* estrépito *m*; *(of people)* jaleo *m*, alboroto *m*

dine [daɪn] *vi* cenar

▶**dine out** *vi* cenar fuera; *Fig* **he'll be able to d. out on that story for weeks!** esa historia le dará tema de conversación para varias semanas

diner ['daɪnə(r)] *n* (a) *(person)* comensal *mf* (b) *(restaurant)* restaurante *m* barato

dingbat ['dɪŋbæt] *n* (a) *Fam* chalado(a) *m,f* (b) *Comptr & Typ* *(carácter m)* dingbat *m*

ding-dong ['dɪŋ'dɒŋ] **1** *n* (a) *(sound)* din don *m* (b) *Fam (fight)* trifulca *f*
  2 *adj (argument, contest)* reñido(a)

dinghy ['dɪŋ(g)ɪ] *n* (**rubber**) **d.** lancha *f* neumática; (**sailing**) **d.** bote *m* de vela

dinginess ['dɪndʒɪnɪs] *n (of room, street)* sordidez *f*; *(of color)* lo sucio, lo deslustrado

dingo ['dɪŋgəʊ] (pl **dingoes**) n dingo m

dingy ['dɪndʒɪ] adj (room, street) sórdido(a); (color) sucio(a), deslustrado(a)

dining ['daɪnɪŋ] n **d. car** (on train) vagón m restaurante; **d. hall** (in school) comedor m; **d. room** comedor m; **d. table** mesa f de comedor

dinky, dinkie ['dɪŋkɪ] adj Pej (insignificant) vulgar, del montón

dinner ['dɪnə(r)] n (midday meal) comida f, almuerzo m; (evening meal) cena f; **to have d.** (at midday) comer, almorzar; (in evening) cenar; **what's for d.?** (midday meal) ¿qué hay de comida?; (evening meal) ¿qué hay de cena?; **d. hour** (at school) hora f de comer; **d. jacket** esmoquin m; **d. party** cena f (en casa con invitados); **d. service** vajilla f

dinnertime ['dɪnətaɪm] n (for midday meal) hora f de comer; (for evening meal) hora f de cenar

dinosaur ['daɪnəsɔ:(r)] n also Fig dinosaurio m

dint [dɪnt] n **by d. of** a fuerza de

diocese ['daɪəsɪs] n Rel diócesis f inv

diode ['daɪəʊd] n Elec diodo m

dioxide [daɪ'ɒksaɪd] n Chem dióxido m

dip [dɪp] **1** n (**a**) (in road) bajada f, pendiente f; (in prices) caída f, descenso m (**b**) Fam (swim) chapuzón m, baño m; **to go for a d.** ir a darse un chapuzón (**c**) (sauce) salsa f fría (para mojar aperitivos)

2 vt (pt & pp **dipped**) (**a**) (immerse) meter (**in(to)** en); (food) mojar (**in(to)** en) (**b**) (lower) bajar

3 vi (road) bajar, descender un poco; (prices) caer, descender; **the sun dipped below the horizon** el sol se hundió en el horizonte

▸**dip into** vt insep (savings, capital) recurrir a, echar mano de; (book, subject) echar un vistazo a

diphtheria [dɪf'θɪərɪə] n Med difteria f

diphthong ['dɪfθɒŋ] n Ling diptongo m

diploma [dɪ'pləʊmə] n diploma m, título m

diplomacy [dɪ'pləʊməsɪ] n also Fig diplomacia f

diplomat ['dɪpləmæt] n diplomático(a) m,f

diplomatic [dɪplə'mætɪk] adj also Fig diplomático(a); **d. corps** cuerpo m diplomático; **d. immunity** inmunidad f diplomática; **d. pouch** valija f diplomática

dipper ['dɪpə(r)] n (**a**) (ladle) cucharón m, cazo m (**b**) **the Big D.** (constellation) la Osa Mayor

dippy ['dɪpɪ] adj Fam (mad) locuelo(a), chiflado(a)

dipsomania [dɪpsə'meɪnɪə] n dipsomanía f

dipsomaniac [dɪpsə'meɪnɪæk] n dipsómano(a) m,f, dipso-maníaco(a) m,f

dipstick ['dɪpstɪk] n (**a**) Aut varilla f del aceite (**b**) Fam (idiot) idiota mf, imbécil mf

dire ['daɪə(r)] adj (consequences) terrible; Fam (bad) chungo(a); **to be in d. need of sth** tener una necesidad acuciante de algo; **to be in d. straits** estar en un serio apuro

direct [dɪ'rekt, daɪ'rekt] **1** adj directo(a); **the d. opposite** justamente lo contrario; **to be a d. descendant of sb** ser descendiente directo(a) de alguien; **to score a d. hit** dar en el blanco, hacer diana; Elec **d. current** corriente f continua; Com **d. mail** propaganda f por correo, correo m directo; **d. marketing** marketing m directo; Gram **d. object** complemento m or objeto m directo; Pol **d. rule** gobierno m directo; Com **d. selling** venta f directa; Gram **d. speech** estilo m directo; Fin **d. taxation** impuestos mpl directos

2 adv (travel, write) directamente; (broadcast) en directo

3 vt (**a**) (remark, gaze, effort) dirigir (**at** a); **can you d. me to the station?** ¿podría indicarme cómo llegar a la estación? (**b**) (company, traffic, movie) dirigir (**c**) (instruct) **to d. sb to do sth** mandar or indicar a alguien que haga algo; **as directed** según las instrucciones

direction [dɪ'rekʃən] n (**a**) (way) dirección f; **in the d. of...**

en dirección a...; **in every d., in all directions** en todas direcciones; Fig **a step in the right d.** un paso hacia el buen camino or en la dirección correcta (**b**) (of movie, play, project) dirección f; **under the d. of...** dirigido(a) por... (**c**) **directions** (to place) indicaciones fpl; **he asked me for directions to the station** me preguntó cómo se llegaba a la estación

directive [dɪ'rektɪv] n directiva f; **a Presidential d.** una directiva del presidente

directly [dɪ'rektlɪ, daɪ'rektlɪ] adv (**a**) (to go, write) directamente; **to be d. descended from sb** ser descendiente directo(a) de alguien (**b**) (opposite, above) justo, directamente (**c**) (frankly) (to answer, speak) directamente, abiertamente (**d**) (soon) pronto, en breve; **I'm coming d.** voy ahora mismo; **I'll come d. after I've finished** vendré en cuanto acabe

directness [dɪ'rektnɪs, daɪ'rektnɪs] n franqueza f

director [dɪ'rektə(r)] n (of company, movie) director(ora) m,f; **d.'s chair** silla f plegable de tela, silla f de director

directorate [dɪ'rektərət] n (post) dirección f; (board) consejo m de administración

directorial [dɪrek'tɔ:rɪəl, daɪrek'tɔ:rɪəl] adj Theat & Cin (career, debut) como director(ora); (work) de director(ora)

directorship [dɪ'rektəʃɪp] n dirección f, puesto m de director(ora)

directory [dɪ'rektərɪ] n (of phone numbers) guía f (telefónica), listín m (de teléfonos), Am directorio m de teléfonos; Comptr directorio m; **(street) d.** callejero m; **d. assistance** (servicio m de) información f telefónica

dirge [dɜ:dʒ] n Fam (depressing tune) = canción sombría y aburrida

dirt [dɜ:t] n (**a**) (mud, dust) suciedad f; **to treat sb like d.** tratar a alguien como a un trapo; **dog d.** excremento m de perro (**b**) (soil) tierra f; **d. road** pista f de tierra (**c**) Fam (scandal) **to dig for d. on sb** buscar material comprometedor acerca de alguien

dirt-cheap ['dɜ:t'tʃi:p] adj & adv Fam tirado(a) de precio

dirty ['dɜ:tɪ] **1** adj (**a**) (unclean) sucio(a); **to get d.** ensuciarse, mancharse; also Fig **to get one's hands d.** mancharse las manos; Fig **the party is washing its d. linen in public** el partido está sacando sus propios trapos sucios a la luz pública, RP el partido está sacando los trapitos al sol

(**b**) (unprincipled, ruthless) sucio(a); **it's a d. business** es un asunto sucio; **to give sb a d. look** fulminar a alguien con la mirada; **d. trick** jugarreta f, mala pasada f; **d. tricks campaign** campaña f de descrédito or difamación; also Fig **d. work** trabajo m sucio

(**c**) (obscene) (movie) pornográfico(a); (book, language) obsceno(a), lascivo(a); **to have a d. mind** tener una mente calenturienta; **d. joke** chiste m verde; **d. old man** viejo m verde; **d. word** palabrota f

2 adv (**a**) (fight, play) sucio (**b**) (obscenely) **to talk d.** decir obscenidades

3 vt ensuciar, manchar

disability [dɪsə'bɪlɪtɪ] n discapacidad f, minusvalía f; **d. insurance** seguro m de incapacidad (a corto plazo)

disable [dɪs'eɪbəl] vt (person) discapacitar, incapacitar; (tank, ship) inutilizar; (alarm system) desactivar

disabled [dɪs'eɪbəld] **1** adj discapacitado(a), minusválido(a); **d. restroom** servicio m or Am baño m or Am lavatorio m para minusválidos

2 npl **the d.** los discapacitados or minusválidos

disabuse [dɪsə'bju:z] vt Formal desengañar (**of** de)

disadvantage [dɪsəd'vɑ:ntɪdʒ] **1** n desventaja f, inconve-niente m; **to be at a d.** estar en desventaja; **to put sb at a d.** poner a alguien en desventaja

2 vt perjudicar

disadvantaged [dɪsəd'vɑ:ntɪdʒd] adj desfavorecido(a)

disaffected [dɪsə'fektɪd] *adj* descontento(a)

disaffection [dɪsə'fekʃən] *n* descontento *m*, desapego *m*

disagree [dɪsə'griː] *vi* (**a**) *(have different opinion)* no estar de acuerdo; **to d. with sb** no estar de acuerdo con alguien (**b**) *Euph (quarrel)* tener una discusión, discutir (**c**) *(not correspond) (reports, figures)* no cuadrar, no coincidir (**d**) *(climate, food)* **to d. with sb** sentarle mal a alguien

disagreeable [dɪsə'griːəbəl] *adj* desagradable

disagreement [dɪsə'griːmənt] *n* (**a**) *(failure to agree)* desacuerdo *m*; **to be in d. with sb** estar en desacuerdo con alguien (**b**) *(quarrel)* discusión *f*; **to have a d. with sb** discutir con alguien (**c**) *(discrepancy)* discrepancia *f*

disallow [dɪsə'laʊ] *vt Formal (objection)* rechazar; *(goal)* anular

disappear [dɪsə'pɪə(r)] *vi* desaparecer

disappearance [dɪsə'pɪərəns] *n* desaparición *f*

disappoint [dɪsə'pɔɪnt] *vt (person)* decepcionar, desilusionar; *(hope, ambition)* frustrar, dar al traste con

disappointed [dɪsə'pɔɪntɪd] *adj (person)* decepcionado(a), desilusionado(a); *(hope, ambition)* frustrado(a); **to be d.** *(person)* estar decepcionado(a) *or* desilusionado(a); **she was d. with the book** el libro le decepcionó

disappointing [dɪsə'pɔɪntɪŋ] *adj* decepcionante

disappointingly [dɪsə'pɔɪntɪŋlɪ] *adv* de manera decepcionante; **she got d. low grades** sacó unas notas decepcionantes

disappointment [dɪsə'pɔɪntmənt] *n* decepción *f*, desilusión *f*; **to be a d.** *(person, movie)* ser decepcionante

disapproval [dɪsə'pruːvəl] *n* desaprobación *f*

disapprove [dɪsə'pruːv] *vi* estar en contra, mostrar desaprobación; **to d. of sth** desaprobar algo

disapproving [dɪsə'pruːvɪŋ] *adj (tone, look)* desaprobatorio(a); **to be d. of sth** desaprobar algo

disapprovingly [dɪsə'pruːvɪŋlɪ] *adv* con desaprobación

disarm [dɪs'ɑːm] **1** *vt also Fig* desarmar
2 *vi* desarmarse

disarmament [dɪs'ɑːməmənt] *n* desarme *m*; **d. talks** conversaciones *fpl* para el desarme

disarming [dɪs'ɑːmɪŋ] *adj (smile)* arrebatador(ora)

disarmingly [dɪs'ɑːmɪŋlɪ] *adv* **she's d. honest/friendly** su franqueza/amabilidad te desarma

disarray [dɪsə'reɪ] *n* desorden *m*; **in d.** *(untidy)* en desorden; *(confused)* sumido(a) en el caos

disassemble [dɪsə'sembəl] *vt* desmontar, desarmar

disaster [dɪ'zɑːstə(r)] *n* desastre *m*, catástrofe *f*; **d. area** zona *f* catastrófica; *Cin* **d. movie** película *f* de catástrofes

disastrous [dɪ'zɑːstrəs] *adj* desastroso(a), catastrófico(a)

disavow [dɪsə'vaʊ] *vt Formal* negar, desmentir

disavowal [dɪsə'vaʊæl] *n Formal* desmentido *m*, mentís *m*

disband [dɪs'bænd] **1** *vt* disolver
2 *vi* disolverse

disbar [dɪs'bɑː(r)] *vt Law* expulsar de la abogacía, inhabilitar como abogado(a)

disbelief [dɪsbɪ'liːf] *n* incredulidad *f*; **in d.** con incredulidad

disbelieve [dɪsbɪ'liːv] *vt* no creer, dudar de

disburse [dɪs'bɜːs] *vt Formal* desembolsar

disbursement [dɪs'bɜːsmənt] *n Formal* desembolso *m*

disc = disk

discard [dɪs'kɑːd] *vt (thing, person)* desechar; *(plan, proposal, possibility)* descartar

discern [dɪ'sɜːn] *vt* distinguir, apreciar

discernible [dɪ'sɜːnəbəl] *adj* perceptible; **there is no d. difference** no hay una diferencia apreciable

discerning [dɪ'sɜːnɪŋ] *adj (audience, customer)* entendido(a); *(taste)* cultivado(a)

discernment [dɪ'sɜːnmənt] *n* discernimiento *m*, criterio *m*

discharge 1 *n* ['dɪstʃɑːdʒ] (**a**) *(of patient)* alta *f*; *(of prisoner)* puesta *f* en libertad; *(of soldier)* licencia *f* (**b**) *(of firearm)* descarga *f*, disparo *m* (**c**) *(of gas, chemical)* emisión *f*; *(of pus, fluid)* supuración *f*
2 *vt* [dɪs'tʃɑːdʒ] (**a**) *(patient)* dar el alta a; *(prisoner)* poner en libertad; *(employee)* despedir; *(soldier)* licenciar (**b**) *(firearm)* descargar, disparar (**c**) *(gas, chemical)* emitir; *(pus, fluid)* supurar (**d**) *(duty)* cumplir; *(debt)* saldar; *(fine)* abonar

disciple [dɪ'saɪpəl] *n* discípulo(a) *m,f*

disciplinary ['dɪsɪplɪnərɪ] *adj* disciplinario(a); **to take d. action against sb** abrirle a alguien un expediente disciplinario

discipline ['dɪsɪplɪn] **1** *n (control, academic subject)* disciplina *f*; **to keep** *or* **maintain d.** guardar la disciplina
2 *vt (punish)* castigar; *(train)* disciplinar; **to d. oneself** disciplinarse

disclaim [dɪs'kleɪm] *vt (deny)* negar

disclaimer [dɪs'kleɪmə(r)] *n* negación *f* de responsabilidad; **to issue a d.** hacer público un comunicado negando toda responsabilidad

disclose [dɪs'kləʊz] *vt* revelar

disclosure [dɪs'kləʊʒə(r)] *n* revelación *f*

disco ['dɪskəʊ] *(pl discos)* *n* discoteca *f*

discography [dɪs'kɒɡrəfɪ] *n* discografía *f*

discolor [dɪs'kʌlə(r)] *vt (fade)* decolorar; *(stain)* teñir, manchar

discomfiture [dɪs'kʌmfɪtʃə(r)] *n Formal* turbación *f*, desconcierto *m*

discomfort [dɪs'kʌmfət] *n (lack of comfort)* incomodidad *f*; *(pain)* molestia *f*, dolor *m*; **to be in d.** sufrir, pasarlo mal

disconcerting [dɪskən'sɜːtɪŋ] *adj (causing confusion, embarrassment)* desconcertante; *(causing anxiety)* preocupante

disconcertingly [dɪskən'sɜːtɪŋlɪ] *adv* de manera desconcertante

disconnect [dɪskə'nekt] *vt (gas, electricity, phone)* cortar, desconectar; *(machine, appliance)* desenchufar, desconectar; **we've been disconnected** nos han cortado el gas/la electricidad/el teléfono

disconsolate [dɪs'kɒnsələt] *adj* desconsolado(a) (**at** por); **to be d. (at)** estar desconsolado(a) (por)

disconsolately [dɪs'kɒnsələtlɪ] *adv* desconsoladamente

discontent [dɪskən'tent] *n* descontento *m*

discontented [dɪskən'tentɪd] *adj* descontento(a); **to be d.** estar descontento(a)

discontinue [dɪskən'tɪnjuː] *vt* suspender, interrumpir; *Com* **discontinued line** restos *mpl* de serie

discontinuous [dɪskən'tɪnjʊəs] *adj (line)* discontinuo(a); *(process, run of events)* intermitente

discord ['dɪskɔːd] *n* discordia *f*

discordant [dɪs'kɔːdənt] *adj (opinions, sound)* discordante, discorde

discotheque ['dɪskətek] *n* discoteca *f*

discount 1 *n* ['dɪskaʊnt] descuento *m*, rebaja *f*; **at a d.** con descuento; **d. card** tarjeta *f* *or* carné *m* de fidelización
2 *vt* (**a**) *(price, goods)* rebajar (**b**) [dɪs'kaʊnt] *(suggestion, possibility)* descartar

discourage [dɪs'kʌrɪdʒ] *vt* (**a**) *(dishearten)* desalentar, desanimar; **to become discouraged** desalentarse, desanimarse (**b**) *(dissuade)* **to d. sb from doing sth** tratar de disuadir a alguien de que haga algo

discouragement [dɪs'kʌrɪdʒmənt] *n* (**a**) *(loss of enthusiasm)* desaliento *m*, desánimo *m* (**b**) *(dissuasion)* intento *m* de disuasión

discouraging [dɪs'kʌrɪdʒɪŋ] *adj* desalentador(ora)

discourse ['dɪskɔːs] *Formal* **1** *n* discurso *m*; **d. analysis** análisis *m inv* del discurso
2 *vi* **to d. (up)on a subject** disertar sobre un tema

discourteous [dɪs'kɜːtɪəs] *adj* descortés

discourtesy [dɪs'kɜːtəsɪ] *n* descortesía *f*

discover [dɪs'kʌvə(r)] *vt* descubrir

discovery [dɪsˈkʌvərɪ] n descubrimiento m; **to make a d.** realizar un descubrimiento

discredit [dɪsˈkredɪt] **1** n descrédito m; **to be a d. to sth/sb** desacreditar algo/a alguien
2 vt desacreditar

discreet [dɪsˈkriːt] adj discreto(a)

discrepancy [dɪsˈkrepənsɪ] n discrepancia f (**between** entre)

discretion [dɪsˈkreʃən] n (tact) discreción f; (judgment) criterio m; **at your d.** a discreción, a voluntad

discretionary [dɪsˈkreʃənərɪ] adj discrecional

discriminate [dɪsˈkrɪmɪneɪt] **1** vt discriminar, distinguir (**from** de)
2 vi **to d. between** discriminar or distinguir entre; **to d. against sb** discriminar a alguien; **to d. in favor of** discriminar a favor de

discriminating [dɪsˈkrɪmɪneɪtɪŋ] adj (audience, customer) entendido(a); (taste) cultivado(a)

discrimination [dɪskrɪmɪˈneɪʃən] n (**a**) (bias) discriminación f; **racial/sexual/religious d.** discriminación racial/sexual/religiosa (**b**) (taste) buen gusto m, refinamiento m (**c**) (differentiation) distinción f, diferenciación f

discriminatory [dɪsˈkrɪmɪnətərɪ] adj discriminatorio(a)

discursive [dɪsˈkɜːsɪv] adj dilatado(a), con muchas digresiones or divagaciones

discus [ˈdɪskəs] n disco m (para lanzamientos)

discuss [dɪsˈkʌs] vt discutir

discussion [dɪsˈkʌʃən] n discusión f; **the matter is under d.** el asunto está siendo discutido

disdain [dɪsˈdeɪn] **1** n desdén m, desprecio m
2 vt desdeñar, despreciar; **to d. to do sth** no dignarse a hacer algo

disdainful [dɪsˈdeɪnfʊl] adj desdeñoso(a)

disease [dɪˈziːz] n enfermedad f

diseased [dɪˈziːzd] adj (plant, limb) enfermo(a); **to be d.** estar afectado(a) por una enfermedad

disembark [dɪsɪmˈbɑːk] vt & vi desembarcar

disembodied [dɪsɪmˈbɒdɪd] adj (voice, presence) inmaterial, incorpóreo(a)

disenchanted [dɪsɪnˈtʃɑːntɪd] adj desencantado(a); **to be d.** estar desencantado(a)

disenchantment [dɪsɪnˈtʃɑːntmənt] n desencanto m

disengage [dɪsɪnˈgeɪdʒ] **1** vt (separate) soltar; (gear) quitar; (clutch) soltar; **to d. oneself from sth** desasirse de algo
2 vi desasirse, soltarse (**from** de); Mil retirarse

disentangle [dɪsɪnˈtæŋgəl] vt desenredar

disfavor [dɪsˈfeɪvə(r)] n **to be in d.** no ser visto(a) con buenos ojos; **to fall into d.** caer en desgracia

disfigure [dɪsˈfɪgə(r)] vt desfigurar

disfigurement [dɪsˈfɪgəmənt] n desfiguración f

disgorge [dɪsˈgɔːdʒ] vt (liquid, sewage) derramar; (people) expulsar; (information) desembuchar

disgrace [dɪsˈgreɪs] **1** n (shame) vergüenza f; **it's a d.!** ¡es una vergüenza or un escándalo!; **he is in d. with the party** el partido está muy disgustado con él; **to resign in d.** dimitir a causa de un escándalo; **he is a d. to his family/country** es una vergüenza or deshonra para su familia/país
2 vt (person) avergonzar; (family, country) deshonrar

disgraceful [dɪsˈgreɪsfʊl] adj vergonzoso(a), indignante; **it's d.!** ¡es una vergüenza!

disgracefully [dɪsˈgreɪsfʊlɪ] adv vergonzosamente; **she was d. late** fue vergonzoso lo tarde que llegó

disgruntled [dɪsˈgrʌntəld] adj contrariado(a), descontento(a); **to be d.** estar contrariado(a) or descontento(a)

disguise [dɪsˈgaɪz] **1** n (costume) disfraz m; **in d.** disfrazado(a)
2 vt (person) disfrazar (**as** de); (one's feelings, the truth) ocultar, disfrazar; **there is no disguising the fact that...** no se puede ocultar el hecho de que...

disgust [dɪsˈgʌst] **1** n asco m, repugnancia f; **to fill sb with d.** dar asco a alguien
2 vt repugnar

disgusted [dɪsˈgʌstɪd] adj indignado(a), asqueado(a); **he was** or **felt d. with himself** sentía asco de sí mismo, estaba indignado consigo mismo

disgusting [dɪsˈgʌstɪŋ] adj (revolting) asqueroso(a), repugnante; (disgraceful) vergonzoso(a)

disgustingly [dɪsˈgʌstɪŋlɪ] adv (sickeningly) **a d. bad meal** una comida asquerosa; Fam **to be d. rich** estar podrido(a) de millones

dish [dɪʃ] **1** n (bowl) (for serving) fuente f; (for cooking) cazuela f; (food) plato m; **dishes** (plates) platos mpl; **to do the dishes** lavar los platos, fregar los cacharros; **d. liquid** or **soap** lavavajillas m inv (detergente); **d. towel** trapo m or paño m de cocina
2 vt Fam **to d. the dirt (on sb)** sacar los trapos sucios (de alguien), RP sacar los trapitos al sol (de alguien)

▸**dish out** vt sep (food, money, advice) repartir

▸**dish up** vt sep (meal) servir

disharmony [dɪsˈhɑːmənɪ] n discordia f

dishcloth [ˈdɪʃklɒθ], **dishrag** [ˈdɪʃræg] n (for washing) bayeta f; (for drying) paño m (de cocina), CAm secador m, Chile paño m de loza, Col limpión m, Méx trapón m, RP repasador m

dishearten [dɪsˈhɑːtən] vt descorazonar, desalentar; **don't get disheartened** trata de no desanimarte

disheartening [dɪsˈhɑːtənɪŋ] adj descorazonador(ora)

disheveled [dɪˈʃevəld] adj (person, appearance) desaliñado(a); **to be d.** estar desaliñado(a)

dishonest [dɪsˈɒnɪst] adj deshonesto(a), poco honrado(a)

dishonesty [dɪsˈɒnɪstɪ] n deshonestidad f, falta f de honradez

dishonor [dɪsˈɒnə(r)] **1** n deshonra f
2 vt deshonrar

dishonorable [dɪsˈɒnərəbəl] adj deshonroso(a)

dishpan [ˈdɪʃpæn] n balde m, palangana f (para fregar los platos)

dishrag = dishcloth

dishtowel [ˈdɪʃtaʊəl] n paño m (de cocina), CAm secador m, Chile paño m de loza, Col limpión m, Méx trapón m, RP repasador m

dishwasher [ˈdɪʃwɒʃə(r)] n (person) lavaplatos mf inv, friegaplatos mf inv; (machine) lavavajillas m inv

dishwater [ˈdɪʃwɒtə(r)] n agua f de fregar (los platos); Fig **this coffee is like d.!** ¡este café está aguado or Esp es puro aguachirle or RP parece caldo de medias!

disillusion [dɪsɪˈluːʒən] **1** vt desilusionar
2 n **= disillusionment**

disillusioned [dɪsɪˈluːʒənd] adj desencantado(a), desilusionado(a); **to be d. (with sb/sth)** estar desencantado(a) (con alguien/algo)

disillusionment [dɪsɪˈluːʒənmənt] n desencanto m, desilusión f (**with** con)

disincentive [dɪsɪnˈsentɪv] n traba f; **it acts as a d. to creativity** constituye una traba para la creatividad

disinclination [dɪsɪŋklɪˈneɪʃən] n falta f de interés (**to do sth** en hacer algo)

disinclined [dɪsɪnˈklaɪnd] adj **to be d. to do sth** no tener ganas de or interés por hacer algo

disinfect [dɪsɪnˈfekt] vt desinfectar

disinfectant [dɪsɪnˈfektənt] n desinfectante m

disinformation [dɪsɪnfəˈmeɪʃən] n desinformación f

disingenuous [dɪsɪnˈdʒenjʊəs] adj falso(a), poco sincero(a)

disingenuousness [dɪsɪnˈdʒenjʊəsnɪs] n falsedad f, falta f de sinceridad

disinherit [dɪsɪnˈherɪt] vt desheredar

disintegrate [dɪsˈɪntɪgreɪt] vi desintegrarse

disintegration [dɪsɪntɪˈgreɪʃən] *n* desintegración *f*

disinterest [dɪsˈɪntərɪst] *n (lack of interest)* desinterés *m*

disinterested [dɪsˈɪntərɪstɪd] *adj* (**a**) *(unbiased)* desinteresado(a) (**b**) *(uninterested)* **he was d. in the movie** no le interesaba la película

disinvestment [dɪsɪnˈvestmənt] *n Fin* desinversión *f*

disjointed [dɪsˈdʒɔɪntɪd] *adj (novel, description)* deshilvanado(a)

disk [dɪsk] *n* (**a**) *Comptr* disco *m*; **d. drive** unidad *f* de disco, disquetera *f* (**b**) *(record)* disco *m*; **d. jockey** pinchadiscos *mf inv* (**c**) *Aut* **d. brake** freno *m* de disco

diskette [dɪsˈket] *n Comptr* disquete *m*

dislike [dɪsˈlaɪk] **1** *n (of things)* aversión *f* (**of** por); *(of people)* antipatía *f* (**of** hacia); **my likes and dislikes** las cosas que me gustan y las que me disgustan
2 *vt* **I d. him/it** no me gusta; **I don't d. him/it** no me disgusta; **I d. them** no me gustan; **I don't d. them** no me disgustan

dislocate [ˈdɪsləkeɪt] *vt* (**a**) *(shoulder, hip)* dislocar; **to d. one's shoulder** dislocarse el hombro (**b**) *(plan, timetable)* trastocar

dislocation [dɪsləˈkeɪʃən] *n* (**a**) *(of shoulder, hip)* dislocación *f* (**b**) *(of plan)* desbaratamiento *m*

dislodge [dɪsˈlɒdʒ] *vt (brick, tile)* soltar; *(something stuck)* sacar; *(opponent)* desplazar, desalojar

disloyal [dɪsˈlɔɪəl] *adj* desleal

disloyalty [dɪsˈlɔɪəltɪ] *n* deslealtad *f*

dismal [ˈdɪzməl] *adj* (**a**) *(place)* sombrío(a), tétrico(a); *(weather)* muy triste; *(future)* oscuro(a) (**b**) *(failure)* horroroso(a); *(performance)* nefasto(a), *Esp* fatal

dismantle [dɪsˈmæntəl] *vt* desmantelar

dismay [dɪsˈmeɪ] **1** *n* consternación *f*; **in d.** con consternación; **(much) to my d.** para mi consternación
2 *vt* consternar

dismayed [dɪsˈmeɪd] *adj* consternado(a)

dismember [dɪsˈmembə(r)] *vt (body)* descuartizar; *(country, company)* desmembrar

dismiss [dɪsˈmɪs] *vt* (**a**) *(from job)* despedir (**b**) *(send away)* **to d. sb** dar a alguien permiso para retirarse; *Mil* **d.!** ¡rompan filas! (**c**) *(thought, theory)* descartar; *(proposal, suggestion)* rechazar; *(threat, danger)* no hacer caso de; *Law (case)* sobreseer; *(appeal)* desestimar; **the suggestion was dismissed as being irrelevant** la sugerencia fue rechazada por no venir al caso (**d**) *(school class)* dejar marchar

dismissal [dɪsˈmɪsəl] *n* (**a**) *(from job)* despido *m* (**b**) *Law (of case)* sobreseimiento *m*; *(of appeal)* desestimación *f*

dismissive [dɪsˈmɪsɪv] *adj* desdeñoso(a), despectivo(a) (**of** hacia *or* respecto a); **he was very d. of my chances** se mostró escéptico en cuanto a mis posibilidades

dismount [dɪsˈmaʊnt] *vi (from horse, bicycle)* desmontar, bajarse (**from** de)

disobedience [dɪsəˈbiːdɪəns] *n* desobediencia *f*

disobedient [dɪsəˈbiːdɪənt] *adj* desobediente

disobey [dɪsəˈbeɪ] *vt* desobedecer

disorder [dɪsˈɔːdə(r)] *n* (**a**) *(confusion, unrest)* desorden *m*; **in d.** en desorden (**b**) *Med* dolencia *f*; **nervous d.** dolencia *f* nerviosa; **personality d.** trastorno *m* de la personalidad

disordered [dɪsˈɔːdəd] *adj (room, mind)* desordenado(a)

disorderly [dɪsˈɔːdəlɪ] *adj* (**a**) *(untidy)* desordenado(a) (**b**) *(unruly)* revoltoso(a); *Law* **d. conduct** escándalo *m* público; *Law* **d. house** casa *f* de prostitución

disorganization [dɪsɔːgənaɪˈzeɪʃən] *n* desorganización *f*

disorganized [dɪsˈɔːgənaɪzd] *adj* desorganizado(a)

disorient [dɪsˈɔːrɪənt], **disorientate** [dɪsˈɔːrɪənteɪt] *vt* desorientar

disorientation [dɪsɔːrɪənˈteɪʃən] *n* desorientación *f*

disown [dɪsˈəʊn] *vt (wife, child)* repudiar; *(country)* renegar de; *(statement)* no reconocer como propio(a)

disparage [dɪsˈpærɪdʒ] *vt* desdeñar, menospreciar

disparaging [dɪsˈpærɪdʒɪŋ] *adj* desdeñoso(a), menospreciativo(a)

disparagingly [dɪsˈpærɪdʒɪŋlɪ] *adv* con desdén, desdeñosamente

disparate [ˈdɪspərɪt] *adj* dispar

disparity [dɪsˈpærɪtɪ] *n* disparidad *f*

dispassionate [dɪsˈpæʃənət] *adj* desapasionado(a)

dispassionately [dɪsˈpæʃənətlɪ] *adv* desapasionadamente, sin apasionamiento

dispatch [dɪsˈpætʃ] **1** *n* (**a**) *(of letter, package)* envío *m* (**b**) *(message)* despacho *m*; *Mil* **he was mentioned in dispatches** apareció mencionado en partes de guerra; *Mil* **d. rider** mensajero(a) *m,f* motorizado(a) (**c**) *Formal (promptness)* **with d.** con celeridad *or* prontitud
2 *vt* (**a**) *(send)* enviar, mandar (**b**) *(kill)* dar muerte a

dispel [dɪsˈpel] (*pt & pp* **dispelled**) *vt (doubt, fear)* disipar

dispensable [dɪsˈpensəbəl] *adj* prescindible

dispensary [dɪsˈpensərɪ] *n Med* dispensario *m*, botiquín *m*

dispensation [dɪspenˈseɪʃən] *n Law & Rel (exemption)* dispensa *f* (**from** de)

dispense [dɪsˈpens] *vt (justice, medication, prescription)* administrar; *(advice)* repartir; *(of vending machine)* expedir
▸**dispense with** *vt insep* prescindir de

dispensing druggist [dɪsˈpensɪŋˈdrʌgɪst] *n* farmacéutico(a) *m,f*

dispersal [dɪsˈpɜːsəl] *n* dispersión *f*

disperse [dɪsˈpɜːs] **1** *vt (seeds, people)* dispersar; *(knowledge, information)* difundir
2 *vi (crowd)* dispersarse; *(darkness, clouds)* disiparse

dispirited [dɪsˈpɪrɪtɪd] *adj* desanimado(a), desalentado(a); **to be d.** estar desanimado(a) *or* desalentado(a)

displace [dɪsˈpleɪs] *vt* (**a**) *(shift)* desplazar; **displaced persons** desplazados *mpl* (**b**) *(supplant)* sustituir

displacement [dɪsˈpleɪsmənt] *n* (**a**) *(of water, people, ship)* desplazamiento *m* (**b**) *(substitution)* **d. (of A by B)** sustitución *f* (de A por B) (**c**) *Psy* **d. activity** actividad *f* sublimadora

display [dɪsˈpleɪ] **1** *n* (**a**) *(of goods)* muestra *f*; *(of handicrafts, paintings)* exposición *f*; **on d.** expuesto(a); **d. cabinet** vitrina *f*; **d. copy** *(of book)* ejemplar *m* de muestra; **d. window** escaparate *m*, *Am* vidriera *f*, *Chile, Col, Méx* vitrina *f* (**b**) *(of emotion, technique)* demostración *f*; *(of sport)* exhibición *f*; **a fireworks d.** un festival *or* castillo de fuegos artificiales (**c**) *Comptr* pantalla *f*
2 *vt* (**a**) *(goods)* disponer; *(on sign, screen)* mostrar (**b**) *(emotion, talent, ignorance)* demostrar, mostrar

displease [dɪsˈpliːz] *vt* disgustar, desagradar; **to be displeased with sb/sth** estar disgustado(a) con alguien/algo

displeasing [dɪsˈpliːzɪŋ] *adj* desagradable

displeasure [dɪsˈpleʒə(r)] *n* disgusto *m*, desagrado *m*; **to incur sb's d.** provocar el enojo de alguien

disposable [dɪsˈpəʊzəbəl] *adj (camera, pen, lighter)* desechable; *(funds)* disponible; **d. income** poder *m* adquisitivo

disposal [dɪsˈpəʊzəl] *n* (**a**) *(of trash)* eliminación *f* (**b**) *(of property)* venta *f* (**c**) *(availability)* **to have sth at one's d.** disponer de algo

dispose [dɪsˈpəʊz] *vt (arrange)* disponer
▸**dispose of** *vt insep* (**a**) *(get rid of)* *(rubbish)* eliminar; *(problem)* acabar con (**b**) *(kill)* dar muerte a

disposed [dɪsˈpəʊzd] *adj (willing)* **to be d. to do sth** estar dispuesto(a) a hacer algo

disposition [dɪspəˈzɪʃən] *n* (**a**) *(temperament)* carácter *m* (**b**) *(inclination)* **to have a d. to do sth** tener tendencia a hacer algo (**c**) *Formal (arrangement)* disposición *f*

dispossess [dɪspəˈzes] *vt* desposeer (**of** de)

dispossessed [dɪspəˈzest] **1** *npl* **the d.** los desposeídos
2 *adj* desposeído(a)

disproportionate [dɪsprə'pɔːʃənət] *adj* desproporciona-do(a)

disproportionately [dɪsprə'pɔːʃənətlɪ] *adv* desproporcionadamente; **a d. large sum of money** una cantidad enorme *or* desmesurada de dinero

disprove [dɪs'pruːv] (*pp* **disproved**, *Law* **disproven** [dɪs'prəʊvən]) *vt* refutar

disputable [dɪs'pjuːtəbəl] *adj* discutible

dispute [dɪs'pjuːt] **1** *n* (*debate*) discusión *f*, debate *m*; (*argument*) pelea *f*, disputa *f*; **the matter in d.** la cuestión debatida; **it's beyond d.** es indiscutible; **it's open to d.** es cuestionable
　　2 *vt* (*subject, claim*) debatir, discutir; **I'm not disputing that** eso no lo discuto
　　3 *vi* discutir (**about** *or* **over** sobre)

disputed [dɪs'pjuːtɪd] *adj* (*decision, fact, claim*) discutido(a), polémico(a)

disqualification [dɪskwɒlɪfɪ'keɪʃən] *n* (*from competition*) descalificación *f*

disqualify [dɪs'kwɒlɪfaɪ] *vt* (*from competition*) descalificar; **to d. sb from doing sth** incapacitar a alguien para hacer algo

disquiet [dɪs'kwaɪət] *n* inquietud *f*, desasosiego *m*

disquieting [dɪs'kwaɪətɪŋ] *adj* inquietante

disregard [dɪsrɪ'gɑːd] **1** *n* indiferencia *f*, menosprecio *m*
　　2 *vt* (*warning, fact*) no tener en cuenta; (*order*) desacatar

disrepair [dɪsrɪ'peə(r)] *n* **in (a state of) d.** deteriorado(a); **to fall into d.** deteriorarse

disreputable [dɪs'repjʊtəbəl] *adj* (*person, behavior*) poco respetable; (*neighborhood, bar*) de mala reputación

disreputably [dɪs'repjʊtəblɪ] *adv* (*to behave*) de forma poco respetable

disrepute [dɪsrɪ'pjuːt] *n* **to bring sth into d.** desprestigiar algo; **to fall into d.** ganar mala fama

disrespect [dɪsrɪ'spekt] *n* irreverencia *f*, falta *f* de respeto; **to treat sb with d.** tratar a alguien irrespetuosamente; **I meant no d.** no pretendía faltar al respeto

disrespectful [dɪsrɪ'spektfʊl] *adj* irrespetuoso(a)

disrupt [dɪs'rʌpt] *vt* (*traffic*) entorpecer, trastornar; (*plan*) trastornar, trastocar; (*meeting*) interrumpir, alterar el desarrollo de; (*life, routine*) alterar

disruption [dɪs'rʌpʃən] *n* (*of traffic*) entorpecimiento *m*, trastorno *m*; (*of plan*) desbaratamiento *m*; (*of meeting*) interrupción *f*; (*of life, routine*) alteración *f*

disruptive [dɪs'rʌptɪv] *adj* **to be d.** ocasionar trastornos; **to have a d. influence on sb** tener una influencia perjudicial sobre alguien

dis(s) [dɪs] *vt Fam* faltar (al respeto) a

dissatisfaction [dɪsætɪs'fækʃən] *n* insatisfacción *f*

dissatisfied [dɪ'sætɪsfaɪd] *adj* insatisfecho(a) (**with** con); **to be d. (with)** estar insatisfecho(a) (con)

dissect [dɪ'sekt] *vt also Fig* diseccionar

dissemble [dɪ'sembəl] *Formal* **1** *vt* ocultar, disimular
　　2 *vi* disimular

disseminate [dɪ'semɪneɪt] *Formal* **1** *vt* propagar, difundir
　　2 *vi* propagarse, difundirse

dissension [dɪ'senʃən] *n Formal* disensión *f*, discordia *f*

dissent [dɪ'sent] **1** *n* discrepancia *f*, disconformidad *f*; **he was booked for d.** fue amonestado por protestar
　　2 *vi* disentir (**from** de)

dissenter [dɪ'sentə(r)] *n* disidente *mf*

dissenting [dɪ'sentɪŋ] *adj* discrepante

dissertation [dɪsə'teɪʃən] *n Univ* (*doctoral*) tesis *f*

disservice [dɪ'sɜːvɪs] *n* **to do sb a d.** perjudicar a alguien

dissidence ['dɪsɪdəns] *n Pol* disidencia *f*

dissident ['dɪsɪdənt] *n & adj* disidente *mf*

dissimilar [dɪ'sɪmɪlə(r)] *adj* distinto(a) (**to** de)

dissimilarity [dɪsɪmɪ'lærɪtɪ] *n* desigualdad *f*, disimilitud *f* (**between** entre)

dissimulate [dɪ'sɪmjʊleɪt] *Formal* **1** *vt* (*feelings*) disimular
　　2 *vi* disimular

dissimulation [dɪsɪmjʊ'leɪʃən] *n Formal* disimulo *m*

dissipate ['dɪsɪpeɪt] **1** *vt* (*fears, doubts*) disipar; (*fortune, one's energy*) derrochar
　　2 *vi* (*mist, doubts*) disiparse

dissipation [dɪsɪ'peɪʃən] *n* (*loose living*) disipación *f*

dissociate [dɪ'səʊsɪeɪt] *vt* disociar; **to d. oneself from sb/sth** desmarcarse de alguien/algo

dissolute ['dɪsəluːt] *adj* disoluto(a)

dissolve [dɪ'zɒlv] **1** *vt* disolver
　　2 *vi* disolverse; **it dissolves in water** es soluble en agua; **to d. into tears** deshacerse en lágrimas

dissonance ['dɪsənəns] *n* (**a**) *Mus* disonancia *f* (**b**) (*disagreement*) discordancia *f*

dissonant ['dɪsənənt] *adj* (**a**) *Mus* disonante (**b**) (*opinions*) discordante

dissuade [dɪ'sweɪd] *vt* **to d. sb from doing sth** disuadir a alguien de hacer algo

distance ['dɪstəns] **1** *n* distancia *f*; **from a d.** desde lejos; **in the d.** en la lejanía; **at a d. of...** a una distancia de...; **within five minutes walking d.** a cinco minutos a pie; **a short d. away** bastante cerca; **some d. away** bastante lejos; **to keep sb at a d.** guardar las distancias con alguien; **to keep one's d.** mantener las distancias; **at this d. in time...** después de tanto tiempo...; **to go the d.** (*in boxing*) aguantar todos los asaltos; **d. learning** educación *f* a distancia
　　2 *vt* **to d. oneself from sb/sth** distanciarse de alguien/algo

distant ['dɪstənt] *adj* (**a**) (*far-off*) distante, lejano(a); **3 miles d.** a 3 millas de distancia; **a d. relative** un pariente lejano; **she had a d. look** tenía la mirada distante *or* perdida; **in the d. past** en el pasado lejano (**b**) (*reserved*) distante

distantly ['dɪstəntlɪ] *adv* (**a**) **d. related** lejanamente emparentado(a) (**b**) (*distractedly*) (*answer, smile*) distraídamente

distaste [dɪs'teɪst] *n* desagrado *m* (**for** por)

distasteful [dɪs'teɪstfʊl] *adj* desagradable

distemper[1] [dɪs'tempə(r)] *n* (*animal disease*) moquillo *m*

distemper[2] *n* (*paint*) (pintura *f* al) temple *m*

distend [dɪs'tend] **1** *vt* hinchar
　　2 *vi* hincharse

distill [dɪs'tɪl] (*pt & pp* **distilled**) *vt* destilar

distillation [dɪstɪ'leɪʃən] *n* (*of water, whiskey*) destilación *f*; (*of information*) condensación *f*, compendio *m*

distillery [dɪs'tɪlərɪ] *n* destilería *f*

distinct [dɪs'tɪŋkt] *adj* (**a**) (*different*) distinto(a); **as d. from** a diferencia de (**b**) (*clear*) (*change, idea, preference*) claro(a) (**c**) (*real*) (*possibility, feeling*) claro(a)

distinction [dɪs'tɪŋkʃən] *n* (**a**) (*difference*) distinción *f*; **to make** *or* **draw a d. between** establecer una distinción entre (**b**) (*honor*) honor *m*; *Ironic* **I had the d. of coming last** me correspondió el honor de ser el último (**c**) (*excellence*) **a writer/scientist of d.** un escritor/científico destacado; **with d.** (*perform, serve*) de manera sobresaliente (**d**) *Sch & Univ* sobresaliente *m*

distinctive [dɪs'tɪŋktɪv] *adj* característico(a)

distinctively [dɪs'tɪŋktɪvlɪ] *adv* de manera característica

distinctly [dɪs'tɪŋktlɪ] *adv* (**a**) (*clearly*) (*speak, hear*) claramente, con claridad; **I d. remember telling you** recuerdo con toda claridad habértelo dicho (**b**) (*decidedly*) (*better, easier*) claramente; (*stupid, ill-mannered*) verdaderamente

distinguish [dɪs'tɪŋgwɪʃ] **1** *vt* (**a**) (*recognize*) distinguir (**b**) (*characterize, differentiate*) distinguir (**from** de); **distinguishing mark** rasgo *m* físico característico (**c**) (*earn praise, honor*) **to d. oneself by...** distinguirse por...
　　2 *vi* **to d. between** distinguir entre

distinguishable [dɪsˈtɪŋgwɪʃəbəl] *adj* (**a**) *(recognizable)* distinguible; **to be d.** distinguirse (**b**) *(differentiable)* diferenciable (**from** de); **the two species are not easily d. from a distance** las dos especies son difíciles de diferenciar *or* distinguir desde lejos

distinguished [dɪsˈtɪŋgwɪʃd] *adj (person, performance, career)* destacado(a); *(air)* distinguido(a)

distort [dɪsˈtɔːt] *vt (shape)* deformar; *(sound)* distorsionar; *Fig (meaning, facts)* distorsionar, tergiversar

distorted [dɪsˈtɔːtɪd] *adj (shape)* deformado(a); *(sound, guitar)* distorsionado(a); *Fig (account)* distorsionado(a), tergiversado(a)

distortion [dɪsˈtɔːʃən] *n (of shape)* deformación *f*; *(of sound)* distorsión *f*; *Fig (of meaning, facts)* distorsión *f*, tergiversación *f*

distract [dɪsˈtrækt] *vt (person, attention)* distraer; **this is distracting us from our main purpose** esto nos está alejando de nuestro objetivo principal; **she is easily distracted** se distrae con facilidad

distracted [dɪsˈtræktɪd] *adj* abstraído(a), ausente; **to be d.** estar abstraído(a) *or* ausente

distracting [dɪsˈtræktɪŋ] *adj* **that noise is very d.** ese ruido distrae mucho

distraction [dɪsˈtrækʃən] *n* (**a**) *(distracting thing)* distracción *f*; **to drive sb to d.** sacar a alguien de quicio (**b**) *(amusement)* entretenimiento *m*, distracción *f*

distraught [dɪsˈtrɔːt] *adj* desconsolado(a), consternado(a); **to be d.** estar desconsolado(a) *or* consternado(a)

distress [dɪsˈtres] **1** *n* sufrimiento *m*, angustia *f*; **to be in d.** estar sufriendo mucho; *(ship)* estar en situación de peligro; **d. signal** señal *f* de socorro
2 *vt (upset)* afligir, angustiar

distressed [dɪsˈtrest] *adj* angustiado(a), afligido(a); **to be d.** estar angustiado(a) *or* afligido(a)

distressing [dɪsˈtresɪŋ] *adj (upsetting)* angustioso(a); *(worrying)* preocupante

distribute [dɪsˈtrɪbjuːt] *vt* distribuir

distribution [dɪstrɪˈbjuːʃən] *n* distribución *f*; **d. of wealth** reparto *m* de la riqueza; *Com* **d. cost** coste *m* de distribución; *Com* **d. network** red *f* de distribución

distributor [dɪsˈtrɪbjʊtə(r)] *n* (**a**) *(person, company)* distribuidor(ora) *m,f* (**b**) *Aut* distribuidor *m*, *Esp* delco® *m*

district [ˈdɪstrɪkt] *n (of country)* comarca *f*; *(of town, city)* barrio *m*; **d. attorney** fiscal *mf* del distrito; **d. court** tribunal *m* federal

distrust [dɪsˈtrʌst] **1** *n* desconfianza *f*
2 *vt* desconfiar de

distrustful [dɪsˈtrʌstfʊl] *adj* desconfiado(a); **to be d. of** desconfiar de

disturb [dɪsˈtɜːb] *vt* (**a**) *(annoy, interrupt) (person)* molestar; *(sleep, concentration)* perturbar; *Law* **to d. the peace** alterar el orden público (**b**) *(worry)* preocupar (**c**) *(disarrange) (papers, room)* desordenar; *(water surface)* agitar

disturbance [dɪsˈtɜːbəns] *n* (**a**) *(nuisance)* molestia *f* (**b**) *(atmospheric, emotional)* perturbación *f* (**c**) *(fight, riot)* disturbio *m*; **to cause** *or* **create a d.** provocar disturbios

disturbed [dɪsˈtɜːbd] *adj (night, sleep)* agitado(a); *(mentally, emotionally)* trastornado(a), perturbado(a); **to be d.** *(mentally, emotionally)* estar trastornado(a) *or* perturbado(a)

disturbing [dɪsˈtɜːbɪŋ] *adj (worrying)* preocupante

disturbingly [dɪsˈtɜːbɪŋlɪ] *adv* **the level of pollution is d. high** el (alto) nivel de contaminación es preocupante

disunity [dɪsˈjuːnɪtɪ] *n* desunión *f*

disuse [dɪsˈjuːs] *n* **to fall into d.** caer en desuso

ditch [dɪtʃ] **1** *n* zanja *f*; *(at roadside)* cuneta *f*; *(as defense)* foso *m*
2 *vt Fam (get rid of) (car, useless object)* deshacerse de; *(girlfriend, boyfriend)* plantar; *(plan, idea)* descartar

dither [ˈdɪðə(r)] *Fam* **1** *n* **to be (all) in a d.** aturullarse
2 *vi* vacilar, estar hecho(a) un lío

ditherer [ˈdɪðərə(r)] *n Fam* **he's such a terrible d.** es superindeciso

ditsy, ditzy [ˈdɪtsɪ] *adj* alocado(a)

ditto [ˈdɪtəʊ] *adv* ídem; *Fam* **I'm hungry — d.** tengo hambre — ídem (de ídem)

ditty [ˈdɪtɪ] *n Fam* tonadilla *f*

ditzy = ditsy

diuretic [daɪjʊˈretɪk] *n & adj* diurético(a)

divan [dɪˈvæn] *n* diván *m*

dive [daɪv] **1** *n* (**a**) *(from poolside, diving board)* salto *m* de cabeza; *(of deep-sea diver, submarine)* inmersión *f* (**b**) *Fam Pej (place)* antro *m*
2 *vi (pt* **dived** *or* **dove** [dəʊv]) *(from poolside, diving board)* tirarse de cabeza; *(scuba-diver)* bucear; *(deep-sea diver, submarine)* sumergirse; *(aircraft)* lanzarse en *Esp* picado *or Am* picada; **to d. for cover** ponerse a cubierto

diver [ˈdaɪvə(r)] *n (from diving board)* saltador(ora) *m,f* de trampolín; *(with scuba apparatus)* submarinista *mf*, buzo *m*; *(deep sea)* buzo *m*

diverge [daɪˈvɜːdʒ] *vi (rays)* divergir; *(roads)* bifurcarse; *(opinions, persons)* discrepar, divergir

divergence [daɪˈvɜːdʒəns] *n* divergencia *f*

divergent [daɪˈvɜːdʒənt], **diverging** [daɪˈvɜːdʒɪŋ] *adj* divergente, discrepante

diverse [daɪˈvɜːs] *adj* diverso(a)

diversification [daɪvɜːsɪfɪˈkeɪʃən] *n Com* diversificación *f*

diversify [daɪˈvɜːsɪfaɪ] **1** *vt* diversificar
2 *vi (company)* diversificarse

diversion [daɪˈvɜːʃən] *n* (**a**) *(of aircraft, funds)* desvío *m*; **to create a d.** distraer la atención (**b**) *(amusement)* distracción *f*

diversity [daɪˈvɜːsɪtɪ] *n* diversidad *f*

divert [daɪˈvɜːt, dɪˈvɜːt] *vt* (**a**) *(aircraft, river, attention)* desviar (**b**) *(amuse)* **to d. oneself** distraerse

divest [daɪˈvest] *vt Formal* **to d. sb of sth** despojar a alguien de algo

divide [dɪˈvaɪd] **1** *n (gulf)* división *f*, separación *f*
2 *vt* (**a**) *(money, food)* repartir (**between** *or* **among** entre); **to d. sth in two/three** dividir algo en dos/tres partes (**b**) *Math* dividir; **d. 346 by 17** dividir 346 entre 17 (**c**) *(separate)* separar (**from** de); **d. and rule** divide y vencerás
3 *vi (road)* bifurcarse; *(group)* dividirse

▶**divide up** *vt sep (share)* repartir

divided [dɪˈvaɪdɪd] *adj* dividido(a); **to be d.** estar dividido(a); **a family d. against itself** una familia dividida; **d. highway** autovía *f*

dividend [ˈdɪvɪdend] *n* dividendo *m*; *Fig* **to pay dividends** resultar beneficioso(a)

divider [dɪˈvaɪdə(r)] *n* (**a**) *(in room) (thin wall)* tabique *m*; *(screen)* mampara *f* (**b**) *Math* **(a pair of) dividers** (un) compás *m* de puntas

dividing [dɪˈvaɪdɪŋ] *adj* **d. line** línea *f* divisoria; **d. wall** muro *m* divisorio

divine [dɪˈvaɪn] **1** *adj (judgment, worship)* divino(a); *Fam* **you look d. in that dress** estás divina con ese vestido
2 *vt* adivinar

diving [ˈdaɪvɪŋ] *n (from poolside, diving board)* salto *m* (de cabeza); *(scuba diving)* submarinismo *m*, buceo *m*; *(deep sea)* buceo *m* en alta mar; **d. bell** campana *f* de buzo; **d. board** trampolín *m*; **d. suit** traje *m* de buceo *or* de hombre rana

divinity [dɪˈvɪnɪtɪ] *n* (**a**) *(divine nature, god)* divinidad *f* (**b**) *(subject)* teología *f* (**c**) **the D.** Dios *m*

divisible [dɪˈvɪzɪbəl] *adj* divisible

division [dɪˈvɪʒən] *n* (**a**) *(separation, in maths)* división *f* (**b**) *(distribution)* reparto *m*; **d. of labor** división *f* del trabajo (**c**) *(discord)* discordia *f* (**d**) *(unit)* división *f*; **first/second d.** *(in league)* primera/segunda división

divisive [dɪˈvaɪsɪv] *adj* disgregador(ora)

divorce [dɪ'vɔːs] **1** *n* divorcio *m*; **to start d. proceedings (against sb)** emprender los trámites de divorcio (contra alguien)

2 *vt* (**a**) *(spouse)* divorciarse de; **to get divorced (from sb)** divorciarse (de alguien) (**b**) *Fig* separar (**from** de)

3 *vi (husband and wife)* divorciarse

divorcé [dɪvɔː'siː] *n* divorciado *m*

divorcée [dɪvɔː'seɪ] *n* divorciada *f*

divulge [daɪ'vʌldʒ] *vt* divulgar, dar a conocer

DIY [diːaɪ'waɪ] *n* (*abbr* **do-it-yourself**) bricolaje *m*

dizzily ['dɪzɪlɪ] *adv* (**a**) *(to rise) (cliffs, prices)* vertiginosamente (**b**) *Fam (to behave, laugh)* atolondradamente

dizzy ['dɪzɪ] *adj* (**a**) *(unsteady) (because of illness)* mareado(a); *(feeling vertigo)* con vértigo; **to be d.** *(because of illness)* estar mareado(a); *(feeling vertigo)* tener *or* sentir vértigo; **to reach the d. heights of government** alcanzar las altas esferas del gobierno; **d. spell** mareo *m* (**b**) *Fam (frivolous)* **a d. blonde** una rubia *or Méx* güera locuela

DJ ['diːdʒeɪ] *n* (*abbr* **disk jockey**) pinchadiscos *mf inv*

Djibouti [dʒɪ'buːtɪ] *n* Yibuti

dl (*abbr* **deciliters**) dl

DMV [diːem'viː] *n* (*abbr* **Department of Motor Vehicles**) Departamento *m* de Vehículos Motorizados

DNA [diːen'eɪ] *n Chem* (*abbr* **deoxyribonucleic acid**) ADN *m*, ácido *m* desoxirribonucleico

do¹ [dəʊ] *n Mus* do *m*

do² [duː] **1** *v aux*

> En el inglés hablado, y en el escrito en estilo coloquial, las formas negativas **do not**, **does not** y **did not** se transforman en **don't**, **doesn't** y **didn't**. Como verbo transitivo **do**, unido a muchos nombres, expresa actividades, como **to do the gardening**, **to do the ironing** y **to do the shopping**. En el presente diccionario, estas estructuras se encuentran bajo los nombres respectivos.

(*3rd person singular* **does** [dʌz], *pt* **did** [dɪd], *pp* **done** [dʌn]) (**a**) *(not translated in negatives and questions)* **I don't speak Spanish** no hablo español; **I didn't see him** no lo vi; **do you speak Spanish?** ¿hablas español?; **did you see him?** ¿lo viste?; **don't you speak Spanish?** ¿no hablas español?; **didn't you see him?** ¿no lo viste?

(**b**) *(for emphasis)* **she DOES speak Spanish!** ¡sí que habla español!; **I DIDN'T see him!** ¡te digo que no lo vi!

(**c**) *(substituting main verb)* **she writes better than I do** escribe mejor que yo; **he has always loved her and still does** siempre la ha querido y todavía la quiere; **if you want to speak to him, do it now** si quieres hablar con él, hazlo ahora; **do you speak Spanish? — no I don't** ¿hablas español? – no; **did you see him? — I did** ¿lo viste? – sí

(**d**) *(in tag questions)* **you speak Spanish, don't you?** tú hablas español, ¿no?; **John lives near here, doesn't he?** John vive cerca de aquí, ¿verdad?; **they said they'd come early, didn't they?** dijeron que vendrían pronto, ¿no?; **you didn't see him, did you?** tú no lo viste, ¿verdad?

2 *vt* (**a**) *(in general)* hacer; **what are you doing?** ¿qué haces?, ¿qué estás haciendo?; **what do you do?** *(what's your job?)* ¿a qué te dedicas?, ¿en qué trabajas?; **what can I do for you?** ¿qué desea?, ¿puedo ayudarle en algo?; **it just isn't done!** *(is not acceptable behavior)* ¡eso no se hace!, ¡eso no está bien!; **the car was doing 100 miles per hour** el coche iba a 100 millas por hora; **they do good food here** aquí hacen muy buena comida; **that hairstyle does nothing for her** ese peinado no le favorece nada; *Fam* **this music doesn't do anything for me** esta música no me dice nada; **to do French/physics** *(at school, university)* estudiar francés/física; **to do the housework** hacer las labores de la casa

(**b**) **to do one's hair** peinarse, arreglarse el pelo; **to do one's teeth** lavarse los dientes

(**c**) *Fam* **to do drugs** tomar drogas

(**d**) **to be done** *(food)* estar hecho(a); **are you done complaining?** ¿has terminado ya de quejarte?; *Fam* **I've been done!** *(cheated)* ¡me han tangado *or* timado!

(**e**) *Fam (prosecute)* **he was done for fraud** lo empapelaron por fraude

3 *vi* (**a**) *(perform, act)* **she did well/badly** le fue bien/mal; **he does well/badly at school** le va bien/mal en el colegio (**b**) *(suffice)* **it will/won't do** será/no será suficiente; **that'll do!** ¡ya basta *or Esp* vale!; **this will never do!** ¡esto es intolerable!; **to make do** arreglárselas, apañárselas (**c**) *(finish)* **hasn't she done yet?** ¿no ha terminado aún?

4 *n* **do's and don'ts** reglas *fpl* básicas

▸**do away with** *vt insep (abolish, kill)* acabar con

▸**do for** *vt insep Fam* **he's done for** está perdido, lo tiene crudo *or* claro

▸**do in** *vt sep Fam* (**a**) *(murder)* cargarse (**b**) *(exhaust)* **I'm absolutely done in** estoy hecho(a) migas

▸**do out of** *vt sep Fam* **to do sb out of sth** *(deprive)* privar a alguien de algo; *(cheat)* tangar *or* estafar algo a alguien

▸**do up 1** *vt sep* (**a**) *(fasten)* abrochar; **do your coat up** abróchate el abrigo (**b**) *(wrap)* envolver (**c**) *(improve appearance of)* remozar, renovar; *Fam* **to do oneself up** *(dress smartly)* arreglarse, *Esp* ponerse guapo(a)

2 *vt (clothes)* abrocharse

▸**do with** *vt insep* (**a**) *(benefit from)* **I could do with a cup of tea** no me vendría mal una taza de té (**b**) *(expressing involvement)* **I want nothing to do with him** no quiero tener nada que ver con él; **I had nothing to do with it** no tuve nada que ver con eso; **it's nothing to do with you** *(not your business)* no es asunto tuyo (**c**) *(stop using)* **to have done with sth** terminar con algo; **are you done with the scissors yet?** ¿has terminado con las tijeras?

▸**do without** *vt insep (manage without)* pasar sin; **I could do without your snide remarks** me sobran *or* puedes ahorrarte tus comentarios sarcásticos

DOA [diːəʊ'eɪ] *adj Med* (*abbr* **dead on arrival**) **he was D. when he arrived at the hospital** ya había muerto, *Esp* ingresó cadáver

DOB (*abbr* **date of birth**) = fecha de nacimiento

doc [dɒk] *n Fam* doctor(ora) *m,f*

docile ['dəʊsaɪl] *adj* dócil

docility [də'sɪlətɪ] *n* docilidad *f*

dock¹ [dɒk] **1** *n (for ships)* muelle *m*; **the docks** el puerto; **d. strike** huelga *f* de estibadores

2 *vi (ship)* atracar; *(two spacecraft)* acoplarse

dock² *n Law* banquillo *m* (de los acusados)

dock³ *vt* (**a**) *(tail)* recortar (**b**) *(wages)* recortar

docker ['dɒkə(r)] *n* estibador *m*

dockyard ['dɒkjɑːd] *n* astillero *m*

doctor ['dɒktə(r)] **1** *n* (**a**) *(medical)* médico(a) *m,f*; **to go to the d.('s)** ir al médico; *Fam Fig* **that's just what the d. ordered** me/le/*etc.* viene que ni pintado (**b**) *Univ* doctor(ora) *m,f*

2 *vt Fam (accounts, evidence)* amañar

doctorate ['dɒktərɪt] *n Univ* doctorado *m*

doctrinaire [dɒktrɪ'neə(r)] *adj* doctrinario(a)

doctrinal [dɒk'traɪnəl] *adj* doctrinal

doctrine ['dɒktrɪn] *n* doctrina *f*

docudrama ['dɒkjʊdrɑːmə] *n* docudrama *m*

document 1 *n* ['dɒkjʊmənt] documento *m*; **d. case** portafolios *m inv*; *Comptr* **d. reader** digitalizador *m*, lector *m* de documentos

2 *vt* ['dɒkjʊment] documentar; **the first documented case** el primer caso registrado *or* documentado

documentary [dɒkjʊ'mentərɪ] **1** *n (TV program)* documental *m*

2 *adj* documental

documentation [dɒkjʊmen'teɪʃən] *n* documentación *f*

dodder ['dɒdə(r)] *vi* renquear, caminar *or Esp* andar con paso vacilante

doddering ['dɒdərɪŋ] *adj (walk)* renqueante, vacilante; **d. fool** viejo *m* chocho

dodge [dɒdʒ] *n* **1** (a) *(movement)* regate *m*, quiebro *m* (**b**) *Fam (trick)* truco *m*; **tax d.** trampa *f* para engañar a Hacienda
   2 *vt (blow, person)* esquivar; *(responsibility, question)* eludir
   3 *vi* apartarse bruscamente

dodo ['dəʊdəʊ] *(pl* **dodos** *or* **dodoes**) *n* dodo *m*; **(as) dead as a d.** muerto(a) y bien muerto(a)

doe [dəʊ] *n (deer)* cierva *f*; *(rabbit)* coneja *f*

does [dʌz] *3rd person singular of* **do**

doesn't ['dʌzənt] = **does not**

doff [dɒf] *vt* to d. one's cap to sb descubrirse ante alguien

dog [dɒg] **1** *n* (a) *(animal)* perro *m*; **d. biscuit** galleta *f* para perros; **d. collar** *(of dog)* collar *m* de perro; *Fam (of cleric)* alzacuello *m*; **d. food** comida *f* para perros; **d. handler** adiestrador(ora) *m,f* de perros; **d. license** licencia *f* del perro; **d. paddle** *(swimming stroke)* estilo *m* perrito; **d. racing** carreras *fpl* de galgos; **d. tag** *(of dog, soldier)* placa *f* de identificación
   (**b**) *Fam (person)* **you lucky d.!** ¡qué potra tienes!; **dirty d.** canalla *mf*, perro(a) *m,f* asqueroso(a)
   (**c**) *Fam Pej (ugly woman)* coco *m*, *Esp* cardo *m*, *Andes, RP* bagre *m*
   (**d**) *(idioms) Fam* **to lead a dog's life** llevar una vida de perros; *Fam* **to make a dog's breakfast** *or* **dinner of sth** hacer una chapuza con algo; *Fam* **it's a d.-eat-d. world** es un mundo de fieras; *Fam* **to go to the dogs** irse a pique, hundirse; *Fam* **to be a d. in the manger** ser como el perro del hortelano, que ni come ni deja comer; *Prov* **you can't teach an old d. new tricks** a perro viejo no hay tus tus; *Prov* **every d. has his day** todos tenemos nuestro momento de gloria
   2 *vt (pt & pp* **dogged**) *(follow)* perseguir, seguir; **to d. sb's footsteps** seguir los pasos de alguien; **she was dogged by misfortune** le perseguía la mala suerte

dog-eared ['dɒgɪəd] *adj (book, page)* ajado(a), con las esquinas dobladas

dogfight ['dɒgfaɪt] *n (between planes)* combate *m* aéreo; *(between people)* lucha *f* encarnizada

dogfish ['dɒgfɪʃ] *n* lija *f*, pintarroja *f*

dogged ['dɒgɪd] *adj* tenaz, perseverante

doggedly ['dɒgɪdlɪ] *adv* tenazmente, con tenacidad

doggedness ['dɒgɪdnɪs] *n* tenacidad *f*

doggerel ['dɒgərəl] *n (comical)* poesía *f* burlesca; *(bad)* ripios *mpl*

doggy ['dɒgɪ] *n Fam* perrito *m*; **d. bag** bolsa *f* con las sobras de la comida

doghouse ['dɒghaʊs] *n Fam* **to be in the d.** haber caído en desgracia

dogma ['dɒgmə] *n* dogma *m*

dogmatic [dɒg'mætɪk] *adj* dogmático(a)

dogmatism ['dɒgmətɪzəm] *n* dogmatismo *m*

do-gooder ['duː'gʊdə(r)] *n Fam Pej* buen(ena) samaritano(a) *m,f*

dog-tired ['dɒg'taɪəd] *adj Fam* hecho(a) polvo

dogwood ['dɒgwʊd] *n* cornejo *m*, cerezo *m* silvestre

doh [dəʊ] *n Mus* do *m*

doily ['dɔɪlɪ] *n* blonda *f*, *RP* carpeta *f*

doing ['duːɪŋ] *n* (a) **this is his d.** esto es obra suya; **it was none of my d.** yo no he tenido nada que ver; **that takes some d.** eso tiene su trabajo *or* no es ninguna tontería (**b**) **doings** actividades *fpl*

do-it-yourself [duːɪtjɔː'self] *n* bricolaje *m*; **a d. enthusiast** un amante del bricolaje

doldrums ['dɒldrəmz] *npl* **to be in the d.** *(person)* estar con

la moral baja, *Am* estar con el ánimo por el piso; *(trade, economy)* estar estancado(a)

▸**dole out** *vt sep Fam* repartir

doleful ['dəʊlfʊl] *adj* triste

doll [dɒl] *n* muñeca *f*

▸**doll up** *vt sep Fam* **to d. oneself up** emperifollarse

dollar ['dɒlə(r)] *n* dólar *m*; **d. bill** billete *m* de un dólar

dollhouse ['dɒlhaʊs] *n* casa *f* de muñecas

dollop ['dɒləp] *n Fam (of ice cream, mashed potato)* cucharada *f*

dolly ['dɒlɪ] *n Fam* muñequita *f*

dolphin ['dɒlfɪn] *n* delfín *m*

dolt [dəʊlt] *n* estúpido(a) *m,f*, idiota *mf*

domain [də'meɪn] *n (lands)* dominios *mpl*; *Comptr* dominio *m*; *Fig (area of influence, expertise)* ámbito *m*, campo *m*; **that is outside my d.** eso queda fuera de mi campo; *Comptr* **d. name** nombre *m* de dominio

dome [dəʊm] *n* cúpula *f*

domestic [də'mestɪk] *adj* (a) *(appliance, pet)* doméstico(a); **d. bliss** felicidad *f* hogareña; **d. servant** criado(a) *m,f*; **d. violence** violencia *f* doméstica (**b**) *(policy)* interior; *(flight, economy)* nacional

domesticate [də'mestɪkeɪt] *vt (animal)* domesticar

domesticated [də'mestɪkeɪtɪd] *adj (animal)* domesticado(a); *Fig Hum* **to be d.** *(person)* estar muy bien enseñado(a)

domestication [dəmestɪ'keɪʃən] *n (of animal)* domesticación *f*

domicile ['dɒmɪsaɪl] *n Law* domicilio *m*

domiciliary [dɒmɪ'sɪlɪərɪ] *adj Formal (visit)* a domicilio; *(care, services)* domiciliario(a)

dominance ['dɒmɪnəns] *n (in general)* predominio *m*, dominación *f*; *(of gene)* dominancia *f*

dominant ['dɒmɪnənt] *adj* dominante

dominate ['dɒmɪneɪt] *vt & vi* dominar

domination [dɒmɪ'neɪʃən] *n* dominio *m*

domineer [dɒmɪ'nɪə(r)] *vi* dominar; **to d. over sb** someter a alguien

domineering [dɒmɪ'nɪərɪŋ] *adj* dominante

Dominica [də'mɪnɪkə] *n* Dominica

Dominican [də'mɪnɪkən] **1** *n (person from Dominican Republic)* dominicano(a) *m,f*
   2 *adj (of Dominican Republic)* dominicano(a); **the D. Republic** la República Dominicana

dominion [də'mɪnjən] *n Literary* dominio *m*

domino ['dɒmɪnəʊ] *(pl* **dominoes** *or* **dominos**) *n* ficha *f* de dominó; **dominoes** *(game)* dominó *m*; *Pol* **d. effect** efecto *m* dominó

don [dɒn] *(pt & pp* **donned**) *vt Formal (hat, clothes)* enfundarse, ponerse

donate [də'neɪt] *vt* donar

donation [də'neɪʃən] *n* donativo *m*, donación *f*; **to make a d.** hacer un donativo

done [dʌn] *pp of* **do**

donkey ['dɒŋkɪ] *n (animal)* burro *m*; *(person)* burro(a) *m,f*; *Fam* **I haven't seen him for d.'s years** no lo he visto desde hace siglos

donor ['dəʊnə(r)] *n* donante *mf*; **d. card** carné *m* de donante

don't [dəʊnt] = **do not**

don't know ['dəʊnt'nəʊ] *n* (a) *(answer)* no sé *m* (**b**) *(person)* = persona que no sabe o no contesta en un cuestionario

donut = **doughnut**

doodad ['duːdæd] *n Fam* chisme *m*, *CAm, Carib, Col* vaina *f*, *RP* coso *m*

doodle ['duːdəl] *Fam* **1** *n* garabato *m*
   2 *vi* garabatear

doom [duːm] **1** *n* fatalidad *f*; **it's not all d. and gloom** no todo es tan terrible

2 *vt* **to be doomed** *(unlucky)* tener mala estrella; *(about to die)* ir hacia una muerte segura; *(plan, marriage, expedition)* estar condenado(a) al fracaso; **to be doomed to do sth** estar fatalmente predestinado(a) a hacer algo

doomsday ['duːmzdeɪ] *n* día *m* del Juicio Final; **till d.** hasta el día del Juicio Final

door [dɔː(r)] *n* puerta *f*; **to see sb to the d.** acompañar a alguien a la puerta *or* a la salida; **to show sb the d.** *(ask to leave)* echar a alguien; **out of doors** al aire libre; **to shut the d. in sb's face** dar a alguien con la puerta en las narices; **she lives two doors away** vive a dos portales de aquí; *Fig* **to lay sth at sb's d.** achacar algo a alguien; **d. handle** manilla *f*, tirador *m*; **d. knocker** aldaba *f*, llamador *m*

doorbell ['dɔːbel] *n* timbre *m*

do-or-die ['duːɔː'daɪ] *adj* **he has a d. approach to any challenge** ante cualquier reto va a por todas

doorjamb = **doorpost**

doorkeeper ['dɔːkiːpə(r)] *n* portero(a) *m,f*

doorknob ['dɔːnɒb] *n* pomo *m*

doorman ['dɔːmən] *n* portero *m*

doormat ['dɔːmæt] *n* felpudo *m*; *Fig* **to treat sb like a d.** tratar como un trapo *or* pisotear a alguien

doorpost ['dɔːpəʊst], **doorjamb** ['dɔːdʒæm] *n* jamba *f*

doorstep ['dɔːstep] *n* escalón *m* de entrada; **he stood on the d.** se quedó en el umbral; *Fig* **on one's d.** *(very near)* en la misma puerta

doorstop ['dɔːstɒp] *n* *(fixed)* tope *m*; *(wedge)* cuña *f*

door-to-door ['dɔːtə'dɔː(r)] **1** *adj Pol* **d. canvassing** = campaña electoral en la que los representantes de los partidos van de casa en casa; *Com* **d. salesman** vendedor *m* a domicilio
2 *adv* **to sell sth d.** vender algo a domicilio

doorway ['dɔːweɪ] *n* puerta *f*, entrada *f*; **in the d.** a *or* en la puerta

dope [dəʊp] **1** *n* (**a**) *Fam (hashish, cannabis)* costo *m*; *(marijuana)* maría *f*; **d. test** *(for athlete)* control *m* or prueba *f* antidoping (**b**) *Fam (idiot)* tonto(a) *m,f*, bobo(a) *m,f*, *Am* sonso(a) *m,f*, *Am* zonzo(a) *m,f*
2 *vt (person, horse)* drogar; *(food, drink)* echar droga en

dopey, dopy ['dəʊpɪ] *adj Fam (stupid)* tonto(a), bobo(a), *Am* sonso(a), *Am* zonzo(a)

doppelgänger ['dɒpəlgæŋə(r)] *n* doble *mf*

dopy = **dopey**

dork [dɔːk] *n Fam* petardo(a) *m,f*

dorm [dɔːm] *n Fam (dormitory)* dormitorio *m*

dormant ['dɔːmənt] **1** *adj (emotions, ideas)* latente; *(volcano)* inactivo(a)
2 *adv* **to lie d.** permanecer latente

dormitory ['dɔːmɪtərɪ] *n* (**a**) dormitorio *m* (**b**) *Univ* ≃ colegio *m* mayor

dormouse ['dɔːmaʊs] *(pl* **dormice** ['dɔːmaɪs]*)* *n* lirón *m*

dorsal ['dɔːsəl] *adj* dorsal

DOS [dɒs] *n Comptr (abbr* **disk operating system***)* DOS *m*

dosage ['dəʊsɪdʒ] *n (amount)* dosis *f*; **to increase the d.** aumentar la dosis

dose [dəʊs] **1** *n* dosis *f inv*; **a d. of flu** una gripe *or Col, Méx* gripa
2 *vt Fam* **to d. oneself (up) with pills** tomarse una fuerte dosis de pastillas

dossier ['dɒsɪeɪ] *n* dossier *m*, expediente *m*

dot [dɒt] **1** *n* punto *m*; **on the d.** en punto; **d. com (company)** empresa *f* punto com; *Comptr* **d. matrix printer** impresora *f* matricial *or* de agujas
2 *vt (pt & pp* **dotted***)* salpicar; **to d. an 'i'** poner el punto sobre una i; **dotted with** salpicado(a) de; *Fig* **to d. the i's (and cross the t's)** dar los últimos toques; **dotted line** línea *f* de puntos; **to sign on the dotted line** estampar la firma

dotage ['dəʊtɪdʒ] *n* **to be in one's d.** estar chocho(a), chochear

▶**dote on, dote upon** [dəʊt] *vt insep* mimar, adorar

dotty ['dɒtɪ] *adj Fam (person)* chalado(a); **a d. idea** una chaladura; **to be d.** estar chalado(a); **he's d. about her** se le cae la baba por ella

double ['dʌbəl] **1** *n* (**a**) *(of person)* doble *mf* (**b**) *(hotel room)* habitación *f* doble (**c**) **doubles** *(in tennis)* dobles *mpl*; **a doubles match** un partido de dobles (**d**) **at** *or* **on the d.** a toda velocidad, corriendo
2 *adj* doble; **a d. gin/whiskey** una ginebra/un whisky doble; **d. m** *(when spelling)* doble eme, dos emes; **d. agent** agente *mf* doble; **d. bass** contrabajo *m*; **d. bed** cama *f* de matrimonio; **d. bill** *(at cinema)* sesión *f* doble; **d. chin** papada *f*; **d. date** cita *f* de dos parejas; *Fam* **to talk d. Dutch** hablar en chino; **d. fault** *(in tennis)* doble falta *f*; **d. figures** números *mpl* de dos cifras; **inflation is now in d. figures** la inflación ha superado la barrera del 10 por ciento; **d. glazing** doble acristalamiento *m*; *Fin* **d. indemnity** = seguro de vida en el que se paga el doble del capital cuando el asegurado muere por accidente; **to lead a d. life** llevar una doble vida; **d. meaning** doble sentido *m*; **d. parking** estacionamiento *m* or *Esp* aparcamiento *m* en doble fila; **d. room** habitación *f* doble; **d. spacing** doble espacio *m*; **d. standard** doble moral *f*; **to do a d. take** reaccionar un instante más tarde
3 *adv* (**a**) *(twice as much)* el doble; **to charge sb d.** cobrar a alguien el doble; **it costs d. what it did last year** cuesta el doble de lo que costaba el año pasado; **to see d.** ver doble (**b**) *(in two)* **to fold sth d.** doblar algo por la mitad; **to be bent d.** estar doblado(a) *or* agachado(a)
4 *vt* (**a**) *(multiply by 2)* duplicar (**b**) *(fold)* doblar por la mitad
5 *vi* (**a**) *(increase)* duplicarse (**b**) **to d. as** *(person)* hacer también de; *(thing)* funcionar también como

▶**double back** *vi* volver (uno) sobre sus pasos

▶**double up** *vi (bend)* doblarse; **to d. up with pain** retorcerse de dolor; **to d. up with laughter** troncharse de risa

double-barreled ['dʌbəl'bærəld] *adj (shotgun)* de dos cañones; *(surname)* compuesto(a)

double-blind ['dʌbəl'blaɪnd] *adj (experiment)* a doble ciego

double-breasted ['dʌbəl'brestɪd] *adj (jacket, suit)* cruzado(a)

double-check ['dʌbəl'tʃek] *vt & vi* comprobar dos veces

double-click ['dʌbəl'klɪk] *Comptr* **1** *n* doble click *m*
2 *vt* hacer doble click en
3 *vi* hacer doble click (**on** en)

double-cross ['dʌbəl'krɒs] *vt* engañar, traicionar

double-dealing ['dʌbəl'diːlɪŋ] *n* doblez *f*, duplicidad *f*

double-edged ['dʌbəl'edʒd] *adj (blade, remark)* de doble filo

double-jointed ['dʌbəl'dʒɔɪntəd] *adj* **to be d.** = tener las articulaciones más flexibles de lo normal de modo que se doblan hacia atrás

double-lock ['dʌbəl'lɒk] *vt* cerrar con dos vueltas (de llave)

double-park ['dʌbəl'pɑːk] **1** *vt* estacionar *or Esp* aparcar en doble fila
2 *vi* estacionarse *or Esp* aparcar en doble fila

double-quick ['dʌbəl'kwɪk] *adv* rapidísimamente

doublethink ['dʌbəlθɪŋk] *n* (asunción *f* de) ideas *fpl* contradictorias

doubly ['dʌblɪ] *adv* doblemente, por partida doble

doubt [daʊt] **1** *n* duda *f*; **to have doubts about sth** tener dudas sobre algo; **to be in d.** *(person)* tener dudas; *(outcome)* ser incierto(a); **when in d.** en caso de duda; **beyond d.** sin lugar a dudas; **no d.** sin duda; **there is no d. that...** no cabe duda de que...; **there is no d. about her guilt** no hay duda alguna acerca de su culpabilidad; **there is some d. about her**

guilt se tienen dudas acerca de su culpabilidad
2 *vt* dudar; **I d. it** lo dudo; **I d. whether that is the case** dudo que sea así; **do you d. me?** ¿acaso dudas de mí?

doubtful ['daʊtfʊl] *adj* (**a**) *(uncertain) (person)* dubitativo(a); *(outcome)* incierto(a); **to be d. about sth** tener dudas acerca de algo; **it is d. whether he will succeed** es dudoso que tenga éxito (**b**) *(questionable)* dudoso(a)

doubtfully ['daʊtfʊlɪ] *adv* con aire dubitativo, sin demasiada convicción

doubting ['daʊtɪŋ] *adj* escéptico(a), incrédulo(a); **a d. Thomas** un(a) escéptico(a) *or* incrédulo(a)

doubtless ['daʊtlɪs] *adv* sin duda, indudablemente

dough [dəʊ] *n* (**a**) *(for bread)* masa *f* (**b**) *Fam (money) Esp* pasta *f*, *Esp, RP* guita *f*, *Am* plata *f*, *Méx* lana *f*

doughnut, donut ['dəʊnʌt] *n (with hole)* dónut *m*; *(without hole)* buñuelo *m*

dour [dʊə(r)] *adj* severo(a), adusto(a)

Douro ['dʊərəʊ] *n* **the D.** el Duero

douse [daʊs] *vt* (**a**) *(soak)* empapar, mojar (**b**) *(extinguish)* apagar

dove[1] [dʌv] *n* paloma *f*

dove[2] [dəʊv] *pt of* **dive**

dovecot(e) ['dʌvkɒt] *n* palomar *m*

dovetail ['dʌvteɪl] *vi (fit closely)* encajar (**with** en *or* con)

dowager ['daʊədʒə(r)] *n* viuda *f (de un noble)* **d. duchess** duquesa *f* viuda

dowdy ['daʊdɪ] *adj* poco atractivo(a)

dowel ['daʊəl] *n (in carpentry)* espiga *f*

down[1] [daʊn] *n (feathers)* plumón *m*

down[2] [daʊn] **1** *prep* **to go d. the street** ir por la calle; **to fall d. the stairs** caerse por las escaleras (abajo); **they sailed d. the river** navegaron río abajo
2 *adv* (**a**) *(motion)* abajo; **I'll be d. in a minute** bajo enseguida; **d. with traitors!** ¡abajo *or* fuera los traidores! (**b**) *(position)* abajo; **d. here/there** aquí/ahí abajo; **further d.** más abajo; **the price is d.** ha bajado el precio; **one d., two to go!** ¡uno menos, ya sólo quedan dos!; **everyone from the boss d.** todos, desde el jefe hacia *or* para abajo (**c**) *(idioms)* **to be d. on sb/sth** haber agarrado *or Esp* cogido manía a alguien/algo; **it's d. to her** *(her decision)* ella decide; *(her achievement)* es gracias a ella; **I'm d. to my last cigarette** sólo me queda un cigarrillo (**d**) *Comptr* **to be d.** no funcionar; **d. time** *(in industry)* paro *m* técnico
3 *adj* (**a**) *(depressed)* deprimido(a) (**b**) **d. payment** pago *m* inicial, *Esp* entrada *f*, *Am* cuota *f* inicial
4 *vt* **to d. an aircraft** derribar un avión; **he downed his beer and left** se terminó la cerveza de un trago y se fue

down-and-out ['daʊnən'aʊt] *Fam* **1** *n (tramp)* vagabundo(a) *m,f*, indigente *mf*
2 *adj* **to be d.** ser indigente

downbeat ['daʊnbiːt] *adj* (**a**) *(gloomy, pessimistic)* triste, pesimista (**b**) *(restrained)* **to be d. about sth** minimizar algo

downcast ['daʊnkɑːst] *adj (eyes)* bajo(a); *(person)* deprimido(a), abatido(a); **to be d.** *(person)* estar deprimido(a) *or* abatido(a)

downer ['daʊnə(r)] *n Fam* (**a**) *(drug)* calmante *m*, depresor *m* (**b**) **what a d.!** *(how depressing)* ¡qué muermo!

downfall ['daʊnfɔːl] *n (of government)* caída *f*; *(of person)* perdición *f*

downgrade ['daʊngreɪd] *vt* degradar, rebajar

downhearted [daʊn'hɑːtɪd] *adj* desanimado(a), abatido(a)

downhill ['daʊn'hɪl] **1** *adj (road)* cuesta abajo; **d. skiing** (esquí *m* de) descenso *m*
2 *adv also Fig* **to go d.** ir cuesta abajo

Downing Street ['daʊnɪŋstriːt] *n* Downing Street

down-in-the-mouth ['daʊnɪnðə'maʊθ] *adj* **to be d.** estar deprimido(a) *or* tristón(ona)

download ['daʊn'ləʊd] *Comptr* **1** *n* descarga *f*
2 *vt* bajar, descargar
3 *vi* descargarse

downloadable [daʊn'ləʊdəbəl] *adj Comptr* descargable; **d. font** fuente *f* cargable

downloading [daʊn'ləʊdɪŋ] *n Comptr* descarga *f*

down-market [daʊn'mɑːkɪt] *adj* popular, barato(a)

downpour ['daʊnpɔː(r)] *n* aguacero *m*, tromba *f* de agua

downright ['daʊnraɪt] **1** *adj (stupidity, dishonesty)* absoluto(a), completo(a); **it's a d. lie!** ¡es completamente falso!
2 *adv (stupid, untrue)* absolutamente, completamente

downshift ['daʊnʃɪft] *vi* (**a**) *(change gear)* reducir (**b**) *(change lifestyle)* relajar el ritmo de vida

downsize ['daʊnsaɪz] *vt Com* hacer reajuste de plantilla en, reducir plantilla en

downsizing ['daʊnsaɪzɪŋ] *n* reajuste *m* de plantillas

Down's Syndrome ['daʊn'sɪndrəʊm] *n* síndrome *m* de Down

downstairs 1 ['daʊnsteəz] *adj* del piso de abajo; **the d. apartment/bathroom** el piso/cuarto de baño de abajo
2 [daʊn'steəz] *adv* **to come/go d.** bajar (la escalera); **he lives d.** vive en el apartamento *or Esp* piso de abajo

downstream [daʊn'striːm] *adv* aguas abajo

downswing ['daʊnswɪŋ] *n Econ* (fase *f* de) contracción *f*, bajón *m*

down-to-earth ['daʊntə'ɜːθ] *adj* práctico(a), realista

downtown ['daʊn'taʊn] **1** *n (city center)* centro *m* (urbano)
2 *adj* del centro; **d. New York** el centro de Nueva York
3 *adv* **he gave me a lift d.** me llevó *or CAm, Méx, Perú* me dio aventón al centro; **to live d.** vivir en el centro

downtrodden ['daʊntrɒdən] *adj* oprimido(a)

downturn ['daʊntɜːn] *n Econ* (fase *f* de) contracción *f*, bajón *m*

downward ['daʊnwəd] **1** *adj (trend)* descendente
2 *adv* hacia abajo

downwards ['daʊnwədz] *adv* hacia abajo

dowry ['daʊrɪ] *n* dote *f*

doze [dəʊz] **1** *n* cabezada *f*, sueñecito *m*; **to have** *or* **take a d.** echar una cabezada
2 *vi* dormitar

▸**doze off** *vi* quedarse traspuesto(a)

dozen ['dʌzən] *n* docena *f*; **a d. eggs** una docena de huevos; **half a d. eggs** media docena de huevos; **86 cents a d.** 86 centavos la docena; *Fam* **dozens of times/people** cientos de veces/personas

dozy ['dəʊzɪ] *adj Fam (sleepy)* amodorrado(a); *(stupid)* bobo(a), idiota

Dr *(abbr* **doctor***)* Dr., Dra., doctor(ora) *m,f*

drab [dræb] *adj (person)* gris, soso(a); *(colors, clothes)* soso(a), insulso(a); *(atmosphere, city)* anodino(a)

drabness ['dræbnɪs] *n (of color, clothes)* sosería *f*; *(of atmosphere)* sosería *f*, insulsez *f*

drachma ['drækmə] *n Formerly* dracma *m*

draconian [drə'kəʊnɪən] *adj* draconiano(a)

draft[1] [drɑːft] **1** *n* (**a**) *(of letter, proposal, novel)* borrador *m* (**b**) *Fin* letra *f* de cambio, giro *m* (**c**) *(conscription)* llamada *f or Am* llamado *m* a filas, reclutamiento *m*; **d. dodger** = persona que se libra de tener que alistarse en el ejército mediante subterfugios
2 *vt* (**a**) *(letter, proposal)* hacer un borrador de; **to d. a bill** redactar un anteproyecto de ley (**b**) *Mil* llamar a filas a, reclutar

▸**draft in** *vt sep (troops, supporters)* movilizar

draft[2] [drɑːft] *n* (**a**) *(wind)* corriente *f* (de aire) (**b**) *(drink)* trago *m*; **on d.** *(beer)* de barril; **d. beer** cerveza *f* de barril

draftboard ['drɑːftbɔːd] *n* tablero *m* de damas

draftee [drɑːf'tiː] *n* recluta *mf (forzoso)*

draft-proof ['drɑːftpruːf] **1** *vt* hacer hermético(a)
  2 *adj* hermético(a)

draft-proofing ['drɑːft'pruːfɪŋ] *n* aislamiento *m* (*contra corrientes*)

draftsman ['drɑːftsmən] *n* delineante *mf*

drafty ['drɑːftɪ] *adj* **this room/house is a bit d.** en este cuarto/en esta casa hay *or* hace bastante corriente

drag [dræg] **1** *n* (**a**) (*air resistance*) resistencia *f* del aire; **d. racing** = carreras de aceleración en coches preparados (**b**) *Fam* (*person*) plomo *m*, pelma *mf*; (*task*) rollo *m*, lata *f*; **the party was a real d.** la fiesta fue un rollazo (**c**) *Fam* (*on cigarette*) chupada *f*, *Esp* calada *f*, *Am* pitada *f*; **to take a d. on a cigarette** dar una chupada a un cigarrillo (**d**) (*women's clothing*) **he was in d.** iba vestido de mujer; **d. artist** *or* **queen** transformista *m*, travestí *m* (*que viste espectacularmente*)
  2 *vt* (*pt & pp* **dragged**) (**a**) (*pull*) arrastrar; *Fig* **they dragged their feet over the decision** se anduvieron con muchos rodeos hasta tomar la decisión; *Fam* **we eventually dragged ourselves away from the party** finalmente y a regañadientes nos fuimos de la fiesta (**b**) (*trawl*) (*pond, canal*) dragar
  3 *vi* (*movie, conversation*) resultar pesado(a); **the meeting dragged to a close** la reunión terminó por fin

▸**drag on** *vi* (*meeting, movie*) durar eternamente

▸**drag out** *vt sep* (*meeting, speech*) alargar innecesariamente

▸**drag up** *vt* (*refer to*) sacar a relucir

dragnet ['drægnet] *n* (*in deep-sea fishing*) red *f* de arrastre *or* barredera; *Fig* (*to catch criminals*) emboscada *f*

dragon ['drægən] *n* (**a**) (*mythological creature*) dragón *m* (**b**) *Fam* (*fearsome woman*) ogro *m*, bruja *f*

dragonfly ['drægənflaɪ] *n* libélula *f*

dragoon [drə'guːn] **1** *n* (*soldier*) dragón *m*
  2 *vt* **to d. sb into doing sth** obligar a alguien a hacer algo

drain [dreɪn] **1** *n* (**a**) (*for water*) desagüe *m*; (*for sewage*) alcantarilla *f*; (*grating*) sumidero *m*; *Fig* **to go down the d.** (*money*) echarse a perder; (*work*) irse al traste (**b**) (*on strength, resources*) merma *f*, mengua *f* (**on** de); **the space program is a d. on the country's resources** el programa espacial se lleva muchos de los recursos del país
  2 *vt* (*liquid*) vaciar, quitar (**from** de); (*sink*) vaciar; (*pond*) desaguar; (*swamp*) drenar; (*pasta, vegetables*) escurrir; *Fig* **to d. wealth from a country** debilitar la economía de un país; *Fig* **to feel drained** estar extenuado(a)
  3 *vi* (*liquid*) irse; (*sink, river*) desaguar; (*washed dishes*) escurrir; **the color drained from her face** se puso pálida, empalideció repentinamente

▸**drain away** *vi* (*liquid*) irse; *Fig* (*strength, enthusiasm*) diluirse, agotarse; *Fig* (*fear, tension*) disiparse

drainage ['dreɪnɪdʒ] *n* (*of soil, land*) drenaje *m*

drainboard ['dreɪnbɔːd] *n* escurridero *m*, escurreplatos *m inv*

drained [dreɪnd] *adj Fig* (*person*) exhausto(a)

drainpipe ['dreɪnpaɪp] *n* tubo *m* de desagüe; **drainpipes** pantalones *mpl* de pitillo

drake [dreɪk] *n* (*male duck*) pato *m*

dram [dræm] *n* (*of whiskey*) chupito *m*

drama ['drɑːmə] *n* (**a**) (*art form*) teatro *m*, drama *m*; (*play*) obra *f* de teatro, drama *m*; *Fig* **to make a d. out of sth** hacer una tragedia de algo; **d. school** escuela *f* de arte dramático (**b**) (*excitement*) dramatismo *m*

dramatic [drə'mætɪk] *adj* (**a**) *Theat* (*actor, work*) dramático(a) (**b**) (*change, reduction*) drástico(a); (*effect*) dramático(a); (*event, scenery*) espectacular

dramatics [drə'mætɪks] *npl* (**a**) *Theat* arte *m* dramático, teatro *m* (**b**) (*behavior*) histrionismo *m*, dramatismo *m* exagerado

dramatist ['dræmətɪst] *n* dramaturgo(a) *m,f*

dramatization [dræmətaɪ'zeɪʃən] *n* dramatización *f*

dramatize ['dræmətaɪz] *vt* (**a**) (*novel*) adaptar para el teatro (**b**) (*exaggerate*) **to d. a situation** dramatizar una situación

drank [dræŋk] *pt of* **drink**

drape [dreɪp] **1** *vt* (*table, coffin*) cubrir (**with** con); **they draped the flag over the coffin** cubrieron el ataúd con la bandera
  2 *n* **drapes** (*curtains*) cortinas *fpl*

drastic ['dræstɪk] *adj* drástico(a)

drat [dræt] *exclam Fam* **d. (it)!** ¡caramba!

dratted ['drætɪd] *adj Fam* dichoso(a), condenado(a)

draught² = **draft²**

draught-proof, draught-proofing = **draft-proof, draft-proofing**

draughtsman = **draftsman**

draughty = **drafty**

draw [drɔː] **1** *n* (**a**) (*in argument*) empate *m* (*in chess*) tablas *fpl* (**b**) (*lottery, for sporting competition*) sorteo *m* (**c**) (*attraction*) atracción *f*
  2 *vt* (*pt* **drew** [druː], *pp* **drawn** [drɔːn]) (**a**) (*picture, diagram, map*) dibujar; **to d. sb's picture** hacer el retrato de alguien
  (**b**) (*pull*) (*cart*) tirar de; (*person*) llevar (**toward** hacia); **he drew her toward him in a passionate embrace** la atrajo hacia él abrazándola apasionadamente; **to d. the curtains** (*open or shut*) correr *or Esp* echar *or RP* cerrar las cortinas; **he barely had time to d. breath** apenas tuvo tiempo de respirar
  (**c**) (*extract*) (*cork, tooth, nail*) sacar (**from** de); (*pistol*) desenfundar; (*sword*) desenvainar; *Fig* (*strength, comfort*) hallar (**from** en); **to d. money from the bank** sacar dinero del banco; **to d. a salary** recibir un sueldo; **to d. blood** hacer sangre; **he drew a knife on me** me sacó un cuchillo; **to d. lots** echar a suertes; **to d. a conclusion from sth** sacar una conclusión de algo; **she refused to be drawn on the issue** eludió dar detalles sobre el asunto; **our members are drawn from all walks of life** nuestros socios proceden de diferentes profesiones; **they were drawn against the champions** (*in competition*) les tocó enfrentarse a los campeones
  (**d**) (*attract*) atraer; **to d. a crowd** atraer a una multitud; **to feel drawn to sb/sth** sentirse atraído(a) hacia alguien/algo; *Fig* **to d. sb's fire** suscitar las críticas *or* iras de alguien
  (**e**) (*tie*) **to d. a chess game with sb** quedar en tablas con alguien
  3 *vi* (**a**) (*illustrate*) dibujar (**b**) (*in game*) empatar (**with** con) (**c**) (*move*) **to d. ahead of sb** adelantar a alguien; **to d. level with sb** ponerse a la altura de alguien; **to d. to an end** llegar al final; **to d. near** acercarse, aproximarse; **to d. to a halt** detenerse, *Am* parar

▸**draw back 1** *vt sep* (*sheet, veil*) retirar
  2 *vi* echarse atrás

▸**draw in** *vi* **the nights are drawing in** las noches se están alargando

▸**draw on 1** *vt insep* (*resources, savings, experience*) recurrir a
  2 *vi* **evening was drawing on** caía la tarde

▸**draw out** *vt sep* (**a**) (*encourage to talk*) **to d. sb out** hacer que alguien hable (**b**) (*prolong*) alargar, prolongar

▸**draw up 1** *vt sep* (**a**) (*pull*) **to d. up a chair** acercar una silla; **she drew herself up to her full height** se levantó cuan larga era (**b**) (*plan, document, will*) redactar
  2 *vi* (*vehicle*) parar, detenerse

drawback ['drɔːbæk] *n* inconveniente *m*

drawbridge ['drɔːbrɪdʒ] *n* puente *m* levadizo

drawer [drɔː(r)] *n* cajón *m*; **chest of drawers** cómoda *f*

drawers [drɔːəz] *npl Old-fashioned* (*for women*) *Esp* bragas *fpl*, *Esp* braga *f*, *CAm, Carib* blúmer *m*, *Andes, Méx, RP* calzón *m*, *CAm, Carib, Méx* pantaleta *f*, *RP* bombacha *f*; (*for men*) calzoncillos *mpl*, *Chile* fundillos *mpl*, *Col* pantaloncillos *mpl*, *Bol, Méx* calzones *mpl*

drawing ['drɔːɪŋ] *n* (**a**) (*illustration*) dibujo *m*; **d. board** tablero *m* de dibujo; *Fig* **back to the d. board!** ¡hay que volver a empezar desde el principio!; **d. paper** papel *m* de dibujo (**b**) **d. room** *(in house)* sala *f* de estar, salón *f* (**c**) **d. power** *(attractive capacity)* poder *m* de convocatoria

drawl [drɔːl] **1** *n* acento *m* cansino
2 *vi* arrastrar los sonidos al hablar

drawn [drɔːn] **1** *adj* **to look d.** tener aspecto demacrado(a); **d. features** facciones *fpl* demacradas
2 *pp of* **draw**

drawstring ['drɔːstrɪŋ] *n* cordón *m*

dread [dred] **1** *n* pavor *m*, terror *m*
2 *vt* **she dreaded telling him** la idea de decírselo le aterraba; **I d. to think!** ¡me da pavor pensarlo!

dreaded ['dredɪd] *adj* temido(a), temible

dreadful ['dredfʊl] *adj* (**a**) *(terrible)* espantoso(a), horroroso(a); **to feel d.** *(ill, embarrassed)* sentirse muy mal *or Esp* fatal; **to look d.** tener un aspecto terrible (**b**) *Fam (for emphasis)* **it's a d. bore!** ¡es un aburrimiento total!; **it's a d. shame!** ¡es una vergüenza absoluta!

dreadfully ['dredfʊlɪ] *adv Fam* (**a**) *(very badly)* espantosamente, *Esp* fatal (**b**) *(very)* terriblemente

dreadlocks ['dredlɒks] *npl* trenzas *fpl* rastafari

dream [driːm] **1** *n* sueño *m*; **to have a d. (about)** soñar (con); **to have bad dreams** tener pesadillas; **a d. come true** un sueño hecho realidad; **it worked like a d.** salió a la perfección; **my d. house** la casa de mis sueños; **d. world** mundo *m* de ensueño
2 *vt* **to d. that...** soñar que...; *Fig* **I never dreamed you would take me seriously** nunca imaginé que me tomarías en serio
3 *vi* soñar; **to d. of** *or* **about** soñar con; *Fam* **I wouldn't d. of it!** ¡jamás se me ocurriría!

▸**dream up** *vt (scheme, excuse)* idear, inventarse

dreamboat ['driːmbəʊt] *n Fam* bombón *m*

dreamer ['driːmə(r)] *n* soñador(ora) *m,f*

dreamlike ['driːmlaɪk] *adj* onírico(a)

dreamy ['driːmɪ] *adj* soñador(ora)

dreary ['drɪərɪ] *adj* deprimente

dredge [dredʒ] *vt (canal, harbor)* dragar; *Fig* **she dredged her memory** rebuscó en su memoria

▸**dredge up** *vt* sacar del agua al dragar; *Fig (scandal, memory)* sacar a relucir

dredger ['dredʒə(r)] *n (boat)* dragador *m*

dregs [dregz] *npl (of drink)* posos *mpl*; *Fig* **the d. of society** la escoria de la sociedad

drench [drentʃ] *vt* empapar (**with** *or* **in** con *or* en); **drenched to the skin** calado(a) hasta los huesos

dress [dres] **1** *n* (**a**) *(for woman)* vestido *m* (**b**) *(clothing)* traje *m*; **to have good/no d. sense** saber/no saber vestirse, tener/no tener estilo para vestir; **d. circle** *(in theater)* piso *m* principal; **d. code** normas *fpl* en el vestir, código *m* vestimentario; **d. rehearsal** *(of play)* ensayo *m* general; **d. shirt** camisa *f* de vestir
2 *vt* (**a**) *(person)* vestir; **to d. oneself, to get dressed** vestirse; **to be dressed in black** ir vestido(a) de negro; **well/badly dressed** bien/mal vestido(a) (**b**) *(wound)* vendar (**c**) *(salad)* aderezar, *Esp* aliñar
3 *vi* vestirse

▸**dress up** *vi (elegantly)* arreglarse, vestirse de etiqueta; *(in fancy dress)* disfrazarse (**as** de)

dresser ['dresə(r)] *n* (**a**) *(in kitchen)* aparador *m* (**b**) *(in bedroom)* cómoda *f* (**c**) *Theat* ayudante *mf* de camerino

dressing ['dresɪŋ] *n* (**a**) **d. gown** bata *f*; **d. room** *Theat* camerino *m*; *Sport* vestuario *m*; **d. table** tocador *m* (**b**) *(for wound)* vendaje *m*, gasa *f* (**c**) *(for salad)* aderezo *m*, *Esp* aliño *m*

dressing-down ['dresɪŋ'daʊn] *n Fam* **to give sb a d.**

regañar a alguien, *Esp* echar un rapapolvo a alguien

dressmaker ['dresmeɪkə(r)] *n* modista *f*

dressmaking ['dresmeɪkɪŋ] *n* corte *m* y confección

dressy [dresɪ] *adj Fam* elegante, puesto(a)

drew [druː] *pt of* **draw**

drib [drɪb] *n* **in dribs and drabs** poco a poco, con cuentagotas

dribble ['drɪbəl] **1** *n (saliva)* baba *f*; *(of blood, oil)* reguero *m*
2 *vi* (**a**) *(person)* babear (**b**) *(liquid)* gotear; *Fig* **to d. in/out** *(people)* entrar/salir poco a poco (**c**) *(in soccer, basketball)* llevar el balón controlado; **to d. past a defender** regatear *or* driblar a un defensa

drier ['draɪə(r)] *n (for hair)* secador *m*; *(for clothes)* secadora *f*

drift [drɪft] **1** *n* (**a**) *(of current)* movimiento *m*, arrastre *m*; *(of business, conversation)* tendencia *f*; *(of events)* curso *m*; **d. net** *(for fishing)* red *f* de deriva (**b**) *(meaning)* *(of person's words)* sentido *m*, idea *f*; *Fam* **I get the d.** ya veo cuál es la idea (**c**) *(of snow)* ventisquero *m*
2 *vi* (**a**) *(boat, economy)* ir a la deriva; *(conversation)* derivar; *(events)* discurrir; *(person)* vagar, errar; **to let things d.** dejar que las cosas vayan a la deriva; **people drifted in and out during the speech** durante el discurso, la gente entraba y salía; **to d. apart** irse separando poco a poco; **to d. into war/crime** ir derivando hacia la guerra/la delincuencia (**b**) *(sand, snow)* amontonarse

drifter ['drɪftə(r)] *n (aimless person)* vagabundo(a) *m,f*

driftwood ['drɪftwʊd] *n* madera *f* flotante

drill [drɪl] **1** *n* (**a**) *(electric tool)* taladradora *f*; *(manual tool)* taladro *m* (manual); *(of dentist)* torno *m*; *(pneumatic)* martillo *m* neumático; **d. bit** broca *f*; **d. hole** *(in wood, brick)* taladro *m*; *(for oil well)* perforación *f* (**b**) *(training)* ejercicio *m*; **fire d.** simulacro *m* de incendio
2 *vt* (**a**) *(well, road)* perforar; **to d. a hole in sth** taladrar un agujero en algo (**b**) *(train) (soldiers)* entrenar; **to d. pupils in pronunciation** hacer practicar la pronunciación a los alumnos; *Fam* **to d. sth into sb** meterle algo en la cabeza a alguien
3 *vi* (**a**) **to d. for oil** hacer perforaciones en búsqueda *or Esp* busca de petróleo (**b**) *(troops)* entrenar, practicar

drink [drɪŋk] **1** *n* bebida *f*; *(alcoholic)* copa *f*; **to have a d.** beber algo; **to go for a d.** ir a tomar algo; *Fam* **the d.** *(the sea)* el mar; **to take to d.** darse a la bebida; **to have a d. problem** tener un problema con la bebida
2 *vt (pt* **drank** [dræŋk], *pp* **drunk** [drʌŋk]) beber; **to d. sb's health** brindar a la salud de alguien; **to d. sb under the table** aguantar bebiendo *or Am* tomando más que alguien
3 *vi* beber, *Am* tomar; **don't d. and drive** si bebes, no conduzcas, *Am* si tomas no manejes; **to d. like a fish** beber *or Am* tomar como un cosaco; **to d. to sb** brindar a la salud de alguien, *Esp* beber a la salud de alguien; **to d. to sth** brindar por algo; *Fig* **to d. in the atmosphere** empaparse del ambiente

▸**drink up 1** *vt sep* beberse todo
2 *vi* **d. up!** *(finish your drink)* ¡termínatelo!

drinkable ['drɪŋkəbəl] *adj (water)* potable; *(wine, beer)* pasable, aceptable

drinker ['drɪŋkə(r)] *n* bebedor(ora) *m,f*; **he's a heavy d.** es un bebedor empedernido

drinking ['drɪŋkɪŋ] *n* **heavy d. is bad for you** beber *or Am* tomar mucho es malo; **his d. companions** sus compañeros de borracheras; **d. chocolate** chocolate *m* a la taza; **d. fountain** fuente *f* de agua potable; **d. straw** pajita *f*, *Col* pitillo *m*, *Méx* popote *m*; **d. water** agua *f* potable

drip [drɪp] **1** *n* (**a**) *(drop)* gota *f*; *(sound)* goteo *m* (**b**) *(in hospital)* gota a gota *m inv*; **she's on a d.** le han puesto suero (**c**) *Fam (weak person)* sosaina *mf*
2 *vt (pt & pp* **dripped**) gotear
3 *vi* gotear; **to be dripping with sweat/blood** estar

empapado(a) en sudor/sangre; *Fig* **to be dripping with jewels** ir cargado(a) de joyas

drip-dry ['drɪp'draɪ] *adj (shirt, fabric)* que no necesita plancha

dripping ['drɪpɪŋ] **1** *n* grasa *m*

2 *adj* **a d. faucet** un grifo *or Chile, Col, Méx* una llave *or RP* una canilla que gotea

3 *adv* **to be d. wet** estar empapado(a)

drippy ['drɪpɪ] *adj* **(a)** *Fam Pej (person)* blandengue **(b)** *(tap, nose)* que gotea

drive [draɪv] **1** *n* **(a)** *(trip)* viaje *m* (en coche *or Am* carro *or CSur* auto); **it's an hour's d. away** está a una hora en coche *or Am* carro *or CSur* auto; **to go for** *or* **take a d.** dar una vuelta en *Esp* coche, dar un paseo en *Am* carro *or CSur* auto

(b) *Aut (of car)* tracción *f*; **four-wheel d.** *(car)* cuatro por cuatro *m inv*, vehículo *m* con tracción a *or Am* en las cuatro ruedas; *(system)* tracción *f* a *or Am* en las cuatro ruedas; **left-hand d.** *(car)* vehículo *m* con el volante al *or Am* del lado izquierdo

(c) *Comptr* unidad *f* de disco

(d) *(in golf)* golpe *m* largo, drive *m*; *(in tennis)* drive *m*, golpe *m* natural

(e) *(of house)* camino *m* de entrada

(f) *(initiative, energy)* brío *m*, empuje *m*

(g) *(campaign)* **sales/membership d.** campaña *f* de ventas/para captar socios

2 *vt (pt* **drove** [drəʊv], *pp* **driven** ['drɪvən]) **(a)** *(car, train)* conducir, *Am* manejar; **to d. sb somewhere** llevar a alguien a algún sitio en coche *or Am* carro *or CSur* auto **(b)** *(direct, guide) (cattle, people)* conducir, guiar; **to d. sb to do sth** empujar a alguien a que haga algo; **to d. prices up/down** hacer que los precios suban/bajen; **to d. sb mad** volver loco(a) a alguien; **to d. oneself too hard** trabajar demasiado; **to d. a hard bargain** ser un/una duro(a) negociador(ora), no regalar nada a nadie **(c)** *(machine)* impulsar, hacer funcionar; **to be driven by electricity** funcionar con electricidad

3 *vi (in car)* conducir, *Am* manejar; **can you d.?** ¿sabes conducir *or Am* manejar?; **to d. to work** ir al trabajo en coche *or Am* carro *or CSur* auto

▸**drive at** *vi* **what are you driving at?** ¿qué estás insinuando?

▸**drive away 1** *vt sep* **(a)** *(in car)* **to d. sb away** llevarse a alguien en un coche *or Am* carro *or CSur* auto **(b)** *(alienate)* **to d. sb away** ahuyentar a alguien

2 *vi (in car)* irse, marcharse *(en coche)*

▸**drive off** *vt sep (repel)* repeler

▸**drive on** *vi (in car)* seguir adelante

drive-by ['draɪvbaɪ] *adj* **d. shooting** *or* **killing** tiroteo *m or* asesinato *m* desde un vehículo

drive-in ['draɪvɪn] *n* **d. (theater)** autocine *m*; **d. (restaurant)** = establecimiento de comida rápida que atiende a los clientes sin que éstos necesiten salir del automóvil

drivel ['drɪvəl] *n Fam Esp* chorradas *fpl, CAm, Méx* babosadas *fpl, Chile* leseras *fpl, Andes, CSur* macanas *fpl*; **to talk d.** decir *Esp* chorradas *o CAm, Méx* babosadas *o Chile* leseras *o Andes, CSur* macanas

driven ['drɪvən] *pp of* **drive**

-driven ['drɪvən] *suffix* **steam-d.** de vapor; **market/consumer-d.** impulsado(a) por el mercado/por los consumidores

driver ['draɪvə(r)] *n* **(a)** *(of car, bus)* conductor(ora) *m,f*; *(of truck)* camionero(a) *m,f*; *(of taxi)* taxista *mf*; *(of train)* maquinista *mf*; **d.'s license** *Esp* carné *m or* permiso *m* de conducir, *Bol, Ecuad, Perú* brevet *m, Carib* licencia *f* de conducir, *Méx* licencia *f* de manejar *or* para conducir, *RP* permiso *m* de conductor, *Urug* libreta *f* de manejar; *Fig* **to be in the d. seat** estar al mando **(b)** *(golf club)* driver *m* **(c)** *Comptr* controlador *m*

drive-through ['draɪvθruː] *n* = establecimiento de comida rápida que atiende a los clientes sin que éstos tengan que salir del automóvil

driveway ['draɪvweɪ] *n* camino *f* de entrada

driving ['draɪvɪŋ] **1** *n (in car)* conducción *f, Am* manejo *m*; **d. teacher** profesor(ora) *m,f* de autoescuela; **d. lessons** clases *fpl* de conducir *or Am* manejar; **d. school** autoescuela *f*; **d. test** examen *m* de conducir *or Am* manejar

2 *adj (rain)* torrencial; **d. force** fuerza *f* motriz

drizzle ['drɪzəl] **1** *n* llovizna *f, Andes, RP* garúa *f*

2 *vi* lloviznar, chispear, *Andes, RP* garuar; **it's drizzling** está lloviznando *or Andes, RP* garuando

drizzly ['drɪzlɪ] *adj (day, weather)* **a d. day** un día de llovizna *or Andes, RP* garúa

droll [drəʊl] *adj* gracioso(a); *Ironic* **oh, very d.!** ¡muy gracioso!

dromedary ['drɒmədərɪ] *n* dromedario *m*

drone [drəʊn] **1** *n* **(a)** *(bee)* zángano *m* **(b)** *(noise)* zumbido *m*

2 *vi* zumbar

▸**drone on** *vi* **to d. on about sth** soltar una perorata sobre algo

drool [druːl] *vi (dribble)* babear; *Fig* **she was drooling at the idea** se le caía la baba con sólo pensarlo

droop [druːp] *vi (head)* inclinarse; *(shoulders)* encorvarse; *(flower)* marchitarse; *Fig (person)* desanimarse

droopy ['druːpɪ] *adj (ears, eyes)* caído(a)

drop [drɒp] **1** *n* **(a)** *(of liquid)* gota *f*; **drops** *(for eyes, nose)* gotas *fpl*; **you've had a d. too much** *(to drink)* llevas una copa de más; **I haven't touched a d. since** desde entonces no he bebido *or Am* tomado ni una gota; *Fig* **it's only a d. in the ocean** no es más que un grano de arena en el desierto **(b)** *(fall, decrease)* caída *f*, descenso *m*; *(by parachute)* suministro *m* aéreo; **a d. of 10 feet** una caída de 10 pies; *Fig* **at the d. of a hat** a la primera *or* las primeras de cambio

2 *vt (pt & pp* **dropped) (a)** *(allow to fall) (accidentally)* dejar caer; *(deliberately)* tirar, dejar caer, *Am salvo RP* botar; *(bomb)* lanzar, tirar; **I've dropped my pen** se me ha caído el boli; *Fam* **to d. sb a line/a card** mandar unas líneas/una postal a alguien; **I'll d. you at the station** *(in car)* te dejaré en la estación; **d. goal** *(in rugby)* gol *m* de bote pronto

(b) *(lower) (prices, one's eyes, voice)* bajar

(c) *(abandon) (subject, idea, plan)* dejar; **to d. sb** *(as friend)* abandonar *or* dejar a alguien; **to d. math/French** dejar las matemáticas/el francés; *Law* **to d. the charges** retirar los cargos

(d) *(omit) (letter, syllable)* saltarse, omitir; *(not pronounce)* no pronunciar; **to d. sb from a team** excluir a alguien de un equipo

(e) *(lose) (points)* perder

3 *vi* **(a)** *(object)* caer, caerse; *(ground)* caer; **to d. out** *(from pocket, briefcase)* caerse; *Fam* **I'm ready** *or* **fit to d.** estoy hecho polvo, *Esp* estoy para el arrastre; *Fam* **people are dropping like flies** la gente está cayendo como moscas; **to d. dead** caerse muerto; *Fam* **d. dead!** ¡muérete!, *RP* ¡morite! **(b)** *(prices, temperature, demand, unemployment)* caer, bajar; *(voice)* bajar; *(wind)* amainar; *(speed)* disminuir

▸**drop around 1** *vt sep (deliver)* **to d. sth around** entregar *or* llevar algo; **I'll d. it around at your place tomorrow** lo dejaré en tu casa mañana

2 *vi (visit)* pasarse

▸**drop by** *vi* **I thought I'd d. by for a chat** se me ocurrió pasarme a charlar *or CAm, Méx* platicar un rato

▸**drop in** *vi* **to d. in on sb** pasar a visitar a alguien

▸**drop off 1** *vt sep (person from car)* dejar

2 *vi* **(a)** *Fam* **to d. off (to sleep)** quedarse traspuesto(a) **(b)** *(membership, attendance)* bajar, disminuir

▸**drop out** *vi (from a contest)* retirarse; *(from society)* marginarse; **to d. out of college** dejar la universidad

drop-dead gorgeous ['drɒpded'gɔːdʒəs] *adj Fam* guapísimo(a); **to be/look d.** estar como un tren *or* para parar un tren

drop-down menu ['drɒpdaʊn'menjuː] *n Comptr* menú *m* desplegable

dropkick ['drɒpkɪk] *n (in football)* (puntapié *m* de) botepronto *m*

droplet ['drɒplɪt] *n* gotita *f*

drop-off ['drɒpɒf] *n* (**a**) *(decrease)* descenso *m* (**b**) *(descent)* descenso *m*

dropout ['drɒpaʊt] *n Fam (from society)* marginado(a) *m,f*; *(from college)* = persona que ha abandonado los estudios; **d. rate** *(from college)* índice *m* de abandono de los estudios

dropper ['drɒpə(r)] *n (for medicine)* cuentagotas *m inv*

droppings ['drɒpɪŋz] *npl* excrementos *mpl*

dross [drɒs] *n Fam (junk, garbage)* porquería *f*, basura *f*

drought [draʊt] *n* sequía *f*

drove [draʊv] **1** *n* **in droves** en manadas
    2 *pt of* **drive**

drown [draʊn] **1** *vt* (**a**) *(kill by drowning)* ahogar; **to d. oneself** ahogarse; **to d. one's sorrows (in drink)** ahogar las penas (en alcohol) (**b**) *(make inaudible)* ahogar
    2 *vi (die by drowning)* ahogarse

▸**drown out** *vt sep (sound)* ahogar

drowse [draʊz] *vi* dormitar

drowsiness ['draʊzɪnɪs] *n* somnolencia *f*, sueño *m*

drowsy ['draʊzɪ] *adj (person)* somnoliento(a), soñoliento(a); *(afternoon)* soporífero(a); **to be d.** estar somnoliento(a)

drudge [drʌdʒ] *n* = persona que tiene un trabajo pesado y aburrido

drudgery ['drʌdʒərɪ] *n* trabajo *m* (duro y) rutinario

drug [drʌg] **1** *n (medicine)* medicamento *m*; *(illegal)* droga *f*; **hard/soft drugs** drogas duras/blandas; **to take drugs** drogarse, tomar drogas; **d. abuse** drogadicción *f*; **d. addict** drogadicto(a) *m,f*, toxicómano(a) *m,f*; **d. dealer** *(large-scale)* narcotraficante *m,f*, traficante *mf* de drogas; *(small-scale)* camello *mf*; **d. squad** brigada *f* de estupefacientes
    2 *vt (pt & pp* **drugged)** drogar; **they had drugged his wine/food** le echaron una droga en el vino/la comida

druggist ['drʌgɪst] *n* farmacéutico(a) *m,f*

drug-sniffing dog ['drʌgsnɪfɪŋdɒg] *n* = perro policía entrenado para detectar drogas o explosivos

drugstore ['drʌgstɔː(r)] *n* = tienda que vende cosméticos, periódicos, medicamentos, *etc.*

druid ['druːɪd] *n* druida *m*

drum [drʌm] **1** *n* (**a**) *(musical instrument)* tambor *m*; **d. kit**, **drums** batería *f* (**b**) *(container)* barril *m*; *(of washing machine)* tambor *m*; *(for oil)* bidón *m*
    2 *vt (pt & pp* **drummed) she was drumming her fingers on the table** estaba tamborileando en la mesa con los dedos; **to d. sth into sb** meterle algo en la cabeza a alguien
    3 *vi (play drums)* tocar la batería; **the rain was drumming on the window panes** la lluvia golpeaba en los cristales

▸**drum up** *vt (support, enthusiasm)* buscar, reunir

drummer ['drʌmə(r)] *n (in pop band)* batería *mf*, *Am* baterista *mf*; *(in military band)* tamborilero(a) *m,f*

drumstick ['drʌmstɪk] *n* (**a**) *(for playing drums)* baqueta *f* (**b**) *(chicken leg)* muslo *m*

drunk [drʌŋk] **1** *n* borracho(a) *m,f*
    2 *adj* borracho(a); **to be d.** estar borracho(a); **to get d.** emborracharse; *Law* **d. and disorderly behavior** estado *m* de embriaguez con conducta violenta; **he was arrested for d. driving** lo detuvieron por conducir *or Am* manejar en estado de embriaguez; *Fig* **d. with power** ebrio(a) de poder
    3 *pp of* **drink**

drunkard ['drʌŋkəd] *n* borracho(a) *m,f*

drunken ['drʌŋkən] *adj (person)* borracho(a); *(party, argument)* acalorado(a) por el alcohol; **d. brawl** trifulca *f* de borrachos; **in a d. stupor** aturdido(a) por el alcohol

drunkenly ['drʌŋkənlɪ] *adv* **he staggered d. down the**

street iba calle abajo tambaleándose por la borrachera

drunkometer [drʌŋ'kɒmɪtə(r)] *n Fam* alcoholímetro *m*

dry [draɪ] **1** *adj* (**a**) *(weather, clothing, wine)* seco(a); **to run** *or* **go d.** secarse; **to be kept d.** *(sign on container)* no mojar; **as d. as a bone** reseco(a); **d. cleaner's** tintorería *f*; **d. cleaning** *(process)* limpieza *f* en seco; *(clothes)* **to collect the d. cleaning** recoger la ropa de la tintorería; *Naut* **d. dock** dique *m* seco; **d. goods** *(drapery)* artículos *mpl* de confección; **d. goods store** mercería *f*; **d. ice** nieve *f* carbónica, hielo *m* seco; **d. land** tierra *f* firme; **d. rot** putrefacción *f* de la madera; **d. run** ensayo *m* (**b**) *(boring) (prose style, person)* aburrido(a), árido(a) (**c**) *(deadpan) (humor)* lacónico(a) (**d**) *(state, town)* que prohíbe la venta de alcohol
    2 *vt* secar; **to d. oneself** secarse; **to d. one's hair** secarse el pelo
    3 *vi* secarse

▸**dry out** *vi* (**a**) *(alcoholic)* dejar el alcohol (**b**) *(moisture, wet thing)* secarse

▸**dry up** *vi* (**a**) *(well, pool)* secarse (**b**) *(funds, conversation, inspiration)* agotarse (**c**) *(actor, public speaker)* quedarse en blanco

dry-clean [draɪ'kliːn] *vt* limpiar en seco

dryer = **drier**

dry-roasted ['draɪrəʊstɪd] *adj (peanuts)* tostado(a)

DTP [diːtiː'piː] *n Comptr (abbr* **desktop publishing)** auto-edición *f*

DTs [diː'tiːz] *npl (abbr* **delirium tremens)** delírium tremens *m inv*; **to have the D.** tener un delírium tremens

dual ['djʊəl] *adj* doble; **to have d. nationality** tener doble nacionalidad; **d. ownership** copropiedad *f*

dual-purpose ['djʊəl'pɜːpəs] *adj* de doble uso

dub [dʌb] *(pt & pp* **dubbed)** *vt* (**a**) *(movie)* doblar (**b**) *(call)* apodar

dubbing ['dʌbɪŋ] *n Cin* doblaje *m*

dubious ['djuːbɪəs] *adj* (**a**) *(uncertain)* **to be d. (about sth)** no estar convencido(a) (de algo) (**b**) *(suspect, questionable)* *(distinction, honor)* dudoso(a); **a d. character** un tipo sospechoso

dubiously ['djuːbɪəslɪ] *adv* (**a**) *(doubtfully)* **he listened d.** escuchaba poco convencido (**b**) *(in suspect manner)* dudosa-mente

Dublin ['dʌblɪn] *n* Dublín

Dubliner ['dʌblɪnə(r)] *n* dublinés(esa) *m,f*

duchess ['dʌtʃɪs] *n* duquesa *f*

duchy ['dʌtʃɪ] *n* ducado *m*

duck [dʌk] **1** *n* pato *m*; **to take to sth like a d. to water** sentirse en algo como pez en el agua; **criticism runs off him like water off a d.'s back** le resbalan las críticas; **d. pond** estanque *m* de patos
    2 *vt* (**a**) *(one's head)* agachar; **to d. sb** *(under water)* hacer una ahogadilla a alguien (**b**) *(avoid)* **to d. the issue** eludir el tema
    3 *vi (to avoid being hit)* agacharse; *(under water)* zambullirse

▸**duck out of** *vt insep* **to d. out of sth/doing sth** zafarse de algo/hacer algo

duck-billed platypus ['dʌkbɪld'plætɪpəs] *n* ornitorrinco *m*

duckling ['dʌklɪŋ] *n* patito *m*

duct [dʌkt] *n (for fuel, air, tears)* conducto *m*

dud [dʌd] *Fam* **1** *n (person)* mamarracho *m*, desastre *m*; *(shell)* proyectil *m* que no estalla
    2 *adj* defectuoso(a); *(banknote)* falso(a)

dude [duːd] *n (man)* tipo *m*, *Esp* tío *m*

due [djuː] **1** *adj* (**a**) *(owed)* pagadero(a); **to fall d.** ser pagadero(a); **are you d. any money from him?** ¿te debe dinero?; **you're d. an apology** mereces *or Am* ameritas una disculpa; **d. to...** *(because of, as result of)* debido a...; *Fin* **d. date** (fecha *f* de) vencimiento *m*
    (**b**) *(merited, proper)* debido(a); **after d. consideration** tras

la debida consideración; **with all d. respect,...** con el debido respeto,...; **in d. course** *(when appropriate)* a su debido tiempo; *(eventually)* al final

(**c**) *(expected)* **the train/he is d. (to arrive) at two o'clock** el tren/él tiene la llegada prevista a las dos; **when is he d.?** ¿cuándo llega?; **she's d. back any minute** volverá en cualquier momento; **when is their baby d.?** ¿para cuándo esperan el niño?; **the movie/book is d. out soon** la película/el libro está a punto de aparecer

2 *n* (**a**) **to give him his d., he did apologize** para ser justos con él, hay que decir que se disculpó (**b**) **dues** *(for membership)* cuota *f*

3 *adv* **d. north/south** justo al *or* hacia el norte/sur

duel ['djʊəl] **1** *n* duelo *m*; **to fight a d.** batirse en duelo
2 *vi* batirse en duelo

duet [dju:'et] *n Mus* dúo *m*; **to sing/play a d.** cantar/tocar un dúo

duffel bag ['dʌfəlbæg] *n* talega *f* de lona

duffer ['dʌfə(r)] *n Fam (incompetent person)* ceporro(a) *m,f*, nulidad *f*; **to be a d. at history/French** ser una nulidad en historia/francés

duffle ['dʌfəl] *n* **d. (coat)** trenca *f*

dug [dʌg] *pt & pp of* **dig**

dugout ['dʌgaʊt] *n* (**a**) *(canoe)* piragua *f*, canoa *f (hecha con un tronco vaciado)* (**b**) *(shelter)* refugio *m* subterráneo; *(in baseball)* foso *m* (del banquillo)

duke [dju:k] *n* duque *m*

dull [dʌl] **1** *adj* (**a**) *(boring) (book, movie, person)* aburrido(a); *(job, life, party)* insulso(a), soso(a); **to be as d. as ditchwater** ser más soso(a) que la calabaza (**b**) *(not intelligent)* tonto(a), torpe, *Am* sonso(a), *Am* zonzo(a) (**c**) *(not sharp) (tool, blade)* romo(a); *(sound, pain)* sordo(a) (**d**) *(not bright) (color, surface)* mate, apagado(a); *(eyes)* apagado(a); *(weather, sky)* gris, triste

2 *vt* (**a**) *(reduce intensity of) (pleasure)* enturbiar; *(the senses)* embotar; *(pain)* mitigar, atenuar; *(sound)* apagar; *(blade)* desafilar, embotar (**b**) *(make less bright) (colors, eyes)* apagar

dullness ['dʌlnɪs] *n* (**a**) *(tedium)* **the d. of the book/speech** lo aburrido que era el libro/discurso (**b**) *(lack of intelligence)* necedad *f*, torpeza *f* (**c**) *(listlessness)* apatía *f* (**d**) *(of tool, blade)* embotamiento *m*; *(of sound, pain)* lo amortiguado (**e**) *(of color, surface, eyes)* falta *f* de brillo

dully ['dʌlɪ] *adv* (**a**) *(boringly)* pesadamente (**b**) *(not brightly)* pálidamente, sin brillo

duly ['dju:lɪ] *adv* (**a**) *(properly)* como corresponde, debidamente; **we were d. worried** estábamos preocupados con razón (**b**) *(as expected)* **he said he'd be punctual and he d. arrived on the stroke of eight** dijo que llegaría puntual y confirmando las previsiones, llegó a las ocho en punto

dumb [dʌm] *adj* (**a**) *(unable to speak)* mudo(a); **to be struck d. with astonishment** quedarse mudo(a) de asombro; **d. animals** los animales indefensos (**b**) *Fam (stupid) (person, action)* bobo(a), estúpido(a); **d. blonde** rubia *f or Méx* güera *f* sin cerebro

dumbbell ['dʌmbel] *n* pesa *f*

dumbfounded [dʌm'faʊndɪd] *adj* boquiabierto(a), pasmado(a)

dumbing (down) ['dʌmɪŋ('daʊn)] *(of population, youth, electorate)* reducción *f* del nivel cultural; *(of newspaper, program)* empobrecimiento *m* de contenidos

dumbstruck ['dʌmstrʌk] *adj* boquiabierto(a), pasmado(a)

dumbwaiter ['dʌmweɪtə(r)] *n (lift)* montaplatos *m inv*

dummy ['dʌmɪ] *n* (**a**) *(in shop window)* maniquí *m*; *(of ventriloquist)* muñeco *m*; *(model of car, plane)* modelo *m*, maqueta *f* (**b**) *Fam (idiot)* idiota *mf*, imbécil *mf*

dump [dʌmp] **1** *n* (**a**) *(for garbage)* vertedero *m*, basurero *m*; *Fam* **what a d.!** ¡qué asco de sitio!, *Esp* ¡qué sitio más cutre!, *RP* ¡qué lugar más terraja!; **d. truck** volquete *m* (**b**) *Mil (store)*

depósito *m* (**c**) *Comptr* (**memory** *or* **storage**) **d.** volcado *m* de memoria

2 *vt* (**a**) *(put down)* soltar, dejar; *(unload)* descargar (**b**) *(dispose of) (garbage, old car)* tirar; *(nuclear, toxic waste)* verter; *Fam (lover, boyfriend, girlfriend)* dejar, dar calabazas a (**c**) *Comptr (memory)* volcar

▸**dump on** *vt insep Fam (criticize) (person)* poner verde a; *(project, suggestion)* dejar por los suelos

dumper ['dʌmpə(r)] *n* **d. (truck)** volquete *m*

dumping ['dʌmpɪŋ] *n* (**a**) **no d.** *(sign)* prohibido arrojar basuras; **d. ground** vertedero *m* (**b**) *Econ* dumping *m*

dumpling ['dʌmplɪŋ] *n (in stew)* = bola de masa hervida; **apple d.** bollo *m* relleno de manzana

dumps [dʌmps] *npl Fam* **to be down in the d.** estar con la moral por los suelos, *Am* estar con el ánimo por el piso

Dumpster® ['dʌmpstə(r)] *n* contenedor *m* (de escombros)

dumpy ['dʌmpɪ] *adj Fam (person, appearance)* rechoncho(a), achaparrado(a)

dunce [dʌns] *n (at school)* burro(a) *m,f*; **d.'s cap** ≃ orejas *fpl* de burro

dune [dju:n] *n* (**sand**) **d.** duna *f*

dung [dʌŋ] *n* estiércol *m*

dungarees [dʌŋgə'ri:z] *npl* (pantalón *m* de) peto *m*; **a pair of d.** unos pantalones de peto

dungeon ['dʌndʒən] *n* mazmorra *f*

dunghill ['dʌŋhɪl] *n* estercolero *m*

dunk [dʌŋk] **1** *n (in basketball)* **d. shot** mate *m*
2 *vt* mojar

dunno [də'nəʊ] *Fam* = **don't know**

duo ['dju:əʊ] *(pl* **duos**) *n* dúo *m*

duodenal [dju:əʊ'di:nəl] *adj (ulcer)* duodenal

duodenum [dju:əʊ'di:nəm] *n* duodeno *m*

dupe [dju:p] **1** *n* primo(a) *m,f*, ingenuo(a) *m,f*
2 *vt* engañar; **to d. sb into doing sth** engañar a alguien para que haga algo

duplex ['dju:pleks] *n & adj* dúplex *m*, duplex *m*

duplicate ['dju:plɪkət] **1** *n (copy)* duplicado *m*, copia *f*; **in d.** por duplicado
2 *adj* duplicado(a)
3 *vt* ['dju:plɪkeɪt] (**a**) *(copy) (document)* duplicar, hacer un duplicado de (**b**) *(repeat) (findings, result)* repetir

duplication [dju:plɪ'keɪʃən] *n* duplicación *f*

duplicity [dju:'plɪsɪtɪ] *n* duplicidad *f*

durability [djʊərə'bɪlɪtɪ] *n* durabilidad *f*

durable ['djʊərəbəl] **1** *adj* duradero(a)
2 *n* (**consumer**) **durables** bienes *mpl* de consumo duraderos

duration [djʊ'reɪʃən] *n* duración *f*; **for the d. (of)** hasta el final (de)

duress [djʊ'res] *n* **under d.** bajo coacción

during ['djʊərɪŋ] *prep* durante

dusk [dʌsk] *n* crepúsculo *m*, anochecer *m*; **at d.** al anochecer

dust [dʌst] **1** *n* (**a**) *(dirt, powder)* polvo *m*; **d. cover** *(for furniture)* funda *f*; **d. cover** *or* **jacket** *(for book)* sobrecubierta *f* (**b**) *(action)* **to give sth a d.** quitar el polvo a algo (**c**) *(idioms)* **once the d. has settled** *(when fuss is over)* cuando haya pasado la tormenta

2 *vt* (**a**) *(clean) (room, furniture)* limpiar el polvo de (**b**) *(sprinkle) (with flour, sugar)* espolvorear (**with** con)

▸**dust down, dust off** *vt sep (furniture)* quitar el polvo a; *Fig (legislation, one's French)* desempolvar

dustcloth ['dʌstklɒθ] *n* trapo *m or* bayeta *f* del polvo

dusting ['dʌstɪŋ] *n* (**a**) *(of room, furniture)* **to do the d.** limpiar *or* quitar el polvo (**b**) *(with sugar)* **give the cake a d. of cocoa** espolvorear el pastel con cacao

dustpan ['dʌstpæn] *n* recogedor *m*; **d. and brush** cepillo *m* y recogedor

dust-up ['dʌstʌp] *n Fam (brawl)* bronca *f*, trifulca *f*; **to have a d. (with sb)** tener una bronca (con alguien)

dusty ['dʌstɪ] *adj* polvoriento(a); **to get d.** llenarse de polvo

Dutch [dʌtʃ] **1** *npl (people)* **the D.** los holandeses
     2 *n (language)* neerlandés *m*
     3 *adj* holandés(esa); **D. courage** = valentía que da el alcohol
     4 *adv Fam* **to go D.** pagar cada uno lo suyo, *Esp* pagar a escote

Dutchman ['dʌtʃmən] *n* holandés *m*

Dutchwoman ['dʌtʃwʊmən] *n* holandesa *f*

dutiful ['djuːtɪfʊl] *adj (son, daughter)* obediente, bien mandado(a)

dutifully ['djuːtɪfʊlɪ] *adv* obedientemente, sin rechistar

duty ['djuːtɪ] *n* **(a)** *(obligation)* deber *m*; **to do one's d.** cumplir (uno) con su deber; **he failed in his d.** faltó a *or* no cumplió con su deber; **I shall make it my d. to…** yo me ocuparé de…; **it is your d. to…** tu deber es…
     (b) *(task)* **duties** tareas *fpl*; **she took up** *or* **assumed her duties** se incorporó a su puesto; **she carried out** *or* **performed her duties well** desempeñó bien su trabajo
     (c) *(of soldier, employee)* **to be on d.** estar de servicio; **to be off d.** estar fuera de servicio; *Mil* **tour of d.** destino *m*; **d. roster** rota *f* de guardias
     (d) *Fin (tax)* derecho *m*, impuesto *m*; **to pay d. on sth** pagar derechos *or* impuestos por algo

duty-free ['djuːtɪ'friː] *adj* exento(a) *or* libre de impuestos; **d. shop** tienda *f* libre de impuestos

DVD [diːviː'diː] *n Comptr (abbr* **Digital Versatile Disc, Digital Video Disc**) DVD *m*; **D. player** reproductor *m* de DVD

DVT [diːviː'tiː] *n (abbr* **deep-vein thrombosis**) TVP *f*

dwarf [dwɔːf] **1** *n (pl* **dwarfs** *or* **dwarves** [dwɔːvz]) enano(a) *m,f*
     2 *adj (plant, tree)* enano(a)
     3 *vt* empequeñecer; **the church is dwarfed by the new skyscraper** el nuevo rascacielos hace pequeña a la iglesia

dweeb [dwiːb] *n Fam* petardo(a) *m,f*

dwell [dwel] *(pt & pp* **dwelled** *or* **dwelt** [dwelt]) *vi Literary (live)* morar
▸**dwell on, dwell upon** *vt insep* **why d. on the negative side of things?** ¿para qué fijarse en el lado negativo de las cosas?; **let's not** *or* **don't let's d. on it** no le demos más vueltas al asunto

dwelling ['dwelɪŋ] *n Formal* **d. (place)** morada *f*; **d. house** residencia *f*

dwelt [dwelt] *pt & pp of* **dwell**

dwindle ['dwɪndəl] *vi* disminuir, reducirse; **to d. (away) to nothing** quedar reducido(a) a nada

dwindling ['dwɪndlɪŋ] *adj (funds, membership)* menguante; *(enthusiasm)* decreciente

dye [daɪ] **1** *n (for clothes, hair)* tinte *m*
     2 *vt* teñir; **to d. sth black/red** teñir algo de negro/rojo; **to d. one's hair** teñirse el pelo

dyed-in-the-wool ['daɪdɪnðə'wʊl] *adj (conservative, Marxist)* acérrimo(a)

dying ['daɪɪŋ] **1** *adj (person)* moribundo(a), agonizante; *(industry, tradition)* en vías de desaparición; **to my d. day** hasta el día de mi muerte; **d. wish** última voluntad *f*; **d. words** últimas palabras *fpl*
     2 *npl* **the d.** los moribundos

dyke = **dike**

dynamic [daɪ'næmɪk] **1** *adj also Fig* dinámico(a)
     2 *n (driving force)* dinámica *f*

dynamics [daɪ'næmɪks] *npl (of change, growth)* dinámica *f*

dynamism ['daɪnəmɪzəm] *n (of person, society)* dinamismo *m*

dynamite ['daɪnəmaɪt] **1** *n* dinamita *f*; *Fig* **his theories were political d.** sus teorías políticas eran pura dinamita; *Fam* **it's d.!** *(marvelous)* ¡es genial!
     2 *vt (building, bridge)* dinamitar

dynamo ['daɪnəməʊ] *(pl* **dynamos**) *n Elec* dinamo *f*

dynastic [dɪ'næstɪk] *adj* dinástico(a)

dynasty ['dɪnəstɪ] *n* dinastía *f*

dysentery ['dɪsəntrɪ] *n* disentería *f*

dysfunction [dɪs'fʌŋkʃən] *n (of organ)* disfunción *f*

dysfunctional [dɪs'fʌŋkʃənəl] *adj (family, relationship)* disfuncional

dyslexia [dɪs'leksɪə] *n* dislexia *f*

dyslexic [dɪs'leksɪk] *adj* disléxico(a)

dystrophy ['dɪstrəfɪ] *n Med* distrofia *f*

E

E, e [i:] *n* (**a**) *(letter)* E, e *f* (**b**) *Mus* mi *m* (**c**) *(abbr* **east**) E, este *m* (**d**) *Sch* suspenso *m*; **to get an E** *(in exam, essay)* obtener una baja calificación (**e**) *Fam (abbr* **ecstasy**) *(drug)* éxtasis *m inv*

each [i:tʃ] **1** *adj* cada; **e. day** cada día; **e. one of us** todos (y cada uno de) nosotros

2 *pron* (**a**) *(both, all)* cada uno; **e. of us** cada uno de nosotros; **we e. earn $300** ganamos cada uno 300 dólares; **peaches at 25 cents e.** melocotones a 25 centavos la pieza *or* cada uno; **a little of e.** un poco de cada (uno) (**b**) *(reciprocal)* **to hate e. other** odiarse; **to kiss e. other** besarse; **to support e. other** apoyarse mutuamente; **we write to e. other** nos escribimos

eager [ˈiːgə(r)] *adj (look, interest)* ávido(a), ansioso(a); *(supporter)* entusiasta; *(desire, hope)* intenso(a); **to be e. for sth** estar ansioso(a) por *or* ávido(a) de algo; **the audience were e. for more** el público seguía pidiendo más; **to be e. to do sth** estar ansioso(a) por hacer algo; **to be e. to please** estar deseando agradar; **they were e. to learn** estaban ávidos *or* ansiosos por aprender; *Fam* **to be an e. beaver** ser muy aplicado(a)

eagerly [ˈiːgəlɪ] *adv* ansiosamente; **e. awaited** ansiado(a), largamente esperado(a)

eagerness [ˈiːgənɪs] *n (impatience)* avidez *f*, ansia *f*; *(enthusiasm)* entusiasmo *m*; **to show e. in doing sth** hacer algo con entusiasmo

eagle [ˈiːgəl] *n* águila *f*

eagle-eyed [i:gəˈlaɪd] *adj* **to be e.** tener vista de lince

ear [ˈɪə(r)] *n* (**a**) *(of person, animal) (external part)* oreja *f*; *(internal part)* oído *m*; **to have an e. for music** tener buen oído para la música; **to have an e. for languages** tener aptitudes para los idiomas; *Med* **e., nose and throat specialist** otorrinolaringólogo(a) *m,f*; **e. lobe** lóbulo *m* de la oreja

(**b**) *(of wheat)* espiga *f*

(**c**) *(idioms)* **to play it by e.** ver qué pasa; **he has the boss's e.** goza de la confianza del jefe; **to keep one's e. to the ground** mantenerse al corriente; **to go in one e. and out the other** *(words, information)* entrar por un oído y salir por el otro; *Fam* **I'm all ears** soy todo oídos; *Fam* **to be up to one's ears in work/debt** estar hasta las *Esp* cejas *or* *Am* narices de trabajo/deudas; *Fam* **to be (thrown) out on one's e.** ser puesto(a) de patitas en la calle; **to reach sb's ears** llegar a los oídos de alguien; **the house was falling down around their ears** la casa se les caía encima

earache [ˈɪəreɪk] *n* dolor *m* de oídos

earbud [ˈɪəbʌd] *n* auricular *m*

eardrum [ˈɪədrʌm] *n* tímpano *m*

-eared [ɪəd] *suffix* **long/short-e.** con orejas largas/cortas

earful [ˈɪəfʊl] *n Fam* **to give sb an e.** *(scold, criticize)* echar un sermón *or Esp* una bronca a alguien

earl [ɜːl] *n* conde *m*

earlier [ˈɜːlɪə(r)] **1** *adj* anterior; **I caught an e. train** tomé *or Esp* cogí un tren anterior; **her e. novels** sus novelas anteriores

2 *adv* **e. (on)** antes; **a few days e.** unos días antes; **no e. than tomorrow** no antes de mañana; **as we saw e.** como vimos anteriormente *or* antes

earliest [ˈɜːlɪəst] **1** *n* **at the e.** como muy pronto; **the e. I can be there is four o'clock** no podré estar ahí antes de las cuatro

2 *adj (opportunity, memory)* primero(a); **at the e. possible moment** lo antes posible; **from the e. times** desde los primeros tiempos

early [ˈɜːlɪ] **1** *adj* (**a**) *(in the day)* temprano(a); **at this e. hour...** a una hora tan temprana...; **in the e. morning** *Esp* por la *or Am* en la *or Arg* a la *or Urug* de mañana temprano; **in the e. afternoon** a primera hora de la tarde; **to have an e. night** acostarse temprano; **to be an e. riser** *or* **bird** ser madrugador(ora); *Prov* **the e. bird catches the worm** a quien madruga, Dios le ayuda

(**b**) *(at beginning of period of time)* temprano(a), primero(a); **an e. goal** un gol temprano *or* tempranero; **the e. days/stages of...** los primeros días/las primeras etapas de...; **in e. summer** a principios del verano; **at an e. age** en una edad temprana; **in the e. 1980s** a principios de los ochenta; **an e. example of...** un ejemplo temprano de...

(**c**) *(ahead of time) (arrival)* antes de tiempo; *(breakfast, lunch)* temprano(a); **to be e.** llegar temprano *or Esp* pronto; **I am half an hour e.** llego media hora antes *or* con media hora de adelanto; **an e. death** una muerte prematura; **e. retirement** jubilación *f* anticipada; *Mil* **e. warning system** sistema *f* de alerta inmediata

(**d**) *(future)* pronto(a); **an e. reply** una pronta respuesta; **at an e. date** en fecha próxima

2 *adv* (**a**) *(in the day)* temprano, *Esp* pronto; **e. in the morning/evening** en las primeras horas de la mañana/tarde; **to get up e.** levantarse temprano; **as e. as possible** lo antes posible, cuanto antes

(**b**) *(at beginning of period of time)* **e. in the year** a primeros de año; **e. on** temprano; **e. in one's life/career** al principio de la vida/carrera profesional

(**c**) *(ahead of time)* temprano, *Esp* pronto; **too e.** demasiado pronto; **they left the party e.** se fueron pronto de la fiesta; **to die e.** morir prematuramente; **to retire e.** jubilarse anticipadamente

earmark [ˈɪəmɑːk] *vt* destinar (**for** a)

earn [ɜːn] *vt (money)* ganar; *(rest, respect)* ganarse; **to e. one's living** ganarse la vida

earner [ˈɜːnə(r)] *n* **(wage) e.** asalariado(a) *m,f*

earnest [ˈɜːnɪst] **1** *adj* serio(a)

2 *n* **in e.** en serio

earnestly [ˈɜːnɪstlɪ] *adv (to speak, discuss, consider)* seriamente, con gravedad; *(to hope, desire, believe)* sinceramente

earnestness [ˈɜːnɪstnɪs] *n* seriedad *f*, gravedad *f*

earning power [ˈɜːnɪŋˈpaʊə(r)] *n* capacidad *f* de ingresos

earnings [ˈɜːnɪŋz] *npl (of person)* ingresos *mpl*; *(of company)* beneficios *mpl*, ganancias *fpl*

earphones [ˈɪəfəʊnz] *npl* auriculares *mpl*

earpiece [ˈɪəpiːs] *n (of telephone)* auricular *m*

earplug ['ɪəplʌg] *n* tapón *m* para los oídos

earring ['ɪərɪŋ] *n Esp* pendiente *m*, *Am* arete *m*

earshot ['ɪəʃɒt] *n* within/out of e. al alcance del/fuera del alcance del oído; **I was within e. of them** yo podía oírles

earsplitting ['ɪəsplɪtɪŋ] *adj* ensordecedor(ora)

earth [ɜːθ] *n* (a) *(planet)* the E. la Tierra; e. mother *(in mythology)* madre tierra *f*, diosa *f* de la fecundidad; *Fig (woman)* madraza *f*; e. sciences ciencias *fpl* de la Tierra (b) *(soil)* tierra *f* (c) *(idioms) Fam* where/why on e....? ¿dónde/por qué diablos...?; to cost the e. costar un ojo de la cara; to promise sb the e. prometer a alguien el oro y el moro; *Fig* to come back to e. (with a bump) bajarse de la nube, bajar a la tierra

earthenware ['ɜːθənweə(r)] *n* loza *f*

earthling ['ɜːθlɪŋ] *n* terrícola *mf*

earthly ['ɜːθlɪ] *adj* (a) *(life, existence)* terrenal (b) *Fam (emphatic)* there's no e. reason no hay razón alguna; she hasn't got an e. (chance) no tiene la menor posibilidad; it's of no e. use no vale absolutamente para nada

earthquake ['ɜːθkweɪk] *n also Fig* terremoto *m*

earth-shattering ['ɜːθʃætərɪŋ] *adj Fam (news, discovery)* extraordinario(a)

earthworks ['ɜːθwɜːks] *n* terraplén *m*

earthworm ['ɜːθwɜːm] *n* lombriz *f (de tierra)*

earthy ['ɜːθɪ] *adj* (a) *(of or like earth)* terroso(a) (b) *(coarse)* grosero(a); *(uninhibited)* directo(a), campechano(a)

earwax ['ɪəwæks] *n* cera *f* de los oídos, cerumen *m*

earwig ['ɪəwɪg] *n* tijereta *f*

ease [iːz] **1** *n* (a) *(facility)* facilidad *f*; with e. con facilidad (b) *(peace)* at e. a gusto; to put sb at e. hacer que alguien se sienta a gusto; to put or set sb's mind at e. tranquilizar a alguien; a life of e. una vida desahogada
    2 *vt* (a) *(alleviate) (pain, anxiety)* calmar (b) *(relax) (pressure, tension)* disminuir (c) *(move carefully, slowly)* she eased the heavy box into the car despacio y con cuidado, trasladó la pesada caja al interior del coche
    3 *vi (pain, pressure)* remitir; the wind/the rain has eased el viento/la lluvia ha amainado un poco

▶**ease off, ease up** *vi (pain)* disminuir, remitir; *(rain)* amainar

easel ['iːzəl] *n* caballete *m*

easily ['iːzɪlɪ] *adv* (a) *(without difficulty, probably)* fácilmente; the information could e. be wrong la información puede muy bien ser errónea; e. the best/biggest sin duda alguna el mejor/mayor; that's e. said eso se dice pronto (b) *(comfortably)* cómodamente, sin dificultad; he's e. 40 *(at least)* andará por los 40 como poco

easiness ['iːzɪnɪs] *n* (a) *(of task)* facilidad *f* (b) *(of manner)* desenvoltura *f*

east [iːst] **1** *n* este *m*; to the e. (of) al este (de); the E. *(Asia)* el Oriente, *(of USA)* el Este
    2 *adj (side)* oriental, este; E. Africa África Oriental; the E. End = el barrio este de Londres; *Formerly* E. Germany Alemania Oriental or del Este; *Old-fashioned* the E. Indies = el archipiélago indonesio, las Indias orientales; the E. Side = el barrio este de Manhattan; e. wind viento *m* de levante
    3 *adv (travel, move)* en dirección este, hacia el este; it's (3 miles) e. of here está (a 3 millas) al este de aquí; to face e. mirar hacia el este

eastbound ['iːstbaʊnd] *adj (train, traffic)* en dirección este; the e. interstate la autopista que va hacia el este

Easter ['iːstə(r)] *n (period)* Semana *f* Santa; *(festival)* Pascua *f*; at E. en Semana Santa; E. egg huevo *m* de Pascua; E. Island la Isla de Pascua; E. Sunday Domingo *m* de Pascua or de Resurrección; E. week Semana Santa

easterly ['iːstəlɪ] **1** *n (wind)* levante *m*
    2 *adj (direction)* (hacia el) este; the most e. point el punto más al este; e. wind viento *m* de levante

eastern ['iːstən] *adj (region)* del este, oriental; *(religion)* oriental; E. Europe Europa Oriental or del Este; E. Standard Time hora *f* oficial en la costa este de los EE.UU.

east-northeast ['iːstnɔːθ'iːst] *adv* en dirección estenordeste or estenoreste

east-southeast ['iːstsaʊθ'iːst] *adv* en dirección estesudeste or estesureste

eastward ['iːstwəd] *adj & adv* hacia el este

eastwards ['iːstwədz] *adv* hacia el este

easy ['iːzɪ] **1** *adj* (a) *(not difficult)* fácil; e. to please fácil de contentar; e. to get on with tratable; it's e. to say... es muy fácil decir...; that's easier said than done es muy fácil decirlo, del dicho al hecho (hay mucho trecho); *Fam* it's as e. as ABC or as pie es pan comido, *RP* es un boleto or una papa; the e. option la solución más fácil; *Fam* e. money dinero *m* fácil; e. on the eye agradable a la vista; *Com* by e. payments, on e. terms con facilidades de pago; *Fam* I'm e.! *(I don't mind)* ¡por mí es igual!, ¡a mí me da lo mismo!
    (b) *(comfortable) (pace, life)* cómodo(a), apacible; *(manners, style)* desenvuelto(a); *Fam* to be on e. street no tener problemas económicos; to have an e. time (of it) tenerlo fácil, no tener que emplearse a fondo; e. chair butaca *f*, sillón *m*; e. listening *(music)* música *f* ligera
    2 *adv* to go e. on sb no ser demasiado duro(a) con alguien; to go e. on sth no pasarse con algo; to take things or it e. tomarse las cosas con calma, tomárselo con calma; take it e.! ¡tranquilo!; e. come, e. go tal como viene, se va

easygoing ['iːzɪ'gəʊɪŋ] *adj (tolerant)* tolerante; *(calm)* tranquilo(a)

eat [iːt] *(pt ate [et, eɪt], pp eaten ['iːtən])* **1** *vt* (a) comer; to e. one's breakfast desayunar (b) *(idioms)* to e. sb out of house and home dejarle la nevera or la despensa vacía a alguien; *Fam* I could e. a horse! ¡tengo un hambre tremenda or Esp canina!; *Fam* he won't e. you! ¡no te va a comer!; *Fam* what's eating you? *(worrying you)* ¿qué te preocupa?, *RP* ¿qué te pica?; to e. one's words tragarse (uno) sus propias palabras; *Fam* if it works, I'll e. my hat si esto funciona, me meto a monja
    2 *vi* comer; *Fig* to have sb eating out of one's hand tener a alguien en *Esp* el bote or *Am* el bolsillo

▶**eat away (at)** *vt insep also Fig* erosionar

▶**eat into** *vt insep (erode)* corroer; *Fig (time)* gastar; *(savings)* mermar

▶**eat out** *vi* salir a comer fuera

▶**eat up 1** *vt sep (food)* terminar (de comer); *(gas, money)* consumir
    2 *vi* e. up! ¡termina (de comer)!

eater ['iːtə(r)] *n* to be a slow/fast e. comer despacio/deprisa

eatery ['iːtərɪ] *n* restaurante *m*

eats [iːts] *npl Fam* comida *f*, *Esp* manduca *f*, *RP* morfi *m*

eau de Cologne ['əʊdəkə'ləʊn] *n* (agua *f* de) colonia *f*

eaves [iːvz] *npl (of house)* alero *m*

eavesdrop ['iːvzdrɒp] *(pt & pp eavesdropped)* *vi* escuchar disimuladamente

ebb [eb] **1** *n (of tide)* reflujo *m*; *Fig* the e. and flow *(of events)* los vaivenes *mpl*; *Fig* to be at a low e. *(person, spirits)* estar en horas bajas; e. tide marea *f* baja, bajamar *f*
    2 *vi (tide)* bajar

▶**ebb away** *vi (water)* bajar; *(strength, enthusiasm)* menguar, disminuir

Ebola virus ['ebələ'vaɪrəs] *n* virus *m* del Ébola

ebony ['ebənɪ] *n* ébano *m*

e-book ['iːbʊk] *n Comptr* libro *m* electrónico

ebullience [ɪ'bʌlɪəns] *n* fogosidad *f*

ebullient [ɪ'bʌlɪənt] *adj* fogoso(a)

EC [iː'siː] *n Formerly (abbr* European Community) CE *f*, Comunidad *f* Europea

eccentric [ek'sentrɪk] n & adj excéntrico(a) m,f
eccentrically [ek'sentrɪklɪ] adv de forma excéntrica, excéntricamente
eccentricity [eksen'trɪsɪtɪ] n excentricidad f
ecclesiastic [ɪkliːzɪ'æstɪk] **1** n clérigo m
 2 adj eclesiástico(a)
ECG [iːsiː'dʒiː] n Med (abbr **electrocardiogram**) ECG m, electrocardiograma m
echelon ['eʃəlɒn] n **the higher echelons** las altas esferas; **the lower echelons** los grados inferiores
echo ['ekəʊ] **1** n (pl **echoes**) also Fig eco m
 2 vt (opinion, words) repetir, hacerse eco de
 3 vi resonar (**with** con)
éclair [eɪ'kleə(r)] n (pastry) petisú m
eclectic [ɪ'klektɪk] adj ecléctico(a)
eclipse [ɪ'klɪps] also Fig **1** n eclipse m
 2 vt eclipsar
eco-friendly ['iːkəʊfrendlɪ] adj ecológico(a)
ecological [iːkə'lɒdʒɪkəl] adj ecológico(a)
ecologist [ɪ'kɒlədʒɪst] n (scientist) ecólogo(a) m,f
ecology [ɪ'kɒlədʒɪ] n ecología f
e-commerce [ɪ'kɒmɜːs] n comercio m electrónico
economic [iːkə'nɒmɪk] adj (**a**) Econ económico(a); **e. migrant** migrante mf (económico) (**b**) (profitable) rentable; **it's more e. to buy in bulk** sale más barato or económico comprar grandes cantidades
economical [iːkə'nɒmɪkəl] adj (cost-effective) económico(a); **he was being e. with the truth** no decía toda la verdad
economically [iːkə'nɒmɪklɪ] adv económicamente
economics [iːkə'nɒmɪks] n economía f; **the e. of a plan** el aspecto económico de un plan
economist [ɪ'kɒnəmɪst] n economista mf
economize [ɪ'kɒnəmaɪz] vi economizar, ahorrar (**on** en)
economy [ɪ'kɒnəmɪ] n economía f; **economies of scale** economías fpl de escala; Av **e. class** clase f turista; **e. drive** (cost-cutting campaign) campaña f de ahorro; **e. measure** medida f de ahorro; **e. size** (of packet) tamaño m económico
ecosystem ['iːkəʊsɪstem] n ecosistema m
ecotax ['iːkəʊtæks] n ecotasa f, impuesto m ecológico
ecoterrorism ['iːkəʊterərɪzəm] n terrorismo m ecológico, ecoterrorismo m
ecoterrorist ['iːkəʊterərɪst] n terrorista mf ecológico(a)
ecotourism ['iːkəʊtɔːrɪzəm] n ecoturismo m, turismo m verde or ecológico
ecowarrior ['iːkəʊwɒrɪə(r)] n militante mf ecologista
ecstasy ['ekstəsɪ] n (emotional state, drug) éxtasis m inv; **he went into ecstasies over the food** se deshacía en elogios a la comida
ecstatic [ek'stætɪk] adj exultante, alborozado(a); **to be e. (about** or **over sth)** estar exultante de alegría (por algo)
ECT [iːsiː'tiː] n Med (abbr **electroconvulsive therapy**) electrochoque m
Ecuador ['ekwədɔː(r)] n Ecuador
Ecuadoran ['ekwədɔːrən], **Ecuadorean, Ecuadorian** [ekwə'dɔːrɪən] n & adj ecuatoriano(a) m,f
ecumenic(al) [iːkjʊ'menɪk(əl)] adj Rel ecuménico(a)
eczema ['eksɪmə] n eccema m
ed [ed] (**a**) (abbr **edition**) ed., edición f (**b**) (abbr **editor**) ed., editor(ora) m,f (**c**) (abbr **edited**) editado(a)
Edam ['iːdæm] n queso m de bola
eddy ['edɪ] **1** n remolino m
 2 vi arremolinarse
edema [ɪ'diːmə] n Med edema m
Eden ['iːdən] n (jardín m del) Edén m
edge [edʒ] **1** n (**a**) (of table, road, forest) borde m; (of page) margen m; (of coin, book) canto m; **at the water's e.** al borde

or a la orilla del agua; Fig **to be on the e. of one's seat** estar (con el alma) en vilo (**b**) (of blade, tool) filo m; Fig **to take the e. off sb's hunger** calmar el hambre a alguien; Fig **it took the e. off their victory** deslustró or enturbió su victoria; Fig **to be on e.** (nervous) estar tenso(a) or nervioso(a); Fig **to set sb on e.** (make nervous) poner los nervios de punta a alguien (**c**) (advantage) ventaja f; **to have the e. (over sb)** llevar ventaja (a alguien)
 2 vt (in sewing) ribetear; **edged with lace** ribeteado(a) con encaje
 3 vi (move slowly) **to e. toward sb/sth** acercarse lentamente a alguien/algo; **to e. past sb** pasar deslizándose junto a alguien; **to e. through the crowd** avanzar lentamente entre la multitud
▸**edge out** vt sep (beat narrowly) batir por muy poco a
edgewise ['edʒwaɪz], **edgeways** ['edʒweɪz] adv de canto, de lado; Fam **I can't get a word in e.** no me dejan meter baza
edginess ['edʒɪnɪs] n (nervousness) estado m de tensión, nerviosismo m
edgy ['edʒɪ] adj (nervous) nervioso(a); **to be e.** estar nervioso(a)
edible ['edɪbəl] adj comestible
edict ['iːdɪkt] n Formal edicto m
edification [edɪfɪ'keɪʃən] n Formal edificación f, instrucción f
edifice ['edɪfɪs] n edificio m
edify ['edɪfaɪ] vt edificar
edifying ['edɪfaɪɪŋ] adj edificante
Edinburgh ['edɪnbrə] n Edimburgo
edit ['edɪt] vt (**a**) (rewrite) corregir; Comptr editar (**b**) (prepare for publication) editar; **edited by...** edición (a cargo) de... (**c**) Cin (cut) montar (**d**) (manage) (newspaper, journal) dirigir
▸**edit out** vt sep eliminar, excluir
editing ['edɪtɪŋ] n Cin montaje m
edition [ɪ'dɪʃən] n edición f
editor ['edɪtə(r)] n (**a**) (of published writings) editor(ora) m,f (**b**) (of movie) montador(ora) m,f (**c**) (of newspaper, journal) director(ora) m,f; (newspaper or TV journalist) redactor(ora) m,f (**d**) Comptr (software) editor m
editorial [edɪ'tɔːrɪəl] **1** n editorial m
 2 adj editorial; **e. staff** (equipo m de) redacción f
EDP [iːdiː'piː] n Comptr (abbr **electronic data processing**) tratamiento m or procesamiento m electrónico de datos
EDT [iːdiː'tiː] n (abbr **Eastern Daylight Time**) = hora en el huso horario del este de los Estados Unidos y Canadá
educate ['edjʊkeɪt] vt educar
educated ['edjʊkeɪtɪd] adj culto(a); **an e. guess** una suposición bien fundada
education [edjʊ'keɪʃən] n (process of learning) educación f, aprendizaje m; (process of teaching) educación f, enseñanza f; (knowledge) educación f, cultura f; **College of E.** Colegio m de Educación; **faculty of E.** facultad f de pedagogía; Fam **it was an e. working over there** trabajar allí fue muy instructivo
educational [edjʊ'keɪʃənəl] adj (system, standards, TV program) educativo(a); (establishment) docente; (experience, visit) instructivo(a); **e. qualifications** títulos mpl académicos
educationally [edjuː'keɪʃənəlɪ] adv pedagógicamente hablando, desde el punto de vista pedagógico; **e. subnormal** con graves problemas de aprendizaje
Edwardian [ed'wɔːdɪən] adj (architecture, furniture) = de la época de Eduardo VII (1901—10)
eek [iːk] exclam Fam ¡ah!
eel [iːl] n anguila f
eerie ['ɪərɪ] adj espeluznante, sobrecogedor(ora)
eerily ['ɪərɪlɪ] adv de forma espeluznante; **it was e. silent** había un silencio sobrecogedor
efface [ɪ'feɪs] vt borrar; **to e. oneself** mantenerse en un segundo plano

effect [ɪ'fekt] **1** n (**a**) (result) efecto m; **to have an e. on** tener efecto en or sobre; **to take e.** (drug, medicine) hacer or surtir efecto; (law) entrar en vigor; **to put sth into e.** llevar algo a la práctica; **in e.** de hecho, en la práctica; **or words to that e.** o algo por el estilo (**b**) (impression) efecto m, impresión f; **for e.** para impresionar (**c**) Formal **personal effects** efectos mpl personales
2 vt Formal (cause) (reconciliation, cure) efectuar, hacer efectivo(a); **to e. a change** efectuar un cambio; **to e. an entry** entrar, penetrar

effective [ɪ'fektɪv] adj (**a**) (efficient, successful) eficaz (**b**) (actual, real) efectivo(a) (**c**) Law (in force) **to be e. (from)** entrar en vigor (desde)

effectively [ɪ'fektɪvlɪ] adv (**a**) (efficiently) eficazmente (**b**) (really) en realidad, de hecho; **they are e. the same** de hecho vienen a ser lo mismo

effectiveness [ɪ'fektɪvnɪs] n eficacia f

effeminate [ɪ'femɪnət] adj afeminado(a)

effervescence [efə'vesəns] n (of liquid, person) efervescencia f

effervescent [efə'vesənt] adj (liquid, person) efervescente

effete [ɪ'fiːt] adj (person, gesture) afectado(a), refinado(a) en exceso

efficacious [efɪ'keɪʃəs] adj Formal eficaz

efficacy ['efɪkəsɪ] n Formal eficacia f

efficiency [ɪ'fɪʃənsɪ] n eficiencia f

efficient [ɪ'fɪʃənt] adj eficiente

efficiently [ɪ'fɪʃəntlɪ] adv con eficiencia, eficientemente

effigy ['efɪdʒɪ] n (statue) efigie f; (for ridicule) monigote m; **to burn sb in e.** quemar un monigote de alguien

effluent ['eflʊənt] n aguas fpl residuales

effort ['efət] n (**a**) (exertion) esfuerzo m; **to make an e. (to do sth)** hacer un esfuerzo (por hacer algo); **to be worth the e.** valer la pena; **put some e. into it!** ¡podrías hacer un esfuerzo! (**b**) (attempt) intento m

effortless ['efətlɪs] adj fácil, cómodo(a)

effortlessly ['efətlɪslɪ] adv sin esfuerzo, fácilmente

effrontery [ɪ'frʌntərɪ] n desfachatez f, descaro m

effusive [ɪ'fjuːsɪv] adj efusivo(a)

effusively [ɪ'fjuːsɪvlɪ] adv efusivamente

EFT [iːef'tiː] n Comptr (abbr **electronic funds transfer**) TEF f, transferencia f electrónica de fondos

EFTA ['eftə] n (abbr **European Free Trade Association**) EFTA f, AELC f, Asociación f Europea de Libre Comercio

EFTPOS ['eftpɒs] n Comptr (abbr **electronic funds transfer at point of sale**) transferencia f (electrónica de fondos) en el punto de venta

EFTS [iːefti:'es] n Comptr (abbr **electronic funds transfer system**) TEF, sistema m de transferencia electrónica de fondos

e.g. [iː'dʒiː] abbr p. ej., por ejemplo

egalitarian [ɪgælɪ'teərɪən] **1** n partidario(a) m,f del igualitarismo
2 adj igualitario(a) m,f

egalitarianism [ɪgælɪ'teərɪənɪzəm] n igualitarismo m

egg [eg] n (**a**) (of animal, food) huevo m, CAm, Méx blanquillo m; **e. cup** huevera f; **e. timer** reloj m de arena (para medir el tiempo que tarda en cocerse un huevo); **e. white** clara f (de huevo); **e. yolk** yema f (de huevo) (**b**) (reproductive cell) óvulo m (**c**) (idioms) **to be a good/bad e.** (person) ser buena/mala gente; **to have e. on one's face** haber quedado en ridículo; Prov **don't put all your eggs in one basket** no te lo juegues todo a una sola carta, Am no pongas todos los huevos en la misma canasta

▸**egg on** vt sep **to e. sb on (to do sth)** incitar a alguien (a hacer algo)

egghead ['eghed] n Hum or Pej lumbrera f, cerebrito m

eggplant ['egplænt] n berenjena f

eggshell ['egʃel] n cáscara f (de huevo)

egis ['iːdʒɪs] n **under the e. of...** bajo los auspicios de...

ego ['iːgəʊ] (pl **egos**) n (self-esteem) amor m propio, autoestima f; Psy ego m, yo m; **he has an enormous e.** tiene un ego descomunal, es un presuntuoso; **to boost sb's e.** dar mucha moral a alguien; Fam **to be on an e. trip** hacer algo por autocomplacerse

egocentric [iːgəʊ'sentrɪk] adj egocéntrico(a)

egocentricity ['iːgəʊsen'trɪsɪtɪ], **egocentrism** ['iːgəʊ'sentrɪzəm] n egocentrismo m

egoist ['iːgəʊɪst] n egoísta mf

egotism ['iːgəʊtɪzəm] n egocentrismo m

egotist ['iːgəʊtɪst] n egocéntrico(a) m,f

egotistic(al) [iːgəʊ'tɪstɪk(əl)] adj egocéntrico(a)

egotistically ['iːgə'tɪstɪklɪ] adv egocéntricamente

Egypt ['iːdʒɪpt] n Egipto

Egyptian [ɪ'dʒɪpʃən] n & adj egipcio(a) m,f

eiderdown ['aɪdədaʊn] n (comforter) edredón m

eight [eɪt] **1** n ocho m; **come at e.** ven a las ocho; **e. and e. are sixteen** ocho y ocho, dieciséis; **there were e. of us** éramos ocho; **all e. of them left** se marcharon los ocho; **the e. of hearts** (in cards) el ocho de corazones
2 adj ocho; **they live at number e.** viven en el número ocho; **chapter/page e.** capítulo/página ocho; **e. hundred** ochocientos(as); **e. hundred men** ochocientos hombres; **e. thousand** ocho mil; **to be e. (years old)** tener ocho años (de edad); **it costs e. dollars** cuesta ocho dólares; **e. o'clock** las ocho; **it's e. minutes to five** son las cinco menos ocho minutos

eighteen [eɪ'tiːn] n & adj dieciocho m; see also **eight**

eighteenth [eɪ'tiːnθ] **1** n (**a**) (fraction) dieciochoavo m, decimoctava parte f (**b**) (in series) decimoctavo(a) m,f (**c**) (of month) dieciocho m
2 adj decimoctavo(a); see also **eleventh**

eighth [eɪtθ] **1** n (**a**) (fraction) octavo m, octava parte f (**b**) (in series) octavo(a) m,f; **Edward the E.** (written) Eduardo VIII; (spoken) Eduardo octavo (**c**) (of month) ocho m; (**on**) **the e. of May** el ocho de mayo; **we're leaving on the e.** nos vamos el (día) ocho
2 adj octavo(a); **the e. century** (written) el siglo VIII; (spoken) el siglo octavo or ocho; Mus **e. note** corchea f

eightieth ['eɪtɪəθ] n & adj octogésimo(a) m,f

eighty ['eɪtɪ] **1** n ochenta m; **e.-one** ochenta y uno(a); **he was doing e. (miles an hour)** (in car) iba a unas ochenta (millas por hora); **in the eighties** (decade) en los (años) ochenta; **to be in one's eighties** tener ochenta y tantos años; **the temperature was in the eighties** (Fahrenheit) hacía alrededor de 30 grados
2 adj ochenta; **about e. cars/passengers** unos ochenta coches/pasajeros; **e. percent of the staff** el ochenta por ciento del personal; **she's about e. (years old)** tiene unos ochenta años; **he will be e. tomorrow** mañana cumple ochenta años

Eire ['eərə] n Formerly Eire m (hoy la República de Irlanda)

either ['aɪðə(r), 'iːðə(r)] **1** adj (**a**) (one or other) cualquiera de los/las dos; **e. candidate may win** puede ganar cualquiera de los (dos) candidatos (**b**) (each of the two) **on e. side** a cada lado; **in e. case** en los dos casos, en cualquier caso
2 pron cualquiera; **e. (of them) will do** me sirve cualquiera (de ellos); **I don't believe e. of them** no creo a ninguno de los dos; **I don't want e. of them** no quiero ninguno
3 conj **e. ... or...** o... o..., (o) bien... o bien...; **e. you or your brother** o tú o tu hermano; **e. come in or go out!** ¡o entras o sales!; **I don't eat e. meat or fish** no como (ni) carne ni pescado
4 adv tampoco; **if you don't go, I won't go e.** si tú no vas,

yo tampoco; **he can't sing, and he can't act e.** no sabe cantar ni tampoco actuar

either-or ['aɪðər'ɔ:(r)] *adj* **to be in an e. situation** tener que elegir (entre lo uno o lo otro)

ejaculate [ɪ'dʒækjʊleɪt] *vi (emit semen)* eyacular

ejaculation [ɪdʒækjʊ'leɪʃən] *n* (**a**) *(of semen)* eyaculación *f* (**b**) *Old-fashioned (exclamation)* exclamación *f*

eject [ɪ'dʒekt] **1** *vt* expulsar
2 *vi (from plane)* eyectarse

ejection [ɪ'dʒekʃən] *n* expulsión *f*; *Av* eyección *f*; *Av* **e. seat** asiento *m* eyectable *or* eyector

ejector seat [ɪ'dʒektəsi:t] *n Av* asiento *m* eyectable *or* eyector

▶**eke out** [i:k] *vt sep* **to e. out a living** ganarse la vida a duras penas

elaborate 1 *adj* [ɪ'læbərət] *(plan, excuse, meal)* elaborado(a); *(drawing, description)* detallado(a)
2 *vt* [ɪ'læbəreɪt] elaborar
3 *vi* dar detalles (**on** sobre)

elaboration [ɪlæbə'reɪʃən] *n* elaboración *f*

élan [eɪ'lɑn] *n Literary* brío *m*

elapse [ɪ'læps] *vi* transcurrir

elastic [ɪ'læstɪk] **1** *n* elástico *m*
2 *adj also Fig* flexible, elástico(a)

elasticity [i:læs'tɪsɪtɪ] *n* elasticidad *f*

elated [ɪ'leɪtɪd] *adj* jubiloso(a), eufórico(a); **to be e. (about sth)** estar jubiloso(a) *or* eufórico(a) (por algo)

elation [ɪ'leɪʃən] *n* júbilo *m*, euforia *f*

elbow ['elbəʊ] **1** *n* codo *m*; **out at the elbows** *(pullover, jacket)* con agujeros en los codos; *Fig* **to give sb the e.** *(employer)* dar la patada a alguien; *(lover)* mandar a alguien a paseo; *Fig* **put some e. grease into it!** ¡dale fuerte! *(al sacar brillo)*
2 *vt* **to e. sb in the ribs** dar un codazo a alguien en las costillas; **to e. sb aside** apartar a alguien de un codazo; **to e. one's way through (a crowd)** abrirse paso a codazos (entre una multitud)

elbowroom ['elbəʊrʊm] *n Fam Fig (freedom)* **to have enough e.** tener un margen de libertad

elder[1] ['eldə(r)] **1** *adj* mayor; **my e. brother** mi hermano mayor; **e. statesman** antiguo mandatario *m (que conserva su prestigio)*
2 *n* (**a**) *(older person)* mayor *mf*; **young people should respect their elders** los jóvenes deberían respetar a sus mayores (**b**) *(of tribe, church)* anciano(a) *m,f*

elder[2] *n (tree)* saúco *m*

elderberry ['eldəberɪ] *n (fruit)* baya *f* de saúco

elderflower ['eldəflaʊə(r)] *n* flor *m* de saúco *m*

elderly ['eldəlɪ] **1** *adj* anciano(a)
2 *npl* **the e.** los ancianos

eldest ['eldɪst] **1** *adj* mayor; **my e. daughter** la mayor de mis hijas, mi hija mayor
2 *n* **the e.** el/la mayor

elect [ɪ'lekt] **1** *adj* electo(a); **the president-e.** el presidente electo
2 *vt* (**a**) *(councilor, MP)* elegir; **to e. sb president, to e. sb to the presidency** elegir a alguien presidente (**b**) *Formal (choose)* **to e. to do sth** elegir hacer algo

election [ɪ'lekʃən] *n* elección *f*; **to hold an e.** celebrar unas elecciones; **to run for e.** presentarse a las elecciones; **e. campaign** campaña *f* electoral

electioneering [ɪlekʃə'nɪərɪŋ] *n* electoralismo *m*

elective [ɪ'lektɪv] *adj (assembly)* electivo(a); *Univ (course)* optativo(a), opcional

elector [ɪ'lektə(r)] *n* elector(ora) *m,f*, votante *mf*

electoral [ɪ'lektərəl] *adj Pol* electoral; **e. college** cuerpo *m* de compromisarios, colegio *m* electoral; **e. reform** reforma *f* electoral

electorate [ɪ'lektərət] *n* electorado *m*

electric [ɪ'lektrɪk] *adj* eléctrico(a); *Fig* **the atmosphere of the meeting was e.** en la reunión el ambiente estaba electrizado; **e. blanket** manta *f* eléctrica; **e. blue** azul *m* eléctrico; **e. chair** silla *f* eléctrica; **e. stove** cocina *f or Col, Méx* estufa *f* eléctrica; **e. eel** anguila *f* eléctrica; **e. fence** valla *f* electrificada, cerca *f* eléctrica; **e. shock** descarga *f* eléctrica

electrical [ɪ'lektrɪkəl] *adj* eléctrico(a); **e. engineering** ingeniería *f* electrónica

electrically [ɪ'lektrɪkəlɪ] *adv* **e. powered** *or* **operated** eléctrico(a); **e. charged** con carga eléctrica

electrician [ɪlek'trɪʃən] *n* electricista *mf*

electricity [ɪlek'trɪsɪtɪ] *n* electricidad *f*

electrification [ɪlektrɪfɪ'keɪʃən] *n* electrificación *f*

electrify [ɪ'lektrɪfaɪ] *vt (supply)* electrificar; *Fig (excite)* electrizar

electrifying [ɪ'lektrɪfaɪɪŋ] *adj Fig* electrizante

electrocardiogram [ɪlektrəʊ'kɑ:dɪəʊɡræm] *n Med* electrocardiograma *m*

electrocardiograph [ɪlektrəʊ'kɑ:dɪəʊɡræf] *n Med* electrocardiógrafo *m*

electrocute [ɪ'lektrəkju:t] *vt* electrocutar; **to e. oneself** electrocutarse

electrocution [ɪlektrə'kju:ʃən] *n* electrocución *f*

electrode [ɪ'lektrəʊd] *n* electrodo *m*

electrolysis [ɪlek'trɒlɪsɪs] *n Chem* electrólisis *f inv*; *(to remove hair)* depilación *f* eléctrica

electrolyte [ɪ'lektrəlaɪt] *n Chem* electrólito *m*, electrolito *m*

electromagnet [ɪlektrəʊ'mæɡnɪt] *n* electroimán *m*

electron [ɪ'lektrɒn] *n* electrón *m*; **e. microscope** microscopio *m* electrónico

electronic [ɪlek'trɒnɪk] *adj* electrónico(a); *Fin* **e. banking** banca *f* electrónica, (servicio *m* de) telebanco; **e. funds transfer** transferencia *f* electrónica de fondos; *Comptr* **e. mail** correo *m* electrónico; *Comptr* **e. office** oficina *f* informatizada *or* electrónica

electronically [ɪlek'trɒnɪklɪ] *adv* electrónicamente

electronics [ɪlek'trɒnɪks] **1** *n* electrónica *f*; **e. company** casa *f* de electrónica; **the e. industry** el sector de la electrónica
2 *npl (of machine)* sistema *m* electrónico

electroplated [ɪ'lektrəpleɪtɪd] *adj* galvanizado(a)

electroshock therapy [ɪlektrəʊ'ʃɒk'θerəpɪ], **electroshock treatment** [ɪlektrəʊ'ʃɒk'tri:tmənt] *n Med* terapia *f or* tratamiento *m* de electrochoque

elegance ['elɪɡəns] *n* elegancia *f*

elegant ['elɪɡənt] *adj (appearance, movement)* elegante; *(reasoning)* lúcido(a)

elegantly ['elɪɡəntlɪ] *adv (dress, move)* elegantemente; **e. arranged/proportioned** armoniosamente dispuesto(a)/proporcionado(a)

elegiac [elə'dʒaɪək] *adj* elegiaco(a), elegíaco(a)

elegy ['elɪdʒɪ] *n* elegía *f*

element ['elɪmənt] *n* (**a**) *(constituent part)* elemento *m*, componente *m*; **this picture has all the elements of a hit movie** esta película contiene todos los ingredientes del éxito (**b**) *(factor)* componente *m*, elemento *m*; **the e. of surprise** el factor sorpresa; **the human e.** el factor humano; **an e. of danger** un factor de peligro (**c**) *(in society)* elemento *m*; **the hooligan e.** los gamberros *(en una multitud, en la sociedad)* (**d**) *Chem* elemento *m* (**e**) *(of kettle, electric fire)* resistencia *f* (**f**) *(force of nature)* **the four elements** los cuatro elementos; **to brave the elements** desafiar a los elementos; **she was in her e.** estaba en su elemento

elemental [elɪ'mentəl] *adj* elemental, primario(a)

elementary [elɪ'mentərɪ] *adj* elemental, básico(a); **e. algebra** álgebra *f* elemental; **e. school** escuela *f* primaria

elephant ['elɪfənt] *n* elefante *m*

elephantine [elɪˈfæntaɪn] *adj (body, size)* mastodóntico(a); *(steps, movement)* pesado(a), de elefante

elevate [ˈelɪveɪt] *vt* elevar

elevated [ˈelɪveɪtɪd] *adj* elevado(a); **to have an e. opinion of oneself** tener un concepto demasiado elevado de uno mismo; **e. railroad** ferrocarril *m or* tren *m* elevado

elevation [elɪˈveɪʃən] *n* (**a**) *(height)* **e. above sea level** altitud *f* (por encima del nivel del mar) (**b**) *(promotion)* ascenso *m*, elevación *f* (**c**) *Archit* alzado *m*

elevator [ˈelɪveɪtə(r)] *n* (**a**) *(for people)* ascensor *m* (**b**) *(for goods)* montacargas *m inv* (**c**) *(on airplane wing)* timón *m* de profundidad

eleven [ɪˈlevən] **1** *n* once *m*; **the Tampa Bay e.** *(football team)* el once de Tampa Bay
2 *adj* once; *see also* **eight**

eleventh [ɪˈlevənθ] **1** *n* (**a**) *(fraction)* onceavo *m*, onceava parte *f* (**b**) *(in series)* undécimo(a) *m,f*; **Louis the E.** *(written)* Luis XI; *(spoken)* Luis once (**c**) *(in month)* once *m*; **(on) the e. of May** el once de mayo; **we're leaving on the e.** nos vamos el (día) once
2 *adj* undécimo(a); *Fig* **at the e. hour** *Esp* en el *or Am* a último momento, *Am* en el último minuto; **the e. century** *(written)* el siglo XI; *(spoken)* el siglo once

elf [elf] *(pl* **elves** [elvz]*) n* elfo *m*

elfin [ˈelfɪn] *adj* delicado(a), angelical

elicit [ɪˈlɪsɪt] *vt (information)* sacar (**from** de), obtener (**from** de); *(reaction, response)* provocar (**from** en)

elide [ɪˈlaɪd] *vt Ling* elidir

eligibility [elɪdʒɪˈbɪlɪti] *n* elegibilidad *f*; **they questioned his e.** cuestionaron si era apto para presentar su candidatura

eligible [ˈelɪdʒəbəl] *adj* **to be e. for sth** reunir los requisitos para algo; **an e. bachelor** un buen partido

eliminate [ɪˈlɪmɪneɪt] *vt* eliminar

elimination [ɪlɪmɪˈneɪʃən] *n* eliminación *f*; **by a process of e.** por (un proceso de) eliminación

elision [ɪˈlɪʒən] *n Ling* elisión *f*

elite [eɪˈliːt] *n* élite *f*

elitism [eɪˈliːtɪzəm] *n* elitismo *m*

elitist [eɪˈliːtɪst] *n & adj* elitista *mf*

elixir [ɪˈlɪksə(r)] *n Literary* elixir *m*

Elizabethan [ɪlɪzəˈbiːθən] *n & adj* isabelino(a) *m,f*

elk [elk] *n* alce *m*

ellipse [ɪˈlɪps] *n Math* elipse *f*

ellipsis [ɪˈlɪpsɪs] *(pl* **ellipses** [ɪˈlɪpsiːz]*) n Gram* elipsis *f inv*

elm [elm] *n* olmo *m*

elocution [eləˈkjuːʃən] *n* dicción *f*

elongate [ˈiːlɒŋgeɪt] *vt* alargar

elope [ɪˈləʊp] *vi* fugarse *(para casarse)*

eloquence [ˈeləkwəns] *n* elocuencia *f*

eloquent [ˈeləkwənt] *adj* elocuente

else [els] *adv* **anyone e.** *(any other person)* cualquier otro(a); *(in negative sentences)* nadie más; **would anyone e. like some coffee?** ¿alguien más quiere café?; **someone e.** *(different person)* otra persona; *(additional person)* alguien más; **everyone e.** todos los demás; **no-one e.** nadie más; **anything e.** cualquier otra cosa; *(in negative sentence)* ninguna otra cosa; **can I get you anything e.?** ¿(desean) alguna cosa más *or* algo más?; **something e.** *(different thing)* otra cosa; *(additional thing)* algo más; **everything e.** todo lo demás; **nothing e.** *(nothing different)* ninguna otra cosa; *(nothing additional)* nada más; **somewhere e.** en/a otro sitio; **anywhere e.** (en/a) cualquier otro sitio; **everywhere e.** (en/a) todos los demás sitios; **nowhere e.** (en/a) ningún otro sitio; **who e. was there?** ¿quién más estaba allí?; **who broke it? — Peter, who e.?** ¿quién lo rompió? — Peter, ¿quién si no? *or* ¿quién va a ser?; **what e.?** ¿qué más?; **where e.?** ¿en/a qué otro sitio?; **when e.?** ¿en qué otro momento?; **how e.?** ¿cómo si no?; **how e. do you think I did it?** ¿cómo piensas si no que lo hice?, *RP* ¿cómo te pensás que lo hice?; **why e.?** ¿por qué si no?; **why e. would I do that?** ¿por qué iba a hacerlo si no?; **little e.** poca cosa más, poco más; **there isn't much e. we can do** no podemos hacer mucho más; **or e.** de lo contrario, si no; **do what I tell you or e.!** ¡como no hagas lo que te digo, te vas a enterar *or* ya verás!

elsewhere [ˈelsweə(r)] *adv* en otro sitio

ELT [iːelˈtiː] *n (abbr* **English Language Teaching***)* enseñanza *f* del inglés

elucidate [ɪˈluːsɪdeɪt] *vt* aclarar, poner en claro

elude [ɪˈluːd] *vt* eludir; **success has eluded us so far** el éxito nos ha rehuido hasta ahora; **his name eludes me** no consigo recordar su nombre

elusive [ɪˈluːsɪv] *adj (enemy, concept)* escurridizo(a)

elver [ˈelvə(r)] *n* angula *f*

elves *pl of* **elf**

emaciated [ɪˈmeɪsɪeɪtɪd] *adj* esquelético(a), raquítico(a); **to be e.** estar esquelético(a) *or* raquítico(a)

e-mail [ˈiːmeɪl] *n* correo *m* electrónico; **e. account** cuenta *f* de correo (electrónico); **e. address** dirección *f* de correo (electrónico)

emanate [ˈemaneɪt] **1** *vt* emanar
2 *vi* emanar (**from** de)

emancipate [ɪˈmænsɪpeɪt] *vt* emancipar

emancipated [ɪˈmænsɪpeɪtɪd] *adj* emancipado(a)

emancipation [ɪmænsɪˈpeɪʃən] *n* emancipación *f*

e-marketing [ˈiːmɑːkɪtɪŋ] *n Comptr* márketing *m* electrónico

emasculate [ɪˈmæskjʊleɪt] *vt Formal (rights, legislation)* desvirtuar; *(group, organization)* debilitar, minar

embalm [ɪmˈbɑːm] *vt* embalsamar

embalmer [ɪmˈbɑːmə(r)] *n* embalsamador(ora) *m,f*

embankment [ɪmˈbæŋkmənt] *n (beside railroad)* terraplén *m*; *(alongside river)* dique *m*

embargo [emˈbɑːgəʊ] **1** *(pl* **embargoes***)* embargo *m*; **to be under (an) e.** estar sometido(a) a embargo; **to put an e. on** imponer un embargo a
2 *vt (pt & pp* **embargoed***)* someter a embargo

embark [ɪmˈbɑːk] *vi* embarcar; *Fig* **to e. (up)on** *(adventure)* embarcarse en

embarrass [ɪmˈbærəs] *vt* avergonzar, abochornar, *Am salvo RP* apenar; **to e. the government** poner en apuros al Gobierno

embarrassed [ɪmˈbærəst] *adj (uncomfortable)* azorado(a), violento(a); *(financially)* apurado(a) (de dinero); **I'm so e. !** me da tanta vergüenza *or Am salvo RP* pena!

embarrassing [ɪmˈbærəsɪŋ] *adj* embarazoso(a), bochornoso(a); **how e.!** ¡qué vergüenza!, *Am salvo RP* ¡qué pena!

embarrassingly [ɪmˈbærəsɪŋlɪ] *adv* bochornosamente; **it was e. easy** resultaba tan sencillo que le hacía a uno sentirse incómodo

embarrassment [ɪmˈbærəsmənt] *n (shame)* vergüenza *f*, *Am salvo RP* pena *f*; *(discomfort)* apuro *m*, embarazo *m*; **much to my e.** para mi bochorno; **to be an e. to sb** ser motivo de vergüenza *or Am salvo RP* pena para alguien

embassy [ˈembəsɪ] *n* embajada *f*; **the Spanish E.** la embajada española *or* de España

embattled [ɪmˈbætəld] *adj* acosado(a); **to be e.** estar acosado(a)

embed [ɪmˈbed] *(pt & pp* **embedded***) vt* (**a**) **to be embedded in sth** estar incrustado(a) en algo; **to be embedded in sb's memory** estar grabado(a) en la memoria de alguien; **embedded journalist** periodista *m,f* incrustado(a) (**b**) *Comptr* incrustar

embellish [ɪmˈbelɪʃ] *vt (room, account)* adornar (**with** con)

embers [ˈembəz] *npl* brasas *fpl*, rescoldos *mpl*

embezzle [ɪm'bezəl] *vt (public money)* malversar; *(private money)* desfalcar

embezzlement [ɪm'bezəlmənt] *n (of public money)* malversación *f*; *(of private money)* desfalco *m*

embezzler [ɪm'bezlə(r)] *n (of public money)* malversador(ora) *m,f*; *(of private money)* desfalcador(ora) *m,f*

embitter [ɪm'bɪtə(r)] *vt (person)* amargar

embittered [ɪm'bɪtəd] *adj* amargado(a)

emblazon [ɪm'bleɪzən] *vt (shield)* blasonar; *Fig (name, headline)* estampar con grandes letras

emblem ['embləm] *n* emblema *m*

emblematic [emblə'mætɪk] *adj* simbólico(a), emblemático(a)

embodiment [ɪm'bɒdɪmənt] *n* encarnación *f*; **she seemed the e. of reasonableness** parecía la sensatez personificada

embody [ɪm'bɒdɪ] *vt* encarnar, representar

embolden [ɪm'bəʊldən] *vt* envalentonar

embolism ['embəlɪzəm] *n Med* embolia *f*

emboss [ɪm'bɒs] *vt (metal, leather)* repujar; *(letter, design)* grabar en relieve; **an embossed letterhead** un membrete en relieve

embrace [ɪm'breɪs] **1** *n* abrazo *m*
  2 *vt (person, belief)* abrazar; *(include)* abarcar
  3 *vi* abrazarse

embroider [ɪm'brɔɪdə(r)] *vt (cloth)* bordar; *Fig (account, report)* adornar

embroidery [ɪm'brɔɪdərɪ] *n* bordado *m*

embroil [ɪm'brɔɪl] *vt* **to be embroiled in sth** estar enredado(a) en algo; **to get embroiled in a debate with sb** enfrascarse *or* enredarse en una discusión con alguien

embryo ['embrɪəʊ] *(pl* **embryos)** *n* embrión *m*; *Fig* **in e.** *(plan, idea)* en estado embrionario

embryonic [embrɪ'ɒnɪk] *adj Biol* embrionario(a); *(plan, idea)* en estado embrionario

emend [ɪ'mend] *vt* corregir

emendation [i:men'deɪʃən] *n* corrección *f*

emerald ['emərəld] *n* esmeralda *f*; **e. (green)** verde *m* esmeralda; **the E. Isle** = Irlanda

emerge [ɪ'mɜːdʒ] *vi (from water)* emerger; *(from behind sth)* salir (**from** de); *Fig (difficulty, truth)* aflorar, surgir; **it later emerged that...** más tarde resultó que...

emergence [ɪ'mɜːdʒəns] *n (of facts, from hiding)* aparición *f*; *(of new state, new leader)* surgimiento *m*

emergency [ɪ'mɜːdʒənsɪ] *n* emergencia *f*; *Med* urgencia *f*; **in an e., in case of e.** en caso de emergencia; **e. brake** freno *m* de mano; **e. exit** salida *f* de emergencia; **e. landing** aterrizaje *m* forzoso; **e. flashers, e. lights** luces *fpl* de emergencia; *Med* **e. room** sala *f* de urgencias; **e. stop** parada *f* en seco *or* de emergencia

emergent [ɪ'mɜːdʒənt] *adj* pujante; **e. nations** países *mpl* emergentes

emery board ['emərɪ'bɔːd] *n* lima *f* de uñas

emetic [ɪ'metɪk] *n* emético *m*, vomitivo *m*

emigrant ['emɪgrənt] *n* emigrante *mf*

emigrate ['emɪgreɪt] *vi* emigrar

emigration [emɪ'greɪʃən] *n* emigración *f*

émigré ['emɪgreɪ] *n* emigrado(a) *m,f*; *Pol* exiliado(a) *m,f*

eminence ['emɪnəns] *n* **(a)** *(importance)* eminencia *f* **(b)** *(title of cardinal)* **Your E.** Su *or* Vuestra Eminencia

eminent ['emɪnənt] *adj (person)* eminente; *(quality)* notable

eminently ['emɪnəntlɪ] *adv* sumamente

emirate ['emɪreɪt] *n* emirato *m*

emissary ['emɪsərɪ] *n* emisario(a) *m,f*

emission [ɪ'mɪʃən] *n* emisión *f*, emanación *f*; **toxic emissions** emanaciones tóxicas

emit [ɪ'mɪt] *(pt & pp* **emitted)** *vt (heat, light, sound)* emitir; *(smell, gas)* desprender, emanar

Emment(h)aler ['eməntɑːlə(r)], **Emment(h)al** ['eməntɑːl] *n* (queso *m*) emental *m or* emmenthal *m*

emoticon [ɪ'mɒtɪkɒn] *n Comptr* emoticono *m*

emotion [ɪ'məʊʃən] *n* emoción *f*

emotional [ɪ'məʊʃənəl] *adj (person)* emotivo(a), sensible; *(problem, reaction)* emocional; *(movie, farewell)* conmovedor(ora), emotivo(a); **to get** *or* **become e.** emocionarse

emotionally [ɪ'məʊʃənəlɪ] *adv* emotivamente; **to be e. involved with sb** tener una relación sentimental con alguien; **e. deprived** privado(a) de cariño

emotive [ɪ'məʊtɪv] *adj (words, plea)* emotivo(a); **an e. issue** un asunto que despierta las más encendidas pasiones

empathize ['empəθaɪz] *vi* identificarse (**with** con)

empathy ['empəθɪ] *n* identificación *f*; **to feel e. for sb** identificarse con alguien

emperor ['empərə(r)] *n* emperador *m*

emphasis ['emfəsɪs] *(pl* **emphases** ['emfəsi:z]) *n* énfasis *m inv*; **to lay** *or* **place e. on sth** hacer hincapié en algo; **the e. is on written work** se hace hincapié en el trabajo escrito

emphasize ['emfəsaɪz] *vt* **(a)** *(point, fact)* hacer hincapié en, subrayar **(b)** *(word, syllable)* acentuar

emphatic [ɪm'fætɪk] *adj (gesture, tone)* enfático(a); *(denial, response)* rotundo(a), categórico(a); *(victory, scoreline)* convincente; **he was quite e. that...** hizo especial hincapié en que...

emphatically [ɪm'fætɪkəlɪ] *adv (to say)* enfáticamente; *(to refuse, deny)* categóricamente; **most e.!** ¡absolutamente!

emphysema [emfɪ'si:mə] *n* enfisema *m*

empire ['empaɪə(r)] *n also Fig* imperio *m*

empire-building ['empaɪə'bɪldɪŋ] *n (within an organization)* acumulación *f* de poder, medro *m* personal

empirical [em'pɪrɪkəl] *adj* empírico(a)

empirically [em'pɪrɪklɪ] *adv* empíricamente

empiricism [em'pɪrɪsɪzəm] *n* empirismo *m*

employ [ɪm'plɔɪ] **1** *n Formal* **to be in sb's e.** trabajar al servicio *or* a las órdenes de alguien
  2 *vt* **(a)** *(workers)* emplear; **to e. oneself (by** *or* **in doing sth)** ocuparse (en hacer algo) **(b)** *(tool, time, force)* emplear, utilizar

employed [ɪm'plɔɪd] *adj* empleado(a), con empleo

employee [em'plɔɪi:] *n* empleado(a) *m,f*; *Com* **e. buyout** = adquisición de una empresa por los empleados

employer [ɪm'plɔɪə(r)] *n (person)* empresario(a) *m,f*, patrono(a) *m,f*; *(company)* empresa *f*

employment [ɪm'plɔɪmənt] *n* **(a)** *(work)* empleo *m*; **to be in e.** tener un (puesto de) trabajo, estar empleado(a); **to be without e.** no tener empleo, estar desempleado(a) *or Am* desocupado(a); *Com* **e. agency** *or* **bureau** agencia *f* de colocaciones **(b)** *(use) (of tool, force)* empleo *m*, uso *m*

empower [ɪm'paʊə(r)] *vt* **to e. sb to do sth** habilitar *or* capacitar a alguien para hacer algo

empowering [ɪm'paʊərɪŋ] *adj* emancipador(ora); **an e. experience** una experiencia que hace sentir fuerte

empress ['emprɪs] *n* emperatriz *f*

emptiness ['emptɪnɪs] *n* vacío *m*

empty ['emptɪ] **1** *adj (container, existence)* vacío(a); *(promise, threat)* vano(a); **on an e. stomach** con el estómago vacío
  2 *vt* vaciar
  3 *vi* vaciarse
  4 *n (bottle)* **empties** cascos *mpl*

▸**empty out** *vt sep (pockets)* vaciar

empty-handed ['emptɪ'hændɪd] *adv* con las manos vacías

empty-headed ['emptɪ'hedɪd] *adj* necio(a), bobo(a); **to be e.** tener la cabeza hueca

EMS [i:em'es] *n (abbr* **emergency medical services)** SME *mpl*, servicios *mpl* médicos de emergencia

emu ['i:mju:] *n (bird)* emú *m*

emulate ['emjʊleɪt] *vt* emular

emulsify [ɪ'mʌlsɪfaɪ] *vt Tech* emulsionar

emulsion [ɪ'mʌlʃən] *n (liquid mixture)* emulsión *f*; **e. (paint)** pintura *f* (al temple)

enable [ɪ'neɪbəl] *vt* (**a**) *(allow)* **to e. sb to do sth** permitir a alguien hacer algo (**b**) *Comptr (function)* ejecutar; *(device)* activar, hacer operativo(a)

enact [ɪ'nækt] *vt* (**a**) *(tragedy, play)* interpretar (**b**) *(law)* promulgar

enamel [ɪ'næməl] **1** *n* esmalte *m*
2 *vt (pt & pp* **enameled)** esmaltar

enamored [ɪ'næməd] *adj* **to be e. of** estar enamorado(a) de; **I'm not greatly e. of** *or* **with the idea** no me entusiasma la idea

encampment [ɪn'kæmpmənt] *n Mil* campamento *m*

encapsulate [ɪn'kæpsjʊleɪt] *vt (summarize)* sintetizar

encase [ɪn'keɪs] *vt (with lining, cover)* revestir; **to be encased in concrete** estar revestido(a) de hormigón *or Am* concreto

enchant [ɪn'tʃɑ:nt] *vt* (**a**) *(charm)* cautivar, encantar; **he was less than enchanted by the idea** la idea no le hacía mucha gracia (**b**) *(put under a spell)* hechizar

enchanting [ɪn'tʃɑ:ntɪŋ] *adj* encantador(ora), cautivador(ora)

enchantingly [ɪn'tʃɑ:ntɪŋlɪ] *adv* con encanto

enchantment [ɪn'tʃɑ:ntmənt] *n* fascinación *f*, encanto *m*

enchantress [ɪn'tʃɑ:ntrɪs] *n (attractive woman)* seductora *f*

enchilada [entʃɪ'lɑ:də] *n Fam* **the whole e.** *(everything)* todo, toda la pesca *or RP* la bola

encircle [ɪn'sɜ:kəl] *vt* rodear

encl (**a**) *(abbr* **enclosure)** material *m* adjunto (**b**) *(abbr* **enclosed)** adjunto(a)

enclave ['enkleɪv] *n* enclave *m*

enclose [ɪn'kləʊz] *vt* (**a**) *(surround)* rodear (**b**) *(include in letter)* adjuntar; **please find enclosed...** le adjunto..., le envío adjunto(a)...

enclosed [ɪŋ'kləʊzd] *adj* (**a**) **an e. space** un espacio cerrado (**b**) *(in letter)* adjunto(a)

enclosure [ɪn'kləʊʒə(r)] *n* (**a**) *(area)* recinto *m*, cercado *m* (**b**) *(in letter)* documento *m* adjunto

encode [en'kəʊd] *vt* cifrar, codificar; *Comptr* codificar

encoding [ɪn'kəʊdɪŋ] *n Comptr* codificación *f*

encompass [ɪn'kʌmpəs] *vt* abarcar, incluir

encore ['ɒŋkɔ:(r)] *n (in theater)* bis *m*; **to call for an e.** pedir un bis; **e.!** ¡otra, otra!

encounter [ɪn'kaʊntə(r)] **1** *n (meeting)* encuentro *m*; *(confrontation)* enfrentamiento *m*
2 *vt (person, difficulty)* encontrarse *or* toparse con

encourage [ɪn'kʌrɪdʒ] *vt (person)* animar; *(growth, belief)* promover, impulsar; **to e. sb to do sth** animar a alguien a hacer algo

encouragement [ɪn'kʌrɪdʒmənt] *n* apoyo *m*, aliento *m*; **to give** *or* **offer sb e.** animar *or* alentar a alguien

encouraging [ɪn'kʌrɪdʒɪŋ] *adj* alentador(ora)

▸**encroach on, encroach upon** [ɪn'krəʊtʃ] *vt insep (rights)* usurpar; *(time, land)* invadir

encrusted [ɪn'krʌstɪd] *adj* **e. with diamonds** con diamantes incrustados; **e. with mud** con barro incrustado

encumber [ɪn'kʌmbə(r)] *vt* **to be encumbered by** *or* **with** estar *or* verse entorpecido(a) por

encumbrance [ɪn'kʌmbrəns] *n* estorbo *m*

encyclical [ɪn'sɪklɪkəl] *n Rel* encíclica *f*

encyclop(a)edia [ɪnsaɪklə'pi:dɪə] *n* enciclopedia *f*

encyclop(a)edic [ɪnsaɪklə'pi:dɪk] *adj* enciclopédico(a)

end [end] **1** *n* (**a**) *(extremity)* extremo *m*; **from one e. to the other** de un extremo al otro; **at the other e. of the line** al otro lado del teléfono; **the financial e. of the business** el lado *or* aspecto financiero del negocio; *Fig* **to come to the e. of the road** *or* **line** llegar al final; **e. to e.** en hilera; **to stand sth on e.** colocar algo de pie *or Am* parado(a); **the deep/shallow e.** *(of swimming pool)* el lado más/menos hondo *or* donde cubre/no cubre

(**b**) *(limit in time, quantity)* final *m*, fin *m*; **for hours/days on e.** por espacio de varias horas/varios días; **to put an e. to sth** poner fin a algo; **to come to an e.** concluir, llegar a su fin; **I am at the e. of my patience** se me está agotando la paciencia; *Fig* **at the e. of the day** en definitiva, al final; **in the e.** al final; **it's not the e. of the world** no es el fin del mundo; *Fam* **no e. of...** la mar de...; **e. product** producto *m* final; *Com & Comptr* **e. user** usuario(a) *m,f* final

(**c**) *(aim, purpose)* fin *m*, propósito *m*; **an e. in itself** un fin en sí mismo; **she attained** *or* **achieved her end(s)** logró lo que se proponía; **to what e.?** ¿con qué fin *or* propósito?; **the e. justifies the means** el fin justifica los medios

(**d**) *(idioms) Fam* **to keep one's e. up** defenderse bien; *Fam* **this job will be the e. of me!** ¡este trabajo va a acabar conmigo!; *Fam* **to make ends meet** llegar a fin de mes; *Fam* **to get hold of the wrong e. of the stick** agarrar el rábano por las hojas, *RP* agarrar para el lado de los tomates; **he can't see beyond the e. of his nose** no ve más allá de sus narices; **we shall never hear the e. of it** nos lo van a recordar mientras vivamos

(**e**) *Sport (in football)* extremo *m*, end *m*; **defensive e.** extremo defensivo, defensive end; **tight e.** extremo cerrado, tight end

2 *vt* terminar, finalizar; **to e. it all** *(commit suicide)* quitarse la vida

3 *vi* terminar, acabar; **I must e. by thanking...** para terminar, debo dar gracias a...

▸**end up** *vi* terminar, acabar; **to e. up doing sth** terminar *or* acabar haciendo algo

endanger [ɪn'deɪndʒə(r)] *vt* poner en peligro; **such work would e. her health** un trabajo así resultaría peligroso para su salud; **an endangered species** una especie amenazada *or* en peligro de extinción

endear [ɪn'dɪə(r)] *vt* **to e. oneself to sb** hacerse querer por alguien; **her outspokenness did not e. her to her boss** su franqueza no le ganó el favor del jefe

endearing [ɪn'dɪərɪŋ] *adj* encantador(ora)

endearingly [ɪn'dɪərɪŋlɪ] *adv* de forma encantadora

endearment [ɪn'dɪəmənt] *n* **words of e.** palabras *fpl* tiernas *or* cariñosas

endeavor [ɪn'devə(r)] **1** *n* esfuerzo *m*
2 *vt* **to e. to do sth** procurar hacer algo

endemic [en'demɪk] *adj* endémico(a)

ending ['endɪŋ] *n (of story)* final *m*, desenlace *m*; *(of word)* terminación *f*

endive ['endaɪv] *n* (**a**) **(curly) e.** escarola *f* (**b**) *(chicory)* endibia *f*, achicoria *f*

endless ['endlɪs] *adj* interminable

endocrine ['endəʊkraɪn] *adj Med* endocrino(a); **e. gland** glándula *f* endocrina

endocrinology [endəʊkraɪ'nɒlədʒɪ] *n* endocrinología *f*

endorphin [en'dɔ:fɪn] *n* endorfina *f*

endorse, indorse [ɪn'dɔ:s] *vt* (**a**) *(document, check)* endosar (**b**) *(approve) (opinion, action)* apoyar, respaldar (**c**) *(commercial product)* promocionar

endorsement [ɪn'dɔ:smənt] *n* (**a**) *(on document, check)* endoso *m* (**b**) *(approval) (of action, opinion)* apoyo *m* (**of** a), respaldo *m* (**of** a)

endow [ɪn'daʊ] *vt* dotar (**with** de)

endowment [ɪn'daʊmənt] *n* (**a**) *Fin* asignación *f*; **e. insurance** seguro *m* de vida mixto *or* de ahorro; **e. policy** póliza *f* de tipo mixto (**b**) *(talent)* dote *f*

endurable [ɪn'djʊərəbəl] *adj* soportable

endurance [ɪn'djʊərəns] *n* resistencia *f*; **beyond e.** a más no poder; **e. test** prueba *f* de resistencia

endure [ɪn'djʊə(r)] **1** *vt* soportar, aguantar
2 *vi (last)* durar

enduring [ɪn'djʊərɪŋ] *adj* duradero(a)

enema ['enəmə] *n* enema *m*

enemy ['enəmɪ] **1** *n* enemigo(a) *m,f*; **she's her own worst e.** su peor enemigo es ella misma
2 *adj (country, ship)* enemigo(a)

energetic [enə'dʒetɪk] *adj* enérgico(a)

energetically [enə'dʒetɪklɪ] *adv* enérgicamente

energize ['enədʒaɪz] *vt (invigorate)* dar energías a

energy ['enədʒɪ] *n* energía *f*; **to save e.** ahorrar energía; **e. crisis** crisis *f* energética

energy-saving ['enədʒɪseɪvɪŋ] *adj* que ahorra energía

enervating ['enəveɪtɪŋ] *adj* debilitante, enervante

enfeeble [ɪn'fiːbəl] *vt* debilitar, enervar

enfold [ɪn'fəʊld] *vt* rodear; **he enfolded her in his arms** la rodeó con sus brazos

enforce [ɪn'fɔːs] *vt (law)* hacer cumplir, aplicar; *(rights)* hacer valer

enforcement [ɪn'fɔːsmənt] *n* aplicación *f*

enfranchise [ɪn'fræntʃaɪz] *vt* otorgar el derecho al voto a

engage [ɪn'geɪdʒ] **1** *vt* (a) *(employ)* contratar (b) *(attention, person)* ocupar; **to e. sb in conversation** entablar conversación con alguien (c) *Mil* **to e. the enemy** entrar en liza con el enemigo (d) *(cog, gear)* engranar; **to e. the clutch** embragar
2 *vi* (a) **to e. in** *(activity, sport)* dedicarse a (b) *(cog wheel)* engranar

engaged [ɪn'geɪdʒd] *adj* (a) *(to be married)* prometido(a); **to be e. (to sb)** estar prometido(a) (a *or* con alguien) (b) *(involved)* **to be e. in doing sth** estar ocupado(a) haciendo algo

engagement [ɪn'geɪdʒmənt] *n* (a) *(to be married)* compromiso *m*; *(period)* noviazgo *m*; **e. ring** anillo *m* de pedida *or* de compromiso (b) *(appointment)* compromiso *m* (c) *(military action)* batalla *f*, combate *m*

engaging [ɪn'geɪdʒɪŋ] *adj* atractivo(a)

engender [ɪn'dʒendə(r)] *vt* engendrar

engine ['endʒɪn] *n* (a) *(of car, plane, ship)* motor *m*; **e. room** sala *f* de máquinas; **e. trouble** avería *f (del motor)* (b) *Rail* locomotora *f*

engineer [endʒɪ'nɪə(r)] **1** *n* ingeniero(a) *mf*; *Naut & Rail* maquinista *mf*
2 *vt (cause, bring about)* urdir

engineering [endʒɪ'nɪərɪŋ] *n* ingeniería *f*

England ['ɪŋglənd] *n* Inglaterra

English ['ɪŋglɪʃ] **1** *n (language)* inglés *m*; **E. class/teacher** clase *f*/profesor(a) *m,f* de inglés
2 *npl (people)* **the E.** los ingleses
3 *adj* inglés(esa); **the E. Channel** el Canal de la Mancha; **E. muffin** tortita *f*

Englishman ['ɪŋglɪʃmən] *n* inglés *m*

English-speaking ['ɪŋglɪʃ'spiːkɪŋ] *adj* anglófono(a), de habla inglesa

Englishwoman ['ɪŋglɪʃwʊmən] *n* inglesa *f*

engrave [ɪn'greɪv] *vt* grabar

engraver [ɪn'greɪvə(r)] *n* grabador(ora) *m,f*

engraving [ɪn'greɪvɪŋ] *n* grabado *m*

engrossed [ɪn'grəʊst] *adj* **to be e. (in)** estar absorto(a) (en)

engrossing [ɪn'grəʊsɪŋ] *adj* absorbente

engulf [ɪn'gʌlf] *vt (of waves, flames)* devorar; **she was engulfed by despair** se sumió en la desesperación

enhance [ɪn'hɑːns] *vt (value, chances)* incrementar, aumentar; *(performance, quality)* mejorar; *(beauty, color)* realzar; *(reputation)* acrecentar, elevar

enigma [ɪ'nɪgmə] *n* enigma *m*

enigmatic [enɪg'mætɪk] *adj* enigmático(a)

enigmatically [enɪg'mætɪklɪ] *adv* enigmáticamente

enjoy [ɪn'dʒɔɪ] *vt* (a) *(take pleasure from)* disfrutar de; **did you e. your meal?** ¿les gustó la comida?; **he enjoys swimming** le gusta nadar; **to e. oneself** divertirse, pasarlo bien (b) *(benefit from)* gozar de, disfrutar de

enjoyable [ɪn'dʒɔɪəbəl] *adj* agradable

enjoyably [ɪn'dʒɔɪəblɪ] *adv* agradablemente; **we spent the weekend most e.** pasamos un fin de semana muy agradable

enjoyment [ɪn'dʒɔɪmənt] *n (pleasure)* disfrute *m*; **to get e. out of sth** disfrutar con algo

enlarge [ɪn'lɑːdʒ] **1** *vt (make larger)* ampliar, agrandar; *(photograph)* ampliar
2 *vi* ampliarse, agrandarse; **to e. (up)on sth** *(explain in greater detail)* explicar algo más detalladamente

enlargement [ɪn'lɑːdʒmənt] *n* ampliación *f*, agrandamiento *m*; *Phot* ampliación *f*

enlighten [ɪn'laɪtən] *vt* aclarar; **can somebody e. me as to what is going on?** ¿podría alguien aclararme qué está ocurriendo?

enlightened [ɪn'laɪtənd] *adj* ilustrado(a), progresista

enlightenment [ɪn'laɪtənmənt] *n (clarification)* aclaración *f*; *Hist* **the E.** la Ilustración

enlist [ɪn'lɪst] **1** *vt (support, help)* conseguir; *Mil (soldier)* alistar; **enlisted man/woman** soldado *mf* raso
2 *vi Mil* alistarse

enliven [ɪn'laɪvən] *vt* animar

en masse ['ɒn'mæs] *adv* en masa

enmesh [ɪn'meʃ] *vt* **to become enmeshed in sth** enredarse en algo

enmity ['enmɪtɪ] *n* enemistad *f*

enormity [ɪ'nɔːmɪtɪ] *n* magnitud *f*

enormous [ɪ'nɔːməs] *adj* enorme, inmenso(a)

enormously [ɪ'nɔːməslɪ] *adv* enormemente, inmensamente

enough [ɪ'nʌf] **1** *adj* suficiente, bastante; **more than e. money/wine** dinero/vino de sobra *or* más que suficiente
2 *pron* **will this be e.?** ¿bastará *or* será bastante con esto?; **I haven't got e.** no tengo suficiente; **more than e.** más que suficiente; **that's e.** *(sufficient)* es suficiente; **that's e.!** *(stop doing that)* ¡basta ya!, *Esp* ¡vale ya!; **e. is e.** ya basta; **e. said!** ¡no me digas más!, ¡ni una palabra más!; **to have e. to live on** tener (lo suficiente) para vivir; **to have had e. of sb/sth** estar harto(a) de alguien/algo
3 *adv* (a) *(sufficiently)* suficientemente, bastante; **good e.** suficientemente bueno(a), suficiente; **she is not strong/tall e.** no es lo bastante fuerte/alta (b) *(reasonably)* bastante; **she's a nice e. girl** la chica es agradable *or Esp* maja; **oddly *or* strangely e.,...** curiosamente,...

en passant [ɒn'pæsɒŋ] *adv* de pasada

enquire = **inquire**

enquiry = **inquiry**

enrage [ɪn'reɪdʒ] *vt* enfurecer, encolerizar

enrapture [ɪn'ræptʃə(r)] *vt* embelesar

enraptured [ɪn'ræptʃəd] *adj* embelesado(a); **to be e.** estar embelesado(a)

enrich [ɪn'rɪtʃ] *vt* enriquecer

enriching [ɪn'rɪtʃɪŋ] *adj* enriquecedor(ora)

enroll [ɪn'rəʊl] **1** *vt* inscribir
2 *vi* inscribirse

enrollment [ɪn'rəʊlmənt] *n* inscripción *f*

ensconce [ɪn'skɒns] *vt* **to e. oneself** aposentarse

ensemble [ɒn'sɒmbəl] *n* conjunto *m*

enshrine [ɪnˈʃraɪn] vt to be enshrined in sth estar amparado(a) por algo

ensign [ˈensaɪn] n (a) (flag) bandera f, enseña f (b) (naval officer) alférez m de fragata

enslave [ɪnˈsleɪv] vt esclavizar

ensnare [ɪnˈsneə(r)] vt (animal, criminal) capturar

ensue [ɪnˈsjuː] vi sucederse, seguir

ensuing [ɪnˈsjuːɪŋ] adj subsiguiente

en suite [ˈɒnˈswiːt] n with an e. bathroom, with bath-room e. con cuarto de baño privado

ensure [ɪnˈʃʊə(r)] vt garantizar

ENT [iːenˈtiː] n Med (abbr **Ear, Nose and Throat**) otorri-nolaringología f; **E. specialist** otorrinolaringólogo(a) m,f

entail [enˈteɪl] vt (a) (involve) implicar, conllevar (b) Law to e. an estate vincular mediante testamento una propiedad

entangle [ɪnˈtæŋgəl] vt to get or become entangled (wires, animal in net) enredarse; to be romantically entangled with sb tener relaciones amorosas con alguien

entanglement [ɪnˈtæŋgəlmənt] n (of wires, cables) enredo m; (love affair, difficult situation) lío m

enter [ˈentə(r)] **1** vt (a) (house, country) entrar en; (race) inscribirse en; (exam) presentarse a; (army, college) ingresar en; to e. a child at school inscribir a un niño en una escuela; to e. sb for a race inscribir a alguien en una carrera; to e. a horse for a race inscribir un caballo para una carrera; it never entered my head that... jamás se me pasó por la cabeza que...; to e. a protest presentar un escrito de protesta (b) Comptr (data) introducir
  2 vi (go in) entrar; to e. for a race inscribirse en una carrera

▸**enter into** vt insep (a) (service, dispute, relationship) empezar, iniciar; to e. into partnership (with sb) asociarse (con alguien); to e. into conversation with sb entablar conversación con alguien (b) (have a part in) money doesn't e. into it el dinero no tiene nada que ver

enterprise [ˈentəpraɪz] n (a) (undertaking) empresa f, iniciativa f; (company) empresa f (b) (initiative) iniciativa f; to show e. tener iniciativa

enterprising [ˈentəpraɪzɪŋ] adj emprendedor(ora)

entertain [entəˈteɪn] **1** vt (a) (amuse) entretener, divertir; to e. guests tener invitados (b) (consider) (opinion) considerar; (fear, suspicion, hope) albergar
  2 vi recibir (invitados)

entertainer [entəˈteɪnə(r)] n artista mf (del espectáculo)

entertaining [entəˈteɪnɪŋ] **1** n to do a lot of e. tener a menudo invitados en casa
  2 adj entretenido(a), divertido(a)

entertainment [entəˈteɪnmənt] n (a) (amusement) entreteni-miento m, diversión f; much to the e. of the crowd para regocijo de la multitud; Com e. allowance gastos mpl de representación (b) Theat espectáculo m; the e. business la industria del espectáculo

enthrall [ɪnˈθrɔːl] vt cautivar, hechizar

enthralling [ɪnˈθrɔːlɪŋ] adj cautivador(ora)

enthuse [ɪnˈθjuːz] **1** vt entusiasmar
  2 vi entusiasmarse (**about** or **over**, por)

enthusiasm [ɪnˈθjuːzɪæzəm] n entusiasmo m

enthusiast [ɪnˈθjuːzɪæst] n entusiasta mf

enthusiastic [ɪnθjuːzɪˈæstɪk] adj (person) entusiasmado(a); (praise) entusiasta; to be e. (about) (person) estar entusias-mado(a) (con)

enthusiastically [ɪnθjuːzɪˈæstɪklɪ] adv con entusiasmo

entice [ɪnˈtaɪs] vt to e. sb to do sth incitar a alguien a hacer algo; he was enticed away from her le incitaron a que la abandonara

enticing [ɪnˈtaɪsɪŋ] adj tentador(ora), atractivo(a)

entire [ɪnˈtaɪə(r)] adj (whole, complete) entero(a); the e. building/country el edificio/país entero; to be in e.

agreement (with sb) estar completamente de acuerdo (con alguien)

entirely [ɪnˈtaɪəlɪ] adv completamente, por entero

entirety [ɪnˈtaɪərətɪ] n integridad f, totalidad f; in its e. en su totalidad, íntegramente

entitle [ɪnˈtaɪtl] vt (a) (allow) to e. sb to do sth autorizar a alguien a hacer algo; to be entitled to (do) sth tener derecho a (hacer) algo (b) (book, song) titular

entitlement [ɪnˈtaɪtəlmənt] n derecho m

entity [ˈentɪtɪ] n ente m, entidad f

entomologist [entəˈmɒlədʒɪst] n entomólogo(a) m,f

entomology [entəˈmɒlədʒɪ] n entomología f

entourage [ɒntuˈrɑːʒ] n séquito m, comitiva f

entrails [ˈentreɪlz] npl entrañas fpl

entrance¹ [ˈentrəns] n (a) (way in, act of entering) entrada f; to gain e. to lograr acceder a, lograr ingresar en; Theat & Fig he made his e. hizo su aparición or entrada (en escena); e. hall vestíbulo m (b) (admission) entrada f, ingreso m; e. examination examen m de ingreso

entrance² [ɪnˈtrɑːns] vt (charm) cautivar, encantar

entrancing [ɪnˈtrɑːnsɪŋ] adj cautivador(ora), encantador(ora)

entrant [ˈentrənt] n participante mf

entrapment [ɪnˈtræpmənt] n Law incitación f al delito

entreat [ɪnˈtriːt] vt rogar, suplicar; to e. sb to do sth suplicar a alguien que haga algo

entreaty [ɪnˈtriːtɪ] n ruego m, súplica f

entrée [ˈɒntreɪ] n Culin plato m principal

entrenched [ɪnˈtrentʃd] adj (custom, attitude) arraigado(a); (person) atrincherado(a); to be e. (custom, attitude) estar arraigado(a); (person) estar atrincherado(a)

entrepreneur [ɒntrəprəˈnɜː(r)] n empresario(a) m,f

entrepreneurial [ɒntrəprəˈnɜːrɪəl] adj empresarial

entropy [ˈentrəpɪ] n entropía f

entrust [ɪnˈtrʌst] vt to e. sb with sth, to e. sth to sb confiar algo a alguien

entry [ˈentrɪ] n (a) (way in, act of entering) entrada f; (into group, organization) ingreso m; to gain e. to lograr introducirse en; she made her e. hizo su entrada (b) (of competitor) participante mf; we had over 1,000 entries for the competition se recibieron más de 1.000 inscripciones para el concurso; e. form (impreso m de) inscripción f (c) (in dictionary, encyclopaedia) entrada f

entwine [ɪnˈtwaɪn] **1** vt entrelazar
  2 vi entrelazarse

enumerate [ɪˈnjuːməreɪt] vt enumerar

enunciate [ɪˈnʌnsɪeɪt] vt (sound, word) articular; (opinion, view) enunciar

envelop [ɪnˈveləp] vt envolver

envelope [ˈenvələʊp, ˈɒnvələʊp] n sobre m

enviable [ˈenvɪəbəl] adj envidiable

envious [ˈenvɪəs] adj envidioso(a); to be or feel e. (of) tener envidia (de)

enviously [ˈenvɪəslɪ] adv con envidia

environment [ɪnˈvaɪrənmənt] n (surroundings) entorno m; the e. el medio ambiente

environmental [ɪnvaɪrənˈmentəl] adj medioambiental; e. damage daños mpl medioambientales; e. disaster catás-trofe f ecológica; e. groups grupos mpl ecologistas; E. Protection Agency = agencia gubernamental estadouni-dense encargada de la protección medioambiental

environmentalist [ɪnvaɪrənˈmentəlɪst] n ecologista mf

environmentally [ɪnvaɪrənˈmentəlɪ] adv ecológicamente, desde el punto de vista ecológico; e. friendly ecológico(a), que no daña el medio ambiente

environs [ɪnˈvaɪrənz] npl inmediaciones fpl, alrededores mpl

envisage [ɪnˈvɪzɪdʒ], **envision** [enˈvɪʒən] vt (foresee) prever;

(imagine) imaginar; **I don't e. any major changes** no preveo ningún cambio importante

envoy ['envɔɪ] *n (diplomat)* enviado(a) *m,f*

envy ['envɪ] **1** *n* envidia *f;* **to be the e. of sb** ser la envidia de alguien

2 *vt (person)* envidiar; **they envied him his success** tenían envidia de *or* envidiaban su éxito

enzyme ['enzaɪm] *n Biol* enzima *m or f*

eon ['iːən] *n* eón; *Fam* **eons ago** hace siglos

EPA [iːpiː'eɪ] *n (abbr* **Environmental Protection Agency**) = agencia gubernamental estadounidense encargada de la protección medioambiental

epaulet ['epəlet] *n Mil* charretera *f*

ephemeral [ɪ'femərəl] *adj* efímero(a)

epic ['epɪk] **1** *n (movie)* película *f* épica; *(poem, novel)* epopeya *f*
2 *adj* épico(a)

epicenter ['epɪsentə(r)] *n* epicentro *m*

epicurean [epɪkjʊ'rɪən] *n & adj* epicúreo(a) *m,f*

epidemic [epɪ'demɪk] *Med & Fig* **1** *n* epidemia *f*
2 *adj* epidémico(a)

epidermis [epɪ'dɜːmɪs] *n Anat* epidermis *f inv*

epidural [epɪ'djʊərəl] *n Med* (anestesia *f)* epidural *f*

epigram ['epɪɡræm] *n* epigrama *m*

epigraph ['epɪɡrɑːf] *n* epígrafe *m*

epilepsy ['epɪlepsɪ] *n* epilepsia *f*

epileptic [epɪ'leptɪk] **1** *n* epiléptico(a) *m,f*
2 *adj* epiléptico(a); **e. fit** ataque *m* epiléptico

epilogue, epilog ['epɪlɒɡ] *n* epílogo *m*

Epiphany [ɪ'pɪfənɪ] *n* Epifanía *f*

episcopal [ɪ'pɪskəpəl] *adj* episcopal; **the E. Church** la Iglesia Episcopal

episcopalian [ɪpɪskə'peɪlɪən] *Rel* **1** *n* **E.** episcopalista *mf*
2 *adj* episcopalista

episode ['epɪsəʊd] *n (part of story, program)* capítulo *m,* episodio *m; (incident)* episodio *m*

epistle [ɪ'pɪsəl] *n also Hum* epístola *f*

epitaph ['epɪtɑːf] *n* epitafio *m*

epithet ['epɪθet] *n* epíteto *m*

epitome [ɪ'pɪtəmɪ] *n* vivo ejemplo *m;* **to be the e. of sth** ser el vivo ejemplo de algo

epitomize [ɪ'pɪtəmaɪz] *vt* reflejar a la perfección, ser el vivo ejemplo de

epoch ['iːpɒk] *n* época *f*

epoch-making ['iːpɒkmeɪkɪŋ] *adj* **an e. change/event** un cambio/acontecimiento que hace/hizo/*etc.* época

eponymous [ɪ'pɒnɪməs] *adj* epónimo(a)

EPS [iːpiː'es] *n Fin (abbr* **earnings per share**) dividendos *mpl* por acción

equable ['ekwəbəl] *adj (person, temper)* ecuánime

equably ['ekwəblɪ] *adv* con ecuanimidad, ecuánimemente

equal ['iːkwəl] **1** *n* igual *mf;* **to treat sb as an e.** tratar a alguien de igual a igual
2 *adj* **(a)** *(identical)* igual; **all things being e.** en condiciones normales; **in e. measure** en igual medida; **on e. terms** en igualdad de condiciones; **e. opportunities** igualdad *f* de oportunidades; **e. pay** igualdad *f* de retribuciones; **e. rights** igualdad *f* de derechos **(b)** *(good enough)* **to be e. to (doing) sth** estar capacitado(a) para (hacer) algo
3 *vt (pt & pp* **equaled**) *(match)* igualar; **four fives e.(s) twenty** cuatro por cinco igual a veinte, cuatro por cinco, veinte

equality [ɪ'kwɒlɪtɪ] *n* igualdad *f*

equalize ['iːkwəlaɪz] **1** *vt* igualar
2 *vi Sport* empatar, igualar el marcador

equalizer ['iːkwəlaɪzə(r)] *n Elec* ecualizador *m; Sport* tanto *m* del empate

equally ['iːkwəlɪ] *adv* **(a)** *(to an equal degree)* igualmente **(b)** *(in equal amounts)* **to share** *or* **divide sth e.** dividir algo en partes iguales

equanimity [ekwə'nɪmɪtɪ] *n* ecuanimidad *f;* **with e.** ecuánimemente

equate [ɪ'kweɪt] *vt* equiparar (**with** con)

equation [ɪ'kweɪʒən] *n Math* ecuación *f*

equator [ɪ'kweɪtə(r)] *n* ecuador *m*

equatorial [ekwə'tɔːrɪəl] *adj* ecuatorial; **E. Guinea** Guinea Ecuatorial

equestrian [ɪ'kwestrɪən] **1** *n* caballista *mf*
2 *adj (statue, ability)* ecuestre

equidistant [ekwɪ'dɪstənt] *adj* equidistante

equilateral [ekwɪ'lætərəl] *adj* equilátero(a)

equilibrium [ekwɪ'lɪbrɪəm] *n* equilibrio *m*

equinox ['ekwɪnɒks] *n* equinoccio *m*

equip [ɪ'kwɪp] *(pt & pp* **equipped**) *vt* **(a)** *(provide with equipment)* equipar; **to e. sb with sth** equipar a alguien con *or* de algo **(b)** *(prepare)* preparar; **to be equipped for…** estar preparado(a) para…

equipment [ɪ'kwɪpmənt] *n (items)* equipo *m;* **e. allowance** gastos *mpl* de equipamiento

equitable ['ekwɪtəbəl] *adj* justo(a), equitativo(a)

equitably ['ekwɪtəblɪ] *adv* equitativamente

equity ['ekwɪtɪ] *n* **(a)** *(fairness)* justicia *f,* equidad *f* **(b)** *Fin (of shareholders)* fondos *mpl* propios, neto *m* patrimonial; *(of company)* capital *m* escriturado *or* social; **equities** acciones *fpl* ordinarias

equivalence [ɪ'kwɪvələns] *n* equivalencia *f*

equivalent [ɪ'kwɪvələnt] **1** *n* equivalente *m*
2 *adj* equivalente (**to** a)

equivocal [ɪ'kwɪvəkəl] *adj* equívoco(a)

equivocally [ɪ'kwɪvəklɪ] *adv* de manera equívoca

equivocate [ɪ'kwɪvəkeɪt] *vi* andarse con rodeos

equivocation [ɪkwɪvə'keɪʃən] *n* evasivas *fpl,* ambigüedades *fpl*

ER [iː'ɑː(r)] *n Med (abbr* **Emergency Room**) (sala *f* de) urgencias *fpl*

era ['ɪərə] *n* era *f*

eradicate [ɪ'rædɪkeɪt] *vt* erradicar

erase [ɪ'reɪs] *vt* borrar

eraser [ɪ'reɪsə(r)] *n* goma *f* (de borrar)

erect [ɪ'rekt] **1** *adj* erguido(a), erecto(a)
2 *vt* erigir

erection [ɪ'rekʃən] *n* **(a)** *(of building)* erección *f,* construcción *f* **(b)** *(erect penis)* erección *f*

ergonomic [iːɡə'nɒmɪk] *adj* ergonómico(a)

ergonomically [ɜːɡə'nɒmɪklɪ] *adv* ergonómicamente; **e. designed** con diseño ergonómico

ergonomics [ɜːɡə'nɒmɪks] *n* ergonomía *f*

Eritrea [erɪ'treɪə] *n* Eritrea

Eritrean [erɪ'treɪən] *n & adj* eritreo(a) *m,f*

ermine ['ɜːmɪn] *n* armiño *m*

erode [ɪ'rəʊd] **1** *vt (rock, soil, metal)* erosionar; *(confidence, power)* erosionar, minar; *(savings, income)* mermar
2 *vi (rock, soil, metal)* erosionarse; *(confidence, power)* minarse; *(savings, income)* mermar

erogenous [ɪ'rɒdʒɪnəs] *adj* erógeno(a); **e. zone** zona *f* erógena

Eros ['ɪərɒs] *n* Eros

erosion [ɪ'rəʊʒən] *n (of rock, soil, metal)* erosión *f; (of confidence, power)* desgaste *m; (of savings, income)* merma *f*

erotic [ɪ'rɒtɪk] *adj* erótico(a)

erotica [ɪ'rɒtɪkə] *npl* obras *fpl* eróticas

erotically [ɪ'rɒtɪklɪ] *adv* eróticamente

eroticism [ɪ'rɒtɪsɪzəm] *n* erotismo *m*

err [ɜː(r)] *vi (make mistake)* cometer un error, errar; **to e. on the side of caution** pecar de prudente; *Prov* **to e. is human** errar es humano

errand ['erənd] *n* recado *m*, *Am* mandado *m*; **to run errands for sb** hacerle los recados *or Am* mandados a alguien; **e. boy** chico *m* de los recados, *RP* cadete *m*

errata [e'rɑːtə] *npl Typ* fe *f* de erratas

erratic [ɪ'rætɪk] *adj (service, performance)* desigual, irregular; *(course, mood)* errático(a)

erratically [ɪ'rætɪklɪ] *adv (to act, behave)* de manera errática, de forma imprevisible; *(to move)* erráticamente

erroneous [ɪ'rəʊnɪəs] *adj* erróneo(a)

error ['erə(r)] *n (mistake)* error *m*; **to make an e.** cometer un error, equivocarse; **in e.** por error; **to see the e. of one's ways** darse cuenta de los propios errores

ersatz ['ɜːzæts] *adj* sucedáneo(a)

erstwhile ['ɜːstwaɪl] *adj Literary* antiguo(a), de otros tiempos

erudite ['erʊdaɪt] *adj* erudito(a)

erudition [erʊ'dɪʃən] *n* erudición *f*

erupt [ɪ'rʌpt] *vi (volcano)* entrar en erupción; *Fig (violence, war)* estallar

eruption [ɪ'rʌpʃən] *n (of volcano)* erupción *f*; *(of anger, noise)* explosión *f*, estallido *m*

escalate ['eskəleɪt] *vi (prices)* aumentar; **to e. into...** *(conflict)* convertirse en...

escalation [eskə'leɪʃən] *n (of prices, conflict)* escalada *f*

escalator ['eskəleɪtə(r)] *n* escalera *f* mecánica

escalope, escal(l)op ['eskəlɒp] *n Culin* escalope *m*

escapade ['eskəpeɪd] *n* aventura *f*, correría *f*

escape [ɪs'keɪp] **1** *n (of person)* huida *f*, evasión *f*; *(of gas, fluid)* escape *m*; **to make one's e.** escapar, huir; *Com* **e. clause** cláusula *f* de escape *or* de salvaguardia; **e. route** *(from fire)* vía *f* de salida (de emergencia); *(of criminal)* vía *f* de escape

2 *vt (danger, punishment)* escapar de, librarse de; **to e. sb's notice** pasar inadvertido(a) a alguien; **her name escapes me** ahora no me sale su nombre

3 *vi (person, gas, fluid)* escaparse **(from** de); **to e. from reality** evadirse de la realidad

escaped [ɪ'skeɪpt] *adj (prisoner)* fugado(a); *(animal)* escapado(a)

escapee [eskeɪ'piː] *n* fugitivo(a) *m,f*

escapism [ɪs'keɪpɪzəm] *n* evasión *f* de la realidad

escapist [ɪs'keɪpɪst] **1** *n* fantasioso(a) *m,f*

2 *adj* de evasión

escapologist [eskə'pɒlədʒɪst] *n* escapista *mf*

escarpment [ɪs'kɑːpmənt] *n* escarpa *f*, escarpadura *f*

eschew [ɪs'tʃuː] *vt* evitar

escort 1 *n* ['eskɔːt] escolta *f*; **under e.** escoltado(a); **e. agency** agencia *f* de acompañantes; *Mil* **e. duty** servicio *m* de escolta

2 *vt* [ɪs'kɔːt] escoltar

escudo [e'skuːdəʊ] *(pl* **escudos**) *n Formerly* escudo *m*

Eskimo ['eskɪməʊ] *(pl* **Eskimos**) *n & adj* esquimal *mf*

ESL [iːes'el] *n (abbr* **English as a Second Language**) = inglés como segunda lengua

esophagus [iː'sɒfəgəs] *(pl* **esophagi** [iː'sɒfəgaɪ]) *n Anat* esófago *m*

esoteric [esəʊ'terɪk] *adj* esotérico(a)

ESP [iːes'piː] *n (abbr* **extrasensory perception**) percepción *f* extrasensorial

espadrille ['espədrɪl] *n* alpargata *f*, zapatilla *f* de esparto

especially [ɪs'peʃəlɪ] *adv* especialmente; **we were e. lucky with the weather** tuvimos especial suerte con el tiempo

Esperanto [espə'ræntəʊ] *n* esperanto *m*

espionage ['espɪənɑːʒ] *n* espionaje *m*

esplanade [esplə'neɪd] *n* paseo *m* marítimo

espouse [ɪs'paʊz] *vt* patrocinar

espresso [es'presəʊ] *(pl* **espressos**) *n* café *m* exprés *or Esp* solo *or Am* negro

Esq *(abbr* **Esquire**) **Derek Wilson, E.** (Sr.) D. Derek Wilson

essay ['eseɪ] *n (at school)* redacción *f*; *(at college)* trabajo *m*

essayist ['eseɪɪst] *n* ensayista *mf*

essence ['esəns] *n (a) (most important part or quality)* esencia *f*; **in e.** esencialmente, en esencia; **the very e. of...** la más pura esencia de...; **time is of the e.** no hay tiempo que perder **(b)** *Culin* esencia *f*; **coffee/vanilla e.** esencia de café/vainilla

essential [ɪ'senʃəl] **1** *npl* **essentials** *(basic foodstuffs)* productos *mpl* primarios *or* de primera necesidad; *(basic issues)* cuestiones *fpl* básicas; **just pack a few essentials** guarda sólo lo imprescindible

2 *adj* **(a)** *(basic)* esencial, básico(a); **e. oil** aceite *m* esencial **(b)** *(indispensable)* esencial, fundamental; **it is e. that...** es fundamental que...

essentially [ɪ'senʃəlɪ] *adv* esencialmente

EST [iːes'tiː] *n (abbr* **Eastern Standard Time**) = hora oficial de la costa este de los EE.UU.

establish [ɪs'tæblɪʃ] *vt* **(a)** *(set up)* establecer; **to e. oneself in business** establecerse en el mundo de los negocios; **to e. a reputation** crearse *or* labrarse una reputación; **they established their right to vote** establecieron su derecho al voto; **the movie established her as an important director** la película la consagró como una gran directora **(b)** *(prove) (fact, sb's innocence)* determinar

established [ɪs'tæblɪʃt] *adj (custom, practice)* establecido(a); *(fact)* probado(a); **the e. church** la religión oficial; **the e. order** el orden establecido

establishment [ɪs'tæblɪʃmənt] *n* **(a) the E.** *(established order)* el sistema, el orden establecido; *(ruling class)* la clase dominante **(b)** *(hotel, restaurant)* establecimiento *m* **(c)** *(of company)* fundación *f*; *(of reputation)* establecimiento *m*; *(of fact)* determinación *f*

estate [ɪs'teɪt] *n* **(a)** *Law (possessions)* posesiones *fpl* **(b)** *(land)* finca *f*

esteem [ɪs'tiːm] **1** *n* estima *f*; **to hold sb in high/low e.** tener a alguien en gran/poca estima

2 *vt* estimar; *Formal* **to e. it an honor that...** considerar un honor que...

esthetic, aesthetic [ɪs'θetɪk] *adj* estético(a)

estimate 1 *n* ['estɪmət] *(calculation)* estimación *f*, cálculo *m* aproximado; *Com* presupuesto *m*; **at a rough e.** aproximadamente

2 *vt* ['estɪmeɪt] estimar; **an estimated cost/value** un coste/valor estimado

estimation [estɪ'meɪʃən] *n* **(a)** *(calculation)* cálculo *m*, estimación *f* **(b)** *(judgment)* juicio *m*, opinión *f*; **she has gone up/down in my e.** ahora la tengo en más/menos estima

Estonia [es'təʊnɪə] *n* Estonia

Estonian [es'təʊnɪən] **1** *n* **(a)** *(person)* estonio(a) *m,f* **(b)** *(language)* estonio *m*

2 *adj* estonio(a)

estranged [ɪs'treɪndʒd] *adj* separado(a); **to be e. (from)** estar separado(a) (de)

estrogen ['iːstrədʒen] *n Biol & Chem* estrógeno *m*

estuary ['estjʊərɪ] *n* estuario *m*

ETA [iːtiː'eɪ] *n Av (abbr* **estimated time of arrival**) hora *f* prevista de llegada

e-tailing ['iːteɪlɪŋ] *n Comptr* venta *f* en Internet

et al [et'æl] *(abbr* **et alii**) et al.

etc [et'setrə] *adv (abbr* **et cetera**) etc., etcétera

etch [etʃ] *vt* grabar (al aguafuerte); *Fig* **the scene was etched in his memory** tenía la escena grabada en la memoria

etching ['etʃɪŋ] *n (picture)* (grabado *m* al) aguafuerte *m*

eternal [ɪ'tɜːnəl] *adj* eterno(a)

eternally [ɪ'tɜːnəlɪ] *adv* eternamente; **I shall be e. grateful**

to you te estaré eternamente agradecido(a)

eternity [ɪ'tɜːnɪtɪ] n eternidad f; Fam **I waited an e.** esperé una eternidad

ether ['iːθə(r)] n éter m

ethereal [ɪ'θɪərɪəl] adj etéreo(a)

ethical ['eθɪkəl] adj ético(a)

ethically ['eθɪklɪ] adv éticamente

ethics ['eθɪks] npl ética f

Ethiopia [iːθɪ'əʊpɪə] n Etiopía

Ethiopian [iːθɪ'əʊpɪən] n & adj etíope mf

ethnic ['eθnɪk] adj étnico(a); **e. cleansing** limpieza f étnica; **e. minority** minoría f étnica

ethnically ['eθnɪklɪ] adv étnicamente

ethnicity ['eθnɪsɪtɪ] n etnicidad f

ethnocentric [eθnəʊ'sentrɪk] adj etnocéntrico(a)

ethnography [eθ'nɒɡrəfɪ] n etnografía f

ethnology [eθ'nɒlədʒɪ] n etnología f

ethos ['iːθɒs] n código m ético, valores mpl (morales)

e-ticket ['iː'tɪkɪt] n Esp billete m or Am boleto m or Am pasaje m electrónico

etiquette ['etɪket] n etiqueta f, protocolo m; **professional e.** ética f profesional

Etruscan [ɪ'trʌskən] n & adj etrusco(a) m,f

etymological [etɪmə'lɒdʒɪkəl] adj etimológico(a)

etymologist [etɪ'mɒlədʒɪst] n etimólogo(a) m,f

etymology [etɪ'mɒlədʒɪ] n etimología f

EU [iː'juː] n (abbr **European Union**) UE f

eucalyptus [juːkə'lɪptəs] n eucalipto m

Eucharist ['juːkərɪst] n **the E.** la Eucaristía

eulogize ['juːlədʒaɪz] vt loar, alabar

eulogy ['juːlədʒɪ] n panegírico m

eunuch ['juːnək] n eunuco m

euphemism ['juːfɪmɪzəm] n eufemismo m

euphemistic [juːfɪ'mɪstɪk] adj eufemístico(a)

euphemistically [juːfɪ'mɪstɪklɪ] adv de manera eufemística, eufemísticamente

euphoria [juː'fɔːrɪə] n euforia f

euphoric [juː'fɔːrɪk] adj eufórico(a); **to be e.** estar eufórico(a)

Eurasian [jʊə'reɪʒən] n & adj eur(o)asiático(a) m,f

eureka [jʊə'riːkə] exclam ¡eureka!

euro ['jʊərəʊ] n (pl **euros**) n Fin (European currency) euro m

Eurocentric [jʊərəʊ'sentrɪk] adj eurocéntrico(a)

Eurodollar ['jʊərəʊdɒlə(r)] n Fin eurodólar m

Euro-MP ['jʊərəʊempiː] n eurodiputado(a) m,f

Europe ['jʊərəp] n Europa

European [jʊərə'piːən] 1 n europeo(a) m,f
2 adj europeo(a); **E. Commission** Comisión f Europea; **E. Court of Human Rights** Tribunal m Europeo de Derechos Humanos; **E. Court of Justice** Tribunal m de Justicia Europeo; **E. Free Trade Association** Asociación f Europea de Libre Comercio; **E. Parliament** Parlamento m Europeo; **E. Union** Unión f Europea

Europhile ['jʊərəʊfaɪl] n & adj europeísta mf

Eustachian tube [juːs'teɪʃən'tjuːb] n Anat trompa f de Eustaquio

euthanasia [juːθə'neɪzɪə] n eutanasia f

evacuate [ɪ'vækjʊeɪt] vt (person, area) evacuar

evacuation [ɪvækjʊ'eɪʃən] n (of people, area) evacuación f

evacuee [ɪvækjʊ'iː] n evacuado(a) m,f

evade [ɪ'veɪd] vt (pursuer) burlar; (blow) esquivar; (question) eludir; **she evaded her responsibilities** rehuyó sus responsabilidades; **to e. tax** evadir impuestos

evaluate [ɪ'væljʊeɪt] vt evaluar

evaluation [ɪvæljʊ'eɪʃən] n evaluación f

evangelical [iːvæn'dʒelɪkəl] n & adj evangélico(a) m,f

evangelism [ɪ'vændʒɪlɪzəm] n evangelismo m

evangelist [ɪ'vændʒɪlɪst] n evangelista mf

evangelize [ɪ'vændʒɪlaɪz] vt & vi evangelizar

evaporate [ɪ'væpəreɪt] 1 vt evaporar; **evaporated milk** leche f concentrada
2 vi (liquid, enthusiasm) evaporarse

evaporation [ɪvæpə'reɪʃən] n evaporación f

evasion [ɪ'veɪʒən] n (escape) (of pursuer, question) evasión f; **(tax) e.** evasión fiscal; **I was met with the usual evasions** me dieron las evasivas de costumbre

evasive [ɪ'veɪsɪv] adj (person, reply) evasivo(a); **to take e. action** Mil maniobrar para evitar el enfrentamiento; Fig quitarse or Andes, RP sacarse de en medio

evasively [ɪ'veɪsɪvlɪ] adv con evasivas

eve [iːv] n (day before) víspera f; **on the e. of...** (en) la víspera de..., en vísperas de...

even ['iːvən] 1 adj (a) (flat) (surface) llano(a), liso(a) (b) (regular) (breathing, pace) regular, constante; (temperature) constante; **to have an e. temper** tener un carácter pacífico; **e. number** número m par (c) (equal) (contest) igualado(a); **to have an e. chance (of doing sth)** tener un cincuenta por ciento de posibilidades (de hacer algo); Fig **to get e. with sb** (take revenge on) vengarse or desquitarse de alguien
2 adv (a) incluso; **e. bigger/more interesting** aún or incluso mayor/más interesante; **I never e. saw it** ni siquiera llegué a verlo; **without e. speaking** sin tan siquiera hablar; **e. as I speak** justo a la vez que estoy hablando (b) (in phrases) **e. if** aunque; **e. now** incluso ahora; **e. so** aun así; **e. then** (still) ya entonces; (nevertheless) aun así; **e. though** aunque, a pesar de que
3 vt (make equal) igualar, equilibrar; **to e. the odds** dar igualdad de oportunidades; **to e. the score** igualar el marcador

▶**even out** 1 vt they aim to **e. out social inequalities** aspiran a eliminar las desigualdades sociales; **with this account you can e. out payments over the year** con esta cuenta, los pagos se reparten equitativamente a lo largo del año
2 vi (differences, workload) equilibrarse

▶**even up** vt sep **to e. things up** igualar or equilibrar las cosas

evenhanded ['iːvən'hændɪd] adj imparcial

evening ['iːvnɪŋ] n (earlier) tarde f; (later) noche f; **tomorrow e.** mañana por la tarde/noche; **yesterday e.** ayer (por la) tarde/noche; Fam **e.!** ¡buenas tardes/noches!, RP ¡nas tardes/noches!; **in the e.** por la tarde/noche; **a musical/cultural e.** una velada musical/cultural; **e. class** clase f nocturna; **e. dress** (for men) traje m de etiqueta; (for women) vestido m or traje m de noche; **e. paper** periódico m vespertino or de la tarde; **e. performance** (of play) sesión f de noche

evenly ['iːvənlɪ] adv (uniformly) uniformemente; (fairly) equitativamente; **to breathe e.** respirar tranquilamente; **to say sth e.** decir algo en tono neutro; **e. matched** en igualdad de condiciones

evensong ['iːvənsɒŋ] n Rel vísperas fpl

event [ɪ'vent] n (a) (occurrence) acontecimiento m; **in the course of events** en el transcurso de los acontecimientos; **in any e.** en cualquier caso; **in the e. of fire** en caso de incendio; **in the e. of her resigning...** en caso de que dimita... (b) (in athletics) prueba f

even-tempered ['iːvən'tempəd] adj ecuánime, sereno(a)

eventful [ɪ'ventful] adj (day, life) agitado(a), azaroso(a)

eventual [ɪ'ventjʊəl] adj final

eventuality [ɪventjʊ'ælɪtɪ] n eventualidad f, posibilidad f; **in that e.** en ese caso; **to be ready for all eventualities** estar preparado(a) or Am alistado(a) para cualquier eventualidad

eventually [ɪ'ventjʊəlɪ] adv finalmente, al final

ever ['evə(r)] adv (a) (always, at any time) **e. since then/1960** desde entonces/1960; **more than e.** más que nunca; **the**

worst/best e. el peor/mejor de todos los tiempos; **all she e. does is criticize** no hace más que criticar; **she was as friendly as e.** estuvo tan amable como siempre; **she's a liar if e. there was one** miente como ella sola, es la más mentirosa del mundo; **she's a genius if e. there was one** es un genio donde los haya; **e. the gentleman, he opened the door for her** caballeroso como siempre, le abrió la puerta

(**b**) *(with negative sense)* **not e.** nunca; **hardly e.** casi nunca; **nothing e. happens** nunca pasa nada; **I don't know if I'll e. meet him again** no sé si lo volveré a ver (alguna vez); **I seldom if e. see her** apenas la veo

(**c**) *(in questions)* alguna vez; **have you e. been to Spain?** ¿has estado (alguna vez) en España?

(**d**) *Fam (intensive)* **e. so pretty** tan guapísima; **e. so expensive** tan carísimo(a); **e. such a lot of money** tantísimo dinero

evergreen ['evəgriːn] **1** *n* árbol *m* (de hoja) perenne
2 *adj* (de hoja) perenne

everlasting [evə'lɑːstɪŋ] *adj* eterno(a), perpetuo(a)

evermore [evə'mɔː(r)] *adv Formal* por siempre (jamás); **for e.** para siempre

every ['evrɪ] *adj* (**a**) *(each, all)* cada; **at e. opportunity** en toda ocasión; **from e. side** de todas partes; **of e. kind** *or* **sort** de todo tipo; **they hung on his e. word** estaban pendientes de cada una de sus palabras; **e. time** siempre, cada vez; **e. one of us** todos y cada uno de nosotros; **e. man for himself!** ¡sálvese quien pueda!

(**b**) *(indicating regular occurrence)* **e. week** todas las semanas; **e. day** todos los días; **e. other** *or* **second day** cada dos días, *Am* día por medio; **e. other line/page** *(one in two)* cada dos líneas/páginas, *Am* línea/página por medio; **e. so often, e. now and again** *or* **then** de vez en cuando

(**c**) *(intensive)* **you have e. right to be angry** tienes todo el derecho a estar *esp Esp* enfadado *or esp Am* enojado; **e. bit as good/as intelligent as...** exactamente igual de bueno/de inteligente que...; **I shall give you e. assistance** te ayudaré en todo

everybody ['evrɪbɒdɪ], **everyone** ['evrɪwʌn] *pron* todo el mundo, todos(as); **e. I know was there** toda la gente que conozco estaba allí; **e. else** todos los demás; **e. who is anybody** toda la gente importante

everyday ['evrɪdeɪ] *adj (event, expression)* cotidiano(a); **for e. use** para uso cotidiano

everyone = everybody

everything ['evrɪθɪŋ] *pron* todo; **e. I did seemed to go wrong** todo lo que hacía parecía salir mal; **e. possible** todo lo posible; **money isn't e.** el dinero no lo es todo

everywhere ['evrɪweə(r)] *adv* por *or* en todas partes; **we looked e.** miramos por todas partes; **e. you go/look** dondequiera que vayas/mires; **e. in France** en toda Francia

evict [ɪ'vɪkt] *vt* desahuciar, desalojar

eviction [ɪ'vɪkʃən] *n* desahucio *m*, desalojo *m*; **e. order** orden *f* de desahucio *or* desalojo

evidence ['evɪdəns] **1** *n* (**a**) pruebas *fpl*; **to be in e.** ser claramente visible; **to show e. of** demostrar, dar prueba de; **there was no e. of his stay in the house** no había pruebas de su paso por la casa (**b**) *Law* pruebas *fpl*; **to give e.** testificar, prestar declaración; **to turn state's e.** = inculpar a un cómplice ante un tribunal a cambio de recibir un trato indulgente
2 *vt Formal* evidenciar, demostrar; **as evidenced by...** como lo demuestra...

evident ['evɪdənt] *adj* evidente; **it was e. that...** era evidente que...

evidently ['evɪdəntlɪ] *adv* evidentemente

evil ['iːvəl] **1** *n* mal *m*; **to speak e. of sb** hablar mal de alguien
2 *adj (person)* malo(a), malvado(a); *(action, practice)* vil, perverso(a); *(influence, effect)* nocivo(a), perjudicial; *(spirit)*

maligno(a); **the e. eye** el mal de ojo

evildoer ['iːvəlduːə(r)] *n Literary* malhechor(ora) *m,f*

evil-looking ['iːvəllʊkɪŋ] *adj* de aspecto siniestro

evil-minded ['iːvəl'maɪndɪd] *adj* perverso(a)

evil-smelling ['iːvəl'smelɪŋ] *adj* maloliente, apestoso(a)

evince [ɪ'vɪns] *vt Formal* evidenciar

evocation [evə'keɪʃən] *n* evocación *f*

evocative [ɪ'vɒkətɪv] *adj* evocador(ora) (**of** de)

evoke [ɪ'vəʊk] *vt* evocar

evolution [iːvə'luːʃən] *n* evolución *f*

evolutionary [iːvə'luːʃənərɪ] *adj* evolutivo(a)

evolve [ɪ'vɒlv] **1** *vt* desarrollar
2 *vi (species)* evolucionar; *(situation)* desarrollarse; **to e. from** *(species)* provenir de; **finding food has evolved into a major problem** encontrar comida se ha convertido en un problema de primer orden

ewe [juː] *n* oveja *f (hembra)*

ex [eks] *n Fam (former spouse, friend, boyfriend)* ex *mf*

ex- [eks] *prefix (former)* ex; **ex-minister/teacher** ex ministro(a)/profesor(ora); **ex-wife/husband** ex mujer/marido, exmujer/exmarido

exacerbate [eg'zæsəbeɪt] *vt* exacerbar

exact [ɪg'zækt] **1** *adj (number, amount)* exacto(a), preciso(a); **at the e. moment when...** en el preciso momento *or* instante en que...; **those were her e. words** esas fueron exactamente sus palabras; **the e. opposite** exactamente lo contrario; **to be e.** para ser exactos; **an e. science** una ciencia exacta
2 *vt (promise, apology)* arrancar (**from** a); *(obedience, respect)* imponer (**from** a); *(tax)* imponer el pago de (**from** a)

exacting [ɪg'zæktɪŋ] *adj (person)* exigente; *(task)* arduo(a); *(standards)* riguroso(a)

exactitude [ɪg'zæktɪtjuːd] *n Formal* exactitud *f*

exactly [ɪg'zæktlɪ] *adv* exactamente; **e.!** ¡exacto!; **not e.** *(not very)* no precisamente; *(as a reply)* no exactamente

exaggerate [ɪg'zædʒəreɪt] *vt & vi* exagerar

exaggerated [ɪg'zædʒəreɪtɪd] *adj* exagerado(a)

exaggeration [ɪgzædʒə'reɪʃən] *n* exageración *f*

exalt [ɪg'zɔːlt] *vt Formal (praise)* exaltar

exalted [ɪg'zɔːltɪd] *adj (high)* elevado(a)

exam [ɪg'zæm] *n* examen *m*; **to take an e.** examinarse, hacer un examen; **e. result** nota *f*, resultado *m*

examination [ɪgzæmɪ'neɪʃən] *n (at school, at college, of records)* examen *m*; **to take an e.** examinarse, hacer un examen; *Educ* **e. board** tribunal *m* (de examen), junta *f* examinadora; *Educ* **e. result** nota *f*, resultado *m*

examine [ɪg'zæmɪn] *vt (evidence, student)* examinar; **to e. one's conscience** hacer examen de conciencia; **examining body** comité *m* de evaluación

examinee [ɪgzæmɪ'niː] *n* examinando(a) *m,f*

examiner [ɪg'zæmɪnə(r)] *n* examinador(ora) *m,f*

example [ɪg'zɑːmpəl] *n* ejemplo *m*; **for e.** por ejemplo; **to set an e.** dar ejemplo; **to make an e. of sb** imponer un castigo ejemplar a alguien; **to follow sb's e.** seguir el ejemplo de alguien; **to lead by e.** predicar con el ejemplo

exasperate [ɪg'zɑːspəreɪt] *vt* exasperar; **to get exasperated** exasperarse

exasperating [ɪg'zɑːspəreɪtɪŋ] *adj* exasperante

exasperatingly [ɪg'zɑːspəreɪtɪŋlɪ] *adv* exasperantemente

exasperation [ɪgzɑːspə'reɪʃən] *n* exasperación *f*

excavate ['ekskəveɪt] *vt* excavar

excavation [ekskə'veɪʃən] *n* excavación *f*

excavator ['ekskəveɪtə(r)] *n (machine)* excavadora *f*

exceed [ɪk'siːd] *vt (amount, number, expectations)* superar, exceder; *(limit)* rebasar

exceedingly [ɪk'siːdɪŋlɪ] *adv* sumamente, extremadamente

excel [ɪkˈsel] (*pt & pp* **excelled**) **1** *vt esp Ironic* **to e. oneself** lucirse

2 *vi* sobresalir (**at** *or* **in** en)

excellence [ˈeksələns] *n* excelencia *f*

excellency [ˈeksələnsɪ] *n* **Your/His E.** Su Excelencia

excellent [ˈeksələnt] *adj* excelente

except [ɪkˈsept] **1** *prep* excepto, salvo; **nobody e. him** nadie salvo él; **e. for** a excepción de, exceptuando; **we would have lost, e. for you** de no ser *or* a no ser por ti, habríamos perdido; **the dress is ready e. for the buttons** menos *or* salvo los botones, el vestido está listo; **he's my best friend, e. for you, of course** es mi mejor amigo, aparte de ti, claro está; **e. that** sólo que; **e. when** salvo cuando

2 *vt* exceptuar, excluir (**from** de); **present company excepted** exceptuando a los aquí presentes; **not excepting…** incluyendo a…

exception [ɪkˈsepʃən] *n* excepción *f*; **to make an e. of sth/ for sb** hacer una excepción con algo/con alguien; **with the e. of…** a excepción (hecha) de…; **without e.** sin excepción; **the e. that proves the rule** la excepción que confirma la regla; **to take e. to sth** (*be offended*) ofenderse por algo; (*object*) censurar algo

exceptionable [ɪkˈsepʃənəbəl] *adj Formal* inaceptable, censurable

exceptional [ɪkˈsepʃənəl] *adj* excepcional

exceptionally [ɪkˈsepʃənəlɪ] *adv* extraordinariamente; **e., more time may be allowed** en casos excepcionales se dará más tiempo

excerpt [ˈeksɜːpt] *n* fragmento *m* (**from** de)

excess [ɪkˈses] *n* exceso *m*; **in e. of** más de; **sums in e. of $1,000** sumas superiores a *or* de más de 1.000 dólares; **to do sth to e.** hacer algo en exceso; **to lead a life of e.** llevar una vida de excesos; **to pay the e.** (*on ticket*) pagar la diferencia *or* el suplemento; **e. baggage** exceso de equipaje

excessive [ɪkˈsesɪv] *adj* excesivo(a)

excessively [ɪkˈsesɪvlɪ] *adv* excesivamente

exchange [ɪksˈtʃeɪndʒ] **1** *n* (**a**) (*of prisoners, ideas*) intercambio *m*; **in e. (for)** a cambio (de); **there was a heated e.** hubo un acalorado intercambio verbal; *Com* **e. of contracts** acto *m* notarial de compraventa; **e. visit** visita *f* de intercambio (**b**) *Fin* (*of currency*) cambio *m*; **e. controls** controles *m* de cambio (monetario); **e. rate** tipo *m* or *Am* tasa *f* de cambio (**c**) (**Stock**) **E.** mercado *m* de valores, bolsa *f* (**d**) (**telephone**) **e.** central *f* telefónica, centralita *f*

2 *vt* intercambiar; (*faulty goods*) descambiar; **to e. sth for sth** cambiar algo por algo; **to e. glances** intercambiar miradas

exchangeable [ɪksˈtʃeɪndʒəbəl] *adj* (*voucher, currency*) canjeable

excise 1 *n* [ˈeksaɪz] **e. (duties)** (*tax*) impuesto *m* sobre el consumo

2 *vt* [ɪkˈsaɪz] (*remove*) extirpar

excitable [ɪkˈsaɪtəbəl] *adj* excitable

excite [ɪkˈsaɪt] *vt* (*person*) entusiasmar, emocionar; (*feeling, passion*) excitar, estimular; (*envy, interest*) suscitar

excited [ɪkˈsaɪtɪd] *adj* entusiasmado(a), emocionado(a); **to get e. (about)** entusiasmarse *or* emocionarse (con)

excitedly [ɪkˈsaɪtɪdlɪ] *adv* con entusiasmo

excitement [ɪkˈsaɪtmənt] *n* emoción *f*; **to avoid e.** evitar las emociones fuertes; **to cause great e.** provocar un gran revuelo

exciting [ɪkˈsaɪtɪŋ] *adj* emocionante, apasionante

exclaim [ɪksˈkleɪm] *vt & vi* exclamar

exclamation [ekskləˈmeɪʃən] *n* exclamación *f*; **e. point** signo *m* de admiración *or* exclamación

exclamatory [eksˈklæmətərɪ] *adj* exclamativo(a)

exclude [ɪksˈkluːd] *vt* excluir; **excluding…** excluyendo…

exclusion [ɪksˈkluːʒən] *n* exclusión *f*; **to the e. of…** haciendo caso omiso de…

exclusive [ɪksˈkluːsɪv] **1** *n* (*in newspaper, on TV*) exclusiva *f*

2 *adj* exclusivo(a); **e. interview** entrevista *f* en exclusiva

3 *adv* **e. of** excluyendo

exclusively [ɪksˈkluːsɪvlɪ] *adv* exclusivamente; (*in newspaper, on TV*) en exclusiva

exclusivity [ekskluːˈsɪvɪtɪ], **exclusiveness** [ɪksˈkluːsɪvnɪs] *n* uso *m* exclusivo, exclusividad *f*

excommunicate [ekskəˈmjuːnɪkeɪt] *vt* excomulgar

excommunication [ekskəmjuːnɪˈkeɪʃən] *n* excomunión *f*

excrement [ˈekskrɪmənt] *n* excremento *m*

excrescence [eksˈkresəns] *n* (*monstrosity*) adefesio *m*

excrete [ɪksˈkriːt] *Formal vt & vi* excretar

excruciating [ɪksˈkruːʃɪeɪtɪŋ] *adj* terrible, espantoso(a)

excruciatingly [ɪksˈkruːʃɪeɪtɪŋlɪ] *adv* terriblemente, espantosamente; **e. painful** terriblemente doloroso(a); *Fam* **e. funny** tremendamente gracioso(a)

excursion [ɪksˈkɜːʃən] *n* excursión *f*

excuse 1 *n* [ɪksˈkjuːs] excusa *f*; **to make an e., to make excuses** disculparse, excusarse; **a poor e. for a car** una porquería de coche

2 *vt* [ɪksˈkjuːz] (**a**) (*forgive*) disculpar, excusar; **e. me!** (*to attract attention*) ¡perdón!, ¡oiga (por favor)!; (*when trying to get past*) ¿me permite?; **e. me?** (*what did you say?*) ¿cómo? (**b**) (*exempt*) eximir (**from** de) (**c**) **to e. oneself** (*give excuse*) disculparse, excusarse

execrable [ˈeksɪkrəbəl] *adj Formal* execrable

execute [ˈeksɪkjuːt] *vt* (*prisoner, command*) ejecutar; (*plan, operation*) llevar a cabo; (*one's duties*) cumplir

execution [eksɪˈkjuːʃən] *n* (*of order, prisoner*) ejecución *f*; (*of duty*) cumplimiento *m*

executioner [eksɪˈkjuːʃənə(r)] *n* verdugo *m*

executive [ɪgˈzekjʊtɪv] **1** *n* (*businessman*) ejecutivo(a) *m,f*; (*committee*) ejecutiva *f*

2 *adj* ejecutivo(a); **an e. car** un coche *or Am* carro *or Chile, RP* auto de lujo; **e. privilege** = exención de la obligación de revelar el contenido de documentos internos por parte del ejecutivo del gobierno

executor [ɪgˈzekjʊtə(r)] *n Law* albacea *mf*

exemplary [ɪgˈzemplərɪ] *adj* ejemplar

exemplify [ɪgˈzemplɪfaɪ] *vt* ilustrar

exempt [ɪgˈzempt] **1** *adj* exento(a) (**from** de)

2 *vt* eximir (**from** de)

exemption [ɪgˈzem(p)ʃən] *n* exención *f* (**from** de)

exercise [ˈeksəsaɪz] **1** *n* (*physical, mental*) ejercicio *m*; (*military*) maniobras *fpl*; **to take e.** hacer ejercicio; **e. bike** bicicleta *f* estática; **e. book** libro *m* de ejercicios; **e. yard** (*in prison*) patio *m* (de ejercicios)

2 *vt* (**a**) (*body, mind*) ejercitar (**b**) (*right, one's influence*) ejercer; **to e. discretion** ser discreto(a); **to e. restraint** controlarse

3 *vi* (*physically*) hacer ejercicio

exert [ɪgˈzɜːt] *vt* (*pressure, influence*) ejercer; **to e. oneself** esforzarse

exertion [ɪgˈzɜːʃən] *n* esfuerzo *m*

exfoliate [eksˈfəʊlɪeɪt] **1** *vt* exfoliar

2 *vi* exfoliarse

exhale [eksˈheɪl] *vi* espirar

exhaust [ɪgˈzɔːst] **1** *n* (**a**) (*on car*) escape *m*; **e. (fumes)** gases *mpl* de la combustión; **e. (pipe)** tubo *m* or *RP* caño *m* de escape (**b**) (*for stove*) **e. (fan)** extractor *m*; **e. hood** campana *f* extractora (de humos)

2 *vt* (*person, resources*) agotar

exhausted [ɪgˈzɔːstɪd] *adj* agotado(a); **to be e.** estar agotado(a)

exhausting [ɪgˈzɔːstɪŋ] *adj* agotador(ora)

exhaustion [ɪgˈzɔːstʃən] *n* agotamiento *m*

exhaustive [ɪgˈzɔːstɪv] *adj* exhaustivo(a)

exhaustively [ɪgˈzɔːstɪvlɪ] *adv* exhaustivamente, de forma exhaustiva

exhibit [ɪgˈzɪbɪt] **1** *n* (*in art exhibition*) obra *f* expuesta; (*in court* *case)* prueba *f* material

2 *vt* **(a)** *(object)* exhibir **(b)** *(painting in exhibition)* exponer **(c)** *(show)* **to e. signs of stress/wear** mostrar signos de estrés/desgaste

exhibition [eksɪ'bɪʃən] *n* exposición *f*; *Fam* **to make an e. of oneself** dar el espectáculo, *Esp* montar el número

exhibitionism [eksɪ'bɪʃənɪzəm] *n* exhibicionismo *m*

exhibitionist [eksɪ'bɪʃənɪst] *n* exhibicionista *mf*

exhibitor [ɪg'zɪbɪtə(r)] *n Art* expositor(ora) *m,f*

exhilarate [ɪg'zɪləreɪt] *vt* entusiasmar, enardecer

exhilarated [ɪg'zɪləreɪtɪd] *adj* eufórico(a), enardecido(a)

exhilarating [ɪg'zɪləreɪtɪŋ] *adj* vivificante, excitante

exhilaration [ɪgzɪlə'reɪʃən] *n* euforia *f*

exhort [ɪg'zɔːt] *vt Formal* exhortar

exhortation [ɪgzɔː'teɪʃən] *n Formal* exhortación *f*

exhume [eks'hjuːm] *vt* exhumar

exile ['eksaɪl] **1** *n* **(a)** *(banishment)* exilio *m*; **in e.** en el exilio **(b)** *(exiled person)* exiliado(a) *m,f*
  2 *vt* exiliar

exist [ɪg'zɪst] *vi* **(a)** *(be in existence)* existir **(b)** *(survive)* sobrevivir **(on** a base de)

existence [ɪg'zɪstəns] *n* existencia *f*; **to be in e.** existir; **to come into e.** nacer, ver la luz; **to go out of e.** desaparecer

existential [egzɪs'tenʃəl] *adj* existencial

existentialism [egzɪs'tenʃəlɪzəm] *n* existencialismo *m*

existentialist [egzɪs'tenʃəlɪst] *n & adj* existencialista *mf*

existing [ɪg'zɪstɪŋ] *adj* actual, existente

exit ['eksɪt] **1** *n* salida *f*; **to make an e.** salir; *Pol* **e. poll** sondeo *m* a la salida de los colegios electorales; **e. visa** visado *m or Am* visa *f* de salida
  2 *vi (leave) & Comptr* salir

exodus ['eksədəs] *n* éxodo *m*

ex officio ['eksə'fɪʃɪəʊ] **1** *adj (member)* en virtud del cargo
  2 *adv* **to act e.** actuar en virtud del cargo

exonerate [ɪg'zɒnəreɪt] *vt* exonerar **(from** *or* **of,** de)

exorbitant [ɪg'zɔːbɪtənt] *adj* exorbitante, exagerado(a)

exorbitantly [ɪg'zɔːbɪtəntlɪ] *adv* exorbitantemente; **it's e. priced** tiene un precio exorbitante

exorcism ['eksɔːsɪzəm] *n* exorcismo *m*

exorcist ['eksɔːsɪst] *n* exorcista *mf*

exorcize ['eksɔːsaɪz] *vt* exorcizar

exotic [ɪg'zɒtɪk] *adj* exótico(a)

exotically [ɪg'zɒtɪklɪ] *adv (dressed, decorated)* de forma exótica

expand [ɪks'pænd] **1** *vt (production, output)* ampliar
  2 *vi (solid, gas)* dilatarse; *(company)* expandirse, extenderse

▶**expand on, expand upon** *vt insep (talk, write at greater length about)* desarrollar

expandable [ɪks'pændəbəl] *adj Comptr* expandible; **4MB e. to 64MB** 4MB expandibles a 64MB

expanded [ɪks'pændɪd] *adj Comptr* ampliado(a); **e. polystyrene** poliestireno *m* expandido

expanding [ɪks'pændɪŋ] *adj (market, company)* en expansión

expanse [eks'pæns] *n (of land, water)* extensión *f*

expansion [ɪks'pænʃən] *n (of solid, gas)* dilatación *f*; *(of production, output)* ampliación *f*; *(of company)* expansión *f*; *Comptr* **e. card** tarjeta *f* de ampliación (de memoria)

expansive [ɪks'pænsɪv] *adj* expansivo(a), comunicativo(a)

expansively [ɪks'pænsɪvlɪ] *adv* de modo muy abierto

expatriate 1 *n* [eks'pætrɪət] *(voluntary)* emigrado(a) *m,f*; *(exile)* expatriado(a) *m,f*
  2 *vt* [eks'pætrɪeɪt] expatriar

expect [ɪks'pekt] **1** *vt* **(a)** *(anticipate)* esperar; **to e. to do sth** esperar hacer algo; **to e. sb to do sth** esperar que alguien haga algo; **I expected as much** ya me lo esperaba; **what do you e. from him?** ¿qué esperas *or* esperabas de él?; **I knew what to e.** ya sabía lo que me esperaba; **to e. the worst** esperarse lo

peor; **as one might e.** como era de esperar; **the movie was better than I expected** la película era mejor de lo que esperaba; **she's expecting a baby** está esperando un hijo
  (b) *(require)* **to e. sb to do sth** esperar de alguien que haga algo; **I e. you to be punctual** confío en que serás puntual; **I don't e. you to be perfect** no pretendo que seas perfecto; **you are expected to answer all the questions** conteste a todas las preguntas; **to e. sth from sb** esperar algo de alguien; **I know what is expected of me** sé qué es lo que se espera de mí; **people e. too much from marriage** la gente espera demasiado del matrimonio
  (c) *(suppose)* **to e. (that)…** suponer (que)…; **I e. so/not** supongo que sí/que no
  2 *vi (be pregnant)* **she's expecting** está en estado

expectancy [ɪks'pektənsɪ] *n* expectación *f*; **life e.** esperanza *f* de vida

expectant [ɪks'pektənt] *adj (air, crowd)* expectante; **e. mother** futura madre *f*

expectation [ekspek'teɪʃən] *n* expectativa *f*; **in (the) e. of sth** en previsión de algo; **to have high expectations of sb/sth** tener muchas esperanzas puestas en alguien/algo; **it came up to/fell short of his expectations** estuvo/no estuvo a la altura de sus expectativas; **contrary to all expectations** contra lo que se esperaba

expected [ɪks'pektɪd] *adj* esperado(a), previsto(a)

expectorant [ɪks'pektərənt] *n Med* expectorante *m*

expediency [ɪks'piːdɪənsɪ] *n* conveniencia *f*

expedient [ɪks'piːdɪənt] **1** *n* recurso *m*
  2 *adj* conveniente, oportuno(a)

expedite ['ekspɪdaɪt] *vt Formal* acelerar, apresurar

expedition [ekspə'dɪʃən] *n* expedición *f*

expeditionary force [ekspə'dɪʃənərɪ'fɔːs] *n Mil* fuerzas *fpl* expedicionarias

expel [ɪks'pel] *(pt & pp* **expelled)** *vt* expulsar

expendable [ɪks'pendəbəl] *adj* prescindible

expenditure [ɪks'pendɪtʃə(r)] *n (of money, energy)* gasto *m*; **public e.** gasto público

expense [ɪks'pens] *n* **(a)** *(cost)* gasto *m*; **at no extra e.** sin costo *or Esp* coste adicional; **at my own e.** a mi costa; **to go to great e.** incurrir en grandes gastos; **no e. was spared to…** no se reparó en gastos para…; **at the e. of one's health/sanity** a costa de perder la salud/cordura; **to make a joke at sb's e.** hacer un chiste a costa de alguien **(b)** *Com* **expenses** gastos *mpl*; **to meet** *or* **cover sb's expenses** correr con *or* costear los gastos de alguien; **all expenses paid** con todos los gastos pagados; **e. account** cuenta *f* de gastos

expensive [ɪks'pensɪv] *adj* caro(a), costoso(a); **to have e. tastes** tener gustos caros; **an e. mistake** un error muy caro

expensively [ɪks'pensɪvlɪ] *adv* caro; **e. dressed/furnished** con ropa cara/muebles caros

experience [ɪks'pɪərɪəns] **1** *n* experiencia *f*; **he still lacks e.** todavía le falta experiencia; **to learn from e.** aprender de la experiencia; **in my e.** según mi experiencia; **she had a nasty e.** le pasó una cosa terrible
  2 *vt* experimentar

experienced [ɪks'pɪərɪənst] *adj* experimentado(a) **(in** en)

experiment [ɪks'perɪmənt] **1** *n* experimento *m*; **to do** *or* **conduct an e.** hacer *or* realizar un experimento; **as an e.** como experimento
  2 *vi* experimentar **(with/on** con)

experimental [ɪksperɪ'mentəl] *adj* experimental

experimentally [ɪksperɪ'mentəlɪ] *adv* de forma experimental, empíricamente

experimentation [ɪksperɪmən'teɪʃən] *n* experimentación *f*

expert ['ekspɜːt] **1** *n* experto(a) *m,f*
  2 *adj* experto(a) **(in** *or* **at** en); **an e. opinion** la opinión de un experto; *Comptr* **e. system** sistema *m* experto; *Law* **e.**

witness perito(a) *m,f*

expertise [eksps:'ti:z] *n* destreza *f*, pericia *f*

expertly ['eksps:tlı] *adv* diestramente, hábilmente

expiate ['ekspıeıt] *vt Formal* expiar

expiration [ekspı'reıʃən] *n (of contract)* vencimiento *m*; **e. date** *(of product)* fecha *f* de caducidad

expire [ıks'paıə(r)] *vi* **(a)** *(law)* caducar; *(deadline)* expirar, vencer **(b)** *Literary (die)* expirar

expiry [ıks'paıərı] *n* vencimiento *m*; **e. date** fecha *f* de caducidad

explain [ıks'pleın] **1** *vt (rule, theory)* explicar; **to e. oneself** explicarse
  2 *vi* explicarse

▸**explain away** *vt sep* justificar, explicar

explanation [eksplə'neıʃən] *n* explicación *f*; **to give an e. of sth** explicar algo

explanatory [ıks'plænətərı] *adj* explicativo(a)

expletive [ıks'pli:tıv] *n* palabrota *f*, *Esp* taco *m*

explicable [eks'plıkəbəl] *adj* explicable

explicit [eks'plısıt] *adj* explícito(a)

explicitly [eks'plısıtlı] *adv* explícitamente

explode [ıks'pləʊd] **1** *vt (bomb)* hacer explotar, explosionar; *Fig (idea, theory)* reventar, desbaratar
  2 *vi (bomb)* explotar, estallar; *Fig (with anger)* estallar

exploit 1 *n* ['eksplɔıt] hazaña *f*, proeza *f*
  2 *vt* [eks'plɔıt] **(a)** *(take unfair advantage of)* explotar **(b)** *(use) (resources, sb's talents)* aprovechar

exploitation [eksplɔı'teıʃən] *n* explotación *f*

exploitative [eks'plɔıtətıv] *adj* explotador(ora)

exploration [eksplə'reıʃən] *n* exploración *f*

exploratory [ıks'plɒrətərı] *adj* exploratorio(a); **e. discussions** *or* **talks** negociaciones *fpl* preliminares; *Med* **e. surgery** cirugía *f* exploratoria

explore [ıks'plɔ:(r)] *vt & vi* explorar

explorer [ıks'plɒrə(r)] *n* explorador(ora) *m,f*

explosion [ıks'pləʊʒən] *n also Fig* explosión *f*, estallido *m*

explosive [ıks'pləʊsıv] **1** *n* explosivo *m*
  2 *adj* explosivo(a); *Fig* **an e. combination** *(of personalities, factors)* una mezcla explosiva

exponent [ıks'pəʊnənt] *n (of theory, art) & Math* exponente *m*; **a leading e. of…** *(supporter)* un destacado defensor de…

exponential [ekspəʊ'nenʃəl] *adj* exponencial; **e. growth/increase** crecimiento *m*/aumento *m* exponencial

export 1 *n* ['ekspɔ:t] **(a)** *(product)* artículo *m* de exportación; **exports** *(of country)* exportaciones *fpl* **(b)** *(exportation)* exportación *f*; **e. duty** derechos *mpl* de exportación; **e. license** permiso *m* de exportación; **e. trade** comercio *m* de exportación
  2 *vt* [eks'pɔ:t] exportar

exportation [ekspɔ:'teıʃən] *n* exportación *f*

exporter [eks'pɔ:tə(r)] *n* exportador(ora) *m,f*

expose [ıks'pəʊz] *vt (gen) & Phot* exponer **(to** a); **to be exposed to criticism** estar expuesto(a) a las críticas; **to e. sb as a traitor** revelar que alguien es un traidor; **a man exposed himself to my sister** a mi hermana le salió al paso un exhibicionista

exposé [eks'pəʊzeı] *n (article)* artículo *m* de denuncia *f*; *(TV program)* programa *m* de denuncia

exposed [ıks'pəʊzd] *adj* expuesto(a); **to be e. (to)** estar expuesto(a) (a)

exposition [ekspə'zıʃən] *n (explanation)* exposición *f*

expostulate [ıks'pɒstjʊleıt] *vi Formal* discutir

exposure [ıks'pəʊʒə(r)] *n* **(a)** *(to air, cold, danger)* exposición *f*; **to die of e.** morir de hipotermia *(a la intemperie)* **(b)** *(publicity)* publicidad *f*; **to get a lot of e.** recibir mucha publicidad **(c)** *(of crime, criminal)* denuncia *f* **(d)** *Phot (time)* (tiempo *m* de)

exposición *f*; *(photograph)* foto *f*; **e. meter** fotómetro *m*

expound [ıks'paʊnd] *vt Formal* explicar, dar cuenta de

express [ıks'pres] **1** *n (train)* (tren *m*) rápido *m*
  2 *adj* **(a)** *(clear) (purpose, instruction)* expreso(a) **(b)** *(rapid)* E. **Mail** = servicio de correo de entrega en 24 horas; **e. train** tren *m* rápido
  3 *adv* **to send a package e.** enviar un paquete urgente
  4 *vt (opinion, emotion)* expresar; **to e. oneself** expresarse

expression [ıks'preʃən] *n (facial, verbal)* expresión *f*; **freedom of e.** libertad *f* de expresión

expressionism [ıks'preʃənızəm] *n* expresionismo *m*

expressionist [ıks'preʃənıst] *n & adj* expresionista *mf*

expressionistic [ıkspreʃə'nıstık] *adj* expresionista

expressionless [ıks'preʃənlıs] *adj (face, voice)* inexpresivo(a)

expressive [ıks'presıv] *adj* expresivo(a)

expressiveness [ık'spresıvnıs] *n* expresividad *f*

expressly [ıks'preslı] *adv* expresamente

expresso [e(k)s'presəʊ] = **espresso**

expropriate [eks'prəʊprıeıt] *vt* expropiar

expropriation [eksprəʊprı'eıʃən] *n* expropiación *f*

expulsion [ıks'pʌlʃən] *n* expulsión *f*

expunge [ıks'pʌndʒ] *vt* borrar, eliminar

expurgate ['ekspɜ:geıt] *vt* expurgar

exquisite ['ekskwızıt] *adj* exquisito(a)

exquisitely [eks'kwızıtlı] *adv* exquisitamente

extant [eks'tænt] *adj Formal* **one of the few e. paintings of that period** una de las pocas pinturas que se conservan de aquel período

extempore [ıks'tempərı] **1** *adj (speech, speaker)* improvisado(a)
  2 *adv* **to speak e.** hablar improvisando

extemporize [ıks'tempəraız] *vi* improvisar

extend [ıks'tend] **1** *vt* **(a)** *(in space)* extender; *(frontier, knowledge)* ampliar; **to e. a house** ampliar una casa **(b)** *(in time) (vacation, contract, deadline)* prolongar **(c)** *(give, offer) (one's hand)* tender; *(support, thanks)* dar; *Fin* **to e. credit to sb** conceder un crédito a alguien
  2 *vi* **(a)** *(in space)* extenderse **(b)** *(in time)* prolongarse

extended family [ıks'tendıd'fæmılı] *n* clan *m* familiar

extension [ıks'tenʃən] *n* **(a)** *(on building)* ampliación *f*; *(of deadline)* prórroga *f*, prolongación *f*; *(for essay)* aplazamiento *m* (de la fecha de entrega) **(b)** *(for telephone)* extensión *f*, *RP* interno *m* **(c)** **e. (cable** *or* **cord)** alargador *m*, alargadera *f*

extensive [ıks'tensıv] *adj (area, knowledge)* extenso(a), amplio(a); *(damage, repairs)* cuantioso(a); **to make e. use of sth** utilizar algo mucho

extensively [ıks'tensıvlı] *adv (to travel, read)* mucho, extensamente; **to use sth e.** utilizar algo mucho

extent [ıks'tent] *n (of lands)* extensión *f*; *(of problem, damage, knowledge)* alcance *m*; **to an e., to a certain e., to some e.** hasta cierto punto, en cierta medida; **to a great e., to a large e.** en gran medida; **to such an e. that…** hasta tal punto que…

extenuating circumstances [ıks'tenjʊeıtıŋ'sɜ:kəmstænsız] *npl* (circunstancias *fpl*) atenuantes *fpl*

exterior [ıks'tıərıə(r)] **1** *n* exterior *m*; **beneath her calm e. she was extremely nervous** bajo su apariencia tranquila estaba sumamente inquieta
  2 *adj* externo(a), exterior

exterminate [ıks'tɜ:mıneıt] *vt* exterminar

extermination [ıkstɜ:mı'neıʃən] *n* exterminio *m*

external [ıks'tɜ:nəl] *adj* externo(a); *Pol* **e. affairs** política *f* exterior; *Univ* **e. degree** licenciatura *f* a distancia; **for e. use only** *(on medicine)* (de) uso tópico

externalize [ıks'tɜ:nəlaız] *vt (feelings, emotions)* exteriorizar

extinct [ıks'tıŋkt] *adj* extinto(a), extinguido(a)

extinction [ıks'tıŋkʃən] *n* extinción *f*

extinguish [ɪks'tɪŋgwɪʃ] vt extinguir; (light, cigarette) apagar

extinguisher [ɪks'tɪŋgwɪʃə(r)] n Esp extintor m, Am extinguidor m

extirpate ['ekstɜːpeɪt] vt Formal extirpar, erradicar

extol(l) [ɪks'təʊl] vt ensalzar

extort [ɪks'tɔːt] vt (money) obtener (mediante extorsión)

extortion [ɪks'tɔːʃən] n extorsión f

extortionate [ɪks'tɔːʃənɪt] adj (demand, price) abusivo(a)

extortionately [ɪks'tɔːʃənɪtlɪ] adv to be e. expensive tener un precio abusivo or exorbitante

extra ['ekstrə] 1 n (on bill) suplemento m, recargo m; (in movie) extra mf
2 adj (a) (additional) adicional; no e. charge sin recargo (b) (spare) de repuesto, de sobra
3 adv be e. careful with the salt ten muchísmo cuidado con la sal; e. fast superrápido; e. large extragrande

extract 1 n ['ekstrækt] (a) (concentrate) extracto m (b) (from book, movie) fragmento m
2 vt [ɪks'trækt] extraer, sacar

extraction [ɪks'trækʃən] n (removal) extracción f; (social, geographical) origen m; she is of Danish e. es de origen danés

extracurricular ['ekstrəkə'rɪkjʊlə(r)] adj Sch extraescolar

extradite ['ekstrədaɪt] vt Law extraditar

extradition [ekstrə'dɪʃən] n Law extradición f

extrajudicial ['ekstrədʒuː'dɪʃəl] adj extrajudicial

extramarital ['ekstrə'mærɪtəl] adj extramarital, adúltero(a)

extraneous [ɪks'treɪnɪəs] adj Formal ajeno(a)

extranet ['ekstrənet] n Comptr extranet m

extraordinarily [ɪks'trɔːdənərɪlɪ] adv extraordinariamente

extraordinary [ɪks'trɔːdənrɪ] adj extraordinario(a); the e. thing is that... lo extraordinario es que...; e. powers poderes mpl extraordinarios, competencias fpl extrordinarias

extrapolate [ɪk'stræpəleɪt] vt & vi extrapolar (from a partir de)

extrapolation [ɪkstræpə'leɪʃən] n extrapolación f

extrasensory perception ['ekstrə'sensərɪpə'sepʃən] n percepción f extrasensorial

extraterrestrial ['ekstrətɪ'restrɪəl] n & adj extraterrestre mf

extravagance [ɪks'trævəgəns] n (a) (excessive spending) derroche m, despilfarro m (b) (expensive purchase) dispendio m

extravagant [ɪks'trævəgənt] adj (person) derrochador(ora); (tastes) caro(a); an e. purchase un despilfarro

extravagantly [ɪks'trævəgəntlɪ] adv dispendiosamente; to live e. vivir a todo lujo

extravaganza [ekstrævə'gænzə] n espectáculo m fastuoso

Extremadura [ekstrəmə'djuːrə] n Extremadura

extreme [ɪks'triːm] 1 n extremo m; to go from one e. to the other pasar de un extremo al otro; to go to extremes recurrir a comportamientos extremos; extremes of temperature temperaturas fpl extremas; in the e. en grado sumo
2 adj extremo(a); Pol the e. left la extrema izquierda; e. sports deportes mpl extremos

extremely [ɪks'triːmlɪ] adv extremadamente, sumamente

extremism [ɪks'triːmɪzəm] n extremismo m

extremist [ɪks'triːmɪst] n & adj extremista mf

extremity [ɪks'tremɪtɪ] n (a) (end) extremo m (b) the extremities (of the body) las extremidades (c) (of situation) gravedad f extrema; (extreme measure) medida f extrema

extricate ['ekstrɪkeɪt] vt sacar, extraer; to e. oneself from (danger, difficulties) escapar or librarse de

extrovert ['ekstrəvɜːt] n & adj extrovertido(a) m,f, extra-vertido(a) m,f

exuberance [ɪg'zjuːbərəns] n euforia f, exultación f

exuberant [ɪg'zjuːbərənt] adj eufórico(a), exultante

exuberantly [ɪg'zjuːbərəntlɪ] adv con euforia, eufóricamente

exude [ɪg'zjuːd] vt (sweat, odor) exudar, rezumar; (health, confidence) rebosar, rezumar

exult [ɪg'zʌlt] vi alborozarse, exultar (in ante)

exultant [ɪg'zʌltənt] adj exultante

exultation [egzʌl'teɪʃən] n júbilo m, euforia f

eye [aɪ] 1 n (a) (of person, needle) ojo m; the e. of the storm el ojo del huracán; to open/close one's eyes abrir/cerrar los ojos; to look sb straight in the e. mirar a alguien a los ojos; as far as the e. can see hasta donde alcanza la vista; e. contact contacto m visual; to establish e. contact with sb mirar a alguien a los ojos, cruzar la mirada con alguien; e. drops (medicine) colirio m; at e. level a la altura de los ojos; e. shadow sombra f de ojos; e. test revisión f ocular or de la vista (b) (idioms) in the eye(s) of the law a (los) ojos de la ley; to be in the public e. estar en (el) candelero; to have an e. for detail/color tener buen ojo para los detalles/el color; to look at sth with a critical e. mirar algo con ojo crítico; to look at sth with an experienced e. mirar algo con ojos de experto; I don't see e. to e. with my boss no veo las cosas igual que (las ve) mi jefe; this is for your eyes only no se lo enseñes a nadie; to keep one's eyes and ears open mantener los ojos y los oídos bien abiertos; to keep one's eyes peeled no perder ojo; to open sb's eyes to sth abrirle a alguien los ojos en relación con algo, hacer ver algo a alguien; to shut or close one's eyes to sth negarse a ver algo, no querer ver algo; to do sth with one's eyes open hacer algo a sabiendas; to catch sb's e. (attract attention) llamar la atención de alguien; to please or delight the e. deleitar la vista; he has eyes in or at the back of his head se entera de todo, RP tiene ojos en la nuca; he has eyes for nobody but her sólo tiene ojos para ella; to set or lay eyes on sth ver algo; I saw it with my own eyes lo vi con mis propios ojos; to run or cast one's e. over sth echar una ojeada a algo; to keep an e. on sth/sb vigilar algo/a alguien; I'll keep an e. out for it/him estaré al tanto de ello/él; to have one's e. on sth/sb (be observing) estar vigilando algo/a alguien; to have one's e. on sth (be intending to buy) tenerle el ojo echado a algo; to have one's eye on sb (be attracted to) haberle echado el ojo a alguien; to make eyes at sb echar miradas lánguidas or miraditas a alguien; with an e. to... con vistas a...; to be up to one's eyes in work/debt estar hasta el cuello de trabajo/deudas; an e. for an e., a tooth for a tooth ojo por ojo, diente por diente
2 vt observar, mirar

▶**eye up** vt sep Fam (ogle) desnudar con la mirada

eyeball ['aɪbɔːl] n globo m ocular

eyebrow ['aɪbraʊ] n ceja f; to raise one's eyebrows (in surprise) arquear las cejas

eye-catching ['aɪkætʃɪŋ] adj llamativo(a)

eyeful ['aɪfʊl] n Fam to get an e. of sth (look at) mirar algo bien

eyeglass ['aɪglɑːs] n monóculo m

eyeglasses ['aɪglɑːsɪz] npl (spectacles) gafas fpl

eyelash ['aɪlæʃ] n pestaña f

eyelid ['aɪlɪd] n párpado m; Fig she didn't so much as bat an e. (didn't show surprise) ni se inmutó

eyeliner ['aɪlaɪnə(r)] n lápiz m de ojos

eye-opener ['aɪəʊpənə(r)] n revelación f

eyepatch ['aɪpætʃ] n parche m

eyeshade ['aɪʃeɪd] n visera f

eyesight ['aɪsaɪt] n vista f; to have good/bad e. estar bien/mal de la vista

eyesore ['aɪsɔː(r)] n (building) engendro m, adefesio m

eyestrain ['aɪstreɪn] n vista f cansada

eyetooth [aɪ'tuːθ] n colmillo m; I'd give my eyeteeth to go with them daría Esp un ojo de la cara or Am todo por ir con ellos

eyewash ['aɪwɒʃ] n (for eye) colirio m, baño m ocular; Fam (nonsense) paparruchas fpl

eyewitness ['aɪwɪtnɪs] n testigo mf ocular

eyrie ['ɪərɪ] n nido m de águila

F

F, f [ef] *n* (**a**) *(letter)* F, f *f* (**b**) *Mus* fa *m* (**c**) *Sch* muy deficiente *m*; **to get an F** *(in exam, essay)* sacar un muy deficiente

F *(abbr* **Fahrenheit**) F, Fahrenheit

fa [fɑː] *n Mus* fa *m*

fable [ˈfeɪbəl] *n* fábula *f*

fabled [ˈfeɪbəld] *adj* legendario(a), fabuloso(a)

fabric [ˈfæbrɪk] *n* (*cloth*) tejido *m*; *Fig* **the f. of society** el tejido social; **f. conditioner** suavizante *m* (para la ropa)

fabricate [ˈfæbrɪkeɪt] *vt* (*story*) inventar; (*evidence*) falsificar

fabulous [ˈfæbjʊləs] *adj* fabuloso(a), magnífico(a)

fabulously [ˈfæbjʊləslɪ] *adv* (*rich*) tremendamente

façade [fæˈsɑːd] *n also Fig* fachada *f*

face [feɪs] **1** *n* (**a**) (*of person*) cara *f*, rostro *m*; *very Fam* **shut your f.!** ¡cierra el pico!, ¡cállate la boca!; **I told him to his f.** se lo dije a *or* en la cara; **I shall never be able to look her in the f. again** nunca podré volver a mirarla a la cara; **to show one's f.** dejarse ver, hacer acto de presencia; **to set one's f. against sth** oponerse cerrilmente a algo; **in the f. of** (*danger, threat*) ante; **f. card** (*playing card*) figura *f*; **f. cloth** toallita *f*; **f. cream** crema *f* facial; **f. mask** (*cosmetic*) mascarilla *f* (facial); (*in ice hockey*) protector *m* facial; **f. pack** mascarilla *f* (facial); **f. powder** polvos *mpl* (para la cara)

(**b**) (*expression*) cara *f*; **to make faces** hacer muecas, poner caras; **to keep a straight f.** quedarse serio(a); **to put a brave f. on it** poner al mal tiempo buena cara

(**c**) (*appearance*) **on the f. of it** a primera vista; **to save f.** salvar las apariencias; **to lose f.** sufrir una humillación; **the changing f. of America** el rostro cambiante de América; **to take sth at f. value** aceptar algo sin darle más vueltas

(**d**) (*surface*) (*of the earth*) superficie *f*, faz *f*; (*of clock*) esfera *f*; (*of coin*) cara *f*; (*of cliff*) ladera *f*; **to disappear off the f. of the earth** desaparecer de la faz de la tierra; **f. up/down** boca arriba/abajo

2 *vt* (**a**) (*confront*) (*difficulty, danger*) afrontar, encarar; **to f. facts** afrontar la realidad; **let's f. it** no nos engañemos; **to be faced with a decision** enfrentarse a una decisión; *Fig* **to f. the music** apechugar con las consecuencias (**b**) (*look toward*) mirar a; **to f. the front** mirar al frente

3 *vi* **to f. north/south** (*building, window*) estar orientado(a) hacia el norte/sur

▶**face up to** *vt insep* (*person, fears*) hacer frente a

-faced [feɪst] *suffix* **round/long-f.** de cara redonda/alargada

faceless [ˈfeɪslɪs] *adj* anónimo(a)

face-lift [ˈfeɪslɪft] *n* (*plastic surgery*) lifting *m*, estiramiento *m* de piel; *Fig* (*of building*) lavado *m* de cara; **to have a f.** hacerse un lifting

face-off [ˈfeɪsɒf] *n* (**a**) (*confrontation*) enfrentamiento *m* (a cara de perro) (**b**) (*in ice hockey*) saque *m* neutral

face-saving [ˈfeɪsseɪvɪŋ] *adj* (*agreement, maneuver*) para salvar las apariencias

facet [ˈfæsɪt] *n* (*of gem, situation*) faceta *f*

facetious [fəˈsiːʃəs] *adj* impertinente

face-to-face [ˈfeɪstəˈfeɪs] **1** *adj* (*meeting*) cara a cara

2 *adv* cara a cara, frente a frente; **to meet sb f.** encontrarse frente a frente con alguien

facial [ˈfeɪʃəl] **1** *n* **to have a f.** hacerse una limpieza de cutis **2** *adj* facial

facile [ˈfæsaɪl] *adj* (*argument, remark*) obvio(a), fácil

facilitate [fəˈsɪlɪteɪt] *vt* facilitar

facilitator [fəˈsɪlɪteɪtə(r)] *n* (*person*) promotor(ora) *m,f*

facility [fəˈsɪlɪtɪ] *n* (**a**) (*ease*) facilidad *f*; **to do sth with great f.** hacer algo con gran facilidad (**b**) **facilities** (*buildings, equipment*) instalaciones *fpl*; (*services*) servicios *mpl*

facsimile [fækˈsɪmɪlɪ] *n* (*copy*) facsímil *m*

fact [fækt] *n* hecho *m*; **in f.** de hecho; **to distinguish f. from fiction** distinguir la realidad de la ficción; **the f. is that…** el hecho es que…; **it's a f. that…** se sabe que…; **to know for a f. (that)…** saber a ciencia cierta (que)…; **it's a f. of life** es una realidad insoslayable *or* un hecho cierto; **the facts of life** (*sexual*) lo referente al sexo y a la reproducción

fact-finding [ˈfæktfaɪndɪŋ] *adj* de investigación

faction [ˈfækʃən] *n* (*group*) facción *f*

factor [ˈfæktə(r)] *n* factor *m*

factorize [ˈfæktəraɪz] *vt Math* factorizar, descomponer en factores

factory [ˈfæktərɪ] *n* fábrica *f*, *Am* planta *f*

factual [ˈfæktʊəl] *adj* basado(a) en hechos

faculty [ˈfækəltɪ] *n* (*of mind, section of university*) facultad *f*; (*staff*) cuerpo *m* docente; **she is still in possession of all her faculties** tiene pleno uso de sus facultades

fad [fæd] *n* moda *f* (**for** de)

fade [feɪd] **1** *vt* desteñir

2 *vi* (*material*) desteñirse, perder color; (*flower*) marchitarse; **to f. from memory** desaparecer de la memoria

▶**fade away** *vi* (*music, hope*) desvanecerse; *Fig* (*person*) evaporarse, desaparecer

▶**fade out** *Cin, TV & Rad* **1** *vt sep* fundir en negro

2 *vi* fundirse en negro; (*music*) apagarse

faded [ˈfeɪdɪd] *adj* (*flower*) marchito(a); (*photograph, garment*) descolorido(a)

fading [ˈfeɪdɪŋ] *adj* (*light*) mortecino(a)

fag [fæg] *n very Fam* (*homosexual*) maricón *m*, *Méx* tortillón *m*, *RP* trolo *m*

faggot [ˈfæɡət] *n* (**a**) (*firewood*) haz *m* de leña (**b**) *very Fam* (*homosexual*) maricón *m*, *Méx* tortillón *m*, *RP* trolo *m*

faggy [ˈfæɡɪ] *adj very Fam* de maricón *or Méx* tortillón *or RP* trolo

Fahrenheit [ˈfærənhaɪt] *adj* Fahrenheit; **70 degrees F.** 70 grados Fahrenheit, ≃ 21 grados centígrados

fail [feɪl] **1** *n* (**a**) (*in exam*) *Esp* suspenso *m*, *Am* reprobado *m* (**b**) **without f.** sin falta

2 *vt* (*exam, candidate*) *Esp* suspender, *Am* reprobar; **to f. a drugs test** dar positivo en un control antidoping; **words f. me** me faltan las palabras; **his nerve failed him** le fallaron los nervios; **I won't f. you** no te fallaré

3 *vi* (*person, plan, business*) fracasar; (*in exam*) *Esp* suspender,

Am reprobar; *(health, brakes)* fallar; *(memory, eyesight)* fallar, debilitarse; **the light was failing** se hacía de noche, estaba oscureciendo; **to f. to do sth** no hacer algo; **I f. to see what the problem is** no acabo de ver cuál es el problema; **if all else fails** en último extremo; **he failed in his duty** no cumplió con su obligación; **it never fails** *(strategy, excuse)* nunca falla; **it never fails to surprise me…** nunca deja de sorprenderme…

failed [feɪld] *adj (attempt, plan)* fallido(a); *(writer, actor)* fracasado(a)

failing ['feɪlɪŋ] **1** *n (fault)* defecto *m*, *Esp* fallo *m*, *Am* falla *f*; **with all her failings** con todos sus *Esp* fallos *or Am* fallas
2 *adj (sight, strength)* debilitado(a)
3 *prep* a falta de; **f. that** en su defecto; **f. all else** en último extremo

fail-safe ['feɪlseɪf] *adj (device)* de seguridad *or* de bloqueo (en caso de *Esp* fallo *or Am* falla); *Fig (plan, excuse)* infalible

failure ['feɪljə(r)] *n (useless person)* inútil *mf*; *(unsuccessful person)* fracasado(a) *m,f*; *(unsuccessful movie, lack of success)* fracaso *m*; *(of machine) Esp* fallo *m*, *Am* falla *f*; *(of company)* quiebra *f*; **f. to keep a promise** incumplimiento *m* de una promesa; **f. to pay a bill** impago *m* de una factura

faint [feɪnt] **1** *n (loss of consciousness)* desmayo *m*
2 *adj (light, sound, smell)* leve, tenue; *(idea, hope, memory)* vago(a), ligero(a); *(chance, possibility)* remoto(a); *(mark, trace)* ligero(a); *(suggestion)* leve; **I haven't got the faintest idea** no tengo ni la más mínima idea; **to feel f.** *(person)* sentirse mareado(a)
3 *vi (lose consciousness)* desmayarse

fainthearted ['feɪnt'hɑːtɪd] *adj* pusilánime

faintly ['feɪntlɪ] *adv* **(a)** *(to hear, see)* apenas; *(to shine)* débilmente; *(to remember)* vagamente **(b)** *(slightly) (uneasy, ridiculous)* ligeramente

fair¹ [feə(r)] *n (trade fair)* feria *f*

fair² **1** *adj* **(a)** *(just)* justo(a); **it's not f.** no es justo; **that's only f., f.'s f.** hay que ser justos; **f. enough!** de acuerdo *or Esp* vale, está bien; **it is only f. to say that…** es justo decir que…; **to be f.,…** para ser justos,…; **by f. means or foul** como sea; *Prov* **all's f. in love and war** en la guerra y en el amor, no hay reglas; **to be f. game** ser un blanco legítimo; **f. play** juego *m* limpio; **they all got their f. share** todos recibieron lo que les correspondía; **we've had our f. share of problems** hemos tenido bastantes problemas; **f. trade** comercio *m* justo
(b) *(quite good)* bastante bueno(a); **a f. amount of…** bastante(s)…; **a f. idea** una idea bastante buena; **f. to middling** normal, regular
(c) *Literary (attractive)* hermoso(a); *Old-fashioned* **the f.** *or* **fairer sex** el bello sexo; **f. weather** buen tiempo
(d) *(light-colored) (hair)* rubio(a), *Méx* güero(a); *(skin)* claro(a)
2 *adv (to act)* justamente; **to play/fight f.** jugar/pelear limpio; **you can't say fairer than that** no se puede pedir más; **to beat sb f. and square** derrotar a alguien con todas las de la ley

fairground ['feəgraʊnd] *n* feria *f*

fair-haired ['feə'heəd] *adj* rubio(a), *Méx* güero(a)

fairly ['feəlɪ] *adv* **(a)** *(justly)* justamente; **to treat sb f.** tratar justamente a alguien; **to play/fight f.** jugar/pelear limpio; **to come by sth f.** conseguir algo limpiamente **(b)** *(quite) (rich, skillful)* bastante; **it is f. certain that…** es bastante probable que…; **he f. lost his temper** perdió por completo los estribos

fair-minded ['feə'maɪndɪd] *adj* imparcial, justo(a)

fairness ['feənɪs] *n (of person)* imparcialidad *f*; *(of decision)* justicia *f*; **in all f.** con toda justicia **(b)** *(of hair)* color *m* rubio; *(of skin)* claridad *f*

fair-sized ['feə'saɪzd] *adj (de tamaño)* considerable

fair-skinned ['feə'skɪnd] *adj* de piel blanca

fairway ['feəweɪ] *n* calle *f (de campo de golf)*

fair-weather friend ['feəweðə'frend] *n* amigo(a) *m,f* sólo para lo bueno

fairy ['feərɪ] *n* hada *f*; **f. godmother** hada madrina; **f. story** *or* **tale** *(magic story)* cuento *m* de hadas; *Fam (lie)* cuento *m* chino, patraña *f*

fairy-tale ['feərɪteɪl] *adj* **a f. ending** un final feliz

faith [feɪθ] *n* fe *f*; **an act of f.** un acto de fe; **to be of the Catholic/Jewish f.** profesar la fe católica/judía; **to keep f. with sb** mantenerse fiel a alguien; **in good/bad f.** de buena/mala fe; **f. healer** = persona que pretende curar a la gente gracias a la fe y la oración

faithful ['feɪθfʊl] **1** *adj (friend, supporter)* fiel, leal; *(copy, account)* fiel
2 *npl* **the f.** los fieles

faithfully ['feɪθfʊlɪ] *adv (loyally, accurately)* fielmente; **Yours f.** *(in formal letter)* (le saluda) atentamente

fake [feɪk] **1** *n (object)* falsificación *f*; *(person)* impostor(ora) *m,f*
2 *adj (passport, banknote)* falso(a); *(beard)* postizo(a)
3 *vt (signature, result)* falsificar; *(illness, death)* simular

falcon ['fɔːlkən] *n* halcón *m*

falconry ['fɔːlkənrɪ] *n* cetrería *f*

Falkland ['fɔːlklənd] *n* **the F. Islands, the Falklands** las (Islas) Malvinas

fall [fɔːl] **1** *n* **(a)** *(of person, prices, besieged city)* caída *f*; **to have a f.** sufrir una caída; **a f. in interest rates** una caída de los tipos de interés; **there has been a heavy f. of snow** ha caído una gran nevada; *Fig* **he's heading for a f.** un día de estos se va a pegar un batacazo; *Fam* **f. guy** chivo *m* expiatorio **(b)** *(autumn)* otoño *m* **(c)** **falls** *(waterfall)* cascada *f*, catarata *f*
2 *vi (pt* **fell** [fel]*, pp* **fallen** ['fɔːlən]*)* **(a)** *(stone, person)* caer; *(price, temperature)* caer, descender; *(empire, government)* caer, sucumbir; *(soldier)* caer, morir; **silence/night fell** se hizo el silencio/de noche; **to f. down a hole** caer por un agujero; **she fell off the ladder** se cayó de la escalera; **Christmas Day falls on a Thursday** el día de Navidad cae en jueves; **my spirits fell** me desmoralicé; **to f. from grace** caer en desgracia; **to f. into a trap** caer en una trampa; **to f. to pieces** *(object)* romperse en pedazos; *Fig (person)* desmoronarse; **to f. flat** *(be disappointing)* no funcionar; **to f. short of doing sth** no llegar a hacer algo; **to f. victim to sth** ser víctima de algo; **the game fell victim to the weather** el partido se suspendió debido al mal tiempo; **the responsibility falls on you** la responsabilidad recae sobre usted; *Formal* **it falls to me to introduce…** es un honor para mí presentarles…
(b) *(become)* **to f. asleep** dormirse; **to f. ill** caer enfermo(a), enfermar, *RP,Ven* enfermarse; **to f. in love** enamorarse; **to f. silent** quedarse callado(a)
(c) *(be classified)* **to f. into two categories** dividirse en dos categorías; **suddenly everything fell into place** de pronto todo encajaba

▸**fall away** *vi (ground)* caer, descender; *(attendance)* declinar

▸**fall back on** *vt insep* **he fell back on his emergency supply** recurrió a sus provisiones de emergencia

▸**fall behind** *vi* quedarse rezagado(a)

▸**fall down** *vi (person, building)* caerse; *Fig (argument, plan)* fallar

▸**fall for** *vt insep Fam* **(a)** *(fall in love with)* enamorarse de **(b)** *(be deceived by) (story)* tragarse; **to f. for it** picar

▸**fall in** *vi* **(a)** *(roof)* hundirse **(b)** *Mil (troops)* formar

▸**fall off** *vi (profits, attendance)* decrecer

▸**fall out** *vi* **(a)** *(quarrel)* reñir **(with** con), pelearse **(with** con) **(b)** *Mil* romper filas

▸**fall over** **1** *vi* tropezar, caerse
2 *vt insep (stumble on)* tropezar con; *Fig* **to f. (all) over oneself to do sth** *(be very keen)* desvivirse por hacer algo

▶**fall through** vi (plan, deal) venirse abajo

fallacious [fə'leɪʃəs] adj falaz

fallacy ['fæləsɪ] n falacia f

fallen ['fɔːlən] **1** npl **the f.** los caídos
2 adj caído(a); Old-fashioned **a f. woman** una mujer perdida
3 pp of **fall**

fallible ['fælɪbəl] adj falible

Fallopian tube [fə'ləupɪən'tjuːb] n Anat trompa f de Falopio

fallout ['fɔːlaut] n Phys lluvia f radiactiva; Fig (from scandal) secuelas fpl

fallow ['fæləu] **1** adj (uncultivated) en barbecho; Fig **a f. period** un período improductivo
2 adv **to lie f.** estar en barbecho

false [fɔːls] adj (a) (incorrect) falso(a); **f. alarm** falsa alarma f; **the ceasefire turned out to be a f. dawn** el alto el fuego se convirtió en una esperanza frustrada; **it's a f. economy** es un falso ahorro; **f. friend** (in foreign language) falso amigo m; **f. modesty** falsa modestia f; Mus & Fig **f. note** nota f falsa; **under f. pretenses** bajo falsas apariencias; **f. start** (in race) salida f nula; **to bear f. witness** presentar falso testimonio (b) (unfaithful) infiel (c) (not real) (beard, nose) postizo(a); **f. teeth** dentadura f postiza, Col, RDom caja f de dientes

falsehood ['fɔːlshud] n (lie) falsedad f

falsely ['fɔːlslɪ] adv (mistakenly) equivocadamente; (insincerely) falsamente

falsetto [fɔːl'setəu] (pl **falsettos**) n Mus falsete m

falsification [fɔːlsɪfɪ'keɪʃən] n falsificación f

falsify ['fɔːlsɪfaɪ] vt (a) (forge) (records, document) falsificar (b) (disprove) (theory) refutar

falter ['fɔːltə(r)] vi vacilar, titubear

fame [feɪm] n fama f; **to seek f. and fortune** buscar fama y fortuna

famed [feɪmd] adj famoso(a), afamado(a)

familiar [fə'mɪlɪə(r)] adj (a) (well-known) familiar; **a f. face** un rostro familiar (b) (informal) familiar, Am confianzudo(a); **to be on f. terms with sb** ser íntimo(a) de alguien; **to get too f. with sb** tomarse demasiada confianza con alguien (c) (acquainted) **to be f. with** estar familiarizado(a) con

familiarity [fəmɪlɪ'ærɪtɪ] n (a) (intimacy) familiaridad f, confianza f; **f. breeds contempt** donde hay confianza da asco (b) (acquaintance) familiaridad f

familiarization [fəmɪlɪərаɪ'zeɪʃən] n familiarización f

familiarize [fə'mɪlɪəraɪz] vt **to f. oneself with sth** familiarizarse con algo; **to f. sb with sth** familiarizar a alguien con algo

family ['fæmɪlɪ] n familia f; **it runs in the f.** es cosa de familia; **to start a f.** empezar a tener hijos; **they treat her as one of the f.** la tratan como si fuera de la familia; Fam **she's in the f. way** está en estado; **f. business** negocio m familiar; **f. doctor** médico m de familia; **f. life** vida f de familia; **f. man** hombre m de familia; **f. name** apellido m; **f. planning** planificación f familiar; **f. resemblance** parecido m de familia; **f. tree** árbol m genealógico

famine ['fæmɪn] n hambruna f; **f. relief** ayuda f humanitaria contra el hambre

famished ['fæmɪʃd] adj **to be f.** estar muerto(a) de hambre

famous ['feɪməs] adj famoso(a)

famously ['feɪməslɪ] adv Fam **to get on f. (with sb)** llevarse genial (con alguien)

fan¹ [fæn] **1** n (cooling device) (hand-held) abanico m; (mechanical) ventilador m; **f. belt** (of car) correa f del ventilador; **f. heater** convector m
2 vt (pt & pp **fanned**) (a) (with fan) abanicar; **to f. oneself** abanicarse (b) (fire, passions) atizar, avivar

▶**fan out** vi (police, soldiers) desplegarse

fan² n (enthusiast) (of music, art, sport) fanático m,f; (of artist, singer) admirador(ora) m,f, fan mf; **I'm not a f. of electric stoves** no soy partidario de las cocinas or Col, Méx, Ven estufas eléctricas; **baseball f.** fan mf de béisbol; **f. club** club m de fans; **f. mail** cartas fpl de fans or de admiradores

fanatic [fə'nætɪk] n fanático(a) m,f

fanatical [fə'nætɪkəl] adj fanático(a)

fanatically [fə'nætɪklɪ] adv con fanatismo, de un modo fanático

fanciable ['fænsɪəbəl] adj Fam atractivo(a), Esp resultón(ona)

fanciful ['fænsɪfʊl] adj (unrealistic) inverosímil

fancily ['fænsɪlɪ] adv extravagantemente, estrafalariamente

fancy ['fænsɪ] **1** n (a) (imagination) fantasía f; **a flight of f.** un delirio (b) (whim) capricho m (c) (liking) **to take a f. to sb/sth** encapricharse de alguien/con algo
2 adj (jewels, hat) de fantasía; (gadget) sofisticado(a); (party) encopetado(a); (hotel) lujoso(a); (food, decoration) con muchas florituras; **f. dress** disfraz m; **f. dress party** fiesta f de disfraces
3 vt (a) Fam (like) **I didn't f. the idea** no me atraía la idea (b) (imagine) imaginar; **to f. (that)…** imaginar que…; **I f. I have seen her before** me parece que la he visto antes; Fam **f. that!** ¡fíjate!, ¡lo que hay que ver!; **f. meeting you here!** ¡qué sorpresa encontrarte aquí! (c) (have good opinion of) **she fancies herself as a writer/musician** se las da de buena escritora/música; **he fancies his chances of getting the job** cree que tiene muchas posibilidades de conseguir el trabajo

fancy-free ['fænsɪ'friː] adj sin compromisos or responsabilidades

fanfare ['fænfeə(r)] n fanfarria f

fang [fæŋ] n colmillo m

fanny ['fænɪ] n Fam (buttocks) culo m; **f. pack** riñonera f

fantasize ['fæntəsaɪz] vi fantasear (**about** sobre)

fantastic [fæn'tæstɪk] adj (a) Fam (excellent) fantástico(a), fabuloso(a) (b) (enormous) (price, size) inmenso(a) (c) (unbelievable) absurdo(a)

fantasy ['fæntəsɪ] n fantasía f; **f. football** = juego en que los participantes escogen su equipo de fútbol ideal de entre los futbolistas de un torneo y luego van sumando puntos según la actuación de éstos en la competición real, Esp ≃ liga f fantástica®

FAO [efeɪ'əu] n (abbr **Food and Agriculture Organization**) FAO f, Organización f para la Agricultura y la Alimentación

far [fɑː(r)] **1** adj lejano(a); **the f. end** el (otro) extremo; Pol **the f. left/right** la extrema izquierda/derecha; **the Far East** el Lejano Oriente m; **Far Eastern** del Lejano Oriente
2 adv (comparative **farther** ['fɑːðə(r)] or **further** ['fɜːðə(r)] superlative **farthest** ['fɑːðɪst] or **furthest** ['fɜːðɪst]) (a) (distance) lejos; **how f. is it to Austin?** ¿a cuánto estamos de Austin?; **f. away** lejos; **f. below/above** muy abajo/arriba; **to go f.** ir lejos; Fig (person) llegar lejos; (money) dar para mucho; Fig **to go so f. as to do sth** llegar al extremo de hacer algo; Fig **to go too f.** ir demasiado lejos; also Fig **f. from…** lejos de…; Fig **f. from it** todo lo contrario; Fig **f. be it from me to criticize, but…** Dios me libre de criticar a nadie, pero…; **f. and wide** or **near** por todas partes; Fig **as f. as I can see** tal y como yo lo veo; **as f. as I know** que yo sepa; **as f. as I'm concerned** en or por lo que a mí respecta; Fig **as f. as possible** en la medida de lo posible
(b) (time) **so f.** hasta el momento; **so f. so good** todo bien de momento; **for as f. back as I can remember** hasta donde alcanzo a recordar; **to work f. into the night** trabajar hasta bien entrada la noche
(c) (much) **by f.** con diferencia, con mucho, RP por lejos; **f. better/worse** mucho mejor/peor; **f. too many** demasiados(as); **f. too much** demasiado; **she's f. too intelligent to do that** es demasiado inteligente para hacer eso; **f. and away the best** el mejor con diferencia or RP por lejos

faraway ['fɑːrəweɪ] *adj (place)* lejano(a); *(look)* ausente

farce [fɑːs] *n also Fig* farsa *f*

farcical ['fɑːsɪkəl] *adj* grotesco(a)

fare [feə(r)] **1** *n* (**a**) *(for journey)* tarifa *f* (**b**) *(taxi passenger)* pasajero(a) *m,f* (**c**) *Formal (food)* comida *f*
 2 *vi* comportarse; **to f. well/badly** *(person, team)* hacerlo bien/mal; *(industry, sector)* comportarse bien/mal; **how did she f.?** ¿cómo le salió?

farewell [feə'wel] *n* despedida *f*, adiós *m*; **to bid sb f.** despedirse de alguien; **to say one's farewells** despedirse; **f. dinner** cena *f* de despedida

far-fetched ['fɑː'fetʃt] *adj (idea, plan)* inverosímil, rebuscado(a)

far-flung ['fɑː'flʌŋ] *adj* (**a**) *(distant)* remoto(a) (**b**) *(widespread)* amplio(a), vasto(a)

farm [fɑːm] **1** *n (small)* granja *f*; *(large)* hacienda *f*, explotación *f* agrícola, *CSur* estancia *f*; **dairy f.** vaquería *f*; **f. animals** animales *mpl* de granja; **f. laborer** trabajador *m* del campo
 2 *vt (land)* cultivar; *(livestock)* criar
 3 *vi (grow crops)* cultivar la tierra

▶**farm out** *vt sep (work)* subcontratar

farmer ['fɑːmə(r)] *n (of small farm)* granjero(a) *m,f*; *(of large farm)* agricultor(ora) *m,f*; **cattle f.** ganadero(a) *m,f (de vacuno)*

farmhouse ['fɑːmhaʊs] *n* granja *f*, casa *f* de campo

farming ['fɑːmɪŋ] *n* agricultura *f*

farmland ['fɑːmlænd] *n* terreno *m* agrícola

farmyard ['fɑːmjɑːd] *n* corral *m*

Faroe ['feɪrəʊ] *n* **the F. Islands, the Faroes** las islas Feroe

far-off ['fɑːrɒf] *adj (place, time)* lejano(a)

far-out [fɑː'raʊt] *adj Fam (strange)* raro(a), **f.!** ¡súper!, *Esp* ¡chachi!

far-reaching ['fɑː'riːtʃɪŋ] *adj (decision, change)* de gran alcance

Farsi ['fɑːsiː] *n (language)* persa *m (moderno)*

farsighted ['fɑː'saɪtɪd] *adj* (**a**) *(shrewd) (person, decision)* previsor(ora), con visión de futuro (**b**) *(long-sighted)* hipermétrope *f*

farsightedness ['fɑː'saɪtɪdnɪs] *n* (**a**) *(of person, decision)* visión *f* de futuro (**b**) *(long-sightedness)* hipermetropía *f*

fart [fɑːt] *very Fam* **1** *n* pedo *m*
 2 *vi* tirarse un pedo, pederse

▶**fart about** *vi very Fam (waste time)* perder el tiempo a lo tonto

farther = **further**

farthest = **furthest**

fascinate ['fæsɪneɪt] *vt* fascinar

fascinating ['fæsɪneɪtɪŋ] *adj* fascinante

fascinatingly ['fæsɪneɪtɪŋlɪ] *adv* fascinantemente, de manera fascinante

fascination [fæsɪ'neɪʃən] *n* fascinación *f*

fascism ['fæʃɪzəm] *n* fascismo *m*

fascist ['fæʃɪst] *n & adj* fascista *mf*

fashion ['fæʃən] **1** *n* (**a**) *(in clothes)* moda *f*; **in f.** de moda; **out of f.** pasado(a) de moda; **to follow f.** seguir la moda; **f. designer** modisto(a) *m,f*; **f. house** casa *f* de moda(s); **f. parade** desfile *m* de moda, desfile *m or* pase *m* de modelos; **f. victim** adicto(a) *m,f* a la moda (**b**) *(manner)* modo *m*, manera *f*; **after a f.** más o menos
 2 *vt (form)* elaborar (**from** con); **he fashioned a small figure from a block of wood** modeló un figurín a partir de un bloque de madera

fashionable ['fæʃənəbəl] *adj* de moda; **to be f.** estar de moda

fashionably ['fæʃnəblɪ] *adv* a la moda

fast[1] [fɑːst] **1** *adj* (**a**) *(rapid)* rápido(a); *Fam* **he pulled a f. one on me** me jugó una mala pasada, *Esp* me la pegó; *Fam Fig* **a f. woman** una mujer fácil *or Esp* casquivana; **f. food** comida *f* rápida; **the f. lane** *(of motorway)* el carril rápido; *Fig* **to live life in the f. lane** llevar un tren de vida frenético (**b**) *(clock, watch)* adelantado(a) (**c**) *(secure) (grip)* firme; *(color)* inalterable, que no destiñe
 2 *adv* (**a**) *(rapidly)* rápido, deprisa; **not so f.!** ¡no tan rápido!; **to play f. and loose with the truth** jugar con la verdad (**b**) *(securely)* firmemente; **to hold f.** sujetarse bien; **f. asleep** profundamente dormido(a)

fast[2] **1** *n* ayuno *m*; **to break one's f.** romper el ayuno; *Rel* **f. day** día *m* de ayuno
 2 *vi* ayunar

fasten ['fɑːsən] **1** *vt (attach)* sujetar; *(door, window)* cerrar, echar el cerrojo a; *Fig (eyes, attention)* fijar; **to f. one's belt/buttons** abrocharse el cinturón/los botones
 2 *vi (garment)* abrocharse

fastener ['fɑːsənə(r)] *n (of garment)* cierre *m*

fast-forward ['fɑːst'fɔːwəd] **1** *n* avance *m* rápido
 2 *vt (cassette)* pasar hacia delante

fastidious [fæ'stɪdɪəs] *adj (fussy)* quisquilloso(a); *(meticulous)* meticuloso(a)

fast-moving ['fɑːst'muːvɪŋ] *adj* veloz, rápido(a)

fast-track ['fɑːsttræk] **1** *n* vía *f* rápida
 2 *vt* hacer por la vía rápida

fat [fæt] **1** *n* (**a**) grasa *f*; **f. content** materia *f* grasa; **f. farm** clínica *f* de adelgazamiento (**b**) *(idioms) Fam* **the fat's in the fire!** ¡la que se va a armar!; **to live off the f. of the land** vivir a cuerpo de rey; *Fam* **to chew the f. (with sb)** estar de charla *or Esp* palique (con alguien)
 2 *adj (person)* gordo(a); *(meat)* graso(a); *Fam (check, salary)* jugoso(a); **to get f.** engordar; *Fig* **to grow f. at the expense of others** *(become rich)* hacerse rico(a) a costa de los demás; *Fam* **a f. lot of good that'll do you!** ¡pues sí que te va a servir de mucho!; *Fam* **f. cat** pez *m* gordo; *Pej* **f. cat executive** = alto ejecutivo con un salario desproporcionado; *Fam* **f. chance!** ¡ni soñarlo!, *Méx* ¡ya mero!

fatal ['feɪtəl] *adj* fatal

fatalist ['feɪtəlɪst] *n* fatalista *mf*

fatalistic [feɪtə'lɪstɪk] *adj* fatalista

fatality [fə'tælɪtɪ] *n (in accident)* víctima *f* mortal

fatally ['feɪtəlɪ] *adv (wounded)* mortalmente

fate [feɪt] *n* destino *m*, sino *m*; **to leave sb to his f.** abandonar a alguien a su suerte; **to suffer/share a similar f.** sufrir/compartir la misma suerte; **a f. worse than death** un sino peor que la muerte

fated ['feɪtɪd] *adj (destined)* predestinado(a)

fateful ['feɪtfʊl] *adj (words, day)* fatídico(a)

father ['fɑːðə(r)] **1** *n (parent, priest)* padre *m*; **f. of six** padre de seis hijos; **from f. to son** de padre a hijo; **he was like a f. to me** fue como un padre para mí; *Prov* **like f., like son** de tal palo, tal astilla; **Our F.** Padre Nuestro; **f. figure** figura *f* paterna
 2 *vt (child)* engendrar; *Fig (idea, invention)* concebir, crear

fatherhood ['fɑːðəhʊd] *n* paternidad *f*

father-in-law ['fɑːðərɪnlɔː] *(pl* **fathers-in-law)** *n* suegro *m*

fatherly ['fɑːðəlɪ] *adj* paternal

father-to-be ['fɑːðətə'biː] *(pl* **fathers-to-be)** *n* futuro padre *m*

fathom ['fæðəm] **1** *n (measurement)* braza *f*
 2 *vt (mystery)* desentrañar; *(person)* entender

▶**fathom out** *vt sep (mystery)* desentrañar; *(person)* entender

fatigue [fə'tiːg] **1** *n* (**a**) *(tiredness)* fatiga *f*, cansancio *m*; **metal f.** fatiga *f* del metal (**b**) *Mil* **f. (duty)** faena *f*; **fatigues** *(military clothing)* traje *m* de faena
 2 *vt (person)* fatigar, cansar

fatso ['fætsəʊ] *(pl* **fatsos)** *n Fam* gordinflón(ona) *m,f*

fatten ['fætən] *vt* engordar, cebar

▶**fatten up** *vt sep* engordar, cebar

fatty ['fætɪ] **1** *n Fam* gordito(a) *m,f*

2 *adj* graso(a); **f. foods** alimentos *mpl* grasos; **f. acid** ácido *m* graso; **f. tissue** tejido *m* adiposo

fatuous ['fætjʊəs] *adj* fatuo(a), necio(a)

fatwa ['fætwɑ:] *n* fatwa *f*

faucet ['fɔ:sɪt] *n Esp* grifo *m*, *Chile, Col, Méx* llave *f*, *RP* canilla *f*

fault [fɔ:lt] **1** *n* (**a**) *(flaw) (of person, product)* defecto *m*; *(of engine)* avería *f*, *Esp* fallo *m*, *Am* falla *f*; **to find f. with** encontrar defectos a; **she's generous to a f.** se pasa de generosa (**b**) *(guilt)* culpa *f*; **to be at f.** tener la culpa; **whose f. is it?** ¿de quién es la culpa?; **it was my f.** fue culpa mía; **through no f. of mine** sin tener yo la culpa (**c**) *(in tennis)* falta *f* (**d**) *(geological)* falla *f*

2 *vt* criticar, poner reparos a; **her attitude can't be faulted** no se puede criticar su actitud

faultless ['fɔ:ltlɪs] *adj* impecable, intachable

faulty ['fɔ:ltɪ] *adj* defectuoso(a)

faun [fɔ:n] *n (mythological creature)* fauno *m*

fauna ['fɔ:nə] *n (animal life)* fauna *f*

favor ['feɪvə(r)] **1** *n* favor *m*; **to be in/out of f. (with)** *(people)* ser visto(a) con buenos/malos ojos (por); *(product, method)* gozar/no gozar de mucha aceptación (entre); **to look on sth/sb with f.** ser partidario(a) de algo/alguien; **to find f. with sb** encontrar aceptación por parte de alguien; **to ask sb a f., to ask a f. of sb** pedir un favor a alguien; **to do sb a f.** hacer un favor a alguien; **in f. of…** *(in preference to)* en favor de…; **to be in f. of sth** estar a favor de algo; **to vote in f. (of)** votar a favor (de); **that's a point in her f.** eso es un punto a su favor; *Fin* **balance in your f.** saldo a su favor

2 *vt* (**a**) *(approve of)* estar a favor de, ser partidario(a) de (**b**) *(bestow favor on)* favorecer

favorable ['feɪvərəbəl] *adj* favorable; **in a f. light** desde una óptica favorable

favorite ['feɪvərɪt] *n & adj* favorito(a) *m,f*

favoritism ['feɪvərɪtɪzəm] *n* favoritismo *m*

fawn[1] [fɔ:n] **1** *n* (**a**) *(deer)* cervatillo *m* (**b**) *(color)* beige *m*, *Esp* beis *m*

2 *adj (color)* beige, *Esp* beis

fawn[2] *vi* adular (**on** a)

fax [fæks] **1** *n (machine)* fax *m*, telefax *m*; *(message)* fax *m*; *Comptr* **f. modem** módem *m* fax; **f. number** número *m* de fax

2 *vt* mandar por fax; **to f. sb** mandar un fax a alguien

faze [feɪz] *vt Fam* desconcertar

FBI [efbiː'aɪ] *n (abbr* **Federal Bureau of Investigation**) FBI *m*

fear [fɪə(r)] **1** *n* miedo *m*, temor *m*; **to be** *or* **go in f. of** tener miedo de; **she was in f. of her life** temía por su vida; *Fam* **to put the f. of God into sb** meter a alguien el miedo en el cuerpo; **for f. of** por miedo a; *Fam* **no f.!** ¡ni pensarlo!, *Méx* ¡ya mero!

2 *vt* temer; **to f. that…** temer(se) que…; **I f. so** eso me temo; **I f. not** me temo que no; **to f. the worst** temerse lo peor

3 *vi* temer (**for** por)

fearful ['fɪəfʊl] *adj* (**a**) *(person)* temeroso(a); **to be f. of…** tener miedo de… (**b**) *(pain, consequence)* terrible, espantoso(a) (**c**) *Fam (noise, expense)* tremendo(a)

fearfully ['fɪəfʊlɪ] *adv* (**a**) *(in fear)* temerosamente, atemorizadamente (**b**) *Fam (extremely)* tremendamente

fearless ['fɪəlɪs] *adj* valiente, arrojado(a)

fearlessness ['fɪəlɪsnɪs] *n* valentía *f*, arrojo *m*

fearsome ['fɪəsəm] *adj* terrible, espantoso(a)

feasibility [fi:zə'bɪlɪtɪ] *n* viabilidad *f*; **f. study** estudio *m* de viabilidad

feasible ['fi:zəbəl] *adj* factible, viable

feast [fi:st] **1** *n* banquete *m*, festín *m*; *Rel* **f. day** fiesta *f* de guardar

2 *vt* **to f. one's eyes on sth** recrear la vista en algo

3 *vi* darse un banquete (**on** *or* **upon** de)

feat [fi:t] *n* hazaña *f*

feather ['feðə(r)] **1** *n* pluma *f*; **you could have knocked me down with a f.** me quedé de piedra; *Fig* **that's a f. in her cap** es un triunfo personal para ella; *Fig* **to make the feathers fly** armar un buen revuelo; **f. bed** colchón *m* de plumas

2 *vt Fig* **to f. one's nest** hacer el agosto

feathered ['feðəd] *adj* con plumas; *Hum* **f. friend** pájaro *m*

featherweight ['feðəweɪt] *n (in boxing)* peso *m* pluma

feathery ['feðərɪ] *adj (sponge, pastry)* ligero(a), liviano(a)

feature ['fi:tʃə(r)] **1** *n* (**a**) *(of face)* rasgo *m*, facción *f*; **features** *(face)* facciones *fpl* (**b**) *(of system, machine)* característica *f* (**c**) **f. (film)** largometraje *m* (**d**) *(in newspaper, on television, radio)* reportaje *m*; **f. writer** articulista *mf*

2 *vt* **a movie featuring…** una película en la que figura…

3 *vi (appear)* figurar, aparecer

feature-length ['fi:tʃəleŋθ] *adj* de larga duración, de largo metraje

featureless ['fi:tʃəlɪs] *adj* uniforme, monótono(a)

Feb *(abbr* **February**) febrero *m*

febrile ['fi:braɪl] *adj Formal (atmosphere, state)* febril

February ['febrʊərɪ] *n* febrero *m*; *see also* **May**

feces ['fi:si:z] *npl* heces *fpl*

feckless ['feklɪs] *adj* abúlico(a), apático(a)

fecklessness ['feklɪsnɪs] *n* abulia *f*, apatía *f*

fed [fed] *pt & pp of* **feed**

federal ['fedərəl] *adj* federal; *Fin* **F. Reserve (System)** Reserva *f* Federal; *Fin* **F. Reserve Board** junta *f* de gobierno de la Reserva Federal

federalism ['fedərəlɪzəm] *n* federalismo *m*

federalist ['fedərəlɪst] *n & adj* federalista *mf*

federally ['fedərəlɪ] *adv* **to be f. funded** estar sufragado(a) con fondos federales

federation [fedə'reɪʃən] *n* federación *f*

fedora [fɪ'dɔ:rə] *n* = sombrero flexible de fieltro

fed up [fed'ʌp] *adj Fam* **to be f. (with)** estar harto(a) (de)

fee [fi:] *n (of lawyer, doctor)* minuta *f*, honorarios *mpl*; *(for entrance)* (precio *m* de) entrada *f*, *Méx* (precio *m* del) boleto *m*; *(for membership)* cuota *f*

feeble ['fi:bəl] *adj (person, light)* débil; *(argument, excuse)* flojo(a), pobre

feebleminded ['fi:bəl'maɪndɪd] *adj* lelo(a)

feebly ['fi:blɪ] *adv* débilmente

feed [fi:d] **1** *n* (**a**) *(animal food)* pienso *m* (**b**) *(for baby) (from breast, bottle)* toma *f*

2 *vt (pt & pp* **fed** [fed]) (**a**) *(give food to)* alimentar, dar de comer a; *(baby) (from breast)* amamantar, dar de mamar a; *(from bottle)* dar el biberón a; *(plant)* echar fertilizante a; **we were well fed** nos dieron muy bien de comer; **to f. one's family** dar de comer a la familia (**b**) *(supply)* **to f. a fire** alimentar un fuego; **to f. coins into a machine** introducir monedas en una máquina; **to f. sb with information** proporcionar información a alguien

3 *vi* alimentarse (**on** de)

feedback ['fi:dbæk] *n Elec* realimentación *f*; *(on microphone)* acoplamiento *m*, feedback *m*; *(response)* reacción *f*

feel [fi:l] **1** *n* (**a**) *(sense of touch)* tacto *m* (**b**) *(sensation)* sensación *f*; **the f. of silk against her skin** el roce de la seda contra su piel; **the movie has an authentic f. to it** la película da sensación de autenticidad (**c**) *(knack)* **she has a real f. for languages** tiene un don especial para los idiomas; **he soon got the f. for it** *Esp* enseguida cogió el truco *or* tranquillo, *Am* enseguida agarró la onda *or RP* le encontró la vuelta

2 *vt (pt & pp* **felt** [felt]) (**a**) *(touch with hand)* tocar, palpar; **to f. one's way** *(in darkness)* andar a tientas; *Fig (in new situation)* familiarizarse (**b**) *(be physically conscious of)* notar; **I felt the**

floor tremble *or* **trembling** noté que el suelo temblaba (**c**) *(experience) (pain, despair)* sentir; **to f. the cold** ser *Esp* friolero(a) *or Am* friolento(a); **I f. it in my bones** *(have intuition)* lo presiento, me da en la nariz (**d**) *(believe)* creer, pensar; **I f. (that)…** me parece que…

3 *vi* (**a**) *(physically) (person)* **to f. ill/tired** sentirse enfermo(a)/cansado(a); **to f. hot/cold** tener calor/frío; **to f. hungry/thirsty** tener hambre/sed; **my foot feels better** tengo mejor el pie; **how do you f.?** ¿cómo te encuentras?; **not to f. like oneself** no sentirse muy bien; **to f. up to doing sth** *(well enough)* sentirse con fuerzas para hacer algo; *(competent enough)* sentirse capaz de hacer algo

(**b**) *(mentally)* **to f. strongly about sth** tener convicciones muy arraigadas sobre algo; **to f. sure (that)…** estar seguro(a) (de que)…; **to f. bad about sth** sentirse mal por algo; **how would you f. if…?** ¿cómo te sentirías si…?; **I f. as if…** me da la sensación de que…; **to f. (like) a new man/woman** sentirse otro/otra; **I felt (like) an idiot** me sentí como un/una idiota; **to f. like doing sth** tener ganas de hacer algo; **I f. like a cup of coffee** *Esp* me apetece *or Carib, Col, Méx* me provoca *or Méx* se me antoja *or CSur* me tomaría un café

(**c**) *(feel sympathy for)* **to f. for sb** sentirlo por alguien; **I really felt for his wife** me daba mucha pena su mujer

(**d**) *(things)* **to f. hard/soft** ser duro(a)/blando(a) al tacto; **it feels soft now** ahora está blando; **to f. hot/cold** estar caliente/frío(a); **it feels like (it's going to) rain** parece que va a llover; **it feels strange/good** es extraño/agradable

(**e**) *(touch with hands)* **to f. in one's pockets** mirarse *or RP* fijarse en los bolsillos *or CAm, Méx, Perú* las bolsas; **he felt on the ground for the key** buscó la llave a tientas por el suelo

feeler ['fiːlə(r)] *n (of insect)* antena *f; (of snail)* cuerno *m; Fig* **to put out feelers** tantear el terreno

feeling ['fiːlɪŋ] *n* (**a**) *(sense of)* **f.** sensibilidad *f;* **to have no f. in one's arm** tener un brazo insensible

(**b**) *(sensation) (of cold, pain)* sensación *f*

(**c**) *(emotion)* sentimiento *m;* **a f. of joy/anger** un sentimiento de alegría/ira; **to speak with f.** hablar apasionadamente; **I know the f.!** ¡sé cómo te sientes!; **I had a f. I might find you here** me daba la sensación *or* tenía la impresión de que te encontraría aquí; **his feelings toward me** sus sentimientos hacia mí; **to hurt sb's feelings** herir los sentimientos de alguien; **to have no feelings** no tener sentimientos; **feelings were running high (about)** estaban los ánimos revueltos (en cuanto a); *Fam* **no hard feelings!** ¡estamos en paz!

(**d**) *(opinion)* opinión *f;* **there is a general f. that…** la impresión general es que…; **my f. is that…** pienso *or* creo que…

(**e**) *(sensitivity)* sensibilidad *f;* **to have a f. for sth** tener sensibilidad para algo

feet [fiːt] *pl of* **foot**

feign [feɪn] *vt (anger, surprise)* simular

feint [feɪnt] **1** *n* amago *m*, finta *f*
2 *vi* **to f. to the left/right** hacer una finta *or* amagar a la izquierda/derecha

feisty ['faɪstɪ] *adj Fam (spirited)* combativo(a), animoso(a)

felicitous [fɪ'lɪsɪtəs] *adj (choice, expression)* feliz, acertado(a)

feline ['fiːlaɪn] **1** *n* felino *m*, félido *m*
2 *adj* felino(a)

fell¹ [fel] *vt (tree)* talar; *(opponent)* derribar

fell² *adj* **at one f. swoop** de un golpe

fell³ *pt of* **fall**

fella ['felə], **feller** ['felə(r)] *n Fam* (**a**) *(man)* tipo *m, Esp* tío *m, RP* flaco *m* (**b**) *(boyfriend)* novio *m, Esp* chorbo *m*

fellow ['feləʊ] *n* (**a**) *(comrade)* compañero(a) *m,f*, camarada *mf;* **f. citizen** conciudadano(a) *m,f;* **f. countryman/country-woman** compatriota *mf;* **f. feeling** (sentimiento *m* de)

solidaridad *f;* **f. passenger/student/worker** compañero(a) *m,f* de viaje/de estudios/de trabajo; *Fig* **f. traveler** *(in politics)* simpatizante *mf* (**b**) *(at college)* profesor(ora) *m,f; (of academy, society)* miembro *m* (**c**) *Fam (man)* tipo *m, Esp* tío *m, RP* flaco *m*

fellowship ['feləʊʃɪp] *n* (**a**) *(friendship)* compañerismo *m*, camaradería *f* (**b**) *(association)* sociedad *f*, asociación *f;* **f. hall** = sala para actividades parroquiales (**c**) *(at college)* beca *f* de investigación

felon ['felən] *n Law* criminal *mf*

felony ['felənɪ] *n Law* crimen *m*, delito *m* grave

felt¹ [felt] *n (fabric)* fieltro *m*

felt² *pt & pp of* **feel**

felt-tip ['felt'tɪp] *n* **f. (pen)** rotulador *m, Méx* plumón *m, RP* marcador *m*

female ['fiːmeɪl] **1** *n (person)* mujer *f; (animal, plant)* hembra *f*
2 *adj (person)* femenino(a); *(animal, plant)* hembra

feminine ['femɪnɪn] **1** *n Gram* femenino *m*
2 *adj* femenino(a)

femininity [femɪ'nɪnɪtɪ] *n* femin(e)idad *f*

feminism ['femɪnɪzəm] *n* feminismo *m*

feminist ['femɪnɪst] *n & adj* feminista *mf*

femur ['fiːmə(r)] *n Anat* fémur *m*

fen [fen] *n (marshy land)* pantano *m*, ciénaga *f;* **the Fens** = tierras bajas del este de Inglaterra, especialmente Norfolk y Cambridgeshire

fence [fens] **1** *n* (**a**) *(barrier)* valla *f*, cerca *f; Fig* **to sit on the f.** no pronunciarse, nadar entre dos aguas; *Fig* **to get off the f.** pronunciarse (**b**) *Fam (receiver of stolen property)* perista *mf*
2 *vi (as sport)* hacer esgrima

▶**fence off** *vt sep* vallar, cercar

fencing ['fensɪŋ] *n (sport)* esgrima *f*

fend [fend] *vi* **to f. for oneself** valerse por sí mismo

▶**fend off** *vt sep (attack)* rechazar; *(blow)* atajar, parar; *(question)* eludir

fender ['fendə(r)] *n* (**a**) *(of car) Esp, RP* guardabarros *mpl, Andes, CAm, Carib* guardafango *m, Méx* salpicadera *f* (**b**) *(for fireplace)* pantalla *f* (de chimenea), parachispas *m inv*

feng shui [fəŋ'ʃweɪ] *n* feng shui *m*

fennel ['fenəl] *n* hinojo *m*

fenugreek ['fenjʊgriːk] *n* alholva *f*, fenogreco *m*

ferment 1 *n* ['fɜːment] *(commotion)* agitación *f;* **in a (state of) f.** agitado(a)
2 *vi* [fə'ment] *(alcoholic drink)* fermentar

fermentation [fɜːmen'teɪʃən] *n* fermentación *f*

fern [fɜːn] *n* helecho *m*

ferocious [fə'rəʊʃəs] *adj* feroz

ferocity [fə'rɒsɪtɪ], **ferociousness** [fə'rəʊʃəsnɪs] *n* ferocidad *f*

ferret ['ferɪt] **1** *n* hurón *m*
2 *vi Fam* **to f. (about) for sth** rebuscar algo

▶**ferret out** *vt sep (object, information)* encontrar, dar con

Ferris wheel ['ferɪs'wiːl] *n* noria *f*

ferrous ['ferəs] *adj* ferroso(a)

ferry ['ferɪ] **1** *n* transbordador *m*, ferry *m*
2 *vt* **to f. sth/sb across a river** pasar algo/a alguien al otro lado de un río; **the injured were ferried to hospital in taxis** los heridos fueron transportados al hospital en taxis

ferryman ['ferɪmən] *n* barquero *m*

fertile ['fɜːtaɪl] *adj also Fig* fértil

fertility [fɜː'tɪlɪtɪ] *n* fertilidad *f;* **f. symbol** símbolo *m* de fertilidad; *Med* **f. treatment** tratamiento *m* de fertilidad

fertilize ['fɜːtɪlaɪz] *vt (animal, plant, egg)* fecundar; *(land)* fertilizar

fertilizer ['fɜːtɪlaɪzə(r)] *n* fertilizante *m*

fervent ['fɜːvənt] *adj* ferviente

fervently ['fɜːvəntlɪ] *adv* fervientemente

fervor ['fɜːvə(r)] *n* fervor *m*

▶**fess up** [fes] *vi Fam (confess)* cantar

fester ['festə(r)] *vi also Fig* enconarse

festival ['festɪvəl] *n* (**a**) *(of arts, music, drama)* festival *m* (**b**) *(public holiday)* festividad *f*

festive ['festɪv] *adj* festivo(a); **in f. mood** con ganas de fiesta; **the f. season** *(Christmas)* la época navideña

festivity [fes'tɪvɪtɪ] *n* regocijo *m*; **the festivities** la celebración, las fiestas

festoon [fes'tuːn] *vt* festonear (**with** con), engalanar (**with** con)

feta ['fetə] *n* **f. (cheese)** queso *m* feta

fetal ['fiːtəl] *adj* fetal; **f. position** posición *f* fetal

fetch [fetʃ] **1** *vt* (**a**) *(bring) (object, liquid)* traer, *Esp* ir a por; *(person)* ir a recoger a; **f.!** *(to dog)* ¡busca! (**b**) *(be sold for)* alcanzar; **it should f. at least $50,000** debería venderse al menos por 50.000 dólares

2 *vi* **to f. and carry for sb** ser el criado de alguien

▶**fetch up** *vi (end up)* ir a parar

fetching ['fetʃɪŋ] *adj* atractivo(a)

fete, fête [feɪt] **1** *n* = fiesta benéfica al aire libre con mercadillo, concursos, actuaciones, etc.

2 *vt* festejar, agasajar

fetid ['fetɪd] *adj* fétido(a)

fetish ['fetɪʃ] *n* fetiche *m*

fetishism ['fetɪʃɪzəm] *n* fetichismo *m*

fetter ['fetə(r)] **1** *vt* poner grilletes a; *Fig* encadenar, atar

2 fetters *npl (on slave, prisoner)* grilletes *mpl*; *Fig (on rights, freedom)* cadenas *fpl*, ataduras *fpl*

fettle ['fetəl] *n* **in good** *or* **fine f.** en plena forma

fetus ['fiːtəs] *n* feto *m*

feud [fjuːd] **1** *n* disputa *f*

2 *vi* estar enemistado(a) (**with** con)

feudal ['fjuːdəl] *adj* feudal

feudalism ['fjuːdəlɪzəm] *n* feudalismo *m*

feuding ['fjuːdɪŋ] *n* altercados *mpl*, reyertas *fpl*

fever ['fiːvə(r)] *n also Fig* fiebre *f*; **to have a f.** tener fiebre; **excitement had risen to f. pitch** los ánimos estaban muy exaltados

feverish ['fiːvərɪʃ] *adj (patient)* con fiebre, febril; *Fig (excitement, atmosphere)* febril

few [fjuː] **1** *n* **the f. who came** los pocos que vinieron

2 *adj* (**a**) *(not many)* pocos(as); **his visits are f. and far between** sólo viene muy de vez en cuando; **every f. minutes/days** cada pocos minutos/días; **he gave too f. examples** dio muy pocos ejemplos; **as f. as a dozen finished the race** tan sólo una docena terminó la carrera; **f. people knew who she was** pocos sabían quién era (**b**) *(some)* **a f.** unos(as) pocos(as), algunos(as); **a good f.** unos cuantos; **quite a f.** bastantes; **in the next f. days** en los próximos días

3 *pron* (**a**) *(not many)* pocos(as); **there are very/too f. of us** somos muy/demasiado pocos; **f. (of them) could speak French** pocos (de ellos) hablaban francés; **f., if any** pocos(as) o ninguno(a), apenas alguno(a) (**b**) *(some)* **a f.** algunos(as); **a f. of the survivors** algunos supervivientes; **a f. of us** algunos de nosotros

fewer ['fjuːə(r)] *(comparative of* **few***)* **1** *adj* menos; **no f. than thirty** no menos de treinta; **f. and f. people** cada vez menos gente

2 *pron* menos *mpl, fpl*; **there are f. (of them) than I thought** hay menos de lo que creía

fewest ['fjuːɪst] *(superlative of* **few***)* **1** *adj* **that hospital reported the f. cases** ese hospital es el que menos casos registró; **take the road which has the f. curves** ve por la carretera que tenga menos curvas

2 *pron* **we received the f.** nosotros somos los que menos recibimos

fez [fez] *(pl* **fezzes***) n* fez *m*

fiancé [fɪ'ɒnseɪ] *n* prometido *m*, novio *m*

fiancée [fɪ'ɒnseɪ] *n* prometida *f*, novia *f*

fiasco [fɪ'æskəʊ] *(pl* **fiascos** *or* **fiascoes***) n* fiasco *m*

fib [fɪb] *Fam* **1** *n* cuento *m*, *Esp* trola *f*; **to tell a f.** contar un cuento, *Esp* meter una trola

2 *vi (pt & pp* **fibbed***)* contar un cuento, *Esp* meter una trola

fibber ['fɪbə(r)] *n Fam* cuentista *mf*, *Am* cuentero(a) *m,f*

fiber ['faɪbə(r)] *n* fibra *f*; **f. optics** transmisión *f* por fibra óptica

fiberglass ['faɪbəglɑːs] *n* fibra *f* de vidrio

fiber-optic [faɪbə'rɒptɪk] *adj* de fibra óptica

fibrous ['faɪbrəs] *adj* fibroso(a)

fickle ['fɪkəl] *adj* inconstante, voluble

fiction ['fɪkʃən] *n (sth invented)* ficción *f*; *(short stories, novels)* (literatura *f* de) ficción *f*; **a work of f.** una obra de ficción

fictional ['fɪkʃənəl] *adj (character)* de ficción; *(scene, account)* novelado(a)

fictitious [fɪk'tɪʃəs] *adj* ficticio(a)

fiddle ['fɪdəl] **1** *n (violin)* violín *m (en música folk)*

2 *vt Fam (cheat)* amañar; **to f. the accounts** amañar la contabilidad, *Méx* hacer una transa con la contabilidad

3 *vi* (**a**) *(play violin)* tocar el violín *(en música folk)* (**b**) *(fidget)* **to f. (about** *or* **around) with sth** juguetear *or* enredar con algo

fiddler ['fɪdlə(r)] *n* violinista *mf (en música folk)*

fiddlesticks ['fɪdəlstɪks] *exclam Old-fashioned* ¡paparruchas!

fidelity [fɪ'delɪtɪ] *n* fidelidad *f*

fidget ['fɪdʒɪt] **1** *n (person)* enredador(ora) *m,f*, trasto *m*

2 *vi* enredar, trastear

fidgety ['fɪdʒɪtɪ] *adj* inquieto(a)

field [fiːld] **1** *n* (**a**) *(of crops) & Comptr* campo *m*; *(for sport)* campo *m*, *Am* cancha *f*; *(of oil, coal)* yacimiento *m*; **she's an expert in her f.** es una experta en su campo; **to work in the f.** *(not in office)* hacer trabajo de campo, trabajar in situ; **f. of vision** campo visual; **f. events** *(in athletics)* pruebas *fpl* de salto y lanzamiento; **f. goal** *(in football, ice hockey)* gol *m* de campo; *(in basketball)* tiro *m* de campo; **f. hockey** hockey *m* sobre hierba *or Am* césped; **f. mouse** ratón *m* de campo; **f. study** *(scientific)* estudio *m* de campo; *Sch & Univ* **f. trip** viaje *m or* salida *f* para *(realizar)* trabajo de campo

(**b**) *Mil* **in the f.** en el campo de batalla; *Fig* **the press had a f. day** la prensa se puso las botas; **f. glasses** prismáticos *mpl*, gemelos *mpl*; **f. gun** cañón *m* de campaña; **f. hospital** hospital *m* de campaña; **f. marshal** mariscal *m* de campo

(**c**) *(in race, contest)* los participantes; *also Fig* **to lead the f.** ir en cabeza

2 *vt* (**a**) *(team)* poner a jugar; *(candidates)* presentar (**b**) **to f. a question** contestar con destreza a una pregunta

fieldwork ['fiːldwɜːk] *n (scientific)* trabajo *m* de campo

fiend [fiːnd] *n (demon)* demonio *m*; **my boss is a f. for punctuality** mi jefe está obsesionado con la puntualidad

fiendish ['fiːndɪʃ] *adj (evil, difficult)* endiablado(a), endemoniado(a)

fiendishly ['fiːndɪʃlɪ] *adv (difficult, clever)* endiabladamente, endemoniadamente

fierce [fɪəs] *adj (animal, look)* fiero(a); *(heat)* abrasador(ora); *(contest, argument, criticism)* encarnizado(a); *(loyalty)* fervoroso(a)

fiercely ['fɪəslɪ] *adv (to glare)* fieramente; *(to fight)* ferozmente; *(to condemn, defend)* vehementemente, apasionadamente; *(to resist)* con furia

fierceness ['fɪəsnɪs] *n (of animal, look)* fiereza *f*; *(of fighting)* encarnizamiento *m*; *(of heat)* intensidad *f*; *(of contest, argument, criticism)* violencia *f*; *(of loyalty)* fervor *m*

fiery ['faɪərɪ] *adj (heat)* achicharrante, abrasador(ora); *(red, sky)* encendido(a); *(taste)* muy picante; *(person, character)* fogoso(a), ardiente

fiesta [fɪ'estə] n fiesta f

fifteen [fɪf'tiːn] **1** n quince m; Sport (rugby team) equipo m
2 adj quince; see also **eight**

fifteenth [fɪf'tiːnθ] **1** n (**a**) (fraction) quinceavo m, quinceava parte f (**b**) (in series) decimoquinto(a) m,f (**c**) (of month) quince m
2 adj decimoquinto(a); see also **eleventh**

fifth [fɪfθ] **1** n (**a**) (fraction) quinto m, quinta parte f (**b**) (in series) quinto(a) m,f (**c**) (of month) cinco m
2 adj quinto(a); **the F. Amendment** la Quinta Enmienda; Pol **f. column** quinta columna f; Fam **to feel like a f. wheel** hacer de carabina or de sujetavelas, Méx hacer mal tercio, RP estar de paleta; see also **eighth**

fiftieth ['fɪftɪəθ] n & adj quincuagésimo(a) m,f

fifty ['fɪftɪ] n & adj cincuenta m; see also **eighty**

fig¹ [fɪg] n (fruit) higo m; Fam **he doesn't give** or **care a f.** le importa un rábano; **f. leaf** (in art) hoja f de parra; Fig **it's just a f. leaf** no es más que una tapadera; **f. tree** higuera f

fig² (abbr **figure**) fig., figura f

fight [faɪt] **1** n (**a**) (physical, verbal) pelea f; (contest, battle) lucha f; (boxing match) combate m; **to start a f. (with sb)** pelearse (con alguien); **to get into a f. (with sb)** pelearse (con alguien); **to give in without a f.** ceder sin oponer resistencia; **to put up a good f.** oponer resistencia (**b**) (spirit) **to show some f.** demostrar espíritu de lucha; **there was no f. left in him** no le quedaban arrestos (**c**) (struggle) lucha f (**for** por); **the f. against cancer** la lucha contra el cáncer
2 vt (pt & pp **fought** [fɔːt]) (person, enemy, rivals) luchar contra; (disease, poverty, fire) luchar contra, combatir; (temptation, desire, decision) luchar contra; (war, battle) librar; Law **she fought her case** defendió su caso (en un juicio); **to f. an election** presentarse a unas elecciones; Fig **to f. sb's battles for them** dar la cara por alguien; **to f. one's way through a crowd** abrirse paso entre una multitud
3 vi (**a**) (physically) luchar, pelearse; (verbally) pelearse, discutir; **to go down fighting** luchar hasta el final; **to f. fair** pelear limpio; **to f. shy of sth** evitar algo (**b**) (struggle) luchar; **to f. for breath** luchar por respirar

▸**fight back 1** vi (retaliate) responder
2 vt sep **to f. back one's tears** tratar de contener las lágrimas

▸**fight off** vt sep (enemy, attack) rechazar, ahuyentar; (illness) librarse de

fighter ['faɪtə(r)] n (in fight) combatiente mf, contendiente mf; (for cause) luchador(ora) m,f; **f. pilot** piloto m de caza; **f. (plane)** caza m; **f. squadron** escuadrón m de cazas

fighter-bomber ['faɪtə'bɒmə(r)] n cazabombardero m

fighting ['faɪtɪŋ] **1** n peleas fpl; Mil luchas fpl
2 adj **to have a f. chance** tener posibilidad de ganar; **to be f. fit** estar en plena forma; **f. forces** fuerzas fpl de combate

figment ['fɪgmənt] n **it's a f. of your imagination** es producto de tu imaginación

figurative ['fɪgərətɪv] adj figurado(a)

figuratively ['fɪgərətɪvlɪ] adv en sentido figurado

figure ['fɪgjə(r)] **1** n (**a**) (number) cifra f; **there must be a mistake in the figures** debe de haber un error en los números; **she's good at figures** se le dan bien los números; **to reach double/three figures** alcanzar valores de dos/tres cifras
(**b**) (body shape) figura f; **to have a good f.** tener buena figura; **a fine f. of a man** un hombre muy bien plantado; **to cut a sorry f.** tener un aspecto lamentable
(**c**) (person) figura f; **a leading f. in local politics** una figura destacada de la política local; **a distinguished f.** una personalidad distinguida
(**d**) (illustration) figura f, ilustración f; **see f. 7 b** ver figura 7 b
(**e**) (expression) **f. of speech** figura f retórica; **I didn't mean it like that, it was just a f. of speech** no quería decir eso, era sólo una manera or forma de hablar
(**f**) Geom figura f; **f. skater** patinador(ora) m,f artístico(a); **f. skating** patinaje m artístico
2 vt pensar, figurarse; **I f. (that) it will take three years** calculo que llevará tres años
3 vi (**a**) (appear) (in list, book) figurar (**b**) Fam (make sense) **that figures!** (es) normal or lógico

▸**figure on** vt insep Fam **to f. on doing sth** contar con hacer algo

▸**figure out** vt sep Fam (amount) calcular; (problem) solventar; **she can't f. you out at all** ¡no te entiende en absoluto!

figurehead ['fɪgəhed] n (on ship) mascarón m de proa; Fig (of country, party) testaferro m

figure-hugging ['fɪgəhʌgɪŋ] adj muy ceñido(a)

Fiji ['fiːdʒiː] n (las islas) Fiyi or Fiji

Fijian [fiː'dʒiːən] **1** n fiyiano(a), m,f, fijiano(a) m,f
2 adj fiyiano(a), fijiano(a)

filament ['fɪləmənt] n Elec filamento m

filch [fɪltʃ] vt Fam afanar, Esp mangar

file¹ [faɪl] **1** n (tool) lima f
2 vt (metal) limar; **to f. one's nails** limarse las uñas

file² **1** n (**a**) (folder) carpeta f; (box) archivo m; (documents) expediente m, ficha f; **to keep** or **have a f. on sb/sth** tener una ficha or un expediente de alguien/algo; **to have sth on f.** tener algo archivado (**b**) Comptr archivo m, fichero m; **f. management** gestión f de archivos or ficheros; **f. manager** administrador m de archivos; **f. server** servidor m de ficheros or archivos
2 vt (**a**) (store) (documents, letters) archivar (**b**) **to f. a claim** presentar una demanda
3 vi **to f. for divorce** presentar una demanda de divorcio

file³ **1** n (line) fila f; **in single f.** en fila india
2 vi **to f. past (sth/sb)** desfilar (ante algo/alguien); **to f. in/out** entrar/salir en fila

filial ['fɪlɪəl] adj filial

filigree ['fɪlɪgriː] n filigrana f

filing ['faɪlɪŋ] n archivación f, archivado m; **f. cabinet** archivador m

Filipino [fɪlɪ'piːnəʊ] **1** n (pl **Filipinos**) filipino(a) m,f
2 adj filipino(a)

fill [fɪl] **1** n **to eat one's f.** comer hasta reventar; Fig **to have had one's f. of sth** estar harto(a) de algo
2 vt (**a**) (container) llenar (**with** de); (gap, hole) rellenar; **to f. sb's glass** llenar el vaso a alguien; **to be filled with admiration/hope** estar lleno(a) de admiración/esperanza; **to f. a vacancy** (employer) cubrir una vacante; **I had a tooth filled** me hicieron un empaste or RP una emplomadura (**b**) (occupy) (time) ocupar
3 vi (become full) llenarse (**with** de or con); **her eyes filled with tears** se le llenaron los ojos de lágrimas

▸**fill in 1** vt sep (**a**) (hole, space, form) rellenar; **to f. in time** matar el tiempo (**b**) Fam (inform) **to f. sb in (on sth)** poner a alguien al tanto (de algo)
2 vi **to f. in for sb** sustituir a alguien

▸**fill out 1** vt sep (form, application) rellenar
2 vi (person) engordar

▸**fill up 1** vt sep (glass) llenar (hasta el borde); Fam **f. her up!** (with gas) ¡lleno, por favor!
2 vi (tank, container) llenarse

fillet ['fɪlɪt] **1** n (of fish) filete m; **f. steak** filete m
2 vt (fish) cortar en filetes

filling ['fɪlɪŋ] **1** n (**a**) (in tooth) empaste m (**b**) (in sandwich, pie) relleno m (**c**) **f. station** gasolinera f, estación f de servicio
2 adj **a f. meal** una comida que llena mucho

filly ['fɪlɪ] n (horse) potra f

film [fɪlm] **1** n (**a**) (thin layer) película f; **a f. of ice** una fina capa de hielo (**b**) *(at cinema)* película *f*; **f. actor/actress** actor *m/* actriz *f* de cine; **f. critic** crítico(a) *m,f* de cine; **f. director** director(ora) *m,f* de cine, cineasta *mf*; **the f. industry** la industria cinematográfica; **f. script** guión *m* de cine; **f. star** estrella *f* de cine; **f. studio** estudio *m* cinematográfico (**c**) *(photographic)* **a (roll of) f.** *(for camera)* un rollo *or* carrete

2 *vt (person, event)* filmar, rodar

3 *vi* rodar

filmgoer ['fɪlmɡəʊə(r)] *n* aficionado(a) *m,f,* al cine, espectador(ora) *m,f* de cine

filmy ['fɪlmɪ] *adj (material)* de gasa

filo pastry ['fiːləʊ'peɪstrɪ] *n* hojaldre *m* griego

filter ['fɪltə(r)] **1** *n (for liquids, on cigarette) & Phot* filtro *m*; **f. coffee** café *m* de filtro; **f. paper** papel *m* de filtro

2 *vt* filtrar

3 *vi (liquid, light)* filtrarse (**through** a través de); **the news soon filtered through** la noticia se filtró rápidamente

filth [fɪlθ] *n (dirt)* porquería *f*; **to talk f.** decir cochinadas

filthy ['fɪlθɪ] **1** *adj* (**a**) *(very dirty)* asqueroso(a) (**b**) *(very bad)* **to be in a f. temper** tener un humor de perros; **he gave me a f. look** me atravesó con la mirada (**c**) *(obscene) (language, jokes)* obsceno(a); *(movie, book)* indecente, *Esp* guarro(a)

2 *adv Fam* **f. rich** asquerosamente rico(a)

filtration [fɪl'treɪʃən] *n Chem* filtración *f*

fin [fɪn] *n (of fish, airplane)* aleta *f*

final ['faɪnəl] **1** *n* (**a**) *(of competition)* final *f*; **to be through to the finals** haber llegado a la fase final (**b**) *Univ* **finals** exámenes *mpl* finales

2 *adj* (**a**) *(last)* último(a); **the f. whistle** el pitido final; **the f. stages** las etapas finales, las últimas etapas; *Fin* **f. demand** último aviso *m* de pago; **f. warning** última advertencia *f* (**b**) *(definitive)* definitivo(a); **the umpire's decision is f.** la decisión del árbitro es definitiva; **and that's f.!** ¡y no hay más que hablar!

finale [fɪ'nɑːlɪ] *n (of concert, play)* final *m*; **grand f.** gran final; **there was a grand f. to the match** el partido tuvo un final apoteósico

finalist ['faɪnəlɪst] *n* finalista *mf*

finality [faɪ'nælɪtɪ] *n (of words, statement)* rotundidad *f*, irrevocabilidad *f*; *(of death)* carácter *m* irreversible

finalization [faɪnəlaɪ'zeɪʃən] *n* ultimación *f*, conclusión *f*

finalize ['faɪnəlaɪz] *vt* ultimar

finally ['faɪnəlɪ] *adv* (**a**) *(lastly)* por último, finalmente; **and f.,...** y por último,... (**b**) *(at last)* por fin, finalmente; **she had f. met him** por fin lo había conocido (**c**) *(irrevocably)* definitivamente; **it hasn't been decided f. yet** todavía no se ha tomado la decisión definitiva

finance [faɪ'næns, fɪ'næns] **1** *n* (**a**) *(subject)* finanzas *fpl*; **f. company** compañía *f* financiera (**b**) **finances** *(funds)* finanzas *fpl*; **his finances are low** se encuentra en una mala situación financiera

2 *vt* financiar

financial [faɪ'nænʃəl, fɪ'nænʃəl] *adj* financiero(a); **f. adviser** asesor(ora) *m,f* financiero(a); **f. control** control *m* financiero; **f. management** gestión *f* financiera; **f. market** mercado *m* financiero; **f. planning** planificación *f* financiera; **f. statement** balance *m* (general)

financially [faɪ'nænʃəlɪ, fɪ'nænʃəlɪ] *adv* económicamente

financier [faɪ'nænsɪə(r)] *n* financiero(a) *m,f*

finch [fɪntʃ] *n* pinzón *m*

find [faɪnd] **1** *n* hallazgo *m*

2 *vt (pt & pp* **found** [faʊnd]) (**a**) *(discover by chance)* encontrar, hallar; **to f. sb at home** *or* **in** encontrar a alguien en casa; **I found her waiting in the hall** me la encontré esperando en la entrada; **leave everything as you found it** deja todo tal y como lo encontraste; **I often f. myself wondering...** a menudo me sorprendo preguntándome...; **they found an**

unexpected supporter in Richard Sanders recibieron el inesperado apoyo de Richard Sanders; **you will f. that I am right** te darás cuenta de que tengo razón; **I was surprised to f. that...** me sorprendió enterarme de que...

(**b**) *(discover by searching)* encontrar, hallar; **to try to f. sth** tratar de encontrar algo; **to f. an answer/a solution** hallar una respuesta/una solución; **the money has been found** han encontrado el dinero; **she was nowhere to be found** no la encontraron por ninguna parte; **to f. a job for sb** encontrarle un trabajo a alguien; **he found something for me to do** me encontró algo que hacer; **he couldn't f. it in his heart to tell her** no halló fuerzas para decírselo; **to f. one's way** orientarse, encontrar el camino; **this leaflet somehow found its way into my bag** no sé cómo ha venido a parar a mi bolso este folleto; **to f. a way to do sth** encontrar la manera de hacer algo; **to f. oneself** *(spiritually)* encontrarse a uno mismo

(**c**) *(experience)* **they will f. it easy/difficult** les resultará *or* lo encontrarán fácil/difícil; **she found it impossible to understand him** le resultó imposible entenderle; **he found it necessary to remind her of her duty** consideró necesario recordarle su obligación; **how did you f. the meal/the exam?** ¿qué te pareció la comida/el examen?; **I found her charming** me pareció muy simpática

(**d**) *Law* **to f. sb guilty/innocent** declarar a alguien culpable/inocente

3 *vi Law* **to f. for/against sb** fallar a favor de/en contra de alguien

▶**find out 1** *vt sep* (**a**) *(discover)* averiguar, descubrir; **we found out that she was French** descubrimos que era francesa (**b**) *(see through)* **to f. sb out** descubrir a alguien; **we've been found out** nos han descubierto

2 *vi* **to f. out about sth** enterarse de algo

finder ['faɪndə(r)] *n* **the f. of the money should contact the police** quien encuentre el dinero ha de llamar a la policía; *Fam* **finders keepers** = si yo lo encontré, es para mí

findings ['faɪndɪŋz] *npl* conclusiones *fpl*

fine¹ [faɪn] **1** *n Law* multa *f*

2 *vt Law* multar, poner una multa a; **to f. sb $100** poner a alguien una multa de 100 dólares

fine² **1** *adj* (**a**) *(excellent) (food, performance)* excelente, exquisito(a); *(weather)* bueno(a); **to appeal to sb's finer feelings** apelar a los más nobles sentimientos de alguien; **she's a f. woman** es una mujer extraordinaria; **the f. arts** las bellas artes; **she's got it down to a f. art** lo hace con los ojos cerrados, lo tiene muy controlado

(**b**) *(thin)* fino(a)

(**c**) *(satisfactory)* bien; **she's f.** está bien; **everything is f.** todo está bien; **that's f. by me** ¡me parece bien!, ¡por mí, *Esp* vale *or Arg* dale *or Méx* órale!

(**d**) *Ironic (great)* **you're a f. one to talk!** ¡mira quién fue a hablar!; **this is another f. mess you've got us into!** ¡en menudo lío nos has vuelto a meter!, *RP* ¡otra vez nos metiste en flor de lío!; **he was in a f. (old) temper!** estaba de un humor de perros

(**e**) *(subtle, delicate)* fino(a); **f. distinction** distinción *f* sutil; **not to put too f. a point on it** hablando en plata; **there's a f. line between eccentricity and madness** la frontera entre la excentricidad y la locura es muy tenue

2 *adv* bien; **she's getting on** *or* **doing f.** le va bien; **they get on f.** se llevan bien

finely ['faɪnlɪ] *adv (skillfully)* acertadamente, hábilmente; **f. balanced** *(contest)* muy equilibrado(a); **f. chopped** picado(a) muy fino(a); **f. tuned** *(engine)* a punto

finery ['faɪnərɪ] *n* galas *fpl*

finesse [fɪ'nes] *n* finura *f*; **he handled the matter with great f.** llevó el asunto con mucha mano izquierda *or* delicadeza

fine-tune ['faɪn'tjuːn] vt poner a punto

fine-tuning ['faɪn'tjuːnɪŋ] n ajuste m

finger ['fɪŋgə(r)] **1** n (**a**) (of hand, glove) dedo m; Fig **to keep one's fingers crossed** cruzar los dedos; **f. bowl** bol m or cuenco m para las manos; **f. buffet** bufé m a base de canapés y aperitivos; **f. food** (snacks) cosas fpl de picar (**b**) (measure) **a f. of brandy** un dedo de coñac (**c**) (idioms) **he's got them (wrapped) around his little f.** los tiene a sus pies; **to have a f. in every pie** estar metido(a) en todo; **don't you dare lay a f. on him** no te atrevas a tocarle un pelo; **she wouldn't lift a f. to help you** no levantaría or movería un dedo por ayudarte; **I can't quite put my f. on it** no consigo dar con ello; **to get one's fingers burned** salir escaldado(a) or escarmentado(a) **2** vt (**a**) (feel) tocar (**b**) Fam (inform on) soplar acerca de, RP pasar el dato de

fingering ['fɪŋgərɪŋ] n Mus digitación f

fingerless ['fɪŋgəlɪs] adj **f. gloves** mitones mpl

fingernail ['fɪŋgəneɪl] n uña f

fingerprint ['fɪŋgəprɪnt] **1** n huella f digital or dactilar **2** vt (person) tomar las huellas digitales or dactilares a

fingertip ['fɪŋgətɪp] n punta f del dedo; **to have sth at one's fingertips** (facts, information) tener algo al alcance de la mano; (subject) conocer algo al dedillo

finicky ['fɪnɪkɪ] adj (fussy) quisquilloso(a); (complicated) trabajoso(a), entretenido(a)

finish ['fɪnɪʃ] **1** n (**a**) (end) (of day, meeting) final m; (of race) meta f; **to be in at the f.** seguir estando hasta el final (**b**) (surface) (of furniture, metalwork) acabado m **2** vt (**a**) (end) terminar, acabar; **to f. doing sth** terminar de hacer algo; **you didn't let me f. (what I was saying)** no me dejaste terminar (lo que estaba diciendo) (**b**) (ruin, kill) (person) acabar con **3** vi terminar, finalizar; **to f. on an optimistic note** finalizar con una nota de optimismo; **to f. fourth** (in race, contest) quedar en cuarto lugar, terminar cuarto(a)

▶**finish off 1** vt sep (**a**) (complete) (task, book) terminar (del todo) (**b**) (use up) acabar (con) (**c**) Fam (kill) terminar con **2** vi terminar

finished ['fɪnɪʃt] adj (**a**) (completed) terminado(a), acabado(a); **the job isn't f. yet** el trabajo no está terminado aún; Fam **he's f.!** ¡está acabado! (**b**) (of high quality) elaborado(a)

finishing ['fɪnɪʃɪŋ] adj **to put the f. touches to sth** dar los últimos (re)toques a algo; **f. line** línea f de meta; **f. school** = escuela privada de etiqueta para señoritas

finite ['faɪnaɪt] adj finito(a); Gram (verb) conjugado(a)

Finland ['fɪnlənd] n Finlandia

Finn [fɪn] n (person) finlandés(esa) m,f

Finnish ['fɪnɪʃ] **1** n (language) finés m, finlandés m **2** adj finlandés(esa)

fir [fɜː(r)] n **f. (tree)** abeto m; **f. cone** piña f

fire ['faɪə(r)] **1** n (**a**) (element, in hearth) fuego m; (large, destructive) incendio m; Fig (enthusiasm) pasión f; **on f.** en llamas, ardiendo; **to cause** or **start a f.** provocar un incendio; **to catch f.** prender; **to set f. to sth, to set sth on f.** prender fuego a algo; **f.!** ¡fuego!; Fig **to play with f.** jugar con fuego; Fig **we'll have to fight f. with f.** a grandes males, grandes remedios; **f. alarm** alarma f contra incendios; **f. department** (cuerpo m de) bomberos mpl; **f. door** puerta f contra incendios; **f. drill** simulacro m de incendio; **f. engine** coche m de bomberos; **f. escape** escalera f de incendios; **f. exit** salida f de incendios; **f. extinguisher** Esp extintor m, Am extinguidor m; **f. fighter** bombero(a) m,f; **f. hazard** = objeto que supone peligro de incendio; **f. hydrant** boca f de incendios; **f. insurance** seguro m contra incendios; **f. regulations** (laws) normativa f contra incendios; (in building) procedimiento m en caso de incendio; **f. sale** venta f de objetos dañados en un incendio; **f. station** parque m de bomberos; **f. truck** coche m de bomberos; **f. warden** = responsable en caso de incendios forestales (**b**) (of rifle, artillery) fuego m; **to open f.** abrir fuego; **to hold one's f.** dejar de disparar; **to come under f.** caer bajo el fuego enemigo; Fig **to be** or **come under f.** (be criticized) recibir muchas críticas **2** vt (**a**) (rifle, bullet, missile) disparar (**at** contra); **to f. a shot** disparar; Fig **to f. a question at sb** lanzar una pregunta a alguien (**b**) Fam (dismiss) despedir; **you're fired!** ¡quedas despedido! (**c**) oil-/gas-fired central heating calefacción f central de petróleo/gas; Fig **to f. sb with enthusiasm** hacer a alguien arder de entusiasmo; Fig **the movie fired his imagination** la película despertó su imaginación (**d**) (pottery) cocer **3** vi (**a**) (with gun) disparar; **f.!** ¡fuego!; Fam Fig **f. away!** (to questioner) ¡adelante! (**b**) (engine) encenderse, Am prenderse

firearm ['faɪərɑːm] n arma f de fuego

firebrand ['faɪəbrænd] n (torch) antorcha f; (agitator) agitador(ora) m,f

firecracker ['faɪəkrækə(r)] n petardo m

firefighting ['faɪəfaɪtɪŋ] adj **f. equipment** equipo m contra incendios

firefly ['faɪəflaɪ] n luciérnaga f

fireguard ['faɪəgɑːd] n pantalla f (de chimenea), parachispas m inv

firelight ['faɪəlaɪt] n luz f del fuego

firelighter ['faɪəlaɪtə(r)] n pastilla f para (encender or Am prender) el fuego

fireman ['faɪəmən] n bombero m

fireplace ['faɪəpleɪs] n chimenea f

firepower ['faɪəpaʊə(r)] n capacidad f ofensiva

fireproof ['faɪəpruːf] adj (clothing, material) ignífugo(a), incombustible

fireside ['faɪəsaɪd] n **by the f.** junto a la chimenea

firewall ['faɪəwɔːl] n Comptr cortafuegos m inv

firewood ['faɪəwʊd] n leña f

firework ['faɪəwɜːk] n fuego m de artificio; **fireworks** fuegos mpl artificiales; Fig **there'll be fireworks** se va a armar una buena; **f. display** (castillo m de) fuegos mpl artificiales

firing ['faɪərɪŋ] n disparos mpl; Fig **to be in the f. line** (be blamed, criticized) estar en la línea de fuego or en el punto de mira; **f. squad** pelotón m de ejecución or de fusilamiento

firm¹ [fɜːm] n (company) empresa f

firm² **1** adj (**a**) (steady, definite) firme; **the f. favorite** el gran favorito; **it is my f. belief that…** creo firmemente que… (**b**) (strict) firme, estricto(a); **to be f. with sb** ser estricto(a) con alguien; **she was polite but f.** se mostró educada, pero firme **2** adv **to stand f.** mantenerse firme; **she held f. to her principles** se mantuvo firme en sus principios

firmly ['fɜːmlɪ] adv (securely, resolutely) con firmeza, firmemente; **I f. believe that…** creo firmemente que…

first [fɜːst] **1** n (**a**) (in series) primero(a) m,f; **we were the f. to arrive** fuimos los primeros en llegar; **it's the f. I've heard of it** es la primera noticia que tengo (de ello), ahora me entero; **Edward the F.** (written) Eduardo I; (spoken) Eduardo primero (**b**) (of month) primero m, Esp uno m; **the f. of May, May f.** (labor holiday) el primero de mayo; **we're leaving on the f.** nos vamos el primero or Esp el (día) uno (**c**) (beginning) **from f. to last** de principio a fin; **from the f.** desde el principio; **at f.** al principio (**d**) (first gear) primera f; **to put the car into f.** meter (la) primera (**e**) (unique event) **it was a f.** fue un acontecimiento sin precedentes **2** adj primero(a); **the f. century** el siglo uno or primero; **for the f. time** por primera vez; **at f. hand** de primera mano; **f.**

things f.! lo primero es lo primero; **I don't know the f. thing about motorbikes** no tengo ni idea de motos; **f. thing in the morning** a primera hora de la mañana; **at f. light** al alba; **at f. sight** a primera vista; **in the f. place** en primer lugar; **on the f. floor** en la planta baja; **the F. World War** la Primera Guerra Mundial; **f. aid** *(skill)* socorrismo *m*; *(treatment)* primeros auxilios *mpl*; **the F. Amendment** la Primera Enmienda; **f. cousin** primo(a) *m,f* carnal; **f. edition** primera edición *f*; *Aut* **f. gear** primera *f*; **the F. Lady** la primera dama; *Naut* **f. mate** segundo *m* de a bordo; **f. name** nombre *m* (de pila); **f. night** *(of play)* (noche *f* del) estreno *m*; *Law* **f. offense** primer delito *m*; *Law* **f. offender** delincuente *mf* sin antecedentes

3 *adv* (**a**) *(firstly)* primero(a); **f. and foremost** ante todo; **f. of all** antes de nada, en primer lugar (**b**) *(for the first time)* por primera vez; **I f. met her in Detroit** la conocí en Detroit (**c**) *(before others)* primero, antes; **you go f.!** *(in queue)* usted está antes; **to come f.** *(in race, contest)* terminar primero; *(in importance)* ser lo primero; **f. come, f. served** por orden de llegada; **ladies f.!** las señoras primero; **to fall head f.** caer de cabeza; **I'd resign f.** *(rather than do sth)* antes dimito

first-aid [fɜːstˈeɪd] *adj* **f. certificate** título *m* de primeros auxilios; **f. box** *or* **kit** botiquín *m* de primeros auxilios

first-born [ˈfɜːstbɔːn] *(pl* **first-born**) *n & adj Literary* primogénito(a) *m,f*

first-class [ˈfɜːstklɑːs] **1** *adj (compartment, ticket)* de primera (clase)

2 *adv* **to travel f.** viajar en primera (clase); **to send a letter f.** enviar una carta urgente

first-degree [ˈfɜːstdɪˈɡriː] *adj* (**a**) *Med (burns)* de primer grado (**b**) *Law (murder)* en primer grado

first-generation [ˈfɜːstdʒenəˈreɪʃən] *adj* de primera generación

first-hand [ˈfɜːsthænd] **1** *adj* de primera mano

2 *adv* de primera mano; **he heard it f.** se lo dijeron a él mismo

firstly [ˈfɜːstlɪ] *adv* en primer lugar

first-rate [fɜːstˈreɪt] *adj* excelente, de primera clase

first-time buyer [ˈfɜːstaɪmˈbaɪə(r)] *n* = persona que compra una vivienda por primera vez

fiscal [ˈfɪskəl] *adj* fiscal; **f. policy** política *f* fiscal; **f. year** año *m* fiscal

fish [fɪʃ] **1** *n* (*pl* **fish** *or* **fishes**) (**a**) *(animal)* pez *m*; *(food)* pescado *m*; **f. cake** pastelillo *m* de pescado; **f. farm** piscifactoría *f*; **f. farming** piscicultura *f*; **f. knife** cuchillo *m* *or* paleta *f* de pescado; **f. slice** pala *f* *or* espátula *f* (de cocina); **f. sticks** palitos *mpl* *or* barritas *fpl* de pescado; **f. tank** acuario *m*

(**b**) *(idioms)* **there are plenty more f. in the sea** con él/ella no se acaba el mundo; **to have other f. to fry** tener algo más importante que hacer; **she felt like a f. out of water** no se sentía en su elemento; **at school/work, he was a big f. in a small pond** le venía pequeña la escuela/la empresa; **neither f. nor fowl** ni chicha ni limoná

2 *vt* (**a**) *(river)* pescar en (**b**) *(remove)* **to f. sth from somewhere** retirar algo de un lugar

3 *vi* (**a**) *(for fish)* pescar (**b**) *Fam* **to f. for compliments** tratar de atraer elogios; **she fished around in her pocket for some change** rebuscó en el bolsillo *or* *CAm, Méx, Perú* la bolsa a ver si tenía monedas

fishbowl [ˈfɪʃbəʊl] *n* pecera *f*

fisherman [ˈfɪʃəmən] *n* pescador *m*

fishhook [ˈfɪʃhʊk] *n* anzuelo *m*

fishing [ˈfɪʃɪŋ] *n* pesca *f*; **to go f.** ir de pesca *or* a pescar; **f. boat** barco *m* pesquero; **f. grounds** caladeros *mpl*; **f. line** sedal *m*; **f. net** red *f* de pesca; **f. port** puerto *m* pesquero; **f. rod** caña *f* de pescar

fishnet [ˈfɪʃnet] *adj* **f. stockings** *or* **tights** medias *fpl* de red *or* de malla

fishy [ˈfɪʃɪ] *adj* (**a**) *(smell, taste)* a pescado (**b**) *Fam (suspicious)* sospechoso(a); **there's something f. going on here** aquí hay gato encerrado

fission [ˈfɪʃən] *n* fisión *f*

fissure [ˈfɪʃə(r)] *n (in mountain, rock)* grieta *f*; *Med* fisura *f*

fist [fɪst] *n* puño *m*; **to shake one's f. at sb** amenazar a alguien con el puño

fistfight [ˈfɪstfaɪt] *n* pelea *f* a puñetazos

fistful [ˈfɪstfʊl] *n* puñado *m*

fisticuffs [ˈfɪstɪkʌfs] *npl* pelea *f* a puñetazos

fit¹ [fɪt] *n* ataque *m*, crisis *f inv*; **(epileptic) f.** ataque *m* de epilepsia, crisis epiléptica; **a f. of coughing** un acceso de tos; *Fam Fig* **to have** *or* **throw a f.** *(get angry)* ponerse hecho(a) una furia; **in a f. of temper** en un arrebato de ira; **a f. of crying** un ataque de llanto; **to do sth by fits and starts** hacer algo a trompicones

fit² **1** *adj* (**a**) *(appropriate)* adecuado(a), apto(a); **f. to eat** comestible; **f. to drink** potable; **a meal f. for a king** una comida digna de un rey; **do as you see** *or* **think f.** haz lo que creas conveniente; **this is no f. way to behave** esta no es manera de comportarse; **that's all he's f. for** no vale para más; **she worked until she was f. to drop** trabajó hasta caer rendida; *Fam* **she was f. to be tied** se subía por las paredes

(**b**) *(healthy)* en forma; **to get/keep f.** ponerse/mantenerse en forma; **he is not yet f. to go back to work** todavía no está en condiciones de volver a trabajar; *Fam* **to be as f. as a fiddle** estar en plena forma

2 *vt* (*pt & pp* **fitted**) (**a**) *(match)* ajustarse a, adecuarse a; **to make the punishment f. the crime** imponer un castigo proporcional al delito (**b**) *(be the right size for)* **it fits me** me sirve, me queda *or* me va bien; **this key fits the lock** esta llave entra (bien) en la cerradura (**c**) *(install)* colocar, poner; **to f. a carpet** colocar una *Esp* moqueta *or Am* alfombra; **the car is fitted with an alarm** el coche viene equipado con alarma (**d**) *(insert)* **to f. sth into sth** introducir *or* encajar algo en algo; **to f. sth onto sth** colocar algo sobre algo; **we can f. another two people inside** podemos meter a dos personas más

3 *vi* (**a**) *(lid, key, plug)* encajar; **to f. (together)** encajar; **to f. into sth** caber en algo (**b**) *(clothes)* quedar bien (de talla)

4 *n* **the skirt is a good/bad f.** la falda *or RP* pollera está bien/mal de talla

▸**fit in 1** *vt sep (in timetable)* **to f. sb in** hacer un hueco a alguien

2 *vi* (**a**) *(go into place)* encajar (**b**) *(person)* **he just didn't f. in** simplemente no encajaba bien (en aquel ambiente)

fitful [ˈfɪtfʊl] *adj (sleep)* intermitente; **to make f. progress** ir progresando por rachas

fitfully [ˈfɪtfʊlɪ] *adv* intermitentemente, a ratos

fitness [ˈfɪtnɪs] *n* (**a**) *(health)* buena forma *f* (**b**) *(suitability)* aptitud *f*

fitting [ˈfɪtɪŋ] **1** *n* (**a**) *(of clothes)* prueba *f*; **f. room** probador *m* (**b**) **fittings** *(of office)* equipamiento *m*; *(of bathroom)* accesorios *mpl*

2 *adj* apropiado(a)

fittingly [ˈfɪtɪŋlɪ] *adv* muy apropiadamente

five [faɪv] **1** *n* cinco *m*; **f.-o'clock shadow** sombra *f* de barba

2 *adj* cinco; *see also* **eight**

five-and-dime [ˈfaɪvənˈdaɪm], **five-and-ten** [ˈfaɪvənˈten] *n* = tienda en la que sólo se venden productos muy baratos

fivefold [ˈfaɪvfəʊld] *adj* quintuplicado(a)

fiver [ˈfaɪvə(r)] *n Fam* cinco dólares *mpl*

fix [fɪks] **1** *n* (**a**) *Fam (difficulty)* **to be in a f.** estar en un lío; **to get into a f.** meterse en un lío (**b**) *(of drug)* pico *m*, *Esp* chute *m* *Fig* **my daily f. of television news** mi dosis diaria de noticias (**c**) *Fam (set-up)* **the match/quiz was a f.** el partido/concurso estaba amañado

2 *vt* (**a**) *(attach securely)* fijar; **to f. sth in one's memory** fijar algo en la memoria; **to f. one's attention on sth** fijar la atención en algo; **to f. one's eyes on sb** fijar la mirada en alguien (**b**) *(decide) (limit, price)* fijar; **nothing is fixed yet** no hay nada fijo todavía (**c**) *(repair)* arreglar (**d**) *(arrange) (meeting)* organizar; **just wait while I f. my hair** espera mientras me peino; *Fam* **I'll f. him!** ¡se va a enterar! (**e**) *Fam (rig) (election, contest) Esp* amañar, *Am* arreglar (**f**) **to f. sb breakfast/a drink** preparar el desayuno/una bebida a alguien

▸ **fix up** *vt sep* (**a**) *(meeting)* preparar; **it's all fixed up** está todo dispuesto (**b**) *(provide)* **I've fixed him up with a date** le he buscado a alguien para que salgan juntos (**c**) *(prepare) (room, apartment)* arreglar, acondicionar

fixated [fik'seitid] *adj* obsesionado(a) (**on** con)

fixation [fik'seiʃən] *n* fijación *f*; **to have a f. about sth** tener una fijación con algo

fixed [fikst] *adj* (**a**) *(price)* fijo(a); **f. assets** activo *m* fijo *or* inmovilizado; **f. costs** costos *mpl or Esp* costes *mpl* fijos; **f. expenses** gastos *mpl* fijos; **f. income** renta *f* fija; **f. rate** *Esp* tipo *m or Am* tasa *f* de interés fijo (**b**) *(definite)* **to have f. ideas** tener ideas fijas; **to have no f. plans** no tener planes definidos (**c**) *Fam* **how are you f. for money/time?** ¿qué tal andas de dinero/tiempo? (**d**) *Fam (election, contest) Esp* amañado(a), *Am* arreglado(a)

fixedly ['fiksidli] *adv* fijamente

fixer ['fiksə(r)] *n Fam* negociador(ora) *m,f*

fixture ['fikstʃə(r)] *n* **bathroom fixtures and fittings** saneamiento *mpl or* sanitarios *mpl* y accesorios; *Fam* **she was something of a f. at his parties** asistía invariablemente a todas sus fiestas

fizz [fiz] **1** *n* (**a**) *(sound)* burbujeo *m* (**b**) *Fam (soft drink)* refresco *m*; *(champagne)* champán *m*
2 *vi* burbujear

▸ **fizzle out** [fizəl] *vi Fam (plan)* quedarse en nada *or Esp* en agua de borrajas; *(enthusiasm, interest)* disiparse

fizziness ['fizinis] *n (of drink)* efervescencia *f*

fizzy ['fizi] *adj (wine)* espumoso(a); *(soft drink)* con gas, con burbujas

fjord [fjɔːd] *n* fiordo *m*

flab [flæb] *n Fam (fat)* grasa *f*

flabbergast ['flæbəgɑːst] *vt Fam* **I was flabbergasted by this news** aluciné *or Esp* flipé con la noticia

flabby ['flæbi] *adj (person)* fofo(a); *Fig (argument, reasoning)* flojo(a)

flaccid ['flæsid] *adj* flác(c)ido(a)

flag [flæg] **1** *n* bandera *f*; *(on boat)* pabellón *m*, bandera *f*; **F. Day** = día de la bandera en Estados Unidos, 14 de junio
2 *vt (pt & pp flagged)* **to f. (down) a taxi** llamar *or* parar a un taxi; **to f. a mistake** señalar un error
3 *vi (person)* desfallecer; *(conversation, interest)* decaer; *(strength)* flaquear

flagellate ['flædʒəleit] *vt* flagelar

flagging ['flægiŋ] **1** *n (on floor)* enlosado *m*
2 *adj (strength, enthusiasm)* debilitado(a); *(conversation, interest)* decreciente

flagpole ['flægpəʊl] *n* asta *f (de bandera)*

flagrant ['fleigrənt] *adj* flagrante

flagrantly ['fleigrəntli] *adv* flagrantemente

flagship ['flægʃip] *n (of fleet)* buque *m* insignia; *Fig (of range of products, policies)* estandarte *m*

flagstone ['flægstəʊn] *n* losa *f*

flag-waving ['flægweiviŋ] *adj* **the streets were full of f. crowds** las calles estaban llenas de multitudes agitando banderas

flail [fleil] **1** *n (agricultural implement)* mayal *m*
2 *vt* agitar; **she flailed her fists at him** trató inútilmente de golpearle
3 *vi* agitarse; **I managed to avoid his flailing fists** conseguí evitar sus puñetazos

▸ **flail around, flail about** *vi (arms, legs)* moverse descontroladamente

flair [fleə(r)] *n* don *m*, dotes *fpl*; **to have a f. for sth** tener dotes para algo; **to do sth with f.** hacer algo con estilo *or* elegancia

flak [flæk] *n* fuego *m* antiaéreo; *Fig* **she got a lot of f. for her decision** su decisión recibió duras críticas; **f. jacket** chaleco *m* antifragmentación

flake [fleik] **1** *n (of snow, cereal)* copo *m*; *(of skin, soap)* escama *f*; *(of paint)* desconchón *m*
2 *vi (skin)* descamarse; *(paint)* desconcharse

▸ **flake out** *vi Fam (fall asleep)* quedarse roque

flaky ['fleiki] *adj* (**a**) *(surface)* desconchado(a); *(skin)* con escamas; **f. pastry** hojaldre *m* (**b**) *Fam (eccentric)* raro(a)

flamboyance [flæm'bɔiəns] *n (of person, manner)* extravagancia *f*; *(of clothes)* vistosidad *f*

flamboyant [flæm'bɔiənt] *adj (person, manner)* extravagante; *(clothes)* vistoso(a)

flame [fleim] **1** *n* llama *f*; *Comptr* llamarada *f*; **to go up in flames** ser pasto de las llamas; **to burst into flames** incendiarse; *Fam* **he's an old f. of mine** es un antiguo amor
2 *vi* (**a**) *(fire)* llamear (**b**) *Comptr* lanzar llamaradas
3 *vt Comptr* lanzar llamaradas a

flamenco [flə'meŋkəʊ] *n* flamenco *m*; **f. dancing** baile *m* flamenco

flameproof ['fleimpruːf] *adj* resistente al fuego

flamethrower ['fleimθrəʊə(r)] *n* lanzallamas *m inv*

flaming ['fleimiŋ] *adj (burning)* en llamas

flamingo [flə'miŋgəʊ] *(pl* **flamingos)** *n* flamenco *m*

flammable ['flæməbəl] *adj* inflamable

flan [flæn] *n* tarta *f*

Flanders ['flɑːndəz] *n* Flandes

flange [flændʒ] *n* pestaña *f*

flank [flæŋk] **1** *n (of person, animal)* costado *m*; *(of beef, mutton)* falda *f*; *(of mountain)* ladera *f*; *(of army)* flanco *m*
2 *vt* flanquear

flannel ['flænəl] *n* (**a**) *(fabric)* franela *f* (**b**) **flannels** *(pants)* pantalones *mpl* de franela; **a pair of f.** unos pantalones de franela

flap [flæp] **1** *n* (**a**) *(of envelope, book cover)* solapa *f*; *(of tent)* puerta *f*; *(of airplane)* alerón *m* (**b**) *Fam (panic)* **to get into a f.** ponerse hecho(a) un manojo de nervios
2 *vt (pt & pp flapped) (wings)* batir; **she flapped her arms excitedly** agitó los brazos con excitación
3 *vi (wings)* aletear; *(flag)* ondear

flapjack ['flæpdʒæk] *n (pancake)* crepe *f*, hojuela *f*

flare [fleə(r)] **1** *n* (**a**) *(signal)* bengala *f*; **f. gun** *or* **pistol** pistola *f* de *or* lanza bengalas (**b**) **flares** *(pants)* pantalones *mpl* de campana; **a pair of flares** unos pantalones de campana
2 *vt* **to f. one's nostrils** hinchar las aletas de la nariz
3 *vi (fire, flame)* llamear; *(temper, trouble)* estallar

▸ **flare up** *vi (fire)* llamear; *(medical condition)* exacerbarse; *(anger, trouble)* estallar

flash [flæʃ] **1** *n* (**a**) *(of light)* destello *m*; **a f. of lightning** un relámpago; **a f. of wit** una ocurrencia; **a f. of inspiration** una inspiración súbita; **in a f.** *(very quickly)* en un abrir y cerrar de ojos; *Fig* **a f. in the pan** un éxito aislado; **f. flood** riada *f*; **f. point** *(of situation)* momento *m* de máxima tensión; *(region)* zona *f* conflictiva (**b**) *(in photography)* flash *m*
2 *adj Fam (showy)* llamativo(a), ostentoso(a)
3 *vt (smile, look)* lanzar (**at** a); *(card, badge)* mostrar, exhibir; **to f. one's headlights at sb** darle las luces a alguien, hacerle señales con los faros a alguien
4 *vi* (**a**) *(light)* destellar; **his eyes flashed with anger** sus ojos lanzaban destellos de ira (**b**) *(move quickly)* **to f. past** pasar a toda velocidad; **it flashed across my mind that...** se me ocurrió de pronto que...; **my life flashed before me** en un instante vi mi vida entera

flashback ['flæʃbæk] n (in novel, movie) escena f retrospectiva

flashily ['flæʃɪlɪ] adv Pej ostentosamente; **f. dressed** con ropa muy llamativa

flashing ['flæʃɪŋ] adj (light) intermitente

flashlight ['flæʃlaɪt] n linterna f

flashy ['flæʃɪ] adj Pej llamativo(a), ostentoso(a)

flask [flɑːsk] n (in chemistry) matraz m; (**hip**) **f.** petaca f; (**thermos**) **f.** termo m

flat [flæt] **1** n (**a**) Fam (flat tire) rueda f desinflada (**b**) **mud flats** marismas fpl; **salt flats** salinas fpl

2 adj (**a**) (surface) llano(a), liso(a), plano(a); (landscape, region) llano(a); (roof) liso(a), plano(a); (nose) chato(a); **to be as f. as a pancake** or **a flounder** estar liso(a) como un plato; Fam (flat-chested) estar plana como una tabla; **to have f. feet** tener los pies planos; **f. racing** carrera f de caballos (sin obstáculos); **f. rate** tarifa f única; **f. tire** rueda f desinflada (**b**) (refusal) rotundo(a) (**c**) (existence, atmosphere) gris, monótono(a); (voice) monótono(a); **this beer is f.** esta cerveza ha perdido el gas or no tiene fuerza (**d**) Mus (a semitone lower) bemol; (out of tune) desafinado(a); **B f.** si m bemol

3 adv (**a**) **he lay f. on the floor** estaba tumbado en el suelo; **to fall f. on one's face** caer de bruces; Fig **the joke fell f.** el chiste no hizo mucha gracia (**b**) (completely) **to turn sb down f.** rechazar a alguien de plano; **in twenty seconds f.** en veinte segundos justos; **to work f. out** trabajar a tope; Fam **to be f. broke** estar sin un Esp duro or Méx quinto, RP estar en lampa y la vía

flat-chested ['flæt'tʃestɪd] adj plana (de pecho)

flatfish ['flætfɪʃ] n pez m (de cuerpo) plano

flat-footed ['flæt'fʊtɪd] adj **to be f.** tener (los) pies planos

flatly ['flætlɪ] adv (refuse, deny) rotundamente, de plano

flat-screen ['flæt'skriːn] adj de pantalla plana

flatten ['flætən] vt (make flat) aplastar; (ground) allanar; (paper) alisar; (building, area) arrasar; Fam (in fight) tumbar

flatter ['flætə(r)] vt (of person) halagar, adular; (of clothes) favorecer; **I felt flattered** me sentí halagado; **to f. oneself** engañarse a sí mismo(a); **she flatters herself that she's a good cook** se piensa que es una buena cocinera; Fam **don't f. yourself!** ¡no te engañes!

flattering ['flætərɪŋ] adj (words) halagador(ora); (clothes, color) favorecedor(ora)

flattery ['flætərɪ] n halagos mpl

flatulence ['flætjʊləns] n Med flatulencia f

flatulent ['flætjʊlənt] adj Med flatulento(a); Fig (speech, style) rimbombante, campanudo(a)

flaunt [flɔːnt] vt hacer ostentación de

flautist ['flɔːtɪst] = **flutist**

flavor ['fleɪvə(r)] **1** n (of food) & Fig sabor m; **her stories have a Mediterranean f.** sus relatos tienen un sabor mediterráneo

2 vt (food) condimentar; **vanilla flavored f.** con sabor a vainilla

flavoring ['fleɪvərɪŋ] n aromatizante m

flavorless ['fleɪvəlɪs] adj insípido(a)

flaw [flɔː] n (in diamond, plan, personality) defecto m, Esp fallo m, Am falla f

flawed [flɔːd] adj defectuoso(a)

flawless ['flɔːlɪs] adj impecable

flax [flæks] n (plant) lino m

flay [fleɪ] vt (flog, criticize) despellejar, desollar

flea [fliː] n (insect) pulga f; Fam **to send sb away with a f. in his ear** echar a alguien una buena reprimenda or Esp bronca, RP dar a alguien un buen rezongo; **f. collar** (collar m) antiparasitario m; **f. market** mercadillo m callejero, rastro m

fleabite ['fliːbaɪt] n picadura f de pulga

flea-bitten ['fliːbɪtən] adj Fam (shabby) mugriento(a)

fleck [flek] **1** n mota f

2 vt motear (**with** de); **flecked with paint** con gotas de pintura

fled [fled] pt & pp of **flee**

fledgling ['fledʒlɪŋ] **1** n (young bird) polluelo m

2 adj Fig (person) novato(a); (company, state) naciente

flee [fliː] (pt & pp **fled** [fled]) vi huir (**from** de)

fleece [fliːs] **1** n (of sheep) vellón m

2 vt Fam (cheat) desplumar

fleecy ['fliːsɪ] adj algodonoso(a)

fleet [fliːt] n (of ships) flota f; (of taxis, buses) flota f, parque m (móvil)

fleet-footed ['fliːt'fʊtɪd] adj Literary alígero(a)

fleeting ['fliːtɪŋ] adj fugaz

fleetingly ['fliːtɪŋlɪ] adv fugazmente, por un momento

Flemish ['flemɪʃ] **1** n (language) flamenco m

2 adj flamenco(a)

flesh [fleʃ] n (of person) carne f; (of fruit) pulpa f; **in the f.** en persona; **to make sb's f. creep** or **crawl** darle escalofríos a alguien; **his own f. and blood** los de su misma sangre; **f. wound** herida f superficial

▸**flesh out** vt sep (plan, remarks) definir, precisar

flesh-colored ['fleʃkʌləd] adj color carne inv

fleshy ['fleʃɪ] adj (limb, fruit) carnoso(a)

flew [fluː] pt of **fly**

flex [fleks] vt flexionar; Fig **they are flexing their muscles** están haciendo una demostración de fuerza

flexibility [fleksɪ'bɪlɪtɪ] n flexibilidad f

flexible ['fleksɪbəl] adj flexible; **f. working hours** horario m de trabajo flexible

flexitime ['fleksɪtaɪm] n horario m flexible

flick [flɪk] **1** n (**a**) (movement) (of finger) toba f; **a f. of the wrist** (in tennis) un golpe de muñeca (**b**) Fam Old-fashioned **the flicks** (cinema) el cine

2 vt (with finger) dar una toba a; (with hands, tail) sacudir; **to f. a switch** pulsar un interruptor; **he flicked the cigarette ash onto the carpet** tiró or Am botó la ceniza del cigarrillo al suelo

▸**flick through** vt insep (book, magazine) hojear

flicker ['flɪkə(r)] **1** n parpadeo m; **a f. of hope** un rayo de esperanza; **a f. of interest** un atisbo de interés

2 vi (flame) parpadear

flier, flyer ['flaɪə(r)] n (**a**) (pilot) piloto mf (**b**) (leaflet) hoja f de propaganda (**c**) Fam (speculative venture) operación f arriesgada

flight [flaɪt] n (**a**) (act of flying) vuelo m; **it's two hours' f. from Seattle** está a dos horas de vuelo desde Seattle; Fig **a f. of fancy** un vuelo de la imaginación; Av **f. attendant** auxiliar mf de vuelo; Av **f. deck** (of plane) cabina f del piloto; Av **f. path** ruta f de vuelo; Av **f. recorder** caja f negra; Av **f. simulator** simulador m de vuelo (**b**) (group of birds) bandada f; (**c**) **f. (of stairs)** tramo m (de escalera); **two flights up from me** dos pisos más arriba (**d**) (escape) huida f, fuga f; **to put sb to f.** poner a alguien en fuga

flightless ['flaɪtlɪs] adj no volador(ora)

flighty ['flaɪtɪ] adj (fickle) inconstante, voluble

flimsily ['flɪmzɪlɪ] adv con poca solidez

flimsy ['flɪmzɪ] adj (structure, fence) endeble; (dress) ligero(a); (excuse, evidence) débil, flojo(a)

flinch [flɪntʃ] vi (with pain) encogerse; **to f. from (doing) sth** (shy away) echarse atrás a la hora de (hacer) algo

fling [flɪŋ] **1** n Fam (affair) aventura f

2 vt (pt & pp **flung** [flʌŋ]) arrojar; **to f. one's arms around sb** abrazar fuertemente a alguien; Fig **to f. oneself into a campaign** meterse de lleno en una campaña

▸**fling out** vt sep (object) tirar, Am botar; (person) echar

flint [flɪnt] n (stone) sílex m inv, pedernal m; (of lighter) piedra f

flinty ['flɪntɪ] adj (soil) silíceo(a); Fig (person) duro(a), despiadado(a); (manner) arisco(a)

flip [flɪp] **1** n **f. chart** flip chart m, pizarra f de conferencia (con bloc); Fam **the f. side** (of record) la cara B; Fig (of situation) la otra cara de la moneda; **f. top** tapa *f* abatible

2 *vt (pt & pp* **flipped) to f. the switch** dar al interruptor; **to f. a coin** lanzar una moneda al aire; *Fam* **to f. one's lid** *or* **wig** *(get angry)* ponerse hecho(a) una fiera, *Esp* cabrearse; *(go mad)* volverse loco *or Esp* majara

3 *vi Fam (get angry)* ponerse hecho(a) una fiera *or Méx* como agua para chocolate; *(go mad)* volverse loco *or Esp* majara

▸**flip through** *vt insep (book, magazine)* hojear, echar un vistazo a

flippant ['flɪpənt] *adj* frívolo(a)

flipper ['flɪpə(r)] *n* aleta *f*

flip-top ['flɪptɒp] *n* abertura *f* con anilla; **f. box** *(for cigarettes)* paquete *m* duro

flirt [flɜːt] **1** *n (man)* ligón *m*, mariposón *m*; *(woman)* ligona *f*, coqueta *f*

2 *vi* flirtear **(with** con), coquetear **(with** con); *Fig* **to f. with danger/an idea** coquetear con el peligro/una idea

flirtatious [flɜːˈteɪʃəs] *adj* coqueto(a)

flit [flɪt] *vi (pt & pp* **flitted) to f. about** *(bird)* revolotear; *Fig* **to f. from one thing to another** saltar de una cosa a otra

float [fləʊt] **1** *n* **(a)** *(on fishing line, net)* flotador *m*, corcho *m*; *(as swimming aid)* flotador *m* **(b)** *(vehicle in procession)* carroza *f*

2 *vt* **(a)** *(ship)* flotar **(b)** *(idea, proposal)* lanzar; **they decided to f. the company** *(on Stock Exchange)* decidieron que la empresa comenzara a cotizar en bolsa

3 *vi (in water, air)* flotar; *Fig* **she floated out of the room** se deslizó fuera de la habitación

floater ['fləʊtə(r)] *n (floating voter)* votante *mf* indeciso(a)

floating ['fləʊtɪŋ] *adj (object, exchange rate)* flotante; *(population)* fluctuante, flotante; *Pol (voter)* indeciso(a)

flock [flɒk] **1** *n (of sheep)* rebaño *m*; *(of birds)* bandada *f*; *Rel (congregation)* rebaño *m*, grey *f*; **a f. of tourists** un grupo multitudinario de turistas

2 *vi (gather)* acudir en masa

flog [flɒg] *(pt & pp* **flogged)** *vt (beat)* azotar; *Fam Fig* **you're flogging a dead horse** te estás esforzando inútilmente; *Fam* **to f. a subject to death** agotar completamente un tema

flogging ['flɒgɪŋ] *n (beating)* azote *m*, flagelación *f*; **he was given a f.** lo azotaron

flood [flʌd] **1** *n* inundación *f*; **the F.** *(in the Bible)* el diluvio (universal); **floods of tears** un mar de lágrimas

2 *vt (land, bathroom, market)* inundar; **to be flooded with complaints/telephone calls** recibir un aluvión de quejas/llamadas *or Am* llamados telefónicos

3 *vi (river)* desbordarse; **the sun's rays came flooding through the window** el sol entraba a raudales por la ventana; **the spectators flooded out of the stadium** los espectadores salían en masa del estadio; **money flooded out of the country** el dinero salió a raudales del país

flood-damaged ['flʌd'dæmɪdʒd] *adj* dañado(a) por inundaciones

floodgate ['flʌdgeɪt] *n* **to open the floodgates to sth** abrir las puertas de par en par a algo

flooding ['flʌdɪŋ] *n* inundaciones *fpl*

floodlight ['flʌdlaɪt] **1** *n* foco *m*

2 *vt (pt & pp* **floodlit** ['flʌdlɪt] *or* **floodlighted)** iluminar con focos

floodlit ['flʌdlɪt] *adj* iluminado(a) con focos

floor [flɔː(r)] **1** *n* **(a)** *(of room, forest)* suelo *m*; *(of Stock Exchange)* parquet *m*; *(of ocean)* fondo *m*; **to give sb the f.** *(in debate)* pasar *or* dar la palabra a alguien; **f. covering** revestimiento *m* para suelos; **f. lamp** lámpara *f* de pie; **f. plan** (plano *m* de) planta *f*; **f. show** espectáculo *m* de variedades; **f. space** superficie *f* comercial, superficie *f* de venta **(b)** *(story) (of building)* piso *m*, planta *f*

2 *vt (knock down)* derribar; *Fig* **the question floored him** la pregunta lo dejó perplejo

floorboard ['flɔːbɔːd] *n* tabla *f* del suelo *(de tarima)*

floozy, floozie ['fluːzɪ] *n Fam* pelandusca *f*

flop [flɒp] **1** *n (failure)* fracaso *m*

2 *vi (pt & pp* **flopped) (a)** *(fall)* dejarse caer **(b)** *(fail)* fracasar

floppy ['flɒpɪ] **1** *adj (ears)* caído(a); *(garments)* flojo(a); *Comptr* **f. disk** disquete *m*

2 *n Comptr* disquete *m*

flora ['flɔːrə] *n (plant life)* flora *f*

floral ['flɔːrəl] *adj* floral; **f. tribute** *(at funeral)* corona *f* de flores

Florence ['flɒrəns] *n* Florencia

florid ['flɒrɪd] *adj (style)* florido(a); *(complexion)* colorado(a)

florist ['flɒrɪst] *n* florista *mf*; **f.'s (shop)** floristería *f*

floss [flɒs] **1** *n* **(dental) f.** hilo *m* dental

2 *vt* **to f. one's teeth** limpiarse los dientes con hilo dental

flotation [fləʊˈteɪʃən] *n Com (of company)* salida *f* a bolsa

flotsam ['flɒtsəm] *n* **f. (and jetsam)** desechos *mpl* arrojados por el mar; *Fig* **the f. of the war/of society** los desechos de la guerra/de la sociedad

flounce [flaʊns] **1** *n (in sewing)* volante *m*, *Chile* vuelo *m*, *RP, Ven* volado *m*

2 *vi* **to f. in/out/off** entrar/salir/irse haciendo aspavientos

flounced [flaʊnst] *adj (skirt)* avolantado(a)

flounder ['flaʊndə(r)] **1** *n (fish)* platija *f*

2 *vi (in water, mud)* debatirse

flour ['flaʊə(r)] **1** *n* harina *f*

2 *vt* enharinar

flourish ['flʌrɪʃ] **1** *n (gesture)* ademán *m* florituresco; *(musical, in writing)* floritura *f*; *(in signature)* rúbrica *f*

2 *vt (brandish)* blandir

3 *vi (thrive) (plant, person)* crecer con vigor; *(business, arts)* florecer

flourishing ['flʌrɪʃɪŋ] *adj (plant)* vigoroso(a), lozano(a); *(business)* próspero(a), floreciente

floury ['flaʊrɪ] *adj (hands, surface)* lleno(a) de harina, enharinado(a); *(roll)* con harina encima; *(in texture)* harinoso(a)

flout [flaʊt] *vt (rule, sb's authority)* desobedecer

flow [fləʊ] **1** *n (of liquid)* flujo *m*; *Fig* **to follow the f. of an argument** seguir el hilo de un razonamiento; *Fig* **to go with the f.** seguir la corriente; **f. chart** organigrama *m*

2 *vi* **(a)** *(water)* correr, fluir; *Fig (ideas, conversation)* fluir; **to f. into the sea** *(river)* desembocar en el mar **(b)** **to f. from** *(be the result of)* derivarse de

flower ['flaʊə(r)] **1** *n* flor *f*; *Fig* **in the first f. of youth** en la flor de la juventud; **f. arranging** arte *m or* decoración *f* floral; **f. bed** parterre *m*; **f. garden** jardín *m* floral; **f. girl** = dama de honor de corta edad que lleva un ramo de flores en una boda; **f. power** movimiento *m* pacifista hippie; **f. seller** florista *mf*; **f. show** exposición *f* de flores

2 *vi (plant)* florecer

flowerpot ['flaʊəpɒt] *n* tiesto *m*, maceta *f*

flowery ['flaʊərɪ] *adj (fabric, dress)* floreado(a); *Fig (prose, compliments)* florido(a)

flowing ['fləʊɪŋ] *adj (hair, movement)* suelto(a)

flown [fləʊn] *pp of* **fly**

flu [fluː] *n* gripe *f*, *Am* gripa *f*; **a dose of the f.** una gripe *or Am* gripa

fluctuate ['flʌktjʊeɪt] *vi* fluctuar

fluctuating ['flʌktjʊeɪtɪŋ] *adj* fluctuante

fluctuation [flʌktjʊˈeɪʃən] *n* fluctuación *f*

flue [fluː] *n (of heater, chimney)* salida *f* de humos

fluency ['fluːənsɪ] *n* fluidez *f*; **f. in French required** *(in job advert)* se requiere dominio del francés

fluent ['fluːənt] *adj* **he is f. in French, he speaks f. French** habla francés con soltura

fluently ['fluːəntlɪ] *adv* con soltura

fluff [flʌf] **1** n pelusa f
2 vt Fam (botch) hacer muy mal; (lines) decir mal

fluffy ['flʌfɪ] adj esponjoso(a)

fluid ['fluːɪd] **1** n fluido m
2 adj fluido(a); **a f. situation** una situación inestable; **f. ounce** onza f líquida (29,6ml)

fluidity [fluːˈɪdɪtɪ] n fluidez f

fluke [fluːk] n Fam (stroke of luck) chiripa f; **by a f.** de chiripa

fluk(e)y ['fluːkɪ] adj Fam (lucky) suertudo(a)

flume [fluːm] n tobogán m

flummox ['flʌməks] vt Fam desconcertar

flung [flʌŋ] pt & pp of **fling**

flunk [flʌŋk] vt & vi Fam Esp catear, Am reprobar, Méx tronar, RP desaprobar

flunkey ['flʌŋkɪ] n Fam Pej lacayo m

fluorescent [fluəˈresənt] adj fluorescente; **f. light** (luz f) fluorescente m

fluoride ['fluəraɪd] n fluoruro m

flurry ['flʌrɪ] n also Fig torbellino m

flush [flʌʃ] **1** n (a) (beginning) **in the first f. of youth** en la primera juventud; **in the first f. of enthusiasm** en el primer momento de entusiasmo (b) (redness of face) rubor m, sonrojo m (c) (in cards) color m
2 adj (a) (even) **the door is f. with the wall** la puerta no sobresale de la pared (b) Fam **to be f. (with money)** (person) estar forrado(a) (de dinero)
3 vt (toilet) **to f. the toilet** tirar de la cadena
4 vi (a) (person) ruborizarse, sonrojarse (b) **the lavatory isn't flushing properly** la cisterna (del váter) no funciona bien
▸**flush out** vt sep (force to emerge) hacer salir

flushed [flʌʃd] adj (face) ruborizado(a); **f. with** (joy, pride) rebosante de; (success) enardecido(a) por

fluster ['flʌstə(r)] **1** vt poner nervioso(a), alterar
2 vi ponerse nervioso(a), alterarse

flute [fluːt] n (musical instrument) flauta f

flutist ['fluːtɪst] n Mus flautista mf

flutter ['flʌtə(r)] **1** n (of wings) aleteo m; (of eyelids) parpadeo m; Fig **in a f. of excitement** en un revuelo de emoción
2 vt **to f. its wings** (bird) batir las alas; **she fluttered her eyelashes at him** lo miró pestañeando con coquetería
3 vi (birds, insects) aletear

flux [flʌks] n **in a state of f.** en constante cambio

fly¹ [flaɪ] n (a) **f.** or **flies** (of pants) bragueta f (b) **f. sheet** (leaflet) hoja f de propaganda

fly² n (insect) mosca f; **he wouldn't hurt a f.** es incapaz de matar una mosca; **they were dropping like flies** caían como moscas; Fig **a f. in the ointment** un pero, Esp una pequeña pega; Fam Fig **there are no flies on him** se las sabe todas; **I wish I could be a f. on the wall** (at interview, meeting) me encantaría espiar por un agujerito

fly³ (pt flew [fluː], pp flown [fləʊn]) **1** vt (a) (plane) pilotar; (goods) mandar por avión; (route, distance) cubrir; **to f. Air India** volar con Air India (b) (kite) volar; **the ship/town hall was flying the Polish flag** la bandera polaca ondeaba en el barco/ayuntamiento; Fig **to f. the flag** (be patriotic) defender el pabellón (del propio país) (c) (flee) huir de, escapar de; Fig **to f. the nest** (child) volar del nido
2 vi (a) (bird, plane) volar; (passenger) ir en avión, volar; **to f. over Boston** sobrevolar Boston; **to f. across the Atlantic** cruzar el Atlántico en avión (b) (flag, hair) ondear (c) (move quickly) ir volando; **I must f.** tengo que salir volando; **the door flew open** la puerta se abrió de golpe; **to f. into a rage** enfurecerse; **to f. at sb** (attack) lanzarse sobre alguien; Fam **to send sth/sb flying** mandar algo/a alguien por los aires; **to f. in the face of reason** ir en contra de la razón
3 n (a) **f. ball** (in baseball) fly m, = bola golpeada hacia lo alto y a lo lojos (b) Fam **on the f.** (ball) por el aire; **to live on the f.** ir siempre escopeteado(a)

▸**fly away** vi (bird) salir volando; (papers) volarse

▸**fly in 1** vt sep (transport by aircraft) traer en avión
2 vi (arrive by aircraft) llegar en avión

flyaway ['flaɪəweɪ] adj (hair) suelto(a)

flyblown ['flaɪbləʊn] adj (a) (food) infestado(a) de moscarda (b) (shabby) mugriento(a)

flyby ['flaɪbaɪ] n desfile m aéreo

fly-by-night ['flaɪbaɪnaɪt] adj Fam Pej (company) nada fiable or Am confiable

flyer = **flier**

flying ['flaɪɪŋ] **1** n **she loves f.** le encanta volar; **f. club** aeroclub m; **f. lessons** lecciones fpl de vuelo; **f. time** horas fpl de vuelo
2 adj (a) (bird) volador(ora); **to pass an exam with f. colors** aprobar un examen con muy buena nota; Av **f. boat** hidroavión m; **f. fish** pez m volador; **f. saucer** platillo m volante (b) (visit) breve

flyleaf ['flaɪliːf] (pl flyleaves ['flaɪliːvz]) n (of book) guarda f

flypaper ['flaɪpeɪpə(r)] n papel m atrapamoscas

flyweight ['flaɪweɪt] n (in boxing) peso m mosca

FM [eˈfem] n Rad (abbr **frequency modulation**) FM f, frecuencia f modulada

foal [fəʊl] **1** n (horse) potro m, potrillo m
2 vi parir

foam [fəʊm] **1** n espuma f; **f. rubber** gomaespuma f
2 vi (sea, beer) hacer espuma; **to f. at the mouth** echar espuma por la boca

foamy ['fəʊmɪ], **foaming** ['fəʊmɪŋ] adj espumoso(a)

fob [fɒb] n cadena f (de reloj), leontina f; **f. watch** reloj m de bolsillo

▸**fob off** (pt & pp fobbed) vt sep Fam **to f. sb off with sth** quitarse a alguien de encima con algo; **to f. sth off on sb** colocarle or endilgarle algo a alguien

focaccia [fəˈkætʃə] n focaccia f

focal ['fəʊkəl] adj focal; **f. length** distancia f focal; **f. point** núcleo m, foco m de atención

focus ['fəʊkəs] **1** n (pl focuses or foci ['fəʊkaɪ]) (of lens, discontent, interest) foco m; **in f.** enfocado(a); **out of f.** desenfocado(a); Com & Pol **f. group** grupo m de discusión
2 vt (pt & pp focussed or focused) (rays of light) enfocar; (one's interest, energy) concentrar (on en); **all eyes were focused on him** todas las miradas estaban centradas en él
3 vi (with eyes) enfocar la vista (on en); Fig **to f. on sth** (debate, speaker) centrarse en algo

fodder ['fɒdə(r)] n (for animal) forraje m

foe [fəʊ] n enemigo(a) m,f

fog [fɒg] n niebla f; Fig **to be in a f.** (confused) estar hecho(a) un lío; Aut **f. light** or **lamp** faro m antiniebla

▸**fog up** (pt & pp fogged) vi (windows) empañarse

fogbound ['fɒgbaʊnd] adj (port, airport) paralizado(a) por la niebla

fogey = **fogy**

foggy ['fɒgɪ] adj neblinoso(a); **a f. day** un día de niebla; **it's f.** hay (mucha) niebla; Fam **I haven't (got) the foggiest (idea)!** no tengo ni la menor idea

foghorn ['fɒghɔːn] n (on ship) sirena f de niebla; **a voice like a f.** una voz estridente, un vozarrón

fogy ['fəʊgɪ] (pl fogies) n Fam **old f.** carroza mf, carcamán mf

foible ['fɔɪbəl] n manía f

foil [fɔɪl] **1** n (a) (metal paper) papel m de aluminio (b) **to act as a f. (to or for)** servir de contrapunto a (a or para) (c) (sword) florete m
2 vt (thwart) frustrar, malograr

foist [fɔɪst] vt imponer (on a)

fold¹ [fəʊld] n (sheep) **f.** redil m

fold² 1 *n* pliegue *m*

2 *vt (cloth, paper)* doblar; *(chair, table)* plegar; **to f. sth in two** *or* **in half** doblar algo por la mitad; **to f. one's arms** cruzarse de brazos

3 *vi* (**a**) *(chair, table)* plegarse (**b**) *Fam (business)* quebrar

▸**fold up 1** *vt sep* doblar

2 *vi (map, chair)* plegarse

-fold [fəʊld] *suffix* **it's a ten/twelve-f. increase** se ha multiplicado por diez/doce

folder ['fəʊldə(r)] *n (file, document wallet)* carpeta *f*; *(ring binder)* carpeta *f* de anillas

folding ['fəʊldɪŋ] *adj (chair, table)* plegable; **f. doors** puertas *fpl* plegables

foldout ['fəʊldaʊt] *n (in a book)* (página *f*) desplegable *m*

foliage ['fəʊlɪdʒ] *n* follaje *m*

folic acid ['fɒlɪk'æsɪd] *n* ácido *m* fólico

folio ['fəʊlɪəʊ] *(pl* **folios)** *n* folio *m*

folk [fəʊk] **1** *npl Fam (people)* gente *f*; **the f. I work with** la gente con la que trabajo; **my/your folks** *(family)* mi/tu familia, mi/tu gente; *(parents)* mis/tus padres

2 *adj (traditional)* **f. dance** baile *m* popular *or* regional; **f. (music)** música *f* folk *or* popular; **f. singer** cantante *mf* de folk; **f. song** canción *f* folk; **f. tale** cuento *m* popular

folklore ['fəʊklɔː(r)] *n* folclor *m*, folclore *m*

follicle ['fɒlɪkəl] *n* folículo *m*

follow ['fɒləʊ] **1** *vt* (**a**) *(person, path, route)* seguir; **I think we're being followed** creo que nos están siguiendo; **the road follows the coast** la carretera va a lo largo de la costa; **to f. one's nose** *(go straight ahead)* seguir todo recto; *(act instinctively)* guiarse por el instinto; **to f. suit** seguir el ejemplo (**b**) *(example, pattern, fashion, instructions)* seguir; *(career)* hacer, seguir (**c**) *(understand)* seguir; **I don't quite f. you** no te sigo bien (**d**) *(pay attention to)* seguir

2 *vi* (**a**) *(come after)* seguir; **proceed as follows** proceda de la siguiente forma (**b**) *(result)* **it follows that...** se sigue *or* deduce que...; **it follows from X that Y** de X se deduce que Y (**c**) *(understand)* entender; **I don't f.** no (lo) entiendo

▸**follow on** *vi* continuar, seguir; **to f. on from my earlier remarks...** a lo anteriormente dicho quisiera añadir *or Am* agregar...

▸**follow through 1** *vt sep* **to f. a project through (to the end)** llevar a cabo un proyecto (hasta el final)

2 *vi* llegar hasta el final

▸**follow up** *vt sep (advantage, success)* acrecentar; *(contact, job opportunity)* hacer un seguimiento de; **to f. up a clue** seguir una pista

follower ['fɒləʊə(r)] *n* seguidor(ora) *m,f*

following ['fɒləʊɪŋ] **1** *n (of team)* seguidores *mpl*; *(of politician, political party)* partidarios *mpl*; *(of TV program)* audiencia *f*; *(of novelist, pop group)* admiradores *mpl*

2 *pron* **the f. is the full list** a continuación figura la lista completa

3 *adj* siguiente; **on the f. day** al día siguiente; **a f. wind** un viento favorable *or* a favor

follow-the-leader ['fɒləʊðə'liːdə(r)] *n* = juego en el que los participantes han de imitar lo que hace el primero de la fila

follow-through ['fɒləʊθruː] *n Sport (of stroke)* acompañamiento *m* (del golpe)

follow-up ['fɒləʊʌp] *n Com* seguimiento *m*

folly ['fɒlɪ] *n* locura *f*

foment [fə'ment] *vt (unrest, ill-feeling)* fomentar

fond [fɒnd] *adj* (**a**) **to be f. of sb** *(like)* tenerle cariño a alguien; **to become f. of sb** encariñarse con alguien; **she was f. of the occasional whiskey** le gustaba tomarse un whisky de vez en cuando (**b**) *(loving)* cariñoso(a); **f. memories** recuerdos *mpl* entrañables (**c**) *(hope, belief)* vano(a)

fondant ['fɒndənt] *n* fondant *m*

fondle ['fɒndəl] *vt* acariciar

fondly ['fɒndlɪ] *adv* (**a**) *(lovingly)* cariñosamente (**b**) *(naively)* **to f. imagine that...** creer ingenuamente que...

fondness ['fɒndnɪs] *n* (**a**) *(affection)* cariño *m* (**for** por), afecto *m* (**for** por) (**b**) *(liking)* afición *f* (**for** a), gusto *m* (**for** por)

fondue ['fɒnduː] *n* fondue *f*

font [fɒnt] *n* (**a**) *Rel* pila *f* bautismal (**b**) *Typ & Comptr* fuente *f*

food [fuːd] *n* comida *f*; **f. and drink** comida y bebida; **to be off one's f.** andar desganado(a); **to give sb f. for thought** servir a alguien como materia de reflexión; *Biol* **f. chain** cadena *f* alimentaria; **f. court** = plaza o zona de un centro comercial dedicada al consumo de comida rápida; **f. industry** industria *f* alimentaria; **f. poisoning** intoxicación *f* alimentaria; **f. processor** robot *m* de cocina

foodie ['fuːdɪ] *n Fam* sibarita *mf* de la cocina

foodstuffs ['fuːdstʌfs] *npl* alimentos *mpl*

fool [fuːl] **1** *n (stupid person)* idiota *mf*; *(jester)* bufón *m*; **to play** *or* **act the f.** hacer el tonto; **to make a f. of sb** poner a alguien en ridículo; **to make a f. of oneself** hacer el ridículo; **I felt such a f.** me sentí como un tonto; **she's no** *or* **nobody's f.** no tiene un pelo de tonta; **they're living in a f.'s paradise** viven en las nubes

2 *vt (deceive)* engañar; **to f. sb into doing sth** engañar a alguien para que haga algo; **you can't f. me** a mí no me engañas; **he's an expert? you could have fooled me!** ¿que es un experto? ¡quién lo hubiera dicho!

3 *vi (act foolishly)* hacer el tonto *or* el indio; **stop fooling!** ¡deja de hacer el tonto!; **I was only fooling** estaba de broma

▸**fool around** *vi* (**a**) *(act foolishly)* hacer el tonto *or* el indio; **to f. around with sth** enredar con algo (**b**) *(waste time)* perder el tiempo (**c**) *Fam (have affair)* tener una aventura (**with** con)

foolhardy ['fuːlhɑːdɪ] *adj* temerario(a)

foolish ['fuːlɪʃ] *adj (stupid)* tonto(a); *(imprudent)* absurdo(a), imprudente; **to do sth f.** hacer una tontería; **to make sb look f.** dejar a alguien en ridículo

foolishly ['fuːlɪʃlɪ] *adv (act)* irreflexivamente

foolproof ['fuːlpruːf] *adj (method, plan)* infalible

foosball ['fuːzbɔːl] *n* fútbol *m* de mesa, *Esp* futbolín *m*, *Arg* metegol *m*, *Chile* taca-taca *m*, *Méx*, *Urug* futbolito *m*

foot [fʊt] *(pl* **feet** [fiːt]) **1** *n* (**a**) *(of person)* pie *m*; *(of animal, chair)* pata *f*; *(of bed)* **f. up** *(rest)* descansar; **to set f. in/on** poner los pies en; **she is on her feet all day** se pasa el día entero de pie *or Am* parada; **to be on one's feet again** *(after illness)* estar recuperado(a); **on f.** a pie, caminando, *Esp* andando; **it was wet under f.** el suelo estaba mojado; **f. bath** baño *m* de pies; *Mil* **f. patrol** patrulla *f* de infantería; **f. pump** bomba *f* de pie; **f. soldier** soldado *mf* de infantería (**b**) *(lower part) (of mountain, stairs, page)* pie *m* (**c**) *(in poetry)* pie *m* (**d**) *(measurement)* pie *m* *(30,48 cm)*; **three f.** *or* **feet six (inches)** tres pies y seis pulgadas *(1,06 m)*; **at 2,000 feet** a dos mil pies *(609,6 m)* (**e**) *(idioms)* **to have one's feet firmly on the ground** tener los pies en la tierra; **to have one f. in the grave** tener un pie en la tumba; **she hasn't put a f. wrong** no ha cometido un solo error; **to put one's f. down** *(be firm) Esp* ponerse serio(a), *Am* no ceder; *(refuse)* negarse *Esp* en redondo *or Am* en rotundamente; *Fam* **to put one's f. in it** meter la pata; **to find one's feet** *(in new surroundings, activity)* familiarizarse; **the job's not much, but it's a f. in the door** el trabajo no es gran cosa, pero supone un primer paso; **to have feet of clay** tener (los) pies de barro; *Fam* **my f.!** ¡ni loco!, *Esp* ¡y un jamón!, *Méx* ¡ni yendo a bailar a Chalma!, *RP* ¡tu abuela!

2 *vt* **to f. the bill** pagar la cuenta

footage ['fʊtɪdʒ] *n Cin* secuencias *fpl*

foot-and-mouth disease [fʊtən'maʊθdɪ'ziːz] *n* glosopeda *f*, fiebre *f* aftosa

football ['fotbɔːl] *n* fútbol *m* americano; *(ball)* balón *m* (de fútbol americano); **f. fan** hincha *mf*, forofo(a) *m,f*; **f. player** futbolista *mf*, jugador(ora) *m,f* de fútbol americano; **f. stadium** estadio *m* de fútbol americano; **f. supporter** hincha *mf*, forofo(a) *m,f*; **f. team** equipo *m* (de fútbol americano)

footbridge ['fotbrɪdʒ] *n* puente *m* peatonal

footer ['fotə(r)] *n Comptr & Typ* pie *m* de página

-footer ['fotə(r)] *suffix* **the boat is a 15-f.** la barca mide seis pies de eslora

foothills ['fothɪlz] *npl* estribaciones *fpl*

foothold ['fothəʊld] *n* punto *m* de apoyo; *Fig* **to gain a f.** afianzarse

footing ['fotɪŋ] *n* **(a) to lose one's f.** *(on hill, ladder)* perder el equilibrio **(b) on an equal f.** de igual a igual; **to be on a friendly f. with sb** tener relaciones amistosas con alguien

footlights ['fotlaɪts] *npl Theat* candilejas *fpl*

footloose ['fotluːs] *adj* libre de ataduras; **to be f. and fancy-free** ser libre como el viento

footman ['fotmən] *n* lacayo *m*

footnote ['fotnəʊt] *n* nota *f* a pie de página

footpath ['fotpɑːθ] *n* sendero *m*, senda *f*

footprint ['fotprɪnt] *n* huella *f*, pisada *f*

footrest ['fotrest] *n (under desk, on motorcycle)* reposapiés *m inv*

footsie ['fotsɪ] *n Fam* **to play f. with sb** = acariciar a alguien con el pie por debajo de la mesa

footsore ['fotsɔː(r)] *adj* con los pies doloridos

footstep ['fotstep] *n* paso *m*; *Fig* **to follow in sb's footsteps** seguir los pasos de alguien

footstool ['fotstuːl] *n* escabel *m*, reposapiés *m inv*

footwear ['fotweə(r)] *n* calzado *m*

footwork ['fotwɜːk] *n (in dancing, sports)* juego *m* de piernas; *Fig* **fancy f.** *(in difficult situation)* malabarismos *mpl*

fop [fɒp] *n Pej* petimetre *m*

foppish ['fɒpɪʃ] *adj Pej* peripuesto(a)

for [fɔː(r), *unstressed* fə(r)] **1** *prep* **(a)** *(reason)* por; **they chose him f. his looks** lo eligieron por su aspecto; **she couldn't sleep f. the pain** no pudo dormir a causa del dolor

(b) *(purpose, destination)* para; **to leave f. France** salir hacia *or* para Francia; **there's no time f. that** no hay tiempo para eso; **it's f. you** es para ti; **what's it f.?** ¿para qué es?; **can you give me something f. the pain?** ¿me puede dar algo para el dolor?

(c) *(in exchange for)* **I bought it f. $10** lo compré por 10 dólares; **you get a lot f. your money** el dinero te da mucho de sí

(d) *(with regard to)* para; **he is big f. his age** es grande para su edad; **as f. him/that,...** en cuanto a él/eso,...; **they sell ten red bikes f. every black one** se venden diez bicicletas de color rojo por cada una de color negro

(e) *(representing)* **A f. Andrew** A de Andrés; **what's the Russian f. "book"?** ¿cómo se dice "libro" en ruso?

(f) *(duration)* durante; **I was there f. a month** pasé un mes allí; **I've been here f. a month** llevo *or* Am tengo un mes aquí; **I will be here f. a month** voy a pasar un mes aquí; **I haven't been there f. a month** hace un mes que no voy (por allí); **we have enough food f. two days** tenemos comida suficiente para dos días

(g) *(point in time)* **f. the first/last time** por primera/última vez; **I need it f. Friday** lo necesito (para) el viernes; **can you do it f. next Monday?** ¿lo puedes hacer para el lunes que viene?

(h) *(in favor of)* **to be f. sth** estar absolutamente a favor de algo; *Fam* **I'm all f. it!** ¡estoy absolutamente a favor!

(i) *(introducing an infinitive clause)* **it is too early f. me to decide** es demasiado pronto para decidirme; **it will be difficult/easy f. her to come** lo va a tener difícil/fácil para

venir; **it took an hour f. us to get there** tardamos *or Am* demoramos una hora en llegar

(j) *(in phrases) Fam* **he's f. it!** ¡se la va a cargar!, *RP* ¡se va a ligar una!; **f. all the good it will do!** ¡para lo que va a servir!; **f. all his wealth, he was still unhappy** a pesar de todo su dinero, no era feliz; **that's men f. you!** ¡los hombres, ya se sabe!

2 *conj Literary (because)* dado que

forage ['fɒrɪdʒ] **1** *n (animal food)* forraje *m*; *Mil* **f. cap** gorra *f* militar

2 *vi* **to f. for** buscar

foray ['fɒreɪ] *n* incursión *f* **(into** en)

forbade, forbad *pt of* **forbid**

forbear [fɔː'beə(r)] **1** *vi (pt* **forbore** [fɔː'bɔː(r)], *pp* **forborne** [fɔː'bɔːn]) *Formal* **to f. from doing sth** abstenerse de hacer algo, contenerse para no hacer algo

2 *n =* **forebear**

forbearance [fɔː'beərəns] *n* paciencia *f*, tolerancia *f*

forbid [fə'bɪd] *(pt* **forbade** [fə'bæd, fə'beɪd] *or* **forbad** [fə'bæd], *pp* **forbidden** [fə'bɪdən]) *vt* prohibir; **to f. sb to do sth** prohibir a alguien que haga algo; **God f.!** ¡Dios no lo quiera!

forbidden [fə'bɪdən] *adj* prohibido(a); **smoking/talking (is) f.** (está) prohibido fumar/hablar

forbidding [fə'bɪdɪŋ] *adj (appearance, look)* severo(a); *(sky)* amenazador(ora); *(landscape)* agreste; *(task)* dificultoso(a)

forbore [fɔː'beə(r)] *pt of* **forbear**

forborne [fɔː'bɔːn] *pp of* **forbear**

force [fɔːs] **1** *n* **(a)** *(strength, violence)* fuerza *f*; **to use f.** emplear la fuerza; **by sheer** *or* **brute f.** por la fuerza

(b) *(power, influence)* fuerza *f*; **the forces of Nature** las fuerzas de la naturaleza; **a f. for good** una fuerza del bien; **f. of circumstance(s)** causas *fpl* de fuerza mayor; **the f. of gravity** la fuerza de la gravedad; **f. of habit** la fuerza de la costumbre; **various forces conspired to bring about his downfall** diversas causas contribuyeron a su caída

(c) *Mil* fuerza *f*; **the (armed) forces** las fuerzas armadas; **the police f.** la policía, el cuerpo de policía; **to join forces (to do sth)** unir fuerzas (para hacer algo); **they turned out in (full) f.** se presentaron en gran número

(d) *(of law)* **to come into f.** entrar en vigor

2 *vt* **(a)** *(compel)* **to f. sb to do sth** *or* **into doing sth** forzar a alguien a hacer algo; **they forced the enemy back** obligaron a retroceder al enemigo; **to f. sth on sb** imponer algo a alguien **(b)** *(use force on) (door, lock)* forzar; **to f. the issue** acelerar las cosas; **to f. sb's hand** forzar a alguien a tomar una decisión; **to f. a car off the road** obligar a un coche a salirse de la carretera; **to f. one's way through a crowd** abrirse paso a través de una multitud; **to f. oneself on sb** *(sexually)* intentar forzar a alguien

▸**force open** *vt sep* forzar

forced [fɔːst] *adj (manner, laugh)* forzado(a); **f. labor** trabajos *mpl* forzados; *Av* **f. landing** aterrizaje *m* forzoso; *Mil* **f. march** marcha *f* forzada

force-feed ['fɔːsfiːd] *(pt & pp* **force-fed** ['fɔːsfed]) *vt* dar de comer a la fuerza

forceful ['fɔːsfol] *adj (person, argument)* poderoso(a)

forceps ['fɔːseps] *npl Med* fórceps *m inv*

forcible ['fɔːsɪbəl] *adj (reminder)* contundente; *Law* **f. entry** allanamiento *m* de morada, *Am* invasión *f* de domicilio

forcibly ['fɔːsɪblɪ] *adv* **(a)** *(by force)* por la fuerza **(b)** *(convincingly)* de manera contundente

ford [fɔːd] **1** *n* vado *m*

2 *vt* vadear

fore [fɔː(r)] **1** *n* **to come to the f.** cobrar importancia

2 *adv Naut* **they searched the ship f. and aft** registraron el barco de proa a popa

forearm ['fɔ:rɑ:m] n antebrazo m

forebear, forbear ['fɔ:beə(r)] n antepasado(a) m,f, ancestro m

foreboding [fɔ:'bəʊdɪŋ] n presentimento m ominoso

forecast ['fɔ:kɑ:st] **1** n pronóstico m; Com previsión f; **the (weather) f.** (prediction) el pronóstico meteorológico; (program) el parte meteorológico, el tiempo
2 vt (pt & pp **forecast(ed)**) pronosticar

foreclose [fɔ:'kləʊz] vt Fin **to f. a mortgage** ejecutar una hipoteca

forecourt ['fɔ:kɔ:t] n (of gas station) explanada f delantera

forefathers ['fɔ:fɑ:ðəz] npl ancestros mpl

forefinger ['fɔ:fɪŋgə(r)] n (dedo m) índice m

forefront ['fɔ:frʌnt] n **to be in the f. (of)** estar a la vanguardia (de)

foregone = **forgone**

foregone ['fɔ:gɒn] **1** adj **the result was a f. conclusion** el resultado ya se conocía de antemano
2 pp of **forgone**

foreground ['fɔ:graʊnd] **1** n primer plano m; **in the f.** (in picture) en primer plano; (issue, person) en primer plano de actualidad, en el candelero
2 vt poner de relieve

forehand ['fɔ:hænd] n (tennis stroke) derecha f

forehead ['fɒrɪd, 'fɔ:hed] n frente f

foreign ['fɒrɪn] adj (a) (from another country) extranjero(a); **f. aid** (to another country) ayuda f al exterior; (from another country) ayuda f extranjera or del exterior; Pol **f. affairs** política f exterior, asuntos mpl exteriores; Journ **f. correspondent** corresponsal mf (en el extranjero); Econ **f. debt** deuda f exterior or externa; Mil **F. Legion** legión f extranjera; Econ **f. trade** comercio m exterior **(b)** (not characteristic of) ajeno(a); Med **f. body** cuerpo m extraño

foreigner ['fɒrɪnə(r)] n extranjero(a) m,f

foreleg ['fɔ:leg] n pata f delantera

foreman ['fɔ:mən] n Ind encargado m; (of jury) presidente m, portavoz m

foremost ['fɔ:məʊst] adj principal

forename ['fɔ:neɪm] n nombre m (de pila)

forensic [fə'rensɪk] adj Law forense; **f. evidence** pruebas fpl forenses; **f. medicine** medicina f forense; **f. scientist** forense mf

foreplay ['fɔ:pleɪ] n juego m amoroso (antes del coito)

forerunner ['fɔ:rʌnə(r)] n predecesor(ora) m,f

foresee [fɔ:'si:] (pt **foresaw** [fɔ:'sɒ], pp **foreseen** [fɔ:'si:n]) vt prever

foreseeable [fɔ:'si:əbəl] adj previsible; **in the f. future** en un futuro próximo or no muy lejano

foreseen pp of **foresee**

foreshadow [fɔ:'ʃædəʊ] vt presagiar, anunciar

foresight ['fɔ:saɪt] n previsión f; **lack of f.** falta f de previsión

foreskin ['fɔ:skɪn] n Anat prepucio m

forest ['fɒrɪst] n bosque m; Fig **she can't see the f. for the trees** los árboles no le dejan ver el bosque; **f. fire** incendio m forestal

forestall [fɔ:'stɔ:l] vt (attempt, criticism, rivals) anticiparse a, adelantarse a

forester ['fɒrɪstə(r)] n guardabosque mf, guarda mf forestal

forestry ['fɒrɪstrɪ] n silvicultura f; **f. worker** trabajador(ora) m,f forestal

foretaste ['fɔ:teɪst] n anticipo m

foretell [fɔ:'tel] (pt & pp **foretold** [fɔ:'təʊld]) vt predecir

forethought ['fɔ:θɔ:t] n previsión f

foretold [fɔ:'təʊld] pt & pp of **foretell**

forever [fə'revə(r)] **1** n Fam **to take f. (to do sth)** tardar un siglo (en hacer algo), Am demorar una eternidad (en hacer algo)
2 adv (until end of time) para siempre; (repeatedly) constantemente; **he was f. changing his mind** siempre estaba cambiando de opinión

forewarn [fɔ:'wɔ:n] vt advertir; Prov **forewarned is forearmed** hombre prevenido vale por dos

forewent pt of **forego**

foreword ['fɔ:wɜ:d] n prólogo m

forfeit ['fɔ:fɪt] n **1** (in game) prenda f; Law sanción f
2 vt (right, property, sb's respect) renunciar a, sacrificar

forfeiture ['fɔ:fɪtʃə(r)] n pérdida f

forgave [fə'geɪv] pt of **forgive**

forge [fɔ:dʒ] **1** n (factory) fundición f; (of blacksmith) forja f, fragua f
2 vt (a) (metal, alliance) forjar (b) (counterfeit) falsificar

▶**forge ahead** vi (make progress) progresar a pasos agigantados; (in competition) tomar la delantera

forged [fɔ:dʒd] adj (banknote, letter) falso(a), falsificado(a)

forgery ['fɔ:dʒərɪ] n falsificación f; **it's a f.** es una falsificación

forget [fə'get] (pt **forgot** [fə'gɒt], pp **forgotten** [fə'gɒtən]) **1** vt olvidar; **to f. to do sth** olvidarse de hacer algo; **to f. how to do sth** olvidar cómo se hace algo; **to be forgotten (by)** caer en el olvido (de); Fam **f. it!** (in reply to apology) olvídalo; (in reply to thanks) no hay de qué; (stop talking about it) dejémoslo; Fam **you can f. the vacation** ya puedes decir adiós a las vacaciones
2 vi olvidarse (**about** de); **before I f.** antes de que se me olvide; **let's f. about it** olvidémoslo

forgetful [fə'getfʊl] adj olvidadizo(a)

forget-me-not [fə'getmɪnɒt] n nomeolvides m inv

forgettable [fə'getəbəl] adj poco memorable

forgivable [fə'gɪvəbəl] adj perdonable

forgivably [fə'gɪvəblɪ] adv comprensiblemente

forgive [fə'gɪv] (pt **forgave** [fə'geɪv], pp **forgiven** [fə'gɪvən])
1 vt perdonar; **to f. sb (for sth)** perdonar (algo) a alguien
2 vi **to f. and forget** perdonar y olvidar

forgiveness [fə'gɪvnɪs] n perdón m; **to ask (sb) for f.** pedir perdón (a alguien)

forgiving [fə'gɪvɪŋ] adj indulgente

forgo, forego [fɔ:'gəʊ] (pt **for(e)went** [fɔ:'went], pp **for(e)gone** [fɔ:'gɒn]) vt renunciar a

forgot [fə'gɒt] pt of **forget**

forgotten [fə'gɒtən] pp of **forget**

fork [fɔ:k] **1** n (a) (for food) tenedor m, Am trinche m (b) (for lifting hay) horca f (c) (in road) bifurcación f; **take the left f.** tomar el desvío a or de la izquierda
2 vi (road) bifurcarse

▶**fork out** Fam **1** vt sep (money) aflojar, Esp apoquinar, RP garpar
2 vi aflojar, Esp apoquinar, RP garpar (**for** por)

forked [fɔ:kt] adj (tongue) bífido(a); (stick) bifurcado(a); **f. lightning** relámpagos mpl (bifurcados)

fork-lift ['fɔ:klɪft] n **f. (truck)** carretilla f elevadora

forlorn [fə'lɔ:n] adj (place) abandonado(a); (look) desamparado(a); (belief, attempt) desesperado(a); **in the f. hope that...** con la vana esperanza de que...

form [fɔ:m] **1** n (a) (shape) forma f; **in the f. of...** en forma de...; **to take the f. of...** consistir en...; **f. and content** forma y fondo or contenido (b) (type) **it's a f. of madness** es una forma de locura; **a f. of address** una fórmula de tratamiento (c) (formality) **as a matter of f., for f.'s sake** por guardar las formas; **it's good/bad f.** es de buena/mala educación (d) (for applications, orders) impreso m, formulario m, Méx forma f; **to fill in** or **out a f.** rellenar un impreso (e) (condition) forma f (física); **to be in (good) f.** estar en (buena) forma (f) (recent performances) (of athlete, player, team) forma f; (in horseracing) reciente historial m
2 vt (in general) formar; (relationship, friendship) establecer;

(plan) concebir; *(obstacle)* constituir; **to f. an idea/opinion** formarse una idea/una opinión; **to f. part of sth** formar parte de algo

   3 *vi* formarse

formal ['fɔːməl] *adj (manner, offer)* formal; **f. dress** traje *m* de etiqueta; **f. education** formación *f* académica

formality [fɔː'mælɪtɪ] *n* formalidad *f*

formalize ['fɔːməlaɪz] *vt* formalizar

formally ['fɔːməlɪ] *adv (with formality)* formalmente; *(officially)* oficialmente

format ['fɔːmæt] **1** *n* formato *m*

   2 *vt (pt & pp* **formatted)** *Comptr* formatear

formation [fɔː'meɪʃən] *n (act, arrangement)* formación *f*; **f. flying** vuelo *m* en formación

formative ['fɔːmətɪv] *adj* formativo(a); **the f. years** el periodo en que se forja la personalidad

formatting ['fɔːmætɪŋ] *n Comptr (of text)* formato *m*

former ['fɔːmə(r)] **1** *adj (pupil, colleague)* antiguo(a); **in a f. life** en una vida anterior; **he is a mere shadow of his f. self** no es más que una sombra de lo que fue

   2 *pron* **the f.** el/la primero(a); *(plural)* los/las primeros(as)

formerly ['fɔːməlɪ] *adv* antiguamente

formidable ['fɔːmɪdəbəl] *adj (opponent, difficulty)* terrible; *(performance, talent)* formidable

formidably ['fɔːmɪdəblɪ] *adv (difficult)* tremendamente; *(talented, thorough)* extraordinariamente

formula ['fɔːmjʊlə] *(pl* **formulas** *or* **formulae** ['fɔːmjʊliː]) *n* **(a)** *(in general)* fórmula *f*; **the f. for success** la clave del éxito; **a peace/pay f.** una fórmula para la paz/de pago; *Sport* **F. One** Fórmula *f* uno **(b)** *(baby milk)* leche *f* maternizada

formulaic [fɔːmjʊ'leɪɪk] *adj* formulario(a)

formulate ['fɔːmjʊleɪt] *vt* formular

fornication [fɔːnɪ'keɪʃən] *n Formal* fornicación *f*

forsake [fə'seɪk] *(pt* **forsook** [fə'sʊk]*, pp* **forsaken** [fə'seɪkən]) *vt Literary* abandonar

forswear [fɔː'sweə(r)] *(pt* **forswore** [fɔː'swɔː(r)]*, pp* **forsworn** [fɔː'swɔːn]) *vt Formal* renunciar a

fort [fɔːt] *n Mil* fortaleza *f*, fuerte *m*; *Fig* **to hold the f.** quedarse al cargo

forte ['fɔːtɪ] *n* fuerte *m*; **punctuality is not his f.** la puntualidad no es su fuerte

forth [fɔːθ] *adv* **to go f.** partir; **and so f.** y así sucesivamente; **to walk back and f.** ir de aquí para allá; **from that day f.** a partir de ese día

forthcoming [fɔːθ'kʌmɪŋ] *adj* **(a)** *(imminent) (election)* próximo(a); *(book)* de próxima aparición **(b)** *(available)* **no money/help was f.** no había dinero/ayuda disponible **(c)** *(informative)* comunicativo(a)

forthright ['fɔːθraɪt] *adj* directo(a), franco(a)

forthwith [fɔːθ'wɪθ] *adv Formal* en el acto

fortieth ['fɔːtɪəθ] *n & adj* cuadragésimo(a) *m,f*

fortification [fɔːtɪfɪ'keɪʃən] *n* fortificación *f*

fortified ['fɔːtɪfaɪd] *adj (a) (town)* fortificado(a) **(b) f. wine** = vino fuerte tipo Oporto o Jerez

fortify ['fɔːtɪfaɪ] *vt Mil* fortificar; **to f. oneself** fortalecerse

fortitude ['fɔːtɪtjuːd] *n* fortaleza *f*, entereza *f*

fortnight ['fɔːtnaɪt] *n* quincena *f*; **a f. today** en quince días; **a f.'s vacation** quince días de vacaciones

fortnightly ['fɔːtnaɪtlɪ] **1** *adj* quincenal

   2 *adv* quincenalmente, cada quince días

fortress ['fɔːtrɪs] *n* fortaleza *f*

fortuitous [fɔː'tjuːɪtəs] *adj* casual, fortuito(a)

fortunate ['fɔːtʃənət] *adj* afortunado(a); **to be f. enough to do sth** tener la suerte de hacer algo

fortunately ['fɔːtʃənətlɪ] *adv* afortunadamente

fortune ['fɔːtʃən] *n* **(a)** *(riches)* fortuna *f*; **to make a** *or* **one's f.**

hacer una fortuna; *Fam* **it cost me a (small) f.** me ha costado una fortuna **(b)** *(luck)* suerte *f*, fortuna *f*; **good/bad f.** buena/mala suerte; **the changing fortunes of . . .** los avatares de . . .; **to tell sb's f.** decir a alguien la buenaventura; **f. cookie** galleta *f* de la suerte

fortune-teller ['fɔːtʃəntelə(r)] *n* adivino(a) *m,f*

forty ['fɔːtɪ] **1** *n* cuarenta *m*

   2 *adj* cuarenta; *Fam* **to have f. winks** echarse una siestecita; *see also* **eighty**

forum ['fɔːrəm] *n* foro *m*; **a f. for debate** un foro de debate

forward ['fɔːwəd] **1** *n Sport* delantero(a) *m,f*

   2 *adj* **(a)** *(position)* delantero(a); *(movement)* hacia delante; *Fin* **f. market** mercado *m* de futuros; **f. planning** planificación *f* (de futuro); **f. roll** *(in gymnastics)* voltereta *f* hacia adelante **(b)** *(impudent, bold)* atrevido(a)

   3 *adv* **(a)** *(of time)* **from this/that day f.** desde este/ese día en adelante; **to put the clocks f.** adelantar los relojes **(b)** *(of direction)* hacia delante **(c)** *(of position)* delante; **we're too far f.** estamos demasiado delante

   4 *vt* **(a)** *(letter)* reexpedir, remitir; **to f. sth to sb** enviar algo a alguien **(b)** *(one's career, interests)* promover

forwarding agent ['fɔːwədɪŋ'eɪdʒənt] *n Com* transitario(a) *m,f*

forward-looking ['fɔːwədlʊkɪŋ] *adj* con visión de futuro, progresista

forwards ['fɔːwədz] *adv* = **forward**

forwent ['fɔːwədz] *adv* = **forewent**

fossil ['fɒs(ɪ)l] *n* fósil *m*; *Fam* **an old f.** *(person)* un carcamal *or Am* carcamán; **f. fuel** combustible *m* fósil

fossilized ['fɒsɪlaɪzd] *adj also Fig* fosilizado(a)

foster ['fɒstə(r)] **1** *adj* **f. child** niño(a) *m,f* en régimen de acogida; **f. parents** familia *f* de acogida; **f. home** hogar *m* de acogida

   2 *vt* **(a)** *(child)* adoptar (temporalmente), acoger **(b)** *(idea, hope, friendship)* fomentar

fostering ['fɒstərɪŋ] *n* acogida *f* familiar *(de un niño)*

fought [fɔːt] *pt & pp of* **fight**

foul [faʊl] **1** *n Sport* falta *f*

   2 *adj* **(a)** *(disgusting) (smell, taste)* asqueroso(a); *(weather)* espantoso(a); **to be in a f. temper** estar de un humor de perros; **to be f. to sb** tratar muy mal *or Esp* fatal a alguien; **f. air** aire *m* viciado; **f. breath** aliento *m* fétido; **f. language** lenguaje *m* soez **(b)** *(illegal) Sport* **f. play** juego *m* sucio; *Law* **f. play is not suspected** no hay sospecha de que exista un acto delictivo

   3 *adv* **(a)** **to smell/taste f.** oler/saber asqueroso(a) *or Esp* fatal **(b)** **to fall f. of the law** tener problemas con la ley

   4 *vt* **(a)** *(make dirty)* ensuciar; *(pollute)* contaminar **(b)** *(entangle)* **weeds had fouled the propeller** unas algas atascaron la hélice **(c)** *Sport* **to f. sb** hacerle (una) falta a alguien

▸**foul up** *vt sep Fam (ruin)* echar a perder, estropear

foul-mouthed ['faʊlmaʊðd] *adj* grosero(a), soez

foul-up ['faʊlʌp] *n Fam* metedura *f or Am* metida *f* de pata

found[1] [faʊnd] *vt* **(a)** *(city, organization)* fundar **(b)** *(suspicions, hope)* fundar, basar (**on** en); **the story is founded on fact** la historia se basa en hechos reales

found[2] *pt & pp of* **find**

foundation [faʊn'deɪʃən] *n* **(a)** *(act of founding, institution)* fundación *f* **(b)** *(basis) (of theory, belief)* fundamento *m*; **the rumor is without f.** el rumor no tiene fundamento **(c)** *Constr* **the foundations** los cimientos; *Fig* **the foundations of modern society** los pilares de la sociedad moderna; *Univ* **f. course** curso *m* introductorio *or* de iniciación; **f. stone** primera piedra *f* **(d)** *(make-up)* **f. (cream)** (crema *f* de) base *f*

founder[1] ['faʊndə(r)] *n (of hospital, school)* fundador(ora) *m,f*

founder[2] *vi (project, talks)* irse a pique (**on** en)

founding father [ˈfaʊndɪŋˈfɑːðə(r)] *n* padre *m* fundador

foundling [ˈfaʊndlɪŋ] *n Old-fashioned* expósito(a) *m,f*

foundry [ˈfaʊndrɪ] *n* fundición *f*

fount [faʊnt] *n Literary & Fig* fuente *f*

fountain [ˈfaʊntɪn] *n* fuente *f*; **f. pen** pluma *f* (estilográfica), *CSur* lapicera *f* fuente

four [fɔː(r)] **1** *n* cuatro *m*; **on all fours** a gatas, a cuatro patas
  2 *adj* cuatro; **the f. winds** los cuatro vientos; **to the f. corners of the earth** a todos los rincones del orbe; *see also* **eight**

four-by-four [ˈfɔːbaɪˈfɔː(r)] *n (vehicle)* todoterreno *m*

four-door [ˈfɔːdɔː(r)] *n* de cuatro puertas; **f. sedan** berlina *f*; **f. hatchback** cinco puertas *m*

four-eyes [ˈfɔːraɪz] *n Fam* cuatro ojos *mf inv, Esp* gafotas *mf inv, Méx* cuatro lámparas *mf inv*

four-figure [ˈfɔːˈfɪɡə(r)] *adj* de cuatro cifras; **a f. sum** una suma de dinero de cuatro cifras

fourfold [ˈfɔːfəʊld] **1** *adj* **a f. increase (in)** cuatro veces más (de)
  2 *adv* cuatro veces

four-legged [ˈfɔːˈleɡɪd] *adj* cuadrúpedo(a); *Hum* **f. friend** amigo *m* cuadrúpedo

four-letter word [ˈfɔːletəˈwɜːd] *n* palabrota *f, Esp* taco *m*

four-ply [ˈfɔːplaɪ] *adj (wool)* de cuatro hebras; *(wood)* de cuatro capas

four-poster [ˈfɔːˈpəʊstə(r)] *n* **f. (bed)** cama *f* de dosel

foursome [ˈfɔːsəm] *n* grupo *m* de cuatro; *(for tennis match, card game)* dos parejas *fpl*

fourteen [ˈfɔːtiːn] *n & adj* catorce *m*; *see also* **eight**

fourteenth [ˈfɔːtiːnθ] **1** *n* **(a)** *(fraction)* catorceavo *m*, catorceava parte *f* **(b)** *(in series)* decimocuarto(a) *m,f* **(c)** *(of month)* catorce *m*
  2 *adj* decimocuarto(a); *see also* **eleventh**

fourth [fɔːθ] **1** *n* **(a)** *(in series)* cuarto(a) *m,f* **(b)** *(of month)* cuarto *m*
  2 *adj* cuarto(a); **the f. estate** *(the press)* el cuarto poder; *see also* **eighth**

fourthly [ˈfɔːθlɪ] *adv* en cuarto lugar

four-wheel drive [ˈfɔːwiːlˈdraɪv] *n* tracción *f* a las cuatro ruedas

fowl [faʊl] *(pl* **fowl)** *n* ave *f* de corral

fox [fɒks] **1** *n* zorro *m*; *Fig* **a sly old f.** *(cunning person)* un viejo zorro; **f. cub** cría *f* de zorro; **f. hunt** caza *f* del zorro
  2 *vt Fam (perplex)* dejar pasmado(a); *(deceive)* burlar, engañar

foxed [fɒkst] *adj (book)* con motas en las páginas

foxglove [ˈfɒksɡlʌv] *n* digital *f*, dedalera *f*

foxhunting [ˈfɒkshʌntɪŋ] *n* caza *f* del zorro

foxtrot [ˈfɒkstrɒt] **1** *n* foxtrot *m*
  2 *vi (pt & pp* **foxtrotted)** bailar el foxtrot

foxy [ˈfɒksɪ] *adj Fam* **(a)** astuto(a), zorro **(b)** sexy

foyer [ˈfɔɪeɪ] *n* vestíbulo *m*

fractal [ˈfræktəl] *n* fractal *m*

fraction [ˈfrækʃən] *n Math* fracción *f*, quebrado *m*; *Fig (small part)* fracción *f*; **a f. too small/large** un poquitín pequeño/grande

fractional [ˈfrækʃənəl] *adj (very small)* ínfimo(a); *(decline, hesitation)* mínimo(a), ligero(a)

fractious [ˈfrækʃəs] *adj* irritable

fracture [ˈfræktʃə(r)] **1** *n* fractura *f*
  2 *vt* fracturar
  3 *vi* fracturarse

fragile [ˈfrædʒaɪl] *adj* frágil

fragility [frəˈdʒɪlɪtɪ] *n* fragilidad *f*

fragment 1 *n* [ˈfræɡmənt] *(of object, story)* fragmento *m*
  2 *vi* [fræɡˈment] *(object)* romperse; *(organization)* fragmentarse

fragmentation [fræɡmenˈteɪʃən] *n (gen) & Comptr* fragmentación *f*

fragrance [ˈfreɪɡrəns] *n* fragancia *f*

fragrant [ˈfreɪɡrənt] *adj* fragante

frail [freɪl] *adj (person)* delicado(a), frágil; *(object, beauty, happiness)* frágil

frailty [ˈfreɪltɪ] *n* fragilidad *f*

frame [freɪm] **1** *n* **(a)** *(of picture, door)* marco *m*; *(of person, animal)* cuerpo *m*; *(of building, bridge)* estructura *f*; *(of bicycle)* cuadro *m*; *(of spectacles)* montura *f* **(b)** *Fig* **f. of mind** humor *m*, estado *m* de ánimo; **f. of reference** marco *m* de referencia
  2 *vt* **(a)** *(picture) also Fig* enmarcar **(b)** *(answer, legislation)* formular **(c)** *Fam (falsely incriminate)* tender una trampa a

framework [ˈfreɪmwɜːk] *n (of structure)* estructura *f*; *Fig (for talks)* marco *m*

franc [fræŋk] *n (currency)* franco *m*; *Formerly* **Belgian/French f.** franco *m* belga/francés; **Swiss f.** franco *m* suizo

France [frɑːns] *n* Francia

franchise [ˈfræntʃaɪz] **1** *n* **(a)** *Com* franquicia *f* **(b)** *Pol* sufragio *m*
  2 *vt Com* franquiciar

Franciscan [frænˈsɪskən] *n & adj* franciscano(a) *m,f*

francophile [ˈfræŋkəfaɪl] *n & adj* francófilo(a) *m,f*

francophobe [ˈfræŋkəfəʊb] *n & adj* francófobo(a) *m,f*

francophone [ˈfræŋkəʊfəʊn] *n & adj* francófono(a) *m,f*

franglais [ˈfrɒŋɡleɪ] *n Hum* francés *m* lleno de anglicismos

Frank [fræŋk] *n Hist* franco(a) *m,f*

frank [fræŋk] *adj (person, answer)* franco(a); **to be f.,...** francamente,...

Frankfurt [ˈfræŋkfɜːt] *n* Fráncfort

frankfurter [ˈfræŋkfɜːtə(r)] *n (sausage)* salchicha *f* de Francfort

frankincense [ˈfræŋkɪnsens] *n* incienso *m*

frankly [ˈfræŋklɪ] *adv* francamente; **f., I couldn't care less** la verdad, me da igual

frantic [ˈfræntɪk] *adj (rush, pace)* frenético(a); **f. with worry** angustiado(a)

frantically [ˈfræntɪklɪ] *adv* frenéticamente

frappé, frappe [ˈfræpeɪ] *n (alchoholic)* = cóctel alcohólico servido con hielo picado; *(milkshake)* batido *m*

fraternal [frəˈtɜːnəl] *adj* fraterno(a), fraternal

fraternity [frəˈtɜːnɪtɪ] *n* **(a)** *(brotherliness)* fraternidad *f*; *(religious group)* hermandad *f*, cofradía *f*; **the medical/banking f.** el gremio médico/de la banca **(b)** *Univ* = asociación de estudiantes que suele funcionar como club social; **f. house** = residencia perteneciente a dicha asociación

fraternize [ˈfrætənaɪz] *vi* confraternizar **(with** con)

fraud [frɔːd] *n* **(a)** *(person)* impostor(ora) *m,f* **(b)** *(deception)* fraude *m*; **to obtain sth by f.** conseguir algo por medios fraudulentos; **f. squad** brigada *f* de delitos económicos, brigada anticorrupción

fraudulence [ˈfrɔːdjʊləns], **fraudulency** [ˈfrɔːdjʊlənsɪ] *n* fraudulencia *f*

fraudulent [ˈfrɔːdjʊlənt] *adj* fraudulento(a)

fraudulently [ˈfrɔːdjʊləntlɪ] *adv* de forma fraudulenta, fraudulentamente

fraught [frɔːt] *adj (situation)* tenso(a), tirante; *(person)* tenso(a); **f. with danger/emotion** cargado(a) de peligro/emoción

fray¹ [freɪ] *n (brawl)* contienda *f*, combate *m*; **to enter the f.** entrar en liza

fray² **1** *vt (material)* deshilachar
  2 *vi (material)* deshilacharse; *(nerves, tempers)* crisparse

frazzle [ˈfræzəl] *n* **to be burned to a f.** estar (totalmente) carbonizado(a)

frazzled [ˈfræzəld] *adj Fam (worn out)* **to be f.** estar hecho(a) polvo *or RP* destruido(a)

freak [fri:k] **1** *n* (**a**) *(strange being)* engendro *m*, monstruo *m*; **by a f. of fortune** por un capricho del destino; **f. show** = espectáculo que consiste en exhibir a personas con extrañas anomalías físicas; **f. storm** tormenta *f* inesperada (**b**) *(enthusiast)* fanático(a) *mf*; *Fam* **jazz/film f.** fanático(a) del jazz/cine

2 *vi* = **freak out**

▸**freak out** *Fam* **1** *vt sep (shock)* alucinar; *(scare)* meter canguelo *or Méx* mello *or RP* cuiqui a

2 *vi (become angry)* ponerse hecho(a) una furia; **I freaked out** *(panicked)* me entró el pánico *or Esp* la neura

freaky ['fri:kɪ] *adj Fam* muy raro(a)

freckle ['frekəl] *n* peca *f*

freckled ['frekəld], **freckly** ['freklɪ] *adj* pecoso(a)

free [fri:] **1** *adj* (**a**) *(unrestricted)* libre (**from** *or* **of** de); **to be f. to do sth** ser libre para hacer algo; **to set sb f.** liberar a alguien; **f. and easy** relajado(a); **feel f. to borrow the car** coge el coche cuando quieras; **feel f. to help yourself to tea** sírvete té si quieres; **she didn't feel f. to...** no se atrevía a...; **as f. as a bird** libre como el viento; **to be a f. agent** *(in general)* poder obrar a su antojo; *(sports player)* tener la carta de libertad; *Fig* **to have a f. hand** *(to make decisions)* tener carta blanca; *Econ* **f. enterprise** empresa *f* libre; **f. fall** *(of parachutist)* caída *f* libre; *(of economy)* caída *f* en *Esp* picado *or Am* picada; **f. kick** *(in soccer)* golpe *m* franco; *Econ* **f. market** libre mercado *m*; **f. speech** libertad *f* de expresión; **she's a f. spirit** no se conforma con una vida convencional; **f. throw** *(in basketball)* tiro *m* libre; **f. trade** libre cambio *m*, libre comercio *m*; **f. trade agreement** acuerdo *m* de libre comercio; **f. verse** verso *m* libre; **f. will** *(generally)* propia voluntad *f*; *(in philosophy, theology)* libre albedrío *m*

(**b**) *(unoccupied)* libre; **I am f. tomorrow** mañana estoy libre; **is this seat f.?** ¿está libre este asiento?; **f. time** tiempo *m* libre

(**c**) *(without charge)* gratuito(a), gratis; **f. gift** obsequio *m* (promocional)

(**d**) *Ironic (generous)* **he is very f. with his advice** es demasiado pródigo a la hora de dar consejos

2 *adv (without charge)* gratis, gratuitamente; **for f.** gratis

3 *vt (pt & pp* **freed** [fri:d]) *(prisoner, funds, mechanism)* liberar (**from** de); *(time, place)* desocupar; *(something stuck)* soltar; **to f. oneself from** *or* **of sth** librarse de algo

freedom ['fri:dəm] *n* libertad *f*; **to have the f. to do sth** tener libertad para hacer algo; **f. of information/speech/worship** libertad de información/expresión/culto; **f. of the press** libertad *f* de prensa; **to give sb the f. of the city** entregar la llave de la ciudad a alguien; **f. fighter** luchador(ora) *m,f* por la libertad

free-for-all ['fri:fərɔːl] *n Fam (fight, discussion)* bronca *f*, gresca *f*, *Méx* agarrón *m*; **it turned into a f.** degeneró en una bronca

freehold ['fri:həʊld] *n Law* propiedad *f* absoluta

freeholder ['fri:həʊldə(r)] *n* propietario(a) *m,f* absoluto(a)

freelance ['fri:lɑːns] **1** *n* (trabajador(ora) *m,f*) autónomo(a) *m,f*, free-lance *mf*

2 *adj* autónomo(a), free-lance

3 *adv* **to work f.** trabajar como autónomo(a) *or* free-lance

4 *vi* trabajar como autónomo(a) *or* free-lance

freelancer ['fri:lɑːnsə(r)] *n* colaborador(ora) *m,f* externo(a), free-lance *mf*

freeloader ['fri:ləʊdə(r)] *n Fam* gorrero(a) *m,f*, *Esp, Méx* gorrón(ona) *m,f*, *RP* garronero(a) *m,f*

freely ['fri:lɪ] *adv (to give, speak)* libremente; **to be f. available** encontrarse fácilmente

Freemason ['fri:meɪsən] *n* masón *m*, francmasón *m*

Freemasonry ['fri:meɪsənrɪ] *n* masonería *f*, francmasonería *f*

free-range ['fri:'reɪndʒ] *adj (egg, chicken)* de corral

freestyle ['fri:staɪl] *n (in swimming)* estilo *m* libre

freethinker [fri:'θɪŋkə(r)] *n* librepensador(ora) *m,f*

freeware ['fri:weə(r)] *n Comptr* freeware *m*, programa *m* de dominio público *(y gratuito)*

freeway ['fri:weɪ] *n* autopista *f*

freewheel [fri:'wi:l] *vi (bicycle)* ir sin pedalear; *(car)* ir en punto muerto

freeze [fri:z] **1** *n (in weather)* helada *f*; **price/wage f.** congelación *f* de los precios/los salarios

2 *vt (pt* **froze** [frəʊz], *pp* **frozen** ['frəʊzən]) *(food, prices)* congelar

3 *vi* (**a**) *(weather)* **it's freezing** *(very cold)* hace un frío espantoso; **it may f. tonight** puede que hiele esta noche (**b**) *(liquid)* congelarse; **to f. to death** morirse de frío; *Fam* **I'm freezing!** ¡me estoy congelando! (**c**) *(person) (stand still)* quedarse paralizado(a); **f.!** ¡quieto(a)!

▸**freeze out** *vt sep Fam* **to f. sb out of the conversation** excluir a alguien de la conversación

▸**freeze over** *vi (pond, river)* helarse

▸**freeze up** *vi (pond, mechanism)* helarse

freeze-dried ['fri:z'draɪd] *adj (coffee, herbs)* liofilizado(a)

freeze-dry ['fri:z'draɪ] *vt* liofilizar

freeze-frame ['fri:z'freɪm] *n Cin* imagen *f* congelada

freezer ['fri:zə(r)] *n (with single compartment, small room)* congelador *m*; *(with two compartments)* combi *m*, *Esp* frigorífico-congelador *m*

freezing ['fri:zɪŋ] *adj (room)* helado(a); *(weather, temperature)* muy frío(a); **f. cold** helado(a)

freight [freɪt] *Com* **1** *n (transport)* transporte *m or* flete *m* de mercancías; *(goods)* flete *m*, carga *f*; *(price)* flete *m*, porte *m*; **f. elevator** montacargas *m inv*; **f. forwarder** transitario(a) *m,f*; **f. train** tren *m* de mercancías

2 *vt (transport)* fletar, transportar; **we'll f. it to you tomorrow** se lo fletaremos mañana

freighter ['freɪtə(r)] *n (ship)* carguero *m*

French [frentʃ] **1** *npl (people)* **the F.** los franceses

2 *n (language)* francés *m*; *Hum* **excuse my F.** *(after swearing)* con perdón; **F. class/teacher** clase *f*/profesor *m* de francés

3 *adj* francés(esa); **F. bread** pan *m* francés *or* de barra; **F. fries** *Esp* patatas *fpl or Am* papas *fpl* fritas; *Mus* **F. horn** trompa *f*; **F. kiss** beso *m* con lengua *or* de tornillo; **F. loaf** barra *f* de pan; **F. window** (puerta *f*) cristalera *f*

Frenchman ['frentʃmən] *n* francés *m*

French-speaking ['frentʃ'spi:kɪŋ] *adj* francófono(a)

Frenchwoman ['frentʃwʊmən] *n* francesa *f*

frenetic [frə'netɪk] *adj* frenético(a)

frenetically [frə'netɪklɪ] *adv* frenéticamente

frenzied ['frenzɪd] *adj* frenético(a); **f. with rage** fuera de sí (de ira); **f. with worry** angustiado(a)

frenzy ['frenzɪ] *n* frenesí *m*; **to work oneself into a f.** ponerse frenético(a)

frequency ['fri:kwənsɪ] *n* frecuencia *f*; *Rad* **f. band** banda *f* de frecuencia

frequent 1 *adj* ['fri:kwənt] frecuente

2 *vt* [frɪ'kwent] frecuentar

frequently ['fri:kwəntlɪ] *adv* con frecuencia

fresco ['freskəʊ] *(pl* **frescos** *or* **frescoes)** *n* fresco *m*

fresh [freʃ] **1** *adj* (**a**) *(food, air)* fresco(a); **it is still f. in my mind** todavía lo tengo fresco en la memoria; **as f. as a daisy** (fresco(a)) como una rosa; **to get some f. air** tomar un poco de aire fresco; **f. troops** tropas *f* de refresco; **f. water** *(not salty)* agua *f* dulce (**b**) *(page, attempt, drink)* nuevo(a); **to make a f. start** empezar de nuevo (**c**) *(original) (approach, writing)* novedoso(a), original (**d**) *Fam (cheeky)* fresco(a); **to get f. with sb** *(sexually)* propasarse con alguien

2 *adv* **f. from...** recién salido(a) de...; **we're f. out of lemons** se nos acaban de terminar los limones

freshen ['freʃən] *vi (wind, weather)* refrescar

▶**freshen up** vi (wash) refrescarse

freshly ['freʃlɪ] adv recién; **f. baked/made/painted** recién horneado/hecho/pintado

freshman ['freʃmən] n Univ novato(a) m,f

freshness ['freʃnɪs] n (of food) frescura f

freshwater ['freʃwɔːtə(r)] adj (fish) de agua dulce

fret[1] [fret] (pt & pp **fretted**) vi (worry) ponerse nervioso(a)

fret[2] n Mus (on guitar) traste m

fretful ['fretfʊl] adj (anxious) inquieto(a)

fretfully ['fretfʊlɪ] adv con mucha desazón, con gran disgusto

Freudian ['frɔɪdɪən] adj freudiano(a); **F. slip** lapsus m inv (linguae)

FRG [efɑːˈdʒiː] n (abbr **Federal Republic of Germany**) RFA f, República f Federal de Alemania

Fri (abbr **Friday**) viernes m inv

friar ['fraɪə(r)] n fraile m; **F. Edmund** Fray Edmund

fricassee [frɪkəˈsiː] n fricasé m

friction ['frɪkʃən] n (rubbing, disagreement) fricción f; Phys rozamiento m; **f. tape** cinta f aislante

Friday ['fraɪdɪ] n viernes m inv; **F. the 13th** ≃ martes y trece; see also **Saturday**

fridge [frɪdʒ] n nevera f, Esp frigorífico m, Méx refrigerador m, RP heladera f

fried [fraɪd] adj frito(a)

friend [frend] n amigo(a) m,f; **to be friends with sb, to be sb's f.** ser amigo de alguien; **to make friends with sb** hacerse amigo de alguien; **to be a f. to sb** ser amigo de alguien, ser un amigo para alguien; **that's what friends are for** para eso están los amigos; **we're just good friends** sólo somos buenos amigos; **he's no f. of mine** no es amigo mío; **to have friends in high places** tener amigos influyentes; **to be a f. of the arts** ser un mecenas de las artes; Prov **a f. in need is a f. indeed** en la adversidad se conoce al amigo

friendless ['frendlɪs] adj **to be f.** no tener amigos; **a f. childhood** una infancia sin amigos

friendliness ['frendlɪnɪs] n amabilidad f, simpatía f

friendly ['frendlɪ] **1** n Sport partido m amistoso

2 adj (person) agradable, amable; (greeting, place) amistoso(a); **to be f. with sb** llevarse bien con alguien; **they became f.** se hicieron amigos(as); **to be on f. terms with sb** llevarse bien con alguien; Mil **f. fire** fuego m del propio bando

friendship ['frendʃɪp] n amistad f; **to form a f. with sb** forjar una amistad con alguien; **to lose sb's f.** perder la amistad de alguien

frier = **fryer**

fries [fraɪz] npl (French) **f.** Esp patatas fpl or Am papas fpl fritas

frieze [friːz] n Art & Archit friso m

frigate ['frɪgət] n fragata f

frigging ['frɪgɪŋ] very Fam **1** adj (for emphasis) Esp puñetero(a), Méx pinche, RP reverendo(a); **shut your f. mouth!** ¡cierra el pico, joder!

2 adv (for emphasis) **I'm f. freezing!** ¡tengo un frío del carajo!

fright [fraɪt] n susto m; **to take f.** asustarse; **to get a f.** darse un susto, asustarse; **to give sb a f.** dar un susto a alguien; Fam **to look a f.** estar horroroso(a)

frighten ['fraɪtən] **1** vt asustar; **to f. sb into doing sth** atemorizar a alguien para que haga algo; Fam **to f. the life** or **the wits out of sb** dar un susto de muerte Esp de muerte or Méx de la madre or RP de miércoles

2 vi **I don't f. easily** no me asusto fácilmente

frightened ['fraɪtənd] adj asustado(a) (**of** de); **to be f. to do sth** tener miedo de hacer algo

frightening ['fraɪtənɪŋ] adj escalofriante, aterrador(ora)

frighteningly ['fraɪtnɪŋlɪ] adv tremendamente, terriblemente

frightful ['fraɪtfʊl] adj espantoso(a)

frightfully ['fraɪtfʊlɪ] adv tremendamente, terriblemente

frigid ['frɪdʒɪd] adj (smile, atmosphere) glacial; (sexually) frígida

frigidity [frɪˈdʒɪdɪtɪ] n (of smile, atmosphere) frialdad f; (sexual) frigidez f

frill [frɪl] n volante m; Fig **without frills** (of ceremony) sin florituras

frilly ['frɪlɪ] adj **f. shirt/skirt** camisa f/falda f de volantes

fringe [frɪndʒ] n (**a**) (on clothes, lampshade) flecos mpl (**b**) (edge) extremo m, borde m; **to be on the fringes of society** ser un/una marginado(a), vivir en la marginalidad; **f. benefits** ventajas fpl adicionales or extras; Pol **f. group** grupo m marginal; **f. theater** teatro m experimental

frisk [frɪsk] **1** vt (search) cachear, registrar

2 vi **to f. about** retozar, corretear

frisky ['frɪskɪ] adj (person) lleno(a) de vitalidad; (animal) retozón(ona), saltarín(ina); **to be f.** (person) estar lleno(a) de vitalidad

fritter ['frɪtə(r)] n Culin buñuelo m; **banana f.** plátano rebozado y frito

▶**fritter away** vt sep (money) despilfarrar; (time) desperdiciar

frivolity [frɪˈvɒlɪtɪ] n frivolidad f

frivolous ['frɪvələs] adj frívolo(a)

frizz [frɪz] **1** n rizos mpl muy pequeños

2 vt rizar (con rizos muy pequeños)

frizzy ['frɪzɪ] adj ensortijado(a)

fro [frəʊ] adv **to go to and f.** ir y venir (de un lado para otro)

frock [frɒk] n (dress) vestido m; **f. coat** levita f

frog [frɒg] n rana f; Fam **to have a f. in one's throat** tener carraspera

frogman ['frɒgmən] n hombre m rana

frogmarch ['frɒgmɑːtʃ] vt llevar por la fuerza

frolic ['frɒlɪk] vi retozar

from [frɒm, unstressed frəm] prep (**a**) (expressing place) de; (expressing specific location or origin) desde; **f. above/the outside** desde arriba/fuera or Am afuera; **there's a great view f. the top** desde la cima la vista es magnífica; **to travel f. Los Angeles to San Francisco** viajar de Los Ángeles a San Francisco; **the train f. Chicago** el tren (procedente) de Chicago; **10 miles f. Barcelona** a 10 millas de Barcelona

(**b**) (expressing time) desde; **f. then (on)** desde entonces; **f. tomorrow** a partir de mañana; **f. morning to** or **till night** de la mañana a la noche; **f. the beginning** desde el principio; **f. six to seven (o'clock)** de (las) seis a (las) siete; **five years f. now** de aquí a cinco años; **to be blind f. birth** ser ciego(a) de nacimiento

(**c**) (expressing range, change) **f.... to...** de... a...; **for children f. seven to nine (years)** para niños de siete a nueve años; **wine f. $4 a bottle** vinos desde 4 dólares la botella

(**d**) (expressing source) de; **I bought it f. a friend** se lo compré a un amigo; **where are you f.?, where do you come f.?** ¿de dónde eres?; **she's f. Portugal** es portuguesa or de Portugal; **to drink f. a cup** beber de una taza or en taza; **a quotation f. the Bible** una cita de la Biblia; **made f. rubber** hecho(a) de goma

(**e**) (expressing removal) **to take sth f. sb** quitar or Andes, RP sacar algo a alguien; **he was banned f. the club** fue expulsado del club

(**f**) (on the basis of) **f. what I heard/saw...** (a juzgar) por lo que yo he oído/visto...; **to act f. conviction** actuar por convicción

frond [frɒnd] n (of fern) fronda f; (of palm) (hoja f de) palma f

front [frʌnt] **1** n (**a**) (not back) parte f delantera; (of building) fachada f; (cover of book) portada f, RP tapa f; **on the f. of the book** en la portada or RP tapa del libro; **at the f. of the book** al principio del libro; **I sat in (the) f.** (of car) me senté delante *or Am* adelante; *Theat* **f. of house** = conjunto de actividades que se desarrollan dentro del teatro y que implican contacto con el público

(**b**) *(outward appearance)* fachada *f*; **his kindness is only a f.** su amabilidad no es más que fachada; **the company is a f. for their arms dealing** la empresa es una tapadera *or RP* pantalla para el tráfico de armas; *Fam* **f. man** *(of pop group)* líder *m*; *(of organization)* cabeza *f* visible

(**c**) *Mil, Pol & Met* frente *m*; *Fig* **to make progress on all fronts** hacer progresos en todos los frentes; *Met* **warm/cold f.** frente cálido/frío

2 in front *adv* **in f.** *(in race, contest)* en cabeza, por delante

3 in front of *prep (in line, opposite)* delante de, *Am* adelante de; *(in presence of)* delante de, en presencia de

4 up front *adv Fam (money)* por adelantado

5 up front *adj* **to be up f. about sth** ser claro(a) en cuanto a algo

6 *adj* delantero(a); *Rail* **f. car** vagón *m* delantero; **f. cover** *(of magazine, book)* portada *f*, *RP* tapa *f*; **f. door** puerta *f* principal; *Mil* **f. line** frente *m* (de batalla); **f. page** *(of newspaper)* portada *f*, primera plana *f*; **f. room** salón *m*, sala *f* de estar; **in the f. row** en la primera fila; *Theat* **to have a f. row seat** tener asiento de primera fila; *Fig* ser espectador privilegiado; **f. seat** *(in car)* asiento *m* delantero *or Am* de adelante; **f. teeth** palas *fpl*; **f. view** vista *f* frontal

7 *vt (government)* encabezar; *(TV program)* presentar; *(organization)* dirigir; *(pop group)* liderar

8 *vi (building)* **the house fronts onto the river** la casa da al río

frontage ['frʌntɪdʒ] *n* fachada *f*

frontal ['frʌntəl] *adj Anat & Mil* frontal

frontier ['frʌntɪə(r)] *n* frontera *f*; **the frontiers of human knowledge** los límites del conocimiento humano; **f. guard** *(person)* guardia *mf* fronterizo(a); **f. town** ciudad *f* fronteriza

frontispiece ['frʌntɪspiːs] *n* frontispicio *m*

front-loading ['frʌnt'ləʊdɪŋ] *adj* de carga frontal

frontrunner ['frʌntrʌnə(r)] *n* favorito(a) *m,f*

frost [frɒst] *n* escarcha *f*; **there was a f.** cayó una helada

▸**frost over, frost up** *vi (window)* cubrirse de escarcha

frostbite ['frɒstbaɪt] *n* congelación *f*

frostbitten ['frɒstbɪtən] *adj (fingers, toes)* con síntomas de congelación; *Fig (very cold)* congelado(a); **his fingers were f.** sus dedos mostraban síntomas de congelación

frosted ['frɒstɪd] *adj (glass)* esmerilado(a)

frostily ['frɒstɪlɪ] *adv* con gelidez *or* frialdad

frosting ['frɒstɪŋ] *n (on cake)* glaseado *m*

frosty ['frɒstɪ] *adj (night, air)* gélido(a), helado(a); *Fig (welcome, smile)* glacial

froth [frɒθ] **1** *n (foam)* espuma *f*

2 *vi* hacer espuma; **he was frothing at the mouth** *(with rage)* echaba espuma por la boca

frothy ['frɒθɪ] *adj* espumoso(a)

frown [fraʊn] **1** *n* **a disapproving f.** el ceño fruncido en señal de desaprobación

2 *vi* fruncir el ceño

▸**frown on, frown upon** *vt insep (disapprove of)* desaprobar

froze [frəʊz] *pt of* **freeze**

frozen ['frəʊzən] **1** *adj* congelado(a); **to be f.** estar congelado(a)

2 *pp of* **freeze**

fructose ['frʌktəʊs] *n* fructosa *f*

frugal ['fruːgəl] *adj* frugal

frugally ['fruːgəlɪ] *adv* frugalmente

fruit [fruːt] *n (for eating)* fruta *f*; *(on plant)* fruto *m*; **to bear f.** *also Fig* dar fruto; **f. bowl** frutero *m*; **f. cocktail** cóctel *m* de frutas, macedonia *f* (de frutas); **f. fly** mosca *f* de la fruta; **f. juice** *Esp* zumo *m or Am* jugo *m* de frutas; **f. salad** macedonia *f* (de frutas); **f. tree** (árbol *m*) frutal *m*

fruitcake ['fruːtkeɪk] *n* bizcocho *m* de frutas; *Fam (mad*

person) chiflado(a), *Esp* chalado(a) *m,f*

fruitful ['fruːtfʊl] *adj (discussion, meeting)* fructífero(a)

fruitfully ['fruːtfʊlɪ] *adv* provechosamente, de modo fructífero

fruition [fruː'ɪʃən] *n* **to come to f.** *(plan, effort)* fructificar

fruitless ['fruːtlɪs] *adj* infructuoso(a)

fruitlessly ['fruːtlɪslɪ] *adv* infructuosamente

fruity ['fruːtɪ] *adj (taste)* afrutado(a); *Fam (voice)* profundo(a)

frump [frʌmp] *n Fam* **she's a f.** es muy rancia en la manera de vestir

frumpish ['frʌmpɪʃ], **frumpy** ['frʌmpɪ] *adj Fam* **to be f.** ser rancio(a) en la manera de vestir

frustrate [frʌs'treɪt] *vt (person, plan)* frustrar

frustrated [frʌs'treɪtɪd] *adj* frustrado(a); **to be f.** estar frustrado(a)

frustrating [frʌs'treɪtɪŋ] *adj* frustrante

frustration [frʌs'treɪʃən] *n (emotion)* frustración *f*

fry [fraɪ] **1** *vt* freír

2 *vi* freírse

fryer, frier ['fraɪə(r)] *n* (**a**) **(deep fat) f.** freidora *f* (**b**) *(chicken)* pollo *m* tierno

frying ['fraɪɪŋ] *n* fritura *f*; **f. pan** sartén *f*; **to jump out of the f. pan into the fire** ir de Guatemala a Guatepeor

frypan ['fraɪpæn] *n* sartén *f*

ft *(abbr* **foot** *or* **feet)** pie *m (30,48 cm)*; **20 ft** 20 pies

FTAA [eftiː'eɪ] *n (abbr* **Free Trade Area of the Americas)** ALCA *f*

FTP [eftiː'piː] *n Comptr (abbr* **File Transfer Protocol)** FTP *m*, protocolo *m* de transferencia de ficheros

fuchsia ['fjuːʃə] *n (plant)* fucsia *f*

fuck [fʌk] *Vulg* **1** *n* (**a**) *(intercourse)* polvo *m*; **to have a f.** echar un polvo, *Esp* follar, *Am* coger, *Méx* chingar, *RP,Ven* clavar (**b**) *(other uses)* **f.!** ¡carajo!, *Esp* ¡joder!; **I don't give a f.** me importa un huevo; **what the f....?** ¿qué coño...?, ¿qué cojones...?; **shut the f. up!** ¡cállate de una puta vez!; **he's as stupid/rich as f.** es más bobo/rico que la hostia; **f. knows why he came!** ¡para qué cojones habrá venido!

2 *vt* (**a**) *(have sex with) Esp* follar, *Am* coger, *Méx* chingar (**b**) *(expressing surprise, contempt, irritation)* **f. it!** ¡carajo!, *Esp* ¡joder!; **f. you!** *Esp* ¡que te den por culo!, *Méx* ¡chinga tu madre!, *RP* ¡andate a la puta que te parió!

3 *vi Esp* follar, *Am* coger, *Méx* chingar

▸**fuck around, fuck about** *vt sep* **to f. sb around** *or* **about** *(treat badly)* joder *or Méx* chingar a alguien

2 *vi (act foolishly)* hacer el *Esp* gilipollas *or Am* pendejo (**with** con)

▸**fuck off** *vi Vulg (go away)* largarse, *RP* tomarse el raje; **f. off!** *Esp* ¡vete a tomar por (el) culo!, *Méx* ¡vete a la chingada!, *RP* ¡andate a la puta que te parió!

▸**fuck up** *vt sep Vulg* **to f. sth up** *(bungle)* joder bien algo

fuck-all ['fʌk'ɔːl] *n Vulg (nothing)* **he's done f. this week** se ha tocado los huevos *or RP* rascado las bolas toda la semana, *Méx* estuvo de huevón toda la semana; **to know f. about sth** no tener ni puta idea de algo

fucked [fʌkt] *adj Vulg* **to be f.** *(exhausted)* estar *Esp* hecho(a) una braga *or Méx* chingado(a) *or RP* hecho(a) una mierda; *(broken)* estar jodido(a)

fucker ['fʌkə(r)] *n Vulg (person)* cabrón(ona) *m,f*, hijo(a) *m,f* de puta *or Méx* de la chingada; *(thing)* **I can't get the f. to start** este hijo (de) puta *or Méx* de la chingada no arranca

fucking ['fʌkɪŋ] *Vulg* **1** *adj* **he's a f. idiot!** ¡es un *Esp* gilipollas *or Am* pendejo *or RP* boludo!; **where's the f. key?** ¿dónde está la puta llave?

2 *adv* **it's f. cold!** ¡hace un frío *Esp* de cojones *or Méx* de la chingada *or RP* de mierda!; **it's f. brilliant!** ¡está de puta madre *or Méx* de la chingada!

fuddy-duddy ['fʌdɪdʌdɪ] *n Fam* **an old f.** un carcamal *or Am* carcamán

fudge [fʌdʒ] **1** *n (sweet)* = dulce de azúcar, leche y mantequilla

2 vt (avoid) **to f. an issue** eludir un asunto, Esp echar balones fuera

3 vi **stop fudging!** ¡déjate de evasivas!

fuel ['fjʊəl] **1** n combustible m; Fig **to add f. to the flames** (situation, crisis) echar leña al fuego; **f. bill** facturas fpl del gas y la electricidad; Aut **f. consumption** consumo m de combustible; Aut **f. gauge** indicador m del nivel de gasolina or RP nafta; Aut **f. injection** inyección f (de combustible); **f. pump** bomba f de (la) gasolina or RP nafta; **f. tank** depósito m de combustible

2 vt Fig (argument, hatred) dar pábulo a, avivar

fuel-efficient ['fjʊəlɪ'fɪʃənt] adj de poco consumo

fugitive ['fjuːdʒɪtɪv] n fugitivo(a) m,f

fugue [fjuːg] n Mus fuga f

fulcrum ['fʌlkrəm] n fulcro m, punto m de apoyo

fulfill, fulfil [fʊl'fɪl] vt (plan, condition, ambition) cumplir; (dream, task) realizar, cumplir; (need, requirement) satisfacer; (function, role) desempeñar; **to feel fulfilled** (person) sentirse realizado(a)

fulfillment, fulfilment [fʊl'fɪlmənt] n (of plan, condition) cumplimiento m; (of ambition, dream, task) realización f, cumplimiento; (of need, requirement) satisfacción f; (of function, role) desempeño m; **to find** or **achieve f.** realizarse, hallar satisfacción

full [fʊl] **1** adj (a) (container, room) lleno(a); (day) completo(a); **to be f. of** estar lleno(a) de; **f. of holes** lleno(a) de agujeros; **to be f. of praise for sb** no tener más que elogios para alguien; **to be f. of oneself** tenérselo muy creído; **f. to the brim** (lleno(a)) hasta el borde; **don't speak with your mouth f.** no hables con la boca llena; **to be f. (up)** (person) estar lleno(a); **on a f. stomach** con el estómago lleno

(**b**) (complete) (amount, support) total; (explanation, recovery) completo(a); **to take f. responsibility for sth** asumir plena responsabilidad por algo; **she gave me the f. story** me lo contó todo; **the f. horror** todo el horror; **the f. implications** todas las implicaciones or Chile, RP implicancias; **to lead a f. life** llevar una vida plena; **I waited two f. hours** or **a f. two hours** esperé dos horas enteras; **to ask for fuller information about sth** pedir más información acerca de algo; **to be in f. bloom** estar reventón(ona) or en pleno florecimiento; **in f. flow** (speaker) en pleno discurso; **to be in f. swing** (party) estar en pleno apogeo; **in f. view** completamente a la vista; **f. board** pensión f completa; Phot **in f. color** a todo color; Rail **f. fare** precio m or tarifa f normal; **f. house** (in theater) lleno m; (in cards) full m; **f. member** miembro m de pleno derecho; **f. moon** luna f llena; **f. name** nombre m y apellido; Theat **f. price** precio m completo

(**c**) (maximum) **at f. blast** (heater, air conditioning) a plena potencia, RP a todo vapor; (radio, TV) a todo volumen; **at f. tilt** a toda pastilla or marcha; (**at) f. speed** a toda velocidad; **at f. stretch** a pleno rendimiento

(**d**) (skirt, sleeve) holgado(a), amplio(a); **a f. figure** (of woman) una figura de formas bien contorneadas; **f. lips** labios mpl carnosos

2 n **to pay in f.** pagar el total; **name in f.** nombre m y apellidos; **to live life to the f.** disfrutar la vida al máximo

3 adv **I know it f. well** lo sé perfectamente; **it hit him f. in the face** le dió en plena cara

fullback ['fʊlbæk] n (in football) fullback mf; (in soccer) (defensa m) lateral m; (in rugby) defensa m de cierre, zaguero m

full-blown [fʊl'bləʊn] adj (war, scandal) declarado(a); (argument) verdadero(a); **to have f. AIDS** haber desarrollado la enfermedad del SIDA (por completo)

full-bodied ['fʊl'bɒdɪd] adj (wine) con cuerpo

full-fledged ['fʊl'fledʒd] adj Fig hecho(a) y derecho(a)

full-grown ['fʊl'grəʊn] adj plenamente desarrollado(a); **to be f.** estar plenamente desarrollado(a)

full-length ['fʊl'leŋθ] adj (portrait, mirror) de cuerpo entero; **f. movie** largometraje m

fullness, fulness ['fʊlnɪs] n **in the f. of time** en su momento

full-on ['fʊl'ɒn] adj Fam (argument) en serio; **to have f. sex** llegar hasta el final

full-page ['fʊl'peɪdʒ] adj (advert, illustration) a toda página

full-scale ['fʊl'skeɪl] adj (**a**) (model) (de) tamaño natural (**b**) (search) exhaustivo(a); **f. war** guerra f a gran escala

full-time ['fʊl'taɪm] **1** adj (job, employment) a tiempo completo; (teacher, housewife) con dedicación exclusiva, de plena dedicación; Fig **looking after the baby is a f. job** cuidar del bebé es un trabajo de plena dedicación

2 adv (work) a tiempo completo

full-timer ['fʊl'taɪmə(r)] n trabajador(ora) m,f or empleado(a) m,f a tiempo completo

fully ['fʊlɪ] adv (**a**) (completely) completamente; **f. grown** hecho(a) y derecho(a) (**b**) (at least) **it takes f. two hours** lleva dos horas largas

fulminate ['fʌlmɪneɪt] vi tronar, arremeter (**against** contra)

fulness = **fullness**

fulsome ['fʊlsəm] adj excesivo(a), exagerado(a); **to be f. in one's praise of sth/sb** alabar algo/a alguien en exceso

fumble ['fʌmbəl] **1** vt **the quarterback fumbled the ball** al quarterback se le escapó la pelota de las manos

2 vi rebuscar; **to f. for words** no encontrar las palabras adecuadas, titubear; **he fumbled with the controls** trató torpemente de accionar los mandos

fume [fjuːm] **1** n fumes humos mpl

2 vi (**a**) (give off fumes) despedir humo (**b**) (be angry) **to be fuming** echar humo (por las orejas)

fumigate ['fjuːmɪgeɪt] vt fumigar

fun [fʌn] n diversión f; **to have f.** divertirse; **it was great f.** fue muy divertido(a); **there'll be f. and games** (trouble) se va a armar una buena; **to make f. of, to poke f. at** burlarse de; **to say sth in f.** decir algo en broma; **to do sth for f., to do sth for the f. of it** hacer algo para divertirse; **to join in the f.** unirse a la diversión; **what f.!** ¡qué divertido!

function ['fʌŋkʃən] **1** n (**a**) (of machine, person, institution) & Math función f; **my f. in life is to…** mi papel consiste en…; Comptr **f. key** tecla f de función (**b**) (celebration) celebración f; (official occasion) acto m; **f. room** salón m de fiestas

2 vi funcionar; **to f. as** servir de, hacer de

functional ['fʌŋkʃənəl] adj (**a**) (practical) funcional (**b**) (operational) **to be f.** estar en funcionamiento or funcionar

functionality [fʌŋkʃə'nælɪtɪ] n funcionalidad f

functionary ['fʌŋkʃənərɪ] n funcionario(a) m,f

fund [fʌnd] **1** n (**a**) (of money) fondo m; **funds** fondos mpl; Fin **f. manager** gestor(ora) m,f financiero(a) or de fondos (**b**) (of information, jokes) fuente f

2 vt Fin financiar

fundamental [fʌndə'mentəl] **1** adj fundamental; **her f. honesty** su honradez inherente

2 n **fundamentals** principios mpl básicos, fundamentos mpl

fundamentalist [fʌndə'mentəlɪst] n Rel integrista mf, fundamentalista mf

fundamentally [fʌndə'mentəlɪ] adv básicamente, fundamentalmente

funding ['fʌndɪŋ] n fondos mpl, financiación f, Am financiamiento m

fund-raiser ['fʌndreɪzə(r)] n (person) recaudador(ora) m,f de fondos; (event) acto m para recaudar fondos

funeral ['fjuːnərəl] n funeral m; Fam **that's your f.!** ¡eso es cosa tuya or tu problema!; **f. director** encargado(a) m,f de la funeraria; **f. home** funeraria f; Mus **f. march** marcha f fúnebre; **f. parlor** funeraria f; **f. procession** cortejo m fúnebre; **f. service** funeral m, honras fpl fúnebres

fungal [ˈfʌŋgəl] *adj* fúngico(a), de los hongos; **a f. infection** una micosis

fungi *pl of* **fungus**

fungicide [ˈfʌŋgɪsaɪd] *n* fungicida *m*

fungus [ˈfʌŋgəs] (*pl* **fungi** [ˈfʌŋgaɪ]) *n (mushroom, toadstool)* hongo *m*; *(on walls) & Med* hongos *mpl*

funk [fʌŋk] *n* (a) *Fam Old-fashioned (fright)* **to be in a f.** estar muerto(a) de miedo; **he got into a f.** le entró mieditis *or Méx* el mello *or RP* el cuiqui (b) *(music)* funk *m*, funky *m*

funky [ˈfʌŋkɪ] *adj Fam (fashionable, excellent)* genial, *Esp* muy guapo(a), *Méx* muy padre

fun-loving [ˈfʌnlʌvɪŋ] *adj* amante de las diversiones

funnel [ˈfʌnəl] **1** *n* (a) *(of locomotive, steamship)* chimenea *f* (b) *(for filling bottle)* embudo *m*
     2 *vt (direct)* canalizar

funnily [ˈfʌnɪlɪ] *adv (strangely)* de forma rara; **f. enough...** curiosamente..., por raro que parezca...

funny [ˈfʌnɪ] **1** *adj* (a) *(amusing)* gracioso(a); **are you trying to be f.?** ¿te estás haciendo el gracioso?; *Ironic* **very f.!** ¡muy gracioso!; **f. bone** hueso *m* de la risa (b) *(strange)* curioso(a), raro(a); **I feel a bit f.** *(ill)* no me siento muy allá; **(that's) f., I thought I'd locked the door** qué curioso, creía que había cerrado la puerta con llave; **(it's) f. you should say that** es curioso que digas eso; **this butter tastes/smells f.** esta mantequilla *or RP* manteca sabe/huele raro; **he went a bit f. in his old age** *(eccentric)* se volvió un poco raro con los años; *Fam* **I don't want any f. business!** ¡nada de trucos!; *Fam* **f. farm** manicomio *m*, *Esp* frenopático *m*
     2 *n* **to make a f.** hacer un chiste; **the funnies** *(in newspaper)* las historietas, *RP* los chistes

fur [fɜː(r)] *n* (a) *(hair)* pelo *m*; *(animal skin)* piel *f*; *Fig* **the f. was flying** se armó la marimorena; **f. coat** abrigo *m* de piel; **f. trade** comercio *m* de pieles (b) *(on tongue)* sarro *m*

furious [ˈfjʊərɪəs] *adj* furioso(a); **to be f.** estar furioso(a); **to be f. with oneself** tirarse de los pelos; **at a f. speed** a una velocidad de vértigo

furiously [ˈfjʊərɪəslɪ] *adv* con furia; **the fire was blazing f.** el fuego ardía con furia

furlong [ˈfɜːlɒŋ] *n (measurement)* = 220 yardas (201.17 metros) *(unidad utilizada en las carreras de caballos)*

furnace [ˈfɜːnɪs] *n* horno *m*

furnish [ˈfɜːnɪʃ] *vt* (a) *(house, apartment)* amueblar (b) *Formal (provide)* proporcionar, suministrar; **to f. sb with sth** proporcionar algo a alguien

furnished [ˈfɜːnɪʃd] *adj (apartment, room)* amueblado(a); **to be f.** estar amueblado(a); **f. accommodation** viviendas *fpl* amuebladas

furnishings [ˈfɜːnɪʃɪŋz] *npl (furniture, fittings)* mobiliario *m*, muebles *mpl*; **soft f.** tapicería *f*

furniture [ˈfɜːnɪtʃə(r)] *n* muebles *mpl*, mobiliario *m*; **a piece of f.** un mueble; **f. polish** abrillantador *m* de muebles, *CSur* lustramuebles *m inv*; **f. store** tienda *f* de muebles; **f. van** camión *m* de mudanzas

furor [fjʊˈrɔː(r)] *n (uproar)* revuelo *m*, escándalo *m*; **to cause a f.** levantar un gran revuelo

furrow [ˈfʌrəʊ] **1** *n (in field, on face)* surco *m*
     2 *vt Literary* **his brow was furrowed with worry** arrugaba la frente con preocupación

furry [ˈfɜːrɪ] *adj (animal)* peludo(a); *(toy)* de peluche; **to have a f. tongue** tener la lengua llena de sarro

further [ˈfɜːðə(r)], **farther** [ˈfɑːðə(r)] *(comparative of* **far**) **1** *adv* (a) más lejos; **I can go no f.** no puedo seguir; **this mustn't go any f.** *(don't tell anyone else)* esto no debe salir de aquí; **I didn't question him any f.** no le pregunté más; **to go no f. into the matter** no profundizar más en el asunto; **by being careful he made his money go f.** siendo cuidadoso pudo sacar más partido a su dinero; **that doesn't get us**

much f. eso no nos ayuda mucho; **f. back** *(in space)* más atrás; *(in time)* antes
     (b) *Formal (moreover)* además; **f. to your recent letter...** en respuesta a su última carta...
     2 *adj* (a) *(more distant)* más alejado(a) (b) *(additional)* nuevo(a), adicional; **upon f. consideration** tras considerarlo de nuevo; **until f. notice** hasta nuevo aviso; **without f. warning** sin más aviso
     3 *vt* promover

furthermore [fɜːðəˈmɔː(r)] *adv Formal* es más

furthermost [ˈfɜːðəməʊst] *adj Literary* último(a), más alejado

furthest [ˈfɜːðɪst], **farthest** [ˈfɑːðɪst] *(superlative of* **far**) **1** *adj* **the f.** el/la más alejado(a), el/la más distante
     2 *adv* más lejos

furtive [ˈfɜːtɪv] *adj* furtivo(a)

fury [ˈfjʊərɪ] *n (of person, storm)* furia *f*; **to be in a f.** estar furioso(a); *Fam* **to work like f.** trabajar como loco(a)

fuse [fjuːz] **1** *n* (a) *Elec* fusible *m*; *Fam Fig* **she blew a f.** *(became angry)* se puso como una fiera; **f. box** cuadro *m* eléctrico, caja *f* de fusibles; **f. wire** fusible *m* (b) *(for dynamite)* mecha *f*; *(in bomb)* espoleta *f*; *Fam Fig* **to have a short f.** *(be short-tempered)* saltar a la mínima, *RP* ser muy calderita
     2 *vt (join, melt)* fundir
     3 *vi* (a) *(metals)* fundirse (b) *(organizations, parties)* fusionarse

fused [fjuːzd] *adj Elec (plug, appliance)* provisto(a) de fusible

fuselage [ˈfjuːzəlɑːʒ] *n* fuselaje *m*

fusillade [fjuːzɪˈleɪd] *n (of bullets)* descarga *f* cerrada; *Fig (of criticism, questions)* lluvia *f*

fusion [ˈfjuːʒən] *n* fusión *f*

fuss [fʌs] **1** *n* alboroto *m*, escándalo *m*; **a lot of f. about or over nothing** mucho ruido y pocas nueces; **I don't see what all the f. is about** no veo a qué viene tanto alboroto; **to make** *or Fam* **kick up a f.** armar un alboroto *or* un escándalo; **he always makes a f. over his grandchildren** se deshace en atenciones cada vez que está con sus nietos
     2 *vi* **to f.** *(about or around)* estar inquieto(a); **stop fussing!** ¡estate quieto!

fussbudget [ˈfʌsbʌdʒɪt], **fusspot** [ˈfʌspɒt] *n Fam* quisquilloso(a) *m,f*

fussily [ˈfʌsɪlɪ] *adv* (a) *(react, comment)* quisquillosamente (b) *(dressed, decorated)* recargadamente

fussiness [ˈfʌsɪnɪs] *n* (a) *(fastidiousness)* meticulosidad *f*, exigencia *f* (b) *(of dress, decoration)* lo recargado

fusspot = **fussbudget**

fussy [ˈfʌsɪ] *adj* (a) *(person)* quisquilloso(a), tiquismiquis; **I'm not f.** *(I don't mind)* me da lo mismo (b) *(dress, decor)* recargado(a)

futile [ˈfjuːtaɪl] *adj (attempt, protest)* inútil, vano(a); *(remark, suggestion)* fútil

futility [fjuːˈtɪlɪtɪ] *n (of attempt, protest)* inutilidad *f*; *(of remark, suggestion)* futilidad *f*

futon [ˈfuːtɒn] *n* futón *m*

future [ˈfjuːtʃə(r)] **1** *n* (a) *(time)* futuro *m*; **in (the) f.** en el futuro; **in the near/distant f.** en un futuro próximo/lejano; **she has a job with a (good) f.** *(prospects)* tiene un trabajo con (mucho) futuro (b) *Fin* **futures** futuros *mpl*; **futures market** mercado *m* de futuros (c) *Gram* **f. (tense)** futuro *m*; **f. perfect (tense)** futuro perfecto
     2 *adj* futuro(a); **at some f. date** en una fecha futura; **for f. reference** para consultar en el futuro

futuristic [ˈfjuːtʃəˈrɪstɪk] *adj* futurista

fuze, fuse [fjuːz] *n (for dynamite)* mecha *f*; *(in bomb)* espoleta *f*

fuzz [fʌz] *n* (a) *(on peach, skin)* pelusa *f* (b) *Fam* **the f.** *(the police)* la poli, *Esp* la pasma, *Méx* los pitufos, *RP* la cana

fuzzy [ˈfʌzɪ] *adj (outline)* borroso(a); *(idea)* vago(a); *(hair)* crespo(a)

FYI *(abbr* **for your information**) para tu información

G

G, g [dʒiː] **1** *n* (**a**) *(letter)* G *f*, g *f* (**b**) *Mus* sol *m*
   2 *adj Cin* ≃ (apta) para todos los públicos

g (*abbr* **gram**) g

gab [gæb] *Fam* **1** *n* **to have the gift of the g.** tener un pico de oro
   2 *vi* (*pt & pp* **gabbed**) *(talk, gossip)* darle al pico; *(to police, press)* dar el soplo, *Méx* soplar, *RP* pasar el dato

gabardine [gæbə'diːn] *n (coat, material)* gabardina *f*

gabble ['gæbəl] **1** *n* vocerío *m*, alboroto *m*
   2 *vi* farfullar

gable ['geɪbəl] *n (of house)* hastial *m*, gablete *m*; **g. end** hastial *m*

Gabon ['gæbən] *n* Gabón

Gabonese [gæbə'niːz] *n & adj* gabonés(esa) *m,f*

▶**gad about** [gæd] *vi Fam* pendonear, zascandilear

gadabout ['gædəbaʊt] *n Fam* pendón *m*, zascandil *mf*

gadfly ['gædflaɪ] *n (insect)* tábano *m*; *Fig (person)* provocador(ora) *m,f*

gadget ['gædʒɪt] *n* artilugio *m*

Gael [geɪl] *n* = persona de origen celta oriunda de Irlanda o el Noroeste de Escocia

Gaelic ['geɪlɪk, 'gælɪk] **1** *n (language)* gaélico *m*
   2 *adj* gaélico(a); *Sport* **G. football** fútbol *m* gaélico, = deporte irlandés a medio camino entre el fútbol y el rugby

gaff [gæf] *n (in fishing)* garfio *m*

gaffe [gæf] *n (blunder)* desliz *m*, metedura *f or Am* metida *f* de pata; **to make a g.** cometer un desliz

gag [gæg] **1** *n* (**a**) *(on mouth)* mordaza *f* (**b**) *Fam (joke)* chiste *m*
   2 *vt* (*pt & pp* **gagged**) *(silence) (person, the press)* amordazar
   3 *vi (retch)* tener arcadas; **to make sb g.** provocar arcadas a alguien

gage [geɪdʒ] = **gauge**

gaggle ['gægəl] *n (of geese)* bandada *f*; *Fig* **a g. of journalists** una manada de periodistas

gaiety ['geɪətɪ] *n* regocijo *m*, alegría *f*

gaily ['geɪlɪ] *adv* alegremente, con alegría

gain [geɪn] **1** *n* (**a**) *(profit)* beneficio *m*, ganancia *f*; **for personal g.** en beneficio propio (**b**) *(increase)* aumento *m* (**in** de)
   2 *vt* (**a**) *(advantage, reputation)* cobrar, ganar; *(victory)* obtener; *(sympathy)* granjearse, ganarse; **to g. access to** *(burglar)* lograr acceder *or* acceso a; **he gained the impression that…** le dio la impresión de que… (**b**) *(increase)* ganar; **to g. weight** ganar peso; **to g. ground on** ganar terreno a; **to g. speed** cobrar velocidad; **to g. time** ganar tiempo
   3 *vi* (**a**) *(benefit)* **to g. by sth** beneficiarse de algo (**b**) *(increase)* **to g. in confidence** cobrar *or* ganar confianza; **to g. in popularity** hacerse cada vez más popular (**c**) *(clock)* adelantar

▶**gain on** *vt insep* **to g. on one's competitors** ganar terreno a los competidores

gainful ['geɪnfʊl] *adj* remunerado(a)

gainfully ['geɪnfʊlɪ] *adv* **to be g. employed** tener un empleo remunerado

gainsay [geɪn'seɪ] (*pt & pp* **gainsaid** [geɪn'sed]) *vt Formal* negar

gait [geɪt] *n* paso *m*, manera *f* de caminar *or Esp* andar

gal [gæl] *n Old-fashioned Fam* moza *f*

gala ['gɑːlə] *n* gala *f*; **g. evening** noche *f* de gala; **g. performance** (actuación *f* de) gala

galactic [gə'læktɪk] *adj* galáctico(a)

Galapagos [gə'læpəgəs] *npl* **the G. (Islands)** las (Islas) Galápagos

galaxy ['gæləksɪ] *n* galaxia *f*; *Fig* **a g. of stars** un elenco de estrellas

gale [geɪl] *n (strong wind)* vendaval *m*; *Fig* **a g. of laughter** un torrente de carcajadas

Galicia [gə'lɪsɪə] *n (in Spain)* Galicia

Galician [gə'lɪsɪən] *n & adj (from Spain)* gallego(a) *m,f*

gall [gɔːl] **1** *n* (**a**) *Med* bilis *f inv*; **g. bladder** vesícula *f* biliar (**b**) *(impudence)* insolencia *f*; **she had the g. to…** tuvo la insolencia de…
   2 *vt (annoy)* irritar, dar rabia a

gallant ['gælənt] *adj (brave)* valiente, intrépido(a); *(attentive)* galante

gallantly ['gæləntlɪ] *adv (bravely)* con coraje, valerosamente; *(attentively)* galantemente, cortésmente

gallantry ['gæləntrɪ] *n (attentiveness)* galantería *f*; *(bravery)* valentía *f*, intrepidez *f*

galleon ['gælɪən] *n* galeón *m*

gallery ['gælərɪ] *n* (**a**) *(art)* **g.** *(for sale)* galería *f* de arte; *(for exhibition)* museo *m* (de arte) (**b**) *(in theater)* galería *f*, paraíso *m*; *Fig* **to play to the g.** *(politician)* actuar para la galería

galley ['gælɪ] (*pl* **galleys**) *n* (**a**) *(ship)* galera *f*; **g. slave** galeote *m* (**b**) *(ship's kitchen)* cocina *f* (**c**) *Typ* **g. (proof)** galerada *f*

Gallic ['gælɪk] *adj (French)* galo(a); *Hist (of Gaul)* galo(a), gálico(a)

gallicism ['gælɪsɪzəm] *n Ling* galicismo *m*

galling ['gɔːlɪŋ] *adj* irritante, mortificante

▶**gallivant around, gallivant about** [gælɪvænt] *vi* pendonear

gallon ['gælən] *n* galón *m* (= *3,785 litros*)

gallop ['gæləp] **1** *n* galope *m*; **at a g.** al galope
   2 *vi* galopar; *Fig* **she galloped through her work** despachó rápidamente su trabajo

gallows ['gæləʊz] *npl* patíbulo *m*, horca *f*; **g. humor** humor *m* negro *or* macabro

gallstone ['gɔːlstəʊn] *n* cálculo *m* biliar

galore [gə'lɔː(r)] *adv Fam* a montones, a patadas

galvanize ['gælvənaɪz] *vt* galvanizar; **to g. sb into action** mover a alguien a la acción

galvanized ['gælvənaɪzd] *adj* galvanizado(a); **g. steel** acero *m* galvanizado

Gambia ['gæmbɪə] *n* **the G.** Gambia

Gambian ['gæmbɪən] *n & adj* gambiano(a) *m,f*, gambio(a) *m,f*

gambit ['gæmbɪt] *n (in chess)* gambito *m*; *(in negotiation, diplomacy)* jugada *f*, maniobra *f*; **opening g.** *(in negotiation, diplomacy)* primer envite *m*

gamble ['gæmbəl] **1** n riesgo m; **to take a g.** arriesgarse

2 vt jugarse; **to g. one's future on sth** jugarse el porvenir por algo

3 vi jugar, apostar dinero; **to g. on sth** *(bet money on)* apostar a algo; *(take risk on)* jugársela confiando en algo, apostar por algo

gambler ['gæmblə(r)] n jugador(ora) m,f

gambling ['gæmblɪŋ] n juego m; **g. debts** deudas fpl de juego; **g. den** timba f, garito m

gambol ['gæmbəl] vi *(lamb, children)* retozar

game [geɪm] **1** n **(a)** *(activity, sport)* juego m; *(of cards, chess)* partida f; *(match)* (of football, baseball, basketball, soccer, tennis, golf) partido m; **g., set, and match** *(in tennis)* juego, set y partido; **games** *(sporting event)* juegos mpl; **politics is just a g. to them** la política no es más que un juego para ellos; **g. plan** plan m or estrategia f de juego; **g. show** concurso m televisivo; **g. theory** teoría f de juegos

(b) *(in hunting)* caza f; **g. reserve** coto m de caza

(c) *(idioms)* **to play the g.** jugar limpio; **two can play at that g.** donde las dan las toman; **to beat sb at his own g.** vencer a alguien con sus propias armas; **to play games with sb** jugar con alguien; **to give the g. away** desvelar el secreto; **what's his g.?** ¿qué pretende?; **I know what your g. is** sé a qué estás jugando; **the g.'s up for him** para él se acabó lo que se daba; **I've been in this g. a long time** llevo mucho tiempo metido en esto

2 adj **(a)** *(brave)* valiente; **to be g. (to do sth)** *(willing)* estar dispuesto(a) (a hacer algo) **(b)** Fam **a g. leg** una pata coja or Andes, RP renga or Esp chula

gamekeeper ['geɪmkiːpə(r)] n guarda mf de caza

gamely ['geɪmlɪ] adv valientemente

gamey = **gamy**

gamma ['gæmə] n *(Greek letter)* gamma f; Phys **g. rays** rayos mpl gamma

gammy ['gæmɪ] adj Fam **a g. leg** una pata coja or Andes, RP renga or Esp chula

gamut ['gæmət] n gama f; **to run the g. of** pasar por toda la gama de

gamy, gamey ['geɪmɪ] adj *(of flavor)* de or a caza

gander ['gændə(r)] n **(a)** *(male goose)* ganso m **(b)** Fam **to take a g. (at)** *(look)* echar un ojo or un vistazo (a)

gang [gæŋ] n *(of criminals)* banda f; *(of children, friends)* pandilla f; *(of workers)* cuadrilla f

▶**gang up** vi **to g. up on sb/with sb** confabularse contra/ con alguien

gang-bang ['gæŋbæŋ] n very Fam *(group rape)* violación f colectiva

Ganges ['gændʒiːz] n **the G.** el Ganges

gangland ['gæŋlænd] n *(underworld)* hampa f; **a g. killing** un ajuste de cuentas entre gángsters

gangling ['gæŋglɪŋ] adj larguirucho(a)

ganglion ['gæŋglɪən] (pl **ganglia** ['gæŋglɪə] or **ganglions**) n Anat ganglio m

gangplank ['gæŋplæŋk] n Naut pasarela f, plancha f

gangrene ['gæŋgriːn] n gangrena f

gangrenous ['gæŋgrɪnəs] adj gangrenoso(a); **to go g.** gangrenarse

gangsta ['gæŋstə] n **(a)** *(music)* **g. (rap)** gangsta m **(b)** *(rapper)* gangsta mf

gangster ['gæŋstə(r)] n gángster m; **g. movie** película f de gángsters

gangway ['gæŋweɪ] n Naut pasarela f, plancha f; **g.!** ¡paso!

gannet ['gænɪt] n *(bird)* alcatraz m; Fam *(greedy person)* glotón(ona) m,f

gantry ['gæntrɪ] n *(for crane)* pórtico m; *(for rocket)* torre f de lanzamiento

gap [gæp] n *(physical opening)* hueco m; *(in mountains)* desfiladero m, paso m; *(in time)* intervalo m; *(in age, ability)* diferencia f; *(in knowledge)* laguna f; *(in text)* espacio m en blanco; **the g. between rich and poor** la brecha entre ricos y pobres; **his death leaves a g. in all of our lives** su muerte deja un vacío en la vida de todos nosotros; Com **a g. in the market** un hueco en el mercado

gape [geɪp] vi **(a)** *(stare)* **to g. (at sth/sb)** mirar (algo/a alguien) con los ojos desorbitados **(b)** **to g. (open)** abrirse

gaping ['geɪpɪŋ] adj *(hole, chasm)* enorme

gappy ['gæpɪ] adj *(account, knowledge)* disperso(a), con muchas lagunas; **to have g. teeth** tener los dientes separados

garage [gæ'rɑːʒ] n *(for storing cars)* garaje m, Am cochera f; *(for repairing cars)* taller m (de reparaciones); **g. sale** = mercadillo en casa de un particular

garb ['gɑːb] n Literary atuendo m, atavío m

garbage ['gɑːbɪdʒ] n **(a)** *(household waste)* basura f; **g. can** cubo m or Am bote m de la basura; **g. collector** basurero(a) m,f; **g. disposal unit** trituradora f de basura; **g. dump** basurero m; **g. heap** montón m de basura; **g. man** basurero m; **g. truck** camión m de la basura **(b)** Fam *(nonsense)* Esp chorradas fpl, Am pendejadas; **he's talking g.** está diciendo Esp chorradas or Am pendejadas

garbanzo [gɑː'bɑːnzəʊ] (pl **garbanzos**) n **g. (bean)** garbanzo m

garble ['gɑːbəl] vt *(story, message)* embrollar

garbled ['gɑːbəld] adj *(story, explanation)* embrollado(a), confuso(a)

garden ['gɑːdən] **1** n jardín m; **g. center** centro m de jardinería; **g. furniture** mobiliario m de jardín; **g. party** recepción f al aire libre; Fig **to lead sb up the g. path** *(mislead)* engatusar a alguien; **g. tools** útiles mpl de jardinería

2 vi cuidar el jardín, trabajar en el jardín

gardener ['gɑːdnə(r)] n jardinero(a) m,f

gardening ['gɑːdnɪŋ] n jardinería f; **to do the g.** cuidar el jardín

gargantuan [gɑː'gæntjʊən] adj *(in general)* colosal; *(meal)* pantagruélico(a)

gargle ['gɑːgəl] vi hacer gárgaras

gargoyle ['gɑːgɔɪl] n gárgola f

garish ['geərɪʃ] adj *(clothes, color)* chillón(ona), estridente; *(light)* deslumbrante

garishly ['geərɪʃlɪ] adv con colores chillones

garland ['gɑːlənd] **1** n guirnalda f

2 vt adornar con guirnaldas

garlic ['gɑːlɪk] n ajo m; **g. bread** pan m de ajo; **g. butter** mantequilla f or Am manteca f aromatizada con ajo; **g. sausage** embutido m al ajo

garment ['gɑːmənt] n prenda f (de vestir)

garnet ['gɑːnɪt] n granate m

garnish ['gɑːnɪʃ] **1** n Culin guarnición f

2 vt guarnecer, adornar (**with** con)

garret ['gærət] n *(attic)* buhardilla f

garrison ['gærɪsən] **1** n guarnición f; **g. duty** servicio m en una guarnición; **g. town** ciudad f con guarnición

2 vt *(troops)* acuartelar

garrote [gə'rɒt] **1** n garrote m vil

2 vt dar garrote vil a

garrulous ['gærʊləs] adj gárrulo(a)

garter ['gɑːtə(r)] n *(for stockings)* liga f; **g. belt** liguero m; **g. snake** culebra f de jaretas

gas [gæs] **1** n **(a)** *(for cooking, heating)* gas m; **to have g.** *(as anesthetic)* recibir anestesia gaseosa; **g. bill** factura f del gas; **g. chamber** cámara f de gas; **g. stove** cocina f or Col, Méx, Ven estufa f de gas; **g. cylinder** bombona f de gas; **g. fire** estufa f de gas; **g. heater** *(for heating)* estufa f de gas; *(for hot water)* calentador m de gas; **g. lamp** lámpara f de gas; **g. main** tubería f del gas, gasoducto m; **g. mask** máscara f antigás; **g. ring** quemador m (**b**) *(gasoline)* gasolina *f*, *RP* nafta *f*; *Fam* **to step on the g.** *(accelerate)* pisar el acelerador; **g. pump** surtidor *m* de gasolina *or RP* nafta; **g. station** gasolinera *f*, estación *f* de servicio; **g. tank** depósito *m* de la gasolina *or RP* nafta

(**c**) *Fam* **what a g.!** ¡qué divertido!

(**d**) *(in stomach, intestines)* gases *mpl*; **to have g.** tener gases

2 *vt* (*pt & pp* **gassed**) gasear

3 *vi Fam (chat)* estar de cháchara *or Esp* palique

gasbag ['gæsbæg] *n Fam* charlatán(ana) *m,f*, cotorra *f*

gaseous ['geɪsɪəs] *adj* gaseoso(a)

gash [gæʃ] **1** *n (wound)* herida *f* (profunda), corte *m* (profundo); *(in wood, metal)* brecha *f*

2 *vt* hacerse una herida en

gasholder ['gæshəʊldə(r)], **gasometer** [gæ'sɒmɪtə(r)] *n* gasómetro *m*

gasket ['gæskɪt] *n Aut* junta *f*; *Fam Fig* **he blew a g.** *(lost his temper)* se salió de sus casillas

gasoline ['gæsəliːn] *n* gasolina *f*, *RP* nafta *f*

gasometer = **gasholder**

gasp [gɑːsp] **1** *n (of surprise)* grito *m* ahogado; **to be at one's last g.** estar en las últimas

2 *vi* lanzar un grito ahogado (**with** *or* **in** de); **to make sb g.** dejar boquiabierto a alguien; **she gasped for breath** *or* **for air** luchaba por respirar

gassy ['gæsɪ] *adj (beer)* con burbujas

gastric ['gæstrɪk] *adj* gástrico(a); **g. flu** gripe *f* gastrointestinal; **g. juices** jugos *mpl* gástricos; **g. ulcer** úlcera *f* gástrica

gastritis [gæs'traɪtɪs] *n* gastritis *f inv*

gastroenteritis [gæstrəʊəntə'raɪtɪs] *n* gastroenteritis *f inv*

gastronomic [gæstrə'nɒmɪk] *adj* gastronómico(a)

gastronomy [gæs'trɒnəmɪ] *n* gastronomía *f*

gasworks ['gæswɜːks] *n* fábrica *f or Am* planta *f* de gas

gate [geɪt] *n* (**a**) *(entrance)* puerta *f*; *(made of metal)* verja *f*; **g. (number) 15** *(in airport)* puerta número 15 (**b**) *Sport (spectators)* entrada *f*; *(takings)* recaudación *f*

gâteau, gateau ['gætəʊ] (*pl* **gâteaux** *or* **gateaux** ['gætəʊz]) *n* pastel *m*, *Esp* tarta *f*, *Col*, *CSur* torta *f*

gate-crash ['geɪtkræʃ] *Fam* **1** *vt* **to g. a party** colarse en una fiesta

2 *vi* colarse

gate-crasher ['geɪtkræʃə(r)] *n Fam* intruso(a) *m,f*

gated ['geɪtɪd] *adj* **g. community** = urbanización protegida con vigilantes

gatehouse ['geɪthaʊs] *n (of park, castle)* casa *f* del guarda; *(of house, estate)* casa *f* del portero

gatekeeper ['geɪtkiːpə(r)] *n (of park, castle)* guarda *mf*; *(of house, estate)* portero(a) *m,f*

gatepost ['geɪtpəʊst] *n* poste *m* (de la verja)

gateway ['geɪtweɪ] *n* entrada *f*; *Fig* **the g. to the East** la vía de entrada a Oriente; *Fig* **the g. to success** la clave del éxito

gather ['gæðə(r)] **1** *vt* (**a**) *(collect)* reunir; *(fruit, flowers)* recoger; **to g. the harvest** recoger la cosecha, cosechar; **he gathered his thoughts** puso en orden sus ideas; **to g. all one's strength to do sth** hacer acopio de fuerzas para hacer algo; **we are gathered here today…** estamos hoy aquí reunidos…; **he gathered her in his arms** la tomó entre sus brazos (**b**) *(accumulate) (dirt, dust)* acumular; *Fig* **to be gathering dust** estar arrinconado(a); **to g. speed** ganar velocidad (**c**) *(conclude, understand)* **to g. that…** deducir que…, entender que…; **as you may already have gathered…** como probablemente ya habrás deducido…; **so I g.** eso parece

2 *vi (people)* reunirse, congregarse; *(things)* acumularse; **a storm is gathering** se está formando una tormenta; **to g. around the fire/the radio** reunirse en torno al fuego/a la radio

▸**gather around, gather round** *vi* formar corro, agruparse

▸**gather together 1** *vt sep (belongings, evidence)* reunir

2 *vi (people)* reunirse

▸**gather up** *vt sep* recoger; **he gathered her up in his arms** la tomó en sus brazos

gathering ['gæðərɪŋ] **1** *n (group)* grupo *m* de personas; *(meeting)* reunión *f*

2 *adj (darkness, speed)* creciente; *also Fig* **the g. storm** la tormenta que se viene preparando

GATT [gæt] *n (abbr* **General Agreement on Tariffs and Trade)** GATT *m*

gauche [gəʊʃ] *adj* torpe, desmañado(a)

gaudily [gɔːdɪlɪ] *adv* con colores chillones

gaudy ['gɔːdɪ] *adj* chillón(ona), llamativo(a)

gauge, gage [geɪdʒ] **1** *n* (**a**) *(size) (of screw, wire, gun)* calibre *m*; *(of railroad track)* ancho *m* de vía (**b**) *(measuring device)* calibrador *m*; **fuel g.** indicador *m* del nivel de gasolina; **pressure g.** manómetro *m*; **the poll is a useful g. of public opinion** los sondeos son un útil indicador de la opinión pública

2 *vt (amount, difficulty)* calcular, precisar

Gaul [gɔːl] *n Hist* (**a**) *(region)* Galia *f* (**b**) *(inhabitant)* galo(a) *m,f*

gaunt [gɔːnt] *adj (person, features)* demacrado(a)

gauntlet ['gɔːntlɪt] *n (glove)* guante *m* (largo); *Hist* guantelete *m*, manopla *f*; *Fig* **to throw** *or* **fling down the g.** *(challenge)* arrojar el guante, *Am* desafiar a alguien; *Fig* **to take up the g.** recoger el guante, aceptar el reto; *Fig* **to run the g. of sth** exponerse a algo

gauze [gɔːz] *n* gasa *f*

gave [geɪv] *pt of* **give**

gavel ['gævəl] *n* martillo *m*, maceta *f (de subastador, juez)*

gawk [gɔːk] *vi Fam* quedarse papando moscas; **to g. at sth/sb** mirar boquiabierto(a) algo/a alguien

gawky ['gɔːkɪ] *adj Fam* desgarbado(a)

gay [geɪ] **1** *adj* (**a**) *(homosexual)* homosexual, gay; **g. rights** derechos *mpl* de los homosexuales (**b**) *esp Old-fashioned (happy)* alegre; **with g. abandon** con alegre despreocupación

2 *n (man)* homosexual *m*, gay *m*; *(woman)* lesbiana *f*

Gaza [gɑːzə] *n* Gaza; **the G. Strip** la Franja de Gaza

gaze [geɪz] **1** *n* mirada *f* (fija); **to meet** *or* **return sb's g.** devolver la mirada a alguien

2 *vi* **to g. at** mirar fijamente *or* embobadamente; **to g. into space** *or* **the middle distance** mirar al vacío

gazelle [gə'zel] *n* gacela *f*

gazette [gə'zet] *n (official journal)* boletín *m* oficial

gazetteer [gæzɪ'tɪə(r)] *n (book)* diccionario *m* geográfico

GB [dʒiː'biː] *n (abbr* **Great Britain)** GB, Gran Bretaña

Gdns *(abbr* **Gardens)** Jardines *(en direcciones)*

GDP [dʒiːdiː'piː] *n Econ (abbr* **gross domestic product)** PIB *m*

gear [gɪə(r)] *n* (**a**) *(on car, bicycle) (speed)* marcha *f*, velocidad *f*; *(mechanism)* engranaje *m*; *Fig* **to put sb's plans out of g.** desbaratar los planes de alguien; **first/second g.** primera *f*/segunda *f* (marcha *or* velocidad) (**b**) *Fam (equipment)* equipo *m*; *(in kitchen)* aparatos *mpl*; *(belongings)* bártulos *mpl* (**c**) *Fam (clothes)* ropa *f*

▸**gear to** *vt sep* **to g. sth to sth** adaptar algo a algo

▸**gear toward** *vt sep* **to be geared toward sth/sb** estar dirigido(a) *or* orientado(a) a algo/alguien

gearbox ['gɪəbɒks] *n* caja *f* de cambios

gearshift ['gɪəʃɪft] *n* palanca *f* de cambios

gee [dʒiː] *exclam* (**a**) *(to horse)* **g. up!** ¡arre! (**b**) **g. (whiz)!** ¡anda!, ¡caramba!

geek [giːk] *n Fam* lelo(a) *m,f*, tontaina *mf*; **a computer g.** un monstruo de la informática

geese *pl of* **goose**

Geiger counter ['gaɪgə(r)] *n* contador *m* Geiger

gel [dʒel] **1** *n (substance)* gel *m*; *(for hair)* gel *m* moldeador, *Esp* gomina *f*
2 *vi (pt & pp* **gelled)** *(liquid)* aglutinarse; *Fig (ideas, plans, team)* cuajar
gelatin(e) [dʒelə'tiːn] *n* gelatina *f*
gelatinous [dʒɪ'lætɪnəs] *adj* gelatinoso(a)
gelding ['geldɪŋ] *n* caballo *m* castrado
gelignite ['dʒelɪgnaɪt] *n* gelignita *f* (explosiva)
gem [dʒem] *n (precious stone)* gema *f*; *Fig* **he's an absolute g.** es una verdadera joya
Gemini [dʒemɪnaɪ] *n (sign of zodiac)* Géminis *m inv*; **to be (a) G.** ser Géminis
gemstone ['dʒemstəʊn] *n* piedra *f* preciosa, gema *f*
gender ['dʒendə(r)] *n* **(a)** *Gram* género *m* **(b)** *(sex)* sexo *m*
gene [dʒiːn] *n Biol* gen *m*; **to have sth in one's genes** *(talent, trait)* llevar algo en los genes *or* en la sangre
genealogical [dʒiːnɪə'lɒdʒɪkəl] *adj* genealógico(a)
genealogy [dʒiːnɪ'ælədʒɪ] *n* genealogía *f*
genera *pl of* **genus**
general ['dʒenərəl] **1** *n* **(a) in g.** en general **(b)** *Mil* general *m*; **g. of the army** capitán(ana) *nm,f* general
2 *adj* general; **as a g. rule** por norma *or* regla general; **in g. terms** en términos generales; **g. anesthetic** anestesia *f* general; **G. Assembly** *(of United Nations)* Asamblea *f* General; **g. delivery** lista *f* de correos; **g. election** elecciones *fpl* generales; **g. knowledge** cultura *f* general; **g. manager** director(ora) *m,f* general; **g. meeting** asamblea *f* general; *Med* **g. practice** medicina *f* general; *Med* **g. practitioner** médico(a) *m,f* de cabecera *or* de familia; **the g. public** el gran público, el público en general; **g. store** tienda *f* *(que vende de todo)*; **g. strike** huelga *f* general
generalist ['dʒenərəlɪst] *n* generalista *mf*
generality [dʒenə'rælɪtɪ] *n* generalidad *f*
generalization [dʒenərəlaɪ'zeɪʃən] *n* generalización *f*
generalize ['dʒenərəlaɪz] **1** *vt* **to become generalized** *(practice, belief)* generalizarse
2 *vi* generalizar
generally ['dʒenrəlɪ] *adv (taken overall)* en general; *(as a general rule)* generalmente, por lo general; **g. speaking** en términos generales
generate ['dʒenəreɪt] *vt (electricity, income)* generar; *(reaction, interest)* provocar
generation [dʒenə'reɪʃən] *n* **(a)** *(of people, computers)* generación *f*; **from g. to g.** de generación en generación; **the younger/older g.** la generación joven/vieja; **g. gap** conflicto *m* generacional **(b)** *(production) (of electricity)* producción *f*
generator ['dʒenəreɪtə(r)] *n Elec* generador *m*
generic [dʒɪ'nerɪk] *adj* genérico(a)
generosity [dʒenə'rɒsɪtɪ] *n* generosidad *f*
generous ['dʒenərəs] *adj* generoso(a)
generously ['dʒenərəslɪ] *adv* generosamente
genesis ['dʒenɪsɪs] *(pl* **geneses** ['dʒenɪsiːz]) *n* génesis *f inv*, origen *m*; **(the Book of) G.** (el Libro *m* del) Génesis *m*
genetic [dʒɪ'netɪk] *adj* genético(a); **g. code** código *m* genético; **g. engineering** ingeniería *f* genética; **g. finger-printing** identificación *f* genética
genetically [dʒɪ'netɪklɪ] *adv* genéticamente; **g. modified** transgénico(a), modificado(a) genéticamente
geneticist [dʒɪ'netɪsɪst] *n* genetista *mf*
genetics [dʒɪ'netɪks] *n* genética *f*
Geneva [dʒɪ'niːvə] *n* Ginebra; **Lake G.** el Lago Leman; **the G. Convention** la Convención de Ginebra
genial ['dʒiːnɪəl] *adj* cordial, amable
geniality [dʒiːnɪ'ælɪtɪ] *n* cordialidad *f*, amabilidad *f*
genially ['dʒiːnɪəlɪ] *adv* cordialmente, amablemente

genie ['dʒiːnɪ] *(pl* **genies** *or* **genii** ['dʒiːnɪaɪ]) *n* duende *m*, genio *m*
genital ['dʒenɪtəl] **1** *adj* genital
2 genitals *npl* (órganos *mpl*) genitales *mpl*
genitalia [dʒenɪ'teɪlɪə] *npl Formal* (órganos *mpl*) genitales *mpl*
genitive ['dʒenɪtɪv] *Gram* **1** *n* genitivo *m*
2 *adj* genitivo(a); **g. case** (caso *m*) genitivo *m*
genius ['dʒiːnɪəs] *n (person)* genio *m*; *(aptitude)* genio *m*, don *m*; **to have a g. for…** tener un don (natural) para…; **man/work of g.** hombre *m*/obra *f* genial
Genoa ['dʒenəʊə] *n* Génova
genocide ['dʒenəsaɪd] *n* genocidio *m*
genre ['ʒɒnrə] *n (of movie, novel)* género *m*
gent [dʒent] *n Fam* **he's a real g.** es todo un caballero
genteel [dʒen'tiːl] *adj (delicate)* fino(a); *Pej* afectado(a); *(respectable)* respetable
Gentile ['dʒentaɪl] *n* gentil *mf*, no judío(a) *m,f*
gentility [dʒen'tɪlɪtɪ] *n* refinamiento *m*, finura *f*; *Pej* afectación *f*, cursilería *f*
gentle ['dʒentəl] *adj (person, manner)* tierno(a), afectuoso(a); *(push, breeze, slope, exercise)* suave; *(hint)* discreto(a); *(rise, fall)* leve; **to be g. with sb/sth** tener cuidado con alguien/algo
gentleman ['dʒentəlmən] *n* caballero *m*; **he's a real g.** es todo un caballero; **a g.'s agreement** un pacto entre caballeros; **Ladies and Gentlemen!** ¡señoras y señores!
gentlemanly ['dʒentəlmənlɪ] *adj* caballeroso(a), cortés
gentleness ['dʒentəlnɪs] *n (of person, nature)* ternura *f*, afectuosidad *f*
gentlewoman ['dʒentəlwʊmən] *n Hist* dama *f*, señora *f*
gently ['dʒentlɪ] *adv (to treat)* con ternura, afectuosamente; *(to move, touch)* con suavidad; *(slowly)* despacio, poco a poco
gentry ['dʒentrɪ] *npl* alta burguesía *f*
genuflect ['dʒenjʊflekt] *vi* hacer una genuflexión
genuine ['dʒenjʊɪn] *adj* **(a)** *(authentic) (manuscript, painting)* genuino(a), auténtico(a) **(b)** *(sincere)* sincero(a); **a g. mistake** un error no intencionado
genuinely ['dʒenjʊɪnlɪ] *adv (sincerely)* realmente
genus ['dʒiːnəs] *(pl* **genuses** *or* **genera** ['dʒenərə]) *n Biol* género *m*
geo- ['dʒiːəʊ] *prefix* geo-
geographer [dʒɪ'ɒgrəfə(r)] *n* geógrafo(a) *m,f*
geographic(al) [dʒɪə'græfɪk(əl)] *adj* geográfico(a)
geography [dʒɪ'ɒgrəfɪ] *n* geografía *f*
geologic(al) [dʒɪə'lɒdʒɪk(əl)] *adj* geológico(a)
geologist [dʒɪ'ɒlədʒɪst] *n* geólogo(a) *m,f*
geology [dʒɪ'ɒlədʒɪ] *n* geología *f*
geometric(al) [dʒɪə'metrɪk(əl)] *adj* geométrico(a)
geometry [dʒɪ'ɒmɪtrɪ] *n* geometría *f*
geophysics [dʒɪəʊ'fɪzɪks] *n* geofísica *f*
geopolitics [dʒɪəʊ'pɒlɪtɪks] *n* geopolítica *f*
Georgia ['dʒɔːdʒɪə] *n (country, US state)* Georgia
Georgian ['dʒɔːdʒɪən] **1** *n* **(a)** *(person)* georgiano(a) *m,f* **(b)** *(language)* georgiano *m*
2 *adj (of country, US state)* georgiano(a)
geothermal [dʒiːəʊ'θɜːməl] *adj* geotérmico(a)
geranium [dʒə'reɪnɪəm] *n* geranio *m*
gerbil ['dʒɜːbɪl] *n* jerbo *m*, gerbo *m*
geriatric [dʒerɪ'ætrɪk] **1** *n Med* anciano(a) *m,f*; *Fam Pej* vejestorio *m*
2 *adj* geriátrico(a)
geriatrics [dʒerɪ'ætrɪks] *n* geriatría *f*
germ [dʒɜːm] *n* **(a)** *Med (micro-organism)* germen *m*, microbio *m*; **g. warfare** guerra *f* bacteriológica **(b)** *Bot & Fig* germen
German ['dʒɜːmən] **1** *n* **(a)** *(person)* alemán(ana) *m,f* **(b)** *(language)* alemán *m*; **G. class/teacher** clase *f*/profesor(ora) *m,f* de alemán

2 *adj* alemán(ana); **G. measles** rubeola *f*; **G. shepherd** pastor *m* alemán

germane [dʒɜː'meɪn] *adj Formal* pertinente; **that's not entirely g. to the matter** eso no concierne mucho al asunto

Germanic [dʒɜː'mænɪk] *adj* germánico(a)

Germany ['dʒɜːmənɪ] *n* Alemania

germ-free ['dʒɜːm'friː] *adj* aséptico(a)

germinate ['dʒɜːmɪneɪt] *vi* germinar

germination [dʒɜːmɪ'neɪʃən] *n* germinación *f*

gerontology [dʒerɒn'tɒlədʒɪ] *n Med* gerontología *f*

gerrymander ['dʒerɪmændə(r)] *vt Pol* = alterar los límites de un distrito electoral para que un partido obtenga mejores resultados

gerund ['dʒerənd] *n Gram* gerundio *m*

gestation [dʒes'teɪʃən] *n Med & Fig* gestación *f*; **g. period** período *m* de gestación

gesticulate [dʒes'tɪkjʊleɪt] *vi* gesticular

gesture ['dʒestʃə(r)] **1** *n also Fig* gesto *m*; *Fig* **as a g. of friendship** en señal de amistad; *Fig* **a hollow** *or* **empty g.** un gesto vacuo *or* para guardar las apariencias

2 *vi (single action)* hacer un gesto; *(repeatedly)* gesticular, hacer gestos; **to g. toward sth** *(point)* señalar *or* indicar hacia algo

get [get] (*pt* **got** [gɒt], *pp* **got** *or* **gotten** ['gɒtən])

> En las expresiones que aparecen bajo (**l**) y (**m**), **get** suele ser opcional. Cuando se omite **get**, **have** no se contrae. Para los casos en que se puede omitir, véase **have**.

1 *vt* **(a)** *(obtain)* conseguir; *(buy)* comprar; **could you g. me some potato chips from the store?** ¿me traes unas patatas fritas de la tienda?; **I can g. you a new video for just $30** te puedo conseguir un vídeo nuevo por sólo 30 dólares; **to g. a job** encontrar trabajo; **to g. the right/wrong answer** dar la respuesta correcta/equivocada

(b) *(receive)* *(present, reply, shock)* recibir; **we can't g. CNN here** aquí no recibimos *or* no llega la CNN; **I got the idea from a book** saqué la idea de un libro; **to g. $28,000 a year** ganar 28.000 dólares anuales; **we don't g. many visitors here** no viene mucha gente por aquí

(c) *(catch)* *(person, disease) Esp* coger; *Am* agarrar; *(train, bus)* tomar, *Fam* coger, *Am* agarrar; *Fam* **I'll g. you for that!** ¡me las pagarás!

(d) *(fetch)* **to g. sth for sb** traerle algo a alguien; **g. me the hammer** tráeme el martillo; **go and g. a doctor** ve a buscar a un médico

(e) *Fam (annoy)* **what gets me is that...** lo que me saca de quicio es que...

(f) *Fam (understand)* **now I g. you!** ¡ahora te entiendo!; **I don't g. your meaning** no entiendo *or* Esp cojo lo que quieres decir; **to g. a joke** pescar *or Esp* coger *or Am* cachar un chiste

(g) *(send)* **to g. sth to sb** mandar *or* enviar algo a alguien; **I got a message to them** les mandé *or* envié un mensaje

(h) *(cause to be in a certain state)* **to g. sth dry/wet** secar/mojar algo; **to g. sth dirty** ensuciar algo; **she got her work finished** terminó su trabajo; **to g. sth fixed** arreglar algo; **you've got him worried** lo has dejado preocupado; **to g. the children to bed** acostar a los niños

(i) *(cause to do)* **she got me to help her** me pidió que la ayudara; **why don't you g. your mother to do it?** ¿por qué no le pides a tu madre que lo haga ella?; **I finally got my mother to do it** por fin conseguí que lo hiciera mi madre; **you can g. them to wrap it for you** puedes pedir que te lo envuelvan; **I can't g. the car to start** no consigo que arranque el coche *or Am* carro *or CSur* auto

(j) *(do gradually)* **to g. to know sb** llegar a conocer a alguien; **you'll g. to like him** te llegará a gustar; **she soon got to thinking that...** pronto empezó a pensar que...

(k) *(have opportunity)* **to g. to do sth** llegar a *or* tener la

ocasión de hacer algo; **you g. to travel a lot in this job** en este trabajo se viaja mucho; **I finally got to see her** por fin pude *or* conseguí verla

(l) *(possess)* *(with* **have**) **they've got a big house** tienen una casa grande; **she hasn't got a car** no tiene coche *or Am* carro *or CSur* auto; **she's got measles/AIDS** tiene (el) sarampión/sida; **we've got a choice** tenemos una alternativa; **I've got something to do** tengo algo que hacer; **what's that got to do with it?** ¿qué tiene eso que ver?

(m) *(must)* *(with* **have**) **I've got to go** me tengo que ir; **have you got to work?** ¿tienes que trabajar?; **it's got to be done** hay que hacerlo

2 *vi* **(a)** *(arrive)* llegar; **to g. home** llegar a casa; **how do you g. there?** ¿cómo se llega?; **he got as far as Chapter Five** llegó hasta el quinto capítulo

(b) *(move)* **to g. in the way** ponerse en medio; **to g. in the way of sb, to g. in sb's way** ponerse delante de alguien; **she got over the wall** sorteó *or* pasó el muro

(c) *(become)* **to g. angry** *esp Esp* enfadarse, *esp Am* enojarse; **to g. better** mejorar; **to g. drunk** emborracharse; **to g. old** envejecer

(d) *(in passive-type constructions)* **to g. broken** romperse; **to g. stolen** ser robado(a)

(e) *(in reflexive-type constructions)* **to g. dressed** vestirse; **to g. married** casarse

(f) *(start)* **to g. going** *(leave)* irse, marcharse; *(start working)* empezar a funcionar; **to g. talking with sb** empezar a hablar con alguien

▸**get about** *vi (person)* moverse; *(news, rumor)* difundirse, trascender

▸**get across** *vt sep* **to g. an idea/a message across** hacer entender una idea/un mensaje; **to g. sth across to sb** hacer que alguien entienda algo

▸**get ahead** *vi* abrirse paso *or* camino

▸**get along** *vi* **(a)** *(leave)* marcharse, irse **(b)** *(progress)* **how are you getting along in your new job?** ¿cómo te va en el nuevo trabajo?; **we can g. along without them** podemos seguir sin ellos **(c)** *(have good relationship)* llevarse bien

▸**get around 1** *vt insep (avoid)* eludir

2 *vi (person)* moverse; *(news, rumor)* difundirse, trascender

▸**get around to, get round to** *vt insep* **to g. around to doing sth** sacar tiempo para hacer algo

▸**get at** *vt insep* **(a)** *(gain access to)* acceder a, llegar a; *(reach)* alcanzar; **to g. at the truth** dar con la verdad **(b)** *(imply)* **what are you getting at?** ¿qué (es lo que) quieres decir? **(c)** *Fam (criticize unfairly)* *(person)* meterse con, *Esp* chinchar

▸**get away** *vi (escape)* irse, escaparse; *(have a vacation)* tomarse unas vacaciones

▸**get away with** *vt insep (crime)* salir impune de; **I don't know how you g. away with speaking to your mother like that** no entiendo cómo tu madre te permite que le hables así; **he got away with a small fine** sólo le han puesto una pequeña multa; *Fig* **that child gets away with murder!** ¡ese niño se sale siempre con la suya!

▸**get back 1** *vt sep (recover)* recuperar

2 *vi (return)* volver, regresar

▸**get back at** *vt insep* **to g. back at sb (for sth)** vengarse de alguien (por algo)

▸**get behind 1** *vt insep (support)* apoyar

2 *vi (become delayed)* atrasarse, quedarse atrás

▸**get by** *vi (manage)* arreglárselas; **to g. by in Spanish** defenderse en español

▸**get down 1** *vt sep* **(a)** *(reduce)* *(weight)* bajar; *(costs, temperature)* reducir **(b)** *(depress)* **to g. sb down** desanimar *or* deprimir a alguien

2 *vi (descend)* bajarse (**from** de)

▸**get down to** *vt insep* ponerse a; **to g. down to doing sth** ponerse a hacer algo; **to g. down to work** poner manos a la obra; **to g. down to the facts** ir (directamente) a los hechos; **when you g. down to it…** en el fondo…

▸**get in 1** *vt sep* (**a**) *(bring inside) (washing)* meter; *(harvest)* recoger (**b**) **I couldn't g. a word in** *(in conversation)* no pude meter baza (**c**) *(stock up with) (food, coal)* hacer acopio de

2 *vi* (**a**) *(arrive) (train, person)* llegar (**b**) *(be elected)* salir elegido(a), ganar las elecciones

▸**get into** *vt insep* (**a**) *(house, car)* entrar en; **to g. into Congress** salir elegido(a) al Congreso; **to g. into trouble** meterse en un lío; *Fam* **I don't know what's got into her** no sé qué mosca le ha picado (**b**) *(clothes, boots)* ponerse (**c**) *Fam* **I really got into it** *(book, activity)* me enganchó muchísimo

▸**get in with** *vt insep (ingratiate oneself with)* congraciarse con

▸**get off 1** *vt sep* (**a**) *(save from punishment)* **to g. sb off** librar *or* salvar a alguien (**b**) **to g. the children off to school** mandar a los niños al colegio; **to g. a baby off to sleep** dormir a un niño

2 *vt insep (bus, train)* bajarse de

3 *vi* (**a**) *(descend from vehicle)* bajarse, apearse; *Fig* **I told him where to g. off** *(rebuked him)* lo mandé a paseo (**b**) *(go unpunished)* librarse (**c**) *(begin)* **to g. off (to sleep)** dormirse, quedarse dormido(a); **to g. off to a good/bad start** empezar con buen/mal pie

▸**get off on** *vt insep Fam* **she really gets off on ordering people about** realmente le mola eso de mandar

▸**get on 1** *vt sep* **to g. one's clothes/pants on** ponerse la ropa/los pantalones

2 *vt insep (board) (train, bus, plane)* montar en, subir a

3 *vi* (**a**) *(board)* montarse, subirse (**b**) *(succeed, progress)* **how are you getting on?** ¿cómo te va?; **I'm getting on well/badly** me va bien/mal; **you'll never g. on in life** *or* **in the world with that attitude!** ¡con esa actitud nunca llegarás a ninguna parte! (**c**) *(have good relationship)* llevarse bien; **to g. on well/badly with sb** llevarse bien/mal con alguien (**d**) **to be getting on (in years)** ser bastante mayor (**e**) *Fam* **to g. it on (with sb)** *(have sex) Esp* enrollarse (con alguien), *Am* coger (con alguien)

▸**get on to** *vt insep* **he must be getting on to fifty** debe de tener cerca de los cincuenta; **it was getting on to midnight** era cerca de medianoche

▸**get onto** *vt insep* (**a**) *(contact)* ponerse en contacto con (**b**) *(move onto subject of)* pasar a (hablar de); **they eventually got onto (the subject of) money** finalmente pasaron a hablar de (asuntos de) dinero

▸**get out 1** *vt sep (tools, books)* sacar; *(nail, splinter)* sacar, extraer; *(stain)* quitar, *Andes, RP* sacar

2 *vi* (**a**) *(leave)* salir (**b**) *(news)* filtrarse; **the secret got out** se descubrió el secreto

▸**get out of** *vt insep (car)* salir *or* bajar de; *(the way)* apartarse de; **to g. out of doing sth** librarse de hacer algo

▸**get over 1** *vt sep (communicate)* hacer llegar, transmitir

2 *vt insep* (**a**) *(cross) (road, river)* cruzar; *(wall, fence)* franquear (**b**) *(recover from) (illness, trauma)* recuperarse de

▸**get over with** *vt sep* **to g. sth over with** terminar con algo

▸**get round 1** *vt insep (avoid)* eludir

2 *vi* = **get about**

▸**get round to** = **get around to**

▸**get through 1** *vt sep (communicate)* **to g. sth through to sb** hacer ver algo a alguien

2 *vt insep* (**a**) *(pass through) (hole, roof)* entrar por (**b**) *(survive) (test, interview)* pasar, superar; *(period of time)* superar, aguantar (**c**) *(finish) (work)* terminar, acabar (**d**) *(consume) (food, drink)* consumir; *(money)* gastar

3 *vi* (**a**) *(arrive) (news, messenger)* llegar (**b**) **to g. through to sb** *(on telephone)* (lograr) comunicarse con alguien; *Fig (communicate with)* conectar con alguien; **the idea had**

finally **got through to him** la idea le entró por fin en la cabeza

▸**get together 1** *vt sep* **to g. some money together** juntar algo de dinero; **let me g. my thoughts together** déjame poner en claro mis ideas

2 *vi (people)* quedar, verse

▸**get up 1** *vt sep* (**a**) *(rouse)* **to g. sb up** levantar *or* despertar a alguien (**b**) *(dress up)* **he got himself up in his best clothes** se puso sus mejores ropas; **to g. oneself up as sb/sth** disfrazarse de alguien/algo (**c**) *very Fam* **he couldn't g. it up** *(achieve erection)* no se le *Esp* empinaba *or Am* paraba

2 *vt insep Fig* **to g. up sb's nose** *(annoy)* fastidiar a alguien, *Esp* tocar a alguien las narices

3 *vi (in morning)* levantarse; *(stand up)* levantarse, ponerse de pie, *Am* pararse

▸**get up to** *vt insep* **what have you been getting up to recently?** ¿qué has estado haciendo últimamente?; **to g. up to mischief** hacer de las suyas; **he's been getting up to his old tricks** ha vuelto a las andadas

getaway ['getəweı] *n* fuga *f*, huida *f*; **to make one's g.** fugarse, escaparse; **g. car** vehículo *m* utilizado en la fuga

get-rich-quick ['get'rɪtʃ'kwɪk] *adj Fam* **a g. scheme** un proyecto para enriquecerse rápidamente

get-together ['get'təgeðə(r)] *n Fam* reunión *f*

get-up ['getʌp] *n Fam (clothes)* indumentaria *f*; *(fancy dress)* disfraz *m*

get-up-and-go [getʌpənd'gəʊ] *n Fam (energy)* dinamismo *m*, iniciativa *f*

get-well card ['get'wel'kɑːd] *adj* = tarjeta con que se desea a un enfermo su mejoría

geyser ['giːzə(r)] *n Geog* géiser *m*

Ghana ['gɑːnə] *n* Ghana

Ghanaian [gɑːˈneɪən] *n & adj* ghanés(esa) *m,f*

ghastly ['gɑːstlɪ] *adj (terrible)* horrible, horroroso(a); **it was all a g. mistake** todo fue un tremendo error; **he looked g.** tenía un aspecto horrible *or Esp* fatal

gherkin ['gɜːkɪn] *n* pepinillo *m*

ghetto ['getəʊ] *(pl* **ghettos***) n* gueto *m*; **g. blaster** *(cassette player)* radiocasete *m* portátil *(de gran tamaño)*

ghettoize ['getəʊaɪz] *vt* marginar (como en un gueto)

ghost [gəʊst] *n* **1** *n* fantasma *m*; *Fig* **the g. of a smile** la sombra de una sonrisa; *Fig* **she doesn't have the g. of a chance** no tiene ni la más remota posibilidad; *Rel* **the Holy G.** el Espíritu Santo; **to give up the g.** pasar a mejor vida; **g. story** relato *m* de fantasmas; **g. town** ciudad *f*/pueblo *m* fantasma

2 *vt* **to g. a book for sb** escribir anónimamente un libro para alguien

ghostly ['gəʊstlɪ] *adj* fantasmal

ghostwrite ['gəʊstraɪt] *vt* **to g. a book for sb** escribir anónimamente un libro para alguien

ghostwriter ['gəʊstraɪtə(r)] *n* negro(a) *m,f*, escritor(ora) *m,f* anónimo(a)

ghoul [guːl] *n (evil spirit)* espíritu *m* maligno; *Fig (morbid person)* espíritu *m* macabro

ghoulish ['guːlɪʃ] *adj (humor, remark)* macabro(a)

GHQ [dʒiːeɪtʃˈkjuː] *n Mil (abbr* **General Headquarters***)* cuartel *m* general

GHz *Elec (abbr* **gigahertz***)* GHz

GI [dʒiːˈaɪ] *n Fam* soldado *m* raso

giant ['dʒaɪənt] **1** *n* gigante(a) *m,f*; **g. killer** *(in sport)* matagigantes *mf inv*

2 *adj* colosal, gigantesco(a); **g. panda** (oso *m*) panda *m*, panda *m* gigante

giantess ['dʒaɪəntes] *n* giganta *f*

gibber ['dʒɪbə(r)] *vi (talk incoherently)* farfullar; *(monkey)* parlotear

gibbering ['dʒɪbərɪŋ] *adj* incoherente, desvariado(a); *Fam* **a g. idiot** un perfecto idiota

gibberish ['dʒɪbərɪʃ] *n (unintelligible speech, writing)* galimatías *m inv*; *(nonsense)* tonterías *fpl*, memeces *fpl*; **to talk g.** decir tonterías *or* memeces

gibbet ['dʒɪbɪt] *n* horca *f*

gibbon ['ɡɪbən] *n* gibón *m*

gibe [dʒaɪb] **1** *n* burla *f*
  2 *vi* **to g. at sb** hacer burla de alguien

giblets ['dʒɪblɪts] *npl* menudillos *mpl*

Gibraltar [dʒɪ'brɔːltə(r)] *n* Gibraltar

giddily ['ɡɪdɪlɪ] *adv (dizzily)* vertiginosamente

giddiness ['ɡɪdɪnɪs] *n (dizziness)* mareo *m*; *(from height)* vértigo *m*

giddy ['ɡɪdɪ] *adj (dizzy)* **to be g.** estar mareado(a); *(from height)* tener vértigo; **g. heights** alturas *fpl*, cumbre *f*

giddyup ['ɡɪdɪʌp] *exclam (to horse)* ¡arre!

GIF [dʒɪf] *n Comptr (abbr* **Graphics Interchange Format**) GIF *m*, formato *m* de intercambio de gráficos

gift [ɡɪft] *n (a) (present)* regalo *m*, obsequio *m*; *Prov* **never look a g. horse in the mouth** a caballo regalado no le mires el diente; **g. shop** tienda *f* de artículos de regalo **(b)** *(talent)* don *m*; **to have a g. for mathematics** tener un don para las matemáticas; **to have the g. of the gab** tener un pico de oro

gifted ['ɡɪftɪd] *adj (talented)* dotado(a); *(unusually talented)* superdotado(a)

gift-wrap ['ɡɪftræp] *vt* envolver con papel de regalo; **would you like it gift-wrapped?** ¿se lo envuelvo para regalo?

gift-wrapped ['ɡɪftræpt] *adj* envuelto(a) para regalo

gig [ɡɪɡ] *n* **(a)** *(carriage)* calesa *f* **(b)** *Fam (pop concert)* actuación *f*, concierto *m*

gigabyte ['dʒɪɡəbaɪt] *n Comptr* gigabyte *m*

gigahertz ['dʒɪɡəhaːts, 'ɡɪɡəhaːts] *n Elec* gigahercio *m*

gigantic [dʒaɪ'ɡæntɪk] *adj* gigantesco(a)

giggle ['ɡɪɡəl] **1** *n* risita *f*, risa *f* floja; **to have (a fit of) the giggles** tener un ataque de risa tonta
  2 *vi* soltar risitas

giggly ['ɡɪɡəlɪ] *adj* **two g. girls at the back of the class** dos niñas soltando risitas al fondo de la clase

gigolo ['dʒɪɡələʊ] *(pl* **gigolos**) *n* gigoló *m*

gild [ɡɪld] *(pt & pp* **gilded** *or* **gilt** [ɡɪlt]) *vt* dorar; *Fig* **to g. the lily** rizar el rizo

gill[1] [ɡɪl] *n* **gills** *(of fish)* branquias *fpl*; *Fig* **to be green around the gills** *(look unwell)* estar pálido(a)

gill[2] [dʒɪl] *n (liquid measure)* cuarto *m* de pinta *(0,142 litros)*

gilt [ɡɪlt] **1** *n* (baño *m*) dorado *m*
  2 *adj* dorado(a)
  3 *pt & pp of* **gild**

gilt-edged ['ɡɪlt'edʒd] *adj Fin* **g. securities** *or* **stock** títulos *mpl or* valores *mpl* de máxima garantía

gimlet ['ɡɪmlɪt] *n (tool)* barrena *f*; **his g. eyes** su mirada *f* penetrante

gimme ['ɡɪmiː] *Fam* = **give me**

gimmick ['ɡɪmɪk] *n* truco *m*, reclamo *m*

gimmicky ['ɡɪmɪkɪ] *adj* artificioso(a)

gin [dʒɪn] *n* ginebra *f*; **g. and tonic** gin-tonic *m*

ginger ['dʒɪndʒə(r)] **1** *n* jengibre *m*; **g. ale** ginger ale *m*; **g. beer** = cerveza de baja graduación o sin alcohol con sabor a jengibre
  2 *adj (hair)* pelirrojo(a)

gingerbread ['dʒɪndʒəbred] *n* pan *m* de jengibre; *(biscuit-like)* galleta *f* de jengibre

gingerly ['dʒɪndʒəlɪ] *adv* con mucho tiento

gingersnap ['dʒɪndʒəsnæp] *n* galleta *f* de jengibre

gingham ['ɡɪŋəm] *n* guinga *f*, = tela de algodón a cuadros

gingivitis [dʒɪndʒɪ'vaɪtɪs] *n Med* gingivitis *f inv*

ginseng ['dʒɪnseŋ] *n* ginseng *m*

giraffe [dʒɪ'rɑːf] *n* jirafa *f*

gird [ɡɜːd] *(pt & pp* **girded** *or* **girt** [ɡɜːt]) *vt Literary* **to g. one's loins** armarse para la batalla

girder ['ɡɜːdə(r)] *n* viga *f*

girdle ['ɡɜːdəl] **1** *n (corset)* faja *f*
  2 *vt Literary* ceñir

girl [ɡɜːl] *n (child, baby)* niña *f*; *(young woman)* chica *f*; **that's my g.!** *(well done)* ¡buena chica!

girlfriend ['ɡɜːlfrend] *n (of boy, man)* novia *f*; *(of girl, woman)* amiga *f*

girlhood ['ɡɜːlhʊd] *n* niñez *f*

girlie, girly ['ɡɜːlɪ] *n Fam* **g. mag** revista *f* de chicas desnudas

girlish ['ɡɜːlɪʃ] *adj* **(a)** *(of girl, young woman)* de niña **(b)** *(man)* afeminado(a)

girly = **girlie**

girt [ɡɜːt] *pt & pp of* **gird**

girth [ɡɜːθ] *n (of tree)* contorno *m*; *(of person)* barriga *f*

gismo = **gizmo**

gist [dʒɪst] *n* esencia *f*; **to get the g. (of sth)** entender el sentido general (de algo)

give [ɡɪv] **1** *vt (pt* **gave** [ɡeɪv], *pp* **given** ['ɡɪvən]) **(a)** *(in general)* dar; *(as present)* regalar; **to g. sth to sb, to g. sb sth** dar algo a alguien; **to g. sb sth to eat** dar algo de comer a alguien; **to g. a child a name** ponerle nombre a un niño; **to g. sb an illness** contagiarle *or* pegarle una enfermedad a alguien; **he was given ten years** le cayeron diez años; **he was given a fine** le pusieron una multa; **g. her my love** dale recuerdos *or Am* cariños de mi parte; **to g. sb a choice** dar a alguien una alternativa; **given the chance again** si se presentara de nuevo la ocasión; **he gave his age as twenty** declaró que tenía veinte años; **she gave me to understand that...** me dio a entender que...; **g. or take a few minutes/dollars** minuto/dólar arriba o abajo
  (b) *(with noun, to form verbal expressions)* **to g. a laugh** soltar una carcajada; **to g. sb a smile** sonreírle a alguien; **to g. sb a fright** dar un susto a alguien; **she gave me a strange look** me lanzó una mirada extraña; **she gave the soup a stir** removió *or* revolvió la sopa
  2 *vi* **(a)** *(donate)* hacer donativos *or Am* donaciones; **please g. generously** por favor, sea generoso en sus donativos *or Am* donaciones; **he gave of his free time to the cause** dedicó gran parte de su tiempo libre a la causa **(b)** *(bend, stretch)* dar de sí; *(break)* ceder, romperse; **she refused to g. on the question of money** se negó a ceder en la cuestión del dinero **(c)** *Fam* **what gives?** ¿qué pasa?
  3 *n* elasticidad *f*

▸**give away** *vt sep* **(a)** *(give for nothing)* regalar **(b)** *(prize)* repartir; **to g. the bride away** llevar a la novia al altar **(c)** *(betray, reveal)* traicionar; **to g. away a secret** revelar un secreto; **his accent gave him away** su acento lo delató

▸**give back** *vt sep* devolver

▸**give in 1** *vt sep (hand over)* entregar
  2 *vi (surrender)* rendirse (**to** a); *(admit defeat)* rendirse, darse por vencido(a)

▸**give off** *vt sep (smell, heat)* despedir

▸**give out 1** *vt sep* **(a)** *(money, food)* repartir; *(information)* divulgar **(b)** *(noise, heat)* emitir
  2 *vi (supplies, patience)* agotarse; *(luck)* acabarse

▸**give over** *vt sep (money, objects)* entregar

▸**give up 1** *vt sep (possessions, activity, hope)* abandonar, renunciar a; **to g. up smoking** dejar de fumar; **to g. up one's job** dejar el trabajo; **to g. sb up for dead** dar a alguien por muerto(a)
  2 *vi (stop trying)* rendirse, darse por vencido(a); **to g. up on sth/sb** *(lose faith, hope in)* dejar algo/a alguien por imposible

▸**give way** *vi* **(a)** *(collapse)* ceder, hundirse **(b)** *(yield) (in argument)* ceder (**to** ante) **(c)** *(be superseded)* verse desbancado(a) (**to** por); **her tears gave way to laughter** las lágrimas dieron paso a la risa

give-and-take ['ɡɪvən'teɪk] *n* toma y daca *m*

giveaway ['gɪvəweɪ] *n Fam* (**a**) *(revelation)* señal *f* reveladora; **it was a dead g.** estaba más claro que el agua (**b**) *(free gift)* obsequio *m*; **g. price** precio *m* de saldo

given ['gɪvən] **1** *adj* (**a**) *(specific) (time, place)* dado(a), determinado(a); **at a g. point** en un momento dado; **g. name** nombre *m* (de pila) (**b**) *(apt, likely)* **to be g. to** ser dado(a) *or* propenso(a) a

2 *conj (considering)* dado(a); **g. the nature of the case** dada la naturaleza del caso

3 *pp of* **give**

gizmo, gismo ['gɪzməʊ] *(pl* **gizmos**) *n Fam* chisme *m*, aparato *m*

gizzard ['gɪzəd] *n* molleja *f*

glacé ['glæsɪ] *adj Culin* confitado(a), escarchado(a), *Col, Méx* cristalizado(a), *RP* abrillantado(a); **g. cherries** cerezas *fpl* confitadas

glacial ['gleɪsɪəl] *adj also Fig* glacial

glacier ['glæsɪə(r)] *n* glaciar *m*

glad [glæd] *adj* alegre, contento(a); **to be g. about sth** estar alegre *or* contento por algo; **to be g. of sth** *(grateful for)* agradecer algo; **to be g. to do sth** estar encantado(a) de hacer algo; *Literary* **g. tidings** buenas nuevas *fpl*; *Fam* **g. rags** ropa *f* elegante

gladden ['glædən] *vt* alegrar, llenar de contento

glade [gleɪd] *n Literary* calvero *m*, claro *m*

gladiator ['glædɪeɪtə(r)] *n* gladiador *m*

gladiolus [glædɪ'əʊləs] *(pl* **gladiolus, gladioli** [glædɪ'əʊlaɪ]) *n* gladiolo *m*

gladly ['glædlɪ] *adv* con mucho gusto

glam [glæm] *n* **g. rock** (música *f)* glam *m*, glam rock *m*

glamor ['glæmə(r)] *n* atractivo *m*, encanto *m*; *Fam* **g. girl** bombón *m*, *Am* muñequita *f*

glamorize ['glæməraɪz] *vt* hacer atractivo(a)

glamorous ['glæmərəs] *adj* atractivo(a)

glamorously ['glæmərəslɪ] *adv* con una elegancia deslumbrante

glance [glɑːns] **1** *n* vistazo *m*, ojeada *f*; **at a g.** de un vistazo; **at first g.** a primera vista

2 *vi* **to g. at** echar una mirada *or* un vistazo a; **to g. through** *(book, magazine)* ojear

▶**glance off** *vt insep (of blow, missile)* rebotar en

glancing ['glɑːnsɪŋ] *adj (blow)* de lado, de refilón

gland [glænd] *n* glándula *f*

glandular ['glændjʊlə(r)] *adj* glandular; *Med* **g. fever** mononucleosis *f inv* infecciosa

glare [gleə(r)] **1** *n* (**a**) *(angry stare)* mirada *f* feroz (**b**) *(bright light)* resplandor *m*; *Fig* **in the full g. of publicity** en el punto de mira de toda la gente

2 *vi (stare angrily)* **to g. at sth/sb** mirar algo/a alguien con furia

glaringly ['gleərɪŋlɪ] *adv* **g. obvious** clarísimo(a), de una claridad meridiana

Glasgow ['glɑːzgəʊ] *n* Glasgow

glass [glɑːs] *n (material)* vidrio *m*, *Esp* cristal *m*; *(vessel)* vaso *m*; *(with stem)* copa *f*; *(glassware)* cristalería *f*; **a g. of wine** un vaso de vino; **g. bottle** botella *f* de vidrio *or Esp* cristal; **g. case** vitrina *f*; *Fig* **g. ceiling** *(in career)* barreras *fpl* laborales *or* profesionales; **g. eye** ojo *m* de vidrio *or Esp* cristal; **g. wool** lana *f* de vidrio

glassblower ['glɑːsbləʊə(r)] *n* soplador(ora) *m,f* de vidrio

glassblowing ['glɑːsbləʊɪŋ] *n* soplado *m* de vidrio

glasses ['glɑːsɪz] *npl (spectacles)* gafas *fpl*, *Am* anteojos *mpl*, *Am* lentes *mpl*

glassful ['glɑːsfʊl] *n* vaso *m*

glassware ['glɑːsweə(r)] *n* cristalería *f*

glassworks ['glɑːswɜːks] *n* fábrica *f* de vidrio

glassy ['glɑːsɪ] *adj (water, lake)* cristalino(a); *(surface)* vítreo(a), bruñido(a); **a g. look** una mirada vidriosa

glassy-eyed ['glɑːsɪ'aɪd] *adj* de mirada vidriosa

glaucoma [glɔː'kəʊmə] *n* glaucoma *m*

glaze [gleɪz] **1** *n (on pottery)* vidriado *m*; *(on pastry)* glaseado *m*

2 *vt* (**a**) *(window)* acristalar (**b**) *(pottery)* vidriar; *(pastry)* glasear

▶**glaze over** *vi (eyes)* velarse

glazed [gleɪzd] *adj* (**a**) *(roof, door)* acristalado(a) (**b**) *(pottery)* vidriado(a)

glazier ['gleɪzɪə(r)] *n* cristalero(a) *m,f* vidriero(a) *m,f*

glazing ['gleɪzɪŋ] *n (glass)* vidrios *mpl*, cristales *mpl*

gleam [gliːm] **1** *n (of light)* destello *m*

2 *vi* resplandecer, relucir

gleaming ['gliːmɪŋ] *adj* resplandeciente, reluciente

glean [gliːn] *vt (information)* averiguar; **to g. information from sth** extraer información de algo

glee [gliː] *n (delight)* regocijo *m*, contento *m*; *(malicious pleasure)* regodeo *m*

gleeful ['gliːfʊl] *adj (happy)* regocijado(a); **to be g.** *(to be maliciously happy)* regodearse

gleefully ['gliːfʊlɪ] *adv (joyfully)* con regocijo; *(maliciously)* con malicia, regodeándose

glen [glen] *n Scot* cañada *f*

glib [glɪb] *adj (salesman, politician)* con mucha labia, *CAm, Ecuad, Méx* labioso(a); *(talk)* simplista; *(excuse, answer)* fácil

glibly ['glɪblɪ] *adv* con labia

glide [glaɪd] *vi (slide)* deslizarse; *Av* planear

glider ['glaɪdə(r)] *n Av* planeador *m*

gliding ['glaɪdɪŋ] *n Av* vuelo *m* sin motor

glimmer ['glɪmə(r)] **1** *n* brillo *m* tenue; *Fig* **g. of hope** resquicio *m* de esperanza; **not the slightest g. of intelligence** ni el más mínimo atisbo de inteligencia

2 *vi (light)* brillar tenuemente; *(water, metal)* relucir

glimpse [glɪmps] **1** *n* vistazo *m* fugaz, atisbo *m*; **to catch a g. of** vislumbrar, entrever; **a g. of the future** un atisbo del futuro

2 *vt* vislumbrar, entrever

glint [glɪnt] **1** *n* centelleo *m*, destello *m*; **with a g. in her eye** con un brillo en los ojos

2 *vi* centellear, lanzar destellos

glisten ['glɪsən] *vi* relucir, brillar

glitter ['glɪtə(r)] **1** *n (sparkle)* brillo *m*, resplandor *m*; *Fig (of occasion)* esplendor *m*, brillantez *f*; **g. rock** (música *f)* glam *m*, glam rock *m*

2 *vi* lanzar destellos; **her eyes glittered with excitement** le brillaban los ojos de emoción; *Prov* **all that glitters is not gold** no es oro todo lo que reluce

glitterati [glɪtə'rɑːtɪ] *npl Fam* famosos *mpl*, *Esp* gente *f* guapa, *Méx* popis *mpl*, *RP* crema *f*

glittering ['glɪtərɪŋ] *adj (jewels)* brillante, resplandeciente; *Fig (occasion, career)* rutilante

glittery ['glɪtərɪ] *adj* llamativo(a), de relumbrón

glitz [glɪts] *n* boato *m*, pompa *f*

glitzy ['glɪtsɪ] *adj Fam (party)* espectacular, despampanante

gloat [gləʊt] *vi (at one's own success)* alardear (**at** *or* **about** de), presumir (**at** *or* **about** de); *(about someone else's misfortune)* regodearse (**about** *or* **over** con *or* de)

global ['gləʊbəl] *adj (comprehensive)* global; *(worldwide)* mundial, global; **g. economy** economía *f* global; **the g. village** la aldea global; **g. warming** cambio *m* climático, calentamiento *m* global

globalism ['gləʊbəlɪzəm] *n* globalismo *m*

globalization [gləʊbəlaɪ'zeɪʃən] *n* mundialización *f*, globalización *f*

globally ['gləʊbəlɪ] *adv* globalmente

globe [gləʊb] *n (sphere)* esfera *f*, bola *f*; *(with map)* globo *m* terráqueo, bola *f* del mundo; **the g.** *(the Earth)* el globo, el planeta; **to travel the g.** viajar por todo el mundo; **g. artichoke** alcachofa *f*, *RP* alcaucil *m*

globetrotter ['gləʊbtrɒtə(r)] *n Fam* trotamundos *mf inv*

globetrotting ['gləʊbtrɒtɪŋ] *n* viajes *mpl* por todo el mundo

globule ['glɒbjuːl] *n* gota *f*

gloom [gluːm] *n* (**a**) *(darkness)* oscuridad *f*, tinieblas *fpl* (**b**) *(melancholy)* abatimiento *m*, tristeza *f*; **to cast** *or* **throw a g. over sth** enturbiar algo (**c**) *(pessimism)* pesimismo *m*

gloomily ['gluːmɪlɪ] *adv (unhappily)* sombríamente, tenebrosamente

gloomy ['gluːmɪ] *adj* (**a**) *(dark)* oscuro(a); **g. weather** tiempo *m* gris (**b**) *(melancholy)* abatido(a), decaído(a); **g. thoughts** pensamientos *mpl* sombríos (**c**) *(pessimistic)* pesimista; **to paint a g. picture (of sth)** hacer un retrato sombrío (de algo), pintar (algo) muy negro

glorify ['glɔːrɪfaɪ] *vt (extoll, glamorize)* glorificar, ensalzar; *Rel* **to g. God** alabar a Dios

glorious ['glɔːrɪəs] *adj* (**a**) *(reign, victory)* glorioso(a) (**b**) *(view, weather)* espléndido(a), magnífico(a)

gloriously ['glɔːrɪəslɪ] *adv* espléndidamente

glory ['glɔːrɪ] *n* (**a**) *(honor)* gloria *f*; **to live on past glories** vivir de glorias pasadas (**b**) *(splendor)* esplendor *m*

▸**glory in** *vt insep* deleitarse *or* regocijarse con

gloss¹ [glɒs] **1** *n (in text)* glosa *f*
2 *vt (text)* glosar, explicar

gloss² *n (of paint, finish)* & *Fig* lustre *m*, brillo *m*; **to take the g. off sth** deslucir algo; **g. paint** pintura *f* (con acabado) brillo

▸**gloss over** *vt insep (difficulty, mistake)* mencionar muy de pasada

glossary ['glɒsərɪ] *n* glosario *m*

glossy ['glɒsɪ] *adj* brillante; **a g. brochure** un folleto en papel cuché; **g. magazine** revista *f* de lujo a todo color; **g. paper** papel *m* cuché

glottal stop ['glɒtəl'stɒp] *n* oclusión *f* glotal

glove [glʌv] *n* guante *m*; *Fig* **the gloves are off** se ha desatado la lucha; *Aut* **g. compartment** guantera *f*

glow [gləʊ] **1** *n (light)* brillo *m*, resplandor *m*; *(on cheeks)* rubor *m*; *Fig* **to have a healthy g.** *(person)* tener buen color; *Fig* **he had a g. of pride/satisfaction** se le iluminaba la cara de orgullo/satisfacción
2 *vi (light, fire)* brillar; *Fig* **to be glowing with health** tener un color muy saludable; *Fig* **he was glowing with pride/ pleasure** la cara se le iluminaba de orgullo/placer

glower ['glaʊə(r)] *vi* **to g. at sb** mirar con furia a alguien

glowing ['gləʊɪŋ] *adj (cigarette, coal)* encendido(a); *Fig (report)* encendido(a), entusiasta; *Fig* **to paint sth in g. colors** pintar algo de color de rosa

glowingly ['gləʊɪŋlɪ] *adv* **to speak g. of sth/sb** hablar elogiosamente de algo/alguien

glowworm ['gləʊwɜːm] *n* luciérnaga *f*

glucose ['gluːkəʊs] *n* glucosa *f*

glue [gluː] **1** *n (in general)* pegamento *m*; *(thicker, for wood, metal)* cola *f*
2 *vt (in general)* pegar; *(wood, metal)* encolar; *Fig* **to be glued to the television** estar pegado(a) a la televisión

glue-sniffer ['gluːsnɪfə(r)] *n* persona *f* que inhala pegamento

glue-sniffing ['gluːsnɪfɪŋ] *n* inhalación *f* de pegamento

glum [glʌm] *adj* abatido(a), triste; **to be g.** estar abatido *or* triste

glumly ['glʌmlɪ] *adv* con abatimiento, con aire sombrío

glut [glʌt] **1** *n Com* saturación *f*
2 *vt (pt & pp* **glutted***)* (**a**) *Com* saturar (**b**) **to g. oneself (on)** saciarse (de), hartarse (de)

gluten ['gluːtən] *n Biochem* gluten *m*

gluten-free ['gluːtən'friː] *adj* sin gluten

glutinous ['gluːtɪnəs] *adj (substance)* viscoso(a), glutinoso(a); *(rice)* apelmazado(a)

glutton ['glʌtən] *n (greedy person)* glotón(ona) *m,f*; *Fig* **she's a g. for work** nunca se harta de trabajar; *Fig* **you're a g. for punishment** eres masoquista

gluttonous ['glʌtənəs] *adj* glotón(ona)

gluttony ['glʌtənɪ] *n* gula *f*, glotonería *f*

glycerin ['glɪsərɪn], **glycerine** ['glɪsəriːn], **glycerol** ['glɪsə-rɒl] *n* glicerina *f*

GM [dʒiːem] **1** *n Com (abbr* **general manager***)* director(ora) *m,f* general
2 *adj (abbr* **genetically modified***)* transgénico(a), modificado(a) genéticamente; **GM food** (alimentos *mpl*) transgénicos *mpl*

GMT [dʒiːemˈtiː] *n (abbr* **Greenwich Mean Time***)* hora *f* del meridiano de Greenwich

gnarled [nɑːld] *adj (tree)* retorcido(a) y nudoso(a); *(hands)* deformado(a)

gnash [næʃ] *vt* **to g. one's teeth** hacer rechinar los dientes

gnat [næt] *n* mosquito *m*

gnaw [nɔː] **1** *vt (of animal)* roer
2 (**a**) *(animal)* **to g. through sth** roer algo (**b**) *Fig (doubt)* **to g. away at sb** corroer a alguien

gnawing ['nɔːɪŋ] *adj (pain)* martirizador(ora); *(doubts)* atenazador(ora)

gnome [nəʊm] *n* gnomo *m*

GNP [dʒiːenˈpiː] *n Econ (abbr* **Gross National Product***)* PNB *m*

gnu [nuː] *n* ñu *m*

go [gəʊ] **1** *n (pl* **goes***)* (**a**) *(turn)* turno *m*; **(it's) your go!** ¡te toca a ti!; **to have a go at doing sth** probar a *or* intentar hacer algo; *Fam* **let's have a go!** ¡vamos a probar *or* intentarlo!; *(let me try)* ¡déjame probar!; **in one go** de una vez (**b**) *(idioms)* **on the go** *(active)* en marcha; **from the word "go"** desde el principio, desde el primer momento; **to make a go of sth** *(succeed)* tener éxito con algo
2 *vi (3rd person singular* **goes** [gəʊz], *pt* **went** [went], *pp* **gone** [gɒn])* (**a**) *(in general)* ir; **to go home** irse a casa; **to go to Spain/the doctor** ir a España/al médico; **the proceeds will go to charity** las ganancias se destinarán a obras de beneficencia; *Mil* **who goes there?** ¿quién va?; *Fig* **where do we go from here?** *(what do we do next?)* y ahora, ¿qué hacemos?; **to go hunting/skiing** ir de caza/a esquiar
(**b**) *(leave) (person)* irse, marcharse; *(train, bus)* salir; **that dog will have to go!** ¡tenemos que librarnos de ese perro!; **we'd better get going** deberíamos irnos *or* salir ya; *Euph* **when I am gone** cuando yo falte
(**c**) *(extend)* **the garden goes down to the river** el jardín llega *or* se extiende hasta el río; **this path goes down to the beach** el camino lleva hasta la playa
(**d**) *(function)* funcionar; *(bell)* sonar; **to keep the conversation going** mantener viva la conversación
(**e**) *(progress)* ir; **to go well/badly** ir bien/mal; **to go wrong** ir mal, *Am* descomponerse, *Andes* malograrse; *Fam* **how's it going?** ¿qué tal?; **if all goes well** si todo va bien; **how does the tune/story go?** ¿cómo es *or* dice la canción/ historia?
(**f**) *(time)* **the time went quickly** el tiempo pasó muy rápido; **it has just gone eight** acaban de dar las ocho; **there are only five minutes to go** sólo quedan cinco minutos
(**g**) *(disappear, deteriorate)* desaparecer; **her sight is going** está perdiendo la vista; **the fuse has gone** se ha fundido el fusible; **the batteries are going** se están acabando las pilas; **most of my money goes on food** la mayor parte del dinero se me va en comida
(**h**) *(forming future)* **to be going to do sth** ir a hacer algo; **I was going to walk there** iba a ir caminando *or* Esp andando; **it's going to rain** va a llover; **I'm going to be a doctor** voy a ser médico

(i) *(match)* ir bien, pegar (**with** con); **these colors go/don't go** estos colores pegan/no pegan

(j) *(be sold)* **it went for \$12** se vendió por 12 dólares

(k) *(fit)* caber; **the piano won't go through the door** el piano no cabe por la puerta; **four into three won't go** tres no es divisible entre cuatro, tres entre cuatro no cabe

(l) *(become)* **to go crazy** volverse loco(a); **to go bad** echarse a perder; **to go red** enrojecer, ponerse rojo(a); **to go cold** enfriarse

(m) *(be the rule)* **what she says goes** ella es la que manda

(n) *Fam (urinate)* mear, *Méx* miar

(o) **to go** *(to take away)* para llevar

3 *vt* **to go it alone** montárselo por su cuenta; **to go one better than sb** superar a alguien

▸**go about 1** *vi (circulate) (person)* ir por ahí; *(rumor)* correr; **there's a bug going about** hay un virus por ahí suelto

2 *vt insep* (a) *(travel) (country)* viajar por (b) *(tackle) (task)* abordar; **to go about doing sth** *(start)* ponerse a hacer algo; **how do I go about getting a license?** ¿qué hay que hacer para conseguir un permiso?

▸**go across 1** *vt insep* cruzar, atravesar

2 *vi* **to go across to Britain** ir a Gran Bretaña

▸**go after** *vt insep (pursue)* ir tras; *Fig (job, prize, person)* estar detrás de, *Esp* ir a por

▸**go against** *vt insep* (a) *(conflict with) (principles, instincts)* ir (en) contra de; **he went against my wishes** actuó en contra de mis deseos (b) *(be unfavorable to)* **the decision went against him** la decisión le fue desfavorable

▸**go ahead** *vi* (a) *(proceed)* seguir adelante; **to go ahead with sth** seguir (adelante) con algo; **may I say something? — go ahead** ¿puedo hablar? — adelante (b) *(go in front)* ir delante

▸**go along** *vi (proceed)* avanzar; **to do sth as one goes along** hacer algo sobre la marcha

▸**go along with** *vt insep* estar de acuerdo con, aceptar; **she wouldn't go along with it** no quiso tomar parte en ello

▸**go around, go round 1** *vi* (a) *(visit)* **I said I'd go around (and see her)** dije que me pasaría (a visitarla); **she's gone around to a friend's** ha ido a casa de un amigo (b) *(circulate) (rumor, cold, flu)* circular (c) *(suffice) (food, drink)* llegar, alcanzar; **there should be enough money to go around** debería llegarnos el dinero

2 *vt insep* **to go around town/the stores** recorrer la ciudad/las tiendas

▸**go at** *vt insep (person)* atacar; *(task)* emprender

▸**go away** *vi (leave)* irse; *(disappear)* desaparecer; **go away!** ¡vete!; **to go away on business** irse en viaje de negocios; **to go away for the weekend** irse a pasar el fin de semana fuera

▸**go back** *vi* (a) *(return)* volver; **to go back to doing sth** volver a hacer algo; **to go back to one's old ways** volver a las andadas (b) *(date back)* **to go back to** remontarse a, datar de; *Fam* **we go back a long way** nos conocemos desde hace mucho tiempo

▸**go back on** *vt insep (promise, one's word)* faltar a

▸**go before 1** *vt insep* **to go before the court** *(defendant)* comparecer ante el juez, ir a juicio; *(case)* verse

2 *vi (precede)* preceder

▸**go by 1** *vi* (a) *(pass)* pasar; **to watch people going by** mirar a la gente que pasa (b) *(elapse) (time)* pasar, transcurrir

2 *vt insep* (a) *(be guided by)* guiarse por; **to go by appearances** fiarse de las apariencias; **to go by the rules** seguir las reglas (b) *(be known by)* **to go by the name of...** ser conocido(a) con el nombre de...

▸**go down 1** *vt insep (descend) (hill, ladder)* bajar por

2 *vi* (a) *(descend)* bajar; *(sun)* ponerse; *(ship)* hundirse; **to go down on one's knees** arrodillarse, ponerse de rodillas; *Fam* **to go down with an illness** agarrar *or Esp* coger una enfermedad (b) *(be defeated)* perder (**to** contra), caer (**to** ante); **I'm not going to go down without a fight** no voy a

rendirme sin luchar (c) *(decrease) (flood, temperature, prices)* descender; *(tire, balloon)* desinflarse (d) *(be received)* **to go down well/badly (with sb)** ser bien/mal acogido(a) por alguien; **he went down in history as a tyrant** pasó a la historia como un tirano

▸**go for** *vt insep* (a) *(attack)* lanzarse contra, atacar; **if you really want the job, go for it!** si realmente te interesa el trabajo, ¡lánzate *or Esp* a por él! (b) *(like)* **she goes for strong types** le van los tipos fuertes (c) *(choose)* escoger, elegir (d) **he has got a lot going for him** tiene mucho a su favor (e) *(apply to)* valer para; **the same goes for you** lo mismo te digo a ti *or* vale para ti

▸**go in** *vi (enter)* entrar; *(fit)* caber; **the sun has gone in** se ha nublado

▸**go in for** *vt insep* (a) *(competition)* tomar parte en (b) **she doesn't go in for cooking/sports** no le atrae la cocina/el deporte

▸**go into** *vt insep* (a) *(enter) (place)* entrar en; *(hospital)* ingresar en; *(career)* entrar en, meterse en (b) *(examine) (question)* tratar; **to go into detail** entrar en detalle

▸**go off 1** *vi* (a) *(leave)* marcharse, irse; **to go off with sb** *(elope)* escaparse con alguien; **to go off with sth** irse con algo, llevarse algo (b) *(gun)* dispararse; *(bomb)* explotar; *(alarm)* saltar, sonar (c) **to go off well** *or* **smoothly** *(event)* salir bien (d) *(be disconnected)* **the lights went off** se fue la luz

2 *vt insep (lose liking for)* **I've gone off the idea** me ha dejado de gustar la idea

▸**go on 1** *vi* (a) *(continue)* seguir (**with** con), continuar (**with** con); **as time went on...** a medida que pasaba el tiempo... (b) *(proceed)* **to go on to sth/to do sth** pasar a algo/a hacer algo (c) *(talk excessively)* hablar sin parar, enrollarse; **to go on about sth** no parar de hablar de algo, enrollarse con algo; **to go on at sb** dar la lata a alguien (d) *(happen)* pasar, ocurrir; **what's going on here?** ¿qué pasa aquí? (e) *(electricity, light, heating)* encenderse, *Am* prenderse

2 *vt insep* (a) *(enter) (boat, train)* subir a (b) *(be guided by)* guiarse por; **the police have nothing to go on** la policía carece de pistas (c) *(approach)* **she's two going on three** tiene dos años, casi tres

▸**go out** *vi* (a) *(leave)* salir; **to go out for a meal** salir a comer fuera; **to go out on strike** ponerse *or* declararse en huelga (b) *(date)* salir; **to go out with sb** salir con alguien (c) *(fire, light)* apagarse (d) *(become unfashionable)* pasar de moda (e) *Sport (be eliminated)* quedar eliminado(a) (f) *TV & Rad (program)* emitirse

▸**go over 1** *vi* (a) *(cross)* **to go over to sb** aproximarse a alguien, acercarse hasta alguien (b) *(switch)* **to go over to a different system** cambiar de sistema; **to go over to the enemy** pasarse a las filas del enemigo (c) *(be received)* **to go over well/badly** tener buena/mala acogida

2 *vt insep* (a) *(road, bridge)* cruzar (b) *(examine) (accounts, report)* estudiar, examinar; **to go over sth in one's mind** repasar algo mentalmente

▸**go round** = **go around**

▸**go through 1** *vi (be completed) (bill)* aprobarse; *(deal, divorce)* consumarse

2 *vt insep* (a) *(penetrate)* atravesar (b) *(suffer)* pasar (por), atravesar; **in spite of all she had gone through** a pesar de todo lo que había pasado (c) *(complete) (formalities)* cumplir con (d) *(examine) (document, accounts)* estudiar, examinar; *(search) (suitcase, house, pockets)* registrar (e) *(use up) (money, food)* acabar con, gastar; **we've gone through six bottles of milk** hemos gastado seis botellas de leche

▸**go through with** *vt insep (carry out)* llevar a término

▸**go together** *vi (harmonize)* pegar, ir bien

▸**go under** *vi (drowning man)* hundirse; *(ship)* naufragar; *(go bankrupt)* quebrar, ir a la quiebra

▸**go up** *vi* (a) *(climb, rise)* subir; *Theat (curtain)* levantarse; **to go** up to bed subir a acostarse; **a shout went up from the crowd** se elevó un grito desde la multitud; *Fig* **to go up in the world** subir peldaños, prosperar **(b)** *(prices, temperature)* subir; **to go up in sb's estimation** crecer *or* aumentar en la estima de alguien **(c)** *(explode)* estallar; **to go up in flames** ser pasto de las llamas

▶**go up to** *vt insep* **(a)** *(approach)* acercarse a, aproximarse a **(b)** *(reach)* **the book only goes up to the end of the war** el libro sólo llega hasta el final de la guerra

▶**go with** *vt insep* **(a)** *(accompany)* ir con; **a company car goes with the job** el puesto lleva aparejado coche de empresa **(b)** *(harmonize with)* pegar con

▶**go without 1** *vi* pasar privaciones; **they haven't got any, so we'll just have to go without** no les quedan, así que habrá que apañárselas (sin ellos)

2 *vt insep (not have)* prescindir de, quedarse sin

goad [gəʊd] **1** *n (remark, criticism)* acicate *m*

2 *vt (sb's curiosity, interest)* suscitar; **to g. sb into doing sth** pinchar a alguien para que haga algo; **he was goaded by these remarks** estos comentarios le sirvieron de acicate

▶**goad on** *vt sep* **to g. sb on** *(motivate)* espolear *or* acicatear a alguien

go-ahead ['gəʊəhed] **1** *n* **to give sb/sth the g.** dar luz verde a alguien/algo

2 *adj (enterprising)* dinámico(ca)

goal [gəʊl] *n* **(a)** *(aim)* objetivo *m*, meta *f*; **to achieve a g.** alcanzar un objetivo **(b)** *(in ice hockey, soccer) (point)* gol *m*; **g. (mouth)** portería *f*, *Am* arco *m*; **g. difference** gol *m* average; **g. kick** *(in soccer)* saque *m* de puerta; **g. line** *(at end of field)* línea *f* de fondo; *(between goalposts)* línea *f* de gol *or* meta; *(in football)* línea *f* de marca; *(in rugby)* línea *f* de marca, *RP* ingoal *m*; **g. scorer** goleador(ora) *m,f*

goalkeeper ['gəʊlkiːpə(r)], *Fam* **goalie** ['gəʊlɪ] *n* portero(a) *m,f*, guardameta *mf*, *Am* arquero(a) *m,f*, *Am* guardavallas *mf inv*, *RP* golero *m,f*

goalkeeping ['gəʊlkiːpɪŋ] *n* defensa *f* de la portería *or Am* del arco

goalless ['gəʊllɪs] *adj (in soccer)* **g. tie** *or* **draw** empate *m* a cero

goalpost ['gəʊlpəʊst] *n (in football, soccer, rugby)* poste *m*; **the goalposts** la portería, la meta, *Am* el arco; *Fig* **to move** *or* **shift the goalposts** cambiar las reglas del juego

goat [gəʊt] *n* cabra *f*; *Fam* **it really gets my g.!** ¡me pone negro(a) *or* a cien *or RP* de la nuca!; **g.'s milk** leche *f* de cabra

goatee [gəʊtiː] *n* perilla *f*

goatherd ['gəʊthɜːd] *n* cabrero(a) *m,f*

goatskin ['gəʊtskɪn] *n* piel *f* de cabra

gobble ['gɒbəl] **1** *vt (eat)* engullir

2 *vi (turkey)* gluglutear

▶**gobble up** *vt sep* engullir; **to g. up one's food** engullir la comida; **to g. up money/resources** *(project)* consumir mucho dinero/muchos recursos

gobbledygook, gobbledegook ['gɒbəldɪguːk] *n Fam* jerigonza *f*, galimatías *m inv*

go-between ['gəʊbɪtwiːn] *n* mediador(ora) *m,f*; **to act** *or* **serve as a g.** actuar como mediador, mediar

goblet ['gɒblɪt] *n* copa *f*

goblin ['gɒblɪn] *n* duende *m*

go-cart ['gəʊkɑːt] *n (child's toy)* coche *m* de juguete; *Sport* kart *m*; **g. racing** carreras *fpl* de karts

God [gɒd] *n* **(a)** Dios *m*; **G. forbid!** ¡Dios no lo quiera!; **G. willing** si Dios quiere; **I wish to G....** ojalá...; **in God's name** por el amor de Dios; *Fam* **oh G.!, my G.!** ¡Dios mío!; *Fam* **for God's sake!** ¡por (el amor de) Dios!; *Fam* **G. knows** sabe Dios; *Fam* **he thinks he's God's gift to women** se cree irresistible para las mujeres **(b)** *Fam Theat* **the gods** *(gallery)* el gallinero

god-awful ['gɒdɔːfəl] *adj Fam* horroroso(a)

godchild ['gɒdtʃaɪld] *n* ahijado(a) *m,f*

goddam(n) ['gɒdæm], **goddamned** ['gɒdæmd] *Fam* **1** *adj* maldito(a), *Esp* dichoso(a), *Méx* pinche; **he's a g. fool!** ¡es un maldito imbécil!

2 *adv* **that was g. stupid!** ¡eso fue una auténtica estupidez!

3 *exclam* **g. (it)!** ¡maldita sea!, *Méx* ¡híjole!, *RP* ¡miércoles!

goddaughter ['gɒddɔːtə(r)] *n* ahijada *f*

goddess ['gɒdɪs] *n* diosa *f*

godfather ['gɒdfɑːðə(r)] *n* padrino *m*

god-fearing ['gɒdfɪrɪŋ] *adj* temeroso(a) de Dios

godforsaken ['gɒdfəseɪkən] *adj* dejado(a) de la mano de Dios

godless ['gɒdlɪs] *adj (person, action)* impío(a)

godlike ['gɒdlaɪk] *adj* divino(a)

godmother ['gɒdmʌðə(r)] *n* madrina *f*

godparent ['gɒdpeərənt] *n* padrino *m*, madrina *f*; **my godparents** mis padrinos

godsend ['gɒdsend] *n* regalo *m* del cielo; **this money is a g. to him** este dinero le viene como llovido del cielo

godson ['gɒdsʌn] *n* ahijado *m*

go-getter ['gəʊgetə(r)] *n Fam* **he's a real g.** es ambicioso y decidido

goggle ['gɒgəl] *vi* mirar con ojos desorbitados; **to g. at sth/sb** mirar algo/a alguien con los ojos como platos

goggle-eyed ['gɒgəlaɪd] *adv Fam* con ojos como platos *or RP* como dos huevos fritos

goggles ['gɒgəlz] *npl* gafas *fpl (para esquí, natación)*; **safety g.** gafas protectoras

go-go dancer ['gəʊgəʊdɑːnsə(r)] *n* gogó *f*

going ['gəʊɪŋ] **1** *n* **(a)** *(progress)* **that's very good g.!** ¡es un buen ritmo!; **it's slow g.** es muy trabajoso(a) **(b)** *(condition of path)* camino *m*; *(in horseracing)* terreno *m*; *Fig* **heavy g.** *(movie, book)* pesado(a); *Fig* **to get out while the g. is good** retirarse mientras las cosas van bien

2 *adj* **(a)** *(functioning)* **a g. concern** *(successful business)* un negocio en marcha y rentable **(b)** *(current)* **the g. price** *or* **rate** la tasa *or* el precio vigente

going-away ['gəʊɪŋəweɪ] *adj* **a g. party/present** una fiesta/un regalo de despedida

going-over ['gəʊɪŋ'əʊvə(r)] *n Fam* **to give sb a g.** *(beating)* dar una paliza *or Esp* tunda a alguien; *(criticism)* echar una reprimenda *or Esp* bronca a alguien, *RP* dar a alguien un buen rezongo; **the auditors gave the accounts a thorough g.** los auditores miraron las cuentas de arriba abajo *or* con lupa

goings-on ['gəʊɪŋzɒn] *npl Fam* asuntos *mpl* turbios, tejemanejes *mpl*

goiter ['gɔɪtə(r)] *n* bocio *m*

gold [gəʊld] **1** *n* oro *m*; **g. bullion** lingotes *mpl* de oro; **g. digger** *Fam (mercenary woman)* cazafortunas *f inv*; **g. dust** oro *m* en polvo; **tickets are like g. dust** es casi imposible conseguir una entrada *or Col, Méx* un boleto; **g. leaf** *or* **foil** pan *m* de oro, oro *m* batido; *Sport* **g. medal** medalla *f* de oro; *also Fig* **g. mine** mina *f* de oro; **g. plate** *(decoration)* baño *m* de oro; *(dishes)* vajilla *f* de oro; *Fin* **g. reserves** reservas *fpl* de oro

2 *adj (of gold)* de oro; *(color)* dorado(a)

golden ['gəʊldən] *adj (made of gold)* de oro; *(gold-colored)* dorado(a); **a g. opportunity** una oportunidad de oro; **the g. boy/girl of...** el chico/la chica de oro de...; **the g. age** la edad de oro; **g. eagle** águila *f* real; **the G. Fleece** el Vellocino de Oro; *Com* **g. handcuffs** contrato *m* blindado; **g. handshake** *(retirement bonus)* gratificación *f* voluntaria por jubilación; **g. hello** = cuantiosa gratificación ofrecida como incentivo para ingresar en una empresa; **g. jubilee** quincuagésimo aniversario *m* (de un reinado); **g. oldie** clásico *m*, viejo éxito *m*; **g. wedding** *(anniversary)* bodas *fpl* de oro

goldfield ['gəʊldfiːld] *n* yacimiento *m* de oro

goldfinch ['gəʊldfɪntʃ] *n* jilguero *m*

goldfish ['gəʊldfɪʃ] *n* pez *m* de colores; **g. bowl** pecera *f*; **it's like living in a g. bowl** es como estar expuesto(a) en un escaparate

gold-plated ['gəʊld'pleɪtɪd] *adj* bañado(a) en oro

gold-rimmed ['gəʊld'rɪmd] *adj (spectacles)* con montura de oro

goldsmith ['gəʊldsmɪθ] *n* orfebre *mf*

golf [gɒlf] *n* golf *m*; **g. ball** pelota *f* de golf; **g. club** *(stick)* palo *m* de golf; *(association)* club *m* de golf; **g. course** campo *m* de golf

golfer ['gɒlfə(r)] *n* jugador(ora) *m,f* de golf, golfista *mf*; **to be a good g.** jugar bien al golf

golfing ['gɒlfɪŋ] *n* **g. vacation** = vacaciones dedicadas a jugar al golf

golly ['gɒlɪ] *exclam Fam Old-fashioned* ¡caramba!

gondola ['gɒndələ] *n* góndola *f*

gondolier [gɒndə'lɪə(r)] *n* gondolero *m*

gone [gɒn] **1** *adj Fam* **to be six months g.** *(pregnant)* estar (embarazada) de seis meses; **to be pretty far g.** *(drunk)* estar como una cuba; **to be g. on sb** *(infatuated)* estar colado(a) por alguien

   2 *pp of* **go**

goner ['gɒnə(r)] *n Fam* **I thought she was a g.** *(thought she would die)* la vi con un pie en la tumba; **I'm a g. if she finds out** *(will be in trouble)* si se entera, me mata

gong [gɒŋ] *n* gong *m*

gonna ['gɒnə] *Fam* = **going to**

gonorrhea [gɒnə'rɪə] *n* gonorrea *f*

goo [guː] *n Fam* **(a)** *(sticky substance)* pringue *f* **(b)** *(sentimentality)* cursilería *f*, *Esp* cursiladas *fpl*

good [gʊd] **1** *n* **(a)** *(in general)* bien *m*; **to do g.** hacer el bien; **he's up to no g.** está tramando algo malo; **to see the g. in sb/sth** ver el lado bueno de alguien/algo

   (b) *(benefit)* bien *m*; **I did it for your own g.** lo hice por tu bien; **it was all to the g.** todo ha sido para bien; **for the g. of his health** por motivos de salud; **for the common g.** por el bien de todos; **it will do you g.** te sentará bien, te vendrá bien; **it won't do any g.** no va a hacer ningún bien; **what's the g. of that?** ¿para qué sirve eso?; **it's no g. complaining** quejarse no sirve de nada; **he's no g.** *(incompetent)* no sirve para nada; *(morally bad)* no es bueno

   2 *adj (comparative* **better** ['betə(r)], *superlative* **best** [best]) **(a)** *(of positive quality)* bueno(a); **it looks g. on you** te queda bien; **she looks g. in that hat** le queda muy bien ese sombrero; **to sound/taste g.** sonar/saber bien; **g. to eat** comestible; **it's g. to see you** me alegro de verte; *Fam* **that's a g. one!** *(I don't believe you)* ¡no me digas!, *Esp* ¡venga ya!; **I suppose he thinks he's too g. for us** debe pensar que es más que nosotros; **if it's g. enough for you, it's g. enough for me** si a ti te sirve *or Esp* vale, a mí también; **to earn g. money** ganar un buen sueldo; **you've got a g. chance** tienes bastantes posibilidades; **to be on to a g. thing** tener entre manos algo bueno; **to have a g. time** pasarlo bien; **to show sb a g. time** sacar a alguien a divertirse por ahí; **all in g. time** todo llegará; **too g. to be true** demasiado bueno para ser verdad; **the g. old days** los viejos tiempos; **g. afternoon!** ¡buenas tardes!; **the G. Book** la Biblia; **he's a g. friend** es un buen amigo; **G. Friday** Viernes *m inv* Santo; *Fam* **g. grief!** ¡madre mía!; **the g. life** la buena vida; **g. looks** atractivo *m*; *Fam* **g. Lord!, g. heavens!, g. gracious!** ¡madre mía!, ¡santo cielo!; **g. morning!** ¡buenos días!; **g. news** buenas noticias *fpl*; **g. night!** ¡buenas noches!, ¡hasta mañana!; **the G. Samaritan** el buen samaritano

   (b) *(advantageous, appropriate)* bueno(a); **a g. opportunity** una buena ocasión; **to be in a g. position to do sth** estar en

una buena posición para hacer algo; **things are looking g.** la cosa tiene buena pinta

   (c) *(beneficial)* bueno(a); **this medicine is very g. for coughs** este medicamento es muy bueno para la tos; **he doesn't know what's g. for him** no sabe lo que le conviene; **to be g. for business** ser bueno para el negocio; **it's a g. thing we were here** menos mal que estábamos aquí; **g. riddance!** ¡ya era hora de que desapareciera!

   (d) *(skillful)* bueno(a); **she is g. at chemistry** se le da bien la química, *Am* es buena en química; **he is g. at languages** se le dan bien los idiomas, *Am* es bueno para los idiomas; **to be g. with one's hands** ser habilidoso(a) con las manos *or Esp* muy manitas; **she is g. with children** se le dan bien los niños; **to be g. in bed** ser bueno(a) en la cama

   (e) *(well-behaved)* bueno(a); **be g.!** *(to child)* ¡sé bueno!, ¡pórtate bien!; **g. conduct** *or* **behavior** buena conducta, buen comportamiento; **to be as g. as gold** ser más bueno(a) que el pan; **to lead a g. life** llevar una vida ejemplar

   (f) *(kind)* amable; **that's very g. of you** es muy amable de tu parte; **he was very g. about it** fue muy comprensivo al respecto; **to do sb a g. turn** hacer un favor a alguien

   (g) *(valid)* **a g. reason** una buena razón; **I have g. reason to believe that...** tengo buenas razones para creer que...; **there is no g. reason why...** no hay razón alguna por la que...; **he's g. for $25,000** *(has in credit)* tiene un activo de 25.000 dólares; *(will contribute)* aportará 25.000 dólares

   (h) *(thorough)* bueno(a); **to have a g. look (at sb/sth)** echar una buena ojeada (a alguien/algo); **to have a g. cry (about)** llorar a gusto (por), *Esp* echarse una buena llantina (por)

   (i) **to make g.** *(person)* prosperar; **he was ordered to make g. the company's losses** fue condenado a indemnizar a la empresa por las pérdidas; **to make g. one's promise** hacer uno buena su promesa; **he made g. his escape** consiguió escapar

   (j) *(at least)* **a g. two hours** dos horas largas, por lo menos dos horas; **a g. deal of** mucho(s), mucha(s); **a g. many** muchos(as)

   3 *adv* **(a)** *(for emphasis)* bien, muy; **a g. long time** un tiempo bien largo, mucho tiempo; **I'll do it when I'm g. and ready** lo haré cuando crea conveniente **(b)** *(as comment, answer)* bien, estupendo; **I feel better today — g.** hoy me encuentro mejor — estupendo *or Méx* padre *or RP* bárbaro

   4 for good *adv (permanently)* para siempre

   5 as good as *adv (almost)* **it's as g. as new** está como nuevo; **he as g. as called me a liar** prácticamente me llamó mentiroso

goodbye, goodby ['gʊd'baɪ] *n* despedida *f*, adiós *m*; **g.!** ¡adiós!; **to say g.** despedirse; **to say g. to sb** decir adiós a alguien, despedir a alguien; **he can say g. to his chances of winning** puede despedirse del triunfo, puede decir adiós al triunfo

good-for-nothing ['gʊdfənʌθɪŋ] **1** *n* inútil *mf*
   2 *adj (person)* inútil

good-hearted [gʊd'hɑːtɪd] *adj (person)* de buen corazón; *(action)* bien intencionado(a)

good-humored [gʊd'hjuːməd] *adj* jovial, distendido(a)

goodie = **goody**

good-looker ['gʊd'lʊkə(r)] *n Fam* **to be a g.** estar bueno(a)

good-looking ['gʊdlʊkɪŋ] *adj Esp* guapo(a), *Am* lindo(a)

good-natured [gʊd'neɪtʃəd] *adj* bondadoso(a)

goodness ['gʊdnɪs] *n* **(a)** *(of person)* bondad *f* **(b)** *(of food)* **if you boil it, you lose all the g.** si lo hierves, pierde todas sus propiedades **(c)** *(in exclamations)* **g. (me)!** ¡santo cielo!; **thank g.!** ¡gracias a Dios!; **for g. sake, be quiet!** ¡por el amor de Dios, cállate!

goodnight [gʊd'naɪt] *n* buenas noches *fpl*; **to say g. (to sb)** dar las buenas noches (a alguien)

goods [gʊdz] *npl* **(a)** *Law* bienes *mpl* **(b)** *(articles)* productos *mpl*, artículos *mpl*; **leather g.** marroquinería *f*, artículos *mpl* de cuero; *Fig* **to deliver the g.** *(keep one's promise)* cumplir (lo prometido); *Fig* **to come up with the g.** cumplir; *Fam* **to have the g. on sb** tener pruebas contra alguien

good-tempered [gʊd'tempəd] *adj* afable

goodwill ['gʊd'wɪl] *n* (**a**) *(benevolence, willingness)* buena voluntad *f*; **to retain sb's g.** conservar el favor de alguien (**b**) *Com* fondo *m* de comercio

goody, goodie ['gʊdɪ] *Fam* **1** *n* (**a**) *(person)* buenazo(a) *m,f*; **the goodies and the baddies** los buenos y los malos (**b**) **goodies** *(food)* golosinas *fpl*
2 *exclam* **g.!** ¡viva!, *Esp* ¡qué chupi!

goody-goody ['gʊdɪgʊdɪ] *n Fam Pej* niño(a) *m,f* modelo

gooey ['guːɪ] *adj Fam* (**a**) *(sticky)* pegajoso(a) (**b**) *(sentimental)* empalagoso(a), sentimentaloide

goof [guːf] *Fam* **1** *n* (**a**) *(blunder)* metedura *f* or *Am* metida *f* de pata (**b**) *(idiot)* bobo(a) *m,f*
2 *vi* meter la pata

▶**goof around, goof about** *vi Fam (mess around)* hacer el bobo

▶**goof off** *Fam* **1** *vt insep* **to g. off work** no ir a trabajar or *Esp* currar
2 *vi* gandulear, holgazanear

goofy ['guːfɪ] *adj Fam (stupid)* bobalicón(ona), *Esp* zampabollos *inv*

goon [guːn] *n Fam* (**a**) *(thug)* matón *m* (**b**) *(stupid person)* bobo(a) *m,f*, lerdo(a) *m,f*

goose [guːs] *(pl* geese [giːs]) *n (bird)* ganso *m*, oca *f*; *Fig* **his g. is cooked** se va a caer con todo el equipo; **to kill the g. that lays the golden egg** matar la gallina de los huevos de oro; **g. bumps, g. pimples,** carne *f* de gallina

gooseberry ['gʊzbərɪ] *n* grosella *f*; **g. bush** grosellero *m*

gooseflesh ['guːsfleʃ] *n* carne *f* de gallina

goose-step ['guːsstep] **1** *n* paso *m* de la oca
2 *vi (pt & pp* goose-stepped) marchar al paso de la oca

gopher ['gəʊfə(r)] *n (ground squirrel)* ardilla *f* de tierra

gore [gɔː(r)] **1** *n (blood)* sangre *f* (derramada)
2 *vt (of bull)* cornear, empitonar

gorge [gɔːdʒ] **1** *n* (**a**) *(valley)* garganta *f*, desfiladero *m* (**b**) *(throat)* **it makes my g. rise** me revuelve el estómago
2 *vt* **to g. oneself (on)** hartarse (de), atiborrarse (de)
3 *vi* hartarse, atiborrarse (**on** de)

gorgeous ['gɔːdʒəs] *adj* (**a**) *(beautiful) (colors, day, sunset)* precioso(a); *(woman, man) Esp* guapísimo(a), *Am* lindísimo(a); *(baby)* precioso(a) (**b**) *(very good) (meal, weather)* estupendo(a), magnífico(a)

gorilla [gə'rɪlə] *n* gorila *m*

gorse [gɔːs] *n* tojo *m*, aulaga *f*

gory ['gɔːrɪ] *adj (movie, crime)* sangriento(a); *(covered in blood)* ensangrentado(a); *Fig & Hum* **in g. detail** con todo lujo de detalles, con pelos y señales

gosh [gɒʃ] *exclam Fam* ¡vaya!, *Esp* ¡jolines!, *Méx* ¡híjole!

goshawk ['gɒshɔːk] *n* azor *m*

gosling ['gɒzlɪŋ] *n* ansarón *m*

gospel ['gɒspəl] *n* evangelio *m*; **St Mark's G., the G. according to St Mark** el evangelio según San Marcos; **to take sth as g.** tomarse algo como si fuera el evangelio; **g. (music)** *(música f)* gospel *m*; **g. singer** cantante *mf* (de) gospel

gossamer ['gɒsəmə(r)] *n* (**a**) *(spider's thread)* (hilos *mpl* de) telaraña *f* (**b**) *(fabric)* gasa *f*

gossip ['gɒsɪp] **1** *n* (**a**) *(person)* chismoso(a) *m,f*, *Esp* cotilla *mf* (**b**) *(talk)* chismorreo *m*, *Esp* cotilleo *m*; **g. column** *(in newspaper)* ecos *mpl* de sociedad; **g. columnist** cronista *mf* de sociedad
2 *vi* chismorrear, *Esp* cotillear

gossipy ['gɒsɪpɪ] *adj* **he's very g.** es muy chismoso or *Esp*

cotilla; **a g. letter** una carta llena de chismorreos or *Esp* cotilleos

got [gɒt] *pt & pp of* **get**

Goth [gɒθ] *n* (**a**) *Hist* godo(a) *m,f* (**b**) *(music fan)* siniestro(a) *m,f*

Gothic ['gɒθɪk] **1** *n (artistic style, language)* gótico *m*
2 *adj* gótico(a); **g. novel** novela *f* gótica

gotta ['gɒtə] *Fam* = **got to**

gotten ['gɒtən] *pp of* **get**

▶**gouge out** [gaʊdʒ] *vt sep (eye)* arrancar; *(hole)* cavar

goulash ['guːlæʃ] *n* gulach *m*

gourd [gʊəd] *n (vegetable, container)* calabaza *f*

gourmand ['gʊəmənd] *n* gourmand *mf*

gourmet ['gʊəmeɪ] *n* gastrónomo(a) *m,f*, gourmet *mf*; **g. cooking** alta or buena cocina *f*

gout [gaʊt] *n (illness)* gota *f*

Gov (**a**) *(abbr* **government**) gobierno *m* (**b**) *(abbr* **governor**) gobernador(ora) *m,f*

govern ['gʌvən] *vt (state, country)* gobernar; *(of scientific law)* regir, determinar; *(emotions)* dominar; **her behavior was governed by a desire for revenge** le movía el deseo de venganza

governess ['gʌvənɪs] *n* institutriz *f*

governing ['gʌvənɪŋ] *adj (party, coalition)* gobernante; *(concept, principle)* rector(a); **g. body** órgano *m* rector

government ['gʌvənmənt] *n* gobierno *m*; **to form a g.** formar gobierno; **g. policy** la política gubernamental

governmental [gʌvən'mentəl] *adj* gubernamental, gubernativo(a)

governor ['gʌvənə(r)] *n (of colony, central bank)* gobernador(ora) *m,f*; **(state) g.** gobernador(ora) *m,f*; **g. general** gobernador general

governorship ['gʌvənəʃɪp] *n* gobernación *f*

Govt *(abbr* **government**) gobierno *m*

gown [gaʊn] *n (of woman)* vestido *m* (largo); *(of magistrate, academic)* toga *f*

GPA [dʒiːpiː'eɪ] *n (abbr* **grade point average**) nota *f* media

gr *(abbr* **gram(s)**) g

grab [græb] **1** *n (movement)* **to make a g. at** *or* **for sth** tratar de agarrar algo; *Fam* **to be up for grabs** estar a disposición de cualquiera
2 *vt (pt & pp* grabbed) **to g. (hold of) sth/sb** agarrar algo/a alguien; **to g. sth off sb** arrebatar algo a alguien; *Fam* **how does that g. you?** ¿qué te parece?; *Fam* **the idea doesn't g. me** no me entusiasma la idea
3 *vi* **to g. at sth/sb** tratar de agarrar algo/a alguien

grace [greɪs] **1** *n* (**a**) *(of movement, dancer, language)* gracia *f*, elegancia *f*
(**b**) *(of manners)* **to do sth with (a) good/bad g.** hacer algo de buena/mala gana; **to have the (good) g. to do sth** tener la delicadeza de hacer algo
(**c**) *(favor)* **to be in/get into sb's good graces** gozar del/ganarse el favor de alguien
(**d**) *Rel* **in a state of g.** en estado de gracia; **to fall from g.** caer en desgracia; **the g. of God** la gracia de Dios; **there, but for the g. of God, go I** siento mucho lo que le ha pasado, nos podría haber pasado a cualquiera
(**e**) *(for payment of a bill)* **to give a debtor seven days' g.** conceder a un moroso una prórroga de siete días
(**f**) *(prayer before meal)* **to say g.** bendecir la mesa
(**g**) *(form of address)* **Your G.** *(bishop)* (Su) Ilustrísima; *(duke, duchess)* (Su) Excelencia
2 *vt* (**a**) *(honor)* honrar (**b**) *(ornament)* adornar

graceful ['greɪsfʊl] *adj (person, movement)* airoso(a), elegante; *(speech, style)* elegante

gracefully ['greɪsfʊlɪ] *adv* con elegancia; **to accept/decline g.** aceptar/declinar cortésmente

graceless ['greɪslɪs] *adj* (**a**) *(inelegant) (person, movement)* falto(a) de gracia, ordinario(a) (**b**) *(rude) (apology, behavior)* grosero(a)

gracious ['greɪʃəs] *adj* (**a**) *(kind, polite)* amable, atento(a); *(in victory)* caballeroso(a) (**b**) *(elegant)* elegante, lujoso(a) (**c**) *(exclamation)* **g. (me)!, good(ness) g.!** ¡santo cielo!, ¡Dios bendito!

graciously ['greɪʃəslɪ] *adv (kindly)* amablemente, cortésmente

graciousness ['greɪʃəsnɪs] *n* (**a**) *(kindness, politeness)* cortesía *f*, gentileza *f* (**b**) *(elegance)* elegancia *f*

gradation [grə'deɪʃən] *n* gradación *f*

grade [greɪd] **1** *n* (**a**) *(rank)* grado *m*, rango *m* (**b**) *(quality)* clase *f*, calidad *f*; **to make the g.** *(be good enough)* dar la talla (**c**) *Sch (mark)* nota *f*; **g. point average** nota *f* media (**d**) *(year at school)* curso *m*; **g. school** escuela *f* primaria (**e**) *Rail* **g. crossing** paso *m* a nivel
2 *vt* (**a**) *(classify)* clasificar (**b**) **to g. essays** calificar los trabajos

gradient ['greɪdɪənt] *n* (**a**) *(of slope)* pendiente *f*; **a g. of 1 in 4, a 1 in 4 g.** una pendiente del 25 por ciento (**b**) *(of temperature)* gradiente *m*, curva *f* de temperaturas

gradual ['grædjʊəl] *adj* gradual

gradualism ['grædjʊəlɪzəm] *n* transformación *f* gradual

gradually ['grædjʊəlɪ] *adv* gradualmente

graduate 1 *n* ['grædjʊət] *Univ* licenciado(a) *m,f*; *(from high school)* ≃ bachiller *mf*
2 *adj (postgraduate)* **g. studies** estudios *mpl* de posgrado
3 *vi* ['grædjʊeɪt] *(from high school)* ≃ sacar el bachillerato; *Fig* **she learned on a cheap violin before graduating to a better instrument** aprendió con un violín corriente antes de pasar a tocar con uno mejor

graduated ['grædʊeɪtɪd] *adj (thermometer)* graduado(a); **g. income tax** impuesto *m* sobre la renta progresivo

graduation [grædjʊ'eɪʃən] *n (from school, college)* graduación *f*; **g. ceremony** ceremonia *f* de graduación

graffiti [græ'fiːtiː] *n (slogans)* pintadas *fpl*; *(art)* graffiti *mpl*

graft¹ [grɑːft] **1** *n (of skin, plant)* injerto *m*
2 *vt (skin, plant)* injertar (**onto** en); *Fig (idea, method)* implantar (**onto** en)

graft² *Fam n (bribery)* corruptelas *fpl*

grain [greɪn] *n* (**a**) *(of wheat, pepper, salt, sand)* grano *m*; **a g. of truth** una pizca de verdad (**b**) *(of photo)* grano *m*; *(of wood, meat)* grano *m*; *Fig* **it goes against the g. for me to do it** hacer eso va contra mi naturaleza

grainy ['greɪnɪ] *adj Phot* granuloso(a), con mucho grano

gram [græm] *n* gramo *m*

grammar ['græmə(r)] *n* gramática *f*; **g. (book)** (método *m* de) gramática *f*

grammarian [grə'meərɪən] *n* gramático(a) *m,f*

grammatical [grə'mætɪkəl] *adj* gramatical

grammatically [grə'mætɪklɪ] *adv* gramaticalmente

gramophone ['græməfəʊn] *n Old-fashioned* gramófono *m*

gramp(s) [græmp(s)] *n Fam* abuelo *m*, yayo *m*

granary ['grænərɪ] *n* granero *m*

grand [grænd] **1** *adj* (**a**) *(imposing)* grandioso(a), imponente; *(plan, scheme)* ambicioso(a); **on a g. scale** a gran escala; **g. finale** final *m* apoteósico, apoteosis *f inv* final; **g. jury** jurado *m* de acusación; **g. larceny** = delito de robo por un valor superior a 500 dólares; **g. master** *(in chess)* gran maestro(a) *m,f*; **g. piano** piano *m* de cola; **g. slam** *(in rugby)* Gran Slam *m*, = conseguir derrotar a los otros cuatro países en el Torneo de las Cinco Naciones **a g. total of $5,000** una suma total de 5.000 dólares
(**b**) *Fam (excellent)* genial, *Am salvo RP* chévere, *Méx* padre, *RP* bárbaro(a)
2 *n Fam (thousand dollars)* mil dólares *mpl*

grandad ['grændæd] *n Fam* abuelito *m*, *Esp* yayo *m*

grandaddy ['grændædɪ] *n Fam* abuelito *m*, *Esp* yayo *m*

grandchild ['græntʃaɪld] *n* nieto(a) *m,f*

granddaughter ['grændɔːtə(r)] *n* nieta *f*

grandeur ['grændjə(r)] *n (of place, building)* grandiosidad *f*; *(personal status)* grandeza *f*

grandfather ['grænfɑːðə(r)] *n* abuelo *m*; **g. clock** reloj *m* de pie

grandiloquence [græn'dɪləkwəns] *n Formal* grandilocuencia *f*

grandiloquent [græn'dɪləkwənt] *adj Formal* grandilocuente

grandiose ['grændɪəʊs] *adj* grandioso(a)

grandly ['grændlɪ] *adv (impressively)* grandiosamente, majestuosamente; *(pompously)* solemnemente

grandma ['grænmɑː] *n Fam* abuelita *f*, *Esp* yaya *f*

grandmother ['grænmʌðə(r)] *n* abuela *f*

grandness ['grændnɪs] *n (of behavior, gesture)* grandilocuencia *f*; *(of lifestyle)* opulencia *f*; *(of appearance)* ostentosidad *f*

grandpa ['grænpɑː] *n Fam* abuelito *m*, *Esp* yayo *m*

grandparent ['grænpeərənt] *n* abuelo(a) *m,f*; **grandparents** abuelos *mpl*

grandson ['grænsʌn] *n* nieto *m*

grandstand ['grænstænd] *n (in stadium)* tribuna *m*; **to have a g. view of sth** presenciar algo desde una posición privilegiada

granite ['grænɪt] *n* granito *m*

granny, grannie ['grænɪ] *n Fam* abuelita *f*, *Esp* yaya *f*; **g. knot** nudo *m* mal hecho

grant [grɑːnt] **1** *n (financial aid)* subvención *f*; *(for student)* beca *f*
2 *vt* (**a**) *(allow) (permission, request)* conceder; **to take sth for granted** dar algo por supuesto *or* por sentado; **she felt that she was being taken for granted** sentía que no la apreciaban debidamente (**b**) *(award) (money, subsidy)* conceder (**c**) *(admit)* reconocer, admitir; **I g. that he's talented, but…** admito que tiene talento, pero…

grant-in-aid ['grɑːntɪn'eɪd] *n* subvención *f*, subsidio *m*

granular ['grænjʊlə(r)] *adj (surface, texture)* granuloso(a)

granulated sugar ['grænjʊleɪtɪd'ʃʊgə(r)] *n* azúcar *m or f* granulado(a)

granule ['grænjʊl] *n* gránulo *m*

grape [greɪp] *n* uva *f*; **g. harvest** vendimia *f*; **g. juice** mosto *m*, *Esp* zumo *m or Am* jugo *m* de uva; **g. picker** vendimiador(ora) *m,f*

grapefruit ['greɪpfruːt] *n* pomelo *m*, *Am* toronja *f*; **g. juice** *Esp* zumo *m or Am* jugo *m* de pomelo

grapevine ['greɪpvaɪn] *n* vid *f*; *(climbing)* parra *f*; *Fam* **I heard on the g. that…** me ha dicho un pajarito que…

graph [grɑːf] *n* gráfico *m*, gráfica *f*; **g. paper** papel *m* cuadriculado

graphic ['græfɪk] *adj* (**a**) *(description, language)* gráfico(a) (**b**) *Art* gráfico(a); **g. artist** artista *mf* gráfico(a); **g. arts** artes *fpl* gráficas; **g. designer** diseñador(ora) *m,f* gráfico(a), grafista *mf*; **g. novel** novela *f* ilustrada (**c**) *Elec* **g. equalizer** ecualizador *m* gráfico

graphically ['græfɪklɪ] *adv (to describe, portray)* gráficamente

graphics ['græfɪks] **1** *n Art* diseño *m* gráfico, grafismo *m*
2 *npl Comptr* gráficos *mpl*

graphite ['græfaɪt] *n* grafito *m*

graphology [græ'fɒlədʒɪ] *n* grafología *f*

grapnel ['græpnəl] *n Naut* rezón *m*

grapple ['græpəl] *vi (fight)* forcejear; **to g. with a problem** debatirse *or* batallar con un problema

grappling hook ['græplɪŋ'hʊk], **grappling iron** ['græplɪŋ'aɪən] *n Naut* rezón *m*

grasp [grɑːsp] **1** *n* (**a**) *(hold)* asimiento *m*; **to wrest sth from**

sb's g. arrancar algo de las manos de alguien; *Fig* **to have sth within one's g.** tener algo al alcance de la mano; *Fig* **the opportunity had slipped from her g.** había dejado escapar la oportunidad **(b)** *(understanding)* comprensión *f*; **to have a good g. of modern history** comprender *or* dominar muy bien la historia moderna

2 *vt* **(a)** *(hold firmly)* agarrar, asir; *Fig* **to g. the opportunity** aprovechar la oportunidad **(b)** *(understand)* comprender

grasping ['grɑːspɪŋ] *adj* avaricioso(a)

grass [grɑːs] *n* **(a)** *(plant)* hierba *f*; *Fig* **she doesn't let the g. grow under her feet** *(is very decisive)* no se dedica a perder el tiempo; *Fig* **the g. roots** *(of organization)* las bases; **g. roots support/opposition** apoyo *m*/oposición *f* de las bases; **g. snake** culebra *f* de agua; **g. widow** = mujer cuyo marido se encuentra ausente **(b)** *(lawn)* césped *m*, hierba *f*; **keep off the g.** *(sign)* prohibido pisar el césped; **g. court** *(in tennis)* pista *f* de hierba **(c)** *Fam (marijuana)* maría *f*, hierba *f*

grasshopper ['grɑːshɒpə(r)] *n* saltamontes *m inv*

grassland ['grɑːslænd] *n* pradera *f*, pastizal *m*

grass-roots ['grɑːsruːts] *adj* bases *fpl*; **g. opinion** la opinión de las bases

grassy ['grɑːsɪ] *adj* poblado(a) de hierba

grate¹ [greɪt] *n (of hearth)* parrilla *f*, rejilla *f*

grate² **1** *vt (cheese, nutmeg)* rallar

2 *vi (machinery)* chirriar, rechinar; **to g. on the ear** *(voice, sound)* chirriar al oído; **it really grates on my nerves** me ataca los nervios

grateful ['greɪtful] *adj* agradecido(a); **to be g.** estar agradecido(a); **I'm g. for all you've done** te agradezco todo lo que has hecho; **I would be g. if you could let me know as soon as possible** le agradecería que me lo comunicara lo antes posible

gratefully ['greɪtfulɪ] *adv* agradecidamente, con agradecimiento

grater ['greɪtə(r)] *n (for cheese, nutmeg)* rallador *m*

gratification [grætɪfɪ'keɪʃən] *n* satisfacción *f*

gratified ['grætɪfaɪd] *adj* **to be g.** estar satisfecho(a) *or* complacido(a)

gratify ['grætɪfaɪ] *vt* satisfacer, complacer

gratifying ['grætɪfaɪɪŋ] *adj* satisfactorio(a), gratificante

grating¹ ['greɪtɪŋ] *adj (noise)* chirriante; *(voice)* chillón(ona)

grating² *n (grille)* reja *f*

gratis ['grɑːtɪs] *adv* gratis

gratitude ['grætɪtjuːd] *n* gratitud *f*

gratuitous [grə'tjuːɪtəs] *adj (unnecessary)* gratuito(a), arbitrario(a)

gratuitously [grə'tjuːɪtəslɪ] *adv* gratuitamente, arbitrariamente

gratuity [grə'tjuːɪtɪ] *n Formal (tip)* propina *f*, gratificación *f*

grave [greɪv] **1** *n* **(a)** tumba *f*, sepultura *f* **(b)** *(idioms)* **to make sb turn in his g.** hacer que alguien se revuelva en su sepultura; **to have one foot in the g.** estar con un pie en la tumba

2 *adj (manner, voice, situation, mistake)* grave

gravedigger ['greɪvdɪgə(r)] *n* sepulturero(a) *m,f*

gravel ['grævəl] *n* grava *f*, gravilla *f*; **g. path** camino *m* de grava; **g. pit** yacimiento *m* de grava, gravera *f*

gravelly ['grævəlɪ] *adj (sand, soil)* pedregoso(a); **a g. voice** una voz cavernosa

gravely ['greɪvlɪ] *adv* gravemente

graven ['greɪvən] *adj (in the Bible)* **g. image** ídolo *m*

graveside ['greɪvsaɪd] *n* pie *m* de la sepultura

gravestone ['greɪvstəʊn] *n* lápida *f*

graveyard ['greɪvjɑːd] *n* cementerio *m*

gravitate ['grævɪteɪt] *vi* **to g. toward** verse atraído(a) por; *Fig* **most of the guests had gravitated toward the bar** casi todos los invitados se habían ido desplazando hacia el bar

gravitational [grævɪ'teɪʃənəl] *adj (force, field)* gravitatorio(a); **g. pull** atracción *f* gravitatoria

gravity ['grævɪtɪ] *n also Fig* gravedad *f*

gravy ['greɪvɪ] *n* jugo *m* de carne; **g. boat** salsera *f*; *Fam* **to be on the g. train** estar apuntado(a) al *Esp* chollo *or Am* chance de la temporada

gray [greɪ] **1** *n (color)* gris *m*

2 *adj* gris; *(hair)* cano(a), gris; *Fig (boring)* gris; **to go g.** *(hair)* encanecer; *Fig* **a g. area** *(unclear)* una cuestión poco clara; **g. hairs** canas *fpl*; **g. matter** *(brain)* materia *f* gris; **g. squirrel** ardilla *f* gris

3 *vi (hair)* encanecer

gray-haired ['greɪheəd] *adj* canoso(a)

graying ['greɪɪŋ] *adj (hair)* encanecido(a); *(population)* envejecido(a)

graze¹ [greɪz] **1** *vt (of farmer) (cattle, herd)* apacentar

2 *vi (cattle)* pastar, pacer

graze² **1** *n* rasguño *m*, arañazo *m*

2 *vt (scrape)* arañar; *(touch lightly)* rozar; **to g. one's knee** hacerse un arañazo en la rodilla

grease [griːs] **1** *n (in cooking, for machine)* grasa *f*; **g. gun** pistola *f* engrasadora

2 *vt (machine)* engrasar, lubricar; *(cake tin)* engrasar; **to g. back one's hair** engominarse el pelo; *Fam* **to g. sb's palm** *(bribe)* untar a alguien, *Andes, RP* coimear a alguien, *CAm, Méx* dar una mordida a alguien; *Fam* **to move like greased lightning** moverse con la velocidad del rayo

greasepaint ['griːspeɪnt] *n Theat* maquillaje *m* de teatro

greasy ['griːsɪ] *adj* **(a)** *(containing, covered in grease)* grasiento(a); *(hair)* graso(a); *(grease-stained)* manchado(a) de grasa; *Fam* **g. spoon** *(cheap restaurant)* restaurante *m* barato **(b)** *Fam (manner)* adulador(ora), *Méx, RP* arrastrado(a)

great [greɪt] **1** *adj* **(a)** *(large, important)* grande, gran *(before singular noun)*; **a g. deal of...** un montón de..., muchísimo(a)...; **to reach a g. age** llegar a una edad avanzada; **to take g. care** poner mucho cuidado; **they are g. friends** son muy buenos amigos; **a g. artist** un/una gran artista; **to be the greatest** ser el mejor

(b) *(in proper names)* **G. Britain** Gran Bretaña; **G. Dane** gran danés *m*; **the G. Lakes** los Grandes Lagos; **Greater New York** el área metropolitana de Nueva York; *Hist* **the G. War** la Primera Guerra Mundial, la guerra del 14

(c) *Fam (very good)* genial, bárbaro(a), *Am salvo RP* chévere, *Méx* padre; **to have a g. time** pasarlo muy bien; **(that's) g.!** ¡genial!, *Am salvo RP* ¡!, *Méx* ¡padre!, *RP* ¡bárbaro(a)!; **he's a g. guy** es un tipo excelente

(d) *(enthusiastic)* **she's a g. traveler** es muy aficionada a viajar; **he's a g. one for having everything planned in advance** nadie como él para tener todo planeado de antemano

2 *n* grande *mf*

3 *adv Fam* **(a)** *(well)* estupendamente; **I feel g.!** ¡me siento estupendamente!; **he's doing g.** *(in health)* se está recuperando muy bien **(b)** *(for emphasis)* **a g. big dog** un perrazo enorme; **you g. fat slob!** ¡so vago!, ¡pedazo de *Andes, Méx* flojo *or RP* haragán!

great-aunt ['greɪt'ɑːnt] *n* tía *f* abuela

greatcoat ['greɪtkəʊt] *n* abrigo *m*, gabán *m*

great-grandchild ['greɪt'græntʃaɪld] *n* bisnieto(a) *m,f*

great-granddaughter ['greɪt'grændɔːtə(r)] *n* bisnieta *f*

great-grandfather ['greɪt'grænfɑːðə(r)] *n* bisabuelo *m*

great-grandmother ['greɪt'grænmʌðə(r)] *n* bisabuela *f*

great-grandparents ['greɪt'grænpeərənts] *npl* bisabuelos *mpl*

great-grandson ['greɪt'grænsʌn] *n* bisnieto *m*

greatly ['greɪtlɪ] *adv (when modifying adjective)* muy; *(when modifying verb)* mucho; **he was g. influenced by his**

father estaba muy influenciado por su padre

great-nephew ['greɪt'nefju:] n sobrino m nieto

greatness ['greɪtnɪs] n (of person) talla f, grandeza f; (of action) grandeza f; **to achieve g.** (writer, politician) alcanzar una gran notoriedad

great-niece ['greɪt'ni:s] n sobrina f nieta

great-uncle ['greɪt'ʌŋkəl] n tío m abuelo

grebe [gri:b] n somormujo m

Grecian ['gri:ʃən] adj helénico(a), griego(a)

Greece [gri:s] n Grecia

greed [gri:d], **greediness** ['gri:dɪnɪs] n (for food) glotonería f, gula f; (for material things) codicia f (**for** de), avidez f (**for** de); (for fame, power) ambición f (**for** de), avidez f (**for** de)

greedily ['gri:dɪlɪ] adv (to eat) con glotonería; (to eye, behave) con avidez

greediness = **greed**

greedy ['gri:dɪ] adj (for food) glotón(a); (for material things) codicioso(a), ávido(a); **to be g. for sth** (knowledge, success) estar ávido(a) de algo

Greek [gri:k] **1** n (**a**) (person) griego(a) m,f (**b**) (language) griego m; **modern G.** griego moderno; Fam **it's all G. to me** me suena a chino
2 adj griego(a)

green [gri:n] **1** n (**a**) (color) verde m (**b**) **greens** (vegetables) verdura f (**c**) (grassy area) (**putting**) **g.** (in golf) green m; **village g.** = en los pueblos, zona de césped de uso público (**d**) Pol (person) ecologista mf, verde mf
2 adj (**a**) (color) verde; **to go** or **turn g.** (traffic lights) cambiar a or ponerse verde; **to be g. with envy** estar muerto(a) de envidia; Fig **to give sb the g. light (to do sth)** dar a alguien luz verde (para hacer algo); **g. bean** Esp judía f verde, Bol, RP chaucha f, Carib, Col habichuela f, Chile poroto m verde, Méx ejote m; **g. belt** (around city) cinturón m verde, pulmón m; **g. card** permiso m de trabajo, carta f verde; **to have a g. thumb** tener buena mano para or Esp con las plantas; **g. onion** cebolleta f, RP cebolla f de verdeo; **g. pepper** pimiento m verde; **the g. revolution** la revolución verde; **g. salad** ensalada f verde; **g. tea** té m verde
(**b**) (young, inexperienced) novato(a); (naive) ingenuo(a)
(**c**) (environmentalist) ecologista, verde; **the G. Party** el partido ecologista or de los verdes

greenback ['gri:nbæk] n Fam billete m (dólar estadounidense), RP verde m

greenbelt ['gri:nbelt] n (around city) cinturón m verde, pulmón m

greenery ['gri:nərɪ] n vegetación f

green-eyed ['gri:naɪd] adj de ojos verdes; Literary **the g. monster** (jealousy) los celos

greenfield ['gri:nfi:ld] n **g. site** (for factory, houses) terreno m edificable (fuera del casco urbano)

greenfly ['gri:nflaɪ] n pulgón m

greengage ['gri:ngeɪdʒ] n (fruit) ciruela f claudia

greenhouse ['gri:nhaʊs] n invernadero m; **the g. effect** el efecto invernadero

Greenland ['gri:nlənd] n Groenlandia

Greenlander ['gri:nləndə(r)] n groenlandés(esa) m,f

green-thumbed ['gri:n'θʌmd] adj con buena mano para las plantas

Greenwich Mean Time ['grenɪtʃ'mi:ntaɪm] n tiempo m universal, hora f del meridiano cero or de Greenwich

greet [gri:t] vt (say hello to) saludar; (welcome) (person, idea) recibir, acoger

greeting ['gri:tɪŋ] n saludo m; **to send greetings to sb** enviar saludos or CAm, Col, Ecuad saludes a alguien; **New Year/birthday greetings** felicitaciones fpl de Año Nuevo/ cumpleaños; **g. card** tarjeta f de felicitación

gregarious [grɪ'geərɪəs] adj sociable

gremlin ['gremlɪn] n Fam duende m

Grenada [grə'neɪdə] n Granada (país)

grenade [grə'neɪd] n (small bomb) granada f

grenadier [grenə'dɪə(r)] n (soldier) granadero m

grenadine ['grenədi:n] n (drink) granadina f

grew ['gru:] pt of **grow**

grey, grey-haired etc = **gray, gray-haired** etc

Greyhound® ['greɪhaʊnd] n **G. (bus)** = autobús de largo recorrido

greyhound ['greɪhaʊnd] n (dog) galgo m; **g. stadium** canódromo m

grid [grɪd] n (**a**) (bars) reja f (**b**) (on map) cuadrícula f; **g. layout** (of town) trazado m cuadricular, planta f cuadriculada; **g. reference** coordenadas fpl (**c**) (for electricity) red f eléctrica

griddle ['grɪdəl] n (for cooking) plancha f

gridiron ['grɪdaɪən] n (**a**) (for cooking) parrilla f (**b**) (football) fútbol m americano; (field) campo m de fútbol americano

gridlock ['grɪdlɒk] n (traffic jam) atasco m, embotellamiento m

grief [gri:f] n dolor m, aflicción f; **to come to g.** venirse abajo; Fam **good g.!** ¡santo Dios!; Fam **to give sb g. (about sth)** (hassle) dar la vara or la lata a alguien (con algo), RP hinchar a alguien (con algo)

grief-stricken ['gri:fstrɪkən] adj afligido(a); **to be g.** estar afligido(a)

grievance ['gri:vəns] n (**a**) (resentment) (sentimiento m de) agravio m (**b**) (complaint) motivo m de queja; Ind **g. procedure** juicio m de faltas

grieve [gri:v] **1** vt **it grieves me to have to tell you that...** lamento tener que decirte que...
2 vi sufrir de aflicción; **to g. for** or **over sb** llorar la muerte de alguien

grieving ['gri:vɪŋ] adj desconsolado(a)

grievous ['gri:vəs] adj Formal grave

grievously ['gri:vəslɪ] adv Formal (seriously) seriamente; **to be g. wounded** estar gravemente herido(a); **you are g. mistaken** estás en un grave error

griffin ['grɪfɪn] n (mythological creature) grifo m

grill [grɪl] **1** n (**a**) (part of oven) grill m; (for open fire) parrilla f; (food) parrillada f; **a mixed g.** una parrillada de carne (**b**) = **grille**
2 vt (**a**) (cook) asar (a la parrilla); **grilled meat** carne f a la parrilla (**b**) Fam (interrogate) acribillar a preguntas

grille, grill [grɪl] n (bars) reja f; Aut (**radiator**) **g.** rejilla f del radiador

grilling ['grɪlɪŋ] n Fam (interrogation) **to give sb a g.** acribillar a alguien a preguntas

grim [grɪm] adj (news, prospects, landscape) desolador(ora); (mood) sombrío(a); (reality) duro(a); (expression, smile) adusto(a); **he showed g. determination** se mostró completamente resuelto; **to hold on like g. death** agarrarse como si le fuera a uno la vida en ello; **to look g.** (serious) tener cara de pocos amigos; (ill) tener muy mala cara; Fam **how do you feel? — pretty g.!** ¿cómo te sientes? — Esp ¡fatal!, Am ¡pésimo!

grimace [grɪ'meɪs] **1** n mueca f
2 vi (once) hacer una mueca; (more than once) hacer muecas

grime [graɪm] n mugre f, porquería f

grimly ['grɪmlɪ] adv (to fight, hold on) con determinación

grimness ['grɪmnɪs] n (of news, report) lo desalentador; (mood) lo sombrío; (of expression, smile) adustez f; (of landscape) desolación f

grimy ['graɪmɪ] adj mugriento(a)

grin [grɪn] **1** n (smile) (amplia) sonrisa f
2 vi (smile) sonreír abiertamente; Fig **to g. and bear it** poner al mal tiempo buena cara

grind [graɪnd] **1** n Fam (**a**) (work) **the daily g.** la rutina diaria,

what a g.! ¡qué rollo de trabajo! (**b**) *(student) Esp* empollón(ona) *m,f, Méx* matado(a) *m,f, RP* traga *mf*

2 *vt (pt & pp* **ground** [graʊnd]) (**a**) *(grain, coffee)* moler; *Fig* **to g. sth/sb under one's heel** hacer añicos algo/a alguien; **to g. one's teeth** hacer rechinar los dientes (**b**) *(polish) (glass)* pulir

3 *vi (wheels, gears)* chirriar; **to g. to a halt** *(vehicle, machine)* detenerse con estrépito; *(project)* acabar estancado(a)

➤**grind down** *vt sep Fig (opposition)* desgastar, minar

➤**grind on** *vi (proceed relentlessly)* proseguir machaconamente

➤**grind out** *vt sep* **to g. out a novel/an essay** escribir una novela/un ensayo con gran dificultad

grinder ['graɪndə(r)] *n (for coffee, pepper)* molinillo *m*; *(crusher)* trituradora *f*; *(for polishing)* pulidora *f*; *(for sharpening)* afilador *m*

grinding ['graɪndɪŋ] *adj (boredom, worry)* insufrible, insoportable; **to come to a g. halt** *(car, machine)* pararse en seco; *(project)* acabar estancado(a); **g. poverty** pobreza *f* absoluta

grindstone ['graɪndstəʊn] *n* muela *f*, piedra *f* de afilar; *Fig* **to keep one's nose to the g.** trabajar como un negro

gringo ['grɪŋɡəʊ] *(pl* **gringos**) *n Fam* gringo(a) *m,f*

grip [grɪp] **1** *n* (**a**) *(hold, grasp)* sujeción *f*; *(in tennis, golf)* sujeción *f*, forma *f* de sujetar; **to have a strong g.** agarrar con fuerza; **to get a g. on sth** *(rope, handle)* agarrar algo; *Fig* **to get to grips with** *(situation)* asimilar; *(subject, method)* llegar a comprender; *Fig* **to get a g. on oneself** dominarse, contenerse; *Fig* **get a g.!** *(control yourself)* ¡no desvaríes!; *Fig* **to have a firm g. on a situation** ejercer un fuerte control sobre una situación; **to lose one's g. (on sth)** *(on rope)* perder el control (de algo); *Fig* **to lose one's g. on reality** perder el contacto con la realidad; *Fig* **to be in the g. of a disease/a crisis** ser presa de una enfermedad/una crisis (**b**) *(handle) (of oar, handlebars)* mango *m* (**c**) *(bag)* bolsa *f* de viaje

2 *vt (pt & pp* **gripped**) *(seize)* agarrar, coger; *(hold)* sujetar; **tires that g. the road** neumáticos *or Col, Méx* llantas *or RP* gomas que se adhieren (bien) a la carretera; *Fig* **to be gripped by panic/fear** ser presa del pánico/miedo; *Fig* **the play gripped the audience** la obra tuvo en vilo al público

3 *vi (tire)* adherirse

gripe [graɪp] **1** *n Fam (complaint)* queja *f*; **what's your g.?** ¿qué tripa se te ha roto?

2 *vi Fam (complain)* quejarse (**about** de)

gripping ['grɪpɪŋ] *adj (book, story)* apasionante

grisly ['grɪzlɪ] *adj* espeluznante, horripilante

grist [grɪst] *n* **it's all g. to his mill** todo lo aprovecha

gristle ['grɪsəl] *n* ternilla *f*

gristly ['grɪslɪ] *adj (meat)* lleno(a) de nervios

grit [grɪt] **1** *n* (**a**) *(gravel)* gravilla *f* (**b**) *(courage, determination)* coraje *m*; **to have a lot of g.** tener mucho coraje

2 *vt (pt & pp* **gritted**) *(clench)* **to g. one's teeth** apretar los dientes

grits [grɪts] *npl* gachas *fpl* de sémola de maíz *or Andes, RP* choclo

gritty ['grɪtɪ] *adj* (**a**) *(sandy)* arenoso(a); **g. soil** guijarral *m* (**b**) *(determined)* valiente, audaz (**c**) **g. realism** realismo *m* descarnado

grizzle ['grɪzəl] *vi (complain)* refunfuñar

grizzled ['grɪzəld] *adj (hair, person) (gray)* canoso(a); *(grayish)* entrecano(a)

grizzly ['grɪzlɪ] **1** *n* **g. (bear)** oso *m* pardo *(norteamericano)*

2 *adj (hair, person)* canoso(a)

groan [grəʊn] **1** *n (of pain, dismay)* gemido *m*; *(of chair, floor)* crujido *m*

2 *vi (in pain, dismay)* gemir; **to g. inwardly** ahogar un gemido; **the shelves groaned under the weight of the books** la estantería estaba hasta arriba de libros

grocer ['grəʊsə(r)] *n* tendero(a) *m,f*

groceries ['grəʊsərɪz] *npl (shopping)* comestibles *mpl*

grocery ['grəʊsərɪ] *n* **g. (store)** *Esp* tienda *f* de alimentación, *CSur* almacén *m*, *Col, Méx* tienda *f* de abarrotes

grog [grɒg] *n Fam (drink)* grog *m*, ponche *m*

groggily ['grɒgɪlɪ] *adv Fam* con aire aturdido

groggy ['grɒgɪ] *adj Fam* atontado(a), grogui; **to be g.** estar atontado(a) *or* grogui

groin [grɔɪn] *n* ingle *f*

groom [gruːm] **1** *n* (**a**) *(of horse)* mozo *m* de cuadra (**b**) *(at wedding)* novio *m*

2 *vt (horse)* almohazar; *Fig (candidate)* preparar

grooming ['gruːmɪŋ] *n (smart, neat appearance)* buena presencia *f*

groove [gruːv] *n (slot)* ranura *f*; *(of record)* surco *m*

groovy ['gruːvɪ] *adj Fam Esp* chachi, *Méx* padre, *RP* bárbaro(a)

grope [grəʊp] **1** *vt* (**a**) **to g. one's way forward** avanzar a tientas (**b**) *Fam (sexually)* meter mano a

2 *vi* **to g. (about) for sth** buscar algo a tientas

gross [grəʊs] **1** *n (quantity)* gruesa *f*, doce docenas *fpl*; **two g.** dos gruesas

2 *adj* (**a**) *(fat)* muy gordo(a) (**b**) *(blatant) (error, ignorance)* craso(a); *(stupidity, indecency, incompetence)* tremendo(a); *Law* **g. negligence** negligencia *f* grave (**c**) *(vulgar) (joke, person)* basto(a), grosero(a) (**d**) *(profit, income)* bruto(a); *Econ* **g. domestic product** producto *m Esp* interior *or Esp* interno bruto; *Com* **g. margin** beneficio *m or* margen *m* bruto; *Econ* **g. national product** producto nacional bruto; **g. weight** peso *m* bruto (**e**) *Fam (disgusting)* asqueroso(a)

3 *vt (profit)* ganar en bruto; **she grosses $40,000 a year** gana 40.000 dólares brutas al año

grossly ['grəʊslɪ] *adv (exaggerated, negligent)* tremendamente, enormemente

grotesque [grəʊ'tesk] *adj* grotesco(a)

grotesquely [grəʊ'tesklɪ] *adv* grotescamente; **he was g. fat** estaba inmensamente gordo

grotto ['grɒtəʊ] *(pl* **grottoes** *or* **grottos**) *n* gruta *f*

grouch [graʊtʃ] *Fam* **1** *n* (**a**) *(person)* gruñón(ona) *m,f* (**b**) *(complaint)* queja *f*

2 *vi* refunfuñar

grouchy ['graʊtʃɪ] *adj Fam* **(to be) g.** *(inherent quality)* (ser) refunfuñón(ona); *(temporary mood)* (estar) enfurruñado(a) *or Am* enojado(a)

ground [graʊnd] **1** *n* (**a**) *(earth)* suelo *m*, tierra *f*; **to sit on the g.** sentarse en el suelo; **above g.** sobre la tierra; **to come above g.** salir a la superficie; **below g.** bajo tierra; **burned to the g.** completamente destruido(a) por el fuego; *Fig* **to get off the g.** *(project)* ponerse en marcha; *Fig* **to work** *or* **drive oneself into the g.** matarse *or Esp* a trabajar *or Am* trabajando; **to go to g.** ocultarse, desaparecer de la circulación; **to run sb to g.** dar por fin con alguien; *Av* **g. control** control *m* de tierra; *Av* **g. crew** personal *m* de tierra; **g. floor** planta *f* baja; *Fig* **to get in on the g. floor** *(project)* estar metido(a) desde el principio; *Mil* **g. forces** ejército *m* de tierra; **g. frost** escarcha *f*; **at g. level** a nivel del suelo; **to establish the g. rules** establecer las normas básicas; **g. staff** personal *m* de mantenimiento (del campo de juego); **g. swell** oleada *f*

(**b**) *(land)* terreno *m*; *Fig* **to find common g. for negotiations** hallar un terreno común para las negociaciones; *Fig* **to be on firm g.** pisar terreno firme; **he's very sure of his g.** está muy seguro de lo que hace/dice; *Fig* **to be on shaky g.** pisar un terreno resbaladizo; *Fig* **to change** *or* **shift one's g.** cambiar la línea de argumentación; *Fig* **to break new** *or* **fresh g.** abrir nuevas vías *or* nuevos caminos; *Fig* **to cover a lot of g.** *(book, lecture)* abarcar mucho; *Fig* **to gain g. on sb** ganarle terreno a alguien; *Fig* **to lose g. to sb** perder terreno ante alguien; *Fig* **to stand** *or* **hold one's g.** mantenerse firme

  (**c**) **grounds** *(of school, hospital)* terrenos *mpl*; *(of country house)* jardines *mpl*

  (**d**) *(reason)* **grounds** motivo *m*, razón *f*; **to have (good) g.** *or* **grounds for doing sth** tener (buenos) motivos para hacer algo; **g.** *or* **grounds for complaint** motivo de queja; **on grounds of ill-health** por motivos de salud; *Law* **grounds for divorce** motivo de divorcio

  (**e**) *Elec* toma *f* de tierra

  2 *adj (coffee, pepper)* molido(a); **g. meat** *Esp, RP* carne *f* picada, *Am* carne *f* molida

  3 *vt* (**a**) *(base)* fundamentar, basar; **their argument is not grounded in fact** su argumento no se basa en hechos reales (**b**) **to g. sb in a subject** *(educate)* enseñar a alguien los principios de una materia (**c**) *Elec (current)* conectar a tierra (**d**) *Av* **the plane was grounded by bad weather** el avión no salió a causa del mal tiempo (**e**) *(prevent from going out)* **her parents grounded her** sus padres la castigaron a quedarse en casa

  4 *pt & pp of* **grind**

groundbreaking ['graʊndbreɪkɪŋ] *adj* innovador(ora)

groundcloth ['graʊndklɒθ] *n (of tent)* suelo *m*

groundhog ['graʊndhɒg] *n* marmota *f*; **G. Day** = 2 de febrero, fecha en la que la marmota sale de su hibernación, según una tradición estadounidense

grounding ['graʊndɪŋ] *n* (**a**) *(basis)* fundamento *m*, base *f* (**b**) *(basic knowledge)* nociones *fpl* elementales, rudimentos *mpl*

groundless ['graʊndlɪs] *adj (suspicion, fear)* infundado(a), inmotivado(a)

groundnut ['graʊndnʌt] *n Esp* cacahuete *m*, *Am* maní *m*, *CAm, Méx* cacahuate *m*; **g. oil** aceite *m* de *Esp* cacahuete *or Am* maní *or CAm, Méx* cacahuate

groundwork ['graʊndwɜːk] *n* **to do** *or* **lay the g.** allanar el camino

group [gruːp] **1** *n* grupo *m*; **g. decision** decisión *f* colectiva; **g. dynamics** dinámica *f* de grupo; **g. photograph** fotografía *f* de grupo; **g. therapy** terapia *f* de grupo

  2 *vt* agrupar

  3 *vi* agruparse

groupie ['gruːpɪ] *n Fam* groupie *mf*, grupi *mf*

grouping ['gruːpɪŋ] *n* agrupación *f*, grupo *m*

grouse¹ [graʊs] *(pl* **grouse**) *n (bird)* lagópodo *m* escocés

grouse² *Fam* **1** *n (complaint)* queja *f*

  2 *vi* quejarse (**about** de)

grout [graʊt] *n (for tiles)* lechada *f*

grove [grəʊv] *n (of trees)* arboleda *f*

grovel ['grɒvəl] *vi (physically)* andar a gatas, gatear; *Fig* **to g. to sb** arrastrarse ante alguien

groveling ['grɒvəlɪŋ] *adj (tone, remark)* servil

grow [grəʊ] *(pt* **grew** [gruː]*, pp* **grown** [grəʊn]) **1** *vt (roses, vegetables)* cultivar; **to g. a beard** dejarse (crecer la) barba; **I've decided to g. my hair long** he decidido dejarme el pelo largo; **g. bag** = bolsa de compost en la que crecen plantas

  2 *vi* (**a**) *(increase in size)* crecer; *Fam* **it'll g. on you** *(music, book)* te irá gustando con el tiempo; **his influence grew** su influencia se acrecentó; **to g. in wisdom/beauty** ganar en sabiduría/belleza (**b**) *(become)* hacerse; **to g. old** envejecer; **to g. big** *or* **bigger** crecer; **to g. angry** *esp Esp* enfadarse, *esp Am* enojarse (**c**) *(come eventually)* **they grew to like the house** les llegó a gustar la casa

▸**grow apart** *vi (people)* distanciarse

▸**grow out of** *vt insep* (**a**) *(become too large for)* **he's grown out of his shoes** se le han quedado pequeños los zapatos (**b**) *(become too old for)* **she grew out of her dolls** dejó de jugar con muñecas al hacerse mayor

▸**grow up** *vi (become adult)* crecer; **I want to be a doctor when I g. up** de mayor quiero ser médico; **we didn't have television when I was growing up** cuando era pequeño no teníamos televisión; *Fam* **g. up!** ¡no seas niño *or Esp* crío!

grower ['grəʊə(r)] *n (person)* cultivador(ora) *m,f*

growing ['grəʊɪŋ] **1** *adj (child)* en edad de crecer; *(town, population)* creciente, en crecimiento; *(debt, discontent)* creciente; **there was a g. fear that…** se extendía el temor de que…

  2 *n Fig* **g. pains** *(of firm, country)* dificultades *fpl* del desarrollo

growl [graʊl] **1** *n (of dog)* gruñido *m*

  2 *vi (dog, person)* gruñir (**at** a)

growling ['graʊlɪŋ] *n (of dog)* gruñidos *mpl*

grown [grəʊn] **1** *adj* adulto(a); **a g. woman** una mujer adulta; **fully g.** completamente desarrollado(a)

  2 *pp of* **grow**

grown-up 1 *n* ['grəʊnʌp] adulto(a) *m,f*; **the grown-ups** los adultos, los mayores

  2 *adj* [grəʊn'ʌp] *(person, attitude)* maduro(a); **he was very g. about it** reaccionó con mucha madurez

growth [grəʊθ] *n* (**a**) *(increase in size)* crecimiento *m*; **a week's g. of beard** una barba de una semana; **a g. area** área de crecimiento; **g. industry** industria *f* en expansión (**b**) *(lump)* bulto *m*

grub [grʌb] *n* (**a**) *(larva)* larva *f*, gusano *m* (**b**) *Fam (food)* comida *f*, *Esp* manduca *f*, *RP* morfi *m*

▸**grub around, grub about** *vi (search)* rebuscar (**for sth** algo)

grubby ['grʌbɪ] *adj* sucio(a), mugriento(a)

grudge [grʌdʒ] **1** *n* rencor *m*, resentimiento *m*; **to bear sb a g.** guardar rencor *or* resentimiento a alguien

  2 *vt* **he paid, but he grudged them every penny** les pagó, pero escatimándoles cada penique; **she grudges him his success** reconoce su éxito a regañadientes

grudging ['grʌdʒɪŋ] *adj* **he felt g. respect for her** sentía respeto por ella a pesar de sí mismo; **to be g. in one's praise** ser reacio(a) a alabar

grudgingly ['grʌdʒɪŋlɪ] *adv* de mala gana, a regañadientes

gruel ['gruːəl] *n (thin porridge)* gachas *fpl* (de avena)

grueling ['gruːəlɪŋ] *adj (journey, experience)* agotador(ora)

gruesome ['gruːsəm] *adj* horripilante, espantoso(a); **in g. detail** sin ahorrar detalles truculentos

gruesomely ['gruːsəmlɪ] *adv* horripilantemente, espantosamente

gruff [grʌf] *adj (tone, manner)* seco(a), hosco(a); *(voice)* áspero(a)

gruffly ['grʌflɪ] *adv* secamente, bruscamente

grumble ['grʌmbəl] **1** *n* queja *f*; **she obeyed without so much as a g.** obedeció sin rechistar

  2 *vi (person)* quejarse (**about** de); *(stomach)* gruñir

grumbler ['grʌmblə(r)] *n* quejica *mf*, gruñón(ona) *m,f*

grumbling ['grʌmblɪŋ] **1** *n* quejas *fpl*

  2 *adj* quejumbroso(a)

grump [grʌmp] *n Fam (person)* gruñón(ona) *m,f*

grumpily ['grʌmpɪlɪ] *adv* de mal humor

grumpiness ['grʌmpɪnɪs] *n* mal genio *m*, malas pulgas *fpl*

grumpy ['grʌmpɪ] *adj* gruñón(ona)

grunge [grʌndʒ] *n (music)* (música *f*) grunge *m*

grungy ['grʌndʒɪ] *adj Fam* asqueroso(a), *Esp* cutre, *Méx* gacho(a), *RP* roñoso(a)

grunt [grʌnt] **1** *n* (**a**) *(of pig, person)* gruñido *m*; **to give a g.** dar un gruñido (**b**) *Fam (foot soldier)* soldado *mf* de infantería

  2 *vi (pig, person)* gruñir

guarantee [gærən'tiː] **1** *n (assurance, document)* garantía *f*; **she gave me her g. that it wouldn't happen again** me aseguró que no volvería a pasar; *Com* **under g.** en garantía

  2 *vt* garantizar; **the watch is guaranteed for two years** el reloj tiene una garantía de dos años; *Fin* **to g. sb against loss**

ofrecer a alguien una garantía contra posibles pérdidas

guaranteed [gærən'ti:d] *adj* garantizado(a)

guarantor [gærən'tɔ:(r)] *n* avalista *mf*, garante *mf*

guard [gɑ:d] **1** *n* (**a**) *(readiness)* **to be on one's g.** estar en guardia; **to put sb on his g.** poner en guardia a alguien; **to put sb off his g.** desarmar a alguien; **to catch sb off his g.** agarrar *or Esp* coger a alguien desprevenido (**b**) *(supervision)* **under g.** bajo custodia; **to be on g. duty** estar de guardia; **g. dog** perro *m* guardián (**c**) *(sentry)* guardia *mf*; *(in prison)* funcionario(a) *m,f* de prisiones, guardián(ana) *m,f*; *Mil (body of sentries)* guardia *f*; **g. of honor** guardia de honor (**d**) *(device) (on machine)* protección *f*; **as a g. against...** como protección contra... (**e**) *(in basketball)* escolta *mf* **2** *vt* (**a**) *(protect)* guardar; **a closely guarded secret** un secreto muy bien guardado (**b**) *(supervise)* vigilar

▸**guard against** *vt insep* evitar

guarded ['gɑ:dɪd] *adj (cautious)* cauteloso(a), cauto(a)

guardedly ['gɑ:dɪdlɪ] *adv* con cautela, cautamente

guardhouse ['gɑ:dhaʊs] *n Mil* cuerpo *m* de guardia; *(prison)* prisión *f* militar

guardian ['gɑ:dɪən] *n (of standards)* guardián(ana) *m,f*; *Law (of minor)* tutor(ora) *m,f*; **g. angel** ángel *m* custodio *or* de la guarda

guardianship ['gɑ:dɪənʃɪp] *n Law* tutela *f*

guardrail ['gɑ:dreɪl] *n* pasamanos *m inv, Esp* barandilla *f*

guardroom ['gɑ:dru:m] *n (guardhouse)* cuerpo *m* de guardia

Guatemala [gwætɪ'mɑ:lə] *n* Guatemala

Guatemalan [gwætɪ'mɑ:lən] *n & adj* guatemalteco(a) *m,f*

guava ['gwɑ:və] *n (fruit)* guayaba *f*; **g. tree** guayabo *m*

gubernatorial [gu:bənə'tɔ:rɪəl] *adj Formal* del/de la gobernador(ora); **a g. candidate/election** un candidato/unas elecciones a gobernador

guerrilla [gə'rɪlə] *n* guerrillero(a) *m,f*; **g. warfare** guerra *f* de guerrillas

guess [ges] **1** *n* conjetura *f*, suposición *f*; **to have** *or* **make a g.** intentar adivinar; **at a g.** a ojo (de buen cubero); **it was a lucky g.** lo he adivinado por casualidad; **it's anybody's g.** no se sabe **2** *vt* (**a**) *(estimate)* adivinar; **g. who I saw!** ¡adivina a quién he visto!; **you've guessed it!** ¡has acertado! (**b**) *(suppose)* suponer; **I g. you're right** supongo que tienes razón **3** *vi* adivinar; **to g. right** acertar; **to g. wrong** equivocarse, no acertar; **to keep sb guessing** tener a alguien en vilo; **to g. at sth** hacer suposiciones *or* conjeturas acerca de algo

guessing game ['gesɪŋ'geɪm] *n* (juego *m* de las) adivinanzas *fpl*

guesstimate ['gestɪmɪt] *n Fam* cálculo *m* a ojo

guesswork ['gesw3:k] *n* conjeturas *fpl*; **it's pure** *or* **sheer g.** son sólo conjeturas

guest [gest] *n (at home, on TV program)* invitado(a) *m,f*; *(at hotel)* huésped *mf*; **be my g.!** ¡por favor!, ¡no faltaba más!; **a g. appearance by...** una aparición como artista invitado(a) de...; **g. artist** artista *mf* invitado(a); **g. room** habitación *f* de los invitados; **g. speaker** orador(ora) *m,f* invitado(a); **g. worker** = extranjero con permiso de trabajo

guff [gʌf] *n Fam* paparruchas *fpl, Esp* chorradas *fpl, Am* pendejadas

guffaw [gʌ'fɔ:] **1** *n* carcajada *f* **2** *vi* carcajearse

GUI ['gu:ɪ] *n Comptr (abbr* **Graphical User Interface)** interfaz *f* gráfica

Guiana [gaɪ'ɑ:nə] *n* (la) Guayana, las Guayanas

guidance ['gaɪdəns] *n* orientación *f*; **under the g. of...** bajo la dirección de...; **for your g.** para su información

guide [gaɪd] **1** *n* (**a**) *(person)* guía *mf*; **g. dog** perro *m* lazarillo (**b**) *(book)* guía *f* (**to** de) (**c**) *(indication)* guía *f*; **as a g.** como guía **2** *vt* guiar; **I will be guided by your advice** me guiaré por tus consejos

guidebook ['gaɪdbʊk] *n* guía *f*

guided ['gaɪdɪd] *adj* **g. missile** misil *m* teledirigido; **g. tour** visita *f* guiada

guideline ['gaɪdlaɪn] *n (indication)* directriz *f*, línea *f* general; **guidelines** directrices *fpl*; **as a general g.** como orientación general

guiding ['gaɪdɪŋ] *adj* **the g. principle of his life** el principio que rige su vida; *Fig* **g. light** guía *mf*

guild [gɪld] *n (of craftsmen, merchants)* gremio *m*

guilder ['gɪldə] *n Formerly (Dutch currency)* florín *m*

guile [gaɪl] *n* astucia *f*

guileless ['gaɪllɪs] *adj* ingenuo(a), cándido(a)

guillemot ['gɪlɪmɒt] *n* arao *m* común

guillotine ['gɪləti:n] **1** *n* guillotina *f* **2** *vt* guillotinar

guilt [gɪlt] *n* (**a**) *(blame)* culpa *f*; **an admission of g.** una declaración de culpabilidad (**b**) *(emotion)* culpabilidad *f*, culpa *f*; **to feel g.** tener sentimientos de culpabilidad; **g. complex** complejo *m* de culpabilidad

guiltily ['gɪltɪlɪ] *adv* con aire culpable

guiltless ['gɪltlɪs] *adj* inocente

guilty ['gɪltɪ] *adj* (**a**) *(of crime)* culpable; **to find sb g./not g.** declarar a alguien culpable/inocente (**b**) *(emotionally)* **to feel g.** sentirse culpable; **g. conscience** remordimientos *mpl* de conciencia; **a g. secret** un secreto vergonzante

Guinea ['gɪnɪ] *n* Guinea

guinea ['gɪnɪ] *n* **g. fowl** pintada *f*, gallina *f* de Guinea; **g. pig** cobaya *m or f*, conejillo *m* de Indias; *Fig* **to be a g. pig** *(for new idea)* hacer de conejillo de Indias

Guinea-Bissau ['gɪnɪbɪ'saʊ] *n* Guinea-Bissau

Guinean [gɪ'neɪən] *n & adj* guineano(a) *m,f*

guise [gaɪz] *n* apariencia *f*; **in** *or* **under the g. of...** bajo la apariencia de...; **in a different g.** con una apariencia diferente

guitar [gɪ'tɑ:(r)] *n* guitarra *f*

guitarist [gɪ'tɑ:rɪst] *n* guitarrista *mf*

gulag ['gu:læg] *n* gulag *m*

gulch [gʌltʃ] *n (valley)* garganta *f*, hoz *f*

gulf [gʌlf] *n* (**a**) *(bay)* golfo *m*; **the G. (of Mexico)** el Golfo de México; **the Persian G.** el Golfo (Pérsico); **the Persian G. War** la guerra del Golfo; **the G. Stream** la corriente del Golfo (**b**) *(between people, ideas)* brecha *f*, abismo *m*

gull [gʌl] *n* gaviota *f*

gullet ['gʌlɪt] *n* esófago *m*

gulley = **gully**

gullibility [gʌlɪ'bɪlɪtɪ] *n* credulidad *f*, ingenuidad *f*

gullible ['gʌlɪbəl] *adj* crédulo(a), ingenuo(a)

gully, gulley ['gʌlɪ] *n* barranco *m*

gulp [gʌlp] **1** *n* trago *m*; **in** *or* **at one g.** de un trago; **"what money?"** he said, **with a g.** "¿qué dinero?" dijo, tragando saliva **2** *vt (swallow)* tragar, engullir **3** *vi (with surprise)* tragar saliva

▸**gulp down** *vt sep (swallow)* tragar, engullir

gum [gʌm] **1** *n* (**a**) *(in mouth)* encía *f*; **g. disease** gingivitis *f inv* (**b**) *(adhesive)* pegamento *m*, goma *f* (**c**) **(chewing) g.** chicle *m* (**d**) *(resin)* **g. arabic** goma *f* arábiga; **g. tree** eucalipto *m* **2** *vt (pt & pp gummed) (stick)* pegar

▸**gum up** *vt sep (mechanism)* pegar

gumboot ['gʌmbu:t] *n* bota *f* de agua *or* goma *or Méx, Ven* caucho

gummed [gʌmd] *adj (label)* engomado(a)

gumption ['gʌmʃən] *n Fam (common sense)* sensatez *f*, sentido *m* común; *(courage)* narices *fpl*, agallas *fpl*

gumshoe ['gʌmʃuː] *n Fam* sabueso *m*, detective *m*

gun [gʌn] **1** *n* (**a**) *(pistol)* pistola *f*; *(rifle)* rifle *m*; *(artillery piece)* cañón *m*; **g. carriage** cureña *f*; **g. laws** legislación *f* sobre armas de fuego; **g. license** licencia *f* de armas (**b**) *(idioms)* *Fam* **big g.** *(important person)* pez *m* gordo; **to be going great guns** ir a pedir de boca; **to stick to one's guns** no dar el brazo a torcer; **to jump the g.** precipitarse

2 *vt (pt & pp* **gunned**) **to g. the engine** dar acelerones

▸**gun down** *vt sep (kill)* matar a tiros

▸**gun for** *vt insep* **he's gunning for us** la tiene tomada con nosotros; **he's gunning for the heavyweight title** aspira al título de los pesos pesados; **she's gunning for my job** tiene las miras puestas en mi trabajo

gunboat ['gʌnbəʊt] *n* cañonera *f*; **g. diplomacy** la diplomacia de los cañones

gundog ['gʌndɒg] *n* perro *m* de caza

gunfight ['gʌnfaɪt] *n* tiroteo *m*

gunfire ['gʌnfaɪə(r)] *n* disparos *mpl*, tiros *mpl*

gung ho [gʌŋ'həʊ] *adj (enthusiastic)* exaltado(a); *(eager for war)* belicoso(a); **to be g. about sth** lanzar las campanas al vuelo con relación a algo

gunk [gʌŋk] *n Fam* porquería *f*, *Esp* pringue *f*

gunman ['gʌnmən] *n* hombre *m* armado

gunner ['gʌnə(r)] *n* artillero *m*

gunpoint ['gʌnpɔɪnt] *n* **at g.** a punta de pistola

gunpowder ['gʌnpaʊdə(r)] *n* pólvora *f*

gunrunner ['gʌnrʌnə(r)] *n* contrabandista *mf* de armas

gunrunning ['gʌnrʌnɪŋ] *n* contrabando *m* de armas

gunship ['gʌnʃɪp] *n* (**helicopter**) **g.** helicóptero *m* de combate

gunshot ['gʌnʃɒt] *n* disparo *m*, tiro *m*; **g. wound** herida *f* de bala

gunsmith ['gʌnsmɪθ] *n* armero *m*

gunwale ['gʌnəl] *n Naut* borda *f*, regala *f*

gurgle ['gɜːgəl] **1** *n (of liquid)* borboteo *m*, gorgoteo *m*; *(of baby)* gorjeo *m*; **a g. of delight** un gorjeo de placer

2 *vi (liquid)* borbotear, gorgotear; *(baby)* gorjear; **to g. with delight** gorjear de placer

gurney ['gɜːnɪ] *n* camilla *f*

guru ['gʊruː] *n also Fig* gurú *m*

gush [gʌʃ] **1** *n (of spring, fountain)* chorro *m*; **a g. of words** un torrente de palabras

2 *vi* (**a**) *(spurt, pour)* manar, correr; **tears gushed from her eyes** derramaba lágrimas a mares (**b**) *Pej (talk effusively)* **to g. about sth** hablar con excesiva efusividad de algo

gushing ['gʌʃɪŋ] *adj Pej (person, praise)* excesivamente efusivo(a)

gusset ['gʌsɪt] *n (of tights, underwear)* escudete *m*

gust [gʌst] **1** *n (of wind, rain, air)* ráfaga *f*

2 *vi (wind)* soplar racheado *or* en ráfagas

gusto ['gʌstəʊ] *n* entusiasmo *m*, ganas *fpl*; **with g.** con muchas ganas

gusty ['gʌstɪ] *adj (wind)* racheado(a); **a g. day/weather** un día/tiempo con viento racheado

gut [gʌt] **1** *n* (**a**) *(intestine)* intestino *m*; *Fam* **guts** *(of person, machine)* tripas *fpl*; *Fam* **to sweat** *or* **work one's guts out** dejarse la piel; *Fam* **she hates my guts** no me puede ver ni en pintura; **a g. feeling** *(intuition)* una intuición, una corazonada; **I have a g. feeling that…** tengo la intuición *or* corazonada de que…; **g. reaction** *(intuitive)* reacción *f* instintiva (**b**) *Fam* **guts** *(courage)* agallas *fpl*, arrestos *mpl*; **I didn't have the guts to tell them** no tuve agallas para decírselo

2 *vt (pt & pp* **gutted**) (**a**) *(fish)* limpiar (**b**) *(building)* **the house had been gutted by the fire** el fuego destruyó por completo el interior de la casa; **she gutted the house and completely redecorated it** dejó la casa totalmente vacía e hizo una reforma completa

gutless ['gʌtlɪs] *adj Fam* cobarde

gutsy ['gʌtsɪ] *adj Fam (brave)* corajudo(a)

gutter ['gʌtə(r)] **1** *n (in street)* cuneta *f*; *(on roof)* canalón *m*; *Fig* **to end up in the g.** terminar en el arroyo; *Fig* **to drag oneself out of the g.** salir del arroyo

2 *vi (flame)* parpadear

guttural ['gʌtərəl] *adj* gutural

guy¹ [gaɪ] *n Fam (man)* tipo *m*, tío *m*; **a great g.** un gran tipo; **a tough g.** un tipo duro; **hi guys!** ¡hola, amigos(as) *or Esp* tíos(as)!

guy² *n* **g. (rope)** *(for tent)* viento *m*

Guyana [gaɪ'ænə] *n* Guyana

Guyanese [gaɪə'niːz] *n & adj* guyanés(esa) *m,f*

guzzle ['gʌzəl] *Fam vt (food)* engullir

gym [dʒɪm] *n (gymnasium)* gimnasio *m*; *(gymnastics)* gimnasia *f*; **g. shoes** zapatillas *fpl* de gimnasia *or* de deporte

gymkhana [jɪŋ'kɑːnɑ] *n* gincana *f* hípica

gymnasium [dʒɪm'neɪzɪəm] *(pl* **gymnasiums** *or* **gymnasia** [dʒɪm'neɪzɪə])* *n* gimnasio *m*

gymnast ['dʒɪmnæst] *n* gimnasta *mf*

gymnastic [dʒɪm'næstɪk] *adj* gimnástico(a)

gymnastics [dʒɪm'næstɪks] **1** *n* gimnasia *f*

2 *npl Fig* **mental g.** gimnasia *f* mental

gynecological [gaɪnɪkə'lɒdʒɪkəl] *adj* ginecológico(a)

gynecologist [gaɪnɪ'kɒlədʒɪst] *n* ginecólogo(a) *m,f*

gynecology [gaɪnɪ'kɒlədʒɪ] *n* ginecología *f*

gypsum ['dʒɪpsəm] *n* yeso *m*

Gypsy ['dʒɪpsɪ] *n* gitano(a) *m,f*; **G. caravan** carromato *m* de gitanos

gyrate [dʒaɪ'reɪt] *vi* rotar, girar

gyration [dʒaɪ'reɪʃən] *n* rotación *f*, giro *m*

gyroscope ['dʒaɪrəskəʊp] *n* giróscopo *m*, giroscopio *m*

H

H, h [eɪtʃ] *n (letter)* H, h *f*; **H-bomb** bomba *f* H

habeas corpus [ˈheɪbɪəsˈkɔːpəs] *n Law* habeas corpus

haberdashery [ˈhæbədæʃərɪ] *n* ropa *f* de caballero; *(shop)* tienda *f* de confección de caballero

habit [ˈhæbɪt] *n* (**a**) *(custom, practice)* hábito *m*, costumbre *f*; **to be in the h. of doing sth** tener la costumbre de hacer algo; **to get into the h. of doing sth** adquirir el hábito de hacer algo; **you must get out of the h. of always blaming other people** tienes que dejar de echar siempre la culpa a los demás; **don't make a h. of it** que no se convierta en una costumbre; **from force of h.** por la fuerza de la costumbre; **a bad/good h.** una mala/buena costumbre (**b**) *Fam (addiction) (to cocaine, heroin)* vicio *m*, hábito *m*; **to kick the h.** dejar el vicio (**c**) *(costume)* hábito *m*

habitable [ˈhæbɪtəbəl] *adj* habitable

habitat [ˈhæbɪtæt] *n* hábitat *m*

habitation [hæbɪˈteɪʃən] *n* (**a**) *(occupation)* habitación *f*; **there were few signs of h.** había pocos rastros de habitantes; **fit/unfit for h.** apto(a)/no apto(a) para su uso como vivienda (**b**) *(dwelling place)* vivienda *f*

habitual [həˈbɪtjʊəl] *adj (generosity, rudeness)* habitual, acostumbrado(a); *(liar, drunk)* habitual

habitually [həˈbɪtjʊəlɪ] *adv* habitualmente

habituate [həˈbɪtjʊeɪt] *vt* habituar (**to** a); **to become habituated to sth** habituarse a algo

hack¹ [hæk] *n Fam* (**a**) *Pej (journalist)* gacetillero(a) *m,f*; *(political activist)* militante *mf*, activista *mf* (**b**) *(taxi)* taxi *m*, *Esp* pelas *m inv*, *RP* tacho *m*

hack² 1 *vt* (**a**) *(cut)* cortar; **to h. sth/sb to pieces** despedazar algo/a alguien a golpes de cuchillo; **to h. one's way through the jungle** abrirse paso a machetazos por la jungla (**b**) *Fam (cope with)* **he can't h. it** no puede con ello

2 *vi* (**a**) *(cut)* **to h. at sth** dar machetazos a algo (**b**) *(cough)* toser con fuerza (**c**) *Comptr* **to h. into a computer system** introducirse ilegalmente en un sistema informático

▸**hack down** *vt sep (tree)* talar, cortar

▸**hack off** *vt sep* (**a**) *(chop off) (branch, limb)* cortar (**b**) *Fam* **to be hacked off (with sb/sth)** estar furioso(a) *or Esp* mosqueado(a) (con alguien/algo)

hacker [ˈhækə(r)] *n Comptr* pirata *mf* informático(a), hacker *mf*

hackles [ˈhækəlz] *npl (of dog)* pelo *m* del cuello; *Fig* **to make sb's h. rise** *(make sb angry)* enfurecer a alguien

hackney cab [ˈhæknɪˈkæb], **hackney carriage** [ˈhæknɪˈkærɪdʒ] *n Formal* taxi *m*

hackneyed [ˈhæknɪd] *adj (language, argument)* manido(a), trillado(a)

hacksaw [ˈhæksɔː] *n* sierra *f* para metales

had [hæd] *pt & pp of* **have**

haddock [ˈhædək] *n* eglefino *m*

hadn't [ˈhædənt] = **had not**

hag [hæg] *n Pej (old woman)* bruja *f*, arpía *f*

haggard [ˈhægəd] *adj* marcado(a) por el cansancio y/o el dolor

haggle [ˈhægəl] *vi* regatear; **to h. about** *or* **over the price of sth** regatear el precio de algo

hagiography [hægɪˈɒgrəfɪ] *n* hagiografía *f*

Hague [heɪg] *n* **the H.** La Haya

hail¹ [heɪl] **1** *n (hailstones)* granizo *m*; *Fig (of blows, bullets, insults)* lluvia *f*

2 *vi* **it's hailing** está granizando

hail² *vt* (**a**) *(attract attention of)* llamar (**b**) *(acclaim)* aclamar (**as** como); **she has been hailed as the greatest novelist of the century** se la ha aclamado como la mejor novelista del siglo

▸**hail from** *vt insep* proceder de

hailstone [ˈheɪlstəʊn] *n (piedra f de)* granizo *m*

hailstorm [ˈheɪlstɔːm] *n* granizada *f*

hair [heə(r)] *n (of head)* pelo *m*, cabello *m*; *(of body)* vello *m*; *(of animal)* pelo *m*; **to have long h.** tener el pelo largo; **to do one's h.** peinarse; **to brush/comb one's h.** cepillarse/peinarse el pelo; **to have** *or* **get one's h. cut** cortarse el pelo; **if you harm** *or* **touch a h. on that child's head…** como le toques un solo pelo a ese niño…; **to make sb's h. stand on end** ponerle a alguien los pelos de punta; *Fam* **to get in sb's h.** dar la lata a alguien; *Fig* **to let one's h. down** *(lose inhibitions)* soltarse el pelo; *Fam* **the h. of the dog** *(for hangover)* = algo de alcohol para quitar la resaca; **h. band** cinta *f (para el pelo)*; **h. dryer** secador *m (de pelo)*; **h. gel** gel *m* moldeador, *Esp* gomina *f*; **h. spray** laca *f (de pelo)*

hairbrush [ˈheəbrʌʃ] *n* cepillo *m*

hairclip [ˈheəklɪp] *n* clipe *m* para el pelo, horquilla *f*

haircut [ˈheəkʌt] *n* corte *m* de pelo; **to have a h.** cortarse el pelo

hairdo [ˈheəduː] *(pl* **hairdos**) *n Fam* peinado *m*

hairdresser [ˈheədresə(r)] *n* peluquero(a) *m,f*; **h.'s** peluquería *f*

hairdressing [ˈheədresɪŋ] *n* peluquería *f*; **h. salon** salón *m* de peluquería

-haired [heəd] *suffix* **curly-h.** de pelo rizado

hairless [ˈheəlɪs] *adj* sin pelo; *(face)* lampiño(a); *(infant, puppy)* pelón(ona)

hairline [ˈheəlaɪn] *n* (**a**) *(of person)* nacimiento *m* del pelo; **to have a receding h.** tener entradas (**b**) **h. crack** *(in pipe, wall)* fisura *f* muy pequeña; **h. fracture** *(of bone)* fisura *f (de hueso)*

hairnet [ˈheənet] *n* redecilla *f* para el pelo

hairpiece [ˈheəpiːs] *n* peluquín *m*

hairpin [ˈheəpɪn] *n* horquilla *f*, *Andes, CAm, Méx,* gancho *m*; **h. bend** *(on road)* curva *f* muy cerrada

hair-raising [ˈheəreɪzɪŋ] *adj* espeluznante

hair's-breadth [ˈheəzbredθ] *n* **by a h.** por un pelo; **to be within a h. of** estar al borde de

hairspray [ˈheəspreɪ] *n* laca *f (de pelo)*

hairstyle [ˈheəstaɪl] *n* peinado *m*

hairy [ˈheərɪ] *adj* (**a**) *(hair-covered)* velludo(a), peludo(a) (**b**) *Fam (scary)* peliagudo(a)

Haiti ['heɪtɪ] *n* Haití

Haitian ['heɪʃən] *n & adj* haitiano(a) *m,f*

hake [heɪk] *n* merluza *f*

halcyon days ['hælsɪən'deɪz] *npl Literary* días *mpl* felices

hale [heɪl] *adj* sano(a); **to be h. and hearty** estar como una rosa

half [hɑːf] **1** *n* (*pl* **halves** [hɑːvz]) (**a**) *(in general)* mitad *f*; **h. an hour** media hora *f*; **h. past twelve** las doce y media; *Sport* **first/second h.** primera/segunda parte *f*, primer/segundo tiempo *m*; **to fold/cut sth in h.** doblar/cortar algo por la mitad; **h. a dozen, a h. dozen** media docena *f*; **h. of them** la mitad (de ellos); **to have h. a mind to do sth** estar tentado(a) de hacer algo; *Hum* **my better** *or* **other h.** mi media naranja; **she is too clever/arrogant by h.** se pasa de lista/arrogante; **she doesn't do things by halves** no le gusta hacer las cosas a medias; **to go halves with sb** pagar *or* ir a medias con alguien

(**b**) *(fraction)* medio *m*; **three and a h.** tres y medio

2 *adj* medio(a); **h. board** media pensión *f*; **h. brother** hermanastro *m*; **h. day** media jornada *f*; **h. hour** media hora *f*; **every h. hour** cada media hora; *Mus* **h. note** blanca *f*; **at h. price** a mitad de precio; **h. volley** media volea *f*

3 *adv* a medias; **to h. do sth** hacer algo a medias; **the bottle was h. full/empty** la botella estaba medio llena/vacía; **you're h. right** tienes razón a medias

half- [hɑːf] *prefix* **h.-naked/asleep/dead** medio desnudo(a)/ dormido(a)/muerto(a)

halfback ['hɑːfbæk] *n (in football)* corredor *m*

half-baked [hɑːf'beɪkt] *adj Fam (theory, plan)* mal concebido(a)

half-breed ['hɑːfbriːd] *n* mestizo(a) *m,f*

half-caste ['hɑːfkɑːst] *n & adj* mestizo(a) *m,f*

half-full ['hɑːf'fʊl] *adj* medio lleno(a)

half-hearted ['hɑːf'hɑːtɪd] *adj (effort, performance)* desganado(a); *(belief, support)* tibio(a)

half-heartedly ['hɑːf'hɑːtɪdlɪ] *adv* sin (muchas) ganas

half-hourly ['hɑːf'aʊəlɪ] *adv* cada media hora

half-jokingly [hɑːf'dʒəʊkɪŋlɪ] *adv (to say, suggest)* medio en broma

half-life ['hɑːflaɪf] *n Phys* media vida *f*

half-marathon [hɑːf'mærəθən] *n* media maratón *f*

half-mast ['hɑːf'mɑːst] *n* **at h.** a media asta

half-open [hɑːf'əʊpən] *adj (eyes, window)* entreabierto(a), entornado(a)

half-sister ['hɑːf'sɪstə(r)] *n* hermanastra *f*

half-size ['hɑːf'saɪz] *n (for clothing)* talla *f* intermedia; *(for shoes)* número *m* intermedio

halftime ['hɑːf'taɪm] *n (of game)* descanso *m*

half-truth ['hɑːf'truːθ] *n* verdad *f* a medias

halfway [hɑːf'weɪ] **1** *adj (point, stage)* intermedio(a); **h. house** *(for former prisoners, addicts)* centro *m* de reinserción; *Fig (compromise)* término *m* medio; **h. line** *(on soccer pitch)* línea *f* divisoria *or* de medio campo

2 *adv* a mitad de camino; *Fig* **to meet sb h.** *(compromise)* llegar a una solución de compromiso con alguien

halfwit ['hɑːfwɪt] *n* bobo(a) *m,f*, *Esp* memo(a) *m,f*

halfwitted [hɑːf'wɪtɪd] *adj (person)* idiota, *Esp* memo(a); **a h. idea** una bobada, *Esp* una memez

half-yearly ['hɑːf'jɪəlɪ] *adj* semestral, bianual

halibut ['hælɪbət] *n* fletán *m*

halitosis [hælɪ'təʊsɪs] *n Med* halitosis *f inv*

hall [hɔːl] *n (a) (entrance room)* vestíbulo *m*; *(corridor)* pasillo *m*; **h. tree** *perchero m (b) (for concerts, meetings) (large room)* salón *m* de actos; *(building)* auditorio *m*

hallmark ['hɔːlmɑːk] *n (on silver)* contraste *m*; *Fig (of idea, plan)* sello *m* característico

hallowed ['hæləʊd] *adj* sagrado(a)

Halloween, Hallowe'en [hæləʊ'iːn] *n* = víspera de Todos los Santos en la que los niños se disfrazan de brujas y fantasmas

hallucinate [hə'luːsɪneɪt] *vi* alucinar, sufrir alucinaciones

hallucination [həluːsɪ'neɪʃən] *n* alucinación *f*

hallucinatory [hə'luːsɪnətərɪ] *adj* alucinatorio(a)

hallucinogen [hə'luːsɪnədʒən] *n* alucinógeno *m*

hallucinogenic [həluːsɪnəʊ'dʒenɪk] *adj* alucinógeno(a)

hallway ['hɔːlweɪ] *n (entrance room)* vestíbulo *m*; *(corridor)* pasillo *m*

halo ['heɪləʊ] *(pl* **halos** *or* **haloes**) *n* halo *m*

halogen ['hælədʒən] *n* halógeno(a); **h. lamp** lámpara *f* halógena

halt [hɒlt] **1** *n* alto *m*, parada *f*; **to come to a h.** detenerse; **to bring sth to a h.** paralizar algo; **to call a h. to sth** interrumpir algo

2 *vt* detener

3 *vi* detenerse

halter ['hɔːltə(r)] *n (a) (for horse)* ronzal *m* (**b**) **h. (top)** *(garment)* top *m* con tiras *or* tirantes que se atan al cuello

halting ['hɔːltɪŋ] *adj (voice, progress)* vacilante, titubeante

haltingly ['hɔːltɪŋlɪ] *adv (to walk)* con paso vacilante; *(to speak)* con la voz entrecortada

halva(h) ['hælvə] *n* halva *f*, = dulce que contiene frutos secos, miel, azafrán y semillas de sésamo

halve [hɑːv] *vt (a) (divide in two)* dividir (en dos); *(cake, fruit)* partir por la mitad (**b**) *(reduce by half)* reducir a la mitad

halves *pl of* **half**

ham [hæm] **1** *n (a) (meat)* jamón *m* (**b**) *Fam (actor)* actor *m* exagerado, actriz *f* exagerada; **h. acting** sobreactuación *f*, histrionismo *m*

2 *vt (pt & pp* **hammed***) Fam (of actor)* **to h. it up** sobreactuar

Hamburg ['hæmbɜːg] *n* Hamburgo

hamburger ['hæmbɜːgə(r)] *n* hamburguesa *f*

ham-handed ['hæm'hændɪd], **ham-fisted** ['hæm'fɪstɪd] *adj Fam (person)* torpe, *Esp* manazas; *(workmanship, attempt)* torpe

hamlet ['hæmlɪt] *n* aldea *f*

hammer ['hæmə(r)] **1** *n (tool) & Sport* martillo *m*; **to come under the h.** *(be auctioned)* salir a subasta; **to go at it h. and tongs** *(argue)* tener una acalorada discusión; *(try hard)* poner mucho empeño *or* esfuerzo; **the h. and sickle** la hoz y el martillo

2 *vt (a) (hit with hammer)* martillear; *(hit with fist)* dar puñetazos a; **to h. a nail into sth** clavar un clavo en algo; **to h. home** *(nail, argument)* remachar; **she hammered home her advantage** se aseguró su ventaja (**b**) *Fam (defeat)* dar una paliza a, *Esp* machacar

▸**hammer away at** *vt insep Fig* **to h. away at a problem** ponerse en serio con un problema

▸**hammer out** *vt sep Fig (agreement)* alcanzar, llegar a

hammering ['hæmərɪŋ] *n (a) (noise)* martilleo *m* (**b**) *Fam (defeat)* paliza *f*

hammock ['hæmək] *n* hamaca *f*

hamper ['hæmpə(r)] **1** *n (a) (for food)* cesta *f*, cesto *m*; **(Christmas) h.** cesta de Navidad (**b**) *(for laundry)* cesta *f or* cesto *m* de la ropa

2 *vt (hinder)* entorpecer

hamster ['hæmstə(r)] *n* hámster *m*

hamstring ['hæmstrɪŋ] **1** *n* tendón *m* de la corva

2 *vt (pt & pp* **hamstrung** ['hæmstrʌŋ]) *(incapacitate)* incapacitar, paralizar

hand [hænd] **1** *n (a) (part of body)* mano *f*; *(of clock, watch)* manecilla *f*; **to hold hands** cogerse de las manos; **h. in h.** (cogidos) de la mano; **to hold sth in one's h.** sostener algo en la mano; **to take sb by the h.** coger a alguien de la mano; **on one's hands and knees** a cuatro patas; **by h.** *(make, wash)* a mano; *(on envelope)* en propia mano; **hands off!** ¡las manos fuera!; **hands up!** ¡manos arriba!; **h. ball** *(offense in soccer)* mano *m*; **h. cream** crema *f* de manos; **h. dryer** *or* **drier** secador *m* de manos, secamanos *m inv*; **h. grenade** granada *f* de mano; **h. luggage** equipaje *m* de mano

  (b) *(worker)* brazo *m*; **to be an old h. at sth** ser veterano(a) en algo

  (c) *(handwriting)* **in his own h.** de su puño y letra

  (d) *(in cards)* mano *f*; *Fig* **to show one's h.** poner las cartas boca arriba *or* sobre la mesa

  (e) *(idioms)* **at h.** a mano; **on h.** disponible; **to have sth to h.** tener algo a mano; **to ask for sb's h. (in marriage)** pedir la mano de alguien; **to be in good hands** estar en buenas manos; **to fall into the wrong hands** caer en malas manos; **it's out of my hands** no está en mi mano; **to change hands** *(money, car)* cambiar de mano; **I had a h. in designing the course** tuve que ver *or* puse de mi parte en el diseño del curso; **to go h. in h. with sth** estar asociado(a) a algo; **to try one's h. at sth** intentar algo alguna vez; **to turn one's h. to sth** dedicarse a algo; **to give** *or* **lend sb a h.** echar una mano a alguien; **to give sb a big h.** *(applaud)* dar un gran aplauso a alguien; **to suffer at sb's hands** sufrir a manos de alguien; **on the one h.** por una parte; **on the other h.** por otra parte; **to have time on one's hands** tener tiempo libre; **to have a situation in h.** tener una situación bajo control; **to take sb in h.** hacerse cargo de alguien; **to get out of h.** escaparse de las manos; **the children got out of h.** los niños se desmandaron; **to dismiss a suggestion out of h.** rechazar una sugerencia sin más ni más; **to have one's hands full** estar completamente ocupado(a); **to have one's hands tied** tener las manos atadas; **to be h. in** *or* **and glove with sb** colaborar estrechamente con alguien; **to live from h. to mouth** vivir de forma precaria; **to lose money h. over fist** perder dinero a raudales; **to make money h. over fist** ganar dinero a espuertas; **to win hands down** ganar con comodidad

  2 *vt* pasar; **to h. sth to sb** pasar algo a alguien; *Fig* **to h. sth to sb on a plate** ponerle algo a alguien en bandeja; *Fig* **you've got to h. it to him** tienes que reconocérselo

▸ **hand around** *vt sep (circulate)* pasar

▸ **hand back** *vt sep (return)* devolver

▸ **hand down** *vt sep (bequeath)* dejar en herencia

▸ **hand in** *vt sep (give)* entregar; *(resignation)* presentar

▸ **hand on** *vt sep* pasar

▸ **hand out** *vt sep (distribute)* repartir

▸ **hand over** *vt sep (give)* dar, entregar; *Fig (control, responsibility)* ceder

handbag ['hændbæg] *n (woman's) Esp* bolso *m*, *Col, CSur* cartera *f*, *Méx* bolsa *f*

handball ['hændbɔːl] *n (game)* balonmano *m*

handbook ['hændbʊk] *n* manual *m*

handbrake ['hændbreɪk] *n (of car)* freno *m* de mano

handcuff ['hændkʌf] *vt* esposar

handcuffs ['hændkʌfs] *npl* esposas *fpl*

handful ['hændfʊl] *n (of sand, rice, people)* puñado *m*; *Fig* **that child is a real h.** ese niño es un terremoto

handgun ['hændgʌn] *n* pistola *f*

handheld ['hænd'held] *adj (camera)* de mano, portátil; **h. computer** *Esp* ordenador *m or Am* computadora *f* de bolsillo

handicap ['hændɪkæp] **1** *n (disadvantage)* desventaja *f*, hándicap *m*; *(disability)* discapacidad *f*, minusvalía *f*; *(in golf, horseracing)* hándicap *m*

  2 *vt (pt & pp* **handicapped)** suponer una desventaja para; **to be handicapped by…** verse perjudicado(a) por…

handicapped ['hændɪkæpt] **1** *adj* discapacitado(a), minusválido(a)

  2 *npl* **the h.** los discapacitados *or* minusválidos

handicraft ['hændɪkrɑːft] *n (skill)* artesanía *f*; *(object)* objeto *m* de artesanía

handiwork ['hændɪwɜːk] *n (craftwork)* trabajos *mpl* manuales, manualidades *fpl*; *Ironic* **this mess looks like Clara's h.!** este desorden parece obra de Clara

handkerchief ['hæŋkətʃɪf] *n* pañuelo *m*

hand-knit ['hænd'nɪt] **1** *n* prenda *f* (de punto) tejida a mano

  2 *vt* tejer a mano

handle ['hændəl] **1** *n (of broom, umbrella, gun, knife)* mango *m*; *(of racket, bat)* empuñadura *f*; *(of suitcase, cup)* asa *f*; *(of door)* manilla *f*; *Fig* **to fly off the h.** *(lose one's temper)* perder los estribos; *Fig* **to get a h. on sth** *(understand)* hacerse una idea clara de algo

  2 *vt* **(a)** *(touch, hold)* manejar, manipular; **h. with care** *(sign)* frágil; **to h. the ball** *(in soccer)* hacer (falta con la) mano; **to h. the ball well/badly** *(in ball sports)* controlar la pelota bien/mal **(b)** *(cope with) (situation, crisis)* hacer frente a, afrontar **(c)** *Com (business, contract, client)* encargarse de

  3 *vi* **h. well** *(car, boat)* responder bien

handlebars ['hændəlbɑːz] *npl (of bicycle, motorbike)* manillar *m*, *Am* manubrio *m*

handmade ['hænd'meɪd] *adj* hecho(a) a mano; **to be h.** estar hecho(a) a mano

hand-me-down ['hændmɪdaʊn] *n Fam* **he wore his brother's hand-me-downs** llevaba ropa heredada de su hermano

handout ['hændaʊt] *n* **(a)** *(donation)* donativo *m*, limosna *f* **(b)** *(leaflet)* hoja *f* informativa

handpick ['hænd'pɪk] *vt* **(a)** *(fruit, vegetables)* escoger **(b)** *(people, team)* seleccionar cuidadosamente

hand-picked ['hænd'pɪkt] *adj* **(a)** *(fruit, vegetables)* escogido(a) **(b)** *(person, team)* cuidadosamente seleccionado(a)

handrail ['hændreɪl] *n* pasamanos *m inv*, baranda *f*, *Esp* barandilla *f*

handset ['hændset] *n (of telephone)* auricular *m*

handsewn ['hænd'səʊn] *adj* cosido(a) a mano

hands-free ['hænz'friː] *adj (phone, dialing)* de manos libres

handshake ['hændʃeɪk] *n* apretón *m* de manos

hands-off ['hæn'zɒf] *adj (approach, style)* no intervencionista

handsome ['hænsəm] *adj* **(a)** *(man)* atractivo, *Esp* guapo, *Am* lindo; *(woman)* distinguida; *(animal)* hermoso(a), bello(a); *(building)* elegante, bello(a) **(b)** *(praise)* generoso(a); *(price, profit)* considerable

handsomely ['hænsəmlɪ] *adv* **(a)** *(dressed, furnished)* elegantemente **(b)** *(praised, paid)* generosamente

hands-on ['hæn'zɒn] *adj* **he has a h. management style** le gusta implicarse en todos los aspectos del negocio; **h. training** formación *f* práctica

handstand ['hændstænd] *n* **to do a h.** hacer el pino

handstitched ['hænd'stɪtʃt] *adj* cosido(a) a mano

hand-to-hand ['hæntə'hænd] *adj* **h. combat** combate *m* cuerpo a cuerpo

hand-to-mouth ['hæntə'maʊθ] **1** *adj* **a h. existence** una existencia precaria

  2 *adv* **to live h.** vivir de forma precaria

handwash ['hændwɒʃ] **1** *vt* lavar a mano

  2 *n* **I'm doing a h.** voy a lavar unas cosas a mano

handwriting ['hændraɪtɪŋ] *n* letra *f*, caligrafía *f*

handwritten ['hændrɪtən] *adj* manuscrito(a), escrito(a) a mano

handy ['hændɪ] *adj* **(a)** *(useful)* práctico(a), útil; **to come in h.** venir bien **(b)** *(within reach)* a mano; **have you got a pen h.?** ¿tienes un bolígrafo a mano? **(c)** *(skillful)* habilidoso(a), *Esp* mañoso(a); **he's very h. in the kitchen** se le da muy bien la cocina *or* cocinar; **she's very h. with a paintbrush** es muy hábil con la brocha

handyman ['hændɪmæn] *n (person good at odd jobs)* persona *f* habilidosa, *Esp* manitas *mf inv*

hang [hæŋ] **1** *n* **(a)** *Fam* **to get the h. of sth** pillar el truco *or*

Esp el tranquillo a algo, *Méx* pescar algo, *RP* agarrar la mano a algo (**b**) **h. glider** ala *f* delta; **to go h. gliding** hacer ala delta

2 *vt* (*pt & pp* **hung** [hʌŋ]) (**a**) *(suspend)* colgar (**b**) **to h. one's head** bajar la cabeza; **he hung his head in shame** bajó la cabeza avergonzado (**c**) (*pt & pp* **hanged**) *(criminal)* ahorcar, colgar (**for** por)

3 *vi* (**a**) *(be suspended)* colgar; **she hung on his every word** estaba totalmente pendiente de sus palabras (**b**) *(be executed)* ser ahorcado(a) *or* colgado(a) (**c**) *(material, clothes)* caer, colgar

▸**hang around, hang about** *vi Fam (wait)* esperar; **he kept me hanging about for hours** me tuvo esperando horas

▸**hang back** *vi (hesitate)* dudar, titubear

▸**hang in** *vi Fam (persevere)* aguantar; **h. in there!** ¡resiste!, ¡aguanta!

▸**hang on 1** *vi* (**a**) *Fam (wait)* esperar (**b**) *(survive)* resistir, aguantar

2 *vt insep (depend on)* depender de; **everything hangs on his answer** todo depende de su respuesta

▸**hang on to** *vt insep (keep)* conservar; **I'd h. on to those documents if I were you** yo, en tu lugar, me quedaría con esos documentos

▸**hang out 1** *vt sep (washing)* tender

2 *vi* (**a**) **his tongue/shirt was hanging out** tenía la lengua/camisa fuera (**b**) *Fam* **to h. out with one's friends** andar por ahí con los amigos; **he usually hangs out in the Bronx Café** normalmente va por el Café Bronx

▸**hang together** *vi (argument, statements)* encajar, concordar

▸**hang up 1** *vt sep (suspend) (hat, picture)* colgar

2 *vi (on telephone)* colgar; **to h. up on sb** colgarle (el teléfono) a alguien

hangar ['hæŋə(r)] *n Av* hangar *m*

hangdog ['hæŋdɒg] *adj* **a h. look** una expresión avergonzada *or Am salvo RP* apenada

hanger ['hæŋə(r)] *n (for clothes)* percha *f*

hanger-on [hæŋə'rɒn] (*pl* **hangers-on**) *n Fam Pej* parásito(a) *m,f*, adlátere *mf*

hanging ['hæŋɪŋ] *n (execution)* ahorcamiento *m*, ejecución *f* en la horca

hangman ['hæŋmən] *n* verdugo *m*

hangnail ['hæŋneɪl] *n* padrastro *m*

hangout ['hæŋaʊt] *n Fam* guarida *f*, sitio *m* predilecto

hangover ['hæŋəʊvə(r)] *n* (**a**) *(from drinking)* resaca *f*, *Guat, Méx* cruda *f* (**b**) *(practice, belief)* vestigio *m*

hang-up ['hæŋʌp] *n Fam (complex)* complejo *m*, paranoia *f*; **to have a h. about sth** estar acomplejado(a) por algo

hanker ['hæŋkə(r)] *vi* **to h. after** *or* **for sth** anhelar algo

hankering ['hæŋkərɪŋ] *n* **to have a h. for sth** sentir anhelo de algo

hankie, hanky ['hæŋkɪ] *n Fam* pañuelo *m*

hanky-panky ['hæŋkɪ'pæŋkɪ] *n Fam* (**a**) *(sexual activity) Esp* ñacañaca *m*, *Méx* cuchi-cuchi *m* (**b**) *(underhand behavior)* chanchullos *mpl*, tejemanejes *mpl*

Hanover ['hænəʊvə(r)] *n* Hanover

haphazard [hæp'hæzəd] *adj (choice, decision)* arbitrario(a), incoherente; *(attempt)* desorganizado(a)

haphazardly [hæp'hæzədlɪ] *adv* a la buena de Dios, descuidadamente

hapless ['hæplɪs] *adj* infortunado(a)

happen ['hæpən] *vi (take place)* pasar, ocurrir, suceder; **it happened ten years ago** pasó hace diez años; **as it happens,...** precisamente..., casualmente...; **what has happened to him?** ¿qué le ha pasado?; **to h. to meet sb** encontrarse con alguien por casualidad; **I h. to know that...** resulta que sé que...

▸**happen on, happen upon** *vt insep* encontrarse con

happening ['hæpənɪŋ] *n* suceso *m*

happily ['hæpɪlɪ] *adv* (**a**) *(with pleasure)* alegremente; **they lived h. ever after** fueron felices y comieron perdices (**b**) *(fortunately)* afortunadamente, por suerte

happiness ['hæpɪnɪs] *n* felicidad *f*

happy ['hæpɪ] *adj* (**a**) *(in a state of contentment)* feliz; *(pleased)* contento(a); *(cheerful)* alegre, feliz; **to be h. with sth** estar contento con algo; **to be h. to do sth** hacer algo con mucho gusto; **to make sb h.** hacer feliz a alguien; **a h. ending** un final feliz; **a h. medium** un (satisfactorio) término medio; **h. birthday/Christmas/New Year!** ¡feliz cumpleaños/Navidad/Año Nuevo! (**b**) *(fortunate) (choice, phrase)* afortunado(a), acertado(a)

happy-go-lucky ['hæpɪgəʊ'lʌkɪ] *adj* despreocupado(a)

Hapsburg, Habsburg ['hæpsbɜːg] *n* **the Hapsburgs** *(in general)* los Habsburgo; *(Spanish royal house)* los Austrias, la casa de Austria

harangue [hə'ræŋ] **1** *n* arenga *f*

2 *vt* arengar, soltar una arenga a; **to h. sb into doing sth** acosar a alguien para que haga algo

harass [hə'ræs, 'hærəs] *vt* acosar, hostigar; **to h. sb into doing sth** acosar a alguien para que haga algo

harassed [hə'ræst, 'hærəst] *adj* agobiado(a)

harassment [hə'ræsmənt, 'hærəsmənt] *n* acoso *m*

harbor ['hɑːbə(r)] **1** *n* puerto *m*

2 *vt (fugitive)* acoger, proteger; *(hope, suspicion)* albergar; **to h. a grudge against sb** guardar rencor a alguien

hard [hɑːd] **1** *adj* (**a**) *(substance)* duro(a); *(fact, evidence)* concreto(a), real; *Fig* **to be as h. as nails** *(unfeeling)* ser insensible, *Esp* ser un hueso; *(tough)* ser duro(a) de pelar; **in h. cash** en metálico; *Comptr* **h. copy** copia *f* impresa, listado *m*; **h. court** *(for tennis)* pista *f* de cemento; *Comptr* **h. disk** disco *m* duro; **h. drugs** drogas *fpl* duras; *Pol* **h. left** izquierda *f* radical; *Comptr* **h. return** retorno *m* manual

(**b**) *(difficult)* difícil; **it's h. to say** no es fácil decir; **to be h. to please** ser muy exigente; **to learn the h. way** aprender a base de equivocarse; **h. of hearing** duro(a) de oído

(**c**) *(harsh) (person, conditions, life)* duro(a); **to be h. on sb** (muy) duro con alguien; **to give sb a h. time** hacérselo pasar mal a alguien; **a h. winter** un invierno muy duro; *Fam* **no h. feelings?** ¿no me guardas rencor?; **to take a h. line on sth** ponerse duro(a) con (respecto a) algo; *Fam* **h. luck!** ¡mala pata *or* suerte!

(**d**) *(intense)* **to be a h. worker** ser muy trabajador(ora); *Law* **h. labor** trabajos *mpl* forzados; *Com* **h. sell** venta *f* agresiva

(**e**) *(water)* duro(a)

(**f**) **h. cider** sidra *f*; **h. liquor** bebida *f* fuerte

2 *adv* (**a**) *(to work)* duro, duramente; *(to think, consider)* detenidamente; *(to push, hit)* fuerte; **to try h.** esforzarse; **to look h. at sb** mirar fijamente a alguien; **to be h. at work** estar muy metido(a) en el trabajo; **it's raining h.** está lloviendo mucho; **to feel h. done by** sentirse injustamente tratado(a); *Fam* **h. up** estar en apuros *or Am* problemas (**b**) *(near)* **h. by** muy cerca de; **to follow h. upon sb** seguir a alguien muy de cerca

hard-and-fast ['hɑːdən'fɑːst] *adj* **there are no h. rules** no hay reglas fijas

hardback, hardcover ['hɑːdbæk] *n (book)* edición *f* de pasta dura

hardball ['hɑːdbɔːl] *n (baseball)* béisbol *m*; *Fig* **to play h. (with sb)** ponerse duro(a) (con alguien), adoptar una línea dura (con alguien)

hard-bitten ['hɑːd'bɪtən] *adj* curtido(a)

hardboard ['hɑːdbɔːd] *n* aglomerado *m*, conglomerado *m*

hard-boiled [hɑːd'bɔɪld] *adj (egg)* duro(a), cocido(a); *Fig (person) (tough)* duro(a), curtido(a)

hard-core ['hɑːdkɔː(r)] *adj (support)* incondicional, acérrimo(a); **h. porn(ography)** porno *m* duro

hardcover = hardback

hard-earned [hɑːdˈɜːnd] *adj* ganado(a) con mucho esfuerzo

harden [ˈhɑːdən] **1** *vt* endurecer; **to h. oneself to sth** insensibilizarse a algo

2 *vi (substance, attitude)* endurecerse

hardened [ˈhɑːdənd] *adj (steel)* endurecido(a), templado(a); *(drinker)* empedernido(a); *(sinner)* impenitente; **a h. criminal** un delincuente habitual

hard-fought [ˈhɑːdˈfɔːt] *adj (election, contest)* (muy) reñido(a), (muy) disputado(a)

hard-headed [ˈhɑːdˈhedɪd] *adj* pragmático(a)

hard-hearted [ˈhɑːdˈhɑːtɪd] *adj* duro(a), insensible

hard-hitting [ˈhɑːdˈhɪtɪŋ] *adj (criticism, report)* contundente

hardiness [ˈhɑːdɪnɪs] *n* fortaleza *f*, reciedumbre *m*

hard-liner [hɑːdˈlaɪnə(r)] *n (politician, activist)* intransigente *mf*, partidario(a) *m,f* de la línea dura

hardly [ˈhɑːdlɪ] *adv (scarcely)* apenas; **h. ever** casi nunca; **h. anyone/anything** casi nadie/nada; **I can h. believe it** me cuesta creerlo

hardness [ˈhɑːdnɪs] *n* **(a)** *(of substance)* dureza *f* **(b)** *(of problem)* dificultad *f*

hard-on [ˈhɑːdɒn] *n Vulg* **to have a h.** *Esp* estar empalmado, *Am* tenerla parada; **he got a h.** se le puso dura, *Esp* se empalmó, *Am* se le paró

hard-pressed [hɑːdˈprest], **hard-pushed** [hɑːdˈpʊʃt] *adj* **to be h. to do sth** tenerlo difícil para hacer algo; **to be h. for time/money** estar (muy) apurado(a) de tiempo/dinero

hardship [ˈhɑːdʃɪp] *n (suffering)* sufrimiento *m*; *(deprivation)* privación *f*; **to live in h.** vivir en la miseria

hardware [ˈhɑːdweə(r)] *n* **(a)** *(tools)* ferretería *f*; **(military) h.** *(weapons)* armamento *m*; **h. store** *(ironmonger's)* ferretería *f* **(b)** *Comptr* hardware *m*, soporte *m* físico

hard-wired [ˈhɑːdˈwaɪəd] *adj Comptr* integrado(a)

hard-won [hɑːdˈwʌn] *adj* ganado(a) a pulso

hardworking [ˈhɑːdˈwɜːkɪŋ] *adj* trabajador(ora)

hardy [ˈhɑːdɪ] *adj (person)* recio(a); *(plant)* resistente (al frío); **a h. perennial** una planta vivaz

hare [heə(r)] *n (animal)* liebre *f*

harebrained [ˈheəbreɪnd] *adj* disparatado(a)

harelip [ˈheəlɪp] *n* labio *m* leporino

harem [hɑːˈriːm] *n* harén *m*

haricot [ˈhærɪkəʊ] *n* **h. (bean)** alubia *f* blanca, *Esp* judía *f* blanca, *Am salvo RP* frijol *m* blanco, *Andes, RP* poroto *m* blanco

hark [hɑːk] *exclam Literary* ¡escucha!

▸**hark back** *vi* **to h. back to sth** recordar algo; **he's always harking back to his youth** siempre está recordando su juventud

harlot [ˈhɑːlət] *n Literary* ramera *f*, meretriz *f*

harm [hɑːm] **1** *n* daño *m*; **to do sb h.** hacer daño a alguien; **to do oneself h.** hacerse daño; **it will do more h. than good** hará más mal que bien; **I see no h. in it** no veo que tenga nada de malo; **there's no h. in trying** no se pierde nada por intentarlo; **you will come to no h.** no sufrirás ningún daño; **out of h.'s way** en lugar seguro

2 *vt (person, animal)* hacer daño a; *(reputation, image, quality)* dañar; *(chances, interests, business)* perjudicar

harmful [ˈhɑːmfʊl] *adj* perjudicial, dañino(a)

harmless [ˈhɑːmlɪs] *adj* inofensivo(a)

harmonica [hɑːˈmɒnɪkə] *n* armónica *f*

harmonics [hɑːˈmɒnɪks] *n* armonía *f*

harmonious [hɑːˈməʊnɪəs] *adj* armonioso(a)

harmoniously [hɑːˈməʊnɪəslɪ] *adv (to live)* en armonía; *(to blend)* armoniosamente

harmonization [hɑːmənaɪˈzeɪʃən] *n* armonización *f*

harmonize [ˈhɑːmənaɪz] *vt & vi* armonizar

harmony [ˈhɑːmənɪ] *n also Fig* armonía *f*; **in h. with** en

armonía con; **to live in h. (with)** vivir en armonía *or* en paz (con)

harness [ˈhɑːnɪs] **1** *n* **(a)** *(of horse)* arreos *mpl*; *(for safety, of parachute)* arnés *m* **(b)** *(idioms)* **to work in h. with sb** trabajar hombro con hombro con alguien; **to die in h.** morir antes de jubilarse

2 *vt (horse)* arrear, aparejar; *(resources)* emplear, hacer uso de

harp [hɑːp] **1** *n* arpa *f*

2 *vi Fam* **to h. on (at sb) about sth** dar la lata (a alguien) con algo, *RP* hinchar (a alguien) con algo

harpist [ˈhɑːpɪst] *n* arpista *mf*

harpoon [hɑːˈpuːn] **1** *n* arpón *m*

2 *vt* arponear

harpsichord [ˈhɑːpsɪkɔːd] *n* clave *m*, clavicémbalo *m*

harpy [ˈhɑːpɪ] *n* arpía *f*

harridan [ˈhærɪdən] *n Literary* vieja *f* gruñona, arpía *f*

harrow [ˈhærəʊ] *n (farm equipment)* grada *f*

harrowing [ˈhærəʊɪŋ] *adj (experience, sight)* angustioso(a)

harry [ˈhærɪ] *vt* acosar

harsh [hɑːʃ] *adj (voice, sound)* áspero(a); *(climate, treatment)* duro(a)

harshly [ˈhɑːʃlɪ] *adv (to answer, speak)* con aspereza; **to treat sb h.** tratar a alguien con dureza

harvest [ˈhɑːvɪst] **1** *n* cosecha *f*

2 *vt* cosechar

has [hæz] *3rd person singular of* **have**

has-been [ˈhæzbiːn] *n Fam Pej* vieja gloria *f*

hash [hæʃ] *n* **(a)** *(stew)* guiso *m* de carne con *Esp* patatas *or Am* papas, *Andes, Méx* ahogado *m* de carne con papas; **h. browns** = fritura de *Esp* patata *or Am* papa y cebolla **(b)** *Fam (hashish)* chocolate *m*, *Esp* costo *m* **(c)** *(symbol)* **h. mark** *Comptr & Typ* signo *m* número; *(on telephone)* almohadilla *f*, numeral *m*; *(in music)* sostenido *m*; *(in football)* hash mark *f* **(d)** *(idioms) Fam* **to make a h. of sth** hacer algo muy mal

hashish [ˈhæʃiːʃ] *n* hachís *m*

hasn't [ˈhæznt] = **has not**

hassle [ˈhæsəl] *Fam* **1** *n* lío *m*, *Esp* follón *m*; **it's too much h.** es demasiado lío; **it's a real h. buying a house** comprarse una casa es un lío *Esp* de aquí te espero *or Méx* de la madre *or RP* que para qué te cuento; **to give sb h.** dar la lata a alguien

2 *vt* dar la lata a a

haste [heɪst] *n* prisa *f*, *Am* apuro *m*; **in h.** a toda prisa, *Am* con apuro; **to make h.** apresurarse, *Am* apurarse; *Prov* **more h. less speed** vísteme despacio que tengo prisa

hasten [ˈheɪsən] **1** *vt* acelerar; **to h. sb's departure** apresurar *or* acelerar la partida de alguien

2 *vi* apresurarse, *Am* apurarse; **I h. to add** me apresuro a añadir

hastily [ˈheɪstɪlɪ] *adv (quickly)* deprisa, apresuradamente; *(rashly)* precipitadamente, apresuradamente; **to judge sth h.** juzgar algo a la ligera

hastiness [ˈheɪstɪnɪs] *n (speed)* celeridad *f*; *(rashness)* precipitación *f*

hasty [ˈheɪstɪ] *adj* apresurado(a); **to jump to a h. conclusion** sacar conclusiones apresuradas

hat [hæt] *n* sombrero *m*; *also Fig* **to take one's h. off to sb** descubrirse ante alguien; *Fig* **to pass the h. around** *(collect money)* pasar la gorra; *Fig* **to throw one's h. in the ring** *(enter contest)* echarse al ruedo; *Fam Fig* **to keep sth under one's h.** no decir ni media de algo a nadie; **h. stand** perchero *m*; **h. trick** *(of goals)* tres goles *mpl (en el mismo partido)*; *(of victories)* tres victorias *fpl* consecutivas

hatch¹ [hætʃ] *n (covering opening)* escotilla *f*; *Fam* **down the h.!** ¡salud!

hatch² [hætʃ] *vt (eggs)* incubar; **to h. a plot** urdir un plan

2 *vi* **the egg hatched** el pollo salió del cascarón

hatchback [ˈhætʃbæk] *n (car)* (3-door) tres puertas *m inv*; (5-door) cinco puertas *m inv*

hatchet [ˈhætʃɪt] n hacha f *(pequeña)*; *Fam* **to do a h. job on sb/sth** *(critic, reviewer)* ensañarse con alguien/algo; *Fam* **h. man** = encargado del trabajo sucio

hatchet-faced [ˈhætʃɪtfeɪst] adj de rostro enjuto y anguloso

hate [heɪt] **1** n *(hatred)* odio m; **h. mail** = cartas que contienen amenazas o fuertes críticas

2 vt odiar, detestar; **he hates to be contradicted** no soporta que le contradigan; *Fam* **I h. to admit it but I think he's right** me cuesta admitirlo, pero creo que tiene razón

hateful [ˈheɪtfʊl] adj odioso(a), detestable

hatpin [ˈhætpɪn] n alfiler m (de sombrero)

hatred [ˈheɪtrɪd] n odio m

haughtily [ˈhɔːtɪlɪ] adv con altanería

haughtiness [ˈhɔːtɪnɪs] n altanería f

haughty [ˈhɔːtɪ] adj altanero(a)

haul [hɔːl] **1** n (**a**) *(fish caught)* captura f; *(loot, of stolen goods)* botín m; *(of drugs)* alijo m (**b**) *Fam (journey)* **it's a long h.** hay un tirón

2 vt (**a**) *(pull)* arrastrar; *Fam* **he was hauled in for questioning** se lo llevaron para interrogarlo; *Fam* **to h. sb over the coals** *(reprimand)* echar una reprimenda or *Esp* una bronca a alguien; **she was hauled up before the principal** la llevaron al despacho del director (**b**) *(transport)* transportar (**c**) *Vulg* **to h. ass** *Esp* ir a toda hostia, *Méx* ir hecho(a) la raya, *RP* ir a los santos pedos

haulage [ˈhɔːlɪdʒ] n *(transportation)* transporte m (de mercancías); *(costs)* portes mpl; **h. firm** empresa f de transportes, transportista m

hauler [ˈhɔːlə(r)] n *(company)* empresa f de transportes, transportista m

haunch [hɔːntʃ] n *(of person)* trasero m; *(of meat)* pierna f; **to sit** or **squat on one's haunches** ponerse en cuclillas

haunt [hɔːnt] **1** n *(favorite place)* lugar m predilecto

2 vt (**a**) *(of ghost) (house)* aparecerse en; *(person)* aparecerse a (**b**) *(of thought, memory)* asaltar; **he was haunted by the fear that…** le asaltaba el temor de que… (**c**) *(frequent)* frecuentar

haunted [ˈhɔːntɪd] adj *(castle, room)* encantado(a); **he has a h. look** tiene una mirada atormentada

haunting [ˈhɔːntɪŋ] adj obsesivo(a)

Havana [həˈvænə] n La Habana; **H. cigar** *(puro m)* habano m

have [hæv]

En el inglés hablado, y en el escrito en estilo coloquial, el verbo auxiliar **have** se contrae de forma que **I have** se transforma en **I've**, **he/she/it has** se transforman en **he's/she's/it's** y **you/we/they have** se transforman en **you've/we've/they've**. Las formas de pasado **I/you/he** *etc* **had** se transforman en **I'd**, **you'd**, **he'd** *etc*. Las formas negativas **has not**, **have not** y **had not** se transforman en **hasn't**, **haven't** y **hadn't**.

1 n **the haves and the h.-nots** los ricos y los pobres

2 vt *(3rd person singular* **has** [hæz], *pt & pp* **had** [hæd]) (**a**) *(in general)* tener; **they've got** or **they h. a big house** tienen una casa grande; **she hasn't got** or **doesn't h. a cat** no tiene gato; **I've got** or **I h. something to do** tengo algo que hacer; **which one will you h.?** ¿cuál prefieres?; **she's got** or **she has measles/AIDS** tiene (el) sarampión/el sida; **she's got** or **she has blue eyes** tiene los ojos azules; **can I h. a beer and a brandy, please?** ¿me daría or *Esp* pone una cerveza y un coñac, (por favor)?; **I'll h. the soup** yo tomaré una sopa; **we've got** or **we h. a choice** tenemos una alternativa; **what's that got to do with it?** ¿qué tiene que ver eso?; **he had me by the throat** me tenía sujeto or cogido por el cuello; **he had them in his power** los tenía en su poder; **you shall h. it back tomorrow** te lo devolveré mañana; *Fam* **I've had it if she finds out!** ¡si se entera, me la cargo!; *Fam* **this coat has had it** este abrigo está para el arrastre, *RP* este saco ya

cumplió; *Fam* **you've been had!** *(you've been cheated)* ¡te han timado!, *Méx* ¡te chingaron!, *RP* ¡te embromaron!; *Fam* **you've got** or **you h. me there!** *(I don't know)* ¡ahí me has *Esp* pillado or *Am* agarrado or *Méx* cachado!

(**b**) *(with noun, to denote activity)* **to h. a bath** darse un baño; **to h. a shave** afeitarse; **to h. breakfast** desayunar; **to h. lunch** comer; **to h. dinner** cenar

(**c**) *(experience)* pasar; **to h. an accident** tener or sufrir un accidente; **to h. a good/bad time** pasarlo bien/mal; **I had a pleasant evening** pasé una agradable velada

(**d**) *(causative)* **I had him do it again** le hice repetirlo; **I'm having my record player repaired** me están arreglando el tocadiscos; **I'll h. you know that…!** te diré que…

(**e**) *(in passive-type constructions)* **to h. one's hair cut** cortarse el pelo; **I had my watch stolen** me robaron el reloj

(**f**) *(allow)* **I will not h. such conduct!** ¡no toleraré ese comportamiento!; **I won't h. you causing trouble!** ¡no permitiré que crees problemas!

(**g**) *(be compelled)* **to h. to do sth** tener que hacer algo; **I h. or I've got to go** me tengo que ir; **do you h. to work?, h. you got to work?** ¿tienes que trabajar?; **it's got** or **it has to be done** hay que hacerlo

(**h**) *(obtain)* **there were no tickets to be had** no quedaban entradas or *Col, Méx* boletos; **I h. it on good authority that…** sé por fuentes fidedignas que…

3 v aux haber; **I/we/they h. seen it** lo he/hemos/han visto; **you h. seen it** *(singular)* lo has visto; *(plural) Esp* lo habéis visto, *Am* lo vieron; **he/she/it has seen it** lo ha visto; **I h. worked here for three years** llevo tres años trabajando aquí; **he has been in prison before — no he hasn't!** ha estado ya antes en la cárcel — ¡no!; **you h. told him, haven't you?** se lo has dicho, ¿no? or ¿verdad?; **you haven't forgotten, h. you?** no te habrás olvidado, ¿no? or ¿verdad?

▶**have in** vt sep *Fam* **to h. it in for sb** tenerla tomada con alguien

▶**have on** vt sep (**a**) *(wear)* llevar puesto; **they had nothing on** estaban desnudos (**b**) *(have arranged)* **he has a lot on this week** esta semana tiene mucho que hacer; **I haven't got anything on on Tuesday** el martes lo tengo libre

▶**have out** vt sep (**a**) *(have extracted)* **I had a tooth out** me sacaron una muela (**b**) *(resolve)* **to h. it out with sb** poner las cosas en claro con alguien

haven [ˈheɪvən] n refugio m

haven't [ˈhævnt] = **have not**

haversack [ˈhævəsæk] n mochila f

havoc [ˈhævək] n estragos mpl; **to cause** or **wreak h.** hacer estragos; **to play h. with** hacer estragos en

Hawaii [həˈwaɪiː] n Hawai

Hawaiian [həˈwaɪən] n & adj hawaiano(a) m,f

hawk[1] [hɔːk] n (**a**) *(bird)* halcón m; **to watch sth/sb like a h.** mirar algo/a alguien con ojos de lince (**b**) *Pol* halcón m, partidario(a) m,f de la línea dura *(en política exterior)*

hawk[2] vt **to h. one's wares** hacer venta ambulante

hawkeyed [ˈhɔːkaɪd] adj con ojos de lince

hawkish [ˈhɔːkɪʃ] adj *Pol* partidario(a) de la línea dura *(en política exterior)*

hawser [ˈhɔːzə(r)] n cable m, estacha f

hawthorn [ˈhɔːθɔːn] n espino m (albar)

hay [heɪ] n heno m; **to make h.** dejar secar la paja; *Fam* **to hit the h.** *(go to bed)* irse al sobre; *Prov* **make h. while the sun shines** aprovecha mientras puedas; **h. fever** fiebre f del heno, alergia f al polen

hayloft [ˈheɪlɒft] n henal m, henil m

hayseed [ˈheɪsiːd] n (**a**) *(seed)* granzas fpl (**b**) *Fam Esp* paleto(a) m,f, *Méx* paisa mf, *RP* pajuerano(a) m,f

haystack [ˈheɪstæk] n almiar m

haywire ['heɪwaɪə(r)] *adv Fam* **to go h.** *(plan)* desbaratarse; *(mechanism)* volverse loco(a)

hazard ['hæzəd] **1** *n (danger)* peligro *m*, riesgo *m*; **a health h.** un peligro para la salud; **a fire h.** una causa potencial de incendio

2 *vt (one's life, fortune)* arriesgar, poner en peligro; *(opinion, guess)* aventurar

hazardous ['hæzədəs] *adj* peligroso(a)

haze [heɪz] **1** *n (of mist)* neblina *f*; *(of doubt, confusion)* nube *f*; **my mind was in a h.** tenía la mente nublada

2 *vt Fam (students, new recruits)* hacer novatadas

hazel ['heɪzəl] *n (color)* color *m* avellana; **h. (tree)** avellano *m*

hazelnut ['heɪzəlnʌt] *n* avellana *f*

hazily ['heɪzɪlɪ] *adv (remember)* vagamente

haziness ['heɪzɪnɪs] *n (of weather)* ambiente *m* neblinoso; *(of memory)* vaguedad *f*

hazing ['heɪzɪŋ] *n Fam (of students, new recruits)* novatadas *fpl*

hazy ['heɪzɪ] *adj (weather)* neblinoso(a); *(memory)* vago(a), confuso(a); **to be h. about sth** no tener algo nada claro

he [hiː] **1** *pron* él; *(usually omitted in Spanish, except for contrast)* **he's Scottish** es escocés; HE **hasn't got it!** ¡él no lo tiene!; *Formal* **he who believes this…** quien se crea *or* aquel que se crea esto…

2 *n* **it's a he** *(animal)* es macho

head [hed] **1** *n* **(a)** *(of person)* cabeza *f*; **a fine h. of hair** una buena cabellera; **to be a h. taller than sb** sacar *or RP* llevar una cabeza a alguien; **from h. to foot** *or* **toe** de la cabeza a los pies; **to stand on one's h.** hacer el pino (con la cabeza sobre el suelo); *Fig* **to stand a situation on its h.** trastornar completamente una situación; **to win by a h.** *(horse)* ganar por una cabeza; *Fig* **h. and shoulders above the other candidates** *(much better than)* está muy por encima de los demás candidatos; *Med* **h. cold** catarro *m*; **h. start** *(advantage)* ventaja *f*

(b) *(intellect, mind)* **to do sums in one's h.** sumar mentalmente; **to have a good h. on one's shoulders** tener la cabeza sobre los hombros; **to have a good h. for business/figures** tener (buena) cabeza para los negocios/los números; **to have a (good) h. for heights** no tener vértigo; **he has taken it into his h. that…** se le ha metido en la cabeza que…; **it never entered my h. that…** nunca se me pasó por la cabeza que…; **to put ideas into sb's h.** meter ideas a alguien en la cabeza; *Fam* **he's not right in the h.** no está bien de la cabeza; *Fam* **h. case** *(lunatic)* chiflado(a) *m,f*

(c) *(of pin, hammer, garlic, list)* cabeza *f*; *(of arrow)* punta *f*; *(of page, stairs)* parte *f* superior; *(of bed, table)* cabecera *f*; *(on beer)* espuma *f*; *(on tape recorder)* cabeza *f* (magnética), cabezal *m*; **a h. of lettuce** una lechuga; **a h. of cabbage** un repollo; **to be at the h. of a list/line** encabezar una lista/cola; **heads or tails?** *(when tossing coin)* ¿cara o cruz?, *Chile, Col* ¿cara o sello?, *Méx* ¿águila o sol?, *RP* ¿cara o ceca?; **to build up a h. of steam** *(person, campaign)* tomar ímpetu; **to come to a h.** *(conflict, situation)* alcanzar un punto crítico

(d) *(person in charge)* *(of family, the Church)* cabeza *mf*; *(of business)* jefe(a) *m,f*; **h. office** sede *f*, central *f*; **h. of state** jefe *m* de Estado; **h. waiter** maître *m*

(e) *(unit)* **to pay $10 per** *or* **a h.** pagar 10 dólares por cabeza; **six h. of cattle** seis cabezas de ganado, seis reses

(f) *(idioms)* **we put our heads together** entre todos nos pusimos a pensar; **they'll have your h. (on a plate) for this** vas a pagar con el pellejo por esto; **to bury** *or* **have one's h. in the sand** adoptar la estrategia del avestruz; **to give sb his h.** *(allow to take decisions)* dar libertad a alguien; **to go over sb's h.** *(appeal to higher authority)* pasar por encima de alguien; *Fam* **to shout one's h. off** desgañitarse, vociferar; **the wine/the praise went to his h.** se le subió a la cabeza el vino/tanto halago; *Prov* **two heads are better**

than one dos mentes discurren más que una sola; **off the top of one's h.** sin pararse a pensar; **it was** *or* **went over my h.** no me di cuenta de nada; **I can't make h. or tail of this** no le encuentro ni pies ni cabeza a esto; *Fam* **to lose one's h.** perder la cabeza *or* los nervios; *Fam* **to keep one's h.** mantener la cabeza en su sitio; *Fam* **to be off one's h.** estar mal de la cabeza *or* como un cencerro; *Vulg* **to give sb h.** *(oral sex)* chupársela *or Esp* hacerle una mamada a alguien

2 *vt* **(a)** *(lead) (organization, campaign)* estar a la cabeza de; *(list, procession)* encabezar **(b)** *(direct)* conducir; **one of the locals headed me in the right direction** un lugareño me indicó el camino **(c)** *(put a title on) (page, chapter)* encabezar, titular **(d)** *(in soccer)* **to h. the ball** cabecear el balón, darle al balón de cabeza

3 *vi (move)* dirigirse; **they were heading out of town** salían de la ciudad

▸**head for** *vt insep* dirigirse a; **you're heading for trouble/disaster** te estás buscando problemas/la ruina

▸**head off 1** *vt sep (prevent)* eludir, evitar

2 *vi (depart)* marcharse

headache ['hedeɪk] *n* dolor *m* de cabeza; *Fig (problem)* quebradero *m* de cabeza

headachy ['hedeɪkɪ] *adj Fam* **I'm feeling a bit h.** me duele un poquillo la cabeza

headband ['hedbænd] *n* cinta *f* para la cabeza

headboard ['hedbɔːd] *n (of bed)* cabecero *m*

headbutt ['hedbʌt] *vt* dar un cabezazo a

headdress ['heddres] *n* tocado *m*

headed ['hedɪd] *adj* **h. (note)paper** papel *m* con membrete

-headed ['hedɪd] *suffix* **a three-h. dragon** un dragón tricéfalo *or* de tres cabezas

header ['hedə(r)] *n* **(a)** *Typ* encabezamiento *m* **(b)** *(in soccer)* cabezazo *m*

headfirst ['hed'fɜːst] *adv* de cabeza

headgear ['hedgɪə(r)] *n* tocado *m*

headhunt ['hedhʌnt] *vt Com* captar, cazar *(altos ejecutivos)*

headhunter ['hedhʌntə(r)] *n Com* cazatalentos *mf inv*

heading ['hedɪŋ] *n (of chapter, article)* encabezamiento *m*; **it comes** *or* **falls under the h. of…** entra dentro de la categoría de…

headlamp ['hedlæmp] *n (on car)* faro *m*

headland ['hedlənd] *n* promontorio *m*

headless ['hedlɪs] *adj (creature, figure)* sin cabeza; *(corpse)* decapitado(a); *Fam* **to run about like a h. chicken** ir *or* andar de aquí para allá sin parar

headlight ['hedlaɪt] *n (on car)* faro *m*

headline ['hedlaɪn] **1** *n (of newspaper, TV news)* titular *m*, *Méx, RP* encabezado *m*; **to hit the headlines** saltar a los titulares; **to be h. news** ser noticia de portada

2 *vt (article, story)* titular

headlock ['hedlɒk] *n* presa *f or* llave *f* de cabeza

headlong ['hedlɒŋ] **1** *adv* de cabeza

2 *adj* **there was a h. rush for the bar** se produjo una estampida hacia el bar

headmaster [hed'mɑːstə(r)] *n Sch* director *m*

headmistress [hed'mɪstrɪs] *n Sch* directora *f*

head-on ['he'dɒn] **1** *adj* de frente; **a h. collision** un choque frontal

2 *adv* de frente; **to meet sb h.** encontrarse con alguien de frente

headphones ['hedfəʊnz] *npl* auriculares *mpl*

headquarters [hed'kwɔːtəz] *npl (of organization)* sede *f*, central *f*; *Mil* cuartel *m* general

headrest ['hedrest] *n* reposacabezas *m inv*

headroom ['hedruːm] *n (under bridge)* gálibo *m*; *(inside car)* altura *f* de la cabeza al techo

headscarf ['hedskɑːf] *n* pañuelo *m* *(para la cabeza)*

headset ['hedset] *n (earphones)* auriculares *mpl*, cascos *mpl*

headstone ['hedstəʊn] *n (on grave)* lápida *f*

headstrong ['hedstrɒŋ] *adj* testarudo(a), cabezota

heads-up ['hed(z)ʌp] **1** *n Fam* **to give sb the h.** informar a alguien
2 *adj* **h. display** *(in aircraft, car)* pantalla *f* virtual a la altura de la vista

headway ['hedweɪ] *n* **to make h.** avanzar

headwind ['hedwɪnd] *n* viento *m* de cara

heady ['hedɪ] *adj (drink, feeling)* embriagador(ora); *(atmosphere, experience, days)* emocionante

heal [hiːl] **1** *vt (wound)* curar; *Fig (differences)* subsanar; *Fig* **wounds which only time would h.** heridas que sólo el tiempo podría cerrar
2 *vi (wound)* **to h. (up** *or* **over)** curarse, sanar

healer ['hiːlə(r)] *n* curandero(a) *m,f*; **time is a great h.** el tiempo todo lo cura

health [helθ] *n* salud *f*; **to be in good/poor h.** estar bien/mal de salud; **the economy is in good h.** la economía goza de buena salud; **the Department of H. and Human Services** el Departamento de Salud y Servicios Humanos; **to drink (to) sb's h.** brindar a la salud de alguien, brindar por alguien; **h. care** atención *f* sanitaria; *Fin* **h. cover** cobertura *f* sanitaria; **h. food** comida *f* integral; **h. hazard** *or* **risk** peligro *m* para la salud; *Fin* **h. insurance** seguro *m* de enfermedad; **h. resort** centro *m* de reposo; **h. spa** clínica *f* de adelgazamiento

healthily ['helθɪlɪ] *adv* de un modo sano

healthy ['helθɪ] *adj (person, climate)* sano(a), saludable; **a h. appetite** un apetito sano; **it is a h. sign that…** es un buen síntoma que…; **he has a h. disrespect for authority** demuestra una saludable falta de respeto ante la autoridad

heap [hiːp] **1** *n* montón *m*; *Fig* **people at the top/bottom of the h.** los de arriba/abajo; *Fam* **we've got heaps of time** tenemos un montón de tiempo; *Fam* **she had heaps of children** tenía montones de hijos
2 *vt* amontonar; **his plate was heaped with food** tenía el plato lleno hasta arriba de comida; **to h. riches/praise/ insults on sb** colmar a alguien de riquezas/alabanzas/insultos

heaped [hiːpt], **heaping** ['hiːpɪŋ] *adj (spoonful)* colmado(a)

hear [hɪə(r)] *(pt & pp* **heard** [hɜːd]) **1** *vt* **(a)** *(perceive)* oír; **to h. sb speak** oír hablar a alguien; **I could hardly h. myself speak** apenas se oía; **she was struggling to make herself heard over the noise** se esforzaba por hacerse oír en medio del ruido; **let's h. it for…** aplaudamos a…; *Fam* **I've heard that one before!** ¡no me vengas con ésas!, *Esp* ¡a otro perro con ese hueso!
(b) *(listen to)* escuchar; **h. me out** escúchame antes; **h.! h.!** *(at meeting)* ¡sí señor!, ¡eso es!; *Law* **to h. a case** ver un caso
(c) *(find out)* oír; **I heard that she was in Spain** he oído (decir) que estaba en España; **I h. you're getting married** tengo entendido que te vas a casar
2 *vi* **I can't h. properly** no oigo bien; **to h. from sb** tener noticias de alguien, saber de alguien; **you'll be hearing from my lawyer!** ¡mi abogado se pondrá en contacto con usted!; **to h. about sth** saber de algo; **they were never heard of again** nunca se supo nada más de ellos; **that's the first I've heard of it!** es la primera noticia que tengo; **I've never heard of such a thing!** ¡nunca he oído hablar de nada semejante!; **I won't h. of it!** ¡no quiero ni oír hablar de ello!

hearing ['hɪərɪŋ] *n* **(a)** *(sense)* oído *m*; **the h. impaired** las personas con discapacidad auditiva **(b)** *(earshot)* **to be within/out of h.** estar/no estar lo suficientemente cerca como para oír **(c)** *(chance to explain)* **to give sb a fair h.** dejar a alguien que se explique; **to condemn sb without a h.** condenar a alguien sin haberlo escuchado antes **(d)** *Law (inquiry)* vista *f*

hearsay ['hɪəseɪ] *n* rumores *mpl*; *Law* **h. evidence** pruebas *fpl* basadas en rumores

hearse [hɜːs] *n* coche *m* fúnebre

heart [hɑːt] *n* **(a)** *(organ)* corazón *m*; **to have h. trouble, to have a weak** *or* **bad h., to have a h. condition** tener problemas cardíacos *or* de corazón; **h. attack** ataque *m* al corazón; **h. disease** cardiopatía *f*; **h. failure** *(condition)* insuficiencia *f* cardíaca; *(cessation of heartbeat)* paro *m* cardíaco; **h. surgery** cirugía *f* cardíaca; **h. transplant** transplante *m* de corazón
(b) *(seat of the emotions)* corazón *m*; **to have a big h.** tener un gran corazón; **a h. of gold** un corazón de oro; **a h. of stone** un corazón duro; **have a h.!** ¡no seas cruel!; **her h.'s in the right place** tiene un gran corazón; **with a heavy h.** con aflicción; **my h. sank at the news** la noticia me dejó hundido; **to have one's h. in one's mouth** tener el corazón en un puño *or Am* en la boca; **to break sb's h.** romperle el corazón a alguien; **to wear one's h. on one's sleeve** no ocultar los sentimientos; **affairs** *or* **matters of the h.** asuntos *mpl or* cosas *fpl* del corazón; *esp Ironic* **my h. bleeds for you** ¡qué pena me das!; **in my h. of hearts** en el fondo (de mi corazón); **from the bottom of one's h.** *(thank, congratulate)* de todo corazón; **he loved her with all his h.** la amaba con toda su alma; **at h.** en el fondo; **to have sb's welfare/interests at h.** preocuparse de veras por el bienestar/los intereses de alguien; **to take sth to h.** tomarse algo a pecho; **he had set his h. on it** lo deseaba con toda el alma; **he's a man after my own h.** es uno de los míos; **to one's h.'s content** hasta saciarse
(c) *(enthusiasm, courage)* **to take/lose h.** animarse/ desanimarse; **he tried to convince them but his h. wasn't in it** trató de convencerlos, pero sin mucho empeño; **I didn't have the h. to tell him** no tuve coraje para decírselo
(d) *(memory)* **by h.** de memoria
(e) *(center)* **the h. of the matter** el meollo del asunto; **in the h. of the forest** en el corazón del bosque
(f) *(in cards)* **hearts** corazones *mpl*

heartache ['hɑːteɪk] *n* dolor *m*, tristeza *f*

heartbeat ['hɑːtbiːt] *n* latido *m* (del corazón)

heartbreak ['hɑːtbreɪk] *n (sorrow)* congoja *f*, pena *f*; *(in love)* desengaño *m* amoroso

heartbreaking ['hɑːtbreɪkɪŋ] *adj* desolador(ora), desgarrador(ora)

heartbroken ['hɑːtbrəʊkən] *adj* abatido(a), descorazonado(a)

heartburn ['hɑːtbɜːn] *n (indigestion)* acidez *f* (de estómago), ardor *m* de estómago

hearten ['hɑːtən] *vt* alentar

heartening ['hɑːtənɪŋ] *adj* alentador(ora)

heartfelt ['hɑːtfelt] *adj* sincero(a)

hearth [hɑːθ] *n* **(a)** *(fireplace)* chimenea *f* **(b)** *(home)* hogar *m*

heartily ['hɑːtɪlɪ] *adv* de todo corazón; **to be h. sick of sth** estar hasta las narices de algo

heartiness ['hɑːtɪnɪs] *n (of person, laughter)* campechanía *f*, jovialidad *f*; *(of welcome)* efusividad *f*, cordialidad *f*; *(of appetite)* voracidad *f*

heartland ['hɑːtlænd] *npl* núcleo *m*; **Britain's industrial h. was devastated by the depression** la recesión asoló el núcleo *or* el corazón industrial de Gran Bretaña

heartless ['hɑːtlɪs] *adj* inhumano(a), despiadado(a)

heartlessly ['hɑːtlɪslɪ] *adv* despiadadamente

heartlessness ['hɑːtlɪsnɪs] *n* crueldad *f*

heartrending ['hɑːtrendɪŋ] *adj* desgarrador(ora)

heart-searching ['hɑːtsɜːtʃɪŋ] *n* **after much h.** tras un profundo examen de conciencia

heart-stopping ['hɑːtstɒpɪŋ] *adj* emocionantísimo(a)

heartstrings ['hɑːtstrɪŋz] *npl* **to tug at sb's h.** tocar la fibra sensible de alguien

heartthrob ['hɑːtθrɒb] *n Fam* ídolo *m*

heart-to-heart [ˈhɑːtəˈhɑːt] **1** *n* to have a h. with sb tener una charla íntima con alguien
2 *adj* íntimo(a)

heartwarming [ˈhɑːtwɔːmɪŋ] *adj* conmovedor(ora)

hearty [ˈhɑːtɪ] *adj* (a) *(person, laugh)* campechano(a), jovial; *(welcome)* cordial, efusivo(a); **my heartiest congratulations** felicidades de todo corazón (b) *(wholehearted) (approval)* caluroso(a); *(dislike)* profundo(a) (c) *(substantial) (meal)* copioso(a); *(appetite)* voraz

heat [hiːt] **1** *n* (a) *(high temperature)* calor *m*; **to cook at a high/moderate/low h.** cocinar a fuego vivo/moderado/ lento; **to turn up the h.** *(on stove)* subir el fuego; *Fam Fig* **to turn up the h. on sb** presionar a alguien; **h. exhaustion** colapso *m* por exceso de calor; **h. loss** pérdida *f* de calor; **h. rash** sarpullido *m* *(por el calor)*; *Med* **h. treatment** termoterapia *f*; **h. wave** ola *f* de calor (b) *(passion)* calor *m*; **in the h. of the moment/of the argument** con el acaloramiento del momento/de la pelea (c) *(of female animal)* **in h.** en celo (d) *(in sport)* serie *f*, eliminatoria *f*
2 *vt* calentar

▸**heat up 1** *vt sep* calentar
2 *vi* calentarse; *Fig (argument, contest)* subir de tono, acalorarse

heated [ˈhiːtɪd] *adj* (a) *(room, building)* caldeado(a); *(swimming pool)* climatizado(a) (b) *(argument)* acalorado(a); **to become h.** *(person)* acalorarse

heatedly [ˈhiːtɪdlɪ] *adv* acaloradamente

heater [ˈhiːtə(r)] *n (radiator)* radiador *m*; *(electric, gas)* estufa *f*

heath [hiːθ] *n* brezal *m*, páramo *m*

heathen [ˈhiːðən] *n* bárbaro(a) *m,f*

heather [ˈheðə(r)] *n* brezo *m*

heating [ˈhiːtɪŋ] *n* calefacción *f*

heatproof [ˈhiːtpruːf] *adj* termorresistente, refractario(a)

heatstroke [ˈhiːtstrəʊk] *n Med* insolación *f*

heave [hiːv] **1** *vt (pull)* tirar de, *Am salvo RP* jalar de; *(push)* empujar; *(lift)* subir; **she heaved herself out of her chair** se levantó de la silla con dificultad; **to h. a sigh of relief** exhalar un suspiro de alivio
2 *vi* (a) **they heaved on the rope** tiraron *or Am salvo RP* jalaron de la cuerda (b) *(deck, ground)* subir y bajar; *(bosom)* palpitar (c) *(retch)* tener arcadas; *(vomit)* vomitar (d) *Naut (pt* **hove** [həʊv]*)* **to h. into view** *(ship)* aparecer; *Fig Hum (person)* aparecer por el horizonte
3 *n (pull)* tirón *m*; *(push)* empujón *m*

▸**heave to** *(pp* **hove** [həʊv]*) vi Naut (ship)* ponerse al pairo

heaven [ˈhevən] *n* cielo *m*; **in h.** en el cielo; *Fig (overjoyed)* en la gloria; **to go to h.** ir al cielo; **this is h.!** ¡esto es la gloria!; **to move h. and earth to do sth** mover *or* remover Roma con Santiago para hacer algo; **the heavens opened** cayó un aguacero; *Fam* **it stinks to high h.** ¡huele que apesta!; **(good) heavens!, heavens above!** ¡madre mía!, ¡Dios mío!; **thank h. (for that)!** ¡gracias a Dios!; **h. knows!** ¡sabe Dios!; **for h.'s sake!** ¡por el amor de Dios!; **h. forbid!** ¡Dios no lo quiera!

heavenly [ˈhevənlɪ] *adj* (a) **h. body** cuerpo *m* celeste (b) *Fam (weather, food)* celestial

heaven-sent [ˈhevənsent] *adj* como caído(a) del cielo; **a h. opportunity** una ocasión de oro

heavily [ˈhevɪlɪ] *adv (to fall, walk, sleep)* pesadamente; **to drink/smoke h.** beber *or Am* tomar/fumar mucho; **it was raining h.** llovía a cántaros, llovía con fuerza; **to rely** *or* **depend h. on sth** depender mucho de algo; **h. built** corpulento(a); **to be h. defeated** perder estrepitosamente; **to be h. taxed** estar sometido(a) a fuertes impuestos

heavy [ˈhevɪ] **1** *adj* (a) *(in weight)* pesado(a); *(food)* pesado(a); **how h. is it?** ¿cuánto pesa?; **a h. blow** un golpe fuerte; **h. industry** industria *f* pesada; **h. metal** *Chem* metal *m* pesado; *(music)* rock *m* duro, heavy metal *m*

(b) *(large, thick) (coat, shoes)* grueso(a)
(c) *(intense) (fighting)* enconado(a); *(rain, showers)* fuerte; *(drinker, smoker)* empedernido(a); **h. losses** grandes pérdidas; **a h. cold** *(illness)* un fuerte resfriado *or RP* resfrío; **to be a h. sleeper** dormir profundamente; *Fig* **to come under h. fire** recibir una lluvia de críticas; **the traffic was very h.** había mucho tráfico
(d) *(oppressive) (smell)* fuerte; *(sky)* cargado(a), plomizo(a); *(fine, sentence)* duro(a); **h. responsibility** gran responsabilidad
(e) *(hard) (work, day)* duro(a); *(breathing)* pesado(a); **the book was h. going** el libro era muy denso; **h. seas** mar *f* gruesa
(f) *Fam (threatening) (situation)* complicado(a), *Esp* chungo(a), *Méx* gacho(a), *RP* fulero(a)
2 *n Fam (thug)* gorila *m*, matón *m*

heavy-duty [hevɪˈdjuːtɪ] *adj* resistente

heavy-handed [hevɪˈhændɪd] *adj* (a) *(clumsy)* torpe (b) *(harsh)* de *or* con mano dura

heavy-hearted [ˈhevɪˈhɑːtɪd] *adj* afligido(a), desconsolado(a)

heavyweight [ˈhevɪweɪt] *n (in boxing) & Fig* peso *m* pesado

Hebrew [ˈhiːbruː] **1** *n (language)* hebreo *m*
2 *adj* hebreo(a); **H. script** escritura *f* hebrea

Hebrides [ˈhebrɪdiːz] *npl* **the H.** las Hébridas

heck [hek] *n Fam* **h.!** ¡vaya, hombre!; **what the h. are you doing here?** ¿qué diablos *or Esp* narices haces aquí?; **what the h.!** *(when taking risk)* ¡qué demonios!; **a h. of a lot** un montón; **not a h. of a lot** no mucho

heckle [ˈhekəl] *vt & vi* interrumpir (con comentarios impertinentes)

heckler [ˈheklə(r)] *n* espectador *m* molesto

heckling [ˈheklɪŋ] *n* interrupciones *fpl* impertinentes

hectare [ˈhektɑː(r)] *n* hectárea *f*

hectic [ˈhektɪk] *adj* ajetreado(a)

hector [ˈhektə(r)] *vt* intimidar; **she tried to h. me into agreeing** trató de intimidarme para que accediera

hectoring [ˈhektərɪŋ] *adj* intimidante, intimidatorio(a)

he'd [hiːd] = **he had, he would**

hedge [hedʒ] **1** *n* (a) *(in field, garden)* seto *m* (b) *(protection)* **a h. against inflation** una protección contra la inflación
2 *vt* (a) *(field)* cercar con un seto (b) **to h. one's bets** cubrirse las espaldas
3 *vi (in discussion)* responder con evasivas

hedgehog [ˈhedʒhɒg] *n* erizo *m*

hedgerow [ˈhedʒrəʊ] *n* seto *m*

hedonism [ˈhedənɪzəm] *n* hedonismo *m*

hedonistic [hedəˈnɪstɪk] *adj* hedonista

heebie-jeebies [hiːbɪˈdʒiːbɪz] *npl Fam* **it gives me the h.** me da canguelo *or Méx* mello *or RP* cuiqui

heed [hiːd] **1** *vt (warning, advice)* prestar atención a, escuchar
2 *n* to pay h. to, to take h. of hacer caso de *or* a; **to pay no h. to, to take no h. of** hacer caso omiso de

heedless [ˈhiːdlɪs] *adj* **to be h. of** hacer caso omiso de

heedlessly [ˈhiːdlɪslɪ] *adv* sin preocuparse, con gran irresponsabilidad

heel [hiːl] **1** *n (of foot, sock)* talón *m*; *(of shoe)* tacón *m*, *Am* taco *m*; **high heels** *(shoes)* zapatos *mpl* de tacón *or Am* taco alto; **he had the police at his heels** la policía le venía pisando los talones; **to take to one's heels** poner pies en polvorosa; **to turn on one's h.** dar media vuelta; *Fam* **to cool one's heels** *(wait)* quedarse esperando un largo rato; *Fig* **to bring sb to h.** meter a alguien en cintura
2 *vt (shoe)* poner un tacón *or Am* taco nuevo a

hefty [ˈheftɪ] *adj Fam (person)* robusto(a), fornido(a); *(suitcase, box)* pesado(a); *(bill, fine)* cuantioso(a)

heifer [ˈhefə(r)] *n (young cow)* novilla *f*, vaquilla *f*

height [haɪt] n (of building, mountain) altura f; (of person) estatura f, altura f; **what h. are you?** ¿cuánto mides?; **to gain/lose h.** (plane) ganar/perder altura; **to be afraid of heights** tener vértigo; **she's at the h. of her powers** está en plenas facultades; **she's at the h. of her career** está en la cumbre de su carrera; **the h. of fashion** el último grito; **it's the h. of madness!** ¡es el colmo de la locura!

heighten ['haɪtən] vt (intensify) intensificar, aumentar

heightened ['haɪtənd] adj (fear, pleasure, tension) mayor

heinous ['heɪnəs] adj Formal (crime) execrable, infame

heir [eə(r)] n heredero m; **to be h. to sth** ser heredero de algo; **the h. to the throne** el heredero al trono; **h. apparent** heredero m forzoso; Fig heredero m natural

heiress ['eərɪs] n heredera f

heirloom ['eəluːm] n reliquia f familiar

heist [haɪst] n Fam golpe m, robo m

held [held] pt & pp of **hold**

helicopter ['helɪkɒptə(r)] n helicóptero m

helipad ['helɪpæd] n helipuerto m

heliport ['helɪpɔːt] n helipuerto m

helium ['hiːlɪəm] n Chem helio m

hell [hel] n (a) infierno m; Fam **h.!** (expressing annoyance) ¡mierda!; **H.'s Angels** (bikers) los ángeles del infierno
  (b) Fam (in phrases) **it was h.** (very difficult or unpleasant) fue un infierno; **to feel like h.** sentirse fatal or muy mal; **to make sb's life h.** amargarle a alguien la vida; **these shoes are giving me h.** estos zapatos me están matando; **all h. broke loose** se armó la gorda or Esp la marimorena; **there'll be h. to pay if…** alguien lo va a pasar muy mal si…; **go to h.!** ¡vete a la mierda! **to run like h.** correr como alma que lleva el diablo; **like h. (I will)!** Esp ¡ni de coña!, Méx ¡ya mero!, RP ¡ni en joda!; **you can wait till h. freezes over** puedes esperar hasta que las ranas críen pelo; **come h. or high water** pase lo que pase; **to go h. for leather** ir a toda mecha; **to do sth for the h. of it** hacer algo porque sí
  (c) Fam (as intensifier) **a h. of a price** un precio altísimo; **he put up a h. of a fight** opuso muchísima resistencia; **to have a h. of a time** (good) pasárselo como Dios or RP como los dioses; (bad) pasarlas negras or Esp moradas; **a h. of a lot of…** Esp una porrada de…, Méx un chorro de…, RP un toco de…; **he's one** or **a h. of a guy** Esp es una pasada de tío, Am es un tipo de primera; **what the h. do you think you're doing?** ¿me quieres decir qué demonios estás haciendo?; **who the h. are you?** ¿y tú quién diablos or Esp leches eres?

he'll [hiːl] = **he will, he shall**

hellbent ['helbent] adj Fam **to be h. on doing sth** tener entre ceja y ceja hacer algo

hellhole ['helhəʊl] n Fam (place) infierno m, agujero m infecto

hellish ['helɪʃ] adj Fam infernal, horroroso(a)

hellishly ['helɪʃlɪ] adv Fam endiabladamente, horrorosamente

hello [he'ləʊ] exclam ¡hola!; (on phone) (when answering) ¿sí?, Esp ¿diga?, Esp ¿dígame?, Am ¿aló?, Carib, RP ¿oigo?, Méx ¿bueno?, RP ¿hola?; (when calling) ¡hola!; **to say h. to sb** saludar a alguien; **h., what's this?** (indicating surprise) caramba, ¿qué es esto?

hell-raiser ['helreɪzə(r)] n Fam camorrista mf

helluva ['heləvə] Fam = **hell of a**

helm [helm] n (of ship) timón m; Fig **to be at the h.** (party, country) estar al frente

helmet ['helmɪt] n casco m

helmsman ['helmzmən] n (on ship) timonel m

help [help] 1 n (a) (aid) ayuda f; **h.!** ¡socorro!; **to be of h. to sb** ser de ayuda para alguien; **thank you, you've been a great h.** gracias, has sido de gran ayuda; **with the h. of sb, with sb's h.** con la ayuda de alguien; **to be beyond h.** no tener remedio; **h. desk** (for queries) servicio m de asistencia; Comptr

h. menu menú m de ayuda (b) (cleaning woman) asistenta f
  2 vt (a) (aid) ayudar; **to h. sb (to) do sth** ayudar a alguien a hacer algo; **to h. sb on/off with his coat** ayudar a alguien a ponerse/quitarse or Am sacarse el abrigo; **can I h. you?** (in shop) ¿en qué puedo servirle?; **to h. one another** ayudarse mutuamente, ayudarse el uno al otro; **to h. oneself to sth** agarrar or Esp coger algo; **h. yourself** sírvete (b) (prevent) **I can't h. it** no lo puedo evitar; **it can't be helped** no queda otro remedio; **I can't h. laughing** no puedo evitar reírme; **she couldn't h. overhearing** no pudo evitar oír (la conversación); **not if I can h. it!** ¡no, si lo puedo evitar!
  3 vi ayudar; **can I h.?** ¿puedo ayudar?

▸**help out** vt sep **to h. sb out** ayudar a alguien

helper ['helpə(r)] n ayudante mf

helpful ['helpfʊl] adj (person) (willing to help) servicial; (advice, book) útil, provechoso(a); **you've been very h.** nos has sido de gran ayuda

helpfully ['helpfʊlɪ] adv **"have you tried asking Sue?"** he suggested h. "¿has probado a preguntar a Sue?" sugirió, tratando de ser útil; **a translation is h. provided** como ayuda se incluye una traducción

helping ['helpɪŋ] 1 n (portion) ración f; **I had a second h. of spaghetti** repetí (de) espagueti
  2 adj **to lend a h. hand** echar una mano

helpless ['helplɪs] adj (powerless) impotente; (defenseless) indefenso(a); **we were h. to prevent it** no pudimos evitarlo; **to be h. with laughter** no poder dejar de reír

helplessly ['helplɪslɪ] adv impotentemente, sin poder hacer nada

helplessness ['helplɪsnɪs] n (a) (powerlessness) impotencia f (b) (defenselessness) indefensión f

helpline ['helplaɪn] n teléfono m de asistencia or ayuda

Helsinki [hel'sɪŋkɪ] n Helsinki

helter-skelter ['heltə'skeltə(r)] adv (in disorder) atropelladamente, a lo loco

hem [hem] 1 n dobladillo m
  2 vt (pt & pp **hemmed**) hacer el dobladillo a
  3 vi **to h. and haw** titubear, vacilar

▸**hem in** vt sep (surround) cercar, rodear

he-man ['hiːmæn] n Fam machote m, Esp hombretón m

hemisphere ['hemɪsfɪə(r)] n hemisferio m

hemline ['hemlaɪn] n bajo m

hemlock ['hemlɒk] n cicuta f

hemoglobin [hiːməʊ'gləʊbɪn] n hemoglobina f

hemophilia [hiːməʊ'fɪlɪə] n hemofilia f

hemophiliac [hiːməʊ'fɪlɪæk] n hemofílico(a) m,f

hemorrhage ['hemərɪdʒ] 1 n (bleeding) hemorragia f; Fig (of people, resources) fuerte pérdida f
  2 vi Med sangrar, sufrir una hemorragia; Fig (of support, funds) decrecer por momentos

hemorrhoids ['hemərɔɪdz] npl Med hemorroides fpl

hemp [hemp] n cáñamo m

hen [hen] n gallina f

hence [hens] adv (a) (thus) de ahí; **h. his anger** de ahí su enfado or Am enojo (b) (from now) desde aquí; **five years h.** de aquí a cinco años

henceforth [hens'fɔːθ], **henceforward** [hens'fɔːwəd] adv Formal en lo sucesivo

henchman ['henʃmən] n Pej sicario m, secuaz m

hencoop ['henkuːp], **hennery** ['henərɪ] n gallinero m

henhouse ['henhaʊs] n gallinero m

henna ['henə] n henna f

hennery ['henərɪ] = **hencoop**

henpecked ['henpekt] adj calzonazos inv

hepatitis [hepə'taɪtɪs] n Med hepatitis f inv

heptagon ['heptəgɒn] n heptágono m

heptathlon [hep'tæθlɒn] *n* heptatlón *m*

her [*unstressed* hə(r), *stressed* hɜ:(r)] **1** *pron* **(a)** *(direct object)* la; **I hate h.** la odio; **I can forgive her son but not** HER puedo perdonar a su hijo, pero no a ella **(b)** *(indirect object)* le; **I gave h. the book** le di el libro; **I gave it to h.** se lo di **(c)** *(after preposition)* ella; **I talked to h.** hablé con ella; **her mother lives near h.** su madre vive cerca de ella **(d)** *(as complement of verb* **to be)** ella; **it's h.!** ¡es ella!; **it was h. who did it** lo hizo ella

2 *possessive adj* **(a)** *(singular)* su; *(plural)* sus; **I took h. car** cogí su coche; *(contrasting with his or theirs)* cogí el coche de ella **(b)** *(for parts of body, clothes)* **h. eyes are blue** tiene los ojos azules; **she hit h. head** se dio un golpe en la cabeza; **she put h. hands in h. pockets** se metió las manos en los bolsillos

herald ['herəld] **1** *n* heraldo *m*
2 *vt* anunciar

heraldic [hə'rældɪk] *adj* heráldico(a)
heraldry ['herəldrɪ] *n* heráldica *f*
herb [ɜ:rb] *n* hierba *f*
herbaceous [ɜ:'beɪʃəs] *adj* herbáceo(a); **h. border** arriate *m* de plantas y flores
herbal ['ɜ:rbəl] *adj* de hierbas; **h. remedies** = remedios a base de hierbas medicinales; **h. tea** infusión *f*
herbalist ['hɜ:bəlɪst] *n* herbolario(a) *m,f*
herbicide ['hɜ:bɪsaɪd] *n* herbicida *m*
herbivore ['hɜ:rbɪvɔ:(r)] *n* herbívoro *m*
herbivorous [hɜ:'bɪvərəs] *adj* herbívoro(a)
herd [hɜ:d] **1** *n* *(of cattle, sheep)* rebaño *m*; *(of horses, elephants)* manada *f*; *(of people)* rebaño *m*, manada *f*; **the h. instinct** el instinto gregario
2 *vt (cattle, people)* conducir
herdsman ['hɜ:dzmən] *n* vaquero(a) *m,f*
here [hɪə(r)] **1** *n* **the h. and now** el aquí y ahora
2 *adv* aquí; **over h.** (por) aquí; **h. it/he is** aquí está; **h.!** *(at roll call)* ¡presente!; **come h.!** ¡ven aquí!; **h.!, come and look at this** ¡ven! echa un vistazo a esto; **she's not h.** no está aquí; **h. she comes** aquí viene; **h. and now** aquí y ahora; **h. and there** aquí y allá; *Fig* **that's neither h. nor there** eso es irrelevante; **what have we h.?** ¿qué es esto?, ¿qué tenemos aquí?; **h.'s what you have to do** esto es lo que tienes que hacer; **h. you are!** *(when giving something)* aquí tienes; **h. goes!** ¡vamos allá!; **h.'s to the future!** ¡por el futuro!
hereafter [hɪər'ɑ:ftə(r)] **1** *adv Formal* en adelante, en lo sucesivo
2 *n Literary* **the h.** el más allá
hereby [hɪə'baɪ] *adv Formal (in writing)* por la presente; *(in speech)* por el presente acto
hereditary [hɪ'redɪtərɪ] *adj* hereditario(a)
heredity [hɪ'redɪtɪ] *n* herencia *f*
heresy ['herəsɪ] *n* herejía *f*
heretic ['herətɪk] *n* hereje *mf*
heretical [hɪ'retɪkəl] *adj* herético(a)
heritage ['herɪtɪdʒ] *n* patrimonio *m*
hermaphrodite [hɜ:'mæfrədaɪt] *n & adj* hermafrodita *mf*
hermetic [hɜ:'metɪk] *adj* hermético(a)
hermetically [hɜ:'metɪklɪ] *adv* herméticamente
hermit ['hɜ:mɪt] *n* ermitaño(a) *m,f*; **h. crab** cangrejo *m* ermitaño
hermitage ['hɜ:mɪtɪdʒ] *n* ermita *f*
hernia ['hɜ:nɪə] *n* hernia *f*
hero ['hɪərəʊ] *(pl* **heroes)** *n* héroe *m*; **h. worship** idolatría *f*
heroic [hɪ'rəʊɪk] *adj* heroico(a)
heroically [hɪ'rəʊɪklɪ] *adv* heroicamente
heroics [hɪ'rəʊɪks] *npl* heroicidades *fpl*
heroin ['herəʊɪn] *n (drug)* heroína *f*; **h. addict** heroinó-mano(a) *m,f*

heroine ['herəʊɪn] *n (female hero)* heroína *f*
heroism ['herəʊɪzəm] *n* heroísmo *m*
heron ['herən] *n* garza *f*
hero-worship ['hɪərəʊwɜ:ʃɪp] *(pt & pp* **hero-worshiped)** *vt* idolatrar
herpes ['hɜ:pi:z] *n* herpes *m inv*
herring ['herɪŋ] *n* arenque *m*
hers [hɜ:z] *possessive pron* **(a)** *(singular)* el suyo *m*, la suya *f*; *(plural)* los suyos *mpl*, las suyas *fpl*; *(to distinguish)* el/la/los/las de ella; **my house is big but h. is bigger** mi casa es grande, pero la suya es mayor; **he didn't have a book, so I gave him h.** no tenía libro, así que le di la de ella **(b)** *(used attributively) (singular)* suyo(a); *(plural)* suyos(as); **this book is h.** este libro es suyo; **a friend of h.** un amigo suyo
herself [hɜ:'self] *pron* **(a)** *(reflexive)* se; **she hurt h.** se hizo daño **(b)** *(emphatic)* ella misma; **she did all the work h.** hizo todo el trabajo ella misma *or* ella sola; **she told me h.** me lo dijo ella misma; **she's not h. today** hoy está un poco rara **(c)** *(after preposition)* ella; **she lives by h.** vive sola; **she bought it for h.** se lo compró para ella; **she talks to h.** habla sola
hertz [hɜ:tz] *(pl* **hertz)** *n Phys* hercio *m*
he's [hi:z] = **he is, he has**
hesitancy ['hezɪtənsɪ] *n* duda *f*, vacilación *f*
hesitant ['hezɪtənt] *adj (speaker, smile, gesture)* vacilante, dubitativo(a); *(speech, voice)* vacilante, titubeante; **to be h. about doing sth** tener dudas a la hora de algo; **I would be h. to...** no me atrevería a...
hesitantly ['hezɪtəntlɪ] *adv (to act, try)* con indecisión, sin demasiada convicción; *(to answer, speak)* con vacilación, de modo vacilante
hesitate ['hezɪteɪt] *vi* dudar, vacilar
hesitation [hezɪ'teɪʃən] *n* vacilación *f*, titubeo *m*; **without h.** sin vacilar
hessian ['hesɪən] *n* arpillera *f*
heterogeneous [hetərə'dʒi:nɪəs] *adj* heterogéneo(a)
heterosexual [hetərəʊ'seksjʊəl] *n & adj* heterosexual *mf*
heuristics [hjʊ'rɪstɪks] *npl* heurística *f*
hew [hju:] *(pp* **hewn** [hju:n] *or* **hewed)** *vt (cut down)* cortar; *(shape)* tallar
hexagon ['heksəgən] *n* hexágono *m*
hexagonal [hek'sægənəl] *adj* hexagonal
hey [heɪ] *exclam* ¡eh!
heyday ['heɪdeɪ] *n* apogeo *m*; **in his/its h.** en su apogeo
hi [haɪ] *exclam Fam* ¡hola!
hiatus [haɪ'eɪtəs] *n (interruption)* interrupción *f*; *(blank space)* laguna *f*
hibernate ['haɪbəneɪt] *vi* hibernar
hibernation [haɪbə'neɪʃən] *n* hibernación *f*
hiccup ['hɪkʌp] **1** *n* hipo *m*; *Fig (minor problem)* traspié *m*, desliz *m*; **to have (the) hiccups** tener hipo
2 *vi (pt & pp* **hiccupped)** *(repeatedly)* tener hipo; *(once)* hipar
hick [hɪk] *n Fam* pueblerino(a) *m,f*, *Esp* paleto(a) *m,f*, *Méx* paisa *mf*, *RP* pajuerano(a) *m,f*
hickey ['hɪkɪ] *(pl* **hickeys** *or* **hickies)** *n Fam (lovebite)* marca *f* (de un beso), *Esp* chupetón *m*, *Am* chupón *m*
hickory ['hɪkərɪ] *n (tree, wood)* nogal *m* americano
hid [hɪd] *pt of* **hide**
hidden ['hɪdən] **1** *adj* oculto(a); **to be h.** estar oculto(a); **h. agenda** objetivo *m* secreto; **h. economy** economía *f* sumergida
2 *pp of* **hide**
hide¹ [haɪd] *vt (pt* **hid** [hɪd], *pp* **hidden** ['hɪdən]) esconder **(from** de); *(emotions, truth)* ocultar; **to have nothing to h.** no tener nada que ocultar; **to h. oneself** esconderse
3 *vi* esconderse **(from** de)

hide² *n* (**a**) *(skin)* piel *f* (**b**) *(idioms)* **to save one's h.** salvar el pellejo; **I haven't seen h. nor hair of her** no le he visto el pelo

hide-and-seek [haɪdən'siːk] *n* escondite *m*, *Am* escondidas *fpl*; **to play h.** jugar al escondite

hidebound ['haɪdbaʊnd] *adj (person, attitude)* rígido(a), inflexible

hideous ['hɪdɪəs] *adj* espantoso(a)

hideously ['hɪdɪəslɪ] *adv* espantosamente

hideout ['haɪdaʊt] *n* guarida *f*, escondite *m*

hidey-hole ['haɪdɪhəʊl] *n Fam* escondite *m*, escondrijo *m*

hiding¹ ['haɪdɪŋ] *n* **to be in h.** estar en la clandestinidad; **to go into/come out of h.** pasar a/salir de la clandestinidad; **h. place** escondite *m*

hiding² *n Fam (beating)* paliza *f*; **to give sb a h.** dar una paliza a alguien

hierarchical [haɪə'rɑːkɪkəl] *adj* jerárquico(a)

hierarchically [haɪə'rɑːkɪkəlɪ] *adv* jerárquicamente

hierarchy ['haɪərɑːkɪ] *n* jerarquía *f*

hieroglyphics [haɪərə'glɪfɪks] *npl* jeroglíficos *mpl*

hi-fi ['haɪfaɪ] *n* alta fidelidad *f*; *(stereo system)* equipo *m* de alta fidelidad

higgledy-piggledy ['hɪɡəldɪ'pɪɡəldɪ] *adv Fam* de cualquier manera, a la buena de Dios

high [haɪ] **1** *n* (**a**) *(peak)* punto *m* álgido; **to reach a new h.** *(in career, performance)* alcanzar nuevas cotas de éxito; *(unemployment, inflation)* alcanzar un nuevo máximo *or* récord; **to be on a h.** *(from drugs)* estar colocado(a); *(from success)* estar ebrio(a) de triunfo; **highs and lows** altibajos *mpl* (**b**) *Met* anticiclón *m*

2 *adj* (**a**) *(mountain, building)* alto(a); **it's 2 feet h.** tiene dos pies de altura; *Fam* **to be left h. and dry** quedarse en la estacada; *Fam* **h. five** palmada *f* en· el aire *(saludo entre dos)*; **h.heels** tacones *mpl or Am* tacos *mpl* altos; **h. jump** salto *m* de altura, *Am* salto *m* alto; **h. jumper** saltador(ora) *m,f* de altura; **h. tide** marea *f* alta; **h. wire** cuerda *f* floja

(**b**) *(price, speed, standards)* alto(a), elevado(a); **to have a h. opinion of sb** tener una buena opinión de alguien; **in h. spirits** muy animado(a); *Aut* **h. beam** luces *fpl* largas *or Am* altas, luces *fpl* de carretera; **h. explosive** explosivo *m* de gran potencia; *Fam* **h. jinks** juerga *f*, jarana *f*; **h. point** momento *m* culminante; *Law* **h. treason** alta traición *f*; **h. winds** viento *m* fuerte

(**c**) *(rank, position)* elevado(a), alto(a); **to act all h. and mighty** comportarse de forma arrogante; **to have a h. profile** ser muy prominente *or* destacado(a); *Mil* **h. command** alto mando *m*; **H. Mass** misa *f* solemne; **h. school** instituto *m* de enseñanza secundaria; **h. society** alta sociedad *f*

(**d**) *(in tone, pitch)* agudo(a); *Fig* **h. note** *(of career, performance)* punto *m* culminante

(**e**) *(of time)* **it's h. time you got yourself a job** ya es hora de que te busques un trabajo; **h. noon** mediodía *m*; **h. summer** pleno verano *m*

(**f**) *(meat)* pasado(a)

(**g**) *Fam* **to be h.** *(on drugs)* estar colocado(a) *or RP* entregado(a); *Fig (on success, excitement)* estar eufórico(a) (**on** de)

3 *adv (to aim, jump)* alto; **to hunt h. and low for sth** buscar algo por todas partes; **feelings were running h.** los ánimos estaban exaltados *or* caldeados

-high [haɪ] *suffix* **shoulder-h.** por los hombros, hasta los hombros, a la altura de los hombros; **waist-h.** por la cintura, hasta la cintura, a la altura de la cintura

highbrow ['haɪbraʊ] *adj (tastes, interests)* intelectual, culto(a)

highchair ['haɪtʃeə(r)] *n* trona *f*

higher education ['haɪəredjʊ'keɪʃən] *n* enseñanza *f* superior

highfalutin [haɪfə'luːtɪn] *adj Fam* pretencioso(a), creído(a)

high-flier, high-flyer ['haɪ'flaɪə(r)] *n (successful person)* persona *f* brillante y ambiciosa

high-flying ['haɪ'flaɪɪŋ] *adj* brillante y ambicioso(a)

high-frequency [haɪ'friːkwənsɪ] *adj* de alta frecuencia

high-handed [haɪ'hændɪd] *adj* despótico(a)

high-handedness ['haɪ'hændɪdnɪs] *n* despotismo *m*

high-heeled ['haɪ'hiːld] *adj* de tacón, *Am* de taco alto

highland ['haɪlənd] *adj* de montaña; **H. fling** = danza individual de ritmo vivo originaria de las Tierras Altas escocesas; **H. games** juegos *mpl* escoceses, = fiesta al aire libre con concursos de música tradicional, deportes rurales, *etc.*, que se celebra en distintas localidades escocesas

highlander ['haɪləndə(r)] *n* (**a**) *(mountain dweller)* montañés(esa) *m,f* (**b**) *(Scottish)* **H.** habitante *mf* de las Tierras Altas de Escocia

Highlands ['haɪləndz] *npl* **the H.** *(of Scotland)* las Tierras Altas de Escocia; **the Kenyan/Guatemalan H.** las zonas montañosas de Kenia/Guatemala

high-level ['haɪlevəl] *adj (talks, delegation)* de alto nivel

highlight ['haɪlaɪt] **1** *n* (**a**) *(of performance, career)* momento *m* cumbre; **highlights** *(of match)* (repetición *f* de las) jugadas *fpl* más interesantes, mejores momentos *mpl* (**b**) *(in hair)* **highlights** reflejos *mpl*, mechas *fpl*

2 *vt (problem, difference)* destacar; *(with pen)* resaltar *(con rotulador fluorescente)*

highlighter ['haɪlaɪtə(r)] *n (pen)* rotulador *m* fluorescente, *Col, RP* resaltador *m*, *Méx* marcador *m*

highly ['haɪlɪ] *adv* (**a**) *(very)* muy; **h. paid** (muy) bien pagado(a); **h. seasoned** muy condimentado(a); **to be h. strung** ser muy nervioso(a) (**b**) **to think h. of sb** tener buena opinión de alguien

high-minded ['haɪ'maɪndɪd] *adj* noble, elevado(a)

Highness ['haɪnɪs] *n* **His/Her Royal H.** Su Alteza Real

high-performance ['haɪpə'fɔːməns] *adj* de alto rendimiento

high-pitched ['haɪpɪtʃt] *adj* agudo(a)

high-powered ['haɪ'paʊəd] *adj (engine, car, telescope)* potente, de gran potencia; *(person, job)* de altos vuelos

high-pressure ['haɪ'preʃə(r)] *adj (substance, container)* a gran presión

high-profile ['haɪ'prəʊfaɪl] *adj (person)* prominente, destacado(a); *(campaign)* de gran alcance

high-resolution ['haɪrezə'luːʃən] *adj (screen, graphics)* de alta resolución

high-rise ['haɪ'raɪz] **1** *n (block of flats)* bloque *m*, torre *f*

2 *adj* **h. building** bloque *m*, torre *f*

high-risk ['haɪrɪsk] *adj (strategy, investment)* de alto riesgo

highroad ['haɪrəʊd] *n Old-fashioned* carretera *f* principal; *Fig* **the h. to success** la vía directa hacia el éxito

high-speed ['haɪ'spiːd] *adj* de alta velocidad

high-spirited ['haɪ'spɪrɪtɪd] *adj* radiante, exultante

high-strung ['haɪ'strʌŋ] *adj* **to be h.** ser muy nervioso(a)

hightail ['haɪteɪl] *vt Fam* **to h. it** largarse corriendo, *Esp, RP* pirarse, pirárselas

high-tech ['haɪ'tek] *adj* de alta tecnología

high-up ['haɪʌp] *adj Fam* importante

highway ['haɪweɪ] *n* carretera *f*; *(freeway)* autopista *f*; **h. patrol** *(organization)* policía *f* de carreteras, *RP* policía *f* caminera; *(unit)* patrulla *f* de carreteras

highwayman ['haɪweɪmən] *n* bandolero *m*, salteador *m* de caminos

hijack ['haɪdʒæk] *vt* secuestrar

hijacker ['haɪdʒækə(r)] *n* secuestrador(ora) *m,f*

hijacking ['haɪdʒækɪŋ] *n* secuestro *m*

hike [haɪk] **1** *n* (**a**) *(walk)* excursión *f*, caminata *f*; **to go on** *or*

for a h. darse una caminata; *Fam* **go take a h.!** ¡vete a paseo! **(b)** *(in prices)* subida *f*

2 *vi (walk)* caminar

3 *vt (prices)* subir

hiker ['haɪkə(r)] *n* excursionista *mf*, senderista *mf*

hiking ['haɪkɪŋ] *n* senderismo *m*; **to go h.** hacer senderismo; **h. boots** botas *fpl* de excursionismo

hilarious [hɪ'leərɪəs] *adj* divertidísimo(a), tronchante

hilariously [hɪ'leərɪəslɪ] *adv* **h. funny** divertidísimo(a), tronchante

hilarity [hɪ'lærɪtɪ] *n* hilaridad *f*

hill [hɪl] *n* **(a)** *(small mountain)* colina *f*, monte *m*; *Fig* **to be over the h.** *(past one's best)* no estar ya para muchos trotes; **h. walking** senderismo *m* **(b)** *(slope)* cuesta *f*; **to go down/up the h.** ir cuesta abajo/arriba

hillbilly ['hɪlbɪlɪ] *n Pej* palurdo(a) *m,f* de la montaña

hillock ['hɪlək] *n* cerro *m*, collado *m*

hillside ['hɪlsaɪd] *n* ladera *f*

hilltop ['hɪltɒp] *n* cima *f*, cumbre *f*

hilly ['hɪlɪ] *adj* con muchas colinas

hilt [hɪlt] *n (of sword, dagger)* puño *m*, empuñadura *f*; *(support)* **to back sb to the h.** apoyar sin reservas a alguien

him [hɪm] *pron* **(a)** *(direct object)* lo; **I hate h.** lo odio; **I can forgive his son but not** HIM puedo perdonar a su hijo, pero no a él **(b)** *(indirect object)* le; **I gave h. the book** le di el libro; **I gave it to h.** se lo di **(c)** *(after preposition)* él; **I talked to h.** hablé con él; **his mother lives near h.** su madre vive cerca de él **(d)** *(as complement of verb to be)* él; **it's h.!** ¡es él!; **it was h. who did it** es él el que lo hizo

Himalayan [hɪmə'leɪən] *adj* himalayo(a)

Himalayas [hɪmə'leɪəz] *npl* **the H.** el Himalaya

himself [hɪm'self] *pron* **(a)** *(reflexive)* se; **he hurt h.** se hizo daño **(b)** *(emphatic)* él mismo; **he did all the work h.** hizo todo el trabajo él (mismo); **he told me h.** me lo dijo él mismo; **he's not h. today** hoy está un poco raro **(c)** *(after preposition)* él; **he lives by h.** vive solo; **he bought it for h.** se lo compró para él; **he talks to h.** habla solo

hind [haɪnd] *adj* trasero(a), de atrás; **h. legs** patas *fpl* traseras

hinder ['hɪndə(r)] *vt (person)* estorbar; *(movements, operation, negotiations)* entorpecer; **his shyness hindered him from making friends** su timidez le impedía hacer amigos

Hindi ['hɪndɪ] *n (language)* hindi *m*

hindquarters ['haɪndkwɔːtəz] *npl* cuartos *mpl* traseros

hindrance ['hɪndrəns] *n (person)* estorbo *m*; *(thing)* impedimento *m*, traba *f*

hindsight ['haɪndsaɪt] *n* retrospección *f*; **with the benefit of h.** con la ventaja que proporciona una mirada retrospectiva

Hindu ['hɪnduː] *n & adj* hindú *mf*

Hinduism ['hɪnduːɪzəm] *n* hinduismo *m*

hinge [hɪndʒ] *n* bisagra *f*

▸**hinge on, hinge upon** *vt insep (depend on)* depender de

hinged [hɪndʒd] *adj* con bisagras, de bisagra

hinky ['hɪŋkɪ] *adj Fam* raro(a)

hint [hɪnt] **1** *n* **(a)** *(allusion)* indirecta *f*, insinuación *f*; **to give** *or* **drop sb a h.** lanzar a alguien una indirecta; **to be able to take a h.** saber pillar *or Esp* coger *or Am* agarrar una indirecta **(b)** *(sign)* rastro *m*; **not a h. of surprise** ni un asomo de sorpresa; **a h. of garlic** un ligero gusto a ajo **(c)** *(piece of advice)* consejo *m*; **to give sb a h.** dar a alguien una pista

2 *vt* **to h. that...** insinuar que...

▸**hint at** *vt insep* aludir a, hacer alusión a

hinterland ['hɪntəlænd] *n* región *f* interior

hip¹ [hɪp] *n* cadera *f*; **h. flask** petaca *f*; **h. joint** articulación *f* de la cadera; **h. pocket** bolsillo *m* trasero

hip² *adj Fam (trendy)* moderno(a), a la última, *Am* de onda

hip-hop ['hɪphɒp] *n Mus* hip-hop *m*

hippo ['hɪpəʊ] *(pl* **hippos***) n Fam* hipopótamo *m*

hippopotamus [hɪpə'pɒtəməs], *(pl* **hippopotamuses** *or* **hippopotami** [hɪpə'pɒtəmaɪ]*) n* hipopótamo *m*

hippy ['hɪpɪ] *n* hippy *mf*

hip-huggers ['hɪp'hʌgərz] *npl* pantalones *mpl* de cintura baja, pantalones *mpl* por la cadera

hire [haɪə(r)] *vt (lawyer, worker)* contratar

hired ['haɪəd] *adj (car, suit)* alquilado(a), *Méx* rentado(a); **h. hand** *(on farm)* jornalero(a) *m,f*

hirsute ['hɜːsjuːt] *adj Literary* hirsuto(a)

his [hɪz] **1** *possessive adj* **(a)** *(singular)* su; *(plural)* sus; **I took h. car** tomé su coche; *(contrasting with hers or theirs)* tomé el coche de él **(b)** *(for parts of body, clothes)* **h. eyes are blue** tiene los ojos azules; **he hit h. head** se dio un golpe en la cabeza; **he put h. hands in h. pockets** se metió las manos en los bolsillos

2 *possessive pron* **(a)** *(singular)* el suyo *m*, la suya *f*; *(plural)* los suyos *mpl*, las suyas *fpl*; *(to distinguish)* el/la/los/las de él; **my house is big but h. is bigger** mi casa es grande, pero la suya es mayor; **she didn't have a book so I gave her h.** ella no tenía libro, así que le di el de él **(b)** *(used attributively) (singular)* suyo(a); *(plural)* suyos(as); **this book is h.** este libro es suyo; **a friend of h.** un amigo suyo

Hispanic [hɪs'pænɪk] **1** *n* hispano(a) *m,f*

2 *adj* hispánico(a), hispano(a)

Hispanist ['hɪspənɪst], **Hispanicist** [hɪs'pænɪsɪst] *n* hispanista *mf*

Hispanophile [hɪs'pænəfaɪl] *n* hispanófilo(a) *m,f*

hiss [hɪs] **1** *n (sound)* silbido *m*; *(to express disapproval)* siseo *m*, *Andes, RP* chistido *m*

2 *vt* sisear

3 *vi* **(a)** *(expressing disapproval)* chistar **(b)** *(snake, steam)* silbar

histogram ['hɪstəgræm] *n* histograma *m*

historian [hɪs'tɔːrɪən] *n* historiador(ora) *m,f*

historic [hɪs'tɒrɪk] *adj* histórico(a)

historical [hɪs'tɒrɪkəl] *adj* histórico(a); **h. drama** *(TV series, movie)* serie *f*/película *f* de época; **h. novel** novela *f* histórica

historically [hɪs'tɒrɪklɪ] *adv* históricamente

history ['hɪstərɪ] *n* historia *f*; **to go down in h. as...** pasar a (los anales de) la historia como...; *Fig* **that's h.** eso pasó a la historia; *Med* **to have a h. of...** tener un historial de...; **h. book** libro *m* de historia; **h. teacher** profesor(ora) *m,f* de historia

histrionic [hɪstrɪ'ɒnɪk] *adj Pej* histriónico(a), teatral

histrionics [hɪstrɪ'ɒnɪks] *npl Pej* histrionismo *m*, teatralidad *f*

hit [hɪt] **1** *n* **(a)** *(blow)* golpe *m*; *(in shooting)* impacto *m*; **to score a direct h.** dar de lleno en el blanco; **h. list** *(of assassination targets)* lista *f* negra; **h. man** asesino *m* a sueldo; **h. squad** banda *f* de asesinos **(b)** *(success)* éxito *m*; **h. (record)** *(disco m de)* éxito *m* **(c)** *(in baseball)* hit *m*, batazo *m* de base **(d)** *Comptr (visit to website)* visita *f*, acceso *m*; *(in search)* aparición *f*

2 *adj (successful)* de mucho éxito

3 *vt (pt & pp* **hit***)* **(a)** *(of person)* golpear; *(of car) (tree, bus)* chocar contra; *Comptr (key)* pulsar; **to h. one's hand (on sth)** darse un golpe en la mano (con algo); **the bullet hit him in the leg** la bala le dio en *or* le alcanzó la pierna; *Fig* **it suddenly hit me that...** de repente me di cuenta de que...; *Fig* **he didn't know what had hit him** no le dio tiempo ni a reaccionar

(b) *(reach)* **to h. a note** llegar a *or* dar una nota; **to h. 90 (miles an hour)** alcanzar las noventa millas por hora; **to have hit an all-time low** *(investment)* haber alcanzado un mínimo histórico; *Fig (relationship)* estar por los suelos

(c) *(affect)* afectar; **to be hard hit** *or* **hit hard by...** verse muy afectado(a) por...

(d) *(arrive at) (barrier, difficulty)* toparse *or* encontrarse con; **the circus hits town tomorrow** el circo llega mañana a la ciudad; **it hits the stores next week** estará a la venta la próxima semana; *Fam* **to h. the road** *(leave)* ponerse en marcha, largarse

4 *vi* golpear

▶**hit back 1** *vt sep* **to h. sb back** devolver el golpe a alguien

2 *vi (return blow)* devolver el golpe; *Fig (with answer, accusation, criticism)* responder

▶**hit off** *vt sep Fam* **to h. it off** caerse bien

▶**hit on, hit upon** *vt insep (idea, solution)* dar con

▶**hit out** *vi (physically)* lanzar golpes (**at** contra); *(verbally)* lanzar ataques (**at** contra)

▶**hit upon** = **hit on**

hit-and-run ['hɪtən'rʌn] *adj* **he was knocked down in a h. accident** lo atropelló un coche que se dio a la fuga; **a h. driver** = conductor que huye tras atropellar a alguien

hitch [hɪtʃ] **1** *n* (a) *(difficulty)* contratiempo *m*; **without a h.** sin ningún contratiempo (b) *(knot)* nudo *m*

2 *vt* (a) *(attach)* enganchar (**to** a); *Fam* **to get hitched** *(marry)* casarse (b) *Fam* **to h. a lift to…** ir en autoestop *or* a dedo a…, *CAm, Méx, Perú* irse de aventón a…

3 *vi Fam* hacer autoestop *or* dedo, *CAm, Méx, Perú* pedir aventón

▶**hitch up** *vt sep (pants, skirt)* subirse

hitchhike ['hɪtʃhaɪk] *vi* hacer autoestop *or* dedo, *CAm, Méx, Perú* pedir aventón

hitchhiker ['hɪtʃhaɪkə(r)] *n* autoestopista *mf*

hi-tech ['haɪ'tek] *adj* de alta tecnología

hither ['hɪðə(r)] *adv Literary* acá; **h. and thither** de acá para allá

hitherto ['hɪðə'tu:] *adv* hasta ahora, hasta la fecha

hit-or-miss ['hɪtɔ:'mɪs] *adj* azaroso(a), al tuntún

HIV [eɪtʃaɪ'vi:] *n (abbr* **human immunodeficiency virus)** VIH *m*, virus *m inv* de la inmunodeficiencia humana; **to be H. positive/negative** ser/no ser seropositivo(a)

hive [haɪv] *n* colmena *f*; *Fig* **a h. of activity** un hervidero de actividad

hiya ['haɪjə] *exclam Fam* **h.!** ¡hola!, ¿qué hay?

HMO [eɪtʃem'əʊ] *n (abbr* **Health Maintenance Organization)** = Organización para el Mantenimiento de la Salud

HMS [eɪtʃem'es] *n Naut (abbr* **Her/His Majesty's Ship)** = título que precede a los nombres de buques de la marina británica

hoard [hɔ:d] **1** *n (of food)* provisión *f*; *(of money)* montón *m*

2 *vt (food)* hacer acopio de; *(money)* atesorar

hoarder ['hɔ:də(r)] *n* acaparador(ora) *m,f*

hoarding ['hɔ:dɪŋ] *n (of food, money)* acaparamiento *m*, acopio *m*

hoarfrost ['hɔ:frɒst] *n* escarcha *f*

hoarse [hɔ:s] *adj* ronco(a); **to be h.** quedarse ronco(a)

hoarsely ['hɔ:slɪ] *adv* con la voz ronca

hoary ['hɔ:rɪ] *adj (old)* viejo(a)

hoax [həʊks] **1** *n* engaño *m*; **to play a h. on sb** engañar a alguien; **h. caller** = persona que realiza falsas alarmas por teléfono

2 *vt* engañar

hobble ['hɒbəl] *vi* cojear, *Andes, RP* renguear

hobby ['hɒbɪ] *n* afición *f*, hobby *m*

hobbyhorse ['hɒbɪhɔ:s] *n (toy)* caballito *m* de juguete; *Fig (favorite subject)* tema *m* favorito

hobnail boot ['hɒbneɪl'bu:t] *n* bota *f* de suela claveteada

hobnob ['hɒbnɒb] *(pt & pp* **hobnobbed)** *vi Fam* **to h. with sb** codearse con alguien

hock¹ [hɒk] *n (wine)* = vino blanco alemán del valle del Rin

hock² *Fam* **1** *n* **in h.** empeñado(a); **to be in h. to the bank** tener una deuda con el banco

2 *vt* empeñar

hockey ['hɒkɪ] *n (on ice)* hockey (sobre hielo); *(on grass)* hockey *m* (sobre hierba *or Am* césped); **h. stick** stick *m*, palo *m* de hockey

hocus-pocus ['həʊkəs'pəʊkəs] *n* camelo *m*, embaucamiento *m*

hodgepodge ['hɒdʒpɒdʒ] *n Fam* revoltijo *m, Esp* batiburrillo *m*

hoe [həʊ] **1** *n* azada *f*, azadón *m*

2 *vt* remover con la azada

hog [hɒg] **1** *n (glutton)* glotón(ona) *m,f*

2 *vt (pt & pp* **hogged)** *Fam* acaparar

Hogmanay [hɒgmə'neɪ] *n Scot* Nochevieja *f*

hogwash ['hɒgwɒʃ] *n Fam* sandeces *fpl*, tonterías *fpl*

hoi polloi [hɔɪpə'lɔɪ] *n* **the h.** el populacho, la plebe

hoist [hɔɪst] **1** *n (device)* aparejo *m* para izar

2 *vt (equipment, person)* subir, izar; *(flag, sail)* izar; *Fig* **she was h. with her own petard** le salió el tiro por la culata

hoity-toity ['hɔɪtɪ'tɔɪtɪ] *adj* altivo(a), engreído(a)

hold [həʊld] **1** *n* (a) *(grip)* **to have h. of sth** tener algo *Esp* cogido *or Am* agarrado; **to catch** *or* **take h. of** agarrarse a; **to let go one's h. on sth** soltar algo; *Fig* **to get h. of sb** *(make contact with)* localizar a alguien; *Fig* **to get h. of sth** *(obtain)* hacerse con algo; **to lose one's h. on reality** perder el contacto con la realidad; *Fig* **to have a h. on** *or* **over sb** tener poder sobre alguien (b) *(in wrestling)* llave *f*; *Fig* **no holds barred** sin límites (c) *(of ship)* bodega *f*

2 *vt (pt & pp* **held** [held]) (a) *(grip)* coger, sujetar, *Am* agarrar; *(embrace)* abrazar; **h. this!** ¡sujeta esto!; **to h. sth/sb tight** coger *or* sujetar algo/a alguien fuerte; **they held hands** estaban agarrados de la mano; **to h. sth in position** sujetar algo sin que se mueva; **to h. sb prisoner** retener a alguien como prisionero; **the police are holding him for questioning** la policía lo tiene retenido para interrogarlo; **to h. sb's interest/attention** mantener el interés/la atención de alguien; **to h. sb to his promise** hacer que alguien cumpla su promesa; **to h. one's breath** contener el aliento; **there's no holding him** no hay quien lo pare; **h. your tongue!** ¡cierra la boca!; *Fam* **h. it!, h. your horses!** ¡para el carro!; *Mus* **to h. a note** sostener una nota; *Tel* **h. the line** espere un momento, no cuelgue

(b) *(keep) (ticket, room)* guardar, reservar; **to h. a town** tener tomada una ciudad; **to h. one's position** mantener la posición; *Fig* **to h. one's ground** mantenerse en sus trece; **to h. one's own** resistir, mantenerse; **to h. one's own against sb** no desmerecer frente a alguien

(c) *(carry)* **to h. one's head high** llevar la cabeza bien alta; **to h. oneself well** mantenerse erguido(a)

(d) *(contain)* contener; **the stadium holds over 20,000** el estadio tiene capacidad *or* cabida para más de 20.000 espectadores; *Fig* **to h. water** *(theory, story)* no hacer agua; **nobody knows what the future holds** nadie sabe lo que deparará el futuro; **it holds no interest for me** no tiene ningún interés para mí

(e) *(conduct) (negotiations, meeting)* llevar a cabo; *(conversation)* mantener

(f) *(possess) (title, rank)* poseer; *(job, position)* ocupar; *(opinion)* mantener; *(record)* ostentar; **she had held office before** ya antes había ocupado un cargo

(g) *(consider)* **to h. sb responsible** hacer a alguien responsable; **to be held in respect** ser respetado(a); **to h. that…** sostener que…

3 *vi* (a) *(rope)* resistir, aguantar; **h. tight!** ¡agárrate bien! (b) *(agreement, weather)* mantenerse; **if your luck holds** si sigues teniendo suerte; **the same holds (true) for everyone** lo mismo es válido para todos

4 on hold *adv* **to put sth on h.** suspender algo temporalmente; *Tel* **to put sb on h.** poner a alguien a la espera

▶**hold against** *vt sep* **to h. sth against sb** tener algo contra alguien

▶**hold back 1** vt sep (person, emotion) contener; (progress, project) impedir el avance de; **he's holding something back** se está guardando algo

2 vi (refrain) contenerse; **to h. back from doing sth** abstenerse de hacer algo

▶**hold down** vt sep (**a**) (restrain) (person) sujetar; (taxes, prices) mantener en un nivel bajo (**b**) **to h. down a job** conservar un trabajo

▶**hold forth** vi explayarse

▶**hold off 1** vt sep (keep at bay) rechazar; **she held off making a decision until she had more information** pospuso su decisión hasta disponer de más datos

2 vi (delay) **the rain is holding off** no se decide a llover

▶**hold on** vi (**a**) (endure) resistir, aguantar (**b**) (wait) esperar; **h. on (a minute)!** ¡espera (un momento)! (**c**) **h. on (tight)!** ¡agárrate (fuerte)!

▶**hold on to** vt insep (**a**) (grip tightly) (to stop oneself from falling) agarrarse a; (to stop something from falling) agarrar; Fig (idea, hope) aferrarse a (**b**) (keep) guardar, conservar

▶**hold out 1** vt sep (one's hand) tender; (hope, opportunity) ofrecer; **I don't h. out much hope that...** tengo pocas esperanzas de que...

2 vi (**a**) (resist) resistir; **to h. out for a better offer** aguantar a la espera de una oferta mejor (**b**) (supplies) durar

▶**hold over** vt sep diferir, posponer

▶**hold together 1** vt sep (party, marriage, alliance) mantener unido(a); (with glue, string, rope) sujetar

2 vi (party, marriage, alliance) mantenerse unido(a)

▶**hold up 1** vt sep (**a**) (support) soportar, aguantar (**b**) (raise) levantar, alzar; Fig **to h. sb up as an example** poner a alguien como ejemplo (**c**) (delay) retrasar (**d**) (rob) atracar

2 vi (theory, alibi) tenerse en pie; (good weather) aguantar; **she's holding up well under the pressure** está aguantando bien las presiones

▶**hold with** vt insep (behavior) aprobar; **I don't h. with his opinions** no estoy de acuerdo con sus opiniones

holdall ['həʊldɔːl] n bolsa f (de viaje o de deporte)

holder ['həʊldə(r)] n (**a**) (of record, trophy, ticket) poseedor(ora) m,f; (of passport, license, permit) titular mf; (of belief, opinion) defensor(ora) m,f (**b**) (device) soporte m

holding ['həʊldɪŋ] n (**a**) (property) propiedad f; (of shares) participación f; Com **h. company** holding m (**b**) Mil **h. operation** maniobra f de contención

holdup ['həʊldʌp] n (**a**) (delay) (in plan) retraso m, Am demora f; (of traffic) retención f (**b**) (armed robbery) atraco m

hole [həʊl] **1** n (**a**) (in roof, clothing) agujero m; (in ground) hoyo m, agujero m; (animal's burrow) madriguera f; (in golf) hoyo m; **to make a h. in sth** hacer un agujero en algo; **the vacation made a h. in their savings** las vacaciones dejaron maltrecha su economía; Fig **to pick holes in sth** (in argument, theory) encontrar defectos en or a algo; **h. in one** (in golf) hoyo m en uno; Fam Fig **to be in a h.** (in difficulty) estar en un brete (**b**) Fam (room, house) cuchitril m; (town) lugar m de mala muerte

2 vt (**a**) (make a hole in) agujerear (**b**) (in golf) **to h. a shot** embocar la bola

▶**hole up** vi Fam (hide) esconderse

holiday ['hɒlɪdeɪ] n (day off) Esp (día m de) fiesta f, Am feriado m; (public holiday) día m festivo, Am día m feriado

holiness ['həʊlɪnɪs] n santidad f; **Your H.** Su Santidad

holistic [həʊˈlɪstɪk] adj holístico(a)

Holland ['hɒlənd] n Holanda

holler ['hɒlə(r)] vi Fam gritar, dar voces

hollow ['hɒləʊ] **1** n hueco m; (in ground) depresión f

2 adj (**a**) (container, log) hueco(a); (cheek, eyes) hundido(a) (**b**) (sound) hueco(a), resonante; **in a h. voice** con voz hueca; **a h. laugh** una risa sardónica (**c**) (promise, guarantee) vacío(a); **h. victory** victoria f deslucida

3 adv (**a**) **to sound h.** sonar a hueco (**b**) Fam **to beat sb (all) h.** dar una (buena) paliza a alguien

▶**hollow out** vt sep ahuecar, vaciar

hollow-eyed ['hɒləʊwaɪd] adj de ojos hundidos

holly ['hɒlɪ] n acebo m

hollyhock ['hɒlɪhɒk] n malvarrosa f

holocaust ['hɒləkɔːst] n holocausto m

hologram ['hɒləgræm] n holograma m

holster ['həʊlstə(r)] n pistolera f

holy ['həʊlɪ] adj santo(a); **the H. Bible** la Sagrada Biblia; Fam **h. cow** or **smoke** or **mackerel!** ¡madre del amor hermoso!; **H. Communion** Sagrada Comunión f; **the H. Father** el Santo Padre; **the H. Ghost** el Espíritu Santo; Fam Pej **H. Joe** meapilas mf inv; **the H. Land** Tierra Santa; **h. orders** sagradas órdenes fpl; **the H. Spirit** el Espíritu Santo; **h. war** guerra f santa; **h. water** agua f bendita; **H. Week** Semana f Santa

homage ['hɒmɪdʒ] n homenaje m; **to pay h. to sth/sb** rendir homenaje a algo/alguien

home [həʊm] **1** n (**a**) (house) casa f; (of animal, plant) hábitat m; (family) hogar m; **at h.** en casa; **to feel at h.** sentirse como en casa; **make yourself at h.** estás en tu casa, ponte cómodo; **to leave h.** (in the morning) salir de casa; (one's parents' home) independizarse, irse de casa; **to be away from h.** estar fuera (de casa); Sport **to be** or **play at h.** jugar en casa; **to have a h. of one's own** tener casa propia; **it's a h. away from h.** es como estar en casa; **to make one's h. in...** asentarse en...; **children's/old people's h.** residencia f infantil/de ancianos; **h. address** domicilio m; **h. banking** telebanco m; **h. cooking** cocina f casera; **h. economics** (school subject) economía f doméstica; **h. improvements** reformas fpl del hogar; **h. life** vida f doméstica; Fin **h. loan** crédito m hipotecario, hipoteca f; **h. movie** vídeo m or Am video m casero or doméstico; **h. owner** propietario(a) m,f de vivienda; Comptr **h. page** portada f de página Web, página f inicial or de inicio; **h. plate** (in baseball) home m, base f meta; **h. run** (in baseball) carrera f completa, home run m, Am jonrón m; **h. shopping** telecompra f; **h. shopping channel** teletienda f; **the h. straight** or **stretch** (in athletics) la recta final; **to tell sb a few h. truths** decirle a alguien cuatro verdades

(**b**) (country, region) tierra f; **at h. and abroad** nacional e internacionalmente; **an example nearer h.** un ejemplo más cercano; **Milan, the h. of fashion** Milán, la meca or la cuna de la moda; **h. front** frente m civil; TV & Journ **h. news** noticias fpl nacionales; Pol **h. rule** autonomía f, autogobierno m

2 adv (**a**) (in general) a casa; **to go/come h.** ir/venir a casa; **to be h.** estar en casa; **to send sb h.** mandar a alguien a casa (**b**) (all the way) **he drove the knife h.** hundió el cuchillo hasta el fondo; **to bring sth h. to sb** dejar bien claro algo a alguien

▶**home in on** vt insep (on target) apuntar a, dirigirse a; (on mistake, evidence) señalar, concentrarse en

homeboy ['həʊmbɔɪ] n Fam (**a**) (man from one's home town, district) paisano(a) m,f (**b**) (friend) amiguete(a) m,f, Esp colega mf, Méx, CAm cuate(a) m,f (**c**) (fellow gang member) compinche mf, Méx, CAm cuate(a) m,f

homebrew ['həʊmbruː] n cerveza f casera

homecoming ['həʊmkʌmɪŋ] n (**a**) (to family, country) regreso m a casa, recepción f (**b**) Sch & Univ fiesta f anual de antiguos alumnos

home-grown ['həʊm'grəʊn] adj (from own garden) de cosecha propia; Fig (not imported) del país

homeland ['həʊmlænd] n tierra f natal, país m

homeless ['həʊmlɪs] **1** adj sin techo, sin hogar

2 npl **the h.** las personas sin techo, los sin techo

homely ['həʊmlɪ] adj (**a**) (ugly) feúcho(a) (**b**) (welcoming) (person, atmosphere) hogareño(a)

homemade ['həʊm'meɪd] *adj* casero(a)

homemaker [həʊm'meɪkə(r)] *n* ama *f* de casa

homeopath ['həʊmɪəʊpæθ] *n* homeópata *mf*

homeopathic [həʊmɪəʊ'pæθɪk] *adj* homeopático(a)

homeopathy [həʊmɪ'ɒpəθɪ] *n* homeopatía *f*

homeroom ['həʊmruːm] *n Sch* = aula donde cada alumno debe presentarse todas las mañanas

homesick ['həʊmsɪk] *adj* nostálgico(a); **to be feel h. (for)** tener nostalgia *or Esp* morriña (de)

homesickness ['həʊmsɪknɪs] *n* nostalgia *f*, *Esp* morriña *f*

homespun ['həʊmspʌn] *adj (wisdom, advice)* de andar por casa, *Am* de entrecasa

homestead ['həʊmsted] *n* finca *f*, hacienda *f*

hometown ['həʊmtaʊn] *n* ciudad *f*/pueblo *m* natal

homeward ['həʊmwəd] **1** *adj* de vuelta a casa
 2 *adv* a casa; **to be h. bound** estar de regreso a casa

homewards ['həʊmwədz] *adv* = **homeward**

homework ['həʊmwɜːk] *n Sch* deberes *mpl*; *also Fig* **to do one's h.** hacer los deberes

homeworker ['həʊmwɜːkə(r)] *n* teletrabajador(ora) *m,f*, persona *f* que trabaja desde su propio domicilio

homicidal [hɒmɪ'saɪdəl] *adj* homicida

homicide ['hɒmɪsaɪd] *n* homicidio *m*

homily ['hɒmɪlɪ] *n Rel* homilía *f*; *Fig* sermón *m*

homing ['həʊmɪŋ] *adj* **h. device** *(of missile)* sistema *m* de guiado pasivo; **h. pigeon** paloma *f* mensajera

homo ['həʊməʊ] *n Fam Pej (homosexual)* marica *m*

homogeneous [hɒmə'dʒiːnɪəs, hə'mɒdʒɪnəs] *adj* homogéneo(a)

homogenize [hɒ'mɒdʒənaɪz] *vt* homogeneizar

homonym ['hɒmənɪm] *n* homónimo *m*

homophobia [hɒmə'fəʊbɪə] *n* homofobia *f*

homophobic [həʊmə'fəʊbɪk] *adj* homófobo(a)

homosexual [hɒmə'seksjʊəl] *n & adj* homosexual *mf*

homosexuality [hɒməseksjʊ'ælɪtɪ] *n* homosexualidad *f*

honcho ['hɒntʃəʊ] *n Fam* **the head h.** el/la mandamás

Honduran [hɒn'djʊərən] *n & adj* hondureño(a) *m,f*

Honduras [hɒn'djʊərəs] *n* Honduras

hone [həʊn] *vt* afilar

honest ['ɒnɪst] *adj (trustworthy)* honrado(a); *(truthful)* sincero(a); **he has an h. face** tiene aspecto de honrado; **the h. truth** la pura verdad; **I don't think he was being h. with me** creo que no me estaba diciendo la verdad; **to be h., I don't know** la verdad es que no lo sé; **to earn an h. living** ganarse honradamente la vida; *esp Hum* **to make an h. woman of sb** *(marry)* llevar a alguien al altar

honestly ['ɒnɪstlɪ] *adv* **(a)** *(legitimately)* honradamente; **to obtain sth h.** conseguir algo honradamente **(b)** *(sincerely)* sinceramente; **I can h. say that...** puedo decir sin faltar a la verdad que...; **h., I'm fine/it doesn't matter** en serio que estoy bien/no importa; **I can't h. remember** la verdad es que no me acuerdo **(c)** *(expressing indignation)* **well h.!** ¡desde luego!, ¡hay que ver!; **h.! some people!** ¡desde luego, hay cada uno por ahí!

honesty ['ɒnɪstɪ] *n (trustworthiness)* honradez *f*; *(truthfulness)* sinceridad *f*; **in all h.** con toda sinceridad; *Prov* **h. is the best policy** lo mejor es decir la verdad

honey ['hʌnɪ] *n* **(a)** *(food)* miel *f* **(b)** *Fam (term of endearment)* cariño *m*, cielo *m*

honeycomb ['hʌnɪkəʊm] **1** *n* panal *m*
 2 *vt* **the mountain is honeycombed with tunnels** el interior de la montaña es un entramado de túneles

honeyed ['hʌnɪd] *adj (voice, words)* meloso(a)

honeymoon ['hʌnɪmuːn] **1** *n* luna *f* de miel, viaje *m* de novios; *Fig* **the h. is over** se acabó el periodo de gracia
 2 *vi* pasar la luna de miel, estar de viaje de novios

honeymooner ['hʌnɪmuːnə(r)] *n* recién casado(a) *m,f* (en viaje de novios); **honeymooners** parejas *fpl* de recién casados (en viaje de novios)

honeysuckle ['hʌnɪsʌkəl] *n* madreselva *f*

Hong Kong ['hɒŋ'kɒŋ] *n* Hong Kong

honk [hɒŋk] **1** *n (of goose)* graznido *m*; *(of car horn)* bocinazo *m*
 2 *vi (goose)* graznar; *(car driver)* tocar la bocina *or* el claxon, dar bocinazos

honky, honkie ['hɒŋkɪ] *n very Fam* = término ofensivo para referirse a un blanco

honky-tonk ['hɒŋkɪtɒŋk] *n Fam* = variedad del ragtime tocada en piano vertical

honor ['ɒnə(r)] **1** *n* **(a)** *(respect)* honor *m*; *(pride)* honra *f*; **in h. of** en honor de; **this is a great h.** es un gran honor; **to have the h. of doing sth** tener el honor de hacer algo; *Hum* **what do I owe this h.?** ¿a qué debo semejante honor *or* privilegio?; **Your H.** *(judge)* Señoría; **h. system** sistema *m* de honor
 (b) *(good name)* honor *m*, honra *f*; **to feel h. bound to do sth** sentirse moralmente obligado(a) a hacer algo; **on my (word of) h.!** ¡palabra de honor!; *Prov* **(there is) h. among thieves** hasta los ladrones tienen sus reglas
 (c) *(award, distinction)* **honors degree** licenciatura *f*; **he was buried with full military honors** fue enterrado con todos los honores militares; *Hum* **to do the honors** *(serve food or drink)* hacer los honores; **h. roll** lista *f* de honor académica
 2 *vt* **(a)** *(person)* honrar; **I felt honored that they had invited me** me honró mucho su invitación **(b)** *(fulfill) (commitment, obligation)* cumplir; *(debt, check)* pagar

honorable ['ɒnərəbəl] *adj* honorable; **h. mention** mención *f* honorífica

honorably ['ɒnərəblɪ] *adv* honorablemente

honorary ['ɒnərərɪ] *adj* honorífico(a), honorario(a); *Univ* **h. degree** título *m* honoris causa

hooch [huːtʃ] *n Fam (liquor)* alcohol *m (destilado clandestinamente)*

hood [hʊd] *n* **(a)** *(of coat, cloak)* capucha *f*; *(car engine cover)* capó *m*, *CAm, Méx* cofre *m*; *(over stove, fireplace)* campana *f* (extractora) **(b)** *Fam (gangster)* matón *m*

hoodlum ['huːdləm] *n Fam* matón *m*

hoodwink ['hʊdwɪŋk] *vt Fam* engañar, *Esp* timar

hoof [huːf] **1** *n (pl* **hooves** [huːvz]) *(of horse)* casco *m*; *(of cattle, deer, sheep)* pezuña *f*
 2 *vt Fam* **to h. it** ir a pata

hoo-ha ['huːhɑː] *n Fam (fuss)* alboroto *m*, *Esp* jaleo *m*

hook [hʊk] **1** *n* **(a)** *(in general)* gancho *m*; *(for coats)* colgador *m*; *(on dress)* corchete *m*; *(for fishing)* anzuelo *m*; *(for hanging pictures)* escarpia *f*, alcayata *f*; **to take the phone off the h.** dejar el teléfono descolgado; *Fam Fig* **to get sb off the h.** *(get out of trouble)* sacar a alguien del apuro; *Fam* **he swallowed it h., line and sinker** *(believed it)* se tragó el anzuelo; *Fam* **by h. or by crook** sea como sea **(b)** *(in boxing)* gancho *m*
 2 *vt* enganchar; **to h. one's legs around sth** rodear algo con las piernas; **to h. a fish** pescar un pez (con anzuelo)

▶**hook up 1** *vt sep TV & Comptr* conectar
 2 *vi* **(a)** *(dress)* abrocharse **(b)** *Comptr* conectar (**with** con *or* a)

hooked [hʊkt] *adj* **(a)** **h. nose** nariz *f* aguileña **(b)** *Fam* **to be h. on sth** estar enganchado(a) a algo

hooker ['hʊkə(r)] *n Fam (prostitute)* fulana *f*, puta *f*

hook(e)y ['hʊkɪ] *n Fam* **to play h.** faltar a clase, *Esp* hacer novillos, *Col* capar clase, *Méx* irse de pinta, *RP* hacerse la rabona

hook-nosed ['hʊknəʊzd] *adj* de nariz aguileña

hooligan ['huːlɪgən] *n* vándalo(a) *m,f*, *Esp* gamberro(a) *m,f*

hooliganism ['huːlɪgənɪzəm] *n* vandalismo *m*, *Esp* gamberrismo *m*

hoop [huːp] *n* aro *m*; *Fig* **to put sb through the hoops** *(test* *thoroughly)* poner a alguien a prueba; *Fam* **to shoot hoops** echar unos tiros

hoopla ['hu:plɑ:] *n (noise, bustle)* alboroto *m*; **there was a lot of h. about the new design** hubo mucho revuelo en torno al nuevo diseño

hooray [hʊ'reɪ] *exclam* ¡hurra!

hoot [hu:t] **1** *n* **(a)** *(of owl)* ululato *m*; *(of horn, factory whistle)* bocinazo *m*; **hoots of laughter** risotadas *fpl*; *Fam Fig* **I don't give a h.** *or* **two hoots** me importa un bledo **(b)** *Fam* **he's a h.!** ¡es divertidísimo!, *Esp* ¡es un cachondo!; **it was a h.!** ¡fue divertidísimo!, *Esp* ¡fue un cachondeo!
2 *vi (owl)* \ululaлr; *(car)* dar bocinazos; *(train)* pitar; **to h. with laughter** reírse a carcajadas

hooves *pl of* **hoof**

hop [hɒp] **1** *n (jump)* salto *m*, brinco *m*; *Fam (on plane)* vuelo *m* corto; *Fam (dance)* baile *m*
2 *vt (pt & pp* **hopped)** *Fam* **h. it!** ¡lárgate!
3 *vi (jump)* saltar, brincar; *(on one leg)* saltar con *or Am* en un pie, saltar a la pata coja; **to h. out of bed** salir de la cama de un salto; *Fam* **h. in!** *(to car)* ¡sube!

▸**hop off** *vi Fam* largarse

hope [həʊp] **1** *n* esperanza *f*; **in the h. of (doing) sth** con la esperanza de (hacer) algo; **in the h. that…** con la esperanza de que…; **there is little h. (of)** hay pocas esperanzas (de); **there is no h. (of)** no hay esperanza(s) (de); **to have (high) hopes of doing sth** tener (grandes) esperanzas de hacer algo; **to get one's hopes up** hacerse ilusiones; **to raise (sb's) hopes** dar esperanzas (a alguien); **she hasn't got a h. of winning** no tiene posibilidad alguna de ganar; *Ironic* **what a h.!, some h.!** ¡no caerá esa breva!; *Fam* **we live in h.!** la esperanza es lo último que se pierde
2 *vt* **to h. to do sth** esperar hacer algo; **I h. to see you again** espero volverte a ver; **I h. (that) your brother is better** espero que tu hermano esté mejor; **I h. you are right** ojalá tengas razón; **we h. and pray that…** ojalá que…; **I h. so** espero que no
3 *vi* esperar; **don't h. for too much** no esperes demasiado; **to h. for the best** esperar (que pase) lo mejor; **we must h. against h.** no debemos perder la esperanza

hopeful ['həʊpfʊl] **1** *n Fam* **a young h.** un/una joven con aspiraciones
2 *adj (situation)* prometedor(ora); **we are h. that…** esperamos que…

hopefully ['həʊpfʊlɪ] *adv* **(a)** *(in a hopeful manner)* esperanzadamente **(b)** *(it is to be hoped)* **h. not** esperemos que no, *Am* ojalá que no; **h. we will have found him by then** con un poco de suerte, para entonces ya lo habremos encontrado

hopeless ['həʊplɪs] *adj* **(a)** *(without hope) (person)* desesperanzado(a), sin esperanza; *(situation)* desesperado(a); **it's h.!** ¡es inútil!; **a h. cause** una causa perdida **(b)** *Fam (very bad)* malísimo(a); **to be h. at math/cooking** ser nulo(a) *or Esp* un(a) negado(a) para las matemáticas/la cocina

hopelessly ['həʊplɪslɪ] *adv* **(a)** *(inconsolably)* desesperanzadamente, sin esperanza **(b)** *(completely)* totalmente; **he was h. in love with her** estaba desesperadamente enamorado de ella

hopping ['hɒpɪŋ] *adv Fam* **to be h. mad** estar hecho(a) una furia, *Méx* estar como agua para chocolate

hops [hɒps] *npl* lúpulo *m*

hopscotch ['hɒpskɒtʃ] *n* tejo *m*, rayuela *f*

horde [hɔ:d] *n (crowd)* multitud *f*, *Am* horda *f*; *(nomadic)* horda *f*

horizon [hə'raɪzən] *n* horizonte *m*; **there is a general election on the h.** hay elecciones generales a la vista

horizontal [hɒrɪ'zɒntəl] **1** *n* horizontal *f*
2 *adj* horizontal

horizontally [hɒrɪ'zɒntəlɪ] *adv* horizontalmente

hormonal [hɔ:'məʊnəl] *adj* hormonal

hormone ['hɔ:məʊn] *n* hormona *f*; *Med* **h. replacement therapy** terapia *f* hormonal sustitutiva

horn [hɔ:n] *n* **(a)** *(of animal)* cuerno *m* **(b)** *(musical instrument)* trompa *f*; *(on car)* bocina *f*, claxon *m*; **to sound one's h.** *(in car)* tocar la bocina *or* el claxon **(c)** *(idioms)* **to be on the horns of a dilemma** estar entre la espada y la pared

horned [hɔ:nd] *adj* con cuernos

hornet ['hɔ:nɪt] *n* avispón *m*; *Fig* **to stir up a h.'s nest** remover un avispero

hornpipe ['hɔ:npaɪp] *n (dance, music)* aire *m* marinero

horn-rimmed ['hɔ:nrɪmd] *adj* **h. spectacles** *or* **glasses** gafas *fpl* de (montura de) concha

horny ['hɔ:nɪ] *adj* **(a)** *(hands)* calloso(a), encallecido(a) **(b)** *very Fam (sexually aroused) Esp, Méx* cachondo(a), *Esp* calentorro(a), *CAm, Col, Méx, Ven* arrecho(a), *RP* caliente

horoscope ['hɒrəskəʊp] *n* horóscopo *m*

horrendous [hɒ'rendəs] *adj* horrendo(a), espantoso(a)

horrendously [hɒ'rendəslɪ] *adv Fam (expensive, complicated)* terriblemente

horrible ['hɒrəbəl] *adj* **(a)** *(unpleasant)* horrible; **how h.!** ¡qué horror! **(b)** *(unkind)* antipático(a); **to be h. to sb** ser muy antipático(a) con alguien

horribly ['hɒrɪblɪ] *adv* espantosamente, horriblemente

horrid ['hɒrɪd] *adj* **(a)** *(unpleasant)* espantoso(a) **(b)** *(unkind)* antipático(a); **to be h. to sb** ser muy antipático con alguien

horrific [hɒ'rɪfɪk] *adj* horrible, espantoso(a)

horrifically [hɒ'rɪfɪklɪ] *adv* de un modo horrible, espantosamente

horrify ['hɒrɪfaɪ] *vt* horrorizar

horrifying ['hɒrɪfaɪɪŋ] *adj* horroroso(a), *Am* aterrorizante

horror ['hɒrə(r)] *n (feeling, terrifying thing)* horror *m*; **to my h. I saw that…** me horroricé al ver que…; **to have a h. of sth** tener pánico *or* horror a algo; *Fam* **that child's a little h.** ese niño es un monstruo; **h. movie** película *f* de terror; **h. story** cuento *m* de terror

horror-stricken ['hɒrəstrɪkən], **horror-struck** ['hɒrəstrʌk] *adj* horrorizado(a)

horse [hɔ:s] *n* **(a)** *(animal, gym apparatus)* caballo *m*; **h. chestnut** *(tree)* castaño *m* de Indias; **h. racing** carreras *fpl* de caballos; **I like h. riding** me gusta montar *or RP* andar a caballo; *Fig* **h. trading** negociaciones *fpl* entre bastidores **(b)** *(idioms)* **to eat like a h.** comer muchísimo *or Esp* como una lima; **to get up on one's high h.** darse ínfulas; **to hear sth from the h.'s mouth** haber oído algo de boca del propio interesado

▸**horse around, horse about** *vi* hacer el indio

horseback ['hɔ:sbæk] *n* **on h.** a caballo

horse-drawn ['hɔ:sdrɔ:n] *adj* de tiro, de caballos

horsefly ['hɔ:sflaɪ] *n* tábano *m*

horsehair ['hɔ:sheə(r)] *n* crin *f*, crines *fpl*; **h. mattress** colchón *m* de crin

horseman ['hɔ:smən] *n* jinete *m*

horsemanship ['hɔ:smənʃɪp] *n* equitación *f*, manejo *m* del caballo

horsemeat ['hɔ:smi:t] *n* carne *f* de caballo

horseplay ['hɔ:spleɪ] *n* retozo *m*, jugueteo *m*

horsepower ['hɔ:spaʊə(r)] *n Tech* caballos *mpl* de vapor

horseradish ['hɔ:srædɪʃ] *n* rábano *m* silvestre

horseshoe ['hɔ:sʃu:] *n* herradura *f*

horsewhip ['hɔ:swɪp] **1** *n* fusta *f*
2 *vt (pt & pp* **horsewhipped)** azotar

horsewoman ['hɔ:swʊmən] *n* amazona *f*

hors(e)y ['hɔ:sɪ] *adj* **(a)** *(horse-like)* caballuno(a) **(b)** *(keen on horses)* aficionado(a) a los caballos

horticultural [hɔ:tɪ'kʌltʃərəl] *adj* hortícola

horticulture ['hɔ:tɪkʌltʃə(r)] *n* horticultura *f*

hosanna [həʊˈzænə] *n* hosanna *m*

hose [həʊz] **1** *n (pipe)* manguera *f*
  2 *vt* regar con manguera

▸**hose down** *vt sep* limpiar con manguera

hosiery [ˈhəʊzɪərɪ] *n* calcetines *mpl* y medias

hospice [ˈhɒspɪs] *n (for the terminally ill)* hospital *m* para enfermos terminales

hospitable [hɒsˈpɪtəbəl] *adj* hospitalario(a)

hospitably [hɒsˈpɪtəblɪ] *adv* hospitalariamente

hospital [ˈhɒspɪtəl] *n* hospital *m*; **h. bed** cama *f* de hospital; **h. care** atención *f* hospitalaria

hospitality [hɒspɪˈtælɪtɪ] *n* hospitalidad *f*

hospitalize [ˈhɒspɪtəlaɪz] *vt* hospitalizar

host¹ [həʊst] **1** *n* (**a**) *(at home, party)* anfitrión(ona) *m,f*; *(on TV)* presentador(ora) *m,f*; **h. country** país *m* anfitrión *or* organizador (**b**) *Biol (of parasite)* huésped *m*
  2 *vt (party)* dar; *(TV show)* presentar; *Comptr (website)* hospedar

host² *n (great number)* **a whole h. of** un sinfín de

host³ *n Rel (consecrated bread)* hostia *f*

hostage [ˈhɒstɪdʒ] *n* rehén *m*; **to take/hold sb h.** tomar/tener a alguien como rehén; *Fig* **that's offering a h. to fortune** eso supone hipotecar el futuro

hostel [ˈhɒstəl] *n* **(youth) h.** albergue *m* juvenil

hosteling [ˈhɒstəlɪŋ] *n* **to go h.** ir de albergues

hostess [ˈhəʊstɪs] *n (in private house)* anfitriona *f*; *(on TV)* azafata *f*; **(air) h.** azafata *f*

hostile [ˈhɒstaɪl, *ˈhɒstaɪl] adj* hostil (**to** a, con); **to be h. to** ser hostil a, mostrarse hostil ante; *Com* **h. takeover bid** OPA *f* hostil

hostility [hɒsˈtɪlɪtɪ] *n* hostilidad *f*; **hostilities** *(war)* hostilidades *fpl*

hosting [ˈhəʊstɪŋ] *n Comptr* hospedaje *m*

hot [hɒt] *adj* (**a**) *(having high temperature)* caliente; *(day, summer, climate)* caluroso(a); **to be h.** *(person)* tener calor; *(thing)* estar caliente; **it's h.** *(weather)* hace calor; **h. dog** perrito *m* caliente, *Col, Méx* perro *m* caliente, *RP* pancho *m*; *Med* **h. flushes** sofocos *mpl*; **h. tub** jacuzzi® *m*
  (**b**) *(spicy)* picante
  (**c**) *(close)* **you're getting h.** *(in guessing game)* caliente, caliente; **to be h. on sb's/sth's trail** estar pisando los talones a alguien/algo
  (**d**) *Fam (good)* **to be h. on sth** *(be knowledgeable about)* estar muy puesto(a) en algo, *RP* estar muy por dentro de algo; *(attach importance to)* ser muy quisquilloso(a) con algo; **it wasn't such a h. idea** no fue una idea tan buena; **how are you? — not so h.** ¿qué tal? — regular
  (**e**) *Fam (sexually attractive)* sexy; *(sexually aroused) Esp, Méx* cachondo(a), *CAm, Col, Méx,Ven* arrecho(a), *RP* alzado(a)
  (**f**) *Fam (stolen)* afanado(a), *Esp* chorizado(a)
  (**g**) **h. pants** minishorts *mpl*
  (**h**) *(idioms)* **h. from the press** *(news)* caliente; *(book)* recién salido(a) (de la imprenta); **too h. to handle** *(issue)* demasiado comprometido(a); **to have a h. temper** tener mal genio; **to get h. under the collar** *(become indignant)* acalorarse; *Fam* **h. air** *(meaningless talk)* palabras *fpl* vanas; *Fam* **it's all h. air** no son más que fanfarronadas; **they're selling like h. cakes** se venden como pan caliente *or Esp* churros *or Esp* rosquillas; **a h. favorite** *(in race)* un(a) gran favorito(a); **h. gossip** chismorreo *m or Esp* cotilleo *m or RP* chusmerío *m* jugoso; *Tel* **h. line** línea *f* directa; **h. news** noticias *fpl* frescas; *Fam* **h. potato** *(controversial issue)* asunto *m* espinoso, *Esp* patata *f* caliente; **to be in the h. seat** ser el responsable; **h. spot** *(trouble spot)* zona *f* conflictiva; *Fam* **to be in h. water** *(in difficult situation)* estar en apuros

hot-air balloon [ˈhɒteəbəˈluːn] *n* globo *m* de aire caliente, aerostato *m*

hotbed [ˈhɒtbed] *n* **a h. of rebellion/intrigue** un foco de rebelión/intrigas

hot-blooded [ˈhɒtˈblʌdɪd] *adj* (**a**) *(passionate)* ardiente (**b**) *(excitable)* irascible

hotel [həʊˈtel] *n* hotel *m*; **h. room** habitación *f (de hotel)*; **h. manager** director(ora) *m,f* de hotel

hotelier [həʊˈteljeɪ] *n* hotelero(a) *m,f*

hotelkeeper [həʊˈtelkiːpə(r)] *n* hotelero(a) *m,f*

hotfoot [ˈhɒtˈfʊt] *Fam* **1** *adv* a la carrera, zumbando
  2 *vt* **to h. it** ir a la carrera, ir zumbando

hothead [ˈhɒthed] *n* impulsivo(a) *m,f*, impetuoso(a) *m,f*

hotheaded [ˈhɒtˈhedɪd] *adj* impulsivo(a), impetuoso(a)

hothouse [ˈhɒthaʊs] *n (glasshouse)* invernadero *m*; *Fig* hervidero *m*

hotly [ˈhɒtlɪ] *adv (to reply, protest)* acaloradamente; **h. contested** reñidamente disputado(a)

hotplate [ˈhɒtpleɪt] *n (on stove)* placa *f*; *(for keeping food warm)* = placa para mantener la comida caliente

hots [hɒts] *npl very Fam* **she had the h. for Fred** Fred la ponía a cien *or* caliente, *RP* estaba recaliente con Fred

hotshot [ˈhɒtʃɒt] *n Fam (expert)* as *m*, *Esp* hacha *m*

hot-tempered [ˈhɒtˈtempəd] *adj* con mal genio

hot-water [hɒtˈwɔːtə(r)] *adj* de agua caliente; **h. bag** *or* **bottle** bolsa *f* de agua caliente

hound [haʊnd] **1** *n (dog)* perro *m* de caza
  2 *vt (persecute)* acosar; **she was hounded by the press** la prensa la acosaba

hour [ˈaʊə(r)] *n* (**a**) *(period of time)* hora *f*; **an h. and a half** una hora y media; **half an h.** media hora; **to pay sb by the h.** pagar a alguien por horas; **to take hours over sth** tardar *or Am* demorar horas en algo; **we've been waiting for hours** llevamos horas esperando; **to work long hours** trabajar muchas horas; **to keep late hours** acostarse muy tarde; **h. hand** *(of watch, clock)* manecilla *f* de las horas (**b**) *(time of day)* **at this h.!** ¡a estas horas!; **till all hours** hasta las tantas; **where were you in my h. of need?** ¿dónde estabas cuando me necesitaba?; **his h. has come** ha llegado su hora

hourglass [ˈaʊəglɑːs] *n* reloj *m* de arena; **an h. figure** una cintura de avispa

hourly [ˈaʊəlɪ] **1** *adj* **at h. intervals** con intervalos de una hora
  2 *adv (every hour)* cada hora; *(at any time)* en cualquier momento

house 1 *n* [haʊs] (**a**) *(dwelling)* casa *f*; *Fig* **to set one's h. in order** poner sus cosas *or* asuntos en orden, *Am* poner la casa en orden; **to get on like a h. on fire** llevarse estupendamente; **the h. of God** la casa del Señor; **the H. of Commons/Lords** la Cámara de los Comunes/Lores; **the Houses of Parliament** el Parlamento británico; **the H. of Representatives** la Cámara de Representantes; **the H. of Stuart/Bourbon** la casa de los Estuardo/los Borbones; *Law* **h. arrest** arresto *m* domiciliario; **h. martin** avión *m* común; **h. painter** pintor(ora) *m,f* de brocha gorda; **h. party** fiesta *f* *(en una casa de campo)*; **h. plant** planta *f* de interior; **h. surgeon** *(in hospital)* cirujano(a) *m,f* residente
  (**b**) *Com (company)* casa *f*, empresa *f*; **banking h.** banco *m*; **publishing h.** (casa *f*) editorial *f*; **h. style** política *f* (de estilo) de la casa
  (**c**) *(restaurant)* **on the h.** por cuenta de la casa; **h. wine** vino *m* de la casa
  (**d**) *Theat* **an empty/a good h.** un público escaso/numeroso
  (**e**) *(music)* (música *f*) house *m*
  2 *vt* [haʊz] *(person, collection, mechanism)* alojar

houseboat [ˈhaʊsbəʊt] *n* barco-vivienda *m*

housebound [ˈhaʊsbaʊnd] *adj* **to be h.** estar confinado(a) en casa

housebreaker [ˈhaʊsbreɪkə(r)] *n* ladrón(ona) *m,f*

housebreaking ['haʊsbreɪkɪŋ] n robos mpl de casas, RP escruche m

housebroken ['haʊsbrəʊkən] adj (pet) = que ya ha aprendido a no hacer sus necesidades en casa

housecoat ['haʊskəʊt] n bata f de (estar en) casa

housefly ['haʊsflaɪ] n mosca f (doméstica)

houseguest ['haʊsgest] n huésped mf, invitado(a) m,f

household ['haʊshəʊld] n hogar m, Esp unidad f familiar; **h. appliance** electrodoméstico m; **h. chores** tareas fpl domésticas; **to be a h. name** (famous person) ser un nombre conocidísimo

householder ['haʊshəʊldə(r)] n ocupante mf de vivienda

house-hunting ['haʊshʌntɪŋ] n búsqueda f de vivienda

househusband ['haʊshʌzbənd] n amo m de casa

housekeeper ['haʊskiːpə(r)] n ama f de llaves

housekeeping ['haʊskiːpɪŋ] n **h. (money)** dinero m para los gastos domésticos

housemaid ['haʊsmeɪd] n doncella f, criada f; **h.'s knee** (inflammation) bursitis f inv de rodilla

house-proud ['haʊspraʊd] adj **she's very h.** es una mujer muy de su casa

house-sit ['haʊssɪt] vi quedarse cuidando la casa (**for** de)

house-to-house ['haʊstəˈhaʊs] adj (search) de casa en casa

housewarming ['haʊswɔːmɪŋ] n **h. (party)** fiesta f de inauguración (de un piso, de una casa)

housewife ['haʊswaɪf] n ama f de casa

housework ['haʊswɜːk] n tareas fpl domésticas

housing ['haʊzɪŋ] n vivienda f; **h. market** mercado m inmobiliario; **h. project** ≃ viviendas fpl de protección oficial

hove pt of **heave**

hovel ['hɒvəl] n Pej Esp chabola f, Méx jacal m, CSur, Ven rancho m

hover ['hɒvə(r)] vi (a) (bird) cernerse, cernirse; (aircraft) permanecer inmóvil en el aire (b) (person) rondar; **she hovered between life and death** se debatía entre la vida y la muerte

hovercraft ['hɒvəkrɑːft] n aerodeslizador m, hovercraft m

how [haʊ] adv (a) (in what way, by what means) cómo; **h. did they find out?** ¿cómo lo averiguaron?; **h. do you pronounce this word?** ¿cómo se pronuncia esta palabra?; **tell me h. he did it** dime cómo lo hizo; Fam **h. come?** ¿cómo es eso?; Fam **and h.!** ¡y cómo!

(b) (to what extent) **h. much** cuánto; **h. many** cuántos(as); **h. many times?** ¿cuántas veces?; **h. often?** ¿con qué frecuencia?; **h. old are you?** ¿cuántos años tienes?; **h. big is it?** ¿cómo es de grande?; **h. long have you been here?** ¿cuánto tiempo llevas or Méx, Ven tienes aquí?; **you know h. useful he is to me** sabes lo útil que me resulta; **h. interested are you in politics?** ¿hasta qué punto te interesa la política?

(c) (greetings, inquiries after health) **h. are you?** ¿cómo estás?, ¿qué tal estás?; Fam **h. are things?** ¿qué tal?; **how's business?** ¿qué tal el negocio?

(d) (in exclamations) qué; **h. pretty she is!** ¡qué guapa es!; **h. disgusting!** ¡qué asqueroso(a)!; **h. she has changed!** ¡cómo ha cambiado!

(e) (in suggestions) **h. about a game of cards?, h. would you like a game of cards?** ¿quieres jugar a las cartas?, ¿te Esp apetece or Carib, Col, Méx provoca jugar a las cartas?; **h. about going out for a meal?, h. would you like to go out for a meal?** ¿quieres salir a comer?, ¿te Esp apetece or Carib, Col, Méx provoca salir a comer?; **h. about it?** ¿qué te parece?; **h. about you?** ¿y tú?

howdy ['haʊdɪ] exclam Fam ¡hola!, ¿qué hay?, CAm, Col, Méx ¡quihubo!

however [haʊˈevə(r)] **1** adv (a) (to whatever degree) **h. clever she is** por muy lista que sea; **h. hard she tried, she couldn't do it** por mucho que lo intentaba no podía hacerlo

(b) (in whatever way) **h. you look at it,...** se mire como se mire,...; **h. did she find out?** pero, ¿cómo se pudo enterar?

2 conj sin embargo, no obstante

howl [haʊl] **1** n (of animal, person) aullido m

2 vi (animal, person) aullar; **to h. with laughter** desternillarse de risa

▸**howl down** vt sep (silence by shouting) acallar con gritos

howler ['haʊlə(r)] n Fam (mistake) error m grave or Esp de bulto

howling ['haʊlɪŋ] **1** n aullidos mpl

2 adj (wolf) aullador(ora); (gale, wind) violento(a), salvaje; Fam **it wasn't exactly a h. success** no fue un éxito clamoroso que digamos

hp [eɪtʃˈpiː] n Tech (abbr **horsepower**) C.V.

HQ [eɪtʃˈkjuː] n (abbr **headquarters**) sede f, central f

hr (abbr **hour**) h.

HRT [eɪtʃɑːˈtiː] n Med (abbr **hormone replacement therapy**) terapia f hormonal sustitutiva

HTML [eɪtʃtiːemˈel] n Comptr (abbr **Hypertext Markup Language**) HTML m

HTTP [eɪtʃtiːtiːˈpiː] n Comptr (abbr **Hypertext Transfer** or **Transport Protocol**) HTTP m

hub [hʌb] n (a) (of wheel) cubo m (b) (of community) centro m (c) **h. (airport)** aeropuerto m principal (con múltiples conexiones)

hubbub ['hʌbʌb] n griterío m, algarabía f

hubby ['hʌbɪ] n Fam (husband) marido m

hubcap ['hʌbkæp] n (of wheel) tapacubos m inv

huckleberry ['hʌkəlbərɪ] n = especie de arándano norteamericano

huddle ['hʌdəl] **1** n (a) (of people, houses) piña f (b) (in football) reunión f en corro or RP ronda

2 vi acurrucarse

▸**huddle together, huddle up** vi apiñarse

Hudson Bay [hʌdsənˈbeɪ] n la bahía de Hudson

hue¹ [hjuː] n (color) tonalidad f

hue² n **h. and cry** revuelo m tremendo; **to raise a h. and cry about sth** poner el grito en el cielo por algo

huff [hʌf] **1** n Fam **to be in a h.** estar mosqueado(a)

2 vi **to h. and puff** (blow) resoplar; Fig (show annoyance) refunfuñar

huffily ['hʌfɪlɪ] adv Fam (sulkily) con tono ofendido or Esp de mosqueo

huffy ['hʌfɪ] adj Fam **to be h.** (in bad mood) estar mosqueado(a); (by nature) ser un/una refunfuñón(ona)

hug [hʌg] **1** n abrazo m; **to give sb a h.** dar un abrazo a alguien

2 vt (pt & pp **hugged**) (a) (embrace) abrazar; **she hugged the child to her** abrazó al niño; **her dress hugged her figure** el vestido se ceñía a su cuerpo (b) Fig (ground, shore) no alejarse de

huge [hjuːdʒ] adj enorme, inmenso(a)

hugely ['hjuːdʒlɪ] adv enormemente

hulk [hʌlk] n (a) (of ship) casco m, carcasa f (b) (large thing) armatoste m; (large person) mole f, mastodonte m

hulking ['hʌlkɪŋ] adj descomunal, mastodóntico(a)

hull [hʌl] **1** n (a) (of ship) casco m (b) (of pea) vaina f

2 vt (peas) desgranar

hullabaloo [hʌləbəˈluː] n Fam jaleo m, alboroto m

hum [hʌm] **1** n zumbido m

2 vt (pt & pp **hummed**) (tune) tararear, canturrear

3 vi (make noise) (person) tararear; (insect, engine) zumbar; **to h. with activity** bullir de actividad

human ['hjuːmən] **1** n ser m humano

2 adj humano(a); **h. being** ser m humano; **h. error** error m humano; **h. interest** interés m humano; **a h. interest story** una historia de interés humano; **h. nature** la naturaleza humana; **h. resources** recursos mpl humanos; **h. rights** derechos mpl humanos; **h. shield** escudo m humano

humane [hjʊˈmeɪn] adj humano(a)

humanely [hjʊˈmeɪnlɪ] *adv* humanamente

humanism [ˈhjuːmənɪzəm] *n* humanismo *m*

humanistic [hjuːməˈnɪstɪk] *adj* humanístico(a)

humanitarian [hjʊmænɪˈteərɪən] **1** *n* persona *f* humanitaria
2 *adj* humanitario(a)

humanity [hjʊˈmænɪtɪ] *n* humanidad *f*; *Univ* **the humanities** humanidades *fpl*, letras *fpl*

humanize [ˈhjuːmənaɪz] *vt* humanizar

humankind [hjʊmənˈkaɪnd] *n* humanidad *f*, raza *f* humana

humanly [ˈhjuːmənlɪ] *adv* humanamente; **to do everything h. possible** hacer todo lo humanamente posible

humble [ˈhʌmbəl] **1** *adj (meek, unpretentious)* humilde; **in my h. opinion** en mi humilde opinión; *Fig* **to eat h. pie** *(admit one was wrong)* tragarse sus palabras
2 *vt (defeat)* humillar, poner en su sitio; **to be humbled (by sth)** sacar una lección de humildad (de algo)

humbling [ˈhʌmbəlɪŋ] *adj* **a h. experience** una lección de humildad

humbly [ˈhʌmblɪ] *adv* humildemente

humbug [ˈhʌmbʌɡ] *n* **(a)** *(nonsense)* tonterías *fpl* **(b)** *(hypocrite)* embaucador(ora) *m,f*

humdinger [ˈhʌmdɪŋə(r)] *n Fam* **a h. of a movie** una película bestial *or* genial *or Méx* padrísima

humdrum [ˈhʌmdrʌm] *adj* anodino(a)

humerus [ˈhjuːmərəs] *n Anat* húmero *m*

humid [ˈhjuːmɪd] *adj* húmedo(a)

humidifier [hjʊˈmɪdɪfaɪə(r)] *n* humidificador *m*

humidity [hjʊˈmɪdɪtɪ] *n* humedad *f*

humiliate [hjʊˈmɪlɪeɪt] *vt* humillar

humiliating [hjʊˈmɪlɪeɪtɪŋ] *adj* humillante

humiliation [hjʊmɪlɪˈeɪʃən] *n* humillación *f*

humility [hjʊˈmɪlɪtɪ] *n* humildad *f*

hummingbird [ˈhʌmɪŋbɜːd] *n* colibrí *m*

hummus [ˈhʊməs] *n* hum(m)us *m inv*, puré *m* de garbanzos

humongous, humungous [hjuːˈmʌŋɡəs] *adj Fam* grandísimo(a), *Esp* gansísimo(a)

humor [ˈhjuːmə(r)] **1** *n (in general)* humor *m*; *(of a situation, a story)* gracia *f*; **sense of h.** sentido *m* del humor; *Formal* **to be in good/bad h.** estar de buen/mal humor
2 *vt (indulge)* complacer

humorless [ˈhjuːmələs] *adj* serio(a), con poco sentido del humor

humorous [ˈhjuːmərəs] *adj (person, remark)* gracioso(a); *(play, magazine)* humorístico(a)

humorously [ˈhjuːmərəslɪ] *adv* con humor, con gracia

hump [hʌmp] **1** *n (on back)* joroba *f*; *(on road)* bache *m (convexo)*
2 *vt Vulg (have sex with)* tirarse a

humpback [ˈhʌmpbæk] *n* **h. whale** yubarta *f*

humungous = humongous

humus [ˈhjuːməs] *n (in soil)* humus *m inv*

hunch [hʌntʃ] **1** *n (intuition)* presentimiento *m*, corazonada *f*
2 *vt* **to h. one's back** encorvar la espalda, encorvar

hunchback [ˈhʌntʃbæk] *n (person)* jorobado(a) *m,f*

hunchbacked [ˈhʌntʃbækt] *adj* jorobado(a)

hundred [ˈhʌndrəd] **1** *n (in general and before "thousand", "million", etc.)* cien *m*; *(before other numbers)* ciento *m*; **one** *or* **a h.** cien; **one** *or* **a h. thousand** cien mil; **a h. and twenty-five books** ciento veinticinco libros; **two h. books** doscientos libros; *Fig* **a h. and one details** mil y un detalles; **to live to be a h.** vivir hasta los cien años; **I've told you hundreds of times** te lo he dicho cientos de veces
2 *adj* cien; **a h. miles an hour** cien millas por hora; **one** *or* **a h. percent** cien por cien, ciento por ciento, *Am* cien por ciento; **to be a h. percent certain** estar seguro(a) al cien por cien *or Am* cien por ciento; **I'm not feeling a h. percent** no me encuentro del todo bien; **the h. meters** *(in track)* los cien metros (lisos); **the H. Years' War** la guerra de los Cien Años

hundredfold [ˈhʌndrədfəʊld] *adv* **to increase a h.** multiplicar por cien

hundredth [ˈhʌndrədθ] **1** *n* **(a)** *(fraction)* centésimo *m*, centésima parte *f* **(b)** *(in series)* centésimo(a) *m,f*
2 *adj* centésimo(a); *Fam* **for the h. time, no!** por enésima vez, ¡no!

hundredweight [ˈhʌndrədweɪt] *n* **(a)** *(metric)* 50 kg **(b)** *(imperial)* = 45,36 kg

hung [hʌŋ] **1** *adj* **h. jury** jurado *m* dividido
2 *pt & pp of* **hang**

Hungarian [hʌŋˈɡeərɪən] **1** *n* **(a)** *(person)* húngaro(a) *m,f* **(b)** *(language)* húngaro *m*
2 *adj* húngaro(a)

Hungary [ˈhʌŋɡərɪ] *n* Hungría

hunger [ˈhʌŋɡə(r)] *n* hambre *f*; **h. strike** huelga *f* de hambre

▸**hunger after, hunger for** *vt insep* ansiar

hungrily [ˈhʌŋɡrɪlɪ] *adv (eat)* vorazmente; *(stare)* con avidez

hungry [ˈhʌŋɡrɪ] *adj* hambriento(a); **to be h.** tener hambre; **to be as h. as a horse** tener un hambre canina; **to be h. for knowledge** tener ansias de conocimiento

hunk [hʌŋk] *n* **(a)** *(large piece of bread, meat)* pedazo *m*, trozo *m* **(b)** *Fam (attractive man)* tipo *m or Esp* tío *m* bueno

hunky [ˈhʌŋkɪ] *adj Fam (man)* fortachón, *Esp* cachas *inv*

hunt [hʌnt] **1** *n (for animals)* caza *f*; *(for person, work)* búsqueda *f*, caza *f*
2 *vt (fox, deer)* cazar; **to h. a criminal** ir tras la pista de un delincuente
3 *vi* **(a)** *(search)* **to h. for** ir en búsqueda *or Esp* busca de **(b)** *(kill animals)* cazar

▸**hunt down** *vt sep (animal)* cazar; *(person)* atrapar, capturar; *(information)* conseguir

▸**hunt out** *vt sep (find) (person)* dar con, lograr encontrar; *(look for) (thing)* buscar

hunted [ˈhʌntɪd] *adj (look, appearance)* angustiado(a)

hunter [ˈhʌntə(r)] *n* cazador(ora) *m,f*

hunter-gatherer [hʌntəˈɡæðərə(r)] *n* cazador-recolector *m*

hunting [ˈhʌntɪŋ] *n* caza *f*; **h. ground** terreno *m* de caza; **h. lodge** refugio *m* de cazadores

huntsman [ˈhʌntsmən] *n (hunter)* cazador *m*

hurdle [ˈhɜːdəl] **1** *n (in race)* valla *f*, *Am* obstáculo *m*; *Fig (obstacle)* obstáculo *m*; *Fig* **to overcome a h.** vencer un obstáculo
2 *vt (obstacle)* saltar

hurdler [ˈhɜːdlə(r)] *n Sport* vallista *mf*

hurdling [ˈhɜːdəlɪŋ] *n Sport* carreras *fpl* de vallas

hurl [hɜːl] *vt (thing)* lanzar; *(insults)* proferir; **to h. oneself at sb** lanzarse contra alguien; **she hurled herself off the bridge** se tiró desde el puente

hurling [ˈhɜːlɪŋ] *n (Irish game)* = hockey irlandés

hurly-burly [ˈhɜːlɪˈbɜːlɪ] *n Fam* tumulto *m*, barullo *m*

hurrah [hʊˈrɑː], **hurray** [hʊˈreɪ] *exclam* ¡hurra!

hurricane [ˈhʌrɪkeɪn] *n* huracán *m*; **h. lamp** farol *m*

hurried [ˈhʌrɪd] *adj* apresurado(a); **to be h.** tener prisa, *Am* estar apurado(a)

hurriedly [ˈhʌrɪdlɪ] *adv* apresuradamente

hurry [ˈhʌrɪ] **1** *n* prisa *f*, *Am* apuro *m*; **to be in a h. (to do sth)** tener prisa *or Am* apuro (por hacer algo); **to do sth in a h.** hacer algo deprisa *or Am* rápido; **to leave in a h.** marcharse apresuradamente; **I won't do that again in a h.** no lo volveré a hacer con prisas; **there's no h.** no corre prisa, *Am* no hay apuro; **what's the h.?** ¿a qué tanta prisa *or Am* tanto apuro?
2 *vt (person)* meter prisa a, apremiar, *Am* apurar; *(work, decision)* apresurar, realizar con prisas; **she was hurried to hospital** la llevaron apresuradamente al hospital
3 *vi* **to h. (to do sth)** apresurarse *or Am* apurarse (a hacer

algo); **to h. into a room** entrar apresuradamente en una habitación; **to h. out of a room** salir apresuradamente de una habitación

▸**hurry along 1** *vt sep (person)* meter prisa a, *Am* apurar

2 *vi* irse rápido; **to h. along toward** precipitarse hacia

▸**hurry back** *vi* volver corriendo

▸**hurry on 1** *vt sep (person)* meter prisa a, *Am* apurar; *(work)* acelerar

2 *vi (proceed quickly) (person)* seguir sin pararse; **to h. on with sth** continuar algo deprisa *or Am* rápido

▸**hurry up 1** *vt sep (person)* meter prisa a, *Am* apurar; *(work)* acelerar

2 *vi* apresurarse, darse prisa, *Am* apurarse; **h. up!** ¡date prisa!, *Am* ¡apúrate!

hurt [hɜːt] **1** *n (emotional)* dolor *m*

2 *adj (emotionally) (person)* dolido(a); *(look)* dolorido(a); *(feelings)* herido(a); **are you h.?** *(after falling)* ¿te has hecho daño?; *(wounded)* ¿estás herido?

3 *vt (pt & pp* **hurt)** **(a)** *(physically)* hacer daño a; *Fig (chances, prospects)* perjudicar; **to h. oneself** hacerse daño; **to h. one's foot** hacerse daño en un pie; **to get h.** hacerse daño; *Fig* **it wouldn't h. him to have to wait** no le va a pasar nada por que espere **(b)** *(emotionally)* herir; **to h. sb's feelings** herir los sentimientos de alguien

4 *vi* **(a)** *(cause pain)* doler; **it hurts** me duele; **where does it h.?** ¿dónde te duele?; **my foot hurts** me duele el pie **(b)** *(emotionally)* resultar doloroso(a), doler

hurtful [ˈhɜːtfʊl] *adj (remark)* hiriente

hurtle [ˈhɜːtəl] *vi* **to h. along** pasar zumbando; **to h. down the street** bajar por la calle a todo correr; **to h. toward** precipitarse hacia

husband [ˈhʌzbənd] **1** *n* marido *m*; **h. and wife** marido y mujer

2 *vt Formal (one's resources)* economizar

husbandry [ˈhʌzbəndrɪ] *n* agricultura *f*; **animal h.** ganadería *f*

hush [hʌʃ] **1** *n (quiet)* silencio *m*; **h.!** ¡silencio!

2 *vt* acallar

▸**hush up** *vt sep (scandal)* echar tierra a

hushed [hʌʃt] *adj* susurrado(a)

hush-hush [ˈhʌʃhʌʃ] *adj Fam* secreto(a)

husk [hʌsk] **1** *n (of seed)* cáscara *f*

2 *vt (grain)* pelar

huskily [ˈhʌskɪlɪ] *adv (hoarsely)* con voz ronca, con tono ronco; *(attractively)* con voz grave

huskiness [ˈhʌskɪnɪs] *n (of voice, sound) (hoarse)* aspereza *f*; *(attractive)* tonalidad *f* grave

husky[1] [ˈhʌskɪ] *adj (voice)* áspero(a); *(attractive)* grave

husky[2] *n (dog)* perro *m* esquimal

hussar [hʊˈzɑː(r)] *n Mil* húsar *m*

hussy [ˈhʌsɪ] *n Old-fashioned or Hum* fresca *f*, pelandusca *f*

hustings [ˈhʌstɪŋz] *npl* mítines *mpl* electorales

hustle [ˈhʌsəl] **1** *n* agitación *f*, bullicio *m*; **h. and bustle** ajetreo *m*, bullicio *m*

2 *vt (shove, push)* empujar; **I was hustled into a small room** me metieron a empujones en un cuartito

hustler [ˈhʌslə(r)] *n Fam (swindler)* estafador(ora) *m,f*, *Esp* timador(ora) *m,f*

hut [hʌt] *n (shed)* cobertizo *m*; *(dwelling)* cabaña *f*, choza *f*

hutch [hʌtʃ] *n (for rabbit)* jaula *f* para conejos

hyacinth [ˈhaɪəsɪnθ] *n* jacinto *m*

hybrid [ˈhaɪbrɪd] **1** *n* híbrido *m*

2 *adj* híbrido(a)

hydrangea [haɪˈdreɪndʒə] *n* hortensia *f*

hydrant [ˈhaɪdrənt] *n* boca *f* de incendio *or* de riego

hydraulic [haɪˈdrɔːlɪk] *adj* hidráulico(a)

hydraulics [haɪˈdrɔːlɪks] *npl* hidráulica *f*

hydrocarbon [haɪdrəʊˈkɑːbən] *n* hidrocarburo *m*

hydrochloric acid [haɪdrəʊˈklɒrɪkˈæsɪd] *n* ácido *m* clorhídrico

hydroelectric [haɪdrəʊɪˈlektrɪk] *adj* hidroeléctrico(a); **h. power** energía *f* hidroeléctrica

hydroelectricity [haɪdrəʊɪlekˈtrɪsɪtɪ] *n* hidroelectricidad *f*

hydrofoil [ˈhaɪdrəfɔɪl] *n (boat)* hidroala *m*, *RP* alíscafo *m*

hydrogen [ˈhaɪdrədʒən] *n Chem* hidrógeno *m*; **h. bomb** bomba *f* de hidrógeno; **h. peroxide** agua *f* oxigenada, *Spec* peróxido *m* de hidrógeno

hydrolysis [haɪˈdrɒlɪsɪs] *n* hidrólisis *f inv*

hydrophobia [haɪdrəˈfəʊbɪə] *n Med (rabies)* hidrofobia *f*, rabia *f*

hydroplane [ˈhaɪdrəpleɪn] *n (boat)* hidroala *m*, *RP* alíscafo *m*

hydrotherapy [haɪdrəʊˈθerəpɪ] *n* hidroterapia *f*

hydroxide [haɪˈdrɒksaɪd] *n* hidróxido *m*

hyena [haɪˈiːnə] *n* hiena *f*

hygiene [ˈhaɪdʒiːn] *n* higiene *f*

hygienic [haɪˈdʒiːnɪk] *adj* higiénico(a)

hygienically [haɪˈdʒiːnɪklɪ] *adv* con higiene, de un modo higiénico

hymen [ˈhaɪmen] *n Anat* himen *m*

hymn [hɪm] *n* himno *m*; **h. book** libro *m* de himnos, himnario *m*

hymnal [ˈhɪmnəl] *n Rel* himnario *m*, libro *m* de himnos

hype [haɪp] *Fam* **1** *n (publicity)* bombo *m*, revuelo *m* publicitario

2 *vt (publicize)* dar mucho bombo a

▸**hype up** *vt sep* **(a)** *(publicize)* dar mucho bombo a **(b)** **to be hyped up** *(excited)* estar hecho(a) un manojo de nervios

hyper [ˈhaɪpə(r)] *adj Fam (overexcited)* acelerado(a)

hyperactive [haɪpəˈræktɪv] *adj* hiperactivo(a)

hyperactivity [haɪpəˈræktɪvɪtɪ] *n* hiperactividad *f*

hyperbola [haɪˈpɜːbələ] *n Math* hipérbola *f*

hyperbole [haɪˈpɜːbəlɪ] *n* hipérbole *f*

hypercritical [haɪpəˈkrɪtɪkəl] *adj* criticón(ona)

hyperlink [ˈhaɪpəlɪŋk] *n Comptr* hiperenlace *m*

hypermarket [ˈhaɪpəmɑːkɪt] *n* hipermercado *m*

hyperopia [haɪpəˈrəʊpɪə] *n Med* hipermetropía *f*

hypersensitive [haɪpəˈsensɪtɪv] *adj* hipersensible, muy susceptible

hypersensitivity [ˈhaɪpəsensɪˈtɪvɪtɪ] *n* hipersensibilidad *f*

hypertension [haɪpəˈtenʃən] *n Med* hipertensión *f*

hypertext [ˈhaɪpətekst] *n Comptr* hipertexto *m*

hyphen [ˈhaɪfən] *n* guión *m*

hyphenate [ˈhaɪfəneɪt] *vt (word)* escribir con guión; **hyphenated American** medio americano(a)

hypnosis [hɪpˈnəʊsɪs] *n* hipnosis *f inv*

hypnotherapy [hɪpnəˈθerəpɪ] *n* terapia *f* hipnótica, hipnoterapia *f*

hypnotic [hɪpˈnɒtɪk] *adj* hipnótico(a)

hypnotism [ˈhɪpnətɪzəm] *n* hipnotismo *m*

hypnotist [ˈhɪpnətɪst] *n* hipnotizador(ora) *m,f*

hypnotize [ˈhɪpnətaɪz] *vt* hipnotizar

hypoallergenic [haɪpəʊæləˈdʒenɪk] *adj* hipoalergénico(a)

hypochondria [haɪpəˈkɒndrɪə] *n Med* hipocondría *f*

hypochondriac [haɪpəˈkɒndrɪæk] *n* hipocondríaco(a) *m,f*

hypocrisy [hɪˈpɒkrɪsɪ] *n* hipocresía *f*

hypocrite [ˈhɪpəkrɪt] *n* hipócrita *mf*

hypocritical [hɪpəˈkrɪtɪkəl] *adj* hipócrita

hypodermic [haɪpəˈdɜːmɪk] **1** *n (jeringuilla f)* hipodérmica *f*

2 *adj* hipodérmico(a)

hypotenuse [haɪˈpɒtənjuːz] *n Math* hipotenusa *f*

hypothermia [haɪpəʊˈθɜːmɪə] *n Med* hipotermia *f*

hypothesis [haɪˈpɒθəsɪs] *(pl* **hypotheses** [haɪˈpɒθəsiːz]) *n* hipótesis *f inv*

hypothesize [haɪˈpɒθəsaɪz] **1** *vt* plantear como hipótesis, conjeturar

2 *vi* plantear hipótesis, conjeturar

hypothetical [haɪpəˈθetɪkəl] *adj* hipotético(a)

hypothetically [haɪpəˈθetɪklɪ] *adv* en teoría, hipotéticamente

hysterectomy [hɪstəˈrektəmɪ] *n Med* histerectomía *f*

hysteria [hɪsˈtɪərɪə] *n* (**a**) *(panic)* histeria *f*, histerismo *m* (**b**) *(laughter)* grandes carcajadas *fpl*, hilaridad *f*

hysterical [hɪsˈterɪkəl] *adj* (**a**) *(uncontrolled)* histérico(a) (**b**) *(very funny)* graciosísimo(a), divertidísimo(a); **h. laughter** carcajadas *fpl* histéricas

hysterically [hɪsˈterɪklɪ] *adv* (**a**) *(uncontrolledly)* histéricamente (**b**) **h. funny** para morirse de risa

hysterics [hɪsˈterɪks] *npl* (**a**) *(panic)* ataque *m* de histeria; **to go into** *or* **have h.** tener un ataque de histeria (**b**) *(laughter)* **we were in h.** nos desternillábamos de risa

Hz *Elec* (*abbr* **Hertz**) Hz

I

I, i [aɪ] *n (letter)* I, i *f*

I *pron* yo *(usually omitted, except for contrast)*; **I'm Scottish** soy escocés; **I haven't got it!** ¡yo no lo tengo!; *Formal* **it was I who did it** yo fui el que lo hizo

IAAF [aɪdʌbəleɪ'ef] *n (abbr* **International Association of Athletics Federations)** IAAF *f*

IAEA [aɪeɪiː'eɪ] *n (abbr* **International Atomic Energy Agency)** AIEA *f*

Iberian [aɪ'biːrɪən] *adj* ibérico(a); **the I. peninsula** la península Ibérica

ibex ['aɪbeks] *n* íbice *m*, cabra *f* montés

ibid ['ɪbɪd] *adv (abbr* **ibidem)** ibíd., ib.

IBM [aɪbiː'em] *n Mil (abbr* **intercontinental ballistic missile)** misil *m* balístico intercontinental

IBRD [aɪbiːɑː'diː] *n (abbr* **International Bank for Reconstruction and Development)** BIRD *m*, Banco *m* Mundial

ICC [aɪsiː'siː] *n (abbr* **International Criminal Court)** CPI *f*, TPI *m*

ice [aɪs] **1** *n* (a) *(frozen water)* hielo *m*; **i. age** glaciación *f*; **i. cream** helado *m*; **i. cube** cubito *m* de hielo; **i. dance** *or* **dancing** patinaje *m* artístico por parejas en la modalidad de danza; **i. floe** témpano *m* (de hielo); **i. hockey** hockey *m* sobre hielo; **i. pack** bolsa *f* de hielo; **i. pick** pico *m* para el hielo; **i. rink** pista *f* de hielo; **i. water** agua *f* con hielo (b) *(idioms)* **to put a project on i.** suspender *or Esp* aparcar un proyecto; **to break the i.** *(socially)* romper el hielo; **to be skating on thin i.** estar jugándosela; **that cuts no i. with me** eso me deja frío
    2 *vt (cake)* glasear

▸**ice over** *vi (pond)* cubrirse de hielo, helarse

▸**ice up** *vi* helarse

iceberg ['aɪsbɜːg] *n* iceberg *m*; **i. lettuce** lechuga *f* iceberg *or* repolluda; *Fig* **that's just the tip of the i.** eso es sólo la punta del iceberg

icebound ['aɪsbaʊnd] *adj (ship, port)* bloqueado(a) por el hielo

icebox ['aɪsbɒks] *n (fridge)* nevera *f*, *RP* heladera *f*, *Méx* refrigerador *m*

icebreaker ['aɪs'breɪkə(r)] *n (ship)* rompehielos *m inv*; *Fig* **this game's a good i.** este juego viene muy bien para romper el hielo

icecap ['aɪskæp] *n (at poles)* casquete *m* polar *or* glaciar

ice-cold ['aɪs'kəʊld] *adj* helado(a)

ice-cream ['aɪskriːm] *adj* **i. cone** helado *m* de cucurucho; **i. parlor** heladería *f*; **i. soda** helado *m* con soda, = helado de mantecado mezclado con agua con gas y algún sabor

iced [aɪst] *adj (cake)* glaseado(a)

Iceland ['aɪslənd] *n* Islandia

Icelander ['aɪsləndə(r)] *n* islandés(esa) *m,f*

Icelandic [aɪs'lændɪk] **1** *n (language)* islandés *m*
    2 *adj* islandés(esa)

ice-skate ['aɪs'skeɪt] **1** *n* patín *m* (de hielo)
    2 *vi* patinar sobre hielo

ice-skating ['aɪs'skeɪtɪŋ] *n* patinaje *m* sobre hielo

icicle ['aɪsɪkəl] *n* carámbano *m*

icing ['aɪsɪŋ] *n (on cake)* glaseado *m*; *Fig* **the i. on the cake** la guinda

icon ['aɪkɒn] *n Art, Comptr & Fig* icono *m*

iconoclastic [aɪkɒnəʊ'klæstɪk] *adj* iconoclasta

ICRC [aɪsiːɑː'siː] *n (abbr* **International Committee of the Red Cross)** CICR *m*

icy ['aɪsɪ] *adj* (a) *(road)* con hielo; *(wind)* helado(a) (b) *Fig (expression, reply)* frío(a)

ID ['aɪ'diː] *n (abbr* **identification)** documentación *f*; **ID card** carné *m* de identidad, *Esp* ≃ DNI *m*

I'd [aɪd] = **I had, I would**

idea [aɪ'diːə] *n* (a) *(individual notion)* idea *f*; **what a good i.!** ¡qué buena idea!; **what put that i. into your head?** ¿qué te metió esa idea en la cabeza?; **the very i.!** ¡es el colmo!, ¡vaya idea!; *Fam* **what's the big i.?** ¿a qué viene esto?
    (b) *(concept)* idea *f*, concepto *m*; **to have an i. that...** tener la sensación de que...; **her i. of a joke is...** su idea de una broma es...; **I had no i. that...** no tenía ni idea de que...; **can you give me an i. of how much it will cost?** ¿puede darme una idea de cuánto va a costar?; **I thought the i. was for them to come here** creí que la idea era que ellos vinieran aquí; **the general i. is to...** la idea general es...

ideal [aɪ'diːəl] *n & adj* ideal *m*

idealism [aɪ'dɪəlɪzəm] *n* idealismo *m*

idealist [aɪ'dɪəlɪst] *n* idealista *mf*

idealistic [aɪdɪə'lɪstɪk] *adj* idealista

idealize [aɪ'dɪəlaɪz] *vt* idealizar

ideally [aɪ'diːəlɪ] *adv* **i., we should all be there** lo ideal sería que estuviéramos todos; **they're i. matched** están hechos el uno para el otro; **i. situated** en una posición ideal

identical [aɪ'dentɪkəl] *adj* idéntico(a); **i. twins** gemelos(as) *mfpl* idénticos(as) *or* monocigóticos(as)

identically [aɪ'dentɪklɪ] *adv* igual, de manera idéntica

identifiable [aɪdentɪ'faɪəbəl] *adj* identificable; **it was not easily i.** no se podía identificar fácilmente

identification [aɪdentɪfɪ'keɪʃən] *n* (a) *(of body, criminal)* identificación *f* (b) *(documents)* documentación *f*

identify [aɪ'dentɪfaɪ] **1** *vt* identificar; **to i. sth with sth** identificar algo con algo
    2 *vi* **to i. with sb/sth** identificarse con alguien/algo

identifying mark [aɪ'dentɪfaɪɪŋ'mɑːk] *n* seña *f* de identidad

Identikit® [aɪ'dentɪkɪt] *n* **I. (picture)** retrato *m* robot

identity [aɪ'dentɪtɪ] *n* identidad *f*; **a case of mistaken i.** un caso de identificación errónea; **i. card** carné *m* de identidad, ≃ DNI *m*; **i. crisis** crisis *f inv* de identidad; **i. theft** robo *m* de identidad

ideological [aɪdɪə'lɒdʒɪkəl] *adj* ideológico(a)

ideologically [aɪdɪə'lɒdʒɪklɪ] *adv* ideológicamente

ideology [aɪdɪ'ɒlədʒɪ] *n* ideología *f*

idiocy ['ɪdɪəsɪ] *n* idiotez *f*, estupidez *f*

idiom ['ɪdɪəm] *n (expression)* modismo *m*, giro *m*; *(dialect)* lenguaje *m*

idiomatic [ɪdɪə'mætɪk] *adj* **his English isn't very i.** su inglés no suena muy natural; **i. expression** modismo *m*, giro *m*

idiomatically [ɪdɪə'mætɪklɪ] *adv* con modismos *or* giros idiomáticos

idiosyncrasy [ɪdɪəʊ'sɪŋkrəsɪ] *n* peculiaridad *f*, particularidad *f*

idiosyncratic [ɪdɪəʊsɪŋ'krætɪk] *adj* peculiar, particular

idiot ['ɪdɪət] *n* idiota *mf*, estúpido(a) *m,f*; **you i.!** ¡idiota!, ¡imbécil!

idiotic [ɪdɪ'ɒtɪk] *adj* idiota, estúpido(a)

idiot-proof ['ɪdɪətpruːf] *Fam* **1** *adj (system, machine)* a prueba de idiotas
  2 *vt* garantizar a prueba de idiotas

idle ['aɪdəl] **1** *adj* **(a)** *(unoccupied) (person)* ocioso(a), desocupado(a); *(factory, machine)* inactivo(a); **an i. moment** un momento libre **(b)** *(lazy)* vago(a) **(c)** *(futile) (threat, boast)* vano(a); *(gossip, rumor)* frívolo(a); **i. curiosity** mera curiosidad
  2 *vi (engine)* estar en punto muerto
▸ **idle away** *vt sep* pasar ociosamente

idleness ['aɪdəlnɪs] *n* **(a)** *(inaction)* ociosidad *f* **(b)** *(laziness)* vagancia *f*

idler ['aɪdlə(r)] *n (lazy person)* vago(a) *m,f*

idly ['aɪdlɪ] *adv* **(a)** *(inactively)* ociosamente; **to stand i. by** estar sin hacer nada **(b)** *(casually)* despreocupadamente

idol ['aɪdəl] *n* ídolo *m*

idolatry [aɪ'dɒlətrɪ] *n* idolatría *f*

idolize ['aɪdəlaɪz] *vt* idolatrar

idyll ['ɪdɪl] *n* idilio *m*

idyllic [ɪ'dɪlɪk] *adj* idílico(a)

i.e. ['aɪ'iː] *(abbr* **id est)** i.e., es decir

if [ɪf] **1** *n* **ifs and buts** pegas *fpl*; **it's a big if** es un gran condicionante
  2 *conj* **(a)** *(conditional)* si; **if I were rich** si fuese rico; **if I were you** si yo en tu lugar; **if the weather's good** si hace buen tiempo **(b)** *(conceding)* si bien; **the movie was good, if rather long** la película fue buena, si bien un poco larga; **if anything it's better** en todo caso, es mejor **(c)** *(whether)* si; **I asked if it was true** pregunté si era verdad **(d)** *(in phrases)* **if not** si no; **if so** en ese caso; **if only!** ¡ojalá!; **if only I had more money!** ¡ojalá tuviera más dinero!; **if and when...** en caso de que...; **he sees them rarely, if at all** *or* **if ever** apenas los ve

iffy ['ɪfɪ] *adj Fam (doubtful)* dudoso(a)

igloo ['ɪgluː] *(pl* **igloos)** *n* iglú *m*

ignite [ɪg'naɪt] **1** *vt (fire, conflict)* prender, encender
  2 *vi (fire, conflict)* prender, encenderse

ignition [ɪg'nɪʃən] *n Aut* encendido *m*, contacto *m*; **i. key** llave *f* de contacto

ignoble [ɪg'nəʊbəl] *adj* innoble, indigno(a)

ignominious [ɪgnə'mɪnɪəs] *adj* ignominioso(a)

ignominiously [ɪgnə'mɪnɪəslɪ] *adv* de forma ignominiosa, ignominiosamente

ignominy ['ɪgnəmɪnɪ] *n* ignominia *f*

ignoramus [ɪgnə'reɪməs] *n* ignorante *mf*

ignorance ['ɪgnərəns] *n* ignorancia *f*; **out of** *or* **through i.** por ignorancia

ignorant ['ɪgnərənt] *adj* ignorante; **to be i. of sth** ignorar algo

ignore [ɪg'nɔː(r)] *vt (person)* no hacer caso a, ignorar; *(warning, advice)* no hacer caso de, ignorar; **just i. him!** ¡no le hagas caso!

iguana [ɪg'wɑːnə] *n* iguana *f*

ilk [ɪlk] *n* **of that i.** por el estilo

I'll [aɪl] = **I will, I shall**

ill¹ [ɪl] **1** *npl* **ills** males *mpl*
  2 *adj* **(a)** *(unwell)* enfermo(a) *or* malo(a); **to be i.** estar enfermo(a) *or* malo(a); **to fall** *or* **be taken i.** caer enfermo(a) *or* malo(a) **(b)** *(bad, poor)* **i. effects** efectos *mpl* indeseables; **i. feeling** rencor *m*; **i. fortune** mala suerte *f or* fortuna *f*; **to be in i. health** tener mala salud; **to be** *or* **feel i. at ease** no sentirse a gusto; **a house of i. repute** *(brothel)* una casa de prostitución; **i. will** rencor *m*
  3 *adv* mal; **I can i. afford it** me lo puedo permitir a duras penas; **to speak/think i. of sb** hablar/pensar mal de alguien

ill² *n (abbr* **illustration)** ilustración *f*

ill-advised ['ɪləd'vaɪzd] *adj* imprudente, desacertado(a); **you'd be i. to complain** harías mal en quejarte

ill-bred ['ɪl'bred] *adj* maleducado(a)

ill-concealed ['ɪlkən'siːld] *adj (disappointment, disgust)* mal disimulado(a)

ill-considered ['ɪlkən'sɪdəd] *adj (remark, decision)* irreflexivo(a), precipitado(a)

ill-disposed ['ɪldɪs'pəʊzd] *adj* **to be i. toward sb** tener mala disposición hacia alguien

illegal [ɪ'liːgəl] *adj* ilegal

illegality [ɪlɪ'gælɪtɪ] *n* ilegalidad *f*

illegible [ɪ'ledʒɪbəl] *adj* ilegible

illegitimacy [ɪlɪ'dʒɪtɪməsɪ] *n* ilegitimidad *f*

illegitimate [ɪlɪ'dʒɪtɪmət] *adj* ilegítimo(a)

ill-equipped ['ɪlɪ'kwɪpd] *adj* mal equipado(a); *Fig* **to be i. to do sth** *(lack skill, experience)* no estar preparado(a) para hacer algo

ill-fated ['ɪl'feɪtɪd] *adj (day, occasion)* aciago(a); *(enterprise)* infausto(a), desdichado(a)

ill-founded ['ɪl'faʊndɪd] *adj* infundado(a)

ill-gotten gains ['ɪlgɒtn'gaɪnz] *npl* ganancias *fpl* obtenidas por medios ilícitos

illiberal [ɪ'lɪbərəl] *adj (narrow-minded)* intolerante

illicit [ɪ'lɪsɪt] *adj* ilícito(a)

ill-informed [ɪlɪn'fɔːmd] *adj* mal informado(a)

ill-intentioned ['ɪlɪn'tenʃənd] *adj* malintencionado(a)

illiteracy [ɪ'lɪtərəsɪ] *n* analfabetismo *m*

illiterate [ɪ'lɪtərət] **1** *adj (unable to read or write)* analfabeto(a); *(usage, style)* analfabeto(a), ignorante
  2 *n* analfabeto(a) *m,f*

ill-mannered ['ɪl'mænəd] *adj* maleducado(a)

ill-natured ['ɪl'neɪtʃəd] *adj* malhumorado(a)

illness ['ɪlnɪs] *n* enfermedad *f*

illogical [ɪ'lɒdʒɪkəl] *adj* ilógico(a)

ill-suited ['ɪl'suːtɪd] *adj (not appropriate)* inadecuado(a) **(to** para)

ill-tempered ['ɪl'tempəd] *adj (person)* malhumorado(a); *(meeting, exchange)* agrio(a); *(match, occasion)* brusco(a), áspero(a)

ill-timed ['ɪl'taɪmd] *adj* inoportuno(a)

ill-treat ['ɪl'triːt] *vt* maltratar

illuminate [ɪ'luːmɪneɪt] *vt* **(a)** *(light up)* iluminar **(b)** *(clarify)* ilustrar

illuminating [ɪ'luːmɪneɪtɪŋ] *adj* ilustrativo(a), iluminador(ora)

illumination [ɪlʊmɪ'neɪʃən] *n* iluminación *f*; *Fig* **his answer provided little i.** su respuesta no resultó muy ilustrativa

ill-use 1 ['ɪl'juːs] maltrato *m*
  2 *vt* ['ɪl'juːz] maltratar; **to feel ill-used** sentirse maltratado(a)

illusion [ɪ'luːʒən] *n* ilusión *f*; **to be under the i. that...** hacerse la ilusión de que...; **I was under no illusions about the risk** no me engañaba en lo referente al peligro

illusory [ɪ'luːsərɪ] *adj* ilusorio(a)

illustrate ['ıləstreıt] *vt also Fig* ilustrar

illustration [ıləs'treıʃən] *n (picture, example)* ilustración *f*

illustrative ['ılʌstrətıv] *adj* ilustrativo(a); **to be i. of sth** ilustrar algo

illustrator ['ıləstreıtə(r)] *n* ilustrador(ora) *m,f*

illustrious [ı'lʌstrıəs] *adj* ilustre, insigne

ILO [aıe'ləʊ] *n (abbr* **International Labor Organization**) OIT *f*, Organización *f* Internacional del Trabajo

I'm [aım] = **I am**

image ['ımıdʒ] *n* imagen *f*; **he's the i. of his father** es la viva imagen *or* el vivo retrato de su padre

image-conscious ['ımıdʒ'kɒnʃəs] *adj* preocupado(a) por la propia imagen

imagery ['ımıdʒərı] *n* imágenes *fpl*

imaginable [ı'mædʒınəbəl] *adj* imaginable; **the best/worst thing i.** lo mejor/peor del mundo

imaginary [ı'mædʒınərı] *adj* imaginario(a), ficticio(a)

imagination [ımædʒı'neıʃən] *n* imaginación *f*; **to have no i.** no tener imaginación

imaginative [ı'mædʒınətıv] *adj* imaginativo(a)

imaginatively [ı'mædʒınətıvlı] *adv* imaginativamente, con imaginación

imagine [ı'mædʒın] *vt* (**a**) *(mentally picture)* imaginar, imaginarse; **to i. sb doing sth** imaginarse a alguien haciendo algo; **you're imagining things** son imaginaciones *or Am* fantasías tuyas; **you must have imagined it** debes de haberlo imaginado (**b**) *(suppose)* imaginar, imaginarse; **I i. that you must be very tired** (me) imagino que debes de estar muy cansado

imbalance [ım'bæləns] *n* desequilibrio *m*

imbecile ['ımbısi:l] *n* imbécil *mf*, idiota *mf*

imbibe [ım'baıb] *vt Formal (drink)* ingerir, beber; *Fig (knowledge, ideas)* absorber, embeber

imbue [ım'bju:] *vt Formal* **to i. sb with sth** inculcar algo a alguien; **to be imbued with sth** estar imbuido(a) de algo

IMF [aıe'mef] *n (abbr* **International Monetary Fund**) FMI *m*

imitate ['ımıteıt] *vt* imitar

imitation [ımı'teıʃən] *n (action, copy)* imitación *f*; **in i. of a** imitación de, imitando a; **i. jewelry** bisutería *f*; **i. leather** *Esp, Méx* piel *f* sintética, *Am salvo Méx* cuero *m* sintético

imitative ['ımıtətıv] *adj* imitativo(a)

imitator ['ımıteıtə(r)] *n* imitador(ora) *m,f*

immaculate [ı'mækjʊlət] *adj (very clean, tidy)* inmaculado(a); *(performance, rendition, taste)* impecable; *Rel* **the I. Conception** la Inmaculada Concepción

immaterial [ımə'tıərıəl] *adj* irrelevante; **that's quite i.** eso no tiene ninguna importancia

immature [ımə'tjʊə(r)] *adj* inmaduro(a)

immaturity [ımə'tjʊərıtı] *n* inmadurez *f*

immeasurable [ı'meʒərəbəl] *adj (size, distance)* inconmensurable; *(change, improvement)* incalculable, inmenso(a)

immeasurably [ı'meʒərəblı] *adv (long, high)* inmensamente, infinitamente; *(better, improved)* infinitamente, sumamente

immediacy [ı'mi:dıəsı] *n* inmediatez *f*, proximidad *f*

immediate [ı'mi:dıət] *adj* inmediato(a); **in the i. future** en un futuro inmediato; **the i. family** la familia más cercana; **in the i. vicinity** en las inmediaciones

immediately [ı'mi:dıətlı] **1** *adv* inmediatamente
2 *conj* **i. I saw her I knew…** en cuanto la vi supe…

immemorial [ımı'mɔ:rıəl] *adj* **from time i.** desde tiempo(s) inmemorial(es)

immense [ı'mens] *adj* inmenso(a)

immensely [ı'menslı] *adv* inmensamente

immensity [ı'mensıtı] *n* inmensidad *f*

immerse [ı'mɜ:s] *vt also Fig* sumergir (**in** en); **to i. oneself in sth** sumergirse en algo

immersion [ı'mɜ:ʃən] *n (in liquid)* inmersión *f*; *(in activity)* enfrascamiento *m*; **i. heater** calentador *m* de agua eléctrico

immigrant ['ımıgrənt] *n & adj* inmigrante *mf*

immigrate ['ımıgreıt] *vi* inmigrar

immigration [ımı'greıʃən] *n* inmigración *f*; **to go through i.** pasar por el control de pasaportes; **i. control** control *m* de pasaportes; **i. officer** agente *mf* de inmigración

imminent ['ımınənt] *adj* inminente

immobile [ı'məʊbaıl] *adj* inmóvil

immobility [ımə'bılıtı] *n* inmovilidad *f*

immobilize [ı'məʊbılaız] *vt* inmovilizar

immoderate [ı'mɒdərət] *adj* desmedido(a)

immodest [ı'mɒdıst] *adj (vain)* inmodesto(a), vanidoso(a); *(indecent)* deshonesto(a), impúdico(a)

immoral [ı'mɒrəl] *adj* inmoral; *Law* **i. earnings** ganancias *fpl* procedentes del proxenetismo

immorality [ımə'rælıtı] *n* inmoralidad *f*

immortal [ı'mɔ:təl] *adj & n* inmortal *mf*

immortality [ımɔ:'tælıtı] *n* inmortalidad *f*

immortalize [ı'mɔ:təlaız] *vt* inmortalizar

immovable [ı'mu:vəbəl] *adj (object)* inamovible, fijo(a); *Fig (opposition)* inflexible

immune [ı'mju:n] *adj* inmune; **to be i. to a disease** ser inmune a una enfermedad; *Fig* **i. to criticism** inmune a la crítica; *Med* **i. system** sistema *m* inmunológico

immunity [ı'mju:nıtı] *n Med* inmunidad *f*; *Law* **i. (from prosecution)** inmunidad *f* (procesal)

immunization [ımjʊnaı'zeıʃən] *n Med* inmunización *f*, vacunación *f*

immunize ['ımjʊnaız] *vt Med* inmunizar

immunodeficiency [ımjʊnəʊdə'fıʃənsı] *n* inmunodeficiencia *f*

immunology [ımjʊ'nɒlədʒı] *n* inmunología *f*

immutable [ı'mju:təbəl] *adj* inmutable

imp [ımp] *n* diablillo *m*

impact 1 *n* ['ımpækt] impacto *m*; **on i.** en el momento del impacto; *Fig* **to make an i. on sb/sth** causar (un) gran impacto en algo/alguien
2 *vt* [ım'pækt] *(collide with)* impactar en, chocar con; *(influence)* repercutir en

impacted [ım'pæktıd] *adj* **to have i. wisdom teeth** tener las muelas del juicio impactadas *or* incluidas

impair [ım'peə(r)] *vt (sight, hearing)* dañar, estropear; *(relations, chances)* perjudicar

impaired [ım'peəd] *adj* defectuoso(a)

impairment [ım'peəmənt] *n (in sight, hearing)* defecto *m*

impale [ım'peıl] *vt* clavar (**on** en)

impart [ım'pɑ:t] *vt Formal (heat, light)* desprender; *(quality)* conferir; *(knowledge)* impartir; *(news)* revelar

impartial [ım'pɑ:ʃəl] *adj* imparcial

impartiality [ımpɑ:ʃı'ælıtı] *n* imparcialidad *f*

impartially [ım'pɑ:ʃəlı] *adv* imparcialmente, de manera imparcial

impassable [ım'pɑ:səbəl] *adj (river, barrier)* infranqueable; *(road)* intransitable

impasse ['æmpɑ:s] *n* punto *m* muerto, callejón *m* sin salida

impassioned [ım'pæʃənd] *adj* apasionado(a)

impassive [ım'pæsıv] *adj* impasible, impertérrito(a)

impassively [ım'pæsıvlı] *adv* impasiblemente

impatience [ım'peıʃəns] *n* impaciencia *f*

impatient [ım'peıʃənt] *adj* impaciente; **to be i. (to do sth)** estar impaciente (por hacer algo); **to get i. (with sb)** impacientarse (con alguien); **to be i. for change** esperar con impaciencia el cambio

impatiently [ım'peıʃəntlı] *adv* impacientemente

impeach [ım'pi:tʃ] *vt Law* iniciar un proceso de destitución *or* un impeachment contra

impeachment [ɪmˈpiːtʃmənt] *n Law* proceso *m* de destitución, impeachment *m*

impeccable [ɪmˈpekəbəl] *adj* impecable

impede [ɪmˈpiːd] *vt* dificultar

impediment [ɪmˈpedɪmənt] *n* impedimento *m*; **(speech) i.** defecto *m* del habla, trastorno *m* del lenguaje

impel [ɪmˈpel] (*pt & pp* **impelled**) *vt* impulsar

impending [ɪmˈpendɪŋ] *adj* inminente

impenetrable [ɪmˈpenɪtrəbəl] *adj (defenses, mystery)* impenetrable

imperative [ɪmˈperətɪv] **1** *n Gram* imperativo *m*
  2 *adj* **(a)** *(need)* imperioso(a), acuciante; **it is i. that he should come** es imprescindible que venga **(b)** *(tone) & Gram* imperativo(a)

imperceptible [ɪmpəˈseptɪbəl] *adj* imperceptible

imperceptibly [ɪmpəˈseptɪblɪ] *adv* imperceptiblemente, de forma imperceptible

imperfect [ɪmˈpɜːfɪkt] **1** *n Gram* imperfecto *m*
  2 *adj (not perfect) & Gram* imperfecto(a)

imperfection [ɪmpəˈfekʃən] *n* imperfección *f*

imperfectly [ɪmˈpɜːfɪktlɪ] *adv* de un modo imperfecto

imperial [ɪmˈpɪərɪəl] *adj* **(a)** *(of empire)* imperial **(b)** *(weights and measures)* británico(a), imperial *(que utiliza pesos y medidas anglosajones la pulgada, la libra, el galón, etc.)*

imperialism [ɪmˈpɪərɪəlɪzəm] *n* imperialismo *m*

imperialist [ɪmˈpɪərɪəlɪst] *n & adj* imperialista *mf*

imperil [ɪmˈperɪl] *vt* poner en peligro

imperious [ɪmˈpɪərɪəs] *adj* imperioso(a), autoritario(a)

imperiously [ɪmˈpɪərɪəslɪ] *adv* imperiosamente

impermanent [ɪmˈpɜːmənənt] *adj* provisional, pasajero(a)

impermeable [ɪmˈpɜːmɪəbəl] *adj* impermeable

impersonal [ɪmˈpɜːsənəl] *adj* impersonal

impersonally [ɪmˈpɜːsənəlɪ] *adv* de forma impersonal

impersonate [ɪmˈpɜːsəneɪt] *vt (pretend to be)* hacerse pasar por; *(do impression of)* imitar, hacer una imitación de

impersonation [ɪmpɜːsəˈneɪʃən] *n (impression)* imitación *f*; **he was sent to prison for i. of a diplomat** fue encarcelado por hacerse pasar por un diplomático

impersonator [ɪmˈpɜːsəneɪtə(r)] *n (impostor)* impostor(ora) *m,f*; *(impressionist)* imitador(ora) *m,f*

impertinence [ɪmˈpɜːtɪnəns] *n* impertinencia *f*

impertinent [ɪmˈpɜːtɪnənt] *adj* impertinente

impertinently [ɪmˈpɜːtɪnəntlɪ] *adv* de un modo impertinente, impertinentemente

imperturbable [ɪmpəˈtɜːbəbəl] *adj* imperturbable

impervious [ɪmˈpɜːvɪəs] *adj (to water)* impermeable; *(to threats, persuasion)* insensible; **she is i. to reason** es imposible que razone

impetuous [ɪmˈpetjʊəs] *adj* impetuoso(a)

impetus [ˈɪmpɪtəs] *n* ímpetu *m*, impulso *m*

▸**impinge on** [ɪmˈpɪndʒ] *vt insep* influir en, repercutir en

impious [ˈɪmpɪəs] *adj* impío(a)

impish [ˈɪmpɪʃ] *adj* travieso(a)

implacable [ɪmˈplækəbəl] *adj* implacable

implant 1 *n* [ˈɪmplɑːnt] *Med* implante *m*
  2 *vt* [ɪmˈplɑːnt] **(a)** *Med* implantar **(b)** *(opinion, belief)* inculcar

implausible [ɪmˈplɔːzɪbəl] *adj* poco convincente

implement 1 *n* [ˈɪmplɪmənt] utensilio *m*
  2 *vt* [ˈɪmplɪment] *(plan, agreement, proposal)* poner en práctica, llevar a cabo

implementation [ɪmplɪmenˈteɪʃən] *n (of plan, agreement, proposal)* puesta *f* en práctica

implicate [ˈɪmplɪkeɪt] *vt* implicar

implication [ɪmplɪˈkeɪʃən] *n (effect)* consecuencia *f*, *Esp* implicación *f*, *Am* implicancia *f*; *(inference)* insinuación *f*; **by i.** indirectamente, implícitamente

implicit [ɪmˈplɪsɪt] *adj* implícito(a); **it was i. in his remarks** estaba implícito en sus comentarios; **i. faith** fe *f* inquebrantable

implied [ɪmˈplaɪd] *adj* implícito(a)

implore [ɪmˈplɔː(r)] *vt* implorar; **to i. sb to do sth** implorar a alguien que haga algo

imploring [ɪmˈplɔːrɪŋ] *adj* implorante

imply [ɪmˈplaɪ] *vt* **(a)** *(insinuate)* insinuar **(b)** *(involve)* implicar

impolite [ɪmpəˈlaɪt] *adj* maleducado(a)

impolitely [ɪmpəˈlaɪtlɪ] *adv* maleducadamente, con mala educación

impoliteness [ɪmpəˈlaɪtnɪs] *n* mala educación *f*

imponderable [ɪmˈpɒndərəbəl] **1** *n* (factor *m*) imponderable *m*
  2 *adj* imponderable

import 1 *n* [ˈɪmpɔːt] **(a)** *(item, activity)* importación *f*; **i. duty** derechos *mpl* de importación *or* de aduana **(b)** *Formal (importance)* significación *f*, importancia *f*
  2 *vt* [ɪmˈpɔːt] *(goods)* importar

importance [ɪmˈpɔːtəns] *n* importancia *f*; **it is of no great i.** no tiene mucha importancia; **to attach i. to sth** dar importancia a algo; **to be full of one's own i.** darse aires, estar pagado(a) de sí mismo(a)

important [ɪmˈpɔːtənt] *adj* importante; **it's not i.** no tiene importancia

importantly [ɪmˈpɔːtəntlɪ] *adv (speak)* dándose importancia; **but, more i....** pero, lo que es más importante...

importation [ɪmpɔːˈteɪʃən] *n (of goods)* importación *f*

importer [ɪmˈpɔːtə(r)] *n* importador(ora) *m,f*

import-export [ˈɪmpɔːtˈekspɔːt] *n* **i. (trade)** importación *f* y exportación, comercio *m* exterior

importune [ɪmˈpɔːtjuːn] *vt Formal (pester)* importunar

impose [ɪmˈpəʊz] *vt (silence, one's will, restrictions)* imponer **(on** a); **to i. a tax on sth** gravar algo con un impuesto; **to i. a fine on sb** poner *or* imponer a alguien una multa

▸**impose on, impose upon** *vt insep (take advantage of)* abusar de

imposing [ɪmˈpəʊzɪŋ] *adj* imponente

imposition [ɪmpəˈzɪʃən] *n* **(a)** *(of tax, fine)* imposición *f* **(b)** *(unfair demand)* abuso *m*

impossibility [ɪmpɒsɪˈbɪlɪtɪ] *n* imposibilidad *f*; **it's a physical i.** es físicamente imposible

impossible [ɪmˈpɒsɪbəl] **1** *n* **the i.** lo imposible; **to ask the i.** pedir lo imposible; **to attempt the i.** intentar lo imposible
  2 *adj* imposible; **an i. position/situation** una posición/ situación insostenible; **to make it i. for sb to do sth** imposibilitar a alguien hacer algo; **it's not i. that...** no es imposible que...; **it's i. to say when we'll finish** es imposible saber cuándo terminaremos; **you're i.!** ¡eres imposible!

impossibly [ɪmˈpɒsɪblɪ] *adv* increíblemente; **he's i. stupid** es increíblemente estúpido; **to behave i.** (com)portarse de forma insoportable

impostor [ɪmˈpɒstə(r)] *n* impostor(ora) *m,f*

impotence [ˈɪmpətəns] *n* impotencia *f*

impotent [ˈɪmpətənt] *adj* impotente

impound [ɪmˈpaʊnd] *vt Law* embargar; *(car)* trasladar al depósito municipal por infracción; **his car has been impounded** se le ha llevado el coche la grúa

impoverish [ɪmˈpɒvərɪʃ] *vt* empobrecer

impoverished [ɪmˈpɒvərɪʃd] *adj* empobrecido(a); **to be i.** estar empobrecido(a)

impoverishment [ɪmˈpɒvərɪʃmənt] *n* empobrecimiento *m*

impracticable [ɪmˈpræktɪkəbəl] *adj* irrealizable, impracticable

impractical [ɪmˈpræktɪkəl] *adj (person, suggestion)* poco práctico(a)

imprecise [ɪmprɪˈsaɪs] *adj* impreciso(a)

imprecision [ɪmprɪˈsɪʒən] *n* imprecisión *f*

impregnable [ɪmˈpregnəbəl] *adj (fortress)* inexpugnable; *Fig (argument)* incontestable

impregnate [ˈɪmpregneɪt] *vt* **(a)** *(fertilize)* fecundar **(b)** *(soak)* impregnar (**with** de)

impresario [ɪmpreˈsɑːrɪəʊ] *(pl* **impresarios)** *n* empresario(a) *m,f or* organizador(ora) *m,f* de espectáculos

impress [ɪmˈpres] *vt* **(a)** *(make an impression on)* impresionar; **she was impressed with** *or* **by it** aquello la impresionó; **to i. sb favorably/unfavorably** causar buena/mala impresión a alguien **(b)** *(emphasize to sb)* **to i. sth on sb** recalcarle a alguien la importancia de algo **(c)** *(imprint)* **to i. sth on sth** imprimir algo en algo; **to i. sth on sb's mind** imprimir algo en la mente de alguien

impression [ɪmˈpreʃən] *n* **(a)** *(effect)* impresión *f*; **to make a good/bad i.** dar buena/mala impresión; **to create a false i.** dar una impresión falsa; **to be under the i. that...** tener la impresión de que...; **to give the i. that...** dar la impresión de que... **(b)** *(imprint) (in wax, snow)* marca *f*, impresión *f* **(c)** *(of book)* impresión *f*, tirada *f* **(d)** *(imitation)* imitación *f*; **to do impressions** hacer imitaciones

impressionable [ɪmˈpreʃənəbəl] *adj* impresionable

impressionism [ɪmˈpreʃənɪzəm] *n Art* impresionismo *m*

impressionist [ɪmˈpreʃənɪst] **1** *n* **(a)** *Art* impresionista *mf* **(b)** *(impersonator)* imitador(ora) *m,f*
2 *adj Art* impresionista

impressionistic [ɪmpreʃəˈnɪstɪk] *adj* impresionista

impressive [ɪmˈpresɪv] *adj* impresionante

impressively [ɪmˈpresɪvlɪ] *adv* de un modo impresionante

imprint 1 *n* [ˈɪmprɪnt] **(a)** *(of seal)* marca *f*; *(of feet)* huella *f* **(b)** *(of publisher)* pie *m* de imprenta
2 *vt* [ɪmˈprɪnt] marcar (**on** en), grabar (**on** en); **her words were imprinted on my memory** sus palabras se me quedaron grabadas en la memoria

imprison [ɪmˈprɪzən] *vt* encarcelar

imprisonment [ɪmˈprɪzənmənt] *n* encarcelamiento *m*

improbability [ɪmprɒbəˈbɪlɪtɪ] *n* *(unlikelihood)* improbabilidad *f*; *(strangeness)* inverosimilitud *f*

improbable [ɪmˈprɒbəl] *adj (unlikely)* improbable; *(strange, unusual)* inverosímil

improbably [ɪmˈprɒbəlɪ] *adv* increíblemente; **i. enough, they turned out to be twin brothers** por inverosímil que parezca, resultó que eran hermanos gemelos

impromptu [ɪmˈprɒmptjuː] **1** *adj (speech, party)* improvisado(a)
2 *adv (unexpectedly)* de improviso; *(ad lib)* improvisadamente

improper [ɪmˈprɒpə(r)] *adj (use, purpose)* impropio(a), incorrecto(a); *(suggestion, behavior)* indecoroso(a); *Law* **i. practices** actuaciones *fpl* irregulares

improperly [ɪmˈprɒpəlɪ] *adv (incorrectly)* incorrectamente; *(inappropriately)* de manera impropia, indecorosamente

impropriety [ɪmprəˈpraɪətɪ] *n (inappropriateness)* impropiedad *f*, incorrección *f*; *(indecency)* falta *f* de decoro; *(unlawfulness)* irregularidad *f*

improve [ɪmˈpruːv] **1** *vt* mejorar; **to i. a property** hacer mejoras en un inmueble; **she was eager to i. her mind** estaba ansiosa por ampliar sus conocimientos
2 *vi* mejorar; **to i. with time** mejorar con el tiempo

▸**improve on, improve upon** *vt insep* mejorar, superar

improved [ɪmˈpruːvd] *adj (system, design)* mejorado(a); **he is much i.** ha mejorado mucho

improvement [ɪmˈpruːvmənt] *n (in situation, quality, behavior)* mejora *f*; *(in health)* mejoría *f*; **to be an i. on** ser mejor que; **there's room for i.** se puede mejorar; **to make improvements (to)** *(home)* hacer reformas (en)

improvident [ɪmˈprɒvɪdənt] *adj Formal* poco previsor(ora), imprudente

improvisation [ɪmprəvaɪˈzeɪʃən] *n* improvisación *f*

improvise [ˈɪmprəvaɪz] *vt & vi* improvisar

imprudent [ɪmˈpruːdənt] *adj* imprudente

impudence [ˈɪmpjʊdəns] *n* desvergüenza *f*, insolencia *f*

impudent [ˈɪmpjʊdənt] *adj* desvergonzado(a), insolente

impugn [ɪmˈpjuːn] *vt Formal* poner en tela de juicio, cuestionar

impulse [ˈɪmpʌls] *n* impulso *m*; **to do sth on i.** hacer algo guiado(a) por un impulso; **i. buying** compra *f* impulsiva

impulsive [ɪmˈpʌlsɪv] *adj* impulsivo(a)

impulsively [ɪmˈpʌlsɪvlɪ] *adv (to buy, act)* impulsivamente

impulsiveness [ɪmˈpʌlsɪvnɪs] *n* impulsividad *f*

impunity [ɪmˈpjuːnɪtɪ] *n* impunidad *f*; **with i.** impunemente

impure [ɪmˈpjʊə(r)] *adj* impuro(a)

impurity [ɪmˈpjʊrɪtɪ] *n* impureza *f*

impute [ɪmˈpjuːt] *vt Formal* **to i. sth to sb** imputar *or* achacar algo a alguien

in¹ *(abbr* **inch** *or* **inches)** pulgada *f (2,54 cm)*

in² [ɪn] **1** *prep* **(a)** *(with place)* en; **in Spain** en España; **to arrive in Spain** llegar a España; **it was cold in the bar** dentro del bar *or* en el bar hacía frío; **those records in the corner are mine** los discos del rincón son míos; **in the rain** bajo la lluvia; **in the sun** al sol; **in bed** en la cama; **in the hospital** en el hospital; **in here** aquí dentro; **in there** allí dentro
(b) *(with expressions of time)* en; **in 1927/April/spring** en 1927/abril/primavera; **he did it in three hours** lo hizo en tres horas; **he'll be here in three hours** llegará dentro de tres horas; **in the morning/afternoon** por la mañana/tarde; **at three o'clock in the afternoon** a las tres de la tarde; **for the first time in years** por primera vez en años *or* desde hace años; **I haven't seen her in years** hace años que no la veo
(c) *(expressing manner)* **in Spanish** en español; **to write in pen/pencil** escribir con bolígrafo/a lápiz; **in a loud/quiet voice** en voz alta/baja; **in this way** de este modo, de esta manera; **dressed in white** vestido(a) de blanco; **in horror/surprise** con horror/sorpresa
(d) *(expressing quantities, denominations, ratios)* **in twos** de dos en dos; **one in ten** uno de cada diez; **2 feet in length/height** dos pies de longitud/altura; **in small/large quantities** en pequeñas/grandes cantidades; **in dollars** en dólares; **he's in his forties** anda por los cuarenta; **the temperature was in the nineties** ≃ hacía (una temperatura de) treinta y tantos grados
(e) *(with gerund)* **he had no difficulty in doing it** no tuvo dificultad en hacerlo; **in saying this, I don't mean to imply that...** no quiero dar a entender con esto que...
(f) *(with field of activity)* **to be in insurance/marketing** dedicarse a los seguros/al marketing
(g) *(in phrases) Fam* **I didn't think she had it in her (to...)** no la creía capaz (de...)
2 *adv* **(a)** *(inside)* dentro; **to go in** entrar
(b) *(not out)* **is your mother in?** ¿está tu madre (en casa)?; **to stay in** quedarse en casa, no salir
(c) *(of train, plane)* **is the train in yet?** ¿ha llegado ya el tren?
(d) *(fashionable)* de moda; **miniskirts are in** se llevan las minifaldas
(e) *(idioms)* **she is in for a surprise** le espera una sorpresa; *Fam* **he's in for it** se va a enterar de lo que es bueno *or Esp* de lo que vale un peine; *Fam* **he's got it in for me** la *Esp* tiene tomada *or Méx* trae conmigo, *RP* se la agarró conmigo; **to be in on a plan** estar al corriente de un plan
3 *adj* **the in crowd** la gente selecta
4 *n* **the ins and outs** los pormenores
5 in that *conj* en el sentido de que

inability [ɪnəˈbɪlɪtɪ] *n* incapacidad *f* **(to do sth** para hacer algo)

inaccessibility [ɪnæksesɪˈbɪlɪtɪ] *n* inaccesibilidad *f*

inaccessible [ɪnækˈsesɪbəl] *adj* inaccesible

inaccuracy [ɪnˈækjʊrəsɪ] *n* inexactitud *f*, imprecisión *f*; **the report was full of inaccuracies** el informe estaba lleno de imprecisiones

inaccurate [ɪnˈækjʊrət] *adj* inexacto(a), impreciso(a)

inaction [ɪnˈækʃən] *n* pasividad *f*, inactividad *f*

inactive [ɪnˈæktɪv] *adj* inactivo(a)

inactivity [ɪnækˈtɪvɪtɪ] *n* inactividad *f*

inadequacy [ɪnˈædɪkwəsɪ] *n* (*of person*) incapacidad *f*; (*of explanation, measures*) insuficiencia *f*

inadequate [ɪnˈædɪkwət] *adj* (**a**) (*insufficient*) insuficiente (**b**) (*not capable*) incapaz, inepto(a); **I feel i.** no me siento competente, *Esp* siento que no doy la talla

inadequately [ɪnˈædɪkwətlɪ] *adv* insuficientemente

inadmissible [ɪnədˈmɪsɪbəl] *adj Law* (*evidence*) inadmisible

inadvertent [ɪnədˈvɜːtənt] *adj* fortuito(a), inintencionado(a)

inadvertently [ɪnədˈvɜːtəntlɪ] *adv* sin querer

inadvisability [ɪnədvaɪzəˈbɪlɪtɪ] *n* **she pointed out the i. of such a move** señaló lo poco aconsejable que era tal paso

inadvisable [ɪnədˈvaɪzəbəl] *adj* poco aconsejable

inalienable [ɪnˈeɪlɪənəbəl] *adj Formal* inalienable

inane [ɪˈneɪn] *adj* necio(a), estúpido(a)

inanimate [ɪnˈænɪmət] *adj* inanimado(a)

inanity [ɪˈnænɪtɪ] *n* necedad *f*, estupidez *f*

inapplicable [ɪnˈæplɪkəbəl] *adj* inaplicable (**to** a); **delete where i.** táchese lo que no proceda

inappropriate [ɪnəˈprəʊprɪət] *adj* (*behavior, remark*) inadecuado(a), improcedente; (*dress*) inadecuado(a), impropio(a); (*present, choice*) inapropiado(a); (*time, moment*) inoportuno(a)

inappropriately [ɪnəˈprəʊprɪətlɪ] *adv* de modo inadecuado; **to be i. dressed** no ir vestido de un modo adecuado; **i. timed** inoportuno(a)

inapt [ɪnˈæpt] *adj* inapropiado(a)

inarticulate [ɪnɑːˈtɪkjʊlɪt] *adj* (*sound*) inarticulado(a); **to be i.** (*person*) expresarse mal; **she was i. with rage** estaba tan *esp Esp* enfadada *or esp Am* enojada que no podía ni hablar

inasmuch as [ɪnəzˈmʌtʃəz] *conj Formal* por cuanto

inattention [ɪnəˈtenʃən] *n* falta *f* de atención

inattentive [ɪnəˈtentɪv] *adj* distraído(a); **to be i. to** no poner suficiente atención a *or* en

inattentively [ɪnəˈtentɪvlɪ] *adv* distraídamente, sin prestar atención

inaudible [ɪnˈɔːdɪbəl] *adj* inaudible

inaudibly [ɪnˈɔːdɪblɪ] *adv* de forma inaudible

inaugural [ɪˈnɔːgjʊrəl] *adj* inaugural

inaugurate [ɪˈnɔːgjʊreɪt] *vt* (*event, scheme*) inaugurar; **the President will be inaugurated in January** el presidente tomará posesión de su cargo en enero

inauguration [ɪnɔːgjʊˈreɪʃən] *n* (*of event, scheme*) inauguración *f*; (*of president*) toma *f* de posesión

inauspicious [ɪnɔːsˈpɪʃəs] *adj* (*circumstances*) desafortunado(a); (*start, moment*) aciago(a)

inauthentic [ɪnɔːˈθentɪk] *adj* no auténtico(a), falso(a)

in-between [ɪnbɪˈtwiːn] *adj* intermedio(a)

inborn [ˈɪnbɔːn] *adj* innato(a)

inbox [ˈɪnbɒks] *n Comptr* buzón *m* de entrada, *Am* casilla *f* de correo de entrada

inbred [ˈɪnˈbred] *adj* (**a**) (*animals, people*) endogámico(a) (**b**) (*innate*) innato(a)

Inc [ɪŋk] *adj Com* (*abbr* **Incorporated**) ≃ S.A.

Inca [ˈɪŋkə] **1** *n* inca *mf*
2 *adj* incaico(a), inca

incalculable [ɪnˈkælkjʊləbəl] *adj* incalculable

incandescent [ɪnkænˈdesənt] *adj* incandescente; *Fig* **to be i. with rage** estar rojo(a) de ira

incantation [ɪnkænˈteɪʃən] *n* conjuro *m*

incapable [ɪnˈkeɪpəbəl] *adj* incapaz (**of doing sth** de hacer algo); **she is i. of kindness/deceit** es incapaz de ser amable/engañar a nadie

incapacitate [ɪnkəˈpæsɪteɪt] *vt* incapacitar

incapacity [ɪnkəˈpæsɪtɪ] *n* incapacidad *f*

in-car [ˈɪnkɑː(r)] *adj* de automóvil; **an i. stereo** un autorradio

incarcerate [ɪnˈkɑːsəreɪt] *vt Formal* encarcelar, recluir

incarceration [ɪnkɑːsəˈreɪʃən] *n Formal* encarcelamiento *m*, reclusión *f*

incarnate [ɪnˈkɑːneɪt] *adj* personificado(a); **beauty i.** belleza personificada; **the devil i.** el diablo en persona

incarnation [ɪnkɑːˈneɪʃən] *n* encarnación *f*

incautious [ɪnˈkɔːʃəs] *adj* incauto(a)

incendiary [ɪnˈsendɪərɪ] **1** *n* (*arsonist*) incendiario(a) *m,f*; (*bomb*) bomba *f* incendiaria
2 *adj* (*bomb, device, remarks*) incendiario(a)

incense¹ [ˈɪnsens] *n* incienso *m*

incense² [ɪnˈsens] *vt* (*anger*) encolerizar, enfurecer

incensed [ɪnˈsenst] *adj* enfurecido(a); **to get** *or* **become i.** enfurecerse

incentive [ɪnˈsentɪv] *n* (*stimulus, payment*) incentivo *m*; **i. plan** plan *m* de incentivos

inception [ɪnˈsepʃən] *n* comienzo *m*, inicio *m*

incessant [ɪnˈsesənt] *adj* incesante, continuo(a)

incest [ˈɪnsest] *n* incesto *m*

incestuous [ɪnˈsestjʊəs] *adj* (*sexually*) incestuoso(a); *Fig* (*environment, group*) endogámico(a)

inch [ɪntʃ] *n* (**a**) pulgada *f* (*2,54 cm*); **i. by i.** palmo a palmo; **the car missed me by inches** el coche no me atropelló por cuestión de centímetros (**b**) (*idioms*) **I know every i. of the town** me conozco la ciudad como la palma de la mano; **he's every i. the gentleman** es todo un caballero; **to be within an i. of doing sth** estar en un tris de hacer algo; **she won't give an i.** no cederá ni un ápice; **give her an i. and she'll take a mile** dale la mano y se tomará el brazo

▸**inch along, inch forward** *vi* avanzar poco a poco

incidence [ˈɪnsɪdəns] *n* incidencia *f* (**of** de)

incident [ˈɪnsɪdənt] *n* incidente *m*

incidental [ɪnsɪˈdentəl] *adj* incidental, accesorio(a); **i. expenses** gastos *mpl* imprevistos; *Cin & Theat* **i. music** música *f* de acompañamiento

incidentally [ɪnsɪˈdentəlɪ] *adv* (*by the way*) por cierto

incinerate [ɪnˈsɪnəreɪt] *vt* incinerar

incineration [ɪnsɪnəˈreɪʃən] *n* incineración *f*

incinerator [ɪnˈsɪnəreɪtə(r)] *n* incineradora *f*

incipient [ɪnˈsɪpɪənt] *adj Formal* incipiente

incision [ɪnˈsɪʒən] *n* incisión *f*

incisive [ɪnˈsaɪsɪv] *adj* (*comment, analysis*) agudo(a), incisivo(a); (*mind*) sagaz, incisivo(a)

incisively [ɪnˈsaɪsɪvlɪ] *adv* (*comment*) con agudeza; (*think*) con sagacidad

incisor [ɪnˈsaɪzə(r)] *n* incisivo *m*

incite [ɪnˈsaɪt] *vt* incitar; **to i. sb to do sth** incitar a alguien a que haga algo

incitement [ɪnˈsaɪtmənt] *n* incitación *f*

incivility [ɪnsɪˈvɪlɪtɪ] *n Formal* descortesía *f*

incl (**a**) (*abbr* **including**) incl. (**b**) (*abbr* **inclusive**) incl.

inclement [ɪnˈklemənt] *adj Formal* (*weather*) inclemente

inclination [ɪnklɪˈneɪʃən] *n* (*desire, angle*) inclinación *f*; **to have no i. to do sth** no sentir ninguna inclinación por *or* a hacer algo; **by i.** por naturaleza

incline 1 *n* [ˈɪnklaɪn] (*slope*) cuesta *f*, pendiente *f*
2 *vt* [ɪnˈklaɪn] (**a**) (*motivate, cause*) inclinar; **her remarks don't i. me to be sympathetic** sus comentarios no me mueven a ser comprensivo (**b**) (*lean*) inclinar; **she inclined her head toward him** inclinó la cabeza hacia él (**c**) (*tend*) **to be inclined to do sth** tener tendencia *or* tender a hacer algo;

I'm inclined to agree with you soy de tu misma opinión
3 *vi* (**a**) *(lean)* inclinarse (**b**) *(tend)* **to i. to** *or* **toward** inclinarse a; **to i. to the belief that...** inclinarse a pensar que...

include [ɪn'kluːd] *vt* incluir; *(in letter)* adjuntar; **my name was not included on the list** mi nombre no figuraba en la lista; **the price does not i. accommodation** el alojamiento no está incluido en el precio

including [ɪn'kluːdɪŋ] *prep* contando, incluyendo; **not i.** sin contar, sin incluir; **$24.99 i. mailing and handling** 24,99 dólares incluyendo gastos de envío

inclusion [ɪn'kluːʒən] *n* inclusión *f*

inclusive [ɪn'kluːsɪv] *adj* **an i. price/sum** un precio/una cifra con todo incluido; **i. of** incluido(a), incluyendo; **i. of sales tax** impuesto de venta incluido; **from the 4th to the 12th of February i.** del 4 al 12 de febrero, ambos inclusive

incognito [ɪnkɒg'niːtəʊ] *adv* de incógnito

incoherence [ɪnkəʊ'hɪərəns] *n* incoherencia *f*

incoherent [ɪnkəʊ'hɪərənt] *adj* incoherente; **he was i. with rage** estaba tan furioso que le fallaban las palabras

incoherently [ɪnkəʊ'hɪərəntlɪ] *adv* incoherentemente

income ['ɪnkʌm] *n (of person) (from work)* ingresos *mpl*; *(from shares, investment)* rendimientos *mpl*, réditos *mpl*; *(from property)* renta *f*; *(in accounts)* ingresos *mpl*; **i. bracket** tramo *m* de renta; **i. tax** impuesto *m* sobre la renta

incoming ['ɪnkʌmɪŋ] *adj (government, president)* entrante; *(tide)* ascendente; **i. flights** vuelos *mpl* de llegada; **the i. missile** el misil que se aproximaba; **i. mail** correo *m* recibido; **i. calls** llamadas *fpl or Am* llamados *mpl* de fuera

incommensurate [ɪnkə'menʃərɪt] *adj* desproporcionado(a) (**with** con relación a, en relación con)

incommunicado [ɪnkəmjuːnɪ'kɑːdəʊ] *adv* **to be held i.** estar incomunicado(a)

in-company ['ɪnkʌmpənɪ] *adj* **i. training** fomación *f* en el lugar de trabajo

incomparable [ɪn'kɒmpərəbəl] *adj* incomparable

incomparably [ɪn'kɒmpərəblɪ] *adv* incomparablemente, infinitamente

incompatibility [ɪnkəmpætɪ'bɪlɪtɪ] *n (gen) & Comptr* incompatibilidad *f*; *(as grounds for divorce)* incompatibilidad *f* de caracteres

incompatible [ɪnkəm'pætɪbəl] *adj (gen) & Comptr* incompatible (**with** con)

incompetence [ɪn'kɒmpɪtəns] *n* incompetencia *f*

incompetent [ɪn'kɒmpɪtənt] *adj* incompetente

incomplete [ɪnkəm'pliːt] *adj* incompleto(a)

incompletely [ɪnkəm'pliːtlɪ] *adv* de forma incompleta

incomprehensible [ɪnkɒmprɪ'hensɪbəl] *adj* incomprensible

incomprehension [ɪnkɒmprɪ'henʃən] *n* incomprensión *f*

inconceivable [ɪnkən'siːvəbəl] *adj* inconcebible

inconclusive [ɪnkən'kluːsɪv] *adj (evidence, investigation)* no concluyente; **the meeting was i.** la reunión no sirvió para aclarar las cosas

incongruity [ɪnkɒn'gruːɪtɪ] *n* incongruencia *f*

incongruous [ɪn'kɒngrʊəs] *adj* incongruente

inconsequential [ɪnkɒnsɪ'kwenʃəl] *adj* trivial, intrascendente

inconsiderate [ɪnkən'sɪdərɪt] *adj* desconsiderado(a)

inconsiderately [ɪnkən'sɪdərɪtlɪ] *adv* desconsideradamente

inconsistency [ɪnkən'sɪstənsɪ] *n (lack of logic, illogical statement)* contradicción *f*, incongruencia *f*; *(uneven quality)* irregularidad *f*

inconsistent [ɪnkən'sɪstənt] *adj (contradictory)* contradictorio(a), incongruente; *(uneven)* irregular; **his words are i. with his conduct** sus palabras no están en consonancia con sus actos

inconsolable [ɪnkən'səʊləbəl] *adj* inconsolable, desconsolado(a)

inconsolably [ɪnkən'səʊləblɪ] *adv* desconsoladamente

inconspicuous [ɪnkən'spɪkjʊəs] *adj* discreto(a); **to be i.** pasar desapercibido(a)

incontestable [ɪnkən'testəbəl] *adj* incontestable, indiscutible

incontinence [ɪn'kɒntɪnəns] *n* incontinencia *f*

incontinent [ɪn'kɒntɪnənt] *adj* incontinente

incontrovertible [ɪnkɒntrə'vɜːtɪbəl] *adj* incontrovertible, indiscutible

inconvenience [ɪnkən'viːnjəns] **1** *n (difficulty)* molestia *f*; *(problem, drawback)* inconveniente *m*; **we apologize for any i.** disculpen las molestias; **to be an i. to sb** suponer una molestia para alguien
2 *vt* causar molestias a

inconvenient [ɪnkən'viːnjənt] *adj (time, request)* inoportuno(a); *(place)* mal situado(a); **I'm afraid 4:30 would be i.** (me temo que) las cuatro y media no me viene bien *or* no es buena hora

inconveniently [ɪnkən'viːnjəntlɪ] *adv* inoportunamente; **the shop is i. situated** la tienda no está en buen sitio *or* no queda muy a mano

incorporate [ɪn'kɔːpəreɪt] *vt* incorporar

incorporated [ɪn'kɔːpəreɪtɪd] *adj (company)* legalmente constituido(a) en sociedad anónima; **Bradley, Wells & Jones, I.** Bradley, Wells & Jones S.A.

incorrect [ɪnkə'rekt] *adj* incorrecto(a)

incorrectly [ɪnkə'rektlɪ] *adv* incorrectamente

incorrigible [ɪn'kɒrɪdʒɪbəl] *adj* incorregible

incorruptible [ɪnkə'rʌptɪbəl] *adj* incorruptible

increase 1 *n* ['ɪnkriːs] aumento *m* (**in** de); *(in price, temperature)* subida *f* (**in** de); **to be on the i.** ir en aumento
2 *vt* [ɪn'kriːs] aumentar; **to i. one's efforts** esforzarse más; **to i. one's speed** acelerar, aumentar la velocidad
3 *vi* aumentar; **to i. in price** subir de precio; **to i. in value** aumentar de valor

increasing [ɪn'kriːsɪŋ] *adj* creciente

increasingly [ɪn'kriːsɪŋlɪ] *adv* cada vez más

incredible [ɪn'kredɪbəl] *adj* (**a**) *(unbelievable)* increíble (**b**) *Fam (excellent)* increíble, extraordinario(a)

incredibly [ɪn'kredɪblɪ] *adv* increíblemente; *Fam* **i. good** increíblemente bueno(a)

incredulity [ɪnkrɪ'djuːlɪtɪ] *n* incredulidad *f*

incredulous [ɪn'kredjʊləs] *adj* incrédulo(a)

incredulously [ɪn'kredjʊləslɪ] *adv* con incredulidad

increment ['ɪnkrɪmənt] *n* incremento *m*

incriminate [ɪn'krɪmɪneɪt] *vt* incriminar

incriminating [ɪn'krɪmɪneɪtɪŋ] *adj* incriminador(ora)

incubate ['ɪnkjʊbeɪt] *vt* incubar

incubation [ɪnkjʊ'beɪʃən] *n* incubación *f*; *Med* **i. period** *(of disease)* período *m* de incubación

incubator ['ɪnkjʊbeɪtə(r)] *n (for eggs, babies)* incubadora *f*

inculcate ['ɪnkʌlkeɪt] *vt Formal* **to i. sth in sb, to i. sb with sth** inculcar algo en alguien

incumbent [ɪn'kʌmbənt] **1** *n* titular *mf*
2 *adj* **to be i. on sb to do sth** incumbir *or* corresponder a alguien hacer algo

incur [ɪn'kɜː(r)] *(pt & pp* **incurred**) *vt (blame, expense)* incurrir en; *(sb's anger)* provocar, incurrir en; *(debt)* contraer

incurable [ɪn'kjʊərəbəl] *adj (disease)* incurable; *(optimist, romantic)* incorregible

incurably [ɪn'kjʊərəblɪ] *adv* **to be i. ill** padecer una enfermedad incurable; **he's i. romantic/optimistic** es un romántico/optimista incorregible

incurious [ɪn'kjʊərɪəs] *adj* poco curioso(a)

incursion [ɪnˈkɜːʃən] n Formal incursión f

indebted [ɪnˈdetɪd] adj (financially) endeudado(a); **to be i. to sb** (financially) estar endeudado(a) con alguien; (for help, advice) estar en deuda con alguien

indebtedness [ɪnˈdetɪdnɪs] n (financial) endeudamiento m; (for help, advice) deuda f (**to** con), agradecimiento m (**to** a)

indecency [ɪnˈdiːsənsɪ] n indecencia f

indecent [ɪnˈdiːsənt] adj indecente, indecoroso(a); **to do sth with i. haste** apresurarse descaradamente a hacer algo; Law **i. assault** abusos mpl deshonestos; Law **i. exposure** exhibicionismo m

indecently [ɪnˈdiːsəntlɪ] adv indecentemente; **to be i. assaulted** ser víctima de abusos deshonestos

indecipherable [ɪndɪˈsaɪfərəbəl] adj indescifrable

indecision [ɪndɪˈsɪʒən] n indecisión f

indecisive [ɪndɪˈsaɪsɪv] adj (person) indeciso(a); (battle, election) no concluyente

indecisively [ɪndɪˈsaɪsɪvlɪ] adv (showing indecision) con indecisión; (inconclusively) sin una conclusión clara

indecorous [ɪnˈdekərəs] adj Formal indigno(a), indecoroso(a)

indeed [ɪnˈdiːd] adv (**a**) (used with "very") very happy **i.** contentísimo(a); **I am very glad i.** me alegro muchísimo; **thank you very much i.** muchísimas gracias (**b**) (in confirmation) efectivamente, ciertamente; **yes i.!** ¡ciertamente!; **i. not!** ¡por supuesto que no!; **you've been to Venice, haven't you? — i. I have!** has estado en Venecia, ¿verdad? — ¡ya lo creo! (**c**) (what is more) es más; **I think so, i. I am sure of it** creo que sí, es más, estoy seguro (**d**) (expressing ironic surprise) **have you i.?** ¿ah, sí?, ¿no me digas?

indefatigable [ɪndɪˈfætɪgəbəl] adj Formal infatigable, incansable

indefatigably [ɪndɪˈfætɪgəblɪ] adv Formal infatigablemente, incansablemente

indefensible [ɪndɪˈfensɪbəl] adj indefendible, injustificable

indefinable [ɪndɪˈfaɪnəbəl] adj indefinible

indefinite [ɪnˈdefɪnɪt] adj (**a**) (period of time, number) indefinido(a) (**b**) (ideas, promises) indefinido(a), vago(a) (**c**) Gram indeterminado(a), indefinido(a); **i. article** artículo m indeterminado or indefinido

indefinitely [ɪnˈdefɪnɪtlɪ] adv indefinidamente

indelible [ɪnˈdelɪbəl] adj also Fig indeleble, imborrable

indelibly [ɪnˈdelɪblɪ] adv also Fig de forma indeleble

indelicate [ɪnˈdelɪkət] adj poco delicado(a), indelicado(a)

indemnify [ɪnˈdemnɪfaɪ] vt **to i. sb for sth** (compensate) indemnizar a alguien por algo; **to i. sb against sth** (give security) asegurar a alguien contra algo

indemnity [ɪnˈdemnɪtɪ] n (guarantee) indemnidad f; (money) indemnización f

indent Typ **1** n [ˈɪndent] sangrado m
  2 vt [ɪnˈdent] sangrar

indentation [ɪndenˈteɪʃən] n (on edge) muesca f; (dent) abolladura f; Typ sangrado m

independence [ɪndɪˈpendəns] n independencia f; **I. Day** el Día de la Independencia

independent [ɪndɪˈpendənt] adj independiente; **to be i. of** ser independiente de

independently [ɪndɪˈpendəntlɪ] adv independientemente (**of** de)

in-depth [ˈɪnˈdepθ] adj a fondo, exhaustivo(a)

indescribable [ɪndɪsˈkraɪbəbəl] adj (pain, beauty) indescriptible

indescribably [ɪndɪsˈkraɪbəblɪ] adv indescriptiblemente

indestructible [ɪndɪsˈtrʌktəbəl] adj indestructible

indeterminate [ɪndɪˈtɜːmɪnət] adj indeterminado(a)

index [ˈɪndeks] **1** n (of book, in library, financial) índice m; **i. finger** (dedo m) índice m

  2 vt (**a**) (book) indizar (**b**) Fin (wages) ajustar según el IPC

India [ˈɪndɪə] n (la) India

Indian [ˈɪndɪən] **1** n (native of India) indio(a) m,f, hindú mf; (Native American) indio(a) m,f, Am indígena mf
  2 adj (from India) indio(a), hindú; (Native American) indio(a), Am indígena; **I. elephant** elefante m asiático; **I. file** fila f india; **I. giver: don't be an I. giver, Tommy!** ¡santa Rita, santa Rita, lo que se da no se quita, Tommy!; **the I. Ocean** el Océano Índico; **I. summer** (in northern hemisphere) veranillo m de San Martín; (in southern hemisphere) veranillo m de San Juan

indicate [ˈɪndɪkeɪt] vt (**a**) (point to) indicar, señalar (**b**) (show) demostrar (**c**) (state) manifestar

indication [ɪndɪˈkeɪʃən] n indicación f; **she gave no i. of her feelings** no manifestó sus sentimientos; **there is every i. that he was speaking the truth** todo parece indicar que dijo la verdad; **all the indications are that...** todo indica que...

indicative [ɪnˈdɪkətɪv] **1** n Gram indicativo m
  2 adj indicativo(a) (**of** de); Gram **i. mood** modo m indicativo

indicator [ˈɪndɪkeɪtə(r)] n (sign) indicador m; **economic indicators** indicadores mpl económicos

indict [ɪnˈdaɪt] vt Law acusar (**for** de)

indictable [ɪnˈdaɪtəbəl] adj Law **i. offense** delito m procesable

indictment [ɪnˈdaɪtmənt] n Law acusación f; Fig **it is an i. of our society** pone en tela de juicio a nuestra sociedad

indie [ˈɪndɪ] adj Fam (film, music, band) independiente, indie

indifference [ɪnˈdɪfərəns] n indiferencia f; **it's a matter of complete i. to me** es un asunto que me trae sin cuidado

indifferent [ɪnˈdɪfərənt] adj (**a**) (not interested) indiferente (**b**) (mediocre) mediocre, regular

indigenous [ɪnˈdɪdʒɪnəs] adj indígena (**to** de)

indigestible [ɪndɪˈdʒestɪbəl] adj indigerible

indigestion [ɪndɪˈdʒestʃən] n indigestión f

indignant [ɪnˈdɪgnənt] adj indignado(a); **to get i. about sth** indignarse por algo

indignation [ɪndɪgˈneɪʃən] n indignación f

indignity [ɪnˈdɪgnɪtɪ] n indignidad f

indigo [ˈɪndɪgəʊ] n & adj añil m

indirect [ɪndɪˈrekt] adj indirecto(a); Com **i. costs** costos or Esp costes mpl indirectos; Gram **i. object** complemento m or objeto m indirecto; Gram **i. speech** estilo m indirecto; **i. tax** impuesto m indirecto

indirectly [ɪndɪˈrektlɪ] adv indirectamente

indiscernible [ɪndɪˈsɜːnɪbəl] adj indiscernible

indiscipline [ɪnˈdɪsɪplɪn] n indisciplina f

indiscreet [ɪndɪsˈkriːt] adj indiscreto(a)

indiscreetly [ɪndɪsˈkriːtlɪ] adv con indiscreción

indiscretion [ɪndɪsˈkreʃən] n indiscreción f

indiscriminate [ɪndɪsˈkrɪmɪnɪt] adj indiscriminado(a); **to be i. in one's praise** hacer elogios indiscriminadamente

indispensable [ɪndɪsˈpensəbəl] adj indispensable, imprescindible

indisposed [ɪndɪsˈpəʊzd] adj Formal (ill) indispuesto(a); **to be i.** hallarse indispuesto

indisposition [ɪndɪspəˈzɪʃən] n Formal (illness) indisposición f

indisputable [ɪndɪsˈpjuːtəbəl] adj indiscutible

indissoluble [ɪndɪˈsɒljʊbəl] adj Formal indisoluble

indistinct [ɪndɪsˈtɪŋkt] adj indistinto(a), impreciso(a)

indistinctly [ɪndɪsˈtɪŋktlɪ] adv (to speak) ininteligiblemente; (to see, remember) de forma imprecisa or confusa

indistinguishable [ɪndɪsˈtɪŋgwɪʃəbəl] adj indistinguible (**from** de)

individual [ɪndɪˈvɪdjʊəl] **1** n (person) individuo m

2 adj (a) (of or for one person, thing) individual (b) (characteristic) personal (c) (single) individual; **the i. hospitals are responsible for running their own affairs** cada hospital lleva sus propios asuntos

individualism [ɪndɪˈvɪdjʊəlɪzəm] n individualismo m

individualist [ɪndɪˈvɪdjʊəlɪst] n individualista mf

individuality [ɪndɪvɪdjʊˈælɪtɪ] n individualidad f

individually [ɪndɪˈvɪdjʊəlɪ] adv individualmente; **he spoke to us all i.** nos habló a todos uno por uno

indivisible [ɪndɪˈvɪzɪbəl] adj indivisible

Indochina [ˈɪndəʊˈtʃaɪnə] n Indochina

indoctrinate [ɪnˈdɒktrɪneɪt] vt adoctrinar; **he indoctrinated his pupils with his prejudices** inculcó sus prejuicios a sus alumnos

indoctrination [ɪndɒktrɪˈneɪʃən] n adoctrinamiento m

indolence [ˈɪndələns] n Formal indolencia f

indolent [ˈɪndələnt] adj Formal indolente

indomitable [ɪnˈdɒmɪtəbəl] adj Formal indómito(a)

Indonesia [ɪndəʊˈniːzɪə] n Indonesia

Indonesian [ɪndəʊˈniːʒən] **1** n (a) (person) indonesio(a) m,f (b) (language) indonesio m
2 adj indonesio(a)

indoor [ˈɪndɔː(r)] adj (plant, photography) de interior; **i. track and field** atletismo m en pista cubierta; **i. (swimming) pool** piscina f or Méx alberca f or RP pileta f cubierta

indoors [ɪnˈdɔːz] adv dentro (de casa); **to go i.** entrar en casa

indorse = **endorse**

induce [ɪnˈdjuːs] vt (a) (persuade) inducir; **to i. sb to do sth** inducir a alguien a hacer algo (b) (cause) provocar; Med **to i. labor** provocar or inducir el parto

inducement [ɪnˈdjuːsmənt] n (incentive) aliciente m, incentivo m

induct [ɪnˈdʌkt] vt (a) (to job, rank) investir (b) Mil reclutar

induction [ɪnˈdʌkʃən] n (a) Med (of labor) inducción f (b) Mil incorporación f a filas

inductive [ɪnˈdʌktɪv] adj (reasoning) inductivo(a)

indulge [ɪnˈdʌldʒ] **1** vt consentir; **they indulged his every whim** le consentían todos los caprichos; **to i. oneself** darse un capricho or un gusto
2 vi **to i. in alcohol** darse a la bebida; **to i. in idle speculation** entregarse a especulaciones vanas

indulgence [ɪnˈdʌldʒəns] n indulgencia f; **I allow myself the occasional i.** de vez en cuando me permito algún lujo

indulgent [ɪnˈdʌldʒənt] adj indulgente (**to** con)

indulgently [ɪnˈdʌldʒəntlɪ] adv con indulgencia

industrial [ɪnˈdʌstrɪəl] adj industrial; **i. disease** enfermedad f laboral; **i. espionage** espionaje m industrial; **i. injury** accidente m laboral; **i. park** polígono m industrial; **i. relations** relaciones fpl laborales; Hist **the I. Revolution** la Revolución Industrial; **i. waste** residuos mpl industriales

industrialist [ɪnˈdʌstrɪəlɪst] n industrial mf

industrialization [ɪndʌstrɪəlaɪˈzeɪʃən] n industrialización f

industrialize [ɪnˈdʌstrɪəlaɪz] vt industrializar

industrialized [ɪnˈdʌstrɪəlaɪzd] adj industrializado(a)

industrious [ɪnˈdʌstrɪəs] adj (pupil, worker) aplicado(a); (research) minucioso(a)

industry [ˈɪndʌstrɪ] n (a) (economic) industria f; **heavy/light i.** industria pesada/ligera; **aircraft/mining/shipping i.** industria aeronáutica/minera/naviera; **tourist i.** sector m turístico; **entertainment i.** industria or sector del espectáculo (b) (hard work) aplicación f

inebriated [ɪnˈiːbrɪeɪtɪd] adj Formal ebrio(a); **to be i.** estar ebrio(a)

inedible [ɪnˈedɪbəl] adj (not edible) incomestible; (unpalatable) incomible

ineffable [ɪnˈefəbəl] adj Formal inefable, indescriptible

ineffective [ɪnɪˈfektɪv] adj ineficaz

ineffectual [ɪnɪˈfektjʊəl] adj (person) inepto(a); (measure) ineficaz

inefficiency [ɪnɪˈfɪʃənsɪ] n ineficiencia f

inefficient [ɪnɪˈfɪʃənt] adj ineficiente

inefficiently [ɪnɪˈfɪʃəntlɪ] adv de forma ineficiente

inelastic [ɪnɪˈlæstɪk] adj (material, principles) rígido(a)

inelegant [ɪnˈelɪgənt] adj poco elegante

inelegantly [ɪnˈelɪgəntlɪ] adv sin elegancia, con poca elegancia

ineligibility [ɪnelɪdʒəˈbɪlɪtɪ] n ausencia f del derecho (**for** a)

ineligible [ɪnˈelɪdʒɪbəl] adj **to be i. for sth** no tener derecho a algo

inept [ɪnˈept] adj (clumsy) inepto(a), incapaz; (inappropriate) inapropiado(a)

ineptitude [ɪnˈeptɪtjuːd] n ineptitud f

ineptly [ɪnˈeptlɪ] adv con bastante ineptitud

inequality [ɪnɪˈkwɒlɪtɪ] n desigualdad f

inequitable [ɪnˈekwɪtəbəl] adj Formal injusto(a), no equitativo(a)

inert [ɪˈnɜːt] adj (motionless) inmóvil; Chem **i. gas** gas m noble or inerte

inertia [ɪˈnɜːʃɪə] n inercia f

inescapable [ɪnɪˈskeɪpəbəl] adj inevitable, ineludible

inessential [ɪnɪˈsenʃəl] adj prescindible

inestimable [ɪnˈestɪməbəl] adj inestimable, inapreciable

inevitability [ɪnevɪtəˈbɪlɪtɪ] n inevitabilidad f

inevitable [ɪnˈevɪtəbəl] adj inevitable

inevitably [ɪnˈevɪtəblɪ] adv inevitablemente

inexact [ɪnɪgˈzækt] adj inexacto(a)

inexcusable [ɪnɪksˈkjuːzəbəl] adj inexcusable, injustificable

inexhaustible [ɪnegˈzɔːstɪbəl] adj inagotable

inexorable [ɪnˈeksərəbəl] adj inexorable

inexpensive [ɪnɪksˈpensɪv] adj económico(a), barato(a)

inexpensively [ɪnɪksˈpensɪvlɪ] adv (to live) con pocos gastos; (to buy, sell) a bajo precio; (to eat) barato

inexperience [ɪnɪksˈpɪərɪəns] n inexperiencia f

inexperienced [ɪnɪksˈpɪərɪənst] adj inexperto(a); **to the i. eye/ear** para el ojo/oído inexperto; **he's i. in handling staff** no tiene experiencia en cuestiones de personal

inexplicable [ɪnɪksˈplɪkəbəl] adj inexplicable

inexpressible [ɪnɪksˈpresɪbəl] adj indescriptible, indecible

inexpressive [ɪnɪksˈpresɪv] adj inexpresivo(a)

inextricably [ɪneksˈtrɪkəblɪ] adv inseparablemente

infallibility [ɪnfælɪˈbɪlɪtɪ] n infalibilidad f

infallible [ɪnˈfælɪbəl] adj infalible

infamous [ˈɪnfəməs] adj infame; **to be i. for sth** ser tristemente famoso(a) por algo

infamy [ˈɪnfəmɪ] n Formal infamia f

infancy [ˈɪnfənsɪ] n (childhood) infancia f; Fig **when medicine was still in its i.** cuando la medicina daba sus primeros pasos

infant [ˈɪnfənt] n (baby) bebé m, Andes guagua f, Andes, RP bebe(a) m; (small child) niño(a) m,f pequeño(a), Andes pelado(a) m,f; Med **i. mortality** mortalidad f infanti;

infanticide [ɪnˈfæntɪsaɪd] n infanticidio m

infantile [ˈɪnfəntaɪl] adj Pej pueril, infantil

infantry [ˈɪnfəntrɪ] n infantería f

infantryman [ˈɪnfəntrɪmən] n soldado m de infantería, infante m

infatuated [ɪnˈfætjʊeɪtɪd] adj **to be i. with** estar prendado(a) or encaprichado(a) de

infatuation [ɪnfætjʊˈeɪʃən] n encaprichamiento m (amoroso)

infect [ɪnˈfekt] vt (with disease) infectar; (with prejudice) emponzoñar; **to become infected** (wound) infectarse; **to i. sb with sth** contagiar algo a alguien; **her enthusiasm**

infected us all nos contagió a todos su entusiasmo

infection [ɪnˈfekʃən] n Med infección f

infectious [ɪnˈfekʃəs] adj (a) (disease) infeccioso(a) (b) (laughter, enthusiasm) contagioso(a)

infer [ɪnˈfɜː(r)] (pt & pp inferred) vt (deduce) inferir (from de), deducir (from de)

inference [ˈɪnfərəns] n inferencia f, deducción f; by i. por deducción

inferior [ɪnˈfɪərɪə(r)] 1 n to be sb's i. ser inferior a alguien
2 adj (in status, quality) inferior (to a)

inferiority [ɪnfɪərɪˈɒrɪtɪ] n inferioridad f; i. complex complejo m de inferioridad

infernal [ɪnˈfɜːnəl] adj (diabolical) infernal, diabólico(a); Fam that i. little man! ¡esa peste de hombre!

inferno [ɪnˈfɜːnəʊ] (pl infernos) n infierno m

infertile [ɪnˈfɜːtaɪl] adj (land) yermo(a); (person) estéril

infertility [ɪnfəˈtɪlɪtɪ] n esterilidad f

infest [ɪnˈfest] vt infestar; to be infested with or by sth estar infestado(a) de algo

infidelity [ɪnfɪˈdelɪtɪ] n infidelidad f

infield [ˈɪnfiːld] n Sport (in baseball) diamante m (interior)

infielder [ˈɪnfiːldə(r)] n Sport (in baseball) jugador m (del diamante) interior

infighting [ˈɪnfaɪtɪŋ] n lucha f interna

infiltrate [ˈɪnfɪltreɪt] 1 vt infiltrar; the organization had been infiltrated by spies se habían infiltrado espías en la organización
2 vi infiltrarse

infiltration [ɪnfɪlˈtreɪʃən] n infiltración f

infiltrator [ˈɪnfɪltreɪtə(r)] n infiltrado(a) m,f

infinite [ˈɪnfɪnɪt] 1 n the i. el infinito
2 adj infinito(a); Rel or Hum in his i. wisdom en su infinita sabiduría

infinitely [ˈɪnfɪnɪtlɪ] adv infinitamente

infinitesimal [ɪnfɪnɪˈtesɪməl] adj infinitesimal

infinitive [ɪnˈfɪnɪtɪv] n Gram infinitivo m; in the i. en infinitivo

infinity [ɪnˈfɪnɪtɪ] n infinito m

infirm [ɪnˈfɜːm] adj achacoso(a)

infirmary [ɪnˈfɜːmərɪ] n (hospital) hospital m, clínica f; (in school, prison) enfermería f

infirmity [ɪnˈfɜːmɪtɪ] n (weakness) debilidad f; the infirmities of old age los achaques de la edad

inflame [ɪnˈfleɪm] vt (a) (desire, curiosity) despertar; (crowd) enardecer (b) (of wound) to become inflamed inflamarse

inflammable [ɪnˈflæməbəl] adj (substance) inflamable; (situation) explosivo(a)

inflammation [ɪnfləˈmeɪʃən] n inflamación f

inflammatory [ɪnˈflæmətrɪ] adj (speech) incendiario(a)

inflatable [ɪnˈfleɪtəbəl] 1 n (rubber dinghy) barca f hinchable
2 adj hinchable

inflate [ɪnˈfleɪt] 1 vt (a) (tire) inflar, hinchar; (sail) hinchar (b) (prices) inflar
2 vi hincharse, inflarse

inflated [ɪnˈfleɪtɪd] adj (balloon, tire) inflado(a), hinchado(a); (prices, salary) desorbitado(a); she has an i. opinion of herself se cree mejor de lo que es

inflation [ɪnˈfleɪʃən] n Econ inflación f

inflationary [ɪnˈfleɪʃənrɪ] adj Econ inflacionista

inflation-proof [ɪnˈfleɪʃənpruːf] adj Econ protegido(a) contra la inflación

inflect [ɪnˈflekt] 1 vt (voice) modular
2 vi Gram (verb) conjugarse; (noun) declinarse

inflection [ɪnˈflekʃən] n (of word) flexión f, terminación f; (in voice) inflexión f

inflexibility [ɪnfleksɪˈbɪlɪtɪ] n rigidez f, inflexibilidad f

inflexible [ɪnˈfleksɪbəl] adj (material, principles) rígido(a), inflexible

inflict [ɪnˈflɪkt] vt (suffering, punishment, defeat) infligir (on a); he was inflicting himself on us teníamos que estar aguantando su presencia

in-flight [ˈɪnflaɪt] adj i. entertainment distracciones fpl ofrecidas durante el vuelo; i. meal comida f (servida) a bordo

influence [ˈɪnfluəns] 1 n influencia f; to be a good/bad i. on sb tener una buena/mala influencia en alguien; to have i. over/with sb tener influencia sobre/con alguien; a man of i. un hombre influyente; under the i. (of drink) bajo los efectos del alcohol
2 vt influir en, influenciar; he is easily influenced se deja influir fácilmente

influential [ɪnfluˈenʃəl] adj influyente

influenza [ɪnfluˈenzə] n gripe f, Col, Méx gripa f

influx [ˈɪnflʌks] n afluencia f

info [ˈɪnfəʊ] n Fam información f

infomercial [ˈɪnfəʊmɜːʃəl] n TV publirreportaje m

inform [ɪnˈfɔːm] 1 vt informar or CAm, Méx reportar (of/about de/sobre); keep me informed of what is happening manténme informado de lo que pase
2 vi to i. on sb delatar a alguien

informal [ɪnˈfɔːməl] adj (dress, manner) informal; (word, language) familiar; (meeting, talks) extraoficial, informal

informality [ɪnfɔːˈmælɪtɪ] n informalidad f

informally [ɪnˈfɔːməlɪ] adv (hold talks, inform) extraoficialmente; (dress, behave) informalmente, de manera informal

informant [ɪnˈfɔːmənt] n (for police) confidente mf; (for study) informante mf

information [ɪnfəˈmeɪʃən] n (a) (news, facts) información f; a piece of i. una información, un dato; for your i. para tu información; i. bureau oficina f de información; i. desk mostrador m de información (b) Comptr i. processing proceso m de datos; i. retrieval recuperación f de la información; i. science informática f; i. society sociedad f de la información; i. superhighway autopista f de la información; i. technology informática f (c) Tel información f, Am informaciones fpl

informative [ɪnˈfɔːmətɪv] adj informativo(a)

informed [ɪnˈfɔːmd] adj (person) informado(a); an i. guess/ decision una conjetura/decisión bien fundada

informer [ɪnˈfɔːmə(r)] n confidente mf

infotainment [ɪnfəʊˈteɪnmənt] n TV programas mpl informativos de entretenimiento

infra dig [ˈɪnfrəˈdɪg] adj Fam Old-fashioned ordinario(a), Esp cutre, Méx gacho(a)

infrared [ɪnfrəˈred] adj Phys infrarrojo(a)

infrastructure [ˈɪnfrəstrʌktʃə(r)] n infraestructura f

infrequent [ɪnˈfriːkwənt] adj infrecuente

infrequently [ɪnˈfriːkwəntlɪ] adv con poca frecuencia, raras veces

infringe [ɪnˈfrɪndʒ] vt (rule) infringir; (right) violar, vulnerar
▸**infringe on** vt insep infringir

infringement [ɪnˈfrɪndʒmənt] n (of rule, law) infracción f; (of right) violación f, vulneración f

infuriate [ɪnˈfjʊərɪeɪt] vt exasperar, enfurecer

infuriating [ɪnˈfjʊərɪeɪtɪŋ] adj exasperante

infuriatingly [ɪnˈfjʊərɪeɪtɪŋlɪ] adv she's an i. nice person es tan buena persona que resulta exasperante

infuse [ɪnˈfjuːz] vt infundir (into en)

infusion [ɪnˈfjuːʒən] n (a) (drink) infusión f (b) (of money, high spirits) inyección f

ingenious [ɪnˈdʒiːnɪəs] adj ingenioso(a)

ingeniously [ɪnˈdʒiːnɪəslɪ] adv ingeniosamente

ingenuity [ɪndʒɪˈnjuːɪtɪ] n ingenio m

ingenuous [ɪnˈdʒenjʊəs] *adj* ingenuo(a)

inglorious [ɪnˈglɔːrɪəs] *adj* vergonzoso(a)

ingot [ˈɪŋgət] *n* lingote *m*

ingrained [ɪnˈgreɪnd] *adj (dirt)* incrustado(a); *(prejudice, habit)* arraigado(a)

ingratiate [ɪnˈgreɪʃɪeɪt] *vt* **to i. oneself (with sb)** congraciarse (con alguien)

ingratiating [ɪnˈgreɪʃɪeɪtɪŋ] *adj* obsequioso(a)

ingratitude [ɪnˈgrætɪtjuːd] *n* ingratitud *f*

ingredient [ɪnˈgriːdɪənt] *n also Fig* ingrediente *m*; *Fig* **the missing i.** lo que falta

ingrown toenail [ˈɪngrəʊnˈtəʊneɪl] *n Med* uña *f* encarnada

inhabit [ɪnˈhæbɪt] *vt* habitar

inhabitable [ɪnˈhæbɪtəbəl] *adj* habitable

inhabitant [ɪnˈhæbɪtənt] *n* habitante *mf*

inhabited [ɪnˈhæbɪtɪd] *adj* habitado(a)

inhale [ɪnˈheɪl] **1** *vt (gas, fumes)* inhalar; *(cigarette smoke)* aspirar
2 *vi* inspirar; *(when smoking)* tragarse el humo

inhaler [ɪnˈheɪlə(r)] *n (for asthmatics)* inhalador *m*

inherent [ɪnˈherənt] *adj* inherente (**in** a)

inherit [ɪnˈherɪt] *vt* heredar (**from** de)

inheritance [ɪnˈherɪtəns] *n* herencia *f*; **i. tax** impuesto *m* sobre sucesiones

inhibit [ɪnˈhɪbɪt] *vt (progress, growth)* impedir, coartar; *(breathing)* inhibir; *(feeling, person)* cohibir, inhibir

inhibited [ɪnˈhɪbɪtɪd] *adj* cohibido(a)

inhibition [ɪnɪˈbɪʃən] *n* inhibición *f*; **to lose one's inhibitions** dejar de sentirse cohibido(a); **to have no inhibitions about doing sth** no sentir ninguna vergüenza *or CAm, Col, Ven* pena a la hora de hacer algo

inhospitable [ɪnhɒˈspɪtəbəl] *adj (person)* inhospitalario(a); *(town, climate)* inhóspito(a)

in-house [ˈɪnˈhaʊs] **1** *adj* **i. staff** personal *m* en plantilla; **i. training** formación *f* en el lugar de trabajo
2 *adv* **the work was done i.** el trabajo se hizo en la misma empresa

inhuman [ɪnˈhjuːmən] *adj* inhumano(a)

inhumane [ɪnhjuːˈmeɪn] *adj* inhumano(a)

inhumanity [ɪnhjuːˈmænɪtɪ] *n* falta *f* de humanidad

inimical [ɪˈnɪmɪkəl] *adj* adverso(a) (**to** a)

inimitable [ɪˈnɪmɪtəbəl] *adj* inimitable

iniquitous [ɪˈnɪkwɪtəs] *adj* inicuo(a)

iniquity [ɪˈnɪkwɪtɪ] *n* iniquidad *f*

initial [ɪˈnɪʃəl] **1** *n* inicial *f*; **initials** iniciales *fpl*
2 *adj* inicial
3 *vt* poner las iniciales en

initially [ɪˈnɪʃəlɪ] *adv* inicialmente

initiate [ɪˈnɪʃɪeɪt] *vt* (**a**) *Formal (begin)* iniciar; *Law* **to i. proceedings (against sb)** emprender una acción legal (contra alguien) (**b**) *(to secret society, gang)* iniciar (**into** en)

initiation [ɪnɪʃɪˈeɪʃən] *n* iniciación *f*; **i. ceremony** ceremonia *f* iniciática *or* de iniciación

initiative [ɪˈnɪʃətɪv] *n* iniciativa *f*; **to take the i.** tomar la iniciativa; **on one's own i.** por iniciativa propia; **she lacks i.** le falta iniciativa

initiator [ɪˈnɪʃɪeɪtə(r)] *n (of scheme, process)* iniciador(ora) *m,f*

inject [ɪnˈdʒekt] *vt (drug, money)* inyectar (**into** en); **to i. sb with a drug** inyectar un medicamento a alguien; *Fig* **to i. sb with enthusiasm** infundir entusiasmo a alguien; *Fig* **to i. new life into sth** infundir nueva vida a algo

injection [ɪnˈdʒekʃən] *n* inyección *f*; **to give sb an i.** poner una inyección a alguien

injudicious [ɪndʒʊˈdɪʃəs] *adj* imprudente, poco juicioso(a)

injunction [ɪnˈdʒʌŋkʃən] *n Law* requerimiento *m* judicial

injure [ˈɪndʒə(r)] *vt (person)* herir, lesionar; *(feelings)* herir; *(reputation, interests)* dañar, perjudicar; **to i. oneself** lesio-narse; **to i. one's leg** lesionarse una pierna

injured [ˈɪndʒəd] **1** *npl* **the i.** los heridos
2 *adj also Fig* herido(a); *(tone, voice)* resentido(a); *Law* **the i. party** la parte perjudicada

injurious [ɪnˈdʒʊrɪəs] *adj* perjudicial (**to** para)

injury [ˈɪndʒərɪ] *n (open wound)* herida *f*; *(broken bone, damaged muscle)* lesión *f*; *(harm)* lesiones *fpl*; **to do oneself an i.** *esp Esp* hacerse daño, *esp Am* lastimarse

injustice [ɪnˈdʒʌstɪs] *n* injusticia *f*; **you do her an i.** estás siendo injusto con ella

ink [ɪŋk] *n* tinta *f*; **i. pad** tampón *m*

ink-jet [ˈɪŋkdʒet] *adj Comptr* **i. printer** impresora *f* de chorro de tinta

inkling [ˈɪŋklɪŋ] *n* **to have an i. of sth** tener una ligera idea de algo; **she had no i. of what they were up to** no tenía ni idea de lo que estaban tramando

inkwell [ˈɪŋkwel] *n* tintero *m*

inky [ˈɪŋkɪ] *adj* (**a**) *(stained with ink)* manchado(a) de tinta (**b**) **i. (black)** negro(a) (como el carbón)

inlaid [ɪnˈleɪd] *adj (with wood)* taraceado(a); *(with jewels)* incrustado(a)

inland [ˈɪnlænd] **1** *adj* interior, del interior
2 *adv (travel)* al interior; *(live)* en el interior

in-laws [ˈɪnlɔːz] *npl* familia *f* política

inlet [ˈɪnlet] *n* (**a**) *(of sea)* ensenada *f* (**b**) *(of pipe, machine)* entrada *f*

in-line [ˈɪnlaɪn] *adj Aut* **i. engine** motor *m* de cilindros en línea; **i. skates** patines *mpl* en línea

inmate [ˈɪnmeɪt] *n (in prison)* recluso(a) *m,f*; *(in mental hospital)* paciente *mf*

inn [ɪn] *n* mesón *m*, posada *f*

innards [ˈɪnədz] *npl* tripas *fpl*

innate [ɪˈneɪt] *adj* innato(a)

innately [ɪˈneɪtlɪ] *adv* por naturaleza

inner [ˈɪnə(r)] *adj* (**a**) *(chamber, lining)* interior; **i. city** = área céntrica y degradada de una ciudad; *Anat* **i. ear** oído *m* interno; **i. tube** cámara *f* (de aire) (**b**) *(thought, feeling)* íntimo(a); **i. peace** paz *f* interior

innermost [ˈɪnəməʊst] *adj* **i. part** parte *f* más interior; **i. thoughts** pensamientos *mpl* más íntimos

inning [ˈɪnɪŋ] *n (in baseball)* turno *m* para batear, *Am* inning *m*

innkeeper [ˈɪnkiːpə(r)] *n* mesonero(a) *m,f*, posadero(a) *m,f*

innocence [ˈɪnəsəns] *n* inocencia *f*

innocent [ˈɪnəsənt] *adj (not guilty, naive)* inocente

innocently [ˈɪnəsəntlɪ] *adv* inocentemente, con inocencia

innocuous [ɪˈnɒkjʊəs] *adj* inocuo(a)

innovate [ˈɪnəveɪt] *vi* innovar

innovation [ɪnəˈveɪʃən] *n* innovación *f*

innovative [ˈɪnəveɪtɪv], **innovatory** [ˈɪnəveɪtərɪ] *adj* innova-dor(ora)

innovator [ˈɪnəveɪtə(r)] *n* innovador(ora) *m,f*

innovatory = **innovative**

innuendo [ɪnjʊˈendəʊ] *(pl* **innuendo(e)s**) *n* indirecta *f*, insinuación *f*; *(in jokes)* doble sentido *m*, juegos *mpl* de palabras *(sobre sexo)*

innumerable [ɪˈnjuːmərəbəl] *adj* innumerable

innumerate [ɪˈnjuːmərət] *adj* falto(a) de conocimientos de aritmética

inoculate [ɪˈnɒkjʊleɪt] *vt* inocular; **to i. sb with sth** inocularle algo a alguien; **to i. sb against sth** vacunar a alguien de algo

inoculation [ɪnɒkjʊˈleɪʃən] *n (action)* vacunación *f*

inoffensive [ɪnəˈfensɪv] *adj* inofensivo(a)

inoperable [ɪnˈɒpərəbəl] *adj Med* **to be i.** no ser operable

inoperative [ɪnˈɒpərətɪv] *adj (rule)* inoperante; **to be i.** *(machine)* no funcionar

inopportune [ɪnˈɒpətjuːn] *adj* inoportuno(a)

inordinate [ɪnˈɔːdɪnət] *adj* desmesurado(a)

inorganic [ɪnɔːˈgænɪk] *adj* inorgánico(a)

inpatient [ˈɪnpeɪʃənt] *n* paciente *mf* interno(a)

input [ˈɪnpʊt] **1** *n Elec* entrada *f*; *Comptr* input *m*, entrada *f* (de información); *(to project)* aportación *f*, aporte *m*
   2 *vt Comptr* **to i. data** introducir datos

inquest [ˈɪnkwest] *n Law* investigación *f*; *(in politics, business)* análisis *m inv*, evaluación *f*; **to hold an i.** *Law (of coroner)* determinar las causas de la muerte; *(in politics, business)* hacer un análisis

inquire, enquire [ɪnˈkwaɪə(r)] *vi* preguntar; **to i. as to** *or* **about...** informarse sobre...; **he inquired why I was there** me preguntó por qué estaba allí; **i. within** *(sign)* razón aquí

▶**inquire after, enquire after** *vt insep* preguntar por

▶**inquire into, enquire into** *vt insep* investigar, indagar

inquiring, enquiring [ɪnˈkwaɪrɪŋ] *adj (mind)* inquisitivo(a); *(look)* de interrogación

inquiry, enquiry [ɪnˈkwaɪrɪ] *n* **(a)** *(official investigation)* investigación *f* (oficial); **to hold an i. (into sth)** realizar una investigación (sobre algo) **(b)** *(request for information)* consulta *f*; **to make inquiries (about sth)** consultar *or* informarse (sobre algo); **i. desk** (mostrador *m* de) información *f*

inquisition [ɪnkwɪˈzɪʃən] *n Hist* **the Spanish I.** la (Santa) Inquisición

inquisitive [ɪnˈkwɪzɪtɪv] *adj (person)* curioso(a); *(mind)* inquisitivo(a); *(look)* de curiosidad

inquisitively [ɪnˈkwɪzɪtɪvlɪ] *adv* con curiosidad

inquisitiveness [ɪnˈkwɪzɪtɪvnɪs] *n* curiosidad *f*

inroads [ˈɪnrəʊdz] *npl* **I had to make i. into my savings** tuve que recurrir a mis propios ahorros; **to make i. into the market** penetrar en el mercado; **the Republicans had made i. into the Democrat vote** los republicanos se habían hecho con parte del voto demócrata

insane [ɪnˈseɪn] *adj (person)* demente, loco(a); *Fam (desire, scheme)* demencial, descabellado(a); **to be i.** *(person)* estar loco(a); **to go i.** trastornarse, volverse loco(a); **to drive sb i.** volver loco(a) a alguien; **to be i. with grief/jealousy** enloquecer de dolor/celos; **i. asylum** manicomio *m*

insanely [ɪnˈseɪnlɪ] *adv* disparatadamente; **i. jealous** loco(a) de celos

insanitary [ɪnˈsænɪtrɪ] *adj* antihigiénico(a)

insanity [ɪnˈsænɪtɪ] *n (of person)* demencia *f*, locura *f*; *Fam (of desire, scheme)* demencialidad *f*, locura *f*

insatiable [ɪnˈseɪʃəbəl] *adj* insaciable

inscribe [ɪnˈskraɪb] *vt (write, engrave)* inscribir

inscription [ɪnˈskrɪpʃən] *n (on stone, coin)* inscripción *f*; *(in book)* dedicatoria *f*

inscrutable [ɪnˈskruːtəbəl] *adj* inescrutable

insect [ˈɪnsekt] *n* insecto *m*; **i. bite** picadura *f* de insecto; **i. repellent** repelente *m* contra insectos

insecticide [ɪnˈsektɪsaɪd] *n* insecticida *m*

insecure [ɪnsɪˈkjʊə(r)] *adj (person)* inseguro(a); *(nail, scaffolding)* poco seguro(a)

insecurely [ɪnsɪˈkjʊəlɪ] *adv (not confidently)* de forma insegura; *(not safely)* de forma poco segura

insecurity [ɪnsɪˈkjʊərɪtɪ] *n* inseguridad *f*

insemination [ɪnsemɪˈneɪʃən] *n* inseminación *f*

insensible [ɪnˈsensɪbəl] *adj Formal* **(a)** *(unconscious)* inconsciente; **to be i.** estar inconsciente **(b)** *(unaware)* **to be i. of sth** no ser consciente de algo

insensitive [ɪnˈsensɪtɪv] *adj* insensible

insensitively [ɪnˈsensɪtɪvlɪ] *adv (tactlessly)* con muy poca sensibilidad

insensitivity [ɪnsensɪˈtɪvɪtɪ] *n* insensibilidad *f*

inseparable [ɪnˈsepərəbəl] *adj* inseparable

insert 1 *n* [ˈɪnsɜːt] *(in magazine)* encarte *m*
   2 *vt* [ɪnˈsɜːt] *(key, finger, coin)* introducir (**into** en); *(clause, advertisement)* insertar (**in** en)

insertion [ɪnˈsɜːʃən] *n* inserción *f*

inset [ˈɪnset] *n (in map, picture)* recuadro *m*

inshore [ɪnˈʃɔː(r)] **1** *adj (navigation)* costero(a); *(fishing)* de bajura
   2 *adv (to sail, blow)* hacia la costa

inside 1 *n* [ˈɪnsaɪd] **(a)** *(of house)* interior *m*; **on/from the i.** en/desde el interior **(b)** *Fam* **insides** *(internal organs)* tripas *fpl*
   2 *adj* [ˈɪnsaɪd] interior; **to have i. information/help** tener información/ayuda confidencial; **to know the i. story** conocer la historia de cerca *or* de primera mano; *Fam* **it must have been an i. job** *(robbery, fraud)* debe de haber sido un trabajo realizado desde dentro *or Am* adentro; **i. left/right** *(in soccer)* interior *m* izquierdo/derecho
   3 *adv* **(a)** *(to be, stay)* dentro, *Am* adentro; *(to look, run)* adentro; **they painted the house i. and out** pintaron la casa por dentro y por fuera; **come i.!** *(to guest)* ¡pasa!; *(to children playing outside)* ¡vamos para dentro! **(b)** *(within oneself)* **i. she was angry** por dentro estaba *esp Esp* enfadada *or esp Am* enojada **(c)** *Fam (in prison) Esp* en chirona, *Andes, Cuba, RP* en cana, *Méx, Ven* en bote
   4 *prep* [ɪnˈsaɪd] **(a)** *(place)* dentro de **(b)** *(with time)* **i. (of) a week/hour** en el espacio de una semana/hora
   5 inside out *adv* **his shirt is i. out** lleva la camisa del revés, *Am* dio vuelta la camiseta; *Fig* **to know sth i. out** saberse algo al dedillo

insider [ɪnˈsaɪdə(r)] *n* = persona que cuenta con información confidencial; *Fin* **i. dealing** *or* **trading** uso *m* de información privilegiada

insidious [ɪnˈsɪdɪəs] *adj* insidioso(a), larvado(a)

insight [ˈɪnsaɪt] *n* **(a)** *(perspicacity)* perspicacia *f*, penetración *f* **(b)** *(understanding)* idea *f* (**into** de); *(revealing comment)* revelación *f*, aclaración *f* (**into** sobre); **to get an i. into sth** hacerse una idea de algo

insignia [ɪnˈsɪgnɪə] *npl* insignias *fpl*

insignificance [ɪnsɪgˈnɪfɪkəns] *n* insignificancia *f*; **my problems pale into i. beside yours** mis problemas son insignificantes comparados con los tuyos

insignificant [ɪnsɪgˈnɪfɪkənt] *adj* insignificante

insincere [ɪnsɪnˈsɪə(r)] *adj* falso(a)

insincerely [ɪnsɪnˈsɪəlɪ] *adv* de un modo poco sincero

insincerity [ɪnsɪnˈserɪtɪ] *n* falsedad *f*, insinceridad *f*

insinuate [ɪnˈsɪnjʊeɪt] *vt (hint)* insinuar; **to i. oneself into sb's favor** ganarse arteramente el favor de alguien

insinuation [ɪnsɪnjʊˈeɪʃən] *n* insinuación *f*

insipid [ɪnˈsɪpɪd] *adj* insípido(a)

insist [ɪnˈsɪst] **1** *vt* **to i. that...** insistir en que...
   2 *vi* insistir; **to i. on sth** *(demand)* exigir algo; *(emphasize)* insistir en algo; **to i. on doing sth** insistir en hacer algo

insistence [ɪnˈsɪstəns] *n* insistencia *f*; **at her i.** ante su insistencia

insistent [ɪnˈsɪstənt] *adj (person, demand)* insistente; **to be i. about sth** insistir sobre *or* en algo

insistently [ɪnˈsɪstəntlɪ] *adv* insistentemente, con insistencia

insofar as [ˈɪnsəʊˈfɑːrəz] *adv* en la medida en que

insole [ˈɪnsəʊl] *n (of shoe)* plantilla *f*

insolence [ˈɪnsələns] *n* insolencia *f*

insolent [ˈɪnsələnt] *adj* insolente

insolently [ˈɪnsələntlɪ] *adv* insolentemente, de un modo insolente

insoluble [ɪnˈsɒljʊbəl] *adj* **(a)** *(substance)* insoluble, indisoluble **(b)** *(problem)* irresoluble

insolvency [ɪnˈsɒlvənsɪ] *n Fin* insolvencia *f*

insolvent [ɪnˈsɒlvənt] *adj Fin* insolvente

insomnia [ɪnˈsɒmnɪə] *n* insomnio *m*

insomniac [ɪnˈsɒmnɪæk] *n* insomne *mf*

inspect [ɪnˈspekt] *vt (passport, luggage, picture)* examinar, inspeccionar; *(school, factory)* inspeccionar; *(troops)* pasar revista a

inspection [ɪnˈspekʃən] *n (of passport, luggage, picture)* examen *m*, inspección *f*; *(of school, factory)* inspección *f*; *(of troops)* revista *f*; **on closer i.** tras un examen más detallado

inspector [ɪnˈspektə(r)] *n (of schools, factories)* inspector(ora) *m,f*

inspiration [ɪnspɪˈreɪʃən] *n* inspiración *f*; **to be an i. to sb** ser una fuente de inspiración para alguien; **to draw i. from sth** inspirarse en algo

inspirational [ɪnspɪˈreɪʃənəl] *adj* inspirador(ora)

inspire [ɪnˈspaɪə(r)] *vt* inspirar; **to i. sb to do sth** inspirar a alguien para hacer algo; **to i. confidence in sb, to i. sb with confidence** inspirar confianza a alguien

inspired [ɪnˈspaɪəd] *adj* inspirado(a)

inspiring [ɪnˈspaɪərɪŋ] *adj* estimulante

instability [ɪnstəˈbɪlɪtɪ] *n* inestabilidad *f*

install [ɪnˈstɔːl] *vt* instalar; **to i. sb in a post** colocar a alguien en un puesto; **to i. oneself in an armchair** instalarse en una butaca

installation [ɪnstəˈleɪʃən] *n* instalación *f*

installment [ɪnˈstɔːlmənt] *n (a) (part payment)* plazo *m*; **to pay by installments** pagar a plazos; *Com* **i. plan** compra *f* a plazos *or Am* en cuotas **(b)** *(of radio, TV program)* episodio *m*; **to publish sth in installments** publicar algo por entregas

instance [ˈɪnstəns] *n (example)* caso *m*; **for i.** por ejemplo; **in the first i.** en primer lugar

instant [ˈɪnstənt] **1** *n (moment)* instante *m*; **do it this i.!** ¡hazlo ahora mismo!; **not an i. too soon** justo a tiempo; **in an i.** en un instante; **the i. I saw him** en cuanto lo vi
2 *adj* instantáneo(a); *Comptr* **i. messaging** mensajería *f* instantánea; *TV* **i. replay** repetición *f* (a cámara lenta)

instantaneous [ɪnstənˈteɪnɪəs] *adj* instantáneo(a)

instantaneously [ɪnstənˈteɪnɪəslɪ] *adv* instantáneamente, al instante

instantly [ˈɪnstəntlɪ] *adv* al instante

instead [ɪnˈsted] *adv* **she couldn't come so he came i.** como ella no podía venir, vino él en su lugar; **I was going to buy the green one but I bought the blue one i.** iba a comprar el verde, pero al final compré el azul; **i. of** en vez de, en lugar de; **i. of doing sth** en lugar *or* vez de hacer algo

instep [ˈɪnstep] *n* empeine *m*

instigate [ˈɪnstɪɡeɪt] *vt (strike, unrest, violence)* instigar; *(inquiry, search, changes)* iniciar

instigation [ɪnstɪˈɡeɪʃən] *n (of strike, unrest, violence)* instigación *f*; **at sb's i.** a instancias de alguien

instigator [ˈɪnstɪɡeɪtə(r)] *n (of strike, unrest, violence)* instigador(ora) *m,f*; *(of inquiry, search, changes)* iniciador(ora) *m,f*

instill [ɪnˈstɪl] *(pt & pp* **instilled**) *vt* inculcar (**in** en)

instinct [ˈɪnstɪŋkt] *n* instinto *m*; **to have an i. for sth** tener buen olfato para algo

instinctive [ɪnˈstɪŋktɪv] *adj* instintivo(a)

institute [ˈɪnstɪtjuːt] **1** *n* instituto *m*
2 *vt (system, procedure)* instaurar; *(search)* emprender; *Law (inquiry)* emprender; *Law* **to i. proceedings (against sb)** emprender una acción legal (contra alguien)

institution [ɪnstɪˈtjuːʃən] *n (a) (organization)* institución *f*; *Fig* **to become a national i.** *(event, TV program)* convertirse en una institución (nacional) **(b)** *(mental hospital)* (hospital *m*) psiquiátrico *m*; *(old people's home)* residencia *f* de ancianos, asilo *m*; *(children's home)* centro *m* de menores

institutional [ɪnstɪˈtjuːʃənəl] *adj* institucional

institutionalize [ɪnstɪˈtjuːʃənəlaɪz] *vt (a) (put in a home)*

internar en un asilo/psiquiátrico; **to become institutionalized** desarrollar una fuerte dependencia institucional *(de la vida carcelaria, hospitalaria, etc.)* **(b)** *(turn into an institution)* institucionalizar; **institutionalized racism** racismo *m* institucionalizado

in-store [ˈɪnstɔː(r)] *adj Mktg* **i. advertising** publicidad *f* en el punto de venta; **i. promotion** promoción *f* en el punto de venta

instruct [ɪnˈstrʌkt] *vt* **(a)** *(teach)* instruir (**in** en) **(b)** *(command)* dar instrucciones a; **to i. sb to do sth** ordenar a alguien que haga algo

instruction [ɪnˈstrʌkʃən] *n* **(a)** *(training)* instrucción *f*, adiestramiento *m*; **we received i. in using the machines** nos enseñaron cómo utilizar las máquinas **(b)** **instructions** instrucciones *fpl*; **instructions for use** instrucciones de uso; **i. manual** manual *m* de instrucciones

instructive [ɪnˈstrʌktɪv] *adj* instructivo(a)

instructor [ɪnˈstrʌktə(r)] *n (teacher)* instructor(ora) *m,f*; *(college lecturer)* profesor(ora) *m,f* de universidad; **driving i.** profesor de autoescuela; **ski i.** monitor(ora) *m,f* de esquí

instrument [ˈɪnstrəmənt] *n Mus Med* instrumento *m*; *Av* **i. board** *or* **panel** tablero *m* de mandos, panel *m* de instrumentos

instrumental [ɪnstrəˈmentəl] **1** *n Mus* (pieza *f*) instrumental *m*
2 *adj* **(a)** fundamental; **she was i. in negotiating the agreement** desempeñó un papel fundamental en la negociación del acuerdo **(b)** *Mus* instrumental

instrumentalist [ɪnstrəˈmentəlɪst] *n (musician)* instrumentista *mf*

instrumentation [ɪnstrəmenˈteɪʃən] *n* instrumentación *f*

insubordinate [ɪnsəˈbɔːdɪnət] *adj* insubordinado(a)

insubordination [ɪnsəbɔːdɪˈneɪʃən] *n* insubordinación *f*

insubstantial [ɪnsəbˈstænʃəl] *adj (structure, argument)* endeble; *(meal)* poco sustancioso; *(book)* intrascendente, insustancial

insufferable [ɪnˈsʌfrəbəl] *adj* insufrible, insoportable

insufficient [ɪnsəˈfɪʃənt] *adj* insuficiente

insufficiently [ɪnsəˈfɪʃəntlɪ] *adv* insuficientemente

insular [ˈɪnsjʊlə(r)] *adj (people, views)* provinciano(a)

insulate [ˈɪnsjʊleɪt] *vt (wire, pipe)* aislar; *Fig* **insulated from the outside world** aislado(a) del mundo exterior

insulation [ɪnsjʊˈleɪʃən] *n* aislamiento *m*

insulator [ˈɪnsjʊleɪtə(r)] *n (material)* aislante *m*; *(device)* aislador *m*

insulin [ˈɪnsjʊlɪn] *n* insulina *f*

insult 1 *n* [ˈɪnsʌlt] *(words, action)* insulto *m*; **to add i. to injury…** para colmo…
2 *vt* [ɪnˈsʌlt] insultar

insulting [ɪnˈsʌltɪŋ] *adj* insultante

insuperable [ɪnˈsuːpərəbəl] *adj* insuperable, infranqueable

insurable [ɪnˈʃʊərəbl] *adj* asegurable

insurance [ɪnˈʃʊərəns] *n* seguro *m*; **to take out i.** hacerse un seguro, asegurarse; **i. broker** agente *mf* libre *or Am* corredor(ora) *m,f* de seguros; **i. claim** reclamación *f or Col, CSur* reclamo *m* al seguro; **i. company** aseguradora *f*, compañía *f* de seguros; **i. policy** póliza *f* de seguros; **i. premium** prima *f* (del seguro)

insure [ɪnˈʃʊə(r)] *vt* asegurar (**against** contra); **to i. one's life** hacerse un seguro de vida

insured [ɪnˈʃʊəd] *adj* asegurado(a); **to be i.** estar asegurado(a); **i. value** valor *m* asegurado

insurer [ɪnˈʃʊərə(r)] *n* asegurador(ora) *m,f*

insurgent [ɪnˈsɜːdʒənt] *n* insurgente *mf*

insurmountable [ɪnsəˈmaʊntəbəl] *adj* insuperable, insalvable

insurrection [ɪnsəˈrekʃən] *n* insurrección *f*

intact [ɪnˈtækt] *adj* intacto(a); **to be i.** estar intacto(a)

intake ['ɪnteɪk] n (of alcohol, calories) ingestión f; (of pupils, recruits) remesa f

intangible [ɪn'tændʒɪbəl] adj intangible

integer ['ɪntɪdʒə(r)] n Math (número m) entero m

integral ['ɪntɪgrəl] adj (essential) esencial; **to be** or **form an i. part of sth** formar parte integrante de algo; Math **i. calculus** cálculo m integral

integrate ['ɪntɪgreɪt] **1** vt integrar (**into** en)
2 vi integrarse

integrated ['ɪntɪgreɪtɪd] adj integrado(a)

integration [ɪntɪ'greɪʃən] n integración f

integrity [ɪn'tegrɪtɪ] n integridad f

intellect ['ɪntɪlekt] n intelecto m

intellectual [ɪntɪ'lektjʊəl] n & adj intelectual mf

intellectually [ɪntɪ'lektjʊəlɪ] adv intelectualmente, desde el punto de vista intelectual

intelligence [ɪn'telɪdʒəns] n (a) (faculty) inteligencia f; Psy **i. quotient** cociente m intelectual; **i. test** test m de inteligencia (b) (information) información f secreta; **i. officer** agente mf de los servicios de inteligencia; **i. service** servicio m de inteligencia

intelligent [ɪn'telɪdʒənt] adj inteligente

intelligentsia [ɪntelɪ'dʒensɪə] n intelectualidad f

intelligible [ɪn'telɪdʒɪbəl] adj inteligible

intemperate [ɪn'tempərət] adj (climate) riguroso(a); (person, behavior) inmoderado(a)

intend [ɪn'tend] vt **to i. to do sth** tener la intención de hacer algo; **to i. sth for sb** (plan to give to) tener pensado dar algo a alguien; **those comments were intended for you** esos comentarios iban por ti or destinados a ti; **was that intended?** ¿ha sido a propósito?; **it was intended as a joke/a compliment** pretendía ser una broma/un cumplido; **I told her to do it, and I i. to be obeyed** le dije que lo hiciera sin rechistar; **I didn't i. her to see it yet** no quería que ella lo viera todavía; **a movie intended for children** una película para niños or dirigida a los niños

intended [ɪn'tendɪd] **1** n Old-fashioned or Hum (future spouse) prometido(a) m,f
2 adj (consequence, outcome) deseado(a); (insult, mistake) intencionado(a)

intense [ɪn'tens] adj intenso(a); (person) muy serio(a)

intensely [ɪn'tenslɪ] adv (strongly, deeply) intensamente; (highly, extremely) enormemente

intensifier [ɪn'tensɪfaɪə(r)] n Gram intensivo m, intensificador m

intensify [ɪn'tensɪfaɪ] **1** vt intensificar
2 vi intensificarse

intensity [ɪn'tensɪtɪ] n intensidad f

intensive [ɪn'tensɪv] adj intensivo(a); Med **i. care** cuidados mpl intensivos, Méx, RP terapia f intensiva

intensively [ɪn'tensɪvlɪ] adv intensivamente

intent [ɪn'tent] **1** n intención f; **to all intents and purposes** a todos los efectos
2 adj (look, expression) intenso(a), concentrado(a); **to be i. on doing sth** estar empeñado(a) en hacer algo

intention [ɪn'tenʃən] n intención f; **to have no i. of doing sth** no tener ninguna intención de hacer algo; **to have every i. of doing sth** tener toda la intención de hacer algo

intentional [ɪn'tenʃənəl] adj intencionado(a)

intentionally [ɪn'tenʃənəlɪ] adv adrede, a propósito

intently [ɪn'tentlɪ] adv (to listen) atentamente; (to look at) intensamente

inter [ɪn'tɜ:(r)] (pt & pp **interred**) vt enterrar

interact [ɪntə'rækt] vi (people) interrelacionarse (**with** con); (factors, events) combinarse (**with** con); Comptr interactuar (**with** con)

interaction [ɪntə'rækʃən] n interacción f

interactive [ɪntə'ræktɪv] adj interactivo(a); Comptr **i. CD** CD m interactivo; **i. television** televisión f interactiva; Comptr **i. video** vídeo m or Am video m interactivo

interbank ['ɪntəbæŋk] adj interbancario(a)

intercede [ɪntə'si:d] vi interceder (**with/for** ante/por)

intercept [ɪntə'sept] vt interceptar

interception [ɪntə'sepʃən] n interceptación f

intercession [ɪntə'seʃən] n intercesión f

interchange 1 n ['ɪntətʃeɪndʒ] (exchange) intercambio m; (on freeway) enlace m, nudo m de carreteras
2 vt [ɪntə'tʃeɪndʒ] intercambiar

interchangeable [ɪntə'tʃeɪndʒəbəl] adj intercambiable

intercity ['ɪntə'sɪtɪ] adj Esp intercity m, Am interurbano m

intercom ['ɪntəkɒm] n interfono m

intercommunicate [ɪntəkə'mju:nɪkeɪt] vi comunicarse

interconnect [ɪntəkə'nekt] vt interconectar

intercontinental [ɪntəkɒntɪ'nentəl] adj intercontinental; Mil **i. ballistic missile** misil m balístico intercontinental

intercourse ['ɪntəkɔ:s] n (a) (sexual) **i.** coito m, cópula f (b) Formal (dealings) trato m; **social i.** relaciones fpl sociales

interdependence ['ɪntədɪ'pendəns] n interdependencia f

interdependent ['ɪntədɪ'pendənt] adj interdependiente

interest ['ɪntrest] **1** n (a) (curiosity) interés m; (hobby) afición f; **of i.** de interés; **to be of i. to sb** interesar a alguien; **to take an i. in sth** interesarse por algo; **to lose i. (in sth)** perder el interés (por algo) (b) (stake) interés m; **to have an i. in sth** (in general) tener interés en or por algo; Fin tener intereses or participación en algo (c) (benefit) **to act in sb's interests** obrar en interés de alguien; **the public i.** el interés general or público; **it's in my i. to do it** me interesa hacerlo; **in the interests of...** en pro de... (d) Fin (on investment) interés m; **i. rate** tipo m or Am tasa f de interés
2 vt interesar; **to i. sb in sth** interesar a alguien en algo; **to be interested in sth** estar interesado(a) en algo, interesarse por algo

interested ['ɪntrestɪd] adj interesado(a)

interest-free ['ɪntrest'fri:] adj (loan, credit) sin intereses

interesting ['ɪntrestɪŋ] adj interesante

interestingly ['ɪntrestɪŋlɪ] adv de manera or forma interesante; **i. enough** curiosamente

interface ['ɪntəfeɪs] n Comptr interface m, interfaz f

interfere [ɪntə'fɪə(r)] vi interferir, entrometerse (**in/with** en); **he's always interfering** siempre está metiéndose donde no le importa; **don't i. with my papers** no enredes en mis papeles; **to i. with sth** (hinder) interferir en or afectar a algo

interference [ɪntə'fɪərəns] n (a) (meddling) intromisión f (b) Rad & TV interferencia f

interfering [ɪntə'fɪərɪŋ] adj entrometido(a)

interim ['ɪntərɪm] **1** n **in the i.** entre tanto, en el ínterin
2 adj (agreement, report) provisional, Am provisorio

interior [ɪn'tɪərɪə(r)] **1** n interior m
2 adj interior; **i. decorator** interiorista mf, Am decorador(ora) m,f de interiores; **i. design** interiorismo m, decoración f de interiores; **Secretary/Department of the I.** Ministro(a)/Ministerio del Interior

interject [ɪntə'dʒekt] vt interponer

interjection [ɪntə'dʒekʃən] n interjección f

interlace [ɪntə'leɪs] vt (entwine) entrelazar; (mix, intersperse) intercalar

interlocking [ɪntə'lɒkɪŋ] adj interconectado(a)

interlocutor [ɪntəlɒ'kju:tə(r)] n Formal interlocutor(ora) m,f

interloper ['ɪntələʊpə(r)] n intruso(a) m,f

interlude ['ɪntəlu:d] n Theat intermedio m; Fig intervalo m

intermarriage [ɪntə'mærɪdʒ] n matrimonio m mixto (entre personas de distintas razas, religiones o comunidades)

intermarry [ɪntə'mærɪ] vi casarse (entre sí) (personas de diferente raza, religión o comunidad); **Catholics and Protestants rarely intermarried** católicos y protestantes raras veces se casaban entre sí

intermediary [ɪntəˈmiːdɪərɪ] n intermediario(a) m,f, mediador(ora) m,f

intermediate [ɪntəˈmiːdɪət] adj intermedio(a)

interment [ɪnˈtɜːmənt] n Formal sepelio m

interminable [ɪnˈtɜːmɪnəbəl] adj interminable

interminably [ɪnˈtɜːmɪnəblɪ] adv interminablemente

intermingle [ɪntəˈmɪŋɡəl] **1** vt mezclar (**with** con)
2 vi mezclarse (**with** con)

intermission [ɪntəˈmɪʃən] n Cin Theat intermedio m, descanso m

intermittent [ɪntəˈmɪtənt] adj intermitente

intermittently [ɪntəˈmɪtəntlɪ] adv de forma intermitente, a intervalos

intern 1 n [ˈɪntɜːn] Med médico(a) m,f interno(a) residente; Com (on work placement) becario(a) m,f
2 vt [ɪnˈtɜːn] recluir

internal [ɪnˈtɜːnəl] adj interno(a); Fin **i. audit** auditoría f interna; Tech **i. combustion engine** motor m de combustión interna; **i. medicine** medicina f interna; **the I. Revenue Service** ≃ Hacienda, Esp ≃ la Agencia Tributaria

internalize [ɪnˈtɜːnəlaɪz] vt interiorizar, Am internalizar

internally [ɪnˈtɜːnəlɪ] adv internamente; **not to be taken i.** (on medicine container) para uso externo

international [ɪntəˈnæʃənəl] **1** n Sport (player) (jugador(ora) m,f) internacional mf; (match) partido m internacional
2 adj internacional; **I. Court of Justice** Tribunal m Internacional de Justicia; **I. Criminal Court** Corte f or Tribunal m Penal International; **I. Date Line** línea f de cambio de fecha; **i. law** derecho m internacional; Fin **I. Monetary Fund** Fondo m Monetario Internacional

internationalize [ɪntəˈnæʃənəlaɪz] vt internacionalizar; **to become internationalized** internacionalizarse

internee [ɪntɜːˈniː] n recluso(a) m,f

Internet [ˈɪntənet] n Comptr **the I.** Internet; **I. address** dirección f de Internet; **I. banking** banca f por Internet; **I. connection** conexión f a Internet

internment [ɪnˈtɜːnmənt] n reclusión f

internship [ˈɪntɜːnʃɪp] n Med Esp ≃ MIR m, Am internado m

interpersonal [ɪntəˈpɜːsənəl] adj interpersonal

interplay [ˈɪntəpleɪ] n interacción f (**of** de)

Interpol [ˈɪntəpɒl] n Interpol f

interpolate [ɪnˈtɜːpəleɪt] vt interpolar

interpose [ɪntəˈpəʊz] vt interponer (**between** entre)

interpret [ɪnˈtɜːprɪt] vt & vi interpretar

interpretation [ɪntəprɪˈteɪʃən] n interpretación f

interpretative [ɪnˈtɜːprɪtətɪv], **interpretive** [ɪnˈtɜːprɪtɪv] adj interpretativo(a); **i. center** centro m de interpretación

interpreter [ɪnˈtɜːprɪtə(r)] n intérprete mf

interpretive = **interpretative**

interracial [ɪntəˈreɪʃəl] adj interracial

interrelated [ɪntərɪˈleɪtɪd] adj interrelacionado(a)

interrogate [ɪnˈterəɡeɪt] vt interrogar

interrogation [ɪnterəˈɡeɪʃən] n interrogatorio m

interrogative [ɪnteˈrɒɡətɪv] **1** n Gram (voice) forma f interrogativa; (word) interrogativo m
2 adj (look, tone) & Gram interrogativo(a)

interrogator [ɪnˈterəɡeɪtə(r)] n interrogador(ora) m,f

interrogatory [ɪntəˈrɒɡətərɪ] adj interrogativo(a)

interrupt [ɪntəˈrʌpt] vt & vi interrumpir

interruption [ɪntəˈrʌpʃən] n interrupción f

intersect [ɪntəˈsekt] **1** vt (of street) cruzar, atravesar
2 vi cruzarse

intersection [ɪntəˈsekʃən] n (of roads) cruce m, intersección f

intersperse [ɪntəˈspɜːs] vt **to be interspersed with sth** estar salpicado(a) de algo

interstate [ɪntəˈsteɪt] **1** n autopista f (que une un estado con otro)
2 adj entre estados

intertwine [ɪntəˈtwaɪn] vt entrelazar (**with** con), entretejer (**with** con); **his fate seemed to be intertwined with hers** sus destinos parecían estar entrelazados

interval [ˈɪntəvəl] n (of time, space) & Mus intervalo m; **at regular intervals** a intervalos regulares; **rainy weather with sunny intervals** tiempo lluvioso con intervalos soleados

intervene [ɪntəˈviːn] vi (person) intervenir; (event) sobrevenir

intervening [ɪntəˈviːnɪŋ] adj (years, months) mediante, transcurrido(a); (miles) intermedio(a); **in the i. period** en el ínterin

intervention [ɪntəˈvenʃən] n intervención f

interview [ˈɪntəvjuː] **1** n entrevista f
2 vt entrevistar

interviewee [ɪntəvjuːˈiː] n entrevistado(a) m,f

interviewer [ˈɪntəvjuːə(r)] n entrevistador(ora) m,f

intestate [ɪnˈtesteɪt] adv Law **to die i.** morir intestado(a)

intestinal [ɪntesˈtaɪnəl] adj intestinal

intestine [ɪnˈtestaɪn] n Anat intestino m; **large/small i.** intestino grueso/delgado

intimacy [ˈɪntɪməsɪ] n (of relationship, atmosphere) intimidad f; Euph (sexual) relaciones fpl (sexuales)

intimate 1 n [ˈɪntɪmət] (close friend, associate) íntimo(a) m,f, allegado(a) m,f
2 adj [ˈɪntɪmət] (friend, restaurant) íntimo(a); **to be i. with sb** (friendly) ser amigo(a) íntimo(a) de alguien; Euph (sexually) tener relaciones (sexuales) con alguien; **to have an i. knowledge of sth** conocer algo a fondo
3 vt [ˈɪntɪmeɪt] Formal dar a entender, sugerir

intimately [ˈɪntɪmətlɪ] adv íntimamente

intimidate [ɪnˈtɪmɪdeɪt] vt intimidar; **to i. sb into doing sth** intimidar a alguien para que haga algo

intimidating [ɪnˈtɪmɪdeɪtɪŋ] adj (experience) imponente, aterrador(ora); (person) avasallador(ora)

intimidation [ɪntɪmɪˈdeɪʃən] n intimidación f

into [ˈɪntʊ] prep (**a**) (with motion, direction) en, dentro de; **to go i. a house** entrar en una casa or Am a una casa; **to get i. a car** subirse a un coche; **she fell i. the water** cayó al agua; **the car crashed i. a tree** el coche chocó contra un árbol
(**b**) (with change) en; **to change i. sth** convertirse en algo; **to grow i. a man** hacerse un hombre; **to translate sth i. English** traducir algo al inglés; **to break sth i. pieces** romper algo en pedazos
(**c**) (regarding) en relación con; **an inquiry i. the accident** una investigación sobre el accidente
(**d**) (with time) **rain continued to fall well i. the summer** siguió lloviendo hasta bien entrado el verano
(**e**) Math **three i. six goes twice** seis entre tres cabe a dos
(**f**) Fam **she's really i. folk music** le gusta or Esp va mucho la música folk; **he's really i. my sister** le gusta un montón or Esp mogollón or Méx un chingo mi hermana

intolerable [ɪnˈtɒlərəbəl] adj (heat, conditions) insoportable; (price, behavior) intolerable

intolerably [ɪnˈtɒlərəblɪ] adv (to behave) de un modo intolerable, muy mal

intolerance [ɪnˈtɒlərəns] n intolerancia f

intolerant [ɪnˈtɒlərənt] adj intolerante (**of** con)

intonation [ɪntəˈneɪʃən] n entonación f

intone [ɪnˈtəʊn] vt decir solemnemente

intoxicated [ɪnˈtɒksɪkeɪtɪd] adj (drunk) **to be i.** estar embriagado(a) or ebrio(a); Fig **i. with power** ebrio de poder

intoxication [ɪntɒksɪˈkeɪʃən] n embriaguez f, ebriedad f

intractable [ɪnˈtræktəbəl] *adj (person)* intratable; *(problem)* arduo(a)

intranet [ˈɪntrənet] *n Comptr* intranet *f*

intransigence [ɪnˈtrænzɪdʒəns] *n Formal* intransigencia *f*

intransigent [ɪnˈtrænzɪdʒənt] *adj Formal* intransigente

intransitive [ɪnˈtrænzɪtɪv] *adj Gram* intransitivo(a)

intrastate [ˈɪntrəˈsteɪt] *adj* intraestatal

intrauterine device [ˈɪntrəˈjuːtəraɪndɪˈvaɪs] *n Med* dispositivo *m* intrauterino, DIU *m*

intravenous [ˈɪntrəˈviːnəs] *adj Med* **i. drip** gota a gota *m*; **i. injection** inyección *f* intravenosa

intravenously [ˈɪntrəˈviːnəslɪ] *adv Med* por vía intravenosa

in-tray [ˈɪntreɪ] *(pl* **in-trays)** *n* = bandeja de trabajos pendientes

intrepid [ɪnˈtrepɪd] *adj* intrépido(a)

intricacy [ˈɪntrɪkəsɪ] *n* complejidad *f*, complicación *f*; **the intricacies of…** los entresijos de…

intricate [ˈɪntrɪkət] *adj* intrincado(a), complicado(a)

intricately [ˈɪntrɪkətlɪ] *adv* intrincadamente, con gran complejidad

intrigue 1 *n* [ˈɪntriːg] intriga *f*
   2 *vt* [ɪnˈtriːg] *(interest)* intrigar
   3 *vi (conspire)* intrigar, conspirar (**against** contra)

intriguing [ɪnˈtriːgɪŋ] *adj* intrigante

intriguingly [ɪnˈtriːgɪŋlɪ] *adv* curiosamente

intrinsic [ɪnˈtrɪnsɪk] *adj* intrínseco(a)

intrinsically [ɪnˈtrɪnsɪklɪ] *adv* intrínsecamente

introduce [ɪntrəˈdjuːs] *vt* **(a)** *(person)* presentar; **to i. oneself** presentarse; **allow me to i. you to Mr. Black** permítame presentarle al Sr. Black; **to i. sb to sth** introducir *or* iniciar a alguien en algo **(b)** *(reform, practice)* introducir; **this custom was introduced by missionaries** esta costumbre la trajeron los misioneros

introduction [ɪntrəˈdʌkʃən] *n* **(a)** *(in general)* introducción *f* **(b)** *(of person)* presentación *f*; **to make the introductions** hacer las presentaciones

introductory [ɪntrəˈdʌktərɪ] *adj* introductorio(a); *Com* **i. price/offer** precio *m*/oferta *f* de lanzamiento

introspection [ɪntrəˈspekʃən] *n* introspección *f*

introspective [ɪntrəˈspektɪv] *adj* introspectivo(a)

introvert [ˈɪntrəvɜːt] *n* introvertido(a) *m,f*

introverted [ɪntrəˈvɜːtɪd] *adj* introvertido(a)

intrude [ɪnˈtruːd] *vi* **(a)** *(impose oneself)* **to i. on sb** molestar *or* importunar a alguien; **I hope I'm not intruding** espero no molestar **(b)** *(interfere)* **her work intrudes on her family life** el trabajo invade su vida familiar; **to i. on sb's privacy** perturbar *or* invadir la intimidad de alguien

intruder [ɪnˈtruːdə(r)] *n* intruso(a) *m,f*

intrusion [ɪnˈtruːʒən] *n* intromisión *f*

intrusive [ɪnˈtruːsɪv] *adj* molesto(a), importuno(a)

intuition [ɪntjuːˈɪʃən] *n* intuición *f*

intuitive [ɪnˈtjuːɪtɪv] *adj* intuitivo(a)

Inuit [ˈɪnʊɪt] *n & adj* inuit *mf*, esquimal *mf*

inundate [ˈɪnʌndeɪt] *vt also Fig* inundar (**with** de)

invade [ɪnˈveɪd] *vt* invadir; **to i. sb's privacy** perturbar *or* invadir la intimidad de alguien

invader [ɪnˈveɪdə(r)] *n* invasor(ora) *m,f*

invalid[1] [ɪnˈvælɪd] *adj (document, argument)* nulo(a)

invalid[2] [ˈɪnvəlɪd] *n (disabled person)* inválido(a) *m,f*; **I'm not an i.!** ¡no soy ningún inválido!

invalidate [ɪnˈvælɪdeɪt] *vt (theory)* invalidar; *(document, contract)* anular, invalidar

invalidity [ɪnvəˈlɪdɪtɪ] *n (of person)* invalidez *f*

invaluable [ɪnˈvæljʊəbəl] *adj* inestimable, inapreciable; **to be i. for sth/to sb** ser de gran valor para algo/para alguien

invariable [ɪnˈveərɪəbəl] *adj* invariable

invariably [ɪnˈveərɪəblɪ] *adv* invariablemente

invasion [ɪnˈveɪʒən] *n* invasión *f*

invasive [ɪnˈveɪsɪv] *adj Med* invasivo(a)

invective [ɪnˈvektɪv] *n* invectivas *fpl*

inveigh [ɪnˈveɪ] *vi Formal* **to i. against** lanzar invectivas contra

inveigle [ɪnˈveɪgəl] *vt* **to i. sb into doing sth** engatusar a alguien para que haga algo

invent [ɪnˈvent] *vt* inventar

invention [ɪnˈvenʃən] *n* **(a)** *(action)* invención *f*; *(thing invented)* invento *m*, invención *f*; *(lie)* invención *f* **(b)** *(creativity)* inventiva *f*

inventive [ɪnˈventɪv] *adj (creative)* inventivo(a), imaginativo(a); *(ingenious)* ingenioso(a)

inventiveness [ɪnˈventɪvnəs] *n* inventiva *f*

inventor [ɪnˈventə(r)] *n* inventor(ora) *m,f*

inventory [ˈɪnventərɪ] *n (list)* inventario *m*; *(stock)* existencias *fpl*

inverse [ɪnˈvɜːs] *adj* inverso(a)

inversion [ɪnˈvɜːʃən] *n* inversión *f*

invert [ɪnˈvɜːt] *vt* invertir

invertebrate [ɪnˈvɜːtɪbrɪt] **1** *n* invertebrado *m*
   2 *adj* invertebrado(a)

inverted [ɪnˈvɜːtɪd] *adj* invertido(a)

invest [ɪnˈvest] **1** *vt* **(a)** *(money, time)* invertir (**in** en) **(b)** *Formal (confer on)* **to i. sb with sth** investir a alguien con algo
   2 *vi* invertir (**in** en)

investigate [ɪnˈvestɪgeɪt] *vt* investigar

investigation [ɪnvestɪˈgeɪʃən] *n* investigación *f*

investigative [ɪnˈvestɪgətɪv] *adj* de investigación, investigador(ora); **i. journalism** periodismo *m* de investigación

investigator [ɪnˈvestɪgeɪtə(r)] *n* investigador(ora) *m,f*

investigatory [ɪnˈvestɪgeɪtərɪ] *adj* de investigación

investment [ɪnˈvestmənt] *n Fin* inversión *f*; **i. account** cuenta *f* de inversiones; **i. analyst** analista *mf* financiero(a) *or* de inversiones; **i. bank** banco *m* de inversiones; **i. income** rendimientos *mpl (de una inversión)*; **i. trust** sociedad *f or* fondo *m* de inversión

investor [ɪnˈvestə(r)] *n* inversor(ora) *m,f*

inveterate [ɪnˈvetərɪt] *adj (gambler, smoker, reader)* empedernido(a); *(liar)* redomado(a)

invidious [ɪnˈvɪdɪəs] *adj (choice, comparison)* odioso(a); **to be in an i. position** estar en una posición ingrata

invigorating [ɪnˈvɪgəreɪt] *adj (bath, air)* tonificante; *(walk)* vigorizante

invincibility [ɪnvɪnsɪˈbɪlɪtɪ] *n* invencibilidad *f*

invincible [ɪnˈvɪnsɪbəl] *adj* invencible

inviolable [ɪnˈvaɪələbəl] *adj Formal* inviolable

inviolate [ɪnˈvaɪələt] *adj Formal* inviolado(a)

invisibility [ɪnvɪzɪˈbɪlɪtɪ] *n* invisibilidad *f*

invisible [ɪnˈvɪzɪbəl] *adj* invisible; *Fin* **i. assets** activos *mpl* invisibles *or* intangibles; *Fin* **i. earnings** (ganancias *fpl*) invisibles *mpl*; **i. ink** tinta *f* simpática *or* invisible

invitation [ɪnvɪˈteɪʃən] *n* invitación *f*

invite 1 *vt* [ɪnˈvaɪt] **(a)** *(guest)* invitar; **to i. sb in/up** invitar a alguien a entrar/subir **(b)** *(request)* **to i. sb to do sth** invitar a alguien a que haga algo; **applications are invited for the post of…** se admiten candidaturas para el puesto de… **(c)** *(trouble, criticism)* buscarse, provocar
   2 *n* [ˈɪnvaɪt] *Fam* invitación *f*

inviting [ɪnˈvaɪtɪŋ] *adj* atractivo(a); *(meal)* apetecible, apetitoso(a)

in vitro fertilization [ɪnˈviːtrəʊfɜːtɪlaɪˈzeɪʃən] *n* fertilización *f or* fecundación *f* in vitro

invoice [ˈɪnvɔɪs] *Com* **1** *n* factura *f*; **to make out an i.** extender *or* hacer una factura

2 vt (goods) facturar; (person, company) mandar la factura a

invoke [ɪnˈvəʊk] vt Formal invocar

involuntarily [ɪnˈvɒləntərəlɪ, ˈɪnvɒlənˈteərəlɪ] adv involuntariamente; **she smiled i.** sonrió sin querer

involuntary [ɪnˈvɒlʌntərɪ] adj involuntario(a)

involve [ɪnˈvɒlv] vt **(a)** (implicate, concern) **to i. sb in sth** implicar or involucrar a alguien en algo; **this doesn't i. you** esto no tiene nada que ver contigo; **we try to i. the parents in the running of the school** intentamos que los padres participen en el manejo de la escuela **(b)** (entail) (work, expense) entrañar, implicar

involved [ɪnˈvɒlvd] adj **(a)** (implicated) **to be i. in sth** (crime, affair) estar implicado(a) or involucrado(a) en algo; **to be i. in an accident** verse envuelto(a) en un accidente; **to be i. in teaching/banking** dedicarse a la enseñanza/la banca **(b)** (emotionally) **to be/get i. with sb** tener una relación (sentimental) con alguien **(c)** (engrossed) **to get i. in a book/movie** enfrascarse en un libro/una película **(d)** (complicated) complicado(a), embrollado(a)

involvement [ɪnˈvɒlvmənt] n **(a)** (participation) participación f (**in** en); (role) relación f (**in** con) **(b)** (commitment) implicación f, compromiso m

invulnerable [ɪnˈvʌlnərəbəl] adj invulnerable

inward [ˈɪnwəd] **1** adj (thoughts) interno(a), interior; (motion) hacia dentro; Econ **i. investment** inversión f del exterior
2 adv hacia dentro

inward-looking [ɪnwədˈlʊkɪŋ] adj (person) introvertido(a); (community) cerrado(a)

inwards [ˈɪnwədz] adv = **inward**

in-your-face [ˈɪnjɔːˈfeɪs] adj Fam (style) descarado(a); (movie, advert) impactante, fuerte

IOC [aɪəʊˈsiː] n (abbr **International Olympic Committee**) COI m, Comité m Olímpico Internacional

iodine [ˈaɪədiːn] n Chem yodo m

ion [ˈaɪən] n ion m

Ionian [aɪˈəʊnɪən] n the I. (Sea) el mar Jónico

ionize [ˈaɪənaɪz] vt ionizar

iota [aɪˈəʊtə] n ápice m; **not an i. of truth** ni un ápice de verdad

IOU [aɪəʊˈjuː] n (= I owe you) pagaré m

IP [aɪˈpiː] n Comptr (abbr **Internet Protocol**) IP **address** dirección f IP

IPA [aɪpiːˈeɪ] n Ling (abbr **International Phonetic Alphabet**) AFI m, Alfabeto m Fonético Internacional

IQ [aɪˈkjuː] n Psy (abbr **intelligence quotient**) cociente m intelectual

Iran [ɪˈrɑːn] n Irán

Iranian [ɪˈreɪnɪən] n & adj iraní mf

Iraq [ɪˈrɑːk] n Irak, Iraq

Iraqi [ɪˈrɑːkɪ] n & adj iraquí mf, irakí mf

irascible [ɪˈræsɪbəl] adj irascible

irate [aɪˈreɪt] adj airado(a), furioso(a)

ire [ˈaɪə(r)] n Literary ira f

Ireland [ˈaɪələnd] n Irlanda

iridium [ɪˈrɪdɪəm] n Chem iridio m

iris [ˈaɪrɪs] n (of eye) iris m inv; (flower) lirio m

Irish [ˈaɪrɪʃ] **1** npl (people) the I. los irlandeses
2 n (language) irlandés m
3 adj irlandés(esa); **I. coffee** café m irlandés; **the I. Sea** el Mar de Irlanda; **I. stew** guiso m de carne con Esp patatas or Am papas

Irishman [ˈaɪrɪʃmən] n irlandés m

Irishwoman [ˈaɪrɪʃwʊmən] n irlandesa f

irk [ɜːk] vt fastidiar, irritar; **I was irked by his attitude** me fastidiaba or irritaba su actitud

irksome [ˈɜːksəm] adj molesto(a), irritante

iron [ˈaɪən] **1** n **(a)** (metal) hierro m; **made of i.** de hierro; **the i. and steel industry** la industria siderúrgica; **he has an i. constitution** está hecho(a) un roble; **a will of i.** una voluntad de hierro; **i. discipline** disciplina f férrea; **the I. Age** la Edad del Hierro; **the I. Curtain** el telón de acero, Am la cortina de hierro; Med **i. lung** pulmón m de acero; **i. ore** mineral m or mena f de hierro **(b)** (for clothes) plancha f; Fig **to have several irons in the fire** andar metido(a) en muchos asuntos **(c)** (in golf) hierro m
2 vt & vi (clothes) planchar

▸**iron out** vt sep (problem, difficulty) allanar, solventar

ironic(al) [aɪˈrɒnɪk(əl)] adj irónico(a)

ironing [ˈaɪənɪŋ] n planchado m, Am planchada f; **to do the i.** planchar; **i. board** tabla f de planchar

irony [ˈaɪrənɪ] n ironía f; **the i. is that...** lo paradójico del asunto es que...

irrational [ɪˈræʃənəl] adj irracional

irrationality [ɪræʃəˈnælɪtɪ] n irracionalidad f

irrationally [ɪˈræʃənəlɪ] adv irracionalmente

irreconcilable [ɪrekənˈsaɪləbəl] adj irreconciliable

irrecoverable [ɪrɪˈkʌvərəbəl] adj irrecuperable

irredeemable [ɪrɪˈdiːməbəl] adj (fault, situation) irremediable

irrefutable [ɪrɪˈfjuːtəbəl] adj irrefutable

irregular [ɪˈregjʊlə(r)] adj irregular

irregularity [ɪregjʊˈlærɪtɪ] n irregularidad f

irrelevance [ɪˈreləvəns], **irrelevancy** [ɪˈreləvənsɪ] n falta f de pertinencia

irrelevant [ɪˈreləvənt] adj carente de pertinencia; **an i. objection/remark** una objeción/un comentario que no viene al caso; **that's i.** eso no viene al caso

irreligious [ɪrɪˈlɪdʒəs] adj irreligioso(a), impío(a)

irremediable [ɪrɪˈmiːdɪəbəl] adj Formal irreparable, irremediable

irreparable [ɪˈrepərəbəl] adj irreparable

irreplaceable [ɪrɪˈpleɪsəbəl] adj irreemplazable

irrepressible [ɪrɪˈpresɪbəl] adj irreprimible

irreproachable [ɪrɪˈprəʊtʃəbəl] adj irreprochable, intachable

irresistible [ɪrɪˈzɪstɪbəl] adj irresistible

irresistibly [ɪrɪˈzɪstɪblɪ] adv irresistiblemente

irresolute [ɪˈrezəluːt] adj Formal irresoluto(a)

irrespective [ɪrɪˈspektɪv] adv **i. of** independientemente de

irresponsible [ɪrɪˈsponsɪbəl] adj irresponsable

irretrievable [ɪrɪˈtriːvəbəl] adj (loss, money) irrecuperable; (mistake, situation, damage) irreparable, irremediable

irretrievably [ɪrɪˈtriːvəblɪ] adv Formal irremediablemente, de forma irremediable

irreverence [ɪˈrevərəns] n irreverencia f, falta f de respeto

irreverent [ɪˈrevərənt] adj irreverente

irreversible [ɪrɪˈvɜːsɪbəl] adj (decision, process) irreversible

irrevocable [ɪˈrevəkəbəl] adj irrevocable

irrigate [ˈɪrɪgeɪt] vt regar

irrigation [ɪrɪˈgeɪʃən] n riego m, irrigación f; **i. canal** or **ditch** acequia f

irritable [ˈɪrɪtəbəl] adj irritable; Med **i. bowel syndrome** colon m irritable

irritably [ˈɪrɪtəblɪ] adv con irritación, irritadamente

irritant [ˈɪrɪtənt] n (to eyes, skin) agente m irritante; (to person, government) molestia f

irritate [ˈɪrɪteɪt] vt (annoy) irritar, fastidiar; Med irritar

irritated [ˈɪrɪteɪtɪd] adj (gen) & Med irritado(a); **don't get i.!** Esp ¡no te enfades!, Am ¡no te enojes!

irritating [ˈɪrɪteɪtɪŋ] adj irritante, exasperante

irritation [ɪrɪˈteɪʃən] n irritación f; **I discovered, to my intense i., that...** me irritó profundamente descubrir que...

IRS [aɪɑːˈres] n (abbr **Internal Revenue Service**) the I.

Hacienda, *Esp* ≃ la Agencia Tributaria, *Méx* ≃ el Servicio de Administración Tributaria

is [ɪz] *3rd person singular of* **be**

ISBN [aɪesːbiːˈen] *n* (*abbr* **International Standard Book Number**) ISBN *m*

ISDN [aɪesdiːˈen] *n Comptr* (*abbr* **integrated services digital network**) RDSI *f*; **ISDN modem** módem *m* RDSI

Islam [ˈɪzlɑːm] *n* (el) Islam

Islamic [ɪzˈlæmɪk] *adj* islámico(a)

island [ˈaɪlənd] *n* (*in sea, river*) isla *f*; (*in road*) isleta *f*

islander [ˈaɪləndə(r)] *n* isleño(a) *m,f*

isle [aɪl] *n* isla *f*; **the I. of Man** la isla de Man; **the I. of Wight** la isla de Wight

isn't [ˈɪzənt] = **is not**

ISO [aɪesˈəʊ] *n* (*abbr* **International Standards Organization**) ISO *f*, Organización *f* Internacional de Normalización

isobar [ˈaɪsəʊbɑː(r)] *n* isobara *f*

isolate [ˈaɪseleɪt] *vt* aislar (**from** de)

isolated [ˈaɪseleɪtɪd] *adj* aislado(a); **to be i. (from)** estar aislado (de)

isolation [aɪseˈleɪʃən] *n* aislamiento *m*; **to deal with sth in i.** tratar algo aisladamente; *Med* **i. ward** pabellón *m* de enfermedades infecciosas

isosceles [aɪˈsɒsɪliːz] *adj* isósceles; **i. triangle** triángulo *m* isósceles

isotope [ˈaɪsətəʊp] *n Phys* isótopo *m*

Israel [ˈɪzreɪəl] *n* Israel

Israeli [ɪzˈreɪlɪ] *n & adj* israelí *mf*

Israelite [ˈɪzrəlaɪt] *n Hist* israelita *mf*

issue [ˈɪʃuː] **1** *n* (**a**) (*topic*) tema *m*, cuestión *f*; **the issues of the day** los temas de actualidad; **that's not the i.** no se trata de eso; **to avoid the i.** evitar el tema; **to confuse the i.** complicar el asunto; **to make an i. of sth** sacar algo de quicio; **at i.** en cuestión; **to take i. with sb** discrepar de alguien (**b**) (*of banknotes, stamps*) emisión *f* (**c**) (*of magazine*) número *m* (**d**) *Formal* (*offspring*) descendencia *f*; *Law* **to die without i.** morir sin dejar descendencia

2 *vt* (*banknote, stamp*) emitir, poner en circulación; (*order*) dar; **to i. sb with sth** proporcionar algo a alguien; **to i. a statement** emitir un comunicado; *Law* **to i. a summons** enviar una citación judicial

3 *vi Formal* (*blood*) manar (**from** de); (*noise*) surgir (**from** de); (*smoke*) brotar (**from** de)

Istanbul [ɪstænˈbʊl] *n* Estambul

isthmus [ˈɪsməs] *n* istmo *m*

IT [aɪˈtiː] *n Comptr* (*abbr* **information technology**) informática *f*

it [ɪt] *pron* (**a**) (*subject*) (*usually omitted in Spanish*) **it is red** es rojo(a); **it escaped** se escapó

(**b**) (*direct object*) lo *m*, la *f*; **I don't want it** no lo/la quiero; **give it to him** dáselo

(**c**) (*indirect object*) le; **give it something to eat** dale algo de comer

(**d**) (*prepositional object*) (*masculine*) él; (*feminine*) ella; (*referring to uncountable nouns*) ello; **from it** de él/ella/ello; **with it** con él/ella/ello; **I don't want to talk about it** no quiero hablar de ello; **put some newspaper under it** pon papel de periódico debajo

(**e**) (*impersonal subject*) **it's raining** está lloviendo, llueve; **it's ten o'clock** son las diez (en punto); **it's cold today** hoy hace frío

(**f**) (*as complement of verb* **to be**) **who is it?** ¿quién es?; **that's it for today** eso es todo por hoy

Italian [ɪˈtælɪən] **1** *n* (**a**) (*person*) italiano(a) *m,f* (**b**) (*language*) italiano *m*; **I. class/teacher** clase *f*/profesor(ora) *m,f* de italiano

2 *adj* italiano(a)

italic [ɪˈtælɪk] *n Typ* **i.(s)** cursiva *f*; **in italics** en cursiva

italicize [ɪˈtælɪsaɪz] *vt* poner en cursiva

Italy [ˈɪtəlɪ] *n* Italia

itch [ɪtʃ] **1** *n* picor *m*; *Fig* **to have an i. to do sth** tener muchas ganas de hacer algo

2 *vi* picar; **my leg is itching** me pica la pierna; *Fig* **to be itching to do sth** tener muchas ganas de hacer algo

itching [ˈɪtʃɪŋ] *n* picor *m*; **i. powder** polvos *mpl* (de) picapica

itchy [ˈɪtʃɪ] *adj* **I've got an i. hand, my hand's i.** me pica la mano; *Fig* **to have i. feet** tener muchas ganas de viajar

it'd [ˈɪtəd] = **it would, it had**

item [ˈaɪtəm] *n* (*in collection*) artículo *m*; (*on list, agenda*) punto *m*; *Journ* noticia *f*; **an i. of clothing** una prenda de vestir; **personal items** objetos *mpl* personales; *Fam* **they're an i.** llevan un montón de tiempo (saliendo) juntos

itemize [ˈaɪtəmaɪz] *vt* (*contents*) hacer una lista de; (*bill*) detallar

iterative [ˈɪtərətɪv] *adj Comptr* iterativo(a)

itinerant [ɪˈtɪnərənt] *adj* ambulante, itinerante

itinerary [aɪˈtɪnərərɪ] *n* itinerario *m*

it'll [ˈɪtəl] = **it will**

its [ɪts] *possessive adj* (**a**) (*singular*) su; (*plural*) sus; **the lion returned to i. den** el león volvió a su guarida (**b**) (*for parts of body, clothes*) **the bear hurt i. paw** el oso se hizo daño en la zarpa; **the plane lost one of i. engines** el avión perdió uno de los motores

it's [ɪts] = **it is, it has**

itself [ɪtˈself] *pron* (**a**) (*reflexive*) se; **the dog hurt i.** el perro se hizo daño (**b**) (*emphatic*) **this method is simplicity i.** este método es la sencillez misma; **the town i. isn't very interesting** la ciudad en sí (misma) no es muy interesante (**c**) (*after preposition*) **by/in i.** por/en sí mismo(a)

IUD [aɪjuːˈdiː] *n Med* (*abbr* **intrauterine device**) DIU *m*, dispositivo *m* intrauterino

I've [aɪv] = **I have**

IVF [aɪviːˈef] *n Med* (*abbr* **in vitro fertilization**) fertilización *f* in vitro

ivory [ˈaɪvərɪ] *n* (*substance*) marfil *m*; (*color*) color *m* marfil; **the I. Coast** la Costa de Marfil; *Fig* **i. tower** torre *f* de marfil

ivy [ˈaɪvɪ] *n* (*plant*) hiedra *f*; **Ivy League** = grupo de universidades de gran prestigio del nordeste de Estados Unidos

J

J, j [dʒeɪ] *n (letter)* J, j *f*

J *Elec (abbr* **Joule(s)**) J

jab [dʒæb] **1** *n (with elbow)* codazo *m; (with finger)* movimiento *m* seco; *(in boxing)* golpe *m* corto

2 *vt (pt & pp* **jabbed**) **he jabbed her in the leg with a pencil** le clavó un lápiz en la pierna; **to j. a finger at sb** señalar a alguien con el dedo

jabber [ˈdʒæbə(r)] *vi Fam* parlotear

Jack [dʒæk] *n (diminutive of* **John***)* **J. Frost** la escarcha, la helada

jack [dʒæk] *n* **(a)** *(person)* **every man j. of them** todo quisque; **he is a j. of all trades** hace *or* sabe hacer un poco de todo **(b)** *(for car)* gato *m* **(c)** *(in cards)* jota *f; (in Spanish cards)* sota *f* **(d)** *Elec (plug)* clavija *f; (socket)* clavijero *m* **(e)** **j. rabbit** *(North American hare)* liebre *f* americana

▸**jack up** *vt sep Fam (price, salaries)* subir

jackal [ˈdʒækəl] *n* chacal *m*

jackass [ˈdʒækæs] *n* **(a)** *(male donkey)* burro *m*, asno *m* **(b)** *Fam (person)* burro(a) *m,f*, animal *mf*

jackboot [ˈdʒækbuːt] *n* bota *f* militar; *Fig* **under the j. of a military dictatorship** bajo el yugo de una dictadura militar

jackdaw [ˈdʒækdɔː] *n* grajilla *f*

jacket [ˈdʒækɪt] *n* **(a)** *(coat) (formal)* chaqueta *f*, americana *f*, *Am* saco *m; (casual)* cazadora *f*, *CSur* campera *f*, *Méx* chamarra *f* **(b)** *(of book)* sobrecubierta *f; (of record)* funda *f* **(c)** *(of boiler)* funda *f*

jackhammer [ˈdʒækhæmə(r)] *n* martillo *m* neumático

jack-in-the-box [ˈdʒækɪnðəbɒks] *n* caja *f* sorpresa

jackknife [ˈdʒæknaɪf] **1** *n* navaja *f*

2 *vi (articulated truck)* hacer la tijera, derrapar por el remolque

jack-o'-lantern [ˈdʒækəˈlæntən] *n (Hallowe'en lantern)* = farolillo hecho con una calabaza hueca y una vela dentro

jackpot [ˈdʒækpɒt] *n (in lottery)* (premio *m*) gordo *m*; **he hit or won the j.** le tocó el gordo

Jacobean [dʒækəˈbiən] *adj* jacobino(a), = relativo al periodo del reinado de Jacobo I de Inglaterra (1603-1625)

Jacobite [ˈdʒækəbaɪt] *n & adj* jacobita *mf*

Jacuzzi® [dʒəˈkuːzɪ] *n* jacuzzi® *m*

jade [dʒeɪd] **1** *n (stone)* jade *m; (color)* verde *m* jade

2 *adj (color)* verde jade

jaded [ˈdʒeɪdɪd] *adj (tired)* agotado(a); *(bored)* harto(a), hastiado(a)

jag [dʒæg] *n Fam* **to go on a (drinking) j.** ir de borrachera; **he had a crying j.** le dio la llorera

jagged [ˈdʒægɪd] *adj (coastline)* accidentado(a); *(crest)* escarpado(a); *(blade)* dentado(a)

jaguar [ˈdʒægwɑː(r)] *n* jaguar *m*

jail [dʒeɪl] **1** *n* cárcel *f*; **to be in j.** estar en la cárcel; **to go to j.** ir a la cárcel

2 *vt* encarcelar

jailbait [ˈdʒeɪlbeɪt] *n very Fam* **she's j.** es menor y puede meterte en líos

jailbird [ˈdʒeɪlbɜːd] *n Fam* preso(a) *m,f* reincidente

jailbreak [ˈdʒeɪlbreɪk] *n* fuga *f*, evasión *f*

jailer, jailor [ˈdʒeɪlə(r)] *n* carcelero(a) *m,f; (of hostages)* captor(ora) *m,f*

jailhouse [ˈdʒeɪlhaʊs] *n* cárcel *f*

jailor = **jailer**

Jakarta [dʒəˈkɑːtə] *n* Yakarta

jalopy [dʒəˈlɒpɪ] *n Fam* cacharro *m*, cafetera *f*

jam¹ [dʒæm] **1** *n* **(a)** *(crowd) (of people)* muchedumbre *f*, multitud *f;* **traffic j.** atasco *m*, embotellamiento *m* **(b)** *Fam (difficult situation)* **to be in/get into a j.** estar/meterse en un aprieto **(c)** *(improvised performance)* **j. (session)** jam-session *f*

2 *vt (pt & pp* **jammed**) **(a)** *(pack tightly) (objects)* embutir **(into** en); *(container)* atestar **(with** de); **traffic jammed the streets** el tráfico colapsaba las calles **(b)** *(block) (radio broadcast, station)* provocar interferencias en; *(switchboard)* bloquear; **the drawer is jammed** el cajón se ha atascado; **he jammed the window open** atrancó la ventana para que se quedara abierta

3 *vi* **(a)** *(drawer, machine)* atascarse, *Am* trancarse; **people jammed into the hall** la gente abarrotaba la sala **(b)** *Mus* improvisar *(con un grupo)*

jam² *n (fruit preserve)* mermelada *f;* **j. jar** tarro *m* de mermelada; **j. tart** pastel *m or Col, CSur* torta *f* de confitura

▸**jam on** *vt sep* **to j. on the brakes** frenar en seco

Jamaica [dʒəˈmeɪkə] *n* Jamaica

Jamaican [dʒəˈmeɪkən] *n & adj* jamaicano(a) *m,f*

jamb [dʒæm] *n (side post of door)* jamba *f*

jamboree [dʒæmbəˈriː] *n (scouts' meeting)* encuentro *m* de boy-scouts; *Fam (celebration)* jolgorio *m*, fiesta *f*

jamming [ˈdʒæmɪŋ] *n Rad* interferencias *fpl*

jammy [ˈdʒæmɪ] *adj (covered with jam)* cubierto(a) de mermelada

jam-packed [ˈdʒæmˈpækd] *adj* **to be j. (with)** estar atestado(a) *or* abarrotado(a) (de)

Jan *(abbr* **January)** ene., enero *m*

jangle [ˈdʒæŋgəl] **1** *n (of keys, chain)* tintineo *m*

2 *vt (keys, chain)* hacer tintinear

3 *vi (keys, chain)* tintinear; *Fig* **her voice made his nerves j.** su voz le ponía los nervios de punta

janitor [ˈdʒænɪtə(r)] *n (caretaker)* conserje *m*, bedel *m*

January [ˈdʒænjʊərɪ] *n* enero *m; see also* **May**

Jap [dʒæp] *n Fam* = término ofensivo para referirse a los japoneses, *RP* ponja *mf*

Japan [dʒəˈpæn] *n* Japón

Japanese [dʒæpəˈniːz] **1** *n* **(a)** *(person)* japonés(esa) *m,f* **(b)** *(language)* japonés *m;* **J. class/teacher** clase *f*/profesor(ora) *m,f* de japonés

2 *npl* **the J.** los japoneses

3 *adj* japonés(esa)

jape [dʒeɪp] *n* broma *f*

jar¹ [dʒɑː(r)] **1** *n (jolt, shock)* sacudida *f;* **the news gave him a nasty j.** la noticia supuso una sorpresa desagradable para él

2 vt (pt & pp **jarred**) (knock) sacudir, golpear; Fig (surprise) alterar, sacudir

3 vi (make unpleasant sound) rechinar; **to j. on the ears** rechinar en los oídos; **to j. on the nerves** crispar los nervios; **to j. (with each other)** (colors) desentonar; (ideas) chocar (entre sí)

jar² n (container) tarro m

jargon ['dʒɑːgən] n Pej jerga f

jarring ['dʒɑːrɪŋ] adj (noise, voice) estridente; (blow) contundente

jasmine ['dʒæzmɪn] n (plant) jazmín m

jaundice ['dʒɔːndɪs] n Med icteria f

jaundiced ['dʒɔːndɪst] adj (attitude, opinion) resentido(a)

jaunt [dʒɔːnt] n excursión f

jauntily ['dʒɔːntɪlɪ] adv desenfadadamente

jauntiness ['dʒɔːntɪnɪs] n desenfado m

jaunty ['dʒɔːntɪ] adj desenfadado(a)

Java ['dʒɑːvə] n Java

javelin ['dʒævlɪn] n jabalina f

jaw [dʒɔː] **1** n mandíbula f; **jaws** (of animal) fauces fpl; (of vice) mordaza f; **the jaws of death** las garras de la muerte

2 vi Fam (chat) charlar, CAm, Méx platicar

jawbone ['dʒɔːbəʊn] n maxilar m inferior

jawbreaker ['dʒɔːbreɪkə(r)] n Fam (**a**) (unpronounceable word, name) trabalenguas m inv (**b**) (candy) caramelo m duro

jay [dʒeɪ] (pl **jays**) n arrendajo m

jaywalker ['dʒeɪwɔːkə(r)] n peatón(ona) m,f imprudente

jaywalking ['dʒeɪwɔːkɪŋ] n imprudencia f peatonal

jazz [dʒæz] n jazz m; Fam **and all that j.** y otras cosas por el estilo, Esp y todo el rollo

▸**jazz up** vt sep Fam (enliven) animar

jazzy ['dʒæzɪ] adj (tune) jazzístico(a); (clothes, pattern) llamativo(a)

jealous ['dʒeləs] adj (**a**) (envious) envidioso(a); **to be j. of sb** tener envidia de alguien (**b**) (possessive) celoso(a)

jealously ['dʒeləslɪ] adv (**a**) (enviously) con envidia (**b**) (possessively) celosamente; **a j. guarded secret** un secreto celosamente guardado

jealousy ['dʒeləsɪ] n (**a**) (envy) envidia f (**b**) (possessiveness) celos mpl

jeans [dʒiːnz] npl (pantalones mpl) vaqueros mpl, Andes, Ven bluyín m, Col bluejeans mpl, Méx pantalones mpl de mezclilla; **a pair of j.** unos (pantalones) vaqueros

jeep [dʒiːp] n todoterreno m, jeep m

jeer [dʒɪə(r)] **1** n (boo) abucheo m; (derision) burla f

2 vt (boo) abuchear; (mock) burlarse de

3 vi (boo) abuchear (**at** a); (mock) burlarse (**at** de)

jeering ['dʒɪərɪŋ] **1** n (booing) abucheo m; (mocking) burlas fpl

2 adj burlón(ona)

jeez [dʒiːz] exclam Fam ¡caray!

jehad = **jihad**

Jehovah [dʒɪ'həʊvə] n Jehová; **J.'s Witness** testigo mf de Jehová

jell [dʒel] vi (liquid) aglutinarse; Fig (ideas, plans, team) cuajar

Jell-O® ['dʒeləʊ] n gelatina f, jalea f

jelly ['dʒelɪ] n (jam) mermelada f, confitura f; **j. roll** brazo m de gitano

jellybean ['dʒelɪbiːn] n pastilla f de goma, Esp gominola f

jellyfish ['dʒelɪfɪʃ] n medusa f

jeopardize ['dʒepədaɪz] vt poner en peligro

jeopardy ['dʒepədɪ] n **in j.** en peligro; **to put sth/sb in j.** poner en peligro algo/a alguien

jerk¹ [dʒɜːk] **1** n (sudden movement) sacudida f; (pull) tirón m; **to give sth a j.** sacudir algo

2 vt (move suddenly) sacudir; (pull) (once) dar un tirón a; (in order to move) mover a tirones

3 vi **to j. forward** (car) dar una sacudida hacia delante; (head)

caer hacia delante; **to j. to a halt** detenerse con una sacudida

▸**jerk off** vi Vulg (masturbate) hacerse una paja

jerk² n Fam (person) majadero(a) m,f

jerkily ['dʒɜːkɪlɪ] adv a trompicones

jerky ['dʒɜːkɪ] adj (movement) brusco(a)

jerrican, jerry can ['dʒerɪkæn] n bidón m

jerry-built ['dʒerɪbɪlt] adj chapucero(a)

Jersey ['dʒɜːzɪ] n (island) Jersey; **J. (cow)** vaca f de Jersey

jersey ['dʒɜːzɪ] (pl **jerseys**) n (garment) suéter m, Esp jersey m, Col saco m, RP pulóver m

Jerusalem [dʒə'ruːsələm] n Jerusalén; **J. artichoke** aguaturma f, cotufa f

jest [dʒest] **1** n **in j.** en broma, de broma; (only) **half in j.** (to speak) medio en broma medio en serio

2 vi bromear

jester ['dʒestə(r)] n bufón m

jesting ['dʒestɪŋ] adj (remark, tone) de broma

Jesuit ['dʒezjʊɪt] n jesuita m

Jesuitical [dʒezjʊ'ɪtɪkəl] adj Pej (argument, reasoning) retorcido(a), sibilino(a)

Jesus ['dʒiːzəs] n Jesús m; **J. Christ** Jesucristo m; Fam **J. (Christ)!** ¡Santo Dios!

jet¹ [dʒet] **1** n (**a**) (plane) reactor m, avión m a reacción; **j. engine** reactor m; **j. fighter** caza m; **j. lag** desfase m horario, jet lag m; **j. propulsion** propulsión f a reacción or a chorro; **the j. set** Esp la jet(-set), Am el jet-set (**b**) (of liquid, steam) chorro m (**c**) (nozzle) boquilla f

2 vi (pt & pp **jetted**) Fam (travel by plane) **to j. in/off** llegar/salir en avión

jet² **1** n (stone) azabache m

2 adj **j. (black)** (negro) azabache

jet-lagged ['dʒetlægd] adj afectado(a) por el desfase horario, con jet lag

jet-powered ['dʒet'paʊəd], **jet-propelled** [dʒetprə'peld] adj a reacción

jet-setter ['dʒetsetə(r)] n miembro m de la jet (set)

Jet Ski® ['dʒetskiː] n moto f náutica or acuática

jettison ['dʒetɪsən] vt also Fig tirar or echar or Am salvo RP botar por la borda

jetty ['dʒetɪ] n malecón m

Jew [dʒuː] n judío(a) m,f; **Jew's** or **Jews' harp** birimbao m, guimbarda f

jewel ['dʒuːəl] n (gem, piece of jewelry) joya f, alhaja f; Fig (person) joya f

jeweler ['dʒuːələ(r)] n joyero(a) m,f; **j.'s (shop)** joyería f

jewelry ['dʒuːəlrɪ] n joyas fpl, alhajas fpl; **a piece of j.** una joya or alhaja

Jewess ['dʒuːes] n Old-fashioned judía f

Jewish ['dʒuːɪʃ] adj judío(a)

Jewry ['dʒuːərɪ] n **New York J.** la comunidad judía neoyorquina

jib¹ [dʒɪb] n (sail) foque m; (of crane) aguilón m

jib² (pt & pp **jibbed**) vi **to j. at doing sth** resistirse a hacer algo

jibe [dʒaɪb] **1** n burla f

2 vi **to j. at sb** hacer burla de alguien

jiffy ['dʒɪfɪ] n Fam **in a j.** en un segundo

jig [dʒɪg] **1** n (dance, music) giga f, jiga f

2 vi (pt & pp **jigged**) (dance) bailar (a ritmo ligero)

jiggery-pokery ['dʒɪgərɪ'pəʊkərɪ] n Fam tejemanejes mpl

jiggle ['dʒɪgəl] **1** vt menear

2 vi menearse

▸**jiggle around, jiggle about** vt sep & vi = **jiggle**

jigsaw ['dʒɪgsɔː] n (**a**) (saw) sierra f de calar or de vaivén, caladora f (**b**) (game) **j. (puzzle)** rompecabezas m inv, puzzle m

jihad, jehad [dʒɪ'hæd] n guerra f santa, yihad f (islámica)

jilt [dʒɪlt] vt (lover, girlfriend) dejar plantado(a)

jimmy ['dʒɪmɪ] n palanqueta f

jingle ['dʒɪŋgəl] **1** n (of bells, keys) tintineo m; Rad & TV melodía f (de un anuncio), sintonía f
2 vt (bells, keys) hacer tintinear
3 vi tintinear

jingoism ['dʒɪŋgəʊɪzəm] n Pej patrioterismo m

jingoistic ['dʒɪŋgəʊ'ɪstɪk] adj Pej patriotero(a)

jinx [dʒɪŋks] Fam **1** n (spell, curse) gafe m; **to put a j. on sth/sb** embrujar algo/a alguien, Esp gafar algo/a alguien, CAm, Carib, Méx echarle la sal a algo/a alguien, RP enyetar algo/a alguien
2 vt **to be jinxed** estar embrujado(a) or Esp gafado(a) or CAm, Carib, Méx salado(a), RP tener yeta

JIT [dʒɪt] adj Ind (abbr **just in time**) **J. production** producción f "justo a tiempo" (con minimización de stocks)

jitters ['dʒɪtəz] npl Fam **the j.** (anxiety) canguelo m, Méx mello m, RP cuiqui m; **I got the j.** me entró canguelo or Méx mello or RP cuiqui

jittery ['dʒɪtərɪ] adj Fam (anxious) histérico(a); **to be/get j.** estar/ponerse histérico(a)

jiujitsu = **jujitsu**

jive [dʒaɪv] **1** n (music, dance) swing m
2 vi (dance) bailar el swing

job [dʒɒb] n (a) (employment) trabajo m, empleo m; (post) (puesto m de) trabajo m, empleo m; **to be out of a j.** estar sin trabajo or empleo; **j. action** huelga f de celo; **Job Center** oficina f de empleo (privada); **j. creation** creación f de empleo; **j. description** responsabilidades fpl del puesto; **to go j. hunting** ponerse a buscar empleo; **j. losses** despidos mpl; **j. offer** oferta f de empleo; **j. opportunities** ofertas fpl de empleo; **j. satisfaction** satisfacción f laboral; **j. security** seguridad f en el trabajo; **j. seeker** persona f en busca de empleo; **j. sharing** empleo compartido; **j. title** cargo m, nombre m del puesto
(b) (piece of work, task) tarea f; **to do a good j.** hacer un buen trabajo; Fig **to do the j.** (serve purpose) servir, funcionar; **it was quite a j. getting her to come** me costó mucho convencerla para que viniera; Com **j. lot** lote m de saldos
(c) (responsibility, duty) tarea f; **I have (been given) the j. of writing the report** me han encargado redactar el informe
(d) Fam (crime) **to do a j.** dar un golpe

jobholder ['dʒɒbhəʊldə(r)] n empleado(a) m,f

jobhunter ['dʒɒbhʌntə(r)] = **job seeker**

jobless ['dʒɒblɪs] **1** npl **the j.** los desempleados, Esp los parados, Am los desocupados
2 adj desempleado(a), Esp parado(a), Am desocupado(a)

job-share ['dʒɒbʃeə(r)] **1** n empleo m compartido
2 vi compartir un empleo

jock [dʒɒk] n Fam (athlete) deportista m

jockey ['dʒɒkɪ] **1** n (pl **jockeys**) jockey m, jinete m
2 vi **to j. for position** luchar por tomar posiciones

Jockey® shorts ['dʒɒkɪʃɔːts] npl calzoncillos mpl, Chile fundillos mpl, Col pantaloncillos mpl, Méx calzones mpl, Méx chones mpl

jockstrap ['dʒɒkstræp] n suspensorio m

jocular ['dʒɒkjʊlə(r)] adj jocoso(a)

jodhpurs ['dʒɒdpəz] npl pantalones mpl de montar

Joe [dʒəʊ] n Fam **he's an ordinary J.** es un tipo del montón; **J. Blow** or **Schmo** or **Six-Pack** el ciudadano de a pie or RP común y silvestre

jog [dʒɒg] **1** n (a) (push) empujoncito m; **to give sb's memory a j.** refrescar la memoria de alguien (b) (run) trote m; **to break into a j.** echar a correr lentamente; **to go for a j.** ir a hacer footing or jogging, ir a correr
2 vt (pt & pp **jogged**) (push) empujar; **to j. sb's memory** refrescar la memoria a alguien
3 vi Sport hacer footing or jogging, correr; **to go jogging** ir a hacer footing or jogging, ir a correr

▶**jog along** vi (run) correr lentamente; Fig (in job) seguir apalancado(a)

jogger ['dʒɒgə(r)] n corredor(ora) m,f de footing or jogging

jogging ['dʒɒgɪŋ] n footing m, jogging m; **to go j.** ir a hacer footing or jogging; **j. pants** pantalones mpl de Esp chándal or RP jogging or Ven mono, Méx pants mpl

joggle ['dʒɒgəl] vt menear

Johannesburg [dʒəʊ'hænɪzbɜːg] n Johan(n)esburgo

john [dʒɒn] n Fam **the j.** (lavatory) el váter

John Bull ['dʒɒn'bʊl] n (Englishman) el inglés de a pie; (England) = la personificación de Inglaterra

join [dʒɔɪn] **1** n juntura f, unión f; (in sewing) costura f
2 vt (a) (unite, connect) unir; **to j. two things/places together** unir dos cosas/lugares; **to j. battle** entablar batalla; **to j. the dots** unir los puntos con una línea; **we joined forces with them** unimos nuestras fuerzas con ellos or a las de ellos (b) (become a member of) (club) ingresar en; (political party, union) afiliarse a; (army) alistarse en; (discussion, game) unirse a; **to j. the line** ponerse a la cola; **may I j. you?** (to sb at table) ¿puedo sentarme contigo?; **to j. sb for a drink** tomarse una copa con alguien (c) (of river, road) desembocar en; **where the river joins the sea** en la desembocadura del río
3 vi (a) (pipes, roads, rivers) juntarse, unirse (b) (enroll) (in club) ingresar; (in political party, union) afiliarse

▶**join in 1** vt insep (game, discussion) participar en
2 vi participar

▶**join up** vi Mil alistarse

joiner ['dʒɔɪnə(r)] n (carpenter) carpintero(a) m,f

joint [dʒɔɪnt] **1** n (a) Anat articulación f; **out of j.** dislocado(a) (b) (in woodwork) junta f, juntura f (c) Fam (nightclub, restaurant) garito m, local m (d) Fam (cannabis cigarette) porro m, canuto m (e) Fam (prison) Esp chirona f, Andes, RP cana f, Méx bote m
2 adj conjunto(a); Fin **j. account** cuenta f indistinta or conjunta; **j. ownership** copropiedad f; **j. stock company** sociedad f anónima; **j. venture** empresa f conjunta or común
3 vt (chicken) trinchar

jointly ['dʒɔɪntlɪ] adv conjuntamente

joist [dʒɔɪst] n (beam) viga f

joke [dʒəʊk] **1** n (a) (funny remark) broma f, chiste m; (funny story) chiste m; (prank, trick) broma; **to tell** or **crack a j.** contar un chiste; **to make a j. about sth** hacer una broma or bromear sobre algo; **to make a j. of sth** pretender que algo era en broma; **to say/do sth for a j.** decir/hacer algo en or de broma; **to play a j. on sb** gastar una broma a alguien; **the j. was on him when he had to...** la broma le salió rana cuando tuvo que...; **she can't take a j.** no sabe aguantar una broma; **that's** or **it's no j.!** ¡no es cosa de broma!; **it's getting beyond a j.** esto ya pasa de castaño oscuro
(b) Fam **to be a j.** (person) ser un/una inútil, no valer Esp un duro or Am ni cinco; (thing) ser de chiste
2 vi bromear; **to j. about sth** bromear acerca de algo; **to j. with sb** bromear con alguien; **I'm not joking** (hablo) en serio; **I was only joking** estaba de broma; **you're joking!, you must be joking!** (expressing surprise) ¡no hablarás en serio!; (expressing refusal) ¡ni hablar!; **joking apart...** bromas aparte..., fuera de broma...

joker ['dʒəʊkə(r)] n (a) (clown) bromista mf, gracioso(a) m,f; (incompetent person) inútil mf (b) (in cards) comodín m; Fig **the j. in the deck** la gran incógnita

jokester ['dʒəʊkstə(r)] n (clown) bromista mf, gracioso(a) m,f

jokey ['dʒəʊkɪ] adj jocoso(a)

jokily ['dʒəʊkɪlɪ] adv en tono de broma

jokingly ['dʒəʊkɪŋlɪ] adv en broma

joky = **jokey**

jolly ['dʒɒlɪ] **1** adj (cheerful) alegre; **the J. Roger** la bandera pirata

2 *vt* **to j. sb into doing sth** animar a alguien a hacer algo; **to j. sb along** animar a alguien

jolt [dʒəʊlt] **1** *n (shake)* sacudida *f; (shock, surprise)* susto *m;* **it gave me a bit of a j.** me dio un buen susto

2 *vt (shake)* sacudir; *(shock, surprise)* sacudir, alterar; **to j. sb into action** empujar a alguien a actuar; **to j. sb out of a depression** hacer salir a alguien de una depresión

3 *vi (shake)* dar sacudidas; **to j. along** *(vehicle)* avanzar a tirones; **to j. to a stop** *(vehicle)* pararse en seco

Jordan [ˈdʒɔːdən] *n (country)* Jordania; **the (River) J.** el Jordán

Jordanian [dʒɔːˈdeɪnɪən] *n & adj* jordano(a) *m,f*

josh [dʒɒʃ] *vt Fam (tease)* tomar el pelo a

joss stick [ˈdʒɒsstɪk] *n* pebete *m*, varilla *f* aromática

jostle [ˈdʒɒsəl] **1** *vt* empujar; **to j. sb out of the way** quitar *or Am* sacar a alguien de en medio a empujones

2 *vi (push)* empujarse; **to j. for position** *(in contest, job)* luchar por tomar posiciones

jot [dʒɒt] *n Fam* **not a j.** ni pizca; **he doesn't care a j.** le importa un comino; **there isn't a j. of truth in what you say** no hay ni un ápice de verdad en lo que dices

▸**jot down** *vt sep* apuntar, anotar

jotter [ˈdʒɒtə(r)] *n* libreta *f*

jottings [ˈdʒɒtɪŋz] *npl* anotaciones *fpl*

joule [dʒuːl] *n Phys* julio *m*

journal [ˈdʒɜːnəl] *n (publication)* revista *f (especializada)*, boletín *m; (diary)* diario *m;* **to keep a j.** llevar *or* escribir un diario

journalese [dʒɜːnəˈliːz] *n Fam Pej* jerga *f* periodística

journalism [ˈdʒɜːnəlɪzəm] *n* periodismo *m*

journalist [ˈdʒɜːnəlɪst] *n* periodista *mf*

journalistic [dʒɜːnəˈlɪstɪk] *adj* periodístico(a)

journey [ˈdʒɜːnɪ] **1** *n (pl* **journeys)** viaje *m;* **a train/plane/boat j.** un viaje en tren/avión/barco; **to make a j.** hacer un viaje; **to set off** *or* **out on a j.** salir de viaje; **to go (away) on a j.** ir(se) de viaje; **to get to** *or* **reach the end of one's j.** llegar al final del viaje

2 *vi* viajar

joust [dʒaʊst] *vi Hist* justar; *(compete)* pugnar, estar en liza

jovial [ˈdʒəʊvɪəl] *adj* jovial

jovially [ˈdʒəʊvɪəlɪ] *adv* jovialmente

jowl [dʒaʊl] *n (jaw)* mandíbula *f; (cheek)* carrillo *m*, mejilla *f*

joy [dʒɔɪ] *(pl* **joys)** *n* **(a)** *(happiness)* alegría *f*, gozo *m;* **to wish sb j.** desear a alguien lo mejor **(b)** *(pleasure)* placer *m*, maravilla *f;* **she's a j. to be with** su compañía es muy placentera; **he's a j. to work for** es una maravilla de jefe

joyful [ˈdʒɔɪfʊl] *adj* alegre

joyfully [ˈdʒɔɪfəlɪ] *adv* alegremente

joyless [ˈdʒɔɪlɪs] *adj* triste

joyous [ˈdʒɔɪəs] *adj* jubiloso(a)

joyride [ˈdʒɔɪraɪd] *n (in stolen car)* **to go for a j.** (ir a) dar una vuelta en un coche *or Am* carro *or esp CSur* auto robado

joyrider [ˈdʒɔɪraɪdə(r)] *n =* persona que roba coches para darse una vuelta por diversión

joystick [ˈdʒɔɪstɪk] *n Av* palanca *f* de mando; *Comptr* joystick *m*

JP [dʒeɪˈpiː] *n Law (abbr* **Justice of the Peace)** juez *mf* de paz

Jr *(abbr* **Junior) Nigel Molesworth, Jr** Nigel Molesworth, hijo

jubilant [ˈdʒuːbɪlənt] *adj (shouts, expression)* de júbilo; *(person, celebration)* jubiloso(a); **to be j. (at** *or* **about** *or* **over sth)** estar encantado(a) (con algo)

jubilation [dʒuːbɪˈleɪʃən] *n* júbilo *m*

jubilee [ˈdʒuːbɪliː] *n* aniversario *m;* **silver/golden j.** vigésimo quinto/quincuagésimo aniversario

Judaic [dʒuːˈdeɪɪk] *adj* judaico(a)

Judaism [ˈdʒuːdeɪɪzəm] *n* judaísmo *m*

Judas [ˈdʒuːdəs] *n (traitor)* judas *mf*

judge [dʒʌdʒ] **1** *n Law* juez *mf*, jueza *f; (in competition)* jurado *m*, juez *m;* **to be a good/poor j. of sth** tener buen ojo para (juzgar) algo; **I will be the j. of that** lo juzgaré por mí mismo

2 *vt* **(a)** *Law (try, give decision about)* juzgar; **to j. a case** juzgar un caso **(b)** *(assess critically)* juzgar, calificar; **to j. sb by** *or* **on sth** juzgar a alguien por algo; **to j. sth/sb a success/failure** calificar algo/a alguien de éxito/fracaso; **to j. it necessary to do sth** juzgar necesario hacer algo **(c)** *(estimate)* estimar, calcular

3 *vi Law Rel* juzgar; **to j. by appearances** juzgar por las apariencias; **as far as I can j.** en mi opinión; **j. for yourself** júzgalo tú mismo, juzga por ti mismo; **judging by…** a juzgar por…

judgment, judgement [ˈdʒʌdʒmənt] *n* **(a)** *(decision)* juicio *m; (of judge, in court)* fallo *m; Law* **to sit in j.** deliberar; *Law* **to pass j.** pronunciar *or* emitir el veredicto; *Fig* **to sit in** *or* **pass j. on sb** emitir juicios sobre alguien; *Rel* **J. Day** el día del Juicio Final

(b) *(opinion)* juicio *m*, parecer *m;* **she gave her j. on the performance** dio su parecer acerca de la actuación; **to form a j.** formarse un juicio

(c) *(discernment)* juicio *m;* **good j.** buen juicio; **to show poor j.** demostrar tener poco juicio; **to trust sb's j.** fiarse (del juicio) de alguien; **in my j.** a mi juicio; **against my better j.** a pesar de no estar plenamente convencido(a)

judgmental, judgemental [dʒʌdʒˈmentəl] *adj* **to be j.** hacer juicios a la ligera

judicial [dʒuːˈdɪʃəl] *adj* judicial

judiciary [dʒuːˈdɪʃɪərɪ] *n (judges)* judicatura *f*, magistratura *f; (branch of authority)* poder *m* judicial

judicious [dʒuːˈdɪʃəs] *adj* juicioso(a)

judiciously [dʒuːˈdɪʃəslɪ] *adv* juiciosamente

judiciousness [dʒuːˈdɪʃnɪs] *n* buen juicio *m*

judo [ˈdʒuːdəʊ] *n* judo *m*

jug [dʒʌg] *n* **(a)** *(for wine, water)* jarra *f* **(b)** *Fam (prison)* **in the j.** en la cárcel *or Esp* chirona *or Andes, RP* la cana *or Méx* el bote

juggernaut [ˈdʒʌgənɔːt] *n (force)* gigante(a) *m,f*, coloso(a) *m,f*

juggle [ˈdʒʌgəl] **1** *vt (balls, figures)* hacer malabarismos *or* juegos malabares con

2 *vi* hacer malabarismos, hacer juegos malabares

juggler [ˈdʒʌglə(r)] *n* malabarista *mf*

jugular [ˈdʒʌgjʊlə(r)] **1** *n* yugular *f; Fig* **to go for the j.** *(in argument)* entrar a degüello

2 *adj* yugular

juice [dʒuːs] *n* **(a)** *(of fruit)* zumo *m*, *Am* jugo *m; (of meat)* jugo *m* **(b)** *Fam (gasoline)* gasolina *f*, *Esp* gasofa *f*, *RP* nafta *f* **(c)** *Fam (alcoholic drink)* bebida *f*, *Méx, RP* chupe *m*

juicer [ˈdʒuːsə(r)] *n* exprimidor *m*

juicy [ˈdʒuːsɪ] *adj also Fig* jugoso(a)

jujitsu, jiujitsu [dʒuːˈdʒɪtsuː] *n* jiu-jitsu *m*

jukebox [ˈdʒuːkbɒks] *n* máquina *f* de discos

Jul *(abbr* **July)** julio *m*

July [dʒuːˈlaɪ] *n* julio *m; see also* **May**

jumble [ˈdʒʌmbəl] **1** *n (of things, ideas, words)* revoltijo *m*, batiburrillo *m;* **in a j.** *(papers)* revueltos; *(ideas)* confusas

2 *vt (things, ideas, words)* revolver

jumbo [ˈdʒʌmbəʊ] *adj* gigante; **j. jet** jumbo *m*

jumbo-sized [ˈdʒʌmbəʊsaɪzd] *adj* de tamaño gigante

jump [dʒʌmp] **1** *n* **(a)** *(leap)* salto *m; Fig* **go take a j.!** ¡vete a freír espárragos!, *RP* ¡andá a freír churros!; *Fig* **to be one j. ahead** ir (un paso) por delante; *Av* **j. jet** reactor *m* de despegue vertical; **j. rope** *Esp* comba *f*, *Am* cuerda *f* de saltar; **j. suit** mono *m (de vestir)* **(b)** *(rise)* salto *m* **(in** en) **(c)** *(fence on racecourse)* obstáculo *m*

2 *vt (hedge, ditch)* saltar; *(word, paragraph, page)* saltarse; **to j. sb** *(attack)* asaltar a alguien; **to j. bail** huir durante la libertad bajo fianza; **to j. the gun** *(in race)* hacer una salida en falso; *Fig* precipitarse; **to j. the lights** *(in car)* saltarse un semáforo, *RP* comerse la luz roja; **to j. the line** colarse; **to j. rope** saltar a la cuerda *or Esp* comba; **to j. ship** desertar, abandonar el barco

3 *vi* (**a**) *(leap) (person, animal)* saltar, brincar; **to j. to one's feet** ponerse en pie de un salto; **to j. for joy** saltar de alegría; **to j. on a train/bus** coger *or* tomar un tren/un autobús; **to j. into a taxi** montar en un taxi; **to j. from a train** tirarse de un tren; **to j. (down) from a wall/tree** dejarse caer desde (lo alto de) un muro/árbol; **to j. out of bed** tirarse de la cama, levantarse (de la cama) de un salto; **to j. to conclusions** sacar conclusiones precipitadas; *Fam* **to j. down sb's throat** ponerse hecho(a) una furia con alguien; *Fig* **to j. out at sb** *(mistake, surprising detail)* saltarle a alguien a la vista

(**b**) *(go directly)* **to j. from one subject to another** saltar de un tema a otro; **the movie then jumps to the present** luego la película da un salto hasta el presente

(**c**) *(rise rapidly) (unemployment)* dispararse, ascender rápidamente

(**d**) *(make a sudden movement)* dar un salto, saltar; **my heart jumped** me dio un vuelco el corazón; **we nearly jumped out of our skins** nos dimos un susto de muerte

▸**jump at** *vt insep* **to j. at an offer/a chance** no dejar escapar una oferta/una oportunidad

▸**jump on** *vt insep Fam (reprimand)* **to j. on sb (for doing sth)** echarse encima de alguien (por haber hecho algo)

jumped-up [ˈdʒʌmpˈtʌp] *adj Fam Pej (recently promoted)* advenedizo(a)

jumper [ˈdʒʌmpə(r)] *n (sleeveless dress) Esp* pichi *m, CSur, Méx* jumper *m*

jumping-off place [ˈdʒʌmpɪŋˈɒfpleɪs], **jumping-off point** [ˈdʒʌmpɪŋˈɒfpɔɪnt] *n* punto *m* de partida

jump-start [ˈdʒʌmpstɑːt] *vt (car)* arrancar utilizando pinzas de batería

jumpy [ˈdʒʌmpɪ] *adj* nervioso(a); **to be j.** estar nervioso(a)

Jun *(abbr* **June)** junio *m*

junction [ˈdʒʌŋkʃən] *n (of roads, railroad lines)* cruce *m*, nudo *m*; *Elec* **j. box** caja *f* de empalmes

juncture [ˈdʒʌŋktʃə(r)] *n* coyuntura *f*; **at this j.** en esta coyuntura

June [dʒuːn] *n* junio *m*; *see also* **May**

jungle [ˈdʒʌŋgəl] *n (forest)* selva *f*, jungla *f*; *Fig* jungla *f*; **j. gym** = estructura de hierro o madera para que trepen los niños

junior [ˈdʒuːnjə(r)] **1** *adj* (**a**) *(in age)* **to be j. to sb** ser más joven que alguien; **Nigel Molesworth J.** Nigel Molesworth hijo; **j. high (school)** *(between 11 and 15)* escuela *f* secundaria (**b**) *(in rank)* de rango inferior; **to be j. to sb** tener un rango inferior al de alguien

2 *n* (**a**) *(in age)* **to be sb's j.** ser más joven que alguien; **he's three years my j.** es tres años menor que yo (**b**) *(in rank)* subalterno(a) *m,f* (**c**) *Sch & Univ* alumno(a) *m,f* de tercero

juniper [ˈdʒuːnɪpə(r)] *n* **j. (tree)** enebro *m*; **j. berry** enebrina *f*, baya *f* de enebro

junk¹ [dʒʌŋk] **1** *n (unwanted objects)* trastos *mpl*; *Fin* **j. bond** bono *m* basura; *Pej* **j. food** comida *f* basura; *Pej* **j. mail** propaganda *f* (postal); **j. shop** cacharrería *f*, baratillo *m*

2 *vt Fam (discard)* deshacerse de

junk² *n (boat)* junco *m*

junket [ˈdʒʌŋkɪt] *n* (**a**) *(food)* cuajada *f* (**b**) *Pej (trip by public official)* = viaje pagado con dinero del contribuyente

junkie, junky [ˈdʒʌŋkɪ] *n Fam (drug addict in general)* drogadicto(a) *m,f, Esp* drogata *mf*; *(heroin addict)* yonqui *mf*; **a game-show j.** un adicto a los concursos

junkman [ˈdʒʌŋkmæn] *n* trapero

junkyard [ˈdʒʌŋkjɑːd] *n (for metal)* chatarrería *f*, depósito *m* de chatarra

junta [ˈdʒʌntə] *n Pej* junta *f* militar

Jupiter [ˈdʒuːpɪtə(r)] *n (planet, god)* Júpiter *m*

jurisdiction [dʒʊərɪsˈdɪkʃən] *n* jurisdicción *f*; **to have j. over**

tener jurisdicción sobre; **within** *or* **under the j. of…** bajo la jurisdicción de…

jurisprudence [dʒʊərɪsˈpruːdəns] *n* jurisprudencia *f*

jurist [ˈdʒʊərɪst] *n Formal (legal expert)* jurista *mf*

juror [ˈdʒʊərə(r)] *n Law (miembro m* del) jurado *m*

jury [ˈdʒʊərɪ] *n Law* jurado *m*; **to be** *or* **serve on the j.** ser miembro del jurado; *Fig* **the j. is still out on the reforms** aún está por ver la conveniencia de las reformas; **j. box** tribuna *f* del jurado; **to do j. service** formar parte de un jurado (popular)

jury-rigging [ˈdʒʊərɪˈrɪgɪŋ] *n* manipulación *f* del jurado

just [dʒʌst] **1** *adj (fair)* justo(a); **it's only j. that…** es justo que…; **he got his j. deserts** recibió su merecido

2 *adv* (**a**) *(exactly)* justamente, justo; **that's j. what I told her** eso es exactamente *or* justo lo que le dije; **that's j. the point!** ¡de eso se trata, precisamente!; **isn't that j. my luck!** ¡vaya mala suerte que tengo!; **it's j. as good/difficult as…** es tan bueno/difícil como…; **j. then** justo entonces; **he's busy j. now** está ocupado en este (preciso) momento; **j. as I was leaving…** justo en el momento en que me iba…; **I can j. see her as a doctor** me la imagino perfectamente como médica

(**b**) *(only)* sólo, solamente; **she's j. a baby** no es más que una niña; **it costs j. $10** sólo cuesta 10 dólares

(**c**) *(barely)* justo; **j. before/after** justo antes/después; **j. over/under $50** poco más/menos de 50 dólares; **j. in time** justo a tiempo; **it's only j. big enough** tiene el tamaño justo; **it's j. enough to live on** llega justo para vivir; **they j. missed the train** perdieron el tren un pelo

(**d**) *(recently)* **to have j. done sth** acabar de hacer algo; **I saw him j. now** lo acabo de ver; **j. yesterday** ayer mismo; **j. last year** tan sólo el año pasado

(**e**) *(simply)* **it was j. wonderful/dreadful!** ¡fue sencillamente maravilloso/horroroso!; **he j. refuses to listen!** ¡es que se niega a escuchar!; **j. ask if you need money** si necesitas dinero, no tienes más que pedirlo

(**f**) *(in threats, exhortations)* **j. (you) try/wait!** ¡inténtalo/espera y verás!; **(that's) j. as well!** ¡menos mal!

3 just about *adv (almost)* casi; **they're j. about the same** son casi iguales; **I can j. about manage** me las puedo arreglar más o menos; **to be j. about to do sth** estar a punto de hacer algo

justice [ˈdʒʌstɪs] *n* (**a**) *(power of law)* justicia *f*; **to bring sb to j.** llevar a alguien a los tribunales (**b**) *(fairness)* justicia *f*; **this photograph doesn't do him j.** esta fotografía no le hace justicia; **not to do oneself j.** no dar lo mejor de sí mismo(a) (**c**) *Law (judge)* juez *mf*, jueza *f*; **j. court** juzgado *m* de instrucción *or* de primera instancia; **J. of the Peace** juez de paz

justifiable [ˈdʒʌstɪfaɪəbəl] *adj* justificable; *Law* **j. homicide** homicidio *m* justificado

justifiably [ˈdʒʌstɪfaɪəblɪ] *adv* justificadamente

justification [dʒʌstɪfɪˈkeɪʃən] *n* justificación *f*; **in j. of** para justificar

justify [ˈdʒʌstɪfaɪ] *vt* (**a**) *(explain)* justificar; **to be justified in doing sth** tener justificación para hacer algo (**b**) *Typ & Comptr* justificar

justly [ˈdʒʌstlɪ] *adv (fairly, rightly)* justamente, con justicia; **j. famous** justamente *or* merecidamente famoso(a)

▸**jut out** [dʒʌt] *(pt & pp* **jutted) 1** *vt sep (chin)* sacar

2 *vi (balcony, rock)* sobresalir

jute [dʒuːt] *n (plant, fiber)* yute *m*

juvenile [ˈdʒuːvɪnaɪl] **1** *adj* (**a**) *(for young people)* juvenil; *Law* **j. court** tribunal *m* (tutelar) de menores; **j. delinquency** delincuencia *f* juvenil; **j. delinquent** delincuente *mf* juvenil (**b**) *Pej (childish)* infantil, pueril

2 *n Law* menor *mf*

juxtapose [dʒʌkstəˈpəʊz] *vt* yuxtaponer

juxtaposition [dʒʌkstəpəˈzɪʃən] *n* yuxtaposición *f*

K

K, k [keɪ] *n* (**a**) *(letter)* K, k *f* (**b**) *(thousand)* **he earns 30K** gana treinta mil

kabob = **kebab**

Kabul [ˈkɑːbʊl] *n* Kabul

Kaffir [ˈkæfə(r)] *n very Fam* = término ofensivo para referirse a los negros, negraco(a) *m,f*

kaftan [ˈkæftæn] *n* caftán *m*

kale [keɪl] *n* col *f* rizada, *CSur* repollo *m* rizado

kaleidoscope [kəˈlaɪdəskəʊp] *n* calidoscopio *m*

kamikaze [kæmɪˈkɑːzɪ] *n & adj also Fig* kamikaze *mf*

kangaroo [kæŋɡəˈruː] (*pl* **kangaroos**) *n* canguro *m*; *Pej* **k. court** tribunal *m* irregular

kaput [kəˈpʊt] *adj Fam* **to be k.** *Esp* estar cascado(a), *esp Am* estar roto(a) *or* estropeado(a)

karaoke [kærɪˈəʊkɪ] *n* karaoke *m*

karate [kəˈrɑːtɪ] *n* kárate *m*; **k. chop** golpe *m* de kárate

karma [ˈkɑːmə] *n Rel* karma *m*; *Fam Fig* **good/bad k.** buenas/malas vibraciones *or Am* ondas, *Esp* buen/mal rollo

Kashmir [kæʃˈmɪə(r)] *n* Cachemira

Kashmiri [kæʃˈmɪərɪ] **1** *n* = habitante *or* nativo(a) de Cachemira
2 *adj* de Cachemira

Katmandu [kætmænˈduː] *n* Katmandú

kayak [ˈkaɪæk] *n* canoa *f*, kayak *m*

Kazakhstan [kæzækˈstɑːn] *n* Kazajistán

kebab [kəˈbæb], **kabob** [kəˈbɒb] *n* brocheta *f*, pincho *m* moruno

kedgeree [kedʒəˈriː] *n* = plato especiado de arroz, pescado y huevo duro

keel [kiːl] *n Naut* quilla *f*; *Fig* **to be on an even k.** *(business, economy)* estar en equilibrio

▶**keel over** *vi (boat)* volcar; *Fam (person)* derrumbarse

keen [kiːn] *adj* (**a**) *(enthusiastic)* entusiasta; **to be k. to do sth** tener muchas ganas de hacer algo; **to be k. for sth to happen** tener muchas ganas de que ocurra algo; **she's k. on Patrick** le gusta Patrick; **he wasn't k. on the idea** no le entusiasmaba la idea; *Fam* **to be as k. as mustard** *(enthusiastic)* estar entusiasmadísimo(a); **to take a k. interest in sth** mostrar gran interés por algo
(**b**) *(acute, perceptive) (mind)* penetrante; *(eyesight)* agudo(a); *(sense of smell)* fino(a); **to have a k. eye for detail** tener buen ojo para el detalle; **to have a k. awareness of sth** ser profundamente consciente de algo
(**c**) *(sharp, intense) (sorrow, regret)* profundo(a); **a k. appetite** un apetito voraz; **a k. blade** una hoja afilada; **k. competition** competencia *f* feroz; **a k. wind** un viento cortante

keenly [ˈkiːnlɪ] *adv (enthusiastically)* con entusiasmo; *(intensely)* profundamente; **a k. contested election** unas elecciones muy reñidas

keep [kiːp] **1** *n* (**a**) *(maintenance)* **to pay for one's k.** pagarse la manutención; **to earn one's k.** ganarse el sustento (**b**) *(of castle)* torre *f* del homenaje
2 *vt (pt & pp* **kept** [kept]) (**a**) *(retain)* quedarse con, guardar; *(store)* guardar; **to k. sth for sb** guardar algo para alguien; **to k. sth from sb** *(information)* ocultar algo a alguien; **to k. one's job** conservar el trabajo; **to k. its shape** *(garment)* no deformarse; **to k. its color** *(garment)* no desteñir; **to k. sb's attention** mantener la atención de alguien; **k. the change** quédese con el cambio
(**b**) *(maintain)* **to k. a diary** llevar un diario; **to k. a note of sth** llevar cuenta de algo; **to k. order** mantener el orden; **to k. a record of sth** registrar algo; **to k. a secret** guardar un secreto
(**c**) *(maintain in a certain condition)* mantener; **to k. sth clean/secret** mantener algo limpio/en secreto; **to k. sb awake** mantener *or* tener despierto(a) a alguien; **to k. sb waiting** tener a alguien esperando
(**d**) *(look after) (animals, shop)* tener; *(mistress)* mantener; **a kept woman** una mujer mantenida; **I've got a family to k.** tengo una familia que mantener
(**e**) *(detain)* entretener, parar; **what kept you?** ¿qué fue lo que te retrasó?
(**f**) *(observe) (promise)* cumplir; **to k. late hours** trasnochar; **she kept her word** mantuvo su palabra
3 *vi* (**a**) *(remain, stay)* mantenerse; **to k. well** mantenerse bien; **how are you keeping?** ¿qué tal estás?; **to k. quiet** estar callado(a) (**b**) *(continue)* **to k. doing sth** *(continue doing)* seguir haciendo algo; **he kept getting into trouble** siempre se estaba metiendo en líos; **to k. straight on** seguir todo recto; **k. (to the) left/right** circular por la izquierda/derecha; **I wish you wouldn't k. saying that** me gustaría que no dijeras eso todo el tiempo (**c**) *(food)* conservarse; *Fig* **it will k.** *(problem)* puede esperar
4 for keeps *adv Fam* para siempre

▶**keep away 1** *vt sep* **to k. sb away from sth** mantener a alguien alejado(a) de algo; **k. that dog away from me!** ¡no me acerques ese perro!
2 *vi* **to k. away from** mantenerse alejado(a) de

▶**keep back 1** *vt sep* (**a**) *(crowd, tears)* contener; **to k. sth back from sb** ocultarle algo a alguien (**b**) *(delay)* entretener; **he was kept back by his lack of qualifications** su falta de titulación le impidió progresar
2 *vi (not approach)* no acercarse

▶**keep down 1** *vt sep* (**a**) **to k. one's voice down** hablar bajo; **to k. one's head down** *(physically)* mantener la cabeza agachada; *Fig* esconder la cabeza; **I can't k. my food down** vomito todo lo que como (**b**) *(repress)* reprimir; *(prices)* mantener bajos
2 *vi (not stand up)* mantenerse cuerpo a tierra

▶**keep from** *vt sep* **to k. sb from doing sth** impedir que alguien haga algo; **to k. sb from his work** no dejar trabajar a alguien

▶**keep in** *vt sep (pupil)* castigar sin salir; **they decided to k. her in overnight** *(in hospital)* decidieron dejarla ingresada hasta el día siguiente

▶**keep in with** *vt insep Fam* **to k. in with sb** cultivar la amistad de alguien

▸**keep off 1** *vt sep* **k. your hands off that!** ¡no toques eso!; **k. your hands off me!** ¡no me toques!

2 *vt insep* **k. off the grass!** *(sign)* prohibido pisar el césped

3 *vi (stay away)* mantenerse al margen

▸**keep on 1** *vt sep (not take off)* dejarse puesto(a); *(not switch off)* dejar encendido(a) *or Am* prendido(a); *(continue to employ)* mantener en el puesto

2 *vi* continuar, seguir; **to k. on doing sth** *(continue doing)* seguir haciendo algo; **she kept on getting into trouble** siempre se estaba metiendo en líos; **to k. on about sth** insistir sobre algo

▸**keep on at** *vt insep Fam* **to k. on at sb (to do sth)** dar la lata a alguien (para que haga algo)

▸**keep out 1** *vt sep (intruders, foreign imports)* impedir el paso a

2 *vi (avoid, stay away from)* **to k. out of sth** no meterse en algo; **to k. out of trouble** no meterse en líos; **to k. out of an argument** mantenerse al margen de una discusión; **k. out** *(sign)* prohibida la entrada, prohibido el paso

▸**keep to 1** *vt sep* **(a)** *(hold)* **to k. sb to a promise** hacer que alguien cumpla una promesa; **to k. delays/costs to a minimum** reducir al mínimo *or* minimizar los retrasos/costes **(b)** *(not reveal)* **to k. sth to oneself** no contar algo; **to k. oneself to oneself** mantenerse apartado(a) del resto

2 *vt insep (promise)* cumplir; **to k. to a subject** ceñirse a un tema; **she kept to her room** se quedó encerrada en su habitación

▸**keep up 1** *vt sep* **(a)** *(custom)* mantener; **to k. up the payments** llevar al día los pagos; **k. it up!** ¡sigue así!; **k. up the good work!** ¡sigue así!; **to k. up appearances** guardar las apariencias **(b)** *(keep awake)* tener en vela

2 *vi* **(a)** *(rain, snow)* continuar **(b)** *(remain level, go at same speed)* no quedarse atrás; **to k. up with sb** seguir el ritmo de alguien; **to k. up with the Joneses** no ser menos que el vecino; **to k. up with events** mantenerse informado(a); **to k. up with the times** adaptarse a los tiempos

keeper ['ki:pə(r)] *n (in zoo, park)* guarda *mf*; *(in museum)* conservador(ora) *m,f*; *(gamekeeper)* guardabosque *m*

keeping ['ki:pɪŋ] *n* **to have sth/sb in one's k.** tener algo/a alguien bajo la custodia de uno; **in k. with…** de acuerdo con…; **out of k. with…** en desacuerdo con…

keepsake ['ki:pseɪk] *n* recuerdo *m*

keg [keg] *n* barrica *f*, barrilete *m*

ken [ken] *n* **to be beyond sb's k.** estar fuera del alcance de alguien

kennel ['kenəl] *n* caseta *f* (del perro)

Kenya ['kenjə, 'ki:njə] *n* Kenia

Kenyan ['kenjən] *n & adj* keniano(a) *m,f*, keniata *mf*

kept [kept] *pt & pp* de **keep**

kernel ['kɜ:nəl] *n (of nut)* pepita *f*; *(of grain)* grano *m*; *Fig (of problem)* núcleo *m*

kerosene, kerosine ['kerəsi:n] *n* queroseno *m*, *Am* querosén *m*; **k. lamp** lámpara *f* de queroseno

kestrel ['kestrəl] *n* cernícalo *m*

ketchup ['ketʃəp] *n* **(tomato) k.** ketchup *m*

kettle [ketəl] *n (for boiling water)* (on stove) tetera *f*; *(electric)* hervidor *m* (eléctrico); **I'll put the k. on** pondré el agua a hervir; *Fam* **that's a different k. of fish** eso es harina de otro costal

kettledrum ['ketəldrʌm] *n* timbal *m*

key [ki:] **1** *n (pl keys)* **(a)** *(of door)* llave *f*; *(of clock, mechanical toy)* cuerda *f*; *(of piano, typewriter)* tecla *f*; *(to problem, situation)* clave *f*, llave *f*; **the k. to happiness/success** la clave de la felicidad/del éxito **(b)** *(answers, guide)* (of map) clave *f*; *(to exercises)* respuestas *fpl* **(c)** *Mus* tono *m*; **major/minor k.** tono mayor/menor; **the k. of C** la clave de do; **to be off k.** estar desafinado(a)

2 *adj (most important)* clave

▸**key in** *vt sep Comptr* teclear, *Am* tipear

keyboard ['ki:bɔ:d] *n (of piano, computer)* teclado *m*; *Mus* **keyboards** teclado *m*, teclados *mpl*; **k. player** teclista *mf*

keycard ['ki:kɑ:d] *n (for door)* tarjeta *f* de acceso

keyhole ['ki:həʊl] *n* (ojo *m* de la) cerradura *f*; **k. surgery** cirugía *f* endoscópica

keynote ['ki:nəʊt] **1** *n* nota *f* dominante

2 *adj (speech, speaker)* principal

keypad ['ki:pæd] *n Comptr* teclado *m* numérico

keyring ['ki:rɪŋ] *n* llavero *m*

keystone ['ki:stəʊn] *n Archit* clave *f* (de un arco); *Fig* piedra *f* angular

keystroke ['ki:strəʊk] *n Comptr* pulsación *f*

kg *(abbr kilogram)* kg *m*

KGB [keɪdʒi:'bi:] *n Formerly* KGB *m*

khaki ['kɑ:kɪ] **1** *n* caqui *m*

2 *adj* caqui *inv*; **k. shorts** pantalones *mpl* cortos caqui; **khakis** portalones de soldado

Khartoum [kɑ:'tu:m] *n* Jartum

kHz *Elec (abbr kilohertz)* kHz *m*

kibbutz [kɪ'bʊts] *(pl* **kibbutzim** [kɪbʊt'si:m]) *n* kibutz *m*

kibosh ['kaɪbɒʃ] *n Fam* **to put the k. on sth** echar algo abajo *or Esp* a pique

kick [kɪk] **1** *n* **(a)** *(with foot)* patada *f*, puntapié *m*; *(of horse)* coz *f*; *(of gun)* retroceso *m*; **to have a k.** *(drink)* estar fuerte *(aunque entre bien)*; **to give sth/sb a k.** dar una patada a algo/alguien; *Fig* **that was a k. in the teeth for him** le sentó como una patada en la boca **(b)** *(thrill)* **to get a k. out of sth** disfrutar con algo; **to get a k. out of doing sth** disfrutar haciendo algo; **to do sth for kicks** hacer algo por gusto, regodearse haciendo algo

2 *vt (once)* dar una patada a; *(several times)* dar patadas a; **to get kicked** *(once)* recibir una patada; *(several times)* recibir patadas; *Vulg* **to k. sb's ass** *(defeat)* dar un buen palizón a alguien; *Vulg* **to k. ass** *(be bossy)* tratar a todo el mundo a patadas; *(be excellent)* ser *Esp* cojonudo(a) *or Am* salvo *RP* chévere *or Méx* padrísimo(a) *or RP* bárbaro(a); *Fam* **to k. the bucket** estirar la pata, *CAm, Méx* doblar *or* liar el petate; *Fig* **to k. a man when he's down** atacar a alguien cuando ya está derrotado; **I could have kicked myself** me hubiera dado de bofetadas, era para tirarme de los pelos; *Fam* **to k. the habit** *(stop taking drugs)* dejar las drogas

3 *vi (once)* dar una patada; *(several times)* dar patadas; *(animal)* dar coces; *(gun)* hacer el retroceso; *Fam* **to k. against sth** *(rebel against)* patalear contra algo

▸**kick around, kick about 1** *vt sep* **to k. a ball around** *or* **about** pelotear, dar patadas a un balón; *Fam* **to k. an idea around** *or* **about** darle vueltas a una idea; **don't let them k. you around** *or* **about** no dejes que te traten a patadas

2 *vi Fam* andar por ahí

▸**kick in** *vt sep (door)* abrir de una patada; *Fam* **to k. sb's head in** romperle la cabeza a alguien

▸**kick off** *vi (in football, soccer)* hacer el saque inicial; *Fam Fig (in meeting, debate)* empezar

▸**kick out** *vt sep Fam* **he was kicked out** *(of job, house)* lo echaron, le dieron la patada

▸**kick up** *vt sep Fam* **to k. up a fuss** armar *or Esp* montar un alboroto; **to k. up one's heels** pasarlo muy bien; **to k. up a row** *or* **a racket** armar *or Esp* montar una bronca

kickback ['kɪkbæk] *n Fam (payment)* **he got a k. for doing it** le *Esp* untaron *or Andes, RP* coimearon *or CAm, Méx* dieron una mordida para que lo hiciera

kickoff ['kɪkɒf] *n (in football, soccer)* saque *m* inicial; *Fam* **for a k.** *(to start with)* para empezar

kick-start ['kɪkstɑ:t] *vt (motorbike, engine)* arrancar a patada (con el pedal); *Fig (economy)* reactivar

kid [kɪd] **1** *n* **(a)** *Fam (child)* niño(a) *m,f*, *esp Esp* crío(a) *m,f*, *Arg* pibe(a) *m,f, Chile* cabro(a) *m,f, Urug* botija *mf*; **my k. brother** mi hermano pequeño; **it's kid's stuff** *(easy, childish)* eso es cosa de niños (**b**) *(young goat)* cabrito *m*; *(skin)* cabritilla *f*; **k. gloves** guantes *mpl* de cabritilla; *Fig* **to handle sb with k. gloves** tratar a alguien con mucho tacto *or Am* guantes de seda

2 *vt (pt & pp* **kidded**) *Fam (fool)* quedarse con, vacilar; **to k. oneself** engañarse

3 *vi Fam* **to be kidding** estar bromeando; **no kidding!** ¿en serio?

kidnap ['kɪdnæp] *vt (pt & pp* **kidnapped**) secuestrar, raptar

kidnapper ['kɪdnæpə(r)] *n* secuestrador(ora) *m,f*, raptor(ora) *m,f*

kidnapping ['kɪdnæpɪŋ] *n* secuestro *m*, rapto *m*

kidney ['kɪdnɪ] *(pl* **kidneys**) *n* riñón *m*; **k. beans** alubias *fpl, Esp* judías *fpl, Am salvo RP* frijoles *mpl, Andes, RP* porotos *mpl*; **k. donor** donante *mf* de riñón; **k. machine** riñón artificial, aparato *m* de diálisis

kill [kɪl] **1** *n (animals killed)* presas *fpl*, caza *f*; *Fig* **to be in at the k.** no perderse el desenlace

2 *vt* (**a**) *(person, animal)* matar; **twelve people were killed** resultaron muertas doce personas; **to k. oneself** matarse; *Fam* **to k. oneself laughing** morirse de risa; *Ironic* **don't k. yourself!** *(to sb not working very hard)* ¡cuidado, no te vayas a herniar!; *Fam* **this one'll k. you** *(joke)* este es buenísimo; **to k. two birds with one stone** matar dos pájaros de un tiro; *Fam* **my feet/these shoes are killing me** los pies/estos zapatos me están matando

(**b**) *(pain)* acabar con; *(sound)* amortiguar; **the speech killed his chances of promotion** el discurso acabó con sus posibilidades de ascenso; *Journ* **to k. a story** = interrumpir la difusión de una noticia; **to k. time** matar el tiempo

▸**kill off** *vt sep* acabar con; **to k. off a character** *(in novel, TV series)* matar a un personaje

killer ['kɪlə(r)] *n* asesino(a) *m,f*; *Fam Fig* **those steps were a k.!** ¡esos escalones me han dejado muerto!; *Fam Fig* **this one's a k.** *(joke)* este es buenísimo; *Fig* **he lacks the k. instinct** *(sportsman)* le falta garra para terminar con su contrincante; **k. whale** orca *f*

killing ['kɪlɪŋ] **1** *n (of person)* asesinato *m*; *(of animals)* matanza *f*; *Fam* **to make a k.** *(on Stock Exchange)* forrarse de dinero

2 *adj* (**a**) *Fam (exhausting)* matador(ora) (**b**) *Fam (very amusing)* desternillante

killjoy ['kɪldʒɔɪ] *(pl* **killjoys**) *n* aguafiestas *mf inv*

kiln [kɪln] *n* horno *m (para cerámica, ladrillos)*

kilo ['kiːləʊ] *(pl* **kilos**) *n* kilo *m*

kilobyte ['kɪləbaɪt] *n Comptr* kilobyte *m*

kilocalorie ['kɪləkælərɪ] *n* kilocaloría *f*

kilogram ['kɪləɡræm] *n* kilogramo *m*

kilohertz ['kɪləhɜːts] *n* kilohercio *m*, kilohertz *m*

kilometer ['kɪləmiːtə(r), kɪ'lɒmətə(r)] *n* kilómetro *m*

kilowatt ['kɪləwɒt] *n* kilovatio *m*; **k.-hour** kilovatio-hora *m*

kilt [kɪlt] *n* falda *f* escocesa

kilter ['kɪltə(r)] *n Fam* **out of k.** *(machine part)* descuajeringado(a), *Esp* escacharrado(a), *Méx* madreado(a); *(schedule)* manga por hombro

kimono [kɪ'məʊnəʊ] *(pl* **kimonos**) *n* quimono *m*, kimono *m*

kin [kɪn] *n* parientes *mpl*, familiares *mpl*; **next of k.** pariente *mf* más cercano(a)

kind¹ [kaɪnd] **1** *n* (**a**) *(class, sort)* clase *f*, tipo *m*; **all kinds of…** toda clase *or* todo tipo de…; **something of the k.** algo así; **nothing of the k.** nada por el estilo; **in a k. of a way** en cierto sentido; **well, it's coffee of a k., I suppose** supongo que debe de ser café, pero no lo parece; **we're two of a k.** estamos hechos de la misma pasta; **it's the only one of its k.** es único en su género; **he's that k. of person** es de esa clase de personas; **this is my k. of party!** ¡este es el estilo de

fiestas que me gusta!; **is this the k. of thing you're looking for?** ¿estás buscando algo así?

(**b**) *Fam* **you look k. of tired** pareces como cansado; **I k. of expected this** me esperaba algo así, me lo temía; **do you like it? — k. of** ¿te gusta? — vaya *or* más o menos; **it was a k. of saucer-shaped thing** era una especie de objeto con forma de plato

2 in kind *adj & adv (payment)* en especie

kind² *adj* amable; **to be k. to sb** ser amable con alguien; **it's very k. of you (to do sth)** es muy amable de tu parte (hacer algo); *Formal* **would you be k. enough to *or* so k. as to…?** ¿le importaría…?; **k. to the skin** *(on detergent, soap package)* no irrita la piel; **by k. permission of…** con el consentimiento de…; **k. words** palabras *fpl* amables

kinda ['kaɪndə] *Fam* = **kind of**

kindergarten ['kɪndəɡɑːtən] *n* jardín *m* de infancia, guardería *f*

kindhearted ['kaɪnd'hɑːtɪd] *adj* bondadoso(a)

kindle ['kɪndəl] *vt (flame, fire)* encender, *Am* prender; *(emotions)* despertar

kindling ['kɪndlɪŋ] *n* leña *f* (menuda)

kindly ['kaɪndlɪ] **1** *adv* amablemente; *(nobly)* generosamente; **to speak k. of sb** hablar bien de alguien; *Formal* **(would you) k. be quiet!** ¿serías tan amable de callarte?; **she didn't take k. to being criticized** no se tomaba bien las críticas

2 *adj* amable

kindness ['kaɪndnɪs] *n* amabilidad *f*; **to show k. to sb** mostrarse amable con alguien; **to do sb a k.** hacer un favor a alguien; *Formal* **would you have the k. to…?** ¿tendría la bondad de…?; **she did it out of the k. of her heart** lo hizo desinteresadamente

kindred ['kɪndrɪd] *adj* por el estilo; **k. spirits** almas *fpl* gemelas

kinetic [kɪ'netɪk] *adj* cinético(a)

king [kɪŋ] *n* rey *m*; **the three Kings** *(in the Bible)* los Reyes Magos; **the k. of the beasts** el rey de la selva

kingdom ['kɪŋdəm] *n* reino *m*; **the k. of Heaven** el Reino de los Cielos; **the animal/plant k.** el reino animal/vegetal; *Fam* **till k. come** hasta el día del Juicio Final; *Fam* **to send sb to k. come** mandar a alguien a otro mundo

kingfisher ['kɪŋfɪʃə(r)] *n* martín *m* pescador

kingpin ['kɪŋpɪn] *n (of organization, company)* eje *m*

king-size(d) ['kɪŋ'saɪz(d)] *adj* (de) tamaño gigante; *(cigarette)* extralargo(a)

kink [kɪŋk] *n (in wire, rope)* retorcimiento *m*; *(in hair)* rizo *m*; *(in character)* manía *f*

kinky ['kɪŋkɪ] *adj* (**a**) *(hair)* rizado(a), *Chile, Col* crespo(a), *Méx* quebrado(a), *RP* enrulado(a) (**b**) *Fam (person)* aberrante, pervertido(a); *(erotic, pornographic)* erótico(a)

kinship ['kɪnʃɪp] *n (family relationship)* parentesco *m*; *(affinity)* afinidad *f*

kinsman ['kɪnzmən] *n Literary* pariente *m*

kinswoman ['kɪnzwʊmən] *n Literary* pariente *f*

kiosk ['kiːɒsk] *n* quiosco *m*, kiosco *m*

kipper ['kɪpə(r)] *n* arenque *m* ahumado

Kirgyzstan, Kirg(h)izstan [kɜːɡɪz'stæn], **Kirg(h)izia** [kɜːˈɡɪzɪə] = **Kyrgyzstan**

Kiribati [kɪrɪ'bætɪ] *n* Kiribati

kirk [kɜːk] *n Scot* iglesia *f*; **the K.** la Iglesia de Escocia

kiss [kɪs] **1** *n* beso *m*; **to give sb a k.** dar un beso a alguien; **to give sb the k. of life** hacer el boca a boca a alguien; *Fig* **the news was the k. of death for the project** la noticia dio el golpe de gracia al proyecto

2 *vt* besar; **to k. sb goodbye/goodnight** dar un beso de despedida/de buenas noches a alguien; **you can k. your chances of promotion goodbye** ya puedes despedirte de tu ascenso

3 *vi* besarse; **to k. and make up** reconciliarse; **to k. and tell** = tener un lío con un(a) famoso(a) y luego contárselo a la prensa

kiss-and-tell [kısən'tel] *adj (journalism)* del corazón; **k. stories/revelations** historias *fpl*/secretos *mpl* de alcoba

kisser ['kısə(r)] *n Fam (mouth)* morros *mpl*, boca *f*

kit [kıt] *n* **(a)** *(for assembly)* kit *m*, modelo *m* para armar; **to make sth from a k.** montar algo; **in k. form** para montar **(b) k. bag** petate *m*

kitchen ['kıtʃın] *n* cocina *f*; **k. knife** cuchillo *m* de cocina; **k. sink** fregadero *m*, *Chile, Col, Méx* lavaplatos *m*, *RP* pileta *f*; *Fam* **he took everything but the k. sink** se llevó hasta el colchón; **k. roll towel** (rollo *m* de) papel *m* de cocina; **k. unit** módulo *m* de cocina

kitchenette [kıtʃı'net] *n* pequeña cocina *f*

kitchenware ['kıtʃınweə(r)] *n* menaje *m*

kite [kaıt] *n* **(a)** *(toy)* cometa *f*, *CAm, Méx* papalote *m*, *Chile* volantín *m*, *Par* pandorga *f*, *Arg* barrilete *m*; *Fig* **to fly a k.** lanzar un globo sonda (para tantear el terreno); *Fam* **go fly a k.!** ¡vete a hacer gárgaras!; *Fam* **to be as high as a k.** ir como una moto **(b)** *(bird)* milano *m*

kith [kıθ] *n Literary* **k. and kin** parientes y amigos *mpl*

kitsch [kıtʃ] *n* kitsch *m*

kitschy ['kıtʃı] *adj* kitsch *inv*

kitten ['kıtən] *n (young cat)* gatito(a) *m,f*

kitty ['kıtı] *n* **(a)** *Fam (cat)* gatito(a) *m,f*, minino(a) *m,f* **(b)** *(for bills)* fondo *m* or caja *f* común; *(in cards)* posturas *fpl*, puesta *f*

kiwi ['ki:wi:] *n* **(a)** *(bird)* kiwi *m*; **k. fruit** kiwi *m* **(b)** *Fam (New Zealander)* **K.** neozelandés(esa) *m,f*

kleptomania [kleptə'meınıə] *n* cleptomanía *f*

kleptomaniac [kleptə'meınıæk] *n* cleptómano(a) *m,f*

klutz [klʌts] *n Fam (clumsy person)* torpe, *Esp* patoso(a) *m,f*

km *(abbr* **kilometer)** km *m*

kmph, km/h *(abbr* **kilometers per hour)** km/h *mpl*

knack [næk] *n* habilidad *f*, maña *f*; **to have the k. of** or **a k. for doing sth** tener habilidad or darse maña para hacer algo; **to get the k. of sth** pillarle or *Esp* cogerle or *Am* agarrarle el truco or el tranquillo a algo

knapsack ['næpsæk] *n* mochila *f*

knave [neıv] *n* **(a)** *(in cards) (American pack)* jota *f*; *(Spanish pack)* sota *f* **(b)** *Literary (scoundrel)* villano *m*

knead [ni:d] *vt (dough)* amasar; *(muscles)* masajear, dar un masaje a

knee [ni:] **1** *n* rodilla *f*; **to go down on one's knees** arrodillarse, ponerse de rodillas; *Fig* **to bring sb to his knees** hacer que alguien hinque la rodilla or se arrodille **2** *vt (hit with knee)* dar un rodillazo a

kneecap ['ni:kæp] *n* rótula *f*

knee-deep ['ni:'di:p] *adj* **she was k. in water** le llegaba el agua por la rodilla; *Fig* **she was k. in work** estaba hasta el cuello de trabajo

knee-high ['ni:'haı] *adj* hasta (la altura de) la rodilla; *Fam* **when I was k. to a grasshopper** cuando era pequeño or canijo or *Am* chiquito

kneejerk ['ni:dʒз:k] *adj (reaction, response)* reflejo(a)

kneel [ni:l] *(pt & pp* **knelt** [nelt]) *vi (go down on one's knees)* arrodillarse, ponerse de rodillas; *(be on one's knees)* estar de rodillas

knee-length ['ni:leŋθ] *adj* hasta la rodilla

kneepad ['ni:pæd] *n* rodillera *f*

knell [nel] *n Literary* tañido *m* fúnebre, toque *m* de difuntos; *Fig* **to toll the (death) k. for sb/sth** suponer el (principio del) fin para alguien/algo

knelt [nelt] *pt & pp of* **kneel**

knew [nju:] *pt of* **know**

knickerbockers ['nıkəbɒkəz], **knickers** ['nıkəz] *npl* bombachos *mpl*

knickknack ['nıknæk] *n Fam* chuchería *f*, baratija *f*

knife [naıf] **1** *n (pl* **knives** [naıvz]) cuchillo *m*; *Fig* **the (long) knives are out for the President** el presidente tiene los días contados; **k. sharpener** afilador *m* de cuchillos; **k. wound** puñalada *f*, cuchillada *f* **2** *vt (stab)* apuñalar, acuchillar

knife-edge ['naıfedʒ] *n Fig* **he has been on a k. all day** *(nervous)* ha estado todo el día con los nervios de punta; *Fig* **the situation/game is balanced on a k.** la situación/el partido pende de un hilo

knifepoint ['naıfpɔınt] *n* **to be robbed at k.** ser robado(a) a punta de cuchillo

knifing ['naıfıŋ] *n* apuñalamiento *m*, acuchillamiento *m*

knight [naıt] **1** *n (person)* caballero *m*; *(in chess)* caballo *m* **2** *vt* ordenar caballero a

knighthood ['naıthʊd] *n (title)* título *m* de caballero

knit [nıt] *(pt & pp* **knitted** or **knit)** **1** *vt (sweater)* tejer; **to k. one's brows** fruncir el ceño **2** *vi* hacer punto

►**knit together** *vi (broken bones)* soldarse

knitted ['nıtəd] *adj* de punto

knitting ['nıtıŋ] *n (item produced)* (labor *f* de) punto *m*, *Am* tejido *m*; **have you finished your k.?** ¿has terminado de hacer punto?, *Am* ¿terminaste el tejido?; **k. machine** *Esp* tricotosa *f*, *Am* máquina *f* de tejer; **k. needle** aguja *f* de punto or *Am* de tejer

knitwear ['nıtweə(r)] *n* prendas *fpl* de punto or *Am* tejidas

knob [nɒb] *n (on a cane)* empuñadura *f*, puño *m*; *(on banisters, door, drawer)* pomo *m*; *(on radio)* botón *m*, mando *m*; **a k. of butter** una nuez de mantequilla or *RP* manteca

knobbly ['nɒblı] *adj* nudoso(a); **k. knees** rodillas *fpl* huesudas

knock [nɒk] **1** *n (blow)* golpe *m*; *(to sb's pride, chances)* revés *m*; **there was a k. at the door** se oyó un golpe en la puerta **2** *vt* **(a)** *(hit)* golpear; **to k. sb to the ground** tumbar a alguien *(a golpes)*; **to k. sb unconscious** dejar a alguien inconsciente; **to k. one's head against sth** golpearse la cabeza contra algo; **to k. a hole in sth** abrir un agujero de un golpe en algo; **to k. holes in an argument** echar por tierra un argumento; **to k. some sense into sb** meter un poco de sentido común en la cabeza a alguien; *Fig* **to k. sth/sb into shape** poner algo/a alguien a punto; *Fam* **to k. on wood** tocar madera **(b)** *Fam (criticize)* poner peros a, criticar **3** *vi* **(a)** *(hit)* dar golpes; **to k. at the door** llamar a la puerta (con los nudillos); **to k. against sth** chocar con or contra algo; **his knees were knocking** le temblaban las rodillas **(b)** *(engine)* golpetear

►**knock around, knock about 1** *vt sep* **(a)** *(person)* maltratar, pegar; **the furniture has been badly knocked around** or **about** los muebles están muy maltratados **(b)** *Fam (idea, suggestion)* dar vueltas a
2 *vt insep Fam* **she's been knocking around** or **about Miami for years** se ha movido por Miami durante años
3 *vi Fam* **has anyone seen my keys knocking around** or **about?** ¿ha visto alguien mis llaves por ahí?

►**knock back** *vt sep Fam* **to k. back a drink** *Esp* atizarse una copa, *Am* hacer fondo blanco con algo de beber

►**knock down** *vt sep* **(a)** *(pedestrian)* atropellar **(b)** *(building)* derribar

►**knock off 1** *vt sep* **(a)** *(cause to fall off)* tirar; **he was knocked off his bike by a car** un coche or *Am* carro or *CSur* auto lo tiró de la bicicleta; *Fam* **to k. sb's head** or **block off** romperle la cabeza a alguien; *Fam* **I managed to get something knocked off the price** conseguí que me rebajaran algo el precio **(b)** *Fam (steal) Esp* mangar, *Am* volar **(c)** *Fam (kill)* asesinar a, *Esp* cepillarse a **(d)** *Fam* **k. it off!** *(stop it)* ¡para ya!

2 *vi (finish work)* terminar de trabajar

▶**knock out** *vt sep* (**a**) *(make unconscious)* dejar sin sentido; *(in boxing match)* dejar fuera de combate; *Fam* **to k. sb's brains/teeth out** partirle la cabeza/la boca a alguien (**b**) *(eliminate from competition)* eliminar (**c**) *Fam (produce quickly) (letter, report, song)* despachar

▶**knock over** *vt sep* (**a**) *(person)* derribar; *(container)* volcar (**b**) *Fam (rob)* atracar

▶**knock up** *vt sep very Fam (make pregnant)* dejar preñada a

knockabout [ˈnɒkəbaʊt] **1** *n* astracanada *f*

2 *adj (comedy, comedian)* bullanguero(a)

knockdown [ˈnɒkdaʊn] *adj Fam (argument)* contundente, *Esp* impepinable; **at a k. price** a un precio de risa

knockdown price [ˈnɒkdaʊnˈpraɪs] *n Fam* **at a k.** a un precio de risa

knocker [ˈnɒkə(r)] *n* (**a**) *(on door)* llamador *m*, aldaba *f* (**b**) *very Fam* **knockers** *(breasts)* domingas *fpl*, *Méx* chichis *fpl*, *RP* lolas *fpl*

knocking [ˈnɒkɪŋ] *n (at door)* golpes *mpl*; *(of engine)* golpeteo *m*

knock-kneed [ˈnɒkˈniːd] *adj* patizambo(a), *Am* chueco(a)

knockout [ˈnɒkaʊt] **1** *n* (**a**) *(in boxing)* K.O. *m*, fuera de combate *m*; *Fig (to chances)* golpe *m* de gracia (**b**) *Fam* **he's/she's a k.** *(attractive)* está imponente

2 *adj* **k. blow** *(in boxing)* golpe *m* que pone fuera de combate; *Fig* **to deliver the k. blow** *(to chances)* asestar el golpe de gracia

knot [nɒt] **1** *n* (**a**) *(in rope, string)* nudo *m*; *(in ribbon)* lazo *m*, lazada *f*; **to tie/untie a k.** atar/desatar un nudo, hacer/deshacer un nudo; *Fam Fig* **to tie the k.** *(get married)* casarse (**b**) *(in wood)* nudo *m* (**c**) *Naut (unit of speed)* nudo *m* (**d**) *(group of people)* corro *m*

2 *vt (pt & pp* **knotted)** *(piece of string)* anudar, atar

knotty [ˈnɒtɪ] *adj Fam (problem)* espinoso(a)

know [nəʊ] **1** *n Fam* **to be in the k.** estar enterado(a), estar en el ajo

2 *vt (pt* **knew** [njuː], *pp* **known** [nəʊn]) (**a**) *(be acquainted with)* conocer; **to get to k. sb** conocer a alguien; **she had long hair when I first knew her** cuando la conocí tenía el pelo largo; **I've never known anything like it** nunca he visto nada igual; **I k. him to say hello to** lo conozco de hola y adiós nada más; **knowing HIM...** conociéndolo...

(**b**) *(have knowledge of)* saber; **to k. that...** saber que...; **to k. the answer** saber la respuesta; **to k. Spanish** saber español; **to k. a lot/a little about sth** saber mucho/poco de algo; **she knows what she is talking about** sabe de lo que está hablando; **to k. how to do sth** saber hacer algo; *Fam* **to k. a thing or two** saber alguna que otra cosa, saber un rato; **to k. one's own mind** tener las ideas claras; **heaven** *or* **God knows!** ¡sabe Dios!

(**c**) *(recognize, distinguish)* distinguir, reconocer; **I knew her by her walk** la distinguí *or* la reconocí por su forma de andar; **he knows a good business opportunity when he sees one** sabe reconocer un buen negocio (cuando lo tiene delante); **to k. right from wrong** distinguir lo bueno de lo malo

3 *vi* saber; **to k. about sth** saber de algo; **to get to k. about sth** enterarse de algo; **I k. of two stores in the area** sé de dos tiendas en la zona; **as far as I k.** que yo sepa; **how should I k.?** ¿cómo voy a saberlo yo?; **you never k.** nunca se sabe; **not that I k. about** que yo sepa, no; **you should k. better than that by now!** ¡a estas alturas ya podías saber que eso no se hace!; *Fam* **it wasn't, you k., quite what I was expecting** en fin, no era lo que me esperaba; **James, you k., my cousin...** James, sí hombre, mi primo...

know-all [ˈnəʊɔːl] = **know-it-all**

know-how [ˈnəʊhaʊ] *n Fam* conocimientos *mpl* prácticos; *Com* técnica *f*, conocimientos *mpl* técnicos

knowing [ˈnəʊɪŋ] **1** *n* **there's no k.** no hay manera de saber

2 *adj (look, smile)* cómplice, de complicidad

know-it-all [ˈnəʊɪtɔːl] *n Fam* sabihondo(a) *m,f*, sabelotodo *mf*

knowledge [ˈnɒlɪdʒ] *n* (**a**) *(awareness)* conocimiento *m*; **(not) to my k.** que yo sepa(, no); **I had no k. of it** no tenía conocimiento de ello; **to have full k. of sth** saber algo perfectamente; **it is common k. that...** todo el mundo sabe que..., de todos es sabido que...; *Formal* **it has come to our k. that...** ha llegado a nuestro conocimiento que... (**b**) *(learning)* conocimientos *mpl*; **to have a k. of several languages** saber varios idiomas; **her k. is immense** tiene unos grandes conocimientos; *Prov* **k. is power** el poder llega por el conocimiento; *Comptr* **k.-based system** sistema *m* experto; **the k. economy** la economía del conocimiento

knowledgeable [ˈnɒlɪdʒəbəl] *adj* entendido(a); **to be k. about sth** ser un (gran) entendido en algo

knowledgeably [ˈnɒlɪdʒəblɪ] *adv* con conocimiento, con erudición

known [nəʊn] **1** *adj* conocido(a)

2 *pp of* **know**

knuckle [ˈnʌkəl] *n* nudillo *m*

▶**knuckle down** *vi Fam* **to k. down (to sth)** ponerse (a algo) en serio

▶**knuckle under** *vi Fam* pasar por el aro, rendirse

knuckle-duster [ˈnʌkəldʌstə(r)] *n* puño *m* americano

KO [ˈkeɪˈəʊ] *Fam* **1** *n (pl* **KO's** [ˈkeɪˈəʊz]) *(in boxing)* K.O. *m*

2 *vt (pp & pt* **KO'd** [ˈkeɪˈəʊd]) *(in boxing)* dejar fuera de combate, noquear

koala [kəʊˈɑːlə] *n* **k. (bear)** koala *m*

kopek [ˈkəʊpek] *n (subdivision of ruble)* kopek *m*, copec *m*

Koran [kəˈrɑːn] *n* **the K.** el Corán

Koranic [kəˈrænɪk] *adj* coránico(a)

Korea [kəˈrɪə] *n* Corea; **North/South K.** Corea del Norte/del Sur

Korean [kəˈrɪən] **1** *n* (**a**) *(person)* coreano(a) *m,f* (**b**) *(language)* coreano *m*

2 *adj* coreano(a); **the K. War** la guerra de Corea

kosher [ˈkəʊʃə(r)] *adj* (**a**) *(in Judaism)* kosher, conforme a la ley judaica; **k. meat** carne *f* kosher (**b**) *Fam (legitimate)* legal

Kosovan [ˈkɒsəvən], **Kosovar** [ˈkɒsəvɑː(r)] **1** *n* kosovar *mf*

2 *adj* kosovar

Kosovo [ˈkɒsəvəʊ] *n* Kosovo

kowtow [kaʊˈtaʊ] *vi also Fig* **to k. to sb** inclinarse ante alguien

kph *(abbr* **kilometers per hour***)* km/h

Kraut [kraʊt] *n Fam* cabeza cuadrada *mf*, = término despectivo para referirse a los alemanes

Kriss Kringle [ˈkrisˈkrɪŋgəl] *n* Papá *m* Noel

krona [ˈkrəʊnə] *n* corona *f* (sueca)

krone [ˈkrəʊnə] *n (Danish/Norwegian currency)* corona *f* (danesa/noruega)

krypton [ˈkrɪptɒn] *n Chem* criptón *m*, kriptón *m*

kudos [ˈkjuːdɒs] *n* gloria *f*, renombre *m*

Kurd [kɜːd] *n & adj* kurdo(a) *m,f*

Kurdish [ˈkɜːdɪʃ] **1** *n (language)* kurdo *m*

2 *adj* kurdo(a)

Kurdistan [kɜːdɪˈstæn] *n* Kurdistán

Kuwait [kʊˈweɪt] *n* Kuwait

Kuwaiti [kʊˈweɪtɪ] *n & adj* kuwaití *mf*

kW *Elec (abbr* **kilowatt***)* kW *m*

kWh *(abbr* **kilowatt-hour***)* kWh

Kyoto [kiːˈəʊtəʊ] *n* Kioto

Kyrgyzstan [kɜːgɪzˈstæn] *n* Kirguizistán

L

L [el] *n (letter)* L, l *f*

l *(abbr* **liter(s))** l, litro(s) *mpl*

LA [el'eɪ] *n (abbr* **Los Angeles**) Los Ángeles

la [lɑː] *n Mus* la

lab [læb] *n Fam (abbr* **laboratory**) laboratorio *m*

label ['leɪbəl] **1** *n* (a) *also Fig* etiqueta *f* (b) *(of record company)* casa *f* discográfica, sello *m* discográfico

　　2 *vt (parcel, bottle)* etiquetar; *(describe)* tildar de; **the bottle was labeled "poison"** la botella tenía una etiqueta que decía "veneno"; **to l. sb a liar** tildar a alguien de mentiroso(a)

labor ['leɪbə(r)] **1** *n* (a) *(work)* trabajo *m*; **l. camp** campo *m* de trabajo (b) *(workers)* mano *f* de obra, trabajadores *mpl*; **l. costs** costos *mpl or Esp* costes *mpl* de mano de obra; **l. dispute** conflicto *m* laboral; **l. force** mano *f* de obra; **l. market** mercado *m* laboral *or* de trabajo; **l. shortage** escasez *f* de mano de obra; **l. union** sindicato *m* (c) *(task)* esfuerzo *m*, tarea *f*; **a l. of love** un trabajo hecho por amor al arte (d) *(childbirth)* parto *m*; **to be in l.** estar de parto; **l. pains** dolores *mpl* del parto

　　2 *vt* **to l. a point** repetir lo mismo una y otra vez

　　3 *vi* (a) *(person)* trabajar afanosamente *(at or over* en); **to l. in vain** trabajar en vano; **to be laboring under a misapprehension/a delusion** tener un malentendido/una falsa ilusión (b) *(engine)* funcionar con dificultad

laboratory [lə'bɒrətrɪ] *n* laboratorio *m*; **l. assistant** ayudante *mf* de laboratorio

labored ['leɪbəd] *adj (breathing)* fatigoso(a), trabajoso(a); *(style)* farragoso(a); *(joke)* pesado(a)

laborer ['leɪbərə(r)] *n* obrero(a) *m,f*

laboring ['leɪbərɪŋ] *adj* **he did a number of l. jobs** trabajó de obrero en varias ocasiones

labor-intensive ['leɪbərɪn'tensɪv] *adj* que absorbe mucha mano de obra

laborious [lə'bɔːrɪəs] *adj (work, explanation)* laborioso(a), arduo(a)

laboriously [lə'bɔːrɪəslɪ] *adv* laboriosamente, arduamente

labor-saving device ['leɪbəseɪvɪŋdɪ'vaɪs] *n* aparato *m* que permite ahorrarse trabajo

labrador ['læbrədɔː(r)] *n (dog)* terranova *m*, labrador *m*

laburnum [lə'bɜːnəm] *n* codeso *m*

labyrinth ['læbərɪnθ] *n* laberinto *m*

labyrinthine [læbə'rɪnθaɪn] *adj* laberíntico(a)

lace [leɪs] **1** *n* (a) *(cloth)* encaje *m*; **l. handkerchief** pañuelo *m* de encaje (b) *(of shoe)* cordón *m*

　　2 *vt* (a) *(shoes)* atar (los cordones de) (b) **to l. a drink** rociar una bebida (con unas gotas de algo fuerte); *Fig* **he laced his story with salacious details** aderezó el relato con detalles obscenos

▸**lace up 1** *vt sep* **to l. one's shoes up** atarse los zapatos

　　2 *vi (shoes, corset)* atarse

lacerate ['læsəreɪt] *vt* lacerar

laceration [læsə'reɪʃən] *n* laceración *f*

lace-up ['leɪsʌp] **1** *n (shoe)* zapato *m* de cordones

　　2 *adj (shoe)* de cordones

lachrymose ['lækrɪməʊs] *adj Literary* lacrimoso(a)

lack [læk] **1** *n* falta *f* (**of** de), carencia *f* (**of** de); **for l. of...** por falta de...

　　2 *vt* carecer de

　　3 *vi* **time was lacking** faltaba tiempo; **she is lacking in confidence/experience** le falta confianza/experiencia; **they l. for nothing** no les falta (de) nada

lackadaisical [lækə'deɪzɪkəl] *adj* dejado(a)

lackey ['lækɪ] (*pl* **lackeys**) *n Pej* lacayo *m*

lackluster ['læklʌstə(r)] *adj (mediocre)* deslucido(a)

laconic [lə'kɒnɪk] *adj* lacónico(a)

lacquer ['lækə(r)] **1** *n* laca *f*

　　2 *vt (wood)* lacar, laquear; *(hair)* aplicar laca a

lacrosse [lə'krɒs] *n Sport* lacrosse *m*

lactose ['læktəʊs] *n Biochem* lactosa *f*

lacuna [lə'kjuːnə] (*pl* **lacunae** [lə'kjuːniː] *or* **lacunas**) *n* laguna *f*

lad [læd] *n Fam* (a) *(boy)* muchacho *m*, chaval *m*, *Arg* pibe *m*, *CAm, Méx* chavo *m*, *Chile* cabro *m* (b) *(young man)* tipo, *Esp* tío *m*

ladder ['lædə(r)] *n* escalera *f*; **the social l.** la escala social; *Fig* **to get one's foot on the l.** dar el primer paso; *Fig* **to reach the top of the l.** llegar a la cumbre

laddie ['lædɪ] *n Fam* muchacho *m*, *CAm, Méx* chavalo *m*

la-de-da = **la-di-da**

laden ['leɪdən] *adj* cargado(a) (**with** de)

la-di-da, la-de-da, lah-di-dah [lɑːdɪ'dɑː] *adj Fam (accent, manner) Esp* pijo(a), *Méx* fresa, *RP* fifí

ladle ['leɪdəl] *n* cucharón *m*, cazo *m*

▸**ladle out** *vt sep (soup)* servir (con el cucharón); *Fig (sympathy, praise)* prodigar

lady ['leɪdɪ] *n* (a) *(woman)* señora *f*; *(in literature, of high status)* dama *f*; **a young l.** *(unmarried)* una señorita; *(married)* una (señora) joven; **an old l.** una señora mayor; **ladies and gentlemen!** ¡señoras y señores!; **he's a ladies' man** es un mujeriego; **the l. of the house** la señora de la casa; **the ladies' room** el baño *or Esp* servicio *m or CSur* toilette *f* de señoras; **l. friend** querida *f*, amiga *f* (b) **Our L.** Nuestra Señora (c) *(title)* **L. Browne** Lady Browne; **L. Luck** la diosa Fortuna

ladybug ['leɪdɪbʌg] *n* mariquita *f*

lady-in-waiting ['leɪdɪn'weɪtɪŋ] (*pl* **ladies-in-waiting**) *n* dama *f* de honor

lady-killer ['leɪdɪkɪlə(r)] *n Fam* castigador *m*, casanova *m*

ladylike ['leɪdɪlaɪk] *adj* femenino(a), propio(a) de una señorita

lag [læg] **1** *n (gap)* intervalo *m*, lapso *m*

　　2 *vt (pt & pp* **lagged**) *(pipes, boiler)* revestir con un aislante

　　3 *vi* **to l. (behind)** quedarse atrás

lager ['lɑːgə(r)] *n* cerveza *f (rubia)*

laggard ['lægəd] *n* rezagado(a) *m,f*

lagoon [ləˈguːn] n laguna f

lah-di-dah = **la-di-da**

laid [leɪd] pt & pp of **lay**

laid-back [leɪdˈbæk] adj Fam tranquilo(a), Esp cachazudo(a)

lain [leɪn] pp of **lie²**

lair [leə(r)] n guarida f

laird [leəd] n Scot terrateniente m

laisser-faire, laissez-faire [leseɪˈfeə(r)] **1** n Econ liberalismo m
2 adj (in general) permisivo(a); Econ liberal

laity [ˈleɪtɪ] n **the l.** el sector laico, los seglares

lake [leɪk] n lago m; **the L. District** la Región de los Lagos (en el noroeste de Inglaterra); **L. Erie** el lago Erie; **L. Geneva** el lago Leman; **L. Huron** el lago Hurón; **L. Michigan** el lago Michigan; **L. Ontario** el lago Ontario; **L. Superior** el lago Superior

lamb [læm] n cordero m; Rel **L. (of God)** Cordero de Dios; **poor l.!** ¡pobrecillo!; **like lambs to the slaughter** como ovejas al matadero; **l. chop** chuleta f de cordero; **l.'s wool** lana f de cordero

lambaste [læmˈbeɪst], **lambast** [læmˈbæst] vt vapulear

lambing [ˈlæmɪŋ] n (tiempo m del) nacimiento m de los corderos

lambskin [ˈlæmskɪn] n piel f de cordero

lambswool [ˈlæmswʊl] **1** n lana f de cordero
2 adj de lana de cordero

lame [leɪm] **1** adj (a) (person, animal) cojo(a); **to be l.** (permanently) ser cojo(a); (temporarily) estar cojo(a); **to go l.** quedarse cojo(a); Pol **a l. duck president** un presidente saliente (cuando ya ha sido elegido su sucesor) (b) (excuse, argument) endeble, pobre
2 vt dejar cojo(a)

lamé [ˈlɑːmeɪ] n lamé m

lamely [ˈleɪmlɪ] adv (to apologize) sin convicción

lament [ləˈment] **1** n lamento m; Mus canto m elegíaco, treno m
2 vt lamentar; **the late lamented Mr. Jones** el llorado difunto Sr. Jones
3 vi lamentarse (**over** de)

lamentable [ləˈmentəbəl] adj lamentable

lamentably [ləˈmentəblɪ] adj lamentablemente

lamentation [læmənˈteɪʃən] n lamentación f

laminate [ˈlæmɪneɪt] n laminado m

laminated [ˈlæmɪneɪtəd] adj (a) (glass) laminado(a); **the wood is l. with plastic** la madera está laminada en plástico (b) (paper, identity card) plastificado(a)

lamp [læmp] n lámpara f

lamplight [ˈlæmplaɪt] n luz f de una lámpara

lampoon [læmˈpuːn] **1** n sátira f
2 vt satirizar

lamppost [ˈlæmppəʊst] n farola f

lamprey [ˈlæmprɪ] (pl **lampreys**) n lamprea f

lampshade [ˈlæmpʃeɪd] n pantalla f (de lámpara)

lampstand [ˈlæmpstænd] n pie m de lámpara

LAN [eleɪˈen] n Comptr (abbr **local area network**) red f de área local

lance [lɑːns] **1** n (weapon) lanza f
2 vt Med sajar, abrir con una lanceta

lance corporal [ˈlɑːnsˈkɔːpərəl] n Mil soldado mf de primera

lancer [ˈlɑːnsə(r)] n (soldier) lancero m

lancet [ˈlɑːnsɪt] n lanceta f

land [lænd] **1** n (a) (in general) tierra f; **on l.** en tierra; **to live off the l.** vivir de la tierra; Literary **he came from a distant l.** venía de una tierra lejana; **he's still in the l. of the living** todavía está en el reino de los vivos; Mil **l. forces** ejército m de tierra; **l. reform** reforma f agraria (b) (property) tierras fpl,

terrenos mpl; **get off my l.!** ¡fuera de mi propiedad!
2 vt (a) (passengers) desembarcar; (cargo) descargar (b) (plane) hacer aterrizar (c) (fish) capturar; Fam **he's just landed a good job** acaba de conseguir un buen trabajo; Fam **that will l. you in prison** eso hará que des con tus huesos en la cárcel; Fam **he was landed with the problem** le endosaron el problema (d) Fam (hit) **I landed him one** le di or Esp aticé un buen tortazo
3 vi (a) (aircraft, pilot) aterrizar, tomar tierra; **we landed in New York** aterrizamos en Nueva York (b) (gymnast, somebody falling) caer; Fig **to l. on one's feet** caer de pie
▶**land up** vi ir a parar (**in** a)

landed [ˈlændɪd] adj **l. gentry** aristocracia f terrateniente; **l. proprietor** terrateniente mf

landfall [ˈlændfɔːl] n Naut **to make l.** arribar a tierra

landfill [ˈlændfɪl] n (technique) enterramiento m de residuos; (refuse) residuos mpl; **l. (site)** vertedero m controlado (en el que se entierran los residuos)

landing [ˈlændɪŋ] n (a) Naut desembarco m; **l. card** tarjeta f de inmigración; **l. craft** lancha f de desembarco (b) Av aterrizaje m; **l. gear** tren m de aterrizaje; **l. lights** luces fpl de aterrizaje; **l. strip** pista f de aterrizaje (c) (of staircase) descansillo m, rellano m

landlady [ˈlændleɪdɪ] n (a) (owner of rented accommodation) casera f, dueña f (b) (woman who runs boarding house) patrona f

landline [ˈlændlaɪn] n (telephone) teléfono m fijo

landlocked [ˈlændlɒkt] adj (country) sin salida al mar, interior

landlord [ˈlændlɔːd] n (a) (owner of rented accommodation) casero m, dueño m (b) (landowner) terrateniente m

landmark [ˈlændmɑːk] n (distinctive feature) punto m de referencia, lugar m señero; Fig (in history) hito m

landmass [ˈlændmæs] n masa f terrestre

landmine [ˈlændmaɪn] n mina f terrestre

landowner [ˈlændəʊnə(r)] n terrateniente mf

landowning [ˈlændəʊnɪŋ] adj **the l. classes** la clase terrateniente

landscape [ˈlændskeɪp] **1** n (land, painting) paisaje m; **l. design** paisajismo m; **l. gardener** paisajista mf; Comptr **l. (orientation)** formato m apaisado; **l. painter** paisajista mf
2 vt ajardinar

landslide [ˈlændslaɪd] n desprendimiento m or corrimiento m de tierras; Pol **to win by a l.** ganar por una mayoría abrumadora

landward [ˈlændwəd] adj Naut más cercano(a) a (la) tierra

lane [leɪn] n (a) (in country) vereda f, camino m; (in town) callejón m (b) (on road) carril m; **traffic is reduced to two lanes** se ha limitado el tráfico a dos carriles (c) (for runner, swimmer) calle f, Andes, RP andarivel m

language [ˈlæŋgwɪdʒ] n (a) (of a people) idioma m, lengua f; Fam Fig **we don't talk the same l.** no hablamos el mismo idioma; **l. laboratory** laboratorio m de idiomas; **l. learning** aprendizaje m de idiomas; **l. teaching** enseñanza f de idiomas (b) (style of speech or writing) lenguaje m; **you should have heard the l. they were using!** ¡tenías que haber oído el lenguaje que empleaban!

languid [ˈlæŋgwɪd] adj lánguido(a)

languidly [ˈlæŋgwɪdlɪ] adv lánguidamente

languish [ˈlæŋgwɪʃ] vi languidecer; **to l. in prison** pudrirse en la cárcel

languor [ˈlæŋgə(r)] n languidez f

languorous [ˈlæŋgərəs] adj lánguido(a)

lank [læŋk] adj (hair) lacio(a)

lanky [ˈlæŋkɪ] adj larguirucho(a)

lanolin(e) [ˈlænəlɪn] n lanolina f

lantern [ˈlæntən] n farol m

lantern-jawed [ˈlæntəndʒɔːd] adj demacrado(a)

Laos [laʊs] n Laos

Laotian ['laʊʃɪən] n & adj laosiano(a) m,f

lap¹ [læp] n regazo m; **to sit on sb's l.** sentarse en el regazo de alguien; Fig **it's in the l. of the gods** está en el aire; Fig **he expects everything to fall into his l.** espera que todo le llueva or Am caiga del cielo; Fig **to live in the l. of luxury** vivir a cuerpo de rey; **l. dancing** striptease m (para un único cliente)

lap² vt (overtake) doblar

lap³ (pt & pp **lapped**) vi (animal) beber a lengüetadas; **to l. against sth** (waves) lamer algo

▸**lap up** vt sep (drink) beberse a lengüetadas; Fam Fig (enjoy) tragarse

lapdog ['læpdɒg] n perrito m faldero

lapel [lə'pel] n solapa f

lapis lazuli ['læpɪs'læzjʊliː] n Geol lapislázuli m

Lapland ['læplænd] n Laponia

Laplander ['læplændə(r)] n lapón(ona) m,f

Lapp [læp] n & adj lapón(ona) m,f

lapse [læps] **1** n (a) (of time) lapso m (b) (in behavior) desliz m; (in standards) bajón m; **a l. in concentration** un momento de distracción

    2 vi (a) (err) tener un desliz; (morally) reincidir; **to l. into silence** sumirse en el silencio; **he soon lapsed back into his old ways** pronto volvió a las andadas (b) (permit, membership) caducar, vencer

lapsed [læpst] adj Rel **a l. Catholic** un/una católico(a) no practicante

laptop ['læptɒp] n Comptr **l. (computer)** Esp ordenador m or Am computadora f portátil

lapwing ['læpwɪŋ] n avefría f

larceny ['lɑːsənɪ] n Law (delito m de) robo m or latrocinio m

larch [lɑːtʃ] n alerce m

lard [lɑːd] **1** n (fat) manteca f or RP grasa f de cerdo

    2 vt Fam (sprinkle) **he larded his writings with quotations** sus escritos estaban recargados de citas

larder ['lɑːdə(r)] n despensa f

large [lɑːdʒ] **1** n **to be at l.** andar suelto(a); **people/the public at l.** la gente/el público en general

    2 adj (a) (in size) grande; **to grow** or **get larger** crecer; **to make sth larger** agrandar algo; **as l. as life** en persona; **larger than life** singular, que se sale de la norma (b) (extensive, significant) **to a l. extent** en gran medida; **a l. part of my job involves…** gran parte de mi trabajo implica…

    3 by and large adv en general

largely ['lɑːdʒlɪ] adv (to a great extent) en gran medida; (mostly) principalmente

large-scale ['lɑːdʒ'skeɪl] adj a gran escala

largess(e) [lɑː'ʒes] n magnanimidad f

lark¹ [lɑːk] n (bird) alondra f; **to be up/rise with the l.** levantarse con el gallo

lark² n (joke) broma f; **to do sth for a l.** hacer algo por diversión; **what a l.!** ¡qué divertido!; **I don't like this fancy dress l.** no me gusta este asunto or Esp rollo or Col, Perú, Ven esta vaina de la fiesta de disfraces

larva ['lɑːvə] (pl **larvas** or **larvae** ['lɑːviː]) n larva f

laryngitis [lærɪn'dʒaɪtɪs] n laringitis f inv

larynx ['lærɪŋks] n laringe f

lasagne [lə'sænjə] n lasaña f

lascivious [lə'sɪvɪəs] adj lascivo(a)

lasciviously [lə'sɪvɪəslɪ] adv lascivamente

laser ['leɪzə(r)] n láser m; **l. beam** rayo m láser; **l. disc** láser disc m; Comptr **l. printer** impresora f láser; Med **l. surgery** cirugía f con láser

lash [læʃ] **1** n (a) (eyelash) pestaña f (b) (blow with whip) latigazo m

    2 vt (a) (with whip) azotar; **to l. (against) sth** (rain, waves) azotar algo (b) (tie) amarrar (**to** a)

    3 vi **the rain** or **it was lashing down** caían chuzos de punta

▸**lash out** vi **to l. out at sb** (physically) atacar or agredir a alguien; (verbally) arremeter contra alguien

lass [læs] n chica f, muchacha f

lassitude ['læsɪtjuːd] n lasitud f

lasso [læ'suː] **1** n (pl **lassos** or **lassoes**) lazo m (para ganado)

    2 vt capturar con lazo, CSur lacear

last¹ [lɑːst] **1** n **the l.** el/la último(a); **the l. but one** el/la penúltimo(a); **we'll never hear the l. of it** nos lo recordará eternamente; **I don't think we've heard the l. of him** creo que volveremos a oír hablar de él; **that's the l. I saw of him** fue la última vez que lo vi; **that's the l. of the wine** es lo último que queda de vino; **to** or **till the l.** hasta el fin; **at (long) l.** por fin

    2 adj (a) (final) último(a); **this is your l. chance** es tu última oportunidad; **you are my l. hope** eres mi última esperanza; **to have the l. word** tener la última palabra; **the l. word in comfort** el no va más en comodidad; **at the l. moment** or **minute** en el último momento or minuto; **l. thing at night** lo último antes de acostarse; **to be on one's l. legs** estar en las últimas; **he's the l. person I'd ask to help me** es la última persona a la que pediría ayuda; **that's the l. thing I'd do in your position** eso es lo último que haría si estuviera en tu lugar; **as a l. resort** como último recurso; Rel **the L. Judgement** el Juicio Final; **l. name** apellido m; Rel **l. rites** extremaunción f; **the l. straw** la gota que colma el vaso

    (b) (most recent) pasado(a), último(a); **the l. time I saw him** la última vez que lo vi; **l. January** en enero pasado; **l. night** anoche; **l. Tuesday** el martes pasado; **l. week** la semana pasada

    3 adv **when I l. saw him** la última vez que lo vi; **to come l.** llegar en último lugar; **to finish l.** terminar el último; (in race) llegar en último lugar; **l. but not least** por último, pero no por ello menos importante

last² n (for shoe) horma f

last³ **1** vt durar; **it will l. me a lifetime** me durará toda la vida; **it has lasted him well** le ha durado bastante

    2 vi durar; **it's too good to l.** es demasiado bueno para que dure; **he won't l. long in that job** no durará mucho en ese trabajo; **she won't l. the night** no llegará a mañana

▸**last out 1** vt sep **to l. the year/the weekend out** llegar a fin de año/al fin de semana

    2 vi (person) aguantar, resistir; (supplies) durar

last-ditch [lɑːst'dɪtʃ] adj último(a), desesperado(a)

lasting ['lɑːstɪŋ] adj duradero(a)

lastly ['lɑːstlɪ] adv por último

last-minute [lɑːst'mɪnɪt] adj de última hora

lat Geog (abbr **latitude**) lat., latitud f

latch [lætʃ] n picaporte m, pestillo m; **to be on the l.** = tener sólo el pestillo echado, no la llave

▸**latch onto** vt insep Fam (a) (attach oneself to) **to l. onto sb** pegarse a alguien; Fig **to l. onto an idea** meterse una idea en la cabeza (b) (understand) **to l. onto sth** darse cuenta or Esp enterarse de algo

latchkey ['lætʃkiː] (pl **latchkeys**) n llave f (de la puerta de entrada); **l. kid** = niño que llega a casa antes que sus padres, que están trabajando

late [leɪt] **1** adj (a) (not on time) retrasado(a); **to be l. (for sth)** llegar tarde (a algo); **the train is ten minutes l.** el tren tiene or lleva diez minutos de retraso or Am demora (b) (far on in time) tarde; **it is getting l.** se está haciendo tarde; **to keep l. hours** trasnochar; **in the l. afternoon** al final de la tarde; **in l. summer** al final del verano; **in l. March** a últimos de marzo; Fig **it's a bit l. in the day to…** ya es un poco tarde para…; **to be in one's l. thirties** tener treinta y muchos años; **in the l. eighties** a finales de los ochenta (c) (dead) difunto(a); **my l. husband** mi difunto marido

2 *adv* (**a**) *(in general)* tarde; **to arrive too l.** llegar demasiado tarde; **he came home very l.** llegó a casa muy tarde; **to work l.** trabajar hasta tarde; **this l. in the day** a estas alturas; **to go to bed/get up l.** acostarse/levantarse tarde; **l. into the night** hasta (altas horas de) la madrugada; **l. in the year** a finales de año; **l. in life** hacia el final de la vida; *Prov* **better l. than never** más vale tarde que nunca (**b**) *(recently)* **as l. as last week** incluso la semana pasada; **of l.** recientemente

latecomer ['leɪtkʌmə(r)] *n* rezagado(a) *m,f*

lately ['leɪtlɪ] *adv* recientemente, últimamente; **until l.** hasta hace poco

lateness ['leɪtnɪs] *n (of person, train)* retraso *m*; **the l. of the hour** lo avanzado de la hora

latent ['leɪtənt] *adj (disease, tendency)* latente; **l. period** periodo *m* de incubación

later ['leɪtə(r)] **1** *adj* posterior; **I caught a l. train** tomé *or Esp* cogí otro tren más tarde; **his l. novels** sus novelas posteriores; **in l. life** en la madurez

2 *adv* **l. (on)** más tarde; **a few days l.** unos días más tarde; **no l. than tomorrow** mañana como muy tarde; **as we shall see l.** como veremos más adelante; *Fam* **see you l.!** ¡hasta luego!

lateral ['lætərəl] *adj* lateral; **l. thinking** pensamiento *m* lateral, = capacidad para darse cuenta de aspectos no inmediatamente evidentes de los problemas

latest ['leɪtɪst] **1** *n* **at the l.** como muy tarde; **the l. I can stay is four o'clock** sólo puedo quedarme hasta las cuatro; **have you heard the l.?** ¿has oído las últimas noticias?

2 *adj* último(a); **her l. work** su última obra; **the l. news** las últimas noticias; **the l. edition** la última edición; **the l. fashions** la última moda

latex ['leɪteks] *n* látex *m*

lathe [leɪð] *n* torno *m*

lather ['læðə(r)] **1** *n* espuma *f*; *Fam* **to work oneself into a l.** ponerse histérico(a)

2 *vt* enjabonar; **to l. one's face** enjabonarse la cara

Latin ['lætɪn] **1** *n* (**a**) *(language)* latín *m* (**b**) *(person)* latino(a) *m,f*

2 *adj* latino(a)

Latin America ['lætɪnə'merɪkə] *n* América Latina, Latinoamérica

Latin American ['lætɪnə'merɪkən] *n & adj* latinoamericano(a) *m,f*

latitude ['lætɪtjuːd] *n* (**a**) *Geog* latitud *f* (**b**) *(freedom)* libertad *f*

latrine [lə'triːn] *n* letrina *f*

latter ['lætə(r)] **1** *adj* (**a**) *(of two)* último(a), segundo(a) (**b**) *(last)* último(a); **the l. half** *or* **part of June** la segunda mitad de junio

2 *n (of two)* **the former…, the l….** aquél…, éste…, el primero…, el segundo…

latter-day ['lætə'deɪ] *adj* moderno(a), de hoy; *Rel* **the L. Saints** los Mormones

latterly ['lætəlɪ] *adv* recientemente, últimamente

lattice ['lætɪs] *n* celosía *f*; **l. window** vidriera *f* de celosía

latticework ['lætɪswɜːk] *n* celosía *f*, enrejado *m*

Latvia ['lætvɪə] *n* Letonia

Latvian ['lætvɪən] **1** *n* (**a**) *(person)* letón(ona) *m,f* (**b**) *(language)* letón *m*

2 *adj* letón(ona)

laudable ['lɔːdəbəl] *adj* loable

laudanum ['lɔːdənəm] *n* láudano *m*

laugh [lɑːf] **1** *n* risa *f*; *Fam* **to do sth for a l.** hacer algo para divertirse *or* por diversión; *Ironic* **that's a l.!** ¡no me hagas reír!; **to have the last l.** ser el último en reír

2 *vi* reírse (**at** de); *Fam* **don't make me l.!** ¡no me hagas reír!; **he'll be laughing on the other side of his face when…**

se llevará un buen chasco cuando…; *Fam* **to l. all the way to the bank** hacer el agosto; *Prov* **he who laughs last laughs best** el que ríe el último ríe mejor

3 *vt* **you'll be laughed out of court** se te reirán en la cara; *Fam* **to l. one's head off, to l. oneself silly** partirse *or Esp* mondarse de risa

▸**laugh off** *vt sep* tomarse a risa

laughable ['lɑːfəbəl] *adj* ridículo(a), risible; *(sum)* irrisorio(a)

laughing ['lɑːfɪŋ] **1** *n* risa *f*

2 *adj (eyes)* risueño(a); **it's no l. matter** no es ninguna tontería; **l. gas** gas *m* hilarante; **l. stock** hazmerreír *m*

laughingly ['lɑːfɪŋlɪ] *adv* (**a**) *(cheerfully)* **he said l.** dijo risueño (**b**) *(inappropriately)* **this noise is l. called music** este ruido algunos lo llaman música

laughter ['lɑːftə(r)] *n* risa *f*

launch [lɔːntʃ] **1** *n* (**a**) *(boat)* lancha *f* (**b**) *(act of launching) (of ship)* botadura *f*; *(of rocket, product)* lanzamiento *m*; **l. pad** plataforma *f* de lanzamiento

2 *vt (ship)* botar; *(rocket, product)* lanzar; *(business, inquiry)* emprender; **to l. sb on a career** *(event)* marcar el inicio de la carrera de alguien

▸**launch into** *vt insep (attack, story)* emprender; *(complaint)* embarcarse en

launcher ['lɔːntʃə(r)] *n (for missiles)* lanzamisiles *m inv*; *(for rocket, spacecraft)* lanzador *m*, lanzacohetes *m inv*

launching pad ['lɔːntʃɪŋ'pæd] *n* plataforma *f* de lanzamiento

launder ['lɔːndə(r)] *vt (clothes)* lavar (y planchar); *Fig (money)* blanquear

launderette [lɔːn'dret], **Laundromat**® ['lɔːndrəmæt] *n* lavandería *f*

laundry ['lɔːndrɪ] *n (dirty clothes)* ropa *f* sucia; *(clean clothes)* ropa *f* limpia, *Esp* colada *f*; **to do the l.** lavar la ropa, *Esp* hacer la colada; **l. basket** cesto *m* de la ropa sucia

laurel ['lɒrəl] *n (tree)* laurel *m*; *Fig* **to rest on one's laurels** dormirse en los laureles; **l. wreath** corona *f* de laurel

lava ['lɑːvə] *n* lava *f*

lavatory ['lævətrɪ] *n (room)* cuarto *m* de baño *m*, servicio *m*, *Am* baño *m*; *(receptacle)* váter *m*, retrete *m*; **to go to the l.** ir al baño; **public l.** servicios *mpl or Esp* aseos *mpl or Am* baños *mpl* públicos; **l. paper** papel *m* higiénico

lavender ['lævɪndə(r)] **1** *n (shrub)* espliego *m*, lavanda *f*; **l. water** agua *f* de lavanda

2 *adj (color)* lila *inv*, violeta *inv*

lavish ['lævɪʃ] **1** *adj* (**a**) *(person)* generoso(a), espléndido(a) (**with** con) (**b**) *(expenditure, decor)* espléndido(a)

2 *vt* **to l. gifts/praise on sb** colmar de regalos/alabanzas a alguien

lavishly ['lævɪʃlɪ] *adv* espléndidamente

law [lɔː] *n* (**a**) *(rule)* ley *f*; **there's no l. against it** no hay ninguna ley que lo prohíba; **the laws of gravity** la ley de la gravedad; **she is a l. unto herself** hace lo que le viene en gana *or* lo que le da la gana; **there's one l. for the rich and another for the poor** hay una ley para el rico y otra para el pobre

(**b**) *(set of rules)* ley *f*; **it's the l.** es la ley; **to break the l.** quebrantar la ley; **to be above the l.** estar por encima de la ley; **you can't take the l. into your own hands** no te puedes tomar la justicia por tu mano; **l. and order** el orden público; **the problem of l. and order** la inseguridad ciudadana; **l. enforcement** mantenimiento *m* de la ley y el orden; **l. firm** bufete *m* de abogados; **l. school** facultad *f* de derecho

(**c**) *(system of justice, subject)* derecho *m*; **to practice l.** ejercer la abogacía

(**d**) *Fam* **the l.** *(police)* la poli

law-abiding ['lɔːəbaɪdɪŋ] *adj* respetuoso(a) con la ley

lawbreaker ['lɔːbreɪkə(r)] *n* delincuente *mf*

lawcourt ['lɔːkɔːt] n juzgado m

lawful ['lɔːful] adj (legal) legal; (rightful) legítimo(a); (not forbidden) lícito(a)

lawless ['lɔːlɪs] adj sin ley; **a l. mob** una muchedumbre anárquica

lawlessness ['lɔːlɪsnɪs] n anarquía f

lawmaker ['lɔːmeɪkə(r)] n legislador(ora) m,f

lawn [lɔːn] n césped m; **l. bowls** bochas fpl inv (inglesas), = juego parecido a la petanca que se juega sobre césped, y en el que las bolas se lanzan a ras de suelo; **l. mower** cortadora f de césped, cortacésped m or f; **l. tennis** tenis m en pista de hierba

lawsuit ['lɔːs(j)uːt] n pleito m

lawyer ['lɔːjə(r)] n abogado(a) m,f

lax [læks] adj (morals, discipline) relajado(a), laxo(a); (person) negligente, poco riguroso(a); (security, standards) descuidado(a), poco riguroso(a)

laxative ['læksətɪv] **1** n laxante m
2 adj laxante

laxity ['læksɪtɪ], **laxness** ['læksnɪs] n (of morals, discipline) laxitud f, Esp relajo m; (of person) negligencia f (**in doing sth** al hacer algo); (of security, standards) falta f de rigor

lay¹ [leɪ] adj Rel laico(a), lego(a); **l. preacher** predicador m laico

lay² **1** n **the l. of the land** (in politics, business) el estado de las cosas
2 vt (pt & pp **laid** [leɪd]) **(a)** (place) dejar, poner; **to l. a book on the table** dejar un libro encima de la mesa; **to l. sb flat** (hit) tumbar a alguien (de un golpe); **to l. sth flat** extender algo; **to l. sb to rest** (bury) dar sepultura a alguien; **to l. one's hands on sth** (find) dar con algo; **she reads everything she can l. her hands on** lee todo lo que cae en sus manos; **if you l. a finger on her…** como le pongas un solo dedo encima…; **to have nowhere to l. one's head** no tener donde caerse muerto; **to l. eyes on sth/sb** ver algo/a alguien; **to l. emphasis on sth** hacer hincapié en algo; **to l. the facts before sb** exponer los hechos a alguien; **to l. claim to sth** reclamar algo; **to l. a curse on sb** echar una maldición a alguien; **to l. the blame on sb** echar la culpa a alguien; **this decision lays bare her true intentions** esta decisión deja claro cuáles son sus verdaderas intenciones; **to l. oneself open to criticism** exponerse a (las) críticas; **to l. sb's fears to rest** apaciguar los temores de alguien
(b) (foundations, carpet, mine) colocar, poner; (cable, trap) tender; **to l. the table** poner la mesa
(c) (egg) poner
(d) **to l. a bet** hacer una apuesta
(e) very Fam **to get laid** Esp, Arg echar un polvo, Am coger
3 vi (bird) poner (huevos)
4 pt of **lie²**

▶**lay aside** vt sep **(a)** (money) reservar, apartar **(b)** (prejudices, doubt) dejar a un lado

▶**lay by** vt sep (money) ahorrar, guardar

▶**lay down** vt sep **(a) to l. down one's arms** dejar or deponer las armas; **he laid down his life for his beliefs** dio su vida por sus creencias **(b)** (principle, rule) establecer; **she's always laying down the law** siempre está dando órdenes

▶**lay in** vt sep (supplies, food) abastecerse de

▶**lay into** vt insep Fam (attack, criticize) arremeter contra

▶**lay off 1** vt sep (make unemployed) despedir (por reducción de plantilla)
2 vt insep Fam (abstain from) dejar; **to l. off drink** dejar la bebida
3 vi Fam **l. off!** ¡déjame en paz!

▶**lay on** vt sep (food, drink) preparar; (party, entertainment) organizar, preparar

▶**lay out** vt sep **(a)** (arrange, display) colocar, disponer; (dead body) amortajar **(b)** (plan) (road) trazar; (town) diseñar el trazado de **(c)** (spend) (money) gastarse

▶**lay over** vi hacer una parada

layer ['leɪə(r)] **1** n (of paint, chocolate) capa f; (of rock) estrato m
2 vt **to have one's hair layered** cortarse el pelo a capas

layered ['leɪəd] adj (hair) a capas

layman ['leɪmən] n Rel laico m, lego m; (non-specialist) profano m, lego m

lay-off ['leɪɒf] (pl **lay-offs**) n despido m (por reducción de plantilla)

layout ['leɪaʊt] n (of town) trazado m; (of house) disposición f; (of text) composición f

layover ['leɪəʊvə(r)] n (on land journey) parada f; (on air journey) escala f

laywoman ['leɪwʊmən] n Rel laica f, lega f; (non-specialist) profana f, lega f

laze [leɪz] vi **to l. (around/about)** holgazanear, gandulear

laziness ['leɪzɪnɪs] n pereza f

lazy ['leɪzɪ] adj (person) perezoso(a); (afternoon) ocioso(a)

lazybones ['leɪzɪbəʊnz] n Fam holgazán(ana) m,f

lb (abbr **pound**) libra f (= 0,45 kg)

LCD [elsiː'diː] n Elec & Comptr (abbr **liquid crystal display**) LCD, pantalla f de cristal líquido

LDC [eldiː'siː] n Econ (abbr **less-developed** or **least-developed country**) país m menos desarrollado

lead¹ [led] n **(a)** (metal) plomo m; **l. poisoning** saturnismo m **(b)** (for pencil) mina f **(c)** (idioms) **to go over like a l. balloon** fracasar estrepitosamente; Fam **they filled him full of l.** le llenaron el cuerpo de plomo; Fam **to swing the l.** escurrir el bulto

lead² [liːd] **1** n **(a)** (advantage) ventaja f; **to be in the l.** ir or estar a la cabeza or en cabeza; **to take** or **go into the l.** ponerse a la or en cabeza; Ind **l. time** (for production) tiempo m or período m de producción; (for delivery) tiempo m de entrega **(b)** (example) ejemplo m; **to give sb a l.** dar un ejemplo a alguien; **to follow sb's l.** seguir el ejemplo de alguien **(c)** (clue) pista f **(d)** (in card game) mano f; **it's your l.** tú eres mano, tú llevas la mano **(e)** Theat & Cin papel m protagonista **(f)** (for dog) correa f **(g)** (cable) cable m
2 vt (pt & pp **led** [led]) **(a)** (show the way to) llevar, conducir; **to l. the way** mostrar el camino; **to l. the conversation away from a subject** llevar la conversación hacia otro tema; **to be easily led** dejarse influir con facilidad; **that leads me to believe that…** eso me hace creer que… **(b) to l. a happy/sad life** tener or llevar una vida feliz/triste **(c)** (team, attack, troops) dirigir **(d)** (be ahead of) **to l. the field** estar or ir a la cabeza; Fig **to l. the field in sth** estar a la cabeza or a la vanguardia en algo; **to l. sb by eight points** llevar a alguien ocho puntos de ventaja
3 vi **(a)** (road) conducir, llevar **(b) to l. to sth** (cause) llevar a algo **(c)** (in competition, race) ir en cabeza; (in card game) salir; **you l. and I'll follow** tú vas delante y yo te sigo

▶**lead away** vt sep **to l. sb away** llevarse a alguien

▶**lead off** vi **(a)** (road, corridor) salir, bifurcarse (**from** de) **(b)** (in discussion) comenzar, empezar

▶**lead up to** vt insep (subject, event) llevar a, conducir a; (of person) ir a referirse a; **the period leading up to the war** el periodo previo or que precedió a la guerra; **what are you leading up to?** ¿a dónde quieres ir a parar (con todo esto)?

leaded ['ledɪd] adj **l. gasoline** gasolina f or RP nafta f con plomo; **l. window** vidriera f (emplomada)

leaden ['ledən] adj (heavy) pesado(a), plúmbeo(a); **a l. sky** un cielo plomizo

leader ['liːdə(r)] n (of group, in race) líder mf; **to be a born l.** ser un líder nato

leadership ['liːdəʃɪp] n (people in charge) dirección f; (position) liderato *m*, liderazgo *m*; *(quality)* capacidad *f* de liderazgo, dotes *fpl* de mando

lead-free [led'fri:] *adj (gasoline, paint)* sin plomo

lead-in ['li:dɪn] *n TV & Rad* presentación *f*

leading ['li:dɪŋ] *adj* (a) *(best, most important)* principal, destacado(a); **one of Europe's l. electronics firms** una de las principales empresas europeas de electrónica; **a l. authority in the field** una destacada autoridad en la materia; **l. light** *(in politics, society)* figura *f* prominente; **l. question** *(seeking to elicit answer)* pregunta *f* capciosa; *Cin & Theat* **l. role** papel *m* protagonista (b) *(team, runner)* líder

leaf [li:f] *(pl* **leaves** [li:vz]) *n* (a) *(of plant, book)* hoja *f*; *Fig* **to turn over a new l.** hacer borrón y cuenta nueva; *Fig* **to take a l. out of sb's book** seguir el ejemplo de alguien (b) *(of table)* hoja *f* abatible

▶**leaf through** *vt insep (book, magazine)* hojear

leaflet ['li:flɪt] **1** *n* folleto *m*; *(political)* octavilla *f*; *(folded)* díptico *m*, panfleto *m*
2 *vt* **to l. an area** repartir folletos en una zona

leafy ['li:fɪ] *adj (tree)* frondoso(a); **l. suburb** zona *f* residencial con arbolado

league [li:g] *n* liga *f*; **l. champions** *(in baseball, soccer)* campeón *m* de liga; **to be in l. with sb** estar coaligado(a) con alguien; *Fig* **to be in a different l.** estar a otro nivel

leak [li:k] **1** *n* (a) *(in bucket)* agujero *m*; *(in pipe)* fuga *f*, escape *m*; *(in roof)* gotera *f*; *(in ship)* vía *f* de agua; *Fam* **to take a l.** echar una meadita (b) *(of liquid, gas)* fuga *f*, escape *m*; *(of information)* filtración *f*
2 *vt (liquid, gas)* tener una fuga *or* un escape de; *(information)* filtrar
3 *vi* (a) *(pipe)* tener una fuga *or* un escape; *(roof)* tener goteras; *(shoe)* calar; *(ship)* hacer agua; **this bucket's leaking** este cubo pierde (b) *(liquid, gas)* salirse, escaparse; *(information)* filtrarse

leakage ['li:kɪdʒ] *n (of liquid, gas)* fuga *f*, escape *m*; *(of information)* filtración *f*

leakproof ['li:kpru:f] *adj* hermético(a)

leaky ['li:kɪ] *adj (bucket)* con agujeros; *(pipe)* con fugas *or* escapes; *(roof)* con goteras; *(shoe)* que cala; *(ship)* que hace agua; *(tap)* que gotea

lean[1] [li:n] *adj* (a) *(person)* delgado(a); *(meat)* magro(a) (b) *(year)* de escasez; *(harvest)* escaso(a)

lean[2] **1** *vt* **to l. sth against sth** apoyar algo contra algo
2 *vi (building)* inclinarse; **to l. on/against sth** apoyarse en/contra algo; *Fig* **to l. on sb** *(rely on)* apoyarse en alguien; *(pressurize)* presionar a alguien; **to l. out of the window** asomarse a la ventana

▶**lean back** *vi* reclinarse

▶**lean over** *vt insep* **he leaned over the fence** se asomó por encima de la valla

leaning ['li:nɪŋ] *n (tendency)* inclinación *f*, tendencia *f*; **to have artistic leanings** tener tendencias *or* inclinaciones artísticas

lean-to ['li:ntu:] *(pl* **lean-tos**) *n (shack)* cobertizo *m*

leap [li:p] **1** *n* salto *m*, brinco *m*; *Fig* **to take a l. in the dark** dar un salto al vacío; *Fig* **to advance by leaps and bounds** avanzar a pasos agigantados; **l. year** año *m* bisiesto
2 *vt (pt & pp* **leaped** *or* **leapt** [lept]) saltar
3 *vi* saltar; **to l. to one's feet** ponerse en pie de un salto; **to l. at the chance** no dejar escapar la oportunidad; **to l. for joy** dar saltos de alegría

leapfrog ['li:pfrɒg] **1** *n* **to play l.** jugar a pídola
2 *vt (pt & pp* **leapfrogged**) saltar por encima de
3 *vi Fig* **to l. over** *(rivals)* pasar por encima de

leapt [lept] *pt & pp of* **leap**

learn [lɜ:n] **1** *vt* (a) *(language, skill)* aprender; *Fig* **he has learned his lesson** ha aprendido la lección (b) *(find out*

about) enterarse de; **we are sorry to l. that...** sentimos mucho haber sabido que...
2 *vi* (a) *(acquire knowledge)* aprender (b) *(find out)* enterarse; **to l. of** *or* **about sth** enterarse de algo

learned ['lɜ:nɪd] *adj* erudito(a)

learner ['lɜ:nə(r)] *n (beginner)* principiante *mf*; *(student)* estudiante *mf*; **to be a quick l.** aprender deprisa; **to be a slow l.** ser lento(a) *(para aprender)*

learning ['lɜ:nɪŋ] *n (process)* aprendizaje *m*; *(knowledge)* conocimientos *mpl*; **l. curve** curva *f* de aprendizaje; **l. disabilities** discapacidad *f* psíquica

lease [li:s] **1** *n Law* (contrato *m* de) arrendamiento *m*; *Fig* **to give sb a new l. on life** dar a alguien una nueva inyección de vida
2 *vt* arrendar (**from/to** de/a)

leasehold ['li:shəʊld] *n* arriendo *m*; **l. property** propiedad *f* arrendada

leaseholder ['li:shəʊldə(r)] *n* arrendatario(a) *m,f*

leash [li:ʃ] *n (for dog)* correa *f*; *Fig* **to keep sb on a tight l.** atar corto a alguien

leasing ['li:sɪŋ] *n Com* leasing *m*, arrendamiento *m*

least [li:st] **1** *n* **the l.** lo menos; **it's the l. I can do** es lo menos que puedo hacer; **that's the l. of my worries** eso es lo que menos me preocupa; **to say the l.** por no decir otra cosa; **not in the l.** en absoluto; **it doesn't matter in the l.** no tiene la menor importancia
2 *adj (superlative of* **little**) *(smallest)* menor; **the l. thing annoys her** la menor cosa le molesta
3 *adv* menos; **the l. interesting/difficult** el menos interesante/difícil; **l. of all her** mucho menos ella; **when I was l. expecting it** cuando menos lo esperaba
4 **at least** *adv* por lo menos, al menos; **at l. as old/expensive as...** por lo menos tan viejo/caro como...; **at the (very) l. they should pay your expenses** como mínimo deberían pagar tus gastos; **he's leaving, at l. that's what I've heard** se marcha, o al menos eso he oído

least-cost ['li:st'kɒst] *n Com* coste *m* mínimo

leather ['leðə(r)] **1** *n* cuero *m*, *Esp, Méx* piel *f*
2 *vt Fam (beat)* cascar, zurrar, *Méx* madrear

leather-bound ['leðəbaʊnd] *adj (book)* encuadernado(a) en cuero *or Esp, Méx* piel

leathery ['leðərɪ] *adj (face, skin)* curtido(a); *(meat)* correoso(a)

leave [li:v] **1** *n* (a) *(permission, vacation)* permiso *m*; **to be on l.** estar de permiso; **to ask l. to do sth** pedir permiso para hacer algo; **to grant** *or* **give sb l. to do sth** conceder *or* dar permiso a alguien para hacer algo; **l. of absence** permiso *m* (b) *(farewell)* **to take one's l. (of sb)** despedirse (de alguien); **to take l. of one's senses** perder el juicio
2 *vt (pt & pp* **left** [left]) (a) *(depart from) (place)* irse de, marcharse de; *(room)* salir de; *(person)* dejar; **he has left San Diego** se ha ido de San Diego; **to l. the table** levantarse de la mesa; **to l. one's job** dejar el trabajo; **the car left the road** el coche salió de la carretera; **his eyes never left her** sus ojos no se apartaban de ella
(b) *(abandon)* abandonar, dejar; **he left his wife** dejó a su mujer
(c) *(put, deposit)* **to l. sth somewhere** *(deliberately)* dejar algo en algún sitio; *(by mistake)* dejarse algo en algún sitio; **take it or l. it** lo tomas o lo dejas; **to l. a message for sb** dejar un recado *or* mensaje para alguien
(d) *(allow to remain)* dejar; **to l. the door open** dejar la puerta abierta; **to l. oneself open to criticism** exponerse a las críticas; **to l. sth unfinished** dejar algo sin terminar; **to l. sb to do sth** dejar a alguien hacer algo; **l. it to me** déjamelo a mí; **it leaves much to be desired** deja mucho que desear; **let's l. it at that** vamos a dejarlo aquí; **I think we should l. (it) well alone** creo que sería mejor no meterse *or* dejar las cosas como están; **l. me alone!** ¡déjame en paz!

(**e**) *(bequeath)* legar, dejar; **he leaves a wife and three children** deja mujer y tres hijos

(**f**) *(remain)* **to be left** quedar; **how many are there left?** ¿cuántos quedan?; **three from seven leaves four** siete menos tres son cuatro

3 *vi (depart)* salir; *(go away)* irse, marcharse

▶**leave behind** *vt sep* **to l. sth behind** dejarse algo; **to l. sb behind** dejar a alguien

▶**leave off 1** *vt insep Fam* **to l. off doing sth** dejar de hacer algo; **to l. off work** dejar el trabajo

2 *vi* **where did we l. off?** ¿dónde lo dejamos?

▶**leave on** *vt sep* **to l. the light/TV on** dejar la luz/televisión encendida *or Am* prendida

▶**leave out** *vt sep* (**a**) *(omit)* omitir (**b**) *(not involve)* **to l. sb out of sth** dejar a alguien al margen de algo; **to feel left out** sentirse excluido(a) (**c**) *(leave ready, available)* **I'll l. your dinner out on the table for you** te dejaré la cena encima de la mesa; **l. the disks out where I can see them** deja los disquetes donde pueda verlos (**d**) *(not put away)* **we l. the car out on the street** dejamos el coche en la calle; **who left the milk out?** ¿quién ha dejado la leche fuera?

▶**leave over** *vt sep* **to be left over** *(food, money)* sobrar

leaven ['levən] *n Culin & Fig* fermento *m*

leave-taking ['li:vteɪkɪŋ] *n* despedida *f*

Lebanese [lebə'ni:z] **1** *npl (people)* **the L.** los libaneses

2 *n & adj* libanés(esa) *m,f*

Lebanon ['lebənən] *n* el Líbano

lech [letʃ] *Fam n (person)* salido(a) *m,f*, sátiro *m*, *Esp, Méx* cachondo(a)

lecher ['letʃə(r)] *n* sátiro *m*, obseso *m*

lecherous ['letʃərəs] *adj* lascivo(a), lujurioso(a)

lecherously ['letʃərəslɪ] *adv* lascivamente

lechery ['letʃərɪ] *n* lascivia *f*, lujuria *f*

lectern ['lektən] *n* atril *m*

lecture ['lektʃə(r)] **1** *n* (**a**) *(public speech)* conferencia *f*; *(college class)* clase *f*; **l. room** sala *f* de conferencias; **l. theater** *(in college)* aula *f*; *(in conference center)* sala *f* de conferencias (**b**) *Fam (reprimand)* sermón *m*; **to give sb a l.** echarle un sermón a alguien, sermonear a alguien

2 *vt Fam (reprimand)* echar un sermón a, sermonear

3 *vi (give public lectures)* dar conferencias; *(at college)* dar *or Am* dictar clases

LED [eli:'di:] *n Elec (abbr* **light-emitting diode)** LED *m*, diodo *m* emisor de luz

led [led] *pt & pp of* **lead**

ledge [ledʒ] *n (shelf)* repisa *f*; *(on cliff)* saliente *m*; *(of window)* alféizar *m (exterior)*; *(on building)* cornisa *f*

ledger ['ledʒə(r)] *n* libro *m* mayor

lee [li:] *n* socaire *m*

leech [li:tʃ] *n* (**a**) *(animal)* sanguijuela *f*; **to cling to sb like a l.** pegarse a alguien como una lapa (**b**) *Pej (parasitical person)* sanguijuela *f*, chupóptero(a) *m,f*

leek [li:k] *n* puerro *m*

leer ['lɪə(r)] **1** *n* mirada *f* impúdica *or* obscena

2 *vi* **to l. at sb** mirar impúdicamente a alguien

lees [li:z] *npl (of wine)* madre *f*, heces *fpl*

leeward ['li:wəd] **1** *n* sotavento *m*

2 *adj* de sotavento; **the L. Islands** las Islas de Sotavento

leeway ['li:weɪ] *n (freedom)* margen *m* de maniobra

left[1] [left] **1** *n* izquierda *f*; **on** *or* **to the l.** a la izquierda; **on my l.** a mano izquierda

2 *adj* izquierdo(a); **the l. wing** *(of party)* la izquierda

3 *adv* a la izquierda; *Fig* **l. and right** por todas partes

left[2] *pt & pp of* **leave**

left-click ['leftklɪk] **1** *vt* hacer click con el botón izquierdo en

2 *vi* hacer click con el botón izquierdo (**on** en)

left-field ['left'fi:ld] *adj Fam (bizarre)* raro(a), extravagante

left-hand ['left'hænd] *adj* de la izquierda; **on the l. side** a la izquierda

left-handed [left'hændɪd] **1** *adj* zurdo(a)

2 *adv* con la izquierda *or* zurda

left-hander [left'hændə(r)] *n (person)* zurdo(a) *m,f*

left-of-center ['leftəv'sentə(r)] *adj Pol* de centroizquierda

leftover ['leftəʊvə(r)] **1** *npl* **leftovers** *(food)* sobras *fpl*

2 *adj (food, paint)* sobrante

left-wing ['leftwɪŋ] *adj* izquierdista, de izquierdas

left-winger ['left'wɪŋə(r)] *n Pol* izquierdista *mf*

leg [leg] **1** *n* (**a**) *(of person)* pierna *f*; *(of animal, table, chair)* pata *f*; *(of pants)* pernera *f*; *Culin (of lamb)* pierna *f*; *Culin (of chicken)* muslo *m*; **l. warmers** calentadores *mpl*, calientapiernas *mpl* (**b**) *(of journey, race)* etapa *f* (**c**) *(idioms)* **to pull sb's l.** tomar el pelo a alguien; **shake a l.!** ¡muévete!; **to show a l.** *(get up)* levantarse; **you don't have a l. to stand on** no tienes a qué agarrarte; **he was given a l. up** *(was helped)* le echaron una mano *or* un cable

2 *vt (pt & pp* **legged)** *Fam* **to l. it** *(hurry)* salir zumbando

legacy ['legəsɪ] *n* legado *m*; **to come into a l.** recibir una herencia

legal ['li:gəl] *adj* legal; **to take l. action (against sb)** presentar una demanda (contra alguien); **l. advice** asesoría *f* jurídica *or* legal; **l. aid** asistencia *f* jurídica de oficio; **l. eagle** *(successful lawyer)* = abogado de éxito, especialmente joven, brillante y dinámico; **l. holiday** día *m* festivo *or Am* feriado; **the l. profession** la profesión jurídica; **l. tender** moneda *f* de curso legal

legality [lɪ'gælɪtɪ] *n* legalidad *f*

legalization [li:gəlaɪ'zeɪʃən] *n* legalización *f*

legalize ['li:gəlaɪz] *vt* legalizar

legally ['li:gəlɪ] *adv* legalmente

legate ['legɪt] *n Rel* nuncio *m*

legation [lɪ'geɪʃən] *n (diplomatic mission)* legación *f*

legend ['ledʒənd] *n* leyenda *f*; **to be a l. in one's own lifetime** ser una leyenda viva

legendary ['ledʒəndərɪ] *adj* legendario(a)

leggings ['legɪŋz] *npl (of woman)* mallas *fpl*; *(of cowboy)* antiparas *fpl*, polainas *fpl*

leggy ['legɪ] *adj (person)* patilargo(a)

legibility [ledʒɪ'bɪlɪtɪ] *n* legibilidad *f*

legible ['ledʒɪbəl] *adj* legible

legion ['li:dʒən] *n* legión *f*

legionary ['li:dʒənərɪ] *n* legionario *m*

legionnaire [li:dʒə'neə(r)] *n* legionario *m*; *Med* **l.'s disease** enfermedad *f* del legionario, legionel(l)a *f*

legislate ['ledʒɪsleɪt] *vi* legislar (**against** en contra de)

legislation [ledʒɪs'leɪʃən] *n* legislación *f*

legislative ['ledʒɪslətɪv] *adj* legislativo(a)

legislator ['ledʒɪsleɪtə(r)] *n* legislador(ora) *m,f*

legislature ['ledʒɪslətjə(r)] *n* legislativo *m*, asamblea *f* legislativa

legitimacy [lɪ'dʒɪtɪməsɪ] *n* legitimidad *f*

legitimate 1 *adj* [lɪ'dʒɪtɪmət] legítimo(a)

2 *vt* [lɪ'dʒɪtɪmeɪt] legitimar

legitimately [lɪ'dʒɪtɪmətlɪ] *adv* legítimamente

legitimize [lɪ'dʒɪtɪmaɪz] *vt* legitimizar

leg-pull ['legpʊl] *n Fam* tomadura *f* de pelo, vacile *m*

legroom ['legrʊm] *n* espacio *m* para las piernas *(en vehículo, en el cine)*

legume ['legju:m] *n Bot* legumbre *f*

leisure ['li:ʒə(r)] *n* ocio *m*; **take these leaflets and read them at your l.** llévate estos folletos y tómate tu tiempo para leerlos; **a life of l.** una vida de ocio; **l. activities** actividades *fpl* para el tiempo libre; **l. center** centro *m* recreativo *or* de ocio

leisurely ['li:ʒəlɪ] *adj (unhurried)* pausado(a), lento(a); *(relaxed)* tranquilo(a), relajado(a)

leisurewear ['leʒəweə(r)] *n* ropa *f* de sport

lemming ['lemɪŋ] *n* lemming *m*; **they followed him like lemmings** le siguieron ciegamente

lemon ['lemən] **1** *n* (**a**) *(fruit)* limón *m*; **l. sole** mendo *m* limón; **l. squeezer** exprimidor *m*, exprimelimones *m inv*; **l. tea** té *m* con limón; **l. tree** limonero *m* (**b**) *(color)* amarillo *m* limón (**c**) *Fam (worthless, useless thing or person)* desastre *m*, *Esp* patata *f*
2 *adj* **l. (colored)** (color) amarillo limón

lemonade [lemə'neɪd] *n (still)* limonada *f*

lemur ['li:mə(r)] *n* lémur *m*

lend [lend] (*pt & pp* **lent** [lent]) *vt (money, book, pen)* prestar; *(dignity, support, credibility)* proporcionar, prestar (**to** a); **to l. sb a (helping) hand** echar una mano a alguien; **to l. an ear** *or* **one's ear to...** escuchar de buena gana a...; **her work doesn't l. itself to dramatization** su obra no se presta a la dramatización

lender ['lendə(r)] *n Fin* prestamista *mf*

lending ['lendɪŋ] *n Fin* préstamos *mpl*, créditos *mpl*; **l. library** biblioteca *f* de préstamo; *Fin* **l. rate** tipo *m or Am* tasa *f* de interés de los préstamos *or* créditos

length [leŋθ] *n* (**a**) *(in space)* longitud *f*; **it's 4 feet in l.** tiene 4 pies de longitud; **to wander the l. and breadth of the country** vagabundear a lo largo y ancho del país
(**b**) *(in time)* duración *f*; **at (great) l.** extensamente, dilatadamente; **a great l. of time** un largo periodo de tiempo; **l. of service** antigüedad *f* en la empresa
(**c**) **to go to the l. of doing sth** llegar incluso a hacer algo; **to go to great lengths to do sth** tomarse muchas molestias para hacer algo; **he would go to any lengths (to do sth)** estaría dispuesto a cualquier cosa (con tal de hacer algo)
(**d**) *(piece) (of wood, string)* trozo *m*, pedazo *m*
(**e**) *(of swimming pool)* largo *m*

lengthen ['leŋθən] **1** *vt* alargar
2 *vi* alargarse

lengthily ['leŋθɪlɪ] *adv* extensamente, dilatadamente

lengthwise ['leŋθwaɪz], **lengthways** ['leŋθweɪz] *adv* a lo largo

lengthy ['leŋθɪ] *adj* largo(a), extenso(a)

lenient ['li:nɪənt] *adj* indulgente, benévolo(a)

leniently ['li:nɪəntlɪ] *adv* con indulgencia, benevolamente

Leningrad ['lenɪŋgræd] *n Formerly* Leningrado

lens [lenz] *n (of glasses)* cristal *m*, lente *f*, *Am* vidrio *m*; *(of camera)* objetivo *m*, lente *f*; *(of eye)* cristalino *m*; **(contact) lenses** *Esp* lentillas *fpl*, *Am* lentes *fpl* de contacto, *Méx* pupilentes *fpl*; **l. cap** tapa *f* del objetivo

Lent [lent] *n Rel* cuaresma *f*

lent [lent] *pt & pp of* **lend**

lentil ['lentɪl] *n* lenteja *f*

Leo ['li:əʊ] *n (sign of zodiac)* Leo *m*; **to be (a) L.** ser Leo

leopard ['lepəd] *n* leopardo *m*

leopard-skin ['lepədskɪn] *adj* de piel de leopardo

leotard ['li:ətɑːd] *n* malla *f*

leper ['lepə(r)] *n* leproso(a) *m,f*; **l. colony** leprosería *f*, lazareto *m*

leprechaun ['leprəkɔːn] *n (Irish fairy)* duende *m*

leprosy ['leprəsɪ] *n* lepra *f*

lesbian ['lezbɪən] **1** *n* lesbiana *f*
2 *adj* lésbico(a), lesbiano(a)

lesion ['li:ʒən] *n* lesión *f*

Lesotho [lɪ'su:tu:] *n* Lesoto *m*

less [les] **1** *adj (comparative of* **little**) menos; **it's l. than a week's work** es menos de una semana de trabajo; **the distance is l. than we thought** la distancia es menor de lo que pensábamos
2 *prep* menos; **a year l. two days** un año menos dos días;

I've got $50, l. what I spent on the train ticket tengo 50 dólares, menos lo que me he gastado en el billete de tren
3 *pron* menos; **I don't think any (the) l. of you** no pienso peor de ti; **I see l. of her nowadays** la veo menos ahora; **in l. than an hour** en menos de una hora; **the l. said about it the better** cuanto menos se hable de ello, mejor; *Fam* **l. of that!** ¡basta ya!
4 *adv* menos; **l. and l.** cada vez menos; **no more, no l.** ni más ni menos; **still l., even l.** todavía menos; **nothing l. than** nada menos que; **she was driving a Rolls, no l.** conducía nada menos que un Rolls; **I expected no l. from you** no esperaba menos de ti; **they haven't got a fridge, much l. a freezer** no tienen nevera y mucho menos congelador

lessen ['lesən] **1** *vt* reducir
2 *vi* disminuir, reducirse

lesser ['lesə(r)] *adj* menor; **the l. of two evils** el mal menor; **to a l. extent** *or* **degree** en menor medida

lesser-known ['lesə'nəʊn] *adj* menos conocido(a)

lesson ['lesən] *n* clase *f*, lección *f*; *Fig* **he has learned his l.** ha aprendido la lección; *Fig* **to teach sb a l.** dar una lección a alguien

lest [lest] *conj Formal* para que no, por si; **l. we forget...** para que no olvidemos,...

let¹ [let] *n (in tennis)* servicio *m* nulo

let² **1** *vt (pt & pp* **let**) (**a**) *(allow)* **to l. sb do sth** dejar a alguien hacer algo; **to l. sb know** decir algo a alguien; **l. me see** *(when answering)* veamos, a ver; *(show me)* déjame ver; **to l. sth pass** *(not criticize, comment on)* dejar pasar algo, pasar algo por alto; **to l. go of sth, to l. sth go** soltar algo; **to l. oneself go** *(lose restraint)* soltarse el pelo; *(stop caring for one's appearance)* abandonarse; **I'm afraid we'll have to l. you go** *(on making somebody unemployed)* me temo que vamos a tener que prescindir de usted; **don't l. it get to you** *or* **get you down** no dejes que eso pueda contigo; **can you l. me have it back tomorrow?** ¿me lo puedes devolver mañana?; **don't l. me see you here again!** ¡que no te vuelva a ver por aquí!; *Math* **l. AB be equal to CD** sea AB igual a CD
(**b**) *(with suggestions)* **let's go!** ¡vamos!; **let's hurry!** ¡deprisa!; **let's not have an argument about it!** ¡no nos peleemos por eso!; **now, don't let's have any nonsense!** ¡bueno, y nada de tonterías!
2 let alone *conj* mucho menos, menos aún

▶ **let by** *vt sep (allow to pass)* **to l. sb by** dejar pasar a alguien

▶ **let down** *vt sep* (**a**) *(hem)* bajar; *(tire)* deshinchar, desinflar; *Fig* **to l. one's hair down** soltarse el pelo (**b**) *Fam (disappoint, fail)* **to l. sb down** fallar a alguien; **the car let us down again** el coche nos dejó tirados otra vez

▶ **let in** *vt sep* (**a**) *(allow to enter)* dejar pasar; **to l. oneself in** *(to house)* entrar; **to l. in the light** dejar que entre la luz; **my shoes are letting in water** me están calando los zapatos (**b**) **to l. sb in on a secret/a plan** contar a alguien un secreto/un plan (**c**) *Fam* **do you know what you are letting yourself in for?** ¿tienes idea de en qué te estás metiendo?

▶ **let into** *vt sep* **who let them into the house?** ¿quién los dejó entrar en la casa?; **I'll l. you into a secret** te contaré un secreto

▶ **let off** *vt sep* (**a**) *(bomb, firework)* hacer explotar; *Fig* **to l. off steam** desfogarse (**b**) *(excuse)* perdonar; **they let him off with a fine** sólo le pusieron una multa

▶ **let on** *vi Fam* **don't l. on that I was there** no digas que estuve allí; **he was more ill than he let on** estaba más enfermo de lo que decía

▶ **let out 1** *vt sep* (**a**) *(release)* dejar salir; **to l. out the air from sth** desinflar *or* deshinchar algo; **to l. out a yell** soltar un grito (**b**) *(jacket, pants)* agrandar (**c**) *(rent out)* alquilar
2 *vi (finish)* terminar, acabar

▶**let up** vi (weather) amainar; **once he's started he never lets up** una vez que empieza ya no se detiene

letch [letʃ] = **lech**

letdown ['letdaʊn] n Fam chasco m, desilusión f

lethal ['li:θəl] adj letal, mortal; Fam **that vodka's l.!** ¡ese vodka es fortísimo!; **l. dose** dosis f inv letal; **l. weapon** arma f mortífera

lethargic [lɪ'θɑ:dʒɪk] adj (drowsy) aletargado(a); (inactive) apático(a)

lethargy ['leθədʒɪ] n (drowsiness) sopor m, letargo m; (inactivity) apatía f

letter ['letə(r)] n (a) (written message) carta f; **l. of acknowledgment** carta de acuse de recibo; Fin **l. of credit** carta de crédito; Fin **l. of exchange** letra f de cambio; **l. bomb** carta bomba; **l. opener** abrecartas m inv (b) (of alphabet) letra f; **the l. of the law** la interpretación literal de la ley; **to obey to the l.** obedecer al pie de la letra (c) **man of letters** hombre m de letras

letterhead ['letəhed] n membrete m

lettuce ['letɪs] n lechuga f

letup ['letʌp] n Fam tregua f, descanso m; **they worked fifteen hours without a l.** trabajaron quince horas sin descanso

leucocyte = **leukocyte**

leukemia [lu:'ki:mɪə] n leucemia f

leukocyte, leucocyte ['lu:kəsaɪt] n Anat leucocito m

level ['levəl] **1** n nivel m; **at eye l.** a la altura de los ojos; **to be on a l. with** estar al mismo nivel or a la misma altura que; Fam **on the l.** honrado(a); **to come down to sb's l.** ponerse al nivel de alguien; **to sink to sb's l.** rebajarse al nivel de alguien; **at ministerial/international l.** a nivel ministerial/internacional

2 adj (a) (not sloping) nivelado(a), liso(a), horizontal; Fig **a l. playing field** igualdad f de condiciones (b) **l. with...** a la altura de...; **to draw l. with** (in race) alcanzar, ponerse a la altura de; (in match) conseguir el empate contra; **she did her l. best** hizo todo lo que estaba en su mano; **a l. spoonful** una cucharada rasa (c) (voice, tone) neutro(a), desapasionado(a); **to keep a l. head** mantener la cabeza fría

3 vt (a) (make level) nivelar; (raze) arrasar (b) (aim) **to l. a blow at sb** propinar or asestar un golpe a alguien; **to l. criticism at sb** dirigir críticas a alguien; **to l. accusations at sb** lanzar acusaciones contra alguien

4 vi Fam **to l. with sb** ser franco(a) con alguien

▶**level off, level out** vi (ground) nivelarse, allanarse; (prices, demand) estabilizarse; Av enderezarse

level-headed ['levəl'hedɪd] adj ecuánime

lever ['levə(r), 'li:və(r)] **1** n palanca f

2 vt **to l. a box open** abrir una caja haciendo palanca

leverage ['li:vərɪdʒ] n Tech apalancamiento m; Fig **to bring l. to bear on** (pressurize) ejercer presión sobre

leveraged buyout ['li:vərɪdʒd'baɪaʊt] n Fin compra f apalancada

levitate ['levɪteɪt] vi levitar

levitation [levɪ'teɪʃən] n levitación f

levity ['levɪtɪ] n frivolidad f

levy ['levɪ] **1** n (tax) impuesto m, tasa f (**on** sobre)

2 vt (tax) aplicar (**on** a)

lewd [lu:d] adj obsceno(a)

lexical ['leksɪkəl] adj léxico(a)

lexicographer [leksɪ'kɒgrəfə(r)] n lexicógrafo(a) m,f

lexicography [leksɪ'kɒgrəfɪ] n lexicografía f

lexicon ['leksɪkən] n (dictionary) lexicón m; (vocabulary) léxico m

ley ['leɪ] n **l. (line)** = línea que una hitos del paisaje y a la que se atribuyen antecedentes prehistóricos

liability [laɪə'bɪlɪtɪ] n (a) Law (responsibility) responsabilidad f

(**for** de); Fin **liabilities** pasivo m, deudas fpl (b) (disadvantage) estorbo m

liable ['laɪəbəl] adj (a) Law (responsible) responsable (**for** de) (b) (to tax, fine) sujeto(a) (**to** a) (c) (likely) propenso(a) (**to** a); **it is l. to explode** puede que explote

liaise [li:'eɪz] vi **to l. with sb (about sth)** trabajar en cooperación con alguien (para algo)

liaison [lɪ'eɪzɒn] n (a) (cooperation) coordinación f; Mil **l. officer** oficial m de enlace (b) (love affair) relación f (amorosa)

liar ['laɪə(r)] n mentiroso(a) m,f

libel ['laɪbəl] Law **1** n libelo m; **l. action** juicio m por libelo; **l. laws** legislación f sobre el libelo

2 vt calumniar

libelous ['laɪbələs] adj calumnioso(a)

liberal ['lɪbərəl] **1** n (a) (tolerant person) liberal mf (b) Pol **L.** liberal mf

2 adj (a) (tolerant) liberal; **l. education** educación f liberal (b) (generous) desprendido(a), generoso(a) (**with** con) (c) (abundant) abundante, generoso(a) (d) Pol **L.** liberal

liberalism ['lɪbərəlɪzəm] n liberalismo m

liberalize ['lɪbərəlaɪz] vt liberalizar

liberally ['lɪbərəlɪ] adv generosamente

liberate ['lɪbəreɪt] vt liberar

liberated ['lɪbəreɪtɪd] adj liberado(a); **a l. woman** una mujer liberada

liberating ['lɪbəreɪtɪŋ] adj liberador(ora)

liberation [lɪbə'reɪʃən] n liberación f; **l. movement** movimiento m de liberación; **l. theology** teología f de la liberación

liberator ['lɪbəreɪtə(r)] n libertador(ora) m,f, liberador(ora) m,f

Liberia [laɪ'bɪərɪə] n Liberia

Liberian [laɪ'bɪərɪən] n & adj liberiano(a) m,f

libertarian [lɪbə'teərɪən] n & adj libertario(a) m,f

liberty ['lɪbətɪ] n libertad f; **at l.** (free) en libertad; **to be at l. to do sth** tener libertad para hacer algo; **to take the l. of doing sth** tomarse la libertad de hacer algo; **to take liberties with** tomarse (excesivas) libertades con; **what a l.!** ¡qué cara más dura!

libido [lɪ'bi:dəʊ] (pl **libidos**) n libido f

Libra ['li:brə] n (sign of zodiac) Libra m; **to be (a) L.** ser Libra

librarian [laɪ'breərɪən] n bibliotecario(a) m,f

library ['laɪbrərɪ] n biblioteca f; Comptr librería f; **film l.** filmoteca f; **music l.** fonoteca f; **l. book** libro m de biblioteca; **l. card** carné m de biblioteca

libretto [lɪ'bretəʊ] (pl **librettos** or **libretti** [lɪ'breti:]) n Mus libreto m

Libya ['lɪbɪə] n Libia

Libyan ['lɪbɪən] n & adj libio(a) m,f

lice pl of **louse**

license ['laɪsəns] **1** n (a) (permit) licencia f, permiso m; Com **under l.** bajo licencia, con autorización; **(driver's) l.** carné m or permiso m de Esp conducir or RP conductor, licencia f Carib de conducir or Méx para conducir; Aut **l. number** (of car) (número m de) matrícula f; Aut **l. plate** (placa f de) matrícula f (b) (freedom) licencia f; (excessive freedom) libertinaje m

2 vt Com autorizar; **to be licensed to carry a gun** tener permiso or licencia de armas

licentious [laɪ'senʃəs] adj licencioso(a)

lichen ['laɪkən] n liquen m

lick [lɪk] **1** n (with tongue) lametazo m, lamedura f; **a l. of paint** una mano de pintura

2 vt (a) (with tongue) lamer; Fig **to l. one's lips** (in anticipation) relamerse; Fig **to l. one's wounds** lamerse las heridas; Fam Fig **to l. sb's boots** darle coba a alguien; Vulg **to l. sb's ass** lamer or RP chupar el culo a alguien; Fam **to l. sth/sb into shape** poner algo/a alguien a punto (b) Fam (defeat) hacer trizas a

licking ['lıkıŋ] *n Fam* **to get** *or* **take a l.** *(physically)* llevarse una buena zurra; *(in game, competition)* llevarse una soberana paliza

licorice ['lıkərıs] *n* regaliz *m*

lid [lıd] *n* **(a)** *(of pot, jar)* tapa *f* **(b)** *(idioms)* **to take the l. off sth** destapar algo; **to keep the l. on sth** mantener oculto algo

lie¹ [laı] **1** *n* mentira *f*; **to tell a l.** decir una mentira, mentir; **to give the l. to sth** desmentir algo; **l. detector** detector *m* de mentiras

2 *vi* mentir; **to l. through one's teeth** mentir descaradamente

lie² *vi* (*pt* **lay** [leı], *pp* **lain** [leın]) **(a)** *(person, animal) (be still)* estar tumbado(a) *or* acostado(a); *(get down)* tumbarse, acostarse; **here lies...** *(on gravestone)* aquí yace...; **to l. in bed** estar en la cama; **I lay awake all night** permanecí despierto toda la noche; **to l. in wait for sb** permanecer *or* estar a la espera de alguien; *Fig* **to l. low** permanecer en un segundo plano

(b) *(object)* estar; **a vast plain lay before us** ante nosotros se extendía una vasta llanura; **to l. in ruins** *(building)* quedar en ruinas; *(career, hopes)* quedar arruinado(a); **the obstacles that l. in our way** los impedimentos que obstaculizan nuestro camino; **the snow did not l.** la nieve no cuajó

(c) *(abstract thing)* **the responsibility lies with the author** la responsabilidad recae sobre el autor; **they know where their true interests l.** saben dónde se hallan sus verdaderos intereses; **the difference lies in that...** la diferencia radica en que...; **a brilliant future lies before her** tiene ante sí un brillante futuro; **what lies behind this uncharacteristic generosity?** ¿qué hay detrás de esta inusual generosidad?

▸**lie around, lie about** *vi (person, thing)* estar tirado(a); **she had left her papers lying around** *or* **about** había dejado sus papeles tirados

▸**lie back** *vi* recostarse

▸**lie down** *vi* echarse, tumbarse; *Fig* **I'm not going to take this lying down** no voy a quedarme de brazos cruzados ante esto

Liechtenstein ['lıktenstaın] *n* Liechtenstein

lieu [lju:, lu:] *n* **in l. of...** en lugar de...

lieutenant [lu:'tenənt] *n Mil* teniente *m*; *Naut* teniente *m* de navío; *(police officer)* oficial *mf* de policía; *Fig (helper)* lugarteniente *mf*; *Mil* **l. colonel** teniente *m* coronel

life [laıf] (*pl* **lives** [laıvz]) *n* **(a)** *(existence)* vida *f*; **to take sb's l.** quitar la vida a alguien; **to take one's own l.** quitarse la vida; **to bring sb back to l.** devolver la vida a alguien; **a matter of l. and death** una cuestión de vida o muerte; **l. after death** la vida después de la muerte; **to risk one's l., to risk l. and limb** arriesgar la vida; **to escape with one's l.** salir con vida; **to lose one's l.** perder la vida; **no lives were lost** no hubo que lamentar víctimas *or* ninguna muerte; **he held on to the rope for dear l.** se aferró a la cuerda con todas sus fuerzas; **run for your lives!** ¡sálvese quien pueda!; *Fam* **not on your l.!** ¡ni en broma!, ¡ni soñarlo!; *Fam* **I couldn't for the l. of me remember** por más que lo intentaba, no conseguía recordar; **from l.** *(to draw, paint)* del natural; **bird l.** aves *fpl*; **plant l.** flora *f*; **l. belt** flotador *m*, salvavidas *m inv*; **l. cycle** ciclo *m* vital; **l. force** fuerza *f* vital; **l. form** forma *f* de vida; **l. jacket** chaleco *m* salvavidas; **l. sciences** ciencias *fpl* naturales *or* biológicas

(b) *(period of existence)* vida *f*; **she worked all her l.** trabajó toda su vida; **never in (all) my l.** (nunca) en mi vida...; **a l. of Tolstoy** una biografía de Tolstói; **to be given a l. sentence,** *Fam* **to get l.** ser condenado(a) a cadena perpetua; *Fin* **l. annuity** renta *f* anual, anualidad *f* vitalicia; *Med* **l. expectancy** esperanza *f* de vida; *Law* **l. imprisonment** cadena *f* perpetua; *Fin* **l. insurance** seguro *m* de vida; **l. member** socio(a) *m,f* vitalicio(a); *Fin* **l. pension** pensión *f* vitalicia; **l. span** vida; **l. story** biografía *f*; **l. subscription** suscripción *f* vitalicia

(c) *(mode of existence)* vida *f*; *Fam* **to live** *or* **lead the l. of Riley** vivir como un rajá; **to make a new l. for oneself** construirse una nueva vida; **the man/woman in your l.** el hombre/la mujer que hay en tu vida; **way of l.** modo *m* de vida; **he makes her l. a misery** le amarga la vida; **to make l. worth living** hacer que la vida merezca la pena; *Fam* **how's l.?** ¿qué tal te va?, ¿cómo va eso?, *CAm, Col, Méx* ¿quihubo?; *Fam* **what a l.!** ¡qué vida esta!; *Fam* **such is l.!, that's l.!** ¡así es la vida!, ¡la vida es así!; *Fam* **this is the l.!** ¡esto es vida!; *Fam* **get a l.!** ¡no tienes nada mejor que hacer?

(d) *(liveliness)* **to come to l.** animarse, cobrar vida; **to bring sb to l.** dar vida a alguien; **to breathe new l. into** *(person, company)* dar nuevos bríos a; **the l. and soul of the party** el alma de la fiesta; **there's l. in the old dog yet** todavía le queda mucha cuerda

lifeblood ['laıfblʌd] *n (blood)* sangre *f*; *Fig (key part)* alma *f*

lifeboat ['laıfbəʊt] *n* **(a)** *(from coast)* lancha *f* de salvamento **(b)** *(on ship)* bote *m* salvavidas

life-giving ['laıfgıvıŋ] *adj* salvador(ora)

lifeguard ['laıfgɑ:d] *n* socorrista *mf*

lifeless ['laıflıs] *adj* sin vida

lifelessly ['laıflıslı] *adv* sin vida

lifelike ['laıflaık] *adj* realista

lifeline ['laıflaın] *n (rope)* cabo *m* (salvavidas); *(means of rescue, survival)* salvavidas *m inv*

lifelong ['laıflɒŋ] *adj* de toda la vida; *Educ* **l. learning** aprendizaje *m* a continuo

life-or-death ['laıfɔ:'deθ] *adj (choice, decision)* de vida o muerte; *(struggle)* a vida o muerte

lifer ['laıfə(r)] *n Fam (prisoner)* condenado(a) *m,f* a cadena perpetua

lifesaver ['laıfseıvə(r)] *n Fam* **it was a l.** *(provided relief)* me salvó la vida

life-saving ['laıfseıvıŋ] *adj* **a l. drug** un medicamento que salva muchas vidas; **he had a l. operation** la operación le salvó la vida

life-size(d) ['laıfsaız(d)] *adj* (de) tamaño natural

lifestyle ['laıfstaıl] *n* estilo *m* de vida

life-support system ['laıfsəpɔ:t'sıstəm], **life-support machine** ['laıfsəpɔ:t'məʃi:n] *n Med* equipo *m* de ventilación *or* respiración asistida

life-threatening ['laıfθretnıŋ] *adj Med* **l. condition** *or* **disease** enfermedad *f* mortífera *or* que puede ocasionar la muerte; **l. situation** situación *f* de peligro mortal

lifetime ['laıftaım] *n* vida *f*; **in my l.** durante mi vida; **it's the chance** *or* **opportunity of a l.** es la oportunidad de mi/tu/su *etc.* vida; **the vacation of a l.** las vacaciones de mi/tu/su *etc.* vida

lift [lıft] **1** *n* **(a)** *(car ride)* **to give sb a l.** llevar a alguien (en el coche), *CAm, Méx, Perú* dar aventón a alguien; **could you give me a l. to the station?** ¿puedes llevarme *or* acercarme a la estación?, *CAm, Méx, Perú* ¿puedes darme aventón hasta la estación? **(b)** *Fam* **that really gave me a l.!** *(cheered me up)* ¡eso me levantó muchísimo los ánimos! **(c)** *Av* sustentación *f*

2 *vt* **(a)** *(one's head, eyes, arm)* levantar; **he won't l. a finger to help** no moverá un dedo para ayudar; **to l. sb (up)** *(after fall)* levantar a alguien; **to l. a child up** coger a un niño en brazos **(b)** *(remove) (restrictions, siege)* levantar **(c)** *Fam (take, steal)* afanar, *Esp* birlar, *Méx* volar

3 *vi (mist, fog)* disiparse

▸**lift off** *vi (rocket)* despegar

lift-off ['lıftɒf] *n (of rocket)* despegue *m*, *Am* decolaje *m*

ligament ['lıgəmənt] *n* ligamento *m*

ligature ['lıgətʃə(r)] *n Med, Mus & Typ* ligadura *f*

light¹ [laıt] **1** *n* **(a)** *(illumination)* luz *f*; **artificial/electric l.**

luz artificial/eléctrica; **by the l. of the moon** a la luz de la luna; **things will look different in the cold l. of day** las cosas se ven distintas a la luz del día; **to be in sb's l.** taparle la luz a alguien; *Comptr* **l. pen** lápiz *m* óptico

(**b**) *(lamp)* luz *f*; **to put** *or* **turn on the l.** encender *or Am* prender la luz; **to put** *or* **turn off the l.** apagar la luz; *Fam* **to go out like a l.** *(fall asleep)* quedarse planchado(a) *or Esp* traspuesto(a); **(traffic) lights** semáforo *m*; **l. bulb** bombilla *f, CAm, Méx, RP* foco *m, RP* lamparita *f, Andes, CAm* bombillo *m*

(**c**) *(fire)* **to set l. to sth** prender fuego a algo; **have you got a l.?** ¿tienes fuego?

(**d**) *(idioms)* **the l. at the end of the tunnel** la luz al final del túnel; **to throw** *or* **cast l. on sth** arrojar luz sobre algo; **to bring sth to l.** sacar algo a la luz; **to come to l.** salir a la luz; **to see sth/sb in a new** *or* **different l.** ver algo/a alguien desde un punto de vista diferente; **in a positive** *or* **favorable l.** desde una óptica positiva *or* favorable; **in the l. of...** *(considering)* a la luz de..., en vista de...

2 *adj* (**a**) *(room)* luminoso(a); **it will soon be l.** pronto será de día (**b**) *(hair, complexion, color)* claro(a)

3 *vt (pt & pp* **lit** [lɪt]*)* (**a**) *(fire)* prender, encender; *(cigarette)* encender (**b**) *(room, street)* iluminar

light² **1** *adj* (**a**) *(not heavy)* ligero(a); **to be l. on one's feet** tener los pies ligeros; **to have a l. meal** tomar una comida ligera; **to be a l. sleeper** tener el sueño ligero; **to have a l. touch** tener delicadeza; *Av* **l. aircraft** avioneta *f; Mil* **l. artillery** artillería *f* ligera; *Mil* **l. infantry** infantería *f* ligera (**b**) *(not strenuous) (job, work)* ligero(a); *(rain)* fina; **a l. sentence** una sentencia benévola (**c**) *(not serious)* alegre; **to make l. of sth** no dar importancia a algo; **l. entertainment** espectáculo *m* de entretenimiento; **l. reading** lectura *f* ligera; **l. verse** poesía *f* ligera

2 *adv* **to travel l.** viajar ligero(a) de equipaje

▶**light on** *(pt & pp* **lighted***) vt insep* dar con; **his eyes lighted on the picture** su mirada se posó en el cuadro

▶**light up** **1** *vt sep* (**a**) *(house, room)* iluminar (**b**) *(cigarette)* encender

2 *vi* (**a**) *(sky)* iluminarse; **his eyes lit up** se le encendieron los ojos (**b**) *Fam (smoker)* encender un cigarrillo

lighten¹ [ˈlaɪtən] **1** *vt (color, hair)* aclarar

2 *vi (sky)* aclararse

lighten² *vt (make less heavy)* aligerar; *Fig* **to l. sb's load** aligerar la carga de alguien

▶**lighten up** *vi Fam* **l. up!** ¡no te pongas así!

▶**lighter** [ˈlaɪtə(r)] *n* encendedor *m, Esp* mechero *m*; **l. fluid** gas *m* (licuado) para mecheros

light-fingered [laɪtˈfɪŋgəd] *adj Fam* largo(a) de manos

light-headed [laɪtˈhedɪd] *adj* **to feel l.** *(dizzy)* estar mareado(a); *(with excitement)* estar exaltado(a)

light-headedness [laɪtˈhedɪdnɪs] *n (dizziness)* mareo *m; (with excitement)* euforia *f*

lighthearted [laɪtˈhɑːtɪd] *adj* alegre

lighthouse [ˈlaɪthaʊs] *n* faro *m*; **l. keeper** farero(a) *m,f*

lighting [ˈlaɪtɪŋ] *n (act, system)* iluminación *f*; **street l.** alumbrado *m* público

lightly [ˈlaɪtlɪ] *adv* ligeramente; **to sleep l.** tener el sueño ligero; **to get off l.** salir bien parado(a); **to speak l. of sth/ sb** hablar a la ligera de algo/alguien; **it was not a decision she took l.** no tomó la decisión a la ligera

lightness [ˈlaɪtnɪs] *n* (**a**) *(brightness)* claridad *f* (**b**) *(in weight)* ligereza *f*

lightning [ˈlaɪtnɪŋ] *n* (**a**) *(bolt)* rayo *m; (sheet)* relámpago *m*; **l. bug** luciérnaga *f*; **l. rod** pararrayos *m inv* (**b**) *(idioms)* **as quick as l., with l. speed** como el rayo; **l. attack** ataque *m* relámpago; **l. strike** huelga *f* relámpago *or* sin previo aviso; **l. visit** visita *f* relámpago

lightweight [ˈlaɪtweɪt] **1** *n (in boxing)* peso *m* ligero; *Fig Pej* **an intellectual l.** un personaje de poca talla intelectual

2 *adj (garment)* ligero(a)

light-year [ˈlaɪtjɪə(r)] *n Astron* año *m* luz

lignite [ˈlɪgnaɪt] *n* lignito *m*

likable, likeable [ˈlaɪkəbəl] *adj* simpático(a)

like¹ [laɪk] **1** *n* **he and his l.** él y los de su clase; **it's not for the likes of me** no es para gente como yo; **music, painting and the l.** música, pintura y cosas así; **I've never seen the l. (of it)** nunca he visto nada parecido *or* nada igual

2 *adj* parecido(a), similar; **they are of l. temperament** tienen un temperamento parecido; **they are as l. as two peas (in a pod)** son como dos gotas de agua

3 *prep* (**a**) *(similar to)* como; **to be l. sb/sth** ser como alguien/algo; **to taste l. sth** saber a algo; **to look l. sb/sth** parecerse a alguien/algo; **what's the weather l.?** ¿qué tiempo hace?; **people l. you** la gente como tú; **you know what she's l.** ya sabes cómo es; **it costs something l. $10** cuesta unas 10 dólares; **that's more l. it** eso está mejor; **we don't have anything l. as many as that** no tenemos tantos, ni muchísimo menos; **there's nothing l. it!** ¡no hay nada igual!; **she is nothing l. as intelligent as you** no es ni mucho menos tan inteligente como tú; **that's not l. him** no es su estilo; **that's just l. him!** ¡es típico de él!; *Prov* **l. father l. son** de tal palo tal astilla

(**b**) *(in the manner of)* como; **just l. anybody else** como todo el mundo; *Fam* **to run l. blazes** *or* **mad** correr como alma que lleva el diablo; *Fam* **don't be l. that** no seas así; **l. this?** ¿así?

(**c**) *(such as)* como (por ejemplo); **take more exercise, l. jogging** haz más ejercicio, como (por ejemplo) correr

4 *adv Fam* **(as) l. as not** casi seguro, seguramente

5 *conj Fam* **do it l. I said** hazlo como te dije; **he looked l. he'd seen a ghost** parecía que *or* como si hubiera visto una aparición; **it's not l. he's ill or anything** no es que esté enfermo

like² **1** *n* **likes** preferencias *fpl*; **likes and dislikes** preferencias y aversiones *fpl*

2 *vt* (**a**) *(in general)* **she likes him/it** le gusta; **she likes them** le gustan; **she likes John** *(as friend)* le cae bien John; *(is attracted to)* le gusta John; **I don't l. him/it** no me gusta; **I don't l. them** no me gustan; **they l. him/it** les gusta; **they l. each other** se gustan; **do you l. Italian food?** ¿te gusta la comida italiana?; **she likes reading** le gusta leer; **she is well liked** es muy querida (por todo el mundo); **I l. to think my father would have agreed** me gusta pensar que mi padre habría estado de acuerdo; **he doesn't l. people to talk about it** no le gusta que la gente hable de ello; *Fam Ironic* **well, I l. that!** ¿qué te parece?, ¡tiene gracia la cosa!

(**b**) *(want)* querer; **what would you l.?** ¿qué quieres?, *Am* ¿qué se te antoja?; **would you l. a cigarette?** ¿quieres un cigarrillo?; **I would very much l. to go** me encantaría ir; **I would l. to know whether...** me gustaría saber si...; **I would l. nothing better than...** nada me gustaría más que...; **you can't always do just as you l.!** ¡no puedes hacer siempre lo que te dé la gana!; **he thinks he can do anything he likes** se cree que puede hacer lo que quiera; **if you l.** si quieres; **when you l.** cuando quieras; **as much/ often/many as you l.** tanto/tan a menudo/tantos como quieras; **I didn't l. to mention it** no quise mencionarlo

-like [laɪk] *suffix* **ghost-l.** fantasmagórico(a); **jelly-l.** gelatinoso(a)

likeable = **likable**

likelihood [ˈlaɪklɪhʊd] *n* probabilidad *f*; **in all l.** con toda probabilidad; **there is little l. of finding it** hay pocas probabilidades de encontrarlo; **the l. is that...** lo más probable es que...

likely [ˈlaɪklɪ] **1** *adj* (**a**) *(probable)* probable; **a l. outcome** un resultado probable; **it's not very l.** no es muy probable; **it's**

more than l. es más que probable; **it's l. to rain** lo más probable es que llueva; **she is l. to come** lo más probable es que venga; *Ironic* **a l. story!** ¡y yo me lo creo! (**b**) *(suitable)* apropiado(a), adecuado(a)

2 *adv* **very l.** muy probablemente; **as l. as not** casi seguro, seguramente; *Fam* **not l.!** ¡ni hablar!

like-minded [laɪk'maɪndɪd] *adj* de mentalidad similar

liken ['laɪkən] *vt* comparar (**to** a *or* con)

likeness ['laɪknɪs] *n* (**a**) *(similarity)* parecido *m*; **a close l.** un parecido muy marcado; **a family l.** un parecido familiar (**b**) *(portrait)* retrato *m*

likewise ['laɪkwaɪz] *adv (similarly)* también, asimismo; **to do l.** hacer lo mismo

liking ['laɪkɪŋ] *n* **it's too sweet for my l.** es demasiado dulce para mi gusto; **is it to your l.?** ¿es de su agrado?; **to have a l. for sth** ser aficionado(a) a algo; **to take a l. to sth** tomar *or Esp* coger gusto a algo, aficionarse a algo; **to take a l. to sb** tomar *or Esp* coger simpatía a alguien

lilac ['laɪlək] **1** *n (tree)* lilo *m*, lila *f; (flower)* lila *f; (color)* lila *m*
2 *adj* lila

lilt [lɪlt] *n* modulación *f*, entonación *f*

lilting ['lɪltɪŋ] *adj* melodioso(a)

lily ['lɪlɪ] *n* lirio *m*; **l. of the valley** lirio *m* de los valles

lily-livered ['lɪlɪlɪvəd] *adj* cobarde, pusilánime

Lima ['liːmə] *n* Lima

lima bean ['liːmə'biːn] *n Esp* judía *f* blanca (limeña), *Am salvo RP* frijol *m* blanco, *Andes, RP* poroto *m* blanco

limb [lɪm] *n* (**a**) *(of body)* miembro *m*; **to tear sb l. from l.** descuartizar a alguien (**b**) *(of tree)* rama *f; Fig* **to be out on a l.** quedarse más solo(a) que la una

limber ['lɪmbə(r)] *adj* flexible

▸**limber up** *vi* precalentar, hacer precalentamiento

limbo ['lɪmbəʊ] *n Rel* limbo *m; Fig* **to be in l.** *(person)* estar perdido(a); *(negotiations, project)* estar en el aire

lime[1] [laɪm] *n (fruit)* lima *f, Méx* limón *m; (citrus tree)* lima *f*, limero *m, Méx* limonero *m; (linden tree)* tilo *m*; **l. juice** *Esp* zumo *m or Am* jugo *m* de lima; **l. green** verde *m* lima

lime[2] *n Chem* cal *f*

limelight ['laɪmlaɪt] *n Fig* **to be in the l.** estar en el candelero

limerick ['lɪmərɪk] *n* = estrofa humorística de cinco versos

limestone ['laɪmstəʊn] *n (roca f)* caliza *f*

limey ['laɪmɪ] *n (pl* **limeys***) n Fam (British person)* = término peyorativo para referirse a un británico

limit ['lɪmɪt] **1** *n* límite *m*; **within limits** dentro de un límite; **to be off limits** estar en una zona de acceso prohibido; **the limits of decency** los límites de la decencia; **to know no limits** no conocer límites; *Fam* **he's/that's the l.!** ¡es el colmo!
2 *vt* limitar; **to l. oneself to sth** limitarse a algo

limitation [lɪmɪ'teɪʃən] *n* limitación *f*; **I know my limitations** conozco mis limitaciones

limited ['lɪmɪtəd] *adj* limitado(a); *(train)* semidirecto(a); *Com* **l. company** sociedad *f* (de responsabilidad) limitada; **l. edition** edición *f* limitada; *Law* **l. liability** responsabilidad *f* limitada

limitless ['lɪmɪtlɪs] *adj* ilimitado(a)

limo ['lɪməʊ] *(pl* **limos***) n Fam* limusina *f*

limousine [lɪmə'ziːn] *n* limusina *f*

limp[1] [lɪmp] **1** *n* cojera *f*; **to have a l.** cojear
2 *vi* cojear

limp[2] *adj (handshake, body)* lánguido(a), flojo(a); *(lettuce)* mustio(a); **to go l.** relajarse

limpet ['lɪmpɪt] *n* lapa *f*; **to stick like a l.** pegarse como una lapa; *Mil* **l. mine** mina *f* lapa, mina *f* magnética

limpid ['lɪmpɪd] *adj* límpido(a), cristalino(a)

limply ['lɪmplɪ] *adv (weakly)* lánguidamente, débilmente

limp-wristed [lɪmp'rɪstɪd] *adj Pej* amariposado(a), afeminado(a)

linchpin, lynchpin ['lɪntʃpɪn] *n (of team, policy)* pieza *f* clave

linden ['lɪndən] *n* **l. (tree)** tilo *m*

line[1] [laɪn] **1** *n* (**a**) *(in general)* línea *f; (on face)* arruga *f; Fig* **to draw the l. at doing sth** no estar dispuesto(a) a hacer algo; **l. drawing** dibujo *m (sin sombreado)*
(**b**) *(row of people or things)* fila *f*; **to stand in a l.** formar una fila; **to stand in l.** hacer cola; *Fig* **to get out of l.** *(be disobedient)* saltarse las normas; **to be in l. with sth** estar de acuerdo con algo; **she is in l. for promotion** la van a ascender; *Fig* **to be on the l.** *(job, reputation)* correr peligro; **l. dancing** baile *m* en línea, = baile al ritmo de música country en el que los participantes se colocan en hileras y dan los mismos pasos
(**c**) *Sport* **l. back** *(in football)* line back *m*; **l. call** *(in tennis)* decisión *f (respecto a si la bola ha entrado o no)*; **l. drive** *(in baseball)* línea *f*, linietazo *m*; **l. of scrimmage** *(in football)* línea *f* de scrimmage
(**d**) *(rope, for washing)* cuerda *f; (for fishing)* sedal *m; (telephone line)* línea *f*
(**e**) *(railroad track)* vía *f; (railroad route)* línea *f*
(**f**) *(direction)* **l. of argument** hilo *m* argumental; **l. of attack** línea *or* plan *m* de ataque; **l. of fire** *also Fig* línea de fuego; **on the same lines as** en la misma línea que; **to be on the right/wrong lines** estar en el buen/mal camino; **along the lines of…** en la (misma) línea que…
(**g**) *(policy)* línea *f*, política *f*; **the party l.** la línea del partido; **to take a firm l. with sb** tener mano dura con alguien
(**h**) *(of text)* línea *f; (of poem, song)* verso *m*; **to drop sb a l.** mandar unas letras *or* escribir a alguien; *Theat* **to learn one's lines** aprenderse el papel; *Fig* **to read between the lines** leer entre líneas
(**i**) *(family)* línea *f*; **male/female l.** línea paterna/materna; **in (a) direct l.** por línea directa
(**j**) *Fam (job)* especialidad *f*; **what l. (of business) are you in?** ¿a qué te dedicas?
(**k**) *Com (of goods)* línea *f*
2 *vt (border)* bordear; **the crowd lined the street** la muchedumbre bordeaba la calle

line[2] *vt (provide with lining)* forrar; *Fig* **to l. one's pockets** *(enrich oneself)* forrarse

▸**line up** **1** *vt sep* (**a**) *(form into a line)* alinear (**b**) *(prepare)* **have you got anyone lined up for the job?** ¿tienes algún candidato firme *or* a alguien pensado para el trabajo?; **have you got anything lined up for this evening?** ¿tienes algo pensado para esta noche?
2 *vi (form a line)* alinearse

lineage ['lɪnɪɪdʒ] *n* linaje *m*

linear ['lɪnɪə(r)] *adj* lineal; *Math* **l. equation** ecuación *f* lineal, *Comptr* **l. programming** programación *f* lineal

lined[1] [laɪnd] *adj (paper)* de rayas, pautado(a); *(face)* arrugado(a)

lined[2] *adj (coat)* forrado(a) (**with** de)

linen ['lɪnɪn] *n* (**a**) *(fabric)* lino *m* (**b**) *(clothes)* ropa *f* blanca; *Fig* **dirty l.** trapos *mpl* sucios; **l. basket** cesto *m* de la ropa sucia

liner ['laɪnə(r)] *n (ship)* transatlántico *m*

lineup ['laɪnʌp] *n (of team)* alineación *f*

linger ['lɪŋɡə(r)] *vi (person)* entretenerse; *(smell, custom)* perdurar, persistir; **to l. behind** rezagarse; **to l. over doing sth** quedarse haciendo algo

lingerie ['lɔːnʒərɪ] *n* lencería *f*, ropa *f* interior femenina

lingo ['lɪŋɡəʊ] *n Fam (language)* idioma *m; (jargon)* jerga *f*

lingua franca ['lɪŋɡwə'fræŋkə] *n* lengua *f or* lingua *f* franca

linguist ['lɪŋɡwɪst] *n (specialist in linguistics)* lingüista *mf; (polyglot)* políglota *mf*

linguistic [lɪŋ'ɡwɪstɪk] *adj* lingüístico(a)

linguistics [lɪŋ'ɡwɪstɪks] *n* lingüística *f*

lining ['laɪnɪŋ] n (of coat) forro m; (of brakes, stomach) revestimiento m

link [lɪŋk] **1** n (**a**) (of chain) eslabón m; (connection) conexión f, nexo m (**between** entre); (between countries, people) lazo m, vínculo m; (road, railroad line) enlace m; Fig **the weak l.** (in argument, team) el punto débil (**b**) **links** Sport campo m de golf (cerca del mar)
2 vt (places) enlazar, comunicar; (facts, events, situations) relacionar; (computers, radio stations) conectar; **she has been linked to** or **with the mafia** ha sido asociada con la mafia; **to l. hands** enlazar las manos
▸**link up 1** vt sep Comptr conectar
2 vi (roads, travelers) encontrarse (**with** con)

inoleum [lɪ'nəʊlɪəm] n linóleo m, sintasol® m

inseed ['lɪnsiːd] n linaza f; **l. oil** aceite m de linaza

intel ['lɪntəl] n dintel m

ion ['laɪən] n león m; **the l.'s share** la mejor parte; **l. cub** cachorro m de león; **l. tamer** domador(ora) m,f de leones

ioness ['laɪənes] n leona f

ionhearted ['laɪənhɑːtɪd] adj valeroso(a), valiente

ip [lɪp] n (**a**) (of mouth) labio m; **to read sb's lips** leer los labios a alguien; **the government is only paying l. service to fighting crime** el Gobierno dice luchar or defiende que lucha contra la delincuencia; **l. gloss** brillo m de labios (**b**) (of jug) pico m (**c**) Fam (impudence) **less of your l.!** ¡no seas impertinente!

iposuction ['lɪpəʊsʌkʃən] n liposucción f

-lipped [lɪpt] suffix **thin/full-l.** de labios finos/gruesos

ippy ['lɪpɪ] Fam adj (cheeky) fresco(a), Esp chulo(a)

ip-read ['lɪpriːd] vi leer los labios

ipstick ['lɪpstɪk] n (substance) carmín m, pintalabios m inv; (stick) lápiz m or Esp barra f de labios, CSur lápiz m rouge, Méx bilet m

ip-sync(h) ['lɪpsɪŋk] vi hacer play-back

iquefy ['lɪkwɪfaɪ] **1** vt licuar
2 vi licuarse

iqueur [lɪ'kjʊə(r)] n licor m

iquid ['lɪkwɪd] **1** n líquido m
2 adj líquido(a); Fin **l. assets** activo m líquido or disponible; **l. crystal display** pantalla f de cristal líquido

iquidate ['lɪkwɪdeɪt] vt (kill) & Fin liquidar

iquidation [lɪkwɪ'deɪʃən] n Fin liquidación f; **to go into l.** (company) ir a la quiebra

iquidity [lɪ'kwɪdɪtɪ] n Fin liquidez f; **l. ratio** coeficiente m or ratio m or f de liquidez

iquidize ['lɪkwɪdaɪz] vt licuar

iquor ['lɪkə(r)] n bebida f alcohólica, alcohol m; **l. store** tienda f de bebidas alcohólicas

ira ['lɪrə] (pl **lire** ['lɪrə]) n Formerly lira f

Lisbon ['lɪzbən] n Lisboa

isp [lɪsp] **1** n ceceo m; **to have a l.** cecear
2 vi cecear

ist¹ [lɪst] **1** n lista f; **l. price** (in catalog) precio m de catálogo
2 vt (enter in list) **his phone number isn't listed in the directory** su número de teléfono no aparece or figura en la guía or Am en el directorio; **to l. names in alphabetical order** poner nombres en orden alfabético; **he listed his demands** enumeró sus exigencias

ist² Naut **1** n escora f
2 vi (ship) escorarse

listen ['lɪsən] vi escuchar; **to l. to sth/sb** escuchar algo/a alguien; **to l. for sth** estar pendiente or a la escucha de algo; **to l. to reason** atender a razones; **he wouldn't l.** no hizo (ningún) caso
▸**listen in** vi escuchar; **to l. in on/to sth** escuchar algo

listener ['lɪsnə(r)] n (**a**) **to be a good l.** saber escuchar (**b**) (to radio program) oyente mf

listeria [lɪ'stɪərɪə] n Med (illness) listeriosis f inv; (bacteria) listeria f

listing ['lɪstɪŋ] n (list) listado m, lista f; **TV listings** (in newspaper) programación f (de televisión)

listless ['lɪstlɪs] adj (lacking energy) desfallecido(a), cansino(a); (lacking enthusiasm) desanimado(a), apático(a)

listlessly ['lɪstlɪslɪ] adv (without energy) cansinamente, lánguidamente; (without enthusiasm) apáticamente

lit [lɪt] pt & pp of **light**

litany ['lɪtənɪ] n (of complaints) letanía f

liter ['liːtə(r)] n litro m

literacy ['lɪtərəsɪ] n alfabetización f; **l. rate** índice m de alfabetización

literal ['lɪtərəl] adj literal

literally ['lɪtərəlɪ] adv literalmente; **to take sth l.** tomar algo al pie de la letra; **it was l. this big!** ¡era sin exagerar así de grande!

literary ['lɪtərərɪ] adj literario(a); **l. agent** agente mf literario(a)

literate ['lɪtərɪt] adj (style) culto(a); **to be l.** (able to read and write) saber leer y escribir

literati [lɪtə'rɑːtɪ] npl Formal literatos mpl, gente f de las letras

literature ['lɪtərɪtʃə(r)] n (fiction, poetry) literatura f; (of academic subject) bibliografía f; Com (leaflets) folletos mpl, prospectos mpl

lithe [laɪð] adj ágil

lithium ['lɪθɪəm] n Chem litio m

lithograph ['lɪθəgræf] n litografía f

Lithuania [lɪθjʊ'eɪnɪə] n Lituania

Lithuanian [lɪθjʊ'eɪnɪən] **1** n (**a**) (person) lituano(a) m,f (**b**) (language) lituano m
2 adj lituano(a)

litigant ['lɪtɪgənt] n Law litigante mf, pleiteante mf

litigate ['lɪtɪgeɪt] vi Law litigar, pleitear

litigation [lɪtɪ'geɪʃən] n Law litigio m, pleito m

litigious [lɪ'tɪdʒəs] adj Formal litigante, litigioso(a)

litmus ['lɪtməs] n **l. paper** papel m de tornasol; Fig **l. test** prueba f definitiva

litter ['lɪtə(r)] n (**a**) (garbage) basura f (**b**) (of animal) camada f (**c**) (for cat) arena f absorbente; **l. box** cama f or bandeja f para la arena del gato
2 vt **to be littered with** estar sembrado(a) or cubierto(a) de

litterbug ['lɪtəbʌg] n Fam = persona que arroja desperdicios en la vía pública

little ['lɪtəl] **1** n poco m; **a l. (bit)** un poco; **to eat l. or nothing** apenas comer; **he knows very l.** no sabe casi nada; **a l. more** un poco más; **a l. hot/slow** un poco caliente/lento(a); **l. by l.** poco a poco; **every l. helps** todo cuenta aunque sea poco
2 adj (**a**) (small) pequeño(a); **a l. girl** una niña pequeña; **a l. house** una casita; **wait a l. while!** ¡espera un poco!; **l. finger** (dedo m) meñique m; **l. toe** meñique m del pie (**b**) (comparative **less** superlative **least**) (not much) poco(a); **a l. money/luck** un poco de dinero/suerte; **there is l. hope/doubt...** quedan pocas esperanzas/dudas...; **it makes l. sense** no tiene mucho sentido
3 adv (comparative **less** superlative **least**) poco; **l. known** poco conocido; **l. more than an hour ago** hace poco más de una hora; **that's l. short of bribery** eso es poco menos que un soborno; **l. did I think that...** poco me podía imaginar que...

littoral ['lɪtərəl] n & adj Geog litoral m

liturgy ['lɪtədʒɪ] n liturgia f

live¹ [laɪv] **1** adj (**a**) (person, animal) vivo(a); Fam **a real l. movie star** un estrella de carne y hueso; **a l. issue** un tema candente (**b**) (TV, radio broadcast) en directo; **l. performance** actuación f en vivo (**c**) (ammunition) (unused) sin utilizar; (not *blank)* real (**d**) *Elec* **l. wire** cable *m* con corriente; *Fig* **she's a l. wire** rebosa energía

2 *adv (to broadcast, perform)* en directo

live² [lɪv] **1** *vt* vivir; **to l. a happy/long life** vivir una vida feliz/larga; **it makes life worth living** hace que merezca la pena vivir; **to l. a lie** vivir en la mentira

2 *vi* vivir; **to l. with sb** vivir con alguien; **as long as I l.** mientras viva; **I want to l. a little** quiero disfrutar un poco de la vida; **he lives by his writing** vive de lo que escribe; **l. and let l.** vive y deja vivir; **you l. and learn** ¡vivir para ver!

▸**live down** *vt sep (mistake, one's past)* relegar al olvido, enterrar; **I'll never l. it down** nunca lograré que se olvide

▸**live off** *vt insep (depend on)* vivir de

▸**live on 1** *vt insep (depend on)* vivir de; **it's not enough to l. on** no da para vivir

2 *vi (continue to live) (person)* sobrevivir, vivir; *(memory)* perdurar

▸**live out** *vt sep* **she lived out her life** *or* **days in poverty/ sadness** acabó sus días sumida en la pobreza/la tristeza; **to l. out a fantasy** vivir *or* realizar una fantasía

▸**live through** *vt insep (war, hard times)* sobrevivir a

▸**live together** *vi* vivir juntos(as)

▸**live up** *vt sep Fam* **to l. it up** pasarlo bien, divertirse

▸**live up to** *vt insep (expectations)* responder a, satisfacer; **to fail to l. up to expectations** no responder a las expectativas; **he lives up to his principles** vive de acuerdo con sus principios

lived-in ['lɪvdɪn] *adj (home, room)* acogedor(ora), con un toque humano; **a l. face** un rostro curtido

live-in ['lɪvɪn] *adj (chauffeur, nanny)* interno(a); **she has a l. lover** su amante vive con ella

livelihood ['laɪvlɪhʊd] *n* sustento *m*; **to earn one's l.** ganarse la vida

liveliness ['laɪvlɪnɪs] *n (of person)* vivacidad *f*, viveza *f*; *(of place, debate)* animación *f*

lively ['laɪvlɪ] *adj (person, place, debate)* animado(a); *(interest)* vivo(a); **a l. mind** una mente despierta; *Fam* **to make things l. for sb** poner las cosas difíciles a alguien; *Fam* **look l.!** ¡vamos, muévete!

▸**liven up** ['laɪvən] **1** *vt sep* animar

2 *vi* animarse

liver ['lɪvə(r)] *n* hígado *m*

livery ['lɪvərɪ] *n* librea *f*

livestock ['laɪvstɒk] *n* ganado *m*

livid ['lɪvɪd] *adj* (**a**) *(angry)* **to be l. (with rage)** estar colérico(a) *or* enfurecido(a) (**b**) *(bluish-gray)* lívido(a), amoratado(a)

living ['lɪvɪŋ] **1** *n* (**a**) *(way of life)* vida *f*; **to be fond of good l.** ser aficionado a la buena vida; **l. conditions** condiciones *fpl* de vida; **l. expenses** gastos *mpl (cotidianos)*; **l. room** sala *f* de estar, salón *m* (**b**) *(livelihood)* sustento *m*; **to earn one's l.** ganarse la vida; **what does he do for a l.?** ¿a qué se dedica?

2 *adj* vivo(a); **she is our finest l. artist** es nuestra mejor artista viva; **there is not a l. soul to be seen** no se ve ni un alma; **the best/worst within l. memory** lo mejor/peor que se recuerda; *Fam* **to scare the l. daylights out of sb** dar un susto de muerte a alguien; *Fam* **to beat the l. daylights out of sb** dar una buena paliza *or Esp* tunda a alguien; **l. will** testamento *m* en vida

lizard ['lɪzəd] *n (small)* lagartija *f*; *(large)* lagarto *m*

llama ['lɑːmə] *n (animal)* llama *f*

lo [ləʊ] *exclam* **lo and behold…** hete aquí que…

load [ləʊd] **1** *n* (**a**) *(burden)* carga *f*; **to share/spread the l.** compartir/repartir el trabajo; **that's a l. off my mind!** ¡me quito *or Am* saco un peso de encima! (**b**) *Fam (lot)* **a l. of, loads of** un montón de; **it's a l. of bull!** *(nonsense)* ¡no son más que tonterías!; *(very bad)* ¡es nefasto(a) *or* de pena!; **we've**

got loads of time tenemos tiempo de sobra

2 *vt & vi* cargar

▸**load up** *vt sep & vi* cargar

loaded ['ləʊdɪd] *adj* (**a**) *(truck, gun)* cargado(a); *(dice,* trucado(a); **to be l.** *(gun)* estar cargado(a); **a l. question** una pregunta capciosa (**b**) *Fam (rich)* **to be l.** estar forrado(a) (**c**) *Fam (drunk) Esp, RP* mamado(a), *Méx* hasta atrás; *(on drugs)* colocado(a), *RP* falopeado(a)

loading ['ləʊdɪŋ] *n (of truck)* carga *f*; **l. zone** zona *f* de carga y descarga

loaf [ləʊf] *(pl* **loaves** [ləʊvz]*) n* pan *m*; **a l. of bread** *(in general)* un pan; *(brick-shaped)* un pan de molde, *Col* un pan tajado, *RP* un pan lactal; *(round and flat)* una hogaza de pan

▸**loaf around, loaf about** *vi* haraganear, gandulear

loafer ['ləʊfə(r)] *n* (**a**) *(person)* haragán(ana) *m,f*, gandul(ula) *m,f* (**b**) *(shoe)* mocasín *m*

loam [ləʊm] *n (soil)* marga *f*

loan [ləʊn] **1** *n* préstamo *m*; **to give sb a l. of sth** prestar algo a alguien; *Fin* **to take out a l.** obtener un préstamo *or* crédito *or Méx* prestamito; *Fam* **l. shark** usurero(a) *m,f*

2 *vt* prestar

loath, loth [ləʊθ] *adj* **to be l. to do sth** ser reacio(a) a hacer algo

loathe [ləʊð] *vt* odiar, detestar; **to l. doing sth** detestar hacer algo

loathing ['ləʊðɪŋ] *n* odio *m*, aborrecimiento *m*

loathsome ['ləʊðsəm] *adj (person, character, behavior)* detestable, odioso(a)

lob [lɒb] **1** *n (in tennis)* globo *m*, lob *m*

2 *vt (pt & pp* **lobbed***) (in tennis)* hacer un globo *or* lob a

lobby ['lɒbɪ] **1** *n* (**a**) *(of hotel)* vestíbulo *m* (**b**) *(pressure group,* grupo *m* de presión, lobby *m*

2 *vt* **to l. a congressman** presionar a un congresista *or Am* congresal

3 *vi* cabildear, presionar; **to l. for/against sth** hacer presión a favor de/en contra de algo

lobbying ['lɒbɪɪŋ] *n Pol* presiones *fpl* políticas

lobbyist ['lɒbɪɪst] *n Pol* miembro *m* de un lobby *or* grupo de presión

lobe [ləʊb] *n (of ear, brain)* lóbulo *m*

lobotomy [lə'bɒtəmɪ] *n* lobotomía *f*

lobster ['lɒbstə(r)] *n (with pincers)* bogavante *m*; **(spiny) l.** langosta *f*; **he was as red as a l.** *(sunburnt)* estaba rojo como un cangrejo; **l. pot** nasa *f*

local ['ləʊkəl] **1** *n (person)* **the locals** los lugareños, los paisanos

2 *adj* local; **l. anesthetic** anestesia *f* local; **l. government** gobierno *m* *or* administración *f* municipal; **l. newspaper** periódico *m* local

locale [ləʊ'kɑːl] *n* emplazamiento *m*, lugar *m*

locality [ləʊ'kælɪtɪ] *n* vecindad *f*, zona *f*

localization [ləʊkəlaɪ'zeɪʃən] *n Comptr* localización *f*

localize ['ləʊkəlaɪz] *vt (restrict)* localizar

locally ['ləʊkəlɪ] *adv* **I live/work l.** vivo/trabajo cerca

locate [ləʊ'keɪt] **1** *vt (find)* localizar; *(situate)* emplazar, ubicar

2 *vi (company)* instalarse, ubicarse

location [ləʊ'keɪʃən] *n* (**a**) *(place)* emplazamiento *m*, ubicación *f*; *Cin* **on l.** en exteriores; *Cin* **l. shot** toma *f* de exteriores (**b**) *(act of finding)* localización *f*

loch [lɒχ] *n Scot (lake)* lago *m*; *(inlet)* ría *f*

lock¹ [lɒk] **1** *n* (**a**) *(on door)* cerradura *f*; **to be under l. and key** estar encerrado(a) bajo siete llaves; *Fig* **l., stock and barrel** *(in its entirety)* íntegramente (**b**) *(in wrestling)* llave *f* inmovilización *f* (**c**) *(on canal)* esclusa *f*

2 *vt (door, padlock)* cerrar; **they were locked in each other's arms** estaban fundidos en un fuerte abrazo; *Fig* **to l horns with sb** enzarzarse en una disputa con alguien

3 vi (door) cerrarse; (car wheels) bloquearse

lock² n (of hair) mechón m; **her golden locks** sus cabellos dorados

▸**lock in** vt sep encerrar

▸**lock out** vt sep dejar fuera; **I locked myself out of my apartment** me dejé las llaves dentro de casa

▸**lock up 1** vt sep (person) encerrar; (valuables) guardar bajo llave; (house) cerrar or dejar cerrado(a) (con llave)
    2 vi cerrar (con llave)

locker ['lɒkə(r)] n (for luggage, in school) taquilla f; **l. room** vestuarios mpl

locket ['lɒkɪt] n guardapelo m

lockjaw ['lɒkdʒɔː] n Old-fashioned tétanos m

lockout ['lɒkaʊt] n cierre m patronal

locksmith ['lɒksmɪθ] n cerrajero(a) m,f

lockup ['lɒkʌp] n Fam (police cells) calabozo m

loco ['ləʊkəʊ] adj (crazy) pirado(a), CSur rayado(a), Méx zafado(a)

locomotion [ləʊkə'məʊʃən] n locomoción f

locomotive [ləʊkə'məʊtɪv] **1** n (train) locomotora f
    2 adj locomotor(ora)

locust ['ləʊkəst] n langosta f

locution [ləʊ'kjuːʃən] n locución f

lodge [lɒdʒ] **1** n (of porter) garita f, portería f; (of gatekeeper) garita f, casa f del guarda; (of beaver) madriguera f; (of masons) logia f
    2 vt (a) (accommodate) hospedar, alojar (b) Law **to l. an appeal** presentar una apelación, apelar
    3 vi (a) (live) hospedarse, alojarse (b) (become fixed) alojarse; **the bullet had lodged in his lung** la bala se le había alojado en el pulmón; **the name had lodged in her memory** el nombre se le quedó grabado en la memoria

lodger ['lɒdʒə(r)] n huésped mf, huéspeda f

lodging ['lɒdʒɪŋ] n alojamiento m; **to take up lodgings** instalarse; **l. house** casa f de huéspedes

loft [lɒft] n (attic) buhardilla f, ático m

lofty ['lɒftɪ] adj (aim, desire) noble, elevado(a)

log [lɒg] **1** n (a) (tree-trunk) tronco m; (firewood) leño m; **to sleep like a l.** dormir como un tronco; **l. cabin** cabaña f; **l. fire** fuego m de leña (b) (record) registro m; (of ship, traveler) diario m de a bordo
    2 vt (pt & pp **logged**) (record) registrar

▸**log in** vi Comptr entrar

▸**log off** vi Comptr salir

▸**log on** = **log in**

▸**log out** = **log off**

logarithm ['lɒgərɪðəm] n logaritmo m

logbook ['lɒgbʊk] n Naut cuaderno m de bitácora

loggerheads ['lɒgəhedz] n Fam **to be at l. with sb** estar peleado(a) or Esp andar a la greña con alguien

logic ['lɒdʒɪk] n lógica f

logical ['lɒdʒɪkəl] adj lógico(a)

logically ['lɒdʒɪklɪ] adv lógicamente

login ['lɒgɪn] n Comptr conexión f; **l. name** nombre m del usuario

logistic(al) [lɒ'dʒɪstɪk(əl)] adj logístico(a)

logistically [lə'dʒɪstɪklɪ] adv logísticamente

logistics [lɒ'dʒɪstɪks] npl logística f

logjam ['lɒgdʒæm] n (in negotiations) punto m muerto

logo ['ləʊgəʊ] n (pl **logos**) n logotipo m

logrolling ['lɒgrəʊlɪŋ] n Pol (exchange of favors) comercio m de favores

loin [lɔɪn] n (a) (of person) **loins** pubis m inv, bajo vientre m (b) (of meat) lomo m

loincloth ['lɔɪnklɒθ] n taparrabos m inv

loiter ['lɔɪtə(r)] vi (delay) entretenerse; (suspiciously) merodear

lollipop ['lɒlɪpɒp] n (disk) piruleta f; (ball) Esp chupachups® m inv; (disk, ball) Chile chupete m, Col colombina f, Andes, CAm, Méx paleta f, RP chupetín m, Ven chupeta f

lollop ['lɒləp] vi Fam **to l. along** avanzar con paso desgarbado

London ['lʌndən] **1** n Londres
    2 adj londinense

Londoner ['lʌndənə(r)] n londinense mf

lone [ləʊn] adj (solitary) solitario(a); **l. parent** madre f soltera, padre m soltero; **the L. Ranger** el Llanero Solitario; Fig **a l. wolf** una persona solitaria

loneliness ['ləʊnlɪnɪs] n soledad f

lonely ['ləʊnlɪ] adj solitario(a); **to feel very l.** sentirse muy solo(a); **l. hearts club** club m de contactos; Journ **l. hearts column** sección f de contactos

loner ['ləʊnə(r)] n solitario(a) m,f

lonesome ['ləʊnsəm] **1** n Fam **to be by one's l.** estar solito
    2 adj solitario(a); **to be l.** (person) estar solo(a)

long¹ [lɒŋ] **1** n **the l. and the short of it is that...** el caso es que...
    2 adj (a) (in size) largo(a); **how l. is the table?** ¿cuánto mide or tiene la mesa de largo?; **it's 4 feet l.** mide or tiene 4 pies de largo; **to go the l. way (around)** ir por el camino más largo; Fig **she'll go a l. way** llegará lejos; Fig **to go a l. way toward doing sth** contribuir mucho a hacer algo; Fam **to be l. on charm/good ideas** estar lleno(a) de or Esp andar sobrado(a) de encanto/buenas ideas; **the l. arm of the law** el largo brazo de la ley; Fig **to have/make a l. face** tener/poner cara triste; **it's a l. shot, but it's our only hope** es difícil que funcione, pero es nuestra única esperanza; **the best by a l. shot** con mucho or de lejos el/la mejor; Fam **not by a l. shot** ni muchísimo menos; **l. johns** calzoncillos mpl largos; **l. jump** salto m de longitud, Chile, Col salto m largo, RP salto m en largo
    (b) (in time) largo(a); **a l. time ago** hace mucho tiempo; **it's been a l. day** ha sido un día muy largo; **the days are getting longer** se están alargando los días; **three days at the longest** tres días como mucho; **it looks like being a l. job** parece que el trabajo va a llevar mucho tiempo; **to take a l. look at sth** mirar algo largamente; **in the l. term** or **run** a largo plazo, a la larga; **to have a l. memory** no olvidar con facilidad; **l. weekend** fin de semana m largo, puente m (corto)
    3 adv (a) (for a long period) durante mucho tiempo, mucho; **I didn't wait l.** no esperé mucho; **I won't stay for l.** no me voy a quedar mucho tiempo; **it won't take l.** no llevará mucho tiempo; **she won't be l.** no tardará or Am demorará mucho; **l. live the King/Queen!** ¡viva el Rey/la Reina!; **as l. as** (providing) mientras, siempre que; **as l. as he is alive,...** mientras viva,...; **to think l. and hard (about sth)** reflexionar profundamente (sobre algo); **I have l. been convinced of it** llevo mucho tiempo convencido de ello; **how l. have you known her?** ¿cuánto (tiempo) hace que la conoces?; Fam **so l.!** ¡hasta luego!; **l. before/after** mucho antes/después; **l. ago** hace mucho (tiempo)
    (b) (for the duration of) **all day/winter l.** todo el día/el invierno, el día/el invierno entero
    (c) (idioms) **I could no longer hear him** ya no lo oía; **I couldn't wait any longer** no podía esperar más; **five minutes longer** cinco minutos más

long² vi **to l. to do sth** desear or anhelar hacer algo; **to l. for the day when...** desear que llegue el día en que...; **to l. for sth to happen** desear que ocurra algo; **a longed-for vacation** unas ansiadas vacaciones

long³ Geog (abbr **longitude**) long., longitud f

longboat ['lɒŋbəʊt] n Hist chalupa f, lancha f de remos

longbow ['lɒŋbəʊ] n arco m

long-distance ['lɒŋ'dɪstəns] **1** adj **a l. (telephone) call** una conferencia; **a l. race** carrera f de fondo; **l. runner** corredor(ora) m,f de fondo
    2 adv **to telephone l.** poner una conferencia

longed-for ['lɒŋdfɔː(r)] *adj* ansiado(a)

longevity [lɒn'dʒevɪtɪ] *n* longevidad *f*

long-forgotten ['lɒŋfə'gɒtən] *adj* olvidado(a)

longhaired ['lɒŋ'heəd] *adj* de pelo largo

longhorn ['lɒŋhɔːn] *n* buey *m* colorado de Tejas

longing ['lɒŋɪŋ] *n (in general)* deseo *m* (**for** de), anhelo *m* (**for** de); *(for home, family, old days)* añoranza *f* (**for** de)

longingly ['lɒŋɪŋlɪ] *adv* con deseo, anhelantemente

longitude ['lɒndʒɪtjuːd] *n* longitud *f (coordenada)*

longitudinal [lɒndʒɪ'tjuːdɪnəl] *adj* longitudinal

long-lived ['lɒŋ'lɪvd] *adj (person)* anciano(a); *(campaign, friendship)* perdurable

long-lost ['lɒŋ'lɒst] *adj* perdido(a) tiempo atrás; **his l. brother returned** regresó su hermano al que no veía desde hacía mucho tiempo

long-range ['lɒŋ'reɪndʒ] *adj (missile)* de largo alcance; *(forecast)* a largo plazo

longshoreman [lɒŋ'ʃɔːmən] *n* estibador *m*

long-sighted [lɒŋ'saɪtɪd] *adj* hipermétrope

long-sleeved [lɒŋ'sliːvd] *adj* de manga larga

long-standing [lɒŋ'stændɪŋ] *adj (arrangement, friendship)* antiguo(a), viejo(a)

long-suffering [lɒŋ'sʌfərɪŋ] *adj* sufrido(a)

long-term ['lɒŋtɜːm] *adj* a largo plazo; **the l. unemployed** los desempleados *or Esp* parados de larga duración; **l. planning** planificación *f* a largo plazo

long-winded [lɒŋ'wɪndɪd] *adj* prolijo(a)

loofah ['luːfə], **luffa** ['lʌfə] *n* esponja *f* vegetal

look [lʊk] **1** *n* (**a**) *(act of looking)* **to have** *or* **take a l. at sth** mirar algo; **to have a l. for sth** buscar algo; **let me have a l.** déjame ver; **to have a l. around the town** (ir a) ver la ciudad; **to have a l. through some magazines** ojear unas revistas

(**b**) *(glance)* mirada *f*; **a suspicious/angry l.** una mirada recelosa/de *esp Esp* enfado *or esp Am* enojo; **we got some very odd looks** nos miraron con cara rara; **if looks could kill...** si las miradas mataran...

(**c**) *(appearance)* aspecto *m*; *Fig* **I don't like the l. of this at all!** no me gusta nada el cariz *or* la pinta que tiene esto; *Fig* **I don't like the l. of him** me da mala espina; **I don't like the l. of those clouds** no me gusta la pinta de esas nubes; **by the l. of it** por lo que parece

(**d**) *(personal appearance)* **(good) looks** atractivo *m*, guapura *f*; **looks don't matter** la belleza no es lo principal

2 *vt* **I can never l. him in the face again** nunca podré volver a mirarlo a la cara; **to l. sb up and down** mirar a alguien de arriba abajo; **l. what you've done!** ¡mira lo que has hecho!; **l. where you're going!** ¡mira por dónde vas!

3 *vi* (**a**) *(in general)* mirar, *Am* ver; **to l. at sth/sb** mirar algo/a alguien; **he's not much to l. at** no es gran cosa, es del montón; *Fig* **to l. the other way** hacer la vista gorda; **I'm just looking, thank you** *(in shop)* sólo estoy mirando; **to l. on the bright side** mirar el lado bueno (de las cosas); **to l. to the future** mirar al futuro; **l. here!** ¡mire usted!; **(now) l.!** ¡mira!; **I don't l. at it that way** yo no lo miro de esa manera; *Prov* **l. before you leap** hay que pensar las cosas dos veces (antes de hacerlas)

(**b**) *(search)* **to l. for sth/sb** buscar algo/a alguien; **we've looked everywhere** hemos buscado *or* mirado *or RP* nos hemos fijado por todas partes

(**c**) *(seem, appear)* parecer; **to l. old/ill** parecer viejo/enfermo; **she looks tired** parece cansada; **things are looking good/bad** las cosas van bien/mal; **he doesn't l. his age** no aparenta la edad que tiene; **to l. the part** dar la talla; **what does she l. like?** ¿cómo es?, ¿qué aspecto tiene?; **to l. like sb** parecerse a alguien; **it looks like** *or* **as if...** parece que *or* como si...; **it looks like rain** parece que

va a llover; **you l. as if you've slept badly** tienes aspecto de haber dormido mal

▶ **look after** *vt insep (person, property, possessions)* cuidar; *(process, arrangements, finances)* hacerse cargo de

▶ **look around, look about** *vi* **I went into the center of town to l. around** fui al centro a dar una vuelta; **I've been looking around for something better** he estado buscando para ver si encontraba algo mejor

▶ **look back** *vi* (**a**) *(in space)* mirar atrás, volver la vista atrás (**b**) *(in time)* **to l. back on sth** recordar algo; **he has never looked back since that day** desde ese día no ha hecho más que progresar

▶ **look down** *vi (from above)* mirar hacia abajo; *(lower one's eyes)* bajar la mirada *or* la vista; *Fig* **to l. down on sb** desdeñar a alguien

▶ **look forward to** *vt insep* **to l. forward to sth** *(party, event)* estar deseando que llegue algo; **I was looking forward to my vacation/a good breakfast** tenía muchas ganas de coger las vacaciones/de un buen desayuno; **I'm looking forward to our next meeting in April** confío en que nuestra próxima reunión de abril será de sumo interés; **I'm sure we're all looking forward to a productive couple of days' work** seguro que vamos a disfrutar de dos días de fructífero trabajo; **to l. forward to doing sth** estar deseando hacer algo, tener muchas ganas de hacer algo; **I l. forward to hearing from you** *(in letter)* quedo a la espera de recibir noticias suyas

▶ **look in** *vi* **to l. in (on sb)** *(visit)* hacer una visita (a alguien)

▶ **look into** *vt insep (investigate)* investigar, examinar

▶ **look on 1** *vt insep (consider)* considerar; **to l. on sth/sb as...** considerar algo/a alguien...; **I l. on her as a friend** la considero una amiga

2 *vi* quedarse mirando

▶ **look out** *vi* mirar; **to l. out of the window** mirar por la ventana; **l. out!** *(be careful)* ¡cuidado!

▶ **look out for** *vt insep* (**a**) *(look for)* buscar (**b**) *(be on guard for)* estar al tanto de

▶ **look over** *vt insep* mirar por encima, repasar

▶ **look through** *vt* (**a**) *(inspect)* examinar (**b**) *(not see)* **she looked straight through me** miró hacia mí, pero no me vio

▶ **look to** *vt insep* (**a**) *(rely on)* **to l. to sb (for sth)** dirigirse a alguien (en busca de algo) (**b**) **we must l. to the future** debemos mirar hacia el futuro

▶ **look up 1** *vt sep (in dictionary, address book)* buscar; **to l. sb up** *(visit)* visitar a alguien

2 *vi (from below)* mirar hacia arriba; *(raise one's eyes)* levantar la mirada *or* la vista; *Fig* **things are looking up** las cosas están mejorando

▶ **look upon** *vt insep (consider)* considerar

▶ **look up to** *vt insep* admirar

look-alike ['lʊkəlaɪk] *n* doble *mf*

looker ['lʊkə(r)] *n Fam* **she's a real l.** es un bombón, es monísima

look-in ['lʊkɪn] *n Fam (chance)* **he won't get a l.** no tendrá ninguna oportunidad

looking-glass ['lʊkɪŋglɑːs] *n Old-fashioned* espejo *m*

lookout ['lʊkaʊt] *n (person)* centinela *mf*, vigilante *mf*; **to keep a l. for sth/sb** estar alerta por si se ve algo/a alguien; **to be on the l. for sth/sb** estar buscando algo/a alguien; **l. post** puesto *m* de vigilancia; **l. tower** atalaya *f*

loom[1] [luːm] *n (for making cloth)* telar *m*

loom[2] *vi* cernerse, cernirse; **dangers l. ahead** los peligros nos acechan; **to l. large** cobrar relevancia; **with the elections/ exams looming large,...** con las elecciones/los exámenes a la vuelta de la esquina,...

loony ['luːnɪ] *Fam* **1** *n* lunático(a) *m,f*, chalado(a) *m,f*, *Méx* zafado(a); **l. bin** loquero *m*, *Esp* frenopático *m*

2 *adj (person)* chalado(a), lunático(a); *(idea)* disparatado(a)

loop [lu:p] **1** *n* bucle *m*

2 *vt (string)* enrollar; **to l. sth around sth** enrollar algo alrededor de algo; *Av* **to l. the l.** rizar el rizo

loophole ['lu:phəʊl] *n (in law)* resquicio *m* legal

loopy ['lu:pɪ] *adj Fam (person)* majareta, chiflado(a); *(idea)* disparatado(a); **to be l.** *(person)* estar chiflado(a) *or Esp* majareta *or Méx* zafado(a)

loose [lu:s] **1** *n* **to be on the l.** andar suelto(a)

2 *adj (tooth, animal, connection)* suelto(a); *(piece of clothing)* suelto(a), holgado(a); *(skin)* colgante; *(alliance, network)* informal; *(translation)* poco exacto(a); *(morals, lifestyle)* disoluto(a); *(sweets, olives)* suelto(a), a granel; **to come l.** aflojarse; **to let sb l. on sth** dar rienda suelta a alguien en algo; **don't let him l. in the kitchen!** ¡no lo dejes suelto en la cocina!; **they let the riot police l. on the crowd** soltaron a los antidisturbios entre la multitud; **to let l. a torrent of abuse** soltar una sarta de improperios; **he's a l. cannon** es un descontrolado, *Am* es un(a) bala perdida; **l. change** (dinero *m*) suelto *m*; **to be at a l. end** no tener nada que hacer; *Fig* **to tie up the l. ends** *(in investigation)* atar cabos sueltos; **l. living** vida *f* disoluta *or* disipada; **l. talk** indiscreciones *fpl*; **a l. woman** una mujer fácil

3 *vt Literary (arrow)* disparar

4 *adv* **to buy sth l.** comprar algo a granel

▶**loose off** *vt (fire)* disparar

loose-fitting ['lu:sfɪtɪŋ] *adj* suelto(a), holgado(a)

loose-leaf ['lu:sli:f] *adj* **l. binder** *or* **folder** cuaderno *m or* carpeta *f* de anillas

loose-limbed ['lu:s'lɪmd] *adj* suelto(a)

loosely ['lu:slɪ] *adv* **(a) l. attached** flojo(a); **l. packed** *(snow, earth)* suelto(a) **(b)** *(roughly)* aproximadamente, vagamente; **l. speaking** hablando en términos generales; **l. translated** traducido(a) muy libremente

loosen ['lu:sən] **1** *vt (screw, knot, belt)* aflojar; *(restrictions)* suavizar; **to l. one's grip** soltar, aflojar la presión; **to l. sb's tongue** soltar la lengua a alguien

2 *vi* aflojarse

▶**loosen up** *vi (relax)* relajarse

loot [lu:t] **1** *n (booty)* botín *m*; *Fam (money) Esp* pasta *f*, *Am* plata *f*, *Méx* lana *f*

2 *vt* saquear

looter ['lu:tə(r)] *n* saqueador(ora) *m,f*

looting ['lu:tɪŋ] *n* saqueo *m*, pillaje *m*

lopsided [lɒp'saɪdɪd] *adj* torcido(a); **a l. grin** una sonrisa torcida

loquacious [lɒ'kweɪʃəs] *adj* locuaz

lord [lɔ:d] **1** *n* **(a)** *(aristocrat)* señor *m*, lord *m* **(b)** *Rel* **the L.** el Señor; **the L.'s Prayer** el padrenuestro; *Fam* **good L.!** ¡Dios mío!; *Fam* **L. knows if…** sabe Dios si…

2 *vt* **to l. it over sb** tratar despóticamente a alguien

lordly ['lɔ:dlɪ] *adj* altanero(a)

lordship ['lɔ:dʃɪp] *n* señoría *f*; **Your L.** (su) Señoría

lore [lɔ:(r)] *n* tradición *f*

Los Angeles [lɒs'ændʒəli:z] *n* Los Ángeles

lose [lu:z] (*pt & pp* **lost** [lɒst]) **1** *vt* **(a)** *(accidentally)* perder; **you have nothing to l.** no tienes nada que perder; **to l. one's voice** quedarse afónico(a); **he had lost interest in his work** había perdido el interés por su trabajo; **it loses something in translation** al traducirlo, pierde algo; **to be lost at sea** desaparecer *or* morir en el mar; **the joke/the irony was lost on him** no entendió el chiste/la ironía; **my watch loses five minutes a day** mi reloj se atrasa cinco minutos al día; **that mistake lost him the match** ese error hizo que perdiera el partido; **to l. one's way, to get lost** perderse; *Fam* **get lost!** ¡lárgate!, ¡piérdete!; **to l. one's balance** perder el equilibrio; **to l. sight of sth/sb** perder

algo/a alguien de vista; *Fam Fig* **you've lost me!** *(I don't understand)* no te sigo

(b) *(deliberately)* **to l. weight** adelgazar, perder peso; **we lost him in the crowd** le dimos esquinazo entre la multitud; **she had lost herself in a book/in her work** se quedó absorta en la lectura de un libro/en su trabajo

2 *vi (in contest)* perder; **to l. in value** perder valor

▶**lose out** *vi* salir perdiendo (**to** en beneficio de); **to l. out on sth** salir perdiendo en algo

loser ['lu:zə(r)] *n (in contest)* perdedor(ora) *m,f*; **to be a good/bad l.** ser buen/mal perdedor(ora); **he's a (born) l.** es un fracasado

losing ['lu:zɪŋ] *adj* **to fight a l. battle** luchar por una causa perdida; **the l. side** los vencidos

loss [lɒs] *n* **(a)** *(in general)* pérdida *f*; **there was great l. of life** hubo muchas víctimas mortales; **to suffer heavy losses** *(casualties)* sufrir muchas bajas (mortales); **it's no great l.** no es una gran pérdida; **without l. of face** sin perder la dignidad; **to be at a l. to explain…** no saber cómo explicar…; **she's never at a l. for an answer** siempre sabe qué contestar **(b)** *(financial)* **losses** pérdidas *fpl*; **to make a l.** tener pérdidas; **to sell at a l.** vender con pérdidas; **to cut one's losses** reducir pérdidas; **l. leader** reclamo *m* de ventas

lost [lɒst] **1** *adj* perdido(a); **to be l.** estar perdido(a); **to seem** *or* **look l.** *(confused)* tener un aire perdido(a); **to give sth/sb up for l.** dar algo/a alguien por perdido(a); **l. cause** causa *f* perdida; **l. and found** objetos *mpl* perdidos; **l. and found office** oficina *f* de objetos perdidos; **l. property** objetos *mpl* perdidos

2 *pt & pp of* **lose**

lot [lɒt] **1** *n* **(a)** *(large quantity)* **a l.** *(singular)* mucho; *(plural)* muchos(as); **a l. of** *(singular)* mucho(a); *(plural)* muchos(as); **a l.** *or* **lots of questions** muchas preguntas; **a l.** *or* **lots of people** mucha gente; **I saw quite a l. of her in Paris** la vi mucho en París; **we had a l.** *or* **lots of fun** nos divertimos mucho; **the l.** todo; **I bought the l.** lo compré todo; *Fam* **listen, you l.!** *Esp* ¡escuchadme bien!, *Am* ¡oigan, ustedes!; *Fam* **that l. next door** los de al lado; *Fam* **he's a bad l.** es un mal bicho

(b) *(destiny)* fortuna *f*, suerte *f*; **to draw** *or* **cast lots for sth** echar algo a suertes; **he was happy with his l.** estaba contento con su suerte; **to throw in one's l. with sb** compartir la suerte de alguien, unir (uno) su suerte a la de alguien

(c) *(piece of land)* terreno *m*; *(at auction)* lote *m*; **in lots** por lotes

2 *adv* **a l.** mucho; **a l. bigger** mucho más grande; **thanks a l.** muchas gracias

loth = **loath**

lotion ['ləʊʃən] *n* loción *f*

lottery ['lɒtərɪ] *n* lotería *f*; *Fig* **it's a l.** es una lotería; **l. ticket** billete *m or Am* boleto *m* de lotería

lotto ['lɒtəʊ] *n (game)* = juego parecido al bingo

lotus ['ləʊtəs] *n* loto *m*; **l. position** posición *f* del loto

loud [laʊd] **1** *adj* **(a)** *(noise, bang, explosion)* fuerte; *(voice, music, radio)* alto(a); *Pej (person)* escandaloso(a); **to be l. in one's praise/condemnation of sth** elogiar/condenar algo rotundamente **(b)** *(color, clothes)* chillón(ona)

2 *adv* alto; **to think out l.** pensar en alto; **louder!** ¡más alto!; **l. and clear** alto y claro

loudly ['laʊdlɪ] *adv* alto

loudmouth ['laʊdmaʊθ] *n Fam* **to be a l.** ser un(a) chismoso(a), *Esp* ser un/una bocazas

loudmouthed ['laʊdmaʊðd] *adj Fam* bocazas *(inv)*

loudness ['laʊdnɪs] *n (of noise, bang, explosion)* fuerza *f*, intensidad *f*; *(of voice, music, radio)* volumen *m* (alto)

loudspeaker [laʊd'spi:kə(r)] *n* altavoz *m*, *Am* altoparlante *m*, *Méx* bocina *f*

lounge [laʊndʒ] **1** *n (in house, hotel)* salón *m*; *(in airport)* sala *f* (de espera)
2 *vi* holgazanear, gandulear
▶**lounge around, lounge about** *vi* holgazanear, gandulear
lounger ['laʊndʒə(r)] *n (chair)* tumbona *f*
louse [laʊs] *(pl lice* [laɪs]*) n* **(a)** *(insect)* piojo *m* **(b)** *Fam (person)* sinvergüenza *mf*, rufián *m*
lousy ['laʊzɪ] *adj Fam* pésimo(a), horroroso(a); **to feel l.** sentirse *Esp* fatal *or Am* pésimo; **a l. trick** una jugarreta; **we had a l. time on vacation** lo pasamos *Esp* fatal *or Am* pésimo durante las vacaciones
lout [laʊt] *n* salvaje *m*, *Esp* gamberro *m*
loutish ['laʊtɪʃ] *adj* grosero(a), *Esp* gamberro(a)
louver, louvre ['luːvə(r)] *n (on door, window)* lama *f*, listón *m*; *(on roof)* lumbrera *f*
louvered, louvred ['luːvəd] *adj* **l. door** puerta *f* (tipo) persiana *or* de listones
lovable, loveable ['lʌvəbəl] *adj* adorable, encantador(ora)
love [lʌv] **1** *n* **(a)** *(between lovers or members of a family)* amor *m*; **to fall in l. with sb** enamorarse de alguien; **to be in l. with sb** estar enamorado(a) de alguien; **to make l. with** *or* **to sb** *(have sex)* hacer el amor con *or* a alguien; *Old-fashioned* **to make l. to sb** *(court)* cortejar a alguien; **the l. of my life** el amor de mi vida; **it was l. at first sight** fue un flechazo; **l. affair** aventura *f* (amorosa); *Euph* **l. child** hijo(a) *m,f* natural; **l. letter** carta *f* de amor; **l. life** vida *f* amorosa; **l. match** matrimonio *m* por amor; **l. nest** nido *m* de amor; **l. song** canción *f* de amor; **l. story** historia *f* de amor
(**b**) *(affection)* cariño *m*; **l. of one's country** cariño por el propio país; **give my l. to your parents** saluda a tus padres de mi parte; **with l. from...** *(at end of letter)* con cariño,...; **Bill sends his l.** Bill manda recuerdos; **there's no l. lost between them** se llevan mal; **I wouldn't do it for l. nor money** no lo haría por nada del mundo
(**c**) *(liking, interest)* afición *f* (**of** *or* **for** a *or* por); **to do sth for the l. of it** hacer algo por gusto *or* afición
(**d**) *(in tennis)* nada; **fifteen l.** quince nada
2 *vt* amar, querer; **I l. you** te quiero; **I l. Chinese food** me encanta la comida china; **they l. to go for walks, they l. going for walks** les encanta ir de paseo; **I'd l. to come** me encantaría ir
loveable = lovable
lovebird ['lʌvbɜːd] *n Fam* **a pair of lovebirds** un par de tortolitos
lovebite ['lʌvbaɪt] *n* chupetón *m*, señal *f* (de un mordisco)
love-hate [lʌv'heɪt] *adj* **a l. relationship** una relación de amor y odio
loveless ['lʌvlɪs] *adj* sin amor, carente de amor
lovelorn ['lʌvlɔːn] *adj Literary or Hum* apesadumbrado(a) *(por amor)*
lovely ['lʌvlɪ] *adj (weather, idea, smell)* estupendo(a); *(curtains, room, garden)* precioso(a), *Am* lindo(a); *(person)* bello(a), *Esp* guapo(a), *Am* lindo(a); **to have a l. time** pasárselo estupendamente; **Clara's coming — oh l.!** viene Clara — *Esp* ¡estupendo!, *Am* salvo *RP* ¡chévere!, *Méx* ¡padre!, *RP* ¡bárbaro!
lovemaking ['lʌvmeɪkɪŋ] *n* relaciones *fpl* sexuales; **a night of passionate l.** una noche de pasión
lover ['lʌvə(r)] *n (of person)* amante *mf*; *(of nature, good food)* amante *mf*, aficionado(a) *mf*
lovesick ['lʌvsɪk] *adj* con mal de amores, enfermo(a) de amor
lovey-dovey ['lʌvɪ'dʌvɪ] *adj Fam* almibarado(a)
loving ['lʌvɪŋ] *adj* cariñoso(a), afectuoso(a)
low¹ [laʊ] **1** *n* **(a)** *Met* zona *f* de bajas presiones **(b)** *(minimum)* mínimo *m*; **to reach a new l.** *(price, popularity)* alcanzar un nuevo mínimo; *(country, reputation)* caer aún más bajo; **an all-time l.** un mínimo histórico

2 *adj* **(a)** *(not high, not loud)* bajo(a); **fuel is getting l.** nos estamos quedando sin combustible; **our stock of food is rather l.** nos queda bastante poca comida; **to cook sth over a l. heat** cocinar algo a fuego lento; *Aut* **to be on l. beam** llevar las luces cortas *or* de cruce puestas; **a l. bow** una reverencia profunda; **of l. birth** de baja extracción; **the lower classes** las clases bajas; *Mil* **lower ranks** soldados *mpl* rasos *or* de rango inferior; **to have a l. opinion of sb** tener mala opinión de alguien; *Fig* **a l. blow** un golpe bajo; **the Low Countries** los Países Bajos; **a l. neckline** un escote amplio; **l. tide** marea *f* baja; **l. water** marea *f* baja
(**b**) *(depressed)* **to feel l.** estar un poco deprimido(a)
(**c**) *(ignoble)* **the lowest of the l.** lo más bajo; **that's a l. trick!** ¡eso es una mala pasada!; **l. life** *(world)* hampa *f*
3 *adv (to hang, aim)* bajo; **to bow l.** hacer una reverencia profunda; **to fly l.** volar bajo; **turn the music/the lights down l.** baja la música/las luces; **we're running l. on fuel/food** nos estamos quedando sin combustible/comida
low² *vi (cattle)* mugir
lowbrow ['laʊbraʊ] *adj (tastes, interests)* vulgar, de las masas; **l. novelist** novelista *mf* populachero(a)
low-budget [laʊ'bʌdʒɪt] *adj (movie, vacation)* de bajo presupuesto
low-calorie [laʊ'kælərɪ] *adj* bajo(a) en calorías
low-cost [laʊ'kɒst] *adj (mortgage)* de bajo costo *or Esp* coste; *(flight)* económico(a)
low-cut [laʊ'kʌt] *adj (dress)* escotado(a)
lowdown ['laʊdaʊn] *Fam n* **to give sb the l. on sth** explicar de pe a pa a alguien los pormenores de algo
lower¹ ['laʊə(r)] *vt (in general)* bajar; *(flag, sail)* arriar; **to l. one's guard** bajar la guardia; **he lowered his voice** bajó la voz; **to l. oneself into sth** entrar en algo; **to l. oneself onto sth** bajar hasta algo; *Fig* **to l. oneself to do sth** rebajarse a hacer algo
lower² ['laʊə(r)] *vi (person)* mirar amenazadoramente; *(sky)* estar tormentoso(a)
lowercase ['laʊə'keɪs] *Typ* **1** *n* minúsculas *fpl*, *Spec* caja *f* baja
2 *adj* en minúsculas, *Spec* en caja baja
lower-class ['laʊə'klɑːs] *adj* de clase baja
low-flying ['laʊ'flaɪɪŋ] *adj* que vuela bajo
low-grade ['laʊ'greɪd] *adj (in quality)* de baja calidad
low-key [laʊ'kiː] *adj* discreto(a)
lowland ['laʊlənd] *adj* de las tierras bajas
lowlands ['laʊləndz] *npl* tierras *fpl* bajas; **the L.** *(of Scotland)* las Tierras Bajas de Escocia
low-level ['laʊ'levəl] *adj* **(a)** *(discussion)* de bajo nivel **(b)** **l. radiation** radiación *f* de baja intensidad
lowly ['laʊlɪ] *adj* humilde
low-lying ['laʊ'laɪɪŋ] *adj (area, mist)* bajo(a)
low-profile ['laʊ'prəʊfaɪl] *adj (talks, visit)* discreto(a); **the police maintained a l. presence throughout** la presencia de la policía fue discreta todo el tiempo
low-spirited ['laʊ'spɪrɪtɪd] *adj* desanimado(a)
low-tar ['laʊ'tɑː(r)] *adj (cigarettes)* bajo(a) en nicotina, de bajo nivel de nicotina
low-tech ['laʊtek] *adj* rudimentario(a), elemental
lox [lɒks] *n* salmón *m* ahumado
loyal ['lɔɪəl] *adj* leal, fiel
loyalist ['lɔɪəlɪst] *n & adj (to government, party)* leal *mf*, adicto(a) *m,f*
loyally ['lɔɪəlɪ] *adv* lealmente, fielmente
loyalty ['lɔɪəltɪ] *n* lealtad *f*, fidelidad *f*; **you'll have to decide where your loyalties lie** tienes que decidir con quién estás; **she had divided loyalties** sus lealtades estaban divididas
lozenge ['lɒzɪndʒ] *n (shape)* rombo *m*; *(cough sweet)* pastilla *f* para la tos
LP [el'piː] *n (abbr* **long-playing record**) LP *m*, elepé *m*

LSD [eles'di:] n (abbr **lysergic acid diethylamide**) LSD m

Lt Mil (abbr **Lieutenant**) Tte., teniente m

Ltd Com (abbr **limited**) ≃ S.L.

lubricant ['lu:brɪkənt] n lubricante m

lubricate ['lu:brɪkeɪt] vt lubricar

lubrication [lu:brɪ'keɪʃən] n lubricación f

lucid ['lu:sɪd] adj lúcido(a)

lucidity [lu:'sɪdɪtɪ] n lucidez f

luck [lʌk] n (chance) suerte f; **(good) l.** (buena) suerte; **bad l.** mala suerte; **he couldn't believe his l.** no podía creerse la suerte que tenía; **to bring sb good/bad l.** traer buena/mala suerte a alguien; **good l.!** ¡(buena) suerte!; **to wish sb l.** desear suerte a alguien; **to be in l.** estar de suerte; **to be out of l.** no tener suerte; **to be down on one's l.** no estar de suerte; **to try one's l.** probar suerte; **to push one's l.** tentar a la suerte; **don't push your l.!** (said in annoyance) ¡no me busques las cosquillas!; **some people have all the l.** hay quien nace con estrella; **just my l.!** ¡qué mala suerte!; **no such l.!** ¡ojalá!; **with any l. he'll still be there** con un poco de suerte, todavía estará allí

▸**luck out** vi Fam (get lucky) tener mucha potra or Méx chance, RP tener mucho tarro

luckily ['lʌkɪlɪ] adv por suerte, afortunadamente

lucky ['lʌkɪ] adj (person) afortunado(a); **to be l.** tener suerte; **to make a l. guess** adivinarlo por casualidad; Fam **(you) l. devil!** ¡qué suertudo(a)!; Ironic **you'll be l.!** ¡ni lo sueñes!; **it's l. you came when you did** fue una suerte que llegaras en ese momento; **she's l. to be alive** tiene suerte de estar con vida; **my l. number** mi número de la suerte; **it's not my l. day** hoy no es mi día (de suerte); **that was l.** ¡qué suerte!; **to strike it l.** tener suerte; **l. charm** amuleto m; **you can thank your l. stars she didn't see you!** ¡da gracias al cielo porque no te vio!

lucrative ['lu:krətɪv] adj lucrativo(a)

lucre ['lu:kə(r)] n Pej or Hum (money) vil metal m; **to do sth for filthy l.** hacer algo por el vil metal

ludicrous ['lu:dɪkrəs] adj ridículo(a)

ludicrously ['lu:dɪkrəslɪ] adv de forma ridícula; **l. cheap/ expensive** increíblemente barato/caro

luffa = **loofah**

lug [lʌg] (pt & pp **lugged**) vt Fam arrastrar, cargar con

luggage ['lʌgɪdʒ] n equipaje m; **a piece of l.** un bulto (de equipaje); **l. label** etiqueta f identificativa del equipaje; **l. locker** taquilla f (para equipaje); **l. rack** (in train, bus) portaequipajes m inv; (on car) baca f

lugubrious [lu:'gu:brɪəs] adj lúgubre

lukewarm ['lu:kwɔ:m] adj (water, response) tibio(a); **she was rather l. about my suggestion** recibió mi sugerencia con bastante tibieza

lull [lʌl] n (in conflict) tregua f; (in conversation) pausa f; Fig **the l. before the storm** la calma que precede a la tormenta

2 vt **to l. sb to sleep** dormir a alguien; **to l. sb into a false sense of security** dar a alguien una falsa sensación de seguridad

lullaby ['lʌləbaɪ] n nana f, canción f de cuna

lumbago [lʌm'beɪgəʊ] n lumbago m

lumbar ['lʌmbə(r)] adj Anat lumbar

lumber ['lʌmbə(r)] **1** n (wood) madera f, maderos mpl

2 vt **to l. sb with sth** hacerle a alguien cargar con algo; **I got lumbered with a huge bill** me hicieron pagar una factura enorme

3 vi **to l. around** or **about** caminar pesadamente

lumbering ['lʌmbərɪŋ] adj (walk) pesado(a)

lumberjack ['lʌmbədʒæk] n leñador(ora) m,f

luminary ['lu:mɪnərɪ] n figura f, lumbrera f

luminosity [lu:mɪ'nɒsɪtɪ] n luminosidad f

luminous ['lu:mɪnəs] adj (in general) luminoso(a); (strip,

roadsign) reflectante; (color, socks) fluorescente, fosforito(a)

lump [lʌmp] **1** n (a) (of earth, sugar) terrón m; (of stone, coal) trozo m; (in sauce) grumo m; (on head) chichón m; (on breast) bulto m; Fig **it brought a l. to my throat** (made me sad) me hizo sentir un nudo en la garganta; Fin **l. sum** pago m único, suma f global (b) Fam (person) zoquete m, Esp tarugo m

2 vt (a) (group) **all such payments were lumped under "additional expenses"** todos esos pagos estaban agrupados bajo el epígrafe de "gastos adicionales"; **you shouldn't l. them together just because they're brothers** no deberías tratarlos de la misma manera sólo porque sean hermanos (b) Fam (endure) **you'll just have to (like it or) l. it!** ¡no te queda más remedio que aguantar!

lumpy ['lʌmpɪ] adj (sauce) grumoso(a), lleno(a) de grumos; (mattress) lleno(a) de bultos

lunacy ['lu:nəsɪ] n locura f, demencia f; Fam **it's sheer l.** ¡es demencial!

lunar ['lu:nə(r)] adj lunar; **l. eclipse** eclipse m de luna; **l. landing** alunizaje m

lunatic ['lu:nətɪk] **1** n loco(a) m,f, lunático(a) m,f; **l. asylum** manicomio m

2 adj (idea, behavior) demencial; **the l. fringe** el sector fanático or intransigente

lunch [lʌntʃ] **1** n comida f, almuerzo m; **to have l.** comer, almorzar; Fam **to be out to l.** (be crazy) estar chiflado(a) or Esp chalado(a); **l. box** or **bucket** tartera f, fiambrera f, Méx, RP vianda f; **l. hour** hora f de comer; **l. pail** tartera f, fiambrera f, Méx, RP vianda f

2 vi comer, almorzar

luncheon ['lʌntʃən] n (a) Formal almuerzo m, comida f (b) **l. meat** fiambre m de lata

lung [lʌŋ] n pulmón m; **to shout at the top of one's lungs** gritar a pleno pulmón; **l. cancer** cáncer m de pulmón

lunge [lʌndʒ] **1** n embestida f, acometida f; **to make a l. for sb/sth** embestir contra alguien/algo

2 vi **to l. at sb (with sth)** embestir contra alguien (con algo)

lungful ['lʌŋfʊl] n **to take a l. of air** llenar los pulmones de aire, inspirar profundamente

lupine ['lu:paɪn], **lupin** ['lu:pɪn] n altramuz m

lurch [lɜ:tʃ] **1** n (of ship, car) bandazo m; **a l. to the right/left** (of politician, party) un giro brusco a la derecha/izquierda; Fam **to leave sb in the l.** dejar a alguien en la estacada

2 vi (ship, car) dar bandazos; (person) tambalearse; **to l. to the left/right** (politician, party) dar un giro brusco a la izquierda/derecha

lure ['lʊə(r)] **1** n (attraction) atractivo m; **she was drawn by the l. of the big city** la sedujo el reclamo de la gran cuidad

2 vt (into trap, ambush) atraer (**into** hasta); **nothing could l. her away from the computer** nada conseguía alejarla Esp del ordenador or Am de la computadora

lurid ['lʊərɪd] adj (a) (sensational) provocador(ora); (shocking) espeluznante; **in l. detail** con macabra precisión (b) (gaudy) chillón(ona)

lurk [lɜ:k] vi estar al acecho; **a doubt still lurked in his mind** su mente todavía albergaba una duda

luscious ['lʌʃəs] adj (woman) voluptuoso(a); (fruit) jugoso(a)

lush [lʌʃ] adj (vegetation, garden) exuberante; (offices, furniture) lujoso(a)

lust [lʌst] n (sexual) lujuria f; Fig (for power, knowledge) sed f, ansia f (**for** de)

▸**lust after** vt insep **to l. after sb** beber los vientos por alguien; **to l. after sth** desvivirse por or ansiar algo

luster ['lʌstə(r)] n lustre m

lustful ['lʌstfʊl] adj lujurioso(a)

lustily ['lʌstɪlɪ] adv con ganas, con fuerza

lustre = **luster**

lustrous ['lʌstrəs] *adj* lustroso(a)

lusty ['lʌstɪ] *adj (person)* lozano(a), vigoroso(a); *(cry)* sonoro(a)

lute [luːt] *n* laúd *m*

Lutheran ['luːθərən] *n & adj* luterano(a) *m,f*

Luxemb(o)urg ['lʌksəmbɜːg] *n* Luxemburgo

Luxemb(o)urger ['lʌksəmbɜːgə(r)] *n* luxemburgués(esa) *m,f*

luxuriant [lʌgˈzjʊərɪənt] *adj* exuberante

luxuriate [lʌgˈzjʊərɪeɪt] *vi* deleitarse (**in** con)

luxurious [lʌgˈzjʊərɪəs] *adj* lujoso(a)

luxury ['lʌkʃərɪ] **1** *n* lujo *m*; **a life of l.** una vida llena de lujos **2** *adj (car, apartment)* de lujo

LW *Rad (abbr* **Long Wave)** LW, OL

lychee [laɪˈtʃiː] *n* lichi *m*

lying ['laɪɪŋ] **1** *n* mentiras *fpl* **2** *adj* mentiroso(a), embustero(a)

lymph [lɪmf] *n Anat* linfa *f*; **l. node** ganglio *m* linfático

lynch [lɪntʃ] *vt* linchar

lynching ['lɪntʃɪŋ] *n* linchamiento *m*

lynchpin = **linchpin**

lynx [lɪŋks] *n* lince *m*

lyre ['laɪə(r)] *n (musical instrument)* lira *f*

lyric ['lɪrɪk] *adj* lírico(a)

lyrical ['lɪrɪkəl] *adj* lírico(a)

lyricism ['lɪrɪsɪzəm] *n* lirismo *m*

lyricist ['lɪrɪsɪst] *n* letrista *mf*

lyrics ['lɪrɪks] *npl* letra *f*

M

M, m [em] *n (letter)* M, m *f*

m (**a**) *(abbr* meter(s)) m, metro *m* (**b**) *(abbr* **mile(s)**) milla *f*

MA [em'eɪ] *n Univ (abbr* **Master of Arts**) máster *m or Am* maestría *f* (en Humanidades); **to have an MA in linguistics** tener un máster en Lingüística; **Frederick Watson, MA** Frederick Watson, licenciado con máster (en letras)

ma [mɑː] *n Fam* mamá *f*

ma'am [mɑːm] *n Old-fashioned* señora *f*

macabre [məˈkɑːbə(r)] *adj* macabro(a)

macaroni [mækəˈrəʊnɪ] *n* macarrones *mpl*; **m. cheese** macarrones con queso

macaroon [mækəˈruːn] *n* mostachón *m*

macaw [məˈkɔː] *n* guacamayo *m*

Mace® [meɪs] *n (spray)* aerosol *m* antivioladores

mace[1] [meɪs] *n (weapon, symbol of office)* maza *f*

mace[2] *n (spice)* macis *f inv*

Macedonia [mæsəˈdəʊnɪə] *n* Macedonia

Macedonian [mæsəˈdəʊnɪən] **1** *n* (**a**) *(person)* macedonio(a) *m,f* (**b**) *(language)* macedonio *m*
2 *adj* macedonio(a)

Mach [mæk] *n Phys* **M. (number)** (número *m* de) Mach *m*

machete [məˈʃetɪ] *n* machete *m*

Machiavellian [mækɪəˈvelɪən] *adj* maquiavélico(a)

machinations [mæʃɪˈneɪʃənz] *npl* maquinaciones *fpl*

machine [məˈʃiːn] **1** *n* máquina *f*; **he's a m.!** ¡es (como) una máquina!; **party/propaganda m.** aparato *m* del partido/propagandístico; *Comptr* **m. code** código *m* máquina; **m. gun** ametralladora *f*; *Comptr* **m. language** lenguaje *m* máquina; **m. shop** taller *m* de máquinas; **m. tool** máquina *f* herramienta; *Comptr* **m. translation** traducción *f* automática
2 *vt* (**a**) *Ind* producir a máquina (**b**) *(with sewing machine)* coser a máquina

machine-gun [məˈʃiːngʌn] *(pt & pp* **machine-gunned**) *vt* ametrallar

machine-readable [məˈʃiːnˈriːdəbəl] *adj Comptr* legible para *Esp* el ordenador *or Am* la computadora

machinery [məˈʃiːnərɪ] *n also Fig* maquinaria *f*

machine-washable [məˈʃiːnˈwɒʃəbəl] *adj* lavable a máquina

machinist [məˈʃiːnɪst] *n (operator)* operario(a) *m,f*

machismo [mæˈtʃɪzməʊ] *n* machismo *m*

macho [ˈmætʃəʊ] *adj (remark, attitude)* muy de macho; **to be m.** *(person)* (presumir de) ser muy macho

macintosh = **mackintosh**

mackerel [ˈmækrəl] *n* caballa *f*

mac(k)intosh [ˈmækɪntɒʃ] *n* impermeable *m*, gabardina *f*

macro [ˈmækrəʊ] *(pl* **macros**) *n Comptr* macro *m or f*; **m. virus** virus *m* de macro

macrobiotic [mækrəʊbaɪˈɒtɪk] *adj* macrobiótico(a); **a m. diet** una dieta macrobiótica

macrobiotics [mækrəʊbaɪˈɒtɪks] *n* macrobiótica *f*

macrocosm [ˈmækrəʊkɒzəm] *n Astron* macrocosmos *m inv*

macroeconomics [ˈmækrəʊiːkəˈnɒmɪks] *n (subject)* macroeconomía *f*

mad [mæd] *adj* (**a**) *(insane) (person)* loco(a); *(idea)* disparatado(a); *(dog)* rabioso(a); **to be m.** *(person)* estar loco(a); **to go m.** volverse loco(a); **as m. as a hatter** más loco(a) que una cabra; **m. with fear** aterrorizado(a); **there was a m. rush for the door** la gente se precipitó como loca hacia la puerta; *Fam* **to run/shout/work like m.** correr/gritar/trabajar como (un/una) loco(a); *Fam* **m. cow disease** el mal *or* la enfermedad de las vacas locas
(**b**) *Fam (enthusiastic)* **to be m. about sth** estar loco(a) por algo
(**c**) *Fam (angry) esp Esp* enfadado(a), *esp Am* enojado(a); **to be m. with** *or* **at sb** estar muy *esp Esp* enfadado(a) *or esp Am* enojado(a) con alguien

Madagascan [mædəˈgæskən] *n & adj* malgache *mf*

Madagascar [mædəˈgæskə(r)] *n* Madagascar

madam [ˈmædəm] *n (as form of address)* señora *f*

madcap [ˈmædkæp] *adj (scheme, idea)* disparatado(a)

madden [ˈmædən] *vt* sacar de quicio, exasperar

maddening [ˈmædənɪŋ] *adj* irritante, exasperante

made [meɪd] *pt & pp of* **make**

Madeira [məˈdɪərə] *n (island)* (la isla de) Madeira; *(wine)* (vino *m* de) Madeira *m*

made-to-measure [ˈmeɪdtəˈmeʒə(r)] **made-to-order** [ˈmeɪdtəˈɔːdə(r)] *adj* a medida

made-up [meɪˈdʌp] *adj* (**a**) *(story, excuse)* inventado(a) (**b**) *(lips)* pintado(a); *(face)* maquillado(a); **to be heavily m.** ir muy maquillado(a)

madhouse [ˈmædhaʊs] *n Fam (lunatic asylum)* manicomio *m*, casa *f* de locos; *Fig* **this place is a m.!** ¡esto es una casa de locos!

madly [ˈmædlɪ] *adv* (**a**) *(insanely)* enloquecidamente (**b**) *(desperately) (to rush, struggle)* como loco(a) (**c**) *Fam (extremely)* tremendamente; **m. in love** locamente enamorado(a)

madman [ˈmædmən] *n* loco *m*, demente *m*

madness [ˈmædnɪs] *n* locura *f*, demencia *f*; **it's sheer m.!** ¡es una locura!

Madrid [məˈdrɪd] *n* Madrid

madwoman [ˈmædwʊmən] *n* loca *f*, demente *f*

maelstrom [ˈmeɪlstrəm] *n also Fig* torbellino *m*

maestro [ˈmaɪstrəʊ] *(pl* **maestros** *or* **maestri** [ˈmaɪstriː]) *n* maestro *m*

mafia [ˈmæfɪə] *n* mafia *f*

mag [mæg] *n Fam* revista *f*

magazine [mægəˈziːn] *n* (**a**) *(publication)* revista *f*; **m. program** *(on radio, TV)* magazine *m*, programa *m* de variedades; **m. rack** revistero *m* (**b**) *(for gun)* recámara *f*; *(ammunition store)* polvorín *m*

magenta [məˈdʒentə] *n & adj* magenta *m*

maggot [ˈmægət] *n* larva *f*, gusano *m*

Maghreb [mæˈgreb] *n* **the M.** el Magreb
Maghrebi [mæˈgrebɪ] *n & adj* magrebí *mf*
Magi [ˈmeɪdʒaɪ] *npl* **the M.** los Reyes Magos
magic [ˈmædʒɪk] **1** *n* magia *f*; **as if by m.** como por arte de magia; **black/white m.** magia negra/blanca
  2 *adj* (**a**) mágico(a); **m. wand** varita *f* mágica (**b**) *Fam (excellent)* genial, *Esp* guay, *Am salvo RP* chévere, *Méx* padrísimo(a), *RP* bárbaro(a)
magical [ˈmædʒɪkəl] *adj* mágico(a)
magically [ˈmædʒɪklɪ] *adv* mágicamente, por arte de magia
magician [məˈdʒɪʃən] *n* mago(a) *m,f*
magisterial [mædʒɪsˈtɪərɪəl] *adj (domineering)* autoritario(a); *(authoritative)* magistral
magistrate [ˈmædʒɪstreɪt] *n Law* juez *mf* de primera instancia; **magistrates' court** juzgado *m* de primera instancia
magna cum laude [ˈmægnəkʊmˈlaʊdeɪ] *adv Univ* **to graduate m.** = licenciarse con matrícula de honor
magnanimity [mægnəˈnɪmɪtɪ] *n* magnanimidad *f*
magnanimous [mægˈnænɪməs] *adj* magnánimo(a)
magnanimously [mægˈnænɪməslɪ] *adv* magnánimamente
magnate [ˈmægneɪt] *n* magnate *mf*
magnesium [mægˈniːzɪəm] *n Chem* magnesio *m*
magnet [ˈmægnɪt] *n* imán *m*; *Fig (for tourists, investors)* foco *m* de atracción
magnetic [mægˈnetɪk] *adj (force, pole)* magnético(a); *Fig (personality)* cautivador(ora); **m. compass** brújula *f*
magnetism [ˈmægnɪtɪzəm] *n also Fig* magnetismo *m*
magnification [mægnɪfɪˈkeɪʃən] *n* ampliación *f*; **a lens with a m. of × 7** una lente de siete aumentos
magnificence [mægˈnɪfɪsəns] *n* magnificencia *f*
magnificent [mægˈnɪfɪsənt] *adj* magnífico(a)
magnify [ˈmægnɪfaɪ] *vt (of lens, telescope)* ampliar, aumentar; *(exaggerate)* magnificar, desorbitar
magnifying glass [ˈmægnɪfaɪɪŋˈglɑːs] *n* lupa *f*
magnitude [ˈmægnɪtjuːd] *n* magnitud *f*; **a problem of the first m.** un problema de primer orden
magnolia [mægˈnəʊlɪə] *n* magnolia *f*
magnum [ˈmægnəm] *n* = botella de vino o champán de 1,5 litros
magpie [ˈmægpaɪ] *n* urraca *f*
maharaja [mɑːhəˈrɑːdʒə] *n* marajá *m*
mahogany [məˈhɒgənɪ] **1** *n (wood)* caoba *f*; *(color)* (color *m*) caoba *m*
  2 *adj* de caoba
maid [meɪd] *n* (**a**) *(servant)* sirvienta *f*; **m. of honor** dama *f* de honor (**b**) *Literary (girl)* doncella *f*
maiden [ˈmeɪdən] **1** *n Literary (girl)* doncella *f*
  2 *adj (flight)* inaugural; **m. aunt** tía *f* soltera; **m. name** apellido *m* de soltera; *Parl* **m. speech** primer discurso *m* como congresista; **m. voyage** viaje *m* inaugural, primer trayecto *m*
mail¹ [meɪl] **1** *n (postal system)* correo *m*; *(letters or parcels received)* correspondencia *f*; **it came in the m.** vino en el correo; *Comptr* **m. bomb** bomba *f* de correo (electrónico); **m. drop** *(letter)* buzón *m*; *(PO box)* apartado *m* de correos, *Am* casilla *f* postal, *Andes, RP* casilla *f* de correos, *Col* apartado *m* aéreo; *Comptr* **m. merge** fusión *f* de correo; *Com* **m. order** venta *f* por correo; **m. train** tren *m* correo; **m. truck** furgoneta *f* del correo
  2 *vt* enviar *or* mandar (por correo)
mail² *n (armor)* malla *f*
mailbag [ˈmeɪlbæg] *n* saca *f* de correos; **she gets a huge m.** *(celebrity, politician)* recibe muchísimas cartas
mailbox [ˈmeɪlbɒks] *n* buzón *m* (de correos); *Comptr* buzón *m*
mailing [ˈmeɪlɪŋ] *n (mailshot)* mailing *m*; **m. list** lista *f* de direcciones *(para envío de publicidad)*

mailman [ˈmeɪlmæn] *n* cartero *m*
maim [meɪm] *vt* lisiar
main [meɪn] **1** *n* (**a**) *(pipe)* (tubería *f*) general *f*; *(cable)* cable *m* principal (**b**) **in the m.** *(generally)* en general
  2 *adj* principal; **the m. thing is to…** lo principal es…; *Journ* **m. article** *(main story)* artículo *m* principal; **m. entrance** entrada *f* principal; *Gram* **m. clause** oración *f* principal; **m. course** plato *m* principal; *Fam* **m. drag** calle *f* principal; *Rail* **m. line** línea *f* principal; **m. road** carretera *f* general; **m. street** calle *f* principal
mainframe [ˈmeɪnfreɪm] *n Comptr Esp* ordenador *m or Am* computadora *f* central
mainland [ˈmeɪnlænd] *n* tierra *f* firme; **m. Europe** la Europa continental; **on the m.** en tierra firme; **he escaped from Alcatraz to the California m.** escapó de Alcatraz hacia la costa californiana
mainline [ˈmeɪnlaɪn] *vi Fam (inject drugs)* picarse, *Esp* chutarse
mainly [ˈmeɪnlɪ] *adv* principalmente; **the accident was caused m. by carelessness** la imprudencia fue la principal causa del accidente; **the passengers were m. Spanish** los pasajeros eran en su mayoría españoles
mainspring [ˈmeɪnsprɪŋ] *n (of clock, watch)* muelle *m* real, resorte *m* principal; *Fig (of change, revolution)* móvil *m* principal
mainstay [ˈmeɪnsteɪ] *n (of economy, philosophy)* pilar *m* fundamental
mainstream [ˈmeɪnstriːm] **1** *n* corriente *f* principal *or* dominante
  2 *adj (politics, ideas, tastes)* convencional; *(movie, literature)* comercial
maintain [meɪnˈteɪn] *vt* mantener; **to m. (that)…** mantener *or* sostener que…
maintainable [meɪnˈteɪnəbəl] *adj (attitude, opinion)* defendible
maintenance [ˈmeɪntənəns] *n* (**a**) *(of car, equipment, roads)* mantenimiento *m*; **m. costs** costos *mpl or Esp* costes *mpl* de mantenimiento (**b**) *Law (alimony)* pensión *f* (alimenticia)
maître d', maitre d' [ˈmeɪtrəˈdiː] *n* maître *mf* (d'hôtel)
maize [meɪz] *n* maíz *m*, *Andes, RP* choclo *m*
Maj *Mil (abbr* **Major***)* comandante *m*
maj *Mus (abbr* **Major***)* mayor
majestic [məˈdʒestɪk] *adj* majestuoso(a)
majesty [ˈmædʒəstɪ] *n* majestuosidad *f*; **His/Her/Your M.** Su Majestad
major [ˈmeɪdʒə(r)] **1** *n* (**a**) *Mil* comandante *mf*; **m. general** general *mf* de división (**b**) *Univ (subject)* especialidad *f*
  2 *adj* (**a**) *(important)* importante, de primer orden; **of m. importance** de enorme importancia; **m. league** *(in baseball)* = liga profesional de béisbol estadounidense; *Fig* **a m. league company** una de las grandes empresas del sector (**b**) *Mus* mayor
  3 *vi Univ* **to m. in** *(subject)* especializarse en
Majorca [məˈjɔːkə] *n* Mallorca
Majorcan [məˈjɔːkən] *n & adj* mallorquín(ina) *m,f*
majority [məˈdʒɒrɪtɪ] *n* (**a**) *(in vote)* mayoría *f*; **to be in a** *or* **the m.** ser mayoría; **m. decision** decisión *f* por mayoría; *Fin* **m. interest** participación *f* mayoritaria; *Pol* **m. leader** = líder de la formación mayoritaria en el senado o el congreso estadounidense; *Pol* **m. rule** gobierno *m* mayoritario; *Law* **m. verdict** veredicto *m* mayoritario; *Pol* **m. vote** votación *f* por mayoría (**b**) *Law (age)* mayoría *f* de edad
make [meɪk] **1** *n* (**a**) *(brand)* marca *f* (**b**) *Fam* **to be on the m.** *(financially)* buscar sólo el propio beneficio; *(sexually)* ir a ligar *or RP* de levante; **to put the m. on sb.** intentar seducir a alguien, *Esp* tirar los tejos a alguien, *Méx* echarle los perros a alguien, *RP* cargar a alguien
  2 *vt (pt & pp* **made** [meɪd]*)* (**a**) *(produce, prepare, perform)* hacer; *(payment, transaction)* realizar, efectuar; *(speech)* pronun-

ciar; *(decision)* tomar; *(mistake)* cometer; **to m. a promise** hacer una promesa; **made in Spain** fabricado(a) en España; **made from** *or* **out of...** hecho(a) con *or* de...; *Fam* **I'll show them what I'm made of** les voy a demostrar quién soy yo; *Fam* **I'm not made of money!** ¡que no soy millonario(a) *or* de oro!; **to m. something of oneself** convertirse en una persona de provecho; **two and two m. four** dos y dos son cuatro; **to m. a choice** elegir; **to m. a difference** cambiar mucho las cosas (a mejor); **it doesn't m. any difference** da lo mismo; **to m. a noise** hacer ruido; **to m. trouble** crear problemas

(b) *(earn) (money)* ganar; **to m. a living** ganarse la vida; **to m. a name for oneself** crearse *or* labrarse una reputación

(c) *(cause to be successful)* **to m. it** *(be successful)* tener éxito, llegar a la cima; **you've got it made** lo tienes todo hecho; **this book made her** este libro le dio la fama; **it's m. or break** es la hora de la verdad; **it made my day** me alegró el día

(d) *(cause to be)* hacer; **to m. sb happy** hacer feliz a alguien; **to m. sb sad** entristecer a alguien; **to m. sb hungry** dar hambre a alguien; **to m. sb tired** cansar a alguien; **that made me angry** eso me *esp Esp* enfadó *or esp Am* enojó; **to m. sb a present of sth** regalar algo a alguien

(e) *(compel)* **to m. sb do sth** hacer que alguien haga algo; **they made us wear suits** nos obligaron a llevar traje; **don't m. me laugh!** ¡no me hagas reír!

(f) *(estimate, calculate)* **what time do you m. it?** ¿qué hora tienes?; **I m. it $50 in total** calculo un total de 50 dólares

(g) *(reach) Fam* **to m. it** *(arrive in time)* llegar (a tiempo); *(finish in time)* **to m. the charts** *(record)* llegar a las listas de éxitos; **to m. the first team** *(be selected)* conseguir entrar en el primer equipo

(h) *(become, be)* ser; **he'll m. a good doctor/singer** será un buen médico/cantante

(i) *(manage to attend) (show, meeting)* llegar a; **I can m. two o'clock** puedo estar allí para las dos

(j) *Fam (have sex with)* **to m. sb, to m. it with sb** hacérselo con alguien

3 *vi* (a) *(act)* **to m. as if** *or* **as though to do sth** hacer como si se fuera a hacer algo (b) *Fam (pretend)* **she makes like she's an expert** se las da de experta (c) **to m. do** arreglárselas; **to m. believe (that)...** imaginarse que... (d) **to m. sure** *or* **certain (of sth)** asegurarse (de algo)

▸**make after** *vt insep* **to m. after sb** *(chase)* salir en persecución de alguien

▸**make for** *vt insep* (a) *(head toward)* dirigirse hacia (b) *(contribute to)* facilitar, contribuir a

▸**make of** *vt sep* **what do you m. of the new manager?** ¿qué te parece el nuevo jefe?; **I don't know what to m. of that remark** no sé cómo interpretar ese comentario

▸**make off** *vi Fam (leave)* largarse

▸**make off with** *vt insep Fam (steal)* largarse con, llevarse

▸**make out 1** *vt sep* (a) *(write) (list)* elaborar, hacer; *(check)* extender (b) *Fam (claim)* **to m. out (that)...** decir *or* pretender que... (c) *(understand, decipher)* entender; *(see)* distinguir; *(hear)* oír

2 *vi Fam (sexually)* meterse mano, *Esp* darse el lote

▸**make over** *vt sep* **she has made the estate over to her granddaughter** ha nombrado a su nieta heredera de sus propiedades

▸**make up 1** *vt sep* (a) *(story, excuses)* inventar (b) *(deficit, loss)* enjugar, recuperar; **I'll m. it up to you later, I promise** te prometo que te recompensaré (por ello) más adelante (c) *(complete) (team, amount)* completar (d) *(form)* formar, componer; **the community is made up primarily of old people** la comunidad se compone de ancianos; **to m. up one's mind** decidirse (e) *(put together) (list)* elaborar, hacer;

(parcel, bed) hacer; *(prescription)* preparar (f) *(apply makeup to)* **to m. oneself up** maquillarse

2 *vi (end quarrel)* reconciliarse

▸**make up for** *vt insep (losses)* compensar; *(lost time)* recuperar; **he bought me flowers to m. up for his behaviour** me compró flores para disculparse por su comportamiento

make-believe ['meɪkbɪliːv] **1** *n* **to live in the land of m.** vivir en un mundo de fantasías

2 *adj* ficticio(a)

makeover ['meɪkəʊvə(r)] *n* renovación *f or* cambio *m* de imagen

maker ['meɪkə(r)] *n* (a) *(manufacturer)* fabricante *mf* (b) *Euph* **to meet one's M.** entregar el alma a Dios

-maker ['meɪkə(r)] *suffix* (a) *(manufacturer)* **furniture/motorcycle-m.** fabricante *mf* de muebles/motocicletas (b) *(machine)* **coffee/ice cream-m.** máquina *f* de café/helados

makeshift ['meɪkʃɪft] *adj* improvisado(a)

makeup ['meɪkʌp] *n* (a) *(cosmetics)* maquillaje *m*; **m. artist** maquillador(ora) *m,f*; **m. bag** bolsa *f* del maquillaje; **m. remover** desmaquillador *m* (b) *(composition) (of team, group)* composición *f*; *(of person)* temperamento *m*, carácter *m*

making ['meɪkɪŋ] *n (of goods)* fabricación *f*, manufactura *f*; **the movie was three years in the m.** llevó tres años realizar la película; **this is history in the m.** se está haciendo historia (aquí y ahora); **a musician in the m.** un músico en ciernes; **the problem is of her own m.** el problema se lo ha buscado ella; **he has the makings of an actor** tiene madera de actor

maladjusted [mælə'dʒʌstɪd] *adj* inadaptado(a)

maladroit [mælə'drɔɪt] *adj* torpe, desacertado(a)

malady ['mælədɪ] *n* mal *m*

Malaga ['mæləgə] *n* Málaga

Malagasy ['mæləgæsɪ] **1** *n (language)* malgache *m*

2 *adj* malgache

malaise [mæ'leɪz] *n* malestar *m*

malaria [mə'leərɪə] *n* malaria *f*

malark(e)y [mə'lɑːkɪ] *n Fam (ridiculous behavior)* payasadas *fpl*, majaderías *fpl*; *(ridiculous explanation)* sandeces *fpl*, majaderías *fpl*

Malawi [mə'lɑːwɪ] *n* Malaui

Malawian [mə'lɑːwɪən] *n & adj* malauita *mf*

Malay [mə'leɪ] *n & adj* malayo(a) *m,f*

Malaysia [mə'leɪzɪə] *n* Malaisia

Malaysian [mə'leɪzɪən] *n & adj* malaisio(a) *m,f*

Maldives ['mɔːldɪvz] *npl* **the M.** las Maldivas

male [meɪl] **1** *n (person)* varón *m*, hombre *m*; *(animal)* macho *m*

2 *adj (person)* masculino(a); *(animal)* macho; **m. chauvinism** machismo *m*; **m. chauvinist** machista *m*; **m. nurse** enfermero *m*

malefactor ['mælɪfæktə(r)] *n Literary* malhechor(ora) *m,f*

malevolence [mə'levələns] *n* malevolencia *f*

malevolent [mə'levələnt] *adj* malévolo(a)

malevolently [mə'levələntlɪ] *adv* malévolamente

malfeasance [mæl'fiːzəns] *n Law* infracción *f*

malformation [mælfɔː'meɪʃən] *n* malformación *f*

malformed [mæl'fɔːmd] *adj (organ, baby)* con malformación, deforme

malfunction [mæl'fʌŋkʃən] **1** *n Esp* fallo *m*, *Am* falla *f*

2 *vi* averiarse

Mali ['mɑːlɪ] *n* Mali

malice ['mælɪs] *n* malicia *f*; *Law* **with m. aforethought** con premeditación y alevosía

malicious [mə'lɪʃəs] *adj* malicioso(a)

maliciously [mə'lɪʃəslɪ] *adv* maliciosamente

malign [mə'laɪn] **1** *adj* perjudicial, pernicioso(a)

2 *vt* difamar

malignant [məˈlɪgnənt] *adj (person, tumor)* maligno(a)

malinger [məˈlɪŋgə(r)] *vi* fingir una enfermedad (para no ir a trabajar)

malingerer [məˈlɪŋgərə(r)] *n* = persona que se finge enferma (para no ir a trabajar)

mall [mɔːl] *n* centro *m* comercial

mallard [ˈmælɑːd] *n* ánade *m* real

malleable [ˈmælɪəbəl] *adj (person, metal)* maleable

mallet [ˈmælɪt] *n* mazo *m*

mallow [ˈmæləʊ] *n (plant)* malva *f*

malnutrition [mælnjuːˈtrɪʃən] *n* desnutrición *f*

malpractice [mælˈpræktɪs] *n* negligencia *f* (profesional); *Law* **m. suit** demanda *f* por negligencia (profesional)

malt [mɔːlt] *n* malta *f*; **m. vinegar** vinagre *m* de malta; **m. whiskey** whisky *m* de malta

Malta [ˈmɔːltə] *n* Malta

Maltese [mɔːlˈtiːz] **1** *n* (**a**) *(person)* maltés(esa) *m,f* (**b**) *(language)* maltés *m*
  2 *npl (people)* **the M.** los malteses
  3 *adj* maltés(esa); **M. cross** cruz *f* de Malta

maltreat [mælˈtriːt] *vt* maltratar

maltreatment [mælˈtriːtmənt] *n* maltrato *m*, malos tratos *mpl*

mammal [ˈmæməl] *n* mamífero *m*

mammary [ˈmæmərɪ] *adj Anat* mamario(a); **m. glands** mamas *fpl*, glándulas *fpl* mamarias

mammography [mæˈmɒgrəfɪ] *n Med* mamografía *f*

mammoth [ˈmæməθ] **1** *n (animal)* mamut *m*
  2 *adj (huge)* gigantesco(a), enorme; *(task)* ingente

mammy [ˈmæmɪ] *n Fam* mamá *f*

man [mæn] **1** *n (pl* **men** [men]) (**a**) *(adult male)* hombre *m*; *Fam* **hey m.!** ¡oye, tío!; **a m.'s jacket/bicycle** una cazadora/bicicleta de hombre; **the army will make a m. of him** el ejército lo hará un hombre; **he took it like a m.** lo aceptó como un hombre; **this will separate the men from the boys** así se verá quién vale de verdad; **to be m. enough to do sth** tener el valor suficiente para hacer algo; **to talk to sb m. to m.** hablar con alguien de hombre a hombre; **he's just the m. for the job** es el hombre indicado (para el trabajo); **to be one's own m.** ser dueño de sí mismo; **he's a man's m.** le gustan las cosas de hombres; **the m. in the street** el hombre de la calle; **a m. of God** un clérigo; **a m. of the world** un hombre de mundo
  (**b**) *(individual, person)* persona *f*, hombre *m*; **any m.** cualquiera; **few men** pocos, pocas personas; **they replied as one m.** respondieron como un solo hombre; **they were patriots to a m.** hasta el último de ellos era un patriota
  (**c**) *Fam (in exclamations)* **m., am I tired!** ¡estoy que me caigo de cansancio!; **hey m., what are you doing?** oye, *Esp* tío *or Am* compadre *or Andes, CAm, Carib, Méx* mano, ¿qué haces?, *RP* ¡parala, loco!
  (**d**) *(husband)* marido *m*; **to live as m. and wife** vivir como marido y mujer
  (**e**) *(humanity)* el hombre
  (**f**) *(employee) (in factory)* empleado(a) *m,f*; *(servant)* criado *m*; *(soldier)* hombre *m*; **our m. in Rome** *(spy)* nuestro agente en Roma; *(diplomat)* nuestro representante en Roma; *(reporter)* nuestro corresponsal en Roma
  (**g**) *(in chess)* pieza *f*; *(in checkers)* ficha *f*
  2 *vt (pt & pp* **manned**) *(machine)* manejar; *(plane, boat)* tripular; *(phone, reception desk)* atender; **a manned flight** un vuelo tripulado

man-about-town [mænəbaʊtˈtaʊn] *n* urbanita *m* sofisticado

manacles [ˈmænəkəlz] *npl (for hands)* esposas *fpl*; *(for feet)* grilletes *mpl*

manage [ˈmænɪdʒ] **1** *vt* (**a**) *(company, hotel, project)* dirigir; *(the*

economy, resources) gestionar, administrar; *(store)* llevar; *Fin* **managed currency** moneda *f* controlada (**b**) *(deal with)* *(situation)* manejar, tratar; **to m. to do sth** conseguir hacer algo; **to know how to m. sb** saber cómo tratar a alguien; **I can't m. three suitcases** no puedo con tres maletas *or Am* valijas; **$100 is the most that I can m.** no puedo dar más de 100 dólares
  2 *vi (cope)* arreglárselas; **to m. without sth/sb** arreglárselas sin algo/alguien; **he'll never m. on his own** no lo podrá hacer él solo

manageable [ˈmænɪdʒəbəl] *adj (object, hair)* manejable; *(level, proportions)* razonable; *(task)* realizable, factible

management [ˈmænɪdʒmənt] *n* (**a**) *(activity) (of company, project)* dirección *f*, gestión *f*; *(of economy, resources)* gestión *f*, administración *f*; **m. consultant** consultor(ora) *m,f* en administración de empresas; **m. studies** estudios *mpl* de gestión empresarial *or* administración de empresas; **m. style** estilo *m* de dirección (**b**) *(managers, employers)* **the m.** la dirección; **under new m.** *(sign)* nuevos propietarios; **m. and unions** la patronal y los sindicatos; **m. buyout** = adquisición de una empresa por sus directivos; **m. team** equipo *m* de dirección

manager [ˈmænɪdʒə(r)] *n (of bank, company)* director *m*; *(of store, bar)* encargado *m*; *(of boxer, singer)* representante *mf*, manager *mf*; *(of baseball, soccer team)* entrenador(ora) *m,f*

managerial [mænɪˈdʒɪərɪəl] *adj* de gestión, directivo(a); **m. skills** capacidad *f* de gestión; **m. staff** directivos *mpl*

managing [ˈmænɪdʒɪŋ] *n* **m. director** director(ora) *m,f* gerente; **m. editor** director(ora) *m,f*

Mandarin [ˈmændərɪn] *n (language)* mandarín *m*

mandarin [ˈmændərɪn] *n* (**a**) *(official)* mandarín *m* (**b**) *(fruit)* mandarina *f*

mandate [ˈmændeɪt] *n* mandato *m*; **to have a m. to do sth** tener autoridad para hacer algo; **to obtain/give a m.** obtener/conferir autoridad *or* permiso

mandatory [ˈmændətərɪ] *adj* obligatorio(a)

man-day [ˈmændeɪ] *n Econ* día-hombre *m*, día *m* de mano de obra

mandible [ˈmændɪbəl] *n* mandíbula *f*

mandolin [ˈmændəlɪn] *n* mandolina *f*

mane [meɪn] *n (of lion)* melena *f*; *(of horse)* crines *fpl*

man-eater [ˈmæniːtə(r)] *n* (**a**) *(animal)* devorador(ora) *m,f* de hombres (**b**) *Fam (woman)* devoradora *f* de hombres

man-eating [ˈmæniːtɪŋ] *adj* devorador(ora) de hombres

maneuver [məˈnuːvə(r)] **1** *n also Fig* maniobra *f*; *Fig* **there wasn't much room for m.** no había mucho margen de maniobra; *Mil* **to be on maneuvers** estar de maniobras
  2 *vt* **we maneuvered the piano up the stairs** subimos el piano con cuidado por la escalera; **he maneuvered the taxi into the space** maniobró para meter el taxi en el hueco
  3 *vi* maniobrar

maneuverable [məˈnuːvrəbəl] *adj* manejable

manful [ˈmænfʊl] *adj (courageous)* valiente

manfully [ˈmænfʊlɪ] *adv* con hombría

manganese [mæŋgəˈniːz] *n Chem* manganeso *m*

mange [meɪndʒ] *n (animal disease)* sarna *f*

manger [ˈmeɪndʒə(r)] *n* pesebre *m*

mangle [ˈmæŋgəl] **1** *n (for clothes)* escurridor *m* de rodillos *(para ropa)*
  2 *vt (body, text, truth)* mutilar

mango [ˈmæŋgəʊ] *(pl* **mangos** *or* **mangoes**) *n* mango *m*

mangrove [ˈmæŋgrəʊv] *n* mangle *m*; **m. swamp** manglar *m*

mangy [ˈmeɪndʒɪ] *adj (animal)* sarnoso(a); *(carpet, coat)* raído(a)

manhandle [ˈmænhændəl] *vt* **they manhandled him into the car** lo metieron en el coche *or Am* carro *or RP* auto a empujones; **they manhandled the piano down the**

stairs acarrearon a duras penas el piano escaleras abajo

manhole ['mænhəʊl] n (boca f de) alcantarilla f; **m. cover** tapa f de alcantarilla

manhood ['mænhʊd] n (**a**) (maturity) madurez f; **to reach m.** alcanzar la madurez (**b**) (masculinity) hombría f; **he proved his m.** demostró su hombría (**c**) (men collectively) American m. los hombres estadounidenses

man-hour ['mænaʊə(r)] n Econ hora-hombre f

manhunt ['mænhʌnt] n caza f del hombre

mania ['meɪnɪə] n (strong interest) pasión f (**for** por); **to have a m. for doing sth** tener pasión por hacer algo

maniac ['meɪnɪæk] n maniaco(a) m,f; **to drive like a m.** Esp conducir or Am manejar como un/una loco(a)

maniacal [mə'naɪəkəl] adj (crazy) maniaco(a); **m. laughter** risa desquiciada

manic ['mænɪk] adj (person) histérico(a); **m. depression** psicosis f inv maniacodepresiva

manic-depressive ['mænɪkdɪ'presɪv] n & adj Psy maniacodepresivo(a) m,f

manicure ['mænɪkjʊə(r)] 1 n manicura f
2 vt **to m. one's nails** hacerse la manicura

manicurist ['mænɪkjʊərɪst] n manicuro(a) m,f

manifest ['mænɪfest] 1 n (of ship, aircraft) manifiesto m
2 adj manifiesto(a), patente; Hist **M. Destiny** (of United States) Destino m Manifiesto
3 vt manifestar

manifestation [mænɪfes'teɪʃən] n manifestación f

manifestly ['mænɪfestlɪ] adv manifiestamente

manifesto [mænɪ'festəʊ] (pl **manifestos** or **manifestoes**) n Pol manifiesto m

manifold ['mænɪfəʊld] adj (numerous) múltiple

manikin = mannequin

Manila [mə'nɪlə] n Manila

mani(l)la envelope [mə'nɪlə'envələʊp] n sobre m marrón de papel manila

manipulate [mə'nɪpjʊleɪt] vt (controls, people, statistics) manipular

manipulation [mənɪpjʊ'leɪʃən] n (of controls, people, statistics) manipulación f

manipulative [mə'nɪpjʊlətɪv] adj Pej manipulador(ora)

mankind [mæn'kaɪnd] n la humanidad

manliness ['mænlɪnɪs] n hombría f, virilidad f

manly ['mænlɪ] adj viril

man-made ['mænmeɪd] adj (fabric, product) sintético(a), artificial; (lake, beach) artificial; **m. disaster** catástrofe f provocada por el hombre

mannequin, man(n)ikin ['mænɪkɪn] n (person) modelo mf, maniquí mf; (dummy) maniquí m

manner ['mænə(r)] n (**a**) (way, method, style) manera f, modo m; **in a m. of speaking** en cierto modo (**b**) (etiquette) (good) **manners** buenos modales mpl; **bad manners** malos modales; **it's bad manners to...** es de mala educación...; **he's got no manners** no tiene modales, es un maleducado (**c**) (type) **all m. of...** toda clase de...; **by no m. of means, not by any m. of means** en absoluto (**d**) (attitude, behavior) actitud f; **I don't like his m.** no me gusta su actitud; **she's got a very unpleasant m.** es muy arisca

mannered ['mænəd] adj afectado(a), amanerado(a)

mannerism ['mænərɪzəm] n tic m, peculiaridad f

mannikin = mannequin

manor ['mænə(r)] n (estate) señorío m; **m. (house)** casa f solariega

manpower ['mænpaʊə(r)] n mano f de obra

mansion ['mænʃən] n mansión f

manslaughter ['mænslɔːtə(r)] n Law homicidio m (involuntario)

mantelpiece ['mæntəlpiːs] n repisa f (de la chimenea)

mantis ['mæntɪs] n mantis f inv religiosa

mantle ['mæntəl] n (of lava, snow) manto m, capa f; (of gas lamp) camisa f, manguito m incandescente; (cloak) capa f; Fig **to take on the m. of office** asumir las responsabilidades del puesto

man-to-man [mæntʊ'mæn] adj & adv de hombre a hombre

mantra ['mæntrə] n mantra m; Fig estribillo m

manual ['mænjʊəl] 1 n (handbook) manual m
2 adj manual

manually ['mænjʊəlɪ] adv a mano, manualmente

manufacture [mænjʊ'fæktʃə(r)] 1 n (act) fabricación f, manufactura f; **manufactures** (products) productos mpl manufacturados
2 vt (cars, clothes) fabricar; Fig (excuse) inventarse; (evidence) sacarse de la manga; **to m. an opportunity to do sth** crear or generar la oportunidad para hacer algo

manufacturer [mænjʊ'fæktʃərə(r)] n Ind fabricante mf

manufacturing [mænjʊ'fæktʃərɪŋ] n Ind fabricación f; **m. capacity** capacidad f de fabricación; **m. industries** industrias fpl manufactureras or de transformación

manure [mə'njʊə(r)] 1 n estiércol m, abono m
2 vt abonar, estercolar

manuscript ['mænjʊskrɪpt] n manuscrito m

many ['menɪ] 1 adj (comparative **more**, superlative **most**) muchos(as); **m. people** mucha gente; **m. times** muchas veces; **there weren't m. houses** no había muchas casas, había pocas casas; **in m. ways** de muchas maneras; **not in so m. words** no exactamente; **so m.** tantos(as); **so m. people** tanta gente; **too m.** demasiados(as); **too m. people** demasiada gente; **how m. times?** ¿cuántas veces?; **I have as m. books as you** tengo tantos libros como tú; **m.'s the time I've done that** lo he hecho muchas veces; Prov **m. hands make light work** cuanta más gente, más llevadero es el trabajo
2 pron muchos(as); **m. of us** muchos de nosotros; **not (very) m.** no muchos(as); **how m.?** ¿cuántos(as)?; **as m. as you like** todos los que quieras; **too m.** demasiados(as); **one of the m. I have known** uno de los muchos que he conocido; Fam **to have had one too m.** llevar una copa de más, haber bebido or Am tomado más de la cuenta

many-colored ['menɪ'kʌləd] adj multicolor

Maori ['maʊrɪ] n & adj maorí mf

map [mæp] 1 n mapa m; Fig **this will put Stonybridge on the m.** esto dará a conocer a Stonybridge; **m. reference** coordenadas fpl
2 vt (pt & pp **mapped**) (region) trazar un mapa de
▸**map out** vt sep (route) indicar en un mapa; (plan, program) proyectar; **she had her career all mapped out** tenía su carrera profesional planeada paso por paso

maple ['meɪpəl] n (tree, wood) arce m; **m. leaf** hoja f de arce; **m. syrup** jarabe m de arce

Mar (abbr **March**) marzo m

mar [mɑː(r)] (pt & pp **marred**) vt deslucir, empañar

maracas [mə'rækəz] npl Mus maracas fpl

marathon ['mærəθən] n maratón m; **a m. speech** un discurso maratoniano; **m. runner** corredor(ora) m,f de maratón

marauder [mə'rɔːdə(r)] n merodeador(ora) m,f

marauding [mə'rɔːdɪŋ] adj (gangs, people) merodeador(ora); **m. animals** animales mpl en busca de su presa

marble ['mɑːbəl] n (**a**) (stone) mármol m (**b**) (glass ball) canica f; **to play marbles** jugar a las canicas; Fam Fig **to lose one's marbles** (go mad) volverse loco(a) or Esp majareta

marbled ['mɑːbəld] adj (paper) jaspeado(a)

March [mɑːtʃ] n marzo m; see also **May**

march [mɑːtʃ] 1 n (of soldiers, demonstrators) marcha f; Fig (of *time, events)* transcurso *m*; **on the m.** en marcha; **m. past** desfile *m*

2 *vt* hacer marchar; **he was marched off to prison** le llevaron (por la fuerza) a la cárcel

3 *vi (soldiers, demonstrators)* marchar; **to m. off** marcharse; **to m. by** *or* **past (sth/sb)** desfilar (ante algo/alguien)

marcher ['mɑːtʃə(r)] *n (demonstrator)* manifestante *mf*

marching orders ['mɑːtʃɪŋ'ɔːdəz] *npl Fam* **to give sb his m.** mandar a paseo a alguien, *Andes, RP* mandar a alguien a bañarse

Mardi Gras ['mɑːdɪgrɑː] *n* martes *m inv* de Carnaval

mare [meə(r)] *n* yegua *f*

margarine [mɑːdʒə'riːn] *n* margarina *f*

margin ['mɑːdʒɪn] *n (gen) & Com* margen *m*; **on the m.(s) of society** en la marginación; **to win by a narrow/an enormous m.** ganar por un estrecho/un amplio margen; **m. of error** margen de error

marginal ['mɑːdʒɪnəl] *adj* **(a)** *(improvement, increase)* marginal **(b)** *(note)* al margen, marginal

marginalize ['mɑːdʒɪnəlaɪz] *vt* marginar

marginally ['mɑːdʒɪnəlɪ] *adv* ligeramente

marigold ['mærɪgəʊld] *n* caléndula *f*

marijuana, marihuana [mærɪ'hwɑːnə] *n* marihuana *f*

marina [mə'riːnə] *n* puerto *m* deportivo

marinade [mærɪ'neɪd] *Culin* **1** *n* adobo *m*

2 *vt & vi* = **marinate**

marinate ['mærɪneɪt] *vt & vi Culin* adobar

marine [mə'riːn] **1** *n (soldier)* marine *mf*, infante *mf* de marina, *Am* fusilero *m* naval; *Fam* **(go) tell it to the marines!** ¡eso cuéntaselo a tu abuela!; **M. Corps** cuerpo *m* de marines, infantería *f* de marina

2 *adj (life, biology)* marino(a); **m. engineering** ingeniería *f* naval

mariner ['mærɪnə(r)] *n Literary* marinero *m*

marionette [mærɪə'net] *n* marioneta *f*

marital ['mærɪtəl] *adj* marital; **m. status** estado *m* civil

maritime ['mærɪtaɪm] *adj* marítimo(a)

marjoram ['mɑːdʒərəm] *n* mejorana *f*

mark¹ [mɑːk] *n Formerly (German currency)* marco *m* (alemán)

mark² **1** *n* **(a)** *(scratch, stain, symbol)* marca *f*

(b) *(sign, proof)* signo *m*, señal *f*; **as a m. of respect** en señal de respeto; **years of imprisonment had left their m. on him** había quedado marcado por años de reclusión; **to make one's m.** *(succeed)* dejar huella, hacerse famoso(a)

(c) *(target)* **his comments hit the m.** dio en el blanco con sus comentarios; **unemployment has passed the three million m.** el número de desempleados *or Am* desocupados ha rebasado la barrera de los tres millones; **her accusation was wide of the m.** su acusación estaba lejos de ser cierta; **he's not up to the m.** no está a la altura de las circunstancias; *Fam* **to be an easy m.** *(dupe)* ser presa fácil

(d) *Sch (score)* nota *f*, calificación *f*; *(point)* punto *m*; **to get good** *or* **high marks** sacar buenas notas

(e) *(in race)* **on your mark(s)! get set! go!** preparados, listos, ¡ya!; **to be quick/slow off the m.** *(in race)* salir rápidamente/lentamente; *Fig* reaccionar con rapidez/lentitud

(f) *(of machine)* **m. II/III** versión *f* II/III

2 *vt* **(a)** *(scratch, stain)* marcar **(b)** *(homework, exam)* corregir, calificar; **to m. sth right/wrong** dar/no dar algo por bueno(a); **it's marked out of ten** está puntuado(a) sobre diez **(c)** *(indicate)* marcar; **this decision marks a change in policy** esta decisión marca un cambio de política; **to m. time** *(musician)* marcar el compás; *Fig (wait)* hacer tiempo **(d)** *(characterize)* marcar, caracterizar; **his comments were marked by their sarcasm** sus comentarios se caracterizaban por el sarcasmo **(e)** *(pay attention to)* **m. my words** fíjate en lo que te digo

▸**mark down** *vt sep* **(a)** *(make note of)* anotar, apuntar; **they had him marked down as a troublemaker** lo tenían fichado como alborotador **(b)** *Com* rebajar

▸**mark off** *vt sep* **(a)** *(divide) (line, road)* delimitar **(b)** *(measure) (distance)* delimitar **(c)** *(check off)* poner una marca en

▸**mark out** *vt sep* **to m. sb out** distinguir a alguien

▸**mark up** *vt sep (price)* subir; *(goods)* subir de precio

markdown ['mɑːkdaʊn] *n (price reduction)* rebaja *f*, reducción *f* (de precio)

marked [mɑːkt] *adj* **(a)** *(difference)* marcado(a); *(improvement)* notable **(b)** **m. cards** cartas *fpl* marcadas; **to be a m. man** tener los días contados

markedly ['mɑːkɪdlɪ] *adv* notablemente, considerablemente

marker ['mɑːkə(r)] *n* **(a)** *(of essay, exam)* examinador(ora) *m,f*, corrector(ora) *m,f* de exámenes; **he's a hard m.** es muy severo al corregir **(b)** **m. (pen)** rotulador *m*, *Col* marcador *m*, *Méx* plumón *m* **(c)** *(indicator)* señal *f*

market ['mɑːkɪt] **1** *n* mercado *m*, *CSur* feria *f*, *CAm, Méx* tianguis *m*; **to put sth on the m.** sacar algo al mercado; *Fin* **m. analyst** analista *mf* de mercados; **m. day** día *m* de mercado; *Econ* **(free) m. economy** economía *f* de (libre) mercado; *Econ* **m. forces** fuerzas *fpl* del mercado; *Com* **m. leader** líder *mf* del mercado; *Fin* **m. maker** creador *m* de mercado; *Econ* **m. price** precio *m* de mercado; *Com* **m. research** estudio *m or* investigación *f* de mercado; *Com* **m. researcher** investigador(ora) *m,f* de mercado; *Com* **m. share** cuota *f* de mercado; **m. square** (plaza *f* del) mercado *m*; *Com* **m. survey** estudio *m* de mercados; **m. town** localidad *f* con mercado

2 *vt* comercializar

marketable ['mɑːkɪtəbəl] *adj* comercializable

marketing ['mɑːkɪtɪŋ] *n Com (study, theory)* marketing *m*, mercadotecnia *f*; *(promotion)* comercialización *f*; **m. campaign** campaña *f* de marketing *or* de publicidad; **m. department** departamento *m* de marketing; **m. manager** director(ora) *m,f* comercial, director(ora) *m,f* de marketing; **m. strategy** estrategia *f* de marketing

marketplace ['mɑːkɪtpleɪs] *n (gen) & Econ* mercado *m*

marking ['mɑːkɪŋ] *n* **(a)** **markings** *(on animal)* marcas *fpl*, manchas *fpl*; *(on plane)* distintivo *m*; **m. ink** tinta *f* indeleble **(b)** *(of essay, exam)* corrección *f*; **I've got a lot of m. to do** tengo que corregir muchos exámenes

marksman ['mɑːksmən] *n* tirador *m*

markup ['mɑːkʌp] *n (on price)* recargo *m*

marmalade ['mɑːməleɪd] *n* mermelada *f* (de naranja)

maroon¹ [mə'ruːn] *n* **(a)** *(color)* granate *m* **(b)** *(firework)* bengala *f* de auxilio *(en el mar)*

maroon² *vt (sailor)* abandonar; *Fig* **we were marooned by the floods** nos quedamos aislados *or* incomunicados por la inundación

marquee [mɑː'kiː] *n (of building)* marquesina *f*

marquis ['mɑːkwɪs] *n* marqués *m*

Marrakech [mærə'keʃ] *n* Marraquech

marriage ['mærɪdʒ] *n (wedding)* boda *f*, *Andes* matrimonio *m*, *RP* casamiento *m*; *(institution, period, relationship)* matrimonio *m*; *Fig (of ideas, organizations)* unión *f*; **m. of convenience** matrimonio *m* de conveniencia; **uncle by m.** tío *m* político; *Fig* **a m. of minds** una perfecta sintonía; **m. certificate** certificado *m or* partida *f* de matrimonio; **m. guidance counselor** consejero(a) *m,f* matrimonial; **m. vows** votos *mpl* matrimoniales

marriageable ['mærɪdʒəbəl] *adj* **a girl of m. age** una muchacha casadera

married ['mærɪd] *adj* casado(a); **to be m.** estar *or Am* ser casado(a); **to get m.** casarse; **a m. couple** un matrimonio; **m. life** vida *f* matrimonial; **m. name** apellido *m* de casada;

Mil **m. quarters** = residencia para oficiales casados y sus familias

marrow ['mærəʊ] *n (of bone)* médula *f*; **to be frozen to the m.** estar helado(a) hasta la médula *or* hasta los tuétanos

marrowbone ['mærəʊbəʊn] *n* hueso *m* de caña

marrowfat ['mærəʊfæt] *n* **m. (pea)** = tipo de guisante grande

marry ['mærɪ] **1** *vt* **(a)** *(get married to)* casarse con; *(of priest, parent)* casar; **will you m. me?** ¿te quieres casar conmigo?; *Fig* **he's married to his job** es esclavo de su trabajo **(b)** *(combine)* casar, combinar; **a style which marries the traditional and the modern** un estilo que combina lo tradicional con lo moderno
    2 *vi* casarse

▶**marry off** *vt sep* casar

Mars [mɑːz] *n (planet, god)* Marte *m*

Marseilles [mɑːˈseɪ] *n* Marsella

marsh [mɑːʃ] *n* pantano *m*, ciénaga *m*

marshal, marshall ['mɑːʃəl] **1** *n* **(a)** *(army officer)* mariscal *m* **(b)** *(police chief)* jefe(a) *m,f* de policía; *(fire chief)* jefe(a) *m,f* de bomberos; *(police officer)* policía *mf*; *(in Wild West)* alguacil *mf* **(c)** *(at race, demonstration)* miembro *m* del servicio de orden
    2 *vt (people, troops)* dirigir; *(arguments, thoughts)* poner en orden

marshland ['mɑːʃlænd] *n* ciénaga *f*, zona *f* pantanosa

marshmallow [mɑːʃˈmæləʊ] *n* **(a)** *(food)* = dulce de consistencia esponjosa **(b)** *(plant)* malvavisco *m*

marshy ['mɑːʃɪ] *adj* pantanoso(a)

marsupial [mɑːˈsuːpɪəl] *n & adj* marsupial *m*

martial ['mɑːʃəl] *adj* marcial; **m. arts** artes *fpl* marciales; **to declare m. law** declarar la ley marcial

Martian ['mɑːʃən] *n & adj* marciano(a) *m,f*

martyr ['mɑːtə(r)] **1** *n* mártir *mf*; *Fig* **to be a m. to rheumatism** estar martirizado(a) por el reúma; *Fig* **to make a m. of oneself** hacerse el/la mártir
    2 *vt* martirizar, hacer mártir

martyrdom ['mɑːtədəm] *n* martirio *m*

marvel ['mɑːvəl] **1** *n* maravilla *f*; **to work marvels** hacer maravillas; **if we survive this it'll be a m.** si salimos de ésta será un milagro; *Fam* **you're a m.!** ¡eres un genio!
    2 *vi* maravillarse **(at** de), asombrarse **(at** de)

marvelous ['mɑːvələs] *adj* maravilloso(a)

marvelously ['mɑːvələslɪ] *adv* maravillosamente

Marxism ['mɑːksɪzəm] *n* marxismo *m*

Marxist ['mɑːksɪst] *n & adj* marxista *mf*

marzipan ['mɑːzɪpæn] *n* mazapán *m*

mascara [mæsˈkɑːrə] *n* rímel *m*

mascot ['mæskət] *n* mascota *f*

masculine ['mæskjʊlɪn] **1** *n Gram* (género *m*) masculino *m*
    2 *adj* masculino(a)

masculinity [mæskjʊˈlɪnɪtɪ] *n* masculinidad *f*

mash [mæʃ] **1** *n (for pigs, poultry)* frangollo *m*
    2 *vt (squash, crush)* machacar; *(vegetables)* majar, hacer puré de

mashed potatoes [mæʃtpəˈteɪtəʊz] *npl* puré *m* de *Esp* patatas *or Am* papas

mask [mɑːsk] **1** *n* máscara *f*, careta *f*; *Fig* **his m. had slipped** se le había caído la máscara
    2 *vt (conceal)* enmascarar

masked [mɑːskt] *adj* enmascarado(a)

masking tape ['mɑːskɪŋteɪp] *n* cinta *f* adhesiva de pintor

masochism ['mæsəkɪzəm] *n* masoquismo *m*

masochist ['mæsəkɪst] *n* masoquista *mf*

masochistic [mæsəˈkɪstɪk] *adj* masoquista

mason ['meɪsən] *n* **(a)** *(builder)* cantero(a) *m,f*, picapedrero(a) *m,f* **(b)** *(freemason)* masón *m*

masonry ['meɪsənrɪ] *n (stonework)* albañilería *f*, obra *f*; **she was hit by a piece of falling m.** le cayó encima un cascote que se había desprendido del edificio

masquerade [mæskəˈreɪd] **1** *n* mascarada *f*
    2 *vi* **to m. as** hacerse pasar por

Mass *n Rel* misa *f*

mass [mæs] **1** *n* **(a)** *(large number)* sinnúmero *m*; *Fam* **I've got masses (of things) to do** tengo un montón de cosas que hacer; *Fam* **there's masses of room** hay muchísimo espacio; **m. grave** fosa *f* común; **m. hysteria** histeria *f* colectiva; **m. media** medios *mpl* de comunicación (de masas); **m. meeting** mítin *m* multitudinario; **m. murderer** asesino(a) *m,f* múltiple; **m. production** fabricación *f* en serie; **m. transit** transporte *m* colectivo *or* público; **m. unemployment** desempleo *m* generalizado *or* masivo, *Am* desocupación *f* generalizada *or* masiva
    (b) *(shapeless substance)* masa *f*
    (c) *Pol* **the masses** las masas
    (d) *Phys* masa *f*
    2 *vi (troops, people)* congregarse, concentrarse; *(clouds)* acumularse

massacre ['mæsəkə(r)] **1** *n* masacre *f*; *Fam Fig* **it was a m.** *(in sport, election)* fue una auténtica paliza
    2 *vt also Fig* masacrar; *Fam Fig* **they were massacred** *(in sport, election)* les dieron un palizón

massage ['mæsɑːʒ] **1** *n* masaje *m*
    2 *vt (body, scalp)* dar un masaje a, masajear

massed [mæst] *adj* **(a)** *(crowds, soldiers)* apelotonado(a) **(b)** *(collective)* **the m. weight of public opinion** el peso de la opinión pública en conjunto

masseur [mæˈsɜː(r)] *n* masajista *m*

masseuse [mæˈsɜːz] *n* masajista *f*

massive ['mæsɪv] *adj* enorme, inmenso(a); *(heart attack, stroke)* muy grave

mass-produce [mæsprəˈdjuːs] *vt Ind* fabricar en serie

mast [mɑːst] *n (of ship)* mástil *m*; *(of radio, TV transmitter)* torre *f*

mastectomy [mæsˈtektəmɪ] *n Med* mastectomía *f*

master ['mɑːstə(r)] **1** *n* **(a)** *(of servants)* señor *m*; *(of ship)* patrón *m*; **the m. of the house** el señor de la casa; **to be one's own m.** ser dueño(a) de sí mismo(a); **to be m. of the situation** ser dueño(a) de la situación; **m. of ceremonies** maestro *m* de ceremonias; **m. bedroom** dormitorio *m or Am* cuarto *m or CAm, Col, Méx* recámara *f* principal; **m. copy** original *m*; *Comptr* **m. file** archivo *m* maestro; **m. key** llave *f* maestra; **m. plan** plan *m* maestro; **m. race** raza *f* superior
    (b) *(skilled person)* maestro(a) *m,f*; *Univ* **M. of Arts/Science** *(degree)* máster *m* en humanidades/ciencias; *(person)* licenciado(a) *m,f* con máster en humanidades/ciencias; **m. carpenter/builder** maestro carpintero/albañil; *Mus* **m. class** clase *f* magistral; **m.'s (degree)** máster *m*; **she has a m.'s (degree) in economics** tiene un máster en *o* de Economía
    (c) *Old-fashioned (young boy)* **M. David Thomas** señorito David Thomas
    (d) *Art* **an old m.** *(painter, painting)* un clásico de la pintura antigua
    2 *vt (one's emotions, foreign language, violin)* dominar

masterful ['mɑːstəfʊl] *adj* autoritario(a)

masterly ['mɑːstəlɪ] *adj* magistral

mastermind ['mɑːstəmaɪnd] **1** *n* cerebro *m*
    2 *vt (project, plot)* dirigir

masterpiece ['mɑːstəpiːs] *n* obra *f* maestra

masterstroke ['mɑːstəstrəʊk] *n* golpe *m* maestro

mastery ['mɑːstərɪ] *n (of territory, subject matter)* dominio *m*

masthead ['mɑːsthed] *n* **(a)** *Naut* tope *m* **(b)** *Journ* cabecera *f*

mastiff ['mæstɪf] *n* mastín *m*

mastitis [mæsˈtaɪtɪs] *n Med* mastitis *f inv*

masturbate ['mæstəbeɪt] **1** *vt* masturbar
2 *vi* masturbarse

masturbation [mæstə'beɪʃən] *n* masturbación *f*

mat [mæt] **1** *n (on floor)* alfombrilla *f*; *(at door)* felpudo *m*; **(table) m.** salvamanteles *m inv*; **(drink) m.** posavasos *m inv*
2 *vi (pt & pp* **matted)** *(hair, fibers)* enredarse

match¹ [mætʃ] *n* fósforo *m, Esp* cerilla *f, Am* cerillo *m*

match² **1** *n* **(a)** *(in sport)* partido *m*; **m. point** *(in tennis)* punto *m* de partido **(b)** *(in design, ability)* **they're a good m.** *(clothes)* pegan, combinan bien; **to be no m. for sb** no ser rival para alguien; **he had met his m.** había encontrado la horma de su zapato **(c)** *(marriage)* **to make a good m.** casarse bien
2 *vt (equal in quality, performance)* igualar, llegar a la altura de; *(pair up)* emparejar; *(of colors, clothes)* pegar con, combinar con; *(of description, account)* coincidir con; **we can't m. their prices** no podemos igualar sus precios; **to m. sb against sb** enfrentar a alguien con alguien; **m. your skill against the experts** mide tu habilidad con los expertos; **to be well matched** *(teams, players)* estar muy igualados(as); **to be a well-matched couple** hacer buena pareja
3 *vi (colors, clothes)* pegar con, combinar con; *(descriptions, stories)* coincidir

▸**match up 1** *vt sep (colors, clothes)* pegar, combinar
2 *vi (clothes, colors)* pegar, combinar; *(explanations)* coincidir; **to m. up to sb's expectations** estar a la altura de las expectativas de alguien

matchbox ['mætʃbɒks] *n* caja *f* de fósforos *or Esp* cerillas *or Am* cerillos

matching ['mætʃɪŋ] *adj* a juego

matchless ['mætʃlɪs] *adj* sin par, sin igual

matchmaker ['mætʃmeɪkə(r)] *n (arranger of marriages)* casamentero(a) *m,f*

matchstick ['mætʃstɪk] *n Esp* cerilla *f, Am* cerillo *m*; **m. man** *or* **figure** monigote *m (dibujo hecho con palotes)*

mate¹ [meɪt] **1** *n* **(a)** *(male animal)* macho *m*; *(female animal)* hembra *f*; *(person)* pareja *f* **(b)** *(on ship)* oficial *m*; **(first) m.** primer oficial *m*
2 *vt (animals)* aparear
3 *vi (animals)* aparearse

mate² *(in chess)* **1** *n* jaque *m* mate
2 *vt* dar jaque mate a

material [mə'tɪərɪəl] **1** *n* **(a)** *(in general)* material *m*; **he isn't officer m.** no tiene madera de oficial **(b)** *(for book)* documentación *f*, material *m*; **reading m.** (material *m* de) lectura *f*, lecturas *fpl*; **she writes all her own m.** *(singer, musician)* ella sola compone toda su música **(c)** *(cloth)* tejido *m*, tela *f* **(d)** *(equipment)* **building materials** material *m* de construcción; **cleaning materials** productos *mpl* de limpieza; **writing materials** objetos *mpl* de papelería *or* escritorio
2 *adj* **(a)** *(physical)* material **(b)** *(important)* sustancial, relevante; **the point is m. to my argument** es un punto pertinente para mi razonamiento

materialism [mə'tɪərɪəlɪzəm] *n* materialismo *m*

materialistic [mətɪərɪə'lɪstɪk] *adj* materialista

materialize [mə'tɪərɪəlaɪz] *vi (hope, something promised)* materializarse; *(spirit)* aparecer

materially [mə'tɪərɪəlɪ] *adv* **(a)** *(in money, goods)* materialmente **(b)** *(appreciably)* sustancialmente

maternal [mə'tɜːnəl] *adj (feelings, instinct, love)* maternal; *(relative, genes)* materno(a)

maternity [mə'tɜːnɪtɪ] *n* maternidad *f*; **m. dress** vestido *m* premamá; **m. hospital** (hospital *m* de) maternidad *f*; **m. leave** baja *f* por maternidad; **m. ward** pabellón *m* de maternidad

math [mæθ] *n* matemáticas *fpl*

mathematical [mæθə'mætɪkəl] *adj* matemático(a)

mathematically [mæθə'mætɪklɪ] *adv* matemáticamente

mathematician [mæθəmə'tɪʃən] *n* matemático(a) *m,f*

mathematics [mæθə'mætɪks] *n (subject)* matemáticas *fpl*; **the m. of the problem is quite complex** el problema entraña una complicada aritmética

matinee, matinée ['mætɪneɪ] *n (of play)* función *f* de tarde; *(of movie)* sesión *f* de tarde, primera sesión *f*; **m. idol** galán *m*

mating ['meɪtɪŋ] *n* apareamiento *m*; **m. call** llamada *f* nupcial; **m. season** época *f* de celo *or* apareamiento

matriarch ['meɪtrɪɑːk] *n* matriarca *f*

matriarchal [meɪtrɪ'ɑːkəl] *adj* matriarcal

matriarchy ['meɪtrɪɑːkɪ] *n* matriarcado *m*

matriculate [mə'trɪkjʊleɪt] *vi (enroll)* matricularse

matriculation [mətrɪkjʊ'leɪʃən] *n (enrollment)* matrícula *f*

matrimonial [mætrɪ'məʊnɪəl] *adj* matrimonial

matrimony ['mætrɪmənɪ] *n* matrimonio *m*

matrix ['meɪtrɪks] *(pl* **matrices** ['meɪtrɪsiːz]*,* **matrixes** ['meɪtrɪksɪz]*) n* matriz *f*

matron ['meɪtrən] *n* **(a)** *(in school)* = mujer a cargo de la enfermería; *(in hospital)* enfermera *f* jefe **(b)** *(older woman)* matrona *f* **(c)** *(in prison)* directora *f*, alcaidesa *f*

matt [mæt] *adj (color, finish)* mate

matted ['mætɪd] *adj (hair)* enredado(a), apelmazado(a)

matter ['mætə(r)] **1** *n* **(a)** *(substance)* materia *f*
(b) *(affair, issue)* asunto *m*, cuestión *f*; **that's a m. of opinion/taste** es cuestión de opinión/gustos; **it's no easy m.** no es asunto fácil; **that's quite another m.** eso es otra cuestión; **within a m. of hours** en cuestión de horas; **he doesn't like it and nor do I for that m.** a él no le gusta y a mí de hecho tampoco; **as a m. of course** automáticamente; **as a m. of fact** de hecho, en realidad; **as matters stand** tal como están las cosas; **to make matters worse...** para colmo de males...; **military/business matters** cuestiones *fpl* militares/de negocios
(c) *(problem)* **what's the m.?** ¿qué pasa?; **what's the m. with you?** ¿qué (es lo que) te pasa?; **there's something the m.** hay algo que no va bien
(d) *(with no)* **no m.!** ¡no importa!; **no m. who/where** quien/donde sea; **no m. how hard I push...** por muy fuerte que empuje...; **no m. who I ask...** pregunte a quien pregunte...; **no m. where I look for it...** por mucho que lo busque...; **no m. what I do...** haga lo que haga...
2 *vi* importar **(to** a); **it doesn't m.** no importa; **nothing else matters** lo demás no importa; **it doesn't m. to me/her** no me/le importa

matter-of-fact ['mætərə'fækt] *adj (tone, voice)* pragmático(a); **he was very m. about it** se lo tomó como si tal cosa

matting ['mætɪŋ] *n* estera *f*

mattress ['mætrɪs] *n* colchón *m*

mature [mə'tjʊə(r)] **1** *adj (person)* maduro(a); *(wine)* de crianza; *(cheese)* curado(a)
2 *vt* madurar; *(wine)* criar
3 *vi (person)* madurar; *(wine)* envejecer, criarse; *Fin (investment)* vencer

maturity [mə'tjʊərɪtɪ] *n* madurez *f*; *Fin* vencimiento *m*

maudlin ['mɔːdlɪn] *adj* llorón(ona), lacrimoso(a); **to be m.** estar llorón(ona) *or* lacrimoso(a)

maul [mɔːl] *vt* **he was mauled by a tiger** fue gravemente herido por un tigre; *Fig* **the book was mauled by the critics** los críticos destrozaron el libro

Maundy ['mɔːndɪ] *n* **M. Thursday** Jueves Santo

Mauritania [mɒrɪ'teɪnɪə] *n* Mauritania

Mauritanian [mɒrɪ'teɪnɪən] *n & adj* mauritano(a) *m,f*

Mauritian [mə'rɪʃən] *n & adj* mauriciano(a) *m,f*

Mauritius [mə'rɪʃəs] *n (isla)* Mauricio

mausoleum [mɔːsə'liːəm] *(pl* **mausoleums** *or* **mausolea** [mɔːsə'liːə]*) n* mausoleo *m*

mauve [məʊv] *n & adj* malva *m*

maverick ['mævərɪk] *n & adj* inconformista *mf*, disidente *mf*

mawkish ['mɔːkɪʃ] *adj Pej* empalagoso(a)

max [mæks] **1** *n* (*abbr* **maximum**) máx., máximo *m*
  2 *vt Fam* **to m. an exam** sacar un sobresaliente
►**max out** *Fam* **1** *vt* **to m. out one's credit card** llegar al límite de la tarjeta de crédito
  2 to m. out on chocolate/booze pasarse con el chocolate/la bebida

maxim ['mæksɪm] *n* máxima *f*

maxima *pl of* **maximum**

maximal ['mæksɪməl] *adj* máximo(a)

maximize ['mæksɪmaɪz] *vt* elevar al máximo, maximizar

maximum ['mæksɪməm] **1** *n* (*pl* **maxima** ['mæksɪmə]) máximo *m*; **to the m.** al máximo; **at the m.** como máximo
  2 *adj* máximo(a); **m. security prison** cárcel *f* de máxima seguridad; **m. speed** velocidad *f* máxima

May [meɪ] *n* mayo *m*; **in M.** en mayo; **at the beginning/end of M.** a principios/finales de mayo; **during M.** en mayo; **each** *or* **every M.** todos los meses *or* cada mes de mayo; **in the middle of M.** a mediados de mayo; **last/next M.** el mayo pasado/próximo; **(on) the first/sixteenth of M.** el uno/dieciséis de mayo; **she was born on the 22nd of M. 1953** nació el 22 de mayo de 1953; **M. Day** el Primero *or* Uno de Mayo

may [meɪ] *v aux* (*3rd person singular* **may**, *pt* **might** [maɪt])

En las expresiones del apartado **(a)**, puede utilizarse **might** sin que se altere apenas el significado.

(a) *(expressing possibility)* **he m. return at any moment** puede volver de un momento a otro; **I m. tell you and I m. not** puede que te lo diga o puede que no; **he m. have lost it** puede que lo haya perdido; **it m. be that...** podría ser que...; **you m. well ask!** ¡eso quisiera saber yo!; **we m. as well go** ya puestos, podíamos ir; **shall we go? — we m. as well** ¿vamos? – bueno *or Esp* vale *or Arg* dale *or Méx* órale
  (b) *Formal (asking for or giving permission)* **m. I come in?** ¿se puede?, ¿puedo pasar?; **if I m. say so** si me permite hacer una observación; **m. I?** *(when borrowing sth)* ¡con permiso!, ¿me permite?
  (c) *(expressing wishes, fears, purpose)* **m. she rest in peace** que en paz descanse; **m. the best man win!** ¡que gane el mejor!; **I fear you m. be right** me temo que tengas razón; **they work long hours so their children m. have a better future** trabajan mucho para que sus hijos tengan un futuro mejor
  (d) *(conceding a fact)* **he m. be very rich, but I still don't like him** tendrá mucho dinero, pero sigue sin caerme bien; **be that as it m., that's as m. be** en cualquier caso

Maya ['maɪə], **Mayan** ['maɪən] *n & adj* maya *mf*

maybe ['meɪbiː] *adv* quizá(s), tal vez; **m. she won't accept** quizá no acepte

Mayday ['meɪdeɪ] *n Av & Naut (distress signal)* SOS *m*, señal *f* de socorro; **M.!** ¡SOS!

mayhem ['meɪhem] *n* alboroto *m*

mayonnaise [meɪə'neɪz] *n* mayonesa *f*

mayor ['meə(r)] *n* alcalde *m*

mayoress ['meərɪs] *n* alcaldesa *f*

maypole ['meɪpəʊl] *n* mayo *m* (*poste*)

maze [meɪz] *n also Fig* laberinto *m*

MBA [embiː'eɪ] *n Univ* (*abbr* **Master of Business Administration**) máster *m* en administración de empresas

MBO [embiː'əʊ] (*pl* **MBOs**) *n Com* **(a)** (*abbr* **management buyout**) = adquisición de una empresa por sus directivos **(b)** (*abbr* **management by objectives**) dirección *f* por objetivos

MC [em'siː] *n* (*abbr* **Master of Ceremonies**) maestro *m* de ceremonias

MD [em'diː] *n Med* (*abbr* **Doctor of Medicine**) doctor(ora) *m,f* en medicina

ME [em'iː] *Med* (*abbr* **myalgic encephalomyelitis**) encefalomielitis *f inv* miálgica

me [*unstressed* mɪ, *stressed* miː] *pron* **(a)** *(object)* me; **she hates me** me odia; **she forgave my brother but not ME** perdonó a mi hermano, pero no a mí; **she gave me the book** me dio el libro **(b)** *(after preposition)* mí; **with me** conmigo **(c)** *(as complement of verb to be)* yo; **it's me!** ¡soy yo! **(d)** *(in interjections)* **who, me?** ¿quién, yo?; **silly me!** ¡qué bobo soy!

meadow ['medəʊ] *n* prado *m*, pradera *f*

meager ['miːgə(r)] *adj* exiguo(a), escaso(a)

meal¹ [miːl] *n* comida *f*; **midday m.** comida *f*, almuerzo *m*; **evening m.** cena *f*; **m. ticket** *(voucher)* vale *m* de comida; *Fam Fig (person)* hermanita *f* de la caridad

meal² *n (flour)* harina *f*

mealtime ['miːltaɪm] *n* hora *f* de comer

mealy ['miːlɪ] *adj* harinoso(a)

mealy-mouthed [miːlɪ'maʊðd] *adj Pej* evasivo(a); **to be m.** andarse con rodeos

mean¹ [miːn] **1** *n (average)* media *f*
  2 *adj (average)* medio(a)

mean² *adj* **(a)** *(miserly)* tacaño(a) **(b)** *(nasty)* malo(a), mezquino(a); **she has a m. streak** a veces tiene muy mala uva; **that was a m. thing to do/say** hacer/decir eso estuvo muy mal *or Esp* fatal *or Am* pésimo; **a m. trick** una jugarreta **(c)** *(poor)* **she's no m. photographer** es muy buena fotógrafa; **it was no m. feat** fue una gran proeza **(d)** *Fam (good)* genial, *Esp* guay, *Am salvo RP* chévere, *Méx* padre, *RP* macanudo(a); **he plays a m. game of pool** juega al billar de vicio

mean³ (*pt & pp* **meant** [ment]) *vt* **(a)** *(signify) (of word, event)* significar; *(of person)* querer decir; **what does the word "tacky" m.?** ¿qué significa *or* qué quiere decir la palabra "tacky"?; **this is Tim, I m. Tom** éste es Tim, digo Tom; **what do you m.?** ¿qué quieres decir?; **it doesn't m. anything** no quiere decir *o* significa nada
  (b) *(speak sincerely)* hablar en serio; **I m. it** lo digo en serio; **you don't m. it!** ¡no lo dirás en serio!
  (c) *(be of importance)* significar (**to** para); **the price means nothing to him** el precio no le preocupa; **it means a lot to me** significa mucho para mí
  (d) *(imply, involve)* significar, suponer; **it would m. having to give up smoking** significaría tener que dejar de fumar
  (e) *(intend)* **to m. to do sth** tener (la) intención de hacer algo; **she means well** lo hace con buena intención; **I m. him no harm** no pretendo hacerle ningún daño; **I m. to succeed** me he propuesto triunfar; **you were meant to ring me first** se suponía que primero me tenías que telefonear; **it's meant to be a good movie** (se supone que) tiene que ser una buena película; **she meant for you to have this ring** quería que esta sortija fuera para ti; **it was meant as a joke/a compliment** pretendía ser una broma/un cumplido; **the bomb was meant for you** la bomba iba destinada a ti; **this portrait is meant to be of the duke** este cuadro pretende ser un retrato del duque; **we were meant for each other** estábamos hechos el uno para el otro

meander [mɪ'ændə(r)] **1** *n* meandro *m*
  2 *vi (river, road)* serpentear; *(person)* vagar, callejear

meaning ['miːnɪŋ] *n* significado *m*, sentido *m*; **to understand sb's m.** entender lo que alguien quiere decir; *Fam* **if you get my m.** sabes por dónde voy ¿no?; **what's the m. of this?** *(expressing indignation)* ¿qué significa esto?; **the m. of life** el sentido de la vida

meaningful ['miːnɪŋfʊl] *adj* significativo(a); **to be m.** tener sentido; **it no longer seemed m. to her** ya no parecía tener sentido para ella

meaningfully ['miːnɪŋfʊlɪ] *adv* **"they left together," she said m.** "se marcharon juntos", dijo intencionadamente

meaningless ['miːnɪŋlɪs] *adj* sin sentido; **to be m.** no tener sentido

meanness ['miːnnɪs] *n* (**a**) *(miserliness)* tacañería *f* (**b**) *(nastiness)* maldad *f*

means [miːnz] **1** *n (method)* medio *m*; **by m. of...** mediante..., por medio de...; **there is no m. of escape** no hay forma de escapar; **by some m. or other** de un modo u otro; **a m. to an end** un medio para conseguir un (determinado) fin; **to use every possible m. to do sth** utilizar cualquier medio para hacer algo; **by all m.** por supuesto; **by no m.** de ningún modo, en absoluto; **m. of production** medios *mpl* de producción; **m. of transportation** medio *m* de transporte
   2 *npl (income, wealth)* medios *mpl*; **a man of m.** un hombre acaudalado *or* de posibles; **I live beyond/within my m.** vivo por encima de/de acuerdo con mis posibilidades; **m. test** *(for benefits)* estimación *f* de ingresos *(para la concesión de un subsidio)*

mean-spirited ['miːn'spɪrɪtɪd] *adj* malintencionado(a)

meant [ment] *pt & pp of* **mean**

meantime ['miːntaɪm], **meanwhile** ['miːnwaɪl] **1** *n* **in the m.** mientras tanto
   2 *adv* mientras tanto

measles ['miːzəlz] *n* sarampión *m*

measly ['miːzlɪ] *adj Fam* ridículo(a), irrisorio(a)

measurable ['meʒərəbəl] *adj* apreciable

measure ['meʒə(r)] **1** *n* (**a**) *(measurement, quantity)* medida *f*; *(means of estimating)* indicador *m*, índice *m*; **this was a m. of how serious the situation was** esto era una muestra *or* un indicador de la gravedad de la situación; **a m. of...** cierto grado de...; **there was a m. of bravado in his words** había cierta fanfarronería en sus palabras; **to get the m. of sb** tomar la medida a alguien; **for good m.** por añadidura; **for good m., he called me a liar** no contento con ello, me llamó *or Am* dijo mentiroso
   (**b**) *(degree)* **in some m.** en cierta medida, hasta cierto punto; **beyond m.** increíblemente; **she has tried my patience beyond m.** ya ha acabado con mi paciencia
   (**c**) *(action, step)* medida *f*; **to take measures** tomar medidas
   (**d**) *Mus* compás *m*
   2 *vt & vi* medir

▸**measure up** *vi* dar la talla (**to** para)

measured ['meʒəd] *adj (movement, step)* medido(a), pausado(a); *(tone, response)* mesurado(a), *Esp* comedido(a)

measurement ['meʒəmənt] *n (quantity, length)* medida *f*

measuring ['meʒərɪŋ] *n* **m. cup** recipiente *m* graduado; **m. spoon** cuchara *f* dosificadora; **m. tape** cinta *f* métrica

meat [miːt] *n* (**a**) *(food)* carne *f*; *Fig* **it was m. and drink to them** era algo que les entusiasmaba; **m. loaf** = pastel de carne picada horneado en un molde (**b**) *Fig (substantial content)* miga *f*

meatball ['miːtbɔːl] *n* albóndiga *f*

meat-eater ['miːtiːtə(r)] *n (animal)* carnívoro(a) *m,f*

meat-eating ['miːtiːtɪŋ] *adj* carnívoro(a)

meaty ['miːtɪ] *adj (taste)* a carne; *(fleshy)* carnoso(a); *Fig (book, movie)* con mucha miga, sustancioso(a)

Mecca ['mekə] *n* La Meca; *Fig* meca *f*

mechanic [mɪ'kænɪk] *n* mecánico(a) *m,f*

mechanical [mɪ'kænɪkəl] *adj also Fig* mecánico(a); **m. engineer** ingeniero(a) *m,f* industrial; **m. engineering** ingeniería *f* industrial; **m. pencil** portaminas *m inv*

mechanically [mɪ'kænɪklɪ] *adv* (**a**) *(by machine)* mecánicamente (**b**) *(unthinkingly)* mecánicamente

mechanics [mɪ'kænɪks] **1** *n* (**a**) *(science)* mecánica *f* (**b**) *(working parts)* mecanismo *m*, mecánica *f*
   2 *npl Fig* **the m. of the electoral system** la mecánica del sistema electoral

mechanism ['mekənɪzəm] *n* mecanismo *m*

mechanize ['mekənaɪz] *vt* mecanizar

mechanized ['mekənaɪzd] *adj* **m. industry** industria *f* mecanizada; **m. troops** tropas *fpl* mecanizadas

MEd [em'ed] *n Univ (abbr* **Master of Education**) *(title)* máster *m* en Pedagogía

medal ['medəl] *n* medalla *f*

medalist ['medəlɪst] *n* medallista *mf*, ganador(ora) *m,f* de medalla; **gold/silver m.** medalla *mf* de oro/plata

medallion [mɪ'dæljən] *n* medallón *m*

meddle ['medəl] *vi* entrometerse (**in** en)

meddler ['medlə(r)] *n* entrometido(a) *m,f*

meddlesome ['medəlsəm] *adj* entrometido(a)

media ['miːdɪə] *n* (**a**) *(TV, press)* medios *mpl* de comunicación; **m. coverage** cobertura *f* informativa; **m. studies** ciencias *fpl* de la información (**b**) *pl of* **medium**

mediaeval = **medieval**

median ['miːdɪən] *Math* **1** *n* (**a**) *Math* mediana *f* (**b**) *Aut* **m. (strip)** mediana *f, Col, Méx* camellón *m*
   2 *adj* mediano(a)

mediate ['miːdɪeɪt] *vi* mediar (**in/between** en/entre)

mediation [miːdɪ'eɪʃən] *n* mediación *f*

mediator ['miːdɪeɪtə(r)] *n* mediador(ora) *m,f*

medic ['medɪk] *n (student)* estudiante *mf* de medicina; *(doctor)* médico(a) *m,f*

Medicaid ['medɪkeɪd] *n* = seguro médico estatal para personas con renta baja

medical ['medɪkəl] **1** *n (physical examination)* reconocimiento *m or* examen *m* médico; **to pass/fail a m.** pasar/no pasar un reconocimiento médico
   2 *adj (record, treatment, profession)* médico(a); *(book, student)* de medicina; **m. advice** consejo *m* médico; **m. examination** examen *m* médico, reconocimiento *m* médico; **m. insurance** seguro *m* médico *or* de enfermedad; **m. practitioner** facultativo(a) *m,f*, médico(a) *m,f*

medically ['medɪklɪ] *adv* **to be m. qualified** tener titulación médica

Medicare ['medɪkeə(r)] *n* = seguro médico para ancianos y algunos discapacitados

medicated ['medɪkeɪtɪd] *adj* medicinal

medication [medɪ'keɪʃən] *n* medicamento *m*, medicina *f*; **to be on m.** tomar medicación

medicinal [me'dɪsɪnəl] *adj* medicinal

medicine ['medɪsɪn] *n* (**a**) *(science)* medicina *f*; **to practice m.** ejercer la medicina; **to study m.** estudiar medicina (**b**) *(drugs)* medicina *f*, medicamento *m*; *Fig* **to give sb a taste of his own m.** pagar a alguien con su misma moneda; **m. chest** *or* **cabinet** (armario *m* del) botiquín *m*; **m. man** *(traditional healer)* hechicero *m* (de la tribu), chamán *m*

medieval, mediaeval [medɪ'iːvəl] *adj* medieval

mediocre [miːdɪ'əʊkə(r)] *adj* mediocre

mediocrity [miːdɪ'ɒkrɪtɪ] *n* mediocridad *f*

meditate ['medɪteɪt] *vi (spiritually)* meditar; *(reflect)* reflexionar, meditar (**on** sobre)

meditation [medɪ'teɪʃən] *n (spiritual)* meditación *f*; *(reflection)* reflexión *f*

meditative ['medɪtətɪv] *adj (person, mood)* meditativo(a), meditabundo(a); *(movie, piece of music)* reflexivo(a)

Mediterranean [medɪtə'reɪnɪən] **1** *n* **the M.** el Mediterráneo
   2 *adj* mediterráneo(a); **the M. Sea** el (mar) Mediterráneo

medium ['miːdɪəm] **1** *n* (**a**) *(pl* **media** ['miːdɪə] *or* **mediums**) *(means of expression, communication)* medio *m*; **through the**

m. of the press a través de la prensa; *Art* **mixed media** técnica *f* mixta (**b**) *(in spiritualism)* médium *mf*

2 *adj* medio(a); **of m. height** de estatura mediana; **in the m. term** a medio plazo; **m. dry** *(wine)* semiseco(a); *Culin* **m. rare** poco hecho(a)

medium-range ['mi:dıəm'reındʃ] *adj (missile)* de medio alcance; *(forecast)* a medio plazo

medium-term ['mi:dıəm'tɜ:m] *adj* a medio plazo

medley ['medlı] *n (mixture)* mezcla *f*; *Mus* popurrí *m*

meek [mi:k] *adj* manso(a), dócil; **to be m. and mild** ser manso(a) como un corderito

meekly ['mi:klı] *adv* dócilmente

meet [mi:t] (*pt & pp* **met** [met]) **1** *n (sports event)* encuentro *m*; *(in track and field)* reunión *f* atlética

2 *vt* (**a**) *(encounter) (by accident)* encontrarse con; *(by arrangement)* encontrarse con, reunirse con; **to m. sb in the street** encontrarse con alguien en la calle; **to arrange to m. sb** quedar con alguien; **to go to m. sb** ir a encontrarse con alguien; **to m. sb at the station** ir a buscar a alguien a la estación; **his eyes met mine** nuestras miradas se encontraron; **a remarkable sight met our eyes** nos topamos con una vista extraordinaria; **there's more to this than meets the eye** es más complicado de lo que parece

(**b**) *(become acquainted with)* conocer; **m. Mr. Jones** le presento al señor Jones; **have you met my husband?** ¿conoces a mi marido?

(**c**) *(join with)* unirse con, juntarse con; **where East meets West** donde se encuentran el Oriente y el Occidente

(**d**) *(satisfy) (demand, need, condition)* satisfacer; *(objection, criticism)* responder a; *(cost, expense)* cubrir; *(order)* servir, cumplir; **to m. a deadline** cumplir (con) un plazo

(**e**) *(encounter) (danger, difficulties)* encontrar, encontrarse; **to m. one's death** encontrar la muerte

3 *vi* (**a**) *(by accident)* encontrarse; *(by arrangement)* quedar, encontrarse; **where shall we m.?** ¿dónde quedamos?; **our eyes met** nuestras miradas se encontraron (**b**) *(become acquainted)* conocerse (**c**) *(society, assembly)* reunirse; **the club meets every Tuesday** el club se reúne todos los martes (**d**) *(rivers, continents)* encontrarse, unirse

▶**meet up** *vi* encontrarse, quedar (**with** con)

▶**meet with** *vt insep (danger, difficulty)* encontrarse con; *(success)* tener; *(accident)* sufrir; **to m. with failure** resultar un fracaso; **to m. with refusal** ser recibido(a) con rechazo

meeting ['mi:tıŋ] *n* (**a**) *(encounter) (by chance)* encuentro *m*; *(prearranged)* cita *f*; **m. place** lugar *m* or punto *m* de encuentro (**b**) *(of committee, delegates)* reunión *f*; **she's in a m.** está en una reunión; **to hold a m.** celebrar una reunión

megabucks ['megəbʌks] *npl Fam* una millonada, *Esp* un pastón, *Méx* un chingo de dinero, *RP* una ponchada de pesos

megabyte ['megəbaıt] *n Comptr* megabyte *m*, mega *m*

megahertz ['megəhɜ:ts] *n Elec* megahercio *m*

megalomania [megələʊ'meınıə] *n* megalomanía *f*

megalomaniac [megələʊ'meınıæk] *n* megalómano(a) *m,f*

megaphone ['megəfəʊn] *n* megáfono *m*

megastar ['megəstɑ:(r)] *n Fam* superestrella *f*

megastore ['megəstɔ:(r)] *n* macrotienda *f*

megaton ['megətʌn] *n* megatón *m*

megawatt ['megəwɒt] *n Elec* megavatio *m*

melancholic [melən'kɒlık] *adj* melancólico(a)

melancholy ['melənkəlı] **1** *n* melancolía *f*

2 *adj* melancólico(a)

melanin ['melənın] *n Physiol* melanina *f*

melanoma [melə'nəʊmə] *n Med* melanoma *m*

melee ['meleı] *n (excited crowd)* turba *f*, enjambre *m*; *(fight)* riña *f*, tumulto *m*

mellifluous [me'lıfluəs] *adj* melifluo(a)

mellow ['meləʊ] **1** *adj (flavor)* delicado(a); *(wine)* añejo(a);

(voice, color) suave; *(person)* apacible, sosegado(a)

2 *vi (flavor)* ganar (con el tiempo); *(wine)* añejarse; *(voice, light)* suavizarse; *(person)* serenarse, sosegarse

melodic [mı'lɒdık] *adj* melódico(a)

melodious [mı'ləʊdıəs] *adj* melodioso(a)

melodrama ['melədrɑ:mə] *n* melodrama *m*

melodramatic [melədrə'mætık] *adj* melodramático(a)

melodramatically [melədrə'mætıklı] *adv* melodramáticamente

melody ['melədı] *n* melodía *f*

melon ['melən] *n (honeydew)* melón *m*; *(watermelon)* sandía *f*

melt [melt] **1** *vt* derretir, fundir; *Fig (sb's resistance)* vencer

2 *vi* derretirse, fundirse; **it melts in the mouth** se funde en la boca; **to m. into thin air** esfumarse

▶**melt away** *vi (snow)* derretirse; *(crowd)* dispersarse, disgregarse; *(objections, opposition)* disiparse, desvanecerse

▶**melt down** *vt sep (metal)* fundir

meltdown ['meltdaʊn] *n Phys (process)* = fusión accidental del núcleo de un reactor; *(leak)* fuga *f* radiactiva

melting ['meltıŋ] *n* **m. point** punto *m* de fusión; *Fig* **m. pot** crisol *m*

member ['membə(r)] **1** *n* (**a**) *(of family, group)* miembro *m*; *(of club)* socio(a) *m,f*; *(of union, party)* afiliado(a) *m,f*, militante *mf*; *Pol* **m. of Congress** congresista *mf*, miembro *m* del congreso (**b**) *(limb, penis)* miembro *m*

2 *adj* **m. country/state** país *m*/estado *m* miembro

membership ['membəʃıp] *n* (**a**) *(state of being a member) (of club)* calidad *f* de socio; *(of party, union)* afiliación *f*; **to renew one's m.** *(of club)* renovar el carné de socio; *(of party, union)* renovar la afiliación; **m. card** carné *m* de socio/afiliado; **m. fee** cuota *f* de socio/afiliado (**b**) *(members) (of club)* socios *mpl*; *(of union, party)* afiliación *f*, afiliados(as) *mfpl*; **a large/small m.** un elevado/escaso número de socios/afiliados

membrane ['membreın] *n* membrana *f*

memento [mı'mentəʊ] (*pl* **mementos** *or* **mementoes**) *n* recuerdo *m*

memo ['meməʊ] (*pl* **memos**) *n* memorándum *m*; *(within office)* nota *f*; **m. pad** bloc *m* de notas

memoir ['memwɑ:(r)] *n (biography)* biografía *f*; *(essay)* memoria *f*; **she's writing her memoirs** está escribiendo sus memorias

memorable ['memərəbəl] *adj* memorable

memorably ['memərəblı] *adv* **as Dante so m. said** como dicen las memorables palabras de Dante

memorandum [memə'rændəm] (*pl* **memorandums** *or* **memoranda** [memə'rændə]) *n* memorándum *m*; *(within office)* nota *f*

memorial [mı'mɔ:rıəl] **1** *n (monument)* monumento *m* conmemorativo

2 *adj* conmemorativo(a); **M. Day** = día de los caídos en la guerra

memorize ['meməraız] *vt* memorizar

memory ['memərı] *n* (**a**) *(faculty) & Comptr* memoria *f*; **to have a good/bad m.** tener buena/mala memoria; **if my m. serves me right** si la memoria no me engaña; **from m.** de memoria; **to commit sth to m.** memorizar algo; **there has been famine here within living m.** aquí todavía se recuerdan épocas de hambre; **m. loss** pérdida *f* de memoria

(**b**) *(thing remembered)* recuerdo *m*; **good/bad memories (of sth)** buenos/malos recuerdos (de algo); **my earliest memories** mis primeros recuerdos; **to have no m. of sth** no recordar algo; **in m. of…** en memoria de…; **to take a trip down m. lane** volver al pasado

men [men] *pl of* **man**

menace ['menıs] **1** *n (threat)* amenaza *f*; *(danger)* peligro *m*; *Fam* **that kid's a m.** este niño es un demonio

2 *vt* amenazar

menacing ['menəsɪŋ] *adj* amenazador(ora)

menagerie [mɪ'nædʒərɪ] *n* colección *f* de animales *(privada)*

mend [mend] **1** *n Fam* **she's on the m.** se está recuperando

2 *vt (repair)* arreglar; *(garment)* coser, remendar; **to m. one's ways** corregirse

3 *vi (broken bone)* soldarse

mendacity [men'dæsɪtɪ] *n Formal* falsedad *f*, mendacidad *f*

menfolk ['menfəʊk] *npl* **the m.** los hombres

menial ['miːnɪəl] **1** *n Pej* lacayo(a) *m,f*

2 *adj* ingrato(a), penoso(a)

meningitis [menɪn'dʒaɪtɪs] *n* meningitis *f inv*

meniscus [mə'nɪskəs] *n Phys & Anat* menisco *m*

menopausal [menə'pɔːzəl] *adj Med or Fam* menopáusico(a)

menopause ['menəpɔːz] *n* menopausia *f*

menstrual ['menstrʊəl] *adj* menstrual; **m. cycle** ciclo *m* menstrual

menstruate ['menstrʊeɪt] *vi* tener la menstruación, menstruar

menstruation [menstrʊ'eɪʃən] *n* menstruación *f*

menswear ['menzweə(r)] *n* ropa *f* de caballero *or* hombre; **m. department** departamento *m or* sección *f* de caballeros

mental ['mentəl] *adj (state, age)* mental; **to make a m. note of sth/to do sth** tratar de acordarse de algo/de hacer algo; **to have a m. block about sth** tener un bloqueo mental con algo; **m. arithmetic** cálculo *m* mental; **to have a m. breakdown** sufrir un ataque de enajenación mental; **m. health** salud *f* mental; **m. hospital** hospital *m* psiquiátrico; **m. illness** enfermedad *f* mental

mentality [men'tælɪtɪ] *n* mentalidad *f*

mentally ['mentəlɪ] *adv* mentalmente; **to be m. handicapped** tener una minusvalía psíquica; **to be m. ill** tener una enfermedad mental

menthol ['menθɒl] *n* mentol *m*; **m. cigarettes** cigarrillos *mpl* mentolados

mention ['menʃən] **1** *n* mención *f*; **to make m. of sth** hacer mención de algo

2 *vt* mencionar; **to m. sb in one's will** mencionar *or* incluir a alguien en el testamento; **not to m....** por no mencionar...; **now that you m. it** ahora que lo dices; **don't m. it!** ¡no hay de qué!

mentor ['mentɔː(r)] *n* mentor(ora) *m,f*

menu ['menjuː] *n* **(a)** *(list of dishes) (at restaurant)* carta *f*, menú *m*; *(for a particular meal)* menú *m* **(b)** *Comptr* menú *m*; **m. bar** barra *f* de menús

meow, miaow [mɪ'aʊ] **1** *n* maullido *m*; **m.!** ¡miau!

2 *vi* maullar

mercantile ['mɜːkəntaɪl] *adj* mercantil

mercenary ['mɜːsɪnərɪ] *n & adj* mercenario(a) *m,f*

merchandise, merchandize ['mɜːtʃəndaɪz] **1** *n* mercancías *fpl*, géneros *mpl*

2 *vt* comercializar

merchandising, merchandizing ['mɜːtʃəndaɪzɪŋ] *n Com* artículos *mpl* de promoción *or* promocionales

merchant ['mɜːtʃənt] *n* comerciante *mf*; **m. bank** banco *m* mercantil *or* de negocios; **m. marine** marina *f* mercante; **m. seaman** marino *m* mercante; **m. ship** buque *m or* barco *m* mercante

merchantman ['mɜːtʃəntmən] *n (ship)* buque *m or* barco *m* mercante

merciful ['mɜːsɪfʊl] *adj* compasivo(a), clemente

mercifully ['mɜːsɪfʊlɪ] *adv (showing mercy)* con compasión; *(fortunately)* afortunadamente

merciless ['mɜːsɪlɪs] *adj* despiadado(a)

mercurial [mɜː'kjʊərɪəl] *adj* voluble, veleidoso(a)

Mercurochrome® [mɜː'kjʊərəkrəʊm] *n* mercurocromo *m*

Mercury ['mɜːkjʊrɪ] *n (planet, god)* Mercurio *m*

mercury ['mɜːkjʊrɪ] *n Chem* mercurio *m*

mercy ['mɜːsɪ] *n* compasión *f*, clemencia *f*; **to have m. on sb** tener compasión *or* apiadarse de alguien; **to beg for m.** suplicar clemencia; **to be at the m. of** estar a merced de; **we should be thankful for small mercies** habría que dar gracias de que las cosas no vayan aún peor; **m. killing** eutanasia *f*

mere [mɪə(r)] *adj* simple, mero(a); **a m. 10 percent of the candidates passed the test** tan sólo un 10 por ciento de los aspirantes superaron la prueba; **the m. mention/presence of...** la sola *or* mera mención/presencia de...; **there was the merest hint of irony in his voice** en su voz había un matiz casi imperceptible de ironía

merely ['mɪəlɪ] *adv* meramente, simplemente

merge [mɜːdʒ] **1** *vt (in general)* fundir; *(companies, organizations)* fusionar; *Comptr (files)* fusionar, unir

2 *vi (in general)* fundirse **(into/with** con); *(companies, banks)* fusionarse; **to m. into the background** perderse de vista

merger ['mɜːdʒə(r)] *n Com* fusión *f*

meridian [mə'rɪdɪən] *n Geog & Astron* meridiano *m*

meringue [mə'ræŋ] *n Culin* merengue *m*

merit ['merɪt] **1** *n (advantage, worth)* mérito *m*; **the merits of peace** las ventajas de la paz; **to judge sth on its merits** juzgar algo por sus méritos; **in order of m.** según los méritos; **m. system** = sistema de contratación y ascenso por méritos

2 *vt* merecer, *Am* ameritar; **we hardly m. a mention in the report** apenas nos mencionan en el informe *or Am* reporte

meritocracy [merɪ'tɒkrəsɪ] *n* meritocracia *f*

meritorious [merɪ'tɔːrɪəs] *adj Formal* meritorio(a)

mermaid ['mɜːmeɪd] *n* sirena *f*

merrily ['merɪlɪ] *adv* alegremente

merriment ['merɪmənt] *n* alegría *f*, regocijo *m*

merry ['merɪ] *adj* **(a)** *(happy)* alegre; **to make merry** festejar; **M. Christmas!** ¡Feliz Navidad!; **the more the merrier** cuantos más, mejor **(b)** *(slightly drunk)* alegre, *Esp* piripi

merry-go-round ['merɪɡəʊraʊnd] *n* tiovivo *m*, carrusel *m*, *RP* calesita *f*

mesh [meʃ] **1** *n (of net, sieve)* malla *f*, red *f*

2 *vi* **(a)** *(gears)* engranarse **(b)** *(proposals)* estar de acuerdo; *(ideas, characters)* encajar

mesmerize ['mezməraɪz] *vt* cautivar

mess [mes] *n* **(a)** *(disorder)* lío *m*, desorden *m*; **the kitchen's a m.** la cocina está toda revuelta; **you look a m.!** ¡estás hecho un desastre!; **to be in a m.** *(room)* estar todo(a) revuelto(a); *Fig (person)* estar en un lío *or* aprieto; *Fig* **to make a m. of sth** *(bungle)* hacer algo desastrosamente **(b)** *(dirt)* porquería *f* **(c)** *Mil* comedor *m*; **m. tin** plato *m* de campaña *or* del rancho

▸mess around, mess about *Fam* **1** *vt sep (treat badly)* traer a maltraer

2 *vi* **(a)** *(fool around, waste time)* hacer el tonto **(b)** *(tinker)* **to m. around** *or* **about with sth** enredar con algo

▸mess up *vt sep Fam (room)* desordenar; *(hair)* revolver; *(plan)* estropear

message ['mesɪdʒ] *n* mensaje *m*; **to leave a m. for sb** dejar un recado *or Am* mensaje a *or* para alguien; *Fam* **to get the m.** enterarse

messaging ['mesədʒɪŋ] *(by cell phone)* mensajería

messenger ['mesɪndʒə(r)] *n* mensajero(a) *m,f*; **m. boy** chico *m* de los recados

Messiah [mɪ'saɪə] *n Rel* Mesías *m inv*

messianic [mesɪ'ænɪk] *adj* mesiánico(a)

messily ['mesɪlɪ] *adv* **to eat m.** ponerse perdido(a) comiendo; *Fig* **to end m.** *(relationship)* terminar mal

Messrs. ['mesəz] *npl (abbr Messieurs)* Sres., señores *mpl*

mess-up ['mesʌp] *n Fam* lío *m*, desastre *m*

messy ['mesɪ] *adj* **(a)** *(dirty)* sucio(a); **to be m.** *(place)* estar sucio(a); *(person)* ser sucio(a) **(b)** *(untidy) (room)* desordenado(a); *(hair)* revuelto(a); *(appearance)* desastroso(a); *(handwriting)* malo(a); *(person)* desaliñado(a) **(c)** *(unpleasantly complex)* lioso(a)

met [met] *pt & pp of* **meet**

metabolic [metəˈbɒlɪk] *adj* metabólico(a)

metabolism [mɪˈtæbəlɪzəm] *n* metabolismo *m*

metabolize [meˈtæbəlaɪz] *vt* metabolizar

metal [ˈmetəl] **1** *n* metal *m*; **m. detector** detector *m* de metales; **m. polish** abrillantador *m* de metales
2 *adj* metálico(a)

metaled [ˈmetəld] *adj (road)* de grava

metallic [mɪˈtælɪk] *adj (sound, voice, taste)* metálico(a); *(paint)* metalizado(a)

metallurgy [meˈtælədʒɪ] *n* metalurgia *f*

metalwork [ˈmetəlwɜːk] *n (craft)* trabajo *m* del metal, metalistería *f*; *(articles)* objetos *mpl* de metal

metamorphosis [metəˈmɔːfəsɪs] *(pl* **metamorphoses** [metəˈmɔːfəsiːz])* *n* metamorfosis *f inv*

metaphor [ˈmetəfə(r)] *n* metáfora *f*

metaphoric(al) [metəˈfɒrɪk(əl)] *adj* metafórico(a)

metaphorically [metəˈfɒrɪklɪ] *adv* metafóricamente

metaphysical [metəˈfɪzɪkəl] *adj* metafísico(a)

metaphysics [metəˈfɪzɪks] *n (subject)* metafísica *f*

▶**mete out** [miːt] *vt sep (punishment)* imponer; *(justice)* aplicar **(to** a)

meteor [ˈmiːtɪə(r)] *n* meteoro *m*, bólido *m*

meteoric [miːtɪˈɒrɪk] *adj* meteórico(a); *Fig* **a m. rise** un ascenso meteórico

meteorite [ˈmiːtɪəraɪt] *n* meteorito *m*

meteorological [miːtɪərəˈlɒdʒɪkəl] *adj* meteorológico(a)

meteorology [miːtɪəˈrɒlədʒɪ] *n* meteorología *f*

meter [ˈmiːtə(r)] *n* **(a)** *(device)* contador *m*; **(gas/electricity) m.** contador (del gas/de la electricidad); **(parking) m.** parquímetro *m*; **m. reading** lectura *f* del contador **(b)** *(measurement)* metro *m* **(c)** *(of poetry)* metro *m*

methadone [ˈmeθədəʊn] *n* metadona *f*

methane [ˈmiːθeɪn] *n Chem* metano *m*

methanol [ˈmeθənɒl] *n* metanol *m*

methinks [miːˈθɪŋks] *adv Archaic or Hum* me parece a mí

method [ˈmeθəd] *n* método *m*; **there's m. in his madness** no está tan loco como parece; *Theat & Cin* **m. acting** interpretación *f* según el método de Stanislavski

methodical [mɪˈθɒdɪkəl] *adj* metódico(a)

Methodism [ˈmeθədɪzəm] *n Rel* metodismo *m*

Methodist [ˈmeθədɪst] *n Rel* metodista *mf*

methodological [meθədəˈlɒdʒɪkəl] *adj* metodológico(a)

methodology [meθəˈdɒlədʒɪ] *n* metodología *f*

methyl [ˈmeθɪl] *n* metilo *m*; **m. alcohol** alcohol *m* metílico

meticulous [mɪˈtɪkjʊləs] *adj* meticuloso(a)

meticulousness [mɪˈtɪkjʊləsnɪs] *n* meticulosidad *f*

metric [ˈmetrɪk] *adj (system)* métrico(a)

metrical [ˈmetrɪkəl] *adj (in poetry)* métrico(a)

metronome [ˈmetrənəʊm] *n Mus* metrónomo *m*

metropolis [mɪˈtrɒpəlɪs] *n* metrópolis *f inv*

metropolitan [metrəˈpɒlɪtən] *adj* metropolitano(a); **the M. Opera** la Ópera Metropolitana (de Nueva York)

mettle [ˈmetəl] *n (courage)* valor *m*, ánimo *m*; **you'll have to be on your m.** tendrás que dar el do de pecho; **she showed her m.** demostró de lo que era capaz

mew [mjuː] **1** *n* maullido *m*
2 *vi* maullar

Mexican [ˈmeksɪkən] **1** *n* mejicano(a) *m,f*, mexicano(a) *m,f*
2 *adj* mejicano(a), mexicano(a); **M. wave** *(in stadium)* ola *f* (mejicana)

Mexico [ˈmeksɪkəʊ] *n* Méjico, México; **M. City** Ciudad de Méjico *or* México

mezzanine [ˈmetsəniːn] *n* **m. (floor)** entreplanta *f*

mezzo-soprano [metsəʊsəˈprɑːnəʊ] *(pl* **mezzo-sopranos)** *n Mus (singer)* mezo-soprano *f*; *(voice)* mezzo-soprano *m*

mg [emˈdʒiː] *n (abbr* **milligram(s))** mg, miligramo *m*

Mgr *Rel (abbr* **monsignor)** Mons., monseñor *m*

MHz *Elec (abbr* **megahertz)** Mhz, megahercio *m*

mi [miː] *n Mus* mi *m*

miaow = **meow**

mica [ˈmaɪkə] *n* mica *f*

mice [maɪs] *pl of* **mouse**

Mickey Mouse [ˈmɪkɪˈmaʊs] *adj Fam Pej (job, qualification)* de tres al cuarto

micro [ˈmaɪkrəʊ] *(pl* **micros)** *n Comptr Esp* microordenador *m, Am* microcomputadora *f*

microbe [ˈmaɪkrəʊb] *n* microbio *m*

microbiology [maɪkrəʊbaɪˈɒlədʒɪ] *n* microbiología *f*

microchip [ˈmaɪkrəʊtʃɪp] *n Comptr* microchip *m*

microcomputer [ˈmaɪkrəʊkəmˌpjuːtə(r)] *n Comptr Esp* microordenador *m, Am* microcomputadora *f*

microcomputing [ˈmaɪkrəʊkəmˌpjuːtɪŋ] *n Comptr* microinformática *f*

microcosm [ˈmaɪkrəʊkɒzəm] *n* microcosmos *m inv*

microelectronics [ˈmaɪkrəʊɪlekˈtrɒnɪks] *n* microelectrónica *f*

microfiche [ˈmaɪkrəʊfiːʃ] *n* microficha *f*

microfilm [ˈmaɪkrəʊfɪlm] **1** *n* microfilm *m*
2 *vt* microfilmar

micrometer [maɪˈkrɒmɪtə(r)] *n* micrómetro *m*

microorganism [ˈmaɪkrəʊˈɔːgənɪzəm] *n* microorganismo *m*

microphone [ˈmaɪkrəfəʊn] *n* micrófono *m*

microprocessor [ˈmaɪkrəʊˈprəʊsesə(r)] *n Comptr* microprocesador *m*

microscope [ˈmaɪkrəskəʊp] *n* microscopio *m*

microscopic [maɪkrəˈskɒpɪk] *adj* microscópico(a)

microscopically [maɪkrəˈskɒpɪklɪ] *adv (to examine)* microscópicamente; **m. small** microscópicamente *or* infinitamente pequeño(a)

microsurgery [maɪkrəʊˈsɜːdʒərɪ] *n* microcirugía *f*

microwave [ˈmaɪkrəʊweɪv] **1** *n Phys* microonda *f*; **m. (oven)** microondas *m inv*
2 *vt* cocinar en el microondas

microwaveable [ˈmaɪkrəʊˈweɪvəbəl] *adj* **it's m.** se puede cocinar en el microondas

mid- [mɪd] *adj* **in m.-ocean** en medio del océano; **in m.-June** a mediados de junio; **she stopped in m.-sentence** se detuvo a mitad de la frase

midair [mɪdˈeə(r)] **1** *n Fig* **to leave sth in m.** dejar algo en el aire
2 *adj (collision, explosion)* en pleno vuelo

mid-Atlantic [ˈmɪdətˈlæntɪk] *adj (accent)* = a medio camino entre el inglés británico y el americano

midday [ˈmɪdˈdeɪ] *n* mediodía *m*; **at m.** a mediodía; **m. meal** comida *f*, almuerzo *m*

middle [ˈmɪdəl] **1** *n* **(a)** *(in general)* medio *m*; **in the m. of the room** en medio de la habitación; **to be in the m. of doing sth** estar ocupado(a) haciendo algo; **he was in the m. of an important conversation** estaba en mitad de una importante conversación; **in the m. of the month** a mediados de mes; **in the m. of the night** en plena noche, en mitad de la noche; *Fig* **to split sth down the m.** dividir algo por la mitad, *RP* partir algo a la mitad; **in the m. of nowhere** en un lugar dejado de la mano de Dios **(b)** *(waist)* cintura *f*
2 *adj (in the middle)* del medio; **m. age** edad *f* madura,

madurez *f*; *Hist* **the M. Ages** la Edad Media; *Pol* **M. America** los estadounidenses tradicionalistas y conservadores; *Mus* **m. C** do *m* central; **the m. class(es)** la clase media; *Fig* **to steer a m. course** *(in politics, diplomacy)* tomar la vía intermedia; **in the m. distance** a media distancia; *Anat* **the m. ear** el oído medio; **the M. East** Oriente *m* Medio; **M. Eastern** de Oriente Medio; **m. finger** (dedo *m*) corazón *m or* mayor *m*; *Pol* **the m. ground** el centro; **m. management** mandos *mpl* intermedios; **m. name** segundo nombre *m*; *Fam* **"generosity" isn't exactly his m. name!** no destaca precisamente por su generosidad; **the M. West** el Medio Oeste *m* (de Estados Unidos)

middle-aged [mɪdəl'eɪdʒd] *adj* de mediana edad

middlebrow ['mɪdəlbrəʊ] *adj (tastes, interests)* del público medio; **a m. novelist** un(a) novelista para el público medio

middle-class [mɪdəl'klɑːs] *adj* de clase media

middleman ['mɪdəlmæn] *n* intermediario *m*

middle-of-the-road ['mɪdləvðə'rəʊd] *adj (policy)* moderado(a); *(music)* convencional

middle-sized ['mɪdəl'saɪzd] *adj* mediano(a)

middleweight ['mɪdəlweɪt] *n (in boxing)* peso *m* medio

middling ['mɪdlɪŋ] *adj* regular

midfield [mɪd'fiːld] *n (in football, soccer)* media *f*, centro *m* del campo; **m. player** *(in soccer)* centrocampista *mf*

midfielder [mɪd'fiːldə(r)] *n (in soccer)* centrocampista *mf*

midge [mɪdʒ] *n* mosquito *m*

midget ['mɪdʒɪt] **1** *n (small person)* enano(a) *m,f*
  2 *adj* en miniatura

Midlands ['mɪdləndz] *npl* **the M.** = la región central de Inglaterra

midlife crisis ['mɪdlaɪf'kraɪsɪs] *n* crisis *f inv* de los cuarenta

midmorning [mɪd'mɔːnɪŋ] *n* media mañana *f*

midnight ['mɪdnaɪt] *n* medianoche *f*; **to burn the m. oil** quedarse hasta muy tarde *(estudiando o trabajando)*

midpoint ['mɪdpɔɪnt] *n* ecuador *m*

midrange ['mɪd'reɪndʒ] *adj Com (computer, car)* de gama media

midriff ['mɪdrɪf] *n* diafragma *m*

midshipman ['mɪdʃɪpmən] *n* guardia *m* marina, guardiamarina *m*

midst [mɪdst] *n* **in the m. of** en medio de; **in our/their m.** entre nosotros/ellos

midstream [mɪd'striːm] *n* **in m.** por el centro del río; *Fig (when speaking)* en mitad del discurso; **to interrupt sb in m.** interrumpir a alguien en plena conversación

midsummer ['mɪdsʌmə(r)] *n* pleno verano *m*; **M. Day** el 24 de junio, San Juan

midterm ['mɪd'tɜːm] *n* **(a)** *Pol* **m. elections** = elecciones a mitad del mandato presidencial **(b)** *Sch & Univ* de mitad de trimestre; **m. exams** exámenes a mitad de semestre

midtown ['mɪdtaʊn] *adj* **a m. apartment** un apartamento *or Esp* piso no muy lejos del centro

midway ['mɪdweɪ] **1** *adj* medio(a)
  2 *adv (in space)* a mitad de camino, a medio camino; *(in time)* hacia la mitad

midweek [mɪd'wiːk] *adv* a mediados de semana; **m. show/flight** representación *f*/vuelo *m* de mitad de semana

Mid-West ['mɪd'west] *n* Medio Oeste *m* (de Estados Unidos)

Mid-Western [mɪd'westən] *adj* del Medio Oeste (de Estados Unidos)

midwife ['mɪdwaɪf] *n* comadrona *f*

midwifery [mɪd'wɪfərɪ] *n* obstetricia *f*

midwinter ['mɪd'wɪntə(r)] *n* pleno invierno *m*

might¹ [maɪt] *n (strength)* fuerza *f*, poder *m*; **with all his m.** *(to work, push)* con todas sus fuerzas; *Prov* **m. is right** quien tiene la fuerza tiene la razón

might² *v aux*

En el inglés hablado, y en el escrito en estilo coloquial, la forma negativa **might not** se transforma en **mightn't**. La forma **might have** se transforma en **might've**. Cuando expresa posibilidad (ver (**a**)), puede utilizarse **may** sin que se altere apenas el significado.

(a) *(expressing possibility)* **it m. be difficult** puede que sea *or* puede ser difícil; **I m. go if I feel like it** puede que vaya si tengo ganas; **it m. be better to ask permission first** sería mejor pedir permiso primero; **you m. want to…** tal vez podrías…; **shall we go? — we m. as well** ¿nos vamos? — bueno, bien *or Esp* vale *or Arg* dale *or Méx* órale; **I wonder what I m. have done to offend him** me pregunto qué le habré hecho para que se ofenda; **I m. as well be talking to myself!** ¡es como si hablara con la pared!

(b) *(as past form of* **may***)* **I knew he m. be angry** ya sabía que se podía *esp Esp* enfadar *or esp Am* enojar; **I was afraid she m. have killed him** tenía miedo de que (ella) lo hubiera matado; **he said he m. be late** dijo que quizá se retrasaría

(c) *Formal (asking for permission)* **m. I have a word with you?** ¿podría hablar un momento con usted?

(d) *(with concessions)* **it m. not be the fastest car in the world, but…** no será el coche más rápido del mundo, pero…

mightily ['maɪtɪlɪ] *adv* **(a)** *(powerfully)* con fuerza **(b)** *Fam* cantidad de, muy; **to be m. relieved** quedarse aliviadísimo(a)

mightn't ['maɪtənt] = **might not**

might've ['maɪtəv] = **might have**

mighty [maɪtɪ] **1** *adj* **(a)** *(powerful)* fuerte, poderoso(a) **(b)** *(large, imposing)* grandioso(a)
  2 *adv Fam* un montón, *Esp* cantidad

migraine ['miːgreɪn] *n* migraña *f*

migrant ['maɪgrənt] **1** *n (person)* emigrante *m,f*, migrante *mf*; *(bird)* ave *f* migratoria
  2 *adj* migratorio(a); **m. worker** trabajador(ora) *m,f* inmigrante

migrate [maɪ'greɪt] *vi* migrar, emigrar

migration [maɪ'greɪʃən] *n* migración *f*, emigración *f*

migratory ['maɪgrətrɪ] *adj* migratorio(a)

mike [maɪk] *n Fam (microphone)* micro *m*, micrófono *m*

Milan [mɪ'læn] *n* Milán

mild [maɪld] *adj (person, remark)* apacible, afable; *(food)* suave; *(punishment, illness, criticism)* leve; *(climate)* benigno(a), suave; *(displeasure, amusement)* ligero(a)

mildew ['mɪldjuː] *n* moho *m*; *(on plants)* añublo *m*

mildly ['maɪldlɪ] *adv* **(a)** *(to say)* con suavidad **(b)** *(moderately)* ligeramente; **to put it m.** por no decir algo peor

mildness ['maɪldnɪs] *n (of person)* afabilidad *f*; *(of weather)* suavidad *f*; *(of criticism)* comedimiento *m*; *(of punishment)* levedad *f*

mile [maɪl] *n (distance)* milla *f* (= 1,6 km); **miles per hour** millas por hora; **he lives miles away** vive a kilómetros de distancia; *Fam Fig* **to be miles away** *(be daydreaming)* estar en Babia; *Fam* **miles better** muchísimo mejor; *Fam* **it stands out a m.** se ve a la legua

mileage ['maɪlɪdʒ] *n* **(a)** *(distance traveled)* ≃ kilómetros *mpl* (recorridos); **m. allowance** ≃ (dieta *f* de) kilometraje *m* **(b)** *(rate of fuel consumption)* consumo *m* (de millas por galón de gasolina); *Fig* **to get a lot of m. out of sth** sacarle mucho partido a algo

milepost ['maɪlpəʊst] *n* mojón *m*

milestone ['maɪlstəʊn] *n (on road)* mojón *m*; *Fig (in career, history)* hito *m*

milieu ['miːljɜː] *n* entorno *m*, medio *m*

militancy ['mɪlɪtənsɪ] *n* militancia *f*

militant ['mɪlɪtənt] **1** *n* militante *mf*, activista *mf*
  2 *adj* militante

militarism ['mɪlɪtərɪzəm] n militarismo m

militaristic [mɪlɪtə'rɪstɪk] adj militarista

military ['mɪlɪtərɪ] **1** n **the m.** el ejército
2 adj militar; **m. academy** academia f militar; **m. man** militar m; **m. police** policía f militar; **m. service** servicio m militar

militate ['mɪlɪteɪt] vi (fact, reason) obrar (**against** en contra de)

militia [mɪ'lɪʃə] n milicia f

militiaman [mɪ'lɪʃəmən] n miliciano m

milk [mɪlk] **1** n leche f; **the m. of human kindness** el don de la amabilidad; **m. of magnesia** magnesia f; **m. bottle** botella f de leche; **m. chocolate** chocolate m con leche; **m. churn** lechera f; **m. jug** jarra f de leche; **m. powder** polvo m de leche; **m. route** = ruta de reparto de leche; **m. shake** batido m, Am licuado m; **m. tooth** diente m de leche
2 vt (cow) ordeñar; Fam Fig **to m. sb dry** (exploit) exprimir a alguien hasta la última gota; Fig **they milked the story for all it was worth** le sacaron todo el jugo posible a la noticia

milking ['mɪlkɪŋ] n ordeño m; **m. machine** ordeñadora f

milkman ['mɪlkmən] n lechero m

milky ['mɪlkɪ] adj (containing too much milk) con demasiada leche; (containing a lot of milk) con mucha leche; (color) lechoso(a); **the M. Way** la Vía Láctea

mill [mɪl] **1** n (a) (grinder) molinillo m; (for flour) molino m; Fam **to put sb through the m.** hacérselas pasar negras or Esp moradas a alguien (b) (textile factory) fábrica f or Am planta f de tejidos
2 vt (grain) moler; (metal) fresar

▶**mill around, mill about** vi (crowd) pulular

millenarian [mɪlə'neərɪən] n & adj milenario(a) m,f

millennial [mɪ'lenɪəl] adj del milenio

millennium [mɪ'lenɪəm] (pl **milleniums** or **millennia** [mɪ'lenɪə]) n milenio m

miller ['mɪlə(r)] n molinero(a) m,f

millet ['mɪlɪt] n mijo m

milligram ['mɪlɪgræm] n miligramo m

milliliter ['mɪlɪliːtə(r)] n mililitro m

millimeter ['mɪlɪmiːtə(r)] n milímetro m

milliner ['mɪlɪnə(r)] n sombrerero(a) m,f

million ['mɪljən] n millón m; **two m. men** dos millones de hombres; Fam **I've told him a m. times** se lo he dicho millones de veces; Fam **thanks a m.!** ¡un millón de gracias!; Fam **she's one in a m.** es única

millionaire [mɪljə'neə(r)] n millonario(a) m,f

millionairess [mɪljə'neərɪs] n millonaria f

millionth ['mɪljənθ] **1** n (a) (fraction) millonésimo m (b) (in series) millonésimo(a) m,f
2 adj millonésimo(a)

millipede ['mɪlɪpiːd] n milpiés m inv

millpond ['mɪlpɒnd] n **as calm as a m.** (water) como una balsa de aceite, totalmente en calma

millstone ['mɪlstəʊn] n muela f, rueda f de molino; Fig **it's a m. around my neck** es una cruz que llevo encima

mime [maɪm] **1** n (performance) mimo m, pantomima f; **m. artist** mimo m
2 vt representar con gestos
3 vi hacer mimo

mimic ['mɪmɪk] **1** n imitador(ora) m,f
2 vt (pt & pp **mimicked**) imitar

mimicry ['mɪmɪkrɪ] n imitación f

min (a) (abbr **minute(s)**) min., minuto m (b) (abbr **minimum**) mín., mínimo m (c) Mus (abbr **Minor**) menor

minaret [mɪnə'ret] n alminar m, minarete m

mince [mɪns] **1** vt (chop up) picar; Fig **she doesn't m. her words** no tiene pelos en la lengua
2 vi (walk) caminar con afectación

mincemeat ['mɪnsmiːt] n (meat) carne f Esp, RP picada or Am molida; (fruit) = relleno a base de fruta escarchada, frutos secos, especias, zumo de limón y grasa animal; Fam Fig **to make m. of sb** hacer trizas or Esp picadillo or RP bolsa a alguien

mincer ['mɪnsə(r)] n picadora f (de carne)

mincing ['mɪnsɪŋ] adj (walk, voice) afectado(a)

mind [maɪnd] **1** n (a) (thoughts) mente f; **to see sth in one's m.'s eye** hacerse una imagen mental de algo; **to bear** or **keep sth in m.** tener algo en cuenta; **it went completely** or **clean out of my m.** se me fue por completo de la cabeza; **to have sth on one's m.** tener algo en la cabeza; **to put** or **set sb's m. at rest** tranquilizar a alguien; **to take sb's m. off sth** quitarle or Am sacarle a alguien algo de la cabeza, hacer que alguien olvide algo; **I couldn't get it off my m.** no podía quitármelo de la cabeza; **it puts me in m. of...** me recuerda...
(b) (opinion) **to my m.** en mi opinión; **to speak one's m.** hablar sin rodeos; **to change one's m. (about sth)** cambiar de opinión (acerca de algo); Fam **I gave him a piece of my m.** le canté las cuarenta; **to be of one m., to be of the same m.** ser de la misma opinión; **to keep an open m. (about sth)** no formarse ideas preconcebidas (respecto a algo)
(c) (will, wants) **she knows her own m.** sabe bien lo que quiere; **to have a m. of one's own** ser capaz de pensar or decidir por sí mismo(a); **to make up one's m.** decidirse; **to be in two minds (about sth)** estar indeciso(a) (acerca de algo); **I've a good m. to do it** me estoy planteando seriamente or tengo en mente hacerlo; **I've half a m. to tell his parents** me entran ganas de decírselo a sus padres; **this computer has a m. of its own** este Esp ordenador or Am computadora hace lo que le da la gana; **to have sth/sb in m.** estar pensando en algo/alguien
(d) (attention) **to keep one's m. on sth** mantenerse concentrado(a) en algo; **your m. is not on the job** no estás concentrado en el trabajo; **I'm sure if you put your m. to it you could do it** estoy seguro de que podrías hacerlo si pusieses tus cinco sentidos (en ello)
(e) (way of thinking) **to have the m. of a three-year-old** tener la mentalidad de un niño de tres años; **you've got a dirty/nasty m.!** ¡qué ideas más cochinas/desagradables tienes!
(f) (reason) **to be out of one's m.** (mad) haber perdido el juicio; **to be bored out of one's m.** estar más aburrido(a) que una ostra; **to be worried out of one's m.** estar muerto(a) de preocupación; **no one in his right m....** nadie en su sano juicio...; **his m. is going** se le va la cabeza
(g) (person) **one of the finest minds of this century** una de las mentes más insignes de este siglo; Prov **great minds think alike** los genios siempre tenemos las mismas ideas
2 vt (a) (concern oneself with) preocuparse de or por; **never m. the car/money** no te preocupes por el coche/dinero; **m. you, I've always thought that...** fíjate, yo siempre he pensado que...
(b) (heed, obey) hacer caso a; **m. your mother!** ¡haz caso a tu madre!
(c) (object to) **I don't m. the cold** el frío no me importa or no me molesta; **what I m. is...** lo que me molesta es...; **I don't m. trying** no me importa intentarlo; **if you don't m. my asking,...** si no te importa que te lo pregunte...; **would you m. not doing that?** ¿te importaría no hacer eso?; **I wouldn't m. a cup of tea** me gustaría tomar una taza de té
(d) (look after) (children, house, store) cuidar
3 vi (a) (object) **do you m.!** (how dare you) ¡oiga usted!; **do you m. if I smoke?** ¿le importa or molesta que fume?; **I don't m.** no me importa; **I don't m. if I do** (accepting sth offered) ¿por qué no? (b) (trouble oneself) **never m.!** ¡es igual!; **never m. about that now** olvídate de eso ahora;

Fam **never you m.!** *(it's none of your business)* ¡no es asunto tuyo!

mind-boggling ['maɪndbɒglɪŋ], **mind-blowing** ['maɪndbləʊɪŋ] *adj Fam* alucinante

minded ['maɪndɪd] *adj* **if you were so m.** si te pusieras (a hacerlo); **he is commercially/mechanically m.** se le da muy bien el comercio/la mecánica

mindful ['maɪndfʊl] *adj* **to be m. of sth** ser consciente de algo

mindless ['maɪndlɪs] *adj (destruction, violence)* gratuito(a), absurdo(a); *(task, job)* mecánico(a)

mindreader ['maɪndriːdə(r)] *n* adivinador(ora) *m,f* del pensamiento; *Fam Hum* **I'm not a m.!** ¡yo no soy ningún adivino!

mine¹ [maɪn] **1** *n* (**a**) *(for coal, tin, diamonds)* mina *f*; *Fig* **a m. of information** una mina *or* un filón de información; **m. shaft** pozo *m* de extracción (**b**) *(bomb)* mina *f*; **m. detector** detector *m* de minas

  2 *vt* (**a**) *(coal, gold)* extraer (**b**) *(place explosive mines in)* minar

  3 *vi* **to m. for coal/gold** extraer carbón/oro

mine² *possessive pron* (**a**) *(singular)* el mío *m*, la mía *f*; *(plural)* los míos *mpl*, las mías *fpl*; **her house is big but m. is bigger** su casa es grande, pero la mía es mayor (**b**) *(used attributively)* *(singular)* mío(a); *(plural)* míos(as); **this book is m.** este libro es mío; **a friend of m.** un amigo mío

minefield ['maɪnfiːld] *n* campo *m* de minas; *Fig (in law, politics)* campo *m* minado, polvorín *m*

miner ['maɪnə(r)] *n* minero(a) *m,f*

mineral ['mɪnərəl] *n* mineral *m*; **m. deposits** depósitos *mpl* minerales; **m. water** agua *f* mineral

mineralogist [mɪnəˈrɒlədʒɪst] *n* mineralogista *mf*

minesweeper ['maɪnswiːpə(r)] *n (ship)* dragaminas *m inv*

mineworker ['maɪnwɜːkə(r)] *n* minero(a) *m,f*

mingle ['mɪŋgəl] **1** *vt* mezclar

  2 *vi (things)* mezclarse; *(person)* alternar; **to m. with the crowd** mezclarse con la multitud

mini ['mɪnɪ] *n (miniskirt)* mini *f*, minifalda *f*

miniature ['mɪnɪtʃə(r)] **1** *n* miniatura *f*

  2 *adj* en miniatura

miniaturize ['mɪnɪtʃəraɪz] *vt* miniaturizar

minibus ['mɪnɪbʌs] *n* microbús *m*

MiniDisc® ['mɪnɪdɪsk] *n Comptr* MiniDisc® *m*

minidress ['mɪnɪdres] *n* minivestido *m*

minimal ['mɪnɪməl] *adj* mínimo(a)

minimalism ['mɪnɪməlɪzəm] *n (in art, music, design)* minimalismo *m*

minimalist ['mɪnɪməlɪst] *n & adj* minimalista *mf*

minimally ['mɪnɪməlɪ] *adv* mínimamente

minimize ['mɪnɪmaɪz] *vt* minimizar, reducir al mínimo

minimum ['mɪnɪməm] **1** *n* mínimo *m*; **to keep sth to a m.** reducir algo al mínimo

  2 *adj* mínimo(a); **m. wage** salario *m* mínimo (interprofesional)

mining ['maɪnɪŋ] *n* minería *f*; **m. area** cuenca *f* minera; **m. engineer** ingeniero(a) *mf* de minas; **the m. industry** el sector minero

minion ['mɪnjən] *n* lacayo *m*, subordinado(a) *m,f*

minipill ['mɪnɪpɪl] *n* = píldora anticonceptiva sin estrógenos

miniseries ['mɪnɪsɪəriːz] *n TV* miniserie *f*

miniskirt ['mɪnɪskɜːt] *n* minifalda *f*

minister ['mɪnɪstə(r)] **1** *n* (**a**) *Pol* ministro(a) *m,f* (**b**) *Rel* ministro *m* de la Iglesia

  2 *vi* **to m. to sb** ocuparse de alguien; **to m. to sb's needs** atender las necesidades de alguien

ministerial [mɪnɪˈstɪərɪəl] *adj Pol* ministerial

ministry ['mɪnɪstrɪ] *n* (**a**) *Pol* ministerio *m* (**b**) *Rel* **to enter the m.** hacerse sacerdote

mink [mɪŋk] *n* visón *m*; **a m. coat** un abrigo de visón

minnow ['mɪnəʊ] *n (fish)* alevín *m*

minor ['maɪnə(r)] **1** *n Law* menor *mf* (de edad)

  2 *adj (lesser)* menor; *(unimportant) (injury, illness)* leve; *(role, problem)* menor; *(detail, repair)* pequeño(a); **of m. importance** de poca importancia; *Mus* **m. key** tono *m* menor; *Sport* **m. league** = liga profesional estadounidense de béisbol de menor importancia que la liga nacional; *Fig* **a m. league company** una empresa de segunda; *Med* **m. operation** operación *f* sencilla

  3 *vi Univ* **to m. in sth** tener algo como asignatura optativa

Minorca [mɪˈnɔːkə] *n* Menorca

Minorcan [mɪˈnɔːkən] *adj* menorquín(ina)

minority [maɪˈnɒrɪtɪ] *n* (**a**) *(of total number)* minoría *f*; **to be in a** *or* **the m.** ser minoría; **m. government** gobierno *m* minoritario; *Fin* **m. interest** participación *f* minoritaria; *Pol* **m. leader** líder *mf* de la oposición; **m. opinion** opinión *f* de la minoría; **m. party** partido *m* minoritario (**b**) *Law (age)* minoría *f* de edad

minstrel ['mɪnstrəl] *n* juglar *m*

mint¹ [mɪnt] *n (plant)* menta *f*; *(sweet)* caramelo *m* de menta; **m. sauce** salsa *f* de menta; **m. tea** *(herbal tea)* infusión *f* de menta

mint² **1** *n* **the (US) M.** ≃ la Casa de la Moneda, *Esp* ≃ la Fábrica Nacional de Moneda y Timbre; *Fam* **to make a m.** montarse en el dólar, *Méx* llenarse de lana, *RP* llenarse de guita; **in m. condition** como nuevo(a)

  2 *vt (coins)* acuñar

minuet [mɪnjʊˈet] *n Mus* minué *m*, minueto *m*

minus ['maɪnəs] **1** *n (sign)* (signo *m*) menos *m*; *(negative aspect)* desventaja *f*, punto *m* negativo

  2 *adj (quantity, number)* negativo(a); *Sch* **B m.** notable *m* bajo; **the m. side** la parte negativa; **m. sign** signo *m* menos

  3 *prep* **ten m. eight leaves two** diez menos ocho igual a dos; **it's m. 12 degrees** hace 12 grados bajo cero; **he managed to escape, but m. his luggage** consiguió escapar, pero sin el equipaje

minuscule ['mɪnəskjuːl] *adj* minúsculo(a), diminuto(a)

minute¹ ['mɪnɪt] **1** *n* (**a**) *(of time)* minuto *m*; **it's ten minutes to three** son las tres menos diez; **it's ten minutes past three** son las tres y diez; **wait a m.!** ¡espera un momento!; **just a m.** un momento; **go downstairs this m.!** ¡baja ahora mismo!; **the m. my back was turned she…** en cuanto me di la vuelta, ella…; **he'll be here any m.** llegará en cualquier momento; **it'll be ready in a m.** estará listo en un minuto *or* momento; **I've just popped in for a m.** sólo me quedaré un momento; **until/at the last m.** hasta/en el último momento; **m. hand** *(of watch)* minutero *m*; **m. steak** filete *m* muy fino

  (**b**) *(note)* nota *f*; **minutes** *(of meeting)* acta *f*, actas *fpl*

  2 *vt (make note of)* hacer constar en acta; **the meeting will be minuted** se levantará acta de la reunión

minute² [maɪˈnjuːt] *adj* (**a**) *(small)* diminuto(a), minúsculo(a); *(increase, improvement)* mínimo(a) (**b**) *(detailed) (examination)* minucioso(a)

minutely [maɪˈnjuːtlɪ] *adv (to examine)* minuciosamente

MIPS *Comptr (abbr* **million instructions per second)** millón *m* de instrucciones por segundo

miracle ['mɪrəkəl] *n* milagro *m*; **to perform** *or* **work miracles** hacer milagros; **by a** *or* **some m.** de milagro, milagrosamente; **it's a m. that…** es un milagro que…; **m. cure** cura *f* milagrosa; **m. worker** persona *f* que hace milagros

miraculous [mɪˈrækjʊləs] *adj* milagroso(a)

mirage ['mɪrɑːʒ] *n also Fig* espejismo *m*

mire [maɪə(r)] *n* lodo *m*, fango *m*

mirror ['mɪrə(r)] **1** *n* espejo *m*; *Fig* **to hold a m. (up) to sth**

dar un fiel reflejo de algo; **m. image** *(exact copy)* reflejo *m* exacto; *(reversed image)* imagen *f* invertida
2 *vt also Fig* reflejar

mirth [mɜːθ] *n* regocijo *m*

mirthless ['mɜːθlɪs] *adj* distante, frío(a)

misadventure [mɪsəd'ventʃə(r)] *n* desventura *f*

misaligned [mɪsə'laɪnd] *adj* desalineado(a)

misanthropic [mɪzən'θrɒpɪk] *adj* misantrópico(a)

misanthropist [mɪ'zænθrəpɪst] *n* misántropo(a) *m,f*

misanthropy [mɪ'zænθrəpɪ] *n* misantropía *f*

misapprehension [mɪsæprɪ'henʃən] *n* malentendido *m*, equívoco *m*; **to be (laboring) under a m.** albergar una falsa impresión

misappropriation ['mɪsəprəʊprɪ'eɪʃən] *n (of private funds)* apropiación *f* indebida; *(of public funds)* malversación *f* (de fondos públicos)

misbegotten [mɪsbɪ'gɒtən] *adj* **(a)** *(plan, decision, idea)* desacertado(a), desafortunado(a) **(b)** *(person)* inútil

misbehave [mɪsbɪ'heɪv] *vi* (com)portarse mal

misbehavior [mɪsbɪ'heɪvjə(r)] *n* mala conducta *f*, mal comportamiento *m*

misc *(abbr* **miscellaneous**) varios

miscalculate [mɪs'kælkjʊleɪt] *vt & vi* calcular mal

miscalculation [mɪskælkjʊ'leɪʃən] *n* error *m* de cálculo

miscarriage [mɪs'kærɪdʒ] *n* **(a)** *Med* aborto *m* (natural *or* espontáneo); **to have a m.** abortar de forma natural **(b)** *Law* **m. of justice** error *m* judicial

miscarry [mɪs'kærɪ] *vi* **(a)** *(pregnant woman)* abortar de forma natural **(b)** *(plan)* fracasar

miscast [mɪs'kɑːst] *vt* **to m. an actor** dar a un actor un papel poco apropiado

miscellaneous [mɪsə'leɪnɪəs] *adj* diverso(a)

miscellany [mɪ'selənɪ] *n* miscelánea *f*

mischief ['mɪstʃɪf] *n* **(a)** *(naughtiness)* travesura *f*; **to be full of m.** ser un/una travieso(a); **to get up to m.** hacer travesuras; **to keep sb out of m.** evitar que alguien haga de las suyas **(b)** *(trouble)* problemas *mpl*; **to make m. (for sb)** crear problemas (a alguien)

mischievous ['mɪstʃɪvəs] *adj (naughty)* travieso(a); *(malicious)* malicioso(a)

mischievously ['mɪstʃɪvəslɪ] *adv (maliciously)* maliciosamente; **he smiled m.** *(naughtily)* sonrió con gesto travieso

misconception [mɪskən'sepʃən] *n* idea *f* equivocada *or* errónea

misconduct [mɪs'kɒndʌkt] *n* conducta *f* poco ética

misconstruction [mɪskən'strʌkʃən] *n Formal* **to be open to m.** ser susceptible de malas interpretaciones

misconstrue [mɪskən'struː] *vt* malinterpretar

misdeed [mɪs'diːd] *n Formal* fechoría *f*

misdemeanor [mɪsdɪ'miːnə(r)] *n Law* falta *f*

misdiagnose [mɪsdaɪəg'nəʊz] *vt Med* diagnosticar erróneamente

misdirect [mɪsdɪ'rekt] *vt* **(a)** *(person)* dar indicaciones equivocadas a; *Law* **to m. the jury** dar instrucciones erróneas al jurado **(b)** *(letter)* mandar a una dirección equivocada

miser ['maɪzə(r)] *n* avaro(a) *m,f*

miserable ['mɪzərəbəl] *adj* **(a)** *(unhappy)* triste, infeliz; **to be m.** estar triste, ser infeliz; **to make sb's life m.** amargar la vida a alguien **(b)** *(unpleasant)* lamentable; *(weather)* horroroso(a) **(c)** *(wretched)* miserable; **I only got a m. $70** sólo me dieron 70 miserables dólares

miserably ['mɪzərəblɪ] *adv* **(a)** *(unhappily)* tristemente **(b)** *(wretchedly)* miserablemente **(c)** *(very badly)* lamentablemente

miserly ['maɪzəlɪ] *adj* avariento(a)

misery ['mɪzərɪ] *n* tristeza *f*, infelicidad *f*; **to make sb's life a**

m. amargar la vida a alguien; **to put an animal out of its m.** terminar con los sufrimientos de un animal; *Hum* **put him out of his m.!** *(by telling him sth)* ¡acaba de una vez con sus sufrimientos!

misfire [mɪs'faɪə(r)] *vi (gun)* encasquillarse; *(plan)* fallar

misfit ['mɪsfɪt] *n (person)* inadaptado(a) *m,f*

misfortune [mɪs'fɔːtʃən] *n* desgracia *f*

misgiving [mɪs'gɪvɪŋ] *n* recelo *m*, duda *f*; **to have misgivings (about sth)** tener recelos (sobre algo); **to have misgivings about doing sth** tener reparos en hacer algo

misgovern [mɪs'gʌvən] *vt* gobernar mal

misguided [mɪs'gaɪdɪd] *adj (person)* confundido(a), equivocado(a); *(advice, decision, attempt)* desacertado(a), desafortunado(a); *(energy, belief, idealism)* mal encaminado(a); **to be m.** *(person)* estar confundido(a) *or* equivocado(a); *(advice, decision, attempt)* ser desacertado(a) *or* desafortunado(a); *(energy, belief, idealism)* ir mal encaminado(a)

mishandle [mɪs'hændəl] *vt (device)* manejar mal; *(situation)* encauzar mal

mishap ['mɪshæp] *n* contratiempo *m*; **without m.** sin ningún contratiempo

mishear [mɪs'hɪə(r)] *(pt & pp* **misheard** [mɪs'hɜːd]) *vt* entender mal

mishmash ['mɪʃmæʃ] *n Fam* batiburrillo *m*, *Am* mejunje *m*

misinterpret [mɪsɪn'tɜːprɪt] *vt* malinterpretar

misinterpretation [mɪsɪntɜːprɪ'teɪʃən] *n* interpretación *f* errónea; **his words are open to m.** sus palabras se prestan a una mala interpretación

misjudge [mɪs'dʒʌdʒ] *vt (distance)* calcular mal; *(person, situation)* juzgar mal

misjudg(e)ment [mɪs'dʒʌdʒmənt] *n* error *m* de apreciación

mislay [mɪs'leɪ] *(pt & pp* **mislaid** [mɪs'leɪd]) *vt* extraviar, perder

mislead [mɪs'liːd] *(pt & pp* **misled** [mɪs'led]) *vt* engañar; **they misled him into thinking that…** le hicieron creer que…

misleading [mɪs'liːdɪŋ] *adj* engañoso(a)

mismanage [mɪs'mænɪdʒ] *vt* administrar *or* gestionar mal

mismanagement [mɪs'mænɪdʒmənt] *n* mala administración *f*, mala gestión *f*

misnomer [mɪs'nəʊmə(r)] *n* denominación *f* impropia

misogynist [mɪ'sɒdʒɪnɪst] *n* misógino(a) *m,f*

misogyny [mɪ'sɒdʒɪnɪ] *n* misoginia *f*

misplace [mɪs'pleɪs] *vt (book, umbrella)* extraviar; *(trust, confidence)* depositar equivocadamente

misprint ['mɪsprɪnt] *n* errata *f* (de imprenta)

mispronounce [mɪsprə'naʊns] *vt* pronunciar mal

mispronunciation [mɪsprənʌnsɪ'eɪʃən] *n* pronunciación *f* incorrecta

misquotation [mɪskwəʊ'teɪʃən] *n* **(a)** *(accidental)* cita *f* errónea **(b)** *(deliberate)* tergiversación *f*

misquote [mɪs'kwəʊt] *vt* **(a)** *(accidentally)* citar equivocadamente **(b)** *(deliberately) (person)* tergiversar las palabras de; *(words)* tergiversar

misread [mɪs'riːd] *(pt & pp* **misread** [mɪs'red]) *vt* **(a)** *(notice, timetable)* leer mal **(b)** *(misinterpret)* malinterpretar

misrepresent [mɪsreprɪ'zent] *vt (person)* tergiversar las palabras de; *(words, facts)* deformar, tergiversar

misrepresentation [mɪsreprɪzen'teɪʃən] *n* deformación *f*, tergiversación *f*

misrule [mɪs'ruːl] *n* desgobierno *m*

Miss [mɪs] *n* señorita *f*; **M. Jones** la señorita Jones; **M. World** Miss Mundo

miss [mɪs] **1** *n Esp* fallo *m*, *Am* falla *f*

2 *vt* **(a)** *(target)* no acertar en; *(shot, penalty) Esp* fallar, *Am* errar; *(bus, train, chance)* perder; *(movie, TV program)* perderse; *Fig* **to m. the boat** *(miss opportunity)* perder el tren; **you've just missed him** se acaba de marchar; **you haven't**

missed much! no te has perdido mucho; **you can't m. the house** la casa no tiene pérdida; **you can't m. the turning** *(in city)* no puedes confundirte de bocacalle; **the boss doesn't m. a thing** al jefe no se le pasa *or* escapa nada

(b) *(not hear) (question, remark)* no oír, perderse; **to m. the point** no entender bien

(c) *(omit) (word, line)* saltarse

(d) *(avoid)* **the car just missed me** el coche *or Am* carro *or CSur* auto no me atropelló por poco; **she just missed being killed** por poco se mata

(e) *(feel lack of)* echar de menos, *esp Am* extrañar; **I m. you** te echo de menos, *esp Am* te extraño

(f) *(lack)* **the table's missing one of its legs** a la mesa le falta una pata

3 *vi* **(a)** *(miss target)* **he shot at me, but missed** me disparó, pero no me dio *or* pero erró **(b)** *(be absent)* **to be missing** faltar; **nothing is missing** no falta nada

▸**miss out 1** *vt sep (omit)* pasar por alto, omitir

2 *vi (not benefit)* **to m. out on sth** perderse algo

missal ['mɪsəl] *n Rel* misal *m*

misshapen [mɪs'ʃeɪpən] *adj* deforme

missile ['mɪsaɪl, 'mɪsəl] *n (rocket)* misil *m*; *(object thrown)* proyectil *m*; **m. launcher** lanzamisiles *m inv*

missing ['mɪsɪŋ] *adj (lost)* perdido(a); *(absent)* ausente; **to be m.** *(person, thing)* faltar; **find the m. word** encuentra la palabra que falta; **m. link** eslabón *m* perdido; **m. person** desaparecido(a) *m,f*

mission ['mɪʃən] *n* **(a)** *(task)* misión *f*; **m. control** centro *m* de control; *Com* **m. statement** declaración *f* de (la) misión, misión *f* **(b)** *(delegation)* delegación *f* **(c)** *Rel* misión *f*; **m. station** misión *f*

missionary ['mɪʃənərɪ] *n Rel* misionero(a) *m,f*; **m. position** *(sexual)* postura *f* del misionero

Mississippi [mɪsɪ'sɪpɪ] *n* Misisipi

missive ['mɪsɪv] *n Formal* misiva *f*

Missouri [mɪ'zʊərɪ] *n* Misuri

misspell ['mɪs'spel] *(pt & pp* **misspelled** *or* **misspelt** ['mɪs'spelt]) *vt* escribir incorrectamente

misspent ['mɪs'spent] *adj* **a m. youth** una juventud malgastada *or* desaprovechada

mist [mɪst] *n (fog)* neblina *f*; *(condensation)* vaho *m*; **sea m.** bruma *f*; **the mists of time** la noche de los tiempos

▸**mist over** *vi (mirror, eyes)* empañarse

▸**mist up** *vi (mirror, glasses)* empañarse

mistakable [mɪs'teɪkəbəl] *adj* confundible **(for** por)

mistake [mɪs'teɪk] **1** *n* error *m*, equivocación *f*; **to make a m.** cometer un error; **make no m.** puedes estar seguro(a); **by m.** por error *or* equivocación; *Fam* **this is hard work and no m.!** no cabe duda de que es un trabajo duro

2 *vt (pt* **mistook** [mɪs'tʊk], *pp* **mistaken** [mɪs'teɪkən]) **(a)** *(misunderstand)* interpretar mal; **I mistook her intentions** interpreté mal sus intenciones **(b)** *(confuse)* confundir **(for** con); **I mistook him for someone else** lo confundí con otra persona; **there's no mistaking a voice like that!** ¡esa voz es inconfundible!

mistaken [mɪs'teɪkən] *adj (belief, impression)* equivocado(a), erróneo(a); **to be m.** *(person)* estar equivocado(a)

Mister ['mɪstə(r)] *n* señor *m*; **M. Jones** el señor Jones

mistime [mɪs'taɪm] *vt* **to m. sth** hacer algo a destiempo

mistletoe ['mɪsəltəʊ] *n* muérdago *m*

mistook [mɪs'tʊk] *pt of* **mistake**

mistranslate [mɪstræns'leɪt] *vt* traducir erróneamente

mistranslation [mɪstræns'leɪʃən] *n* error *m* de traducción, mala traducción *f*

mistreat [mɪs'triːt] *vt* maltratar

mistress ['mɪstrɪs] *n* **(a)** *(of servant, house)* señora *f*, ama *f* **(b)** *(lover)* querida *f*, amante *f*

mistrial [mɪs'traɪəl] *n Law* juicio *m* nulo

mistrust [mɪs'trʌst] **1** *n* desconfianza *f*

2 *vt* desconfiar de

mistrustful [mɪs'trʌstfʊl] *adj* desconfiado(a); **to be m. of...** desconfiar de...

misty ['mɪstɪ] *adj (place, weather)* neblinoso(a); *(at sea or seaside)* brumoso(a); *(form)* borroso(a)

misunderstand [mɪsʌndə'stænd] *(pt & pp* **misunderstood** [mɪsʌndə'stʊd]) *vt* entender mal

misunderstanding [mɪsʌndə'stændɪŋ] *n* **(a)** *(misconception)* malentendido *m*, confusión *f*; **there's been a m. about the time** ha habido un malentendido con la hora **(b)** *(disagreement)* desacuerdo *m*, diferencias *fpl*

misuse 1 *n* [mɪs'juːs] uso *m* indebido

2 *vt* [mɪs'juːz] usar indebidamente

mite [maɪt] *n* **(a)** *(bug)* ácaro *m* **(b)** *Fam (a little bit)* **it's a m. expensive** es un poquitín *or Esp* pelín caro

miter, mitre ['maɪtə(r)] *n Rel* mitra *f*

mitigate ['mɪtɪgeɪt] *vt (effect, suffering)* atenuar, mitigar; *(pain)* aliviar, mitigar; *Law* **mitigating circumstances** circunstancias *fpl* atenuantes

mitigation [mɪtɪ'geɪʃən] *n* atenuación *f*; *Law* **in m.** como atenuante

mitre = **miter**

mitt [mɪt] *n* **(a)** *(mitten)* manopla *f*; **baseball m.** guante *m* de béisbol **(b)** *Fam (hand)* **mitts** garras *fpl, Esp* zarpas *fpl*

mitten ['mɪtən] *n (glove)* manopla *f*; *(fingerless)* mitón *m*

mix [mɪks] **1** *n (gen) & Mus* mezcla *f*

2 *vt* mezclar; *(drink)* preparar; **to m. business with pleasure** mezclar el placer con los negocios

3 *vi* **(a)** *(blend)* mezclarse; *(combine well)* compaginar bien **(b)** *(socially)* relacionarse **(with** con)

▸**mix up** *vt sep* **(a)** *(ingredients)* mezclar **(b)** *(confuse) (one's papers)* revolver, desordenar; *(people, dates)* confundir **(c)** *Fam (in situation, relationship)* **to be mixed up in sth** andar metido(a) en algo; **to get mixed up with sb** liarse con alguien

mix-and-match ['mɪksən'mætʃ] *adj* **m. clothes** coordinados *mpl*

mixed ['mɪkst] *adj (assorted)* variado(a); **it was a m. blessing** tuvo su lado bueno y su lado malo; *Fam* **it was a m. bag** había de todo; **to have m. feelings (about sth)** tener sentimientos contradictorios (respecto a algo); **m. doubles** *(in tennis)* dobles *mpl* mixtos; **m. grill/salad** parrillada *f/* ensalada *f* mixta; **m. marriage** = matrimonio entre personas de distintas razas o religiones

mixed-media ['mɪkst'miːdɪə] *adj* multimedia *inv*

mixed-up [mɪks'tʌp] *adj Fam (person)* desorientado(a), confuso(a)

mixer ['mɪksə(r)] *n* **(a)** *(for cooking)* batidora *f* **(b)** *Cin & Mus (mixing board)* mesa *f* de mezclas **(c)** *(in drink)* refresco *m (para mezcla alcohólica)* **(d)** *(socially)* **to be a good m.** ser muy abierto(a) con la gente

mixing ['mɪksɪŋ] *n* **m. bowl** cuenco *m*, bol *m*; *Cin & Mus* **m. board** mesa *f* de mezclas

mixture ['mɪkstʃə(r)] *n* mezcla *f*

mix-up ['mɪksʌp] *n* confusión *f*; **there was a m. over the dates** hubo una confusión con las fechas

mktg *Com (abbr* **marketing**) marketing *m*

ml *(abbr* **milliliter(s)**) ml, mililitro *m*

mm *(abbr* **millimeter(s)**) mm, milímetro *m*

mnemonic [nɪ'mɒnɪk] *n* recurso *m* mnemotécnico

MO [em'əʊ] *n (abbr* **money order**) transferencia *f*, giro *m*

moan [məʊn] **1** *n* **(a)** *(sound)* gemido *m* **(b)** *(complaint)* queja *f*

2 *vi* **(a)** *(make sound)* gemir **(b)** *(complain)* quejarse **(about** de)

moaner ['məʊnə(r)] *n* quejica *mf, Am* quejoso(a) *m,f*

moat [məʊt] *n* foso *m*

mob [mɒb] **1** n (crowd) turba f, horda f; Fam **the Mob** (the Mafia) la Mafia; **m. rule** la ley de la calle
2 vt (pt & pp **mobbed**) **to be mobbed by fans** ser asediado(a) por una multitud de admiradores

mobile ['məʊbaɪl] **1** n (hanging ornament) móvil m
2 adj móvil; **m. home** (caravan) caravana f, RP casa f rodante

mobility [məʊ'bɪlɪtɪ] n movilidad f

mobilize ['məʊbɪlaɪz] vt (troops, support) movilizar

mobster ['mɒbstə(r)] n Fam gángster m

moccasin ['mɒkəsɪn] n mocasín m

mocha ['mɒkə] **1** n (type of coffee) (café m) moca f; (flavor) moca f
2 adj (coffee, flavor) de moca

mock [mɒk] **1** adj fingido(a), simulado(a); **m. battle** simulacro m de batalla
2 vt (ridicule) burlarse de

mockery ['mɒkərɪ] n (a) (ridicule) burlas fpl (b) (travesty) farsa f; **to make a m. of sth/sb** poner algo/a alguien en ridículo

mockingbird ['mɒkɪŋbɜːd] n sinsonte m

mock-up ['mɒkʌp] n reproducción f, modelo m (de tamaño natural)

modal ['məʊdəl] **1** n verbo m modal
2 adj **m. verb** verbo m modal

mode [məʊd] n (a) (manner) modo m; **m. of transportation** medio m de transporte (b) Comptr & Tech modalidad f, función f (c) Math moda f

model ['mɒdəl] **1** n (a) (small version) maqueta f; **m. aircraft** maqueta de avión; **m. kit** kit m de montaje (b) (example) modelo m; **this is our latest m.** este es nuestro último modelo (c) (paragon) modelo m; **to take sb as one's m.** tomar a alguien como modelo; **m. pupil** alumno(a) m,f modélico(a) or modelo (d) (person) (fashion model, for artist) modelo mf
2 vt (a) **to m. oneself on sb** seguir el ejemplo de alguien (b) Comptr simular por Esp ordenador or Am computadora
3 vi (artist's model) posar; (fashion model) hacer or trabajar de modelo

modeling ['mɒdəlɪŋ] n (a) (of model planes, boats) **he's into m.** su hobby es hacer maquetas (b) (in fashion show, for magazine) trabajo m de modelo (c) Comptr modelado m

modem ['məʊdem] n Comptr módem m

moderate ['mɒdərɪt] **1** n Pol moderado(a) m,f
2 adj moderado(a); **to be a m. drinker** beber or Am tomar moderadamente
3 vt ['mɒdəreɪt] (one's demands, zeal) moderar
4 vi Formal (at meeting) moderar, hacer de moderador

moderately ['mɒdərɪtlɪ] adv (to eat, drink) moderadamente, con moderación; (reasonably) medianamente, moderadamente

moderation [mɒdə'reɪʃən] n moderación f; **in m.** con moderación

modern ['mɒdən] adj moderno(a); **m. languages** lenguas fpl modernas

modernism ['mɒdənɪzəm] n modernismo m

modernist ['mɒdənɪst] n & adj modernista mf

modernity [mɒ'dɜːnɪtɪ] n modernidad f

modernization [mɒdənaɪ'zeɪʃən] n modernización f

modernize ['mɒdənaɪz] **1** vt modernizar
2 vi modernizarse

modest ['mɒdɪst] adj (a) (not boastful) modesto(a) (b) (moderate) (requirement, increase) modesto(a), moderado(a) (c) (chaste) recatado(a)

modestly ['mɒdɪstlɪ] adv (a) (not boastfully) modestamente (b) (moderately) moderadamente (c) (chastely) recatadamente

modesty ['mɒdɪstɪ] n (a) (humility) modestia f; **false m.** falsa modestia (b) (moderation) (of requirement, increase) modestia f, moderación f (c) (chastity) recato m

modicum ['mɒdɪkəm] n **a m. of...** un mínimo de...

modification [mɒdɪfɪ'keɪʃən] n modificación f; **to make modifications to sth** modificar algo

modify ['mɒdɪfaɪ] vt modificar

modular ['mɒdjʊlə(r)] adj por módulos

modulate ['mɒdjʊleɪt] vt modular

modulation [mɒdjʊ'leɪʃən] n modulación f

module ['mɒdjuːl] n módulo m

modus operandi ['məʊdəsɒpə'rændaɪ] n Formal modus m operandi

mogul ['məʊgəl] n (magnate) magnate mf

mohair ['məʊheə(r)] n mohair m; **m. sweater** suéter m or Esp jersey m or Col saco m or RP pulóver m de mohair

Mohammed [məʊ'hæmɪd] pr n Mahoma

moist [mɔɪst] adj húmedo(a)

moisten ['mɔɪsən] vt humedecer

moisture ['mɔɪstʃə(r)] n humedad f

moisturize ['mɔɪstʃəraɪz] vt (skin) hidratar

moisturizer ['mɔɪstʃəraɪzə(r)] n crema f hidratante

molar ['məʊlə(r)] n muela f, molar m

molasses [mə'læsɪz] n melaza f

mold¹ [məʊld] n (fungus) moho m

mold² **1** n (in art, cooking) molde m; Fig **cast in the same m.** cortado(a) por el mismo patrón; Fig **a star in the John Wayne m.** un actor del estilo de John Wayne; Fig **to break the m.** romper moldes or el molde
2 vt (plastic, person's character) moldear

Moldavia [mɒl'deɪvɪə], **Moldova** [mɒl'dəʊvə] n Moldavia

Moldavian [mɒl'deɪvɪən], **Moldovan** [mɒl'dəʊvən] n & adj moldavo(a) m,f

molder ['məʊldə(r)] vi desmoronarse

molding ['məʊldɪŋ] n Archit moldura f

moldy ['məʊldɪ] adj mohoso(a)

mole¹ [məʊl] n (birthmark) lunar m

mole² n (animal, spy) topo m

molecular [mə'lekjʊlə(r)] adj molecular

molecule ['mɒlɪkjuːl] n molécula f

molehill ['məʊlhɪl] n topera f

moleskin ['məʊlskɪn] **1** n (fur) piel f de topo; (cotton fabric) piel f de melocotón
2 adj de piel de melocotón

molest [mə'lest] vt (pester) molestar, importunar; (sexually) abusar (sexualmente) de

molestation [mɒle'steɪʃən] n (a) (sexual) abuso m sexual (b) (pestering) hostigamiento m; (more violently) agresión f

mollify ['mɒlɪfaɪ] vt apaciguar

mollusk, mollusc ['mɒləsk] n molusco m

mollycoddle ['mɒlɪkɒdəl] vt Fam mimar

molt [məʊlt] vi (animal) mudar el pelo; (bird) mudar el plumaje

molten ['məʊltən] adj fundido(a)

mom [mɒm] n Fam mamá f, mami f

MOMA ['məʊmə] n (abbr **Museum of Modern Art**) Museo m de Arte Moderno (de Nueva York)

moment ['məʊmənt] n (a) (instant) momento m; **a m. ago** hace un momento; **at the m.** (right now) en este momento; (these days) actualmente; **at the last m.** en el último momento; **for the m.** por el momento; **in a m.** enseguida; **at any m.** en cualquier momento; **wait a m.!, one m.!** ¡espera un momento!; **I haven't a m. to spare** no tengo ni un minuto; **tell him the m. he arrives** díselo en cuanto llegue; **without a m.'s hesitation** sin dudarlo un momento; **to live for the m.** vivir el presente; **the man of the m.** el hombre del momento; **the m. of truth** la hora de la verdad; **he has his moments** tiene sus buenos golpes; **the book has its moments** el libro tiene sus (buenos) momentos
(b) (importance) **of great/little m.** de mucha/poca importancia

momentary ['məʊməntərɪ] *adj* momentáneo(a)

momentous [məʊ'mentəs] *adj* muy importante, trascendental

momentum [məʊ'mentəm] *n Phys* momento *m* (lineal); **to gather/lose m.** *(car, campaign)* cobrar/perder impulso

Mon *(abbr Monday)* lunes *m inv*

Monaco ['mɒnɑ:kəʊ] *n* Mónaco

monarch ['mɒnək] *n* monarca *mf*

monarchist ['mɒnəkɪst] *n* monárquico(a) *m,f*

monarchy ['mɒnəkɪ] *n* monarquía *f*

monastery ['mɒnəstrɪ] *n* monasterio *m*

monastic [mə'næstɪk] *adj* monástico(a)

monasticism [mə'næstɪsɪzəm] *n* vida *f* monástica

Monday ['mʌndɪ] *n* lunes *m inv*; *Fam* **M. morning quarterback** estratega *mf* de salón *(sobre todo el que comenta los resultados deportivos); see also* **Saturday**

monetarism ['mʌnɪtərɪzəm] *n* monetarismo *m*

monetarist ['mʌnɪtərɪst] *n & adj* monetarista *mf*

monetary ['mʌnɪtərɪ] *adj* monetario(a); **m. policy** política *f* monetaria

money ['mʌnɪ] *n* dinero *m*; **to do sth for m.** hacer algo por dinero; **to make m.** *(person)* ganar *or* hacer dinero; *(business)* dar dinero; **to be worth a lot of m.** *(thing)* valer mucho dinero; *(person)* tener mucho dinero; **there's no m. in it** no es un buen negocio; *Fam* **to be in the m.** haber ganado mucha plata, *Esp* haberse hecho con un montón de pasta, *Méx* haber hecho un chorro de lana, *RP* haber juntado un toco de guita; *Fam* **to be on the m.** *(accurate)* dar en el clavo; **we really got our m.'s worth** desde luego, valía la pena pagar ese dinero; **the Government must put its m. where its mouth is** el Gobierno debe demostrar con hechos lo que mantiene; *Fam* **to spend m. like water** gastar dinero a espuertas *or Am* a patadas; *Fam* **m. doesn't grow on trees!** ¡el dinero no se encuentra así como así!, *RP* ¡la plata no cae del cielo!; **for my m....** para mí..., en mi opinión...; **m. belt** = cinturón donde se puede guardar el dinero; *Fin* **m. market** mercado *m* monetario; *Econ* **m. supply** oferta *f or* masa *f* monetaria

money-back ['mʌnɪ'bæk] *n* **m. guarantee** garantía *f* de devolución del dinero si el producto no es satisfactorio

moneybags ['mʌnɪbægz] *n Fam (person)* ricachón(ona) *m,f*

moneyed ['mʌnɪd] *adj* adinerado(a), pudiente

money-grubbing ['mʌnɪɡrʌbɪŋ] *adj Fam* tacaño(a), rata

moneylender ['mʌnɪlendə(r)] *n* prestamista *mf*

moneymaker ['mʌnɪmeɪkə(r)] *n (store, business, product)* negocio *m* rentable

moneymaking ['mʌnɪmeɪkɪŋ] *adj* rentable, lucrativo(a)

Mongol ['mɒŋɡəl] *Hist* **1** *n* mongol(ola) *m,f*
  2 *adj* mongol(ola); **the M. Hordes** las hordas mongolas

mongol ['mɒŋɡəl] *n Old-fashioned (person with Down's Syndrome)* mongólico(a) *m,f*

Mongolia [mɒŋ'ɡəʊlɪə] *n* Mongolia

Mongolian [mɒŋ'ɡəʊlɪən] *n & adj* mongol(ola) *m,f*

mongoose ['mɒŋɡu:s] *n* mangosta *f*

mongrel ['mʌŋɡrəl] *n (dog)* perro *m* cruzado

monitor ['mɒnɪtə(r)] **1** *n* **(a)** *(supervisor)* supervisor(ora) *m,f*
  (b) *TV* pantalla *f*; *Comptr* monitor *m*
  2 *vt* controlar

monk [mʌŋk] *n* monje *m*

monkey ['mʌŋkɪ] *n* **(a)** *(animal)* mono *m*; *Fam* **to make a m. out of sb** tomarle el pelo a alguien; **m. bars** = en los parques, estructura de hierro o madera para que trepen los niños; *Fam* **m. business** bribonadas *fpl*; **m. puzzle (tree)** araucaria *f*; **m. wrench** llave *f* inglesa **(b)** *(naughty child)* diablillo *m*

▸**monkey around, monkey about** *vi Fam (fool around)* hacer el indio **(with** con)

monkfish ['mʌŋkfɪʃ] *n* rape *m*

mono ['mɒnəʊ] *n* **in m.** *(sound recording)* en mono(aural)

monochrome ['mɒnəkrəʊm] *adj Art* monocromo(a), monocromático(a); *Phot* en blanco y negro

monocle ['mɒnəkəl] *n* monóculo *m*

monogamous [mɒ'nɒɡəməs] *adj* monógamo(a)

monogamy [mɒ'nɒɡəmɪ] *n* monogamia *f*

monogram ['mɒnəɡræm] *n* monograma *m*

monograph ['mɒnəɡræf] *n* monografía *f*

monolingual [mɒnəʊ'lɪŋɡwəl] *adj* monolingüe

monolith ['mɒnəlɪθ] *n* monolito *m*

monolithic [mɒnə'lɪθɪk] *adj* monolítico(a)

monologue, monolog ['mɒnəlɒɡ] *n* monólogo *m*

monopolistic [mənɒpə'lɪstɪk] *adj* monopolístico(a)

monopolization [mənɒpəlaɪ'zeɪʃən] *n (of market)* monopolización *f*; *(of conversation, attention)* monopolización *f*

monopolize [mə'nɒpəlaɪz] *vt* monopolizar; *Fig* **she monopolized him for the evening** lo acaparó *or* monopolizó toda la noche

monopoly [mə'nɒpəlɪ] *n also Fig* monopolio *m*; **to have a m. on sth** tener el monopolio *or* la exclusiva de algo

monorail ['mɒnəʊreɪl] *n* monorraíl *m*

monosemic [mɒnə'si:mɪk] *adj Ling* monosémico(a)

monosyllabic [mɒnəʊsɪ'læbɪk] *adj (word)* monosílabo(a), monosilábico(a); *(person, reply)* lacónico(a)

monosyllable ['mɒnəʊsɪləbəl] *n* monosílabo *m*

monotheism ['mɒnəθɪɪzəm] *n* monoteísmo *m*

monotone ['mɒnətəʊn] *n* **to speak in a m.** hablar con voz monótona

monotonous [mə'nɒtənəs] *adj* monótono(a)

monotony [mə'nɒtənɪ] *n* monotonía *f*

Monsignor [mɒn'si:njə(r)] *n* monseñor *m*

monsoon [mɒn'su:n] *n* monzón *m*

monster ['mɒnstə(r)] **1** *n* monstruo *m*
  2 *adj Fam (enormous)* monstruoso(a)

monstrosity [mɒn'strɒsɪtɪ] *n* monstruosidad *f*

monstrous ['mɒnstrəs] *adj (repugnant, enormous)* monstruoso(a); **it is m. that...** es una monstruosidad que...

monstrously ['mɒnstrəslɪ] *adv* monstruosamente

montage [mɒn'tɑ:ʒ] *n Cin & Phot* montaje *m*

month [mʌnθ] *n* mes *m*; **in the m. of August** en el mes de agosto; **in the summer/winter months** en los meses de verano/invierno; **a m. ago** hace un mes; **a ten-m.-old baby** un bebé *or Andes* una guagua *or RP* un nene de diez meses; **once a m.** una vez al mes; *Fam* **never in a m. of Sundays** ni aunque viva cien años

monthly ['mʌnθlɪ] **1** *n (magazine)* revista *f* mensual
  2 *adj* mensual; **m. installment** plazo *m* mensual; **m. payment** mensualidad *f*
  3 *adv* mensualmente

Montreal [mɒntri:'ɔ:l] *n* Montreal

Montserrat [mɒntsə'ræt] *n* (la isla de) Monserrat

monument ['mɒnjʊmənt] *n* monumento *m*

monumental [mɒnjʊ'mentəl] *adj (large, impressive)* monumental; **of m. significance** de enorme trascendencia; **m. ignorance** ignorancia *f* supina

moo [mu:] **1** *n (pl* **moos)** mugido *m*; **m.!** ¡mu!
  2 *vi* mugir

▸**mooch around, mooch about** [mu:tʃ] *vi Fam* zascandilear, zangolotear

mood [mu:d] *n* **(a)** *(state of mind)* humor *m*; **the m. of the public/electorate** el sentir del gran público/del electorado; **to be in a good/bad m.** estar de buen/mal humor; **she's in one of her moods** está otra vez de mal humor; **I'm not in the m. (for)** no estoy de humor (para); **he's in no m. for jokes** no está de humor para chistes; **m. swing** cambio *m* repentino de humor **(b)** *Gram* modo *m*

moodily ['muːdɪlɪ] *adv* malhumoradamente

moodiness ['muːdɪnɪs] *n* (**a**) *(sulkiness)* mal humor (**b**) *(changeability)* volubilidad *f*, cambios *mpl* de humor

moody ['muːdɪ] *adj* (**a**) *(sulky)* malhumorado(a); **to be m.** *(permanently)* tener mal humor; *(temporarily)* estar malhumorado(a) *or* de mal humor (**b**) *(changeable)* voluble, variable

moon [muːn] **1** *n* luna *f*; **the M.** la Luna; *Fam* **to ask for the m.** pedir la luna; *Fam* **to promise sb the m.** prometer a alguien el oro y el moro; *Fam* **to be over the m.** estar encantado(a); **m. landing** alunizaje *m*
2 *vi Fam (expose one's buttocks)* enseñar el culo
▶**moon around, moon about** *vi* vagar, andar mirando a las musarañas

moonbeam ['muːnbiːm] *n* rayo *m* de luna

moonlight ['muːnlaɪt] **1** *n* luz *f* de la luna; **in the m., by m.** a la luz de la luna
2 *vi Fam (have an additional job)* estar pluriempleado(a)

moonlighting ['muːnlaɪtɪŋ] *n Fam* pluriempleo *m*

moonlit ['muːnlɪt] *adj* iluminado(a) por la luna

moonshine ['muːnʃaɪn] *n Fam* (**a**) *(nonsense)* sandeces *fpl* (**b**) *(illegal alcohol)* = alcohol destilado ilegalmente

Moor [mʊə(r)] *n* moro(a) *m,f*

moor[1] [mʊə(r)] *n (heath)* páramo *m*

moor[2] *vt (ship)* atracar

moorhen ['mɔːhen] *n (water bird)* polla *f* de agua

mooring ['mʊərɪŋ] *n (place)* atracadero *m*; **moorings** amarras *fpl*

Moorish ['mʊərɪʃ] *adj* moro(a)

moorland ['mʊələnd] *n* páramo *m*

moose [muːs] *(pl* **moose** *) n (elk)* alce *m*

moot [muːt] **1** *adj* **it's a m. point** es discutible
2 *vt (propose, suggest)* **it was mooted that...** se sugirió que...

mop [mɒp] **1** *n (for floor)* fregona *f*; *Fam* **a m. of hair** una mata de pelo
2 *vt (pt & pp* **mopped**) **to m. the floor** fregar el suelo, pasarle la fregona al suelo; **to m. one's brow** enjugarse la frente
▶**mop up** *vt sep (liquid)* limpiar, enjugar; *Fig (enemy forces)* terminar con, limpiar

▶**mope around, mope about** [məʊp] *vi* andar como alma en pena

moped ['məʊped] *n (motorbike)* ciclomotor *m*

mopping-up operation ['mɒpɪŋ'ʌpɒpə'reɪʃən] *n (of enemy forces)* operación *f* de limpieza

moral ['mɒrəl] **1** *n* (**a**) *(of story)* moraleja *f* (**b**) **morals** moral *f*, moralidad *f*
2 *adj* moral; **to give sb m. support** dar apoyo moral a alguien; **he is lacking in m. fiber** carece de solidez *or* talla moral; **the m. majority** la mayoría moral; **m. victory** victoria *f* moral

morale [mɒ'rɑːl] *n* moral *f*; **his m. is very low/high** tiene la moral muy baja/alta; **to be good/bad for m.** ser bueno/malo para la moral; **a m. booster** una inyección de moral

moralist ['mɒrəlɪst] *n* moralista *mf*

moralistic [mɒrə'lɪstɪk] *adj* moralista

morality [mə'rælɪtɪ] *n* moralidad *f*

moralize ['mɒrəlaɪz] *vi* moralizar

moralizing ['mɒrəlaɪzɪŋ] **1** *n* moralización *f*
2 *adj* moralizador(ora), moralizante

morally ['mɒrəlɪ] *adv* moralmente; **m. right/wrong** moralmente aceptable/inaceptable

morass [mə'ræs] *n (marsh)* pantano *m*, cenagal *m*; *Fig (of detail, despair)* marasmo *m*, laberinto *m*

moratorium [mɒrə'tɔːrɪəm] *(pl* **moratoriums** *or* **moratoria** [mɒrə'tɔːrɪə]) *n* moratoria *f* (**on** en)

morbid ['mɔːbɪd] *adj* morboso(a)

morbidly ['mɔːbɪdlɪ] *adv* morbosamente

mordant ['mɔːdənt] *adj Formal (sarcasm, wit)* mordaz

more [mɔː(r)] *(comparative of* **many, much**) **1** *pron* más; **there are m. of us** nosotros somos más; **there's no m.** ya no hay *or* queda más; **do you want (any or some) m.?** ¿quieres más?; **what m. can I say?** ¿qué más puedo decir?; **he knows m. than you (do)** él sabe más que tú; **we should see m. of each other** deberíamos vernos más; **it's just m. of the same** es más de lo mismo; **what is m.,...** lo que es más,...; **let us say no m. about it** el asunto queda olvidado; **the m. I hear about this, the less I like it** cuanto más sé del asunto, menos me gusta
2 *adj* más; **m. water/children** más agua/niños; **m. than a hundred people** más de cien personas; **one m. week** una semana más; **is there any m. bread?** ¿hay *or* queda más pan?; **to have some m. wine** tomar un poco más de vino; **I have no m. money** no me queda dinero; **there are m. and m. accidents** cada vez hay más accidentes; **there are two m. questions to go** quedan dos preguntas (más)
3 *adv* (**a**) *(to form comparative of adjective or adverb)* más; **m. interesting (than)** más interesante (que); **he became m. and m. drunk** cada vez estaba más borracho; **this made things all the m. difficult** esto *Esp* ponía *or Am* hacía las cosas aún más difíciles; **m. easily** más fácilmente
(**b**) *(with verbs) (to eat, exercise)* más; **I would think m. of her if...** tendría mejor opinión de ella si...; **(the) m.'s the pity** es una lástima; **he was m. surprised than annoyed** más que molesto estaba sorprendido; **I'm m. than satisfied** estoy más que satisfecho; **I like her m. than I used to** me cae mejor que antes; **that's m. like it!** ¡eso está mejor!; **m. or less** más o menos
(**c**) *(in time)* **once m.** una vez más, otra vez; **he doesn't drink any m.** ha dejado la bebida; *Euph* **he is no m.** ha pasado a mejor vida

morello [mə'reləʊ] *(pl* **morellos**) *n* **m. (cherry)** guinda *f*

moreover [mɔː'rəʊvə(r)] *adv* además, (lo que) es más

mores [mɔː'reɪz] *npl Formal* costumbres *fpl*

morgue [mɔːg] *n* depósito *m* de cadáveres; *Fig* **this place is like a m.** este sitio parece un entierro

moribund ['mɒrɪbʌnd] *adj* agonizante, moribundo(a)

Mormon ['mɔːmən] *n Rel* mormón(ona) *m,f*

morn [mɔːn] *n Literary* mañana *f*

morning ['mɔːnɪŋ] *n* mañana *f*; **this m.** esta mañana; **tomorrow m.** mañana por la mañana; **yesterday m.** ayer por la mañana; **the next m., the m. after** la mañana siguiente; **the m. before** la mañana anterior; **the m. after (the night before)** la resaca (de la noche anterior); **m., noon and night** (mañana,) día y noche; **(early) in the m.** por la mañana (temprano); **on Wednesday m.** el miércoles por la mañana; **good m.!,** *Fam* **m.!** ¡buenos días!; **m. dress** chaqué *m*; **m. sickness** náuseas *fpl* matutinas del embarazo; **m. star** lucero *m* del alba

morning-after pill ['mɔːnɪŋ'ɑːftəpɪl] *n* píldora *f* del día siguiente

Moroccan [mə'rɒkən] *n & adj* marroquí *mf*

Morocco [mə'rɒkəʊ] *n* Marruecos

moron ['mɔːrɒn] *n Fam* subnormal *mf*, *Am* zonzo(a) *m,f*

moronic [mə'rɒnɪk] *adj Fam (person)* subnormal, *Am* zonzo(a); *(expression, behavior)* de subnormal, *Am* zonzo(a); **a m. comment** una memez

morose [mə'rəʊs] *adj* hosco(a), huraño(a)

morphine ['mɔːfiːn] *n* morfina *f*

morrow ['mɒrəʊ] *n* (**a**) *Literary (next day)* día *m* siguiente; **on the m.** mañana, al siguiente día (**b**) *Archaic or Literary (morning)* mañana *f*

Morse [mɔːs] *n* **in M.** en (código) morse; **M. code** código *m* morse

morsel ['mɔːsəl] *n* pedacito *m*

mortal ['mɔːtəl] **1** *n* mortal *mf*; *Ironic* **he doesn't speak to mere mortals like us!** ¡no habla con los simples mortales como nosotros!
  2 *adj* mortal; **m. enemy** enemigo *m* mortal; **m. remains** restos *mpl* mortales; **m. sin** pecado *m* mortal; **m. wound** herida *f* mortal

mortality [mɔː'tælɪtɪ] *n (of person, death rate)* mortalidad *f*

mortally ['mɔːtəlɪ] *adv* **m. wounded** herido(a) de muerte; **m. offended** ultrajado(a)

mortar ['mɔːtə(r)] *n* **(a)** *(in construction)* argamasa *f*, mortero *m* **(b)** *(for grinding)* **pestle and m.** almirez *m*, mortero *m* **(c)** *(missile)* mortero *m*

mortgage ['mɔːgɪdʒ] **1** *n* hipoteca *f*; **m. (re)payments** plazos *mpl* de la hipoteca; **m. broker** agente *mf* hipotecario(a); **m. lender** entidad *f* de préstamo hipotecario; **m. rate** tipo *m* (de interés) hipotecario, *Am* tasa *f* de interés hipotecaria
  2 *vt (property, one's future)* hipotecar

mortice = **mortise**

mortician [mɔː'tɪʃən] *n (undertaker)* encargado(a) *m,f* de funeraria

mortification [mɔːtɪfɪ'keɪʃən] *n Rel* mortificación *f*; *Fig (embarrassment)* bochorno *m*

mortify ['mɔːtɪfaɪ] *vt Rel* mortificar; **I was mortified** me sentí abochornado

mortise, mortice ['mɔːtɪs] *n (in carpentry)* muesca *f*, mortaja *f*; **m. lock** cerradura *f* embutida *or* de pestillo

mortuary ['mɔːtjʊərɪ] *n* depósito *m* de cadáveres

mosaic [məʊ'zeɪɪk] *n* mosaico *m*

Moscow ['mɒskəʊ] *n* Moscú

Moses ['məʊzɪz] *pr n* Moisés

Moslem ['mɒzlem] *n & adj* musulmán(ana) *m,f*

mosque [mɒsk] *n* mezquita *f*

mosquito [məs'kiːtəʊ] *(pl* **mosquitoes)** *n* mosquito *m*, *Am* zancudo *m*; **m. bite** picadura *f* de mosquito; **m. net** mosquitera *f*, mosquitero *m*

moss [mɒs] *n* musgo *m*

most [məʊst] *(superlative of* **many, much) 1** *pron* **m. of my friends** la mayoría de *or* casi todos mis amigos; **m. of the time** la mayor parte del *or* casi todo el tiempo; **at m., at the (very) m.** como mucho; **to make the m. of an opportunity** aprovechar al máximo una oportunidad; **he is more interesting than m.** es más interesante que la mayoría; **he earns the m.** él es el que más (dinero) gana
  2 *adj* **(a)** *(the majority of)* la mayoría de; **m. women** la mayoría de las mujeres **(b)** *(greatest amount of)* **the m.** más; **he has (the) m. money** él es el que más dinero tiene; **for the m. part** en su mayor parte
  3 *adv* **(a)** *(to form superlative of adjectives and adverbs)* el/la más; **the m. beautiful woman** la mujer más bella; **the m. interesting book** el libro más interesante; **these are the m. expensive** éstos son los más caros; **those who have answered m. accurately** los que mejor hayan contestado **(b)** *(with verbs)* **the one who works m. is...** el/la que trabaja más es...; **who do you like m.?** ¿quién te cae mejor?; **what I want m.** lo que más deseo; **that's what worries me (the) m.** eso es lo que más me preocupa **(c)** *(very)* muy, sumamente; **m. unhappy** muy desgraciado(a) **(d)** *Fam (almost)* casi; **I go there m. every day** voy ahí casi todos los días

most-favored nation ['məʊst'feɪvəd'neɪʃən] *n Econ* nación *f* más favorecida; **m. status** estatus *m inv* de nación más favorecida

mostly ['məʊstlɪ] *adv* **(a)** *(in the main)* principalmente, sobre todo **(b)** *(most often)* casi siempre

motel [məʊ'tel] *n* motel *m*

moth [mɒθ] *n* polilla *f*

mothball ['mɒθbɔːl] *n* bola *f* de naftalina; *Fig* **to put a project in mothballs** aparcar un proyecto

moth-eaten ['mɒθiːtən] *adj* apolillado(a)

mother ['mʌðə(r)] **1** *n* **(a)** *(parent)* madre *f*; **m. of six** madre de seis hijos; **M.'s Day** Día *m* de la Madre; **m. country** madre patria *f*; **M. Nature** la madre naturaleza; *Rel* **M. Superior** madre superiora; **m. tongue** lengua *f* materna **(b)** *very Fam* cabrón(ona) *m,f*; **the m.'s broken down again** el cabrón (de él) ha vuelto a estropearse
  2 *vt* mimar

motherboard ['mʌðəbɔːd] *n Comptr* placa *f* madre

motherfucker ['mʌðəfʌkə(r)] *n Vulg* **(a)** *(person)* hijo(a) *m,f* de puta, *Méx* hijo(a) *m,f* de la chingada **(b)** *(thing)* **the m. won't start** este puto coche *or Am* carro *or Chile, RP* auto no arranca

motherhood ['mʌðəhʊd] *n* maternidad *f*

mother-in-law ['mʌðərɪnlɔː] *(pl* **mothers-in-law)** *n* suegra *f*

motherland ['mʌðəlænd] *n* tierra *f* natal

mother-of-pearl ['mʌðərəv'pɜːl] *n* nácar *m*

mother-to-be ['mʌðətə'biː] *(pl* **mothers-to-be)** *n* futura madre *f*

motif [məʊ'tiːf] *n* motivo *m*

motion ['məʊʃən] **1** *n* **(a)** *(movement)* movimiento *m*; **to set sth in m.** poner algo en marcha; *Fig* **to go through the motions** hacer las cosas mecánicamente; **to go through the motions of doing sth** cumplir con el formulismo de hacer algo; **m. picture** película *f*; **m. sickness** mareo *m (del viajero)* **(b)** *(in meeting, debate)* moción *f*; **to propose/second a m.** proponer/apoyar una moción; **the m. was carried** la moción fue aprobada
  2 *vt* **to m. sb to do sth** indicar a alguien (con un gesto) que haga algo
  3 *vi* **to m. to sb to do sth** indicar a alguien (con un gesto) que haga algo

motionless ['məʊʃənlɪs] *adj* inmóvil; **to remain m.** permanecer inmóvil

motivate ['məʊtɪveɪt] *vt* motivar

motivating ['məʊtɪveɪtɪŋ] *adj* estimulante, alentador(ora)

motivation [məʊtɪ'veɪʃən] *n* motivación *f*

motivational [məʊtɪ'veɪʃənəl] *adj Psy* **m. research** estudio *m* de la psicología del consumidor

motive ['məʊtɪv] **1** *n (reason)* motivo *m*, razón *f*; *Law* móvil *m*
  2 *adj* **m. force** fuerza *f* motriz

motiveless ['məʊtɪvlɪs] *adj (crime)* sin motivo

motley ['mɒtlɪ] *adj* heterogéneo(a), abigarrado(a); **m. crew** grupo *m* heterogéneo

motocross ['məʊtəkrɒs] *n* motocross *m*

motor ['məʊtə(r)] **1** *n (engine)* motor *m*; **m. home** *(caravan)* autocaravana *f*, rulot *f*, *RP* casa *f* rodante; **m. inn** *or* **lodge** motel *m*; *Med* **m. neurone disease** enfermedad *f* de la motoneurona *or* neurona motora; **m. racing** carreras *fpl* de coches *or Am* carros *or CSur* autos; **m. vehicle** vehículo *m* de motor
  2 *vi Old-fashioned (travel by car)* viajar en automóvil; *Fam* **he was really motoring** *(going fast)* iba a toda mecha

motorbike ['məʊtəbaɪk] *n* moto *f*

motorboat ['məʊtəbəʊt] *n (lancha f)* motora *f*

motorcade ['məʊtəkeɪd] *n* desfile *m* de coches *or Am* carros *or CSur* autos

motorcycle ['məʊtəsaɪkəl] *n* motocicleta *f*

motorcyclist ['məʊtəsaɪklɪst] *n* motociclista *mf*

motoring ['məʊtərɪŋ] *n* automovilismo *m*

motorist ['məʊtərɪst] *n* conductor(ora) *m,f*, automovilista *mf*

motorize ['məʊtəraɪz] *vt* motorizar

motorized ['məʊtəraɪzd] *adj Mil* motorizado(a)

Motown ['məʊtaʊn] *n (pop music)* música *f* Motown

mottled ['mɒtəld] *adj (complexion)* con manchas rojizas; *(coat, surface)* moteado(a)

motto ['mɒtəʊ] *(pl mottoes) n* lema *m*

mound [maʊnd] *n (hill)* colina *f; (of earth, sand, in baseball)* montículo *m*

mount¹ [maʊnt] *n (mountain)* monte *m;* **M. Sinai** el Monte Sinaí; **M. Vesuvius** el Vesubio

mount² *n* **(a)** *(for painting, color slide)* soporte *m* **(b)** *(horse)* montura *f*

2 *vt* **(a)** *(bicycle, horse)* montar en, subirse a; *(stairs, ladder)* subir **(b)** *(photograph, gun)* montar; **to m. an exhibition** montar una exposición; **to m. an offensive** realizar una ofensiva; **to m. guard** montar guardia

3 *vi* **(a)** *(get onto horse)* montar, montarse **(b)** *(opposition, tension)* aumentar, crecer

mount up *vi (cost, debts)* aumentar, crecer

mountain ['maʊntɪn] *n* montaña *f; Fig* **a m. of work** una montaña de trabajo; **to make a m. out of a molehill** hacer una montaña de un grano de arena; **m. bike** bicicleta *f* de montaña; **m. climbing** montañismo *m*, alpinismo *m*, *Am* andinismo *m*; **m. goat** *(in general)* cabra *f* montés; *(American variety)* rebeco *m* blanco, cabra *f* de las nieves *or* de las Montañas Rocosas; **m. lion** puma *m*; **m. range** cadena *f* montañosa, cordillera *f*; **m. rescue team** equipo *m* de rescate de montaña; **M. Standard Time** = hora oficial en la zona de las Montañas Rocosas en los Estados Unidos

mountaineer [maʊntɪ'nɪə(r)] *n* montañero(a) *m,f*, alpinista *mf*, *Am* andinista *mf*

mountaineering [maʊntɪ'nɪərɪŋ] *n* montañismo *m*, alpinismo *m*, *Am* andinismo *m*

mountainous ['maʊntɪnəs] *adj* montañoso(a)

mountainside ['maʊntɪnsaɪd] *n* ladera *f*

mounted ['maʊntɪd] *adj* montado(a); **the m. police** la policía montada

mounting ['maʊntɪŋ] **1** *n (for engine, gun)* soporte *m*

2 *adj (cost, opposition)* creciente

mourn ['mɔːn] **1** *vt* llorar la muerte de

2 *vi* **to m. for sb** llorar la muerte de alguien

mourner ['mɔːnə(r)] *n* doliente *mf*

mournful ['mɔːnfʊl] *adj* fúnebre, lúgubre

mourning ['mɔːnɪŋ] *n* duelo *m*, luto *m*; **to be in m. (for sb)** guardar luto (por alguien); **to go into m.** ponerse de luto

mouse [maʊs] *(pl* **mice** [maɪs]) *n* **(a)** *(animal)* ratón *m* **(b)** *Comptr Esp* ratón *m*, *Am* mouse *m*; **m. button** botón *m* del *Esp* ratón *or Am* mouse; **m. pad** alfombrilla *f*

mousetrap ['maʊstræp] *n* ratonera *f*

mousse [muːs] *n (dessert)* mousse *m or f; (for hair)* espuma *f*

mousy ['maʊsɪ] *adj* **(a)** *(hair)* parduzco(a) **(b)** *(person, manner)* apocado(a), tímido(a)

mouth 1 *n* [maʊθ] *(of person, animal, tunnel)* boca *f; (of river)* desembocadura *f;* **we have seven mouths to feed** tenemos siete bocas que alimentar; *Fam* **keep your m. shut about this** no digas ni mu *or Esp* ni pío de esto; *Fam* **to have a big m.** ser un(a) bocazas *or Am* chusmo(a); *Fam* **he's all m.** todo lo hace de boquilla *or Méx* de dientes para afuera *or RP* de boca para afuera; **to put words into sb's m.** poner palabras en boca de alguien; **m. organ** armónica *f*; **m. ulcer** llaga *f* en la boca

2 *vt* [maʊð] *(without sincerity)* decir mecánicamente; *(silently)* decir moviendo sólo los labios

mouthful ['maʊθfʊl] *n (of food)* bocado *m; (of drink)* trago *m; Fam Fig* **that's quite a m.!** *(long name, word)* ¡qué *or Esp* menudo trabalenguas!; **you said a m.!** ¡qué razón tienes!, ¡y que lo digas!

mouthpiece ['maʊθpiːs] *n* **(a)** *(of musical instrument)*

boquilla *f; (of telephone)* micrófono *m* **(b)** *(of government, political party)* portavoz *mf*

mouth-to-mouth ['maʊθtə'maʊθ] *adj* **m. resuscitation** *(respiración f)* boca a boca *m;* **to give sb m. resuscitation** hacer el boca a boca a alguien

mouthwash ['maʊθwɒʃ] *n* elixir *m* (bucal)

mouthwatering ['maʊθwɔːtərɪŋ] *adj* muy apetecible

movable, moveable ['muːvəbəl] *adj* móvil; *Rel* **a m. feast** una fiesta movible

move [muːv] **1** *n* **(a)** *(motion)* movimiento *m;* **we must make a m.** debemos irnos; **to make a m. toward sth/sb** hacer amago de dirigirse hacia algo/alguien; **on the m.** *(traveling)* de viaje; *(active, busy)* en marcha, en movimiento; *Fam* **get a m. on!** ¡date prisa!, *Am* ¡apúrate!

(b) *(action, step)* paso *m;* **to make the first m.** dar el primer paso

(c) *(from home)* mudanza *f*, traslado *m; (in job)* cambio *m*

(d) *(in board games)* movimiento *m*, jugada *f; (in sport)* jugada *f;* **(it's) your m.** te toca (jugar), tú mueves

2 *vt* **(a)** *(shift) (person, object, chesspiece)* mover; *(employee)* trasladar; *(postpone)* trasladar; **could you m. your bag out of the way?** ¿puedes quitar *or Am* sacar tu bolsa de en medio?; **m. your chair a bit closer** acerca la silla un poco; **to m. home** mudarse de casa; **to m. jobs** *(within company, sector)* cambiar de trabajo; *Fam* **m. yourself! we're going to be late!** ¡muévete, que vamos a llegar tarde!

(b) *(influence)* **I won't be moved** no voy a cambiar de opinión; **I felt moved to protest** me sentí impulsado a protestar

(c) *(affect emotionally)* conmover; **to m. sb to anger** enfurecer a alguien; **to m. sb to tears** hacer saltar las lágrimas a alguien

(d) *(in debate) (resolution)* proponer, *Am* mocionar; **I m. that…** propongo *or Am* mociono que…

3 *vi* **(a)** *(change position)* moverse; *(progress, advance)* avanzar; **to get things moving** poner las cosas en marcha; **don't m.!** ¡no te muevas!; **I can't m.** *(I'm stuck)* ¡no puedo moverme!; **could you m., please?** ¿podría apartarse, por favor?; *Fam* **come on, m.!** ¡venga *or Méx* ándale, muévete!, *RP* ¡dale, movete!

(b) *(act)* moverse, actuar; **to m. to do sth** moverse *or* actuar para hacer algo

(c) *(to new home, office)* mudarse; **to m. to another job** cambiar de trabajo; **to m. to the country** irse a vivir al campo

(d) *(in games)* mover

▶**move along 1** *vt sep (crowd)* dispersar; **he was moved along by the police** la policía lo echó de allí

2 *vi* **it's time we were moving along** es hora de marcharse

▶**move around, move about 1** *vt sep (furniture)* mover; *(employee)* trasladar

2 *vi* moverse; **I heard somebody moving about upstairs** oí a alguien trajinar arriba; **he moves around a lot** *(in job)* se mueve mucho

▶**move away 1** *vt sep* apartar, retirar

2 *vi (from window, person)* apartarse, retirarse; *(from house)* mudarse

▶**move back 1** *vt sep (further away)* hacer retroceder; *(to former position)* devolver a su sitio

2 *vi (retreat)* retirarse; *(to former position)* volver

▶**move forward 1** *vt sep (meeting)* adelantar

2 *vi (person, car)* avanzar

▶**move in** *vi (take up residence)* instalarse, mudarse; **to m. in with sb** irse a vivir con alguien

▶**move off** *vi (person)* marcharse, irse; *(car, train, procession)* partir

▶**move on 1** *vt sep (crowd)* dispersar; **he was moved on by the police** la policía lo echó de allí

2 vi (**a**) (person, line) avanzar; **time's moving on** no queda mucho tiempo; **it's time we were moving on** es hora de marcharse; **things have moved on since then** las cosas han cambiado mucho desde entonces (**b**) (change subject) cambiar de tema; **to m. on to** pasar a (hablar de)

▸**move out** vi (move house) mudarse; **my boyfriend moved out last week** mi novio me dejó y se fue de casa la semana pasada

▸**move over** vi (make room) echarse a un lado, correrse; **to m. over to a new system** pasar a un nuevo sistema; **m over!** ¡apártate!, ¡córrete!

▸**move up** vi (**a**) (make room) echarse a un lado, correrse (**b**) (be promoted) ascender

moveable = movable

movement ['mu:vmənt] n (gen) & Mus movimiento m; **free m. of people and goods,...** la libre circulación de personas y mercancías,...; **to watch sb's movements** seguir los movimientos de alguien; **the armor made m. very difficult** la armadura dificultaba el movimiento; **a political m.** un movimiento político; (**bowel**) **m.** evacuación f (del vientre)

mover ['mu:və(r)] n (**a**) (in debate) ponente mf; **the movers and shakers** (in politics) los que mueven los hilos (**b**) **he's a beautiful m.** (dancer, footballer) se mueve con mucha elegancia

movie ['mu:vɪ] n película f; **to go to the movies** ir al cine; **she's in the movies** es actriz de cine; **m. actor/actress** actor m/actriz f de cine; **m. camera** cámara f cinematográfica or de cine; **m. house** cine m; **m. industry** industria f cinematográfica or del cine; **m. projector** proyector m cinematográfico; **m. star** estrella f de cine; **m. theater** cine m

moviegoer ['mu:vɪɡəʊə(r)] n asiduo(a) m,f al cine

moving ['mu:vɪŋ] adj (**a**) (train, vehicle) en movimiento; **m. staircase** escalera f mecánica (**b**) (causing motion) **the m. spirit** la fuerza impulsora (**c**) (description, story) conmovedor(ora) (**d**) **m. firm** empresa f de portes y mudanzas

mow [məʊ] vt (pp mowed or mown [məʊn]) (lawn) cortar; (hay) segar

▸**mow down** vt sep (slaughter) segar la vida de

Mozambican [məʊzæm'bi:kən] n & adj mozambiqueño(a) m,f

Mozambique [məʊzæm'bi:k] n Mozambique

MP [em'pi:] n Mil (abbr **Military Police(man)**) (force) policía f militar; (agent) policía mf militar

MP3 [empi:'θri:] n (abbr **MPEG-1 Audio Layer-3**) MP3 m; **M. player** reproductor m de MP3

MPEG ['empeɡ] n Comptr (abbr **Moving Pictures Expert Group**) MPEG m

mpg [empi:'dʒi:] n Aut (abbr **miles per gallon**) ≃ litros mpl a los cien, = consumo del coche medido en millas por galón de combustible

mph [empi:'eɪtʃ] n (abbr **miles per hour**) millas fpl por hora

Mr. ['mɪstə(r)] n (abbr **Mister**) Sr., señor m; **Mr. Jones** el Sr. Jones; **Mr. Right** (ideal man) el hombre ideal

Mrs. ['mɪsɪz] n (abbr **Missus**) Sra., señora f; **Mrs. Jones** la Sra. Jones

MS (abbr **manuscript**) ms., manuscrito m

Ms. [mɪz] n (non-specific as to marital status) Sra.

Ms. es el equivalente femenino de **Mr.**, y se utiliza para dirigirse a una mujer sin precisar su estado civil.

ms (abbr **milliseconds**) ms, milisegundos mpl

MSc [emes'si:] n Univ (abbr **Master of Science**) máster m or Am maestría f en Ciencias; **to have an M. in chemistry** tener un máster en Química; **Fiona Watson, M.** Fiona Watson, licenciada con máster en Ciencias

MSG [emes'dʒi:] n (abbr **monosodium glutamate**) glutamato m monosódico

MST [emes'ti:] n (abbr **Mountain Standard Time**) = hora oficial en la zona de las Montañas Rocosas en los Estados Unidos

Mt (abbr **Mount**) monte m

much [mʌtʃ] (comparative **more** superlative **most**) **1** pron mucho; **there is not m. left** no queda mucho; **it's not worth m.** no vale mucho, no tiene mucho valor; **m. has happened since you left** han pasado muchas cosas desde que te fuiste; **she made m. of the fact that...** le dio mucha importancia al hecho de que...; **I'll say this m. for him,** he's very polite tengo que admitir que es muy amable; **I don't think m. of him** no lo tengo en gran estima; **it didn't come as m. of a surprise** no fue ninguna sorpresa; **she isn't m. of a singer** no es gran cosa como cantante; **in the end it cost as m. again** al final costó el doble; **twice as m.** el doble; **I thought/expected as m.** era lo que pensaba/me esperaba; **as m. as possible** todo lo posible; **it was as m. as we could do to stand upright** apenas podíamos mantenernos en pie; **he left without so m. as saying goodbye** se marchó sin siquiera decir adiós; **he has drunk so m. that...** ha bebido or Am tomado tanto que...; **so m. the better** tanto mejor; **so m. so that...** tanto es así que...; **so m. for her promises of help!** ¡y me/nos etc había prometido su ayuda!; **I've got too m.** tengo demasiado; Fam **that's a bit m.!** ¡eso es pasarse!

2 adj

Normalmente, sólo se usa en estructuras negativas e interrogativas, salvo en lenguaje formal.

mucho(a); **how m. money?** ¿cuánto dinero?; **there isn't m. traffic** no hay mucho tráfico; **too m. time** demasiado tiempo; **so m. time** tanto tiempo; **as m. time as you like** tanto tiempo como quieras, todo el tiempo que quieras; Formal **m. work still needs to be done** aún queda mucho trabajo por hacer

3 adv mucho; **I don't like it m.** no me gusta mucho; **m. as I'd like to, I can't go** por mucho que quiera, no puedo ir; **m. better/worse** mucho mejor/peor; **m. the best/largest** con mucho el mejor/más grande; **thank you very m.** muchas gracias; **it's/he's m. the same (as before)** no ha cambiado mucho; **m. to my astonishment** para mi estupefacción; **m. too good** demasiado bueno; **m. as I like him, I don't really trust him** aunque me cae muy bien, no me fío de él; **the result was m. as I expected** resultó más o menos como esperaba; **so m.** tanto; **too m.** demasiado; **they charged me $10 too m.** me cobraron 10 dólares de más; **this is too m.!** ¡esto ya es el colmo!

muchness ['mʌtʃnɪs] n Fam **they're much of a m.** son prácticamente iguales

muck [mʌk] n (dirt) mugre f, porquería f; (manure) estiércol m; Fam (bad food) bazofia f

▸**muck up** vt sep Fam (make dirty) ensuciar; (spoil) echar a perder

muckraking ['mʌkreɪkɪŋ] n Fam (in journalism) búsqueda del escándalo

mucky ['mʌkɪ] adj Fam mugriento(a)

mucous ['mju:kəs] adj mucoso(a)

mucus ['mju:kəs] n mocos mpl, mucosidad f

mud [mʌd] n barro m; Fig **to throw m. at sb** difamar a or desacreditar a alguien; Fam **his name is m.** tiene muy mala fama; **m. hut** choza f de barro

mudbank ['mʌdbæŋk] n barrizal m, cenagal m

muddle ['mʌdəl] **1** n lío m; **to be in a m.** (things, person) estar hecho(a) un lío; **to get into a m.** (things) liarse; (person) hacerse un lío; **there was a m. over the dates** hubo un lío con las fechas

2 vt (**a**) (put in disorder) desordenar; (mix up) confundir (**b**) (bewilder) liar; **to get muddled** hacerse un lío

▸**muddle along** vi ir tirando

▶**muddle through** *vi* arreglárselas; **we'll m. through somehow** ya nos las arreglaremos

▶**muddle up** *vt sep* (**a**) *(put in disorder)* desordenar; *(mix up)* confundir (**b**) *(bewilder)* liar; **to get muddled up** hacerse un lío

muddleheaded [mʌdəl'hedɪd] *adj (person, decision)* atolondrado(a)

muddy ['mʌdɪ] **1** *adj (path)* embarrado(a), enfangado(a); *(water)* turbio(a); *(jacket, hands)* lleno(a) de barro; *(color, complexion)* terroso(a)
2 *vt* manchar de barro; *Fig* **to m. the waters** enturbiar el asunto

mudflat ['mʌdflæt] *n* marisma *f*

mudpack ['mʌdpæk] *n* mascarilla *f* de barro

mudslinging ['mʌdslɪŋɪŋ] *n Fam* **the debate degenerated into m.** el debate degeneró en meras descalificaciones

muesli ['mjuːzlɪ] *n* muesli *m*

muezzin [muː'ezɪn] *n Rel* almuecín *m*

muff¹ [mʌf] *vt Fam (catch)* fallar; *(chance, opportunity)* echar a perder; *(job, task)* hacer de pena; **he muffed the line** se lió con la frase

muff² *n (for hands)* manguito *m*

muffin ['mʌfɪn] *n* ≃ magdalena *f*

muffle [mʌfəl] *vt* (**a**) *(deaden sound of)* amortiguar (**b**) **to m. oneself up** abrigarse bien

muffled ['mʌfəld] *adj (sound, footstep)* apagado(a)

muffler ['mʌflə(r)] *n* (**a**) *(scarf)* bufanda *f* (**b**) *(of car)* silenciador *m*

mufti ['mʌftɪ] *n Fam* **in m.** *(soldier)* de paisano

mug [mʌg] **1** *n* (**a**) *(cup)* taza *f* alta (**b**) *Fam (face)* jeta *f*; **m. shot** foto *f* para ficha policial
2 *vt (pt & pp mugged) (attack)* atracar

mugger ['mʌgə(r)] *n* atracador(ora) *m,f*

mugging ['mʌgɪŋ] *n* atraco *m*

muggy ['mʌgɪ] *adj* bochornoso(a); **it's m.** hace mucho bochorno

Muhammad [mə'hæmɪd] *pr n* Mahoma

mujahideen [muːdʒɪhæ'dɪn] *n* mujahidín *m*

mulatto [mjuː'lætəʊ] (*pl* **mulattoes** *or* **mulattos**) *n* mulato(a) *m,f*

mulberry ['mʌlbərɪ] *n (fruit)* mora *f*; *(tree)* morera *f*

mulch [mʌltʃ] *n* mantillo *m*, *Col* capote *m*

mule [mjuːl] *n* (**a**) *(animal)* mulo(a) *m,f* (**b**) *(drug smuggler)* correo *m*, *RP* mula *f*

▶**mull over** [mʌl] *vt sep (consider)* **to m. sth over** darle vueltas a algo

mulled wine ['mʌld'waɪn] *n* = vino con azúcar y especias que se toma caliente

mullet ['mʌlɪt] *n* **gray m.** mújol *m*; **red m.** salmonete *m*

multi-access ['mʌltɪ'ækses] *adj Comptr* multiusuario *inv*, de acceso múltiple

multichannel [mʌltɪ'tʃænəl] *adj (TV)* multicanal

multicolored [mʌltɪkʌləd] *adj* multicolor

multicultural [mʌltɪ'kʌltʃərəl] *adj* multicultural

multidisciplinary ['mʌltɪdɪsɪ'plɪnərɪ] *adj Educ* multidisciplinar

multiethnic ['mʌltɪ'eθnɪk] *adj* multiétnico(a)

multifaceted ['mʌltɪ'fæsɪtɪd] *adj* múltiple, con múltiples facetas

multifarious [mʌltɪ'feərɪəs] *adj* múltiple

multifunctional [mʌltɪ'fʌŋkʃənəl] *adj* multifuncional

multilateral [mʌltɪ'lætərəl] *adj* multilateral

multilingual [mʌltɪ'lɪŋgwəl] *adj* (**a**) *(person)* polígloto(a) (**b**) *(dictionary, document)* multilingüe

multimedia [mʌltɪ'miːdɪə] **1** *n* multimedia *f*
2 *adj* multimedia *inv*

multimillion [mʌltɪ'mɪljən] *adj* **a m. dollar project** un proyecto multimillonario

multimillionaire [mʌltɪmɪlɪə'neə(r)] *n* multimillonario(a) *m,f*

multinational [mʌltɪ'næʃənəl] *n & adj* multinacional *f*

multiparty [mʌltɪ'pɑːtɪ] *adj* **m. democracy/system** democracia *f*/sistema *m* pluripartidista

multiple ['mʌltɪpəl] **1** *n Math* múltiplo *m*
2 *adj* múltiple; *Med* **m. sclerosis** esclerosis *f inv* múltiple

multiple-choice ['mʌltɪpl'tʃɔɪs] *adj* **m. exam/question** examen *m*/pregunta *f* (de) tipo test

multiplex ['mʌltɪpleks] *n* multicine *m*

multiplication [mʌltɪplɪ'keɪʃən] *n* multiplicación *f*; **m. table** tabla *f* de multiplicar

multiplicity [mʌltɪ'plɪsɪtɪ] *n* multiplicidad *f*, diversidad *f*

multiplier ['mʌltɪplaɪə(r)] *n Math & Phys* multiplicador *m*

multiply ['mʌltɪplaɪ] **1** *vt* multiplicar (**by** por)
2 *vi (reproduce)* multiplicarse

multiprocessor [mʌltɪ'prəʊsesə(r)] *n Comptr* multiprocesador *m*

multiprogramming [mʌltɪ'prəʊgræmɪŋ] *n Comptr* multiprogramación *f*

multipurpose [mʌltɪ'pɜːpəs] *adj* multiusos

multiracial [mʌltɪ'reɪʃəl] *adj* multirracial

multistory [mʌltɪ'stɔːrɪ] *adj* de varios pisos *or* plantas; **m. parking garage** estacionamiento *m or Esp* aparcamiento *m or Col* parqueadero *m* de varias plantas

multitasking ['mʌltɪ'tɑːskɪŋ] *n* (**a**) *Comptr* multitarea *f* (**b**) *Ind* movilidad *f* funcional

multitude ['mʌltɪtjuːd] *n (large number, crowd)* multitud *f*; **a m. of** multitud de

multitudinous [mʌltɪ'tjuːdɪnəs] *adj Fam* multitudinario(a)

multiuser ['mʌltɪ'juːsə(r)] *adj Comptr* multiusuario *inv*; **m. system** sistema *m* multiusuario

mum [mʌm] *Fam adv* **to keep m. (about sth)** no decir ni pío *or* ni mu (sobre algo)

mumble ['mʌmbəl] **1** *n* murmullo *m*
2 *vt & vi* murmurar, musitar

mumbo jumbo ['mʌmbəʊ'dʒʌmbəʊ] *n (nonsense)* palabrería *f*, monsergas *fpl*; *(jargon)* jerigonza *f*, jerga *f*

mummify ['mʌmɪfaɪ] *vt* momificar

mummy ['mʌmɪ] *n (embalmed body)* momia *f*

mumps [mʌmps] *n (illness)* paperas *fpl*

munch [mʌntʃ] *vt* ronzar, mascar

munchies ['mʌntʃɪz] *npl Fam* (**a**) *(snacks)* cosillas *fpl* de picar, *Méx* antojitos *mpl* (**b**) *(desire to eat)* **to have the m.** tener un poquillo de hambre

mundane [mʌn'deɪn] *adj* banal

municipal [mjuː'nɪsɪpəl] *adj* municipal

municipality [mjuːnɪsɪ'pælɪtɪ] *n* municipio *m*

munitions [mjuː'nɪʃənz] *npl* municiones *fpl*, armamento *m*

mural ['mjʊərəl] *n* mural *m*

Murcian ['mɜːsɪən] *n & adj* murciano(a) *m,f*

murder ['mɜːdə(r)] **1** *n* (**a**) *(killing)* asesinato *m*; *Fig* **she gets away with m.** se le consiente cualquier cosa; **m. case** causa *f* de *or* juicio *m* por asesinato; **m. inquiry** investigación *f* de un asesinato; *Fam (difficult task)* tortura *f*; **finding a parking place on a Saturday is m.** buscar estacionamiento *or Esp* aparcamiento el sábado es una tortura
2 *vt* (**a**) *(kill)* asesinar; *Fam Fig* **I'll m. you (for that)!** ¡te voy a matar! (**b**) *(ruin) (song, tune)* destrozar

murderer ['mɜːdərə(r)] *n* asesino(a) *m,f*

murky ['mɜːkɪ] *adj (weather, sky)* oscuro(a), sombrío(a); *(details, past)* tenebroso(a)

murmur ['mɜːmə(r)] **1** *n* murmullo *m*; **to do sth without a m.** hacer algo sin rechistar
2 *vi* murmurar

Murphy ['mɜːfɪ] n **M. bed** cama f plegable, mueble m cama; Fam **M.'s law** la ley de Murphy, = aquello de que si algo puede ir mal, ten por seguro que lo hará

muscle ['mʌsəl] n músculo m; **she didn't move a m.** no movió un solo músculo; Fig **political m.** pujanza f política

▶**muscle in** vi entrometerse (**on** en)

muscleman ['mʌsəlmæn] n forzudo m, hércules m inv

Muscovite ['mʌskəvaɪt] n & adj moscovita mf

muscular ['mʌskjʊlə(r)] adj (tissue) muscular; (person) musculoso(a); Med **m. dystrophy** distrofia f muscular

Muse [mjuːz] n musa f

muse [mjuːz] vi reflexionar, cavilar (**on** or **about** sobre)

museum [mjuːˈzɪəm] n museo m; also Hum **m. piece** pieza f de museo

mush [mʌʃ] n (**a**) (pulp) masa f, puré m (**b**) Fam (sentimentality) ñoñeces fpl, sensiblerías fpl

mushroom ['mʌʃrʊm] **1** n Bot hongo m, Esp seta f; Culin (wild mushroom) Esp seta f, Am hongo m; (button mushroom) champiñón m; **m. cloud** hongo m atómico
2 vi (costs, prices) dispararse; (town) expandirse, extenderse

mushy ['mʌʃɪ] adj (pulpy) blando(a), pastoso(a); Fam (sentimental) ñoño(a), sensiblero(a)

music ['mjuːzɪk] n música f; **to set words to m.** poner música a la letra; Fig **those words were m. to her ears** esas palabras le sonaban a música celestial; **m. box** caja f de música; **m. piracy** piratería f musical; **m. stand** atril m; **m. teacher** profesor(ora) m,f de música; **m. video** vídeo m or Am video m musical

musical ['mjuːzɪkəl] **1** n (show, movie) musical m
2 adj (tuneful) musical; (musically gifted) con talento musical; **m. chairs** juego m de las sillas; Fig **to play m. chairs** andar constantemente cambiando de puesto; **m. instrument** instrumento m musical

musically ['mjuːzɪklɪ] adv (sing) armoniosamente; **m. gifted** con talento para la música

musician [mjuːˈzɪʃən] n músico(a) m,f

musicologist [mjuːzɪˈkɒlədʒɪst] n musicólogo(a) m,f

musings ['mjuːzɪŋz] npl reflexiones fpl, cavilaciones fpl

musk [mʌsk] n almizcle m

musket ['mʌskɪt] n mosquete m

musketeer [mʌskɪˈtɪə(r)] n mosquetero m

muskrat ['mʌskræt] n rata f almizclada

musky ['mʌskɪ] adj almizclado(a), almizcleño(a); **a m. smell** un olor a almizcle

Muslim ['mʌzlɪm] n & adj musulmán(ana) m,f

muslin ['mʌzlɪn] n muselina f

muss [mʌs] n Fam **to m. (up)** (hair) revolver

mussel ['mʌsəl] n mejillón m; **m. bed** vivero m de mejillones

must [mʌst] **1** n Fam (**a**) (necessity) **to be a m.** ser imprescindible (**b**) (thing not to be missed) **this movie's a m.** esta película hay que verla or no hay que perdérsela
2 modal aux v (**a**) (expressing obligation) tener que, deber; **you m. do it** tienes que hacerlo, debes hacerlo; **you m. be ready at four o'clock** tienes que estar listo a las cuatro; **you mustn't tell anyone** no se lo digas a nadie; **this plant m. be watered daily** esta planta hay que regarla todos los días; **I m. say I thought it was pretty good** la verdad es que me pareció bastante bueno; **will you come with me? — if I m.** ¿vendrás conmigo? — si no queda más remedio; **take it if you m.** llévatelo or Esp cógelo si tanta falta te hace; **m. you be so silly?** ¡mira que eres tonto!
(**b**) (suggesting, inviting) tener que; **you m. come and visit us** tienes que venir a vernos; **we m. go out for a drink sometime** tenemos que quedar algún día para tomar algo
(**c**) (expressing probability) deber de; **you m. be hungry** debes de tener hambre; **it m. be interesting working there** debe de ser interesante trabajar allí; **I m. have made a**

mistake debo de haberme equivocado; **you m. be joking!** ¡no lo dirás en serio!

mustache ['mʌstæʃ] n bigote m

mustachioed [məˈstɑːʃɪəʊd] adj con bigotes, bigotudo(a)

mustard ['mʌstəd] n mostaza f; Fam Fig **she couldn't cut the m.** no consiguió dar la talla; **m. gas** gas m mostaza

muster ['mʌstə(r)] **1** n Fig **it was good enough to pass m.** era pasable
2 vt (gather) reunir; **to m. one's strength/courage** hacer acopio de fuerzas/valor

musty ['mʌstɪ] adj **to have a m. smell** (room) oler a cerrado; (clothes) oler a humedad

mutable ['mjuːtəbəl] adj Formal mudable, mutable

mutant ['mjuːtənt] n & adj mutante mf

mutate [mjuːˈteɪt] vi mutarse (**into** en), transformarse (**into** en)

mutation [mjuːˈteɪʃən] n mutación f

mute [mjuːt] **1** n (**a**) (person) mudo(a) m,f (**b**) Mus sordina f
2 adj (silent) mudo(a)

muted ['mjuːtɪd] adj (sound) apagado(a); (protest, criticism) débil

mutely ['mjuːtlɪ] adv (to stare, gaze) en silencio

mutilate ['mjuːtɪleɪt] vt mutilar

mutilation [mjuːtɪˈleɪʃən] n mutilación f

mutineer [mjuːtɪˈnɪə(r)] n amotinado(a) m,f

mutinous ['mjuːtɪnəs] adj (rebellious) rebelde; (taking part in mutiny) amotinado(a)

mutiny ['mjuːtɪnɪ] **1** n motín m
2 vi amotinarse

mutt [mʌt] n Fam (dog) chucho m, RP pichicho m

mutter ['mʌtə(r)] **1** n murmullo m
2 vt & vi murmurar

mutton ['mʌtən] n (meat of sheep) carnero m

mutual ['mjuːtʃʊəl] adj (reciprocal) mutuo(a); (shared) común; **the feeling is m.** el sentimiento es mutuo; **a m. friend** un amigo común; Fin **m. benefit society** mutua f, mutualidad f; Fin **m. fund** fondo m de inversión mobiliaria

mutually ['mjuːtʃʊəlɪ] adv mutuamente; **to be m. exclusive** excluirse mutuamente

muzzle ['mʌzəl] **1** n (**a**) (dog's snout) hocico m; (device for dog) bozal m (**b**) (of gun) boca f
2 vt (dog) poner un bozal a; Fig (person, press) amordazar

MW (**a**) Rad (abbr **Medium Wave**) OM, onda f media (**b**) Elec (abbr **Megawatts**) MW, megavatios mpl

my [maɪ] possessive adj (**a**) (singular) mi; (plural) mis; **my dog** mi perro; **my parents** mis padres; **it wasn't MY idea** ¡no fue idea mía! (**b**) (for parts of body, clothes) (translated by definite article) **my eyes are blue** tengo los ojos azules; **I hit my head** me di un golpe en la cabeza; **I put my hands in my pockets** me metí las manos en los bolsillos or CAm, Méx, Perú las bolsas (**c**) **(oh) my!** ¡madre mía!, ¡jesús!

Myanmar [maɪænˈmɑː(r)] n (official name of Burma) Myanmar

mynah ['maɪnə] n **m. (bird)** miná f, = estornino hablador de la India

myopia [maɪˈəʊpɪə] n also Fig miopía f

myopic [maɪˈɒpɪk] adj miope; Fig corto(a) de miras

myriad ['mɪrɪəd] adj Literary **there are m. examples** hay una miríada or un sinnúmero de ejemplos

myrrh [mɜː(r)] n mirra f

myrtle ['mɜːtəl] n (shrub) mirto m, arrayán m

myself [maɪˈself] pron (**a**) (reflexive) me; **I hurt m.** me hice daño (**b**) (emphatic) (male) yo mismo; (female) yo misma; **I did all the work m.** yo mismo or yo solo hice todo el trabajo; **I told her m.** se lo dije yo mismo; **I'm not quite m. today** me siento un poco raro hoy, Esp hoy no estoy muy allá (**c**) (after preposition) mí; **I bought it for m.** lo compré para mí; **I live by m.** vivo solo; **I realized I was talking to**

m. me di cuenta de que estaba hablando solo

mysterious [mɪsˈtɪərɪəs] *adj* misterioso(a); **to be m. about sth** andarse con muchos misterios acerca de algo

mysteriously [mɪsˈtɪərɪəslɪ] *adv* misteriosamente

mystery [ˈmɪstərɪ] **1** *n* misterio *m*; **it's a m. to me** es un misterio para mí

  2 *adj (guest, prize)* sorpresa *inv*; *(benefactor, witness)* anónimo(a), desconocido(a)

mystic [ˈmɪstɪk] *n* místico(a) *m,f*

mystical [ˈmɪstɪkəl] *adj* místico(a)

mysticism [ˈmɪstɪsɪzəm] *n* misticismo *m*

mystification [mɪstɪfɪˈkeɪʃən] *n (bewilderment)* estupefacción *f*, desconcierto *m*; *(deliberate confusion)* artimaña *f*, ardid *m*

mystify [ˈmɪstɪfaɪ] *vt* dejar estupefacto(a) *or* perplejo(a), desconcertar; **I was mystified** me quedé estupefacto

mystique [mɪsˈtiːk] *n* aureola *f* de misterio

myth [mɪθ] *n* mito *m*

mythical [ˈmɪθɪkəl] *adj* mítico(a)

mythological [mɪθəˈlɒdʒɪkəl] *adj* mitológico(a)

mythology [mɪˈθɒlədʒɪ] *n* mitología *f*

myxomatosis [mɪksəməˈtəʊsɪs] *n* mixomatosis *f inv*

N

N, n [en] *n* (**a**) *(letter)* N, n *f* (**b**) *(abbr* **north**) N

NAACP [eneɪeɪsiːˈpiː] *n* (*abbr* **National Association for the Advancement of Colored People**) = asociación americana para la defensa de los derechos de la gente de color

naan [nɑːn] *n* **n. (bread)** = clase de pan indio en forma de hogaza aplanada

nab [næb] (*pt & pp* **nabbed**) *vt Fam* (**a**) *(catch, arrest)* pescar, *Esp* trincar (**b**) *(steal)* birlar

nadir [ˈneɪdɪə(r)] *n Astron* nadir *m*; *Fig* **to reach a n.** *(party, career)* tocar fondo

NAFTA [ˈnæftə] *n* (*abbr* **North American Free Trade Agreement**) NAFTA *m*, TLC *m*

nag¹ [næg] *n Fam (horse)* rocín *m*, jamelgo *m*

nag² **1** *n (person)* pesado(a) *m,f*, latoso(a) *m,f*

2 *vt* (*pt & pp* **nagged**) *(of person)* fastidiar, *Esp* dar la lata a; *(of doubt)* asaltar; **to n. sb into doing sth** dar la lata a alguien para que haga algo

3 *vi* fastidiar, dar la lata; **to n. at sb to do sth** dar la lata a alguien para que haga algo; **her conscience was nagging at her to go to the police** tenía remordimientos de conciencia que le impulsaban a acudir a la policía

nagging [ˈnægɪŋ] **1** *n* regañinas *fpl*

2 *adj* persistente

nail [neɪl] **1** *n* (**a**) *(in carpentry)* clavo *m*; *Fig* **it was another n. in his coffin** era otro clavo más en su ataúd; *Fig* **to hit the n. on the head** dar en el clavo (**b**) *(of finger, toe)* uña *f*; **n. file** lima *f* de uñas; **n. scissors** tijeras *fpl* de manicura; **n. polish** laca *f* or esmalte *m* de uñas; **n. polish remover** quitaesmaltes *m inv*

2 *vt* (**a**) *clavar*; **he nailed the lid shut** fijó la tapa con clavos; *Fig* **he stood nailed to the spot** se quedó clavado (**b**) *(idioms) Fam* **to n. sb for a crime** emplumar or empapelar a alguien por un delito; *Fam* **to n. a lie** desterrar una falsedad

▸**nail down** *vt sep (fasten)* fijar con clavos; *Fam Fig* **to n. sb down to a date/price** hacer que alguien se comprometa a dar una fecha concreta/un precio concreto

nail-biting [ˈneɪlbaɪtɪŋ] *adj Fam (contest, finish)* de infarto, emocionantísimo(a); **after a n. few hours, the hostages were released** después de varias horas de tensa espera liberaron a los rehenes

nailbrush [ˈneɪlbrʌʃ] *n* cepillo *m* de uñas

naive [naɪˈiːv] *adj* ingenuo(a)

naively [naɪˈiːvlɪ] *adv* ingenuamente

naivety [naɪˈiːvətɪ] *n* ingenuidad *f*

naked [ˈneɪkɪd] *adj* desnudo(a); **to be n.** estar desnudo(a); **a n. flame** una llama (sin protección); **n. aggression** agresión *f* abierta or alevosa; **visible to the n. eye** visible a simple vista

nakedness [ˈneɪkədnɪs] *n* desnudez *f*

namby-pamby [ˈnæmbɪˈpæmbɪ] *n & adj Fam* ñoño(a) *m,f*

name [neɪm] **1** *n* (**a**) *(of person)* nombre *m*; **my n. is…** me llamo…; **what's your n.?** ¿cómo te llamas?; **to mention sb by n.** mencionar a alguien por su nombre; **to take sb's n.** *(note down)* anotar or tomar el nombre de alguien; **a big n. in the theater** una figura del teatro; **to put one's n. down (for** **sth)** apuntarse (a algo); **to go by** or **under the n. of…** ser conocido(a) como…; **in the n. of…** en nombre de…; **in the n. of God** or **Heaven!, in God's** or **Heaven's n.!** ¡por el amor de Dios!; **he was President in all but n.** él era el Presidente de hecho; **to call sb names** poner verde or insultar a alguien; **he hasn't got a penny to his n.** no tiene ni un centavo or *Esp* duro or *RP* peso; **last n.** apellido *m*

(**b**) *(reputation)* nombre *m*, reputación *f*; **she has a good/ bad n.** tiene buena/mala fama; **to have a n. for prompt and efficient service** tener fama de ofrecer un servicio bueno y rápido; **to make a n. for oneself (as)** hacerse un nombre (como)

2 *vt* (**a**) *(give name to)* poner nombre a, bautizar; **they named her Paula** le pusieron or llamaron Paula; **to n. sb for** or **after sb** poner a alguien el nombre de alguien (**b**) *(appoint)* nombrar (**c**) *(designate, identify)* nombrar; **to n. names** dar nombres concretos; **n. your price** di or pon un precio

name-calling [ˈneɪmkɔːlɪŋ] *n* improperios *mpl*, insultos *mpl*

name-dropper [ˈneɪmdrɒpə(r)] *n Fam* **she's a terrible n.** se las da de conocer a muchos famosos

name-dropping [ˈneɪmdrɒpɪŋ] *n Fam* **there was a lot of n. in his speech** en el discurso se las daba de conocer a muchos famosos

nameless [ˈneɪmlɪs] *adj (person)* anónimo(a); **someone who shall remain n.** alguien que permanecerá en el anonimato

namely [ˈneɪmlɪ] *adv* a saber, es decir

nameplate [ˈneɪmpleɪt] *n* placa *f* con el nombre

namesake [ˈneɪmseɪk] *n* tocayo(a) *m,f*

Namibia [nəˈmɪbɪə] *n* Namibia

Namibian [nəˈmɪbɪən] *n & adj* namibio(a) *m,f*

nancy [ˈnænsɪ] *n very Fam* **n. (boy)** *(homosexual)* mariquita *m*, marica *m*; *(effeminate man)* mariposón *m*

nanny [ˈnænɪ] *n* (**a**) *(nursemaid)* niñera *f* (**b**) **n. goat** cabra *f*

nanosecond [ˈnænəʊsekənd] *n Phys* nanosegundo *m*

nanotechnology [ˈnænəʊtekˈnɒlədʒɪ] *n* nanotecnología *f*

nap¹ [næp] **1** *n (sleep)* cabezada *f*, siesta *f*; **to take** or **have a n.** echar una cabezada or una siesta

2 *vi* (*pt & pp* **napped**) echar una cabezada or una siesta; *Fig* **they were caught napping** los *Esp* cogieron or *Am* agarraron desprevenidos

nap² *n (of cloth)* pelusa *f*, lanilla *f*

napalm [ˈneɪpɑːm] *n* napalm *m*

nape [neɪp] *n* **n. (of the neck)** nuca *f*

naphthalene [ˈnæfθəliːn] *n* naftalina *f*

napkin [ˈnæpkɪn] *n* (**a**) **(table) n.** servilleta *f*; **n. ring** servilletero *m* (aro) (**b**) *(sanitary napkin)* compresa *f*, *Am* toalla *f* higiénica

Naples [ˈneɪpəlz] *n* Nápoles

Napoleonic [nəpəʊlɪˈɒnɪk] *adj* napoleónico(a); **the N. Wars** las guerras napoleónicas

narc [nɑːk] *n Fam* estupa *mf (agente de la brigada de estupefacientes)*

narcissus [nɑːˈsɪsəs] (*pl* **narcissus, narcissi** [nɑːˈsɪsaɪ] *or* **narcissuses**) *n (flower)* narciso *m*

narcosis [nɑːˈkəʊsɪs] *n Med* narcosis *f inv*

narcotic [nɑːˈkɒtɪk] **1** *n* narcótico *m*, estupefaciente *m*; **narcotics agent** agente *mf* (de la brigada) de estupefacientes; **narcotics squad** brigada *f* antidroga *or* de estupefacientes
2 *adj* narcótico(a), estupefaciente

narrate [nəˈreɪt] *vt* narrar

narrative [ˈnærətɪv] **1** *n (story)* narración *f*
2 *adj* narrativo(a)

narrator [nəˈreɪtə(r)] *n* narrador(ora) *m,f*

narrow [ˈnærəʊ] **1** *adj* estrecho(a); *(majority)* escaso(a); **to grow** *or* **become n.** estrecharse, angostarse; **to have a n. mind** ser estrecho(a) de miras; **to have a n. escape** librarse por los pelos; **by a n. margin** *(to win, lose)* por un estrecho margen; **in the narrowest sense** en el sentido mas estricto; **to take a n. view of sth** enfocar algo desde un punto de vista muy limitado; **n. boat** barcaza *f*; **n. gauge** vía *f* estrecha
2 *vt* **to n. one's eyes** *(in suspicion, anger)* entornar los ojos *or* la mirada
3 *vi (road)* estrecharse

▶ **narrow down** *vt sep (choice, possibilities)* limitar, reducir

narrowly [ˈnærəʊlɪ] *adv* **(a)** *(to interpret)* estrictamente, al pie de la letra **(b)** *(only just)* por poco

narrow-minded [ˈnærəʊˈmaɪndɪd] *adj* estrecho(a) de miras

narrow-mindedness [ˈnærəʊˈmaɪndɪdnɪs] *n (of person)* estrechez *f* de miras, cerrazón *f*; *(of attitude, opinions)* cerrazón *f*

narrowness [ˈnærəʊnɪs] *n* estrechez *f*; *(of majority)* escaso margen *m*

NASA [ˈnæsə] *n (abbr* **National Aeronautics and Space Administration)** la NASA, = agencia aeroespacial norteamericana

nasal [ˈneɪzəl] *adj* nasal; **to have a n. voice** tener la voz nasal

nastily [ˈnɑːstɪlɪ] *adv (to act, behave, remark)* con mala intención, desagradablemente; **to fall n.** tener una mala caída

nastiness [ˈnɑːstɪnɪs] *n (of person, remark)* mala intención *f*

nasturtium [nəˈstɜːʃəm] *n* capuchina *f*

nasty [ˈnɑːstɪ] *adj (taste, experience, person)* desagradable; *(remark)* malintencionado(a); *(book, movie, crime)* repugnante; *(shock)* desagradable; *(problem)* espinoso(a), peliagudo(a); **a n. accident** un accidente grave; **a n. cut** una herida muy fea; **a n. fall** una mala caída; **to be n. to sb** ser antipático(a) con alguien; **to turn n.** *(situation, weather)* ponerse feo(a); **hiding her clothes was a really n. thing to do** esconderle la ropa fue una broma demasiado pesada; *Fig* **his behavior left (me with) a n. taste in the mouth** comportamiento me dejó muy mal sabor de boca; **you've got a n. mind!** ¡qué mal pensado eres!

nation [ˈneɪʃən] *n* nación *f*; **n. state** estado-nación *m*

national [ˈnæʃənəl] **1** *n* **(a)** *(person)* ciudadano(a) *m,f*, súbdito(a) *m,f* **(b)** *(newspaper)* periódico *m* (de ámbito) nacional
2 *adj* nacional; **n. anthem** himno *m* nacional; **the n. debt** la deuda pública; **N. Guard** Guardia *f* Nacional; **n. holiday** día *m* festivo *or Am* feriado; **n. park** parque *m* nacional; **n. military service** *(in army)* servicio *m* militar; **N. Rifle Association** = asociación estadounidense que se opone a cualquier restricción en el uso de armas de fuego; **n. security** seguridad *f* nacional; **N. Security Adviser** asesor(ora) *m,f* en materia de seguridad nacional; **N. Security Council** Consejo *m* de Seguridad Nacional; **N. Socialism** nacionalsocialismo *m*

nationalism [ˈnæʃənəlɪzəm] *n* nacionalismo *m*

nationalist [ˈnæʃənəlɪst] *n & adj* nacionalista *mf*

nationalistic [næʃənəˈlɪstɪk] *adj* nacionalista

nationality [næʃəˈnælɪtɪ] *n* nacionalidad *f*

nationalization [næʃənəlaɪˈzeɪʃən] *n* nacionalización *f*

nationalize [ˈnæʃənəlaɪz] *vt* nacionalizar

nationally [ˈnæʃənəlɪ] *adv* en el ámbito nacional; **to be n. renowned** ser conocido(a) en todo el país

nationhood [ˈneɪʃənhʊd] *n* estatus *m inv* de nación

nationwide [ˈneɪʃənwaɪd] **1** *adj* de ámbito nacional
2 *adv* en todo el país; **to be broadcast n.** ser transmitido(a) a todo el país

native [ˈneɪtɪv] **1** *n (of country, town)* natural *mf*, nativo(a) *m,f*; **I am a n. of Tampa** soy natural de Tampa; **the koala is a n. of Australia** el koala es originario de Australia; **she speaks English like a n.** su inglés es perfecto
2 *adj* natal, nativo(a); **he returned to his n. London** regresó a su Londres natal; **N. American** indio(a) *m,f* americano(a); **n. land** tierra *f* natal; **n. language** lengua *f* materna; **n. speaker** hablante *mf* nativo(a); **I'm not a n. speaker of Spanish** mi lengua materna no es el español

Nativity [nəˈtɪvɪtɪ] *n Rel* **the N.** la Natividad; **N. play** auto *m* navideño *or* de Navidad

NATO [ˈneɪtəʊ] *n (abbr* **North Atlantic Treaty Organization)** OTAN *f*

natty [ˈnætɪ] *adj Fam (person, dress)* fino(a), elegante

natural [ˈnætʃərəl] **1** *n* **he's a n. as an actor** es un actor nato
2 *adj* **(a)** *(color, taste)* natural; **death from n. causes** muerte *f* natural; **n. childbirth** parto *m* natural; **n. disaster** catástrofe *f* natural; **n. gas** gas *m* natural; **n. history** historia *f* natural; **n. mother** madre *f* biológica; **n. resources** recursos *mpl* naturales; **n. sciences** ciencias *fpl* naturales; **n. selection** selección *f* natural
(b) *(normal, to be expected)* natural, lógico(a); **it's only n. that you should want to be here** es natural que quieras estar aquí; **one's** *or* **the n. reaction is to...** la reacción más normal es. . .
(c) *(unaffected)* natural, espontáneo(a)

naturalism [ˈnætʃərəlɪzəm] *n* naturalismo *m*

naturalist [ˈnætʃərəlɪst] *n* naturalista *mf*

naturalistic [nætʃərəˈlɪstɪk] *adj* naturalista

naturalization [nætʃərəlaɪˈzeɪʃən] *n* naturalización *f*

naturalize [ˈnætʃərəlaɪz] *vt* naturalizar, nacionalizar

naturally [ˈnætʃərəlɪ] *adv (obviously, logically)* naturalmente; *(in one's nature)* por naturaleza; *(unaffectedly)* con naturalidad; **to come n. to sb** ser innato(a) en alguien

nature [ˈneɪtʃə(r)] *n* **(a)** *(the natural world)* naturaleza *f*; **to let n. take its course** dejar que la naturaleza siga su curso; **n. lover** amante *mf* de la naturaleza; **n. reserve** reserva *f* natural; **n. trail** senda *f* natural, ruta *f* ecológica
(b) *(character) (of thing)* naturaleza *f*; *(of person)* naturaleza *f*, carácter *m*; **to have a jealous n.** tener un carácter celoso; **it's not in her n.** no es su carácter, no es propio de ella; **to be shy by n.** ser tímido(a) por naturaleza
(c) *(sort)* género *m*, clase *f*; **problems of this n.** problemas de este género; *Formal* **what is the n. of your complaint?** ¿cuál es el motivo de su queja?

naturism [ˈneɪtʃərɪzəm] *n* naturismo *m*, nudismo *m*

naught [nɔːt] *n* **(a)** *Literary (nothing)* nada *f*; **his plans came to n.** sus planes (se) quedaron en nada **(b)** cero *m*

naughtily [ˈnɔːtɪlɪ] *adv* **to behave n.** portarse mal

naughtiness [ˈnɔːtɪnɪs] *n (disobedience, mischievousness)* travesura *f*; *(sexual impropriety)* picardía *f*

naughty [ˈnɔːtɪ] *adj (child)* malo(a), travieso(a); *(word, picture, magazine)* picante

Nauru [ˈnaʊruː] *n* Nauru

nausea [ˈnɔːzɪə] *n* náuseas *fpl*

nauseate [ˈnɔːzɪeɪt] *vt* dar *or* provocar náuseas a

nauseating [ˈnɔːzɪeɪtɪŋ] *adj* nauseabundo(a)

nauseatingly [ˈnɔːzɪeɪtɪŋlɪ] *adv* repugnantemente; **she was n. smug** su engreimiento era repugnante

nauseous ['nɔːzɪəs] *adj* nauseabundo(a); **to feel n.** sentir *or* tener náuseas

nautical ['nɔːtɪkəl] *adj* náutico(a); **n. mile** milla *f* marina *or* náutica

naval ['neɪvəl] *adj* naval; **n. battle** batalla *f* naval; **n. officer** oficial *mf* de marina

Navarre [nə'vɑː] *n* Navarra

Navarrese [nævɑː'riːz] *adj* navarro(a)

nave [neɪv] *n Archit (of church)* nave *f* central

navel ['neɪvəl] *n* ombligo *m*

navigable ['nævɪgəbəl] *adj* navegable

navigate ['nævɪgeɪt] **1** *vt (seas)* surcar, navegar por; *(ship)* gobernar, pilotar

2 *vi* navegar; **I'll drive if you n.** *(in car)* yo conduzco *or Am* manejo si tú haces de copiloto

navigation [nævɪ'geɪʃən] *n* navegación *f*

navigational [nævɪ'geɪʃənəl] *adj* **n. equipment** equipo *m* de navegación

navigator ['nævɪgeɪtə(r)] *n Naut* oficial *m* de derrota; *Av* piloto *m* navegante

navy ['neɪvɪ] *n* marina *f*, armada *f*; **n. (blue)** azul *m* marino

Nazi ['nɑːtsɪ] *n & adj* nazi *mf*

Nazism ['nɑːtsɪzəm] *n* nazismo *m*

NB [en'biː] *(abbr* **nota bene)** N.B.

NBA [enbiː'eɪ] *(abbr* **National Basketball Association)** NBA *f*

NBC [enbiː'siː] *(abbr* **National Broadcasting Company)** NBC *f*

NCO [ensiː'əʊ] *(pl* **NCOs)** *n Mil (abbr* **noncommissioned officer)** suboficial *mf*

NE *(abbr* **northeast)** NE

Neanderthal [nɪ'ændətɑːl] **1** *n* (**a**) hombre *m* de Neandert(h)al (**b**) *Fam (coarse person)* troglodita *mf*

2 *adj* (**a**) **N. man** el hombre de Neandert(h)al (**b**) *Fam (attitude, behavior)* cavernícola

Neapolitan [nɪːə'pɒlɪtən] *n & adj* napolitano(a) *m,f*

near [nɪə(r)] **1** *adj* cercano(a), próximo(a); **to the nearest foot** en número redondo de pies; **in the n. future** en un futuro próximo; **it was a n. thing** poco faltó; **this is the nearest thing we have to a conference room** esto es lo más parecido que tenemos a una sala de reuniones; **the N. East** (el) Cercano Oriente, *Esp* (el) Oriente Próximo

2 *adv* cerca; **to be n.** estar cerca; **n. at hand** *(thing)* a mano; *(event)* cercano(a); **they were n. to giving up** estuvieron a punto de abandonar; **n. to tears** a punto de (echarse a) llorar; **n. to despair** próximo(a) a la desesperación; **she's nowhere n. finished** le falta mucho para terminar; **a n. total failure** un fracaso casi absoluto

3 *prep* cerca de; **n. Madrid/downtown** cerca de Madrid/del centro; **her birthday is n. Christmas** su cumpleaños cae por Navidad; **he came n. (to) being run over** estuvo a punto de ser atropellado; **nobody comes anywhere n. her** *(in skill, performance)* nadie se le puede comparar; **he's nowhere n. it!** *(with guess)* ¡no tiene ni idea!

4 *n* **my nearest and dearest** mis (parientes) más allegados

5 *vt* acercarse a, aproximarse a; **to be nearing completion** estar próximo(a) a finalizarse

near- [nɪə(r)] *prefix* **n.-complete** casi completo(a); **n.-perfect** casi perfecto(a)

nearby 1 ['nɪəbaɪ] *adj* cercano(a)

2 [nɪə'baɪ] *adv* cerca

nearly ['nɪəlɪ] *adv (almost)* casi; **we're n. there** *(finished)* ya casi hemos terminado; *(at destination)* ya casi hemos llegado; **he very n. died** estuvo a punto de morir; **not n. enough money/time** muy poco dinero/tiempo; **n. new** casi como nuevo(a); **it's not n. so beautiful as I remember** no es ni de lejos tan bonito como lo recuerdo

nearsighted [nɪə'saɪtɪd] *adj* corto(a) de vista, miope

neat [niːt] *adj* (**a**) *(person) (in habits)* ordenado(a); *(in appearance)* aseado(a), pulcro(a); *(room, house)* pulcro(a), ordenado(a); *(handwriting)* claro(a), nítido(a); *(solution)* certero(a), hábil; **he's a n. worker** es un trabajador esmerado (**b** *(whiskey, vodka)* seco(a), solo(a) (**c**) *Fam (good)* genial, fenomenal

▸**neaten up** ['niːtən] *vt sep (hair, garden)* arreglar

neatly ['niːtlɪ] *adv* (**a**) *(carefully)* cuidadosamente, con esmero (**b**) *(skillfully)* **she n. avoided the subject** eludió hábilmente el tema

neatness ['niːtnɪs] *n (of appearance)* pulcritud *f*; *(of work)* esmero *m*; *(of solution)* acierto *m*, habilidad *f*; *(of handwriting)* nitidez *f*; *(of room, house)* pulcritud *f*

nebula ['nebjʊlə] *n Astron* nebulosa *f*

nebulous ['nebjʊləs] *adj (vague)* nebuloso(a)

necessarily [nesɪ'serəlɪ] *adv* necesariamente; **it's not n. the case** no tiene por qué ser necesariamente así

necessary ['nesɪsərɪ] **1** *n Fam* **to do the n.** hacer lo necesario

2 *adj (indispensable)* necesario(a), preciso(a); **it is n. to remind them** hay que recordárselo; **to do what is n.** hacer lo necesario; **if n.** si es preciso *or* necesario; **when(ever) n.** cuando sea necesario *or* preciso; **a n. evil** un mal necesario

necessitate [nɪ'sesɪteɪt] *vt Formal* hacer necesario(a), precisar

necessity [nɪ'sesɪtɪ] *n (need)* necesidad *f*; **of n.** por fuerza, necesariamente; **necessities** *(things needed)* necesidades *fpl*; *Prov* **n. is the mother of invention** la necesidad aviva el ingenio

neck [nek] **1** *n* (**a**) *(of person, dress, bottle)* cuello *m*; *(of animal)* pescuezo *m*; *(of guitar)* mástil *m*; *(of violin)* mango *m*; *(of land)* istmo *m*; **high n.** *(of dress)* cuello alto; **low n.** *(of dress)* escote *m* (**b**) *(idioms) Fam* **to risk one's n.** jugarse el pellejo; *Fam* **he got it in the n.** *(was severely punished)* se le cayó el pelo; *Fam* **he's in it up to his n.** está metido hasta el cuello; **to finish n. and n.** llegar igualados(as); *Fam* **to stick one's n. out** *(take risk)* arriesgarse; *Fam* **what are you doing in this n. of the woods?** ¿qué haces tú por estos andurriales?

2 *vi Fam (couple) Esp* morrearse, *Am* manosearse

necklace ['neklɪs] *n* collar *m*

neckline ['neklaɪn] *n* escote *m*

necktie ['nektaɪ] *n* corbata *f*

necromancy ['nekrəʊmænsɪ] *n Formal* nigromancia *f*, necromancia *f*

nectar ['nektə(r)] *n* néctar *m*

nectarine ['nektəriːn] *n* nectarina *f*

née, nee [neɪ] *adj* de soltera; **Mrs. Gutteridge, n. Bard** la Sra. Gutteridge, de soltera Bard

need [niːd] **1** *n* necesidad *f* (**for** de); **to attend to sb's needs** atender las necesidades de alguien; **there is no n. to...** no hace falta...; **if n. be, in case of n.** si fuera necesario; **to be in n.** *(poor, destitute)* estar necesitado(a); **to be in n. of sth** necesitar algo; **in time of n.** en los momentos de necesidad; **their n. is greater than mine** ellos están más necesitados que yo

2 *vt (of person)* necesitar; **to n. to do sth** tener que hacer algo; **you'll n. to take more money** te hará falta más dinero; **I didn't n. to be reminded of it** no hizo falta que nadie me lo recordara; **his hair needs cutting** le hace falta un corte de pelo; **the flashlight needs a new battery** hay que cambiarle la pila a la linterna; **this work needs a lot of patience** este trabajo requiere mucha paciencia; *Ironic* **that's all I n.!** ¡sólo me faltaba eso!

3 *modal aux v*

Cuando se emplea como verbo modal sólo existe una forma, y los auxiliares **do/does** no se usan: **he need only worry about himself**; **need she go?**; **it needn't matter**

you needn't worry, I'll be fine! no te preocupes, no me va a pasar nada; **you needn't wait** no hace falta que me esperes; **n. I say more?** no hace falta decir más, ya se sabe

needful ['ni:dfʊl] n Fam **to do the n.** hacer lo necesario; **the n.** (money) Esp la pasta, Am la plata, Méx la lana

needle ['ni:dəl] **1** n (for sewing, of compass, of pine-tree) aguja f; **it's like looking for a n. in a haystack** es como buscar una aguja en un pajar; Fam Fig **to give sb the n.** (annoy) fastidiar a alguien
2 vt Fam pinchar, picar

needlecraft ['ni:dəlkrɑːft] n costura f

needless ['ni:dlɪs] adj innecesario(a); **n. to say,...** ni que decir tiene que..., huelga decir que...

needlessly ['ni:dlɪslɪ] adv innecesariamente

needlework ['ni:dəlwɜːk] n (sewing) costura f; (embroidery) bordado m

need-to-know [ni:dtə'nəʊ] adj **information is given on a n. basis** se proporciona la información sólo a las personas que se considere que la necesitan

needy ['ni:dɪ] **1** npl **the n.** los necesitados
2 adj (person) necesitado(a); **to be n.** estar necesitado(a)

ne'er [neə(r)] adv Literary nunca, jamás

ne'er-do-well ['neədʊwel] n & adj inútil mf

nefarious [nɪ'feərɪəs] adj infame

negate [nɪ'geɪt] vt (work, effect) invalidar, anular

negation [nɪ'geɪʃən] n negación f

negative ['negətɪv] **1** n (a) Gram negación f, forma f negativa; **to answer in the n.** dar una respuesta negativa (b) Phot negativo m
2 adj negativo(a); **don't be so n.!** ¡no seas tan negativo!; Fin **n. cash flow** cash flow m or flujo m de caja negativo; Fin **n. equity** = depreciación del valor de mercado de una propiedad por debajo de su valor en hipoteca; **n. sign** (minus) signo m negativo

negatively ['negətɪvlɪ] adv negativamente

negativity [negə'tɪvɪtɪ] n negatividad f

neglect [nɪ'glekt] **1** n (of garden, person, machine) abandono m, descuido m; (of duty, responsibilities) incumplimiento m; **from or through n.** por negligencia
2 vt (a) (not care for) (child, one's health) descuidar, desatender; **to n. oneself** descuidarse (b) (ignore) (duty, responsibilities) incumplir; (post) abandonar; (one's work) tener abandonado(a); **to n. to do sth** dejar de hacer algo

neglectful [nɪ'glektfʊl] adj descuidado(a), negligente; **to be n. of sth/sb** descuidar or desatender algo/a alguien

negligee, négligée ['neglɪʒeɪ] n salto m de cama, negligé m

negligence ['neglɪdʒəns] n negligencia f

negligent ['neglɪdʒənt] adj negligente

negligently ['neglɪdʒəntlɪ] adv negligentemente

negligible ['neglɪdʒɪbəl] adj insignificante

negotiable [nɪ'gəʊʃəbəl] adj (demand, salary) negociable; **not n.** (obstacle) infranqueable; (path) intransitable; (demand) no negociable, innegociable

negotiate [nɪ'gəʊʃɪeɪt] **1** vt (a) (price, treaty) negociar; **price to be negotiated** precio a convenir (b) (obstacle) salvar, franquear
2 vi negociar

negotiating [nɪ'gəʊʃɪeɪtɪŋ] adj negociador(ora); **the n. table** la mesa de negociaciones

negotiation [nɪgəʊʃɪ'eɪʃən] n negociación f; **under n.** en proceso de negociación; **negotiations** negociaciones

negotiator [nɪ'gəʊʃɪeɪtə(r)] n negociador(ora) m,f

Negress ['ni:grɪs] n Old-fashioned negra f

Negro ['ni:grəʊ] Old-fashioned **1** n (pl **Negroes**) negro(a) m,f
2 adj negro(a); **N. spiritual** (song) espiritual m negro

neigh [neɪ] **1** n relincho m
2 vi relinchar

neighbor ['neɪbə(r)] n vecino(a) m,f; **to be a good n.** ser un buen vecino; Rel **love thy n. as thyself** ama a tu prójimo como a ti mismo

neighborhood ['neɪbəhʊd] n (a) (district) barrio m; (people) vecindario m; **n. watch** vigilancia f vecinal (b) (vicinity) cercanías fpl; **to live in the (immediate) n. of...** vivir en las cercanías de...; **a figure in the n. of $2,000** una cantidad que ronda las 2.000 dólares

neighboring ['neɪbərɪŋ] adj vecino(a)

neighborliness ['neɪbəlɪnɪs] n buena vecindad f

neighborly ['neɪbəlɪ] adj (person) amable (con los vecinos); **to be n.** ser buen(a) vecino(a)

neither ['naɪðə(r), 'niːðə(r)] **1** adv **n. ... nor...** ni... ni...; **n. (the) one nor the other** ni uno ni otro; **that's n. here nor there** eso no viene al caso
2 conj **do I** yo tampoco; **if you don't go n. shall I** si tú no vas, yo tampoco; **the money wasn't available and n. were the facilities** no había ni dinero ni instalaciones
3 adj ninguno(a); **n. driver was injured** ninguno de los conductores resultó herido
4 pron ninguno(a); **which do you want? — n. (of them)** ¿cuál quieres? — ninguno; **n. of my brothers can come** no puede venir ninguno de mis hermanos

nemesis ['neməsɪs] n Literary verdugo m

neo- ['ni:əʊ] prefix neo-

neoclassical [ni:əʊ'klæsɪkəl] adj neoclásico(a)

neoclassicism [ni:əʊ'klæsɪsɪzəm] n neoclasicismo m

neofascism ['ni:əʊ'fæʃɪzəm] n neofascismo m

neofascist [nɪəʊ'fæʃɪst] n & adj neofascista mf

neolithic [ni:əʊ'lɪθɪk] adj neolítico(a)

neologism [nɪ'plədʒɪzəm] n neologismo m

neon ['ni:ɒn] n Chem neón m; **n. light** luz f de neón; **n. sign** letrero m or rótulo m de neón

neonatal ['ni:əʊ'neɪtəl] adj neonatal

neo-Nazi ['ni:əʊ'nɑːtsɪ] n & adj neonazi mf

Nepal [nɪ'pɔːl] n Nepal

Nepalese [nepə'liːz], **Nepali** [ne'pɔːlɪ] **1** n (a) (person) nepalés(esa) m,f, nepalí mf (b) (language) nepalés m, nepalí m
2 adj nepalés(esa), nepalí

nephew ['nefjuː] n sobrino m

nepotism ['nepətɪzəm] n nepotismo m

Neptune ['neptjuːn] n (planet, god) Neptuno

nerd [nɜːd] n Fam (a) (boring person) petardo(a) m,f, RP nerd mf; **a computer n.** un tipo raro obsesionado con los Esp ordenadores or Am computadoras (b) (as insult) bobo(a) m,f, gil mf

nerdy [nɜːdɪ] adj Fam de petardo(a) or RP nerd

nerve [nɜːv] **1** n (a) Anat nervio m; Fam **she gets on my nerves!** ¡me saca de quicio!; **her nerves were in a terrible state** tenía los nervios destrozados; Anat **n. cell** neurona f; Fig **n. center** (of organization) centro m neurálgico; **n. ending** terminación f nerviosa; **n. gas** gas m nervioso (b) (courage) sangre f fría; **to have nerves of steel** tener nervios de acero; **to keep/lose one's n.** mantener/perder la calma (c) Fam (cheek) cara f dura, descaro m; **what a n.!** ¡qué cara más dura!; **you've got a n.!** ¡qué cara tienes!
2 vt **to n. oneself to do sth** templar los nervios para hacer algo

nerve-(w)racking ['nɜːvrækɪŋ] adj angustioso(a)

nervous ['nɜːvəs] adj (a) (apprehensive) inquieto(a), nervioso(a); **to be n.** (by nature) ser nervioso(a); (temporarily) estar nervioso(a); **he was n. about (doing) it** le ponía nervioso (hacerlo) (b) **n. breakdown** crisis f inv nerviosa; **n. energy** nervio m; **n. exhaustion** agotamiento m nervioso; **n. system** sistema m nervioso

nervously ['nɜːvəslɪ] adv nerviosamente

nervousness ['nɜːvəsnɪs] n (of speaker, performer) nerviosismo m

nervy ['nɜːvɪ] *adj Fam* (**a**) *(tense)* nervioso(a); **to be n.** estar nervioso(a) (**b**) *(cheeky)* caradura, fresco(a) (**c**) *(brave)* con agallas, valiente

nest [nest] **1** *n (of bird, bandits)* nido *m*; *(of ants)* hormiguero *m*; *(of wasps)* avispero *m*; *Fig* **to fly the n.** dejar el nido, irse de casa; **n. of tables** mesas *fpl* nido; *Fig* **n. egg** ahorrillos *mpl*
2 *vi* anidar

nesting ['nestɪŋ] *n* **n. box** caja *f* nido

nestle ['nesəl] *vi (person)* acomodarse; **to n. up to sb** recostarse en alguien

nestling ['neslɪŋ] *n (young bird)* polluelo *m*

Net [net] *n Fam Comptr (Internet)* **the N.** la Red; **N. user** internauta *mf*, cibernauta *mf*

net¹ [net] **1** *n* red *f*; *Fig* **to slip through the n.** *(mistake)* colarse; *(criminal)* escaparse; **n. curtain** visillo *m*
2 *vt (pt & pp* **netted**) *(capture) (animals)* capturar, apresar; *(drugs)* incautarse de; *(donations)* recoger; *(reward)* embolsarse

net² **1** *adj (weight, price, profit)* neto(a); **n. revenue** facturación *f*
2 *vt (pt & pp* **netted**) *(earn)* **to n. $2,000** ganar 2.000 dólares netos *or* limpios

netball ['netbɔːl] *n* nétbol *m*, = modalidad de baloncesto para mujeres

Netherlands ['neðələndz] *npl* **the N.** los Países Bajos

nethermost ['neðəməʊst] *adj Literary* inferior

netiquette ['netɪket] *n Comptr* netiqueta *f*

netizen ['netɪzən] *n Comptr* ciudadano(a) *m,f* de la Red, ciuredano(a) *m,f*

netting ['netɪŋ] *n* red *f*, malla *f*

nettle ['netəl] **1** *n (plant)* ortiga *f*
2 *vt (irritate)* irritar, fastidiar

network ['netwɜːk] **1** *n (gen) & Comptr* red *f*; *TV* cadena *f*; **n. computer** *Esp* ordenador *m or Am* computadora *f* de red
2 *vi (establish contacts)* establecer contactos

networking ['netwɜːkɪŋ] *n Com* establecimiento *m* de contactos profesionales

neural ['njʊərəl] *adj Anat* neural

neuralgia [njʊ'rældʒə] *n Med* neuralgia *f*

neurologist [njʊə'rɒlədʒɪst] *n Med* neurólogo(a) *m,f*

neurology [njʊə'rɒlədʒɪ] *n Med* neurología *f*

neuron ['njʊərɒn] *n Anat* neurona *f*

neurosis [njʊ'rəʊsɪs] *(pl* **neuroses** [njʊ'rəʊsiːz]) *n* neurosis *f inv*

neurosurgeon ['njʊərəʊ'sɜːdʒən] *n* neurocirujano(a) *m,f*

neurosurgery [njʊərəʊ'sɜːdʒərɪ] *n Med* neurocirugía *f*

neurotic [njʊ'rɒtɪk] **1** *n* neurótico(a) *m,f*
2 *adj* neurótico(a), paranoico(a); **to be/get n. about sth** estar/ponerse neurótico(a) *or* paranoico(a) por algo

neuter ['njuːtə(r)] **1** *n Gram (género m)* neutro *m*
2 *adj Gram* neutro(a)
3 *vt (animal)* castrar

neutral ['njuːtrəl] **1** *n* (**a**) *(country)* nación *f* neutral; **to be a n.** ser neutral (**b**) *Aut* **in n.** en punto muerto
2 *adj* (**a**) *Pol* neutral (**b**) *(color)* neutro(a); **n. shoe polish** crema *f* (de calzado) incolora

neutrality [njuː'trælɪtɪ] *n* neutralidad *f*

neutralization ['njuːtrəlaɪ'zeɪʃən] *n* neutralización *f*

neutralize ['njuːtrəlaɪz] *vt* neutralizar

neutrino [njʊ'triːnəʊ] *n Phys* neutrino *m*

neutron ['njuːtrɒn] *n Phys* neutrón *m*; **n. bomb** bomba *f* de neutrones

never ['nevə(r)] *adv* nunca; **n. again!** ¡nunca más!; **n. mind!** ¡no importa!; **she n. said a word** no dijo ni una palabra; **I've n. met him** no lo conozco de *or Méx, RP* para nada; **I n. expected this** jamás hubiera esperado esto; **he n. even congratulated me** ni siquiera me felicitó; *Fam* **well I n.!** ¡no me digas!

never-ending [nevər'endɪŋ] *adj* interminable

nevertheless [nevəðə'les] *adv (however)* no obstante, sin embargo; *(despite everything)* de todas maneras, a pesar de todo

new [njuː] *adj* (**a**) *(not old, recent)* nuevo(a); **we need a n. dishwasher** nos hace falta otro lavavajillas *or* un lavavajillas nuevo; **what's n.?** *(greeting)* ¿qué tal?, *CAm, Col, Méx, Ven* ¡qué hubo!; **that's nothing n.!** no es ninguna novedad; **she's n. to this work** es la primera vez que trabaja en esto; **to be n. to a town** ser nuevo(a) en *or* acabar de mudarse a una ciudad; **n. man** hombre *m* moderno *(que ayuda en casa, etc.)*; **n. moon** luna *f* nueva; **n. town** = ciudad satélite de nueva planta creada para descongestionar un núcleo urbano
(**b**) *(in proper names)* **N. Age** = movimiento que gira en torno a las ciencias ocultas, medicinas alternativas, religiones orientales, etc.; **N. Delhi** Nueva Delhi; **N. England** Nueva Inglaterra; **N. Guinea** Nueva Guinea; **N. Hampshire** Nueva Hampshire; **N. Jersey** Nueva Jersey; **N. Mexico** Nuevo México; **N. Orleans** Nueva Orleans; **N. South Wales** Nueva Gales del Sur; **the N. Testament** el Nuevo Testamento; **the N. World** el Nuevo Mundo; **N. Year** año *m* nuevo; **N. Year's Day** día *m* de año nuevo; **N. Year's Eve** Nochevieja *f*; **N. Year's resolutions** = buenos propósitos para el año nuevo; **N. York** Nueva York; **N. Yorker** neoyorquino(a) *m,f*; **N. Zealand** Nueva Zelanda; **N. Zealander** neozelandés(esa) *m,f*, neocelandés(esa) *m,f*

newbie ['njuːbɪ] *n Fam Comptr* novato(a) *m,f*

newborn ['njuːbɔːn] *adj* recién nacido(a); **n. baby** (bebé *m*) recién nacido *m*

newcomer ['njuːkʌmə(r)] *n* recién llegado(a) *m,f* (**to** a)

newfangled ['njuːfæŋɡəld] *adj Pej* moderno(a); **I don't hold with those n. ideas** yo no comulgo con esas moderneces

Newfoundland ['njuːfəndlænd] *n* Terranova

newly ['njuːlɪ] *adv* recién, recientemente; *Econ* **n. industrialized country** país *m* de reciente industrialización

newlyweds ['njuːlɪwedz] *npl* recién casados *mpl*

newness ['njuːnɪs] *n (of design)* novedad *f*; **because of her n. to the job** por ser nueva en el trabajo

news [njuːz] *n* noticias *fpl*; *(TV program)* telediario *m*, *Am* noticiero *m*, *Andes, RP* noticioso *m*; *(radio program)* noticiario *m*, informativo *m*, *Am* noticiero *m*, *Andes, RP* noticioso *m*; **a piece of n.** una noticia; **to be in the n.** ser noticia; **good/bad n.** buenas/malas noticias; *Fam* **he's bad n.** es un tipo de cuidado, tiene mucho peligro; *Fam* **that's n. to me!** ¡(pues) ahora me entero!; *Prov* **no n. is good n.** si no hay noticias, es que todo va bien; **n. agency** agencia *f* de noticias; **n. bulletin** boletín *m* de noticias; **n. conference** rueda *f* de prensa; **n. flash** noticia *f* de última hora *or* de alcance; **n. item** noticia *f*; **n. report** crónica *f* (informativa), artículo *m*; **n. service** servicios *mpl* informativos

newscaster ['njuːzkɑːstə(r)] *n* locutor(ora) *m,f or* presentador(ora) *m,f* de informativos

newsgroup ['njuːzgruːp] *n Comptr* grupo *m* de noticias

newsletter ['njuːzletə(r)] *n* boletín *m* informativo

newsmagazine ['njuːzmæɡəziːn] *n* revista *f* de noticias

newsman ['njuːzmæn] *n (reporter)* periodista *m*

newspaper ['njuːzpeɪpə(r)] *n* periódico *m*; *(daily)* periódico, diario *m*; **wrapped in n.** envuelto(a) en papel de periódico; **n. report** artículo *m* periodístico

newspaperman ['njuːzpeɪpəmæn] *n (reporter)* periodista *m*, hombre *m* de prensa; *(proprietor)* propietario *m* de un periódico, hombre *m* de prensa

newspaperwoman ['njuːzpeɪpəwʊmən] *n (reporter)* periodista *f*; *(proprietor)* propietaria *f* de un periódico

newsprint ['njuːzprɪnt] *n* papel *m* de periódico

newsreel ['njuːzriːl] *n* noticiario *m* cinematográfico, ≃ nodo *m*

newsroom ['njuːzruːm] *n* (sala *f* de) redacción *f*

newsstand ['nju:zstænd] *n* quiosco *m*, puesto *m* de periódicos

newswoman ['nju:zwʊmən] *n (reporter)* periodista *f*

newsworthy ['nju:zwɜ:ðɪ] *adj* de interés periodístico

newt [nju:t] *n* tritón *m*

next [nekst] **1** *adj* **(a)** *(in space)* siguiente; *(room, house)* de al lado; **n. door** (en la casa de) al lado
(b) *(in time, order)* siguiente; **n. week/month** la semana/el mes que viene; **the n. chapter/page** el capítulo/la página siguiente; **the n. time I see him** la próxima vez que lo vea; **it's the n. station** es la próxima estación; **the n. turning on the right** el primer desvío a la derecha; **your name is n. on the list** tu nombre es el siguiente de la lista; **ask the n. person you meet** pregunta a la primera persona que te encuentres; **who's n.?, whose turn is it n.?** ¿quién es el siguiente?, ¿a quién le toca?; **the n. size up/down** una talla más/menos, *RP* el talle siguiente/anterior
2 *adv* **(a)** *(in space)* **to be n. to** estar al lado de; **I can't bear wool n. to my skin** no soporto el contacto de la lana (en la piel)
(b) *(in time, order)* después, luego; **what shall we do n.?** ¿qué hacemos ahora?; **what did you do n.?** ¿qué hiciste después *or* a continuación?; **she'll be asking me to give up my job n.!** ¡ya sólo falta que me pida que deje el trabajo!; **when shall we meet n.?** ¿cuándo nos volveremos a ver?; **n. to my dog I like my sister best** después de mi perro, a quien más quiero es a mi hermana; **if we can't do that, the n. best thing would be to…** si eso no se puede hacer, siempre podríamos…; **the n. fastest after the Ferrari was…** el (siguiente) más rápido después del Ferrari fue…; **who is the n. oldest/youngest after Mark?** ¿quién es el más viejo/joven después de Mark?; **I got it for n. to nothing** lo compré por casi nada; **there is n. to no evidence** no hay apenas pruebas; **in n. to no time** en un abrir y cerrar de ojos
3 *pron* the n. el/la siguiente; **the year after n.** el año siguiente al que viene; **(the) n. to arrive was Carmen** la siguiente en llegar fue Carmen; **n. please!** ¡el siguiente, por favor!; **n. of kin** familiares *mpl or* parientes *mpl* más próximo

next-door ['neks'dɔ:(r)] *adj* de al lado; **the n. neighbors** los vecinos de al lado

NFC [efef'si:] *n (abbr **National Football Conference**)* = una de las conferencias que forman la liga nacional de la NFL

NFL [enef'el] *n (abbr **National Football League**)* = una de las dos ligas nacionales de fútbol americano

NGO [endʒi:'əʊ] *(pl **NGOs**) n (abbr **nongovernmental organization**)* ONG *f*

NHL [enef'el] *n (abbr **National Hockey League**)* = liga estadounidense de hockey sobre hielo

nib [nɪb] *n (of pen)* plumilla *f*

nibble ['nɪbəl] **1** *n* **to have a n. at sth** dar un mordisquito a *or* mordisquear algo; **nibbles** *(snacks)* algo *m* de picar, *Méx* antojitos *mpl*
2 *vt* mordisquear

Nicaragua [nɪkə'rægjʊə] *n* Nicaragua

Nicaraguan [nɪkə'rægjʊən] *n & adj* nicaragüense *mf*

nice [naɪs] *adj* **(a)** *(pleasant)* agradable; *(good)* bueno(a); *(attractive) Esp* bonito(a), *Am* lindo(a); *(friendly)* simpático(a), *Esp* majo(a), *RP* dulce; **to be n. to sb** ser amable con alguien; **to have a n. time** pasarlo bien; **have a n. day!** ¡adiós, buenos días!, ¡que pase un buen día!, *RP* ¡que lo pase bien!; **it was n. of her to…** fue muy amable de su parte…; *Ironic* **we ARE in a n. mess!** ¡nos hemos metido en un buen lío!; *Ironic* **that's a n. way to behave!** *¡Esp* bonita *or Am* linda manera de comportarse!
(b) *(intensive)* **n. and easy** muy fácil; **n. and handy** muy conveniente; **a n. warm bath** un buen baño calentito

nice-looking ['naɪslʊkɪŋ] *adj Esp* guapo(a), *Am* lindo(a)

nicely ['naɪslɪ] *adv* **(a)** *(politely) (to behave)* bien, correctamente; *(to ask)* con educación **(b)** *(well)* bien; **to be doing n.** ir bien; **she has done very n. (for herself)** le han ido muy bien las cosas

nicety ['naɪsɪtɪ] *n* **niceties** detalles *mpl*, sutilezas *fpl*; **to a n.** con suma precisión *or* exactitud

niche [ni:ʃ] *n* hornacina *f*, nicho *m*; *Com* **n. market** nicho *m* de mercado; *Com* **n. marketing** marketing *m* de nichos *or* segmentación

nick [nɪk] *n* **(a)** *(in wood)* muesca *f*; *(on face)* corte *m* **(b) in the n. of time** justo a tiempo
2 *vt (cut) (object)* hacer un corte *or* una muesca en; **to n. one's face** cortarse la cara

nickel ['nɪkəl] *n (metal)* níquel *m*; *(coin)* moneda *f* de cinco centavos

nicknack ['nɪknæk] *n Fam* chuchería *f*, baratija *f*

nickname ['nɪkneɪm] **1** *n* apodo *m*, mote *m*
2 *vt* apodar; **he was nicknamed "Tank"** lo apodaron "Tank"

nicotine ['nɪkəti:n] *n* nicotina *f*; **n. patch** parche *m* de nicotina

niece [ni:s] *n* sobrina *f*

nifty ['nɪftɪ] *adj Fam* **(a)** *(clever) (idea, device)* ingenioso(a) **(b)** *(agile) (person, footwork)* ágil

Niger ['naɪdʒə] *n* Níger

Nigeria [naɪ'dʒɪərɪə] *n* Nigeria

Nigerian [naɪ'dʒɪərɪən] *n & adj* nigeriano(a) *m,f*

niggardly ['nɪgədlɪ] *adj* mísero(a)

nigger ['nɪgə(r)] *n very Fam* = término generalmente ofensivo para referirse a un negro, *RP* grone *m*

niggle ['nɪgəl] **1** *vt* incomodar, fastidiar; **there is still something that is niggling me** todavía hay algo que me provoca desazón
2 *vi (be overfussy)* **to n. about details** ser muy quisquilloso(a); **to n. (away) at sb** dar la tabarra a alguien

niggling ['nɪgəlɪŋ] *adj (details)* de poca monta, insignificante; *(pain)* molesto(a); *(doubt)* inquietante

nigh [naɪ] *adv* **(a)** *Literary* cerca; **the end is n.!** ¡el fin está cerca! **(b) well n. impossible** *(almost)* casi *or* prácticamente imposible

night [naɪt] *n* noche *f*; **at n.** por la noche; **late at n.** bien entrada la noche; **all n.** toda la noche; **last n.** anoche; **tomorrow n.** mañana por la noche; **on Thursday n.** el jueves por la noche; **good n.!** ¡buenas noches!; **to have a n. out** salir por la noche; **to make a n. of it** salir toda la noche; *Fig* **n. bird** noctámbulo(a) *m,f*, trasnochador(ora) *m,f*; **n. flight** vuelo *m* nocturno; *Fig* **n. owl** noctámbulo(a) *m,f*, trasnochador(ora) *m,f*; **n. school** escuela *f* nocturna; **n. shift** turno *m* de noche; **to have good/bad n. vision** ver bien/mal de noche

nightcap ['naɪtkæp] *n* **(a)** *(hat)* gorro *m* de dormir **(b)** *(drink)* copa *f* antes de acostarse

nightclub ['naɪtklʌb] *n* sala *f* de fiestas, discoteca *f*

nightclubbing ['naɪtklʌbɪŋ] *n* **to go n.** ir de discotecas

nightdress ['naɪtdres] *n* camisón *m*

nightfall ['naɪtfɔ:l] *n* anochecer *m*; **at n.** al anochecer

nightgown ['naɪtgaʊn] *n* camisón *m*

nightie ['naɪtɪ] *n Fam* camisón *m*

nightingale ['naɪtɪŋgeɪl] *n* ruiseñor *m*

nightjar ['naɪtdʒɑ:(r)] *n (bird)* chotacabras *m inv*

nightlife ['naɪtlaɪf] *n* vida *f* nocturna, ambiente *m* nocturno

nightlong ['naɪtlɒŋ] *adj* **n. celebrations/vigil** fiesta *f*/ vigilia *f* durante toda la noche

nightly ['naɪtlɪ] **1** *adj* **his n. stroll** su paseo de cada noche; **twice n. flights** dos vuelos cada noche
2 *adv* todas las noches

nightmare ['naɪtmeə(r)] *n also Fig* pesadilla *f*

nightmarish ['naɪtmeərɪʃ] *adj* de pesadilla

nightshirt ['naɪtʃɜːt] *n* camisa *f* de dormir

nightstick ['naɪtstɪk] *n* porra *f*

nighttime ['naɪttaɪm] **1** *n* noche *f*; **at n.** por la noche, durante la noche

  2 *adj* nocturno(a)

nihilist ['naɪɪlɪst] *n* nihilista *mf*

nihilistic [naɪ(h)ɪ'lɪstɪk] *adj* nihilista

nil [nɪl] *n* cero *m*

Nile [naɪl] *n* **the N.** el Nilo

nimble ['nɪmbəl] *adj* ágil; **to have n. feet** *(footballer)* tener un buen juego de piernas

nimbly ['nɪmblɪ] *adv* con agilidad

nincompoop ['nɪŋkəmpuːp] *n Fam* bobo(a) *m,f*, *Esp* percebe *mf*

nine [naɪn] **1** *n* nueve *m*; **a n.-to-five job** un trabajo de oficina *(de nueve a cinco)*; *Fam* **to be dressed up to the nines** ir de punta en blanco

  2 *adj* nueve; *Fig* **n. times out of ten** la mayoría de las veces; **to have n. lives** tener siete vidas (como los gatos); *see also* **eight**

nineteen [naɪn'tiːn] **1** *n* diecinueve *m*

  2 *adj* diecinueve; *see also* **eight**

nineteenth [naɪn'tiːnθ] **1** *n* **(a)** *(fraction)* diecinueveavo *m*, diecinueveava parte *f* **(b)** *(in series)* decimonoveno(a) *m,f* **(c)** *(of month)* diecinueve *m*

  2 *adj* decimonoveno(a); *Fam* **the n. hole** *(of golf course)* el bar; *see also* **eleventh**

ninetieth ['naɪntɪθ] *n & adj* nonagésimo(a) *m,f*

nine-to-five ['naɪntə'faɪv] **1** *adj* **a n. job** un trabajo de oficina *(de nueve a cinco)*

  2 *adv* **to work n.** trabajar de nueve a cinco, tener horario de oficina

ninety ['naɪntɪ] **1** *n* noventa *m*

  2 *adj* noventa; **n.-nine times out of a hundred** el noventa y nueve por ciento de las veces; *see also* **eighty**

ninth [naɪnθ] **1** *n* **(a)** *(fraction)* noveno *m*, novena parte *f* **(b)** *(in series)* noveno(a) *m,f* **(c)** *(of month)* nueve *m*

  2 *adj* noveno(a); *see also* **eighth**

nip [nɪp] **1** *n* **(a)** *(pinch)* pellizco *m*; *(with teeth)* bocado *m*, mordisquillo *m*; *Fam* **it was n. and tuck right until the end** fueron muy igualados hasta el final **(b)** **there's a n. in the air** hace fresco **(c)** *Fam (of liquor)* chupito *m*, copita *f*

  2 *vt* *(pt & pp* **nipped)** **(a)** *(pinch)* pellizcar; *(with teeth)* mordisquear; *Fam Fig* **to n. sth in the bud** cortar algo de raíz **(b)** *(of cold, frost)* helar **(c)** *Fam (steal)* afanar, *Esp* mangar

  3 *vi (sting)* escocer

nipple ['nɪpəl] *n (female)* pezón *m*; *(male)* tetilla *f*; *(on baby's bottle)* tetilla *f*, tetina *f*

nippy ['nɪpɪ] *adj Fam* **(a)** *(quick)* ligero(a), rápido(a) **(b)** *(cold)* fresco(a); **it's a bit n. today** hoy hace un poco de fresco

nit [nɪt] *n (insect)* piojo *m*; *(insect's egg)* liendre *f*

nit-pick ['nɪtpɪk] *vi Fam* poner peros *or Esp* pegas, ser un(a) quisquilloso(a)

nit-picker ['nɪtpɪkə(r)] *n Fam* quisquilloso(a) *m,f*

nit-picking ['nɪtpɪkɪŋ] *Fam* **1** *n* critiqueo *m* por nimiedades, *Esp* puñetería *f*

  2 *adj* quisquilloso(a)

nitrate ['naɪtreɪt] *n* nitrato *m*

nitric ['naɪtrɪk] *adj* nítrico(a)

nitrogen ['naɪtrədʒən] *n* nitrógeno *m*

nitroglycerin(e) [naɪtrəʊ'glɪsəriːn] *n* nitroglicerina *f*

nitrous ['naɪtrəs] *adj* nitroso(a)

nitty-gritty ['nɪtɪ'grɪtɪ] *n Fam* meollo *m*; **to get down to the n.** ir al grano, ir al meollo del asunto

nitwit ['nɪtwɪt] *n Fam* idiota *mf*, bobo(a) *m,f*

NNE *(abbr* **north-northeast)** NNE, nornordeste

NNW *(abbr* **north-northwest)** NNO, nornoroeste

No, no *(abbr* **number)** n°, núm., número

no [nəʊ] **1** *adv* **(a)** *(interjection)* no; **to say no** decir que no; **she won't take no for an answer** no para hasta salirse con la suya **(b)** *(not)* no; **he's no cleverer than her** no es más listo que ella; **no more/less than $100** no más/menos de 100 dólares

  2 *adj* **there is no bread** no hay pan; **he's no friend of mine** no es amigo mío; **I am in no way surprised** no me sorprende en absoluto; **there's no denying it** no se puede negar; **there's no pleasing him** no hay forma de agradarle; **no smoking** *(sign)* prohibido fumar; *Fam* **no way!** ¡ni hablar!, *Esp* ¡de eso nada!, *Am* ¡para nada!

  3 *n (pl* **noes)** *Pol* **ayes and noes** votos a favor y en contra

Noah's ark ['nəʊəz'ɑːk] *n* el arca de Noé

Nobel Prize ['nəʊbel'praɪz] *n* Premio *m* Nobel

nobility [nəʊ'bɪlɪtɪ] *n* nobleza *f*

noble ['nəʊbəl] **1** *n* noble *mf*

  2 *adj (birth, person)* noble; *(sentiment, act)* noble, magnánimo(a); *(building, sight)* grandioso(a)

nobleman ['nəʊbəlmən] *n* noble *m*

noble-minded [nəʊbəl'maɪndɪd] *adj* noble

noblewoman ['nəʊbəlwʊmən] *n* noble *f*

nobly ['nəʊblɪ] *adv* generosamente, noblemente

nobody ['nəʊbədɪ] **1** *n* **he's/she's a n.** es un/una don nadie

  2 *pron* nadie; **n. spoke to me** nadie me dirigió la palabra; **n. else** nadie más; **he is n.'s fool** no tiene un pelo de tonto; **if you don't have money, you're n.** si no tienes dinero, no eres nadie

no-brainer ['nəʊ'breɪnə(r)] *n Fam* **it's a n.** está tirado

nocturnal [nɒk'tɜːnəl] *adj* nocturno(a)

nod [nɒd] **1** *n (greeting)* saludo *m* (con la cabeza); *(in agreement)* señal *f* de asentimiento *(con la cabeza)*; **to give sth/sb the n.** dar el consentimiento para algo/a alguien

  2 *vt* *(pt & pp* **nodded)** **(a)** **to n. one's head** *(in assent)* asentir con la cabeza; *(in greeting)* saludar con la cabeza; *(as signal)* hacer una señal con la cabeza; **to n. one's approval** dar la aprobación con una inclinación de cabeza

  3 *vi* **to n. in agreement** asentir con la cabeza

▸**nod off** *vi Fam* quedarse dormido(a), dormirse

nodding ['nɒdɪŋ] *adj* **to have a n. acquaintance with sth/ sb** conocer un poco algo/a alguien; *Fam* **n. donkey** *(oil-pump)* = tipo de bomba para extraer petróleo

node [nəʊd] *n* nudo *m*; *Med* nodo *m*, nódulo *m*

nodule ['nɒdjuːl] *n* nódulo *m*

no-fault ['nəʊ'fɔːlt] *adj Law* **n. compensation** seguro *m* a todo riesgo; **n. divorce** divorcio *m* de mutuo acuerdo

no-fly zone [nəʊ'flaɪzəʊn] *n* zona *f* de exclusión aérea

no-frills [nəʊ'frɪlz] *adj* sin florituras

no-go area ['nəʊ'gəʊ'eərɪə] *n* zona *f* prohibida

no-good ['nəʊgʊd] *Fam adj* inútil

no-holds-barred ['nəʊ'həʊldz'bɑːd] *adj (report, documentary)* a fondo, sin restricciones

noise [nɔɪz] *n* ruido *m*; **to make a n.** *(individual sound)* hacer un ruido; *(racket)* hacer ruido; **to make noises about doing sth** andar diciendo que uno va a hacer algo; *Fig* **a big n.** un pez gordo

noiselessly ['nɔɪzlɪslɪ] *adv* silenciosamente

noisily ['nɔɪzɪlɪ] *adv* ruidosamente

noisy ['nɔɪzɪ] *adj* ruidoso(a)

nomad ['nəʊmæd] *n & adj* nómada *mf*

nomadic [nəʊ'mædɪk] *adj* nómada

no man's land ['nəʊmænzlænd] *n also Fig* tierra *f* de nadie

nomenclature [nəʊ'menklətʃə(r)] *n* nomenclatura *f*

nominal ['nɒmɪnəl] *adj* nominal; *(price, amount)* simbólico(a)

nominally ['nɒmɪnəlɪ] *adv* nominalmente

nominate ['nɒmɪneɪt] *vt (propose)* proponer; *(appoint)* nombrar

nomination [nɒmɪ'neɪʃən] *n (proposal)* nominación *f*; *(appointment)* nombramiento *m*

nominative ['nɒmɪnətɪv] **1** *n* nominativo *m*
2 *adj* nominativo(a)

nominee [nɒmɪ'niː] *n* candidato(a) *m,f*

non- [nɒn] *prefix* no

nonacceptance ['nɒnək'septəns] *n* no aceptación *f*

nonaddictive ['nɒnə'dɪktɪv] *adj* que no crea adicción

nonaggression pact [nɒnə'greʃən'pækt] *n Pol* pacto *m* de no agresión

nonalcoholic [nɒnælkə'hɒlɪk] *adj* sin alcohol

nonaligned [nɒnə'laɪnd] *adj Pol* no alineado(a)

nonattendance [nɒnə'tendəns] *n* ausencia *f*

nonbinding ['nɒn'baɪndɪŋ] *adj* no vinculante

nonbiodegradable ['nɒnbaɪəʊdɪ'greɪdəbəl] *adj* no biodegradable

nonchalance [nɒnʃə'lɑːns] *n* indiferencia *f*, despreocupación *f*

nonchalant [nɒnʃə'lɑːnt] *adj* indiferente, despreocupado(a)

nonchalantly [nɒnʃə'lɑːntlɪ] *adv* con indiferencia *or* despreocupación

noncombatant [nɒn'kɒmbətənt] *n & adj Mil* no combatiente *mf*

noncommissioned officer ['nɒnkəmɪʃənd'ɒfɪsə(r)] *n Mil* suboficial *mf*

noncommittal [nɒnkə'mɪtəl] *adj (answer)* evasivo(a); **to be n.** responder con evasivas

noncompliance ['nɒnkəm'plaɪəns] *n Formal* incumplimiento *m* **(with** de)

nonconformist [nɒnkən'fɔːmɪst] *n & adj* inconformista *mf*

nondairy ['nɒndeərɪ] *adj* no lácteo(a)

nondeductible [nɒndɪ'dʌktɪbəl] *adj Fin* no desgravable

nondescript [nɒndɪ'skrɪpt] *adj* anodino(a)

none [nʌn] **1** *pron (not any)* nada; *(not one)* ninguno(a); **n. of us/them** ninguno de nosotros/ellos; **n. of this concerns me** nada de esto me concierne; **it was n. other than the President** no era otro que el propio Presidente; **there was n. left** no quedaba nada; **there were n. left** no quedaba ninguno; *Fam* **we'll have n. of that!** ¡eso no te lo consiento!
2 *adv* **his answer left me n. the wiser** su respuesta no me aclaró nada; **she was n. too happy about the situation** la situación no le hacía ninguna gracia; **n. too soon** justo a tiempo

nonentity [nɒ'nentɪtɪ] *n* nulidad *f*

nonessential [nɒnɪ'senʃəl] **1** *n* **nonessentials** lo accesorio
2 *adj* accesorio(a), prescindible

nonetheless [nʌnðə'les] *adv (however)* no obstante, sin embargo; *(despite everything)* de todas maneras, a pesar de todo

nonevent [nɒnɪ'vent] *n* chasco *m*; **the party turned out to be a bit of a n.** al final la fiesta no fue nada especial

nonexecutive director [nɒnɪg'zekjʊtɪvdaɪ'rektə(r)] *n* director(ora) *m,f* no ejecutivo(a)

nonexistent [nɒnɪg'zɪstənt] *adj* inexistente

nonfat ['nɒnfæt] *adj (food)* sin grasa

nonfiction [nɒn'fɪkʃən] *n* no ficción *f*

nonflammable [nɒn'flæməbəl] *adj* incombustible, ininflamable

non-habit-forming ['nɒn'hæbɪtfɔːmɪŋ] *adj* que no crea adicción

nonintervention ['nɒnɪntə'venʃən] *n* no intervención *f*

nonlinear [nɒn'lɪnɪə(r)] *adj Comptr* **n. programming** programación *f* no lineal

nonnative ['nɒn'neɪtɪv] *adj* no nativo(a); **n. speaker** hablante *mf* no nativo

nonnegotiable [nɒnnɪ'gəʊʃɪəbəl] *adj* no negociable

nonnuclear [nɒn'njuːklɪə(r)] *adj (war)* convencional; *(energy)* no nuclear; *(country)* sin armamento nuclear

no-no ['nəʊnəʊ] *n Fam* **that's a n.** eso ni se te ocurra

no-nonsense [nəʊ'nɒnsəns] *adj (approach)* serio(a) y directo(a); *(implement, gadget)* práctico(a), funcional

nonpartisan [nɒn'pɑːtɪzæn] *adj* imparcial

nonpayment [nɒn'peɪmənt] *n* impago *m*

nonperson [nɒn'pɜːsən] *(pl* **nonpersons)** *n* **politically, she became a n.** políticamente hablando, dejó de existir

nonplus(s)ed [nɒn'plʌst] *adj* perplejo(a), anonadado(a)

nonprofit [nɒn'prɒfɪt] *adj* sin ánimo de lucro

nonracial [nɒn'reɪʃəl] *adj* no racista

nonrefundable ['nɒnriː'fʌndəbəl] *adj (deposit)* a fondo perdido, sin posibilidad de reembolso

nonresident [nɒn'rezɪdənt] *n (of country, hotel)* no residente *mf*

nonreturnable [nɒnrɪ'tɜːnəbəl] *adj* no retornable

nonsectarian ['nɒnsek'teərɪən] *adj* no sectario(a)

nonsense ['nɒnsəns] *n* tonterías *fpl*, disparates *mpl*; **n.!** ¡tonterías!; **to talk (a lot of) n.** decir (muchos) disparates; **to make a n. of sth** echar por tierra algo

nonsensical [nɒn'sensɪkəl] *adj* absurdo(a), disparatado(a)

non sequitur [nɒn'sekwɪtə(r)] *n* incongruencia *f*

nonsexist [nɒn'seksɪst] *adj* no sexista

nonsmoker [nɒn'sməʊkə(r)] *n* no fumador(ora) *m,f*

nonsmoking ['nɒnsməʊkɪŋ] *adj (area, carriage)* de no fumadores; **this is a n. flight** no está permitido fumar en este vuelo

nonspecialist [nɒn'speʃəlɪst] **1** *n* profano(a) *m,f*
2 *adj* no especializado(a)

nonstandard ['nɒn'stændəd] *adj* **(a)** *Ling* no normativo(a) **(b)** *(product, size)* fuera de lo común

nonstarter [nɒn'stɑːtə(r)] *n* **the project's a n.** es un proyecto inviable

nonstick ['nɒn'stɪk] *adj* antiadherente

nonstop ['nɒn'stɒp] **1** *adj (journey, flight)* directo(a), sin escalas
2 *adv* sin parar, ininterrumpidamente; *(fly)* directo

nontariff barrier ['nɒn'tærɪf'bærɪə(r)] *n Econ* barrera *f* no arancelaria

nontransferable ['nɒntræns'fɜːrəbəl] *adj* intransferible

nonverbal [nɒn'vɜːbəl] *adj* no verbal; **n. communication** comunicación *f* no verbal

nonviolent [nɒn'vaɪələnt] *adj* no violento(a)

noodle ['nuːdəl] *n* **(a)** *(pasta)* **noodles** tallarines *mpl (chinos)* **(c)** *Fam (head)* coco *m*, mollera *f*

nook [nʊk] *n* rincón *m*, recoveco *m*; **nooks and crannies** recovecos *mpl*

nooky, nookie ['nʊkɪ] *n Fam* marcha *f* para el cuerpo, ñacañaca *m*; **to get one's n.** echar un polvete *or Méx* caldito

noon [nuːn] *n* mediodía *m*; **at n.** al mediodía

noonday ['nuːndeɪ] *n* **the n. sun** el sol del mediodía

no one ['nəʊwʌn] *pron* = **nobody**

noose [nuːs] *n (loop)* nudo *m* corredizo; *(rope)* soga *f*; *Fig* **to put one's head in a n.** meterse en la boca del lobo

nope [nəʊp] *adv Fam* no

nor [nɔː(r)] *conj* ni; **neither... n.** ni... ni; **he neither drinks n. smokes** ni fuma ni bebe *or Am* toma; **n. do I** yo tampoco, ni yo

Nordic ['nɔːdɪk] *adj* nórdico(a)

norm [nɔːm] *n* norma *f*; **to deviate from the n.** salirse de la norma

normal ['nɔːməl] **1** *n* **above/below n.** *(temperature, rate)* por encima/por debajo de lo normal; **things quickly got back to n. after the strike** las cosas volvieron pronto a la normalidad después de la huelga
2 *adj* normal

normality [nɔːˈmælɪtɪ], **normalcy** [ˈnɔːməlsɪ] *n* normalidad *f*

normalization [nɔːməlaɪˈzeɪʃən] *n* normalización *f*

normalize [ˈnɔːməlaɪz] **1** *vt* normalizar
2 *vi* normalizarse

normally [ˈnɔːməlɪ] *adv* normalmente

Norman [ˈnɔːmən] *n & adj* normando(a) *m,f*

Normandy [ˈnɔːməndɪ] *n* Normandía

north [nɔːθ] **1** *n* norte *m*; **to the n. (of)** al norte (de); **the N.-South divide** la división Norte-Sur
2 *adj (direction, side)* norte; **n. London** el norte de Londres; **n. wind** viento *m* del norte; **N. Africa** África del Norte; **N. African** norteafricano(a) *m,f*; **N. America** Norteamérica; **N. American** norteamericano(a) *m,f*; **N. Carolina** Carolina del Norte; **N. Dakota** Dakota del Norte; **the N. Pole** el Polo Norte; **the N. Sea** el Mar del Norte
3 *adv* al norte; **to face n.** estar orientado(a) al norte; **to go n.** ir hacia el norte

northbound [ˈnɔːθbaʊnd] *adj (train, traffic)* en dirección norte; **the n. freeway** el carril que va hacia el norte

northeast [nɔːˈθiːst] **1** *n* nordeste *m*, noreste *m*
2 *adj (side)* nordeste, noreste; **n. wind** viento *m* del nordeste
3 *adv (to go, move)* hacia el nordeste; *(to be situated, face)* al nordeste

northeasterly [nɔːˈθiːstəlɪ] **1** *n (wind)* viento *m* del nordeste
2 *adj (direction)* nordeste; **n. wind** viento *m* del nordeste

northeastern [nɔːˈθiːstən] *adj (region)* del nordeste

northerly [ˈnɔːðəlɪ] **1** *n (wind)* viento *m* del norte
2 *adj (direction)* norte; **the most n. point** el punto más septentrional; **n. wind** viento *m* del norte

northern [ˈnɔːðən] *adj (region, accent)* del norte, norteño(a); **n. Spain** el norte de España; **n. hemisphere** hemisferio *m* norte; **N. Ireland** Irlanda del Norte; **N. Irish** norirlandés(esa); **n. lights** aurora *f* boreal

northerner [ˈnɔːðənə(r)] *n* norteño(a) *m,f*

north-facing [ˈnɔːθˈfeɪsɪŋ] *adj* orientado(a) al norte

North Korea [ˈnɔːθkəˈriːə] *n* Corea del Norte

North Korean [ˈnɔːθkəˈriːən] *n & adj* norcoreano(a) *m,f*

north-northeast [nɔːθnɔːˈθiːst] *adv* en dirección nornordeste

north-northwest [nɔːθnɔːˈθwest] *adv* en dirección nornoroeste

northward [ˈnɔːθwəd] *adj & adv* hacia el norte

northwards [ˈnɔːθwədz] *adv* hacia el norte

northwest [nɔːθˈwest] **1** *n* noroeste *m*
2 *adj (side)* noroeste; **n. wind** viento *m* del noroeste
3 *adv (to go, move)* hacia el noroeste; *(to be situated, face)* al noroeste

northwesterly [nɔːθˈwestəlɪ] **1** *n (wind)* viento *m* del noroeste
2 *adj (direction)* noroeste; **n. wind** viento *m* del noroeste

northwestern [nɔːθˈwestən] *adj (region)* del noroeste

Norway [ˈnɔːweɪ] *n* Noruega

Norwegian [nɔːˈwiːdʒən] **1** *n* **(a)** *(person)* noruego(a) *m,f* **(b)** *(language)* noruego *m*
2 *adj* noruego(a)

nose [nəʊz] *n* **(a)** *(of person)* nariz *f*; *(of animal)* hocico *m*; **her n. is bleeding** está sangrando por la nariz; **to blow one's n.** sonarse la nariz; **to hold one's n.** taparse la nariz; **to have a n. job** *(cosmetic surgery)* operarse la nariz
(b) *(of vehicle, plane, missile)* morro *m*
(c) *(idioms)* **it's right under your n.** lo tienes delante de las narices; **to turn one's n. up at sth** hacerle ascos a algo; **she walked by with her n. in the air** pasó con gesto engreído; **to look down one's n. at sb** mirar a alguien por encima del hombro; **she paid through the n. for it** le costó un ojo de la cara; **to get up sb's n.** poner negro(a) a alguien; **they are**

leading them by the n. les están manejando a su antojo; **to keep one's n. clean** no meterse en líos; **to have a n. for sth** tener olfato para algo; **to poke one's n. into other people's business** meter las narices en los asuntos de otros; **to put sb's n. out of joint** hacerle un feo a alguien

▸**nose around, nose about** *vi Fam* curiosear

nosebleed [ˈnəʊzbliːd] *n* **to have a n.** sangrar por la nariz

-nosed [nəʊzd] *suffix* **red-n.** con la nariz colorada

nosedive [ˈnəʊzdaɪv] **1** *n (of plane) Esp* picado *m*, *Am* picada *f*; *(of prices)* caída *f* en *Esp* picado *or Am* picada
2 *vi (plane)* hacer *Esp* un picado *or Am* una picada; *(prices)* caer en *Esp* picado *or Am* picada

nosey = **nosy**

no-show [nəʊˈʃəʊ] *n (for flight)* pasajero *m* (con reserva) no presentado; *(at theater)* reserva *f* no cubierta

nosiness [ˈnəʊzɪnɪs] *n* curiosidad *f*, entrometimiento *m*

no-smoking [nəʊˈsməʊkɪŋ] *adj (area)* de *or* para no fumadores; **this is a n. flight** en este vuelo está prohibido fumar

nostalgia [nɒsˈtældʒɪə] *n* nostalgia *f* (**for** de)

nostalgic [nɒsˈtældʒɪk] *adj* nostálgico(a)

nostalgically [nɒsˈtældʒɪklɪ] *adv* con nostalgia

nostril [ˈnɒstrɪl] *n* orificio *m* nasal, ventana *f* de la nariz

nosy, nosey [ˈnəʊzɪ] *adj Fam* entrometido(a)

not [nɒt] *adv*

En el inglés hablado, y en el escrito en estilo coloquial, **not** se contrae después de verbos modales y auxiliares.

no; **n. me/him** yo/él no; **I don't know** no sé; **don't move!** ¡no te muevas!; **whether she likes it or n.** le guste o no; **I think/hope n.** creo/espero que no; **she asked me n. to tell him** me pidió que no se lo dijera; **n. wishing to cause an argument, he said nothing** como no deseaba provocar una discusión, no dijo nada; **you understand, don't you?** entiendes, ¿no?; **n. at all** en absoluto; **thank you so much! — n. at all!** ¡muchísimas gracias! — ¡de nada! *or* ¡no hay de qué!; **n. always** no siempre; **n. any more** ya no; **n. even** ni siquiera; **n. only... but also...** no sólo... sino también...; **n. yet** todavía no, aún no; **n. that I minded** no es que me importara; **n. that it matters** no es que importe

notable [ˈnəʊtəbəl] *adj* notable; **to be n. for sth** destacar por algo

notably [ˈnəʊtəblɪ] *adv (especially)* en particular, en especial; *(noticeably)* notablemente

notary [ˈnəʊtərɪ] *n Law* **n. (public)** notario(a) *m,f*, *Am* escribano(a) *m,f*

notation [nəʊˈteɪʃən] *n* notación *f*

notch [nɒtʃ] **1** *n* **(a)** *(in stick)* muesca *f* **(b)** *(grade, level)* punto *m*, grado *m*; **she's a n. above the rest** está por encima de los demás
2 *vt (once)* hacer una muesca en; *(several times)* hacer muescas en

▸**notch up** *vt sep (victory, sale)* apuntarse

note [nəʊt] **1** *n* **(a)** *(short letter, at foot of page, record)* nota *f*; **(lecture) notes** apuntes *mpl* de clase; **to take** *or* **make a n. of sth** tomar nota de algo; **to take n. of sth/sb** *(notice)* fijarse en algo/alguien **(b)** *(musical)* nota *f*; *Fig (of doubt, anger)* nota *f*, tono *m*; **on a lighter n.** pasando a cosas menos serias **(c)** *(of)* **n.** excepcional, destacable
2 *vt (notice)* notar; *(mention)* señalar; *(error, mistake)* advertir; *(fact)* darse cuenta de; **please n. that...** tenga en cuenta que...

▸**note down** *vt sep* anotar, apuntar

notebook [ˈnəʊtbʊk] *n* libreta *f*; *(bigger)* cuaderno *m*; *Comptr Esp* ordenador *m or Am* computadora *f* portátil

noted [ˈnəʊtɪd] *adj* destacado(a); **to be n. for sth** destacar por algo

notepad [ˈnəʊtpæd] *n* bloc *m* de notas

notepaper ['nəʊtpeɪpə(r)] *n* papel *m* de carta
noteworthy ['nəʊtwɜːðɪ] *adj* digno(a) de mención
not-for-profit ['nɒtfə'prɒfɪt] *adj* sin ánimo de lucro
nothing ['nʌθɪŋ] **1** *pron* nada; **n. happened** no pasó nada; **say n. about it** no digas nada (de esto); **to say n. of...** por no hablar de...; **he was n. if not discreet** desde luego fue muy discreto; **n. new/remarkable** nada nuevo/especial; **n. else** nada más; **n. but** tan sólo; **you've caused me n. but trouble** no me has traído (nada) más que problemas; **buy n. but the best** compre sólo lo mejor; **n. much** no mucho, poca cosa; **there is n. more to be said** no hay (nada) más que decir; **there's n. like a nice steak!** ¡no hay nada como un buen filete!; **as a pianist he has n. on his brother** como pianista, no tiene ni punto de comparación con su hermano; **there's n. in it** *(it's untrue)* es falso; **he thinks n. of telling lies to get what he wants** no le importa mentir para conseguir sus propósitos; *Fam* **there's n. to it** no tiene ningún misterio; **$1,000 is n. to her** para ella 1.000 dólares no son nada; **I have n. to do** no tengo nada que hacer; **to have n. to do with sth/sb** no tener nada que ver con algo/alguien; **we have n. to do with the neighbors** no tenemos trato con los vecinos; **that's n. to do with you** no tiene nada que ver contigo; **to get angry/worried for** *or* **about n.** *esp Esp* enfadarse *or esp Am* enojarse/preocuparse por nada; **to do sth for n.** *(in vain)* hacer algo para nada; *(with no reason)* hacer algo porque sí; *(free of charge)* hacer algo gratis
2 *n* **to come to n.** quedar en nada; **a hundred dollars? — a mere n.!** ¿cien dólares? – ¡una bagatela!
3 *adv* **she looks n. like her sister** no se parece en nada a su hermana; **it was n. like as difficult as they said** no era ni mucho menos tan difícil como decían
notice ['nəʊtɪs] **1** *n* (a) *(warning)* aviso *m*; **to give sb n. of sth** avisar a alguien de algo, notificar algo a alguien; **without (prior) n.** sin previo aviso; **until further n.** hasta nuevo aviso; **at short n.** en poco tiempo, con poca antelación; **at a moment's n.** enseguida; **to give (one's) n., to hand in one's n.** *(resign)* presentar la dimisión, despedirse; **to give sb (their) n.** *(make redundant)* despedir a alguien; **to give sb a month's n.** *(of redundancy)* comunicarle a alguien el despido con un mes de antelación; *(to move out)* darle a alguien un plazo de un mes para abandonar el inmueble
(b) *(attention)* **to take n. of sth/sb** prestar atención a algo/alguien; **to take no n. (of)** no hacer caso (de); **to attract n.** llamar la atención; **the fact escaped everyone's n.** el hecho pasó inadvertido a todo el mundo; **it has come to my n. that...** ha llegado a mi conocimiento que...
(c) *(sign)* cartel *m*
(d) *Theat* crítica *f*, reseña *f*
2 *vt (realize)* darse cuenta de; *(sense)* notar; *(observe)* fijarse en; **I noticed he was uncomfortable** me di cuenta de que estaba incómodo; **have you noticed anything strange in her behavior?** ¿has notado algo extraño en su comportamiento?; **I noticed a man yawning at the back** me fijé en un hombre al fondo que bostezaba; **to be noticed, to get oneself noticed** llamar la atención
3 *vi* darse cuenta
noticeable ['nəʊtɪsəbəl] *adj (change, difference)* apreciable, notable; **barely n.** apenas perceptible; **it was very n. that...** se notaba claramente que...
noticeably ['nəʊtɪsəblɪ] *adv* claramente, notablemente
notifiable [nəʊtɪ'faɪəbəl] *adj (disease)* notificable
notification [nəʊtɪfɪ'keɪʃən] *n* notificación *f*; **to give sb n. of sth** notificar algo a alguien
notify ['nəʊtɪfaɪ] *vt* notificar; **to n. sb of sth** notificar algo a alguien
notion ['nəʊʃən] *n* (a) *(idea, concept)* idea *f*, noción *f*; **to have no n. of sth** no tener noción de algo; **I have a n. that...** me

parece que...; **to have a n. to do sth** tener el capricho de hacer algo (b) **notions** *(sewing materials)* cosas *fpl* de costura; **notions store** mercería *f*
notoriety [nəʊtə'raɪətɪ] *n* mala fama *f*
notorious [nəʊ'tɔːrɪəs] *adj Pej* (tristemente) famoso(a) *or* célebre; **he's n. for his bad temper** todo el mundo conoce su mal humor
notoriously [nəʊ'tɔːrɪəslɪ] *adv* **it is n. difficult/bad** es de sobra conocido lo difícil/malo que es
notwithstanding [nɒtwɪθ'stændɪŋ] *Formal* **1** *prep* a pesar de, pese a
2 *adv* no obstante, sin embargo
nougat ['nuːgɑː] *n* = tipo de dulce con frutos secos
noun [naʊn] *n Gram* sustantivo *m*, nombre *m*; **proper n.** nombre propio
nourish ['nʌrɪʃ] *vt (person, animal)* nutrir, alimentar; *(feeling, hope)* abrigar, albergar; **to be well nourished** estar bien alimentado(a)
nourishing ['nʌrɪʃɪŋ] *adj* nutritivo(a)
nourishment ['nʌrɪʃmənt] *n (food)* alimentos *mpl*; *(nourishing quality)* alimento *m*, alimentación *f*
Nov *(abbr* **noviembre**) noviembre *m*
Nova Scotia ['nəʊvə'skəʊʃə] *n* Nueva Escocia
novel ['nɒvəl] **1** *n* novela *f*
2 *adj (original)* novedoso(a), original
novelist ['nɒvəlɪst] *n* novelista *mf*
novelty ['nɒvəltɪ] *n (newness)* novedad *f*; *(cheap toy)* baratija *f*; **the n. will soon wear off** pronto dejará de ser una novedad; **it has a certain n. value** tiene un cierto atractivo por ser nuevo
November [nəʊ'vembə(r)] *n* noviembre *m*; *see also* **May**
novice ['nɒvɪs] *n (beginner)* principiante *mf*, novato(a) *m,f*; *Rel* novicio(a) *m,f*
now [naʊ] **1** *adv* (a) *(at this moment)* ahora; *(these days)* hoy (en) día; **what shall we do n.?** ¿y ahora qué hacemos?; *Fam* **it's n. or never** ahora o nunca; **that'll do for n.** ya basta por ahora *or* por el momento; **it's two years n. since his mother died** hace dos años que murió su madre; **he won't be long n.** no tardará mucho, *Am* no demorará mucho más; **n. is the time to...** ahora es el momento de...; **any minute n.** en cualquier momento; **any day n.** cualquier día de estos; **right n.** ahora mismo; **(every) n. and then, (every) n. and again** de vez en cuando; **up to** *or* **until n.** hasta ahora; **from n. on** a partir de ahora; **in three days from n.** de aquí a tres días; **he ought to be here by n.** ya debería haber llegado; **and n. for some music** y a continuación, un poco de música
(b) *(to introduce statement, question)* **n., there are two ways of interpreting this** ahora bien, lo podemos interpretar de dos maneras; **well n., what's happened here?** vamos a ver, ¿qué ha pasado?
(c) *(as reproof)* **come n.!** ¡venga, hombre/mujer!, *Am* ¡pero qué cosa!; **n., n.! stop quarreling!** *Esp* ¡hala, hala! *or Am* ¡bueno, bueno! ¡basta de peleas!
2 *conj* **n. (that) I'm older I think differently** ahora que soy más viejo *or Am* grande, ya no pienso igual; **n. (that) you mention it,...** ahora que lo dices,...
nowadays ['naʊədeɪz] *adv* hoy (en) día, actualmente
nowhere ['nəʊweə(r)] **1** *n* **in the middle of n.** en un lugar dejado de la mano de Dios; **he came from n. to win the race** remontó desde atrás y ganó la carrera
2 *adv (posición)* en/a ningún lugar, en/a ninguna parte; **n. else** en/a ningún otro lugar; **she was n. to be found** no se la podía encontrar por ninguna parte; **qualifications alone will get you n.** sólo con los estudios no irás a ninguna parte; **it's n. near the shopping center** no queda nada cerca del centro comercial; **the rest were n.** *(in contest)* los demás

quedaron muy por detrás; *Fam* **we're getting n. fast** estamos perdiendo el tiempo

noxious ['nɒkʃəs] *adj* nocivo(a)

nozzle ['nɒzəl] *n* boquilla *f*

nr (*abbr* **near**) cerca de

NRA [enɑːˈreɪ] *n* (*abbr* **National Rifle Association**) = asociación estadounidense que se opone a cualquier restricción en el uso de armas de fuego

nth [enθ] *adj Fam* enésimo(a); **for the n. time** por enésima vez

nuance ['njuːɒns] *n* matiz *m*

nub [nʌb] *n* **the n. of the matter** *or* **issue** el quid de la cuestión

nubile ['njuːbaɪl] *adj* (*attractive*) de buen ver

nuclear ['njuːklɪə(r)] *adj* nuclear; **n. disarmament** desarme *m* nuclear; **n. energy** energía *f* nuclear; **n. family** familia *f* nuclear; **n. physics** física *f* nuclear; **n. power** energía *f* nuclear *or* atómica; **n. power station** central *f* nuclear; **n. war(fare)** guerra *f* nuclear *or* atómica; **n. warhead** cabeza *f* nuclear; **n. waste** residuos *mpl* nucleares; **n. weapon** arma *f* nuclear *or* atómica; **n. winter** invierno *m* nuclear

nuclear-free zone ['njuːklɪəfriːˈzəʊn] *n* zona *f* desnuclearizada

nuclear-powered ['njuːklɪəˈpaʊəd] *adj* nuclear; **n. submarine** submarino *m* nuclear

nucleic [njuːˈkliːɪk] *adj* nucleico(a); **n. acid** ácido *m* nucleico

nucleus ['njuːklɪəs] (*pl* **nuclei** ['njuːklɪaɪ]) *n also Fig* núcleo *m*

nude [njuːd] **1** *n* desnudo *m*; **in the n.** desnudo(a)
2 *adj* desnudo(a); **to be n.** estar desnudo(a)

nudge [nʌdʒ] **1** *n* (*push*) empujón *m*; (*with elbow*) codazo *m*
2 *vt* (*push*) dar un empujón a; (*elbow*) dar un codazo a

nudist ['njuːdɪst] *n* nudista *mf*; **n. camp/colony** campamento *m*/colonia *f* nudista

nudity ['njuːdɪtɪ] *n* desnudez *f*

nugatory ['njuːgətɒrɪ] *adj* fútil

nugget ['nʌgɪt] *n* (*of gold*) pepita *f*; *Fig* **a few useful nuggets of information** unas cuantas informaciones útiles

nuisance ['njuːsəns] *n* (*annoying thing*) pesadez *f*, molestia *f*; (*annoying person*) pesado(a) *m,f*; **to make a n. of oneself** dar la lata; **what a n.!, that's a n.!** ¡qué contrariedad!; **n. call** llamada *f* (telefónica) molesta, *Am* llamado *m* (telefónico) molesto

nuke [njuːk] *vt Fam* atacar con armas nucleares

null [nʌl] *adj* nulo(a); **n. and void** nulo(a) y sin valor

nullify ['nʌlɪfaɪ] *vt* anular, invalidar

numb [nʌm] **1** *adj* entumecido(a); **to be n.** estar entumecido(a); **to go n.** entumecerse; **n. with cold** entumecido(a) por el frío; **n. with fear** paralizado(a) por el miedo
2 *vt* (*of cold, grief*) entumecer; (*of terror*) paralizar

number ['nʌmbə(r)] **1** *n* (a) número *m*; **a large n. of** gran número de; **their supporters were present in small/ great numbers** un pequeño/gran número de sus partidarios hizo acto de presencia; **I live at n. 40** vivo en el (número) 40; **(telephone) n.** número (de teléfono *or Am* telefónico); *Comptr* **n. crunching** cálculos *mpl*; **to be n. one** ser el número uno; *Fam* **to look after n. one** cuidarse de los propios intereses; **numbers (game** *or* **racket)** lotería *f* ilegal
(b) (*song*) tema *m*, canción *f*
(c) (*idioms*) **he's my n. two** (*subordinate*) es mi segundo (de a bordo); *Fam* **I've got your n.!** ¡te tengo calado!; *Fam* **his n.'s up** le ha llegado la hora; *Fam* **that car is a nice little n.** ¡vaya cochazo!, *Méx* ¡qué carro más padre!, *CSur* ¡flor de auto!
2 *vt* (a) (*assign number to*) numerar (b) (*count*) contar; (*amount to*) sumar; **his days are numbered** tiene los días contados; **he numbers her among his friends** la cuenta entre sus amigos

numbering ['nʌmbərɪŋ] *n* numeración *f*

numbly ['nʌmlɪ] *adv* (*answer, stare*) sin poder reaccionar

numbness ['nʌmnɪs] *n* (*of fingers*) entumecimiento *m*; (*from grief*) aturdimiento *m*; (*from fear*) parálisis *f inv*

numbskull ['nʌmskʌl] *n Fam* idiota *mf*, *Esp* majadero(a) *m,f*

numeracy ['njuːmərəsɪ] *n* conocimiento *m* de aritmética

numeral ['njuːmərəl] *n* número *m*

numerate ['njuːmərət] *adj* **to be n.** tener un conocimiento básico de aritmética

numerator ['njuːməreɪtə(r)] *n Math* numerador *m*

numeric(al) [njuːˈmerɪk(əl)] *adj* numérico(a); *Comptr* **n. keypad** teclado *m* numérico

numerically [njuːˈmerɪklɪ] *adv* en número, numéricamente

numerous ['njuːmərəs] *adj* numeroso(a); **on n. occasions** en numerosas ocasiones

nun [nʌn] *n* monja *f*

nunnery ['nʌnərɪ] *n* convento *m*

nuptial ['nʌpʃəl] **1** *npl* **nuptials** boda *f*, esponsales *mpl*
2 *adj* nupcial

nurse [nɜːs] **1** *n* (a) (*medical*) enfermera *f*; **(male) n.** enfermero *m* (b) (*looking after children*) niñera *f*
2 *vt* (*look after*) cuidar, atender; (*suckle*) amamantar, dar de mamar a; *Fig* (*feeling, hope*) guardar, abrigar; **she nursed him back to health** lo cuidó hasta que se restableció; *Fig* **to n. a grievance** guardar rencor

nursery ['nɜːsərɪ] *n* (a) (*establishment*) guardería *f*; (*room in house*) cuarto *m* de los niños; **n. rhyme** poema *m* or canción *f* infantil; **n. school** centro *m* de preescolar, parvulario *m* (b) (*for plants*) vivero *m*, semillero *m*

nursing ['nɜːsɪŋ] *n* (*profession*) enfermería *f*; (*care given by a nurse*) cuidados *mpl*, atención *f* sanitaria; **n. home** (*for old people, war veterans*) residencia *f*; **n. staff** personal *m* sanitario

nurture ['nɜːtʃə(r)] *vt* (a) (*feed*) (*children, plants*) nutrir, alimentar; (*plan, scheme*) alimentar (b) (*bring up*) criar

nut [nʌt] *n* (a) (*food*) fruto *m* seco; (*walnut*) nuez *f*; (*peanut*) *Esp* cacahuete *m*, *Andes, Carib, RP* maní *m*, *CAm, Méx* cacahuate *m*; (*hazelnut*) avellana *f*; (*almond*) almendra *f*; **nuts and raisins** frutos *mpl* secos; *Fig* **a hard** *or* **tough n.** (*person*) un hueso (duro de roer); *Fig* **a tough** *or* **hard n. to crack** (*problem*) un hueso duro de roer
(b) *Fam* (*head*) coco *m*; **to be off one's n.** estar mal de la azotea
(c) *Fam* (*mad person*) chiflado(a) *m,f*, *Esp* chalado(a) *m,f*; **a jazz/tennis n.** un(a) loco(a) del jazz/tenis
(d) (*for fastening bolt*) tuerca *f*; *Fig* **the nuts and bolts** los aspectos prácticos
(e) *very Fam* (*testicle*) **nuts** huevos *mpl*, *Méx* albóndigas *fpl*

nutcase ['nʌtkeɪs] *n Fam* chalado(a) *m,f*

nutcrackers ['nʌtkrækəz] *npl* cascanueces *m inv*; **a pair of n.** un cascanueces

nuthouse ['nʌthaʊs] *n Fam* manicomio *m*, loquero *m*

nutmeg ['nʌtmeg] *n* nuez *f* moscada

nutrient ['njuːtrɪənt] **1** *n* **nutrients** sustancias *fpl* nutritivas
2 *adj* nutritivo(a)

nutrition [njuːˈtrɪʃən] *n* nutrición *f*

nutritional [njuːˈtrɪʃənəl] *adj* nutritivo(a)

nutritious [njuːˈtrɪʃəs] *adj* nutritivo(a), alimenticio(a)

nuts [nʌts] *adj Fam* (*mad*) chiflado(a), *Esp* majara; **to be n.** estar chiflado(a) *or Esp* majara; **to be n. about** (*be very keen on*) estar loco(a) por

nutshell ['nʌtʃel] *n* cáscara *f* (de fruto seco); *Fig* **in a n....** en una palabra...

nutty ['nʌtɪ] *adj* (a) (*in taste*) **to have a n. taste** saber a avellana/nuez/etc (b) *Fam* (*mad*) chiflado(a), chalado(a); **to be n.** estar chiflado(a) *or* chalado(a)

nuzzle ['nʌzəl] **1** *vt (of dog, cat)* acariciar con el morro *or* hocico; *(of person)* acurrucarse contra
   2 *vi* **to n. against sb** *(person)* acurrucarse contra alguien

NW *(abbr* **northwest***)* NO

NY [en'waɪ] *n (abbr* **New York***)* Nueva York

NYC [enwaɪ'siː] *n (abbr* **New York City***)* (ciudad *f* de) Nueva York

nylon ['naɪlɒn] *n (textile)* nylon *m*, nailon *m*

nylons ['naɪlɒnz] *npl (stockings)* medias *fpl* de nylon; **a pair of n.** unas medias de nylon

nymph [nɪmf] *n* ninfa *f*

nymphomania [nɪmfəʊ'meɪnɪə] *n* ninfomanía *f*

nymphomaniac [nɪmfəʊ'meɪnɪæk] *n* ninfómana *f*

NYSE [enwaɪes'iː] *n St Exch (abbr* **New York Stock Exchange***)* Bolsa *f* de Nueva York

NZ *(abbr* **New Zealand***)* Nueva Zelanda

O

O, o [əʊ] *n* (**a**) *(letter)* O, o *f* (**b**) *(zero)* cero *m*

oaf [əʊf] *n* tarugo *m*, zote *m*

oak [əʊk] *n* roble *m*; **o. apple** agalla *f* de roble

oar [ɔː(r)] *n* remo *m*; *Fig* **to put one's o. in** meter las narices

oarsman [ˈɔːzmən] *n* remero *m*

OAS [əʊeɪˈes] *n* *(abbr* **Organization of American States***)* OEA *f*, Organización *f* de Estados Americanos

oasis [əʊˈeɪsɪs] *(pl* **oases** [əʊˈeɪsiːz]*)* *n* oasis *m inv*; *Fig* **an o. of calm** un oasis de tranquilidad

oat [əʊt] **1** *n* (**a**) *(plant)* avena *f*; **o. bran** salvado *m* de avena (**b**) *(food)* **an o. cookie** una galleta de avena

2 oats *npl* (**a**) *(food)* copos *mpl* de avena (**b**) *Fam* **to be feeling one's oats** *(be full of energy)* estar en plena forma

oatcake [ˈəʊtkeɪk] *n* galleta *f* (salada) de avena

oath [əʊθ] *n* (**a**) *(pledge)* juramento *m*; **o. of allegiance** juramento de adhesión; **to take** *or* **swear an o.** prestar juramento, jurar; *Law* **on** *or* **under o.** bajo juramento (**b**) *(swearword)* juramento *m*, palabrota *f*

oatmeal [ˈəʊtmiːl] *n* harina *f* de avena

obdurate [ˈɒbdjʊrɪt] *adj* obstinado(a)

obedience [əˈbiːdɪəns] *n* obediencia *f*

obedient [əˈbiːdɪənt] *adj* obediente

obelisk [ˈɒbəlɪsk] *n* obelisco *m*

obese [əʊˈbiːs] *adj* obeso(a)

obesity [əʊˈbiːsɪtɪ] *n* obesidad *f*

obey [əˈbeɪ] **1** *vt (person, order)* obedecer; **to o. the law** obedecer las leyes

2 *vi* obedecer

obfuscation [ɒbfəˈskeɪʃən] *n* oscurecimiento *m*

obituary [əˈbɪtjʊərɪ] *n* nota *f* necrológica, necrología *f*; **o. column** sección *f* de necrológicas; **o. notice** nota necrológica

object 1 *n* [ˈɒbdʒɪkt] (**a**) *(thing)* objeto *m* (**b**) *(focus)* **he was the o. of their admiration** él era el objeto de su admiración; *Fig* **to give sb an o. lesson in sth** dar a alguien una lección magistral de algo (**c**) *(purpose, aim)* objeto *m*, propósito *m*; **the o. of the exercise is to...** el ejercicio tiene por objeto... (**d**) *(obstacle)* **expense is no o.** el gasto no es ningún inconveniente (**e**) *Gram* **direct/indirect o.** complemento *m* or objeto *m* directo/indirecto

2 *vi* [əbˈdʒekt] oponerse (**to** a); **I o. to doing that** me indigna tener que hacer eso

objection [əbˈdʒekʃən] *n* objeción *f*, reparo *m*; **to raise objections** poner objeciones *or* reparos; **I see no o.** no veo ningún inconveniente

objectionable [əbˈdʒekʃənəbəl] *adj (behavior)* reprobable; **he made himself thoroughly o.** se puso muy desagradable

objective [əbˈdʒektɪv] **1** *n (aim, goal)* objetivo *m*

2 *adj (impartial)* objetivo(a)

objectively [əbˈdʒektɪvlɪ] *adv* objetivamente

objectivity [ɒbdʒekˈtɪvɪtɪ] *n* objetividad *f*

obligation [ɒblɪˈgeɪʃən] *n* obligación *f*; **to be under an o. to**

sb tener una obligación para con alguien; **to be under an o. to do sth** estar obligado(a) a hacer algo

obligatory [ɒˈblɪgətərɪ] *adj* obligatorio(a)

oblige [əˈblaɪdʒ] *vt* (**a**) *(compel)* obligar; **to be obliged to do sth** estar obligado(a) a hacer algo (**b**) *(do a favor for)* hacer un favor a (**c**) **to be obliged to sb** *(be grateful)* estarle agradecido(a) a alguien; **I would be obliged if you would...** te estaría muy agradecido si...; **much obliged** muy agradecido(a)

obliging [əˈblaɪdʒɪŋ] *adj* atento(a)

obligingly [əˈblaɪdʒɪŋlɪ] *adv* atentamente

oblique [əˈbliːk] *adj (line, angle)* oblicuo(a); *(reference, hint)* indirecto(a)

obliterate [əˈblɪtəreɪt] *vt* (**a**) *(erase)* borrar; *Fig (the past)* suprimir (**b**) *(destroy)* asolar, arrasar

oblivion [əˈblɪvɪən] *n* olvido *m*; **to sink into o.** caer en el olvido

oblivious [əˈblɪvɪəs] *adj* inconsciente; **o. to the pain/risks** ajeno(a) al dolor/a los riesgos; **I was o. of** *or* **to what was going on** no era consciente de lo que estaba pasando

oblong [ˈɒblɒŋ] **1** *n* rectángulo *m*

2 *adj* rectangular

obnoxious [əbˈnɒkʃəs] *adj (person, action)* perverso(a)

oboe [ˈəʊbəʊ] *n* oboe *m*

oboist [ˈəʊbəʊɪst] *n Mus* oboe *mf*

obscene [əbˈsiːn] *adj (indecent)* obsceno(a); *Fig (profits, prices)* escandaloso(a)

obscenely [əbˈsiːnlɪ] *adv* obscenamente; **o. rich** escandalosamente rico(a)

obscenity [əbˈsenɪtɪ] *n* obscenidad *f*

obscure [əbˈskjʊə(r)] **1** *adj (author, book, background)* oscuro(a); *(remark, argument)* oscuro(a), enigmático(a); *(feeling, sensation)* vago(a), oscuro(a)

2 *vt* (**a**) *(hide from view)* ocultar (**b**) *(make unclear)* oscurecer

obscurely [əbˈskjʊəlɪ] *adv (to feel, see)* vagamente; *(to speak)* confusamente

obscurity [əbˈskjʊərɪtɪ] *n* oscuridad *f*

obsequious [əbˈsiːkwɪəs] *adj* servil

obsequiousness [əbˈsiːkwɪəsnɪs] *n* servilismo *m*

observable [əbˈzɜːvəbəl] *adj* observable, apreciable

observance [əbˈzɜːvəns] *n (of law, custom)* observancia *f*, acatamiento *m*; **religious observances** prácticas *fpl* religiosas

observant [əbˈzɜːvənt] *adj* observador(ora)

observation [ɒbzəˈveɪʃən] *n* (**a**) *(act of observing)* observación *f*; *(by police)* vigilancia *f*; *(gen)* & *Med* **to keep sb under o.** tener a alguien en *or* bajo observación; **to escape o.** pasar inadvertido(a); *Rail* **o. car** = vagón con grandes ventanales; *Mil* **o. post** puesto *m* de observación (**b**) *(remark)* observación *f*, comentario *m*; **to make an o.** hacer una observación *or* un comentario

observational [ɒbzəˈveɪʃənəl] *adj (study, techniques)* de observación

observatory [əbˈzɜːvətərɪ] n observatorio m

observe [əbˈzɜːv] vt (a) (watch) observar (b) (notice) advertir (c) (say) **to o. that...** señalar or observar que... (d) (law, customs) observar, acatar; **to o. the Sabbath** guardar el descanso sabático

observer [əbˈzɜːvə(r)] n observador(ora) m,f

obsess [əbˈses] vt obsesionar; **to be obsessed with** or **by sth/sb** estar obsesionado(a) con or por algo/alguien

obsession [əbˈseʃən] n obsesión f

obsessive [əbˈsesɪv] adj obsesivo(a)

obsessively [əbˈsesɪvlɪ] adv obsesivamente

obsolescence [ɒbsəˈlesəns] n obsolescencia f

obsolete [ˈɒbsəliːt] adj obsoleto(a)

obstacle [ˈɒbstəkəl] n obstáculo m; **to put obstacles in sb's way** ponerle a alguien obstáculos en el camino; also Fig **o. course** carrera f de obstáculos

obstetric(al) [ɒbˈstetrɪk(əl)] adj Med obstétrico(a)

obstetrician [ɒbsteˈtrɪʃən] n Med obstetra mf, tocólogo(a) m,f

obstetrics [ɒbˈstetrɪks] n Med obstetricia f, tocología f

obstinacy [ˈɒbstɪnəsɪ] n obstinación f, terquedad f

obstinate [ˈɒbstɪnɪt] adj (person) obstinado(a), terco(a); (resistance) tenaz, obstinado(a); (illness) pertinaz; **to be o. about sth** obstinarse en algo

obstreperous [əbˈstrepərəs] adj alborotado(a); **to get o. (about sth)** alborotarse (por algo)

obstruct [əbˈstrʌkt] vt (a) (block) (road, pipe) obstruir, bloquear; (view) impedir (b) (hinder) obstaculizar, entorpecer; **to o. a bill** (in Congress) entorpecer la aprobación de un proyecto de ley; Law **to o. the course of justice** obstaculizar or entorpecer la acción de la justicia

obstruction [əbˈstrʌkʃən] n (a) (action) (of street) obstrucción f (b) (blockage) atasco m; **to cause an o.** (on road) provocar un atasco

obstructive [əbˈstrʌktɪv] adj (behavior, tactics) obstruccionista; **to be o.** (person) poner impedimentos

obtain [əbˈteɪn] **1** vt (information, money) obtener, conseguir
2 vi Formal (practice, rule) prevalecer

obtainable [əbˈteɪnəbəl] adj **easily o.** fácilmente obtenible; **only o. on prescription** sólo disponible con receta médica

obtrusive [əbˈtruːsɪv] adj (a) (person) entrometido(a); (behavior) molesto(a) (b) (smell) penetrante

obtuse [əbˈtjuːs] adj (a) Math obtuso(a) (b) (person, mind) obtuso(a), duro(a) de mollera; **you're being deliberately o.** no estás queriendo entender

obverse [ˈɒbvɜːs] **1** n (of medal) anverso m; Fig **the o. is sometimes true** a veces se da el caso contrario
2 adj opuesto(a)

obviate [ˈɒbvɪeɪt] vt Formal (difficulty, danger) evitar; **this would o. the need to...** esto evitaría la necesidad de...

obvious [ˈɒbvɪəs] **1** n **to state the o.** constatar lo evidente
2 adj obvio(a), evidente; **it was the o. thing to do** hacer eso era lo más lógico

obviously [ˈɒbvɪəslɪ] adv (a) (in an obvious way) obviamente, evidentemente; **she o. likes you** está claro que le gustas (b) (of course) desde luego, por supuesto; **o. not** claro que no

occasion [əˈkeɪʒən] **1** n (a) (time) ocasión f; **on one o.** en una ocasión; **on several occasions** en varias ocasiones; **on o.** (occasionally) en ocasiones (b) (event) acontecimiento m; **on the o. of...** con ocasión de...; **a sense of o.** un ambiente de gala (c) (opportunity) ocasión f, oportunidad f; **on the first o.** a la primera oportunidad; **I'd like to take this o. to...** me gustaría aprovechar esta oportunidad para... (d) Formal (cause) motivo m; **to have o. to do sth** tener motivos para hacer algo; **o. for complaint** motivo de queja
2 vt Formal (fear, surprise) ocasionar, causar

occasional [əˈkeɪʒənəl] adj ocasional, esporádico(a); **o.**

showers chubascos mpl ocasionales; **o. table** mesita f auxiliar

occasionally [əˈkeɪʒənəlɪ] adv ocasionalmente, de vez en cuando

occidental [ɒksɪˈdentəl] adj occidental

occlusion [əˈkluːʒən], **occluded front** [əˈkluːdɪdˈfrʌnt] n Met frente m ocluido

occult [ɒˈkʌlt] **1** n **the o.** lo oculto
2 adj oculto(a)

occupant [ˈɒkjʊpənt] n (of house, car) ocupante mf; (of job) titular mf

occupation [ɒkjʊˈpeɪʃən] n (a) (profession) profesión f, ocupación f (b) (pastime) pasatiempo m (c) (of house, land) ocupación f

occupational [ɒkjʊˈpeɪʃənəl] adj profesional, laboral; **o. disease** enfermedad f profesional; **o. hazard** gaje m del oficio; **o. therapy** terapia f ocupacional

occupied [ˈɒkjʊpaɪd] adj (a) (house) ocupado(a) (b) (busy) ocupado(a), atareado(a); **to be o. with sth** estar ocupado(a) con algo; **to keep sb o.** tener ocupado(a) a alguien

occupy [ˈɒkjʊpaɪ] vt (house, sb's attention) ocupar; **she occupies her time in studying** ocupa su tiempo estudiando, dedica su tiempo a estudiar

occur [əˈkɜː(r)] (pt & pp **occurred**) vi (a) (event) suceder, ocurrir; (opportunity) darse, surgir; **his name occurs several times in the report** su nombre aparece varias veces en el informe or Am reporte (b) (idea) **when did the idea o. to you?** ¿cuándo se te ocurrió esa idea?

occurrence [əˈkʌrəns] n (a) (event) suceso m; **it's an everyday o.** sucede todos los días (b) (incidence) (of disease) incidencia f; **to be of frequent o.** ocurrir con frecuencia

ocean [ˈəʊʃən] n océano m; Fam **oceans of** la mar de; **o. liner** transatlántico m

ocean-going [ˈəʊʃəngəʊɪŋ] adj (vessel) marítimo(a)

Oceania [əʊʃɪˈeɪnɪə] n Oceanía

oceanic [əʊʃɪˈænɪk] adj oceánico(a)

oceanography [əʊʃəˈnɒgrəfɪ] n oceanografía f

ocelot [ˈɒsəlɒt] n ocelote m

ocher, ochre [ˈəʊkə(r)] n & adj ocre m

o'clock [əˈklɒk] adv (it's) **one o.** (es) la una; (it's) **two/three o.** (son) las dos/tres; **at four o.** a las cuatro

OCR [əʊsiːˈɑː(r)] n Comptr (a) (abbr **optical character reader**) lector m óptico de caracteres (b) (abbr **optical character recognition**) reconocimiento m óptico de caracteres

Oct (abbr **October**) octubre m

octagon [ˈɒktəgən] n octógono m, octágono m

octagonal [ɒkˈtægənəl] adj octogonal, octagonal

octane [ˈɒkteɪn] n Chem octano m; **o. number** octanaje m

octave [ˈɒktɪv] n Mus octava f

October [ɒkˈtəʊbə(r)] n octubre m; see also **May**

octogenarian [ɒktədʒɪˈneərɪən] n & adj octogenario(a) m,f

octopus [ˈɒktəpəs] n pulpo m

oculist [ˈɒkjʊlɪst] n oculista mf

OD [əʊˈdiː] (pt & pp **OD'd**, **OD'ed**) vi Fam meterse una sobredosis; Fig **I think I've rather OD'd on pizza** creo que me he pasado con la pizza

odd [ɒd] **1** adj (a) (strange) raro(a), extraño(a) (b) Math (number) impar; **to be the o. man out** ser el bicho raro (c) (one of a pair) **an o. sock** un calcetín desparejado (d) (occasional) ocasional; **I smoke the o. cigarette** me fumo un cigarrillo de cuando en cuando; **you've made the o. mistake** has cometido algún que otro error; **o. jobs** chapuzas fpl, trabajillos mpl (caseros)
2 adv **a hundred o. sheep** ciento y pico ovejas; **twenty o. dollars** veintitantos dólares

oddball [ˈɒdbɔːl] Fam n & adj excéntrico(a) m,f, raro(a) m,f

oddity ['ɒdɪtɪ] n (a) (strangeness) rareza f (b) (person) bicho m raro; (thing) rareza f; **it's just one of his little oddities** no es más que otra de sus rarezas

oddly ['ɒdlɪ] adv extrañamente, de manera rara; **o. enough** aunque parezca raro

oddness ['ɒdnɪs] n (strangeness) rareza f

odds [ɒdz] npl (a) (probability) probabilidades fpl; (in betting) apuestas fpl; **this horse has a o. of 7-1** las apuestas para este caballo están en or son de 7 a 1; **the o. are that...** lo más probable es que...; **the o. are against him** tiene pocas posibilidades; **the o. are in his favor** tiene muchas posibilidades; **to succeed against the o.** triunfar a pesar de las dificultades (b) **to be at o. with sb** (disagree) estar peleado(a) con alguien (c) Fam **o. and ends** cosillas fpl, chismes mpl

odds-on [ɒd'zɒn] adj (horse) **o. favorite** favorito(a) m,f claro(a) or indiscutible; Fam **it's o. that...** es casi seguro que...

ode [əʊd] n oda f

odious ['əʊdɪəs] adj odioso(a), aborrecible

odium ['əʊdɪəm] n Formal odio m, aborrecimiento m

odometer [əʊ'dɒmɪtə(r)] n (in car) ≃ cuentakilómetros m inv

odor ['əʊdə(r)] n (smell) olor m; (unpleasant smell) mal olor m, tufo m; Fig **to be in good/bad o. with sb** estar a bien/mal con alguien

odorless ['əʊdəlɪs] adj inodoro(a)

Odyssey ['ɒdɪsɪ] n odisea f

OECD [əʊiːsiː'diː] n (abbr **Organization for Economic Cooperation and Development**) OCDE f, Organización f para la Cooperación y el Desarrollo Económico

Oedipal ['iːdɪpəl] adj edípico(a)

o'er ['əʊə(r)] prep & adv Literary por

of [ɒv, unstressed əv] prep de; **made of wood** de madera; **to be guilty/capable of...** ser culpable/capaz de...; **to be proud/tired of...** estar orgulloso(a)/cansado(a) de...; **a bag of potatoes** una bolsa de Esp patatas or Am papas; **a bottle of wine** una botella de vino; **a friend of mine** un amigo mío; **a car of her own** su propio coche; **the two of us** los dos, nosotros dos; **how much of it do you want?** ¿cuánto quiere?; **a drop of 20 percent** una bajada del 20 por ciento; **there were four of us** éramos cuatro; **he of all people should know that...** él más que nadie debería saber que...; **it was clever of her to do it** fue muy lista en hacerlo; **the husband of the President** el marido de la presidenta; **the University of Alabama** la Universidad de Alabama; **a girl of ten** una niña de diez años; **fear of spiders** miedo a las arañas; **it was very kind of you** fue muy amable de tu parte; **the 4th of October** el 4 de octubre; **of an evening** por la noche; **a quarter of one** la una menos cuarto

off [ɒf] **1** adv (a) (away) **the meeting is only two weeks o.** sólo quedan dos semanas para la reunión; **five miles o.** a cinco millas (de distancia); **I must be o.** tengo que irme; **I'm o. to Tucson** me voy a Tucson; **o. you go!** ¡andando!

(b) (indicating removal) **to take one's coat** quitarse el abrigo; **the handle has come o.** se ha soltado el asa; **o. and on, on and o.** (intermittently) a intervalos, intermitentemente

(c) (with prices) **20 percent/$5 o.** una rebaja del 20 por ciento/de 5 dólares

(d) (away from work, school) **to have time o.** tener tiempo libre

2 prep (a) (away from) **o. the coast** cerca de la costa; **a street o. the main road** una calle que sale de la principal; **o. the record** extraoficialmente

(b) (indicating removal from) **to fall/jump o. sth** caerse/ saltar de algo; **the handle has come o. the saucepan** se ha desprendido el mango de la cacerola

(c) (with prices) **20 percent/$5 o. the price** una rebaja del 20 por ciento/de 5 dólares

(d) (absent from) **to be o. work/school** faltar al trabajo/ colegio; **Jane's o. work today** Jane no viene hoy a trabajar

(e) (not liking) **she's been o. her food lately** últimamente no está comiendo bien or está sin apetito or Esp está desganada

(f) Fam (from) **to buy/borrow sth o. sb** comprar/pedir prestado algo a alguien; **I got some useful advice o. him** me dio algunos consejos útiles

3 adj (a) (not functioning) (light, TV) apagado(a); (water, electricity) desconectado(a)

(b) (canceled) **the wedding is o.** se ha cancelado la boda; **the deal is o.** el acuerdo se ha roto

(c) (absent from work, school) **to be o.** faltar; **Jane's o. today** Jane no viene hoy a trabajar/a clase

(d) (food) pasado(a); (milk) cortado(a); (meat) malo(a), RP estropeado(a)

(e) (unsuccessful) **to have an o. day** tener un mal día

(f) (in tourism) **the o. season** la temporada baja

(g) (describing situation) **to be well/badly o.** tener mucho/ poco dinero; **you'd be better o. staying where you are** será mejor or más vale que te quedes donde estás

offal ['ɒfəl] n Culin asaduras fpl

offbeat [ɒf'biːt] adj Fam (unconventional) inusual, original

off-chance ['ɒftʃɑːns] n **on the o.** por si acaso

off-color [ɒf'kʌlə(r)] adj (a) (unwell) indispuesto(a) (b) (joke) fuera de tono

off-duty ['ɒf'djuːtɪ] adj (soldier) de permiso; (policeman) fuera de servicio

offend [ə'fend] **1** vt ofender; **to be offended (at or by sth)** ofenderse or sentirse ofendido(a) (por algo)

2 vi Law delinquir; **to o. against good taste** atentar contra el buen gusto

offended [ə'fendɪd] adj (insulted) ofendido(a)

offender [ə'fendə(r)] n Law delincuente mf

offending [ə'fendɪŋ] adj (causing a problem) enojoso(a)

offense [ə'fens] n (a) Law delito m, infracción f; **petty minor o.** infracción leve (b) (annoyance, displeasure) ofensa f; **to cause o.** ofender; **to take o.** sentirse ofendido(a) (at por), ofenderse (at por) (c) Sport (attackers) atacantes mfpl, línea f de ataque

offensive [ə'fensɪv] **1** n Mil & Fig ofensiva f; **to take the o.** pasar a la ofensiva; **to be on the o.** estar en plena ofensiva

2 adj (word, action) ofensivo(a); **to be o. to sb** mostrarse ofensivo(a) con alguien

offensively [ə'fensɪvlɪ] adv (a) (insultingly) de manera insultante or ofensiva (b) (on the attack) ofensivamente

offer ['ɒfə(r)] **1** n oferta f; **to make sb an o. (for sth)** hacer a alguien una oferta (por algo); **on o.** (reduced) de oferta; (available) disponible; **o. of marriage** propuesta f de matrimonio

2 vt ofrecer; **to o. sb sth, to o. sth to sb** ofrecer algo a alguien; **to o. to do sth** ofrecerse a hacer algo; Law **to o. a plea of guilty/innocent** declararse culpable/inocente

▶**offer up** vt sep (prayers) ofrecer

offering ['ɒfərɪŋ] n entrega f; Rel ofrenda f

offhand [ɒf'hænd] **1** adj desconsiderado(a); **to be o. (with sb)** mostrarse desconsiderado(a) (con alguien)

2 adv (immediately) **I don't know o.** ahora mismo, no lo sé

offhanded [ɒf'hændɪd] adj desconsiderado(a)

offhandedly [ɒf'hændɪdlɪ] adv (casually) indiferentemente

office ['ɒfɪs] n (a) (place) oficina f; (of doctor, dentist) consulta f; **the manager's o.** el despacho or la oficina del jefe; **o. boy** chico m de los recados; **o. building** bloque m de oficinas; **o. hours** horas fpl or horario m de oficina; **o. work** trabajo m de oficina; **o. worker** oficinista mf (b) Pol (position) cargo m; **to hold o.** ocupar un cargo; **to be out of o.** (political party) estar en la oposición (c) Formal **I got the apartment through the good offices of Philip** conseguí el piso gracias a los buenos oficios de Philip

officeholder ['ɒfɪshəʊldə(r)] n titular mf de (un) cargo

officer ['ɒfɪsə(r)] n (army) oficial mf; (police) agente mf; (in local government) inspector(ora) m,f

official [ə'fɪʃəl] **1** n (in public sector) funcionario(a) m,f; (in labor union) representante mf
  2 adj oficial

officialdom [ə'fɪʃəldəm] n Pej (bureaucracy) los funcionarios, la administración

officialese [əfɪʃə'liːz] n Pej jerga f administrativa

officially [ə'fɪʃəlɪ] adv oficialmente

officiate [ə'fɪʃɪeɪt] vi Rel celebrar (el oficio) (**at** en)

officious [ə'fɪʃəs] adj excesivamente celoso(a) or diligente

officiously [ə'fɪʃəslɪ] adv con excesiva diligencia

offing ['ɒfɪŋ] n (**to be**) **in the o.** (ser) inminente

off-key ['ɒf'kiː] Mus **1** adj desafinado(a)
  2 adv desafinadamente

off-line ['ɒflaɪn] adj Comptr (processing) fuera de línea; (printer) desconectado(a)

off-load [ɒf'ləʊd] vt (surplus goods) colocar; **to o. sth onto sb** colocarle algo a alguien; **to o. blame onto sb** descargar la culpa en alguien

off-peak ['ɒf'piːk] adj (electricity, travel) en horas valle; (vacations) en temporada baja; (phone call) en horas de tarifa reducida

off-piste ['ɒfpiːst] adj & adv fuera de pista

offprint ['ɒfprɪnt] n Typ separata f

off-putting ['ɒfpʊtɪŋ] adj desagradable; **I find his manner rather o.** sus modales me resultan desagradables

off-ramp ['ɒfræmp] n carril m de deceleración or de salida

off-road ['ɒfrəʊd] adj (driving) fuera de pista; **an o. vehicle** un (vehículo) todoterreno

offscreen ['ɒf'skriːn] adj Cin & TV **their o. relationship mirrored their love affair in the movie** su relación detrás de la cámara era un reflejo de su aventura amorosa en la película

off-season ['ɒfsiːzən] adj (rate) de temporada baja

offset ['ɒfset] **1** n Typ (process) offset m
  2 vt (pt & pp **offset**) compensar

offshoot ['ɒfʃʊt] n (of tree) vástago m; (of family) rama f; (of political party, artistic movement) ramificación f

offshore ['ɒfʃɔː(r)] **1** adv cerca de la costa
  2 adj (island) cercano(a) a la costa; **o. oil rig** plataforma f petrolífera (en el mar); **o. fund** fondo m colocado en paraíso fiscal; Fin **o. investment** inversión f en un paraíso fiscal

offside ['ɒfsaɪd] **1** n Aut lado m del conductor
  2 adj (a) Aut del lado del conductor (b) [ɒf'saɪd] (in football, hockey, soccer, rugby) (en) fuera de juego

offspring ['ɒfsprɪŋ] npl (young of an animal) crías fpl; (children) hijos mpl, descendencia f

offstage [ɒf'steɪdʒ] Theat **1** adv fuera del escenario
  2 adj de fuera del escenario

off-the-cuff [ɒfðə'kʌf] adj (remark) espontáneo(a), improvisado(a)

off-the-record [ɒfðə'rekɔːd] adj extraoficial, oficioso(a)

off-the-wall [ɒfðə'wɔːl] adj Fam estrafalario(a)

off-white ['ɒf'waɪt] **1** n tono m blancuzco, blanco m marfil
  2 adj blancuzco(a)

oft- [ɒft] prefix **o.-repeated** muy repetido(a); **o.-quoted** muy citado(a)

often ['ɒfən, 'ɒftən] adv a menudo, frecuentemente; **how o.?** (how many times) ¿cuántas veces?; (how frequently) ¿cada cuánto tiempo?, ¿con qué frecuencia?; **as o. as not** la mitad de las veces; **more o. than not** muchas veces; **every so o.** de vez en cuando, cada cierto tiempo

ogle ['əʊgəl] vt **to o. sb** comerse a alguien con los ojos

ogre ['əʊgə(r)] n also Fig ogro m

ogress ['əʊgrɪs] n (frightening woman) ogro m

oh [əʊ] exclam (expressing surprise) ¡oh!; **oh no!** ¡oh, no!

ohm [əʊm] n Elec ohmio m

oho [əʊ'həʊ] exclam (expressing triumph, surprise) ¡ajajá!

oil [ɔɪl] **1** n (for cooking, lubricating) aceite m; (petroleum) petróleo m; Fig **to pour o. on troubled waters** calmar los ánimos; **o. company** compañía f petrolera; **o. drum** bidón m de petróleo; **o. field** yacimiento m petrolífero; **o. lamp** lámpara f de aceite; **o. paint** pintura f al óleo; **o. painting** óleo m; **o. pan** cárter m; **o. refinery** refinería f de petróleo; **o. rig** plataforma f petrolífera; **o. slick** marea f negra; **o. tanker** petrolero m; **o. well** pozo m petrolífero or de petróleo
  2 vt (machine) engrasar, lubricar; Fig **to o. the wheels** allanar el terreno

oilcan ['ɔɪlkæn] n (for applying oil) aceitera f; (large container) lata f de aceite

oiled [ɔɪld] adj (a) (machine) engrasado(a) (b) Fam (**well**) **o.** (drunk) (bien) puesto(a) or mamado(a)

oil-fired ['ɔɪlfaɪəd] adj **o. central heating** calefacción f central de petróleo

oilskin ['ɔɪlskɪn] n (fabric) hule m; **oilskins** chubasquero m, impermeable m

oily ['ɔɪlɪ] adj (a) (hands, rag) grasiento(a); (skin, hair) graso(a); (food) grasiento(a), aceitoso(a) (b) Pej (manner) empalagoso(a)

oink [ɔɪŋk] vi (pig) gruñir

ointment ['ɔɪntmənt] n ungüento m, pomada f

OK, okay ['əʊ'keɪ] **1** exclam de acuerdo, Esp vale, Am ok, Méx ándale; **OK, OK! I'll do it now** ¡bueno, de acuerdo or Esp vale or Am ok or Méx ándale!, ya lo hago
  2 adj bien; **that's OK by** or **with me** (a mí) me parece bien; **is it OK to wear jeans?** ¿está bien si voy con vaqueros?; **no, it is NOT OK!** no, no está bien; **it's more than OK** está pero que muy bien; Fam **she was OK about it** (didn't react badly) se lo tomó bastante bien; Fam **he's an OK sort of guy** es un tipo Esp legal or Méx, RP derecho; **are we OK for time?** ¿vamos bien de tiempo?
  3 n **to give (sb) the OK** dar permiso (a alguien)
  4 vt (pt & pp **OK'd** or **okayed**) Fam (proposal, plan) dar el visto bueno a

Okie ['əʊkɪ] n Fam = campesino de Oklahoma

okra ['ɒkrə] n quingombó m, okra f

old [əʊld] **1** npl **the o.** los ancianos, las personas mayores
  2 adj (a) (not young, not new) (person) anciano(a), viejo(a); Méx, RP grande; (furniture, car, custom) viejo(a); **an o. man** un anciano, un viejo; **an o. woman** una anciana, una vieja; **o. people, o. folk(s)** los ancianos, las personas mayores; **to go over o. ground** volver sobre un asunto muy trillado; **to be an o. hand at sth** tener larga experiencia en algo; Fam **to be o. hat** estar muy visto(a), Esp estar más visto(a) que el tebeo; Fig **he's one of the o. school** es de la vieja escuela; **o. age** la vejez; **O. Glory** = la bandera estadounidense; **the O. Testament** el Antiguo Testamento; **o. wives' tale** cuento m de viejas
    (b) (referring to person's age) **how o. are you?** ¿cuántos años tienes?; **to be five years o.** tener cinco años; **at six years o.** a los seis años (de edad); **a two-year-o. (child)** un niño de dos años; **to grow** or **get older** hacerse mayor; **when you're older** cuando seas mayor; **you're o. enough to do that yourself** ya eres mayorcito para hacerlo tú mismo
    (c) (former) antiguo(a); **in the o. days** antes, antiguamente; **an o. flame** un antiguo amor, Am un ex amor
    (d) (long-standing) **an o. friend (of mine)** un viejo amigo (mío); **o. habits die hard** es difícil abandonar las costumbres de toda la vida
    (e) Fam (intensifier) **any o. how** de cualquier manera; **any o. thing** cualquier cosa
    (f) Fam (affectionate) **o. Fred** el bueno de Fred; **o. fellow** or **boy** (addressing sb) muchacho; **my** or **the o. man** (husband)

mi *or* el pariente, *Méx* mi *or* el viejo, *RP* el don *or* el viejo; *(father)* mi *or* el viejo, *Méx* mi *or* el jefe; **my** *or* **the o. woman** *or* **lady** *(wife)* mi *or* la parienta, *Méx* mi *or* la vieja, *RP* la dueña *or* la vieja

old-fashioned [əʊld'fæʃənd] **1** *adj (outdated)* anticuado(a); *(from former times)* tradicional, antiguo(a); **the o. way** a la antigua

2 *n* = cóctel hecho con whisky, fruta, azúcar, licor amargo y soda

old-timer [əʊld'taɪmə(r)] *n Fam* (a) *(experienced person)* veterano(a) *m,f* (b) *(form of address)* abuelo(a) *m,f*

old-world ['əʊld'wɜːld] *adj (courtesy, charm)* del pasado, de antes

oleander [əʊlɪ'ændə(r)] *n* adelfa *f*

olfactory [ɒl'fæktərɪ] *adj Anat* olfativo(a)

oligarchy ['ɒlɪgɑːkɪ] *n* oligarquía *f*

olive ['ɒlɪv] **1** *n (fruit)* aceituna *f*; *(tree)* olivo *m*; *Fig* **to hold out the o.** branch hacer un gesto de paz; **o. grove** olivar *m*; **o. oil** aceite *m* de oliva

2 *adj (skin)* aceitunado(a); **o. (green)** verde oliva

Olympic [ə'lɪmpɪk] **1** *npl* **the Olympics** las Olimpiadas, los Juegos Olímpicos

2 *adj* olímpico(a); **the O. Games** los Juegos Olímpicos

Oman [əʊ'mɑːn] *n* Omán

Omani [əʊ'mɑːnɪ] *n & adj* omaní *mf*

ombudsman ['ɒmbʊdzmən] *n* defensor(ora) *m,f* del pueblo

omelet ['ɒmlɪt] *n* tortilla *f* (francesa); **ham/cheese o.** tortilla de jamón/queso

omen ['əʊmen] *n* presagio *m*, augurio *m*

ominous ['ɒmɪnəs] *adj* siniestro(a); **an o.-looking sky** un cielo amenazador; **an emergency meeting?, that sounds o.** ¿una reunión de emergencia?, eso no presagia nada bueno

ominously ['ɒmɪnəslɪ] *adv* siniestramente, amenazadoramente

omission [əʊ'mɪʃən] *n* omisión *f*

omit [əʊ'mɪt] *(pt & pp* **omitted)** *vt* omitir; **to o. to do sth** no hacer algo

omnibus ['ɒmnɪbəs] *n* (a) *(book)* recopilación *f*, antología *f* (b) *Old-fashioned (bus)* ómnibus *m inv* (c) *Pol* **o. bill** = proyecto de ley que engloba medidas diversas

omnipotence [ɒm'nɪpətəns] *n* omnipotencia *f*

omnipotent [ɒm'nɪpətənt] *adj* omnipotente

omnipresent [ɒmnɪ'prezənt] *adj* omnipresente

omniscience [ɒm'nɪsɪəns] *n* omnisciencia *f*

omniscient [ɒm'nɪsɪənt] *adj* omnisciente

omnivorous [ɒm'nɪvərəs] *adj* omnívoro(a); *Fig (reader)* insaciable

on [ɒn] **1** *prep* (a) *(position)* en; **on the table** encima de *or* sobre la mesa, en la mesa; **on the second floor** en el segundo piso; **on the wall** en la pared; **on page 4** en la página 4; **on the right/left** a la derecha/izquierda; **on foot** a pie; **on horseback** a caballo; **on (the) television** en la televisión; **to be on a committee** formar parte de un comité; **I haven't got any money on me** no llevo nada de dinero encima, *Am* no tengo nada de plata encima

(b) *(direction)* **to fall on sth** caerse encima de *or* sobre *or Am* arriba de algo

(c) *(time)* **on the 15th** el día 15; **on Sunday** el domingo; **on Christmas Day** el día de Navidad; **on that occasion** en aquella ocasión

(d) *(about)* sobre, acerca de; **a book on France** un libro sobre Francia

(e) *(introducing a gerund)* **on completing the test, you should…** después de terminar la prueba, tienes que…; **on discovering the corpse, she screamed** al descubrir el cadáver, dio un grito

(f) *(indicating use, support)* **to live on $200 a week** vivir con 200 dólares a la semana; **it runs on lead-free gas** usa *or* lleva

gasolina sin plomo; **to play sth on the guitar** tocar algo en *or Esp* a la guitarra; **the drinks are on me** las bebidas corren de mi cuenta; **I'm on antibiotics** estoy tomando antibióticos; **to be on drugs** tomar drogas

2 *adj* (a) *(in operation) (light, television, engine)* encendido(a), *Am* prendido(a); **in the "on" position** en posición de encendido *or Am* prendido (b) *(taking place)* **what's on?** *(on TV)* ¿qué hay en la tele?; *(at movie theater)* ¿qué película pasan *or* dan *or Esp* echan?; **is the meeting still on?** ¿sigue en pie lo de la reunión?; **I've got a lot on at the moment** *(am very busy)* ahora estoy muy ocupado (c) *(on duty)* de servicio; **who's on this evening?** ¿quién está de servicio esta noche?

3 *adv* (a) *(as clothing)* **she had a red dress on** llevaba un vestido rojo; **he had nothing on** estaba desnudo; **to put sth on** ponerse algo (b) *(in time)* **earlier on** antes; **later on** más tarde; **from that day on** desde aquel día, a partir de aquel día; **on and off, off and on** *(intermittently)* a intervalos, intermitentemente (c) *(expressing continuation)* **to read/ work on** seguir leyendo/trabajando; **he went on and on about it** no dejaba de hablar de ello

onboard ['ɒnbɔːd] *adj* de a bordo; **o. computer** *Esp* ordenador *m or Am* computadora *f* de a bordo

once [wʌns] **1** *adv* (a) *(on one occasion)* una vez; **more than o.** más de una vez; **o. a week** una vez a la semana; **o. or twice** una o dos veces; **o. in a while** de vez en cuando; **o. more, o. again** otra vez, una vez más; **you've called me stupid o. too often** ya me has llamado estúpido demasiadas veces; **o. and for all** de una vez por todas; **a o.-in-a-lifetime opportunity** una ocasión única, una ocasión que sólo se presenta una vez en la vida (b) *(formerly)* una vez, en otro tiempo; **o. upon a time there was a princess** érase una vez una princesa

2 *conj* una vez que; **o. he reached home, he collapsed** una vez en casa, se derrumbó; **o. he finishes we can leave** cuando termine, nos podremos marchar

3 at once *adv (immediately)* inmediatamente, ahora mismo; *(at the same time)* al mismo tiempo, a la vez

once-over ['wʌnsəʊvə(r)] *n Fam* **to give sth the o.** dar a algo un repaso; **to give sb the o.** mirar a alguien de arriba a abajo

oncologist [ɒŋ'kɒlədʒɪst] *n* oncólogo(a) *m,f*

oncoming ['ɒnkʌmɪŋ] *adj (traffic)* en dirección contraria

one [wʌn] **1** *n* uno *m*; **there's only o. left** sólo queda uno; **the guests arrived in ones and twos** poco a poco fueron llegando los invitados; **to be at o. with sb** coincidir plenamente con alguien; **to have o. for the road** *(final drink)* tomar la última *or Esp* la espuela; **he's had o. too many** *(drink)* lleva *or Esp* ha tomado una copa de más; *Fam* **to get o. up on sb** quedar por encima de alguien

2 *pron* (a) *(identifying)* **this o.** éste(a); **that o.** ése(a), aquél/élla); **these ones** éstos(as); **those ones** ésos(as), aquéllos(as); **which o. do you want?** ¿cuál quieres?; **the o. I told you about** el/la que te dije; **the big/red o.** el grande/rojo; **the ones with the long sleeves** los/las de manga larga; **that's a difficult o.!** ¡qué difícil!

(b) *(indefinite)* **I haven't got a pencil, have you got o.?** no tengo lápiz, ¿tienes tú (uno)?; **he is o. of us** es uno de los nuestros; **she is o. of the family** es de la familia; **o. of my friends** uno de mis amigos; **o. of these days** uno de estos; **any o. of us** cualquiera de nosotros; **it is just o. of those things** son cosas que pasan; **o. after the other** uno tras otro; **o. at a time** de uno en uno, *Am* uno por uno; **o. by o.** de uno en uno, uno por uno

(c) *(particular person)* **to act like o. possessed** actuar como un/una poseso(a); **I, for o., do not believe it** yo, desde luego, no me lo creo; **I'm not o. to complain** yo no soy de los que se quejan; **he's not a great o. for parties** no le gustan *or Esp* van mucho las fiestas

(d) *(impersonal)* **o. never knows** nunca se sabe; **it is enough to make o. weep** basta para hacerle llorar a uno(a)

3 *adj* **(a)** *(number)* un(a); **chapter o.** capítulo *m* primero; **page o.** primera página *f*; **to be o. (year old)** tener un año; **they live at number o.** viven en el número uno; **o. o'clock** la una; **come at o.** ven a la una; **o. or two people** una o dos personas; **o. stormy evening in January** una tarde tormentosa de enero; **o. day we shall be free** algún día seremos libres; **for o. thing,...** para empezar,...

(b) *(single)* un(a) único(a), un(a) solo(a); **he did it with o. end in mind** lo hizo con un solo propósito; **her o. worry** su única preocupación; **my o. and only suit** mi único traje; **they are o. and the same thing** son una o la misma cosa; **we'll manage o. way or another** nos las arreglaremos de una forma u otra; **as o. man** como un solo hombre; *Fam* **it's all o. to me** me da igual **(c)** *Fam (for emphasis)* **that's o. big problem you've got there** menudo problema tienes ahí

one-armed ['wʌnɑːmd] *adj (person)* manco(a)

one-dimensional ['wʌndaɪ'menʃənəl] *adj Geom* unidimensional; *(character)* superficial

one-eyed ['wʌnaɪd] *adj* tuerto(a)

one-horse town ['wʌnhɔːs'taʊn] *n Fam* pueblo *m* de mala muerte

one-legged [wʌn'legɪd] *adj* cojo(a)

one-liner [wʌn'laɪnə(r)] *n Fam (joke)* golpe *m*

one-man ['wʌnmæn] *adj (job)* individual, de una sola persona; **o. band** hombre *m* orquesta; **o. show** espectáculo *m* en solitario; *Fig* **this company/team is a o. show** el funcionamiento de esta empresa/de este equipo gira en torno a un solo hombre

one-night stand ['wʌnnaɪt'stænd] *n Fam (of performer)* representación *f* única; *(of musician)* concierto *m* único; *(sexual encounter)* ligue *m* or *RP* levante *m* de una noche

one-on-one ['wʌnɒn'wʌn] **1** *adj* cara a cara; **o. tuition** clases *fpl* particulares

2 *adv* **to go o. with sb** enfrentarse en un mano a mano con alguien

one-parent family ['wʌnpeərənt'fæmɪlɪ] *n* familia *f* monoparental

one-party ['wʌn'pɑːtɪ] *adj* unipartidista

one-piece swimsuit ['wʌnpiːs'swɪmsuːt] *n* bañador *m* or *RP* malla *f* de una pieza

onerous ['əʊnərəs] *adj* oneroso(a)

oneself [wʌn'self] *pron* **(a)** *(reflexive)* **to look after o.** cuidarse; **to trust o.** confiar en uno(a) mismo(a); **to feel o. again** volver a sentirse el/la de siempre **(b)** *(emphatic)* uno(a) mismo(a), uno(a) solo(a); **to do sth all by o.** hacer algo uno(a) solo(a); **to see (sth) for o.** ver (algo) uno(a) mismo(a)

one-sided [wʌn'saɪdɪd] *adj* **(a)** *(unequal)* desnivelado(a), desigual **(b)** *(biased)* parcial

one-time ['wʌntaɪm] *adj* antiguo(a); **her o. lover** su ex amante

one-to-one ['wʌntə'wʌn] *adj (discussion)* cara a cara; **o. tuition** clases *fpl* particulares

one-track ['wʌntræk] *adj* **to have a o. mind** *(be obsessed with one thing)* estar obsesionado(a) con una cosa, no pensar más que en una cosa; *(be obsessed with sex)* no pensar más que en el sexo

one-two [wʌn'tuː] *n* **(a)** *(in soccer, field hockey)* pared *f*; **to play a o.** hacer la pared **(b)** *(in boxing)* izquierdazo *m* seguido de derechazo

one-upmanship [wʌn'ʌpmənʃɪp] *n Fam* **it was pure o.** todo era por quedar por encima de los demás

one-way ['wʌnweɪ] *adj (ticket)* de ida; *(street, traffic)* de sentido único

ongoing ['ɒngəʊɪŋ] *adj* en curso

onion ['ʌnjən] *n* cebolla *f*; **o. soup** sopa *f* de cebolla

online ['ɒn'laɪn] *adj Comptr* en línea, on line; **to be o.** *(person)* estar conectado(a) (a Internet); **o. banking** banca *f* electrónica; **o. retailer** minorista *mf* online or en línea, tienda *f* virtual; **o. store** tienda *f* virtual

onlooker ['ɒnlʊkə(r)] *n* curioso(a) *m,f*

only ['əʊnlɪ] **1** *adj* único(a); **o. child** hijo(a) *m,f* único(a); **you are not the o. one** no eres el único; **the o. thing that worries me is...** lo único que me preocupa es...

2 *adv* solamente, sólo; **I o. touched it** no hice más que tocarlo; **it's o. natural** es (más que) natural; **I shall be o. too pleased to come** me encantará acudir; **if o. they knew!, if they o. knew!** ¡si ellos supieran!; **not o...., but also...** no sólo..., sino también...; **I saw her o. yesterday** la vi ayer mismo; **I o. just managed it** por poco no lo consigo; **it's o. me** (sólo) soy yo

3 *conj* sólo que, pero; **I would do it o. I haven't the time** lo haría, sólo que no tengo tiempo

on-off switch, on/off switch ['ɒn'ɒfswɪtʃ] *n* interruptor *m*

onomatopoeia [ɒnəmætə'piːə] *n* onomatopeya *f*

onomatopoeic [ɒnəmætə'piːɪk] *adj* onomatopéyico(a)

on-ramp ['ɒnræmp] *n* carril *m* de aceleración or de incorporación

onrush ['ɒnrʌʃ] *n (of emotions)* arrebato *m*; *(of people)* oleada *f*

onset ['ɒnset] *n* irrupción *f*; **the o. of a disease** el desencadenamiento or inicio de una enfermedad; **the o. of war** el estallido de la guerra

on-site ['ɒn'saɪt] *adj & adv* in situ

onslaught ['ɒnslɔːt] *n* acometida *f*

onstage 1 *adj* ['ɒnsteɪdʒ] de escena

2 *adv* [ɒn'steɪdʒ] en escena

onto ['ɒntu, *unstressed* 'ɒntə] *prep* sobre, encima de; **to jump o. sth** saltar sobre algo; **to fall o. sth** caerse encima de algo; **to be o. a good thing** habérselo montado bien; **I think the police are o. us** creo que la policía anda detrás de nosotros

onus ['əʊnəs] *n* responsabilidad *f*; **the o. is on the government to resolve the problem** la resolución del problema es incumbencia del Gobierno; *Law* **o. of proof** peso *m* de la prueba, onus probandi *m*

onward ['ɒnwəd] **1** *adj (motion)* hacia delante

2 *adv* **from tomorrow o.** a partir de mañana; **from this time o.** (de ahora) en adelante

onwards ['ɒnwədz] *adv* = **onward**

onyx ['ɒnɪks] *n* ónice *m*

oodles ['uːdəlz] *npl Fam* **o. of time/money** una porrada or un chorro or *Col* un jurgo or *RP* un toco de tiempo/dinero

oomph [ʊmf] *n Fam (energy)* garra *f*, *Esp* marcha *f*

oops [uːps] *exclam (to child)* ¡arriba!, *Esp* ¡aúpa!; *(after mistake)* ¡uy!, ¡oh!

ooze [uːz] **1** *n* **(a)** *(mud)* fango *m* **(b)** *(flow)* flujo *m*

2 *vt (liquid)* rezumar; **to o. charm** rezumar encanto; **to o. confidence** rebosar confianza

3 *vi* rezumar, brotar; **to o. with confidence** rebosar confianza

op [ɒp] *n Fam (medical operation)* operación *f*

opal ['əʊpəl] *n* ópalo *m*

opaque [əʊ'peɪk] *adj (glass)* opaco(a); *Fig (difficult to understand)* oscuro(a), poco claro(a)

op cit [ɒp'sɪt] *n (abbr* **opere citato***)* op. cit., en la obra citada

OPEC ['əʊpek] *n (abbr* **Organization of Petroleum Exporting Countries***)* OPEP *f*

op-ed ['ɒped] *n (in newspaper)* **an o. (piece)** un artículo de opinión, un artículo firmado; **the o. page** la sección de artículos de opinión

open ['əʊpən] **1** *n* **(a) in the o.** *(outside)* al aire libre; *(not hidden)* a la vista; **to bring sth out into the o.** *(problem, disagreement)* sacar a relucir algo; **to come out into the o.**

about sth desvelar algo (**b**) *(sporting competition)* open *m*, abierto *m*

2 *adj* (**a**) *(in general)* abierto(a); **to be o.** estar abierto(a); **o. from nine to five** abierto(a) de nueve a cinco; **o. to the public** abierto(a) al público; **o. all night** abierto(a) toda la noche *or* las veinticuatro horas; **o. late** abierto(a) hasta tarde; **let's leave the matter o.** dejemos el asunto ahí pendiente de momento; **a career o. to very few** una profesión reservada a unos pocos; **o. to traffic** abierto(a) al tráfico; **membership is o. to people over eighteen** pueden hacerse socios los mayores de dieciocho años; **two possibilities are o. to us** tenemos dos opciones; **o. to the elements** expuesto(a) a las inclemencias del tiempo; **to be o. to doubt** ser dudoso(a) *or* cuestionable; **to be o. to ridicule** exponerse a quedar en ridículo; **to be o. to suggestions** estar abierto(a) a sugerencias; **in the o. air** al aire libre; **to welcome sb with o. arms** recibir a alguien con los brazos abiertos; **o. country** campo *m* abierto; *Law* **in o. court** en juicio público, en vista pública; **o. house** jornada *f* de puertas abiertas; **o. invitation** *(to guests)* invitación *f* permanente; *Fig (to thieves)* invitación clara; *Econ* **o. market** mercado *m* libre; **to keep an o. mind (on sth)** mantenerse libre de prejuicios (acerca de algo); **o. sandwich** = rebanada de pan con algo de comer encima; **the o. sea** mar *m* abierto; **o. season** *(for hunting)* temporada *f* (de caza); *Fig* **to declare o. season on sth/sb** abrir la veda de *or* contra algo/alguien; **o. spaces** *(parks)* zonas *fpl* *or Am* áreas *fpl* verdes; **o. ticket** billete *m* *or Am* boleto *m* *or* pasaje *m* abierto; **o. wound** herida *f* abierta

(**b**) *(person, manner)* abierto(a); *(preference, dislike)* claro(a), manifiesto(a); *(conflict)* abierto(a); **to be o. with sb** ser franco(a) con alguien; **to be o. about sth** ser muy claro(a) *or* sincero(a) con respecto a algo; **o. letter** *(in newspaper)* carta *f* abierta; **o. secret** secreto *m* a voces

3 *adv* **to cut sth o.** abrir algo de un corte; **the door flew o.** la puerta se abrió con violencia

4 *vt (in general)* abrir; *(negotiations, conversation)* entablar, iniciar; **to o. a hole in sth** abrir *or* practicar un agujero en algo; **to o. fire (on sb)** hacer *or* abrir fuego (sobre alguien); **he opened his heart to her** se sinceró con ella

5 *vi (door, window, flower)* abrirse; *(store, bank)* abrir; *(meeting, negotiations)* abrirse, dar comienzo; **to o. late** *(store)* abrir hasta tarde; **the kitchen opens onto the garden** la cocina da al jardín; **the play opens with a death scene** la obra comienza con una escena de muerte; **the movie opens next week** la película se estrena la semana que viene; **o. wide!** *(at dentist's)* ¡abre bien la boca!

▸**open out 1** *vt sep (sheet of paper)* abrir, desdoblar

2 *vi (flower)* abrirse; *(view, prospects)* abrirse, extenderse; *(road, valley)* ensancharse, abrirse

▸**open up 1** *vt sep (new store, business)* abrir; **to o. up opportunities for** abrir las puertas a, presentar nuevas oportunidades para

2 *vi (storekeeper, new store)* abrir; *(flower, new market)* abrirse; *Fig (person)* abrirse, sincerarse; **this is the police, o. up!** ¡policía, abran la puerta!

open-air [ˈəʊpəˈneə(r)] *adj (restaurant, market)* al aire libre

open-and-shut [ˈəʊpənənˈʃʌt] *n* **an o. case** un caso elemental *or* claro

opencast [ˈəʊpənˈkɑːst] *adj (mine)* a cielo abierto

open-door policy [ˈəʊpənˈdɔːpɒlɪsɪ] *n* política *f* permisiva *or* de puertas abiertas

open-ended [ˈəʊpənˈendɪd] *adj (contract)* indefinido(a); *(question)* abierto(a); *(discussion)* sin restricciones

open-heart surgery [ˈəʊpənˈhɑːtˈsɜːdʒərɪ] *n* cirugía *f* a corazón abierto

opening [ˈəʊpənɪŋ] **1** *n* (**a**) *(of play, new era)* principio *m*; *(of negotiations)* apertura *f*; *(of Parliament)* sesión *f* inaugural (**b**) *(gap)* abertura *f*, agujero *m* (**c**) *(of cave, tunnel)* entrada *f* (**d**)

(opportunity) oportunidad *f*; *(job)* puesto *m* vacante

2 *adj* **o. address** *or* **speech** *(in court case)* presentación *f* del caso; **o. batter** *(in baseball)* bateador *m* inicial; **o. ceremony** ceremonia *f* inaugural *or* de apertura; **o. gambit** *(in chess)* gambito *m* de salida; *(in conversation, negotiation)* táctica *f* inicial; **o. hours** horario *m* de apertura

openly [ˈəʊpənlɪ] *adv* abiertamente

open-minded [əʊpənˈmaɪndɪd] *adj* de mentalidad abierta

open-mindedness [əʊpənˈmaɪndɪdnɪs] *n* mentalidad *f* abierta

open-mouthed [əʊpənˈmaʊðd] *adj* boquiabierto(a)

openness [ˈəʊpənnɪs] *n (frankness)* franqueza *f*

open-plan [ˈəʊpənplæn] *adj (office)* de planta abierta

opera [ˈɒpərə] *n* ópera *f*; **o. glasses** prismáticos *mpl*, gemelos *mpl (de teatro)*; **o. house** (teatro *m* de la) ópera; **o. singer** cantante *mf* de ópera

operable [ˈɒpərəbəl] *adj Med* operable

operagoer [ˈɒprəɡəʊə(r)] *n* **as regular operagoers will know...** como los asiduos *or* aficionados a la ópera ya sabrán...

operate [ˈɒpəreɪt] **1** *vt (machine)* manejar, hacer funcionar; *(brakes)* accionar; *(service)* proporcionar; **to be operated by electricity** funcionar con electricidad

2 *vi* (**a**) *(machine)* funcionar; *(company)* actuar, operar; **we o. in most of Kentucky** desarrollamos nuestra actividad en la mayor parte de Kentucky (**b**) *Med* operar; **to o. on sb (for)** operar a alguien (de); **to be operated on** ser operado(a)

operatic [ɒpəˈrætɪk] *adj* operístico(a)

operating [ˈɒpəreɪtɪŋ] *adj* **o. costs** costos *mpl or Esp* costes *mpl* de explotación; **o. room** quirófano *m*; *Comptr* **o. system** sistema *m* operativo; *Med* **o. table** mesa *f* de operaciones

operation [ɒpəˈreɪʃən] *n* (**a**) *(of machine)* funcionamiento *m*; **to be in o.** *(machine)* estar funcionando; *(system, law)* estar en vigor; **to come into o.** *(law)* entrar en vigor (**b**) *(process)* tarea *f*, operación *f*; **a firm's operations** las operaciones *or* actividades de una empresa (**c**) *Med* operación *f*; **to have an o. (for sth)** operarse (de algo) (**d**) *Mil* operación *f*; **operations room** centro *m* de control

operational [ɒpəˈreɪʃənəl] *adj* operativo(a); **it should be o. next year** debería entrar en funcionamiento el año que viene

operative [ˈɒpərətɪv] **1** *n (manual worker)* operario(a) *m,f*; *(spy)* agente *mf*

2 *adj (law, rule)* vigente; **to become o.** *(law)* entrar en vigor; **the o. word** la palabra clave

operator [ˈɒpəreɪtə(r)] *n* (**a**) *(of machine)* operario(a) *m,f* (**b**) *Tel* telefonista *mf*, operador(ora) *m,f* (**c**) *Fam* **he's a pretty smooth o.** *(with women)* se las lleva de calle; *(in business)* es un lince *or* un hacha para los negocios

operetta [ɒpəˈretə] *n Mus* opereta *f*

ophthalmology [ɒfθælˈmɒlədʒɪ] *n Med* oftalmología *f*

opinion [əˈpɪnjən] *n* opinión *f*; **in my o.** en mi opinión; **to be of the o. that...** ser de la opinión de que...; **to ask sb's o.** pedir la opinión de alguien; **to form an o. of sth/sb** formarse una opinión sobre algo/alguien; **to have a high/low o. of sb** tener (una) buena/mala opinión de alguien; **what is your o. of him?** ¿qué opinas de él?; **o. poll** *or* **survey** sondeo *m* de opinión, encuesta *f*

opinionated [əˈpɪnjəneɪtɪd] *adj* dogmático(a); **to be o.** creer a toda costa que uno lleva la razón

opium [ˈəʊpɪəm] *n* opio *m*; **o. addict** adicto(a) *m,f* al opio; **o. den** fumadero *m* de opio

Oporto [ɒˈpɔːtəʊ] *n* Oporto

opossum [əˈpɒsəm] *n* zarigüeya *f*

opp *(abbr* **opposite**) en la página opuesta

opponent [əˈpəʊnənt] *n (in game, politics)* adversario(a) *m,f*, oponente *mf*; *(of policy, system)* opositor(ora) *m,f*

opportune [ˈɒpətjuːn] *adj* oportuno(a)

opportunism [ɒpəˈtjuːnɪzəm] *n* oportunismo *m*

opportunist [ɒpəˈtjuːnɪst] *n & adj* oportunista *mf*

opportunistic [ɒpətjʊˈnɪstɪk] *n* oportunista; *Med* **o. infection** infección *f* oportunista

opportunity [ɒpəˈtjuːnɪtɪ] *n* oportunidad *f*, ocasión *f*; **to have the o. of doing sth** *or* **to do sth** tener la oportunidad *or* ocasión de hacer algo; **at every o.** a la mínima oportunidad; **at the first** *or* **earliest o.** a la primera oportunidad; **if I get an o.** si tengo ocasión *or* oportunidad; **the o. of a lifetime** una oportunidad única en la vida; **a job with opportunities** un trabajo con buenas perspectivas

oppose [əˈpəʊz] *vt* oponerse a; **to be opposed to sth** estar en contra de algo; **we should act now as opposed to waiting till later** deberíamos actuar ya en lugar de esperar más; **I'm referring to my real father as opposed to my stepfather** me refiero a mi verdadero padre y no a mi padrastro

opposing [əˈpəʊzɪŋ] *adj* opuesto(a), contrario(a)

opposite [ˈɒpəzɪt] **1** *n* the o. of... lo contrario de...
   2 *adj* (**a**) *(page, shore)* opuesto(a); **the o. side of the street** el otro lado de la calle (**b**) *(opinion)* contrario(a); **in the o. direction** en dirección contaria; **the o. sex** el sexo opuesto
   3 *adv* enfrente; **the house o.** la casa de enfrente
   4 *prep* enfrente de

opposition [ɒpəˈzɪʃən] *n* (**a**) *(resistance)* oposición *f*; **to meet with o.** encontrar oposición (**b**) *(contrast)* **to act in o. to...** actuar en contra de... (**c**) *(opponents)* **the o.** los contrincantes, los adversarios; *Pol* **to be in o.** estar en la oposición

oppress [əˈpres] *vt (treat cruelly)* oprimir

oppressed [əˈprest] **1** *npl* **the o.** los oprimidos
   2 *adj (people, nation)* oprimido(a)

oppression [əˈpreʃən] *n* (**a**) *(of a people)* opresión *f* (**b**) *(of the mind)* agobio *m*, desasosiego *m*

oppressive [əˈpresɪv] *adj* (**a**) *(law, regime)* opresor(ora), opresivo(a) (**b**) *(atmosphere)* agobiante; *(heat)* sofocante

oppressively [əˈpresɪvlɪ] *adv (govern)* opresivamente; **it was o. hot** hacía un calor agobiante

opt [ɒpt] **1** *vt* **to o. to do sth** optar por hacer algo
   2 *vi* **to o. for...** optar por...

▸**opt out** *vi* **they opted out of the project** decidieron no participar en el proyecto

optic [ˈɒptɪk] *adj* óptico(a); **o. nerve** nervio *m* óptico

optical [ˈɒptɪkəl] *adj* óptico(a); *Comptr* **o. character reader** lector *m* óptico de caracteres; *Comptr* **o. character recognition** reconocimiento *m* óptico de caracteres; *Comptr* **o. disk** disco *m* óptico; **o. fiber** fibra *f* óptica; **o. illusion** ilusión *f* óptica

optician [ɒpˈtɪʃən] *n* óptico(a) *m,f*

optics [ˈɒptɪks] *n (subject)* óptica *f*

optimal [ˈɒptɪməl] *adj* óptimo(a)

optimism [ˈɒptɪmɪzəm] *n* optimismo *m*

optimist [ˈɒptɪmɪst] *n* optimista *mf*

optimistic [ɒptɪˈmɪstɪk] *adj* optimista

optimistically [ɒptɪˈmɪstɪklɪ] *adv* con optimismo

optimize [ˈɒptɪmaɪz] *vt* optimizar

optimum [ˈɒptɪməm] **1** *n* nivel *m* óptimo
   2 *adj* óptimo(a)

option [ˈɒpʃən] *n* (**a**) *(choice)* opción *f*; **to have the o. of doing sth** tener la opción de hacer algo; **to have no o.** no tener opción; **a soft** *or* **easy o.** una opción cómoda *or* fácil; **to leave** *or* **keep one's options open** dejar abiertas varias opciones (**b**) *Fin* opción *f* (**c**) *Sch & Univ* (asignatura *f*) optativa *f*

optional [ˈɒpʃənəl] *adj* optativo(a); **o. extras** accesorios *mpl* opcionales; *Sch* **o. subject** asignatura *f* optativa

optionally [ˈɒpʃənəlɪ] *adv* opcionalmente

optometry [ɒpˈtɒmətrɪ] *n Med* optometría *f*

opt-out [ˈɒptaʊt] **1** *n* autoexclusión *f*
   2 *adj* **o. clause** cláusula *f* de exclusión *or* de no participación

opulent [ˈɒpjʊlənt] *adj* opulento(a)

OR *n* [əʊˈɑː(r)] *(abbr* **operating room**) quirófano *m*, sala *f* de operaciones; **OR nurse** instrumentista *mf*

or [ɔː(r), *unstressed* ə(r)] *conj* (**a**) o; *(before* **o** *or* **ho**) u; **an hour or so** alrededor de una hora; **did she do it or not?** ¿lo hizo o no?; **keep still or I'll shoot!** ¡quieto o disparo!; **snow or no snow, she was determined to go** con nieve o sin ella, estaba decidida a ir (**b**) *(with negative)* ni; **she didn't write or phone** no escribió ni llamó

oracle [ˈɒrəkəl] *n* oráculo *m*

oral [ˈɔːrəl] **1** *n (exam)* (examen *m*) oral *m*
   2 *adj (tradition, history, skills)* oral; *(agreement)* verbal; *Sch* **o. examination** examen *m* oral; **o. sex** sexo *m* oral

orally [ˈɔːrəlɪ] *adv* oralmente; **to take medicine o.** tomar un medicamento por vía oral

orange [ˈɒrɪndʒ] **1** *n (fruit)* naranja *f*; *(color)* naranja *m*; **o. blossom** flor *f* de azahar; **o. grove** naranjal *m*; **o. juice** *Esp* zumo *m or Am* jugo *m* de naranja; **o. peel** peladura *f* de naranja; **o. tree** naranjo *m*
   2 *adj (color)* naranja, anaranjado(a)

orang(o)utan [əˈræŋətæn], **orangoutang** [əˈræŋəˈtæŋ] *n* orangután *m*

oration [ɔːˈreɪʃən] *n* alocución *f*, discurso *m*

orator [ˈɒrətə(r)] *n* orador(ora) *m,f*

oratorical [ɒrəˈtɒrɪkəl] *adj* oratorio(a)

oratory¹ [ˈɒrətərɪ] *n (art of speaking)* oratoria *f*

oratory² *n Rel (chapel)* oratorio *m*, capilla *f*

orb [ɔːb] *n Literary* esfera *f*

orbit [ˈɔːbɪt] **1** *n* (**a**) *(of planet)* órbita *f*; **in o.** en órbita; **to go into o.** entrar en órbita (**b**) *(scope)* órbita *f*, ámbito *m*
   2 *vt* girar alrededor de
   3 *vi* estar en órbita

orbital [ˈɔːbɪtəl] *adj Astron* orbital

orchard [ˈɔːtʃəd] *n* huerto *m* (de frutales); **(apple) o.** huerto de manzanos, manzanal *m*

orchestra [ˈɔːkɪstrə] *n* (**a**) *(musicians)* orquesta *f*; *Theat* **o. pit** orquesta, foso *m* (**b**) *(in theater)* platea *f*, patio *m* de butacas

orchestral [ɔːˈkestrəl] *adj* orquestal

orchestrate [ˈɔːkɪstreɪt] *vt also Fig* orquestar

orchid [ˈɔːkɪd] *n* orquídea *f*

ordain [ɔːˈdeɪn] *vt* (**a**) *Formal (decree)* decretar, disponer; **fate ordained that we should meet** el destino dispuso que nos encontráramos (**b**) *Rel (priest)* ordenar

ordeal [ɔːˈdiːl] *n* calvario *m*

order [ˈɔːdə(r)] **1** *n* (**a**) *(instruction)* orden *f*; **to give sb an o.** dar una orden a alguien; **to obey** *or* **follow orders** obedecer *or* cumplir órdenes; **to be under orders (to do sth)** tener órdenes (de hacer algo); **I don't take orders from you/anyone** yo no acepto órdenes tuyas/de nadie; *Fin* **pay to the o. of L. Black** páguese a L. Black
   (**b**) *Com* pedido *m*; **to place an o. (with sb)** hacer un pedido (a alguien); **to have sth on o.** haber hecho un pedido de algo; **to make sth to o.** hacer algo por encargo; **o. form** hoja *f* de pedido
   (**c**) *(peace, tidiness)* orden *m*; **to restore o.** restablecer el orden; *Fig* **to set one's own house in o.** poner (uno) orden en su vida
   (**d**) *(condition)* **out of o.** averiado(a), estropeado(a); **in (good) working** *or* **running o.** en buen estado de funcionamiento
   (**e**) *(in meeting)* **to call sb to o.** llamar a alguien al orden; **to rule a question out of o.** declarar improcedente una pregunta; *Fam* **that's out of o.!** ¡eso no está bien!, *Esp* ¡eso no es de recibo!; *Fig* **I think a celebration is in o.** creo que

se impone celebrarlo; *Rel* **o. of service** orden *m* ritual *or* litúrgico

(**f**) *(system)* orden *m*; **the new world o.** el nuevo orden mundial

(**g**) *(sequence)* orden *m*; **in the right/wrong o.** bien/mal ordenado(a); **in o.** en orden; **out of o.** desordenado(a); **in o. of age/size** por orden de edad/tamaño

(**h**) *(degree)* orden *m*; **of the highest o.** de primer orden; **in the o. of…** del orden de…; **on the o. of…** como…; **the higher/lower orders** *(social classes)* las capas altas/bajas de la sociedad

(**i**) *Rel* orden *f*; **to take holy orders** ordenarse sacerdote

(**j**) **in o. to do sth** para hacer algo; **in o. that they understand** para que comprendan

2 *vt* (**a**) *(instruct)* **to o. sb to do sth** mandar *or* ordenar a alguien hacer algo; *Law* **he was ordered to pay costs** el juez le ordenó pagar las costas (**b**) *Com* pedir, encargar; *(in restaurant)* pedir (**c**) *(arrange)* ordenar, poner en orden; **to o. sth according to size/age** ordenar algo de acuerdo con el tamaño/la edad

3 *vi (in restaurant)* pedir

▸**order around, order about** *vt sep* **to o. sb around** *or* **about** mangonear a alguien, no parar de dar órdenes a alguien

▸**order in** *vt sep (supplies)* encargar; *(troops)* solicitar el envío de

ordered ['ɔːdəd] *adj (organized)* ordenado(a)

orderly ['ɔːdəlɪ] **1** *n* celador(ora) *m,f*

2 *adj (tidy, methodical)* ordenado(a); **in an o. fashion** de forma ordenada

ordinal ['ɔːdɪnəl] *n & adj* ordinal *m*

ordinance ['ɔːdɪnəns] *n Formal (decree)* ordenanza *f*, decreto *m*

ordinarily ['ɔːdɪnərɪlɪ, ɔːdən'erəlɪ] *adv* normalmente

ordinary ['ɔːdɪnərɪ] **1** *n* **out of the o.** fuera de lo normal

2 *adj (normal)* normal; *(mediocre)* común, ordinario(a); **an o. Englishman** un inglés medio; **she was just an o. tourist** no era más que una simple turista; **this is no o. car** es un coche fuera de lo normal; **in the o. course of events** si las cosas siguen su curso normal

ordination [ɔːdɪ'neɪʃən] *n Rel* ordenación *f*

ordnance ['ɔːdnəns] *n Mil (supplies)* pertrechos *mpl*; *(guns)* armamento *m*; **o. factory** fábrica *f or Am* planta *f* de armamento

ore [ɔː(r)] *n* mineral *m*; **iron/aluminum o.** mineral de hierro/aluminio

oregano [ɒ'regənəʊ] *n* orégano *m*

Oregon ['ɒrɪgən] *n* Oregón

organ ['ɔːgən] *n* (**a**) *Anat & Mus* órgano *m*; **o. donor** donante *mf* de órganos; **o. transplant** transplante *m* de órganos (**b**) *(newspaper, journal)* órgano *m* (de difusión)

organ-grinder ['ɔːgəngraɪndə(r)] *n* organillero(a) *m,f*

organic [ɔː'gænɪk] *adj (disease, function)* orgánico(a); *(farming, gardening)* biológico(a), ecológico(a)

organism ['ɔːgənɪzəm] *n* organismo *m*

organist ['ɔːgənɪst] *n* organista *mf*

organization [ɔːgənaɪ'zeɪʃən] *n* organización *f*

organize ['ɔːgənaɪz] **1** *vt* organizar; **they organized accommodations for me** se encargaron de buscarme alojamiento

2 *vi (workers)* organizarse; *(form union)* constituirse en sindicato

organizer ['ɔːgənaɪzə(r)] *n* (**a**) *(person)* organizador(ora) *m,f* (**b**) *(diary)* agenda *f*

orgasm ['ɔːgæzəm] *n* orgasmo *m*; **to have an o.** tener un orgasmo

orgasmic [ɔː'gæzmɪk] *adj Fam (smell, taste)* orgásmico(a)

orgy ['ɔːdʒɪ] *n* orgía *f*; *Fig* **an o. of violence** una masacre

orient ['ɔːrɪənt] **1** *n* **the O.** (el) Oriente

2 *vt* = **orientate**

oriental [ɔːrɪ'entəl] **1** *n Old-fashioned (person)* **an O.** un/una oriental

2 *adj* oriental

orientate ['ɔːrɪənteɪt] *vt* orientar; **to o. oneself** orientarse

orientation [ɔːrɪən'teɪʃən] *n* orientación *f*; **o. course** curso *m* orientativo

-oriented ['ɔːrɪəntɪd], **-orientated** ['ɔːrɪənteɪtɪd] *suffi* **she's very work-o.** el trabajo ocupa un lugar fundamenta en su vida; **youth-o.** enfocado(a) hacia los jóvenes

orienteering [ɒrɪən'tɪərɪŋ] *n* orientación *f (deporte de aventura)*

orifice ['ɒrɪfɪs] *n* orificio *m*

origin ['ɒrɪdʒɪn] *n* origen *m*; **country of o.** país *m* de origen; **o** **Greek o.** de origen griego

original [ə'rɪdʒɪnəl] **1** *n (painting, document)* original *m*; **to read Tolstoy in the o.** leer a Tolstói en el idioma original

2 *adj (first, innovative)* original; *Rel* **o. sin** pecado *m* original

originality [ərɪdʒɪ'nælɪtɪ] *n* originalidad *f*

originally [ə'rɪdʒɪnəlɪ] *adv* (**a**) *(initially)* originariamente, en un principio; **where do you come from o.?** ¿cuál es tu lugar de origen? (**b**) *(in an innovative way)* originalmente, de forma original

originate [ə'rɪdʒɪneɪt] **1** *vt* crear, promover

2 *vi* originarse; **to o. from…** *(person)* proceder de…; **to o in…** *(river)* nacer en…; *(custom)* proceder *or* surgir de…

Orkney ['ɔːknɪ] *n* **the O. Islands, the Orkneys** las (Islas) Orcadas

ornament 1 *n* ['ɔːnəmənt] adorno *m*

2 *vt* ['ɔːnəment] *(room)* decorar; *(style)* adornar

ornamental [ɔːnə'mentəl] *adj* ornamental, decorativo(a); **purely o.** meramente decorativo(a)

ornate [ɔː'neɪt] *adj (building, surroundings)* ornamentado(a) *(style)* recargado(a)

ornery ['ɔːnərɪ] *adj Fam* gruñón(ona), cascarrabias *inv*

ornithology [ɔːnɪ'θɒlədʒɪ] *n* ornitología *f*

orphan ['ɔːfən] **1** *n* huérfano(a) *m,f*; **to be left an o.** queda huérfano(a)

2 *adj* **an o. child** un niño huérfano

3 *vt* **to be orphaned** quedar huérfano(a)

orphanage ['ɔːfənɪdʒ] *n* orfanato *m*

orthodontics [ɔːθə'dɒntɪks] *n* ortodoncia *f*

orthodontist [ɔːθə'dɒntɪst] *n* ortodontista *mf*

orthodox ['ɔːθədɒks] *adj* ortodoxo(a)

orthodoxy ['ɔːθədɒksɪ] *n* ortodoxia *f*

orthopedic, orthopaedic [ɔːθə'piːdɪk] *adj Med* ortopédico(a)

orthopedics, orthopaedics [ɔːθə'piːdɪks] *n Med* ortopedia *f*

Oscar® ['ɒskə(r)] *n* Oscar *m*

oscillate ['ɒsɪleɪt] *vi* oscilar; **he oscillated between hope and despair** pasaba de la esperanza a la desesperación

Oslo ['ɒzləʊ] *n* Oslo

osmosis [ɒz'məʊsɪs] *n also Fig* ósmosis *f inv*, osmosis *f inv*

osprey ['ɒspreɪ] *n* águila *f* pescadora

ossify ['ɒsɪfaɪ] *vi Anat* osificarse; *Fig (person, system)* anquilosarse

ostensible [ɒs'tensɪbəl] *adj* aparente

ostensibly [ɒ'stensɪblɪ] *adv* aparentemente

ostentation [ɒsten'teɪʃən] *n* ostentación *f*

ostentatious [ɒsten'teɪʃəs] *adj* ostentoso(a)

ostentatiously [ɒsten'teɪʃəslɪ] *adv* ostentosamente

osteoarthritis [ɒstɪəʊɑː'θraɪtɪs] *n Med* osteoartritis *f inv* artritis *f inv* ósea

osteopath ['ɒstɪəpæθ] *n Med* osteópata *mf*

ostracism ['ɒstrəsɪzəm] *n* ostracismo *m*

ostracize ['ɒstrəsaɪz] *vt* aislar, condenar al ostracismo

ostrich ['ɒstrɪtʃ] *n* avestruz *m*

other ['ʌðə(r)] **1** *adj* otro(a); **the o. one** el otro/la otra; **every o. day/week** cada dos días/semanas; **I work every o. day/month** trabajo un día/mes sí, un día/mes no; **the o. day** el otro día; **the o. four** los otros cuatro; **o. people seem to like it** parece que a otros les gusta; **o. people's property** propiedad ajena; **any o. book** cualquier otro libro; **somebody o. than me should do it** debería hacerlo alguien que no sea yo

2 *pron* **the o.** el otro/la otra; **one after the o.** uno tras otro; **(the) others** (los/las) otros(as); **some laughed, others wept** unos reían y otros lloraban; **somewhere or o.** en algún sitio; **someone or o.** no sé quién, alguien; **some woman or o.** no sé qué mujer, una mujer; **something or o.** no sé qué, algo; **somehow or o.** de la manera que sea, sea como sea; **somehow or o., we arrived on time** nos las arreglamos para llegar a tiempo

3 *adv* **the color's odd, o. than that, it's perfect** el color es un poco raro, pero, por lo demás, resulta perfecto; **she never speaks of him o. than admiringly** siempre habla de él con admiración

otherwise ['ʌðəwaɪz] **1** *adv* (**a**) *(differently)* de otra manera; **he could not do o.** no pudo hacer otra cosa; **to think o.** pensar de otra manera; **to be o. engaged** tener otros asuntos que resolver; **except where o. stated** excepto donde se indique lo contrario (**b**) *(apart from that)* por lo demás

2 *conj* si no, de lo contrario

otherworldly [ʌðə'wɜːldlɪ] *adj (person)* místico(a); *(religion, experience)* sobrenatural

Ottawa ['ɒtəwə] *n* Ottawa

otter ['ɒtə(r)] *n* nutria *f*

Ottoman ['ɒtəmən] *Hist n & adj* otomano(a) *m,f*

ottoman ['ɒtəmən] *n (piece of furniture)* canapé *m*, otomana *f*

ouch [aʊtʃ] *exclam (expressing pain)* ¡ay!

ought [ɔːt] *v aux*

En el inglés hablado, y en el escrito en estilo coloquial, la forma negativa **ought not** se transforma en **oughtn't**.

(**a**) *(expressing obligation, desirability)* deber, tener que; **I o. to be going** tendría que irme ya; **you oughtn't to worry so much** no deberías preocuparte tanto; **I thought I o. to let you know about it** me pareció que deberías saberlo; **he had drunk more than he o. to** había bebido *or Am* tomado más de la cuenta; **this o. to have been done before** esto se tenía que haber hecho antes; **they o. not to have waited** no tenían que haber esperado

(**b**) *(expressing probability)* **they o. to be in Paris by now** a estas horas tendrían que estar ya en París; **you o. to be able to get $150 for the painting** deberías conseguir al menos 150 dólares por el cuadro

oughtn't ['ɔːtənt] = **ought not**

ounce [aʊns] *n (measurement)* onza *f*; **if you had an o. of sense** si tuvieras dos dedos de frente

our ['aʊə(r)] *possessive adj* (**a**) *(singular)* nuestro(a); *(plural)* nuestros(as) (**b**) *(for parts of body, clothes) (translated by definite article)* **someone stole o. clothes** nos robaron la ropa

ours ['aʊəz] *possessive pron* (**a**) *(singular)* el nuestro *m*, la nuestra *f*; *(plural)* los nuestros *mpl*, las nuestras *fpl*; **their house is big but o. is bigger** su casa es grande, pero la nuestra es mayor (**b**) *(used attributively) (singular)* nuestro *m*, nuestra *f*; *(plural)* nuestros *mpl*, nuestras *fpl*; **this book is o.** este libro es nuestro; **a friend of o.** un amigo nuestro

ourselves [aʊə'selvz] *pron* (**a**) *(reflexive)* nos; **we both hurt o.** los dos nos hicimos daño (**b**) *(emphatic)* nosotros mismos *or* solos *mpl*, nosotras mismas *or* solas *fpl*; **we did all the work o.** hicimos todo el trabajo nosotros solos; **we o. do not believe it** nosotros mismos no nos lo creemos (**c**) *(after preposition)* nosotros *mpl*, nosotras *fpl*; **we shouldn't talk**

about o. no deberíamos hablar sobre nosotros; **we shouldn't fight among o.** no deberíamos pelearnos entre nosotros; **we were all by o.** estábamos nosotros solos

oust [aʊst] *vt* desbancar; **to o. sb from his post** destituir a alguien, separar a alguien de su cargo

out [aʊt] **1** *adv* (**a**) *(outside, not in, not at home)* fuera; **he's o.** está fuera; **I was only o. for a minute** sólo salí un momento; **o. here** aquí fuera; **it's cold o. there** hace frío (ahí) fuera; **to go o.** salir; **to stay o. late** salir hasta muy tarde; **the tide is o.** la marea está baja; **o.!** *(in tennis)* ¡out!

(**b**) *(not concealed)* **the secret is o.** se ha desvelado el secreto; **he's o.** *(openly gay)* es homosexual declarado; **the sun is o.** ha salido el sol, hace sol; **the tulips are o. early this year** los tulipanes han salido *or* florecido muy pronto este año

(**c**) *(published)* **to come o.** salir; **her new book will be o. next week** la semana que viene sale su nuevo libro

(**d**) *(not in fashion)* **to be o.** no *Esp* llevarse *or Am* usarse

(**e**) *(indicating intention)* **to be o. to do sth** pretender hacer algo; **to be o. for money/a good time** ir en busca de dinero/diversión; *Fam* **to be o. to get sb** ir detrás de alguien, *Esp* ir a por alguien

(**f**) *(unconscious, asleep)* **to be o. cold** *(unconscious)* estar inconsciente; *Fam* **to be o. for the count** *(asleep)* estar roque *or Am* planchado(a); *Fam* **I was o. like a light** caí redondo en la cama

(**g**) *(extinguished) (fire, light)* apagado(a)

(**h**) **to be o.** *(on strike)* estar en huelga

(**i**) *(indicating completion)* **before the week is o.** antes de que termine la semana

(**j**) *Law* **the jury is o.** el jurado está deliberando

(**k**) *(unacceptable)* **that's o.** eso es imposible

2 *prep (through)* **to look o. the window** mirar por la ventana

3 *vt Fam* revelar la homosexualidad de

4 out of *prep (outside)* **to go o. of the office** salir de la oficina; **to throw sth o. of the window** tirar *or Am salvo RP* botar algo por la ventana; **keep o. of direct sunlight** manténgase a resguardo de los rayos del sol; **to be o. of the country** estar fuera del país; **o. of doors** fuera; **to sleep o. of doors** dormir al raso; **o. of danger** fuera de peligro; **to be o. of power** estar en la oposición

5 out of *prep (lacking)* **I'm o. of cash/ideas** me he quedado sin dinero/ideas

6 out of *prep (from)* de; **to get sth o. of sth/sb** sacar algo de algo/a alguien; **three days o. of four** tres días de cada cuatro; **twenty o. of twenty** *(mark)* veinte sobre *or* de veinte; **he built a hut o. of sticks** construyó una choza con palos; **it's made o. of plasticine** está hecho de plastilina; **she paid for it o. of her own money** lo pagó de *or* con su dinero; **o. of friendship/curiosity** por amistad/curiosidad

7 out of *prep (in phrases) Fam* **to be o. of it** *(dazed)* estar atontado(a); **to feel o. of it** *(excluded)* no sentirse integrado(a)

outage ['aʊtɪdʒ] *n* (**a**) *(power cut)* apagón *m*, corte *m* de luz (**b**) *Com (missing goods)* faltante *m*

out-and-out [aʊtə'naʊt] *adj (villain, reactionary)* consumado(a), redomado(a); *(success, failure)* rotundo(a), absoluto(a)

outback ['aʊtbæk] *n* **the o.** el interior despoblado de Australia

outbid ['aʊt'bɪd] *(pt & pp* **outbid***) vt* sobrepasar *(en una puja)*; **to o. sb** sobresar la puja de alguien

outboard ['aʊtbɔːd] **1** *n (motor)* fueraborda *m*

2 *adj* **o. motor** motor *m* (de) fueraborda

outbreak ['aʊtbreɪk] *n (of hostilities)* comienzo *m*; *(of epidemic, violence)* brote *m*; *(of war, conflict)* estallido *m*

outbuilding ['aʊtbɪldɪŋ] *n* dependencia *f*

outburst ['aʊtbɜːst] *n* arrebato *m*, arranque *m*

outcast ['aʊtkɑːst] *n* paria *mf*, marginado(a) *m,f*

outclass [aʊt'klɑːs] *vt* superar (ampliamente)

outcome ['aʊtkʌm] *n* resultado *m*

outcrop ['aʊtkrɒp] *n (of rock)* afloramiento *m*

outcry ['aʊtkraɪ] *n (protest)* protesta *f*; **to raise an o. (against)** protestar (en contra de)

outdated [aʊt'deɪtɪd] *adj* anticuado(a)

outdistance [aʊt'dɪstəns] *vt* dejar atrás

outdo [aʊt'duː] *(pt* **outdid** [aʊt'dɪd], *pp* **outdone** [aʊt'dʌn]) *vt (person)* superar, sobrepasar; **not to be outdone,...** para no ser menos,...

outdoor ['aʊtdɔː(r)] *adj* al aire libre; **she's an o. person** le gusta salir al aire libre; **the o. life** la vida al aire libre; **o. swimming pool** piscina *f or Méx* alberca *f or RP* pileta *f* descubierta

outdoors [aʊt'dɔːz] **1** *n* **the great o.** la naturaleza, el campo **2** *adv* fuera; **the wedding will be held o.** la boda se celebrará al aire libre; **to sleep o.** dormir al raso

outer ['aʊtə(r)] *adj* exterior; **o. door** puerta *f* exterior; **o. Los Angeles** la periferia de Los Ángeles; **O. Mongolia** Mongolia Exterior; **o. space** el espacio exterior

outermost ['aʊtəməʊst] *adj (layer)* exterior

outfit ['aʊtfɪt] *n* **(a)** *(clothes)* traje *m* **(b)** *Fam (organization)* grupo *m*

outflank [aʊt'flæŋk] *vt Mil* sorprender por la espalda; *Fig (outmaneuver)* superar

outflow ['aʊtfləʊ] *n (of liquid, currency)* salida *f*, fuga *f*

outgoing [aʊt'gəʊɪŋ] *adj* **(a)** *(departing)* saliente **(b)** *(sociable)* abierto(a), extrovertido(a)

outgrow [aʊt'grəʊ] *(pt* **outgrew** [aʊt'gruː], *pp* **outgrown** [aʊt'grəʊn]) *vt (toys)* hacerse demasiado mayor para; **he's outgrown the jacket** se le ha quedado pequeña la chaqueta; **he should have outgrown that habit by now** ya no tiene edad para esas cosas; **to have outgrown one's friends** tener ya poco en común *or* poco que ver con los amigos

outhouse ['aʊthaʊs] *n* dependencia *f*

outing ['aʊtɪŋ] *n* **(a)** *(excursion)* excursión *f* **(b)** *(of homosexual)* = hecho de revelar la homosexualidad de alguien, generalmente un personaje célebre

outlandish [aʊt'lændɪʃ] *adj* estrafalario(a), extravagante

outlast [aʊt'lɑːst] *vt* sobrevivir a

outlaw ['aʊtlɔː] **1** *n* proscrito(a) *m,f* **2** *vt (custom)* prohibir; *(person)* proscribir

outlay ['aʊtleɪ] *n (expense)* desembolso *m*

outlet ['aʊtlet] *n* **(a)** *(for water)* desagüe *m*; *(for steam)* salida *f*; *(for talents, energy)* válvula *f* de escape **(b)** *(store)* punto *m* de venta

outline ['aʊtlaɪn] **1** *n (shape)* silueta *f*, contorno *m*; *(drawing)* esbozo *m*, bosquejo *m*; *(of play, novel)* resumen *m*; *(of plan, policy)* líneas *fpl* maestras; **a rough o.** *(of plan, proposal)* un esbozo, una idea aproximada; **in o.** a grandes rasgos **2** *vt (shape)* perfilar; *(plot of novel)* resumir; *(plan, policy)* exponer a grandes rasgos

outlive [aʊt'lɪv] *vt* sobrevivir a; **to have outlived its usefulness** *(machine, theory)* haber dejado de ser útil *or* de servir

outlook ['aʊtlʊk] *n* **(a)** *(prospect)* perspectiva *f*; *(of weather)* previsión *f*; **the o. is gloomy** *(for economy)* las previsiones son muy malas **(b)** *(attitude)* punto *m* de vista, visión *f*; **o. on life** visión de la vida

outlying ['aʊtlaɪŋ] *adj* periférico(a)

outmaneuver [aʊtmə'nuːvə(r)] *vt Mil* superar a base de estrategia; *(in politics, sport)* superar

outmoded [aʊt'məʊdɪd] *adj* anticuado(a)

outnumber [aʊt'nʌmbə(r)] *vt (the enemy)* superar en número; **we were outnumbered** eran más que nosotros

out-of-court ['aʊtəv'kɔːt] *adj* **an o. settlement** un acuerdo sin acudir a los tribunales

out-of-pocket expenses ['aʊtəv'pɒkɪtɪk'spensɪz] *npl* gastos *mpl* extras

out-of-the-ordinary [aʊtəvðə'ɔːdɪnərɪ] *adj* fuera de lo normal

out-of-the-way [aʊtəvðə'weɪ] *adj (remote)* apartado(a), remoto(a); *(unusual)* fuera de lo común

out-of-work ['aʊtəv'wɜːk] *adj* sin trabajo, desempleado(a)

outpatient ['aʊtpeɪʃənt] *n* paciente *mf* externo(a)

outperform ['aʊtpə'fɔːm] *vt* rendir más que, ofrecer un mejor rendimiento que

outplacement ['aʊtpleɪsmənt] *n* recolocación *f*, = asesoramiento dirigido a facilitar la recolocación de empleados, generalmente subvencionado por la empresa que los despide

outpost ['aʊtpəʊst] *n Mil* enclave *m*; *Fig* **the last o. of civilization** el último baluarte de la civilización

output ['aʊtpʊt] **1** *n (of goods, of author)* producción *f*; *(of data, information)* información *f* producida; *(of generator)* potencia *f* (de salida) **2** *vt (pt & pp* **output)** producir

outrage ['aʊtreɪdʒ] **1** *n* **(a)** *(act)* ultraje *m*; **it's an o.!** ¡es un escándalo! **(b)** *(indignation)* indignación *f* **2** *vt (make indignant)* indignar, ultrajar; **I am outraged** estoy indignado

outrageous [aʊt'reɪdʒəs] *adj (cruelty)* atroz; *(price, conduct)* escandaloso(a); *(clothes, haircut)* estrambótico(a)

outrageously [aʊt'reɪdʒəslɪ] *adv (cruel)* espantosamente, terriblemente; *(expensive, to behave)* escandalosamente; *(to dress)* estrambóticamente

outreach 1 *n* ['aʊtriːtʃ] **o. worker** = trabajador social que presta asistencia a personas que pudiendo necesitarla no la solicitan **2** *vt* [aʊt'riːtʃ] *(exceed)* exceder, superar

outright 1 *adv* [aʊt'raɪt] **(a)** *(completely)* (*ban, win*) completamente; **to buy sth o.** comprar algo (con) dinero en mano; **he was killed o.** murió en el acto **(b)** *(bluntly)* **I told him o. what I thought of him** le dije claramente lo que pensaba de él; **to refuse o.** negarse rotundamente **2** *adj* ['aʊtraɪt] total, absoluto(a); **an o. failure** un fracaso total, un rotundo fracaso; **the o. winner** el campeón absoluto

outrun [aʊt'rʌn] *(pt* **outran** [aʊt'ræn], *pp* **outrun)** *vt (run faster than)* correr más rápido que

outsell [aʊt'sel] *vt* superar en ventas

outset ['aʊtset] *n* principio *m*; **at the o.** al principio; **from the o.** desde el principio

outshine [aʊt'ʃaɪn] *(pt & pp* **outshone** [aʊt'ʃɒn]) *vt (surpass)* eclipsar

outside ['aʊtsaɪd, aʊt'saɪd] **1** *n (of book, building)* exterior *m*; **on the o.** por fuera *or Am* afuera; **from the o.** desde fuera *or Am* afuera; **at the o.** *(of estimate)* a lo sumo **2** *adj (help, influence, world)* exterior; **there's an o. chance** existe una posibilidad remota **3** *adv* fuera; **to go o.** salir afuera; **from o.** desde fuera *or Am* afuera **4** *prep* **(a)** *(physically)* fuera de; **I'll meet you o. the movie theater** nos vemos a la entrada del cine; **o. office hours** fuera de horas de oficina **(b)** *(apart from)* aparte de; **o. (of) a few friends** aparte de unos pocos amigos

outsider [aʊt'saɪdə(r)] *n* **(a)** *(socially)* extraño(a) *m,f* **(b)** *(in election, race, competition)* **he's an o.** no figura entre los favoritos

outsize(d) ['aʊtsaɪz(d)] *adj (clothes)* de talla especial; *(appetite, ego)* desmedido(a)

outskirts ['aʊtskɜːts] *npl (of city)* afueras *fpl*

outsmart [aʊt'smɑːt] *vt* superar en astucia, burlar

outsourcing ['aʊtsɔːsɪŋ] *n Com* externalización *f*, subcontratación *f*, *Am* tercerización *f*, *Am* terciarización *f*

outspend [aʊt'spend] *vt* gastar más que

outspoken [aʊt'spəʊkən] *adj* directo(a), abierto(a)

outspokenness [aʊt'spəʊkənnɪs] *n* franqueza *f*

outstanding [aʊt'stændɪŋ] *adj* (**a**) *(remarkable) (feature, incident)* notable, destacado(a); *(person)* excepcional (**b**) *(unresolved, unpaid)* pendiente

outstandingly [aʊt'stændɪŋlɪ] *adv* extraordinariamente

outstay [aʊt'steɪ] *vt* **to o. one's welcome** abusar de la hospitalidad, quedarse más tiempo del apropiado

outstretched ['aʊtstretʃt] *adj* extendido(a), estirado(a); **with o. arms** con los brazos extendidos

outstrip [aʊt'strɪp] (*pt & pp* **outstripped**) *vt* superar, aventajar

outtake ['aʊtteɪk] *n Cin & TV* = escena o secuencia que se elimina de la versión montada de una película o vídeo

out-tray ['aʊttreɪ] *n* bandeja *f* de trabajos terminados

outward ['aʊtwəd] **1** *adj* (**a**) *(journey, flight)* de ida; **o. voyage** *or* **journey** viaje *m* de ida (**b**) *(external)* externo(a)
   2 *adv* hacia fuera

outwardly ['aʊtwədlɪ] *adv* aparentemente, en apariencia; **o. calm** aparentemente tranquilo(a)

outwards ['aʊtwədz] *adv* = **outward**

outweigh [aʊt'weɪ] *vt (be more important than)* tener más peso que

outwit [aʊt'wɪt] (*pt & pp* **outwitted**) *vt* ser más astuto(a) que, burlar

outworker ['aʊtwɜːkə(r)] *n* trabajador(ora) *m,f* a domicilio *or* externo(a)

outworn [aʊt'wɔːn] *adj (theories, ideas)* anticuado(a)

ova ['əʊvə] *n pl of* **ovum**

oval ['əʊvəl] **1** *n* óvalo *m*
   2 *adj* oval, ovalado(a); **the O. Office** el despacho oval

ovarian [əʊ'veərɪən] *adj Anat* ovárico(a); **o. cancer** cáncer *m* de ovario

ovary ['əʊvərɪ] *n Anat* ovario *m*

ovation [əʊ'veɪʃən] *n* ovación *f*; **the audience gave her a standing o.** el público puesto en pie le dedicó una calurosa ovación

oven ['ʌvən] *n* horno *m*; **electric/gas o.** horno eléctrico/de gas; **o. gloves** manoplas *fpl* de cocina

ovenproof ['ʌvənpruːf] *adj* refractario(a)

oven-ready ['ʌvənredɪ] *adj (chicken)* listo(a) para hornear

ovenware ['ʌvənweə(r)] *n* accesorios *mpl* para el horno

over ['əʊvə(r)] **1** *n (in cricket)* = serie de seis lanzamientos en la misma dirección
   2 *prep* (**a**) *(above, on top of)* sobre, encima de, *Am* arriba de; **to put a blanket o. sb** cubrir a alguien con una manta; **all o. Spain** por toda España; **all o. the world** por todo el mundo; **to throw sth o. the wall** tirar *or* lanzar *or Am salvo RP* botar algo por encima de la tapia; **to read o. sb's shoulder** leer por encima del hombro de alguien; **directly o. our heads** justo encima de nosotros; *Fig* **the lecture was way o. my head** no me enteré de nada de la conferencia; **I couldn't hear her o. the noise** no podía oírla por el ruido
   (**b**) *(across)* **to go o. the road** cruzar la calle; **to live o. the road** vivir al *or Am* del otro lado de la calle; **o. the border** al *or Am* del otro lado de la frontera; **the bridge o. the river** el puente sobre el río
   (**c**) *(about)* **to laugh o. sth** reírse de algo; **to fight o. sth** pelear por algo; **we had trouble o. the tickets** tuvimos problemas con las entradas *or Am* los boletos
   (**d**) *(in excess of)* más de; **o. and above** además de, más allá de; **he's o. fifty** tiene más de cincuenta años; **children o. five** los niños mayores de cinco años
   (**e**) *(during)* durante; **o. Christmas/the weekend** durante la Navidad/el fin de semana; **o. the last three years** (durante) los tres últimos años; **to discuss sth o. lunch** hablar de algo durante la comida

(**f**) *(recovered from)* **I'm o. the flu/the disappointment** ya se me ha pasado la gripe *or Méx* gripa/la desilusión
   3 *adv* (**a**) *(across)* **o. here/there** aquí/allí, *Am* acá/allá; **he led me o. to the window** me llevó hasta la ventana; **to cross o.** *(the street)* cruzar; **I asked him o. (to my house)** lo invité a mi casa
   (**b**) *(down)* **to fall o.** caerse; **to bend o.** agacharse; **to push sth o.** tirar algo, *CSur* voltear algo
   (**c**) *(everywhere)* **famous the world o.** famoso(a) en el mundo entero
   (**d**) *(indicating repetition)* **three times o.** tres veces; **o. and o. again** una y otra vez; **all o. again** otra vez desde el principio
   (**e**) *(in excess)* **children of five and o.** niños mayores de cinco años; **there was $5 left o.** sobraron *or* quedaron 5 dólares
   (**f**) *(on radio)* **o. (and out)** cambio (y corto)
   4 *adj (finished)* **it is (all) o.** todo ha terminado; **the danger is o.** ha pasado el peligro; **to get sth o. (and done) with** terminar algo de una vez por todas

overabundant [əʊvərə'bʌndənt] *adj* superabundante

overachiever [əʊvərə'tʃiːvə(r)] *n* = persona que rinde más de lo normal

overact [əʊvər'ækt] *vi* sobreactuar

overactive [əʊvər'æktɪv] *adj* hiperactivo(a)

overall ['əʊvərɔːl] **1** *adj* total, global
   2 *adv* en general; **England came third o.** Inglaterra quedó tercera en la clasificación general

overanxious [əʊvər'æŋkʃəs] *adj* excesivamente preocupado(a)

overawe [əʊvər'ɔː] *vt* intimidar, cohibir; **to be overawed by sth/sb** quedarse anonadado(a) por algo/alguien

overbalance [əʊvə'bæləns] *vi* perder el equilibrio

overbearing [əʊvə'beərɪŋ] *adj* imperioso(a), despótico(a)

overblown [əʊvə'bləʊn] *adj* exagerado(a)

overboard ['əʊvəbɔːd] *adv* por la borda; **to fall o.** caer por la borda, caer al agua; **man o.!** ¡hombre al agua!; *Fig* **to go o. (about)** entusiasmarse mucho (con)

overbook ['əʊvə'bʊk] *vt (flight, vacation)* = aceptar un número de reservas mayor que el de plazas disponibles; **they've overbooked this flight** este vuelo tiene overbooking

overbooking [əʊvə'bʊkɪŋ] *n* overbooking *m*, = venta de más plazas de las disponibles

overcapacity ['əʊvəkə'pæsɪtɪ] *n Ind* capacidad *f* excesiva de producción

overcast ['əʊvəkɑːst] *adj (sky, day)* nublado(a); **to be o.** estar nublado(a)

overcautious [əʊvə'kɔːʃəs] *adj* demasiado cauteloso(a)

overcharge [əʊvə'tʃɑːdʒ] *vt* (**a**) *(for goods, services)* **to o. sb (for sth)** cobrar de más a alguien (por algo); **he overcharged me by $5** me cobró cinco dólares de más (**b**) *Elec (battery)* sobrecargar

overcoat ['əʊvəkəʊt] *n* abrigo *m*

overcome [əʊvə'kʌm] (*pt* **overcame** [əʊvə'keɪm], *pp* **overcome**) *vt (defeat) (an opponent, one's fears)* vencer; *(problem, obstacle)* superar; **to be o. with** *or* **by grief** sucumbir al dolor; **I was quite o.** estaba totalmente abrumado(a), me embargaba la emoción

overcompensate [əʊvə'kɒmpenseɪt] *vi* **to o. for sth** compensar algo en exceso

overcomplicate [əʊvə'kɒmplɪkeɪt] *vt* complicar en exceso

overconfident [əʊvə'kɒnfɪdənt] *adj* demasiado confiado(a)

overcook [əʊvə'kʊk] *vt* cocinar demasiado, pasar mucho

overcrowded [əʊvə'kraʊdəd] *adj (room)* atestado(a); *(area, region)* superpoblado(a); **the problem of o. classrooms** el problema de la masificación de las aulas

overcrowding [əʊvə'kraʊdɪŋ] *n (of slums, prisons)* hacinamiento *m*; *(of classrooms)* masificación *f*; *(of city, region)* superpoblación *f*

overdeveloped [əʊvədɪ'veləpt] *adj* hiperdesarrollado(a); *Phot* sobrerrevelado(a)

overdo [əʊvə'duː] (*pt* **overdid** [əʊvə'dɪd], *pp* **overdone** [əʊvə'dʌn]) *vt* (**a**) *(exaggerate)* exagerar; **to o. it** *(work too hard)* trabajar demasiado (**b**) *(do or have too much of)* pasarse con; **to o. the salt/make-up** pasarse con la sal/el maquillaje

overdone ['əʊvədʌn] *adj (food)* demasiado hecho(a), pasado(a)

overdose ['əʊvədəʊs] **1** *n* sobredosis *f inv*
   2 *vi* tomar una sobredosis; **to o. on drugs** tomar una sobredosis de drogas; *Fig* **to o. on chocolate** darse un atracón de chocolate

overdraft ['əʊvədrɑːft] *n Fin (amount borrowed)* saldo *m* negativo *or* deudor; **to arrange an o.** acordar un (límite de) descubierto; **o. limit** límite *m* de descubierto

overdrawn [əʊvə'drɔːn] *adj Fin (account)* en descubierto; **to be $100 o.** tener un descubierto de 100 dólares

overdressed [əʊvə'drest] *adj* demasiado trajeado(a)

overdrive ['əʊvədraɪv] *n (in car)* superdirecta *f; Fig* **to go into o.** entregarse a una actividad frenética

overdue [əʊvə'djuː] *adj* **to be o.** *(person, train)* retrasarse, venir con retraso *or Am* demora; *(bill)* estar sin pagar; *(library book)* haber rebasado el plazo de préstamo *or Méx* prestamiento; **this measure is long o.** esta medida debía haberse adoptado hace tiempo

overeat [əʊvər'iːt] (*pt* **overate** [əʊvər'eɪt], *pp* **overeaten** [əʊvər'iːtən]) *vi* comer demasiado

overemphasize [əʊvər'emfəsaɪz] *vt* hacer excesivo hincapié en, recalcar en exceso

overenthusiastic [əʊvərɪnθjuːzɪ'æstɪk] *adj* excesivamente entusiasta

overestimate [əʊvər'estɪmeɪt] *vt* sobreestimar

overexcited [əʊvərɪk'saɪtɪd] *adj* demasiado emocionado(a) *or* entusiasmado(a)

overexcitement [əʊvərɪk'saɪtmənt] *n* emoción *f* excesiva, entusiasmo *m* excesivo

overexpose [əʊvərɪks'pəʊz] *vt Phot* sobreexponer

overexposure ['əʊvərɪk'spəʊʒə(r)] *n (of film)* sobreexposición *f*; **to suffer from o.** *(issue, public figure)* = aparecer demasiado en los medios de comunicación

overextended [əʊvərɪk'stendɪd] *adj Fin* insolvente, con alto grado de pasivo

overfamiliar [əʊvəfə'mɪlɪə(r)] *adj* (**a**) *(too intimate, disrespectful)* confianzudo(a); **to be o. with sb** ser demasiado confianzudo(a) con alguien, tomarse demasiadas libertades con alguien (**b**) *(conversant)* **I'm not o. with the system** no estoy muy familiarizado con el sistema

overflow 1 *n* ['əʊvəfləʊ] *(of population)* exceso *m* de población; **o. (pipe)** rebosadero *m*, desagüe *m*
   2 *vi* [əʊvə'fləʊ] *(river)* desbordarse; *(liquid, cup)* rebosar; **to o. with joy** estar rebosante de felicidad

overfull [əʊvə'fʊl] *adj* repleto(a), saturado(a)

overground 1 *adj* ['əʊvəgraʊnd] de superficie; **an o. rail link** un enlace ferroviario de superficie
   2 *adv* [əʊvə'graʊnd] por la superficie

overgrown [əʊvə'grəʊn] *adj* **o. with weeds** *(garden)* invadido(a) por las malas hierbas; **he's like an o. schoolboy** es como un niño grande

overhang 1 *n* ['əʊvəhæŋ] *(of roof)* alero *m*, voladizo *m*; *(on mountain)* saliente *m*
   2 *vt* [əʊvə'hæŋ] (*pt & pp* **overhung** [əʊvə'hʌŋ]) *(of balcony, rocks)* colgar sobre

overhanging ['əʊvəhæŋɪŋ] *adj (ledge, balcony)* sobresaliente; **we walked under the o. branches** caminamos bajo las crecidas ramas de los árboles

overhaul 1 ['əʊvəhɔːl] *n (of machine, policy)* revisión *f*
   2 *vt* [əʊvə'hɔːl] (**a**) *(machine, policy)* revisar (**b**) *(overtake)* adelantar

overhead ['əʊvəhed] **1** *n Com* gastos *mpl* generales
   2 *adj (cable)* aéreo(a); **o. projector** retroproyector *m*, proyector *m* de transparencias
   3 *adv* [əʊvə'hed] (por) arriba; **a plane flew o.** un avión sobrevoló nuestras cabezas

overhear [əʊvə'hɪə(r)] (*pt & pp* **overheard** [əʊvə'hɜːd]) *vt* oír *or* escuchar casualmente

overheat [əʊvə'hiːt] *vi (engine, economy)* recalentarse

overheated [əʊvə'hiːtɪd] *adj (engine, economy)* recalentado(a); *Fig (argument, person)* acalorado(a), agitado(a)

overindulge [əʊvərɪn'dʌldʒ] **1** *vt (child)* consentir; **to o. oneself** *(drink, eat to excess)* atiborrarse, empacharse
   2 *vi* atiborrarse, empacharse

overindulgence [əʊvərɪn'dʌldʒəns] *n* (**a**) *(toward person)* indulgencia *f* excesiva (**b**) *(in food and drink)* exceso *m*; **a lifetime of o.** una vida de excesos

overindulgent ['əʊvərɪn'dʌldʒənt] *adj* (**a**) *(toward person)* demasiado indulgente (**b**) *(in food and drink)* **an o. weekend** un fin de semana de excesos

overjoyed [əʊvə'dʒɔɪd] *adj* contentísimo(a); **to be o. at sth** estar contentísimo(a) con algo; **he was o. to hear that they were coming** le encantó saber que venían

overkill ['əʊvəkɪl] *n* **there's a danger of o.** se corre el peligro de caer en el exceso; **media o.** *(on TV, in newspapers)* cobertura *f* informativa exagerada

overland 1 *adv* [əʊvə'lænd] por tierra
   2 *adj* ['əʊvəlænd] terrestre

overlap 1 *n* ['əʊvəlæp] *(of planks, tiles)* superposición *f*, solapamiento *m*; *(between two areas of work, knowledge)* coincidencia *f*
   2 *vi* [əʊvə'læp] (*pt & pp* **overlapped**) *(planks, tiles)* superponerse *or* solaparse (**with** con); *(categories, theories)* tener puntos en común (**with** con); *(periods of time)* coincidir (**with** con)

overleaf [əʊvə'liːf] *adv* al dorso; **see o.** véase al dorso

overload 1 *n* ['əʊvələʊd] *Elec* sobrecarga *f*
   2 *vt* [əʊvə'ləʊd] *(machine, person)* sobrecargar

overlong [əʊvə'lɒŋ] *adj* demasiado largo(a)

overlook [əʊvə'lʊk] *vt* (**a**) *(look out over)* dar a; **the town is overlooked by the castle** el castillo domina la ciudad (**b**) *(fail to notice)* pasar por alto, no darse cuenta de (**c**) *(disregard)* pasar por alto, no tener en cuenta

overly ['əʊvəlɪ] *adv* excesivamente, demasiado; **not o.** no excesivamente, no demasiado

overmanning [əʊvə'mænɪŋ] *n Ind* exceso *m* de empleados

overmuch [əʊvə'mʌtʃ] *adv* en exceso

overnight 1 *adv* [əʊvə'naɪt] (**a**) *(during the night)* durante la noche; **to stay o.** quedarse a pasar la noche (**b**) *(suddenly)* de la noche a la mañana, de un día para otro
   2 *adj* ['əʊvənaɪt] (**a**) *(for one night)* de una noche; **o. bag** bolso *m* de viaje; **o. train/flight** tren *m*/vuelo *m* nocturno; **o. stay** *Esp, Méx* estancia *f or Am* estadía *f* de una noche (**b**) *(sudden)* repentino(a)

overoptimistic [əʊvərɒptɪ'mɪstɪk] *adj* demasiado optimista

overpaid [əʊvə'peɪd] *adj* **to be o.** ganar demasiado (dinero), estar demasiado bien pagado(a)

overpass ['əʊvəpɑːs] *n* paso *m* elevado

overpayment [əʊvə'peɪmənt] *n (of taxes, employee)* pago *m* excesivo

overpopulation [əʊvəpɒpjʊ'leɪʃən] *n* superpoblación *f*

overpower [əʊvə'paʊə(r)] *vt* vencer, dominar

overpowering [əʊvə'paʊərɪŋ] *adj (emotion, heat)* tremendo(a), desmesurado(a); *(smell, taste)* fortísimo(a), intensísimo(a); *(desire)* irrefrenable, irreprimible

overpriced [əʊvə'praɪst] adj excesivamente caro(a)

overproduction [əʊvəprə'dʌkʃən] n Econ superproducción f

overqualified [əʊvə'kwɒlɪfaɪd] adj **to be o. (for a job)** tener más títulos de los necesarios (para un trabajo)

overrate [əʊvə'reɪt] vt sobrevalorar

overrated [əʊvə'reɪtɪd] adj sobrevalorado(a)

overreach [əʊvə'riːtʃ] vt **to o. oneself** extralimitarse

overreact [əʊvərɪ'ækt] vi reaccionar exageradamente

overreaction [əʊvərɪ'ækʃən] n reacción f exagerada or excesiva

override [əʊvə'raɪd] (pt **overrode** [əʊvə'rəʊd], pp **overridden** [əʊvə'rɪdən]) vt (a) (objections, wishes, regulations) hacer caso omiso de (b) (take precedence over) anteponerse a; Tech (controls) anular

overriding [əʊvə'raɪdɪŋ] adj primordial

overrule [əʊvə'ruːl] vt (opinion) desautorizar; Law (decision) anular, invalidar; **she was overruled by her boss** su jefe la desautorizó

overrun 1 n ['əʊvərʌn] Com **(cost) o.** costos mpl or Esp costes mpl superiores a los previstos

2 vt [əʊvə'rʌn] (pt **overran** [əʊvə'ræn], pp **overrun**) (a) (country) invadir; **the house was o. with mice** los ratones habían invadido la casa (b) (allotted time) rebasar, excederse de; **to o. a budget** salirse de un presupuesto

3 vi (exceed allotted time) alargarse más de la cuenta, rebasar el tiempo previsto

overseas 1 adj ['əʊvəsiːz] extranjero(a); (trade, debt) exterior; **o. possessions** territorios mpl de ultramar

2 adv [əʊvə'siːz] fuera del país

oversee [əʊvə'siː] (pt **oversaw** [əʊvə'sɔː], pp **overseen** [əʊvə'siːn]) vt supervisar

overseer ['əʊvəsɪə(r)] n Old-fashioned supervisor(ora) m,f

oversensitive [əʊvə'sensɪtɪv] adj susceptible

oversexed [əʊvə'sekst] adj libidinoso(a), lujurioso(a)

overshadow [əʊvə'ʃædəʊ] vt (person, success) eclipsar; (occasion) deslucir

overshoe ['əʊvəʃuː] n chanclo m

overshoot [əʊvə'ʃuːt] (pt & pp **overshot** [əʊvə'ʃɒt]) vt pasar de largo, pasarse; Av **to o. the runway** salirse de la pista

oversight ['əʊvəsaɪt] n descuido m, omisión f; **through** or **by an o.** por descuido

oversimplify [əʊvə'sɪmplɪfaɪ] vt simplificar en exceso

oversized ['əʊvəsaɪzd] adj enorme

oversleep [əʊvə'sliːp] (pt & pp **overslept** [əʊvə'slept]) vi quedarse dormido(a)

overspend [əʊvə'spend] (pt & pp **overspent** [əʊvə'spent]) **1** vt **to o. one's budget** salirse del presupuesto

2 vi gastar de más; **to o. by $100** gastar cien dólares de más

overspill ['əʊvəspɪl] n (of population) exceso m de población

overstaffing [əʊvə'stɑːfɪŋ] n exceso m de personal

overstate [əʊvə'steɪt] vt exagerar

overstatement [əʊvə'steɪtmənt] n exageración f

overstay [əʊvə'steɪ] vt **to o. one's welcome** abusar de la hospitalidad, quedarse más tiempo del apropiado

overstep [əʊvə'step] vt traspasar, saltarse; Fig **to o. the mark** (exceed one's powers) pasarse de la raya

oversubscribed [əʊvəsəb'skraɪbd] adj Fin **the share offer was (five times) o.** la demanda superó (en cinco veces) la oferta de venta de acciones

overt [əʊ'vɜːt] adj claro(a), ostensible; **do you have to be so o. about it?** ¿tienes que mostrarlo tan a las claras?

overtake [əʊvə'teɪk] (pt **overtook** [əʊvə'tʊk], pp **overtaken** [əʊvə'teɪkən]) vt (car) adelantar; (competitor in race) rebasar; **they had been overtaken by events** se habían visto superados por los acontecimientos

over-the-counter ['əʊvəðə'kaʊntə(r)] adj & adv (medicine) sin receta

overthrow 1 n ['əʊvəθrəʊ] derrocamiento m

2 vt [əʊvə'θrəʊ] (pt **overthrew** [əʊvə'θruː], pp **overthrown** [əʊvə'θrəʊn]) derrocar

overtime ['əʊvətaɪm] **1** n (a) Ind (work) horas fpl extraordinarias or extras; **o. pay** horas fpl extra(s) (b) (in basketball, football) prórroga f

2 adv Ind **to work o.** hacer horas extras; Fig **your imagination is working o.** se te está disparando la imaginación

overtly [əʊ'vɜːtlɪ] adv abiertamente, claramente

overtone ['əʊvətəʊn] n (of sadness, bitterness) tinte m, matiz m

overture ['əʊvətjʊə(r)] n Mus obertura f; Fig **to make overtures to sb** hacer proposiciones a or tener contactos con alguien

overturn [əʊvə'tɜːn] **1** vt (table, boat) volcar; (government) derribar; (bill) rechazar

2 vi volcar

overuse 1 n [əʊvə'juːs] uso m excesivo, abuso m

2 vt [əʊvə'juːz] abusar de

overvalue [əʊvə'væljuː] vt (currency, house) sobrevalorar; (person's abilities) sobreestimar

overview ['əʊvəvjuː] n visión f general

overweight [əʊvə'weɪt] adj **to be o.** tener exceso de peso; **to be 10 pounds o.** tener 10 libras de más

overwhelm [əʊvə'welm] vt (enemy, opponent) arrollar; **to be overwhelmed with joy** no caber en sí de alegría; **overwhelmed by grief/with work** abrumado(a) por la pena/el trabajo

overwhelming [əʊvə'welmɪŋ] adj (need, desire) acuciante; (pressure) abrumador(ora); (defeat, majority) aplastante

overwhelmingly [əʊvə'welmɪŋlɪ] adv **to vote o. in favor of sth** aprobar algo por mayoría aplastante

overwork [əʊvə'wɜːk] **1** n exceso m de trabajo

2 vt (person) hacer trabajar en exceso

3 vi trabajar en exceso

overwrite Comptr **1** n ['əʊvəraɪt] **o. mode** función f de "sobreescribir"

2 vt [əʊvə'raɪt] sobreescribir

overwrought [əʊvə'rɔːt] adj muy alterado(a), muy nervioso(a); **to get o. (about sth)** alterarse mucho (por algo)

overzealous [əʊvə'zeləs] adj demasiado celoso(a)

ovulate ['ɒvjʊleɪt] vi Biol ovular

ovulation [ɒvjʊ'leɪʃən] n Biol ovulación f

ovum ['əʊvəm] (pl **ova** ['əʊvə]) n Biol óvulo m

ow [aʊ] exclam ¡ay!

owe [əʊ] vt deber; **to o. sb sth, to o. sth to sb** deber algo a alguien; **to o. sb an apology** deber disculpas a alguien; **to o. it to oneself to do sth** deber hacer algo, tener merecido hacer algo, Am ameritar hacer algo; **I o. my life to you** te debo la vida

owing ['əʊɪŋ] adj **the money o. to me** el dinero que se me adeuda; **o. to** (because of) debido a

owl [aʊl] n **(short-eared) o.** búho m, CAm, Méx tecolote m; **(barn) o.** lechuza f

own [əʊn] **1** adj propio(a); **her o. money** su propio dinero; **I saw it with my o. eyes** lo vi con mis propios ojos; **I do my o. accounts** llevo mi propia contabilidad; **in one's o. right** por derecho propio; **o. goal** (in soccer) autogol m, gol m en propia meta or Esp puerta or Am propio arco

2 pron (a) (of possession) **my o.** el/la mío(a); **it's my o.** es mío(a); **I have money of my o.** tengo dinero propio or Am mío; **a child of his o.** un hijo suyo; **he made that expression/part his o.** hizo suya esa expresión/suyo ese papel; **she has a copy of her o.** tiene un ejemplar para ella; **for reasons of his o.** por razones privadas

(b) *(idioms)* **to do sth on one's o.** *(without company)* hacer algo solo(a); *(on one's own initiative)* hacer algo por cuenta propia; **I am (all) on my o.** estoy solo; **you're on your o.!** *(I won't support you)* ¡conmigo no cuentes!; **he has come into his o. since being promoted** desde que lo ascendieron ha demostrado su verdadera valía *or* sus verdaderas posibilidades; **to get one's o. back (on sb)** vengarse (de alguien), tomarse la revancha (contra alguien); **he looks after his o.** *(friends, relatives)* cuida de los suyos; **she managed to hold her o.** consiguió defenderse

3 *vt* **(a)** *(property)* poseer; **who owns this land?** ¿de quién es esta tierra?, ¿quién es el propietario de esta tierra?; **he behaves as if he owned the place** se comporta como si fuera el dueño **(b)** *(admit)* Old-fashioned **to o. (that)...** reconocer que...

▶**own up** *vi (confess)* **to o. up (to sth)** confesar (algo)

owner ['əʊnə(r)] *n* dueño(a) *m,f*, propietario(a) *m,f*; **cars parked here at owners' risk** *(sign)* estacionamiento *or Esp* aparcamiento permitido bajo responsabilidad del propietario

ownership ['əʊnəʃɪp] *n* propiedad *f*; **under new o.** *(sign)* nuevos propietarios; **to be in private/public o.** ser de propiedad privada/pública

ox [ɒks] (*pl* **oxen** ['ɒksən]) *n* buey *m*

oxide ['ɒksaɪd] *n Chem* óxido *m*

oxidize ['ɒksɪdaɪz] *Chem* **1** *vt* oxidar
2 *vi* oxidarse

oxtail ['ɒksteɪl] *n* rabo *m* de buey

oxyacetylene [ɒksɪə'setɪliːn] *n Chem* oxiacetileno *m*; **o. torch** soplete *m* (oxiacetilénico)

oxygen ['ɒksɪdʒən] *n Chem* oxígeno *m*; **o. bottle** *or* **cylinder** bombona *f* de oxígeno; **o. mask** mascarilla *f* de oxígeno

oxygenation [ɒksɪdʒə'neɪʃən] *n Chem & Physiol* oxigenación *f*

oxymoron [ɒksɪ'mɔːrɒn] *n* oxímoron *m*, = figura del lenguaje consistente en yuxtaponer dos palabras aparentemente contradictorias

oyster ['ɔɪstə(r)] *n* ostra *f*; *Fig* **the world is your o.** el mundo es tuyo, te vas a comer el mundo; **o. bed** criadero *m* de ostras

oystercatcher ['ɔɪstəkætʃə(r)] *n (bird)* ostrero *m*

oz (*abbr* **ounce(s)**) onza(s) *fpl*

ozone ['əʊzəʊn] *n Chem* ozono *m*; **o. layer** capa *f* de ozono

ozone-friendly ['əʊzəʊn'frendlɪ] *adj* no perjudicial para la capa de ozono

P

P, p [piː] *n (letter)* P, p *f; Fam* **to mind one's P's and Q's** comportarse (con educación)

PA [ˈpiːˈeɪ] *n* (**a**) *(abbr* **public address**) megafonía *f;* **a message came over the PA (system)** dieron un mensaje por megafonía (**b**) *Com (abbr* **personal assistant**) secretario(a) *m,f* personal

pa [pɑː] *n Fam (dad)* papá *m*

p.a. *(abbr* **per annum**) anual, al año

PAC [piːeɪˈsiː] *n Pol (abbr* **Political Action Committee**) = grupo de presión estadounidense para el apoyo de causas políticas

pace [peɪs] **1** *n* (**a**) *(step)* paso *m; Fig* **to put sb through his paces** poner a alguien a prueba (**b**) *(speed)* ritmo *m,* paso *m;* **at a slow p.** lentamente; **at a fast p.** rápidamente; **to set the p.** marcar el paso, imponer el ritmo; **to force the p.** forzar el ritmo; **to keep p. with sb** seguirle el ritmo a alguien
2 *vt (room, street)* caminar por; **to p. oneself** controlar el ritmo
3 *vi* caminar; **to p. up and down** caminar de un lado a otro

pacemaker [ˈpeɪsmeɪkə(r)] *n* (**a**) *Sport* liebre *f* (**b**) *(for heart)* marcapasos *m inv*

Pacific [pəˈsɪfɪk] *adj* **the P. (Ocean)** el (océano) Pacífico; **the P. Rim** = los países que bordean el Pacífico, sobre todo los asiáticos; **P. Standard Time** = hora oficial de la costa del Pacífico en Estados Unidos

pacifier [ˈpæsɪfaɪə(r)] *n (for baby)* chupete *m*

pacifism [ˈpæsɪfɪzəm] *n* pacifismo *m*

pacifist [ˈpæsɪfɪst] *n & adj* pacifista *mf*

pacify [ˈpæsɪfaɪ] *vt (country)* pacificar; *(person)* apaciguar

pack [pæk] **1** *n* (**a**) *(rucksack)* mochila *f;* **p. animal** bestia *f* de carga (**b**) *(small box) (of cigarettes)* paquete *m; (of playing cards)* baraja *f* (**c**) *(group) (of thieves, photographers)* pandilla *f; (of runners, cyclists)* pelotón *m; (of wolves)* manada *f;* **a p. of lies** una sarta de mentiras; **p. ice** banco *m* de hielo
2 *vt* (**a**) *(put into box)* empaquetar; *(items for sale)* envasar; *(in cotton wool, newspaper)* envolver; **did you p. my toothbrush?** ¿metiste mi cepillo de dientes (en la maleta)? (**b**) *(cram) (earth into hole)* meter; *(passengers into bus, train)* apiñar; **we were packed in like sardines** estábamos como sardinas en lata (**c**) *(fill) (hole, box)* llenar (**with** de); **to p. one's suitcase** hacer la maleta *or RP* valija; *Fig* **to p. one's bags** *(leave)* hacer las maletas *or RP* valijas (**d**) **to p. a punch** *(fighter, drink)* pegar duro
3 *vi* (**a**) *(prepare luggage)* hacer el equipaje; *Fam Fig* **to send sb packing** *(send away)* mandar a alguien a paseo (**b**) *(cram)* **to p. into a room** apiñarse en una habitación

pack in *Fam vt (job, course)* dejar; **p. it in!** *(stop complaining)* ¡deja de protestar *or* de dar la murga!

pack off *vt sep Fam (send)* mandar

pack up *vt sep (belongings)* recoger

package [ˈpækɪdʒ] **1** *n (parcel)* paquete *m; (pay deal, contract)* paquete *m; Com* **p. deal** acuerdo *m* global; **p. store** tienda *f* de bebidas alcohólicas *or* de licores; **p. tour** paquete *m* turístico, viaje *m* organizado
2 *vt (goods)* envasar; *Fig* **to p. sb** *(pop star, politician)* vender a alguien

packaging [ˈpækɪdʒɪŋ] *n (for transport, freight)* embalaje *m; (of product)* envasado *m*

packed [pækt] *adj* (**a**) *(crowded)* abarrotado(a) (**b**) **p. lunch** comida *f* preparada de casa *(para excursión, trabajo, colegio)*

packer [ˈpækə(r)] *n* empaquetador(ora) *m,f,* embalador(ora) *m,f*

packet [ˈpækɪt] *n* (**a**) *(of seeds, stamps)* paquete *m; (bag)* bolsa *f* (**b**) *Comptr* paquete *m;* **p. switching** conmutación *f* de paquetes

packhorse [ˈpækhɔːs] *n* caballo *m* de carga

packing [ˈpækɪŋ] *n* (**a**) *(packing material)* embalaje *m;* **p. case** cajón *m* (**b**) *(for vacation)* **to do one's p.** hacer el equipaje

pact [pækt] *n* pacto *m;* **to make a p. with sb** hacer un pacto con alguien

pad [pæd] **1** *n* (**a**) *(for protection, of dog's feet)* almohadilla *f; (of cotton wool)* tampón *m; (for helicopters)* plataforma *f;* **(writing) pad** bloc *m* (**b**) *Fam (home)* casa *f, Esp* queli *f*
2 *vt (pt & pp* **padded**) *(stuff)* acolchar *or* almohadillar (**with** con)
3 *vi* **to p. around** caminar con suavidad

▶ **pad out** *vt sep (speech, essay)* rellenar

padded [ˈpædɪd] *adj (door, wall)* acolchado(a), almohadillado(a); **with p. shoulders** con hombreras; **p. cell** celda *f* acolchada

padding [ˈpædɪŋ] *n (material)* relleno *m; (of cotton)* guata *f; Fig (in speech, essay)* paja *f,* relleno *m*

paddle [ˈpædl] **1** *n* (**a**) *(for canoe)* canalete *m,* remo *m; (of paddle boat)* pala *f;* **p. boat** barco *m* (de vapor) de ruedas (**b**) *(for table tennis)* pala *f* (**c**) *(walk in water)* **to go for a p.** dar un paseo por el agua *or* la orilla
2 *vt* (**a**) *(canoe)* remar en; *Fig* **to p. one's own canoe** arreglárselas solo(a) (**b**) *(smack)* pegar
3 *vi* (**a**) *(in canoe)* remar (**b**) *(duck)* nadar (**c**) *(walk in water)* dar un paseo por el agua *or* la orilla

paddling pool [ˈpædlɪŋˈpuːl] *n (inflatable)* piscina *f* hinchable, *Méx* alberca *f or RP* pileta *f* inflable; *(in park)* piscina *f* para niños

paddock [ˈpædək] *n (field)* cercado *m,* potrero *m*

Paddy [ˈpædɪ] *n Fam* irlandés *m*

paddy [ˈpædɪ] *n* (**a**) **p. (field)** arrozal *m* (**b**) *Fam* **p. wagon** *(police van)* furgón *m* policial, *Arg* celular *m*

padlock [ˈpædlɒk] **1** *n* candado *m*
2 *vt* cerrar con candado

padre [ˈpɑːdreɪ] *n Fam (military chaplain)* capellán *m*

pagan [ˈpeɪgən] *n & adj* pagano(a) *m,f*

paganism [ˈpeɪgənɪzəm] *n* paganismo *m*

page[1] [peɪdʒ] *n* página *f;* **on p. 6** en la página 6; *Fig* **a glorious p. in our history** una página gloriosa de nuestra historia

page[2] **1** *n (servant, at wedding)* paje *m*
2 *vt (call) (by loudspeaker)* avisar por megafonía; *(by electronic device)* llamar por el buscapersonas *or Esp* busca *or Méx* localizador *or RP* radiomensaje

pageant ['pædʒənt] *n (procession)* desfile *m*, procesión *f*; *(of historical events)* representación *f* de escenas históricas

pageantry ['pædʒəntrɪ] *n* pompa *f*, esplendor *m*

pageboy ['peɪdʒbɔɪ] *n (servant, at wedding)* paje *m*; **p. (haircut)** *(hairstyle)* corte *m* estilo paje

pager ['peɪdʒə(r)] *n* buscapersonas *m inv*, *Esp* busca *m*, *Méx* localizador *m*, *RP* radiomensaje *m*

paginate ['pædʒɪneɪt] *vt Comptr* paginar

pagination [pædʒɪ'neɪʃən] *n Comptr* paginación *f*

pagoda [pə'gəʊdə] *n* pagoda *f*

paid [peɪd] **1** *adj (person, work)* remunerado(a); **p. vacations** vacaciones *fpl* pagadas
  2 *pt & pp of* **pay**

pail [peɪl] *n (bucket)* cubo *m*

pain [peɪn] **1** *n* (a) *(physical)* dolor *m*; *(mental)* sufrimiento *m*, pena *f*; **to cause sb p.** *(physical)* dolerle a alguien; *(mental)* afligir *or* hacer sufrir a alguien; **to be in p.** estar sufriendo; **I have a p. in my leg** me duele una pierna
  (b) *(trouble)* **to take pains to do sth, to be at great pains to do sth** tomarse muchas molestias para hacer algo; **for my pains** por mi esfuerzo
  (c) *Formal* **on p. of death** so pena de muerte
  (d) *(idioms) Fam* **he's a p. (in the neck)** es un plomazo *or* pelmazo *or Méx* sangrón; *Vulg* **it's a p. in the ass** es *Esp* un coñazo *or Méx* una chingadera *or RP* un embole; *Fam* **cooking can be a p.** a veces resulta una lata cocinar
  2 *vt* afligir, hacer sufrir

pained [peɪnd] *adj (look, expression)* afligido(a), de pena

painful ['peɪnfʊl] *adj (physically, mentally)* doloroso(a); *(part of body)* dolorido(a); **is it p. here?** ¿te duele aquí?; **it's p. to watch them** resulta penoso mirarlos

painfully ['peɪnfʊlɪ] *adv (to walk, move)* con dolor; *Fig (extremely)* tremendamente; **she fell p.** tuvo una caída dolorosa

painkiller ['peɪnkɪlə(r)] *n* analgésico *m*

painless ['peɪnlɪs] *adj (not painful)* indoloro(a); *Fig (easy)* fácil, muy llevadero(a)

painstaking ['peɪnzteɪkɪŋ] *adj (person, research)* meticuloso(a), concienzudo(a); *(care)* esmerado(a)

paint [peɪnt] **1** *n* pintura *f*; **wet p.** *(sign)* recién pintado; **p. gun** pistola *f (para pintar)*; **p. remover** decapante *m*
  2 *vt (picture, person, room)* pintar; *Fam* **to p. one's face** *(put on make-up)* pintarse; **to p. one's nails** pintarse las uñas; *Fig* **to p. a favorable picture (of)** dar una visión favorable (de); *Fig* **to p. the town red** irse de juerga
  3 *vi* pintar

paintball ['peɪntbɔːl] *n* paintball *m*, juegos *mpl* de guerra con pintura

paintbox ['peɪntbɒks] *n* caja *f* de acuarelas

paintbrush ['peɪntbrʌʃ] *n (of artist)* pincel *m*; *(of decorator)* brocha *f*

painter ['peɪntə(r)] *n (artist)* pintor(ora) *m,f*; *(decorator)* pintor(ora) *m,f* (de brocha gorda)

painting ['peɪntɪŋ] *n (picture)* cuadro *m*, pintura *f*; *(activity)* pintura *f*; **p. and decorating** pintura y decoración

paintwork ['peɪntwɜːk] *n (of car, room)* pintura *f*

pair [peə(r)] **1** *n (of shoes, gloves)* par *m*; *(of people, cards)* pareja *f*; **a p. of glasses** unas gafas; **a p. of scissors** unas tijeras; **a p. of pants** unos pantalones
  2 *vt (people, animals)* emparejar (**with** con)

▶**pair off 1** *vt sep (people)* emparejar
  2 *vi (people)* emparejarse

▶**pair up** *vi* hacer pareja, emparejarse

pajamas [pə'dʒɑːməz] *npl* pijama *m*, *Am* piyama *m or f*; **a pair of p.** un pijama *or Am* piyama

Pakistan [pɑːkɪ'stɑːn] *n* Paquistán

Pakistani [pɑːkɪ'stɑːnɪ] *n & adj* paquistaní *mf*

pal [pæl] *n Fam* amiguete(a) *m,f*, *Esp* colega *mf*; **look here, p.** ¡mira, *Esp* tío *or Am* compadre!

palace ['pælɪs] *n* palacio *m*

palatable ['pælətəbəl] *adj (food)* apetitoso(a); *Fig (suggestion)* aceptable

palate ['pælɪt] *n (in mouth)* paladar *m*

palatial [pə'leɪʃəl] *adj* suntuoso(a), señorial

palaver [pə'lɑːvə(r)] *n Fam (fuss)* lío *m*, *Esp* follón *m*; **what a p.!** ¡vaya lío *or Esp* follón!

pale[1] [peɪl] **1** *adj (skin)* pálido(a); *(color)* claro(a); **to turn p. (with fright)** palidecer (de miedo); *Fig* **a p. imitation of sth** un pálido remedo de algo
  2 *vi (person)* palidecer; **to p. into insignificance** reducirse hasta la insignificancia

pale[2] *n (of fence)* estaca *f*; *Fig* **to be/go beyond the p.** pasarse de la raya

paleness ['peɪlnɪs] *n* palidez *f*

Palestine ['pælɪstaɪn] *n* Palestina

Palestinian [pælɪ'stɪnɪən] *n & adj* palestino(a) *m,f*

palette ['pælɪt] *n Art* paleta *f*; **p. knife** espátula *f*

paling ['peɪlɪŋ] *n (fence)* cerca *f*, estacada *f*

palisade [pælɪ'seɪd] *n (fence)* empalizada *f*

pall[1] [pɔːl] *n (of smoke)* cortina *f*, manto *m*

pall[2] *vi (become uninteresting)* decaer

pallbearer ['pɔːlbeərə(r)] *n* portador(ora) *m,f* del féretro

pallet[1] ['pælɪt] *n (bed)* jergón *m*

pallet[2] *n Ind (wooden platform)* palet *m*, palé *m*

palliative ['pælɪətɪv] *n* paliativo *m*

pallid ['pælɪd] *adj* pálido(a)

pallor ['pælə(r)] *n* lividez *f*

pally ['pælɪ] *adj Fam* **to be p. with sb** comportarse amistosamente con alguien

palm[1] [pɑːm] *n* **p. (tree)** palmera *f*; **p. (leaf)** palma *f*; **P. Sunday** Domingo *m* de Ramos

palm[2] *n (of hand)* palma *f*; *Fig* **to have sb in the p. of one's hand** tener a alguien en el bolsillo

▶**palm off** *vt sep* **to p. sth off onto sb** endilgar algo a alguien

palmistry ['pɑːmɪstrɪ] *n* quiromancia *f*

palmtop ['pɑːmtɒp] *n Comptr* palmtop *m*, asistente *m* personal

palomino [pælə'miːnəʊ] *(pl* **palominos)** *n (horse)* = caballo alazán de crin y cola blancas

palpable ['pælpəbəl] *adj* palpable

palpate [pæl'peɪt] *vt Med* explorar

palpitate ['pælpɪteɪt] *vi (heart)* palpitar; **to p. with fear/excitement** estar estremecido(a) de miedo/emoción

palpitations [pælpɪ'teɪʃənz] *npl* palpitaciones *fpl*

paltry ['pɔːltrɪ] *adj* miserable

pamper ['pæmpə(r)] *vt (person)* mimar, consentir; **to p. oneself** darse lujos

pamphlet ['pæmflɪt] *n (informative)* folleto *m*; *(controversial)* panfleto *m*

pan[1] [pæn] **1** *n (for cooking)* cacerola *f*, cazuela *f*; *(frying pan)* sartén *f*; *(of scales)* platillo *m*
  2 *vi (pt & pp* **panned)** **to p. for gold** extraer oro

pan[2] *(pt & pp* **panned)** *vt Fam (criticize)* vapulear, *Esp* poner por los suelos

▶**pan out** *vi Fam (turn out)* salir; **let's see how things p. out** a ver cómo salen las cosas

panacea [pænə'sɪə] *n* panacea *f*

panache [pə'næʃ] *n* gracia *f*, garbo *m*

Pan-African [pæn'æfrɪkən] *adj* panafricano(a)

Panama ['pænəmɑː] *n* Panamá; **the P. Canal** el canal de Panamá; **P. (hat)** *(sombrero m)* panamá *m*

Panamanian [pænə'meɪnɪən] *n & adj* panameño(a) *m,f*

Pan-American [pænə'merɪkən] *adj* panamericano(a)

pancake ['pænkeɪk] n crepe f, torta f

pancreas ['pæŋkrɪəs] n Anat páncreas m inv

panda ['pændə] n (oso m) panda m

pandemic [pæn'demɪk] n Med pandemia f

pandemonium [pændɪ'məʊnɪəm] n **there was p., p. broke out** se armó un auténtico pandemónium; **to cause p.** sembrar el caos

pander ['pændə(r)] vi **to p. to sb** complacer a alguien; **to p. to sb's views** someterse a la opinión de alguien

pane [peɪn] n **p. (of glass)** hoja f de vidrio or Esp cristal

panel ['pænəl] n (a) (on wall, of door) panel m; (of switches, lights) panel m, tablero m (b) (at interview, of experts) panel m, equipo m; **p. discussion** debate m, mesa f redonda

paneling ['pænəlɪŋ] n (on wall) paneles mpl

panelist ['pænəlɪst] n (on radio, TV program) participante mf (en un debate)

pan-fry ['pæn'fraɪ] vt freír a la sartén

pang [pæŋ] n (of hunger, jealousy) punzada f

panhandle ['pænhændəl] **1** n (of state) = península de forma estrecha y alargada unida a un territorio de mayor tamaño
2 vi Fam (beg) mendigar

panic ['pænɪk] **1** n pánico m; **in a p.** aterrorizado(a); **to get into a p. (over sth)** aterrorizarse (por algo); **the crowd was thrown into a p.** cundió el pánico entre la multitud; **p. attack** ataque m de pánico; **p. button** botón m de alarma; Fin **p. buying/selling** compra f/venta f provocada por el pánico
2 vt (pt & pp **panicked**) aterrorizar; **to p. sb into doing sth** aterrorizar a alguien para que haga algo
3 vi aterrorizarse; **don't p.!** ¡que no cunda el pánico!

panicky ['pænɪkɪ] adj Fam (reaction) de pánico; **she got p.** le entró el pánico

panic-stricken ['pænɪkstrɪkən] adj aterrorizado(a); **to be p.** estar aterrorizado(a)

pannier, panier ['pænɪə(r)] n (on animal, bicycle) alforja f

panoply ['pænəplɪ] n boato m

panorama [pænə'rɑːmə] n panorama m

panoramic [pænə'ræmɪk] adj panorámico(a)

panpipes ['pænpaɪps] npl Mus siringa f, flauta f de Pan

pansy ['pænzɪ] n (a) (flower) pensamiento m (b) Fam (effeminate man) mariposón m, mariquita m

pant[1] [pænt] vi jadear; **to p. for breath** resollar (intentando recobrar el aliento)

pant[2] adj **p. leg** pernera f

pantheon ['pænθɪən] n also Fig panteón m

panther ['pænθə(r)] n pantera f

panties ['pæntɪz] npl Esp bragas fpl, Chile, Col, Méx calzones mpl, Ecuad follones mpl, RP bombacha f

pantry ['pæntrɪ] n despensa f

pants [pænts] npl pantalones mpl; Fam **to scare the p. off sb** hacer que a alguien le entre el canguelo or Méx mello; Fam **she's the one who wears the p.** ella es la que lleva los pantalones en casa; Fam **he was caught with his p. down** lo pillaron en bragas

pantsuit ['pæntsuːt] n traje m de chaqueta y pantalón (para mujer)

panty ['pæntɪ] n **p. hose** medias fpl, pantis mpl; **p. liner** protege-slips m inv, RP, Ven protector m diario

Pap [pæp] n Med **P. smear** or **test** citología f

pap [pæp] n Fam Pej (nonsense) bobadas fpl

papa ['pɑːpə] n papá m, papi m

papacy ['peɪpəsɪ] n papado m

papal ['peɪpəl] adj papal

paparazzo [pæpə'rætsəʊ] (pl **paparazzi** [pæpə'rætsiː]) n paparazzi mf

papaya [pə'paɪə], **papaw** ['pɔːpɔː] n (fruit) papaya f; (tree) papayo m

paper ['peɪpə(r)] **1** n (a) (material) papel m; **a piece of p.** un papel; Fig **on p.** (in theory) sobre el papel; **p. airplane** avión m de papel; **p. bag** bolsa f de papel; **p. cup** vaso m de papel; Comptr **p. feed** sistema m de alimentación de papel; **p. knife** abrecartas m inv; **p. mill** fábrica f or Am planta f de papel, papelera f; **p. money** papel m moneda; **p. towel** toallita f de papel; Comptr **p. tray** bandeja f del papel
(b) **papers** (documents) papeles mpl, documentación f
(c) (examination) examen m
(d) (scholarly study, report) estudio m, trabajo m; **to read** or **give a p.** leer or presentar una ponencia
(e) (newspaper) periódico m; **p. boy/girl** repartidor(ora) m,f de periódicos; **to do a p. route** hacer el reparto de periódicos a domicilio
2 vt (wall, room) empapelar

paperback ['peɪpəbæk] n libro m or edición f en rústica

paperclip ['peɪpəklɪp] n clip m

paperless ['peɪpəlɪs] adj **the p. office** la oficina completamente informatizada

paper-thin ['peɪpə'θɪn] adj muy fino(a)

paperweight ['peɪpəweɪt] n pisapapeles m inv

paperwork ['peɪpəwɜːk] n papeleo m

papery ['peɪpərɪ] adj apergaminado(a)

papier-mâché ['pæpjeɪ'mæʃeɪ] n cartón m piedra

Papuan ['pæpjʊən] n & adj papú mf, papúa mf

Papua New Guinea ['pæpjʊənjuː'gɪniː] n Papúa Nueva Guinea

papyrus [pə'paɪrəs] n papiro m

par [pɑː(r)] n (a) (equality) **to be on a p. with** estar al mismo nivel que (b) (in golf) par m; **a p.-three (hole)** un (hoyo de) par tres; Fig **that's about p. for the course** es lo que cabe esperar (c) Fin **above p.** sobre la par; **below p.** bajo par; Fig **to feel below p.** no encontrarse muy allá

parable ['pærəbəl] n parábola f

parabola [pə'ræbələ] n parábola f

parabolic [pærə'bɒlɪk] adj parabólico(a)

parachute ['pærəʃuːt] **1** n paracaídas m inv; **p. jump** salto m en paracaídas
2 vt (person, supplies) lanzar en paracaídas
3 vi saltar en paracaídas

parachuting ['pærəʃuːtɪŋ] n paracaidismo m; **to go p.** hacer paracaidismo

parachutist ['pærəʃuːtɪst] n paracaidista mf

parade [pə'reɪd] **1** n (procession) desfile m; **on p.** (troops) pasando revista; **a p. of stores** una hilera de tiendas; **p. ground** plaza f de armas
2 vt (troops) pasar revista a; (riches, knowledge) ostentar
3 vi (troops) desfilar; **to p. around** or **about** desfilar

paradigm ['pærədaɪm] n paradigma m

paradise ['pærədaɪs] n paraíso m; **bird of p.** ave f del Paraíso

paradox ['pærədɒks] n paradoja f

paradoxical [pærə'dɒksɪkəl] adj paradójico(a)

paragliding ['pærəglaɪdɪŋ] n parapente m; **to go p.** ir a hacer parapente

paragon ['pærəgən] n dechado m; **a p. of virtue** un dechado de virtudes

paragraph ['pærəgræf] n párrafo m

Paraguay ['pærəgwaɪ] n Paraguay

Paraguayan [pærə'gwaɪən] n & adj paraguayo(a) m,f

parakeet ['pærəkiːt] n periquito m

paralegal [pærə'liːgəl] n ayudante mf de un abogado, RP procurador(ora) m,f

parallel ['pærəlel] **1** n Math (línea f) paralela f; Geog paralelo m; Fig (analogy) paralelismo m; **to draw a p. between two things** establecer un paralelismo entre dos cosas; **without p.** sin parangón

2 *adj* paralelo(a); **to be** *or* **run p. to sth** ser *or* ir paralelo(a) a algo; **p. bars** barras *fpl* paralelas; *Comptr* **p. cable** cable *m* paralelo; *Elec* **p. circuits** circuitos *mpl* en paralelo; **p. lines** líneas *fpl* paralelas; *Comptr* **p. port** puerto *m* paralelo; *Comptr* **p. processing** procesado *m* en paralelo; **p. turn** *(in skiing)* giro *m* en paralelo

3 *vt (be similar to)* asemajarse a

parallelogram [pærə'leləgræm] *n* paralelogramo *m*

paralysis [pə'ræləsɪs] *n* parálisis *f inv*

paralytic [pærə'lɪtɪk] *adj Med* paralítico(a)

paralyze ['pærəlaɪz] *vt* paralizar; **to be paralyzed by fear** estar paralizado(a) por el miedo

paramedic [pærə'medɪk] *n* auxiliar *mf* sanitario(a)

parameter [pə'ræmɪtə(r)] *n* parámetro *m*

paramilitary [pærə'mɪlɪtrɪ] *adj* paramilitar

paramount ['pærəmaʊnt] *adj* primordial, vital; **it is of p. importance** es de capital *or* suma importancia

paranoia [pærə'nɔɪə] *n* paranoia *f*

paranoid ['pærənɔɪd] *adj* paranoico(a) (**about** por *or* con)

paranormal [pærə'nɔ:məl] **1** *n* **the p.** lo paranormal

2 *adj* paranormal

parapet ['pærəpet] *n* parapeto *m*

paraphernalia [pærəfə'neɪlɪə] *npl* parafernalia *f*

paraphrase ['pærəfreɪz] **1** *n* paráfrasis *f inv*

2 *vt* parafrasear

paraplegic [pærə'pli:dʒɪk] *n & adj* parapléjico(a) *m,f*

parasailing ['pærəseɪlɪŋ] *n* = especie de parapente con esquís acuáticos y a remolque de una lancha motora

parasite ['pærəsaɪt] *n also Fig* parásito *m*

parasitic [pærə'sɪtɪk] *adj also Fig* parásito(a)

parasol ['pærəsɒl] *n* sombrilla *f*

paratrooper ['pærətru:pə(r)] *n* (soldado *m*) paracaidista *m*

parboil ['pɑ:bɔɪl] *vt* cocer a medias, sancochar

parcel ['pɑ:səl] *n (package)* paquete *m*; *(of land)* parcela *f*; **p. bomb** paquete *m* bomba; **p. post** (servicio *m* de) paquete *m* postal *or Andes, RP* encomienda *f*

▸**parcel out** *vt sep (land)* parcelar; *(money)* dividir en lotes

▸**parcel up** *vt sep (wrap up)* embalar, empaquetar

Parcheesi® [pɑ:'tʃi:zɪ] *n* ≃ parchís *m*

parchment ['pɑ:tʃmənt] *n* pergamino *m*; **p. paper** papel *m* pergamino

pardon ['pɑ:dən] **1** *n (forgiveness)* perdón *m*; *Law* indulto *m*; **(I beg your) p.?** *(what did you say?)* ¿cómo dice?; **I beg your p.!** *(in apology)* ¡discúlpeme!

2 *vt (action, person)* perdonar, excusar; *Law* indultar; **p. me?** *(what did you say?)* ¿cómo dice?; **p. me!** *(in apology)* ¡discúlpeme!

pardonable ['pɑ:dənəbəl] *adj (mistake, behavior)* perdonable, excusable

pare [peə(r)] *vt (vegetable)* pelar; *(nails)* cortar; *(expenses)* recortar

▸**pare down** *vt sep (expenses)* recortar

parent ['peərənt] *n (father)* padre *m*; *(mother)* madre *f*; **parents** padres *mpl*; **p. company** empresa *f* matriz; **P.-Teacher Association** = asociación de padres de alumnos y profesores, ≃ APA *f*

parentage ['peərəntɪdʒ] *n* origen *m*, familia *f*

parental [pə'rentəl] *adj* de los padres

parenthesis [pə'renθəsɪs] *(pl* **parentheses** [pə'renθəsi:z]) *n* paréntesis *m inv*; **in parentheses** entre paréntesis

parenthood ['peərənthʊd] *n (fatherhood)* paternidad *f*; *(motherhood)* maternidad *f*; **the joys of p.** las satisfacciones que trae tener hijos

parenting ['peərəntɪŋ] *n* **p. skills** capacidad *f* para cuidar de los hijos

pariah [pə'raɪə] *n* paria *mf*

Paris ['pærɪs] *n* París

parish ['pærɪʃ] *n* parroquia *f*, feligresía *f*; **p. church** iglesia *f* parroquial; **p. council** concejo *m*

parishioner [pə'rɪʃənə(r)] *n* feligrés(esa) *m,f*, parroquiano(a) *m,f*

Parisian [pə'rɪzɪən] *n & adj* parisino(a) *m,f*

parity ['pærɪtɪ] *n* paridad *f*; **to achieve p.** *(of pay, output,* equipararse

park [pɑ:k] **1** *n* parque *m*

2 *vt* estacionar, *Esp* aparcar; *Fam* **to p. oneself in front of the TV** apoltronarse *or Am* echarse enfrente de la televisión

3 *vi* estacionar, *Esp* aparcar, *Am* estacionarse, *Am salvo RP* parquearse

parka ['pɑ:kə] *n* parka *f*

park-and-ride ['pɑ:kən'raɪd] *n* = sistema de estacionamientos en la periferia de una ciudad conectados con el centro por transporte público

parking ['pɑ:kɪŋ] *n* estacionamiento *m*, *Esp* aparcamiento *m*, *Col* parqueadero *m*; **no p.** *(sign)* prohibido estacionar *or Esp* aparcar, estacionamiento prohibido; **p. attendant** vigilante *mf* de estacionamiento *or Esp* aparcamiento; **p. lights** *(on car,* luces *fpl* de estacionamiento; **p. lot** *Esp* aparcamiento *m*, *R* playa *f* de estacionamiento, *Col* parqueadero *m*; **p. meter** parquímetro *m*; **p. space** estacionamiento *m*, *Esp* aparca miento *m*, sitio *m or* hueco *m* para estacionar; **p. ticket** multa *f* de estacionamiento; **p. zone** área *f* de estacionamiento *or Esp* aparcamiento *(señalizada)*

Parkinson's disease ['pɑ:kɪnsənzdɪ'zi:z] *n* (síndrome *m* de) Parkinson *m*

parkland ['pɑ:klænd] *n* zonas *fpl* verdes, parque *m*

parkway ['pɑ:kweɪ] *n* bulevar *m*, avenida *f*

parlance ['pɑ:ləns] *n* in scientific/political p. en la jerga científica/política; **in common p.** en el habla común

parlay ['pɑ:lɪ] *vt (winnings)* volver a apostar *(el dinero gastado en una apuesta)*; *Fig (money, talent)* convertir, transformar

parley [pɑ:lɪ] *vi* parlamentar (**with** con)

parliament ['pɑ:ləmənt] *n* (**a**) *(law-making body)* parlament *m* (**b**) *(period between elections)* legislatura *f*

parliamentarian [pɑ:ləmen'teərɪən] *n* parlamentario(a) *m,f*

parliamentary [pɑ:lə'mentərɪ] *adj* parlamentario(a)

parlor ['pɑ:lə(r)] *n (in house)* salón *m*; **beauty p.** salón *m* de belleza

Parmesan [pɑ:mɪ'zæn] *n* **P. (cheese)** queso *m* parmesano

parochial [pə'rəʊkɪəl] *adj Rel* parroquial; *Fig Pej (narrow minded)* provinciano(a), corto(a) de miras; **p. school** colegi *m* privado religioso

parochialism [pə'rəʊkɪəlɪzəm] *n Pej (of mentality)* provin cialismo *m*, estrechez *f* de miras

parody ['pærədɪ] **1** *n* parodia *f* (**of** de)

2 *vt* parodiar

parole [pə'rəʊl] **1** *n Law* libertad *f* bajo palabra; **to be (out** on p. estar en libertad bajo palabra; **p. board** junta *f* de libertad condicional; **p. officer** = asistente social que supervisa a un preso en libertad bajo palabra y ante quien se presenta periódicamente

2 *vt Law* poner en libertad bajo palabra

paroxysm ['pærəksɪzəm] *n (of anger, guilt, jealousy)* arrebato *m*, ataque *m*; **to be in paroxysms of laughter** tener un ataque de risa

parquet ['pɑ:keɪ] *n* **p. (floor)** (suelo *m* de) parqué *m*

parrot ['pærət] **1** *n* loro *m*

2 *vt* repetir como un loro

parry ['pærɪ] *vt (blow)* parar, desviar; *(question)* esquivar, eludi

parse [pɑ:z] *vt* (**a**) *Gram (word)* analizar gramaticalmente (**b** *Comptr & Ling (sentence)* analizar sintácticamente

parser ['pɑ:zə(r)] *n Comptr* analizador *m* sintáctico

parsimonious [pɑ:sɪ'məʊnɪəs] *adj (mean)* tacaño(a), míse ro(a)

parsley ['pɑːslɪ] *n* perejil *m*

parsnip ['pɑːsnɪp] *n* pastinaca *f*, chirivía *f*

parson ['pɑːsən] *n* párroco *m*

parsonage ['pɑːsənɪdʒ] *n* casa *f* parroquial

part [pɑːt] **1** *n* (a) *(portion, element)* parte *f; (of machine)* pieza *f;* **the parts of the body** las partes del cuerpo; **parts of speech** categorías *fpl* gramaticales; **(spare) parts** recambios *mpl*, piezas *fpl* de recambio, *Am* refacciones *fpl, Col, Cuba, RP* repuestos *mpl*; **p. two** *(of TV or radio series)* segunda parte; **in that p. of the world** en esa parte del mundo; **in these parts** por aquí; **good in parts** bueno(a) a ratos; **the worst p. was when she started laughing** lo peor fue cuando empezó a reírse; **the difficult p. is remembering** lo difícil es acordarse; **for the best** *or* **greater p. of five years** durante casi cinco años; **the greater p. of the population** la mayor parte de la población; **to be** *or* **form p. of sth** ser *or* formar parte de algo; **it's all p. of growing up** forma parte del proceso de crecimiento; **it is p. and parcel of...** es parte integrante de...; **in p.** en parte, parcialmente; **for the most p.** en su mayor parte; **in p. exchange** como parte del pago; **p. owner** copropietario(a) *m,f*

(b) *(role)* papel *m; Theat* **to play a p.** interpretar un papel; **to take p. (in sth)** participar *or* tomar parte (en algo); **to have** *or* **play a large p. in sth** tener un papel importante en algo; **I want no p. of** *or* **in it** no quiero tener nada que ver con eso

(c) *(side)* **to take sb's p.** tomar partido por *or* ponerse de parte de alguien; **on the p. of...** por parte de...; **for my p.** por mi parte

(d) *(in hair)* raya *f, Col, Méx,Ven* carrera *f*

2 *adv* **she's p. Spanish** es medio española; **it's p. silk, p. cotton** es de seda y algodón

3 *vt (fighters, lovers)* separar; *(curtains)* abrir, descorrer; **to p. one's hair** hacerse raya *or Col, Méx,Ven* carrera (en el pelo); **to p. company** separarse

4 *vi (separate)* separarse; **to p. (as) friends** quedar como amigos; **to p. with sth** desprenderse de algo

partake [pɑːˈteɪk] *(pt* **partook** [pɑːˈtʊk], *pp* **partaken** [pɑːˈteɪkən]) *vi Formal* (a) *(drink)* **to p. of** tomar, ingerir (b) *(have quality)* **to p. of** participar de, tener parte de

partial ['pɑːʃəl] *adj* (a) *(incomplete, biased)* parcial; *Astron* **p. eclipse** eclipse *m* parcial (b) *(fond)* **she is p. to wine** le gusta el vino

partially ['pɑːʃəlɪ] *adv (in part, with bias)* parcialmente; **p. sighted** con visión parcial

participant [pɑːˈtɪsɪpənt] *n & adj* participante *mf*

participate [pɑːˈtɪsɪpeɪt] *vi* participar (**in** en)

participation [pɑːtɪsɪˈpeɪʃən] *n* participación *f* (**in** en)

participatory [pɑːtɪsɪˈpeɪtərɪ] *adj* participativo(a)

participle ['pɑːtɪsɪpəl] *n Gram* participio *m*; **past p.** participio pasado *or* pasivo; **present p.** participio de presente *or* activo

particle ['pɑːtɪkəl] *n* partícula *f*; **p. accelerator** acelerador *m* de partículas; **p. physics** física *f* de partículas

particular [pəˈtɪkjʊlə(r)] **1** *n* detalle *m*, pormenor *m*; **alike in every p.** iguales en todos los aspectos; **to go into particulars** entrar en detalles; **to take down sb's particulars** tomar los datos de alguien

2 *adj* (a) *(specific)* particular, específico(a); **which p. person did you have in mind?** ¿en quién pensabas en concreto?; **for no p. reason** por ninguna razón en particular *or* en especial (b) *(special)* particular, especial; **he is a p. friend of mine** es un amigo mío muy querido; **to take p. care over sth** tener especial cuidado con algo (c) *(exacting)* exigente; **to be p. about sth** ser exigente con algo; **I'm not p.** me da lo mismo

3 in particular *adv (specifically)* en particular; **I didn't notice anything in p.** no noté nada de particular

particularly [pəˈtɪkjʊləlɪ] *adv (especially)* particularmente, especialmente; **not p.** no especialmente; **it's cold here, p.**

at night aquí hace frío, sobre todo por la noche

parting ['pɑːtɪŋ] *n* despedida *f*, partida *f*; **they had come to the p. of the ways** había llegado la hora de despedirse *or* el momento de la despedida; **p. shot** = comentario hiriente a modo de despedida; **p. words** palabras *fpl* de despedida

partisan [pɑːtɪˈzæn] **1** *n (during 2nd World War)* partisano(a) *m,f; (supporter)* partidario(a) *m,f* (**of** de)

2 *adj (biased)* parcial

partition [pɑːˈtɪʃən] **1** *n (in room)* tabique *m*

2 *vt (country)* dividir

▸**partition off** *vt sep (room)* dividir con un tabique *or* con tabiques

partly ['pɑːtlɪ] *adv* en parte, parcialmente

partner ['pɑːtnə(r)] **1** *n (in company)* socio(a) *m,f; (in tennis)* compañero(a) *m,f; (in dancing)* pareja *f; (lover)* compañero(a) *m,f*, pareja *f*; **p. in crime** cómplice *mf*

2 *vt (in games, in dancing)* hacer pareja con

partnership ['pɑːtnəʃɪp] *n* asociación *f*, sociedad *f*; **to enter** *or* **go into p. (with sb)** formar sociedad *or* asociarse (con alguien)

partridge ['pɑːtrɪdʒ] *n* perdiz *f*

part-time [pɑːt'taɪm] *adj & adv* a tiempo parcial

part-timer [pɑːt'taɪmə(r)] *n* trabajador(ora) *m,f* a tiempo parcial

partway ['pɑːtweɪ] *adv* **I'm p. through it** *(book, task)* voy por la mitad; **this will go p. toward covering the costs** esto sufragará parte de los gastos

party ['pɑːtɪ] **1** *n* (a) *(political)* partido *m*; **a p. member, a member of the p.** un miembro del partido; **to follow** *or* **toe the p. line** seguir la línea del partido (b) *(celebration)* fiesta *f*; **to have** *or* **throw a p.** dar *or* celebrar una fiesta; *Fig* **the p.'s over** se acabó la fiesta; *Fam* **he's a p. animal** le gustan *or Esp* van las fiestas; *Fam* **p. pooper** aguafiestas *mf inv* (c) *(group)* grupo *m; Tel* **p. line** línea *f* compartida, party-line *f*; **p. wall** *(in house)* pared *f* medianera (d) *Law (participant)* parte *f*; **I would never be p. to such a thing** nunca tomaría parte en algo semejante

2 *vi Fam (celebrate)* estar de marcha

partygoer ['pɑːtɪɡəʊə(r)] *n* **the streets were full of partygoers** las calles estaban llenas de gente que acudía a fiestas

pass¹ [pɑːs] *n (over mountains)* paso *m*, desfiladero *m*

pass² **1** *n* (a) *(permit)* pase *m*; **rail/bus p.** abono *m* de tren/ autobús (b) *(in sport)* pase *m* (c) **the aircraft made two low passes over the village** el avión pasó dos veces sobre el pueblo a baja altura; *Fam* **to make a p. at sb** tirar los tejos a alguien

2 *vt* (a) *(go past) (person)* pasar junto a; *(destination)* pasarse, saltarse; *(frontier)* pasar; *(car, runner)* pasar, adelantar; **I often p. him in the street** me cruzo con él a menudo en la calle

(b) *(exam, candidate, bill)* aprobar; **to p. history** aprobar historia

(c) *(give) & Sport* pasar; **p. me the salt, please** ¿me pasas la sal?

(d) **to p. the time** *(person)* pasar el tiempo; **it passes the time** sirve para matar el tiempo

(e) *Law* **to p. sentence** dictar sentencia; **to p. judgment on sb** juzgar a alguien

(f) **to p. water** orinar; **to p. wind** ventosear, expulsar ventosidades

3 *vi* (a) *(go past)* pasar; *(overtake)* adelantar, pasar; **to let sb p., to allow sb to p.** dejar pasar a alguien; **to p. from one person to another** pasar de una persona a otra; **to p. unobserved** pasar desapercibido(a); **let it p.!** ¡no hagas caso!; **p.!** *(when answering question)* ¡paso!; **I think I'll p. on the potatoes** no voy a tomar patatas (b) *(time)* pasar, transcurrir (c) *(go away)* pasar (d) *Literary (take place)* **it came to p. that...** aconteció que... (e) *(in exam)* aprobar

▶**pass away** *vi Euph* fallecer

▶**pass down** *vt sep (knowledge, tradition)* pasar, transmitir

▶**pass for** *vt insep* pasar por

▶**pass off** 1 *vt sep* **to p. sth off as sth** hacer pasar algo por algo; **to p. oneself off as** hacerse pasar por; **he tried to p. it off as a joke** intentó hacer ver que había sido una broma

2 *vi* **everything passed off well** todo fue bien

▶**pass on** 1 *vt sep (object)* pasar, hacer circular; *(news, information)* pasar, transmitir; *(disease)* contagiar

2 *vi Euph* fallecer

▶**pass out** *vi (faint)* desvanecerse, desmayarse

▶**pass over** *vt sep* **to p. sb over (for promotion)** olvidar a alguien (para el ascenso)

▶**pass through** 1 *vt insep (city, area)* pasar por

2 *vi* **I was just passing through** pasaba por aquí

▶**pass up** *vt sep (opportunity)* dejar pasar

passable ['pɑːsəbəl] *adj* (a) *(of acceptable quality)* pasable, aceptable (b) *(road, bridge)* practicable, transitable

passage ['pæsɪdʒ] *n* (a) *(journey)* viaje *m*, travesía *f*; **the p. of time** el paso del tiempo; **to work one's p.** *(on ship)* = costearse el pasaje trabajando durante la travesía (b) *(corridor)* corredor *m*, pasillo *m*; *(alley)* pasaje *m*, callejón *m* (c) *(from book, piece of music)* pasaje *m*

passageway ['pæsɪdʒweɪ] *n (corridor)* corredor *m*, pasillo *m*; *(alley)* pasaje *m*, callejón *m*

passé [pɑːˈseɪ] *adj* pasado(a) de moda

passenger ['pæsəndʒə(r)] *n* pasajero(a) *m,f*; **p. seat** asiento *m* del copiloto

passerby [pɑːsəˈbaɪ] *(pl* **passersby** [pɑːsəzˈbaɪ]) *n* viandante *mf*

passing ['pɑːsɪŋ] 1 *n* (a) *(going past)* paso *m*; **in p.** de pasada; **p. place** *(on road)* apartadero *m* *(en la carretera)* (b) *(of time)* paso *m*, transcurso *m* (c) *(death)* fallecimiento *m*

2 *adj (car)* que pasa; *(remark)* de pasada; *(whim, fancy)* pasajero(a)

passion ['pæʃən] *n (emotion, desire)* pasión *f*; *(anger, vehemence)* ira *f*; **to have a p. for sth** sentir pasión por algo; **in a fit of p.** *(anger)* en un arrebato de ira; **she hates him with a p.** lo odia con toda su alma; *Law* **crime of p.** crimen *m* pasional; *Rel* **the P. (of Christ)** la Pasión (de Cristo); **p. fruit** granadilla *f*, fruta *f* de la pasión

passionate ['pæʃənɪt] *adj (lover, embrace)* apasionado(a); *(speech, advocate)* vehemente, apasionado(a)

passive ['pæsɪv] 1 *n Gram* (voz *f*) pasiva *f*

2 *adj* pasivo(a); **p. resistance** resistencia *f* pasiva; **p. smoking** tabaquismo *m* pasivo

passive-aggressive ['pæsɪvəˈgresɪv] *adj* pasivo(a)-agresivo(a)

passively ['pæsɪvlɪ] *adv* pasivamente

passkey ['pɑːskiː] *n* llave *f* maestra

Passover ['pɑːsəʊvə(r)] *n Rel* Pascua *f* judía

passport ['pɑːspɔːt] *n* pasaporte *m*

password ['pɑːswɜːd] *n Mil & Comptr* contraseña *f*

past [pɑːst] 1 *n* pasado *m*; **in the p.** en el pasado; *Gram* en pasado; **it is a thing of the p.** es (una) cosa del pasado; **to live in the p.** vivir en el pasado

2 *adj* pasado(a); **those days are p.** esos días han pasado; **in times p.** en otros tiempos, en tiempos pasados; **to be a p. master at sth** ser un/una maestro(a) consumado(a) en algo; **the p. week** la última semana; *Gram* **p. participle** participio *m* pasado *or* pasivo; **p. perfect** pasado pluscuamperfecto

3 *prep (beyond)* **a little p. the bridge** poco después del puente, justo pasado el puente; **to walk p. the house** pasar por delante de la casa; **it is p. four (o'clock)** son más de las cuatro; **half p. four** las cuatro y media; **a quarter p. four** las cuatro y cuarto; **twenty p. four** las cuatro y veinte; **I'm p. caring** ya no me trae sin cuidado; *Fam* **to be p. it** estar para el

arrastre; *Fam* **I wouldn't put it p. her** ella es muy capaz (de hacerlo)

4 *adv* **to walk** *or* **go p.** pasar (caminando); **to run p.** pasar corriendo

pasta ['pæstə] *n* pasta *f*

paste [peɪst] 1 *n* (a) *(smooth substance)* pasta *f*, crema *f* (b) *(glue) (for paper)* pegamento *m*; *(for wallpaper)* engrudo *m*, cola *f*

2 *vt (glue)* pegar

pastel ['pæstəl] 1 *n (crayon)* pastel *m*; *(drawing)* dibujo *m* al pastel

2 *adj* pastel

pasteurization [pɑːstjəraɪˈzeɪʃən] *n* pasteurización *f*

pasteurize ['pɑːstjəraɪz] *vt* pasteurizar; **pasteurized milk** leche *f* pasteurizada

pastiche [pæˈstiːʃ] *n* pastiche *m*

pastille, pastil ['pæstɪl] *n* pastilla *f*

pastime ['pɑːstaɪm] *n* pasatiempo *m*, afición *f*

pasting ['peɪstɪŋ] *n Fam (beating)* paliza *f*, tunda *f*; **to give sb a p.** dar una paliza a alguien

pastor ['pɑːstə(r)] *n Rel* pastor *m*

pastoral [pɑːˈstɔːrəl] *adj* (a) *(rural)* pastoril, pastoral (b) *(work, activities)* pastoral; **p. care** tutoría *f* y orientación *f* individual

pastry ['peɪstrɪ] *n (dough)* masa *f*; *(cake)* pastel *m*, *Col, CSur* torta *f*; **p. cook** pastelero(a) *m,f*

pasture ['pɑːstʃə(r)] *n* pasto *m*; *Fig* **to put sb out to p.** jubilar a alguien

pasty ['peɪstɪ] *adj (face, complexion)* pálido(a), descolorido(a)

pasty-faced ['peɪstɪfeɪst] *adj* pálido(a)

pat [pæt] 1 *n* (a) *(tap)* palmadita *f*; *Fig* **to give sb a p. on the back** felicitar a alguien (b) *(of butter)* porción *f*

2 *adj (answer, explanation)* fácil, rápido(a)

3 *adv* **to know** *or* **have sth down p.** saber algo de memoria

4 *vt (pt & pp* **patted**) *(tap)* **to p. sb on the head** dar palmaditas a alguien en la cabeza; *Fig* **to p. sb on the back** dar a alguien unas palmaditas en la espalda

Patagonia [pætəˈgəʊnɪə] *n* la Patagonia

patch [pætʃ] 1 *n* (a) *(of cloth)* remiendo *m*; **(eye) p.** parche *m* (en el ojo) (b) *(of color, light)* mancha *f*; **a p. of blue sky** un claro *m* (c) *(of land)* parcela *f*, terreno *m*

2 *vt (hole, garment)* remendar, poner un parche en

▶**patch up** *vt sep Fam (wounded person)* hacer una cura *or Méx, RP* curación de urgencia a; *(marriage, friendship)* arreglar; **we've patched things up** *(after quarrel)* hemos hecho las paces

patchwork ['pætʃwɜːk] *n (in sewing)* labor *f* de retazo, patchwork *m*; *(of ideas, policies)* mosaico *m*; **p. quilt** edredón *m* de retazos *or* de patchwork

patchy ['pætʃɪ] *adj (novel, economic recovery)* desigual

pâté, pate ['pæteɪ] *n* paté *m*

patent ['pætənt] 1 *n* patente *f*; **to take out a p. on sth** patentar algo; *Com* **p. applied for, p. pending** patente solicitada, en espera de patente

2 *adj* (a) *(patented)* patentado(a); **p. leather** charol *m*; **p. medicine** específico *m*, especialidad *f* farmacéutica (b) *(evident)* patente, evidente

3 *vt* patentar

patently ['pætəntlɪ] *adv* evidentemente, patentemente

paternal [pəˈtɜːnəl] *adj (feelings)* paternal; *(duty, responsibilities)* paterno(a)

paternally [pəˈtɜːnəlɪ] *adv* paternalmente

paternity [pəˈtɜːnɪtɪ] *n* paternidad *f*; *Law* **p. suit** juicio *m* para determinar la paternidad; **p. test** prueba *f* de (la) paternidad

path [pɑːθ] *n (route)* camino *m*, sendero *m*; *(of rocket, planet, bird)* trayectoria *f*; *(of inquiry, to success)* vía *f*, camino *m*; **he killed everyone in his p.** mató a todo el que encontró a su paso; **their paths had crossed before** sus caminos ya se habían cruzado antes

pathetic [pə'θetɪk] *adj (feeble)* penoso(a); *(touching)* patético(a), conmovedor(ora)

pathetically [pə'θetɪklɪ] *adv (feebly)* penosamente, lastimosamente; *(touchingly)* patéticamente, conmovedoramente; **p. bad** penoso(a)

pathological [pæθə'lɒdʒɪkəl] *adj* patológico(a)

pathologist [pə'θɒlədʒɪst] *n (forensic scientist)* forense *mf*, médico(a) *m,f* forense

pathology [pə'θɒlədʒɪ] *n* patología *f*

pathos ['peɪθɒs] *n* patetismo *m*

pathway ['pɑːθweɪ] *n* camino *m*

patience ['peɪʃəns] *n* paciencia *f*; **to try** *or* **tax sb's p.** poner a prueba la paciencia de alguien; **to exhaust sb's p.** acabar con *or* agotar la paciencia de alguien; **to lose one's p. (with sb)** perder la paciencia (con alguien); **I've no p. with him** me exaspera

patient ['peɪʃənt] **1** *n* paciente *mf*
  2 *adj* paciente; **to be p. with sb** ser paciente con alguien, tener paciencia con alguien

patiently ['peɪʃəntlɪ] *adv* pacientemente

patio ['pætɪəʊ] *(pl* **patios***) n* = área pavimentada contigua a una casa, utilizada para solazarse o comer al aire libre

patriarch ['peɪtrɪɑːk] *n* patriarca *m*

patriarchal [peɪtrɪ'ɑːkəl] *adj* patriarcal

patriarchy ['peɪtrɪɑːkɪ] *n* patriarcado *m*

patrician [pə'trɪʃən] **1** *n* patricio *m*
  2 *adj* **(a)** *(upper-class)* patricio(a) **(b)** *(haughty)* altanero(a)

patrimony ['pætrɪmənɪ] *n* patrimonio *m*

patriot ['pætrɪət, 'peɪtrɪət] *n* patriota *mf*

patriotic [pætrɪ'ɒtɪk, peɪtrɪ'ɒtɪk] *adj* patriótico(a)

patriotically [pætrɪ'ɒtɪklɪ, peɪtrɪ'ɒtɪklɪ] *adv* patrióticamente

patriotism ['pætrɪətɪzəm, 'peɪtrɪətɪzəm] *n* patriotismo *m*

patrol [pə'trəʊl] **1** *n* patrulla *f*; **to be on p.** patrullar; **p. car** coche *m* *or Am* carro *m* *or CSur* auto *m* patrulla; **p. wagon** *(police van)* furgón *m* celular *or* policial
  2 *vt (pt & pp* **patrolled***) (area, border)* patrullar
  3 *vi* patrullar; **to p. up and down** ir y venir

patrolman [pə'trəʊlmæn] *n* patrullero *m*, policía *m*

patron ['peɪtrən] *n* **(a)** *(of artist)* mecenas *mf inv*; *(of charity)* patrocinador(ora) *m,f*; **p. saint** patrón(ona) *m,f*, santo(a) *m,f* patrón(ona) **(b)** *(of store)* cliente(a) *m,f*

patronage ['pætrənɪdʒ] *n* **(a)** *(of arts)* mecenazgo *m*; *(of charity)* patrocinio *m*; **under the p. of...** bajo *or* con el patrocinio de... **(b)** *Pej* clientelismo *m*; **political p.** clientelismo político

patronize ['pætrənaɪz] *vt* **(a)** *(artist)* patrocinar; *(store, restaurant)* frecuentar **(b)** *(treat condescendingly)* tratar con condescendencia *or* paternalismo

patronizing ['pætrənaɪzɪŋ] *adj* condescendiente, paternalista

patronizingly ['pætrənaɪzɪŋlɪ] *adv* con condescendencia

patsy ['pætsɪ] *n Fam* **(a)** *(gullible person)* pringado(a) *m,f* **(b)** *(scapegoat)* chivo *m* expiatorio

patter[1] ['pætə(r)] **1** *n (of footsteps)* correteo *m*; *(of rain)* repiqueteo *m*
  2 *vi (rain)* repiquetear, tamborilear; **he pattered along the corridor** pasó correteando por el pasillo

patter[2] *n Fam (talk)* labia *f*

pattern ['pætən] **1** *n* **(a)** *(design)* dibujo *m*; *(on dress, cloth)* estampado *m*, dibujo *m*; **p. book** muestrario *m* **(b)** *(of events)* evolución *f*; *(of behavior)* pauta *f*; **the evening followed the usual p.** la noche transcurrió como de costumbre **(c)** *(in sewing, knitting)* patrón *m* **(d)** *(norm)* pauta *f*, norma *f*; **to set a p.** marcar la pauta
  2 *vt (model)* **to p. sth on sth** imitar algo tomando algo como modelo

patterned ['pætənd] *adj* estampado(a)

paunch [pɔːntʃ] *n* barriga *f*, panza *f*, *Chile* guata *f*; **to have a p.** tener barriga

pauper ['pɔːpə(r)] *n* indigente *mf*; **p.'s grave** fosa *f* común

pause [pɔːz] **1** *n (in music, conversation)* pausa *f*; *(rest)* pausa *f*, descanso *m*
  2 *vi (when working)* parar, descansar; *(when speaking)* hacer una pausa; **to p. for breath** hacer una pausa *or* detenerse para tomar aliento

pave [peɪv] *vt (road)* pavimentar; *Fig* **to p. the way for sth/sb** preparar el terreno para algo/alguien

pavement ['peɪvmənt] *n (roadway)* calzada *f*

pavilion [pə'vɪlɪən] *n* pabellón *m*

paving ['peɪvɪŋ] *n (surface)* pavimento *m*; **p. stone** losa *f*

paw [pɔː] **1** *n (of cat, lion, bear)* garra *f*, pata *f*; *(of dog)* pata *f*; *Fam* **paws off!** ¡no se toca!
  2 *vt (of animal)* tocar con la pata; **to p. the ground** piafar

pawn[1] [pɔːn] **1** *n* **p. ticket** resguardo *m* de la casa de empeños
  2 *vt* empeñar

pawn[2] *n (chess piece)* peón *m*; *Fig* títere *m*

pawnbroker ['pɔːnbrəʊkə(r)] *n* prestamista *mf (de casa de empeños)*

pawnshop ['pɔːnʃɒp] *n* casa *f* de empeños

pawpaw = **papaya**

pay [peɪ] **1** *n* sueldo *m*, paga *f*; **the pay's good/bad** el sueldo es bueno/malo; **to be in sb's p.** estar a sueldo de alguien; *also Fig* **to hit** *or* **strike p. dirt** hallar un filón; **p. check** cheque *m* del sueldo; **p. phone** teléfono *m* de monedas; **p. raise** aumento *m* de sueldo; **p. slip** nómina *f (documento)*
  2 *vt (pt & pp* **paid** [peɪd]*)* **(a)** *(person, money, bill)* pagar; **I paid $5 for it** me costó 5 dólares; **to be well/badly paid** estar bien/mal pagado(a); **I wouldn't do it if you paid me** no lo haría ni aunque me pagaras; **he insisted on paying his (own) way** se empeñó en pagarlo de su propio dinero *or* costeárselo él mismo; **to p. cash** pagar en efectivo; **to p. money into sb's account** *Esp* ingresar *or Am* depositar dinero en la cuenta de alguien
  (b) *(give)* **to p. attention** prestar atención; **to p. sb a compliment** hacerle un cumplido a alguien; **to p. sb a visit** hacer una visita a alguien; **to p. homage to sb** rendir homenaje a alguien; **she paid her respects to the President** presentó sus respetos al presidente
  (c) *(profit)* **it will p. you to do it** te conviene hacerlo
  3 *vi* **(a)** *(give payment)* pagar; **to p. for sth** pagar algo; **to p. through the nose** pagar un ojo de la cara *or Esp* un riñón; **who's paying?** ¿quién paga?; **to p. by check** pagar con un cheque **(b)** *(be profitable)* **it wouldn't p.** no sería rentable, no merecería la pena; **it pays to be honest** conviene ser honrado

▸**pay back** *vt sep (person)* devolver el dinero a; *(money)* devolver; *(loan)* amortizar; *Fig* **I'll p. you back for this!** *(take revenge)* ¡me las pagarás por esto!

▸**pay off 1** *vt sep* **(a)** *(debt)* saldar, liquidar; *(mortgage)* amortizar, redimir; *Fam* **to p. sb off** *(bribe)* sobornar *or* untar a alguien, *Méx* dar una mordida a alguien, *RP* coimear a alguien **(b)** *(worker)* hacer el finiquito a
  2 *vi (efforts)* dar fruto

▸**pay out 1** *vt sep* **(a)** *(money)* gastar **(b)** *(pt* **payed***) (rope)* soltar poco a poco
  2 *vi* pagar

▸**pay up** *vi* pagar

payable ['peɪəbəl] *adj* pagadero(a); **to make a check p. to sb** extender un cheque a favor de alguien

pay-as-you-go ['peɪəzjʊ'gəʊ] *n (with cellphone)* prepago *m*

payback ['peɪbæk] *n* **(a)** *Fin* recuperación *f*, reembolso *m*; **p. period** periodo *m* de amortización *or* reembolso **(b)** *Fam (revenge)* venganza *f*, revancha *f*

payday ['peɪdeɪ] n día m de pago

payee [peɪ'iː] n beneficiario(a) m,f

paying ['peɪɪŋ] adj **p. guest** huésped(eda) m,f de pago

payload ['peɪləʊd] n (of vehicle, spacecraft) carga f útil; (of missile) carga f explosiva

paymaster ['peɪmɑːstə(r)] n oficial m pagador; **the terrorists' p.** la mano negra que financia a los terroristas

payment ['peɪmənt] n (act of paying, amount paid) pago m; **to make a p.** efectuar un pago; **to stop p. on a check** revocar un cheque; **on p. of $100** previo pago de 100 dólares; **p. by installments** pago a plazos; **p. in full** liquidación f

payoff ['peɪɒf] n Fam (a) (bribe) soborno m, Méx mordida f, RP coima f (b) (reward) compensación f

payola [peɪ'əʊlə] n Fam = soborno, especialmente a un presentador radiofónico para que promocione un disco determinado

pay-per-view ['peɪpə'vjuː] 1 n pago m por visión
2 adj **p. channel** canal m de pago por visión; **p. television** televisión f a la carta

payroll ['peɪrəʊl] n Com plantilla f, nómina f (de empleados); **to be on the p.** estar en plantilla or nómina

PBS [piːbiː'es] n (abbr **Public Broadcasting Service**) = canal público de televisión, con información no comercial y educativa

PC ['piː'siː] 1 n (abbr **personal computer**) PC m, ordenador m or Am computadora f personal
2 adj (abbr **politically correct**) políticamente correcto(a)

pc (abbr **postcard**) (tarjeta f) postal f

PDQ [piːdiː'kjuː] adv Fam (abbr **Pretty Damn(ed) Quick**) por la vía rápida, rapidito

PE ['piː'iː] n Sch (abbr **physical education**) educación f física

pea [piː] n Esp guisante m, Am arveja f, Carib, Méx chícharo m; **like two peas in a pod** como dos gotas de agua

peace [piːs] n paz f; **at p.** en paz; **to make (one's) p. with sb** hacer las paces con alguien; **p. and quiet** paz y tranquilidad; **for the sake of p. and quiet** para tener la fiesta en paz; **p. of mind** tranquilidad f de espíritu, sosiego m; Law **to keep/disturb the p.** mantener/alterar el orden (público); **p. campaigner** pacifista mf; **P. Corps** = organización gubernamental estadounidense de ayuda al desarrollo con cooperantes sobre el terreno; **p. movement** pacifismo m, movimiento m pacifista; **p. negotiations** negociaciones fpl de paz; **p. offering** oferta f de paz; **p. talks** conversaciones fpl de paz; **p. treaty** tratado m de paz

peaceable ['piːsəbəl] adj pacífico(a)

peaceful ['piːsful] adj (calm) tranquilo(a), sosegado(a); (non-violent) pacífico(a)

peacekeeper ['piːskiːpə(r)] n (soldier) soldado m de las fuerzas de pacificación; (country, organization) fuerza f de pacificación

peacekeeping ['piːskiːpɪŋ] n mantenimiento m de la paz; **p. forces** fuerzas fpl de pacificación or interposición

peace-loving ['piːslʌvɪŋ] adj amante de la paz

peacetime ['piːstaɪm] n tiempo m de paz

peach [piːtʃ] n (fruit) melocotón m, Am durazno m; Fam **she's a p.** es monísima; **p. melba** copa f Melba, = postre a base de melocotón, helado de vainilla y jarabe de frambuesa; **p. tree** melocotonero m, Am duraznero m

peacock ['piːkɒk] n pavo m real

peak [piːk] 1 n (a) (summit of mountain) cima f, cumbre f; (mountain) pico m (b) (of price, inflation, success) punto m máximo, (máximo) apogeo m; **in p. condition** en condiciones óptimas; **p. period** horas fpl punta; **p. season** temporada f alta (c) (of cap) visera f
2 vi alcanzar el punto máximo

peal [piːl] n (of bells) repique m; **p. of thunder** trueno m; **peals of laughter** risotadas fpl, carcajadas fpl

peal out vi (bells) repicar

peanut ['piːnʌt] n cacahuete m, Andes, Carib, RP maní m, CAm, Méx cacahuate m; Fam Fig **peanuts** (small sum of money) calderilla f; **p. butter** mantequilla f or crema f de cacahuete or Andes, Carib, RP maní m or CAm, Méx cacahuate; **p. gallery** (in theater) gallinero m; **p. oil** aceite m de cacahuete or Andes, Carib, RP maní or CAm, Méx cacahuate

pear [peə(r)] n (fruit) pera f; **p. tree** peral m

pearl [pɜːl] n (a) perla f; **p. diver** pescador(ora) m,f de perlas **p. necklace** collar m de perlas (b) (idioms) **pearls of wisdom** perlas de sabiduría; **it was like casting pearls before swine** era como echar margaritas a los cerdos

pearly ['pɜːlɪ] adj perlado(a); **the P. Gates** las puertas del cielo

pear-shaped ['peəʃeɪpt] adj (figure) en forma de pera

peasant ['pezənt] n campesino(a) m,f; Pej (uncultured person) cateto(a) m,f, Esp paleto(a) m,f

peashooter ['piːʃuːtə(r)] n cerbatana f

peat [piːt] n turba f; **p. bog** turbera f

pebble ['pebəl] n guijarro m; **p. beach** playa f pedregosa

pebbly ['peblɪ] adj pedregoso(a)

pecan [pɪ'kæn] n pacana f

peccary ['pekərɪ] n pecarí m

peck [pek] 1 n (a) (of bird) picotazo m (b) Fam (kiss) besito m; **to give sb a p. on the cheek** dar un besito a alguien en la mejilla
2 vt (a) (of bird) picotear (b) Fam (kiss) **to p. sb on the cheek** dar un besito a alguien en la mejilla

pecs [peks] npl Fam (pectoral muscles) pectorales mpl

pectin ['pektɪn] n Chem pectina f

pectoral ['pektərəl] Anat 1 npl **pectorals** pectorales mpl
2 adj pectoral

peculiar [pɪ'kjuːlɪə(r)] adj (a) (strange) raro(a); **how p.!** ¡qué raro!; **she is a little p.** es un poco rara; **to feel p.** (unwell) sentirse mal (b) (particular) **to be p.** to característico(a) or peculiar de; **this species is p. to Spain** es una especie autóctona de España

peculiarity [pɪkjuːlɪ'ærɪtɪ] n (strangeness) rareza f; (unusual characteristic) peculiaridad f

peculiarly [pɪ'kjuːlɪəlɪ] adv (a) (strangely) extrañamente (b) (especially) particularmente

pecuniary [pɪ'kjuːnɪərɪ] adj Formal pecuniario(a)

pedagogic(al) [pedə'gɒdʒɪk(əl)] adj pedagógico(a)

pedagogy ['pedəgɒdʒɪ] n pedagogía f

pedal ['pedəl] 1 n pedal m; **p. boat** patín m; **p. car** cochecito m de pedales; **p. trash can** cubo m or Am bote m (de basura) con pedal
2 vt **to p. a bicycle** dar pedales a la bicicleta
3 vi pedalear

pedant ['pedənt] n puntilloso(a) m,f, = persona excesivamente preocupada por los detalles

pedantic [pɪ'dæntɪk] adj puntilloso(a)

pedantically [pɪ'dæntɪklɪ] adv puntillosamente

pedantry ['pedəntrɪ] n escrupulosidad f, meticulosidad f exagerada

peddle ['pedəl] vt (goods) vender de puerta en puerta; (ideas, theories) difundir; **to p. drugs** trapichear con drogas

peddler ['pedlə(r)] n (of goods) vendedor(ora) m,f ambulante, mercachifle mf; (of ideas, theories) divulgador(ora) m,f, propagador(ora) m,f; (of drugs) camello m

pederast ['pedəræst] n Formal pederasta m

pedestal ['pedɪstəl] n pedestal m; Fig **to put sb on a p.** poner a alguien en un pedestal; **p. lamp** lámpara f de pie

pedestrian [pɪ'destrɪən] 1 n peatón(ona) m,f; **p. crossing** paso m de peatones; **p. mall** zona f peatonal
2 adj (unimaginative) prosaico(a), pedestre

pedestrianize [pɪ'destrɪənaɪz] vt **to p. a road** hacer peatonal una calle

pediatric [pi:dr'ætrɪk] *adj Med* pediátrico(a)

pediatrician [pi:dɪə'trɪʃən] *n Med* pediatra *mf*

pediatrics [pi:dr'ætrɪks] *n Med* pediatría *f*

pedicure ['pedɪkjʊə(r)] *n* pedicura *f*; **to have a p.** hacerse la pedicura

pedigree ['pedɪgri:] **1** *n (of dog) & Fig* pedigrí *m*; *(ancestry)* linaje *m*; *Fig* **his p. as a democrat is open to question** su pedigrí democrático es discutible

2 *adj (dog)* con pedigrí

pedophile ['pi:dəʊfaɪl] *n* pedófilo(a) *m,f*

pedophilia [pi:də'fɪlɪə] *n* pederastia *f*

pee [pi:] *Fam* **1** *n* pis *m*; **to have a p.** hacer pis, mear

2 *vi* hacer pis, mear

peek [pi:k] **1** *n* vistazo *m*, ojeada *f*; **to take** *or* **have a p. (at sth)** echar un vistazo *or* una ojeada (a algo)

2 *vi* echar un vistazo *or* una ojeada (**at** a)

peel [pi:l] **1** *n (on fruit, vegetable)* piel *f*; *(after peeling)* monda *f*, peladura *f*

2 *vt (fruit, vegetable)* pelar; **to keep one's eyes peeled** tener los ojos bien abiertos

3 *vi (paint)* levantarse; *(sunburnt skin, person)* pelarse

▶**peel off 1** *vt sep (skin of fruit, vegetable)* pelar; *(one's clothes)* quitarse, despojarse de, *Am* sacarse

2 *vi (paint)* levantarse; *(sunburnt skin)* pelarse

peelings ['pi:lɪŋz] *npl (of potato, carrot)* mondas *fpl*, peladuras *fpl*

peep¹ [pi:p] **1** *n (furtive glance)* vistazo *m*, ojeada *f*; **to have** *or* **take a p. at sth** echar un vistazo *or* una ojeada a algo

2 *vi* echar una ojeada (**at** a); **to p. through the keyhole** mirar *or* espiar por el ojo de la cerradura; **to p. out from behind sth** asomar por detrás de algo

peep² *n (sound)* pitido *m*; *Fam* **I don't want to hear another p. out of you** no quiero volver a oírte decir ni pío

peephole ['pi:phəʊl] *n* mirilla *f*

Peeping Tom ['pi:pɪŋ'tɒm] *n Fam* mirón(ona) *m,f*

peer¹ [pɪə(r)] *n* igual *m*; *Formal* **without p.** sin igual, sin par; **he started smoking because of p. pressure** empezó a fumar por influencia de la gente de su entorno; **his p. group** (la gente de) su entorno

peer² *vi* **to p. at sth/sb** mirar con esfuerzo algo/a alguien; **to p. over a wall** atisbar por encima de un muro

peerage ['pɪərɪdʒ] *n (rank)* título *m* de par; **the p.** *(peers)* los pares

peerless ['pɪəlɪs] *adj* sin igual, sin par

peeve [pi:v] *vt Fam* fastidiar; **to be peeved about sth** estar fastidiado(a) *or* molesto(a) por algo

peevish ['pi:vɪʃ] *adj* irritable, malhumorado(a)

peewit, pewit ['pi:wɪt] *n* avefría *f*

peg [peg] **1** *n (pin for fastening)* clavija *f*; *(for coat, hat)* colgador *m*; **(tent) p.** clavija *f*, estaquilla *f*; **to take sb down a p. (or two)** bajarle a alguien los humos

2 *vt (pt & pp pegged)* **(a)** *(fasten)* **to p. sth in place** fijar algo con clavijas **(b)** *(prices)* fijar; **to p. sth to the rate of inflation** ajustar algo al índice de la inflación **(c)** *Fam (identify)* **to p. sb as a troublemaker** encasillar a alguien como un alborotador

▶**peg out** *vi Fam (die)* estirar la pata, *Méx, CAm* petatearse

pejorative [pɪ'dʒɒrətɪv] *adj* peyorativo(a)

Pekinese [pi:kɪ'ni:z] *n (perro m)* pequinés *m*

Peking [pi:'kɪŋ] *n* Pekín

pelican ['pelɪkən] *n (bird)* pelícano *m*

pellet ['pelɪt] *n (of paper, bread, clay)* bolita *f*; *(for gun)* perdigón *m*

pell-mell ['pel'mel] *adv* desordenadamente, en tropel

pelmet ['pelmɪt] *n (of wood)* galería *f (para cortinas)*; *(of cloth)* cenefa *f*

pelt¹ [pelt] *n (animal skin)* piel *f*, pellejo *m*

pelt² **1** *vt* **to p. sb with stones** lanzar a alguien una lluvia de piedras, apedrear a alguien

2 *vi* **(a)** *Fam (rain)* **it was pelting down** diluviaba, *Esp* caían chuzos de punta **(b)** *(go fast)* ir disparado(a); **he came pelting along the corridor** venía disparado por el pasillo

pelvic ['pelvɪk] *adj* pélvico(a)

pelvis ['pelvɪs] *n* pelvis *f inv*

pen¹ [pen] **1** *n (for writing)* pluma *f (estilográfica)*; *(ballpoint)* bolígrafo *m*, *CSur* lapicera *f*, *Col, Ecuad* esferográfico *m*, *Carib, Méx* pluma *f*, *RP* birome *m*; **to put p. to paper** ponerse a escribir; **p. pal** amigo(a) *m,f* por correspondencia; **p. name** seudónimo *m*

2 *vt (pt & pp penned)* escribir

pen² *n* **(a)** *(for sheep)* redil *m*; *(for cattle)* corral *m* **(b)** *Fam (prison) Esp* trullo *m*, *Andes, Col, RP* cana *f*, *Méx* bote *m*

▶**pen in** *vt sep (animals, people)* encerrar

penal ['pi:nəl] *adj* penal; **p. code** código *m* penal; **p. colony** colonia *f* penitenciaria; **p. servitude** trabajos *mpl* forzados

penalize ['pi:nəlaɪz] *vt* penalizar; **to p. sb for doing sth** penalizar a alguien por hacer algo

penalty ['penltɪ] *n* **(a)** *(punishment) (fine)* sanción *f*; *(for serious crime)* pena *f*, castigo *m*; **to impose a p. on sb** imponer un castigo a alguien; **on** *or* **under p. of death** so pena de muerte; **to pay the p.** pagar las consecuencias; *Com* **p. clause** cláusula *f* de penalización **(b)** *(in soccer)* penalti *m*, penalty *m*, *Am* penal *m*; *Sport* **p. area** área *f* de castigo; **p. kick** *(in soccer)* (lanzamiento *m* de) penalti *or Am* penal; **p. shootout** *(in soccer)* lanzamiento *m or* tanda *f* de penaltis *or Am* penales

penance ['penəns] *n also Fig* penitencia *f*; **to do p. (for sth)** hacer penitencia (por algo)

penchant ['pɒnʃɒn] *n* inclinación *f*, propensión *f*; **to have a p. for (doing) sth** tener propensión a (hacer) algo

pencil ['pensəl] **1** *n* lápiz *m*; **p. case** plumier *m*; **p. drawing** dibujo *m* a lápiz; **p. sharpener** sacapuntas *m inv*

2 *vt (draw)* dibujar a lápiz; *(write)* redactar *(con lápiz)*

▶**pencil in** *vt sep (provisionally decide)* apuntar provisionalmente

pendant ['pendənt] *n* colgante *m*

pending ['pendɪŋ] **1** *adj (unresolved)* pendiente; **to be p.** estar pendiente

2 *prep* a la espera de; **p. the outcome** a la espera del resultado

pendulum ['pendjʊləm] *n* péndulo *m*

penetrate ['penɪtreɪt] **1** *vt* **(a)** *(object, body, wall)* penetrar; *(area, market, group)* penetrar en, adentrarse en **(b)** *(enemy, rival group)* infiltrarse en

2 *vi* penetrar

penetrating ['penɪtreɪtɪŋ] *adj (sound, voice, cold)* penetrante; *(mind)* perspicaz, penetrante

penetratingly ['penɪtreɪtɪŋlɪ] *adv (loudly) (to scream, shout)* ensordecedoramente; *(acutely)* perspicazmente

penetration [penɪ'treɪʃən] *n* penetración *f*

penetrative ['penɪtrətɪv] *adj (sex)* con penetración

penguin ['peŋgwɪn] *n* pingüino *m*

penicillin [penɪ'sɪlɪn] *n* penicilina *f*

peninsula [pɪ'nɪnsjʊlə] *n* península *f*

peninsular [pɪ'nɪnsjʊlə(r)] *adj* peninsular; *Hist* **the P. War** la Guerra de la Independencia (española)

penis ['pi:nɪs] *(pl* **penises** [pi:nɪsɪz]*) n* pene *m*

penitence ['penɪtəns] *n* arrepentimiento *m*

penitent ['penɪtənt] **1** *n* penitente *mf*

2 *adj* arrepentido(a)

penitential [penɪ'tenʃəl] *adj* penitencial

penitentiary [penɪ'tenʃərɪ] *n* prisión *f*, cárcel *f*

penknife ['pennaɪf] *n* navaja *f*, cortaplumas *m inv*

pennant ['penənt] *n* banderín *m*

penniless ['penɪlɪs] *adj* **to be p.** estar sin un centavo *or Esp* duro

Pennsylvania [pensɪl'veɪnɪə] *n* Pensilvania

penny ['penɪ] *n* (**a**) *(cent)* centavo *m* (**b**) *(idioms)* **they haven't a p. to their name** no tienen ni una perra gorda *or Esp* ni un duro; **a p. for your thoughts** dime en qué estás pensando; **he keeps turning up like a bad p.** no hay forma de perderlo de vista *or* de quitárselo de encima

penny-pinching ['penɪpɪntʃɪŋ] *adj (person)* agarrado(a), tacaño(a); *(ways, habits)* mezquino(a)

pension ['penʃən] *n* pensión *f*; **to be on a p.** cobrar una pensión; **p. fund** fondo *m* de pensiones

▸**pension off** *vt sep* jubilar

pensionable ['penʃənəbəl] *adj* **of p. age** en edad de jubilación

pensioner ['penʃənə(r)] *n* pensionista *mf*, jubilado(a) *m,f*

pensive ['pensɪv] *adj* pensativo(a); **to be p.** estar pensativo(a)

pensively ['pensɪvlɪ] *adv* pensativamente

pentagon ['pentəgən] *n* pentágono *m*; **the P.** *(building)* el Pentágono

pentagonal [pen'tægənəl] *adj* pentagonal

pentathlon [pen'tæθlən] *n* pentatlón *m* (moderno)

Pentecost ['pentɪkɒst] *n Rel* Pentecostés *m*

penthouse ['penthaʊs] *n* ático *m*

pent-up [pen'tʌp] *adj* contenido(a)

penultimate [pe'nʌltɪmɪt] *adj* penúltimo(a)

penury ['penjʊrɪ] *n* miseria *f*, penuria *f*

peony ['piːənɪ] *n* peonía *f*

people ['piːpəl] **1** *npl* (**a**) *(plural of* person*) (as group)* gente *f*; *(as individuals)* personas *fpl*; **other p.** otras personas; **most p.** la mayoría de la gente; **old p.** los viejos, los mayores; **young p.** los jóvenes; **there were five p. in the room** había cinco personas en la habitación; **he's one of those p. who...** es una de esas personas que...; **p. say that...** se dice que...; **p. mover** *(car)* monovolumen *m*

(**b**) *(citizens)* pueblo *m*, ciudadanía *f*; **the common p.** la gente corriente *or* común; **a man of the p.** un hombre del pueblo; **p. power** poder *m* popular; **P.'s Republic** República *f* Popular; **the P.'s Republic of China** la República Popular China

(**c**) *Fam (family)* **my/his p.** mi/su gente

2 *n (nation)* pueblo *m*; **the Scottish p.** el pueblo escocés

3 *vt* poblar

pep [pep] *n Fam* ánimo *m*, energía *f*; **p. pill** estimulante *m*; **p. rally** asamblea *f* de preparación; **she gave us a p. talk** nos dirigió unas palabras de ánimo

▸**pep up** *(pt & pp* **pepped)** *vt sep Fam (person, event)* animar; *(dish)* alegrar

pepper ['pepə(r)] **1** *n (spice)* pimienta *f*; *(vegetable)* pimiento *m*, *CAm, Méx* chile *m*, *Andes, RP* ají *m*, *Col, Ven* pimentón *m*; **black/white p.** pimienta negra/blanca; **green/red p.** pimiento verde/rojo; **p. mill** molinillo *m* de pimienta

2 *vt (in cooking)* sazonar con pimienta; *Fig* **to p. sth with bullets** acribillar a balazos algo

pepperbox ['pepəbɒks] *n* pimentero *m*

peppercorn ['pepəkɔːn] *n* grano *m* de pimienta

peppermint ['pepəmɪnt] *n (plant)* hierbabuena *f*; *(flavor)* menta *f*; *(sweet)* caramelo *m* de menta

peppery ['pepərɪ] *adj* (**a**) *(spicy)* **to be too p.** tener demasiada pimienta (**b**) *(irritable)* picajoso(a), irascible

peptic ulcer ['peptɪk'ʌlsə(r)] *n Med* úlcera *f* gastroduodenal

per [pɜː(r)] *prep* por; **p. day** al día, por día; **100 miles p. hour** 100 millas por hora; *Formal* **as p. your instructions** según sus instrucciones; **as p. usual** como de costumbre; **p. annum** al año, por año; **p. capita** per cápita; **p. se** en sí, per se

perceive [pə'siːv] *vt* (**a**) *(notice) (sound, light, smell)* percibir; *(difference)* apreciar, distinguir (**b**) *(understand) (truth, importance)* apreciar, entender (**c**) *(view)* **to p. sth/sb as...** ver *or* juzgar algo/a alguien como...

percent, per cent [pə'sent] **1** *n* porcentaje *m*, tanto *m* por ciento; **forty p. of women** el cuarenta por ciento de las mujeres; **a ten p. increase** un aumento del diez por ciento

2 *adv* por ciento

percentage [pə'sentɪdʒ] *n* porcentaje *m*, tanto *m* por ciento; **to receive a p. on all sales** percibir un tanto por ciento de todas las ventas

perceptible [pə'septɪbəl] *adj* perceptible

perceptibly [pə'septɪblɪ] *adv* sensiblemente

perception [pə'sepʃən] *n* (**a**) *(with senses)* percepción *f* (**b**) *(of difference, importance, facts)* apreciación *f* (**c**) *(discernment)* perspicacia *f*

perceptive [pə'septɪv] *adj* atinado(a), perspicaz

perceptiveness [pə'septɪvnɪs] *n* perspicacia *f*

perch[1] [pɜːtʃ] **1** *n (for bird)* percha *f*; *Fam (seat, position)* atalaya *f*; *Fam Fig* **to knock sb off his p.** bajarle los humos a alguien

2 *vi (bird)* posarse; **he perched on the edge of the table** *(person)* se sentó en el borde de la mesa

perch[2] *n (fish)* perca *f*

percolate ['pɜːkəleɪt] **1** *vt (coffee)* hacer *(con la cafetera)*; **percolated coffee** café *m* de cafetera

2 *vi* filtrarse

percolator ['pɜːkəleɪtə(r)] *n* cafetera *f* (de filtro)

percussion [pə'kʌʃən] *n Mus* percusión *f*; **p. instruments** instrumentos *mpl* de percusión

percussionist [pə'kʌʃənɪst] *n Mus* percusionista *mf*

peregrine falcon ['perɪgrɪn'fɔːlkən] *n* halcón *m* peregrino

peremptory [pə'remptərɪ] *adj (person, manner, voice)* imperioso(a); *(command)* perentorio(a)

perennial [pə'renɪəl] **1** *n Bot* planta *f* perenne

2 *adj (plant)* (de hoja) perenne; *(problems, beauty)* eterno(a)

perfect 1 *adj* ['pɜːfɪkt] (**a**) *(excellent, flawless)* perfecto(a); **no one's p.** nadie es perfecto; **Tuesday would be p.** el martes me vendría muy bien; *Mus* **to have p. pitch** tener una entonación perfecta (**b**) *(complete)* **it makes p. sense** es del todo razonable; **he's a p. stranger to me** no lo conozco de nada; **he's a p. fool** es un perfecto idiota; **he's a p. gentleman** es un perfecto caballero (**c**) *Gram* perfecto(a); **future p.** futuro *m* perfecto; **past p.** pretérito *m* pluscuamperfecto

2 *vt* [pə'fekt] perfeccionar

perfection [pə'fekʃən] *n* perfección *f*

perfectionism [pə'fekʃənɪzəm] *n* perfeccionismo *m*

perfectionist [pə'fekʃənɪst] *n* perfeccionista *mf*

perfectly ['pɜːfɪktlɪ] *adv (faultlessly)* perfectamente; *(absolutely)* completamente; **it's p. obvious** resulta totalmente evidente; **she's p. right** tiene toda la razón

perfidious [pə'fɪdɪəs] *adj Literary* pérfido(a)

perfidy ['pɜːfɪdɪ] *n Literary* perfidia *f*

perforate ['pɜːfəreɪt] *vt* perforar

perforated ['pɜːfəreɪtɪd] *adj* perforado(a); **p. line** línea *f* perforada; *Med* **p. ulcer** úlcera *f* perforada

perforation [pɜːfə'reɪʃən] *n (hole, on stamp)* perforación *f*

perform [pə'fɔːm] **1** *vt (miracle, operation, service)* realizar, efectuar; *(one's duty)* cumplir; *(play)* representar; *(role, piece of music)* interpretar

2 *vi (actor)* actuar; *(singer)* interpretar, cantar; *(machine, car)* funcionar, comportarse

performance [pə'fɔːməns] *n* (**a**) *(of task)* realización *f*, ejecución *f*; *(of duty)* cumplimiento *m*; **p. appraisal** evaluación *f* del rendimiento (**b**) *(of actor, sportsperson)* actuación *f*; *(of pupil, economy)* comportamiento *m*; *(of machine, car)* rendimiento *m*, prestaciones *fpl* (**c**) *(of play)* representación *f*; *Fam Fig* **to make a p. (about sth)** *(fuss)* armar un escándalo *or Esp* montar una escena (por algo)

performance-enhancing [pə'fɔːmənsen'hɑːnsɪŋ] *adj* que mejora el rendimiento

performance-related [pə'fɔ:mənsrɪ'leɪtɪd] *adj* según el rendimiento

performer [pə'fɔ:mə(r)] *n* intérprete *mf*

performing [pə'fɔ:mɪŋ] *adj (dog, seal)* amaestrado(a); **p. arts** artes *fpl* interpretativas

perfume 1 *n* ['pɜ:fju:m] *(of flowers)* aroma *m*, fragancia *f; (for person)* perfume *m*; **p. counter** sección *f* de perfumería
    2 *vt* [pə'fju:m] perfumar

perfumed ['pɜ:fju:md] *adj* perfumado(a)

perfumery [pə'fju:mərɪ] *n* perfumería *f*

perfunctory [pə'fʌŋktərɪ] *adj (glance, smile)* rutinario(a), superficial; *(letter, instructions, examination)* somero(a)

perhaps [pə'hæps] *adv* quizá, quizás, tal vez, *Am* talvez; **p. so/not** quizá sí/no; **p. she'll come** quizá venga

peril ['perɪl] *n* peligro *m*, riesgo *m*; **in p. of her life** a riesgo de (perder) su vida; **at your p.** por tu cuenta y riesgo

perilous ['perɪləs] *adj* peligroso(a)

perilously ['perɪləslɪ] *adv* peligrosamente; **we came p. close to a collision** estuvimos en un tris de chocar

perimeter [pə'rɪmɪtə(r)] *n* perímetro *m*; **p. fence** valla *f* exterior

period ['pɪərɪəd] *n* (**a**) *(stretch of time)* periodo *m*, período *m*; **for a p. of three months** durante un periodo de tres meses; **within the agreed p.** dentro del plazo acordado; **sunny periods** intervalos *mpl* de sol (**b**) *Sch* clase *f*; **a French p.** una clase de francés (**c**) *(menstruation)* periodo *m*, regla *f*; **to have one's p.** tener el periodo *or* la regla; **p. pains** dolores *mpl* menstruales (**d**) *(historical age)* época *f*, periodo *m*; **p. dress/furniture** traje *m*/muebles *mpl* de época; *TV* **p. drama** drama *m* (televisivo) de época (**e**) *(full stop)* punto *m*

periodic [pɪərɪ'ɒdɪk] *adj* periódico(a); *Chem* **p. table** tabla *f* periódica

periodical [pɪərɪ'ɒdɪkəl] *n* publicación *f* periódica, boletín *m*

periodically [pɪərɪ'ɒdɪklɪ] *adv* periódicamente

peripheral [pə'rɪfərəl] **1** *npl Comptr* **peripherals** periféricos *mpl*
    2 *adj (area, vision)* periférico(a); *(issue, importance)* secundario(a)

periphery [pə'rɪfərɪ] *n* periferia *f*

periphrasis [pə'rɪfrəsɪs] *(pl* **periphrases** [pə'rɪfrəsi:z]) *n* perífrasis *f inv*

periscope ['perɪskəʊp] *n* periscopio *m*

perish ['perɪʃ] *vi* (**a**) *(person)* perecer; **p. the thought!** ¡Dios no lo quiera! (**b**) *(rubber, leather)* estropearse

perishable ['perɪʃəbəl] **1** *npl* **perishables** productos *mpl* perecederos
    2 *adj* perecedero(a)

peritonitis [perɪtə'naɪtɪs] *n Med* peritonitis *f inv*

perjure ['pɜ:dʒə(r)] *vt Law* **to p. oneself** perjurar

perjurer ['pɜ:dʒərə(r)] *n Law* perjuro(a) *m,f*

perjury ['pɜ:dʒərɪ] *n Law* perjurio *m*; **to commit p.** cometer perjurio

▶**perk up** [pɜ:k] *Fam* **1** *vt sep* animar, levantar el ánimo a
    2 *vi* animarse

perky ['pɜ:kɪ] *adj Fam* animado(a); **to be p.** estar animado(a)

perm [pɜ:m] **1** *n (hairdo)* permanente *f*; **to have a p.** llevar una permanente
    2 *vt* **to have one's hair permed** hacerse la permanente

permanence ['pɜ:mənəns] *n* permanencia *f*

permanent ['pɜ:mənənt] *adj* permanente; *(employee, job)* fijo(a); **p. address** domicilio *m* fijo, residencia *f* habitual; **p. wave** *(hairdo)* permanente *f*

permeate ['pɜ:mɪeɪt] **1** *vt* impregnar
    2 *vi* **to p. through sth** *(liquid)* filtrarse a través de algo; *(fear, suspicion)* extenderse por algo

permissible [pə'mɪsɪbəl] *adj* admisible, permisible

permission [pə'mɪʃən] *n* permiso *m*; **to ask for p. to do sth** pedir permiso para hacer algo; **to give sb p. to do sth** dar a alguien permiso para hacer algo; **with your p.** con (su) permiso

permissive [pə'mɪsɪv] *adj* permisivo(a)

permit 1 *n* ['pɜ:mɪt] *(for fishing, imports, exports)* licencia *f; (for parking, work, residence)* permiso *m*; **p. holders only** *(sign)* estacionamiento reservado
    2 *vt* [pə'mɪt] *(pt & pp* **permitted**) permitir; **to p. sb to do sth** permitir a alguien hacer algo
    3 *vi* **weather permitting** si el tiempo lo permite

permutation [pɜ:mjʊ'teɪʃən] *n* permutación *f*

pernicious [pə'nɪʃəs] *adj* pernicioso(a)

peroxide [pə'rɒksaɪd] *n Chem* peróxido *m*; **p. blonde** *(woman)* rubia *f* oxigenada *or Esp* de bote

perpendicular [pɜ:pən'dɪkjʊlə(r)] **1** *n* perpendicular *f*
    2 *adj* perpendicular

perpetrate ['pɜ:pɪtreɪt] *vt (crime, deception)* perpetrar

perpetrator ['pɜ:pɪtreɪtə(r)] *n* autor(ora) *m,f*

perpetual [pə'petjʊəl] *adj (eternal)* perpetuo(a); *(constant)* continuo(a), constante; *Phys* **p. motion** movimiento *m* perpetuo

perpetually [pə'petjʊəlɪ] *adv (eternally)* perpetuamente; *(constantly)* continuamente, constantemente

perpetuate [pə'petjʊeɪt] *vt Formal* perpetuar

perpetuity [pɜ:pɪ'tju:ɪtɪ] *n Formal* **in p.** a perpetuidad

perplex [pə'pleks] *vt* dejar perplejo(a)

perplexing [pə'pleksɪŋ] *adj* desconcertante

perplexity [pə'pleksɪtɪ] *n* perplejidad *f*, desconcierto *m*

persecute ['pɜ:sɪkju:t] *vt (for political or religious reasons)* perseguir; *(harass)* acosar, atormentar

persecution [pɜ:sɪ'kju:ʃən] *n* persecución *f; Psy* **p. complex** manía *f* persecutoria

persecutor ['pɜ:sɪkju:tə(r)] *n* perseguidor(ora) *m,f*

perseverance [pɜ:sɪ'vɪərəns] *n* perseverancia *f*

persevere [pɜ:sɪ'vɪə(r)] *vi* perseverar (**with** en); **to p. in doing sth** seguir haciendo algo con perseverancia

Persia ['pɜ:ʒə] *n Formerly* Persia

Persian ['pɜ:ʒən] **1** *n* (**a**) *(person)* persa *mf* (**b**) *(language)* persa *m*
    2 *adj* persa; **the P. Gulf** el Golfo Pérsico

persimmon ['pɜ:sɪmən] *n* caqui *m (fruta)*

persist [pə'sɪst] *vi (person)* persistir, perseverar; *(fog, fever)* persistir; *(belief)* persistir, subsistir; **to p. in doing sth** empeñarse en hacer algo; **to p. in one's belief that...** empeñarse en creer que...; **to p. in one's efforts (to do sth)** no cejar en el empeño (de hacer algo)

persistence [pə'sɪstəns] *n (of person)* empeño *m*, persistencia *f; (of pain, belief, rumors)* persistencia *f*

persistent [pə'sɪstənt] *adj (person)* persistente, insistente; *(rain, pain)* pertinaz; *(doubts, rumors)* persistente; **p. offender** delincuente *mf* habitual

persistently [pə'sɪstəntlɪ] *adv (constantly)* constantemente; *(repeatedly)* repetidamente

persnickety [pə'snɪkɪtɪ] *adj Fam (person)* quisquilloso(a); *(task)* engorroso(a)

person ['pɜ:sən] *(pl* **people** ['pi:pəl], *Formal* **persons**) *n* persona *f*; **in p.** en persona; **to have sth on one's p.** llevar algo encima; *Gram* **in the first/second/third p.** en primera/segunda/tercera persona; *Law* **by a p. or persons unknown** por uno o varios desconocidos

personable ['pɜ:sənəbəl] *adj* agradable

personage ['pɜ:sənɪdʒ] *n* personaje *m*

personal ['pɜ:sənəl] **1** *adj* personal; **to make a p. appearance** hacer acto de presencia; **for p. reasons** por motivos personales; **don't be p., don't make p. remarks** no hagas comentarios de índole personal; **it's nothing p., but...** no es nada personal, pero...; **she's a p. friend of**

the president es amiga personal del presidente; **p. ad** *(in newspaper, magazine)* anuncio *m* personal (por palabras); **p. assistant** secretario(a) *m,f* personal; **p. best** *(in sport)* plusmarca *f* (personal), récord *m* personal; **p. column** *(in newspaper, magazine)* sección *f* de anuncios personales *or* de contactos; *Comptr* **p. computer** *Esp* ordenador *m or Am* computadora *f* personal; **p. effects** efectos *mpl* personales; **p. foul** *(in basketball)* (falta *f*) personal; **p. growth** desarrollo *m* personal; **p. hygiene** aseo *m* personal; **p. loan** préstamo *m or* crédito *m or Méx* prestamiento *m* personal; **p. organizer** agenda *f*; *Gram* **p. pronoun** pronombre *m* personal; **p. stereo** walkman® *m*; **p. trainer** preparador(ora) *m,f* físico(a) personal

2 *n (advertisement)* anuncio *m* en la sección de contactos

personality [pɜːsə'nælɪtɪ] *n* personalidad *f*; **p. cult** culto *m* a la personalidad; *Psy* **p. disorder** trastorno *m* de la personalidad

personally ['pɜːsənəlɪ] *adv (in my opinion)* personalmente; *(to visit, talk to, know)* en persona; **p., I think…** personalmente, creo…; **don't take it p.** no te lo tomes como algo personal; **I will hold you p. responsible if she gets hurt** si se hace daño te pediré cuentas a ti personalmente

personification [pɜːsɒnɪfɪ'keɪʃən] *n* personificación *f*; **to be the p. of meanness** ser la tacañería personificada

personify [pɜː'sɒnɪfaɪ] *vt* personificar

personnel [pɜːsə'nel] *n* personal *m*; **p. (department)** departamento *m* de personal; **p. manager** director(ora) *m,f or* jefe(a) *m,f* de personal

perspective [pə'spektɪv] *n* perspectiva *f*; **to see things in p.** ver las cosas con perspectiva; **to put sth into p.** ver algo con perspectiva

Perspex® ['pɜːspeks] *n* perspex® *m*, plexiglás® *m*

perspicacious [pɜːspɪ'keɪʃəs] *adj Formal* perspicaz

perspicacity [pɜːspɪ'kæsɪtɪ] *n Formal* perspicacia *f*

perspiration [pɜːspə'reɪʃən] *n* transpiración *f*, sudor *m*

perspire [pə'spaɪə(r)] *vi* transpirar, sudar

persuade [pə'sweɪd] *vt* persuadir; **to p. sb to do sth** persuadir a alguien para que haga algo; **to p. sb not to do sth** disuadir a alguien de que haga algo

persuasion [pə'sweɪʒən] *n* **(a)** *(act, ability)* persuasión *f*; **powers of p.** poder *m* de persuasión **(b)** *(beliefs)* convicciones *fpl*

persuasive [pə'sweɪzɪv] *adj (person, argument)* persuasivo(a)

persuasively [pə'sweɪzɪvlɪ] *adv* persuasivamente

persuasiveness [pə'sweɪzɪvnəs] *n (of person, argument)* persuasión *f*

pert [pɜːt] *adj* **(a)** *(young woman)* pizpireta **(b)** *(nose, breasts, bottom)* respingón(ona)

pertain [pə'teɪn] *vi Formal* **to p. to** *(be relevant to)* concernir a; *(belong to)* pertenecer a

pertinent ['pɜːtɪnənt] *adj* pertinente; **to be p. to** concernir a

pertly ['pɜːtlɪ] *adv (to reply)* con descaro *or* atrevimiento

perturb [pə'tɜːb] *vt* inquietar, perturbar

perturbing [pə'tɜːbɪŋ] *adj* inquietante, perturbador(ora)

Peru [pə'ruː] *n* Perú

perusal [pə'ruːzəl] *n Formal* lectura *f*

peruse [pə'ruːz] *vt (read carefully)* leer con detenimiento; *(read quickly)* ojear

Peruvian [pə'ruːvɪən] *n & adj* peruano(a) *m,f*

pervade [pɜː'veɪd] *vt* impregnar

pervasive [pɜː'veɪsɪv] *adj (smell)* penetrante; *(influence)* poderoso(a)

perverse [pə'vɜːs] *adj* **(a)** *(contrary)* aberrante; *(stubborn)* terco(a), cabezota; **he's just being p.** simplemente está llevando la contraria; **she takes a p. delight in causing harm** disfruta de lo lindo haciendo daño **(b)** *(sexually deviant)* pervertido(a)

perversely [pə'vɜːslɪ] *adv* **p. enough, I quite enjoyed it** paradójicamente, me gustó

perverseness [pə'vɜːsnɪs] *n* **he did it out of sheer p.** lo hizo por llevar la contraria

perversion [pə'vɜːʒən] *n (sexual)* perversión *f*; *(of the truth)* deformación *f*, tergiversación *f*; *(of justice)* distorsión *f*, corrupción *f*

pervert 1 *n* ['pɜːvɜːt] **(sexual) p.** pervertido(a) *m,f* (sexual)
2 *vt* [pə'vɜːt] *(corrupt)* pervertir; *(distort)* tergiversar; *Law* **to p. the course of justice** obstaculizar el curso de la justicia

peseta [pə'seɪtə] *n Formerly* peseta *f*

pesky ['peskɪ] *adj Fam* plomo(a), latoso(a), *Méx* sangrón(ona), *RP* hinchón(ona)

peso ['peɪsəʊ] *(pl* **pesos***) n (Argentinian, Mexican currency)* peso *m*

pessary ['pesərɪ] *n Med* pesario *m*

pessimism ['pesɪmɪzəm] *n* pesimismo *m*

pessimist ['pesɪmɪst] *n* pesimista *mf*

pessimistic [pesɪ'mɪstɪk] *adj* pesimista

pest [pest] *n* **(a)** *(vermin, insects)* plaga *f*; **p. control** métodos *mpl* para combatir las plagas **(b)** *Fam (nuisance)* plomazo *m*, *Esp* latazo *m*

pester ['pestə(r)] *vt* molestar, *Esp* incordiar; **to p. sb to do sth** dar la lata *or* incordiar a alguien para que haga algo; **to p. sb into doing sth** conseguir que alguien haga algo a fuerza de darle la lata *or* incordiarle

pesticide ['pestɪsaɪd] *n* pesticida *m*

pestilence ['pestɪləns] *n Literary* pestilencia *f*, peste *f*

pestilential [pestɪ'lenʃəl] *adj Literary* pestilente

pestle ['pesəl] *n* mano *f* del mortero; **p. and mortar** mortero *m*, almirez *m*

pet [pet] **1** *n* **(a)** *(animal)* animal *m* doméstico *or* de compañía; **p. food** comida *f* para animales domésticos; **p. shop** pajarería *f* **(b)** *(favorite)* **mother's/teacher's p.** preferido(a) *m,f* de mamá/del profesor; **my p.!** ¡mi tesoro!; **my p. hate** lo que más odio; **p. name** *(diminutive)* apelativo *m or* nombre *m* cariñoso; **p. subject** tema *m* favorito
2 *vt (pt & pp* **petted***) (stroke, pat) (person, dog)* acariciar
3 *vi Fam (sexually) Esp* darse *or* pegarse el lote, *Am* manosearse

petal ['petəl] *n* pétalo *m*

peter ['piːtə(r)] *n Fam (penis)* pilila *f*, pito *m*
▸**peter out** *vi (conversation, enthusiasm)* decaer, declinar; *(path, stream)* extinguirse, desaparecer

petite [pə'tiːt] *adj* menudo(a)

petition [pɪ'tɪʃən] **1** *n (request, document)* petición *f*, súplica *f*; *(list of names)* lista *f* de firmas recogidas; *Law* **p. for a divorce** demanda *f* de divorcio
2 *vt (court, sovereign)* presentar una petición *or Am* un pedido a
3 *vi* **to p. for sth** solicitar algo; *Law* **to p. for divorce** presentar una demanda de divorcio

petitioner [pɪ'tɪʃənə(r)] *n* peticionario(a) *m,f*

petrify ['petrɪfaɪ] *vt Geol* petrificar; *(with fear)* petrificar, paralizar

petrochemical [petrəʊ'kemɪkəl] **1** *npl* **petrochemicals** productos *mpl* petroquímicos
2 *adj* petroquímico(a)

petroleum [pə'trəʊlɪəm] *n* petróleo *m*; **p. jelly** vaselina *f*

petticoat ['petɪkəʊt] *n (from waist down)* enaguas *fpl*; *(full-length)* combinación *f*

petty ['petɪ] *adj* **(a)** *(insignificant)* insignificante; **p. cash** caja *f* para gastos menores; **p. crime** delitos *mpl* menores; *Law* **p. larceny** = delito de robo por un valor inferior a los 500 dólares; *Naut* **p. officer** suboficial *mf* de marina **(b)** *(small-minded)* mezquino(a)

petty-minded ['petɪ'maɪndɪd] *adj* mezquino(a)

petulance ['petjʊləns] *n* **a fit of p.** una rabieta

petulant ['petjʊlənt] *adj (person)* caprichoso(a); **with a p. gesture** con un gesto de niño caprichoso

petulantly ['petjʊləntlɪ] *adv* caprichosamente

petunia [pɪ'tjuːnɪə] *n* petunia *f*

pew [pjuː] *n* banco *m*

pewit = **peewit**

pewter ['pjuːtə(r)] *n* peltre *m*

PGA [piːdʒiː'eɪ] *n (abbr* **Professional Golfers' Association)** PGA *f*, asociación *f* de golfistas profesionales

pH [piː'eɪtʃ] *n Chem* pH *m*

phalanx ['fælæŋks] *n Mil & Hist* falange *f*; *Fig (of officials, journalists)* pelotón *m*

phallic ['fælɪk] *adj* fálico(a); **p. symbol** símbolo *m* fálico

phallus ['fæləs] *n* falo *m*

phantasm ['fæntæzəm] *n* fantasma *m*, espectro *m*

phantom ['fæntəm] *n* fantasma *m*; **p. pregnancy** embarazo *m* psicológico

Pharaoh ['feərəʊ] *n* faraón *m*

pharmaceutical [fɑːmə'sjuːtɪkəl] **1** *npl* **pharmaceuticals** productos *mpl* farmacéuticos
  2 *adj* farmacéutico(a)

pharmacist ['fɑːməsɪst] *n* farmacéutico(a) *m,f*

pharmacological [fɑːməkə'lɒdʒɪkəl] *adj* farmacológico(a)

pharmacologist [fɑːmə'kɒlədʒɪst] *n* farmacólogo(a) *m,f*

pharmacology [fɑːmə'kɒlədʒɪ] *n* farmacología *f*

pharmacy ['fɑːməsɪ] *n* farmacia *f*

pharyngitis [færɪn'dʒaɪtɪs] *n Med* faringitis *f inv*

pharynx ['færɪŋks] *n* faringe *f*

phase [feɪz] *n* fase *f*, etapa *f*; **it's just a p. (he's going through)** ya se le pasará; **out of p.** desfasado(a)

► **phase in** *vt sep* introducir gradualmente *or* escalonadamente

► **phase out** *vt sep* eliminar gradualmente *or* escalonadamente

phased [feɪzd] *adj (gradual)* gradual; *(in stages)* escalonado(a)

phase-out ['feɪzaʊt] *n* eliminación *f* progresiva

PhD [piːeɪtʃ'diː] *n Univ (abbr* **Doctor of Philosophy)** *(person)* doctor(ora) *m,f*; *(degree)* doctorado *m*

pheasant ['fezənt] *n* faisán *m*

phenomenal [fɪ'nɒmɪnəl] *adj* fenomenal, extraordinario(a)

phenomenally [fɪ'nɒmɪnəlɪ] *adv* fenomenalmente, extraordinariamente

phenomenon [fɪ'nɒmɪnən] *(pl* **phenomena** [fɪ'nɒmɪnə] *or* **phenomenons)** *n* fenómeno *m*

pheromone ['ferəməʊn] *n* feromona *f*

phew [fjuː] *exclam* ¡uf!

phial ['faɪəl] *n* ampolla *f*, vial *m*

Philadelphian [fɪlə'delfɪən] **1** *n* persona de Filadelfia
  2 *adj* de Filadelfia

philanderer [fɪ'lændərə(r)] *n Pej* donjuán *m*

philandering [fɪ'lændərɪŋ] *Pej* **1** *n* líos *mpl* amorosos
  2 *adj* mujeriego(a)

philanthropic [fɪlən'θrɒpɪk] *adj* filantrópico(a)

philanthropist [fɪ'lænθrəpɪst] *n* filántropo(a) *m,f*

philanthropy [fɪ'lænθrəpɪ] *n* filantropía *f*

philatelist [fɪ'lætəlɪst] *n* filatelista *mf*

philately [fɪ'lætəlɪ] *n* filatelia *f*

philharmonic [fɪlə'mɒnɪk] *Mus* **1** *n* filarmónica *f*
  2 *adj* filarmónico(a)

Philippines ['fɪlɪpiːnz] *npl* **the P.** las Filipinas

philologist [fɪ'lɒlədʒɪst] *n* filólogo(a) *m,f*

philology [fɪ'lɒlədʒɪ] *n* filología *f*

philosopher [fɪ'lɒsəfə(r)] *n* filósofo(a) *m,f*

philosophic(al) [fɪlə'sɒfɪk(əl)] *adj (person, attitude)* filosófico(a); **to be p. about sth** tomarse algo con filosofía

philosophically [fɪlə'sɒfɪklɪ] *adv* **(a)** *(argue)* filosóficamente **(b)** *(calmly, dispassionately)* con filosofía

philosophize [fɪ'lɒsəfaɪz] *vi* filosofar

philosophy [fɪ'lɒsəfɪ] *n* filosofía *f*; **my p. is...** mi filosofía es...

phishing ['fɪʃɪŋ] *n Comptr* phishing *m*

phlegm [flem] *n (mucus, composure)* flema *f*

phlegmatic [fleg'mætɪk] *adj* flemático(a)

phobia ['fəʊbɪə] *n* fobia *f*

phobic ['fəʊbɪk] *adj* **she's a bit p. about spiders** le tiene fobia a las arañas

phoenix ['fiːnɪks] *n* fénix *m inv*; **to rise like a p.** renacer de las propias cenizas

phone [fəʊn] **1** *n* teléfono *m*; **to be on the p.** *(talking)* estar al teléfono; *(have a telephone)* tener teléfono; **p. bill** factura *f* del teléfono; **p. book** guía *f* telefónica *or* de teléfonos, *Am* directorio *m* de teléfonos; **p. booth** cabina *f* telefónica; **p. call** llamada *f* telefónica, *Am* llamado *m* telefónico; **p. card** tarjeta *f* telefónica; **p. number** número *m* de teléfono
  2 *vt* **to p. sb** telefonear a alguien, llamar a alguien (por teléfono), *Am* hablar a alguien (por teléfono)
  3 *vi* telefonear, llamar (por teléfono); **to p. home** llamar a casa (por teléfono)

phone-in ['fəʊnɪn] *n Rad & TV* **p. (program)** = programa con llamadas de los televidentes/oyentes

phoneme ['fəʊniːm] *n Ling* fonema *m*

phonetic [fə'netɪk] *adj Ling* fonético(a); **p. alphabet** alfabeto *m* fonético

phonetically [fə'netɪklɪ] *adv* fonéticamente

phonetics [fə'netɪks] *n Ling* fonética *f*

phoney = **phony**

phonograph ['fəʊnəgrɑːf] *n* **(a)** *Old-fashioned* gramófono *m* **(b)** *(early form of gramophone)* fonógrafo *m*

phony, phoney ['fəʊnɪ] *Fam* **1** *n (pl* **phonies, phoneys)** *(person)* falso(a) *m,f*, farsante *mf*
  2 *adj* falso(a)

phosphate ['fɒsfeɪt] *n* fosfato *m*

phosphorescent [fɒsfə'resənt] *adj* fosforescente

phosphorus ['fɒsfərəs] *n Chem* fósforo *m*

photo ['fəʊtəʊ] *(pl* **photos)** *n* foto *f*; **p. album** álbum *m* de fotos; **p. booth** fotomatón *m*; **p. finish** *(in race)* foto-finish *f*; **p. opportunity** = ocasión de aparecer fotografiado dando una buena imagen

photocopier ['fəʊtəʊkɒpɪə(r)] *n* fotocopiadora *f*

photocopy ['fəʊtəʊkɒpɪ] **1** *n* fotocopia *f*
  2 *vt* fotocopiar

photocopying ['fəʊtəʊkɒpɪɪŋ] *n* fotocopiado *m*; **there's some p. to do** hay que hacer algunas fotocopias

photoelectric [fəʊtəʊɪ'lektrɪk] *adj* fotoeléctrico(a); **p. cell** célula *f* fotoeléctrica

photogenic [fəʊtə'dʒenɪk] *adj* fotogénico(a)

photograph ['fəʊtəgræf] **1** *n* fotografía *f*; **to take sb's p.** sacarle una fotografía a alguien; **p. album** álbum *m* de fotografías
  2 *vt* fotografiar

photographer [fə'tɒgrəfə(r)] *n* fotógrafo(a) *m,f*

photographic [fəʊtə'græfɪk] *adj* fotográfico(a); **to have a p. memory** tener memoria fotográfica

photographically [fəʊtə'græfɪklɪ] *adv* fotográficamente

photography [fə'tɒgrəfɪ] *n* fotografía *f*

photosensitive [fəʊtəʊ'sensɪtɪv] *adj* fotosensible

Photostat® ['fəʊtəʊstæt] *n* (fotocopia *f* de) fotostato *m*

photosynthesis [fəʊtəʊ'sɪnθɪsɪs] *n Bot* fotosíntesis *f inv*

photosynthesize [fəʊtəʊ'sɪnθɪsaɪz] *vt Bot* fotosintetizar

phrasal verb ['freɪzəl'vɜːb] *n Gram* verbo *m* regido por preposición/adverbio

phrase [freɪz] **1** *n* frase *f*; **p. book** manual *m or* guía *f* de conversación
  2 *vt* expresar; *Mus* frasear

phraseology [freɪzɪ'ɒlədʒɪ] *n* fraseología *f*

phrasing ['freɪzɪŋ] *n* (a) *(expressing)* expresión *f* (b) *Mus* fraseo *m*

phylum ['faɪləm] *n* Biol & Zool filum *m*, tipo *m*

phys ed ['fɪz'ed] *n* Educ (abbr **physical education**) educación *f* física

physical ['fɪzɪkəl] 1 *n (examination)* chequeo *m*, examen *m* or reconocimiento *m* médico

2 *adj* físico(a); **p. education** educación *f* física; **p. exercise** or **training** ejercicios *mpl* físicos; **p. fitness** buena forma *f* física; **p. geography** geografía *f* física; **a p. impossibility** una imposibilidad física or material; **p. sciences** ciencias *fpl* físicas; **p. therapy** fisioterapia *f*

physically ['fɪzɪklɪ] *adv* físicamente; **p. fit** en buena forma física; **the p. handicapped** los discapacitados físicos

physician [fɪ'zɪʃən] *n* médico(a) *m,f*

physicist ['fɪzɪsɪst] *n* físico(a) *m,f*

physics ['fɪzɪks] *n* física *f*

physiognomy [fɪzɪ'ɒnəmɪ] *n Formal* fis(i)onomía *f*

physiological [fɪzɪə'lɒdʒɪkəl] *adj* fisiológico(a)

physiologist [fɪzɪ'ɒlədʒɪst] *n* fisiólogo(a) *m,f*

physiology [fɪzɪ'ɒlədʒɪ] *n* fisiología *f*

physiotherapist [fɪzɪəʊ'θerəpɪst] *n* fisioterapeuta *mf*

physiotherapy [fɪzɪəʊ'θerəpɪ] *n* fisioterapia *f*

physique [fɪ'ziːk] *n* físico *m*

pi [paɪ] *n Math* pi *m*

pianist ['pɪənɪst] *n* pianista *mf*

piano [pɪ'ænəʊ] *(pl* **pianos**) *n* piano *m*; **p. concerto** concierto *m* para piano y orquesta; **p. stool** escabel *m*, taburete *m* de piano; **p. tuner** afinador(ora) *m,f* de pianos

pic [pɪk] *n Fam* foto *f*

piccolo ['pɪkələʊ] *(pl* **piccolos**) *n* flautín *m*, piccolo *m*

pick [pɪk] 1 *n* (a) *(tool)* pico *m* (b) *(choice)* **we had first p.** nos dejaron elegir los primeros; **take your p.** escoge a tu gusto; **the p. of the bunch** el/la mejor de todos(as)

2 *vt* (a) *(choose)* escoger, elegir; *(team)* seleccionar; **to p. a fight with sb** buscar pelea con alguien

(b) *(flowers, fruit)* recoger, *Esp* coger

(c) *(other uses)* **to p. a lock** forzar una cerradura; **to p. a guitar** puntear; **to p. one's nose** meterse el dedo en or hurgarse la nariz; **to p. one's teeth** escarbarse los dientes; **to p. a spot/a scab** arrancarse un grano/una costra; **to p. sb's pocket** robar algo del bolsillo de alguien; **she picked a hole in her jumper** se hizo un punto en el jersey (tirando); *Fig* **to p. holes in sth** *(in argument, theory)* sacar fallos a algo, *Am* encontrar fallas a algo; **to p. sb's brains** aprovechar los conocimientos de alguien; **to have a bone to p. with sb** tener que ajustar cuentas con alguien

3 *vi* **we can't afford to p. and choose** no podemos andar eligiendo

▶**pick off** *vt sep (remove)* retirar; *(of gunman, sniper)* ir abatiendo (uno por uno)

▶**pick on** *vt insep (bully)* meterse con

▶**pick out** *vt sep* (a) *(remove)* quitar, *Am* sacar (b) *(select)* elegir, escoger (c) *(recognize)* reconocer

▶**pick up 1** *vt sep* (a) *(lift up)* recoger, *Esp* coger; **to p. up the phone** descolgar el teléfono; **to p. up survivors** rescatar supervivientes; *Fig* **to p. oneself up** *(after defeat)* recuperarse; *Fig* **to p. up the pieces** empezar de nuevo *(tras un fracaso)*; *also Fig* **to p. up the bill** or **tab** pagar la cuenta

(b) *(collect)* recoger; *(arrest)* detener

(c) *(acquire, learn)* aprender; **to p. up speed** ganar velocidad

(d) *(radio station)* sintonizar; *(message)* captar, recibir

(e) *(notice)* percatarse de

(f) *(discussion)* reanudar

(g) *(make better)* **that will p. you up** eso te reconfortará

(h) *Fam* **to p. sb up** *(find sexual partner)* ligarse or *RP* levantar a alguien

2 *vi* (a) *(improve)* mejorar; **business is picking up** el negocio se va animando (b) *(continue)* **let's p. up where we left off** vamos a seguir por donde estábamos

pickax ['pɪkæks] *n* pico *m*

picket ['pɪkɪt] 1 *n* (a) *(in strike, of guards)* piquete *m*; **p. line** piquete *m* (b) *(stake)* estaca *f*; **p. fence** cerca *f*, estacada *f*

2 *vt (during strike)* hacer piquetes en

pickings ['pɪkɪŋz] *npl* botín *m*; **rich p.** pingües beneficios *mpl*

pickle ['pɪkəl] 1 *n* **pickles** variantes *mpl*, encurtidos *mpl*; *Fam Fig* **to be in a bit of a p.** estar en un buen lío

2 *vt* encurtir; **pickled cabbage/onions** col *f*/cebolletas *fpl* en vinagre

pick-me-up ['pɪkmɪʌp] *n Fam* reconstituyente *m*, tónico *m*

pickpocket ['pɪkpɒkɪt] *n* carterista *mf*

pickup ['pɪkʌp] *n* (a) **p. (truck)** camioneta *f*; **p. point** *(for goods, passengers)* lugar *m* de recogida (b) *Fam (improvement)* recuperación *f* (c) *Fam (sexual partner)* ligue *m*, *RP, Ven* levante *m*; **p. line** frase *f* típica para ligar

picky ['pɪkɪ] *adj Fam* exigente, escrupuloso(a)

picnic ['pɪknɪk] 1 *n* picnic *m*, comida *f* campestre; **to go on a p.** ir de picnic; *Fam Fig* **it was no p.** *(wasn't easy)* tuvo bemoles, se las trajo; **p. basket** or **hamper** cesta *f* de merienda

2 *vi (pt & pp* **picnicked**) ir de picnic

picnicker ['pɪknɪkə(r)] *n* excursionista *mf*

Pict [pɪkt] *n Hist* picto(a) *m,f*

pictorial [pɪk'tɔːrɪəl] *adj* gráfico(a), ilustrado(a)

picture ['pɪktʃə(r)] 1 *n* (a) *(painting)* cuadro *m*, pintura *f*; *(drawing)* dibujo *m*; *(in book)* ilustración *f*; *(photograph)* fotografía *f*; *(on TV, in mind)* imagen *f*; **he's the p. of health** es la viva imagen de la salud; *Fig* **the political/economic p.** el panorama político/económico; *Fig* **to put sb in the p.** poner a alguien al tanto or en situación; *Fam Fig* **I get the p.** ya veo, ya entiendo; **p. book** libro *m* ilustrado; **p. frame** marco *m*; **p. gallery** pinacoteca *f*; **p. messaging** mensajería *f* de imágenes; **p. postcard** postal *f*; **p. window** ventanal *m*

(b) *Fam (movie)* película *f*

2 *vt* (a) *(imagine)* imaginarse; **I can't p. him as a teacher** no me lo imagino (trabajando) de profesor (b) *(represent, portray)* retratar

picturesque [pɪktʃə'resk] *adj* pintoresco(a)

pidgin ['pɪdʒɪn] *n* lengua *f* híbrida, (lengua *f)* pidgin *m*; **p. English** = mezcla de inglés con un idioma local

pie [paɪ] *n (of meat, fish)* empanada *f*, pastel *m*, *Col, CSur* torta *f*; *(of fruit)* tarta *f*; *Fam* **p. in the sky** castillos *mpl* en el aire; **p. chart** gráfico *m* de sectores

piece [piːs] *n* (a) *(of paper, meat, cake)* trozo *m*, pedazo *m*; *(of cloth, music)* pieza *f*; *(newspaper article)* artículo *m*; **a p. of advice** un consejo; *Fig* **it was a p. of cake** *(very easy)* estaba tirado or chupado; **a p. of carelessness** un descuido; **a p. of clothing** una prenda (de vestir); **a p. of furniture** un mueble; **a p. of land** un terreno; **that was a p. of (good) luck!** ¡fue (una) suerte!; **a p. of luggage** un bulto (de equipaje); **a p. of news** una noticia; **p. rate** *(pay)* tarifa *f* a destajo

(b) *(in games, of jigsaw puzzle)* pieza *f*; *(in dominoes, checkers)* ficha *f*

(c) *(coin)* **five/fifty cent p.** moneda *f* de cinco/cincuenta centavos

(d) *(of artillery)* pieza *f*; *Fam (gun)* pipa *f*, *Am* fierro *m*

(e) *(idioms)* **they are all of a p.** están cortados por el mismo patrón; **to be still in one p.** estar sano(a) y salvo(a); **to give sb a p. of one's mind** cantar las cuarenta a alguien; **he said his p.** dijo lo que pensaba; **p. by p.** paso por paso, poco a poco; *Fig* **to go to pieces** derrumbarse; **to fall to pieces** caerse a pedazos; **to take sth to pieces** desmontar algo

▶**piece together** *vt sep (parts)* montar; *(broken object)* recomponer; *(facts)* reconstruir; *(evidence)* componer

piecemeal ['piːsmiːl] **1** *adj* deslavazado(a), poco sistemático(a)
 2 *adv* deslavazadamente, desordenadamente

piecework ['piːswɜːk] *n* (trabajo *m* a) destajo *m*

pieceworker ['piːswɜːkə(r)] *n* trabajador(ora) *m,f* a destajo

pied-à-terre ['pjeɪdæ'teə(r)] *n* = segunda vivienda, a menudo en una ciudad o un país diferente

pier [pɪə(r)] *n (landing stage)* muelle *m*, embarcadero *m*; *(with seaside amusements)* malecón *m*; *(of bridge)* pilar *m*

pierce [pɪəs] *vt* perforar; **to have one's ears pierced** hacerse agujeros en las orejas

piercing ['pɪəsɪŋ] **1** *n (for body adornment)* piercing *m*
 2 *adj (voice, sound, look)* penetrante; *(wind)* cortante

piety ['paɪətɪ] *n* piedad *f*

pig [pɪg] **1** *n* (a) *(animal)* cerdo *m*, puerco *m*, *Am* chancho *m* (b) *Fam (greedy person)* comilón(ona) *m,f*, glotón(ona) *m,f*, *Am* chancho *m*; *(unpleasant person)* cerdo(a) *m,f*, asqueroso(a) *m,f*, *Am* chancho *m* (c) *very Fam (policeman) Esp* madero *m*, *Andes, Pan* paco *m*, *Méx* tamarindo *m*, *RP* cana *m* (d) *Fam (idioms)* **to buy a p. in a poke** recibir gato por liebre; **to make a p. of oneself** ponerse hasta las orejas de comida; **pigs might fly!** ¡que te crees tú eso!, *Esp* ¡y yo soy la reina de los mares!, *Méx* ¡y yo soy el presidente de la República!, *RP* ¡y yo soy Gardel!
 2 *vt (pt & pp* **pigged)** *Fam* **to p. oneself** ponerse las botas (comiendo)
 ► **pig out** *vi Fam* ponerse las botas (comiendo)

pigeon ['pɪdʒɪn] *n* paloma *f*

pigeonhole ['pɪdʒɪnhəʊl] **1** *n* casillero *m*, casilla *f*
 2 *vt* encasillar

piggy ['pɪgɪ] *Fam* **1** *n* cerdito(a) *m,f*, *Am* chanchito(a) *m,f*; **p. bank** hucha *f*, *Am* alcancía *f (en forma de cerdito)*
 2 *adj* **p. eyes** ojillos *mpl* de cerdo

piggyback ['pɪgɪbæk] *n* **to give sb a p.** llevar a alguien a cuestas

pigheaded [pɪg'hedɪd] *adj* cabezota, testarudo(a)

piglet ['pɪglɪt] *n* cochinillo *m*, cerdito *m*

pigment ['pɪgmənt] *n* pigmento *m*

pigmentation [pɪgmən'teɪʃən] *n* pigmentación *f*

pigmy = **pygmy**

pigpen ['pɪgpen], **pigsty** ['pɪgstaɪ] *n also Fig* pocilga *f*

pigtail ['pɪgteɪl] *n (plaited)* trenza *f*; *(loose)* coleta *f*

pike¹ [paɪk] *n (weapon)* pica *f*

pike² *n (fish)* lucio *m*

Pilates® [pɪ'lɑːteɪz] *n* Pilates® *n*

pilchard ['pɪltʃəd] *n* sardina *f*

pile [paɪl] **1** *n* (a) *(heap)* pila *f*, montón *m*; **to put in(to) a p.**, **to make a p. of** apilar; *Fam* **she made her p. in property** se forró *or Méx* se llenó de lana *or RP* se llenó de guita con el negocio inmobiliario; *Fam* **to have piles of** *or* **a p. of work to do** tener un montón de trabajo que hacer; *Fam Fig* **to be at the top/bottom of the p.** estar en lo más alto/bajo de la escala (b) *(of carpet)* pelo *m* (c) *Phys* **(atomic) p.** pila *f* atómica (d) *(building)* mansión *f*; *(column, pillar)* pilar *m*; **p. driver** martinete *m*
 2 *vt* amontonar, apilar; **they piled food onto my plate** me llenaron el plato de comida
 3 *vi Fam* **to p. into a car** meterse atropelladamente en un coche *or Am* carro *or CSur* auto
 ► **pile in** *vi* meterse atropelladamente
 ► **pile on** *vt sep* **to p. on the pressure** aumentar la presión al máximo
 ► **pile out** *vi* salir atropelladamente
 ► **pile up** *vi (dirty clothes, work)* acumularse, apilarse

piles [paɪlz] *npl (hemorrhoids)* almorranas *fpl*

pileup ['paɪlʌp] *n Fam (of cars)* choque *m* masivo

pilfer ['pɪlfə(r)] *vt & vi* hurtar, *Esp* sisar

pilgrim ['pɪlgrɪm] *n* peregrino(a) *m,f*

pilgrimage ['pɪlgrɪmɪdʒ] *n* peregrinación *f*, peregrinaje *m*; **to go on a p., to make a p.** hacer una peregrinación

pill [pɪl] *n* pastilla *f*, píldora *f*; **the p.** *(contraceptive)* la píldora; **to be on the p.** tomar la píldora

pillage ['pɪlɪdʒ] **1** *n* pillaje *m*, saqueo *m*
 2 *vt & vi* saquear

pillar ['pɪlə(r)] *n (of building)* pilar *m*; *(of fire)* columna *f*; *Fig* **a p. of society/the Church** uno de los pilares de la sociedad/la Iglesia; **from p. to post** de la Ceca a la Meca; **to be a p. of strength** ser como una roca

pillion ['pɪljən] *n* **p. (seat)** asiento *m* trasero

pillory ['pɪlərɪ] **1** *n* picota *f*
 2 *vt (ridicule)* poner en la picota

pillow ['pɪləʊ] *n* almohada *f*

pillowcase ['pɪləʊkeɪs], **pillowslip** ['pɪləʊslɪp] *n* funda *f* de almohada

pilot ['paɪlət] **1** *n (of plane, ship)* piloto *mf*; *TV* **p. (program)** programa *m* piloto; **p. light** piloto *m*; **p. scheme/study** proyecto *m*/estudio *m* piloto
 2 *vt (plane, ship)* pilotar

pimp [pɪmp] *n* proxeneta *m*, *Esp* chulo *m*, *RP* cafiolo *m*

pimple ['pɪmpəl] *n* grano *m*

pimply ['pɪmplɪ] *adj* lleno(a) de granos

PIN [pɪn] *n Fin (abbr* **personal identification number)** P. **(number)** PIN *m*

pin [pɪn] **1** *n (for sewing)* alfiler *m*; *(bolt)* clavija *f*; *(of grenade)* seguro *m*; *Med* clavo *m*; **you could have heard a p. drop** se oía el vuelo de una mosca; *Fam* **pins and needles** hormigueo *m*; **(firing) p.** percutor *m*; **(safety) p.** *(for fastening clothes)* imperdible *m*, *Am* alfiler *m* de gancho, *CAm, Méx* seguro *m*; **p. money** dinero *m* extra
 2 *vt (pt & pp* **pinned)** *(fasten with pin)* clavar; *(hold still)* sujetar, atrapar; **to p. sb against** *or* **to a wall** atrapar a alguien contra una pared; **to p. the blame on sb** cargar la culpa a alguien; **he pinned his hopes on them** puso *or* cifró sus esperanzas en ellos
 ► **pin down** *vt sep* (a) *(trap)* atrapar, sujetar (b) *(identify)* identificar (c) *(force to be definite)* **we tried to p. him down to a date** intentamos que se comprometiera a dar una fecha
 ► **pin up** *vt sep (notice)* clavar; *(hair)* recoger; *(hem)* coger *or* prender con alfileres

pinafore ['pɪnəfɔː(r)] *n* **p. dress** *Esp* pichi *m*, *CSur, Méx* jumper *m*

pinball ['pɪnbɔːl] *n* **to play p.** jugar a la máquina *or* al flíper; **p. machine** máquina *f* de bolas, flíper *m*

pincer ['pɪnsə(r)] *n (of crab, insect)* pinza *f*; *Mil* **p. movement** movimiento *m* de tenaza

pincers ['pɪnsəz] *npl (tool)* tenazas *fpl*

pinch [pɪntʃ] **1** *n* (a) *(action)* pellizco *m*; *(small amount)* pizca *f*, pellizco *m*; **to give sb a p.** dar un pellizco a alguien (b) *(idioms)* **to feel the p.** pasar estrecheces; **to take sth with a p. of salt** no tomarse algo muy en serio, no dar demasiado crédito a algo
 2 *vt (nip)* pellizcar; **these shoes p. my feet** estos zapatos me aprietan
 3 *vi (shoes)* apretar

pinch-hit ['pɪntʃ'hɪt] *vi* (a) *(in baseball)* = sustituir a un bateador en un momento decisivo del partido (b) *Fig (substitute)* **to p. for sb** sustituir a alguien *(en una emergencia)*

pincushion ['pɪnkʊʃən] *n* acerico *m*, alfiletero *m*

pine¹ [paɪn] *n (tree, wood)* pino *m*; **p. cone** piña *f*; **p. forest** pinar *m*; **p. needle** aguja *f* de pino; **p. nut** piñón *m*

pine² *vi* **to p. for sth/sb** echar de menos *or* añorar algo/a alguien, *Am* extrañar algo/a alguien
 ► **pine away** *vi* consumirse de pena

pineapple ['paɪnæpəl] *n* piña *f*, *RP* ananá *m*

ping [pɪŋ] **1** *n* sonido *m* metálico
 2 *vi* sonar

Ping-Pong® [ˈpɪŋpɒŋ] n pimpón m, ping-pong m

pinhead [ˈpɪnhed] n Fam (stupid person) majadero(a) m,f

pinion [ˈpɪnjən] **1** n (cogwheel) piñón m
   2 vt (restrain) inmovilizar, sujetar; **to p. sb to the ground** inmovilizar a alguien en el suelo

pink [pɪŋk] **1** n (**a**) (color m) rosa m; Fam **to be in the p.** (be well) estar como una rosa (**b**) (flower) clavel m
   2 adj rosa; **to turn p.** sonrojarse; Fam **to get a p. slip** ser despedido(a); **the p. dollar** = el poder adquisitivo de los homosexuales; **p. gin** pink gin m, ginebra f con angostura

pinkeye [ˈpɪŋkaɪ] n conjuntivitis f inv

pinkie, pinky [ˈpɪŋkɪ] n (dedo m) meñique m

pinnacle [ˈpɪnəkəl] n (of mountain, fame, career) cima f, cumbre f

pinpoint [ˈpɪnpɔɪnt] vt señalar, precisar

pinprick [ˈpɪnprɪk] n pinchazo m

pinstripe [ˈpɪnstraɪp] adj de raya diplomática; **p. suit** traje m de raya diplomática

pint [paɪnt] n (measurement) pinta f (0,57 litros)

pinto bean [ˈpɪntəʊˈbiːn] n alubia f pinta, Am frijol m or CSur poroto m pinto

pint-size(d) [ˈpaɪntsaɪz(d)] adj Fam diminuto(a), pequeña-jo(a)

pinup [ˈpɪnʌp] n Fam (**a**) (poster) **pinups** posters mpl de chicas ligeritas de ropa (**b**) (woman) modelo f de revista (erótica)

pioneer [paɪəˈnɪə(r)] **1** n also Fig pionero(a) m,f
   2 vt iniciar, promover

pioneering [paɪəˈnɪərɪŋ] adj pionero(a)

pious [ˈpaɪəs] adj pío(a), piadoso(a); **a p. hope** una vana ilusión

piously [ˈpaɪəslɪ] adv piadosamente

pip [pɪp] n (**a**) (of fruit) pepita f (**b**) (on card, die) punto m

pipe [paɪp] **1** n (**a**) (tube) tubería f; (musical instrument) flauta f; **the pipes** (bagpipes) la gaita; **p. band** grupo m de gaiteros (**b**) (for smoking) pipa f; **to smoke a p.** fumarse una pipa; Fam Fig **put that in your p. and smoke it!** Esp ¡toma del frasco, Carrasco!, Am ¡tómate esa!; **p. cleaner** desatascador m; **p. dream** sueño m imposible
   2 vt (water, oil) conducir mediante tuberías

▸**pipe down** vi Fam cerrar el pico, callarse

▸**pipe up** vi hacerse oír

pipeline [ˈpaɪplaɪn] n tubería f, conducto m; **oil p.** oleoducto m; Fig **there are several projects in the p.** hay en preparación varios proyectos

piper [ˈpaɪpə(r)] n (bagpipe player) gaitero(a) m,f; Prov **he who pays the p. calls the tune** el que paga, manda

pipette [pɪˈpet] n pipeta f

piping [ˈpaɪpɪŋ] **1** n (**a**) (pipes) tuberías fpl, tubos mpl (**b**) (sound of bagpipes) (sonido m de) gaitas fpl (**c**) (on uniform) ribetes mpl
   2 adj (sound) agudo(a); **a p. voice** una voz de pito
   3 adv **p. hot** caliente, calentito(a)

pipsqueak [ˈpɪpskwiːk] n Fam pelagatos mf inv

piquant [ˈpiːkənt] adj fuerte, picante

pique [piːk] n **1** n rabia f; **in a fit of p.** en una rabieta
   2 vt molestar

piracy [ˈpaɪrəsɪ] n (gen) & Com piratería f

piranha [pɪˈrɑːnə] n piraña f

pirate [ˈpaɪrɪt] n pirata mf; **p. edition** edición f pirata; **p. radio** radio f pirata

pirouette [pɪrʊˈet] **1** n pirueta f
   2 vi hacer piruetas

Pisa [ˈpiːzə] n Pisa

Pisces [ˈpaɪsiːz] n (sign of zodiac) Piscis m inv; **to be (a) P.** ser Piscis

piss [pɪs] very Fam **1** n (urine) meada f; **to have a p.** mear, echar

una meada; **p. artist** (useless person) puto(a) inútil m,f; (drunk) borrachuzo(a) m,f, Am borrachón(ona) m,f
   2 vt **to p. oneself** mearse encima, mearse en los pantalones
   3 vi mear

▸**piss around, piss about** vi very Fam (behave foolishly) hacer el Esp gilipollas or Am pendejo; (waste time) tocarse los huevos

▸**piss off** very Fam vt sep (annoy) joder, cabrear, Méx fregar; **to be pissed off (with)** estar cabreado(a) (con), Méx estar enchilado(a) (con)

pissed [pɪst] adj very Fam (angry) cabreado(a); **to be p.** estar cabreado(a)

pisser [ˈpɪsə(r)] n very Fam (**a**) (annoying situation) ¡qué putada!, Col, RP ¡qué cagada!, Méx ¡es una chingadera! (**b**) (penis) verga f, Esp picha f, Chile pico m, Méx pájaro m, RP pija f

pistachio [pɪˈstɑːʃɪəʊ] (pl pistachios) n (nut) pistacho m; (tree) alfóncigo m, pistachero m

piste [piːst] n (ski slope) pista f

pistol [ˈpɪstəl] n (gun) pistola f; **p. shot** disparo m (de pistola), pistoletazo m

piston [ˈpɪstən] n émbolo m, pistón m

pit[1] [pɪt] n (**a**) (hole in ground) hoyo m; (coal mine) mina f; **the news hit him in the p. of his stomach** la noticia le dolió en lo más profundo; Fam **it's/he's the pits!** ¡es penoso! (**b**) Theat foso m (de la orquesta); **the pits** (in motor racing) los boxes; **p. stop** (in motor race) parada f en boxes; (in journey) parada f (**c**) (on metal, glass) marca f; (on skin) picadura f (**d**) St Exch corro m

pit[2] **1** n (of cherry) hueso m, pipo m, RP carozo m; (of peach, plum) hueso m, RP carozo m
   2 vt (cherry, olive) deshuesar

pit[3] vt (pt & pp pitted) **to p. sb against sb** enfrentar a alguien con alguien; **to p. oneself against sb** enfrentarse con alguien; **she pitted her wits against them** midió su ingenio con el de ellos

pita [ˈpɪtə] n **p. (bread)** pan m (de) pita

pit-a-pat [ˈpɪtəˈpæt], **pitter-patter** [ˈpɪtəˈpætə(r)] **1** n (of rain) tamborileo m, repiqueteo m; (of feet, heart) golpeteo m
   2 adv **to go p.** (rain) repiquetear; (feet, heart) golpetear

pitch[1] [pɪtʃ] n (tar) brea f

pitch[2] **1** n (**a**) (for sport) campo m (**b**) Mus (of note) tono m; Fig **to reach such a p. that...** llegar a tal punto que...; **p. pipe** diapasón m (**c**) (talk) (sales) **p.** charla f para vender (**d**) (slope) (of roof, ceiling) pendiente f
   2 vt (**a**) (throw) lanzar (**b**) (aim) **our new model is pitched to appeal to executives** nuestro nuevo modelo está diseñado para atraer a ejecutivos; **he pitched the talk at the right level** le imprimió a la charla or CAm, Méx plática el tono or nivel apropiado (**c**) (set up) (tent) montar
   3 vi (ship, plane) cabecear, tambalearse

▸**pitch in** vi colaborar, echar una mano

pitch-black [pɪtʃˈblæk] adj oscuro(a) como boca de lobo

pitched [pɪtʃt] adj (**a**) (sloping) en pendiente (**b**) **p. battle** batalla f campal

pitcher[1] [ˈpɪtʃə(r)] n (jug) jarra f; (large and made of clay) cántaro m

pitcher[2] n (in baseball) lanzador(ora) m,f

pitchfork [ˈpɪtʃfɔːk] n horca f

piteous [ˈpɪtɪəs] adj penoso(a), patético(a)

pitfall [ˈpɪtfɔːl] n (danger) peligro m, riesgo m

pith [pɪθ] n (of orange) piel f blanca; (of argument, idea) meollo m; **p. helmet** salacot m

pithy [ˈpɪθɪ] adj (style, story) sustancioso(a), enjundioso(a)

pitiable [ˈpɪtɪəbəl] adj lamentable

pitiful [ˈpɪtɪfʊl] adj (arousing pity) lastimoso(a); (deplorable) lamentable, deplorable

pitifully [ˈpɪtɪfʊlɪ] adv (arousing pity) lastimosamente; (deplor-

ably) deplorablemente, lamentablemente

pitiless ['pɪtɪlɪs] *adj* despiadado(a)

pitilessly ['pɪtɪlɪslɪ] *adv* despiadadamente

pittance ['pɪtəns] *n* miseria *f*

pitter-patter = pit-a-pat

pituitary gland [pɪ'tjuːɪtərɪ'glænd] *n* Anat hipófisis *f inv*; glándula *f* pituitaria

pity ['pɪtɪ] **1** *n* (**a**) *(compassion)* piedad *f*, compasión *f*; **to take** *or* **have p. (on sb)** apiadarse *or* compadecerse (de alguien); **to show no p.** no mostrar compasión; **for p.'s sake!** ¡por el amor de Dios! (**b**) *(misfortune)* **it's a p. that…** es una lástima *or* una pena que…; **what a p.!** ¡qué pena!, ¡qué lástima!; **more's the p.** por desgracia

  2 *vt* compadecer

pitying ['pɪtɪɪŋ] *adj* compasivo(a)

pityingly ['pɪtɪɪŋlɪ] *adv* compasivamente, con compasión

pivot ['pɪvət] **1** *n* *(of turning mechanism)* eje *m*, pivote *m*; *(key person)* eje *m*

  2 *vi (turning mechanism)* pivotar (**on** sobre); *(plan)* girar (**on** *or* **around** en torno a)

pivotal ['pɪvətəl] *adj* crucial

pixel ['pɪksəl] *n* Comptr píxel *m*, elemento *m* de imagen

pixie ['pɪksɪ] *n* duende *m*

pizza ['piːtsə] *n* pizza *f*; **p. parlor** pizzería *f*

PJs ['piːdʒeɪz] *npl* Fam pijama *m*, Am piyama *m or f*

Pk *(abbr* **Park***)* parque *m*

pkt *(abbr* **packet***)* paquete *m*

Pl *(abbr* **Place***)* C/, calle *f*

placard ['plækɑːd] *n* pancarta *f*

placate [plə'keɪt] *vt* aplacar

place [pleɪs] **1** *n* (**a**) *(location)* lugar *m*, sitio *m*; *(in street names)* calle *f*; **to move from one p. to another** ir de un lugar a otro; **a good p. to meet people** un buen sitio para conocer (a) gente; **I'm looking for a p. to live** estoy buscando casa; **can you recommend a p. to eat?** ¿me puedes recomendar un restaurante?; **this is no p. for you** este no es lugar para ti; **I can't be in two places at once!** ¡no puedo estar en dos sitios a la vez!; *Fam* **she has worked all over the p.** ha trabajado en mil sitios; *Fig* **his explanation was all over the p.** su explicación fue muy liosa; *Fam* **my hair is all over the p.** llevo el pelo hecho un desastre; **at the interview he was all over the p.** en la entrevista no dio pie con bola *or Esp* una a derechas; *Fam Fig* **to go places** *(be successful)* llegar lejos; **p. of birth/death** lugar de nacimiento/defunción; **p. kick** *(in football, rugby)* puntapié *m* colocado; **p. name** topónimo *m*; **p. of work/residence** lugar de trabajo/residencia; **p. of worship** templo *m*

  (**b**) *(assigned to person)* puesto *m*; *(assigned to thing)* sitio *m*; *(at college, on course)* plaza *f*; **to find a p. for sb** *(job)* encontrar colocación a alguien; **there's a time and a p. for everything** cada cosa a su tiempo; **to hold sth in p.** sujetar algo; **he had lost his p.** *(in a book)* había perdido la página por la que iba; **to take p.** tener lugar; **to take sb's p.** ocupar el puesto de alguien; *Fig* **out of p.** *(person, remark)* fuera de lugar

  (**c**) *Fam (residence)* casa *f*; **a little p. in the country** una casita en el campo; **your p. or mine?** ¿en tu casa o en la mía?

  (**d**) *(seat)* sitio *m*, asiento *m*; **to keep sb's p. in a line** guardarle a alguien el sitio en una cola; **to set** *or* **lay an extra p. at table** poner un cubierto *or* servicio más en la mesa; **to change places with sb** cambiarle el sitio a alguien; *Fig* **put yourself in my p.** ponte en mi lugar; **p. mat** mantel *m* individual

  (**e**) *(in competition, society)* puesto *m*, lugar *m*; **in first/second p.** en primer/segundo lugar; **in the first p.…** en primer lugar…; **in the second p.…** en segundo lugar…; **I don't know why they gave him the job in the first p.** no sé

cómo se les ocurrió darle el trabajo; **you have to know your p.** hay que saber estar (en su sitio); **to put sb in his p.** poner a alguien en su sitio

  (**f**) *Math* **to three decimal places** con tres (cifras) decimales

  2 *vt* (**a**) *(put)* colocar, poner; **the house is well placed** la casa está bien situada; **to be well placed to do sth** estar en una buena posición para hacer algo; **I know his face but I can't p. him** conozco su cara, pero no sé de qué

  (**b**) *Com & Fin* **to p. an order (with sb)** hacer un pedido (a alguien); **to p. a contract with sb** conceder un contrato a alguien; **to p. a bet (on sth)** hacer una apuesta (por algo)

  (**c**) *(find a job for)* colocar

  (**d**) *(classify)* situar, colocar; **to be placed third** clasificarse en tercer lugar

placebo [plæ'siːbəʊ] *(pl* **placebos***) n also Fig* placebo *m*

placement ['pleɪsmənt] *n (for trainee, student)* colocación *f* en prácticas

placenta [plə'sentə] *(pl* **placentas** *or* **placentae** [plə'sentiː]*) n* placenta *f*

placid ['plæsɪd] *adj* plácido(a)

placing ['pleɪsɪŋ] *n (act of putting)* colocación *f*; *(situation, position)* ubicación *f*, posición *f*

plagiarism ['pleɪdʒərɪzəm] *n* plagio *m*

plagiarize ['pleɪdʒəraɪz] *vt* plagiar

plague [pleɪg] **1** *n (disease)* peste *f*; *(of insects, frogs)* plaga *f*; **to avoid sb like the p.** huir de alguien como de la peste

  2 *vt (of person)* molestar, fastidiar; *(of problem)* fastidiar; **to p. sb with questions** asediar a alguien a *or* con preguntas

plaice [pleɪs] *(pl* **plaice***) n (fish)* solla *f*, platija *f*

plaid [plæd] *n (fabric)* tela *f* escocesa

plain [pleɪn] **1** *n* llanura *f*

  2 *adj* (**a**) *(clear, unambiguous)* claro(a); **to make sth p. to sb** dejar claro algo a alguien; **I'll be quite p. with you** voy a ser claro con usted; *Fam* **it's as p. as the nose on your face** está más claro que el agua; **in p. English** en lenguaje llano; **a p. answer** una respuesta directa *or* clara; *Fig* **it was p. sailing** fue pan comido; **p. speaking** franqueza *f*; **the p. truth** la verdad pura y simple (**b**) *(simple) (style, garment)* sencillo(a); *Fam* **that's just p. foolishness** es pura tontería; **p. chocolate** chocolate *m* amargo; **in p. clothes** *(policeman)* de paisano; **p. flour** harina *f* sin levadura (**c**) *(not beautiful)* feo(a); **a p. Jane** un patito feo

plainly ['pleɪnlɪ] *adv* (**a**) *(clearly)* claramente; **to speak p.** hablar con franqueza (**b**) *(simply) (to live, dress)* con sencillez

plainness ['pleɪnnɪs] *n (of style, expression, food)* sencillez *f*; *(of looks)* falta *f* de atractivo

plainspoken [pleɪn'spəʊkən] *adj* franco(a), directo(a)

plaintiff ['pleɪntɪf] *n Law* demandante *mf*

plaintive ['pleɪntɪv] *adj* lastimero(a)

plaintively ['pleɪntɪvlɪ] *adv* lastimosamente

plait [plæt] **1** *n* trenza *f*

  2 *vt* trenzar

plan [plæn] **1** *n* (**a**) *(proposal, intention)* plan *m*; **a change of p.** un cambio de planes; **everything went according to p.** todo fue según lo previsto; **the best p. would be to…** lo mejor sería…; **what are your plans for the summer?** ¿qué planes tienes para el verano?; **to have other plans** tener otras cosas que hacer (**b**) *(of building, town)* plano *m*; *(of essay, novel)* esquema *m*

  2 *vt (pt & pp* **planned***)* (**a**) *(arrange)* planear; **to p. to do sth** planear hacer algo; **it all went as planned** todo fue según lo previsto (**b**) *(design) (building)* proyectar; *(economy)* planificar

  3 *vi* hacer planes; **to p. for the future** hacer planes para el futuro

▶**plan out** *vt sep* planificar

plane¹ [pleɪn] *n (surface, level)* plano *m*

plane² n (airplane) avión m; **by p.** en avión; **p. ticket** billete m or Am boleto m or Am pasaje m de avión

plane³ 1 n (tool) cepillo m
2 vt cepillar

plane⁴ n **p. (tree)** plátano m

planet ['plænɪt] n planeta m

planetarium [plænɪ'teərɪəm] (pl **planetariums** or **planetaria** [plænɪ'teərɪə]) n planetario m

planetary ['plænɪtərɪ] adj planetario(a)

plank [plæŋk] n (of wood) tablón m; Fig (central element) punto m principal; (of political platform) elemento m

plankton ['plæŋktən] n plancton m

planner ['plænə(r)] n encargado(a) m,f de la planificación; (town planner) urbanista mf

planning ['plænɪŋ] n planificación f; (town planning) urbanismo m; **it's still at the p. stage** aún está en fase de estudio

plant [plɑːnt] **1** n (a) (living thing) planta f; **p. life** flora f (b) Ind (equipment) maquinaria f; (factory) fábrica f, planta f; **p. leasing** alquiler m de equipo; **p. maintenance** mantenimiento m de la planta
2 vt (tree, flower) plantar; (crops, field) sembrar; (bomb) colocar; **to p. an idea in sb's mind** inculcar una idea a alguien; Fam **to p. sth on sb** endosar algo a alguien

plantain ['plæntɪn] n (a) (wild plant) llantén m (b) (similar to banana) (fruit) plátano m, RP banana f; (tree) platanero m

plantation [plæn'teɪʃən] n plantación f

planter ['plɑːntə(r)] n (person) plantador(ora) m,f; (machine) sembradora f; **p.'s punch** = ponche de ron y frutas con hielo molido

plaque [plɑːk] n (a) (bronze, marble) placa f (b) (on teeth) placa f dental (bacteriana)

plasma ['plæzmə] n plasma m; Comptr **p. screen** pantalla f de plasma

plaster ['plɑːstə(r)] **1** n (on wall) yeso m; **p. of Paris** escayola f; **to put a leg in p.** escayolar una pierna; **p. cast** escayola f
2 vt (a) (wall) enyesar, enlucir (b) (cover) cubrir (**with** de); **plastered with mud** embarrado(a), cubierto(a) de barro; **his name was plastered over the front pages** su nombre aparecía en los titulares or Méx, RP encabezados de todas las portadas

plasterboard ['plɑːstəbɔːd] n pladur® m

plastered ['plæstəd] adj Fam (drunk) trompa; **to be p.** estar trompa

plasterer ['plɑːstərə(r)] n enlucidor(ora) m,f

plastic ['plæstɪk] **1** n plástico m
2 adj (cup, bag) de plástico; **p. bullet** bala f de goma; **p. explosive** (explosivo m) plástico m; **p. surgeon** cirujano(a) m,f plástico(a); **p. surgery** cirugía f plástica; **p. wrap** plástico m transparente (para envolver alimentos)

plasticity [plæs'tɪsɪtɪ] n (of material) plasticidad f; Fig (of mind) ductilidad f, adaptabilidad f

plate [pleɪt] **1** n (a) (for food) plato m; (for church offering) platillo m; Fam Fig **to hand sth to sb on a p.** poner algo en bandeja a alguien; **p. rack** escurreplatos m inv (b) (sheet of metal, glass, plastic) placa f; **gold/silver p.** oro m/plata f chapado(a); **p. glass** vidrio m para cristaleras
2 vt (with gold) dorar; (with silver) platear

plateau ['plætəʊ] n Geog meseta f; Fig **to reach a p.** (career, economy) estabilizarse

platform ['plætfɔːm] n (a) (raised flat surface) plataforma f; (in train station) (where passengers stand) andén m; (where train stops) vía f; Rail **p. 4** vía 4; **p. shoes** zapatos mpl de plataforma; **p. soles** suelas fpl de plataforma (b) (at meeting) tribuna f; (political program) programa m

platinum ['plætɪnəm] n Chem platino m; **p. blond hair** pelo m rubio platino

platitude ['plætɪtjuːd] n tópico m, trivialidad f

platonic [plə'tɒnɪk] adj platónico(a)

platoon [plə'tuːn] n Mil pelotón m

platter ['plætə(r)] n (serving plate) fuente f

platypus ['plætɪpəs] n ornitorrinco m

plausibility [plɔːzɪ'bɪlɪtɪ] n plausibilidad f

plausible ['plɔːzəbəl] adj (excuse, argument) plausible

play [pleɪ] **1** n (a) (drama) obra f (de teatro) (b) (of children) juego m; **at p.** jugando; **p. on words** juego de palabras (c) (in sport) juego m; **p. began at one o'clock** el juego comenzó a la una; **in p.** en juego; **out of p.** fuera del campo; Fig **to come into p.** entrar en juego; Fig **to make a p. for sth** tratar de conseguir algo (d) Tech juego m
2 vt (a) (game, sport) jugar a; (opponent) jugar contra; **to p. center** jugar de centro; **to p. soccer/chess** jugar al fútbol/ajedrez; **to p. sb at sth** jugar contra alguien a algo; **he decided not to p. Sanders** decidió no sacar a Sanders; **to p. a shot** (in golf, pool) dar un golpe, hacer un tiro; **to p. a card** jugar una carta; Fig **stop playing games!** ¡basta ya de juegos!; Fig **to p. ball** (co-operate) cooperar; **to p. the Stock Exchange** jugar a la bolsa; **to p. a joke** or **a trick on sb** gastarle una broma a alguien
(b) (in play, movie) interpretar; **to p. Macbeth** interpretar a Macbeth; Fig **to p. an important part (in sth)** desempeñar un papel importante (en algo); Fig **to p. no part in sth** (person) no tomar parte en algo; (thing, feeling) no tener nada que ver con algo; Fig **to p. the fool** hacer el tonto
(c) (musical instrument, piece) tocar; (record, CD, tape) poner
3 vi (a) (children) jugar; (animals) retozar; **to p. with sth** (pen, hair) juguetear con algo; Fig **to p. with an idea** darle vueltas a una idea; Fig **to p. with fire** jugar con fuego; Fam Fig **what's she playing at?** ¿a qué juega?
(b) (sportsperson) jugar; **to p. fair/dirty** jugar limpio/sucio; **to p. for money** jugar por or con dinero; Fig **to p. for time** intentar ganar tiempo; Fig **to p. into sb's hands** hacerle el juego a alguien, facilitarle las cosas a alguien; Fig **to p. safe** ir a lo seguro, no arriesgarse
(c) (musical instrument) sonar; (musician) tocar
(d) (actor) actuar; (movie) exhibirse; (play) representarse

▸**play around, play about** vi juguetear, jugar

▸**play along** vi seguir la corriente (**with** a)

▸**play back** vt sep **to p. back a recording** reproducir una grabación

▸**play down** vt sep restar importancia a

▸**play off** vt sep **she played her two enemies off against each other** enfrentó a sus dos enemigos entre sí

▸**play on 1** vt insep (exploit) (feelings, fears) aprovecharse de
2 vi (continue to play) (musician) seguir tocando; (sportsperson) seguir jugando

▸**play out** vt sep **the drama being played out before them** la tragedia que se desarrolla ante sus ojos

playacting ['pleɪæktɪŋ] n teatro m, cuento m

playback ['pleɪbæk] n reproducción f

playboy ['pleɪbɔɪ] n vividor m, playboy m

player ['pleɪə(r)] n (sportsperson) jugador(ora) m,f; (musician) intérprete mf; (actor) actor m, actriz f, intérprete mf

playful ['pleɪfʊl] adj (person, animal, mood) juguetón(ona); (remark) de or en broma

playfulness ['pleɪfʊlnɪs] n (of smile, remark, suggestion) carácter m juguetón

playground ['pleɪgraʊnd] n (at school) patio m de recreo; (in park) zona f de juegos

playgroup ['pleɪgruːp] n escuela f infantil, guardería f

playhouse ['pleɪhaʊs] n (theater) teatro m

playing ['pleɪɪŋ] n **p. card** carta f, naipe m; **p. field** campo m de juego

playmate ['pleɪmeɪt] n compañero(a) m,f de juegos

play-off ['pleɪɒf] n Sport (partido m de) desempate m

playpen ['pleɪpen] *n* parque *m*, corral *m*

playroom ['pleɪruːm] *n* cuarto *m* de juegos

plaything ['pleɪθɪŋ] *n* juguete *m*

playtime ['pleɪtaɪm] *n (at school)* recreo *m*

playwright ['pleɪraɪt] *n* dramaturgo(a) *m,f*, autor(ora) *m,f* teatral

plaza ['plɑːzə] *n (shopping center)* centro *m* comercial

plea [pliː] *n* (a) *(appeal)* petición *f*, súplica *f*, *Am* pedido *m*; **to make a p. for sth** suplicar algo (b) *(excuse)* excusa *f*; **on the p. that…** alegando que… (c) *Law* declaración *f*; **to enter a p. of guilty/not guilty** declararse culpable/inocente; **p. bargaining** = negociación extrajudicial entre el abogado y el fiscal por la que el acusado acepta su culpabilidad en cierto grado a cambio de no ser juzgado por un delito más grave

plead [pliːd] *(pt & pp* **pled** [pled]) **1** *vt Law* **to p. sb's case** *(lawyer)* defender a alguien; *Law* **to p. insanity** alegar enajenamiento de las facultades mentales; **to p. ignorance** alegar desconocimiento

2 *vi* **to p. with sb (to do sth)** implorar a alguien (que haga algo); *Law* **to p. guilty/not guilty** declararse culpable/ inocente

pleading ['pliːdɪŋ] *adj* suplicante

pleadingly ['pliːdɪŋlɪ] *adv (to look, ask)* suplicantemente

pleasant ['plezənt] *adj (remark, place, weather)* agradable; *(person)* agradable, simpático(a); *(surprise)* grato(a), agradable

pleasantly ['plezəntlɪ] *adv (to smile, behave)* con simpatía; **to be p. surprised** estar gratamente sorprendido(a)

pleasantry ['plezəntrɪ] *n (joke)* broma *f*; **to exchange pleasantries** *(polite remarks)* intercambiar cumplidos

please [pliːz] **1** *adv* por favor; **p. don't cry** no llores, por favor; **p. tell me…** dime…; **may I? — p. do** ¿puedo? — por favor *or* no faltaba más; **p. sit down** tome asiento, por favor; **p. don't interrupt!** ¡no interrumpas!; **yes, p.!** ¡sí!

2 *vt (give pleasure to)* complacer, agradar; **you can't p. everybody** no se puede complacer a todo el mundo; **p. yourself!** ¡como quieras!; **to be easy/hard to p.** ser fácil/ difícil de complacer; **p. God!** ¡ojalá!

3 *vi* (a) *(like)* **he does as he pleases** hace lo que quiere; **this way, if you p.** por aquí, por favor; **and then, if you p., he blamed me for it!** ¡y luego, por si fuera poco, me echó la culpa a mí! (b) *(give pleasure)* agradar, complacer; **to be eager to p.** estar ansioso(a) por agradar

pleased [pliːzd] *adj (happy)* contento(a); **to be p.** *(happy)* estar contento(a); **to be p. with sth/sb** *(satisfied)* estar satisfecho(a) *or* contento(a) con algo/alguien; **to be p. to do sth** alegrarse de hacer algo; **to be p. for sb** alegrarse por alguien; **he was as p. as Punch** estaba encantado de la vida; **he's very p. with himself** está muy satisfecho *or* pagado de sí mismo; **p. to meet you** encantado(a) (de conocerle); **I'm p. to say that…** tengo el gusto de comunicarles que…

pleasurable ['pleʒərəbəl] *adj* agradable, grato(a)

pleasure ['pleʒə(r)] *n* (a) *(contentment)* satisfacción *f*, placer *m*; **he took p. in informing them that they had been sacked** disfrutó mucho comunicándoles que habían sido despedidos; **it gave me great p.** fue un auténtico placer para mí; **with p.** con (mucho) gusto; **(it's) my p.!** ¡no hay de qué!; *Formal* **I have p. in informing you that…** tengo el gusto de *or* me complace informarles de que… (b) *(enjoyment)* placer *m*; **p. boat** barco *m* de recreo; **p. trip** viaje *m* de placer (c) *(will)* voluntad *f*; **at sb's p.** según disponga alguien

pleat [pliːt] *n (in sewing)* pliegue *m*

pleated ['pliːtɪd] *adj (skirt)* plisado(a)

pleb [pleb] *n Hist* **the plebs** la plebe

plebeian [plə'biːən] *n & adj* plebeyo(a) *m,f*

plebiscite ['plebɪsɪt] *n* plebiscito *m*

plectrum ['plektrəm] *n Mus* púa *f*, plectro *m*

pled [pled] *pt & pp of* **plead**

pledge [pledʒ] **1** *n* (a) *(promise)* promesa *f*; **the P. of Allegiance** la Jura de la Bandera *(en colegios estadounidenses)* (b) *(token)* prenda *f*

2 *vt (promise)* prometer; **to p. one's allegiance to the king** jurar fidelidad al rey; **to p. money** *(in radio, television appeal)* prometer hacer un donativo (de dinero)

plenary ['pliːnərɪ] *adj* plenario(a); **p. assembly** asamblea *f* plenaria; **p. (session)** sesión *f* plenaria

plenipotentiary [plenɪpə'tenʃərɪ] **1** *n* embajador(ora) *m,f* plenipotenciario(a)

2 *adj* plenipotenciario(a)

plentiful ['plentɪfʊl] *adj* abundante

plenty ['plentɪ] **1** *n* abundancia *f*; **land of p.** tierra *f* de la abundancia

2 *pron* **p. of time/money** mucho tiempo/dinero; **p. of food** mucha comida; **p. of books** muchos libros; **that's p.** es (más que) suficiente

3 *adv Fam* **it's p. big enough** es grande más que de sobra

plethora ['pleθərə] *n* plétora *f*

pleurisy ['plʊərɪsɪ] *n* pleuresía *f*

Plexiglas® ['pleksɪɡlɑːs] *n* plexiglás® *m*

pliability [plaɪə'bɪlɪtɪ], **pliancy** ['plaɪənsɪ] *n (of material)* maleabilidad *f*; *(of person)* flexibilidad *f*, ductilidad *f*

pliable ['plaɪəbəl], **pliant** ['plaɪənt] *adj (wood, plastic)* flexible; *(person)* influenciable

pliers ['plaɪəz] *npl* alicates *mpl*; **a pair of p.** unos alicates

plight [plaɪt] *n* trance *m*, situación *f* comprometida

plinth [plɪnθ] *n* pedestal *m*

PLO [piːe'ləʊ] *n (abbr* **Palestine Liberation Organization)** OLP *f*

plod [plɒd] *(pt & pp* **plodded)** *vi* (a) *(walk)* caminar con paso lento; **to p. on** seguir caminando *(con lentitud o esfuerzo)* (b) *(work)* **to p. (away)** trabajar pacientemente

plodding ['plɒdɪŋ] *adj (walk, rhythm, style)* lento(a) y cansino(a); *(worker)* laborioso(a) pero lento(a)

plonk [plɒŋk] **1** *n (sound)* golpe *m* (seco), ruido *m* (sordo)

2 *vt Fam* **to p. sth down** dejar *or* poner algo de golpe; **to p. oneself down in an armchair** dejarse caer (de golpe) en una butaca

plop [plɒp] **1** *n* glu(p) *m*, = sonido de algo al hundirse en un líquido

2 *vi (pt & pp* **plopped)** caer haciendo glup

plot [plɒt] **1** *n* (a) *(conspiracy)* trama *f*, complot *m* (b) *(of play, novel)* trama *f*, argumento *m*; *Fig* **the p. thickens** el asunto se complica (c) *(land)* terreno *m*; **(vegetable) p.** huerta *f*, huerto *m*

2 *vt (pt & pp* **plotted)** (a) *(plan)* tramar, planear; **to p. to do sth** tramar *or* planear hacer algo; **to p. a movie/novel** trazar el argumento de una película/novela (b) *(draw) (curve)* trazar; *(progress, development)* representar; **to p. a course** planear *or* trazar una ruta (en el mapa)

3 *vi (conspire)* confabularse, conspirar

plotter ['plɒtə(r)] *n (conspirator)* conspirador(ora) *m,f*

plotting ['plɒtɪŋ] *n (conspiring)* tramas *fpl*, complots *mpl*

plover ['plʌvə(r)] *n* chorlito *m*

plow [plaʊ] **1** *n* arado *m*; **the P.** *(constellation)* la Osa Mayor

2 *vt (field, furrow)* arar, labrar; *Fig* **to p. profits back into a company** reinvertir beneficios en una empresa

3 *vi* arar, labrar; *Fig* **to p. through sth** *(work, reading)* tomarse el trabajo de hacer algo; *Fig* **to p. into sth** *(of vehicle)* estrellarse contra algo

▶**plow on** *vi* esforzarse en seguir adelante (**with** con)

▶**plow up** *vt sep (field)* roturar; **the park had been plowed up by vehicles** los vehículos dejaron el parque lleno de surcos

plowman ['plaʊmən] *n* labrador *m*

ploy [plɔɪ] *n* estratagema *f*

pluck [plʌk] **1** *n (courage)* coraje *m*, valor *m*

2 *vt (hair, feathers)* arrancar; *(flower)* coger; *(chicken)* desplumar; **to p. one's eyebrows** depilarse las cejas; **they were plucked from danger by a helicopter** un helicóptero les sacó del peligro; **to p. a guitar** puntear (a la guitarra)

3 *vi* **to p. at sb's sleeve** tirar a alguien de la manga

▸**pluck up** *vt sep* **to p. up the courage to do sth** armarse de valor para hacer algo

pluckily ['plʌkɪlɪ] *adv* valientemente

plucky ['plʌkɪ] *adj* valiente

plug [plʌg] **1** *n* (**a**) *(for sink)* tapón *m* (**b**) *(electrical)* enchufe *m*; *Aut* (**spark**) **p.** bujía *f*; *Fam Fig* **to pull the p. on sth** acabar con algo (**c**) *(of tobacco)* rollo *m* (de tabaco de mascar) (**d**) *Fam (publicity)* publicidad *f*; **to give sth a p.** hacer publicidad de *or* promocionar algo

2 *vt (pt & pp* **plugged**) (**a**) *(block)* tapar, taponar; **to p. a leak** tapar una fuga (**b**) *Fam (promote)* hacer publicidad de, promocionar

▸**plug away** *vi Fam* trabajar con tesón (**at** en)

▸**plug in** *vt sep* enchufar

plug-and-play ['plʌgən'pleɪ] *adj Comptr* para enchufar y usar

plug-in ['plʌgɪn] *n Comptr* dispositivo *m* opcional

plum [plʌm] **1** *n (fruit)* ciruela *f*; **p. pudding** = pudín con pasas y otras frutas; **p. tree** ciruelo *m*

2 *adj* (**a**) *(color)* morado(a) (**b**) *Fam (very good)* **a p. job** un *Esp* chollo *or Méx* churro (de trabajo), *RP* un laburazo

plumage ['plu:mɪdʒ] *n* plumaje *m*

plumb [plʌm] **1** *n* **p. (line)** plomada *f*; **out of p.** torcido(a)

2 *adv* (**a**) *(exactly)* de lleno, directamente; **p. in the center** en todo *or* justo en el centro (**b**) *(utterly)* totalmente, completamente; **he's p. crazy** está totalmente *or* completamente loco

3 *vt (sea)* sondar; *Fig* **to p. the depths of** abismarse *or* sumergirse en las profundidades de

plumber ['plʌmə(r)] *n* fontanero(a) *m,f, Méx, RP, Ven* plomero(a) *m,f*

plumbing ['plʌmɪŋ] *n* (**a**) *(job)* fontanería *f, Méx, RP, Ven* plomería *f* (**b**) *(system)* cañerías *fpl*

plume [plu:m] *n (single feather)* pluma *f*; *(on hat)* penacho *m*; *(of smoke)* nube *f*, penacho *m*

plummet ['plʌmɪt] *vi also Fig* desplomarse, caer en picado, *Am* caer en picada

plump [plʌmp] **1** *adj* rechoncho(a)

2 *vt* **to p. oneself into an armchair** dejarse caer en una butaca

▸**plump down** *vt sep* dejar *or* poner de golpe; **she plumped herself down on the sofa** se dejó caer en el sofá

▸**plump for** *vt insep Fam (choose)* decidirse por

plunder ['plʌndə(r)] **1** *n (action)* saqueo *m*, pillaje *m*; *(loot)* botín *m*

2 *vt* saquear, expoliar

plunge [plʌndʒ] **1** *n (dive)* zambullida *f*; *Fig (decrease)* desplome *m*; *Fam Fig* **to take the p.** dar el paso (decisivo)

2 *vt* sumergir (**into** en); **to p. a knife into sb's back** hundir a alguien un cuchillo en la espalda; **to p. sb into despair** sumir a alguien en la desesperación

3 *vi (into water)* zambullirse (**into** en); *Fig (decrease)* desplomarse; **she plunged to her death** murió tras caer al vacío

plunger ['plʌndʒə(r)] *n (of syringe)* émbolo *m*; *(for clearing sink)* desatascador *m*

plunging ['plʌndʒɪŋ] *adj (prices)* en picado, *Am* en picada; **p. neckline** escote *m* pronunciado

pluperfect [plu:'pɜ:fɪkt] *n Gram* pluscuamperfecto *m*

plural ['plʊərəl] *n & adj Gram* plural *m*

pluralism ['plʊərəlɪzəm] *n* pluralismo *m*

pluralist ['plʊərəlɪst] *n & adj* pluralista *mf*

plurality [plʊə'rælɪtɪ] *n* (**a**) *(variety)* pluralidad *f* (**b**) **a p. of** la mayoría relativa de

plus [plʌs] **1** *n (pl* **plusses** ['plʌsɪz]) (**a**) *(sign)* signo *m* más (**b**) *(advantage)* ventaja *f*

2 *adj* **on the p. side the bicycle is light** esta bicicleta tiene la ventaja de ser ligera; **fifteen p.** de quince para arriba, más de quince; **I got a C p.** saqué un aprobado alto

3 *prep* más; **seven p. nine** siete más nueve; **two floors p. an attic** dos pisos y una buhardilla

plush [plʌʃ] **1** *n Tex* felpa *f*

2 *adj Fam* lujoso(a), *Esp* muy puesto(a)

Pluto ['plu:təʊ] *n (planet, god)* Plutón

plutonium [plu:'təʊnɪəm] *n Chem* plutonio *m*

ply[1] [plaɪ] *n* **three-p.** *(wood, paper handkerchief, tire)* de tres capas

ply[2] **1** *vt* **to p. one's trade** ejercer su oficio; **to p. sb with questions** acribillar a alguien a preguntas; **to p. sb with drink** ofrecer bebida insistentemente a alguien

2 *vi* **to p. between** cubrir la ruta entre

plywood ['plaɪwʊd] *n* contrachapado *m*

PM [pi:'em] *n (abbr* **Prime Minister**) primer(era) ministro(a) *m,f*

pm [pi:'em] *adv (abbr* **post meridiem**) p.m., post meridiem; **6 pm** las 6 de la tarde

PMS [pi:em'es] *n (abbr* **premenstrual syndrome**) síndrome *m* premenstrual

pneumatic [nju:'mætɪk] *adj* neumático(a); **p. drill** martillo *m* neumático; **p. tire** neumático *m*

pneumonia [nju:'məʊnɪə] *n* pulmonía *f*, neumonía *f*

PO [pi:'əʊ] *n (abbr* **Post Office**) oficina *f* de correos

poach[1] [pəʊtʃ] *vt Culin (eggs)* escalfar; *(fish)* cocer; **poached eggs** huevos *mpl* escalfados

poach[2] *vt* (**a**) *(catch illegally)* **to p. fish/game** pescar/cazar furtivamente (**b**) *(employee)* robar

poacher ['pəʊtʃə(r)] *n (of fish)* pescador *m* furtivo; *(of game)* cazador *m* furtivo

pocket ['pɒkɪt] **1** *n* (**a**) *(in pants, jacket)* bolsillo *m*, *CAm, Méx, Perú* bolsa *f*; **to go through sb's pockets** buscar en los bolsillos de alguien; **prices to suit every p.** precios para todos los bolsillos; **to be out of p.** haber perdido dinero; **I paid for the presents out of my own p.** pagué los regalos de mi propio bolsillo; *Fig* **to line one's pockets** llenarse los bolsillos, forrarse; *Fig* **to have sb in one's p.** tener a alguien metido en el bolsillo; **p. calculator** calculadora *f* de bolsillo

(**b**) *(in snooker, pool)* agujero *m*, tronera *f*

(**c**) *(of air, gas)* bolsa *f*; *(of resistance, rebellion)* foco *m*

2 *vt (put in pocket)* meter en el bolsillo; *Fam (steal)* afanar, *Esp* embolsarse

pocketbook ['pɒkɪtbʊk] *n (wallet)* cartera *f*; *(handbag) Esp* bolso *m*, *Col, CSur* cartera *f*, *Méx* bolsa *f*

pocketknife ['pɒkɪtnaɪf] *n* navaja *f*, cortaplumas *m inv*

pockmarked ['pɒkmɑ:kt] *adj (face)* picado(a) (de viruelas); *(surface)* acribillado(a)

pod [pɒd] *n (of plant)* vaina *f*

podia ['pəʊdɪə] *pl of* **podium**

podiatrist [pə'daɪətrɪst] *n* podólogo(a) *m,f*

podiatry [pə'daɪətrɪ] *n* podología *f*

podium ['pəʊdɪəm] *(pl* **podiums** *or* **podia** ['pəʊdɪə]) *n* podio *m*

Podunk ['pəʊdʌnk] *n* pueblo *m* de mala muerte

poem ['pəʊɪm] *n* poema *m*

poet ['pəʊɪt] *n (male)* poeta *m*; *(female)* poetisa *f*, poeta *f*

poetic [pəʊ'etɪk] *adj* poético(a); **it was p. justice that she should be replaced by someone she herself had sacked** fue una ironía del destino que la reemplazaran por alguien a quien ella había despedido anteriormente; **p. license** licencia *f* poética

poetical [pəʊ'etɪkəl] *adj* poético(a)

poetically [pəʊ'etɪklɪ] *adv* de manera poética, poéticamente

poetry ['pəʊɪtrɪ] *n* poesía *f*; **p. in motion** poesía en movimiento; **p. reading** recital *m* de poesía

poignancy ['pɔɪnjənsɪ] *n* patetismo *m*

poignant ['pɔɪnjənt] *adj* patético(a), conmovedor(ora)

poignantly ['pɔɪnjəntlɪ] *adv* de modo conmovedor

point [pɔɪnt] **1** *n* (**a**) *(in space)* punto *m*; **p. of contact** punto de contacto; **p. of sale** punto de venta; **p. of view** punto de vista
  (**b**) *(in time)* instante *m*, momento *m*; **at this p. in time** en este preciso instante; **at this p. the phone rang** en ese instante sonó el teléfono; **to be on the p. of doing sth** estar a punto de hacer algo; **to reach the p. of no return** llegar a un punto sin retorno; **outspoken to the p. of rudeness** franco(a) hasta lindar con la grosería
  (**c**) *(of argument, discussion)* punto *m*; **the p. is,…** la cuestión es que…; **I accept your p.** estoy de acuerdo con lo que dices; **she has a p.** no le falta razón; **he made several interesting points** hizo varias observaciones *or* puntualizaciones muy interesantes; **to get to the p.** ir al grano; **that's beside the p.** eso no viene al caso; **that's not the p.** no es esa la cuestión; **what's the p.?** ¿para qué?; **to make a p. of doing sth** preocuparse de *or* procurar hacer algo; **there is no p. in waiting any longer** no vale la pena seguir esperando; **in p. of fact** en realidad; **her remarks were very much to the p.** sus comentarios fueron muy pertinentes; **it has its good points** tiene sus cosas buenas; **up to a p.** hasta cierto punto; **not to put too fine a p. on it…** hablando en plata…; **a p. of grammar/law** una cuestión gramatical/legal; **p. of order** cuestión *f* de procedimiento *or* de forma
  (**d**) *(punctuation mark)* punto *m*; *Math* **(decimal) p.** coma *f* (decimal); **three p. five** tres coma cinco
  (**e**) *(in game)* punto *m*, tanto *m*; *(in exam)* punto *m*; **to win on points** ganar por puntos
  (**f**) *(on compass, thermometer)* grado *m*; *Fin (on stockmarket)* entero *m*, punto *m*
  (**g**) *(of needle, pencil, sword)* punta *f*; **to end in a p.** acabar en punta
  (**h**) *(of land)* punta *f*, cabo *m*
  2 *vt (aim)* dirigir; **to p. a gun at sb** apuntar con un arma a alguien; *Fig* **to p. the finger at sb** *(accuse)* señalar (con el dedo) a alguien; *Fam* **just p. me in the right direction** *(show how to do)* basta con que me digas cómo hacerlo más o menos; **to p. the way** indicar el camino; *Fig* indicar el rumbo a seguir
  3 *vi* **to p. at sth/sb** *(with finger)* señalar algo/a alguien; **to p. north** señalar al norte; **the hour hand is pointing to ten** *Esp* la manecilla horaria *or Am* el horario indica las diez; **to be pointing toward sth** estar mirando hacia algo, estar en dirección a algo; **this points to the fact that…** esto nos lleva al hecho de que…; **all the evidence points to suicide** todas las pruebas sugieren que se trata de un suicidio

▶**point out** *vt sep (error)* hacer notar, indicar; *(fact)* recalcar; **to p. sth/sb out (to sb)** señalar algo/a alguien (a alguien); **to p. out to sb the advantages of sth** mostrar a alguien las ventajas de algo; **might I p. out that…?** ¿puedo hacer notar que…?

▶**point up** *vt sep (highlight)* subrayar

point-blank ['pɔɪnt'blæŋk] **1** *adj (refusal, denial)* rotundo(a), tajante; **at p. range** a bocajarro, a quemarropa
  2 *adv (to fire)* a bocajarro, a quemarropa; **he asked me p. whether…** me preguntó de sopetón si…; **to deny sth p.** negar algo en redondo; **to refuse p.** negarse en redondo *or* de plano

pointed ['pɔɪntɪd] *adj* (**a**) *(sharp)* puntiagudo(a) (**b**) *(remark)* intencionado(a)

pointedly ['pɔɪntɪdlɪ] *adv* intencionadamente, con intención

pointer ['pɔɪntə(r)] *n* (**a**) *(indicator)* indicador *m*; *(stick)* puntero *m* (**b**) *Fam (advice)* indicación *f* (**c**) *(dog)* perro *m* de muestra, pointer *m*

pointless ['pɔɪntlɪs] *adj* sin sentido; **to be p.** no tener sentido

poise [pɔɪz] *n (balance)* equilibrio *m*; *(composure)* compostura *f*, aplomo *m*

poised [pɔɪzd] *adj* (**a**) *(composed)* equilibrado(a) (**b**) *(ready)* **to be p. to do sth** estar preparado(a) para hacer algo (**c**) *(suspended)* suspendido(a)

poison ['pɔɪzən] **1** *n* veneno *m*; **p. gas** gas *m* tóxico; **p. ivy** zumaque *m*; **p. pen letter** anónimo *m* malicioso
  2 *vt* (**a**) *(person, food) (intentionally)* envenenar; *(accidentally)* intoxicar; **to p. sb's mind (against sb)** enemistar *or* encizañar a alguien (con alguien) (**b**) *(pollute)* contaminar

poisoning ['pɔɪzənɪŋ] *n* (**a**) *(of person, food) (intentional)* envenenamiento *m*; *(accidental)* intoxicación *f*; **to die of p.** *(intentional)* morir envenenado(a); *(accidental)* morir por intoxicación (**b**) *(pollution)* contaminación *f*

poisonous ['pɔɪzənəs] *adj (snake, plant, mushroom)* venenoso(a); *(chemical, fumes)* tóxico(a); *(remark)* envenenado(a); *(rumor, doctrine)* nocivo(a), dañino(a)

poke [pəʊk] **1** *n* golpe *m (con la punta de un objeto)*; **she gave him a p. with her umbrella** le dio con la punta del paraguas
  2 *vt* **to p. sb with one's finger/a stick** dar a alguien con la punta del dedo/de un palo; **to p. sb in the ribs** *(with elbow)* dar a alguien un codazo en las costillas; **to p. a hole in sth** hacer un agujero en algo; **to p. the fire** atizar el fuego; *Fig* **to p. one's nose into other people's business** meter las narices en asuntos ajenos; **to p. fun at sth/sb** reírse de algo/alguien
  3 *vi* **to p. at sth (with one's finger/a stick)** dar un golpe a algo (con la punta del dedo/de un palo)

▶**poke around, poke about** *vi (search)* rebuscar; *(be nosy)* fisgonear, fisgar

▶**poke out 1** *vt sep* **to p. one's head out (of) the window** asomar la cabeza por la ventana; **to p. one's tongue out** sacar la lengua; **be careful! you nearly poked my eye out!** ¡ten cuidado! ¡casi me sacas un ojo!
  2 *vi (protrude)* asomar, sobresalir

poker[1] ['pəʊkə(r)] *n (for fire)* atizador *m*

poker[2] *n (card game)* póquer *m*

poker-faced ['pəʊkəfeɪst] *adj* con cara de póquer

poky, pokey ['pəʊkɪ] **1** *n Fam (prison)* cárcel *f*, *Esp* trullo *m*, *Andes, RP* cana *f*, *Méx* bote *m*
  2 *adj* (**a**) *(cramped)* **a p. room** un cuchitril, un cuartucho (**b**) *(slow)* **to be p.** *(move)* ir a paso de tortuga; *(act)* ser pachorra

pol [pɒl] *n Fam* politico(a) *m,f*

Poland ['pəʊlənd] *n* Polonia

polar ['pəʊlə(r)] *adj* polar; **p. bear** oso *m* polar *or* blanco

polarity [pəʊ'lærɪtɪ] *n* polaridad *f*

polarization [pəʊlərɪ'zeɪʃən] *n* polarización *f*

polarize ['pəʊləraɪz] **1** *vt* polarizar
  2 *vi* polarizarse

Polaroid® ['pəʊlərɔɪd] *n (camera)* polaroid® *f*; *(photo)* foto *f* instantánea

Pole [pəʊl] *n* polaco(a) *m,f*

pole[1] [pəʊl] *n (for supporting)* poste *m*; *(for jumping, punting)* pértiga *f*; *(for flag, tent)* mástil *m*; *Sport* **p. vault** salto *m* con pértiga

pole[2] *n Elec & Geog* polo *m*; **North/South P.** Polo Norte/Sur; *Fig* **to be poles apart** estar en polos opuestos; **P. Star** estrella *f* polar

poleax(e) ['pəʊlæks] *vt (physically)* noquear, tumbar de un golpe; *(emotionally)* dejar anonadado(a)

polecat ['pəʊlkæt] *n* turón *m*

polemic [pə'lemɪk] *n (controversy)* polémica *f*; *(speech, article)* diatriba *f*

polemical [pə'lemɪkəl] *adj* polémico(a)

polemicist [pə'lemɪsɪst] *n* polemista *mf*

polestar ['pəʊlstɑː(r)] *n* estrella *f* polar

police [pə'liːs] **1** *npl* **the p.** la policía; **two hundred p.** doscientos policías; **p. academy** academia *f* de policía; **p. car** coche *m or Am* carro *or CSur* auto de policía; **p. chief** jefe *m* de policía; **p. commissioner** = ciudadano que preside un consejo civil encargado de supervisar la actuación de la policía; **p. department** jefatura *f* de policía; **p. dog** perro *m* policía; **p. force** cuerpo *m* de policía; **p. officer** (agente *mf* de) policía *mf*; **p. record** antecedentes *mpl* policiales; **p. state** estado *m* policial; **p. station** comisaría *f* de policía

2 *vt* vigilar, custodiar; *Fig* vigilar, supervisar; **the streets are not properly policed these days** no hay suficientes policías en la calle hoy en día

policeman [pə'liːsmən] *n* policía *m*

policewoman [pə'liːswʊmən] *n* (mujer *f*) policía *f*

policy ['pɒlɪsɪ] *n* **(a)** *(of government, personal)* política *f*; **foreign p.** política exterior; **it's a matter of p.** es una cuestión de política; **it's a good/bad p.** es/no es conveniente; **p. statement** declaración *f* de principios **(b)** *Fin* **(insurance) p.** póliza *f* (de seguros); **p. holder** asegurado(a) *m,f*

polio ['pəʊlɪəʊ] *n* poliomielitis *f inv*, polio *f*

Polish ['pəʊlɪʃ] **1** *n (language)* polaco *m*

2 *adj* polaco(a)

polish ['pɒlɪʃ] **1** *n* **(a)** *(finish, shine)* brillo *m*; **to give sth a p.** dar *or* sacar brillo a algo **(b)** *(for shoes)* betún *m*, crema *f* (para calzado); *(for furniture, floors)* cera *f*; *(for metal)* abrillantador *m*; *(for nails)* esmalte *m*, laca *f* **(c)** *(refinement)* acabado *m*, refinamiento *m*

2 *vt* **(a)** *(wood, metal, stone)* pulir; *(shoes)* dar brillo a, limpiar; *(floor)* encerar **(b)** *(improve)* pulir, perfeccionar

▸**polish off** *vt sep Fam (food)* zamparse; *(drink)* cepillarse, *Esp* pimplarse, *RP* mandarse; *(work, opponent)* acabar con, *Esp* cepillarse

polished ['pɒlɪʃt] *adj (wood, metal, stone)* pulido(a); *(shoes)* brillante, limpio(a); *(floor)* encerado(a); *(manners)* refinado(a); *(style)* acabado(a), pulido(a)

polite [pə'laɪt] *adj* educado(a), cortés; **to be p. to sb** ser amable *or* educado(a) con alguien; **it's not p. to...** no es de buena educación...; **in p. society** entre gente educada

politely [pə'laɪtlɪ] *adv* educadamente, cortésmente

politeness [pə'laɪtnɪs] *n* educación *f*, cortesía *f*

politic ['pɒlɪtɪk] *adj Formal* prudente

political [pə'lɪtɪkəl] *adj* político(a); **he isn't very p.** no le va mucho la política; **p. asylum** asilo *m* político; **p. correctness** lo políticamente correcto; **p. prisoner** preso(a) *m,f* político(a); **p. science** ciencias *fpl* políticas, politología *f*

politically [pə'lɪtɪklɪ] *adv* políticamente; **p. motivated** por motivos políticos; **p. correct** políticamente correcto(a)

politician [pɒlɪ'tɪʃən] *n* político(a) *m,f*

politicization [pəlɪtɪsaɪ'zeɪʃən] *n* politización *f*

politicize [pə'lɪtɪsaɪz] *vt* politizar

politics ['pɒlɪtɪks] **1** *n* política *f*

2 *npl* **(a)** *(views)* ideas *fpl* políticas **(b)** **office p.** intrigas *fpl* de oficina

polka ['pɒlkə] *n* polca *f*; **a p. dot tie** una corbata de lunares

poll [pəʊl] **1** *n (voting)* votación *f*; **(opinion) p.** *(survey)* sondeo *m or* encuesta *f* (de opinión); **to go to the polls** acudir a las urnas

2 *vt (votes)* obtener; *(people)* sondear

pollen ['pɒlən] *n* polen *m*; **p. count** concentración *f* de polen en el aire

pollinate ['pɒlɪneɪt] *vt* polinizar

polling ['pəʊlɪŋ] *n* votación *f*; **p. booth** cabina *f* electoral; **p. day** jornada *f* electoral; **p. station** colegio *m* electoral

pollster ['pəʊlstə(r)] *n* encuestador(ora) *m,f*

pollutant [pə'luːtənt] *n* (sustancia *f*) contaminante *m*

pollute [pə'luːt] *vt* contaminar

polluter [pə'luːtə(r)] *n* (company) empresa *f* contaminante; *(industry)* industria *f* contaminante

pollution [pə'luːʃən] *n* contaminación *f*

Pollyanna [pɒlɪ'ænə] *n* **she's a real P.** es ingenuamente optimista

polo ['pəʊləʊ] *n (sport)* polo *m*

poltergeist ['pɒltəgaɪst] *n* espíritu *m or* fuerza *f* paranormal, poltergeist *m*

polyester [pɒlɪ'estə(r)] *n* poliéster *m*

polyethylene [pɒlɪ'eθəliːn] *n* polietileno *m*

polygamous [pə'lɪgəməs] *adj* polígamo(a)

polygamy [pə'lɪgəmɪ] *n* poligamia *f*

polyglot ['pɒlɪglɒt] *n & adj* políglota(a) *m,f*

polygon ['pɒlɪgən] *n* polígono *m*

polymer ['pɒlɪmə(r)] *n Chem* polímero *m*

Polynesia [pɒlɪ'niːzɪə] *n* Polinesia

Polynesian [pɒlɪ'niːzɪən] *n & adj* polinesio(a) *m,f*

polyp ['pɒlɪp] *n Med* pólipo *m*

polyphonic [pɒlɪ'fɒnɪk] *adj Mus* polifónico(a)

polysemy [pə'lɪsɪmɪ] *n Ling* polisemia *f*

polystyrene [pɒlɪ'staɪriːn] *n* poliestireno *m*

polyunsaturated [pɒlɪʌn'sætjʊreɪtɪd] *adj* poliinsaturado(a)

polyurethane [pɒlɪ'jʊərɪθeɪn] *n* poliuretano *m*

pomegranate ['pɒmɪgrænɪt] *n (fruit)* granada *f*; **p. (tree)** granado *m*

pomp [pɒmp] *n* pompa *f*, boato *m*; **p. and circumstance** pompa y circunstancia

pom-pom ['pɒmpɒm], **pompon** ['pɒmpɒn] *n (on hat, used by cheerleader)* pompón *m*

pomposity [pɒm'pɒsɪtɪ] *n* pretenciosidad *f*, pedantería *f*

pompous ['pɒmpəs] *adj (person)* pretencioso(a), pedante; *(language, remark)* altisonante, grandilocuente; *(style, speech)* pomposo(a), altisonante

pompously ['pɒmpəslɪ] *adv* pomposamente

poncho ['pɒntʃəʊ] *(pl ponchos)* *n* poncho *m*

pond [pɒnd] *n* estanque *m*

ponder ['pɒndə(r)] **1** *vt* considerar

2 *vi* **to p. over** *or* **on sth** reflexionar sobre algo

ponderous ['pɒndərəs] *adj (person, movement)* pesado(a), cansino(a); *(progress)* ralentizado(a), muy lento(a); *(piece of writing)* cargante, pesado(a)

pontiff ['pɒntɪf] *n* pontífice *m*

pontificate¹ [pɒn'tɪfɪkət] *n Rel* pontificado *m*

pontificate² [pɒn'tɪfɪkeɪt] *vi* pontificar

pontoon [pɒn'tuːn] *n (float)* pontón *m*; **p. bridge** puente *m* de pontones

pony ['pəʊnɪ] *n* poni *m*; *Fam* **the ponies** las carreras (de caballos)

▸**pony up** *vi Fam (pay up)* poner dinero, *Esp* apoquinar, *RP* garpar

ponytail ['pəʊnɪteɪl] *n (hairstyle)* coleta *f*

pooch [puːtʃ] *n Fam* chucho *m*

poodle ['puːdəl] *n* caniche *m*

pooh [puː] *exclam (at a smell)* ¡puaj!; *(scornful)* ¡bah!

pooh-pooh ['puː'puː] *vt* **to p. a suggestion** despreciar una sugerencia

pool¹ [puːl] *n (pond)* charca *f*; *(puddle, of blood)* charco *m*; **(swimming) p.** piscina *f*, *Méx* alberca *f*, *RP* pileta *f*

pool² **1** *n (group)* conjunto *m*; *(of money)* fondo *m* común; **car p.** parque *m* móvil, flota *f* de automóviles

2 *vt (ideas, resources)* poner en común

pool³ *n (game)* billar *m* americano; **p. table** mesa *f* de billar americano

poop [puːp] *n Fam* **1** *n* **(a)** *(feces)* cacas *fpl*; **to take a p.** hacer caca **(b)** *(information)* información *f*, datos *mpl*

2 *vi* hacer(se) caca

pooped [puːpt] *adj Fam* hecho(a) migas *or* polvo

poor [pʊə(r)] **1** *npl* **the p.** los pobres

2 *adj* (**a**) *(not rich)* pobre; **the abacus is the p. man's calculator** el ábaco es la calculadora de los pobres (**b**) *(inferior)* malo(a); *(chances, reward)* escaso(a); **to be in p. health** estar mal de salud; **to have a p. memory** tener mala memoria; **to be p. at math** no ser bueno(a) en matemáticas; **to be a p. sailor** marearse siempre en los barcos; **the light is p.** hay poca luz; **to be a p. loser** ser un(a) mal perdedor(ora); **in p. taste** de mal gusto (**c**) *(expressing pity)* **p. creature** *or* **thing!** ¡pobrecillo(a)!; **p. (old) Tim!** ¡pobre Tim!

poorly ['pʊəlɪ] **1** *adv* mal; **p. dressed** mal vestido(a); **to be p. off** ser pobre
2 *adj* enfermo(a); **to be p.** estar enfermo

pop[1] [pɒp] **1** *n (music)* (música *f*) pop *m*
2 *adj* **p. art** arte *m* pop; **p. group** grupo *m* (de música) pop; **p. music** música *f* pop; **p. singer** cantante *mf* pop; **p. song** canción *f* pop

pop[2] *n (father)* papá *m*

pop[3] **1** *n* (**a**) *(sound)* pequeño estallido *m* (**b**) *Fam (fizzy drink)* gaseosa *f*
2 *vt (pt & pp* **popped**) (**a**) *(burst)* hacer explotar (**b**) *Fam (put quickly)* **to p. sth into a drawer** poner *or* echar algo en un cajón; **to p. one's head out of the window** asomar la cabeza por la ventana; *Fam* **he decided to p. the question** decidió pedirle que se casara con él; **to p. pills** atiborrarse de pastillas
3 *vi* (**a**) *(burst)* estallar, explotar; *(cork)* saltar; **my ears popped** se me destaponaron los oídos (**b**) *Fam (go quickly)* **we popped over to Jamaica for the weekend** el fin de semana hicimos una escapada a Jamaica

▶**pop in** *vi Fam* pasarse un momento *(por casa de alguien)*
▶**pop off** *vi Fam (die)* estirar la pata, *Esp* irse al otro barrio, *Méx* patatearse
▶**pop out** *vi Fam (go out)* salir

pop. *(abbr* **population**) población *f*
popcorn ['pɒpkɔːn] *n* palomitas *fpl* de maíz, *RP* pochoclo *m*
pope [pəʊp] *n* papa *m*
pop-eyed ['pɒpaɪd] *adj Fam* de ojos saltones
popgun ['pɒpɡʌn] *n* pistola *f* de juguete *(de aire comprimido)*
poplar ['pɒplə(r)] *n* álamo *m*
poplin ['pɒplɪn] *n (cloth)* popelina *f*, popelín *m*
poppy ['pɒpɪ] *n* amapola *f*; **p. seed** semilla *f* de amapola
poppycock ['pɒpɪkɒk] *n Fam (nonsense) Esp* majaderías *fpl*, *Am* zonceras *fpl*
Popsicle® ['pɒpsɪkəl] *n* polo *m*, *Am* paleta *f* helada, *Arg* palito *m* de agua
populace ['pɒpjʊləs] *n Formal* **the p.** el pueblo, la plebe
popular ['pɒpjʊlə(r)] *adj (in general)* popular; *(newspapers, TV programs)* de masas; **you won't make yourself very p. doing that** no va a sentar nada bien que hagas eso; **she is p. with her colleagues** cae bien a sus compañeros; **by p. demand** a petición *or Am* pedido popular *or* del público; **contrary to p. belief** en contra de lo que comúnmente se cree
popularity [pɒpjʊ'lærɪtɪ] *n* popularidad *f*; **p. rating** índice *m* de popularidad
popularization [pɒpjʊləraɪ'zeɪʃən] *n* popularización *f*
popularize ['pɒpjʊləraɪz] *vt (make popular)* popularizar; *(make easy to understand)* divulgar
popularly ['pɒpjʊləlɪ] *adv* comúnmente, popularmente; **it is p. believed that…** todo el mundo cree que…
populate ['pɒpjʊleɪt] *vt* poblar; **sparsely populated** *(region)* poco poblado(a)
population [pɒpjʊ'leɪʃən] *n* población *f*; **p. explosion** explosión *f* demográfica
populism ['pɒpjʊlɪzəm] *n* populismo *m*
populist ['pɒpjʊlɪst] *n & adj* populista *mf*
populous ['pɒpjʊləs] *adj* populoso(a)
pop-up menu ['pɒpʌp'menjuː] *n Comptr* menú *m* desplegable

porcelain ['pɔːslɪn] *n* porcelana *f*; **p. ware** porcelana
porch [pɔːtʃ] *n (veranda)* porche *m*
porcupine ['pɔːkjʊpaɪn] *n* puerco *m* espín
pore [pɔː(r)] *n* poro *m*
▶**pore over** *vt insep* leer atentamente, estudiar con detenimiento
pork [pɔːk] *n (carne f de) cerdo *m or Am* chancho *m*; *Fam* **p. barrel politics** = política de adjudicación de contratas estatales que benefician a la zona del que las concede; **p. chop** chuleta *f* de cerdo; **p. pie** empanada *f* de carne de cerdo
porn [pɔːn] *n Fam* porno *m*; **soft/hard p.** porno blando/duro
porno ['pɔːnəʊ] *adj Fam* porno
pornographer [pɔː'nɒɡrəfə(r)] *n* pornógrafo(a) *m,f*
pornographic [pɔːnə'ɡræfɪk] *adj* pornográfico(a)
pornography [pɔː'nɒɡrəfɪ] *n* pornografía *f*
porosity [pɔː'rɒsɪtɪ] *n* porosidad *f*
porous ['pɔːrəs] *adj* poroso(a)
porpoise ['pɔːpəs] *n* marsopa *f*
porridge ['pɒrɪdʒ] *n* gachas *fpl* de avena
port[1] [pɔːt] *n (harbor, town)* puerto *m*; **in p.** en puerto; *also Fig* **p. of call** escala *f*; *Prov* **any p. in a storm** en casos extremos, se olvidan los remilgos; **P. of Spain** Puerto España
port[2] *n Naut (left-hand side)* babor *m*
port[3] *n (drink)* (vino *m* de) oporto *m*
port[4] *n Comptr* puerto *m*; **parallel/serial p.** puerto paralelo/ (en) serie
portable ['pɔːtəbəl] *adj* portátil
portal ['pɔːtəl] *n* (**a**) *Formal (entrance)* pórtico *m* (**b**) *Comptr (Web page)* portal *m*
Port-au-Prince [pɔːtəʊ'prɛs] *n* Puerto Príncipe
portcullis [pɔːt'kʌlɪs] *n* rastrillo *m (reja)*
portend [pɔː'tend] *vt Formal* augurar
portent ['pɔːtent] *n Formal (omen)* augurio *m*
portentous [pɔː'tentəs] *adj Formal (significant)* decisivo(a), relevante; *(threatening)* de mal agüero
porter ['pɔːtə(r)] *n (at station)* mozo *m* de equipaje; *(at hotel)* portero(a) *m,f*, conserje *mf*; *(in hospital)* celador(ora) *m,f*; *(in sleeping-car)* mozo *m*
portfolio [pɔːt'fəʊliəʊ] *(pl* **portfolios**) *n (for documents, drawings)* cartera *f*; *(of person's work)* carpeta *f*; *Fin* **stock p.** cartera de valores
porthole ['pɔːthəʊl] *n Naut* portilla *f*, ojo *m* de buey
portion ['pɔːʃən] *n (share)* parte *f*, porción *f*; *(of food)* ración *f*, porción *f*
▶**portion out** *vt sep* repartir
portly ['pɔːtlɪ] *adj* corpulento(a)
portrait ['pɔːtreɪt] *n also Fig* retrato *m*; **he had his p. painted** le pintaron un retrato; **p. gallery** galería *f* de retratos; *Comptr* **p. (orientation)** formato *m* vertical *or* de retrato; **p. painter** retratista *mf*
portray [pɔː'treɪ] *vt (of painting, writer, book)* retratar, describir; *(of actor)* interpretar (el papel de)
portrayal [pɔː'treɪəl] *n (description)* descripción *f*, representación *f*; *(by actor)* interpretación *f*
Portugal ['pɔːtjʊɡəl] *n* Portugal
Portuguese [pɔːtjʊ'ɡiːz] **1** *n* (**a**) *(pl* **Portuguese**) *(person)* portugués(esa) *m,f* (**b**) *(language)* portugués *m*
2 *adj* portugués(esa)
POS [piːəʊ'es] *n Com (abbr* **point of sale**) punto *m* de venta
pose [pəʊz] **1** *n* (**a**) *(position)* postura *f*, posición *f* (**b**) *Pej (affectation)* pose *f*; **it's just a p.** no es más que una pose
2 *vt (problem, question)* plantear; *(danger, threat)* suponer
3 *vi (for portrait)* posar; *Pej (behave affectedly)* tomar *or* hacer poses; **to p. as** *(pretend to be)* hacerse pasar por
poser ['pəʊzə(r)] *n Fam (difficult question)* rompecabezas *m inv*
posh [pɒʃ] *Fam adj (person, accent) Esp* pijo(a), *Méx* fresa, *RP*

(con)cheto(a); *(restaurant, area, clothes)* elegante

position [pə'zɪʃən] **1** *n* (**a**) *(physical posture)* posición *f*; **in a horizontal/vertical p.** en posición horizontal/vertical; **in the on/off p.** *(switch, lever)* (en la posición de) encendido *or Am* prendido/apagado

(**b**) *(opinion)* postura *f*, posición *f*

(**c**) *(place)* posición *f*, lugar *m*; *(in sport)* posición *f*; **in p.** en su sitio; **out of p.** fuera de su sitio

(**d**) *(situation)* posición *f*, situación *f*; **to be in a strong p.** estar en una buena posición; **put yourself in my p.** ponte en mi lugar *or* situación; **to be in a p. to do sth** estar en condiciones de hacer algo; **to be in no p. to do sth** no estar en condiciones de hacer algo

(**e**) *Formal (job)* puesto *m*, empleo *m*; **a p. of responsibility** un puesto de responsabilidad

2 *vt (place) (object)* colocar, situar; *(troops)* apostar; **to p. oneself** colocarse, situarse; **to be well/poorly positioned to do sth** estar en una buena/mala posición para hacer algo

positioning [pə'zɪʃənɪŋ] *n Com* posicionamiento *m*

positive ['pozɪtɪv] *adj* (**a**) *(answer)* afirmativo(a); *(evidence, proof)* concluyente; *Med* **the test was p.** la prueba ha dado positivo; **on the p. side** como aspecto positivo (**b**) *(constructive) (person, philosophy)* positivo(a); **p. thinking** actitud *f* positiva (**c**) *(certain)* (completamente) seguro(a); **to be p. about sth** estar completamente seguro(a) de algo (**d**) *(for emphasis)* **it's a p. disgrace** es una verdadera vergüenza (**e**) *Math & Elec* positivo(a)

positively ['pozɪtɪvlɪ] *adv* (**a**) *(answer)* afirmativamente; *(think, react)* positivamente (**b**) *(for emphasis)* verdaderamente, realmente; *Fam* **p. not** de ninguna manera

posse ['posɪ] *n (to catch criminal)* partida *f or* cuadrilla *f* (de persecución); *Fig (group)* banda *f*, cuadrilla *f*

possess [pə'zes] *vt* (**a**) *(property, quality, faculty)* poseer (**b**) **possessed by fear/rage** embargado(a) por el miedo/la rabia; **what possessed you to do that?** ¿qué te impulsó a hacer eso?

possession [pə'zeʃən] *n (ownership, thing possessed)* posesión *f*; **to be in p. of sth** estar en posesión de algo; **in full p. of his senses *or* faculties** en plena posesión de sus facultades (mentales)

possessive [pə'zesɪv] **1** *n Gram* posesivo *m*

2 *adj (parent, lover) & Gram* posesivo(a); **to be p. of *or* about sth/sb** ser posesivo con algo/alguien

possessor [pə'zesə(r)] *n* poseedor(ora) *m,f*

possibility [posɪ'bɪlɪtɪ] *n* posibilidad *f*; **to be within/outside the bounds of p.** entrar/no entrar dentro de lo posible; **that is a distinct p.** es una posibilidad real; **to allow for all possibilities** prepararse para cualquier eventualidad

possible ['posɪbəl] **1** *n (person)* candidato(a) *m,f* posible

2 *adj* posible; **to make sth p.** hacer posible algo; **if p.** si es posible; **it is p. that he will come** es posible que venga; **as much as p.** cuanto sea posible; **I want you to try, as much as p., to behave** quiero que, en la medida de lo posible, intentes portarte bien; **as soon as p.** cuanto antes; **whenever/wherever p.** cuando/donde sea posible; **anything's p.** todo es posible

possibly ['posɪblɪ] *adv* (**a**) *(perhaps)* posiblemente; **will you go? – p.** ¿irás? – puede *or* quizá; **p. not** puede que no (**b**) *(for emphasis)* **I can't p. do it** me resulta de todo punto imposible hacerlo; **I'll do all I p. can** haré todo lo que esté en mi mano; **how could you p. do such a thing?** ¿cómo se te ocurrió hacer semejante cosa?

possum ['posəm] *n* zarigüeya *f*

post¹ [pəʊst] *n* (**a**) *(wooden stake)* poste *m* (**b**) *(job, military position)* puesto *m*; **to be/die at one's p.** estar/morir al pie del cañón; **p. exchange** = tienda en una base militar

post² *vt (affix)* poner, pegar; *(on bulletin board)* anunciar, pegar;

Comptr enviar a; **p. no bills** *(sign)* prohibido fijar carteles

post³ 1 *n* **p. office** oficina *f* de correos; **the P. Office** *(government department) Esp* Correos *m inv*, *Am* Correo *m*

2 *vt (letter)* enviar *or* mandar (por correo); *Fam Fig* **I'll keep you posted** te mantendré informado(a)

postage ['pəʊstɪdʒ] *n* franqueo *m*; **p. and handling** gastos *mpl* de envío; **p. paid** franqueo pagado; **p. stamp** sello *m* (de correos), *Am* estampilla *f*

postal ['pəʊstəl] *adj* postal; **p. vote** voto *m* por correo

postcard ['pəʊstkɑːd] *n* (tarjeta *f*) postal *f*

postdate [pəʊst'deɪt] *vt* extender con fecha posterior

poster ['pəʊstə(r)] *n (for advertising)* cartel *m*, póster *m*; *(of painting, pop group)* póster *m*; **p. paint** témpera *f*

posterior [pos'tɪərɪə(r)] *n Hum (buttocks)* trasero *m*, posaderas *fpl*

posterity [pos'terɪtɪ] *n* posteridad *f*

postfeminism [pəʊst'femɪnɪzəm] *n* pos(t)feminismo *m*

postfeminist [pəʊst'femɪnɪst] *n & adj* pos(t)feminista *mf*

postgraduate [pəʊst'grædjʊɪt] **1** *n* estudiante *mf* de posgrado

2 *adj* de posgrado; **p. studies** estudios *mpl* de posgrado

posthaste ['pəʊst'heɪst] *adv* a toda prisa

posthumous ['postjʊməs] *adj* póstumo(a)

posthumously ['postjʊməslɪ] *adv* póstumamente

Postimpressionism ['pəʊstɪm'preʃənɪzəm] *n* postimpresionismo *m*

Postimpressionist ['pəʊstɪm'preʃənɪst] *n & adj* postimpresionista *mf*

posting ['pəʊstɪŋ] *n* (**a**) *Mil* destino *m* (**b**) *Comptr* destino *m*

Post-it® ['pəʊstɪt] *n* **P. (note)** post-it® *m*

postmark ['pəʊstmɑːk] *n* matasellos *m inv*

postmaster ['pəʊstmɑːstə(r)] *n* funcionario *m* de correos

postmistress ['pəʊstmɪstrɪs] *n* funcionaria *f* de correos

postmodern [pəʊst'modən] *adj* posmoderno(a)

postmodernism [pəʊst'modənɪzəm] *n* posmodernismo *m*

postmodernist [pəʊst'modənɪst] *n & adj* posmoderno(a) *m,f*

postmortem [pəʊst'mɔːtəm] *n* autopsia *f*

postnatal [pəʊst'neɪtəl] *adj Med* posparto, puerperal; **p. depression** depresión *f* puerperal *or* posparto

postoperative [pəʊst'opərətɪv] *adj Med* pos(t)operatorio(a)

postpaid ['pəʊst'peɪd] **1** *adj* con el franqueo pagado

2 *adv* libre de gastos de envío

postpone [pəʊst'pəʊn] *vt* aplazar, posponer

postponement [pəʊst'pəʊnmənt] *n* aplazamiento *m*

postscript ['pəʊsskrɪpt] *n* posdata *f*

post-traumatic stress disorder ['pəʊsttrɔː'mætɪk'stresdɪs'ɔːdə(r)] *n Med* síndrome *m* de estrés postraumático

postulate ['postjʊleɪt] *vt* postular

posture ['postʃə(r)] **1** *n* postura *f*; **to have good/bad p.** tener (una) buena/mala postura

2 *vi* tomar *or* hacer poses

postwar ['pəʊst'wɔː(r)] *adj* de posguerra; **the p. period** la posguerra

posy ['pəʊzɪ] *n* ramillete *m*, ramo *m*

pot [pot] **1** *n* (**a**) *(container)* bote *m*; *(for cooking)* cacerola *f*, olla *f*; *(for tea)* tetera *f*; *(for coffee)* cafetera *f*; **pots and pans** cazos *mpl* y ollas; **I'd like a p. of tea** quiero un té (de tetera); *Fam* **pots of money** montones de dinero; *Fam* **to go to p.** irse al garete *or Am* al diablo; **p. plant** planta *f* de interior (**b**) *Fam (marijuana)* maría *f*

2 *vt (pt & pp **potted**) (butter, meat)* envasar; *(plant)* plantar (en tiesto)

potash ['potæʃ] *n* potasa *f*

potassium [pə'tæsɪəm] *n* potasio *m*

potato [pə'teɪtəʊ] *(pl potatoes) n Esp* patata *f*, *Am* papa *f*; **p.**

chips *Esp* patatas *fpl or Am* papas *fpl* fritas *(de bolsa)*; **p. peeler** *Esp* pelapatatas *m inv, Am* pelapapas *m inv*; **p. salad** ensalada *f* de *Esp* patatas *or Am* papas

potbellied [pɒt'belɪd] *adj (from over-eating)* barrigón(ona); *(from malnourishment)* con el vientre hinchado

potency ['pəʊtənsɪ] *n* potencia *f*

potent ['pəʊtənt] *adj* potente

potentate ['pəʊtənteɪt] *n* soberano *m* absoluto

potential [pə'tenʃəl] **1** *n* potencial *m*; **to have p.** tener potencial; **she failed to fulfill her p.** no llegó a explotar todo su potencial
2 *adj* potencial

potentially [pə'tenʃəlɪ] *adv* en potencia

pothole ['pɒthəʊl] *n (in road)* bache *m*

potion ['pəʊʃən] *n* poción *f*

potluck ['pɒt'lʌk] *n Fam* **to take p.** aceptar lo que haya

potpie ['pɒtpaɪ] *n* = plato consistente en carne y verdura cubierto de pasta y hervido u horneado en una olla

potpourri [pəʊ'pʊərɪ] *n (of flowers, music)* popurrí *m*

potted ['pɒtɪd] *adj* **(a)** *(food)* en conserva **(b)** *(drunk)* borracho(a), *Esp, RP* mamado(a), *Méx* hasta atrás

potter ['pɒtə(r)] *n* alfarero(a) *m,f*, ceramista *mf*; **p.'s wheel** torno *m* (de alfarero)

pottery ['pɒtərɪ] *n (art, place)* alfarería *f*; *(objects)* cerámica *f*, alfarería *f*

potty ['pɒtɪ] *n* orinal *m*; **p. training** = proceso de enseñar a un niño a usar el orinal

potty-train ['pɒtɪtreɪn] *vt* enseñar a utilizar el orinal a

potty-trained ['pɒtɪtreɪnd] *adj* **he/she is p.** ya no necesita pañales

pouch [paʊtʃ] *n* **(a)** *(for money)* saquito *m*; *(for tobacco)* petaca *f*; *(for ammunition)* cebador *m* **(b)** *(of marsupial)* marsupio *m*

pouf(fe) [puːf] *n* puf *m*

poulterer ['pəʊltərə(r)] *n* pollero(a) *m,f*

poultice ['pəʊltɪs] *n* cataplasma *f*

poultry ['pəʊltrɪ] *n (birds)* aves *fpl* de corral; *(meat)* carne *f* de ave *or* pollería; **p. farm** granja *f* avícola; **p. farmer** avicultor(ora) *m,f*

pounce [paʊns] *vi* abalanzarse (**on** sobre)

pound¹ [paʊnd] *n* **(a)** *(unit of weight)* libra *f* (= 0,454 kg) **(b)** *(British currency)* libra *f* (esterlina); **p. coin** moneda *f* de una libra; **p. sign** símbolo *m* de la libra; **p. sterling** libra esterlina

pound² *n (for dogs)* perrera *f*; *(for cars)* depósito *m* de coches

pound³ 1 *vt (crush)* machacar; *(with artillery)* atacar; **to p. sth to pieces** destrozar algo a golpes; **to p. sb into submission** someter a alguien por la fuerza
2 *vi (drum)* redoblar; *(heart)* latir, palpitar; **to p. at** *or* **on sth** aporrear algo; **my head is pounding** tengo la cabeza a punto de estallar

-pounder ['paʊndə(r)] *suffix* **a fifteen-p.** *(fish)* un ejemplar de quince libras; **a six/twenty-five-p.** *(gun)* una pieza de seis/veinticinco libras

pounding ['paʊndɪŋ] *n* **to give sb a p.** dar una buena tunda a alguien

pour [pɔː(r)] **1** *vt* verter (**into** en); **to p. sb a drink** servir una bebida a alguien; **to p. money into a project** invertir un dineral en un proyecto
2 *vi* brotar, fluir; **it's pouring (with rain)** llueve a cántaros; **sweat was pouring off him** le chorreaba el sudor; **tourists were pouring into the palace** entraban al palacio turistas a espuertas

▸**pour in 1** *vt sep (liquid)* verter
2 *vi (liquid)* entrar a raudales; *(people, letters)* llegar a raudales

▸**pour out 1** *vt sep (coffee, tea)* servir; *Fig (anger, grief)* desahogar
2 *vi (liquid)* salirse; *Fig (people)* salir a raudales

pouring ['pɔːrɪŋ] *adj (rain)* torrencial

pout [paʊt] **1** *n (in annoyance)* mohín *m*; *(seductive)* mueca *f* seductora (con los labios)
2 *vi (in annoyance)* hacer un mohín, ponerse de morros; *(seductively)* fruncir los labios con aire seductor

POV [piːəʊ'viː] *n TV & Cin (abbr* **point of view**) punto *m* de vista

poverty ['pɒvətɪ] *n* pobreza *f*; *Fig (of ideas)* escasez *f*, pobreza *f*; **to live in p.** vivir en la pobreza; **p. line** umbral *m* de pobreza

poverty-stricken ['pɒvətɪstrɪkən] *adj* empobrecido(a), depauperado(a)

POW [piːəʊ'dʌbəljuː] *n (abbr* **prisoner of war**) prisionero(a) *m,f* de guerra

powder ['paʊdə(r)] **1** *n* polvo *m*; **(face) p.** polvos *mpl*; *Fam* **to take a p.** *(disappear)* poner los pies en polvorosa; *Fig* **p. keg** polvorín *m*; **p. puff** borla *f*; **p. room** *(toilet)* baño *m or Esp* servicios *mpl or CSur* toilette *m* de señoras
2 *vt* **to p. sth with sugar** espolvorear azúcar sobre algo; **to p. one's face** empolvarse la cara; *Euph* **to p. one's nose** ir al tocador

powdered ['paʊdəd] *adj (milk)* en polvo; **p. sugar** azúcar *m Esp, Méx* glas *or Esp* de lustre *or Chile* flor *or Col* pulverizado *or RP* impalpable

powdery ['paʊdərɪ] *adj (substance)* arenoso(a); *(snow)* en polvo; *(apple, potato)* harinoso(a)

power ['paʊə(r)] **1** *n* **(a)** *(authority)* poder *m*; **to come to p.** subir al poder; **to be in/out of p.** estar/no estar en el poder; **to be in sb's p.** estar en poder de alguien; **he had them in his p.** los tenía en su poder; **p. base** bastión *f* de popularidad; **p. struggle** lucha *f* por el poder
(b) *(capacity)* capacidad *f*, facultad *f*; **to have the p. to do sth** tener la facultad de hacer algo; **she did everything in her p. to help** hizo todo lo que estuvo en su mano para ayudar; **it is beyond my p.** no está en mi mano; **to be at the height** *or* **peak of one's powers** estar en plenas facultades; *Fam* **that'll do you a p. of good** eso te sentará estupendamente; **powers of concentration** capacidad *f* de concentración; **powers of persuasion** poder *m* de persuasión; **the p. of speech** la facultad del habla; **p. of life and death over sb** poder para decidir sobre la vida de alguien
(c) *(physical strength)* potencia *f*; *Aut* **p. steering** *Esp* dirección *f* asistida, *Esp* servodirección *f*, *Am* dirección *f* hidráulica
(d) *(powerful person)* autoridad *f*; *(powerful group, nation)* potencia *f*; **the great powers** las grandes potencias; *Fig* **the p. behind the throne** el/la que maneja los hilos; **the powers that be** las autoridades
(e) *Law* competencia *f*; **p. of attorney** poder *m* (notarial)
(f) *(electricity)* electricidad *f*; *(energy)* energía *f*; **wind p.** energía eólica; **p. cut** corte *m* de corriente *or* del fluido eléctrico; **p. mower** cortadora *f* de césped automática; **p. pack** alimentador *m* de corriente; **p. plant** central *f or Andes, RP* usina *f* eléctrica; **p. station** central *f or Andes, RP* usina *f* eléctrica; **p. tool** herramienta *f* eléctrica
(g) *Math* potencia *f*; **three to the p. of ten** tres elevado a diez
2 *vt (provide with power)* propulsar; **powered by two engines** con dos motores

-powered ['paʊəd] *suffix* **steam-p.** de *or* a vapor, accionado(a) por vapor de agua; **wind-p.** de viento, alimentado(a) por el viento

powerful ['paʊəfʊl] *adj (muscles, engine, voice)* potente; *(country, politician)* poderoso(a); *(drug, smell)* fuerte; *(speech, image)* conmovedor(ora)

powerfully ['paʊəfʊlɪ] *adv (with great strength)* con fuerza; *(to argue)* convincentemente; *(to speak)* de forma conmovedora

powerhouse ['paʊəhaʊs] *n Fam (person)* motor *m*

powerless ['paʊəlɪs] *adj* impotente; **to be p. to react** no tener capacidad para *or* no ser capaz de reaccionar

PR [piː'ɑ(r)] n (a) (abbr **public relations**) relaciones fpl públicas (b) Pol (abbr **proportional representation**) representación f proporcional (c) (abbr **Puerto Rico**) Puerto Rico

practicability [præktɪkə'bɪlɪtɪ] n (feasibility) viabilidad f

practicable ['præktɪkəbəl] adj (feasible) factible, viable

practical ['præktɪkəl] **1** n (lesson) (clase f) práctica f; (exam) examen m práctico

2 adj (a) (mind, solution) práctico(a); **he's very p.** es muy práctico; **for all p. purposes** a efectos prácticos; **p. joke** broma f (pesada); **to play a p. joke on sb** gastar una broma a alguien; **p. joker** bromista mf; **p. nurse** enfermero(a) m,f auxiliar (b) (virtual) **it's a p. certainty** es prácticamente seguro

practicality [præktɪ'kælɪtɪ] n (of suggestion, plan) viabilidad f; **practicalities** aspectos mpl prácticos

practically ['præktɪklɪ] adv prácticamente

practice ['præktɪs] **1** n (a) (action, exercise) práctica f; (in sport) entrenamiento m; **in p.** en la práctica; **to put an idea into p.** poner en práctica una idea; **to be out of p.** estar desentrenado(a); Prov **p. makes perfect** se aprende a base de práctica; **p. game** partido m de entrenamiento

(b) (of profession) ejercicio m, práctica f; **medical p.** (place) consulta f médica, consultorio m médico; (group of doctors) = grupo de médicos que comparten un consultorio; **legal p.** (place, legal firm) bufete m de abogados

(c) (custom) práctica f; **to make a p. of doing sth** tomar por costumbre hacer algo; **it's the usual p.** es el procedimiento habitual; **to be good/bad p.** ser una buena/mala costumbre

2 vt (a) (musical instrument, language) practicar (b) (medicine, law) ejercer (c) (religion, custom) practicar; **to p. what one preaches** predicar con el ejemplo

3 vi (a) (musician) practicar; (sportsperson) entrenar (b) (doctor, lawyer) ejercer

practiced ['præktɪst] adj experto(a) (**at** en)

practicing ['præktɪsɪŋ] adj (doctor, lawyer) en ejercicio, en activo; (Christian) practicante

pragmatic [præg'mætɪk] adj pragmático(a)

pragmatics [præg'mætɪks] n Ling pragmática f

pragmatism ['prægmətɪzəm] n pragmatismo m

pragmatist ['prægmətɪst] n pragmático(a) m,f

Prague [prɑːg] n Praga

prairie ['preərɪ] n pradera f; **p. dog** perro m de las praderas; **p. schooner** = carromato típico de los colonos del oeste americano

praise [preɪz] **1** n elogio m, alabanza f; **in p. of** en alabanza de; **to sing the praises of** prodigar alabanzas a; **I have nothing but p. for him** no tengo más que elogios para él

2 vt elogiar, alabar; **to p. God** alabar a Dios; **to p. sb to the skies** poner a alguien por las nubes

praiseworthy ['preɪzwɜːðɪ] adj encomiable

prance [prɑːns] vi (horse) encabritarse; (person) dar brincos, brincar; **to p. in/out** entrar/salir dando brincos

prank [præŋk] n broma f (pesada), jugarreta f; **to play a p. on sb** gastarle una broma a alguien

prate [preɪt] vi Formal perorar

prattle ['prætəl] **1** n charla f, parloteo m

2 vi charlar, parlotear (**about** de or acerca de)

prawn [prɔːn] n gamba f, Am camarón m

pray [preɪ] vi rezar, orar; **to p. to God** rezar a Dios; **to p. for sth/sb** rezar por algo/alguien; Fig **to p. for good weather/ rain** rezar para que haga buen tiempo/llueva

prayer [preə(r)] n oración f; **to say one's prayers** rezar las oraciones; **to say a p.** rezar una oración; **her p. had been answered** sus súplicas habían sido atendidas; Fam Fig **he doesn't have a p.** (has no chance) no tiene ninguna posibilidad, no tiene nada que hacer; **p. beads** rosario m; **p.**

book devocionario m; **p. mat** = esterilla que utilizan los musulmanes para el rezo; **p. meeting** = reunión de creyentes, generalmente protestantes, para rezar en grupo

praying mantis ['preɪŋ'mæntɪs] n mantis f inv religiosa

preach [priːtʃ] **1** vt predicar

2 vi predicar; Fig **you're preaching to the converted** estás evangelizando en un convento

preacher ['priːtʃə(r)] n predicador(ora) m,f

preamble ['priːæmbəl] n Formal preámbulo m

prearranged [priːə'reɪndʒd] adj acordado(a) de antemano

precancerous [priː'kænsərəs] adj Med precanceroso(a)

precarious [prɪ'keərɪəs] adj precario(a)

precariously [prɪ'keərɪəslɪ] adv precariamente; **p. balanced** (object, situation) en equilibrio precario

precariousness [prɪ'keərɪəsnɪs] n precariedad f

precaution [prɪ'kɔːʃən] n precaución f; **to take precautions** tomar precauciones; (use contraceptive) usar anticonceptivos; **as a p.** como (medida de) precaución

precautionary [prɪ'kɔːʃənərɪ] adj preventivo(a)

precede [prɪ'siːd] vt (in time, space, importance) preceder a; **in the weeks preceding her departure** durante las semanas previas a su partida

precedence ['presɪdəns] n prioridad f, precedencia f; **in order of p.** por orden de precedencia; **to take p. over** tener prioridad sobre

precedent ['presɪdənt] n precedente m; **to create** or **set a p.** sentar (un) precedente; **without p.** sin precedentes

preceding [prɪ'siːdɪŋ] adj precedente, anterior

precept ['priːsept] n precepto m

precinct ['priːsɪŋkt] n (administrative, police division) distrito m; (police station) comisaría f (de policía)

precious ['preʃəs] **1** n (term of endearment) **my p.!** ¡mi cielo!

2 adj (a) (valuable) precioso(a), valioso(a); (secret, possession) preciado(a); **this photo is very p. to me** esta foto tiene mucho valor para mí; Ironic **you and your p. books!** ¡tú y tus dichosos libros! (b) Pej (affected) afectado(a)

3 adv Fam (for emphasis) **p. little** poquísimo; **p. few** poquísimos(as)

precipice ['presɪpɪs] n precipicio m

precipitate 1 [prɪ'sɪpɪtɪt] Chem precipitado m

2 adj Formal precipitado(a)

3 vt [prɪ'sɪpɪteɪt] (hasten) precipitar

precipitately [prɪ'sɪpɪtətlɪ] adv precipitadamente

precipitation [prɪsɪpɪ'teɪʃən] n Met precipitaciones fpl; **annual p.** pluviosidad f anual

precipitous [prɪ'sɪpɪtəs] adj (steep) empinado(a)

precipitously [prɪ'sɪpɪtəslɪ] adv (steeply) abruptamente, pronunciadamente

précis ['preɪsiː] (pl **précis** ['preɪsiːz]) n resumen m

precise [prɪ'saɪs] adj (a) (exact) preciso(a); **to be p.** para ser exactos; **at the p. moment when...** en el preciso momento en que... (b) (meticulous) meticuloso(a)

precisely [prɪ'saɪslɪ] adv precisamente; **at six (o'clock) p.** a las seis en punto; **p.!** ¡exactamente!

precision [prɪ'sɪʒən] n precisión f; Mil **p. bombing** bombardeo m de precisión; **p. instrument** instrumento m de precisión

preclude [prɪ'kluːd] vt excluir; **to p. sb from doing sth, to p. sb's doing sth** impedir a alguien hacer algo

precocious [prɪ'kəʊʃəs] adj precoz

precociousness [prɪ'kəʊʃəsnɪs], **precocity** [prɪ'kɒsɪtɪ] n precocidad f

preconceived [priːkən'siːvd] adj (idea) preconcebido(a)

preconception [priːkən'sepʃən] n idea f preconcebida; (prejudice) prejuicio m

precondition [priːkən'dɪʃən] n condición f previa

precooked [pri:'kʊkt] *adj* precocinado(a)

precursor [prɪ'kɜːsə(r)] *n* precursor(ora) *m,f*

predate [pri:'deɪt] *vt* (**a**) *(precede)* preceder a, anteceder a (**b**) *(put earlier date on)* antedatar

predator ['predətə(r)] *n* (*animal)* predador(ora) *m,f*, depredador(ora) *m,f; (person)* aprovechado(a) *m,f*, buitre *mf*

predatory ['predətərɪ] *adj (animal)* predador(ora), depredador(ora); *(person)* aprovechado(a)

predecessor ['pri:dɪsesə(r)] *n* predecesor(ora) *m,f*

predestination [pri:destɪ'neɪʃən] *n* predestinación *f*

predestine [pri:'destɪn] *vt* predestinar; **to be predestined to do sth** estar predestinado(a) a hacer algo

predetermine [pri:dɪ'tɜːmɪn] *vt* predeterminar

predicament [prɪ'dɪkəmənt] *n (unpleasant situation)* aprieto *m*, apuro *m; (difficult choice)* dilema *m*, conflicto *m;* **to be in an awkward p.** estar en un brete

predicate 1 *n* ['predɪkət] *Gram* predicado *m*
2 *vt* ['predɪkeɪt] **to be predicated on sth** fundarse *or* basarse en algo

predict [prɪ'dɪkt] *vt* predecir

predictability [prɪdɪktə'bɪlɪtɪ] *n* predicibilidad *f*

predictable [prɪ'dɪktəbəl] *adj (foreseeable)* predecible, previsible; *(unoriginal)* poco original; *Fam* **you're so p.!** ¡siempre estás con lo mismo!

predictably [prɪ'dɪktəblɪ] *adv* previsiblemente; **p., he arrived an hour late** como era de prever, llegó con una hora de retraso *or Am* demora

prediction [prɪ'dɪkʃən] *n* predicción *f*

predispose [pri:dɪs'pəʊz] *vt* predisponer; **I was not predisposed to believe her** no estaba predispuesto a creerla

predisposition [pri:dɪspə'zɪʃən] *n* predisposición *f* (**to** *or* **toward** a)

predominance [prɪ'dɒmɪnəns] *n* predominio *m*

predominant [prɪ'dɒmɪnənt] *adj* predominante

predominantly [prɪ'dɒmɪnəntlɪ] *adv* predominantemente

predominate [prɪ'dɒmɪneɪt] *vi* predominar

preeminence [prɪ'emɪnəns] *n* preeminencia *f*

preeminent [prɪ'emɪnənt] *adj* preeminente

preeminently [prɪ'emɪnəntlɪ] *adv (mainly)* sobre todo, por encima de todo

preempt [prɪ'empt] *vt* adelantarse a; **he was preempted by a rival** se le adelantó uno de sus rivales

preemptive [prɪ'emptɪv] *adj Fin* **p. bid** licitación *f or* oferta *f* preferente; *Mil* **p. strike** ataque *m* preventivo

preen [pri:n] *vt* **to p. itself** *(bird)* atusarse las plumas; **to p. oneself** *(person)* acicalarse

preestablished [pri:ɪs'tæblɪʃt] *adj* preestablecido(a)

prefab ['pri:fæb] *n Fam (house)* casa *f* prefabricada

prefabricated [pri:'fæbrɪkeɪtɪd] *adj* prefabricado(a)

preface ['prefɪs] **1** *n (of book)* prefacio *m*, prólogo *m; (to speech)* preámbulo *m*
2 *vt* **she prefaced her speech with an anecdote** abrió su discurso con una anécdota

prefect ['pri:fekt] *n (administrator)* prefecto *m*

prefer [prɪ'fɜː(r)] *(pt & pp* **preferred)** *vt* (**a**) *(favor)* preferir; **I p. wine to beer** prefiero el vino a la cerveza; **I p. her to her sister** me cae mejor ella que su hermana; **I would p. to stay at home** preferiría quedarme en casa (**b**) *Law* **to p. charges** presentar cargos

preferable ['prefərəbəl] *adj* preferible

preferably ['prefərəblɪ] *adv* preferiblemente

preference ['prefərəns] *n* preferencia *f;* **to give sb p., to give p. to sb** dar preferencia a alguien; **I have no p.** me da lo mismo; **in p. to...** antes que..., en lugar de...; **in order of p.** por orden de preferencia

preferential [prefə'renʃəl] *adj* preferente

preferred [prɪ'fɜːd] *adj* preferido(a), favorito(a); *St Exch* **p. stock** acciones *fpl* preferentes *or* privilegiadas

prefigure [pri:'fɪgə(r)] *vt* prefigurar

prefix ['pri:fɪks] *n* prefijo *m*

pregnancy ['pregnənsɪ] *n* embarazo *m;* **p. test** prueba *f* de embarazo

pregnant ['pregnənt] *adj* (**a**) *(woman)* embarazada; *(animal)* preñada; **to be p.** *(woman)* estar embarazada; *(animal)* estar preñada; **she's three months p.** está (embarazada) de tres meses (**b**) *Literary* **p. with** *(situation, remark)* preñado(a) *or* cargado(a) de; **a p. silence** un silencio significativo

preheat [pri:'hi:t] *vt* precalentar

prehensile [prɪ'hensaɪl] *adj* prensil

prehistoric [pri:hɪs'tɒrɪk] *adj* prehistórico(a)

prehistory [pri:'hɪstərɪ] *n* prehistoria *f*

prejudge [pri:'dʒʌdʒ] *vt* prejuzgar

prejudice ['predʒʊdɪs] **1** *n* (**a**) *(bias)* prejuicio *m* (**b**) *Law* **without p. to** sin perjuicio *or* menoscabo de
2 *vt* (**a**) *(bias)* predisponer (**against/in favor of** en contra de/a favor de) (**b**) *(harm)* perjudicar

prejudiced ['predʒʊdɪst] *adj* **to be p.** tener prejuicios; **to be p. against/in favor of** estar predispuesto(a) en contra de/a favor de

prejudicial [predʒʊ'dɪʃəl] *adj* perjudicial (**to** para)

preliminary [prɪ'lɪmɪnərɪ] **1** *n* preludio *m;* **preliminaries** *(to investigation, meeting)* preliminares *mpl*
2 *adj* preliminar

prelude ['prelju:d] *n* preludio *m* (**to** de *or* a)

premarital [pri:'mærɪtəl] *adj* prematrimonial

premature ['premətjʊə(r)] *adj* prematuro(a); *Fam* **you're being a bit p.!** ¡te estás adelantando un poco!; **p. ejaculation** eyaculación *f* precoz

prematurely ['premətjʊəlɪ] *adv* prematuramente

premeditated [pri:'medɪteɪtɪd] *adj* premeditado(a)

premeditation [pri:medɪ'teɪʃən] *n* premeditación *f*

premenstrual [pri:'menstrʊəl] *adj Med* **p. syndrome** síndrome *m* premenstrual; **p. tension** tensión *f* premenstrual

premier ['premɪə(r)] **1** *n (prime minister)* jefe(a) *m,f* del Gobierno, primer(era) ministro(a) *m,f*
2 *adj* primero(a)

premiere ['premɪeə(r)] *n (of play, movie)* estreno *m*

premise ['premɪs] **1** *n (of argument, theory)* premisa *f*
2 *vt* **to be premised on...** partir del supuesto *or* de la premisa de que...

premises ['premɪsɪz] *npl (of factory)* instalaciones *fpl; (of store)* local *m*, locales *mpl;* **business p.** locales comerciales; **on/off the p.** dentro/fuera del establecimiento; **to see sb off the p.** sacar a alguien del establecimiento

premium ['pri:mɪəm] *n* (**a**) *Fin (for insurance)* prima *f; (additional sum)* recargo *m;* **to sell sth at a p.** vender algo por encima de su valor (**b**) *(fuel)* gasolina *f* súper (**c**) *(idioms)* **to be at a p.** *(be scarce)* estar muy cotizado(a); **to put a p. on sth** conceder una importancia especial a algo

premonition [pri:mə'nɪʃən] *n* presentimiento *m*, premonición *f;* **to have a p. that...** tener el presentimiento de que...

prenatal [pri:'neɪtəl] *adj* prenatal

prenuptial ['pri:'nʌpʃəl] *adj* prenupcial; **p. agreement** acuerdo *m* prenupcial

preoccupation [pri:ɒkjʊ'peɪʃən] *n* preocupación *f* (**with** por)

preoccupied [pri:'ɒkjʊpaɪd] *adj* preocupado(a); **to be p. with** *or* **by sth** estar preocupado(a) por algo

preoccupy [pri:'ɒkjʊpaɪ] *vt* preocupar

prep [prep] *adj* **p. (school)** = escuela privada de enseñanza secundaria y preparación para estudios superiores

prepaid [pri:'peɪd] *adj (envelope)* franqueado(a), con franqueo pagado

preparation [prepə'reɪʃən] n (**a**) (act of preparing) preparación f; **preparations** (for ceremony, party) preparativos mpl (**b**) (medicine) preparado m

preparatory [prɪ'pærətərɪ] adj preparatorio(a); Formal **p. to (doing) sth** antes de (hacer) algo; **p. school** = escuela privada de enseñanza secundaria y preparación para estudios superiores

prepare [prɪ'peə(r)] **1** vt preparar
2 vi prepararse (**for** para); **to p. to do sth** prepararse or Am alistarse para hacer algo

prepared [prɪ'peəd] adj (**a**) (willing) **to be p. to do sth** estar dispuesto(a) a hacer algo (**b**) (ready) **to be p. for sth** estar preparado(a) para algo (**c**) (made in advance) **a p. statement** una declaración preparada (de antemano)

preparedness [prɪ'peərɪdnɪs] n preparación f

prepayment [priː'peɪmənt] n pago m (por) adelantado

preponderance [prɪ'pɒndərəns] n preponderancia f, predominio m

preposition [prepə'zɪʃən] n preposición f

prepositional [prepə'zɪʃənəl] adj preposicional

prepossessing [priːpə'zesɪŋ] adj atractivo(a), agradable

preposterous [prɪ'pɒstərəs] adj absurdo(a), ridículo(a)

preposterously [prɪ'pɒstərəslɪ] adv absurdamente, ridículamente

preppy, preppie ['prepɪ] adj Fam Esp pijo(a), Méx fresa, RP (con)cheto(a)

preprogram(m)ed [priː'prəʊɡræmd] adj Comptr preprogramado(a)

prequel ['priːkwəl] n = película o libro que desarrolla una historia o se refiere a eventos que preceden a otros contenidos en una obra ya existente

prerecord [priːrɪ'kɔːd] vt pregrabar

prerecorded [priːrɪ'kɔːdɪd] adj pregrabado(a)

prerequisite [priː'rekwɪzɪt] n requisito m previo (**of/for** para)

prerogative [prɪ'rɒɡətɪv] n prerrogativa f

Pres. (abbr **president**) presidente(a) m,f

presage ['presɪdʒ] Literary **1** n presagio m
2 vt presagiar

Presbyterian [prezbɪ'tɪərɪən] n & adj presbiteriano(a) m,f

presbytery ['prezbɪt(ə)rɪ] n presbiterio m

preschool [priː'skuːl] adj preescolar

preschooler ['priːskuːlə(r)] n niño(a) m,f en edad preescolar

prescribe [prɪ'skraɪb] vt (**a**) (medicine) recetar (**b**) (punishment, solution) prescribir; **in the prescribed manner** de la forma prescrita

prescription [prɪ'skrɪpʃən] n receta f; **available only on p.** sólo con receta médica; **p. charge** precio m de un medicamento con receta

preselect ['priːsə'lekt] vt (tracks, channels) preseleccionar

presence ['prezəns] n presencia f; **in the p. of** en presencia de; **to have p.** tener mucha presencia; **she made her p. felt** hizo sentir su presencia; **p. of mind** presencia de ánimo

present¹ ['prezənt] **1** n **the p.** el presente; **up to the p.** hasta la fecha, hasta ahora; **at p.** (now) en estos momentos; (these days) actualmente; **for the p.** de momento, por el momento
2 adj (**a**) (in attendance) presente; **to be p. (at)** estar presente (en); **those p.** los presentes (**b**) (current) actual; **at the p. time** or **moment** en estos momentos; **in the p. case** en este caso; Gram **p. perfect** pretérito m perfecto; Gram **the p. tense** el (tiempo) presente; **p. participle** participio m de presente or activo

present² **1** n ['prezənt] (gift) regalo m; **to give sb a p.** regalar algo a alguien; **birthday/Christmas p.** regalo de cumpleaños/Navidad
2 vt [prɪ'zent] (**a**) (introduce, put forward) presentar; **if the opportunity presents itself** si se presenta la ocasión (**b**)

(give) entregar; **to p. sth to sb, to p. sb with sth** (gift) regalar algo a alguien; (award, certificate) otorgar or entregar algo a alguien (**c**) Mil **p. arms!** ¡presenten armas!

presentable [prɪ'zentəbəl] adj presentable; **to make oneself p.** ponerse presentable

presentation [prezən'teɪʃən] n (**a**) (of person) presentación (**b**) (of gift, award) entrega f; **to make a p. to sb** (give present) hacer (entrega de) un obsequio a alguien; (give award) otorgar or entregar un premio a alguien (**c**) (formal talk) **to give a p** hacer una exposición, dar una charla (con la ayuda de gráficos, diapositivas, etc.) (**d**) **on p. of** (passport, coupon) con la presentación de,

present-day ['prezənt'deɪ] adj actual

presentiment [prɪ'zentɪmənt] n premonición f, presentimiento m

presently ['prezəntlɪ] adv (**a**) (soon) pronto; (soon afterward poco después (**b**) (now) actualmente

preservation [prezə'veɪʃən] n (**a**) (maintenance) conservación f, mantenimiento m (**b**) (protection) (of species, building, conservación f, protección f

preservative [prɪ'zɜːvətɪv] n conservante m

preserve [prɪ'zɜːv] **1** n (**a**) (jam) confitura f, mermelada f (**b** (in hunting) coto m de caza (**c**) (area of dominance) territorio m **engineering is no longer a male p.** la ingeniería ya no es un mundo exclusivamente masculino
2 vt (**a**) (maintain) conservar, mantener (**b**) (leather, wood conservar (**c**) (fruit) confitar, poner en conserva (**d**) (protect conservar, proteger (**from** de); **saints p. us!** ¡que Dios no proteja or ampare!

preshrunk [priː'ʃrʌŋk] adj lavado(a) previamente

preside [prɪ'zaɪd] vi presidir; **to p. over a meeting** presidir una reunión; **he presided over the decline of the empire** él estuvo al mando durante el declive del imperio

presidency ['prezɪdənsɪ] n presidencia f; (of college) rectorado m

president ['prezɪdənt] n (of country, company) presidente(a) m,f; (of college) rector(ora) m,f; **Presidents' Day** Día m de los presidentes, = fiesta que conmemora los nacimientos de Washington y Lincoln, el tercer lunes de febrero

presidential [prezɪ'denʃəl] adj presidencial

press [pres] **1** n (**a**) (act of pushing) **at the p. of a button...** a pulsar un botón...; Hist **p. gang** = grupo de marineros que se encargaba de reclutar por la fuerza a gente para la Armada
(**b**) (newspapers) **the p.** la prensa; **to get a good/bad p.** tener buena/mala prensa; **p. agency** agencia f de noticias; **p. box** tribuna f de prensa or periodistas; **p. clipping** recorte m de prensa; **p. conference** rueda f or conferencia f de prensa; **p. kit** carpeta f or dossier m de prensa; **p. officer** jefe(a) m,f de prensa; **p. photographer** fotógrafo(a) m,f de prensa; **p. release** comunicado m or nota f de prensa; **p. secretary** secretario(a) m,f de prensa
(**c**) (machine) prensa f; (printing) **p.** imprenta f; **to go to p** (newspaper) entrar en prensa
2 vt (**a**) (button, switch) apretar; (into clay, cement) presiona (**into** sobre); **he pressed the note into my hand** me puso el billete en la mano
(**b**) (squeeze) apretar; (juice, lemon) exprimir; (grapes, olives, flowers) prensar
(**c**) (iron) planchar
(**d**) (pressurize) presionar; **to p. sb to do sth** presionar a alguien para que haga algo; **to be pressed for time/money** estar apurado(a) de tiempo/dinero
(**e**) (force) **to p. sth on sb** obligar a alguien a aceptar algo; **to p. home one's advantage** sacar (uno) el máximo partido a su ventaja; **to p. one's attentions on sb** prodigar excesivas atenciones a alguien
(**f**) Law **to p. charges (against sb)** presentar cargos (contra alguien)

3 *vi (push)* empujar; *(crowd)* apelotonarse

▸**press ahead** = press on

▸**press for** *vt insep (demand)* exigir

▸**press on** *vi* seguir adelante

pressing ['presɪŋ] *adj (urgent)* apremiante

pressure ['preʃə(r)] **1** *n* presión *f*; **to put p. on sb (to do sth)** presionar a alguien (para que haga algo); **to be under p.** estar presionado(a); **p. of work** estrés *m* laboral; **p. cooker** olla *f* a presión; **p. gauge** manómetro *m*; **p. group** grupo *m* de presión; *Med* **p. point** punto *m* de presión

2 *vt* **to p. sb to do sth** presionar a alguien para que haga algo

pressurize ['preʃəraɪz] *vt* **(a)** *Tech (container)* presurizar **(b)** *(person)* **to p. sb (into doing sth)** presionar a alguien (para que haga algo)

pressurized ['preʃəraɪzd] *adj Tech* presurizado(a)

prestige [pres'tiːʒ] *n* prestigio *m*

prestigious [pres'tɪdʒəs] *adj* prestigioso(a)

presumably [prɪ'zjuːməblɪ] *adv* presumiblemente, según cabe suponer; **p. she'll come** cabe suponer que vendrá

presume [prɪ'zjuːm] **1** *vt* **(a)** *(suppose)* suponer; **I p. so** supongo (que sí) **(b)** **to p. to do sth** tomarse la libertad de hacer algo

2 *vi (be cheeky)* pasarse de listo(a); **I don't want to p. on you** no quiero abusar de su generosidad

presumed [prɪ'zjuːmd] *adj* **twenty people are missing, p. dead** han desaparecido veinte personas, por cuyas vidas se teme; **everyone is p. innocent until proven guilty** todo el mundo es inocente hasta que no se demuestre lo contrario

presumption [prɪ'zʌmpʃən] *n* **(a)** *(assumption)* suposición *f*, supuesto *m*; *Law* **p. of innocence** presunción *f* de inocencia **(b)** *(arrogance)* presunción *f*, osadía *f*

presumptuous [prɪ'zʌmptjʊəs] *adj* presuntuoso(a), osado(a)

presuppose [priːsə'pəʊz] *vt* presuponer

presupposition [priːsʌpə'zɪʃən] *n* supuesto *m*, suposición *f*

pretend [prɪ'tend] **1** *vt* **(a)** *(feign)* fingir, simular; **to p. to be ill** fingir que se está enfermo(a); **to p. to do sth** fingir hacer algo; **they pretended that nothing had happened** hicieron como si no hubiera pasado nada **(b)** *(claim)* pretender

2 *vi (put on an act)* fingir

3 *adj Fam* de mentira; **p. money** dinero *m* de mentira; **a p. slap** un amago de bofetada

pretense [prɪ'tens] *n* fingimiento *m*; **he says… but it's all a p.** dice que… pero es mentira; **to make a p. of doing sth** aparentar hacer algo; **he made no p. of his skepticism** no trató de ocultar su escepticismo

pretension [prɪ'tenʃən] *n* pretensión *f*

pretentious [prɪ'tenʃəs] *adj* pretencioso(a)

pretentiousness [prɪ'tenʃəsnəs] *n* pretenciosidad *f*

preterit(e) ['pretərɪt] *n Gram* **the p.** el pretérito

pretext ['priːtekst] *n* pretexto *m*; **under** *or* **on the p. of doing sth** con el pretexto de hacer algo

Pretoria [prɪ'tɔːrɪə] *n* Pretoria

prettiness ['prɪtɪnɪs] *n* lo bonito

pretty ['prɪtɪ] **1** *adj (person, thing)* bonito(a), *Am* lindo(a); **it's not a p. sight** es un espectáculo lamentable; *Fam* **to cost a p. penny** costar un riñón

2 *adv* **(a)** *(fairly)* bastante; **they're p. much the same** son poco más o menos lo mismo **(b)** *Fam* **to be sitting p.** encontrarse en una situación ventajosa

pretzel ['pretzəl] *n* palito *m* salado *(alargado o en forma de 8)*

prevail [prɪ'veɪl] *vi* **(a)** *(be successful)* prevalecer **(over** sobre**)**; **let us hope that justice prevails** esperemos que se imponga la justicia **(b)** *(persuade)* **to p. upon sb to do sth** convencer a alguien para que haga algo **(c)** *(predominate)* predominar; **in the conditions now prevailing** en las circunstancias actuales

prevailing [prɪ'veɪlɪŋ] *adj* predominante

prevalent ['prevələnt] *adj* frecuente, corriente

prevaricate [prɪ'værɪkeɪt] *vi* dar rodeos, andar con evasivas

prevarication [prɪværɪ'keɪʃən] *n* rodeos *mpl*, evasivas *fpl*

prevent [prɪ'vent] *vt* evitar, impedir; **to p. sb from doing sth** evitar *or* impedir que alguien haga algo; **to p. sth from happening** evitar *or* impedir que pase algo

preventable [prɪ'ventəbəl] *adj* evitable

preventative = preventive

prevention [prɪ'venʃən] *n* prevención *f*; *Prov* **p. is better than cure** más vale prevenir que curar

preventive [prɪ'ventɪv], **preventative** [prɪ'ventətɪv] *adj* **p. medicine** medicina *f* preventiva; **p. measures** medidas *fpl* preventivas

preview ['priːvjuː] **1** *n (of play, movie)* preestreno *m*; *(of TV program)* avance *m*

2 *vt* **the movie was previewed** hubo un preestreno de la película

previous ['priːvɪəs] **1** *adj* previo(a), anterior; **the p. day** el día anterior; **p. engagement** compromiso *m* previo; *Law* **p. convictions** antecedentes *mpl* penales

2 *adv* **p. to** con anterioridad a

previously ['priːvɪəslɪ] *adv* anteriormente; **three days p.** tres días antes

prewar ['priːwɔː(r)] *adj* de preguerra

prey [preɪ] *n* presa *f*; *Fig* **to be a p. to** ser presa (fácil) para *or* de; **to fall p. to** caer *or* ser víctima de

▸**prey on, prey upon** *vt insep (of animal)* alimentarse de; *(of opportunist)* aprovecharse de, cebarse en; **something is preying on his mind** está atormentado por algo

price [praɪs] **1** *n* precio *m*; **to rise** *or* **increase in p.** subir de precio; **at any p.** a toda costa; **not at any p.** por nada del mundo; *Fig* **to pay the p. (for sth)** pagar el precio (de algo); *Fig* **it's too high a p. (to pay)** es un precio demasiado alto *or* caro; **to put** *or* **set a p. on sb's head** poner precio a la cabeza de alguien; *Fig* **everyone has his p.** todos tenemos un precio; *Fam* **what p. patriotism now?** ¿de qué ha servido tanto patriotismo?; **p. cut** reducción *f* de precios; **p. freeze** congelación *f* de precios; **p. increase** subida *f* de precios; **p. index** índice *m* de precios; **p. list** lista *f* de precios; **p. range** escala *f* de precios; **that's outside my p. range** eso no está a mi alcance; **p. tag** etiqueta *f* del precio; **p. war** guerra *f* de precios

2 *vt (decide cost of)* poner precio a; **the toy is priced at $10** el precio del juguete es de 10 dólares; **to p. oneself out of the market** perder mercado por pedir precios demasiado elevados

price-cutting ['praɪs'kʌtɪŋ] *n Com* reducción *f* de precios

-priced [praɪst] *suffix* **high-p.** caro(a); **low-p.** barato(a)

price-fixing ['praɪs'fɪksɪŋ] *n Com* fijación *f* de precios

priceless ['praɪslɪs] *adj* **(a)** *(invaluable)* de valor incalculable **(b)** *Fam (funny)* graciosísimo(a)

pricey, pricy ['praɪsɪ] *adj Fam* carillo(a)

prick [prɪk] **1** *n* **(a)** *(of needle)* pinchazo *m*; **pricks of conscience** remordimientos *mpl* de conciencia **(b)** *Vulg (penis) Esp* polla *f*, *Am* verga *f*, *Chile* pico *m*, *Chile* penca *f*, *Méx* pito *m*, *RP* pija *f* **(c)** *Vulg (person) Esp* gilipollas *mf inv*, *Am* pendejo(a) *m,f*, *RP* forro *m*

2 *vt (make holes in)* pinchar; **to p. one's finger** pincharse el dedo; **to p. a hole in sth** hacer un agujero en algo

▸**prick up** *vt sep* **to p. up one's ears** *(dog)* aguzar las orejas; *(person)* aguzar el oído *or* los oídos

prickle ['prɪkəl] **1** *n* **(a)** *(of hedgehog)* púa *f*; *(of plant)* espina *f*, pincho *m* **(b)** *(sensation)* hormigueo *m*

2 *vi (skin)* hormiguear

prickly ['prɪklɪ] *adj* **(a)** *(animal)* cubierto(a) de púas; *(plant)* espinoso(a); *Fig (person)* susceptible, irritable; **p. pear** *(tree)* chumbera *f*, nopal *m*; *(fruit)* higo *m* chumbo, *Am* tuna *f* **(b)**

(sensation) hormigueante; **p. heat** = erupción cutánea producida por el calor

pricy = pricey

pride [praɪd] **1** n **(a)** *(satisfaction)* orgullo m; *(self-esteem)* amor m propio; *Pej (vanity)* soberbia f, orgullo m; **to take p. in sth** enorgullecerse de algo **(b)** *(person, thing)* **he is the p. of the family** es el orgullo de la familia; **the p. of my collection** la joya de mi colección; **she's his p. and joy** ella es su mayor orgullo; **to have p. of place** ocupar el lugar preferente **(c)** *(of lions)* manada f
  2 vt **to p. oneself on sth** enorgullecerse de algo

priest [priːst] n sacerdote m

priestess ['priːstɪs] n sacerdotisa f

priesthood ['priːsthʊd] n sacerdocio m; **to enter the p.** ordenarse sacerdote

prig [prɪɡ] n puritano(a) m,f, mojigato(a) m,f

priggish ['prɪɡɪʃ] adj puritano(a), mojigato(a)

prim [prɪm] adj **p. (and proper)** remilgado(a)

primacy ['praɪməsɪ] n primacía f

prima facie ['praɪmə'feɪʃɪ] **1** adj Law **p. case** caso m prima facie
  2 adv a primera vista

primarily [praɪ'merɪlɪ] adv principalmente

primary ['praɪmərɪ] **1** n *(in election)* elecciones fpl primarias
  2 adj **(a)** *(main)* principal; **p. colors** colores mpl primarios **(b)** *(initial)* **p. education** enseñanza f primaria; **p. school** escuela f primaria

primate ['praɪmeɪt] n **(a)** *(animal)* primate m **(b)** Rel primado m

prime [praɪm] **1** n *(best time)* **the p. of life** la flor de la vida; **she was in her p.** estaba en sus mejores años; **she is past her p.** su mejor momento ha pasado
  2 adj **(a)** *(principal)* principal, primordial; *(importance)* capital; **p. minister** primer(era) ministro(a) m,f; **p. ministership** or **ministry** mandato m de primer ministro; Math **p. number** número m primo; **p. time** *(on TV)* franja f *(horaria)* de máxima audiencia **(b)** *(excellent)* óptimo(a), excelente; **a p. example (of)** un ejemplo palmario (de); **p. quality** calidad f suprema
  3 vt **(a)** *(prepare) (engine, pump)* cebar; *(surface)* imprimar **(b)** *(provide with information)* **to p. sb for sth** preparar or instruir a alguien para algo

primer¹ ['praɪmə(r)] n *(paint)* tapaporos m inv

primer² n *(textbook)* texto m elemental

primeval [praɪ'miːvəl] adj primigenio(a), primitivo(a); **p. forests** bosques mpl vírgenes

primitive ['prɪmɪtɪv] adj primitivo(a)

primly ['prɪmlɪ] adv con remilgo

primordial [praɪ'mɔːdɪəl] adj primigenio(a), primitivo(a); **p. soup** sustancia f primigenia

primrose ['prɪmrəʊz] n *(plant)* primavera f; **p. yellow** amarillo m claro

primula ['prɪmjʊlə] n prímula f

Primus® **(stove)** ['praɪməs('stəʊv)] n infiernillo m, camping-gas m inv, Am primus m inv

prince [prɪns] n príncipe m; **the P. of Wales** el Príncipe de Gales; **P. Charming** príncipe m azul; **p. regent** príncipe m regente

princely ['prɪnslɪ] adj *(splendid)* magnífico(a); also Ironic **a p. sum** una bonita suma

princess [prɪn'ses] n princesa f

principal ['prɪnsɪpəl] **1** n *(of school)* director(ora) m,f
  2 adj principal

principality [prɪnsɪ'pælɪtɪ] n principado m

principle ['prɪnsɪpəl] n principio m; **in p.** en principio; **on p.** por principios

principled ['prɪnsɪpəld] adj *(person, behavior)* ejemplar, de grandes principios

print [prɪnt] **1** n **(a)** *(of fingers, feet)* huella f **(b)** *(printed matter)*

---

in p. impreso(a); **out of p., no longer in p.** agotado(a); **to appear in p.** aparecer impreso(a); **p. run** *(of books, newspapers)* tirada f, Am tiraje m **(c)** *(characters)* caracteres mpl; Fig **the small p.** *(in contract)* la letra pequeña **(d)** *(engraving)* grabado m; *(photographic copy)* copia f; *(textile)* estampado m
  2 vt **(a)** *(book)* imprimir; *(newspaper)* publicar; **the image had printed itself on her memory** se le quedó la imagen grabada en la memoria **(b)** *(write clearly)* escribir claramente *(con las letras separadas)* **(c)** *(in photography)* **to p. a negative** sacar copias de un negativo
  3 vi *(write clearly)* escribir con claridad

▸**print out** vt sep Comptr imprimir

printed ['prɪntɪd] adj impreso(a); Elec **p. circuit** circuito m impreso; **p. matter** impresos mpl

printer ['prɪntə(r)] n *(person)* impresor(ora) m,f; *(machine)* impresora f

printing ['prɪntɪŋ] n *(process, action)* impresión f; *(industry)* imprenta f, artes fpl gráficas; **first/second p.** primera/ segunda impresión; **p. error** errata f *(de imprenta)*; **p. press** imprenta

printout ['prɪntaʊt] n Comptr listado m, copia f en papel

prior¹ ['praɪə(r)] **1** adj previo(a); **to have p. knowledge of sth** tener conocimiento previo de algo
  2 adv **p. to** con anterioridad a

prior² n Rel prior m

prioritize [praɪ'ɒrɪtaɪz] vt dar prioridad a

priority [praɪ'ɒrɪtɪ] n prioridad f; **to have** or **take p. over sth/sb** tener prioridad respecto a algo/alguien; **we need to get our priorities right** tenemos que establecer un orden de prioridades; **you should get your priorities right!** ¡tienes que darte cuenta de lo que es verdaderamente importante!

priory ['praɪərɪ] n Rel priorato m

prism ['prɪzəm] n prisma m

prison ['prɪzən] n cárcel f, prisión f; **p. camp** campo m de prisioneros; **p. officer** funcionario(a) m,f de prisiones

prisoner ['prɪzənə(r)] n *(in jail)* recluso(a) m,f; *(captive,* prisionero(a) m,f; **to hold/take sb p.** tener/hacer prisionero(a) a alguien; Fig **to take no prisoners** no andarse con chiquitas; **p. of war** prisionero(a) m,f de guerra

prissy ['prɪsɪ] adj Fam remilgado(a)

pristine ['prɪstiːn] adj prístino(a), inmaculado(a)

privacy ['prɪvəsɪ, 'praɪvəsɪ] n intimidad f; **in the p. of one's own home** en la intimidad del hogar

private ['praɪvɪt] **1** n **(a)** **in p.** en privado **(b)** *(soldier)* soldado m raso; **p. first class** = rango del ejército de los Estados Unidos que se encuentra entre soldado raso y cabo
  2 adj **(a)** *(personal)* privado(a), personal; **p. life** vida privada; Fam **p. parts** partes fpl pudendas
  (b) *(secret)* privado(a); **p. and confidential** privado y confidencial; **can we go somewhere p.?** ¿podemos ir a un lugar donde estemos a solas?
  (c) *(for personal use)* particular; **a p. house** una casa particular; **p. lessons** clases fpl particulares; Tel **p. line** línea f privada; **p. office** oficina f particular; **p. secretary** secretario(a) m,f personal
  (d) *(not state-run)* privado(a); **p. detective** or **investigator** o Fam **eye** detective mf or investigador(ora) m,f privado(a); **p. education** enseñanza f privada; **p. enterprise** empresa privada; **p. school** colegio m privado
  (e) *(not for the public)* **a p. party** una fiesta particular o privada; **p. property** propiedad f privada; **p. road** carretera f particular

privately ['praɪvɪtlɪ] adv *(in private)* en privado; **she was p. educated** fue a un colegio privado; **p. owned** en manos privadas

privation [praɪ'veɪʃən] n privación f
privatization [praɪvɪtaɪ'zeɪʃən] n privatización f
privatize ['praɪvɪtaɪz] vt privatizar
privet ['prɪvɪt] n alheña f
privilege ['prɪvɪlɪdʒ] **1** n privilegio m; **to have the p. of doing sth** tener el privilegio de hacer algo
2 vt **to be privileged to do sth** tener el privilegio de hacer algo
privy ['prɪvɪ] **1** n Old-fashioned (toilet) retrete m, excusado m
2 adj Formal **to be p. to sth** estar enterado(a) de algo
prize¹ [praɪz] **1** n (award) premio m; **to win a p.** ganar un premio; Fig **no prizes for guessing who did it** es evidente quién lo hizo; **p. day** día m de la entrega de premios; **p. draw** rifa f; **p. money** (dinero m del) premio m; **he won p. money of $60,000** ganó un premio en metálico de 60.000 dólares
2 vt (value) apreciar
prize² = **pry²**
prizefight ['praɪzfaɪt] n combate m profesional de boxeo
prizefighter ['praɪzfaɪtə(r)] n boxeador m profesional
prizegiving ['praɪzgɪvɪŋ] n entrega f de premios
prizewinner ['praɪzwɪnə(r)] n premiado(a) m,f
prizewinning ['praɪzwɪnɪŋ] adj premiado(a)
pro¹ [prəʊ] (pl **pros**) Fam **1** n (professional) profesional mf, Méx profesionista mf
2 adj profesional; **p. football** fútbol m americano profesional
pro² **1** n (pl **pros**) **the pros and cons** los pros y los contras
2 prep **to be p. sth** estar a favor de algo
proactive [prəʊ'æktɪv] adj **to be p.** tomar la iniciativa
pro-am ['prəʊ'æm] n Sport torneo m abierto para profesionales y aficionados
probability [prɒbə'bɪlɪtɪ] n probabilidad f; **in all p.** con toda probabilidad
probable ['prɒbəbəl] adj probable
probably ['prɒbəblɪ] adv probablemente
probation [prə'beɪʃən] n (in job) periodo m de prueba; Law libertad f condicional; **on p.** (in job) a prueba; Law en libertad condicional; **p. officer** = asistente social que ayuda y supervisa a un preso en libertad condicional
probationary [prə'beɪʃənərɪ] adj de prueba
probationer [prə'beɪʃənə(r)] n (in job) trabajador(ora) m,f en periodo de prueba
probe [prəʊb] **1** n (a) (instrument) sonda f; (space) **p.** sonda espacial (b) Fam (inquiry) investigación f
2 vt (a) Med sondar; (feel) tantear (b) (investigate) investigar
3 vi **to p. into** (past, private life) escarbar en
probity ['prəʊbɪtɪ] n Formal probidad f
problem ['prɒbləm] n problema m; **he's a p.** es problemático; Fam **no p.!** ¡claro (que sí)!; **p. area** (in town) zona f problemática; (in project) asunto m problemático; **p. child** niño(a) m,f problemático(a) or difícil
problematic(al) [prɒblɪ'mætɪk(əl)] adj problemático(a)
problem-solving ['prɒbləmsɒlvɪŋ] **1** n resolución f de problemas
2 adj **p. skills** habilidades fpl para la resolución de problemas
procedure [prə'siːdʒə(r)] n procedimiento m
proceed [prə'siːd] vt **to p. to do sth** proceder a hacer algo, ponerse a hacer algo
2 vi (a) (go on) proseguir; **to p. with sth** seguir adelante con algo; **to p. with caution** proceder con cautela; **how shall we p.?** ¿cómo hemos de proceder? (b) (result) **to p. from** proceder de
proceedings [prə'siːdɪŋz] npl (a) (events) acto m (b) Law proceso m, pleito m; **to start p. against sb** entablar un pleito contra alguien
proceeds ['prəʊsiːdz] npl recaudación f
process¹ ['prəʊses] **1** n proceso m; **by a p. of elimination**

por eliminación; **he failed, and lost all his money in the p.** al fracasar, perdió todo su dinero; **to be in the p. of doing sth** estar haciendo algo
2 vt (raw material, waste, information) procesar; (request) tramitar; (film) revelar; **processed** or **p. cheese** queso m fundido; **processed food** alimentos mpl manipulados or procesados
process² [prə'ses] vi (walk in procession) desfilar
processing ['prəʊsesɪŋ] n (of raw material, waste, information) procesamiento m; (of request) tramitación f; (of photographs) revelado m; Comptr **p. language** lenguaje m de programación; Comptr **p. speed** velocidad f de proceso
procession [prə'seʃən] n procesión f; **in p.** en fila
processor ['prəʊsesə(r)] n Comptr procesador m
pro-choice ['prəʊ'tʃɔɪs] adj = en favor del derecho de la mujer a decidir en materia de aborto
proclaim [prə'kleɪm] vt (one's innocence, guilt) proclamar; **to p. a state of emergency** declarar el estado de emergencia
proclamation [prɒklə'meɪʃən] n proclamación f
proclivity [prəʊ'klɪvɪtɪ] n Formal propensión f, proclividad f (**for** a)
procrastinate [prəʊ'kræstɪneɪt] vi andarse con dilaciones, retrasar las cosas
procrastination [prəʊkræstɪ'neɪʃən] n dilaciones fpl, demora f
procreate ['prəʊkrɪeɪt] vi Formal reproducirse, procrear
procreation [prəʊkrɪ'eɪʃən] n Formal procreación f
procure [prə'kjʊə(r)] vt obtener, conseguir; **to p. sth for sb** procurarle algo a alguien; **to p. sth for oneself** hacerse con algo
procurement [prə'kjʊəmənt] n obtención f
prod [prɒd] **1** n **to give sth/sb a p.** dar un empujón a algo/alguien; Fig **he needs a p.** necesita que lo espoleen
2 vt (pt & pp **prodded**) (poke) empujar; Fig **to p. sb into doing sth** espolear a alguien para que haga algo
prodigal ['prɒdɪgəl] adj pródigo(a)
prodigious [prə'dɪdʒəs] adj prodigioso(a)
prodigy ['prɒdɪdʒɪ] n prodigio m
produce 1 n ['prɒdjuːs] (food) productos mpl del campo; **agricultural/dairy p.** productos agrícolas/lácteos; **p. of Spain** producto de España
2 vt [prə'djuːs] (a) (create) (food, goods) producir; (effect, reaction) producir, provocar (b) (present) (ticket, passport) presentar, mostrar; (documents, alibi) presentar; **she produced a $10 bill** sacó un billete de 10 dólares (c) (play) montar; (movie, radio or TV program) producir
producer [prə'djuːsə(r)] n (a) (of crops, goods) productor(ora) m,f (b) (of movie, play, radio or TV program) productor(ora) m,f
product ['prɒdʌkt] n producto m; Com **p. development** desarrollo m del producto; Mktg **p. placement** colocación f de producto
production [prə'dʌkʃən] n (a) (manufacture) producción f; **to go into p.** empezar a fabricarse; **it went out of p. years ago** hace años que dejó de fabricarse; **p. costs** costos mpl or Esp costes mpl de producción; **p. line** cadena f de producción; **p. manager** jefe(a) m,f de producción; **p. process** proceso m de producción; **p. target** objetivo m de producción (b) (play) montaje m; (movie, radio or TV program) producción f
productive [prə'dʌktɪv] adj productivo(a)
productivity [prɒdʌk'tɪvɪtɪ] n Ind productividad f; **p. agreement** acuerdo m sobre productividad; **p. bonus** plus m de productividad; **p. drive** campaña f de productividad
profane [prə'feɪn] **1** adj (a) (language) blasfemo(a) (b) Rel (secular) profano(a)
2 vt profanar
profanity [prə'fænɪtɪ] n (a) (oath) blasfemia f (b) (blasphemous nature) grosería f

profess [prə'fes] *vt* (**a**) *(declare)* manifestar (**b**) *(claim)* proclamar; **he professes to be a socialist** se dice socialista; **I don't p. to be an expert, but...** no pretendo ser un experto, pero...

professed [prə'fest] *adj* (**a**) *(self-declared)* declarado(a) (**b**) *(pretended)* supuesto(a), pretendido(a)

profession [prə'feʃən] *n* (**a**) *(occupation)* profesión *f*; **by p.** de profesión; **the teaching p.** el profesorado (**b**) *(declaration)* manifestación *f*

professional [prə'feʃənəl] **1** *n* profesional *mf*, *Méx* profesionista *mf*
2 *adj (paid, competent)* profesional; *(soldier)* de carrera; *(army)* profesional; **they made a very p. job of the repair** hicieron la reparación con gran profesionalidad; **to turn** *or* **go p.** *(sportsperson)* hacerse profesional *or Méx* profesionista; **to take p. advice on sth** pedir asesoramiento sobre algo a un profesional *or Méx* profesionista; **p. misconduct** violación *f* de la ética profesional

professionalism [prə'feʃənəlɪzəm] *n* (**a**) *(professional approach)* profesionalidad *f* (**b**) *(in sports)* profesionalismo *m*

professor [prə'fesə(r)] *n Univ* profesor(ora) *m,f*

proffer ['prɒfə(r)] *vt Formal (advice)* brindar; *(opinion)* ofrecer, dar; *(thanks)* dar; *(hand, object)* tender

proficiency [prə'fɪʃənsɪ] *n* competencia *f* (**in** *or* **at** en), aptitud *f* (**in** *or* **at** para)

proficient [prə'fɪʃənt] *adj* competente (**in** *or* **at** en)

profile ['prəʊfaɪl] **1** *n* (**a**) *(side view, outline)* perfil *m*; **to keep a low p.** mantenerse en un segundo plano (**b**) *(description)* retrato *m*
2 *vt (describe)* retratar

profit ['prɒfɪt] **1** *n* (**a**) *(of company, on deal)* beneficio *m*; **at a p.** con beneficios; **to make a p.** obtener *or* sacar beneficios; *Com* **p. center** centro *m* de beneficios; **p. and loss account** cuenta *f* de pérdidas y ganancias; **p. margin** margen *m* de beneficios; **p. sharing** participación *f* en los beneficios (**b**) *(advantage)* provecho *m*
2 *vi* **to p. by** *or* **from** sacar provecho de

profitability [prɒfɪtə'bɪlɪtɪ] *n* rentabilidad *f*

profitable ['prɒfɪtəbəl] *adj (company, deal)* rentable; *(experience)* provechoso(a)

profitably ['prɒfɪtəblɪ] *adv (trade, operate)* con beneficios; *(use one's time)* provechosamente

profiteer [prɒfɪ'tɪə(r)] *Pej* **1** *n* desaprensivo(a) *m,f*, especulador(ora) *m,f*
2 *vi* especular

profit-making ['prɒfɪtmeɪkɪŋ] *adj* con ánimo de lucro, lucrativo(a)

profligate ['prɒflɪgət] *adj Formal* derrochador(ora)

profound [prə'faʊnd] *adj* profundo(a)

profundity [prə'fʌndɪtɪ] *n* profundidad *f*

profuse [prə'fjuːs] *adj* profuso(a); **he offered p. apologies/thanks** se prodigó en disculpas/agradecimientos

profusely [prə'fjuːslɪ] *adv (to apologize, thank)* cumplidamente; *(to sweat, bleed)* profusamente

profusion [prə'fjuːʒən] *n* profusión *f*

progeny ['prɒdʒɪnɪ] *n Formal* progenie *f*, prole *f*

prognosis [prɒg'nəʊsɪs] *(pl* **prognoses** [prɒg'nəʊsiːz]*) n Med & Fig* pronóstico *m*

program¹ ['prəʊgræm] *Comptr* **1** *n* programa *m*
2 *vt & vi (pt & pp* **program(m)ed**) programar

program² ['prəʊgræm] **1** *n (on TV, for play, of political party)* programa *m*; **what's the p. for today?** ¿qué programa tenemos para hoy?; **p. seller** vendedor(ora) *m,f* de programas
2 *vt* programar; **to p. sth to do sth** programar algo para que haga algo

program(m)able [prəʊ'græməbəl] *adj* programable; **p. calculator** calculadora *f* programable

program(m)ed ['prəʊgræmd] *n Educ* **p. instruction** *or* **learning** enseñanza *f* programada

program(m)er ['prəʊgræmə(r)] *n Comptr* programador(ora) *m,f*

progress 1 *n* ['prəʊgres] (**a**) *(improvement)* progreso *m*; **to make p. (in sth)** hacer progresos (en algo) (**b**) *(movement)* avance *m*, progreso *m*; **in p.** en curso; **a p. report on the project** un informe *or Am* reporte sobre la marcha del proyecto
2 *vi* [prə'gres] (**a**) *(improve)* progresar; **the patient is progressing satisfactorily** el paciente evoluciona satisfactoriamente (**b**) *(advance)* avanzar

progression [prə'greʃən] *n* evolución *f*, progresión *f*

progressive [prə'gresɪv] **1** *n* progresista *mf*
2 *adj* (**a**) *(increasing)* progresivo(a); **p. disease** enfermedad *f* degenerativa (**b**) *(forward-looking)* progresista

progressively [prə'gresɪvlɪ] *adv* progresivamente

prohibit [prə'hɪbɪt] *vt (forbid)* prohibir; **to p. sb from doing sth** prohibir a alguien que haga algo; **smoking prohibited** *(sign)* prohibido fumar; **it is prohibited by law** lo prohíbe la ley

prohibition [prəʊɪ'bɪʃən] *n* prohibición *f*; *Hist* **P.** la Ley Seca

prohibitive [prə'hɪbɪtɪv] *adj* prohibitivo(a)

prohibitively [prə'hɪbɪtɪvlɪ] *adv* **p. expensive** de precio prohibitivo

project 1 *n* ['prɒdʒekt] *(undertaking, plan)* proyecto *m*; *(at school, college)* trabajo *m*; *Com* **p. manager** jefe(a) *m,f* de proyecto
2 *vt* [prə'dʒekt] (**a**) *(plan)* proyectar, planear (**b**) *(propel)* proyectar; **to p. one's voice** proyectar la voz
3 *vi (protrude)* sobresalir, proyectarse

projected [prə'dʒektɪd] *adj* proyectado(a)

projectile [prə'dʒektaɪl] *n* proyectil *m*

projection [prə'dʒekʃən] *n* (**a**) *(of movie, in mapmaking, psychological)* proyección *f*; *Cin* **p. room** sala *f* de proyección (**b**) *(prediction)* estimación *f*, pronóstico *m* (**c**) *(protruding part)* proyección *f*, saliente *m*

projectionist [prə'dʒekʃənɪst] *n* proyeccionista *mf*

projector [prə'dʒektə(r)] *n* proyector *m*

prolapse ['prəʊlæps] *n Med* prolapso *m*

proletarian [prəʊlɪ'teərɪən] *n & adj* proletario(a) *m,f*

proletariat [prəʊlɪ'teərɪət] *n* proletariado *m*

pro-life ['prəʊ'laɪf] *adj* pro vida, antiabortista

proliferate [prə'lɪfəreɪt] *vi* proliferar

proliferation [prəlɪfə'reɪʃən] *n* proliferación *f*

prolific [prə'lɪfɪk] *adj* prolífico(a)

prolix ['prəʊlɪks] *adj Formal* prolijo(a)

prologue, prolog ['prəʊlɒg] *n* prólogo *m*

prolong [prə'lɒŋ] *vt* prolongar

prolongation [prəʊlɒŋ'geɪʃən] *n (of life, time)* prolongación *f*

prolonged [prə'lɒŋd] *adj* prolongado(a)

prom [prɒm] *n* baile *m* de fin de curso

promenade ['prɒmənɑːd] **1** *n (in public place)* paseo *m*; **p. deck** *(on ship)* cubierta *f* de paseo
2 *vi* pasear

prominence ['prɒmɪnəns] *n* (**a**) *(of land, physical feature)* prominencia *f* (**b**) *(of issue, person)* relevancia *f*, importancia *f*; **to give sth p.** destacar algo; **to come to p.** empezar a descollar *or* sobresalir; **to occupy a position of some p.** ocupar un puesto de cierto relieve

prominent ['prɒmɪnənt] *adj* (**a**) *(projecting)* prominente (**b**) *(conspicuous)* visible, destacado(a); *(important)* renombrado(a), prominente

prominently ['prɒmɪnentlɪ] *adv* visiblemente; **to figure p. in sth** tener un papel relevante *or* destacar en algo

promiscuity [prɒmɪs'kjuːɪtɪ] *n* promiscuidad *f*

promiscuous [prə'mɪskjʊəs] *adj* promiscuo(a)

promise ['prɒmɪs] **1** *n* (**a**) *(pledge)* promesa *f*; **to make a p.** hacer la promesa; **to keep/break one's p.** mantener/romper la promesa (**b**) *(potential)* buenas perspectivas *fpl*; **to show p.** ser prometedor(ora); **she never fulfilled her early p.** nunca llegó tan lejos como parecía prometer

2 *vt* prometer; **to p. to do sth** prometer hacer algo; **to p. sth to sb, to p. sb sth** prometerle algo a alguien; **he promised me he'd do it** me prometió que lo haría; **it promises to be hot** promete hacer calor

promising ['prɒmɪsɪŋ] *adj* prometedor(ora)

promisingly ['prɒmɪsɪŋlɪ] *adv* de manera prometedora

promontory ['prɒməntərɪ] *n* promontorio *m*

promote [prə'məʊt] *vt* (**a**) *(raise in rank)* ascender; **to be promoted** *(officer, employee)* ser ascendido(a) (**b**) *(encourage)* fomentar, promover; **to p. sb's interests** favorecer los intereses de alguien (**c**) *Com* promocionar

promoter [prə'məʊtə(r)] *n* *(of theory, cause, boxing match)* promotor(ora) *m,f*; *(of show)* organizador(ora) *m,f*

promotion [prə'məʊʃən] *n* (**a**) *(of employee, officer, soccer team)* ascenso *m* (**b**) *(of product, plan)* promoción *f*

promotional [prə'məʊʃənəl] *adj (literature, campaign)* promocional

prompt [prɒmpt] **1** *n* (**a**) **to give an actor a p.** dar el pie a un actor (**b**) *Comptr (short phrase)* mensaje *m* (al usuario); **return to the C:\ p.** volver a C:\

2 *adj* (**a**) *(swift)* rápido(a); **p. payment** pronto pago *m* (**b**) *(punctual)* puntual

3 *adv* **at three o'clock p.** a las tres en punto

4 *vt* (**a**) *(cause)* provocar, suscitar; **to p. sb to do sth** provocar que alguien haga algo, impulsar a alguien a hacer algo (**b**) *Theat* apuntar (**c**) *(encourage) (interviewee)* ayudar a seguir

prompter ['prɒmptə(r)] *n Theat* apuntador(ora) *m,f*

prompting ['prɒmptɪŋ] *n (persuasion)* persuasión *f*, insistencia *f*; **to do sth at sb's p.** acceder a hacer algo ante la insistencia de alguien; **the promptings of his conscience** los dictados de su conciencia

promptly ['prɒmptlɪ] *adv (rapidly)* sin demora; *(punctually)* con puntualidad; *(immediately)* inmediatamente

prone [prəʊn] *adj* (**a**) *(inclined)* **to be p. to (do) sth** ser propenso(a) a (hacer) algo (**b**) *Formal (lying face down)* boca abajo

prong [prɒŋ] *n (of fork)* diente *m*

pronghorn ['prɒŋhɔːn] *n* antílope *m* americano

pronoun ['prəʊnaʊn] *n Gram* pronombre *m*

pronounce [prə'naʊns] **1** *vt* (**a**) *(word)* pronunciar; **this letter is not pronounced** esta letra no se pronuncia (**b**) *(declare) (opinion)* manifestar; **to p. that...** manifestar que...; **to p. oneself for/against sth** pronunciarse a favor de/en contra de algo; **he was pronounced dead/innocent** fue declarado muerto/inocente; *Law* **to p. sentence** dictar sentencia

2 *vi* **to p. on** pronunciarse sobre; **to p. for/against sb** emitir un dictamen a favor de/en contra de alguien

pronounced [prə'naʊnst] *adj* pronunciado(a), acusado(a)

pronouncement [prə'naʊnsmənt] *n Formal* declaración *f*, manifestación *f*

pronto ['prɒntəʊ] *adv Fam* enseguida, ya

pronunciation [prənʌnsɪ'eɪʃən] *n* pronunciación *f*

proof [pruːf] **1** *n* (**a**) *(evidence)* prueba *f*; **to give p. of sth** probar algo; **p. of identity** documento *m* de identidad; **p. of purchase** tíquet *m* or justificante *m* de compra; **to put sth to the p.** poner algo a prueba; *Prov* **the p. of the pudding is in the eating** el movimiento se demuestra caminando or *Esp* andando (**b**) *Typ* prueba *f* (**c**) *(of alcohol)* **40 degrees p.** de 40 grados

2 *adj (resistant)* **to be p. against sth** ser resistente a algo

proofread ['pruːfriːd] *vt Typ* corregir pruebas de

proofreader ['pruːfriːdə(r)] *n Typ* corrector(ora) *m,f* de pruebas

proofreading ['pruːfriːdɪŋ] *n Typ* corrección *f* de pruebas

prop [prɒp] **1** *n* (**a**) *(physical support)* puntal *m*; *(emotional support)* apoyo *m*, sostén *m* (**b**) *(in theater)* accesorio *m*; **props** atrezo *m*

2 *vt (pt & pp* **propped)** apoyar (**against** contra)

▸**prop up** *vt sep (building, tunnel)* apuntalar; *Fig (economy, regime)* apoyar; **to p. sth up against sth** apoyar algo contra or en algo

propaganda [prɒpə'gændə] *n* propaganda *f*

propagate ['prɒpəgeɪt] **1** *vt (plant, theory)* propagar

2 *vi (plant)* propagarse

propagation [prɒpə'geɪʃən] *n* propagación *f*

propane ['prəʊpeɪn] *n Chem* propano *m*

propel [prə'pel] *(pt & pp* **propelled)** *vt* propulsar; **to p. sth/sb along** propulsar algo/a alguien; **propelled by ambition** impulsado(a) por la ambición

propellant, propellent [prə'pelənt] *n (for rocket)* propulsante *m*, combustible *m*; *(for aerosol)* propelente *m*

propeller [prə'pelə(r)] *n* hélice *f*

propensity [prə'pensɪtɪ] *n* tendencia *f*, propensión *f*

proper ['prɒpə(r)] *adj* (**a**) *(correct)* correcto(a); *(real)* verdadero(a); **he isn't a p. doctor** no es médico de verdad; **to get a p. night's sleep** dormir bien toda la noche; **we're still not in Chicago p.** todavía no estamos en Chicago propiamente dicho; *Gram* **p. name** nombre *m* propio; *Gram* **p. noun** nombre *m* propio (**b**) *(appropriate) (time, place)* adecuado(a), apropiado(a) (**c**) *(characteristic)* **p. to** propio(a) de

properly ['prɒpəlɪ] *adv* (**a**) *(correctly)* bien (**b**) *(suitably)* apropiadamente

property ['prɒpətɪ] *n* (**a**) *(possessions)* propiedades *fpl*; *(land, house)* propiedad *f*, inmueble *m*; **p. bubble** burbuja *f* inmobiliaria; **p. developer** promotor(ora) *m,f* inmobiliario(a); **p. market** mercado *m* inmobiliario; **p. tax** impuesto *m* sobre el patrimonio (**b**) *(quality)* propiedad *f*

prophecy ['prɒfɪsɪ] *n* profecía *f*

prophesy ['prɒfɪsaɪ] *vt* profetizar

prophet ['prɒfɪt] *n* profeta *m*

prophetic [prə'fetɪk] *adj* profético(a)

prophylactic [prɒfɪ'læktɪk] *Med* **1** *n* profiláctico *m*; *(condom)* preservativo *m*, profiláctico *m*

2 *adj* profiláctico(a)

propitiate [prə'pɪʃɪeɪt] *vt Formal* propiciar

propitious [prə'pɪʃəs] *adj Formal* propicio(a)

proportion [prə'pɔːʃən] **1** *n* (**a**) *(relationship)* proporción *f*; **in p.** proporcionado(a); **out of p.** desproporcionado(a); **in p. to...** en proporción a...; **the payment is out of all p. to the work involved** lo que se paga no es proporcional al trabajo que supone; **to lose all sense of p.** perder el sentido de la medida; **to get sth out of p.** exagerar algo (**b**) *(part, amount)* proporción *f*, parte *f* (**c**) **proportions** *(dimensions)* proporciones *fpl*

2 *vt* proporcionar

proportional [prə'pɔːʃənəl] *adj* proporcional (**to** a); *Pol* **p. representation** representación *f* proporcional

proportionally [prə'pɔːʃənəlɪ] *adv* proporcionalmente

proportionate [prə'pɔːʃənɪt] *adj* proporcional (**to** a)

proportionately [prə'pɔːʃənɪtlɪ] *adv* en proporción

proposal [prə'pəʊzəl] *n (offer)* propuesta *f*; *(plan)* proyecto *m*; **p. (of marriage)** propuesta or proposición *f* de matrimonio

propose [prə'pəʊz] **1** *vt* proponer; **to p. to do sth, to p. doing sth** *(suggest)* proponer hacer algo; *(intend)* proponerse hacer algo; **to p. a toast** proponer un brindis

2 *vi* **he proposed to her** le pidió que se casara con él

proposition [prɒpə'zɪʃən] **1** *n* (**a**) *(offer)* propuesta *f*; *Fam* **it's not a paying p.** no es rentable (**b**) *(in logic, argument)* proposición *f*
2 *vt* hacer proposiciones a
propound [prə'paʊnd] *vt Formal* exponer
proprietary [prə'praɪətərɪ] *adj (air, attitude)* de propietario(a), posesivo(a); *Com (brand)* registrado(a)
proprietor [prə'praɪətə(r)] *n* propietario(a) *m,f*
propriety [prə'praɪətɪ] *n* decoro *m*; **the proprieties** *(etiquette)* las convenciones
propulsion [prə'pʌlʃən] *n* propulsión *f*
pro rata ['prəʊ'rɑːtə] **1** *adj* prorrateado(a)
2 *adv* de forma prorrateada
prosaic [prəʊ'zeɪɪk] *adj* prosaico(a)
prosaically [prəʊ'zeɪɪklɪ] *adv* prosaicamente
proscribe [prəʊ'skraɪb] *vt* proscribir, excluir
prose [prəʊz] *n* prosa *f*; *(translation in exam)* (prueba *f* de) traducción *f* inversa
prosecute ['prɒsɪkjuːt] *Law* **1** *vt* procesar
2 *vi (lawyer)* ejercer de acusación
prosecuting attorney ['prɒsɪkjuːtɪŋə'tɜːnɪ] *n* fiscal *m*
prosecution [prɒsɪ'kjuːʃən] *n Law (proceedings)* proceso *m*, juicio *m*; **the p.** la acusación
prosecutor ['prɒsɪkjuːtə(r)] *n Law* fiscal *mf*; **public p.** fiscal *mf* (del Estado)
prospect 1 *n* ['prɒspekt] (**a**) *(expectation, thought)* perspectiva *f* (**b**) *(chance, likelihood)* posibilidad *f*; **there is very little p. of it** es muy poco probable; **there is no p. of agreement** no hay posibilidad *or* perspectivas de acuerdo; **future prospects** perspectivas *fpl* de futuro; **a job with prospects of advancement** un trabajo con buenas perspectivas de futuro (**c**) *(view)* vista *f*, panorámica *f*
2 *vi* [prə'spekt] **to p. for gold** hacer prospecciones en busca de oro
prospective [prə'spektɪv] *adj (future)* futuro(a); *(potential)* posible, potencial
prospector [prə'spektə(r)] *n* **oil/gold p.** buscador(ora) *m,f* de petróleo/oro
prospectus [prə'spektəs] *n* folleto *m*, prospecto *m*
prosper ['prɒspə(r)] *vi* prosperar
prosperity [prɒs'perɪtɪ] *n* prosperidad *f*
prosperous ['prɒspərəs] *adj* próspero(a)
prostate ['prɒsteɪt] *n Anat* **p. (gland)** próstata *f*
prosthesis [prɒs'θiːsɪs] *(pl* **prostheses** [prɒs'θiːsiːz]) *n* prótesis *f inv*
prosthetic [prɒs'θetɪk] *adj* artificial; **p. limb** prótesis *f*
prostitute ['prɒstɪtjuːt] **1** *n* prostituta *f*; **male p.** prostituto *m*
2 *vt also Fig* **to p. oneself** prostituirse
prostitution [prɒstɪ'tjuːʃən] *n* prostitución *f*
prostrate 1 *adj* ['prɒstreɪt] *(lying down)* postrado(a), tendido(a) boca abajo; *Fig* **p. with grief** postrado(a) por el dolor
2 *vt* [prə'streɪt] **to p. oneself (before)** postrarse (ante)
protagonist [prə'tægənɪst] *n (main character)* protagonista *mf*; *(of idea, theory)* abanderado(a) *m,f*, promotor(ora) *m,f*
protect [prə'tekt] *vt* proteger (**from** *or* **against** de *or* contra); **a protected species** una especie protegida
protection [prə'tekʃən] *n* protección *f*; **p. money** extorsión *f* *or* impuesto *m* *(a cambio de protección)*; **p. racket** red *f* de extorsión
protectionism [prə'tekʃənɪzəm] *n Econ* proteccionismo *m*
protective [prə'tektɪv] *adj* protector(ora); **p. custody** detención *f* cautelar *(para protección del detenido)*
protectively [prə'tektɪvlɪ] *adv (to behave, act)* de manera protectora
protector [prə'tektə(r)] *n (device)* protector *m*; *(person)* protector(ora) *m,f*

protégé ['prɒteʒeɪ] *n* protegido(a) *m,f*
protein ['prəʊtiːn] *n* proteína *f*
protest 1 *n* ['prəʊtest] protesta *f*; **to make a p.** protestar; **to do sth under p.** hacer algo de mal grado; **she resigned in p.** dimitió en señal de protesta; **p. song** canción *f* protesta; **p. vote** voto *m* de castigo
2 *vt* [prə'test] (**a**) *(object to)* protestar en contra de (**b**) *(one's innocence, love)* declarar, manifestar; **to p. that…** declarar *or* manifestar que…
3 *vi* protestar (**about/against** por/en contra de)
Protestant ['prɒtɪstənt] *n & adj* protestante *mf*
Protestantism ['prɒtɪstəntɪzəm] *n* protestantismo *m*
protestation [prɒtes'teɪʃən] *n* declaración *f*, manifestación *f*
protester [prə'testə(r)] *n* manifestante *mf*
protocol ['prəʊtəkɒl] *n* protocolo *m*
proton ['prəʊtɒn] *n Phys* protón *m*
prototype ['prəʊtətaɪp] *n* prototipo *m*
protracted [prə'træktɪd] *adj* prolongado(a)
protractor [prə'træktə(r)] *n* transportador *m*
protrude [prə'truːd] *vi* sobresalir
protruding [prə'truːdɪŋ] *adj (ledge)* saliente; *(jaw, teeth)* prominente
protuberance [prə'tjuːbərəns] *n Formal* protuberancia *f*
protuberant [prə'tjuːbərənt] *adj Formal* protuberante
proud [praʊd] **1** *adj (in general)* orgulloso(a); *(arrogant)* orgulloso(a), soberbio(a); *(noble)* orgulloso(a), digno(a); **to be p. of (having done) sth** estar orgulloso(a) de (haber hecho) algo; **a p. moment** un momento de gran satisfacción; **to be as p. as a peacock** estar orgullosísimo(a)
2 *adv* **you've done us p.** lo has hecho muy bien; **to do oneself p.** hacerlo muy bien
proudly ['praʊdlɪ] *adv* orgullosamente, con orgullo; *(arrogantly)* con soberbia
prove [pruːv] *(pp* **proven** ['pruːvən, 'prəʊvən] *or* **proved**) **1** *vt (demonstrate)* demostrar, probar; **to p. sb wrong/guilty** demostrar que alguien está equivocado(a)/es culpable; **she wanted a chance to p. herself** quería una oportunidad para demostrar su valía
2 *vi* **to p. (to be) correct** resultar (ser) correcto(a)
provenance ['prɒvənəns] *n Formal* procedencia *f*, origen *m*
proverb ['prɒvɜːb] *n* refrán *m*, proverbio *m*
proverbial [prə'vɜːbɪəl] *adj* proverbial
provide [prə'vaɪd] *vt* (**a**) *(supply)* suministrar, proporcionar; *(service, support)* prestar, proporcionar; **to p. sb with sth** suministrar *or* proporcionar algo a alguien (**b**) *(stipulate)* establecer
▸**provide against** *vt insep (danger, possibility)* prepararse *or Am* alistarse para
▸**provide for** *vt insep* (**a**) *(support)* mantener (**b**) *Formal (allow for)* prever
provided [prə'vaɪdɪd] *conj* **p. (that)** siempre que, a condición de que
providence ['prɒvɪdəns] *n* providencia *f*
provident ['prɒvɪdənt] *adj (foresighted, thrifty)* previsor(ora)
providential [prɒvɪ'denʃəl] *adj Formal* providencial
providently ['prɒvɪdəntlɪ] *adv Formal* previsoramente
provider [prə'vaɪdə(r)] *n* proveedor(ora) *m,f*, abastecedor(ora) *m,f*
providing [prə'vaɪdɪŋ] *conj* **p. (that)** siempre que, a condición de que
province ['prɒvɪns] *n* (**a**) *(of country)* provincia *f*; **in the provinces** en provincias (**b**) *(domain)* terreno *m*, campo *m* de acción
provincial [prə'vɪnʃəl] *adj* provincial; *Pej (parochial)* provinciano(a)
provision [prə'vɪʒən] *n* (**a**) **provisions** *(supplies)* provisiones

fpl (**b**) *(supplying) (of money, water)* suministro *m*, abastecimiento *m*; *(of services)* prestación *f* (**c**) *(allowance)* **to make p. for sth** prever algo, tener en cuenta algo; **the law makes no p. for a case of this kind** la ley no contempla un caso de este tipo (**d**) *(in treaty, contract)* estipulación *f*, disposición *f*

provisional [prə'vɪʒənəl] *adj* provisional

provisionally [prə'vɪʒənəlɪ] *adv* provisionalmente

proviso [prə'vaɪzəʊ] *(pl* **provisos, provisoes)** *n* condición *f*; **with the p. that…** a condición de que…

provocation [prɒvə'keɪʃən] *n* provocación *f*; **at the slightest p.** a la menor provocación; **without p.** sin mediar provocación

provocative [prə'vɒkətɪv] *adj (polemical)* provocador(ora); *(sexually)* provocativo(a)

provoke [prə'vəʊk] *vt (incite)* provocar; **to p. sb into doing sth** empujar a alguien a hacer algo; **to p. sb to anger** provocar la ira de alguien

provoking [prə'vəʊkɪŋ] *adj (irritating)* irritante, enojoso(a)

prow [praʊ] *n (of ship)* proa *f*

prowess ['praʊɪs] *n (skill)* proezas *fpl*

prowl [praʊl] **1** *n* **to be on the p.** *(person, animal)* merodear; **to be on the p. for sth** andar a la caza de algo; **p. car** coche *m or Am* carro *m or CSur* auto *m* patrulla
2 *vt (streets, area)* merodear por
3 *vi* merodear

prowler ['praʊlə(r)] *n* merodeador(ora) *m,f*

proximity [prɒk'sɪmɪtɪ] *n* cercanía *f*, proximidad *f*; **in close p. to** muy cerca de

proxy ['prɒksɪ] *n (person)* apoderado(a) *m,f*; *(power)* poder *m*; **to vote by p.** votar por poderes

Prozac® ['prəʊzæk] *n* Prozac® *m*

prude [pruːd] *n* mojigato(a) *m,f*

prudence ['pruːdəns] *n* prudencia *f*

prudent ['pruːdənt] *adj* prudente

prudery ['pruːdərɪ], **prudishness** ['pruːdɪʃnɪs] *n* mojigatería *f*

prudish ['pruːdɪʃ] *adj* mojigato(a), pacato(a)

prudishness = **prudery**

prune¹ [pruːn] *n (fruit)* ciruela *f* pasa

prune² *vt (bush, tree)* podar; *Fig (article)* recortar

pruning ['pruːnɪŋ] *n (of bush, tree)* poda *f*; *(of article, budget, staff)* recorte *m*, reducción *f*; **p. knife** podadera *f*

prurient ['prʊərɪənt] *adj* procaz, lascivo(a)

Prussia ['prʌʃə] *n* Prusia

Prussian ['prʌʃən] *n & adj* prusiano(a) *m,f*

pry¹ [praɪ] *vi* entrometerse, husmear; **to p. into sth** entrometerse en algo

pry² [praɪ], **prize** [praɪz] *vt* **to p. sth off** arrancar algo; **to p. sth open** forzar algo; **to p. sth out of sb** *(secret, truth)* arrancarle algo a alguien

prying ['praɪɪŋ] *adj* entrometido(a)

PS [piː'es] *n (abbr* **postscript)** P.D.

psalm [sɑːm] *n* salmo *m*

pseudo- ['sjuːdəʊ] *prefix* seudo-, pseudo-

pseudonym ['sjuːdənɪm] *n* seudónimo *m*

psoriasis [sə'raɪəsɪs] *n* soriasis *f*

PST [piːes'tiː] *n (abbr* **Pacific Standard Time)** = hora oficial de la costa del Pacífico en Estados Unidos

psyche ['saɪkɪ] *n* psique *f*, psiquis *f inv*

psyche out [saɪk] *vt sep Fam (unnerve)* hacer guerra psicológica a, poner nervioso(a)

psyche up *vt sep Fam* **to p. sb up** mentalizar a alguien; **to p. oneself up (for sth)** mentalizarse (para algo)

psychedelic [saɪkə'delɪk] *adj* psicodélico(a)

psychiatric [saɪkɪ'ætrɪk] *adj* psiquiátrico(a)

psychiatrist [saɪ'kaɪətrɪst] *n* psiquiatra *mf*

psychiatry [saɪ'kaɪətrɪ] *n* psiquiatría *f*

psychic ['saɪkɪk] **1** *n* médium *mf inv*
2 *adj (phenomena, experiences)* paranormal, extrasensorial; *(person)* vidente; **to have p. powers** tener poderes paranormales; *Fam* **I'm not p.!** ¡no soy un adivino!

psycho ['saɪkəʊ] *(pl* **psychos)** *n Fam (crazy person)* psicópata *mf*

psychoanalysis [saɪkəʊə'nælɪsɪs] *n* psicoanálisis *m inv*

psychoanalyst [saɪkəʊ'ænəlɪst] *n* psicoanalista *mf*

psychoanalyze [saɪkəʊ'ænəlaɪz] *vt* psicoanalizar

psycholinguistics ['saɪkəʊlɪŋ'gwɪstɪks] *n* psicolingüística *f*

psychological [saɪkə'lɒdʒɪkəl] *adj* psicológico(a); **I have a p. block about driving** conducir me produce un bloqueo psicológico; **p. warfare** guerra *f* psicológica

psychologically ['saɪkə'lɒdʒɪklɪ] *adv* psicológicamente

psychologist [saɪ'kɒlədʒɪst] *n* psicólogo(a) *m,f*

psychology [saɪ'kɒlədʒɪ] *n* psicología *f*

psychometric [saɪkə'metrɪk] *adj* psicométrico(a)

psychopath ['saɪkəʊpæθ] *n* psicópata *mf*

psychopathic ['saɪkəʊ'pæθɪk] *adj* psicopático(a)

psychosis [saɪ'kəʊsɪs] *(pl* **psychoses** [saɪ'kəʊsiːz]) *n* psicosis *f inv*

psychosomatic [saɪkəʊsə'mætɪk] *adj* psicosomático(a)

psychotherapist [saɪkəʊ'θerəpɪst] *n* psicoterapeuta *mf*

psychotherapy [saɪkəʊ'θerəpɪ] *n* psicoterapia *f*

psychotic [saɪ'kɒtɪk] *n & adj* psicótico(a) *m,f*

PT [piː'tiː] *n (abbr* **physical training)** educación *f* física

PTA [piːtiː'eɪ] *n Sch (abbr* **Parent-Teacher Association)** = asociación de padres de alumnos y profesores, ≃ APA *f*

ptarmigan ['tɑːmɪgən] *n* perdiz *f* nival

PTO [piːtiː'əʊ] *(abbr* **please turn over)** sigue

pub [pʌb] *n* pub *m*

puberty ['pjuːbətɪ] *n* pubertad *f*

pubic ['pjuːbɪk] *adj* pubiano(a)

public ['pʌblɪk] **1** *n* **the (general) p.** el público en general, el gran público; **in p.** en público
2 *adj* público(a); **to go p.** *(company)* pasar a cotizar en Bolsa; **to go p. with sth** *(reveal information)* manifestar públicamente algo; **to make sth p.** hacer público(a) algo; **to make a p. appearance** hacer *or* efectuar una aparición pública; **to be in the p. domain** ser del dominio público; **at p. expense** con dinero público; **to be in the p. eye** estar expuesto(a) a la opinión pública; **in the p. interest** en favor del interés general; **p. access television** = sistema de televisión que permite a sus usuarios emitir sus propios programas; **p. assistance** ayudas *fpl* estatales; **p. debt** deuda *f* pública; *Com* **p. enterprise** empresa *f* pública; **p. health** salud *f* pública; **p. inquiry** investigación *f (de puertas abiertas)*; **p. opinion** la opinión pública; *Law* **p. prosecutor** fiscal *mf* (del Estado); **p. relations** relaciones *fpl* públicas; **p. school** colegio *m* público; **p. sector** sector *m* público; **p. speaking** oratoria *f*; **p. spending** gasto *m* público; **p. transportation** transporte *m* público; *Com* **p. utility** (empresa *f* de) servicio *m* público

public-address system ['pʌblɪkə'dres'sɪstəm] *n* (sistema *m* de) megafonía *f*

publication [pʌblɪ'keɪʃən] *n* publicación *f*

publicity [pʌb'lɪsɪtɪ] *n* publicidad *f*; **p. campaign** campaña *f* publicitaria *or* de publicidad; **p. stunt** artimaña *f* publicitaria

publicity-seeking [pʌb'lɪsɪtɪ'siːkɪŋ] *adj* en busca de publicidad

publicize ['pʌblɪsaɪz] *vt* hacer público(a); **a much publicized dispute** un enfrentamiento muy aireado por los medios de comunicación

publicly ['pʌblɪklɪ] *adv* públicamente; **p. owned** de titularidad pública

public-spirited ['pʌblɪk'spɪrɪtɪd] *adj* cívico(a)

publish ['pʌblɪʃ] *vt* publicar

publishable ['pʌblɪʃəbl] *adj* publicable

publisher ['pʌblɪʃə(r)] *n (person)* editor(ora) *m,f; (company)* editorial *f*

publishing ['pʌblɪʃɪŋ] *n* industria *f* editorial; **p. house** editorial *f*

pucker ['pʌkə(r)] **1** *vt* **to p. one's lips** fruncir los labios
    2 *vi (face)* arrugarse; *(lips)* fruncirse

pudding ['pʊdɪŋ] *n (sweet)* budín *m*, pudín *m; (savory)* pastel *m*, *Col, CSur* torta *f*; **p. bowl** bol *m*

puddle ['pʌdəl] *n* charco *m*

pudgy ['pʌdʒɪ] *adj* rechoncho(a), regordete(a)

puerile ['pjʊəraɪl] *adj Pej* pueril

Puerto Rican [pweətəʊ'riːkən] *n & adj* puertorriqueño(a) *m,f*

Puerto Rico [pweətəʊ'riːkəʊ] *n* Puerto Rico

puff [pʌf] **1** *n (of breath)* bocanada *f; (of air)* soplo *m; (of smoke)* nube *f; (of cigarette)* chupada *f, Esp* calada *f, Am* pitada *f*; **p. pastry** hojaldre *m*
    2 *vt* **to p. smoke into sb's face** echar una bocanada de humo a la cara de alguien
    3 *vi (person)* resoplar, jadear; **to p. along** *(steam engine)* avanzar echando humo; **to p. on a cigarette** dar chupadas *or Esp* caladas *or Am* pitadas a un cigarrillo

▸**puff out** *vt sep (cheeks, chest)* inflar, hinchar

▸**puff up** *vt sep (cheeks)* inflar, hinchar; **he was puffed up with pride** no cabía en sí de orgullo

puffer ['pʌfə(r)] *n* **p. (fish)** pez *m* globo

puffin ['pʌfɪn] *n* frailecillo *m*

puffy ['pʌfɪ] *adj* hinchado(a)

pug [pʌg] *n (dog)* dogo *m*; **p.-nosed** chato(a)

pugnacious [pʌg'neɪʃəs] *adj* combativo(a)

puke [pjuːk] *Fam* **1** *n* papa *f*, vomitona *f*
    2 *vt* devolver
    3 *vi* echar la papa, devolver

Pulitzer ['pʊlɪtsər] *n* **the P. (prize)** el (premio) Pulitzer

pull [pʊl] **1** *n* **(a)** *(act of pulling)* tirón *m, Am salvo RP* jalón *m; (of water current)* fuerza *f*; **to give sth a p.** dar un tirón *or Am salvo RP* un jalón a algo; **to take a p. at a bottle** echar un trago de una botella; *Com* **p. date** fecha *f* límite de venta **(b)** *Fam (influence)* influencia *f*; **to have a lot of p.** ser muy influyente
    2 *vt* **(a)** *(tug)* tirar de; *(trigger)* apretar; **to p. sth open/shut** abrir/cerrar algo de un tirón *or Am salvo RP* un jalón; **to p. a muscle** sufrir un tirón en un músculo; *also Fig* **to p. sth to pieces** hacer trizas algo
    (b) *(attract)* atraer
    (c) *(extract) (tooth, cork)* sacar; **to p. a gun on sb** sacar un arma y apuntar a alguien
    (d) *Fam (withdraw)* retirar
    (e) *(idioms) Fam* **to p. a bank job** atracar un banco; **to p. a face** hacer una mueca; *Fam* **to p. sb's leg** tomarle el pelo a alguien; *Fam* **talking to her is like pulling teeth** hay que sacarle las cosas con sacacorchos; **she's not pulling her weight** no arrima el hombro (como los demás); *Fam* **to p. a fast one on sb** hacer una jugarreta *or* engañar a alguien
    3 *vi* tirar, *Am salvo RP* jalar **(at** *or* **on** de); **to p. clear of sth** dejar algo atrás

▸**pull ahead** *vi (in race, election)* tomar la delantera, ponerse en cabeza

▸**pull apart** *vt sep also Fig* hacer trizas

▸**pull away** *vi (from station)* alejarse; *(from curb, embrace)* apartarse

▸**pull back 1** *vt sep (curtains)* descorrer
    2 *vi (person)* echarse atrás; *(troops)* retirarse

▸**pull down** *vt sep (demolish)* demoler, derribar

▸**pull in 1** *vt sep* **(a)** *(rope, fishing line)* recoger **(b)** *(money)* sacar;

to p. sb in for questioning detener a alguien para interrogarlo **(c)** *(attract)* atraer
    2 *vi* **(a)** *(car)* parar; *(train, bus)* llegar

▸**pull off** *vt sep* **(a)** *(clothes)* quitar, *Am* sacar; **she pulled off her T-shirt** se quitó *or Am* sacó la camiseta **(b)** *Fam (succeed in doing)* sacar adelante; **he pulled it off** lo consiguió

▸**pull on** *vt sep (clothes)* ponerse

▸**pull out 1** *vt sep (tooth)* sacar, arrancar; *Fam Fig* **to p. out all the stops** tocar todos los registros
    2 *vi* **(a)** *(train)* salir; **he pulled out into the stream of traffic** se incorporó al tráfico **(b)** *(race, agreement)* **to p. out (of sth)** retirarse (de algo)

▸**pull over** *vi (driver)* parar en *Esp* el arcén *or Chile* la berma *or Méx* el acotamiento *or RP* la banquina *or Ven* el hombrillo

▸**pull through** *vi (recover)* recuperarse, salir adelante

▸**pull together 1** *vt sep* **to p. oneself together** serenarse
    2 *vi* juntar esfuerzos

▸**pull up 1** *vt sep* **to p. sb up (short)** *(stop)* parar a alguien en seco; *Fig* **to p. one's socks up** espabilar
    2 *vi (car)* parar

pull-down menu ['pʊldaʊn'menjuː] *n Comptr* menú *m* desplegable

pullet ['pʊlɪt] *n* polla *f*, gallina *f* joven

pulley ['pʊlɪ] *n* polea *f*

pullout ['pʊlaʊt] *n (in newspaper, magazine)* suplemento *m*

pullover ['pʊləʊvə(r)] *n* suéter *m*, pulóver *m, Esp* jersey *m*

pull-up ['pʊlʌp] *n (exercise)* flexión *f (colgando de una barra con los brazos)*

pulmonary ['pʌlmənərɪ] *adj* pulmonar

pulp [pʌlp] **1** *n (of fruit)* pulpa *f*, carne *f*; **to reduce sth to (a) p.** reducir algo a (una) pasta; *Fam* **to beat sb to a p.** hacer picadillo *or* papilla a alguien; **p. fiction** literatura *f* barata *or* de baja estofa, novelas *fpl* de tiros
    2 *vt* hacer pasta de papel con

pulpit ['pʊlpɪt] *n* púlpito *m*

pulsate [pʌl'seɪt] *vi* palpitar

pulse¹ [pʌls] *n (of blood)* pulso *m; (of light, sound)* impulso *m*; **to feel** *or* **take sb's p.** tomar el pulso a alguien

pulse² *n (pea, bean, lentil)* legumbre *f*

pulverize ['pʌlvəraɪz] *vt* pulverizar; *Fam Fig* **to p. sb** *(beat up, defeat heavily)* dar una paliza a alguien

puma ['pjuːmə] *n* puma *m*

pumice ['pʌmɪs] *n* **p. (stone)** piedra *f* pómez

pummel ['pʌməl] *vt* aporrear

pump¹ [pʌmp] *n (ballet shoe)* zapatilla *f* de ballet; *(flat shoe)* zapato *m* de salón

pump² **1** *n (machine)* bomba *f; (at gas station)* surtidor *m*
    2 *vt* bombear; **to p. sb's stomach** hacer un lavado de estómago a alguien; *Fig* **to p. money into sth** inyectar una gran cantidad de dinero en algo; *Fam* **to p. sb for information** sonsacar a alguien; **to p. sb's hand** dar un enérgico apretón de manos a alguien; *Fam* **to p. iron** *(do weightlifting)* hacer pesas
    3 *vi (heart, machine)* bombear

▸**pump out** *vt sep (music, information)* emitir

▸**pump up** *vt sep* inflar

pumpkin ['pʌmpkɪn] *n* calabaza *f, Andes, RP* zapallo *m, Carib, Col* ahuyama *f*

pun [pʌn] *n* juego *m* de palabras

punch¹ [pʌntʃ] **1** *n (tool)* punzón *m*; **(ticket) p.** canceladora *f* de billetes
    2 *vt (metal)* perforar; *(ticket)* picar
    3 *vi* **to p. in/out** *(at work)* fichar *or Am* marcar tarjeta (a la entrada/salida)

punch² **1** *n* **(a)** *(blow)* puñetazo *m; Fig* **he didn't pull his punches** no tuvo pelos en la lengua, se despachó a gusto **(b)** *(energy)* garra *f*; **p. line** *(of joke)* final *m* del chiste *m*, golpe *m*; **he**

had forgotten the p. line había olvidado cómo acababa el chiste
  2 *vt* (**a**) *(hit)* dar *or* pegar un puñetazo a; **to p. sb in the face/on the nose** pegarle a alguien un puñetazo en la cara/en la nariz (**b**) *(cattle)* conducir, guiar

punch³ *n (drink)* ponche *m*

Punch and Judy show ['pʌntʃən'dʒuːdɪʃəʊ] *n* = espectáculo de títeres de la cachiporra representado en una feria o junto al mar

punchbag ['pʌntʃbæg] *n* saco *m* (de boxeo)

punch-drunk ['pʌntʃdrʌŋk] *adj (dazed)* aturdido(a); *(boxer)* sonado(a)

punchy ['pʌntʃɪ] *adj Fam* con garra

punctilious [pʌŋk'tɪlɪəs] *adj* puntilloso(a)

punctual ['pʌŋktjʊəl] *adj* puntual

punctuality [pʌŋktjʊ'ælɪtɪ] *n* puntualidad *f*

punctually ['pʌŋktjʊəlɪ] *adv* puntualmente

punctuate ['pʌŋktjʊeɪt] *vt (sentence, writing)* puntuar; *Fig* **her speech was punctuated with applause** su discurso se vio interrumpido en ocasiones por aplausos

punctuation [pʌŋktjʊ'eɪʃən] *n* puntuación *f*; **p. mark** signo *m* de puntuación

puncture ['pʌŋktʃə(r)] **1** *n (in tire)* pinchazo *m*, *CAm, Carib, Méx* ponchadura *f*; *(in skin)* punción *f*; *(in metal)* perforación *f*; **to have a p.** tener un pinchazo *or CAm, Carib, Méx* una ponchadura
  2 *vt (tire)* pinchar, *CAm, Carib, Méx* ponchar; *(metal, lung)* perforar; *(blister, abscess)* punzar

pundit ['pʌndɪt] *n* experto(a) *m,f*

pungent ['pʌndʒənt] *adj (smell, taste)* acre; *(style, wit)* mordaz

punish ['pʌnɪʃ] *vt* castigar; **to p. sb for doing sth** castigar a alguien por hacer algo

punishment ['pʌnɪʃmənt] *n* castigo *m*; **to make the p. fit the crime** hacer que el castigo guarde proporción con el delito; **to take a lot of p.** *(boxer)* recibir muchos golpes; *(clothing, paint)* aguantar mucho trote

punitive ['pjuːnɪtɪv] *adj* de castigo, punitivo(a)

punk [pʌŋk] *n* punk *mf*, punki *mf*; **p. (rock)** (música *f*) punk *m*

punt¹ [pʌnt] **1** *n* batea *f (impulsada con pértiga)*
  2 *vi* **to go punting** pasear en batea por un río

punt² [pʊnt] **1** *n (in football, rugby)* patada *f* larga de volea
  2 *vt* dar una patada larga de volea a

puny ['pjuːnɪ] *adj* enclenque

pup [pʌp] *n* (**a**) *(of dog)* cachorro *m*; *(of seal)* cría *f* (**b**) **p. tent** tienda *f* individual

pupil¹ ['pjuːpəl] *n (student)* alumno(a) *m,f*

pupil² *n (of eye)* pupila *f*

puppet ['pʌpɪt] *n also Fig* títere *m*, marioneta *f*; *Fig* **p. government** gobierno *m* títere; **p. show** (espectáculo *m* de) guiñol *m*

puppetry ['pʌpɪtrɪ] *n* arte *m* del titiritero *or* marionetista

puppy ['pʌpɪ] *n* cachorro *m*; **p. fat** obesidad *f* infantil; **p. love** amor *m* de adolescente

purchase ['pɜːtʃɪs] **1** *n* (**a**) *(action, thing bought)* adquisición *f*, compra *f*; **p. price** precio *m* de compra (**b**) *(grip)* **to get a p. on sth** agarrarse *or* asirse a algo
  2 *vt* adquirir, comprar

purchaser ['pɜːtʃəsə(r)] *n* comprador(ora) *m,f*

purchasing ['pɜːtʃəsɪŋ] *n* **p. manager** jefe(a) *m,f* de compras; **p. power** poder *m* adquisitivo

pure [pjʊə(r)] *adj* puro(a); **p. silk** pura seda *f*; **p. wool** pura lana *f* virgen; **p. mathematics** matemáticas *fpl* puras

purebred ['pjʊəbred] *adj (dog)* de raza; *(horse)* purasangre

puree, purée ['pjʊəreɪ] **1** *n* puré *m*
  2 *vt* hacer puré

purely ['pjʊəlɪ] *adv* puramente; **p. by chance** por pura casualidad; **p. and simply** lisa y llanamente

purgatory ['pɜːgətərɪ] *n Rel* purgatorio *m*

purge [pɜːdʒ] **1** *n* purga *f*
  2 *vt* purgar

purification [pjʊərɪfɪ'keɪʃən] *n* purificación *f*; *(of water)* depuración *f*

purify ['pjʊərɪfaɪ] *vt* purificar; *(water)* depurar

purist ['pjʊərɪst] *n* purista *mf*

puritan ['pjʊərɪtən] *n* (**a**) *(strict person)* puritano(a) *m,f* (**b**) *Hist* **P.** puritano(a) *m,f*

puritanical [pjʊərɪ'tænɪkəl] *adj* puritano(a)

purity ['pjʊərɪtɪ] *n* pureza *f*

purl [pɜːl] **1** *n* punto *m* del revés
  2 *vi* hacer punto del revés

purloin [pɜː'lɔɪn] *vt* sustraer

purple ['pɜːpəl] **1** *n* morado *m*
  2 *adj* morado(a); **to turn** *or* **go p.** *(with embarrassment, anger)* enrojecer; *Mil* **P. Heart** = medalla concedida a los heridos en combate; **p. prose** prosa *f* recargada

purport *Formal* **1** *n* ['pɜːpɔːt] sentido *m*, significado *m*
  2 *vt* [pɜː'pɔːt] **to p. to be sth** pretender ser algo

purportedly [pə'pɔːtɪdlɪ] *adv Formal* supuestamente

purpose ['pɜːpəs] *n* (**a**) *(object, aim)* propósito *m*, objeto *m*; **on p.** adrede, a propósito; **to no p.** en vano; **what is the p. of your visit?** ¿cuál es el objeto de su visita?; **they have a real sense of p.** saben lo que quieren (conseguir) (**b**) *(use)* finalidad *f*; **to serve a p.** tener una utilidad *or* finalidad; **to serve no p.** no servir para nada; **to serve sb's p.(s)** ser útil a los propósitos de alguien; **for all practical purposes** a efectos prácticos; **for the purposes of** a efectos de

purpose-built ['pɜːpəs'bɪlt] *adj* construido(a) al efecto

purposeful ['pɜːpəsfʊl] *adj* decidido(a)

purposefully ['pɜːpəsfʊlɪ] *adv (determinedly)* resueltamente

purposeless ['pɜːpəslɪs] *adj (life)* sin objetivo; *(act, violence)* gratuito(a)

purposely ['pɜːpəslɪ] *adv* adrede, a propósito

purr [pɜː(r)] **1** *n (of cat)* ronroneo *m*; *(of machine)* rumor *m*, zumbido *m*
  2 *vi (cat)* ronronear

purse [pɜːs] **1** *n (handbag) Esp* bolso *m*, *Col, CSur* cartera *f*, *Méx* bolsa *f*; **the public p.** el erario público; *Fig* **to hold the p. strings** llevar las riendas del gasto
  2 *vt* **to p. one's lips** fruncir los labios

pursue [pə'sjuː] *vt* (**a**) *(person, animal)* perseguir; *(pleasure, knowledge, happiness)* buscar (**b**) *(studies, inquiry)* proseguir, continuar; *(course of action)* seguir; *(profession)* ejercer

pursuer [pə'sjuːə(r)] *n* perseguidor(ora) *m,f*

pursuit [pə'sjuːt] *n* (**a**) *(of person, animal)* persecución *f*; *(of pleasure, knowledge, happiness)* busca *f*, búsqueda *f*; **to be in p. of** ir en busca de; **he came with two policemen in hot p.** venía con dos policías pisándole los talones (**b**) *(activity)* ocupación *f*; **(leisure) pursuits** aficiones *fpl*

purvey [pə'veɪ] *vt Formal (goods)* proveer, abastecer; *(lies, rumors)* difundir

purveyor [pə'veɪə(r)] *n Formal* proveedor(ora) *m,f*

pus [pʌs] *n* pus *m*

push [pʊʃ] **1** *n* (**a**) *(act of pushing)* empujón *m*, *CAm, Méx* aventón *m*; **to give sth/sb a p.** dar un empujón a algo/alguien; *Fam* **when p. comes to shove...** a la hora de la verdad... (**b**) *Mil (attack)* ofensiva *f*; **sales p.** campaña *f* de ventas; **to make a p. for sth** tratar de conseguir algo
  2 *vt* (**a**) *(in general)* empujar; *(button)* apretar, pulsar; **to p. the door shut/open** cerrar/abrir la puerta empujándola; **P.** *(sign)* empujar, empuje; **to p. sb out of the way** apartar a alguien un empujón *or CAm, Méx* aventón; **to p. one's way through the crowd** abrirse paso a empujones entre la gente; *Fig* **don't p. yourself too hard** no te pases en el esfuerzo; *Fig* **to p. sb into doing sth** forzar a alguien a

hacer algo; **to p. one's luck** tentar a la suerte; **don't p. your luck!** *(said in annoyance)* ¡no me busques!, *Esp* ¡no me busques las cosquillas!; **to be pushed for time** estar apurado(a) *or RP* corto(a) de tiempo

(**b**) *(sell, promote) (goods)* promocionar; *(theory)* defender

(**c**) *Fam (drugs)* pasar, trapichear con, *RP* transar

(**d**) *Fam* **he's pushing sixty** ronda los sesenta

3 *vi (in general)* empujar; *(move forward)* avanzar (a empujones); **he pushed past me** se me coló a empujones; **to p. forward** empujar hacia delante

▸**push around, push about** *vt sep Fam Fig (bully)* abusar de

▸**push ahead** *vi* seguir adelante (**with** con)

▸**push aside** *vt sep* apartar (de un empujón); *Fig (reject)* dejar a un lado

▸**push in** *vi (in line)* colarse

▸**push off** *vi Fam* **p. off!** ¡lárgate!

▸**push on** *vi (continue)* seguir, continuar; **to p. on with sth** seguir adelante con algo

▸**push over** *vt sep* derribar

▸**push through** *vt sep (reform, law)* hacer aprobar *(con urgencia)*

push-button ['puʃ'bʌtən] *adj* de teclas, de botones

pusher ['puʃə(r)] *n Fam* **(drug) p.** camello *m*, *Am* dealer *m*

pushover ['puʃəuvə(r)] *n Fam* **it's a p.** es pan comido; **I'm a p.** no sé decir que no

push-up ['puʃʌp] *n* flexión *f* (de brazos)

pushy ['puʃɪ] *adj Fam* avasallador(ora)

puss [pus] *n Fam (cat)* gatito *m*, minino *m*

pussy ['pusɪ] *n Fam (cat)* gatito *m*, minino *m*; **p. willow** sauce *m* blanco

pussycat ['pusɪkæt] *n* gatito *m*, minino *m*

pussyfoot ['pusɪfut] *vi Fam* **to p. around** *or* **about** andarse con rodeos

pustule ['pʌstjuːl] *n* pústula *f*

put [put] *(pt & pp* **put)** **1** *vt* (**a**) *(place)* poner; *(carefully)* colocar; **to p. sth into sth** meter algo en algo; **to p. one's arms around sth/sb** rodear algo/a alguien con los brazos; **she put her head around the door** asomó la cabeza por la puerta; **to p. a man on the moon** enviar un hombre a la Luna; **to p. a limit on sth** poner un límite a algo; *Fam* **p. 'er there!** *(shake hands)* ¡choca esos cinco!, ¡chócala!; *Fig* **to p. oneself into sb's hands** ponerse en manos de alguien; *Fig* **to p. sb in his place** poner a alguien en su sitio; *Fig* **p. yourself in my position** ponte en mi lugar; **to p. a matter right** arreglar una cuestión; **to p. money on a horse** apostar a un caballo; **to p. a lot of work into sth** trabajar intensamente en algo; **to p. a stop to sth** poner fin a algo; **to p. a child to bed** acostar a un niño; **to p. sb to the test** poner a alguien a prueba

(**b**) *(present)* **to p. a question to sb** hacer una pregunta a alguien; **to p. a proposal to sb** presentar una propuesta a alguien; **I p. it to you that…** *(in court case)* ¿no es cierto que…?

(**c**) *(express)* **to p. sth well/badly** expresar algo bien/mal; **I couldn't have put it better myself** nadie lo hubiera dicho mejor; **to p. it bluntly** hablando claro; **to p. it mildly** por no decir otra cosa; **how shall I p. it?** ¿cómo lo diría?

(**d**) *(estimate)* calcular (**at** en); **I would p. her age at forty** yo diría que tiene unos cuarenta años

2 *vi* **to p. to sea** zarpar

▸**put about 1** *vt sep (rumor)* difundir; **to p. it about that…** difundir el rumor de que…

2 *vi (ship)* cambiar de rumbo

▸**put across** *vt sep (message, idea)* transmitir, hacer llegar; **to p. oneself across well/badly** hacerse entender bien/mal

▸**put aside** *vt sep* (**a**) *(reserve)* apartar; **we'll p. it aside for you** *(in store)* se lo dejamos apartado (**b**) *(save) (money)* ahorrar (**c**) *(problem, fact)* dejar a un lado

▸**put away** *vt sep* (**a**) *(tidy away)* ordenar, recoger; **p your money/wallet away** guarda tu dinero/cartera (**b**) *Fam (imprison)* encerrar (**c**) *Fam (eat, drink)* **he can really p. it away!** ¡cómo traga!

▸**put back** *vt sep* (**a**) *(replace)* devolver a su sitio (**b**) *(clock)* retrasar, atrasar; *Fig* **that puts the clock back ten years** esto nos devuelve a la misma situación de hace diez años

▸**put by** *vt sep (save)* ahorrar

▸**put down** *vt sep* (**a**) *(set down)* dejar; **I couldn't p. the book down** *(book)* no me podía despegar del libro (**b**) *(revolt, opposition)* reprimir, ahogar (**c**) *(write)* poner por escrito; **to p. sth down in writing** poner algo por escrito; **to p. one's name down for sth** apuntarse a *or* inscribirse en algo (**d**) *(attribute)* **to p. sth down to sth** achacar *or* atribuir algo a algo (**e**) *(criticize)* **to p. sb down** dejar a alguien en mal lugar; **to p. oneself down** menospreciarse

▸**put forward** *vt sep* (**a**) *(plan, theory, candidate)* proponer; *(proposal)* presentar (**b**) *(clock, time of meeting)* adelantar

▸**put in 1** *vt sep* (**a**) *(install)* poner, instalar (**b**) *(claim, protest)* presentar; **to p. in a (good) word for sb** decir algo en favor de alguien (**c**) *(time, work)* invertir, dedicar

2 *vi (ship)* atracar, hacer escala

▸**put off** *vt sep* (**a**) *(postpone)* aplazar, posponer; **to p. off doing sth** dejar algo para más tarde (**b**) *(cause to dislike)* desagradar, resultar desagradable a; **that meal put me off seafood** después de aquella comida dejó de gustarme el marisco (**c**) *(distract)* distraer (**d**) *(discourage)* **to p. sb off doing sth** quitarle *or Am* sacarle a alguien las ganas de hacer algo (**e**) *(make wait)* tener esperando

▸**put on** *vt sep* (**a**) *(clothes)* ponerse; **he put his pants on** se puso el pantalón; **to p. on one's makeup** ponerse el maquillaje, maquillarse; **to p. on an act** fingir; **to p. on an accent** poner *or* simular un acento; **to p. on weight** engordar (**b**) *(light, TV, heating)* encender, *Am* prender; *(music, videotape)* poner; **to p. the kettle on** poner el agua a hervir *(en el hervidor de agua)* (**c**) *(play, show)* representar, hacer (**d**) *Fam (fool)* **to p. sb on** tomarle el pelo *or Esp, Carib, Méx* vacilar a alguien; **you're putting me on!** ¡me estás tomando el pelo *or Esp, Carib, Méx* vacilando!

▸**put out 1** *vt sep* (**a**) *(fire, light)* apagar (**b**) *(place outside)* sacar (**c**) *(extend)* **to p. out one's hand** tender la mano (**d**) *(arrange for use)* dejar preparado(a) (**e**) *(report, statement)* emitir (**f**) *(annoy)* **to be put out** estar disgustado(a) (**g**) *(inconvenience)* molestar; **to p. oneself out (for sb)** molestarse (por alguien) (**h**) *(dislocate)* **to p. one's shoulder/knee out** dislocarse el hombro/la rodilla

2 *vi very Fam (have sex willingly)* acostarse, meterse en la cama (**for** con)

▸**put through** *vt sep* (**a**) *(on phone)* **to p. sb through to sb** poner *or* pasar a alguien con alguien (**b**) *(subject to)* **to p. sb through sth** someter a alguien a algo; **he put her through hell** le ha hecho pasar las de Caín

▸**put together** *vt sep (machine, furniture)* montar; *(file, report, meal, team)* confeccionar; **she's more intelligent than the rest of them put together** ella es más lista que todos los demás juntos; *Fig* **to p. two and two together** atar cabos

▸**put up** *vt sep* (**a**) *(ladder)* situar; *(tent)* montar; *(building, barricade, fence)* levantar, construir; *(painting, notice)* colocar, poner; *(statue)* erigir, poner; *(umbrella)* abrir; **to p. up one's hand** levantar la mano; **to p. one's hair up** recogerse el pelo (**b**) *(increase)* elevar, subir (**c**) *(provide accommodation for)* alojar (**d**) *(provide) (money)* aportar; *(candidate)* presentar; **to p. sth up for sale** poner algo a la venta; **to p. up a fight** *or* **struggle** ofrecer resistencia

▸**put upon** *vt insep* **to feel put upon** sentirse utilizado(a)

▶**put up to** *vt sep* **to p. sb up to doing sth** animar a alguien a hacer algo

▶**put up with** *vt insep* aguantar, soportar

putative ['pju:tətɪv] *adj Formal* presunto(a), supuesto(a); *Law (father)* putativo(a)

put-down ['pʊtdaʊn] *n Fam* desaire *m*

put-on ['pʊtɒn] **1** *n Fam* **is that one of your put-ons?** ¿me estás tomando el pelo *or Esp, Carib, Méx* vacilando?
   2 *adj* fingido(a), simulado(a)

putrefy ['pju:trɪfaɪ] *vi* pudrirse

putrid ['pju:trɪd] *adj* putrefacto(a), pútrido(a)

putsch [pʊtʃ] *n* pronunciamiento *m* (militar)

putt [pʌt] **1** *n (in golf)* golpe *m* corto *(con el putter)*
   2 *vi (in golf)* golpear en corto *(con el putter)*

putter ['pʌtə(r)] *n (golf club)* putter *m*

putty ['pʌtɪ] *n* masilla *f; Fig* **he's p. in her hands** hace lo que quiere con él

put-up job ['pʊtʌp'dʒɒb] *n Fam* pufo *m*, apaño *m*

puzzle ['pʌzl] **1** *n* (**a**) *(game)* rompecabezas *m inv*; *(mental)* acertijo *m*; **p. book** libro *m* de pasatiempos (**b**) *(mystery)* enigma *m*

   2 *vt (person)* desconcertar, dejar perplejo(a)

▶**puzzle out** *vt sep* desentrañar

▶**puzzle over** *vt insep* dar vueltas a

puzzled ['pʌzəld] *adj* perplejo(a)

puzzling ['pʌzlɪŋ] *adj* desconcertante

PVC [pi:vi:'si:] *n (abbr* **polyvinyl chloride**) PVC *m*

PX [pi:'eks] *n (abbr* **post exchange**) *Mil* cooperativa *f* militar, economato *m* militar

pygmy, pigmy ['pɪgmɪ] *n* pigmeo(a) *m,f*

pylon ['paɪlən] *n* torre *f* (de alta tensión)

pyramid ['pɪrəmɪd] *n* pirámide *f*

pyre ['paɪə(r)] *n* pira *f*

Pyrenean [pɪrə'nɪən] *adj* pirenaico(a)

Pyrenees [pɪrə'ni:z] *npl* **the P.** los Pirineos

Pyrex® ['paɪreks] *n* pyrex® *m;* **P. dish** fuente *f* de pyrex®

pyromaniac [paɪrəʊ'meɪnɪæk] *n* pirómano(a) *m,f*

pyrotechnics [paɪrəʊ'teknɪks] **1** *n (science)* pirotecnia *f*
   2 *npl (fireworks display)* fuegos *mpl* artificiales; *Fig (in speech, writing)* malabarismos *mpl*, virguerías *fpl*

python ['paɪθən] *n* (serpiente *f*) pitón *m or f*

Q

Q, q [kjuː] n (letter) Q, q f
Qatar [kæˈtɑː(r)] n Qatar
Qatari [kæˈtɑːrɪ] **1** n persona de Qatar
    2 adj de Qatar
QED [kjuːiːˈdiː] (abbr **quod erat demonstrandum**) QED, lo que había que demostrar
Q-tip® [ˈkjuːtɪp] n bastoncillo m (de algodón)
qty Com (abbr **quantity**) cantidad f
quack [kwæk] **1** n (of duck) graznido m
    2 vi (duck) graznar
quad [kwɒd] n Fam (of school, college) patio m
quadrangle [ˈkwɒdræŋɡəl] n (a) (shape) cuadrilátero m, cuadrángulo m (b) (of school, college) patio m
quadrant [ˈkwɒdrənt] n cuadrante m
quadraphonic, quadriphonic [kwɒdrəˈfɒnɪk] adj cuadrafónico(a)
quadratic equation [kwɒˈdrætɪkɪˈkweɪʒən] n Math ecuación f de segundo grado
quadrilateral [kwɒdrɪˈlætərəl] **1** n cuadrilátero m
    2 adj cuadrilátero(a)
quadriphonic = **quadraphonic**
quadriplegic [kwɒdrɪˈpliːdʒɪk] n & adj tetrapléjico(a) m,f
quadruped [ˈkwɒdrʊped] n cuadrúpedo m
quadruple [kwɒˈdruːpəl] **1** adj cuádruple, cuádruplo(a)
    2 vt cuadruplicar
    3 vi cuadruplicarse
quadruplet [kwɒˈdruːplɪt] n cuatrillizo(a) m,f
quaff [kwɒf] vt Literary trasegar, ingerir a grandes tragos
quagmire [ˈkwæɡmaɪə(r)] n (bog) barrizal m, lodazal m; Fig (difficult situation) atolladero m
quail¹ [kweɪl] (pl **quail**) n (bird) codorniz f
quail² vi (person) amedrentarse, amilanarse
quaint [kweɪnt] adj (picturesque) pintoresco(a); (old-fashioned) anticuado(a) y singular
quaintly [ˈkweɪntlɪ] adv (in a picturesque way) pintorescamente; (in an old-fashioned way) de forma anticuada y singular
quake [kweɪk] **1** n Fam (earthquake) terremoto m
    2 vi temblar, estremecerse; **to q. in one's boots** temblar de miedo
Quaker [ˈkweɪkə(r)] n Rel cuáquero(a) m,f
qualification [kwɒlɪfɪˈkeɪʃən] n (a) (skill) aptitud f, capacidad f (b) (requirement) requisito m (c) (modification) condición f, reserva f (d) (for competition) clasificación f
qualified [ˈkwɒlɪfaɪd] adj (a) (competent) capaz, capacitado(a); **to be q. to do sth** (be competent) estar capacitado(a) para hacer algo (b) (modified) limitado(a), parcial
qualifier [ˈkwɒlɪfaɪə(r)] n (a) (person, team) clasificado(a) m,f; (game) partido m de clasificación, eliminatoria f (b) Gram calificador m, modificador m
qualify [ˈkwɒlɪfaɪ] **1** vt (a) (make competent) **to q. sb to do sth** capacitar a alguien para hacer algo (b) (modify) matizar

    2 vi (a) (in competition) clasificarse (b) (be eligible) **to q. for sth** tener derecho a algo
qualifying [ˈkwɒlɪfaɪɪŋ] adj (round, game) eliminatorio(a)
qualitative [ˈkwɒlɪtətɪv] adj cualitativo(a)
qualitatively [ˈkwɒlɪtətɪvlɪ] adv cualitativamente
quality [ˈkwɒlɪtɪ] n (a) (excellence, standard) calidad f; **of good/poor q.** de buena/mala calidad; **q. of life** calidad de vida; **q. circle** círculo m de calidad; **q. control** control m de calidad; **q. goods** artículos mpl de calidad; **q. time** = tiempo que uno reserva para disfrutar de la pareja, la familia, los amigos, etc., y alejarse de las preocupaciones laborales y domésticas (b) (characteristic, feature) cualidad f
qualm [kwɑːm] n escrúpulo m, reparo m; **to have no qualms about doing sth** no tener ningún escrúpulo or reparo en hacer algo
quandary [ˈkwɒndərɪ] n dilema m; **to be in a q. (about sth)** estar en un dilema (acerca de algo)
quanta [ˈkwɒntə] pl of **quantum**
quantifiable [kwɒntɪˈfaɪəbəl] adj cuantificable; **a q. amount** una cantidad cuantificable
quantifier [ˈkwɒntɪfaɪə(r)] n Math cuantificador m
quantify [ˈkwɒntɪfaɪ] vt cuantificar
quantitative [ˈkwɒntɪtətɪv] adj cuantitativo(a)
quantity [ˈkwɒntɪtɪ] n cantidad f
quantum [ˈkwɒntəm] (pl **quanta** [ˈkwɒntə]) n Phys cuanto m; Fig **q. leap** paso m de gigante; **q. mechanics** mecánica f cuántica; **q. theory** teoría f cuántica
quarantine [ˈkwɒrəntiːn] **1** n cuarentena f; **to be in q.** estar en cuarentena
    2 vt poner en cuarentena
quark [kwɑːk] n Phys quark m
quarrel [ˈkwɒrəl] **1** n (a) (argument) pelea f, discusión f; **to have a q.** pelearse; **to pick a q. with sb** buscar pelea con alguien (b) (disagreement) discrepancia f, desacuerdo m; **to have no q. with sb** no tener discrepancia alguna con alguien
    2 vi (a) (argue) pelearse, discutir (**with** con) (b) (disagree) **to q. with sth** discrepar de algo
quarreling [ˈkwɒrəlɪŋ] n peleas fpl, discusiones fpl
quarrelsome [ˈkwɒrəlsəm] adj peleón(ona)
quarry¹ [ˈkwɒrɪ] n (prey) & Fig presa f
quarry² **1** n (for stone) cantera f
    2 vt (hill) excavar; (stone) extraer
quart [kwɔːt] n (liquid measurement) cuarto m de galón (= 0,946 l)
quarter [ˈkwɔːtə(r)] **1** n (a) (fraction, of orange, of moon) cuarto m; **he ate a q. of the cake** se comió una or la cuarta parte del pastel; **a q. of a century** un cuarto de siglo; **a q. of an hour** un cuarto de hora; **a q. (of a pound)** un cuarto de libra (= 113,5 g); **three quarters** tres cuartos; **three quarters of all women** las tres cuartas partes de las mujeres; **three and a q. (ounces)** tres (onzas) y cuarto; **the bottle was still a q. full** quedaba aún un cuarto de botella
    (b) (in telling time) **it's/at a q. of six** son/a las seis menos

cuarto; **it's a q. to** son menos cuarto; **it's/at (a) q. after six** son/a las seis y cuarto; **it's (a) q. after** son y cuarto
(**c**) *(three-month period)* trimestre *m*
(**d**) *(area)* barrio *m*
(**e**) *(group)* **in some quarters** en algunos círculos; **help came from an unexpected q.** la ayuda llegó por el lado que menos se esperaba
(**f**) *Mil* **quarters** *(lodgings)* alojamiento *m*; **officer quarters** residencia *f* de oficiales
(**g**) *(mercy)* **to give no q.** no dar cuartel
(**h**) *(coin)* cuarto *m* de dólar (**i**) *Mus* **q. note** negra *f*
2 *vt* (**a**) *(divide into four)* dividir en cuatro partes (**b**) *Mil (troops)* acantonar, alojar

quarterback ['kwɔːtəbæk] *n* quarterback *m (en fútbol americano, jugador que dirige el ataque)*

quarterdeck ['kwɔːtədek] *n (of ship)* alcázar *m*, cubierta *f* de popa

quarterfinal [kwɔːtə'faɪnəl] *n (game)* enfrentamiento *m* de cuartos de final; **the quarterfinals** los cuartos de final

quarterfinalist ['kwɔːtə'faɪnəlɪst] *n* cuartofinalista *mf*

quarterly ['kwɔːtəlɪ] **1** *n* publicación *f* trimestral
2 *adj* trimestral
3 *adv* trimestralmente

quartermaster ['kwɔːtəmɑːstə(r)] *n Mil* oficial *m* de intendencia; **Q. Corps** ≃ intendencia *f*

quartet [kwɔː'tet] *n* cuarteto *m*

quarto ['kwɔːtəʊ] *(pl* **quartos***)* *n* pliego *m* en cuarto

quartz [kwɔːts] *n* cuarzo *m*; **q. watch** reloj *m* de cuarzo

quasar ['kweɪzɑː(r)] *n Astron* cuásar *m*, quasar *m*

quash [kwɒʃ] *vt (revolt)* sofocar; *(objection)* acallar; *Law (sentence)* revocar, anular

quaver ['kweɪvə(r)] **1** *n (in voice)* temblor *m*
2 *vi (voice)* temblar

quay [kiː] *n* muelle *m*

quayside ['kiːsaɪd] *n* muelles *mpl*

queasiness ['kwiːzɪnɪs] *n* mareo *m*

queasy ['kwiːzɪ] *adj* **to feel q.** estar mareado(a), tener mal cuerpo

Quebec [kwɪ'bek] *n* (provincia *f* de) Quebec; **Q. City** Quebec (capital)

queen [kwiːn] *n* (**a**) *(of country)* reina *f*; *(in cards, chess)* dama *f*, reina *f*; **q. bee** abeja *f* reina (**b**) *Fam Pej (homosexual)* marica *m*, maricón *m*

queen-size ['kwiːnsaɪz] *adj (bed)* grande

queer ['kwɪə(r)] **1** *n Fam Pej (male homosexual)* marica *m*, maricón *m*
2 *adj* (**a**) *(strange)* raro(a), extraño(a) (**b**) *(suspicious)* raro(a), sospechoso(a) (**c**) *Fam (unwell)* **to feel q.** encontrarse mal (**d**) *Fam Pej (homosexual)* marica, maricón; **q. cinema** cine *m* gay

quell [kwel] *vt (revolt)* sofocar; *(doubt, worry, passion)* apagar

quench [kwentʃ] *vt (thirst, fire)* apagar

querulous ['kwerʊləs] *adj* lastimero(a), quejumbroso(a)

query ['kwɪərɪ] **1** *n* duda *f*, pregunta *f*; *(on phone line, to expert, at information desk)* consulta *f*; **to raise a q. about sth** *(call into question)* poner en duda algo; *Comptr* **q. language** lenguaje *m* de consulta (estructurado)
2 *vt (question) (invoice)* reclamar contra; *(decision)* cuestionar; **to q. if** *or* **whether…** poner en duda si…

quest [kwest] *Literary* **1** *n* búsqueda *f* (**for** de); **to go** *or* **be in q. of sth** ir en búsqueda *or Esp* busca de algo
2 *vi* **to q. after** *or* **for sth** ir en búsqueda *or Esp* busca de algo

question ['kwestʃən] **1** *n* (**a**) *(interrogation)* pregunta *f*; **to ask (sb) a q.** hacer una pregunta (a alguien); **q. mark** signo *m* de interrogación; *Fig* **a q. mark hangs over the future of the project** el futuro del proyecto está en el aire
(**b**) *(doubt)* duda *f*; **there is no q. about it** no cabe duda (al respecto); **to call sth into q.** poner algo en duda; **beyond q.**

fuera de (toda) duda; **to be open to q.** ser cuestionable; **without q.** sin duda (**c**) *(matter)* cuestión *f*; **it is a q. of…** se trata de…; **there is no q. of our agreeing to that** en ningún caso vamos a estar conformes con eso; **that's out of the q.!** ¡es imposible!; **it's only a q. of time** sólo es cuestión de tiempo; **the matter/person in q.** el asunto/individuo en cuestión
2 *vt* (**a**) *(ask questions to) (for inquiry)* interrogar; *(for survey)* encuestar; **she was questioned on her views** *(in interview)* le pidieron su opinión (**b**) *(cast doubt on)* cuestionar, poner en duda

questionable ['kwestʃənəbəl] *adj* cuestionable, dudoso(a)

questioning ['kwestʃənɪŋ] **1** *n (interrogation)* interrogatorio *m*; **he was held for q. by the police** la policía lo detuvo para interrogarlo
2 *adj (look, mind)* inquisitivo(a)

questioningly ['kwestʃənɪŋlɪ] *adv* inquisitivamente

questionnaire [kwestʃə'neə(r)] *n* cuestionario *m*

quibble ['kwɪbəl] **1** *n* pega *f* insignificante, pequeñez *f*
2 *vi* poner pegas (**about** *or* **over** a); **let's not q.** no vamos a discutir por una tontería

quiche [kiːʃ] *n* quiche *m or f*

quick [kwɪk] **1** *n* **to bite one's nails to the q.** morderse las uñas hasta hacerse daño; *Fig* **to cut sb to the q.** herir a alguien en lo más profundo
2 *adj* (**a**) *(rapid)* rápido(a); **to have a q. bath** darse un baño rápido; **to have a q. drink** tomarse algo rápidamente; **that was q.!** ¡qué rápido!; **be q.!** ¡date prisa!, *Am* ¡apúrate!; **to be q. to do sth** no tardar *or Am* demorar en hacer algo; **to be q. to criticize** apresurarse a criticar; **to be q. off the mark** *(to act)* no perder el tiempo; *(to understand)* ser muy espabilado(a); **to have a q. temper** tener mal genio (**b**) *(clever)* listo(a), despierto(a)
3 *adv Fam (to run, talk, think)* rápido; **as q. as a flash** en un suspiro, *Esp* como una exhalación

quicken ['kwɪkən] **1** *vt* (**a**) *(make faster)* acelerar; **to q. one's pace** apretar *or* acelerar el paso (**b**) *(imagination)* estimular; *(interest)* despertar
2 *vi* (**a**) *(pace)* acelerarse; **his pulse quickened** se le aceleró el pulso (**b**) *(imagination)* estimularse; *(interest)* despertarse

quickfire ['kwɪkfaɪə(r)] *adj* rápido(a)

quickie ['kwɪkɪ] *Fam* **1** *n* **to have a q.** *(drink)* tomar una copa rápida; *(sex)* echar uno rápido
2 *adj* **q. divorce** divorcio *m* por la vía rápida

quicklime ['kwɪklaɪm] *n* cal *f* viva

quickly ['kwɪklɪ] *adv* rápidamente, rápido, deprisa; **I q. realized that…** enseguida me di cuenta de que…

quickness ['kwɪknɪs] *n (speed)* rapidez *f*; *(of mind)* agudeza *f*

quicksand ['kwɪksænd] *n* arenas *fpl* movedizas

quicksilver ['kwɪksɪlvə(r)] *n Old-fashioned (mercury)* azogue *m*

quick-tempered ['kwɪk'tempəd] *adj* irascible; **to be q.** tener mal genio

quick-witted ['kwɪk'wɪtɪd] *adj* agudo(a)

quiescent [kwɪ'esənt] *adj Literary* inactivo(a), pasivo(a)

quiet ['kwaɪət] **1** *n* silencio *m*, tranquilidad *f*; **the q. of the countryside** la paz del campo; *Fam* **to do sth on the q.** hacer algo a escondidas *or Esp* a la chita callando
2 *adj* (**a**) *(not loud) (person, music)* tranquilo(a); *(voice)* bajo(a); *(engine)* silencioso(a); **to keep sb q.** hacer callar a alguien; **to keep q.** *(make no noise)* no hacer ruido; *(say nothing)* estar callado(a); **to keep q. about sth** guardar silencio *or* no decir nada sobre algo; **to keep sth q.** mantener algo en secreto; **be q.!** ¡cállate!; **q. please!** ¡silencio, por favor!; **as q. as a mouse** *(person)* callado(a) como un muerto
(**b**) *(discreet)* discreto(a); **to have a q. laugh at sth/sb** reírse para sus adentros de algo/alguien

(**c**) *(peaceful)* tranquilo(a); **a q. wedding** una boda íntima *or* discreta

(**d**) *(business, market)* inactivo(a), poco animado(a)

▸**quiet down** = quieten down

quieten ['kwaɪətən] *vt* tranquilizar

▸**quieten down 1** *vt sep (make silent)* hacer callar; *(make calm)* tranquilizar, calmar

2 *vi (become silent)* callarse; *(become calm)* tranquilizarse, calmarse

quietly ['kwaɪətlɪ] *adv* (**a**) *(silently)* silenciosamente, sin hacer ruido (**b**) *(discreetly)* discretamente; **to be q. determined** estar interiormente resuelto(a); **to be q. confident** estar íntimamente convencido(a)

quietness ['kwaɪətnɪs] *n (of place)* silencio *m*, calma *f*; *(of person, manner)* tranquilidad *f*

quill [kwɪl] *n (feather, pen)* pluma *f*; *(of porcupine)* púa *f*

quilt [kwɪlt] **1** *n* edredón *m*

2 *vt (garment)* acolchar; **quilted jacket** chaqueta *f* acolchada

quince [kwɪns] *n* membrillo *m*; **q. jelly** dulce *m* de membrillo

quinine ['kwɪniːn] *n* quinina *f*

quintessence [kwɪn'tesəns] *n Formal* quintaesencia *f*

quintessential [kwɪntɪ'senʃəl] *adj Formal* arquetípico(a), prototípico(a); **Holmes is the q. Englishman** Holmes es el inglés por excelencia, Holmes es la quintaesencia de lo inglés

quintessentially [kwɪntɪ'senʃəlɪ] *adv Formal* prototípicamente, esencialmente

quintet [kwɪn'tet] *n* quinteto *m*

quintuplet [kwɪn'tjuːplɪt] *n* quintillizo(a) *m,f*

quip [kwɪp] **1** *n* broma *f*, chiste *m*

2 *vi (pt & pp quipped)* bromear

quirk [kwɜːk] *n* (**a**) *(of character)* manía *f* (**b**) *(of fate, nature)* capricho *m*; **by a q. of fate** por un capricho del destino

quirky ['kwɜːkɪ] *adj* peculiar

quisling ['kwɪzlɪŋ] *n* traidor(ora) *m,f*

quit [kwɪt] **1** *vt (pt & pp quit or quitted) (person, place)* abandonar, dejar; *Comptr* salir de; **to q. one's job** dejar el trabajo; **to q. doing sth** dejar de hacer algo

2 *vi (give up)* abandonar; *(resign)* dimitir; *Comptr* salir

3 *adj* **to be q. of** librarse *or* deshacerse de

quite [kwaɪt] *adv* (**a**) *(entirely)* completamente, totalmente; **that's not q. true** no es del todo cierto; **I'm not q. ready** no estoy del todo listo; **it's not q. what I wanted** no es exactamente lo que yo quería; **I can't q. see what you mean** no alcanzo a ver qué quieres decir; **q. enough** más que suficiente; **that's q. enough of that!** ¡ya es más que

suficiente!; **q. apart from the fact that...** sin mencionar el hecho de que...; **that's q. all right** *(it doesn't matter)* no importa; *(you're welcome)* no hay de qué; **you know q. well what I mean!** ¡sabes muy bien lo que quiero decir!; **I q. understand** lo entiendo perfectamente

(**b**) *(fairly)* bastante; **I q. like him** me gusta bastante; **q. a lot of problems** bastantes problemas

(**c**) *(for emphasis)* **it was q. a surprise** fue toda una sorpresa; **it's been q. a day!** ¡menudo día!; **that movie is q. something** ¡menuda película!

quits [kwɪts] *adj* **to be q. (with sb)** estar en paz (con alguien); **let's call it q.** vamos a dejarlo así

quiver¹ ['kwɪvə(r)] *n (for arrows)* carcaj *m*, aljaba *f*

quiver² **1** *n (tremble)* estremecimiento *m*

2 *vi (tremble)* estremecerse (**with** de)

quivering ['kwɪvərɪŋ] *adj* tembloroso(a), trémulo(a)

quixotic [kwɪk'sɒtɪk] *adj* quijotesco(a)

quiz [kwɪz] **1** *n (pl quizzes)* (**a**) *(competition, game)* concurso *m*; **q. (show)** programa *m* concurso (**b**) *(test)* examen *m*, control *m*

2 *vt (pt & pp quizzed)* interrogar

quizzical ['kwɪzɪkəl] *adj (look, air)* interrogador(ora), de interrogación

quizzically ['kwɪzɪklɪ] *adv* con aire dubitativo

Quorn® [kwɔːn] *n* = tipo de proteína vegetal utilizada como sustituto de la carne

quorum ['kwɔːrəm] *n* quórum *m inv*

quota ['kwəʊtə] *n (share)* cupo *m*, cuota *f*

quotable ['kwəʊtəbəl] *adj (remark, writer, book)* que se presta a ser citado(a)

quotation [kwəʊ'teɪʃən] *n* (**a**) *(from author)* cita *f*; **q. marks** comillas *fpl* (**b**) *Com (for work)* presupuesto *m*

quote [kwəʊt] **1** *n Fam* (**a**) *(from author)* cita *f*; **in quotes** *(in quotation marks)* entre comillas (**b**) *Com (for work)* presupuesto *m*

2 *vt* (**a**) *(author, passage)* citar; **he was quoted as saying that...** se le atribuye haber dicho que...; **in reply please q. this number** en su contestación por favor indique este número (**b**) *Com (price)* dar un presupuesto de; **he quoted me a price of $100** me dio un presupuesto de 100 dólares, fijó un precio de 100 dólares; *Fin* **quoted company** empresa *f* cotizada en Bolsa

quotient ['kwəʊʃənt] *n Math* cociente *m*

Quran [kə'rɑːn] *n* **the Q.** el Corán

Quranic [kə'rænɪk] *adj* coránico(a)

R

R, r [ɑ:(r)] n (letter) R, r f; Fam **the three R's** lectura, escritura y aritmética

R Pol (abbr **Republican**) republicano(a)

rabbi ['ræbaɪ] n Rel rabino m

rabbit ['ræbɪt] n conejo m; **r. hole** madriguera f; **r. hutch** conejera f

rabble ['ræbəl] n multitud f; **r. rouser** agitador(ora) m,f (de masas)

rabid ['ræbɪd] adj (**a**) (animal) rabioso(a) (**b**) (person, emotion) furibundo(a)

rabies ['reɪbi:z] n rabia f, hidrofobia f

raccoon [rə'ku:n] n mapache m

race[1] [reɪs] **1** n (contest) carrera f; **the hundred meters r.** los cien metros lisos; Fig **a r. against time** una carrera contrarreloj; **the races** (horseraces) las carreras

2 vt (**a**) (athlete) correr con or contra; **I'll r. you home!** ¡te echo una carrera hasta casa! (**b**) (horse) hacer correr (en carreras)

3 vi (**a**) (athlete, horse) correr, competir (**b**) (move quickly) correr; **to r. in/out** entrar/salir corriendo; **to r. down the street** correr calle abajo; **to r. by** (time) pasar volando (**c**) (engine) acelerarse; (pulse, heart) palpitar aceleradamente

race[2] n (of people, animals) raza f; **the human r.** la raza humana; **r. relations** relaciones fpl interraciales

racecourse ['reɪskɔ:s] n hipódromo m

racehorse ['reɪshɔ:s] n caballo m de carreras

racer ['reɪsə(r)] n (person) corredor(ora) m,f; (bicycle) bicicleta f de carreras

racetrack ['reɪstræk] n (for athletes) pista f; (for cars) circuito m; (for horses) hipódromo m

racial ['reɪʃəl] adj racial; **r. discrimination** discriminación f racial

racially ['reɪʃəlɪ] adv racialmente; **r. prejudiced** con prejuicios raciales

racing ['reɪsɪŋ] **1** n carreras fpl

2 adj **r. bicycle** bicicleta f de carreras; **r. car** coche m or Am carro m or CSur auto m de carreras

racism ['reɪsɪzəm] n racismo m

racist ['reɪsɪst] n & adj racista mf

rack [ræk] **1** n (**a**) (for bottles) botellero m; (for plates) escurreplatos m inv; (for magazines) revistero m; (for goods in store) expositor m; (for luggage) portaequipajes m inv; Tech **r. and pinion** engranaje m de piñón y cremallera (**b**) (for torture) potro m; Fig **to be on the r.** estar contra las cuerdas (**c**) (idioms) **to go to r. and ruin** venirse abajo

2 vt (torment) torturar, atormentar; **to be racked with pain** estar atormentado(a) por el dolor; **to r. one's brains** devanarse los sesos

racket[1] ['rækɪt] n (for tennis) raqueta f

racket[2] n (**a**) Fam (noise) estruendo m, Esp jaleo m; **to make a r.** armar alboroto or Esp jaleo (**b**) (criminal activity) negocio m mafioso; (swindling) estafa f

racketeer [rækɪ'tɪə(r)] n (criminal) mafioso(a) m,f; (swindler) estafador(ora) m,f

racketeering [rækɪ'tɪərɪŋ] n negocios mpl mafiosos; (swindling) estafas fpl

racquet ['rækɪt] n (for tennis) raqueta f

racy ['reɪsɪ] adj (risqué) atrevido(a); (lively) vívido(a)

radar ['reɪdɑ:(r)] n radar m; **r. operator** operador(ora) m,f de radar; **r. screen** pantalla f de radar

radial ['reɪdɪəl] **1** n (tire) neumático m or Col, Méx llanta f or Arg goma f (de cubierta) radial

2 adj radial

radiance ['reɪdɪəns] n (of light) resplandor m; (of person, smile) esplendor m

radiant ['reɪdɪənt] adj (light, person, smile) radiante, resplandeciente; **to be r. (with)** (person, smile) estar radiante (de)

radiantly ['reɪdɪəntlɪ] adv (to shine, glow) radiantemente; **r. beautiful** de una belleza radiante

radiate ['reɪdɪeɪt] **1** vt (heat, light) irradiar; Fig (happiness, enthusiasm) irradiar; (health) rebosar

2 vi irradiar (**from** de or desde)

radiation [reɪdɪ'eɪʃən] n radiación f

radiator ['reɪdɪeɪtə(r)] n (heater) radiador m

radical ['rædɪkəl] n & adj radical mf

radicalism ['rædɪkəlɪzəm] n radicalismo m

radii ['reɪdɪaɪ] pl of **radius**

radio ['reɪdɪəʊ] **1** n (pl radios) radio f; **r. cassette (recorder)** radiocasete m; **r. station** emisora f de radio; **r. wave** onda f de radio

2 vt (information) transmitir por radio; (person) comunicar por radio con

3 vi **to r. for help** pedir ayuda por radio

radioactive [reɪdɪəʊ'æktɪv] adj radiactivo(a); **r. waste** residuos mpl radiactivos

radioactivity [reɪdɪəʊæk'tɪvɪtɪ] n radiactividad f

radio-controlled [reɪdɪəʊkən'trəʊld] adj teledirigido(a)

radiograph ['reɪdɪəʊgrɑ:f] n radiografía f

radiographer [reɪdɪ'ɒgrəfə(r)] n técnico(a) m,f especialista en rayos X

radiography [reɪdɪ'ɒgrəfɪ] n radiografía f

radiologist [reɪdɪ'ɒlədʒɪst] n radiólogo(a) m,f

radiology [reɪdɪ'ɒlədʒɪ] n radiología f

radiotherapy [reɪdɪəʊ'θerəpɪ] n radioterapia f

radish ['rædɪʃ] n rábano m

radium ['reɪdɪəm] n Chem radio m

radius ['reɪdɪəs] (pl radii ['reɪdɪaɪ]) n radio m; **within a r. of** en un radio de

radon ['reɪdɒn] n Chem radón m

RAF [ɑ:reɪ'ef] n (abbr **Royal Air Force**) RAF f, fuerzas fpl aéreas británicas

raffia ['ræfɪə] n rafia f

raffish ['ræfɪʃ] adj pícaro(a)

raffle ['ræfəl] **1** n rifa f; **r. ticket** boleto m de rifa

2 vt rifar

raft [rɑ:ft] n balsa f

rafter ['rɑːftə(r)] *n* viga *f* (de tejado); *Constr* cabrio *m*

rafting ['rɑːftɪŋ] *n* rafting *m*; **to go r.** hacer rafting

rag [ræg] *n* (**a**) *(piece of cloth)* trapo *m*; **rags** *(clothes)* harapos *mpl*; **to go from rags to riches** salir de la miseria y pasar a la riqueza; **r. doll** muñeca *f* de trapo; *Fam* **the r. trade** la industria de la moda (**b**) *Fam Pej (newspaper)* periodicucho *m*

ragamuffin ['rægəmʌfɪn] *n* golfillo(a) *m,f*, pilluelo(a) *m,f*

ragbag ['rægbæg] *n* batiburrillo *m*

rage [reɪdʒ] **1** *n* (**a**) *(fury)* cólera *f*, ira *f*; **to be in a r.** estar hecho(a) una furia (**b**) *Fam (fashion)* **to be all the r.** *(music, style)* hacer furor

2 *vi* (**a**) **to r. about sth** despotricar contra algo; **to r. against** *or* **at sb/sth** encolerizarse con alguien/algo (**b**) *(sea)* embravecerse, encresparse; *(epidemic, war)* recrudecerse

ragged ['rægɪd] *adj (clothes)* raído(a); *(edge)* irregular; *(person)* andrajoso(a); *Fam* **she had run herself r.** se había quedado molida

raging ['reɪdʒɪŋ] *adj* (**a**) *(person)* furioso(a); **to be in a r. temper** estar hecho(a) una furia (**b**) *(sea)* embravecido(a), encrespado(a); *(fire)* pavoroso(a); *(fever, thirst, headache)* atroz

ragwort ['rægwɜːt] *n* hierba *f* cana

raid [reɪd] **1** *n* *(on bank)* atraco *m*; *(by army)* incursión *f*; *(by police)* redada *f*

2 *vt (of robbers)* atracar, asaltar; *(of army)* hacer una incursión en; *(of police)* hacer una redada en; *Fig* **to r. the fridge** saquear la nevera *or RP* la heladera *or Méx* el refrigerador

raider ['reɪdə(r)] *n (criminal)* atracador(ora) *m,f*

rail¹ [reɪl] *n* (**a**) *(of stairway, balcony)* baranda *f*, *Esp* barandilla *f* (**b**) *(train system)* ferrocarril *m*, tren *m*; *(track)* riel *m*, carril *m*; **by r.** en tren; **r. network** red *f* ferroviaria; **r. strike** huelga *f* ferroviaria *or* de trenes

rail² *vi* **to r. at** *or* **against sth** protestar airadamente contra algo

railcar ['reɪlkɑː(r)] *n* vagón *m*

railings ['reɪlɪŋz] *npl* verja *f*

railroad ['reɪlrəʊd] **1** *n (system)* (red *f* de) ferrocarril *m*; *(track)* vía *f* férrea; **r. car** vagón *m* (de tren); **r. crossing** paso *m* a nivel; **r. line** *(track)* vía *f* (férrea); *(route)* línea *f* de tren; **r. network** red *f* ferroviaria; **r. station** estación *f* de trenes *or* de ferrocarril; **r. system** red *f* ferroviaria; **r. track** vía *f* (férrea); **r. worker** ferroviario(a) *m,f*

2 *vt Fam* **to r. sb into doing sth** avasallar a alguien para que haga algo; **to r. a bill through Congress** imponer un proyecto de ley al Congreso

railway ['reɪlweɪ] *n* = **railroad**

rain [reɪn] **1** *n* lluvia *f*; **in the r.** bajo la lluvia; **it looks like r.** parece que va a llover; **the rains** las lluvias; **come r. or shine** *(whatever the weather)* llueva o truene; *(whatever the circumstances)* sea como sea, pase lo que pase; **r. check** *(at sporting event)* = entrada para asistir más tarde a un encuentro suspendido por la lluvia; *Fam* **I'll take a r. check on that** lo dejaré para otra vez; **r. cloud** nube *f* de lluvia, nubarrón *m*; **r. dance** danza *f* de la lluvia; **r. forest** selva *f* tropical

2 *vt* **to r. blows/gifts on sb** hacer llover los golpes/los regalos sobre alguien

3 *vi* llover; **it's raining** está lloviendo; *Fam* **it's raining cats and dogs** está lloviendo a cántaros *or* a mares; *Prov* **when it rains, it pours** las desgracias nunca vienen solas

rainbow ['reɪnbəʊ] *n* arco *m* iris; **r. coalition** = coalición de partidos minoritarios; **r. trout** trucha *f* arco iris

raincoat ['reɪnkəʊt] *n* impermeable *m*

raindrop ['reɪndrɒp] *n* gota *f* de lluvia

rainfall ['reɪnfɔːl] *n* pluviosidad *f*

rainproof ['reɪnpruːf] *adj* impermeable

rainstorm ['reɪnstɔːm] *n* aguacero *m*

rainwater ['reɪnwɔːtə(r)] *n* agua *f* de lluvia

rainy ['reɪnɪ] *adj* lluvioso(a); *Fig* **to save sth for a r. day**

guardar algo para cuando haga falta; **the r. season** la estación de las lluvias

raise [reɪz] **1** *n (pay increase)* aumento *m* (de sueldo)

2 *vt* (**a**) *(lift)* levantar; **to r. one's voice** alzar *or* levantar la voz; **to r. one's glass to one's lips** llevarse el vaso a los labios; *also Fig* **to r. one's hat to sb** quitarse *or Am* sacarse el sombrero ante alguien; *Fig* **the audience raised the roof** *(in theater)* el teatro (literalmente) se vino abajo

(**b**) *(price, standard)* aumentar, elevar; *Fig* **to r. the stakes** forzar la situación

(**c**) *(problem, subject)* plantear

(**d**) *(smile, laugh)* provocar; *(fears, doubts)* levantar, sembrar; **I don't want to r. your hopes** no quisiera darte falsas esperanzas; **to r. the alarm** dar la voz de alarma; **to r. hell** *or* **Cain** poner el grito en el cielo

(**e**) *(money)* reunir, recaudar

(**f**) *(children, cattle)* criar; *(crops)* cultivar

(**g**) *(blockade, embargo)* levantar

(**h**) *(statue)* erigir

raised [reɪzd] *adj* (**a**) *(elevated) (ground, platform)* elevado(a) (**b**) *(embossed)* con relieve

raisin ['reɪzən] *n* (uva *f*) pasa *f*

rake [reɪk] **1** *n* (**a**) *(garden tool)* rastrillo *m*; **to be as thin as a r.** estar en los huesos (**b**) *(dissolute man)* crápula *m*, calavera *m*

2 *vt (leaves, soil)* rastrillar; **to r. one's memory** escarbar en la memoria

▸**rake around, rake about** *vi (search)* rebuscar

▸**rake in** *vt sep Fam (money)* amasar; **she's raking it in!** ¡se está forrando!, *Méx* ¡se está llenando de lana!

▸**rake off** *vt sep Fam (money)* llevarse

▸**rake over** *vt sep (subject, the past)* remover

rakish ['reɪkɪʃ] *adj (dissolute)* licencioso(a), disoluto(a); *(charm, smile)* desenvuelto(a); **to wear one's hat at a r. angle** llevar el sombrero ladeado con un aire de desenfado

rally ['rælɪ] **1** *n* (**a**) *(protest gathering)* concentración *f* (de protesta) (**b**) *(in tennis)* intercambio *m* de golpes, peloteo *m* (**c**) *(car race)* rally *m*; **r. driver** piloto *m* de rallys

2 *vt (troops)* reagrupar; *(support)* reunir, recabar; **to r. sb's spirits** elevar el ánimo a alguien; **rallying cry** consigna *f*, grito *m* de guerra

3 *vi (recover)* recuperarse; **to r. to sb's defense** salir en defensa de alguien; **to r. around** agruparse

▸**rally round** *vt insep also Fig* **to r. round the flag** agruparse en torno a la bandera

RAM [ræm] *n Comptr (abbr* **random access memory**) (memoria *f*) RAM *f*, memoria *f* de acceso aleatorio

ram [ræm] **1** *n* (**a**) *(animal)* carnero *m* (**b**) *(implement)* (battering) **r.** ariete *m*

2 *vt (pt & pp* **rammed**) (**a**) *(crash into)* embestir; *(of ship)* abordar (**b**) *(force into place)* embutir, apretar; *Fam* **she's always ramming her views down my throat** siempre está tratando de inculcarme a la fuerza sus ideas

Ramadan [ræmə'dæn] *n Rel* ramadán *m*

ramble ['ræmbəl] **1** *n (walk)* excursión *f*, caminata *f*

2 *vi* (**a**) *(walk)* caminar, marchar (**b**) *(digress)* divagar

▸**ramble on** *vi* divagar constantemente; **to r. on about sth** divagar sobre algo

rambler ['ræmblə(r)] *n (walker)* excursionista *mf*, senderista *mf*

rambling ['ræmblɪŋ] **1** *n* (**a**) *(walking)* **to go r.** ir de excursión, hacer senderismo (**b**) **ramblings** *(words)* divagaciones *fpl*, digresiones *fpl*

2 *adj* (**a**) *(letter, speech)* inconexo(a) (**b**) *(house)* laberíntico(a); **r. rose** rosal *m* trepador

rambunctious [ræm'bʌŋkʃəs] *adj Fam* bullicioso(a)

ramification [ræmɪfɪ'keɪʃən] *n* ramificación *f*

ramp [ræmp] *n* (**a**) *(to ease access)* rampa *f*; *(to plane, ship)* escalerilla f (b) (to join freeway) carril m de incorporación or aceleración; (to exit freeway) carril m de salida or deceleración

rampage 1 n ['ræmpeɪdʒ] **to go on the r.** ir arrasando con todo

2 vi [ræm'peɪdʒ] **to r. about** ir en desbandada

rampant ['ræmpənt] adj incontrolado(a)

rampart ['ræmpɑːt] n muralla f

ramrod ['ræmrɒd] n (for rifle) baqueta f; Fig **r. straight** con la espalda recta

ramshackle ['ræmʃækəl] adj destartalado(a)

ran [ræn] pt of **run**

ranch [rɑːntʃ] n rancho m; **r. dressing** = aderezo para ensalada con leche y mayonesa; **r. hand** peón(ona) m,f, jornalero(a) m,f; **r. house** (on ranch) casa f (en un rancho); (bungalow) bungalow m

rancher ['rɑːntʃə(r)] n ranchero(a) m,f

rancid ['rænsɪd] adj rancio(a); **to go r.** ponerse rancio(a)

rancor ['ræŋkə(r)] n acritud f, resentimiento m

rand [rænd] n rand m

random ['rændəm] **1** n **at r.** al azar

2 adj (choice, sample) al azar; Comptr **r. access memory** memoria f de acceso aleatorio; **r. sampling** muestreo m aleatorio, pruebas fpl aleatorias

rang [ræŋ] pt of **ring²**

range [reɪndʒ] **1** n (a) (of weapon, telescope, hearing) alcance m; (of ship, plane) autonomía f; **out of r.** fuera del alcance; **within r.** al alcance; **r. finder** telémetro m (b) (of prices, colors, products) gama f; (of instrument, voice) registro m; (of knowledge) amplitud f; (of research) ámbito m (c) (of hills, mountains) cordillera f (d) (practice area) (shooting) **r.** campo m de tiro (e) (stove) fogón m, cocina f or Col, Méx, Ven estufa f de carbón

2 vt (arrange in row) (troops, books) alinear; **to r. oneself with/against sb** alinearse con/en contra de alguien (b) (travel) recorrer

3 vi (a) (extend) **ages ranging from ten to ninety** edades comprendidas entre los diez y los noventa años; **during the summer temperatures r. from 70 to 86 degrees** durante el verano las temperaturas oscilan entre los 70 y los 86 grados (b) **to r. over** (include) abarcar, comprender

ranger ['reɪndʒə(r)] n (in forest) guardabosques mf inv; Mil comando m

Rangoon [ræn'guːn] n Rangún

rangy ['reɪndʒɪ] adj (limb) largo(a); (person) patilargo(a)

rank¹ [ræŋk] **1** n (a) (status) rango m; Fig **she pulled r. on him** le recordó quién mandaba (allí) (b) (row) fila f; Mil **the ranks** la tropa; Fig **to rise from the ranks** ascender de soldado a oficial; Fig **the ranks of the unemployed** las filas del paro; Fig **to break ranks (with)** desmarcarse (de); Fig **to close ranks** cerrar filas

2 vt clasificar (among entre or dentro de); **to r. sth/sb as** catalogar algo/a alguien como

3 vi figurar (among entre or dentro de); **that ranks as one of the best films I've seen** es una de las mejores películas que he visto; **to r. above/below sb** tener un rango superior/inferior al de alguien; **this ranks as a major disaster** esto constituye un desastre de primer orden

rank² adj (a) (foul-smelling) pestilente (b) (absolute) total; **she's a r. outsider** no es más que una comparsa, no tiene muchas posibilidades

rank-and-file [ræŋkən'faɪl] n **the r.** (in army) la tropa; (of political party) las bases

ranking ['ræŋkɪŋ] n (classification) clasificación f

rankle ['ræŋkəl] **1** vt doler

2 vi doler

ransack ['rænsæk] vt (house, desk) revolver, poner patas arriba; (store, town) saquear

ransom ['rænsəm] **1** n rescate m; **to hold sb to r.** pedir un rescate por alguien; Fig **to be held to r. by sb** estar a merced de alguien

2 vt rescatar, pagar el rescate de

rant [rænt] vi Fam despotricar (about/at acerca de/contra); **to r. and rave (about sth/at sb)** poner el grito en el cielo (por algo/ante alguien)

rap [ræp] n **1** (a) (sharp blow) golpe m; Fig **to give sb a r. over the knuckles** echar un Esp rapapolvo or Méx un buen regaño or RP un buen reto a alguien; Fam **to take the r. for sth** (blame, punishment) pagar el pato por algo (b) (music) rap m

2 vt (pt & pp rapped) (strike) dar un golpe a; Fig **to r. sb's knuckles, to r. sb over the knuckles** echar un Esp rapapolvo or Méx un buen regaño or RP un buen reto a alguien

3 vi (chat) charlar, CAm, Méx platicar

rapacious [rə'peɪʃəs] adj rapaz

rapaciousness [rə'peɪʃəsnɪs], **rapacity** [rə'pæsɪtɪ] n (of person) rapacidad f; (of appetite) voracidad f

rape¹ [reɪp] **1** n (crime) violación f; Fig (of countryside, environment) destrucción f

2 vt violar

rape² n (crop) colza f

rapid ['ræpɪd] adj rápido(a); Physiol **r. eye movement** movimientos mpl oculares rápidos; **r. reaction force** fuerza f de intervención rápida; **r. transit** transporte m urbano rápido

rapidity [rə'pɪdɪtɪ] n rapidez f, celeridad f

rapidly ['ræpɪdlɪ] adv rápidamente

rapids ['ræpɪdz] npl (in river) rápidos mpl

rapier ['reɪpɪə(r)] n estoque m

rapist ['reɪpɪst] n violador m

rappel [rə'pel] **1** n rápel m

2 vi hacer rápel

rapper ['ræpə(r)] n rapero(a) m,f

rapport [ræ'pɔː(r)] n buena relación f; **to have a good r. (with sb)** entenderse or llevarse muy bien (con alguien)

rapt [ræpt] adj (attention, look) extasiado(a); **to be r. in contemplation** estar absorto(a) en la contemplación

rapture ['ræptʃə(r)] n gozo m; **to be in raptures** estar encantado(a); **to go into raptures over** estar embelesado(a) con

rapturous ['ræptʃərəs] adj (cries, applause) arrebatado(a); (reception, welcome) clamoroso(a)

rapturously ['ræptʃərəslɪ] adv (to praise, applaud) con entusiasmo

rare [reə(r)] adj (a) (uncommon) raro(a); **to have a r. gift (for sth)** tener un don especial (para algo) (b) (steak) muy poco hecho(a)

rarefied ['reərɪfaɪd] adj (air, gas) rarificado(a), enrarecido(a); Fig (atmosphere, ideas) exclusivista, encopetado(a)

rarely ['reəlɪ] adv raras veces, raramente

raring ['reərɪŋ] adj **to be r. to do sth** estar deseando hacer algo; **to be r. to go** estar deseando empezar

rarity ['reərɪtɪ] n rareza f; **to be/become a r.** ser/convertirse en una rareza or un caso especial; **r. value** rareza

rascal ['rɑːskəl] n (child) pillo(a) m,f; Old-fashioned or Hum (scoundrel) bribón(ona) m,f

rash¹ [ræʃ] n (a) (on skin) erupción f, sarpullido m (b) (of complaints, letters) alud f, avalancha f

rash² adj (person) impulsivo(a); (action, remark) imprudente

rasher ['ræʃə(r)] n **r. (of bacon)** loncha f de tocino or Esp beicon

rashly ['ræʃlɪ] adv impulsivamente, precipitadamente

rasp [rɑːsp] **1** n (a) (tool) lima f gruesa, escofina f (b) (sound) chirrido m

2 vt (say hoarsely) bufar, carraspear

raspberry ['rɑːzbərɪ] n (fruit) frambuesa f; (plant) frambueso m; Fam Fig **to blow a r. at sb** hacerle una pedorreta a alguien; **r. jam** mermelada f de frambuesa

Rastafarian [ræstə'feəriən], *Fam* **Rasta** ['ræstə] *n & adj* rastafari *mf*

rat [ræt] **1** *n* (**a**) *(animal)* rata *f*; **r. poison** matarratas *m inv*, raticida *m*; **r. trap** ratonera *f*, trampa *f* para ratas (**b**) *Fam (scoundrel)* miserable *mf*, canalla *mf* (**c**) *Fam (informer)* soplón(ona) *m,f*, *Esp* chivato(a) *m,f* (**d**) *(idioms)* **I smell a r.** aquí hay gato encerrado; **to get out of the r. race** huir de la lucha frenética por escalar peldaños en la sociedad; *very Fam* **I don't give a r.'s ass** me importa un huevo, *Esp* me la suda
2 *vi (pt & pp* **ratted**) *Fam (inform)* cantar; **to r. on sb** delatar a alguien

ratchet ['rætʃɪt] *n* trinquete *m*; **r. (wheel)** rueda *f* de trinquete
▶**ratchet up** *vt sep (increase)* hacer subir, incrementar

rate [reɪt] **1** *n* (**a**) *(of inflation, crime, divorce, unemployment)* índice *m*, tasa *f*; *(of interest)* tipo *m*, *Am* tasa *f*; *Fin* **r. of return** tasa *f* de rentabilidad (**b**) *(speed)* ritmo *m*; **at this r.** a este paso; **at any r.** *(anyway)* en cualquier caso; *(at least)* por lo menos (**c**) *(price, charge)* tarifa *f*
2 *vt* (**a**) *(classify)* clasificar (**among** entre *or* dentro de); **to r. sth/sb as** catalogar algo/a alguien como; **to r. sb/sth highly** tener una buena opinión de alguien/algo; **I don't really r. their chances** no les doy muchas posibilidades (**b**) *(deserve)* merecer; **to r. a mention** ser digno(a) de mención
3 *vi* **to r. as** figurar como

rather ['rɑːðə(r)] *adv* (**a**) *(preferably)* **I'd r. stay** preferiría quedarme; **I'd r. not go** preferiría no ir; **r. you than me!** ¡no quisiera estar en tu lugar! (**b**) *(more exactly)* más bien; **he seemed tired or, r., bored** parecía cansado o, más bien, aburrido (**c**) *(quite)* bastante; *(very)* muy; **I r. liked it** me gustó mucho (**d**) *(instead of)* **r. than him** en vez *or* lugar de él; **r. than staying** en vez *or* lugar de quedarse

ratification [rætɪfɪ'keɪʃən] *n* ratificación *f*

ratify ['rætɪfaɪ] *vt* ratificar

rating ['reɪtɪŋ] *n* *(classification)* puesto *m*, clasificación *f*; **the ratings** *(for TV, radio)* los índices de audiencia

ratio ['reɪʃɪəʊ] *(pl* **ratios**) *n* proporción *f*, razón *f*; **in a r. of four to one** en una proporción de cuatro a uno

ration ['ræʃən, 'reɪʃən] **1** *n* ración *f*; **rations** *(supplies)* (raciones *fpl* de) víveres *mpl*; **r. book** cartilla *f* de racionamiento
2 *vt* racionar

rational ['ræʃənəl] *adj (sensible)* racional; *(sane)* lúcido(a)

rationalism ['ræʃənəlɪzəm] *n* racionalismo *m*

rationalist ['ræʃənəlɪst] *n* racionalista *mf*

rationalistic [ræʃənə'lɪstɪk] *adj* racionalista

rationality [ræʃə'nælɪtɪ] *n* racionalidad *f*

rationalization [ræʃənəlaɪ'zeɪʃən] *n* racionalización *f*

rationalize ['ræʃənəlaɪz] *vt* racionalizar

rationally ['ræʃənəlɪ] *adv (sensibly)* racionalmente; *(sanely)* lúcidamente

rationing ['ræʃənɪŋ] *n* racionamiento *m*

rattle ['rætəl] **1** *n* (**a**) *(for baby)* sonajero *m* (**b**) *(noise) (of train)* traqueteo *m*; *(of gunfire)* tableteo *m*; *(of chains)* crujido *m*; *(of glass, coins, keys)* tintineo *m*; *(of door, window)* golpeteo *m*
2 *vt* (**a**) *(chains, keys)* hacer entrechocar; *(door, window)* sacudir (**b**) *Fam (make nervous)* **to be rattled by sth** perder la calma a causa de algo
3 *vi (chains)* crujir; *(glass, keys, coins)* tintinear; *(door, window)* golpetear
▶**rattle off** *vt sep Fam (say quickly)* soltar de un tirón; *(write quickly)* garabatear
▶**rattle on** *vi Fam* parlotear, *Esp* cascar

rattlesnake ['rætəlsneɪk] *n* serpiente *f* de cascabel

rattling ['rætlɪŋ] *n* *(noise) (of train)* traqueteo *m*; *(of chains)* crujido *m*; *(of door, window)* golpeteo *m*

raucous ['rɔːkəs] *adj (voice, laughter, cry)* estridente; *(rowdy)* ruidoso(a)

raucously ['rɔːkəslɪ] *adv* estridentemente

raunchy ['rɔːntʃɪ] *adj Fam (lyrics, movie, novel)* picante, procaz; *(dress)* provocativo(a), sexy

ravage ['rævɪdʒ] **1** *vt* arrasar; **the city had been ravaged by war** la ciudad había sido arrasada *or* asolada por la guerra; **his face was ravaged by illness** la enfermedad había hecho estragos en su cara
2 ravages *npl* estragos *mpl*

rave [reɪv] **1** *n (party)* macrofiesta *f* (tecno)
2 *adj* **r. notice** *or* **review** *(for play)* crítica *f* entusiasta
3 *vi (deliriously)* desvariar; **to r. about sb/sth** *(enthusiastically)* deshacerse en elogios sobre alguien/algo

raven ['reɪvən] **1** *n (bird)* cuervo *m*
2 *adj (color)* azabache

ravenous ['rævənəs] *adj (animal, person)* hambriento(a) *m,f*; **to be r.** tener un hambre canina

ravine [rə'viːn] *n* barranco *m*

raving ['reɪvɪŋ] *adj* (**a**) *(delirious)* **to be r. mad** estar como una cabra; **a r. lunatic** un loco de atar (**b**) *(success)* clamoroso(a); *(beauty)* arrebatador(ora)

ravish ['rævɪʃ] *vt* (**a**) *Literary (delight)* deslumbrar, cautivar (**b**) *Old-fashioned (rape)* forzar, violar

ravishing ['rævɪʃɪŋ] *adj* deslumbrante, cautivador(ora); **she's a r. beauty** es de una belleza deslumbrante

ravishingly ['rævɪʃɪŋlɪ] *adv* **r. beautiful** de una belleza deslumbrante

raw [rɔː] *adj* (**a**) *(food, silk)* crudo(a); *(sugar)* sin refinar; *(statistics)* en bruto; **to be r.** *(meat, vegetables)* estar crudo(a); **r. materials** materias *fpl* primas; **r. recruit** recluta *m* novato (**b**) *(skin)* agrietado(a); *Fig* **to get a r. deal** ser tratado(a) injustamente; *Fig* **to touch a r. nerve** dar en lo más vivo (**c**) *(weather, wind)* crudo(a)

ray¹ [reɪ] *n (of light, sun)* rayo *m*; **a r. of hope** un rayo de esperanza
ray² *n (fish)* raya *f*

rayon ['reɪɒn] *n (fabric)* rayón *m*

raze [reɪz] *vt* arrasar; **to r. sth to the ground** arrasar totalmente algo

razor ['reɪzə(r)] *n* navaja *f* de afeitar; *(electric)* maquinilla *f* de afeitar; **r. blade** cuchilla *f* de afeitar; **r. clam** navaja *f (molusco)*

razor-sharp ['reɪzəʃɑːp] *adj (knife)* muy afilado(a); *Fig (intelligence)* agudo(a); *(wit)* afilado(a)

razzmatazz ['ræzmətæz] *n Fam* oropel *m*, fastuosidad *f*

R & B ['ɑːrən'biː] *n (abbr* **rhythm and blues**) rhythm and blues *m*

RC [ɑː'siː] *n & adj (abbr* **Roman Catholic**) católico(a) *m,f* romano(a)

R & D [ɑːrən'diː] *n Com (abbr* **research and development**) I+D, investigación *f* y desarrollo

Rd *(abbr* **Road**) C/, calle *f*

RDA [ɑːdiː'eɪ] *n (abbr* **recommended daily allowance**) cantidad *f* diaria recomendada

re¹ [riː] *prep* con referencia a; **re your letter...** con referencia a *or* en relación con su carta...; **re: 2004 sales figures** REF: cifras de ventas de 2004
re² [reɪ] *n Mus* re *m*

reach [riːtʃ] **1** *n* (**a**) *(accessibility)* alcance *m*; **within r.** al alcance; **out of r.** fuera del alcance (**b**) **the upper reaches of a river** la cabecera *or* el curso alto de un río; **the furthest reaches of the empire** los últimos confines del imperio
2 *vt* (**a**) *(manage to touch)* alcanzar; *(conclusion, decision, destination)* llegar a; *(agreement, stage, level)* alcanzar, llegar a; **the news didn't r. him** no le llegó la noticia (**b**) *(contact) (by phone)* contactar con *or Am* a; **to r. a wider audience** llegar a un público más amplio (**c**) *(stretch as far as) (one's shoulder, waist)* llegar a
3 *vi (forest, property)* extenderse; *(noise, voice)* oírse; **to r. for sth** (tratar de) alcanzar algo; *Fig* **to r. for the sky** *or* **the stars** apuntar a lo más alto

▶**reach out** *vi* **to r. out for sth** extender el brazo para agarrar *or Esp* coger algo

reachable ['riːtʃəbəl] *adj (place)* accesible; *(goal, objective)* asequible, alcanzable

react [rɪ'ækt] *vi* reaccionar (**against/to** contra/ante)

reaction [rɪ'ækʃən] *n* reacción *f*

reactionary [rɪ'ækʃənərɪ] *n & adj* reaccionario(a) *m,f*

reactivate [rɪ'æktɪveɪt] *vt* reactivar

reactive [rɪ'æktɪv] *adj* reactivo(a)

reactor [rɪ'æktə(r)] *n* reactor *m*

read [riːd] **1** *n* **this book's a good r.** este libro se lee muy bien *or* es muy entretenido
2 *vt (pt & pp* **read** [red]) **(a)** *(book, newspaper, letter)* leer; **to r. Italian** leer en italiano; **do you r. me?** *(on radio)* ¿me recibes? **(b)** *(interpret)* interpretar; **to r. sb's mind** adivinar los pensamientos a alguien; **it can be read in two ways** tiene una doble lectura; **to r. the future** adivinar el futuro **(c)** *(say aloud) (letter, poem)* leer (en voz alta) **(d)** *(of dial, thermometer)* marcar; **the sign read "No Entry"** el letrero decía "prohibida la entrada"
3 *vi* **(a)** *(person)* leer; **to r. aloud** leer en alto *or* en voz alta; *Fig* **to r. between the lines** leer entre líneas **(b)** *(text)* **to r. well/ badly** estar bien/mal escrito(a)
▶**read out** *vt sep* leer (en voz alta)
▶**read up on** *vt insep* empaparse de, leer mucho sobre

readable ['riːdəbəl] *adj (book)* ameno(a); *(handwriting)* legible

reader ['riːdə(r)] *n* **(a)** *(person)* lector(ora) *m,f* **(b)** *(reading book)* libro *m* de lectura

readily ['redɪlɪ] *adv (willingly)* de buena gana; *(easily)* fácilmente

reading ['riːdɪŋ] *n* **(a)** *(action, pastime)* lectura *f*; **r. age** nivel *m* de lectura; **r. glasses** gafas *fpl* para leer; **r. list** *f* de lecturas **(b)** *(measurement)* **to take a r. from the gas meter** leer el contador del gas **(c)** *(interpretation)* interpretación *f*, lectura *f*

readjust [riːə'dʒʌst] **1** *vt* reajustar; *(clothing, device, object)* ajustar
2 *vi* adaptarse de nuevo

readjustment [riːə'dʒʌstmənt] *n* reajuste *m*

readme file ['riːdmiː'faɪl] *n Comptr (documento m)* léeme *m*

readmit [riːəd'mɪt] *vt* readmitir (**to** en)

read-only ['riːd'əʊnlɪ] *adj Comptr* **r. file** archivo *m* de sólo lectura; **r. memory** memoria *f* de sólo lectura

readvertize [riː'ædvətaɪz] *vt* **to r. a post** volver a anunciar una oferta de empleo

ready ['redɪ] **1** *n* **at the r.** a mano
2 *adj* **(a)** *(prepared)* listo(a); **to be r. (to do sth)** estar listo(a) *or* preparado(a) (para hacer algo); **we were r. to give up** estuvimos a punto de darnos por vencidos; **to get (oneself) r.** *(prepared)* prepararse *or Am* alistarse; *(smarten up)* arreglarse; **to get sth r.** preparar algo; **r.!, steady!, go!** preparados, listos, ¡ya!; **r. cash** dinero *m* en efectivo **(b)** *(willing)* dispuesto(a); **to be r. to do sth** estar dispuesto(a) a hacer algo **(c)** *(quick)* rápido(a); **to have a r. wit** ser muy despierto(a)
3 *vt (prepare)* preparar; **to r. oneself for action** prepararse *or Am* alistarse para la acción

ready-made [redɪ'meɪd] *adj (clothes)* de confección, confeccionado(a); **r. food** platos *mpl* precocinados; **a r. phrase** una frase hecha

ready-to-wear ['redɪtə'weə(r)] *adj* de confección

reaffirm [riːə'fɜːm] *vt* reafirmar

real [rɪəl] **1** *adj* **(a)** *(danger, fear, effort)* real; *(authentic) (gold, leather)* auténtico(a); **r. flowers** flores *fpl* naturales; **the r. reason** el verdadero motivo; **a r. friend** un amigo de verdad **(b)** *(actual)* real; **the r. world** el mundo real; **what does that mean in r. terms?** ¿qué significado tiene a efectos prácticos?; *Com* **r. estate** bienes *mpl* inmuebles; **r. estate**

agent agente *mf* inmobiliario(a); **r. estate developer** *Esp* promotor(ora) *m,f* inmobiliario, *Am* constructor(ora) *m,f*; **r. property** bienes *mpl* inmuebles **(c)** *(for emphasis)* **a r. idiot** un tonto de remate; **a r. disaster** un perfecto desastre
2 *adv Fam (very)* muy; **it's r. good** es superbueno(a)

realism ['rɪəlɪzəm] *n* realismo *m*

realist ['rɪəlɪst] *n* realista *mf*

realistic [rɪə'lɪstɪk] *adj* realista

reality [rɪ'ælɪtɪ] *n* realidad *f*; **in r.** en realidad; **r. TV** la televisión de los reality-shows

realization [rɪəlaɪ'zeɪʃən] *n* **this r. frightened her** al darse cuenta se asustó; **the r. of what he meant was slow in coming** tardó *or Am* demoró en darse cuenta de lo que quería decir

realize ['rɪəlaɪz] *vt* **(a)** *(become aware of)* darse cuenta de; **I r. he's busy, but...** ya sé que está ocupado, pero... **(b)** *(ambition, dream)* realizar; **our fears were realized** nuestros temores se vieron confirmados

real-life ['rɪəllaɪf] *adj* de la vida real; **his r. wife** su mujer en la vida real

really ['rɪəlɪ] *adv (truly)* de verdad; *(very)* realmente, verdaderamente; **is it r. true?** ¿es eso verdad *or* cierto?; **r.?** ¿de verdad?, ¿en serio?; **this is r. not all that bad** esto no está pero que nada mal

realm [relm] *n* **(a)** *(kingdom)* reino *m* **(b)** *(field)* ámbito *m*, dominio *m*; **within/beyond the realms of possibility** dentro de/fuera de lo posible

realtor ['rɪəltə(r)] *n* agente *mf* inmobiliario(a)

realty ['rɪəltɪ] *n* bienes *mpl* inmuebles

ream [riːm] *n (of paper)* resma *f*; *Fig* **reams of** toneladas *fpl* de

reanimate [riː'ænɪmeɪt] *vt* reanimar

reap [riːp] *vt* recolectar, cosechar; **to r. the benefits (of)** cosechar los beneficios (de)

reaper ['riːpə(r)] *n (machine)* cosechadora *f*

reappear [riːə'pɪə(r)] *vi* reaparecer

reappearance [riːə'pɪərəns] *n* reaparición *f*

reapply [riːə'plaɪ] *vi (for job)* volver a presentar solicitud *or* presentarse

reappoint [riːə'pɔɪnt] *vt* volver a nombrar

reappraise [riːə'preɪz] *vt* reconsiderar

rear[1] [rɪə(r)] *n* **(a)** *(back part)* parte *f* trasera; *(of military column)* retaguardia *f*; **at the r. of** *(inside)* al fondo de; *(behind)* detrás de; **in the r.** detrás, en la parte de atrás; **to bring up the r.** *(in race)* ser el farolillo rojo; **r. admiral** contralmirante *m*; **r. entrance** puerta *f* trasera; *Mil* **r. guard** retaguardia *f*; **r. legs** *(of animal)* patas *fpl* traseras; **r. lights** *(of car)* luces *fpl* traseras; **r. window** *(of car)* luneta *f*, ventana *f* trasera **(b)** *Fam (buttocks)* trasero *m*

rear[2] *vt* **(a)** *(child, livestock)* criar **(b)** *(one's head)* levantar; **fascism has reared its ugly head** el fascismo ha levantado su repugnante cabeza
▶**rear up** *vi (horse)* encabritarse

rearguard ['rɪəgɑːd] *adj also Fig* **to fight a r. action** emprender un último intento a la desesperada

rearm [riː'ɑːm] **1** *vt* rearmar
2 *vi* rearmarse

rearmament [riː'ɑːməmənt] *n* rearme *m*

rearrange [riːə'reɪndʒ] *vt (books, furniture)* reordenar; *(appointment)* cambiar

rearview mirror ['rɪəvjuː'mɪrə(r)] *n (espejo m)* retrovisor *m*

rearwheel drive ['rɪəwiːl'draɪv] *n* tracción *f* trasera

reason ['riːzən] **1** *n* **(a)** *(cause, motive)* razón *f*, motivo *m* (**for** de); **for reasons of health** por razones de salud; **for one r. or another** por un motivo u otro; **for no particular r.** sin *or* por ningún motivo en especial; **that's no r. for giving up!** ¡eso no es motivo para darse por vencido!; **I don't know the r. why** no sé por qué; *Ironic* **for reasons best known to**

himself por razones que a mí se me escapan; **give me one good r. why I should!** ¿y por qué razón debería hacerlo?

(b) *(sanity, common sense)* razón *f*; **to listen to** *or* **see r.** atender a razones, *Am* atender razones; **it stands to r.** es lógico *or* evidente; **within r.** dentro de lo razonable

2 *vt* **to r. that...** argumentar que...

3 *vi* razonar **(about** sobre); **to r. with sb** razonar con alguien

reasonable ['riːzənəbəl] *adj (fair, sensible, moderate)* razonable; *(acceptable)* aceptable, razonable; **the weather/meal was r.** el tiempo/la comida fue aceptable; **be r.!** ¡sé razonable!

reasonably ['riːzənəblɪ] *adv* **(a)** *(behave, act)* razonablemente **(b)** *(quite)* bastante, razonablemente

reasoning ['riːzənɪŋ] *n (thinking)* razonamiento *m*

reassemble [riːə'sembəl] **1** *vt (people)* reagrupar; *(machine)* volver a montar

2 *vi (people)* reagruparse

reassert ['riːə'sɜːt] *vt (authority)* reafirmar, volver a imponer; **her distrust of men reasserted itself** se reafirmó su desconfianza de los hombres

reassess [riːə'ses] *vt* **(a)** *(policy, situation)* replantearse **(b)** *Fin (tax)* revisar; *(property)* volver a tasar

reassign [riːə'saɪn] *vt (employee)* destinar **(to** a); *(work, project)* reasignar **(to** a)

reassurance [riːə'ʃʊərəns] *n (comfort)* consuelo *m*; *(guarantee)* garantía *f*

reassure [riːə'ʃʊə(r)] *vt* confortar, tranquilizar; **to feel reassured** sentirse más tranquilo(a); **he reassured them that he would be there** les aseguró que estaría allí

reassuring [riːə'ʃʊərɪŋ] *adj* tranquilizador(ora), confortante

reassuringly [riːə'ʃʊərɪŋlɪ] *adv* de modo tranquilizador; **a r. solid keyboard** un teclado bien sólido

reawaken [riːə'weɪkən] **1** *vt* volver a despertar

2 *vi (person)* volver a despertarse

reawakening [riːə'weɪkənɪŋ] *n (of interest, curiosity)* renacimiento *m*; **the r. of national pride** el rebrote del orgullo nacionalista

rebate ['riːbeɪt] *n Fin (refund)* devolución *f*, reembolso *m*; *(discount)* bonificación *f*

rebel 1 *n* ['rebəl] rebelde *mf*; **r. leader** cabecilla *mf* rebelde *or* de la rebelión

2 *vi* [rɪ'bel] *(pt & pp* **rebelled)** rebelarse **(against** contra)

rebellion [rɪ'beljən] *n* rebelión *f*

rebellious [rɪ'beljəs] *adj* rebelde

rebirth [riː'bɜːθ] *n (renewal)* resurgimiento *m*

reboot [riː'buːt] *vt & vi Comptr* reinicializar

reborn [riː'bɔːn] *adj* **to be r.** renacer

rebound 1 *n* ['riːbaʊnd] *(of ball)* rebote *m*; *Fig* **she married him on the r.** se casó con él después de una decepción amorosa

2 *vi* [rɪ'baʊnd] *(ball)* rebotar; *Fig* **to r. on sb** *(joke, lie)* volverse en contra de alguien

rebuff [rɪ'bʌf] **1** *n (slight)* desaire *m*, desplante *m*; *(rejection)* rechazo *m*; **to meet with a r.** *(person, suggestion)* ser rechazado(a)

2 *vt (slight)* desairar; *(reject)* rechazar

rebuild [riː'bɪld] *(pt & pp* **rebuilt** [riː'bɪlt]) *vt & vi* reconstruir

rebuke [rɪ'bjuːk] **1** *n* reprensión *f*, reprimenda *f*

2 *vt* reprender

rebut [rɪ'bʌt] *(pt & pp* **rebutted)** *vt* refutar

rebuttal [rɪ'bʌtəl] *n* refutación *f*

recalcitrant [rɪ'kælsɪtrənt] *adj* recalcitrante

recall 1 *n* ['riːkɔːl] *(memory)* memoria *f*; **lost beyond r.** perdido(a) irremisiblemente

2 *vt* [rɪ'kɔːl] **(a)** *(remember)* recordar; **to r. doing sth** recordar haber hecho algo **(b)** *(defective goods)* retirar del mercado; *(library book)* reclamar

recant [rɪ'kænt] **1** *vt (opinion)* retractarse de

2 *vi (change opinion)* retractarse; *Rel* abjurar

recap ['riːkæp] **1** *n* **(a)** *(summary)* recapitulación *f* **(b)** *(tire)* neumático *m* recauchutado, *Col, Méx* llanta *f or Arg* goma *f* recauchutada

2 *vi (pt & pp* **recapped)** **(a)** *(summarize)* recapitular **(b)** *(tire)* recauchutar

recapitulate [riːkə'pɪtjʊleɪt] *vt & vi* recapitular

recapture [riː'kæptʃə(r)] **1** *n (of criminal)* nueva captura *f*, segunda detención *f*; *(of town, territory)* reconquista *f*; **he escaped r. for nearly a year** no lo volvieron a capturar hasta pasado casi un año

2 *vt* **(a)** *(criminal)* volver a detener; *(town, territory)* reconquistar **(b)** *(memory, atmosphere)* recuperar; *(one's youth)* revivir

recede [rɪ'siːd] *vi (tide, coastline)* retroceder; **to have a receding chin** tener la barbilla hundida; **to have a receding hairline** tener entradas

receipt [rɪ'siːt] *n* **(a)** *(act of receiving)* recibo *m*; **to be in r. of sth** haber recibido algo **(b)** *(proof of payment)* recibo *m*; **receipts** *(at box office)* recaudación *f*

receive [rɪ'siːv] *vt* recibir; **to r. stolen goods** comerciar con *or* receptar bienes robados; **it was well/badly received** *(movie, proposal)* fue bien/mal acogido(a); **to r. sb into the Church** recibir a alguien en el seno de la Iglesia

received [rɪ'siːvd] *adj (idea, opinion)* común, aceptado(a)

receiver [rɪ'siːvə(r)] *n* **(a)** *(of stolen goods)* perista *mf*; *Law* receptador(ora) *m,f* **(b)** *(of telephone)* auricular *m*, *RP, Ven* tubo *m*; **to pick up the r.** descolgar el teléfono; **to replace the r.** colgar el teléfono **(c)** *(of radio set)* receptor *m* **(d)** *Fin* **to call in the receivers** declararse en quiebra, poner la empresa en manos de la administración judicial **(e)** *(in football)* receptor *m*, receiver *m*

receivership [rɪ'siːvəʃɪp] *n Fin* **to go into r.** declararse en quiebra

receiving [rɪ'siːvɪŋ] **1** *n (of stolen goods)* receptación *f*

2 *adj Fam* **to be on the r. end (of sth)** ser la víctima (de algo)

recent ['riːsənt] *adj* reciente; **in r. months** en los últimos meses; **in r. times** recientemente; **her most r. novel** su última *or* su más reciente novela

recently ['riːsəntlɪ] *adv* recientemente, hace poco; **as r. as yesterday** ayer sin ir más lejos; **until quite r.** hasta hace muy poco

receptacle [rɪ'septəkəl] *n* receptáculo *m*

reception [rɪ'sepʃən] *n* **(a)** *(of guests, new members)* recibimiento *m*; *(of announcement, new movie)* recibimiento *m*, acogida *f*; **to get a warm r.** ser acogido(a) calurosamente **(b)** *(party)* recepción *f*; **(wedding) r.** banquete *m* de boda *or Andes* matrimonio *or RP* casamiento *m* **(c)** *(in hotel)* **r. (desk)** recepción *f* **(d)** *(of radio, TV program)* recepción *f*

receptionist [rɪ'sepʃənɪst] *n* recepcionista *mf*

receptive [rɪ'septɪv] *adj* receptivo(a)

recess ['riːses] *n* **(a)** *(of Congress)* período *m* vacacional; *(in trial)* descanso *m* **(b)** *(in wall)* hueco *m*; *(of mind, past)* recoveco *m* **(c)** *Sch (play period)* recreo *m*

recession [rɪ'seʃən] *n Econ* recesión *f*

recharge [riː'tʃɑːdʒ] *vt (battery)* recargar; *Fig* **to r. one's batteries** recargar las baterías

rechargeable [riː'tʃɑːdʒəbəl] *adj* recargable

recidivism [rɪ'sɪdɪvɪzəm] *n Law* reincidencia *f*

recipe ['resɪpɪ] *n also Fig* receta *f*; **a r. for disaster/success** la receta para el desastre/el éxito; **r. book** recetario *m* (de cocina)

recipient [rɪ'sɪpɪənt] *n (of gift, letter)* destinatario(a) *m,f*; *(of check, award, honor)* receptor(ora) *m,f*

reciprocal [rɪ'sɪprəkəl] *adj* recíproco(a)

reciprocate [rɪˈsɪprəkeɪt] **1** *vt* corresponder a **2** *vi* corresponder

reciprocity [resɪˈprɒsɪtɪ] *n Formal* reciprocidad *f*

recital [rɪˈsaɪtəl] *n (of poetry, music)* recital *m; (of facts)* perorata *f*

recitation [resɪˈteɪʃən] *n (of poem)* recitación *f*

recite [rɪˈsaɪt] **1** *vt (poem)* recitar; *(complaints, details)* enumerar **2** *vi* recitar

reckless [ˈreklɪs] *adj (decision, behavior)* imprudente; *(driving)* temerario(a); **r. driver** conductor(ora) *m,f* temerario(a)

recklessly [ˈreklɪslɪ] *adv (to decide, behave)* imprudentemente; *(to drive)* de modo temerario

reckon [ˈrekən] **1** *vt* (**a**) *(consider)* considerar; **he is reckoned to be...** está considerado como... (**b**) *(calculate)* calcular (**c**) *Fam (think)* **to r. (that)** creer que **2** *vi* calcular

▶ **reckon on** *vt insep* contar con; **you should r. on there being about thirty people there** debes contar con que habrá por lo menos treinta personas

▶ **reckon with** *vt insep* contar con; **she's someone to be reckoned with** es una mujer de armas tomar

reckoning [ˈrekənɪŋ] *n* **by my r.** según mis cálculos; **day of r.** hora *f* de la verdad

reclaim [rɪˈkleɪm] *vt (lost property, expenses)* reclamar; *(waste materials)* recuperar; **to r. land from the sea** ganar terreno al mar

reclamation [rekləˈmeɪʃən] *n (of waste materials)* recuperación *f;* **land r. project** proyecto *m* para ganar terreno al mar

reclassify [riːˈklæsɪfaɪ] *vt* reclasificar

recline [rɪˈklaɪn] *vi* reclinarse

reclining [rɪˈklaɪnɪŋ] *adj* **in a r. position** reclinado(a); **r. seat** asiento *m* reclinable

recluse [rɪˈkluːs] *n* solitario(a) *m,f*

recognition [rekəɡˈnɪʃən] *n* reconocimiento *m;* **to have changed beyond** *or* **out of all r.** estar irreconocible; **in r. of** en reconocimiento a

recognizable [rekəɡˈnaɪzəbəl] *adj* reconocible

recognizably [rekəɡˈnaɪzəblɪ] *adv* claramente

recognize [ˈrekəɡnaɪz] *vt* reconocer

recognized [ˈrekəɡnaɪzd] *adj (government)* legítimo(a); *(method)* reconocido(a); *(qualification)* homologado(a); **to be a r. authority (on sth)** ser una autoridad reconocida (en algo)

recoil 1 *n* [ˈriːkɔɪl] *(of gun)* retroceso *m* **2** *vi* [rɪˈkɔɪl] *(gun, person)* retroceder

recollect [rekəˈlekt] *vt* recordar

recollection [rekəˈlekʃən] *n* recuerdo *m;* **to the best of my r.** en lo que alcanzo a recordar

recommend [rekəˈmend] *vt* (**a**) *(praise)* recomendar; **to r. sth to sb** recomendar algo a alguien; **the proposal has a lot to r. it** la propuesta presenta muchas ventajas (**b**) *(advise)* recomendar, aconsejar; **to r. sb to do sth** recomendar a alguien hacer algo; *Com* **recommended retail price** precio *m* recomendado de venta al público

recommendable [rekəˈmendəbəl] *adj* recomendable

recommendation [rekəmenˈdeɪʃən] *n* recomendación *f;* **on my/her r.** recomendado(a) por mí/por ella

recompense [ˈrekəmpens] **1** *n* recompensa *f;* **in r. for** como recompensa por **2** *vt* recompensar (**for** por)

reconcilable [rekənˈsaɪləbəl] *adj (people)* reconciliable; *(opinions, accounts)* conciliable

reconcile [ˈrekənsaɪl] *vt* (**a**) *(people)* reconciliar; **to be reconciled with sb** reconciliarse con alguien; **to be reconciled to sth** estar resignado(a) a algo (**b**) *(facts, differences, opinions)* conciliar

reconciliation [rekənsɪlɪˈeɪʃən] *n* (**a**) *(of people)* reconciliación *f* (**b**) *(of differences, opinions)* conciliación *f*

reconditioned [riːkənˈdɪʃənd] *adj (TV, washing machine)* reparado(a)

reconnaissance [rɪˈkɒnɪsəns] *n Mil* reconocimiento *m;* **r. flight** vuelo *m* de reconocimiento

reconquer [riːˈkɒŋkə(r)] *vt* reconquistar

reconquest [riːˈkɒŋkwest] *n* reconquista *f*

reconsider [riːkənˈsɪdə(r)] *vt* reconsiderar

reconsideration [ˈriːkənsɪdəˈreɪʃən] *n* reconsideración *f*

reconstitute [riːˈkɒnstɪtjuːt] *vt (organization, committee)* reconstituir; *(dried food)* rehidratar

reconstruct [riːkənˈstrʌkt] *vt* reconstruir

reconstruction [riːkənˈstrʌkʃən] *n* reconstrucción *f*

record [ˈrekɔːd] **1** *n* (**a**) *(account)* registro *m;* **to keep a r. of sth** anotar algo; **to put sth on r.** dejar constancia (escrita) de algo; **the coldest winter on r.** el invierno más frío del que se tiene constancia; **to be on r. as saying that...** haber declarado públicamente que...; **off the r.** *(say)* confidencialmente; **(just) for the r.** para que conste; **to put** *or* **set the r. straight** poner las cosas en claro *or* en su sitio (**b**) *(personal history)* historial *m; (of criminal)* antecedentes *mpl* penales; **to have a good/bad safety r.** tener un buen/mal historial en materia de seguridad; **he has a r.** *(of criminal)* tiene antecedentes; **academic r.** expediente *m* académico; *Med* **case r.** historial *m* (clínico) (**c**) *(musical)* disco *m;* **to make a r.** grabar un disco; **r. company** compañía *f* discográfica; **r. player** tocadiscos *m inv* (**d**) *(best performance)* récord *m;* **to set a r.** establecer un récord; **to hold the r.** tener el récord; **to break** *or* **beat the r.** batir el récord; **r. holder** plusmarquista *mf* (**e**) *Comptr* registro *m* **2** *adj* **in r. time** en tiempo récord; **unemployment is at a r. high/low** el desempleo *or* *Am* la desocupación ha alcanzado un máximo/mínimo histórico **3** *vt* [rɪˈkɔːd] (**a**) *(on video, cassette)* grabar (**b**) *(write down)* anotar

record-breaking [ˈrekɔːdbreɪkɪŋ] *adj* récord *inv;* **to have r. sales** batir todos los récords de ventas

recorded [rɪˈkɔːdɪd] *adj* (**a**) *(message, program, tape)* grabado(a) (**b**) *(documented)* documentado(a); **throughout r. history** a lo largo del periodo histórico del que se tienen documentos escritos

recorder [rɪˈkɔːdə(r)] *n* (**a**) **(tape) r.** grabadora *f,* magnetófono *m* (**b**) *(musical instrument)* flauta *f* dulce, flauta *f* de pico

recording [rɪˈkɔːdɪŋ] *n (on tape)* grabación *f;* **r. studio** estudio *m* de grabación

recount[1] [ˈriːkaʊnt] *n (in election)* segundo recuento *m*

recount[2] [rɪˈkaʊnt] *vt (relate)* relatar

recoup [rɪˈkuːp] *vt* recuperar, resarcirse de

recourse [rɪˈkɔːs] *n* recurso *m;* **to have r. to** recurrir a

recover [rɪˈkʌvə(r)] **1** *vt (gen)* & *Comptr* recuperar **2** *vi (from illness, setback)* recuperarse

recoverable [rɪˈkʌvərəbəl] *adj* recuperable

recovery [rɪˈkʌvərɪ] *n* (**a**) *(of lost object)* recuperación *f* (**b**) *(from illness, of economy)* recuperación *f;* **to make a r.** recuperarse; **r. position** posición *f* de recuperación

re-create [riːkrɪˈeɪt] *vt* recrear

recreation [rekrɪˈeɪʃən] *n (leisure)* ocio *m,* esparcimiento *m; Sch (break)* recreo *m;* **to do sth for r.** hacer algo como pasatiempo; **r. room** sala *f* de recreo

recreational [rekrɪˈeɪʃənəl] *adj* recreativo(a); **r. drug** = droga de consumo esporádico y por diversión; **r. vehicle** autocaravana *f,* casa *f* caravana

recrimination [rɪkrɪmɪˈneɪʃən] *n* recriminación *f,* reproche *m*

recruit [rɪˈkruːt] **1** *n (soldier)* recluta *mf; (new employee, member)* nuevo miembro *m* **2** *vt (soldier)* reclutar; *(employee)* contratar; *(member)* enrolar, reclutar

recruiter [rɪˈkruːtə(r)] *n (of soldier)* encargado(a) *m,f* del reclutamiento; *(of employee)* encargado(a) *m,f* de la contratación

recruiting [rɪˈkruːtɪŋ] *n* reclutamiento *m*; **r. sergeant** sargento *m* encargado del reclutamiento

recruitment [rɪˈkruːtmənt] *n (of soldier)* reclutamiento *m*; *(of employee)* contratación *f*; *(of new member)* enrolamiento *m*, reclutamiento *m*

rectangle [ˈrektæŋgəl] *n* rectángulo *m*

rectangular [rekˈtæŋgjʊlə(r)] *adj* rectangular

rectify [ˈrektɪfaɪ] *vt* rectificar

rectitude [ˈrektɪtjuːd] *n Formal* rectitud *f*, integridad *f*

rector [ˈrektə(r)] *n* **(a)** *Rel* párroco *m* **(b)** *(of college)* rector(ora) *m,f*; *(of school)* director(ora) *m,f*

rectory [ˈrektərɪ] *n Rel* rectoría *f*

rectum [ˈrektəm] *n Anat* recto *m*

recumbent [rɪˈkʌmbənt] *adj Formal* yacente

recuperate [rɪˈkuːpəreɪt] **1** *vt (one's strength, money)* recuperar **2** *vi (person)* recuperarse

recuperation [rɪkuːpəˈreɪʃən] *n* recuperación *f*

recur [rɪˈkɜː(r)] *(pt & pp* **recurred***)* *vi (event, problem)* repetirse; *(illness)* reaparecer

recurrence [rɪˈkʌrəns] *n (of event, problem)* repetición *f*; *(of illness)* reaparición *f*

recurrent [rɪˈkʌrənt] *adj* recurrente

recurring [rɪˈkɜːrɪŋ] *adj (problem)* recurrente, reiterativo(a); *Math* **six point six** *n* seis coma seis período *or* periódico (puro); **a r. nightmare** una pesadilla recurrente

recyclable [riːˈsaɪkləbəl] *adj* reciclable

recycle [riːˈsaɪkəl] *vt* reciclar; **recycled paper/glass** papel *m*/vidrio *m* reciclado; *Comptr* **r. bin** papelera *f* de reciclaje

recycling [riːˈsaɪklɪŋ] *n* reciclaje *m*, reciclado *m*; **r. plant** planta *f* de reciclaje

red [red] **1** *n (color)* rojo *m*; *Fam Fig* **to see r.** *(become angry)* ponerse hecho(a) una furia; **to be in the r.** *(be in debt)* estar en números rojos **2** *adj* rojo(a); **to have r. hair** ser pelirrojo(a); **to turn** *or* **go r.** *(sky)* ponerse rojo; *(person)* ponerse colorado(a); **to be as r. as a beet** estar más rojo que un tomate *or Méx* jitomate; **r. alert** alerta *f* roja; *Hist* **the Red Army** el Ejército Rojo; *Fig* **to roll out the r. carpet for sb** recibir a alguien con todos los honores; *Physiol* **r. corpuscle** glóbulo *m* rojo, hematíe *m*; **Red Cross** Cruz *f* Roja; *Fig* **r. herring** *(distraction)* señuelo *m* *(para desviar la atención)*; *(misleading clue)* pista *f* falsa; **r. light** semáforo *m* (en) rojo; **to go through a r. light** saltarse un semáforo en rojo; **r. meat** carne *f* roja; **r. pepper** pimiento *m* rojo *or* colorado; **(Little) Red Riding Hood** Caperucita *f* Roja; **the Red Sea** el Mar Rojo; **r. tape** burocracia *f*, papeleo *m* (burocrático); **r. wine** vino *m* tinto

red-blooded [redˈblʌdɪd] *adj* **a r. male** un macho de pelo en pecho

redcurrant [ˈredkʌrənt] *n* grosella *f* (roja)

redden [ˈredən] **1** *vt* enrojecer **2** *vi (sky)* ponerse rojo(a); *(person)* ponerse colorado(a)

reddish [ˈredɪʃ] *adj (light, color)* rojizo(a)

redecorate [riːˈdekəreɪt] *vt (repaint)* pintar de nuevo; *(repaper)* empapelar de nuevo

redeem [rɪˈdiːm] *vt* **(a)** *(pawned item)* desempeñar; *(bond)* amortizar; *(share)* rescatar; *(gift token, coupon)* canjear; **to r. a mortgage** amortizar una hipoteca **(b)** *(sinner)* redimir; *Fig* **he redeemed himself by scoring the equalizer** subsanó su error al marcar el gol del empate

redeemable [rɪˈdiːməbəl] *adj* **(a)** *(bond)* amortizable; *(share)* rescatable **(b)** *(sinner)* redimible

Redeemer [rɪˈdiːmə(r)] *n Rel* **the R.** el Redentor

redeeming [rɪˈdiːmɪŋ] *adj* **he has no r. features** no se salva por ningún lado, no tiene nada que lo salve

redemption [rɪˈdempʃən] *n Rel* redención *f*; *also Fig* **to be beyond** *or* **past r.** no tener salvación

redeploy [riːdɪˈplɔɪ] *vt (troops, resources)* redistribuir, reorganizar

redeployment [riːdɪˈplɔɪmənt] *n* redistribución *f*, reorganización *f*

redevelop [riːdɪˈveləp] *vt (land)* reconvertir; *(town)* reedificar

red-eye [ˈredaɪ] *n* **(a)** *Phot* ojos *mpl* rojos **(b)** *Fam (whiskey)* whisky *m* de poca calidad **(c)** *Fam (overnight flight)* vuelo *m* nocturno

red-eyed [ˈredˈaɪd] *adj* **to be r.** tener los ojos rojos

red-faced [ˈredˈfeɪst] *adj (naturally)* sonrosado(a); *(with anger)* sulfurado(a); *(with embarrassment)* ruborizado(a)

red-handed [ˈredˈhændɪd] *adv* **he was caught r.** lo *Esp* cogieron *or Am* agarraron con las manos en la masa

redhead [ˈredhed] *n* pelirrojo(a) *m,f*

redheaded [redˈhedɪd] *adj* pelirrojo(a)

red-hot [redˈhɒt] *adj* **(a)** *(very hot)* al rojo vivo, candente **(b)** *Fam* **to be r. (on sth)** *(very good)* ser un genio para algo, *Esp, Méx* ser un hacha (en algo); **r. news** noticias *fpl* de candente actualidad

redial *Tel* **1** *n* [ˈriːdaɪəl] **r. (feature)** (botón *m* de) rellamada *f* **2** *vt* [riːˈdaɪəl] *(number)* volver a marcar *or Andes, RP* discar **3** *vi* volver a marcar *or Andes, RP* discar (el número)

redid [riːˈdɪd] *pt of* **redo**

redirect [riːdɪˈrekt, riːdaɪˈrekt] *vt (letter)* reexpedir; *(plane, traffic)* desviar; **to r. one's energies (toward sth)** reorientar los esfuerzos (hacia algo)

rediscover [riːdɪsˈkʌvə(r)] *vt* redescubrir

rediscovery [riːdɪˈskʌvərɪ] *n* redescubrimiento *m*

redistribute [riːˈdɪstrɪbjuːt] *vt* redistribuir

redistribution [riːdɪstrɪˈbjuːʃən] *n* redistribución *f*

red-letter day [ˈredˈletədeɪ] *n* jornada *f* memorable

red-light district [ˈredˈlaɪtˈdɪstrɪkt] *n Esp* barrio *m* chino, *Am* zona *f* roja, *Andes* barrio *m* de tolerancia

redneck [ˈrednek] *n Pej* ≈ sureño racista y reaccionario, de baja extracción social

redo [riːˈduː] *(pt* **redid** [riːˈdɪd]*, pp* **redone** [riːˈdʌn]*) vt* rehacer

redolent [ˈredələnt] *adj* **to be r. of** *(smell of)* oler a; *(be suggestive of)* tener reminiscencias de

redone [riːˈdʌn] *pp of* **redo**

redouble [riːˈdʌbəl] *vt* redoblar; **to r. one's efforts** redoblar los esfuerzos

redraft [riːˈdrɑːft] *vt* redactar de nuevo, reescribir

redress [rɪˈdres] **1** *n (of grievance)* reparación *f*; **to seek r.** exigir reparación **2** *vt (injustice, grievance)* reparar; **to r. the balance** reestablecer el equilibrio

redskin [ˈredskɪn] *n Old-fashioned* piel roja *mf*

reduce [rɪˈdjuːs] *vt* **(a)** *(make smaller, lower)* reducir; *(price, product)* rebajar; **to r. a sauce** reducir una salsa; **to r. speed** reducir la velocidad **(b)** *(bring to a certain state)* **to r. sth to ashes/dust** reducir algo a cenizas/polvo; **to r. sb to silence** reducir a alguien al silencio; **his words reduced her to tears** sus palabras le hicieron llorar; **to be reduced to doing sth** no tener más remedio que hacer algo

reduced [rɪˈdjuːst] *adj (smaller)* reducido(a); **on a r. scale** a escala reducida; **at r. prices** a precios reducidos; **to live in r. circumstances** haber venido a menos

reduction [rɪˈdʌkʃən] *n* reducción *f*; *(of price, product)* rebaja *f*

reductive [rɪˈdʌktɪv] *adj* reductor(ora)

redundant [rɪˈdʌndənt] *adj (superfluous)* superfluo(a), innecesario(a); *(words, information)* redundante

redwood [ˈredwʊd] *n* secuoya *f*, secoya *f*

reed [riːd] *n* **(a)** *(plant)* caña *f* **(b)** *Mus (of instrument)* lengüeta *f*

reef [riːf] *n* arrecife *m*

reek [ri:k] **1** n peste f, tufo m
2 vi also Fig apestar (**of** a)

reel [ri:l] **1** n (**a**) (for tape, cable, fishing line) carrete m, bobina f; (of movie) rollo m (**b**) (dance, music) = danza escocesa o irlandesa
2 vi (sway) tambalearse; **my head is reeling** me da vueltas la cabeza

▶**reel off** vt sep (names, statistics) soltar de un tirón

reelect [ri:ɪ'lekt] vt Pol reelegir

reelection [ri:ɪ'lekʃən] n reelección f

reemerge ['ri:ɪ'mɜːdʒ] vi (from water, room, hiding) reaparecer, salir; **he has reemerged as a major contender** ha reaparecido como un candidato de primera fila

reemergence ['ri:ɪ'mɜːdʒəns] n (from water, room, hiding) reaparición f, salida f; **the r. of this problem in recent years** la reaparición de este problema en los últimos años

reenact [ri:ɪ'nækt] vt (crime, battle) reconstruir

reenter [ri:'entə(r)] **1** vt (room, country) volver a entrar en; **to r. the job market** reinsertarse en el or reincorporarse al mercado de trabajo
2 vi volver a entrar; **to r. for an examination** volver a examinarse

reestablish [ri:ɪ'stæblɪʃ] vt restablecer

reexamination ['ri:ɪgzæmɪ'neɪʃən] n (**a**) (of question, case) reexamen m (**b**) Law (of witness) segundo interrogatorio m

reexamine [ri:ɪg'zæmɪn] vt (**a**) (of question, case) reexaminar (**b**) Law (witness) interrogar por segunda vez

ref [ref] n (**a**) (abbr **reference**) **r. number** n° ref., número m de referencia (**b**) Fam (referee) árbitro m

refectory [rɪ'fektərɪ] n (in monastery) refectorio m

refer [rɪ'fɜː(r)] (pt & pp **referred**) vt remitir; **to r. a matter to sb** remitir un asunto a alguien; **to r. a patient to a specialist** enviar a un paciente al especialista

▶**refer to** vt insep (**a**) (consult) consultar (**b**) (allude to, mention) referirse a; **who are you referring to?** ¿a quién te estás refiriendo?; **referred to as…** conocido(a) como…; **he never refers to it** nunca hace referencia al asunto (**c**) (apply to) referirse a, ser aplicable a

referee [refə'ri:] **1** n árbitro m
2 vt & vi arbitrar

reference ['refərəns] n (**a**) (consultation) consulta f; (source) referencia f; **for r. only** (book) para consulta en sala; **to keep sth for future r.** guardar algo para su posterior consulta; **r. book/work** libro m/obra f de consulta; **r. number** número m de referencia; **r. point, point of r.** punto m de referencia (**b**) (allusion) referencia f, alusión f; **with r. to…** con referencia a… (**c**) (from employer) informe m, referencia f

referendum [refə'rendəm] n referéndum m; **to hold a r.** celebrar un referéndum

refill 1 n ['ri:fɪl] (for notebook, pen) recambio m; **would you like a r.?** (of drink) ¿quieres otra copa?
2 vt [ri:'fɪl] (glass) volver a llenar; (lighter, pen) recargar

refine [rɪ'faɪn] vt (sugar, petroleum) refinar; (technique, machine) perfeccionar

refined [rɪ'faɪnd] adj (**a**) (petroleum, sugar) refinado(a) (**b**) (person, taste) refinado(a), sofisticado(a)

refinement [rɪ'faɪnmənt] n (**a**) (of manners, taste, person) refinamiento m (**b**) (of technique) sofisticación f; **to make refinements to sth** perfeccionar algo

refinery [rɪ'faɪnərɪ] n refinería f

refit 1 n ['ri:fɪt] (of ship) reparación f
2 vt [ri:'fɪt] (pt & pp **refitted**) (ship) reparar

reflate [ri:'fleɪt] vt Econ reflacionar

reflation [ri:'fleɪʃən] n Econ reflación f

reflect [rɪ'flekt] **1** vt (**a**) (image, light) reflejar; **to be reflected** reflejarse (**b**) (mood, personality) reflejar (**c**) (think) **to r. that…** considerar que…

2 vi (**a**) (think) reflexionar (**on** sobre) (**b**) **to r. well/badly on sb** dejar en buen/mal lugar a alguien

reflection [rɪ'flekʃən] n (**a**) (reflected image) reflejo m; Fig **an accurate r. of the situation** un fiel reflejo de la situación; Fig **the termination of the project is no r. on your own performance** la cancelación del proyecto no significa que tú no lo hayas hecho bien (**b**) (thought) reflexión f; **on r.** después de pensarlo

reflective [rɪ'flektɪv] adj (**a**) (surface) reflectante (**b**) (person) reflexivo(a)

reflector [rɪ'flektə(r)] n (on bicycle, vehicle) reflectante m, catadióptrico m

reflex ['ri:fleks] **1** n reflejo m
2 adj reflejo(a); **r. action** acto m reflejo; **r. camera** (cámara f) réflex f inv

reflexive [rɪ'fleksɪv] adj Gram reflexivo(a); **r. verb** verbo m reflexivo

reflexively [rɪ'fleksɪvlɪ] adv Gram reflexivamente

reforestation [ri:fɒrɪ'steɪʃən] n reforestación f, repoblación f forestal

reform [rɪ'fɔːm] **1** n reforma f; **r. school** reformatorio m
2 vt (improve) reformar; **he's a reformed character** se ha reformado completamente
3 vi reformarse

re-form ['ri:'fɔːm] vi (organization, pop group) volver a unirse

reformat ['ri:'fɔːmæt] (pt & pp **reformatted**) vt Comptr (disk) volver a formatear

reformation [refə'meɪʃən] n reforma f; Hist **the R.** la Reforma

reformatory [rɪ'fɔːmətərɪ] n reformatorio m

reformer [rɪ'fɔːmə(r)] n reformador(ora) m,f

reformist [rɪ'fɔːmɪst] n & adj reformista mf

refract [rɪ'frækt] vt (light) refractar

refraction [rɪ'frækʃən] n Phys refracción f

refrain [rɪ'freɪn] **1** n (musical) estribillo m; Fig (repeated comment) cantinela f
2 vi abstenerse (**from** de); **to r. from comment** abstenerse de hacer comentarios; **please r. from talking/smoking** (sign) se ruega guardar silencio/no fumar

refreeze [ri:'fri:z] vt volver a congelar

refresh [rɪ'freʃ] vt refrescar; Comptr regenerar; **to r. oneself** refrescarse; **to r. one's memory** refrescar la memoria; **to r. sb's glass** (top up) llenarle el vaso a alguien

refreshing [rɪ'freʃɪŋ] adj (breeze, drink) refrescante

refreshingly [rɪ'freʃɪŋlɪ] adv **he's r. honest** da gusto su honradez

refreshments [rɪ'freʃmənts] npl refrigerio m

refrigerate [rɪ'frɪdʒəreɪt] vt refrigerar, conservar en (la) nevera or Esp (el) frigorífico or Méx (el) refrigerador or RP (la) heladera

refrigeration [rɪfrɪdʒə'reɪʃən] n **keep under r.** manténgase en la nevera or Esp el frigorífico or Méx el refrigerador or RP la heladera

refrigerator [rɪ'frɪdʒəreɪtə(r)] n (domestic) nevera f, Esp frigorífico m, RP heladera f, Méx refrigerador m; (industrial) cámara f frigorífica m

refuel [ri:'fjʊəl] **1** vt (ship, aircraft) repostar combustible a
2 vi (ship, aircraft) repostar

refueling [ri:'fjʊəlɪŋ] n repostaje m; **r. plane/ship** avión m/barco m nodriza; **r. stop** escala f técnica or de repostaje

refuge ['refjuːdʒ] n (from danger, weather) refugio m; **to seek r.** buscar refugio; **to take r.** refugiarse

refugee [refjʊ'dʒiː] n refugiado(a) m,f; **r. camp** campo m de refugiados

refund 1 n ['ri:fʌnd] reintegro m, reembolso m
2 vt [ri:'fʌnd] reembolsar

refundable [ri:'fʌndəbəl] adj reembolsable

refurbish [riː'fɜːbɪʃ] *vt (flat, restaurant)* remodelar

refusal [rɪ'fjuːzəl] *n* negativa *f*; **to give a flat r.** negarse rotundamente; **to meet with a r.** ser rechazado(a); **that's its third r.** *(horse)* ha rehusado por tercera vez; **to have first r. (on sth)** tener opción de compra (sobre algo)

refuse¹ ['refjuːs] *n (rubbish)* basura *f*; **r. collection** recogida *f* de basuras; **r. disposal** eliminación *f* de basuras

refuse² [rɪ'fjuːz] **1** *vt (invitation, offer, request)* rechazar; **to r. to do sth** negarse a hacer algo; **to r. sb sth** denegar algo a alguien

2 *vi (person)* negarse; *(horse)* rehusar

refutation [refjʊ'teɪʃən] *n* refutación *f*

refute [rɪ'fjuːt] *vt (argument, theory)* refutar; *(allegation)* desmentir, negar

regain [rɪ'geɪn] *vt* **(a)** *(get back)* recuperar; **to r. consciousness** recobrar *or* recuperar el conocimiento; **to r. the lead** *(in contest)* volver a ponerse en cabeza **(b)** *(reach again) (shore, seat)* volver a alcanzar

regal ['riːgəl] *adj* regio(a)

regale [rɪ'geɪl] *vt* divertir, entretener (**with** con)

regalia [rɪ'geɪlɪə] *npl* galas *fpl*; **in full r.** con toda la parafernalia

regard [rɪ'gɑːd] **1** *n* **(a)** *(admiration)* admiración *f*, estima *f*; **to hold sb in high/low r.** tener mucha/poca estima a alguien **(b)** *(consideration)* consideración *f*; **out of r. for** por consideración hacia; **without r. to** *(safety, rules)* sin (ninguna) consideración por; *(gender, race)* independientemente de; **don't pay any r. to what she says** no hagas caso de lo que diga **(c)** *(connection)* **in this r.** en este sentido; **in all regards** en todos los sentidos *or* aspectos; **with r. to** en cuanto a, con respecto a **(d) regards** *(good wishes)* saludos *mpl*, *CAm, Col, Ecuad* saludes *fpl*; **give her my regards** salúdala de mi parte

2 *vt* **(a)** *(admire, respect)* **I r. him highly** tengo un alto concepto de él **(b)** *(consider)* **to r. sth/sb as…** considerar algo/a alguien…; **to r. sth/sb with suspicion** tener recelo de algo/alguien **(c)** *(concern)* concernir; **as regards…** en lo referente *or* concerniente a…

regarding [rɪ'gɑːdɪŋ] *prep* con respecto a, en cuanto a

regardless [rɪ'gɑːdlɪs] *adv* **(a)** *(despite everything)* a pesar de todo **(b) r. of** *(without considering)* sin tener en cuenta; **r. of the expense** cueste lo que cueste

regatta [rɪ'gætə] *n* regata *f*

regency ['riːdʒənsɪ] *n* regencia *f*

regenerate [rɪ'dʒenəreɪt] **1** *vt* regenerar

2 *vi* regenerarse

regeneration [rɪdʒenə'reɪʃən] *n* regeneración *f*

regent ['riːdʒənt] *adj* regente

reggae ['regeɪ] *n Mus* reggae *m*

regime [reɪ'ʒiːm] *n (political)* régimen *m*

regiment ['redʒɪmənt] **1** *n (in army)* regimiento *m*

2 *vt* someter a severa disciplina

regimental [redʒɪ'mentəl] *adj (band, flag)* de regimiento

regimentation [redʒɪmen'teɪʃən] *n* severa disciplina *f*

region ['riːdʒən] *n* región *f*; **in the r. of** *(approximately)* alrededor de, del orden de

regional ['riːdʒənəl] *adj* regional

regionalism ['riːdʒənəlɪzəm] *n* regionalismo *m*

regionally ['riːdʒənəlɪ] *adv* regionalmente, por regiones

register ['redʒɪstə(r)] **1** *n (record) & Mus, Ling* registro *m*; **r. of births, marriages and deaths** registro *m* civil; **r. of voters** censo *m* electoral; **(cash) r.** caja *f* registradora

2 *vt* **(a)** *(record) (member)* inscribir; *(student)* matricular; *(birth, marriage, death)* registrar; *(complaint, protest)* presentar **(b)** *(show) (temperature, speed)* registrar; *(astonishment, displeasure)* denotar, mostrar **(c)** *(realize) (fact, problem)* darse cuenta de, enterarse de **(d)** *(achieve) (progress)* realizar

3 *vi* **(a)** *(for course)* matricularse; *(at hotel)* inscribirse, registrarse; *(voter)* inscribirse (en el censo) **(b)** *Fam (fact)* **it didn't r. with him** no se enteró

registered ['redʒɪstəd] *adj* **r. mail** correo *m* certificado *(con derecho a indemnización)*; **r. trademark** marca *f* registrada; *Comptr* **r. user** usuario(a) *m,f* registrado(a)

registrar ['redʒɪstrɑː(r)] *n* **(a)** *(record keeper)* registrador(ora) *m,f* **(b)** *(of college)* secretario(a) *m,f*

registration [redʒɪs'treɪʃən] *n (of student)* matriculación *f*; *(of voter)* inscripción *f* (en el censo); *(of birth, death, marriage)* registro *m*

regress [rɪ'gres] *vi* involucionar, sufrir una regresión

regression [rɪ'greʃən] *n* regresión *f*

regressive [rɪ'gresɪv] *adj* regresivo(a)

regret [rɪ'gret] **1** *n (remorse)* remordimiento *m*; *(sadness)* pesar *m*; **she sent her regrets** mandó sus disculpas *or* excusas

2 *vt (pt & pp* **regretted***)* sentir, lamentar; **to r. doing** *or* **having done sth** arrepentirse de *or* lamentar haber hecho algo; **I r. to (have to) inform you that…** siento (tener que) comunicarte que…

regretful [rɪ'gretfʊl] *adj (remorseful)* arrepentido(a); *(sad)* apesadumbrado(a), pesaroso(a)

regrettable [rɪ'gretəbəl] *adj* lamentable

regroup [riː'gruːp] **1** *vt* reagrupar

2 *vi* reagruparse

regular ['regjʊlə(r)] **1** *n* **(a)** *(in bar, restaurant)* habitual *mf*, parroquiano(a) *m,f* **(b)** *(gas)* súper *f*

2 *adj* **(a)** *(features, pulse, verb)* regular; **on a r. basis** con regularidad, regularmente; **as r. as clockwork** como un reloj, con una regularidad cronométrica **(b)** *(normal, habitual)* habitual; *(in size)* normal, mediano(a) **(c)** *(army)* regular **(d)** *Fam (for emphasis)* verdadero(a), auténtico(a); **a r. mess** un verdadero *or* auténtico desastre **(e)** *Fam (decent)* **a r. guy** *Esp* un tío legal, *Am* un tipo derecho

regularity [regjʊ'lærɪtɪ] *n* regularidad *f*

regulate ['regjʊleɪt] *vt* regular

regulation [regjʊ'leɪʃən] **1** *n* **(a)** *(action)* regulación *f* **(b)** *(rule)* regla *f*, norma *f*; **regulations** reglamento *m*, normas *fpl*

2 *adj (size, dress)* reglamentario(a)

regulator ['regjʊleɪtə(r)] *n (device)* regulador *m*; *(regulatory body)* organismo *m* regulador

regulatory [regjʊ'leɪtərɪ] *adj* regulador(ora)

regurgitate [rɪ'gɜːdʒɪteɪt] *vt* regurgitar

rehab ['riːhæb] *n Fam* rehabilitación *f*; **r. center** centro *m* de rehabilitación

rehabilitate [riːhə'bɪlɪteɪt] *vt* rehabilitar

rehabilitation [riːhəbɪlɪ'teɪʃən] *n* rehabilitación *f*

rehash 1 ['riːhæʃ] *n* refrito *m*

2 *vt* [riː'hæʃ] hacer un refrito con

rehearsal [rɪ'hɜːsəl] *n* ensayo *m*

rehearse [rɪ'hɜːs] *vt & vi* ensayar

reheat ['riː'hiːt] *vt* recalentar

rehouse [riː'haʊz] *vt* realojar

reign [reɪn] **1** *n* reinado *m*

2 *vi* reinar

reigning ['reɪnɪŋ] *adj (monarch)* reinante; *(champion)* actual

reimburse [riːɪm'bɜːs] *vt* reembolsar

rein [reɪn] *n also Fig* rienda *f*; *Fig* **to give sb free r. to do sth** dar carta blanca a alguien para hacer algo; *Fig* **to give free r. to one's imagination** dar rienda suelta a la imaginación; *Fig* **to keep a tight r. on sth** llevar algo muy controlado; **to keep a tight r. on sb** atar corto a alguien

reincarnate [riːɪn'kɑːneɪt] *vt* **to be reincarnated** reencarnarse

reincarnation [riːɪnkɑː'neɪʃən] *n* reencarnación *f*

reindeer ['reɪndɪə(r)] *n* reno *m*

reinforce [riːɪn'fɔːs] *vt* reforzar; **reinforced concrete**

hormigón *m or Am* concreto *m* armado

reinforcement [riːɪnˈfɔːsmənt] *n* refuerzo *m*; *Mil* **reinforcements** refuerzos *mpl*

reinsert [riːɪnˈsɜːt] *vt* volver a introducir

reinstate [riːɪnˈsteɪt] *vt (person in job)* restituir (en el puesto); *(clause)* reincorporar; *(law, practice)* reinstaurar

reinsurance [riːɪnˈʃʊərəns] *n* reaseguro *m*

reinsure [riːɪnˈʃʊə(r)] *vt* reasegurar

reintegrate [riːˈɪntɪgreɪt] *vt* reintegrar; *(into society)* reinsertar

reintegration [riːɪntəˈgreɪʃən] *n* reintegración *f*; *(into society)* reinserción *f* (social)

reinvent [riːɪnˈvent] *vt* **to r. the wheel** reinventar la rueda, = perder el tiempo haciendo algo que ya está hecho

reinvest [riːɪnˈvest] *vt* reinvertir

reissue [riːˈɪʃuː] **1** *n (of book, record)* reedición *f*; *(of bank note)* nueva emisión *f*
2 *vt (book, record)* reeditar; *(bank note)* emitir de nuevo

reiterate [riːˈɪtəreɪt] *vt* reiterar

reiteration [riːɪtəˈreɪʃən] *n* reiteración *f*

reject 1 *n* [ˈriːdʒekt] *(object)* artículo *m* con tara *or* defectuoso; *Fam (person)* inútil *mf*, inepto(a) *m,f*
2 *vt* [rɪˈdʒekt] rechazar; **to feel rejected** sentirse rechazado(a)

rejection [rɪˈdʒekʃən] *n* rechazo *m*; **to meet with r.** ser rechazado(a)

rejoice [rɪˈdʒɔɪs] *vi* alegrarse

rejoicing [rɪˈdʒɔɪsɪŋ] *n* regocijo *m*, alegría *f*

rejoin¹ [riːˈdʒɔɪn] *vt* **(a)** *(join again) (party, firm)* reincorporarse a **(b)** *(meet again)* reunirse con

rejoin² [rɪˈdʒɔɪn] *vt & vi (retort)* replicar

rejoinder [rɪˈdʒɔɪndə(r)] *n* réplica *f*

rejuvenate [rɪˈdʒuːvɪneɪt] *vt* rejuvenecer

rekindle [riːˈkɪndəl] *vt (fire, enthusiasm, hope)* reavivar

relapse *Med* **1** *n* [ˈriːlæps] recaída *f*
2 *vi* [rɪˈlæps] recaer, sufrir una recaída

relate [rɪˈleɪt] **1** *vt* **(a)** *(narrate)* relatar, narrar **(b)** *(connect) (two facts, ideas)* relacionar
2 *vi* **(a) to r. to** *(be relevant to)* estar relacionado(a) con **(b) to r. to** *(understand)* comprender, entender; **she doesn't r. to other children very well** no se entiende mucho con los demás niños

related [rɪˈleɪtɪd] *adj (linked)* relacionado(a); **to be r. to sb** *(of same family)* ser pariente de alguien

-related [rɪˈleɪtɪd] *suffix* **business-r. activities** actividades de carácter empresarial; **defense-r. industries** industrias relacionadas con la defensa

relation [rɪˈleɪʃən] *n* **(a)** *(relative)* pariente *mf* **(b)** *(connection)* relación *f*; **to bear no r. to** no guardar relacion con; **in r. to** en relación a

relational [rɪˈleɪʃənəl] *adj Comptr* **r. database** base *f* de datos relacional

relationship [rɪˈleɪʃənʃɪp] *n* **(a)** *(between people, countries)* relación *f*; *(kinship)* parentesco *m*; **to have a good/bad r. with sb** llevarse bien/mal con alguien **(b)** *(connection)* relación *f*

relative [ˈrelətɪv] **1** *n (person)* pariente *mf*
2 *adj (comparative)* relativo(a); **r. to** con relación a; *Gram* **r. clause** oración *f* relativa

relatively [ˈrelətɪvlɪ] *adv* relativamente

relativism [ˈrelətɪvɪzəm] *n Phil* relativismo *m*

relativist [ˈrelətɪvɪst] *n & adj* relativista *mf*

relativity [reləˈtɪvɪtɪ] *n Phys* relatividad *f*

relax [rɪˈlæks] **1** *vt (person, muscles, discipline)* relajar; **to r. one's grip** dejar de apretar
2 *vi (person, muscles, discipline)* relajarse; **r.!** *(calm down)* ¡tranquilízate!

relaxation [riːlækˈseɪʃən] *n (of person, muscles, discipline)* relajación *f*; **a form of r.** una forma de relajarse

relaxed [rɪˈlækst] *adj (atmosphere, person)* relajado(a)

relaxing [rɪˈlæksɪŋ] *adj* relajante

relay 1 *n* [ˈriːleɪ] *(of workers)* relevo *m*, turno *m*; **to work in relays** trabajar por turnos; **r. (race)** carrera *f* de relevos; *Rad & TV* **r. station** repetidor *m*
2 *vt* [rɪˈleɪ] *Rad TV* retransmitir; *(information)* pasar

release [rɪˈliːs] **1** *n* **(a)** *(of prisoner)* liberación *f*; *(of gas)* emisión *f*; *(from care, worry)* alivio *m* **(b)** *(of book, record)* publicación *f*; *(of movie)* estreno *m*; **new releases** *(records)* novedades *fpl* (discográficas); **to be on general r.** *(movie)* estar en cartel
2 *vt* **(a)** *(prisoner)* liberar, soltar; *(gas, fumes)* desprender, emitir; *(balloon, bomb, brake)* soltar; *(funds)* desbloquear; **to r. sb from an obligation** liberar a alguien de una obligación; **to r. sb's hand** soltar la mano a alguien **(b)** *(book, record)* publicar; *(movie)* estrenar; *(news, information)* hacer público(a)

relegate [ˈrelɪgeɪt] *vt* relegar

relegation [relɪˈgeɪʃən] *n (of person)* relegación *f*

relent [rɪˈlent] *vi (storm, wind)* amainar; *(person)* ceder, ablandarse

relentless [rɪˈlentlɪs] *adj* implacable

relevance [ˈreləvəns] *n* pertinencia *f*; **to have no r. to sth** no tener nada que ver con algo

relevant [ˈreləvənt] *adj* pertinente; **that's not r.** eso no viene al caso; **the r. chapters** los capítulos correspondientes; **the r. facts** los hechos que vienen al caso; **the r. authorities** la autoridad competente; **her ideas are still r. today** sus ideas siguen teniendo vigencia

reliability [rɪlaɪəˈbɪlɪtɪ] *n* fiabilidad *f*, *Am* confiabilidad

reliable [rɪˈlaɪəbəl] *adj (person, machine)* fiable, *Am* confiable; *(information)* fidedigno(a), fiable, *Am* confiable; **from a r. source** de fuentes fidedignas

reliably [rɪˈlaɪəblɪ] *adv* **to be r. informed that...** saber de buena fuente que...

reliance [rɪˈlaɪəns] *n (dependence)* dependencia *f* (**on** de); *(trust)* confianza *f* (**on** en)

reliant [rɪˈlaɪənt] *adj* **to be r. on** depender de

relic [ˈrelɪk] *n Rel & Fig* reliquia *f*

relief [rɪˈliːf] *n* **(a)** *(in general)* alivio *m*; **to bring r. to sb** aliviar a alguien; **that's a r.!** ¡qué alivio!; **much to my r.** para mi tranquilidad **(b)** *(help)* ayuda *f*, auxilio *m*; **r. fund** fondo *m* de ayuda **(c)** *(state benefit)* **to be on r.** cobrar un subsidio **(d)** *(replacement)* relevo *m*; **r. pitcher** lanzador(ora) *m,f* sustituto(a) **(e)** *(of besieged city, troops)* liberación *f* **(f)** *Art* relieve *m*; **in r.** en relieve; **to throw sth into r.** poner algo de relieve; **r. map** mapa *m* de relieve

relieve [rɪˈliːv] *vt* **(a)** *(alleviate) (pain, anxiety, problem)* aliviar; *(tension, boredom)* atenuar, mitigar; **to feel relieved** sentirse aliviado(a); *Euph* **he relieved himself** hizo sus necesidades **(b)** *(replace)* relevar **(c)** *(liberate) (city)* liberar; **to r. sb from a duty** liberar a alguien de una obligación; *Hum* **to r. sb of his wallet** birlarle a alguien la cartera

religion [rɪˈlɪdʒən] *n* religión *f*

religious [rɪˈlɪdʒəs] *adj* religioso(a)

religiously [rɪˈlɪdʒəslɪ] *adv also Fig* religiosamente

relinquish [rɪˈlɪŋkwɪʃ] *vt* renunciar a; **to r. one's hold on sth** renunciar a algo

relish [ˈrelɪʃ] **1** *n* **(a)** *(pleasure)* deleite *m*, goce *m*; **to do sth with r.** hacer algo con gran deleite **(b)** *(pickle)* salsa *f* condimentada
2 *vt* gozar con, deleitarse en; **I didn't r. the idea** no me entusiasmaba la idea

relive [riːˈlɪv] *vt* revivir

reload [riːˈləʊd] **1** *vt (gun, camera)* volver a cargar
2 *vi* volver a cargar el arma, recargar

relocate [riːləʊˈkeɪt] **1** *vt* trasladar
2 *vi* mudarse, trasladarse

relocation [riːləʊˈkeɪʃən] n traslado m

reluctance [rɪˈlʌktəns] n resistencia f, reticencia f; **to do sth with r.** hacer algo a regañadientes

reluctant [rɪˈlʌktənt] adj reacio(a), reticente; **to be r. to do sth** ser reacio(a) a hacer algo

▶**rely on, rely upon** [rɪˈlaɪ] vt insep **(a)** (count on) contar con; **I'm relying on you to do it** cuento con que vas a hacerlo **(b)** (be dependent on) depender de

REM [ɑːriːˈem] n (abbr **rapid eye movement**) (fase f) REM m, movimientos mpl oculares rápidos

remain [rɪˈmeɪn] vi **(a)** (stay behind) permanecer, quedarse **(b)** (be left) quedar; **it remains to be seen** queda or está por ver **(c)** (continue to be) seguir siendo; **to r. silent** permanecer callado(a); **to r. faithful to** permanecer fiel a

remainder [rɪˈmeɪndə(r)] n resto m

remaindered [rɪˈmeɪndɜːd] adj **r. books** libros mpl de saldo

remaining [rɪˈmeɪnɪŋ] adj restante

remains [rɪˈmeɪnz] npl (of meal) sobras fpl, restos mpl; (of civilization, fortune) restos mpl; (of old building) ruinas fpl; (of person) restos mpl (mortales); **human r.** restos mpl humanos

remake [ˈriːmeɪk] n (of movie) nueva versión f

remark [rɪˈmɑːk] **1** n (comment) comentario m; **to make** or **pass a r.** hacer un comentario
2 vt comentar, observar

remarkable [rɪˈmɑːkəbəl] adj (impressive) notable, excepcional; (surprising) insólito(a), sorprendente

remarkably [rɪˈmɑːkəblɪ] adv (impressively) excepcionalmente, extraordinariamente, (surprisingly) curiosamente, sorprendentemente

remarriage [riːˈmærɪdʒ] n segundo matrimonio m, segundas nupcias fpl

remarry [riːˈmærɪ] vi volver a casarse

remedial [rɪˈmiːdɪəl] adj correctivo(a); **r. education** educación f especial; **r. teacher** profesor(ora) m,f de educación especial

remedy [ˈremɪdɪ] **1** n remedio m; **it's past r.** ya no tiene remedio
2 vt poner remedio a, remediar

remember [rɪˈmembə(r)] **1** vt **(a)** (recall) recordar, acordarse de; **to r. doing sth** recordar haber hecho algo; **to r. to do sth** acordarse de hacer algo; **to r. that...** recordar que...; **a night to r.** una noche inolvidable; **r. me to your father!** dale recuerdos a tu padre de mi parte **(b)** (commemorate) recordar
2 vi recordar, acordarse; **as far as I r.** según recuerdo, por lo que yo recuerdo

remembrance [rɪˈmembrəns] n Formal (memory) recuerdo m; **in r. of** en recuerdo or conmemoración de

remind [rɪˈmaɪnd] vt recordar (of a); **to r. sb to do sth** recordar a alguien que haga algo; **that reminds me... did you get the cheese?** eso me recuerda or ahora que recuerdo... ¿has comprado el queso?

reminder [rɪˈmaɪndə(r)] n aviso m

reminisce [remɪˈnɪs] vi **to r. about sth** rememorar algo

reminiscence [remɪˈnɪsəns] n rememoración f, remembranza f

reminiscent [remɪˈnɪsənt] adj **to be r. of** evocar, tener reminiscencias de

remiss [rɪˈmɪs] adj negligente, descuidado(a); **it was very r. of him** fue muy descuidado por su parte

remission [rɪˈmɪʃən] n **(a)** Law reducción f de la pena **(b)** (of disease) **to be in r.** haber remitido

remit 1 n [ˈriːmɪt] cometido m; **that goes beyond/comes within our r.** eso está fuera de/dentro de nuestro ámbito de actuación
2 vt [rɪˈmɪt] (pt & pp **remitted**) (payment) remitir, girar

remittance [rɪˈmɪtəns] n Fin giro m, envío m de dinero

remnant [ˈremnənt] n (of banquet, building) resto m; (of civilization, dignity) vestigio m; (of cloth) retal m

remonstrate [ˈremənstreɪt] vi quejarse, protestar; **to r. with sb** tratar de hacer entrar en razón a alguien; **she remonstrated with him over his decision** trató de convencerle de que cambiara su decisión

remorse [rɪˈmɔːs] n remordimientos mpl; **without r.** sin remordimientos; **to feel r.** tener remordimientos

remorseful [rɪˈmɔːsfʊl] adj lleno(a) de remordimientos; **to be r.** tener remordimientos

remorsefully [rɪˈmɔːsfʊlɪ] adv con remordimiento

remorseless [rɪˈmɔːslɪs] adj (merciless) despiadado(a); (relentless) implacable

remortgage [riːˈmɔːgɪdʒ] vt (house, property) volver a hipotecar

remote [rɪˈməʊt] adj **(a)** (far-off) remoto(a), lejano(a); Rad & TV **r. broadcast** emisión f desde fuera del estudio; **r. control** telemando m, mando m a distancia **(b)** (aloof) distante **(c)** (slight) (chance, possibility) remoto(a); **I haven't the remotest idea** no tengo ni la más remota idea

remote-controlled [rɪˈməʊtkənˈtrəʊld] adj teledirigido(a)

remotely [rɪˈməʊtlɪ] adv **(a)** (distantly) remotamente, lejanamente **(b)** (slightly) remotamente; **not r.** ni remotamente, ni de lejos

removal [rɪˈmuːvəl] n (of politician, official) destitución f; (of control, doubt, threat, stain) eliminación f

remove [rɪˈmuːv] vt **(a)** (take away) (thing) quitar, retirar; (doubt) despejar; (control, threat) eliminar; (stain) quitar; (politician, official) destituir; **to r. a child from school** no llevar más a un niño al colegio **(b)** (take off) (bandage, covering, tire) quitar, Am sacar; **to r. one's coat** quitarse or Am sacarse el abrigo

remover [rɪˈmuːvə(r)] n **paint r.** decapante m; **nail polish r.** quitaesmaltes m inv

remunerate [rɪˈmjuːnəreɪt] vt Formal remunerar, retribuir

remuneration [rɪmjuːnəˈreɪʃən] n Formal remuneración f, retribución f; **r. package** paquete m de beneficios

remunerative [rɪˈmjuːnərətɪv] adj Formal remunerado(a)

renaissance [rɪˈneɪsəns] n renacimiento m; **the R.** el Renacimiento

renal [ˈriːnəl] adj Anat renal

rename [riːˈneɪm] vt cambiar el nombre a

rend [rend] (pt & pp **rent** [rent]) vt Literary (tear) desgarrar; **the country was rent by civil war** el país quedó destrozado por la guerra civil

render [ˈrendə(r)] vt **(a)** Formal (give) **to r. homage to sb** rendir homenaje a alguien; **for services rendered** por los servicios prestados **(b)** (cause to be) dejar; **the news rendered her speechless** la noticia la dejó sin habla **(c)** (translate) traducir; **to r. sth into French** traducir algo al francés

rendezvous [ˈrɒndɪvuː] **1** n (pl **rendezvous** [ˈrɒndɪvuːz]) (meeting) cita f; (meeting place) lugar m de encuentro
2 vi encontrarse, reunirse

rendition [renˈdɪʃən] n interpretación f

renegade [ˈrenɪgeɪd] n renegado(a) m,f

renege [rɪˈneɪg] vi **to r. on a promise** incumplir una promesa

renew [rɪˈnjuː] vt (passport, membership) renovar; (attempts, calls, attacks) renovar, reanudar; (relations, friendship) reanudar

renewable [rɪˈnjuːəbəl] adj renovable; **r. energy source** fuente f de energía renovable

renewal [rɪˈnjuːəl] n (of passport, membership) renovación f; (of attempts, calls, attacks) reanudación f

rennet [ˈrenɪt] n Culin cuajo m

renounce [rɪˈnaʊns] vt renunciar a

renovate [ˈrenəveɪt] vt renovar, restaurar

renovation [renəˈveɪʃən] n renovación f, restauración f

renown [rɪˈnaʊn] n fama f, renombre m

renowned [rɪˈnaʊnd] adj célebre, renombrado(a)

rent¹ [rent] **1** n (for apartment, house) alquiler m; **for r.** en alquiler; **how much r. do you pay?** ¿cuánto pagas de alquiler?
   2 vt (house, video, car) alquilar, Méx rentar

rent² pt & pp of **rend**

rental [ˈrentəl] n alquiler m

rent-free [rentˈfriː] **1** adj exento(a) del pago de alquiler
   2 adv sin pagar alquiler

reoccupy [riːˈɒkjʊpaɪ] vt ocupar de nuevo

reopen [riːˈəʊpən] **1** vt (frontier, investigation) reabrir; (talks) reanudar; Fig **to r. old wounds** abrir viejas heridas
   2 vi (store, theater) volver a abrir; **school reopens on the 21st of August** las clases se reanudan el 21 de agosto

reopening [riːˈəʊpənɪŋ] n (of store, theater, frontier, investigation) reapertura f; (of talks) reanudación f

reorder [riːˈɔːdə(r)] vt Com pedir de nuevo

reorganization [riːɔːgənaɪˈzeɪʃən] n reorganización f

reorganize [riːˈɔːgənaɪz] vt reorganizar

rep [rep] n Fam (salesperson) representante mf, comercial mf

repackage [riːˈpækɪdʒ] vt (goods) reempaquetar, reembalar; Fig (renew image of) renovar la imagen de

repaid [riːˈpeɪd] pt & pp of **repay**

repaint [riːˈpeɪnt] vt repintar

repair [rɪˈpeə(r)] **1** n (of watch, car, machine) reparación f; (of shoes, clothes) arreglo m; **to be beyond r.** no poderse arreglar; **to be in good/bad r.** estar en buen/mal estado; **to be under r.** estar en reparación; **r. shop** taller m
   2 vt (watch, car, machine) reparar; (shoes, clothes, road) arreglar

repairman [rɪˈpeəmæn] n técnico m

reparation [repəˈreɪʃən] n (a) Formal compensación f, reparación f; **to make r. for sth** compensar por algo (b) (after war) **reparations** indemnizaciones fpl (de guerra)

repartee [repɑːˈtiː] n pulso m verbal a base de agudezas

repast [rɪˈpɑːst] n Literary colación f, comida f

repatriate [riːˈpætrieɪt] vt repatriar

repatriation [riːpætrɪˈeɪʃən] n repatriación f

repay [riːˈpeɪ] (pt & pp **repaid** [riːˈpeɪd]) vt (a) (money) devolver; (person) pagar; (debt) saldar (b) (person for kindness, help) recompensar; (kindness, loyalty) pagar

repayable [riːˈpeɪəbəl] adj (loan) pagadero(a), a devolver (**over** en)

repayment [riːˈpeɪmənt] n pago m, devolución f; **r. plan** plan m de amortización

repeal [rɪˈpiːl] vt (law, regulation) derogar, abrogar

repeat [rɪˈpiːt] **1** n (of event, TV program) repetición f; Com **the success of a business depends on r. orders** el éxito de un negocio depende de la renovación de pedidos
   2 vt repetir; **to r. oneself** repetirse; **don't r. this, but...** no se lo cuentes a nadie, pero...

repeated [rɪˈpiːtɪd] adj repetido(a)

repeatedly [rɪˈpiːtɪdlɪ] adv repetidas veces, repetidamente

repel [rɪˈpel] (pt & pp **repelled**) vt (throw back) repeler, rechazar; (disgust) repeler, repugnar

repellent [rɪˈpelənt] **1** n (for insects) repelente m (antiinsectos)
   2 adj repelente

repent [rɪˈpent] **1** vt arrepentirse de
   2 vi arrepentirse (**of** de)

repentance [rɪˈpentəns] n arrepentimiento m

repentant [rɪˈpentənt] adj arrepentido(a); **to be r.** estar arrepentido(a)

repercussion [riːpəˈkʌʃən] n repercusión f

repertoire [ˈrepətwɑː(r)] n repertorio m

repertory [ˈrepətərɪ] n Theat **r. company** compañía f de repertorio

repetition [repɪˈtɪʃən] n repetición f

repetitious [repɪˈtɪʃəs] adj repetitivo(a)

repetitive [rɪˈpetɪtɪv] adj (style, job) repetitivo(a); **r. strain** or **stress injury** lesión f por esfuerzo or movimiento repetitivo

rephrase [riːˈfreɪz] vt reformular, expresar de forma diferente

replace [rɪˈpleɪs] vt (a) (put back) volver a poner, devolver; **to r. the receiver** colgar (el teléfono) (b) (substitute for) sustituir, reemplazar (**with/by** por); (tire, broken part) (re)cambiar

replacement [rɪˈpleɪsmənt] n (a) (act of putting back) devolución f; (act of substituting) sustitución f; (of tire, broken part) (re)cambio m; Fin **r. cost** costo m or Esp coste m de sustitución; **r. parts** piezas fpl de recambio; **r. value** valor m de reposición (b) (for person) sustituto(a) m,f

replay 1 n [ˈriːpleɪ] (of soccer match) repetición f (del partido); **(instant) r.** (on TV) repetición f (de la jugada)
   2 vt [riːˈpleɪ] (match) jugar de nuevo

replenish [rɪˈplenɪʃ] vt (cup, tank) rellenar; **to r. one's supplies** surtirse de provisiones

replete [rɪˈpliːt] adj Formal repleto(a) (**with** de)

replica [ˈreplɪkə] n réplica f

replicate [ˈreplɪkeɪt] vt reproducir

reply [rɪˈplaɪ] **1** n respuesta f, contestación f; **in r.** en or como respuesta; **there was no r.** (to telephone) no contestaban, no había nadie
   2 vi responder, contestar; **to r. to a letter** contestar a una carta

report [rɪˈpɔːt] **1** n (a) (account) informe m, Am reporte m; (in newspaper, on radio, television) reportaje m; **there are reports that...** circula el rumor or corre la voz de que...; Sch **r. (card)** boletín m de evaluación, RP carné m de notas or calificaciones (b) (sound) estallido m, explosión f
   2 vt (information) informar de; (accident, theft) dar parte de; **the incident was reported in the local press** la prensa local informó del incidente; **it is reported that the Secretary of State is about to resign** se ha informado or CAm, Méx reportado de la inminente dimisión del secretario de Estado; **to r. sb missing** denunciar la desaparición de alguien; **to r. sb to the police** denunciar a alguien a la policía; **she reported her findings to him** le informó de or le dio a conocer sus hallazgos
   3 vi (a) (present oneself) presentarse; **to r. for duty** presentarse para el servicio (b) (give account) informar; (journalist) informar (**on** sobre); **she reported to her boss** informó a su jefe (c) (be accountable) **to r. to sb** ser responsable ante alguien

reported [rɪˈpɔːtɪd] adj **there have been several r. sightings** se tienen noticias de varios avistamientos; Gram **r. speech** el estilo indirecto

reportedly [rɪˈpɔːtɪdlɪ] adv según se dice; **he is r. resident in Paris** según se dice, reside en París

reporter [rɪˈpɔːtə(r)] n reportero(a) m,f

repose [rɪˈpəʊz] Formal **1** n reposo m
   2 vi reposar

repository [rɪˈpɒzɪtərɪ] n (for books, furniture) depósito m; (of knowledge) arsenal m, depositario(a) m,f

repossess [riːpəˈzes] vt Fin embargar (definitivamente)

reprehensible [reprɪˈhensəbəl] adj censurable, recriminable

reprehensibly [reprɪˈhensɪblɪ] adv de un modo censurable or recriminable

represent [reprɪˈzent] vt (depict, symbolize) representar; (describe) presentar, describir; **to r. a company** representar a una empresa; **this represents a great improvement** esto representa una gran mejora

representation [reprɪzenˈteɪʃən] n (of facts, in Congress) representación f; Formal **to make representations (to sb)** presentar una protesta (ante alguien)

representational [reprɪzenˈteɪʃənəl] adj Art figurativo(a)

representative [reprɪˈzentətɪv] **1** *n* (**a**) *(of company, on committee)* representante *mf* (**b**) *Pol* representante *mf*, diputado(a) *m,f*
 2 *adj* representativo(a)

repress [rɪˈpres] *vt* reprimir

repressed [rɪˈprest] *adj* **to be r.** estar reprimido(a)

repression [rɪˈpreʃən] *n* represión *f*

repressive [rɪˈpresɪv] *adj* represivo(a)

reprieve [rɪˈpriːv] **1** *n Law* indulto *m*; *Fig* **to win a r.** *(project, company)* salvarse de momento
 2 *vt Law* indultar; *Fig (project, company)* salvar de momento

reprimand [ˈreprɪmɑːnd] **1** *n* reprimenda *f*
 2 *vt* reprender

reprint 1 *n* [ˈriːprɪnt] reimpresión *f*
 2 *vt* [riːˈprɪnt] reimprimir

reprisal [rɪˈpraɪzəl] *n* represalia *f*; **to take reprisals** tomar represalias; **in r. for** en represalia por

reproach [rɪˈprəʊtʃ] **1** *n* reproche *m*; **beyond** or **above r.** irreprochable, intachable
 2 *vt* hacer reproches a; **to r. sb for (doing) sth** reprochar (el haber hecho) algo a alguien; **to r. oneself for sth** reprocharse algo

reproachful [rɪˈprəʊtʃfʊl] *adj (tone, look)* de reproche

reproachfully [rɪˈprəʊtʃfʊlɪ] *adv* de manera reprobatoria

reprobate [ˈreprəbeɪt] *n* granujilla *mf*, tunante *mf*

reprocess [riːˈprəʊses] *vt* reprocesar, volver a tratar

reprocessing [riːˈprəʊsesɪŋ] *n* reprocesado *m*; **r. plant** planta *f* de reprocesado

reproduce [riːprəˈdjuːs] **1** *vt* reproducir
 2 *vi* reproducirse

reproduction [riːprəˈdʌkʃən] *n* reproducción *f*; **r. furniture** reproducciones *fpl* de muebles antiguos

reproductive [riːprəˈdʌktɪv] *adj Biol* reproductor(ora); **r. organs** órganos *mpl* reproductores

reproof [rɪˈpruːf] *n Formal* reprobación *f*, desaprobación *f*

reprove [rɪˈpruːv] *vt Formal* recriminar, reprobar

reproving [rɪˈpruːvɪŋ] *adj Formal* de reprobación, reprobatorio(a)

reprovingly [rɪˈpruːvɪŋlɪ] *adv* de manera reprobatoria

reptile [ˈreptaɪl] *n* reptil *m*

reptilian [ˈreptɪlɪən] *adj also Fig* de reptil

republic [rɪˈpʌblɪk] *n* república *f*

Republican [rɪˈpʌblɪkən] **1** *n* republicano(a) *m,f*; **the Republicans** *(party)* los republicanos, el partido republicano
 2 *adj (politician, voter)* republicano(a)

republican [rɪˈpʌblɪkən] *n & adj* republicano(a) *m,f*

republicanism [rɪˈpʌblɪkənɪzəm] *n* republicanismo *m*

repudiate [rɪˈpjuːdɪeɪt] *vt Formal (offer)* rechazar; *(rumor, remark)* desmentir

repudiation [rɪpjuːdɪˈeɪʃən] *n (of offer)* rechazo *m*; *(of rumor, remark)* desmentido *m*

repugnance [rɪˈpʌgnəns] *n* repugnancia *f*

repugnant [rɪˈpʌgnənt] *adj* repugnante

repulse [rɪˈpʌls] *vt (army, attack)* rechazar; **I am repulsed by your heartlessness** me repulsa tu crueldad

repulsive [rɪˈpʌlsɪv] *adj* repulsivo(a)

repulsively [rɪˈpʌlsɪvlɪ] *adv* de manera repulsiva

reputable [ˈrepjʊtəbəl] *adj* reputado(a), acreditado(a)

reputation [repjuːˈteɪʃən] *n (of person, store)* reputación *f*; **to have a good/bad r.** tener buena/mala reputación *or* fama; **to have a r. for frankness** tener fama de franco(a); **they lived up to their r.** hicieron honor a su reputación

repute [rɪˈpjuːt] **1** *n Formal* reputación *f*, fama *f*; **of r.** de prestigio; **to be held in high r.** estar muy bien considerado(a)
 2 *vt* **to be reputed to be wealthy/a genius** tener fama de rico/de ser un genio; **the reputed author of the work** el supuesto autor de la obra

reputedly [rɪˈpjuːtɪdlɪ] *adv* según parece, según se dice

request [rɪˈkwest] **1** *n* petición *f*, solicitud *f*, *Am* pedido *m*; **to make a r. (for sth)** hacer una petición *or Am* un pedido (de algo); **available on r.** disponible mediante solicitud; **by popular r.** a petición *or Am* pedido del público
 2 *vt* pedir, solicitar; **to r. sb to do sth** pedir *or* solicitar a alguien que haga algo; **passengers are requested not to smoke** se ruega a los señores pasajeros se abstengan de fumar; **as requested** como se solicitaba

requiem [ˈrekwɪəm] *n Mus* réquiem *m*; *Rel* **r. (mass)** misa *f* de difuntos

require [rɪˈkwaɪə(r)] *vt* requerir, necesitar; **you are required to…** se le pide que…; **if required** si es necesario; **when required** cuando sea necesario

requirement [rɪˈkwaɪəmənt] *n* requisito *m*

requisite [ˈrekwɪzɪt] **1** *adj* necesario(a), requerido(a); **without the r. care** sin el debido cuidado
 2 requisites *npl (necessary conditions)* requisitos *mpl*; *(objects)* accesorios *mpl*, artículos *mpl*

requisition [rekwɪˈzɪʃən] *vt (supplies)* requisar

rerelease [ˈriːrɪˈliːs] **1** *n (movie)* reestreno *m*; *(record)* relanzamiento *m*
 2 *vt (movie)* reestrenar; *(record)* relanzar

rerun [ˈriːrʌn] *n (on TV)* reposición *f*; *(of situation, conflict)* repetición *f*

resale [riːˈseɪl] *n* reventa *f*

reschedule [riːˈskedʒuːl] *vt (meeting, flight)* volver a programar; *(debt)* renegociar

rescind [rɪˈsɪnd] *vt Law (law)* derogar; *(contract)* rescindir

rescue [ˈreskjuː] **1** *n* rescate *m*; **to come to sb's r.** acudir al rescate de alguien; **r. services** servicios *mpl* de salvamento
 2 *vt* rescatar

rescuer [ˈreskjuːə(r)] *n* salvador(ora) *m,f*

research [rɪˈsɜːtʃ] **1** *n* investigación *f*; **to do r. into sth** investigar algo; **r. and development** investigación y desarrollo; **r. assistant** ayudante *mf* de investigación; **r. laboratory** laboratorio *m* de investigación
 2 *vt* investigar; **a well-researched book** un libro muy bien documentado
 3 *vi* investigar; **to r. into sth** investigar algo

researcher [rɪˈsɜːtʃə(r)] *n* investigador(ora) *m,f*

resemblance [rɪˈzembləns] *n* parecido *m*, similitud *f*; **to bear a r. to sb/sth** guardar parecido con alguien/algo

resemble [rɪˈzembəl] *vt* parecerse a

resent [rɪˈzent] *vt* sentirse molesto(a) por; **I r. his interference** me parece mal que se entrometa; **I r. being treated like an idiot** me molesta que me traten como a un imbécil; **I r. that!** ¡eso no me parece nada bien!; **they obviously resented my presence** evidentemente, les molestaba mi presencia

resentful [rɪˈzentfʊl] *adj* resentido(a); **to be** or **feel r.** estar resentido(a)

resentment [rɪˈzentmənt] *n* resentimiento *m*; **to feel r. toward sb** tener resentimiento hacia alguien

reservation [rezəˈveɪʃən] *n* (**a**) *(booking)* reserva, *Am* reservación *f*; **to make a r.** hacer una reserva; **r. desk** mostrador *m* de reservas (**b**) *(doubt)* reserva *f*; **without r.** sin reservas (**c**) **(Indian) r.** reserva *f* india

reserve [rɪˈzɜːv] **1** *n* (**a**) *(supply)* reserva *f*; **to keep sth in r.** reservar algo, tener algo en reserva; **he drew on his reserves** echó mano de sus reservas (**b**) *Sport* reserva *mf*; *Mil* **the reserves** la reserva (**c**) *(for birds, game)* reserva *f*; **game r.** coto *m* de caza; **nature r.** reserva natural (**d**) *(reticence)* reserva *f*; **without r.** sin reservas (**e**) *Fin* **r. bank** = uno de los doce bancos que forman la Reserva Federal estadounidense

2 *vt* *(book, keep)* reservar; **to r. the right to do sth** reservarse el derecho a hacer algo; **to r. one's strength** ahorrar *or* reservar fuerzas; **to r. judgment (on sth)** reservarse la opinión (sobre algo)

reserved [rɪˈzɜːvd] *adj* reservado(a)

reservist [rɪˈzɜːvɪst] *n Mil* reservista *mf*

reservoir [ˈrezəvwɑː(r)] *n (lake)* embalse *m*, pantano *m*; *Fig (of strength, courage)* reserva *f*, cúmulo *m*

reset [riːˈset] *(pt & pp* **reset**) *vt (watch)* ajustar; *(counter)* poner a cero; *Med (bone)* colocar en su sitio; *Comptr* **r. button** *or* **switch** botón *m* para reinicializar

reshape [riːˈʃeɪp] *vt (plans, future)* rehacer, reorganizar; *(party, industry)* reestructurar, remodelar

reshuffle [ˈriːʃʌfəl] *n Pol* **(Cabinet) r.** reajuste *m or* remodelación *f* del Gabinete (ministerial)

reside [rɪˈzaɪd] *vi (a) (person)* residir **(b)** *(power, quality)* **to r. in** residir en, radicar en

residence [ˈrezɪdəns] *n* **(a)** *(stay)* estancia *f*; **she took up r. in El Paso** fijó su residencia en El Paso; **place of r.** lugar *m* de residencia; **r. permit** permiso *m* de residencia **(b)** *Formal (home)* residencia *f*

resident [ˈrezɪdənt] **1** *n (of country, street)* residente *mf*; *(of hotel)* residente *mf*, huésped *mf*; **residents' association** asociación *f* de vecinos

2 *adj* residente; **to be r. in Wichita** residir en Wichita

residential [rezɪˈdenʃəl] *adj* residencial

residual [rɪˈzɪdjʊəl] *adj* residual

residue [ˈrezɪdjuː] *n (remainder)* resto *m*, residuo *m*; *Chem* residuo *m*

resign [rɪˈzaɪn] **1** *vt (job, position)* dimitir de, renunciar a; **to r. oneself to (doing) sth** resignarse a (hacer) algo

2 *vi* dimitir

resignation [rezɪgˈneɪʃən] *n* **(a)** *(from job)* dimisión *f*; **to hand in one's r.** presentar la dimisión **(b)** *(attitude)* resignación *f*

resilience [rɪˈzɪliəns] *n (of material, metal)* elasticidad *f*; *(of person)* capacidad *f* de recuperación

resilient [rɪˈzɪliənt] *adj (material, metal)* elástico(a); **to be r.** *(person, economy)* tener capacidad de recuperación

resin [ˈrezɪn] *n* resina *f*

resist [rɪˈzɪst] **1** *vt* resistir; *Law* **to r. arrest** resistirse a la autoridad; **I couldn't r. telling him** no pude resistir la tentación de decírselo; **I can't r. chocolates** los bombones me resultan irresistibles

2 *vi* resistir

resistance [rɪˈzɪstəns] *n* resistencia *f*; **to put up** *or* **offer r.** oponer *or* ofrecer resistencia; **to meet with no r.** no encontrar resistencia; **to take the line of least r.** tomar el camino más fácil; **r. fighter** miembro *m* de la resistencia

resistant [rɪˈzɪstənt] *adj* **to be r. to sth** *(change, suggestion)* mostrarse remiso(a) a aceptar algo, mostrar resistencia a algo; *(disease)* ser resistente a algo

-resistant [rɪˈzɪstənt] *suffix* anti; **rust-r.** antioxidante; **stain-r.** antimanchas

resistor [rɪˈzɪstə(r)] *n Elec* resistencia *f (componente)*

resolute [ˈrezəluːt] *adj* resuelto(a), decidido(a)

resolution [rezəˈluːʃən] *n* **(a)** *(decision) (of individual)* determinación *f*; *(of committee)* resolución *f* **(b)** *(firmness)* resolución *f*, decisión *f* **(c)** *(solution)* resolución *f*, solución *f*

resolve [rɪˈzɒlv] **1** *n* determinación *f*; **to make a firm r. to do sth** resolver firmemente hacer algo

2 *vt* **(a)** *(decide)* **to r. to do sth** resolver hacer algo **(b)** *(solve)* resolver, solucionar

3 *vi* **to r. on/against doing sth** tomar la resolución de hacer/no hacer algo

resonance [ˈrezənəns] *n (of voice)* resonancia *f*

resonant [ˈrezənənt] *adj* resonante

resonate [ˈrezəneɪt] *vi* resonar

resort [rɪˈzɔːt] **1** *n* **(a)** *(recourse)* recurso *m*; **to have r. to sth** recurrir a algo; **as a last r.** como último recurso **(b)** *(vacation place)* centro *m* turístico, lugar *m* de veraneo

2 *vi* **to r. to** recurrir a

resound [rɪˈzaʊnd] *vi (voice)* resonar, retumbar; **the stadium resounded with applause** el estadio resonaba con los aplausos

resounding [rɪˈzaʊndɪŋ] *adj (crash)* estruendoso(a); *(applause)* sonoro(a), clamoroso(a); *(success, failure)* rotundo(a), clamoroso(a)

resoundingly [rɪˈzaʊndɪŋlɪ] *adv (to defeat)* rotundamente; **to be r. successful** tener un éxito rotundo

resource [rɪˈzɔːs] **1** *n* recurso *m*; **to be left to one's own resources** tener que arreglárselas solo(a); **r. management** gestión *f* de recursos

2 *vt (project)* financiar

resourceful [rɪˈzɔːsfʊl] *adj* ingenioso(a), lleno(a) de recursos

respect [rɪˈspekt] **1** *n* **(a)** *(admiration, consideration)* respeto *m*; **to have r. for sth/sb** respetar algo/a alguien; **out of r. for…** por respeto hacia…; **to treat mountains with r.** respetar la montaña; **with all due r.…** con el debido respeto…; **to pay one's last respects** decir el último adiós **(b)** *(aspect)* sentido *m*, aspecto *m*; **in some/certain respects** en algunos/ciertos aspectos; **in all respects, in every r.** en todos los sentidos; **with r. to, in r. of** con respecto a

2 *vt* respetar

respectability [rɪspektəˈbɪlɪtɪ] *n* respetabilidad *f*

respectable [rɪˈspektəbəl] *adj* **(a)** *(honorable, decent)* respetable **(b)** *(fairly large)* considerable, respetable; *(fairly good)* decente

respectably [rɪˈspektəblɪ] *adv* **(a)** *(in a respectable manner)* respetablemente **(b)** *(fairly well)* decentemente, pasablemente

respected [rɪˈspektɪd] *adj* respetado(a)

respecter [rɪˈspektə(r)] *n* **death is no r. of persons** la muerte no hace distinciones

respectful [rɪˈspektfʊl] *adj* respetuoso(a)

respective [rɪˈspektɪv] *adj* respectivo(a)

respectively [rɪˈspektɪvlɪ] *adv* respectivamente

respiration [respɪˈreɪʃən] *n* respiración *f*

respiratory [rɪˈspɪrɪtərɪ] *adj Anat* respiratorio(a)

respite [ˈrespaɪt] *n* respiro *m*, tregua *f*; **to work without r.** trabajar sin tregua; **they gave her no r.** no le concedieron un momento de respiro, no le dieron cuartel

resplendent [rɪˈsplendənt] *adj* resplandeciente; **to be r.** estar resplandeciente

respond [rɪˈspɒnd] *vi* responder; *Med* **to r. to treatment** responder al tratamiento

respondent [rɪˈspɒndənt] *n* **(a)** *Law* demandado(a) *m,f* **(b)** *(to questionnaire)* encuestado(a) *m,f*

response [rɪˈspɒns] *n* respuesta *f*; **in r. to** en respuesta a; **r. time** tiempo *m* de respuesta

responsibility [rɪspɒnsɪˈbɪlɪtɪ] *n* responsabilidad *f* **(for** de); **to take** *or* **accept full r. for sth** asumir toda la responsabilidad de algo; **answering the phone is his r., not mine** contestar el teléfono le corresponde a él, no a mí

responsible [rɪˈspɒnsɪbəl] *adj (trustworthy, accountable)* responsable; **to be r. for** ser responsable de; **to hold sb r.** considerar a alguien responsable; **a r. job** un puesto de responsabilidad

responsive [rɪˈspɒnsɪv] *adj* **to be r.** *(to criticism, praise, idea, suggestion)* ser receptivo(a), responder bien; *(willing to participate)* demostrar interés; **to be r. to treatment** responder (bien) al tratamiento

rest[1] [rest] **1** *n* **(a)** *(repose)* descanso *m*; **to have** *or* **take a r.** descansar, tomarse un descanso; *Euph* **to be at r.** *(be dead)* descansar en paz; **to put** *or* **set sb's mind at r.** tranquilizar a alguien; *Fam* **give it a r., will you!** ¿quieres parar de una vez?, *RP* ¡parala de una buena vez!; **to come to r.** detenerse; **r. area** *(on highway)* área *f* de descanso; **r. room** baño *m*, *Esp* servicios *mpl*, *CSur* toilette *m* **(b)** *(support)* soporte *m*, apoyo *m* **(c)** *Mus (pause)* silencio *m*

2 *vt* **(a)** *(cause to repose)* **to r. one's eyes/legs** descansar los ojos/las piernas; **God r. his soul!** ¡Dios lo tenga en su gloria! **(b)** *(lean)* apoyar **(on** en) **(c)** *(base) (argument, theory)* apoyar **(on** en), basar **(on** en); *(one's hopes, confidence)* depositar **(on** en); *Fig* **I r. my case!** ¡he dicho!

3 *vi* **(a)** *(relax)* descansar; **I won't r. until...** no descansaré hasta...; **to r. on** *(of structure, argument)* descansar en *or* sobre, apoyarse en *or* sobre; **r. in peace** *(on gravestone)* descanse en paz **(b)** *(remain)* **there the matter rests** así ha quedado la cosa; **I won't let it r. at that** esto no va a quedar así; **r. assured (that)** puedes estar seguro(a) (de que); **to r. with sb** *(decision, responsibility)* corresponderle a alguien

rest² *n* **the r.** *(remainder)* el resto; *(others)* el resto, los demás; **the r. of us** los demás

restaurant ['restrɒnt] *n* restaurante *m*

restful ['restfʊl] *adj* tranquilo(a), reposado(a)

restive ['restɪv] *adj* inquieto(a), nervioso(a)

restless ['restlɪs] *adj (fidgety)* inquieto(a), agitado(a); *(dissatisfied)* descontento(a); **I've had a r. night** he pasado una noche agitada

restlessness ['restlɪsnɪs] *n (fidgeting, nervousness)* inquietud *f*, agitación *f*; **the audience was showing signs of r.** el público comenzaba a dar muestras de impaciencia

restoration [restə'reɪʃən] *n (of building, furniture, monarchy)* restauración *f*; *(of communications, law and order)* restablecimiento *m*; *(of lost property, fortune)* restitución *f*

restore [rɪ'stɔː(r)] *vt (building, furniture, monarchy)* restaurar; *(communications, law and order)* restablecer; *(confidence)* devolver; *(property, fortune)* restituir; **to r. sb to health/ strength** devolver la salud/la fuerza a alguien

restrain [rɪ'streɪn] *vt (person, crowd, dog, one's curiosity)* contener; *(passions, anger)* reprimir, dominar; **to r. sb from doing sth** impedir a alguien que haga algo; **to r. oneself** contenerse, controlarse

restrained [rɪ'streɪnd] *adj (person)* comedido(a); *(response, emotion)* contenido(a)

restraint [rɪ'streɪnt] *n* **(a)** *(moderation)* dominio *m* de sí mismo(a), comedimiento *m*; **to urge r.** pedir moderación **(b)** *(restriction)* restricción *f*, limitación *f*; **without r.** sin restricciones

restrict [rɪ'strɪkt] *vt (person, freedom)* restringir, limitar; **to r. oneself to...** limitarse a...

restricted [rɪ'strɪktɪd] *adj* restringido(a), limitado(a); **r. area** zona *f* de acceso restringido; **r. document** documento *m* confidencial

restriction [rɪ'strɪkʃən] *n* restricción *f*, limitación *f*; **to place restrictions on sth** poner trabas a algo

restrictive [rɪ'strɪktɪv] *adj* restrictivo(a); *Ind* **r. practices** prácticas *fpl* restrictivas

restructure [riː'strʌktʃə(r)] *vt* reestructurar

restructuring [riː'strʌktʃərɪŋ] *n Ind* reestructuración *f*, reconversión *f*

restyle ['riː'staɪl] *vt (car)* rediseñar, cambiar el diseño de; *(hair, clothes)* cambiar el estilo de

result [rɪ'zʌlt] **1** *n* resultado *m*; **as a r.** como consecuencia *or* resultado; **as a r. of...** como consecuencia *or* resultado de...; **the r. is that...** el caso es que...; **to yield** *or* **show results** dar resultado

2 *vi* **to r. from** resultar de; **to r. in sth** tener algo como resultado

resultant [rɪ'zʌltənt] *adj* resultante

resume¹ [rɪzjuːm] **1** *vt (relations, work)* reanudar

2 *vi* continuar

résumé, resume² ['rezjumeɪ] *n (summary)* resumen *m*; *(curriculum vitae)* currículum (vitae) *m*

resumption [rɪ'zʌmpʃən] *n* reanudación *f*

resurface [riː'sɜːfɪs] **1** *vt (road)* rehacer el firme de

2 *vi (submarine)* volver a la superficie; *Fig (person)* reaparecer

resurgence [rɪ'sɜːdʒəns] *n* resurgimiento *m*

resurgent [rɪ'sɜːdʒənt] *adj* renaciente, resurgente

resurrect [rezə'rekt] *vt (the dead, fashion, argument)* resucitar

resurrection [rezə'rekʃən] *n (of conflict, accusation)* reavivamiento *m*; *Rel* **the R.** la Resurrección

resuscitate [rɪ'sʌsɪteɪt] *vt (person)* reanimar, hacer revivir; *(scheme, career)* resucitar

retail ['riːteɪl] **1** *n Com (selling, trade)* venta *f* al por menor, *Am* menoreo *m*; **r. outlet** punto *m* de venta; **r. price** precio *m* de venta (al público)

2 *vt (goods)* vender al por menor; *(gossip)* contar

3 *vi* **it retails at $9,995** su precio de venta al público es 9.995 dólares

retailer ['riːteɪlə(r)] *n Com* minorista *mf*

retain [rɪ'teɪn] *vt* **(a)** *(keep)* conservar; *(heat)* retener **(b)** *(hold in place)* sujetar; **retaining wall** muro *m* de contención **(c)** *(remember)* retener

retainer [rɪ'teɪnə(r)] *n* **(a)** *(fee)* anticipo *m* **(b)** *(servant)* criado(a) *m,f* (de toda la vida)

retake 1 *n* ['riːteɪk] **(a)** *(of exam)* repesca *f* **(b)** *Cin (of scene)* nueva toma *f*; **to do a r.** repetir una toma

2 *vt* [riː'teɪk] **(a)** *(exam)* volver a presentarse a **(b)** *Cin (scene)* volver a rodar

retaliate [rɪ'tælieɪt] *vi* desquitarse, tomarse la revancha

retaliation [rɪtæli'eɪʃən] *n* represalias *fpl*; **in r. (for sth)** como represalia (por algo)

retaliatory [rɪ'tæliətəri] *adj* como *or* en represalia

retard [rɪ'tɑːd] *vt (delay)* retrasar

retardant [rɪ'tɑːdənt] **1** *n* retardador *m*

2 *adj* retardador(ora), retardante

retarded [rɪ'tɑːdɪd] *adj* **to be (mentally) r.** ser retrasado(a) mental

retch [retʃ] *vi* tener arcadas

retention [rɪ'tenʃən] *n (of custom, practice)* conservación *f*, preservación *f*; *(of fact, impression)* retención *f*

retentive [rɪ'tentɪv] *adj (memory, person)* retentivo(a)

rethink 1 *n* ['riːθɪŋk] **to have a r. (about sth)** hacerse un replanteamiento (de algo)

2 *vt* [riː'θɪŋk] *(pt & pp* **rethought** [riː'θɔːt]*)* replantear(se)

reticent ['retɪsənt] *adj* reservado(a)

retina ['retɪnə] *n Anat* retina *f*

retinue ['retɪnjuː] *n* comitiva *f*, séquito *m*

retire [rɪ'taɪə(r)] **1** *vt* jubilar

2 *vi* **(a)** *(employee)* jubilarse **(b)** *(withdraw)* retirarse **(c)** *Formal (to bed)* retirarse (a descansar)

retired [rɪ'taɪəd] *adj (from job)* jubilado(a); *(from military)* retirado(a); **to be r.** *(from job)* estar jubilado(a)

retiree [rɪtaɪə'riː] *n* jubilado(a) *m,f*

retirement [rɪ'taɪəmənt] *n (act)* jubilación *f*; *(period)* retiro *m*; **to take early r.** tomar la jubilación anticipada; **he came out of r.** salió de su retiro; **(of) r. age** (en) edad *f* de jubilación; **r. pension** pensión *f* de jubilación; **r. plan** plan *m* de jubilación

retiring [rɪ'taɪərɪŋ] *adj* **(a)** *(reserved)* retraído(a), reservado(a) **(b)** *(official)* saliente *(por jubilación)*

retort [rɪ'tɔːt] **1** *n (answer)* réplica *f*

2 *vt & vi* replicar

retrace [rɪ'treɪs] *vt* **they retraced their steps** volvieron sobre sus pasos

retract [rɪ'trækt] **1** *vt* **(a)** *(statement, offer)* retractarse de **(b)** *(claws)* retraer; *(undercarriage)* replegar

2 *vi* **(a)** *(person)* retractarse **(b)** *(claws)* retraerse; *(undercarriage)* replegarse

retractable [rɪ'træktəbəl] *adj (antenna, tip of instrument)* retráctil; *(undercarriage)* replegable

retrain [riː'treɪn] **1** *vt (employee)* reciclar
2 *vi (employee)* reciclarse

retraining [riː'treɪnɪŋ] *n* reciclaje *m* profesional

retread ['riːtred] *n Aut* neumático *m* recauchutado, *Col, Méx* llanta *f* or *Arg* goma *f* recauchutada

retreat [rɪ'triːt] **1** *n* (**a**) *(withdrawal)* retirada *f*; **to beat a r.** batirse en retirada (**b**) *(place)* retiro *m*, refugio *m*
2 *vi* retirarse

retrial [riː'traɪəl] *n Law* nuevo juicio *m*

retribution [retrɪ'bjuːʃən] *n* represalias *fpl*

retrieve [rɪ'triːv] *vt (gen) & Comptr* recuperar

retriever [rɪ'triːvə(r)] *n (dog)* perro *m* cobrador

retro ['retrəʊ] *adj* retro

retroactive [retrəʊ'æktɪv] *adj Formal* retroactivo(a)

retrograde ['retrəgreɪd] *adj (movement, step)* retrógrado(a)

retrospect ['retrəspekt] *n* **in r.** retrospectivamente

retrospective [retrə'spektɪv] **1** *n (exhibition)* retrospectiva *f*
2 *adj* retrospectivo(a)

retry [riː'traɪ] **1** *vt Law* volver a procesar a
2 *vi Comptr* reintentar

return [rɪ'tɜːn] **1** *n* (**a**) *(of person, peace, season)* vuelta *f*, regreso *m*; *Com (of goods)* devolución *f*; *(of tennis service)* resto *m*; **on my r.** a mi vuelta *or* regreso; **by r. mail** a vuelta de correo; **in r.** a cambio; **to do sth in r.** corresponder con algo; **many happy returns of the day!** ¡felicidades!, ¡feliz cumpleaños!; **r. journey** viaje *m* de vuelta; **r. game** *(soccer)* partido *m* de vuelta (**b**) *Fin (profit)* rendimiento *m*; **to bring a good r.** proporcionar buenos dividendos; **r. on investment** rendimiento de las inversiones
2 *vt* (**a**) *(give or send back)* devolver; **to r. a compliment/favor** devolver *or RP* retribuir un cumplido/favor; **to r. sb's love** corresponder al amor de alguien; **r. to sender** *(on letter)* devolver al remitente; **to r. the serve** *(in tennis)* restar, devolver el servicio; **to r. sb's call** devolver una llamada a alguien, *Am* llamar a alguien en respuesta a su llamado; *Law* **to r. a verdict of guilty/not guilty** pronunciar un veredicto de culpable/inocente (**b**) *Com & Fin (profit)* rendir, proporcionar
3 *vi (come or go back)* volver, regresar; **to r. to work** volver al trabajo

returnable [rɪ'tɜːnəbəl] *adj (bottle)* retornable; **sale items are not r.** no se admite la devolución de artículos rebajados

reunification [riːjuːnɪfɪ'keɪʃən] *n* reunificación *f*

reunify [riː'juːnɪfaɪ] *vt* reunificar

reunion [riː'juːnɪən] *n* reunión *f*

reunite [riːjʊ'naɪt] **1** *vt* reunir; **to be reunited (with sb)** reencontrarse *or* volver a reunirse (con alguien)
2 *vi* reunirse

reusable [riː'juːzəbəl] *adj* reutilizable

reuse [riː'juːz] *vt* volver a utilizar, reutilizar

Rev *n Rel (abbr* **Reverend)** **R. Gray** el reverendo Gray

rev [rev] *Aut vt (pt & pp* **revved)** **to r. the engine** revolucionar *or* acelerar el motor

revalue [riː'væljuː] *vt Fin* revalorizar

revamp [riː'væmp] *vt Fam* renovar

reveal [rɪ'viːl] *vt* revelar; **it has been revealed that...** se ha dado a conocer que...

revealing [rɪ'viːlɪŋ] *adj (sign, comment)* revelador(ora); *(dress)* insinuante

revealingly [rɪ'viːlɪŋlɪ] *adv (significantly)* significativamente; **r., not one of them speaks a foreign language** es significativo que ninguno (de ellos) hable otro idioma

revel ['revəl] *vi* estar de juerga; **to r. in sth** deleitarse con algo

revelation [revə'leɪʃən] *n* revelación *f*; **(the Book of) Revelations** el Apocalipsis

reveler ['revələ(r)] *n* juerguista *mf*

revenge [rɪ'vendʒ] **1** *n* venganza *f*; **to take r. (on sb)** vengarse (de alguien); **to do sth out of r.** hacer algo por venganza; *Prov* **r. is sweet** la venganza es un placer de dioses
2 *vt* **to be revenged** vengarse

revenue ['revənjuː] *n Fin* ingresos *mpl*

reverberate [rɪ'vɜːbəreɪt] *vi* (**a**) *(sound)* reverberar; **the stadium reverberated with applause** el estadio resonaba con los aplausos (**b**) *(news, rumor)* repercutir

reverberation [rɪvɜːbə'reɪʃən] *n* (**a**) *(sound)* reverberación *f* (**b**) *(news, rumor)* repercusión *f*

revere [rɪ'vɪə(r)] *vt* reverenciar, venerar

reverence ['revərəns] *n* reverencia *f*, veneración *f*

Reverend ['revərənd] *Rel n* reverendo *m*; **Right R.** reverendísimo

reverent ['revərənt] *adj* reverente

reverential [revə'renʃəl] *adj* reverente

reverently ['revərəntlɪ] *adv* con reverencia

reverie ['revərɪ] *n* ensoñación *f*

reversal [rɪ'vɜːsəl] *n (of opinion, policy, roles)* inversión *f*; *Law (of decision)* revocación *f*; **to suffer a r.** sufrir un revés

reverse [rɪ'vɜːs] **1** *n* (**a**) *(opposite)* **the r.** lo contrario; **quite the r.!** ¡todo lo contrario! (**b**) *(other side) (of coin)* reverso *m*; *(of fabric)* revés *m*; *(of sheet of paper)* dorso *m* (**c**) *(defeat, misfortune)* revés *m* (**d**) *Aut (gear)* marcha *f* atrás; **he put the car into r.** puso *or* metió la marcha atrás
2 *adj* contrario(a), inverso(a); **in r. order** en orden inverso; **the r. side** *(of fabric)* el revés; *(of sheet of paper)* el dorso; *Aut* **r. gear** marcha *f* atrás
3 *vt (order, situation, trend)* invertir; **the roles are reversed** se han invertido los papeles; **she reversed the car into the road** salió a la carretera marcha atrás

reversible [rɪ'vɜːsəbəl] *adj* (**a**) *(jacket)* reversible (**b**) *(decree, decision)* revocable; *(surgery)* reversible; **the decision is not r.** la decisión es irrevocable

revert [rɪ'vɜːt] *vi* (**a**) *(return)* volver; **he soon reverted to type** pronto volvió a su antiguo ser (**b**) *Law (property)* revertir

review [rɪ'vjuː] **1** *n* (**a**) *(of policy, situation)* revisión *f*; **to be under r.** estar siendo revisado(a) (**b**) *(of book, play, movie)* crítica *f*, reseña *f* (**c**) *Mil* revista *f*
2 *vt* (**a**) *(policy, situation)* revisar (**b**) *(book, play, movie)* hacer una crítica de, reseñar (**c**) *Mil (troops)* pasar revista a
3 *vi (for test)* repasar

reviewer [rɪ'vjuːə(r)] *n (of book, play, movie)* crítico(a) *m,f*

revile [rɪ'vaɪl] *vt Formal* denigrar, vilipendiar

revise [rɪ'vaɪz] *vt (text, law)* revisar; **to r. one's opinion of sb** cambiar de opinión sobre alguien

revision [rɪ'vɪʒən] *n (of text)* revisión *f*

revisionism [rɪ'vɪʒənɪzəm] *n Pol* revisionismo *m*

revisionist [rɪ'vɪʒənɪst] *n & adj* revisionista *mf*

revisit [rɪ'vɪzɪt] *vt* volver a visitar

revitalize [rɪ'vaɪtəlaɪz] *vt* reanimar, revitalizar

revival [rɪ'vaɪvəl] *n (of person)* reanimación *f*; *(of industry)* reactivación *f*; *(of hope)* recuperación *f*; *(of custom, fashion)* resurgimiento *f*; *(of play)* reposición *f*, nuevo montaje *m*

revive [rɪ'vaɪv] **1** *vt (person)* reanimar; *(industry)* reactivar; *(hopes)* recuperar; *(custom, fashion)* hacer resurgir
2 *vi (person)* reanimarse; *(industry)* reactivarse; *(hopes)* renacer; *(custom, fashion)* revivir

revocation [revə'keɪʃən] *n Formal* revocación *f*

revoke [rɪ'vəʊk] *vt Formal (law)* derogar; *(decision, privilege)* revocar

revolt [rɪ'vəʊlt] **1** *n* rebelión *f*; **to be in r.** rebelarse
2 *vt (disgust)* repugnar; **to be revolted by sth** sentir asco por algo
3 *vi (rebel)* rebelarse

revolting [rɪ'vəʊltɪŋ] *adj (disgusting)* repugnante, asqueroso(a)

revoltingly [rɪ'vəʊltɪŋlɪ] *adv (disgustingly)* asquerosamente, repugnantemente

revolution [revə'lu:ʃən] *n* (**a**) *(radical change)* revolución *f* (**b**) *(turn)* vuelta *f*, giro *m*

revolutionary [revə'lu:ʃənərɪ] *n & adj* revolucionario(a) *m,f*

revolutionize [revə'lu:ʃənaɪz] *vt* revolucionar

revolve [rɪ'vɒlv] *vi* girar (**around** en torno a)

revolver [rɪ'vɒlvə(r)] *n* revólver *m*

revolving [rɪ'vɒlvɪŋ] *adj* giratorio(a)

revue [rɪ'vju:] *n Theat* revista *f*

revulsion [rɪ'vʌlʃən] *n* repugnancia *f*

reward [rɪ'wɔːd] **1** *n* recompensa *f*
     2 *vt* recompensar

rewarding [rɪ'wɔːdɪŋ] *adj* gratificante

rewind [ri:'waɪnd] *(pt & pp* **rewound** [ri:'waʊnd]) *vt (tape, film)* rebobinar

rewire [ri:'waɪə(r)] *vt (house)* renovar la instalación eléctrica de

reword [ri:'wɜːd] *vt* reformular, expresar de otra manera

rework [ri:'wɜːk] *vt (idea, text)* rehacer, reelaborar

reworking [ri:'wɜːkɪŋ] *n (of idea, text)* reelaboración *f*

rewound [ri:'waʊnd] *pt & pp of* **rewind**

rewrite [ri:'raɪt] *(pt* **rewrote** [ri:'rəʊt], *pp* **rewritten** [ri:'rɪtən]) *vt* reescribir

Reykjavik ['rekjəvɪk] *n* Reikiavik

rhapsodic(al) [ræp'sɒdɪk(əl)] *adj (prose, description)* enardecido(a)

rhapsodize ['ræpsədaɪz] *vi* deshacerse en elogios (**over** *or* **about** sobre)

rhapsody ['ræpsədɪ] *n Mus* rapsodia *f*; **to go into rhapsodies over sth** deshacerse en elogios sobre algo

rhesus ['ri:səs] *n* (**a**) *Med* **r. factor** factor *m* Rh; **r. positive/ negative** Rh *m* positivo/negativo (**b**) **r. monkey** macaco *m* (de la India)

rhetoric ['retərɪk] *n also Fig* retórica *f*

rhetorical [rɪ'tɒrɪkəl] *adj* retórico(a); **r. question** pregunta *f* retórica

rhetorically [rɪ'tɒrɪklɪ] *adv* retóricamente

rheumatic [ru:'mætɪk] *adj Med* reumático(a); **r. fever** fiebre *f* reumática

rheumatism ['ru:mətɪzəm] *n* reumatismo *m*, reúma *m*

rheumatoid arthritis ['ru:mətɔɪdɑː'θraɪtɪs] *Med n* artritis *f inv* reumatoide

Rhine [raɪn] *n* **the R.** el Rin

rhinestone ['raɪnstəʊn] *n* diamante *m* de imitación

rhino ['raɪnəʊ] *(pl* **rhinos**) *n Fam* rinoceronte *m*

rhinoceros [raɪ'nɒsərəs] *n* rinoceronte *m*

rhizome ['raɪzəʊm] *n Bot* rizoma *m*

Rhodes [rəʊdz] *n* Rodas

rhododendron [rəʊdə'dendrən] *n* rododendro *m*

rhomboid ['rɒmbɔɪd] *n* romboide *m*

rhombus ['rɒmbəs] *n* rombo *m*

Rhone [rəʊn] *n* **the R.** el Ródano

rhubarb ['ru:bɑːb] *n* ruibarbo *m*; **r. jam** confitura *f* de ruibarbo

rhyme [raɪm] **1** *n* rima *f*; **to speak in r.** hablar en verso; **without r. or reason** sin venir a cuento
     2 *vi* rimar

rhythm ['rɪðəm] *n* ritmo *m*; **r. guitar** guitarra *f* rítmica; **r. method** *(of contraception)* método *m* (de) Ogino

rhythmic(al) ['rɪðmɪk(əl)] *adj* rítmico(a)

rhythmically ['rɪðmɪklɪ] *adv* rítmicamente, con ritmo

rib [rɪb] **1** *n* (**a**) *(of person, animal)* costilla *f*; **r. cage** caja *f* torácica; **r. roast** costilla *f* asada, *Arg* bife *m* de chorizo, *Méx* trozo *m* de rosbif (**b**) *(of umbrella)* varilla *f*

     2 *vt (pt & pp* **ribbed**) *Fam (tease)* tomar el pelo a

ribald ['rɪbəld, 'raɪbəld] *adj (joke, song)* procaz; *(language,* grosero(a)

ribbed [rɪbd] *adj (pullover)* acanalado(a)

ribbing ['rɪbɪŋ] *n* (**a**) *(on pullover)* cordoncillos *mpl* (**b**) *Fam (teasing)* tomadura *f* de pelo

ribbon ['rɪbən] *n (for hair, typewriter)* cinta *f*; *(of land)* franja *f* faja *f*; **torn to ribbons** hecho(a) jirones

riboflavin(e) [raɪbəʊ'fleɪvɪn] *n Chem* riboflavina *f*, vitamina B_2

rice [raɪs] *n* arroz *m*; **r. field** *or* **paddy** arrozal *m*; **r. pudding** arroz con leche; **r. wine** vino *m* de arroz

rich [rɪtʃ] **1** *npl* **the r.** los ricos; **riches** riquezas *fpl*
     2 *adj (person, country)* rico(a); *(food)* sustancioso(a) *(chocolate)* extrafino(a); *(soil)* fértil; *(harvest, supply)* abundante; *(color, voice)* profundo(a); **to become r.** hacerse rico; **to be r. in…** ser rico(a) en…; **I'll only have a small piece, this cake's very r.** sólo tomaré un trocito de pastel porque llena mucho; *Fam* **that's a bit r.!** ¡esa sí que es buena!

-rich [rɪtʃ] *suffix* **vitamin-r. foods** alimentos ricos en vitaminas

richly ['rɪtʃlɪ] *adv (furnished, ornamented)* lujosamente; **r. deserved** merecidísimo(a)

Richter Scale ['rɪktə'skeɪl] *n* escala *f* de Richter

rick [rɪk] *n (of hay, straw)* almiar *m*

rickets ['rɪkɪts] *npl Med* raquitismo *m*

rickety ['rɪkɪtɪ] *adj Fam (furniture, staircase)* desvencijado(a) *(alliance, alibi)* precario(a)

ricochet ['rɪkəʃeɪ] **1** *n* bala *f* rebotada
     2 *vi (pt & pp* **ricocheted** ['rɪkəʃeɪd] *or* **ricochetted** ['rɪkəʃetɪd]) rebotar

rid [rɪd] *(pt & pp* **rid**) *vt* **to r. sb of sth** librar a alguien de algo; **to r. oneself of sth, to get rid of sth** deshacerse de algo

riddance ['rɪdəns] *n Fam* **good r.!** ¡ya era hora (de que se fuera)!

ridden ['rɪdən] *pp of* **ride**

-ridden ['rɪdən] *suffix* **flea-r.** infectado(a) de pulgas; **a disease-r. town** una población azotada por las enfermedades

riddle ['rɪdəl] **1** *n (puzzle)* acertijo *m*, adivinanza *f*; *(mystery)* enigma *m*
     2 *vt* **to r. sb with bullets** acribillar a alguien a balazos; **riddled with mistakes** plagado(a) de errores

ride [raɪd] **1** *n* (**a**) *(on bicycle, in car, on horse)* paseo *m*; **to give sb a r.** *(in car)* llevar a alguien (en coche), *CAm, Méx, Perú* dar aventón *or Cuba* botella *or Perú* una jalada *or Ven* cola a alguien; **to go for a r.** ir a dar una vuelta (en coche/a bicicleta/a caballo); **I have a r. coming** me van a llevar en coche *or Am* carro *or CSur* auto; **it's only a short r. away** está a poca distancia; *Fig* **she was given a rough r.** *(by interviewer, critics)* se las hicieron pasar negras *or Esp* moradas; *Fig* **to take sb for a r.** engañar a alguien como a un chino, tomar a alguien el pelo, *RP* venderle un buzón a alguien
     (**b**) *(attraction at amusement park)* atracción *f*, *Am* juego *m*
     2 *vt (pt* **rode** [rəʊd], *pp* **ridden** ['rɪdən]) **to r. a horse/a bicycle** montar *or Am* andar a caballo/en bicicleta; **to r. the bus/train** viajar en autobús/tren
     3 *vi (on horse, bicycle)* **can you r.?** ¿sabes *Esp* montar *or Am* andar?; **I rode into town** fui a la ciudad en bicicleta/a caballo; *Fig* **to be riding high** atravesar un buen momento; *Fig* **to let sth r.** dejar pasar algo

▶**ride out** *vt sep (problem, crisis)* soportar, aguantar; **to r. out the storm** capear el temporal

rider ['raɪdə(r)] *n (on horse) (man)* jinete *m*; *(woman)* amazona *f*; *(on bicycle)* ciclista *mf*; *(on motorbike)* motorista *mf*

ridge [rɪdʒ] *n (of mountain)* cresta *f*; *(of roof)* caballete *m* cumbrera *f*; *(on surface)* rugosidad *f*; *Met* **r. of high pressure** zona *f* de altas presiones

ridicule ['rɪdɪkjuːl] **1** *n* burlas *fpl*, mofa *f*; **to hold sth/sb up to r.** poner algo/a alguien en ridículo
  2 *vt* ridiculizar, poner en ridículo

ridiculous [rɪ'dɪkjʊləs] *adj* ridículo(a); **to make sb look r.** poner en ridículo *or* ridiculizar a alguien; **to make oneself r.** hacer el ridículo

ridiculousness [rɪ'dɪkjʊləsnɪs] *n* lo ridículo

riding ['raɪdɪŋ] *n* equitación *f*, monta *f*; **r. boots** botas *fpl* de montar; **r. crop** *or* **whip** fusta *f*; **r. school** escuela *f* hípica

rife [raɪf] *adj* **to be r.** reinar, imperar; **the text is r. with errors** el texto está plagado de errores

riffraff ['rɪfræf] *n* gentuza *f*

rifle[1] ['raɪfəl] *n* rifle *m*, fusil *m*; **r. range** campo *m* de tiro; **r. shot** disparo *m* de rifle

rifle[2] *vt* (*house, office*) revolver (*en busca de algo*); (*pockets, drawer*) rebuscar en

rifleman ['raɪfəlmən] *n* fusilero *m*

rift [rɪft] *n* (*in earth, rock*) grieta *f*, brecha *f*; (*in relationship*) desavenencia *f*; (*in political party*) escisión *f*

rig [rɪg] **1** *n* (**a**) (*of ship*) aparejo *m* (**b**) (**oil**) **r.** (*on land*) torre *f* de perforación (petrolífera); (*at sea*) plataforma *f* petrolífera (**c**) *Fam* (*outfit*) vestimenta *f* (**d**) *Fam* (*truck*) camión *m*
  2 *vt* (*pt & pp* **rigged**) (**a**) (*ship*) aparejar (**b**) *Fam* (*election*) amañar

▸**rig out** *vt sep Fam* **to be rigged out in…** estar vestido(a) con…

▸**rig up** *vt sep* improvisar, *Esp* apañar

Riga ['riːgə] *n* Riga

rigamarole = **rigmarole**

rigging ['rɪgɪŋ] *n Naut* jarcias *fpl*, cordaje *m*

right [raɪt] **1** *n* (**a**) (*morality*) bien *m*; **to know r. from wrong** distinguir lo que está bien de lo que está mal; **to be in the r.** tener razón; **to set things to rights** poner las cosas en orden
  (**b**) (*entitlement*) derecho *m*; **to have the r. to do sth** tener derecho a hacer algo; **to be within one's rights to do sth** tener todo el derecho a hacer algo; **by rights** en justicia; **by r.** por derecho propio; **to be famous in one's own r.** ser famoso(a) por méritos propios *or* por derecho propio; **the r. to vote** el derecho al voto; **r. of way** (*on land*) derecho de paso; (*on road*) prioridad *f*
  (**c**) (*right-hand side*) derecha *f*; **on** *or* **to the r.** a la derecha; **on my r.** a mi derecha; *Pol* **the r.** la derecha; **a r. to the jaw** (*in boxing*) un derechazo en la mandíbula
  2 *adj* (**a**) (*correct*) correcto(a); **that was the r. thing to do** eso es lo que había que hacer; **are you sure that's the r. time?** ¿seguro que es ésa la hora?; **my watch is r.** mi reloj va *or Am* marcha *or RP* anda bien; **to be r.** (*person*) tener razón; **you were r. not to say anything** hiciste bien en no decir nada; **to stay on the r. side of sb** seguir a buenas con alguien
  (**b**) (*morally good*) **it's not r.** no está bien; **to do the r. thing** hacer lo (que es) debido
  (**c**) (*appropriate*) (*place, time, action*) apropiado(a); **to wait for the r. moment** esperar el momento oportuno; **to know the r. people** tener buenos contactos; **to be in the r. place at the r. time** estar en el lugar y en el momento adecuados
  (**d**) (*mentally, physically well*) **I'm not feeling quite r.** no me siento muy bien; **to be as r. as rain** estar como una rosa; **no one in his r. mind…** nadie en su sano juicio… **he's not quite r. in the head** no está muy bien de la cabeza
  (**e**) (*right-hand*) derecho(a); **on the r. side** a la derecha; **r. hand** mano *f* derecha; *Pol* **the r. wing** la derecha
  (**f**) *Math* **r. angle** ángulo *m* recto
  3 *adv* (**a**) (*straight*) directamente; **he drove r. into the wall** chocó de frente *or* directamente contra la pared; **to put things r.** arreglar las cosas; **to put sb r.** sacar a alguien de su error
  (**b**) (*immediately*) **r. away** en seguida, inmediatamente, *CAm,*

Méx ahorita, *Chile* al tiro; **I'll be r. back** vuelvo en seguida; **r. now** ahora mismo
  (**c**) (*completely*) **the bullet went r. through his arm** la bala le atravesó el brazo de parte a parte; **to go r. up to sb** acercarse justo hasta donde está alguien; **he turned r. round** se dio media vuelta, *RP* se dio vuelta; **r. at the top/back** arriba/detrás del todo
  (**d**) (*exactly*) **r. here/there** aquí/ahí mismo; **r. behind/in the middle** justo detrás *or Am* atrás/en medio; *Fig* **to be r. behind sb** (*support*) apoyar plenamente a alguien
  (**e**) (*to answer, guess*) correctamente, bien; **to understand/remember r.** entender/recordar bien
  (**f**) (*well*) **it was a mistake, r. enough** de acuerdo, fue un error
  (**g**) (*to look, turn*) a la derecha; *Fig* **left, r. and center** por todas partes
  4 *vt* (**a**) (*put upright*) (*boat, car*) enderezar, poner derecho(a) (**b**) (*redress*) **to r. a wrong** terminar con una injusticia
  5 *exclam* (**a**) (*expressing agreement*) ¡de acuerdo!, *Esp* ¡vale!, *Méx* ¡órale!, *RP* ¡está bien! (**b**) (*when ready to begin*) *Esp* ¡venga!, *Am* ¡bueno!

right-angled ['raɪtæŋgəld] *adj* (*triangle*) rectángulo(a); (*corner, bend*) en ángulo recto

right-click ['raɪtklɪk] *Comptr* **1** *vt* hacer clic con el botón derecho en
  2 *vi* hacer clic con el botón derecho (**on** en)

righteous ['raɪtʃəs] *adj* (*person*) virtuoso(a); (*indignation*) justo(a)

rightful ['raɪtfʊl] *adj* legítimo(a)

right-hand ['raɪthænd] *adj* **on the r. side** a la derecha; *Aut* **r. drive** (*vehicle*) vehículo *m* con el volante a la derecha; **to be sb's r. man** ser la mano derecha de alguien

right-handed [raɪt'hændɪd] **1** *adj* diestro(a)
  2 *adv* con la mano derecha

right-hander [raɪt'hændə(r)] *n* (*person*) diestro(a) *m,f*

rightly ['raɪtlɪ] *adv* correctamente; **I don't r. know why…** no sé muy bien por qué…; **r. or wrongly** para bien o para mal; **…and r. so** …y con razón; **he was r. angry** se *esp Esp* enfadó *or esp Am* enojó y con razón

right-minded [raɪt'maɪndɪd], **right-thinking** [raɪt'θɪŋkɪŋ] *adj* **any r. person would have done the same** cualquier persona de bien hubiera hecho lo mismo

right-of-center ['raɪtəv'sentə(r)] *adj Pol* de centro derecha

right-thinking = **right-minded**

right-to-life ['raɪttə'laɪf] *adj* antiaborto *inv*, pro vida *inv*

right-wing [raɪt'wɪŋ] *adj Pol* derechista, de derechas

right-winger [raɪt'wɪŋə(r)] *n Pol* derechista *mf*

rigid ['rɪdʒɪd] *adj* rígido(a); **she's very r. in her ideas** es de ideas muy rígidas

rigidity [rɪ'dʒɪdɪtɪ] *n* rigidez *f*

rigmarole ['rɪgmərəʊl], **rigamarole** ['rɪgəmərəʊl] *n Fam* (*process*) engorro *m*, *Esp* latazo *m*; (*speech*) rollo *m*, galimatías *m inv*

rigor ['rɪgə(r)] *n* rigor *m*

rigor mortis ['rɪgə'mɔːtɪs] *n Med* rigidez *f* cadavérica, rigor *m* mortis

rigorous ['rɪgərəs] *adj* riguroso(a)

rile [raɪl] *vt Fam* (*annoy*) fastidiar, irritar, *Am* enojar

rim [rɪm] *n* (*of cup, bowl*) borde *m*; (*of wheel*) llanta *f*; (*of spectacles*) montura *f*

rimless ['rɪmlɪs] *adj* (*spectacles*) sin montura (*pero con patillas*)

-rimmed [rɪmd] *suffix* **gold/steel-r.** (*spectacles*) con montura dorada/de metal, *RP* con armazón dorado/de metal; **to have red-r. eyes** tener los ojos inyectados en sangre

rind [raɪnd] *n* (*of fruit*) cáscara *f*; (*of cheese, bacon*) corteza *f*

ring[1] [rɪŋ] **1** *n* (**a**) (*for finger*) anillo *m*; (*with gem*) sortija *f*; (*for keys*) llavero *m*; (*plain metal band*) aro *m*; (*for curtains*) anilla *f*;

the rings *(in gymnastics)* las anillas; **r. binder** archivador *m or* carpeta *f* de anillas; **r. finger** (dedo *m*) anular *m* **(b)** *(of people, chairs)* corro *m*, círculo *m*; *(on stove)* fuego *m*, quemador *m*; *(stain)* cerco *m*; **to have rings under one's eyes** tener ojeras; *Fig* **to run rings around sb** darle mil vueltas a alguien **(c)** *(for boxing, wrestling)* cuadrilátero *m*, ring *m* **(d)** *(of spies, criminals)* red *f*

2 *vt (surround)* rodear

ring² **1** *n (sound) (of bell)* timbrazo *m*; *(of small bell, coins)* tintineo *m*; **there was a r. at the door** sonó el timbre de la puerta; **to have the r. of truth** ser verosímil; **the name has a familiar r. to it** el nombre me suena

2 *vt (pt* **rang** [ræŋ], *pp* **rung** [rʌŋ]) *(bell, alarm)* hacer sonar; *Fig* **that rings a bell** *(sounds familiar)* eso me suena

3 *vi* **(a)** *(bell, telephone)* sonar; **to r. at the door** llamar al timbre de la puerta; *Fig* **to r. true/false** tener pinta de ser verdad/mentira **(b)** *(resonate) (street, room)* resonar; **my ears were ringing** me zumbaban los oídos

▸**ring out** *vi (voice, shout)* resonar

▸**ring up** *vt sep (on cash register)* teclear; **the concert rang up a profit of...** el concierto recaudó unos beneficios de...

ring-fence ['rɪŋ'fens] **1** *n (round field)* cerca *f (que rodea una propiedad)*

2 *vt Fin* proteger

ringleader ['rɪŋliːdə(r)] *n* cabecilla *mf*

ringlet ['rɪŋlɪt] *n* tirabuzón *m*

ringmaster ['rɪŋmɑːstə(r)] *n* director *m* de circo

ringside ['rɪŋsaɪd] *n* **a r. seat** *(in boxing)* un asiento de primera fila; *Fig (close view)* una visión muy cercana

ringtone ['rɪŋtə(r)] *n* melodía *f*

ringworm ['rɪŋwɜːm] *n Med* tiña *f*

rink [rɪŋk] *n* pista *f* de patinaje

rinky-dink ['rɪŋkɪdɪŋk] *adj Fam* **(a)** *(cheap)* ordinario(a), *Esp* cutre, *Méx* naco(a), *RP* groncho(a) **(b)** *(small-time)* de poca importancia *or Esp* monta

rinse [rɪns] **1** *n* **to give sth a r.** enjuagar *or Esp* aclarar algo

2 *vt (clothes, dishes)* enjuagar, *Esp* aclarar; **to r. one's hands** enjuagarse las manos

▸**rinse out** *vt sep (cup)* enjuagar; *(clothes)* enjuagar, *Esp* aclarar; **to r. out one's mouth** enjuagarse la boca

Rio (de Janeiro) ['riːəʊ(dɪdʒə'neərəʊ)] *n* Río de Janeiro

riot ['raɪət] **1** *n (uprising)* disturbio *m*, algarada *f*; **a r. of color** una explosión de colores; **the children ran r. while their parents were away** los niños se desmandaron cuando no estaban sus padres; **her imagination was running r.** su imaginación se había desbocado; **to read sb the r. act** poner los puntos sobre las íes a alguien, *Esp* leerle la cartilla a alguien; **r. police** policía *f* antidisturbios; **r. squad** brigada *f* antidisturbios

2 *vi (crowd)* causar *or* provocar disturbios; *(prisoners)* amotinarse

rioter ['raɪətə(r)] *n* alborotador(ora) *m,f*

riotous ['raɪətəs] *adj (party, occasion, living)* desenfrenado(a); **a r. success** un éxito arrasador

riotously ['raɪətəslɪ] *adv* **r. funny** de morirse de risa

RIP [ɑːraɪ'piː] *(abbr* **Rest In Peace)** R.I.P., Q.E.P.D.

rip [rɪp] **1** *n (in cloth, paper)* desgarrón *m*, rasgadura *f*

2 *vt (pt & pp* **ripped)** *(cloth, paper)* rasgar; **to r. sth to pieces** hacer jirones algo; *Fig (performance, argument)* hacer añicos algo

3 *vi* **(a)** *(cloth, paper)* rasgarse **(b)** *Fam* **to let r.** *(while driving)* pisar a fondo; *(in performance)* darlo todo, entregarse; **to let r. (at sb)** *(shout at)* echar una bronca (a alguien)

▸**rip off** *vt sep* **(a)** *(tear)* arrancar; **he ripped off his shirt** se desembarazó de su camisa **(b)** *Fam (swindle)* **to r. sb off** clavar *or Esp* timar a alguien; **that sketch was ripped off from another comedian** ese sketch está copiado de otro humorista

▸**rip open** *vt sep* abrir de un tirón

ripe [raɪp] *adj (fruit)* maduro(a); *(cheese)* curado(a); **to be r.** estar maduro(a); **to live to a r. old age** vivir hasta una edad avanzada; **the time is r. for...** ha llegado el momento de...

ripen ['raɪpən] *vi* madurar

rip-off ['rɪpɒf] *n Fam* timo *m*; **what a r.!** ¡menudo robo!

riposte [rɪ'pɒst] *n (reply)* réplica *f*

ripple [rɪpəl] **1** *n (on water)* onda *f*, ondulación *f*; *(of excitement)* asomo *m*; *(of applause)* murmullo *m*

2 *vi (water)* ondular; *(laughter, applause)* extenderse

rise [raɪz] **1** *n* **(a)** *(in price, temperature, pressure)* aumento *m*, subida *f* (**in** de); **to be on the r.** ir en aumento; **the r. and fall** el ascenso y la caída, el esplendor y la decadencia **(b)** *(of leader, party)* ascenso *m*; **her r. to power** su ascenso *or* acceso al poder; **to give r. to sth** dar pie a algo; *Fam* **to get a r. out of sb** conseguir mosquear a alguien **(c)** *(in ground)* subida *f*, cuesta *f*

2 *vi (pt* **rose** [rəʊz], *pp* **risen** ['rɪzən]) **(a)** *(get up)* levantarse; **to r. early/late** levantarse temprano/tarde; *Fam* **r. and shine!** ¡arriba!

(b) *(road, ground)* subir, elevarse; *(smoke, balloon)* ascender, subir; *(sun, moon)* salir; *(in society)* ascender; **a murmur rose from the crowd** un murmullo se elevó entre la multitud; **to r. to the occasion** estar a la altura de las circunstancias; **to r. to power** ascender *or* acceder al poder; **to r. in sb's esteem** ganarse la estima de alguien

(c) *(temperature, price)* aumentar, subir; *(voice)* elevarse, subir; *(hope)* aumentar; *(dough)* fermentar, subir; **my spirits rose** se me levantó el ánimo

(d) *(revolt)* levantarse; **to r. in arms** levantarse en armas; **to r. in protest (against sth)** alzarse en protesta (contra algo)

▸**rise above** *vt insep (problem, criticism)* remontar, superar; **he rose above his limitations** superó sus limitaciones

▸**rise up** *vi (revolt)* levantarse; **to r. up in arms** levantarse en armas; **to r. up in protest (against sth)** alzarse en protesta (contra algo)

risible ['rɪzɪbəl] *adj* risible

rising ['raɪzɪŋ] **1** *n (revolt)* revuelta *f*, levantamiento *m*

2 *adj (sun)* naciente; *(prices, temperature)* en aumento, ascendente; *(artist, politician)* en alza; *Fig* **r. star** valor *m* en alza, estrella *f* en ciernes

risk [rɪsk] **1** *n* riesgo *m*, peligro *m*; **at r.** en peligro; **at the r. of...** a riesgo de...; **to run the r. of...** correr el riesgo de...; **to take risks** arriesgarse, correr riesgos; **r. assessment** evaluación *f* de riesgos; *Fin* **r. capital** capital *m* (de) riesgo; **r. management** gestión *f* de riesgos

2 *vt* poner en peligro; **to r. one's neck** jugarse el cuello; **we can't r. it** no podemos correr ese riesgo; **to r. defeat** correr el riesgo de *or* arriesgarse a ser derrotado(a)

risky ['rɪskɪ] *adj* arriesgado(a)

risotto [rɪ'zɒtəʊ] *(pl* **risottos)** *n* risotto *m*, = guiso italiano a base de arroz, verduras, etc.

risqué [rɪs'keɪ] *adj (humor)* atrevido(a), subido(a) de tono

rissole ['rɪsəʊl] *n* = pequeña masa frita, generalmente redonda, de carne o verduras

rite [raɪt] *n Rel* rito *m*; **the last rites** la extremaunción

ritual ['rɪtjʊəl] **1** *n* ritual *m*

2 *adj* ritual

ritualistic [rɪtjʊə'lɪstɪk] *adj (following a pattern)* ritual; *Rel* ritualista

ritzy ['rɪtsɪ] *adj Fam* lujoso(a)

rival ['raɪvəl] **1** *n & adj* rival *mf*

2 *vt* rivalizar con

rivalry ['raɪvəlrɪ] *n* rivalidad *f*

river ['rɪvə(r)] *n* río *m*; **a r. of blood** un río de sangre; **r. traffic** tráfico *m* fluvial

riverbed ['rɪvəbed] *n* lecho *m* (del río)

riverside ['rɪvəsaɪd] n ribera f, orilla f (del río); **r. villa** mansión f a la orilla del río

rivet ['rɪvɪt] **1** n remache m

2 vt remachar; **to be absolutely riveted** (fascinated) estar completamente fascinado(a); Fig **to be riveted to the spot** quedarse clavado(a)

riveting ['rɪvɪtɪŋ] adj (fascinating) fascinante

RNA [ɑːren'eɪ] Biol (abbr **ribonucleic acid**) ARN m, ácido m ribonucleico

roach [rəʊtʃ] n (a) (fish) rubio m, rutilo m (b) Fam (cockroach) cucaracha f, Chile barata f

road [rəʊd] n (in general) carretera f; (in town) calle f; (path, track) camino m; **they live across** or **over the r.** viven al otro lado de la calle, viven enfrente; **by r.** por carretera; **to be off the r.** (vehicle) estar averiado(a); **down** or **up the r.** un poco más lejos, por o en la misma calle; **a few years down the r.** dentro de unos años; **after three hours on the r.** después de tres horas en la carretera o de camino; **to be on the r.** (salesman) estar de viaje (de ventas); (pop group) estar de gira; also Fig **somewhere along the r.** en algún punto o momento; Fam **let's have one for the r.** vamos a tomar la última o la espuela; **to be on the r. to recovery** estar en vías de recuperación; **to be on the right r.** ir por (el) buen camino; Fam **let's get this show on the r.!** ¡en marcha!, ¡vamos allá!; **to come to the end of the r.** (relationship) acabar; **r. accident** accidente m de carretera; **r. conditions** estado m de las carreteras; Fam **r. hog** conductor(ora) m,f temerario(a), loco(a) m,f del volante; **r. manager** mánager mf or organizador(ora) m,f de una gira; **r. map** mapa m de carreteras; **r. rage** violencia f en carretera o al volante; **r. repairs** obras fpl (en la calzada); **r. sign** señal f de tráfico; **r. tax** impuesto m de circulación; **r. test** prueba f en carretera; **r. works** obras fpl (en la calzada)

roadblock ['rəʊdblɒk] n control m de carretera

roadside ['rəʊdsaɪd] n borde m de la carretera; **r. bar/hotel** bar m/hotel m de carretera

road test ['rəʊdtest] vt (car) probar en carretera

roadway ['rəʊdweɪ] n calzada f

roadworthy ['rəʊdwɜːðɪ] adj (vehicle) en condiciones de circular

roam [rəʊm] **1** vt (streets, the world) vagar por, recorrer

2 vi **to r. (about)** vagar

roar [rɔː(r)] **1** n (of person) grito m, rugido m; (of animal, sea, wind, crowd) rugido m; (of traffic, engine) estruendo m

2 vi (in general) rugir; (person) vociferar, rugir; **to r. with laughter** reírse a carcajadas

roaring ['rɔːrɪŋ] adj **a r. fire** un fuego muy vivo; **the store was doing a r. business** el negocio iba viento en popa; **it was a r. success** fue un éxito clamoroso

roast [rəʊst] **1** n (piece of meat) asado m

2 adj asado(a)

3 vt (a) (meat) asar; (nuts, coffee) tostar (b) Fam (criticize) desollar

roasting ['rəʊstɪŋ] Fam **1** n **to give sb a r.** echar una regañina or Esp bronca a alguien; (criticize) poner a parir a alguien, Méx viborear a alguien, RP dejar por el piso a alguien

2 adj **r.(-hot)** abrasador(ora), achicharrante; **it's r. in here** aquí te achicharras

rob [rɒb] (pt & pp **robbed**) vt (person, bank) atracar; (house) robar; **to r. sb of sth** robar algo a alguien

robber ['rɒbə(r)] n atracador(ora) m,f

robbery ['rɒbərɪ] n atraco m

robe [rəʊb] n (of priest) sotana f; (of judge) toga f; (dressing gown) bata f, batín m

robin ['rɒbɪn] n petirrojo m

robot ['rəʊbɒt] n robot m

robotic [rəʊ'bɒtɪk] adj de robot

robotics [rəʊ'bɒtɪks] n robótica f

robust [rəʊ'bʌst] adj (person) robusto(a); (material, suitcase) resistente; (defense, speech) enérgico(a)

rock [rɒk] **1** n (a) (substance, large stone) roca f; Fig **to be on the rocks** (marriage, company) estar al borde del naufragio; **on the rocks** (whiskey) con hielo; **to reach** or **hit r. bottom** tocar fondo; **the R. (of Gibraltar)** el Peñón (de Gibraltar); **r. candy** azúcar m or f cande; **r. climbing** escalada f; **r. face** pared f (de roca); **r. garden** jardín m de rocalla; **r. pool** charca f (en las rocas de la playa); **r. salt** sal f gema

(b) Fam (diamond) pedrusco m, diamante m

(c) (rocking motion) **to give sth a r.** mecer algo

(d) (music) rock m; **r. and roll** rock and roll m; **r. concert** concierto m de rock; **r. group** grupo m de rock; **r. singer** cantante mf de rock

2 vt (boat, chair) mecer, balancear; (building) (of earthquake, explosion) sacudir; **to r. a baby to sleep** mecer a un niño hasta que se quede dormido; Fig **to r. the boat** (create problems) complicar el asunto; **the country was rocked by these revelations** estas revelaciones conmocionaron al país

3 vi (sway) balancearse; (building) estremecerse; **to r. (backward and forward) in one's chair** mecerse en la silla; **to r. with laughter** reírse a carcajadas

rockabilly ['rɒkəbɪlɪ] n rockabilly m

rock-bottom ['rɒkbɒtəm] adj (prices) mínimo(a)

rocker ['rɒkə(r)] n (a) (chair) mecedora f; Fam **she's off her r.** le falta un tornillo (b) (musician, fan) roquero(a) m,f

rockery ['rɒkərɪ] n (in garden) jardín m de rocalla

rocket¹ ['rɒkɪt] **1** n cohete m; Fam **it isn't r. science** no se trata de descubrir América; **r. launcher** lanzacohetes m inv

2 vi (prices) dispararse

rocket² n (salad plant) oruga f, roqueta f

rockfall ['rɒkfɔːl] n desprendimiento m (de piedras)

rock-hard [rɒk'hɑːd] adj duro(a) como una piedra

Rockies ['rɒkɪz] npl **the R.** las Montañas Rocosas

rocking ['rɒkɪŋ] adj **r. chair** mecedora f; **r. horse** caballo m de balancín

rock-solid [rɒk'sɒlɪd] adj (support) sólido(a) como una piedra

rocky ['rɒkɪ] adj (a) (path, soil) pedregoso(a); **the R. Mountains** las Montañas Rocosas (b) (unstable) (marriage, relationship, economy) inestable

rod [rɒd] n (wooden) vara f; (metal) barra f; (for fishing) caña f (de pescar); Fig **to rule with a r. of iron** gobernar con mano de hierro

rode [rəʊd] pt of **ride**

rodent ['rəʊdənt] n roedor m

rodeo ['rəʊdɪəʊ] n rodeo m

roe¹ [rəʊ] n **r. (deer)** corzo m

roe² n (of fish) huevas fpl

roger ['rɒdʒə(r)] exclam **r.!** (in radio message) ¡recibido!

rogue [rəʊg] n (dishonest) granuja mf, bribón(ona) m,f; (mischievous) truhán(ana) m,f, pícaro(a) m,f; **r. elephant** elefante m solitario; **r. state** estado m delincuente or canalla

roguish ['rəʊgɪʃ] adj (smile, look) pícaro(a), picarón(ona)

role [rəʊl] n Cin, Theat & Fig papel m; Fig **to play an important r.** desempeñar un papel importante; **r. model** ejemplo m, modelo m a seguir

role-playing ['rəʊlpleɪɪŋ] n juego m de roles

roll [rəʊl] **1** n (a) (of paper, film) rollo m; (of fat, flesh) Esp michelín m, Méx llanta f, RP rollo m; (of banknotes) fajo m (b) (bread) panecillo m, Méx bolillo m; **ham/cheese r.** bocadillo m or Am sándwich m de jamón/queso (c) (noise) (of drum) redoble m; (of thunder) retumbo m (d) (movement) (of ship) balanceo m; Fam **to be on a r.** llevar una buena racha (e) (list) lista f; **to take a r. call** pasar lista; Mil **r. of honor** lista de los caídos en la guerra

2 *vt* (**a**) *(ball)* hacer rodar; **to r. sth along the ground** hacer rodar algo por el suelo; **to r. one's eyes** poner los ojos en blanco; **to r. one's r's** marcar las erres al hablar; **the animal rolled itself into a ball** el animal se hizo una bola *or* se enroscó (**b**) *(road, lawn)* apisonar; *(metal)* laminar (**c**) *(cigarette)* liar; *(paper, carpet)* enrollar

3 *vi* (**a**) *(ball)* rodar; *(ship)* balancearse; *(cine camera)* rodar; *Fig* **heads will r.** van a rodar cabezas; *Fam* **to be rolling in money, to be rolling in it** nadar en la abundancia, *Esp* estar montado(a) en el dólar; *Fig* **to start the ball rolling** poner las cosas en marcha (**b**) *(thunder)* retumbar

▶**roll back** *vt sep* **to r. back the enemy** hacer retroceder al enemigo

▶**roll over** *vi* *(several times)* dar vueltas; *(once) (person)* darse la vuelta; *(car)* dar una vuelta (de campana)

▶**roll up 1** *vt sep (map)* enrollar; *(pants)* remangar, arremangar; *(blind, car window)* subir; **to r. sth up in paper** envolver algo con papel; **r. up one's sleeves** remangarse *or* arremangarse la camisa
    2 *vi Fam (arrive)* llegar

rolled ['rəʊld] *adj* **r. gold** metal *m* laminado en oro; **r. oats** copos *mpl* de avena

rolled-up [rəʊl'dʌp] *adj (sleeves, pants)* remangado(a), arremangado(a); *(umbrella)* cerrado(a); *(newspaper)* enrollado(a)

roller ['rəʊlə(r)] *n (for paint, garden, in machine)* rodillo *m*; *(for hair)* rulo *m*, *Chile* tubo *m*, *RP* rulero *m*, *Ven* rollo *m*; **r. coaster** montaña *f* rusa; **r. skates** patines *mpl* (de ruedas)

Rollerblades® ['rəʊləbleɪdz] *npl* patines *mpl* en línea

Rollerblading® ['rəʊləbleɪdɪŋ] *n* **to go R.** patinar *(con patines en línea)*

roller-skate ['rəʊləskeɪt] *vi* patinar (sobre ruedas)

roller-skating ['rəʊləskeɪtɪŋ] *n* **to go r.** ir a patinar (sobre ruedas)

rolling ['rəʊlɪŋ] *adj (hills, fields)* ondulado(a); *(sea, waves)* ondulante; *(thunder)* retumbante; **r. mill** *(for steel)* laminadora *f*; **r. pin** rodillo *m* (de cocina); *Rail* **r. stock** material *m* móvil *or* rodante

roll-on ['rəʊlɒn] *adj* (**a**) **r. (deodorant)** desodorante *m* de bola (**b**) *Naut* **r. roll-off ferry** transbordador *m*, ferry *m (con trasbordo horizontal)*

rolltop desk ['rəʊltɒp'desk] *n* buró *m*

roly-poly ['rəʊlɪ'pəʊlɪ] *adj Fam (plump)* rechoncho(a)

ROM [rɒm] *n Comptr (abbr* **read-only memory)** (memoria *f*) ROM *f*

romaine [rəʊ'meɪn] *n* **r. (lettuce)** lechuga *f* romana

Roman ['rəʊmən] **1** *n* romano(a) *m,f*
    2 *adj* romano(a); **R. alphabet** alfabeto *m* latino; *Rel* **R. Catholic** católico(a) (romano(a)); **R. nose** nariz *f* aguileña; **R. numerals** números *mpl* romanos

roman ['rəʊmən] *n Typ* (caracteres *mpl* en) redonda *f*

romance ['rəʊmæns, rə'mæns] *n* (**a**) *(book)* novela *f* rosa; *(movie)* película *f* romántica *or* de amor (**b**) *(love affair)* romance *m*, aventura *f* (amorosa) (**c**) *(charm)* encanto *m*

Romania, Rumania [rə'meɪnɪə] *n* Rumanía

Romanian, Rumanian [rə'meɪnɪən] **1** *n* (**a**) *(person)* rumano(a) *m,f* (**b**) *(language)* rumano *m*
    2 *adj* rumano(a)

romantic [rə'mæntɪk] *n & adj* romántico(a) *m,f*

romantically [rə'mæntɪklɪ] *adv* de manera romántica; **to be r. involved with sb** tener un romance con alguien

romanticism [rə'mæntɪsɪzəm] *n (of person, in art)* romanticismo *m*

romanticize [rə'mæntɪsaɪz] *vt (idea, incident)* idealizar; **to r. war** rodear la guerra de un halo romántico

Romany ['rəʊmənɪ] **1** *n* (**a**) *(person)* romaní *mf*, gitano(a) *m,f* (**b**) *(language)* romaní *m*; *(in Spain)* caló *m*
    2 *adj* romaní, gitano(a)

rom-com ['rɒmkɒm] *n* comedia *f* romántica

Rome [rəʊm] *n* Roma; *Prov* **R. wasn't built in a day** no se ganó Zamora en una hora; *Prov* **when in R.(, do as the Romans do)** (allá) donde fueres haz lo que vieres

romp [rɒmp] **1** *n* **to have a r.** juguetear; **the play is an enjoyable r.** la obra es un divertimiento agradable
    2 *vi* **to r. (around** *or* **about)** juguetear; **to r. through an examination** sacar un examen con toda facilidad

romper ['rɒmpə(r)] *n* **r. suit, rompers** pelele *m*

roof [ru:f] **1** *n (of building)* tejado *m*; *(of car, tunnel, cave)* techo *m*; **to have a r. over one's head** tener un techo *or* sitio donde dormir; **to live under one** *or* **the same r.** vivir bajo el mismo techo; *Fam* **to hit the r.** *(person)* ponerse hecho(a) una furia; *Fam* **to go through the r.** *(inflation, prices)* ponerse por las nubes; **the r. of the mouth** el paladar, el cielo de la boca; **r. garden** azotea *f* con jardín *or* ajardinada; *Aut* **r. rack** baca *f*
    2 *vt* techar, cubrir

roofing ['ru:fɪŋ] *n* **r. material** *(for making roofs)* techumbre *f*; *(for covering roofs)* revestimiento *m* de tejados

rooftop ['ru:ftɒp] *n* tejado *m*; *Fig* **to shout sth from the rooftops** proclamar algo a los cuatro vientos

rook [rʊk] *n (bird)* grajo *m*; *(in chess)* torre *f*

rookery ['rʊkərɪ] *n* colonia *f* de grajos

rookie ['rʊkɪ] *n Fam* novato(a) *m,f*

room [ru:m] *n* (**a**) *(in house)* habitación *f*, cuarto *m*; *(in hotel)* habitación *f*; *(bedroom)* dormitorio *m*, *Am* cuarto *m*, *CAm, Col, Méx* recámara *f*; *(large, public)* sala *f*; **double/single r.** habitación doble/individual; **r. and board** pensión *f* completa; **r. service** servicio *m* de habitaciones; **r. temperature** temperatura *f* ambiente
    (**b**) *(space)* espacio *m*, sitio *m*, *Am* lugar *m*, *Andes* campo *m*; **there's no r.** no hay sitio *or Am* lugar *or Andes* campo; **to make r. (for sb)** hacer sitio *or Am* lugar *or Andes* campo (para *or* a alguien); **is there r. for one more?** ¿cabe uno más?; **there's no r. for doubt** no hay lugar a dudas; **there is r. for improvement** se puede mejorar

-room [ru:m] *suffix* **two/three/four-r.** de dos/tres/cuatro habitaciones

roomer ['ru:mə(r)] *n* huésped *mf*, huéspeda *f*

roomful ['ru:mfʊl] *n* habitación *f* llena, cuarto *m* lleno

roomie ['ru:mɪ] *n Fam* compañero(a) *m,f* de cuarto *or* habitación

rooming house ['ru:mɪŋhaʊs] *n* casa *f* de huéspedes, pensión *f*

roommate ['ru:mmeɪt] *n* compañero(a) *m,f* de cuarto *or* habitación

roomy ['ru:mɪ] *adj* espacioso(a)

roost [ru:st] **1** *n* percha *f*, palo *m*; **to rule the r.** manejar el cotarro
    2 *vi* estar posado(a) *(para dormir)*; *Fig* **his actions have come home to r.** ahora está sufriendo las consecuencias de sus actos

rooster ['ru:stə(r)] *n* gallo *m*

root [ru:t] **1** *n* (**a**) *(of plant, tooth, word)* raíz *f*; **to pull sth up by the roots** arrancar algo de raíz; **to take r.** *(plant, idea)* arraigar; **they destroyed the party r. and branch** destrozaron el partido por completo; *Fig* **to put down roots** echar raíces; *Fig* **to get back to one's roots** volver a las raíces; **r. beer** = bebida gaseosa sin alcohol elaborada con extractos de plantas; **r. crops** tubérculos *mpl* (comestibles); **r. vegetables** tubérculos *mpl*
    (**b**) *(origin)* raíz *f*; **the conflict has its roots in the past** el conflicto hunde sus raíces en el pasado; *Prov* **money is the r. of all evil** el dinero es la raíz de todos los males
    2 *vt* **to be rooted to the spot** quedarse de una pieza
    3 *vi* (**a**) **to r. around** *or* **about (for sth)** rebuscar (algo) (**b**) **to r. for sb** apoyar a alguien

▸**root out** vt sep (racism, crime) cortar de raíz

rope [rəʊp] 1 n (a) (thick, for hanging) soga f; (thinner) cuerda f; Naut cabo m, maroma f; (of pearls) sarta f; **r. ladder** escalera f de cuerda (b) (idioms) **to be on the ropes** estar contra las cuerdas; **to learn the ropes** ponerse al tanto (con un trabajo); **to show sb the ropes** poner a alguien al tanto; **to give sb plenty of r.** dar gran libertad de movimientos a alguien

2 vt (a) (fasten) atar (**to** a); **they roped themselves together** (for climbing) se encordaron (b) (cattle, horses) atrapar con el lazo, CSur lacear

▸**rope in** vt sep Fam **to r. sb in(to doing sth)** liar a alguien (para hacer algo)

▸**rope off** vt sep acordonar

rop(e)y ['rəʊpɪ] adj Fam (unreliable) flojo(a); (ill) pachucho(a), Am flojo(a)

rosary ['rəʊzərɪ] n Rel rosario m; **to say one's r.** rezar el rosario

rose [rəʊz] 1 n (a) (flower) rosa f; (on watering can, shower) alcachofa f; **r. bed** macizo m de rosas; **r. garden** rosaleda f, jardín m de rosas, Méx, CSur rosedal m; **r. grower** cultivador(ora) m,f de rosas; **r. hip** escaramujo m; Archit **r. window** rosetón m (b) (idioms) **life is not a bed of roses** la vida no es un lecho or camino de rosas; **to come up roses** salir a pedir de boca

2 adj (color) rosa

3 pt of **rise**

rosé ['rəʊzeɪ] n (wine) rosado m

rosebud ['rəʊzbʌd] n capullo m de rosa

rosebush ['rəʊzbʊʃ] n rosal m

rose-colored ['rəʊzkʌləd], **rose-tinted** ['rəʊztɪntɪd] adj rosado(a), color de rosa; **to see things through r. glasses** or **spectacles** ver las cosas de color de rosa

rosemary ['rəʊzmərɪ] n romero m

rose-tinted = **rose-colored**

rosette [rəʊ'zet] n (badge of honor) escarapela f

rose-water ['rəʊzwɔːtə(r)] n agua f de rosas

rosewood ['rəʊzwʊd] n palo m de rosa

roster ['rɒstə(r)] n lista f

rostrum ['rɒstrəm] n estrado m

rosy ['rəʊzɪ] adj (pink) rosa, rosado(a); (cheeks, complexion) sonrosado(a); Fig (future) (de) color de rosa

rot [rɒt] 1 n (in house, wood) podredumbre f; Fig **the r. has set in** el mal ha empezado a arraigar; Fig **to stop the r.** impedir que la situación siga degenerando

2 vt (pt & pp **rotted**) pudrir

3 vi pudrirse; **to r. in prison** pudrirse en la cárcel

rotary ['rəʊtərɪ] 1 n (traffic circle) rotonda f

2 adj (movement) rotatorio(a), giratorio(a); **r. pump** bomba f rotatoria

rotate [rəʊ'teɪt] 1 vt (a) (turn) hacer girar (b) (alternate) (duties, crops) alternar

2 vi (a) (turn) girar (b) (in job) turnarse, rotar

rotating [rəʊ'teɪtɪŋ] adj (a) (turning) giratorio(a) (b) (alternating) **on a r. basis** en forma rotativa or rotatoria

rotation [rəʊ'teɪʃən] n (a) (circular movement) rotación f (b) (in job) rotación f, alternancia f; **by** or **in r.** por turno (rotatorio); **crop r.** rotación de cultivos

rote [rəʊt] n **r. learning** aprendizaje m memorístico; **to learn sth by r.** aprender algo de memoria or de corrido

rotor ['rəʊtə(r)] n rotor m

rotten ['rɒtən] adj (a) (wood, egg, fruit) podrido(a); **to be r.** estar podrido (b) (bad, of poor quality) malísimo(a); **I feel r.** (ill) me siento Esp fatal or Am pésimo; **I feel r. about what happened** (sorry) siento en el alma lo que pasó; **what r. luck!** ¡qué mala pata!; **a r. trick** una canallada

rotting ['rɒtɪŋ] adj podrido(a), que se está pudriendo

rotund [rəʊ'tʌnd] adj orondo(a), rollizo(a)

rouge [ruːʒ] n colorete m

rough [rʌf] 1 n (a) (in golf) matojos mpl (b) Fam Old-fashioned (hooligan) matón m (c) (difficulty) **to take the r. with the smooth** estar a las duras y a las maduras, Am estar para las buenas y las malas (d) Fig **she is a diamond in the r.** vale mucho, aunque no tenga muchos modales

2 adj (a) (surface, skin) áspero(a); (terrain) accidentado(a) (b) (unrefined) (manners, speech) tosco(a); **r. draft** borrador m; **r. sketch** bosquejo m

(c) (violent, not gentle) bruto(a); **to receive r. treatment** ser maltratado(a); **a r. crossing** una travesía difícil; **r. sea(s)** mar f brava, mar m embravecido

(d) (harsh) (voice) ronco(a); (wine) peleón(ona); (spirits) de garrafa; Fam **it was r. on her** fue muy duro para ella; **r. justice** injusticia f

(e) (approximate) (calculation, estimate) aproximado(a); **at a r. guess** a ojo; **I've got a r. idea of what he wants** tengo una vaga idea de or sé más o menos lo que quiere

3 adv **to play r.** jugar duro; Fam **to sleep r.** dormir a la intemperie or Esp al raso

4 vt Fam **we had to r. it** nos las arreglamos or Esp apañamos como pudimos

▸**rough up** vt sep Fam **to r. sb up** dar a alguien una paliza

roughage ['rʌfɪdʒ] n fibra f

rough-and-ready [rʌfən'redɪ] adj rudimentario(a); (person) basto(a), tosco(a)

rough-and-tumble [rʌfən'tʌmbl] n riña f, rifirrafe m; **the r. of politics** la brega de la política

roughhouse ['rʌfhaʊs] 1 n bronca f, trifulca f

2 vt tratar a lo bruto (generalmente en broma)

3 vi armar jaleo, RP hacer quilombo

roughly ['rʌflɪ] adv (a) (violently) brutalmente; **to treat sb r.** tratar a alguien con brutalidad (b) (crudely) groseramente (c) (approximately) aproximadamente; **r. (speaking)** aproximadamente

roughness ['rʌfnɪs] n (a) (of surface, skin) aspereza f (b) (of sea) embravecimiento m, agitación f (c) (violent behavior) brutalidad f

roughshod ['rʌfʃɒd] adv **to ride r. over sth** pisotear algo

rough-spoken [rʌf'spəʊkən] adj malhablado(a)

roulette [ruː'let] n (game) ruleta f; **r. table** mesa f de ruleta; **r. wheel** ruleta f

round [raʊnd] 1 n (a) (stage of tournament) vuelta f, ronda f (eliminatoria); (in boxing) asalto m, round m; (of golf) recorrido m (del campo); **the first r. of the elections** la primera vuelta de las elecciones; **to get through to the next r.** pasar a la siguiente ronda

(b) (of talks, visits) ronda f; (of drinks) ronda f, Am vuelta f; **it's my r.** me toca pagar esta ronda or Am vuelta; **a r. of applause** una ovación, Am una salva de palmas

(c) **to do one's rounds** (doctor) (visit patients at home) hacer las visitas (a los pacientes); (in hospital) hacer la ronda de visitas en sala; **the daily r.** (of tasks) las tareas cotidianas; **one of the rumors doing the rounds** uno de los rumores que corren

(d) Mil (bullet) bala f

(e) Mus (canon) m

2 adj (a) (in shape) redondo(a); **to have r. shoulders** tener las espaldas cargadas; **r. table (conference)** mesa f redonda; **r. trip** viaje m de ida y vuelta (b) (number) redondo(a); **a r. dozen** una docena justa; **in r. figures** en números redondos

3 adv (surrounding) alrededor; **all (the) year r.** durante todo el año

4 prep (a) (position) alrededor de; **r. the table** en torno a la mesa; **r. here** por aquí (b) (motion) **to look r. the room** mirar por toda la habitación; **to travel r. the world** viajar por todo el mundo; **to go r. an obstacle** rodear un obstáculo; **to go r. the corner** doblar la esquina; **it's just r. the corner** está a la vuelta de la esquina, RP queda a la vuelta (c) (approximately) **r.**

about alrededor de, aproximadamente; **r. about midday** a eso del mediodía

5 vt (**a**) (make round) redondear (**b**) (move round) (obstacle) rodear; (corner) doblar (**c**) (figures) **to r. up/down** redondear al alza/a la baja

▸**round off** vt sep (conclude) rematar, concluir

▸**round up** vt sep (cattle) recoger; (criminals, suspects) detener

roundabout ['raʊndəbaʊt] adj (approach, route) indirecto(a); **to lead up to a question in a r. way** preguntar algo después de un largo preámbulo

round-eyed ['raʊndaɪd] adj (surprised) atónito(a), con los ojos muy abiertos or como platos

roundly ['raʊndlɪ] adv (praise, condemn) con rotundidad

round-trip ['raʊnd'trɪp] adj (ticket) de ida y vuelta

roundup ['raʊndʌp] n (of criminals) redada f; (on TV, radio) resumen m

rouse [raʊz] vt (from sleep) despertar; (make more active) incitar; **to r. oneself (to do sth)** animarse (a hacer algo); **to r. sb to action** empujar a alguien a la acción; **to r. sb to anger** encolerizar a alguien

rousing ['raʊzɪŋ] adj (music, speech) estimulante; (welcome, send-off, cheers) entusiasta

rout [raʊt] **1** n derrota f aplastante

2 vt arrollar, aplastar

route [ruːt] **1** n (of traveler) ruta f, itinerario m; (of plane, ship) ruta f; (of parade) itinerario m; (to failure, success) vía f (**to** hacia); **bus r.** línea f de autobús

2 vt hacer pasar, dirigir; **the train was routed through Birmingham** hicieron pasar el tren por Birmingham

router ['ruːtə(r)] n Comptr router m, direccionador m

routine [ruː'tiːn] **1** n (**a**) (habit) rutina f; **the daily r.** la rutina diaria (**b**) (of performer, comedian) número m; Fam Fig **don't give me that r.** no me vengas con ese cuento (**c**) Comptr rutina f

2 adj (**a**) (normal) habitual; **r. inquiries** investigación f rutinaria (**b**) (dull) rutinario(a), monótono(a)

routinely [ruː'tiːnlɪ] adv habitualmente

roux [ruː] (pl **roux** [ruːz]) n Culin roux m, = espesante de salsas a base de harina y mantequilla

rove [rəʊv] **1** vt vagar por

2 vi vagar; **his eyes roved around the room** sus ojos recorrieron la habitación

row[1] [rəʊ] n hilera f; (of seats) fila f; **in a r.** en hilera, en fila; **two Sundays in a r.** dos domingos seguidos; **in the front r.** (of seats) en primera fila; **r. house** casa f adosada

row[2] **1** n (in boat) paseo m en barca; **to go for a r.** darse un paseo en barca

2 vt **to r. a boat** llevar una barca remando; **he rowed us across the river** nos llevó al otro lado del río en barca

3 vi remar

row[3] [raʊ] **1** n (**a**) (noise) jaleo m, alboroto m; (protest) escándalo m (**b**) (quarrel) bronca f, trifulca f; **to have a r. (with sb)** tener una bronca (con alguien)

2 vi discutir

rowan ['raʊən] n serbal m

rowboat ['rəʊbəʊt] n bote m or barca f de remos

rowdy ['raʊdɪ] **1** n alborotador(ora) m,f

2 adj (noisy) ruidoso(a); (disorderly) alborotador(ora)

rower ['rəʊə(r)] n remero(a) m,f

rowing ['rəʊɪŋ] n remo m; **r. machine** banco m de remo

royal ['rɔɪəl] **1** n Fam **the Royals** la familia real

2 adj real; (splendid) magnífico(a); **His/Her R. Highness** Su Alteza Real; **r. blue** azul m real (intenso y más claro que el marino); **the R. Family** la Familia Real; **r. jelly** jalea f real

royalist ['rɔɪəlɪst] n & adj monárquico(a) m,f

royally ['rɔɪəlɪ] adv (entertain, welcome) con magnificencia

royalty ['rɔɪəltɪ] n (**a**) (rank, position) realeza f (**b**) **royalties**

(for author, singer) derechos mpl de autor

rpm [ɑːpiː'em] n Aut (abbr **revolutions per minute**) rpm, revoluciones fpl por minuto

R & R [ɑːrən'ɑː(r)] n Mil (abbr **rest and recreation**) permiso m

RSA [ɑːres'eɪ] n (abbr **Republic of South Africa**) República f de Sudáfrica

RSVP [ɑːresviː'piː] (abbr **répondez s'il vous plaît**) (on invitation) se ruega contestación

rub [rʌb] **1** n to give sth a r. frotar algo; Fig **there's the r.!** ¡ahí está el problema!

2 vt (pt & pp **rubbed**) frotar; **to r. one's hands together** frotarse las manos; Fig **to r. shoulders with** codearse con; Fam **to r. sb up the wrong way** caer mal a alguien; Fam **there's no need to r. it in!** ¡no tienes por qué restregármelo por las narices!

3 vi (straps, shoes) rozar (**against** contra)

▸**rub off 1** vt sep (dirt, stains) limpiar, eliminar (frotando); (writing) borrar

2 vi borrarse; Fig **to r. off on sb** (manners, enthusiasm) influir en or contagiarse a alguien

▸**rub out** vt sep (**a**) (erase) borrar (**b**) Fam (murder) acabar con, Esp cepillarse a

rubber ['rʌbə(r)] n (**a**) (substance) goma f, Am hule m; **r. ball** pelota f de goma; **r. band** goma (elástica); **r. boot** bota f de agua or goma or Méx, Ven caucho; **r. dinghy** lancha f neumática; **r. gloves** guantes mpl de goma; **r. plant** ficus m inv; **r. ring** (swimming aid) flotador m (aro); **r. stamp** tampón m de goma (**b**) Fam (condom) goma f, Méx impermeable m, RP forro m (**c**) **rubbers** (boots) botas fpl de agua or goma or Méx, Ven caucho

rubber-stamp [rʌbə'stæmp] vt Fig (approve) dar el visto bueno a

rubbery ['rʌbərɪ] adj correoso(a)

rubbish ['rʌbɪʃ] n (refuse, junk) basura f

rubble ['rʌbəl] n escombros mpl

rube [ruːb] n Fam palurdo(a) m,f, Esp paleto(a) m,f, Col, Méx indio(a) m,f, RP pajuerano(a) m,f

rubella [ruː'belə] n Med rubeola f

ruble ['ruːbəl] n (Russian currency) rublo m

rubric ['ruːbrɪk] n (set of instructions) directrices fpl, normas fpl

ruby ['ruːbɪ] **1** n rubí m

2 adj (color) rojo(a) intenso(a) or rubí

ruck n (in cloth) arruga f

▸**ruck up** vi (sheet, dress) arrugarse

rucksack ['rʌksæk] n macuto m, mochila f

ructions ['rʌkʃənz] npl Fam bronca f, jaleo m; **there'll be r.** va a armar la gorda

rudder ['rʌdə(r)] n (on boat, plane) timón m

ruddy ['rʌdɪ] adj (complexion) rubicundo(a); (sky) rojizo(a), arrebolado(a)

rude [ruːd] adj (**a**) (impolite) maleducado(a), grosero(a) (**b**) (indecent) de mal gusto, ordinario(a); **a r. joke** un chiste verde (**c**) (primitive) tosco(a) (**d**) (shock, surprise) duro(a); **to receive a r. awakening** llevarse una desagradable sorpresa (**e**) (vigorous) **to be in r. health** estar rebosante de salud

rudeness ['ruːdnɪs] n (**a**) (impoliteness) mala educación f, grosería f (**b**) (indecency) (of joke, story) ordinariez f, mal gusto m

rudimentary [ruːdɪ'mentərɪ] adj rudimentario(a)

rudiments ['ruːdɪmənts] npl rudimentos mpl, fundamentos mpl

rue [ruː] vt Formal lamentar, deplorar

rueful ['ruːfʊl] adj compungido(a)

ruefully ['ruːfəlɪ] adv con arrepentimiento y pesar

ruff [rʌf] n (on costume) golilla f

ruffian ['rʌfɪən] n Old-fashioned rufián m

ruffle ['rʌfəl] vt (disturb) (water surface) rizar; (hair) despeinar, to **r. sb's feathers** hacer *esp Esp* enfadar *or esp Am* enojar a alguien; to **r. sb's composure** hacer perder la calma a alguien

ruffled ['rʌfəld] *adj* **the decision caused a few r. feathers** la decisión molestó a unos cuantos

rug [rʌg] *n* (a) *(carpet)* alfombra *f*; *Fig* **to pull the r. from under sb's feet** dejar a alguien en la estacada (b) *Fam (hairpiece)* peluquín *m*

rugby ['rʌgbɪ] *n* rugby *m*

rugged ['rʌgɪd] *adj* (a) *(ground, country)* irregular, accidentado(a); **r. features** rasgos *mpl* recios (b) *(manner)* rudo(a), tosco(a)

ruin ['ruːɪn] **1** *n* ruina *f*; **to fall into r.(s)** quedar en ruinas; **it will be the r. of him** será su ruina; **r. is staring us in the face** estamos a punto de perderlo todo

2 *vt* arruinar; **to r. one's health/eyesight** arruinarse la salud/la vista; **we're ruined** estamos arruinados; **the meal's ruined** se ha echado a perder la comida; **tourism has ruined the town** el turismo ha echado a perder la ciudad

ruined ['ruːɪnd] *adj (building)* en ruinas

ruinous ['ruːɪnəs] *adj (expense)* ruinoso(a); **in a r. condition** en un estado ruinoso

ruinously ['ruːɪnəslɪ] *adv* **r. expensive** extraordinariamente caro

rule [ruːl] **1** *n* (a) *(principle, regulation)* regla *f*, norma *f*; **as a r.** por norma, por regla general; **to make it a r. to do sth** tener por costumbre *or* norma hacer algo; **rules and regulations** normativa *f*, reglamento *m*; **it's against the rules** va contra las normas; **as a r. of thumb** por regla general; **r. book** reglamento *m* (b) *(government)* gobierno *m*; **under British r.** bajo dominio *or* gobierno británico; **the r. of law** el imperio de la ley (c) *(for measuring)* regla *f*

2 *vt* (a) *(country, people)* gobernar; **don't let him r. your life** no le dejes que gobierne *or* controle tu vida (b) *(decide, decree)* decretar, determinar (c) *(paper)* rayar; **ruled paper** papel *m* rayado *or* pautado

3 *vi* (a) *(monarch)* reinar (b) *(judge)* decidir, fallar; **to r. in favor of/against sb** fallar a favor de/en contra de alguien

▶**rule out** *vt sep* descartar, excluir

ruler ['ruːlə(r)] *n* (a) *(of country)* gobernante *mf* (b) *(for measuring)* regla *f*

ruling ['ruːlɪŋ] **1** *n (of judge, umpire)* fallo *m*, decisión *f*

2 *adj (passion, consideration)* predominante, primordial; *(party)* gobernante, en el poder; **the r. classes** las clases dirigentes

rum [rʌm] *n (drink)* ron *m*

Rumania = Romania

Rumanian = Romanian

rumble ['rʌmbəl] **1** *n* (a) *(of thunder, gunfire)* rugido *m*, retumbo *m*; *(of cart)* fragor *m*, estrépito *m*; *(of stomach)* gruñido *m*; **rumbles of discontent** murmullos *mpl* de insatisfacción (b) *Fam (fight)* riña *f* callejera

2 *vi* (a) *(thunder)* retumbar; *(stomach)* gruñir; **to r. past** pasar rugiendo (b) *Fam (fight)* pelearse

rumbling ['rʌmblɪŋ] *n* **there were rumblings of discontent among the workers** los trabajadores comenzaban a mostrar su descontento

ruminant ['ruːmɪnənt] *n Zool* rumiante *m*

ruminate ['ruːmɪneɪt] *vi Formal* **to r. about** *or* **on sth** meditar acerca de algo

ruminative ['ruːmɪnətɪv] *adj* pensativo(a), meditabundo(a)

rummage ['rʌmɪdʒ] *vi* **he rummaged through my suitcase** rebuscó en *or* revolvió mi maleta *or Am* valija; **r. sale** *(in store)* liquidación *f* de saldos; *(for charity)* mercadillo *m* *or* rastrillo *m* benéfico

rumor ['ruːmə(r)] **1** *n* rumor *m*; **r. has it that...** según los rumores,...; **there's a r. going around that...** corren rumores de que...

2 *vt* **it is rumored that...** se rumorea que...; **he is rumored to be about to resign** se rumorea que está a punto de dimitir

rump [rʌmp] *n* (a) *(of animal)* cuartos *mpl* traseros; *Fam (of person)* trasero *m*; **r. steak** filete *m* de lomo (b) *(of political party, assembly)* resto *m (tras escisión)*

rumple ['rʌmpəl] *vt (crease)* arrugar; *(hair)* despeinar

rumpus ['rʌmpəs] *n Fam (noise)* jaleo *m*, bronca *f*, *Esp* follón *m*; **to kick up** *or* **cause a r.** armar un jaleo *or* una bronca *or Esp* un follón; **r. room** cuarto *m* de juegos

run [rʌn] **1** *n* (a) *(act of running)* carrera *f*; **at a r.** corriendo, *RP* a las corridas; **to go for a r.** ir a correr; **to be on the r.** *(prisoner, suspect)* estar fugado(a) *or* en fuga; *Fig* **we've got them on the r.** los tenemos contra las cuerdas; **to give sb the r. of the house** poner la casa a disposición de alguien; *Fam* **to make a r. for it** salir corriendo *or Esp* por piernas; *Fam* **to give sb a r. for his money** hacer sudar (la camiseta) a alguien; *Fam* **to have the runs** estar suelto(a), tener cagalera

(b) *(trip) (in car)* vuelta *f*; **to go for a r.** ir a dar una vuelta (en coche)

(c) *Com (of book)* tirada *f*; *(of product)* partida *f*, tanda *f*

(d) *(sequence, series)* serie *f*; *(in cards)* escalera *f*; **a r. of good/bad luck** una racha de buena/mala suerte; **in the long r.** a la larga, a largo plazo; **in the short r.** a corto plazo; **in the ordinary r. of things** en condiciones normales

(e) *Fin (on bank, stock exchange)* retirada *f* masiva de fondos; **a r. on the dollar** una fuerte presión sobre el dólar

(f) *(in baseball, cricket)* carrera *f*

(g) *(in stocking)* carrera *f*

(h) *(for skier)* pista *f*

(i) *(for chickens, rabbits)* corral *m*

(j) *Mus* carrerilla *f*

2 *vt (pt ran [ræn], pp run)* (a) *(distance)* correr, recorrer; **to r. a race** correr (en) una carrera; **to r. an errand** hacer un recado *or Am* mandado; **to allow things to r. their course** dejar que las cosas sigan su curso; **to r. sb close** quedarse a un paso de vencer a alguien; *Fam* **we were run off our feet** no tuvimos ni un momento de descanso

(b) *(drive)* **to r. sb to the airport** llevar a alguien al aeropuerto, dar *CAm, Méx* aventón *or Cuba* botella a alguien hasta el aeropuerto

(c) *(smuggle) (drugs, arms)* pasar de contrabando

(d) *(operate) (machine, engine)* hacer funcionar; *(test, experiment)* hacer, realizar, *Esp* efectuar; *Comptr (program)* ejecutar; **this car is expensive to r.** este coche consume mucho

(e) *(manage) (business, hotel)* dirigir, llevar; **stop trying to r. my life for me!** ¡deja de dirigir mi vida!; *Fig* **who's running the show?** ¿quién está a cargo de esto?

(f) *(pass) (cables, pipes)* hacer pasar; **to r. one's fingers over sth** pasar la mano por algo, *Esp* acariciar algo; **he ran his fingers through his hair** se pasó los dedos entre los cabellos; **she ran her eye over the page** echó una ojeada a la página

(g) *(water)* dejar correr; **to r. a bath** preparar un baño

(h) **to r. a temperature** tener fiebre; **to r. a deficit** tener déficit; **to r. an article** publicar un artículo

3 *vi* (a) *(person)* correr; **to r. up/down the street** subir/bajar la calle corriendo; **to r. around** *or* **about** correr de acá para allá; **I'll just r. across** *or* **around to the store** voy en un momento a la tienda; **to r. after sb** correr detrás *or Am* atrás de alguien; **to r. for help** correr en búsqueda *or Esp* busca de ayuda; **to r. out** *(exit)* salir corriendo; *Fig* **to r. out on sb** abandonar a alguien

(b) *(flee)* escapar corriendo; **r. for it!, r. for your lives!** ¡corre!, *Esp* ¡huye!, *Am* ¡sálvese quien pueda!

(c) *(compete in race)* correr; **to r. for Congress** presentarse a las elecciones al Congreso (**d**) *(flow)* correr; **the river runs into a lake** el río desemboca en un lago; **my nose is running** me moquea *or RP* chorrea la nariz, tengo mocos; **my blood ran cold** se me heló la sangre en las venas

(**e**) **to r. aground** *(ship)* encallar, embarrancar; *Fig (project, economy)* irse al traste, malograrse

(**f**) *(last, extend) (contract, lease)* durar; *(play)* estar en cartel; **it runs in the family** es cosa de familia; **a murmur ran through the crowd** se extendió un murmullo entre la multitud; **that song keeps running through my head** no se me va esa canción de la cabeza; **the total ran to $2,000** el total ascendió a 2.000 dólares

(**g**) *(bus, train)* circular; **to be running late** *(bus, person)* ir con retraso, *Am* estar atrasado(a) *or* demorado(a)

(**h**) *(operate) (machine)* funcionar (**on** con); **the engine's running** el motor está en marcha; **the software won't r. on this machine** el programa no funciona en *Esp* este ordenador *or Am* esta computadora; **things are running smoothly** las cosas marchan bien

(**i**) *(pass) (road, railway)* ir; **the line runs along the coast** la línea de tren discurre paralela a la costa

(**j**) **feelings** *or* **tempers are running high** los ánimos están revueltos; **supplies are running low** se están agotando las reservas; **the river had run dry** el río se había secado

(**k**) *(color, dye)* desteñir

▸**run away** *vi (person)* escapar, huir; **to r. away from home** escaparse de casa; *Fig* **to r. away from the facts** no querer ver los hechos; *Fig* **don't r. away with the idea that…** no vayas a pensar que…

▸**run down 1** *vt sep* (**a**) *(in car)* atropellar (**b**) *(find)* localizar, encontrar (**c**) *(criticize)* menospreciar, criticar (**d**) *(reduce) (production, stocks)* reducir, disminuir; *(industry, factory)* desmantelar

2 *vi (battery)* agotarse

▸**run in** *vt sep Fam (arrest)* detener

▸**run into** *vt insep* (**a**) *(collide with)* chocar con *or* contra; **to r. into difficulties** tropezar con problemas (**b**) *(meet by chance)* encontrarse con

▸**run off 1** *vt sep (print)* tirar

2 *vi* echar a correr, salir corriendo; **to r. off with the cash** escapar con el dinero; **to r. off with sb** escaparse con alguien

▸**run on** *vi (meeting)* continuar; *Fam (talk a lot)* hablar sin parar

▸**run out** *vi (lease, contract)* vencer, cumplirse; *(money, supplies)* agotarse; **to r. out of sth** quedarse sin algo; *Fig* **to r. out of steam** *(person)* quedarse sin fuerzas; *(project)* perder empuje

▸**run over 1** *vt sep (in car)* atropellar

2 *vt insep (rehearse, check)* ensayar, repasar

3 *vi (speech, TV program)* durar demasiado

▸**run up** *vt sep* (**a**) *(debts)* acumular (**b**) *(flag)* izar (**c**) *(clothes)* hacerse, coser

runaround ['rʌnəraʊnd] *n Fam* **to give sb the r.** enredar a alguien

runaway ['rʌnəweɪ] **1** *n* fugitivo(a) *m,f*

2 *adj (prisoner, slave)* fugitivo(a); *(train, truck)* incontrolado(a); *(inflation)* galopante; *(victory, success)* apabullante

rundown ['rʌndaʊn] *n (summary)* resumen *m*, informe *m*, *Am* reporte *m*; **to give sb a r.** poner a alguien al tanto

run-down [rʌn'daʊn] *adj (building)* ruinoso(a); *(person)* pachucho(a), débil

rung [rʌŋ] **1** *n (of ladder)* peldaño *m*, escalón *m*; *Fig* **the bottom r.** *(in organization)* el escalón más bajo

2 *pp of* **ring²**

run-in ['rʌnɪn] *n Fam* **to have a r. with sb** tener una pelea *or* una riña con alguien

runner ['rʌnə(r)] *n* (**a**) *(athlete)* corredor(ora) *m,f*; *(messenger)* mensajero(a) *m,f*, recadero(a) *m,f* (**b**) *(on sleigh)* patín *m* (**c**) *(carpet)* alfombra *f* estrecha (para escaleras)

runner-up [rʌnə'rʌp] *(pl* **runners-up)** *n* subcampeón(ona) *m,f*

running ['rʌnɪŋ] **1** *n* (**a**) *(competition, race)* **to be out of/in the r.** no tener/tener posibilidades de ganar; **to make all the r.** *(in contest)* ocupar el primer puesto desde el principio; *Pol* **r. mate** candidato(a) *m,f* a la vicepresidencia; **r. shoe** zapatilla *f* deportiva; **r. track** pista *f* (de atletismo) (**b**) *(operation) (of machine, car)* funcionamiento *m*; **r. costs** costos *mpl or Esp* costes *mpl* de mantenimiento (**c**) *(management) (of hotel, restaurant)* dirección *f*, gestión *f*

2 *adj (battle, feud)* continuo(a), constante; *Aut* **r. board** estribo *m*; **r. commentary** comentario *m* en directo; **r. sore** llaga *f* supurante; **r. total** total *m* actualizado; **r. water** agua *f* corriente

runny ['rʌnɪ] *adj (sauce, custard)* demasiado líquido(a); *(honey)* fluido(a); **to have a r. nose** tener mocos, moquear

runoff ['rʌnɒf] *n* desempate *m*

run-of-the-mill [rʌnəvðə'mɪl] *adj* corriente y moliente

run-on ['rʌnɒn] *n (in printed matter)* texto *m* seguido *or* corrido

runt [rʌnt] *n* (**a**) *(of litter)* cachorro *m* más pequeño (**b**) *(weak person)* enano(a) *m,f*, pigmeo(a) *m,f*

run-up ['rʌnʌp] *n (before jump)* carrerilla *f*

runway ['rʌnweɪ] *n* (**a**) *(for takeoff)* pista *f* de despegue *or Am* decolaje; *(for landing)* pista *f* de aterrizaje (**b**) *(at fashion show)* pasarela *f*

rupee [ruː'piː] *n (Indian currency)* rupia *f*

rupture ['rʌptʃə(r)] **1** *n (breaking)* ruptura *f*; *Med* hernia *f*

2 *vt (relations, container)* romper; *Med* **to r. oneself** herniarse

3 *vi (container, pipeline)* romperse

rural ['rʊərəl] *adj* rural

ruse [ruːz] *n* artimaña *f*, ardid *m*

rush¹ [rʌʃ] *n (plant)* **rushes** juncos *mpl*; **r. matting** estera *f* de junco

rush² **1** *n* (**a**) *(hurry)* prisa *f*, *Am* apuro *m*; **to be in a r.** tener prisa, *Am* estar apurado(a); **there's no r.** no hay prisa *or Am* apuro; **to make a r. for sth** apresurarse a alcanzar algo; **to make a r. at sb** abalanzarse hacia alguien; **the r. hour** *Esp* la hora *f* punta, *Am* la hora *f* pico; **a r. job** una chapuza (**b**) *(surge) (of air)* ráfaga *f*; *(of water)* chorro *m*; *(of requests)* ola *f* (**c**) *(demand)* demanda *f*; **there's been a r. on sugar** ha habido una fuerte demanda de azúcar (**d**) *Cin* **rushes** primeras pruebas *fpl*

2 *vt* (**a**) *(hurry) (task)* realizar a toda prisa; *(person)* apresurar; **don't r. me!** ¡no me metas prisa!, *Am* ¡no me apures!; **to r. sb into doing sth** meter prisa *or Am* apurar a alguien para que haga algo; **to be rushed off one's feet** no tener un momento de descanso (**b**) *(transport quickly)* llevar apresuradamente; **she was rushed to hospital** la llevaron al hospital a toda prisa (**c**) *(attack)* arremeter contra

3 *vi (move fast)* precipitarse; *(hurry)* apresurarse, *Am* apurarse; **I must r.** (me voy que) tengo mucha prisa *or Am* estoy muy apurado(a); **the blood rushed to his cheeks** se le subieron los colores; **she rushed into marriage** se casó demasiado apresuradamente

▸**rush around, rush about** *vi* trajinar (de acá para allá)

▸**rush in** *vi (enter)* entrar a toda prisa

▸**rush off** *vi (flee)* irse corriendo

▸**rush out 1** *vt sep (book)* sacar a toda prisa

2 *vi (exit)* salir apresuradamente

▸**rush through 1** *vt sep* **to r. a bill/decision through** aprobar un proyecto de ley/tomar una decisión a toda prisa

2 *vt insep (book, meal, work)* despachar con rapidez

rusk [rʌsk] *n* = galleta dura y crujiente para niños que comienzan a masticar

russet ['rʌsɪt] **1** *n (color)* castaño *m* rojizo

2 *adj* rojizo(a)

Russia ['rʌʃə] *n* Rusia

Russian ['rʌʃən] **1** *n* (**a**) *(person)* ruso(a) *m,f* (**b**) *(language)* ruso *m*; **R. class/teacher** clase *f*/profesor(ora) *m,f* de ruso
2 *adj* ruso(a); **R. roulette** ruleta *f* rusa

rust [rʌst] **1** *n* óxido *m*, herrumbre *f*
2 *adj (color)* color teja *inv*
3 *vi* oxidarse

rusted ['rʌstɪd] *adj* oxidado(a)

rustic ['rʌstɪk] *adj* rústico(a)

rustle¹ ['rʌsəl] **1** *n (of leaves)* susurro *m*; *(of paper)* crujido *m*
2 *vt (leaves)* hacer susurrar; *(paper)* hacer crujir
3 *vi (leaves)* susurrar; *(paper)* crujir

rustle² *vt (cattle)* robar

▶**rustle up** *vt sep Fam (meal, snack)* improvisar, *Esp* apañar; **to r. up support** reunir apoyo

rustler ['rʌslə(r)] *n (cattle thief)* cuatrero(a) *m,f*, ladrón(ona) *m,f* de ganado

rustproof ['rʌstpruːf] *adj* inoxidable

rusty ['rʌstɪ] *adj* (**a**) *(metal)* oxidado(a); *Fig* **my French is a bit r.** hace mucho que no practico mi francés (**b**) *(color)* color teja *inv*

rut¹ [rʌt] *n (groove)* rodada *f*; *Fig* **to be in a r.** *(routine)* estar apalancado(a) *or* estancado(a)

rut² **1** *n (of stag)* celo *m*
2 *vi (pt & pp* **rutted)** *(stag)* estar en celo

rutabaga [ruːtəˈbeɪgə] *n* colinabo *m*

ruthless ['ruːθlɪs] *adj* despiadado(a); **with r. efficiency** con rigurosa eficacia

rutted ['rʌtɪd] *adj* **a badly r. road** una carretera llena de grandes surcos *or* rodadas

RV [ɑːˈviː] *n (abbr* **recreational vehicle**) autocaravana *f*, casa *f or* coche *m* caravana

Rwanda [rəˈwændə] *n* Ruanda

Rwandan [rəˈwændən] *n & adj* ruandés(esa) *m,f*

rye [raɪ] *n* centeno *m*; **r. (bread)** pan *m* de centeno; **r. (whisky)** whisky *m* de centeno

S

S, s [es] n (a) (letter) S, s f (b) (abbr **south**) S

Sabbath ['sæbəθ] n (Jewish) Sabbat m, sábado m judío; (Christian) domingo m; (witches') **S.** aquelarre m; **S. day observance** cumplimiento m del descanso sabático/dominical

sabbatical [sə'bætɪkəl] Univ **1** n **to be on s.** estar en excedencia
 2 adj **s. year/term** año m/trimestre m sabático or de excedencia

saber ['seɪbə(r)] n sable m

saber-toothed tiger n ['seɪbətu:θt'taɪgə(r)] tigre m dientes de sable

sable ['seɪbəl] **1** n (animal) marta f cebellina; **s. coat** abrigo m de marta
 2 adj Literary (black) prieto(a), negro(a)

sabotage ['sæbətɑːʒ] **1** n sabotaje m
 2 vt sabotear

saboteur [sæbə'tɜː(r)] n saboteador(ora) m,f

sac [sæk] n Biol bolsa f, saco m

saccharin ['sækərɪn] n sacarina f

saccharine ['sækərɪn] adj Pej (smile, movie) empalagoso(a)

sachet ['sæʃeɪ] n sobrecito m

sack¹ [sæk] **1** n (a) (bag) saco m; Fam **to hit the s.** (go to bed) meterse en el sobre, Esp irse a la piltra (b) Fam (dismissal) **to give sb the s.** echar a alguien; **he got the s.** lo echaron
 2 vt Fam (dismiss from job) echar, despedir

sack² **1** n (plundering) saqueo m
 2 vt (town) saquear

sacking ['sækɪŋ] n (a) (textile) arpillera f, tela f de saco (b) Fam (dismissal) despido m

sacrament ['sækrəmənt] n Rel sacramento m; **to take** or **receive the sacraments** tomar or recibir los sacramentos

sacred ['seɪkrɪd] adj (place, book) sagrado(a); (duty, vow) solemne; **s. to the memory of...** consagrado(a) a la memoria de...; **is nothing s.?** ¿es que ya no se respeta nada?; Fig **to be a s. cow** ser sacrosanto(a)

sacrifice ['sækrɪfaɪs] **1** n (act, offering) sacrificio m; **to make sacrifices** sacrificarse, hacer sacrificios
 2 vt sacrificar; **to s. oneself** sacrificarse

sacrificial [sækrɪ'fɪʃəl] adj de sacrificio; Fig **s. lamb** or **victim** chivo m expiatorio

sacrilege ['sækrɪlɪdʒ] n also Fig sacrilegio m

sacrilegious [sækrɪ'lɪdʒəs] adj also Fig sacrílego(a)

sacristan ['sækrɪstən] n Rel sacristán m

sacrosanct ['sækrəʊsæŋkt] adj sacrosanto(a)

SAD [sæd] n Med (abbr **Seasonal Affective Disorder**) trastorno m afectivo estacional

sad [sæd] adj (a) (unhappy, depressing) triste; **to become s.** entristecerse; **to make sb s.** entristecer a alguien (b) Fam (pathetic) lamentable, penoso(a)

sadden ['sædən] vt entristecer

saddle ['sædəl] **1** n (on horse) silla f (de montar); (on bicycle) sillín m; **in the s.** a caballo; Fig **to be in the s.** (be in charge) llevar las riendas
 2 vt (horse) ensillar; Fam Fig **to s. sb with sth** encajar or Esp, Méx encasquetar algo a alguien

saddlebag ['sædəlbæg] n (for horse) alforja f; (for bicycle) cartera f

sadism ['seɪdɪzəm] n sadismo m

sadist ['seɪdɪst] n sádico(a) m,f

sadistic [sə'dɪstɪk] adj sádico(a)

sadly ['sædlɪ] adv (to reply, smile) tristemente; **you're s. mistaken** estás muy equivocado(a); **he is s. missed** lo echamos mucho de menos, Am lo extrañamos mucho; **s., this is so** así es, por desgracia

sadness ['sædnɪs] n tristeza f

sadomasochism [seɪdəʊ'mæsəkɪzəm] n sadomasoquismo m

sadomasochist [seɪdəʊ'mæsəkɪst] n sadomasoquista mf

sadomasochistic ['seɪdəʊmæsə'kɪstɪk] adj sadomasoquista

safari [sə'fɑːrɪ] n safari m; **on s.** de safari; **s. jacket** sahariana f; **s. park** safari park m

safe [seɪf] **1** n (for money) caja f fuerte
 2 adj (house, activity) seguro(a); (choice, topic of conversation) prudente; **s. from sth** a salvo de algo; **s. and sound** sano(a) y salvo(a); **it is s. to say that...** se puede decir sin temor a equivocarse que...; **it's a pretty s. assumption** or **bet that...** es prácticamente seguro que...; **at a s. distance** a una distancia prudencial; **to wish sb a s. journey** desear a alguien un feliz viaje or un viaje sin percances; **to be on the s. side** para mayor seguridad; Prov **better s. than sorry** más vale prevenir (que curar); **s. driver discount** descuento m por no siniestralidad; **s. house** piso m franco; **s. seat** (in politics) escaño m seguro; **s. sex** sexo m seguro or sin riesgo
 3 adv **to play (it) s.** ser precavido(a)

safe-conduct [seɪf'kɒndʌkt] n salvoconducto m

safeguard ['seɪfgɑːd] **1** n salvaguardia f, garantía f
 2 vt (sb's interests, rights) salvaguardar
 3 vi **to s. against sth** salvaguardarse or protegerse de algo

safekeeping [seɪf'kiːpɪŋ] n **in s.** bajo custodia

safely ['seɪflɪ] adv (a) (without risk) sin riesgos; **once we're s. home** cuando estemos tranquilos en casa; **drive s.!** ¡conduce or Am maneja con cuidado!; **to arrive s.** llegar sano(a) y salvo(a) (b) (with certainty) con certeza; **I can s. say that...** puedo decir sin temor a equivocarme que...

safety ['seɪftɪ] n seguridad f; (on gun) seguro m; (football player) safety m; **for s.'s sake** para mayor seguridad; **she's very s. conscious** tiene muy en cuenta la seguridad; Prov **there's s. in numbers** en compañía está uno más seguro; **s. belt** cinturón m de seguridad; **s. glass** vidrio m de seguridad; **s. matches** fósforos mpl or Esp cerillas fpl or Am cerillos mpl de seguridad; **s. measures** medidas fpl de seguridad; **s. net** red f (de seguridad); Fig red f asistencial (del Estado); Fig **to fall**

through the s. net quedar excluido(a) de la red asistencial; **s. pin** imperdible m, Am alfiler m de gancho, CAm, Méx seguro m; also Fig **s. valve** válvula f de escape

saffron ['sæfrən] **1** n azafrán m
2 adj (de color) azafrán

sag [sæg] (pt & pp **sagged**) vi (roof, bridge) hundirse, ceder; (flesh, rope) colgar; (confidence, support) decaer

saga ['sɑːgə] n (story) saga f; Fig **a s. of corruption** una historia interminable de corrupción

sagacious [sə'geɪʃəs] adj Formal sagaz

sagacity [sə'gæsɪtɪ] n Formal sagacidad f

sage¹ [seɪdʒ] **1** n (wise man) sabio m
2 adj (person, conduct) sabio(a)

sage² n (herb) salvia f

saggy ['sægɪ] adj (mattress) hundido(a); (bottom) flácido(a), fofo(a); (breasts) caído(a)

Sagittarius [sædʒɪ'teərɪəs] n (sign of zodiac) Sagitario m; **to be (a) S.** ser Sagitario

Sahara [sə'hɑːrə] n **the S. (Desert)** el (desierto del) Sahara

said [sed] pt & pp of **say**

sail [seɪl] **1** n (on boat) vela f; (of windmill) aspa f; **to set s. (for)** zarpar (con rumbo a); **to go for a s.** hacer una excursión en velero
2 vt (a) (boat) gobernar (b) (ocean) navegar por
3 vi (ship, person) navegar; (start voyage) zarpar; **the clouds sailed by** las nubes avanzaban suavemente; **his book sailed out of the window** su libro salió volando por la ventana; Fam **to s. through an examination** pasar un examen con mucha facilidad or Esp con la gorra or RP de taquito

sailboarder ['seɪlbɔːdə(r)] n windsurfista mf

sailboarding ['seɪlbɔːdɪŋ] n windsurf m

sailing ['seɪlɪŋ] n (activity) (navegación f a) vela f; (departure) salida f; **s. ship** barco m de vela

sailor ['seɪlə(r)] n marinero m; **to be a bad s.** no soportar bien los viajes por mar; **s. suit** traje m de marinero

saint [seɪnt] n santo(a) m,f; **All Saints' (Day)** día m de Todos los Santos; **S. Bernard** (dog) San Bernardo m; **s.'s day** onomástica f, santo m

sainthood ['seɪnthʊd] n santidad f

saintly ['seɪntlɪ] adj santo(a)

sake [seɪk] n **for the s. of sb, for sb's s.** por (el bien de) alguien; **for God's** or **goodness'** or **heaven's s.** por (el amor de) Dios; **for the s. of peace** para que haya paz; **for old times' s.** por los viejos tiempos; **this is talking for talking's s.** es hablar por hablar; **for the s. of argument...** como hipótesis...

salable, saleable ['seɪləbəl] adj vendible

salacious [sə'leɪʃəs] adj salaz

salad ['sæləd] n ensalada f; **s. bar** (restaurant) bar m de ensaladas; (area) mostrador m de ensaladas; **s. bowl** ensaladera f; Fig **s. days** tiempos mpl mozos; **s. dressing** aderezo m or Esp aliño m para la ensalada

salamander ['sæləmændə(r)] n salamandra f

salami [sə'lɑːmɪ] n salami m, Am salame m

salaried ['sælərɪd] adj asalariado(a)

salary ['sælərɪ] n salario m, sueldo m; **s. earner** asalariado(a) m,f; **s. grade** nivel m or grado m salarial; **s. scale** escala f salarial

sale [seɪl] n (a) (action of selling) venta f; **for s.** (available) en venta; (sign) se vende; **to put sth up for s.** poner algo en venta; **on s.** a la venta; **sales department** departamento m de ventas; **sales drive** promoción f de ventas; **sales force** personal m de ventas; **sales manager** jefe(a) m,f de ventas; **sales pitch** estrategia f de ventas; **s. slip** recibo m; **sales tax** impuesto m de venta
(b) (turnover) **sales** ventas fpl; **sales figures** cifra f de ventas; **sales forecast** previsión f de ventas; **sales target** objetivo m de ventas

(c) (auction) subasta f; **book s.** mercadillo m de libros
(d) (with reduced prices) rebajas fpl; **the sales** las rebajas; **s. price** precio m rebajado; **there's a s. on at Woolworths** están de rebajas en Woolworths

saleable = **salable**

salesclerk ['seɪlzklɜːk] n dependiente(a) m,f, vendedor(ora) m,f

salesgirl ['seɪlzɡɜːl] n dependienta f

salesman ['seɪlzmən] n (for company) comercial m, vendedor m; (in store) dependiente m, vendedor m

salesmanship ['seɪlzmənʃɪp] n habilidad f para vender

salesperson ['seɪlzpɜːsən] n (for company) comercial mf, vendedor(ora) m,f; (in store) dependiente(a) m,f, vendedor(ora) m,f

salesroom ['seɪlzruːm] n (for auctions) sala f de subastas

saleswoman ['seɪlzwʊmən] n (for company) comercial f, vendedora f; (in store) dependienta f, vendedora f

salient ['seɪlɪənt] adj (feature, fault) relevante, sobresaliente; **s. points** puntos mpl más sobresalientes

saline ['seɪlaɪn] adj salino(a); Med **s. drip** gota a gota m de suero (fisiológico); **s. solution** solución f salina

saliva [sə'laɪvə] n saliva f

salivate ['sælɪveɪt] vi salivar, segregar saliva; Fig **he was salivating** se le hacía la boca agua

sallow ['sæləʊ] adj (complexion) amarillento(a), demacrado(a)

▸**sally forth** ['sælɪ] vi Literary partir con determinación

salmon ['sæmən] (pl **salmon**) n salmón m; **s. (pink)** color m salmón; **s. trout** trucha f asalmonada

salmonella [sælmə'nelə] n (bacteria) salmonella f; (illness) salmonelosis f inv

salon ['sælɒn] n (beauty) **s.** salón m de belleza; **(hair-dressing) s.** (salón m de) peluquería f

saloon [sə'luːn] n (room) sala f, salón m; (bar) bar m

salt [sɔːlt] **1** n (a) (substance) sal f; **(bath) salts** sales fpl de baño; **s. mine** mina f de sal, salina f (b) Fam (sailor) **an old s.** un lobo de mar (c) (idioms) **to take a story with a pinch** or **grain of s.** no creerse del todo una historia; **no journalist worth his s....** ningún periodista que se precie...; **to rub s. in sb's wounds** removerle la herida a alguien; **the s. of the earth** la sal de la tierra
2 adj **s. cod** bacalao m (salado); **s. water** agua f salada
3 vt (food) salar; (roads) esparcir sal en

▸**salt away** vt sep (money) ahorrar or guardar en secreto

saltcellar ['sɔːltselə(r)] n salero m

salt-free ['sɔːltfriː] adj sin sal

saltpeter [sɒlt'piːtə(r)] n salitre m

saltshaker ['sɔːltʃeɪkə(r)] n salero m

saltwater ['sɔːltwɔːtə(r)] adj **s. lake** lago m de agua salada; **s. fish** pez m de agua salada

salty ['sɔːltɪ] adj salado(a)

salubrious [sə'luːbrɪəs] adj Formal (hygienic) salubre; (respectable) acomodado(a), respetable

salutary ['sæljʊtərɪ] adj saludable; **to have a s. effect on sb** tener un efecto saludable sobre alguien

salute [sə'luːt] **1** n saludo m; **a ten-gun s.** una salva de diez cañonazos; **to take the s.** pasar revista a las tropas (en desfile)
2 vt saludar; Fig **to s. sb's achievements** rendir homenaje a los logros de alguien
3 vi saludar

salvage ['sælvɪdʒ] **1** n (a) (of ship) rescate m, salvamento m; (of waste material) recuperación f; **s. vessel** buque m de salvamento (b) (objects salvaged) material m rescatado
2 vt also Fig salvar, rescatar

salvation [sæl'veɪʃən] n salvación f; **S. Army** Ejército m de Salvación

salve [sælv] vt **to s. one's conscience** descargar la conciencia

salver ['sælvə(r)] n (tray) bandeja f, fuente f

salvo ['sælvəʊ] (*pl* **salvos** *or* **salvoes**) *n also Fig* salva *f*
Samaritan [sə'mærɪtən] *n* **the Good S.** el Buen Samaritano; **the Samaritans** los Samaritanos, *Esp* ≃ el Teléfono de la Esperanza
same [seɪm] **1** *adj* **the s. man** el mismo hombre; **the s. woman** la misma mujer; **the s. children** los mismos niños; **the s. one** el (la) mismo(a); **the house isn't the s. without her** la casa no es la misma sin ella; **in the s. way** del mismo modo, de igual forma; **to go the s. way** ir por el mismo camino; **the** *or* **that very s. day** el *or* ese mismo día; **it all amounts** *or* **comes to the s. thing** todo viene a ser lo mismo; **at the s. time** *(simultaneously)* al mismo tiempo; *(nevertheless)* sin embargo
    2 *pron* **the s.** lo mismo; **it's the s. everywhere** es igual en todas partes; **if it's all the s. to you** si no te importa; *Fam* **(the) s. again?** *(in bar)* ¿(otra de) lo mismo?; *Fam* **s. here!** *(I agree)* estoy de acuerdo; *(I did the same thing)* yo también; **(the) s. to you!** ¡igualmente!; **I would have done the s.** yo hubiera hecho lo mismo
    3 *adv* **to think/taste the s.** pensar/saber igual; **all the s.** *(nevertheless)* de todas maneras
same-day ['seɪmdeɪ] *adj Com* **s. delivery** entrega *f* en el día
sameness ['seɪmnɪs] *n* uniformidad *f*
Samoa [sə'məʊə] *n* Samoa
Samoan [sə'məʊən] **1** *n* (**a**) *(person)* samoano(a) *m,f* (**b**) *(language)* samoano *m*
    2 *adj* samoano(a)
sample ['sɑ:mpəl] **1** *n* muestra *f*; *Med* **to take a s.** tomar una muestra
    2 *vt* (**a**) *(public opinion)* sondear; *(food, experience)* probar (**b**) *Mus* samplear
sampling ['sɑ:mplɪŋ] *n Mus* sampleado *m*
sanatarium [sænə'teərɪəm], **sanitarium** [sænɪ'teərɪəm] (*pl* **sanatoriums** *or* **sanatoria** [sænə'tɔ:rɪə], **sanitariums** *or* **sanitaria** [sænɪ'teərɪə]) *n* sanatorio *m*
sanctify ['sæŋ(k)tɪfaɪ] *vt* santificar
sanctimonious [sæŋ(k)tɪ'məʊnɪəs] *adj* mojigato(a)
sanction ['sæŋ(k)ʃən] **1** *n* (**a**) *(penalty)* sanción *f*; **(economic) sanctions** sanciones *fpl* económicas (**b**) *Formal (consent)* sanción *f*
    2 *vt Formal (authorize)* sancionar, autorizar
sanctity ['sæŋ(k)tɪtɪ] *n* *(of life)* carácter *m* sagrado; *(of home)* santidad *f*
sanctuary ['sæŋ(k)tj(ʊ)ərɪ] *n Rel* santuario *m*; *(for fugitive, refugee)* asilo *m*, refugio *m*; *(for birds, wildlife)* santuario *m*; **to seek s.** buscar refugio
sand [sænd] **1** *n* arena *f*; **s. castle** castillo *m* de arena; **s. dune** duna *f*
    2 *vt* (**a**) *(smooth with sandpaper)* lijar (**b**) *(cover with sand)* enarenar
sandal ['sændəl] *n* sandalia *f*, *Andes, CAm* ojota *f*, *Méx* guarache *m*
sandbag ['sændbæg] *n* saco *m* terrero *or m* de arena, *RP* bolsa *f* de arena
sandbank ['sændbæŋk] *n* banco *m* de arena
sandblast ['sændblɑ:st] *vt* limpiar con chorro de arena
sandbox ['sændbɒks] *n* recinto *m* de arena
sander ['sændə(r)] *n* acuchillador(ora) *m,f* de suelos
sandpaper ['sændpeɪpə(r)] **1** *n* (papel *m* de) lija *f*
    2 *vt* lijar
sandstone ['sændstəʊn] *n* arenisca *f*
sandstorm ['sændstɔ:m] *n* tormenta *f* de arena
sandwich ['sændwɪtʃ] **1** *n* *(with sliced bread)* sándwich *m*; *(with French bread) Esp* bocadillo *m*, *Am* sándwich *m*, *CSur* sándwiche *m*, *Col* sánduche *m*, *Méx* torta *f*; **s. filling** relleno *m*
    2 *vt* intercalar; **to be sandwiched (between)** estar encajonado(a) (entre)

sandy ['sændɪ] *adj* (**a**) *(earth, beach)* arenoso(a) (**b**) *(hair)* rubio(a) rojizo(a)
sane [seɪn] *adj (not mad)* cuerdo(a); *(sensible)* juicioso(a), sensato(a)
sanely ['seɪnlɪ] *adv (sensibly)* sensatamente
San Franciscan ['sænfrən'sɪskən] **1** *n* persona de San Francisco
    2 *adj* de San Francisco
San Francisco ['sænfrən'sɪskəʊ] *n* San Francisco
sang [sæŋ] *pt of* **sing**
sangfroid ['sɒŋ'frwɑ:] *n* sangre *f* fría
sanguine ['sæŋgwɪn] *adj Formal (optimistic)* optimista
sanitarium = **sanatorium**
sanitary ['sænɪtərɪ] *adj (clean)* higiénico(a); *(relating to hygiene)* sanitario(a); **s. inspector** inspector(ora) *m,f* de sanidad; **s. napkin** compresa *f*, *Am* toalla *f* higiénica
sanitation [sænɪ'teɪʃən] *n* saneamiento *m*, instalaciones *fpl* sanitarias; **s. worker** recolector(ora) *m,f* de residuos, basurero *m,f*
sanitize ['sænɪtaɪz] *vt (document, biography)* mutilar, meter la tijera a; **a sanitized account of events** un relato de los hechos demasiado aséptico
sanity ['sænɪtɪ] *n* cordura *f*
sank [sæŋk] *pt of* **sink**
San Marino [sænmə'ri:nəʊ] *n* San Marino
Santa (Claus) ['sæntɪ('klɔ:z)] *n* Papá *m* Noel
Santiago [sæntɪ'ɑ:geʊ] *n* Santiago de Chile
São Tomé and Principe ['saʊtə'meɪən'prɪnsɪpeɪ] *n* Santo Tomé y Príncipe
sap¹ [sæp] *n (of plant)* savia *f*
sap² *n Fam (gullible person)* papanatas *mf inv*, *Esp* pardillo(a) *m,f*
sap³ (*pt & pp* **sapped**) *vt (undermine) & Fig* minar, debilitar
saphead ['sæphed] *n Fam* bobo(a) *m,f*, *Esp* memo(a) *m,f*
sapling ['sæplɪŋ] *n* pimpollo *m*, árbol *m* joven
sapper ['sæpə(r)] *n Mil* zapador *m*
sapphire ['sæfaɪə(r)] *n (precious stone)* zafiro *m*; *(color)* azul *m* zafiro
Saragossa [særə'gɒsə] *n* Zaragoza
Sarajevo [særə'jeɪvəʊ] *n* Sarajevo
Saran wrap® [sə'ræn'ræp] *n* plástico *m* transparente *(para envolver alimentos)*
sarcasm ['sɑ:kæzəm] *n* sarcasmo *m*
sarcastic [sɑ:'kæstɪk] *adj* sarcástico(a)
sarcastically [sɑ:'kæstɪklɪ] *adv* sarcásticamente
sarcophagus [sɑ:'kɒfəgəs] (*pl* **sarcophaguses** *or* **sarcophagi** [sɑ:'kɒfəgaɪ]) *n* sarcófago *m*
sardine [sɑ:'di:n] *n* sardina *f*; **packed in like sardines** como sardinas en lata
Sardinia [sɑ:'dɪnɪə] *n* Cerdeña
Sardinian [sɑ:'dɪnɪən] *n & adj* sardo(a) *m,f*
sardonic [sɑ:'dɒnɪk] *adj* sardónico(a)
sardonically [sɑ:'dɒnɪklɪ] *adv* sardónicamente
sari ['sɑ:rɪ] *n* sari *m*
sartorial [sɑ:'tɔ:rɪəl] *adj Formal* del vestir; **s. elegance** elegancia *f* en el vestir
SASE [eseɪes'i:] *n (abbr* **self-addressed stamped envelope***)* sobre *m* franqueado con la dirección del remitente
sash [sæʃ] *n (on dress)* faja *f*, fajín *m*; **s. cord** cordón *m* (de las ventanas de guillotina); **s. window** ventana *f* de guillotina
sass [sæs] *Fam* **1** *n* frescura *f*, impertinencia *f*
    2 *vt* **don't you. s. me!** ¡a ver cómo me hablas!
sassy ['sæsɪ] *adj* (**a**) *(cheeky)* fresco(a), impertinente (**b**) *(in style)* que da la nota, muy llamativo(a)
SAT [sæt] *(abbr* **scholastic aptitude test***)* = examen que realizan al final de la enseñanza secundaria los alumnos que quieren ir a la universidad

Sat (*abbr* **Saturday**) sábado *m*

sat [sæt] *pt & pp of* **sit**

Satan ['seɪtən] *n* Satanás *m*, Satán *m*

satanic [sə'tænɪk] *adj* satánico(a)

Satanism ['seɪtənɪzəm] *n* satanismo *m*

Satanist ['seɪtənɪst] *n* practicante *mf* del satanismo

satchel ['sætʃəl] *n* cartera *f* (de colegial)

sate [seɪt] *vt Formal* saciar

satellite ['sætəlaɪt] *n* satélite *m*; **s. dish** (antena *f*) parabólica *f*; **s. (state)** estado *m* satélite; **s. television** televisión *f* vía satélite; **s. (city)** ciudad *f* satélite

satiate ['seɪʃɪeɪt] *vt Formal* saciar

satin ['sætɪn] *n* (*cloth*) satén *m*, raso *m*; **s. finish** (*of paper, paint*) (acabado *m*) satinado *m*

satire ['sætaɪə(r)] *n* sátira *f*

satirical [sə'tɪrɪkəl] *adj* satírico(a)

satirically [sə'tɪrɪklɪ] *adv* satíricamente

satirist ['sætɪrɪst] *n* escritor(ora) *m,f* de sátiras

satirize ['sætɪraɪz] *vt* satirizar

satisfaction [sætɪs'fækʃən] *n* satisfacción *f*; **it gives me great s. to know that...** me satisface enormemente saber que...

satisfactorily [sætɪs'fæktrɪlɪ] *adv* satisfactoriamente

satisfactory [sætɪs'fæktərɪ] *adj* (*result, standard, condition*) satisfactorio(a); *Sch* **I got "s." for my work** saqué un aprobado en el trabajo

satisfied ['sætɪsfaɪd] *adj* satisfecho(a); **to be s.** estar satisfecho; **I am s. that he is telling the truth** ahora estoy convencido de que dice la verdad

satisfy ['sætɪsfaɪ] *vt* (*person, curiosity*) satisfacer; (*condition*) satisfacer, cumplir; **to s. the examiners** aprobar el examen

saturate ['sætʃəreɪt] *vt* (*soak*) empapar (**with** de *or* en); *Fig* saturar (**with** de); **to s. the market** saturar el mercado; **saturated fats** grasas *fpl* saturadas

saturation [sætʃə'reɪʃən] *n* (*soaking*) empapamiento *m*; *Fig* saturación *f*; *Mil* **s. bombing** bombardeo *m* intensivo; **to reach s. point** llegar al punto de saturación

Saturday ['sætədɪ] *n* sábado *m*; **this S.** este sábado; **on S.** el sábado; **on S. morning/night** el sábado por la mañana/por la noche; **on S. afternoon/evening** el sábado por la tarde/noche; **on Saturdays** los sábados; **every S.** todos los sábados; **every other S.** cada dos sábados, un sábado sí y otro no; **last S.** el sábado pasado; **the S. before last** hace dos sábados; **next S.** el sábado que viene; **the S. after next, a week on S.** dentro de dos sábados, del sábado en ocho días; **the following S.** el sábado siguiente; **S.'s paper** el periódico del sábado; **the S. movie** la película del sábado; *Fam* **S. night special** (*gun*) pistola *f* barata

Saturn ['sætɜːn] *n* (*planet, god*) Saturno *m*

sauce [sɔːs] *n* (a) (*for food*) salsa *f*; **tomato/cheese s.** salsa de tomate *or Méx* jitomate/de queso; **s. boat** salsera *f* (b) *Fam* (*alcohol*) bebida *f*, *Esp* priva *f*, *Méx* chupe *m*, *RP* chupi *m*

saucepan ['sɔːspən] *n* cazo *m*

saucer ['sɔːsə(r)] *n* platillo *m*

saucy ['sɔːsɪ] *adj Fam* (*impertinent*) descarado(a); (*risqué*) picante, subido(a) de tono

Saudi ['saʊdɪ] **1** *n* (*person*) saudí *mf*; *Fam* (*country*) Arabia Saudí
2 *adj* saudí

Saudi Arabia ['saʊdɪə'reɪbɪə] *n* Arabia Saudí

Saudi Arabian ['saʊdɪə'reɪbɪən] *n & adj* saudí *mf*

sauna ['sɔːnə] *n* sauna *f*, *Am* sauna *m or f*

saunter ['sɔːntə(r)] **1** *n* paseo *m* (con aire desenfadado)
2 *vi* **to s. (along)** pasear (con aire desenfadado)

sausage ['sɒsɪdʒ] *n* salchicha *f*; (*cured*) ≃ salchichón *m*, ≃ chorizo *m*; *Fam* **s. dog** perro *m* salchicha; **s. meat** carne *f* de embutido

sauté, saute ['səʊteɪ] *Culin* **1** *adj* salteado(a)
2 *vt* saltear

savage ['sævɪdʒ] **1** *n Old-fashioned* salvaje *mf*
2 *adj* (*animal, person*) salvaje; (*attack*) salvaje, feroz; (*criticism*) virulento(a)
3 *vt* (*attack physically*) atacar salvajemente; *Fig* (*criticize*) criticar con saña *or* virulencia

savagely ['sævɪdʒlɪ] *adv* (*beat, attack*) salvajemente; (*criticize*) con virulencia

savanna(h) [sə'vænə] *n* sabana *f*

save¹ [seɪv] *prep Formal* (*except*) salvo, a excepción de

save² **1** *vt* (a) (*rescue*) (*person, animal*) salvar; **to s. sb's life** salvarle la vida a alguien; *Fam* **she can't sing to s. her life** no tiene ni idea de cantar; *Fam* **to s. one's (own) neck** *or* **skin** salvar el pellejo; **to s. sb from falling** evitar que alguien se caiga; **to s. a shot** parar un disparo; **to s. the situation** salvar la situación; **to s. one's soul** salvar el alma; **God s. the King/the Queen!** ¡Dios salve al Rey/a la Reina!
(b) (*keep for future*) guardar; (*money*) ahorrar; *Comptr* guardar, salvar; (*on screen*) archivar, guardar; **to s. oneself for sth** reservarse para algo; **I am saving my strength** estoy ahorrando fuerzas
(c) (*not waste*) (*time, money, space*) ahorrar; **this will s. us having to do it again** esto nos evitará *or* ahorrará tener que hacerlo de nuevo; **s. your breath** no te esfuerces, ahórrate las palabras; **I saved $10 by buying it there** me ahorré 10 dólares por comprarlo ahí
2 *vi* **to s. for sth** ahorrar para algo; **s. on heating costs by insulating your house** aísle su casa y ahorre en calefacción
3 *n* (*goalkeeper*) parada *f*; **to make a s.** hacer una parada

▸**save up** *vt sep* ahorrar (**for** para)

saver ['seɪvə(r)] *n Fin* ahorrador(ora) *m,f*, *RP* ahorrista *mf*

-saver [-'seɪvə] *suffix* **it's a real money-s.** sale bastante más barato

saving ['seɪvɪŋ] **1** *n* (a) (*economy*) ahorro *m*; **to make savings** ahorrar, economizar (b) *Fin* **savings** ahorros *mpl*; **she lived off her savings** vivía de sus ahorros; **savings account** cuenta *f* de ahorros; **savings bank** caja *f* de ahorros; **savings bond** bono *m* de ahorro; **savings and loan association** ≃ caja *f* de ahorros
2 *adj* **her s. grace** lo único que le salva

savior ['seɪvjə(r)] *n* salvador(ora) *m,f*; *Rel* **the S.** el Salvador

savor ['seɪvə(r)] **1** *n* (*interest, enjoyment*) sabor *m*
2 *vt* saborear
3 *vi* **s. of** oler a

savory ['seɪvərɪ] *adj* (a) (*food*) (*appetizing*) sabroso(a); (*not sweet*) salado(a) (b) (*conduct*) **not very s.** no muy edificante

savoy [sə'vɔɪ] *n* **s. (cabbage)** col *f* rizada *or* de Milán, *CSur* repollo *m* rizado *or* de Milán

saw¹ [sɔː] **1** *n* (*tool*) sierra *f*
2 *vt* (*pp* **sawed** *or* **sawn** [sɔːn]) serrar

▸**saw off** *vt sep* serrar, cortar (con sierra)

▸**saw up** *vt sep* serrar en trozos

saw² *pt of* **see**

sawdust ['sɔːdʌst] *n* serrín *m*

sawed-off ['sɔːdɒf] *adj* **s. shotgun** escopeta *f* de cañones recortados, recortada *f*

sawmill ['sɔːmɪl] *n* aserradero *m*, serrería *f*

sawn [sɔːn] *pp of* **saw¹**

sax [sæks] *n Fam* (*saxophone*) saxo *m*

Saxon ['sæksən] **1** *n* (a) (*person*) sajón(ona) *m,f* (b) (*language*) sajón *m*
2 *adj* sajón(ona)

Saxony ['sæksənɪ] *n* Sajonia

saxophone ['sæksəfəʊn] *n* saxofón *m*; **s. player** saxofonista *mf*

saxophonist [sæk'sɒfənɪst] *n* saxofonista *mf*

say [seɪ] **1** *n* he wasn't allowed to have his s. no le dejaron expresar su opinión; **I had no s. in the matter** no tuve ni voz ni voto en el asunto

2 *vt* (*pt & pp* **said** [sed]) decir; **to s. sth to sb** decir algo a alguien; **to s. sth again** repetir algo; **to s. mass** decir misa; **to s. a prayer** rezar una oración; **it says…** (*text, sign*) dice…, pone…; **my watch says four o'clock** en mi reloj pone las cuatro en punto; **"good morning," she said** "buenos días" dijo; **he said that you were here** dijo que estabas aquí; **to s. hello (to sb)** saludar (a alguien); **to s. goodbye (to sb)** despedirse (de alguien); **to s. yes to an offer/a proposal** aceptar una oferta/una propuesta; **to s. no to an offer/a proposal** rechazar una oferta/una propuesta; **I wouldn't s. no to a cup of coffee** me tomaría un café; **he didn't s. a word** no dijo nada; **it's (not) for him to s.** (no) le corresponde a él decidir; **there's no saying what might happen if…** es imposible decir lo que ocurriría si…; **what have you got to s. for yourself?** ¿qué tienes que decir a tu favor?; **there's a lot to be said for…** hay mucho que decir a favor de…; **you're honest, I'll s. that for you** eres honrado, eso sí *or* eso hay que reconocerlo; **it says a lot about her that…** dice mucho de ella que…; **don't s. you've forgotten already!** ¡no me digas que ya te has olvidado!; **you can s. that again!** ¡y que lo digas!; **need I s. more?** está claro ¿no?; **they s. that…, it is said that…** dicen que…, se dice que…; **it is difficult to s. (when/where/which…)** es difícil decir (cuándo/dónde/cuál…); **if I had, s., $100,000** si yo tuviera, digamos, 100.000 dólares; **countries such as Germany, s., or France** países como Alemania, por poner un caso *or* ejemplo, o Francia

3 *vi* **I'm not saying** no te lo digo; **as they s., as people s.** como se dice, como dice la gente; **I s.!** (*expressing surprise*) ¡caramba!; (*to attract attention*) ¡oiga!; **I'll s.!** ¡ya lo creo!; *Fam* **you don't s.!** ¡no me digas!

saying ['seɪɪŋ] *n* dicho *m*; **as the s. goes** como dice el refrán

S/C (*abbr* **self-contained**) independiente

scab [skæb] *n* (**a**) (*on skin*) costra *f*, postilla *f* (**b**) *Fam* (*strikebreaker*) esquirol *m*, *Am* rompehuelgas *mf inv*, *RP* carnero *m*

scabbard ['skæbəd] *n* vaina *f*

scabies ['skeɪbiːz] *n* sarna *f*

scaffold ['skæfəld] *n* (*outside building*) andamio *m*; (*for execution*) patíbulo *m*

scaffolding ['skæfəldɪŋ] *n* andamiaje *m*

scalawag [skæləwæg], **scallywag** ['skælɪwæg] *n* *Fam* granuja *mf*

scald [skɔːld] **1** *n* escaldadura *f*
2 *vt* escaldar

scalding ['skɔːldɪŋ] *adj* **to be s. (hot)** estar ardiendo, escaldar

scale¹ [skeɪl] **1** *n* (**a**) (*on fish, reptile*) escama *f* (**b**) (*in pipes, kettle*) incrustación *f* (de cal)
2 *vt* (**a**) (*fish*) escamar, descamar (**b**) (*teeth*) limpiar, quitar *or* *Am* sacar el sarro a; (*boiler, pipe*) desincrustar

scale² *n* (**a**) (*instrument, pay rates*) escala *f*; **on a s. of one to ten** en una escala de uno a diez (**b**) (*of problem, changes*) escala *f*, magnitud *f*; (*of map, drawing*) escala *f*; **to s.** a escala; **s. model** modelo *m* a escala, maqueta *f* (**c**) *Mus* escala *f* (**d**) **scales** (*for weighing*) balanza *f*; **a pair** *or* **set of (kitchen) scales** una balanza (de cocina); **(bathroom) scales** báscula *f* (de baño)

▶**scale down** *vt sep* (*demands, expectations*) reducir

▶**scale up** *vt sep* (*prices, demands*) aumentar

scale³ *vt* (*climb*) escalar

scallion ['skælɪən] *n* (*spring onion*) cebolleta *f*

scallop, scollop ['skæləp, 'skɒləp] *n* (**a**) (*shellfish*) vieira *f* (**b**) (*in sewing*) festón *m*

scallywag = **scalawag**

scalp [skælp] **1** *n* (*skin of head*) cuero *m* cabelludo; (*as war trophy*) cabellera *f*
2 *vt* (**a**) (*in Indian war*) cortar la cabellera a (**b**) *Fam* (*tickets, securities*) revender

scalpel ['skælpəl] *n* *Med* bisturí *m*

scalper ['skælpə(r)] *n* *Fam* (*of tickets, securities*) revendedor(ora) *m,f*

scaly ['skeɪlɪ] *adj* (*fish*) con escamas; (*skin*) escamoso(a)

scam [skæm] *n* *Fam* chanchullo *m*, *Esp* pufo *m*

scamp [skæmp] *n* (*rascal*) granuja *mf*

scamper ['skæmpə(r)] *vi* ir dando brincos

▶**scamper away, scamper off** *vi* salir dando brincos

scampi ['skæmpɪ] *n* gambas *fpl* rebozadas

scan [skæn] **1** *vt* (*pt & pp* **scanned**) (**a**) (*examine closely*) (*face, crowd*) escrutar, escudriñar; (*the horizon*) otear, escudriñar; *Med* hacer un escáner a (**b**) (*glance at*) (*newspaper, list*) ojear (**c**) *Comptr* escanear
2 *n* (**a**) *Med* escáner *m* (**b**) *Comptr* escaneo *m*

scandal ['skændəl] *n* (**a**) (*outrage*) escándalo *m*; **financial/political s.** escándalo financiero/político; **it's a s.!** ¡es un escándalo!; **to create** *or* **cause a s.** provocar *or* ocasionar un escándalo (**b**) (*gossip*) chismorreo *m*, *Esp* cotilleo *m*

scandalize ['skændəlaɪz] *vt* escandalizar

scandalous ['skændələs] *adj* escandaloso(a)

scandalously ['skændələslɪ] *adv* escandalosamente

Scandinavia [skændɪ'neɪvɪə] *n* Escandinavia

Scandinavian [skændɪ'neɪvɪən] *n & adj* escandinavo(a) *m,f*

scanner ['skænə(r)] *n* *Comptr & Med* escáner *m*

scant [skænt] *adj* escaso(a)

scantily ['skæntɪlɪ] *adv* apenas; **s. dressed** *or* **clad** ligero(a) de ropa

scanty ['skæntɪ] *adj* (*dress*) exiguo(a); (*information*) escaso(a)

scapegoat ['skeɪpgəʊt] *n* chivo *m* expiatorio

scar [skɑː(r)] **1** *n* cicatriz *f*; *Fig* (*emotional*) cicatriz *f*, huella *f*; **s. tissue** tejido *m* cicatrizal
2 *vt* (*pt & pp* **scarred**) dejar cicatrices en; *also Fig* **to be scarred for life** quedar marcado(a) de por vida
3 *vi* (*wound*) cicatrizar

scarce [skeəs] *adj* escaso(a); *Fam* **to make oneself s.** esfumarse, poner (los) pies en polvorosa

scarcely ['skeəslɪ] *adv* apenas; **she could s. speak** apenas podía hablar; **s. ever/any/anyone** casi nunca/ninguno/nadie; **it is s. likely that…** es muy improbable que…

scarcity ['skeəsɪtɪ], **scarceness** ['skeəsnɪs] *n* escasez *f*

scare ['skeə(r)] **1** *n* **a safety/pollution s.** una alarma (social) por razones de seguridad/contaminación; **you gave me an awful s.** me has dado un susto tremendo
2 *vt* asustar; *Fam* **to s. the life out of sb, to s. the living daylights out of sb** pegarle un susto de muerte a alguien
3 *vi* asustarse

▶**scare away, scare off** *vt sep* ahuyentar

scarecrow ['skeəkrəʊ] *n* espantapájaros *m inv*

scared [skeəd] *adj* asustado(a); **to be s.** estar asustado(a); **to be s. of** tener miedo de; **to be s. stiff, to be s. to death** estar muerto(a) de miedo

scaremongering ['skeəmʌŋgərɪŋ] *n* alarmismo *m*

scarf [skɑːf] (*pl* **scarves** [skɑːvz]) *n* (*woolen*) bufanda *f*; (*of silk, for head*) pañuelo *m*

scarlet ['skɑːlɪt] **1** *n* (*color m*) escarlata *m*
2 *adj* escarlata; *Fig* **to go** *or* **turn s.** (*with anger, embarrassment*) ponerse colorado(a); **s. fever** escarlatina *f*

scarves [skɑːvz] *pl of* **scarf**

scary ['skeərɪ] *adj* *Fam* (*noise, situation*) aterrador(ora), espantoso(a); (*movie, book*) de miedo

scat [skæt] *exclam* *Fam* ¡lárgate!, *Esp* ¡largo!

scathing ['skeɪðɪŋ] *adj* (*remark, sarcasm*) mordaz, cáustico(a);

she was s. about the security arrangements criticó con mordacidad las medidas de seguridad

scathingly ['skeɪðɪŋlɪ] *adv (remark, speak)* con mordacidad

scatological [skætə'lɒdʒɪkəl] *adj* escatológico(a)

scatter ['skætə(r)] **1** *vt (clouds, demonstrators)* dispersar; *(corn, seed)* esparcir; **to s. crumbs/papers all over the place** dejar todo lleno *or* sembrado de migas/papeles
2 *vi (crowd)* dispersarse

scatterbrain ['skætəbreɪn] *n Fam* despistado(a) *m,f*

scattergun ['skætəɡʌn] *n* escopeta *f*

scavenge ['skævɪndʒ] **1** *vt* rebuscar (entre los desperdicios)
2 *vi* **to s. for sth** rebuscar algo entre los desperdicios; **to s. in the garbage cans** rebuscar en los cubos de basura

scavenger ['skævɪndʒə(r)] *n (animal)* (animal *m*) carroñero *m*

scenario [sɪ'nɑːrɪəʊ] *(pl* **scenarios)** *n* **(a)** *(of movie)* argumento *m* **(b)** *(situation)* situación *f* hipotética; **a likely s. is...** puede muy bien ocurrir que...

scene [siːn] *n* **(a)** *Theat & Cin* escena *f; also Fig* **a touching/terrifying s.** una escena conmovedora/aterradora; *Fig* **behind the scenes** entre bastidores; **a s. of devastation** una escena de destrucción; **I can picture the s.** me puedo imaginar la escena; *Theat* **s. shifter** tramoyista *mf*
(b) *(event)* escenario *m*; **a change of s. would do him good** un cambio de aires le vendría bien; **to arrive** *or* **come on the s.** aparecer (en escena); **the s. of the crime/accident** el escenario *or* lugar del crimen/accidente
(c) *(fuss)* **to make a s.** hacer una escena, *Esp* montar un número
(d) *(world)* **the political/sporting s.** el panorama político/deportivo; *Fam* **it's not my s.** no me va mucho

scenery ['siːnərɪ] *n* **(a)** *(in play)* decorado *m* **(b)** *(landscape)* paisaje *m*; *Fam* **you need a change of s.** necesitas un cambio de aires

scenic ['siːnɪk] *adj (picturesque)* pintoresco(a); **s. railway** *(train)* tren *m* turístico; **s. route** ruta *f* turística

scent [sent] **1** *n* **(a)** *(smell)* aroma *m*, olor *m* **(b)** *(perfume)* perfume *m* **(c)** *(in hunting)* rastro *m*; **to pick up the s.** seguir el rastro; **to be on the s. of** seguir el rastro de; **to lose the s.** perder el rastro; **he threw his pursuers off the s.** despistó a sus perseguidores
2 *vt* **(a)** *(smell)* olfatear, localizar el rastro de; *Fig* **to s. danger** olerse el peligro **(b)** *(perfume)* perfumar

scepter ['septə(r)] *n* cetro *m*

skeptic ['skeptɪk] *n* escéptico(a) *m,f*

skeptical ['skeptɪkəl] *adj* escéptico(a)

skeptically ['skeptɪklɪ] *adv* escépticamente, con escepticismo

skepticism ['skeptɪsɪzəm] *n* escepticismo *m*

schedule ['skedjuːl] **1** *n* **(a)** *(plan)* programa *m*, plan *m*; **on s.** *(train, bus)* de acuerdo con el horario previsto; **behind/ahead of s.** detrás de/por delante de lo programado *or* previsto; **everything went according to s.** todo fue según las previsiones; **I work to a very tight s.** tengo que cumplir unos plazos muy estrictos **(b)** *Com (list of prices)* lista *f or* catálogo *m* de precios
2 *vt* programar; **we're scheduled to arrive at 21.45** está previsto que lleguemos a las 21:45

scheduled ['skedjuːld] *adj (services)* programado(a); **s. flight** vuelo *m* regular; **at the s. time** a la hora prevista

schematic [skɪ'mætɪk] *adj* esquemático(a)

scheme [skiːm] **1** *n (arrangement, system)* sistema *m*, método *m*; *(plan)* plan *m*, proyecto *m*; *(plot)* intriga *f*; **in the (greater) s. of things** desde una perspectiva general, en un plano global
2 *vi Pej* intrigar

schilling ['ʃɪlɪŋ] *n Formerly (Austrian currency)* chelín *m*

schism ['s(k)ɪzəm] *n* cisma *m*

schizoid ['skɪtsɔɪd] *n & adj* esquizoide *mf*

schizophrenia [skɪtsəʊ'friːnɪə] *n* esquizofrenia *f*

schizophrenic [skɪtsəʊ'frenɪk] *n & adj* esquizofrénico(a) *m,f*

schmaltzy ['ʃmɔːltsɪ] *adj Fam* sensiblero(a), *Esp* ñoño(a)

schmuck ['ʃmʌk] *n Fam* lelo(a) *m,f*

scholar ['skɒlə(r)] *n (learned person)* erudito(a) *m,f*

scholarly ['skɒləlɪ] *adj* erudito(a)

scholarship ['skɒləʃɪp] *n* **(a)** *(learning)* erudición *f* **(b)** *Educ (grant)* beca *f*

scholastic [skə'læstɪk] *adj Formal* académico(a)

school¹ [skuːl] **1** *n* **(a)** *(for children)* (up to 14) colegio *m*, escuela *f*; *(from 14 to 18)* instituto *m*; *(of dance, languages etc) (private)* escuela *f*, academia *f*; **to go to s.** ir al colegio; **I went to** *or* **was at s. with him** fuimos juntos al colegio; **there is no s. tomorrow** mañana no hay colegio *or* clase; **when does s. start?** ¿cuándo empiezan las clases?; **s. of art** escuela *f* de bellas artes; **of s. age** en edad escolar; **s. board** junta *f* escolar; **s. book** libro *m* de texto (escolar); **s. bus** autobús *m* escolar; **s. day** día *m* de colegio; **s. friend** amigo(a) *m,f* del colegio; **s. hours** horas *fpl* de clase; **s. uniform** uniforme *m* escolar; **s. vacation** vacaciones *f* escolares; **s. year** año *m* escolar *or* académico
(b) *(college, university)* universidad *f*
(c) *(college department)* facultad *f*
(d) *(of artists, thinkers)* escuela *f*; **s. of thought** corriente *f or* escuela de pensamiento; *Fig* **he's one of the old s.** es de la vieja escuela
2 *vt (educate)* educar; *(train) (child, mind)* instruir, adiestrar; **to s. sb in sth** instruir a alguien en algo

school² *n (of fish)* banco *m*

schoolbag ['skuːlbæɡ] *n* cartera *f*

schoolboy ['skuːlbɔɪ] *n* colegial *m*

schoolchild ['skuːltʃaɪld] *n* colegial(ala) *m,f*

schoolfellow ['skuːlfeləʊ] *n* compañero(a) *m,f* de colegio

schoolgirl ['skuːlɡɜːl] *n* colegiala *f*

schooling ['skuːlɪŋ] *n* enseñanza *f or* educación *f* escolar

schoolmaster ['skuːlmɑːstə(r)] *n Formal (primary)* maestro *m*; *(secondary)* profesor *m*

schoolmate ['skuːlmeɪt] *n* compañero(a) *m,f* de colegio

schoolmistress ['skuːlmɪstrɪs] *n Formal (primary)* maestra *f*; *(secondary)* profesora *f*

schoolroom ['skuːlruːm] *n* aula *f*, clase *f*

schoolteacher ['skuːltiːtʃə(r)] *n (primary)* maestro(a) *m,f*; *(secondary)* profesor(ora) *m,f*

schoolyard ['skuːljɑːd] *n* patio *m* de recreo

schooner ['skuːnə(r)] *n* **(a)** *(ship)* goleta *f* **(b)** *(glass)* catavino *m*, copa *f* (de jerez)

sciatic [saɪ'ætɪk] *adj* ciático(a); **s. nerve** nervio *m* ciático

sciatica [saɪ'ætɪkə] *n Med* ciática *f*

science ['saɪəns] *n* ciencia *f*; **s. class** clase *f* de ciencias; **s. fiction** ciencia ficción *f*; **s. teacher** profesor(ora) *m,f* de ciencias

scientific [saɪən'tɪfɪk] *adj* científico(a)

scientifically [saɪən'tɪfɪklɪ] *adv* científicamente

scientist ['saɪəntɪst] *n* científico(a) *m,f*

sci-fi ['saɪfaɪ] *Fam* **1** *n* ciencia ficción *f*
2 *adj* de ciencia ficción

scimitar ['sɪmɪtə(r)] *n* cimitarra *f*

scintillating ['sɪntɪleɪtɪŋ] *adj (conversation)* chispeante; *(performance)* brillante

scissors ['sɪzəz] *npl* tijeras *fpl*; **a pair of s.** unas tijeras

sclerosis [sklɪə'rəʊsɪs] *n Med* esclerosis *f inv*

scoff [skɒf] *vi (mock)* mofarse (**at** de)

scold [skəʊld] *vt* reñir, regañar

scollop = scallop

scone [skɒn, skəʊn] *n* = bollo pequeño, redondo y bastante seco, a veces con pasas

scoop [sku:p] **1** *n* **(a)** *(utensil) (for flour, mashed potato)* paleta *f*; *(for ice cream)* pinzas *fpl* de cuchara; *(for sugar)* cucharilla *f* plana **(b)** *(portion) (of ice cream)* bola *f*; *(of mashed potato)* paletada *f* **(c)** *Journ* primicia *f*
2 *vt* **to s. a story** obtener una primicia

▶**scoop up** *vt sep (with hands)* recoger ahuecando las manos; *(with spoon)* tomar una cucharada de; **he scooped up the papers in his arms** recogió los papeles entre sus brazos

scoot [sku:t] *vi Fam* **to s. (off** *or* **away)** salir disparado(a)

scooter ['sku:tə(r)] *n (for child)* patinete *m*; **(motor) s.** escúter *m*, Vespa® *f*

scope [skəʊp] *n* ámbito *m*, alcance *m*; **to give s. for…** *(interpretation, explanation)* permitir (la posibilidad de)…; **to give free s. to one's imagination** dar rienda suelta a la imaginación

scorch [skɔ:tʃ] **1** *n* **s. (mark)** (marca *f* de) quemadura *f*
2 *vt* chamuscar; **scorched earth policy** *(retreating army)* política *f* de tierra quemada

scorcher ['skɔ:tʃə(r)] *n Fam (hot day)* día *m* (de calor) abrasador

scorching ['skɔ:tʃɪŋ] *adj* abrasador(ora)

score [skɔ:(r)] **1** *n* **(a)** *(total) (in sport)* resultado *m*; *(in quiz)* puntuación *f*; **there was still no s.** no se había movido el marcador; **what's the s.?** ¿cómo van?; **to keep the s.** llevar el tanteo; *Fam Fig* **to know the s.** conocer el percal
(b) *(line)* arañazo *m*
(c) *(quarrel)* **to have a s. to settle with sb** tener una cuenta que saldar con alguien
(d) *(reason, grounds)* **don't worry on that s.** no te preocupes en ese aspecto; **on that s. alone** sólo por eso
(e) *Mus* partitura *f*; *(for movie)* banda *f* sonora original
(f) *Old-fashioned (twenty)* **a s.** una veintena; *Fam* **scores** *(a lot)* montones *mpl*
2 *vt* **(a)** *(in sport) (goal)* marcar; *(point, run)* anotar; *Fig (success, victory)* apuntarse; **to s. a hit** *(hit target)* hacer blanco; *Fig (person, movie)* acertar **(b)** *(cut line in)* marcar con una raya *or* estría; **she scored her name on a tree** grabó su nombre en un árbol **(c)** *Fam (buy)* **to s. drugs** conseguir *or Esp* pillar droga
3 *vi* **(a)** *(get a goal, run)* marcar; *Fig* **her proposal scores on cost** el punto fuerte de su propuesta son los costes **(b)** *Fam (sexually)* ligar; *(buy drugs)* conseguir *or Esp* pillar droga

scoreboard ['skɔ:bɔ:d] *n* marcador *m*

scorecard ['skɔ:kɑ:d] *n* tarjeta *f* de puntuación

scorer ['skɔ:rə(r)] *n* **(a)** *(player) (in basketball, football, rugby)* anotador(ora) *m,f*; *(in soccer, hockey)* goleador(ora) *m,f* **(b)** *(score keeper)* encargado(a) *m,f* del marcador

scoring ['skɔ:rɪŋ] *n* **(a)** *(in sport)* **to open the s.** abrir el marcador **(b)** *(orchestration)* orquestación *f*

scorn [skɔ:n] **1** *n* desprecio *m*, desdén *m*; **to pour s. on sth** hablar de algo con desdén
2 *vt* despreciar, desdeñar; **to s. to do sth** no dignarse a hacer algo

scornful ['skɔ:nfʊl] *adj* despreciativo(a), desdeñoso(a); **to be s. of sth** despreciar *or* desdeñar algo

scornfully ['skɔ:nfʊlɪ] *adv* con desdén, con aire despreciativo

Scorpio ['skɔ:pɪəʊ] *n (sign of zodiac)* Escorpio *m*, Escorpión *m*; **to be (a) S.** ser Escorpio *or* Escorpión

scorpion ['skɔ:pɪən] *n* escorpión *m*, alacrán *m*

Scot [skɒt] *n* escocés(esa) *m,f*

Scotch [skɒtʃ] **1** *n (whiskey)* whisky *m* escocés
2 *adj* **S. broth** = caldo típico escocés; **S. tape**® cinta *f* adhesiva, *Esp* celo *m*, *CAm, Méx* Durex® *m*; **S. whiskey** whisky *m* escocés

scotch [skɒtʃ] *vt (rumor)* desmentir

scot-free ['skɒt'fri:] *adj Fam* **to get off s.** quedar impune

Scotland ['skɒtlənd] *n* Escocia

Scots [skɒts] **1** *n (dialect)* (dialecto *m*) escocés *m*
2 *adj* escocés(esa)

Scotsman ['skɒtsmən] *n* escocés *m*

Scotswoman ['skɒtswʊmən] *n* escocesa *f*

Scottie dog ['skɒtɪ'dɒg] *n Fam* terrier *m* escocés

Scottish ['skɒtɪʃ] *adj* escocés(esa); **S. terrier** terrier *m* escocés

scoundrel ['skaʊndrəl] *n (wicked person)* bellaco(a) *m,f*, canalla *mf*; *Fam (rascal)* granujilla *mf*

scour ['skaʊə(r)] *vt* **(a)** *(pot, surface)* restregar **(b)** *(area)* peinar; *(house)* registrar, rebuscar en

scourer ['skaʊərə(r)] *n* estropajo *m*

scourge [skɜ:dʒ] *n* azote *m*

scouring pad ['skaʊərɪŋpæd] *n* estropajo *m*

scout [skaʊt] **1** *n* **(a)** *Mil (person)* explorador(ora) *m,f*; **(Boy) S.** boy-scout *m*, escultista *m*; **(talent) s.** cazatalentos *mf inv* **(b)** *(action)* **to have a s. around (for sth)** buscar (algo)
2 *vi* **to s. ahead** reconocer el terreno; **to s. for talent** ir a la caza de talentos

scoutmaster ['skaʊtmɑ:stə(r)] *n* jefe *m* de boy-scouts *or* escultistas

scowl [skaʊl] **1** *n* **to give sb a s.** mirar a alguien con cara de *esp Esp* enfado *or esp Am* enojo
2 *vi* fruncir el ceño, poner cara de *esp Esp* enfado *or esp Am* enojo

scowling ['skaʊlɪŋ] *adj (look)* severo(a)

scrabble ['skræbəl] *vi* **to s. around** *or* **about for sth** buscar algo a tientas

scraggy ['skrægɪ] *adj* raquítico(a), esquelético(a)

scram [skræm] *(pt & pp* **scrammed)** *vi Fam* largarse, *Esp, RP* pirarse; **s.!** ¡fuera!, ¡largo!

scramble ['skræmbəl] **1** *n (rush)* desbandada *f*; *(struggle)* lucha *f* **(for** por); **it was a short s. to the top** para alcanzar la cumbre había que trepar un poco
2 *vt Tel (signal)* codificar
3 *vi* **to s. for sth** luchar por algo; **to s. up a hill** trepar por una colina

scrambled eggs ['skræmbəld'egz] *npl* huevos *mpl* revueltos

scrambling ['skræmblɪŋ] *n* **(a)** *(sport)* motocross *m* **(b)** *(in rock climbing)* ascenso *m* trepando

scrap[1] [skræp] **1** *n* **(a)** *(of material)* trozo *m*; *(of information)* fragmento *m*; **a s. of evidence** un indicio; **to tear sth into scraps** hacer trizas algo; **scraps** *(of food)* sobras *fpl*; **there isn't a s. of truth in what she says** no hay ni rastro de verdad en lo que dice; **s. heap** montón *m* de chatarra; *Fig* **to be on the s. heap** *(person)* estar excluido(a) del mundo laboral; *(idea)* quedar descartado(a); **s. paper** papel *m* usado **(b)** **s. (metal)** chatarra *f*; **to sell sth for s.** vender algo para chatarra; **s. dealer** chatarrero(a) *m,f*
2 *vt (pt & pp* **scrapped)** *(car)* mandar a la chatarra; *(submarine, missile)* desmantelar; *(project)* descartar, abandonar

scrap[2] *Fam* **1** *n (fight)* bronca *f*, pelea *f*; **to have a s., to get into a s.** pelearse
2 *vi (pt & pp* **scrapped)** *(fight)* pelearse

scrapbook ['skræpbʊk] *n* álbum *m* de recortes

scrape [skreɪp] **1** *n* **(a)** *(action)* rascada *f*; *(mark)* arañazo *m*; *(on skin)* arañazo *m*, rasguño *m*; *(sound)* chirrido *m*; **to give sth a s.** rascar algo **(b)** *Fam* **to get into a s.** meterse en un lío *or Esp* fregado
2 *vt (scratch) (side of car)* rayar, arañar; *(dirt, wallpaper)* rascar, arrancar; *(vegetables)* raspar; **to s. one's knee** arañarse *or* rasguñarse la rodilla; **to s. one's shoes** restregar los zapatos; **to s. one's plate clean** rebañar el plato; *Fig* **to s. the bottom of the barrel** tener que recurrir a lo peor; *Fig* **I just s. a living** me gano la vida como puedo
3 *vi* **(a)** *(make sound)* chirriar; **she was scraping away on her fiddle** rascaba el violín con un sonido chirriante **(b)** *(barely manage)* **to s. home** *(in contest)* ganar a duras penas; **to s. into college** entrar en la universidad por los pelos

▸**scrape through** vt insep (exam) aprobar por los pelos

▸**scrape together** vt sep (money, resources) reunir a duras penas

scraper ['skreɪpə(r)] n (tool) rasqueta f

scrappy ['skræpɪ] adj (knowledge, performance) deslavazado(a)

scratch [skrætʃ] **1** n (a) (on skin, record, furniture) arañazo m; **it's just a s.** no es más que un rasguño or arañazo; **he came out of it without a s.** salió sin un rasguño (b) (action) **to give one's nose a s.** rascarse la nariz; **s. card** tarjeta f de rasca y gana, boleto m de lotería instantánea, Am raspadito m, Arg raspadita f; **s. pad** bloc m de borrador; **s. paper** papel m usado (c) Fam (idioms) **to start from s.** partir de cero; **to come up to s.** dar la talla; **to bring sth/sb up to s.** poner algo/a alguien a punto

2 adj (meal, team) improvisado(a), de circunstancias

3 vt (a) (skin) arañar; (glass, record) rayar; **to s. oneself** rascarse; **to s. one's nose** rascarse la nariz; **he scratched his name on the card** garabateó su nombre en la tarjeta; Fig **you s. my back and I'll s. yours** hoy por ti y mañana por mí; Fig **we've only scratched the surface of the problem** no hemos hecho más que empezar a tratar el problema (b) (remove) **to s. sb's name from a list** quitar or Am sacar a alguien de una lista

4 vi (oneself) rascarse; (thorns) picar; (new clothes) rascar, raspar; **the dog was scratching at the door** el perro estaba arañando la puerta

▸**scratch out** vt sep (number, name) tachar; Fig **to s. sb's eyes out** arrancarle a alguien los ojos

scratchy ['skrætʃɪ] adj (garment, towel) áspero(a); (record) con muchos arañazos

scrawl [skrɔːl] **1** n garabatos mpl

2 vt garabatear

3 vi hacer garabatos

scrawny ['skrɔːnɪ] adj esquelético(a), raquítico(a)

scream [skriːm] **1** n (a) (of person) grito m, chillido m; **to let out a s.** soltar un grito; **screams of laughter** carcajadas fpl (b) Fam (good fun) **it was a s.** fue para morirse de risa or Esp para mondarse; **he's a s.** es la monda

2 vt gritar; **to s. abuse** lanzar improperios or insultos; **the headlines screamed "guilty"** los titulares or Méx, RP encabezados clamaban "culpable"

3 vi gritar, chillar; **jets screamed overhead** los reactores pasaron con estruendo; **to s. in pain** gritar de dolor; **to s. with laughter** reírse a carcajadas

screaming ['skriːmɪŋ] n gritos mpl, chillidos mpl

screamingly ['skriːmɪŋlɪ] adv Fam **s. funny** Esp para mondarse de risa, Am chistosísimo(a)

scree [skriː] n pedruscos mpl

screech [skriːtʃ] **1** n (of bird, person) chillido m; (of brakes) chirrido m; **a s. of laughter** una carcajada

2 vt chillar; **to s. an order** dar una orden con un chillido

3 vi (bird, person) chillar; (brakes) chirriar, rechinar; **the car screeched to a halt** el coche se detuvo chirriando

screen [skriːn] **1** n (a) (barrier) mampara f; (folding) biombo m (b) (of TV, cinema, computer) pantalla f; **the big/small s.** la gran/pequeña pantalla; **s. actor/actress** actor m/actriz f de cine; Comptr **s. memory** memoria f en pantalla; Comptr **s. saver** salvapantallas m; Cin **s. test** prueba f (de cámara)

2 vt (a) (protect) proteger; **to s. sth from view** ocultar algo a la vista (b) (show) (movie) proyectar (c) (filter) (staff, applicants) examinar, controlar; (information) filtrar

screening ['skriːnɪŋ] n (a) (of movie) proyección f; **first s.** estreno m (b) (of staff, applicants) examen m, control m

screenplay ['skriːnpleɪ] n Cin guión m

screenwriter ['skriːnraɪtə(r)] n Cin guionista mf

screw [skruː] **1** n (a) (for fixing) tornillo m; Fam Fig **she's got a s. loose** le falta un tornillo; Fam Fig **to put the screws on sb**

apretar las clavijas a alguien; **s. top** (of bottle, jar) tapón m de rosca (b) (propeller) hélice f (c) Fam (prison officer) carcelero m, Esp boqueras m inv (d) Vulg (sexual intercourse) polvo m; **to have a s.** echar un polvo, Am coger

2 vt (a) (fix) atornillar (**on** or **onto** a); **to s. one's face into a smile** sonreír forzadamente; Fam **they'll s. you for every penny you've got** van a sacarte hasta el último céntimo (b) Vulg (have sex with) Esp follar, Am coger; **s. you!** Esp ¡que te den por culo!, Méx ¡vete a la chingada!, RP ¡andate a la puta que te parió!

3 vi Vulg (have sex) joder, Esp follar, Am coger

▸**screw around** vi (a) Vulg Esp follar or Am coger con todo el mundo (b) Fam (waste time) rascarla, RP boludear

▸**screw on 1** vt sep (with screw) atornillar; (lid, top) enroscar; Fam **he's got his head screwed on** tiene la cabeza en su sitio

2 vi (lid, top) enroscarse

▸**screw up** Fam **1** vt (spoil) jorobar; **his parents really screwed him up** sus padres lo dejaron bien tarado

2 vi don't s. up this time esta vez no vayas a jorobarla

screwball 1 n (a) (person) cabeza mf loca, RP tiro m al aire (b) (in baseball) tirabuzón m, lanzamiento m de tornillo

2 adj Fam chiflado(a); **s. comedy** comedia f disparatada

screwdriver ['skruːdraɪvə(r)] n Esp, Carib, RP destornillador m, Andes, CAm desatornillador m, Méx desarmador m

screwed-up ['skruːd'ʌp] adj Fam trastornado(a), hecho(a) polvo

screwy ['skruːɪ] adj Fam (person) rarísimo(a); (idea) descabellado(a)

scribble ['skrɪbəl] **1** n garabatos mpl; **I can't read this s.** no entiendo estos garabatos

2 vt **to s. sth (down)** garabatear algo

3 vi hacer garabatos

scribbling ['skrɪblɪŋ] n scribblings Fam (inferior writings) garabatos mpl

scribe [skraɪb] n escribano(a) m,f, amanuense mf

scrimmage ['skrɪmɪdʒ] n (a) (fight) tumulto m, alboroto m (b) (in football) scrimmage m

scrimp [skrɪmp] vi **to s. (and save)** economizar, hacer economías

scrip [skrɪp] n (a) St Exch resguardo m provisional; **s. issue** emisión m de acciones liberadas (b) Fam (prescription) receta f

script [skrɪpt] n (a) (for play, movie) guión m; (in exam) ejercicio m (escrito), examen m (b) (handwriting) caligrafía f, letra f

scriptural ['skrɪptʃərəl] adj bíblico(a)

Scripture ['skrɪptʃə(r)] n (Holy) S., the Scriptures la Sagrada Escritura

scriptwriter ['skrɪptraɪtə(r)] n TV & Cin guionista mf

scroll [skrəʊl] **1** n (a) (of paper, parchment) rollo m (b) Archit voluta f

2 vi Comptr desplazar el cursor; **to s. through** (text) recorrer

▸**scroll down** vi Comptr bajar el cursor

▸**scroll up** vi Comptr subir el cursor

scrolling ['skrəʊlɪŋ] n Comptr desplazamiento m por la pantalla

scrotum ['skrəʊtəm] n escroto m

scrounge [skraʊndʒ] Fam **1** vt **to s. sth from** or **off sb** gorrear or Esp, Méx gorronear or RP garronear algo a alguien

2 vi **to s. around** andar gorreando or Esp, Méx gorroneando or RP garroneando; **to s. off sb** vivir a costa de alguien, Esp, Méx vivir de alguien por la gorra

scrounger ['skraʊndʒə(r)] n Fam gorrero(a) m,f, Esp, Méx gorrón(ona) m,f, RP garronero(a) m,f

scrub [skrʌb] **1** n (a) (bushes) maleza f, matorral m (b) (wash)

to give sth a (good) s. fregar (bien) algo; **s. brush** cepillo *m* de fregar (**c**) *Sport (team)* equipo *m* reserva; *(player)* reserva *mf*
2 *vt (pt & pp* **scrubbed**) (**a**) *(floor, pots)* fregar; **to s. one's hands** lavarse bien las manos (**b**) *Fam (cancel)* borrar

▶**scrub up** *vi Med* lavarse bien las manos

scrubber ['skrʌbə(r)] *n (for dishes)* estropajo *m*

scrubbing brush ['skrʌbɪŋ'brʌʃ] *n* cepillo *m* de fregar

scrubland ['skrʌblænd] *n* monte *m* bajo, matorral *m*

scruff [skrʌf] *n* **the s. of the neck** el cogote

scruffily ['skrʌfɪlɪ] *adv* **to be s. dressed** vestir andrajosamente *or* con desaliño

scruffy ['skrʌfɪ] *adj (person)* desaliñado(a), zarrapastroso(a); *(clothes)* andrajoso(a)

scrum [skrʌm] *n (in rugby) Esp* melé *f*, *Am* scrum *f*; **s. half** *Esp* medio (de) melé *mf*, *Am* medio scrum *mf*

scrumptious ['skrʌm(p)ʃəs] *adj Fam (food)* riquísimo(a), de chuparse los dedos

scrunch [skrʌn(t)ʃ] **1** *vt (paper)* estrujar; *(can)* aplastar
2 *vi (make sound)* crujir

scruple ['skru:pəl] **1** *n* escrúpulo *m*; **to have no scruples** no tener escrúpulos
2 *vi* **not to s. to do sth** no tener escrúpulos en hacer algo

scrupulous ['skru:pjʊləs] *adj* escrupuloso(a)

scrupulously ['skru:pjʊləslɪ] *adv* escrupulosamente

scrutinize ['skru:tɪnaɪz] *vt (document, votes)* escrutar

scrutiny ['skru:tɪnɪ] *n (of document, votes)* escrutinio *m*; **to come under s.** ser cuidadosamente examinado(a)

scuba ['sku:bə] *n* **s. diver** submarinista *mf* buceador(ora) *m,f (con botellas de oxígeno)*; **to go s. diving** hacer submarinismo

scuff [skʌf] **1** *n* **s. mark** rozadura *f*, rasguño *m*
2 *vt* rozar

scuffle ['skʌfəl] **1** *n* riña *f*, reyerta *f*
2 *vi* reñir, pelear

sculpt [skʌlpt] *vt & vi* esculpir

sculptor ['skʌlptə(r)] *n* escultor(ora) *m,f*

sculptural ['skʌlptʃərəl] *adj* escultórico(a)

sculpture ['skʌlptʃə(r)] **1** *n* escultura *f*
2 *vt* esculpir

scum [skʌm] *n* (**a**) *(layer of dirt)* capa *f* de suciedad; *(froth)* espuma *f* (**b**) *(worthless people)* escoria *f*; **the s. of the earth** la escoria de la sociedad

scumbag [skʌmbæg] *n very Fam (person)* cerdo(a) *m,f*, mamón(ona) *m,f*

scummy ['skʌmɪ] *adj Fam (dirty, worthless)* asqueroso(a)

scupper ['skʌpə(r)] *vt (ship, project)* hundir

scurrilous ['skʌrɪləs] *adj* ultrajante, denigrante

scurry ['skʌrɪ] *vi (dash)* corretear apresuradamente

▶**scurry away, scurry off** *vi* escabullirse

scurvy ['skɜ:vɪ] *n Med* escorbuto *m*

scuttle¹ ['skʌtəl] **1** *n (coal)* **s.** cajón *m* para el carbón
2 *vt (ship)* barrenar, taladrar; *(plan)* hundir

scuttle² *vi (run)* corretear

▶**scuttle away, scuttle off** *vi* escabullirse

scuzzball ['skʌzbɔ:l] *n Fam (filthy person)* piojoso(a) *m,f*

scythe [saɪð] **1** *n* guadaña *f*
2 *vt* segar

SE [e'si:] *n (abbr* **southeast**) SE

sea [si:] *n* mar *m or f*; **by the s.** junto al mar; **to go by s.** ir en barco; **to go to s.** *(become a sailor)* enrolarse de marinero; *Fig* **a s. of people** un mar de gente; **heavy** *or* **rough seas** mar *f* gruesa; **on the high seas, out at s.** en alta mar; **to find** *or* **get one's s. legs** acostumbrarse al mar *(no marearse)*; *Fig* **to be at s.** estar totalmente perdido(a), no saber uno por dónde anda; **s. air** aire *m* del mar; **s. anemone** anémona *f* de mar; **s. bass** lubina *f*; **s. battle** batalla *f* naval; **s. bream** besugo *m*; **s. breeze** brisa *f* marina; *Fam* **(old) s. dog** (viejo) lobo *m* de

mar; **s. horse** hipocampo *m*, caballito *m* de mar; *Naut* **s. lane** ruta *f* marítima; **s. level** nivel *m* del mar; **s. lion** león *m* marino; **s. monster** monstruo *m* marino; **s. power** *(country)* potencia *f* naval; **s. salt** sal *f* marina; **s. urchin** erizo *m* de mar; **s. voyage** travesía *f*, viaje *m* por mar

seabag ['si:bæg] *n* macuto *m (cilíndrico)*

seabed ['si:bed] *n* fondo *m* del mar, lecho *m* marino

Seabee ['si:bi:] *n* = ingeniero de campo de la Marina estadounidense

seaboard ['si:bɔ:d] *n* litoral *m*, costa *f*

seaborne ['si:bɔ:n] *adj* marítimo(a)

seafarer ['si:feərə(r)] *n* marino(a) *m,f*, marinero(a) *m,f*

seafaring ['si:feərɪŋ] *adj* marinero(a)

seafood ['si:fu:d] *n* marisco *m*, *Am* mariscos *mpl*

seafront ['si:frʌnt] *n* paseo *m* marítimo

seagoing ['si:gəʊɪŋ] *adj* marítimo(a)

seagull ['si:gʌl] *n* gaviota *f*

SEAL [si:l] *n (soldier)* = miembro de la unidad élite de operaciones especiales de la Armada

seal¹ [si:l] *n (animal)* foca *f*

seal² **1** *n* (**a**) *(stamp)* sello *m*; **to give one's s. of approval to sth** dar el visto bueno a algo; **to set the s. on sth** *(alliance, friendship, defeat)* sellar algo; *(fate)* determinar algo (**b**) *(on machine, pipes, connection)* junta *f*; *(on bottle, box, letter)* precinto *m*
2 *vt (with official seal)* sellar; *(close) (envelope, frontier)* precintar, cerrar; *(jar, joint)* precintar, cerrar herméticamente; *(fate)* determinar; **my lips are sealed** soy una tumba

▶**seal in** *vt sep* encerrar

▶**seal off** *vt sep* impedir el paso a

sealing ['si:lɪŋ] *n (hunting of seals)* caza *f* de focas

sealing wax ['si:lɪŋ'wæks] *n* lacre *m*

sealskin ['si:lskɪn] *n* piel *f* de foca

seam [si:m] *n* (**a**) *(of garment)* costura *f*; *(in metalwork)* unión *f*, juntura *f*; **to be coming apart at the seams** *(clothing)* estar descosiéndose; *Fig (plan, organization)* estar desmoronándose (**b**) *(of coal)* filón *m*, veta *f*

seaman ['si:mən] *n Naut* marino *m*

seamanship ['si:mənʃɪp] *n Naut* náutica *f*, navegación *f*

seamstress ['semstrɪs] *n* costurera *f*

seamy ['si:mɪ] *adj* sórdido(a)

seance ['seɪɒns] *n* sesión *f* de espiritismo

seaplane ['si:pleɪn] *n* hidroavión *m*

seaport ['si:pɔ:t] *n* puerto *m* de mar

sear [sɪə(r)] *vt (skin)* quemar, abrasar; *Fig* **the image was seared on his memory** la imagen le quedó grabada a fuego en la memoria

search [sɜ:tʃ] **1** *n* búsqueda *f*; **to be in s. of** ir en búsqueda *or Esp* busca de; **to make a s. of** rastrear; *Comptr* **to do a s.** hacer una búsqueda; *Comptr* **s. engine** motor *m* de búsqueda; **s. party** equipo *m* de búsqueda; *Law* **s. warrant** orden *f* de registro
2 *vt (person, place)* registrar; *Comptr (file, directory)* buscar en; *Fam* **s. me!** ¡ni idea!, ¡yo qué sé!
3 *vi* buscar; **to s. after** *or* **for sth** buscar algo; *Comptr* **s. and replace** buscar y reemplazar

searching ['sɜ:tʃɪŋ] *adj (gaze)* escrutador(ora); *(question)* incisiva

searchingly ['sɜ:tʃɪŋlɪ] *adv (to gaze)* con mirada escrutadora; *(to question)* de manera incisiva

searchlight ['sɜ:tʃlaɪt] *n* reflector *m*

searing ['sɪərɪŋ] *adj (pain)* punzante; *(heat)* abrasador(ora); *(criticism, indictment)* incisivo(a)

seascape ['si:skeɪp] *n Art* marina *f*

seashell ['si:ʃel] *n* concha *f*

seashore ['si:ʃɔ:(r)] *n* orilla *f* del mar

seasick ['siːsɪk] *adj* **to be s.** estar mareado(a); **to get s.** marearse

seasickness ['siːsɪknɪs] *n* mareo *m (en barco)*

seaside ['siːsaɪd] *n* playa *f;* **at the s.** en la playa; **s. resort** centro *m* turístico costero

season[1] ['siːzən] *n (period of year)* estación *f; (for sports, activity)* temporada *f; (of movies)* ciclo *m;* **S.'s Greetings** Felices Fiestas; **in s.** *(food)* en temporada; **the high s.** *(for tourism)* la temporada alta; **s. ticket** abono *m*

season[2] *vt* **(a)** *(dish)* condimentar, sazonar **(b)** *(wood)* curar

seasonable ['siːzənəbəl] *adj* **(a) s. weather** tiempo *m* propio de la época **(b)** *(help, advice)* oportuno(a)

seasonal ['siːzənəl] *adj (changes)* estacional; *(commerce)* de temporada; **s. adjustment** fluctuación *f or* ajuste *m* estacional; **s. worker** temporero(a) *m,f,* trabajador(ora) *m,f* temporero(a)

seasonally ['siːzənəlɪ] *adv* **s. adjusted** desestacionaliza-do(a), con ajuste estacional

seasoned ['siːzənd] *adj* **(a)** *(food)* condimentado(a), sazona-do(a) **(b)** *(wood)* curado(a) **(c)** *(person)* experimentado(a); **a s. soldier** un soldado veterano

seasoning ['siːzənɪŋ] *n Culin* condimento *m*

seat [siːt] **1** *n* **(a)** *(chair, on bus, train, plane)* asiento *m; (in theater)* butaca *f; (in stadium)* localidad *f,* asiento *m; (in Congress)* escaño *m;* **to take a s.** tomar asiento, sentarse; **s. belt** cinturón *m* de seguridad **(b)** *(part) (of chair, toilet)* asiento *m; (of pants)* parte *f* del trasero **(c)** *(center) (of government)* sede *f;* **a s. of learning** un centro de enseñanza

2 *vt* **(a)** *(cause to sit)* sentar; **to remain seated** permanecer sentado(a); *Formal* **please be seated** por favor, tome asiento **(b)** *(accommodate)* **the bus seats thirty** el autobús tiene capacidad *o* cabida para treinta pasajeros sentados; **this table seats twelve** en esta mesa caben doce personas

seating ['siːtɪŋ] *n (seats)* asientos *mpl;* **s. capacity** *(at cinema, stadium)* aforo *m (de personas sentadas); (on bus, plane)* número *m* de plazas (sentadas)

seaway ['siːweɪ] *n* ruta *f* marítima

seaweed ['siːwiːd] *n* algas *fpl* marinas; **a piece of s.** un alga

seaworthy ['siːwɜːðɪ] *adj (ship)* en condiciones de navegar

sebaceous [sɪ'beɪʃəs] *adj* sebáceo(a)

sec[1] *(abbr* **seconds)** s., segundos *mpl*

sec[2] [sek] *n Fam (moment)* **just a s.!** ¡un momentín!

secede [sɪ'siːd] *vi* escindirse, separarse **(from** de)

secession [sɪ'seʃən] *n* secesión *f,* escisión *f*

secluded [sɪ'kluːdɪd] *adj* apartado(a), retirado(a)

seclusion [sɪ'kluːʒən] *n* retiro *m;* **to live in s.** vivir reclui-do(a)

second[1] ['sekənd] *n (time)* segundo *m;* **I won't be a s.** no tardo *or Am* demoro nada; **just a s.** un momento, un segundo; **s. hand** *(of clock)* segundero *m*

second[2] **1** *n* **(a)** *(in series)* segundo(a) *m,f;* **Edward the S.** *(written)* Eduardo II; *(spoken)* Eduardo segundo; **she was s.** quedó (en) segunda (posición); **s. in command** segundo de a bordo **(b)** *(of month)* **the s. of May** el dos de mayo; **we're leaving on the s.** nos marchamos el (día) dos **(c)** *Com* **seconds** *(defective goods)* artículos *mpl* defectuosos **(d)** *(in duel)* padrino *m; (in boxing)* ayudante *m* del preparador **(e) s. (gear)** segunda *f* **(f)** *Fam (at meal)* **anyone for seconds?** ¿alguien quiere repetir?

2 *adj* segundo(a); **the s. century** el siglo dos *or* segundo; **twenty-s.** vigésimo segundo(a), vigésimosegundo(a); *Fig* **to take s. place (to sb)** quedar por debajo (de alguien); **to be s. to none** no tener rival; **the s. largest city in the world** la segunda ciudad más grande del mundo; **a s. Picasso/ Churchill** un nuevo Picasso/Churchill; **on s. thoughts** pensándolo bien; **to have s. thoughts (about sth)** tener

alguna duda (sobre algo); *Fig* **to play s. fiddle to sb** hacer de comparsa de alguien; **lying is s. nature to her** las mentiras le salen automáticamente; **she got her s. wind** entraron energías renovadas, se recuperó; **s. base** *(in baseball) (place)* segunda base *f; (player)* segunda base *mf;* **s. chance** segunda oportunidad *f;* **s. childhood** senilidad *f;* **s. class** *(on train)* segunda *f* (clase); *Rel* **the S. Coming** el Segundo Adveni-miento; **s. cousin** primo(a) *m,f* segundo(a); **s. floor** primer piso *m;* **s. language** segunda lengua *f;* **s. name** apellido *m; Law* **s. offense** reincidencia *f;* **s. opinion** segunda opinión *f; Gram* **(in the) s. person** (en) segunda persona *f;* **s. sight** clarividencia *f;* **s. violin** segundo violín *m;* **the S. World War** la Segunda Guerra Mundial

second[3] *vt (motion, speaker)* secundar

secondary ['sekəndərɪ] *adj* secundario(a); *Educ* **s. education** enseñanza *f* secundaria; *Educ* **s. school** instituto *m (de enseñanza secundaria)*

second-best ['sekənd'best] **1** *n* segunda opción *f;* **to be content with s.** conformarse con una segunda opción

2 *adv* **to come off s.** caer derrotado(a)

second-class ['sekənd'klɑːs] **1** *adj* **(a)** *(postage)* **s. mail** = en el Reino Unido, servicio postal de segunda clase, más barato y lento que la primera clase **(b)** *(inferior)* de segunda; **s. citizen** ciudadano(a) *m,f* de segunda (clase)

2 *adv* **to travel s.** viajar en segunda

seconder ['sekəndə(r)] *n* **the s. of a motion** la persona que secunda una moción

second-generation ['sekəndʒenə'reɪʃən] *adj (immigrant, computer)* de segunda generación

second-guess ['sekənd'ges] *vt* predecir, anticiparse a

secondhand ['sekənd'hænd] **1** *adj (car, clothes)* de segunda mano

2 *adv (to buy)* de segunda mano; **to hear news s.** enterarse de una noticia a través de terceros

secondly ['sekəndlɪ] *adv* en segundo lugar

second-rate [sekənd'reɪt] *adj* de segunda (categoría)

second-string [sekənd'strɪŋ] *adj (substitute)* suplente, reserva; *(second-rate)* de segunda (categoría)

secrecy ['siːkrɪsɪ] *n* confidencialidad *f;* **in s.** en secreto; **to swear sb to s.** hacer jurar a alguien que guardará el secreto

secret ['siːkrɪt] **1** *n* secreto *m;* **to do sth in s.** hacer algo en secreto; **I make no s. of it** no pretendo que sea un secreto; **to let sb into a s.** revelar *or* contar un secreto a alguien

2 *adj* secreto(a); **to keep sth s. from sb** ocultar algo a alguien; **s. agent** agente *mf* secreto(a); **s. police** policía *f* secreta; **the S. Service** los servicios secretos; *also Fig* **s. weapon** arma *f* secreta

secretarial ['sekrə'teərɪəl] *adj (work)* administrativo(a); **s. college** escuela *f* de secretariado; **s. course** curso *m* de secretariado

secretariat [sekrə'teərɪət] *n Pol* secretaría *f*

secretary ['sekrətərɪ] *n* **(a)** *(in office)* secretario(a) *m,f* **(b)** *Pol* ministro(a) *m,f;* **S. of the Interior** ≃ Ministro(a) *m,f* del Medio Ambiente; **S. of State** secretario(a) *m,f* de Estado

secretary-general ['sekrətərɪ'dʒenərəl] *(pl* **secretaries-general)** *n Pol* secretario(a) *m,f* general

secrete [sɪ'kriːt] *vt* **(a)** *(discharge)* secretar, segregar **(b)** *(hide)* ocultar

secretion [sɪ'kriːʃən] *n* secreción *f*

secretive ['siːkrɪtɪv] *adj* reservado(a); **to be s. about sth** ser reservado(a) respecto a algo

secretively ['siːkrɪtɪvlɪ] *adv (behave)* muy en secreto

secretly ['siːkrɪtlɪ] *adv* en secreto

sect [sekt] *n* secta *f*

sectarian [sek'teərɪən] *adj* sectario(a)

sectarianism [sek'teərɪənɪzəm] *n* sectarismo *m*

section ['sekʃən] **1** *n* sección *f; Mus* **the brass/string s.** la sección de metal/cuerda; **all sections of society** todos los sectores de la sociedad

2 *vt (cut)* seccionar

sectional ['sekʃənəl] *adj* (**a**) *(interests, rivalries)* particular (**b**) **a s. drawing** una sección, un corte

sector ['sektə(r)] *n* sector *m*; **public/private s.** sector *m* público/privado

secular ['sekjʊlə(r)] *adj* *(history, art)* secular; *(music)* profano(a); *(education)* laico(a)

secularize ['sekjʊləraɪz] *vt* secularizar

secure [sɪ'kjʊə(r)] **1** *adj* (**a**) *(free from anxiety)* seguro(a); **s. in the knowledge that...** con la conciencia tranquila sabiendo que... (**b**) *(investment, place, foothold)* seguro(a); *(foundations)* firme, seguro(a); **to make sth s.** asegurar algo

2 *vt* (**a**) *(make safe) (region)* proteger; *(future)* asegurar (**b**) *(fasten) (load)* asegurar, afianzar; *(door, window)* cerrar bien (**c**) *(obtain) (support, promise, loan)* conseguir

secured [sɪ'kjʊəd] *adj* *(debt, loan)* garantizado(a)

securely [sɪ'kjʊəlɪ] *adv* (**a**) *(safely)* a buen recaudo (**b**) *(firmly)* firmemente; **the door was s. fastened** la puerta estaba firmemente cerrada

security [sɪ'kjʊərɪtɪ] *n* (**a**) *(stability, safety)* seguridad *f*; **s. of tenure** cargo *m* vitalicio; **S. Council** Consejo *m* de Seguridad; **s. forces** fuerzas *fpl* de seguridad; **s. guard** guarda *mf* jurado(a); **s. officer** agente *mf* de seguridad; **s. risk** peligro *m* para la seguridad del Estado *(persona)* (**b**) *Fin (for loan)* garantía *f*, aval *m* (**c**) *Fin* **securities** valores *mpl*

sedan [sɪ'dæn] *n* (**a**) *Aut* turismo *m* (**b**) **s. chair** silla *f* de manos

sedate [sɪ'deɪt] **1** *adj* sosegado(a), sereno(a)

2 *vt* sedar

sedately [sɪ'deɪtlɪ] *adv* sosegadamente

sedation [sɪ'deɪʃən] *n* **under s.** sedado(a)

sedative ['sedətɪv] *n* sedante *m*

sedentary ['sedəntrɪ] *adj* sedentario(a)

sediment ['sedɪmənt] *n* sedimento *m*

sedition [sɪ'dɪʃən] *n* sedición *f*

seditious [sɪ'dɪʃəs] *adj* sedicioso(a)

seduce [sɪ'djuːs] *vt (sexually)* seducir; *Fig* **to s. sb into doing sth** inducir a alguien a hacer algo

seducer [sɪ'djuːsə(r)] *n* seductor(ora) *m,f*

seduction [sɪ'dʌkʃən] *n* seducción *f*

seductive [sɪ'dʌktɪv] *adj* seductor(ora); **a s. offer** una oferta tentadora

seductively [sɪ'dʌktɪvlɪ] *adv* seductoramente

see¹ [siː] *n Rel* sede *f* (episcopal)

see² (*pt* saw [sɔː], *pp* seen [siːn]) **1** *vt* (**a**) *(with eyes, perceive)* ver; **to s. sb do** *or* **doing sth** ver a alguien hacer algo; **did you s. that program last night?** ¿viste anoche ese programa?; **now s. what you've done!** ¡mira lo que has hecho!; **to s. the sights** hacer turismo; **s. page 50** ver *or* véase pág. 50; **to be seeing things** *(hallucinate)* ver visiones; **it has to be seen to be believed** hay que verlo para creerlo; **I can't s. a way out of this problem** no le veo solución a este problema; **could you s. your way to lending me the money?** ¿crees que podrías prestarme el dinero?; **to s. sense** *or* **reason** atender a razones; **these years saw many changes** estos años fueron testigos de muchos cambios; **I don't know what you s. in her** no sé qué ves en ella; **it remains to be seen whether...** está por ver si...; **I can't s. any** *or* **the sense in continuing this discussion** creo que no tiene sentido continuar esta discusión; **this is how I s. it** yo lo veo así

(**b**) *(understand)* ver, entender; **I s. what you mean** ya veo lo que quieres decir; **I don't s. the need for...** no veo qué necesidad hay de...; **I don't s. the point** no creo que tenga sentido

(**c**) *(envisage, imagine)* creer, imaginarse; **what do you s.**

happening next? ¿qué crees que ocurrirá a continuación?; **I can't s. them accepting this** no creo que vayan a aceptar esto; **I can't s. you as a boxer** no te imagino como *or* de boxeador

(**d**) *(investigate, inquire)* **I'll s. what I can do** veré qué puedo hacer; **let's s. what happens if...** veamos qué ocurre si...

(**e**) *(make sure)* **I shall s. (to it) that he comes** me encargaré de que venga; **s. (to it) that you don't miss the train!** ¡asegúrate de no perder el tren!; *Fam* **he'll s. you (all) right** él te echará una mano

(**f**) *(meet) (person)* ver; *(doctor, solicitor)* ver, visitar; **I'm seeing Bill tomorrow** mañana voy a ver a Bill; **s. you soon!** ¡hasta pronto!

(**g**) *(escort, accompany)* acompañar; **to s. sb home/to the door** acompañar a alguien a casa/a la puerta

2 *vi* (**a**) *(with eyes)* ver; **as far as the eye can s.** hasta donde alcanza la vista; **s. for yourself** míralo tú mismo; **we shall s.** ya veremos (**b**) *(understand)* entender, ver; **as far as I can s.** a mi entender; **ah, I s.!** ¡ah, ya veo! (**c**) *(examine, consider)* **let me s., let's s.** veamos; **can we go to the beach? — we'll s.** ¿podemos ir a la playa? — ya veremos (**d**) *(find out)* **I'll go and s.** voy a ver

▶**see about** *vt insep* (**a**) *(deal with)* encargarse *or* ocuparse de (**b**) *(consider)* ver, pensar; *Fam* **we'll (soon) s. about that!** ¡eso está por ver!

▶**see after** *vt insep (person, possessions)* cuidar

▶**see in** *vt sep* **to s. the New Year in** recibir el Año Nuevo

▶**see off** *vt sep (say goodbye to)* despedir

▶**see out** *vt sep (escort to door)* acompañar a la puerta; **I'll s. myself out** ya conozco el camino (de salida), gracias

▶**see through 1** *vt sep (project, policy)* **to s. sth through** sacar algo adelante

2 *vt insep (not be deceived by) (person)* ver las intenciones de; *(plan, lies)* percatarse de

▶**see to** *vt insep (deal with)* ocuparse de; **to get sth seen to** hacer que alguien se ocupe de algo; **I'll s. to it that you're not disturbed** me aseguraré *or* encargaré de que nadie te moleste

seed [siːd] **1** *n* (**a**) *(for sowing)* semilla *f*; *(of fruit)* pepita *f*; **the price of s.** el precio de las semillas; **to go** *or* **run to s.** *(plant)* granar; *Fig* **to sow (the) seeds of discord/doubt** sembrar la discordia/la duda; **s. corn** simiente *f* de trigo; *Fig* inversión *f* de futuro; **s. merchant** vendedor *m* de semillas; **s. potatoes** *Esp* patatas *fpl* *or* *Am* papas *fpl* de siembra (**b**) *Literary (semen)* semilla *f*, semen *m* (**c**) *Sport (in tournament)* cabeza *mf* de serie

2 *vt* (**a**) *(remove seeds from)* despepitar (**b**) *Sport (in tournament)* **seeded players/teams** jugadores *mpl*/equipos *mpl* seleccionados como cabezas de serie; **he's seeded 5th** es la cabeza de serie número 5

3 *vi (plant)* dar semilla, granar

seedless ['siːdlɪs] *adj* sin pepitas

seedling ['siːdlɪŋ] *n* plantón *m*

seedy ['siːdɪ] *adj* (**a**) *(shabby) (person, appearance, hotel)* miserable, cutre (**b**) *Fam (unwell)* **to feel s.** estar malo(a) *or* *Esp* pachucho(a) *or* *Col* maluco(a)

seeing ['siːɪŋ] **1** *n* **s. is believing** ver para creer

2 *conj* **s. that** *or* **as** *or* **how...** en vista de que..., ya que...; **s. it's so simple, why don't you do it yourself?** ya que es tan sencillo, ¿por qué no lo haces tú mismo?

Seeing Eye® dog ['siːmaɪ'dɒg] *n* perro *m* lazarillo

seek [siːk] (*pt & pp* sought [sɔːt]) *vt* (**a**) *(look for) (thing lost, job)* buscar; *(friendship, promotion)* tratar de conseguir; **to s. one's fortune** buscar fortuna (**b**) *(request)* **to s. sth from sb** pedir algo a alguien; **to s. sb's help/advice** pedir ayuda/consejo a alguien (**c**) *(try)* **to s. to do sth** procurar hacer algo

▶**seek out** *vt sep (person)* ir en búsqueda *or* *Esp* busca de

seeker ['siːkə(r)] *n* buscador(ora) *m,f*

seem [si:m] *vi* parecer; **to s. tired** parecer cansado(a); **do what seems best** haz lo que te parezca mejor; **it seemed like a dream** parecía un sueño; **it doesn't s. right** no me parece bien; **I s. to have dropped your vase** creo que he tirado tu jarrón; **I can't s. to get it right** no consigo que me salga bien; **it seems (that)…, it would s. (that)…** parece que…; **it seems likely that…** parece probable que…; **it seems to me that…** me parece que…; **it seems** *or* **would s. so** parece que sí; **it seems** *or* **would s. not** parece que no

seeming ['si:mɪŋ] *adj* aparente

seemingly ['si:mɪŋlɪ] *adv* aparentemente

seemly ['si:mlɪ] *adj Formal* correcto(a), apropiado(a)

seen [si:n] *pp of* **see²**

seep [si:p] *vi* **to s. into sth** filtrarse en algo

seepage ['si:pɪdʒ] *n* filtración *f*

seer [sɪə(r)] *n Literary* adivino(a) *m,f*, profeta *m*

seesaw ['si:sɔ:] **1** *n* balancín *m (columpio)*
    2 *vi (prices, mood)* fluctuar

seethe [si:ð] *vi (liquid)* borbotar; **to be seething (with anger)** estar a punto de estallar (de cólera)

see-through ['si:θru:] *adj* transparente

segment 1 *n* ['segmənt] *(of circle, worm)* segmento *m*; *(of orange)* gajo *m*
    2 *vt* [seg'ment] segmentar

segmentation [segmen'teɪʃən] *n Econ* segmentación *f*

segmented [seg'mentɪd] *adj Econ* segmentado(a)

segregate ['segrɪgeɪt] *vt* segregar **(from** de)

segregated ['segrɪgeɪtɪd] *adj (school, beach)* segregado(a)

segregation [segrɪ'geɪʃən] *n* segregación *f*

segregationist [segrɪ'geɪʃənɪst] *n & adj* segregacionista *mf*

Seine [seɪn] *n* **the S.** el Sena

seismic ['saɪzmɪk] *adj* sísmico(a)

seismograph ['saɪzməgræf] *n* sismógrafo *m*

seismology [saɪz'mɒlədʒɪ] *n* sismología *f*

seize [si:z] *vt* **(a)** *(grab)* agarrar, *Esp* coger; **to s. hold of sth** agarrar algo; **to s. the opportunity of doing sth** aprovechar la oportunidad de hacer algo **(b)** *(take for oneself) (city, territory)* tomar; *Law (drugs, stolen goods)* incautarse de

▸**seize on, seize upon** *vt insep* aprovecharse de

▸**seize up** *vi (engine, machine)* atascarse

seizure ['si:ʒə(r)] *n* **(a)** *(of land, city)* toma *f*; *Law (of property, goods)* incautación *f* **(b)** *Med* ataque *m*

seldom ['seldəm] *adv* rara vez, raras veces

select [sɪ'lekt] **1** *adj* selecto(a)
    2 *vt* seleccionar

selected [sɪ'lektɪd] *adj* seleccionado(a); **s. works** obras *fpl* escogidas

selection [sɪ'lekʃən] *n* **(a)** *(act of choosing)* selección *f*; **to make a s.** realizar una selección **(b)** *(range)* gama *f* **(c)** *(thing chosen)* elección *f*

selective [sɪ'lektɪv] *adj* selectivo(a); **to be s. (about sth)** ser selectivo (con algo)

selectively [sɪ'lektɪvlɪ] *adv* con un criterio selectivo

self [self] *(pl* **selves** [selvz]*) n* **(a)** **he's quite his old s. again** ha vuelto a ser él mismo; **she is a shadow of her former s.** no es ni sombra de lo que era; **she was her usual cheerful s.** se mostró alegre como siempre **(b)** *Psy* **the s.** el yo, el ser

self-absorbed ['selfəb'zɔ:bd] *adj* ensimismado(a)

self-addressed envelope ['selfə'drest'envələʊp] *n* sobre *m* dirigido a uno mismo

self-appointed ['selfə'pɔɪntɪd] *adj* autodesignado(a), autoproclamado(a)

self-assured ['selfə'ʃʊəd] *adj* seguro(a) de sí mismo(a); **to be s.** estar seguro de sí mismo

self-awareness ['selfə'weənɪs] *n* conocimiento *m* de sí mismo(a)

self-catering ['self'keɪtərɪŋ] *adj (vacation, accommodation)* sin servicio de comidas

self-centered ['self'sentəd] *adj* egoísta

self-confessed ['selfkən'fest] *adj* confeso(a)

self-confidence ['self'kɒnfɪdəns] *n* confianza *f* en sí mismo(a)

self-confident ['self'kɒnfɪdənt] *adj* lleno(a) de confianza en sí mismo(a)

self-confidently ['self'kɒnfɪdəntlɪ] *adv* con gran confianza or seguridad

self-congratulatory ['selfkəngrætjʊ'leɪtərɪ] *adj* de autosatisfacción

self-conscious ['self'kɒnʃəs] *adj* cohibido(a)

self-consciously ['self'kɒnʃəslɪ] *adv (with embarrassment)* con inhibición, tímidamente; *(affectedly)* afectadamente, con afectación

self-contained ['selfkən'teɪnd] *adj (person, apartment)* independiente

self-contradictory ['selfkɒntrə'dɪktərɪ] *adj* contradictorio(a)

self-control ['selfkən'trəʊl] *n* autocontrol *m*

self-deception ['selfdɪ'sepʃən] *n* autoengaño *m*

self-defeating ['selfdɪ'fi:tɪŋ] *adj* contraproducente

self-defense ['selfdɪ'fens] *n (judo, karate etc)* defensa *f* personal; *(nonviolent action)* autodefensa *f*; **in s.** en defensa propia, en legítima defensa

self-denial ['selfdɪ'naɪəl] *n* abnegación *f*

self-deprecating ['self'deprɪkeɪtɪŋ] *adj* **he's famous for his s. humor** siempre se ríe de sí mismo

self-destruct ['selfdɪ'strʌkt] *vi* autodestruirse

self-destructive ['selfdɪs'trʌktɪv] *adj* autodestructivo(a)

self-determination ['selfdɪtɜ:mɪ'neɪʃən] *n* autodeterminación *f*

self-discipline ['self'dɪsɪplɪn] *n* autodisciplina *f*

self-disciplined ['self'dɪsɪplɪnd] *adj* autodisciplinado(a)

self-doubt ['self'daʊt] *n* falta *f* de confianza (en uno mismo)

self-effacing ['selfɪ'feɪsɪŋ] *adj* modesto(a), humilde

self-employed ['selfɪm'plɔɪd] *adj* autónomo(a)

self-esteem [selfɪ'sti:m] *n* **to have high/low s.** tener mucho/poco amor propio, tener mucha/poca autoestima

self-evident ['self'evɪdənt] *adj* evidente, obvio(a)

self-explanatory ['selfɪk'splænətərɪ] *adj* **to be s.** estar muy claro(a), hablar por sí mismo(a)

self-expression ['selfɪk'spreʃən] *n* autoexpresión *f*

self-fulfilling ['selffʊl'fɪlɪŋ] *adj (prophecy, prediction)* determinante

self-governing ['self'gʌvənɪŋ] *adj* autónomo(a)

self-government ['self'gʌvənmənt] *n* autogobierno *m*, autonomía *f*

self-help ['self'help] *n* autoayuda *f*; **s. group** grupo *m* de apoyo

self-image ['self'ɪmɪdʒ] *n* imagen *f* de sí mismo(a)

self-importance ['selfɪm'pɔ:təns] *n* engreimiento *m*, presunción *f*

self-important ['selfɪm'pɔ:tənt] *adj* engreído(a), presuntuoso(a)

self-improvement ['selfɪm'pru:vmənt] *n* autosuperación *f*

self-induced ['selfɪn'dju:st] *adj (hysteria, illness)* provocado(a) por uno mismo

self-indulgence ['selfɪn'dʌldʒəns] *n* autocomplacencia *f*

self-indulgent ['selfɪn'dʌldʒənt] *adj* autocomplaciente

self-inflicted ['selfɪn'flɪktɪd] *adj* autoinfligido(a)

self-interest ['self'ɪntrest] *n* interés *m* propio

self-interested ['self'ɪntrestɪd] *adj* egoísta

selfish ['selfɪʃ] *adj* egoísta

selfishness ['selfɪʃnɪs] *n* egoísmo *m*

self-justification ['selfdʒʌstɪfɪ'keɪʃən] n autojustificación f

self-knowledge ['self'nɒlɪdʒ] n conocimiento m de sí mismo(a)

selfless ['selflɪs] adj desinteresado(a), desprendido(a)

selflessly ['selflɪslɪ] adv desinteresadamente, de manera desinteresada

self-made man ['selfmeɪd'mæn] n hombre m hecho a sí mismo

self-pity ['self'pɪtɪ] n autocompasión f

self-pitying ['self'pɪtɪɪŋ] adj autocompasivo(a)

self-portrait ['self'pɔːtreɪt] n autorretrato m

self-possessed ['selfpə'zest] adj sereno(a), dueño(a) de sí mismo(a)

self-possession ['selfpə'zeʃən] n serenidad f, autocontrol m

self-preservation ['selfprezə'veɪʃən] n propia conservación f; **instinct for s.** instinto m de conservación

self-reliant ['selfrɪ'laɪənt] adj autosuficiente

self-respect ['selfrɪ'spekt] n amor m propio, dignidad f

self-restraint ['selfrɪ'streɪnt] n autodominio m, autocontrol m

self-righteous ['self'raɪtʃəs] adj santurrón(ona)

self-righteousness ['self'raɪtʃəsnɪs] n santurronería f

self-rising flour ['selfraɪzɪŋ'flaʊə(r)] n Esp harina f con levadura, Am harina f con polvos de hornear, RP harina f leudante

selfsame ['selfseɪm] adj mismísimo(a)

self-satisfied ['self'sætɪsfaɪd] adj satisfecho(a) or pagado(a) de sí mismo(a); **to be s.** estar satisfecho or pagado de sí mismo

self-service ['self'sɜːvɪs] **1** n autoservicio m
2 adj de autoservicio

self-starter ['self'stɑːtə(r)] n (person) persona f con iniciativa

self-styled ['selfstaɪld] adj (president, king) autoproclamado(a); (philosopher, expert) pretendido(a), sedicente

self-sufficiency ['selfsə'fɪʃənsɪ] n autosuficiencia f

self-sufficient ['selfsə'fɪʃənt] adj autosuficiente

self-taught ['self'tɔːt] adj autodidacto(a)

sell [sel] (pt & pp sold [səʊld]) **1** vt vender; **to s. sb sth, to s. sth to sb** vender algo a alguien; **to s. sth at a loss/a profit** vender algo con pérdida/ganancia; **scandal sells newspapers** las noticias escandalosas venden bien; Fig **to s. oneself** venderse; Fig **to s. sb an idea** vender una idea a alguien; Fig **to s. sb down the river** traicionar or vender a alguien
2 vi (product) venderse (**for** a); **to s. like hot cakes** venderse como rosquillas

▸**sell off** vt sep (property, stock) liquidar

▸**sell out 1** vt sep (a) **the concert is sold out** no quedan entradas or Am boletos para el concierto (b) (betray) vender, traicionar
2 vi (a) **they have sold out of tickets** se han agotado las entradas or Am los boletos (b) (betray beliefs) venderse

seller ['selə(r)] n vendedor(ora) m,f; Econ **sellers' market** mercado m de vendedores

selling ['selɪŋ] n venta f; **s. point** ventaja f (de un producto); **s. price** precio m de venta

sell-off ['selɒf] n (of state-owned company) privatización f

sellout ['selaʊt] n (a) (play, concert) lleno m (b) (betrayal) traición f

semantic [sɪ'mæntɪk] adj semántico(a)

semantics [sɪ'mæntɪks] n semántica f; Fig **let's not worry about s.** dejemos a un lado los matices

semaphore ['seməfɔː(r)] n código m alfabético de banderas

semblance ['sembləns] n apariencia f

semen ['siːmen] n semen m

semester [sɪ'mestə(r)] n Univ semestre m

semi ['semɪ] n Fam (abbr **semitrailer**) semirremolque m

semiautomatic ['semɪɔːtə'mætɪk] adj semiautomático(a)

semicircle ['semɪsɜːkəl] n semicírculo m

semicircular [semɪ'sɜːkjʊlə(r)] adj semicircular

semicolon ['semɪ'kəʊlən] n punto m y coma

semiconductor ['semɪkən'dʌktə(r)] n Elec semiconductor m

semiconscious ['semɪ'kɒnʃəs] adj semiconsciente

semidetached ['semɪdɪ'tætʃt] **1** n (house) chalet m semiadosado
2 adj semiadosado(a)

semifinal ['semɪ'faɪnəl] n semifinal f

semifinalist ['semɪ'faɪnəlɪst] n semifinalista mf

seminal ['semɪnəl] adj (very important) trascendental

seminar ['semɪnɑː(r)] n seminario m

seminary ['semɪnərɪ] n seminario m

semiprecious ['semɪ'preʃəs] adj **s. stone** piedra f fina or semipreciosa

Semite ['siːmaɪt] n semita mf

Semitic [sɪ'mɪtɪk] adj semita, semítico(a)

semitrailer ['semɪtreɪlə(r)] n semirremolque m

semitropical ['semɪ'trɒpɪkəl] adj subtropical

semivowel [semɪ'vaʊəl] n semivocal f

semolina [semə'liːnə] n sémola f

senate ['senɪt] n **the S.** el Senado

senator ['senətə(r)] n senador(ora) m,f

send [send] (pt & pp sent [sent]) vt (letter, message, person) mandar, enviar; **to s. word to sb (that...)** mandar el recado a alguien (de que...); **to s. sb to prison** enviar a alguien a prisión; **to s. sb on an errand** mandar a alguien a (hacer) un recado; **to s. sth/sb flying** mandar or lanzar algo/a alguien por los aires; **that sent him into fits of laughter** aquello le provocó un ataque de risa

▸**send away 1** vt sep **to s. sb away** mandar a alguien que se marche
2 vi **to s. away for sth** pedir algo por correo

▸**send back** vt sep (purchase, order of food) devolver

▸**send for** vt insep (help, supplies) mandar traer; (doctor) mandar llamar

▸**send in** vt sep (application, troops, supplies) enviar

▸**send off 1** vt sep (a) (letter, order) mandar, enviar (b) Sport expulsar
2 vi **to s. off for sth** pedir algo por correo

▸**send on** vt sep (a) (send ahead) **we had our belongings sent on** enviamos nuestras pertenencias a nuestro destino antes de partir (b) (forward after use) enviar más tarde

▸**send out 1** vt sep (letters, invitations) mandar, enviar; (radio signals) emitir
2 vi **to s. out for sth** pedir que traigan algo

sender ['sendə(r)] n remitente mf

send-off ['sendɒf] n Fam despedida f

Senegal [senɪ'gɔːl] n Senegal

Senegalese [senɪgə'liːz] n & adj senegalés(esa) m,f

senile ['siːnaɪl] adj senil; Med **s. dementia** demencia f senil

senility [sɪ'nɪlɪtɪ] n senilidad f

senior ['siːnjə(r)] **1** n (a) **to be sb's s.** (in age) ser mayor que alguien; (in rank) ser el superior de alguien; **she is three years his s.** ella es tres años mayor que él (b) (student) estudiante mf de último curso (c) (senior citizen) persona f de la tercera edad
2 adj (a) (in age) mayor; **Thomas Smith, S.** Thomas Smith, padre; **s. citizen** persona f de la tercera edad (b) (in rank, position) superior; **s. officer** oficial m superior; **s. partner** (in company) socio m principal (c) Sch de los últimos cursos

seniority [siːnɪ'ɒrɪtɪ] n (in age, length of service) antigüedad f; (in rank) rango m, categoría f

sensation [sen'seɪʃən] n (a) (feeling) sensación f; **burning s.** quemazón f (b) (excitement) **to be a s.** ser todo un éxito; **to cause a s.** causar sensación

sensational [sen'seɪʃənəl] adj (**a**) (exaggerated) tremendista, sensacionalista (**b**) (excellent) extraordinario(a), sensacional

sensationalism [sen'seɪʃənəlɪzəm] n sensacionalismo m

sensationally [sen'seɪʃənəlɪ] adv (**a**) (exaggeratedly) con sensacionalismo (**b**) (excellently) de maravilla, Esp estupendamente; **s. successful** de tremendo éxito

sense [sens] **1** n (**a**) (faculty) sentido m; **to come to one's senses** (recover consciousness) recobrar el conocimiento or sentido; (see reason) entrar en razón; **s. of smell/hearing** sentido del olfato/oído; **to lose all s. of time** perder la noción del tiempo; **s. of direction** sentido de la orientación; **s. of duty** sentido del deber; **s. of humor** sentido del humor (**b**) (feeling) sensación f; **a s. of achievement** la sensación de haber logrado algo (**c**) (rationality, common sense) sensatez f, buen juicio m; **good s.** buen juicio; **there's no s. in staying** no tiene sentido quedarse (**d**) (meaning) sentido m; **to make (no) s.** (no) tener sentido; **to make s. of sth** entender algo; **in a s.** en cierto sentido; **in the s. that...** en el sentido de que...
2 vt (perceive) notar, percibir; **to s. that...** tener la sensación de que...

senseless ['senslɪs] adj (**a**) (unconscious) inconsciente (**b**) (pointless) absurdo(a)

senselessly ['senslɪslɪ] adv (pointlessly) de forma absurda, sin sentido

sensibility [sensɪ'bɪlɪtɪ] n (of artist) sensibilidad f; **to offend sb's sensibilities** (feelings) herir la sensibilidad de alguien

sensible ['sensɪbəl] adj (**a**) (rational) (person, decision) sensato(a); **the s. thing to do** lo sensato, lo que tiene sentido (hacer) (**b**) (practical) (clothes, shoes) práctico(a) (**c**) Formal (aware) **to be s. of sth** ser consciente de algo

sensibly ['sensɪblɪ] adv (rationally) sensatamente

sensitive ['sensɪtɪv] adj (in general) sensible (**to** a); (touchy) susceptible

sensitively ['sensɪtɪvlɪ] adv (tactfully) con delicadeza, con tacto

sensitivity [sensɪ'tɪvɪtɪ] n sensibilidad f

sensitize ['sensɪtaɪz] vt sensibilizar (**to** acerca de or ante)

sensor ['sensə(r)] n sensor m

sensory ['sensərɪ] adj sensorial; **s. organs** órganos mpl sensoriales

sensual ['sensjʊəl] adj sensual

sensuality [sensjʊ'ælɪtɪ] n sensualidad f

sensuous ['sensjʊəs] adj sensual

sent [sent] pt & pp of **send**

sentence ['sentəns] **1** n (**a**) Gram oración f, frase f (**b**) Law sentencia f; **to pass s.** dictar sentencia
2 vt Law sentenciar (**to** a)

sententious [sen'tenʃəs] adj Formal sentencioso(a)

sentient ['sentɪənt] adj sensitivo(a), sensible

sentiment ['sentɪmənt] n (**a**) (opinion) parecer m; **public s.** el sentir popular (**b**) (sentimentality) sentimentalismo m

sentimental [sentɪ'mentəl] adj sentimental

sentimentalist [sentɪ'mentəlɪst] n sentimental mf

sentimentality [sentɪmen'tælɪtɪ] n sentimentalismo m

sentimentalize [sentɪ'mentəlaɪz] vt tratar con sentimentalismo

sentimentally [sentɪ'mentəlɪ] adv sentimentalmente; **to be s. attached to sb** tener una relación sentimental con alguien; **to be s. attached to sth** tener cariño a algo

sentry ['sentrɪ] n Mil centinela m; **to be on s. duty** estar de guardia; **s. box** garita f

Seoul [səʊl] n Seúl

Sep (abbr **September**) septiembre m

separable ['sepərəbəl] adj separable

separate 1 adj ['sepərət] (parts, box, room) separado(a);

(occasion, attempt) distinto(a); (organization) independiente; **the two issues are quite s.** son dos cuestiones bien distintas; **fish and meat should be kept s.** hay que guardar la carne y el pescado por separado; **to lead s. lives** vivir separados(as); also Fig **they went their s. ways** siguieron cada uno su camino
2 vt ['sepəreɪt] separar (**from** de)
3 vi separarse (**from** de)

separated ['sepəreɪtɪd] adj separado(a); **he is s. from his wife** está separado de su mujer

separation [sepə'reɪʃən] n separación f

separatism ['sepərətɪzəm] n Pol separatismo m

separatist ['sepərətɪst] n Pol separatista mf

sepia ['siːpɪə] n (color) (color m) sepia m

sepsis ['sepsɪs] n Med sepsis f inv, infección f

Sept (abbr **September**) septiembre m

September [sep'tembə(r)] n septiembre m; see also **May**

septet [sep'tet] n Mus septeto m

septic ['septɪk] adj séptico(a); **to become s.** infectarse; **s. tank** fosa f séptica

septicemia [septɪ'siːmɪə] n Med septicemia f

sepulcher ['sepəlkə(r)] n Literary sepulcro m

sequel ['siːkwəl] n (**a**) (book, movie) continuación f (**to** de) (**b**) (result) secuela f

sequence ['siːkwəns] n (**a**) (order) sucesión f, secuencia f; **in s.** en sucesión or orden; **out of s.** desordenado(a) (**b**) (of numbers, events) serie f; (in movie) secuencia f

sequencer ['siːkwənsə(r)] n Mus secuenciador m

sequential [sɪ'kwenʃəl] adj secuencial

sequestrate ['sekwəstreɪt] vt Law embargar

sequestration [siːkwe'streɪʃən] n Law embargo m

sequin ['siːkwɪn] n lentejuela f

sequoia [sɪ'kwɔɪə] n sec(u)oya f

Serb [sɜːb] n & adj serbio(a) m,f

Serbia ['sɜːbɪə] n Serbia

Serbian ['sɜːb(ɪ)ən] n & adj serbio(a) m,f

Serbo-Croatian ['sɜːbəʊkrəʊ'eɪʃən] n (language) serbocroata m

serenade [serə'neɪd] **1** n serenata f
2 vt dar una serenata a

serendipity [serən'dɪpɪtɪ] n = don para realizar hallazgos afortunados

serene [sɪ'riːn] adj sereno(a)

serenity [sɪ'renɪtɪ] n serenidad f

serf [sɜːf] n Hist siervo(a) m,f (de la gleba)

serfdom ['sɜːfdəm] n Hist servidumbre f

serge [sɜːdʒ] n sarga f

sergeant ['sɑːdʒənt] n Mil sargento mf; (in police) ≃ oficial mf de policía; Mil **s. major** sargento mf primero

serial ['sɪərɪəl] **1** n (in magazine) novela f por entregas, folletín m; (on TV) serial m
2 adj en serie; **s. killer** asesino(a) m,f en serie; **s. killing** asesinato m en serie; **s. number** número m de serie; Comptr **s. port** puerto m (en) serie

serialization [sɪərɪəlaɪ'zeɪʃən] n (in newspaper, magazine) publicación f por entregas; (on TV) serialización f, adaptación f al formato de serie

serialize ['sɪərɪəlaɪz] vt (in newspaper, magazine) publicar por entregas; (on TV) emitir en forma de serial

series ['sɪərɪz] n serie f

serious ['sɪərɪəs] adj (**a**) (person) serio(a); **to be s. about doing sth** estar decidido(a) a hacer algo; **are you s.?** ¿lo dices en serio?; **it wasn't a s. suggestion** no lo decía en serio (**b**) (grave) (situation, problem, injury) serio(a), grave (**c**) Fam (for emphasis) **s. money** cantidad de dinero

seriously ['sɪərɪəslɪ] adv (**a**) (in earnest) seriamente, en serio;

to take sth/sb s. tomar algo/a alguien en serio; **to take oneself too s.** tomarse demasiado en serio (**b**) *(gravely)* seriamente, gravemente; **s. ill** seriamente *or* gravemente enfermo(a) (**c**) *Fam (very)* cantidad de

sermon ['sɜːmən] *n also Fig* sermón *m*

serpent ['sɜːpənt] *n Literary* sierpe *f*, serpiente *f*

serpentine ['sɜːpəntaɪn] *adj Literary* serpenteante, serpentino(a)

serrated [se'reɪtɪd] *adj* dentado(a)

serum ['sɪərəm] *n Med* suero *m*

servant ['sɜːvənt] *n (in household)* criado(a) *m,f*, sirviente(a) *m,f*; *(of leader, country)* servidor(ora) *m,f*

serve [sɜːv] **1** *n (in tennis)* servicio *m*; **(it's) your s.!** ¡tú sacas!

2 *vt* (**a**) *(be faithful to) (master, cause)* servir, estar al servicio de; **to s. one's own interests** actuar en interés propio

(**b**) *(be useful to)* servir; **it doesn't s. my purpose** no me sirve; **it has served me well** me ha hecho un buen servicio *or* apaño; **if my memory serves me right** si mal no recuerdo

(**c**) *(complete) (prison sentence, term of office)* cumplir; *(apprenticeship)* realizar, hacer

(**d**) *(customer)* atender; **are you being served?** ¿le están atendiendo?

(**e**) *(meal, drink)* servir; **to s. lunch/dinner** servir el almuerzo/la cena; **serves four** *(on packet, in recipe)* para cuatro raciones

(**f**) *Law* **to s. sb with a summons** citar a alguien

(**g**) **it serves her right!** ¡se lo merece!, ¡lo tiene bien merecido!

3 *vi* (**a**) *(carry out duty)* servir; **to s. in a government** ser miembro de un gobierno (**b**) **to s. as…** *(be used as)* servir de…; **to s. as an example** servir de ejemplo (**c**) *(in store)* atender, despachar (**d**) *(with food, drink)* **s. chilled** *(on wine)* sírvase bien frío (**e**) *(in tennis)* servir, sacar

▸**serve up** *vt sep (food)* servir; *Fig* ofrecer

server ['sɜːvə(r)] *n* (**a**) *(in tennis)* jugador(ora) *m,f* al servicio (**b**) *(tray)* bandeja *f* (**c**) *Comptr* servidor *m*

service ['sɜːvɪs] **1** *n* (**a**) *(with army, firm)* servicio *m*; *Mil* **the services** las fuerzas armadas; **to do sb a s.** hacer un favor a alguien; **to be at sb's s.** estar al servicio de alguien; **to be of s. to sb** serle a alguien de utilidad; **he offered his services** ofreció sus servicios

(**b**) *Old-fashioned (of servant)* **to be in s.** servir; **to go into s.** entrar a servir

(**c**) *(in store, restaurant)* servicio *m*; **s. is included** el servicio está incluido; **s. not included** servicio no incluido; **s. charge** *(tarifa f por)* servicio *m*; **s. industry** industria *f* de servicios

(**d**) *(system)* **postal/air/train s.** servicios *mpl* postales/aéreos/de ferrocarril

(**e**) *(maintenance)* revisión *f*; **s. station** *(on motorway)* estación *f* de servicio

(**f**) *Rel* oficio *m*, servicio *m*

(**g**) **tea/dinner s.** servicio *m* de té/de mesa

(**h**) *(in tennis)* saque *m*, servicio *m*; **s. line** línea *f* de saque *or* servicio

2 *vt (car, computer, TV)* revisar; *Fin (loan, debt)* amortizar los intereses de

serviceable ['sɜːvɪsəbəl] *adj* (**a**) *(in working order)* en buen uso (**b**) *(useful)* útil, práctico(a)

serviceman ['sɜːvɪsmən] *n Mil* militar *m*

servicewoman ['sɜːvɪswʊmən] *n Mil* militar *f*

servicing ['sɜːvɪsɪŋ] *n (of heating, car)* revisión *f*; *(of loan, debt)* servicio *m*

servile ['sɜːvaɪl] *adj* servil

serving ['sɜːvɪŋ] *n (portion)* ración *f*; **s. spoon** cuchara *f* de servir

servitude ['sɜːvɪtjuːd] *n* esclavitud *f*

servo ['sɜːvəʊ] **1** *n (pl* **servos)** *Fam (servomechanism)* servomecanismo *m*

2 *adj Aut* **s. brake** servofreno *m*

sesame ['sesəmɪ] *n* **s. oil** aceite *m* de sésamo *or* de ajonjolí; **s. seeds** *(semillas fpl* de) sésamo *m*; **open s.!** ¡ábrete, sésamo!

session ['seʃən] *n* (**a**) *(period of activity)* sesión *f*; *Mus* **s. musician** músico *m* de sesión (**b**) *(meeting)* reunión *f*; **to be in s.** estar reunido(a) (**c**) *Sch & Univ (term)* trimestre *m*; *(year)* curso *m*

set [set] **1** *n* (**a**) *(of keys, boxes, chess pieces, pans)* juego *m*; *(of problems, rules, symptoms) & Math* conjunto *m*; *(of stamps, picture cards, books)* serie *f*, colección *f*; **s. of teeth** dentadura *f* (**b**) *(of people)* grupo *m*, círculo *m* (**c**) *Sch* **top/bottom s.** = grupo de los alumnos más/menos aventajados en cada asignatura a los que se enseña por separado (**d**) *(TV, radio)* aparato *m*, receptor *m*; **television s.** televisor *m* (**e**) *Theat & TV (scenery)* decorado *m*; *Cin* plató *m* (**f**) *(in tennis)* set *m*; **s. point** punto *m* de set

2 *adj* (**a**) *(fixed) (ideas, price)* fijo(a); **to be s. in one's ways** tener hábitos fijos; **s. lunch** menú *m* (del día); **s. phrase** frase *f* hecha; **s. piece** *(in play, movie)* = escena clásica e impactante; *(in sport)* jugada *f* ensayada (a balón parado) (**b**) *(ready)* **to be (all) s. for sth/to do sth** estar preparado(a) para algo/para hacer algo (**c**) *(determined)* **to be (dead) s. on doing sth** estar empeñado(a) en hacer algo; **to be (dead) s. against sth** oponerse totalmente a algo

3 *vt (pt & pp* **set)** (**a**) *(place)* colocar; *(jewel)* engastar; **to s. the table** poner la mesa; **to s. a trap (for sb)** tender una trampa (a alguien); **the novel/movie is set in Kansas** la novela/película transcurre *or* se desarrolla en Kansas

(**b**) *(fix) (date, day, limit, price)* fijar; *(task, problem)* dar, encargar; *(record)* establecer; *(watch, clock)* poner en hora; **to s. a value on sth** poner precio *or* asignar un valor a algo; **s. the alarm clock for 8 a.m.** pon el despertador a las ocho; **to s. the scene for sb** poner a alguien en situación

(**c**) *(cause to start)* **that set me thinking** eso me hizo pensar; **to s. sb free** dejar libre *or* poner en libertad a alguien; **to s. sth on fire** prender fuego a algo; **her performance set people talking** su actuación dio que hablar (a la gente)

(**d**) *Med (bone, fracture)* recomponer

4 *vi* (**a**) *(sun, moon)* ponerse; **we saw the sun setting** vimos la puesta de sol (**b**) *(become firm) (jelly)* cuajar; *(concrete)* endurecerse; *(broken bone)* soldarse

▸**set about** *vt insep (task, job)* emprender; *(problem, situation)* abordar; **to s. about doing sth** empezar a hacer algo

▸**set against** *vt sep* (**a**) *(cause to oppose)* **to s. sb against sb** enemistar a alguien con alguien (**b**) *(compare)* **to s. sth against sth** comparar algo con algo (**c**) *(deduct)* **to s. expenses against tax** deducir gastos de los impuestos

▸**set apart** *vt sep* distinguir (**from** de)

▸**set aside** *vt sep* (**a**) *(job, task)* dejar (a un lado) (**b**) *(save) (money)* ahorrar; *(time)* reservar

▸**set back** *vt sep* (**a**) *(delay)* retrasar (**b**) *Fam (cost)* costar

▸**set by** *vt sep (reserve)* apartar

▸**set down** *vt sep (put down) (object)* dejar; *(passenger)* dejar (bajar); **to s. sth down in writing** poner algo por escrito

▸**set forth** *vi Literary (depart)* partir

▸**set in** *vi (fog, winter)* instalarse; *(night)* caer; *(mood, infection)* arraigar

▸**set off 1** *vt sep* (**a**) *(bomb, alarm)* accionar; *(argument, chain of events)* desencadenar (**b**) *(enhance) (color, feature)* realzar

2 *vi (depart)* salir

▸**set out 1** *vt sep (arrange)* disponer; *(ideas)* exponer

2 *vi* (**a**) *(depart)* salir (**b**) *(in job, task)* empezar, comenzar (**c**) *(intend)* **to s. out to do sth** pretender hacer algo

▸**set to** *vi* (**a**) *(start working)* empezar *or* ponerse a trabajar (**b**) *Fam (start arguing)* meterse *or Esp* enzarzarse en una pelea

▸**set up 1** *vt sep* (**a**) *(erect) (statue)* erigir; *(tent, barrier)* montar (**b**) *(arrange, organize) (meeting, group)* organizar; *(system, company)* establecer; **to s. up house** *or* **home** instalarse; *Fam* **I've been set up!** *(I've been framed)* ¡me han tendido una trampa!

2 *vi(establish oneself)* establecerse (**as** de *or* como); **to s. up in business** montar un negocio

▶**set upon** *vt insep (attack)* atacar

setback ['setbæk] *n* contratiempo *m*, revés *m*

settee [se'ti:] *n* sofá *m*

setter ['setə(r)] *n (dog)* setter *m*

setting ['setɪŋ] **1** *n* (**a**) *(of story, festival)* escenario *m*, marco *m* (**b**) *(of sun)* puesta *f* (de sol) (**c**) *(on machine)* posición *f*; **highest s.** máximo *m*; **lowest s.** mínimo *m* (**d**) **s. lotion** fijador *m*

2 *adj (sun, star)* poniente

settle ['setəl] **1** *vt* (**a**) *(put in place)* colocar, poner; **she had settled herself in an armchair** se había instalado cómodamente en un sillón; **to s. the children for the night** acostar a los niños (**b**) *(nerves)* calmar; **I took something to s. my stomach** tomé algo que me asentara el estómago (**c**) *(day, venue)* fijar (**d**) *(problem, dispute)* resolver; *(account, debt)* liquidar, saldar; **she settled her affairs** resolvió sus asuntos; *Fam* **that settles it!** ¡no se hable más!; *Law* **to s. a matter out of court** llegar a un acuerdo extrajudicial (**e**) *(colonize)* colonizar

2 *vi* (**a**) *(bird, insect, dust)* posarse (**on** en *or* sobre); *(liquid, beer)* reposar (**b**) *(person, family)* asentarse (**in** en); *(crowd, situation)* apaciguarse, tranquilizarse; **to s. into an armchair** instalarse en un sillón; *Law* **to s. (out of court)** llegar a un acuerdo extrajudicial

▶**settle down 1** *vt sep* (**a**) *(make comfortable)* acomodar (**b**) *(make calm)* calmar, tranquilizar

2 *vi* (**a**) *(make oneself comfortable)* acomodarse, instalarse; **to s. down to work** concentrarse en el trabajo (**b**) *(adopt regular life)* sentar la cabeza (**c**) *(situation, excitement)* tranquilizarse, calmarse

▶**settle for** *vt insep (accept)* conformarse con

▶**settle in** *vi (become established)* establecerse

▶**settle on** *vt insep (decide on, choose)* decidirse por

▶**settle up** *vi (pay bill, debt)* pagar

settled ['setəld] *adj (stable)* estable

settlement ['setəlmənt] *n* (**a**) *(of problem, dispute)* resolución *f*; *Com (of account, debt)* liquidación *f*; **to reach a s.** llegar a un acuerdo (**b**) *(town, village) (recently built)* asentamiento *m*; *(in isolated area)* poblado *m*

settler ['setlə(r)] *n* colono *m*

set-top box ['settɒp'bɒks] *n TV* descodificador *m*

setup ['setʌp] *n* (**a**) *Fam (organization, arrangement)* sistema *m*, montaje *m* (**b**) *Fam (trap, trick)* montaje *m*, trampa *f* (**c**) *Comptr* **s. CD-ROM** CD-ROM *m* de instalación

seven ['sevən] **1** *n* siete *m*

2 *adj* siete; *Rel* **the s. deadly sins** los siete pecados capitales; *Literary* **to sail the s. seas** surcar los siete mares; *see also* **eight**

seventeen [sevən'ti:n] *n & adj* diecisiete *m*; *see also* **eight**

seventeenth [sevən'ti:nθ] **1** *n* (**a**) *(fraction)* diecisieteavo *m*, decimoséptima parte *f* (**b**) *(in series)* decimoséptimo(a) *m,f* (**c**) *(of month)* diecisiete *m*

2 *adj* decimoséptimo(a); *see also* **eleventh**

seventh ['sevənθ] **1** *n* (**a**) *(fraction)* séptimo *m*, séptima parte *f* (**b**) *(in series)* séptimo(a) *m,f* (**c**) *(of month)* siete *m*

2 *adj* séptimo(a); **to be in s. heaven** estar en el séptimo cielo; *see also* **eighth**

seventieth ['sevəntɪɪθ] *n & adj* septuagésimo(a) *m,f*

seventy ['sevəntɪ] *n & adj* setenta *m*; *see also* **eighty**

sever ['sevə(r)] *vt also Fig* cortar

several ['sevərəl] **1** *adj* varios(as)

2 *pron* varios(as) *m,fpl*; **s. of us/them** varios de nosotros/ellos

severance ['sevərəns] *n* ruptura *f*; *Ind* **s. pay** indemnización *f* por despido

severe [sɪ'vɪə(r)] *adj* (**a**) *(harsh) (person, punishment, criticism)* severo(a) (**b**) *(pain)* fuerte, intenso(a); *(illness)* grave (**c**) *(austere) (style, architecture)* sobrio(a)

severely [sɪ'vɪəlɪ] *adj* (**a**) *(harshly)* con severidad (**b**) *(injured, ill)* gravemente (**c**) *(austerely)* con sobriedad

severity [sɪ'verɪtɪ] *n* (**a**) *(harshness) (of person, punishment, criticism)* severidad *f* (**b**) *(of pain)* intensidad *f*; *(of illness)* gravedad *f* (**c**) *(austerity) (of style, architecture)* sobriedad *f*

Seville [se'vɪl] *n* Sevilla

sew [səʊ] (*pp* **sewn** [səʊn]) *vt & vi* coser

▶**sew up** *vt sep (hole, wound)* coser; *Fam* **it's all sewn up** está todo arreglado

sewage ['su:ɪdʒ] *n* aguas *fpl* residuales; **s. disposal** depuración *f* de aguas residuales; **s. works** depuradora *f*; **s. system** alcantarillado *m*

sewer ['su:ə(r)] *n (pipe)* alcantarilla *f*, cloaca *f*; **main s.** colector *m*

sewing machine ['səʊɪŋməʃi:n] *n* máquina *f* de coser

sewn [səʊn] *pp of* **sew**

sex [seks] *n* sexo *m*; **to have s. with sb** hacer el amor con alguien, acostarse con alguien; **s. appeal** atractivo *m* sexual; **s. change** cambio *m* de sexo; **s. education** educación *f* sexual; **s. life** vida *f* sexual; **s. maniac** obseso(a) *m,f* (sexual); **s. offender** autor(ora) *m,f* de un delito sexual; **s. shop** sex shop *f*; **s. symbol** símbolo *m* sexual, sex symbol *mf*

sexagenarian [seksədʒɪ'neərɪən] *n* sexagenario(a) *m,f*

sexism ['seksɪzəm] *n* sexismo *m*

sexist ['seksɪst] *n & adj* sexista *mf*

sexologist [sek'sɒlədʒɪst] *n* sexólogo(a) *m,f*

sextant ['sekstənt] *n Naut* sextante *m*

sextet [seks'tet] *n Mus* sexteto *m*

sexton ['sekstən] *n Rel* sacristán *m*

sexual ['seksjʊəl] *adj* sexual; **s. abuse** abuso *m* sexual, abusos *mpl* deshonestos; **s. discrimination** discriminación *f* sexual; **s. harassment** acoso *m* sexual; **s. intercourse** relaciones *fpl* sexuales, el acto sexual; **s. reproduction** reproducción *f* sexual

sexuality [seksjʊ'ælɪtɪ] *n* sexualidad *f*

sexually ['seksjʊəlɪ] *adv* sexualmente; **s. transmitted disease** enfermedad *f* de transmisión sexual

sexy ['seksɪ] *adj* sexy; *Fig (car, idea, object)* muy atractivo(a)

Seychelles [seɪ'ʃelz] *npl* **the S.** las (islas) Seychelles

Sgt *Mil (abbr* **Sergeant**) sargento *mf*

sh [ʃ] *exclam* ¡chsss!, ¡sssh!

shabbily ['ʃæbɪlɪ] *adv* (**a**) *(furnished)* cochambrosamente; *(dressed)* desaliñadamente, desastradamente (**b**) *(to behave)* ruinmente, con mezquindad; **he was treated very s.** lo trataron muy mal *or Esp* fatal

shabbiness ['ʃæbɪnɪs] *n* (**a**) *(of appearance)* desaliño *m*; *(of furniture)* aspecto *m* cochambroso (**b**) *(of conduct, treatment)* ruindad *f*, mezquindad *f*

shabby ['ʃæbɪ] *adj* (**a**) *(clothing)* raído(a), desgastado(a); *(appearance)* desaliñado(a), desastrado(a); *(furniture, house)* cochambroso(a) (**b**) *(conduct, behavior)* ruin, mezquino(a); **s. trick** mala jugada *f* or pasada *f*

shack [ʃæk] *n* casucha *f*, *Esp* chabola *f*, *CSur, Ven* rancho *m*

▶**shack up** *vi Fam* **to s. up with sb** arrejuntarse *or* vivir arrejuntado(a) con alguien

shackle ['ʃækəl] **1** *n* **shackles** grilletes *mpl*

2 *vt (prisoner)* poner grilletes a; *Fig* **to be shackled by convention** ser prisionero(a) de los convencionalismos

shade [ʃeɪd] **1** *n* (**a**) *(shadow)* sombra *f*; **in the s.** a la sombra; *Fig* **to put sb in the s.** hacer sombra *or* eclipsar a alguien; **shades of 1968...** *(reminders)* esto recuerda a 1968... (**b**) *(nuance) (of color)* tono *m*, tonalidad *f*; *(of opinion)* matiz *m*; **a**

s. better/longer ligeramente mejor/más largo(a) (**c**) *Literary (ghost)* espíritu *m*, fantasma *m* (**d**) *Fam* **shades** *(sunglasses)* gafas *fpl or Am* anteojos *mpl* de sol

2 *vt (protect from sun)* dar sombra a, proteger del sol

▸**shade in** *vt sep (part of drawing)* sombrear

shaded ['ʃeɪdɪd] *adj* sombreado(a)

shading ['ʃeɪdɪŋ] *n (on drawing, map)* sombreado *m*

shadow ['ʃædəʊ] **1** *n also Fig* sombra *f*; **to cast a s.** proyectar una sombra; *Fig* **the news cast a s. over the occasion** la noticia vino a ensombrecer el acto; **without a s. of doubt** sin sombra de duda; **to have shadows under one's eyes** tener ojeras

2 *vt (follow)* seguir

shadowy ['ʃædəʊɪ] *adj (vague)* vago(a), impreciso(a); *(dark)* oscuro(a), sombrío(a); **a s. form** una figura en la oscuridad

shady ['ʃeɪdɪ] *adj* (**a**) *(garden, lane)* sombreado(a), umbrío(a) (**b**) *Fam (suspicious) (person)* sospechoso(a), siniestro(a); *(transaction)* turbio(a), oscuro(a)

shaft [ʃɑːft] *n* (**a**) *(of spear)* asta *f*, vara *f*; *(of golf club)* vara *f*, barra *f*; *(of tool)* mango *m*; *(of light)* rayo *m* (**b**) *(of mine)* pozo *m*; *(for lift)* hueco *m* (**c**) *(in engine, machine)* eje *m*

shag [ʃæg] *n (tobacco)* picadura *f*

shaggy ['ʃægɪ] *adj (hairy)* peludo(a), *Esp* lanoso(a); *Fam* **s. dog story** chiste *m* interminable *(con final flojo)*

shah [ʃɑː] *n* sha *m*

shake [ʃeɪk] **1** *n* (**a**) *(action)* sacudida *f*; **a s. of the head** *(to say no)* un movimiento negativo de la cabeza; *(with resignation)* un gesto de resignación con la cabeza; *Fam* **he got the shakes** le entró el tembleque; **with a s. in his voice** con la voz temblorosa; *Fam* **in two shakes** en un pispás; *Fam* **to be no great shakes** no ser gran cosa (**b**) **(milk) s.** batido *m*

2 *vt (pt* **shook** [ʃʊk], *pp* **shaken** ['ʃeɪkən]) *(person, duster)* sacudir; *(branch, box, bottle)* agitar; *(building)* sacudir, hacer temblar; *(dice)* menear, agitar; *(shock emotionally)* conmocionar; *Fig* **to s. sb's faith** quebrantar la fe de alguien; **to s. one's head** *(to say no)* negar con la cabeza; *(in disbelief)* hacer un gesto de incredulidad con la cabeza; **to s. one's fist at sb** amenazar a alguien con el puño; **to s. hands with sb** estrechar *or* dar la mano a alguien; **to s. hands on a deal** sellar un trato con un apretón de manos

3 *vi* (**a**) *(person, building, voice)* temblar; **to s. with fear/rage** temblar de miedo/rabia; **to be shaking like a leaf** temblar como un flan (**b**) *Fam* **to s. on it** cerrar el trato con un apretón de manos

▸**shake off** *vt sep (illness, depression)* salir de, quitarse *or Am* sacarse de encima; *(pursuer)* librarse de

▸**shake up** *vt sep* (**a**) *(upset)* trastornar (**b**) *(reorganize) (system)* reorganizar

Shakespearian [ʃeɪk'spɪərɪən] *adj* shakespeariano(a)

shake-up ['ʃeɪkʌp] *n Fam (reorganization)* reorganización *f*

shakily ['ʃeɪkɪlɪ] *adv (to walk, write, speak)* temblorosamente

shaky ['ʃeɪkɪ] *adj (table, ladder)* inestable, inseguro(a); *(handwriting, voice)* tembloroso(a); *(health, position)* débil, precario(a); **his English is s.** habla un inglés precario

shale [ʃeɪl] *n (rock)* esquisto *m*

shall *[stressed* ʃæl, *unstressed* ʃəl] *modal aux v*

En el inglés hablado, y en el escrito en estilo coloquial, el verbo **shall** se contrae de manera que **I/you/he** *etc* **shall** se transforman en **I'll/you'll/he'll** *etc*. La forma negativa **shall not** se transforma en **shan't**.

(**a**) *(with first person) (expressing intentions, promises, predictions)* **I s. be there if I can** si puedo, estaré allí; **I shan't say this more than once** esto no lo voy a repetir; **we s. take note of your comments** tendremos en cuenta tus comentarios; **as we s. see** como veremos

(**b**) *Formal (with 2nd and 3rd person) (expressing determination)*

you s. pay for this! ¡me las pagarás *or* vas a pagar!; **they s. not pass** no pasarán

(**c**) *(making suggestions, offers)* **s. I open the window?** ¿abro la ventana?; **s. I make some coffee?** ¿preparo café?

(**d**) *(indicating rule)* **all members s. be entitled to vote** todos los socios tendrán derecho al voto; **the term "company property" s. be understood to include…** se entiende que el término "propiedad de la empresa" comprende…

shallot [ʃə'lɒt] *n* chalota *f*

shallow ['ʃæləʊ] *adj* (**a**) *(water)* poco profundo(a); *(dish)* llano(a) (**b**) *(person, mind)* superficial, poco profundo(a)

shallowness ['ʃæləʊnɪs] *n* (**a**) *(of water)* poca profundidad *f* (**b**) *(of person, mind)* superficialidad *f*

sham [ʃæm] **1** *n (trial, election)* farsa *f*; *(person)* farsante *mf*

2 *adj (illness, emotion)* fingido(a)

3 *vt & pp* **shammed** *(feign)* fingir, simular

4 *vi* fingir

shamble ['ʃæmbəl] *vi* **to s. along** caminar arrastrando los pies

shambles ['ʃæmbəlz] *n (disorder)* desastre *m*, desorden *m*; **this place is a s.!** ¡esto es un desorden!; *Fam* **what a s.!** ¡qué desastre!

shambolic [ʃæm'bɒlɪk] *adj Fam* desastroso(a)

shame [ʃeɪm] **1** *n* (**a**) *(disgrace, guilt)* vergüenza *f*, *Am salvo RP* pena *f*; **to my s.** para mi vergüenza; **to have no s.** no tener vergüenza; **s. on you!** ¡debería darte vergüenza!; **to put sb to s.** dejar a alguien en mal lugar (**b**) *(pity)* pena *f*; **it would be a s. to…** sería una pena…; **what a s.!** ¡qué pena!

2 *vt* (**a**) *(cause to feel ashamed)* avergonzar, *Am salvo RP* apenar; **to s. sb into doing sth** avergonzar a alguien para que haga algo (**b**) *(bring shame on)* deshonrar, dejar en mal lugar

shamefaced ['ʃeɪmfeɪst] *adj* avergonzado(a), *Am salvo RP* apenado(a)

shameful ['ʃeɪmfʊl] *adj* vergonzoso(a)

shamefully ['ʃeɪmfəlɪ] *adv* vergonzosamente

shameless ['ʃeɪmlɪs] *adj* desvergonzado(a); **he/she is s. about doing it** no le da ninguna vergüenza *or Am salvo RP* pena hacerlo

shamelessly ['ʃeɪmlɪslɪ] *adv* con desvergüenza, con descaro

shammy ['ʃæmɪ] *n* **s. (leather)** gamuza *f*

shampoo [ʃæm'puː] **1** *n* champú *m*

2 *vt* **to s. one's hair** lavarse el pelo con champú

shamrock ['ʃæmrɒk] *n* trébol *m*

shank [ʃæŋk] *n (of person)* espinilla *f*; *(of horse)* caña *f*; *(of lamb, beef)* pierna *f*

shan't [ʃɑːnt] = **shall not**

shanty[1] ['ʃæntɪ] *n (hut)* casucha *f*, *Esp* chabola *f*, *CSur, Ven* rancho *m*

shanty[2] *n (song)* saloma *f (marinera)*

shantytown ['ʃæntɪtaʊn] *n Esp* barrio *m* de chabolas, *Am* barriada *f*, *Perú* pueblo *m* joven, *Arg, Bol* villa *f* miseria, *Chile* callampa *f*, *Méx* ciudad *f* perdida, *Urug* cantegril *m*

shape [ʃeɪp] **1** *n* (**a**) *(form)* forma *f*; **what s. is it?** ¿qué forma tiene?; **to be the same s. as…** tener la misma forma que…; **to take s.** *(plan)* tomar forma; **they won't accept change in any s. or form** no aceptarán absolutamente ningún tipo de cambio; *Fig* **in the s. of…** en forma de… (**b**) *(condition)* **to be in good/bad s.** *(person)* estar/no estar en forma; *(company, economy)* estar en buenas/malas condiciones; **to get into/keep in s.** *(person)* ponerse/mantenerse en forma; **to be out of s.** no estar en forma

2 *vt* (**a**) *(clay)* modelar, moldear; *(wood)* tallar (**b**) *(character, attitude)* moldear, modelar; *(events)* dar forma a

▸**shape up** *vi* (**a**) *(progress)* **how is she shaping up in her new job?** ¿qué tal se está adaptando a su nuevo trabajo?;

he is shaping up well va haciendo progresos (**b**) *(improve oneself)* enmendarse; **you'd better s. up or ship out!** ¡o te espabilas, o te largas!

shapeless ['ʃeɪplɪs] *adj* informe

shapelessness ['ʃeɪplɪsnɪs] *n* falta *f* de forma

shapely ['ʃeɪplɪ] *adj* **she's very s.** tiene muy buen tipo

shard [ʃɑːd] *n (of pottery)* fragmento *m; (of glass)* esquirla *f*

share [ʃeə(r)] **1** *n* (**a**) *(portion)* parte *f;* **in equal shares** en *or* a partes iguales; **to have a s. in sth** participar en algo; **he doesn't do his s.** no hace lo que le corresponde; **you've had your fair s. of problems/luck** has tenido bastantes problemas/bastante suerte (**b**) *Fin* acción *f;* **s. capital** capital *m* social; **s. certificate** título *m* de acción; **s. price** cotización *f*

2 *vt (secret, opinion, profit)* compartir

3 *vi* compartir; **to s. in sth** participar de algo; **s. and s. alike!** ¡hay que compartir las cosas!

▶**share out** *vt sep* repartir

sharecropper ['ʃeəkrɒpə(r)] *n* aparcero(a) *m,f*

shareholder ['ʃeəhəʊldə(r)] *n Fin* accionista *mf*

shareholding ['ʃeəhəʊldɪŋ] *n Fin* participación *f* accionarial

shark [ʃɑːk] *n* (**a**) *(fish)* tiburón *m* (**b**) *(ruthless person)* buitre *mf*

sharp [ʃɑːp] **1** *n (in music)* sostenido *m*

2 *adj* (**a**) *(knife, point, features)* afilado(a), *Am* filoso(a); *(needle, pencil)* puntiagudo(a); **to be s.** *(knife)* estar afilado; *Fig* **to be at the s. end of sth** tener que enfrentarse cara a cara con algo (**b**) *(angle, bend)* cerrado(a); *(rise, fall)* pronunciado(a); *(sight, hearing)* agudo(a) (**c**) *(outline, focus, photograph)* nítido(a); *(contrast)* acusado(a), fuerte (**d**) *(intelligent)* agudo(a), despierto(a) (**e**) *(harsh) (retort, words, person)* mordaz, seco(a); **a s. tongue** una lengua afilada *or* viperina (**f**) *(taste, sauce)* ácido(a); *(sound, pain)* agudo(a); *(wind, frost)* cortante, intenso(a) (**g**) *(in music)* sostenido(a); **C s.** do *m* sostenido

3 *adv* (**a**) *(punctually)* en punto; **at four o'clock s.** a las cuatro en punto (**b**) *(immediately)* **to turn s. left/right** girar repentinamente a la izquierda/derecha (**c**) *(idioms) Fam* **look s.!** ¡espabila!

sharpen ['ʃɑːpən] *vt* (**a**) *(knife, tool)* afilar; *(pencil)* sacar punta a (**b**) *(pain, desire)* agudizar; **to s. one's wits** agudizar el ingenio

sharpener ['ʃɑːpənə(r)] *n (for knife)* afilador *m; (for pencil)* sacapuntas *m inv,* afilalápices *m inv*

sharp-eyed ['ʃɑːpaɪd] *adj* observador(ora)

sharply ['ʃɑːplɪ] *adv* (**a**) *(contrast)* acusadamente; **to bring sth s. into focus** enfocar algo nítidamente (**b**) *(rise, fall)* pronunciadamente; *(brake)* en seco

sharpness ['ʃɑːpnɪs] *n* (**a**) *(of knife)* agudeza *f* (**b**) *(of contours, photograph)* nitidez *f; (of mind, hearing, sight)* agudeza *f* (**c**) *(of voice, words)* mordacidad *f* (**d**) *(of pain)* agudeza *f; (of wind)* intensidad *f*

sharpshooter ['ʃɑːpʃuːtə(r)] *n* tirador(ora) *m,f* de élite

sharp-sighted [ʃɑːp'saɪtɪd] *adj* observador(ora)

sharp-tongued [ʃɑːp'tʌŋd] *adj* mordaz

shat [ʃæt] *pt & pp of* **shit**

shatter ['ʃætə(r)] **1** *vt* (**a**) *(glass, bone)* hacer añicos (**b**) *(hopes)* echar por tierra; *(silence)* romper; *(health, nerves)* destrozar

2 *vi (glass, windshield)* hacerse añicos

shattered ['ʃætəd] *adj Fam* **to be s.** *(stunned)* quedarse destrozado(a)

shattering ['ʃætərɪŋ] *adj* (**a**) *(blow, defeat, news)* demoledor(ora), devastador(ora) (**b**) *Fam (exhausting)* agotador(ora), matador(ora)

shatterproof ['ʃætəpruːf] *adj* inastillable

shave [ʃeɪv] **1** *n* afeitado *m;* **to have a s.** afeitarse; *Fig* **that was a close s.!** ¡ha faltado un pelo!

2 *vt* (**a**) afeitar; **to s. one's face** afeitarse; **to s. one's legs** afeitarse las piernas (**b**) *(wood)* cepillar

3 *vi* afeitarse

▶**shave off** *vt sep* afeitar; **he shaved his beard off** se afeitó la barba

shaven ['ʃeɪvən] *adj* afeitado(a)

shaver ['ʃeɪvə(r)] *n* maquinilla *f* (de afeitar) eléctrica

shaving ['ʃeɪvɪŋ] *n* (**a**) **s. brush** brocha *f* de afeitar; **s. foam** espuma *f* de afeitar (**b**) *(piece of wood, metal)* viruta *f*

shawl [ʃɔːl] *n* chal *m, Am* rebozo *m*

she [ʃiː] **1** *pron* ella; *(usually omitted in Spanish, except for contrast)* **she's Scottish** es escocesa; **SHE hasn't got it!** ¡ella no lo tiene!

2 *n* **it's a s.** *(animal)* es hembra

sheaf [ʃiːf] *(pl* **sheaves** [ʃiːvz]*) n (of corn)* gavilla *f; (of papers)* manojo *m*

shear [ʃɪə(r)] *(pp* **sheared** *or* **shorn** [ʃɔːn]*)* **1** *vt (sheep)* esquilar; *Fig* **to be shorn of sth** verse despojado(a) de algo

2 *vi (cut)* **to s. through sth** atravesar *or* cortar algo

shears ['ʃɪəz] *npl (for garden)* tijeras *fpl* de podar

sheath [ʃiːθ] *n* (**a**) *(for cable, knife)* funda *f;* **s. knife** cuchillo *m* de monte (**b**) *(contraceptive)* condón *m*

shed[1] [ʃed] *n (in garden)* cobertizo *m; (in factory)* nave *f, Andes, Carib, RP* galpón *m*

shed[2] *(pt & pp* **shed**) *vt (leaves)* perder; *(tears, blood)* derramar; **to s. light on sth** arrojar luz sobre algo; **to s. its skin** *(snake)* mudar la piel; **to s. weight** perder peso

she'd [ʃiːd] = **she had, she would**

sheen [ʃiːn] *n* lustre *m,* brillo *m*

sheep [ʃiːp] *(pl* **sheep**) *n* oveja *f;* **s. farming** ganadería *f* ovina

sheepdog ['ʃiːpdɒg] *n* perro *m* pastor

sheepfold ['ʃiːpfəʊld] *n* redil *m*

sheepish ['ʃiːpɪʃ] *adj* avergonzado(a), azarado(a)

sheepskin ['ʃiːpskɪn] *n* piel *f* de oveja; **s. jacket** zamarra *f*

sheer [ʃɪə(r)] *adj* (**a**) *(pure, total)* puro(a), verdadero(a); **it's s. madness** es una verdadera locura (**b**) *(steep)* empinado(a), escarpado(a) (**c**) *(stockings, fabric)* fino(a), transparente

sheet [ʃiːt] *n (on bed)* sábana *f; (of paper, glass)* hoja *f; (of ice)* capa *f; (of metal)* lámina *f; (of flame)* cortina *f; Comptr* **s. feeder** alimentador *m* de hojas sueltas; **s. lightning** relámpagos *mpl* (difusos); **s. metal** chapa *f* (de metal); **s. music** partituras *fpl* sueltas

sheetfeed ['ʃiːtfiːd] *n Comptr* alimentador *m* de hojas sueltas

sheik(h) [ʃeɪk] *n* jeque *m*

shekel ['ʃekəl] *n (Israeli currency)* shekel *m*

shelf [ʃelf] *(pl* **shelves** [ʃelvz]*) n* (**a**) *(in cupboard, bookcase)* estante *m,* balda *f;* **(set of) shelves** estantería *f; Fig* **to be left on the s.** quedarse para vestir santos; *Com* **s. life** *(of goods)* vida *f* útil, vida *f* en estantería *or* expositor (**b**) *(cliff, rock face)* plataforma *f,* saliente *m*

shell [ʃel] **1** *n* (**a**) *(of snail, oyster, on beach)* concha *f; (of lobster, tortoise)* caparazón *m; (of egg, nut)* cáscara *f; Fig* **she soon came out of her s.** rápidamente salió de su concha *or* caparazón (**b**) *(of building)* esqueleto *m,* armazón *m or f* (**c**) *(bomb)* proyectil *m;* **s. shock** neurosis *f inv* de guerra

2 *vt* (**a**) *(nuts, eggs)* pelar; *(peas)* desgranar (**b**) *(bombard)* atacar con fuego de artillería

▶**shell out** *Fam* **1** *vt sep (money)* poner, *Esp* apoquinar

2 *vi* poner, *Esp* apoquinar; **to s. out for sth** pagar algo

she'll [ʃiːl] = **she will, she shall**

shellfire ['ʃelfaɪə(r)] *n* fuego *m* de artillería

shellfish ['ʃelfɪʃ] *n (crustacean)* crustáceo *m; (mollusk)* molusco *m; (food)* marisco *m, Am* mariscos *mpl*

shelling ['ʃelɪŋ] *n* ataque *m* de artillería

shellproof ['ʃelpruːf] *adj* a prueba de bombas

shell-shocked ['ʃelʃɒkt] *adj (soldier)* que sufre neurosis de guerra; *Fig* **to feel s.** sentirse traumatizado(a)

shelter ['ʃeltə(r)] **1** *n (place, protection)* refugio *m*; **to take s.** refugiarse
2 *vt* resguardar (**from** de), refugiar (**from** de)
3 *vi* resguardarse (**from** de), refugiarse (**from** de)
sheltered ['ʃeltəd] *adj* resguardado(a); **he had a s. childhood** fue un niño muy protegido
shelve [ʃelv] *vt (postpone)* aparcar, posponer
shelving ['ʃelvɪŋ] *n* estanterías *fpl*
shepherd ['ʃepəd] **1** *n* pastor *m*; **s.'s pie** = pastel de carne picada y puré de *Esp* patatas *or Am* papas
2 *vt (sheep)* pastorear; *Fig (people)* dirigir *(en grupo)*
shepherdess [ʃepə'des] *n* pastora *f*
sherbet ['ʃɜːbət] *n (dessert)* sorbete *m*
sheriff ['ʃerɪf] *n* sheriff *m*
sherry ['ʃerɪ] *n (vino m de)* jerez *m*
she's [ʃiːz] = she is, she has
Shetland ['ʃetlənd] *n* **the S. Islands, the Shetlands** las Islas Shetland; **S. pony** pony *m* de Shetland
Shia ['ʃiːə] **1** *n (person)* chiíta *mf; (religion)* chiísmo *m*
2 *adj* chiíta
shield [ʃiːld] **1** *n (of knight)* escudo *m; (police badge, trophy)* placa *f; Fig (protection)* protección *f*
2 *vt (protect)* proteger (**from** de); **to s. one's eyes** protegerse los ojos
shift [ʃɪft] **1** *n* **(a)** *(change)* cambio *m*; **a s. in meaning** un cambio de significado; **a s. to the right/left** *(in politics)* un desplazamiento hacia la derecha/izquierda; **s. key** *(on typewriter, computer)* tecla *f* de mayúsculas; *Aut* **s. stick** (palanca *f* de) cambios *mpl* **(b)** *Ind* turno *m*; **to work (in) shifts** trabajar por turnos; **s. worker** trabajador(ora) *m,f* por turnos **(c) s. (dress)** vestido *m* recto
2 *vt* **(a)** *(move)* mover; *(stain)* eliminar; **to s. the blame onto sb** echar la culpa a alguien; *Aut* **to s. gear** cambiar de marcha **(b)** *Fam (sell)* vender, despachar
3 *vi (move)* moverse; *(change)* cambiar; *Fam (move quickly)* ir a toda máquina *or Esp* mecha
shiftless ['ʃɪftlɪs] *adj* holgazán(ana)
shiftwork ['ʃɪftwɜːk] *n Ind* trabajo *m* por turnos
shifty ['ʃɪftɪ] *adj (person)* sospechoso(a); *(look)* furtivo(a)
Shiite ['ʃiːaɪt] *n & adj* chiíta *mf*
shilling ['ʃɪlɪŋ] *n* chelín *m*
shimmer ['ʃɪmə(r)] **1** *n* brillo *m* trémulo
2 *vi* rielar
shimmering ['ʃɪmərɪŋ] *adj* con brillo trémulo
shin [ʃɪn] *n* espinilla *f, RP* canilla *f*; **s. guard** *or* **pad** espinillera *f, RP* canillera *f*
shinbone ['ʃɪnbəʊn] *n* tibia *f*
shindig ['ʃɪndɪg], **shindy** ['ʃɪndɪ] *n Fam (din) Esp* jaleo *m, Esp* follón *m, Am* lío *m*; **to kick up a s.** armar un *Esp* jaleo *or Am* lío
shine [ʃaɪn] **1** *n* **(a)** *(change)* brillo *m*, lustre *m*; **to give one's shoes a s.** sacar brillo a los zapatos **(b)** *(idioms)* **to take the s. off sth** empañar *or* deslucir algo; *Fam* **to take a s. to sb** tomar cariño a alguien
2 *vt (pt & pp* **shone** [ʃɒn]) **(a) to s. a flashlight on sth** enfocar una linterna hacia algo **(b)** *(pt & pp* **shined** [ʃaɪnd]) *(polish)* lustrar, sacar brillo a
3 *vi* brillar; *Fig* **to s. at sth** destacar en algo; **her face shone with joy** estaba resplandeciente de alegría
shiner ['ʃaɪnə(r)] *n Fam (black eye)* ojo *m* morado *or Esp* a la virulé
shingle ['ʃɪŋgəl] *n* **(a)** *(wooden tile)* teja *f* de madera **(b)** *(pebbles)* guijarros *mpl*
shingles ['ʃɪŋgəlz] *n (disease)* herpes *m inv*; **to have s.** tener un herpes
shining ['ʃaɪnɪŋ] *adj* brillante, reluciente; *Fig* **a s. example (of)** un ejemplo señero *or* brillante (de)
shinny ['ʃɪnɪ] *vi (climb)* **to s. up/down a tree** trepar a/bajar de un árbol

shiny ['ʃaɪnɪ] *adj* brillante, reluciente
ship [ʃɪp] **1** *n* barco *m*, buque *m*; **to go by s.** ir en barco; *Fig* **when my s. comes in** cuando me haga rico(a)
2 *vt (pt & pp* **shipped**) *(transport by sea, rail)* fletar, transportar; *(take on board)* cargar
▸**ship off** *vt sep Fam* mandar
shipboard ['ʃɪpbɔːd] *n Naut* **on s.** a bordo
shipbuilder ['ʃɪpbɪldə(r)] *n* constructor *m* naval *or* de buques
shipbuilding ['ʃɪpbɪldɪŋ] *n* construcción *f* naval; **the s. industry** la industria naval
shipload ['ʃɪpləʊd] *n* cargamento *m*, carga *f; Fig* **by the s.** a montones
shipmate ['ʃɪpmeɪt] *n Naut* compañero *m* de tripulación
shipment ['ʃɪpmənt] *n* flete *m*, cargamento *m*
shipowner ['ʃɪpəʊnə(r)] *n* armador(ora) *m,f*, naviero(a) *m,f*
shipping ['ʃɪpɪŋ] *n (ships)* navíos *mpl*, buques *mpl*; **s. agent** *(person)* agente *mf* marítimo(a), consignatario(a) *m,f; (company)* compañía *f* naviera; **s. lane** ruta *f* de navegación
shipshape ['ʃɪpʃeɪp] *adj* ordenado(a), en perfecto orden
shipwreck ['ʃɪprek] **1** *n* naufragio *m*
2 *vt* **to be shipwrecked** naufragar
shipwrecked ['ʃɪprekt] *adj* náufrago(a)
shipwright ['ʃɪpraɪt] *n Naut* carpintero *m* de ribera
shipyard ['ʃɪpjɑːd] *n* astillero *m*
shire ['ʃaɪə(r)] *n* condado *m*; **s. horse** (caballo *m*) percherón *m*
shirk [ʃɜːk] **1** *vt (obligation, task)* eludir
2 *vi (avoid work)* gandulear
shirker ['ʃɜːkə(r)] *n Fam* vago(a) *m,f*, gandul(ula) *m,f, Andes, Méx* flojo(a) *m,f, RP* vagoneta *mf*
shirt [ʃɜːt] *n* camisa *f; Fam* **keep your s. on!** ¡no te sulfures!
shirtmaker ['ʃɜːtmeɪkə(r)] *n* camisero(a) *m,f*
shirtsleeves ['ʃɜːtsliːvz] *npl* **to be in s.** estar en mangas de camisa
shirttail ['ʃɜːtteɪl] *n* faldón *m* de la camisa
shit [ʃɪt] *Vulg* **1** *n* **(a)** *(excrement)* mierda *f; (mess)* porquería *f*, mierda *f*; **to take a s.** cagar
(b) *(nasty person)* cabrón(ona) *m,f*, hijo(a) *m,f* de puta
(c) *(idioms)* **to talk s.** decir *Esp* gilipolleces *or Am* pendejadas; **he's in the s.** está jodidísimo, *Esp* tiene un marrón que te cagas; **he doesn't give a s.** le importa un huevo; **he doesn't do s.** se está tocando los huevos constantemente; **to beat** *or* **kick the s. out of sb** dar una paliza *or Méx* chinga a alguien, *Esp* inflar a alguien a hostias; **to scare the s. out of sb** hacer cagarse de miedo a alguien, *Esp* acojonar a alguien, *Méx* sacar un pedo a alguien, *RP* hacer que alguien se cague hasta las patas
2 *vt (pt & pp* **shit** *or* **shat** [ʃæt]) **to s. oneself** *(defecate)* cagarse (encima); *(be scared)* cagarse *or Esp* jiñarse de miedo
3 *vi* cagar
4 *exclam* **s.!** ¡mierda!, *RP* ¡la puta!
shitless ['ʃɪtlɪs] *adj Vulg* **to scare sb s.** hacer cagarse de miedo a alguien, *Esp* acojonar a alguien, *Méx* sacar un pedo a alguien, *RP* hacer que alguien se cague hasta las patas; **to be scared s.** estar cagado(a) de miedo, *Esp* estar acojonado(a); **to be scared s. (of sth/sb)** acojonarle a uno (algo/alguien)
shitload ['ʃɪtləʊd] *n Vulg* **he bought shitloads of** *or* **(whole) s. of books** compró una porrada *or Esp* un huevo *or Méx* un chingo de libros
shitty ['ʃɪtɪ] *adj Vulg (weather, job)* de mierda, *Esp* chungo(a), *RP* chotísimo(a); *(behavior, remark)* muy cabrón(ona); **to feel s.** sentirse de puta pena *or Méx* de la chingada *or RP* para la mierda
shiver ['ʃɪvə(r)] **1** *n (of cold, fear)* escalofrío *m*; **it sent shivers down my spine** me produjo *or* dio escalofríos
2 *vi (with cold)* tiritar (**with** de); *(with fear)* temblar (**with** de)
shivery ['ʃɪvərɪ] *adj (cold)* tembloroso(a); *(feverish)* con escalofríos
shoal [ʃəʊl] *n (of fish)* banco *m; Fig (of people)* manada *f*

shock¹ [ʃɒk] n **a s. of hair** una mata de pelo, una pelambrera

shock² **1** n (a) *(impact)* sacudida f; *(of earthquake)* temblor m; **s. (absorber)** amortiguador m; **s. tactics** *(in campaign)* táctica f sensacionalista; *Mil* **s. troops** tropas fpl de choque; *also Fig* **s. wave** onda f expansiva (b) *(surprise)* susto m; *(emotional blow)* conmoción f; **I got a real s. when…** me quedé de piedra cuando…; **to be in s.** estar conmocionado(a) (c) *(electric)* calambrazo m, descarga f (eléctrica); **s. therapy** terapia f de electrochoque

2 vt *(surprise, startle)* dejar boquiabierto(a), dar un susto a; *(scandalize)* escandalizar; **to s. sb into doing sth** amedrentar a alguien para que haga algo

shocked [ʃɒkt] adj *(startled)* conmocionado(a), impactado(a); *(scandalized)* escandalizado(a)

shocker ['ʃɒkə(r)] n *(news, event)* *(surprising)* bombazo m, escándalo m; *(very bad)* desastre m

shocking ['ʃɒkɪŋ] adj (a) *(scandalous)* escandaloso(a); **s. pink** rosa m chillón (b) *(very bad)* *(weather)* de perros; *(pain)* insoportable

shockingly ['ʃɒkɪŋlɪ] adv escandalosamente

shockproof ['ʃɒkpruːf] adj *(watch)* antichoque

shod [ʃɒd] pt & pp of **shoe**

shoddy ['ʃɒdɪ] adj *(goods)* de pacotilla; *(workmanship)* chapucero(a); *(conduct)* miserable

shoe [ʃuː] **1** n zapato m; *(horseshoe)* herradura f; **a pair of shoes** unos zapatos, un par de zapatos; *Fig* **I wouldn't like to be in his shoes** no me gustaría estar en su pellejo; *Fig* **put yourself in my shoes** ponte en mi lugar; **s. polish** betún m, crema f (para calzado); **s. store** zapatería f

2 vt *(pt & pp* **shod** [ʃɒd]) *(horse)* herrar

shoebrush ['ʃuːbrʌʃ] n cepillo m *(para zapatos)*

shoehorn ['ʃuːhɔːn] n calzador m

shoelace ['ʃuːleɪs] n cordón m (de zapato)

shoemaker ['ʃuːmeɪkə(r)] n zapatero(a) m,f

shoeshine ['ʃuːʃaɪn] n *(person)* limpiabotas mf inv

shoestring ['ʃuːstrɪŋ] n (a) *Fam* **on a s.** *(cheaply)* *Esp* con cuatro perras, *Am* sin mucha plata or *Méx* lana, *RP* con dos mangos (b) cordón m (de zapato)

shone [ʃɒn] pt & pp of **shine**

shoo [ʃuː] exclam **s.!** ¡fuera!

▸**shoo away, shoo off** vt sep espantar

shoo-in ['ʃuːɪn] n *Fam* **he was a s. for the leadership election** tenía asegurada la elección como líder

shook [ʃʊk] pt of **shake**

shoot [ʃuːt] **1** n (a) *(of plant)* retoño m, vástago m (b) *(hunting party)* cacería f

2 *(pt & pp* **shot** [ʃɒt]) vt (a) *(fire)* *(bullet)* disparar; *(arrow)* lanzar, tirar; **to s. a glance at sb** lanzar una mirada a alguien (b) **to s. sb** *(wound)* disparar a alguien; *(kill)* matar de un tiro a alguien; *(execute)* fusilar a alguien; **she was shot in the arm** le dieron un tiro en el brazo; **to s. rabbits/grouse** cazar conejos/urogallos; *Fig* **to s. oneself in the foot** tirar (uno) piedras contra su propio tejado (c) *(movie, TV program)* rodar (d) *(pass rapidly)* **to s. the rapids** salvar or atravesar los rápidos (e) *(play)* **to s. dice/pool** jugar a los dados/al billar americano (f) *Fam* **to s. the breeze** or **the bull** *(chat)* estar de cháchara or *Esp* palique or *Méx* plática

3 vi (a) *(with gun)* disparar **(at** a); *(in soccer)* tirar, chutar (b) *(move rapidly)* ir a escape, ir como una exhalación; **he shot into/out of the house** entró en/salió de la casa como una exhalación; **the pain shot up his left side** le daban punzadas de dolor en el costado izquierdo

4 exclam *Fam* ¡miércoles!, ¡mecachis!, *Méx* ¡chin!

▸**shoot down** vt sep *(person)* abatir (a tiros); *(plane)* derribar

▸**shoot off** vi *(leave quickly)* salir a escape

▸**shoot out** vi *(emerge quickly)* aparecer de pronto

▸**shoot up** vi (a) *(plants, children)* crecer con rapidez; *(buildings)* levantarse con rapidez (b) *(rocket)* elevarse a gran velocidad; *(prices)* dispararse (c) *Fam (inject drugs)* pincharse, *Esp* chutarse

shooting ['ʃuːtɪŋ] **1** n (a) *(gunfire)* tiroteo m; *(incident)* ataque m con disparos; *(killing)* asesinato m (con arma de fuego) (b) *(at targets)* tiro m al blanco; *(at birds, animals)* caza f; **s. stick** bastón m asiento (c) *(of movie, TV program)* rodaje m

2 adj **s. star** estrella f fugaz

shoot-out ['ʃuːtaʊt] n *(gunfight)* tiroteo m; **penalty s.** *(in soccer)* lanzamiento m or tanda f de penaltis or *Am* penales

shop [ʃɒp] **1** n (a) *(for goods)* tienda f (b) *Fam* **to do a s.** *(do shopping)* hacer la compra or *Am* las compras (c) *(workshop)* taller m (d) *Fam (idioms)* **to talk s.** hablar del trabajo or *Esp* del curro or *CAm, Méx, Perú* de la chamba or *RP* del laburo

2 vi comprar, hacer compra(s); **to go shopping** ir de compras; **to s. around** comparar precios (en diferentes establecimientos)

shopaholic [ʃɒpə'hɒlɪk] n *Fam* consumista mf

shopgirl ['ʃɒpgɜːl] n dependienta f

shopkeeper ['ʃɒpkiːpə(r)] n tendero(a) m,f

shoplift ['ʃɒplɪft] vt & vi robar en las tiendas

shoplifter ['ʃɒplɪftə(r)] n ratero(a) m,f (en comercios)

shoplifting ['ʃɒplɪftɪŋ] n hurtos mpl (en comercios)

shopper ['ʃɒpə(r)] n comprador(ora) m,f

shopping ['ʃɒpɪŋ] n *(activity)* compra f, *Am* compras fpl; *(purchases)* compras fpl; **to do the s.** hacer la compra or *Am* las compras; **s. bag** bolsa f de la compra; **s. basket** or **cart** *(in store, for Internet shopping)* cesta f de la compra; **s. center** centro m comercial; **s. channel** canal m de compras, teletienda f; **s. list** lista f de la compra; **s. mall** parque m comercial

shopwindow [ʃɒp'wɪndəʊ] n escaparate m, *Am* vidriera f, *Am* vitrina f

shore [ʃɔː(r)] n *(of sea, lake)* orilla f; **on s.** en tierra; **to go on s.** *(from ship)* bajar a tierra

▸**shore up** vt sep also Fig apuntalar

shoreline ['ʃɔːlaɪn] n orilla f

shorn [ʃɔːn] pp of **shear**

short [ʃɔːt] **1** n *Fam* (a) *(short movie)* corto m, cortometraje m (b) *(short circuit)* cortocircuito m

2 adj (a) *(physically)* corto(a); *(person)* bajo(a), *Méx* chaparro(a), *RP* petiso(a); **Bill is s. for William** Bill es el diminutivo de William; **to have a s. temper** or **fuse** tener el genio muy vivo; **s. list** lista f de seleccionados; **s. story** cuento m

(b) *(in time)* corto(a), breve; **in s.** en resumen, en pocas palabras; **in s. order** inmediatamente; **the s. answer is "no"** en pocas palabras, la respuesta es "no"; **to make s. work of sb/sth** dar buena cuenta de alguien/algo; **s. and sweet** conciso(a) y al grano

(c) *(abrupt)* seco(a); **to be s. with sb** ser seco(a) con alguien

(d) *(insufficient, lacking)* escaso(a); **to be in s. supply** *(money, water)* escasear; **to be s. of** andar escaso(a) de; **the change was 50 cents s.** faltaban 50 centavos en la vuelta or *Am* el vuelto; **it's little** or **not far s. of…** *(almost)* le falta poco para ser…; **he's not far s. of forty** anda cerca de los cuarenta; **it was little s. of miraculous that she survived** fue poco menos que un milagro que sobreviviera

(e) *Elec* **s. circuit** cortocircuito m

3 adv (a) *(suddenly)* **to stop s.** pararse en seco; **to bring sb up s.** dejar paralizado(a) a alguien

(b) *(in length, duration)* **they stopped s. of…** no llegaron a…; **to cut sth/sb s.** interrumpir algo/a alguien

(c) *(without)* **to go s.** pasar privaciones; **to go s. of sth** andar escaso(a) de algo (**d**) *(to express insufficiency)* **we are running s. of coffee** se nos está terminando el café; **to fall s.** quedarse corto(a); **to fall s. of** *(target, standard, expectations)* no alcanzar; *Fig* **to sell sth/sb s.** *(underestimate)* infravalorar algo/a alguien; **I was caught s.** me entraron muchas ganas de ir al cuarto de baño

shortage ['ʃɔːtɪdʒ] *n* escasez *f*, carestía *f*; **gas/food s.** escasez de gasolina *or RP* nafta/alimentos; **he has no s. of ideas** no le faltan ideas

shortbread ['ʃɔːtbred] *n* ≃ mantecada *f*, = especie de galleta elaborada con mantequilla

shortcake ['ʃɔːtkeɪk] *n (cake)* = bizcocho que generalmente lleva fruta y nata batida

shortchange ['ʃɔːt(t)ʃeɪndʒ] *vt (in store)* devolver de menos a; *Fig (cheat)* timar

short-circuit [ʃɔːt'sɜːkɪt] **1** *vt (electrical)* producir un cortocircuito en; *Fig (bypass)* saltarse
2 *vi* tener un cortocircuito

shortcomings ['ʃɔːtkʌmɪŋz] *npl* defectos *mpl*

shortcut ['ʃɔːtkʌt] *n also Fig* atajo *m*

shorten ['ʃɔːtən] *vt (skirt, text)* acortar; *(visit, task)* abreviar

shortfall ['ʃɔːtfɔːl] *n* déficit *m*

shorthaired ['ʃɔːtheəd] *adj* de pelo corto

shorthand ['ʃɔːthænd] *n* taquigrafía *f*; **s. typist** taquimeca-nógrafo(a) *m,f*

short-haul ['ʃɔːthɔːl] *adj* de corto recorrido

short-list ['ʃɔːtlɪst] *vt* **to be short-listed (for sth)** estar seleccionado(a) (para algo)

short-lived [ʃɔːt'lɪvd] *adj (success, rejoicing)* efímero(a)

shortly ['ʃɔːtlɪ] *adv* (**a**) *(soon)* en seguida, pronto; **s. after(ward)** poco después (**b**) *(abruptly)* secamente, brusca-mente

short-order cook ['ʃɔːtɔːdə'kʊk] *n* = cocinero que prepara platos rápidos *or RP* minutas

short-range ['ʃɔːtreɪndʒ] *adj (missile)* de corto alcance

shorts [ʃɔːts] *npl (short pants)* pantalones *mpl* cortos; *(under-pants)* calzoncillos *mpl*, *Chile* fundillos *mpl*, *Col* pantaloncillos *mpl*, *Méx* calzones *mpl*

shortsighted [ʃɔːt'saɪtɪd] *adj* miope, corto(a) de vista; *Fig* corto(a) de miras

shortsightedness [ʃɔːt'saɪtɪdnɪs] *n* miopía *f*; *Fig* estrechez *f* de miras

short-sleeved ['ʃɔːt'sliːvd] *adj* de manga corta

short-stay ['ʃɔːtsteɪ] *adj (parking lot)* para estancias breves

shortstop ['ʃɔːtstɒp] *n (in baseball)* = jugador que intenta interceptar bolas entre la segunda y tercera base

short-tempered [ʃɔːt'tempəd] *adj* **to be s.** tener mal genio

short-term ['ʃɔːttɜːm] *adj (solution, loan)* a corto plazo; **s. contract** contrato *m* temporal

shorty ['ʃɔːtɪ] *n Fam* retaco(a) *m,f*, canijo(a) *m,f*, *Méx* chaparrito(a) *m,f*, *RP* retacón(ona) *m,f*

shot [ʃɒt] **1** *n* (**a**) *(act of firing, sound)* tiro *m*, disparo *m*; **to fire a s.** disparar; *Fig* **like a s.** *(without hesitation)* al instante; *Fig* **my answer was a s. in the dark** respondí al azar *or* a ciegas; *Fig* **to call the shots** dirigir el cotarro; **s. put** lanzamiento *m* de peso *or Am* de bala
(**b**) *(marksman)* **he is a good/bad s.** es un buen/mal tirador
(**c**) *(in soccer)* tiro *m*, chut(e) *m*; *(in basketball)* tiro *m*, lanzamiento *m*
(**d**) *(photograph)* foto *f*; *(of movie, TV program)* toma *f*
(**e**) *Fam (injection)* inyección *f*
(**f**) *(attempt)* intento *m*, intentona *f*; **to have a s. at sth/at doing sth** intentar algo/hacer algo
(**g**) *(drink)* chupito *m*, dedal *m*; **s. glass** vaso *m* para chupitos
2 *pt & pp of* **shoot**

shotgun ['ʃɒtgʌn] *n* escopeta *f*; *Fam* **to have a s. wedding** casarse por haber metido la pata, *Esp* casarse de penalti, *RP* casarse de apuro

should [ʃʊd] *modal aux v*

La forma negativa **should not** se transforma en **shouldn't**.

(**a**) *(expressing obligations, recommendations, instructions)* **you s. do it at once** deberías hacerlo inmediatamente; **you shouldn't laugh at him** no deberías reírte de él; **you s. have come earlier** deberías haber venido antes; **he shouldn't have told them** no debería habérselo dicho; **a present?, oh you shouldn't have!** ¿un regalo? ¡no tenías que haberte molestado!; **you s. have seen the expression on his face!** ¡tendrías que haber visto la cara que puso!; **you s. read the instructions carefully** lea detenidamente las instrucciones

(**b**) *(expressing probability)* **the weather s. improve from now on** a partir de ahora, el tiempo debería mejorar; **she s. have arrived by this time** a estas horas ya debe de haber llegado

(**c**) *(in exclamations, in rhetorical questions)* **why s. you suspect me?** ¿por qué habrías de sospechar de mí?; **who s. I meet but Martin!** y ¿a quién me encontré? ¡a Martin!; **he apologized — I s. think so, too!** se disculpó — ¡es lo mínimo que podía hacer!

(**d**) *(in subordinate clauses)* **he ordered that they s. be released** ordenó que los liberaran; **she insisted that he s. wear his hair short** insistió en que llevase el pelo corto

(**e**) *(in conditional clauses)* **if he s. come** *or Formal* **s. he come, let me know** si viene, avísame; **if you s. have any difficulty, phone this number** si tuviera algún problema, llame a este número

(**f**) *(expressing opinions, preferences)* **I s. like a drink** me gustaría *or Esp* apetecería tomar algo; **we s. want to know if there was anything seriously wrong** si algo va muy mal, nos gustaría saberlo; **I s. imagine he was rather angry!** ¡me imagino que estaría bastante *esp Esp* enfadado *or esp Am* enojado!; **I shouldn't be surprised if...** no me sorprendería que...

shoulder ['ʃəʊldə(r)] **1** *n* (**a**) *(of person)* hombro *m*; **s. to s.** hombro con hombro; *Fig* **to rub shoulders with sb** codearse con alguien; *Fig* **to be looking over one's s.** estar inquieto(a); *Fig* **to cry on sb's s.** coger a alguien de paño de lágrimas; **s. bag** bolsa *f* de bandolera; **s. blade** omóplato *m*; **s. pad** hombrera *f*; **s. strap** *(of garment)* tirante *m*, *CSur* bretel *m*; *(of bag)* correa *f* (**b**) *(of meat)* paletilla *f* (**c**) *(along road) Esp* arcén *m*, *Méx* acotamiento *m*, *RP* banquina *f*, *Ven* hombrillo *m*
2 *vt* (**a**) *(push)* **to s. one's way through a crowd** abrirse paso a empujones entre la multitud; **to s. sb aside** apartar a alguien de un empujón (del hombro) (**b**) *(put on shoulder)* echarse al hombro; *Fig (responsibility)* asumir

shouldn't [ʃʊdnt] = **should not**

shout [ʃaʊt] **1** *n* grito *m*; **shouts of laughter** carcajadas *fpl*
2 *vt* gritar; **to s. sth at sb** gritarle algo a alguien
3 *vi* gritar; **to s. at sb** gritar a alguien; **to s. for help** gritar pidiendo ayuda; *Fig* **to have something to s. about** tener algo que celebrar

▸ **shout down** *vt sep* **to s. sb down** impedir con gritos que alguien hable

shouting ['ʃaʊtɪŋ] *n* griterío *m*, gritos *mpl*

shove [ʃʌv] **1** *n* empujón *m*; **to give sth/sb a s.** dar un empujón a algo/alguien
2 *vt & vi* empujar

▸ **shove around** *vt sep Fam (bully)* abusar de

▸ **shove off** *vi Fam (leave)* largarse

shovel ['ʃʌvəl] **1** *n* pala *f*
2 *vt* echar a paladas; *Fam* **to s. food into one's mouth** atiborrarse de comida

shovelful ['ʃʌvəlfʊl] *n* palada *f*

show [ʃəʊ] **1** *n* (**a**) *(exhibition)* exposición *f*, muestra *f*; **to be**

on s. exhibirse, estar expuesto(a); **to put sth on s.** exponer algo; **s. apartment** apartamento *m or Esp* piso *or Arg* departamento *m* piloto; **s. house** casa *f* piloto; **s. jumper** jinete *m*/amazona *f* de pruebas de saltos; **s. jumping** prueba *f* de saltos (de equitación); *Pej* **s. trial** juicio *m* ejemplarizante

(**b**) *(concert, play)* espectáculo *m*; *(on TV, radio)* programa *m*; *Fig* **to run the s.** dirigir el cotarro; **s. business** el mundo del espectáculo

(**c**) *(act of showing)* demostración *f*; **s. of hands** votación *f* a mano alzada; **it's all s.** es pura fachada; **to do sth for s.** hacer algo por alardear; *Fam* **good s.!** *(well done)* ¡bien hecho!

2 *vt (pp* **shown** [ʃəʊn]) (**a**) *(display)* mostrar, enseñar; *(picture)* exponer, exhibir; *(courage, talent)* mostrar, demostrar; **to s. sb sth, to s. sth to sb** enseñar *or* mostrar algo a alguien; *Fig* **to s. one's cards** *or* **one's hand** mostrar las verdaderas intenciones; **they had nothing to s. for all their work** trabajaron mucho para nada; **he won't s. his face here again** no volverá a dejarse ver por aquí; **to s. oneself** dejarse ver; **to s. a profit/a loss** registrar *or* arrojar beneficios/pérdidas; **you're showing your age** estás hecho un carcamal; **to s. oneself to be…** demostrar ser…

(**b**) *(indicate)* mostrar; *(time, temperature)* indicar, señalar

(**c**) *(prove, demonstrate)* mostrar, demostrar; **it goes to s. that…** eso viene a demostrar que…

(**d**) *(teach)* enseñar; **to s. sb how to do sth** enseñar a alguien a hacer algo

(**e**) *(movie)* proyectar; *(TV program)* emitir, poner; **they are showing a Clint Eastwood movie tonight** esta noche ponen *or* echan una película de Clint Eastwood

(**f**) *(escort, lead)* **to s. sb the way** mostrar a alguien el camino; **to s. sb to his room** llevar a alguien a su habitación; **to s. sb around the town** enseñarle la ciudad a alguien

3 *vi* (**a**) *(be visible)* notarse (**b**) *(movie)* **what's showing this week?** ¿qué ponen *or* echan esta semana?; **"now showing at a theater near you"** ahora en pantalla

▶**show in** *vt sep (escort in)* acompañar hasta dentro

▶**show off 1** *vt sep* alardear de

2 *vi* alardear, fanfarronear

▶**show out** *vt sep (escort out)* acompañar hasta la puerta

▶**show up 1** *vt sep* (**a**) *(reveal)* descubrir, poner al descubierto (**b**) *(embarrass)* poner en evidencia

2 *vi* (**a**) *(stand out)* destacar; **the marks s. up under infrared light** la luz infrarroja revela las marcas (**b**) *Fam (arrive)* aparecer, presentarse

show-and-tell [ˈʃəʊənˈtel] *n* = ejercicio escolar en que un alumno lleva a la clase un objeto de su elección y habla sobre él

showbiz [ˈʃəʊbɪz] *n Fam* la farándula, el mundo del espectáculo

showcase [ˈʃəʊkeɪs] *n (for displaying objects)* vitrina *f*; *Fig (for talents, work)* escaparate *m*

showdown [ˈʃəʊdaʊn] *n* discusión *f* cara a cara

shower [ˈʃaʊə(r)] **1** *n* (**a**) *(of rain)* chubasco *m*, chaparrón *m*; *(of stones, insults)* lluvia *f* (**b**) *(for washing)* ducha *f*, *Col, Méx, Ven* regadera *f*; **to have** *or* **take a s.** ducharse, darse una ducha; **s. cap** gorro *m* de baño; **s. curtain** cortinas *fpl* de ducha; **s. gel** gel *m* de ducha; **s. head** alcachofa *f* (de ducha) (**c**) *(party)* = fiesta celebrada en honor a una persona que se va a casar o que va a tener un bebé, y a la que todos los invitados traen un regalo

2 *vt* **to s. sb with sth, to s. sth on sb** colmar a alguien de algo

3 *vi (take a shower)* ducharse

showery [ˈʃaʊərɪ] *adj* lluvioso(a)

showgirl [ˈʃəʊgɜl] *n* chica *f* de revista

showily [ˈʃəʊɪlɪ] *adv* llamativamente

showing [ˈʃəʊɪŋ] *n (exhibition)* exposición *f*, muestra *f*; *(of movie)* pase *m*, proyección *f*

showman [ˈʃəʊmən] *n (entertaining person)* showman *m*

showmanship [ˈʃəʊmənʃɪp] *n* espectacularidad *f*

shown [ʃəʊn] *pp of* **show**

show-off [ˈʃəʊof] *n Fam* fanfarrón(ona) *m,f, Esp* fantasma *mf*

showpiece [ˈʃəʊpiːs] *n* pieza *f* principal *(de una colección)*

showroom [ˈʃəʊruːm] *n* sala *f* de exposición

show-stopper [ˈʃəʊstopə(r)] *n Fam* **it was a real s.** fue una auténtica sensación

showy [ˈʃəʊɪ] *adj* llamativo(a)

shrank [ʃræŋk] *pt of* **shrink**

shrapnel [ˈʃræpnəl] *n* metralla *f*

shred [ʃred] **1** *n* jirón *m*; **in shreds** hecho(a) jirones; *also Fig* **to tear sth to shreds** hacer trizas algo; *Fig* **there isn't a s. of evidence** no hay ni rastro de pruebas

2 *vt (pt & pp* **shredded**) *(documents)* hacer tiras, triturar; *(food)* cortar en tiras

shredder [ˈʃredə(r)] *n (for paper)* trituradora *f* de documentos

shrew [ʃruː] *n* (**a**) *(animal)* musaraña *f* (**b**) *(nagging woman)* bruja *f*

shrewd [ʃruːd] *adj (person)* astuto(a); *(decision)* inteligente, astuto(a)

shrewdly [ˈʃruːdlɪ] *adv* astutamente

shriek [ˈʃriːk] **1** *n* alarido *m*, chillido *m*; **shrieks of laughter** carcajadas *fpl*; **to give a s.** soltar un alarido *or* chillido

2 *vt* chillar

3 *vi* chillar; **to s. with laughter** reírse a carcajadas

shrift [ʃrɪft] *n* **to give sb short s.** prestar escasa atención a alguien

shrill [ʃrɪl] *adj* estridente, agudo(a)

shrimp [ʃrɪmp] *n* gamba *f*

shrine [ʃraɪn] *n (tomb)* sepulcro *m*; *(place) & Fig* santuario *m*

shrink [ʃrɪŋk] **1** *n Fam (psychiatrist)* psiquiatra *mf*

2 *vt (pt* **shrank** [ʃræŋk] *or* **shrunk** [ʃrʌŋk], *pp* **shrunk** *or* **shrunken** [ˈʃrʌŋkən]) encoger

3 *vi* (**a**) *(material)* encoger(se); *(income, budget)* reducirse, disminuir (**b**) *(move back)* **to s. from sth** retroceder ante algo; **to s. from doing sth** no atreverse a hacer algo

shrinkage [ˈʃrɪŋkɪdʒ] *n (of material)* encogimiento *m*; *Fig (in sales, profits)* reducción *f*

shrink-wrapped [ʃrɪŋkˈræpt] *adj* empaquetado(a) con plástico (de polietileno) adherente

shrivel [ˈʃrɪvəl] **1** *vt* marchitar

2 *vi* marchitarse

▶**shrivel up** *vi* secarse

shroud [ʃraʊd] **1** *n* mortaja *f*, sudario *m*; *Fig (of mystery)* halo *m*; *(of darkness)* manto *m*

2 *vt (obscure)* envolver; **to be shrouded in sth** estar envuelto(a) en algo

Shrove Tuesday [ˈʃrəʊvˈtjuːzdɪ] *n* Martes *m inv* de Carnaval

shrub [ʃrʌb] *n* arbusto *m*

shrug [ʃrʌg] **1** *n* encogimiento *m* de hombros

2 *vt (pt & pp* **shrugged**) **to s. one's shoulders** encogerse de hombros

3 *vi* **to s.** encogerse de hombros

▶**shrug off** *vt sep* quitar importancia a

shrunk [ʃrʌŋk] *pt & pp of* **shrink**

shrunken [ˈʃrʌŋkən] **1** *adj* encogido(a)

2 *pp of* **shrink**

shudder [ˈʃʌdə(r)] **1** *n (of person)* estremecimiento *m*; *Fam* **it gives me the shudders** me pone los pelos de punta

2 *vi (person)* estremecerse; *(vehicle)* dar una sacudida; **I s. to think of it** me estremezco sólo de pensarlo

shuffle [ˈʃʌfəl] **1** *n* (**a**) **to walk with a s.** caminar arrastrando los pies (**b**) **to give the cards a s.** barajar *or* mezclar las cartas

2 *vt (papers)* revolver; *(cards)* barajar

3 *vi (when walking)* arrastrar los pies

shun [ʃʌn] *(pt & pp* **shunned**) *vt* rehuir, evitar

shunt [ʃʌnt] *vt (train, car)* cambiar de vía; *Fam Fig* **we were shunted into another room** nos hicieron pasar a otra habitación

shush [ʃʌʃ] **1** *vt* hacer callar
2 *exclam* **s.!** ¡chsss!, ¡sssh!

shut [ʃʌt] **1** *adj* cerrado(a); **to be s.** estar cerrado; *Fam* **to keep one's mouth s.** no decir ni pío
2 *vt (pt & pp* **shut)** cerrar; **to s. the door on sb** dar a alguien con la puerta en las narices; **to s. one's finger in the door** pillarse un dedo con la puerta; *Fam* **s. your mouth!** ¡cierra el pico!
3 *vi (door)* cerrarse; *(store)* cerrar
▶**shut down 1** *vt sep* cerrar por completo; *(production)* suspender
2 *vi* cerrar por completo
▶**shut in** *vt sep (confine)* encerrar
▶**shut off** *vt sep* **(a)** *(electricity, water, funds, flow of arms)* cortar; *(engine)* apagar **(b)** *(road, exit)* cortar **(c)** *(isolate)* **to s. oneself off (from)** aislarse (de)
▶**shut out** *vt sep* **(a)** *(exclude) (person)* excluir; *(light, view)* tapar **(b)** *(keep outside)* dejar fuera; **to s. oneself out** quedarse fuera sin llaves
▶**shut up 1** *vt sep* **(a)** *(confine)* encerrar **(b)** *(close)* cerrar **(c)** *Fam (silence)* hacer callar
2 *vi Fam (be quiet)* callarse

shutdown [ʃʌtdaʊn] *n (of factory)* cierre *m*
shut-eye [ʃʌtaɪ] *n Fam* **to get some s.** echar un sueñecito *or* una cabezadita
shutoff [ʃʌtɒf] *n (device)* válvula *f* de cierre; *Elec* interruptor *m*
shutter [ʃʌtə(r)] *n* **(a)** *(on window)* contraventana *f*; *(of store)* persiana *f*; **to put up the shutters** *(of store)* cerrar **(b)** *(of camera)* obturador *m*; **s. release** disparador *m*; **s. speed** tiempo *m* de exposición
shuttered [ʃʌtəd] *adj (with shutters fitted)* con contraventanas; *(with shutters closed)* con las persianas cerradas
shuttle [ʃʌtəl] **1** *n* **(a)** *(train, bus)* servicio *m* regular *(entre dos puntos)*; *(plane)* avión *m* (de puente aéreo); *(space vehicle)* transbordador *m* espacial; **s. service** *(of planes)* puente *m* aéreo; *(of trains, buses)* servicio regular **(b)** *(in badminton)* volante *m*
2 *vt* **to s. sb back and forth** trasladar a alguien de acá para allá
3 *vi* **to s. between A and B** ir y venir entre A y B
shuttlecock [ʃʌtəlkɒk] *n* volante *m*
shy [ʃaɪ] **1** *adj* tímido(a); **to be s. of sb** tener miedo de alguien; **to be s. of doing sth** mostrarse remiso(a) a hacer algo
2 *vi (horse)* asustarse **(at** de)
▶**shy away** *vi* **to s. away from doing sth** no atreverse a hacer algo; **to s. away from sth** eludir algo
shyly [ʃaɪlɪ] *adv* tímidamente, con timidez
Siamese [saɪəˈmiːz] **1** *n (pl* **Siamese)** *(cat)* (gato *m*) siamés *m*
2 *adj* siamés(esa); **S. cat** gato *m* siamés; **S. twins** hermanos(as) *m,fpl* siameses(esas)
Siberia [saɪˈbɪərɪə] *n* Siberia
Siberian [saɪˈbɪərɪən] *adj* siberiano(a)
sibling [sɪblɪŋ] *n (brother)* hermano *m*; *(sister)* hermana *f*; **s. rivalry** rivalidad *f* entre hermanos
sic [sɪk] *adv* sic
Sicilian [sɪˈsɪlɪən] *n & adj* siciliano(a) *m,f*
Sicily [sɪsɪlɪ] *n* Sicilia
sick [sɪk] **1** *npl* **the s.** los enfermos
2 *adj* **(a)** *(ill)* enfermo(a); **to be s.** *(be ill)* estar enfermo; *(vomit)* vomitar, devolver; **to feel s.** sentirse mal; **to make oneself s.** *(deliberately)* provocarse el vómito; **you're going to make yourself s.!** ¡te vas a empachar!; *Fig* **it makes me s.!** ¡me pone enfermo(a)!; *Fig* **to be worried s.** estar muerto(a) de preocupación; **s. bay** enfermería *f*; **s. leave** baja *f* por enfermedad; **s. note** certificado *m* de baja *(por enfermedad)*; **s. pay** paga *f* por enfermedad
(b) *(fed up)* **to be s. of sb/sth** estar harto(a) de alguien/algo; **to grow s. of sth** hartarse de algo; **to be s. and tired of sb/sth, to be s. to death of sb/sth** estar hasta la coronilla de alguien/algo
(c) *(cruel) (humor, joke)* morboso(a), macabro(a); *(person)* retorcido(a); **to have a s. mind** tener una mente retorcida, ser retorcido
sicken [sɪkən] **1** *vt (make ill)* (hacer) enfermar; *(disgust)* poner enfermo(a)
2 *vi* ponerse enfermo(a), enfermar
sickening [sɪkənɪŋ] *adj (disgusting)* repugnante; *Fam (annoying)* irritante, exasperante
sickeningly [sɪkənɪŋlɪ] *adv* asquerosamente; **s., she won all the prizes** qué asco, ganó todos los premios
sickle [sɪkəl] *n* hoz *f*
sickly [sɪklɪ] *adj* **(a)** *(person, complexion)* enfermizo(a); *(plant)* marchito(a); *(color, light)* pálido(a), desvaído(a); *(smile)* falso(a) **(b)** *(taste, sentiment)* empalagoso(a); **s. sweet** empalagoso(a), dulzarrón(ona)
sickness [sɪknɪs] *n (illness)* enfermedad *f*; *(nausea)* mareo *m*
sickroom [sɪkruːm] *n* habitación *f* del enfermo
side [saɪd] **1** *n* **(a)** *(of person)* costado *m*; *(of animal)* ijada *f*; **by sb's s.** al lado de alguien; **s. by s.** uno al lado del otro; *Fam* **to split one's sides (laughing)** partirse de risa
(b) *(part) (of house, box, triangle, square)* lado *m*; *(of river)* orilla *f*, margen *m or f*; *(of road)* borde *m*, margen *m or f*; *(of mountain)* ladera *f*; **on the south s. (of the city)** en la parte sur (de la ciudad); **s. door/entrance** puerta *f*/entrada *f* lateral
(c) *(of record, paper)* cara *f*
(d) *(adjacent area)* lado *m*; **on this/that s. (of)** a este/ese lado (de); **on the other s. (of sth)** al otro lado (de algo); **on both sides** a ambos lados; **on all sides, on every s.** por todos (los) lados; **from all sides, from every s.** desde todas partes; **to move from s. to s.** moverse de un lado a otro; **the left-hand s.** la izquierda; **the right-hand s.** la derecha; **to stand on** *or* **to one s.** mantenerse al margen; **s. dish** plato *m* de acompañamiento *or* guarnición; **s. salad** ensalada *f* de acompañamiento *or* guarnición; **s. view** vista *f* lateral
(e) *(of situation, argument, personality)* lado *m*, aspecto *m*; **to look on the bright/gloomy s. (of things)** mirar el lado positivo/negativo (de las cosas); **to hear** *or* **look at both sides of the question** considerar las dos caras de una situación
(f) *(in game)* equipo *m*; *(in dispute)* parte *f*, bando *m*; **to be on sb's s.** *(defending)* estar de parte de alguien; *(in game)* estar en el equipo de alguien; **to take sides** tomar partido; **he's on our s.** está de nuestro lado; **to change sides** cambiar de bando
(g) *(secondary part)* **s. effects** efectos *mpl* secundarios; **s. issue** cuestión *f* secundaria; **s. order** ración *f (como acompañamiento)*; **s. road** carretera *f* secundaria; **s. street** bocacalle *f*
(h) *(idioms)* **on his mother's s.** *(of family)* por línea materna; **to put sth to one s.** dejar algo a un lado; **to take sb to one s.** llevar a alguien aparte; **to be on the wrong s. of forty** pasar de los cuarenta; **to get on the right s. of sb** caer en gracia a alguien, complacer a alguien; **to get on the wrong s. of sb** ganarse la antipatía de alguien; **it's a bit on the expensive/long s.** es un poco caro/largo; **he does a bit of gardening on the s.** hace algunos trabajos extras de jardinería
2 *vi* **to s. with** ponerse del lado de; **to s. against** ponerse en contra de
sideboard [saɪdbɔːd] *n* aparador *m*
sideburns [saɪdbɜːnz] *npl* patillas *fpl*
sidecar [saɪdkɑː(r)] *n* sidecar *m*
-sided [-saɪdɪd] *suffix* **three/many-s.** de tres/múltiples caras

sidekick ['saɪdkɪk] *n Fam* compinche *mf*

sidelight ['saɪdlaɪt] *n Aut* luz *f* de posición

sideline ['saɪdlaɪn] *n* (**a**) *(of football field, basketball court)* línea *f* de banda; *Fig* **to sit on the sidelines** quedarse al margen (**b**) *Com (business)* negocio *m* subsidiario; *(job)* segundo empleo *m*

sidesaddle ['saɪdsædəl] **1** *n* jamugas *fpl*, silla *f* de amazona
2 *adv* **to ride s.** montar a mujeriegas

sideshow ['saɪdʃəʊ] *n (at fair)* barraca *f* (de feria); *Fig* cuestión *f* menor *or* secundaria

sidesplitting ['saɪdsplɪtɪŋ] *adj Fam* desternillante, divertidísimo(a)

sidestep ['saɪdstep] *(pt & pp* **sidestepped**) **1** *vt (tackle)* esquivar, evitar; *(player)* regatear; *Fig (question)* soslayar, eludir
2 *vi (in boxing)* esquivar

sideswipe ['saɪdswaɪp] *n* **to take a s. at sb/sth** meterse de pasada con alguien/algo

sidetrack ['saɪdtræk] *vt* desviar

sidewalk ['saɪdwɔːk] *n* acera *f*, *CSur* vereda *f*, *CAm, Méx* banqueta *f*; **s. cafe** café *m* con terraza

sideway(s) ['saɪdweɪ(z)] **1** *adj (look)* de reojo; *(movement)* lateral
2 *adv* de lado

siding ['saɪdɪŋ] *n (on railway)* apartadero *m*; *(not connected to main track)* vía *f* muerta

sidle ['saɪdəl] *vi* **to s. up to sb** *(hesitantly)* acercarse tímidamente a alguien; *(furtively)* acerarse furtivamente a alguien

siege [siːdʒ] *n* asedio *m*, sitio *m*; **to lay s. to a town** sitiar una ciudad; **under s.** sitiado(a); **s. mentality** manía *f* persecutoria

Sierra Leone [sɪˈerəlɪˈəʊn] *n* Sierra Leona

sieve [sɪv] **1** *n (with coarse mesh)* criba *f*, cedazo *m*; *(with fine mesh)* tamiz *m*; *(in kitchen)* colador *m*; *Fam* **to have a memory like a s.** tener una memoria pésima *or* de mosquito
2 *vt (with coarse mesh)* cribar, cerner; *(with fine mesh)* tamizar; *(in kitchen)* colar

sift [sɪft] **1** *vt (flour, sugar)* tamizar
2 *vi (search)* **to s. through sth** examinar algo concienzudamente

sigh [saɪ] **1** *n* suspiro *m*
2 *vi* suspirar; *(wind)* susurrar

sight [saɪt] **1** *n* (**a**) *(faculty)* vista *f*; **to lose one's s.** perder la vista
(**b**) *(act of seeing)* **to catch s. of sth/sb** ver algo/a alguien; **to lose s. of sth/sb** perder de vista algo/a alguien; **I hate the s. of him** no lo puedo ni ver; **I can't stand the s. of blood** no soporto ver la sangre; **to shoot sb on s.** disparar contra alguien en cuanto se lo ve; **at first s.** a primera vista; **it was love at first s.** fue un flechazo; **to know sb by s.** conocer a alguien de vista; **to buy sth s. unseen** comprar algo a ciegas
(**c**) *(range of vision)* **to come into s.** aparecer; **to be within s. (of)** *(able to see)* estar a la vista (de); *Fig (of victory, the end)* estar a un paso (de); **to keep sb in s.** no perder de vista a alguien; **to put sth out of s.** esconder algo; **to keep out of s.** no dejarse ver; *Prov* **out of s., out of mind** ojos que no ven, corazón que no siente
(**d**) *(of instrument)* visor *m*; *(of gun)* mira *f*; *Fig* **to have sth/sb in one's sights** tener algo/a alguien en el punto de mira; *Fig* **to have *or* set one's sights on sth/sb** tener las miras puestas en algo/alguien
(**e**) *(spectacle)* espectáculo *m*; *Fam* **you're/it's a s. for sore eyes!** ¡dichosos los ojos que te/lo ven!; *Fam* **you look a s.!** *(mess)* ¡menuda cómo te has puesto!; *(ridiculous)* ¡vaya facha *or* pinta que tienes!; **the sights** *(of city)* los lugares de interés
(**f**) *Fam (for emphasis)* **a (damn) s. longer/harder** muchísimo más largo/duro
2 *vt (see)* avistar, ver

sighted ['saɪtɪd] **1** *npl* **the s.** las personas sin discapacidades visuales
2 *adj (person)* sin discapacidades visuales

sighting ['saɪtɪŋ] *n* **several sightings have been reported** ha sido visto(a) en varias ocasiones

sightless ['saɪtlɪs] *adj* ciego(a)

sight-read ['saɪtriːd] *(pt & pp* **sight-read** ['saɪtred]) *vt & vi* repentizar

sightseeing ['saɪtsiːɪŋ] *n* visitas *fpl* turísticas; **to go s.** hacer turismo

sightseer ['saɪtsiːə(r)] *n* turista *mf*

sign [saɪn] **1** *n* (**a**) *(gesture)* seña *f*; **to make a s. to sb** hacer una seña a alguien; **s. language** lenguaje *m* por señas
(**b**) *(indication)* indicio *m*, señal *f*; **it's a sure s. that...** es un indicio inequívoco de que...; **a good/bad s.** una buena/mala señal; **a s. of the times** un signo de los tiempos que corren; **there's no s. of an improvement** no hay indicios de mejoría; **there is no s. of him/it** no hay ni rastro de él/ello; **he gave no s. of having heard** no dio muestras de haberlo oído; **all the signs are that...** todo parece indicar que...; **the equipment showed signs of having been used** el equipo tenía aspecto de haber sido utilizado
(**c**) *(notice)* cartel *m*; *(of pub, store)* letrero *m*, rótulo *m*; *(on road)* señal *f* (de tráfico); **follow the signs for Omaha** sigue las indicaciones para Omaha
(**d**) *(symbol)* signo *m*; **plus/minus s.** signo más/menos; **s. of the zodiac** signo del zodíaco
2 *vt* (**a**) *(write signature on)* firmar (**b**) *(in sign language)* indicar (con señas) (**c**) *(in sport)* fichar
3 *vi* (**a**) *(write signature)* firmar (**b**) *(in sport)* fichar (**for** por)

▶**sign away** *vt sep (rights)* ceder (por escrito)

▶**sign for** *vt insep (delivery, equipment)* firmar el acuse de recibo de

▶**sign in** *vi (in factory)* fichar, *Am* marcar tarjeta; *(in hotel)* registrarse

▶**sign off** *vi* (**a**) *(radio, TV host)* despedir la emisión (**b**) *(close letter)* despedirse, terminar

▶**sign out 1** *vt sep* **to s. sth out** *(book, equipment)* registrar *or* consignar el préstamo de algo
2 *vi* firmar a la salida

▶**sign up** *vi* (**a**) *(register)* apuntarse (**for** a) (**b**) *(soldier)* alistarse

signal ['sɪgnəl] **1** *n* señal *f*; *Fig* **to send the wrong signals** dar una impresión equivocada; *Rail* **s. tower** sala *f* de agujas, puesto *m* de señales; **s. flare** bengala *f*; **s. rocket** cohete *m* de señales
2 *vt* (**a**) *(send message to)* indicar (mediante señales) a; **to s. sb to do sth** hacerle una señal a alguien de *or* para que haga algo (**b**) *(be sign of)* señalar
3 *vi* **s. to me if you need help** hazme una seña si necesitas ayuda; **she signaled for the bill** pidió la cuenta con una seña *or* haciendo señas; *Aut* **he didn't s. before he turned** no dio la indicación de que iba a torcer

signaling ['sɪgnəlɪŋ] *n Rail* señalización *f*; **s. failure** *Esp* fallo *m or Am* falla *f* en el sistema de señales

signalman ['sɪgnəlmən] *n Rail* guardavía *m*

signatory ['sɪgnətərɪ] *n* signatario(a) *m,f*

signature ['sɪgnətʃə(r)] *n* firma *f*; **s. tune** *(of radio, TV program)* sintonía *f*

signboard ['saɪnbɔːd] *n* letrero *m*

signet ring ['sɪgnɪt'rɪŋ] *n* sello *m (sortija)*

significance [sɪgˈnɪfɪkəns] *n* (**a**) *(importance)* importancia *f*; **of no/of great s.** de ninguna/de gran importancia (**b**) *(meaning)* significado *m*

significant [sɪgˈnɪfɪkənt] *adj (important)* considerable, importante; *(meaningful)* significativo(a); **s. other** media naranja *f*

significantly [sɪgˈnɪfɪkəntlɪ] *adv* (**a**) *(appreciably)* sensiblemente (**b**) *(meaningfully)* significativamente; **s., no one**

mentioned it es significativo que nadie lo mencionara

signify ['sɪgnɪfaɪ] vt (**a**) *(indicate)* señalar; *(constitute)* suponer, representar (**b**) *(mean)* significar

signpost ['saɪnpəʊst] **1** n also Fig señal f, indicación f
2 vt señalizar; Fig señalar

signwriter ['saɪnraɪtə(r)] n rotulista mf

Sikh [siːk] n & adj sij mf

silage ['saɪlɪdʒ] n forraje m

silence ['saɪləns] **1** n silencio m; **to listen/watch in s.** escuchar/observar en silencio; Prov **s. is golden** en boca cerrada no entran moscas
2 vt hacer callar

silencer ['saɪlənsə(r)] n *(on gun)* silenciador m

silent ['saɪlənt] adj *(person, place)* silencioso(a); *(not pronounced) (letter)* mudo(a); **to be s.** *(not talk)* estar callado(a); **she's rather s.** *(by nature)* es muy callada; **to fall s.** quedarse en silencio; **to remain** or **keep silent** permanecer callado(a); **s. movie** película f muda; **the s. majority** la mayoría silenciosa; Com **s. partner** socio(a) m,f capitalista; **s. protest** protesta f silenciosa

silently ['saɪləntlɪ] adv *(not speaking)* en silencio; *(without noise)* sin hacer ruido, silenciosamente

silhouette [sɪluː'et] **1** n silueta f
2 vt **she was silhouetted against the light** la luz dibujaba su silueta, su silueta se recortaba al trasluz

silica ['sɪlɪkə] n sílice f

silicon ['sɪlɪkən] n silicio m; **s. chip** chip m de silicio

silk [sɪlk] n seda f; **s. screen printing** serigrafía f

silkworm ['sɪlkwɜːm] n gusano m de (la) seda

silky ['sɪlkɪ] adj sedoso(a); *(voice)* meloso(a)

sill [sɪl] n *(of window)* alféizar m

silliness ['sɪlɪnɪs] n tontería f, estupidez f; **stop this s.!** ¡ya basta de tonterías!

silly ['sɪlɪ] **1** adj tonto(a), estúpido(a); **the s. thing is that…** lo más ridículo es que…; **to make sb look s.** poner a alguien en ridículo; **to say/do something s.** decir/hacer una tontería; **to laugh/worry oneself s.** morirse de la risa/de preocupación; **to knock sb s.** dejar a alguien atontado de un mamporro
2 n Fam idiota mf

silo ['saɪləʊ] *(pl* **silos**) n silo m

silt [sɪlt] n limo m, sedimentos mpl fluviales

▶**silt up** vi encenagarse

silver ['sɪlvə(r)] **1** n (**a**) *(metal)* plata f; Prov **every cloud has a s. lining** no hay mal que por bien no venga; **s. haired** con el pelo blanco; **s. (medal)** medalla f de plata; **s. plate** *(coating)* baño m de plata; *(articles)* objetos mpl plateados; **the s. screen** la pantalla grande; **s. wedding** bodas fpl de plata (**b**) *(silverware)* (objetos mpl de) plata f
2 adj (**a**) *(made of silver)* de plata (**b**) **s.(-colored)** plateado(a)

silver-plated [sɪlvə'pleɪtɪd] adj con baño de plata

silversmith ['sɪlvəsmɪθ] n platero(a) m,f

silverware ['sɪlvəweə(r)] n (objetos mpl de) plata f

silverwork ['sɪlvəwɜːk] n *(trabajo m de)* platería f

silvery ['sɪlvərɪ] adj *(color)* plateado(a); *(sound)* argentino(a)

SIM [sɪm] n *(abbr* **subscriber identity module**) **S. card** *(in cell phone)* tarjeta f SIM

simian ['sɪmɪən] adj simiesco(a)

similar ['sɪmɪlə(r)] adj parecido(a) (**to** a); **s. in appearance/size** de parecido aspecto/tamaño

similarity [sɪmɪ'lærɪtɪ] n parecido m, similitud f

similarly ['sɪmɪləlɪ] adv (**a**) *(in the same way)* igual, de la misma manera (**b**) *(likewise)* igualmente, del mismo modo

simile ['sɪmɪlɪ] n símil m

simmer ['sɪmə(r)] **1** n at a **s.** a fuego lento
2 vt cocer a fuego lento

3 vi cocerse a fuego lento; Fig *(revolt, discontent)* fraguarse; **she was simmering with rage** estaba a punto de explotar

▶**simmer down** vi calmarse, tranquilizarse

simper ['sɪmpə(r)] vi sonreír con afectación

simple ['sɪmpəl] adj (**a**) *(uncomplicated)* sencillo(a); **it's as s. as that** es así de sencillo; **in s. terms** sencillamente; **the s. truth** la pura verdad (**b**) *(naive)* inocente, cándido(a); **he's a bit s.** es un poco simplón (**c**) *(not compound)* Fin **s. interest** interés m simple; Gram **s. tense** tiempo m simple

simpleminded [sɪmpəl'maɪndɪd] adj *(person)* simplón(ona); *(ideas, belief)* ingenuo(a)

simpleton ['sɪmpəltən] n simple mf, papanatas mf inv

simplicity [sɪm'plɪsɪtɪ] n sencillez f; **it's s. itself** es de lo más sencillo

simplification [sɪmplɪfɪ'keɪʃən] n simplificación f

simplify ['sɪmplɪfaɪ] vt simplificar

simplistic [sɪm'plɪstɪk] adj simplista

simplistically [sɪm'plɪstɪklɪ] adv simplísticamente

simply ['sɪmplɪ] adv (**a**) *(in simple manner)* con sencillez (**b**) *(absolutely)* sencillamente (**c**) *(just)* sólo; **it's s. a question of time** sólo es una cuestión de tiempo; **she s. had to snap her fingers and…** sólo con chasquear los dedos…

simulate ['sɪmjʊleɪt] vt simular

simulated ['sɪmjʊleɪtɪd] adj *(leather, marble)* de imitación; *(surprise, anger)* fingido(a), simulado(a)

simulation [sɪmjʊ'leɪʃən] n simulación f

simulcast ['saɪməlkæst] vt retransmitir simultáneamente

simultaneous [sɪməl'teɪnɪəs] adj simultáneo(a); **s. broadcast** retransmisión f simultánea; **s. translation** traducción simultánea

simultaneously [sɪməl'teɪnɪəslɪ] adv simultáneamente

sin [sɪn] **1** n pecado m; Old-fashioned or Hum **to be living in s.** vivir en pecado; Fam **it would be a s. to…** sería un pecado…
2 vi *(pt & pp* **sinned**) pecar

since [sɪns] **1** prep desde; **s. his death** desde su muerte; **s. June/1993** desde junio/1993; **s. then** desde entonces
2 adv desde entonces; **long s.** hace mucho
3 conj (**a**) *(in time)* desde que; **it's a long time s. I saw her** ha pasado mucho tiempo desde que la vi (**b**) *(because)* ya que

sincere [sɪn'sɪə(r)] adj sincero(a)

sincerely [sɪn'sɪəlɪ] adv sinceramente; **Yours s., S. yours** *(ending letter)* Atentamente

sincerity [sɪn'serɪtɪ] n sinceridad f; **in all s.** con toda sinceridad

sinecure ['saɪnɪkjʊə(r)] n sinecura f

sinew ['sɪnjuː] n tendón m

sinewy ['sɪnjuːɪ] adj *(person, muscles)* fibroso(a); *(hands)* nervudo(a)

sinful ['sɪnfʊl] adj *(person)* pecador(ora); *(act, life)* pecaminoso(a); *(waste)* escandaloso(a)

sing [sɪŋ] *(pt* **sang** [sæŋ], *pp* **sung** [sʌŋ]) **1** vt *(song)* cantar; **to s. sb to sleep** arrullar a alguien
2 vi *(person, bird)* cantar; *(kettle)* pitar

▶**sing out** vi *(sing loudly)* cantar en voz alta

Singapore [sɪŋə'pɔː(r)] n Singapur

Singaporean [sɪŋə'pɔːrɪən] n & adj singapurense mf

singe [sɪndʒ] vt chamuscar

singer ['sɪŋə(r)] n cantante mf; **s. songwriter** or **s./song writer** cantautor(ora) m,f

Singhalese = Sinhalese

singing ['sɪŋɪŋ] n canto m; **his s. is awful** canta fatal; **s. lessons** clases fpl de canto; **to have a fine s. voice** tener buena voz

single ['sɪŋgəl] **1** n (**a**) *(record)* sencillo m, single m (**b**) *(hotel room)* habitación f sencilla or individual (**c**) **singles** *(in tennis)* (modalidad f de) individuales mpl

2 adj (**a**) (just one) único(a), solo(a); **every s. day** todos los días; **not a s. one** ni uno solo; **I haven't seen a s. soul** no he visto ni un alma; **don't say a s. word** no digas ni una (sola) palabra; Fin **s. currency** moneda f única; Econ **s. market** mercado m único (**b**) (not double) **in s. figures** por debajo de diez; **in s. file** en fila india; **s. bed** cama f individual; **s. room** habitación f sencilla or individual (**c**) (not married) soltero(a); **s. mother** madre f soltera; **s. parent** padre m/madre f soltero(a); **s. parent family** familia f monoparental

▶**single out** vt sep señalar, distinguir; **she was singled out for special praise** fue distinguida con una mención especial

single-breasted ['sɪŋɡəl'brestɪd] adj (jacket, suit) recto(a), no cruzado(a)

single-handed ['sɪŋɡəl'hændɪd] adj & adv en solitario, sin ayuda

single-handedly ['sɪŋɡəl'hændɪdlɪ] adv = **single-handed**

single-minded ['sɪŋɡəl'maɪndɪd] adj resuelto(a), determinado(a)

single-mindedly ['sɪŋɡəl'maɪndɪdlɪ] adv con determinación, con empeño

single-sex school ['sɪŋɡəl'seks'skuːl] n (for girls) colegio m para niñas; (for boys) colegio m para niños

single-track railroad ['sɪŋɡəl'træk'reɪlrəʊd] n vía f única

singly ['sɪŋɡlɪ] adv individualmente, uno(a) por uno(a)

singsong ['sɪŋsɒŋ] **1** n (voice, tone) **he spoke in a s.** habló con voz cantarina
2 adj (voice, tone) cantarín(ina)

singular ['sɪŋɡjʊlə(r)] **1** n Gram singular m; **in the s.** en singular
2 adj (**a**) Gram singular (**b**) (remarkable) singular, excepcional

singularly ['sɪŋɡjʊləlɪ] adv singularmente, excepcionalmente

Sinhalese [sɪnə'liːz], **Singhalese** [sɪŋə'liːz] **1** n (**a**) (person) cingalés(esa) m,f (**b**) (language) cingalés m
2 adj cingalés(esa)

sinister ['sɪnɪstə(r)] adj siniestro(a)

sink[1] [sɪŋk] n (in kitchen) fregadero m; (in bathroom) lavabo m, Am lavamanos m inv

sink[2] (pt **sank** [sæŋk], pp **sunk** [sʌŋk]) **1** vt (**a**) (ship) hundir; **to be sunk in thought** estar abstraído(a); Fam Fig **to be sunk** (in trouble) estar perdido(a) (**b**) (well) cavar; (shaft) excavar; **to s. one's teeth into sth** hundir or hincar los dientes en algo; **to s. money into a project** invertir mucho dinero en un proyecto
2 vi (in water, mud) hundirse; **her heart sank** se le cayó el alma a los pies; **his spirits sank** se desanimó; **to s. into sb's memory** quedar grabado(a) en la memoria de alguien; **to s. into oblivion** sumirse en el olvido; **to s. into a deep sleep** sumirse en un sueño profundo; **to s. into an armchair** hundirse en un sillón; **to s. to the ground** ir cayendo al suelo; **he has sunk in my estimation** ha perdido gran parte de mi estima; **how could you s. so low?** ¿cómo pudiste caer tan bajo?

▶**sink in** vi (liquid) penetrar, calar; (information) calar; Fig **it hasn't sunk in yet** todavía no lo he or lo tengo asumido

sinker ['sɪŋkə(r)] n Fam (doughnut) donut m

sinking ['sɪŋkɪŋ] **1** n (**a**) (of ship) hundimiento m (**b**) Fin **s. fund** fondo m de amortización
2 adj **with a s. heart** con creciente desánimo; **to get that s. feeling** empezar a preocuparse

sinner ['sɪnə(r)] n pecador(ora) m,f

sinuous ['sɪnjʊəs] adj sinuoso(a)

sinus ['saɪnəs] n seno m (nasal); **s. infection** sinusitis f inv

sinusitis [saɪnə'saɪtɪs] n sinusitis f inv

sip [sɪp] **1** n sorbo m; **to take a s. (of sth)** dar un sorbo (a algo)
2 vt (pt & pp **sipped**) sorber, beber a sorbos
3 vi **she sipped at her drink** bebió un sorbo

siphon, syphon ['saɪfən] **1** n sifón m
2 vt bombear

▶**siphon off** vt sep (liquid) sacar a sifón; Fig (money, supplies) desviar

sir [sɜː(r)] n (**a**) (form of address) señor m; **Dear S.** (in letter) Estimado señor, Muy señor mío; **Dear Sirs** Estimados señores, Muy señores míos (**b**) (title) **S. Cedric** sir Cedric (título nobiliario masculino)

sire ['saɪə(r)] **1** n (**a**) (of animal) padre m (**b**) Old-fashioned (address to sovereign) señor m, majestad m
2 vt engendrar

siren ['saɪərən] n sirena f

sirloin ['sɜːlɔɪn] n **s. (steak)** solomillo m

sisal ['saɪzəl] n (plant) pita f; (material) sisal m

sissy ['sɪsɪ] n Fam (weak male) blandengue m, llorica m; (effeminate male) mariquita m

sister ['sɪstə(r)] n (**a**) (sibling) hermana f; **s. company** empresa f asociada; **s. ship** buque m gemelo; **s. city** ciudad f hermanada (**b**) (nun) hermana f; **S. Teresa** sor Teresa, la hermana Teresa

sisterhood ['sɪstəhʊd] n (**a**) (community of nuns) hermandad f, congregación f (**b**) (solidarity) hermandad f (entre mujeres)

sister-in-law ['sɪstərɪn'lɔː] (pl **sisters-in-law**) n cuñada f

sisterly ['sɪstəlɪ] adj de hermana

sit [sɪt] (pt & pp **sat** [sæt]) **1** vt **to s. a child on one's knee** sentar a un niño en el regazo
2 vi (**a**) (person) (be seated) estar sentado(a); (sit down) sentarse; **s.!** (to dog) ¡siéntate!; **don't just s. there!** ¡no te quedes ahí (sentado) sin hacer nada!; Fam **to s. tight** quedarse quieto(a) (**b**) (assembly, court) reunirse; **to s. on a jury** formar parte de un jurado (**c**) (object) **to be sitting on the radiator** estar encima del radiador

▶**sit around, sit about** vi gandulear, holgazanear

▶**sit back** vi (**a**) (lean back) **to s. back in one's chair** recostarse en la silla (**b**) Fam (relax) relajarse; (not intervene) quedarse de brazos cruzados

▶**sit down 1** vt sep **to s. sb down** sentar a alguien; Fam **s. yourself down!** ¡siéntate!
2 vi sentarse; **to be sitting down** estar sentado(a)

▶**sit in** vi (at meeting) estar presente (**on** en) (como observador)

▶**sit on** vt insep Fam (**a**) (not deal with) no tocar (**b**) (repress) hacer la vida imposible a

▶**sit out 1** vt sep (not participate in) saltarse
2 vi (in yard) sentarse fuera

▶**sit through** vt insep aguantar

▶**sit up** vi (**a**) (straighten one's back) sentarse derecho(a); (from lying position) incorporarse; Fig **he made them s. up and take notice** les hizo reaccionar y que se fijaran en él (**b**) (not go to bed) **to s. up (late)** quedarse levantado(a) hasta tarde

sitar ['sɪtɑː(r)] n Mus sitar m

sitcom ['sɪtkɒm] n TV telecomedia f (de situación)

site [saɪt] **1** n (**a**) (position) lugar m; (archaeological) yacimiento m; (of monument, building, complex) emplazamiento m (**b**) (building) **s.** obra f (**c**) Comptr sitio m; **s. map** mapa m del sitio
2 vt emplazar, ubicar; **to be sited** estar situado(a)

sit-in ['sɪtɪn] n encierro m

sitting ['sɪtɪŋ] **1** n (of committee, for portrait) sesión f; (for meal) turno m; **at one s.** de una sentada
2 adj (**a**) (seated) sentado(a); Fam Fig **to be a s. duck** or **target** ser un blanco fácil (**b**) Pol **the s. member** (in Congress) el/la actual miembro del Congreso

situate ['sɪtjʊeɪt] vt situar, ubicar

situated ['sɪtjʊeɪtɪd] adj situado(a)

situation [sɪtjʊ'eɪʃən] n (**a**) (circumstances) situación f; **s. comedy** (on TV) telecomedia f (de situación) (**b**) (job) colocación f; **situations vacant/wanted** ofertas fpl/demandas fpl de empleo (**c**) (location) situación f, ubicación f

sit-up ['sɪtʌp] n **to do sit-ups** hacer abdominales

six [sɪks] **1** *n* seis *m*; *Fam* **it's s. of one and half a dozen of the other** viene a ser lo mismo; **at sixes and sevens** hecho(a) un lío
2 *adj* seis; *see also* **eight**

six-figure ['sɪks'fɪgə(r)] *adj* **a s. sum** una cantidad (de dinero) de seis cifras

six-pack ['sɪkspæk] *n* (**a**) *(beer)* paquete *m or* pack *m* de seis cervezas (**b**) *Fam (stomach muscles) (of man)* abdominales *mpl*

six-shooter ['sɪkʃuːtə(r)] *n* revólver *m (de seis disparos)*

sixteen [sɪks'tiːn] *n & adj* dieciséis *m*; *see also* **eight**

sixteenth [sɪks'tiːnθ] **1** *n* (**a**) *(fraction)* dieciseisavo *m*, decimosexta parte *f*; *Mus* **s. note** semicorchea *f* (**b**) *(in series)* decimosexto(a) *m,f* (**c**) *(of month)* dieciséis *m*
2 *adj* decimosexto(a); *see also* **eleventh**

sixth [sɪksθ] **1** *n* (**a**) *(fraction)* sexto *m*, sexta parte *f* (**b**) *(in series)* sexto(a) *m,f* (**c**) *(of month)* seis *m*
2 *adj* sexto(a); **s. sense** sexto sentido *m*; *see also* **eighth**

sixtieth ['sɪkstɪɪθ] *n & adj* sexagésimo(a) *m,f*

sixty ['sɪkstɪ] *n & adj* sesenta *m*; *see also* **eighty**

sixty-fourth note ['sɪkstɪfɔːθ'nəʊt] *n Mus* semifusa *f*

size [saɪz] *n* (**a**) *(of person)* talla *f*, tamaño *m*; *(of place, object)* tamaño *m*; *(of problem, undertaking)* envergadura *f*, dimensiones *fpl*; *Fam* **that's about the s. of it** así están las cosas (**b**) *(of clothes)* talla *f*; *(of shoes)* número *m*; **what s. do you take?**, **what s. are you?** *(of clothes)* ¿qué talla usas *or* gastas?; *(of shoes)* ¿qué número calzas?; **s. 10 shoes** ≃ zapatos del número 44; **to try sth (on) for s.** probarse algo para ver qué tal queda de talla

▸**size up** *vt sep (situation)* calibrar; *(person)* analizar

sizeable ['saɪzəbəl] *adj* considerable

sizzle ['sɪzəl] **1** *n* crepitación *f*
2 *vi* crepitar

sizzling ['sɪzlɪŋ] *adj* (**a**) *(sputtering)* chisporroteante (**b**) *Fam (hot) (day)* achicharrante, abrasador(ora)

skate¹ [skeɪt] *n (fish)* raya *f*

skate² **1** *n* patín *m*
2 *vi* patinar; *Fig* **to s. around sth** evitar algo; **to be skating on thin ice** pisar un terreno peligroso

skateboard ['skeɪtbɔːd] *n* monopatín *m*, skate(board) *m*

skateboarding ['skeɪtbɔːdɪŋ] *n* skate(board) *m*

skater ['skeɪtə(r)] *n* patinador(ora) *m,f*

skating ['skeɪtɪŋ] *n* patinaje *m*; **s. rink** pista *f* de patinaje

skeletal ['skelɪtəl] *adj* esquelético(a)

skeleton ['skelɪtən] *n* *(of person)* esqueleto *m*; *(of building)* esqueleto *m*, estructura *f*; *Fig* **a s. in the closet** un secreto vergonzante; **s. crew** tripulación *f* mínima; **s. key** llave *f* maestra; **s. staff** personal *m* mínimo

sketch [sketʃ] **1** *n* (**a**) *(drawing, description)* esbozo *m*, bosquejo *m*; **s. map** esquema *m*, croquis *m inv*; **s. pad** bloc *m* de dibujo (**b**) *(on stage, TV)* episodio *m*, sketch *m*
2 *vt also Fig* esbozar

▸**sketch in** *vt sep also Fig* esbozar

▸**sketch out** *vt sep (plan)* hacer un esquema de

sketchbook ['sketʃbʊk] *n* cuaderno *m* de dibujo

sketchily ['sketʃɪlɪ] *adv* someramente, superficialmente

sketchy ['sketʃɪ] *adj* somero(a), vago(a)

skew [skjuː] **1** *n* **on the s.** ladeado(a), torcido(a)
2 *vt (distort)* distorsionar

skewed [skjuːd] *adj (distorted)* sesgado(a)

skewer ['skjuːə(r)] **1** *n* brocheta *f*
2 *vt* ensartar, espetar

skew-gee ['skjuː'dʒiː] *Fam* **1** *adj* torcido(a)
2 *adv* de lado

ski [skiː] **1** *n* esquí *m*; **a pair of skis** unos esquís; **s. boots** botas *fpl* de esquí; **s. instructor** monitor(ora) *m,f* de esquí; **s. jump** salto *m* de esquí; **s. jumper** saltador(ora) *m,f* de esquí; **s. lift** remonte *m*, telesquí *m*; **s. pants** pantalones *mpl* de esquí; **s. resort** estación *f* de esquí; **s. run** *or* **slope** pista *f* de esquí; **s. stick** bastón *m* de esquí
2 *vi (pt & pp* **skied***)* esquiar

skid [skɪd] **1** *n* (**a**) *(of car)* patinazo *m*; **to go into a s.** patinar (**b**) *(idioms) Fam* **to put the skids under sth/sb** ocasionar la ruina de algo/alguien; *Fam* **to be on the skids** estar yéndose a pique; *Fam* **to be on s. row** pordiosear, vivir en la indigencia
2 *vi (pt & pp* **skidded***)* patinar

skidmark ['skɪdmɑːk] *n* marca *f* de neumáticos

skier ['skiːə(r)] *n* esquiador(ora) *m,f*

skiing ['skiːɪŋ] *n* esquí *m*; **to go s.** ir a esquiar; **s. vacation** vacaciones *fpl* de esquí; **s. instructor** monitor(ora) *m,f* de esquí

skill [skɪl] *n (ability)* destreza *f*, habilidad *f*; *(talent)* talento *m*, aptitud *f*; *(technique)* técnica *f*, capacidad *f*

skilled [skɪld] *adj (person)* experto(a), capacitado(a); *(work)* especializado(a); **she's s. in resolving such problems** se le da muy bien resolver ese tipo de problemas; **s. worker** trabajador(ora) *m,f* cualificado(a)

skillet ['skɪlɪt] *n* sartén *f*

skillful ['skɪlfʊl] *adj* hábil, habilidoso(a)

skillfully ['skɪlfʊlɪ] *adv* hábilmente

skim [skɪm] *(pt & pp* **skimmed***)* **1** *vt* (**a**) *(milk) Esp* quitar la nata a, *Am* sacar la crema a; *(soup)* espumar (**b**) *(surface)* rozar apenas; **to s. stones (on water)** hacer cabrillas *or* la rana (en el agua)
2 *vi* **to s. along** *or* **over the ground** pasar rozando el suelo

▸**skim off** *vt sep (fat, cream)* retirar; *Fig (money)* quedarse con

▸**skim through** *vt insep (novel, document)* echar una ojeada a

skim milk ['skɪm'mɪlk], **skimmed milk** ['skɪmd'mɪlk] *n* leche *f* desnatada *or* descremada

skimp [skɪmp] **1** *vt* escatimar
2 *vi* **to s. on sth** escatimar algo

skimpily ['skɪmpɪlɪ] *adv* **s. dressed** ligero(a) de ropa; **the book deals rather s. with the economic background** el libro trata de manera un tanto superficial el trasfondo económico

skimpy ['skɪmpɪ] *adj (meal)* exiguo(a), escaso(a); *(clothes)* exiguo(a)

skin [skɪn] **1** *n* (**a**) *(of person, animal, fruit)* piel *f*; *(on milk, sauce)* nata *f*; **to be all s. and bone** estar en los huesos; *Fam* **I nearly jumped out of my s.** casi me muero del susto; **by the s. of one's teeth** por los pelos; **to save one's (own) s.** salvar el pellejo; *Fam* **to get under sb's s.** poner histérico(a) a alguien; *Fam* **it's no s. off my nose** me *Esp* trae *or Am* tiene sin cuidado *or* al fresco; **s. cancer** cáncer *m* de piel; **s. complaint** afección *f* cutánea; **s. cream** crema *f* para la piel; **s. disease** enfermedad *f* cutánea; **s. diving** buceo *m* a pulmón libre; *Fam* **s. flick** *(porn movie)* película *f* porno; *Med* **s. graft** injerto *m* de piel
(**b**) *Fam (skinhead)* cabeza *mf* rapada
2 *vt (pt & pp* **skinned***)* *(animal)* despellejar, desollar; *(tomato)* pelar; **to s. one's knees** arañarse las rodillas

skinflint ['skɪnflɪnt] *n Fam* rata *mf*, roñoso(a) *m,f*

skinhead ['skɪnhed] *n* cabeza *mf* rapada

skinny ['skɪnɪ] *adj* flaco(a)

skintight ['skɪntaɪt] *adj* muy ajustado(a)

skip [skɪp] **1** *n* brinco *m*
2 *vt (pt & pp* **skipped***)* *(meal, page, stage)* saltarse
3 *vi (lambs, children)* brincar; *(with rope)* saltar a la cuerda *or Esp* comba

skipper ['skɪpə(r)] **1** *n (of ship)* patrón(ona) *m,f*, capitán(ana) *m,f*; *(of team)* capitán(ana) *m,f*
2 *vt Fam* capitanear

skipping ['skɪpɪŋ] *n (saltos mpl a la)* cuerda *f or Esp* comba

skirmish ['skɜːmɪʃ] **1** *n Mil* escaramuza *f*; *Fig* refriega *f*, trifulca *f*
2 *vi* pelear, luchar

skirt [skɜːt] **1** n falda f, CSur pollera f

2 vt (village, hill) bordear, rodear

skirt around, skirt round vt insep (village, hill) bordear, rodear; **to s. around** or **round a problem** eludir or evadir un problema

skit [skɪt] n parodia f

kittish ['skɪtɪʃ] adj (person) locuelo(a), juguetón(ona)

kittle ['skɪtəl] n bolo m; **to have a game of skittles** echar una partida de bolos

kulduggery = skullduggery

kulk [skʌlk] vi (hide) esconderse; (move furtively) merodear

kull [skʌl] n cráneo m; **the s. and crossbones** la calavera y las tibias

kullcap ['skʌlkæp] n casquete m; (of priest) solideo m

kul(l)duggery [skʌl'dʌɡərɪ] n tejemanejes mpl

kunk [skʌŋk] n (animal) mofeta f; Fam Pej (person) miserable mf, Esp perro m

ky [skaɪ] n cielo m; Fam **the s.'s the limit** podemos conseguir cualquier cosa que nos propongamos; Fam **to praise sb to the skies** poner a alguien por las nubes; **s. high** (price, costs) altísimo(a)

ky-blue [skaɪ'bluː] adj azul celeste

kydiver ['skaɪdaɪvə(r)] n = persona que practica la caída libre (en paracaídas)

kydiving ['skaɪdaɪvɪŋ] n caída f libre (en paracaídas)

kylark ['skaɪlɑːk] n alondra f

kylight ['skaɪlaɪt] n claraboya f

kyline ['skaɪlaɪn] n (horizon) horizonte m; (of city) silueta f, contorno m

kyscraper ['skaɪskreɪpə(r)] n rascacielos m inv

lab [slæb] n (of stone, concrete) losa f; (of cake, meat) trozo m; (of chocolate) tableta f; (in mortuary) mesa f de amortajamiento

lack [slæk] **1** n **to take up the s.** (in rope) tensar la cuerda; Fig **I'm fed up with having to take up your s.** estoy harto de tener que encargarme de tu trabajo

2 adj (a) (not tight) flojo(a); **to be s.** estar flojo(a); **trade is s.** el negocio está flojo; **s. periods** períodos mpl de poca actividad (b) (careless) dejado(a)

3 vi Fam vaguear

slack off vi (a) (diminish) aflojar (b) (avoid work) gandulear

lacken ['slækən] **1** vt (pace, rope) aflojar

2 vi (person) flojear; (rope) destensarse; (speed) reducirse, disminuir; (storm, wind) amainar, aflojar; (energy, enthusiasm) atenuarse, disminuir

slacken off vi (diminish) aflojar

lacker ['slækə(r)] n Fam vago(a) m,f, tirado(a) m,f, Méx flojo(a) m,f

lackness ['slæknɪs] n (a) (negligence, laziness) dejadez f (b) (of rope) distensión f (c) (of business) atonía f, inactividad f

lacks [slæks] npl (pants) pantalones mpl

lain [sleɪn] **1** npl **the s.** las bajas, los fallecidos

2 pp of **slay**

lake [sleɪk] vt Literary **to s. one's thirst** apagar or calmar la sed

lalom ['slɑːləm] n eslalon m

lam [slæm] **1** n (a) (of door) portazo m (b) (in basketball) **s. dunk** mate m

2 vt (pt & pp **slammed**) (a) (door, lid, drawer) cerrar de un golpe; **to s. the door in sb's face** dar con la puerta en las narices a alguien; **to s. sth down** dejar caer or estampar algo de un golpe; **to s. on the brakes** pisar el freno de golpe (b) Fam (criticize) criticar, poner verde a, Méx viborear, RP verdulear

3 vi (door) cerrarse de golpe, dar un portazo

lander ['slɑːndə(r)] **1** n difamación f

2 vt difamar

landerous ['slɑːndərəs] adj difamatorio(a)

slang [slæŋ] n argot m

slant [slɑːnt] **1** n (a) (slope) inclinación f (b) (emphasis, bias) sesgo m, orientación f; **she put a favorable s. on the information** le dio un cariz or sesgo favorable a la información

2 vt (a) (set at angle) inclinar (b) (bias) enfocar subjetivamente

3 vi (slope) estar inclinado(a)

slanting ['slɑːntɪŋ] adj inclinado(a)

slap [slæp] **1** n (with hand) bofetada f, cachete m; also Fig **a s. in the face** una bofetada; Fig **a s. on the wrist** (reprimand) un tirón de orejas

2 adv Fam **s. in the middle** en todo el medio

3 vt (pt & pp **slapped**) dar una palmada en; **to s. sb's face, to s. sb in the face** abofetear a alguien; **to s. sb on the back** dar a alguien una palmada en la espalda; Fig **to s. sb down** hacer callar a alguien; **to s. some paint on sth** dar una mano de pintura a algo

slapdash ['slæpdæʃ] adj chapucero(a)

slapstick ['slæpstɪk] n **s. (comedy)** = comedia visual disparatada

slash [slæʃ] **1** n (a) (cut) tajo m, corte m (b) Typ barra f

2 vt (cut) cortar; (reduce) recortar fuertemente; **prices slashed** (sign) precios por los suelos

slat [slæt] n listón m, tablilla f

slate [sleɪt] n (stone) pizarra f; Fig **to wipe the s. clean** hacer borrón y cuenta nueva; (writing) **s.** pizarra f; **s. gray** gris m pizarra; **s. quarry** pizarral m

slaughter ['slɔːtə(r)] **1** n (of animals) sacrificio m; (of people) matanza f

2 vt (animals) sacrificar; (people) matar; Fam (defeat heavily) dar una paliza a, Esp machacar

slaughterhouse ['slɔːtəhaʊs] n matadero m

Slav [slɑːv] n eslavo(a) m,f

slave [sleɪv] **1** n esclavo(a) m,f; Fam Fig **s. driver** negrero(a) m,f, tirano(a) m,f; **s. labor** trabajo m de esclavos; **s. trade** comercio m or trata f de esclavos

2 vi trabajar como un negro; **I've been slaving over a hot stove all day!** ¡me he pasado el día bregando en la cocina!

slaver ['slævə(r)] vi babear

slavery ['sleɪvərɪ] n esclavitud f

Slavic ['slɑːvɪk] adj eslavo(a)

slavish ['sleɪvɪʃ] adj servil

slavishly ['sleɪvɪʃlɪ] adv de un modo servil, servilmente; **to copy sth s.** copiar algo punto por punto

Slavonic [slə'vɒnɪk] adj eslavo(a)

slay [sleɪ] (pt **slew** [sluː], pp **slain** [sleɪn]) vt (kill) dar muerte a

sleaze [sliːz] n Fam corrupción f

sleazy ['sliːzɪ] adj Fam (place, bar, hotel) de mala muerte, Esp cutre, Méx gacho(a); (government, politician) corrupto(a); (affair, reputation) escandaloso(a) y sórdido(a)

sled [sled], **sledge** [sledʒ] **1** n trineo m

2 vi montar en trineo

sledgehammer ['sledʒhæmə(r)] n mazo m, maza f; Fig **to use a s. to crack a nut** matar moscas a cañonazos

sleek [sliːk] adj (hair) liso(a) y brillante; (manner) bien plantado(a)

▸**sleek down** vt sep **to s. down one's hair** alisarse el pelo

sleep [sliːp] **1** n (a) (rest) sueño m; **to go to s.** dormirse; **to put sb to s.** (anesthetize) dormir a alguien; **to put an animal to s.** (kill) sacrificar un animal (para evitar que sufra); **to send sb to s.** (bore) dar sueño or aburrir a alguien; **I'm not losing any s. over it** no me quita el sueño; **to walk/talk in one's s.** caminar/hablar en sueños; **my foot has gone to s.** se me ha dormido el pie (b) (in eye) legañas fpl

2 vi (pt & pp **slept** [slept]) dormir; **s. well!** ¡que duermas bien!, ¡que descanses!; Euph **to s. with sb** acostarse con alguien; **I slept through the alarm** no oí el despertador;

I'll s. on it lo consultaré con la almohada; **to s. rough** dormir a la intemperie

3 *vt* **the cottage sleeps four** la casa puede albergar a cuatro personas; **I haven't slept a wink all night** no he pegado ojo en toda la noche

▸**sleep around** *vi Fam* acostarse con unos y con otros

▸**sleep in** *vi* quedarse durmiendo hasta tarde

▸**sleep off** *vt sep* **to s. off a hangover** dormir la mona

▸**sleep together** *vi* acostarse juntos

sleeper ['sliːpə(r)] *n* **(a)** **to be a light/heavy s.** tener el sueño ligero/profundo **(b)** *Rail (train)* tren *m* de literas **(c)** *Fam (movie, book, album)* = película, libro o disco de escasas ventas al principio, pero que más tarde produce beneficios inesperadamente

sleepily ['sliːpɪlɪ] *adv* soñolientamente

sleepiness ['sliːpɪnɪs] *n* somnolencia *f*

sleeping ['sliːpɪŋ] **1** *n* **s. arrangements** distribución *f* de (las) camas; **s. bag** saco *m* de dormir, *Col, Méx* sleeping (bag) *m*, *RP* bolsa *f* de dormir; **s. car** *(on train)* coche *m* cama; **s. pill** somnífero *m*, pastilla *f* para dormir

2 *adj* dormido(a); *Fig* **to let s. dogs lie** no enturbiar las aguas

sleepless ['sliːplɪs] *adj* **to have a s. night** pasar una noche en blanco

sleepwalk ['sliːpwɔːk] *vi* caminar dormido(a) *or* sonámbulo(a)

sleepwalker ['sliːpwɔːkə(r)] *n* sonámbulo(a) *m,f*

sleepwalking ['sliːpwɔːkɪŋ] *n* sonambulismo *m*

sleepy ['sliːpɪ] *adj* adormilado(a), soñoliento(a); **to be** *or* **feel s.** tener sueño

sleet [sliːt] **1** *n* aguanieve *f*

2 *vi* **it's sleeting** está cayendo aguanieve

sleeve [sliːv] *n* **(a)** *(of shirt, jacket)* manga *f*; *Fig* **he's still got something up his s.** aún le queda algo escondido en la manga **(b)** *(of record)* funda *f* (de papel)

sleeveless ['sliːvlɪs] *adj* sin mangas

sleigh [sleɪ] *n* trineo *m*

sleight [slaɪt] *n* **s. of hand** trucos *mpl*, juegos *mpl* de manos; *Fig* **by s. of hand** con tejemanejes, por arte de birlibirloque

slender ['slendə(r)] *adj* **(a)** *(person, waist, figure)* esbelto(a) **(b)** *(hope)* remoto(a); *(income, majority)* escaso(a); **of s. means** de pocos recursos

slept [slept] *pt & pp of* **sleep**

sleuth [sluːθ] *n Fam* sabueso *m*, detective *mf*

slew [sluː] *pt of* **slay**

slice [slaɪs] **1** *n* *(of bread)* rebanada *f*; *(of cheese, ham)* loncha *f*; *(of beef)* tajada *f*; *(of salami, cucumber)* rodaja *f*; *(of cake)* trozo *m*, porción *f*; *Fig* **a s. of the profits** un pedazo *or* una porción del pastel *or Am* de la torta

2 *vt* **(a)** *(bread)* partir en rebanadas; *(cheese, ham)* partir en lonchas; *(beef)* partir; *(salami, cucumber)* partir en rodajas; *(cake)* trocear, dividir; **to s. sth in two** *or* **in half** dividir algo en dos *or* por la mitad **(b)** *(in golf)* golpear mal

▸**slice off** *vt sep* cortar

▸**slice through** *vt insep* atravesar, cortar

▸**slice up** *vt sep* repartir, dividir

sliced bread ['slaɪst'bred] *n* pan *m* de molde *or RP* pan *m* lactal en rebanadas; *Fam* **it's the best thing since s.** es lo mejor del mundo

slick [slɪk] **1** *n* *(oil)* **s.** marea *f* negra

2 *adj* **(a)** *(campaign)* hábil; *(performance, production)* perfecto(a) **(b)** *Pej (salesman)* **to be s.** tener mucha labia **(c)** *(surface, tire)* resbaladizo(a)

▸**slick back** *vt sep* **to s. one's hair back** alisarse el pelo

slickly ['slɪklɪ] *adv (marketed, organized)* hábilmente

slide [slaɪd] **1** *n* **(a)** *(fall) (land)* desprendimiento *m*, deslizamiento *m*; *(in prices, popularity)* caída *f*, desplome *m* **(in** de);

Math **s. rule** regla *f* de cálculo **(b)** *(in playground)* tobogán *m* **(c)** *(photographic)* diapositiva *f*; *(for microscope)* portaobjetos *m inv*; **s. projector** proyector *m* de diapositivas; *(gen) & Comptr* **s. show** proyección *f* de diapositivas

2 *vt* *(pt & pp* **slid** [slɪd]) pasar, deslizar; **to s. the lid off** quitar *or Am* sacar la tapa corriéndola *or* deslizándola

3 *vi* **(a)** *(slip)* resbalar; **the door slid open** la puerta se abrió deslizándose; **to s. down a rope** deslizarse por una cuerda *Fig* **to let things s.** dejar que las cosas vayan a peor **(b)** *(move quietly)* deslizarse

sliding ['slaɪdɪŋ] *adj* corredero(a); **s. door** puerta *f* corredera **s. scale** escala *f* móvil

slight [slaɪt] **1** *n (affront)* desaire *m*

2 *adj* **(a)** *(small, unimportant)* ligero(a), pequeño(a); **not the slightest danger/interest** ni el más mínimo peligro/interés **not in the slightest** en lo más mínimo **(b)** *(person)* menudo(a)

3 *vt* desairar

slightly ['slaɪtlɪ] *adv* **(a)** *(to a small degree)* ligeramente, un poco **(b)** **s. built** menudo(a)

slily = **slyly**

slim [slɪm] **1** *adj (person)* delgado(a); *(book)* fino(a), delgado(a) *(chance, hope)* pequeño(a); *(majority)* escaso(a)

2 *vi (pt & pp* **slimmed**) adelgazar

▸**slim down 1** *vt sep (budget)* reducir, recortar; *(company)* reducir plantilla en

2 *vi* **(a)** *(person)* adelgazar, perder peso **(b)** *(company)* reducir plantilla

slime [slaɪm] *n (mud)* lodo *m*, cieno *m*; *(of snail, slug)* baba *f*

slimline ['slɪmlaɪn] *adj (phone, calculator)* extraplano(a)

slimmer ['slɪmə(r)] *n* persona *f* que está a régimen

slimming ['slɪmɪŋ] *n* adelgazamiento *m*; **s. can be bad for you** adelgazar puede ser perjudicial; **s. product** producto *m* para adelgazar

slimy ['slaɪmɪ] *adj (frog, snail)* viscoso(a); *(person)* pegajoso(a) empalagoso(a)

sling [slɪŋ] **1** *n* **(a)** *(for injured arm)* cabestrillo *m* **(b)** *(weapon)* honda *f*

2 *vt (pt & pp* **slung** [slʌŋ]) *(throw)* lanzar, arrojar; **to s. sth over one's shoulder** echarse algo a la espalda

▸**sling out** *vt sep Fam (throw away)* tirar, *Am* botar; *(person)* echar

slingshot ['slɪŋʃɒt] *n* tirachinas *m inv*

slink [slɪŋk] *(pt & pp* **slinked** *or* **slunk** [slʌŋk]) *vi* **to s. off** *or* **away** marcharse subrepticiamente

slinky ['slɪŋkɪ] *adj* **a s. dress** un vestido que marca las curvas

slip [slɪp] **1** *n* **(a)** *(fall)* resbalón *m*; *(landslide)* corrimiento *m* deslizamiento *m*; *(in prices, standards)* derrumbamiento *m* caída *f* **(b)** *(error)* desliz *m*; **s. of the pen** lapsus *m in* (calami); **s. of the tongue** lapsus *m inv* (linguae) **(c) to give sb the s.** dar esquinazo a alguien **(d)** *(paper)* papeleta *f*; *(form* hoja *f* **(e) a s. of a girl** una chavalina; **a s. of a boy** un chavalín **(f)** *(garment)* combinación *f*; **(pillow) s.** funda *f* (de almohada)

2 *vt (pt & pp* **slipped**) **(a)** *(leave)* **his name has slipped my mind** se me ha ido su nombre de la cabeza; **the ship slipped its moorings** el barco se soltó del amarre **(b)** *(put)* deslizar **he slipped on/off his shoes** se puso/se quitó los zapatos **to s. sth into the conversation** deslizar algo en la conversación **(c) to have slipped a disk** tener una vértebra dislocada, tener una hernia discal

3 *vi* **(a)** *(slide)* resbalar; **his foot slipped** le resbaló un pie *also Fig* **to s. from sb's hands** *or* **grasp** escapársele de las manos a alguien; *Fig* **to s. through sb's fingers** escapársele de las manos a alguien; **to let one's guard s.** bajar la guardia **to let one's concentration s.** desconcentrarse

(b) *(move quickly)* **to s. into sth** *(bed)* meterse en algo; *(room* colarse en algo; *(clothes, shoes)* ponerse algo; **to s. out of** *(clothes)* quitarse, *Am* sacarse; **I'll just s. around to the post office** voy un momento a correos

(**c**) *(make mistake)* tener un desliz, cometer un error; **you're slipping** estás fallando

(**d**) **she let s. a few swear words** se le escaparon unas cuantas palabrotas; **he let it s. that he would be resigning** se le escapó que iba a dimitir

▸**slip away** *vi (leave)* desaparecer, desvanecerse

▸**slip by** *vi (time, years)* pasar

▸**slip out** *vi (escape)* escaparse; **to s. out to the store** salir un momento a la tienda

▸**slip through** *vi (mistake, saboteur)* colarse

▸**slip up** *vi (make mistake)* tener un desliz, cometer un error

slip-on ['slɪpɒn] **1** *n Fam* **slip-ons** zapatos *mpl* sin cordones
2 *adj* **s. shoes** zapatos *mpl* sin cordones

slipper ['slɪpə(r)] *n* zapatilla *f*

slippery ['slɪpərɪ] *adj* resbaladizo(a), escurridizo(a); *(person)* tramposo(a); *Fig* **to be on a s. slope** caer cuesta abajo

slippy ['slɪpɪ] *adj* resbaladizo(a), escurridizo(a)

slipshod ['slɪpʃɒd] *adj* chapucero(a)

slipstream ['slɪpstriːm] *n* estela *f*

slipup ['slɪpʌp] *n* (pequeño) error *m*, desliz *m*

slipway ['slɪpweɪ] *n Naut* grada *f*

slit [slɪt] **1** *n (below door)* rendija *f*; *(of dress, in paper)* corte *m*, raja *f*
2 *vt (pt & pp* **slit**) hacer una abertura en; **to s. sth open** abrir algo rajándolo; **to s. sb's throat** degollar a alguien

slither ['slɪðə(r)] *vi* deslizarse

sliver ['slɪvə(r)] *n (of ham, cheese)* lonchita *f*; *(of glass)* esquirla *f*

slob [slɒb] *n Fam (untidy person)* cerdo(a) *m,f*, *Esp* guarro(a) *m,f*; *(lazy person)* dejado(a) *m,f*, tirado(a) *m,f*

slobber ['slɒbə(r)] *vi* babear

sloe [sləʊ] *n (fruit)* endrina *f*; **s. gin** licor *m* de endrinas, ≃ pacharán *m*

slog [slɒg] *Fam* **1** *n* **it was a bit of a s.** fue un aburrimiento *or Esp* tostonazo (de trabajo); **it's a long s.** *(walk)* hay un buen trecho *or Esp* una buena tirada
2 *vi (pt & pp* **slogged**) *(work hard)* trabajar como un/una negro(a), *Esp* dar el callo

slogan ['sləʊgən] *n* eslogan *m*

sloop [sluːp] *n (ship)* balandro *m*

slop [slɒp] **1** *n (a) (pig food)* desperdicios *mpl* (para los cerdos); *Pej (bad food)* bazofia *f* (**b**) *Fam (sentimentality)* cursilerías *fpl*
2 *vt (pt & pp* **slopped**) derramar
3 *vi* derramarse

slope [sləʊp] **1** *n* cuesta *f*, pendiente *f*
2 *vi* caer, inclinarse

sloping ['sləʊpɪŋ] *adj (roof, ground)* en cuesta, inclinado(a); *(handwriting)* inclinado(a); *(shoulders)* caído(a)

sloppily ['slɒpɪlɪ] *adv (work)* chapuceramente; *(dress)* descuidadamente

sloppy ['slɒpɪ] *adj* (**a**) *(careless)* chapucero(a), descuidado(a) (**b**) *Fam (sentimental)* almibarado(a)

slosh [slɒʃ] *vi (liquid)* chapotear

sloshed [slɒʃt] *adj Fam* como una cuba, *Esp, RP* mamado(a), *Col* caído(a) (de la perra), *Méx* ahogado(a)

slot [slɒt] **1** *n (in box, machine, computer)* ranura *f*; *(in schedule, list)* hueco *m*; **s. machine** *(for vending)* máquina *f* expendedora; *(for gambling)* (máquina *f*) tragaperras *f inv*
2 *vt (pt & pp* **slotted**) *(part)* introducir

▸**slot in** *vt sep (into schedule)* hacer un hueco a

sloth [sləʊθ] *n* (**a**) *(laziness)* pereza *f* (**b**) *(animal)* perezoso *m*

slothful ['sləʊθfʊl] *adj* perezoso(a) *m,f*

slouch [slaʊtʃ] **1** *n Fam* **he's no s. in the kitchen** es un hacha en la cocina

2 *vi (on chair)* repantigarse; **he slouched out of the room** salió de la habitación caminando encorvado; **don't s.!** ¡ponte derecho!

slough [slʌf] *vt* **to s. its skin** *(reptile)* mudar de piel *or* de camisa

Slovak ['sləʊvæk] **1** *n* (**a**) *(person)* eslovaco(a) *m,f* (**b**) *(language)* eslovaco *m*
2 *adj* eslovaco(a)

Slovakia [sləʊ'vækɪə] *n* Eslovaquia

Slovakian [sləʊ'vækɪən] *n & adj* eslovaco(a) *m,f*

Slovene ['sləʊviːn], **Slovenian** [sləʊ'viːnɪən] **1** *n* (**a**) *(person)* esloveno(a) *m,f* (**b**) *(language)* esloveno *m*
2 *adj* esloveno(a)

Slovenia [sləʊ'viːnɪə] *n* Eslovenia

Slovenian = **Slovene**

slovenly ['slʌvənlɪ] *adj (untidy)* desastrado(a); *(careless)* descuidado(a)

slow [sləʊ] **1** *adj* (**a**) *(not fast)* lento(a); **to be s. to do sth** tardar *or Am* demorar en hacer algo; **business is s.** el negocio está flojo; **my watch is s.** mi reloj va atrasado; *Culin* **in a s. oven** a horno moderado; **we're making s. progress** avanzamos muy poco; **she's a s. worker** trabaja despacio; *Aut* **s. lane** carril *m* lento; *Cin & TV* **(in) s. motion** a cámara lenta; **s. train** tren *m* lento (**b**) *(stupid)* corto(a) *or* lento(a) de entendederas
2 *adv* despacio, lentamente
3 *vi* aminorar la velocidad; **to s. to a halt** ir aminorando la velocidad hasta detenerse

▸**slow down, slow up 1** *vt sep* retrasar
2 *vi* aminorar la velocidad

slowly ['sləʊlɪ] *adv* despacio, lentamente; **s. but surely** lento, pero seguro

slow-moving ['sləʊ'muːvɪŋ] *adj (person, car, line, river)* lento(a); *(movie, plot)* lento(a)

slowness ['sləʊnɪs] *n* lentitud *f*

slowpoke ['sləʊpəʊk] *Fam* tortuga *f*

slow-witted ['sləʊ'wɪtɪd] *adj* torpe, obtuso(a)

slowworm ['sləʊwɜːm] *n* lución *m*

SLR [esel'ɑː(r)] *n Phot (abbr* **single-lens reflex**) (cámara *f*) réflex *f inv* monoobjetivo

sludge [slʌdʒ] *n* fango *m*, lodo *m*

slug [slʌg] **1** *n* (**a**) *(mollusc)* babosa *f* (**b**) *Fam (bullet)* bala *f* (**c**) *Fam (of drink)* trago *m*
2 *vt (pt & pp* **slugged**) *Fam (hit)* dar un tortazo *or Esp* castañazo a

sluggish ['slʌgɪʃ] *adj (person)* aletargado(a); *(response)* lento(a), retardado(a); *(market, business)* inactivo(a), flojo(a); **at a s. pace** con paso cansino

sluggishly ['slʌgɪʃlɪ] *adv (to move)* lentamente, despacio; *(to respond)* con lentitud, con retardo

sluice [sluːs] **1** *n* canal *m*; **s. (gate)** esclusa *f*, compuerta *f*
2 *vt* **to s. sth down** *or* **out** enjuagar algo

slum [slʌm] **1** *n (district)* barrio *m* bajo; *(on outskirts)* arrabal *m*, suburbio *m*; *(house)* tugurio *m*; **s. landlord** casero *m* que alquila *or Méx* renta tugurios
2 *vt (pt & pp* **slummed**) **to s. it** ir de pobre, llevar vida de pobre

slumber ['slʌmbə(r)] **1** *n* (**a**) *Literary* sueño *m* (**b**) **s. party** = fiesta de adolescentes que se quedan a dormir en casa de quien la organiza
2 *vi* dormir

slump [slʌmp] **1** *n (in prices, sales)* desplome *m*, caída *f*; *(economic depression)* crisis *f inv*, recesión *f*
2 *vi (person)* caer, desplomarse; *(economy)* hundirse; *(prices)* desplomarse

slung [slʌŋ] *pt & pp of* **sling**

slunk [slʌŋk] *pt & pp of* **slink**

slur [slɜ:(r)] **1** *n* (**a**) *(insult)* agravio *m*, injuria *f*; **to cast a s. on sb's reputation** manchar la reputación de alguien (**b**) *(in speech)* **there was a s. in her voice** hablaba arrastrando las palabras
2 *vt* (*pt & pp* **slurred**) pronunciar con dificultad

slurp [slɜ:p] *vt & vi* sorber

slush [slʌʃ] *n* (**a**) *(snow)* nieve *f* sucia *(medio derretida)* (**b**) *Fam Pol* **s. fund** fondos *mpl* para corrupción *or Esp* corruptelas (**c**) *Fam (sentimentality)* sensiblería *f*

slut [slʌt] *n Fam (promiscuous woman)* puta *f*

sluttish ['slʌtɪʃ] *adj (behavior)* de fulana

sly [slaɪ] **1** *n* **on the s.** subrepticiamente, a hurtadillas
2 *adj* (**a**) *(cunning)* astuto(a), artero(a) (**b**) *(dishonest)* desaprensivo(a) (**c**) *(mischievous)* malicioso(a)

slyly, slily ['slaɪlɪ] *adv* (**a**) *(cunningly)* astutamente (**b**) *(nastily)* de manera desaprensiva (**c**) *(mischievously)* maliciosamente

S & M [esən'em], **S/M** [es'em] *n (abbr* **sado-masochism)** sado *m*

smack [smæk] **1** *n* (**a**) *(blow)* (on bottom) azote *m*; *(in face)* bofetada *f*; *(sound)* chasquido *m*; **a s. in the face** una bofetada (**b**) *Fam (heroin)* caballo *m* (**c**) *Fam (kiss)* besote *m*, besazo *m*
2 *adv Fam* **to bump s. into a tree** chocar de lleno con un árbol
3 *vt (hit)* (on bottom) dar un azote a; *(in face)* dar una bofetada a; **to s. one's lips** relamerse

▶ **smack of** *vt insep (suggest)* oler a

smacker ['smækə(r)] *n Fam* (**a**) *(big kiss)* besazo *m* (**b**) **fifty smackers** *(dollars)* cincuenta dólares *mpl*

small [smɔ:l] **1** *n* **the s. of the back** la región lumbar, los riñones
2 *adj* (**a**) *(not large)* pequeño(a), *Am* chico(a); **to make sth smaller** empequeñecer algo; **it made me feel s.** hizo que me sintiera muy poca cosa *or* me avergonzara de mí mismo; **to have a s. appetite** tener poco apetito; **the s. hours** la madrugada; *Journ* **s. ads** anuncios *mpl* breves *or* por palabras; **s. arms** armas *fpl* cortas; **s. business** pequeña empresa *f*; **s. businessman** pequeño empresario *m*; **s. letters** (letras *fpl*) minúsculas *fpl*; **the s. print** la letra pequeña; **the s. screen** la pequeña pantalla; **s. talk** charla *f* insustancial
(**b**) *(not important)* pequeño(a); **it's s. wonder that...** no es de extrañar que...; **it's no s. achievement** es un logro nada despreciable; **in a s. way** a pequeña escala; *Fam* **it's s. beer** *or* **potatoes** es una nadería *or Am* zoncera, es cosa de niños; **s. change** cambio *m*, suelto *m*, *Am* vuelto *m*; **s. fry** gente *f* de poca monta
3 *adv (write)* con letra pequeña; **to chop sth up s.** cortar algo en trozos pequeños; **to think s.** plantearse las cosas a pequeña escala

small-minded [smɔ:l'maɪndɪd] *adj* mezquino(a)

smallness ['smɔ:lnɪs] *n* pequeñez *f*, pequeño tamaño *m*

smallpox ['smɔ:lpɒks] *n* viruela *f*

small-scale ['smɔ:lskeɪl] *adj* a pequeña escala

small-time ['smɔ:ltaɪm] *adj Fam* de poca monta

small-town ['smɔ:l'taʊn] *adj (parochial)* provinciano(a), de pueblo

smarmy ['smɑ:mɪ] *adj Pej* zalamero(a)

smart [smɑ:t] **1** *adj* (**a**) *(clever)* inteligente; *(sharp)* agudo(a), listo(a); **don't try to get s. with me** no te hagas el listo (conmigo); **the s. money is on Jones to win the election** los entendidos en la materia creen que Jones ganará las elecciones; *Fam* **s. aleck** sabelotodo *mf*, *Esp* listillo(a) *m,f*, *Méx, RP* vivo(a) *m,f*; **s. bomb** bomba *f* teledirigida; **s. card** tarjeta *f* inteligente
(**b**) *(elegant)* elegante; **the s. set** la gente guapa; **to be a s. dresser** vestir elegantemente
(**c**) *(quick)* rápido(a); **look s. (about it)!** ¡date prisa!, *Am* ¡apúrate!

(**d**) *Fam (excellent)* genial, *Esp* molón(ona), *Am* salvo *RP* chévere, *Col* tenaz, *Méx* padrísimo(a); *(pretty)* mono(a)
2 *vi (sting) (wound, graze)* escocer; *(person)* resentirse, dolerse

▶ **smarten up** ['smɑ:tən] **1** *vt sep (place)* arreglar; **to s. oneself up** acicalarse
2 *vi (behave more cleverly)* espabilarse

smartly ['smɑ:tlɪ] *adv* (**a**) *(cleverly)* con inteligencia (**b**) *(elegantly)* elegantemente (**c**) *(quickly)* rápidamente, con rapidez; *(sharply)* secamente

smarty-pants ['smɑ:tɪpænts] *(pl* **smarty-pants)** *n Fam* sabelotodo *mf*, *Esp* listillo(a) *m,f*, *Méx, RP* vivo(a) *m,f*

smash [smæʃ] **1** *n* (**a**) *(blow)* golpe *m*, batacazo *m*; *(noise)* estruendo *m*; *(collision)* choque *m*; *(in tennis)* mate *m*, smash *m*; **s. (hit)** *(record, movie)* gran éxito *m*
2 *vt* (**a**) **to s. sth (to pieces)** hacer algo pedazos *or* añicos; **to s. sth against sth** destrozar algo contra algo; **to s. sth open** abrir algo de un golpetazo; **to s. down a door** derribar una puerta (**b**) *(ruin) (hopes, chances, resistance)* acabar con; **to s. a drugs ring** desarticular una red de narcotraficantes; **she smashed the world record** pulverizó el récord mundial
3 *vi* (**a**) *(collide)* **to s. into sth** empotrarse en algo, chocar contra algo (**b**) **to s. (into pieces)** estallar (en mil pedazos)

▶ **smash up** *vt sep* destrozar

smash-and-grab raid [smæʃən'græb'reɪd] *n* = rotura de un escaparate para robar artículos expuestos en él

smashed ['smæʃt] *adj Fam (drunk)* como una cuba, *Esp, RP* mamado(a), *Col* caído(a) (de la perra), *Méx* ahogado(a)

smashing ['smæʃɪŋ] *adj (blow)* violento(a), potente

smattering ['smætərɪŋ] *n* nociones *fpl*

smear [smɪə(r)] **1** *n* (**a**) *(stain)* mancha *f*; *Med* **s. test** citología *f* (**b**) *(slander)* calumnia *f*; **s. campaign** campaña *f* de difamación
2 *vt* (**a**) *(stain)* embadurnar, untar; *(smudge)* emborronar (**b**) *(slander)* difamar, calumniar

smell [smel] **1** *n* (**a**) *(odor)* olor *m*; **there's a bad s.** huele mal; **to have a s. of sth** oler algo (**b**) *(sense)* olfato *m*
2 *vt* (*pt & pp* **smelled** *or* **smelt** [smelt]) oler; *Fig (danger)* oler, presentir; *Fig* **I s. a rat** aquí hay gato encerrado
3 *vi* oler; *(stink)* apestar; **to s. of sth** oler a algo; **to s. nice/ horrible** oler bien/muy mal *or Esp* fatal

smelly ['smelɪ] *adj* apestoso(a); **to be s.** apestar

smelt [smelt] **1** *vt (ore)* fundir
2 *pt & pp of* **smell**

smile [smaɪl] **1** *n* sonrisa *f*; **to give sb a s.** sonreírle a alguien; **she was all smiles** estaba muy contenta; **to take** *or* **wipe the s. off sb's face** borrarle la sonrisa a alguien
2 *vi* sonreír; **to s. at sb** sonreírle a alguien; **fortune smiled on them** les sonrió la fortuna; **s.!** *(for photograph)* sonría, por favor

smiling ['smaɪlɪŋ] *adj* sonriente

smirk [smɜ:k] **1** *n* sonrisa *f* complacida *(despreciativa)*
2 *vi* sonreír con satisfacción *(despreciativa)*

smite [smaɪt] *(pt* **smote** [sməʊt], *pp* **smitten** ['smɪtən]) *vt* (**a**) *Literary (strike)* golpear (**b**) **they were smitten with terror/ remorse** les asaltó el pánico/el remordimiento

smith [smɪθ] *n* herrero *m*

smithereens [smɪðə'ri:nz] *npl* **to smash sth to s.** hacer algo añicos; **to blow sth to s.** hacer saltar algo en mil pedazos

smithy ['smɪðɪ] *n (forge)* fragua *f*

smitten ['smɪtən] **1** *adj (in love)* enamorado(a) (**with** de), colado(a) (**with** por)
2 *pp of* **smite**

smock [smɒk] *n* blusón *m*

smog [smɒg] *n* niebla *f* tóxica, hongo *m* de contaminación

smoke [sməʊk] **1** *n* humo *m*; **to have a s.** fumarse un cigarrillo; *Fig* **to go up in s.** esfumarse, desvanecerse; *Fig* **s. and mirrors** espejismos; *Prov* **there's no s. without fire**

cuando el río suena, agua lleva; **s. bomb** bomba *f* de humo; **s. detector** detector *m* de humo; *also Fig* **s. screen** cortina *f* de humo; **s. signals** señales *fpl* de humo

2 *vt* (**a**) *(cigarette)* fumar; **to s. a pipe** fumar en pipa (**b**) *(meat, fish)* ahumar

3 *vi* (**a**) *(person)* fumar (**b**) *(chimney, oil)* echar humo

▸**smoke out** *vt sep (insects)* ahuyentar con humo; *Fig (rebels)* sacar de su escondite

smoked [sməʊkt] *adj* ahumado(a); **s. glass** vidrio *m or Esp* cristal *m* ahumado

smokeless ['sməʊklɪs] *adj* **s. tobacco** rapé *m*

smoker ['sməʊkə(r)] *n* fumador(ora) *m,f*; **to be a heavy s.** ser un/una fumador(ora) empedernido(a); **s.'s cough** tos *f* de fumador

smoking ['sməʊkɪŋ] *n* **s. can damage your health** el tabaco perjudica seriamente la salud; **no s.** *(sign)* prohibido fumar; *Fig* **s. gun** *(proof)* pistola *f* humeante; **s. jacket** batín *m*; **s. room** salón *m* de fumar

smoky ['sməʊkɪ] *adj (atmosphere, room)* lleno(a) de humo; *(fire, lamp)* humeante; *(surface, taste)* ahumado(a)

smolder ['sməʊldə(r)] *vi (fire)* arder con rescoldo; *Fig* **to s. with anger/passion** arder de ira/pasión

smoldering ['sməʊldərɪŋ] *adj (fire)* humeante, con rescoldo; *(anger, passion)* ardiente, encendido(a)

smooch [smuːtʃ] *vi Fam* besuquearse

smooth [smuːð] **1** *adj* (**a**) *(not rough) (paper, skin)* liso(a), suave; *(road, surface)* llano(a), liso(a); *(sea)* en calma; *(sauce)* homogéneo(a); *(wine, whiskey)* suave; *(style)* fluido(a); *(flight, crossing)* tranquilo(a), cómodo(a); **a s. shave** un afeitado suave (**b**) *(person, manner)* meloso(a); **he's a s. talker** tiene el don de la palabra; **to be a s. operator** ser un águila, saber cómo llevarse el gato al agua (**c**) *(without problems)* sin contratiempos

2 *vt* alisar; **to s. the way for sb/sth** allanarle el camino a alguien/algo

▸**smooth back** *vt sep* **to s. back one's hair** alisarse el pelo hacia atrás

▸**smooth down** *vt sep* alisar

▸**smooth out** *vt sep (map, sheets, crease)* estirar, alisar; *Fig (difficulty)* allanar, resolver

▸**smooth over** *vt sep* **to s. over difficulties** mitigar las dificultades; **to s. things over** dulcificar las cosas

smoothie ['smuːðɪ] *n* (**a**) *Fam Pej (person)* zalamero(a) *m,f* (**b**) *(drink)* = zumo de fruta con yogur

smoothly ['smuːðlɪ] *adv* **to go s.** transcurrir sin contratiempos

smoothness ['smuːðnɪs] *n (of paper, skin, wine, whiskey)* suavidad *f*; *(of road, surface)* lisura *f*; *(of sauce)* homogeneidad *f*

smooth-talking ['smuːð'tɔːkɪŋ] *n* con mucha labia

smoothy ['smuːðɪ] *n Fam Pej (person)* zalamero(a) *m,f*

smote [sməʊt] *pt of* **smite**

smother ['smʌðə(r)] *vt* (**a**) *(person)* ahogar, asfixiar; *(fire)* ahogar; *(cry, yawn)* contener, ahogar; **to s. sb with kisses** colmar a alguien de besos (**b**) *(cover)* **to s. sth in sth** cubrir algo de algo

SMS [esem'es] *n (abbr* **short message service***) (service)* SMS *m*; *(message)* mensaje *m* SMS *or* de texto

smudge [smʌdʒ] **1** *n* mancha *f*; *(of ink)* borrón *m*

2 *vt (ink, paper)* emborronar; *(lipstick)* correr; *(drawing)* difuminar

3 *vi (ink, lipstick)* correrse

smug [smʌg] *adj* engreído(a), petulante

smuggle ['smʌgəl] *vt (arms, drugs)* pasar de contrabando; **to s. sth into/out of the country** introducir algo al país/sacar algo del país de contrabando; **to s. sb in/out** meter/sacar a alguien clandestinamente

smuggler ['smʌglə(r)] *n* contrabandista *mf*

smuggling ['smʌglɪŋ] *n* contrabando *m*

smugly ['smʌglɪ] *adv* con petulancia, con aires de suficiencia

smut [smʌt] *n* (**a**) *(soot)* hollín *m*, carbonilla *f* (**b**) *(obscenity)* cochinadas *fpl*

smutty ['smʌtɪ] *adj* (**a**) *(dirty)* tiznado(a) (**b**) *(obscene)* verde, cochino(a)

snack [snæk] **1** *n* tentempié *m*, *Esp* piscolabis *m inv*, *Méx* botana *f*; **s. bar** cafetería *f*

2 *vi* **to s. (on sth)** tomarse un tentempié *or* piscolabis (de algo)

snag [snæg] **1** *n (problem)* problema *m*, inconveniente *m*

2 *vt (pt & pp* **snagged***)* **to s. one's dress on sth** engancharse el vestido en *or* con algo

snail [sneɪl] *n* caracol *m*; **at a s.'s pace** a paso de tortuga; *Fam* **s. mail** correo *m* caracol, correo *m* tradicional

snake [sneɪk] **1** *n (big)* serpiente *f*; *(small)* culebra *f*; *Fig* **a s. in the grass** un judas; **s. charmer** encantador(ora) *m,f* de serpientes

2 *vi (road, river)* serpentear

snakebite ['sneɪkbaɪt] *n (bite)* mordedura *f* de serpiente

snakeskin ['sneɪkskɪn] *n* piel *f* de serpiente

snap [snæp] **1** *n* (**a**) *(bite)* mordisco *m* al aire (**b**) *(sound)* chasquido *m* (**c**) *(of weather)* **cold s.** ola *f* de frío (**d**) *Fam (photograph)* foto *f* (**e**) *Fam (easy task)* **it's a s.!** ¡está chupado!, ¡es pan comido! (**f**) **s. fastener** broche *m* (presión)

2 *adj (judgment, decision)* en el acto, súbito; **to call a s. election** adelantar las elecciones para aprovechar una circunstancia favorable

3 *vt (pt & pp* **snapped***)* (**a**) *(break)* romper, partir; **to s. sth in two** partir algo en dos (**b**) *(make noise with)* **to s. one's fingers** chasquear los dedos (**c**) *(say sharply)* espetar (**d**) *Fam (take photograph of)* fotografiar

4 *vi* (**a**) *(break cleanly)* romperse, partirse; *(break noisily)* quebrarse, romperse (con un chasquido) (**b**) *(bite)* **the dog snapped at him** el perro intentó morderle; **to s. shut** *(jaws, lid)* cerrarse de golpe (**c**) *(speak abruptly)* **to s. at sb** hablar en mal tono a alguien (**d**) *(idioms)* **to s. out of it** *(depression, apathy)* recuperar el ánimo; **s. out of it!** *(sulk)* ¡alegra esa cara!, *Esp* ¡anímate, hombre!

▸**snap off 1** *vt sep* (**a**) *(break)* partir, arrancar (**b**) *Fam Fig* **to s. sb's head off** soltarle un bufido a alguien, gruñir a alguien

2 *vi* partirse, desprenderse

▸**snap up** *vt sep* (**a**) *(seize in jaws)* agarrar, morder (**b**) *Fam (buy, take quickly)* atrapar, *Esp* pillar, *Esp* hacerse con

snapdragon ['snæpdrægən] *n (boca f de)* dragón *m (planta)*

snappy ['snæpɪ] *adj (style, prose)* chispeante; *(slogan)* agudo(a), ingenioso(a); **to be a s. dresser** vestirse muy bien; *Fam* **make it s.!** *(be quick)* ¡rapidito!

snapshot ['snæpʃɒt] *n Fam (photograph)* foto *f*

snare [sneə(r)] **1** *n also Fig* trampa *f*; **s. drum** *(in military band)* tambor *m*; *(in rock music)* caja *f*

2 *vt (animal)* cazar *(con trampa)*; *Fig* **the police snared the criminals** la policía atrapó a los delincuentes *(tendiéndoles una trampa)*

snarl [snɑːl] **1** *n (of dog)* gruñido *m*; *(of lion, person)* rugido *m*

2 *vi (dog)* gruñir; *(lion)* rugir; **to s. at sb** *(person)* gruñirle a alguien

▸**snarl up** *vi* atascarse

snatch [snætʃ] **1** *n (of music, conversation)* retazo *m*; **to sleep in snatches** dormir a ratos

2 *vt* (**a**) *(grab)* **to s. sth (from sb)** arrebatar algo (a alguien); **to s. something to eat** comer algo apresuradamente; **to s. some sleep** aprovechar para dormir un poco (**b**) *(wallet, handbag)* robar (con tirón); *(person)* secuestrar

3 *vi* **to s. at sth** intentar agarrar *or Esp* coger algo

▸**snatch away** *vt sep* arrebatar

snazzy ['snæzɪ] *adj Fam* vistoso(a) y elegante, *Esp* chulo(a)

sneak [sni:k] **1** *adj* **to get a s. preview of sth** tener un anticipo en exclusiva de algo

2 *vt* (*pt & pp* **sneaked, snuck** [snʌk]) **to s. sth past sb** pasar algo por delante de alguien sin que se dé cuenta; **to s. sb in/out** introducir/sacar a alguien a hurtadillas; **to s. a glance at sb** mirar furtivamente a alguien; **she sneaked her boyfriend into her bedroom** coló a su novio en su dormitorio *or Am* cuarto

3 *vi* (*move furtively*) deslizarse; **to s. past sb** colarse sin ser visto(a) por alguien; **to s. in/out** entrar/salir a hurtadillas

▸**sneak away, sneak off** *vi* escaparse, escabullirse

sneaker ['sni:kə(r)] *n* (*sports shoe*) playera *f*, zapatilla *f* de deporte

sneaky ['sni:kɪ] *adj Fam* ladino(a), artero(a)

sneer ['snɪə(r)] **1** *n* (*expression*) mueca *f* desdeñosa

2 *vt* decir con desprecio

3 *vi* **to s. at sb/sth** burlarse de alguien/algo

sneering ['snɪərɪŋ] **1** *n* burlas *fpl*

2 *adj* burlón(ona)

sneeze [sni:z] **1** *n* estornudo *m*

2 *vi* estornudar; *Fam Fig* **it's not to be sneezed at** no es moco de pavo

snicker ['snɪkə(r)] **1** *n* risilla *f* burlona

2 *vi* burlarse, reírse

snide [snaɪd] *adj* malicioso(a)

sniff [snɪf] **1** *n* **to take a s. at sth** olfatear algo; **with a s. of disgust** con un aire disgustado

2 *vt* (**a**) (*smell*) oler, olfatear; (*detect*) olfatear, detectar (**b**) (*inhale*) (*air*) aspirar; (*cocaine, glue*) esnifar

3 *vi* (*inhale*) inspirar; (*disdainfully*) hacer un gesto de desprecio; *Fam* **it's not to be sniffed at** no es moco de pavo

▸**sniff out** *vt sep* (*of dog*) encontrar olfateando; *Fig* (*of investigator*) descubrir, dar con

sniffle ['snɪfəl] **1** *n* (*slight cold*) **to have the sniffles** tener un ligero resfriado

2 *vi* (**a**) (*sniff repeatedly*) sorber (**b**) (*cry quietly*) gimotear

sniffy ['snɪfɪ] *adj Fam* (*disdainful*) desdeñoso(a); **to be s. about sth** tratar algo con desprecio

snifter ['snɪftə(r)] *n Fam Old-fashioned* (*drink*) trago *m*, copita *f*

snigger ['snɪgə(r)] **1** *n* risilla *f* burlona

2 *vi* reírse burlonamente

sniggering ['snɪgərɪŋ] *n* risitas *fpl* burlonas

snip [snɪp] **1** *n* (*cut*) corte *m*

2 *vt* (*pt & pp* **snipped**) cortar

▸**snip off** *vt sep* cortar

snipe[1] [snaɪp] (*pl* **snipe**) *n* (*bird*) agachadiza *f*

snipe[2] *vi* (*shoot*) disparar (*desde un escondite*); **to s. at sb** disparar a alguien; *Fig* (*criticize*) criticar a alguien

sniper ['snaɪpə(r)] *n* (*rifleman*) francotirador(ora) *m,f*

snippet ['snɪpɪt] *n* (*of information, conversation*) retazo *m*; **a s. of news** un fragmento de una noticia

snitch [snɪtʃ] *Fam* **1** *n* (*informer*) soplón(ona) *m,f*, *Esp* chivato(a) *m,f*

2 *vi* **to s. on sb** *Esp* chivarse de alguien, *Col* sapear *or Méx* soplar *or RP* botonear a alguien

snivel ['snɪvəl] *vi* lloriquear, gimotear

sniveling ['snɪvəlɪŋ] *adj* llorica

snob [snɒb] *n* presuntuoso(a) *m,f*

snobbery ['snɒbərɪ] *n* presuntuosidad *f*

snobbish ['snɒbɪʃ] *adj* presuntuoso(a)

snooker ['snu:kə(r)] **1** *n* (*game*) snooker *m*, billar *m* inglés

2 *vt* **to s. sb** (*trap*) acorralar a alguien

snoop [snu:p] *Fam* **1** *n* (**a**) (*person*) fisgón(ona) *m,f* (**b**) (*look*) **to have a s. (around)** fisgonear, *Esp* fisgar

2 *vi* fisgonear, *Esp* fisgar

snooper ['snu:pə(r)] *n Fam* fisgón(ona) *m,f*

snooty ['snu:tɪ] *adj Fam* presuntuoso(a)

snooze [snu:z] *Fam* **1** *n Esp* siestecilla *f*, *Am* siestita *f*; **to have a s.** echarse una *Esp* siestecilla *or Am* siestita; **s. button** (*on alarm clock*) = botón para la función de dormitar

2 *vi* echarse una *Esp* siestecilla *or Am* siestita

snore [snɔ:(r)] **1** *n* ronquido *m*

2 *vi* roncar

snoring ['snɔ:rɪŋ] *n* ronquidos *mpl*

snorkel ['snɔ:kəl] **1** *n* snorkel *m*, tubo *m* para buceo

2 *vi* bucear con tubo *or* snorkel

snort [snɔ:t] **1** *n* (*of person, horse*) bufido *m*, resoplido *m*

2 *vt Fam* (*drugs*) esnifar

3 *vi* (*person, horse*) resoplar, bufar

snot [snɒt] *n Fam* mocos *mpl*

snotty ['snɒtɪ] *adj Fam* (**a**) (*nose, handkerchief*) con mocos (**b**) (*arrogant*) creído(a), petulante

snotty-nosed ['snɒtɪ'nəʊzd] *adj Fam* (**a**) (*child*) mocoso(a) (**b**) (*arrogant*) creído(a), petulante

snout [snaʊt] *n* (*of animal*) hocico *m*, morro *m*; *Fam* (*of person*) napias *fpl*

snow [snəʊ] **1** *n* nieve *f*; **s. blindness** deslumbramiento *m* por la nieve; **s. boot** bota *f* de esquí; **s. line** límite *m* de las nieves perpetuas; **s. pea** tirabeque *m*

2 *vi* nevar; **it's snowing** está nevando

▸**snow in** *vt sep* **to be snowed in** estar aislado(a) por la nieve

▸**snow under** *vt sep* **to be snowed under** (*with work*) estar desbordado(a); (*with invitations, offers*) no dar abasto

snowball ['snəʊbɔ:l] **1** *n* bola *f* de nieve; **s. fight** guerra *f* de bolas de nieve; *Fam* **she hasn't a s.'s chance (in hell)** lo tiene muy crudo

2 *vi* (*problems*) multiplicarse; (*project*) crecer vertiginosamente

Snowbike® ['snəʊbaɪk] *n* motoesquí *m*

snowboard ['snəʊbɔ:d] *n* snowboard *m*

snowboarder ['snəʊbɔ:də(r)] *n* persona *f* que practica el snowboard

snowboarding ['snəʊbɔ:dɪŋ] *n* snowboard *m*; **to go s.** hacer snowboard

snowbound ['snəʊbaʊnd] *adj* aislado(a) a causa de la nieve

snowcapped ['snəʊkæpt] *adj* cubierto(a) de nieve

snowdrift ['snəʊdrɪft] *n* nevero *m*, ventisquero *m*

snowdrop ['snəʊdrɒp] *n* (*flower*) campanilla *f* de invierno

snowfall ['snəʊfɔ:l] *n* nevada *f*

snowflake ['snəʊfleɪk] *n* copo *m* de nieve

snowman ['snəʊmæn] *n* muñeco *m* de nieve

snowmobile ['snəʊməbi:l] *n* motonieve *f*, moto *f* de nieve

snowplow ['snəʊplaʊ] *n* quitanieves *f inv*

snowshoe ['snəʊʃu:] *n* raqueta *f* (*de nieve*)

snowstorm ['snəʊstɔ:m] *n* ventisca *f*, tormenta *f* de nieve

snowsuit ['snəʊsu:t] *n* traje *m* de esquí

Snow White ['snəʊ'waɪt] *pr n* **S. and the Seven Dwarfs** Blancanieves y los siete enanitos

snowy ['snəʊɪ] *adj* (*landscape, field*) nevado(a); (*weather, day*) nevoso(a), de nieve

snub [snʌb] **1** *n* desaire *m*

2 *vt* (*pt & pp* **snubbed**) desairar

snub nose ['snʌb'nəʊz] *n* nariz *f* respingona

snub-nosed ['snʌb'nəʊzd] *adj* (**a**) (*person*) de nariz respingona (**b**) (*revolver*) corto(a)

snuck [snʌk] *pt & pp of* **sneak**

snuff [snʌf] **1** *n* rapé *m*

2 *vt* (*candle*) apagar

▸**snuff out** *vt sep* (*candle*) apagar; (*life, opposition*) truncar, cercenar

snuffbox ['snʌfbɒks] *n* tabaquera *f*, caja *f* para el rapé

snuffle ['snʌfəl] **1** *n* (*sniff*) resoplido *m*

2 *vi* (*sniff*) sorber

snug [snʌg] *adj* (**a**) (*cozy*) **I'm nice and s. by the fire** estoy muy a gusto delante de la chimenea; **this bed's very s.** se está muy a gusto en esta cama (**b**) *(tight-fitting)* ajustado(a)

▸**snuggle up** ['snʌɡəl] *vi* **to s. up to sb** acurrucarse contra alguien

snugly ['snʌɡlɪ] *adv (comfortably)* a gusto, confortablemente; **to fit s.** quedar ajustado(a)

so¹ [səʊ] **1** *adv* (**a**) *(to such an extent)* tan; **it isn't so very old** no es tan viejo; **he's not so clever as she is** él no es tan listo como ella; **so many children** tantos niños; **so much money** tanto dinero; **would you be so kind as to…?** ¿sería tan amable de…?; **it was difficult, so much so that…** ha sido difícil, tanto (es así) que…; **a little girl so high** una niña así de alta; **I was so hungry I had three helpings** tenía tantísima hambre que me serví tres veces (**b**) *(intensive)* **it's so easy** es facilísimo, es muy fácil; **we enjoyed ourselves so much!** ¡nos hemos divertido muchísimo!; **I was so disappointed** me llevé una decepción enorme; **we're so pleased you could come!** ¡qué bien que hayas podido venir!; *Fam* **I so don't want to go there** no me apetece ir ni de coña

(**c**) *(expressing agreement)* **you're late — so I am!** llegas tarde — ¡pues sí!; **that's Bill Clinton! — so it is!** ¡mira, Bill Clinton! — ¡anda, es verdad!

(**d**) *(referring to statement already mentioned)* **I hope/think/ suppose so** espero/creo/supongo que sí, eso espero/creo/ supongo; **so I believe** eso creo; **I'm not very organized — so I see!** no me organizo muy bien — ¡ya lo veo!; **so be it!** ¡así sea!; **is that so?** ¿ah, sí?, ¿de verdad?; **if so,…** si es así,…

(**e**) *(also)* **so am I** yo también; **so do we** nosotros también; **so can they** ellos también (pueden); **so is my brother** mi hermano también

(**f**) *(in this way)* así; **do it so** hazlo así; **and so on, and so forth** y cosas así, etcétera

2 *conj* (**a**) *(because of this)* así que; **she has a bad temper, so be careful** tiene mal genio, así que ten cuidado; **he wasn't there, so I came back again** como no estaba, me volví

(**b**) *(introducing remark)* **so that's what it is!** ¡así que es eso!; **so you're not coming?** entonces ¿no vienes?; **so what do we do now?** y ahora ¿qué hacemos?; **so (what)?** ¿y (qué)?

3 so as to *conj* para; **we hurried so as not to be late** nos dimos prisa *or Am* nos apuramos para no llegar tarde

4 so (that) *conj* para que; **she sat down so (that) I could see better** se sentó para que yo viera mejor; **we hurried so (that) we wouldn't be late** nos dimos prisa *or Am* nos apuramos para no llegar tarde

so² *n Mus* sol *m*

soak [səʊk] **1** *vt (leave in water)* poner en remojo; *(make very wet)* empapar (**with** en *or* de)

2 *vi (food, clothes)* estar en remojo; **to leave sth to s.** dejar algo en remojo

▸**soak in** *vi* impregnarse

▸**soak up** *vt sep (liquid)* absorber; *Fig* **to s. up the sun** tostarse al sol

soaked [səʊkt] *adj* empapado(a); **to be s.** estar empapado(a); **s. to the skin** calado(a) hasta los huesos

so-and-so ['səʊənsəʊ] *(pl* **so-and-sos**) *n Fam* (**a**) *(unspecified person)* fulanito(a) *m,f*; **Mr. S.** don fulanito de tal (**b**) *(unpleasant person)* hijo(a) *m,f* de mala madre

soap [səʊp] **1** *n* jabón *m*; **a bar of s.** una pastilla de jabón; **s. (opera)** telenovela *f*, culebrón *m*; **s. flakes** jabón *m* en escamas; **s. powder** detergente *m* en polvo

2 *vt* enjabonar

soapbox ['səʊpbɒks] *n* tribuna *f* improvisada

soapdish ['səʊpdɪʃ] *n* jabonera *f*

soapsuds ['səʊpsʌdz] *npl* espuma *f* (de jabón)

soapy ['səʊpɪ] *adj (water)* jabonoso(a); *(hands, face)* enjabona-do(a); *(taste, smell)* a jabón

soar [sɔː(r)] *vi (bird, plane)* remontarse, remontar el vuelo; *Fig*

(building) elevarse, alzarse; *Fig (hopes, prices)* desorbitarse, dispararse

soaring ['sɔːrɪŋ] *adj (hopes, prices)* desorbitado(a); *(building)* altísimo(a)

SOB [esəʊ'biː] *n Fam (abbr* **son of a bitch**) hijo(a) *m,f* de su madre

sob [sɒb] **1** *n* sollozo *m*; *Fam* **s. story** dramón *m*

2 *vi (pt & pp* **sobbed**) sollozar

sobbing ['sɒbɪŋ] *n* sollozos *mpl*, llanto *m*

sober ['səʊbə(r)] *adj* (**a**) *(not drunk)* sobrio(a), sereno(a) (**b**) *(sensible)* serio(a)

▸**sober up 1** *vt sep* quitar *or Am* sacar la borrachera a

2 *vi* **by the next day he had sobered up** al día siguiente ya se le había pasado la borrachera

sobering ['səʊbərɪŋ] *adj* **it's a s. thought** da mucho que pensar

soberly ['səʊbəlɪ] *adv* con sobriedad

sobriety [səʊ'braɪətɪ] *n* seriedad *f*

soc *(abbr* **society**) asociación *f*

so-called ['səʊ'kɔːld] *adj (generally known as)* (así) llamado(a); *(wrongly known as)* mal llamado(a)

soccer ['sɒkə(r)] *n* fútbol *m*; **s. game** partido *m* de fútbol

sociable ['səʊʃəbəl] *adj* sociable

social ['səʊʃəl] **1** *adj* social; **s. class** clase *f* social; **s. climber** arribista *mf*; *Pol* **s. democrat** socialdemócrata *mf*; **s. life** vida *f* social; **s. outcast** marginado(a) *m,f*; **s. sciences** ciencias *fpl* sociales; **S. Security** seguridad *f* social; **the s. services** los servicios sociales; **s. studies** (ciencias *fpl*) sociales *fpl*; **s. work** asistencia *f* or trabajo *m* social; **s. worker** asistente *mf* or trabajador(ora) *m,f* social

2 *n (party)* reunión *f*, fiesta *f*

socialism ['səʊʃəlɪzəm] *n* socialismo *m*

socialist ['səʊʃəlɪst] *n & adj* socialista *mf*

socialite ['səʊʃəlaɪt] *n* personaje *m* de la vida mundana

socialize ['səʊʃəlaɪz] *vi* alternar; **to s. with sb** tener trato *or* alternar con alguien

socializing ['səʊʃəlaɪzɪŋ] *n* trato *m* social, relaciones *fpl* sociales; **they do a lot of s.** hacen mucha vida social

socially ['səʊʃəlɪ] *adv* socialmente; **we don't see each other s.** no tenemos relación fuera del trabajo

society [sə'saɪətɪ] *n (in general)* sociedad *f*; *(club)* asociación *f*, sociedad *f*; **(high) s.** la alta sociedad

socioeconomic [səʊsɪəʊiːkə'nɒmɪk] *adj* socioeconó-mico(a)

sociolinguistics ['səʊsɪəʊlɪŋ'ɡwɪstɪks] *n* sociolingüística *f*

sociological [səʊsɪəʊ'lɒdʒɪkəl] *adj* sociológico(a)

sociologist [səʊsɪ'ɒlədʒɪst] *n* sociólogo(a) *m,f*

sociology [səʊsɪ'ɒlədʒɪ] *n* sociología *f*

sock [sɒk] **1** *n* (**a**) *(garment)* calcetín *m* (**b**) *Fam (blow)* puñetazo *m*

2 *vt Fam (hit)* dar un puñetazo a; *Fig* **s. it to them!** ¡a por ellos!, ¡valor y al toro!

socket ['sɒkɪt] *n (of eye)* cuenca *f*; *(for plug)* enchufe *m (toma de corriente)*

sod [sɒd] *n (of earth)* tepe *m*

soda ['səʊdə] *n* (**a**) **s. (water)** (agua *f* de) seltz *m*, soda *f*; **s. siphon** sifón *m* (**b**) *(fizzy drink)* refresco *m (gaseoso)*; **s. fountain** puesto *m* de helados y refrescos, *Carib, Chile, Col, Méx* fuente *f* de soda (**c**) *Chem* sosa *f*

sodden ['sɒdən] *adj* empapado(a); **to be s.** estar empa-pado(a)

sodium ['səʊdɪəm] *n Chem* sodio *m*; **s. bicarbonate** bicarbonato *m* sódico *or* de sodio; **s. chloride** cloruro *m* de sodio

sodomize ['sɒdəmaɪz] *vt* sodomizar

sodomy ['sɒdəmɪ] *n* sodomía *f*

sofa ['səʊfə] *n* sofá *m*; **s. bed** sofá-cama *m*

Sofia [səʊ'fiːə] *n* Sofía

soft [sɒft] *adj* (**a**) *(in texture) (ground, rock, cheese)* blando(a); *(pillow, carpet, fabric)* suave; **s. goods** = artículos y materiales de decoración del tipo cortinas, cojines, alfombras, etc.; **s. shoulder** *(beside road) Esp* arcén *m or Esp* acotamiento *or RP* banquina *f or Ven* hombrillo *m* sin estabilizar; *Anat* **s. tissue** tejido *m* blando; **s. top** *(car)* descapotable *m, Am* convertible *m*; **s. toy** peluche *m (muñeco)*

(**b**) *(not harsh, not strong) (voice, rain, color)* suave; **s. currency** divisa *f* débil; **s. drinks** refrescos *mpl*; **s. drugs** drogas *fpl* blandas; *Phot* **in s. focus** ligeramente velado(a) *or* difuminado(a); *Fin* **s. loan** crédito *m* blando; *Com* **s. sell** venta *f* no agresiva

(**c**) *(not strict)* blando(a); **to have a s. spot for sb** tener debilidad por alguien; **to have a s. heart** ser muy blando(a)

(**d**) *Fam (stupid)* tonto(a)

(**e**) *(easy) (job, life)* fácil; *Fam* **to be a s. touch** ser un poco primo(a) *or Am* bobito(a); **s. option** opción *f* fácil

(**f**) *Comptr* **s. copy** copia *f* en formato electrónico; **s. return** retorno *m* automático

softback = **softcover**

softball ['sɒftbɔːl] *n* = juego parecido al béisbol jugado en un campo más pequeño y con una pelota más blanda

soft-boiled ['sɒftbɔɪld] *adj (egg)* pasado(a) por agua

soft-core ['sɒftkɔː(r)] *adj (pornography)* blando(a)

softcover ['sɒftkʌvə(r)], **softback** ['sɒftbæk] *n* libro *m* de tapa blanda *or* en rústica

soften ['sɒfən] **1** *vt (wax, butter, leather)* ablandar, reblandecer; *(light, contrast, skin)* suavizar; *Fig* **to s. the blow** amortiguar el golpe

2 *vi (wax, butter)* ablandarse; *Fig (person)* ceder, ablandarse; *Fig (opinions, resolve, stance)* suavizarse

▸**soften up** *vt sep Fam (before attack)* debilitar; *(before request)* ablandar

softener ['sɒfənə(r)] *n* suavizante *m*

softening ['sɒfnɪŋ] *n (of attitude, expression, voice)* relajamiento *m*

softhearted [sɒft'hɑːtɪd] *adj* bondadoso(a), de buen corazón

softie = **softy**

softly ['sɒftlɪ] *adv (talk)* suavemente; *(walk)* con suavidad; **to be s. lit** tener una iluminación tenue *or* suave

softness ['sɒftnɪs] *n (of ground)* blandura *f*; *(of skin, voice, fabric)* suavidad *f*

soft-pedal [sɒft'pedəl] *vt (minimize)* restar importancia a

soft-soap ['sɒft'səʊp] *vt Fam* dar coba a

soft-spoken [sɒft'spəʊkən] *adj* de voz suave

software ['sɒftweə(r)] *n Comptr* soporte *m* lógico, software *m*; **s. engineer** ingeniero(a) *m,f* de programas; **s. package** paquete *m* de software

softy, softie ['sɒftɪ] *n Fam (gentle person)* buenazo(a) *m,f*; *(coward)* gallina *mf*

soggy ['sɒgɪ] *adj* empapado(a); **to be s.** estar empapado(a)

soil [sɔɪl] **1** *n (earth)* tierra *f*; **the s.** el suelo, el terreno; **on Texas s.** en suelo tejano

2 *vt (clothes, sheet)* manchar, ensuciar; *Fig* **to s. one's hands** mancharse las manos

sol [sɒl] *n Mus* sol *m*

solace ['sɒləs] *n Literary* consuelo *m*

solar ['səʊlə(r)] *adj (system, energy)* solar; **s. eclipse** eclipse *m* de sol; **s. plexus** plexo *m* solar; **s. power** energía *f* solar

solar-powered ['səʊlə'paʊəd] *adj* por energía solar, alimentado(a) por energía solar

sold [səʊld] *pt & pp of* **sell**

solder ['səʊldə(r)] **1** *n* soldadura *f*

2 *vt* soldar

soldering iron ['səʊldərɪŋ'aɪən] *n* soldador *m*

soldier ['səʊldʒə(r)] **1** *n* soldado *m*; **an old s.** un veterano, un excombatiente

2 *vi* servir como soldado

▸**soldier on** *vi* seguir adelante pese a todo

sole¹ [səʊl] **1** *n (of foot)* planta *f*; *(of shoe)* suela *f*

2 *vt (shoe)* poner suelas a

sole² *n (fish)* lenguado *m*

sole³ *adj (only)* único(a); *Com* **s. agent** agente *mf* en exclusiva

solely ['səʊllɪ] *adv* únicamente

solemn ['sɒləm] *adj* solemne

solemnity [sə'lemnɪtɪ] *n* solemnidad *f*

sol-fa [sɒl'fɑː] *n Mus* solfa *f*

solicit [sə'lɪsɪt] **1** *vt Formal (request)* solicitar

2 *vi (prostitute)* abordar clientes

soliciting [sə'lɪsɪtɪŋ] *n (by prostitutes)* ejercicio *m* de la prostitución en las calles

solicitous [sə'lɪsɪtəs] *adj Formal* solícito(a)

solid ['sɒlɪd] **1** *n* sólido *m*; **solids** *(food)* alimentos *mpl* sólidos

2 *adj* (**a**) *(not liquid)* sólido(a); *Fig (support)* fuerte, sólido(a); *Fig* **he's a s. worker** un trabajador de fiar; **s. fuel** combustible *m* sólido (**b**) *(not hollow)* macizo(a); **s. gold** oro *m* macizo; **s. silver** plata *f* maciza

3 *adv* **ten hours s.** diez horas sin interrupción; **the hall was packed s.** la sala estaba atestada de gente; **to be s. with sb** llevarse bien con alguien

solidarity [sɒlɪ'dærɪtɪ] *n* solidaridad *f*

solidify [sə'lɪdɪfaɪ] *vi* solidificarse

solidity [sə'lɪdɪtɪ] *n* solidez *f*

solidly ['sɒlɪdlɪ] *adv (firmly)* sólidamente; *(without interruption)* sin interrupción; *(vote)* unánimemente

solid-state ['sɒlɪd'steɪt] *adj Elec* de estado sólido, de componentes sólidos

soliloquy [sə'lɪləkwɪ] *n* soliloquio *m*

solitaire [sɒlɪ'teə(r)] *n (game, jewelry)* solitario *m*

solitary ['sɒlɪtərɪ] *adj* solitario(a); **s. confinement** aislamiento *m*, incomunicación *f*; **to be in s. confinement** estar incomunicado(a)

solitude ['sɒlɪtjuːd] *n* soledad *f*

solo ['səʊləʊ] **1** *n (pl* **solos**) *(musical)* solo *m*

2 *adj (performance)* en solitario; **s. flight** vuelo *m* en solitario

3 *adv* en solitario; **to go s.** *(musician)* iniciar una carrera en solitario; *(business partner)* montar el propio negocio

soloist ['səʊləʊɪst] *n* solista *mf*

Solomon Islands ['sɒləmən'aɪləndz] *npl* **the S.** las Islas Salomón

solstice ['sɒlstɪs] *n* solsticio *m*

solubility [sɒljʊ'bɪlətɪ] *n* solubilidad *f*

soluble ['sɒljʊbəl] *adj* soluble

solution [sə'luːʃən] *n* solución *f*

solve [sɒlv] *vt* resolver

solvency ['sɒlvənsɪ] *n* solvencia *f*

solvent ['sɒlvənt] **1** *n* disolvente *m*; **s. abuse** inhalación *f* de disolventes *(pegamento y otros)*

2 *adj (financially)* solvente

Somali [sə'mɑːlɪ] *n & adj* somalí *mf*

Somalia [sə'mɑːlɪə] *n* Somalia

somber ['sɒmbə(r)] *adj (color)* oscuro(a); *(person, mood)* sombrío(a)

some [sʌm] **1** *pron* (**a**) *(people)* algunos(as); **s. believe that...** hay quien cree que...; **s. of my friends** algunos amigos míos; **they went off, s. one way, s. another** unos se fueron en una dirección y otros en otra (**b**) *(a certain number)* unos(as), algunos(as); *(a certain quantity)* algo; **s. are more difficult than others** unos son más difíciles que otros; **there is s. left** queda algo; **there are s. left** quedan algunos; **give me s.** *(a few)* dame unos(as) cuantos(as); *(a bit)* dame un poco; **s. of the time** parte del tiempo

2 *adj* **(a)** *(certain quantity or number)* **there are s. apples in the kitchen** hay manzanas en la cocina; *(a few)* hay algunas *or* unas pocas manzanas en la cocina; **to drink s. water** beber agua; **I ate s. fruit** comí fruta; **would you like s. wine?** ¿te apetece vino?; *(a bit)* ¿quieres un poco de vino?; **I felt s. uneasiness** sentí un cierto malestar; **in s. ways** en cierto modo; **to s. extent** hasta cierto punto

(b) *(as opposed to other)* **s. people say…** hay quien dice…; **s. mornings I don't feel like getting up** algunas mañanas no me apetece levantarme

(c) *(considerable)* **for s. time** durante un buen rato; **s. distance away** bastante lejos; **s. miles away** a bastantes millas

(d) *(unspecified)* algún(una); **for s. reason or other** por una razón u otra, por alguna razón; **at s. time in the future** en algún momento futuro; **in s. book or other** en no sé qué libro, en algún libro; **s. fool left the door open** algún idiota dejó la puerta abierta

(e) *Fam (intensive)* **that was s. storm/meal!** ¡qué *or Esp* menuda tormenta/comida!; *Ironic* **s. hope** *or* **chance!** ¡ni lo sueñes!

3 *adv* **(a)** *(approximately)* unos(as); **s. fifteen minutes** unos quince minutos **(b)** *(slightly)* algo, un poco; **shall I turn it up s.?** ¿lo subo algo *or* un poco?

somebody ['sʌmbədɪ], **someone** ['sʌmwʌn] **1** *n* **she thinks she's s.** se cree alguien; **I want to be s.** quiero ser alguien

2 *pron* alguien; **s. told me that…** me dijeron que…; **he's s. you can trust** se puede confiar en él; **s. else** otra persona

someday ['sʌmdeɪ] *adv* algún día; **he'll come s.** algún día vendrá

somehow ['sʌmhaʊ] *adv* **(a)** *(in some way or other)* de alguna manera; **we'll get the money s. (or other)** de un modo u otro conseguiremos el dinero **(b)** *(for some reason or other)* por alguna razón

someone = **somebody**

somersault ['sʌməsɔːlt] **1** *n (of person)* salto *m* mortal

2 *vi (person)* dar un salto mortal/saltos mortales; *(car)* dar una vuelta de campana/vueltas de campana

something ['sʌmθɪŋ] **1** *n* **I've brought you a little s.** te he traído una cosilla

2 *pron* **(a)** *(in general)* algo; **s. or other** alguna cosa; **there's s. about him I don't like** hay algo en él que no me gusta; **s. tells me she'll be there** algo me dice que estará allí; **s. to drink/to read** algo de beber/para leer; **s. to live for** una razón para vivir; **I've got s. else to do after I finish this** aún me queda algo que hacer después de esto; **he's s. in publishing** tiene un puesto importante en el mundo editorial; **in the year eleven hundred and s.** en el año mil ciento y algo; **she's eighty s.** tiene ochenta y tantos años; **at least he apologized — that's s.!** al menos pidió disculpas — ¡eso ya es algo!; **there's s. in what you say** tienes algo de razón; **she has s. to do with what happened** está relacionada con lo que ocurrió; **that was quite s.!** ¡fue impresionante!; **she's got a cold or s.** tiene un resfriado o algo así

(b) *(certain degree)* **there's been s. of an improvement** se ha producido una cierta mejora; **she's s. of a miser** es un poco tacaña; **it's s. like a guinea pig** es algo así como un conejillo de Indias

3 *adv Fam (intensifying)* **it hurt s. awful** dolía horrores *or Méx* un chorro, *Esp* dolía (una) cosa mala

sometime ['sʌmtaɪm] *adv* algún día, alguna vez; **see you s.** ya nos veremos; **s. last week** un día de la semana pasada; **s. before Christmas** en algún momento antes de Navidad; **s. soon** un día de estos; **s. or other** tarde o temprano

sometimes ['sʌmtaɪmz] *adv* a veces

somewhat ['sʌmwɒt] *adv* un poco, un tanto

somewhere ['sʌmweə(r)] *adv* **(a)** *(in some place)* en algún sitio, en alguna parte; *(to some place)* a algún sitio, a alguna parte; **it must be s. else** debe de estar en otra parte; **why don't you go s. else?** ¿por qué no te vas a otro sitio?; **s. in Spain** en (algún lugar de) España; **s. or other** en algún sitio; *Fig* **now we're getting s.!** ¡ya parece que las cosas marchan! **(b)** *(approximately)* **he is s. around fifty** tiene unos cincuenta años; **it costs s. in the region of $500** cuesta alrededor de 500 dólares; **s. around four o'clock** a eso de las cuatro

somnolent ['sɒmnələnt] *adj Formal* somnoliento(a)

son [sʌn] *n* hijo *m*; **youngest/eldest s.** hijo *m* menor/mayor; *very Fam* **s. of a bitch** *(person)* hijo *m* de perra, *Méx* hijo *m* de la chingada; *Fam Euph* **s. of a gun** *(person)* sinvergüenza, granuja

sonar ['səʊnɑː(r)] *n* sonar *m*

sonata [sə'nɑːtə] *n* sonata *f*

song [sɒŋ] *n* **(a)** canción *f*; **to burst** *or* **break into s.** ponerse a cantar **(b)** *(idioms)* **to buy sth for a s.** comprar algo por cuatro perras gordas; **to make a s. and dance (about sth)** montar un número (a cuenta de algo)

songbird ['sɒŋbɜːd] *n* pájaro *m* cantor

songbook ['sɒŋbʊk] *n* libro *m* de canciones

songwriter ['sɒŋraɪtə(r)] *n* compositor(ora) *m,f*; *(of lyrics only)* letrista *mf*

sonic ['sɒnɪk] *adj (of sound)* del sonido; *(of speed of sound)* sónico(a); *Av* **s. boom** estampido *m* sónico *(al rebasar la barrera del sonido)*

son-in-law ['sʌnɪnlɔː] *n (pl* **sons-in-law**) yerno *m*

sonnet ['sɒnɪt] *n* soneto *m*

sonny ['sʌnɪ] *n Fam* hijo *m*, pequeño *m*

sonorous ['sɒnərəs] *adj* sonoro(a)

soon [suːn] *adv* **(a)** *(within a short time)* pronto; **it will s. be Friday** pronto será viernes; **see you s.!** ¡hasta pronto!; **s. after(ward)** poco después; **s. after four** poco después de las cuatro; **no sooner had she left than…** en cuanto se fue…

(b) *(early)* pronto; **must you leave so s.?** ¿tienes que irte tan pronto?; **it's too s. to tell** aún no se puede saber; **none too s.** en buena hora; **how s. can you get here?** ¿cuánto tardarás *or Am* demorarás en llegar?; **sooner or later** tarde o temprano; **the sooner the better** cuanto antes mejor; **as s. as** tan pronto como; **as s. as possible** lo antes posible

(c) *(expressing preference)* **I would just as s. stay** preferiría quedarme; **I would sooner do it alone** preferiría hacerlo yo solo

soot [sʊt] *n* hollín *m*

soothe [suːð] *vt (pain, burn)* aliviar, calmar; *(person, anger)* calmar

soothing ['suːðɪŋ] *adj (relaxing)* relajante, sedante

soothsayer ['suːθseɪə(r)] *n* adivino(a) *m,f*

sooty ['sʊtɪ] *adj (covered in soot)* tiznado(a); *(black)* negro(a)

SOP [sɒp] *n (abbr* **standard operating procedure**) PNT *m*

sop [sɒp] *n (concession)* pequeña concesión *f* (**to** a)

sophist ['sɒfɪst] *n* sofista *mf*

sophisticated [sə'fɪstɪkeɪtɪd] *adj* sofisticado(a)

sophistication [səfɪstɪ'keɪʃən] *n* sofisticación *f*

sophistry ['sɒfɪstrɪ] *n* sofismas *mpl*, sofistería *f*

sophomore ['sɒfəmɔː(r)] *n Univ & Sch* = estudiante de segundo curso

soporific [sɒpə'rɪfɪk] *adj Formal* soporífero(a)

sopping ['ʃɒpɪŋ] *adj* **to be s. (wet)** estar empapado(a)

soppy ['sɒpɪ] *adj Fam* sensiblero(a), *Esp* ñoño(a)

soprano [sə'prɑːnəʊ] *(pl* **sopranos**) *n (singer)* soprano *mf*; **s. voice** (voz *f* de) soprano *m*

sorbet ['sɔːbeɪ] *n* sorbete *m*

sorcerer ['sɔːsərə(r)] *n* brujo *m*, hechicero *m*

sorceress ['sɔːsərɪs] *n* bruja *f*, hechicera *f*

sorcery ['sɔːsərɪ] *n* brujería *f*, hechicería *f*

sordid ['sɔːdɪd] *adj* sórdido(a)

sore [sɔː(r)] **1** *n* (*wound*) llaga *f*, úlcera *f*

2 *adj* (**a**) (*painful*) dolorido(a); **his feet were s.** tenía los pies doloridos; **to have a s. throat** tener dolor de garganta; **I've got a s. leg/back** me duele la pierna/la espalda (**b**) *Fam* (*annoyed*) *esp Esp* enfadado(a) (**about** por), molesto(a) (**about** por), *esp Am* enojado(a) (**about** por); **it's a s. point (with him)** es un tema delicado (para él)

sorely ['sɔːlɪ] *adv* (*greatly*) enormemente; **she will be s. missed** se la echará muchísimo de menos, *Am* se la extrañará muchísimo; **to be s. in need of sth** necesitar algo desesperadamente; **s. tempted** enormemente tentado(a)

sorority [sə'rɒrɪtɪ] *n Univ* = asociación femenina de estudiantes que suele funcionar como club social

sorrow ['sɒrəʊ] *n* pesar *m*, pena *f*; **to my great s.** con gran pesar mío

sorrowful ['sɒrəfʊl] *adj* afligido(a), apenado(a)

sorrowfully ['sɒrəflɪ] *adv* tristemente

sorry ['sɒrɪ] *adj* (**a**) (*regretful, disappointed*) **to be s. about sth** lamentar *or* sentir algo; **I'm s.** (*regretful*) lo lamento, lo siento; (*apology*) lo siento; **to keep you waiting** siento haberle hecho esperar; **s.!** (*apology*) ¡perdón!; **s.?** (*what?*) ¿perdón?, ¿cómo dice(s)?; **to say s. (to sb)** pedir perdón (a alguien); **she's s. she did it** siente mucho haberlo hecho; **I'm s. to hear that…** lamento saber que…; *Fam* **you'll be s.!** ¡te arrepentirás!

(**b**) (*sympathetic*) **to feel s. for sb** sentir pena *or* lástima por alguien; **he felt s. for himself** se compadecía de sí mismo

(**c**) (*pathetic*) lamentable; **to be a s. sight** ofrecer un espectáculo lamentable

sort [sɔːt] **1** *n* (**a**) (*kind*) clase *f*, tipo *m*; **what s. of tree is it?** ¿qué clase de árbol es éste?; **all sorts of** todo tipo de; **that s. of thing** ese tipo de cosas; **she's that s. of person** ella es así; **something of the s.** algo por el estilo; **did you leave this window open? — I did nothing of the s.!** ¿has dejado la ventana abierta? — ¡qué va!; **he's so arrogant! — he's nothing of the s.!** ¡es tan arrogante! — ¡qué va a ser arrogante!; **it takes all sorts** de todo tiene que haber; *Fam* **she's a good s.** es buena gente; **she's not the s. to give in easily** no es de las que se rinden fácilmente; **we don't want your s. here** no queremos gente como tú por aquí; **to be out of sorts** no encontrarse muy allá; **coffee of a s.** café, por llamarlo de alguna forma; **he's a writer of sorts** se le podría llamar escritor

(**b**) (*to organize*) **to have a s. through sth** revisar algo

2 sort of *adv Fam* (*a little*) un poco; (*in a way*) en cierto modo; **this is s. of embarrassing** esto es un poco embarazoso; **I s. of expected it** en cierto modo ya me lo esperaba; **do you like it? — s. of** ¿te gusta? — bueno, más o menos

3 *vt* (*classify*) ordenar, clasificar; *Comptr* ordenar

▸**sort out** *vt sep* (**a**) (*organize*) ordenar; **she sorted out the clothes she wanted to keep** separó la ropa que no quería tirar *or Am* botar (**b**) (*problem*) arreglar

sorta ['sɔːtə] *Fam* = **sort of**

sortie ['sɔːtiː] *n Mil & Fig* incursión *f*

sorting ['sɔːtɪŋ] *n* selección *f*, clasificación *f*

SOS [esəʊ'es] *n* S.O.S. *m*

so-so ['səʊsəʊ] *adj* regular; **it was only s.** fue regularcillo

soufflé ['suːfleɪ] *n* suflé *m*; **cheese s.** suflé de queso

sought [sɔːt] *pt & pp of* **seek**

sought-after ['sɔːtɑːftə(r)] *adj* solicitado(a)

soul [səʊl] *n* (**a**) (*spirit*) alma *f*; **to sell one's s.** venderse,

vender el alma; *Fig* **she's the s. of discretion** es la discreción en persona; *Fig* **it lacks s.** le falta gancho *or* garra; **All Souls' Day** el día de (los) difuntos; **s. mate** alma *f* gemela (**b**) (*person*) alma *f*; **not a s.** ni un alma; **he's a good s.** es (una) buena persona; **poor s.!** ¡pobrecillo! (**c**) (*music*) soul *m*; **s. food** = comida tradicional de los negros del sur de Estados Unidos

soul-destroying ['səʊldɪstrɔɪɪŋ] *adj* desmoralizador(ora)

soulful ['səʊlfʊl] *adj* emotivo(a), conmovedor(ora)

soulless ['səʊllɪs] *adj* (*person*) inhumano(a), desalmado(a); (*place*) impersonal

soul-searching ['səʊlsɜːtʃɪŋ] *n* examen *m* de conciencia, reflexión *f*

sound¹ [saʊnd] **1** *n* (*in general*) sonido *m*; (*individual noise*) ruido *m*; **not a s. could be heard** no se oía nada; **he likes the s. of his own voice** le gusta escucharse a sí mismo; **to turn the s. up/down** (*on TV, radio*) subir/bajar el volumen; *Fig* **I don't like the s. of it** no me gusta nada como suena; **he's angry, by the s. of it** parece que está *esp Esp* enfadado *or esp Am* enojado; **s. barrier** barrera *f* del sonido; **s. bite** frase *f* lapidaria (*en medios de comunicación*); *Comptr* **s. card** tarjeta *f* de sonido; **s. effects** efectos *mpl* sonoros *or* de sonido; **s. engineer** ingeniero(a) *m,f* de sonido; **s. system** equipo *m* de sonido; **s. track** banda *f* sonora; **s. wave** onda *f* sonora

2 *vt* (**a**) (*trumpet*) tocar; (*alarm*) hacer sonar; **to s. one's horn** tocar el claxon *or* la bocina; *Fig* **to s. the alarm** dar la voz de alarma (**b**) (*pronounce*) pronunciar; **the "h" is not sounded** la "h" no se pronuncia

3 *vi* (**a**) (*make sound*) (*trumpet, bell*) sonar (**b**) (*seem*) parecer; **she sounds French** suena francesa; **that sounds like trouble!** eso suena a que puede haber problemas; **that sounds like a good idea** eso me parece muy buena idea; **from what people say, he sounds (like) a nice guy** por lo que dicen, parece buena gente *or Esp* un tipo majo; **it sounds like Mozart** suena a *or* parece Mozart; **how does that s. to you?** (*referring to suggestion*) ¿a ti qué te parece?

▸**sound off** *vi Fam* despotricar (**about** de)

▸**sound out** *vt sep* sondear, tantear (**about** acerca de)

sound² **1** *adj* (**a**) (*healthy*) sano(a); (*solid*) sólido(a); (*in good condition*) en buen estado; **he is of s. mind** tiene pleno uso de sus facultades mentales (**b**) (*argument, reasoning*) sólido(a); **a s. piece of advice** un consejo sensato; **it makes good s. sense** parece de lo más razonable (**c**) (*reliable*) (*investment, business*) seguro(a), sólido(a); (*person*) competente

2 *adv* **to be s. asleep** estar profundamente dormido(a)

-sounding [-'saʊndɪŋ] *suffix* **a foreign-s. name** un nombre que suena extranjero

sounding board ['saʊndɪŋ'bɔːd] *n* (*on pulpit, stage*) tornavoz *m*; *Fig* **I used John as a s.** puse a prueba mis ideas contándoselas a John

soundings ['saʊndɪŋz] *npl Fig* **to take s.** tantear *or* sondear el terreno

soundly ['saʊndlɪ] *adv* (**a**) (*solidly*) sólidamente (**b**) (*logically*) razonablemente (**c**) (*thoroughly*) **to sleep s.** dormir profundamente; **to thrash sb s.** dar a alguien una buena paliza

soundproof ['saʊndpruːf] **1** *adj* insonorizado(a)

2 *vt* insonorizar

soundproofing ['saʊndpruːfɪŋ] *n* insonorización *f*, aislamiento *m* acústico

soup [suːp] *n* sopa *f*; *Fam Fig* **to be in the s.** estar en un aprieto; **s. kitchen** comedor *m* popular; **s. ladle** cucharón *m*; **s. plate** plato *m* hondo *or* sopero; **s. spoon** cuchara *f* sopera

▸**soup up** *vt sep Fam* (*engine*) trucar

sour ['saʊə(r)] **1** *adj* (*fruit, wine*) ácido(a), agrio(a); (*milk*) agrio(a), cortado(a); *Fig* (*person*) agrio(a), áspero(a); **to turn s.** (*milk*) cortarse, agriarse; *Fig* (*situation, relationship*) agriarse, echarse a perder; **s. cream** *Esp* nata *f* agria, *Am* crema *f* de leche agria; *Fig* **it's (a case of) s. grapes** es cuestión de despecho

2 *vt (milk)* cortar, agriar; *Fig (atmosphere, relationship)* agriar, echar a perder

3 *vi (milk)* cortarse, agriarse; *Fig (atmosphere, relationship)* agriarse, echarse a perder

source [sɔːs] *n (of river)* nacimiento *m*; *(of light, information)* fuente *f*; *(of infection, discontent)* foco *m*; *Comptr* **s. program** programa *f* fuente

sourly ['saʊəlɪ] *adv* con acritud, agriamente

souse [saʊs] *vt* empapar

south [saʊθ] **1** *n* sur *m*; **to the s. (of)** al sur (de); **the S.** *(region)* el Sur; *(the southern states)* los estados del sur

2 *adj (direction, side)* (del) sur; **s. wind** viento *m* del sur; **S. Africa** Sudáfrica; **S. African** sudafricano(a) *m,f*; **S. America** Sudamérica, América del Sur; **S. American** sudamericano(a) *m,f*; **S. Carolina** Carolina del Sur; **the S. China Sea** el mar de China (meridional); **S. Dakota** Dakota del Sur; **S. Korea** Corea del Sur; **S. Korean** surcoreano(a) *m,f*; **the S. Pole** el Polo Sur

3 *adv* hacia el sur, en dirección sur; **to face s.** *(house)* estar orientado(a) al sur

southbound ['saʊθbaʊnd] *adj (train, traffic)* en dirección sur; **the s. lanes** la calzada en dirección sur

southeast [saʊθ'iːst] **1** *n* sudeste *m*, sureste *m*

2 *adj (side)* sudeste; *(wind)* del sudeste

3 *adv* al sudeste, en dirección sudeste

southeasterly [saʊθ'iːstəlɪ] **1** *n (wind)* viento *m* del sudeste

2 *adj (direction)* sudeste; **s. wind** viento *m* del sudeste

southeastern [saʊθ'iːstən] *adj (region)* del sudeste

southerly ['sʌðəlɪ] **1** *n (wind)* viento *m* del sur

2 *adj (direction)* sur; *(wind)* del sur; **the most s. point** el punto más meridional

southern ['sʌðən] *adj* **(a)** *(region, accent)* del sur, meridional; **s. Spain** el sur de España, la España meridional; **the s. hemisphere** el hemisferio sur **(b)** *(in Civil War)* **S.** sureño, del Sur

Southerner, southerner ['sʌðənə(r)] *n* sureño(a) *m,f*

southernmost ['sʌðənməʊst] *adj* más al sur, más meridional

south-facing ['saʊθ'feɪsɪŋ] *adj* orientado(a) al sur

south-southeast ['saʊθsaʊθ'iːst] *adv* en dirección sursudeste

south-southwest ['saʊθsaʊθ'west] *adv* en dirección sursudoeste

southward ['saʊθwəd] *adj & adv* hacia el sur

southwards ['saʊθwədz] *adv* hacia el sur

southwest [saʊθ'west] **1** *n* sudoeste *m*, suroeste *m*

2 *adj (side)* sudoeste; *(wind)* del sudoeste

3 *adv* hacia el sudoeste, en dirección sudoeste

southwesterly [saʊθ'westəlɪ] **1** *n (wind)* (viento *m* del) sudoeste *m*

2 *adj (direction)* sudoeste; *(wind)* del sudoeste

3 *adv* hacia el sudoeste

southwestern [saʊθ'westən] *adj (region)* del sudoeste

souvenir [suːvə'nɪə(r)] *n* recuerdo *m*

sovereign ['sɒvrɪn] *n & adj* soberano(a) *m,f*

sovereignty ['sɒvrəntɪ] *n* soberanía *f*

Soviet ['səʊvɪet] **1** *n (person)* soviético(a) *m,f*

2 *adj* soviético(a); *Formerly* **the S. Union** la Unión Soviética

sow¹ [səʊ] *(pt* **sowed** [səʊd], *pp* **sown** [səʊn] *or* **sowed)** *vt (seeds) & Fig* sembrar; **to s. a field with wheat** sembrar trigo en un campo

sow² [saʊ] *n (female pig)* cerda *f*, puerca *f*, *Am* chancha *f*

sown [səʊn] *pp of* **sow¹**

soy [sɔɪ], **soya** ['sɔɪə] *n* soja *f*

soybean ['sɔɪbiːn] *n* semilla *f* de soja

soy sauce [sɔɪ'sɔːs] *n* (salsa *f* de) soja *f*

sozzled ['sɒzəld] *adj Fam (drunk)* **to be s.** estar como una cuba *or Esp* mamado(a) *or Col* caído(a) de la perra *or Méx* ahogado(a) *or RP* en pedo; **to get s.** agarrarse un pedo

spa [spɑː] *n* balneario *m*

space [speɪs] **1** *n* **(a)** *(room)* espacio *m*, sitio *m*; **to stare into s.** mirar al vacío; **to take up a lot of s.** ocupar mucho espacio *or* sitio

(b) *(individual place)* sitio *m*; *(on printed form)* espacio *m* (en blanco); **wide open spaces** grandes extensiones *fpl*; **a parking s.** un sitio para estacionar *or Esp* aparcar; **s. bar** *(on keyboard)* barra *f* espaciadora

(c) *(period of time)* espacio *m*, intervalo *m*; **in the s. of a year** en el espacio de un año

(d) *(outer space)* espacio *m*; **the s. age** la era espacial; *Fam* **he's a bit of a s. cadet** está un poco colgado, anda siempre como alucinado; **s. rocket** cohete *m* espacial; **s. shuttle** transbordador *m* espacial; **s. suit** traje *m* espacial; **s. travel** viajes *mpl* espaciales

(e) *(gap) (in timetable)* hueco *m*

2 *vt* espaciar

▸**space out** *vt sep (arrange with gaps)* espaciar, separar; *Fam* **to be spaced out** *(dazed)* estar atontado(a)

space-age ['speɪseɪdʒ] *adj* de la era espacial

spacecraft ['speɪskrɑːft] *n* nave *f* espacial, astronave *f*

spaceman ['speɪsmæn] *n* astronauta *m*

space-saving ['speɪs'seɪvɪŋ] *adj* que ahorra *or* permite ahorrar espacio

spaceship ['speɪsʃɪp] *n* nave *f* espacial

spacing ['speɪsɪŋ] *n* espacio *m*; *Typ* **double s.** doble espacio

spacious ['speɪʃəs] *adj* espacioso(a)

spade [speɪd] *n* **(a)** *(tool)* pala *f*; **to call a s. a s.** llamar a las cosas por su nombre, llamar al pan pan y al vino vino **(b)** *(in cards)* **spades** picas *fpl*

spaghetti [spə'getɪ] *n* espaguetis *mpl*

Spain [speɪn] *n* España

Spam® [spæm] *n* = fiambre de cerdo en conserva

spam [spæm] *Comptr* **1** *n* correo *m* basura

2 *vt* enviar correo basura a

3 *vi* enviar correo basura

spammer ['spæmə(r)] *Comptr n* = persona que envía correo basura

spamming ['spæmɪŋ] *Comptr n* envío *m* correo basura

span [spæn] **1** *n* **(a)** *(of hand)* palmo *m*; *(of wing)* envergadura *f* **(b)** *(of arch)* luz *f*, vano *m*; *(of bridge)* arcada *f*, ojo *m* **(c)** *(of time)* período *m*, lapso *m* **(d)** *(of knowledge, interests)* repertorio *m*, gama *f*

2 *vt (pt & pp* **spanned)** *(of bridge)* atravesar, cruzar; *Fig (of life, knowledge)* abarcar

Spanglish ['spæŋglɪʃ] *n* spanglish *m*

Spaniard ['spænɪəd] *n* español(ola) *m,f*

spaniel ['spænjəl] *n* spaniel *m*

Spanish ['spænɪʃ] **1** *npl (people)* **the S.** los españoles

2 *n (language)* español *m*, castellano *m*; **S. class/teacher** clase *f*/profesor(ora) *m,f* de español

3 *adj* español(ola); **the S. Armada** la Armada Invencible; **the S. Civil War** la guerra civil española; **the S. Inquisition** la (Santa) Inquisición; **S. moss** musgo *m* negro; **S. omelet** tortilla *f* española *or Esp* patatas *or Am* papas

spank [spæŋk] **1** *n* **to give sb a s.** darle un azote a alguien

2 *vt* dar unos azotes a, azotar

spanking ['spæŋkɪŋ] **1** *n* azotaina *f*, zurra *f*; **to give sb a s.** dar a alguien una azotaina

2 *adv Fam* **s. new** flamante; **they had a s. good time** se lo pasaron bomba *or* en grande

spar¹ [spɑː(r)] *n (on ship)* palo *m*, verga *f*

spar² (*pt & pp* **sparred**) *vi* **to s. with sb** (*in boxing*) entrenar con alguien como sparring; (*argue*) discutir en tono cordial con alguien

spare ['speə(r)] **1** *n* (*spare part*) (pieza *f* de) recambio *m or* repuesto *m*; (*tire*) rueda *f* de repuesto *or RP* de auxilio, *Méx* llanta *f* de refacción

　2 *adj* (**a**) (*available*) de más; (*surplus*) sobrante; **do you have a s. pen?** ¿tienes un bolígrafo de sobra?; **a s. moment** un rato libre; **s. parts** recambios *mpl*, piezas *fpl* de recambio; **s. room** habitación *f* de invitados; **s. time** tiempo *m* libre; **s. tire** rueda *f* de repuesto; **s. wheel** rueda *f* de repuesto *or* recambio *or RP* auxilio, *Méx* llanta *f* de refacción (**b**) (*frugal*) (*meal, style, room*) sobrio(a), sencillo(a)

　3 *vt* (**a**) (*go without*) **to have no time to s.** no tener ni un minuto libre, no poder entretenerse; **they arrived with five minutes to s.** llegaron cinco minutos antes; **can you s. the time?** ¿tienes tiempo?; **can you s. me a few moments?** ¿tienes un rato?, ¿me puedes dedicar unos minutos?; **could you s. me some milk?** ¿puedes dejarme un poco de leche?; **to s. a thought for sb** acordarse de alguien

　(**b**) (*in negative constructions*) **to s. no expense/effort** no reparar en gastos/esfuerzos

　(**c**) (*save*) **to s. sb the trouble of doing sth** ahorrar a alguien las molestias de hacer algo; **s. me the details!** ¡ahórrame los detalles!

　(**d**) (*show mercy toward*) apiadarse de; **to s. sb's life** perdonarle la vida a alguien; **to s. sb's feelings** ahorrar sufrimientos a alguien

spareribs ['speərɪbz] *npl* costillas *fpl* de cerdo *or* puerco *or Am* chancho

sparing ['speərɪŋ] *adj* parco(a) (**with** en)

sparingly ['speərɪŋlɪ] *adv* con moderación, parcamente

spark [spɑːk] **1** *n* (*electrical, from fire*) chispa *f*; *Fig* **sparks flew** salían chispas; *Fig* **he hasn't a s. of imagination** no tiene ni gota *or* chispa de imaginación; *Aut* **s. plug** bujía *f*

　2 *vi* echar chispas

▸**spark off** *vt sep* desencadenar

sparkle ['spɑːkəl] **1** *n* (*of light, eyes, diamond*) destello *m*; *Fig* (*of person*) chispa *f*; *Fig* **the s. had gone out of their marriage** su matrimonio ya no tenía ninguna chispa

　2 *vi* (*light, eyes, diamond*) destellar; *Fig* (*person, conversation*) brillar, ser chispeante

sparkler ['spɑːklə(r)] *n* (*firework*) bengala *f*

sparkling ['spɑːklɪŋ] *adj* (*light, eyes, diamond*) centelleante, brillante; *Fig* (*conversation*) chispeante; **s. wine** vino *m* espumoso

sparring ['spɑːrɪŋ] *n* **s. match** (*debate*) contienda *f* dialéctica amistosa; **s. partner** (*in boxing*) sparring *m*; *Fig* contertulio(a) *m,f*

sparrow ['spærəʊ] *n* gorrión *m*; **s. hawk** gavilán *m*

sparse [spɑːs] *adj* (*population*) disperso(a); (*information*) somero(a), escaso(a); (*hair*) ralo(a)

sparsely ['spɑːslɪ] *adv* (*populated*) poco, dispersamente; (*covered*) escasamente, someramente; **s. furnished** poco amueblado(a)

Spartan ['spɑːtən] *n & adj also Fig* espartano(a) *m,f*

spasm ['spæzəm] *n Med* espasmo *m*; *Fig* (*of coughing, jealousy*) acceso *m*; *Fig* (*of activity*) arranque *m*

spasmodic [spæz'mɒdɪk] *adj* (*irregular*) intermitente, con altibajos; *Med* espasmódico(a)

spasmodically [spæz'mɒdɪklɪ] *adv* (*irregularly*) intermitentemente

spastic ['spæstɪk] *n* (**a**) *Med* enfermo(a) *m,f* de parálisis cerebral (**b**) *very Fam* (*idiot*) subnormal *m,f*

spat¹ [spæt] *n Fam* (*quarrel*) rifirrafe *m*, bronca *f*

spat² *pt & pp of* **spit²**

spate [speɪt] *n* (*of letters, crimes*) oleada *f*; **to be in full s.** (*river*)

estar *or* bajar muy crecido; *Fig* (*speaker*) estar en plena arenga

spatial ['speɪʃəl] *adj* espacial

spatter ['spætə(r)] *vt* salpicar (**with** de)

spatula ['spætjʊlə] *n* espátula *f*

spawn [spɔːn] **1** *n* (*of frog, fish*) hueva *f*

　2 *vt* (*give rise to*) generar

　3 *vi* (*fish*) desovar

speak [spiːk] (*pt* **spoke** [spəʊk], *pp* **spoken** ['spəʊkən]) **1** *vt* (**a**) (*utter*) pronunciar; **she always speaks her mind** siempre dice lo que piensa; **to s. the truth** decir la verdad (**b**) (*language*) hablar; **to s. Spanish** hablar español; **Spanish spoken** (*sign*) se habla español

　2 *vi* (**a**) (*talk*) hablar, *esp Am* conversar, *Méx* platicar; **to s. to sb (about)** hablar *or esp Am* conversar *or Méx* platicar con alguien (de); **they're not speaking** (*to each other*) no se hablan; **I'll s. to him about it** hablaré con él al respecto; **I know her to s. to** la conozco lo bastante como para hablar con ella; **legally/morally speaking** (hablando) en términos legales/morales; **so to s.** por así decirlo; **who's speaking?** (*on phone*) ¿con quién hablo?; **Mr. Curry? — yes, speaking** ¿el señor Curry? – sí, soy yo

　(**b**) (*give a speech*) dar una charla; **he spoke on the subject of…** el tema de su charla fue…

　3 *n* **computer/advertising s.** jerga *f* informática/publicitaria

▸**speak for** *vt insep* **to s. for sb** (*on behalf of*) hablar en nombre de alguien; **s for yourself!** ¡no pluralices!, ¡eso lo dices tú!; **the facts s. for themselves** los hechos hablan por sí solos *or* mismos

▸**speak out** *vi* hablar abiertamente (**against** en contra de)

▸**speak up** *vi* hablar más alto, levantar la voz; **to s. up for sb** hablar en favor de alguien

speakerphone ['spiːkəfəʊn] *n* manos libres *m inv*

speaker ['spiːkə(r)] *n* (**a**) (*person*) (*in conversation, on radio*) interlocutor(ora) *m,f*; (*at meeting*) orador(ora) *m,f*; (*at conference*) conferenciante *mf*, orador(ora) *m,f*, *Am* conferencista *mf*; (*of language*) hablante *mf*; **she's a good s.** es (una) buena oradora; **the S.** el/la presidente(a) de la Cámara de Representantes (**b**) (*loudspeaker*) altavoz *m*, *Am* altoparlante *m*, *Am* parlante *m*, *Méx* bocina *f*

speaking ['spiːkɪŋ] *adj* (*doll, robot*) parlante; *Theat & Cin* **a s. part** un papel con diálogo

-speaking [-'spiːkɪŋ] *suffix* (**a**) (*person*) **they're both German/Spanish-s.** los dos son germanohablantes/hispanohablantes (**b**) (*country*) **French/English-s. countries** países francófonos/anglófonos

spear ['spɪə(r)] **1** *n* (*for thrusting*) lanza *f*; (*for throwing*) jabalina *f*

　2 *vt* (*food*) pinchar

spearhead ['spɪəhed] **1** *n also Fig* punta *f* de lanza

　2 *vt* (*attack, campaign*) encabezar

spearmint ['spɪəmɪnt] *n* (*plant*) hierbabuena *f*; (*flavor*) menta *f*

spec [spek] *n Fam* **to do sth on s.** hacer algo por si acaso

special ['speʃəl] **1** *n* (*on menu*) plato *m* del día

　2 *adj* especial; **it's nothing s.** no es nada del otro mundo; **what's so s. about the 19th of November?** ¿qué tiene de especial el 19 de noviembre?; **s. agent** agente *mf* especial; **s. delivery** envío *m* urgente, *Esp* ≃ postal exprés *m*; *Cin* **s. effects** efectos *mpl* especiales; **s. needs** necesidades *fpl* educativas especiales; **s. offer** oferta *f* especial; *Pol* **s. powers** competencias *fpl* extraordinarias

specialism ['speʃəlɪzəm] *n* (*subject*) especialidad *f*

specialist ['speʃəlɪst] **1** *n* especialista *mf*; *Med* **heart s.** cardiólogo(a) *m,f*; *Med* **cancer s.** oncólogo(a) *m,f*

　2 *adj* (*knowledge*) especializado(a); **s. subject** especialidad *f*

speciality [speʃɪ'ælɪtɪ] *n* especialidad *f*

specialization [speʃəlaɪ'zeɪʃən] *n* especialización *f*

specialize ['speʃəlaız] vi especializarse (**in** en)

specialized ['speʃəlaızd] adj especializado(a)

specially ['speʃəlı] adv (in particular) especialmente; **they had a cake s. made** les hicieron un pastel para la ocasión

specialty ['speʃəltı] n especialidad f

species ['spiːʃiːz] (pl **species**) n especie f

specific [spɪ'sɪfɪk] **1** n **specifics** detalles mpl
   2 adj (case, task, sequence) específico(a); (command, instructions) preciso(a), concreto(a); **to be s.,...** para ser más precisos,...; **to be s. about sth** ser claro(a) respecto a algo; **could you be more s.?** ¿podrías especificar or concretar más?; Phys **s. gravity** peso m específico

specifically [spɪ'sɪfɪkəlı] adv (**a**) (expressly) específicamente (**b**) (precisely) precisamente, concretamente

specification [spesɪfɪ'keɪʃən] n especificación f; **specifications** (of machine) especificaciones fpl or características fpl técnicas

specify ['spesɪfaı] vt especificar

specimen ['spesɪmɪn] n (of mineral, handwriting, blood) muestra f; Fam **he's an odd s.** es un bicho raro; **s. copy** ejemplar m de muestra

specious ['spiːʃəs] adj engañoso(a), especioso(a)

speck [spek] n (of dust, dirt) mota f; (of paint, ink) gotita f

speckled ['spekəld] adj moteado(a)

specs [speks] npl Fam (spectacles) gafas fpl; **a pair of s.** unas gafas

spectacle ['spektəkəl] n (**a**) (show, sight) espectáculo m; **to make a s. of oneself** dar el espectáculo, dar el número (**b**) **spectacles** gafas fpl, Am lentes fpl, Am anteojos mpl; **a pair of spectacles** unas gafas; **s. case** (hard) estuche m de gafas; (soft) funda f de gafas

spectacular [spek'tækjʊlə(r)] **1** n Theat espectáculo m grandioso
   2 adj espectacular

spectacularly [spek'tækjʊləlı] adv espectacularmente, de forma espectacular; **to fail s.** fracasar estrepitosamente

spectator [spek'teɪtə(r)] n espectador(ora) m,f; **the spectators** el público, los espectadores; **s. sport** deporte m de masas

specter ['spektə(r)] n espectro m

spectra ['spektrə] pl of **spectrum**

spectrum ['spektrəm] (pl **spectra** ['spektrə]) n also Fig espectro m

speculate ['spekjʊleɪt] vi especular (**about** sobre)

speculation [spekjʊ'leɪʃən] n especulación f

speculative ['spekjʊlətɪv] adj especulativo(a)

speculator ['spekjʊleɪtə(r)] n Fin especulador(ora) m,f

sped [sped] pt & pp of **speed**

speech [spiːtʃ] n (**a**) (faculty) habla f; **s. defect** or **impediment** defecto m del habla or de dicción; **s. therapist** logopeda mf; **s. therapy** logopedia f (**b**) (language) habla f, lenguaje m (**c**) (of politician, at conference) discurso m; Theat parlamento m; **to give** or **make a s.** dar or pronunciar un discurso (**d**) Gram **part of s.** categoría f gramatical; **direct/indirect s.** estilo m directo/indirecto

speechless ['spiːtʃlɪs] adj sin habla; **to be left s.** quedarse sin habla

speechmaking ['spiːtʃmeɪkɪŋ] n (public speaking) oratoria f, arte m de hablar en público

speechwriter ['spiːtʃraɪtə(r)] n redactor(ora) m,f de discursos

speed [spiːd] **1** n (**a**) (rate of movement) velocidad f; (quickness) rapidez f; **the s. of light/of sound** la velocidad de la luz/del sonido; **at s.** a gran velocidad; **to gather** or **pick up s.** ganar or cobrar velocidad; **to lose s.** perder velocidad; **s. bump** Esp resalto m (de moderación de velocidad), Arg despertador m, Méx tope m; **s. camera** cámara f de control de velocidad;

Fam **s. cop** policía mf de tráfico or RP caminera (en carretera); **s. dating** speed dating m, citas fpl rápidas; **s. dialing** marcado m rápido; **s. limit** límite m de velocidad; **s. trap** radar m (de control de velocidad)
   (**b**) (gear) marcha f, velocidad f; **a five-s. gearbox** una caja de cambios de cinco marchas (**c**) Fam (amphetamine) anfetas fpl, speed m
   2 vi (**a**) (pt & pp **sped** [sped] or **speeded**) (go fast) avanzar rápidamente; (hurry) precipitarse (**b**) Aut (exceed speed limit) sobrepasar el límite de velocidad; **I was caught speeding** Esp me cogieron conduciendo demasiado deprisa, Am me agarraron manejando demasiado deprisa (**c**) Fam (be under effect of amphetamines) **to be speeding** estar or ir puesto(a) de speed

▶**speed off** vi salir disparado(a)

▶**speed up 1** vt sep (process) acelerar; (person) apresurar
   2 vi (car) acelerar; (process) acelerarse; (person) apresurarse, Am apurarse

speedboat ['spiːdbəʊt] n motora f, planeadora f

speedily ['spiːdɪlı] adv rápidamente

speeding ['spiːdɪŋ] n Aut **I was stopped for s.** me pararon por exceso de velocidad

speedometer [spiː'dɒmɪtə(r)] n Aut velocímetro m

speedway ['spiːdweɪ] n carreras fpl de motos

speedy ['spiːdɪ] adj rápido(a); **to wish sb a s. recovery** desearle a alguien una pronta recuperación

spell¹ [spel] n hechizo m, encantamiento m; **to cast a s. over sb** hechizar or encantar a alguien; Fig **to break the s.** romper la magia del momento; Fig **to be under a s.** estar hechizado(a); Fig **to be under sb's s.** estar cautivado(a) or hipnotizado(a) por alguien

spell² n (**a**) (period) período m, temporada f; **a cold s.** una ola de frío; **sunny spells** intervalos mpl soleados; **a good/bad s.** una buena/mala racha (**b**) (turn) turno m; **she offered to do a s. at the wheel** se ofreció para conducir or Am manejar un rato

spell³ 1 vt (**a**) (write correctly) deletrear; **how do you s. it?** ¿cómo se escribe? (**b**) (signify) suponer; **to s. disaster** suponer un desastre
   2 vi escribir sin faltas; **he can't s.** tiene muchas faltas de ortografía

▶**spell out** vt sep (explain explicitly) explicar claramente; **do I have to s. it out for you?** ¿cómo te lo tengo que decir?

spellbinding ['spelbaɪndɪŋ] adj cautivador(ora), fascinante

spellbound ['spelbaʊnd] adj hechizado(a)

spell-checker ['speltʃekə(r)] n Comptr corrector m ortográfico

speller ['spelə(r)] n (book) manual m de ortografía

spelling ['spelɪŋ] n ortografía f; **to be good/bad at s.** tener buena/mala ortografía; **s. bee** concurso m de ortografía; **s. mistake** falta f de ortografía

spelunker [spɪ'lʌŋkə(r)] n espeleólogo(a) m,f

spelunking [spe'lʌŋkɪŋ] n espeleología f

spend [spend] (pt & pp **spent** [spent]) vt (**a**) (money) gastar (**on** en) (**b**) (time) pasar; **to s. time on sth** dedicar tiempo a algo

spender ['spendə(r)] n **to be a high/low s.** gastar mucho/poco

spending ['spendɪŋ] n gasto m; **consumer s.** gasto m or consumo m privado; **public s.** gasto m público; **s. money** dinero m para gastos; **s. power** poder m adquisitivo; **to go on a s. spree** salir a gastar a lo loco

spendthrift ['spendθrɪft] n despilfarrador(ora) m,f, manirroto(a) m,f

spent [spent] **1** adj (fuel, ammunition) usado(a); **to be a s. force** ser una fuerza devaluada
   2 pt & pp of **spend**

sperm [spɜːm] n esperma m, semen m; **s. bank** banco m de semen; **s. donor** donante m de semen; **s. whale** cachalote m

spermicide ['spɜːmɪsaɪd] n espermicida m

spew [spjuː] vt & vi Fam (vomit) devolver, vomitar

sphere [sfɪə(r)] n also Fig esfera f; **that's outside my s.** eso está fuera de mi ámbito; **s. of influence** ámbito m de influencia

spherical ['sferɪkəl] adj esférico(a)

sphincter ['sfɪŋktə(r)] n Anat esfínter m

sphinx [sfɪŋks] n esfinge f

spic, spick [spɪk] n very Fam = término ofensivo para referirse a un latino

spice [spaɪs] **1** n (seasoning) especia f; Fig chispa f; **s. rack** especiero m
2 vt (food) sazonar, especiar

▸**spice up** vt (make more exciting) dar chispa a

spick¹ [spɪk] **1** adj **s. and span** como los chorros del oro, impecable

spick² = spic

spicy ['spaɪsɪ] adj (food) (seasoned with spices) especiado(a), sazonado(a); (hot) picante; Fig (story, gossip) jugoso(a), picante

spider ['spaɪdə(r)] n araña f; **s. web** tela f de araña, telaraña f; **s. crab** centollo m, centolla f; **s. monkey** mono m araña; **s. plant** cinta f

spiel [spiːl] n Fam rollo m

spike [spaɪk] **1** n pincho m; **spikes** (running shoes) zapatillas fpl de clavos
2 vt **to s. sb's guns** (spoil plans) chafarle los planes a alguien; **to s. sb's drink** añadir licor a la bebida de alguien

spiked [spaɪkt] adj (shoes) con clavos

spiky ['spaɪkɪ] adj espinoso(a); **s. hair** pelo m de punta

spill [spɪl] **1** vt (liquid, salt) derramar; Fig **to s. the beans** Esp descubrir el pastel, Am destapar la olla
2 vi (liquid) derramarse
3 n **to take a s.** (fall) tener una caída

▸**spill over** vi (liquid) rebosar; Fig (conflict) extenderse (**into** a)

spillage ['spɪlɪdʒ] n derrame m

spilled [spɪlt] pt & pp of spill

spin [spɪn] **1** n (turning movement) giro m; (on ball) efecto m; (on news story) sesgo m; **to go into a s.** (car) dar vueltas; (plane) entrar en barrena; **to go for a s.** (in car) ir a dar una vuelta; **to put s. on a ball** dar efecto a una pelota; **s. doctor** asesor(ora) m,f político(a) (para dar buena prensa a un partido o político); **s. dryer** centrifugadora f
2 vt (pt & pp spun [spʌn]) (a) (wool, cotton) hilar (b) (wheel, top) (hacer) girar; Fig **to s. one's wheels** perder el tiempo; **to s. a coin** echar a cara o cruz or Chile, Col cara o sello or Méx águila o sol or RP cara o seca (c) (spin-dry) centrifugar
3 vi (wheel, spinning top, dancer) dar vueltas, girar; **my head's spinning** me da vueltas la cabeza; **the room's spinning** todo me da vueltas

▸**spin out** vi (vehicle, driver) descontrolarse

spinach ['spɪnɪtʃ] n espinacas fpl

spinal ['spaɪnəl] adj Anat espinal; **s. column** columna f vertebral; **s. cord** médula f espinal; Med **s. injury** lesión f de columna

spindle ['spɪndəl] n huso m

spindly ['spɪndlɪ] adj larguirucho(a)

spin-dry ['spɪn'draɪ] vt centrifugar

spine [spaɪn] n (a) (backbone) columna f vertebral (b) (book) lomo m (c) (spike) (of plant, fish) espina f

spineless ['spaɪnlɪs] adj (weak) pusilánime, débil

spinning top ['spɪnɪŋ'tɒp] n peonza f

spinning wheel ['spɪnɪŋ'wiːl] n rueca f

spin-off ['spɪnɒf] n (a) (by-product) (producto m) derivado m, subproducto m (b) (TV program) secuela f televisiva (c) Fin (of company) escisión f

spinster ['spɪnstə(r)] n Old-fashioned solterona f

spiny ['spaɪnɪ] adj espinoso(a); **s. lobster** langosta f

spiral ['spaɪərəl] **1** n espiral f; **s. staircase** escalera f de caracol
2 vi (smoke) ascender en espiral; (prices) subir vertiginosamente

spire ['spaɪə(r)] n (of church) aguja f

spirit ['spɪrɪt] n (a) (ghost, person) espíritu m; **the Holy S.** el Espíritu Santo
(b) (mood, attitude) espíritu m; **that was not the s. of the agreement** ese no era el espíritu del acuerdo; **she entered into the s. of the occasion** se puso a tono con la ocasión, participó del acontecimiento; Fam **that's the s.!** ¡eso es!
(c) (courage) valor m, coraje m; (energy) brío m; **to show s.** mostrar valor or coraje; **to break sb's s.** desmoralizar a alguien; **to be in good/poor spirits** tener la moral alta/baja; **to say sth with s.** decir algo con arrestos
(d) **spirits** (drinks) licores mpl; **s. lamp** lámpara f de alcohol; **s. level** (instrument) nivel m de burbuja

▸**spirit away, spirit off** vt sep hacer desaparecer

spirited ['spɪrɪtɪd] adj (person) valeroso(a), con arrestos; (defense, reply) enérgico(a)

spiritual ['spɪrɪtjʊəl] **1** n Mus (song) (African-American) **s.** espiritual m negro
2 adj Rel espiritual; **France is my s. home** Francia es mi patria espiritual

spiritualism ['spɪrɪtjʊəlɪzəm] n espiritismo m

spirituality [spɪrɪtjʊˈælɪtɪ] n espiritualidad f

spiritually ['spɪrɪtjʊəlɪ] adv espiritualmente

spit¹ [spɪt] n (a) (for cooking) espetón m, asador m (b) (of land) lengua f

spit² **1** n (saliva) saliva f; Fam **s. and polish** limpieza f, pulcritud f
2 (pt & pp spat [spæt], spit) vt escupir
3 vi (person, cat) escupir; (hot fat) saltar

▸**spit out** vt sep escupir; Fam **s it out!** (say what you want to) ¡suéltalo!

spite [spaɪt] **1** n (a) (malice) rencor m; **out of s.** por rencor (b) **in s. of...** a pesar de...
2 vt fastidiar

spiteful ['spaɪtfʊl] adj rencoroso(a)

spitefully ['spaɪtfʊlɪ] adv maliciosamente

spitting ['spɪtɪŋ] n Fam Hum **to be in or within s. distance (of)** estar a un paso (de); Fam **he's the s. image of his father** es el vivo retrato de su padre

spittle ['spɪtəl] n saliva f, baba f

splash [splæʃ] **1** n (a) (of liquid) salpicadura f; **there was a loud s.** se oyó un fuerte ruido de algo cayendo al agua; **to fall into the water with a s.** caer al agua salpicando; Fam Fig **to make a s.** causar sensación (b) (of color) mancha f (c) Comptr **s. page** preportada f, splash page f
2 vt salpicar; **a photo was splashed across the front page** publicaron una gran foto en la portada
3 vi (water, waves) salpicar; (children) chapotear

▸**splash down** vi (spacecraft) amerizar

splashy ['splæʃɪ] adj Fam llamativo(a), ostentoso(a)

splat [splæt] **1** n ruido m sordo
2 adv **to go s. into the wall** hacer "plaf" contra la pared

splatter ['splætə(r)] **1** n salpicadura f
2 vt **to s. sb with mud** salpicar a alguien de barro

splay [spleɪ] vt extender

spleen [spliːn] n (a) Anat bazo m (b) Formal (anger) rabia f, ira f; **she vented her s. on him** descargó toda su rabia sobre él

splendid ['splendɪd] adj espléndido(a)

splendor ['splendə(r)] n esplendor m

splice [splaɪs] vt (a) (rope, tape, movie) empalmar (b) Fam **to get spliced** (marry) casarse

spliff [splɪf] n Fam porro m, canuto m

splint [splɪnt] *n (for broken limb)* tablilla *f*; **in splints** entablillado(a)

splinter ['splɪntə(r)] **1** *n (of wood, bone)* astilla *f*; *(of glass)* esquirla *f*; *Pol* **s. group** grupo *m* disidente
2 *vt* astillar
3 *vi* astillarse; *Fig (political party)* escindirse

split [splɪt] **1** *n (in wood)* grieta *f*; *(in group)* escisión *f*; *(in garment)* raja *f*; **to do the splits** abrirse totalmente de piernas
2 *adj* partido(a); **s. ends** *(in hair)* puntas *fpl* abiertas; **s. peas** guisantes *mpl* or *Méx* chícharos *mpl* secos partidos, *Am* arvejas *fpl* secas partidas; **s. personality** doble personalidad *f*; **s. screen** pantalla *f* partida; **in a s. second** en una fracción de segundo; **s. ticket** voto *m* dividido
3 *vt (pt & pp* **split***) (wood, cloth)* rajar; *(amount of money, group)* dividir; **to s. one's head open** hacerse una brecha en la cabeza; *Fam* **to s. one's sides laughing** partirse *or Esp* troncharse de risa; *Fig* **to s. hairs** buscarle tres pies al gato; **to s. the vote** dividir el voto; **to s. the difference** dejarlo en la mitad
4 *vi* **(a)** *(wood, cloth)* rajarse; *(political party)* escindirse; *Fam* **my head's splitting** me va a estallar la cabeza **(b)** *Fam (leave)* abrirse, *Esp, RP* pirarse, *Méx, RP* rajarse

▸**split up 1** *vt sep (money, work)* dividir; *(couple, people fighting)* separar
2 *vi (couple)* separarse

split-second ['splɪtsekənd] *adj (decision)* instantáneo(a); *(timing)* al milímetro

splitting ['splɪtɪŋ] *adj (headache)* atroz

splurge [splɜːdʒ] *Fam* **1** *n* derroche *m*
2 *vt* derrochar

splutter ['splʌtə(r)] *vi (person)* farfullar; *(engine, candle)* chisporrotear

spoil [spɔɪl] **1** *vt (pt & pp* **spoiled** *or* **spoilt** [spɔɪlt]) **(a)** *(ruin)* estropear; **to s. sb's fun** aguarle la fiesta a alguien; **to s. sb's appetite** quitarle *or Am* sacarle las ganas de comer a alguien; *Pol* **spoiled ballot** voto *m* nulo, papeleta *f* nula, *Méx, RP* boleta *f* nula **(b)** *(indulge) (person)* mimar, consentir; **a spoiled child** un niño/una niña mimado(a); **to be spoiled for choice** tener mucho donde elegir
2 *vi* **(a)** *(fruit, fish)* estropearse **(b)** **to be spoiling for a fight** tener ganas de pelea

spoils [spɔɪlz] *npl (of war, crime)* botín *m*; **to claim one's share of the s.** reclamar una parte del botín

spoilsport ['spɔɪlspɔːt] *n Fam* aguafiestas *mf inv*

spoilt [spɔɪlt] *pt & pp of* **spoil**

spoke¹ [spəʊk] *n (of wheel)* radio *m*

spoke² *pt of* **speak**

spoken ['spəʊkən] *pp of* **speak**

spokesman ['spəʊksmən] *n* portavoz *m*

spokesperson ['spəʊkspɜːsən] *n* portavoz *mf*

spokeswoman ['spəʊkswʊmən] *n* portavoz *f*

sponge [spʌndʒ] **1** *n* esponja *f*; *Fig* **to throw in the s.** tirar la toalla; **s. cake** bizcocho *m*
2 *vt* **(a)** *(wash)* limpiar *(con una esponja)* **(b)** *Fam (scrounge)* **to s. sth off** *or* **from sb** gorrear *or Esp, Méx* gorronear *or RP* garronear algo a alguien
3 *vi Fam (scrounge) Esp, Méx* vivir de gorra, *RP* vivir de arriba

▸**sponge down** *vt sep (wash)* lavar *(con una esponja)*

▸**sponge off** *vt insep Fam (scrounge from)* vivir a costa de

sponger ['spʌndʒə(r)] *n Fam* gorrero(a) *m,f*, *Esp, Méx* gorrón(ona) *m,f*, *RP* garronero(a) *m,f*

spongy ['spʌndʒɪ] *adj* esponjoso(a)

sponsor ['spɒnsə(r)] **1** *n (of team, exhibition)* patrocinador(ora) *m,f*; *(of student, club member) (man)* padrino *m*; *(woman)* madrina *f*
2 *vt (team, exhibition)* patrocinar, financiar; *(student)* subvencionar; *(club member)* apadrinar

sponsorship ['spɒnsəʃɪp] *n (of athlete, team, festival)* patrocinio *m*, financiación *f*, *Am* financiamiento *m*; *(of candidate)* apoyo *m* (**of** a); **s. deal** *(of athlete, team)* contrato *m* con un patrocinador

spontaneity [spɒntə'neɪtɪ] *n* espontaneidad *f*

spontaneous [spɒn'teɪnɪəs] *adj* espontáneo(a)

spoof [spuːf] *n Fam* **(a)** *(parody)* parodia *f*, burla *f* **(b)** *(hoax)* broma *f*

spook [spuːk] *n Fam* **(a)** *(ghost)* fantasma *m* **(b)** *(spy)* espía *mf*

spooky ['spuːkɪ] *adj Fam* espeluznante, escalofriante

spool [spuːl] *n (of film, thread)* carrete *m*

spoon [spuːn] **1** *n* cuchara *f*; *(spoonful)* cucharada *f*
2 *vt* **to s. sauce onto sth** rociar salsa sobre algo con una cuchara; **he spooned the soup into the baby's mouth** dio la sopa al bebé con una cuchara

spoon-feed ['spuːnfiːd] *(pt & pp* **spoon-fed** ['spuːnfed]) *vt (help too much)* dar las cosas hechas *or* masticadas a

spoonful ['spuːnfʊl] *n* cucharada *f*

sporadic [spə'rædɪk] *adj* esporádico(a)

sporadically [spə'rædɪklɪ] *n* esporádicamente

spore [spɔː(r)] *n (of fungus)* espora *f*

sport [spɔːt] **1** *n* **(a)** *(activity)* deporte *m*; **to be good at sports** ser buen/buena deportista **(b)** *Fam (person)* **to be a (good) s.** *Esp* ser un(a) tío(a) grande, *Am* ser buena gente; **to be a bad s.** *(bad loser)* ser mal perdedor, *Esp* tener mal perder
2 *vt (wear)* lucir, llevar

sporting ['spɔːtɪŋ] *adj (related to sport, fair)* deportivo(a); **to give sb a s. chance** dar una oportunidad seria a alguien

sports [spɔːts] *adj* **s. car** coche *m or Am* carro *m or CSur* auto *m* deportivo; **s. center** polideportivo *m*; **s. facility** campo *m* de deportes; **s. lottery** quinielas *fpl*; *Journ* **s. page** página *f* de deportes; **s. store** tienda *f* de deportes

sportscast ['spɔːtskɑːst] *n* retransmisión *f* deportiva

sportsman ['spɔːtsmən] *n* deportista *m*

sportsmanlike ['spɔːtsmənlaɪk] *adj* deportivo(a)

sportsmanship ['spɔːtsmənʃɪp] *n* deportividad *f*

sportsperson ['spɔːtspɜːsən] *n* deportista *mf*

sportswoman ['spɔːtswʊmən] *n* deportista *f*

sport-utility vehicle ['spɔːtjuː'tɪlɪtɪ'viːɪkəl] *n* todoterreno *m*

spot [spɒt] **1** *n* **(a)** *(place)* lugar *m*, sitio *m*; *Fam* **to put sb on the s.** poner a alguien en un aprieto; *Fam* **to be in a (tight) s.** estar en un aprieto; **s. check** inspección *f* al azar; *Fin* **s. price** precio *m* al contado **(b)** *(stain)* mancha *f* **(c)** *(pimple)* grano *m* **(d)** *(on shirt, tie, leopard)* lunar *m* **(e)** *Theat (spotlight)* foco *m* **(f)** *TV & Rad (in schedule)* espacio *m*
2 *vt (pt & pp* **spotted***)* **(a)** *(stain, mark)* salpicar **(b)** *(notice) (person, object, mistake)* localizar, ver; **to s. sb doing sth** ver a alguien hacer algo

spotless ['spɒtlɪs] *adj also Fig* inmaculado(a)

spotlessly ['spɒtlɪslɪ] *adv* inmaculadamente

spotlight ['spɒtlaɪt] *n* foco *m*, reflector *m*; *Fig* **to be in the s.** estar en el candelero

spotter plane ['spɒtə'pleɪn] *n* avión *m* de reconocimiento

spotty ['spɒtɪ] *adj* **(a)** *(pimply)* con acné **(b)** *(patchy) (performance)* desigual

spouse [spaʊz] *n* cónyuge *mf*

spout [spaʊt] **1** *n* **(a)** *(of kettle)* pitorro *m* **(b)** *(jet of liquid)* chorro *m*
2 *vt (liquid)* chorrear; *Fam Fig (speech, nonsense)* soltar
3 *vi (liquid)* chorrear; *Fam Fig (person)* largar, enrollarse

sprain [spreɪn] **1** *n (injury)* torcedura *f*, esguince *m*
2 *vt* **to s. one's ankle/wrist** torcerse el tobillo/la muñeca

sprang [spræŋ] *pt of* **spring**

sprat [spræt] *n* **(a)** *(fish)* espadín *m* **(b)** *(insignificant person)* pelagatos *m inv*

sprawl [sprɔːl] *vi (person)* despatarrarse; *(city)* extenderse

sprawling ['sprɔːlɪŋ] *adj (person)* despatarrado(a); *(city)* desperdigado(a)

spray¹ [spreɪ] *n (of flowers)* ramo *m*

spray² **1** *n* (**a**) *(liquid)* rociada *f*; *(from sea)* rocío *m* del mar, roción *m* (**b**) *(act of spraying)* rociada *f*; **to give sth a s.** *(flowers, crops)* rociar algo; *(room)* rociar algo con ambientador (**c**) *(device)* aerosol *m*, spray *m*; *(for perfume)* atomizador *m*; **s. can** aerosol, spray; **s. gun** *(for paint)* pistola *f* (pulverizadora); **s. paint** pintura *f* en aerosol

2 *vt (liquid, room, crops)* rociar

spray-on ['spreɪɒn] *adj* en aerosol

spray-paint ['spreɪpeɪnt] *vt (with spray can)* pintar con aerosol; *(with spray gun)* pintar a pistola

spread [spred] **1** *n* (**a**) *(of wings, sails)* envergadura *f* (**b**) *(of products, ages)* gama *f* (**c**) *(of doctrine)* difusión *f*; *(of disease)* propagación *f* (**d**) *Fam (big meal)* banquete *m*, comilona *f* (**e**) *(in newspaper)* **a full-page s.** una plana entera; **a two-page s.** una página doble (**f**) *(paste)* **cheese s.** queso *m* para untar; **chocolate s.** crema *f* de cacao

2 *vt (pt & pp spread)* (**a**) *(extend)* **to s. one's arms/legs** extender los brazos/las piernas; *Fig* **to s. one's wings** emprender el vuelo (**b**) *(distribute)* *(sand, straw)* extender, esparcir; *(terror)* sembrar; *(disease)* propagar; *(news, lies)* difundir; **to s. work/payments over several months** distribuir el trabajo/los pagos a lo largo de varios meses (**c**) *(apply)* *(butter, ointment)* untar; **to s. a surface with sth** untar algo en una superficie

3 *vi (forest)* extenderse; *(news)* difundirse; *(disease)* propagarse

▸**spread out 1** *vt sep (map, newspaper)* desplegar, extender

2 *vi (person)* *(on floor, bed)* estirarse; *(search party)* desplegarse

spreadsheet ['spredʃiːt] *n Comptr* hoja *f* de cálculo

spree [spriː] *n Fam* **to go on a s.** *(go drinking)* ir de juerga; **to go on a shopping/spending s.** salir a comprar/gastar a lo loco

sprig [sprɪg] *n* ramita *f*

sprightly ['spraɪtlɪ] *adj* vivaz, vivaracho(a)

spring [sprɪŋ] **1** *n* (**a**) *(of water)* manantial *m* (**b**) *(season)* primavera *f*; **in (the) s.** en primavera; **s. onion** cebolleta *f*, *RP* cebolla *f* de verdeo; **s. roll** rollo *m* or rollito *m* de primavera, *RP* arrollado *m* or arrolladito *m* primavera; **s. tide** marea *f* viva *(de primavera)* (**c**) *(leap)* brinco *m*, salto *m* (**d**) *(elasticity)* elasticidad *f*; **he walked with a s. in his step** caminaba con paso alegre (**e**) *(device)* *(in watch)* resorte *m*; *(in car)* ballesta *f*; *(in mattress)* muelle *m*

2 *vt (pt sprang* [spræŋ] *or sprung* [sprʌŋ], *pp sprung)* (**a**) *(reveal unexpectedly)* **to s. sth on sb** soltarle algo a alguien (**b**) *(develop)* **to s. a leak** *(container)* empezar a tener una fuga; *(boat)* empezar a hacer agua (**c**) *Fam* **to s. sb out of jail** ayudar a alguien a escapar de la cárcel

3 *vi* (**a**) *(jump)* brincar, saltar; **to s. to one's feet** levantarse de un brinco; **to s. into action** entrar en acción; **to s. to sb's defense** lanzarse a la defensa de alguien; **the lid sprang open** la tapa se abrió de pronto; **to s. to mind** venir(se) a la cabeza (**b**) *(originate, come into being)* **to s. from** provenir de, proceder de; **to s. into existence** aparecer de pronto; *Fam* **where did you s. from?** ¿de dónde has salido?

▸**spring up** *vi* (**a**) *(jump to one's feet)* levantarse de un brinco (**b**) *(appear suddenly)* brotar, surgir (de la noche a la mañana)

springboard ['sprɪŋbɔːd] *n also Fig* trampolín *m*

spring-clean [sprɪŋ'kliːn] *vt (house)* limpiar a fondo

spring-cleaning [sprɪŋ'kliːnɪŋ] *n* limpieza *f* a fondo; **to do the s.** hacer una limpieza a fondo

springtime ['sprɪŋtaɪm] *n* primavera *f*

springy ['sprɪŋɪ] *adj (material)* elástico(a); *(ground, mattress)* mullido(a)

sprinkle ['sprɪŋkəl] *vt (with liquid)* rociar (**with** con); *(with salt, flour)* espolvorear (**with** con)

sprinkler ['sprɪŋklə(r)] *n (for lawns)* aspersor *m*; *(as fire prevention)* rociador *m* antiincendios

sprinkling ['sprɪŋklɪŋ] *n* pizca *f*, poco *m*; **there was a s. of new faces** había unas cuantas caras nuevas

sprint [sprɪnt] **1** *n (fast run)* carrera *f*; *(running race)* carrera *f* de velocidad

2 *vi (run fast)* correr a toda velocidad

sprinter ['sprɪntə(r)] *n* velocista *mf*, esprínter *mf*

sprocket ['sprɒkɪt] *n* diente *m* (de engranaje); **s. (wheel)** rueda *f* dentada

sprout [spraʊt] **1** *n (of plant)* brote *m*; **(Brussels) sprouts** coles *fpl* or *CSur* repollitos *mpl* de Bruselas

2 *vt Fam* **to s. a mustache/a beard** dejarse crecer el bigote/la barba; **he's starting to s. a beard** *(for first time)* le está saliendo barba

3 *vi (leaves, hair)* brotar

▸**sprout up** *vi (plant, child)* crecer rápidamente; *(new buildings, suburbs)* surgir (de la noche a la mañana)

spruce¹ [spruːs] *n (tree)* picea *f*

spruce² *adj (tidy)* pulcro(a); *(smart)* elegante

▸**spruce up** *vt sep (room)* adecentar; **to s. oneself up** arreglarse, acicalarse

sprung [sprʌŋ] **1** *adj* de muelles

2 *pp of* **spring**

spry [spraɪ] *adj* vivaz, vivaracho(a)

spun [spʌn] **1** *adj* **s. silk** hilado *m* de seda

2 *pp of* **spin**

spunk [spʌŋk] *n Fam (courage)* agallas *fpl*, arrestos *mpl*

spur [spɜː(r)] **1** *n* (**a**) *(for riding)* espuela *f*; *Fig (stimulus)* acicate *m*, incentivo *m*; *Fig* **he won his spurs** demostró su valía; **on the s. of the moment** sin pararse a pensar (**b**) *(of land, rock)* estribación *f*

2 *vt (pt & pp spurred)* *(horse)* espolear; *Fig* **to s. sb on (to do sth)** espolear a alguien (para que haga algo); *Fig* **to s. sb into action** hacer que alguien pase a la acción

spurious ['spjʊərɪəs] *adj* falso(a), espurio(a)

spurn [spɜːn] *vt* desdeñar

spurt [spɜːt] **1** *n (of liquid)* chorro *m*; *(of action, energy)* arranque *m*; *(of speed)* arrancada *f*; **to put on a s.** acelerar

2 *vt* lanzar chorros de

3 *vi (liquid)* chorrear

sputter ['spʌtə(r)] *vi (fire, flame, candle)* crepitar; *(motor)* pegar explosiones

spy [spaɪ] **1** *n* espía *mf*; **s. plane** avión *m* espía or de espionaje; **s. ring** red *f* de espionaje; **s. satellite** satélite *m* espía or de espionaje

2 *vt (notice)* ver; **she had spied a flaw in his reasoning** había captado un error en su razonamiento

3 *vi* espiar; **to s. on sb** espiar a alguien

▸**spy out** *vt sep* **to s. out the land** reconocer el terreno

Sq *(abbr* **Square***)* Pl., Plaza *f*

sq *Math (abbr* **square***)* cuadrado(a)

sq ft *(abbr* **square foot** *or* **feet***)* pie(s) *mpl* cuadrado(s)

squabble ['skwɒbəl] **1** *n* riña *f*, pelea *f*

2 *vi* reñir, pelear

squabbling ['skwɒblɪŋ] *n* riñas *fpl*, peleas *fpl*

squad [skwɒd] *n* (**a**) *(of workmen)* brigada *f*, cuadrilla *f* (**b**) *(of athletes, football players)* lista *f* de convocados; **the first-team s.** el primer equipo (**c**) *(of soldiers)* escuadra *f*; *(of police force)* brigada *f*; **s. car** coche *m* or *Am* carro *m* or *CSur* auto *m* patrulla

squadron ['skwɒdrən] *n Mil (of planes)* escuadrón *m*; *(of ships)* escuadra *f*

squalid ['skwɒlɪd] *adj (dirty)* mugriento(a), inmundo(a); *(sordid)* sórdido(a)

squall [skwɔːl] **1** *n (of wind)* turbión *m*, ventarrón *m*

2 *vi (cry)* berrear

squalor ['skwɒlə(r)] *n (dirtiness)* inmundicia *f; (poverty)* miseria *f*

squander ['skwɒndə(r)] *vt (money, time, talents)* despilfarrar, malgastar; *(opportunity)* desperdiciar

square [skweə(r)] **1** *n* (**a**) *(shape)* cuadrado *m; (on chessboard, checkerboard)* casilla *f; (on map)* recuadro *m; Fig* **to be back to s. one** haber vuelto al punto de partida (**b**) *Math* cuadrado *m* (**c**) *(of city, town)* plaza *f; (smaller)* plazoleta *f* (**d**) *Old-fashioned Fam (unfashionable)* carca *mf*
2 *adj* (**a**) *(in shape)* cuadrado(a); **s. bracket** corchete *m;* **s. dance** baile *m* de figuras *or* en cuadrilla (**b**) *(right-angled)* **s. corner** esquina *f* en ángulo recto (**c**) *Math (meter, centimeter)* cuadrado(a); **s. root** raíz *f* cuadrada (**d**) *Old-fashioned Fam (unfashionable)* carca (**e**) *(idioms)* **to be s. with sb** *(honest)* ser claro(a) con alguien; **that makes us s.** *(having settled debt)* estamos en paz; **she felt like a s. peg in a round hole** se sentía fuera de lugar; **a s. deal** un trato justo; **a s. meal** una buena comida
3 *adv* directamente; **she hit him s. on the jaw** le dio de lleno en la mandíbula
4 *vt* (**a**) *(make square)* cuadrar; *Math (number)* elevar al cuadrado; **squared paper** papel *m* cuadriculado (**b**) *(settle)* **to s. accounts with sb** arreglar cuentas con alguien; **how do you s. it with your convictions?** ¿cómo lo haces encajar con tus convicciones?
5 *vi (agree)* cuadrar, concordar
▸**square up** *vi* (**a**) *(settle debts)* hacer *or* saldar cuentas (**b**) *(fighters)* ponerse en guardia; *Fig* **to s. up to a problem/an opponent** hacer frente a un problema/un adversario

squarely ['skweəlɪ] *adv* (**a**) *(directly)* directamente (**b**) *(honestly)* con franqueza

squash¹ [skwɒʃ] **1** *n* (**a**) *(crush)* apretones *mpl* (**b**) *(sport)* squash *m;* **s. court** pista *f or* cancha *f* de squash
2 *vt* aplastar
▸**squash up** *vi* apretujarse, apretarse

squash² *n (vegetable)* calabacera *f,* cucurbitácea *f*

squat [skwɒt] **1** *adj (person)* chaparro(a), achaparrado(a); *(object, building)* muy bajo(a)
2 *vi (pt & pp* **squatted***)* (**a**) *(crouch down)* agacharse, ponerse de cuclillas (**b**) *(occupy dwelling illegally)* ocupar una vivienda ilegalmente

squatter ['skwɒtə(r)] *n* ocupante *mf* ilegal

squaw [skwɔ:] *n =* mujer india norteamericana

squawk [skwɔ:k] **1** *n (of bird)* graznido *m*
2 *vi (bird)* graznar; *Fam (person, baby)* chillar

squeak [skwi:k] **1** *n (of animal, person)* chillido *m; (of door, hinges)* chirrido *m; Fam* **I don't want to hear another s. out of you** no quiero oírte decir ni pío
2 *vi (animal, person)* chillar; *(door, wheel)* chirriar, rechinar; *(shoes)* crujir

squeaky ['skwi:kɪ] *adj (voice)* chillón(ona); *(door, wheel)* chirriante; *(shoes)* que crujen; **s. clean** *(person, image)* impoluto(a)

squeal [skwi:l] **1** *n* chillido *m*
2 *vt* chillar
3 *vi* (**a**) chillar; *Fam* **to s. about sth** *(complain)* quejarse de algo (**b**) *Fam (inform)* **to s. (on sb)** dar el soplo (sobre alguien)

squeamish ['skwi:mɪʃ] *adj* aprensivo(a), escrupuloso(a); **to be s. about sth** ser (muy) aprensivo(a) con algo; **I'm very s. about blood** la sangre me da mucha aprensión

squeeze [skwi:z] **1** *n* apretón *m,* apretujón *m;* **to give sb a s.** *(hug)* dar un achuchón a alguien; **a s. of lemon** un chorrito de limón; *Fam* **we all got in but it was a tight s.** cupimos todos, pero tuvimos que apretujarnos bastante; *Fam* **to put the s. on sb** *(pressurize)* apretarle las tuercas a alguien
2 *vt* (**a**) *(in general)* apretar; *(sponge)* estrujar; *(lemon)* exprimir; **to s. sb's hand** dar a alguien un apretón de manos; **to s. sth into a box** meter algo en una caja apretando; **I think we can just s. you in** creo que te podemos hacer un hueco (**b**) *Fig (put pressure on)* presionar

3 *vi* **to s. into a place** meterse a duras penas en un sitio; **s. up a bit!** ¡apretaos *or* correos un poco más!
▸**squeeze out** *vt sep (juice)* exprimir

squelch [skweltʃ] *vi* chapotear; **to s. through the mud** atravesar el lodo chapoteando

squib [skwɪb] *n (firework)* petardo *m*

squid [skwɪd] (*pl* **squid**) *n (animal)* calamar *m; (food)* calamares *mpl*

squiggle ['skwɪgəl] *n (scrawl, doodle)* garabato *m; (wavy line)* línea *f* serpenteante

squiggly ['skwɪglɪ] *adj* ondulante, serpenteante

squint [skwɪnt] **1** *n (eye defect)* **to have a s.** tener estrabismo, ser estrábico(a)
2 *vi* (**a**) *(have an eye defect)* tener estrabismo (**b**) *(narrow one's eyes)* entrecerrar *or* entornar los ojos; **to s. at sth/sb** *(look sideways)* mirar algo/a alguien de reojo

squire ['skwaɪə(r)] *n Hist* escudero *m*

squirm [skwɜ:m] *vi (wriggle)* retorcerse; *(with embarrassment)* ruborizarse, avergonzarse; *Am* apenarse

squirrel ['skwɪrəl] *n* ardilla *f*

squirt [skwɜ:t] **1** *n* (**a**) *(of liquid)* chorro *m* (**b**) *Fam (insignificant person)* mequetrefe *mf*
2 *vt (liquid)* lanzar un chorro de
3 *vi (liquid)* **to s. out** chorrear

squishy ['skwɪʃɪ] *adj (fruit, mess)* blando(a) y húmedo(a); *(sound)* de chapoteo

Sr *(abbr* **Senior***)* Thomas Smith, **Sr** Thomas Smith, padre

Sri Lanka [sri:'læŋkə] *n* Sri Lanka

Sri Lankan [sri:'læŋkən] *n & adj* esrilanqués(esa) *m,f*

SSE *(abbr* **south-southeast***)* SSE, sursudeste

SSW *(abbr* **south-southwest***)* SSO, sursudoeste

St (**a**) *(abbr* **Street***)* c/, calle *f* (**b**) *(abbr* **Saint***)* S., San *m,* Santa *f;* **St Kitts and Nevis** *(island group)* San Cristóbal y Nevis; **St Lucia** *(island)* Santa Lucía; **St Vincent and the Grenadines** *(island group)* San Vicente y las Granadinas; **St Petersburg** San Petersburgo

stab [stæb] **1** *n (with knife)* cuchillada *f,* puñalada *f; Fig (of pain, envy)* punzada *f; Fam* **to have a s. at sth/doing sth** intentar algo/hacer algo
2 *vt (pt & pp* **stabbed***) (with knife)* acuchillar, apuñalar; *(food)* pinchar, ensartar; **to s. sb to death** matar a alguien a puñaladas; *Fig* **to s. sb in the back** darle a alguien una puñalada por la espalda

stabbing ['stæbɪŋ] **1** *n (attack)* apuñalamiento *m*
2 *adj (pain)* punzante

stability [stə'bɪlɪtɪ] *n* estabilidad *f*

stabilize ['steɪbɪlaɪz] **1** *vt* estabilizar
2 *vi* estabilizarse

stabilizer ['steɪbɪlaɪzə(r)] *n (on bicycle)* estabiciclo *m,* estabilizador *m (para bicicleta infantil)*

stable¹ ['steɪbəl] **1** *n (for horses)* cuadra *f,* establo *m; Fig* **to lock the s. door after the horse has bolted** tomar medidas demasiado tarde
2 *vt (keep in stable)* guardar en cuadra

stable² *adj (marriage, job)* estable; *(person)* equilibrado(a); *(object, structure, instrument)* fijo(a), seguro(a); *(medical condition)* estacionario(a)

stack [stæk] **1** *n* (**a**) *(of wood, plates)* pila *f,* montón *m; (of hay)* almiar *m; Fam* **stacks of time/money** un montón de tiempo/dinero (**b**) *(chimney)* chimenea *f*
2 *vt (wood, plates)* apilar; **the odds were stacked against them** tenían todo en contra de ellos
▸**stack up 1** *vt sep* apilar
2 *vi* (**a**) *(mount up)* **the evidence was stacking up against him** se iban amontonando pruebas contra él (**b**) *(compare)* **our product stacks up well against theirs** nuestro producto compite a un buen nivel respecto del suyo

stadium ['steɪdɪəm] *n* estadio *m*

staff [stɑːf] **1** *n* (**a**) *(stick)* bastón *m*; *(of shepherd)* cayado *m* (**b**) *(personnel)* personal *m*, plantilla *f*; **teaching/nursing s.** personal docente/de enfermería; *Mil* **general s.** estado *m* mayor; *Med* **s. nurse** enfermero(a) *m,f* (**c**) *Mus* (*pl* **staffs** *or* **staves** [steɪvz]) pentagrama *m*

2 *vt* proveer de personal; **the office is staffed by volunteers** la oficina se nutre de personal voluntario; **the desk is staffed at all times** el mostrador está atendido en todo momento

staffer ['stæfə(r)] *n Fam* empleado(a) *m,f*

stag [stæg] *n (animal)* ciervo *m*; **s. beetle** ciervo *m* volante; **s. night** *or* **party** despedida *f* de soltero

stage [steɪdʒ] **1** *n* (**a**) *(platform)* *(in theater)* escenario *m*; *(more generally)* estrado *m*; **to go on the s.** hacerse actor *m*/actriz *f*; *Fig* **to set the s. for sth** preparar el terreno para algo; **s. designer** escenógrafo(a) *m,f*; **s. directions** acotaciones *fpl*; **s. door** entrada *f* de artistas; **s. fright** miedo *m* escénico; **s. manager** director(ora) *m,f* de escena, regidor(ora) *m,f*; **s. name** nombre *m* artístico; **s. whisper** aparte *m* (**b**) *(phase)* etapa *f*, fase *f*; **at this s. in…** en esta fase de…; **to do sth in stages** hacer algo por etapas; **s. (coach)** diligencia *f*

2 *vt (play)* llevar a escena, representar; *Fig (demonstration, invasion)* llevar a cabo

stagehand ['steɪdʒhænd] *n Theat* tramoyista *mf*, sacasillas *mf inv*

stage-manage ['steɪdʒ'mænɪdʒ] *vt Theat* dirigir; *Fig (event, demonstration)* orquestar

stagestruck ['steɪdʒstrʌk] *adj Theat* **to be s.** estar enamorado(a) de las tablas

stagflation [stæg'fleɪʃən] *n Econ* estanflación *f*

stagger ['stægə(r)] **1** *vt* (**a**) *(astound)* dejar anonadado(a) (**b**) *(work, vacations)* escalonar

2 *vi (stumble)* tambalearse; **to s. along** ir tambaleándose; **to s. to one's feet** levantarse tambaleándose

stagnant ['stægnənt] *adj* estancado(a)

stagnate [stæg'neɪt] *vi* estancarse

stagnation [stæg'neɪʃən] *n* estancamiento *m*

staid [steɪd] *adj* formal, estirado(a)

stain [steɪn] **1** *n (mark)* mancha *f*; *(dye)* tinte *m*; **stained glass** vidrio *m* de colores; **s. remover** quitamanchas *m inv*

2 *vt (mark)* manchar; *(dye)* teñir

-stained [-steɪnd] *suffix* **nicotine/sweat-s.** manchado(a) de nicotina/sudor

stained-glass ['steɪndɡlɑːs] *adj* **s. window** vidriera *f*

stainless steel ['steɪnlɪs'stiːl] *n* acero *m* inoxidable

stair ['steə(r)] *n (single step)* escalón *m*, peldaño *m*; **s.(s)** escalera(s) *fpl*

staircase ['steəkeɪs] *n* escalera *f*

stake [steɪk] **1** *n* (**a**) *(piece of wood, metal)* estaca *f*; *(for plant)* guía *f*, rodrigón *m*; **to be burned at the s.** morir quemado(a) en la hoguera (**b**) *(bet)* apuesta *f*; **to be at s.** estar en juego (**c**) *(share)* **to have a s. in sth** *(interest)* tener intereses en algo; *(shareholding)* tener una participación (accionarial) en algo

2 *vt* (**a**) *(bet) (money)* apostar (**on** a); *Fig (one's reputation, job)* jugarse (**on** en); **I'd s. my life on it** pondría la mano en el fuego por ello (**b**) **to s. a claim (to sth)** reivindicar el derecho (a algo)

stakeholder ['steɪkhəʊldə(r)] *n* parte *f* interesada, partícipe *mf*

stakeout ['steɪkaʊt] *n* **to be on s.** montar vigilancia

stalactite ['stæləktaɪt] *n* estalactita *f*

stalagmite ['stæləgmaɪt] *n* estalagmita *f*

stale [steɪl] *adj* (**a**) *(bread)* revenido(a), pasado(a); *(air)* viciado(a); *(smell)* rancio(a) (**b**) *(ideas, jokes)* manido(a); *(social life, relationship)* anquilosado(a); **to get s.** *(person)* anquilosarse

stalemate ['steɪlmeɪt] *n (in chess, negotiations)* tablas *fpl*; **to reach a s.** llegar a un punto muerto

stalk¹ [stɔːk] **1** *vt (track)* seguir con sigilo; *(obsessively)* acechar

2 *vi (walk angrily)* **she stalked out of the room** salió *esp Esp* enfadada *or esp Am* enojada de la habitación

stalk² *n (of plant, flower)* tallo *m*; *(of fruit)* rabo *m*

stalker ['stɔːkə(r)] *n* = persona que sigue o vigila obsesivamente a otra

stall [stɔːl] **1** *n* (**a**) *(in stable)* casilla *f* (**b**) *(in market)* puesto *m*

2 *vt (hold off)* retener

3 *vi* (**a**) *(car)* pararse, *Esp* calarse; *Fig (campaign)* estancarse, quedarse estancado(a) (**b**) *(delay)* demorarse; **to s. (for time)** (intentar) ganar tiempo

stalling ['stɔːlɪŋ] *n* evasivas *fpl*, rodeos *mpl*; **s. tactics** tácticas *fpl* dilatorias

stallion ['stælɪən] *n* (caballo *m*) semental *m*

stalwart ['stɔːlwət] **1** *n* incondicional *mf*

2 *adj* enérgico(a)

stamen ['steɪmən] *n Bot* estambre *m*

stamina ['stæmɪnə] *n* resistencia *f*, aguante *m*

stammer ['stæmə(r)] **1** *n* tartamudeo *m*

2 *vt* balbucir

3 *vi* tartamudear

▶**stammer out** *vt insep* balbucir, farfullar

stamp [stæmp] **1** *n (on letter, mark)* sello *m*, *Am* estampilla *f*, *CAm, Méx* timbre *m*; *(device)* tampón *m*; *(on legal documents)* póliza *f*, timbre *m*; *Fig* **to bear the s. of genius** tener el sello *or* la marca inconfundible del genio; *Fig* **s. of approval** aprobación *f*, beneplácito *m*; **s. album** álbum *m* de sellos; **s. collector** coleccionista *mf* de sellos; *Fin* **s. duty** *or* **tax** póliza *f*, = impuesto de transmisiones patrimoniales; **s. machine** máquina *f* expendedora de sellos

2 *vt* (**a**) *(put mark on)* estampar; **a stamped addressed envelope** un sobre franqueado y con el domicilio (**b**) **to s. one's foot** patear

3 *vi* **to s. upstairs** subir ruidosamente las escaleras; **he stamped off in a rage** se marchó *esp Esp* enfadado *or esp Am* enojado

▶**stamp out** *vt sep (resistance, dissent)* acabar *or* terminar con

stampede [stæm'piːd] **1** *n* estampida *f*, desbandada *f*; **there was a s. for the door** hubo una desbandada hacia la puerta

2 *vt* lanzar en estampida

3 *vi* salir de estampida

stance [stæns] *n (physical position, view)* postura *f*

stand [stænd] **1** *n* (**a**) *(view)* postura *f*; **to take a s.** adoptar una postura (**b**) *(of lamp)* soporte *m*; *(for books, postcards)* expositor *m* (**c**) *(stall) (in open air)* puesto *m*, tenderete *m*; *(at exhibition)* stand *m*, puesto *m*; **newspaper s.** quiosco *m* (de periódicos) (**d**) *(grandstand)* **s.(s)** gradas *fpl*, *Esp* graderío *m* (**e**) *(witness box)* estrado *m*; **to take the s.** subir al estrado (**f**) *(taxi line)* parada *f* de taxis

2 *vt (pt & pp* **stood** [stʊd]*)* (**a**) *(place)* colocar; **he stood the ladder against the wall** apoyó la escalera contra la pared (**b**) *(endure)* soportar; **he can't s. her** no la soporta; **to s. comparison with** poder compararse con; **to s. one's ground** mantenerse firme (**c**) *(pay for)* **to s. sb a drink** invitar a alguien a una copa (**d**) *(have)* **to s. a chance (of doing sth)** tener posibilidades (de hacer algo); **he doesn't s. a chance!** ¡no tiene ninguna posibilidad! (**e**) *Law* **to s. trial** ser procesado(a)

3 *vi* (**a**) *(person) (get up)* ponerse de pie, levantarse, *Am* pararse; *(be upright)* estar de pie *or Am* parado(a); *(remain upright)* quedarse de pie *or Am* parado(a); **to s. on one's head** hacer el pino; **I could hardly s.** casi no me tenía en pie; **don't just s. there!** ¡no te quedes ahí parado(a)!; **to s. fast** *or* **firm** mantenerse firme; **to s. still** *(person)* quedarse quieto(a); *(time)* detenerse (**b**) *(building)* estar situado(a) *or* ubicado(a); *(object)* estar colocado(a)

(**c**) *(be in situation)* **the debt/inflation stands at…** la deuda/la inflación asciende a *or* se sitúa en…; **to s. in need of…** tener necesidad de…; **you s. in danger of getting killed** corres el peligro de que te maten; **you s. to lose/gain $5,000** puedes perder/ganar 5.000 dólares; **it stands to reason that…** se cae por su propio peso que…

(**d**) *(remain motionless) (liquid)* reposar

(**e**) *(idioms)* **we're standing right behind you** estamos de tu lado; **to s. on one's own two feet** ser autosuficiente; **I don't know where I s.** no sé a qué atenerme; **to know how things s.** saber cómo están las cosas; **I s. corrected** corrijo lo dicho; **the offer still stands** la oferta sigue en pie

▸**stand aside** *vi (move aside)* hacerse a un lado

▸**stand back** *vi (move away)* alejarse (**from** de)

▸**stand by 1** *vt insep* (**a**) *(friend)* apoyar (**b**) *(promise, prediction)* mantener

2 *vi* (**a**) *(be ready)* estar preparado(a) (**for** para) (**b**) *(not get involved)* mantenerse al margen, quedarse sin hacer nada

▸**stand down** *vi* (**a**) *(retire)* retirarse (**b**) *(leave witness box)* bajar del estrado

▸**stand for** *vt insep* (**a**) *(mean)* significar, querer decir; *(represent)* representar (**b**) *(tolerate)* aguantar, soportar

▸**stand out** *vi* (**a**) *(be prominent)* destacar; *Fam* **it stands out a mile!** ¡se nota *or* se ve a la legua! (**b**) **to s. out against sth** *(oppose)* oponerse a algo

▸**stand up 1** *vt sep Fam* **to s. sb up** *(on date)* dar plantón a alguien

2 *vi* (**a**) *(get up)* levantarse, ponerse de pie, *Am* pararse; *(be upright)* estar de pie; *(remain upright)* quedarse de pie *or Am* parado(a); *Fig* **to s. up for sth/sb** defender algo/a alguien; *Fig* **to s. up to sb** hacer frente a alguien (**b**) *(argument, theory)* sostenerse; **it'll never s. up in court** eso no serviría como prueba en un juicio

stand-alone ['stændələʊn] *adj Comptr* independiente, autónomo(a)

standard ['stændəd] **1** *n* (**a**) *(for weight, measurement)* norma *f*; *(to judge performance, success)* criterio *m*, patrón *m*; *Fin* **gold/dollar s.** patrón *m* oro/dólar (**b**) *(required level)* nivel *m*; **to be up to/below s.** estar al nivel/por debajo del nivel exigido; **to have high/low standards** *(at work)* ser muy/poco exigente; *(morally)* tener muchos/pocos principios; **s. of living** nivel *m* de vida (**c**) *(flag)* estandarte *m*

2 *adj* (**a**) *(length, width, measure)* estándar; *Math* **s. deviation** desviación *f* típica *or* estándar; **s. size** tamaño *m* estándar *or* normal (**b**) *(usual)* habitual; **headrests are fitted as s.** los reposacabezas vienen con el equipamiento de serie; **S. English** inglés *m* normativo; **it is s. practice** es la práctica habitual; **s. time** hora *f* oficial

standard-bearer ['stændədbeərə(r)] *n also Fig* abanderado(a) *m,f*

standardization [stændədaɪ'zeɪʃən] *n* normalización *f*, estandarización *f*

standardize ['stændədaɪz] *vt* normalizar, estandarizar

standby ['stændbaɪ] *n* (**a**) *(money, fuel, food)* reserva *f*; **to have sth as a s.** tener algo de reserva; **to be on s.** *(troops, emergency services)* estar en alerta (**b**) *(for air travel)* **to be on s.** estar en lista de espera; **s. passenger** pasajero(a) *m,f* en lista de espera; **s. ticket** billete *m or Am* boleto *m* de lista de espera

stand-in ['stændɪn] *n* suplente *mf*, sustituto(a) *m,f*

standing ['stændɪŋ] **1** *n* (**a**) *(position, status)* posición *f*, reputación *f* (**b**) **friends of long s.** amigos de hace mucho tiempo; **an agreement of long s.** un acuerdo que viene de lejos

2 *adj* (**a**) *(upright)* vertical, derecho(a); **s. ovation** ovación *f* cerrada (del público puesto) en pie; **s. room only** *(on train)* sólo pasajeros de pie (**b**) *(permanent)* permanente; **s. army**

ejército *m* permanente; **you have a s. invitation** estás invitado a venir cuando quieras; **it's a s. joke in the office** es una de las bromas de siempre en la oficina; **s. charges** *(on bill)* tarifa *f* fija

stand-off ['stændɒf] *n* (**a**) *(deadlock)* punto *m* muerto (**b**) *Sport (tie)* empate *m*

standoffish [stænd'ɒfɪʃ] *adj Fam* distante

standpoint ['stændpɔɪnt] *n* punto *m* de vista

standstill ['stændstɪl] *n* **to be at a s.** estar detenido(a); **to come to a s.** pararse, detenerse; **to bring sth to a s.** paralizar algo

stand-up ['stændʌp] **1** *n (comedy)* = humorismo que consiste en salir solo al escenario con un micrófono y contar chistes

2 *adj* (**a**) *(comedian)* de micrófono, = que basa su actuación en contar chistes al público solo desde el escenario (**b**) *(passionate)* **a s. argument** una violenta discusión; **a s. fight** una batalla campal, una pelea salvaje (**c**) *(decent, honest)* decente

stank [stæŋk] *pt of* **stink**

stanza ['stænzə] *n* estrofa *f*

staple¹ ['steɪpəl] **1** *n* grapa *f*, *Chile* corchete *m*, *RP* ganchito *m*; **s. gun** grapadora *f or Am* engrapadora *f or Chile* corchetera *f or RP* abrochadora *f* industrial

2 *vt* grapar, *Am* engrapar, *Chile* corchetear, *RP* abrochar

staple² *n (basic food)* alimento *m* básico; *Fig* **such stories are a s. of the tabloid press** esas historias son el pan de cada día en la prensa amarilla

stapler ['steɪplə(r)] *n* grapadora *f*, *Am* engrapadora *f*, *Chile* corchetera *f*, *RP* abrochadora *f*

star [stɑ:(r)] **1** *n* (**a**) *(heavenly body, famous person)* estrella *f*; **the Stars and Stripes** la bandera americana; **to reach for the stars** *(aspire)* apuntar al cielo; **to see stars** *(after blow to head)* ver las estrellas; **movie** *or* **film s.** estrella de cine; **s. fruit** carambola *f (fruto)*; **s. player** estrella *f or* figura *f* del equipo; **s. sign** signo *m* del zodiaco; **s. turn** atracción *f* principal, actuación *f* estelar (**b**) *Fam* **stars** *(horoscope)* horóscopo *m*

2 *vt (pt & pp* **starred***) (actor)* estar protagonizado(a) por

3 *vi* **to s. in a movie** protagonizar una película

starboard ['stɑ:bəd] *n Naut* estribor *m*

starch [stɑ:tʃ] **1** *n (for shirts)* almidón *m*; *(in food)* fécula *f*

2 *vt (shirt)* almidonar

starchy ['stɑ:tʃɪ] *adj* (**a**) *(food)* feculento(a) (**b**) *Fam (person, manner)* estirado(a), rígido(a)

stardom ['stɑ:dəm] *n* estrellato *m*

stare [steə(r)] **1** *n* mirada *f* fija

2 *vt* **the answer was staring me in the face** tenía la solución delante de las narices

3 *vi* **to s. (at sth/sb)** mirar fijamente (algo/a alguien); **to s. into the distance** mirar al vacío; **it's rude to s.** es de mala educación quedarse mirando (con descaro)

starfish ['stɑ:fɪʃ] *n* estrella *f* de mar

staring ['steərɪŋ] *adj* **he had s. eyes** tenía la mirada fija

stark [stɑ:k] **1** *adj (contrast)* claro(a); *(light, colors)* frío(a); *(truth, facts)* crudo(a); *(landscape)* desolado(a)

2 *adv* **s. naked** completamente desnudo(a); **s. raving mad** completamente loco(a)

starkly ['stɑ:klɪ] *adv* claramente, inequívocamente

starlet ['stɑ:lɪt] *n (young actress)* actriz *f* incipiente

starlight ['stɑ:laɪt] *n* luz *f* de las estrellas

starling ['stɑ:lɪŋ] *n* estornino *m*

starlit ['stɑ:lɪt] *adj* iluminado(a) por las estrellas

starry ['stɑ:rɪ] *adj* estrellado(a)

starry-eyed [stɑ:rɪ'aɪd] *adj* cándido(a), idealista; *(lovers)* embelesado(a), embobado(a)

start [stɑ:t] **1** *n* (**a**) *(beginning)* principio *m*, comienzo *m*; *(starting place, of race)* salida *f*; **for a s.** para empezar; **at the s.** al principio; **at the s. of the month** a principios de mes; **from the s.** desde el principio; **from s. to finish** de principio a fin; **to make a s. on sth** empezar con algo; **he lent her $500 to give her a s.** le prestó 500 dólares para ayudarla a empezar; **to give sb a 60 meter(s) s.** *(in race)* dar a alguien una ventaja de 60 metros **(b)** *(sudden movement)* susto *m*, sobresalto *m*; **to wake with a s.** despertarse sobresaltado(a); **to give sb a s.** *(frighten)* sobresaltar a alguien, dar un susto a alguien

2 *vt* **(a)** *(begin)* empezar, comenzar; *(conversation, talks)* entablar, iniciar; *(fashion, rumor)* promover, poner en circulación; *(fire)* ocasionar, provocar; *(business)* montar; **to s. school** empezar el colegio; **to s. doing sth, to s. to do sth** ponerse *or* empezar a hacer algo; **it's just started raining** acaba de ponerse *or* empezar a llover; **to get started** empezar **(b)** *(cause to start)* *(machine, engine, car)* arrancar, poner en marcha

3 *vi* **(a)** *(begin)* empezar, comenzar; **to s. at the beginning** empezar por el principio; **to s. by doing sth** comenzar haciendo algo; **she had started as a doctor** había comenzado trabajando como médica; **to s. with** para empezar; **to s. on sth** empezar algo; **now don't YOU s.!** ¡no empieces!, ¡no empecemos! **(b)** *(be frightened)* sobresaltarse; **to s. awake** despertarse sobresaltado(a) **(c)** *(begin journey)* salir, partir **(d)** *(car, engine)* arrancar

▶**start off 1** *vt sep (argument, debate)* suscitar, provocar; **to s. sb off** *(in business)* dar un primer empujón a alguien; *(on a subject)* dar cuerda a alguien

2 *vi (begin)* empezar, comenzar; *(on journey)* salir; **to s. off by doing sth** comenzar haciendo algo

▶**start out** *vi (begin)* empezar; *(on journey)* salir, partir

▶**start up 1** *vt sep (car, machine)* arrancar, poner en marcha; *(business)* montar, poner

2 *vi (engine)* arrancar, ponerse en marcha; **to s. up in business** poner *or* montar un negocio

starter ['stɑ:tə(r)] *n* **(a)** *Sport (competitor)* competidor(ora) *m,f*; *(official)* juez *mf* de salida **(b) to be a late s.** *(child)* llevar retraso *or Am* demora (en el aprendizaje); **to be a slow s.** tardar *or Am* demorar en ponerse en marcha **(c)** *(device)* motor *m* de arranque **(d) for starters** *(for a start)* para empezar

starting ['stɑ:tɪŋ] *n Sport* **s. block** tacos *mpl or* puesto *m* de salida; *Sport* **s. line** línea *f* de salida; *Sport* **s. pistol** *(gun)* pistola *f* para dar la salida; **s. point** *or* **place** punto *m* de partida; **s. price** *(in betting)* precio *m* de las apuestas a la salida; **s. salary** salario *m or* sueldo *m* inicial

startle ['stɑ:təl] *vt* sobresaltar

startled ['stɑ:təld] *adj (look, cry)* de sobresalto; **to look/ seem s.** parecer sobresaltado(a)

startling ['stɑ:tlɪŋ] *adj (noise)* que sobresalta; *(news, event)* sorprendente

start-up ['stɑ:tʌp] *n Com* puesta *f* en marcha; **s. costs** gastos *mpl* de puesta en marcha

starvation [stɑ:'veɪʃən] *n* inanición *f*; **to die of s.** morir de inanición; **s. diet** dieta *f* miserable; **s. wages** salario *m* mísero

starve [stɑ:v] **1** *vt* privar de alimentos; **to s. sb to death** matar a alguien de inanición; *Fig* **to be starved of sth** estar privado(a) de algo

2 *vi (lack food)* pasar mucha hambre; **to s. (to death)** morir de inanición; *Fam* **I'm starving** me muero de hambre

starving ['stɑ:vɪŋ] *adj* famélico(a), hambriento(a)

stash [stæʃ] *Fam* **1** *n* alijo *m*

2 *vt (hide)* poner a buen recaudo

state [steɪt] **1** *n* **(a)** *(condition, situation)* estado *m*; **I am not in a fit s. to travel** no estoy en condiciones de viajar; **a s. of emergency** estado de emergencia; **s. of health** estado *m* de salud; **s. of mind** estado *m* anímico; **in a s. of terror** aterrorizado(a); **in a s. of shock** en estado de shock; **to be in a terrible s.** estar en un estado terrible; **to lie in s.** *(before funeral)* yacer en la capilla ardiente; **the S. of the Union Address** el discurso sobre el estado de la nación

(b) *(country, administrative region)* estado *m*; *Fam* **the States** *(the USA)* (los) Estados Unidos; **s. control** control *m* estatal; *Pol* **S. Department** Departamento *m* de Estado, = Ministerio de Asuntos *or Am* Relaciones Exteriores estadounidense; **s. highway** ≃ carretera *f* nacional; **s. occasions** ceremonias *fpl* de gala; **states' rights** = derechos de los que goza cada estado de Estados Unidos; **s. secret** secreto *m* de Estado; **s. sector** sector *m* público; **s. visit** viaje *m* oficial *or* de Estado

2 *vt (declare)* declarar; *(one's name and address)* indicar; *(reasons, demands, objections)* exponer; **to s. the obvious** decir una obviedad; **as stated earlier/above** como se hizo constar antes/más arriba

stated ['steɪtɪd] *adj (intentions)* expreso(a); *(purpose, amount)* indicado(a); *(date, time, price)* fijado(a)

Statehouse ['steɪthaʊs] *n* Congreso *m* *(de un estado)*

stateless ['steɪtlɪs] *adj* apátrida

stately ['steɪtlɪ] *adj* imponente, majestuoso(a); **s. home** casa *f* solariega

statement ['steɪtmənt] *n (of opinion)* declaración *f*; *(from bank)* extracto *m* (bancario); **a s. of the facts** una exposición de los hechos; **to make a s.** *(spokesperson)* hacer una declaración; *(witness)* prestar declaración; *Fig (lifestyle, behavior)* decir algo de sí mismo(a)

state-of-the-art [steɪtəvðɪ'ɑ:t] *adj* de vanguardia; **s. technology** tecnología *f* punta

state-owned ['steɪt'əʊnd] *adj* público(a), estatal

state-run ['steɪtrʌn] *adj* estatal

statesman ['steɪtsmən] *n* estadista *m*, hombre *m* de Estado

statesmanlike ['steɪtsmənlaɪk] *adj (behavior, speech)* digno(a) de un gran hombre de Estado; **he's not very s.** le falta la gravedad propia de un hombre de Estado

static ['stætɪk] **1** *n (electricity)* electricidad *f* estática; *(on radio, TV)* interferencias *fpl*

2 *adj* estático(a); **s. electricity** electricidad *f* estática

station ['steɪʃən] **1** *n* **(a)** *(for trains, buses)* estación *f*; **s. wagon** *(car)* ranchera *f* **(b)** *(post)* puesto *m*; **(police) s.** comisaría *f* (de policía); **(radio) s.** emisora *f* (de radio); **(television) s.** canal *m* (de televisión); **s. house** *(of police)* comisaría *f* (of firemen) parque *m* de bomberos **(c)** *(social condition)* posición *f*; **to have ideas above one's s.** tener demasiadas aspiraciones

2 *vt (person)* colocar; *(soldier, troops)* apostar

stationary ['steɪʃənərɪ] *adj (not moving)* inmóvil; **to remain s.** permanecer inmóvil

stationer ['steɪʃənə(r)] *n* **s.'s (store)** papelería *f*

stationery ['steɪʃənərɪ] *n (writing materials)* artículos *mpl* de papelería; *(writing paper)* papel *m* de carta

stationmaster ['steɪʃənmɑ:stə(r)] *n* jefe *m* de estación

statistic [stə'tɪstɪk] *n* estadística *f*, dato *m* estadístico; **statistics** *(facts)* estadísticas *fpl*; *(science)* estadística *f*

statistical [stə'tɪstɪkəl] *adj* estadístico(a)

statistically [stə'tɪstɪklɪ] *adv* estadísticamente

statistician [stætɪs'tɪʃən] *n* estadístico(a) *m,f*

stats [stæts] *npl Fam* estadísticas *fpl*

statue ['stætju:] *n* estatua *f*

statuesque [stætjʊ'esk] *adj* escultural

statuette [stætjʊ'et] *n* estatuilla *f*

stature ['stætʃə(r)] *n (physical build)* estatura *f*; *(reputation)* talla *f*, estatura *f*

status ['steɪtəs] *n (in society, profession)* categoría *f*, posición *f*; *(prestige)* categoría *f*, prestigio *m*; *Law* estado *m*; *Comptr* **s. line** línea *f* de estado; **'s. report** informe *m* de la situación; **s. symbol** señal *f* de prestigio

status quo ['steɪtəs'kwəʊ] *n* statu quo *m*

statute ['stætju:t] *n* estatuto *m*; **by s.** por ley; **s. book** legislación *f*, código *m* de leyes

statutory ['stætjʊtərɪ] *adj* legal, reglamentario(a); **s. duty**

obligación *f* legal; *Law* **s. rape** relaciones *fpl* sexuales con un(a) menor

staunch¹ [stɔ:ntʃ] *adj (resolute)* fiel, leal

staunch² *vt (blood)* cortar; *(wound)* restañar

staunchly ['stɔ:ntʃlɪ] *adv* firmemente, fielmente

stave [steɪv] *n* (**a**) *(of barrel)* duela *f* (**b**) *Mus* pentagrama *m*

▶**stave in** *(pt & pp* **staved** *or* **stove** [stəʊv]) *vt sep* romper, quebrar

▶**stave off** *vt sep (problem, disaster)* aplazar, retrasar; **to s. off one's hunger** espantar el hambre

staves [steɪvz] *pl of* **staff**

stay [steɪ] **1** *n* (**a**) *(visit) Esp, Méx* estancia *f, Am* estadía *f* (**b**) *Law* **s. of execution** aplazamiento *m* de sentencia

2 *vt (endure)* **to s. the course** *or* **distance** aguantar hasta el final

3 *vi* (**a**) *(not move, remain)* permanecer, quedarse; **s. where you are!** ¡no te muevas de donde estás!; *Fam* **to s. put** no moverse; **to s. still** quedarse quieto(a); **it looks like cell phones are here to s.** parece que los teléfonos móviles no son una moda pasajera; **I can't s. long** no puedo quedarme mucho tiempo (**b**) *(reside temporarily)* quedarse; **I'm staying at a hotel** estoy (alojado) en un hotel; **to s. with sb** estar (alojado) en casa de alguien

▶**stay away** *vi* mantenerse alejado(a) (**from** de)

▶**stay in** *vi (not go out)* quedarse en casa

▶**stay on** *vi (remain longer)* quedarse

▶**stay out** *vi* (**a**) *(stay outside)* quedarse *or* permanecer fuera; **to s. out all night** estar fuera toda la noche (**b**) *(not interfere)* **to s. out of sth** mantenerse al margen de algo; **s out of this!** ¡no te metas en esto!

▶**stay up** *vi (not go to bed)* quedarse levantado(a)

staying power ['steɪɪŋ'paʊə(r)] *n* resistencia *f*

STD [esti:'di:] *n* *(abbr* **sexually transmitted disease)** enfermedad *f* de transmisión sexual

stead [sted] *n* **it will stand you in good s.** te será de gran utilidad; **in sb's s.** en lugar de alguien

steadfast ['stedfɑ:st] *adj* firme

Steadicam® ['stedɪkæm] *n Cin* steadycam® *f*

steadily ['stedɪlɪ] *adv (change, grow)* constantemente; *(work)* a buen ritmo; *(walk)* con paso firme; *(look)* fijamente; *(breathe)* con regularidad

steady ['stedɪ] **1** *adj* (**a**) *(stable)* firme, estable; **in a s. voice** con voz tranquila (**b**) *(regular) (rate, growth, pace)* constante; *(progress)* continuo(a); *(income)* regular; *(pulse)* constante, regular; **s. girlfriend/boyfriend** novia *f*/novio *m* estable; **to have a s. job** tener un trabajo fijo; **to drive at a s. 55 mph** conducir a una velocidad constante de 55 millas por hora

2 *adv* **they are going s.** son novios formales; **s.!** ¡tranquilo!

3 *vt* estabilizar, afianzar; **to s. oneself** *(physically)* afianzarse; *(mentally)* reunir fuerzas; **to s. one's nerves** tranquilizarse

steak [steɪk] *n (beef)* filete *m*, bistec *m, RP* bife *m; (of fish)* filete *m*; **s. house** parrilla *f, RP* churrasquería *f*

steal [sti:l] *(pt* **stole** [stəʊl], *pp* **stolen** ['stəʊlən]) **1** *vt* (**a**) robar; **to s. sth from sb** robar algo a alguien (**b**) *(idioms)* **to s. a glance at sb** dirigir una mirada furtiva a alguien; **to s. the show** acaparar toda la atención

2 *vi* (**a**) *(rob)* robar (**b**) *(move quietly)* **to s. away/in/out** alejarse/entrar/salir furtivamente; **to s. up on sb** acercarse furtivamente a alguien; **middle age steals up on you** cuando te quieres dar cuenta, eres una persona de mediana edad

stealth [stelθ] *n* sigilo *m*; **s. bomber** avión *m or* bombardero *m* invisible; **s. tax** impuesto *m* oculto

stealthily ['stelθɪlɪ] *adv* subrepticiamente, furtivamente

stealthy ['stelθɪ] *adj* subrepticio(a), furtivo(a)

steam [sti:m] **1** *n* (**a**) vapor *m*; *(on window, mirror)* vaho *m*; **s.**

bath baño *m* de vapor; **s. engine** máquina *f* de vapor; **s. iron** plancha *f* de vapor; **s. shovel** excavadora *f* (**b**) *(idioms)* **to run out of s.** *(lose momentum)* perder fuelle; **to let off s.** desfogarse; **she did it under her own s.** lo hizo por sus propios medios

2 *vt Culin* cocinar al vapor; **to s. open an envelope** abrir un sobre exponiéndolo al vapor

3 *vi (give off steam)* despedir vapor

▶**steam up 1** *vt sep* **to get all steamed up (about sth)** *(person)* acalorarse

2 *vi (window, glasses)* empañarse

steamer ['sti:mə(r)] *n* (**a**) *(ship)* barco *m* de vapor (**b**) *Culin (pot)* olla *f* para cocinar al vapor

steamroller ['sti:mrəʊlə(r)] **1** *n Constr* apisonadora *f*

2 *vt* **to s. sb into doing sth** forzar a alguien a hacer algo

steamship ['sti:mʃɪp] *n* barco *m* de vapor

steamy ['sti:mɪ] *adj* (**a**) *(room)* lleno(a) de vapor (**b**) *Fam (novel, movie)* erótico(a)

steel [sti:l] **1** *n* acero *m*; **nerves of s.** nervios *mpl* de acero; **the s. industry** la industria del acero; **s. band** *(musical)* = grupo de percusión caribeño que utiliza bidones de metal; **s. mill** fundición *f* de acero; **s. wool** estropajo *m* de acero

2 *vt* **to s. oneself to do sth** armarse de valor para hacer algo; **to s. oneself against sth** armarse de valor para enfrentarse con algo

steelworker ['sti:lwɜ:kə(r)] *n* trabajador(ora) *m,f* del acero

steelworks ['sti:lwɜ:ks] *n* acería *f*

steep¹ [sti:p] *adj* (**a**) *(path, hill, climb)* empinado(a); *(rise, fall)* pronunciado(a) (**b**) *Fam (expensive)* abusivo(a)

steep² *vt (clothes)* dejar en remojo; *(food)* macerar; **to be steeped in history** rezumar historia

steeple ['sti:pəl] *n (of church)* torre *f*

steeplechase ['sti:pəltʃeɪs] *n Sport* carrera *f* de obstáculos

steeplejack ['sti:pəldʒæk] *n* = persona que arregla torres y chimeneas

steer¹ [stɪə(r)] **1** *vt (car)* conducir, *Am* manejar; *(ship)* gobernar; **to s. sb out of trouble** sacar a alguien de un aprieto

2 *vi (person)* conducir, *Am* manejar; *(ship, car)* manejarse; **to s. for sth** llevar rumbo a algo; **to s. clear of sth/sb** evitar algo/a alguien

steer² *n (bull)* buey *m*

steering ['stɪərɪŋ] *n (mechanism)* dirección *f; Aut* **s. column** columna *f* de dirección; *Pol* **s. committee** comisión *f* directiva; *Aut* **s. wheel** volante *m, Andes* timón *m*

stem [stem] **1** *n (of plant)* tallo *m; (of glass)* pie *m; (of tobacco pipe)* tubo *m; (of word)* raíz *f; Biol* **s. cell** célula *f* madre

2 *vt (pt & pp* **stemmed)** *(halt)* contener

3 *vi* **to s. from** derivarse de

stench [stentʃ] *n* pestilencia *f*

stencil ['stensəl] **1** *n* (**a**) *Art* plantilla *f* (**b**) *(for typing)* cliché *m*, clisé *m*

2 *vt* estarcir

stenographer [stə'nɒɡrəfə(r)] *n* taquígrafo(a) *m,f*

step [step] **1** *n* (**a**) *(movement, sound)* paso *m*; **to take a s.** dar un paso; **at every s.** a cada paso; **s. by s.** paso a paso; *also Fig* **to watch one's s.** mirar dónde se pone el pie; **every s. of the way** en todo momento; **to keep (in) s.** *(in dance)* seguir el ritmo; *Fig* **to be out of s. (with sth)** no estar en consonancia (con algo)

(**b**) *(action, measure)* medida *f*; **to take steps (to do sth)** tomar medidas (para hacer algo); **the next s. is to...** el siguiente paso es...; **a s. in the right direction** un avance, un adelanto

(**c**) *(of staircase)* escalón *m*, peldaño *m; (of stepladder)* peldaño *m; (on outside of building)* escalón *m;* **(flight of) steps** (tramo *m* de) escalera *f* (**d**) *(exercise)* **s. (aerobics)** step *m*, aerobic *m* con escalón; **s. class** clase *f* de step

(**e**) *Mus* tono *m*

2 *vi (pt & pp stepped) (take a step)* dar un paso; *(walk)* caminar; **to s. on sb's foot** pisarle un pie a alguien; **s. this way** pasa por aquí; *Fam* **to s. on it** *(hurry up)* aligerar, darse prisa, *Am* apurarse

▸**step back** *vi* **to s. back from a situation** dar un paso atrás para considerar una situación objetivamente

▸**step forward** *vi (volunteer)* presentarse, ofrecerse

▸**step in** *vi (referee, government)* intervenir

▸**step up** *vt sep (production, pace)* aumentar

stepbrother ['stepbrʌðə(r)] *n* hermanastro *m*

step-by-step ['stepbaɪ'step] *adj (guide, explanation)* paso a paso; *(approach)* progresivo(a), gradual

stepchild ['steptʃaɪld] *n* hijastro(a) *m,f*

stepdaughter ['stepdɔ:tə(r)] *n* hijastra *f*

stepfather ['stepfɑ:ðə(r)] *n* padrastro *m*

stepladder ['steplædə(r)] *n* escalera *f* de tijera

stepmother ['stepmʌðə(r)] *n* madrastra *f*

stepparent ['steppeərənt] *n (man)* padrastro *m*; *(woman)* madrastra *f*; **stepparents** padrastros *mpl*

steppe [step] *n* estepa *f*

stepsister ['stepsɪstə(r)] *n* hermanastra *f*

stepson ['stepsʌn] *n* hijastro *m*

stereo ['steriəʊ] **1** *n (pl stereos) (equipment)* equipo *m* de música; *(sound)* estéreo *m*, sonido *m* estereofónico; **in s.** en estéreo

2 *adj* estéreo, estereofónico(a)

stereophonic [steriə'fɒnɪk] *adj* estereofónico(a)

stereoscopic [steriəʊ'skɒpɪk] *adj (vision)* estereoscópico(a)

stereotype ['steriətaɪp] **1** *n* estereotipo *m*

2 *vt* estereotipar

stereotyped ['steriətaɪpt] *adj* estereotipado(a)

stereotypical [steriə'tɪpɪkəl] *adj* estereotipado(a)

sterile ['steraɪl] *adj* estéril

sterility [stə'rɪlɪti] *n* esterilidad *f*

sterilization [sterɪlaɪ'zeɪʃən] *n* esterilización *f*

sterilize ['sterɪlaɪz] *vt* esterilizar

sterilized ['sterəlaɪzd] *adj (germ-free)* esterilizado(a)

sterling ['stɜ:lɪŋ] **1** *n (British currency)* libra *f* esterlina

2 *adj* (**a**) *(silver)* de ley (**b**) *(effort, quality)* admirable, excelente

stern[1] [stɜ:n] *adj (person, look)* severo(a); **we are made of sterner stuff** somos más duros de pelar de lo que parece

stern[2] *n Naut* popa *f*

sternum ['stɜ:nəm] *n Anat* esternón *m*

steroid ['stɪərɔɪd] *n* esteroide *m*

stethoscope ['steθəskəʊp] *n Med* fonendoscopio *m*, estetoscopio *m*

stevedore ['sti:vədɔ:(r)] *n* estibador *m*

stew [stju:] **1** *n Culin* guiso *m*; *Fam Fig* **to be in a s.** *(person)* estar hecho(a) un manojo de nervios

2 *vt (meat)* guisar, cocer; *(fruit)* cocer para compota

3 *vi (meat)* guisarse, cocer; *Fam* **to let sb s. (in his own juice)** dejar a alguien que sufra

steward ['stjʊəd] *n (on estate)* administrador *m*; *(on plane)* auxiliar *m* de vuelo; *(on ship)* camarero *m*; *(at concert, demonstration)* auxiliar *mf* de la organización; *(in athletics)* juez *mf*

stewardess [stjʊə'des] *n (on plane)* auxiliar *f* de vuelo, azafata *f*, *Am* aeromoza *f*; *(on ship)* camarera *f*

stewed [stju:d] *adj* **s. beef** carne *f* de vaca guisada; **s. fruit** compota *f*

stick[1] [stɪk] *n* (**a**) *(of wood)* palo *m*; *(for walking)* bastón *m*; *(of chewing gum, glue, deodorant)* barra *f*; *(of dynamite)* cartucho *m*; *(of celery, rhubarb)* tallo *m*, rama *f*; *Fam Fig* **to get hold of the**

wrong end of the s. coger el rábano por las hojas; *Fam* **he lives out in the sticks** vive en el quinto infierno *or Esp* pino; **s. insect** insecto *m* palo (**b**) *Aut* **s. shift** *(system)* palanca *f* de cambio manual

stick[2] *(pt & pp stuck* [stʌk]) **1** *vt* (**a**) *(insert)* **to s. sth in(to) sth** clavar algo en algo (**b**) *Fam (put)* poner; **s. your things over there** pon tus bártulos por ahí (**c**) *(attach with glue)* pegar (**on** a)

2 *vi* (**a**) *(adhere)* pegarse; **the name stuck** el nombre tuvo éxito, se quedó con el nombre; *Fig* **to s. to one's guns** mantenerse en sus trece; **to s. to the facts** atenerse a los hechos; **she stuck to her principles** fue fiel a sus principios (**b**) *(become jammed)* atascarse; **it sticks in my throat** se me atraganta

▸**stick around** *vi Fam* quedarse

▸**stick at** *vt insep (persevere with)* perseverar en; **to s. at nothing** no reparar en nada

▸**stick by** *vt insep (friend)* apoyar; *(promise, statement)* mantener

▸**stick out 1** *vt sep* (**a**) *(cause to protrude)* sacar; **she stuck her tongue out at me** me sacó la lengua; *Fam* **to s. one's neck out** arriesgar el pellejo (**b**) *Fam (endure)* **to s. it out** aguantar

2 *vi* (**a**) *(protrude)* sobresalir (**b**) *Fam (be noticeable)* verse a la legua, *Esp* cantar; **it sticks out a mile** se ve a la legua; **it sticks out like a sore thumb** se ve a la legua, *Esp* canta un montón

▸**stick together 1** *vt sep* pegar

2 *vi* (**a**) *(with glue)* pegarse (**b**) *(friends)* apoyarse

▸**stick up 1** *vt sep (sign, poster)* pegar; *Fam* **s. 'em up!** ¡manos arriba!

2 *vi (point upward) (building)* sobresalir; **her hair sticks up** tiene el pelo de punta

▸**stick up for** *vt insep (person, rights)* defender

▸**stick with** *vt insep (not give up)* seguir con

sticker ['stɪkə(r)] *n (with information, price)* etiqueta *f*; *(with slogan, picture)* pegatina *f*; **s. price** precio *m* de catálogo

stickiness ['stɪkɪnɪs] *n (of material)* pegajosidad *f*; *(of weather)* bochorno *m*

sticking point ['stɪkɪŋ'pɔɪnt] *n* escollo *m*

stick-in-the-mud ['stɪkɪnðəmʌd] *n Fam* carroza *mf*

stickleback ['stɪkəlbæk] *n* espinoso *m* (de agua dulce)

stickler ['stɪklə(r)] *n* **to be a s. for sth** ser un/una maniático(a) de algo

stick-on ['stɪkɒn] *adj* adhesivo(a)

stickup ['stɪkʌp] *n Fam (robbery)* atraco *m* (a mano armada)

sticky ['stɪki] *adj* (**a**) *(substance)* pegajoso(a); *(climate, weather)* bochornoso(a); *(label)* adhesivo(a) (**b**) *Fam (awkward)* problemático(a); **to come to a s. end** tener un final sangriento

stiff [stɪf] *adj* (**a**) *(rigid)* tieso(a), rígido(a); *(paste)* consistente; **as s. as a board** tieso(a) como un palo; **to be bored/scared/frozen s.** estar muerto(a) de aburrimiento/miedo/frío (**b**) *(joint)* agarrotado(a), anquilosado(a); **to be s.** *(person)* tener agujetas; **to have a s. neck** tener tortícolis (**c**) *(handle, hinge, drawer)* duro(a) (**d**) *(severe) (fine, competition, prison sentence)* duro(a); *(exam, test)* difícil; *(breeze, drink)* fuerte; **s. resistance** gran resistencia *f* (**e**) *(formal) (person, manner)* rígido(a), estirado(a); *(smile)* forzado(a)

stiffen ['stɪfən] **1** *vt (fabric, paper)* aprestar, endurecer; *(paste)* espesar; *(resolve, resistance)* reforzar

2 *vi (limb, joint, person)* agarrotarse; *(opposition)* endurecerse

stiffly ['stɪfli] *adv (to bow)* con rigidez; *(to answer, greet)* forzadamente

stifle ['staɪfəl] *vt (person)* ahogar, asfixiar; *(cries, yawn)* ahogar, reprimir; *(rebellion)* sofocar

stifling ['staɪflɪŋ] *adj* sofocante, asfixiante

stigma ['stɪgmə] *n (disgrace)* estigma *m*, deshonra *f*

stigmata [stɪg'mɑːtə] *npl (of saint)* estigmas *mpl*

stigmatize ['stɪgmətaɪz] *vt* estigmatizar

stile [staɪl] *n (in fence, hedge)* escalones *mpl*

stiletto [stɪ'letəʊ] *(pl* **stilettos***) n (dagger)* estilete *m; (shoe)* zapato *m* de tacón *or Am* taco de aguja; **s. heels** tacones *mpl or Am* tacos *mpl* de aguja

still¹ [stɪl] **1** *n* (**a**) **in the s. of the night** en el silencio de la noche (**b**) *Cin* fotograma *m*
   2 *adj (motionless)* quieto(a); *(calm)* sereno(a); *(silent)* silencioso(a); *(orange juice)* natural; *(mineral water)* sin gas; *Art* **s. life** bodegón *m*, naturaleza *f* muerta; *Prov* **s. waters run deep** tras una fachada silenciosa se ocultan fuertes emociones
   3 *adv* **to be/stand s.** estar quieto(a)
   4 *vt (person)* calmar, tranquilizar; **to s. sb's fears** ahuyentar los temores de alguien

still² *adv* (**a**) *(up to given point in time)* todavía, aún, *Am* siempre; **I s. think/say that...** sigo creyendo/diciendo que...; **I s. have $50** aún me quedan 50 dólares (**b**) *(even)* todavía, aún; **s. more/better** aún más/mejor (**c**) *(nonetheless)* de todas formas, aún así

still³ *n (distilling equipment)* alambique *m*

stillbirth ['stɪlbɜːθ] *n* nacimiento *m* de un niño muerto

stillborn ['stɪlbɔːn] *adj* **the child was s.** el niño nació muerto

stillness ['stɪlnɪs] *n* calma *f*, quietud *f*

stilt [stɪlt] *n (for walking)* zanco *m; (for building)* poste *m*, pilote *m*

stilted ['stɪltɪd] *adj (style, manner)* forzado(a)

Stilton ['stɪltən] *n* **S. (cheese)** queso *m* Stilton

stimulant ['stɪmjʊlənt] *n* estimulante *m*

stimulate ['stɪmjʊleɪt] *vt (person, mind, appetite)* estimular; *(enthusiasm, interest)* suscitar

stimulating ['stɪmjʊleɪtɪŋ] *adj* estimulante

stimulation [stɪmjʊ'leɪʃən] *n (action)* estimulación *f; (result)* estímulo *m*

stimulus ['stɪmjʊləs] *(pl* **stimuli** ['stɪmjʊlaɪ]*) n* estímulo *m*

sting [stɪŋ] **1** *n* (**a**) *(of bee, scorpion) (organ)* aguijón *m; (wound)* picadura *f; Fig* **to take the s. out of sth** hacer algo menos traumático(a) (**b**) *(sensation)* escozor *m*
   2 *vt (pt & pp* **stung** [stʌŋ]*) (of bee)* picar; *(of nettle)* pinchar; *Fig (of remark)* herir; *Fig* **to s. sb into action** espolear a alguien para que pase a la acción; *Fam Fig* **they stung him for $10** le clavaron 10 dólares
   3 *vi (eyes, skin)* escocer

stinging ['stɪŋɪŋ] *adj (pain)* punzante; *(remark, criticism)* hiriente, despiadado(a); **s. nettle** ortiga *f*

stingray ['stɪŋreɪ] *n* pastinaca *f (pez)*

stingy ['stɪndʒɪ] *adj (person)* tacaño(a), rácano(a); *(portion)* raquítico(a); **to be s. with food/praise** ser tacaño(a) con la comida/los elogios

stink ['stɪŋk] **1** *n (smell)* peste *f*, hedor *m; Fig* **to raise** *or* **make** *or* **kick up a s. (about sth)** montar un escándalo (por algo)
   2 *vi (pt* **stank** [stæŋk] *or* **stunk** [stʌŋk], *pp* **stunk**) apestar (**of** a); *Fam Fig* **this movie stinks!** ¡esta película no vale un pimiento *or Am* nada!; *Fam Fig* **to s. of corruption** apestar a corrupción

stinkbomb ['stɪŋkbɒm] *n* bomba *f* fétida

stinker ['stɪŋkə(r)] *n Fam (person)* mamón(ona) *m,f, Méx* mamila *mf, RP* choto(a) *m,f;* **to be a real s.** *(movie, question, exam)* ser muy *Esp* chungo(a) *or Am* feo(a)

stinking ['stɪŋkɪŋ] **1** *adj* apestoso(a)
   2 *adv Fam* **to be s. drunk** estar como una cuba; **to be s. rich** estar podrido(a) de dinero, *Méx* tener un chorro de lana

stint [stɪnt] **1** *n (period)* período *m;* **to take a s. at the wheel** tomar el relevo al volante; **he had a two-year s. in the army** sirvió por un período de dos años en el ejército
   2 *vt* escatimar; **to s. oneself** privarse de algunas cosas *(en beneficio de otras personas)*
   3 *vi* **to s. on sth** escatimar algo

stipend ['staɪpend] *n Rel & Univ* estipendio *m*

stipulate ['stɪpjʊleɪt] *vt* estipular

stipulation [stɪpjʊ'leɪʃən] *n* estipulación *f*

stir [stɜː(r)] **1** *n* (**a**) *(action)* **to give sth a s.** remover *or* revolver algo (**b**) *(excitement)* **to cause a s.** causar (un gran) revuelo
   2 *vt (pt & pp* **stirred**) (**a**) *(liquid, mixture)* remover, revolver; *(leaves)* agitar; *Fam* **s. yourself!** ¡muévete! (**b**) *(move emotionally) (person)* conmover, emocionar (**c**) *(arouse) (emotion)* provocar; *(curiosity)* despertar; **to s. sb to do sth** mover a alguien a hacer algo
   3 *vi (move)* moverse

▸**stir up** *vt sep* (**a**) *(dust, leaves)* levantar (**b**) *(incite) (rebellion, dissent, anger)* provocar; *(workers, crowd)* agitar; **to s. things up** soliviantar los ánimos

stir-fry ['stɜːfraɪ] *Culin* **1** *n* = salteado de (carne y) verduras típico de la cocina china
   2 *vt* saltear, rehogar a fuego vivo

stirring ['stɜːrɪŋ] **1** *n* **the first stirrings of...** los primeros indicios de...
   2 *adj (speech, movie)* emotivo(a), emocionante

stirrup ['stɪrəp] *n* estribo *m*

stitch [stɪtʃ] **1** *n* (**a**) *(in sewing)* puntada *f; (in knitting)* punto *m; Med* punto *m* (de sutura); *Fam* **she didn't have a s. on** estaba en cueros *or* en pelotas; *Prov* **a s. in time saves nine** una puntada a tiempo ahorra ciento (**b**) *(sharp pain)* **to have a s.** tener flato (**c**) *Fam* **we were in stitches** *(laughing)* nos partíamos (de risa)
   2 *vt (clothing)* coser; *Med* suturar, coser

stoat [stəʊt] *n* armiño *m*

stock [stɒk] **1** *n* (**a**) *(supply)* reservas *fpl; Com* existencias *fpl;* **the red ones are out of s.** los rojos están agotados; **the red ones are in s.** nos quedan rojos en almacén; *Fig* **to take s.** hacer balance; *Com* **s. control** control *m* de existencias; *Com* **s. list** inventario *m*
      (**b**) *(livestock)* ganado *m*
      (**c**) *Fin (share)* valor *m; (total share value)* capital *m* en) acciones *fpl;* **stocks and shares** valores *mpl; Fig* **her s. is going up/down** está ganando/perdiendo crédito; **s. certificate** título *m* de acción; **s. exchange** bolsa *f* (de valores); **s. market** mercado *m* de valores; **s. options** opciones *fpl* sobre acciones
      (**d**) *(descent)* ascendencia *f*, origen *m;* **she's of German s.** es de origen alemán
      (**e**) *(of rifle)* culata *f*
      (**f**) **stocks** *(for punishment)* picota *f*
      (**g**) *(in cooking)* caldo *m*
      (**h**) **s. car** *(for racing)* stock-car *m*, = automóvil adaptado para carreras en pista de tierra con muchos choques
   2 *adj (argument, excuse)* tópico(a)
   3 *vt* (**a**) *(have in stock) (goods)* tener (existencias de) (**b**) *(supply) (store)* surtir (**with** de), abastecer (**with** de); **the store is well stocked** la tienda está bien surtida

▸**stock up** *vi* aprovisionarse (**with** de)

stockade [stɒ'keɪd] *n* empalizada *f*

stockbroker ['stɒkbrəʊkə(r)] *n Fin* corredor(ora) *m,f* de Bolsa

stockholder ['stɒkhəʊldə(r)] *n Fin* accionista *mf*

Stockholm ['stɒkhəʊm] *n* Estocolmo

stocking ['stɒkɪŋ] *n* media *f*

stockpile ['stɒkpaɪl] **1** *n* reservas *fpl*
   2 *vt* acumular, hacer acopio de

stockroom ['stɒkruːm] *n* almacén *m*

stock-still ['stɒk'stɪl] *adv* **to stand s.** quedarse inmóvil

stocktaking ['stɒkteɪkɪŋ] *n Com* inventario *m* (de existencias); *Fig* **a s. exercise** un balance provisional

stocky ['stɒkɪ] *adj* chaparro(a)

stodgy ['stɒdʒɪ] *adj (food, book, person)* pesado(a)

stoic ['stəʊɪk] n estoico(a) m,f
stoical ['stəʊɪkəl] adj estoico(a)
stoically ['stəʊɪklɪ] adv estoicamente
stoicism ['stəʊɪsɪzəm] n estoicismo m
stoke [stəʊk] vt (add fuel to) alimentar
STOL [stɒl] n Av (abbr **short takeoff and landing**) despegue m or Am decolaje m y aterrizaje rápido or en corto
stole[1] [stəʊl] n (garment) estola f
stole[2] pt of **steal**
stolen ['stəʊlən] **1** adj (car, property) robado(a)
  2 pp of **steal**
stolid ['stɒlɪd] adj imperturbable
stomach ['stʌmək] **1** n estómago m; **on an empty s.** con el estómago vacío; Fig **it turns my s.** me revuelve el estómago; Fig **to have no s. for sth** no tener estómago para algo; **to have (a) s. ache** tener dolor de estómago; Med **s. pump** sonda f gástrica
  2 vt (tolerate) soportar
stomp [stɒmp] vi dar fuertes pisadas; **to s. in/out** entrar/salir airadamente
stone [stəʊn] **1** n (**a**) (material, piece of rock) piedra f; (on grave) lápida f; Fig **to leave no s. unturned** remover Roma con Santiago; Fig **a s.'s throw from here** a un tiro de piedra (de aquí); **the S. Age** la Edad de Piedra (**b**) (of fruit) hueso m, RP carozo m
  2 adj de piedra
  3 vt (**a**) (fruit) deshuesar (**b**) (person) apedrear; **he was stoned to death** murió lapidado
stone-cold ['stəʊn'kəʊld] adj helado(a)
stoned [stəʊnd] adj Fam (on drugs) colocado(a); **to be s.** estar colocado(a)
stone-dead ['stəʊn'ded] adj Fam **to be s.** estar tieso(a) or seco(a); **to kill sb s.** dejar a alguien tieso(a) or seco(a)
stone-deaf ['stəʊn'def] adj Fam sordo(a) como una tapia; **to be s.** estar sordo(a) como una tapia
stonemason ['stəʊnmeɪsən] n cantero(a) m,f (que labra la piedra)
stonewall ['stəʊn'wɔːl] vi (in inquiry) entorpecer, andarse con evasivas
stoneware ['stəʊnweə(r)] n (cerámica f de) gres m
stonework ['stəʊnwɜːk] n obra f de cantería
stonily ['stəʊnɪlɪ] adv con frialdad, insensiblemente
stony ['stəʊnɪ] adj (ground, beach) pedregoso(a); Fig (look, silence) glacial
stony-faced ['stəʊnɪ'feɪst] adj impertérrito(a), impasible
stood [stʊd] pt & pp of **stand**
stooge [stuːdʒ] n (comedian's fall-guy) comparsa mf; (minion) títere m, secuaz mf
stool [stuːl] n (**a**) (seat) banqueta f; (with short legs) taburete m; Fig **to fall between two stools** quedarse nadando entre dos aguas; Fam **s. pigeon** soplón(ona) m,f (**b**) Med (feces) heces fpl
stoop[1] [stuːp] **1** n **to have a s.** ser cargado(a) de espaldas; **to walk with a s.** caminar encorvado(a)
  2 vi (bend down) agacharse, agachar el cuerpo; Fig **to s. to (doing) sth** rebajarse a (hacer) algo; **I never thought they'd s. so low as to...** nunca pensé que caerían tan bajo como para...
stoop[2] n (porch) porche m
stop [stɒp] **1** n (**a**) (halt) parada f; **to put a s. to sth** poner fin a algo; **to come to a s.** detenerse; Aut **s. sign** (señal f de) stop m (**b**) (pause) (in work, journey) parada f; (of plane) escala f; **to make a s.** parar, detenerse; **ten minutes' s.** una parada de diez minutos (**c**) (stopping place) parada f (**d**) (in telegram) stop m (**e**) Mus (on organ) registro m; Fig **to pull out all the stops** tocar todos los registros
  2 vt (pt & pp **stopped**) (**a**) (halt) (person, vehicle) parar, detener; (conversation) interrumpir; (corruption, abuse) poner

fin a; (check) bloquear; **s., thief!** ¡al ladrón! (**b**) (cease) parar; **to s. doing sth** dejar de hacer algo; **to s. smoking/drinking** dejar de fumar/de beber (**c**) (prevent) impedir; **to s. sb (from) doing sth** impedir que alguien haga algo; **I couldn't s. myself** no podía parar (**d**) (fill in) (hole, gap) taponar
  3 vi (**a**) (halt) (moving person, vehicle) parar(se), detenerse (**b**) (cease) (speaker, worker) parar; **the rain has stopped** ha dejado de llover; **the pain has stopped** ya no me duele; **she did not s. at that** no se contentó con eso; **he'll s. at nothing** no se detendrá ante nada; **to s. short** or **dead** pararse en seco (**c**) (stay) quedarse
▸**stop by** vi (visit briefly) pasarse; **I'll s. by at your place tomorrow** me pasaré mañana por tu casa
▸**stop off** vi (stay briefly) parar, hacer una parada
▸**stop over** vi Av hacer escala
▸**stop up** vt sep (hole) taponar, tapar; (sink, pipe) atascar
stopcock ['stɒpkɒk] n llave f de paso
stopgap ['stɒpgæp] n (thing) recambio m, repuesto m (provisional); (person) sustituto(a) m,f (temporal); **s. measure** medida f provisional
stoplight ['stɒplaɪt] n Aut semáforo m
stopover ['stɒpəʊvə(r)] n Av escala f
stoppage ['stɒpɪdʒ] n (of flow, traffic) retención f, detención f; (of work) interrupción f; (as protest) paro m
stopper ['stɒpə(r)] n tapón m
stopwatch ['stɒpwɒtʃ] n cronómetro m
storage ['stɔːrɪdʒ] n almacenamiento m, almacenaje m; **in s.** en almacén; **to put sth into s.** almacenar algo; **s. charges** gastos mpl de almacenaje; **s. space** sitio m or espacio m para guardar cosas; **s. tank** depósito m
store [stɔː(r)] **1** n (**a**) (supply) (of goods) reserva f, provisión f; Fig (of knowledge) caudal m, cúmulo m; **stores** (supplies) reservas fpl (**b**) (warehouse) almacén m (**c**) (business) tienda f; **s. card** tarjeta f de compra (a crédito); **s. detective** vigilante m de paisano (de establecimiento comercial) (**d**) (idioms) **to hold** or **keep sth in s.** tener algo guardado(a) or reservado(a); **I have a surprise in s. for her** le tengo reservada or guardada una sorpresa; **to set** or **lay great s. by sth** dar mucha importancia a algo
  2 vt (put in storage) almacenar; (electricity, heat) acumular; (keep) guardar; **s. in a cool place** consérvese en lugar fresco
▸**store up** vt sep acumular
storehouse ['stɔːhaʊs] n almacén m
storekeeper ['stɔːkiːpə(r)] n tendero(a) m,f
storeroom ['stɔːruːm] n (in office, factory) almacén m; (at home) trastero m
stork [stɔːk] n cigüeña f
storm [stɔːm] **1** n (**a**) (bad weather) tormenta f; **s. clouds** nubes fpl de tormenta; **s. door** doble puerta f, contrapuerta f; **s. window** contraventana f (**b**) (scandal) tormenta f; (of insults, protest) aluvión m (**c**) Mil **to take a town/a fortress by s.** tomar una ciudad/una fortaleza por asalto; Fig **he took the audience by s.** tuvo un éxito arrasador entre el público; **s. troops** tropas fpl de asalto
  2 vt (town, fortress) asaltar
  3 vi (person) enfurecerse; **to s. at sb** echar la bronca a alguien; **to s. in/out** salir/entrar airadamente
stormy ['stɔːmɪ] adj also Fig tormentoso(a)
story[1] ['stɔːrɪ] n (**a**) (account) (fictional) cuento m; (factual) historia f; Fig **to tell stories** (lie) contar cuentos (**b**) (plot) (of novel, play) argumento m; **s. line** argumento m (in newspaper) artículo m (**d**) (idioms) **that is quite another s.** eso ya es otra cosa; **it's the same old s.** es la historia de siempre; Fam **it's the s. of my life!** ¡siempre me pasa lo mismo!; **it's a long s.** es muy largo de contar; **to cut a long s. short, ...** para resumir, ...

story² ['stɔːrɪ] (*pl* **stories**) *n* piso *m*, planta *f*; **a four-s. building** un edificio de cuatro plantas

storybook ['stɔːrɪbʊk] *n* libro *m* de cuentos

storyteller ['stɔːrɪtelə(r)] *n* narrador(ora) *m,f*

stout [staʊt] **1** *n* (*beer*) cerveza *f* negra

2 *adj* (**a**) (*fat*) (*person*) rechoncho(a) (**b**) (*solid*) (*door, shoes*) resistente (**c**) (*brave*) (*person, resistance*) valeroso(a)

stouthearted [staʊt'hɑːtɪd] *adj Literary* denodado(a), valeroso(a)

stoutly ['staʊtlɪ] *adv* (*resist*) denodadamente; (*maintain*) a toda costa

stove¹ [staʊv] *n* (*for cooking*) cocina *f*, *Col, Méx, Ven* estufa *f*; (*for heating*) estufa *f*

stove² *pt & pp of* **stave**

stow [staʊ] *vt* (*put away*) guardar; *Naut* estibar

➤**stow away** *vi* (*on ship*) ir or viajar de polizón

stowaway ['staʊəweɪ] *n* polizón *m*

straddle ['strædəl] *vt* sentarse a horcajadas en

strafe [streɪf] *vt Mil* ametrallar desde el aire

straggle ['strægəl] *vi* (*lag behind*) rezagarse; (*spread untidily*) desparramarse

straggler ['stræglə(r)] *n* rezagado(a) *m,f*

straggly ['stræglɪ] *adj* (*hair*) desordenado(a)

straight [streɪt] **1** *n* (**a**) **to keep to the s. and narrow** seguir por el buen camino (**b**) (*in horse race*) recta *f*

2 *adj* (**a**) (*not curved*) (*line, back*) recto(a); (*hair*) liso(a); (*tie, skirt, picture*) derecho(a); **to keep a s. face** contener la sonrisa; **to put things** or **matters s.** aclarar las cosas; **to put sb s.** aclararle las cosas a alguien

(**b**) (*consecutive*) consecutivo(a); **three s. wins** tres victorias consecutivas; **s. flush** (*in cards*) escalera *f* de color

(**c**) (*honest*) (*person, answer*) franco(a); **to be s. with sb** ser franco(a) con alguien

(**d**) (*conventional*) convencional; *Theat* **s. man** actor *m* (con papel) serio

(**e**) *Fam* (*heterosexual*) heterosexual

(**f**) (*undiluted*) solo(a); **to drink s. vodkas** beber vodka a palo seco

3 *adv* (**a**) (*in straight line*) recto, en línea recta; **sit up s.!** ¡siéntate derecho!; **to look s. ahead** mirar hacia adelante; **go s. on** sigue todo recto or derecho; **to see/think s.** ver/pensar con claridad; *Fig* **to go s.** (*criminal*) reformarse (**b**) (*immediately*) inmediatamente, en seguida; **s. away** or **off** inmediatamente (**c**) (*directly*) directamente; **to cut s. through sth** atravesar algo; **to come** or **get s. to the point** ir directamente al grano; **to come s. out with sth** decir algo sin rodeos

straightaway ['streɪtəweɪ] *adv* inmediatamente, *Méx* ahorita, *Andes, CSur* al tiro

straighten ['streɪtən] *vt* (*bent nail, rod*) enderezar; (*picture, tie*) poner derecho(a); **to s. one's back** enderezar la espalda

➤**straighten out** *vt sep* (*problem*) resolver; (*one's affairs*) poner en orden

straight-faced ['streɪt'feɪst] *adj* con la cara seria

straightforward [streɪt'fɔːwəd] *adj* (*honest*) franco(a); (*simple*) sencillo(a)

straightforwardly [streɪt'fɔːwədlɪ] *adv* (*honestly*) con franqueza, claramente; (*simply*) de forma sencilla, con sencillez

strain¹ [streɪn] **1** *n* (**a**) (*on rope, beam*) (*from pressure, pushing*) presión *f*; (*from tension, pulling*) tensión *f*; (*on economy*) tensión *f*; (*on friendship*) tirantez *f*; (*of muscle*) distensión *f*; (*of ankle*) torcedura *f*; **to put a s. on** (*economy, friendship*) crear tensiones en (**b**) (*mental stress*) agobio *m*; **to be under a lot of s.** estar muy agobiado(a)

2 *vt* (**a**) (*put strain on*) (*rope*) tensar; (*economy, friendship*) crear tensiones en; **to s. a muscle** distenderse un músculo; **to s. one's ankle** torcerse el tobillo; **to s. one's back** hacerse daño en la espalda; **to s. one's ears** aguzar el oído (**b**) *Culin* (*liquid*) colar; (*vegetables*) escurrir

3 *vi* **to s. at a rope/door** tirar de una cuerda/puerta; *Fig* **to be straining at the leash (to do sth)** estar impaciente (por hacer algo)

strain² *n* (*variety*) (*of virus*) cepa *f*; (*of plant*) variedad *f*; **a s. of madness** (*streak*) un toque de locura; **in the same s.** en la misma línea

strained [streɪnd] *adj* (*muscle*) distendido(a); (*atmosphere, conversation, relations*) tenso(a), tirante

strainer ['streɪnə(r)] *n* colador *m*

strait [streɪt] *n* estrecho *m*; **the Straits of Florida/ Gibraltar** el estrecho de Florida/Gibraltar; *Fig* **to be in dire** or **desperate straits** estar en serios aprietos

straitlaced ['streɪt'leɪst] *adj* mojigato(a)

strand¹ [strænd] *vt* (*ship*) varar; **to be stranded** quedar varado(a)

strand² *n* (*of rope*) cabo *m*; (*of cotton*) hebra *f*; (*of hair*) pequeño mechón *m*; *Fig* (*of plot*) hilo *m* (argumental)

strange [streɪndʒ] *adj* (**a**) (*odd*) (*person, behavior*) raro(a), extraño(a); **it felt s. to be back in Canada** se hacía raro estar de nuevo en Canadá (**b**) (*unfamiliar*) (*person, place*) desconocido(a), extraño(a)

strangely ['streɪndʒlɪ] *adv* (*behave, dress*) de modo extraño; **s. familiar** extrañamente familiar; **s. enough,...** aunque parezca raro or extraño,...

strangeness ['streɪndʒnɪs] *n* (**a**) (*oddness*) rareza *f* (**b**) (*unfamiliarity*) lo desconocido

stranger ['streɪndʒə(r)] *n* (*unknown person*) desconocido(a) *m,f*, extraño(a) *m,f*; (*person from other place*) forastero(a) *m,f*

strangle ['stræŋgəl] *vt* (*person, economy*) estrangular

stranglehold ['stræŋgəlhəʊld] *n* (*control*) **to have a s. on sb/sth** tener un control absoluto sobre alguien/algo

strangling ['stræŋglɪŋ] *n* (**a**) (*asphyxiation*) asfixia *f* (**b**) (*case of murder by strangulation*) estrangulamiento *m*

strangulation [stræŋgjʊ'leɪʃən] *n* estrangulamiento *m*

strap [stræp] **1** *n* (*of watch, bag*) correa *f*; (*of shoe*) tira *f*; (*on dress, bra*) tirante *m*, *Am* bretel *m*

2 *vt* (*pt & pp* **strapped**) **to s. sth to sth** sujetar algo con correas a algo

➤**strap in** *vt sep* abrocharse; **to s. oneself in** abrocharse or ponerse el cinturón (de seguridad)

strapless ['stræplɪs] *adj* (*dress, bra*) sin tirantes or *Am* breteles

strapping ['stræpɪŋ] *adj* fornido(a)

Strasbourg ['stræzbɜːg] *n* Estrasburgo

strata ['strɑːtə] *pl of* **stratum**

strategic [strə'tiːdʒɪk] *adj* estratégico(a)

strategically [strə'tiːdʒɪklɪ] *adv* estratégicamente

strategist ['strætədʒɪst] *n* estratega *mf*

strategy ['strætɪdʒɪ] *n* estrategia *f*

stratification [strætɪfɪ'keɪʃən] *n* estratificación *f*

stratosphere ['strætəsfɪə(r)] *n* estratosfera *f*

stratum ['strɑːtəm] (*pl* **strata** ['strɑːtə]) *n also Fig* estrato *m*

straw [strɔː] *n* paja *f*; (*for drinking*) pajita *f*, *Méx* popote *m*; *Fig* **to clutch** or **grasp at straws** agarrarse a un clavo ardiendo; *Fig* **that's the last s.** (eso) es la gota que colma el vaso; *Fig* **s. man** hombre *m* de paja; **s. vote** sondeo *m* informal

strawberry ['strɔːbərɪ] *n* fresa *f*, *CSur* frutilla *f*; **s. jam** mermelada *f* de fresa or *CSur* frutilla; **s. blonde** rubio(a) bermejo(a)

straw-colored ['strɔːkʌləd] *adj* pajizo(a)

strawhat [strɔː'hæt] *n* sombrero *m* de paja

stray [streɪ] **1** *n* (*dog*) perro *m* callejero; (*cat*) gato *m* callejero

2 *adj* (*dog, cat*) callejero(a); (*bullet*) perdido(a)

3 *vi* **to s. from** (*person*) desviarse de; (*animal*) descarriarse de; **to s. from the point** divagar

streak [striːk] **1** *n (stripe)* raya *f*, lista *f*; *(in hair)* mecha *f*; **a s. of lightning** un rayo; **a s. of luck** una racha de suerte; **winning/losing s.** racha *f* de ganar/de perder; **to have a cruel s.** tener un vena de crueldad

2 *vt* **streaked with dirt** manchado(a); **streaked with tears** cubierto(a) de lágrimas; **his hair is streaked with silver** tiene mechones grises; **to have one's hair streaked** hacerse mechas en el pelo

3 *vi* **(a)** *(move quickly)* **to s. off** salir disparado(a); **to s. past** pasar a toda velocidad **(b)** *Fam (run naked)* hacer streaking

streaker ['striːkə(r)] *n Fam* persona *f* que hace streaking

streaky ['striːkɪ] *adj (surface, pattern)* veteado(a)

stream [striːm] **1** *n* **(a)** *(brook)* arroyo *m*, riachuelo *m* **(b)** *(of light, blood, water)* chorro *m*; *(of tears, insults)* torrente *m*; *(of people)* oleada *f*; **to come on s.** *(industrial plant)* entrar en funcionamiento

2 *vt (spurt)* chorrear

3 *vi* **(a)** **the water streamed out** el agua salía a chorros; **people streamed into the stadium** la gente entraba en masa al estadio; **his eyes were streaming** le lloraban los ojos **(b)** *(hair, banner)* ondear

streamer ['striːmə(r)] *n* serpentina *f*

streamline ['striːmlaɪn] *vt (vehicle)* hacer más aerodinámico(a); *(system, department)* racionalizar

streamlined ['striːmlaɪnd] *adj (vehicle)* aerodinámico(a); *(system, department)* racionalizado(a)

streamlining ['striːmlaɪnɪŋ] *n (of vehicle)* aerodinamismo *m*; *(of system, department)* racionalización *f*

street [striːt] *n* **(a)** *(in town)* calle *f*; **on the s.** en la calle; **s. fighting** peleas *fpl* callejeras; **s. map** plano *m* de calles; *(book)* callejero *m*; **s. market** mercado *m* en la calle; **s. sweeper** barrendero(a) *m,f*; **s. theater** teatro *m* callejero; **s. value** *(of drugs)* valor *m* en la calle **(b)** *(idioms)* **to walk the streets** *(prostitute)* hacer la calle; **the man in the s.** el hombre de la calle; *Fam* **to have s. cred** tener buena imagen en la calle

streetcar ['striːtkɑː(r)] *n* tranvía *m*

streetlamp ['striːtlæmp], **streetlight** ['striːtlaɪt] *n* farola *f*

streetsmart = **streetwise**

streetwalker ['striːtwɔːkə(r)] *n* prostituta *f*

streetwise ['striːtwaɪz], **streetsmart** ['striːtsmɑːt] *adj* espabilado(a), *RP* canchero(a)

strength [streŋθ] *n* **(a)** *(power) (of person)* fuerza *f*; *(of nail, rope)* resistencia *f*; *(of currency)* fortaleza *f*; *(of emotion, light, sound)* intensidad *f*; *(of alcohol)* graduación *f*; **to be at full s.** *(department, regiment)* tener el cupo completo; **to be under s.** *(department, regiment)* estar por debajo del cupo; **in s.** en gran número; **to go from s. to s.** ir cada vez mejor; **on the s. of . . .** atendiendo a . . . **(b)** *(strong point)* punto *m* fuerte

strengthen ['streŋθən] **1** *vt (wall, building)* reforzar; *(muscles)* fortalecer; *(friendship)* consolidar; *(determination)* reafirmar; *(position)* reforzar, afianzar

2 *vi (friendship)* consolidarse; *(determination)* reafirmarse; *(currency)* fortalecerse

strenuous ['strenjʊəs] *adj (activity, lifestyle)* agotador(ora); *(effort)* denodado(a); *(opposition)* enérgico(a); *(denial)* tajante

strenuously ['strenjʊəslɪ] *adv (campaign)* enérgicamente; *(resist)* denodadamente; *(deny)* tajantemente

strep throat ['strep'θrəʊt] *n Fam* inflamación *f* de la garganta

stress [stres] **1** *n* **(a)** *(tension) (physical)* presión *f*; *(mental)* estrés *m*; **to be under a lot of s.** estar sometido(a) a mucho estrés; **a s. factor** un factor de estrés **(b)** *(emphasis)* énfasis *m*; *Ling* acento *m*; **to put s. on sth** hacer hincapié en algo

2 *vt (emphasize)* subrayar, hacer hincapié en

3 *vi Fam* estresarse

stressed-out ['strest'aʊt] *adj Fam* agobiado(a), estresado(a)

stressful ['stresfʊl] *adj* estresante

stretch [stretʃ] **1** *n* **(a)** *(of body)* **to have a s.** estirarse; **by no**

s. of the imagination de ningún modo; **s. marks** estrías *fpl* **(b)** *(of water, land)* extensión *f*; *(of road)* tramo *m*; *(of time, silence)* período *m*; **at one s.** de una vez **(c)** *(capacity)* **at full s.** *(factory)* a pleno rendimiento

2 *vt* **(a)** *(extend) (elastic, belt)* estirar; *(arm, hand)* estirar, extender; **to s. the truth** apurar *or* forzar las cosas **(b)** *(put demands on) (person)* exigir mucho a; *(resources)* mermar mucho; *(sb's patience)* abusar de; **we're fully stretched at the moment** en este momento estamos trabajando al límite (de nuestras posibilidades) **(c)** *(make last) (income, supplies)* estirar

3 *vi* **(a)** *(rope, rubber band, person)* estirarse **(b)** *(road, time)* extenderse **(c)** *(resources, budget)* dar de sí **(to** para)

▶**stretch out 1** *vt sep* **(a)** *(extend)* **to s. out one's arm** estirar el brazo; **to s. out one's hand** tender la mano **(b)** *(resources, budget)* estirar

2 *vi* **(a)** *(person)* tenderse **(b)** *(road, time)* extenderse

stretcher ['stretʃə(r)] *n* camilla *f*

stretcher-bearer ['stretʃəbeərə(r)] *n* camillero(a) *m,f*

stretchy ['stretʃɪ] *adj* elástico(a)

strew [struː] *(pp* **strewed** *or* **strewn** [struːn]) *vt (objects)* dispersar (**over** *or* **around** por); *(surface)* cubrir (**with** de)

stricken ['strɪkən] *adj (with grief, guilt)* afligido(a) (**with** por); *(with illness, by disaster)* gravemente afectado(a) (**with/by** por)

strict [strɪkt] *adj* **(a)** *(person, instruction, discipline)* estricto(a); **s. morals** moral *f* estricta; **a s. Muslim** un musulmán ortodoxo **(b)** *(meaning, minimum)* estricto(a); **in strictest confidence** en el más riguroso secreto

strictly ['strɪktlɪ] *adv* **(a)** *(severely)* estrictamente **(b)** *(exactly)* rigurosamente; **s. speaking** en un sentido estricto; **not s. true** no del todo *or* rigurosamente cierto

strictness ['strɪktnɪs] *n (of discipline, rules)* rigor *m*

stridden ['strɪdən] *pp of* **stride**

stride [straɪd] **1** *n* **(a)** zancada *f* **(b)** *(idioms)* **to make great strides** progresar a pasos agigantados; **to take sth in one's s.** asumir algo bien; **to get into one's s.** agarrar *or Esp* coger el ritmo

2 *vi (pt* **strode** [strəʊd], *pp* **stridden** ['strɪdən]) **to s. in/ out/off** entrar/salir/alejarse a grandes zancadas

strident ['straɪdənt] *adj* estridente

strife [straɪf] *n* conflictos *mpl*

strike [straɪk] **1** *n* **(a)** *Ind* huelga *f*; **teachers'/miners' s.** huelga de profesores/de mineros; **to be on s.** estar en huelga; **to go on s.** declararse en huelga; **s. fund** caja *f* de resistencia; **s. pay** subsidio *m* de huelga **(b)** *(discovery) (of ore, oil)* descubrimiento *m* **(c)** *(blow)* golpe *m*; *Mil* ataque *m* **(d)** *(in baseball)* strike *m*

2 *vt (pt & pp* **struck** [strʌk]) **(a)** *(hit)* golpear; **to s. sb in the face** golpear a alguien en la cara; **to s. sb a blow** pegar un golpe a alguien; *Fig* **to s. a blow for freedom** romper una lanza a favor de la libertad; **the clock struck ten** el reloj dio las diez; *Fig* **to s. the right note** *(speech, remark)* calar hondo; *Fig* **to s. the wrong note** *(speech, remark)* dar una nota discordante; **to s. terror into sb** aterrorizar a alguien; **to be struck dumb** quedarse mudo(a), no poder articular palabra; **he was struck dead by a heart attack** murió de un ataque cardíaco; **the child/the tree was struck by lightning** el niño/el árbol fue alcanzado por un rayo

(b) *(collide with)* chocar contra; **her head struck the floor** su cabeza chocó contra el suelo

(c) *(match)* encender, *Am* prender

(d) *(mint) (coin, medal)* acuñar

(e) *(impress, surprise)* chocar, sorprender; **what struck me was her voice** lo que me chocó mucho fue su voz

(f) *(occur to)* **it strikes me that . . .** se me ocurre que . . .

(g) *(seem to)* parecer; **it doesn't s. me as being very difficult** no me parece muy difícil; **he strikes me as a**

reasonable person me da la impresión de que es una persona razonable

(h) *(discover) (gold, oil)* descubrir; *Fam* **to s. it rich** hacerse rico(a); *Fam* **to s. it lucky** tener suerte

(i) *(reach)* **to s. a bargain** *or* **deal** hacer un trato; **to s. a balance** encontrar un equilibrio

(j) *(go on strike against)* **workers voted to s. the company** los trabajadores de la empresa votaron ir a la huelga

3 vi (a) *(attack) (enemy, criminal)* atacar; *(disaster, earthquake)* sobrevenir; *(clock)* dar las horas; **s. while the iron is hot** aprovecha ahora que estás a tiempo (b) *(go on strike)* hacer huelga, declararse en huelga; *(be on strike)* estar en huelga

▸**strike back** *vi (retaliate)* devolver el ataque

▸**strike down** *vt sep* (a) *(of disease)* abatir, abatirse sobre; *(of lightning, bullet)* alcanzar (b) *Law* revocar

▸**strike off** *vt sep (doctor, lawyer)* expulsar del colegio profesional

▸**strike out1** *vt sep* (a) *(delete)* tachar (b) *(in baseball)* eliminar a *(por cometer tres strikes)*, *Am* ponchar
  2 vi (a) *(hit out)* **to s. out at sb** arremeter contra alguien (b) *(leave)* partir (**for** hacia); **to s. out in a new direction** tomar un nuevo rumbo; **to s. out on one's own** independizarse (c) *(in baseball)* quedar eliminado(a) *(por cometer tres strikes)*, *Am* poncharse

▸**strike up** *vt sep (song)* arrancar con; *(friendship, conversation)* trabar, iniciar

strikebreaker ['straɪkbreɪkə(r)] *n* esquirol *mf*

striker ['straɪkə(r)] *n* (a) *(striking worker)* huelguista *mf* (b) *(in soccer)* delantero(a) *m,f*

striking ['straɪkɪŋ] *adj* (a) *(noticeable, surprising)* chocante, sorprendente; *(impressive)* deslumbrante (b) *(worker)* en huelga

strikingly ['straɪkɪŋlɪ] *adv (obvious, similar, original)* sorprendentemente

string [strɪŋ] **1** *n* (a) *(substance)* cuerda *f*; **a (piece of) s.** una cuerda (b) *(of violin, tennis racket, bow)* cuerda *f*; *(of puppet)* hilo *m*; *Mus* **the strings** la sección de cuerda, las cuerdas; *Fig* **to have more than one s. to one's bow** tener varios recursos; *Fig* **with no strings attached** sin compromiso; *Fig* **to pull strings** mover hilos; *Mus* **s. quartet** cuarteto *m* de cuerda (c) *(of pearls, beads)* sarta *f*; *(of islands)* rosario *m*; *(of words, stores, defeats)* serie *f*; *Comptr* cadena *f*
  2 *vt* (*pp & pt* **strung** [strʌŋ]) (a) *(violin, tennis racket, bow)* encordar (b) *(pearls, beads)* ensartar

▸**string along** *vt sep Fam* dar falsas esperanzas a

▸**string up** *vt sep Fam (criminal)* ahorcar

stringed [strɪŋd] *adj (instrument)* de cuerda

stringent ['strɪndʒənt] *adj* riguroso(a), estricto(a)

strip¹ [strɪp] *n (of cloth, paper, metal)* tira *f*; *(of land)* franja *f*; *Fam* **to tear sb off a s.** echar un rapapolvo a alguien, *Méx* repelar a alguien, *RP* pegar un levante a alguien; **s. lighting** iluminación *f* con fluorescentes

strip² **1** *n* **to do a s.** *(undress)* hacer un striptease; **s. club** club *m* de striptease; **s. poker** strip póquer *m*; **s. show** (espectáculo *m* de) striptease *m*
  2 *vt* (*pt & pp* **stripped**) *(person)* desnudar; *(bed)* deshacer; *(paint, wallpaper)* rascar, quitar, *Am* sacar; **to s. sb of sth** despojar a alguien de algo
  3 *vi (undress)* desnudarse

▸**strip off** **1** *vt sep (paint, wallpaper)* rascar, quitar, *Am* sacar
  2 *vi (undress)* desnudarse, desvestirse

stripe [straɪp] *n* (a) *(on cloth, animal's coat)* raya *f*, lista *f* (b) *(indicating rank)* galón *m*

striped [straɪpt] *adj* a rayas

stripling ['strɪplɪŋ] *n* mozalbete *m*

stripper ['strɪpə(r)] *n (striptease artist)* artista *mf* de striptease

strip-search ['strɪpsɜːtʃ] **1** *n* registro *m* integral
  2 *vt* **to s. sb** someter a alguien a un registro integral

striptease ['strɪptiːz] *n* striptease *m*

strive [straɪv] (*pt* **strove** [strəʊv], *pp* **striven** ['strɪvən]) *vi* esforzarse; **to s. to do sth** esforzarse por hacer algo; **to s. for** *or* **after sth** luchar por algo

strobe [strəʊb] *n Phys* estroboscopio *m*; **s. lighting** luces *fpl* estroboscópicas (de discoteca)

strode [strəʊd] *pt of* **stride**

stroke [strəʊk] **1** *n* (a) *(blow, tennis shot)* golpe *m*; *(in rowing)* palada *f*; *(movement in swimming)* brazada *f*; *(swimming style)* estilo *m*; **a brush s.** *Art* una pincelada; *(of decorator)* un brochazo; **on the s. of nine** al dar las nueve (b) *(caress)* caricia *f*; **to give sth/sb a s.** acariciar algo/a alguien (c) *Med* derrame *m* cerebral, apoplejía *f* (d) *(idioms)* **she hasn't done a s. of work** no ha dado ni golpe; **a s. of luck** un golpe de suerte; **a s. of genius** una genialidad; **at a s.** de un golpe
  2 *vt (caress)* acariciar

stroll [strəʊl] **1** *n* paseo *m*; **to go for a s.** ir a dar un paseo
  2 *vi* caminar

strong [strɒŋ] **1** *adj* (a) *(physically or mentally powerful)* fuerte; *(friendship, argument)* sólido(a) (b) *(intense) (color, light)* intenso(a); *(smell, drink, measures, language)* fuerte; *(resemblance, accent)* marcado(a); *(belief, support)* firme; *(possibility)* serio(a); **s. point** (punto *m*) fuerte *m* (c) *(durable) (rope, cloth, shoes)* fuerte, resistente; **s. room** cámara *f* acorazada (d) *(good)* *(candidate)* firme; *(team)* fuerte; **she's s. at physics** la física es uno de sus fuertes
  2 *adv* **to be still going s.** estar todavía en forma
  3 *npl* **the s.** los fuertes

strong-arm tactics ['strɒŋɑːm'tæktɪks] *npl* mano *f* dura

strongbox ['strɒŋbɒks] *n* caja *f* fuerte

stronghold ['strɒŋhəʊld] *n (fortress)* fortaleza *f*; *Fig (of political party, religion)* baluarte *m*, bastión *m*

strongly ['strɒŋlɪ] *adv (oppose, endorse)* rotundamente, fuertemente; *(believe)* firmemente; **s. built** sólidamente construido(a); **a s. worded letter** una carta escrita en un tono fuerte; **he feels very s. about it** (es un tema que) le preocupa mucho

strongman ['strɒŋmæn] *n (in circus)* forzudo *m*; *Fig (dictator)* dictador *m*

strong-minded [strɒŋ'maɪndɪd] *adj* decidido(a), resuelto(a)

strongroom ['strɒŋruːm] *n* cámara *f* acorazada

strong-willed [strɒŋ'wɪld] *adj* tenaz, tozudo(a)

strontium ['strɒntɪəm] *n Chem* estroncio *m*

strop [strɒp] *n (leather strap)* asentador *m*

strove [strəʊv] *pt of* **strive**

struck [strʌk] *pt & pp of* **strike**

structural ['strʌktʃərəl] *adj* estructural; **s. damage** daños *mpl* estructurales; **s. survey** peritaje *m* or tasación *f* de estructuras

structuralism ['strʌktʃərəlɪzəm] *n* estructuralismo *m*

structuralist ['strʌktʃərəlɪst] *n & adj* estructuralista *mf*

structurally ['strʌktʃərəlɪ] *adv* estructuralmente

structure ['strʌktʃə(r)] **1** *n* (a) *(in general)* estructura *f* (b) *(building, monument)* construcción *f*
  2 *vt* estructurar, articular

structured ['strʌktʃəd] *adj* estructurado(a); *Comptr* **s. query language** lenguaje *m* estructurado de consulta

struggle ['strʌɡəl] **1** *n (effort)* lucha *f* (**for** por); *(physical fight)* forcejeo *m*; **without a s.** sin oponer resistencia; **life is a s.** la vida es una lucha constante
  2 *vi (try hard)* luchar (**for** por); *(fight physically)* forcejear; **to s. to do sth** luchar por hacer algo; **to be struggling** *(person, company)* estar pasándolo muy mal

strum [strʌm] (*pt & pp* **strummed**) *vt (guitar)* rasguear

strung [strʌŋ] *pt & pp of* **string**

strung out ['strʌŋ'aʊt] *adj Fam (tense)* tenso(a), agobiado(a); *(addicted)* enganchado(a) (**on** a)

strut¹ [strʌt] *n (for frame)* riostra *f*; *Av* montante *m*

strut² (*pt & pp* **strutted**) *vi* pavonearse; **to s. in/out** entrar/salir pavoneándose

strychnine ['strɪkniːn] *n* estricnina *f*

stub [stʌb] **1** *n (of pencil)* punta *f* final; *(of cigarette)* colilla *f*; *(of check)* matriz *f*
   2 *vt (pt & pp* **stubbed**) **to s. one's toe (on** *or* **against sth)** darse un golpe en el dedo gordo (contra algo)
▸**stub out** *vt sep (cigarette)* apagar, aplastar

stubble ['stʌbəl] *n* **(a)** *(in field)* rastrojo *m* **(b)** *(on face)* barba *f* de unos días

stubbly ['stʌblɪ] *adj (beard)* de unos días; *(chin)* con pelillos

stubborn ['stʌbən] *adj (person)* testarudo(a), terco(a); *(determination, resistance)* obstinado(a), pertinaz; *(stain, infection)* pertinaz; **as s. as a mule** terco(a) como una mula

stubbornness ['stʌbənnɪs] *n (of person)* testarudez *f*; *(of determination, resistance)* obstinación *f*

stubby ['stʌbɪ] *adj* regordete(a)

stucco ['stʌkəʊ] *n* estuco *m*

stuck [stʌk] **1** *adj* **to get s.** atascarse; **to be s. for sth** no tener algo; *Fam* **to be s. with sb/sth** tener que cargar con alguien/algo
   2 *pt & pp of* **stick²**

stuck-up ['stʌk'ʌp] *adj Fam* creído(a), engreído(a)

stud¹ [stʌd] *n (fastener)* automático *m*, corchete *m*; *(for decoration)* tachón *m*; *(on football, baseball, soccer boots) Esp* taco *m*, *RP* tapón *m*; *(earring) Esp* pendiente *m*, *Am* arete *m*

stud² *n* **(a)** *(farm)* cuadra *f*; *(stallion)* semental *m* **(b)** *Fam (man)* semental *m*

student ['stjuːdənt] *n (at college)* estudiante *mf*; *(at school)* alumno(a) *m,f*, estudiante *mf*; **law/medical s.** estudiante de derecho/medicina; **the s. body** el cuerpo estudiantil; **s. card** carné *m* de estudiante; *Aut* **s. driver** conductor(ora) *m,f* en prácticas; **s. life** la vida estudiantil; **s. loan** préstamo *m* para estudiantes; **s. nurse** estudiante *mf* de enfermería; **s. teacher** profesor(ora) *m,f* en prácticas; **s. union** *(association)* = en una universidad, asociación que organiza actividades, asesora y representa a los alumnos; *(place)* = edificio para los alumnos que cuenta con bares, discoteca, servicios y oficinas

studied ['stʌdɪd] *adj (manner, attitude)* estudiado(a)

studio ['stjuːdɪəʊ] (*pl* **studios**) *n (of TV, movie company)* estudio *m*, plató *m*; *(of artist, photographer, for recording music)* estudio *m*; *TV* **s. audience** público *m* en estudio; **s. apartment** *(apartamento m)* estudio *m*

studious ['stjuːdɪəs] *adj* estudioso(a)

study ['stʌdɪ] **1** *n* **(a)** *(investigation)* estudio *m*, investigación *f*; *(written report)* estudio *m*, informe *m*, *Am* reporte *m*; **to make a s. of sth** realizar un estudio sobre algo; **s. group** grupo *m* de estudio; **s. hall** *(room)* sala *f* de estudios; *(period)* hora *f* de estudio; **s. tour** viaje *m* de estudio **(b)** *(artist)* estudio *m* **(c)** *(room)* *(cuarto m de)* estudio *m*
   2 *vt & vi* estudiar

stuff [stʌf] **1** *n (substance)* cosa *f*; *(objects, possessions)* cosas *fpl*; **what's this s.?** ¿qué es esto?; **he reads all that intellectual s.** se dedica a leer todas esas cosas de intelectuales; *Fam* **this wine is good s.** es bueno este vino; *Fam* **she writes good s.** escribe bien; *Fam* **he knows his s.** conoce bien el tema; *Fam* **that's the s.!** ¡sí señor!, ¡eso es!
   2 *vt (fill)* rellenar; *(cushion)* forrar, rellenar; *(pockets)* llenar; *(dead animal)* disecar; **to s. sth into sth** meter algo dentro de algo; *Fam* **to s. oneself** *or* **one's face** atiborrarse, *Esp* ponerse las botas

stuffed [stʌft] *adj (pepper, mushroom, olive)* relleno(a); *(toy)* de peluche; *(animal)* disecado(a)

stuffily [stʌft] *adj (to say, reply)* petulantemente, altaneramente

stuffing ['stʌfɪŋ] *n (for furniture, chicken)* relleno *m*; *Fam* **to**

knock the s. out of sb *(news, disappointment)* dejar a alguien con la moral por los suelos, *Am* dejar a alguien los ánimos por el piso

stuffy ['stʌfɪ] *adj* **(a)** *(room)* cargado(a) **(b)** *(person)* estirado(a)

stultifying ['stʌltɪfaɪɪŋ] *adj* tedioso(a)

stumble ['stʌmbəl] **1** *n* tropezón *m*
   2 *vi (when walking)* tropezar, toparse; *Fig (when speaking)* trastabillar
▸**stumble across** *vt insep (find)* tropezar con, toparse con

stump [stʌmp] **1** *n* **(a)** *(of tree)* tocón *m*; *(of arm, leg)* muñón *m* **(b)** *Fam* **to be on the s.** *(politician)* estar de campaña electoral
   2 *vt (baffle)* dejar perplejo(a); **to be stumped for an answer** no saber qué contestar

stumpy ['stʌmpɪ] *adj* rechoncho(a)

stun [stʌn] (*pt & pp* **stunned**) *vt (make unconscious)* dejar sin sentido; *Fig (shock)* dejar de piedra

stung [stʌŋ] *pt & pp of* **sting**

stunk [stʌŋk] *pt & pp of* **stink**

stunned [stʌnd] *adj (person, expression)* atónito(a); **they watched in s. silence** miraban en silencio, estupefactos

stunning ['stʌnɪŋ] *adj (blow)* contundente; *(performance)* soberbio(a); *(woman, outfit)* imponente

stunningly ['stʌnɪŋlɪ] *adv* **a s. good-looking man/beautiful woman** un hombre/una mujer imponente

stunt¹ [stʌnt] *vt (person, growth)* atrofiar

stunt² *n (in movie)* escena *f* peligrosa; *(for publicity)* truco *m* publicitario; **s. man** especialista *m*, doble *m*; **s. woman** especialista *f*, doble *f*

stupefaction [stjuːpɪ'fækʃən] *n* estupefacción *f*

stupefied ['stjuːpɪfaɪd] *adj* **(a)** *(tired, bored)* hastiado(a) **(b)** *(amazed)* estupefacto(a)

stupefy ['stjuːpɪfaɪ] *vt (of alcohol, drugs, news)* aturdir, ofuscar; *(of behavior)* dejar perplejo(a)

stupefying ['stjuːpɪfaɪɪŋ] *adj (boring)* embotante; *(amazing)* asombroso(a)

stupendous [stjuː'pendəs] *adj* estupendo(a), extraordinario(a)

stupid ['stjuːpɪd] *adj* estúpido(a), idiota; **don't be s.!** ¡no seas estúpido!; **how s. of me!** ¡qué tonto(a) soy!; **what a s. thing to do!** ¡menuda estupidez!

stupidity [stjuː'pɪdɪtɪ] *n* estupidez *f*, imbecilidad *f*

stupidly ['stjuːpɪdlɪ] *adv* tontamente

stupor ['stjuːpə(r)] *n* aturdimiento *m*

sturdy ['stɜːdɪ] *adj (person)* robusto(a); *(object)* resistente; *(opposition, resistance)* firme, sólido(a)

sturgeon ['stɜːdʒən] *n* esturión *m*

stutter ['stʌtə(r)] **1** *n* tartamudeo *m*
   2 *vi* tartamudear

sty¹ [staɪ] *n (pigsty) & Fig* pocilga *f*

sty², stye [staɪ] *n Med* orzuelo *m*

style [staɪl] **1** *n* **(a)** *(manner, design, sophistication)* estilo *m*; **she has s.** tiene estilo; **to live in s.** vivir con lujo **(b)** *(fashion, mode)* moda *f*; **to be in s.** estar de moda
   2 *vt (design)* diseñar; *(hair)* peinar

-style [-staɪl] *suffix* **a sixties-s. haircut** un corte de pelo al estilo de los (años) sesenta

styli ['staɪlaɪ] *pl of* **stylus**

styling ['staɪlɪŋ] *n* diseño *m*; **s. gel** gel *m* moldeador; **s. mousse** espuma *f* (moldeadora)

stylish ['staɪlɪʃ] *adj* elegante

stylishly ['staɪlɪʃlɪ] *adv (dress)* elegantemente, con estilo; *(write)* efectista

stylishness ['staɪlɪʃnɪs] *n (of person, clothes, hotel, area)* elegancia *f*; *(of book, movie)* efectismo *m*

stylist ['staɪlɪst] *n (hairdresser)* peluquero(a) *m,f*, estilista *mf*

stylistic [staɪ'lɪstɪk] *adj* estilístico(a)

stylistically [staɪˈlɪstɪklɪ] *adv* desde el punto de vista estilístico

stylized [ˈstaɪəlaɪzd] *adj* convencional, estereotipado(a)

stylus [ˈstaɪləs] (*pl* **styluses** *or* **styli** [staɪlaɪ]) *n (for engraving)* estilo *m*, punzón *m*; *(on record player)* aguja *f*

stymie [ˈstaɪmɪ] *vt Fam* bloquear

Styrofoam® [ˈstaɪrəfəʊm] *n* espuma *f* de poliestireno

suave [swɑːv] *adj* fino(a), cortés; *Pej* zalamero(a), lisonjero(a)

sub [sʌb] *Fam* **1** *n* (**a**) *(substitute)* suplente *mf* (**b**) *(submarine)* submarino *m* (**c**) *Fam (sandwich) Esp* flauta *f*, = sándwich hecho con una barra de pan larga y estrecha
2 *vi (substitute)* **to s. for sb** reemplazar *or* sustituir a alguien

subcommittee [ˈsʌbkəmɪtɪ] *n* subcomité *m*

subconscious [sʌbˈkɒnʃəs] *n & adj* subconsciente *m*

subcontinent [sʌbˈkɒntɪnənt] *n* subcontinente *m*; **the (Indian) S.** el subcontinente asiático *or* indio

subcontract *Com* **1** *n* [sʌbˈkɒntrækt] subcontrata *f*
2 *vt* [ˈsʌbkəntrækt] subcontratar

subcontracting [ˈsʌbkəntræktɪŋ] *n* subcontratación *f*; **we do a lot of s. for larger firms** hacemos muchas subcontratas para grandes empresas

subcontractor [ˈsʌbkəntræktə(r)] *n Com* subcontratista *mf*

subculture [ˈsʌbkʌltʃə(r)] *n* subcultura *f*

subcutaneous [sʌbkjʊˈteɪnɪəs] *adj* subcutáneo(a)

subdivision [ˈsʌbdɪvɪʒən] *n* subdivisión *f*

subdue [səbˈdjuː] *vt (enemy)* someter, subyugar; *(resistance)* doblegar; *(emotions)* dominar, controlar

subdued [səbˈdjuːd] *adj (person, voice, tone)* apagado(a); *(light, sound)* tenue

subentry [sʌbˈentrɪ] *n Typ* subentrada *f*

subhuman [sʌbˈhjuːmən] **1** *n* bestia *mf*
2 *adj* infrahumano(a)

subject [ˈsʌbdʒɪkt] **1** *n* (**a**) *(of conversation, book, painting, photograph)* tema *m*; *(at school, college)* asignatura *f*, materia *f*; **while we are on the s.** ya que hablamos del tema; **to change the s.** cambiar de tema; **s. matter** *(of letter, book)* tema *m*, asunto *m* (**b**) *Gram* sujeto *m* (**c**) *(of monarch)* súbdito(a) *m,f*
2 *adj* (**a**) *(state, country)* sometido(a) (**b**) *(prone)* **to be s. to illness/jealousy/depression** ser propenso(a) a las enfermedades/los celos/la depresión; **to be s. to delay/a fine of $50** estar sujeto(a) a retrasos *or Am* demoras/una multa de 50 dólares (**c**) **s. to** *(dependent on)* sujeto(a) a
3 *vt* [səbˈdʒekt] (**a**) *(subjugate) (people, nation)* someter, subyugar (**b**) *(force to undergo)* **to s. sb to sth** someter a alguien a algo

subjective [səbˈdʒektɪv] *adj* subjetivo(a)

subjectivity [sʌbdʒekˈtɪvɪtɪ] *n* subjetividad *f*

sub judice [sʌbˈdʒuːdɪsɪ] *adj Law* sub iudice, sub júdice

subjugate [ˈsʌbdʒʊgeɪt] *vt (people, nation)* someter, subyugar

subjunctive [səbˈdʒʌŋktɪv] *Gram* **1** *n* subjuntivo *m*
2 *adj* subjuntivo(a)

sublet [sʌbˈlet] (*pt & pp* **sublet**) *vt* subarrendar

sublimate [ˈsʌblɪmeɪt] *vt* sublimar

sublimation [sʌblɪˈmeɪʃən] *n (of desire)* sublimación *f*

sublime [səˈblaɪm] **1** *n* **from the s. to the ridiculous** de lo sublime a lo ridículo
2 *adj (beauty)* sublime; *Ironic (ignorance)* supino(a), sumo(a)

subliminal [sʌbˈlɪmɪnəl] *adj Psy* subliminal

submachine gun [sʌbməˈʃiːngʌn] *n* metralleta *f*

submarine [sʌbməˈriːn] *n* (**a**) *(vessel)* submarino *m* (**b**) *Fam* **s. (sandwich)** *Esp* flauta *f*, = sándwich hecho con una barra de pan larga y estrecha

submerge [səbˈmɜːdʒ] **1** *vt (immerse)* sumergir; *(flood)* inundar; *Fig* **to s. oneself in one's work** encerrarse en el trabajo
2 *vi (submarine, diver)* sumergirse

submerged [səbˈmɜːdʒd] *adj (field)* anegado(a); *(submarine)* sumergido(a); *(reef, volcano)* submarino(a)

submersible [səbˈmɜːsɪbəl] *n* sumergible *m*

submersion [səbˈmɜːʃən] *n* inmersión *f*

submission [səbˈmɪʃən] *n* (**a**) *(to person's will, authority)* sumisión *f*; **to starve sb into s.** someter a alguien dejándole sin comer; **to beat sb into s.** someter a alguien a golpes (**b**) *(of documents)* entrega *f* (**c**) *(report)* ponencia *f*, presentación *f*

submissive [səbˈmɪsɪv] *adj* sumiso(a)

submissively [səbˈmɪsɪvlɪ] *adv* de forma sumisa

submissiveness [səbˈmɪsɪvnɪs] *n* sumisión *f*

submit [səbˈmɪt] **1** *vt* presentar; **to s. sth for approval/inspection** presentar algo para su aprobación/inspección
2 *vi (to person, authority)* someterse (**to** a)

subnormal [sʌbˈnɔːməl] *adj* subnormal

subordinate 1 *n* [səˈbɔːdɪnət] subordinado(a) *m,f*
2 *adj (rank, role)* secundario(a), inferior; **to be s. to sb** estar subordinado(a) a alguien; *Gram* **s. clause** oración *f* subordinada
3 *vt* [səˈbɔːdɪneɪt] subordinar

subordination [səbɔːdɪˈneɪʃən] *n* subordinación *f*

subplot [ˈsʌbplɒt] *n* trama *f* secundaria

subpoena [səˈpiːnə] *Law* **1** *n* citación *f*
2 *vt* citar

subprogram [ˈsʌbprəʊgræm] *n Comptr* subprograma *m*

subscribe [səbˈskraɪb] *vi* (**a**) **to s. to** *(newspaper, magazine)* suscribirse a; *(to charity)* dar donativos a; *(to telephone, Internet service)* abonarse a (**b**) **to s. to** *(opinion, theory)* suscribir

subscriber [səbˈskraɪbə(r)] *n (to newspaper, magazine)* suscriptor(ora) *m,f*; *(to telephone, Internet service)* abonado(a) *m,f*; *(to charity)* donador(ora) *m,f*

subscript [ˈsʌbskrɪpt] *n Typ* subíndice *m*; **s. "a"** "a" escrita como subíndice

subscription [sʌbˈskrɪpʃən] *n (to newspaper, magazine)* suscripción *f*; *(to club)* cuota *f*; *(to charity)* donativo *m*

subsection [ˈsʌbsekʃən] *n* apartado *m*

subsequent [ˈsʌbsɪkwənt] *adj* posterior

subservient [sʌbˈsɜːvɪənt] *adj* servil

subset [ˈsʌbset] *n* subconjunto *m*

subside [səbˈsaɪd] *vi (ground, building)* hundirse; *(water)* bajar (de nivel); *(blister, bump)* bajar, deshincharse; *(storm)* amainar; *(excitement, fever)* calmarse

subsidence [səbˈsaɪdəns] *n (of ground, building)* hundimiento *m*; *(of water)* bajada *f*

subsidiarity [sʌbsɪdɪˈærɪtɪ] *n* subsidiariedad *f*

subsidiary [sʌbˈsɪdɪərɪ] **1** *n (company)* filial *f*
2 *adj* secundario(a)

subsidize [ˈsʌbsɪdaɪz] *vt* subvencionar

subsidy [ˈsʌbsɪdɪ] *n* subvención *f*

subsistence [səbˈsɪstəns] *n* subsistencia *f*; *Com* **s. allowance** dietas *fpl*; **s. wage** salario *m* exiguo

subspecies [ˈsʌbspiːʃiːz] *n* subespecie *f*

substance [ˈsʌbstəns] *n* (**a**) *(matter)* sustancia *f*; *Formal* **s. abuse** abuso *m* de narcóticos (**b**) *(essential element) (of article, argument)* esencia *f*; **I agree in s.** esencialmente, estoy de acuerdo (**c**) *(solidity, worth)* consistencia *f*; **the accusations lack s.** las acusaciones son inconsistentes

substandard [sʌbˈstændəd] *adj* deficiente

substantial [səbˈstænʃəl] *adj* (**a**) *(significant) (progress, difference)* sustancial, significativo(a); *(reason, evidence)* de peso; **a s. number of...** una cantidad considerable de... (**b**) *(meal)* abundante; *(structure)* sólido(a); *(book)* enjundioso(a) (**c**) *(sum of money, profit)* sustancioso(a), considerable

substantially [səbˈstænʃəlɪ] *adv* (**a**) *(considerably) (better, worse)* significativamente, considerablemente (**b**) *(for the most part)* esencialmente (**c**) *(solidly)* firmemente

substantiate [səb'stænʃɪeɪt] *vt (statement, claim)* probar

substantive ['sʌbstəntɪv] **1** *n Gram* sustantivo *m*
2 *adj (measures, issue)* significativo(a)

substitute ['sʌbstɪtjuːt] **1** *n (thing)* sustituto *m; (person)* sustituto(a) *m,f; Sport* suplente *mf;* **coffee s.** sucedáneo *m* de café; **to do s. teaching** hacer suplencias de profesor; **s. teacher** profesor(ora) *m,f* suplente
2 *vt* sustituir, reemplazar (**for** por)
3 *vi* **to s. for sb** sustituir *or* reemplazar a alguien

substitution [sʌbstɪ'tjuːʃən] *n* sustitución *f; Sport* sustitución *f,* cambio *m*

subsume [sʌb'sjuːm] *vt Formal* englobar, incluir

subterfuge ['sʌbtəfjuːdʒ] *n (trickery)* subterfugios *mpl*

subterranean [sʌbtə'reɪnɪən] *adj* subterráneo(a)

subtitle ['sʌbtaɪtəl] *TV & Cin* **1** *n* subtítulo *m*
2 *vt* subtitular

subtitled ['sʌbtaɪtəld] *adj (movie)* subtitulado(a)

subtitling ['sʌbtaɪtlɪŋ] *n* subtitulación *f*

subtle ['sʌtəl] *adj* sutil

subtlety ['sʌtəltɪ] *n* sutileza *f*

subtly ['sʌtlɪ] *adv* sutilmente

subtotal ['sʌbtəʊtəl] *n* subtotal *m*

subtract [səb'trækt] *vt* restar, sustraer

subtraction [səb'trækʃən] *n* resta *f,* sustracción *f*

subtropical [sʌb'trɒpɪkəl] *adj* subtropical

suburb ['sʌbɜːb] *n* = zona residencial en la periferia de una ciudad; **the suburbs** las zonas residenciales de la periferia

suburban [sə'bɜːbən] *adj (attitudes, life)* aburguesado(a); **s. train** tren *m* de cercanías

suburbia [sə'bɜːbɪə] *n* zonas *fpl* residenciales de la periferia

subversion [səb'vɜːʃən] *n* subversión *f*

subversive [səb'vɜːsɪv] *n & adj* subversivo(a) *m,f*

subvert [səb'vɜːt] *vt* subvertir

subway ['sʌbweɪ] *n (underground railway)* metro *m, RP* subte *m*

sub-zero [sʌb'zɪərəʊ] *adj* bajo cero

succeed [sək'siːd] **1** *vt (follow)* suceder a
2 *vi* (**a**) *(be successful) (person)* tener éxito; *(plan)* tener éxito, funcionar; *(in life)* triunfar; **to s. in doing sth** conseguir *or* lograr hacer algo (**b**) **to s. to the throne** suceder al *or* en el trono

succeeding [sək'siːdɪŋ] *adj (following)* siguiente

success [sək'ses] *n* éxito *m;* **to be a s.** ser un éxito; **without s.** sin éxito; **to meet with s.** tener éxito; **s. story** éxito *m*

successful [sək'sesfʊl] *adj (person)* con éxito; *(attempt, negotiations)* fructífero(a); *(project, movie, novel)* exitoso(a); **one of Britain's most s. authors** uno de los autores británicos de más éxito; **s. applicants** los candidatos elegidos; **to be s.** *(person, project)* tener éxito; **to be s. in doing sth** conseguir *or* lograr hacer algo

successfully [sək'sesfəlɪ] *adv* con éxito

succession [sək'seʃən] *n* sucesión *f;* **for two years in s.** dos años consecutivos

successive [sək'sesɪv] *adj* sucesivo(a)

successively [sək'sesɪvlɪ] *adv* sucesivamente

successor [sək'sesə(r)] *n* sucesor(ora) *m,f*

succinct [sʌk'sɪŋkt] *adj* sucinto(a), escueto(a)

succulent ['sʌkjʊlənt] **1** *n Bot* planta *f* carnosa *or* suculenta
2 *adj (delicious)* suculento(a)

succumb [sə'kʌm] *vi* sucumbir (**to** a)

such [sʌtʃ] **1** *pron* **if s. were the case** en tal caso; **and s.** y otros(as) por el estilo; **s. is life!** ¡así es la vida!; **philosophy as s. is not taught in our schools** la filosofía, como tal (asignatura), no se enseña en nuestros colegios; **the text as s. is fine but...** el texto en sí está bien pero...; **I wasn't scared as s.** asustado, lo que se dice asustado, no estaba
2 *adj* tal; **s. a man** un hombre así, semejante hombre; **s.**

ignorance tamaña *or* semejante ignorancia; **animals s. as the lion or the tiger** animales tales como el león o el tigre; **did you ever see s. a thing!** ¡has visto alguna vez algo parecido *or* semejante?; **do you have s. a thing as a screwdriver?** ¿no tendrás un destornillador?; **how can you tell s. lies?** ¿cómo puedes mentir de esa manera?; **their problems are s. that...** sus problemas son tales *or* de tal calibre que...; **there's the church, s. as it is** ahí está la iglesia, que *or* aunque no es gran cosa; **there is no s. thing** eso no existe; **I said no s. thing** yo no dije tal cosa *or* nada de eso; **on s. and s. a day** tal día; **in s. a way that...** de tal forma *or* forma tal que... *Formal* **until s. time as may be convenient** en tanto resulte conveniente
3 *adv* tan; **I had never seen s. a big house** nunca había visto una casa tan grande; **I had never heard s. good music** nunca había escuchado una música tan buena; **it was s. a long time ago** pasó hace tanto tiempo; **we had s. a good time!** ¡nos lo pasamos tan bien!

suchlike ['sʌtʃlaɪk] *pron* **and s.** y similares

suck [sʌk] **1** *vt (lollipop)* chupar; *(liquid)* succionar; *(mother's milk)* mamar; *(air)* aspirar; **to s. one's thumb** chuparse el dedo
2 *vi very Fam* **that movie/idea sucks!** ¡esa película/idea es una caca!

▸**suck in** *vt sep (gas)* aspirar; *(liquid)* succionar; *Fig* **to get sucked into sth** *(situation)* caer en algo

▸**suck up 1** *vt sep (liquid)* succionar; *(dust)* aspirar
2 *vi Fam* **to s. up to sb** *Esp* hacer la pelota a *or Méx* lambisconear a *or CSur* chuparle las medias a alguien

sucker ['sʌkə(r)] *n* (**a**) *(of octopus)* ventosa *f; (of plant)* chupón *m,* vástago *m* (**b**) *Fam (gullible person)* pringado(a) *m,f,* primo(a) *m,f;* **he's a s. for blondes** las rubias le chiflan

suckle ['sʌkəl] **1** *vt (child, young)* amamantar
2 *vi (baby, animal)* mamar

sucrose ['suːkrəʊs] *n* sacarosa *f*

suction ['sʌkʃən] *n* succión *f*

Sudan [suː'dæn] *n* Sudán

Sudanese [suːdə'niːz] *n & adj* sudanés(esa) *m,f*

sudden ['sʌdən] *adj* repentino(a), súbito(a); **all of a s.** de repente; **it was all very s.** fue todo muy precipitado; *Fig* **s. death** *(in game, contest)* muerte *f* súbita

suddenly ['sʌdənlɪ] *adv* de repente, de pronto

suddenness ['sʌdənnɪs] *n* **the s. of her death/decision** lo repentino de su muerte/decisión

suds [sʌdz] *npl (of soap)* espuma *f* (de jabón)

sue [suː] **1** *vt Law* demandar (**for** por)
2 *vi* (**a**) *Law* **to s. for divorce** solicitar el divorcio (**b**) **to s. for peace** pedir la paz

suede [sweɪd] *n* ante *m*

suet ['suːɪt] *n* sebo *m,* unto *m*

Suez ['suːɪz] *n* **the S. Canal** el Canal de Suez

suffer ['sʌfə(r)] **1** *vt* (**a**) *(loss, defeat, consequences)* sufrir; *(pain, sorrow)* sufrir, padecer (**b**) *(tolerate)* aguantar, soportar; **she doesn't s. fools gladly** no les da ningún cuartel a los tontos
2 *vi* sufrir (**from** de); **your health/work will s.** se resentirá tu salud/trabajo

sufferance ['sʌfərəns] *n* **to admit sb on s.** tolerar la presencia de alguien

sufferer ['sʌfərə(r)] *n* enfermo(a) *m,f;* **a cancer s.** un enfermo de cáncer

suffering ['sʌfərɪŋ] *n* sufrimiento *m*

suffice [sə'faɪs] *vi Formal* bastar, ser suficiente

sufficiency [sə'fɪʃənsɪ] *n Formal* cantidad *f* suficiente

sufficient [sə'fɪʃənt] *adj* suficiente; **to be s.** bastar, ser suficiente; **$5 should be s.** debería bastar con 5 dólares

sufficiently [sə'fɪʃəntlɪ] *adv* suficientemente, bastante; **to be s. big** ser (lo) suficiente *or* lo bastante grande

suffix ['sʌfɪks] *n Gram* sufijo *m*
suffocate ['sʌfəkeɪt] **1** *vt* asfixiar; *Fig* sofocar
2 *vi* asfixiarse
suffocating ['sʌfəkeɪtɪŋ] *adj* asfixiante
suffocation [sʌfə'keɪʃən] *n* asfixia *f*
suffrage ['sʌfrɪdʒ] *n Pol* sufragio *m*, derecho *m* de voto; **universal/women's s.** sufragio *m* universal/femenino
suffragette [sʌfrə'dʒet] *n Hist* sufragista *f*
suffuse [sə'fjuːz] *vt Literary* **suffused with light** bañado(a) de luz
sugar ['ʃʊgə(r)] **1** *n* (**a**) *(food)* azúcar *m or f*; **two sugars, please** dos (cucharaditas) de azúcar, por favor; **s. almond** peladilla *f*; **s. beet** remolacha *f* (azucarera), *Méx* betabel *m* (azucarero); **s. bowl** azucarero *m*; **s. cane** caña *f* de azúcar; *Fam* **s. daddy** = hombre maduro que tiene una joven mantenida; **s. lump** terrón *m* de azúcar, azucarillo *m*; **s. plantation** plantación *f* de azúcar; **s. refinery** azucarera *f*, refinería *f* de azúcar (**b**) *Fam (term of address)* cielo *m*, cariño *m*
2 *vt (coffee, tea)* echar azúcar a; *Fig* **to s. the pill** dorar la píldora
sugarcane ['ʃʊgəkeɪn] *n* caña *f* de azúcar
sugarcoated [ʃʊgə'kəʊtɪd] *adj (pills, sweets)* azucarado(a); *(almonds)* garrapiñado(a)
sugar-free [ʃʊgə'friː] *adj* sin azúcar
sugary ['ʃʊgərɪ] *adj* (**a**) *(containing sugar)* azucarado(a) (**b**) *(smile, tone)* almibarado(a)
suggest [sə'dʒest] *vt* (**a**) *(propose)* sugerir; **to s. (that)...** sugerir que...; **I s. (that) we discuss it tomorrow** sugiero que lo discutamos mañana (**b**) *(insinuate, imply)* sugerir, denotar; **her expression suggested a lack of interest** su expresión denotaba falta de interés
suggestible [sə'dʒestɪbəl] *adj* sugestionable
suggestion [sə'dʒestʃən] *n* (**a**) *(proposal)* sugerencia *f*; **to make a s.** hacer una sugerencia; **s. box** buzón *m* de sugerencias (**b**) *(insinuation, hint)* indicio *m*; **there is no s. that he might be guilty** no hay indicios de que pueda ser culpable; **she has just a s. of a foreign accent** tiene un ligerísimo acento extranjero
suggestive [sə'dʒestɪv] *adj* (**a**) *(reminiscent, thought-provoking)* sugerente; **to be s. of sth** sugerir algo (**b**) *(erotic)* insinuante
suggestively [sə'dʒestɪvlɪ] *adv (leer, move)* de forma insinuante
suicidal [sʊɪ'saɪdəl] *adj* suicida
suicide ['sʊɪsaɪd] *n* suicidio *m*; **to commit s.** suicidarse; **s. bomber** terrorista *mf* suicida; **s. mission** misión *f* suicida; **s. note** = nota que deja un suicida
suit [suːt] **1** *n* (**a**) *(clothing)* traje *m*, *Andes, RP* terno *m*; **s. of armor** armadura *f* (**b**) *(in cards)* palo *m*; *Fig* **to follow s.** seguir el ejemplo; *Fig* **politeness is not his strong s.** la amabilidad no es su fuerte (**c**) *Law* pleito *m*, demanda *f*
2 *vt* (**a**) *(of clothes, colors)* sentar bien a; **blue/this hat suits you** el azul/este sombrero te sienta bien (**b**) *(of arrangement, time, job)* convenir a, venir bien a; **to be suited to** *or* **for sth** *(purpose, job)* ser indicado(a) para algo; **they are well suited to each other** están hechos el uno para el otro; **s. yourself** haz lo que quieras (**c**) *(adapt)* adecuar
suit up *vi* ponerse el traje
suitability [suːtə'bɪlɪtɪ] *n (of arrangement, comment)* conveniencia *f*
suitable ['suːtəbəl] *adj* adecuado(a), apropiado(a); **the movie is not s. for children** la película no es apta para menores
suitably ['suːtəblɪ] *adv (behave, dress)* adecuadamente; **she was s. impressed** estaba impresionada como correspondía
suitcase ['suːtkeɪs] *n* maleta *f*, *Méx* petaca *f*, *RP* valija *f*
suite [swiːt] *n* (**a**) *(of rooms)* suite *f*; **(three-piece) s.** tresillo *m*,

conjunto *m* de sofá y (dos) sillones (**b**) *Mus* suite *f*
suitor ['suːtə(r)] *n* (**a**) *(admirer)* pretendiente *m* (**b**) *Law* demandante *mf*
sulfate ['sʌlfeɪt] *n Chem* sulfato *m*
sulfide ['sʌlfaɪd] *n Chem* sulfuro *m*
sulfur ['sʌlfə(r)] *n Chem* azufre *m*; **s. dioxide** dióxido *m* de azufre
sulfuric [sʌl'fjʊərɪk] *adj Chem* sulfúrico(a); **s. acid** ácido *m* sulfúrico
sulk [sʌlk] **1** *n* **to be in a s.** estar enfurruñado(a)
2 *vi* enfurruñarse
sulkily ['sʌlkɪlɪ] *adv* enrabietadamente
sulky ['sʌlkɪ] *adj* enfurruñado(a), enrabietado(a)
sullen ['sʌlən] *adj* huraño(a), hosco(a)
sullenly ['sʌlənlɪ] *adv* hoscamente
sully ['sʌlɪ] *vt Literary (reputation)* manchar; *Fig* **to s. one's hands (with sth)** mancharse las manos (con algo)
sultan ['sʌltən] *n* sultán *m*
sultry ['sʌltrɪ] *adj (heat, weather)* bochornoso(a), sofocante; *(look, smile)* sensual
sum [sʌm] *n (amount of money, mathematical problem)* suma *f*; **to do sums** hacer cuentas; **in s.** en suma; **the s. of my efforts** el resultado de mis esfuerzos; **s. total** (suma) total *m*
▸**sum up** *(pt & pp* **summed)** **1** *vt sep* (**a**) *(summarize)* resumir (**b**) *(assess quickly)* evaluar
2 *vi (summarize)* resumir; *(in debate, trial)* recapitular
summarily ['sʌmərɪlɪ] *adv* sumariamente
summarize ['sʌməraɪz] *vt* resumir
summary ['sʌmərɪ] **1** *n* resumen *m*; *TV & Rad* **news s.** resumen *m* de noticias
2 *adj (brief)* sumario(a); **s. dismissal** despido *m* inmediato
summer ['sʌmə(r)] **1** *n* verano *m*; **in (the) s.** en verano; **s. vacations** vacaciones *fpl* de verano; **s. school** escuela *f* de verano
2 *vi* veranear
summerhouse ['sʌməhaʊs] *n (in garden)* glorieta *f*, cenador *m*
summertime ['sʌmətaɪm] *n* verano *m*
summery ['sʌmərɪ] *adj* veraniego(a)
summing-up [sʌmɪŋ'ʌp] *n Law* recapitulación *f*, conclusiones *fpl*
summit ['sʌmɪt] *n* (**a**) *(of mountain, career, power)* cima *f*, cumbre *f* (**b**) *(meeting)* cumbre *f*; **to hold a s.** celebrar una (reunión en la) cumbre
summon ['sʌmən] *vt (police, doctor)* llamar; *(help)* pedir; *(meeting)* convocar; *Law (witness)* citar
▸**summon up** *vt sep (courage)* armarse de; *(support)* reunir; **to s. up one's strength** hacer acopio de fuerzas
summons ['sʌmənz] **1** *n (pl* **summonses** ['sʌmənzɪz]) citación *f*
2 *vt Law* citar
sump [sʌmp] *n (cesspool)* pozo *m* negro
sumptuous ['sʌm(p)tjʊəs] *adj* suntuoso(a)
sumptuously ['sʌm(p)tjʊəslɪ] *adv* suntuosamente
Sun *(abbr* **Sunday)** domingo *m*
sun [sʌn] **1** *n* sol *m*; **in the s.** al sol; **you've caught the s.** te ha dado el sol; **everything under the s.** todo lo habido y por haber; **s. hat** pamela *f*; **s. lamp** lámpara *f* de rayos UVA; **s. lotion** loción *f* bronceadora; *Aut* **s. shield** *or* **visor** parasol *m*
2 *vt (pt & pp* **sunned)** **to s. oneself** tomar el sol
sunbaked ['sʌnbeɪkt] *adj* abrasado(a), agostado(a)
sunbathe ['sʌnbeɪð] *vi* tomar el sol
sunbathing ['sʌnbeɪðɪŋ] *n* baños *mpl* de sol; **to do some s.** tomar el sol
sunbeam ['sʌnbiːm] *n* rayo *m* de sol

sunblock ['sʌnblɒk] n bloqueador m solar
sunburn ['sʌnbɜ:n] n quemadura f (de sol)
sunburned ['sʌnbɜ:nd], **sunburnt** ['sʌnbɜ:nt] adj quemado(a) (por el sol)
sundae ['sʌndeɪ] n helado m con fruta y nueces
Sunday ['sʌndeɪ] n domingo m; **S. best** traje m de los domingos; **S. paper** periódico m dominical or del domingo; Rel **S. school** catequesis f inv dominical; see also **Saturday**
sundial ['sʌndaɪəl] n reloj m de sol
sundown ['sʌndaʊn] n puesta f de sol, atardecer m; **at s.** al atardecer
sun-drenched ['sʌndrenʃt] adj bañado(a) de sol
sun-dried ['sʌndraɪd] adj secado(a) al sol; **s. tomatoes** tomates mpl or Méx jitomates mpl secos
sundry ['sʌndrɪ] **1** n (a) **all and s.** todo quisque (b) **sundries** (items) artículos mpl varios; (costs) gastos mpl diversos
  2 adj diversos(as)
sunflower ['sʌnflaʊə(r)] n girasol m; **s. oil** aceite m de girasol; **s. seeds** (as snack) pipas fpl (de girasol)
sung [sʌŋ] pp of **sing**
sunglasses ['sʌnglɑ:sɪz] npl gafas fpl or Am anteojos mpl de sol
sunk [sʌŋk] pp of **sink**[2]
sunken ['sʌŋkən] adj (ship, eyes) hundido(a); (rock) sumergido(a)
sunlamp ['sʌnlæmp] n lámpara f de rayos UVA
sunlight ['sʌnlaɪt] n (luz f del) sol m; **in the s.** al sol
sunlit ['sʌnlɪt] adj soleado(a)
Sunni ['sʊnɪ] n (person) sunnita mf; (religion) sunnismo m
sunny ['sʌnɪ] adj (a) (day, place) soleado(a); **it's s.** hace sol (b) (face, personality) radiante
sunrise ['sʌnraɪz] n amanecer m; **at s.** al amanecer; Econ **s. industry** industria f de tecnología punta
sunroof ['sʌnru:f] n Aut techo m solar
sunset ['sʌnset] n puesta f de sol, atardecer m; **at s.** al atardecer
sunshade ['sʌnʃeɪd] n (for table) sombrilla f
sunshine ['sʌnʃaɪn] n sol m; **five hours' s.** cinco horas de sol
sunspot ['sʌnspɒt] n (a) Astron mancha f solar (b) Fam (vacation resort) lugar m (costero) de veraneo
sunstroke ['sʌnstrəʊk] n Med insolación f
suntan ['sʌntæn] n bronceado m; **s. lotion** loción f bronceadora
sun-up ['sʌnʌp] n amanecer m
sup [sʌp] (pt & pp **supped**) vt beber a sorbos
super ['su:pə(r)] **1** n (a) (gas) (gasolina f or RP nafta f) súper f (b) (of apartment building) portero(a) m,f
  2 adj Fam (excellent) genial, Am salvo RP chévere, Méx padre, RP bárbaro(a)
superabundant [su:pərə'bʌndənt] adj superabundante
superannuated [su:pər'ænjʊeɪtɪd] adj (a) (job, post) con plan de jubilación incluido (b) (obsolete) anticuado(a), obsoleto(a)
superannuation [su:pərænjʊ'eɪʃən] n Fin pensión f (de jubilación)
superb [su:'pɜ:b] adj excelente
supercharger ['su:pətʃɑ:dʒə(r)] n Aut & Av sobrealimentador m
supercilious [su:pə'sɪlɪəs] adj arrogante, altanero(a)
superconductor [su:pəkən'dʌktə(r)] n Phys superconductor m
super-duper ['su:pə'du:pə(r)] adj Fam genial, Esp superguay, Am salvo RP cheverísimo(a), Méx padrísimo(a), RP regenial
superego ['su:pəri:gəʊ] (pl **superegos**) n Psy superyó m, superego m
superficial [su:pə'fɪʃəl] adj superficial
superficiality [su:pəfɪʃɪ'ælɪtɪ] n superficialidad f
superficially [su:pə'fɪʃəlɪ] adv superficialmente

superfluous [su:'pɜ:flʊəs] adj superfluo(a)
superhuman [su:pə'hju:mən] adj sobrehumano(a)
superimpose [su:pərɪm'pəʊz] vt superponer
superintend [su:pərɪn'tend] vt supervisar
superintendent [su:pərɪn'tendənt] n (supervisor) supervisor(ora) m,f, director(ora) m,f; (police officer) comisario(a) m,f jefe; (of apartment building) portero(a) m,f
superior [su:'pɪərɪə(r)] **1** n (senior) superior m; **to be sb's s.** ser el superior de alguien
  2 adj (a) (better, more senior) superior (b) (arrogant) arrogante; **a s. smile** una sonrisa (con aires) de superioridad
superiority [su:pɪərɪ'ɒrɪtɪ] n superioridad f
superlative [su:'pɜ:lətɪv] **1** n Gram superlativo m
  2 adj (a) (excellent) excelente (b) Gram superlativo(a)
superlatively [su:'pɜ:lətɪvlɪ] adv extremadamente, extraordinariamente
superman ['su:pəmæn] n superhombre m
supermarket ['su:pəmɑ:kɪt] n supermercado m
supernatural [su:pə'nætʃərəl] **1** n **the s.** lo sobrenatural
  2 adj sobrenatural
superpower ['su:pəpaʊə(r)] n superpotencia f
superscript ['su:pəskrɪpt] n Typ superíndice m; **s. "a"** "a" escrita como superíndice
supersede [su:pə'si:d] vt sustituir
supersonic [su:pə'sɒnɪk] adj Av supersónico(a)
superstar ['su:pəstɑ:(r)] n superestrella f
superstition [su:pə'stɪʃən] n superstición f
superstitious [su:pə'stɪʃəs] adj supersticioso(a)
superstitiously [su:pə'stɪʃəslɪ] adv supersticiosamente
superstore ['su:pəstɔ:(r)] n Com hipermercado m, gran superficie f
superstructure ['su:pəstrʌktʃə(r)] n superestructura f
supertanker ['su:pətæŋkə(r)] n Naut superpetrolero m
supervise ['su:pəvaɪz] vt (children) vigilar; (work, workers) supervisar
supervision [su:pə'vɪʒən] n (of children) vigilancia f; (of work, workers) supervisión f
supervisor ['su:pəvaɪzə(r)] n supervisor(ora) m,f; (of apartment building) portero(a) m,f
supervisory [su:pə'vaɪzərɪ] adj de supervisión; **in a s. capacity** en calidad de supervisor(ora)
superwoman ['su:pəwʊmən] n Fam supermujer f
supine ['su:paɪn] Formal **1** adj tumbado(a) de espaldas; Fig (inactive) pasivo(a)
  2 adv **to lie s.** yacer de espaldas
supper ['sʌpə(r)] n (evening meal) cena f; (snack before going to bed) = refrigerio que se toma antes de ir a la cama; **to have s.** cenar; **we had fish for s.** cenamos pescado
suppertime ['sʌpətaɪm] n hora f de cenar
supplant [sə'plɑ:nt] vt desbancar; **she supplanted her rival** arrebató el puesto a su rival
supple ['sʌpəl] adj flexible
supplement ['sʌplɪmənt] **1** n (a) (addition) complemento m, (b) (extra charge) suplemento m (c) (of newspaper, book) suplemento m
  2 vt complementar
supplementary [sʌplɪ'mentərɪ] adj complementario(a) suplementario(a)
supplication [sʌplɪ'keɪʃən] n súplica f
supplier [sə'plaɪə(r)] n proveedor m
supply [sə'plaɪ] **1** n abastecimiento m, suministro m; **a week's/a month's s. (of sth)** reservas fpl (de algo) para una semana/un mes; **gas is in short s.** escasean los suministro de gasolina; Econ **s. and demand** la oferta y la demanda; M **s. lines** líneas fpl de abastecimiento; Naut **s. ship** buque m nodriza

2 *vt* **to s. sb with sth, to s. sth to sb** suministrar algo a alguien; **to s. sb's needs** satisfacer las necesidades de alguien

support [sə'pɔːt] **1** *n* (**a**) *(backing)* apoyo *m*; **to give s. to sth/sb** apoyar algo/a alguien; **in s. of...** en apoyo de...; **my son is my only means of s.** mi hijo es mi único sostén económico; *Mus* **s. band** teloneros *mpl* (**b**) *(person, thing supporting)* soporte *m*

2 *vt* (**a**) *(hold up)* sostener, soportar; **I supported him with my arm** lo sujeté con mi brazo (**b**) *(encourage, aid)* apoyar; **to s. a team** ser seguidor(ora) de un equipo; **which team do you s.?** ¿de qué equipo eres? (**c**) *(sustain)* mantener; **to s. oneself** ganarse la vida, mantenerse

supporter [sə'pɔːtə(r)] *n* *(of opinion, party)* partidario(a) *m,f*; *(of team)* seguidor(ora) *m,f*

supporting [sə'pɔːtɪŋ] *adj* **s. band** teloneros *mpl*; *Cin & Theat* **s. cast** actores *mpl* de reparto *or* secundarios

supportive [sə'pɔːtɪv] *adj* **he was s.** apoyó mucho, fue muy comprensivo

suppose [sə'pəʊz] *vt* suponer; **I s. so** supongo (que sí); **I s. not** supongo que no; **s.** *or* **supposing he came back** supongamos *or* suponiendo que volviera; **I don't s. you'd consider sharing it?** ¿considerarías la posibilidad de compartirlo?; **s. we change the subject?** ¿qué te parece si cambiamos de tema?

supposed [sə'pəʊzd] *adj* (**a**) *(meant)* **to be s. to do sth** tener que hacer algo; **you were s. to wash the dishes** tenías que fregar los platos; **you're not s. to smoke in here** aquí dentro no se puede fumar; **there's s. to be a meeting today** se supone que hoy hay reunión (**b**) *(reputed)* **the movie's s. to be very good** se supone que es una película muy buena

supposition [sʌpə'zɪʃən] *n* suposición *f*; **on the s. that...** dando por supuesto que...

suppository [sə'pɒzɪtrɪ] *n* *Med* supositorio *m*

suppress [sə'pres] *vt* *(revolt)* reprimir, sofocar; *(fact, evidence)* ocultar; *(feelings, emotions, smile)* reprimir; *(cough)* ahogar

suppressed [sə'prest] *adj* *(emotion)* reprimido(a)

suppression [sə'preʃən] *n* *(of revolt, feelings, emotions)* represión *f*; *(of fact, evidence)* ocultación *f*

suppurate ['sʌpjʊreɪt] *vi* *Med* supurar

supranational [suːprə'næʃənəl] *adj* supranacional

supremacy [sʊ'preməsɪ] *n* supremacía *f*

supreme [sʊ'priːm] *adj* supremo(a); **to make the s. sacrifice** dar *or* entregar la vida; **to reign s.** *(person)* no tener rival; *(justice, ideology)* imperar; *Mil* **S. Commander** comandante *m* en jefe; *Law* **S. Court** Tribunal *m* Supremo, *Am* Corte *f* Suprema

supremely [sʊ'priːmlɪ] *adv* sumamente

surcharge ['sɜːtʃɑːdʒ] **1** *n* recargo *m*

2 *vt* cobrar con recargo a

sure [ʃʊə(r)] **1** *adj* seguro(a); **to be s. of** *or* **about sth** estar seguro(a) de algo; **she is very s. of herself** está muy segura de sí misma; **to make s. of sth** asegurarse de algo; **to make s. (that)...** asegurarse de que...; **she's s. to win** ganará sin duda; **for s.** con (toda) seguridad; *Fam* **s. thing!** ¡desde luego!

2 *adv* (**a**) *Fam (really)* **it s. is cold** menudo frío que hace; **are you tired — I s. am** ¿estás cansado? — ya lo creo *or* y tanto (**b**) *(yes)* claro

3 sure enough *adv* **s. enough he was there** efectivamente estaba allí

sure-footed [ʃʊə'fʊtɪd] *adj* **to be s.** moverse con paso seguro

surely ['ʃʊəlɪ] *adv* (**a**) *(certainly)* seguramente, sin duda; **s. you don't believe that!** ¡no me digas que te crees eso!; **s. not!** ¡no me digas! (**b**) *(in a sure manner)* **slowly but s.** lento pero seguro

sureness ['ʃʊənɪs] *n* (**a**) *(certainty)* certeza *f*, certidumbre *f* (**b**) *(steadiness) (of aim)* lo certero; *Fig* **he handled the problem**

with great s. of touch se enfrentó al problema con gran aplomo

surety ['ʃʊərətɪ] *n* *Law (money)* fianza *f*, garantía *f*; **to stand s. (for sb)** ser fiador(ora) *m,f or* garante *mf* (de alguien)

surf [sɜːf] **1** *n* oleaje *m*

2 *vt* *Comptr* **to s. the Net** navegar por Internet

3 *vi* *Sport* hacer surf

surface ['sɜːfɪs] **1** *n* (**a**) *(exterior, face)* superficie *f*; *Fig* **on the s.** a primera vista; **by s. mail** por correo terrestre; **s. area** área *f*, superficie *f*; *Phys* **s. tension** tensión *f* superficial; **s. water** aguas *fpl* superficiales (**b**) *(area)* área *f*, superficie *f*

2 *vt* *(road)* pavimentar, revestir

3 *vi* *(submarine, whale)* salir a la superficie; *Fig (person, emotion)* surgir, aparecer

surface-to-air missile ['sɜːfɪstʊeə'mɪsaɪl] *n* *Mil* misil *m* superficie-aire *or* tierra-aire

surface-to-surface missile ['sɜːfɪstə'sɜːfɪs'mɪsaɪl] *n* *Mil* misil *m* superficie-superficie *or* tierra-tierra

surfboard ['sɜːfbɔːd] *n* tabla *f* de surf

surfboarding ['sɜːfbɔːdɪŋ] *n* surf *m*; **to go s.** hacer surf

surfeit ['sɜːfɪt] *n* exceso *m*

surfer ['sɜːfə(r)] *n* surfista *mf*

surfing ['sɜːfɪŋ] *n* surf *m*

surge [sɜːdʒ] **1** *n* *(of electricity)* sobrecarga *f* (temporal); *(of enthusiasm, support)* oleada *f*

2 *vi* *(electricity)* experimentar una sobrecarga (temporal); *(sea)* encresparse; *(crowd)* abalanzarse

surgeon ['sɜːdʒən] *n* cirujano(a) *m,f*; **S. General** director(ora) *m,f* general de sanidad pública

surgery ['sɜːdʒərɪ] *n* cirugía *f*; **to perform s. on sb** realizar una operación a alguien

surgical ['sɜːdʒɪkəl] *adj* quirúrgico(a); *Fig* **with s. precision** con una precisión milimétrica; **s. instruments** instrumental *m* quirúrgico; *Mil* **s. strike** ataque *m* controlado *(de objetivos específicos)*

surgically ['sɜːdʒɪklɪ] *adv* quirúrgicamente

Surinam [sʊrɪ'næm] *n* Surinam

surly ['sɜːlɪ] *adj* hosco(a), arisco(a)

surmise [sɜː'maɪz] *vt* presumir, figurarse

surmount [sɜː'maʊnt] *vt* *(obstacle, difficulty)* vencer, superar

surname ['sɜːneɪm] *n* apellido *m*

surpass [sɜː'pɑːs] *vt* *(rival)* aventajar, sobrepasar; *(expectation, record)* superar

surplice ['sɜːplɪs] *n* *Rel* sobrepelliz *f*

surplus ['sɜːpləs] **1** *n* *Econ (of goods)* excedente *m*; *(of trade, budget)* superávit *m inv*

2 *adj* *(items)* excedente; **to be s. to requirements** sobrar

surprise [sə'praɪz] **1** *n* sorpresa *f*; **to take sb by s.** *Esp* coger *or Am* agarrar a alguien por sorpresa; **to give sb a s.** dar una sorpresa a alguien; **what a s.!** ¡qué sorpresa!; **it was no s.** no fue ninguna sorpresa; **to my great s., much to my s.** para mi sorpresa

2 *adj* *(attack)* (por) sorpresa; *(defeat)* sorpresivo(a); **s. party** fiesta *f* sorpresa

3 *vt* (**a**) *(astonish)* sorprender; **I was pleasantly surprised** me sorprendió gratamente; **I'm not surprised that...** no me extraña que... (**b**) *(catch unawares)* *Esp* coger *or Am* agarrar por sorpresa

surprising [sə'praɪzɪŋ] *adj* sorprendente

surprisingly [sə'praɪzɪŋlɪ] *adv* sorprendentemente; **s. enough** sorprendentemente; **not s.** como era de esperar

surreal [sə'rɪəl] *adj* surrealista

surrealism [sə'rɪəlɪzəm] *n* *Art* surrealismo *m*

surrealist [sə'rɪəlɪst] *n & adj* surrealista *mf*

surrealistic [sərɪə'lɪstɪk] *adj* surrealista

surrender [sə'rendə(r)] **1** *n* *(of army)* rendición *f*; *(of weapons)* entrega *f*; **no s.!** ¡no nos rendiremos!; *Fin* **s. value** valor *m* de rescate

2 *vt (fortress, town)* rendir, entregar; *(right, possessions)* renunciar a; *(advantage)* perder; **to s. control of sth** entregar el control de algo

3 *vi* rendirse

surreptitious [sʌrəp'tɪʃəs] *adj* subrepticio(a), clandestino(a)

surreptitiously [sʌrəp'tɪʃəslɪ] *adv* subrepticiamente, clandestinamente

surrogacy ['sʌrəgəsɪ] *n Med* alquiler *m* de úteros

surrogate ['sʌrəgət] *n* sustituto(a) *m,f;* **s. mother** madre *f* de alquiler

surround [sə'raʊnd] **1** *n* marco *m*

2 *vt* rodear; **surrounded by...** rodeado(a) de *or* por...

surrounding [sə'raʊndɪŋ] **1** *adj* circundante

2 surroundings *npl* entorno *m*

surtax ['sɜːtæks] *Fin* **1** *n* impuesto *m* adicional

2 *vt* aplicar un impuesto adicional a

surveillance [sɜː'veɪləns] *n* vigilancia *f;* **under s.** bajo vigilancia

survey 1 *n* ['sɜːveɪ] **(a)** *(of subject, situation)* estudio *m;* *(of opinions)* encuesta *f* **(b)** *(of building)* tasación *f,* peritaje *m;* *(of land)* estudio *m* topográfico

2 *vt* [sə'veɪ] **(a)** *(topic, subject)* estudiar **(b)** *(building)* tasar, peritar; *(land)* medir

surveying [sə'veɪɪŋ] *n (building)* tasación *f,* peritaje *m;* *(land)* agrimensura *f*

surveyor [sə'veɪə(r)] *n (of building)* tasador(ora) *m,f or* perito(a) *m,f* de la propiedad; *(of land)* agrimensor(ora) *m,f*

survival [sə'vaɪvəl] *n* **(a)** *(continued existence)* supervivencia *f; also Fig* **the s. of the fittest** la supervivencia del más apto; **s. kit** equipo *m* de supervivencia **(b)** *(relic)* vestigio *m*

survive [sə'vaɪv] **1** *vt* sobrevivir a

2 *vi* sobrevivir; **my pay is barely enough to s. on** mi sueldo apenas llega para sobrevivir

surviving [sə'vaɪvɪŋ] *adj* superviviente

survivor [sə'vaɪvə(r)] *n* superviviente *mf*

susceptibility [səseptɪ'bɪlɪtɪ] *n (to criticism, pressure)* sensibilidad *f* **(to** a); *(to illness)* propensión *f* **(to** a)

susceptible [sə'septɪbəl] *adj (to criticism, pressure)* sensible **(to** a); *(to illness)* propenso(a) **(to** a)

sushi ['suːʃɪ] *n* sushi *m*

suspect ['sʌspekt] **1** *n* sospechoso(a) *m,f*

2 *adj* sospechoso(a)

3 *vt* [sə'spekt] **(a)** *(person)* sospechar de; **to s. sb of having done sth** sospechar que alguien ha hecho algo **(b)** *(have intuition of) (motives)* recelar de; **to s. the truth** sospechar (cuál es la verdad) **(c)** *(consider likely)* **I s. you're right** sospecho que tienes razón; **I suspected as much!** ¡ya me lo imaginaba!

suspected [sə'spektɪd] *adj* supuesto(a); **a s. murderer** un presunto asesino

suspend [sə'spend] *vt* **(a)** *(hang)* suspender, colgar **(from** de) **(b)** *(service, employee)* suspender; **he was suspended from school** lo expulsaron temporalmente del colegio

suspended [sə'spendɪd] *adj* suspendido(a); **s. animation** muerte *f* aparente; *Law* **to give sb a s. sentence** conceder a alguien una suspensión *or* remisión condicional de la pena

suspender [sə'spendə(r)] *n* **suspenders** *(for pants)* tirantes *mpl*

suspense [sə'spens] *n (uncertainty)* incertidumbre *f; (in movie) Esp* suspense *m, Am* suspenso *m;* **to keep sb in s.** tener a alguien en suspenso

suspension [sə'spenʃən] *n* **(a)** *(of car)* suspensión *f;* **s. bridge** puente *m* colgante **(b)** *(of service, employee)* suspensión *f; (from school)* expulsión *f* (temporal)

suspicion [sə'spɪʃən] *n* **(a)** *(belief of guilt)* sospecha *f;* **to be under s.** estar bajo sospecha; **to be above s.** estar libre de sospecha; **I have my suspicions about him** tengo mis

sospechas sobre él; **to arouse s.** despertar sospechas **(b)** *(small amount)* asomo *m*

suspicious [sə'spɪʃəs] *adj* **(a)** *(arousing suspicion) (fact, behavior, circumstances)* sospechoso(a) **(b)** *(having suspicions) (person, mind)* receloso(a) **(of** or **about** de); **his behavior made me s.** su comportamiento me hizo sospechar

suspiciously [sə'spɪʃəslɪ] *adv (behave)* sospechosamente; *(watch, ask)* recelosamente, con suspicacia; **s. similar** sospechosamente similares

sustain [sə'steɪn] *vt* **(a)** *(weight, growth, life)* sostener; *Law* **objection sustained** se admite la protesta **(b)** *(loss, attack)* sufrir

sustainable [sə'steɪnəbl] *adj* sostenible; **s. development** desarrollo *m* sostenible

sustained [sə'steɪnd] *adj* continuo(a); **s. applause** aplauso *m* prolongado

sustenance ['sʌstɪnəns] *n* sustento *m;* **means of s.** medio *m* de vida

suture ['suːtʃə(r)] *n Med* sutura *f*

SUV [esjuː'viː] *n (abbr* **sport-utility vehicle)** todoterreno *m*

SW *n* **(a)** *(abbr* **southwest)** SO, sudoeste *m* **(b)** *Rad (abbr* **shortwave)** SW, OC, onda *f* corta

swab [swɒb] **1** *n Med (cotton wool)* torunda *f*

2 *vt (pt & pp* **swabbed)** *(clean) (wound)* limpiar; *(floor)* fregar

swag [swæg] *n Fam (of thief)* botín *m*

swagger ['swægə(r)] **1** *n* pavoneo *m*

2 *vi (strut)* pavonearse; **to s. in/out** entrar/salir pavoneándose

swallow¹ ['swɒləʊ] **1** *n (of drink)* trago *m; (of food)* bocado *m*

2 *vt* **(a)** *(food, drink)* tragar, tragarse; **to s. sth whole** tragar algo sin masticar; *Fig* **to s. one's pride** tragarse el orgullo **(b)** *Fam (believe)* tragarse

3 *vi* tragar; **to s. hard** *(when nervous, afraid)* tragar saliva

▶ **swallow up** *vt sep (company, country)* absorber

swallow² *n (bird)* golondrina *f; Prov* **one s. doesn't make a summer** una golondrina no hace verano

swam [swæm] *pt of* **swim**

swamp [swɒmp] **1** *n* pantano *m;* **s. fever** *(malaria)* paludismo *m,* malaria *f*

2 *vt (flood)* anegar, inundar; *Fig* **to be swamped with work** estar desbordado(a) de trabajo

swan [swɒn] *n* cisne *m; Fig* **s. song** canto *m* de cisne

swank [swæŋk] *Fam* **1** *n (ostentation)* fanfarronería *f (ostentatious person)* fanfarrón(ona) *m,f,* figurón *m*

2 *vi* fanfarronear

swanky ['swæŋkɪ] *adj Fam (person) (boastful)* fanfarrón(ona) *(posh) Esp* pijo(a), *Méx* fresa; *(restaurant, hotel)* fastuoso(a) pomposo(a)

swap [swɒp] **1** *n* trueque *m,* intercambio *m;* **to do a s.** hacer un trueque

2 *vt (pt & pp* **swapped)** **to s. sth for sth** cambiar algo por algo; **to s. places with sb** *(change seat)* cambiarse de sitio con alguien; *Fig* intercambiar papeles con alguien; **to s. insults/ideas** intercambiar insultos/ideas

3 *vi* hacer un intercambio

swarm [swɔːm] **1** *n (of bees)* enjambre *m; (of people)* nube *f* enjambre *m*

2 *vi (bees)* volar en enjambre; *(people)* apelotonarse, ir en masa; **Orlando was swarming with tourists** Orlando era un hervidero de turistas

swarthy ['swɔːðɪ] *adj* moreno(a), atezado(a)

swashbuckling ['swɒʃbʌklɪŋ] *adj (hero)* intrépido(a) *(movie, story)* de espadachines

swastika ['swɒstɪkə] *n* esvástica *f,* cruz *f* gamada

SWAT [swɒt] *n (abbr* **Special Weapons and Tactics)** *Esp* ≃ GEO *m,* = unidad armada de la policía estadounidense especializada en intervenciones peligrosas

swat [swɒt] (*pt & pp* **swatted**) *vt* aplastar

swathe [sweɪð] **1** *n* faja *f*, banda *f*; *Fig* **the cannons had cut great swathes through the troops** los cañones hicieron estragos en las tropas

2 *vt* **to s. sth in bandages** vendar algo, envolver algo en vendajes

sway [sweɪ] **1** *n* (**a**) *(movement)* vaivén *m*, balanceo *m* (**b**) *(control, power)* dominio *m*; **he was under her s.** estaba bajo la férula *or* el yugo de ella; **to hold s. over sth** ejercer dominio sobre algo

2 *vt (influence, persuade)* hacer cambiar (de opinión)

3 *vi* balancearse; **to s. from side to side** balancearse de un lado a otro

Swazi ['swɑːzɪ] **1** *n* (**a**) *(person)* suazi *mf* (**b**) *(language)* suazi *m*

2 *adj* suazi

Swaziland ['swɑːzɪlænd] *n* Suazilandia

swear [sweə(r)] (*pt* **swore** [swɔː(r)], *pp* **sworn** [swɔːn]) **1** *vt (vow)* jurar; **to s. to do sth** jurar hacer algo; *Law* **to s. an oath** prestar juramento

2 *vi (use swearwords)* jurar, decir palabrotas; **to s. at sb** insultar a alguien

swear by *vt insep (have confidence in)* confiar en

▸**swear in** *vt sep Law (jury, witness)* tomar juramento a

swearing ['sweərɪŋ] *n* palabrotas *fpl*; **s. is naughty** decir palabrotas es de mala educación

swearword ['sweəwɜːd] *n* palabrota *f*, *Esp* taco *m*

sweat [swet] **1** *n (perspiration)* sudor *m*; *Fam* **no s.!** ¡no hay problema!; **s. gland** glándula *f* sudorípara

2 *vt* sudar; *Fam* **to s. buckets** sudar a chorros; *Fig* **to s. blood** sudar tinta

3 *vi* (**a**) *(perspire)* sudar; *Fam* **to s. like a pig** sudar como un cerdo (**b**) *Fam Fig (worry)* sufrir, angustiarse; **I'm going to make him s.** voy a dejarle que sufra

sweatband ['swetbænd] *n (on head)* banda *f (para la frente)*; *(on wrist)* muñequera *f*

sweater ['swetə(r)] *n* suéter *m*, *Esp* jersey *m*, *Col* saco *m*, *RP* pulóver *m*

sweating ['swetɪŋ] *n* transpiración *f*, sudoración *f*

sweatshirt ['swetʃɜːt] *n* sudadera *f*, *Col*, *RP* buzo *m*

sweatshop ['swetʃɒp] *n* = fábrica donde se explota al trabajador

sweaty ['swetɪ] *adj* sudoroso(a); **to be s.** estar sudoroso(a); **s. smell** olor *m* a sudor

Swede [swiːd] *n (person)* sueco(a) *m,f*

Sweden ['swiːdən] *n* Suecia

Swedish ['swiːdɪʃ] **1** *npl (people)* **the S.** los suecos

2 *n (language)* sueco *m*

3 *adj* sueco(a)

weep [swiːp] **1** *n* (**a**) *(action)* barrido *m*, *Am* barrida *f*; *Fig* **at one s.** de una pasada; *Fig* **to make a clean s.** *(replace staff)* quitar de en medio personal; *(of prizes)* arrasar (**b**) *(movement)* **with a s. of the arm** moviendo el brazo extendido (**c**) *(extent)* *(of land, knowledge)* extensión *f*; *(of road, river)* curva *f*

2 *vt (pt & pp* **swept** [swept]) (**a**) *(floor, street)* barrer; *(chimney)* deshollinar; **a wave swept him overboard** lo arrastró una ola y cayó al mar (**b**) *(idioms)* **to s. sth under the carpet** soterrar algo; **to s. the board** *(in competition)* arrasar; **the latest craze to s. the country** la última moda que está haciendo furor en todo el país; *Fig* **he swept her off her feet** se enamoró perdidamente de él

3 *vi* (**a**) *(with broom)* barrer (**b**) *(move rapidly)* **to s. in/out** entrar/salir con gallardía; **to s. to power** subir al poder de forma arrasadora

sweep aside *vt sep (opposition)* barrer; *(criticism)* hacer caso omiso de

sweep away *vt sep (remove)* barrer

▸**sweep up 1** *vt sep (dust, leaves)* barrer

2 *vi (clean up)* limpiar

sweeper ['swiːpə(r)] *n* (**a**) **(carpet) s.** cepillo *m* mecánico (**b**) *(soccer player)* líbero *m*

sweeping ['swiːpɪŋ] *adj (gesture)* amplio(a); *(statement)* (demasiado) generalizador(ora); *(change)* radical

sweepstake ['swiːpsteɪk] *n* porra *f (juego)*

sweet [swiːt] *adj* (**a**) *(taste, wine)* dulce; *(smell)* fragante; *(sound)* suave, dulce; **to taste s.** saber dulce; **as s. as honey** dulce como la miel; *Fig* **the s. smell of success** las mieles del éxito; **to have a s. tooth** ser goloso(a); **s. corn** maíz *m* tierno, *Andes, RP* choclo *m*, *Méx* elote *m*; *Bot* **s. pea** guisante *m* de olor; **s. potato** batata *f*, *Esp, Cuba, Urug* boniato *m*, *CAm, Méx* camote *m*; *Bot* **s. william** minutisa *f* (**b**) *(charming)* rico(a), mono(a); **that's very s. of you** eres muy amable; **to whisper s. nothings to sb** susurrar palabras de amor a alguien

sweet-and-sour ['swiːtən'saʊə(r)] *adj* agridulce; **s. pork** cerdo *m* agridulce

sweetbreads ['swiːtbredz] *npl* mollejas *fpl*

sweeten ['swiːtən] *vt (food)* endulzar; *Fig* **to s. sb's temper** aplacar el mal humor de alguien

sweetener ['swiːtənə(r)] *n* (**a**) *(in food)* edulcorante *m* (**b**) *Fam (bribe)* propina *f*

sweetheart ['swiːthɑːt] *n* novio(a) *m,f*

sweetie ['swiːtɪ] *n Fam (darling)* cariño *m*; **he's such a s.** es un encanto

sweetly ['swiːtlɪ] *adv (sing, smile)* con dulzura

sweetness ['swiːtnɪs] *n* dulzura *f*, dulzor *m*; **to be all s. and light** estar de lo más amable

sweet-talk ['swiːt'tɔːk] *vt Fam* **to s. sb into doing sth** convencer a alguien con halagos de que haga algo

sweet-tempered [swiːt'tempəd] *adj* apacible

swell [swel] **1** *vt (pp* **swollen** ['swəʊlən] *or* **swelled**) *(numbers, crowd)* aumentar

2 *vi (part of body)* hincharse; *(number, crowd)* aumentar, crecer; **to s. with pride** henchirse de orgullo

3 *n (of sea)* mar *m* de fondo

4 *adj Fam (excellent)* genial, *Méx* padre, *RP* bárbaro(a)

▸**swell up** *vi (part of body)* hincharse

swelling ['swelɪŋ] *n* hinchazón *f*

sweltering ['sweltərɪŋ] *adj* asfixiante, sofocante

swept [swept] *pt & pp of* **sweep**

swerve [swɜːv] **1** *n (of car)* giro *m or* desplazamiento *m* brusco; *(of player)* regate *m*

2 *vi (car)* desplazarse bruscamente; *(driver)* dar un volantazo; *(player)* regatear; *(ball)* ir con efecto

swift [swɪft] **1** *n (bird)* vencejo *m*

2 *adj (runner, horse)* veloz, rápido(a); *(reaction, reply)* rápido(a), pronto(a)

swift-footed ['swɪftfʊtɪd] *adj* rápido(a)

swiftly ['swɪftlɪ] *adv (move)* velozmente, rápidamente; *(react)* con rapidez, con prontitud

swiftness ['swɪftnɪs] *n (of movement, reply)* rapidez *f*

swig [swɪg] *Fam* **1** *n* trago *m*; **he took a s. from the bottle** dio un trago de la botella

2 *vt(pt & pp* **swigged**) *Esp* pimplar, *Am* tomar

swill [swɪl] **1** *n (food) (for pigs)* sobras *fpl* para los cerdos *or* puercos *or Am* chanchos; *Pej (for people)* bazofia *f*, *Esp* bodrio *m*

2 *vt Fam (drink)* trasegar, tragar

swim [swɪm] **1** *n* baño *m*; **to go for or have a s.** ir a nadar, ir a darse un baño

2 *vt (pt* **swam** [swæm], *pp* **swum** [swʌm]) nadar; **to s. the breaststroke** *Esp* nadar a braza, *Am* nadar pecho; **to s. the Channel** atravesar el Canal de la Mancha a nado

3 *vi* (**a**) *(in water)* nadar; **to go swimming** ir a nadar; **to s. across a river** atravesar un río a nado; *Fig* **to s. with the**

tide seguir la corriente (**b**) *(be dizzy)* **my head is swimming** me da vueltas la cabeza

swimmer ['swɪmə(r)] *n* nadador(ora) *m,f*

swimming ['swɪmɪŋ] *n* natación *f*; **s. lesson** clase *f* de natación; **s. pool** piscina *f*, *Méx* alberca *f*, *RP* pileta *f*; **s. suit** traje *m* de baño, *Esp* bañador *m*, *Ecuad, Perú, RP* malla *f*; **s. trunks** traje *m* de baño *(de hombre)*, *Esp* bañador *m (de hombre)*, *Ecuad, Perú, RP* malla *f (de hombre)*

swimmingly ['swɪmɪŋlɪ] *adv Fam* como la seda

swimsuit ['swɪmsuːt] *n* traje *m* de baño, *Esp* bañador *m*, *Ecuad, Perú, RP* malla *f*

swimwear ['swɪmweə(r)] *n* moda *f* de baño

swindle ['swɪndəl] **1** *n* timo *m*, estafa *f*
  2 *vt* timar, estafar; **to s. sb out of sth** estafarle algo a alguien

swindler ['swɪndlə(r)] *n* timador(ora) *m,f*, estafador(ora) *m,f*

swine [swaɪn] *(pl* **swine**) *n* (**a**) *(pig)* cerdo *m*, puerco *m*, *Am* chancho *m*; **s. fever** peste *f* porcina (**b**) *Fam (unpleasant person)* cerdo(a) *m,f*, canalla *mf*

swing [swɪŋ] **1** *n* (**a**) *(movement) (of rope, chain)* vaivén *m*, balanceo *m*; *(of pendulum)* oscilación *f*; *(in baseball, golf)* swing *m*; *Fam* **to take a s. at sb** intentar darle un golpe a alguien; **to be in full s.** ir a toda marcha; *Fam* **to get into the s. of things** agarrar *or Esp* coger el ritmo (**b**) *(change) (in opinion, in mood)* cambio *m* repentino (**in** de) (**c**) *(in playground)* columpio *m*
  2 *vt (pt & pp* **swung** [swʌŋ]) *(one's arms, baseball bat, racquet, ax)* balancear; **to s. one's hips** menear las caderas; **to s. sth/ sb onto one's shoulder** echarse algo/a alguien al hombro; *Fam* **to s. a deal** cerrar un trato; *Fam* **to s. it so that...** *(arrange things)* arreglar las cosas para que...
  3 *vi* (**a**) *(move to and fro)* balancearse; *(on playground swing)* columpiarse; **to s. open** *(door)* abrirse; **to s. into action** entrar en acción; *Fam* **he should s. for this** *(be hanged)* deberían colgarlo por esto; *Fam* **the party was really swinging** la fiesta estaba muy animada (**b**) *(change direction)* girar, torcer; **to s. around** dar media vuelta

swipe [swaɪp] **1** *n (with fist or stick)* **to take a s. at sb** dirigir un golpe a alguien; *Fig* **the program takes a s. at the rich and famous** el programa dirige sus ataques contra los ricos y famosos
  2 *vt Fam (steal)* afanar, birlar, *Méx* bajar
  3 *vi* **to s. at sb/sth** intentar dar un golpe a alguien/algo

swirl [swɜːl] **1** *n (of cream)* rizo *m*; *(of smoke)* voluta *f*; *(of leaves, dust)* remolino *m*
  2 *vt* revolver
  3 *vi* arremolinarse

swish [swɪʃ] **1** *n* (**a**) *(sound) (of cane, whip)* silbido *m*; *(of dress, silk)* frufrú *m*, (sonido *m* del) roce *m* (**b**) *Fam (effeminate homosexual)* mariquita *m*
  2 *adj Fam (elegant, smart)* distinguido(a), refinado(a)
  3 *vt (cane, whip)* hacer silbar; **to s. its tail** *(animal)* menear *or* agitar la cola
  4 *vi (dress, silk)* sonar al rozar; *(cane, whip)* silbar

Swiss [swɪs] **1** *npl* **the S.** los suizos
  2 *adj* suizo(a); **S. chard** acelga *f*; **S. cheese** queso *m* suizo; **S. cheese plant** costilla *f* de hombre *m*

switch [swɪtʃ] **1** *n* (**a**) *(electrical)* interruptor *m* (**b**) *(in policy, opinion)* cambio *m*, viraje *m*; **to make a s.** hacer un cambio (**c**) *(stick)* vara *f*
  2 *vt* (**a**) *(change)* cambiar (**to** a); *(transfer)* trasladar; **to s. channels/jobs** cambiar de cadena/trabajo; **they switched their attention to something else** dirigieron su atención a otra cosa (**b**) *(exchange)* intercambiar
  3 *vi (change)* cambiar (**to** a); **to s. from gas to electricity** cambiar el gas por la electricidad, pasarse del gas a la electricidad

▸**switch off 1** *vt sep (appliance, heating)* apagar
  2 *vi* (**a**) *(appliance, heating)* apagarse (**b**) *Fam (person)* desconectar

▸**switch on 1** *vt sep (appliance, heating)* encender, *Am* prender
  2 *vi (appliance, heating)* encenderse, *Am* prenderse

▸**switch over** *vi (change TV channel)* cambiar de cadena; **to s. over to gas** pasarse *or* cambiar al gas

switchback ['swɪtʃbæk] *n (road)* carretera *f* en zigzag

switchblade ['swɪtʃbleɪd] *n* navaja *f* automática

switchboard ['swɪtʃbɔːd] *n* centralita *f*, *Am* conmutador *m*; **s. operator** telefonista *mf*

switcher ['swɪtʃə(r)] *n TV & Cin (machine)* mezclador *m* de imagen

switch-hitter ['swɪtʃhɪtə(r)] *n* (**a**) *(in baseball)* bateador(ora) *m,f* ambidextro(a) (**b**) *very Fam (bisexual)* bisexual *mf*, *RP* bi *mf*

switchman ['swɪtʃmən] *n Rail* guardagujas *m inv*

Switzerland ['swɪtsələnd] *n* Suiza

swivel ['swɪvəl] **1** *n* cabeza *f* giratoria; **s. chair** silla *f* giratoria
  2 *vi* girar

swollen ['swəʊlən] *pp of* **swell**

swoon [swuːn] **1** *n* desmayo *m*, desvanecimiento *m*
  2 *vi* desmayarse, desvanecerse

swoop [swuːp] **1** *n (of bird, plane)* (vuelo *m* en) picado *m*; *(of police)* redada *f*
  2 *vi (bird, plane)* volar en *Esp* picado *or Am* picada; *(police)* hacer una redada

sword [sɔːd] *n* espada *f*; **s. dance** danza *f* del sable

swordfish ['sɔːdfɪʃ] *n* pez *m* espada

swore [swɔː(r)] *pt of* **swear**

sworn [swɔːn] **1** *adj* **s. enemy** enemigo(a) *m,f* encarnizado(a)
  2 *pp of* **swear**

swum [swʌm] *pp of* **swim**

swung [swʌŋ] *pt & pp of* **swing**

sycamore ['sɪkəmɔː(r)] *n (plane tree)* plátano *m*

sycophant ['sɪkəfənt] *n* adulador(ora) *m,f*

sycophantic [sɪkə'fæntɪk] *adj* adulador(ora)

Sydney ['sɪdnɪ] *n* Sidney

syllable ['sɪləbəl] *n* sílaba *f*

syllabus ['sɪləbəs] *n* programa *m* de estudios, currículo *m*

sylphlike ['sɪlflaɪk] *adj Hum (woman)* delgada; *(figure)* de sílfide

symbiosis [sɪmbaɪ'əʊsɪs] *n* simbiosis *f inv*

symbiotic [sɪmb(a)ɪ'ɒtɪk] *adj* simbiótico(a)

symbol ['sɪmbəl] *n* símbolo *m*

symbolic [sɪm'bɒlɪk] *adj* simbólico(a)

symbolically [sɪm'bɒlɪklɪ] *adv* simbólicamente, de forma simbólica

symbolism ['sɪmbəlɪzəm] *n Art* simbolismo *m*

symbolist ['sɪmbəlɪst] *n & adj Art* simbolista *mf*

symbolize ['sɪmbəlaɪz] *vt* simbolizar

symmetrical [sɪ'metrɪkəl] *adj* simétrico(a)

symmetrically [sɪ'metrɪklɪ] *adv* simétricamente

symmetry ['sɪmɪtrɪ] *n* simetría *f*

sympathetic [sɪmpə'θetɪk] *adj* comprensivo(a); **to be s. to a proposal/cause** simpatizar con una propuesta/causa; **a s. audience** un público bien dispuesto

sympathetically [sɪmpə'θetɪklɪ] *adv (with understanding)* comprensivamente; *(in favorable light)* con indulgencia

sympathize ['sɪmpəθaɪz] *vi* (**a**) *(show sympathy)* compadecerse (**with** de) (**b**) **to s. (with sth/sb)** *(understand)* comprender (algo/a alguien); *(agree)* estar a favor (de algo/ alguien)

sympathizer ['sɪmpəθaɪzə(r)] *n (political)* simpatizante *mf*

sympathy ['sɪmpəθɪ] *n* (**a**) *(pity, compassion)* compasión *f*; *Formal* **you have my deepest s.** le doy mi más sincero pésame (**b**) *(understanding)* comprensión *f*; *(support)* apoyo *m*, solidaridad *f*; **to feel s. for sb** simpatizar con alguien; *Ind* **s. strike** huelga *f* de solidaridad *or* apoyo

symphony ['sɪmfənɪ] *n Mus* sinfonía *f*; **s. orchestra** orquesta *f* sinfónica

symposium [sɪm'pəʊzɪəm] (*pl* **symposia** [sɪm'pəʊzɪə]) *n* simposio *m*

symptom ['sɪm(p)təm] *n also Fig* síntoma *m*

symptomatic [sɪm(p)tə'mætɪk] *adj* sintomático(a) (**of** de)

synagog(ue) ['sɪnəgɒg] *n* sinagoga *f*

sync(h) [sɪŋk] *n Fam* sincronización *f*; **to be in/out of s. with...** estar/no estar en sintonía con...

synchronization [sɪŋkrənaɪ'zeɪʃən] *n* sincronización *f*

synchronize ['sɪŋkrənaɪz] *vt* sincronizar

syncopation [sɪŋkə'peɪʃən] *n Mus* síncopa *f*

syndicalism ['sɪndɪkəlɪzəm] *n Pol* sindicalismo *m* (revolucionario)

syndicalist ['sɪndɪkəlɪst] *n Pol* sindicalista *m* (revolucionario(a))

syndicate 1 *n* ['sɪndɪkət] *Com* agrupación *f*; **crime s.** organización *f* criminal
2 *vt* ['sɪndɪkeɪt] *Journ* sindicar, = difundir conjuntamente en diferentes medios; **syndicated columnist** = columnista que publica simultáneamente en varios medios

syndication [sɪndɪ'keɪʃən] *n Journ* sindicación *f* de contenidos

syndrome ['sɪndrəʊm] *n Med & Fig* síndrome *m*

synergy ['sɪnədʒɪ] *n* sinergia *f*

synod ['sɪnəd] *n Rel* sínodo *m*

synonym ['sɪnənɪm] *n* sinónimo *m*

synonymous [sɪ'nɒnɪməs] *adj* sinónimo(a) (**with** de)

synopsis [sɪ'nɒpsɪs] (*pl* **synopses** [sɪ'nɒpsiːz]) *n* sinopsis *f inv*, resumen *m*

syntax ['sɪntæks] *n Ling* sintaxis *f inv*; *Comptr* **s. error** error *m* de sintaxis

synth [sɪnθ] *n Fam* sintetizador *m*

synthesis ['sɪnθɪsɪs] (*pl* **syntheses** ['sɪnθɪsiːz]) *n* síntesis *f inv*

synthesize ['sɪnθəsaɪz] *vt* sintetizar

synthesizer ['sɪnθəsaɪzə(r)] *n* sintetizador *m*

synthetic [sɪn'θetɪk] **1** *n* **synthetics** fibras *fpl* sintéticas
2 *adj* sintético(a)

synthetically [sɪn'θetɪklɪ] *adv* sintéticamente

syphilis ['sɪfɪlɪs] *n* sífilis *f inv*

syphon = **siphon**

Syria ['sɪrɪə] *n* Siria

Syrian ['sɪrɪən] *n & adj* sirio(a) *m,f*

syringe [sɪ'rɪndʒ] **1** *n* jeringuilla *f*
2 *vt Med (ears)* destaponar

syrup ['sɪrəp] *n (of sugar)* almíbar *m*; *(medicinal)* jarabe *m*

syrupy ['sɪrəpɪ] *adj (smile, music)* almibarado(a)

sysop ['sɪsɒp] *n Comptr (abbr* **systems operator**) operador *m* de sistemas

system ['sɪstəm] *n* **(a)** *(structure, method)* sistema *m*; **the s.** *(established order)* el sistema; *Fam* **it was a shock to the s.** fue todo un trauma; *Fam* **to get sth/sb out of one's s.** quitarse *or Am* sacarse algo/a alguien de la cabeza **(b)** *Comptr* **systems analysis** análisis *m inv* de sistemas; **systems analyst** analista *mf* de sistemas; **s. disk** disco *m* de sistema; **s. error** error *m* del sistema

systematic [sɪstə'mætɪk] *adj* sistemático(a)

systematically [sɪstə'mætɪklɪ] *adv* sistemáticamente

systematize ['sɪstəmətaɪz] *vt* sistematizar

T

T, t [tiː] *n* (**a**) *(letter)* T, t *f* (**b**) *(idioms)* **that's you to a T** *(of impersonation)* es clavado a ti; **it suits me to a T** me viene como anillo al dedo

t *(abbr* **ton(s)**) tonelada(s) *fpl (= 907 kg)*

tab [tæb] *n* (**a**) *(on garment)* etiqueta *f*; *Fam* **to keep tabs on sth/sb** vigilar de cerca algo/a alguien (**b**) *(on typewriter, word processor)* tabulador *m*; **t. (key)** tecla *f* de tabular, tabulador *m* (**c**) *(on can of drink)* anilla *f* (**d**) *Fam (bill)* cuenta *f* (**e**) *Fam (of drug)* pasti *f*, pastilla *f*; *(for curtains)* anilla *f*

tabby ['tæbɪ] *n* **t. (cat)** gato *m* atigrado

tabernacle ['tæbənækəl] *n (church)* tabernáculo *m*; *(on altar)* sagrario *m*

table ['teɪbəl] **1** *n* (**a**) *(furniture)* mesa *f*; **to lay** *or* **set the t.** poner la mesa; **to clear the t.** recoger la mesa; **at t.** a la mesa; **t. dancing** striptease *m (en el que las bailarinas se acercan a las mesas)*; **t. lamp** lámpara *f* de mesa; **t. linen** mantelería *f*; **t. manners** modales *mpl* (en la mesa); **t. mat** salvamanteles *m inv*; **t. salt** sal *f* de mesa; **t. tennis** ping-pong *m*, tenis *m* de mesa; **t. wine** vino *m* de mesa

(**b**) *(of facts, figures)* tabla *f*; **t. of contents** índice *m*; *Math* **twelve times t.** tabla *f* (de multiplicar) del doce

(**c**) *(idioms)* **the offer is still on the t.** la oferta está aún sobre la mesa; **to turn the tables on sb** cambiarle *or* volverle las tornas a alguien

2 *vt* **to t. a motion/proposal** *(postpone)* posponer la discusión de una moción/propuesta

tablecloth ['teɪbəlklɒθ] *n* mantel *m*

tablespoon ['teɪbəlspuːn] *n (utensil)* cuchara *f* de servir; **a t. of flour** una cucharada (grande) de harina

tablespoonful ['teɪbəlspuːnfʊl] *n* cucharada *f* (grande)

tablet ['tæblɪt] *n* (**a**) *(pill)* comprimido *m*, pastilla *f* (**b**) *(inscribed stone)* lápida *f*

tableware ['teɪbəlweə(r)] *n* servicio *m* de mesa, vajilla *f*

tabloid ['tæblɔɪd] *n (newspaper)* diario *m* popular *or* sensacionalista (de formato tabloide); **the t. press** la prensa popular *or* sensacionalista

taboo [tə'buː] **1** *n (pl* **taboos)** tabú *m*
2 *adj* tabú

tabular ['tæbjʊlə(r)] *adj* **in t. form** en forma tabular

tabulate ['tæbjʊleɪt] *vt (arrange in table)* tabular

tachometer [tæ'kɒmɪtə(r)] *n Aut* tacómetro *m*

tacit ['tæsɪt] *adj* tácito(a)

tacitly ['tæsɪtlɪ] *adv* tácitamente

taciturn ['tæsɪtɜːn] *adj* taciturno(a), retraído(a)

tack [tæk] **1** *n* (**a**) *(small nail)* tachuela *f* (**b**) *Naut* bordada *f*; *Fig* **to change t.** cambiar de enfoque

2 *vt* (**a**) *(fasten)* **to t. (down)** clavar; *Fig* **to t. sth on** *(add)* añadir algo a posteriori (**b**) *(in sewing)* **to t. up a hem** hilvanar un dobladillo

3 *vi Naut* dar bordadas

tackle ['tækəl] **1** *n* (**a**) *(equipment)* equipo *m*; **(fishing) t.** aparejos *mpl* de pesca (**b**) *(challenge) (in soccer)* entrada *f*; *(in football, rugby)* placaje *m*, *Am* tackle *m* (**c**) *(position in football)* tackle *m*

2 *vt* (**a**) *(deal with)* abordar; **to t. sb about sth** *(confront)* abordar a alguien para tratar algo (**b**) *(in soccer)* entrar a; *(in football, rugby)* hacer un placaje a, *Am* tacklear

tacky ['tækɪ] *adj* (**a**) *(sticky)* pegajoso(a) (**b**) *Fam (tasteless)* chabacano(a), ordinario(a), *Esp* hortera, *Méx* gacho(a), *RP* mersa

tact [tækt] *n* tacto *m*, discreción *f*

tactful ['tæktfʊl] *adj* discreto(a), diplomático(a)

tactic ['tæktɪk] *n* táctica *f*

tactical ['tæktɪkəl] *adj* táctico(a); *Pol* **t. voting** voto *m* útil

tactically ['tæktɪklɪ] *adv* tácticamente

tactician [tæk'tɪʃən] *n* táctico(a) *m,f*

tactile ['tæktaɪl] *adj* táctil

tactless ['tæktlɪs] *adj* falto(a) de tacto, indiscreto(a)

tactlessly ['tæktlɪslɪ] *adv* indiscretamente, sin tacto alguno

tad [tæd] *n Fam* **a t. short** un poquitín *or Esp* pelín *or Am* chiquitín corto(a)

tadpole ['tædpəʊl] *n* renacuajo *m*

Tadzhikistan = Tajikistan

taffeta ['tæfɪtə] *n* tafetán *m*

taffy ['tæfɪ] *n (small sweet)* (caramelo *m* de) tofe *m*; *(substance)* caramelo *m*; **t. apple** manzana *f* de caramelo

tag [tæg] **1** *n* (**a**) *(label)* etiqueta *f*; *Gram* **t. question** cláusula *f* final interrogativa (**b**) *(game)* **to play t.** jugar a pillarse *or* al corre que te pillo

2 *vt (pt & pp* **tagged)** *(label)* etiquetar

▸**tag along** *vi* pegarse; **to t. along with sb** pegarse a alguien

▸**tag on** *vt sep* añadir (a posteriori)

Tagus ['teɪgəs] *n* **the T.** el Tajo

Tahiti [tə'hiːtɪ] *n* Tahití

Tahitian [tə'hiːʃən] *n & adj* tahitiano(a) *m,f*

tai chi [taɪ'tʃiː] *n* tai-chi *m*

tail [teɪl] **1** *n* (**a**) *(of bird, fish, plane)* cola *f*; *(of mammal, reptile)* rabo *m*, cola *f*; *(of shirt)* faldón *m*; **tails** *(of coin)* cruz *f*, *Andes, Ven* sello *m*, *Méx* sol *m*, *RP* ceca *f*; **tails, t. coat** frac *m* (**b**) *(idioms)* **with his t. between his legs** con el rabo entre las piernas; *Fam* **to put a t. on sb** ponerle a alguien un vigilante que le sigue a todas partes; *Fam* **to turn t.** salir corriendo *or Esp* por piernas; **t. end** *(of conversation, movie)* final *m*

2 *vt Fam (follow)* seguir a todas partes

▸**tail away, tail off** *vi (attendance)* decrecer; *(performance)* decaer; *(voice)* desvanecerse

tailgate ['teɪlgeɪt] **1** *n Aut* puerta *f* trasera

2 *vt Esp* conducir *or Am* manejar pegado a, pisar los talones a

taillight ['teɪllaɪt] *n Aut* faro *m* trasero

tailor ['teɪlə(r)] **1** *n* sastre *m*; **t.'s dummy** maniquí *m*; **t.'s (store)** sastrería *f*

2 *vt (suit)* confeccionar; *Fig (speech, policy)* adaptar (**to** a)

tailor-made ['teɪləmeɪd] *adj (suit)* hecho(a) a medida; *Fig* **the job was t. for her** el trabajo parecía hecho a su medida

tailplane ['teɪlpleɪn] *n Av* plano *m* de cola

tailspin ['teɪlspɪn] *n Av* barrena *f*; *Fig* **to go into a t.** entrar en barrena

tailwind ['teɪlwɪnd] *n* viento *m* de cola

taint [teɪnt] **1** *n* impureza *f*, contaminación *f*; *Fig* tara *f*
2 *vt* (*contaminate*) contaminar; *Fig* manchar

Taiwan [taɪ'wɑːn] *n* Taiwán

Taiwanese [taɪwə'niːz] *n & adj* taiwanés(esa) *m,f*

Tajikistan, Tadzhikistan [tɑːdʒɪkɪ'stɑːn] *n* Tayikistán

take [teɪk] **1** *vt* (*pt* **took** [tʊk], *pp* **taken** ['teɪkən]) (**a**) (*grasp*) tomar, coger, *Am* agarrar; **to t. hold of sth** agarrar algo; **to t. sb by the arm** tomar *o* coger a alguien del brazo; **to t. sb in one's arms** tomar *o* coger en brazos a alguien; **to t. the opportunity to do sth** aprovechar la oportunidad para hacer algo
(**b**) (*remove, steal*) tomar, coger; **to t. sth away from sb** quitarle algo a alguien; **to t. sth out of sth** sacar algo de algo
(**c**) (*tolerate*) (*heat, pressure*) soportar, aguantar; **she can't t. a joke** no sabe aguantar una broma; **I can't t. (it) anymore** no lo aguanto más
(**d**) (*lead, carry*) llevar; **to t. sb home/to the station** llevar a alguien a casa/a la estación; **to t. sb to court** llevar a alguien a juicio; **to t. flowers to sb, to t. sb flowers** llevarle flores a alguien; **to t. the dog for a walk** sacar a pasear al perro; **her job takes her all over the world** su trabajo le hace viajar por todo el mundo; **if you can get the money we'll t. it from there** si consigues el dinero, entonces veremos
(**e**) (*get on*) (*bus, road*) tomar; **t. the first turning on the left** gira por la primera a la izquierda
(**f**) (*require*) (*effort, dedication, strength*) requerir; **it took four of us to carry him** hicimos falta cuatro para llevarlo; **it takes courage to...** hace falta valor para...; **how long does it t.?** ¿cuánto tiempo lleva?; **learning a language takes a long time** aprender un idioma lleva mucho tiempo; **it took me an hour to get here** tardé una hora en llegar; **that will t. some explaining** eso va a ser complicado de explicar
(**g**) (*adopt*) (*precautions, measures*) tomar; **to t. legal advice** consultar a un abogado; **to t. sth as an example** tomar algo como ejemplo
(**h**) (*record*) (*temperature, notes*) tomar; **to t. sb's details** tomar los datos de alguien
(**i**) (*capture*) (*town*) tomar; (*chess, checker piece*) comer(se); **to t. power** hacerse con el poder; **to t. first prize** ganar el primer premio
(**j**) (*assume*) **I t. it that...** supongo que...
(**k**) (*accept*) aceptar; **will you t. a check?** ¿se puede pagar con cheque?; **I'll t. the red one** me quedo con el rojo; **does this machine t. quarters?** ¿esta máquina acepta monedas de 25 centavos?; **my car only takes diesel** mi coche sólo funciona con gasóleo; **this bus takes fifty passengers** en este autobús caben cincuenta pasajeros; **t. it or leave it!** ¡lo tomas o lo dejas!; **to t. sth well/badly** tomarse algo bien/mal; **to t. sth the wrong way** malentender algo; **you can t. it from me that...** créeme cuando te digo que...
(**l**) (*exam, subject, course*) hacer (**m**) (*in phrases*) **to t. a bath** darse un baño; **to t. drugs** tomar drogas; **to t. fright** asustarse; **to be taken ill** ponerse enfermo(a); **to t. a look at sth** echar un vistazo a algo; **to t. a photograph of sth/sb** hacer *o* sacar una fotografía a algo/alguien; **to t. a seat** sentarse, tomar asiento; **to t. a walk** dar un paseo
2 *vi* (*be successful*) (*fire*) prender; (*plant cutting*) arraigar; (*innovation*) cuajar; (*dye*) coger
3 *n* (**a**) (*recording*) (*of movie, music*) toma *f* (**b**) (*money*) recaudación *f*; *Fam* **to be on the t.** engordar el bolsillo

▸**take after** *vt insep* (*resemble*) parecerse a

▸**take apart** *vt* (*machine, engine*) desmontar; (*argument*) destrozar

▸**take away 1** *vt sep* (*remove*) quitar, *Am* sacar; *Math* restar (**from** de); **the men are coming to t. away the rubbish tomorrow** los hombres vendrán a llevarse la basura mañana; **to t. sth away from sb** quitar *or Am* sacar algo a alguien

2 *vi* **to t. away from the pleasure/value of sth** restar placer/valor a algo

▸**take back** *vt sep* (**a**) (*return*) devolver; **that takes me back to my childhood** eso me hace volver a la infancia (**b**) (*accept again*) (*former employee*) readmitir; (*faulty goods*) admitir (devolución de); **she's a fool to t. him back** es tonta por dejarle volver (**c**) (*withdraw*) retirar; **t. that back!** ¡retira eso!

▸**take down** *vt sep* (**a**) (*remove*) (*from shelf*) bajar; (*poster, curtains*) quitar, *Am* sacar (**b**) (*lower*) **to t. down one's pants** bajarse los pantalones; *Fam* **to t. sb down a peg or notch or two** bajarle los humos a alguien (**c**) (*dismantle*) (*tent, scaffolding*) desmontar; (*wall, barricade*) desmantelar (**d**) (*record*) anotar, apuntar; (*notes*) tomar

▸**take for** *vt sep* **I took him for somebody else** lo tomé por *or* confundí con otro; **what do you t. me for?** ¿por quién me tomas?

▸**take in** *vt sep* (**a**) (*lead, carry*) (*person*) conducir dentro; (*harvest, washing*) recoger (**b**) (*orphan*) recoger, adoptar; (*lodgers*) admitir (**c**) (*garment*) meter (**d**) (*include*) abarcar, cubrir; **the tour takes in all the major sights** el recorrido cubre todos los principales puntos de interés (**e**) (*understand*) asimilar; **to t. in the situation** hacerse cargo de la situación (**f**) (*deceive*) engañar, embaucar

▸**take off 1** *vt sep* (**a**) (*remove*) (*clothes, makeup*) quitarse, *Am* sacarse; (*lid, sheets*) quitar, *Am* sacar; **t. your feet off the table!** ¡quita *or Am* saca los pies de la mesa!; **he never took his eyes off us** no apartó la mirada de nosotros; **he took $10 off (the price)** rebajó 10 dólares (del precio); **to t. sth off sb's hands** quitar *or Am* sacar algo de las manos a alguien; **to t. years off sb** (*clothes, diet*) quitar *or Am* sacarle a alguien años de encima (**b**) (*lead*) (*person*) llevar; **to t. oneself off** retirarse (**c**) (*not work*) **to t. the day off** tomarse el día libre

2 *vi* (**a**) (*leave*) (*plane*) despegar, *Am* decolar; *Fam* (*person*) marcharse, irse (**b**) *Fam* (*succeed*) empezar a cuajar; **it never took off** nunca cuajó

▸**take on** *vt sep* (**a**) (*task, responsibility*) aceptar; (*problem, opponent*) enfrentarse a; (*fuel*) repostar; (*supplies*) reponer (**b**) (*hire*) (*worker*) contratar (**c**) (*acquire*) tomar, adquirir

▸**take out** *vt sep* (**a**) (*remove*) sacar; **her job really takes it out of her** su trabajo la deja totalmente agotada; **to t. it out on sb** pagarla *or* desahogarse con alguien (**b**) (*person*) sacar; **to t. sb out for a meal/to a restaurant** llevar a alguien a comer/a un restaurante (**c**) (*obtain*) (*license*) sacarse; (*insurance policy*) contratar, suscribir; **to t. out a subscription** suscribirse

▸**take over 1** *vt sep* (**a**) (*become responsible for*) hacerse cargo de (**b**) (*take control of*) (*place*) tomar; (*company*) absorber, adquirir

2 *vi* (**a**) (*assume power*) tomar posesión (**b**) (*relieve*) tomar el relevo (**from** de)

▸**take to** *vt insep* (**a**) (*go to*) **to t. to one's heels** darse a la fuga; **to t. to one's bed** meterse en la cama; **to t. to the hills** echarse al monte (**b**) (*adopt habit*) **to t. to doing sth** adquirir la costumbre de hacer algo, empezar a hacer algo; **to t. to drink** darse a la bebida (**c**) (*like*) **I took to them** me cayeron bien

▸**take up 1** *vt sep* (**a**) (*carry*) subir (**b**) (*lead*) (*person*) llevar, subir (**c**) (*lift*) (*carpet, floorboards, paving stones*) levantar (**d**) (*shorten*) (*skirt, hem*) subir, acortar (**e**) (*accept*) (*challenge, offer, suggestion*) aceptar; **to t. sb up on an offer** aceptar una oferta de alguien (**f**) (*discuss*) (*subject, problem*) discutir (**with** con) (**g**) (*assume*) (*position*) tomar; (*post, duties*) asumir (**h**) (*hobby, studies*) **she's taken up fencing/psychology** ha empezado a practicar esgrima/estudiar psicología; **we t. up the story just after...** retomamos la historia justo después de... (**i**) (*occupy*) (*space, time, attention*) ocupar

2 *vi* **to t. up with sb** trabar amistad con alguien

▸**take upon** *vt sep* **she took it upon herself to tell him**

my secret decidió por su cuenta contarle mi secreto

take-home pay ['teɪkhəʊm'peɪ] *n* salario *m* neto

taken ['teɪkən] **1** *adj* (**a**) *(occupied)* **is this seat t.?** ¿está ocupado este asiento? (**b**) *(impressed)* **I was very t. with him/it** me impresionó mucho
   2 *pp of* **take**

takeoff ['teɪkɒf] *n* (**a**) *(imitation)* imitación *f*; **to do a t. of sb** imitar a alguien (**b**) *(of plane, economy)* despegue *m*, *Am* decolaje *m*

takeout ['teɪkaʊt] **1** *n (food)* comida *f* para llevar
   2 *adj (food)* para llevar

takeover ['teɪkəʊvə(r)] *n* (**a**) *Com (of company)* absorción *f*, adquisición *f*; **t. bid** oferta *f* pública de adquisición (de acciones), OPA *f* (**b**) *Pol* ocupación *f*

taker ['teɪkə(r)] *n* **there were no takers** nadie aceptó la oferta

taking ['teɪkɪŋ] *n* **it's yours for the t.** está a tu disposición

talc [tælk] *n* talco *m*

talcum powder ['tælkəm'paʊdə(r)] *n* polvos *mpl* de talco

tale [teɪl] *n* (**a**) *(story)* historia *f*; *(legend)* cuento *m*; **she lived to tell the t.** vivió para contarlo (**b**) *(lie)* cuento *m*, patraña *f*; **to tell tales (about sb)** contar patrañas (sobre alguien)

talent ['tælənt] *n (ability)* talento *m*, dotes *fpl*; *(person with ability)* talento *m*; *Mus & Sport* **t. scout** cazatalentos *mf inv*

talented ['tæləntɪd] *adj* con talento

talisman ['tælɪzmən] *n* talismán *m*

talk [tɔːk] **1** *n* (**a**) *(conversation)* conversación *f*, charla *f*, *CAm, Méx* plática *f*; **to have a t. with sb** hablar con alguien; *Fam* **to be all t. (and no action)** hablar mucho (y no hacer nada); *TV & Rad* **t. show** programa *m* de entrevistas (**b**) **talks** *(negotiations)* conversaciones *fpl* (**c**) *(gossip)* habladurías *fpl*; *(speculation)* especulaciones *fpl*; **there is some t. of his returning** se dice que va a volver; **it's the t. of the town** es la comidilla local (**d**) *(lecture)* conferencia *f*, charla *f*
   2 *vt* (**a**) *(speak) (Spanish, German)* hablar; **to t. nonsense** decir tonterías; **to t. politics** hablar de política; **to t. (common) sense** hablar con sensatez; **to t. (some) sense into sb** hacer entrar en razón a alguien; **she can t. her way out of anything** sabe salir con palabras de cualquier situación (**b**) *(convince)* **to t. sb into/out of doing sth** persuadir a alguien para que haga/para que no haga algo
   3 *vi* (**a**) *(speak)* hablar (**to/about** con/de), *CAm, Méx* platicar (**to/about** con/de); **to t. to oneself** hablar solo(a); **to t. of or about doing sth** hablar de hacer algo; **talking of embarrassing situations,...** hablando de situaciones embarazosas,...; **to t. big** farolear; *Fam* **now you're talking!** ¡así se habla!; *Fam* **you can t.!** ¡mira quién fue a hablar!; **to make a prisoner t.** hacer hablar a un prisionero; **what are you talking about?** ¡pero qué dices!; **I don't know what you're talking about** no sé de qué me hablas (**b**) *(gossip)* cotillear, murmurar (**c**) *(give lecture)* dar una conferencia (**on** sobre)

▸**talk back** *vi* responder, replicar

▸**talk down** *vi* **to t. down to sb** hablar con aires de superioridad a alguien

▸**talk over** *vt sep* hablar de, tratar de

talkative ['tɔːkətɪv] *adj* hablador(ora), locuaz

talker ['tɔːkə(r)] *n* hablador(ora) *m,f*

talking ['tɔːkɪŋ] *adj* **t. book** audiolibro *m*, = cinta grabada con la lectura de un libro; **t. point** tema *m* de conversación

talking-to ['tɔːkɪntuː] *(pl* **talking-tos**) *n Fam* sermón *m*, *Esp* rapapolvo *m*; **to give sb a t.** echarle a alguien un buen sermón *or Esp* rapapolvo

tall [tɔːl] **1** *adj* alto(a); **how t. are you?** ¿cuánto mides?; **I'm six foot t.** mido un metro ochenta; *Fig* **that's a t. order** eso es mucho pedir; *Fig* **a t. story** un cuento chino
   2 *adv* **to walk** *or* **stand t.** andar con la cabeza bien alta

Tallin(n) ['tælɪn] *n* Tallin(n)

tallness ['tɔːlnɪs] *n* altura *f*

tallow ['tæləʊ] *n* sebo *m*

tally ['tælɪ] **1** *n* cuenta *f*; **to keep a t. of sth** llevar la cuenta de algo
   2 *vi (figures, report)* encajar, concordar

talon ['tælən] *n* garra *f*

tamarind ['tæmərɪnd] *n* tamarindo *m*

tambourine [tæmbə'riːn] *n Mus* pandereta *f*

tame [teɪm] **1** *adj* (**a**) *(not timid or vicious)* manso(a); *(domesticated)* domesticado(a) (**b**) *(unadventurous)* soso(a)
   2 *vt (lion, tiger)* domar; *Fig (emotion)* dominar

tamely ['teɪmlɪ] *adv (accept, agree to)* dócilmente; **t. worded** pusilánime, blando(a)

Tamil ['tæmɪl] **1** *n* (**a**) *(person)* tamil *mf* (**b**) *(language)* tamil *m*
   2 *adj* tamil

▸**tamper with** ['tæmpə(r)] *vt insep (documents, records)* manipular, falsear

tampon ['tæmpɒn] *n* tampón *m*

tan¹ [tæn] *n Math (abbr* **tangent**) tangente *f*

tan² **1** *n (color)* marrón *m* claro; *(from sun)* bronceado *m*, *Esp* moreno *m*
   2 *adj (color)* marrón claro
   3 *vt (pt & pp* **tanned**) *(leather)* curtir; *(of sun) (skin)* broncear, tostar; *Fam* **to t. sb, to t. sb's hide** dar una paliza *or Esp* zurra a alguien
   4 *vi (person, skin)* broncearse, ponerse moreno(a)

tandem ['tændəm] *n (bicycle)* tándem *m*; *Fig* **to do sth in t. (with sb)** hacer algo en conjunto *or Esp* al alimón (con alguien)

tang [tæŋ] *n (taste)* sabor *m* fuerte; *(smell)* olor *m* penetrante

tangent ['tændʒənt] *n Math* tangente *f*; *Fig* **to go off at a t.** salirse por la tangente

tangerine [tændʒə'riːn] **1** *n (fruit)* mandarina *f*; *(color)* mandarina *m*
   2 *adj (color)* naranja, mandarina

tangible ['tændʒɪbəl] *adj* tangible, palpable; *Fin* **t. assets** (activo *m*) inmovilizado *m*

tangibly ['tændʒɪblɪ] *adv* claramente

Tangier(s) [tæn'dʒɪə(z)] *n* Tánger

tangle ['tæŋgəl] **1** *n (of threads, hair)* maraña *f*, lío *m*; *also Fig* **to be in a t.** estar hecho(a) un lío; **to get into a t.** enredarse; *Fig* hacerse un lío
   2 *vt* **to get tangled up (in sth)** quedarse enredado(a) (en algo); *Fig* verse involucrado(a) (en algo)

▸**tangle with** *vt insep Fam (quarrel, fight with)* buscarse un lío con

tangled ['tæŋgəld] *adj* enredado(a), enmarañado(a)

tango ['tæŋgəʊ] **1** *n (pl* **tangos**) *(dance)* tango *m*
   2 *vi* bailar el tango; *Fam* **it takes two to t.** tiene que haber sido cosa de dos

tangy ['tæŋɪ] *adj (taste)* ligeramente ácido(a); *(smell)* penetrante

tank [tæŋk] *n* (**a**) *(container)* depósito *m*; *(on truck, train)* cisterna *f* (**b**) *Mil* tanque *m*, carro *m* de combate (**c**) *Fam (cell)* celda *f*

▸**tank along** *vi Fam* ir a toda máquina *or Esp* pastilla

tankard ['tæŋkəd] *n* jarra *f*, bock *m*

tanker ['tæŋkə(r)] *n (ship) (in general)* buque *m* cisterna; *(for oil)* petrolero *m*; *(truck)* camión *m* cisterna

tanned [tænd] *adj* moreno(a), bronceado(a); **to be t.** estar moreno(a) *or* bronceado(a)

tanner ['tænə(r)] *n* curtidor(ora) *m,f*

tannery ['tænərɪ] *n* curtiduría *f*, tenería *f*

tannin ['tænɪn] *n* tanino *m*

tanning ['tænɪŋ] *n* (**a**) *(of skin)* bronceado *m*; **t. lotion** crema *f* bronceadora; **t. studio** salón *m* de bronceado, solarium *m* (**b**) *(of hides)* curtido *m*

tantalize ['tæntəlaɪz] *vt* poner los dientes largos a (**with** con)

tantalizing ['tæntəlaɪzɪŋ] *adj* sugerente

tantalizingly ['tæntəlaɪzɪŋlɪ] *adv* de forma sugerente

tantamount ['tæntəmaʊnt] *adj* equivalente; **to be t. to** equivaler a

tantrum ['tæntrəm] *n* rabieta *f*; **to throw a t.** agarrar *or Esp* coger una rabieta

Tanzania [tænzə'nɪə] *n* Tanzania

Tanzanian [tænzə'nɪən] *n & adj* tanzano(a) *m,f*

tap¹ [tæp] **1** *n* **to put a t. on the phone** intervenir *or* pinchar el teléfono

2 *vt (pt & pp* **tapped)** *(tree)* sangrar; *(resources)* aprovechar, explotar; *(phone)* intervenir, pinchar; *Fam* **to t. sb for money** sacar dinero a alguien

tap² **1** *n* (**a**) *(light blow)* golpecito *m*; **to give sth a t.** darle un golpecito a algo; **to give sb a t. on the shoulder** darle un golpecito en el hombro a alguien (**b**) **t. dancing** claqué *m*

2 *vt (pt & pp* **tapped)** dar un golpecito a; **I tapped him on the shoulder** le di un golpecito en el hombro

3 *vi* **to t. at** *or* **on the door** llamar suavemente a la puerta

tape [teɪp] **1** *n* (**a**) *(ribbon)* cinta *f*; **(adhesive** *or* **Scotch**®**) t.** cinta adhesiva; *Sport* **the (finishing) t.** la (cinta de) meta; **t. (measure)** cinta *f* métrica (**b**) *(for recording, cassette)* cinta *f* (magnetofónica); **t. head** cabezal *m* (de casete *or* cinta); **t. recorder** casete *m*; **t. recording** grabación *f* (magnetofónica)

2 *vt* (**a**) *(stick with tape)* pegar con cinta adhesiva (**b**) *(record)* grabar

▶**tape up** *vt sep (bandage up)* poner una venda a, vendar

taper ['teɪpə(r)] **1** *n (candle)* candela *f*

2 *vi* estrecharse; *(to a point)* acabar en punta

▶**taper off** *vi (object)* estrecharse; *(production, numbers)* disminuir

tape-record ['teɪprɪkɔːd] *vt* grabar (en cinta)

tapestry ['tæpɪstrɪ] *n (cloth)* tapiz *m*; *(art)* tapicería *f*

tapeworm ['teɪpwɜːm] *n* tenia *f*, solitaria *f*

tapioca [tæpɪ'əʊkə] *n* tapioca *f*

tapping ['tæpɪŋ] *n (sound)* golpeteo *m*

tar [tɑː(r)] **1** *n* (**a**) *(substance)* alquitrán *m* (**b**) *Old-fashioned Fam (sailor)* marinero *m*

2 *vt (pt & pp* **tarred)** alquitranar; **to t. and feather sb** emplumar a alguien; *Fig* **we have all been tarred with the same brush** nos han metido a todos en el mismo saco

tarantula [tə'ræntjʊlə] *n* tarántula *f*

tardily ['tɑːdɪlɪ] *adv Formal (late)* tardíamente; *(slowly)* lentamente

tardy ['tɑːdɪ] *adj Formal (late)* tardío(a); *(slow)* lento(a)

target ['tɑːgɪt] **1** *n (of bullet, missile, joke)* blanco *m*, objetivo *m*; *Fig (aim, goal)* objetivo *m*, meta *f*; *Fig* **to set oneself a t.** trazarse una meta; **to be on t.** ir según lo previsto; **to be on t. to do sth** ir camino de hacer algo; *TV & Rad* **t. audience** audiencia *f* a la que está orientada la emisión; **t. language** *(in translating)* lengua *f* de destino *or* llegada; **t. market** mercado *m* objeto *or* objetivo; *Sport* **t. practice** prácticas *fpl* de tiro

2 *vt* (**a**) *(aim)* **to t. sth at sth** *(missile)* apuntar algo hacia *or* a algo; *Fig (campaign, TV program, benefits)* destinar algo a algo (**b**) *(aim at)* apuntar a, tener como objetivo

tariff ['tærɪf] *n (tax)* arancel *m*; *(price list)* tarifa *f*; **t. barrier** barrera *f* arancelaria

Tarmac® ['tɑːmæk] **1** *n* asfalto *m*; *Av (runway)* pista *f*

2 *vt (pt & pp* **Tarmacked)** asfaltar

tarnish ['tɑːnɪʃ] **1** *vt (metal, reputation)* empañar

2 *vi (metal)* empañarse, deslucirse

tarot ['tærəʊ] *n* tarot *m*

tarpaulin [tɑː'pɔːlɪn], *Fam* **tarp** [tɑːp] *n* lona *f* impermeable, hule *m*

tarragon ['tærəgən] *n* estragón *m*

tart [tɑːt] **1** *n* (**a**) *(cake) (large)* tarta *f*, pastel *m*; *(small)* pastelillo *m* (**b**) *Fam Pej (promiscuous woman)* zorra *f*; *(prostitute)* fulana *f*, *Méx* piruja *f*

2 *adj (in taste)* agrio(a); *(tone)* áspero(a)

tartan ['tɑːtən] *n* tartán *m*, tela *f* escocesa; **t. tie/jacket** corbata *f* /chaqueta *f* de tela escocesa

Tartar ['tɑːtə(r)] *n* tártaro(a) *m,f*

tartar ['tɑːtə(r)] *n (on teeth)* sarro *m*

tartar(e) sauce ['tɑːtə'sɔːs] *n* salsa *f* tártara

tartly ['tɑːtlɪ] *adv* ásperamente

tarty ['tɑːtɪ] *adj Fam (clothes)* de fulana

task [tɑːsk] *n* tarea *f*; **to take sb to t. for (doing) sth** reprender a alguien por (haber hecho) algo; **t. force** *Mil* destacamento *m*; *Fig (committee)* equipo *m* de trabajo

taskmaster ['tɑːskmɑːstə(r)] *n* **he is a hard t.** es muy exigente

Tasmania [tæz'meɪnɪə] *n* Tasmania

Tasmanian [tæz'meɪnɪən] *n & adj* tasmano(a) *m,f*

Tasman Sea ['tæzmən'siː] *n* **the T.** el Mar de Tasmania

tassel ['tæsəl] *n* borla *f*

taste [teɪst] **1** *n* (**a**) *(flavor)* sabor *m*, gusto *m*; **(sense of) t.** (sentido *m* del) gusto; *Anat* **t. bud** papila *f* gustativa (**b**) *(sample)* **to have a t. of sth** probar algo; **a t. of things to come** una muestra de lo que vendrá; **to give sb a t. of his own medicine** pagar a alguien con su misma moneda (**c**) *(liking)* afición *f*, gusto *m*; **to acquire** *or* **develop a t. for sth** aficionarse a algo; **add sugar to t.** añada azúcar a su gusto; **it's a matter of t.** es una cuestión de gustos; **violent films are not to my t.** las películas violentas no son de mi gusto (**d**) *(judgment)* gusto *m*; **in bad** *or* **poor t.** de mal gusto

2 *vt* (**a**) *(detect flavor of)* notar (un sabor a) (**b**) *(sample)* probar; *(wine)* catar; *Fig* **to t. success/despair** probar el éxito/la desesperación

3 *vi* saber, tener sabor (**of** a); **it tastes fine to me** a mí me sabe bien

tasteful ['teɪstfʊl] *adj* de buen gusto

tastefully ['teɪstfəlɪ] *adv* con buen gusto

tasteless ['teɪstlɪs] *adj* (**a**) *(food)* insípido(a) (**b**) *(remark, clothes)* de mal gusto

tastelessly ['teɪstlɪslɪ] *adv (decorated)* con poco gusto

taster ['teɪstə(r)] *n (person)* catador(ora) *m,f*

tasty ['teɪstɪ] *adj (delicious)* sabroso(a), rico(a)

tattered ['tætəd] *adj* andrajoso(a)

tatters ['tætəz] *npl* **to be in t.** *(clothes)* estar hecho(a) jirones; *Fig (ruined)* haber quedado arruinado(a)

tattle ['tætəl] **1** *n* habladurías *fpl*, chismes *mpl*

2 *vi* chismorrear, *Am* chismear, *Col, Méx* chismosear

tattletale ['tætəlteɪl] *n (person)* acusica *mf*, *Esp* chivato(a) *m,f*

tattoo¹ [tə'tuː] *(pl* **tattoos**) *n* (**a**) *(on drum)* retreta *f* (**b**) *(military show)* exhibición *f* militar

tattoo² **1** *n (pl* **tattoos)** *(design)* tatuaje *m*

2 *vt* tatuar

tatty ['tætɪ] *adj Fam* ajado(a), *Esp* sobado(a)

taught [tɔːt] *pt & pp of* **teach**

taunt [tɔːnt] **1** *n (words)* pulla *f*

2 *vt* mofarse de, hacer mofa de

taunting ['tɔːntɪŋ] **1** *n* pullas *fpl*

2 *adj* hiriente, burlón(ona)

Taurus ['tɔːrəs] *n (sign of zodiac)* tauro *m*; **to be (a) T.** ser tauro

taut [tɔːt] *adj* tenso(a)

tauten ['tɔːtən] **1** *vt* tensar

2 *vi* tensarse

tautness ['tɔːtnɪs] *n* tensión *f*

tautological [tɔːtə'lɒdʒɪkəl] *adj* tautológico(a)

tautology [tɔː'tɒlədʒɪ] *n* tautología *f*

tavern ['tævən] *n Literary* taberna *f*

tawdry ['tɔːdrɪ] *adj (conduct, motive)* oscuro(a), sórdido(a); *(decor, jewelry)* de oropel

tawny ['tɔːnɪ] *adj* leonado(a); **t. owl** cárabo *m*

tax [tæks] **1** *n* impuesto *m*, tributo *m*; *(taxation)* impuestos *mpl*; **to pay t.** ser un/una contribuyente, pagar impuestos; **t. bracket** banda *f* impositiva, tramo *m* impositivo; **t. break** ventaja *f* fiscal; **t. code** código *m* impositivo; **t. collector** recaudador(ora) *m,f* de impuestos; **t. cut** reducción *f* fiscal; **t. evasion** fraude *m* or evasión *f* fiscal; **t. exile** *(person)* exiliado(a) *m,f* fiscal; **t. form** declaración *f* de la renta; **t. free** libre de impuestos; **t. haven** paraíso *m* fiscal; **t. incentive** incentivo *m* fiscal; **t. rebate** devolución *f* fiscal; **t. relief** desgravación *f* fiscal; **t. return** declaración *f* de la renta; **t. system** sistema *m* impositivo

2 *vt* (**a**) *Fin (goods, income)* gravar; *(people)* cobrar impuestos a (**b**) *(resources, patience, knowledge)* poner a prueba (**c**) *Formal (accuse)* **he was taxed with having lied** se le imputó haber mentido

taxable ['tæksəbəl] *adj* gravable, imponible; **t. income** ingresos *mpl* sujetos a gravamen, ≃ base *f* imponible

taxation [tæk'seɪʃən] *n (system)* fiscalidad *f*, sistema *m* fiscal or tributario; **an increase in t.** un aumento de los impuestos

tax-deductible [tæksdɪ'dʌktɪbəl] *adj* desgravable

tax-free ['tæks'friː] **1** *adj* libre de impuestos

2 *adv* sin pagar impuestos

taxi ['tæksɪ] **1** *n* taxi *m*; **t. driver** taxista *mf*; **t. stand** parada *f* de taxis

2 *vi (aircraft)* rodar

taxidermist ['tæksɪdɜːmɪst] *n* taxidermista *mf*

taxing ['tæksɪŋ] *adj* difícil, arduo(a)

taxonomy [tæk'sɒnəmɪ] *n* taxonomía *f*

taxpayer ['tækspeɪə(r)] *n* contribuyente *mf*

TB [tiː'biː] *n (tuberculosis)* tuberculosis *f inv*

tea [tiː] *n (plant, drink)* té *m*; *(herbal infusion)* infusión *f*, té *m*; **t. bag** bolsita *f* de té; **t. caddy** lata *f* de té; **t. leaves** *(dry)* hojas *fpl* de té; *(in bottom of cup)* posos *mpl* de té; **a t. party** una reunión para tomar el té; **t. service** or **set** servicio *m* de té; **t. strainer** colador *m (pequeño)*

teach [tiːtʃ] *(pt & pp* taught [tɔːt]) **1** *vt* enseñar; **to t. sb sth**, **to t. sth to sb** enseñar algo a alguien; **to t. sb (how) to do sth** enseñarle a alguien a hacer algo; **he taught me Spanish at school** me daba clase de español en el colegio; **she taught herself to play the piano** aprendió (ella) sola a tocar el piano; **to t. school** ser profesor(a); *Fig* **to t. sb a lesson** darle una lección a alguien; *Fam* **that'll t. him!** ¡así aprenderá!

2 *vi* enseñar, dar clase(s)

teacher ['tiːtʃə(r)] *n (at primary school)* maestro(a) *m,f*; *(at secondary school, college)* profesor(ora) *m,f*; **French t.** profesor(ora) *m,f* de francés; **teachers college** escuela *f* de magisterio; **t.'s pet** favorito(a) *m,f* del profesor; **t. training** estudios *mpl* de magisterio, formación *f* pedagógica

teaching ['tiːtʃɪŋ] *n* (**a**) *(profession, action)* enseñanza *f*, docencia *f*; **t. practice** prácticas *fpl* de enseñanza; **t. staff** profesorado *m*, personal *m* docente (**b**) *(doctrine)* enseñanza *f*

teacup ['tiːkʌp] *n* taza *f* de té

teak [tiːk] *n* teca *f*

team [tiːm] *n (of players, workers)* equipo *m*; *(of horses)* tiro *m*; *(of oxen)* yunta *f*; **a t. effort** una labor de equipo; **t. game** juego *m* de equipo; **t. player** buen(a) trabajador(ora) *m,f* en equipo; **t. spirit** espíritu *m* de equipo

▶ **team up** *vi* unirse (**with** a)

teammate ['tiːmmeɪt] *n Sport* compañero(a) *m,f* de equipo

teamster ['tiːmstə(r)] *n (truck driver)* camionero(a) *m,f*

teamwork ['tiːmwɜːk] *n* trabajo *m* en or de equipo

teapot ['tiːpɒt] *n* tetera *f*

tear¹ [tɪə(r)] *n* lágrima *f*; **in tears** llorando; *Anat* **t. duct**

conducto *m* lacrimal; **t. gas** gas *m* lacrimógeno

tear² [teə(r)] **1** *n* desgarrón *m*; *(of muscle)* desgarro *m*

2 *vt (pt* tore [tɔː(r)], *pp* torn [tɔːn]) *(rip)* rasgar; *(snatch)* arrancar; **to t. sth in two** *or* **in half** romper algo en dos; *also Fig* **to t. sth to pieces** hacer trizas algo; *Fig* **to t. sb to pieces** hacer trizas a alguien; **she was torn between going and staying** tenía unas dudas tremendas sobre si irse o quedarse

3 *vi* (**a**) *(material)* rasgarse; *(muscle)* desgarrarse (**b**) **to t. at sth** *(rip)* desgarrar algo (**c**) *(move quickly)* **to t. along/past** ir/ pasar muy deprisa

▶ **tear apart** *vt sep (person)* destruir; *(party, country)* desmembrar

▶ **tear away 1** *vt sep* (**a**) *(remove by tearing)* arrancar (**b**) **to t. oneself away from sth** despegarse de algo

2 *vi* alejarse muy deprisa

▶ **tear down** *vt sep (building, statue)* derribar; *(poster)* arrancar; *(reputation)* destrozar

▶ **tear into** *vt insep* **to t. into sb** *(physically)* arrojarse sobre alguien; *(verbally)* arremeter contra alguien

▶ **tear off 1** *vt sep (detach by tearing)* arrancar

2 *vi (run away)* salir pitando

▶ **tear out** *vt sep* arrancar; *Fig* **to t. one's hair out** tirarse de los pelos

▶ **tear up** *vt sep (document, photo)* romper, rasgar; *(plant, floorboards)* arrancar

tearaway ['teərəweɪ] *n* alborotador(ora) *m,f*, *Esp* elemento(a) *m,f*

teardrop ['tɪədrɒp] *n* lágrima *f*

tearful ['tɪəfʊl] *adj (person)* lloroso(a); *(goodbye, reunion)* lacrimoso(a)

tearfully ['tɪəfəlɪ] *adv* entre lágrimas, lacrimosamente

tearing ['teərɪŋ] *adj Fam* **to be in a t. hurry** tener muchísima prisa, *Am* tener muchísimo apuro

tearjerker ['tɪədʒɜːkə(r)] *n Fam* **to be a real t.** *(movie, book)* ser lacrimógeno(a)

tearoom ['tiːruːm] *n* salón *m* de té

tearstained ['tɪəsteɪnd] *adj* **her face was t.** tenía un rastro de lágrimas en la cara

tease [tiːz] **1** *n (person)* guasón(ona) *m,f*, bromista *mf*

2 *vt* tomar el pelo a *(about* por)

3 *vi* bromear; **I was only teasing!** ¡sólo era una broma!

▶ **tease out** *vt sep (information)* sonsacar, extraer

teaser ['tiːzə(r)] *n Fam (problem)* rompecabezas *m inv*

teasing ['tiːzɪŋ] *n* burlas *fpl*, pitorreo *m*

teaspoon ['tiːspuːn] *n* cucharilla *f*; **a t. of sugar** una cucharadita de azúcar

teaspoonful ['tiːspuːnfʊl] *n* cucharadita *f* (de las de café)

teat [tiːt] *n (of animal)* teta *f*

teatime ['tiːtaɪm] *n (in afternoon)* hora *f* del té

techie ['tekɪ] *n Fam Comptr (person)* experto(a) *m,f* en informática

technical ['teknɪkəl] *adj* técnico(a); *Sch* **t. drawing** dibujo *m* técnico; **t. foul** *(in basketball)* (falta *f*) técnica *f*; **t. hitch** fallo *m* técnico, *Am* falla *f* técnica

technicality [teknɪ'kælɪtɪ] *n* detalle *m* técnico

technically ['teknɪklɪ] *adv* técnicamente; **t., they are still married** estrictamente hablando, siguen casados

technician [tek'nɪʃən] *n* técnico(a) *m,f*

technique [tek'niːk] *n* técnica *f*

technocrat ['teknəkræt] *n* tecnócrata *mf*

technological [teknə'lɒdʒɪkəl] *adj* tecnológico(a)

technology [tek'nɒlədʒɪ] *n* tecnología *f*

teddy ['tedɪ] *n* (**a**) *(toy)* **t. bear** osito *m* de peluche (**b**) *(underwear)* body *m*

tedious ['tiːdɪəs] *adj* tedioso(a)

tedium ['tiːdɪəm] *n* tedio *m*

tee [tiː] *n (in golf) (peg)* tee *m; (area)* salida *f* (del hoyo), tee *m;* **t. shirt** camiseta *f, Chile* polera *f, Méx* playera *f, RP* remera *f*

▶**tee off 1** *vi (in golf)* dar el primer golpe

2 *vt sep Fam (annoy)* mosquear, poner negro(a); **to be teed off about sth** estar mosqueado(a) por algo

teem [tiːm] *vi* **(a)** *(rain)* **it was teeming (down)** llovía a cántaros **(b) to t. with** *(insects, ideas)* rebosar de

teeming ['tiːmɪŋ] *adj (streets)* atestado(a); *(crowds)* numeroso(a)

teenage ['tiːneɪdʒ] *adj* adolescente

teenager ['tiːneɪdʒə(r)] *n* adolescente *mf*

teen idol ['tiːn'aɪdəl] *n Fam* ídolo *m* juvenil

teens [tiːnz] *npl* adolescencia *f;* **to be in one's t.** ser (un) adolescente

teensy(-weensy) ['tiːnzɪ('wiːnzɪ)], **teeny(-weeny)** ['tiːnɪ('wiːnɪ)] *adj Fam* **a t. bit of…** un poquitín *or Am* un chiquitín de…

teenybopper ['tiːnɪbɒpə(r)] *n Fam* = quinceañera seguidora de la música pop y sus modas

teeny(-weeny) = **teensy(-weensy)**

teeter ['tiːtə(r)] *vi* tambalearse; *Fig* **to t. on the brink of** tambalearse al borde de

teeth [tiːθ] *pl of* **tooth**

teethe [tiːð] *vi* **to be teething** estar echando los dientes

teething ['tiːðɪŋ] *n* dentición *f; Fig* **t. troubles** *(of project)* problemas *mpl* de partida

teetotaler [tiːˈtəʊtələ(r)] *n* abstemio(a) *m,f*

TEFL ['tefəl] *n (abbr* **Teaching English as a Foreign Language)** enseñanza *f* del inglés como idioma extranjero

Teh(e)ran [teəˈrɑːn] *n* Teherán

tel *(abbr* **telephone)** tel, teléfono *m*

telecommunication(s) [telɪkəmjuːnɪˈkeɪʃən(z)] *n* telecomunicaciones *fpl*

telecommute ['telɪkəmjuːt] *vi* teletrabajar

telecommuting ['telɪkəˈmjuːtɪŋ] *n* teletrabajo *m*

teleconference [telɪˈkɒnfərəns] *n* teleconferencia *f*

teleconferencing ['telɪˈkɒnfərənsɪŋ] *n* teleconferencias *fpl*

telegenic [telɪˈdʒenɪk] *adj* telegénico(a)

telegram ['telɪgræm] *n* telegrama *m*

telegraph ['telɪgrɑːf] **1** *n* telégrafo *m;* **t. pole** poste *m* telegráfico; **t. wire** tendido *m* telegráfico

2 *vt* telegrafiar

telegraphic [telɪˈgræfɪk] *adj* telegráfico(a)

telemarketing [telɪˈmɑːkɪtɪŋ] *n Com* telemarketing *m,* ventas *fpl* por teléfono

telepathic [telɪˈpæθɪk] *adj* telepático(a)

telepathy [tɪˈlepəθɪ] *n* telepatía *f*

telephone ['telɪfəʊn] **1** *n* teléfono *m;* **to be on the t.** *(be subscriber)* tener teléfono; *(be speaking)* estar hablando por teléfono; **to speak to sb on the t.** hablar con alguien por teléfono; *Com* **t. banking** telebanca *f,* banca *f* telefónica; **t. book** guía *f* telefónica, listín *m* de teléfonos, *Am* directorio *m* de teléfonos; **t. booth** cabina *f* telefónica; **t. call** llamada *f* telefónica; **t. directory** guía *f* telefónica, listín *m* de teléfonos, *Am* directorio *m* de teléfonos; **t. number** número *m* de teléfono; **t. pole** poste *m* de telégrafos

2 *vt* **to t. sb** telefonear a alguien, llamar a alguien (por teléfono), *RP* hablar a alguien por teléfono

3 *vi* telefonear, llamar (por teléfono)

telephoto lens [telɪˈfəʊtəʊˈlenz] *adj* teleobjetivo *m*

teleprinter ['telɪprɪntə(r)] *n* teletipo *m,* teleimpresor *m*

telesales [telɪˈseɪlz] *npl Com* televentas *fpl,* ventas *fpl* por teléfono

telescope ['telɪskəʊp] **1** *n* telescopio *m; Naut* catalejo *m*

2 *vi* plegarse (como un telescopio)

telescopic [telɪsˈkɒpɪk] *adj* **(a)** *(relating to vision)* telescópico(a); **t. sight** *(of rifle)* mira *f* telescópica **(b)** *(expanding) (ladder)* extensible; *(umbrella)* plegable

teletext ['telɪtekst] *n TV* teletexto *m*

televangelist [telɪˈvændʒəlɪst] *n* predicador *m* evangelista televisivo

televise ['telɪvaɪz] *vt* televisar

television [telɪˈvɪʒən] *n* televisión *f;* **on t.** en *or* por (la) televisión; **to watch t.** ver la televisión; **it makes good t.** es muy televisivo; **t. camera** cámara *f* de televisión; **t. program** programa *m* de televisión; **t. screen** pantalla *f* de televisión; **t. set** televisor *m*

teleworking ['telɪwɜːkɪŋ] *n* teletrabajo *m inv*

telex ['teleks] **1** *n* télex *m inv*

2 *vt (message)* enviar por télex

tell [tel] *(pt & pp* **told** [təʊld]) **1** *vt* **(a)** *(say)* decir; *(story, joke, secret)* contar; **to t. sb sth, to t. sth to sb** contarle algo a alguien; **to t. the truth/a lie** decir la verdad/una mentira; **to t. you the truth…** a decir verdad…; **can you t. me the way to the station?** ¿me puede decir cómo se va a la estación?; **we are told that…** se dice que…; **I told you so!** ¡te lo dije!; **you're telling me!** ¡a mí me lo vas a contar!; **let me t. you, I was frightened!** te confieso que estaba asustado; **to t. the time** *(clock)* indicar *or* dar la hora; **to t. sb the time** *(person)* decir la hora a alguien; **his expression told us the answer** la expresión de su cara nos reveló la respuesta

(b) *(discern) (attitude, mood)* ver, saber; **we couldn't t. if he was angry or not** no se sabía si estaba *esp Esp* enfadado *or esp Am* enojado o no; **you can t. she's lived abroad** se nota que ha vivido en el extranjero; **there's no telling what she'll do next** no hay manera de saber qué hará a continuación

(c) *(distinguish)* distinguir **(from** de); **to t. two people/things apart** distinguir entre dos personas/cosas; **to t. right from wrong** distinguir lo que está bien de lo que está mal; **I can't t. the difference** no veo la diferencia

(d) *(order)* **to t. sb to do sth** mandar a alguien hacer algo, decir a alguien que haga algo; **do as you are told!** ¡haz lo que te dicen *or* mandan!; **I'm not asking you, I'm telling you!** no es una petición *or Am* pedido, ¡es una orden!; **she wouldn't be told** no hacía caso de lo que le decían

(e) *Pol (count)* escrutar; **all told** en total

2 *vi* **(a)** *(say)* **please don't t.!** ¡no te chives!; **that would be telling!** ¡eso sería contar demasiado! **(b)** *(discern)* **it's difficult** *or* **hard to t.** es difícil de saber; **it's too early to t.** es demasiado pronto para saberlo; **you never can t.** nunca se sabe **(c)** *(have effect)* hacerse notar

▶**tell off** *vt sep Fam (scold)* **to t. sb off (for)** echar una reprimenda *or Esp* bronca a alguien (por), dar *Méx* una jalada *or RP* un rezongo a alguien (por)

▶**tell on** *vt insep Fam (inform on)* **he told on me to the teacher** le fue contando lo que yo había hecho al profesor

teller ['telə(r)] *n* **(a)** *(of votes)* escrutador(ora) *m,f* **(b)** *(in bank)* cajero(a) *m,f;* **t. machine** cajero *m* automático

telling ['telɪŋ] **1** *n (of story)* narración *f,* relato *m;* **it loses nothing in the t.** no pierde nada al contarlo

2 *adj (blow, contribution)* decisivo(a); *(argument)* contundente

telltale ['telteɪl] **1** *n (person)* acusica *mf, Esp* chivato(a) *m,f*

2 *adj (sign, odor)* revelador(ora)

temerity [tɪˈmerɪtɪ] *n* osadía *f,* atrevimiento *m;* **to have the t. to do sth** tener la osadía de hacer algo

temp [temp] *Fam* **1** *n* trabajador(ora) *m,f* temporal (administrativo(a)); **to be a t.** hacer trabajo temporal de administrativo(a)

2 *vi* hacer trabajo temporal de administrativo(a)

temper ['tempə(r)] **1** *n (character)* carácter *m; (mood)* humor *m; (bad mood)* mal humor; **to be in a good/(bad) t.** estar de buen/mal humor; **to keep one's t.** mantener la calma; **to lose one's t.** perder los estribos; **to have a short t.** tener mal genio; **to fly into a t.** ponerse hecho(a) una furia; *Fam* **t., t.!** ¡calma, calma!; **t. tantrum** rabieta *f*

2 *vt* (**a**) *(steel)* templar (**b**) *(action)* moderar, mitigar

temperament ['tempərəmənt] *n* temperamento *m*

temperamental [tempərə'mentəl] *adj (person)* temperamental; *Fig (machine)* caprichoso(a)

temperamentally [temprə'mentəlɪ] *adv* de forma temperamental, temperamentalmente; **to be t. unsuited to sth** no tener el temperamento adecuado para algo, no tener madera de algo

temperance ['tempərəns] *n* (**a**) *(moderation)* moderación *f*, sobriedad *f* (**b**) *(abstinence from alcohol)* abstinencia *f* (del alcohol); *Hist* **t. movement** liga *f* antialcohólica

temperate ['tempərət] *adj* (**a**) *Geog (climate, zone)* templado(a) (**b**) *(language, criticism)* moderado(a)

temperature ['tempərətʃə(r)] *n* temperatura *f*; **to take sb's t.** tomar la temperatura a alguien; **to have** *or* **to run a t.** tener fiebre

tempered ['tempəd] *adj (steel)* templado(a); **t. glass** vidrio *m* reforzado

tempest ['tempɪst] *n Literary* tempestad *f*; **it was a t. in a teapot** fue una tormenta en un vaso de agua

tempestuous [tem'pestjʊəs] *adj* tempestuoso(a), tormentoso(a)

template ['templɪt] *n (gen)* & *Comptr* plantilla *f*

temple[1] ['tempəl] *n (place of worship)* templo *m*

temple[2] *n (side of head)* sien *f*

tempo ['tempəʊ] *(pl* **tempos***)* *n Mus* tempo *m*

temporal ['tempərəl] *adj* (**a**) *(power)* temporal, terrenal (**b**) *Gram* temporal

temporarily [tempə'rerɪlɪ] *adv* temporalmente, *Am* temporariamente

temporary ['tempərərɪ] *adj (in general)* temporal, *Am* temporario(a); *(office, arrangement, repairs)* provisional, *Am* temporario(a); **t. job** trabajo *m* temporal

tempt [tem(p)t] *vt* tentar; **to t. sb to do sth** tentar a alguien a hacer algo; **I'm tempted to accept** me siento tentado de aceptar; **to t. fate** tentar (a) la suerte

temptation [tem(p)'teɪʃən] *n* tentación *f*

tempting ['tem(p)tɪŋ] *adj* tentador(ora)

temptress ['tem(p)trɪs] *n Literary* seductora *f*, mujer *f* fatal

ten [ten] **1** *n* diez *m*; **t. to one he'll find out** me apuesto el cuello a que lo descubrirá

2 *adj* diez; **the T. Commandments** los Diez Mandamientos; *see also* **eight**

tenable ['tenəbəl] *adj* sostenible

tenacious [te'neɪʃəs] *adj* tenaz

tenaciously [tə'neɪʃəslɪ] *adv* tenazmente, con tenacidad

tenacity [te'næsɪtɪ] *n* tenacidad *f*

tenancy ['tenənsɪ] *n Law (right)* arrendamiento *m*, alquiler *m*; *(period)* periodo *m* de alquiler; **t. agreement** contrato *m* de alquiler *or* arrendamiento

tenant ['tenənt] *n (of house)* inquilino(a) *m,f*; *(of land)* arrendatario(a) *m,f*

tend[1] [tend] *vt (look after)* cuidar (de)

tend[2] *vi* tender (**toward** hacia); **to t. to do sth** soler hacer algo

▸ **tend to** *vt insep (look after)* atender a

tendency ['tendənsɪ] *n (trend)* tendencia *f*; *(leaning)* inclinación *f*; **to have a t. to (do) sth** tener tendencia a (hacer) algo

tendentious [ten'denʃəs] *adj Formal* tendencioso(a)

tender[1] ['tendə(r)] *n Naut* barcaza *f*; *Rail* ténder *m*

tender[2] *adj* (**a**) *(gentle, affectionate)* cariñoso(a), afectuoso(a) (**b**) *(sensitive)* muy sensible; *Fig* **at the t. age of…** a la tierna edad de… (**c**) *(meat)* tierno(a)

tender[3] **1** *n Com (bid)* oferta *f*; **to make** *or* **put in a t.** hacer *or* presentar una oferta

2 *vt Formal (offer) (one's services, money)* ofrecer; **to t. one's resignation** presentar la dimisión

3 *vi Com* **to t. for a contract** presentarse a una licitación de contrata

tenderhearted [tendə'hɑːtɪd] *adj* bondadoso(a)

tenderly ['tendəlɪ] *adv (affectionately)* cariñosamente, afectuosamente

tenderness ['tendənɪs] *n* (**a**) *(affection)* ternura *f*, cariño *m* (**b**) *(pain)* dolor *m* (**c**) *(of meat)* blandura *f*, terneza *f*

tendon ['tendən] *n Anat* tendón *m*

tendril ['tendrɪl] *n Bot* zarcillo *m*

tenement ['tenɪmənt] *n* **t. (building)** bloque *m* de apartamentos *or Esp* pisos *or Arg* departamentos

tenet ['tenɪt] *n* principio *m*, postulado *m*

tenfold ['tenfəʊld] **1** *adj* **a t. increase** un aumento por diez

2 *adv* diez veces

tenner ['tenə(r)] *n Fam (ten-dollar bill)* billete *m* de diez dólares

tennis ['tenɪs] *n* tenis *m*; **to play t.** jugar al tenis; **t. ball** pelota *f* de tenis; **t. club** club *m* de tenis; **t. court** pista *f or* cancha *f* de tenis; *Med* **t. elbow** codo *m* de tenista; **t. player** tenista *mf*; **t. racket** *or* **racquet** raqueta *f* de tenis; **t. shoe** zapatilla *f* de tenis

tenor ['tenə(r)] *n* (**a**) *Mus* tenor *m*; **t. sax(ophone)** saxo *m* tenor (**b**) *(content, sense)* tenor *m*

tenpin bowling ['tenpɪn'bəʊlɪŋ] *n* bolos *mpl*

tense[1] [tens] *n Gram* tiempo *m*; **in the present/future t.** en (tiempo) presente/futuro

tense[2] **1** *adj* tenso(a); **my neck was very t.** tenía el cuello muy tenso

2 *vt* tensar; **to t. oneself** ponerse tenso(a)

3 *vi* tensarse, ponerse tenso(a)

▸ **tense up** *vi* ponerse tenso(a)

tensely ['tenslɪ] *adv (nervously)* tensamente

tension ['tenʃən] *n* tensión *f*

tent [tent] *n* tienda *f* de campaña, *Am* carpa *f*; **t. peg** piqueta *f*, clavija *f*; **t. pole** mástil *m* (de tienda *or Am* carpa)

tentacle ['tentəkəl] *n* tentáculo *m*

tentative ['tentətɪv] *adj (person)* vacilante, titubeante; *(arrangement, conclusions)* provisional

tentatively ['tentətɪvlɪ] *adv (hesitantly)* con vacilación, con titubeo; *(provisionally)* provisionalmente

tenterhooks ['tentəhʊks] *npl* **to be on t.** estar sobre ascuas; **to keep sb on t.** tener a alguien sobre ascuas

tenth [tenθ] **1** *n* (**a**) *(fraction)* décimo *m*, décima parte *f* (**b**) *(in series)* décimo(a) *m,f* (**c**) *(of month)* diez *m*

2 *adj* décimo(a); *see also* **eighth**

tenuous ['tenjʊəs] *adj (connection)* vago(a), tenue; *(argument)* flojo(a), débil; *(comparison)* traído(a) por los pelos

tenuousness ['tenjʊəsnɪs] *n (of connection)* vaguedad *f*; *(of argument)* falta *f* de solidez; *(of comparison)* falta *f* de conexión

tenure ['tenjə(r)] *n (of land)* arriendo *m*; *(of office)* ocupación *f*; *Univ* titularidad *f*; **to have t.** ser profesor(ora) numerario(a) *or* titular

tepid ['tepɪd] *adj also Fig* tibio(a); **to be t.** *(water)* estar tibio(a)

term [tɜːm] **1** *n* (**a**) *(word, expression)* término *m*; **I told her in no uncertain terms** se lo dije en términos claros; **in terms of salary/pollution** en cuanto a salario/contaminación

(**b**) *(relations)* **I'm on good/bad terms with her** me llevo bien/mal con ella; **to be on friendly terms with sb** llevarse bien con alguien; **not to be on speaking terms** no hablarse; **to come to terms with sth** llegar a aceptar algo

(**c**) *Com* **terms** *(of contract)* términos *mpl*, condiciones *fpl*; **terms of reference** *(of commission)* competencias *fpl*; **terms of payment** condiciones *fpl* de pago

(**d**) *Sch* & *Univ (of three months)* trimestre *m*; *(of four months)* cuatrimestre *m*; **t. of office** *(of politician)* mandato *m*; **a t. of imprisonment** un periodo de reclusión; **in the long/short**

t. a largo/corto plazo; **her pregnancy has reached (full) t.** (ella) ha salido de cuentas; *Univ* **t. paper** trabajo *m* de fin de trimestre
  2 *vt* denominar, llamar

terminal ['tɜːmɪnəl] **1** *n* (**a**) *Elec (of battery)* polo *m* (**b**) *(rail, bus, air)* terminal *f* (**c**) *Comptr* terminal *m*
  2 *adj (phase, illness)* terminal

terminally ['tɜːmɪnəlɪ] *adv* **to be t. ill** estar en la fase terminal de una enfermedad; **t. ill patient** enfermo(a) *m,f* terminal

terminate ['tɜːmɪneɪt] **1** *vt* (**a**) *(contract)* rescindir; *(project)* suspender (**b**) *(pregnancy)* interrumpir
  2 *vi* (**a**) *(contract)* finalizar (**b**) *(bus, train)* **the train terminates here** esta es la última parada del tren

termination [tɜːmɪ'neɪʃən] *n (of contract)* rescisión *f*; *(of project)* suspensión *f*; **t. (of pregnancy)** interrupción *f* (del embarazo)

terminology [tɜːmɪ'nɒlədʒɪ] *n* terminología *f*

terminus ['tɜːmɪnəs] *n* (**a**) *(final stop) (of bus)* última parada *f*, final *m* de trayecto (**b**) *(building) (of bus, train)* (estación *f*) terminal *f*

termite ['tɜːmaɪt] *n* termes *m inv*, termita *f*

tern [tɜːn] *n* charrán *m* común

Terr *(abbr* **Terrace**) = nombre que recibe una calle con casas adosadas

terrace ['terɪs] *n* (**a**) *(outside cafe, hotel)* terraza *f* (**b**) *(on hillside)* terraza *f*

terraced ['terɪst] *adj (hillside)* en terrazas

terracotta ['terə'kɒtə] *n* terracota *f*

terrain [tə'reɪn] *n* terreno *m*

terrapin ['terəpɪn] *n* tortuga *f* acuática

terrestrial [tɪ'restrɪəl] *adj* terrestre; **t. television** *or* **TV** televisión *f* (por vía) terrestre

terrible ['terəbəl] *adj (shocking)* horrible, terrible; *(of poor quality)* horroroso(a); **I'm t. at French** se me da muy mal *or Esp* fatal el francés

terribly ['terəblɪ] *adv* (**a**) *(badly)* tremendamente mal, *Esp* fatal (**b**) *Fam (very)* tremendamente

terrier ['terɪə(r)] *n (dog)* terrier *m*; *Fig (persistent person)* batallador(ora) *m,f*

terrific [tə'rɪfɪk] *adj Fam* (**a**) *(very good) (food, book, weather, performance)* estupendo(a), genial, *Am salvo RP* chévere, *Méx* padre, *RP* bárbaro(a) (**b**) *(very great) (amount, size, speed, shock)* tremendo(a)

terrifically [tə'rɪfɪklɪ] *adv Fam (very)* tremendamente; **it was t. hot** hacía un calor tremendo

terrified ['terɪfaɪd] *adj* aterrorizado(a), aterrado(a); **to be t. of** tener terror a

terrify ['terɪfaɪ] *vt* aterrar, aterrorizar

terrifying ['terɪfaɪɪŋ] *adj* aterrador(ora)

terrifyingly ['terɪfaɪɪŋlɪ] *adv* aterradoramente

territorial [terɪ'tɔːrɪəl] *adj* territorial; **t. waters** aguas *fpl* territoriales

territory ['terɪtərɪ] *n* territorio *m*; *Fig (area of activity)* ámbito *m*

terror ['terə(r)] *n (fear)* terror *m*; **a reign of t.** un imperio del terror; *Fam* **that child is a t.** ese niño es un demonio *or* diablo

terrorism ['terərɪzəm] *n* terrorismo *m*

terrorist ['terərɪst] *n & adj* terrorista *mf*

terrorize ['terəraɪz] *vt* aterrorizar

terror-stricken ['terəstrɪkən], **terror-struck** ['terəstrʌk] *adj* aterrado(a); **to be t.** estar aterrado(a)

terse [tɜːs] *adj* tajante, seco(a)

terseness ['tɜːsnɪs] *n* sequedad *f*

TESL ['tesəl] *n (abbr* **Teaching English as a Second Language**) enseñanza *f* del inglés como segunda lengua

TESOL ['tiːsəl] *n (abbr* **Teaching English to Speakers of**

Other Languages) enseñanza *f* del inglés a hablantes de otras lenguas

test [test] **1** *n* (**a**) *(trial, check)* prueba *f*; **to put sth/sb to the t.** poner algo/a alguien a prueba; **to pass the t.** superar la prueba; **to stand the t. of time** resistir la prueba del tiempo; **t. ban** suspensión *f* de pruebas nucleares; **t. bed** banco *m* de pruebas; *Law* **t. case** resolución *f* judicial que sienta jurisprudencia; **t. drive** prueba *f* de carretera; **t. flight** vuelo *m* de prueba; **t. pilot** piloto *mf* de pruebas; **t. run** *(trial)* prueba *f*, ensayo *m*; **t. tube** probeta *f*
  (**b**) *(examination)* examen *m*; **driving t.** examen *m* de *Esp* conducir *or Am* manejar; **eye t.** revisión *f* de la vista; **blood t.** análisis *m inv* de sangre; **French t.** prueba *f or* control *m* de francés
  2 *vt* (**a**) *(examine) (pupil)* examinar; *(sight, hearing)* revisar; **to t. sb's knowledge** poner a prueba los conocimientos de alguien; **to t. sb for drugs/Aids** hacer a alguien la prueba antidoping/del sida (**b**) *(try out) (object, system)* probar
  3 *vi* **to t. for Aids** hacerse la prueba del sida; **to t. positive/negative** *(for drugs, Aids)* dar positivo/negativo

▸**test out** *vt sep (idea, scheme)* poner a prueba

testament ['testəmənt] *n* (**a**) *Law (will)* testamento *m* (**b**) *(tribute)* testimonio *m*; **to be a t. to** dar testimonio de (**c**) *Rel* **the Old/New T.** el Antiguo/Nuevo Testamento

test-drive ['testdraɪv] *vt Aut* probar en carretera

testicle ['testɪkəl] *n Anat* testículo *m*

testify ['testɪfaɪ] *Law* **1** *vt* **to t. that...** testificar *or* atestiguar que...
  2 *vi* testificar, declarar (**for/against** a favor de/en contra de); *Fig* **to t. to sth** *(be proof of)* atestiguar algo

testily ['testɪlɪ] *adv* irritadamente

testimonial [testɪ'məʊnɪəl] *n (character reference)* referencias *fpl*

testimony ['testɪmənɪ] *n Law* testimonio *m*; **to bear t. to sth** atestiguar algo

testing ['testɪŋ] **1** *n (of machine, bridge)* prueba *f*; **t. ground** campo *m* de pruebas
  2 *adj (problem)* difícil, arduo(a)

testis ['testɪs] *(pl* **testes** ['testiːz]) *n Anat* testículo *m*

testosterone [tes'tɒstərəʊn] *n Biol* testosterona *f*

test-tube baby ['testtjuːb'beɪbɪ] *n* niño(a) *m,f* probeta

testy ['testɪ] *adj (person, mood)* irritable; *(tone, manner)* susceptible; **to be t.** *(by nature)* ser irritable; *(temporarily)* estar irritable *or* irritado(a)

tetanus ['tetənəs] *n Med* tétanos *m inv*

tetchy ['tetʃɪ] *adj Fam* susceptible, irritable; **to be t.** estar susceptible

tether ['teðə(r)] **1** *n (for tying animal)* correa *f*, atadura *f*; *Fig* **to be at the end of one's t.** estar al borde de la desesperación
  2 *vt (animal)* atar

Texan ['teksən] *n & adj* tejano(a) *m,f*

Texas ['teksəs] *n* Texas, Tejas

text [tekst] **1** *n* texto *m*; *Comptr* **t. editor** editor *m* de textos; **t. message** *(sent by cell phone)* mensaje *m* de texto; **t. messaging** *(on cell phones)* mensajería *f* de texto
  2 *vt (send text message to)* enviar un mensaje de texto a
  3 *vi (send text messages)* enviar mensajes de texto

textbook ['tekstbʊk] *n* libro *m* de texto; *Fig* **a t. example** un ejemplo modélico *or* de libro

textile ['tekstaɪl] **1** *n* tejido *m*; **textiles** *(industry)* la industria textil
  2 *adj* textil

textual ['tekstjʊəl] *adj* textual

texture ['tekstʃə(r)] *n* textura *f*

Thai [taɪ] **1** *n* (**a**) *(person)* tailandés(esa) *m,f* (**b**) *(language)* tailandés *m*
  2 *adj* tailandés(esa)

Thailand ['taɪlænd] *n* Tailandia

Thames [temz] *n* **the T.** el Támesis

than [ðæn *unstressed* ðən] *conj (in general)* que; *(with numbers, amounts)* de; **he's taller t. me** *or Formal* **I** es más alto que yo; **he was taller t. I had expected** era más alto de lo que me esperaba; **she stands a better chance of winning t. she did last year** tiene más posibilidades de ganar (de las) que (tuvo) el año pasado; **he is more t. a friend** es más que un amigo; **more/less t. ten** más/menos de diez; **more t. once** más de una vez

thank [θæŋk] *vt* dar las gracias a; **I thanked everybody** se lo agradecí a todo el mundo; **to t. sb for sth** agradecer algo a alguien, dar las gracias a alguien por algo; **to t. sb for doing sth.** agradecer a alguien que haya hecho algo, dar gracias a alguien por haber hecho algo; **t. God!** ¡gracias a Dios!; **t. you** gracias; **t. you very much** muchas gracias; **no, t. you** no, gracias; **t. you for coming** gracias por venir; *Ironic* **I'll t. you to mind your own business!** te agradecería que te ocuparas de tus asuntos; *Ironic* **we have Michael to t. for this** esto se lo tenemos que agradecer a Michael

thankful ['θæŋkfʊl] *adj* agradecido(a); **to be t. that...** dar gracias de que...

thankfully ['θæŋkfəlɪ] *adv* afortunadamente

thankless ['θæŋklɪs] *adj* ingrato(a)

thanks [θæŋks] *npl* gracias *fpl*; **t.!** ¡gracias!; *Fam* **no t.** no, gracias; **t. for coming** gracias por venir; *Fam* **t. for nothing!** ¡gracias por nada!; **to give t. to sb for sth** darle a alguien las gracias por algo; **give him my t.** dale las gracias de mi parte; **t. to him/to his help** gracias a él/a su ayuda; **no t. to you/them!** a pesar de ti/ellos

thanksgiving [θæŋks'gɪvɪŋ] *n* agradecimiento *m*; **T. (Day)** día *m* de acción de gracias *(el cuarto jueves de noviembre)*

thank you ['θæŋkjʊ] *n* agradecimiento *m*; **to say t. to sb** dar las gracias a alguien; **t. letter** carta *f* de agradecimiento; *see also* **thank**

that [ðæt] **1** *demonstrative adj (pl* **those** [ðəʊz]) *(masculine)* ese; *(further away)* aquel; *(feminine)* esa; *(further away)* aquella; **t. man standing in front of you** ese hombre (que está) delante de ti; **t. man right at the back** aquel hombre del fondo; **compare t. edition with these two** compara esa edición con estas dos; **t. one** *(masculine)* ése; *(further away)* aquél; *(feminine)* ésa; *(further away)* aquélla; **at t. time** en aquella época; **t. fool of a teacher** ese *or* aquel profesor tan tonto; **well, how's t. leg of yours?** a ver, ¿cómo va esa pierna?; **what about t. drink you owe me?** ¿qué pasa con esa copa que me debes?

2 *demonstrative pron (pl* **those**) *(in near to middle distance) (indefinite)* eso; *(masculine)* ése; *(feminine)* ésa; *(further away) (indefinite)* aquello; *(masculine)* aquél; *(feminine)* aquélla; **give me t.** dame eso; **this is new and t.'s old** éste es nuevo y ése es viejo; **what's t.?** ¿qué es eso?; **who's t.?** *(pointing)* ¿quién es ése/ésa?; *(who are you?)* ¿quién es?; **who's t. at the back in the blue coat?** ¿quién es aquél del fondo con el abrigo azul?; **is t. all the luggage you're taking?** ¿es ése todo el equipaje que llevas?; **t.'s where he lives** ahí es donde vive; **all t. about my family** lo de *or* aquello de mi familia; **t. was two years ago** eso fue hace dos años; **t.'s strange!** ¡qué raro!, ¡es extraño!; **with t. she turned and left** con eso, dio media vuelta y se marchó; **what do you mean by t.?** ¿qué quieres decir con eso?; **it was a long journey and a tedious one at t.** fue un viaje largo y, encima, tedioso; **can you run as fast as t.?** ¿puedes correr así de deprisa?; **t.'s right!, t.'s it!** ¡eso es!; **t.'s all** eso es todo; **t.'s t.!** ¡ya está!; **t. will do** eso valdrá; **t.'s enough of t.!** ¡ya basta!

3 *adv* **(a)** *(in comparisons)* así de; **t. high** así de alto; **can you run t. fast?** ¿puedes correr así de deprisa?; **t. many** tantos(as); **t. much** tanto **(b)** *(so, very)* tan; **is she t. tall?** ¿tan alta es?

4 [*unstressed* ðət] *relative pron*

El pronombre relativo **that** puede omitirse salvo cuando es sujeto de la oración subordinada.

(a) que; **the letter t. came yesterday** la carta que llegó ayer; **the letter t. I sent you** la carta que te envié; **you're the only person t. can help me** eres la única persona que puede ayudarme **(b)** *(with following preposition)* que; **the envelope t. I put it in** el sobre en que lo guardé; **the woman t. we're talking about** la mujer de quien *or* de la que estamos hablando; **the person t. I gave it to** la persona a quien *or* a la que se lo di **(c)** *(when)* que; **the last time t. I saw him** la última vez que lo vi; **the day t. I left** el día (en) que me fui

5 [*unstressed* ðət] *conj*

---

that se puede omitir cuando introduce una oración subordinada.

(a) *(introducing subordinate clause)* que; **she said t. she would come** dijo que vendría; **I'll see to it t. everything is ready** me ocuparé de que todo esté listo **(b)** *Literary (in exclamations)* **t. it should have come to this!** ¡que hayamos tenido que llegar a esto!; **oh t. it were possible!** ¡ojalá fuese posible!

thataway ['ðætəweɪ] *adv Fam* por ahí

thatch [θætʃ] **1** *n (on roof)* paja *f*; *Fam (of hair)* mata *f*

2 *vt (roof)* cubrir con paja; **thatched cottage** casa *f* de campo con techo de paja; **thatched roof** techo *m* de paja

thaw [θɔː] **1** *n* deshielo *m*; *Fig* **a t. in relations** una mejora de las relaciones

2 *vt* fundir, derretir; *(food)* descongelar

3 *vi (snow, ice)* derretirse, fundirse; *(food)* descongelarse; *Fig (person, manner)* relajarse

▸**thaw out** *vi (lake)* deshelarse; *(food)* descongelarse; *(person) (in front of fire)* entrar en calor

the [*before consonant sounds* ðə, *before vowel sounds* ðɪ, *stressed* ðiː] *definite art* **(a)** *(singular) (masculine)* el; *(feminine)* la; *(plural) (masculine)* los; *(feminine)* las; **t. book** el libro; **t. table** la mesa; **t. books** los libros; **t. tables** las mesas; **to/from t. airport** al/del aeropuerto; **t. good/beautiful** *(as concepts)* lo bueno/bello; **I'll see him in t. summer** lo veré en verano; **she's got t. measles/the flu** tiene (el) sarampión/(la) gripe; **t. best** el/la mejor; **t. longest** el/la más largo(a)

(b) *(specifying)* **t. reason I asked is...** el motivo de mi pregunta es...; **I was absent at t. time** yo no estaba en ese momento; **t. Europe of today** la Europa actual; **t. minute I saw her** en cuanto la vi; *Fam* **how's t. knee?** ¿qué tal esa rodilla?

(c) *(denoting class, group)* **t. poor/blind** los pobres/ciegos; **t. Wilsons** los Wilson

(d) *(with titles)* **Edward t. Eighth** Eduardo octavo; **Catherine t. Great** Catalina la Grande

(e) *(proportions, rates)* **to be paid by t. hour** cobrar por horas; **35 miles to t. gallon** 35 millas por *or* el galón

(f) *(in exclamations)* **t. arrogance/stupidity of it!** ¡qué arrogancia/estupidez!; **$200 for a shirt! t. man's mad!** ¡200 dólares por una camisa! ¡ese tipo está loco!

(g) [*stressed* ðiː] **not THE Professor Branestawm?** ¿no será el famosísimo Profesor Branestawm?; **it's THE diet for the new century** es el régimen del siglo veintiuno

(h) *(in comparisons)* **t. sooner t. better** cuanto antes, mejor; **t. less we argue, t. more work we'll get done** cuanto menos discutamos, más trabajaremos; **I was all t. more puzzled by his calmness** lo que más me extrañaba era su tranquilidad; **she felt all t. better for having told him** se sentía mucho mejor por habérselo dicho

(i) *(with dates)* **t. sixties** los sesenta; **t. eighteen hundreds** el siglo diecinueve

theater ['θɪətə(r)] *n* teatro *m*; *Mil* **t. of war** escenario *m* de guerra; **t. company** compañía *f* de teatro

theatergoer ['θɪətəgəʊə(r)] *n* aficionado(a) *m,f* al teatro

theatrical [θɪ'ætrɪkəl] *adj also Fig* teatral; **t. company** compañía *f* teatral

thee [ðiː] *pron Literary & Rel (plural)* os; *(singular)* te; *(after preposition) (plural)* vos; *(singular)* ti

theft [θeft] *n* robo *m; (not as serious)* hurto *m*

theftproof ['θeftpruːf] *adj (vehicle, door)* a prueba de robo, antirrobo

their ['ðeə(r)] *possessive adj* **(a)** *(singular)* su; *(plural)* sus; **we went to t. house** *(not yours or ours)* fuimos a casa de ellos **(b)** *(for parts of body, clothes) (translated by definite article)* **t. eyes are blue** tienen los ojos azules; **they both forgot t. hats** los dos se olvidaron el sombrero **(c)** *(indefinite use)* su; **somebody called but they didn't leave t. name** ha llamado alguien, pero no ha dejado su nombre; **someone's left t. umbrella** alguien se ha dejado el paraguas

theirs ['ðeəz] *possessive pron* **(a)** *(singular)* el suyo/la suya; *(plural)* los suyos/las suyas; **our house is big but t. is bigger** nuestra casa es grande, pero la suya es mayor **(b)** *(used attributively) (singular)* suyo/suya; *(plural)* suyos/suyas; **this book is t.** este libro es suyo; **a friend of t.** un amigo suyo **(c)** *(indefinite use)* **if anyone hasn't got t. they can use mine** si alguien no tiene el suyo, puede usar el mío

them [ðem *unstressed*, ðəm] *pron* **(a)** *(direct object)* los/las; **I hate t.** los odio; **I can forgive their son but not** THEM puedo perdonar a su hijo, pero no a ellos **(b)** *(indirect object)* les; **I gave t. the book** les di el libro; **I gave it to t.** se lo di **(c)** *(after preposition)* ellos/ellas; **I'm thinking of t.** estoy pensando en ellos **(d)** *(as complement of verb to be)* ellos/ellas; **it's t.!** ¡son ellos!; **it was t. who did it** fueron ellos los que lo hicieron **(e)** *(indefinite use)* **if anyone comes, tell t....** si viene alguien, dile que...

thematic [θiː'mætɪk] *adj* temático(a)

theme [θiːm] *n* **(a)** *(subject)* tema *m*, asunto *m*; **t. park** parque *m* temático **(b)** *(in literature, music)* tema *m*; *TV & Rad* **t. song** *or* **tune** sintonía *f*

themselves [ðəm'selvz, *stressed* ðem'selvz] *pron* **(a)** *(reflexive)* se; **they've hurt t.** se han hecho daño **(b)** *(emphatic)* **they did all the work t.** hicieron todo el trabajo ellos mismos *or* ellos solos; **they told me t.** me lo dijeron ellos mismos **(c)** *(after preposition)* **they were all by t.** estaban ellos solos; **they were talking about t.** estaban hablando de sí mismos; **they were fighting among t.** se estaban peleando entre ellos

then [ðen] **1** *adv* **(a)** *(at that time)* entonces; **it was better t.** era mejor entonces; **before t.** antes (de eso); **since/until t.** desde/hasta entonces; **by t.** para entonces; **t. and there** en aquel instante, al momento **(b)** *(next)* luego; **what t.?** y luego, ¿qué?; **and t. there's the cost** y luego está el coste **(c)** *(in that case)* entonces; **if you don't like it, t. choose another one** si no te gusta, elige otro **(d)** *(therefore)* entonces; **you already knew, t.?** entonces, ¿ya lo sabías?

2 *adj* **the t. President** el entonces presidente

thence [ðens] *adv Formal* **(a)** *(from there)* de allí, de ahí; **we went to Paris and t. to Rome** fuimos a París y de ahí a Roma **(b)** *(because of that)* de ahí

theologian [θiːə'ləʊdʒ(ɪ)ən] *n* teólogo(a) *m,f*

theological [θiːə'lɒdʒɪkəl] *adj* teológico(a)

theology [θiː'ɒlədʒɪ] *n* teología *f*

theorem ['θɪərəm] *n Math* teorema *m*

theoretical [θɪə'retɪkəl] *adj* teórico(a)

theoretically [θɪə'retɪklɪ] *adv (relating to theory)* en la teoría, teóricamente; *(hypothetically)* en teoría, teóricamente; **it's t. possible** en teoría es posible

theoretician [θiːərɪ'tɪʃən] *n* teórico(a) *m,f*

theorist ['θɪərɪst] *n* teórico(a) *m,f*

theorize ['θɪərаɪz] *vi* teorizar

theory ['θɪərɪ] *n* teoría *f*; **in t.** en teoría

therapeutic [θerə'pjuːtɪk] *adj also Fig* terapéutico(a)

therapist ['θerəpɪst] *n* terapeuta *mf*

therapy ['θerəpɪ] *n* terapia *f*

there [ðeə(r), *unstressed* ðə(r)] **1** *pron* **t. is, t. are** hay; **t. was, t. were** había/hubo; **t. will be** habrá; **t.'s a page missing** falta una página; **t. are** *or Fam* **t.'s two slices left** quedan dos lonchas; **t. isn't any** no hay; **t. are four of us** somos cuatro; **t. comes a time when...** llega un momento en que...

2 *adv* **(a)** *(referring to place)* ahí; *(more distant) (at precise point)* allí; *(more vaguely)* allá; **the keys aren't t.** las llaves no están ahí/allí; **who's t.?** *(after knock on door)* ¿quién es?; **up/down t.** ahí arriba/abajo; **I'm going t. tomorrow** voy para allá mañana; **we went to Paris and from t. to Rome** fuimos a París, y de allí a Roma; **somewhere near t.** por allí cerca; **put it over t.** ponlo ahí; **give me that book t.** dame ese libro de ahí; **do we have time to get t. and back?** ¿tenemos tiempo de ir (allí) y volver?; **t. and then** en aquel instante, al momento; **hey! you t.!** ¡oye, tú!; **t. they are!** ¡ahí están!; **t. she goes!** ¡va por ahí!; **t. you are!** *(when giving sb sth)* ¡ahí tienes!; *Fam* **he's not all t.** no está bien de la cabeza

(b) *(at that point)* **we'll stop t. for today** lo dejamos aquí por hoy; **t.'s the difficulty** ahí está la dificultad; *Fam* **t. you have me!, you've got me t.!** *(I don't know the answer)* ¡ahí me has pillado!

3 *exclam* **t. now, that's done!** ¡hala, ya está!; **t. (you are), I told you so** ¿ves?, ya te lo dije; **t., t.! don't worry!** ¡venga, no te preocupes!

thereabouts ['ðeərə'baʊts] *adv* **(a)** *(with place)* **(or) t.** (o) por ahí **(b)** *(with number, quantity, distance)* **or t.** más o menos, (o) por ahí

thereafter [ðeər'ɑːftə(r)] *adv Formal* en lo sucesivo, a partir de ahí

thereby ['ðeəbaɪ] *adv Formal* así, de ese modo; **t. hangs a tale!** y el asunto tiene miga

therefore ['ðeəfɔː(r)] *adv* por (lo) tanto, por consiguiente; **I think, t. I am** pienso, luego existo

thermal ['θɜːməl] **1** *n Met* corriente *f* de aire ascendente, (corriente *f*) térmica *f*

2 *adj* térmico(a); **t. energy** energía *f* térmica; *Comptr* **t. paper** papel *m* térmico; *Geol* **t. springs** aguas *fpl* termales; **t. underwear** ropa *f* interior térmica

thermodynamics [θɜːməʊdaɪ'næmɪks] *n Phys* termodinámica *f*

thermoelectric [θɜːməʊɪ'lektrɪk] *adj* termoeléctrico(a)

thermometer [θə'mɒmɪtə(r)] *n* termómetro *m*

thermos ['θɜːməs] *n* **t. (flask)** termo *m*

thermostat ['θɜːməstæt] *n* termostato *m*

thesaurus [θɪ'sɔːrəs] *n* diccionario *m* de sinónimos

these [ðiːz] *(plural of* **this)** **1** *adj* estos(as); **t. ones** éstos

2 *pron* éstos(as); **t. are the ones I want** éstos son los que quiero

thesis ['θiːsɪs] *(pl* **theses** ['θiːsiːz]) *n* tesis *f inv*

thespian ['θespɪən] *n Literary* actor *m*, actriz *f*

they [ðeɪ] *pron* **(a)** *(personal use)* ellos *mpl*, ellas *fpl (usually omitted, except for contrast)*; **t.'re Canadian** son canadienses; THEY **haven't got it!** ¡ellos no lo tienen!; **t. alone know** sólo ellos lo saben **(b)** *(indefinite use)* **nobody ever admits t.'ve lied** la gente nunca reconoce que ha mentido; **t. say that...** dicen que...

they'd [ðeɪd] = **they had, they would**

they'll [ðeɪl] = **they will, they shall**

they're [ðeə(r)] = **they are**

they've [ðeɪv] = **they have**

thick [θɪk] **1** *n* **in the t. of the forest** en la espesura del bosque; **in the t. of it** *or* **of things** en primera línea;

through t. and thin para lo bueno y para lo malo

2 *adj* **(a)** *(in size)* grueso(a); **the wall is a foot t.** el muro tiene un pie de espesor

(b) *(mist, smoke)* denso(a); *(forest)* espeso(a); *(hair)* poblado(a); *(beard)* poblado(a), tupido(a); *(accent)* acusado(a), marcado(a); **a voice t. with emotion** una voz quebrada por la emoción; **the air was t. with smoke** un humo espeso invadía el aire; **the snow was t. on the ground** había una espesa capa de nieve; *Fig* **to be t. on the ground** *(plentiful)* ser abundante

(c) *(soup, sauce, paint)* espeso(a)

(d) *Fam (stupid)* corto(a), lerdo(a)

(e) *(idioms)* **to have a t. skin** tener mucha correa *or* mucho aguante *(ante críticas o insultos)*; *Fam* **they're as t. as thieves** son uña y carne, *Esp* están a partir un piñón

3 *adv* **to cut the bread t.** cortar el pan en rebanadas gruesas; **to spread the butter t.** untar mucha mantequilla; *Fam* **to lay it on a bit t.** cargar las tintas; **to come t. and fast** llegar a raudales

thicken ['θɪkən] **1** *vt (sauce)* espesar

2 *vi (fog, smoke, sauce)* espesarse; *Hum* **the plot thickens** la cosa se complica

thickener ['θɪknə(r)] *n* espesante *m*

thicket ['θɪkɪt] *n* matorral *m*

thickhead ['θɪkhed] *n Fam* burro(a) *m,f*, tarugo(a) *m,f*

thickly ['θɪklɪ] *adv* **(a)** **t. cut slices of cheese** lonchas de queso gruesas; **to spread butter t.** untar una gruesa capa de mantequilla **(b)** *(to speak)* con la voz quebrada

thickness ['θɪknɪs] *n* **(a)** *(of wall, lips, layer)* grosor *m* **(b)** *(of forest, hair, beard)* espesura *f* **(c)** *(of sauce)* consistencia *f*

thickset ['θɪk'set] *adj (person)* chaparro(a)

thick-skinned [θɪk'skɪnd] *adj Fig* **to be t.** tener mucha correa *or* mucho aguante *(ante críticas o insultos)*

thief [θiːf] *(pl* **thieves** [θiːvz]*) n* ladrón(ona) *m,f*

thieve [θiːv] *vt & vi* robar

thieving ['θiːvɪŋ] **1** *n* robo *m*

2 *adj* ladrón(ona)

thigh [θaɪ] *n* muslo *m*

thighbone ['θaɪbəʊn] *n* fémur *m*

thimble ['θɪmbəl] *n* dedal *m*

thin [θɪn] **1** *adj* **(a)** *(not thick)* delgado(a), fino(a); *(person, face, arm)* delgado(a); *(paper, slice, layer)* fino(a); *(blanket, clothing)* ligero(a), fino(a); **to grow** *or* **become thinner** *(person)* adelgazar

(b) *(sparse) (hair, beard)* ralo(a), escaso(a); *(crowd, vegetation)* escaso(a), disperso(a); *(fog, mist)* ligero(a), tenue

(c) *(soup)* claro(a); *(paint, sauce)* aguado(a)

(d) *(voice)* atiplado(a)

(e) *(idioms)* **to be as t. as a rail** estar como un *or* hecho(a) un palillo; **he had vanished into t. air** había desaparecido como por arte de magia; **they saw this demand as the t. end of the wedge** consideraron que esta demanda era sólo el principio (y luego pedirían más); **to have a t. skin** ser muy susceptible; **to have a t. time (of it)** estar en horas bajas; **to be t. on the ground** *(scarce)* ser escaso(a)

2 *adv* **to slice sth t.** cortar algo en rodajas finas; **to spread sth t.** *(butter, jam)* untar una capa fina de algo; **our resources are spread very t.** los recursos que tenemos son insuficientes

3 *vt (pt & pp* **thinned***) (paint)* diluir, aclarar; *(sauce)* aclarar, aguar

4 *vi (crowd)* dispersarse; *(fog, mist)* despejarse; **his hair is thinning** está empezando a perder pelo

thine [ðaɪn] *Literary & Rel* **1** *adj* tu

2 *pron* tuyo

thing [θɪŋ] *n* **(a)** *(object)* cosa *f*; *Fam* **what's that t.?** ¿qué es ese chisme?; **my/your things** *(clothes)* mi/tu ropa; *(belongings)* mis/tus cosas

(b) *Fam (person)* **poor t.!** ¡pobre!; **you lucky t.!** ¡vaya suerte que tienes!; **you silly t.!** ¡qué bobo eres!

(c) *(action, remark, fact)* cosa *f*; **things are going badly** las cosas van mal; *Fam* **how are things?, how's things?** ¿qué tal van las cosas?, ¿cómo te va?; **that was a silly t. to do/ say** hacer/decir eso fue una tontería; **you take things too seriously** te tomas las cosas demasiado en serio; **for one t.** para empezar; **what with one t. and another** entre unas cosas y otras; **it's just one of those things** cosas que pasan; **the t. is,...** el caso es que...; **it's the only t. we can do** es lo único que podemos hacer; **the important t. is that...** lo importante es que...; **that's quite another t.** eso es algo completamente distinto; **I don't know a t. about algebra** no tengo ni idea de álgebra; **to know a t. or two (about)** saber bastante (de)

(d) *(idioms)* **she has a t. about...** *(likes)* le mola cantidad *or* le priva...; *(dislikes)* le tiene manía a...; **she's got a t. about tidiness/punctuality** es muy maniática con la limpieza/ puntualidad; **the latest t. in shoes** lo último en zapatos

thingamajig ['θɪŋəmɪdʒɪg], **thingamabob** ['θɪŋəmɪbɒb], **thingummy** ['θɪŋəmɪ] *n Fam (object)* chisme *m*, *CAm, Carib, Col* vaina *f*, *RP* coso *m*; *(person)* fulanito(a) *m,f*, mengano(a) *m,f*

think [θɪŋk] **1** *vt (pt & pp* **thought** [θɔːt]*) (a) (have in mind)* **to t. that...** pensar que...; **to t. evil/kind thoughts** tener pensamientos malévolos/benévolos; **what are you thinking?** ¿en qué estás pensando?; **did you t. to bring any money?** ¿se te ha ocurrido traer algo de dinero?

(b) *(believe, have as opinion)* creer, pensar; **he thinks he knows everything** se cree que lo sabe todo; **who do you t. you are?** ¿quién te has creído que eres?; **anyone would t. she was asleep** cualquiera hubiera creído que está dormida; **who'd have thought it!** ¡quién lo hubiera pensado!; **all this is very sad, don't you t.?** todo esto es muy triste, ¿no crees?; **it is thought that...** se cree que...; **they were thought to be rich** se les creía *or* consideraba ricos; **I t. so** creo que sí; **I t. not** no creo; **I thought so, I thought as much** ya me lo figuraba; **I should t. so too!** ¡menos mal!; **I shouldn't t. so** no creo; *Fam* **that's what you t.!** eso es lo que tú te crees

(c) *(imagine)* imaginarse; **I (really) can't t. what/where/ why...** no se me ocurre qué/dónde/por qué...; **t. what we could do with all that money!** ¡imagínate lo que podríamos hacer con todo ese dinero!; **to t. that he's only twenty!** ¡y pensar que sólo tiene veinte años!

2 *vi* pensar; **to t. ahead** planear con anticipación; **to t. aloud** pensar en voz alta; **to t. (long and) hard** pensárselo muy bien; *Fam* **to t. big** ser ambicioso(a); **I did it without thinking** lo hice sin darme cuenta; **if you t. I'll help you do it, you can t. again!** ¡vas listo si crees que te voy a ayudar!; **it makes you t.** da que pensar; **to t. on one's feet** improvisar, discurrir sobre la marcha

3 *n* **to have a t.** pensárselo; *Fam* **you've got another t. coming!** ¡estás muy equivocado!

▸**think about** *vt insep* **(a)** *(in general)* pensar en; **to t. about doing sth** pensar en hacer algo; **it's quite cheap when you t. about it** si lo piensas bien, sale bastante barato; **I'll t. about it** me lo pensaré; **that will give them something to t. about** eso les hará reflexionar; **I'd t. twice about that, if I were you** yo, en tu lugar, me lo pensaría dos veces **(b)** *(take into account)* tener en cuenta; **I've got my family to t. about** debo tener en cuenta a mi familia **(c)** *(have opinion about)* opinar de, pensar de

▸**think back to** *vt insep* recordar

▸**think of** *vt insep* **(a)** *(take into account)* pensar en, tener en cuenta; **I can't t. of everything!** ¡no puedo ocuparme de *or* estar en todo!

(b) *(have in mind)* pensar en; **to t. of doing sth** pensar en hacer algo; **what were you thinking of giving her?** ¿qué estabas pensando regalarle?; **come to t. of it, I DID see her that night** ahora que caigo *or* que lo pienso, sí que la vi aquella noche; **just t. of it... a vacation in the Caribbean!** ¡imagínate unas vacaciones en el Caribe!

(**c**) *(recall)* recordar; **I can't t. of the answer** no se me ocurre cuál es la respuesta

(**d**) *(have opinion about)* opinar de, pensar de; **to t. well/badly of sb** tener buena/mala opinión de alguien; **I don't t. much of the idea** la idea no me parece muy buena

▸**think out** *vt sep* meditar

▸**think over** *vt sep* reflexionar sobre, pensar sobre; **I'll t. it over** me lo pensaré

▸**think through** *vt sep* pensar *or* meditar bien

▸**think up** *vt sep* idear; *(excuse)* inventar

thinker ['θɪŋkə(r)] *n* pensador(ora) *m,f*

thinking ['θɪŋkɪŋ] **1** *n* (**a**) *(process of thought)* pensamiento *m*; **to do some t.** pensar un poco (**b**) *(opinion)* opinión *f*, parecer *m*; **to my (way of) t.** en mi opinión

2 *adj* **the t. man's cover girl** una belleza con cerebro

think-tank ['θɪŋktæŋk] *n* grupo *m* de expertos, equipo *m* de cerebros

thinly ['θɪnlɪ] *adv* **to spread sth t.** extender una capa fina de algo; **to slice sth t.** cortar algo en rodajas finas; **t. populated** escasamente poblado(a)

thinner ['θɪnə(r)] *n* disolvente *m*

thinness ['θɪnnɪs] *n* (**a**) *(of person, face, arms)* delgadez *f*; *(of paper, slice, layer)* finura *f*; *(of blanket, clothing)* ligereza *f* (**b**) *(of liquid)* fluidez *f*

third [θɜːd] **1** *n* (**a**) *(fraction)* tercio *m* (**b**) *(in series)* tercero(a) *m,f*; **Edward the T.** *(written)* Eduardo III; *(spoken)* Eduardo tercero (**c**) *(of month)* tres *m*; **the t. of May** el tres de mayo; **we're leaving on the t.** nos vamos el (día) tres (**d**) *Mus* tercera *f*

2 *adj* tercero(a); *(before masculine singular noun)* tercer; **the t. century** el siglo tercero *or* tres; **I was t. in the race** llegué el tercero en la carrera; **t. base** *(in baseball)* *(place)* tercera base *f*; *(player)* tercera base *mf*; *Fam* **to give sb the t. degree** someter a alguien a un duro interrogatorio; *Law* **t. party** tercero *m*; **t. party cover** seguro *m* a terceros; **the T. World** el Tercer Mundo

third-degree ['θɜːdɪ'griː] *adj Med* **t. burns** quemaduras *fpl* de tercer grado

thirdly ['θɜːdlɪ] *adv* en tercer lugar

third-rate ['θɜːd'reɪt] *adj (mediocre)* de tercera (categoría)

Third-World ['θɜːd'wɜːld] *adj* del tercer mundo, tercermundista

thirst [θɜːst] **1** *n* sed *f*; *Fig* **the t. for knowledge** la sed de conocimientos

2 *vi (for knowledge, revenge)* tener sed (**for** de)

thirsty ['θɜːstɪ] *adj* sediento(a) (**for** de); **to be t.** tener sed; *Fam* **all this talking is t. work** tanto hablar da sed

thirteen [θɜː'tiːn] *n & adj* trece *m*; *see also* **eight**

thirteenth [θɜː'tiːnθ] **1** *n* (**a**) *(fraction)* treceavo *m*, treceava parte *f* (**b**) *(in series)* decimotercero(a) *m,f* (**c**) *(of month)* trece *m*

2 *adj* decimotercero(a); *(before masculine singular noun)* decimotercer; *see also* **eleventh**

thirtieth ['θɜːtɪɪθ] **1** *n* (**a**) *(in series)* trigésimo(a) *m,f* (**b**) *(of month)* treinta *m*; **(on) the t. of May** el treinta de mayo; **we're leaving on the t.** nos vamos el (día) treinta

2 *adj* trigésimo(a)

thirty ['θɜːtɪ] *n & adj* treinta *m*; *see also* **eighty**

thirty-first ['θɜːtɪ'fɜːst] **1** *n* (**a**) *(in series)* trigésimo(a) *m,f* primero(a) (**b**) *(of month)* treinta y uno *m*

2 *adj* trigésimo(a) primero(a); *(before masculine singular noun)* trigésimo primer

thirty-one ['θɜːtɪ'wʌn] **1** *n* treinta y uno *m*

2 *adj* treinta y uno(a); *(before masculine noun)* treinta y un

this [ðɪs] **1** *demonstrative adj (pl* **these** [ðiːz]) este(a); **t. one** éste(a); **t. book** este libro; **t. question** esta pregunta; **I saw him t. morning** lo he visto esta mañana

2 *demonstrative pron (pl* **these**) éste(a); *(indefinite)* esto; **who's t.?** ¿quién es éste?; **what's t.?** ¿qué es esto?; **t. is Jason Wallace** *(introducing another person)* te presento a Jason Wallace; *(introducing self on telephone)* soy Jason Wallace; **t. is ridiculous!** ¡esto es ridículo!; **t. is what she told me** eso es lo que ella me dijo; **t. is where I live** aquí es donde vivo, vivo aquí; **listen to t.** escucha esto; **drink some of t.** toma un poco (de esto); **what's t. I hear about you resigning?** ¿qué es eso de que vas a dimitir?; **do it like t.** hazlo así; **in a case like t.** en un caso así; *Fam* **we talked about t. and that** hablamos de todo un poco

3 *adv* **t. high/far** tan alto/lejos; *(gesturing with hands)* así de alto/lejos; **t. much is certain,...** esto es cierto,...

thistle ['θɪsəl] *n* cardo *m*

thither ['ðɪðə(r)] *adv* **to run hither and t.** correr de aquí para allá

thong [θɒŋ] *n* (**a**) *(for fastening)* correa *f* (**b**) *(swimwear, underwear)* tanga *m* (**c**) *(sandal)* chancleta *f*, chancla *f*

thorax ['θɔːræks] *n Anat* tórax *m inv*

thorn [θɔːn] *n* espina *f*; *Fig* **to be a t. in sb's flesh** *or* **side** no dar tregua a alguien

thorny ['θɔːnɪ] *adj also Fig* espinoso(a)

thorough ['θʌrə] *adj (search, person)* minucioso(a); *(knowledge)* profundo(a); **to do** *or* **make a t. job of it** hacerlo con mucho esmero; **a t. scoundrel** un perfecto canalla

thoroughbred ['θʌrəbred] *n & adj (horse)* purasangre *m*

thoroughfare ['θʌrəfeə(r)] *n* vía *f* (pública)

thoroughgoing ['θʌrəgəʊɪŋ] *adj (search, revision, inspection)* minucioso(a), concienzudo(a); *(knowledge)* profundo(a)

thoroughly ['θʌrəlɪ] *adv* (**a**) *(with thoroughness)* minuciosamente, concienzudamente (**b**) *(entirely)* completamente

thoroughness ['θʌrənɪs] *n* minuciosidad *f*

those [ðəʊz] *(plural of* **that**) **1** *adj* esos(as); *(further away)* aquellos(as); **t. ones** ésos(as); *(further away)* aquéllos(as)

2 *pron* ésos(as); *(further away)* aquéllos(as); **t. of us who remember the war** aquéllos *or* los que recordamos la guerra; **t. of us who were present** los que estuvimos presentes

thou [ðaʊ] *pron Literary & Rel* tú

though [ðəʊ] **1** *conj* aunque; **t. I say so myself** aunque no esté bien que yo lo diga; **strange t. it may seem** aunque parezca raro; **even t. you'll laugh at me** aunque te rías de mí; **as t.** como si

2 *adv* sin embargo

thought [θɔːt] **1** *n* (**a**) *(thinking)* pensamiento *m*; *(idea)* idea *f*; **that's** *or* **there's a t.!** ¡qué buena idea!; **it's quite a t.!** *(pleasant)* ¡sería genial!; *(unpleasant)* ¡sería horrible!; **what a kind t.!** ¡qué detalle tan amable!; **the mere t. of it** sólo (de) pensar en ello; **I didn't give it another t.** no me lo pensé dos veces; **what are your thoughts on the matter?** ¿qué es lo que piensas del asunto?

(**b**) *(reflection)* reflexión *f*; **after much t.** tras mucho reflexionar; **to give a great deal of t. to sth** reflexionar mucho sobre algo; **she was deep** *or* **lost in t.** estaba sumida en sus pensamientos

(**c**) *(intention)* **I had no t. of offending you** no tenía intención de ofenderte; **you must give up all t.(s) of seeing him** olvida la idea de verlo

2 *pt & pp of* **think**

thoughtful ['θɔːtfʊl] *adj* (**a**) *(pensive) (person)* pensativo(a), meditabundo(a); *(book, writer)* ponderado(a), concienzudo(a) (**b**) *(considerate)* considerado(a), atento(a)

thoughtfully ['θɔːtfəlɪ] *adv (considerately)* consideradamente

thoughtless ['θɔːtlɪs] *adj (inconsiderate)* desconsiderado(a)

thoughtlessly ['θɔːtlɪslɪ] *adv (inconsiderately)* desconsideradamente, con falta de consideración

thought-out ['θɔːt'aʊt] *adj* **well/poorly t.** *(plan, scheme)* bien/mal meditado(a)

thought-provoking ['θɔːtprəvəʊkɪŋ] *adj* intelectualmente estimulante

thousand ['θaʊzənd] **1** *n a or* one t. mil; **three t.** tres mil; **thousands of people** millares *or* miles de personas; **in thousands** a millares; *Fam* **to have a t. and one things to do** tener mil cosas que hacer; **she's one in a t.** hay pocas como ella
2 *adj* mil; **a t. years** mil años

thousandth ['θaʊzən(t)θ] **1** *n* (a) *(fraction)* milésima *f*, milésima parte *f* (b) *(in series)* milésimo(a) *m,f*
2 *adj* milésimo(a)

thrash [θræʃ] *vt also Fig* dar una paliza a
▶**thrash around, thrash about 1** *vt sep* **to t. one's arms and legs around** agitar con violencia los brazos y las piernas
2 *vi (move furiously)* agitarse *or* revolverse (con violencia)
▶**thrash out** *vt sep (solution)* alcanzar por fin; **they are still thrashing out an agreement** todavía están luchando por alcanzar un acuerdo

thread [θred] **1** *n* (a) *(of cotton, nylon)* hilo *m*; **a (piece of) t.** un hilo; *Fig* **to hang by a t.** pender de un hilo; **to lose the t. of the conversation** perder el hilo de la conversación (b) *(of screw, bolt)* rosca *f*
2 *vt (needle)* enhebrar; *(beads)* ensartar; **to t. one's way between the cars** avanzar sorteando los coches

threadbare ['θredbeə(r)] *adj (clothes, carpet)* raído(a); *Fig (argument, joke)* trillado(a)

threat [θret] *n* amenaza *f*

threaten ['θretən] **1** *vt* amenazar; **to t. to do sth** amenazar con hacer algo; **to t. sb with sth** amenazar a alguien con algo
2 *vi* amenazar

threatening ['θretənɪŋ] *adj* amenazante, amenazador(ora)

threateningly ['θretənɪŋlɪ] *adv (look)* con aire amenazador; *(say)* en tono amenazado

three [θriː] *n & adj* tres *m; see also* **eight**

three-cornered [θriː'kɔːnəd] *adj* triangular; **t. hat** sombrero *m* de tres picos

three-course meal ['θriːkɔːs'miːl] *n* comida *f* de tres platos

three-dimensional [θriːdaɪ'menʃənəl] *adj* tridimensional

threefold ['θriːfəʊld] **1** *adj* triplicado(a), por tres
2 *adv* tres veces; **to increase t.** triplicarse

three-legged [θriː'legɪd] *adj (stool)* de tres patas; **t. race** = carrera por parejas con un pie atado

three-piece ['θriːpiːs] *adj* **t. suit** terno *m*; **t. suite** tresillo *m*, sofá *m* y dos sillones

three-point turn ['θriːpɔɪnt'tɜːn] *n Aut* cambio *m* de sentido con marcha atrás

three-quarters [θriː'kwɔːtəz] **1** *pron (amount)* tres cuartos *mpl*, tres cuartas *fpl* partes
2 *adv* **t. full/finished** lleno(a)/terminado(a) en sus tres cuartas partes

threescore ['θriːskɔː(r)] *adj Literary* sesenta; **t. (years) and ten** setenta (años)

threesome ['θriːsəm] *n* trío *m*; **we went as a t.** fuimos los tres juntos

three-wheeler [θriː'wiːlə(r)] *n (car)* automóvil *m* de tres ruedas; *(tricycle)* triciclo *m*

thresh [θreʃ] *vt* trillar

threshold ['θreʃəʊld] *n also Fig* umbral *m*; **to cross the t.** franquear el umbral; **to be on the t. (of)** estar en el umbral *or* en puertas (de)

threw [θruː] *pt of* **throw**

thrice [θraɪs] *adv Literary* tres veces

thrift [θrɪft] *n* ahorro *m*, frugalidad *f*

thriftless ['θrɪftlɪs] *adj* derrochador(ora)

thrifty ['θrɪftɪ] *adj (person)* ahorrativo(a); *(meal)* frugal

thrill [θrɪl] **1** *n (excitement)* emoción *f*; *(trembling)* estremecimiento *m*; **he gets a t. out of ordering people about** disfruta dando órdenes a la gente
2 *vt* encantar, entusiasmar
3 *vi Literary* estremecerse

thrilled [θrɪld] *adj* **he was t. with his present** estaba entusiasmado con su regalo; **I'm t. for you** me alegro muchísimo por ti

thriller ['θrɪlə(r)] *n (novel)* novela *f* de *Esp* suspense *or Am* suspenso, thriller *m*; *(movie)* película *f* de *Esp* suspense *or Am* suspenso, thriller *m*

thrilling ['θrɪlɪŋ] *adj* apasionante, emocionante

thrive [θraɪv] *(pt* thrived *or* throve [θrəʊv]) *vi (person, plant)* medrar; *(business)* prosperar; **to t. on other people's misfortunes** aprovecharse de las desgracias ajenas; **some people t. on stress** algunas personas se crecen con el estrés

thriving ['θraɪvɪŋ] *adj (plant)* lozano(a); *(person)* mejor que nunca; *(business)* próspero(a), floreciente

throat [θrəʊt] *n* (a) garganta *f*; **to grab sb by the t.** agarrar a alguien por el cuello; **to clear one's t.** carraspear, aclararse la garganta (b) *Fam (idioms)* **to ram** *or* **shove sth down sb's t.** hacerle tragar algo a alguien; **there's no need to jump down my t.!** ¡no hay motivo para que me eches así los perros!; **they're always at each other's throats** siempre se están tirando los trastos (a la cabeza)

throaty ['θrəʊtɪ] *adj (cough, voice)* ronco(a)

throb [θrɒb] **1** *n (of heart)* palpitación *f*, latido *m*; *(of engine)* zumbido *m*
2 *vi (pt & pp* throbbed) *(heart)* palpitar, latir; *(engine)* zumbar; *(drums)* retumbar; **my head is throbbing** me late la cabeza de dolor

throbbing ['θrɒbɪŋ] *adj (rhythm)* vibrante, palpitante; *(engine, machine)* vibrante; *(heart)* palpitante; *(pain)* punzante

throes [θrəʊz] *npl* **the t. of death, death t.** la agonía de la muerte; **we're in the t. of moving house** estamos pasando la agonía de mudarnos de casa

thrombosis [θrɒm'bəʊsɪs] *n Med* trombosis *f inv*

throne [θrəʊn] *n* trono *m*

throng [θrɒŋ] **1** *n* muchedumbre *f*, gentío *m*
2 *vt* atestar, abarrotar
3 *vi (gather)* aglomerarse, apelotonarse; **to t. around sb** apiñarse en torno a alguien; **people thronged to the new multiplex** la gente acudió en masa al nuevo cine multisalas

throttle ['θrɒtəl] **1** *n Aut* estrangulador *m*; **at full t.** a toda velocidad
2 *vt (strangle)* estrangular

through [θruː] **1** *prep* (a) *(with place)* a través de; **to go t. a tunnel** atravesar un túnel, pasar a través de un túnel; **we went t. Belgium** atravesamos Bélgica; **to look t. a hole** mirar por un agujero; **she came in t. the window** entró por la ventana
(b) *(in the course of)* **all t. his life** durante toda su vida; **halfway t. a book/a movie** a mitad de un libro/una película; *Fam* **he's been t. a lot** ha pasado mucho; **to get t. sth** *(finish)* terminar algo
(c) *(by means of)* por; **to send sth t. the mail** mandar algo por correo; **I found out t. my brother** me enteré por mi hermano
(d) *(because of)* por; **t. ignorance/carelessness** por ignorancia/descuido
(e) **Tuesday t. Thursday** desde el martes hasta el jueves inclusive
2 *adv* (a) *(to other side)* **to go t.** *(of bullet, nail)* traspasar, pasar al otro lado; **to let sb t.** dejar pasar a alguien; **to get t. to the**

final llegar or pasar a la final (**b**) (from start to finish) **to sleep all night t.** dormir de un tirón; **to read a book right t.** leerse un libro de principio a fin; **t. and t.** de la cabeza a los pies (**c**) (in contact) **to get t. to sb** (on phone) conseguir contactar or comunicar con alguien; Fam (make oneself understood) comunicarse con alguien; **I'll put you t. to him** (on phone) le pongo or paso con él

3 adj (**a**) (finished) **to be t. with sth/sb** haber terminado con algo/alguien (**b**) (direct) **t. ticket** billete m directo; **t. train** tren m directo

throughout [θruː'aʊt] **1** prep (place) por todo(a); (time) durante todo(a), a lo largo de todo(a); **t. the country** por todo el país; **t. her life** durante toda su vida

2 adv (place) en su totalidad; (time) en todo momento

throughput ['θruːpʊt] n Com rendimiento m

throve [θrəʊv] pt of **thrive**

throw [θrəʊ] **1** vt (pt **threw** [θruː], pp **thrown** [θrəʊn]) (**a**) (with hands) (in general) tirar, Am aventar; (ball, javelin) lanzar; **the rioters began throwing stones** los alborotadores empezaron a arrojar piedras; **to t. sth at sth/sb** tirarle algo a algo/alguien; **to t. sth in sb's face** arrojar algo a alguien en la cara; Fig echar en cara algo a alguien; **to t. (sb) forward/ backward** lanzar (a alguien) hacia delante/atrás; **to t. oneself into** (river) tirarse a; Fig (undertaking, work) entregarse a; **to t. oneself on sb's mercy** ponerse a merced de alguien; **she threw herself at him** prácticamente se echó en sus brazos; **to t. sb into confusion** sumir a alguien en la confusión; **to t. a switch** dar al interruptor; **to t. open the door** abrir la puerta de golpe; Fam **she tends to t. her weight about** tiende a abusar de su autoridad

(**b**) (glance) lanzar

(**c**) (image, shadow) proyectar; Fig **to t. light on sth** arrojar luz sobre algo

(**d**) (have) **to t. a fit** (get angry) ponerse hecho(a) una furia; Fam **to t. a party** dar una fiesta

(**e**) Sport (in wrestling) derribar; **the horse threw its rider** el caballo desmontó al jinete

(**f**) Fam (disconcert) desconcertar

2 n (of dice, darts) tirada f; (of ball, javelin, discus) lanzamiento m; (in wrestling) derribo m

▸**throw away** vt sep (**a**) (discard) tirar, Am botar (**b**) (opportunity, life, money) desperdiciar

▸**throw in** vt sep (**a**) (into a place) echar, tirar; Fig **to t. in one's hand** or **one's cards** or **the towel** tirar la toalla; Fig **he threw in his lot with the rebels** unió su destino al de los rebeldes (**b**) (add) añadir; (include as extra) incluir (como extra)

▸**throw out** vt sep (**a**) (eject) (person) echar; (thing) tirar; (proposal) rechazar; **to t. sb out of work** echar a alguien del trabajo (**b**) (emit) (light, heat) despedir

▸**throw together** vt sep (assemble or gather hurriedly) juntar a la carrera; (make hurriedly) pergeñar; **chance had thrown us together** el azar quiso que nos conociéramos

▸**throw up 1** vt sep (**a**) (raise) **to t. up one's hands** (in horror, dismay) echarse las manos a la cabeza (**b**) (reveal) (facts, information) poner de manifiesto (**c**) (abandon) (career) abandonar

2 vi Fam (vomit) devolver, echar la papilla

throwaway ['θrəʊəweɪ] adj (disposable) desechable; **a t. line** or **remark** un comentario insustancial or pasajero

throwback ['θrəʊbæk] n Biol regresión f, salto m atrás; Fig retorno m

throw-in ['θrəʊɪn] n (in basketball, soccer) saque m de banda, Andes, RP saque m de costado

thrown [θrəʊn] pp of **throw**

thru [θruː] prep & adv Fam = **through**

thrush¹ [θrʌʃ] n (bird) tordo m, zorzal m

thrush² n (disease) candidiasis f inv

thrust [θrʌst] **1** n (**a**) (with knife) cuchillada f; (in fencing)

estocada f; (of army) ofensiva f (**b**) (of argument) sentido m, objetivo m; **the main t. of his argument was that...** lo que pretendía demostrar con su argumento era que... (**c**) Av empuje m

2 vt (pt & pp **thrust**) hundir (**into** en); **she t. the letter into my hands** me echó la carta en las manos; **he was suddenly t. into a position of responsibility** se vio de repente en un puesto de responsabilidad

▸**thrust aside** vt sep rechazar, apartar

▸**thrust forward** vt sep (push forward) empujar (hacia delante); Fig **to t. oneself forward** (for job, to gain attention) hacerse notar

▸**thrust on** vt sep **fame was t. on him** la fama le cayó encima; **he t. himself on them** tuvieron que cargar con él

▸**thrust out** vt sep (one's arm, leg) extender de golpe

▸**thrust upon** = **thrust on**

thruway ['θruːweɪ] n Aut autopista f

thud [θʌd] **1** n golpe m sordo

2 vi (pt & pp **thudded**) hacer un ruido sordo

thug [θʌg] n matón m

thumb [θʌm] **1** n pulgar m; Fig **she's got him under her t.** lo tiene completamente dominado; Fam **he's all thumbs** es un torpe or Esp manazas; Fam **to give sth/sb the thumbs up** dar el visto bueno a algo/alguien; Fam **to give sth/sb the thumbs down** no dar el visto bueno a algo/alguien

2 vt **to t. one's nose at sb** hacerle burla a alguien; Fam **to t. a lift** or **ride** hacer dedo, CAm, Méx, Perú pedir aventón; **I thumbed a ride to Abilene** fui a Abilene a dedo; **a well-thumbed book** un libro manoseado

3 vi **to t. through sth** hojear algo

thumbnail ['θʌmneɪl] n uña f del pulgar; **t. sketch** reseña f, descripción f somera

thumbprint ['θʌmprɪnt] n huella f del pulgar

thumbtack ['θʌmtæk] n Esp chincheta f, Am chinche m

thump [θʌmp] **1** n (blow) porrazo m; (sound) ruido m seco

2 vt (hit) dar un porrazo a

3 vi (**a**) (on table, door) golpear (**b**) (walk heavily) **I could hear him thumping around upstairs** lo oía dar fuertes pisadas en el apartamento or Esp piso de arriba (**c**) (heart) **my heart was thumping** el corazón me latía con fuerza

thumping ['θʌmpɪŋ] Fam **1** adj enorme, tremendo(a)

2 adv **a t. great book/house** un pedazo de libro/casa, un libro/una casa de aquí te espero

thunder ['θʌndə(r)] **1** n truenos mpl; **with a face like t.** con el rostro encendido por la ira

2 vi (**a**) (during storm) tronar; (guns, waves) retumbar; **to t. along** (train, truck) pasar con estrépito (**b**) (speaker) tronar, vociferar

thunderbolt ['θʌndəbəʊlt] n rayo m; Fig (news) mazazo m

thunderclap ['θʌndəklæp] n trueno m

thundercloud ['θʌndəklaʊd] n nube f de tormenta

thundering ['θʌndərɪŋ] adj (very large) tremendo(a), enorme; **to be in a t. rage** estar hecho(a) una furia

thunderous ['θʌndərəs] adj (voice, applause) atronador(ora)

thunderstorm ['θʌndəstɔːm] n tormenta f

thunderstruck ['θʌndəstrʌk] adj pasmado(a), atónito(a)

Thur (abbr **Thursday**) jueves m inv

Thursday ['θɜːzdeɪ] n jueves m inv; see also **Saturday**

thus [ðʌs] adv Formal (**a**) (in this way) así, de este modo (**b**) (therefore) por consiguiente (**c**) **t. far** (up to now) hasta el momento; (up to here) hasta aquí

thwart [θwɔːt] vt (person, plan) frustrar

thy [ðaɪ] adj Literary & Rel tu; **love t. neighbor** amarás al prójimo

thyme [taɪm] n tomillo m

thyroid ['θaɪrɔɪd] Anat **1** n (glándula f) tiroides m inv

2 adj tiroideo(a)

thyself [ðaɪˈself] *pron Literary & Rel* tú mismo; **for t.** para ti mismo(a)

ti [tiː] *n Mus* si *m*

tiara [tɪˈɑːrə] *n (jewelry)* diadema *f; (of Pope)* tiara *f*

Tibet [tɪˈbet] *n* (el) Tíbet

Tibetan [tɪˈbetən] **1** *n* **(a)** *(person)* tibetano(a) *m,f* **(b)** *(language)* tibetano *m*
    2 *adj* tibetano(a)

tibia [ˈtɪbɪə] *n Anat* tibia *f*

tic [tɪk] *n Med* tic *m;* **a nervous t.** un tic nervioso

tick¹ [tɪk] *n (parasite)* garrapata *f*

tick² **1** *n* **(a)** *(of clock)* tictac *m* **(b)** *(mark)* marca *f*, señal *f* de visto bueno
    2 *vi (clock)* hacer tictac; **the minutes are ticking by** *or* **away** los minutos pasan; *Fam* **I don't know what makes him t.** no sé qué es lo que le mueve
    3 *vt (mark)* marcar

▸**tick off** *vt sep* **(a)** *(on list)* marcar con una señal de visto bueno **(b)** *Fam (irritate)* fastidiar

ticker tape [ˈtɪkəteɪp] *n* cinta *f* de cotizaciones (bursátiles); **a t. parade** un desfile de recibimiento multitudinario

ticket [ˈtɪkɪt] **1** *n* **(a)** *(for train, plane, lottery)* billete *m, Am* boleto *m, esp Am* pasaje *m; (for theater, cinema)* entrada *f, Col, Méx* boleto *m;* **(parking) t.** multa *f* de aparcamiento; **I got a (parking) t.** me pusieron una multa (de aparcamiento); **t. office** taquilla *f, Am* boletería *f;* **t. window** ventanilla *f* **(b)** *(label)* **(price) t.** etiqueta *f* (de precio) **(c)** *Pol (list of candidates)* candidatura *f;* **she ran on an anticorruption t.** se presentó bajo la bandera de la anticorrupción **(d)** *Fam* **it was just the t.!** ¡era justo lo que necesitaba!
    2 *vt* **(a)** *(goods)* etiquetar **(b)** *(mark out)* distinguir; **to be ticketed for sth** estar destinado(a) a algo

ticking [ˈtɪkɪŋ] *n* **(a)** *(of clock)* tictac *m* **(b)** *Tex* terliz *m*, cutí *m (para colchones)*

tickle [ˈtɪkəl] **1** *n* cosquillas *fpl;* **to have a t. in one's throat** tener picor de garganta
    2 *vt* **(a)** hacer cosquillas a **(b)** *(amuse)* divertir; **to t. sb's fancy** atraer *or Esp* apetecer *or Carib, Col, Méx* provocar *or Méx* antojársele a alguien; **to be tickled pink** estar encantado(a)
    3 *vi* hacer cosquillas

tickling [ˈtɪklɪŋ] *adj* **I felt a t. sensation in my feet** sentía cosquilleo en los pies

ticklish [ˈtɪklɪʃ] *adj* **(a)** *(person)* **to be t.** tener cosquillas **(b)** *Fam (situation, problem)* delicado(a), peliagudo(a), *Méx* pelón(ona)

tickly [ˈtɪklɪ] *adj Fam* **a t. blanket/beard** una manta/barba que pica; **I've got a t. throat** tengo la garganta tomada, me pica la garganta

tic-tac-toe, tick-tack-toe [tɪktækˈtəʊ] *n* tres en raya *m*

tidal [ˈtaɪdəl] *adj* **the river is t. up to Trenton** la marea llega hasta Trenton; **t. energy** energía *f* mareomotriz; **t. wave** maremoto *m*

tidbit [ˈtɪdbɪt] *n (snack)* tentempié *m*, refrigerio *m; Fig* **a t. of gossip** un chismorreo *or Esp* cotilleo; **a t. of information** una noticia

tiddlywinks [ˈtɪdlɪwɪŋks], **tiddledywinks** [ˈtɪdəldɪwɪŋks] *n (juego m* de la) pulga *f*

tide [taɪd] *n* marea *f; Fig (of events)* rumbo *m*, curso *m;* **high/low t.** marea alta/baja; *Fig* **to go against the t.** ir contra (la) corriente; *Fig* **the rising t. of discontent** la creciente ola de descontento; *Fig* **the t. has turned** se han vuelto las tornas

▸**tide over** *vt sep* **to t. sb over** *(of money)* sacar a alguien del apuro; **I lent him some money to t. him over till payday** le presté un poco de dinero para que llegara hasta el día de cobro

tidemark [ˈtaɪdmɑːk] *n (mark left by tide)* línea *f* de la marea

tidings [ˈtaɪdɪŋz] *npl Literary* nuevas *fpl*, noticias *fpl*

tidy [ˈtaɪdɪ] **1** *adj* **(a)** *(room, habits)* ordenado(a); *(appearance)* arreglado(a), aseado(a); *(mind)* metódico(a) **(b)** *Fam (considerable)* considerable
    2 *vt (room)* ordenar; *(garden, hair)* arreglar

▸**tidy up** *vi* recoger

tie [taɪ] **1** *n* **(a)** *(link)* lazo *m*, vínculo *m* **(b)** *(item of clothing)* corbata *f* **(c)** *Sport (draw)* empate *m* **(d)** *Rail* traviesa *f*
    2 *vt (shoelace, piece of string)* atar; **to t. sth to sth** atar algo a algo; **to t. a knot** atar *or* hacer un nudo; *Fig* **to have one's hands tied** *(have no alternative)* tener las manos atadas; *Fig* **he was tied to his desk** estaba atado a su trabajo; *Fig* **she felt tied by a sense of duty** se sentía obligada por sentido del deber
    3 *vi (in race, contest)* empatar

▸**tie back** *vt sep (hair, curtains)* recoger

▸**tie down** *vt sep (immobilize)* atar; *Fig* **children t. you down** los hijos atan mucho; *Fig* **I don't want to be tied down to a specific date** no quiero comprometerme a una fecha concreta

▸**tie in** *vi (facts, story)* encajar, concordar

▸**tie on** *vt* atar

▸**tie up** *vt sep* **(a)** *(animal, parcel)* atar; *(boat)* amarrar; *Fig (deal)* cerrar; **my capital is tied up in property** tengo mi capital invertido en bienes inmuebles **(b)** **to be tied up** *(busy)* estar muy ocupado(a)

tiebreak(er) [ˈtaɪbreɪk(ər)] *n (in tennis)* tie-break *m*, muerte *f* súbita; *(in quiz, competition)* desempate *m*

tie-in [ˈtaɪɪn] *n* **(a)** *(link)* relación *f* (**with** con) **(b)** **a movie/TV t. =** producto a veces promocional relacionado con una nueva película o programa televisivo

tiepin [ˈtaɪpɪn] *n* alfiler *m* de corbata

tier [tɪə(r)] *n (of theater)* fila *f; (of stadium)* grada *f; (of wedding cake)* piso *m; (administrative)* nivel *m*

TIFF [tɪf] *n Comptr (abbr* **Tagged Image File Format**) TIFF

tiff [tɪf] *n Fam* riña *f*, desavenencia *f*

tiger [ˈtaɪgə(r)] *n* tigre *m*

tight [taɪt] **1** *adj* **(a)** *(clothes)* ajustado(a), estrecho(a); *(knot, screw)* apretado(a); *Fig (bend)* cerrado(a); *Fig (restrictions)* severo(a); **to be a t. fit** *(clothes)* quedar muy justo(a); **to keep a t. hold on sth** tener algo bien agarrado(a); **we're a bit t. for time** vamos un poco cortos *or* justos de tiempo; *Fig* **to be in a t. spot** *or* **corner** estar en un aprieto; *Fig* **to run a t. ship** llevar el timón con mano firme; **to work to a t. schedule** trabajar con un calendario estricto
    (b) *(race, finish)* reñido(a); *Fam* **money's a bit t. at the moment** ahora mismo ando un poco justo de dinero
    (c) *Fam (stingy)* agarrado(a), roñoso(a)
    (d) *Fam (drunk)* alegre, *Esp* piripi
    2 *adv (hold, squeeze)* con fuerza; *(seal, shut)* bien; **hold t.!** ¡agárrate fuerte!; **sleep t.!** ¡que descanses!

tighten [ˈtaɪtən] **1** *vt (screw, knot)* apretar; *(rope)* tensar; *(restrictions, security)* intensificar; *(conditions, rules)* endurecer; **to t. one's grip on** *(rope, handle)* asir con más fuerza; *Fig* **he tightened his grip on the organization** incrementó su control sobre la organización; *Fig* **to t. one's belt** apretarse el cinturón
    2 *vi (knot)* apretarse; *(grip)* intensificarse; *(rope)* tensarse

▸**tighten up** *vt sep (screw)* apretar; *(restrictions, security)* intensificar

tight-fisted [taɪtˈfɪstɪd] *adj Fam* agarrado(a), rata

tight-fitting [taɪtˈfɪtɪŋ] *adj (item of clothing)* ajustado(a), ceñido(a); **you need a t. lid for the saucepan** te hace falta una tapa que encaje *or* ajuste bien en la cacerola

tight-knit [ˈtaɪtˈnɪt] *adj (community)* muy integrado(a)

tight-lipped [ˈtaɪtˈlɪpt] *adj* **to be t. (about sth)** *(silent)* no soltar prenda (sobre algo); *(angry)* estar enfurruñado(a) (por algo)

tightly ['taɪtlɪ] *adv (hold, squeeze)* con fuerza; *(seal, close)* bien

tightness ['taɪtnɪs] *n (of link, clothing)* estrechez *f*; *(of regulations, security)* rigidez *f*

tightrope ['taɪtrəʊp] *n* cuerda *f* floja; *Fig* **to be walking a t.** estar en la cuerda floja; **t. walker** funambulista *mf*

tigress ['taɪgrɪs] *n* tigresa *f*

'til [tɪl] = **until**

tile [taɪl] **1** *n (on roof)* teja *f*; *(on floor)* baldosa *f*; *(on wall)* azulejo *m*
2 *vt (put tiles on) (roof)* tejar; *(floor)* embaldosar; *(walls)* poner azulejos en, *Esp* alicatar

tiled [taɪld] *adj (roof)* de tejas; *(floor)* embaldosado(a); *(wall)* con azulejos, *Esp* alicatado(a)

tiler ['taɪlə(r)] *n (of roof)* techador(ora) *m,f*; *(of floor)* solador(ora) *m,f*; *(of wall)* = albañil que coloca azulejos, *Esp* alicatador(ora) *m,f*

till¹ [tɪl] *vt (field)* labrar

till² *n (cash register)* caja *f* (registradora); *Fig* **to be caught with one's hand** *or* **fingers in the t.** ser atrapado(a) haciendo un desfalco

till³ = **until**

tiller ['tɪlə(r)] *n (on boat)* caña *f* del timón

tilt [tɪlt] **1** *n* **(a)** *(angle)* inclinación *f* **(b)** *(speed)* **at full t.** a toda marcha
2 *vt also Fig* inclinar; **to t. one's head** inclinar la cabeza
3 *vi* **(a)** *(incline)* inclinarse; **to t. forward/backward** inclinarse hacia delante/hacia atrás **(b)** **to t. at windmills** arremeter contra molinos de viento
▶**tilt over** *vi (fall)* venirse abajo

timber ['tɪmbə(r)] *n (wood)* madera *f* (de construcción); **t.!** ¡árbol va!

time [taɪm] **1** *n* **(a)** *(in general)* tiempo *m*; **in t.** *(eventually)* con el tiempo; **in t. for sth/to do sth** a tiempo para algo/para hacer algo; **in good t.** *(early)* con tiempo; **she'll do it in her own good t.** lo hará a su ritmo; **all in good t.!** cada cosa a su (debido) tiempo, todo se andará; **he did it in his own t.** *(out of working hours)* lo hizo fuera de las horas de trabajo; *(at his own pace)* lo hizo a su aire *or* ritmo; **when I have the t.** cuando tenga tiempo; **now my t. is my own** ahora tengo todo el tiempo del mundo; **to take one's t. (doing sth)** tomarse (uno) su tiempo (para hacer algo); **you took your t.!** ¡has tardado mucho!; **it takes t.** lleva tiempo; **I've no t. for him** no me cae nada bien; **in no t. at all, in next to no t.** en un abrir y cerrar de ojos; **t. is getting on** no queda mucho tiempo; **t.'s up!** ¡se acabó el tiempo!; *Fam* **to do t.** *(go to prison)* pasar una temporada a la sombra; **if I had my t. over again** si pudiera vivir otra vez; **t. will tell** el tiempo lo dirá; *Prov* **t. is money** el tiempo es oro; *Fig* **to be sitting on a t. bomb** estar (sentado(a)) sobre un volcán; **t. frame** plazo *m* de tiempo; **t. travel** viajes *mpl* en el tiempo; *Fig* **to be in a t. warp** seguir anclado(a) en el pasado

(b) *(period)* **in a short t.** dentro de poco; **in a long t.** desde hace (mucho) tiempo; **in three weeks' t.** dentro de tres semanas; **to take a long t. over sth/to do sth** tomarse mucho tiempo para algo/para hacer algo; **for some t.** durante bastante tiempo; **for the t. being** por ahora, por el momento; **to have a good t.** pasárselo bien; **to give sb a hard t.** hacer pasar a alguien un mal rato

(c) *(age)* época *f*; **before my t.** antes de mi época; **to be ahead of one's t.** estar por delante de su tiempo, ser un(a) adelantado(a) de su tiempo; **she was a good singer in her t.** en sus tiempos fue una gran cantante; **to move with the times** ir con los tiempos; **she's seen a few things in her t.** ella ha visto unas cuantas cosas en su vida; **t. capsule** = recipiente que contiene objetos propios de una época y que se entierra para que futuras generaciones puedan conocer cómo se vivía entonces

(d) *(moment)* momento *m*; **I didn't know it at the t.** en aquel momento *or* entonces no lo sabía; **at that t.** en aquel momento *or* entonces; **at the present t.** en el momento presente; **at one t. it was different** hubo un tiempo en que era distinto; **at no t.** en ningún momento; **at the same t.** al mismo tiempo; **at all times** en todo momento; **this t. next year** el año que viene por estas fechas; **from that t. (onward)** desde entonces (en adelante); **at that t. of (the) year** por aquellas fechas; **the t. for talking is past** la ocasión de hablar ya ha pasado; *Fam* **it's high t.!** ¡ya era hora!

(e) *(on clock)* hora *f*; **what's the t.?** ¿qué hora es?; **the t. is six o'clock** son las seis (en punto); **to pass the t. of day with sb** charlar un rato con alguien; **this t. tomorrow** mañana a estas horas; **on t.** a la hora en punto; **to be on t.** llegar a la hora; **I was just in t. to see it** llegué justo a tiempo para verlo; **it is t. we left** es hora de que nos vayamos; **there's a t. check every five minutes** *(on radio)* dan la hora cada cinco minutos; **t. difference** diferencia *f* horaria; **t. lag** lapso *m*; **t. lapse** lapso *m* (de tiempo); *Ind* **t. sheet** ficha *f* de horas trabajadas; **t. signal** señal *f* horaria; **t. switch** temporizador *m*

(f) *(occasion)* vez *f*; **at times** a veces; **every t.** siempre; **every t. she looks at me** cada vez que me mira; **from t. to t.** de vez en cuando; **t. and t. again, t. after t.** una y otra vez

(g) *(in multiplication)* **four times two is eight** cuatro por dos son ocho; **three times as big (as)** tres veces mayor (que)

(h) *Mus* tiempo *m*; **to keep t.** llevar el ritmo *or* compás

(i) *Sport* tiempo *m* muerto; *Fig* descanso *m*

2 *vt* **(a)** *(meeting, visit)* programar **(b)** *(remark, action)* **well timed** oportuno(a); **badly timed** inoportuno(a) **(c)** *(person, race)* cronometrar

time-consuming ['taɪmkənsjuːmɪŋ] *adj* **a t. task** una tarea que lleva mucho tiempo; **to be t.** llevar mucho tiempo

time-honored ['taɪmɒnəd] *adj* ancestral

timekeeping ['taɪmkiːpɪŋ] *n Ind (in factory)* control *m* de puntualidad

timely ['taɪmlɪ] *adj* oportuno(a)

time-out ['taɪmaʊt] *n Sport* tiempo *m* muerto; *Fig* descanso *m*

timepiece ['taɪmpiːs] *n* reloj *m*

timer ['taɪmə(r)] *n (device)* temporizador *m*

time-saver ['taɪmseɪvə(r)] *n* **the dishwasher is a great t.** el lavavajillas (te) ahorra mucho tiempo

time-saving ['taɪmseɪvɪŋ] *adj (device, method)* que ahorra tiempo

timescale ['taɪmskeɪl] *n* plazo *m* (de tiempo)

time-sharing ['taɪmʃeərɪŋ], **time-share** ['taɪmʃeə(r)] *n* multipropiedad *f*, copropiedad *f*

timespan ['taɪmspæn] *n* plazo *m*

timetable ['taɪmteɪbəl] **1** *n (for buses, trains, school)* horario *m*; *(for event, project)* programa *m*; **to work to a t.** tener un horario de trabajo
2 *vt* programar

time-wasting ['taɪmweɪstɪŋ] *n* pérdida *f* de tiempo

timid ['tɪmɪd] *adj* tímido(a)

timidity [tɪ'mɪdɪtɪ] *n* timidez *f*

timidly ['tɪmɪdlɪ] *adv* tímidamente

timing ['taɪmɪŋ] *n* **(a)** *(of announcement, election)* (elección *f* del) momento *m*, oportunidad *f*; **they questioned the t. of the election** la fecha de las elecciones fue polémica **(b)** *(of remark, action)* **how's that for t.!** we've finished one day before the deadline ¡qué te parece! hemos terminado un día antes de la fecha límite; **her remarks were good/bad t.** sus comentarios vinieron en buen/mal momento **(c)** *(of musician)* compás *m*, (sentido *m* del) ritmo *m*; **the comedian's t. was perfect** el humorista hizo un uso perfecto de las pausas y del ritmo

timorous ['tɪmərəs] *adj* timorato(a), temeroso(a)

TIN [tiːaɪˈen] *n* (*abbr* **taxpayer identification number**) = número de identificación fiscal

tin [tɪn] *n* (**a**) (*metal*) estaño *m*; **t. mine** mina *f* de estaño; **t. plate** hojalata *f*; **t. soldier** soldadito *m* de plomo; **t. whistle** flautín *m* (**b**) (*mold*) molde *m*; **cake t.** molde *m* (*para bizcocho, plum-cake, etc*) (**c**) (*can*) lata *f*, *Am* tarro *m*

tinder [ˈtɪndə(r)] *n* yesca *f*

tinderbox [ˈtɪndəbɒks] *n* (*explosive situation*) **the country is a t.** el país es un polvorín

tinfoil [ˈtɪnˈfɔɪl] *n* papel *m* (de) aluminio

ting-a-ling [ˈtɪŋəlɪŋ] *n & adv* tilín *m*

tinge [tɪndʒ] **1** *n* (*of color, emotion*) matiz *m*
2 *vt* **tinged with** (*color*) con un matiz de; (*emotion*) teñido(a) de

tingle [ˈtɪŋɡəl] **1** *n* (*physical sensation*) hormigueo *m*; (*of fear, excitement*) estremecimiento *m*
2 *vi* **my hands are tingling** siento un hormigueo en las manos; **to t. with fear/excitement** estremecerse de miedo/emoción

tingling [ˈtɪŋɡlɪŋ] *n* (*of skin*) hormigueo *m*

tinker [ˈtɪŋkə(r)] **1** *n* quincallero(a) *m,f*, chamarilero(a) *m,f*
2 *vi* enredar (**with** con)

tinkle [ˈtɪŋkəl] **1** *n* (*of bell*) tintineo *m*
2 *vi* tintinear

tinnitus [tɪnˈaɪtəs] *n Med* zumbido *m* de oídos

tinny [ˈtɪnɪ] *adj* (*sound*) metálico(a)

tinsel [ˈtɪnsəl] *n* espumillón *m*

tint [tɪnt] **1** *n* (*color*) matiz *m*; (*in hair*) tinte *m*
2 *vt* (*hair*) teñir

tiny [ˈtaɪnɪ] *adj* diminuto(a), minúsculo(a); **a t. bit** un poquitín

tip¹ [tɪp] **1** *n* (*end*) punta *f*; **on the tips of one's toes** de puntillas; **to have sth on the t. of one's tongue** tener algo en la punta de la lengua; *Fig* **the t. of the iceberg** la punta del iceberg
2 *vt* (*pt & pp* **tipped**) **tipped with steel** con la punta de acero

tip² **1** *n* (**a**) (*payment*) propina *f* (**b**) (*piece of advice*) consejo *m*
2 *vt* (*pt & pp* **tipped**) (*give money to*) dar (una) propina a

tip³ *vt* (*pt & pp* **tipped**) (**a**) (*pour*) verter (**b**) **to t. the scales at 195 lb** pesar 95 libras; *Fig* **to t. the scales** *or* **balance (in sb's favor)** inclinar la balanza (a favor de alguien)

▸ **tip off** *vt sep* (*warn*) avisar, prevenir

▸ **tip out** *vt sep* vaciar

▸ **tip over 1** *vt sep* volcar
2 *vi* volcarse

▸ **tip up 1** *vt sep* inclinar
2 *vi* inclinarse

tip-off [ˈtɪpɒf] *n* soplo *m*

-tipped [tɪpt] *suffix* **a steel-t. cane** un bastón con (la) contera de acero; **the bird has black-t. wings** el pájaro tiene alas de puntas negras, el pájaro tiene las alas negras por los extremos

tipple [ˈtɪpəl] *Fam* **1** *n* (*drink*) bebida *f* preferida; **what's your t.?** ¿qué bebes *or Am* tomas?
2 *vi* beber, empinar el codo, *Am* tomar

tipsy [ˈtɪpsɪ] *adj* achispado(a); **to be t.** estar achispado(a)

tiptoe [ˈtɪptəʊ] **1** *n* **on t.** de puntillas
2 *vi* caminar *or Esp* andar de puntillas; **to t. in/out** entrar/salir de puntillas

tiptop [ˈtɪptɒp] *adj* inmejorable, perfecto(a); **in t. condition** en inmejorables condiciones

tirade [taɪˈreɪd] *n* invectiva *f*, diatriba *f*

tire¹ [ˈtaɪə(r)] **1** *vt* cansar, fatigar
2 *vi* cansarse, fatigarse; **to t. of (doing) sth** cansarse de (hacer) algo

▸ **tire out** *vt sep* (*exhaust*) agotar, fatigar

tire² [ˈtaɪə(r)] *n* neumático *m*, *Am* llanta *f*, *Arg* goma *f*; **t. marks** rodada *f*; **t. pressure** presión *f* de los neumáticos *or* de las ruedas

tired [ˈtaɪəd] *adj* cansado(a), fatigado(a); **to be t.** estar cansado(a) *or* fatigado(a); **to be t. of (doing) sth** estar cansado(a) de (hacer) algo; *Fig* **a t. old cliché** un lugar común muy manido

tireless [ˈtaɪəlɪs] *adj* incansable, infatigable

tirelessly [ˈtaɪəlɪslɪ] *adv* incansablemente, infatigablemente

tiresome [ˈtaɪəsəm] *adj* pesado(a)

tiring [ˈtaɪərɪŋ] *adj* agotador(ora)

tissue [ˈtɪsjuː] *n* (**a**) *Biol* tejido *m* (**b**) (*paper handkerchief*) Kleenex® *m inv*, pañuelo *m* de papel; *Fig* **a t. of lies** una sarta de mentiras; **t. paper** papel *m* de seda

tit¹ [tɪt] *n* (*bird*) herrerillo *m*, paro *m*

tit² *n* **t. for tat** donde las dan, las toman; **to give sb t. for tat** pagar a alguien con la misma moneda

tit³ *n very Fam* (*breast*) teta *f*, *Méx* chichi *f*, *RP* lola *f*

titanic [taɪˈtænɪk] *adj* (*conflict, struggle*) titánico(a), descomunal

titanium [taɪˈteɪnɪəm] *n Chem* titanio *m*

tit-for-tat [tɪtfəˈtæt] *adj Fam* como represalia

titillate [ˈtɪtɪleɪt] *vt* excitar

titillation [tɪtɪˈleɪʃən] *n* provocación *f*, excitación *f*

title [ˈtaɪtl] **1** *n* (**a**) (*of book, chapter*) título *m*; **they publish ten titles a month** publican diez títulos al mes; **t. page** portada *f*; *Cin & Theat* **t. rôle** papel *m* principal; *Mus* **t. track** (*of album*) canción *f* que da título al disco (**b**) (*of person*) título *m* (**c**) *Sport* título *m*; **t. fight** combate *m* por el título (**d**) *Law* (*to property*) título *m* de propiedad (**e**) *Cin & TV* **the titles** los títulos (de crédito)
2 *vt* titular

titled [ˈtaɪtld] *adj* (*person*) con título nobiliario

titleholder [ˈtaɪtlhəʊldə(r)] *n Sport* campeón(ona) *m,f*

titter [ˈtɪtə(r)] **1** *n* risilla *f*
2 *vi* reírse tontamente

tittle-tattle [ˈtɪtltætl] *Fam* **1** *n* habladurías *fpl*, chismes *mpl*
2 *vi* chismorrear, *Am* chismear, *Col, Méx* chismosear

titular [ˈtɪtjʊlə(r)] *adj* nominal

tizzy [ˈtɪzɪ] *n Fam* **to get into a t.** ponerse histérico(a)

TLC [tiːelˈsiː] *n Fam* (*abbr* **tender loving care**) cariño *m*

TNT [tiːenˈtiː] *n Chem* (*abbr* **trinitrotoluene**) TNT *m*, trinitrotolueno *m*

to [tuː, *unstressed* tə] **1** *prep* (**a**) (*toward*) a; **to go to France** ir a Francia; **to go to church/to school** ir a misa/al colegio; **to the front** hacia el frente; **to the left/right** a la izquierda/derecha
(**b**) (*until*) hasta; **to this day** hasta el día de hoy; **to count (up) to ten** contar hasta diez; **a year to the day** hoy hace exactamente un año
(**c**) (*expressing indirect object*) a; **to give sth to sb** dar algo a alguien; **give it to me** dámelo; **to speak to sb** hablar con alguien
(**d**) (*with result*) **to my surprise/joy** para mi sorpresa/alegría; **to my horror, I discovered that...** cuál no sería mi horror al descubrir que...
(**e**) (*expressing a proportion*) a; **by six votes to four** por seis votos a cuatro; **there are 100 yen to the dollar** el dólar está a 100 yenes
2 *particle* (**a**) (*with the infinitive*) **to go** ir; **I have a lot to do** tengo mucho que hacer; **I have nothing to do** no tengo nada que hacer; **he came to help me** vino a ayudarme; **she's old enough to go to school** ya tiene edad para ir al colegio; **it's too hot to drink** está demasiado caliente para beberlo; **I want him to know** quiero que lo sepa (**b**) (*representing verb*) **I want to** quiero hacerlo; **you ought to** deberías hacerlo; **I was told to** me dijeron que lo hiciera

toad [təʊd] *n* (*animal*) sapo *m*; *Fam Pej* (*person*) gusano *m*

toadstool [ˈtəʊdstuːl] *n Esp* seta *f* venenosa, *Am* hongo *m* venenoso

toady ['təʊdɪ] *Fam* **1** *n Esp* pelotillero(a) *m,f*, *Am* arrastrado(a) *m,f*, *Col* cepillero(a) *m,f*, *Méx* lambiscón(ona) *m,f*, *CSur* chupamedias *mf inv*

2 *vi* **to t. to sb** *Esp* hacer la pelota a alguien, *Méx* lambisconear a alguien, *CSur* chupar las medias a alguien

toast [təʊst] **1** *n* (**a**) *(toasted bread)* pan *m* tostado; **a slice** *or* **piece of t.** una tostada; **t. rack** portatostadas *m inv* (**b**) *(tribute)* brindis *m inv*; **to drink a t. to sb** hacer un brindis a la salud de alguien

2 *vt* (**a**) *(bread)* tostar; **toasted cheese** tostada *f* de queso; **toasted sandwich** sándwich *m* (caliente) (**b**) *(tribute)* brindar a la salud de

toaster ['təʊstə(r)] *n* tostador *m*

tobacco [tə'bækəʊ] *n* tabaco *m*; **t. pouch** petaca *f*

tobacconist [tə'bækənɪst] *n* estanquero(a) *m,f*

toboggan [tə'bɒgən] **1** *n* tobogán *m (trineo)*

2 *vi* tirarse por el tobogán *(pista de nieve)*

today [tə'deɪ] **1** *n* hoy; **t.'s date/paper** la fecha/el periódico de hoy

2 *adv* hoy; **a week ago t.** hace (hoy) una semana

toddle ['tɒdəl] *vi (infant)* dar los primeros pasos; *Fam* **he toddled off** se largó

toddler ['tɒdlə(r)] *n* niño(a) *m,f* pequeño(a) *(que aprende a caminar)*

to die for [tə'daɪfɔː(r)] *adj Fam* **it's t.** está que te mueres

to-do [tə'duː] *(pl* **to-dos**) *n Fam* revuelo *m*

toe [təʊ] *n* (**a**) *(of foot)* dedo *m* del pie; *(of sock, shoe)* puntera *f*; **big t.** dedo *m* gordo del pie; **little t.** meñique *m* del pie (**b**) *(idioms)* **to be on one's toes** estar alerta; **to keep sb on his toes** no dar tregua a alguien

toehold ['təʊhəʊld] *n (in climbing)* punto *m* de apoyo; *Fig* **to gain a t. in the market** lograr introducirse en el mercado

toenail ['təʊneɪl] *n* uña *f* del pie; **t. clipper(s)** cortaúñas *m inv*

tofu ['təʊfuː] *n Culin* tofu *m*

together [tə'geðə(r)] **1** *adv* juntos(as); **t. with** junto con; **all t.** todos(as) juntos(as); **to go** *or* **belong t.** ir juntos(as); **to act t.** obrar al unísono; **to get t. again** *(couple, partners)* volver a juntarse

2 *adj Fam* equilibrado(a)

togetherness [tə'geðənɪs] *n* unidad *f*, unión *f*

toggle ['tɒgəl] **1** *n (on coat)* botón *m* de trenca; *Comptr* **t. key** *or* **switch** = combinación de teclas que permite pasar de una aplicación a otra

2 *vi Comptr* = abrir y cerrar una función o pantalla con la misma tecla; **you can t. between the two applications** puedes pasar de una aplicación a otra pulsando una tecla

Togo ['təʊgəʊ] *n* Togo

Togolese [təʊgəʊ'liːz] *n & adj* togolés(esa) *m,f*

togs [tɒgz] *npl Fam (clothes)* ropa *f*

toil [tɔɪl] **1** *n Literary* esfuerzo *m*

2 *vi (work hard)* trabajar con afán; **to t. away at sth** esforzarse mucho en algo; **to t. up a hill** subir penosamente una montaña

toiler ['tɔɪlə(r)] *n* trabajador(ora) *m,f* incansable

toilet ['tɔɪlɪt] *n* (**a**) *(bowl)* váter *m*, inodoro *m*; **to go to the t.** *(in house)* ir al baño; *(in public place)* ir al baño *or Esp* al servicio *or CSur* a la toilette; **t. humor** humor *m* escatológico; **t. paper** papel *m* higiénico *or Chile* confort; **t. roll** rollo *m* de papel higiénico; **t. seat** asiento *m* del váter (**b**) *Old-fashioned (washing and dressing)* aseo *m* personal; **t. bag** bolsa *f* de aseo; **t. soap** jabón *m* de tocador

toiletries ['tɔɪlɪtrɪz] *npl* artículos *mpl* de tocador

token ['təʊkən] **1** *n* (**a**) *(indication)* señal *f*, muestra *f*; **as a t. of respect** como señal *or* muestra de respeto; **by the same t.** de la misma manera (**b**) *(for vending machine)* ficha *f*; *(paper)* vale *m*

2 *adj (resistance, effort)* simbólico(a); **I don't want to be the**

t. woman on the committee no quiero estar en la comisión para cubrir el porcentaje femenino

Tokyo ['təʊkɪəʊ] *n* Tokio

told [təʊld] *pt & pp of* **tell**

tolerable ['tɒlərəbəl] *adj* (**a**) *(pain, discomfort)* soportable, tolerable (**b**) *(behavior, effort)* aceptable

tolerance ['tɒlərəns] *n* tolerancia *f*; **to have a high/low t. for sth** ser muy/poco tolerante con algo

tolerant ['tɒlərənt] *adj* tolerante

tolerantly ['tɒlərəntlɪ] *adv* con tolerancia

tolerate ['tɒləreɪt] *vt* tolerar

toleration [tɒlə'reɪʃən] *n* tolerancia *f*

toll[1] [təʊl] *n* (**a**) *(charge)* peaje *m*, *Méx* cuota *f*; **t. bridge** puente *m* de peaje *or Méx* cuota; **t. road** carretera *f* de peaje *or Méx* cuota (**b**) *(of dead, injured)* **the disease had taken its t.** la enfermedad había hecho estragos; **the death t. has risen to a hundred** el número de víctimas ha ascendido a cien

toll[2] **1** *vt (bell)* tañer

2 *vi (bell)* doblar; **to t. for the dead** tocar a muerto

toll-free [təʊl'friː] **1** *adj* **t. number** (número *m* de) teléfono *m* gratuito

2 *adv (call)* gratuitamente

Tom [tɒm] *n Fam* **every T., Dick or Harry** cualquier mequetrefe

tom [tɒm] *n Fam (cat)* gato *m* (macho); *(turkey)* pavo *m* (macho)

tomahawk ['tɒməhɔːk] *n* hacha *f* india

tomato [tə'meɪtəʊ] *(pl* **tomatoes**) *n* (**a**) *(fruit)* tomate *m*, *Méx* jitomate *m*; **t. juice** *Esp* zumo *m or Am* jugo *m* de tomate *or Méx* jitomate; **t. ketchup** (tomate) ketchup *m*, catchup *m*; **t. sauce** *(for pasta)* (salsa *f* de) tomate *or Méx* jitomate; *(ketchup)* (tomate) ketchup *m*, catchup *m*; **t. soup** crema *f* de tomate *or Méx* jitomate (**b**) *Fam (beautiful woman)* **she's a real t.** está buenísima

tomb [tuːm] *n* tumba *f*

tomboy ['tɒmbɔɪ] *n* niña *f* poco femenina

tombstone ['tuːmstəʊn] *n* lápida *f*

tomcat ['tɒmkæt] *n* gato *m* (macho)

tome [təʊm] *n Formal* tomo *m*, volumen *m*

tomfoolery [tɒm'fuːlərɪ] *n Fam* tonterías *fpl*, *Esp* niñerías *fpl*

tomorrow [tə'mɒrəʊ] **1** *n* mañana *m*; **the day after t.** pasado mañana; **t. is another day** mañana será otro día; *Fam* **she was eating like there was no t.** comía como si se fuese a acabar el mundo

2 *adv* mañana; **t. morning/evening** mañana por la mañana/tarde; *Fig* **what will the world be like t.?** ¿cómo será el mundo en el futuro?

tom-tom ['tɒmtɒm] *n Mus* tam-tam *m inv*

ton [tʌn] *n* (**a**) *(weight)* tonelada *f* (aproximada) *(= 907 kg)* (**b**) *(idioms) Fam* **this suitcase weighs a t.** esta maleta pesa un quintal *or* una tonelada; *Fam* **tons of...** *(lots of)* montones de...; *Fam* **he'll come down on you like a t. of bricks** te va a poner a caldo

tone [təʊn] *n (sound, color)* tono *m*; *(on phone)* señal *f*, tono *m*; *(quality of sound)* timbre *m*; **t. of voice** tono *m* de voz; *Fig* **to raise/lower the t.** *(of place, occasion)* elevar/bajar el tono

▶**tone down** *vt sep (color)* rebajar el tono de; *Fig (remarks)* bajar el tono de

▶**tone up** *vt sep (muscles)* tonificar, entonar

tone-deaf [təʊn'def] *adj* **to be t.** tener mal oído

toner ['təʊnə(r)] *n (for printer)* tóner *m*

Tonga ['tɒŋə] *n* Tonga

Tongan ['tɒŋgən] **1** *n* (**a**) *(person)* tongano(a) *m,f* (**b**) *(language)* tongano *m*

2 *adj* de Tonga, tongano(a)

tongs [tɒŋz] *npl (for coal, heavy objects)* tenazas *fpl*; *(for food, smaller objects)* pinzas *fpl*; **a pair of t.** unas tenazas/pinzas

tongue [tʌŋ] *n* (**a**) *(in mouth, of land, flame)* lengua *f*; *(of shoe)* lengüeta *f*; *(language)* idioma *m*, lengua *f*; **to stick one's t. out** sacar la lengua; **t. twister** trabalenguas *m inv* **(b)** *(idioms)* **hold your t.!** ¡calla la boca!; **have you lost your t.?** ¿se te ha comido la lengua el gato?; **to say sth t. in cheek** decir algo en broma

tongue-tied ['tʌŋtaɪd] *adj* mudo(a); **to be t.** quedarse mudo(a)

tonic ['tɒnɪk] *n* tónico *m*, reconstituyente *m*; **t. (water)** (agua *f*) tónica *f*

tonight [tə'naɪt] *n & adv* esta noche

tonnage ['tʌnɪdʒ] *n Naut (of ship)* tonelaje *m*

tonne [tʌn] *n* tonelada *f* (métrica)

tonsil ['tɒnsəl] *n* amígdala *f*; **to have one's tonsils out** operarse de las amígdalas

tonsillitis [tɒnsɪ'laɪtɪs] *n Med* amigdalitis *f inv*

too [tuː] *adv* **(a)** *(excessively)* demasiado; **it's t. difficult** es demasiado difícil; **t. much** demasiado; **I know her all** *or* **only t. well** la conozco demasiado bien; **you're t. kind** es usted muy amable; **he's not t. well today** no se encuentra muy *or* demasiado bien hoy; **t. bad!** *(bad luck)* ¡qué se le va a hacer!; *(that's your problem)* ¡mala suerte!; **it's t. bad you weren't here earlier** es una pena que no estuvieras aquí antes

(**b**) *(also)* también

(**c**) *(moreover)* además

(**d**) *Fam (for emphasis)* **I'm not rich! — you are t.!** ¡no soy rico! — ¡claro que sí!; **you will t. behave!** ¡ya lo creo que te vas a portar bien!

took [tʊk] *pt of* **take**

tool [tuːl] *n* **(a)** *(implement)* herramienta *f*; **(set of) tools** herramienta *f*; **t. bag** bolsa *f* de herramientas; **t. kit** juego *m* de herramientas **(b)** *(means, instrument)* instrumento *m*

toolbar ['tuːlbɑː(r)] *n Comptr* barra *f* de herramientas

toolbox ['tuːlbɒks] *n (gen) & Comptr* paleta *f* de herramientas

toolshed ['tuːlʃed] *n* cobertizo *m* para los aperos

toot [tuːt] **1** *n* bocinazo *m*

2 *vt (horn, trumpet)* tocar

tooth [tuːθ] *(pl* **teeth** [tiːθ]*) n* **(a)** *(of person, saw)* diente *m*; *(molar)* muela *f*; *(of comb)* púa *f*; **(set of) teeth** dentadura *f*; **to cut a t.** echar un diente; **he had a t. out** le sacaron una muela; **t. decay** caries *f inv* **(b)** *(idioms)* **to lie through one's teeth** mentir como un/una bellaco(a); **in the teeth of opposition** haciendo frente a la oposición; **armed to the teeth** armado(a) hasta los dientes; **to fight t. and nail** luchar con uñas y dientes; *Fam* **to get one's teeth into sth** hincar el diente a algo; *Fam* **long in the t.** entrado(a) en años

toothache ['tuːθeɪk] *n* dolor *m* de muelas

toothbrush ['tuːθbrʌʃ] *n* cepillo *m* de dientes

toothless ['tuːθlɪs] *adj* desdentado(a); *Fig* inoperante, ineficaz

toothpaste ['tuːθpeɪst] *n* dentífrico *m*, pasta *f* de dientes

toothpick ['tuːθpɪk] *n* palillo *m* (de dientes)

toothy ['tuːθɪ] *adj* **a t. grin** una sonrisa que enseña todos los dientes

top¹ [tɒp] *n (spinning top)* peonza *f*

top² **1** *n* **(a)** *(highest part)* parte *f* superior, parte *f* de arriba; *(of tree)* copa *f*; *(of mountain)* cima *f*; *(of list)* cabeza *f*; **at the t. of the stairs** en lo alto de la escalera; **to be (at the) t. of the class** ser el/la primero(a); **from t. to bottom** de arriba abajo; **at the t. of one's voice** a grito pelado; *Mil* **to go over the t.** entrar en acción; *Fig* pasarse de la raya; *Fig* **to make it to the t.** llegar a la cumbre

(**b**) *(lid)* tapa *f*; *(of bottle)* tapón *m*; *(of pen)* capucha *f*

(**c**) *(upper surface)* superficie *f*

(**d**) *(garment) (T-shirt)* camiseta *f*; *(blouse)* blusa *f*

(**e**) *Fam Old-fashioned* **it's (the) tops** *(excellent)* es pistonudo(a)

2 *adj* **(a)** *(highest)* de más arriba, más alto(a); *(in pile)* de encima; **the t. people** *(in society)* la flor y nata; *(in an organization)* los jefes; *Fam* **the t. brass** *(army officers)* los altos mandos; **t. coat** *(of paint)* última mano *f*; *Fam Fig* **t. dog** mandamás *mf*; **to be on t. form** estar en plena forma; **t. hat** sombrero *m* de copa; **t. speed** velocidad *f* máxima; *Fig* **at t. speed** a toda velocidad

(**b**) *(best, major)* mejor, más importante; **the t. ten** *(in general)* los diez mejores; *(in music charts)* el top diez, los diez primeros; *Fam* **to pay top d. (for sth)** pagar *Esp* un pastón *or Méx* un chorro de lana *or RP* un vagón de guita (por algo)

3 *vt (pt & pp* **topped***)* **(a)** *(place on top of)* cubrir (**with** de); **to t. it all** para colmo **(b)** *(exceed)* superar, sobrepasar **(c)** *(be at top of) (list, class)* encabezar; **to t. the bill** encabezar el cartel

4 on top *adv* encima; *Fig* **to come out on t.** salir victorioso(a)

5 on top of *prep (above)* encima de, sobre; *(in addition to)* además de; *Fig* **to be on t. of sth** tener algo bajo control; **you mustn't let things get on t. of you** no debes dejar que las cosas te agobien; **to be on t. of the world** estar en la gloria

top-down [tɒp'daʊn] *adj* **a t. management style** un estilo de dirección jerárquico

top-flight ['tɒpflaɪt] *adj* de primera (categoría)

top-heavy [tɒp'hevɪ] *adj (structure)* sobrecargado(a) en la parte superior; *Fig (organization)* con demasiados altos cargos

topic ['tɒpɪk] *n* tema *m*, asunto *m*

topical ['tɒpɪkəl] *adj* actual, de actualidad

topless ['tɒplɪs] *adj (person)* en topless; *(beach, bar)* de topless

top-level ['tɒplevəl] *adj* de alto nivel

topmost ['tɒpməʊst] *adj* superior, más alto(a); *(in pile)* de encima

top-of-the-line ['tɒpəvðə'laɪn] *adj* de gama alta; **it is our t. model** es el modelo más alto de la gama

topography [tə'pɒgrəfɪ] *n* topografía *f*

topping ['tɒpɪŋ] *n (for pizza)* ingrediente *m*; **cake with cream t.** pastel *m* con *Esp* nata *or Am* crema de leche encima

topple ['tɒpəl] **1** *vt (person, structure, government)* derribar

2 *vi (person, government)* derrumbarse

top-secret ['tɒp'siːkrɪt] *adj* altamente confidencial

topsoil ['tɒpsɔɪl] *n (capa f superficial del) suelo m*

topsy-turvy [tɒpsɪ'tɜːvɪ] *adj (untidy)* manga por hombro; *(confused)* enrevesado(a); **the whole world's turned t.** el mundo entero está patas arriba

torch [tɔːtʃ] **1** *n (burning stick)* antorcha *f*; *Fig* **to carry a t. for sb** estar enamorado(a) *or* prendado(a) de alguien

2 *vt* incendiar

torchlight ['tɔːtʃlaɪt] *n* **by t.** con luz de linterna; **t. procession** procesión *f* de antorchas

tore [tɔː] *pt of* **tear**

torment 1 *n* ['tɔːment] tormento *m*; **to be in t.** sufrir

2 *vt* [tɔː'ment] *(cause extreme suffering)* atormentar; *(annoy)* hacer rabiar a

tormentor [tɔː'mentə(r)] *n* torturador(ora) *m,f*

torn [tɔːn] *pp of* **tear**

tornado [tɔː'neɪdəʊ] *(pl* **tornadoes***) n* tornado *m*

Toronto [tə'rɒntəʊ] *n* Toronto

torpedo [tɔː'piːdəʊ] **1** *n (pl* **torpedoes***) Naut* torpedo *m*; **t. boat** (barco *m*) torpedero *m*

2 *vt also Fig* torpedear

torpid ['tɔːpɪd] *adj* aletargado(a)

torpor ['tɔːpə(r)] *n* letargo *m*

torrent ['tɒrənt] *n* torrente *m*; **it's raining in torrents** llueve torrencialmente; **a t. of abuse** un torrente de insultos

torrential [tə'renʃəl] *adj* torrencial

torrid ['tɒrɪd] *adj (weather)* tórrido(a); *(affair)* ardiente, apasionado(a)

torso ['tɔːsəʊ] (pl **torsos**) n torso m

tortoise ['tɔːtəs] n tortuga f (terrestre)

tortoiseshell ['tɔːtəsʃel] n carey m; **t. (cat)** = gato con manchas negras y marrones

tortuous ['tɔːtjʊəs] adj (path) tortuoso(a); (explanation) enrevesado(a)

torture ['tɔːtʃə(r)] **1** n tortura f; Fig **it was sheer t.!** ¡fue una auténtica tortura!, ¡fue un tormento!; **t. chamber** cámara f de torturas

   2 vt torturar; Fig atormentar

toss [tɒs] **1** n (of ball) lanzamiento m; (of head) sacudida f; **to decide sth on the t. of a coin** decidir algo a cara o cruz or Chile, Col a sello or Méx águila o sol or RP cara o seca

   2 vt (ball) lanzar; (salad) remover; **to t. sth to sb** echar algo a alguien; **to t. a coin** echar a cara o cruz or Chile, Col cara o sello or Méx águila o sol or RP cara o seca; **to t. one's head** sacudir la cabeza; **to t. a pancake** dar la vuelta a una crepe lanzándola por el aire; **the ship was tossed by the sea** el mar sacudía or zarandeaba el barco

   3 vi **to t. (up) for sth** jugarse algo a cara o cruz or Chile, Col cara o sello or Méx águila o sol or RP cara o seca; **to t. and turn in bed** dar vueltas en la cama

▸**toss around, toss about** vt sep (ball) lanzar; (ship) zarandear; Fig (idea) barajar

▸**toss off** vt sep Fam (write quickly) escribir rápidamente

▸**toss out** vt sep tirar

toss-up ['tɒsʌp] n **to have a t.** decidir a cara o cruz or Chile, Col cara o sello or Méx águila o sol or RP cara o seca; Fam **it's a t. between the bar and the movie** igual vamos al pub que vamos al cine; **it's a t. whether he'll say yes or no** lo mismo dice que sí o dice que no

tot[1] [tɒt] n (child) niño(a) m,f pequeño(a)

total ['təʊtəl] **1** n total m; **in t.** en total

   2 adj total; Astron **t. eclipse** eclipse m total; **t. failure** rotundo fracaso m

   3 vt (**a**) (amount to) ascender a (**b**) (count up) sumar (**c**) Fam (car) cargarse, Esp jeringar, Méx dar en la madre, RP hacer bolsa

totalitarian [təʊtælɪ'teərɪən] adj totalitario(a)

totalitarianism [təʊtælɪ'teərɪənɪzəm] n totalitarismo m

totality [təʊ'tælɪtɪ] n totalidad f, conjunto m

totally ['təʊtəlɪ] adv totalmente, completamente

tote[1] [təʊt] n (in betting) totalizador m

tote[2] vt Fam (carry) pasear, cargar con; (gun) portar

totem pole ['təʊtəm'pəʊl] n tótem m

totter ['tɒtə(r)] vi (person, government) tambalearse; **to t. in/out** entrar/salir tambaleándose

tottering ['tɒtərɪŋ] adj tambaleante

toucan ['tuːkæn] n tucán m

touch [tʌtʃ] **1** n (**a**) (act of touching) toque m; (lighter) roce m; **I felt a t. on my arm** noté que me tocaban el brazo; **it was t. and go whether…** no era seguro si…; Fam **to be an easy** or **soft t.** (financially) ser desprendido(a), ser dadivoso(a)

   (**b**) (sense, feel) tacto m; **hard/soft to the t.** duro(a)/blando(a) al tacto

   (**c**) (detail) toque m; **there were some nice touches in the movie** la película tenía algunos buenos detalles; Fig **he's lost his t.** ha perdido facultades

   (**d**) (small amount) toque m, pizca f; **a t. (too) strong/short** un poquito fuerte/corto(a); **a t. of flu** una ligera gripe

   (**e**) (communication) **to be/get in t. with sb** estar/ponerse en contacto con alguien; **to stay in/lose t. with sb** mantener/perder el contacto con alguien; **to lose t. with reality** desconectarse de la realidad

   (**f**) (in soccer, rugby) **the ball has gone into t.** la pelota se ha ido fuera

   2 vt (**a**) (physically) tocar; (affect) afectar; **to t. bottom** (ship, economy) tocar fondo; **I never t. wine** nunca pruebo el vino;

the law can't t. her la ley no puede tocarla; Fig **there's nothing to t. it** no tiene rival (**b**) (emotionally) conmover

▸**touch down** vi (plane) aterrizar

▸**touch on** vt insep tocar, mencionar

▸**touch up** vt sep (picture) retocar

touchdown ['tʌtʃdaʊn] n (**a**) (of plane) aterrizaje m (**b**) (in football) ensayo m

touché [tuː'ʃeɪ] exclam **t.!** (in fencing) ¡touché!; Hum ¡touché!, ¡es verdad!

touched [tʌtʃt] adj (**a**) (emotionally moved) conmovido(a) (**b**) Fam (mad) Esp tocado(a) del ala, Am zafado(a)

touching ['tʌtʃɪŋ] adj (moving) conmovedor(ora)

touchingly ['tʌtʃɪŋlɪ] adv de un modo conmovedor

touchline ['tʌtʃlaɪn] n (in soccer, rugby) línea f de banda

touch(-sensitive) screen ['tʌtʃ('sensɪtɪv)'skriːn] n Comptr pantalla f táctil

touchstone ['tʌtʃstəʊn] n piedra f de toque

touch-tone telephone ['tʌtʃtəʊn'teləfəʊn] n teléfono m de tonos or de marcado por tonos

touch-typing ['tʌtʃtaɪpɪŋ] n mecanografía f al tacto

touchy ['tʌtʃɪ] adj (subject) espinoso(a), peliagudo(a); (person) susceptible

tough [tʌf] **1** n matón m

   2 adj (**a**) (material, person) resistente, fuerte; (meat, rule, policy) duro(a); Fam **a t. guy** un tipo duro; **to get t. (with sb)** ponerse duro(a) (con alguien) (**b**) (difficult) difícil; (unfair) injusto(a); Fam **t. luck!** ¡mala suerte!

   3 adv **to act t.** hacerse el/la duro(a)

toughen ['tʌfən] vt endurecer

toughness ['tʌfnɪs] n (**a**) (of meat, task, skin, conditions) dureza f; (of material) resistencia f (**b**) (of person) (strength) fortaleza f; (hardness) dureza f

toupee ['tuːpeɪ] n bisoñé m

tour [tʊə(r)] **1** n (of tourist) recorrido m, viaje m; (by pop group, theater company) gira f; (by tourist) hacer un recorrido turístico; **to go on a t.** (pop group, theater company) irse de gira; Mil **t. of duty** periodo m de servicio en el extranjero; **t. of inspection** (recorrido m de) inspección f; **t. guide** (person) guía mf turístico(a); **t. operator** tour operador m, operador m turístico

   2 vt (country, hospital) recorrer; (of pop group, theater company) ir de gira por

   3 vi (tourist) hacer turismo; (pop group, theater company) estar de gira

tour de force ['tʊədə'fɔːs] n tour de force m, creación f magistral

tourism ['tʊərɪzəm] n turismo m

tourist ['tʊərɪst] n turista mf; **t. attraction** atracción f turística; Av **t. class** clase f turista; **t. guide** (person) guía mf turístico(a); **t. (information) office** oficina f de turismo; Fam **t. trap** sitio m para turistas

tournament ['tʊənəmənt], **tourney** ['tʊənɪ] n torneo m

tourniquet ['tʊənɪkeɪ] n Med torniquete m

tousle ['taʊzəl] vt revolver; **tousled hair** pelo m revuelto

tout [taʊt] **1** vt (goods) tratar de vender

   2 vi **to t. for votes** tratar de captar votos

tow [təʊ] **1** n **to give sth/sb a t.** remolcar algo/a alguien; Fam **to have someone in t.** llevar a alguien detrás; **t. bar** (on automobile) barra f de remolque; **t. truck** grúa f (automóvil)

   2 vt remolcar, llevar a remolque; **the vehicle was towed away** la grúa se llevó el vehículo

toward(s) [tə'wɔːd(z)] prep hacia; **her feelings t. me** sus sentimientos por or hacia mí; **they behaved strangely t. us** se comportaron de un modo extraño con nosotros; **to contribute t. the cost of…** contribuir al coste de…; **15 percent of the budget will go t. improving safety** el 15 por ciento del presupuesto estará dedicado a mejoras en la seguridad; **this money can go t. your new bicycle** este dinero puede ser para tu bicicleta nueva

towaway zone ['təʊəweɪ'zəʊn] *n* = zona de estacionamiento prohibido de la que se retiran los vehículos

towel ['taʊəl] **1** *n* toalla *f*; *Fig* **to throw in the t.** tirar la toalla; **t. bar** toallero *m*
  2 *vt* **to t. oneself (dry)** secarse (con la toalla)

toweling ['taʊəlɪŋ] *n* toalla *f*; **t. bathrobe** albornoz *m*

tower ['taʊə(r)] **1** *n* torre *f*; *Fig* **she's a t. of strength** es un apoyo sólido como una roca; *Comptr* **t. system** torre *f*
  2 *vi* **to t. above** *or* **over sth** elevarse por encima de algo; **to t. above** *or* **over sb** verse mucho más alto que alguien

towering ['taʊərɪŋ] *adj* colosal

town [taʊn] *n* *(big)* ciudad *f*; *(smaller)* pueblo *m*; **to go into t.** ir al centro (de la ciudad); **he's out of t.** está fuera (de la ciudad); *Fam Fig* **to go to t.** tirar la casa por la ventana; *(in explanation, description)* explayarse; **t. center** centro *m* urbano; **t. clerk** secretario(a) *m,f* del ayuntamiento; **t. hall** ayuntamiento *m*; **t. planner** urbanista *mf*; **t. planning** urbanismo *m*

townsfolk ['taʊnzfəʊk] *npl* habitantes *mpl*, ciudadanos *mpl*

township ['taʊnʃɪp] *n* = en Sudáfrica, área urbana en la que se concentra la población negra

townspeople ['taʊnzpiːpəl] *npl* habitantes *mpl*

towrope ['təʊrəʊp] *n* cuerda *f* para remolcar

toxic ['tɒksɪk] *adj Med* tóxico(a); *Med* **t. shock syndrome** síndrome *m* del shock tóxico

toxicity [tɒk'sɪsɪtɪ] *n* toxicidad *f*

toxin ['tɒksɪn] *n Med* toxina *f*

toy [tɔɪ] **1** *n* juguete *m*; **t. soldier** soldadito *m* de juguete; **t. store** juguetería *f*
  2 *vi* **to t. with sb** jugar con alguien; **to t. with an idea** darle vueltas a una idea; **to t. with sb's affections** jugar con los sentimientos de alguien

TQM [tiːkjuː'em] *n Com* (*abbr* **total quality management**) gestión *f* de calidad total

trace [treɪs] **1** *n* (**a**) *(sign)* rastro *m*, pista *f*; **without (a) t.** sin dejar rastro (**b**) *(small amount)* rastro *m*, huella *f*; *Chem* **t. element** oligoelemento *m* (**c**) *(path)* senda *f*
  2 *vt* (**a**) *(draw)* trazar; *(with tracing paper)* calcar (**b**) *(track)* *(person)* seguir la pista *or* el rastro a; *Fig (development, history)* trazar (**c**) *(find)* localizar

traceable ['treɪsəbəl] *adj* localizable

trachea [trə'kiːə] (*pl* **tracheae** [trə'kiiː] *or* **tracheas**) *n Anat* tráquea *f*

tracheotomy [trækɪ'ɒtəmɪ] *n* traqueotomía *f*; **to perform a t. (on sb)** hacer una traqueotomía (a alguien)

track [træk] **1** *n* (**a**) *(single mark)* huella *f*; *(set of marks)* rastro *m*; **tire tracks** rodada *f*; **to be on the right/wrong t.** ir por (el) buen/mal camino; **to keep t. of sb** seguirle la pista a alguien; **to keep t. of** *(movements, developments)* estar al tanto de; **I've lost t. of her** le he perdido la pista; **I've lost t. of how much money I've spent** he perdido la cuenta del dinero que llevo gastado; *Fam* **to make tracks** largarse, *Esp, RP* pirarse; **to stop sb in his tracks** hacer que alguien se pare en seco
  (**b**) *(path)* senda *f*, camino *m*; *(for running)* pista *f*; *Sport* **t. events** pruebas *fpl* en pista, carreras *fpl* de atletismo; **t. record** *(previous performance)* historial *m*, antecedentes *mpl*; **t. shoes** zapatillas *fpl* de deporte
  (**c**) *(on record, CD)* corte *m*, canción *f*
  (**d**) *(of tank, tractor)* oruga *f*
  (**e**) *(railroad line)* vía *f*; *Fig* **from the wrong side of the tracks** de origen humilde
  2 *vt* rastrear

▸**track down** *vt sep (locate)* localizar

tracked [trækt] *adj (vehicle)* de oruga

tracker ['trækə(r)] *n (person)* rastreador(ora) *m,f*; **t. dog** perro *m* rastreador

tracking ['trækɪŋ] *n* (**a**) *(following)* *(of person, plane, satellite,* seguimiento *m*; **t. device** dispositivo *m* de seguimiento; *Cin* **t. shot** travelling *m*; **t. station** *(for satellites)* estación *f* de seguimiento (**b**) *Sch* = sistema de división del alumnado en grupos por niveles de aptitud (**c**) *Comptr* tracking *m*, espacio *m* entre palabras

tracksuit ['træks(j)uːt] *n Esp* chándal *m*, *Méx* pants *mpl*, *RP* jogging *m*; **t. pants** pantalones *mpl* de *Esp* chándal *or RP* jogging, *Méx* pants *mpl*; **t. jacket** chaqueta *f* de *Esp* chándal *or Méx* pants *or RP* jogging

tract¹ [trækt] *n* (**a**) *(of land)* tramo *m* (**b**) *Anat* **respiratory t.** vías *fpl* respiratorias; **digestive t.** aparato *m* digestivo

tract² *n (pamphlet)* panfleto *m*

tractable ['træktəbəl] *adj (person, animal)* dócil, manejable

traction ['trækʃən] *n (force)* tracción *f*; *Med* **to have one's leg in t.** tener la pierna en alto *(por lesión)*; **t. engine** locomotora *f* de tracción

tractor ['træktə(r)] *n (vehicle)* tractor *m*; *Comptr* **t. feed** alimentación *f* automática de papel *(por arrastre)*

trade [treɪd] **1** *n* (**a**) *(commerce)* comercio *m* (**in** de); **t. association** asociación *f* gremial; **t. deficit** déficit *m* comercial; **t. discount** descuento *m* comercial; **t. embargo** embargo *m* comercial; **t. fair** feria *f* (de muestras); **t. gap** déficit *m* de la balanza comercial; **t. name** *(of product)* nombre *m* comercial; *(of company)* razón *f* social; **t. secret** secreto *m* de la casa; *Geog* **t. winds** vientos *mpl* alisios
  (**b**) *(swap)* intercambio *m*; **to do a t.** hacer un intercambio
  (**c**) *(profession)* oficio *m*; **he's a plumber by t.** su oficio es el de fontanero; **t. union** sindicato *m*; **t. unionism** sindicalismo *m*; **t. unionist** sindicalista *mf*
  2 *vt* **to t. sth (for sth)** intercambiar algo (por algo); **to t. places with sb** cambiarse de sitio con alguien; **to t. insults/blows** intercambiar insultos/golpes
  3 *vi* comerciar

▸**trade in** *vt sep* entregar como parte del pago

▸**trade on** *vt insep (exploit)* aprovecharse de

trade-in ['treɪdɪn] *n Com* = artículo de segunda mano que se entrega como parte del pago

trademark ['treɪdmɑːk] *n Com* marca *f* comercial *or* registrada; *Fig* sello *m* personal

trade-off ['treɪdɒf] *n* **a t. between speed and accuracy** un término medio *or* una solución a medio camino entre la velocidad y la precisión

trader ['treɪdə(r)] *n* comerciante *mf*

tradesman ['treɪdzmən] *n* pequeño comerciante *m*, tendero *m*; **tradesmen's entrance** entrada *f* de servicio

trading ['treɪdɪŋ] *n* **t. floor** *(in stock exchange)* parquet *m*; **t. partner** socio(a) *m,f* comercial; **t. post** = establecimiento comercial en zonas remotas o de colonos; **t. stamp** cupón *m*, vale *m*

tradition [trə'dɪʃən] *n* tradición *f*

traditional [trə'dɪʃənəl] *adj* tradicional

traditionalist [trə'dɪʃənəlɪst] *n & adj* tradicionalista *mf*

traffic ['træfɪk] *n* **1** (**a**) *(vehicles)* tráfico *m*; **road/air t.** tráfico *m* rodado/aéreo; **t. calming measures** medidas *fpl* para reducir la velocidad del tráfico; **t. circle** rotonda *f*, *Esp* glorieta *f*; **t. cone** cono *m* de señalización; *Fam* **t. cop** policía *m or Esp* guardia *mf* de tráfico; **t. island** refugio *m*, isleta *f*; **t. jam** atasco *m*, embotellamiento *m*; **t. policeman** policía *m* de tráfico (**b**) *(trade)* *(in drugs, slaves)* tráfico *m* (**in** de)
  2 *vt* traficar con
  3 *vi* traficar

tragedy ['trædʒɪdɪ] *n* tragedia *f*

tragic ['trædʒɪk] *adj* trágico(a)

tragically ['trædʒɪklɪ] *adv* trágicamente

tragicomic [trædʒɪ'kɒmɪk] *adj* tragicómico(a)

trail [treɪl] **1** *n* (**a**) *(of smoke, blood)* rastro *m*; **to pick up the t.** encontrar el rastro; **to be on the t. of sth/sb** estar sobre la pista de algo/alguien (**b**) *(path)* camino *m*, senda *f*; **t. bike** moto *f* de trial *or* motocross

2 *vt* (**a**) *(drag)* arrastrar (**b**) *(follow)* seguir la pista de (**c**) *(in competition, game)* ir por detrás de

3 *vi* (**a**) *(drag)* arrastrar (**b**) *(move slowly)* avanzar con paso cansino; **to t. in and out** entrar y salir con desgana (**c**) *(be losing)* ir perdiendo

trail away, trail off *vi* ir debilitándose

trailblazer ['treɪlbleɪzə(r)] *n* innovador(ora) *m,f*, pionero(a) *m,f*

trailer ['treɪlə(r)] *n* (**a**) *(vehicle)* remolque *m*, tráiler *m*; *(caravan)* caravana *f*, roulotte *f*; **t. park** camping *m* para caravanas *or* roulottes; *Fam Pej* **t. trash** = personas de clase humilde que viven en campings para caravanas (**b**) *Cin (for movie)* avance *m*, tráiler *m*

train [treɪn] **1** *n* (**a**) *(means of transport)* tren *m*; **by t.** en tren (**b**) *(series)* concatenación *f*, serie *f*; **t. of thought** pensamientos *mpl* (**c**) *(retinue)* séquito *m* (**d**) *(of dress)* cola *f*

2 *vt* (**a**) *(person)* formar, adiestrar; *(animal, ear)* adiestrar, educar; *(in sport)* entrenar; **to t. sb for sth/to do sth** adiestrar a alguien para algo/para hacer algo (**b**) *(gun, telescope)* dirigir (**on** hacia)

3 *vi (athlete, soldier)* entrenar(se); **to t. as a nurse/teacher** estudiar para (ser) enfermero(a)/maestro(a)

trained [treɪnd] *adj* experto(a); *Hum* **her husband is very well t.!** ¡qué marido tan apañado tiene!

trainee [treɪ'niː] *n* aprendiz(iza) *m,f*; *(at lawyer's)* pasante *mf*; *(at accountant's)* contable *mf or Am* contador(ora) *m,f* en prácticas

trainer ['treɪnə(r)] *n* (**a**) *(of athletes, football team, racehorses)* entrenador(ora) *m,f* (**b**) *Av* **t. (aircraft)** avión *m* de entrenamiento

training ['treɪnɪŋ] *n (for job)* formación *f*; *(in sport)* entrenamiento *m*; **to be in t.** estar entrenando; **to be out of t.** estar desentrenado(a); *Mil* **t. camp** campamento *m* de instrucción; **t. course** cursillo *m* de formación; **t. officer** jefe(a) *m,f* de formación

trainload ['treɪnləʊd] *n* **a t. of…** un tren cargado de…

traipse [treɪps] *vi Fam* dar vueltas y vueltas, *Esp* estar en danza; **to t. round the shops** patearse las tiendas

trait [treɪt] *n* rasgo *m*

traitor ['treɪtə(r)] *n* traidor(ora) *m,f*

trajectory [trə'dʒektərɪ] *n* trayectoria *f*

tramp [træmp] **1** *n* (**a**) *(vagabond)* vagabundo(a) *m,f* (**b**) *Fam (immoral woman)* fulana *f*, *Méx* piruja *f*, *RP* reventada *f* (**c**) **t. (steamer)** carguero *m* (**d**) *(walk)* caminata *f*

2 *vt* **to t. the streets** recorrer a pie las calles

3 *vi* caminar con pasos pesados, marchar; **she tramped up the road** subió la carretera caminando con pasos pesados

trample ['træmpəl] **1** *vt* pisotear

2 *vt also Fig* **to t. on sth/sb** pisotear algo/a alguien

trampoline [træmpə'liːn] *n* cama *f* elástica

trance [trɑːns] *n* trance *m*; **to go into a t.** entrar en trance

tranquil ['træŋkwɪl] *adj* tranquilo(a)

tranquility [træŋ'kwɪlɪtɪ] *n* tranquilidad *f*

tranquilizer ['træŋkwɪlaɪzə(r)] *n* tranquilizante *m*

transaction [træn'zækʃən] *n* transacción *f*

transatlantic [trænzət'læntɪk] *adj* transatlántico(a)

transcend [træn'send] *vt* ir más allá de, superar

transcendental [trænsen'dentəl] *adj* trascendental; **t. meditation** meditación *f* trascendental

transcontinental [trænzkɒntɪ'nentəl] *adj* transcontinental

transcribe [træn'skraɪb] *vt* transcribir

transcript ['trænskrɪpt] *n* (**a**) *(of speech, tapes)* transcripción *f* (**b**) *Sch & Univ* expediente *m* académico

transcription [træns'krɪpʃən] *n (of speech, tapes)* transcripción *f*

transfer 1 *n* ['trænsfɜː(r)] (**a**) *(move) (of employee, department, prisoners)* traslado *m*; *(of money, funds)* transferencia *f*; *(of baseball, soccer player)* traspaso *m*; **t. of power** traspaso *m* de poderes; **t. fee** *(for footballer)* (ficha *f* de) traspaso *m*; **to be on the t. list** *(footballer)* ser transferible; **t. lounge** *(in airport)* sala *f* de tránsito; **t. passengers** pasajeros *mpl* en tránsito; *Comptr* **t. speed** velocidad *f* de transmisión (**b**) *(sticker)* calcomanía *f*

2 *vt* [træns'fɜː(r)] *(employee, department, prisoners)* trasladar; *(funds)* transferir; *(footballer, power)* traspasar; *(attention, affection)* trasladar

3 *vi (within organization)* trasladarse; *(between planes, trains)* hacer transbordo

transferable [træns'fɜːrəbəl] *adj* transferible; **not t.** intransferible

transfigure [træns'fɪɡə(r)] *vt* transfigurar

transfix [træns'fɪks] *vt (pierce)* atravesar; *Fig* **they were transfixed with fear** estaban paralizados por el miedo

transform [træns'fɔːm] *vt* transformar

transformation [trænsfə'meɪʃən] *n* transformación *f*

transformer [træns'fɔːmə(r)] *n Elec* transformador *m*

transfusion [træns'fjuːʒən] *n* **(blood) t.** transfusión *f* (de sangre)

transgress [trænz'ɡres] *Formal* **1** *vt (law)* transgredir, infringir

2 *vi (violate law)* infringir la ley; *(sin)* pecar

transience ['trænzɪəns] *n* transitoriedad *f*

transient ['trænzɪənt] *adj* pasajero(a), transitorio(a)

transistor [træn'zɪstə(r)] *n Elec* transistor *m*

transit ['trænsɪt] *n* tránsito *m*; **in t.** en tránsito; **t. camp** campo *m* provisional; **t. visa** visado *m or Am* visa *f* de tránsito

transition [træn'zɪʃən] *n* transición *f*; **t. period** periodo *m* de transición

transitional [træn'zɪʃənəl] *adj* de transición

transitive ['trænzɪtɪv] *adj Gram* transitivo(a)

transitory ['trænsɪtərɪ] *adj* transitorio(a)

translate [træns'leɪt] **1** *vt* traducir (**from/into** de/a)

2 *vi (person)* traducir; *(word, expression)* traducirse (**as** por); **this word doesn't t.** esta palabra no tiene traducción

translation [træns'leɪʃən] *n* traducción *f*

translator [træns'leɪtə(r)] *n* traductor(ora) *m,f*

transliterate [trænz'lɪtəreɪt] *vt Ling* transliterar

translucent [trænz'luːsənt] *adj* translúcido(a)

transmission [trænz'mɪʃən] *n (action)* transmisión *f*; *TV & Rad (program)* programa *m*, emisión *f*; *Aut* **t. shaft** árbol *m* de transmisión

transmit [trænz'mɪt] *vt* transmitir

transmitter [trænz'mɪtə(r)] *n (emitter)* emisora *f*; *(relay station)* repetidor *m*

transparent [træns'pærənt] *adj* transparente; *Fig* **a t. lie** una mentira flagrante

transpire [træns'paɪə(r)] **1** *vt (become apparent)* **it transpired that…** se supo que…

2 *vi (happen)* ocurrir, pasar

transplant 1 *n* ['trænsplɑːnt] *Med* transplante *m*

2 *vt* [træns'plɑːnt] (**a**) *Med (organ)* transplantar (**b**) *(population)* trasladar

transplantation [trænsplɑːn'teɪʃən] *n* trasplante *m*

transport 1 *n* ['trænspɔːt] transporte *m*; **t. plane** avión *m* de transporte; **t. ship** buque *m* de transporte

2 *vt* [træns'pɔːt] transportar

transportation [trænspɔː'teɪʃən] *n* transporte *m*; *Hist (as punishment)* deportación *f*; **road/rail t.** transporte *m* por carretera/ferrocarril; **t. costs** gastos *mpl* de transporte

transporter [træns'pɔːtə(r)] *n (vehicle)* camión *m* para el transporte de vehículos

transpose [træns'pəʊz] *vt (words)* invertir; *Typ* transponer; *(music)* transportar

transsexual [træn(z)'seksjʊəl] *n* transexual *mf*

Transvaal ['trɑːnzvɑːl] *n* **the T.** la región de Transvaal

transverse ['trænzvɜːs] *adj* transversal

transvestism [trænz'vestɪzəm] *n* travestismo *m*

transvestite [trænz'vestaɪt] *n* travestido(a) *m,f*, travesti *mf*, *Esp* travestí *mf*

trap [træp] **1** *n* **(a)** *(in hunting) & Fig* trampa *f*; **to set a t.** tender *or* poner una trampa **(for** a); **to walk** *or* **fall straight into the t.** caer en la trampa **(b)** *Fam (mouth)* **shut your t.!** ¡cierra el pico!

2 *vt (pt & pp* **trapped)** *(animal, person)* atrapar; **to t. sb into saying/doing sth** engañar a alguien para que diga/haga algo

trapdoor ['træpdɔː(r)] *n* trampilla *f*

trapeze [trə'piːz] *n* trapecio *m*; **t. artist** trapecista *mf*

trapezium [trə'piːzɪəm] *(pl* **trapeziums** *or* **trapezia** [trə'piːzɪə]) *n Geom* trapezoide *m*

trapezoid ['træpəzɔɪd] *n* trapecio *m*

trapper ['træpə(r)] *n (hunter)* trampero *m*

trappings ['træpɪŋz] *npl (of power, success)* parafernalia *f*

trash [træʃ] **1** *n (worthless objects)* bazofia *f*, basura *f*; *(refuse)* basura *f*; *Fam* **that book/movie is a load of t.** ese libro/esa película es pura bazofia; **t. can** cubo *m* de la basura

2 *vt Fam (vandalize)* destrozar

trashy ['træʃɪ] *adj Fam* de pacotilla, *Esp* cutre, *Méx* gacho(a), *RP* groncho(a)

trauma ['trɔːmə] *n Med* traumatismo *m*; *Psy* trauma *m*

traumatic [trɔː'mætɪk] *adj* traumático(a)

traumatize ['trɔːmətaɪz] *vt* traumatizar

travail ['træveɪl] *n Literary* penalidad *f*, calamidad *f*

travel ['trævəl] **1** *n* viajes *mpl*; **on my travels** en mis viajes; **t. agency** agencia *f* de viajes; **t. agent** empleado(a) *m,f* de una agencia de viajes; **t. card** abono *m* de transportes; **t. documents** documentación *f* para el viaje; **t. expenses** gastos *mpl* de viaje; **t. insurance** seguro *m* de (asistencia en) viaje; **t. sickness** mareo *m*; **t. writer** autor(ora) *m,f* de libros de viajes

2 *vt (road, country)* viajar por

3 *vi (person)* viajar; *(vehicle)* circular; *(sound, light, electricity)* propagarse; **news travels fast round here** por aquí las noticias vuelan

traveler ['trævələ(r)] *n* viajero(a) *m,f*

traveling ['trævəlɪŋ] **1** *n* viajes *mpl*; **t. bag** bolsa *f* de viaje; **t. companion** compañero(a) *m,f* de viaje; **t. expenses** gastos *mpl* de viaje

2 *adj (performer)* ambulante; **t. salesman** viajante *m* (de comercio)

traverse ['trævəs] *vt Literary* atravesar, cruzar

travesty ['trævəstɪ] **1** *n* parodia *f* burda

2 *vt* parodiar (burdamente)

trawl [trɔːl] **1** *n* **(a)** *(net)* red *f* de arrastre **(b)** *(search)* rastreo *m*; **he had a t. through the records** hizo un rastreo de los archivos

2 *vt* **(a)** *(sea)* hacer pesca de arrastre en **(b)** *(search through)* rastrear

3 *vi* **(a)** *(fish)* hacer pesca de arrastre **(b)** *(search)* **to t. through sth** rebuscar en *or* rastrear algo

trawler ['trɔːlə(r)] *n (ship)* barco *m* arrastrero

tray [treɪ] *n* bandeja *f*

treacherous ['tretʃərəs] *adj (person, road)* traicionero(a)

treachery ['tretʃərɪ] *n* traición *f*

treacle ['triːkəl] *n* melaza *f*

tread [tred] **1** *n* **(a)** *(sound of footstep)* pisadas *fpl*, pasos *mpl* **(b)** *(of tire)* banda *f* de rodadura, dibujo *m* **(c)** *(of stair)* huella *f* (del peldaño)

2 *vt (pt* **treaded** *or* **trod** [trɒd], *pp* **trodden** ['trɒdən])

(ground, grapes) pisar; *(path)* recorrer; **to t. sth underfoot** pisotear algo; **to t. sth into the carpet** ensuciar la *Esp* moqueta *or Am* alfombra con algo pegado al zapato; **to t. the boards** *(appear on stage)* pisar las tablas; **to t. water** flotar moviendo las piernas; *Fig* estar en un punto muerto

3 *vi* andar; **to t. on sth** pisar algo; **to t. on sb's toes** pisar (el pie) a alguien; *Fig* meterse en los asuntos de alguien; *Fig* **to t. carefully** *or* **warily** andar con pies de plomo

treadmill ['tredmɪl] *n (in gym)* cinta *f* de carreras *or* de correr, tapiz *m* rodante; *Hist (in prison)* noria *f*; *Fig (routine)* rutina *f*

treason ['triːzən] *n* traición *f*

treasonable ['triːzənəbəl] *adj (offense, act)* de alta traición

treasure ['treʒə(r)] **1** *n* also Fig tesoro *m*; **t. hunt** juego *m* de las pistas; **t. trove** *Law* tesoro *m* encontrado; *Fig* tesoro *m*

2 *vt* apreciar mucho, tener en gran estima; **my most treasured possession** mi más preciado bien

treasurer ['treʒərə(r)] *n* tesorero(a) *m,f*

treasury ['treʒərɪ] *n* tesorería *f*; **the Department of the T.** tesoro (público), ≃ (el Ministerio de) Economía; *Fin* **t. bonds** bonos *mpl* del tesoro; **T. note** pagaré *m* del tesoro; **t. stock** autocartera *f*

treat [triːt] **1** *n (pleasure)* placer *m*; *(gift)* regalo *m*; **to give oneself a t.** darse un capricho; **it's my t.** *(I'm paying)* yo invito; **you've got a real t. in store** te espera *or Esp* aguarda una agradable sorpresa

2 *vt* **(a)** *(person, illness, metal)* tratar; **to t. sth as a joke** tomarse algo a broma; **you t. this place like a hotel!** ¡te comportas como si esto fuera un hotel! **(b)** *(give as a present)* **to t. sb to sth** invitar a alguien a algo; **I'll t. you** te invito; **to t. oneself to sth** darse el capricho de comprarse algo; *Ironic* **she treated us to one of her tantrums** nos deleitó con una de sus rabietas

3 *vi Formal (negotiate)* negociar **(with** con)

treatise ['triːtɪz] *n* tratado *m*

treatment ['triːtmənt] *n (of prisoner)* trato *m*; *(of patient, machine, matter)* tratamiento *m*; **preferential t.** trato *m* de favor; *Fam* **to give sb the t.** *(beat up)* dar una paliza *or Esp* un buen repaso a alguien

treaty ['triːtɪ] *n (international)* tratado *m*; *(between individuals)* pacto *m*

treble ['trebəl] **1** *n Mus (person, voice)* soprano *m*, tiple *m*

2 *adj (triple)* triple; *Mus* **t. clef** clave *f* de sol

3 *vt (value, number)* triplicar

4 *vi* triplicarse

tree [triː] *n* árbol *m*; *Fig* **to get to the top of the t.** llegar a lo más alto; **t. house** cabaña *f* en (la copa de) un árbol; **t. trunk** tronco *m* (de árbol)

treetop ['triːtɒp] *n* copa *f* de árbol

trek [trek] **1** *n (long walk)* caminata *f*; *(long journey)* largo camino *m*

2 *vi* **to t. over the hills** recorrer las montañas; **to t. home** recorrer el largo camino hasta casa; *Fam* **to t. to the stores** darse una caminata hasta las tiendas

trellis ['trelɪs] *n* espaldar *m*, guía *f*

tremble ['trembəl] **1** *n* temblor *m*

2 *vi (vibrate)* temblar

trembling ['tremblɪŋ] *adj (body, hands)* tembloroso(a)

tremendous [trɪ'mendəs] *adj (amount, size, noise)* tremendo(a); *(book, vacation, writer)* extraordinario(a), estupendo(a), *Am* salvo *RP* chévere, *Méx* padre, *RP* bárbaro(a)

tremendously [trɪ'mendəslɪ] *adv (very)* enormemente, tremendamente

tremor ['tremə(r)] *n (of person)* temblor *m*; *(earthquake)* temblor de tierra

tremulous ['tremjʊləs] *adj* trémulo(a)

trench [tren(t)ʃ] *n (ditch)* zanja *f*; *Mil* trinchera *f*; **t. coat** trinchera; **t. warfare** guerra *f* de trincheras

renchant ['tren(t)ʃənt] *adj* mordaz

rend [trend] *n* tendencia *f*; **to set/start a t.** establecer/iniciar una tendencia

rendily ['trendɪlɪ] *adv (to dress)* a la última (moda)

rendsetter ['trendsetə(r)] *n* pionero(a) *m,f*

rendy ['trendɪ] *Fam* **1** *n Pej (person)* modernillo(a) *m,f*, *RP* modernoso(a) *m,f*
  2 *adj (clothes, style)* de moda; *(person)* moderno(a)

repidation [trepɪ'deɪʃən] *n Formal* inquietud *f*, miedo *m*

respass ['trespəs] *vi Law* entrar sin autorización

respasser ['trespəsə(r)] *n Law* intruso(a) *m,f*; **trespassers will be prosecuted** *(sign)* prohibido el paso (bajo sanción)

resses ['tresɪz] *npl Literary (hair)* melena *f*, cabellera *f*

restle ['tresəl] *n* caballete *m*; **t. table** mesa *f* de caballetes

riage ['triːɑːʒ] *n* selección *f* de prioridades *(en la atención a víctimas de guerra, catástrofes, etc.)*

rial ['traɪəl] *n* **(a)** *Law* juicio *m*; **to bring sb to t.** llevar a alguien a juicio; **to be on t.** estar siendo juzgado(a) **(b)** *(test)* ensayo *m*, prueba *f*; **on t.** a prueba; **t. and error** ensayo y error, tanteo *m*; **by t. and error** probando hasta dar con la solución; **t. period** periodo *m* de prueba; **t. run** ensayo *m*; **t. separation** *(of married couple)* separación *f* de prueba **(c)** *(ordeal)* dura prueba *f*; **my boss is a real t.!** ¡aguantar a mi jefe es un verdadero calvario!

riangle ['traɪæŋgəl] *n* triángulo *m*

riangular [traɪ'æŋgjʊlə(r)] *adj* triangular

ribal ['traɪbəl] *adj* tribal

ribalism ['traɪbəlɪzəm] *n Pol* tribalismo *m*

ribe [traɪb] *n* tribu *f*

ribesman ['traɪbzmən] *n* miembro *m* de una tribu

ribulation [trɪbjʊ'leɪʃən] *n Formal* tribulación *f*

ribunal [tr(a)ɪ'bjuːnəl] *n Law* tribunal *m*

ributary ['trɪbjʊtərɪ] **1** *n (of river)* afluente *m*
  2 *adj* tributario(a)

ribute ['trɪbjuːt] *n (homage)* tributo *m*; **to pay t. to** rendir tributo a

rice [traɪs] *n* **in a t.** en un santiamén

riceps ['traɪseps] *n Anat* tríceps *m inv*

rick [trɪk] **1** *n* **(a)** *(ruse, deceitful behavior, by magician)* truco *m*; *(practical joke)* broma *f*; **to play a t. on sb** gastar una broma a alguien; **to obtain sth by a t.** conseguir algo con engaños; **a nasty t.** una jugarreta; **t. photography** fotografía *f* trucada; **t. question** pregunta *f* con trampa; **t. or treat** = frase que pronuncian los niños que van de casa en casa en la noche de Halloween cuando se les abre la puerta
  (b) *(in card game)* mano *f*, baza *f*; **to take** or **make a t.** ganar una mano
  (c) *(idioms)* **he's been up to his old tricks again** ha vuelto a las andadas; **that should do the t.** esto debería servir; **she knows all the tricks** se las sabe todas; **the tricks of the trade** los trucos del oficio; **she doesn't miss a t.** no se le pasa una; *Fam* **how's tricks?** ¿qué pasa?, *Esp* ¿cómo lo llevas?
  2 *vt (person)* engañar; **to t. sb into doing sth** engañar a alguien para que haga algo; **to t. sb out of sth** quitar *or Am* sacarle algo a alguien a base de engaños

rickery ['trɪkərɪ] *n* engaños *mpl*, trampas *fpl*; **by t.** con malas artes

rickle ['trɪkəl] **1** *n (of blood, water) (thin stream)* hilo *m*, reguero *m*; *(drops)* goteo *m*; *Fig (of complaints, letters)* goteo *m*
  2 *vt (liquid)* derramar un hilo de
  3 *vi (liquid)* **water/blood trickled down** corría un hilo de agua/sangre; **to t. in/out** *(people)* ir entrando/saliendo poco a poco; **news is beginning to t. through** la noticia está empezando a filtrarse

rickle-down theory ['trɪkəl'daʊnθɪərɪ] *n* = teoría según la cual la riqueza de unos pocos termina por revertir en toda la sociedad

trickster ['trɪkstə(r)] *n* timador(ora) *m,f*

tricky ['trɪkɪ] *adj (task, situation, subject)* delicado(a); *(question)* difícil; *Fam* **he's a t. customer** es un elemento de cuidado *or* un pájaro (de cuenta)

tricycle ['traɪsɪkəl] *n* triciclo *m*

trident ['traɪdənt] *n* tridente *m*

tried-and-tested ['traɪdən'testɪd] *adj* probado(a)

trier ['traɪə(r)] *n Fam* **to be a t.** tener mucho tesón

trifle ['traɪfəl] *n (insignificant thing)* nadería *f*; **a t. wide/short** un poquito ancho(a)/corto(a)

▸**trifle with** *vt insep* jugar con; **a person not to be trifled with** una persona que hay que respetar

trifling ['traɪflɪŋ] *adj* insignificante

trigger ['trɪgə(r)] **1** *n (of gun)* gatillo *m*; *Fig (of change, decision)* factor *m* desencadenante, detonante *m*; *Fam* **to be t. happy** tener el gatillo demasiado ligero
  2 *vt (reaction)* desencadenar

▸**trigger off** *vt sep* desencadenar

trigonometry [trɪgə'nɒmɪtrɪ] *n Math* trigonometría *f*

trilingual [traɪ'lɪŋgwəl] *adj (person)* trilingüe; *(document, conference)* trilingüe, en tres idiomas

trill [trɪl] **1** *n* trino *m*
  2 *vi* trinar

trillion ['trɪljən] *n (million million)* billón *m*; *Fam* **I've got trillions of things to do!** ¡tengo millones de cosas que hacer!

trilogy ['trɪlədʒɪ] *n* trilogía *f*

trim [trɪm] **1** *n* **(a)** *(of hair, hedge)* recorte *m* **(b)** **to be/keep in t.** *(keep fit)* estar/mantenerse en forma
  2 *adj (neat)* aseado(a); **to have a t. figure** *(person)* tener buen tipo
  3 *vt (pt & pp* **trimmed)** **(a)** *(cut) (hair, hedge, expenditure)* recortar; *(meat)* quitar *or Am* sacar la grasa a **(b)** *(decorate)* ribetear **(with** con)

▸**trim down** *vt sep (text, expenditure)* recortar; *(company)* racionalizar

trimester ['traɪmestə(r)] *n* trimestre *m*

trimming ['trɪmɪŋ] *n (on clothes)* adorno *m*; *(on edge)* ribete *m*; *Culin* **turkey with all the trimmings** pavo *m* con la guarnición clásica *(patatas asadas, coles de bruselas, jugo de carne, etc)*

Trinidad and Tobago ['trɪnɪdædəntə'beɪgəʊ] *n* Trinidad y Tobago

Trinity ['trɪnɪtɪ] *n Rel* trinidad *f*

trinket ['trɪŋkɪt] *n* baratija *f*, chuchería *f*

trio ['triːəʊ] *(pl* **trios)** *n* trío *m*

trip [trɪp] **1** *n* **(a)** *(journey)* viaje *m* **(b)** *Fam (on drugs)* viaje *m*, *Esp* flipe *m* **(c)** *(causing stumble)* zancadilla *f*; **t. switch** interruptor *m* diferencial; **t. wire** = cable tendido para hacer tropezar a quien pase
  2 *vt (pt & pp* **tripped)** **(a)** *(cause to stumble)* poner la zancadilla a **(b)** *(switch)* hacer saltar
  3 *vi* **(a)** *(stumble)* tropezar **(b)** *(step lightly)* brincar, danzar; **to t. off the tongue** *(word, name)* pronunciarse fácilmente **(c)** *Fam (on drugs)* **to be tripping** ir puesto(a), *Esp* flipar, *Col* ir pingo(a), *Méx* ir trabado(a), *RP* ir falopeado(a)

▸**trip over 1** *vt insep* tropezar con
  2 *vi* tropezar

▸**trip up 1** *vt sep (cause to fall)* poner la zancadilla a; *Fig (cause to make mistake)* confundir
  2 *vi (stumble)* tropezar

tripe [traɪp] *n Culin* mondongo *m*, *Esp* callos *mpl*, *Chile* chunchules *mpl*; *Fam (nonsense)* tonterías *fpl*, bobadas *fpl*

triple ['trɪpəl] **1** *adj* triple; **t. jump** triple salto *m*
  2 *adv* **t. the amount** el triple
  3 *vt* triplicar, multiplicar por tres
  4 *vi* triplicarse, multiplicarse por tres

triplet ['trɪplɪt] n (**a**) (child) trillizo(a) m,f (**b**) Mus tresillo m

triplicate ['trɪplɪkət] n **in t.** por triplicado

tripod ['traɪpɒd] n trípode m

Tripoli ['trɪpəlɪ] n Trípoli

trite [traɪt] adj manido(a)

triumph ['traɪəmf] **1** n triunfo m; **in t.** triunfalmente
  2 vi triunfar (**over** sobre)

triumphalist [traɪˈʌmfəlɪst] adj triunfalista

triumphant [traɪˈʌmfənt] adj triunfante

triumvirate [traɪˈʌmvɪrɪt] n triunvirato m

trivet ['trɪvɪt] n (on table) salvamanteles m inv (de metal)

trivia ['trɪvɪə] npl trivialidades fpl; **t. quiz** concurso m de preguntas triviales

trivial ['trɪvɪəl] adj trivial

trivialize ['trɪvɪəlaɪz] vt trivializar

trod [trɒd] pt of **tread**

trodden ['trɒdən] pp of **tread**

Trojan ['trəʊdʒən] Hist **1** n troyano(a) m,f
  2 adj troyano(a); **T. Horse** caballo m de Troya; **the T. War** la guerra de Troya

troll [trəʊl] n troll m, trasgo m

trolley ['trɒlɪ] n **t. (car)** tranvía m

trolleybus ['trɒlɪbʌs] n trolebús m

trollop ['trɒləp] n Old-fashioned or Hum (promiscuous woman) fulana f, Esp pendón m

trombone [trɒmˈbəʊn] n Mus trombón m

trombonist [trɒmˈbəʊnɪst] n Mus trombonista mf

troop [truːp] **1** n (**a**) troops (soldiers) tropas fpl; **t. carrier** vehículo m para el transporte de tropas (**b**) (of people) grupo m, batallón m
  2 vi to **t. in/out** entrar/salir con paso cansino

trooper ['truːpə(r)] n (soldier) soldado m (de caballería o división acorazada); (mounted policeman) policía mf a caballo; Fam **to swear like a t.** jurar como un carretero

trophy ['trəʊfɪ] n trofeo m

tropic ['trɒpɪk] n trópico m; **the tropics** los trópicos

tropical ['trɒpɪkəl] adj tropical

trot [trɒt] **1** n trote m; **at a t.** al trote
  2 vi (pt & pp **trotted**) (horse) trotar; (person) correr a paso lento

▶**trot out** vt sep Fam (excuses, information) salir con

Trotskyism ['trɒtskɪɪzəm] n trotskismo m

Trotskyist ['trɒtskɪɪst], **Trotskyite** ['trɒtskɪaɪt] n & adj trotskista mf

trotter ['trɒtə(r)] n Culin (of pig) pata f, manita f

trouble ['trʌbəl] **1** n (**a**) (problem) problema m; (inconvenience) molestia f; **to go to the t. of doing sth** tomarse la molestia de hacer algo; **what's** or **what seems to be the t.?** ¿cuál es el problema?; **the t. is that…** el problema es que…; **to have t. with sth/sb** tener problemas con algo/alguien; **to have t. doing sth** tener dificultades para hacer algo; **it has been nothing but t.** no ha traído nada más que problemas; **to be in t.** (in difficulty) tener problemas; (in bad books of) estar en un lío (**with** con); **to get into t.** meterse en líos; **to get sb out of t.** sacar a alguien de un apuro; **to keep out of t.** no meterse en líos; **to make t.** causar problemas; **it's more t. than it's worth** no da más que problemas; **her troubles are over** se han acabado los problemas; **it's not worth the t.** no merece la pena; **(it's) no t.** no es molestia; Fam **man/woman t.** mal m de amores
  (**b**) (disorder, unrest) conflicto m; **t. spot** punto m conflictivo
  2 vt (worry) preocupar, inquietar; (inconvenience) molestar
  3 vi **to t. to do sth** tomarse la molestia de hacer algo

troubled ['trʌbld] adj (person, look) preocupado(a), inquieto(a); (period, region) agitado(a)

trouble-free ['trʌbəlfriː] adj (installation, operation) senci-

llo(a), sin complicaciones; (stay, vacation, period) tranquilo(a)

troublemaker ['trʌbəlmeɪkə(r)] n alborotador(ora) m,f

troubleshooter ['trʌbəlʃuːtə(r)] n (for organizational problems) = experto contratado para localizar y resolver problemas financieros, estructurales, etc; (for machines) técnico(a) m,f (en averías)

troublesome ['trʌbəlsəm] adj problemático(a)

trough [trɒf] n (**a**) (for food) comedero m; (for drink) abrevadero m (**b**) (of wave) seno m; (on graph) depresión f (**c**) (in weather front) banda f de bajas presiones

trounce [traʊns] vt aplastar, arrollar

troupe [truːp] n (of actors, dancers) compañía f

trousers ['traʊzəz] npl pantalones mpl; **a pair of t.** unos pantalones

trousseau ['truːsəʊ] n ajuar m

trout [traʊt] (pl **trout**) n trucha f

trowel ['traʊəl] n (for gardening) pala f de jardinero, desplantador m; (for building) llana f, paleta f

truancy ['truːənsɪ] n ausentismo or Esp absentismo m escola

truant ['truːənt] n niño(a) m,f que falta a clase or Esp hac novillos or Col capa clase or Méx se va de pinta or RP se hace l rabona; **to play t.** faltar a clase, Esp hacer novillos, Col capa clase, Méx irse de pinta, RP hacerse la rabona

truce [truːs] n also Fig tregua f; **to call a t.** hacer una tregua

truck [trʌk] **1** n (**a**) (truck) camión m; **t. driver** camionero(a m,f, CAm, Méx trailero(a) m,f; **t. stop** bar m de carretera (**b** (produce) productos mpl; **t. farm** explotación f agrícola; **t farmer** horticultor(ora) m,f (**c**) Fam **I'll have no t. wit him/it** no pienso tener nada que ver con él/ello
  2 vt (goods) transportar en camión
  3 vi (drive a truck) Esp conducir or Am manejar un camión

trucker ['trʌkə(r)] n (truck driver) camionero(a) m,f, CAm, Mé trailero(a) m,f

truckload ['trʌkləʊd] n **a t. of…** un camión cargado de…

truculent ['trʌkjʊlənt] adj agresivo(a), airado(a)

trudge [trʌdʒ] **1** n (long walk) caminata f
  2 vi caminar fatigosamente

true [truː] **1** adj (**a**) (factually correct) cierto(a), verdadero(a); **i is t. that…** es cierto or verdad que…; **to come t.** (wish hacerse realidad, realizarse; **this also holds t. for…** est también vale para…; **how t.!** ¡cuánta razón llevas!
  (**b**) (real) (reason, feelings) verdadero(a); **t. north** norte r geográfico
  (**c**) (faithful) leal, fiel; **to be t. to sb** ser leal a alguien; **she wa t. to her principles** era fiel a sus principios; **t. to life** fiel a l realidad; **t. to form** or **type** como era de esperar; **t. love** amc m verdadero
  (**d**) (accurate) exacto(a); **his aim was t.** acertó, dio en e blanco
  2 n **out of t.** torcido(a)

truffle ['trʌfəl] n (fungus, chocolate) trufa f

truism ['truːɪzəm] n perogrullada f

truly ['truːlɪ] adv verdaderamente, realmente; **yours t.** (at en of letter) atentamente; Fam (myself) este menda, un servidor

trump [trʌmp] **1** n (in cards) triunfo m, pinta f; **what trumps?** ¿(en) qué pintan?; **spades are trumps** pinta picas; Fig **she played her t. card** jugó su mejor baza or el a que escondía en la manga; Fam Fig **she came up trumps** di la sorpresa
  2 vt (in cards) ganar arrastrando

▶**trump up** vt sep (charge, accusation) inventar

trumpet ['trʌmpɪt] **1** n trompeta f; Fig **to blow one's own t** echarse flores
  2 vt (success, achievements) pregonar
  3 vi (elephant) barritar

trumpeter ['trʌmpɪtə(r)] n trompetista mf

truncate [trʌnˈkeɪt] vt truncar

truncated [trʌŋ'keɪtɪd] *adj* truncado(a); **it was published in a t. form** fue publicado en una versión abreviada

trundle ['trʌndəl] **1** *vt (push)* empujar lentamente
2 *vi (vehicle)* rodar
3 *n* **t. bed** carriola *f (cama)*

trunk [trʌŋk] *n* **(a)** *(of tree, body)* tronco *m* **(b)** *(case)* baúl *m* **(c)** *(of car)* maletero *m*, *CAm, Méx* cajuela *f*, *RP* baúl *m* **(d)** *(of elephant)* trompa *f* **(e) trunks** *(swimsuit)* traje *m* de baño *(de hombre)*, *Esp* bañador *m (de hombre)*, *Ecuad, Perú, RP* malla *f (de hombre)*

truss [trʌs] **1** *n Med* braguero *m*
2 *vt (tie up)* atar
▸**truss up** *vt sep* atar

trust [trʌst] **1** *n* **(a)** *(belief)* confianza *f*; **he put his t. in them** depositó su confianza en ellos; **to take sth on t.** dar por cierto(a) algo **(b)** *Law* **in t.** en fideicomiso; **t. deed** contrato *m or* escritura *f* de fideicomiso; *Fin* **t. fund** fondo *m* en fideicomiso **(c)** *Com (group of companies)* trust *m*
2 *vt* **(a)** *(believe in)* confiar en; **to t. sb to do sth** confiar en que alguien haga algo; **to t. sb with sth** confiar algo a alguien; *Fam* **t. him to say that!** ¡típico de él! **(b)** *Formal* **to t. (that)…** confiar en que…
3 *vi* **to t. in sth/sb** tener confianza *or* confiar en algo/alguien; **to t. to luck** confiar en la suerte

trusted ['trʌstɪd] *adj* de confianza; *Comptr* **t. third party** *(for Internet transactions)* tercero *m* de confianza

trustee [trʌs'ti:] *n Law (of fund, property)* fideicomisario(a) *m,f*; *(of charity, institution)* miembro *m* del consejo de administración

trusting ['trʌstɪŋ] *adj* confiado(a)

trustworthiness ['trʌstwɜ:ðɪnɪs] *n (of person)* honradez *f*, *Am* confiabilidad *f*; *(of source)* fiabilidad *f*, *Am* confiabilidad *f*

trustworthy ['trʌstwɜ:ðɪ] *adj (person)* fiable, de confianza, *Am* confiable; *(source)* fidedigno(a), fiable, *Am* confiable

trusty ['trʌstɪ] *adj* fiel

truth [tru:θ] *n* verdad *f*; **to tell the t.** decir la verdad

truthful ['tru:θfʊl] *adj (person)* sincero(a); *(story)* veraz, verídico(a)

truthfully ['tru:θfʊlɪ] *adv* con sinceridad, sinceramente

truthfulness ['tru:θfʊlnɪs] *n* verdad *f*; **in all t.** con toda sinceridad

try [traɪ] **1** *n* **(a)** *(attempt)* intento *m*; **to give sth a t.** intentar algo; **to have a t. at doing sth** probar a hacer algo; **it's worth a t.** merece la pena intentarlo **(b)** *(in rugby)* ensayo *m*
2 *vt* **(a)** *(sample)* probar; **I'll t. anything once** estoy dispuesto a probar todo una vez **(b)** *(attempt)* intentar; **to t. to do sth**, *Fam* **to t. and do sth** tratar de *or* intentar hacer algo; **have you tried the pharmacist's?** ¿has probado en la farmacia? **(c)** *Law (case)* ver; *(person)* juzgar **(d)** *(test) (person, patience)* poner a prueba
3 *vi* intentarlo; **he didn't really t.** no lo intentó de veras; **you must t. harder** debes esforzarte más; **just you t.!** ¡inténtalo y verás!
▸**try on** *vt sep (clothes)* probarse
▸**try out** *vt sep (method, machine)* ensayar, probar; **to t. sth out on sb** probar algo con alguien

trying ['traɪɪŋ] *adj (person, experience)* difícil; **these are t. times** corren tiempos duros

tryout ['traɪaʊt] *n* prueba *f*; **he was given a t.** le hicieron una prueba

tsar, tsarist = **czar, czarist**

tsetse ['t(s)etsɪ] *n* **t. (fly)** mosca *f* tse-tsé

T-shirt ['ti:ʃɜ:t] *n* camiseta *f*, *Chile* polera *f*, *Méx* playera *f*, *RP* remera *f*

TTP [ti:ti:'pi:] *n Comptr (abbr* **trusted third party**) *(for Internet transactions)* tercero *m* de confianza

tub [tʌb] *n* **(a)** *(for washing clothes)* tina *f*; *(bath)* bañera *f*, *Am* tina *f*, *Am* bañadera *f* **(b)** *(for ice cream)* tarrina *f* **(c)** *Fam (boat)* cascarón *m*

tuba ['tju:bə] *n Mus* tuba *f*

tubby ['tʌbɪ] *adj Fam (person)* rechoncho(a)

tube [tju:b] *n* **(a)** *(pipe, container)* tubo *m*; *Fam* **to go down the tubes** irse a pique **(b)** *Fam (TV)* **the t.** la tele

tuber ['tju:bə(r)] *n Bot* tubérculo *m*

tubercular [tjʊ'bɜ:kjʊlə(r)] *adj Med* tuberculoso(a)

tuberculosis [tjʊbɜ:kjʊ'ləʊsɪs] *n* tuberculosis *f inv*

tubing ['tju:bɪŋ] *n (tubes)* tuberías *fpl*; **a piece of rubber/glass t.** un tubo de goma/vidrio

tubular ['tju:bjʊlə(r)] *adj* tubular; *Mus* **t. bells** campanas *fpl* tubulares

tuck [tʌk] **1** *n (in sewing)* pinza *f*, pliegue *m*
2 *vt* **to t. one's pants into one's socks** remeterse los pantalones en los calcetines; **he tucked his briefcase under his arm** se encajó la cartera bajo el brazo; **to t. sb up in bed** arropar a alguien en la cama; **to t. sth into a drawer** guardar algo en un cajón
▸**tuck in 1** *vt sep (sheets)* remeter; *(children in bed)* arropar
2 *vi Fam (eat)* manducar *or Esp, Ven* papear sin cortarse; **t in!** ¡come, come!
▸**tuck into** *vt insep Fam (meal)* manducar *or Esp, Ven* papear con ganas

Tudor ['tju:də(r)] **1** *n Hist* **the Tudors** los Tudor
2 *adj* Tudor

Tue(s) *(abbr* **Tuesday**) martes *m inv*

Tuesday ['tju:zdɪ] *n* martes *m inv; see also* **Saturday**

tuft [tʌft] *n (of hair)* mechón *m*; *(of grass)* mata *f*

tug [tʌg] **1** *n* **(a)** *(pull)* tirón *m*; **to give sth a t.** dar un tirón a algo; **t. of war** *(game)* = juego en el que dos equipos tiran de una soga; *Fig* lucha *f* a brazo partido **(b)** *Naut* remolcador *m*
2 *vt (pt & pp* **tugged**) *(rope, handle)* tirar de; *Naut* remolcar
3 *vi* **to t. at sth** dar un tirón a algo

tugboat ['tʌgbəʊt] *n* remolcador *m*

tuition [tjʊ'ɪʃən] *n* **(a)** *(instruction)* clases *fpl* **(b)** *Univ* **t. (fees)** matrícula *f*

tulip ['tju:lɪp] *n* tulipán *m*

tum [tʌm] *n (in children's language)* tripita *f*, barriga *f*, *Chile* guata *f*

tumble ['tʌmbəl] **1** *n (fall)* caída *f*, revolcón *m*; **to take a t.** *(person)* caer, caerse; *Fig (prices)* caer en *Esp* picado *or Am* picada; **t. dryer** secadora *f*
2 *vi (person)* caer, caerse; *Fig (prices)* caer en *Esp* picado *or Am* picada
▸**tumble down** *vi* desmoronarse

tumbledown ['tʌmbəldaʊn] *adj (house)* ruinoso(a), en ruinas

tumbler ['tʌmblə(r)] *n* vaso *m*

tumescent [tjʊ'mesənt] *adj Formal* tumefacto(a)

tummy ['tʌmɪ] *n Fam* tripita *f*, barriga *f*, *Chile* guata *f*; **to have (a) t. ache** tener dolor de tripa

tumor ['tju:mə(r)] *n Med* tumor *m*

tumult ['tju:mʌlt] *n* tumulto *m*

tumultuous [tjʊ'mʌltjʊəs] *adj* tumultuoso(a)

tuna ['tju:nə] *n* atún *m*

tundra ['tʌndrə] *n* tundra *f*

tune [tju:n] **1** *n* **(a)** *(melody)* melodía *f*; **I can't sing in t.** desafino al cantar; **to be out of t.** *(instrument)* estar desafinado(a); *(person)* desafinar **(b)** *(idioms)* **to be in t. with one's surroundings** estar a tono con el entorno; **to call the t.** llevar la batuta; **to change one's t.** cambiar de actitud; **to the t. of** por valor de
2 *vt (musical instrument)* afinar; *(engine)* poner a punto; *(TV, radio)* sintonizar
▸**tune in** *vi Rad & TV* **to t. in to sth** sintonizar (con) algo; **make sure you t. in next week** vuelva a sintonizarnos la próxima semana

tuneful ['tju:nfʊl] *adj* melodioso(a)

tunefully ['tju:nfʊlɪ] *adv* melodiosamente

tuneless ['tju:nlɪs] *adj* sin melodía

tunelessly ['tju:nlɪslɪ] *adv* sin melodía, desafinadamente

tuner ['tju:nə(r)] *n Rad & TV* sintonizador *m*

tungsten ['tʌŋstən] *n Chem* tungsteno *m*; **t. steel** acero *m* de tungsteno

tunic ['tju:nɪk] *n* túnica *f*

tuning ['tju:nɪŋ] *n* (**a**) *(of musical instrument)* afinamiento *m*, afinación *f*; **t. fork** diapasón *m* (**b**) *(of car engine)* puesta *f* a punto

Tunis ['tju:nɪs] *n* Túnez *(ciudad)*

Tunisia [tju:'nɪzɪə] *n* Túnez *(país)*

Tunisian [tju:'nɪzɪən] *n & adj* tunecino(a) *m,f*

tunnel ['tʌnəl] **1** *n* túnel *m*; *Fig* **t. vision** estrechez *f* de miras
   2 *vt* **to t. one's way out of prison** escapar de la cárcel haciendo un túnel
   3 *vi* abrir un túnel

Tupperware® ['tʌpəweə(r)] *n* tupperware® *m*

turban ['tɜ:bən] *n* turbante *m*

turbine ['tɜ:baɪn] *n* turbina *f*

turbocharged ['tɜ:bəʊtʃɑ:dʒd] *adj* turbo *inv*

turbocharger ['tɜ:bəʊtʃɑ:dʒə(r)] *n* turbo *m*, turbocompresor *m*

turbojet ['tɜ:bəʊdʒet] *n (engine, plane)* turborreactor *m*

turboprop ['tɜ:bəʊprɒp] *n (engine)* turbopropulsor *m*, turbohélice *f*; *(plane)* avión *m* turbopropulsado

turbot ['tɜ:bət] *n* rodaballo *m*

turbulence ['tɜ:bjʊləns] *n* turbulencia *f*

turbulent ['tɜ:bjʊlənt] *adj* turbulento(a)

turd [tɜ:d] *n Fam* (**a**) *(excrement)* cagada *f*, mierda *f* (**b**) *(person) Esp* gilipollas *mf inv*, *Am* pendejo(a) *m,f*, *RP* boludo(a) *m,f*

tureen [tjʊə'ri:n] *n* sopera *f*

turf [tɜ:f] **1** *n* *(surface)* césped *m*; *Fam (territory)* territorio *m*; **a piece of t.** un tepe
   2 *vt* cubrir de césped

Turk [tɜ:k] *n* turco(a) *m,f*

Turkey ['tɜ:kɪ] *n* Turquía

turkey ['tɜ:kɪ] *n* (**a**) *(bird)* pavo *m*, *Méx* guajolote *m*; *(meat)* pavo *m* (**b**) *Fam (bad play, movie)* fracaso *m*

Turkish ['tɜ:kɪʃ] **1** *n (language)* turco *m*
   2 *adj* turco(a); **T. bath** baño *m* turco; **T. delight** delicias *fpl* turcas, = dulce gelatinoso recubierto de azúcar en polvo

Turkmenistan [tɜ:kmenɪ'stɑ:n] *n* Turkmenistán

turmeric ['tɜ:mərɪk] *n* cúrcuma *f*

turmoil ['tɜ:mɔɪl] *n* (estado *m* de) confusión *f* or agitación *f*; **the country is in (a) t.** reina la confusión en el país; **his mind was in t.** tenía la mente trastornada

turn [tɜ:n] **1** *n* (**a**) *(of wheel, screw)* vuelta *f*; **the meat is done to a t.** la carne está en su punto
   (**b**) *(change of direction)* giro *m*; *(in road)* curva *f*; **no right t.** *(on sign)* prohibido girar a la derecha; *Fig* **at every t.** a cada paso; **to take a t. for the better/worse** cambiar a mejor/peor; **events took an unexpected t.** los acontecimientos tomaron un cariz *or* rumbo inesperado; **at the t. of the year/century** hacia finales de año/siglo; **the t. of the tide** el cambio de marea; *Fig* el punto de inflexión; *Aut* **t. signal** intermitente *m*, *Bol* guiñador *m*, *Chile* señalizador *m*, *Col, Ecuad, Méx* direccional *m or f*, *Urug* señalero *m*
   (**c**) *(in game, line)* turno *m*; **it's my t.** me toca a mí; **to take turns (at doing sth)** turnarse (para hacer algo); **in t.** a su vez
   (**d**) *Fam (fit)* ataque *m*; *Fig* **it gave me quite a t.** me dio un buen susto
   (**e**) *Theat* número *m*
   (**f**) *(service)* **to do sb a good t.** hacer un favor a alguien; **one good t. deserves another** amor con amor se paga
   (**g**) **t. of phrase** *(way of expressing oneself)* modo *m* de expresión

   2 *vt* (**a**) *(cause to move) (wheel, handle)* girar; *(page)* pasar; *(key, omelet)* dar la vuelta a; **to t. one's head/eyes** volver la cabeza/la vista; *Fam Fig* **without turning a hair** sin pestañear; *Fam Fig* **success has turned her head** el éxito se le ha subido a la cabeza; **the sight/story turned my stomach** la visión/historia me revolvió las tripas
   (**b**) *(direct)* **to t. one's attention/one's thoughts to...** centrar la atención/los pensamientos en...; **to t. the conversation to...** encauzar la conversación hacia...
   (**c**) *(go round)* **to t. the corner** doblar *or Am* voltear la esquina; *Fig* superar la crisis; **she's turned forty** ha cumplido cuarenta años
   (**d**) *(change, convert)* **to t. sth into sth** convertir algo en algo; **to t. sth green/black** poner *or* volver algo verde/negro(a); **to t. sb against sb** volver a alguien contra alguien
   (**e**) *(on lathe)* tornear

   3 *vi* (**a**) *(rotate) (wheel)* girar; *(person)* volverse; **she turned to me** se volvió hacia mí; *Fig* **to t. to sb (for help/advice)** acudir a alguien (en busca de ayuda/consejo); **to t. to the right/the left** torcer *or* doblar a la derecha/la izquierda; **my thoughts often t. to this subject** pienso en este asunto a menudo
   (**b**) *(change)* **her luck has turned** ha cambiado su suerte; **to t. against sb** volverse contra alguien; **to t. nasty** *(person)* ponerse agresivo(a); *(situation)* ponerse feo(a); **to t. red** *(sky, water)* ponerse rojo(a), enrojecer; *(person)* ponerse colorado(a); **to t. sour** *(milk)* cortarse, agriarse; *Fig (relationship)* deteriorarse

▸**turn around 1** *vt sep (car, table)* dar la vuelta a; *(economy, situation, company)* enderezar
   2 *vi (person)* darse la vuelta

▸**turn away 1** *vt sep (refuse entry)* prohibir la entrada a; *(reject)* rechazar
   2 *vi (look away)* desviar la mirada

▸**turn back 1** *vt sep* **to t. sb back** hacer volver a alguien; **to t. the clocks back** atrasar los relojes; *Fig* retroceder en el tiempo, regresar al pasado
   2 *vi* **he turned back** volvió sobre sus pasos; **t. back to page 12** volvamos a la página 12

▸**turn down** *vt sep* (**a**) *(volume, heat)* bajar (**b**) *(request, application, person)* rechazar

▸**turn in 1** *vt sep (lost property)* entregar; *(person)* entregar a la policía
   2 *vi Fam* irse a dormir

▸**turn into** *vt insep* convertirse en

▸**turn off 1** *vt sep* (**a**) *(water, gas)* cerrar; *(light, TV)* apagar (**b**) *Fam* **to t. sb off** cortar el rollo a alguien
   2 *vi (leave road, path)* salir

▸**turn on 1** *vt sep* (**a**) *(water, gas)* abrir; *(light, TV, engine)* encender, *Am* prender (**b**) *Fam (excite)* entusiasmar; *(sexually)* excitar, *Esp, Méx* poner cachondo(a) a
   2 *vt insep* (**a**) *(attack)* volverse contra (**b**) *(depend on)* **it all turns on...** todo depende de...

▸**turn out 1** *vt sep* (**a**) *(eject)* echar (**b**) *(pocket, container)* vaciar (**c**) *(light)* apagar; *(gas)* cerrar (**d**) *(produce)* producir; **to be well turned out** *(person)* ir muy arreglado(a)
   2 *vi* (**a**) *(appear, attend)* acudir, presentarse (**b**) *(result)* salir; **to t. out well/badly** salir bien/mal; **he turned out to be a cousin of mine** resultó ser primo mío; **it turns out that...** resulta que...

▸**turn over 1** *vt sep* (**a**) *(turn)* dar la vuelta a; **to t. sth over in one's mind** dar vueltas a algo; *Fig* **to t. over a new leaf** hacer borrón y cuenta nueva (**b**) *(hand in)* **to t. sth/sb over to sb** entregar algo/a alguien a alguien
   2 *vi* (**a**) *(person)* darse la vuelta; *(car)* volcarse (**b**) *(change TV channels)* cambiar de cadena

▸**turn up 1** *vt sep* (**a**) *(pants)* meter (de abajo); **to t. one's collar up** subirse el cuello (**b**) *(volume, heat)* subir

2 vi *(person, lost object)* aparecer; **something is sure to t. up** seguro que algo aparecerá

turnabout ['tɜːnəbaʊt] *n (in situation, opinion)* vuelco *m*, giro *m*

turnaround ['tɜːnəraʊnd] *n* (**a**) *(in situation, opinion)* vuelco *m*, giro *m* (**b**) *Com* **t. time** tiempo *m* de espera *(de pedidos)*

turncoat ['tɜːnkəʊt] *n Esp* chaquetero(a) *m,f*, *Am* oportunista *mf*, *RP* camaleón *m*

turning ['tɜːnɪŋ] *n* (**a**) *(off road) (in country)* giro *m*, desviación *f*; *(in town)* bocacalle *f* (**b**) **t. circle** *(of car)* (capacidad *f* de) giro *m*; *Fig* **t. point** punto *m* de inflexión

turnip ['tɜːnɪp] *n* nabo *m*

turnoff ['tɜːnɒf] *n* (**a**) *(on road)* salida *f*, desviación *f* (**b**) *Fam* **it's a t.** me corta el rollo

turn-on ['tɜːnɒn] *n Fam* **it's a t. for him** *(sexually)* le vuelve loco, *Esp* le pone a cien

turnout ['tɜːnaʊt] *n (attendance)* concurrencia *f*, asistencia *f*; *(for election)* (índice *m* de) participación *f*

turnover ['tɜːnəʊvə(r)] *n* (**a**) *Com* volumen *m* de negocio, facturación *f* (**b**) *Culin* **apple t.** = especie de empanada de hojaldre rellena de compota de manzana

turnpike ['tɜːnpaɪk] *n (road)* autopista *f* de peaje

turnstile ['tɜːnstaɪl] *n* torniquete *m* or torno *m* (de entrada)

turntable ['tɜːnteɪbəl] *n (for record)* plato *m*, giradiscos *m inv*

turpentine ['tɜːpəntaɪn] *n* trementina *f*

turquoise ['tɜːkwɔɪz] **1** *n (color)* (azul *m*) turquesa *m*; *(stone)* turquesa *f*
2 *adj* turquesa

turret ['tʌrɪt] *n (on building)* torrecilla *f*; **(gun) t.** torreta *f*

turtle ['tɜːtəl] *n* tortuga *f*; **to turn t.** *(ship)* volcar; **t. dove** tórtola *f*; **t. soup** sopa *f* de tortuga

turtleneck ['tɜːtəlnek] *n* cuello *m* alto; **t. sweater** suéter *m* or *Esp* jersey *m* de cuello alto

Tuscan ['tʌskən] *adj* toscano(a)

Tuscany ['tʌskənɪ] *n* (la) Toscana

tusk [tʌsk] *n* colmillo *m*

tussle ['tʌsəl] **1** *n* pelea *f*; **to have a t. with sb** tener una pelea con alguien
2 *vi* **to t. (with sb for sth)** pelearse (con alguien por algo)

tutor ['tjuːtə(r)] **1** *n* private **t.** profesor(ora) *m,f* particular
2 *vt* **to t. sb in French** dar clases particulares de francés a alguien

Tuvalu [tuːˈvɑːluː] *n* (las islas) Tuvalu

tuxedo [tʌkˈsiːdəʊ] *(pl* **tuxedos)** *n* esmoquin *m*

TV [tiːˈviː] *n (television)* televisión *f*; **TV dinner** = menú completo precocinado y congelado que sólo necesita calentarse en el mismo envase; **TV program** programa *m* de televisión

TVP® [tiːviːˈpiː] *n Culin (abbr* **textured vegetable protein)** proteína *f* vegetal texturizada, = alimento proteínico a base de soja texturizada que se utiliza como sustituto de la carne

twaddle ['twɒdəl] *n Fam* tonterías *fpl*, sandeces *fpl*

twang [twæŋ] **1** *n (sound)* sonido *m* vibrante; **nasal t.** entonación *f* nasal
2 *vi (string)* producir un sonido vibrante

tweak [twiːk] **1** *n* **to give sb's ear a t.** dar a alguien un tirón de orejas; *Fam* **to give sth a t.** *(statistics, text)* hacer un pequeño ajuste en algo
2 *vt (nose, ear)* pellizcar

tweed [twiːd] *n Tex* tweed *m*; **tweeds** *(suit)* traje *m* de tweed

tweet [twiːt] **1** *n* pío *m*, gorjeo *m*
2 *vi* piar, gorjear

tweezers ['twiːzəz] *npl* pinzas *fpl*; **a pair of t.** unas pinzas

twelfth [twelfθ] **1** *n* (**a**) *(fraction)* doceavo *m*, doceava parte *f* (**b**) *(in series)* duodécimo(a) *m,f* (**c**) *(of month)* doce *m*
2 *adj* duodécimo(a); **T. Night** noche *f* de Reyes; *see also* **eleventh**

twelve [twelv] *n & adj* doce *m*; *see also* **eight**

twentieth ['twentɪɪθ] **1** *n* (**a**) *(fraction)* veinteavo *m*, vigésima parte *f* (**b**) *(in series)* vigésimo(a) *m,f* (**c**) *(of month)* veinte *m*
2 *adj* vigésimo(a); *see also* **eleventh**

twenty ['twentɪ] *n & adj* veinte *m*; *see also* **eighty**

twenty-first ['twentɪˈfɜːst] **1** *n* (**a**) *(in series)* vigésimo(a) primero(a) (**b**) *(of month)* veintiuno *m*
2 *adj* vigésimo(a) primero(a); *(before masculine singular noun)* vigésimo primer

twenty-one ['twentɪˈwʌn] **1** *n* veintiuno *m*
2 *adj* veintiuno(a); *(before masculine singular noun)* veintiún

twerp [twɜːp] *n Fam* lerdo(a) *m,f*, *Esp* memo(a) *m,f*

twice [twaɪs] *adv* dos veces; **t. as big as…** el doble de grande que…; **t. as slow** el doble de lento(a); **it would cost t. as much** costaría el doble; **t. over** dos veces; **to think t. before doing sth** pensárselo dos veces antes de hacer algo; **he didn't have to be asked t.** no hubo que pedírselo dos veces

twiddle ['twɪdəl] **1** *vt (knob, dial)* dar vueltas a, girar; *Fig* **to t. one's thumbs** holgazanear
2 *vi* **to t. with sth** juguetear *or* trastear con algo

twig [twɪg] *n (small branch)* ramita *f*

twilight ['twaɪlaɪt] *n* crepúsculo *m*

twin [twɪn] **1** *n* gemelo(a) *m,f*; **t. brother** hermano *m* gemelo; **t. sister** hermana *f* gemela
2 *adj (paired)* parejo(a); **t. beds** camas *fpl* gemelas; **t.-engine(d) aircraft** (avión *m*) bimotor *m*

twine [twaɪn] **1** *n (string)* cordel *m*
2 *vt* **to t. one's arms around sth/sb** rodear algo/a alguien con los brazos

twinge [twɪndʒ] *n (of pain)* punzada *f*; **a t. of conscience** un remordimiento (de conciencia)

twinkle ['twɪŋkəl] **1** *n (of stars, lights)* parpadeo *m*; *(of eyes)* brillo *m*
2 *vi (star, light)* parpadear; *(eyes)* brillar

twinkling ['twɪŋklɪŋ] *n* **in the t. of an eye** en un abrir y cerrar de ojos

twirl [twɜːl] **1** *n (movement)* giro *m*, vuelta *f*
2 *vt* hacer girar; **he twirled his mustache** se retorció el bigote
3 *vi (person)* girar sobre sí mismo(a)

twist [twɪst] **1** *n* (**a**) *(action)* **to give sth a t.** retorcer algo; **with a t. of the wrist** con un giro de muñeca (**b**) *(movement)* **twists and turns** *(of road)* vueltas *fpl* y revueltas; *Fig (of events)* avatares *mpl* (**c**) *(in story, plot)* giro *m* inesperado (**d**) *(piece)* **a t. of lemon** un trozo de peladura de limón (**e**) *(dance)* twist *m*
2 *vt (thread, rope)* retorcer; *(sb's words, meaning of text)* tergiversar; **to t. one's ankle** torcerse el tobillo; **to t. sb's arm** retorcerle el brazo a alguien; *Fig* presionar a alguien; *Fig* **to t. the knife in the wound** remover la herida
3 *vi* (**a**) *(smoke)* elevarse en espirales; *(road)* torcer; **to t. and turn** *(road)* serpentear (**b**) *(dance)* bailar el twist

▸**twist off 1** *vt sep (lid)* desenroscar
2 *vi (lid)* desenroscarse

twisted ['twɪstɪd] *adj also Fig* retorcido(a)

twister ['twɪstə(r)] *n (tornado)* tornado *m*

twitch [twɪtʃ] **1** *n* (**a**) *(pull)* tirón *m* (**b**) **to have a nervous t.** tener un tic nervioso
2 *vt (pull)* dar un tirón a
3 *vi (face)* contraerse

twitchy ['twɪtʃɪ] *adj Fam* tenso(a), nervioso(a)

twitter ['twɪtə(r)] **1** *n (of birds)* gorjeo *m*; *Fam* **to be in a t.** *(excited)* estar agitado(a)
2 *vi (bird)* gorjear; *Fig (person)* parlotear

two [tuː] **1** *n (pl* **twos)** dos *m*; **to break/fold sth in t.** romper/doblar algo en dos; **to walk in twos, to walk t. by**

t. caminar de dos en dos; *Fig* **to put t. and t. together** atar cabos; *Fam* **that makes t. of us** ya somos dos; **t. percent milk** leche *f* semidesnatada

2 *adj* dos; *see also* **eight**

two-bit ['tuː'bɪt] *adj Fam (insignificant)* de tres al cuarto, *RP* de morondanga

two-dimensional [tuːd(a)ɪ'menʃənəl] *adj* bidimensional; *Fig (character, movie)* superficial, plano(a)

two-faced ['tuːfeɪst] *adj* falso(a), hipócrita

twofold ['tuːfəʊld] *adj* doble; **a t. rise** una subida del doble, una duplicación

two-legged [tuː'legɪd] *adj* bípedo(a)

two-piece ['tuːpiːs] *adj* **t. suit** traje *m*; **t. swimsuit** biquini *m*

twosome ['tuːsəm] *n* dúo *m*

two-time ['tuːtaɪm] *vt Fam* **to t. sb** engañar *or Esp Fam* pegársela a alguien

two-way ['tuːweɪ] *adj* **t. mirror** luna *f* de efecto espía *or* espejo; **t. radio** aparato *m* emisor y receptor de radio

tycoon [taɪ'kuːn] *n* magnate *m*

type [taɪp] **1** *n* **(a)** *(kind)* tipo *m*, clase *f*; *Fam* **he's not my t.** no es mi tipo **(b)** *Typ* tipo *m* (de imprenta); **in bold t.** en negrita

2 *vt (with typewriter)* mecanografiar; *(with word processor)* escribir *or* introducir en *Esp* el ordenador *or Am* la computadora

3 *vi* escribir a máquina

▸ **type up** *vt sep (with typewriter)* escribir a máquina; *(with word processor)* escribir en *Esp* el ordenador *or Am* la computadora

typecast ['taɪpkɑːst] *(pt & pp* **typecast**) *vt* encasillar

typeface ['taɪpfeɪs] *n* tipo *m* de imprenta

typescript ['taɪpskrɪpt] *n* copia *f* mecanografiada

typesetter ['taɪpsetə(r)] *n (person)* tipógrafo(a) *m,f*

typesetting ['taɪpsetɪŋ] *n* composición *f* (tipográfica)

typewriter ['taɪpraɪtə(r)] *n* máquina *f* de escribir

typewritten ['taɪprɪtən] *adj* escrito(a) a máquina, mecanografiado(a)

typhoid ['taɪfɔɪd] *n Med* **t. (fever)** fiebre *f* tifoidea

typhoon [taɪ'fuːn] *n* tifón *m*

typhus ['taɪfəs] *n Med* tifus *m inv*

typical ['tɪpɪkəl] *adj* típico(a); **isn't that t. (of him/her)!** ¡típico (de él/ella)!

typify ['tɪpɪfaɪ] *vt (exemplify)* tipificar; *(sum up)* caracterizar

typing ['taɪpɪŋ] *n (by typewriter)* mecanografía *f*; *(by word processor)* introducción *f* (de datos) en *Esp* el ordenador *or Am* la computadora; **t. error** error *m* mecanográfico; **t. paper** papel *m* para escribir a máquina; **t. pool** sección *f* de mecanografía; **t. speed** velocidad *f* de mecanografiado

typist ['taɪpɪst] *n* mecanógrafo(a) *m,f*

typographic(al) [taɪpə'græfɪk(əl)] *adj* tipográfico(a)

typography [taɪ'pɒgrəfɪ] *n* tipografía *f*

tyrannical [tɪ'rænɪkəl] *adj* tiránico(a)

tyrannize ['tɪrənaɪz] *vt* tiranizar

tyranny ['tɪrənɪ] *n* tiranía *f*

tyrant ['taɪrənt] *n* tirano(a) *m,f*

tzar, tzarist = **czar, czarist**

U

U, u [ju:] *n (letter)* U, u *f*

UAE [ju:eɪ'i:] *n (abbr* **United Arab Emirates**) EAU *mpl,* Emiratos *mpl* Árabes Unidos

U-bend ['ju:bend] *n* sifón *m*

ubiquitous [ju:'bɪkwɪtəs] *adj* ubicuo(a)

U-boat ['ju:bəʊt] *n* submarino *m (alemán)*

udder ['ʌdə(r)] *n* ubre *f*

UFO ['ju:fəʊ] *(pl* **UFOs**) *n (abbr* **unidentified flying object**) OVNI *m*

Uganda [ju:'gændə] *n* Uganda

Ugandan [ju:'gændən] *n & adj* ugandés(esa) *m,f*

ugh [ʌχ] *exclam* ¡puaj!

ugly ['ʌglɪ] *adj* **(a)** *(in appearance)* feo(a); *Fig* **u. duckling** patito *m* feo **(b)** *(unpleasant)* desagradable

UHF [ju:eɪtʃ'ef] *n Rad (abbr* **ultrahigh frequency**) UHF *m or f*

uh-huh [ʌ'hʌ] *exclam Fam* **u.!** ¡ajá!

UHT [ju:eɪtʃ'ti:] *adj (abbr* **ultra high temperature**) U. milk leche *f* uperisada *or* UHT

UK [ju:'keɪ] *n (abbr* **United Kingdom**) Reino *m* Unido

ukelele = **ukulele**

Ukraine [ju:'kreɪn] *n* Ucrania

Ukrainian [ju:'kreɪnɪən] **1** *n* **(a)** *(person)* ucraniano(a) *m,f* **(b)** *(language)* ucraniano *m*
2 *adj* ucraniano(a)

ukulele, ukelele [ju:kə'leɪlɪ] *n* ukelele *m*

ulcer ['ʌlsə(r)] *n* úlcera *f*

ulcerate ['ʌlsəreɪt] **1** *vt* ulcerar
2 *vi* ulcerarse

ulna ['ʌlnə] *n Anat* cúbito *m*

Ulster ['ʌlstə(r)] *n* el Ulster

ulterior [ʌl'tɪərɪə(r)] *adj* **u. motive** motivo *m* encubierto

ultimate ['ʌltɪmət] **1** *n Fam* **the u. in hi-fi equipment** el último grito *or Esp* el no va más en alta fidelidad
2 *adj* **(a)** *(last)* *(responsibility, decision)* final, último(a) **(b)** *(supreme, best)* **the u. deterrent** la medida disuasoria *or Am* disuasiva definitiva; **the u. vacation** las vacaciones soñadas

ultimately ['ʌltɪmɪtlɪ] *adv* **(a)** *(finally)* finalmente, en última instancia **(b)** *(basically)* básicamente

ultimatum [ʌltɪ'meɪtəm] *n* ultimátum *m*

ultra- ['ʌltrə] *prefix* ultra-

ultramarine [ʌltrəmə'ri:n] *n* azul *m* de ultramar

ultramodern [ʌltrə'mɒdən] *adj* ultramoderno(a)

ultrasound ['ʌltrəsaʊnd] *n Med* ultrasonido *m*; **an u. scan** una ecografía

ultraviolet [ʌltrə'vaɪələt] *adj* ultravioleta

umbilical cord [ʌm'bɪlɪkəl'kɔ:d] *n* cordón *m* umbilical

umbrage ['ʌmbrɪdʒ] *n* **to take u. (at sth)** sentirse ofendido(a) (por algo)

umbrella [ʌm'brelə] *n* paraguas *m inv; Col* sombrilla *f; Fig* **under the u. of...** al amparo de..., bajo la protección de...; **u. organization** organización *f* aglutinante; **u. stand** paragüero *m*

umpire ['ʌmpaɪə(r)] **1** *n (in tennis)* juez *mf* de silla; *(in baseball, cricket)* árbitro(a) *m,f*
2 *vt* arbitrar

umpteen [ʌmp'ti:n] *adj Fam* **to have u. things to do** tener montones de cosas que hacer

umpteenth [ʌmp'ti:nθ] *adj Fam* enésimo(a); **for the u. time** por enésima vez

UN [ju:'en] *n (abbr* **United Nations**) ONU *f*

unabashed [ʌnə'bæʃt] *adj* descarado(a); **to be u. (by *or* at)** no sentir vergüenza *or Am* pena (de *or* por)

unable [ʌn'eɪbəl] *adj* **to be u. to do sth** *(owing to lack of skill, knowledge)* ser incapaz de hacer algo; *(owing to lack of time, money)* no poder hacer algo

unabridged [ʌnə'brɪdʒd] *adj* íntegro(a)

unacceptable [ʌnək'septəbəl] *adj* inadmisible, inaceptable

unacceptably [ʌnək'septəblɪ] *adv* inadmisiblemente

unaccompanied [ʌnə'kʌmpənɪd] **1** *adj* *(child)* no acompañado(a); *(violin, singer)* solo(a), sin acompañamiento
2 *adv* **to travel u.** viajar solo(a); **to play/sing u.** tocar/cantar sin acompañamiento

unaccomplished [ʌnə'kʌmplɪʃt] *adj (unimpressive)* mediocre

unaccountable [ʌnə'kaʊntəbəl] *adj* **(a)** *(not answerable)* **to be u. (to sb)** no tener que rendir cuentas (a alguien) **(b)** *(puzzling)* inexplicable

unaccustomed [ʌnə'kʌstəmd] *adj* **(a)** **to be u. to sth** no estar acostumbrado(a) a algo **(b)** *(not usual)* inusual, desacostumbrado(a)

unacknowledged [ʌnək'nɒlɪdʒd] **1** *adj* no reconocido(a)
2 *adv* **to go u.** *(talent, achievement)* no ser reconocido(a)

unadulterated [ʌnə'dʌltəreɪtɪd] *adj* **(a)** *(food)* natural, no adulterado(a) **(b)** *(joy)* absoluto(a)

unadventurous [ʌnəd'ventʃərəs] *adj (person)* poco atrevido(a), convencional; *(decision, choice)* poco arriesgado(a)

unadvisable [ʌnəd'vaɪzəbəl] *adj* desaconsejable

unaffected [ʌnə'fektɪd] *adj* **(a)** *(sincere)* *(person, style, joy)* espontáneo(a) **(b)** *(not touched)* **he was u.** no se vio afectado

unaffiliated [ʌnə'fɪleɪtɪd] *adj* no afiliado(a)

unafraid [ʌnə'freɪd] *adj* **to be u. of sth/sb** no temer algo/a alguien

unaided [ʌn'eɪdɪd] *adv* sin ayuda

unaltered [ʌn'ɔ:ltəd] *adj* **to remain u.** *(weather, opinion)* permanecer igual

unambiguous [ʌnæm'bɪgjʊəs] *adj* explícito(a), claro(a)

unambitious [ʌnæm'bɪʃəs] *adj (person, project)* poco ambicioso(a)

un-American [ʌnə'merɪkən] *adj (not typical of America)* poco americano(a); *(against America)* antiamericano(a)

unanimity [ju:nə'nɪmɪtɪ] *n* unanimidad *f*

unanimous [jʊ'nænɪməs] *adj* unánime

unanimously [jʊ'nænɪməslɪ] *adv* unánimemente

unannounced [ʌnə'naʊnst] **1** *adj (arrival)* no anunciado(a)

2 *adv* **to arrive u.** llegar sin previo aviso

unanswerable [ʌnˈɑːnsərəbəl] *adj* incontestable

unanswered [ʌnˈɑːnsəd] **1** *adj (question, letter)* no contestado(a)

2 *adv* **to go u.** *(question, letter)* quedar sin respuesta

unappealing [ʌnəˈpiːlɪŋ] *adj* poco atractivo(a)

unappetizing [ʌnˈæpɪtaɪzɪŋ] *adj* poco apetitoso(a)

unappreciated [ʌnəˈpriːʃɪeɪtɪd] *adj (effort, contribution)* no reconocido(a); **to feel u.** sentirse poco valorado(a)

unapproachable [ʌnəˈprəʊtʃəbəl] *adj (person, manner)* inaccesible

unarguably [ʌnˈɑːgjʊəblɪ] *adv* indiscutiblemente

unarmed [ʌnˈɑːmd] *adj* desarmado(a); **u. combat** combate *m* sin armas

unashamed [ʌnəˈʃeɪmd] *adj* descarado(a); **he was completely u. about it** no le dio ninguna vergüenza *or Am* pena

unashamedly [ʌnəˈʃeɪmɪdlɪ] *adv (brazenly)* descaradamente

unassailable [ʌnəˈseɪləbəl] *adj (castle, position)* inexpugnable; *(argument, theory)* irrebatible

unassuming [ʌnəˈsjuːmɪŋ] *adj* modesto(a)

unattached [ʌnəˈtætʃt] *adj* suelto(a); **to be u.** *(without partner)* no tener pareja

unattainable [ʌnəˈteɪnəbəl] *adj* inalcanzable

unattractive [ʌnəˈtræktɪv] *adj* poco atractivo(a)

unauthorized [ʌnˈɔːθəraɪzd] *adj* no autorizado(a)

unavailable [ʌnəˈveɪləbəl] *adj* **to be u.** no estar disponible

unavailing [ʌnəˈveɪlɪŋ] *adj (effort)* inútil, vano(a)

unavoidable [ʌnəˈvɔɪdəbəl] *adj* inevitable

unaware [ʌnəˈweə(r)] *adj* inconsciente; **to be u. of sth** no ser consciente de algo

unawares [ʌnəˈweəz] *adv* **to catch sb u.** agarrar *or Esp* coger a alguien desprevenido(a)

unbalanced [ʌnˈbælənst] *adj (person)* desequilibrado(a); *(report)* sesgado(a), parcial

unbearable [ʌnˈbeərəbəl] *adj* insoportable

unbeatable [ʌnˈbiːtəbəl] *adj (team, position)* invencible, imbatible; *(product, value, price)* insuperable

unbeaten [ʌnˈbiːtən] *adj* invicto(a)

unbecoming [ʌnbɪˈkʌmɪŋ] *adj (behavior)* impropio(a) (**to** de); *(dress)* poco favorecedor(ora)

unbeknown(st) [ʌnbɪˈnəʊn(st)] *adv* **u. to me** sin mi conocimiento

unbelievable [ʌnbɪˈliːvəbəl] *adj* increíble

unbending [ʌnˈbendɪŋ] *adj* inflexible

unbiased [ʌnˈbaɪəst] *adj* imparcial

unblock [ʌnˈblɒk] *vt (sink, pipe)* desatascar; *(road)* desbloquear

unborn [ˈʌnbɔːn] *adj* **u. child** niño *m* (aún) no nacido

unbounded [ʌnˈbaʊndɪd] *adj* ilimitado(a)

unbreakable [ʌnˈbreɪkəbəl] *adj (plate, toy)* irrompible; *Fig (spirit, alliance)* inquebrantable

unbridled [ʌnˈbraɪdəld] *adj (passion, aggression)* desatado(a)

unbroken [ʌnˈbrəʊkən] *adj* **(a)** *(not broken)* intacto(a) **(b)** *(uninterrupted)* ininterrumpido(a)

unburden [ʌnˈbɜːdən] *vt* **to u. oneself to sb** desahogarse con alguien

unbusinesslike [ʌnˈbɪznɪslaɪk] *adj* poco profesional

unbutton [ʌnˈbʌtən] *vt* desabrochar, desabotonar; **to u. one's shirt** desabrocharse la camisa

uncalled-for [ʌnˈkɔːldfɔː(r)] *adj* **to be u.** *(behavior, remark)* estar fuera de lugar

uncannily [ʌnˈkænɪlɪ] *adv* asombrosamente; **u. accurate** de una precisión asombrosa

uncanny [ʌnˈkænɪ] *adj (coincidence, similarity, resemblance)* asombroso(a), extraño(a); *(knack, ability)* inexplicable

uncaring [ʌnˈkeərɪŋ] *adj* desafecto(a), indiferente; **an u. mother** una madre poco afectuosa

unceasing [ʌnˈsiːsɪŋ] *adj* constante, incesante

uncensored [ʌnˈsensəd] *adj* sin censurar, íntegro(a)

uncertain [ʌnˈsɜːtən] *adj (future)* incierto(a); **to be u. about sth** no estar seguro(a) de algo; **it is u. if… if…** no se sabe si…; **in no u. terms** en términos bien claros

uncertainly [ʌnˈsɜːtənlɪ] *adv (to smile, enter)* de forma vacilante; **…he said u.** …dijo vacilante *or* inseguro

uncertainty [ʌnˈsɜːtəntɪ] *n* **(a)** *(insecurity)* incertidumbre *f* **(b)** *(doubt)* duda *f*

unchallenged [ʌnˈtʃælɪndʒd] **1** *adj (assumption, accusation)* no cuestionado(a)

2 *adv* **to let sth pass u.** dejar pasar algo

unchanged [ʌnˈtʃeɪndʒd] *adj* igual, sin cambios; **to remain u.** no haber cambiado

unchanging [ʌnˈtʃeɪndʒɪŋ] *adj* inmutable

uncharacteristic [ʌnkærəktəˈrɪstɪk] *adj* atípico(a), poco característico(a)

uncharacteristically [ʌnkærəktəˈrɪstɪklɪ] *adv* **he was u. generous/cheerful** mostraba una generosidad/alegría atípica *or* poco normal en él

uncharitable [ʌnˈtʃærɪtəbəl] *adj* cruel

uncharted [ʌnˈtʃɑːtɪd] *adj* desconocido(a), inexplorado(a)

unchecked [ʌnˈtʃekt] **1** *adj* **(a)** *(not restrained)* incontrolado(a) **(b)** *(not verified)* sin comprobar

2 *adv* **to go u.** *(corruption, epidemic)* avanzar sin freno

uncivil [ʌnˈsɪv(ɪ)l] *adj* maleducado(a), descortés

uncivilized [ʌnˈsɪvɪlaɪzd] *adj* poco civilizado(a), incivilizado(a); **at an u. hour** a una hora intempestiva

unclaimed [ʌnˈkleɪmd] *adj (money, baggage)* no reclamado(a); **to go u.** *(money, baggage)* no ser reclamado por nadie

uncle [ˈʌŋkəl] *n* tío *m*; **U. Sam** el Tío Sam

unclean [ʌnˈkliːn] *adj* sucio(a)

unclear [ʌnˈklɪə(r)] *adj* poco claro(a); **I'm still u. about what happened** todavía no tengo muy claro lo que pasó

unclothed [ʌnˈkləʊðd] *adj* desvestido(a), desnudo(a)

uncluttered [ʌnˈklʌtə(d)] *adj* despejado(a)

uncoil [ʌnˈkɔɪl] *vt* desenrollar

uncombed [ʌnˈkəʊmd] *adj* despeinado(a)

uncomfortable [ʌnˈkʌmfətəbəl] *adj* incómodo(a); **to be u.** *(physically)* estar incómodo(a); *(ill-at-ease)* sentirse incómodo(a); **there was an u. silence** se produjo un silencio embarazoso *or* incómodo

uncommitted [ʌnkəˈmɪtɪd] *adj (voter)* indeciso(a); *(funds)* no comprometido(a)

uncommon [ʌnˈkɒmən] *adj* inusual

uncommunicative [ʌnkəˈmjuːnɪkətɪv] *adj* reservado(a), poco comunicativo(a)

uncomplaining [ʌnkəmˈpleɪnɪŋ] *adj* **she accepted the extra work with u. resignation** aceptó el trabajo extra resignada y sin quejarse

uncomplicated [ʌnˈkɒmplɪkeɪtɪd] *adj* sencillo(a)

uncomplimentary [ʌnkɒmplɪˈmentərɪ] *adj* poco elogioso(a)

uncomprehending [ʌnkɒmprɪˈhendɪŋ] *adj* **to be u. of sth** no entender algo; **with an u. look** con cara de no haber comprendido

uncomprehendingly [ʌnkɒmprɪˈhendɪŋlɪ] *adv* con un gesto de incomprensión

uncompromising [ʌnˈkɒmprəmaɪzɪŋ] *adj (person, opposition)* intransigente; *(resolute)* inquebrantable

uncompromisingly [ʌnkɒmprəˈmaɪzɪŋlɪ] *adv* sin concesiones, de manera inquebrantable

unconcealed [ʌnkənˈsiːld] *adj* indisimulado(a), manifiesto(a)

unconcerned [ʌnkənˈsɜːnd] **1** *adj* indiferente; **to be u. about sth** no preocuparse por algo

2 *adv* **to watch/wait u.** mirar/esperar con indiferencia

unconditional [ʌnkən'dɪʃənəl] *adj* incondicional; **u. surrender** rendición *f* incondicional

unconditionally [ʌnkən'dɪʃənəlɪ] *adv (to support)* incondicionalmente; *(to surrender, accept)* sin condiciones

unconfirmed [ʌnkən'fɜːmd] *adj* no confirmado(a)

unconnected [ʌnkə'nektɪd] *adj* inconexo(a), sin relación; **two u. facts** dos hechos independientes

unconscious [ʌn'kɒnʃəs] **1** *n Psy* **the u.** el inconsciente
2 *adj* **(a)** *(not awake)* inconsciente; **to be u.** estar inconsciente **(b)** *(unintentional)* inintencionado(a); **to be u. of sth** no ser consciente de algo

unconsciously [ʌn'kɒnʃəslɪ] *adv* inconscientemente

unconsciousness [ʌn'kɒnʃəsnɪs] *n* inconsciencia *f*; **he lapsed into u.** perdió el conocimiento, se quedó inconsciente

unconstitutional [ʌnkɒnstɪ'tjuːʃənəl] *adj* inconstitucional, anticonstitucional

uncontaminated [ʌnkən'tæmɪnetɪd] *adj* sin contaminar

uncontested [ʌnkən'testɪd] *adj (right, superiority)* indisputado(a); *Pol* **u. seat** escaño *m* con un solo candidato

uncontrollable [ʌnkən'trəʊləbəl] *adj* incontrolable

uncontrollably [ʌnkən'trəʊləblɪ] *adv* incontrolablemente; **they laughed u.** no podían parar de reírse

uncontroversial [ʌnkɒntrə'vɜːʃəl] *adj* anodino(a), nada polémico(a)

unconventional [ʌnkən'venʃənəl] *adj* poco convencional

unconventionally [ʌnkən'venʃənəlɪ] *adv* de forma poco convencional

unconvinced [ʌnkən'vɪnst] *adj* **to be u.** no estar convencido(a); **I remain u.** sigo sin convencerme

unconvincing [ʌnkən'vɪnsɪŋ] *adj* poco convincente

unconvincingly [ʌnkən'vɪnsɪŋlɪ] *adv (to argue, lie, perform)* de forma poco convincente

uncooked [ʌn'kʊkt] *adj* crudo(a)

uncool [ʌn'kuːl] *adj Fam (unfashionable)* poco enrollado(a), *Méx* nada suave, *RP* nada copado(a), *Ven* aguado(a)

uncooperative [ʌnkəʊ'ɒpərətɪv] *adj* **to be u.** no estar dispuesto(a) a cooperar

uncoordinated [ʌnkəʊ'ɔːdɪneɪtɪd] *adj (efforts)* descoordinado(a); *(person)* falto(a) de coordinación, torpe

uncork [ʌn'kɔːk] *vt* descorchar

uncorroborated [ʌnkə'rɒbəreɪtɪd] *adj* no confirmado(a)

uncountable [ʌn'kaʊntəbəl] *adj Gram* incontable

uncouth [ʌn'kuːθ] *adj* basto(a)

uncover [ʌn'kʌvə(r)] *vt* destapar; *Fig (evidence, plot)* descubrir

uncritical [ʌn'krɪtɪkəl] *adj* poco crítico(a); **to be u. of sb/sth** no ser crítico(a) con alguien/algo

UNCTAD ['ʌŋktæd] *n (abbr* **United Nations Conference on Trade and Development)** UNCTAD *f*

unction ['ʌŋkʃən] *n* **(a)** *(of manner)* untuosidad *f*, empalago *m* **(b)** *Rel* unción *f*; **extreme u.** extremaunción *f*

unctuous ['ʌŋktjʊəs] *adj Pej* untuoso(a), empalagoso(a)

uncultivated [ʌn'kʌltɪveɪtɪd] *adj* **(a)** *(land)* sin cultivar **(b)** *(person)* inculto(a)

uncultured [ʌn'kʌltʃəd] *adj* inculto(a)

uncut [ʌn'kʌt] *adj (gem)* en bruto; *(text, movie)* íntegro(a)

undamaged [ʌn'dæmɪdʒd] *adj* intacto(a)

undated [ʌn'deɪtɪd] *adj* no fechado(a)

undaunted [ʌn'dɔːntɪd] *adj* imperturbable; **to be u. by sth** no amilanarse *or* arredrarse por algo

undecided [ʌndɪ'saɪdɪd] *adj* **(a)** *(question, problem)* sin resolver; **that's still u.** todavía está por decidir **(b)** *(person)* indeciso(a); **to be u. about sth** estar indeciso(a) sobre algo

undefeated [ʌndɪ'fiːtɪd] *adj* invicto(a)

undefended [ʌndɪ'fendɪd] *adj* indefenso(a)

undemanding [ʌndɪ'mɑːndɪŋ] *adj (job)* fácil, que exige poco esfuerzo; *(person)* poco exigente

undemocratic [ʌndemə'krætɪk] *adj* antidemocrático(a)

undemonstrative [ʌndɪ'mɒnstrətɪv] *adj* reservado(a)

undeniable [ʌndɪ'naɪəbəl] *adj* innegable

undeniably [ʌndɪ'naɪəblɪ] *adv* innegablemente

under ['ʌndə(r)] **1** *prep* **(a)** *(beneath)* debajo de, bajo, *Am* abajo de; *(with verbs of motion)* bajo; **u. the table/the stairs** debajo de la mesa/las escaleras; **to walk u. a ladder** pasar por debajo de una escalera; *Fam* **to be/feel u. the weather** *(ill)* estar/encontrarse pachucho(a)
(b) *(less than)* menos de; **in u. ten minutes** en menos de diez minutos; **he's u. thirty** tiene menos de treinta años; **to be u. age** ser menor de edad; **children u. five** niños de menos de cinco años
(c) *(having control of)* **he has a hundred men u. him** tiene cien hombres a su cargo; **Spain u. Franco** la España de Franco
(d) *(subject to)* **to be u. orders to do sth** tener órdenes de hacer algo; **u. the terms of the agreement** según el acuerdo; **u. these conditions/circumstances** en estas condiciones/circunstancias
(e) *(in the process of)* **u. construction/observation** en construcción/observación; **the matter is u. investigation** se está investigando el asunto; **to get u. way** *(meeting, campaign)* ponerse en marcha, arrancar; **to be u. way** *(meeting, campaign)* estar en marcha
2 *adv* **(a)** *(underneath)* debajo, *Am* abajo; *(underwater)* bajo el agua, debajo *or Am* abajo del agua; **to go u.** *(ship, company)* hundirse **(b)** *(less)* **for $5 or u.** por 5 dólares o menos; **children of seven and u.** niños menores de ocho años

underachiever [ʌndərə'tʃiːvə(r)] *n* persona *f* que rinde por debajo de sus posibilidades

underage [ʌndər'eɪdʒ] *adj* **u. drinking** consumo *m* de alcohol por menores; **u. sex** relaciones *fpl* sexuales entre menores

undercarriage ['ʌndəkærɪdʒ] *n Av* tren *m* de aterrizaje

undercharge [ʌndə'tʃɑːdʒ] *vt* cobrar de menos

underclass ['ʌndəklɑːs] *n* clase *f* marginal

underclothes ['ʌndəkləʊðz] *npl* ropa *f* interior

underclothing ['ʌndəkləʊðɪŋ] *n* ropa *f* interior

undercoat ['ʌndəkəʊt] *n* primera mano *f (de pintura)*

undercook [ʌndə'kʊk] *vt* **to be undercooked** no estar lo suficientemente hecho(a)

undercover ['ʌndəkʌvə(r)] **1** *adj (agent, investigation)* secreto(a)
2 *adv* **to work u.** trabajar en secreto

undercurrent ['ʌndəkʌrənt] *n (in sea)* corriente *f* submarina; *Fig (of emotion, unrest)* corriente *f* subyacente

undercut ['ʌndəkʌt] *(pt & pp* **undercut)** *vt Com* **to u. the competition** vender a precios más baratos que los de la competencia

underdeveloped [ʌndədɪ'veləpt] *adj (economy, country)* subdesarrollado(a)

underdog ['ʌndədɒg] *n* **(a)** *(in contest)* = competidor o equipo considerado probable perdedor; **Boston is the u.** Boston tiene menos posibilidades de ganar **(b)** *(in society)* **the underdogs** los débiles y oprimidos

underestimate 1 *n* [ʌndər'estɪmɪt] infravaloración *f*
2 *vt* [ʌndər'estɪmeɪt] infravalorar, subestimar

underestimation [ʌndərestɪ'meɪʃən] *n* infravaloración *f*

underexposed ['ʌndərɪks'pəʊzd] *adj Phot* subexpuesto(a)

underfed [ʌndə'fed] *adj* desnutrido(a), malnutrido(a)

underfoot [ʌndə'fʊt] *adv* **it's wet u.** el suelo está mojado; **to trample sth u.** pisotear algo

underfunding [ʌndə'fʌndɪŋ] *n* escasez *f* de fondos

undergarment ['ʌndəgɑːmənt] *n* prenda *f* (de ropa) interior

undergo [ʌndə'gəʊ] (*pt* **underwent** [ʌndə'went], *pp* **undergone** [ʌndə'gɒn]) *vi* (*change*) experimentar; (*test*) ser sometido(a) a; (*pain*) sufrir; **to u. treatment** (*patient*) recibir tratamiento

undergraduate [ʌndə'grædjʊɪt] *n* estudiante *mf* universitario(a) (*sin licenciatura*)

underground ['ʌndəgraʊnd] **1** *n* (*resistance movement*) resistencia *f* (clandestina)
2 *adj* (*cables, passage*) subterráneo(a) (**b**) (*movement, newspaper*) clandestino(a)
3 *adv* (*to work, live*) bajo tierra; *Fig* **to go u.** pasar a la clandestinidad

undergrowth ['ʌndəgrəʊθ] *n* maleza *f*

underhand [ʌndə'hænd] *adj* turbio(a), poco honrado(a)

underlain [ʌndə'leɪn] *pp of* **underlie**

underlay ['ʌndəleɪ] *n* (*for carpet*) refuerzo *m* (*debajo de las moquetas*)

underlie [ʌndə'laɪ] (*pt* **underlay** [ʌndə'leɪ], *pp* **underlain** [ʌndə'leɪn])
2 *vt* subyacer tras *or* bajo
3 *pt of* **underlie**

underline [ʌndə'laɪn] *vt also Fig* subrayar

underlying [ʌndə'laɪɪŋ] *adj* subyacente

undermanning [ʌndə'mænɪŋ] *n Ind* insuficiencia *f* de personal

undermentioned ['ʌndəmenʃənd] *adj Formal* abajo mencionado(a) *or* citado(a)

undermine [ʌndə'maɪn] *vt* (*weaken*) minar, socavar

underneath [ʌndə'niːθ] **1** *n* parte *f* inferior *or* de abajo
2 *prep* debajo de, bajo; (*with verbs of motion*) bajo; **he crawled u. the fence** se arrastró por debajo de la valla
3 *adv* debajo

undernourished [ʌndə'nʌrɪʃt] *adj* desnutrido(a)

underpaid [ʌndə'peɪd] *adj* mal pagado(a)

underpants ['ʌndəpænts] *npl* calzoncillos *mpl*, *Chile* fundillos *mpl*, *Col* pantaloncillos *mpl*, *Méx* calzones *mpl*, *Méx* chones *mpl*

underpass ['ʌndəpɑːs] *n* (*for cars, pedestrians*) paso *m* subterráneo

underperform [ʌndəpə'fɔːm] *vi Fin* rendir por debajo de sus posibilidades

underpin [ʌndə'pɪn] (*pt & pp* **underpinned**) *vt* (*support*) sustentar

underpopulated [ʌndə'pɒpjʊleɪtɪd] *adj* poco poblado(a)

underprivileged [ʌndə'prɪvɪlɪdʒd] *adj* desfavorecido(a)

underqualified [ʌndə'kwɒlɪfaɪd] *adj* **to be u.** no estar suficientemente cualificado(a)

underrate [ʌndə'reɪt] *vt* subestimar, infravalorar

undersecretary [ʌndə'sekrətrɪ] *n* subsecretario(a) *m,f*

undershirt ['ʌndəʃɜːt] *n* camiseta *f*

underside ['ʌndəsaɪd] *n* parte *f* inferior

undersized [ʌndə'saɪzd] *adj* demasiado pequeño(a)

underskirt ['ʌndəskɜːt] *n* enaguas *fpl*

understaffed [ʌndə'stɑːft] *adj* **to be u.** no tener suficiente personal

understand [ʌndə'stænd] (*pt & pp* **understood** [ʌndə-'stʊd]) **1** *vt* (**a**) (*comprehend*) entender, comprender; **they u. each other** se entienden mutuamente; **what I can't u. is why...** lo que no llego a entender es por qué...; **is that understood?** ¿entendido? (**b**) (*believe, assume*) **I u. that...** tengo entendido que...; **to give sb to u. that...** dar a entender a alguien que...; **are we to u. that ...?** ¿quiere eso decir que...?, ¿debemos entender (con eso) que...?; **it was understood that few of us would survive** se entendía *or* se daba por sabido que pocos sobreviviríamos
2 *vi* entender, comprender

understandable [ʌndə'stændəbəl] *adj* comprensible

understandably [ʌndə'stændəblɪ] *adv* comprensiblemente

understanding [ʌndə'stændɪŋ] **1** *n* (**a**) (*comprehension*) comprensión *f*; **it's beyond all u.** no tiene ninguna lógica, es incomprensible (**b**) (*sympathy*) comprensión *f* (**c**) (*agreement*) acuerdo *m*; **to come to** *or* **to reach an u.** llegar a un acuerdo; **on the u. that...** a condición de que...
2 *adj* comprensivo(a)

understandingly [ʌndə'stændɪŋlɪ] *adv* **he smiled at me u.** me sonrió comprensivo

understated [ʌndə'steɪtɪd] *adj* (*clothes, design*) discreto(a)

understatement [ʌndə'steɪtmənt] *n* **that's an u.!** ¡eso es quedarse corto!

understood [ʌndə'stʊd] *pt & pp of* **understand**

understudy ['ʌndəstʌdɪ] *n Theat* suplente *mf*, actor(triz) *m,f* suplente

undertake [ʌndə'teɪk] (*pt* **undertook** [ʌndə'tʊk], *pp* **undertaken** [ʌndə'teɪkən]) *vt* emprender; **to u. to do sth** encargarse de hacer algo

undertaker ['ʌndəteɪkə(r)] *n* encargado(a) *m,f* de una funeraria

undertaking [ʌndə'teɪkɪŋ] *n* (**a**) (*enterprise*) empresa *f*, proyecto *m* (**b**) (*promise*) compromiso *m*; **she gave me her u. that she would do it** me dijo que se comprometía a hacerlo

undertone ['ʌndətəʊn] *n* (*low voice*) voz *f* baja; *Fig* (*hint, suggestion*) tono *m*

undertook ['ʌndə'tʊk] *pt of* **undertake**

undertow ['ʌndətəʊ] *n* resaca *f*

undervalue [ʌndə'væljuː] *vt also Fig* infravalorar

underwater 1 *adj* ['ʌndəwɔːtə(r)] submarino(a)
2 *adv* [ʌndə'wɔːtə(r)] **to swim u.** bucear

underwear ['ʌndəweə(r)] *n* ropa *f* interior

underweight [ʌndə'weɪt] *adj* **to be u.** (*person*) estar muy flaco(a)

underwent [ʌndə'went] *pt of* **undergo**

underworld ['ʌndəwɜːld] *n* (**a**) (*in mythology*) **the U.** el Hades (**b**) (*of criminals*) **the u.** el hampa

underwrite ['ʌndəraɪt] (*pt* **underwrote** [ʌndə'rəʊt], *pp* **underwritten** [ʌndə'rɪtn]) *vt Fin* asegurar; *Fig* (*pay for*) financiar

underwriter ['ʌndəraɪtə(r)] *n Fin* (*in insurance*) asegurador(ora) *m,f*

undeserved [ʌndɪ'zɜːvd] *adj* inmerecido(a)

undeservedly [ʌndɪ'zɜːvɪdlɪ] *adv* inmerecidamente

undeserving [ʌndɪ'zɜːvɪŋ] *adj* indigno(a); **to be u. of sth** no merecer algo

undesirable [ʌndɪ'zaɪərəbəl] *n & adj* indeseable *mf*

undetected [ʌndɪ'tektɪd] **1** *adj* no detectado(a)
2 *adv* **to go u.** no ser detectado(a)

undetermined [ʌndɪ'tɜːmɪnd] *adj* indeterminado(a); **to be u.** (*cause*) no estar determinado(a)

undeterred [ʌndɪ'tɜːd] **1** *adj* **to be u. by sth** no desanimarse por algo
2 *adv* **he carried on u.** siguió sin arredrarse

undeveloped [ʌndɪ'veləpt] *adj* no desarrollado(a); *Phot* (*film*) sin revelar; **u. land** tierra *f* sin explotar

undid [ʌn'dɪd] *pt of* **undo**

undigested [ʌnd(a)ɪ'dʒestɪd] *adj also Fig* no digerido(a)

undignified [ʌn'dɪgnɪfaɪd] *adj* poco digno(a), indecoroso(a)

undiluted [ʌndaɪ'luːtɪd] *adj* (*liquid*) no diluido(a); *Fig* (*pleasure*) puro(a), absoluto(a)

undiminished [ʌndɪ'mɪnɪʃt] *adj* no disminuido(a); **to remain u.** no haber disminuido

undiplomatic [ʌndɪplə'mætɪk] *adj* poco diplomático(a)

undisciplined [ʌn'dɪsɪplɪnd] *adj* indisciplinado(a)

undisclosed [ʌndɪs'kləʊzd] *adj* no revelado(a)

undiscovered [ʌndɪsˈkʌvəd] **1** adj sin descubrir
2 adv **to go/remain u.** estar/permanecer sin descubrir

undiscriminating [ʌndɪsˈkrɪmɪneɪtɪŋ] adj **to be u.** no hacer distinciones, no distinguir

undisguised [ʌndɪsˈgaɪzd] adj no disimulado(a)

undisputed [ʌndɪsˈpju:tɪd] adj indiscutible

undistinguished [ʌndɪsˈtɪŋgwɪʃt] adj mediocre

undisturbed [ʌndɪsˈtɜ:bd] adj (sleep) tranquilo(a); **she left his papers u.** dejó sus papeles tal como estaban

undivided [ʌndɪˈvaɪdɪd] adj **he gave me his u. attention** me prestó toda su atención

undo [ʌnˈdu:] (pt undid [ʌnˈdɪd], pp undone [ʌnˈdʌn]) vt **(a)** (mistake) corregir; (damage) reparar; Comptr (command) deshacer **(b)** (knot) deshacer; (button) desabrochar; (parcel, zipper) abrir; (shoelaces) desatar

undoing [ʌnˈdu:ɪŋ] n perdición f

undone [ʌnˈdʌn] **1** adj **(a)** (loose) (jacket, buttons) desabrochado(a); (laces) desatado(a); **to come u.** (jacket, buttons) desabrocharse; (laces) desatarse **(b)** (incomplete) sin hacer; **to leave sth u.** dejar algo sin hacer
2 pp of **undo**

undoubted [ʌnˈdaʊtɪd] adj indudable

undoubtedly [ʌnˈdaʊtɪdlɪ] adv indudablemente

undreamed-of [ʌnˈdri:mdɒv], **undreamt-of** [ʌnˈdremtɒv] adj inimaginable

undress [ʌnˈdres] **1** n **in a state of u.** desvestido(a), desnudo(a)
2 vt desvestir, desnudar; **to get undressed** desvestirse, desnudarse
3 vi desvestirse, desnudarse

undrinkable [ʌnˈdrɪŋkəbəl] adj imbebible

undue [ʌnˈdju:] adj excesivo(a)

undulate [ˈʌndjʊleɪt] vi ondular

undulating [ˈʌndjʊleɪtɪŋ] adj ondulante

undulation [ʌndjʊˈleɪʃən] n ondulación f

unduly [ʌnˈdju:lɪ] adv excesivamente

undying [ʌnˈdaɪɪŋ] adj eterno(a)

unearned [ʌnˈɜ:nd] adj (reward, punishment) inmerecido(a); Fin **u. income** rendimientos mpl del capital, renta f no salarial

unearth [ʌnˈɜ:θ] vt (buried object) desenterrar; Fig (information, secret) descubrir

unearthly [ʌnˈɜ:θlɪ] adj **(a)** (supernatural) sobrenatural **(b)** Fam **at an u. hour** a una hora intempestiva; **an u. din** or **racket** un ruido espantoso; **for some u. reason** por algún motivo incomprensible

unease [ʌnˈi:z] n inquietud f, desasosiego m

uneasily [ʌnˈi:zɪlɪ] adv con inquietud

uneasy [ʌnˈi:zɪ] adj (person) inquieto(a); (sleep) agitado(a); **to be u. (about sth)** estar inquieto(a) (por algo)

uneconomic [ʌni:kəˈnɒmɪk] adj carente de rentabilidad, antieconómico(a)

uneconomical [ʌni:kəˈnɒmɪkəl] adj (wasteful, inefficient) ineficaz desde el punto de vista económico, poco rentable

uneducated [ʌnˈedjʊkeɪtɪd] adj inculto(a)

unelectable [ʌnɪˈlektəbəl] adj (party, person) inelegible

unemotional [ʌnɪˈməʊʃənəl] adj (person) frío(a), impasible

unemployable [ʌnɪmˈplɔɪəbəl] adj **to be u.** no ser apto(a) para trabajar

unemployed [ʌnɪmˈplɔɪd] **1** npl **the u.** los desempleados, Esp los parados, Am los desocupados
2 adj (person) desempleado(a), Esp parado(a), Am desocupado(a); **to be u.** estar desempleado(a) or Esp en (el) paro or Am desocupado(a)

unemployment [ʌnɪmˈplɔɪmənt] n desempleo m, Esp paro m, Am desocupación f; **u. stands at 10 percent** el índice or la tasa de desempleo or Esp de paro or Am de la desocupación se

sitúa en el 10 por ciento; **u. benefit** or **compensation** subsidio m de desempleo or Am de desocupación

unending [ʌnˈendɪŋ] adj interminable

unendurable [ʌnɪnˈdjʊərəbəl] adj insoportable

unenlightened [ʌnɪnˈlaɪtənd] adj (person, decision) retrógrado(a)

unenlightening [ʌnɪnˈlaɪtnɪŋ] adj poco ilustrativo(a)

unenterprising [ʌnˈentəpraɪzɪŋ] adj poco emprendedor(ora)

unenthusiastic [ʌnɪnθ(j)u:zɪˈæstɪk] adj (reaction, response) tibio(a); (person) poco entusiasta

unenthusiastically [ʌnɪnθju:zɪˈæstɪklɪ] adv sin entusiasmo

unenviable [ʌnˈenvɪəbəl] adj desagradable, nada envidiable

unequal [ʌnˈi:kwəl] adj desigual; **an u. struggle** una lucha desigual; **he was u. to the challenge** no estuvo a la altura de lo exigido

unequaled [ʌnˈi:kwəld] adj sin par

unequivocal [ʌnɪˈkwɪvəkəl] adj Formal inequívoco(a)

unequivocally [ʌnɪˈkwɪvəklɪ] adv Formal inequívocamente, de modo inequívoco

unerring [ʌnˈɜ:rɪŋ] adj infalible

UNESCO [ju:ˈneskəʊ] n (abbr **United Nations Educational, Scientific and Cultural Organization**) UNESCO f

unethical [ʌnˈeθɪkəl] adj poco ético(a)

uneven [ʌnˈi:vən] adj (surface, road, breathing) irregular; (performance) desigual

unevenly [ʌnˈi:vənlɪ] adv (divided, spread) de forma desigual; **to be u. matched** no estar de igual a igual, tener niveles muy distintos

uneventful [ʌnɪˈventfʊl] adj sin incidentes

unexceptionable [ʌnɪkˈsepʃənəbəl] adj irreprochable

unexceptional [ʌnɪkˈsepʃənəl] adj mediocre; **to be u.** no tener nada de especial

unexciting [ʌnɪkˈsaɪtɪŋ] adj anodino(a), insulso(a)

unexpected [ʌnɪksˈpektɪd] adj inesperado(a)

unexplained [ʌnɪksˈpleɪnd] adj inexplicado(a)

unexplored [ʌnɪksˈplɔ:d] adj inexplorado(a)

unfailing [ʌnˈfeɪlɪŋ] adj (hope, courage) firme, inconmovible; (punctuality) infalible; (patience, good humor) inagotable

unfailingly [ʌnˈfeɪlɪŋlɪ] adv indefectiblemente

unfair [ʌnˈfeə(r)] adj injusto(a); **to be u. to sb** ser injusto(a) con alguien; Com **u. competition** competencia f desleal

unfairly [ʌnˈfeəlɪ] adv injustamente

unfairness [ʌnˈfeənɪs] n injusticia f

unfaithful [ʌnˈfeɪθfʊl] adj **to be u. (to sb)** ser infiel (a alguien)

unfamiliar [ʌnfəˈmɪlɪə(r)] adj extraño(a), desconocido(a); **to be u. with sth** no estar familiarizado(a) con algo; **I'm u. with that name** desconozco ese nombre

unfashionable [ʌnˈfæʃənəbəl] adj **to be u.** no estar de moda; **to become u.** pasar de moda

unfasten [ʌnˈfɑ:sən] vt (knot) desatar, deshacer; (door) abrir; **to u. one's belt** desabrocharse el cinturón

unfathomable [ʌnˈfæðəməbəl] adj insondable

unfavorable [ʌnˈfeɪvərəbəl] adj desfavorable

unfavorably [ʌnˈfeɪvərəblɪ] adv desfavorablemente

unfeeling [ʌnˈfi:lɪŋ] adj insensible

unfinished [ʌnˈfɪnɪʃt] adj inacabado(a); **to leave sth u.** dejar algo sin terminar; **u. business** asuntos mpl pendientes

unfit [ʌnˈfɪt] adj **(a)** (unsuitable) inadecuado(a), inapropiado(a); **to be u. for sth** no ser apto(a) para algo **(b)** (in poor physical condition) bajo(a) de forma; (injured) lesionado(a)

unflagging [ʌnˈflægɪŋ] adj infatigable

unflappable [ʌnˈflæpəbəl] adj impasible, imperturbable

unflattering [ʌnˈflætərɪŋ] *adj* poco favorecedor(ora)

unflinching [ʌnˈflɪnʃɪŋ] *adj (resolve, courage)* a toda prueba; *(loyalty, support)* inquebrantable

unfold [ʌnˈfəʊld] **1** *vt* (**a**) *(newspaper, map)* desdoblar (**b**) *(story, proposal)* revelar
2 *vi (story, events)* desarrollarse

unforced [ʌnˈfɔːst] *adj (natural)* espontáneo(a); **u. error** error *m* no forzado

unforeseeable [ʌnfəˈsiːəbəl] *adj* imprevisible

unforeseen [ʌnfɔːˈsiːn] *adj* imprevisto(a)

unforgettable [ʌnfəˈgetəbəl] *adj* inolvidable

unforgivable [ʌnfəˈgɪvəbəl] *adj* imperdonable

unforgivably [ʌnfəˈgɪvəblɪ] *adv* imperdonablemente

unforgiving [ʌnfəˈgɪvɪŋ] *adj* implacable

unforthcoming [ʌnfɔːˈkʌmɪŋ] *adj* reservado(a)

unfortunate [ʌnˈfɔːtʃənɪt] *adj (person, choice, remark, mistake)* desafortunado(a); *(accident, event)* desgraciado(a)

unfortunately [ʌnfɔːtʃənɪtlɪ] *adv* desgraciadamente

unfounded [ʌnˈfaʊndɪd] *adj* infundado(a)

unfriendly [ʌnˈfrendlɪ] *adj (person)* arisco(a), antipático(a); *(reception)* hostil

unfulfilled [ʌnfʊlˈfɪld] *adj (promise)* incumplido(a); *(desire, ambition)* insatisfecho(a); *(potential)* desaprovechado(a); **to feel u.** sentirse insatisfecho(a)

unfunny [ʌnˈfʌnɪ] *adj* **to be u.** no tener ninguna gracia

unfurl [ʌnˈfɜːl] **1** *vt (flag, sails)* desplegar
2 *vi* desplegarse

unfurnished [ʌnˈfɜːnɪʃt] *adj* sin amueblar; **u. accommodation** vivienda *f* sin amueblar

ungainly [ʌnˈgeɪnlɪ] *adj* desgarbado(a), torpe

ungodly [ʌnˈgɒdlɪ] *adj* impío(a), blasfemo(a); *Fig* **at an u. hour** a una hora intempestiva

ungovernable [ʌnˈgʌvənəbəl] *adj (people, country)* ingobernable; *(feelings)* incontrolable

ungracious [ʌnˈgreɪʃəs] *adj* descortés

ungrammatical [ʌngrəˈmætɪkəl] *adj* incorrecto(a) (gramaticalmente)

ungrateful [ʌnˈgreɪtfʊl] *adj* desagradecido(a)

ungratefully [ʌnˈgreɪtfʊlɪ] *adv* con desagradecimiento

ungrudging [ʌnˈgrʌdʒɪŋ] *adj* **to be u. in one's praise/support** no escatimar elogios/apoyo

unguarded [ʌnˈgɑːdɪd] *adj* (**a**) *(place)* desprotegido(a) (**b**) *(remark)* imprudente; **in an u. moment** en un momento de despiste

unhampered [ʌnˈhæmpəd] *adj* libre (**by** de)

unhappily [ʌnˈhæpɪlɪ] *adv* (**a**) *(unfortunately)* desgraciadamente (**b**) *(sadly)* tristemente

unhappiness [ʌnˈhæpɪnɪs] *n* infelicidad *f*, desdicha *f*

unhappy [ʌnˈhæpɪ] *adj* (**a**) *(sad) (person, childhood, marriage)* infeliz; *(day, ending, face)* triste; **to be u.** *(person)* ser infeliz (**b**) *(worried)* **I'm u. about leaving the child alone** me preocupa dejar al niño solo (**c**) *(not pleased)* **to be u. with sth** estar descontento(a) *or* no estar contento(a) con algo (**d**) *(unfortunate) (choice, state of affairs)* desgraciado(a), desafortunado(a)

unharmed [ʌnˈhɑːmd] *adj (person)* indemne, ileso(a); *(object)* intacto(a)

UNHCR [juːeneɪtˈsiːˈɑː(r)] *n (abbr* **United Nations High Commission for Refugees**) ACNUR *m*

unhealthily [ʌnˈhelθɪlɪ] *adv* de forma poco saludable

unhealthy [ʌnˈhelθɪ] *adj (ill)* enfermizo(a); *(unwholesome)* insano(a), malsano(a)

unheard-of [ʌnˈhɜːdɒv] *adj* inaudito(a); **that was u. in my youth** eso era impensable cuando yo era joven

unheeded [ʌnˈhiːdɪd] *adj* desoído(a), desatendido(a); **to go u.** ser ignorado(a), caer en saco roto

unhelpful [ʌnˈhelpfʊl] *adj (person)* poco servicial; *(criticism, advice)* poco constructivo(a)

unhesitating [ʌnˈhezɪteɪtɪŋ] *adj (support)* decidido(a); *(reply)* inmediato(a)

unhindered [ʌnˈhɪndəd] **1** *adj* **he was u. by any doubts** no tuvo ninguna duda
2 *adv* **to work u.** trabajar sin estorbos

unhinged [ʌnˈhɪndʒd] *adj (mad)* trastornado(a)

unholy [ʌnˈhəʊlɪ] *adj* profano(a); *(words)* blasfemo(a); *(thoughts)* impuro(a); *Fam* **an u. mess/noise** un desorden/ruido espantoso; **u. alliance** alianza *f* contra natura

UNHRC [juːeneɪtˈʃɑːˈsiː] *n (abbr* **United Nations Human Rights Commission**) UNHRC *f*

unhurt [ʌnˈhɜːt] *adj* ileso(a); **to be u.** *(after accident)* salir ileso

unhygienic [ʌnhaɪˈdʒiːnɪk] *adj* antihigiénico(a)

UNICEF [ˈjuːnɪsef] *n (abbr* **United Nations International Children's Emergency Fund**) UNICEF *m or f*

unicorn [ˈjuːnɪkɔːn] *n* unicornio *m*

unidentified [ʌnaɪˈdentɪfaɪd] *adj* no identificado(a); **u. flying object** objeto *m* volador no identificado

unification [juːnɪfɪˈkeɪʃən] *n* unificación *f*

uniform [ˈjuːnɪfɔːm] **1** *n* uniforme *m*
2 *adj (color, size)* uniforme; *(temperature)* constante

uniformity [juːnɪˈfɔːmɪtɪ] *n* uniformidad *f*

uniformly [ˈjuːnɪfɔːmlɪ] *adv* uniformemente

unify [ˈjuːnɪfaɪ] **1** *vt* unificar
2 *vi* unificarse

unilateral [juːnɪˈlætərəl] *adj* unilateral

unilaterally [juːnɪˈlætərəlɪ] *adv* unilateralmente

unimaginable [ʌnɪˈmædʒɪnəbəl] *adj* inimaginable

unimaginative [ʌnɪˈmædʒɪnətɪv] *adj* **to be u.** *(person)* tener poca imaginación; *(book, meal, choice)* ser muy poco original, no tener originalidad

unimpaired [ʌnɪmˈpeəd] *adj* indemne; **her faculties remained u.** no había perdido facultades

unimportant [ʌnɪmˈpɔːtənt] *adj* **to be u.** no importar

unimpressed [ʌnɪmˈprest] *adj* **to be u. by sth** no quedar convencido(a) con algo

uninformed [ʌnɪnˈfɔːmd] *adj* desinformado(a); **to be u. about sth** no estar informado(a) de algo

uninhabitable [ʌnɪnˈhæbɪtəbəl] *adj* inhabitable

uninhabited [ʌnɪnˈhæbɪtɪd] *adj* desierto(a)

uninhibited [ʌnɪnˈhɪbɪtɪd] *adj* desinhibido(a)

uninitiated [ʌnɪˈnɪʃɪeɪtɪd] **1** *npl* **to the u.** para los profanos (en la materia)
2 *adj* no iniciado(a), profano(a)

uninspiring [ʌnɪnˈspaɪərɪŋ] *adj* anodino(a)

unintelligible [ʌnɪnˈtelɪdʒɪbəl] *adj* ininteligible

unintended [ʌnɪnˈtendɪd] *adj* no deseado(a)

unintentional [ʌnɪnˈtenʃənəl] *adj* inintencionado(a); **it was u.** fue sin querer

uninterested [ʌnˈɪntərestɪd] *adj* poco interesado(a); **he was completely u.** no le interesaba en absoluto

uninteresting [ʌnˈɪntərestɪŋ] *adj* sin interés, anodino(a)

uninterrupted [ʌnɪntəˈrʌptɪd] *adj* constante, ininterrumpido(a)

uninvited [ʌnɪnˈvaɪtɪd] **1** *adj (comment, advice)* no solicitado(a); **there were a few u. guests** algunos de los presentes no habían sido invitados
2 *adv* **to arrive u.** llegar sin haber sido invitado(a)

uninviting [ʌnɪnˈvaɪtɪŋ] *adj (place)* inhóspito(a); *(food)* nada apetitoso(a); *(prospect)* desagradable

union [ˈjuːnjən] *n* (**a**) *(of countries)* unión *f*; **U. Jack** bandera *f* del Reino Unido (**b**) *(marriage)* enlace *m* (**c**) *Ind* sindicato *m* (**d**) **u. suit** calzoncillos *mpl* largos

unionism [ˈjuːnjənɪzəm] *n* (**a**) *(labor unionism)* sindicalismo *m* (**b**) *(in Northern Ireland)* unionismo *m*

unionist ['ju:njənɪst] n (**a**) *(supporter of trade union)* sindicalista mf (**b**) *Hist* U. unionista mf (**c**) *(in Northern Ireland)* U. unionista mf *(partidario de que Irlanda del Norte siga formando parte del Reino Unido)*

unionize ['ju:njənaɪz] vt sindicar

unique [ju:'ni:k] adj único(a); **to be u. to** ser exclusivo(a) de; **u. selling point** or **proposition** argumento m diferenciador

unisex ['ju:nɪseks] adj unisex inv

unison ['ju:nɪsən] n **in u.** al unísono

unit ['ju:nɪt] n *(in general)* unidad f; *(in hospital)* unidad f, servicio m; *(in army)* sección f, unidad f; **(kitchen) u.** módulo m (de cocina); **u. of measurement** unidad f de medida; *Com* **u. price** precio m por unidad; *Fin* **u. trust** sociedad f de inversión mobiliaria

unitary ['ju:nɪtərɪ] adj unitario(a)

unite [ju:'naɪt] **1** vt unir
    2 vi unirse

united [ju:'naɪtɪd] adj unido(a); **the U. Arab Emirates** los Emiratos Árabes Unidos; **the U. Kingdom (of Great Britain and Northern Ireland)** el Reino Unido (de Gran Bretaña e Irlanda del Norte); **the U. Nations** las Naciones Unidas; **the U. States (of America)** los Estados Unidos (de América)

unity ['ju:nɪtɪ] n unidad f

univ *(abbr* **university)** univ., universidad f

universal [ju:nɪ'vɜ:səl] adj universal; **u. suffrage** sufragio m universal

universally [ju:nɪ'vɜ:səlɪ] adv universalmente

universe ['ju:nɪvɜ:s] n universo m

university [ju:nɪ'vɜ:sɪtɪ] n universidad f; **u. professor** profesor(ora) m,f de universidad; **u. student** estudiante mf universitario(a)

UNIX ['ju:nɪks] n Comptr *(abbr* **Uniplexed Information and Computing System)** UNIX m

unjust [ʌn'dʒʌst] adj injusto(a)

unjustifiable [ʌndʒʌstɪ'faɪəbəl] adj injustificable

unjustifiably [ʌn'dʒʌstɪfaɪəblɪ] adv injustificablemente, sin justificación

unjustified [ʌn'dʒʌstɪfaɪd] adj injustificado(a)

unjustly [ʌn'dʒʌstlɪ] adv injustamente

unkempt [ʌn'kem(p)t] adj *(hair)* revuelto(a); *(beard, appearance)* descuidado(a)

unkind [ʌn'kaɪnd] adj *(unpleasant)* antipático(a), desagradable; *(uncharitable)* cruel; **to be u. (to sb)** ser antipático(a) or desagradable (con alguien)

unkindly [ʌn'kaɪndlɪ] adv *(harshly)* con dureza, duramente; **to behave u. toward sb** estar desagradable con alguien

unknowingly [ʌn'nəʊɪŋlɪ] adv inconscientemente, inadvertidamente

unknown [ʌn'nəʊn] **1** n *(person)* desconocido(a) m,f; **the u.** *(place, things)* lo desconocido
    2 adj desconocido(a); *Fig* **an u. quantity** una incógnita; **the U. Soldier** el soldado desconocido
    3 adv **u. to the rest of us** sin que lo supiéramos los demás

unlace [ʌn'leɪs] vt desatar

unladylike [ʌn'leɪdɪlaɪk] adj impropio(a) de una señora

unlawful [ʌn'lɔ:fʊl] adj ilegal, ilícito(a)

unlawfully [ʌn'lɔ:fʊlɪ] adv ilegalmente, ilícitamente

unleaded [ʌn'ledɪd] **1** n gasolina f or RP nafta f sin plomo
    2 adj **u. gasoline** gasolina f or RP nafta f sin plomo

unleash [ʌn'li:ʃ] vt *(dogs)* soltar; *Fig (forces, criticism)* desencadenar

unleavened [ʌn'levənd] adj **u. bread** pan m ázimo

unless [ʌn'les] conj a no ser que, a menos que; **u. I hear to the contrary** en tanto no se me indique lo contrario; **u. I'm mistaken** si no me equivoco

unlike [ʌn'laɪk] prep **to be u. sb/sth** no parecerse a alguien/algo; **he's not u. his sister** se parece bastante a su hermana; **u. his father,...** a diferencia de su padre,...; **it's u. him to do such a thing** no es propio de él hacer algo así

unlikelihood [ʌn'laɪklɪhʊd] n improbabilidad f

unlikely [ʌn'laɪklɪ] adj improbable; **it's u. to happen** no es probable que suceda; **he's u. to do it** no es probable que lo haga; **in the u. event of an accident** en el hipotético caso de un accidente

unlimited [ʌn'lɪmɪtɪd] adj ilimitado(a), sin límites; **to be u.** no tener límite; **with u. mileage** *(hired car)* sin límite de kilometraje

unlisted [ʌn'lɪstɪd] adj (**a**) *Fin* **u. company** compañía f que no cotiza en bolsa; **u. securities** títulos mpl no cotizados (**b**) *(phone number)* que no figura en la guía (telefónica)

unlit [ʌn'lɪt] adj *(fire, cigarette)* sin encender, *Am* sin prender; *(place)* sin iluminar

unload [ʌn'ləʊd] **1** vt *(boat, gun, goods)* descargar; *Fig* **he always unloads his problems onto me** siempre me viene con sus problemas
    2 vi *(truck, ship)* descargar

unlock [ʌn'lɒk] vt *(door)* abrir; *Fig (mystery)* desvelar

unlovable [ʌn'lʌvəbəl] adj desagradable

unloved [ʌn'lʌvd] adj **to feel u.** no sentirse querido(a)

unlovely [ʌn'lʌvlɪ] adj poco atractivo(a), nada agraciado(a)

unlucky [ʌn'lʌkɪ] adj *(person)* sin suerte; *(coincidence)* desafortunado(a); *(day)* funesto(a), aciago(a); *(number, color)* que da mala suerte; **to be u.** *(have bad luck)* tener mala suerte; *(bring bad luck)* traer or dar mala suerte; **I was u. enough to miss the train** tuve la mala suerte de perder el tren

unmanageable [ʌn'mænɪdʒəbəl] adj *(person)* rebelde, díscolo(a); *(situation)* ingobernable; *(hair)* rebelde

unmanly [ʌn'mænlɪ] adj *(effeminate)* poco viril; *(cowardly)* pusilánime

unmanned [ʌn'mænd] adj *(spacecraft)* no tripulado(a)

unmarked [ʌn'mɑ:kt] adj (**a**) *(without scratches, cuts) (person)* incólume; *(object, surface)* inmaculado(a); *(police car)* camuflado(a) (**b**) *(uncorrected)* sin corregir

unmarried [ʌn'mærɪd] adj *(person)* soltero(a); **an u. couple** una pareja no casada, una pareja de hecho

unmask [ʌn'mɑ:sk] vt *(criminal)* desenmascarar; *(plot)* descubrir

unmentionable [ʌn'menʃənəbəl] **1** adj *(subject)* vedado(a), innombrable
    2 unmentionables npl *(underwear)* calzoncillos mpl

unmistakable [ʌnmɪs'teɪkəbəl] adj inconfundible

unmistakably [ʌnmɪs'teɪkəblɪ] adv indudablemente, sin lugar a dudas

unmitigated [ʌn'mɪtɪgeɪtɪd] adj *(support, disaster)* completo(a), absoluto(a)

unmoved [ʌn'mu:vd] **1** adj **she was u. by his appeal** su llamamiento no logró conmoverla
    2 adv **to watch/listen u.** observar/escuchar impertérrito(a)

unnamed [ʌn'neɪmd] adj no mencionado(a)

unnatural [ʌn'nætʃərəl] adj (**a**) *(abnormal)* anormal, antinatural; **it's u. to...** no es normal... (**b**) *(affected)* afectado(a)

unnaturally [ʌn'nætʃərəlɪ] adv (**a**) *(abnormally)* anormalmente (**b**) *(affectedly)* con poca naturalidad

unnecessarily [ʌnnesɪ'serɪlɪ] adv innecesariamente; **we don't want to worry them u.** no queremos preocuparles sin necesidad

unnecessary [ʌn'nesɪsərɪ] adj innecesario(a)

unnerve [ʌn'nɜ:v] vt poner nervioso(a), desconcertar

unnerving [ʌn'nɜ:vɪŋ] adj desconcertante

unnoticed [ʌn'nəʊtɪst] **1** adj inadvertido(a)
    2 adv **to pass** or **go u.** pasar desapercibido(a) or inadvertido(a)

unobservant [ʌnəb'zɜ:vənt] *adj* **to be u.** ser poco observador(ora)

unobserved [ʌnəb'zɜ:vd] *adv* **to do sth u.** hacer algo sin ser visto(a)

unobstructed [ʌnəb'strʌktɪd] *adj (exit, view)* despejado(a)

unobtainable [ʌnəb'teɪnəbəl] *adj* **to be u.** no poderse obtener, ser inasequible; *(on phone)* no estar disponible

unobtrusive [ʌnəb'tru:sɪv] *adj* discreto(a)

unoccupied [ʌn'ɒkjʊpaɪd] *adj (seat)* libre; *(house, person)* desocupado(a)

unofficial [ʌnə'fɪʃəl] *adj* extraoficial; **to be u.** no ser oficial; **in an u. capacity** extraoficialmente, de forma oficiosa; *Ind* **u. strike** huelga *f* no apoyada por los sindicatos

unofficially [ʌnə'fɪʃəlɪ] *adv* extraoficialmente, de forma no oficial

unopened [ʌn'əʊpənd] *adj* sin abrir

unopposed [ʌnə'pəʊzd] **1** *adj* **to be u.** no tener oposición
   2 *adv* **to go u.** no encontrar oposición

unorthodox [ʌn'ɔ:θədɒks] *adj* poco ortodoxo(a)

unpack [ʌn'pæk] **1** *vt (suitcase)* deshacer, *Am* desempacar; *(box, contents)* desembalar
   2 *vi* deshacer el equipaje

unpaid [ʌn'peɪd] *adj* **(a)** *(work, volunteer)* no retribuido(a) **(b)** *(bill, debt)* impagado(a)

unpalatable [ʌn'pælətəbəl] *adj (food)* intragable; *Fig (truth)* desagradable, crudo(a)

unparalleled [ʌn'pærəleld] *adj (growth, decline)* sin precedentes; *(success)* sin igual; **a place of u. beauty** un lugar de una belleza incomparable

unpardonable [ʌn'pɑ:dənəbəl] *adj* imperdonable

unpatriotic [ʌnpeɪtrɪ'ɒtɪk] *adj* antipatriótico(a)

unperturbed [ʌnpə'tɜ:bd] **1** *adj* **to be u. by sth** no ser afectado(a) por algo
   2 *adv* **to remain u.** permanecer impasible

unplanned [ʌn'plænd] *adj* espontáneo(a); *(result, visit)* imprevisto(a); **an u. pregnancy** un embarazo no planeado

unpleasant [ʌn'plezənt] *adj* desagradable

unpleasantly [ʌn'plezəntlɪ] *adv* desagradablemente

unpleasantness [ʌn'plezəntnɪs] *n* **the u. of...** lo desagradable de...; **to cause u.** provocar mal ambiente

unplug [ʌn'plʌg] *(pt & pp* **unplugged***) vt* desenchufar

unplugged [ʌn'plʌgd] *adj Mus* desenchufado(a), acústico(a)

unpolished [ʌn'pɒlɪʃt] *adj (shoes, surface)* deslustrado(a); *Fig (performance)* deslucido(a); *(style)* tosco(a)

unpolluted [ʌnpə'lu:tɪd] *adj* no contaminado(a), limpio(a)

unpopular [ʌn'pɒpjʊlə(r)] *adj (politician, decision)* impopular; **he was u. with his colleagues** sus compañeros no le tenían mucho aprecio

unpopularity [ʌnpɒpjʊ'lærɪtɪ] *n* impopularidad *f*

unprecedented [ʌn'presɪdentɪd] *adj* sin precedente(s)

unpredictable [ʌnprɪ'dɪktəbəl] *adj* imprevisible, impredecible

unpredictably [ʌnprə'dɪktəblɪ] *adv* de manera imprevisible *or* impredecible

unprejudiced [ʌn'predʒʊdɪst] *adj (view, person)* libre de prejuicios; **to be u.** no tener prejuicios

unprepared [ʌnprɪ'peəd] *adj (speech)* improvisado(a); **to be u. for sth** *(person)* no estar preparado(a) para algo

unprepossessing [ʌnpri:pə'zesɪŋ] *adj* poco atractivo(a)

unpresentable [ʌnprɪ'zentəbəl] *adj* impresentable

unpretentious [ʌnprɪ'tenʃəs] *adj* modesto(a), sencillo(a)

unprincipled [ʌn'prɪnsɪpəld] *adj* sin principios; **to be u.** no tener principios

unprintable [ʌn'prɪntəbəl] *adj (offensive)* impublicable

unproductive [ʌnprə'dʌktɪv] *adj (land, work)* improductivo(a); *(meeting, conversation, effort)* infructuoso(a)

unprofessional [ʌnprə'feʃənəl] *adj* poco profesional

unprofitable [ʌn'prɒfɪtəbəl] *adj (company)* poco rentable *(meeting)* infructuoso(a), poco productivo(a)

unpromising [ʌn'prɒmɪsɪŋ] *adj* poco prometedor(ora)

unpronounceable [ʌnprə'naʊnsəbəl] *adj* impronunciable

unprotected [ʌnprə'tektɪd] *adj* desprotegido(a)

unprovoked [ʌnprə'vəʊkt] *adj* espontáneo(a), no provoca do(a)

unpublished [ʌn'pʌblɪʃt] *adj* inédito(a)

unpunished [ʌn'pʌnɪʃt] **1** *adj* impune
   2 *adv* **to go u.** quedar impune

unputdownable [ʌnpʊt'daʊnəbəl] *adj Fam (book)* absor bente, que se lee de una sentada

unqualified [ʌn'kwɒlɪfaɪd] *adj* **(a)** *(doctor, teacher)* sir titulación; **I'm quite u. to talk about it** no estoy cualifica do para hablar de ello **(b)** *(support, disaster)* completo(a) absoluto(a)

unquestionable [ʌn'kwestʃənəbəl] *adj* indiscutible, indu dable

unquestionably [ʌn'kwestʃənəblɪ] *adv* indiscutiblemente indudablemente

unquestioning [ʌn'kwestʃənɪŋ] *adj (trust, obedience)* cie go(a); *(support)* incondicional

unravel [ʌn'rævəl] **1** *vt (wool)* deshacer; *Fig (plot, mystery* desentrañar
   2 *vi (wool)* deshacerse; *Fig (plan)* desbaratarse; *Fig (mystery* desentrañarse

unreadable [ʌn'ri:dəbəl] *adj* ilegible

unreal [ʌn'rɪəl] *adj* irreal

unrealistic [ʌnrɪə'lɪstɪk] *adj* poco realista

unreasonable [ʌn'ri:zənəbəl] *adj (person)* poco razonable irrazonable; *(demand)* absurdo(a), disparatado(a); *(price* exorbitante, desorbitado(a)

unreasonably [ʌn'ri:zənəblɪ] *adv (to behave)* de forma poco razonable; *(to demand)* de forma absurda; **not u.** no sin razón

unrecognizable [ʌnrekəg'naɪzəbl] *adj* irreconocible

unrecognized [ʌn'rekəgnaɪzd] **1** *adj (talent, government)* ne reconocido(a)
   2 *adv* **to go u.** *(talent, famous person)* pasar desapercibido(a)

unrecorded [ʌnrɪ'kɔ:dɪd] *adj* no registrado(a)

unrefined [ʌnrɪ'faɪnd] *adj* **(a)** *(sugar, gas)* sin refinar **(b** *(person, taste)* poco refinado(a)

unregistered [ʌn'redʒɪstəd] *adj (worker, immigrant)* sir papeles; *(voter)* no inscrito(a)

unrelated [ʌnrɪ'leɪtɪd] *adj* **(a)** *(events)* inconexo(a) **(b)** *(people* no emparentado(a)

unrelenting [ʌnrɪ'lentɪŋ] *adj* implacable

unreliability ['ʌnrɪlaɪə'bɪlətɪ] *n (of method, machine, statistics* falta *f* de fiabilidad; *(of person)* informalidad *f*

unreliable [ʌnrɪ'laɪəbəl] *adj (method, machine)* poco fiable *(statistics)* poco fidedigno(a), poco fiable; *(person)* informal

unrelieved [ʌnrɪ'li:vd] *adj (boredom, ugliness)* absoluto; *(pain* sin alivio

unremarkable [ʌnrɪ'mɑ:kəbəl] *adj* corriente

unremitting [ʌnrɪ'mɪtɪŋ] *adj* incesante, continuo(a)

unrepentant [ʌnrɪ'pentənt] *adj* impenitente; **to be u about** no arrepentirse de

unreported [ʌnrɪ'pɔ:tɪd] **1** *adj* **an u. incident/problem** ur incidente/problema del que no se ha informado *or CAm, Mé* reportado
   2 *adv* **many crimes go u.** muchos delitos no se denuncia *or CAm, Méx* reportan

unrepresentative [ʌnreprɪ'zentətɪv] *adj* no representati vo(a)

unrepresented [ʌnreprɪ'zentɪd] *adj* no representado(a), si representación

unrequited love [ˌʌnrɪkwaɪtɪd'lʌv] *n* amor *m* no correspondido

unreserved [ˌʌnrɪ'zɜːvd] *adj* (**a**) *(praise, support)* sin reservas (**b**) *(seat, table)* libre, no reservado(a)

unreservedly [ˌʌnrɪ'zɜːvɪdlɪ] *adv (to praise, support)* sin reservas; *(to apologize)* profusamente

unresponsive [ˌʌnrɪ'spɒnsɪv] *adj* indiferente (**to** ante); **the patient was u. to the treatment** el paciente no respondió al tratamiento

unrest [ʌn'rest] *n (unease)* malestar *m*; *(disturbances)* desórdenes *mpl*, disturbios *mpl*; *(in labor relations)* conflictividad *f*

unrestricted [ˌʌnrɪ'strɪktɪd] *adj* ilimitado(a), absoluto(a)

unrewarding [ˌʌnrɪ'wɔːdɪŋ] *adj (financially)* poco rentable; *(intellectually)* ingrato(a), poco gratificante

unripe [ʌn'raɪp] *adj* verde; **to be u.** estar verde

unrivaled [ʌn'raɪvəld] *adj (person, brilliance, beauty)* incomparable; **to be u.** ser inigualable

unroll [ʌn'rəʊl] *vt* desenrollar

unromantic [ˌʌnrə'mæntɪk] *adj* poco romántico(a)

unruffled [ʌn'rʌfəld] *adj* sereno(a), imperturbable

unruly [ʌn'ruːlɪ] *adj (hair)* rebelde; *(children, mob, behavior)* revoltoso(a)

unsaddle [ʌn'sædəl] *vt (horse)* desensillar

unsafe [ʌn'seɪf] *adj* (**a**) *(dangerous)* peligroso(a) (**b**) *(at risk)* inseguro(a), en peligro

unsaid [ʌn'sed] *adj* **to leave sth u.** no decir algo; **it's better left u.** mejor no decirlo

unsalted [ʌn'sɔːltɪd] *adj* sin sal

unsatisfactory [ˌʌnsætɪs'fæktərɪ] *adj* insatisfactorio(a)

unsatisfied [ʌn'sætɪsfaɪd] *adj* insatisfecho(a)

unsatisfying [ʌn'sætɪsfaɪɪŋ] *adj (explanation)* insatisfactorio(a); *(ending, meal)* decepcionante; *(experience)* poco gratificante

unsavory [ʌn'seɪvərɪ] *adj (person, reputation)* indeseable

unscathed [ʌn'skeɪðd] *adj* ileso(a)

unscheduled [ʌn'skedjuːld] *adj* no programado(a), imprevisto(a)

unscientific [ˌʌnsaɪən'tɪfɪk] *adj* poco científico(a)

unscramble [ʌn'skræmbəl] *vt* descifrar

unscrew [ʌn'skruː] **1** *vt* desatornillar
2 *vi* desatornillarse

unscrupulous [ʌn'skruːpjʊləs] *adj* poco escrupuloso(a)

unscrupulously [ʌn'skruːpjʊləslɪ] *adv* sin escrúpulos

unseat [ʌn'siːt] *vt also Fig* derribar

unseemly [ʌn'siːmlɪ] *adj* indigno(a)

unseen [ʌn'siːn] *adj* invisible; **u. by the guards** sin ser visto por los guardias

unselfconscious [ˌʌnself'kɒnʃəs] *adj* natural

unselfish [ʌn'selfɪʃ] *adj* desinteresado(a), generoso(a)

unsentimental [ˌʌnsentɪ'mentəl] *adj* desapasionado(a)

unsettle [ʌn'setəl] *vt (make nervous)* desasosegar, intranquilizar

unsettled [ʌn'setəld] *adj* (**a**) *(restless)* inquieto(a) (**b**) *(unresolved)* sin resolver (**c**) *(unpaid)* sin pagar

unshak(e)able [ʌn'ʃeɪkəbəl] *adj (belief, determination)* inquebrantable

unsightly [ʌn'saɪtlɪ] *adj* feo(a), horrible

unsigned [ʌn'saɪnd] *adj (contract)* sin firmar; *(band)* sin contrato

unskilled [ʌn'skɪld] *adj (worker)* no cualificado(a); **he is u. at such work** se le da mal ese tipo de trabajos

unskillful [ʌn'skɪlfʊl] *adj* torpe, desmañado(a)

unsociable [ʌn'səʊʃəbəl] *adj* insociable

unsold [ʌn'səʊld] *adj* sin vender

unsolicited [ˌʌnsə'lɪsɪtɪd] *adj* no solicitado(a); **the advice was u.** nadie había pedido ese consejo

unsolved [ʌn'sɒlvd] *adj* sin resolver

unsophisticated [ˌʌnsə'fɪstɪkeɪtɪd] *adj* sencillo(a), simple

unsound [ʌn'saʊnd] *adj* (**a**) *(health)* frágil; *Law* **to be of u. mind** no estar en plena posesión de las facultades mentales (**b**) *(decision, advice)* desacertado(a); *Fin (investment)* poco seguro(a)

unsparing [ʌn'speərɪŋ] *adj* **to be u. of one's time/in one's efforts** no escatimar tiempo/esfuerzo

unspeakable [ʌn'spiːkəbəl] *adj (conditions, squalor)* inefable; *(pain)* indecible

unspecified [ʌn'spesɪfaɪd] *adj* sin especificar

unspoiled [ʌn'spɔɪld], **unspoilt** [ʌn'spɔɪlt] *adj* intacto(a)

unspoken [ʌn'spəʊkən] *adj (fear)* oculto(a), no expresado(a); *(threat)* velado(a); *(agreement)* tácito(a)

unsporting [ʌn'spɔːtɪŋ], **unsportsmanlike** [ʌn'spɔːtsmənlaɪk] *adj* antideportivo(a)

unstable [ʌn'steɪbəl] *adj (structure, government)* inestable

unsteadily [ʌn'stedɪlɪ] *adv (to move, walk)* con paso inseguro; *(to speak)* con voz temblorosa

unsteady [ʌn'stedɪ] *adj (table, chair)* inestable, inseguro(a); *(hand, voice)* tembloroso(a); **he was u. on his feet** se tambaleaba

unstinting [ʌn'stɪntɪŋ] *adj (praise, effort)* generoso(a), pródigo(a); **to be u. in one's praise (of sb/sth)** no escatimar elogios (a alguien/algo)

unstressed [ʌn'strest] *adj Ling* no acentuado(a), sin acento

unsubstantiated [ˌʌnsəb'stænʃɪeɪtɪd] *adj (accusation, rumor)* no probado(a)

unsuccessful [ˌʌnsək'sesfʊl] *adj (person)* fracasado(a); *(attempt, project)* fallido(a); **to be u.** *(person, project)* no tener éxito

unsuccessfully [ˌʌnsək'sesfəlɪ] *adv* sin éxito

unsuitable [ʌn's(j)uːtəbəl] *adj (arrangement, behavior, climate)* inadecuado(a), inapropiado(a) (**for** para); *(time)* inoportuno(a) (**for** para); **he's u. for the job** no es la persona adecuada *or* apropiada para el trabajo; **this movie is u. for children** esta película no es apta para menores

unsuitably [ʌn's(j)uːtəblɪ] *adv* inadecuadamente

unsuited [ʌn'suːtɪd] *adj* **to be u. to sth** ser poco indicado(a) para algo

unsupported [ˌʌnsə'pɔːtɪd] *adj* (**a**) *(statement, charges)* infundado(a) (**b**) *(structure)* **to be u.** no tener apoyo

unsure [ʌn'ʃʊə(r)] *adj* inseguro(a); **to be u. of** *or* **about sth** tener dudas acerca de algo

unsurpassed [ˌʌnsə'pɑːst] *adj* sin igual, insuperable; **to be u.** ser insuperable

unsurprisingly [ˌʌnsə'praɪzɪŋlɪ] *adv* **u., this suggestion was rejected** lógicamente *or* como era de esperar, la sugerencia fue rechazada

unsuspected [ˌʌnsəs'pektɪd] *adj* insospechado(a); **her treason was u. by her superiors** sus superiores nunca sospecharon de su traición

unsuspecting [ˌʌnsəs'pektɪŋ] *adj* confiado(a)

unsweetened [ʌn'swiːtnd] *adj (without sugar)* sin azúcar; *(without sweeteners)* sin edulcorantes

unswerving [ʌn'swɜːvɪŋ] *adj* inquebrantable

unsympathetic [ˌʌnsɪmpə'θetɪk] *adj* poco comprensivo(a) (**to** con); **they are u. to such requests** suelen rechazar ese tipo de peticiones

unsympathetically [ˌʌnsɪmpə'θetɪklɪ] *adv (to speak, behave, react)* de forma poco comprensiva

unsystematic [ˌʌnsɪstə'mætɪk] *adj* poco sistemático(a)

untainted [ʌn'teɪntɪd] *adj* impoluto(a); **u. by corruption** sin mancha de corrupción

untalented [ʌn'tæləntɪd] *adj* sin talento

untamed [ʌn'teɪmd] *adj (animal)* salvaje

untangle [ʌnˈtæŋgəl] *vt* desenredar, desenmarañar

untapped [ʌnˈtæpt] *adj* sin explotar

untenable [ʌnˈtenəbəl] *adj* insostenible

untested [ʌnˈtestɪd] *adj* **to be u.** no haber sido puesto(a) a prueba

unthinkable [ʌnˈθɪŋkəbəl] *adj* impensable

unthought-of [ʌnˈθɔːtɒv] *adj* **an u. possibility** una posibilidad en la que no se había pensado

untidiness [ʌnˈtaɪdɪnɪs] *n* desorden *m*

untidy [ʌnˈtaɪdɪ] *adj* *(person, place)* desordenado(a); **to be u.** *(place)* estar desordenado(a)

untie [ʌnˈtaɪ] *vt* desatar; **to u. a knot** desatar *or* deshacer un nudo

until [ʌnˈtɪl] **1** *prep* hasta; **u. ten o'clock** hasta las diez; **u. now** hasta ahora; **not u. tomorrow** hasta mañana, no
2 *conj* hasta que; **u. she gets back** hasta que vuelva; **we waited u. the rain stopped** esperamos a que escampara, **he won't come u. he's invited** no vendrá mientras no lo invitemos

untimely [ʌnˈtaɪmlɪ] *adj* inoportuno(a); *(death)* prematuro(a)

untiring [ʌnˈtaɪərɪŋ] *adj* incansable

untitled [ˈʌnˈtaɪtəld] *adj (painting)* sin título

untold [ʌnˈtəʊld] *adj (wealth, beauty)* inconmensurable

untouchable [ʌnˈtʌtʃəbəl] *n & adj* intocable *mf*

untouched [ʌnˈtʌtʃt] *adj* intacto(a); **u. by human hand** no tocado(a) por la mano del hombre; **he left the meal u.** dejó la comida intacta

untoward [ʌntəˈwɔːd] *adj (unlucky)* desafortunado(a); *(unusual)* inusual, fuera de lo común

untrained [ʌnˈtreɪnd] *adj (person)* sin preparación; *(animal)* sin adiestrar

untranslatable [ʌntrænsˈleɪtəbəl] *adj* intraducible

untried [ʌnˈtraɪd] *adj* **(a) to be u.** *(system, person)* no haber sido puesto(a) a prueba **(b)** *Law (person, case)* pendiente de juicio

untroubled [ʌnˈtrʌbəld] *adj* tranquilo(a), despreocupado(a); **to be u. (by)** no estar afectado(a) (por)

untrue [ʌnˈtruː] *adj* **(a)** *(false)* falso(a) **(b)** *(unfaithful)* desleal **(to** a)

untrustworthy [ʌnˈtrʌstwɜːðɪ] *adj (person)* indigno(a) de confianza; *(information)* poco fiable

untruth [ʌnˈtruːθ] *n* falsedad *f*

untruthful [ʌnˈtruːθfʊl] *adj (person)* embustero(a), mentiroso(a); *(story, reply)* falso(a)

unusable [ʌnˈjuːzəbəl] *adj* inutilizable, inservible

unused [ʌnˈjuːzd] *adj* **(a)** *(not in use)* sin usar **(b)** *(never yet used)* sin estrenar **(c)** [ʌnˈjuːst] **to be u. to sth** no estar acostumbrado(a) a algo

unusual [ʌnˈjuːʒʊəl] *adj (not common)* inusual; *(strange)* extraño; **it's not u. for him to take two hours for lunch** no es nada raro que tarde dos horas en almorzar; **it's u. of her not to notice** es raro que no se dé cuenta

unusually [ʌnˈjuːʒʊəlɪ] *adv (abnormally)* insólitamente; *(very)* extraordinariamente

unvaried [ʌnˈveərɪd] *adj* monótono(a), uniforme

unvarnished [ʌnˈvɑːnɪʃt] *adj* sin barnizar; *Fig* **the u. truth** la verdad desnuda

unveil [ʌnˈveɪl] *vt (statue, plaque)* descubrir; *Fig (product, plan)* revelar, desvelar

unverifiable [ʌnˈverɪfaɪəbəl] *adj* inverificable

unvoiced [ʌnˈvɔɪst] *adj* **(a)** *Ling* sordo(a) **(b)** *(unspoken)* no expresado(a); **an u. fear** un temor oculto

unwanted [ʌnˈwɒntɪd] *adj (attentions, responsibility, baby)* no deseado(a); *(clothes, trinkets)* desechado(a)

unwarranted [ʌnˈwɒrəntɪd] *adj* injustificado(a)

unwary [ʌnˈweərɪ] *adj* incauto(a)

unwavering [ʌnˈweɪvərɪŋ] *adj (loyalty, support)* inquebrantable; *(gaze)* fijo(a); *(concentration)* intenso(a)

unwelcome [ʌnˈwelkəm] *adj (visit, visitor)* inoportuno(a); *(news)* desagradable; **to make sb feel u.** hacer que alguien se sienta incómodo

unwell [ʌnˈwel] *adj* indispuesto(a), enfermo(a); **to be u.** estar indispuesto(a) *or* enfermo(a)

unwholesome [ʌnˈhəʊlsəm] *adj (food, climate)* insalubre

unwieldy [ʌnˈwiːldɪ] *adj (tool)* poco manejable; *(object)* aparatoso(a); *Fig (system)* aparatoso(a)

unwilling [ʌnˈwɪlɪŋ] *adj* reacio(a); **to be u. to do sth** ser reacio(a) a hacer algo

unwillingly [ʌnˈwɪlɪŋlɪ] *adv* de mala gana

unwillingness [ʌnˈwɪlɪŋnɪs] *n* mala gana *f*

unwind [ʌnˈwaɪnd] *(pt & pp* **unwound** [ʌnˈwaʊnd]) **1** *vt* desenrollar
2 *vi* **(a)** *(string, wool)* desenrollarse **(b)** *Fam (relax)* relajarse, desconectar

unwise [ʌnˈwaɪz] *adj* imprudente

unwisely [ʌnˈwaɪzlɪ] *adv* imprudentemente, con mal criterio

unwitting [ʌnˈwɪtɪŋ] *adj* involuntario(a)

unworkable [ʌnˈwɜːkəbəl] *adj* impracticable

unworthy [ʌnˈwɜːðɪ] *adj* indigno(a) (**of** de)

unwound [ʌnˈwaʊnd] *pt of* **unwind**

unwrap [ʌnˈræp] *(pt & pp* **unwrapped**) *vt* desenvolver

unwritten [ʌnˈrɪtən] *adj (language, law)* no escrito(a); *(agreement)* tácito(a), verbal

unyielding [ʌnˈjiːldɪŋ] *adj* inflexible

unzip [ʌnzɪp] *(pt & pp* **unzipped**) *vt* abrir la cremallera *or Am* el cierre de; *Comptr (file)* descomprimir; **to u. one's pants** bajarse la cremallera *or Am* el cierre de los pantalones

up [ʌp] **1** *adv* **(a)** *(with motion)* hacia arriba; **to come/go up** subir; **to put one's hand up** levantar la mano; **to go up north** ir hacia el norte; **to go up to sb** acercarse a alguien; **to put a poster up** pegar un cartel **(b)** *(with position)* arriba; **up here/there** aquí/allí arriba; **up above** arriba; **further up** más arriba; **the sun was up** ya había salido el sol; **prices are up** los precios han subido **(c)** *(ahead)* **to be one goal/five points up** ir ganando por *or* de un gol/cinco puntos
2 *prep* **(a)** *(with motion)* **to go up the stairs** subir las escaleras; **to walk up the street** caminar *or Esp* andar por la calle; **to climb up a hill** subir *or* escalar una colina; *Vulg* **up yours!** ¡vete a la mierda! **(b)** *(with position)* **up a tree/ladder** en lo alto de un árbol/una escalera; **she lives up the street from me** vive en mi misma calle; **to be up against sth** *(confronted with)* enfrentarse a algo
3 *adj* **(a)** *(out of bed)* **he isn't up** no está levantado; **I was up all night** pasé toda la noche levantado; **to be up and about** *(in morning)* estar levantado(a); *(after illness)* estar recuperado(a) **(b)** *Fam (wrong)* **what's up?** ¿qué pasa?; **what's up with you/him?** ¿qué te/le pasa?; **something's up** algo pasa *or* ocurre **(c)** *(finished)* **your time's up** se te ha terminado el tiempo; **the two weeks were nearly up** ya casi habían transcurrido las dos semanas **(d)** *(idioms)* **to be up and running** *(machine, project)* estar en marcha
4 *n Fam* **life's ups and downs** los altibajos de la vida; **to be on the up and up** *(honest)* ser *Esp* legal *or Am* recto(a)
5 *vt (pt & pp* **upped**) *Fam (price)* subir
6 *vi Fam* **to up and leave** *or* **go** *Esp* coger y marcharse, *Am* agarrar e irse
7 **up to** *prep* **(a)** *(until, as far as)* hasta; **up to now** hasta ahora; **up to $100 a week** hasta 100 dólares semanales; **up to the age of seven** hasta los siete años
(b) *(equal to)* **he's not up to the job** no está a la altura del puesto; **I don't feel up to it** no me siento en condiciones de hacerlo; *Fam* **it's not up to much** *(not very good)* no es gran cosa

(c) *(doing)* **what have you been up to?** ¿qué has estado haciendo?; **I'm sure he's up to something!** ¡estoy seguro de que prepara algo!; **what are the children up to?** ¿qué están tramando los niños?

(d) *(indicating responsibility, decision)* **it's up to you to do it** te corresponde a ti hacerlo; **it's up to you whether you tell her** depende de ti si se lo dices o no

up-and-coming [ˈʌpəndˈkʌmɪŋ] *adj* prometedor(ora)

upbeat [ˈʌpbiːt] *adj (optimistic)* optimista

upbraid [ʌpˈbreɪd] *vt* recriminar; **to u. sb for sth** recriminar algo a alguien

upbringing [ˈʌpbrɪŋɪŋ] *n* crianza *f*, educación *f*

update 1 *n* [ˈʌpdeɪt] actualización *f*
2 *vt* [ʌpˈdeɪt] actualizar; **to u. sb on sth** poner a alguien al corriente de algo

upend [ʌpˈend] *vt (turn upside down)* poner boca abajo; *(knock over)* derribar

up-front [ʌpˈfrʌnt] **1** *adj Fam (frank)* claro(a), franco(a)
2 *adv (to pay)* por adelantado

upgradable [ʌpˈgreɪdəbəl] *adj Comptr (hardware, system)* actualizable; *(memory)* ampliable

upgrade 1 *n* [ˈʌpgreɪd] *Comptr* actualización *f*
2 *vt* [ʌpˈgreɪd] *(improve)* modernizar; *(promote)* ascender

upheaval [ʌpˈhiːvəl] *n* trastorno *m*, conmoción *f*; **political u.** conmoción política; **emotional u.** trastornos *mpl* emocionales

upheld [ʌpˈheld] *pt & pp of* **uphold**

uphill [ˈʌphɪl] **1** *adj (road)* cuesta arriba; *Fig (struggle)* duro(a), arduo(a)
2 *adv* cuesta arriba

uphold [ʌpˈhəʊld] *(pt & pp* **upheld** [ʌpˈheld]) *vt (opinion, principle)* defender; *(decision)* apoyar, corroborar; **to u. the law** hacer respetar la ley

upholstered [ʌpˈhəʊlstəd] *adj* tapizado(a)

upholstery [ʌpˈhəʊlstərɪ] *n* tapicería *f*

upkeep [ˈʌpkiːp] *n* mantenimiento *m*

uplift 1 *n* [ˈʌplɪft] subida *f* de ánimo; **to give sth/sb an u.** animar algo/a alguien
2 [ʌpˈlɪft] *vt (emotionally)* animar, levantar el espíritu a

uplifting [ʌpˈlɪftɪŋ] *adj* estimulante

upload [ˈʌpləʊd] *vt Comptr* cargar, subir

upmarket [ˈʌpmɑːkɪt] *adj* de categoría

upon [əˈpɒn] *prep* en, sobre; **u. realizing what had happened…** al darse cuenta de lo ocurrido…; *Old-fashioned* **u. my word!** ¡caramba!

upper [ˈʌpə(r)] **1** *n (of shoe)* empeine *m*
2 *adj* superior; *Typ* **u. case** mayúsculas *fpl*; **u. class** clase *f* alta; **to gain the u. hand** tomar la delantera; **the U. House** la Cámara Alta; **u. limit** límite *m* superior, tope *m*

upper-class [ˈʌpəˈklɑːs] *adj* de clase alta

upper-crust [ʌpəˈkrʌst] *adj Fam (person, accent)* de clase alta

uppermost [ˈʌpəməʊst] *adj (in position)* superior; *Fig* **it was u. in my mind** era una cuestión prioritaria para mí

uppity [ˈʌpɪtɪ] *adj Fam* creído(a), engreído(a); **to get u.** darse aires

upright [ˈʌpraɪt] **1** *n (beam)* poste *m*, montante *m*
2 *adj* **(a)** *(vertical)* vertical, derecho(a); **u. piano** piano *m* vertical **(b)** *(honest)* honrado(a)
3 *adv* **to put/place sth u.** poner/colocar algo derecho

uprising [ʌpˈraɪzɪŋ] *n* levantamiento *m*

uproar [ˈʌprɔː(r)] *n (noise)* alboroto *m*; *(protest)* escándalo *m*, polémica *f*; **the meeting was in an u.** se armó un gran alboroto en la reunión

uproarious [ʌpˈrɔːrɪəs] *adj (noisy)* escandaloso(a); *(funny)* divertidísimo(a)

uproot [ʌpˈruːt] *vt* desarraigar

upscale [ˈʌpskeɪl] *adj (neighborhood, restaurant)* elegante

upset 1 *n* [ˈʌpset] *(disturbance)* trastorno *m*; *(surprise)* resultado *m* inesperado; **to have a stomach u.** tener el estómago mal
2 *vt* [ʌpˈset] *(pt & pp* **upset**) **(a)** *(liquid, container)* tirar, volcar **(b)** *(person)* disgustar; *(plans, schedule)* trastornar, alterar; **the least thing upsets him** se disgusta por cualquier cosa
3 *adj* [ʌpˈset] *(unhappy)* disgustado(a); **to be u. about sth** estar disgustado por algo; **to have an u. stomach** tener el estómago mal

upsetting [ʌpˈsetɪŋ] *adj* desagradable

upshot [ˈʌpʃɒt] *n* resultado *m*

upside down [ˈʌpsaɪdˈdaʊn] **1** *adj* al *or* del revés
2 *adv* **to hang u.** *(person, animal)* colgar cabeza abajo; **to turn sth u.** poner algo del revés; *Fig* poner algo patas arriba

upstage [ʌpˈsteɪdʒ] **1** *adv Theat (move)* hacia el fondo de la escena; **to be** *or* **stand u. of sb** estar en segundo plano respecto a alguien
2 *vt Theat & Fig* dejar en segundo plano

upstairs [ʌpˈsteəz] **1** *n* **the u.** el piso de arriba
2 *adv* arriba; **I ran u.** subí (al piso de) arriba corriendo
3 *adj* **u. neighbors** vecinos *mpl* de arriba

upstanding [ʌpˈstændɪŋ] *adj (honest)* honrado(a), recto(a)

upstart [ˈʌpstɑːt] *n* advenedizo(a) *m,f*

upstream [ˈʌpstriːm] *adv* río arriba

upsurge [ˈʌpsɜːdʒ] *n* aumento *m*, incremento *m*

upswing [ˈʌpswɪŋ] *n (improvement)* mejora *f*, alza *f*

uptake [ˈʌpteɪk] *n Fam* **to be quick/slow on the u.** ser/no ser muy espabilado(a)

uptight [ʌpˈtaɪt] *adj Fam (nervous)* tenso(a); *(straitlaced)* estrecho(a)

up-to-date [ʌptəˈdeɪt] *adj (news, information)* reciente, actual; *(method, approach)* moderno(a); **to bring sb u. (on sth)** poner a alguien al día (sobre algo)

upturn [ˈʌptɜːn] *n* mejora *f* (**in** de)

upturned [ˈʌptɜːnd] *adj (bucket, box) (face down)* boca abajo; *(on its side)* volcado(a); *(nose)* respingón(ona)

upward [ˈʌpwəd] **1** *adj* hacia arriba; **u. mobility** ascenso *m* en la escala social
2 *adv* = **upward(s)**

upward-compatible [ˈʌpwədkəmˈpætɪbəl] *adj Comptr* compatible con versiones posteriores

upwardly mobile [ˈʌpwədlɪˈməʊbaɪl] *adj* = que va ascendiendo en la escala social

upward(s) [ˈʌpwədz] *adv* hacia arriba; **to look u.** mirar hacia arriba; **from $100 u.** a partir de 100 dólares; **u. of** por encima de

Urals [ˈjʊərəlz] *npl* **the U.** los Urales

uranium [jʊˈreɪnɪəm] *n Chem* uranio *m*

Uranus [jʊˈreɪnəs, ˈjʊərənəs] *n (planet)* Urano

urban [ˈɜːbən] *adj* urbano(a); **u. legend** *or* **myth** leyenda *f* popular; **u. renewal** remodelación *f* urbana; **u. sprawl** aglomeración *f* urbana

urbane [ɜːˈbeɪn] *adj* cortés, comedido(a)

urbanization [ɜːbənaɪˈzeɪʃən] *n (process)* urbanización *f*

urchin [ˈɜːtʃɪn] *n (child)* pilluelo(a) *m,f*, golfillo(a) *m,f*

urethra [jʊˈriːθrə] *n Anat* uretra *f*

urge [ɜːdʒ] **1** *n* impulso *m*, deseo *m* irresistible; **to have** *or* **feel an u. to do sth** sentir la necesidad de hacer algo; **sexual urges** impulsos *mpl* sexuales
2 *vt* **(a)** *(encourage)* **to u. sb to do sth** instar a alguien a hacer algo **(b)** *(recommend)* rogar, pedir encarecidamente **(c)** *(goad, incite)* **he urged his men into battle** incitó a sus hombres a entrar en batalla; **to u. a horse forward** espolear a un caballo

▸**urge on** *vt sep* alentar, animar; **to u. sb on to do sth** animar a alguien a hacer algo

urgency [ˈɜːdʒənsɪ] *n* urgencia *f*; **it's a matter of u.** es muy urgente

urgent ['ɜːdʒənt] *adj* urgente; **to be in u. need of sth** necesitar algo urgentemente; **this is u.** es urgente

urgently ['ɜːdʒəntlɪ] *adv* urgentemente

urinal [jə'raɪnəl] *n* urinario *m*

urinary ['jʊərɪnərɪ] *adj Anat* urinario(a)

urinate ['jʊərɪneɪt] *vi* orinar

urine ['jʊərɪn] *n* orina *f*

urn [ɜːn] *n* urna *f*; **(coffee/tea) u.** = recipiente grande de metal con un grifo para el café/té

urology [jʊ'rɒlədʒɪ] *n Med* urología *f*

Uruguay ['jʊərəgwaɪ] *n* Uruguay

Uruguayan [jʊərə'gwaɪən] *n & adj* uruguayo(a) *m,f*

US [juː'es] **1** *n* (*abbr* **United States**) EE.UU. *mpl*
2 *adj* estadounidense

us [*stressed* ʌs, *unstressed* əs] *pron* (**a**) (*object*) nos; **she forgave our son but not** us perdonó a nuestro hijo, pero no a nosotros; **she gave us the book** nos dio el libro; **she gave it to us** nos lo dio (**b**) (*after preposition*) nosotros (**c**) (*as complement of verb* **to be**) nosotros; **it's us!** ¡somos nosotros!

USA [juːes'eɪ] *n* (**a**) (*abbr* **United States of America**) EE.UU. *mpl* (**b**) (*abbr* **United States Army**) ejército *m* de los Estados Unidos

usable, useable ['juːzəbəl] *adj* utilizable; **it's no longer u.** ya no sirve

USAF [juːeseɪ'ef] *n* (*abbr* **United States Air Force**) fuerzas *fpl* aéreas de los Estados Unidos

usage ['juːsɪdʒ] *n* (**a**) (*use*) & *Gram* uso *m* (**b**) (*custom*) uso *m*, costumbre *f*

USB [juːes'biː] *n Comptr* (*abbr* **Universal Serial Bus**) USB *m*

USCG [juːessiː'dʒiː] *n* (*abbr* **United States Coast Guard**) = guardacostas de los Estados Unidos

use 1 *n* [juːs] (**a**) (*utilization*) uso *m*, utilización *f*; **to make (good) u. of sth** hacer (buen) uso de algo; **to be in u.** estar en uso, usarse; **not to be in u., to be out of u.** (*method, site*) estar en desuso; **out of u.** (*sign*) no funciona; **directions** *or* **instructions for u.** instrucciones *fpl* de uso
 (**b**) (*ability, permission to use*) **she has full u. of her faculties** está en plena posesión de sus facultades; **to have the u. of the bathroom** poder usar el cuarto de baño (**c**) (*usefulness*) **to be of u.** ser útil; **can I be of any u. to you?** ¿te puedo ser útil en algo?; **it's not much u.** no sirve de mucho; *Fam* **he's no u.** es un inútil; **to have no u. for sth** no tener necesidad de algo; **it's no u. crying** llorar no sirve de nada; **it's no u., I can't do it!** ¡es inútil, no puedo hacerlo!; **what's the u. of worrying?** ¿de qué sirve preocuparse?
 2 *vt* [juːz] (**a**) (*utilize*) usar, utilizar; **to u. force/diplomacy** hacer uso de la fuerza/la diplomacia; **he used every means at his disposal** empleó todos los medios a su alcance; **u. your head!** ¡piensa un poco!; *Fam* **I could u. some sleep** no me vendría mal dormir un poco (**b**) (*exploit*) utilizar; **I feel I've been used** me siento utilizado (**c**) (*consume*) (*drugs*) consumir; (*gas, electricity*) funcionar con; **who has used all the coffee?** ¿quién ha gastado todo el café?
 3 *v aux* **used to** ['juːstə]

Como verbo auxiliar, aparece siempre en la forma **used to**. Se traduce al español por el verbo principal en pretérito imperfecto, o por el pretérito imperfecto de **soler** más infinitivo.

we used to live abroad antes vivíamos en el extranjero; **I used not to** *or* **didn't use to like him** antes no me caía bien; **I used to eat there a lot** solía comer allí muy a menudo; **things aren't what they used to be** las cosas ya no son lo que eran; **do you travel much? — I used to** ¿viajas mucho? — antes sí

▶**use up** *vt sep* (*food, fuel*) acabar; (*money, ideas*) agotar

useable = **usable**

used [juːzd] *adj* (**a**) (*secondhand*) usado(a); (*car, book*) usado(a), de ocasión (**b**) [juːst] (*accustomed*) **to be u. to (doing) sth** estar acostumbrado(a) a (hacer) algo; **to get u. to sth/sb** acostumbrarse a algo/alguien (**c**) (*exploited*) **to feel u.** sentirse utilizado(a) *or* manipulado(a)

useful ['juːsfʊl] *adj* útil; **to make oneself u.** ayudar

usefully ['juːsfəlɪ] *adv* (*profitably*) provechosamente

usefulness ['juːsfʊlnɪs] *n* utilidad *f*; **it has outlived its u.** ha dejado de ser útil

useless ['juːslɪs] *adj* (**a**) (*not useful*) inservible; **to be u.** (*system, method*) no servir para nada; **to be worse than u.** no servir de nada (**b**) (*incompetent*) **to be u. (at sth)** ser un/una inútil (para algo) (**c**) (*futile*) inútil

uselessly ['juːslɪslɪ] *adv* inútilmente

user ['juːzə(r)] *n* (*of road, dictionary, computer*) usuario(a) *m,f*; *Fam* (*of drugs*) consumidor(ora) *m,f*; *Comptr* **u. interface** interfaz *m or f* de usuario; *Comptr* **u. name** nombre *m* de usuario

user-friendly [juːzə'frendlɪ] *adj* (*gen*) & *Comptr* de fácil manejo

usher ['ʌʃə(r)] **1** *n* (*in court*) ujier *m*; (*in theater*) acomodador *m*; (*at wedding*) = persona encargada de indicar a los invitados dónde deben sentarse
 2 *vt* **to u. sb in** hacer pasar a alguien; **to u. sb out** acompañar a alguien afuera

usherette [ʌʃə'ret] *n* (*in theater*) acomodadora *f*

USMC [juːesem'siː] *n* (*abbr* **United States Marine Corps**) = cuerpo de infantería de marina de Estados Unidos

USN [juːes'en] *n* (*abbr* **United States Navy**) armada *f* estadounidense

USP [juːes'piː] *n Com* (*abbr* **unique selling point** *or* **proposition**) argumento *m* diferenciador

USS [juːes'es] *n Naut* (*abbr* **United States Ship**) = título que precede a los nombres de buques de la marina estado-unidense

USSR [juːeses'ɑː(r)] *n Formerly* (*abbr* **Union of Soviet Socialist Republics**) URSS *f*

usual ['juːʒʊəl] **1** *n Fam* (*in bar*) **the u.** lo de siempre
 2 *adj* habitual, acostumbrado(a); **at the u. time** a la hora de siempre; **you're not your u. cheery self today** hoy no estás tan alegre como de costumbre; **it's not u. for him to be this late** no suele llegar tan tarde; **earlier/later than u.** más pronto/tarde de lo normal; **as u.** como de costumbre

usually ['juːʒʊəlɪ] *adv* habitualmente, normalmente; **he was more than u. polite** estuvo más amable que de costumbre

usurer ['juːʒərə(r)] *n* usurero(a) *m,f*

usurp [juː'zɜːp] *vt* usurpar

usurper [jʊ'zɜːpə(r)] *n* usurpador(ora) *m,f*

usury ['juːʒʊrɪ] *n* usura *f*

utensil [juː'tensəl] *n* utensilio *m*; **kitchen utensils** utensilios *mpl* de cocina

uterus ['juːtərəs] *n Anat* útero *m*

utilitarian [juːtɪlɪ'teərɪən] **1** *n* (*in philosophy*) utilitarista *mf*
 2 *adj* (**a**) (*approach*) pragmático(a); (*design*) funcional, práctico(a) (**b**) (*in philosophy*) utilitarista

utilitarianism [juːtɪlɪ'teərɪənɪzəm] *n* utilitarismo *m*

utility [juː'tɪlɪtɪ] *n* (**a**) (*usefulness*) utilidad *f*; *Comptr* **u. program** utilidad *f*; **u. room** = cuarto utilizado para planchar, lavar, etc. (**b**) (**public) u.** servicio *m* público; **utilities** (*stocks, bonds*) acciones *fpl* en empresas públicas (**c**) **utilities** (*service charges*) servicio *m*

utilization [juːtɪlaɪ'zeɪʃən] *n* utilización *f*, empleo *m*

utilize ['juːtɪlaɪz] *vt* utilizar

utmost ['ʌtməʊst], **uttermost** ['ʌtəməʊst] **1** *n* **to the u.** al máximo; **she did her u. to persuade them** hizo todo lo que pudo para convencerlos
 2 *adj* (**a**) (*greatest*) sumo(a); **with the u. contempt** con el

mayor desprecio; **it is of the u. importance that...** es de suma importancia que...; **with the u. ease** con suma facilidad (**b**) *(furthest)* **the u. ends of the earth** los últimos confines de la tierra

utopia [juːˈtəʊpɪə] *n* utopía *f*

utopian [juːˈtəʊpɪən] *n & adj* utópico(a) *m,f*

utter[1] [ˈʌtə(r)] *adj* total, completo(a); **it's u. madness** es una auténtica locura; **the movie is u. rubbish** la película es una verdadera porquería

utter[2] *vt (cry)* lanzar, dar; *(word)* decir, pronunciar

utterance [ˈʌtərəns] *n (act)* pronunciación *f*, mención *f*; *(words spoken)* expresión *f*; **to give u. to sth** manifestar *or* expresar algo

utterly [ˈʌtəlɪ] *adv* completamente, totalmente

uttermost = utmost

U-turn [ˈjuːtɜːn] *n (in car)* cambio *m* de sentido; *Fig* giro *m* radical *or* de 180 grados; **to do a U.** *(in car)* cambiar de sentido

UV [juːˈviː] *adj Phys (abbr* **ultraviolet***)* ultravioleta; **UV rays** rayos *mpl* ultravioleta

uvula [ˈjuːvjələ] *n Anat* úvula *f*

Uzbekistan [ʊzbekɪˈstɑːn] *n* Uzbekistán

V

V, v [viː] *n* (**a**) *(letter)* V, v *f*; **V sign** *(for victory)* uve *f* de la victoria (**b**) *(abbr* **very**) muy (**c**) *(abbr* **versus**) contra (**d**) *(abbr* **verse**) *(pl* **vv**) versículo *m*

V *Elec (abbr* **volt**) V, voltio *m*; **240 V** 240 V

VA [viːˈeɪ] *n (abbr* **Veterans Administration**) = organismo estadounidense que se ocupa de los veteranos de guerra

vacancy [ˈveɪkənsɪ] *n* (**a**) *(position, job)* (puesto *m*) vacante *f*; **to fill a v.** cubrir una vacante (**b**) *(at hotel)* habitación *f* libre; **no vacancies** *(sign)* completo

vacant [ˈveɪkənt] *adj* (**a**) *(seat, space)* libre; *(job)* vacante; **to be v.** *(seat, space)* estar libre (**b**) *(expression, look)* vacío(a), inexpresivo(a)

vacantly [ˈveɪkəntlɪ] *adv (absentmindedly)* distraídamente

vacate [vəˈkeɪt] *vt (seat, apartment)* dejar libre; *(one's post)* dejar vacante

vacation [vəˈkeɪʃən] **1** *n* vacaciones *fpl*; **to take a v.** tomarse unas vacaciones
2 *vi* pasar las vacaciones; *(in summer)* veranear

vacationer [vəˈkeɪʃənə(r)] *n* turista *mf*; *(in summer)* veraneante *mf*

vaccinate [ˈvæksɪneɪt] *vt Med* vacunar

vaccination [væksɪˈneɪʃən] *n Med* vacunación *f*

vaccine [ˈvæksiːn] *n Med* vacuna *f*

vacillate [ˈvæsɪleɪt] *vi* vacilar, titubear (**between** entre)

vacuous [ˈvækjʊəs] *adj (remark, book, person)* vacuo(a), vacío(a); *(look, expression)* vacío(a), vago(a)

vacuum [ˈvækjʊm] **1** *n Phys* vacío *m*; **v. bottle** termo *m*; **v. cleaner** aspiradora *f*, aspirador *m*
2 *vt* pasar la aspiradora por

vacuum-packed [vækjʊmˈpækt] *adj* envasado(a) al vacío

vagabond [ˈvægəbɒnd] *n* vagabundo(a) *m,f*

vagary [ˈveɪgərɪ] *n* **the vagaries of...** los avatares *or* caprichos de...

vagina [vəˈdʒaɪnə] *n* vagina *f*

vaginal [vəˈdʒaɪnəl] *adj* vaginal

vagrancy [ˈveɪgrənsɪ] *n Law* vagabundeo *m*

vagrant [ˈveɪgrənt] *n* mendigo(a) *m,f*, vagabundo(a) *m,f*

vague [veɪg] *adj (idea, feeling)* vago(a); *(shape, outline)* vago(a), borroso(a); **I haven't the vaguest idea** no tengo ni la más remota idea; **he was rather v. about it** no precisó mucho; **to bear a v. resemblance to sth/sb** parecerse *or* recordar vagamente a algo/alguien

vaguely [ˈveɪglɪ] *adv* vagamente

vagueness [ˈveɪgnɪs] *n* vaguedad *f*

vain [veɪn] **1** *n* **in v.** en vano
2 *adj* (**a**) *(conceited)* vanidoso(a), vano(a) (**b**) *(hopeless)* vano(a)

vale [veɪl] *n Literary* valle *m*; *Fig* **v. of tears** valle de lágrimas

valence [ˈveɪləns] *n Chem* valencia *f*

Valencia [vəˈlensɪə] *n* Valencia

Valencian [vəˈlensɪən] *n & adj* valenciano(a) *m,f*

valentine [ˈvæləntaɪn] *n* **v. (card)** = tarjeta para el día de los enamorados; **V.'s Day** día *m* de San Valentín, día *m* de los enamorados

valet [ˈvæleɪ] *n* ayuda *m* de cámara; **v. parking** servicio *m* de aparcacoches

valiant [ˈvælɪənt] *adj Literary* valeroso(a)

valiantly [ˈvælɪəntlɪ] *adv* valerosamente

valid [ˈvælɪd] *adj* válido(a); **v. for six months** válido durante seis meses; **no longer v.** caducado(a)

validate [ˈvælɪdeɪt] *vt* validar

validation [vælɪˈdeɪʃən] *n* validación *f*

validity [vəˈlɪdɪtɪ] *n* validez *f*

valise [væˈliːz] *n (small suitcase)* maleta *f* de fin de semana

valley [ˈvælɪ] *(pl* **valleys**) *n* valle *m*

valor [ˈvælə(r)] *n Literary* valor *m*

valuable [ˈvæljʊəbəl] **1** *n* **valuables** objetos *mpl* de valor
2 *adj* valioso(a)

valuation [væljʊˈeɪʃən] *n* (**a**) *(act)* tasación *f* (**b**) *(price)* valoración *f*

value [ˈvæljuː] **1** *n* (**a**) *(worth)* valor *m*; **to be of v.** tener valor; **of great/little v.** muy/poco valioso(a); **of no v.** sin valor; **to be good/poor v. (for money)** tener buena/mala relación calidad-precio; **to set a v. on sth** poner precio a algo; **to the v. of...** hasta un valor de...; **to make a v. judgment** hacer un juicio de valor (**b**) *(principle)* **values** valores *mpl*
2 *vt* (**a**) *(evaluate)* valorar, tasar; **to get sth valued** pedir una valoración de algo (**b**) *(appreciate)* apreciar

valued [ˈvæljuːd] *adj (friend)* estimado(a), apreciado(a); *(contribution)* valioso(a)

valueless [ˈvæljʊlɪs] *adj* sin valor

valve [vælv] *n Anat & Tech* válvula *f*; *Mus* pistón *m*

vampire [ˈvæmpaɪə(r)] *n* vampiro *m*; **v. bat** vampiro *m*

van [væn] *n Aut* camioneta *f*, furgoneta *f*; **v. driver** conductor(ora) *m,f* de camioneta

Vancouver [vænˈkuːvə(r)] *n* Vancouver

vandal [ˈvændəl] *n* vándalo *m*, *Esp* gamberro(a) *m,f*

vandalism [ˈvændəlɪzəm] *n* vandalismo *m*, *Esp* gamberrismo *m*

vandalize [ˈvændəlaɪz] *vt* destrozar

vane [veɪn] *n (for indicating wind direction)* veleta *f*

vanguard [ˈvængɑːd] *n* vanguardia *f*; **to be in the v.** ir en vanguardia, estar a la vanguardia

vanilla [vəˈnɪlə] *n* vainilla *f*

vanish [ˈvænɪʃ] *vi* desaparecer; **to v. into thin air** esfumarse

vanishing [ˈvænɪʃɪŋ] *adj* **to do a v. act** *(disappear)* desaparecer; **v. point** punto *m* de fuga

vanity [ˈvænɪtɪ] *n* vanidad *f*; **v. case** bolsa *f* de aseo

vanquish [ˈvæŋkwɪʃ] *vt Literary* vencer, derrotar

vantage point [ˈvɑːntɪdʒ'pɔɪnt] *n* atalaya *f*; *Fig* posición *f* aventajada

Vanuatu [vænuːˈætuː] *n* Vanuatu

vapid [ˈvæpɪd] *adj* vacuo(a), insustancial

vapor [ˈveɪpə(r)] *n* vapor *m*; **v. trail** *(from plane)* estela *f*

vaporize ['veɪpəraɪz] **1** vt evaporar
    2 vi evaporarse

vaporizer ['veɪpəraɪzə(r)] n (**a**) (for water) vaporizador m; (for perfume) pulverizador m, vaporizador m (**b**) Med (inhaler) inhalador m

variable ['veərɪəbəl] **1** n variable f
    2 adj variable; Ind **v. costs** costes mpl variables

variance ['veərɪəns] n **to be at v. with sth/sb** discrepar de algo/alguien

variant ['veərɪənt] **1** n variante f
    2 adj alternativo(a); **v. spelling** variante f ortográfica

variation [veərɪ'eɪʃən] n variación f

varicose vein ['værɪkəʊs'veɪn] n Med variz f, vena f varicosa

varied ['veərɪːd] adj variado(a)

variety [və'raɪətɪ] n (**a**) (diversity) variedad f; **a v. of reasons** diversos motivos; Prov **v. is the spice of life** en la variedad está el gusto (**b**) (of plant) variedad f (**c**) Theat variedades fpl; **v. show** espectáculo m de variedades

various ['veərɪəs] adj (different) diversos(as), diferentes; (several) varios(as); **at v. times** en distintas ocasiones

variously ['veərɪəslɪ] adv **v. described as a hero or a bandit** descrito por unos como héroe y por otros como bandido

varnish ['vɑːnɪʃ] **1** n (for wood, oil painting) barniz m
    2 vt (wood) barnizar

varnish over vt sep Fig maquillar

vary ['veərɪ] **1** vt variar
    2 vi variar (**in** de); **opinions v.** hay diversas opiniones

varying ['veərɪɪŋ] adj diverso(a), variado(a)

vase [veɪs] n jarrón m

vasectomy [və'sektəmɪ] n Med vasectomía f

Vaseline® ['væsəliːn] n vaselina® f

vast [vɑːst] adj (area) vasto(a); (majority, number) inmenso(a)

vastly ['vɑːstlɪ] adv enormemente

vat [væt] n (container) tina f, cuba f

Vatican ['vætɪkən] n **the V.** el Vaticano; **V. City** Ciudad f del Vaticano

vaudeville ['vɔːdəvɪl] n Theat vodevil m

vault¹ [vɔːlt] n (**a**) Archit bóveda f (**b**) (cellar) sótano m; (for burial) cripta f; (of bank) cámara f acorazada, Am bóveda f de seguridad

vault² vt & vi saltar

vaulted ['vɔːltɪd] adj (ceiling) abovedado(a)

vaulting horse ['vɔːltɪŋ'hɔːs] n plinto m

vaunt [vɔːnt] vt cacarear; **his much vaunted reputation as...** su cacareada reputación de...

VC [viː'siː] n (abbr **Vice-Chairman**) vicepresidente(a) m,f

VCR [viːsiː'ɑː(r)] n (abbr **videocassette recorder**) (aparato m or reproductor m de) vídeo m or Am video m

VD [viː'diː] n (abbr **venereal disease**) enfermedad f venérea

VDU [viːdiː'juː] n Comptr (abbr **visual display unit**) monitor m

veal [viːl] n (carne f de) ternera f

vector ['vektə(r)] n Math & Med vector m

veer ['vɪə(r)] vi torcer, girar; **to v. to the left/right** torcer a la izquierda/derecha; Fig **the party has veered to the left** el partido ha dado un giro a la izquierda

veer around vi (wind) cambiar de dirección

vegan ['viːgən] n vegetariano(a) m,f estricto(a) (que no come ningún producto de origen animal)

vegeburger ['vedʒɪbɜːgə(r)] n hamburguesa f vegetariana

vegetable ['vedʒtəbəl] n (**a**) (plant) hortaliza f; **vegetables** verdura f, verduras fpl; **eat up your vegetables** cómete la verdura; **v. garden** huerto m; **v. oil** aceite m vegetal (**b**) (brain-damaged person) vegetal m

vegetarian [vedʒɪ'teərɪən] n & adj vegetariano(a) m,f

vegetate ['vedʒɪteɪt] vi vegetar

vegetation [vedʒɪ'teɪʃən] n vegetación f

vehemence ['viːɪməns] n vehemencia f

vehement ['viːɪmənt] adj vehemente

vehicle ['viːɪkəl] n also Fig vehículo m

vehicular [vɪ'hɪkjʊlə(r)] adj de vehículos; **v. traffic** tráfico m de vehículos

veil [veɪl] **1** n velo m; Fig **a v. of smoke** una cortina de humo; Fig **to draw a v. over sth** correr un tupido velo sobre algo; Fig **under a v. of secrecy** rodeado(a) de un halo de secreto or misterio
    2 vt cubrir con un velo; Fig **veiled in secrecy** rodeado(a) de un halo de secreto or misterio

veiled [veɪld] adj (**a**) (wearing veil) **to be v.** llevar velo (**b**) (threat, allusion) velado(a)

vein [veɪn] n (**a**) Anat vena f; (of leaf) nervio m (**b**) (in rock) filón m, veta f; (in wood, marble) veta f (**c**) (idioms) **in a lighter v.** en un tono más ligero; **in a similar v.** en la misma vena, en el mismo tono

Velcro® ['velkrəʊ] n velcro® m

vellum ['veləm] n pergamino m, vitela f; **v. (paper)** papel m pergamino

velocity [vɪ'lɒsɪtɪ] n velocidad f

velvet ['velvɪt] n terciopelo m; **v. jacket** chaqueta f de terciopelo

velveteen [velvɪ'tiːn] n pana f lisa

velvety ['velvɪtɪ] adj aterciopelado(a)

venal ['viːnəl] adj corrupto(a)

vendetta [ven'detə] n **to carry on a v. against sb** llevar a cabo una campaña para destruir a alguien

vending machine ['vendɪŋmə'ʃiːn] n máquina f expende-dora

vendor ['vendɔː(r)] n vendedor(ora) m,f

veneer [və'nɪə(r)] n laminado m, chapa f; Fig fachada f, pátina f

venerable ['venərəbəl] adj venerable

venerate ['venəreɪt] vt venerar

veneration [venə'reɪʃən] n veneración f

venereal [vɪ'nɪərɪəl] adj venéreo(a); **v. disease** enfermedad f venérea

Venetian [vɪ'niːʃən] **1** n veneciano(a) m,f
    2 adj veneciano(a); **V. blind** persiana f veneciana

Venezuela [vene'zweɪlə] n Venezuela

Venezuelan [vene'zweɪlən] n & adj venezolano(a) m,f

vengeance ['vendʒəns] n venganza f; **to take v. on sb** vengarse de alguien; Fig **the problem has returned with a v.** el problema se ha presentado de nuevo con agravantes

vengeful ['vendʒfʊl] adj vengativo(a)

venial ['viːnɪəl] adj (sin) venial; (error) leve

Venice ['venɪs] n Venecia

venison ['venɪsən] n (carne f de) venado m

venom ['venəm] n also Fig veneno m

venomous ['venəməs] adj venenoso(a); Fig (look, criticism) envenenado(a), ponzoñoso(a)

vent [vent] **1** n (orificio m de) ventilación f; Fig **she gave v. to her feelings** se desahogó, dio rienda suelta a sus sentimientos
    2 vt **she vented her anger on him** descargó su ira sobre él

ventilate ['ventɪleɪt] vt ventilar

ventilation [ventɪ'leɪʃən] n ventilación f

ventilator ['ventɪleɪtə(r)] n ventilador m

ventriloquism [ven'trɪləkwɪzəm] n ventriloquía f

ventriloquist [ven'trɪləkwɪst] n ventrílocuo(a) m,f; **v.'s dummy** muñeco m de ventrílocuo

venture ['ventʃə(r)] **1** n (undertaking) aventura f, iniciativa f; (in business) empresa f, operación f; Fin **v. capital** capital m de riesgo
    2 vt (stake) arriesgar; (comment) aventurar; **to v. to do sth**

aventurarse a hacer algo; *Prov* **nothing ventured, nothing gained** el que no se arriesga no pasa la mar

3 *vi* aventurarse

▶**venture on, venture upon** *vt insep* aventurarse en, meterse en

venue ['venjuː] *n (for meeting)* lugar *m; (for concert)* local *m,* sala *f; (for football, basketball, soccer game)* estadio *m*

Venus ['viːnəs] *n (goddess)* Venus *f; (planet)* Venus *m*

veracity [vəˈræsɪtɪ] *n Formal* veracidad *f*

veranda(h) [vəˈrændə] *n* porche *m,* galería *f*

verb [vɜːb] *n* verbo *m*

verbal ['vɜːbəl] *adj* verbal; **v. abuse** insultos *mpl*

verbalize ['vɜːbəlaɪz] *vt* expresar con palabras

verbally ['vɜːbəlɪ] *adv* de palabra

verbatim [vɜːˈbeɪtɪm] **1** *adj* literal

2 *adv* literalmente

verbiage ['vɜːbɪdʒ] *n* palabrería *f,* verborrea *f*

verbose [vɜːˈbəʊs] *adj* verboso(a), prolijo(a)

verbosity [vɜːˈbɒsɪtɪ] *n* verbosidad *f,* verborrea *f*

verdict ['vɜːdɪkt] *n Law & Fig* veredicto *m;* **to return a v. of guilty/not guilty** pronunciar un veredicto de culpabilidad/inocencia; **what's your v. on the play?** ¿qué te ha parecido la obra?

verge [vɜːdʒ] *n (edge)* borde *m,* margen *m; Fig* **on the v. of…** al borde de…; *Fig* **to be on the v. of doing sth** estar a punto de hacer algo

▶**verge on** *vt insep* rayar en; **verging on…** rayano(a) *or* rayando en; **she was verging on hysteria** estaba al borde de la histeria

verger ['vɜːdʒə(r)] *n (in Episcopal Church)* sacristán *m*

verifiable [verɪˈfaɪəbəl] *adj* verificable

verification [verɪfɪˈkeɪʃən] *n* verificación *f*

verify ['verɪfaɪ] *vt* verificar

verisimilitude [verɪsɪˈmɪlɪtjuːd] *n Formal* verosimilitud *f*

veritable ['verɪtəbəl] *adj Formal* verdadero(a)

vermilion [vəˈmɪljən] **1** *n* bermellón *m*

2 *adj* bermejo(a)

vermin ['vɜːmɪn] *npl (insects)* bichos *mpl,* sabandijas *fpl; (bigger animals)* alimañas *fpl; Fig (people)* escoria *f,* gentuza *f*

vermouth ['vɜːməθ] *n* vermú *m,* vermut *m*

vernacular [vəˈnækjʊlə(r)] **1** *n Ling* lengua *f* vernácula; *(spoken language)* lenguaje *m* de la calle; **in the local v.** en el habla local

2 *adj* vernáculo(a)

verruca [veˈruːkə] *n Med* verruga *f (especialmente en las plantas de los pies)*

versatile ['vɜːsətaɪl] *adj (person)* polifacético(a), versátil; *(object)* polivalente, versátil

versatility [vɜːsəˈtɪlɪtɪ] *n (of person)* carácter *m* polifacético, versatilidad *f; (of object)* polivalencia *f*

verse [vɜːs] *n (a) (poetry)* poesía *f,* verso *m (b) (stanza)* estrofa *f (c) (of Bible)* versículo *m*

versed [vɜːst] *adj* **to be v. in sth** estar versado(a) en algo

version ['vɜːʃən] *n* versión *f;* **the economy/deluxe v.** *(of car, computer)* el modelo económico/de lujo

verso ['vɜːsəʊ] *n Typ (of page)* verso *m*

versus ['vɜːsəs] *prep Law & Sport* contra

vertebra ['vɜːtɪbrə] *(pl* **vertebras** *or* **vertebrae** ['vɜːtɪbriː]*) n Anat* vértebra *f*

vertebral column ['vɜːtɪbrəl'kɒləm] *n Anat (spine)* columna *f* vertebral

vertebrate ['vɜːtɪbrɪt] *n & adj* vertebrado(a) *m,f*

vertex ['vɜːteks] *(pl* **vertexes** *or* **vertices** ['vɜːtɪsiːz]*) n Math* vértice *m*

vertical ['vɜːtɪkəl] *n & adj* vertical *f*

vertically ['vɜːtɪklɪ] *adv* verticalmente

vertices ['vɜːtɪsiːz] *pl of* **vertex**

vertigo ['vɜːtɪɡəʊ] *n Med* vértigo *m*

verve [vɜːv] *n* nervio *m,* energía *f*

very ['verɪ] **1** *adv (a) (extremely)* muy; **v. good/little** muy bueno/poco; **v. much** mucho; **it isn't v. difficult** no es muy difícil; **are you hungry? — yes, v.** ¿tienes hambre? — sí, mucha; *Rad* **v. high frequency** frecuencia *f* muy alta **(b)** *(emphatic use)* **the v. first/best** el primero/el mejor de todos; **at the v. most** como muy mucho; **at the v. least/latest** como muy poco/muy tarde; **the v. same day** justo ese mismo día; **I v. nearly died** estuve en un tris de morir; **the v. next day** precisamente el día siguiente

2 *adj (emphatic use)* **in this v. house** en esta misma casa; **this v. day** este mismo día; **those were his v. words** esas fueron sus palabras exactas; **at the v. beginning** al principio del todo; **the v. thought of it was enough to turn my stomach** sólo de pensarlo se me revolvía el estómago

vessel ['vesəl] *n (a) Naut* buque *m,* navío *m (b) (receptacle,* vasija *f,* recipiente *m (c) Anat* vaso *m*

vest [vest] *n* chaleco *m*

vested ['vestɪd] *adj* **to have a v. interest in sth/in doing sth** tener intereses creados en algo/en hacer algo

vestibule ['vestɪbjuːl] *n* vestíbulo *m*

vestige ['vestɪdʒ] *n* vestigio *m*

vestments ['vestmənts] *npl Rel* vestiduras *fpl (sacerdotales)*

vest-pocket ['vest'pɒkɪt] *adj (a) (book, camera, pistol)* de bolsillo **(b)** *(farm, park)* minúsculo(a)

vestry ['vestrɪ] *n Rel* sacristía *f*

vet¹ [vet] *n* veterinario(a) *m,f*

vet² *(pt & pp* **vetted***) vt (person)* someter a investigación, *(application)* investigar; *(speech, book, movie)* inspeccionar, examinar

vet³ *n Fam Mil (veteran)* excombatiente *mf,* veterano(a) *m,f*

veteran ['vetərən] **1** *n Mil* excombatiente *mf,* veterano(a) *m,f; Fig* veterano(a) *m,f*

2 *adj* veterano(a)

veterinarian [vetərɪˈneərɪən] *n* veterinario(a) *m,f*

veterinary ['vetərɪnərɪ] *adj* veterinario(a); **v. medicine** veterinaria *f*

veto ['viːtəʊ] **1** *n (pl* **vetoes***)* veto *m;* **right** *or* **power of v.** derecho *m* de veto; **to impose a v. on sth** vetar algo

2 *vt* vetar

vetting ['vetɪŋ] *n* investigación *f (del historial)* personal

vex [veks] *vt (annoy)* molestar, disgustar; *(anger) esp Esp* enfadar, *esp Am* enojar

vexation [vekˈseɪʃən] *n (annoyance)* disgusto *m,* molestia *f, (anger) esp Esp* enfado *m, esp Am* enojo *m*

vexatious [vekˈseɪʃəs] *adj Formal* molesto(a)

vexed [vekst] *adj (a) (annoyed)* molesto(a), disgustado(a), *(angry) esp Esp* enfadado(a), *esp Am* enojado(a) **(b)** *(much debated)* **a v. question** una cuestión controvertida

VHF [viːeɪtʃˈef] *adj Rad (abbr* **very high frequency***)* VHF *f*

VHS [viːeɪtʃˈes] *n TV (abbr* **video home system***)* VHS *m*

via ['vaɪə] *prep (travel)* vía; *(using)* a través de

viability [vaɪəˈbɪlɪtɪ] *n* viabilidad *f*

viable ['vaɪəbəl] *adj* viable

viaduct ['vaɪədʌkt] *n* viaducto *m*

Viagra® [vaɪˈæɡrə] *n* Viagra® *m or f*

vibes [vaɪbz] *npl Fam* vibraciones *fpl, Esp* rollo *m, Am* onda *f;* **good/bad v.** buen/mal rollo

vibrant ['vaɪbrənt] *adj (scene, city)* animado(a); *(colors)* vivo(a), brillante; *(personality)* pujante

vibrate [vaɪˈbreɪt] *vi* vibrar

vibration [vaɪˈbreɪʃən] *n* vibración *f*

vibrator [vaɪˈbreɪtə(r)] *n* vibrador *m*

vicar ['vɪkə(r)] *n (in Church of England)* párroco *m*

vicarage ['vɪkərɪdʒ] *n (in Episcopal Church)* casa *f* del párroco

vicarious [vɪ'keərɪəs] *adj* indirecto(a)

vicariously [vɪ'keərɪəslɪ] *adv* indirectamente

vice¹ [vaɪs] *n (immorality)* vicio *m*; **the V. Squad** la brigada antivicio

vice² *n (for wood or metalwork)* torno *m or* tornillo de banco

vice-chairman [vaɪs'tʃeəmən] *n* vicepresidente *m*

vice-chairwoman [vaɪs'tʃeəwʊmən] *n* vicepresidenta *f*

vice-president [vaɪs'prezɪdənt] *n* (a) *(of country)* vicepresidente(a) *m,f* (b) *Com (of company)* vicepresidente(a) *m,f*

viceroy ['vaɪsrɔɪ] *(pl* **viceroys**) *n* virrey *m*

vice versa [vaɪs'vɜːsə] *adv* viceversa

vicinity [vɪ'sɪnɪtɪ] *n* cercanías *fpl*, inmediaciones *fpl*; **in the v.** en las cercanías; **a sum in the v. of $25,000** una cantidad que ronda los 25.000 dólares

vicious ['vɪʃəs] *adj* (a) *(violent) (blow, kick, attack)* brutal; *(struggle, fight)* feroz; *(person)* cruel (b) *(malicious, cruel) (comment, criticism)* despiadado(a); *(gossip)* malintencionado(a); *(person)* cruel; **a v. circle** un círculo vicioso

viciously ['vɪʃəslɪ] *adv (to attack, kick)* brutalmente, con saña; *(to criticize)* despiadadamente; *(to gossip)* con mala intención

vicissitude [vɪ'sɪsɪtjuːd] *n Formal* vicisitud *f*

victim ['vɪktɪm] *n* víctima *f*; **to be the v. of** ser víctima de; **to fall v. to sb's charms** caer rendido(a) ante los encantos de alguien

victimization [vɪktɪmaɪ'zeɪʃən] *n* persecución *f*, trato *m* injusto

victimize ['vɪktɪmaɪz] *vt* perseguir, tratar injustamente; **he was victimized at school** en la escuela se metían con él

victor ['vɪktə(r)] *n* vencedor(ora) *m,f*

Victorian [vɪk'tɔːrɪən] *n & adj* victoriano(a) *m,f*

victorious [vɪk'tɔːrɪəs] *adj* victorioso(a); **to be v. over sb** triunfar sobre alguien

victory ['vɪktərɪ] *n* victoria *f*; **v. celebrations** celebración *f* de la victoria

victuals ['vɪtəlz] *npl Old-fashioned (food)* vituallas *fpl*

video ['vɪdɪəʊ] **1** *n (pl* **videos**) *(medium)* vídeo *m, Am* video *m*; *(cassette)* cinta *f* de vídeo; *(recorder)* (aparato *m* de) vídeo *m*; **to have sth on v.** tener algo (grabado) en vídeo; **v. camera** cámara *f* de vídeo; **v. clip** videoclip *m*, vídeo *m*; **v. recorder** (aparato *m* de) vídeo; **v. game** videojuego *m*

2 *vt* (a) *(record)* grabar (en vídeo *or Am* video) (b) *(movie)* hacer un vídeo *or Am* video de

videocassette ['vɪdɪəʊkə'set] *n* cinta *f* de vídeo *or Am* video; **v. recorder** (aparato *m or* reproductor *m* de) vídeo *m or Am* video *m*

videoconferencing ['vɪdɪəʊkɒnfrənsɪŋ] *n* videoconferencias *fpl*

videotape ['vɪdɪəʊteɪp] *n* cinta *f* de vídeo *or Am* video

vie [vaɪ] *(pt & pp* **vied** [vaɪd]) *vi* **to v. with sb (for sth/to do sth)** rivalizar con alguien (por algo/para hacer algo)

Vienna [vɪ'enə] *n* Viena

Viennese [vɪə'niːz] *n & adj* vienés(esa) *m,f*

Vietnam [vɪet'næm] *n* Vietnam; **the V. War** la guerra de Vietnam

Vietnamese [vɪetnə'miːz] **1** *n* (a) *(person)* vietnamita *mf* (b) *(language)* vietnamita *m*

2 *npl* **the V.** los vietnamitas

3 *adj* vietnamita

view [vjuː] **1** *n* (a) *(sight)* vista *f*; **in v.** a la vista; **in full v. of** delante de, a la vista de; **out of v.** fuera de la vista (b) *(scene, prospect)* vista *f*; **a room with a v.** una habitación con vistas; **to have a good v. of sth** tener una buena vista de algo; *Fig* **in v. of…** *(considering)* en vista de… (c) *(opinion)* opinión *f*; **in my v.** en mi opinión, a mi parecer (d) *(intention)* **with this in v.** teniendo esto en cuenta; **with a v. to doing sth** con vistas a hacer algo

2 *vt* (a) *(inspect, look at)* ver (b) *(consider)* ver, considerar; **she viewed it as a mistake** lo veía *or* consideraba un error; **to v. sth with horror/delight** contemplar algo con horror/placer

viewer ['vjuːə(r)] *n* (a) *TV* telespectador(ora) *m,f*, televidente *mf* (b) *Phot (for slides)* visor *m*

viewfinder ['vjuːfaɪndə(r)] *n Phot* visor *m*

viewing ['vjuːɪŋ] *n* (a) *(of movie, TV program)* **for home v.** para ver en casa; **this program is essential v.** no te debes/se debe perder este programa (b) *(of house)* visita *f*

viewpoint ['vjuːpɔɪnt] *n* punto *m* de vista

vigil ['vɪdʒɪl] *n* vigilia *f*; **to keep v.** observar vigilia

vigilance ['vɪdʒɪləns] *n* vigilancia *f*

vigilant ['vɪdʒɪlənt] *adj* alerta

vigilante [vɪdʒɪ'læntɪ] *n* miembro *m* de una patrulla de vecinos

vignette [vɪn'jet] *n Phot* viñeta *f*; *Fig (picture)* escena *f*; *(in writing)* retrato *m*, semblanza *f*

vigor ['vɪgə(r)] *n (of person)* vigor *m*; *(of denial, criticism)* rotundidad *f*, fuerza *f*

vigorous ['vɪgərəs] *adj* (a) *(strong and healthy)* vigoroso(a) (b) *(energetic)* enérgico(a); *(lifestyle)* dinámico(a); *(exercise)* intenso(a) (c) *(forceful)* fuerte

vigorously ['vɪgərəslɪ] *adv* enérgicamente

Viking ['vaɪkɪŋ] *n & adj* vikingo(a) *m,f*

vile [vaɪl] *adj (despicable)* vil; *Fam (awful)* horroroso(a), espantoso(a)

vilification [vɪlɪfɪ'keɪʃən] *n* vilipendio *m*

vilify ['vɪlɪfaɪ] *vt* vilipendiar, denigrar

villa ['vɪlə] *n (in country)* villa *f*

village ['vɪlɪdʒ] *n* pueblo *m*; *(smaller)* aldea *f*; **v. idiot** tonto(a) *m,f* del pueblo

villager ['vɪlɪdʒə(r)] *n* lugareño(a) *m,f*

villain ['vɪlən] *n (scoundrel)* canalla *mf*, villano(a) *m,f*; *Theat & Cin* malo *m*; *Hum* **the v. of the piece** el malo de la película

villainous ['vɪlənəs] *adj* vil, infame

villainy ['vɪlənɪ] *n* villanía *f*, infamia *f*

Vilnius ['vɪlnɪʌs] *n* Vilna, Vilnius

vindicate ['vɪndɪkeɪt] *vt (decision, action)* justificar; *(person)* dar la razón a

vindication [vɪndɪ'keɪʃən] *n (of decision, action)* justificación *f*; *(of person)* rehabilitación *f*

vindictive [vɪn'dɪktɪv] *adj* vengativo(a)

vindictively [vɪn'dɪktɪvlɪ] *adv* de un modo vengativo

vine [vaɪn] *n (in vineyard)* vid *f*; *(decorative)* parra *f*

vinegar ['vɪnɪgə(r)] *n* vinagre *m*

vineyard ['vɪnjəd] *n* viñedo *m*

vintage ['vɪntɪdʒ] *n (crop)* cosecha *f*; *Fig* **a v. year for comedy** un año excepcional en cuanto a comedias; **v. car** coche *m* antiguo *or* de época *(de entre 1919 y 1930)*; **v. wine** vino *m* de buena cosecha

vinyl ['vaɪnɪl] *n* vinilo *m*

viola [vɪ'əʊlə] *n* viola *f*

violate ['vaɪəleɪt] *vt (rule, law, agreement)* violar

violation [vaɪə'leɪʃən] *n (of rule, law, agreement)* violación *f*

violence ['vaɪələns] *n* violencia *f*

violent ['vaɪələnt] *adj* violento(a); **to take a v. dislike to sb** tomar *or Esp* coger una enorme antipatía a alguien

violently ['vaɪələntlɪ] *adv* violentamente; **to be v. ill** vomitar muchísimo

violet ['vaɪələt] **1** *n (plant)* violeta *f*; *(color)* violeta *m*

2 *adj* **v.(-colored)** (de color) violeta

violin [vaɪə'lɪn] *n* violín *m*

violinist [vaɪə'lɪnɪst] *n* violinista *mf*

VIP [viːaɪ'piː] *n (abbr* **very important person**) VIP *mf*; **V. lounge** sala *f* VIP; **to get V. treatment** recibir tratamiento de persona importante

viper ['vaɪpə(r)] *n* víbora *f*

viral ['vaɪrəl] *adj Med* vírico(a), viral

virgin ['vɜːdʒɪn] **1** *n* virgen *mf*; **the (Blessed) V.** la (Santísima) Virgen; **the V. Islands** las Islas Vírgenes

    2 *adj* virgen

virginal ['vɜːdʒɪnəl] *adj* virginal

Virginia [vɜːˈdʒɪnjə] *n* Virginia

virginity [vəˈdʒɪnɪtɪ] *n* virginidad *f*

Virgo ['vɜːgəʊ] *n (sign of zodiac)* virgo *m*; **to be (a) V.** ser virgo

virile ['vɪraɪl] *adj* viril

virility [vɪˈrɪlɪtɪ] *n* virilidad *f*

virology [vaɪˈrɒlədʒɪ] *n Med* virología *f*

virtual ['vɜːtjʊəl] *adj* virtual; **the v. extinction of the wild variety** la práctica desaparición de la variedad silvestre; **it's a v. impossibility** es virtualmente imposible; **the organization was in a state of v. collapse** la organización se hallaba prácticamente al borde del hundimiento; *Comptr* **v. reality** realidad *f* virtual

virtually ['vɜːtjʊəlɪ] *adv* virtualmente, prácticamente

virtue ['vɜːtjuː] *n* virtud *f*; **by v. of** en virtud de; **to make a v. of necessity** hacer de la necesidad una virtud; **it has the added v. of being quicker** cuenta con la virtud añadida de ser más rápido(a)

virtuosity [vɜːtjʊˈɒsɪtɪ] *n* virtuosismo *m*

virtuoso [vɜːtjʊˈəʊzəʊ] *(pl* **virtuosos** *or* **virtuosi** [vɜːtjʊˈəʊziː]*) n Mus* virtuoso(a) *m,f*

virtuous ['vɜːtjʊəs] *adj* virtuoso(a)

virulent ['vɪr(j)ʊlənt] *adj* virulento(a)

virus ['vaɪrəs] *n Med & Comptr* virus *m inv*; *Comptr* **v. check** detección *f* de virus

visa ['viːzə] *n* visado *m*, *Am* visa *f*

vis-à-vis ['viːzɑːviː] *prep (in comparison with)* en comparación con, frente a; *(in relation to)* en relación con, con relación *or* respecto a

visceral ['vɪsərəl] *adj* visceral

viscount ['vaɪkaʊnt] *n* vizconde *m*

viscous ['vɪskəs] *adj* viscoso(a)

visibility [vɪzɪˈbɪlɪtɪ] *n* visibilidad *f*; **v. was down to a few yards** no se veía más allá de unos pocos metros

visible ['vɪzɪbəl] *adj* visible

visibly ['vɪzɪblɪ] *adv* visiblemente

vision ['vɪʒən] *n* **(a)** *(eyesight)* visión *f*, vista *f*; **to have good/ poor v.** estar bien/mal de la vista **(b)** *(plan)* concepto *m*, imagen *f*; **man/woman of v.** hombre *m*/mujer *f* con visión de futuro **(c)** *(apparition)* visión *f*, aparición *f*; **to have** *or* **see visions** ver visiones; **I had visions of being left homeless** ya me veía en la calle

visionary ['vɪʒənərɪ] *n & adj* visionario(a) *m,f*

visit ['vɪzɪt] **1** *n* visita *f*; **to pay sb a v.** hacer una visita a alguien; **to be on a v.** estar de visita

    2 *vt* visitar

    3 *vi* **to be visiting** estar de visita

visiting ['vɪzɪtɪŋ] **1** *n* **v. card** tarjeta *f* de visita; **v. hours** horas *fpl* de visita, horario *m* de visita(s); *Law* **v. rights** *(of divorced parent)* derecho *m* de visita (a los hijos)

    2 *adj (team)* visitante; **v. lecturer** profesor(ora) *m,f* invitado(a)

visitor ['vɪzɪtə(r)] *n (guest, in hospital)* visita *f*; *(tourist)* turista *mf*, visitante *mf*; **visitors' book** libro *m* de visitas

visor ['vaɪzə(r)] *n (of helmet, cap)* visera *f*

vista ['vɪstə] *n* vista *f*, panorama *m*; *Fig* horizonte *m*

visual ['vɪʒʊəl] *adj* visual; **the v. arts** las artes plásticas; **v. aids** medios *mpl* visuales; *Comptr* **v. display unit** monitor *m*

visualize ['vɪʒʊəlaɪz] *vt (imagine)* visualizar; *(foresee)* prever

visually ['vɪʒʊəlɪ] *adv* visualmente; **the v. handicapped** las personas con discapacidades visuales

vital ['vaɪtəl] *adj* **(a)** *(essential)* vital; **v. organ** órgano *m* vital; **v.**

statistics *Hum (of woman)* medidas *fpl* **(b)** *(vigorous)* vital, lleno(a) de vida

vitality [vaɪˈtælɪtɪ] *n* vitalidad *f*

vitally ['vaɪtəlɪ] *adv* **supplies are v. needed** se necesitar suministros urgentemente; **v. important** de importancia vita

vitamin ['vaɪtəmɪn] *n* vitamina *f*; **with added vitamins** enriquecido(a) con vitaminas

vitreous ['vɪtrɪəs] *adj* **v. enamel** esmalte *m* (vítreo); *Anat* **v humor** humor *m* vítreo

vitriol ['vɪtrɪəl] *n (acid)* vitriolo *m*; *Fig (nasty remarks* causticidad *f*

vitriolic [vɪtrɪˈɒlɪk] *adj* cáustico(a), corrosivo(a)

vittles ['vɪtəlz] *npl* vituallas *fpl*

vituperative [vɪˈtjuːpərətɪv] *adj Formal* injurioso(a)

vivacious [vɪˈveɪʃəs] *adj* vivaracho(a), vivaz

vivacity [vɪˈvæsɪtɪ] *n* vivacidad *f*

vivid ['vɪvɪd] *adj (description, memory, impression)* vívido(a) *(imagination)* muy vivo(a); *(colors)* vivo(a)

vividly ['vɪvɪdlɪ] *adv (remember, describe)* vívidamente

vivisection [vɪvɪˈsekʃən] *n* vivisección *f*

vixen ['vɪksən] *n* zorra *f*

viz [vɪz] *adv (abbr* **videlicet**) a saber

VOA [viːəʊˈeɪ] *n (abbr* **Voice of America**) = cadena de radio exterior estadounidense

vocab ['vəʊkæb] *n Fam* vocabulario *m*

vocabulary [vəˈkæbjʊlərɪ] *n* vocabulario *m*

vocal ['vəʊkəl] **1** *n Mus* **vocals** voces *fpl*; **on vocals** como vocalista

    2 (a) *adj (music)* vocal; *Anat* **v. cords** cuerdas *fpl* vocales **(b** *(outspoken)* vehemente, explícito(a); **to be very v. in one's criticism** expresar las críticas muy a las claras

vocalist ['vəʊkəlɪst] *n Mus* vocalista *mf*

vocation [vəʊˈkeɪʃən] *n* vocación *f*; **to have a v. (for sth)** tener vocación (para algo)

vocational [vəʊˈkeɪʃənəl] *adj (course, qualification)* de formación profesional; **v. training** formación *f* profesional

vocative ['vɒkətɪv] *Gram* **1** *n* vocativo *m*

    2 *adj* vocativo(a)

vociferous [vəˈsɪfərəs] *adj* ruidoso(a), vehemente

vociferously [vəˈsɪfərəslɪ] *adv* ruidosamente, vehemente mente

vodka ['vɒdkə] *n* vodka *m*

vogue [vəʊg] *n* **to be in v.** estar en boga

voice [vɔɪs] **1** *n* **(a)** *(of person)* voz *f*; **to raise/lower one's v** levantar/bajar la voz; **at the top of one's v.** a voz en grito; **to lose one's v.** quedarse afónico(a); **v. box** laringe *f*; *Comptr* **v recognition** reconocimiento *m* de voz **(b)** *Gram* **active/ passive v.** voz activa/pasiva **(c)** *(idioms)* **the v. of reason** la voz de la razón; **with one v.** unánimemente; **to make one's v. heard** hacerse oír; **to give v. to one's feelings** expresar *o* manifestar los sentimientos; **these reforms would give small parties a v.** estas reformas darían voz a los partidos minoritarios

    2 *vt* **(a)** *(opinion, feelings)* expresar **(b)** *Ling (consonant* sonorizar

voiced [vɔɪst] *adj Ling* sonoro(a)

voiceless ['vɔɪslɪs] *adj Ling* sordo(a)

voicemail ['vɔɪsmeɪl] *adj Comptr* buzón *m* de voz

voice-over ['vɔɪsəʊvə(r)] *n Cin & TV* voz *f* en off

void [vɔɪd] **1** *n* vacío *m*

    2 *adj* **(a)** **v. of** carente de **(b)** *Law (deed, contract)* **(null and) v** nulo(a) y sin valor

volatile ['vɒlətaɪl] *adj* **(a)** *(person)* temperamental; *(situation, economy, market)* inestable, muy cambiante **(b)** *Chem* volátil

volcanic [vɒlˈkænɪk] *adj* volcánico(a)

volcano [vɒlˈkeɪnəʊ] *(pl* **volcano(e)s**) *n* volcán *m*

vole [vəʊl] n ratón m de campo

volition [və'lɪʃən] n Formal **of one's own v.** por propia voluntad

volley ['vɒlɪ] (pl **volleys**) n (**a**) (of gunfire) ráfaga f; (of blows, stones) lluvia f; Fig (of insults) torrente m (**b**) (in tennis, soccer) volea f

volleyball ['vɒlɪbɔːl] n voleibol m, balonvolea m

volt [vəʊlt] n Elec voltio m

voltage ['vəʊltɪdʒ] n Elec voltaje m

volte-face ['vɒltfɑːs] n viraje m or giro m radical

voluble ['vɒljʊbəl] adj locuaz

volubly ['vɒljʊblɪ] adv con locuacidad

volume ['vɒljuːm] n volumen m; Fig **to speak volumes** decir mucho; **to turn the v. up/down** (on TV, radio) subir/bajar el volumen; **v. control** mando m del volumen

voluminous [və'ljuːmɪnəs] adj voluminoso(a)

voluntarily [vɒlʌn'teərɪlɪ] adv voluntariamente

voluntary ['vɒləntərɪ] adj voluntario(a); **v. layoff** despido m voluntario; **to do v. work** trabajar como voluntario(a)

volunteer [vɒlən'tɪə(r)] **1** n voluntario(a) m,f
2 vt (information, advice) ofrecer (voluntariamente); **to v. to do sth** ofrecerse a hacer algo
3 vi ofrecerse (voluntariamente)

voluptuous [və'lʌptjʊəs] adj voluptuoso(a)

vomit ['vɒmɪt] **1** n vómito m
2 vt & vi vomitar

voodoo ['vuːduː] n vudú m

voracious [və'reɪʃəs] adj voraz

voraciously [və'reɪʃəslɪ] adv (to eat, read) vorazmente

vortex ['vɔːteks] (pl **vortexes** or **vortices** ['vɔːtɪsiːz]) n torbellino m, remolino m; Fig vorágine f

vote [vəʊt] **1** n (choice) voto m; (voting) votación f; **to put sth to the v., to take a v. on sth** someter algo a votación; **to have the v.** tener derecho de voto; **they got 52 percent of the v.** obtuvieron un 52 por ciento de los votos; **v. of confidence** voto de confianza; **v. of no confidence** moción f de censura; **to propose a v. of thanks for sb** pedir el agradecimiento para alguien

2 vt **to v. Democrat/Republican** votar a los demócratas/republicanos; **to v. to do sth** votar hacer algo; **to v. a proposal down** rechazar una propuesta en votación; **to v. sb in** elegir a alguien (en votación); **I v. (that) we go** voto por ir; **they voted the vacation a success** coincidieron en que las vacaciones habían sido un éxito
3 vi votar (**for/against** por/en contra de); **to v. yes/no** votar a favor/en contra; **to v. on sth** someter algo a votación

voter ['vəʊtə(r)] n votante mf

voting ['vəʊtɪŋ] **1** n votación f; **v. booth** cabina f electoral
2 adj (member) con voto

votive ['vəʊtɪv] adj Rel votivo(a)

▶**vouch for** [vaʊtʃ] vt insep (person) responder de; (quality, truth) dar fe de

vow [vaʊ] **1** n Rel voto m; (promise) promesa f; **to make a v. to do sth** prometer solemnemente hacer algo; **to take a v. of poverty/silence** hacer voto de pobreza/silencio
2 vt prometer solemnemente, jurar; **to v. to do sth** jurar hacer algo

vowel ['vaʊəl] n vocal f; **v. sound** sonido m vocálico

voyage ['vɔɪdʒ] n viaje m (largo, marítimo o espacial)

voyager ['vɔɪdʒə(r)] n viajero(a) m,f

voyeur [vɔɪ'jɜː(r)] n voyeur mf

voyeuristic [vɔɪjɜː'rɪstɪk] adj voyeurista

vs (abbr **versus**) contra

VTOL [viːtiːəʊ'el] n Av (abbr **vertical takeoff and landing**) despegue m or Am decolaje m (y aterrizaje) vertical

VTR [viːtiːˈɑː(r)] n TV (abbr **videotape recorder**) (aparato m de) vídeo m or Am video m

vulgar ['vʌlgə(r)] adj (rude) vulgar, grosero(a); (in poor taste) ordinario(a), chabacano(a); (habit) grosero(a); **don't be v.!** ¡no seas grosero!

vulgarity [vʌl'gærɪtɪ] n (rudeness) vulgaridad f, grosería f; (poor taste) ordinariez f, chabacanería f

vulnerability [vʌlnərə'bɪlɪtɪ] n vulnerabilidad f

vulnerable ['vʌlnərəbəl] adj vulnerable

vulture ['vʌltʃə(r)] n buitre m

vulva ['vʌlvə] n vulva f

W

W, w ['dʌbəljuː] *n* (**a**) *(letter)* W, w *f* (**b**) *(abbr* **west**) O, oeste *m*

W *Elec (abbr* **watts**) W, vatios *m*

wacky ['wækɪ] *adj Fam (person, behavior, dress sense)* estrafalario(a); *(sense of humor, comedian)* estrambótico(a)

wad [wɒd] *n (of cotton)* bolita *f*; *(of paper)* taco *m*; *(of bank notes)* fajo *m*

wadding ['wɒdɪŋ] *n (for packing)* relleno *m*

waddle ['wɒdəl] *vi* caminar *or Esp* andar como un pato, anadear

wade [weɪd] *vi (in water)* caminar en el agua; **to w. across a stream** vadear un riachuelo; *Fig* **to w. in** entrometerse

▸**wade into** *vt insep Fig (task)* acometer; *(person)* arremeter contra

wader ['weɪdə(r)] *n* (**a**) *(bird)* (ave *f*) zancuda *f* (**b**) *(boots)* **waders** botas *fpl* altas de agua

wafer ['weɪfə(r)] *n (cracker)* barquillo *m*; *Rel* hostia *f*

wafer-thin [weɪfə'θɪn] *adj* muy fino(a); *Fig (majority)* ajustado(a)

waffle ['wɒfəl] *n (food) Esp* gofre *m*; *Am* wafle *m*

waft [wɒft] **1** *vt* llevar, hacer flotar
2 *vi* flotar

wag[1] [wæg] **1** *n (action)* meneo *m*; **with a w. of its tail** meneando la cola
2 *vt (pt & pp* **wagged**) menear, agitar; **to w. one's finger at sb** advertir a alguien con el dedo
3 *vi* menearse; *Fam* **tongues will w.** van a correr rumores

wag[2] *n Fam (joker)* bromista *mf*, guasón(ona) *m,f*

wage [weɪdʒ] **1** *n (pay)* **w.(s)** salario *m*, sueldo *m*; **daily w.** jornal *m*; **w. claim** reivindicación *f* salarial; **w. cut** recorte *m* salarial; **w. differential** diferencia *f* salarial; **w. earner** asalariado(a) *m,f*; **w. freeze** congelación *f* salarial; **w. scale** escala *f* salarial
2 *vt* **to w. war (on)** librar una guerra (contra); **to w. a campaign against smoking** emprender una campaña contra el tabaco

wager ['weɪdʒə(r)] *Formal* **1** *n* apuesta *f*
2 *vt* apostar, apostarse

waggle ['wægəl] **1** *vt* menear
2 *vi* menearse

wagon ['wægən] *n (horse-drawn)* carro *m*; *Fig* **to be on the w.** *(alcoholic)* haber dejado de beber *or Am* tomar

waif [weɪf] *n* niño(a) *m,f* abandonado(a)

wail [weɪl] **1** *n (of person)* quejido *m*, gemido *m*; *(of siren)* sonido *m*, aullido *m*
2 *vi (person)* gemir; *(siren)* sonar, aullar

waist [weɪst] *n* cintura *f*

waistband ['weɪstbænd] *n* cinturilla *f*

waist-deep ['weɪs'diːp] *adj* **she was w. in water** le llegaba el agua por la cintura

-waisted ['weɪstɪd] *suffix* **a low/high-w. dress** un vestido de cintura baja/alta, un vestido bajo/alto de cintura

waistline ['weɪstlaɪn] *n* cintura *f*; **to watch one's w.** cuidar la línea

wait [weɪt] **1** *n* espera *f*; **we had a long w.** esperamos mucho;

it was worth the w. mereció la pena esperar; **to lie in w. for sb** acechar a alguien
2 *vt* (**a**) *(wait for)* **you must w. your turn** debes esperar tu turno (**b**) *(serve at)* **to w. table(s)** servir mesas
3 *vi* esperar; **to w. for sth/sb** esperar algo/a alguien; **to wait for sth to happen** esperar a que ocurra algo; **to keep sb waiting** tener a alguien esperando; **I can't w. to see her** estoy impaciente por verla; **repairs while you w.** *(sign)* arreglos en el acto; **we must w. and see** tendremos que esperar a ver (qué pasa)

▸**wait around, wait about** *vi* esperar

▸**wait on** *vt insep (serve)* servir; **to w. on sb hand and foot** traérselo todo en bandeja a alguien

▸**wait up** *vi* **to w. up for sb** esperar a alguien levantado(a)

waiter ['weɪtə(r)] *n* camarero *m*, *Andes, RP* mozo *m*, *Chile, Ven* mesonero *m*, *Col, Guat, Méx, Salv* mesero *m*

waiting ['weɪtɪŋ] *n* espera *f*; **they are playing a w. game** están dejando que transcurra el tiempo a ver qué pasa; **w. list** lista *f* de espera; **w. room** sala *f* de espera

waitress ['weɪtrɪs] *n* camarera *f*, *Andes, RP* moza *f*, *Chile, Ven* mesonera *f*, *Col, Guat, Méx, Salv* mesera *f*

waive [weɪv] *vt (rights, claim)* renunciar a; *(rule)* no aplicar

wake[1] [weɪk] *n (of ship)* estela *f*; *Fig* **in the w. of sth** a raíz de algo; *Fig* **to follow in sb's w.** seguir los pasos de alguien

wake[2] *n (on night before funeral)* velatorio *m*, *Am* velorio *m*

wake[3] *(pt* **waked** *or* **woke** [wəʊk], *pp* **woken** ['wəʊkən]) **1** *v...* despertar
2 *vi* despertarse

▸**wake up 1** *vt sep* despertar
2 *vi* despertarse; *Fig* **to w. up to the truth** abrir los ojos a la realidad

wakeful ['weɪkfʊl] *adj* (**a**) *(sleepless)* desvelado(a); **to be w...** estar desvelado(a); **to have a w. night** pasar la noche en vela (**b**) *(vigilant)* alerta; **to be w.** estar alerta

waken ['weɪkən] *vt* despertar

waking ['weɪkɪŋ] *adj* de vigilia, sin dormir; **w. hours** horas *fp...* que uno pasa despierto, horas *fpl* de vigilia

Wales [weɪlz] *n* (País *m* de) Gales

walk [wɔːk] **1** *n* (**a**) *(short)* paseo *m*; *(long)* caminata *f*; **it's a ten-minute w. away** está a diez minutos de camino (de aquí); **to go for a w.** ir a dar un paseo (**b**) *(gait)* andares *mpl...* manera *f* de caminar *or Esp* andar (**c**) *(speed)* **at a w.** al paso paseando (**d**) *(path)* paseo *m*, sendero *m* (**e**) *(profession condition)* **people from all walks of life** gente de toda condición (**f**) *(in baseball)* paso *m* a primera base *(caminando)*
2 *vt* **to w. the dog** sacar *o* pasear al perro; **to w. sb home** acompañar a alguien a casa; **to w. the streets** caminar por las calles; *Euph (prostitute)* hacer la calle
3 *vi* (**a**) *(move on foot)* caminar, *Esp* andar; *(as opposed to riding driving)* ir andando *or* caminando; *(for exercise, pleasure)* pasear caminar; **to w. home** ir caminando *or Esp* andando a casa (**b** *(in baseball)* = avanzar a una base cuando el pítcher comete cuatro bolas

▸ **walk away** *vi* irse (caminando *or Esp* andando); *Fig* **to w. away from trouble** evitar los problemas; *Fig* **to w. away with a prize** salir premiado(a), llevarse un premio

▸ **walk in** *vi* entrar

▸ **walk into** *vt insep* (**a**) *(enter)* entrar en (**b**) *(collide with)* chocar con

▸ **walk off** *vi* marcharse; **to w. off with sth** *(steal, win easily)* llevarse algo

▸ **walk out** *vi* salir; *Ind (go on strike)* ponerse *or* declararse en huelga; **to w. out on sb** *(leave)* dejar *or* abandonar a alguien

▸ **walk over** *vt insep Fam* **to w. all over sb** pisotear a alguien

walker ['wɔːkə(r)] *n* caminante *mf*

walkie-talkie [wɔːkɪ'tɔːkɪ] *n Rad* walkie-talkie *m*

walk-in ['wɔːkɪn] *adj* **w. closet** armario *m* vestidor; **w. pantry** despensa *f*

walking ['wɔːkɪŋ] **1** *n* **I like w.** me gusta caminar *or Esp* andar; **we do a lot of w.** caminamos *or Esp* andamos mucho; **w. shoes** botas *fpl (de senderismo)*; **w. stick** bastón *m*
2 *adj* **at w. pace** al paso, paseando; *Fam* **she's a w. encyclopedia** es una enciclopedia ambulante *or* andante; **the w. wounded** los heridos que aún pueden andar

Walkman® ['wɔːkmən] *n* walkman® *m*

walk-on part ['wɔːkɒn'pɑːt] *n Cin & Theat* papel *m* de figurante

walkout ['wɔːkaʊt] *n (strike)* huelga *f*; *(from meeting)* abandono *m* (en señal de protesta)

walkover ['wɔːkəʊvə(r)] *n Fam* **it was a w.** fue pan comido *or* un paseo

walkway ['wɔːkweɪ] *n (between buildings)* pasadizo *m*, pasaje *m*

wall [wɔːl] *n* (**a**) *(interior)* pared *f*; *(exterior, freestanding)* muro *m*; *(of garden, around building)* tapia *f*; *(of town, city)* muralla *f*; **the Great W. of China** la Gran Muralla china; **w. cupboard** alacena *f*; **w. hanging** tapiz *m* (**b**) *(idioms)* **a w. of silence** un muro de silencio; **to go to the w.** irse al traste; *Fam* **to drive sb up the w.** hacer que alguien se suba por las paredes

▸ **wall in** *vt sep (surround with wall)* tapiar; *(enclose)* encerrar

▸ **wall off** *vt sep* separar con un muro

▸ **wall up** *vt sep* condenar, tapiar

wallaby ['wɒləbɪ] *n* wallaby *m*, valabí *m*

wallet ['wɒlɪt] *n* cartera *f*

wallflower ['wɔːlflaʊə(r)] *n (plant)* alhelí *m*; *Fig* **to be a w.** no tener con quien bailar

Walloon [wɒ'luːn] *n & adj* valón(ona) *m,f*

wallop ['wɒləp] *Fam* **1** *n* tortazo *m*, *Méx* madrazo *m*
2 *vt* dar un tortazo *or Méx* madrazo a

walloping ['wɒləpɪŋ] *Fam* **1** *n* paliza *f*
2 *adv (for emphasis)* **a w. great pay raise** *Esp* una subida de sueldo de aquí te espero, *Am* un aumento de sueldo que para qué te cuento

wallow ['wɒləʊ] *vi* revolcarse; **to w. in self-pity** recrearse *or* regodearse en la autocompasión

wallpaper ['wɔːlpeɪpə(r)] **1** *n (on walls)* papel *m* pintado; *Comptr* papel *m* tapiz
2 *vt* empapelar

wall-to-wall ['wɔːltəwɔːl] *adj* **w. carpeting** *Esp* enmoquetado *m*, *Esp* moqueta *f*, *Am* alfombra *f*; *Fig* **w. coverage** cobertura *f* total

walnut ['wɔːlnʌt] *n (fruit)* nuez *f*; *(tree, wood)* nogal *m*

walrus ['wɔːlrəs] *n* morsa *f*

waltz [wɔːls] **1** *n* vals *m*
2 *vi* bailar el vals; *Fam* **she waltzed into the room** entró en la habitación como si tal cosa; *Fam* **to w. off with sth** largarse con algo

WAN ['dʌbəljuːeɪ'en] *n Comptr (abbr* **wide area network***)* red *f* de área extensa

wan [wɒn] *adj* macilento(a), pálido(a)

wand [wɒnd] *n* varita *f*

wander ['wɒndə(r)] **1** *n* vuelta *f*
2 *vt (streets, world)* vagar por
3 *vi* (**a**) *(roam, stray)* vagar (**around** por); **she had wandered from the path** se había alejado del camino (**b**) *(verbally, mentally)* distraerse; **to w. from the subject** desviarse del tema, divagar; **my thoughts were wandering** mi mente empezaba a divagar

wanderer ['wɒndərə(r)] *n* trotamundos *mf inv*

wandering ['wɒndərɪŋ] *adj (person, life)* errante, errabundo(a); *(tribe)* nómada

wane [weɪn] **1** *n* **to be on the w.** *(moon)* ir menguando; *Fig (popularity, enthusiasm, power)* ir decayendo
2 *vi (moon)* menguar; *(popularity, enthusiasm, power)* ir decayendo

wangle ['wæŋgəl] *vt Fam* agenciarse; **he wangled it so that…** se las arregló *or Esp* apañó para que…; **could you w. me a ticket?** ¿podrías comprarme *or Esp* pillarme una entrada?

want [wɒnt] **1** *vt* (**a**) *(wish, desire)* querer; **to w. to do sth** querer hacer algo; **to w. sb to do sth** querer que alguien haga algo; **she knows what she wants** sabe lo que quiere; **that's the last thing we w.!** ¡sólo nos faltaba eso!; **I know when I'm not wanted** sé perfectamente cuándo estoy de más; **what does he w. with me?** ¿qué quiere de mí?
(**b**) *(need)* necesitar; **you w. to be careful with him** hay que tener cuidado con él
(**c**) *(seek)* **he's wanted by the police** lo busca la policía; **you're wanted on the phone** te llaman por teléfono; **wanted, a good cook** *(advertisement)* se necesita buen cocinero
2 *vi* **he wants for nothing** no le falta de nada
3 *n* (**a**) *(need)* necesidad *f*; **w. ad** demanda *f* (**b**) *(lack)* falta *f*, carencia *f* (**of** de); **for w. of anything better to do** a falta de algo mejor que hacer; **it wasn't for w. of trying** no será porque no lo intentamos

wanting ['wɒntɪŋ] *adj* **he is w. in intelligence** le falta inteligencia; **to be found w.** no dar la talla

wanton ['wɒntən] *adj* (**a**) *(unjustified)* injustificado(a), sin sentido; *(cruelty)* gratuito(a) (**b**) *(unrestrained)* descontrolado(a); *(sexually)* lascivo(a)

WAP [wæp] *n Comptr (abbr* **Wireless Application Protocol***)* WAP *m*; **W. phone** teléfono *m* WAP

war [wɔː(r)] *n* guerra *f*; **to be at w. (with)** estar en guerra (con); **to go to w. (with/over)** entrar en guerra (con/por); *Fig* **a w. of words** una batalla dialéctica, un combate verbal; *Fam Fig* **you look as if you've been in the wars** parece que volvieras de la guerra; **w. criminal** criminal *mf* de guerra; **w. cry** grito *m* de guerra; **w. games** *Mil* maniobras *fpl*; *(with model soldiers)* juegos *mpl* de estrategia (militar); **w. memorial** monumento *m* a los caídos (en la guerra); **w. veteran** excombatiente *mf*

warble ['wɔːbəl] **1** *n* trino *m*
2 *vi* trinar

warbler ['wɔːblə(r)] *n* curruca *f*

ward [wɔːd] *n* (**a**) *(in hospital)* sala *f* (**b**) *(electoral division)* distrito *m* electoral (**c**) *Law* **w. of court** pupilo(a) *m,f* bajo tutela

▸ **ward off** *vt sep (blow)* rechazar, parar; *(danger)* ahuyentar, prevenir

warden ['wɔːdən] *n (of park)* guarda *mf*; *(of institution)* guardián(ana) *m,f*, vigilante *mf*; *(of prison)* director(ora) *m,f*, alcaide(esa) *m,f*

wardrobe ['wɔːdrəʊb] *n* (**a**) *(cupboard)* armario *m*, ropero *m* (**b**) *(clothes)* guardarropa *m*; **to have a large w.** tener un amplio guardarropa (**c**) *Theat (costumes)* vestuario *m*

warehouse ['weəhaʊs] *n* almacén *m*

wares [weəz] *npl* mercaderías *fpl*, mercancías *fpl*

warfare ['wɔːfeə(r)] *n* guerra *f*

warhead ['wɔːhed] *n* ojiva *f*

warhorse ['wɔːhɔːs] *n Fig* **an old w.** un veterano, un perro viejo

warily ['weərɪlɪ] *adv* cautelosamente

wariness ['weərɪnɪs] *n* cautela *f*, precaución *f*

warlike ['wɔːlaɪk] *adj* agresivo(a), belicoso(a)

warlord ['wɔːlɔːd] *n* señor *m* de la guerra

warm [wɔːm] **1** *adj (iron, oven, bath)* caliente; *(water, soup)* templado(a); *(weather, welcome, color)* cálido(a); *(garment)* de abrigo; **it's w.** *(weather)* hace calor; **to be w.** *(person)* tener calor; *Fig (in personality)* ser cálido(a) o afectuoso(a); **to get w.** *(person)* entrar en calor; *(room, water)* calentarse; **you're getting warmer** *(in guessing game)* caliente, caliente

   2 *vt* calentar; **to w. oneself by the fire** calentarse al lado del fuego

   3 *vi* **to w. to sb** *(take liking to)* tomar afecto o cariño a alguien

▸**warm up 1** *vt sep (food)* calentar

   2 *vi (dancer, athlete)* calentar, hacer calentamiento; *(engine, radio)* calentarse

warm-blooded [wɔːm'blʌdɪd] *adj* de sangre caliente

warmhearted [wɔːm'hɑːtɪd] *adj* cariñoso(a), amable

warmly ['wɔːmlɪ] *adv* **(a) w. dressed** abrigado(a) **(b)** *(to applaud)* calurosamente; *(to thank)* de todo corazón

warmonger ['wɔːmʌŋgə(r)] *n* belicista *mf*

warmongering ['wɔːmʌŋgərɪŋ] **1** *n (activities)* actividad *f* bélica; *(attitude)* belicismo *m*

   2 *adj* belicista

warmth [wɔːmθ] *n (heat)* calor *m*; *Fig (of welcome)* calidez *f*, calor *m*; *(of person's character)* calidez *f*, afectuosidad *f*; *(affection)* cariño *m*

warm-up ['wɔːmʌp] *n (of dancer, athlete)* calentamiento *m*

warn [wɔːn] *vt* **(a)** *(caution)* advertir; **to w. sb about sth** advertir a alguien de algo; **to w. sb against sth** prevenir a alguien contra algo; **he warned her not to go** le advirtió que no fuese; **you have been warned!** ¡quedas advertido! **(b)** *(alert, inform)* avisar, advertir; **she had been warned in advance** la habían avisado de antemano

warning ['wɔːnɪŋ] *n* **(a)** *(caution)* advertencia *f*, aviso *m*; **to give sb a w.** hacer una advertencia a alguien; *Fig* **w. sign** señal *f* de alarma **(b)** *(advance notice)* aviso *m*; **without w.** sin previo aviso

warp [wɔːp] **1** *vt* **(a)** *(wood, metal)* alabear, combar **(b)** *(person, mind)* corromper, pervertir

   2 *vi (wood, metal)* alabearse, combarse

warpath ['wɔːpɑːθ] *n Fam* **to be on the w.** estar en pie de guerra

warped [wɔːpt] *adj* **(a)** *(wood, metal)* alabeado(a), combado(a) **(b)** *(person, mind)* degenerado(a), pervertido(a)

warrant ['wɒrənt] **1** *n Law* mandamiento *m* o orden *f* judicial; *Mil* **w. officer** ≃ subteniente *mf*

   2 *vt (justify)* justificar; *(deserve)* merecer

warranty ['wɒrəntɪ] *n Com* garantía *f*; **under w.** en garantía

warren ['wɒrən] *n (of rabbit)* red *f* de madrigueras; *Fig* laberinto *m*

warring ['wɔːrɪŋ] *adj* beligerante

warrior ['wɒrɪə(r)] *n* guerrero(a) *m,f*

Warsaw ['wɔːsɔː] *n* Varsovia; *Formerly* **W. Pact** Pacto *m* de Varsovia

warship ['wɔːʃɪp] *n* buque *m* de guerra

wart [wɔːt] *n* verruga *f*; **a biography of Walt Whitman, warts and all** una biografía de Walt Whitman que muestra lo bueno y lo menos bueno

warthog ['wɔːthɒg] *n* facóquero *m*

wartime ['wɔːtaɪm] *n* tiempos *mpl* de guerra; **in w.** en tiempos de guerra

wary ['weərɪ] *adj* cauteloso(a), precavido(a); **to be w. of sth/sb** recelar de algo/alguien

was [wɒz] *pt of* **be**

wash [wɒʃ] **1** *n* **(a)** *(action)* lavado *m*; **to give sth a w.** lavar algo; **give the floor a good w.** friega bien el suelo; **your jeans are in the w.** *(are going to be washed)* tus vaqueros están para lavar; *(are being washed)* tus vaqueros están lavándose; *Fig* **it will all come out in the w.** *(be all right)* todo se arreglará **(b)** *(of ship)* estela *f*

   2 *vt* **(a)** *(clean)* lavar; *(floor)* fregar; **to w. oneself** lavarse; **to w. one's face/one's hands** lavarse la cara/las manos; **to w. the dishes** fregar o lavar los platos; *Fig* **to w. one's hands of sth** lavarse las manos en cuanto a algo **(b)** **the cargo was washed ashore** el mar arrastró el cargamento hasta la costa; **he was washed overboard** un golpe de mar lo tiró o *Am* botó del barco

   3 *vi (wash oneself)* lavarse; *Fam* **that won't w.!** *(won't be believed)* ¡eso no se lo cree nadie!, *Esp* ¡eso no va a colar!

▸**wash away** *vt sep* **(a)** *(bridge)* arrastrar **(b)** *(dirt)* quitar, *Am* sacar

▸**wash down** *vt sep (food)* regar, rociar

▸**wash off** *vt sep* lavar, quitar o *Am* sacar lavando

▸**wash out** *vt sep* **(a)** *(cup, bottle)* enjuagar **(b)** **to be completely washed out** *(exhausted)* estar completamente agotado(a)

▸**wash up 1** *vt sep (bring ashore) (of sea)* arrastrar hasta la playa

   2 *vi (wash oneself)* lavarse

washbasin ['wɒʃbeɪsən] *n* lavabo *m*, *Am* lavamanos *m inv*

washboard ['wɒʃbɔːd] *n* tabla *f* de lavar

washbowl ['wɒʃbəʊl] *n* palangana *f*

washcloth ['wɒʃklɒθ] *n (face cloth)* toallita *f* (para la cara)

washer ['wɒʃə(r)] *n* **(a)** *Fam (washing machine)* lavadora *f*, *RP* lavarropas *m inv* **(b)** *(for screw)* arandela *f*; *(rubber)* zapata *f*, junta *f*

washing ['wɒʃɪŋ] *n* **(a)** *(action)* **to do the w.** lavar la ropa; **w. machine** lavadora *f*, *RP* lavarropas *m inv*; **w. powder** jabón *m* o detergente *m* (en polvo) **(b)** *(dirty clothes)* ropa *f* sucia; *(clean clothes)* ropa *f* limpia

Washington, DC ['wɒʃɪŋtən'diː'siː] *n* Washington, DC *(capital federal)*

washout ['wɒʃaʊt] *n Fam* fracaso *m*, desastre *m*

washrag ['wɒʃræg] *n (face cloth)* toallita *f* (para la cara)

washroom ['wɒʃruːm] *n* lavabo *m*, baño *m*, *Esp* servicios *mpl*, *CSur* toilette *f*

wasn't [wɒznt] = **was not**

WASP [wɒsp] *n (abbr* **white Anglo-Saxon Protestant)** WASP *mf*, = persona de raza blanca, origen anglosajón y protestante

wasp [wɒsp] *n* avispa *f*

waspish ['wɒspɪʃ] *adj* mordaz, hiriente

wastage ['weɪstɪdʒ] *n* desperdicio *m*, despilfarro *m*

waste [weɪst] **1** *n* **(a)** *(of money, time)* pérdida *f*, derroche *m*; *(of effort)* desperdicio *m*; **to go to w.** desperdiciarse **(b)** *(trash)* desechos *mpl*; *(radioactive, toxic)* residuos *mpl*; **household w.** basura *f*; **w. pipe** tubo *m* de desagüe **(c)** **wastes** *(desert)* erial *m*, desierto *m*

   2 *adj (heat, water)* residual; *(fuel)* de desecho; **w. product** *Ind* producto *m* o material *m* de desecho; *Physiol* excrementos *mpl*

   3 *vt (squander) (money, energy)* malgastar, derrochar; *(time)* perder; *(opportunity, food)* desperdiciar; **she wasted no time (in) telling me** no le faltó tiempo para decírmelo; *Prov* **w. not, want not** no malgastes y nada te faltará

▸**waste away** *vi* consumirse

wastebasket ['weɪstbɑːskɪt] *n* papelera *f*, cesto *m* de los papeles, *Arg*, *Méx* cesto *m*, *Méx* bote *m*

wasted ['weɪstɪd] *adj (effort, opportunity)* desperdiciado(a), desaprovechado(a)

wasteful ['weɪstfʊl] *adj* **to be w.** *(process, practice)* ser un despilfarro; *(person)* ser despilfarrador(ora)

wasteland ['weɪstlænd] *n* yermo *m*, erial *m*

wastepaper [weɪst'peɪpə(r)] *n* papeles *mpl* viejos; **w. basket** papelera *f*, *Arg, Méx* cesto *m*, *Méx* bote *m*

waster ['weɪstə(r)] *n Fam (idle person)* inútil *mf*

wasting disease ['weɪstɪŋdɪ'ziːz] *n* = enfermedad debilitante que consume los tejidos

watch [wɒtʃ] **1** *n* **(a)** *(timepiece)* reloj *m* **(b)** *(period of guard duty)* turno *m* de vigilancia; *(guard)* guardia *f*; **to be on w.** estar de guardia; **to keep a close w. on sth/sb** vigilar de cerca algo/a alguien

   2 *vt* **(a)** *(observe)* mirar, observar; *(movie, match, program)* ver; **to w. television** ver la televisión; **to w. sb doing sth** ver *or* observar a alguien hacer algo; **we are being watched** nos están observando **(b)** *(keep an eye on) (children, luggage)* vigilar **(c)** *(be careful of)* tener cuidado con, vigilar; **w. your language!** ¡cuidado con ese lenguaje!; *Fam* **w. it!** ¡ojo (con lo que haces)!, ¡cuidado!

   3 *vi* mirar, observar

▸**watch out** *vi* tener cuidado; **w. out!** ¡cuidado!; **to w. out for sth** estar al atento por si aparece algo

▸**watch over** *vt insep* vigilar

watchdog ['wɒtʃdɒg] *n* perro *m* guardián; *Fig* organismo *m* regulador

watchful ['wɒtʃfʊl] *adj* vigilante, alerta

watchmaker ['wɒtʃmeɪkə(r)] *n* relojero(a) *m,f*

watchman ['wɒtʃmən] *n* vigilante *m*

watchtower ['wɒtʃtaʊə(r)] *n* atalaya *f*

watchword ['wɒtʃwɜːd] *n* consigna *f*

water ['wɔːtə(r)] **1** *n* **(a)** agua *f*; *Med* **w. on the brain** hidrocefalia *f*; **w. bed** cama *f* de agua; **w. biscuit** galleta *f* *(cracker)* sin sal; **w. chestnut** castaña *f* de agua; **w. cooler** refrigerador *m* del agua; **w. gun** pistola *f* de agua; **w. heater** calentador *m* de agua; **w. level** nivel *m* del agua; **w. lily** nenúfar *m*; **w. meter** contador *m* del agua; **w. pistol** pistola *f* de agua; **w. polo** waterpolo *m*; **w. power** energía *f* hidráulica; **w. rat** rata *f* de agua; **w. skiing** esquí *m* acuático; **w. wings** manguitos *mpl*, flotadores *mpl*

   (b) **waters** *(of country, river, lake)* aguas *fpl*

   (c) *(of pregnant woman)* **her waters broke** rompió aguas

   (d) *(idioms)* **to spend money like w.** gastar dinero a manos llenas; **the argument doesn't hold w.** ese argumento no se tiene en pie; **to keep one's head above w.** mantenerse a flote; **that's all w. over the dam now** todo eso es agua pasada

   2 *vt* **(a)** *(fields, plants)* regar **(b)** *(horse)* dar de beber a

   3 *vi (eyes)* llorar, empañarse; **my eyes are watering** me lloran los ojos; **it makes my mouth w.** me hace la boca agua

▸**water down** *vt sep (dilute)* aguar, diluir; *Fig (criticism, legislation)* atenuar, dulcificar

waterborne ['wɔːtəbɔːn] *adj (goods) (by sea)* transportado(a) por mar; *(by river)* transportado(a) por río; *(disease)* transmitido(a) por el agua

watercolor ['wɔːtəkʌlə(r)] *n Art* acuarela *f*

watercourse ['wɔːtəkɔːs] *n (river)* curso *m* de agua

watercress ['wɔːtəkres] *n* berros *mpl*

waterfall ['wɔːtəfɔːl] *n* cascada *f*, catarata *f*

waterfowl ['wɔːtəfaʊl] *(pl* **waterfowl**) *n* ave *f* acuática

waterfront ['wɔːtəfrʌnt] *n (promenade)* paseo *m* marítimo; **a w. development** = viviendas u oficinas frente al mar, a un río o a un lago

watering ['wɔːtərɪŋ] *n* riego *m*; **w. can** regadera *f*; **w. hole** *(for animals)* bebedero *m*; *Fam (bar)* bar *m*

waterline ['wɔːtəlaɪn] *n* línea *f* de flotación

waterlogged ['wɔːtəlɒgd] *adj (shoes, clothes)* empapado(a); *(land)* anegado(a); *(pitch)* (totalmente) encharcado(a)

watermark ['wɔːtəmɑːk] *n (in paper)* filigrana *f*

watermelon ['wɔːtəmelən] *n* sandía *f*

waterproof ['wɔːtəpruːf] **1** *n* impermeable *m*

   2 *adj* impermeable

   3 *vt* impermeabilizar

water-resistant ['wɔːtərɪsɪstənt] *adj (watch)* sumergible; *(fabric)* impermeable

watershed ['wɔːtəʃed] *n Geog* línea *f* divisoria de aguas; *(turning point)* punto *m* de inflexión

waterside ['wɔːtəsaɪd] *n* ribera *f*, orilla *f*

water-ski ['wɔːtəskiː] *vi* hacer esquí acuático

watertight ['wɔːtətaɪt] *adj (seal)* hermético(a); *(compartment)* estanco(a); *Fig (argument, alibi)* irrefutable

waterway ['wɔːtəweɪ] *n* curso *m* de agua navegable

waterworks ['wɔːtəwɜːks] *n* **(a)** *(for treating water)* central *f* de abastecimiento de agua **(b)** *Fam (tears)* **to turn on the w.** ponerse a llorar (a voluntad)

watery ['wɔːtərɪ] *adj (soup, beer)* aguado(a); *(eyes)* lloroso(a), acuoso(a); *(color)* pálido(a), claro(a)

watt [wɒt] *n Elec* vatio *m*

wattage ['wɒtɪdʒ] *n Elec* potencia *f* en vatios

wave [weɪv] **1** *n* **(a)** *(of water)* ola *f*; *(of troops, crime)* oleada *f*; *(in hair) & Phys* onda *f*; *(of emotion)* arranque *m*; *Fig* **to make waves** alborotar, armar jaleo; *Rad* **w. band** banda *f* de frecuencias; **w. power** energía *f* de las olas **(b)** *(gesture)* saludo *m* (con la mano)

   2 *vt* **(a)** *(flag, stick)* agitar; **to w. one's arms about** agitar los brazos; **to w. goodbye to sb** decir adiós a alguien con la mano **(b)** **to have one's hair waved** ondularse el pelo

   3 *vi* **(a)** *(person)* saludar (con la mano); **to w. to sb** saludar a alguien con la mano **(b)** *(flag)* ondear

▸**wave aside** *vt sep (objection, criticism)* rechazar, desechar

wavelength ['weɪvleŋθ] *n Rad* longitud *f* de onda; *Fig* **we're not on the same w.** no estamos en la misma onda

waver ['weɪvə(r)] *vi (person)* vacilar, titubear; *(voice)* temblar; *(courage)* flaquear

waverer ['weɪvərə(r)] *n* indeciso(a) *m,f*

wavy ['weɪvɪ] *adj* ondulado(a)

wax¹ [wæks] **1** *n (for candles, polishing)* cera *f*; *(in ear)* cera *f*, cerumen *m*

   2 *vt* **(a)** *(polish)* encerar **(b)** **to have one's legs waxed** hacerse la cera en las piernas

wax² *vi* **(a)** *(moon)* crecer **(b)** *(become)* **to w. lyrical** ponerse lírico(a)

waxed [wækst] *adj (cloth, paper)* encerado(a)

waxen ['wæksən] *adj (complexion)* céreo(a)

waxwork ['wækswɜːk] *n* **w. (dummy)** figura *f* de cera; **waxworks** museo *m* de cera

way [weɪ] **1** *n* **(a)** *(route) also Fig* camino *m*; **to go the wrong w.** equivocarse de camino; **the w. to the station** el camino de la estación; **to ask the w.** preguntar cómo se va; **to show sb the w.** indicar el camino a alguien; **to lose one's w.** perderse; **to find one's w. to a place** llegar a un sitio; *Fig* to **find a w. out of a problem** encontrar la solución a un problema; **to know one's w. about** conocer la zona; **on the w.** en el camino; *Fam* **they've got a baby on the w.** van a tener un bebé; *Fig* **she is well on the w. to success** va camino del éxito; **he was on his w. to Seville** iba camino *Esp* de *or Am* a Sevilla; **I must be on my w.** debo irme ya; **out of the w.** retirado(a), apartado(a); *Fig* **he went out of his w. to help her** se esforzó por ayudarla; **the w. in** la entrada; **the w. out** la salida; **to make one's w. to a place** dirigirse a un lugar; **to make one's w. through the crowd** abrirse paso entre la multitud; *Fig* **to make one's w. in the world** abrirse camino en el mundo; *also Fig* **to make w. for sb/sth** dejar vía libre a alguien/algo; **to lead the w.** mostrar el camino; *Fig* marcar la pauta; **to stand in sb's w.** cerrar el paso a alguien; *Fig* interponerse en el camino de alguien; *also Fig* **to be in the w.** estar en medio; *also Fig* **to get in the w.** ponerse en medio; *also Fig* **to get out of the w.** quitarse de en medio; *also Fig* **to keep out of the w.** mantenerse alejado(a)

(b) *(distance)* **to go a part of/all the w.** hacer parte del/todo el camino; *Fig* **I'm with you all the w.** tienes todo mi apoyo; **to be a long w. from** estar muy lejos de; **we've still got a long w. to go** todavía nos queda mucho camino por delante; **to be a little/long w. off** *(in distance)* estar un poco/muy lejos; *(when guessing)* andar un poco/muy descaminado(a)

(c) *(direction)* dirección *f*; **which w....?** ¿en qué dirección...?; **this/that w.** por aquí/allí; *Fig* **to look the other w.** *(ignore sth)* hacer la vista gorda; *Fam* **down our w.** en mi tierra; **if the chance comes your w.** si se te presenta la ocasión; **trust should work both ways** la confianza debe ser mutua; **we split the money three ways** dividimos el dinero en tres partes

(d) *(manner)* modo *m*, manera *f*; **in this w.** de esta manera; **this/that w.** así; **she prefers to do things (in) her own w.** prefiere hacer las cosas a su manera; **I don't like the w. things are going** no me gusta cómo van las cosas; **one w. or another** de un modo u otro; *Fam* **w. to go!** ¡bien hecho!; **to my w. of thinking** para mí, a mi parecer; **to find a w. of doing sth** hallar un modo de hacer algo; **to get into the w. of doing sth** acostumbrarse a hacer algo; **he has a w. with children** se le dan bien los niños; **he got his w.** se salió con la suya; **to get used to sb's ways** acostumbrarse a la manera de ser de alguien

(e) *(respect)* sentido *m*; **in a w.** en cierto sentido; **in every w.** en todos los sentidos; **in no w.** de ningún modo

(f) *(state, condition)* **to be in a good/bad w.** *(business)* marchar bien/mal; **to be in a bad w.** *(person)* estar mal

2 *adv Fam* mucho; **w. back in the 1920s** allá en los años 20; **we go w. back** nos conocemos desde hace mucho (tiempo); **w. ahead** mucho más adelante; **w. down South** muy al sur; **your guess was w. out** ibas muy desencaminado; **it was w. too easy** fue exageradamente fácil

3 **by the way** *adv* a propósito, por cierto

4 **by way of** *prep (via)* **we went by w. of Amsterdam** fuimos por *or* vía Amsterdam, pasamos por Amsterdam; **by w. of an introduction/a warning** a modo de introducción/advertencia

wayfarer ['weɪfeərə(r)] *n* caminante *mf*

waylay [weɪ'leɪ] *(pt & pp* **waylaid** [weɪ'leɪd]) *vt (attack)* atracar, asaltar; *Fig (stop)* abordar, detener

way-out [weɪ'aʊt] *adj Fam* extravagante

wayside ['weɪsaɪd] *n* borde *m* de la carretera; *Fig* **to fall by the w.** irse a paseo

wayward ['weɪwəd] *adj* rebelde, desmandado(a)

WBA ['dʌbəljuːbiː'eɪ] *n (abbr* **World Boxing Association)** Asociación *f* Mundial de Boxeo

WBC ['dʌbəljuːbiː'siː] *n (abbr* **World Boxing Council)** Consejo *m* Mundial de Boxeo

we [wiː] *pron* nosotros(as); *(usually omitted, except for contrast)* **we're Americans** somos estadounidenses; **WE haven't got it!** ¡nosotros no lo tenemos!; **as we say in New York** como decimos en Nueva York; **we Spanish are...** (nosotros) los españoles somos...

weak [wiːk] *adj (person, currency, character, excuse)* débil; *(tea, coffee)* flojo(a); **to grow w.** debilitarse; **to have a w. heart** estar mal del corazón; **to be w. at physics** estar flojo en física; *Fig* **she went w. at the knees** le empezaron a temblar las piernas; *Fig* **w. spot** punto *m* débil

weaken ['wiːkən] **1** *vt* debilitar

2 *vi* debilitarse

weak-kneed [wiːk'niːd] *adj Fig* débil de carácter, pusilánime

weakling ['wiːklɪŋ] *n* enclenque *mf*, canijo(a) *m,f*

weakly ['wiːklɪ] *adv* débilmente

weakness ['wiːknɪs] *n* debilidad *f*; *(weak point)* punto *m* débil, defecto *m*; **to have a w. for sth/sb** sentir *or* tener debilidad por algo/alguien

weak-willed [wiːk'wɪld] *adj* sin fuerza de voluntad

weal [wiːl] *n (mark on skin)* señal *f*, verdugón *m*

wealth [welθ] *n* riqueza *f*; *Fig* abundancia *f*, profusión *f*

wealthy ['welθɪ] **1** *npl* **the w.** los ricos

2 *adj* rico(a), pudiente

wean [wiːn] *vt (baby)* destetar; *Fig* **to w. sb from** *or* **off a bad habit** quitar *or Am* sacarle una mala costumbre a alguien

weapon ['wepən] *n* arma *f*; **weapons of mass destruction** armas *fpl* de destrucción masiva

wear [weə(r)] **1** *n* (a) *(clothing)* ropa *f*; **evening/casual w.** ropa de noche/de esport (b) *(use)* uso *m*; **to get a lot of w. out of sth** aprovechar mucho algo; *Fam* **to be the worse for w.** estar para el arrastre; *Fam* **it was none the worse for w.** tampoco estaba tan mal; **w. and tear** deterioro *m*, desgaste *m*

2 *vt (pt* **wore** [wɔː(r)], *pp* **worn** [wɔːn]) (a) *(garment, glasses)* llevar; **what are you going to w.?** ¿qué te vas a poner?; **to w. black** ir de negro; **to w. one's hair long** llevar el pelo largo (b) *(erode)* desgastar; **to w. a hole in sth** terminar haciendo un agujero en algo

3 *vi (clothing)* **to w. thin** *(clothes)* gastarse, desgastarse; **my patience is wearing thin** se me está acabando la paciencia; **that joke is wearing thin** esa broma ha dejado de tener gracia; **that excuse is wearing thin** esa excusa ya no sirve; **to w. well** *(clothing, person, movie)* envejecer bien

▸**wear away 1** *vt sep* gastar, desgastar

2 *vi* desgastarse

▸**wear down 1** *vt sep* gastar, desgastar; *Fig* **to w. sb down** agotar *or* extenuar a alguien

2 *vi* desgastarse

▸**wear off** *vi (pain, effect)* pasar

▸**wear on** *vi (time)* transcurrir, pasar

▸**wear out** *vt sep* gastar, desgastar; **to w. oneself out** agotarse

wearily ['wɪərɪlɪ] *adv (walk)* cansinamente; *(lean, sit down)* con aire de cansancio; *(sigh)* fatigosamente

wearisome ['wɪərɪsəm] *adj (boring)* tedioso(a); *(tiring)* fatigoso(a); *(annoying)* exasperante

weary ['wɪərɪ] **1** *adj* cansado(a); **to be w. of sth** estar hastiado(a) de algo; **to grow w. of sth** hartarse de algo

2 *vt (tire)* fatigar, cansar; *(annoy)* hartar

3 *vi* cansarse, hartarse (**of** de)

weasel ['wiːzəl] *n* comadreja *f*

weather ['weðə(r)] **1** *n* tiempo *m*; **what's the w. like?** ¿qué (tal) tiempo hace?; **the w. is good/bad** hace buen/mal tiempo; **in this w.** con este tiempo; **w. permitting** si el tiempo lo permite; **to be under the w.** *(ill)* estar pocho(a); **w. chart** mapa *m* del tiempo; **w. forecast** pronóstico *m* meteorológico *or* del tiempo; **w. forecaster** meteorólogo(a) *m,f*; **w. map** mapa *m* del tiempo; **w. station** estación *f* meteorológica, observatorio *m* meteorológico; **w. vane** veleta *f*

2 *vt (rock)* erosionar; *Fig* **to w. the storm** capear el temporal

3 *vi (rock)* erosionarse

weatherbeaten ['weðəbiːtən] *adj (person, face)* curtido(a); *(cliff, rock)* erosionado(a)

weathercock ['weðəkɒk] *n* veleta *f*

weatherman ['weðəmæn] *n* hombre *m* del tiempo

weatherproof ['weðəpruːf] *adj* resistente (a las inclemencias del tiempo)

weave [wiːv] **1** *n (pattern)* tejido *m*

2 *vt (pt* **weaved** *or* **wove** [wəʊv], *pp* **weaved** *or* **woven** ['wəʊvən]) tejer; *Fig* **a skillfully woven plot** una trama muy bien urdida

3 *vi* tejer; *Fig* **to w. through the traffic** avanzar zigzagueando entre el tráfico

weaver ['wiːvə(r)] *n* tejedor(ora) *m,f*

weaving ['wiːvɪŋ] *n Tex* tejeduría *f*

web [web] *n* (**a**) *(of spider)* telaraña *f*, tela *f* de araña; *Fig (of lies, intrigue)* trama *f* (**b**) *(of duck, frog)* membrana *f* interdigital (**c**) *Comptr* **the Web** la Web; **W. designer** diseñador(ora) *m,f* de páginas web; **W. page** página *f* web; **W. site** sitio *m* Web

webbed [webd] *adj (foot)* palmeado(a)

webbing ['webɪŋ] *n (on chair, bed)* cinchas *fpl*

webcam ['webkæm] *n* cámara *f* web

web-footed [web'fʊtɪd] *adj (bird)* palmípedo(a); *(animal)* con membrana interdigital

weblog ['weblɒg] *n Comptr* weblog *m*, bitácora *f*

Webmaster ['webmɑːstə(r)] *n Comptr* administrador(ora) *m,f* de (sitio) web, webmaster *mf*

Wed *(abbr* **Wednesday)** miércoles *m inv*

wed [wed] *(pt & pp* **wedded)** **1** *vt* casarse con; *Fig* **to be wedded to** *(an idea, principle)* aferrarse a; *(one's work)* entregarse en cuerpo y alma a
2 *vi* desposarse, casarse

we'd [wiːd] = **we had, we would**

wedding ['wedɪŋ] *n* boda *f*, *Andes* matrimonio *m*, *RP* casamiento *m*; **w. cake** tarta *f* or pastel *m* de boda, *Andes* torta *f* de matrimonio, *RP* torta *f* de casamiento; **w. day** día *m* de la boda *or Andes* del matrimonio *or RP* del casamiento; **w. dress** traje *m or* vestido *m* de novia; **w. night** noche *f* de bodas; **w. ring** alianza *f*, anillo *m* de boda *or Andes* matrimonio *or RP* casamiento

wedge [wedʒ] **1** *n (for door, wheel)* cuña *f*, calzo *m*; *(of cake)* trozo *m*; *Fig* **it has driven a w. between them** los ha enemistado
2 *vt (insert)* encajar; **to w. a door open** calzar una puerta para dejarla abierta

wedlock ['wedlɒk] *n Law* matrimonio *m*; **to be born out of w.** nacer fuera del matrimonio

Wednesday ['wenzdɪ] *n* miércoles *m inv*; *see also* **Saturday**

wee [wiː] *adj Fam* pequeño(a); **a w. bit** un poquito

weed [wiːd] **1** *n (plant)* mala hierba *f*; **w. killer** herbicida *f*
2 *vt (garden)* escardar

▶**weed out** *vt sep Fig (people, applications)* descartar; *(mistakes)* eliminar

weedy ['wiːdɪ] *adj Pej (person)* enclenque

week [wiːk] *n* semana *f*; **next w.** la semana que viene; **last w.** la semana pasada; **every w.** todas las semanas; **once/twice a w.** una vez/dos veces a la semana; **within a w.** en el plazo de una semana; **in a w., in a w.'s time** dentro de una semana; **I haven't seen her for** *or* **in weeks** no la he visto desde hace semanas; **w. in w. out** semana tras semana; **a w. from tomorrow/Tuesday** de mañana/del martes en ocho días

weekday ['wiːkdeɪ] *n* día *m* entre semana, día *m* laborable; **weekdays only** sólo laborables

weekend [wiːk'end] *n* fin *m* de semana; **on the w.** el fin de semana; **w. break** vacaciones *fpl* de fin de semana

weekly ['wiːklɪ] **1** *adj* semanal
2 *adv* semanalmente
3 *n (newspaper)* semanario *m*

weeknight ['wiːknaɪt] *n* noche *f* de entre semana

weep [wiːp] **1** *vt (pt & pp* **wept** [wept]) **to w. tears of joy/anger** llorar de alegría/rabia
2 *vi (person)* llorar

weeping ['wiːpɪŋ] **1** *n* llanto *m*
2 *adj (loroso(a)*; **w. willow** sauce *m* llorón

weepy ['wiːpɪ] *adj Fam (book, movie, ending)* lacrimógeno(a), *Chile* cebollero(a); **to be w.** *(person)* estar lloroso(a)

wee(-)wee ['wiːwiː] *n Fam* **to do a w.** *(urinate)* hacer pis *or* pipí

weft [weft] *n Tex* trama *f*

weigh [weɪ] **1** *vt* (**a**) *(measure)* pesar (**b**) *(consider)* sopesar; **he weighed his words carefully** midió bien sus palabras; **to w. one thing against another** sopesar una cosa frente a otra (**c**) *Naut* **to w. anchor** levar anclas
2 *vi* pesar; **it weighs 2 pounds** pesa 2 libras; **how much do you w.?** ¿cuánto pesas?; **it's weighing on my conscience** me pesa en la conciencia; **her experience weighed in her favor** su experiencia inclinó la balanza a su favor

▶**weigh down** *vt sep* cargar; *Fig* **to be weighed down with grief** estar abrumado(a) por la pena

▶**weigh in** *vi* (**a**) *(boxer, jockey)* **to w. in at...** dar un peso de... (**b**) *Fam (join in)* meter baza

▶**weigh out** *vt sep* pesar

▶**weigh up** *vt sep (situation, chances)* sopesar

weighbridge ['weɪbrɪdʒ] *n* báscula *f* de puente

weight [weɪt] **1** *n* (**a**) *(of person, object)* peso *m*; **they're the same w.** pesan lo mismo; **to lose w.** adelgazar, perder peso; **to put on w.** engordar, ganar peso; **to have a w. problem** tener un problema de peso (**b**) *(for scales, of clock)* pesa *f*; **weights and measures** pesos *mpl* y medidas; **w. lifter** levantador(ora) *m,f* de pesos; **w. lifting** halterofilia *f*, levantamiento *m* de pesos; **w. training** gimnasia *f* con pesas (**c**) *(load)* peso *m*, carga *f* (**d**) *(idioms)* **that's a w. off my mind** me he quitado *or Am* sacado un peso de encima; **to carry w.** influir, tener peso
2 *vt (bias)* **the system is weighted in his favor** el sistema se inclina a su favor

▶**weight down** *vt sep* sujetar *(con un peso)*

weightless ['weɪtlɪs] *adj* ingrávido(a)

weight-watcher ['weɪtwɒtʃə(r)] *n* persona *f* a dieta

weighty ['weɪtɪ] *adj (load, object)* pesado(a); *Fig (problem, matter)* grave; *(reason)* de peso

weir [wɪə(r)] *n* presa *f*

weird [wɪəd] *adj* extraño(a), raro(a)

weirdo ['wɪədəʊ] *(pl* **weirdos)** *n Fam* bicho *m* raro

welcome ['welkəm] **1** *n* bienvenida *f*
2 *adj (person)* bienvenido(a); *(news, change)* grato(a); **to make sb w.** ser hospitalario(a) con alguien; **I don't feel w. here** siento que no soy bienvenido(a) aquí; **you're always w.** siempre serás bienvenido; **w. home!** ¡bienvenido a casa!; **you're w. to borrow it** tómalo *or Esp* cógelo prestado cuando quieras
3 *vt (person)* dar la bienvenida a; *(news, change)* acoger favorablemente; **we w. this change** este cambio nos parece muy positivo; **to w. the opportunity to do sth** alegrarse de tener la oportunidad de hacer algo

welcoming ['welkəmɪŋ] *adj (person, attitude)* afable, hospitalario(a)

weld [weld] **1** *n* soldadura *f*
2 *vt* soldar

welder ['weldə(r)] *n* soldador(ora) *m,f*

welding ['weldɪŋ] *n* soldadura *f*

welfare ['welfeə(r)] *n* (**a**) bienestar *m*; **w. work** trabajo *m* social (**b**) *(social security)* **to be on w.** recibir un subsidio del Estado

well¹ [wel] *n (for water, oil)* pozo *m*; *(for lift, stairs)* hueco *m*

▶**well up** *vi (tears)* brotar

well² *(comparative* **better** ['betə(r)], *superlative* **best** [best]) **1** *adj* **to be w.** estar bien; **to get w.** ponerse bien; **how are you? — w., thank you** ¿cómo estás? — bien, gracias; **it is just as w.** menos mal; **that's all very w., but...** todo eso está muy bien, pero...
2 *adv* (**a**) *(satisfactorily)* bien; **to speak w. of sb** hablar bien de alguien; **I did as w. as I could** lo hice lo mejor que pude; **to be doing w.** *(after operation)* irse recuperando; **w. done!** ¡bien

hecho!; **you would do w. to say nothing** harías bien en no decir nada; **to come out of sth w.** salir bien parado(a) de algo; **he apologized, as w. he might** se disculpó, y no era para menos; **very w.!** *(OK)* ¡muy bien!, *Esp* ¡vale!, *Méx* ¡órale!

(**b**) *(for emphasis)* bien; **I know her w.** la conozco bien; **it is w. known that...** todo el mundo sabe que...; **it's w. worth trying** bien vale la pena intentarlo; **she's w. able to look after herself** es muy capaz de valerse por sí misma; **I can w. believe it** no me extraña nada; **I am w. aware of that** soy perfectamente consciente de eso; **w. before/after** mucho antes/después; **to leave w. enough alone** dejar las cosas como están

(**c**) *(also)* **as w.** también; **as w. as** *(in addition to)* además de

3 *exclam* **w., who was it?** ¿y bien? ¿quién era?; **w., here we are (at last)!** bueno, ¡por fin hemos llegado!; **w., w.!** ¡vaya, vaya!; **w. I never!** ¡caramba!; **w., that's life!** en fin, ¡así es la vida!

we'll [wiːl] = **we will, we shall**

well-adjusted [welə'dʒʌstɪd] *adj (person)* equilibrado(a)

well-advised [welad'vaizd] *adj* sensato(a), prudente; **you'd be w. to stay indoors today** hoy lo mejor sería no salir de casa

well-argued [wel'ɑːgjuːd] *adj* bien argumentado(a)

well-attended [welə'tendɪd] *adj* muy concurrido(a); **the meeting was w.** a la reunión acudió *or* asistió mucha gente

well-balanced [wel'bælənst] *adj (person, diet)* equilibrado(a)

well-behaved [welbɪ'heɪvd] *adj* (bien) educado(a); **to be w.** portarse bien

well-being ['welbiːɪŋ] *n* bienestar *m*

well-built [wel'bɪlt] *adj (building)* bien construido(a); *(person)* fornido(a)

well-chosen [wel'tʃəʊzən] *adj* acertado(a)

well-deserved [weldɪ'zɜːvd] *adj* (bien) merecido(a)

well-disposed [weldɪs'pəʊzd] *adj* **to be w. toward sb** tener buena disposición hacia alguien

well-dressed [wel'drest] *adj* elegante; **to be w.** ir bien vestido(a)

well-earned [wel'ɜːnd] *adj* (bien) merecido(a)

well-educated [wel'edjʊkeɪtɪd] *adj* culto(a), instruido(a)

well-fed [wel'fed] *adj* bien alimentado(a)

well-founded [wel'faʊndɪd] *adj (suspicion, fear)* fundado(a)

well-heeled [wel'hiːld] *adj Fam* ricachón(ona), forrado(a), *Esp* con pelas, *Am* con plata

well-informed [welɪn'fɔːmd] *adj* (bien) informado(a)

well-intentioned [welɪn'tenʃənd] *adj* bienintencionado(a)

well-kept [wel'kept] *adj (garden)* cuidado(a); *(secret)* bien guardado(a)

well-known [wel'nəʊn] *adj* conocido(a), famoso(a)

well-loved [wel'lʌvd] *adj* muy querido(a)

well-made [wel'meɪd] *adj* bien hecho(a)

well-meaning [wel'miːnɪŋ] *adj* bienintencionado(a)

well-meant [wel'ment] *adj* bienintencionado(a)

well-nigh ['welnaɪ] *adv* casi, prácticamente

well-off [wel'ɒf] *adj (wealthy)* acomodado(a), rico(a); *Fig* **you don't know when you're w.** no sabes lo afortunado que eres

well-paid [wel'peɪd] *adj* bien pagado(a)

well-read [wel'red] *adj* leído(a), = que ha leído mucho

well-spoken [wel'spəʊkən] *adj* bienhablado(a)

well-timed [wel'taɪmd] *adj* oportuno(a)

well-to-do [weltə'duː] *adj* acomodado(a), próspero(a)

well-versed [wel'vɜːst] *adj* **to be w. in sth** estar muy ducho(a) *or* versado(a) en algo

wellwisher ['welwɪʃə(r)] *n* simpatizante *mf*, admirador(ora) *m,f*

well-worn [wel'wɔːn] *adj (garment)* gastado(a); *(argument)* manido(a).

well-written [wel'rɪtən] *adj* bien escrito(a)

Welsh [welʃ] **1** *npl (people)* **the W.** los galeses

2 *n (language)* galés *m*

3 *adj* galés(esa); **W. Assembly** Asamblea *f* de Gales, Parlamento *m* de Gales

welt [welt] *n (mark on skin)* señal *f*, verdugón *m*

welter ['weltə(r)] *n* **a w. of...** un barullo de...

welterweight ['weltəweɪt] *n Sport* peso *m* wélter *m*

wench [wentʃ] *n Old-fashioned or Hum* moza *f*

wend [wend] *vt Literary* **they wended their way homeward** con paso cansino pusieron rumbo a casa

went [went] *pt of* **go**

wept [wept] *pt & pp of* **weep**

were [wɜː(r)] *pt of* **be**

we're [wɪə(r)] = **we are**

weren't [wɜːnt] = **were not**

werewolf ['wɪəwʊlf] *n* hombre *m* lobo

west [west] **1** *n* oeste *m*; **to the w. (of)** al oeste (de); **the W. of Spain** el oeste de España; **the W.** Occidente

2 *adj (side, coast)* oeste, occidental; **W. Africa** África Occidental; **W. African** africano(a) *m,f* occidental; **the W. Bank** Cisjordania; **the W. End** *(of London)* = zona de Londres famosa por sus comercios y teatros; *Formerly* **W. Germany** Alemania Occidental; **W. Indian** antillano(a) *m,f*; **the W. Indies** las Antillas; **the W. Side** = el barrio oeste de Manhattan; **W. Virginia** Virginia Occidental; **w. wind** viento *m* de poniente *or* del oeste

3 *adv* hacia el oeste, en dirección oeste; **to face w.** dar *or* mirar al oeste; *Fig* **to go w.** *(TV, car)* romperse, estropearse

westbound ['westbaʊnd] *adj (train, traffic)* en dirección oeste; **the w. lane** el carril que va hacia el oeste

westerly ['westəlɪ] **1** *n (wind)* viento *m* de poniente *or* del oeste

2 *adj (direction)* hacia el oeste; **the most w. point** el punto más occidental; **w. wind** viento *m* de poniente *or* del oeste

western ['westən] **1** *n (movie)* película *f* del oeste, western *m*; *(novel)* novela *f* del oeste

2 *adj* occidental; **w. Spain** la España occidental; **W. Europe** Europa occidental; **the w. hemisphere** el hemisferio occidental

westernization [westənaɪ'zeɪʃən] *n* occidentalización *f*

westernized ['westənaɪzd] *adj* occidentalizado(a)

westernmost ['westənməʊst] *adj* más occidental

Western Samoa ['westənsə'məʊə] *n* Samoa Occidental

Western Samoan ['westənsə'məʊən] *n & adj* samoano(a) *m,f* occidental

Westminster [west'mɪnstə(r)] *n (as seat of administration)* Westminster, el parlamento británico

west-northwest ['westnɔː'west] *adv* en dirección oesnoroeste

west-southwest ['westsaʊθ'west] *adv* en dirección oesuroeste

westward ['westwəd] *adj & adv* hacia el oeste

westwards ['westwədz] *adv* hacia el oeste

wet [wet] **1** *adj (damp)* húmedo(a); *(soaked)* mojado(a); *(weather)* lluvioso(a); **to be w.** *(damp)* estar húmedo(a); *(soaked)* estar mojado(a); *(ink, paint)* estar fresco(a); **to get w.** mojarse; *Fig* **w. blanket** aguafiestas *mf inv*; **w. dream** polución *f* nocturna, *Am* orgasmo *m* nocturno; **w. paint** *(sign)* recién pintado; **w. suit** traje *m* de submarinismo

2 *vt (pt & pp* **wet** *or* **wetted)** *(dampen)* humedecer; *(soak)* mojar; **to w. the bed** mojar la cama, orinarse en la cama; **to w. oneself** mearse encima

3 *n (dampness)* humedad *f*; *(rain)* lluvia *f*

we've [wiːv] = **we have**

whack [wæk] *Fam* **1** *n* (**a**) *(blow)* porrazo *m*, *Méx* madrazo *m* (**b**) *(share)* parte *f* (**c**) **out of w.** averiado(a), estropeado(a)

2 *vt* (**a**) *(hit)* dar un porrazo *or Méx* madrazo a; **to w. sb on** *or*

over the head dar un porrazo *or Méx* madrazo a alguien en la cabeza **(b)** *Fam (murder)* liquidar, *Esp* cepillarse, *Esp* cargarse

whacked-out [wæk'aʊt] *adj Fam (exhausted)* derrengado(a), molido(a)

whacking ['wækɪŋ] *Fam adv* **a w. great increase/fine** un incremento/una multa bestial

whale [weɪl] *n* ballena *f*; *Fam* **we had a w. of a time** nos lo pasamos bomba

whaler ['weɪlə(r)] *n (person, vessel)* ballenero *m*

whaling ['weɪlɪŋ] *n* caza *f* de ballenas

wharf [wɔːf] *(pl* **wharves** [wɔːvz]*) n* embarcadero *m*

what [wɒt] **1** *adj* **(a)** *(in questions)* qué; **w. sort do you want?** ¿qué tipo quieres?; **tell me w. books you want** dime qué libros quieres; **w. color/size is it?** ¿de qué color/talla *or RP* talle es?; **w. good is that?** ¿de qué sirve eso? **(b)** *(in relative constructions)* **he took it** cogió lo poco que me quedaba; **I'll give you w. money I have** te daré todo el dinero que tengo

2 *pron* **(a)** *(in questions)* qué; **w. do you want?** ¿qué quieres?; **w. are you doing here?** ¿qué haces aquí?; **w.'s that?** ¿qué es eso?; **w.'s that to you?** ¿a ti qué te importa?; **w.'s to be done about this problem?** ¿qué podríamos hacer para resolver este problema?; **w. did I tell you?** ¿qué te dije?; **w. will people say?** ¿qué va a decir la gente?; **w.'s the Spanish for "dog"?** ¿cómo se dice "dog" en español?; **w.'s he/she/it like?** ¿cómo es?; **w. about the money I lent you?** ¿y el dinero que te presté?; **w. about a game of bridge?** ¿*Esp* te apetece *or Carib, Col, Méx* te provoca *or Méx* se te antoja *or CSur* querés echar una partida de bridge?; **w. about me?** ¿y yo qué?; **if that doesn't work, w. then?** y si eso no funciona, ¿qué?; *Fam* **so w.?**, **w. of it?** ¿y qué?; *Fam* **d'you think I'm mad or w.?** ¿te crees que estoy loco o qué?; *Fam* **paper, pens, pencils, and w.** *or* **w. have you** papel, bolígrafos, lápices y toda la pesca

(b) *(relative)* qué; **I don't know w. has happened** no sé qué ha pasado; **w. is most remarkable is that...** lo más sorprendente es que...; **w. I like is a good detective story** lo que más me gusta son las novelas policíacas; *Fam* **he knows w.'s w.** tiene la cabeza *Esp* sobre los hombros *or Am* bien puesta; *Fam* **to give sb w. for** darle a alguien para el pelo

(c) w. for? *(for what purpose)* ¿para qué?; *(why)* ¿por qué?; **w.'s that for?** ¿para qué es eso?; **w. did he do that for?** ¿por qué hizo eso?; **tell me w. you're crying for** dime por qué lloras

(d) *(in exclamations)* **w. an idea!** ¡menuda idea!; **w. a fool he is!** ¡qué tonto es!; **w. a lot of people!** ¡cuánta gente!

3 *exclam* **w.?** you didn't check the dates? ¿qué? ¿que no comprobaste las fechas?; **w. next (I ask myself)!** ¡(me pregunto) con qué saldrán ahora!

whatchamacallit ['wɒtʃəmakɔːlɪt] *n Fam* chisme *m, CAm, Carib, Col* vaina *f, RP* coso *m*

what-d'ye-call-her ['wɒtʃəkɔːlə(r)] *n Fam (person)* fulanita *f*, menganita *f*

what-d'ye-call-him ['wɒtʃəkɔːlɪm] *n Fam (person)* fulanito *m*, menganito *m*

what-d'ye-call-it ['wɒtʃəkɔːlɪt] *n Fam (thing)* chisme *m, CAm, Carib, Col* vaina *f, RP* coso *m*

whatever [wɒt'evə(r)] **1** *pron* **w. it is, w. it may be** sea lo que sea; **w. happens** pase lo que pase; **do w. you like** haz lo que quieras; **w. you say** *(expressing acquiescence)* lo que tú digas; **give him w. he wants** dale lo que quiera; **w. does that mean?** ¿y eso qué significa?

2 *adj* **(a)** *(no matter what)* **I regret w. harm I may have done** pido disculpas por el daño que pueda haber ocasionado; **pay w. price they ask** paga el precio que sea **(b)** *(emphatic)* **for no reason w.** sin motivo alguno; **none/nothing w.** absolutamente ninguno(a)/nada

what's-her-name ['wɒtsəneɪm], **what's-his-name** ['wɒtsɪzneɪm], **what's-its-name** ['wɒtsɪtsneɪm] *n Fam* = **what-d'ye-call-her/him/it**

whatsit ['wɒtsɪt] *n Fam* chisme *m, CAm, Carib, Col* vaina *f, RP* coso *m*

whatsoever [wɒtsəʊ'evə(r)] *adj* **for no reason w.** sin motivo alguno; **none/nothing w.** absolutamente ninguno(a)/nada

wheat [wiːt] *n* trigo *m*; **w. germ** germen *m* de trigo

wheaten ['wiːtən] *adj (loaf, roll)* de trigo

wheatfield ['wiːtfiːld] *n* trigal *m*

wheedle ['wiːdəl] *vt sep* **to w. sth out of sb** sacar algo a alguien con halagos; **to w. sb into doing sth** hacerle zalamerías a alguien para que haga algo

wheel [wiːl] **1** *n* **(a)** *(on car, trolley)* rueda *f*; **the w. of fortune** la rueda de la fortuna **(b)** *(for steering)* volante *m, Andes* timón *m*; *(of boat)* timón *m*; **to be at** *or* **behind the w.** ir al volante

2 *vt (push)* empujar, hacer rodar

3 *vi (turn)* girar, dar vueltas

wheelbarrow ['wiːlbærəʊ] *n* carretilla *f*

wheelbase ['wiːlbeɪs] *n Aut* distancia *f* entre ejes, batalla *f*

wheelchair ['wiːltʃeə(r)] *n* silla *f* de ruedas

-wheeled [wiːld] *suffix* **two/three/etc-w.** de dos/tres/*etc* ruedas

wheeling ['wiːlɪŋ] *n* **w. and dealing** tejemanejes *mpl*

wheeze [wiːz] **1** *n (noise)* resuello *m*, resoplido *m*

2 *vi (breathe heavily)* resollar, resoplar

whelk [welk] *n* bu(c)cino *m*

whelp [welp] *n (dog)* cachorro *m*; *(person)* mocoso(a) *m,f*

when [wen] **1** *adv (in questions)* cuándo; **w. will you come?** ¿cuándo vienes?; **tell me w. it happened** dime cuándo ocurrió; **until w. can you stay?** ¿hasta cuándo te puedes quedar?; *Fam* **say w.!** *(when pouring drink)* ¡dime basta!

2 *conj* **(a)** *(with time)* cuando; **I had just gone to bed w. the phone rang** acababa de acostarme cuando sonó el teléfono; **tell me w. you've finished** avísame cuando hayas terminado; **what's the good of talking w. you never listen?** ¿de qué sirve hablarte si nunca escuchas? **(b)** *(whereas)* cuando

whence [wens] *adv Literary* de dónde

whenever [wen'evə(r)] **1** *conj* **(a)** *(every time that)* cada vez que; **I go w. I can** voy siempre que puedo **(b)** *(no matter when)* **come w. you like** ven cuando quieras

2 *adv (referring to unspecified time)* cuando sea; **Sunday, Monday, or w.** el domingo, el lunes o cuando sea **(b)** *(in questions)* cuándo; **w. did you find the time to do all that?** ¿de dónde sacaste tiempo para hacer todo eso?

where [weə(r)] **1** *adv (in questions)* dónde; **w. are you going?** ¿adónde *or* dónde vas?; **w. does he come from?** ¿de dónde es?; **w. am I?** ¿dónde estoy?; **tell me w. she is** dime dónde está; **w. did I go wrong?** ¿en qué *or* dónde me equivoqué?; **w. would we be if...?** ¿dónde estaríamos si...?

2 *conj* donde; **I'll stay w. I am** me quedaré donde estoy; **go w. you like** ve a donde quieras; **that is w. you are mistaken** ahí es donde te equivocas; **the house w. I was born** la casa donde nací; **near w. I live** cerca de donde vivo; **they went to Paris, w. they stayed a week** fueron a París, donde permanecieron una semana; **w. there is disagreement, seek legal advice** en caso de disputa, pide asesoría jurídica

whereabouts 1 *npl* ['weərəbaʊts] *(location)* **nobody knows her w., her w. are unknown** está en paradero desconocido

2 *adv* [weərə'baʊts] *(where)* dónde

whereas [weə'ræz] *conj* **(a)** *(on the other hand)* mientras que **(b)** *Law* considerando que

whereby [weə'baɪ] *adv Formal* por el/la cual

whereupon [weərə'pɒn] *conj Literary* tras lo cual

wherever [weə'revə(r)] **1** *conj* (**a**) *(everywhere that)* allá donde, dondequiera que; **I see him w. I go** vaya donde vaya, siempre lo veo; **w. possible** (allá) donde sea posible (**b**) *(no matter where)* dondequiera que; **we'll go w. you want** iremos donde quieras

    2 *adv* (**a**) *(referring to unknown or unspecified place)* en cualquier parte; **at home, in the office, or w.** en casa, en la oficina o donde sea; **it's in Auburn, w. that is** está en Auburn, dondequiera que quede eso (**b**) *(in questions)* **w. can he be?** ¿dónde puede estar?

wherewithal ['weərwɪðɔ:l] *n* **the w. (to do sth)** los medios (para hacer algo)

whet [wet] (*pt & pp* **whetted**) *vt (tool, blade)* afilar; *(appetite)* despertar, abrir

whether ['weðə(r)] *conj* (**a**) *(indirect question)* si; **I don't know w. it's true** no sé si es verdad (**b**) *(conditional)* **w. she comes or not we shall leave** nos iremos, venga ella o no; **w. or not this is true** sea eso verdad o no

whew [hju:] *exclam* (**a**) *(relief, fatigue)* ¡uf! (**b**) *(astonishment)* ¡hala!

whey [weɪ] *n* suero *m*

which [wɪtʃ] **1** *adj* (**a**) *(in questions)* qué; **w. color do you like best?** ¿qué color te gusta más?; **w. way do we go?** ¿hacia dónde vamos?; **w. one(s)?** ¿cuál(es)? (**b**) *(in relative constructions)* **I was there for a week, during w. time…** estuve allí una semana, durante la cual…; **she came at noon, by w. time I had left** llegó a mediodía, para entonces yo ya me había marchado

    2 *pron* (**a**) *(in questions) (singular)* cuál; *(plural)* cuáles; **w. have you chosen?** ¿cuál has escogido?; **w. of the two is prettier?** ¿cuál de las dos es más bonita?; **w. of them is going?** ¿cuál de ellos va?; **I can never remember w. is w.** nunca me acuerdo de cuál es cuál

    (**b**) *(relative) (singular)* que, el/la cual; *(plural)* que, los/las cuales; **the house w. is for sale** la casa que está en venta; **the house, w. has been empty for years** la casa, que lleva años vacía

    (**c**) *(referring back to whole clause)* lo cual; **he's getting married, w. surprises me** se va a casar, lo cual *or* cosa que me sorprende; **she was back in Florida, w. annoyed me** estaba de vuelta en Florida, lo cual me molestó

    (**d**) *(with prepositions)* **the house of w. I am speaking** la casa de la que estoy hablando; **the countries w. we are going to** los países a los que vamos a ir; **the town w. we live in** la ciudad en (la) que vivimos; **I was shocked by the anger with w. she said this** me sorprendió el *esp Esp* enfado *or esp Am* enojo con (el) que dijo esto; **after w. he went out** tras lo cual, salió

whichever [wɪtʃ'evə(r)] **1** *adj* **take w. book you like best** toma *or Esp* coge el libro que prefieras; **w. way we do it there'll be problems** lo hagamos como lo hagamos habrá problemas

    2 *pron* cualquiera; **w. you choose, it will be a bargain** elijas el que elijas, será una ganga; **the 30th or the last Friday, w. comes first** el día 30 o el último viernes, lo que venga antes

whiff [wɪf] *n (smell)* olorcillo *m* (**of** a); **she caught a w. of it** le llegó el olorcillo; *Fig* **a w. of scandal** un tufillo a escándalo

while [waɪl] **1** *n* (**a**) *(time)* rato *m*; **after a w.** después de un rato; **for a w.** (durante) un rato; **in a w.** dentro de un rato; **a short** *or* **little w. ago** hace un rato; **a good w., quite a w.** un buen rato; **once in a w.** de vez en cuando (**b**) **it's not worth my w.** no me merece la pena; **I'll make it worth your w.** te recompensaré

    2 *conj* (**a**) *(during the time that)* mientras; **w. reading I fell asleep** me quedé dormido mientras leía; **it won't happen w. I'm in charge!** ¡esto no ocurrirá mientras yo esté al

cargo! (**b**) *(although)* si bien; **w. I admit it's difficult,…** bien admito que es difícil,… (**c**) *(whereas)* mientras que; **one wore white, w. the other was all in black** uno iba de blanco, mientras que el otro vestía todo de negro

▸**while away** *vt sep (time)* matar, pasar

whim [wɪm] *n* capricho *m*; **to do sth on a w.** hacer algo por capricho

whimper ['wɪmpə(r)] **1** *n* gimoteo *m*; *Fig* **without a w.** sin rechistar

    2 *vi* gemir, gimotear

whimsical ['wɪmzɪkəl] *adj (person, behavior)* caprichoso(a), *(remark, story)* curioso(a), inusual

whine [waɪn] **1** *n (of person, animal)* gemido *m*; *(of machine)* chirrido *m*

    2 *vi (in pain)* gimotear; *(complain)* quejarse (**about** de)

whinny ['wɪnɪ] **1** *n* relincho *m*

    2 *vi* relinchar

whip [wɪp] **1** *n* (**a**) *(for punishment)* látigo *m*; *(for horse)* fusta *f* (**b**) *(in Congress)* = encargado de mantener la disciplina de partido en el Congreso

    2 *vt (pt & pp* **whipped**) (**a**) *(lash, hit)* azotar; *(horse)* fustigar; **whipped cream** *Esp* nata *f* montada, *Am* crema *f* batida; *Fig* **he whipped the crowd into a frenzy** exaltó al gentío (**b**) *Fam (defeat)* dar una paliza a

▸**whip off** *vt sep Fam (clothes)* quitarse, *Am* sacarse

▸**whip out** *vt sep Fam* sacar rápidamente

▸**whip up** *vt sep* **to w. up one's audience** entusiasmar al público; **to w. up support (for sth)** recabar apoyo (para algo); *Fam* **I'll w. you up something to eat** te prepararé algo de comer

whiplash ['wɪplæʃ] *n* **w. (injury)** esguince *m* cervical *(lesión cervical por acción de la inercia)*

whippersnapper ['wɪpəsnæpə(r)] *n Fam* mocoso(a) *m,f*

whippet ['wɪpɪt] *n* lebrel *m*

whipping ['wɪpɪŋ] *n* azotes *mpl*; **to give sb a w.** *(punish)* azotar a alguien; **w. boy** cabeza *mf* de turco; **w. cream** *Esp* nata *f* para montar, *Am* crema *f* para batir

whirl [wɜ:l] **1** *n* remolino *m*; **a w. of activity** un torbellino de actividad; **the social w.** el torbellino de la vida social; *Fam* **my head's in a w.** tengo una gran confusión mental; *Fam* **let's give it a w.** probémoslo

    2 *vt* **to w. sth/sb around** hacer girar algo/a alguien

    3 *vi (dust, smoke, leaves)* arremolinarse; *(person)* girar vertiginosamente; **my head's whirling** me da vueltas la cabeza

▸**whirl along** *vi (car, train)* avanzar rápidamente

▸**whirl around** *vi* volverse *or* darse la vuelta rápidamente

whirlpool ['wɜ:lpu:l] *n* remolino *m*

whirlwind ['wɜ:lwɪnd] *n* torbellino *m*; **w. romance** romance *m* arrebatado; **w. tour** visita *f* relámpago

whirr [wɜ:(r)] **1** *n* zumbido *m*

    2 *vi* zumbar

whisk [wɪsk] **1** *n Culin* batidor *m* (manual)

    2 *vt* (**a**) *(eggs)* batir (**b**) *(move quickly)* **he was whisked into hospital** lo llevaron al hospital a toda prisa

    3 *vi (move quickly)* **she whisked past me** pasó zumbando a mi lado

▸**whisk away, whisk off** *vt sep* llevarse rápidamente

whisker ['wɪskə(r)] *n* **whiskers** *(of cat, mouse)* bigotes *mpl*; *(of man)* patillas *fpl*; *Fam* **to win by a w.** ganar por un pelo

whiskey ['wɪskɪ] *n* whisky *m*

whisper ['wɪspə(r)] **1** *n* susurro *m*; **to speak in a w.** hablar en voz baja *or Am* despacio; **and remember, not a w. of it to anyone!** y recuerda, ¡ni una palabra a nadie!

    2 *vt* **to w. sth to sb** susurrar algo a alguien

    3 *vi* susurrar; **stop whispering at the back of the class!** ¡vale ya de cuchichear ahí atrás!

whist [wɪst] *n (cardgame)* whist *m*

whistle ['wɪsəl] **1** *n* (**a**) *(noise)* silbido *m* (**b**) *(musical instrument)* pífano *m*, flautín *m*; *(of referee, policeman)* silbato *m*, pito *m*

2 *vt (tune)* silbar

3 *vi* silbar; **the bullet whistled past his ear** la bala le pasó silbando junto al oído; *Fam* **he can w. for his money** puede esperar sentado su dinero

whistle-blower ['wɪsəlbləʊə(r)] *n (in company, government)* denunciante *mf (de ilegalidades o corruptelas)*

whistle-stop tour ['wɪsəlstɒp'tʊə(r)] *n* **a w. of Europe** un recorrido rápido por Europa

Whit [wɪt] *n* Pentecostés *m*; **W. Sunday** domingo *m* de Pentecostés

whit [wɪt] *n* **not a w.** ni pizca; **it won't make a w. of a difference** va a dar exactamente igual

white [waɪt] **1** *n* (**a**) *(color, of eyes)* blanco *m* (**b**) *(person)* blanco(a) *m,f* (**c**) *(of egg)* clara *f*

2 *adj* blanco(a); **to turn** or **go w.** ponerse blanco(a), empalidecer; **w. with fear** pálido(a) de miedo; **w. as a ghost** or **sheet** blanco(a) como la nieve; **w. chocolate** chocolate *m* blanco; *Fig* **w. elephant** mamotreto *m* inútil; **w. fish** pescado *m* blanco; **w. flag** bandera *f* blanca; **w. flour** harina *f* (refinada); **w. heat** calor *m* blanco, rojo *m* blanco; **the W. House** la Casa Blanca; **w. lie** mentira *f* piadosa; **a w. man** un hombre blanco; **w. meat** carne *f* blanca; **w. sauce** (salsa *f*) bechamel *f*, *Col, CSur* salsa *f* blanca; **w. tie** *(formal dress)* frac *m* y *Esp* pajarita blanca or *Méx* corbata de moño blanca or *RP* moñito blanco; *Fam Pej* **w. trash** gentuza *f* blanca

whitebait ['waɪtbeɪt] *n* **deep-fried w.** pescaditos *mpl* fritos

white-collar worker ['waɪt'kɒlə'wɜːkə(r)] *n* oficinista *mf*, administrativo(a) *m,f*

white-haired ['waɪt'heəd] *adj* canoso(a)

Whitehall ['waɪthɔːl] *n* = calle de Londres donde se encuentra la administración central británica

white-hot ['waɪt'hɒt] *adj* candente

white-knuckle [waɪt'nʌkəl] *adj* **w. ride** atracción *f* que pone los pelos de punta

whiteness ['waɪtnɪs] *n* blancura *f*

whitewash ['waɪtwɒʃ] **1** *n* cal *f*, lechada *f*; *Fig* encubrimiento *m*

2 *vt* encalar; *Fig* encubrir

whither ['wɪðə(r)] *adv Literary* adónde

whiting ['waɪtɪŋ] *n (fish)* pescadilla *f*

whitish ['waɪtɪʃ] *adj* blancuzco(a), blanquecino(a)

Whitsun ['wɪtsən] *n* Pentecostés *m*

whittle ['wɪtəl] *vt (carve)* tallar; *(sharpen)* sacar punta a, pelar; *Fig* **to w. sth down** ir reduciendo algo

▸**whittle away** *vt sep* **his savings had been gradually whittled away** sus ahorros se habían visto mermados gradualmente

whiz [wɪz] **1** *n Fam (expert)* genio *m* (**at** de); **w. kid** joven *mf* prodigio

2 *vi (bullet)* zumbar, silbar; *(person, car)* ir corriendo, ir zumbando; **to w. past** pasar zumbando; **he whizzed through the work** hizo el trabajo a toda velocidad

WHO [dʌbəlju:eɪtʃ'əʊ] *n (abbr* **World Health Organization)** OMS *f*

who [hu:] *pron* (**a**) *(in questions) (singular)* quién; *(plural)* quiénes; **w. is it?** ¿quién es?; **w. with?** ¿con quién?; **w. is it for?** ¿para quién es?; **who's speaking?** *(on phone)* ¿de parte de quién?; **w. did you say was there?** ¿quién has dicho que estaba allí?; **w. does he think he is?** ¿quién se cree que es? (**b**) *(relative)* que; **the people w. came yesterday** las personas que vinieron ayer; **those w. have already paid can leave** los que ya hayan pagado pueden marcharse; **Louise's father, w. is a doctor, was there** estuvo allí el padre de Louise, que es médico

whodun(n)it [hu:'dʌnɪt] *n Fam (book)* novela *f* de *Esp*

suspense or *Am* suspenso; *(movie)* película *f* de *Esp* suspense or *Am* suspenso *(centrada en la resolución de un caso de asesinato)*

whoever [hu:'evə(r)] *pron* (**a**) *(anyone that)* quienquiera; **w. finds it may keep it** quienquiera que or quien lo encuentre, puede quedarse con ello (**b**) *(no matter who)* **w. you are, speak!** habla, quienquiera que seas; **w. wrote that letter** el que escribió esa carta; *Fam* **ask Simon or Chris or w.** pregúntale a Simon, a Chris o a quien sea (**c**) *(in questions)* **w. can that be?** ¿quién puede ser?

whole [həʊl] **1** *n* totalidad *f*; **the w. of the village** todo el pueblo; **as a w.** en conjunto; **on the w.** en general

2 *adj* (**a**) *(entire, intact)* entero(a); **he swallowed it w.** se lo tragó entero; **to tell the w. truth** decir toda la verdad; **the w. world** todo el mundo; **to last a w. week** durar toda una semana; **w. milk** leche *f* entera; *Mus* **w. note** semibreve *f*, *Am* redonda *f*; **w. wheat bread** pan *m* integral (**b**) *Fam* **the w. lot of them** todos ellos; **for a w. lot of reasons** por un montón de razones

whole-food ['həʊlfu:d] *n* alimentos *mpl* integrales; **w. restaurant** restaurante *m* macrobiótico

wholehearted [həʊl'hɑːtɪd] *adj (support, agreement)* incondicional, sin reservas

wholeheartedly [həʊl'hɑːtɪdlɪ] *adv (to support, agree)* incondicionalmente, sin reservas

wholesale ['həʊlseɪl] **1** *n Com* compraventa *f* al por mayor, *Am* mayoreo *m*

2 *adj (price, dealer)* al por mayor; *Fig (rejection)* rotundo(a); *(slaughter)* indiscriminado(a)

3 *adv Com* al por mayor; *Fig (reject)* rotundamente

wholesaler ['həʊlseɪlə(r)] *n* mayorista *mf*

wholesome ['həʊlsəm] *adj* sano(a), saludable

wholly ['həʊllɪ] *adv* enteramente, completamente

whom [hu:m] *pron*

> En la actualidad, sólo aparece en contextos formales. **Whom** se puede sustituir por **who** en todos los casos salvo cuando va después de preposición.

(**a**) *(in questions) (singular)* quién; *(plural)* quiénes; **w. did you see?** ¿a quién viste?; **to w. were you speaking?** ¿con quién estabas hablando? (**b**) *(relative)* que; **the woman w. you saw** la mujer que viste; **the man to w. you gave the money** el hombre al que diste el dinero; **somebody to w. he could talk** alguien con quien pudiera hablar; **the person of w. we were speaking** la persona de la que hablábamos; **the men, both of w. were quite young,...** los dos hombres, que eran bastante jóvenes,...

whoop [wu:p] **1** *n* grito *m*, alarido *m*

2 *vi (shout)* gritar

whoopee [wʊ'pi:] **1** *n Fam* **to make w.** *(have fun)* pasarlo genial or *Esp* teta

2 *exclam* ¡yupi!, ¡yuju!

whooping cough ['hu:pɪŋ'kɒf] *n* tos *f* ferina

whoops [wʊps] *exclam* ¡huy!

whopper ['wɒpə(r)] *n Fam (huge thing)* enormidad *f*, *Esp* pasada *f (de grande)*; *(lie)* trola *f*, bola *f*

whopping ['wɒpɪŋ] *Fam adj* **w. (great)** enorme

whore [hɔː(r)] *n Fam* puta *f*

whorehouse ['hɔːhaʊs] *n Fam* casa *f* de putas, burdel *m*

whose [hu:z] **1** *possessive pron (in questions) (singular)* de quién; *(plural)* de quiénes; **w. are these gloves?** ¿de quién son estos guantes?; **tell me w. they are** dime de quién son

2 *possessive adj* (**a**) *(in questions) (singular)* de quién; *(plural)* de quiénes; **w. daughter are you?** ¿de quién eres hija?; **w. fault is it?** ¿de quién es la culpa? (**b**) *(relative)* cuyo(a); **the pupil w. work I showed you** el alumno cuyo trabajo te enseñé; **the man to w. wife I gave the money** el hombre a cuya esposa entregué el dinero

why [waɪ] **1** adv **(a)** (in questions) por qué; **w. didn't you say so?** ¿por qué no lo dijiste?; **w. not?** ¿por qué no?; **w. get angry?** ¿para qué esp Esp enfadarse or esp Am enojarse? **(b)** (in suggestions) por qué; **w. don't you phone him?** ¿por qué no lo llamas?; **w. don't I come with you?** ¿y si voy contigo?

2 conj (relative) por qué; **I'll tell you w. I don't like her** te diré por qué no me gusta; **that is w. I didn't say anything** (es) por eso (por lo que) no dije nada; **the reason w....** la razón por la que...

3 n **the whys and wherefores (of sth)** el cómo y por qué (de algo)

4 exclam **w., it's David!** ¡vaya, si es David!

wick [wɪk] n (of lamp, candle) pabilo m

wicked ['wɪkɪd] adj **(a)** (evil) perverso(a), malo(a); (dreadful) horroroso(a), horrible; **a w. sense of humor** un sentido del humor muy pícaro **(b)** Fam (excellent) genial, Esp guay, Am salvo RP chévere, Col tenaz, Méx muy padre, Ven arrecho(a), RP bárbaro(a)

wickedness ['wɪkɪdnɪs] n maldad f, perversidad f

wicker ['wɪkə(r)] n mimbre m; **w. chairs** asientos mpl de mimbre

wickerwork ['wɪkəwɜːk] n (baskets) cestería f

wicket ['wɪkɪt] n (in cricket) (stumps) palos mpl

wicketkeeper ['wɪkɪtkiːpə(r)] n (in cricket) cátcher mf

wide [waɪd] **1** adj **(a)** (broad) ancho(a); **it's 4 feet w.** tiene 4 pies de ancho; **how w. is it?** ¿qué ancho tiene?, ¿cuánto mide de ancho?; **in the whole w. world** de todo el ancho mundo; Comptr **w. area network** red f de área extensa; **w. receiver** (in football) receptor(ora) m,f, receiver mf **(b)** (range, experience, gap) amplio(a), extenso(a)

2 adv **to open sth w.** (eyes, mouth) abrir algo mucho; (door) abrir algo de par en par; **to be w. open to criticism** estar muy expuesto(a) a la crítica; **w. apart** muy separado(a); **to be w. awake** estar completamente despierto(a); **the shot went w.** el tiro salió desviado; **his guess was w. of the mark** su conjetura estaba totalmente descaminada

wide-angle ['waɪdæŋɡəl] adj Phot **w. lens** gran angular m

wide-eyed ['waɪdaɪd] adj con los ojos muy abiertos or como platos

widely ['waɪdlɪ] adv **(a)** (generally) en general; **she is w. expected to resign** en general se espera que dimita; **w. known** ampliamente conocido; **it is w. believed that...** existe la creencia generalizada de que... **(b)** (at a distance) **w. spaced** muy espaciado(a) **(c)** (a lot) **to travel w.** viajar mucho; **opinions differ w.** hay muchas y muy diversas opiniones

widen ['waɪdən] **1** vt (road, garment) ensanchar, ampliar; Fig (influence, limits) ampliar, extender

2 vi (river) ensancharse; (gap) acrecentarse

▸ **widen out** vi ensancharse

wide-ranging [waɪd'reɪndʒɪŋ] adj amplio(a), extenso(a)

widespread ['waɪdspred] adj extendido(a), generalizado(a)

widow ['wɪdəʊ] **1** n viuda f; **she was left a w. at the age of thirty** quedó viuda a los treinta (años); **w.'s pension** pensión f de viudedad

2 vt **to be widowed** enviudar, quedarse viudo(a)

widowed ['wɪdəʊd] adj viudo(a)

widower ['wɪdəʊə(r)] n viudo m

width [wɪdθ] n anchura f; (in swimming pool) ancho m

wield [wiːld] vt **(a)** (sword) blandir, empuñar; (pen) manejar **(b)** (power, influence) ejercer

wife [waɪf] (pl wives [waɪvz]) n mujer f, esposa f; Fam **the w.** Esp la parienta, Am la vieja, RP la doña

wifely ['waɪflɪ] adj de esposa, conyugal

wig [wɪɡ] n peluca f

wiggle ['wɪɡəl] **1** n meneo m

2 vt menear

3 vi menearse

wiggly ['wɪɡlɪ] adj Fam (line) ondulado(a)

wigwam ['wɪɡwæm] n tipi m, tienda f india

wild [waɪld] **1** adj **(a)** (not domesticated) (plant) silvestre; (animal) salvaje; (countryside) agreste; **w. flowers** flores fpl silvestres; **a w. goose chase** una búsqueda inútil; Fam **w. horses wouldn't drag it out of me** no me lo sacarán Esp ni a tiros or Am ni que me maten; Fig **to sow one's w. oats** darse la gran vida de joven; **w. rice** arroz m salvaje or silvestre; **the W. West** el salvaje oeste (americano)

(b) (unrestrained) (wind) furioso(a); (weather) desapacible, desabrido(a); (person, enthusiasm) descontrolado(a), desenfrenado(a); (promise, rumor) descabellado(a); **w. eyes** ojos mpl desorbitados; **to drive sb w.** poner a alguien fuera de sí

(c) (random) (estimate) descabellado(a); **it was just a w. guess** fue un intento de acertar al tuntún; **w. card** Comptr comodín m; Sport invitado(a) m,f por la organización; Fig incógnita f

(d) Fam (enthusiastic) **to be w. about sb/sth** estar loco(a) por alguien/algo; **I'm not w. about it** no me entusiasma mucho

2 adv **to grow w.** (plant) crecer silvestre; **to run w.** (children, criminals) estar descontrolado(a); **the audience went w.** el público se desmeleno or enfervorizó

3 n **in the w.** (animal) en estado salvaje; **in the wilds of Alaska** en los remotos parajes de Alaska

wildcat ['waɪldkæt] n **(a)** (animal) gato m montés **(b)** Ind **w. strike** huelga f salvaje

wildcatter ['waɪldkætə(r)] n buscador(ora) m,f de petróleo

wilderness ['wɪldənɪs] n desierto m, yermo m; Fig **his years in the w.** los años que pasó en el ostracismo

wildfire ['waɪldfaɪə(r)] n **to spread like w.** extenderse como un reguero de pólvora

wildfowl ['waɪldfaʊl] (pl wildfowl) n aves fpl de caza

wildlife ['waɪldlaɪf] n fauna f; **w. park** parque m natural; TV **w. program** programa m de animales

wildly ['waɪldlɪ] adv **(a)** (behave) descontroladamente; (cheer, applaud) enfervorizadamente, vehementemente; **to rush about w.** ir de aquí para allá como un(a) loco(a) **(b)** (at random) al azar **(c)** (for emphasis) (expensive, funny, enthusiastic) enormemente, tremendamente; **w. inaccurate** disparatado(a); **w. exaggerated** exageradísimo(a)

wildness ['waɪldnɪs] n **(a)** (of country, animal) estado m salvaje **(b)** (of wind, waves) furia f, violencia f; (of applause) fervor m, vehemencia f; (of ideas, words) extravagancia f, excentricidad f

will¹ [wɪl] **1** n **(a)** (resolve, determination) voluntad f; **at w.** a voluntad; **the w. to live** las ganas de vivir; **to show good w.** demostrar tener buena voluntad; **with the best w. in the world** con la mejor voluntad del mundo; **he imposed his w. on them** les impuso su voluntad; **this computer has a w. of its own** Esp este ordenador or Am esta computadora hace lo que le da la gana; Prov **where there's a w. there's a way** quien la sigue, la consigue

(b) Law testamento m; **the last w. and testament of...** la última voluntad de...; **to make one's w.** hacer testamento

2 vt **(a)** **he was willing her to win** deseaba vehementemente que ganara; **she was willing herself to do it** apeló a toda su fuerza de voluntad para hacerlo **(b)** (leave in one's will) **to w. sth to sb** legar algo a alguien

will² modal aux v

En el inglés hablado, y en el escrito en estilo coloquial, el verbo **will** se contrae de manera que **I/you/he** etc **will** se transforman en **I'll, you'll, he'll** etc. La forma negativa **will not** se transforma en **won't**.

(a) (expressing future tense) **I'll do it tomorrow** lo haré mañana; **it won't take long** no llevará or Am demorará mucho tiempo; **persuading the parents w. be difficult** va a ser difícil convencer a los padres; **you'll write to me, won't you?** me escribirás, ¿verdad?; **you won't forget, w. you?** no te olvides, por favor; **w. you be there? — yes I w./no I won't** ¿vas a ir? — sí/no

(b) (expressing wish, determination) **I won't allow it!** ¡no lo permitiré!; **w. you help me?** ¿me ayudas?; **she won't let me see him** no me deja verlo; **won't you sit down?** ¿no se quiere sentar?; **be quiet for a minute, w. you?** estate callado un momento, ¿quieres?; **if she** WILL **insist on doing everything herself...** como insiste en hacerlo todo ella...; WILL **you go away!** ¡quieres hacer el favor de irte!; **it won't open** no se abre

(c) (expressing general truth) **the restaurant w. seat a hundred people** el restaurante puede albergar a cien personas; **these things w. happen** son cosas que pasan

(d) (conjecture) **you'll be tired** debes de estar cansado; **they'll be home by now** ya deben de haber llegado a casa

willful ['wɪlfʊl] adj (a) (stubborn) obstinado(a), tozudo(a) (b) (deliberate) premeditado(a), deliberado(a); Law **w. murder** asesinato m premeditado

willfully ['wɪlfəlɪ] adv (a) (stubbornly) obstinadamente, tozudamente (b) (deliberately) deliberadamente

willies ['wɪlɪz] npl Fam **to have the w.** tener canguelo; **this place gives me the w.** este lugar me da canguelo

willing ['wɪlɪŋ] adj (assistant) muy dispuesto(a); (accomplice) voluntario(a); **she was a w. participant** participó de muy buena gana; **to be w. to do sth** estar dispuesto(a) a hacer algo, hacer algo de buena gana; **God w.** si Dios quiere

willingly ['wɪlɪŋlɪ] adv de buena gana, gustosamente; **I would w. help** ayudaría gustoso

willingness ['wɪlɪŋnɪs] n buena disposición f

will-o'-the-wisp [wɪləðə'wɪsp] n (light) fuego m fatuo; Fig (elusive aim) quimera f

willow ['wɪləʊ] n **w. (tree)** sauce m

willpower ['wɪlpaʊə(r)] n fuerza f de voluntad

willy-nilly ['wɪlɪ'nɪlɪ] adv (like it or not) a la fuerza, quieras o no; (haphazardly) a la buena de Dios

wilt [wɪlt] vi (plant) marchitarse; Fig (person) flaquear, resentirse

wily ['waɪlɪ] adj astuto(a), taimado(a)

WIMP [wɪmp] Comptr n (abbr **windows, icons, menus and pointing device** or **pointer**) W. (interface) interfaz m or f WIMP

wimp [wɪmp] n Fam (physically) debilucho(a) m,f; (lacking character) blandengue mf

wimpish ['wɪmpɪʃ] adj Fam blandengue

win [wɪn] **1** n victoria f, triunfo m

2 vt (pt & pp **won** [wʌn]) (battle, race, prize, election) ganar; (popularity, recognition) obtener, ganar; (confidence, love) ganarse; (parliamentary seat) obtener, sacar; **to w. an argument** salir victorioso(a) en una discusión; **to w. money off** or **from sb** ganarle dinero a alguien; Fam **you can't w. them all, you w. some you lose some** a veces se gana y a veces se pierde

3 vi ganar; Fam **you (just) can't w.** no hay forma de salir ganando; **OK, you w.!** de acuerdo or Esp vale, tú ganas

▸**win around** vt sep convencer, ganarse (el apoyo de)
▸**win back** vt sep recuperar
▸**win out, win through** vi (succeed) triunfar
▸**win over** vt sep convencer, ganarse (el apoyo de)

wince [wɪns] **1** n (of pain) mueca f de dolor; (of embarrassment) gesto m de bochorno

2 vi (with pain) hacer una mueca de dolor; (with embarrassment) hacer un gesto de bochorno

winch [wɪntʃ] **1** n torno m, cabrestante m

2 vt levantar con un torno or cabrestante

wind¹ [wɪnd] **1** n (a) (air current) viento m; **to sail into** or **against the w.** navegar contra el viento; Fig **to sail close to the w.** lindar con lo prohibido; **w. energy** energía f eólica; **w. farm** parque m eólico, central f eólica; **w. instrument** instrumento m de viento; **w. power** energía f eólica; Av **w. sock** manga f (catavientos); **w. tunnel** túnel m aerodinámico

(b) (breath) aliento m, resuello m; **let me get my w. back** deja que recupere el aliento

(c) (abdominal) gases mpl, flatulencia f; **to break w.** soltar una ventosidad; **the baby's got w.** el bebé tiene gases

(d) (idioms) **to take the w. out of sb's sails** bajar la moral a alguien; **to get w. of sth** enterarse de algo

2 vt **to w. sb** (with punch) dejar a alguien sin respiración

wind² [waɪnd] (pt & pp **wound** [waʊnd]) **1** vt (a) (thread, string) enrollar (b) (handle) dar vueltas a; (clock, watch) dar cuerda a; **to w. a tape on/back** pasar rápidamente/rebobinar una cinta

2 vi (path, river) serpentear, zigzaguear; **the road winds up/down the hill** la carretera sube/baja la colina haciendo eses

▸**wind around** vt sep **to w. sth around sth** enrollar algo alrededor de algo

▸**wind down** **1** vt sep (a) (car window) bajar, abrir (b) (reduce) (production) ir reduciendo; (company) ir reduciendo la actividad de

2 vi (a) (party, meeting) ir concluyendo (b) Fam (person) relajarse

▸**wind up 1** vt sep (a) (car window) subir, cerrar (b) (bring to an end) (meeting, business) concluir

2 vi (a) (end speech, meeting) concluir (b) Fam (end up) terminar

windbag ['wɪndbæg] n Fam charlatán(ana) m,f

windbreak ['wɪndbreɪk] n pantalla f contra el viento

Windbreaker® ['wɪndbreɪkə(r)] n (jacket) cazadora f, CSur campera f, Méx chamarra f

windchill factor ['wɪndtʃɪlfæktə(r)] n índice m de enfriamiento (del aire)

winder ['waɪndə(r)] n (on watch) cuerda f; (on car door) manivela f

windfall ['wɪndfɔːl] n (of fruit) fruta f caída; Fig (of money) dinero m caído del cielo; Fin **w. profits** (of company) beneficio m inesperado

winding ['waɪndɪŋ] adj (path, stream) serpenteante, zigzagueante; **w. staircase** escalera f de caracol

windmill ['wɪndmɪl] n molino m de viento

window ['wɪndəʊ] n (a) (of house) & Comptr ventana f; (of vehicle) ventana f, ventanilla f; (of store) escaparate m, Am vidriera f, Chile, Col, Méx vitrina f; (at bank, ticket office) ventanilla f; **w. box** jardinera f; **w. cleaner** limpiacristales mf inv; **w. dressing** (in store) escaparatismo m; Fig presentación f engañosa de los hechos; **w. frame** marco m de ventana; **w. ledge** alféizar m, antepecho m (cornisa exterior); **w. seat** asiento m de ventana

(b) (idioms) **to provide a w. on sth** dar una idea de algo; **w. of opportunity** período m favorable; Fam **that's my vacation out of the w.** ya me he quedado sin vacaciones

windowpane ['wɪndəʊpeɪn] n vidrio m or Esp cristal m (de ventana)

window-shopping ['wɪndəʊʃɒpɪŋ] n **to go w.** ir a ver escaparates

windowsill ['wɪndəʊsɪl] n alféizar m, antepecho m

windpipe ['wɪndpaɪp] n tráquea f

windshield ['wɪndʃiːld] n parabrisas m inv; **w. wiper** limpiaparabrisas m inv

windsurf ['wɪndsɜːf] vi hacer windsurf, hacer tabla a vela

windsurfing ['wɪndsɜːfɪŋ] n **to go w.** ir a hacer windsurf or tabla a vela

windswept ['wɪndswept] *adj (hillside, scene)* azotado(a) por el viento; **w. hair** pelo revuelto por el viento

windward ['wɪndwəd] *adj* de barlovento; **the W. Islands** las Islas de Barlovento

windy¹ ['wɪndɪ] *adj (day)* ventoso(a); *(place)* expuesto(a) al viento; **it's w.** hace viento

windy² ['waɪndɪ] *adj (road)* serpenteante, zigzagueante

wine [waɪn] **1** *n* vino *m*; **red/white w.** vino tinto/blanco; **w. bar** bar *m (de cierta elegancia, especializado en vinos y con una pequeña carta de comidas)*; **w. bottle** botella *f* de vino; **w. cellar** bodega *f*; **w. grower** viticultor(ora) *m,f*; **w. list** carta *f* de vinos; **w. rack** botellero *m*; **w. tasting** cata *f* de vinos; **w. vinegar** vinagre *m* de vino

2 *vt* **to w. and dine sb** agasajar a alguien

wineglass ['waɪnglɑːs] *n* copa *f* de vino

wing [wɪŋ] **1** *n* **(a)** *(of bird, plane)* ala *f*; *Fig* **to take sb under one's w.** poner a alguien bajo la propia tutela, apadrinar a alguien; *Fig* **to spread** *or* **stretch one's wings** remontar el vuelo, echarse al ruedo; **w. nut** palomilla *f*

(b) *(of building, hospital)* ala *f*

(c) *(in soccer, rugby) (area)* banda *f*; *(player)* extremo *mf*, lateral *mf*; **w. forward** *(in rugby)* ala *m* delantero

(d) *(in theater)* **the wings** los bastidores; **to be waiting in the wings** *(actor)* esperar entre bastidores; *Fig* esperar su oportunidad

(e) *Pol* **the left/right w.** la izquierda/derecha

(f) *(in Air Force)* **a fighter/bomber w.** un ala de cazas/ bombarderos

2 *vt* **(a)** *(injure) (bird)* herir en el ala; *(person)* herir en el brazo **(b)** *Fam (improvise)* **to w. it** improvisar **(c)** *(fly) (bird)* **to w. its way toward** volar hacia; *Fig* **my report should be winging its way toward you** mi informe *or Am* reporte ya está en camino

winger ['wɪŋə(r)] *n (in soccer, rugby)* extremo *mf*, lateral *mf*

wingspan ['wɪŋspæn] *n* envergadura *f* (de alas)

wink [wɪŋk] **1** *n* guiño *m*; **to give sb a w.** guiñarle un ojo a alguien; *Fam* **I didn't sleep a w.** no pegué ojo

2 *vi* guiñar, hacer un guiño; *(star, light)* titilar

▸**wink at** *vt insep (person)* guiñar a, hacer un guiño a; *Fig (abuse, illegal practice)* hacer la vista gorda ante

winkle ['wɪŋkəl] *n (mollusk)* bígaro *m*

winner ['wɪnə(r)] *n* vencedor(ora) *m,f*, ganador(ora) *m,f*; **this book will be a w.** este libro será un éxito; **to be on to a w.** tener un éxito entre manos

winning ['wɪnɪŋ] **1** *adj* **(a)** *(victorious) (team, person)* ganador(ora), vencedor(ora); *(basket, goal, run, touchdown)* de la victoria; *(ticket, number)* premiado(a); **w. post** meta *f*; **w. streak** racha *f* de suerte **(b)** *(attractive)* encantador(ora), atractivo(a)

2 *npl* **winnings** ganancias *fpl*

winnow ['wɪnəʊ] *vt (grain)* aventar

wino ['waɪnəʊ] *(pl* **winos)** *n Fam (alcoholic)* borracho(a) *m,f*

winsome ['wɪnsəm] *adj* encantador(ora), atractivo(a)

winter ['wɪntə(r)] **1** *n* invierno *m*; **in (the) w.** en invierno; **w. break** vacaciones *fpl* de invierno; **w. clothing** ropa *f* de invierno

2 *vi* pasar el invierno

wintertime ['wɪntətaɪm] *n* invierno *m*

wint(e)ry ['wɪntərɪ] *adj (weather)* invernal; *Fig (smile)* gélido(a), glacial

wipe [waɪp] **1** *n* **(a)** *(action)* **to give sth a w.** limpiar algo con un paño, pasar el paño a algo **(b)** *(moist tissue)* toallita *f* húmeda

2 *vt* **(a)** *(table, plate)* pasar un paño por *or* a; **to w. one's nose** limpiarse la nariz; **he wiped his hands on the towel** se secó las manos con la toalla; **to w. one's shoes on the mat** limpiarse los zapatos en el felpudo; *Fam* **to w. up the floor with sb** dar una paliza a alguien **(b)** *(recording tape)* borrar

▸**wipe away** *vt sep (tears)* enjugar; *(mark)* limpiar, quitar, *Am* sacar

▸**wipe off 1** *vt sep* limpiar; *Fam* **that'll w. the smile off his face!** ¡eso le borrará la sonrisa de la cara!

2 *vi (stain)* salir, quitarse

▸**wipe out** *vt sep* **(a)** *(erase) (memory)* borrar; *(debt)* saldar **(b)** *(destroy) (family, species)* hacer desaparecer

▸**wipe up** *vt sep* limpiar

wiper ['waɪpə(r)] *n Aut* limpiaparabrisas *m inv*

wire ['waɪə(r)] **1** *n* **(a)** *(in general)* alambre *m*; *(electrical)* cable *m*; **w. brush** cepillo *m* de púas metálicas; **w. fence** alambrada *f*; **w. mesh** malla *f or* tela *f* metálica **(b)** *(telegram)* telegrama *m* **(c)** *(idioms) Fam* **we got our wires crossed** tuvimos un cruce de cables y no nos entendimos; **the contest went right down to the w.** el desenlace del concurso no se decidió hasta el último momento

2 *vt* **(a)** *(house)* cablear, tender el cableado de; **to w. sth to sth** *(connect electrically)* conectar algo a algo (con un cable); *(attach with wire)* sujetar algo a algo con un alambre **(b)** *(send telegram to)* mandar un telegrama a

wirecutters ['waɪəkʌtəz] *npl* cizallas *fpl*; **a pair of w.** unas cizallas

wired [waɪəd] *adj Fam* **(a)** *(highly strung)* tenso(a) **(b)** *(after taking drugs)* muy acelerado(a), *Esp* espídico(a)

wireless ['waɪəlɪs] *adj Comptr* wireless, inalámbrico(a)

wire-puller ['waɪəpʊlə(r)] *n* = persona que mueve los hilos

wiretap ['waɪətæp] **1** *n* escucha *f* telefónica

2 *vt* intervenir

wiretapping ['waɪətæpɪŋ] *n Tel* intervención *f* de la línea

wiring ['waɪərɪŋ] *n (electrical)* instalación *f* eléctrica

wiry ['waɪərɪ] *adj* **(a)** *(hair)* basto(a) y rizado(a) *or Méx* quebrado(a) **(b)** *(person)* fibroso(a)

wisdom ['wɪzdəm] *n (knowledge)* sabiduría *f*; *(judgment)* sensatez *f*, cordura *f*; **w. tooth** muela *f* del juicio

wise [waɪz] *adj (knowledgeable)* sabio(a); *(sensible)* sensato(a), prudente; *Am* **w. man** un sabio; *Fam Pej* **a w. guy** un sabelotodo; **the Three W. Men** los Reyes Magos; **it wouldn't be w. to do it** no sería aconsejable hacerlo; **to be w. after the event** verlo todo claro a posteriori; **to be none the wiser** no haber sacado nada en claro; *Fam* **to get w. to a fact** percatarse de un hecho; *Fam* **to get w. to sb** calar a alguien

▸**wise up** *Fam vi* **to w. up to sb** calar a alguien; **to w. up to the fact that…** aceptar el hecho de que…; **w. up!** ¡espabílate!

-wise [waɪz] *suffix Fam (with reference to)* **health/salary-w.** en cuanto a la salud/al salario

wisecrack ['waɪzkræk] *Fam* **1** *n* chiste *m*, salida *f* ingeniosa

2 *vi* soltar un chiste *or* una salida ingeniosa

wisely ['waɪzlɪ] *adv (prudently)* sensatamente

wish [wɪʃ] **1** *n* **(a)** *(desire)* deseo *m*; **to make a w.** pedir un deseo; **to have no w. to do sth** no tener ningún deseo de hacer algo; **to do sth against sb's wishes** hacer algo en contra de los deseos de alguien **(b)** *(greeting)* **(with) best wishes** *(in letter, on card)* un saludo cordial *or* afectuoso; **they send you their best wishes** te envían saludos *or CAm, Col, Ecuad* saludes

2 *vt* **(a)** *(want)* desear, querer; **to w. to do sth** desear hacer algo; **it is to be wished that…** sería deseable que…; **to w. sb well** desearle a alguien lo mejor; **to w. sb luck/a pleasant journey** desear a alguien suerte/un buen viaje **(b)** *(want something impossible, unlikely)* **I w. I had seen it!** ¡ojalá lo hubiera visto!; **I w. I hadn't left so early** ojalá no me hubiera marchado tan pronto; **w. you were here!** *(on postcard)* te echo de menos, *Am* te extraño

3 *vi* **to w. for sth** desear algo; **what more could you w. for?** ¿qué más se puede pedir *or* desear?; **as you w.** como quieras

wishbone ['wɪʃbəʊn] *n* espoleta *f (hueso de ave)*

wishful ['wɪʃfʊl] *adj* **that's just w. thinking** no son más que ilusiones

wishy-washy ['wɪʃɪwɒʃɪ] *adj Fam* vacilante

wisp [wɪsp] *n (of straw)* brizna *f; (of hair, wool)* mechón *m; (of smoke)* voluta *f; (of cloud)* jirón *m*

wistful ['wɪstfʊl] *adj* nostálgico(a)

wistfully ['wɪstfʊlɪ] *adv* con nostalgia

wit [wɪt] *n* **(a)** *(intelligence, presence of mind)* inteligencia *f*, lucidez *f;* **he hasn't the w. to see it** no tiene la lucidez suficiente para verlo; **to have quick wits** tener rapidez mental; **to have lost one's wits** haber perdido la razón; **to have/keep one's wits about one** ser/estar espabilado(a); **to be at one's wit's end** estar al borde de la desesperación; **to live by one's wits** ser un pícaro; **to scare sb out of his wits** dar un susto de muerte a alguien **(b)** *(humor)* ingenio *m*, agudeza *f* **(c)** *(witty person)* ingenioso(a) *m,f*

witch [wɪtʃ] *n* bruja *f;* **w. doctor** hechicero *m*, curandero *m; Pol* **w. hunt** caza *f* de brujas

witchcraft ['wɪtʃkrɑːft] *n* brujería *f*

with [wɪð] *prep* con; **w. me** conmigo; **w. you** contigo; **w. himself/herself** consigo; **to travel/work w. sb** viajar/ trabajar con alguien; **he is staying w. friends** se queda con *or* en casa de unos amigos; **a girl w. blue eyes** una chica de ojos azules; **I was left w. nobody to talk to** me quedé sin nadie con quien hablar; **this problem will always be w. us** siempre tendremos este problema; **she came in w. a suitcase** entró con una maleta en la mano; **I'm w. you** *(I support you)* estoy contigo; **I'm not w. you** *(I don't understand)* no te sigo; *Fam* **to be w. it** *(fashionable) (person)* ser enrollado(a) *or Méx* suave *or RP* copado(a); *(clothing)* estar en la onda; **a smile** con una sonrisa, sonriendo

withdraw [wɪð'drɔː] *(pt* **withdrew** [wɪð'druː], *pp* **withdrawn** [wɪð'drɔːn]) **1** *vt* retirar; *(money)* sacar **(from** de)
2 *vi* retirarse; **to w. in favor of sb** dejar paso a alguien; **she withdrew into herself** se encerró en sí misma

withdrawal [wɪð'drɔːəl] *n (of support, accusation)* retirada *f;* **to make a w.** *(from bank)* efectuar un reintegro; **w. symptoms** síndrome *m* de abstinencia

withdrawn [wɪð'drɔːn] **1** *adj* retraído(a)
2 *pp of* **withdraw**

withdrew [wɪð'druː] *pt of* **withdraw**

wither ['wɪðə(r)] *vi (plant)* marchitarse; *(limb)* atrofiarse

withered ['wɪðəd] *adj (plant)* marchito(a); *(limb)* atrofiado(a)

withering ['wɪðərɪŋ] *adj (look)* fulminante; *(tone)* mordaz

withhold [wɪð'həʊld] *(pt & pp* **withheld** [wɪð'held]) *vt (consent, help)* negar **(from** a); *(money)* retener **(from** a); *(information, the truth)* ocultar **(from** a)

within [wɪð'ɪn] **1** *prep* **(a)** *(inside)* dentro de; **problems w. the party** problemas en el seno del partido
(b) *(not beyond)* **he lives w. a few miles of downtown** vive a pocas millas del centro; **w. a radius of ten miles** en un radio de diez millas; **w. limits** dentro de un orden, hasta cierto punto; **w. reason** dentro de lo razonable; **w. sight** a la vista; *Fam* **to come w. an inch of doing sth** estar en un tris de hacer algo; **w. the law** dentro de la legalidad
(c) *(time)* en menos de; **w. an hour** en menos de una hora; **w. the next five years** *(during) (in future)* durante los próximos cinco años; *(in past)* durante los cinco años siguientes; *(before end of)* dentro de un plazo de cinco años; **they died w. a few days of each other** murieron con pocos días de diferencia
2 *adv* **from w.** desde dentro

without [wɪð'aʊt] **1** *prep* sin; **w. any money/difficulty** sin dinero/dificultad; **a journey w. end** un viaje sin fin; **w. doing sth** sin hacer algo; **it goes w. saying that...** huelga decir que...; **to do** *or* **go w. sth** pasar sin algo
2 *adv* **(a) she went w. so that her children would have**

enough to eat ella se quedaba sin comer para que sus hijos tuvieran suficiente **(b)** *Formal* **from w.** desde fuera *or Am* afuera

withstand [wɪð'stænd] *(pt & pp* **withstood** [wɪð'stʊd]) *vt* soportar, aguantar

witless ['wɪtlɪs] *adj (person, remark)* necio(a), simple; **to scare sb w.** helar la sangre en las venas a alguien

witness ['wɪtnɪs] **1** *n* **(a)** *Law* testigo *mf;* **to call sb as a w.** llamar a alguien a testificar; **w. for the defense/prosecution** testigo de descargo/de cargo; **w. box** estrado *m* del testigo **(b)** *(testimony)* **to bear w. (to sth)** dar testimonio (de algo)
2 *vt (scene)* ser testigo de, presenciar; *Law* **to w. sb's signature** firmar en calidad de testigo de alguien
3 *vi Law* **to w. to sth** dar testimonio de algo

witticism ['wɪtɪsɪzəm] *n* ocurrencia *f*, agudeza *f*

wittily ['wɪtɪlɪ] *adv* ingeniosamente

wittingly ['wɪtɪŋlɪ] *adv (intentionally)* adrede, intencionadamente

witty ['wɪtɪ] *adj* ingenioso(a), agudo(a)

wives [waɪvz] *pl of* **wife**

wizard ['wɪzəd] *n* brujo *m*, mago *m; Fig* genio *m*

wizened ['wɪzənd] *adj* marchito(a), arrugado(a)

wk *(abbr* **week**) semana *f*

WMD [estiː'diː] *npl (abbr* **weapons of mass destruction)** armas *fpl* de destrucción masiva

wobble ['wɒbəl] *vi (chair, table)* tambalearse, cojear; *(jelly)* temblar, agitarse

wobbly ['wɒblɪ] *adj (chair, table)* cojo(a); *(shelf, ladder)* tambaleante; **to be w. (on one's legs)** tambalearse, andar con paso inseguro

woe [wəʊ] *n Literary* infortunio *m*, desdicha *f;* **he gave me a tale of w.** me contó una sarta de desgracias

woebegone ['wəʊbɪgɒn] *adj (look, expression)* desconsolado(a)

woeful ['wəʊfʊl] *adj* **(a)** *(sad)* apesadumbrado(a), afligido(a) **(b)** *(terrible)* penoso(a), deplorable; **w. ignorance** una ignorancia supina

woefully ['wəʊfʊlɪ] *adv* **(a)** *(sadly)* apesadumbradamente, con pesadumbre **(b)** *(extremely)* terriblemente, extremadamente

wok [wɒk] *n* wok *m*, = sartén china con forma de cuenco

woke [wəʊk] *pt of* **wake**³

woken ['wəʊkən] *pp of* **wake**³

wolf [wʊlf] *(pl* **wolves** [wʊlvz]) *n* **(a)** *(animal)* lobo *m;* **w. cub** lobezno *m*, lobato *m* **(b)** *(idioms)* **to earn enough to keep the w. from the door** ganar lo suficiente como para ir tirando; **to throw sb to the wolves** arrojar a alguien a las fieras; **a w. in sheep's clothing** un lobo con piel de cordero; **to cry w.** dar una falsa voz de alarma

▶**wolf down** *vt sep* tragar, engullir

woman ['wʊmən] *(pl* **women** ['wɪmɪn]) *n* mujer *f;* **don't be such an old w.!** *(said to man)* ¡no seas tan quejica!; **w. driver** conductora *f;* **women's page** páginas *fpl* femeninas; **women's magazine** revista *f* femenina; **women's lib** *or* **liberation** la liberación de la mujer; **the women's movement** el movimiento feminista; *Euph* **women's problems** *(gynecological)* problemas *mpl* femeninos; **women's rights** los derechos de la mujer; **women's shelter** centro *m* de acogida para mujeres (maltratadas)

womanizer ['wʊmənaɪzə(r)] *n* mujeriego *m*

womanly ['wʊmənlɪ] *adj* femenino(a)

womb [wuːm] *n* matriz *f*, útero *m*

women ['wɪmɪn] *pl of* **woman**

womenfolk ['wɪmɪnfəʊk] *n* mujeres *fpl*

won [wʌn] *pt & pp of* **win**

wonder ['wʌndə(r)] **1** *n* **(a)** *(miracle)* milagro *m;* **to work** *or* **do**

wonders hacer milagros; **it's a w. (that) he hasn't lost it** es un milagro *or* es increíble que no lo haya perdido; **no w. the plan failed** no es de extrañar que el plan haya fracasado; **w. drug** droga milagrosa (**b**) *(astonishment)* asombro *m*; **in w.** con asombro

2 *vt* preguntarse; **one wonders whether…** me pregunto si…; **I was wondering if you were free tonight** se me ocurre que quizá no tengas nada que hacer esta noche

3 *vi* (**a**) *(be curious)* tener curiosidad, pensar; **to w. about sth** preguntarse por algo; **I w. about her sometimes** hay veces que no la entiendo (**b**) *Literary (be amazed)* asombrarse (**at** de)

wonderful ['wʌndəfʊl] *adj* maravilloso(a)

wondrous ['wʌndrəs] *adj* maravilloso(a)

wont [wəʊnt] *Formal* **1** *n* costumbre *f*; **as is his w.** como acostumbra

2 *adj* **to be w. to do sth** ser dado(a) a hacer algo

won't [wəʊnt] = **will not**

woo [wu:] *vt* (**a**) *Literary (woman)* cortejar (**b**) *(supporters, investors)* atraer

wood [wʊd] *n* (**a**) *(material)* madera *f*; *(for fire)* leña *f*; **made of w.** de madera; **w. carving** *(object)* talla *f* (en madera); **w. louse** cochinilla *f* (**b**) *(forest)* bosque *m*; **the woods** el bosque (**c**) *(idioms)* **we're not out of the woods yet** todavía no hemos salido del túnel

woodbine ['wʊdbaɪn] *n (plant)* madreselva *f*

woodchip ['wʊdtʃɪp] *n* = papel pintado con trocitos de madera para dar textura

woodcock ['wʊdkɒk] *n* becada *f*, chocha *f*

woodcut ['wʊdkʌt] *n* grabado *m* en madera, xilografía *f*

woodcutter ['wʊdkʌtə(r)] *n* leñador(ora) *m,f*

wooded ['wʊdɪd] *adj* cubierto(a) de árboles, boscoso(a)

wooden ['wʊdən] *adj (made of wood)* de madera; *Fig (unexpressive)* envarado(a), acartonado(a); **w. spoon** cuchara *f* de palo

woodland ['wʊdlənd] *n* bosque *m*

woodlouse ['wʊdlaʊs] *(pl* **woodlice** ['wʊdlaɪs]*) n* cochinilla *f*

woodpecker ['wʊdpekə(r)] *n* pájaro *m* carpintero

woodpile ['wʊdpaɪl] *n* montón *m* de leña

woodshed ['wʊdʃed] *n* leñera *f*

woodwind ['wʊdwɪnd] *n Mus (section of orchestra)* sección *f* de (instrumentos de) viento de madera; **w. instrument** instrumento *m* de viento de madera

woodwork ['wʊdwɜːk] *n* (**a**) *(craft)* carpintería *f* (**b**) *(of house, room)* madera *f*, carpintería *f*; *Fig* **to come** *or* **crawl out of the w.** salir de las sombras, surgir de la nada

woodworm ['wʊdwɜːm] *n* carcoma *f*

woof [wʊf] *exclam (of dog)* ¡guau!

wool [wʊl] *n* lana *f*; *Fam* **to pull the w. over sb's eyes** embaucar *or Esp* dar el pego a alguien

woolen ['wʊlən] **1** *adj (dress)* de lana

2 *npl* **woolens** prendas *fpl* de lana

woolly ['wʊlɪ] *adj (sweater)* de lana; *Fig (idea, theory)* confuso(a)

wop [wɒp] *n very Fam* = término despectivo para referirse a personas de origen italiano

word [wɜːd] **1** *n* (**a**) *(in general)* palabra *f*; **w. for w.** al pie de la letra; **in a w.** en una palabra; **in other words** en otras palabras; **not in so many words** no con esas palabras; **not a w.** ni una (sola) palabra; **she said it in her own words** lo dijo con sus propias palabras; **I can't put it into words** no lo puedo expresar con palabras; **he's a man of few words** es hombre de pocas palabras; **I couldn't get a w. in (edgewise)** no pude meter baza; **the W. of God** la palabra de Dios; **I'll take your w. for it** daré por cierto lo que (me) dices; **to take sb at his w.** no poner en duda lo que alguien dice; **without a w.** sin mediar palabra; **it was too ridiculous for words** no se puede imaginar nada más ridículo;

my w.! ¡Virgen Santa!; *Comptr* **w. processing** tratamiento *m* de textos; *Comptr* **w. processor** procesador *m* de textos

(**b**) *(remarks, conversation)* **to have a w. with sb** hablar con alguien; **to have words with sb** discutir con alguien; **to give sb the w.** dar un aviso a alguien; **you're putting words into my mouth** me estás atribuyendo cosas que no he dicho; **you've taken the words (right) out of my mouth** me has quitado *or Am* sacado la palabra de la boca; **to put in a good w. for sb** decir algo en favor de alguien; **he never has a good w. for anyone** nunca tiene buenas palabras para nadie; **a w. of warning** una advertencia; **a w. of advice** un consejo

(**c**) *(news)* **to receive w. from sb** tener noticias de alguien; **to send sb w. of sth** avisar a alguien de algo; **the w. is that…** se rumorea que…; **by w. of mouth** de palabra

(**d**) *(promise)* **w. of honor** palabra *f* de honor; **she gave me her w.** me dio su palabra; **I always keep my w.** yo siempre mantengo mi palabra; **he broke** *or* **went back on his w.** no cumplió con su palabra

(**e**) **words** *(lyrics)* letra *f*

2 *vt* expresar; *(in writing)* redactar

word-for-word [wɜːdfə'wɜːd] *adj* literal

wording ['wɜːdɪŋ] *n* **to change the w. of sth** redactar algo de otra forma; **the w. was ambiguous** estaba redactado de forma ambigua

word-of-mouth [wɜːdəv'maʊθ] *adj* boca a boca; *Mktg* **w. advertising** publicidad *f* boca a boca

wordy ['wɜːdɪ] *adj* verboso(a)

wore [wɔː(r)] *pt of* **wear**

work [wɜːk] **1** *n* (**a**) *(labor)* trabajo *m*; **to be at w. (on sth)** estar trabajando (en algo); **to get to w.** ponerse a trabajar; **w. in progress** *(sign)* trabajos en curso; **the w. ethic** la ética del trabajo; *Comptr* **w. station** estación *f* de trabajo

(**b**) *(employment)* trabajo *m*, empleo *m*; **to look for w.** buscar empleo *or* trabajo; **to be out of w.** no tener trabajo, *Esp* estar parado(a); **w. experience** *(previous employment)* experiencia *f* laboral; **w. hours** horario *m* de trabajo; **w. permit** permiso *m* de trabajo

(**c**) *(tasks)* trabajo *m*; **to have w. to do** tener trabajo (que hacer); **it will take a lot of w.** costará mucho trabajo; **to put a lot of w. into sth** poner mucho esfuerzo en algo; **let's get down to w.!** ¡manos a la obra!; **to have one's w. cut out** tenerlo bastante difícil; **to make quick** *or* **short w. of sth** despachar algo en seguida; **it's all in a day's w.** es el pan nuestro de cada día; **good** *or* **nice w.!** ¡buen trabajo!

(**d**) *(product, achievement)* obra *f*; **a w. of art** una obra de arte; **is this all your own w.?** ¿lo has hecho todo tú mismo?

(**e**) **works** *(construction)* obras *fpl*

(**f**) **works** *(mechanism)* mecanismo *m*

(**g**) *Fam* **the works** *(everything)* todo; **to give sb the works** *(beating)* dar una paliza a alguien; *(luxury treatment)* tratar a alguien a cuerpo de rey

2 *vt* (**a**) **to w. sb hard** hacer trabajar mucho a alguien; **to w. oneself to death** matarse a trabajar; **to w. one's passage** pagarse el pasaje trabajando en el barco

(**b**) *(operate) (machine)* manejar, hacer funcionar

(**c**) *(bring about) (miracle, cure)* hacer, obrar; **to w. a change on sth/sb** operar un cambio en algo/alguien; **I'll w. it** *or* **things so that they pay in advance** lo arreglaré de forma que paguen por adelantado

(**d**) *(move)* **to w. one's hands free** lograr soltarse las manos; **to w. one's way through a book** ir avanzando en la lectura de un libro

(**e**) *(exploit) (mine, quarry)* explotar; *(land)* labrar

3 *vi* (**a**) *(person)* trabajar; **to w. for sb** trabajar para alguien; **her age works against her/in her favor** la edad juega en su contra/en su favor (**b**) *(function) (machine, system)* funcionar (**c**) *(have effect) (medicine)* hacer efecto; *(plan, method)* funcionar

▸**work in** *vt sep (include)* añadir, incluir

▸**work off** *vt sep* **he worked off 5 pounds** perdió 5 libras haciendo ejercicio; **she worked off her anger** desahogó su enfado

▸**work on 1** *vt insep* **to w. on sth** trabajar en algo **2** *vi (continue to work)* seguir trabajando

▸**work out 1** *vt sep (cost, total)* calcular; **to w. out the answer** dar con la solución; **to w. out how to do sth** dar con la manera de hacer algo; **I'm sure we can w. this thing out** estoy seguro de que lo podemos arreglar **2** *vi* (**a**) *(problem, situation)* **it all worked out in the end** al final todo salió bien; **to w. out well/badly (for sb)** salir bien/mal (a alguien) (**b**) *(total)* salir; **it works out at $150 a head** sale a 150 dólares por cabeza (**c**) *(exercise)* hacer ejercicios

▸**work up** *vt sep* (**a**) *(develop)* **to w. up enthusiasm/ interest for sth** ir entusiasmándose con/interesándose por algo; **he had worked up an appetite** ya le había entrado el apetito (**b**) *(excite)* **to get worked up (about sth)** alterarse (por algo)

▸**work up to** *vt insep* prepararse *or Am* alistarse para

workable ['wɜːkəbəl] *adj* factible

workaday ['wɜːkədeɪ] *adj* corriente, de todos los días

workaholic [wɜːkə'hɒlɪk] *n Fam* **to be a w.** estar obsesionado(a) con el trabajo

workbench ['wɜːkbentʃ] *n* banco *m* de carpintero

workday ['wɜːkdeɪ] *n* jornada *f* laboral

worker ['wɜːkə(r)] *n* trabajador(ora) *m,f*; **to be a fast/slow w.** trabajar rápido/lento; **w. bee** abeja *f* obrera; **w. compensation** indemnización *f* laboral; **w. participation** participación *f* (de los trabajadores) en la empresa

workforce ['wɜːkfɔːs] *n (working population)* población *f* activa; *(employees)* trabajadores *mpl*, mano *f* de obra

workhouse ['wɜːkhaʊs] *n* correccional *m*

working ['wɜːkɪŋ] **1** *n* (**a**) *(operation) (of machine)* funcionamiento *m* (**b**) **workings** *(mechanism)* mecanismo *m*, maquinaria *f* **2** *adj (person)* con trabajo, trabajador(ora); **to have a w. knowledge of French** tener un conocimiento básico de francés; **to be in w. order** funcionar bien; **w. agreement** acuerdo *m* tácito; **the w. class** la clase trabajadora *or* obrera; **w. clothes/conditions** ropa *f*/ condiciones *fpl* de trabajo; **w. day** jornada *f* laboral; **w. hours** horario *m* de trabajo; **w. life** vida *f* laboral; **w. lunch** almuerzo *m* de trabajo; **w. majority** mayoría *f* suficiente; **w. model** prototipo *m*; **w. population** población *f* activa

working-class ['wɜːkɪŋ'klɑːs] *adj* de clase obrera

workload ['wɜːkləʊd] *n* cantidad *f* de trabajo

workman ['wɜːkmən] *n* obrero *m*

workmanlike ['wɜːkmənlaɪk] *adj* competente, profesional

workmanship ['wɜːkmənʃɪp] *n* confección *f*, factura *f*; **a fine piece of w.** un trabajo excelente

workout ['wɜːkaʊt] *n* sesión *f* de ejercicios

workplace ['wɜːkpleɪs] *n* lugar *m* de trabajo

worksheet ['wɜːkʃiːt] *n (detailing work plan)* hoja *f* de trabajo; *(of exercises)* hoja *f* de ejercicios

workshop ['wɜːkʃɒp] *n also Fig* taller *m*

workweek ['wɜːkwiːk] *n* semana *f* laboral

world [wɜːld] *n* (**a**) *(the earth)* mundo *m*; **the best/biggest in the w.** el mejor/más grande del mundo; **to go around the w.** dar la vuelta al mundo; **the w. over, all over the w.** en todas partes; **the W. Bank** el Banco Mundial; **w. champion** campeón(ona) *m,f* mundial; **the W. Cup** *(soccer)* el Mundial (de fútbol), los Mundiales (de fútbol); **w.'s fair** exposición *f* universal; **w. map** mapamundi *m*; **w. music** música *f* étnica; **w. record** récord *m* mundial *or* del mundo; **W. Series** = final a siete partidos entre los dos campeones de las ligas de béisbol en Estados Unidos; **w. war** guerra *f* mundial; **W. War One/Two**

la Primera/Segunda Guerra Mundial; **the W. Wide Web** la (World Wide) Web (**b**) *(sphere of activity)* mundo *m*; **the literary/business w.** el mundo literario/de los negocios (**c**) *(society)* **a man of the w.** un hombre de mundo; **to go up in the w.** prosperar; **to come down in the w.** venir a menos; **he's got the w. at his feet** tiene el mundo a sus pies; **w. view** visión *f* del mundo (**d**) *(for emphasis)* **that will do you the w. of good** te vendrá la mar de bien; **there's a w. of difference between the two parties** los dos partidos no tienen nada que ver (el uno con el otro); **she thinks the w. of him** lo quiere como a nada en el mundo; **they carried on for all the w. as if nothing had happened** siguieron tranquilamente como si nada hubiera pasado (**e**) *(idioms)* **he's not long for this w.** le queda poco, está con un pie en la tumba; **to bring a child into the w.** traer un niño al mundo; **he wants to have the best of both worlds** él quiere tenerlo todo (y eso no es posible); **she lives in a w. of her own** vive en su propio mundo; *Fam* **it's out of this w.** es una maravilla; **not for (anything in) the w.** ni por todo el oro del mundo; **it's a small w.!** ¡el mundo es un pañuelo!; **what is the w. coming to?** ¿adónde vamos a ir a parar?

world-beater ['wɜːldbiːtə(r)] *n (sportsperson)* fuera de serie *mf*; *(product)* producto *m* fuera de serie

world-famous ['wɜːld'feɪməs] *adj* mundialmente famoso(a)

worldly ['wɜːldlɪ] *adj (pleasure)* mundano(a), terrenal; **w. goods** bienes *mpl* terrenales; **w. wisdom** gramática *f* parda

worldly-wise ['wɜːldlɪ'waɪz] *adj* **to be w.** tener mucha experiencia *or* en la vida

world-weary ['wɜːldwɪərɪ] *adj* hastiado(a) (del mundo)

worldwide ['wɜːldwaɪd] **1** *adj* mundial **2** *adv* en todo el mundo

worm [wɜːm] **1** *n (gen) & Comptr* gusano *m*; *(earthworm)* lombriz *f* (de tierra); *Med* **to have worms** tener lombrices; *Fig* **he's a w.** es un miserable *or* un gusano; *Fig* **the w. has turned!** ¡finalmente el perro enseña los dientes! **2** *vt* (**a**) *(cat, dog)* administrar vermífugos a (**b**) **she wormed her way out of the situation** las ingenió para salir del paso; *Pej* **to w. oneself into sb's favor/confidence** ganarse el favor/la confianza de alguien; **to w. a secret out of sb** sonsacar un secreto a alguien

worm-eaten ['wɜːmiːtən] *adj (wood)* carcomido(a); *(fruit)* agusanado(a)

worn [wɔːn] *pp of* **wear**

worried ['wʌrɪd] *adj* preocupado(a); **to be w. (about)** estar preocupado(a) (por)

worriedly ['wʌrɪdlɪ] *adv* con preocupación

worrier ['wʌrɪə(r)] *n* **to be a w.** preocuparse por todo

worry ['wʌrɪ] **1** *n* preocupación *f*; **it's causing me a lot of w.** me tiene muy preocupado; **that's the least of my worries** eso es lo que menos me preocupa **2** *vt (cause anxiety to)* preocupar; **it doesn't w. me** no me preocupa; **to w. oneself sick (about sth)** angustiarse (por algo) **3** *vi* preocuparse (**about** de); **not to w.!** ¡no pasa nada!; **don't (you) w. about me** no te preocupes por mí; **there's** *or* **it's nothing to w. about** no hay de qué preocuparse

worrying ['wʌrɪɪŋ] *adj* preocupante

worryingly ['wʌrɪɪŋlɪ] *adv* preocupantemente, de forma preocupante

worse [wɜːs] **1** *adj (comparative of* **bad***)* peor (**than** que); **there's nothing w. than...** no hay nada peor que...; **to get w.** empeorar; **it could have been w.** podría haber sido peor; **to make matters w.** empeorar las cosas; **to go from bad to w.** ir de mal en peor; **I'm none the w. for it** no me afectó en nada; **so much the w. for them!** ¡peor para ellos!; **she was the w. for drink** estaba bastante bebida; *Fam* **to be**

the w. for wear *(car, book, drunk person)* estar para el arrastre; **I can't go, w. luck!** ¡no puedo ir, qué fastidio!

2 *adv (comparative of* **badly)** peor; **you could do (a lot) w. than accept their offer** harías bien en aceptar su oferta; **I don't think any w. of her for it** no tengo peor concepto de ella por eso; **he is w. off than before** las cosas le van peor que antes

3 *n* **there was w. to come** lo peor no había llegado aún; **I've seen w.** he visto cosas peores; **a change for the w.** un cambio a peor

worsen ['wɜːsən] *vt & vi* empeorar

worship ['wɜːʃɪp] **1** *n (of deity)* adoración *f* (**of** de), culto *m* (**of** a); *(of person)* adoración *f* (**for** por); **place of w.** templo *m*

2 *vt (deity)* adorar, rendir culto a; *(person)* adorar; *(money)* rendir culto a

worst [wɜːst] **1** *adj (superlative of* **bad)** peor; **the w. book** el peor libro; **the w. movie** la peor película; **his w. mistake** su error más grave; **the w. thing was…** lo peor fue…

2 *adv (superlative of* **badly)** peor; **w. of all,…** y lo que es peor,…; **the elderly are the w. off** los ancianos son los que peor están; **he came off w.** (él) llevó la peor parte, él fue quien salió peor

3 *n* **he's the w. of them all** es el peor de todos; **the w. that could happen** lo peor que podría suceder; **the w. of it is that…** lo peor de todo es que…; **he's prepared for the w.** está preparado para lo peor; **at the w., if it comes to the w.** en el peor de los casos; **the w. is yet to come** lo peor está aún por llegar; **do your w.!** ¡aquí te espero!, *Esp* ¡ven a por mí si puedes!; **the w. is over** ya ha pasado lo peor

worst-case scenario ['wɜːstkeɪsɪˈnɑːrɪəʊ] *(pl* **worst-case scenarios)** *n* **this is a w.** esto es lo que ocurriría en el peor de los casos

worsted ['wʊstɪd] *n Tex* estameña *f*

worth [wɜːθ] **1** *n* valor *m*; **give me $30 w. of gasoline** póngame 30 dólares de gasolina *or RP* nafta; **to get one's money's w.** sacar partido al *or* del dinero

2 *prep* **(a)** *(having a value of)* **to be w. a lot of money** valer mucho dinero; **how much is it w.?** ¿qué valor tiene?; **that's my opinion, for what it's w.** esa es mi opinión, si sirve de algo; **he's w. at least 50 million** tiene por lo menos 50 millones; **he was pulling for all he was w.** tiraba con todas sus fuerzas **(b)** *(meriting)* **the museum is w. a visit** merece la pena visitar el museo; **this book is not w. buying** no merece la pena comprar este libro; **it is/isn't w. it** merece/no merece la pena; **it's w. thinking about** es algo a tener en cuenta

worthless ['wɜːθlɪs] *adj* **to be w.** *(thing)* no valer nada, no tener ningún valor; **he's completely w.** es un perfecto inútil

worthlessness ['wɜːθlɪsnɪs] *n* falta *f* de valor, insignificancia *f*

worthwhile [wɜːθ'waɪl] *adj* **to be w.** merecer *or* valer la pena

worthy ['wɜːðɪ] **1** *n* **the town worthies** los notables *or* las fuerzas vivas de la ciudad

2 *adj (person, life)* virtuoso(a); **to be w. of sth** merecer algo; **w. of respect** digno(a) de respeto

would [wʊd] *modal aux v*

En el inglés hablado, y en el escrito en estilo coloquial, el verbo **would** se contrae de manera que **I/you/he** etc **would** se transforman en **I'd, you'd, he'd** etc. La forma negativa **would not** se transforma en **wouldn't**.

(a) *(expressing conditional tense)* **she w. come if you invited her** si la invitases, vendría; **had he let go** *or* **if he had let go, he w. have fallen** si (se) hubiera soltado, se habría caído; **they w. never agree to such conditions** nunca aceptarían unas condiciones así; **w. you do it? — yes I w./ no I wouldn't** ¿lo harías? — sí/no; **you wouldn't do it, w. you?** tú no lo harías, ¿verdad?

(b) *(expressing wish, determination)* **I wouldn't do it for anything** no lo haría por nada del mundo; **she wouldn't let me speak to him** no me dejaba hablar con él; **what w. you have me do?** ¿qué quieres que haga?; **the wound wouldn't heal** la herida no cicatrizaba; **w. you pass the mustard please?** ¿me pasas la mostaza, por favor?; **w. you like a drink?** ¿tienes ganas de *or Esp* te apetece *or Andes, Méx, Ven* te provoca *or Méx* se te antoja tomar algo?; **be quiet, w. you!** haz el favor de callarte, ¿quieres?

(c) *(for emphasis)* **you WOULD insist on going!** ¡pero tú tenías que insistir en ir!; **I forgot — you WOULD** se me olvidó — ¡cómo no!

(d) *(expressing past habit)* **she w. often return home exhausted** solía volver agotada a casa; **there w. always be some left over** siempre sobraba algo

(e) *(in reported speech)* **she told me she w. be there** me dijo que estaría allí; **I said I w. do it** dije que lo haría

(f) *(conjecture)* **w. that be my pen you're using?** ¿no será ese bolígrafo que estás usando el mío?; **that w. have been before your time** eso debe de haber sido antes de tu época; **I wouldn't know** no sé

would-be ['wʊdbiː] *adj* **a w. actor/politician** un aspirante a actor/político

wouldn't [wʊdnt] = **would not**

wound¹ [wuːnd] **1** *n* herida *f*

2 *vt also Fig* herir

wound² [waʊnd] *pt & pp of* **wind²**

wounded ['wuːndɪd] **1** *npl* **the w.** los heridos

2 *adj* herido(a); **to be w.** estar herido(a)

wounding ['wuːndɪŋ] *adj* hiriente

wove [wəʊv] *pt of* **weave**

woven ['wəʊvən] *pp of* **weave**

wow [waʊ] *Fam* **vt** encandilar

2 *exclam* ¡hala!, *RP* ¡uau!

WP [dʌbəljuːˈpiː] *n Comptr* **(a)** *(abbr* **word processor)** procesador *m* de textos **(b)** *(abbr* **word processing)** tratamiento *m* de textos

wpm [dʌbəljuːpiːˈem] *(abbr* **words per minute)** palabras *fpl* por minuto

wrangle ['ræŋɡəl] **1** *n* disputa *f*

2 *vi* pelear **(about** *or* **over** por), reñir **(about** *or* **over** por)

wrap [ræp] **1** *n* **(a)** *(shawl)* chal *m*; *Fig* **to keep sth under wraps** mantener algo en secreto **(b)** *(sandwich)* wrap *m*, = tortilla de harina rellena y enrollada

2 *vt (pt & pp* **wrapped)** envolver **(in** con); **she wrapped the bandage around his head** le puso la venda alrededor de la cabeza; *Fig* **wrapped in mystery** rodeado(a) de misterio

▸**wrap up 1** *vt sep* **(a)** *(parcel, present)* envolver; *Fig* **to be wrapped up in sth** *(absorbed)* estar absorto(a) en algo **(b)** *Fam (bring to an end)* poner punto final a

2 *vi (dress warmly)* abrigarse

wraparound ['ræpəraʊnd] **1** *n* **(a)** *(skirt)* falda *for RP* pollera *f* cruzada **(b)** *Comptr* contorneo *m*

2 *adj (skirt)* cruzado(a)

wrapper ['ræpə(r)] *n* envoltorio *m*

wrapping ['ræpɪŋ] *n* envoltura *f*, envoltorio *m*; **w. paper** papel *m* de envolver

wrath [rɒθ] *n Literary* ira *f*

wreak [riːk] *vt* **to w. havoc** causar estragos; **to w. vengeance on sb** vengarse de alguien

wreath [riːθ] *n (of flowers)* corona *f* (de flores)

wreathe [riːð] *vt* coronar

wreck [rek] **1** *n (ship)* restos *mpl* del naufragio; *(car, train, plane)* restos *mpl* del accidente; *Fig* **to be a physical w.** estar destrozado(a) físicamente; *Fig* **to be a nervous w.** tener los nervios destrozados

2 vt (*ship*) hundir; (*car, room, house*) destrozar; *Fig* (*plans, hopes, happiness*) dar al traste con; *Fig* (*marriage, career*) destruir, arruinar; **to w. one's health** destrozarse la salud

wreckage ['rekɪdʒ] n (*of ship*) restos mpl del naufragio; (*of car, train, plane*) restos mpl del accidente

wrecker ['rekə(r)] n (*salvage vehicle*) grúa f

wren [ren] n chochín m

wrench [rentʃ] **1** n (**a**) (*pull*) tirón m; (*to ankle, shoulder*) torcedura f; *Fig* **it was a w. to leave** me partía el corazón tener que irme (**b**) (*tool*) llave f; (*adjustable tool*) llave f inglesa

    2 vt **to w. one's ankle/one's shoulder** torcerse un tobillo/un hombro; **to w. sth out of sb's hands** arrancarle algo a alguien de las manos

wrest [rest] vt **to w. sth from sb** arrebatar or arrancar algo a alguien

wrestle ['resəl] vi luchar; *Fig* **to w. with a problem** lidiar con un problema

wrestler ['reslə(r)] n luchador(ora) m,f (de lucha libre)

wrestling ['reslɪŋ] n lucha f libre; **w. match** combate m de lucha libre

wretch [retʃ] n miserable mf

wretched ['retʃɪd] adj (**a**) (*very bad*) horrible, inmundo(a) (**b**) (*unhappy*) abatido(a) (**c**) (*for emphasis*) **I can't find the w. umbrella!** ¡no encuentro el maldito paraguas!

wriggle ['rɪgəl] **1** vt **to w. one's way out of a situation** lograr escurrir el bulto (de una situación)

    2 vi **to w. (around)** menearse; **to w. out of sth/of doing sth** escaquearse de algo/de hacer algo

wring [rɪŋ] (pt & pp **wrung** [rʌŋ]) vt (*clothes*) escurrir, estrujar; **to w. one's hands** retorcerse las manos; *Fam* **I'd like to w. his neck** me gustaría retorcerle el pescuezo; *Fig* **to w. sth from sb** sacarle algo a alguien

wringer ['rɪŋə(r)] n escurridor m de rodillos; *Fam Fig* **to put sb through the w.** hacer pasar un mal trago a alguien

wringing ['rɪŋɪŋ] adj **to be w. (wet)** estar empapado(a)

wrinkle ['rɪŋkəl] **1** n arruga f

    2 vi arrugarse

wrinkled ['rɪŋkəld] adj arrugado(a)

wrinkly ['rɪŋklɪ] adj arrugado(a)

wrist [rɪst] n muñeca f

wristwatch ['rɪstwɒtʃ] n reloj m (de pulsera)

writ [rɪt] n *Law* mandato m judicial; **to serve a w. on sb** entregar un mandato judicial a alguien

write [raɪt] (pt **wrote** [rəʊt], pp **written** ['rɪtən]) **1** vt (*answer, name, letter*) escribir; (*check*) extender; **to w. sb** escribir a alguien; **she had guilt written all over her face** su rostro era el vivo retrato de la culpabilidad

    2 vi escribir; **to w. for a newspaper** escribir or colaborar en un periódico; *Fam* **that's nothing to w. home about** eso no es nada del otro mundo

▸**write away for** vt insep **to w. away for sth** escribir pidiendo algo

▸**write back** vi responder, contestar (*por carta*)

▸**write down** vt sep escribir, anotar

▸**write in 1** vt sep (*name, answer*) escribir

    2 vi (*send letter*) escribir

▸**write off 1** vt sep (**a**) (*debt*) condonar (**b**) *Fam* (*person*) descartar; **to w. sb off as a has-been** considerar que alguien está acabado

    2 vi **to w. off for sth** escribir pidiendo algo

▸**write out** vt sep (*instructions, recipe*) escribir, copiar; (*check*) extender

▸**write up** vt sep (*notes, thesis*) redactar; (*diary, journal*) poner al día

write-off ['raɪtɒf] n (*of debt*) condonación f

write-protected ['raɪtprə'tektɪd] adj *Comptr* protegido(a) contra escritura

writer ['raɪtə(r)] n (*by profession*) escritor(ora) m,f; (*of article,*

book) autor(ora) m,f; **w.'s block** bloqueo m mental (*al escribir*)

write-up ['raɪtʌp] n (*review*) crítica f

writhe [raɪð] vi retorcerse

writing ['raɪtɪŋ] n (**a**) (*action*) escritura f; (*profession*) literatura f; **w. desk** escritorio m; **w. paper** papel m de escribir (**b**) (*handwriting*) letra f, escritura f (**c**) (*thing written*) (*literature*) literatura f; (*written words*) escritura f; **in w.** por escrito; *Fig* **the w. is on the wall for him** tiene los días contados

written ['rɪtən] **1** adj escrito(a); **w. consent** consentimiento m por escrito; **w. examination** examen m escrito

    2 pp of **write**

wrong [rɒŋ] **1** n (*immoral actions*) mal m; **to know right from w.** distinguir el bien del mal; **he can do no w.** lo hace todo bien; **to do sb w.** agraviar a alguien; **to right a w.** deshacer un entuerto; *Prov* **two wrongs don't make a right** vengándose no se consigue nada; **to be in the w.** ser el/la culpable

    2 adj (**a**) (*morally bad*) malo(a); **stealing is w.** robar está mal; **it was w. of you not to tell me** hiciste mal en no decírmelo (**b**) (*incorrect, mistaken*) incorrecto(a), erróneo(a); **to be w.** (*person*) estar equivocado(a), equivocarse; (*answer*) ser incorrecto(a) or erróneo(a); **my watch is w.** mi reloj va mal; **you chose the w. moment** no escogiste el momento oportuno; **don't get the w. idea** no te equivoques; **I did/said the w. thing** hice/dije lo que no debía; **to drive on the w. side of the road** conducir or Am manejar por el lado contrario de la carretera; *Fig* **to start** or **get off on the w. foot** empezar con mal pie; *Fig* **to go about it the w. way** hacerlo mal; *Fig* **to get on the w. side of sb** ponerse a mal con alguien; *Fig* **to back the w. horse** apostar por el perdedor; **you have the w. number** (*on phone*) se ha equivocado de número

    (**c**) (*amiss*) **what's w.?** ¿qué pasa?; **what's w. with you?** ¿qué te pasa?; **is anything w.?** ¿pasa algo?; *Fam* **to be w. in the head** estar *Esp* chiflado(a) or Am zafado(a) or RP rayado(a); **there's something w. with this machine** a este aparato le pasa algo

    3 adv (**a**) (*morally*) mal; **he admitted he had done w.** admitió que había hecho mal (**b**) (*incorrectly*) mal; **to go w.** (*plan*) salir mal; (*make mistake*) equivocarse; **to guess w.** no acertar, equivocarse; **don't get me w., I like her** no me malentiendas, (ella) me cae bien

    4 vt agraviar, tratar injustamente

wrongdoer ['rɒŋduːə(r)] n malhechor(ora) m,f

wrongdoing ['rɒŋduːɪŋ] n (*immoral actions*) desmanes mpl; (*crime*) delito m, delincuencia f

wrongful ['rɒŋfʊl] adj injusto(a); **w. dismissal** despido m improcedente

wrongfully ['rɒŋfʊlɪ] adv injustamente

wrong-headed [rɒŋ'hedɪd] adj empecinado(a)

wrongly ['rɒŋlɪ] adv (**a**) (*unjustly*) injustamente (**b**) (*incorrectly*) erróneamente

wrote [rəʊt] pt of **write**

wrought-iron ['rɔːt'aɪən] adj de hierro forjado

wrought-up ['rɔːt'ʌp] adj **to be w. (about sth)** estar muy alterado(a) (por algo)

wrung [rʌŋ] pt & pp of **wring**

wry [raɪ] adj irónico(a)

wt (*abbr* **weight**) peso m

WTO ['dʌbəljuːtiː'əʊ] n (*abbr* **World Trade Organization**) OMC f

WW (*abbr* **World War**) **WWI/II** la Primera/Segunda Guerra Mundial

WWF ['dʌbəljuːdʌbəljuː'ef] n (*abbr* **Worldwide Fund for Nature**) WWF m, Fondo m Mundial para la Naturaleza

WWW n (*abbr* **World Wide Web**) WWW f

WYSIWYG ['wɪzɪwɪg] n *Comptr* (*abbr* **What You See Is What You Get**) WYSIWYG, = se imprime lo que ves

X

X, x [eks] *n (letter)* X, x *f*; **for x number of years** durante un número x de años, durante x años; *Biol* **X chromosome** cromosoma *m* X

x-axis ['eksæksɪs] *n Math* eje *m* de abscisas, abcisa *f*

xenon ['zenɒn] *n Chem* xenón *m*

xenophobia [zenə'fəʊbɪə] *n* xenofobia *f*

xenophobic [zenə'fəʊbɪk] *adj* xenófobo(a)

Xerox® ['zɪərɒks] *n* fotocopia *f*, xerocopia *f*

xerox ['zɪərɒks] *vt* fotocopiar

XL *(abbr* **extra large)** XL, (talla *f*) muy grande

Xmas ['krɪsməs, 'eksməs] *n (abbr* **Christmas)** Navidad *f*

X-rated ['eksreɪtɪd] *adj Fam* fuerte; **X. movie** *(pornographic)* película *f* X

X-ray ['eksreɪ] **1** *n (pl* **X-rays)** *(radiation)* rayo *m* X; *(picture)* radiografía *f*; **X. examination** examen *m* por rayos X; **to have an X.** hacerse una radiografía
   2 *vt* radiografiar

xylophone ['zaɪləfəʊn] *n* xilófono *m*, xilofón *m*

Y

Y, y [waɪ] *n (letter)* Y, y *f*; *Biol* **Y chromosome** cromosoma *m* Y

yacht [jɒt] *n (sailing boat)* velero *m*; *(large private boat)* yate *m*; **y. club** club *m* náutico; **y. race** regata *f*

yachting ['jɒtɪŋ] *n* (navegación *f* a) vela *f*

yachtsman ['jɒtsmən] *n (in race)* tripulante *m*; *(round-the-world)* navegante *m*

yak [jæk] *n* yak *m*, yac *m*

yam [jæm] *n (vegetable)* ñame *m*; *(sweet potato)* batata *f*, *Esp* boniato *m*, *Am* camote *m*

Yank [jæŋk], **Yankee** ['jæŋkɪ] *n Fam (person from northern states)* = estadounidense procedente del norte del país; *(US citizen)* yanqui *mf*

yank [jæŋk] **1** *n Fam* **to give sth a y.** dar un tirón a algo
   2 *vt Fam* **to y. the door open** abrir la puerta de un tirón; **to y. sth out** arrancar algo de un tirón

yap [jæp] *(pt & pp yapped)* *vi (dog)* ladrar *(de forma aguda)*; *Fam (person)* chacharear, parlotear

yard¹ [jɑːd] *n (measurement)* yarda *f (0,914 m)*

yard² *n* **(a)** *(of farm)* corral *m* **(b)** *(for working)* taller *m (al aire libre)*; **(ship) y.** astillero *m* **(c)** *(for storage)* almacén *m*, depósito *m (al aire libre)*; **(builder's) y.** almacén de materiales de construcción

yardstick ['jɑːdstɪk] *n (standard)* patrón *m* (de medida)

yarn [jɑːn] *n* **(a)** *Tex* hilo *m* **(b)** *Fam (story)* batallita *f*; **to spin a y.** contar batallitas

yawn [jɔːn] **1** *n* bostezo *m*; *Fam (boring thing)* pesadez *f*, latazo *m*
   2 *vi* **(a)** *(person)* bostezar **(b)** *(chasm)* abrirse

y-axis ['waɪæksɪs] *n Math* eje *m* de ordenadas, ordenada *f*

yds *(abbr* **yards***)* yardas *fpl*

ye [jiː] **1** *pron Literary* = **you**
   2 *definite art Hum* = **the**

yea [jeɪ] *n* **yeas and nays** votos *mpl* a favor y en contra
   2 *adv Literary* = **yes**

yeah [jeə] *adv Fam* sí; **oh y.?** *(in disbelief, challenging)* ¿ah, sí?

year [jɪə(r)] *n* año *m*; *(at school, college)* curso *m*; **in the y. 1931** en el año 1931; **this y.** este año; **last y.** el año pasado; **next y.** el año que viene; **every y.** todos los años; **twice a y.** dos veces al año; **to earn $20,000 a y.** ganar 20.000 dólares al año; **to be ten years old** tener diez años; **he got five years** *(prison sentence)* le cayeron cinco años; **for many years** durante muchos años; **y. in y. out** año tras año; **over the years** con el paso de los años; **years ago** hace años; **it's years since I saw him, I haven't seen him for** *or* **in years** hace años que no lo veo; **from his earliest years** desde temprana edad; **to be getting on in years** empezar a hacerse viejo(a)

yearbook ['jɪəbʊk] *n* anuario *m*

year-end [jɪə'end] **1** *n* final *m* or fin *m* de año; **at the y.** al final del año, a final(es) de año
   2 *adj Fin (accounts)* de cierre de ejercicio; *(profits, losses)* al final del año, al cierre del ejercicio

yearlong ['jɪəlɒŋ] *adj* **y. wait** una espera de un año

yearly ['jɪəlɪ] **1** *adj* anual

2 *adv* anualmente, cada año; **twice y.** dos veces al año

yearn [jɜːn] *vi* **to y. for sth/to do sth** anhelar algo/hacer algo

yearning ['jɜːnɪŋ] *n* anhelo *m*

year-round ['jɪəraʊnd] **1** *adj* de todo el año
   2 *adv* todo el año

yeast [jiːst] *n* levadura *f*

yell [jel] **1** *n* grito *m*; **to give a y.** dar un grito
   2 *vt & vi* gritar

yellow ['jeləʊ] **1** *n* amarillo *m*
   2 *adj* **(a)** *(in color)* amarillo(a); **to turn** *or* **go y.** amarillear, ponerse amarillo; **y. card** *(in soccer)* tarjeta *f* amarilla; *Med* **y. fever** fiebre *f* amarilla; *Tel* **the Y. Pages** las páginas amarillas; **the Y. River** el río Amarillo *or* Huango Ho **(b)** *Fam (cowardly)* cagueta, gallina
   3 *vi* amarillear, ponerse amarillo(a)

yelp [jelp] **1** *n* aullido *m*
   2 *vi* aullar

Yemen ['jemən] *n* Yemen

Yemeni ['jemənɪ] *n & adj* yemení *mf*

yen¹ [jen] *(pl* **yen***)* *n (Japanese currency)* yen *m*

yen² *n* **to have a y. for sth/to do sth** tener muchas ganas de algo/de hacer algo

Yerevan [jerə'væn] *n* Ereván

yes [jes] **1** *n* sí *m*
   2 *adv* sí; **he said y.** dijo que sí; **didn't you hear me? —** y., **I did** ¿no me has oído? — sí; **y.?** *(to sb waiting to speak)* ¿sí?; *(answering phone)* ¿sí?, *Esp* ¿diga?, *Esp* ¿dígame?, *Andes, Carib* ¿aló?, *Col, Méx* ¿bueno?, *RP* ¿hola?

yes-man ['jesmæn] *n* adulador(ora) *m,f*, cobista *mf*

yesterday ['jestədeɪ] **1** *n* ayer *m*
   2 *adv* ayer; **the day before y.** anteayer; **y. morning/evening** ayer por la mañana/por la tarde

yet [jet] **1** *adv* **(a)** *(still)* todavía, aún; **I haven't finished y.** todavía no he terminado; **don't go y.** no te vayas todavía; **I'll catch her y.!** ¡ya la atraparé!; **as y.** hasta ahora, por el momento; **not y.** todavía no; **y. again** una vez más; **y. more** aún más; **y. another mistake** otro error más **(b)** *(in questions)* ya; **have they decided y.?** ¿han decidido ya?
   2 *conj* aunque, sin embargo; **small y. strong** pequeño aunque fuerte; **and y. I like him** y, sin embargo, me gusta

yeti ['jetɪ] *n* yeti *m*

yew [juː] *n* tejo *m*

Yiddish ['jɪdɪʃ] *n & adj* yiddish *m*, yídish *m*

yield [jiːld] **1** *n (of field)* cosecha *f*; *(of mine, interest)* rendimiento *m*; *Fin (profit)* beneficio *m*
   2 *vt* **(a)** *(results, interest)* proporcionar; **to y. a profit** proporcionar beneficios **(b)** *(territory)* ceder; *(right)* conceder
   3 *vi* **(a)** *(surrender)* rendirse **(b)** **to y. to temptation** ceder a la tentación **(b)** **y.** *(traffic sign)* ceda el paso

yippee [jɪ'piː] *exclam* ¡yupi!, ¡viva!

YMCA [waɪemsiː'eɪ] *n (abbr* **Young Men's Christian Association***)* ACJ *f*, Asociación *f* Cristiana de Jóvenes *(que regenta hostales económicos)*

yoga [ˈjəʊɡə] n yoga m
yog(h)urt [ˈjɒɡət] n yogur m
yoke [jəʊk] **1** n (**a**) (for oxen) & Fig yugo m (**b**) (for carrying) balancín m
2 vt (oxen) uncir (al yugo); Fig **to be yoked to…** estar uncido al yugo de…
yokel [ˈjəʊkəl] n Pej or Hum palurdo(a) m,f, Esp paleto(a) m,f
yolk [jəʊk] n yema f (de huevo)
yonder [ˈjɒndə(r)] adv (**over**) y. allá
you [juː] pron

In Spanish, the formal form **usted** takes a third person singular verb and **ustedes** takes a third person plural verb. In many Latin American countries, **ustedes** is the standard form of the second person plural and is not considered formal.

(**a**) (subject) (usually omitted in Spanish, except for contrast) (singular) tú, esp RP vos, Formal usted; (plural) Esp vosotros(as), Am or Formal ustedes; **y. seem happy** (singular) pareces feliz, Formal parece feliz; (plural) Esp parecéis felices, Am or Formal parecen felices; **have you got it?** (singular) ¿lo tienes tú?, Formal ¿lo tiene usted?; (plural) Esp ¿lo tenéis vosotros?, Am or Formal ¿lo tienen ustedes?
(**b**) (direct object) (singular) te, Formal lo(la); (plural) Esp os, Am or Formal los(las); **I can understand your son but not you** (singular) a tu hijo lo entiendo, pero a ti no, Formal a su hijo lo entiendo, pero a usted no; (plural) Esp a vuestro hijo lo entiendo, pero a vosotros no, Am or Formal a su hijo lo entiendo, pero a ustedes no
(**c**) (indirect object) (singular) te, Formal le; (plural) Esp os, Am or Formal les; **I gave y. the book** (singular) te di el libro, Formal le di el libro; (plural) Esp os di el libro, Am or Formal les di el libro; **I told y.** (singular) te lo dije, Formal se lo dije; (plural) Esp os lo dije, Am or Formal se lo dije
(**d**) (after preposition) (singular) ti, Formal usted; (plural) Esp vosotros(as), Am or Formal ustedes; **I'm thinking of y.** (singular) pienso en ti, Formal pienso en usted; (plural) Esp pienso en vosotros, Am or Formal pienso en ustedes; **with y.** (singular) contigo, Formal con usted; (plural) Esp con vosotros, Am or Formal con ustedes
(**e**) (impersonal) **y. don't do that kind of thing** esas cosas no se hacen; **y. never know** nunca se sabe; **exercise is good for y.** es bueno hacer ejercicio; **y. have to be careful with him** hay que or uno tiene que tener cuidado con él
(**f**) (as complement of verb to be) **oh, it's y.!** (singular) ¡ah, eres tú!, Formal ¡ah, es usted!; (plural) Esp ¡ah, sois vosotros!, Am or Formal ¡ah, son ustedes!; **it was y. who did it** (singular) fuiste tú quien lo hiciste, Formal fue usted quien lo hizo; (plural) Esp fuisteis vosotros quienes lo hicisteis, Am or Formal fueron ustedes quienes lo hicieron
(**g**) (with interjections) **poor old y.!** ¡pobrecito!; **y. idiot!** ¡idiota!; **don't y. forget!** ¡no te olvides!
(**h**) (in apposition) **y. men are all the same!** ¡todos los hombres Esp sois or Am son iguales!
(**i**) (with imperative) **y. sit down here** (singular) tú siéntate aquí; (plural) Esp ustedes sentaos aquí, Am ustedes siéntense acá; **don't y. dare!** ¡ni se te ocurra!
you-all [juːˈɔl, jɔl] pron Fam (in Southern states) Esp vosotros, LAm ustedes
you'd [juːd] = you had, you would
you-know-what [juːnəʊˈwɒt] n Fam Euph **does he know about the y.?** ¿está al corriente de… ya sabes?; **they were doing y.** estaban haciendo ya sabes qué or lo que te dije
you-know-who [juːnəʊˈhuː] n **he was talking to y.** estaba hablando ya sabes con quién
you'll [juːl] = you will, you shall
young [jʌŋ] **1** npl (**a**) (people) **the y.** los jóvenes (**b**) (animals) crías fpl

2 adj (person) joven; (appearance) juvenil; **she's (two years) younger than me** es (dos años) menor que yo; **you're only y. once** sólo se es joven una vez en la vida; **y. man** (chico m) joven m; **y. woman** (chica f) joven f; **when I was a y. man** cuando era joven; **in his younger days** en su juventud; **the night is y.!** ¡la noche es joven!; **y. people** los jóvenes, la gente joven; **y. in spirit** or **at heart** joven de espíritu
youngster [ˈjʌŋstə(r)] n joven mf
your [jɔː(r)] possessive adj (**a**) (of one person) tu, Formal su; **y. house** tu/su casa; **y. books** tus/sus libros; **it wasn't YOUR idea!** ¡no fue idea tuya!
(**b**) (of more than one person) Esp vuestro(a), Am or Formal su; **y. house** Esp vuestra casa, Am or Formal su casa; **y. books** Esp vuestros libros, Am or Formal sus libros; **it wasn't YOUR idea!** Esp ¡no fue idea vuestra!, Am or Formal ¡no fue idea suya or de ustedes!
(**c**) (for parts of body, clothes) (translated by definite article) **did you hit y. head?** ¿te has dado un golpe en la cabeza?; **why did you put y. hand in y. pocket?** ¿por qué te has metido la mano en el bolsillo?
(**d**) (impersonal) **you should buy y. ticket first** hay que comprar el billete antes; **smoking is bad for y. health** el tabaco perjudica la salud; Fam **y. average Frenchman** el francés medio
you're [jɔː(r)] = you are
yours [jɔːz] possessive pron

In Spanish, the forms **tuyo(a)**, **suyo(a)** and **vuestro(a)** require a definite article in the singular and in the plural when they are the subject of the phrase.

(**a**) (of one person) (singular) tuyo(a) m,f; (plural) tuyos(as) m,fpl; (formal: singular) suyo(a) m,f; (formal: plural) suyos(as) m,fpl; **my house is big but y. is bigger** mi casa es grande, pero la tuya/suya es mayor; **this book is y.** este libro es tuyo/suyo; **these books are y.** estos libros son tuyos/suyos; **a friend of y.** un amigo tuyo/suyo; **where's that brother of y.?** ¿dónde anda ese hermano tuyo?; **y. (sincerely/faithfully)** atentamente
(**b**) (of more than one person) (singular) Esp vuestro(a), Am or Formal suyo(a); (plural) Esp vuestros(as), Am or Formal suyos(as); **this book is y.** este libro es vuestro/suyo; **these books are y.** estos libros son vuestros/suyos
yourself [jɔːˈself] pron (**a**) (reflexive) te, Formal se; **have you hurt y.?** ¿te has hecho daño?, Formal ¿se ha hecho daño?
(**b**) (emphatic) tú mismo m, tú misma f, Formal usted mismo m, usted misma f; **did you do all the work y.?** ¿has hecho todo el trabajo tú solo?, Formal ¿ha hecho todo el trabajo usted solo?; **you told me y.** me lo dijiste tú mismo, Formal me lo dijo usted mismo; **you're not y. today** hoy no se te nota nada bien
(**c**) (after preposition) ti, Formal usted; **did you do this by y.?** ¿lo has hecho tú solo?, Formal ¿lo ha hecho usted solo?; **do you live by y.?** ¿vives solo?, Formal ¿vive solo?; **did you buy it for y.?** ¿te lo has comprado para ti?, Formal ¿se lo ha comprado para usted?
yourselves [jɔːˈselvz] pron (**a**) (reflexive) Esp os, Am or Formal se; **have you hurt y.?** Esp ¿os habéis hecho daño?, Am or Formal ¿se han hecho daño?
(**b**) (emphatic) Esp vosotros(as) mismos(as), Am or Formal ustedes mismos(as); **did you do all the work y.?** Esp ¿habéis hecho todo el trabajo vosotros solos?, Am or Formal ¿han hecho todo el trabajo ustedes solos?; **you told me y.** Esp me lo dijisteis vosotros mismos, Am or Formal me lo dijeron ustedes mismos
(**c**) (after preposition) Esp vosotros(as), Am or Formal ustedes; **did you do this by y.?** Esp ¿lo habéis hecho vosotros solos?, Am or Formal ¿lo han hecho ustedes solos?; **did you**

buy it for **y.?** *Esp* ¿os lo habéis comprado para vosotros?, *Am or Formal* ¿se lo han comprado para ustedes?; **share the money among y.** *Esp* repartíos el dinero, *Am or Formal* repártanse el dinero

outh [juːθ] *n* (**a**) *(period)* juventud *f*; **in his early y.** en su (primera) juventud (**b**) *(young man)* joven *m* (**c**) *(young people)* juventud *f*; **y. club** club *m* juvenil; **y. hostel** albergue *m* juvenil

outhful ['juːθful] *adj (person)* joven; *(looks, enthusiasm)* juvenil

ou've [juːv] = **you have**

owl [jaʊl] **1** *n* aullido *m*, chillido *m*
   2 *vi* aullar, chillar

o-yo ['jəʊjəʊ] *(pl* **yo-yos)** *n* yoyó *m*

r *(abbr* **year)** año *m*

uan [juːˈæn] *n (Chinese currency)* yuan *m*

yucca ['jʌkə] *n* yuca *f*

yuck [jʌk] *exclam Fam* ¡puaj!, ¡aj!

yucky ['jʌkɪ] *adj Fam* asqueroso(a)

Yugoslav ['juːgəʊslɑːv] *n & adj* yugoslavo(a) *m,f*

Yugoslavia [juːgəʊˈslɑːvɪə] *n Formerly* Yugoslavia

Yugoslavian [juːgəʊˈslɑːvɪən] *adj* yugoslavo(a)

yuletide ['juːltaɪd] *n* Navidad *f*

yummy ['jʌmɪ] *adj Fam* rico(a)

yuppie ['jʌpɪ] *n* yupi *mf*; **a y. restaurant** un restaurante de yupis; *Fam* **y. flu** la gripe *or Am* gripa del yupi *(encefalomielitis miálgica)*

YWCA [waɪdʌbəljuːsiːˈeɪ] *n (abbr* **Young Women's Christian Association)** ACJ *f*, Asociación *f* Cristiana de Jóvenes *(que regenta hostales económicos)*

Z

Z, z [ziː] *n (letter)* Z, z *f*; *Fam* **to catch some z's** echar una cabezada *or* un sueñecito, echarse una siestecita

Zaire [zɑːˈɪə(r)] *n Formerly* Zaire

Zairean [zɑːˈɪərɪən] *n & adj* zaireño(a) *m,f*

Zambia [ˈzæmbɪə] *n* Zambia

Zambian [ˈzæmbɪən] *n & adj* zambiano(a) *m,f*

zany [ˈzeɪnɪ] *adj Fam (humor, movie)* disparatado(a); *(person) Esp* chiflado(a), *Am* zafado(a), *RP* rayado(a)

zap [zæp] *(pt & pp* **zapped)** *Fam* vt **(a)** *(destroy, disable)* fulminar **(b)** *Comptr (delete)* borrar

zapper [ˈzæpə(r)] *n Fam (TV remote control)* mando *m* a distancia, telemando *m*

zeal [ziːl] *n* celo *m*

zealot [ˈzelət] *n* fanático(a) *m,f*

zealous [ˈzeləs] *adj* celoso(a)

zealously [ˈzeləslɪ] *adv* celosamente

zebra [ˈziːbrə, ˈzebrə] *n* cebra *f*

zee [ziː] *n (letter)* zeta *f*

zenith [ˈzenɪθ] *n Astron & Fig* cenit *m*; **she was at the z. of her influence** su influencia estaba en el punto más alto

zephyr [ˈzefə(r)] *n* céfiro *m*

zero [ˈzɪərəʊ] **1** *n (pl* **zeros)** cero *m*; **22 degrees below z.** 22 grados bajo cero; *Mil* **z. hour** hora *f* cero *or* H; **z. tolerance** tolerancia *f* cero, inflexibilidad *f* absoluta

2 *adj Fam* nulo(a); **to have z. charm** no tener el más mínimo encanto

3 *vi* **to z. in on sth** apuntar hacia algo

zest [zest] *n* **(a)** *(enjoyment)* goce *m*, deleite *m* **(b)** *Culin (of orange, lemon)* piel *f*, cáscara *f*

zigzag [ˈzɪgzæg] **1** *n* zigzag *m*

2 *vi (pt & pp* **zigzagged)** zigzaguear

zilch [zɪltʃ] *n Fam* nada de nada; **there's z. on TV** no hay nada de nada en la tele

Zimbabwe [zɪmˈbɑːbweɪ] *n* Zimbabue

Zimbabwean [zɪmˈbɑːbweɪən] *n & adj* zimbabuense *mf*, zimbabuo(a) *m,f*

zinc [zɪŋk] *n* cinc *m*, zinc *m*

Zionism [ˈzaɪənɪzəm] *n* sionismo *m*

Zionist [ˈzaɪənɪst] *n & adj* sionista *mf*

zip [zɪp] *n* **(a)** *Fam (vigor)* nervio *m*, brío *m* **(b)** **z. code** código *m* postal **(c)** *Comptr* **Zip® disk** disco *m* Zip®; **z. file** archivo *m* zip

2 *vi (pt & pp* **zipped)** **to z. past** *(car, bullet)* pasar zumbando

▸**zip through** *vt insep Fam* **I zipped through the last chapters** me cepillé en un momento los últimos capítulos

▸**zip up 1** *vt sep (clothes, bag)* cerrar la cremallera *or Am* el cierre de

2 *vi* cerrarse con cremallera *or Am* cierre

zipper [ˈzɪpə(r)] *n* cremallera *f*, *Am* cierre *m*

zippy [ˈzɪpɪ] *adj Fam* animado(a)

zither [ˈzɪðə(r)] *n Mus* cítara *f*

zodiac [ˈzəʊdɪæk] *n* zodiaco *m*, zodíaco *m*

zombie [ˈzɒmbɪ] *n* zombi *mf*

zone [zəʊn] **1** *n* zona *f*

2 *vt (city, area)* dividir en zonas

zonked (out) [zɒŋkt(ˈaʊt)] *adj Fam* **to be z.** *(exhausted)* estar molido(a) *or* hecho(a) polvo; *(drugged)* estar colocado(a) *or Col* trabado(a) *or Méx* pingo(a) *or RP* falopeado(a); *(drunk)* estar mamado(a) *or Esp, Méx* pedo

zoo [zuː] *n (pl* **zoos)** *n* zoo *m*, zoológico *m*

zoological [zʊəˈlɒdʒɪkəl] *adj* zoológico(a); **z. garden(s)** parque *m* zoológico

zoologist [zʊˈɒlədʒɪst] *n* zoólogo(a) *m,f*

zoology [zʊˈɒlədʒɪ] *n* zoología *f*

zoom [zuːm] *n* **(a)** *(noise)* zumbido *m* **(b)** *Phot* **z. lens** zoom *m*

2 *vi* **to z. along/past** ir/pasar zumbando *or* a toda velocidad

▸**zoom in** *vi Cin TV* enfocar en primer plano

zucchini [zuːˈkiːnɪ] *n (pl* **zucchini** *or* **zucchinis)** *n* calabacín *m*

Zulu [ˈzuːluː] *n & adj* zulú *mf*

zygote [ˈzaɪgəʊt] *n Biol* zigoto *m*, cigoto *m*